THE CONCISE OXFORD FRENCH DICTIONARY

THE CONCISE OXFORD FRENCH DICTIONARY

SECOND EDITION

FRENCH–ENGLISH
Edited by H. Ferrar

ENGLISH–FRENCH
Edited by J. A. Hutchinson and J.-D. Biard

CLARENDON PRESS · OXFORD
1980

Oxford University Press, Walton Street, Oxford OX2 6DP

OXFORD LONDON GLASGOW
NEW YORK TORONTO MELBOURNE WELLINGTON
KUALA LUMPUR SINGAPORE HONG KONG TOKYO
DELHI BOMBAY CALCUTTA MADRAS KARACHI
NAIROBI DAR ES SALAAM CAPE TOWN

Published in the United States of America, by
Oxford University Press, New York

Concise Oxford French–English Dictionary
first published 1934

Concise Oxford English–French Dictionary
first published 1940

Second edition 1980

British Library Cataloguing in Publication Data

The concise Oxford French dictionary. – 2nd ed.
1. French language – Dictionaries – English
2. English language – Dictionaries – French
I. Ferrar, Henry   II. Hutchinson, Joyce Agnes
III. Biard, Jean Dominique
443'.2'1   PC2640   80–40695

ISBN 0–19–864126–5

Typesetting by William Clowes (Beccles) Limited, Beccles and London
Printed in Great Britain at the University Press, Oxford
by Eric Buckley, Printer to the University

THE CONCISE OXFORD FRENCH–ENGLISH DICTIONARY

First edited by
Abel and Marguerite Chevalley

SECOND EDITION

edited by H. Ferrar
Head of Modern Languages,
Radley College

PREFACE

THE first edition of the *Concise Oxford French–English Dictionary* appeared in 1934. The forty-five years intervening have not lightened the task of the lexicographer. First, and obviously, there is the very large backlog of vocabulary necessary to describe everything new that has been invented, discovered, experienced, or become a subject of discussion since 1934. Secondly, such is the nature of the environment that more and more technical terms have become a necessary part of everyday vocabulary. Thirdly, in an era of mass-communication many new words are overexposed and thereby worked to death in less time than it takes to revise a dictionary. Under these circumstances the preparation of the second edition has called for rewriting rather than revision and, in some areas, for a basically new approach.

Nearly 3000 completely new vocabulary items have been inserted, and an even larger number of new translations has appeared under existing headwords. Many existing translations have had to be updated, rephrased, or even honourably superannuated.

The accelerating pace of change has imposed another limitation. Dr. Chevalley, in his Introduction to the first edition, upheld the principle that: 'A dictionary . . . can always translate an idiom by an idiom, a gallicism by the corresponding anglicism, a popular or slang term by a term of the same order and tint, a metaphor by a metaphor of approximately the same power'. The manifest archaism of many of Dr. Chevalley's idioms and popular and slang expressions indicates, sadly, that this is no longer possible, except on a very short-term basis, thereby giving a clear warning to succeeding editors. In the colloquial field at any rate, the search for modernity invites premature obsolescence. We have therefore adopted a cautious approach in this area. With metaphors and idioms this has mainly taken the form of preferring the well-tried to the latest. In the case of popular and slang expressions, interjections, and expletives we have, on occasion, felt compelled to indicate the sense and quality rather than offer an exact English equivalent. Similarly uninspiring reasons have compelled us to say goodbye to the illustrations. The splendid numbered diagrams of an Imperial Airways biplane and of the Mauretania have not been reprinted.

Other changes have been made necessary by the pressure of new material. The scholarly etymologies have, with great regret, been taken out, and some reduction in the number of examples has been found desirable as well as necessary. A feature that commends itself in the first edition is that there is virtually no 'compression', that is, each headword is a separate entry. While the increased amount of material in the second edition has necessitated some compression, we have tried to keep this to a minimum and to maintain the essential visibility of information.

In most other respects the special qualities of the original dictionary have been retained. The process of revising the original text compiled by the Chevalleys inspires increasing respect. Quite apart from the manifest scholarship, two features stand out in particular. It is in the first place an unusually comprehensive work. So much material has been incorporated in what is still a concise volume that there is a very good chance of finding both the French word and the appropriate English translation. This is achieved in the first edition, and, it is hoped, similarly in the second, by supplying a relatively large number of possible renderings. The final selection remains, of course, with the user, in the light of his knowledge of the English language.

The other feature that must have contributed to the popularity of the first edition is what could be described as 'usability'. The answer, if there at all, could be found without going round too many corners. The second edition tries hard to maintain this quality. It is not often necessary to look in more than one place for the solution. Proper names, abbreviations, and acronyms are not listed separately but appear in the main alphabetical sequence. The only exception to this practice is the conjugation of irregular and defective verbs, which is given separately in the Introduction.

The basic aims and scope of the second edition correspond to those of the original. It seeks to provide a translation of most of the words and expressions likely to be encountered from Corneille to the pages of a contemporary newspaper. In addition the present volume endeavours to keep pace with the expanded technical vocabulary which is now required by the informed general reader.

It is difficult to acknowledge adequately the valuable and abundant help received from several quarters. Dr. Joyce Hutchinson very kindly spared the time from the compilation of the English–French section to prepare the original material for letters A, B, C and E, and has been very helpful in this respect and in the supply of miscellaneous information. Mrs. Joan Pusey, besides preparing the original material for letter D, has devoted many months of hard work and her very considerable experience in lexicography to the checking of material and to the reading of galley proofs. Thanks are also due to Mrs. Joyce Reid and Mrs. Dorothy Eagle, who each read a substantial section of the galley proofs and made many valuable suggestions.

Dr. J.-D. Biard of Exeter University has very kindly read all the proofs with a particular eye to the French portions of the text, and virtually all his helpful emendations have been incorporated. Mention must also be made of Mr. A. S. Treves, whose original and scholarly notes have been available to those concerned with the first half of the dictionary. Grateful thanks are also due to the Cultural Attaché at the French Embassy in London who supplied copies of the *Journal Officiel* of 18 January 1973 and of 9 November 1976 containing lists of French words to be preferred to (mainly technical) anglicisms. We have included a number of these approved words, while prudently retaining some of the proscribed anglicisms. We were also fortunate to have been given the opportunity to make use of a number of items of French vocabulary collected by Librairie Larousse and made available to us by courtesy of Mme Françoise Dubois-Charlier.

Finally an anonymous nod in the direction of Radley College Common Room, many of whose members have allowed themselves to be button-holed on a wide variety of detailed points and who have contributed, from their special knowledge, to the accuracy of the terminology.

H. F.

INTRODUCTION

A. STRUCTURE OF ENTRIES

Feminine Forms
Feminine forms of nouns and adjectives are shown e.g., **ami, -e, bon, -ne, act-eur, -rice, heureu-x, -se**.

Plural Forms
Plural forms are not indicated for words whose singular ends in **-s** or **-x**, nor for simple (i.e. not compound) words which add **-s** for the plural. With compound words the plural is not normally given where this is formed by adding **-s** to both components. The plural of other compound words has been given in most cases. Where there is doubt, it may, as general guidance, be assumed that any component of a compound which is not itself a noun or an adjective will not take plural **-s**.

Other plural forms of simple words are shown e.g., **jeu** (pl. **-x**), **cheval** (pl. **aux**), **oeil** (pl. **yeux**).

Swung Dash
To save space, the swung dash ~ has been used in the dictionary entries. It normally represents the headword, or that part of it which precedes a hyphen.

Pronunciation
The pronunciation is given in phonetic symbols between square brackets.

B. SYMBOLS

Phonetic Symbols
The following are used. In the specimen words given below the letter or letters relevant to the symbol are printed in bold type.

[a]	m**a**l, l**a**tte	[œ]	n**eu**f, p**eu**r
[ɑ]	p**a**s, p**a**sse	[œ̃]	**un**, h**um**ble
[ɑ̃]	**en**f**an**t, c**am**p	[j]	p**i**ed, **y**eux, fi**ll**e
[e]	**é**t**é**, all**er**	[u]	t**ou**t, r**ou**te
[ɛ]	p**è**re, n**e**tte, jou**et**, all**ait**	[y]	p**u**, m**u**r
[ɛ̃]	v**in**, p**ain**	[w]	**ou**i, j**ou**er
[ə]	d**e**, pr**e**mier	[wa]	m**oi**, n**oi**r, b**oî**te
[i]	n**i**, f**i**ne	[ɥ]	l**u**i, h**u**ile, m**u**et
[o]	s**o**t, b**eau**	[b]	**b**al, ro**b**e
[ɔ]	n**o**te, h**o**mme	[d]	**d**ame, su**d**
[ɔ̃]	r**on**de, r**om**pre	[f]	**f**ait, **ph**rase
[ø]	f**eu**, cr**eux**	[g]	**g**ant, se**c**ond

[ɲ]	di**gn**e, oi**gn**on	[r]	**r**ose, tou**r**
[k]	**qu**i, **c**roire, ro**c**	[s]	**s**i, soi**x**ante
[ks]	se**x**e, e**xc**ès	[ʃ]	**ch**ou, lâ**ch**e, **sch**iste
[l]	**l**ong, seu**l**, vi**ll**e	[t]	**t**as, pa**tt**e
[m]	**m**ot, ra**m**e	[v]	**v**in, ca**v**e
[n]	**n**ez, auto**mn**e	[z]	**z**èle, ro**s**e
[ŋ]	campi**ng**	[ʒ]	**j**e, **g**ens
[p]	**p**is, ca**p**e, o**b**tenir		

Other Symbols

~ the use of the swung dash is explained in Section A above

= represents 'equals', 'is equivalent to', '(approximately) corresponds to'

⇧ indicates that this headword does not, or may not, mean the same as an English word with the same or similar spelling,
e.g. under **bribe**, ⇧ not 'bribe'
under **fastidieux**, ⇧ not 'fastidious'

'h an apostrophe before the initial **h** of a headword indicates that it is aspirated

C. TABLES OF VERBS

Irregular Verbs

Where a compound verb is not listed, it may be assumed that it is conjugated in full in the same way as the simple verb.

Tenses not shown

(a) The *Imperf. Indic.*, *Fut.* and *Imperat.* are assumed to be formed regularly. If this is not the case, the form is given under Remarks.

(b) The *Condit.* and *Imperf. Subjunc.* are not shown, except where there is doubt.

Pattern

Infin.	*Pres. Indic.*	*Pres. Subjunc.*	Remarks
Pres. Part. *Past Part.* *Past Hist(oric)*	(in full)	(1st sing., 1st pl., 3rd pl.)	

abattre AS BATTRE

absoudre	abs-ous	absolv-e	*Past Part. fem.*:
absolvant	-ous	-ions	absoute
absous	-out	-ent	
absolus	-olvons		
	-olvez		
	-olvent		

abstraire as TRAIRE

accroître as CROÎTRE, but circumflex only in group *-ît*

acquérir	acqu-iers	acqu-ière	*Fut.*:
acquérant	-iers	-érions	acquerrai
acquis	-iert	-ièrent	
acquis	-érons		
	-érez		
	-ièrent		

aller	vais	aille	*Fut.*: irai
allant	vas	allions	*2nd sing.*
allé	va	aillent	*Imperat.*: va
allai	allons		(*but* vas-y)
	allez		
	vont		

apercevoir as RECEVOIR

assaillir	assaill-e	assaill-e	
assaillant	-es	-ions	
assailli	-e	-ent	
assaillis	-ons		
	-ez		
	-ent		

asseoir	ass-ieds	assey-e	*Imperf.*:
asseyant	-ieds	-ions	asseyais
(assoyant)	-ied	-ent	(assoyais)
assis	(ass-ois	(ass-oie	*Fut.*: assiérai
assis	-ois	-oyions	(assoirai)
	-oit)	-oient)	*Imperat.*:
	assey-ons		assieds
	-ez		(assois), etc.
	-ent		
	(ass-oyons		
	-oyez		
	-oient)		

atteindre as PEINDRE

avoir	ai	aie	*Imperat.*: aie
ayant	as	aies	ayons
eu	a	ait	ayez
eus	avons	ayons	*Fut.* aurai
	avez	ayez	
	ont	aient	

battre regular except *sing. Pres. Indic.*: bats, bats, bat

boire	boi-s	boive
buvant	-s	buvions
bu	-t	boivent
bus	buv-ons	
	-ez	
	boivent	

bouillir	bou-s
bouillant	-s
bouilli	-t
bouillis	bouill-ons
	-ez
	-ent

ceindre as PEINDRE

circoncire as DIRE, but *2nd pl. Pres. Indic.* and *Imperat.*: circoncisez; *Past Part.*: circoncis.

concevoir as RECEVOIR

conclure	conclu-s	conclu-e
concluant	-s	-ions
conclu	-t	-ent
conclus	-ons	
	-ez	
	-ent	

conduire	condui-s	conduis-e
conduisant	-s	-ions
conduit	-t	-ent
conduisis	-sons	
	-sez	
	-sent	

confire as SUFFIRE, but *Past Part.*: confit

connaître	conn-ais	connaiss-e	*Fut.*: connaîtrai
connaissant	-ais	-ions	
connu	-aît	-ent	
connus	-aissons		
	-aissez		
	-aissent		

conquérir as ACQUÉRIR

construire as CONDUIRE

contraindre as CRAINDRE

contredire as DIRE, but *2nd pl. Pres. Indic.* and *Imperat.*: contredisez.

coudre	cou-ds	cous-e	
cousant	-ds	-ions	
cousu	-d	-ent	
cousis	-sons		
	-sez		
	-sent		

courir	cour-s	cour-e	*Fut.*: courrai
courant	-s	-ions	
couru	-t	-ent	
courus	-ons		
	-ez		
	-ent		

couvrir as OUVRIR

craindre	crain-s	craign-e
craignant	-s	-ions
craint	-t	-ent
craignis	craign-ons	
	-ez	
	-ent	

croire	croi-s	croie
croyant	-s	croyions
cru	-t	croient
crus	croy-ons	
	-ez	
	croient	

croître	croî-s	croiss-e
croissant	-s	-ions
crû	-t	-ent
crûs	croiss-ons	
	-ez	
	-ent	

cueillir as ASSAILLIR, but *Fut.*: cueillerai.

cuire as CONDUIRE

décevoir as RECEVOIR

déchoir	déch-ois	déch-oie	*Fut.*: déchoirai;
(none)	-ois	-oyions	also (obs.):
déchu	-oit	-oient	*Pres. Indic.*:
déchus	-oyons		déchet
	-oyez		*Fut.*: décherrai
	-oient		

décrire as ÉCRIRE

décroître as CROÎTRE (for circumflex see ACCROÎTRE)

dédire as DIRE, but *2nd pl. Pres. Indic.* and *Imperat.*: dédisez.

défaillir as ASSAILLIR

devoir	doi-s	doive	*Past Part.*:
devant	-s	devions	*fem.*: due,
dû	-t	doivent	dues; *masc. pl.*:
dus	dev-ons		dus
	-ez		*Fut.*: devrai
	doivent		

dire	di-s	dis-e	
disant	-s	-ions	
dit	-t	-ent	
dis	disons		
	dites		
	disent		

dissoudre as ABSOUDRE

distraire as TRAIRE

dormir	dor-s	dorm-e	
dormant	-s	-ions	
dormi	-t	-ent	
dormis	dorm-ons		
	-ez		
	-ent		

écrire	écri-s	écriv-e	
écrivant	-s	-ions	
écrit	-t	-ent	
écrivis	écriv-ons		
	-ez		
	-ent		

élire as LIRE

émouvoir as MOUVOIR, but *Past Part.*: ému, émue.

(**s'**)**enquérir** as ACQUÉRIR

(**s'**)**ensuivre** as SUIVRE (but found only in 3rd persons)

envoyer regular, except *Fut.*: enverrai

éteindre as PEINDRE

être	suis	soi-s	*Imperat.*: sois
étant	es	-s	soyons
été	est	-t	soyez
fus	sommes	soy-ons	
	êtes	-ez	
	sont	soient	

exclure as CONCLURE

extraire as TRAIRE

faire	fai-s	fass-e	*Fut.*: ferai
faisant	-s	-ions	
fait	-t	-ent	
fis	faisons		
	faites		
	font		

falloir	faut	faille	*Fut.*: faudra
(impers.)			
(none)			
fallu			
fallut			

feindre as PEINDRE

fuir	fui-s	fuie
fuyant	-s	fuyions
fui	-t	fuient
fuis	fuy-ons	
	-ez	
	fuient	

geindre as PEINDRE

haïr as regular **-ir** verb, but *sing. Pres. Indic.*: hais, hais, hait.

inscrire as ÉCRIRE

interdire as DIRE but *2nd pl. Pres. Indic.* and *Imperat.*: interdisez.

introduire as CONDUIRE

joindre	join-s	joign-e
joignant	-s	-ions
joint	-t	-ent
joignis	joign-ons	
	-ez	
	-ent	

lire	li-s	lis-e
lisant	-s	-ions
lu	-t	-ent
lus	lis-ons	
	-ez	
	-ent	

luire as NUIRE

maudire as **-ir** verb, except *Past Part.*: maudit

médire as DIRE but *2nd pl. Pres. Indic.* and *Imperat.*: médisez

mentir as DORMIR (*Pres. Indic.*: je mens, etc.)

mettre	me-ts	mett-e
mettant	-ts	-ions
mis	-t	-ent
mis	mett-ons	
	-ez	
	-ent	

moudre	mou-ds	moul-e
moulant	-ds	-ions
moulu	-d	-ent
moulus	moul-ons	
	-ez	
	-ent	

mourir	meur-s	meure	*Fut.*: mourrai
mourant	-s	mourions	
mort	-t	meurent	
mourus	mour-ons		
	-ez		
	meurent		

mouvoir	meu-s	meuve	*Past Part.*:
mouvant	-s	mouvions	*fem.* mue,
mû	-t	meuvent	mues;
mus	mouv-ons		*masc.pl.*: mus
	-ez		
	meuvent		

naître	nais	naiss-e	*Fut.*: naîtrai
naissant	nais	-ions	
né	naît	-ent	
naquis	naiss-ons		
	-ez		
	-ent		

nuire as CONDUIRE but *Past Part.*: nui

offrir as OUVRIR (*Pres.Indic.*: offre, etc.; *Past Part.*: offert.)

ouvrir	ouvr-e	ouvr-e
ouvrant	-es	-ions
ouvert	-e	-ent
ouvris	-ons	
	-ez	
	-ent	

paître as CONNAÎTRE but no *Past Part.* or *Past Hist.*

paraître as CONNAÎTRE

partir as DORMIR (*Pres.Indic.*: pars, etc.)

peindre	pein-s	peign-e
peignant	-s	-ions
peint	-t	-ent
peignis	peign-ons	
	-ez	
	-ent	

percevoir as RECEVOIR

plaindre as CRAINDRE

plaire plaisant plu (invar.) plus	plais plais plaît plais-ons -ez -ent	plais-e -ions -ent	
pleuvoir (impers.) pleuvant plu plut	pleut	pleuve	also (fig. and pers.) *Imperat.*: pleus pleuvons pleuvez; *Pres. Indic.*: pleuvent

pourvoir as VOIR but *Past Hist.*: pourvus; *Fut.*: pourvoirai.

pouvoir pouvant pu pus	peux (or) puis peux peut pouv-ons -ez peuvent	puiss-e -ions -ent	No *Imperat.*, but *Pres. Subjunc.* used optatively; e.g. *puissiez-vous réussir* = may you succeed; *Fut.*: pourrai
prendre prenant pris pris	pren-ds -ds -d -ons -ez prennent	prenne prenions prennent	

prédire as DIRE but *2nd pl. Pres. Indic.* and *Imperat.*: prédisez

prévaloir as VALOIR but *Pres. Subjunct.*: prévale, etc.

prévoir as VOIR but *Fut.*: prévoirai

produire as CONDUIRE

recevoir recevant reçu reçus	reç-ois -ois -oit recev-ons -ez reçoivent	reçoive recevions reçoivent	*Fut.*: recevrai

réduire as CONDUIRE

renaître as NAÎTRE (but found only in Compound Tenses)

repaître as CONNAÎTRE

(**se**) **repentir** as DORMIR (*Pres. Indic.*: je me repens, etc.)

requérir as ACQUÉRIR

résoudre as ABSOUDRE, but *Past Part.*: résolu (occ.: résous, résoute)

ressortir (= go out again) as SORTIR

ressortir (= come under the jurisdiction (*de*, of)) as regular **-ir** verb

restreindre as PEINDRE

rire	ri-s	ri-e
riant	-s	-ions
ri	-t	-ent
ris	-ons	
	-ez	
	-ent	

rompre regular except *Pres. Indic.*: il rompt

savoir	sai-s	sach-e	*Imperf.*: savais;
sachant	-s	-ions	*Fut.*: saurai
su	-t	-ent	
sus	sav-ons		
	-ez		
	-ent		

sentir as DORMIR (*Pres. Indic.*: sens, etc.)

servir as DORMIR (*Pres. Indic.*: sers, etc.)

sortir as DORMIR (*Pres. Indic.*: sors, etc.)

souffrir as OUVRIR (*Pres. Indic.*: souffre, etc.; *Past Part.*: souffert)

soustraire as TRAIRE

suffire	suffi-s	suffis-e
suffisant	-s	-ions
suffi	-t	-ent
suffis	-sons	
	-sez	
	-sent	

suivre	sui-s	suiv-e	
suivant	-s	-ions	
suivi	-t	-ent	
suivis	-vons		
	-vez		
	-vent		
surseoir	sursoi-s	sursoie	*Fut.*: surseoirai
sursoyant	-s	sursoyions	
sursis	-t	sursoient	
sursis	sursoy-ons		
	-ez		
	sursoient		

taire as PLAIRE, but *Pres. Indic.*: il tait; *Past Part. fem.*: tue

teindre as PEINDRE

tenir as VENIR

traduire as CONDUIRE

traire	trai-s	traie	
trayant	-s	trayions	
trait	-t	traient	
(none)	tray-ons		
	-ez		
	traient		

tressaillir as ASSAILLIR

vaincre	vain-cs	vainqu-e	
vainquant	-cs	-ions	
vaincu	-c	-ent	
vainquis	-quons		
	-quez		
	-quent		
valoir	vau-x	vaille	*Fut.*: vaudrai
valant	-x	valions	
valu	-t	vaillent	
valus	val-ons		
	-ez		
	-ent		

venir venant venu vins	vien-s -s -t ven-ons -ez viennent	vienne venions viennent	*Fut.*: viendrai *3rd sing. Imperf. Subjunc.*; vînt
vêtir vêtant vêtu vêtis	vê-ts -ts -t -tons -tez -tent	vêt-e -ions -ent	
vivre vivant vécu vécus	vi-s -s -t viv-ons -ez -ent	viv-e -ions -ent	
voir voyant vu vis	voi-s -s -t voy-ons -ez voient	voie voyions voient	*Fut.*: verrai
vouloir voulant voulu voulus	veu-x -x -t voul-ons -ez veulent	veuille voulions veuillent	*Imperat.*: regular, or: veuille veuillons veuillez; *Fut.*: voudrai

DEFECTIVE VERBS

These verbs are only found in the tenses and persons listed below. (Very rare forms have been omitted.)

accroire *Infin.* only.

attraire *Infin.* only.

braire *Pres. Indic.*: brait, braient; *Fut.*: braira.

bruire *Pres. Part.*: bruissant; *Pres. Indic.*: bruit; *Imperf.*: bruiss-ait, -aient.

chaloir *Pres. Indic.*: chaut.

choir *Past Part.*: chu; *Pres. Indic.*: choi-s, -s, -t, -ent; *Past Hist.*: chut.

clore *Pres. Part.*: closant; *Past Part.*: clos; *Pres. Indic.*: clos, clos, clôt, closent; *Imperat.*: clos; *Fut.* and *Condit.* clorai(s), etc.; *Pres. Subjunc.*: close, etc.

échoir *Pres. Part.*: échéant; *Past Part.*: échu; *Past Hist.*: échut; *Fut.*: échoira; (or obs.) écherra; *Condit.*: échoir-ait, -aient; (or obs.) écherr-ait, -aient.

écloper *Past Part.*: éclopé

éclore *Past Part.*: éclos; *Pres. Indic.*: éclot, éclosent; *Fut.*: éclor-a, -ont; *Condit.*: éclor-ait, -aient; *Pres. Subjunc.*: éclos-e, -ent.

enclore as CLORE.

faillir Compound Tenses and *Past Part.*: failli; *Fut.* and *Condit.*: faillirai(s), etc.; *Past Hist.* faillis, etc.

férir *Past Part.*: féru.

forfaire *Past Part.*: forfait.

frire *Pres. Indic.* fri-s, -s, -t; Compound Tenses and *Past Part.*: frit.

gésir *Pres. Part.*: gisant; *Pres. Indic.*: gis, gis, gît, gis-ons, -ez, -ent; *Imperf.*: gisais, etc.

oindre *Past Part.*: oint (but see also POINDRE).

poindre *Pres. Indic.*: point; *Fut.*: poindra; also in proverb: *poignez vilain, il vous oindra.*

promouvoir *Pres. Part.*: promouvant; Compound Tenses and *Past Part.*: promu.

quérir *Infin.* only.

ravoir (fam.) *Fut.* and *Condit.* raurai(s), etc.

seoir *Pres. Part.*: seyant; *Past Part.*: sis; *Pres. Indic.*: sied, siéent; *Pres. Subjunc.*: siée, siéent; *Imperf.*: sey-ait, -aient; *Fut.*: siéra; *Condit.*: siér-ait, -aient.

D. ABBREVIATIONS USED IN THE DICTIONARY

abbrev. abbreviation, acronym
adj. adjective, etc.
admin./istration
adv./erb(ial)
aeron./autics
agric./ulture
alg./ebra
anat./omy
anc./ient
ant./iquity
anthrop./ology
approx./imately
arch./itecture
archaeol./ogy
arith./metic
art./icle
artill./ery
astrol./ogy
astron./omy
astronaut./ics

bibl./ical
biochem./istry
biol./ogy
bookb./inding
book-keep./ing
bot./any
build./ing
butch./ery

c./entury
carp./entry
Cath. Roman Catholic
cent./ury
chem./istry
child. children's, childish
cin./ema
civ./il(ian)
comm./erce
comp./ound
conch./ology
condit./ional
conj./unction
constr./uction
cook./ery
crust./acea

danc./ing
def./inite
dem./onstrative
dial./ect
diplom./acy
dressm./aking

econ./omics
eccles./iastic
electr. electricity, electronics
Eng./lish
eng./ineering
engr./aving
ent./omology
esp./ecially
ethn./ology
euphem./ism
exc./ept

f./eminine
falc./onry
fam./iliar
fem./inine
fenc./ing
feud./al
fig./urative(ly)
fin./ance
fish./ing
forest./ry
fort./ification
Fr./ench
fut./ure

g./ram(s)
G.B. Great Britain
geog./raphy
geol./ogy
geom./etry
Gr./eek
gram./mar
gymn./astics

herald./ry
hist./ory
horol./ogy
hort./iculture
hunt./ing
hydr./aulics

i./ntransitive
ichth./yology
imperat./ive
imperf./ect
impers./onal(ly)
ind./efinite
indic./ative
indust./ry
infin./itive
int./errogative(ly)
interj./ection
invar./iable

iron./ically
irreg./ular(ly)

join./ery

kg kilogram(s)
km kilometre(s)

lang. language, linguistics
lit./eral(ly)
Lit. literature, literary
liturg./ical
loc./ution
log./ic

m./asculine
masc./uline
mason./ry
math./ematics
mech./anics
med./icine
metall./urgy
meteor./ology
mil./itary
min./eralogy
mod./ern
moll./usca
mus./ic
myth./ology

naut./ical
nav./al
needlew./ork
neg./ative
num./eral

obj./ect
obs. obsolete, obsolescent, archaic
occ./asionally
onom./atopoeic
opp./osite
opt./ics
ord./inal
ornith./ology

p./erson(al)
p.p. past participle
paint./ing
palaeont./ology
parl./iament(ary)
part./iciple

pathol./ogy
pej./orative
pers./on(al)
pharm./acy, etc.
phil./osophy
phon./etics
photo./graphy, etc.
phys./ics
physiol./ogy
pl./ural
poet./ic(al)
pol./itics
pop./ular
poss./essive
prep./osition
pres./ent
print./ing
pron./oun
pros./ody
psychol./ogy

qch. quelque chose
qn. quelqu'un

rail./way
rel./ative
relig./ion
refl./exive
rhet./oric
rid./ing
Rom./an

s. substantive, noun
sci./ence
sculpt./ure
sing./ular
s.o. someone
sth. something
subjunc./tive
surg./ery
surv./eying

t./ransitive
techn./ical
teleph./ony, etc.
text./ile(s)
theatr./ical
theol./ogy
TV television
typ./ography

U.K. United Kingdom
U.S. United States (of America)
usu./ally

v./erb
vet./erinary
vulg./ar

zool./ogy

A

A, a [ɑ] *s.m.* the letter A, a; *ne savoir ni a ni b,* to be hopelessly ignorant; *prouver par a plus b,* to demonstrate mathematically, to prove conclusively.

a [a] 3rd sing. pres. indic. AVOIR.

à [a] *prep.* (contracts with the definite articles *le* and *les* to *au* and *aux* respectively). **1.** (place: 'to', 'into', 'at', 'in', 'on') ~ *la gare,* to or at the station; ~ *Paris,* to or in Paris; *au Japon,* to or in Japan; ~ *droite,* to or on the right; ~ *terre,* to or on the ground; *monter au grenier,* to go up into the attic; *au toit,* to or on the roof; *au mur,* on or against the wall; ~ *la campagne,* to or in the country; ~ *sa chambre,* to or in one's room; *au deuxième étage,* to or on the second floor; ~ *bord,* on board, *au bord,* to or at the edge; *porter* ~ *la main,* to carry in one's hand; *avoir mal au pied,* to have a pain in one's foot; *c'est* ~ *quelle distance?,* how far is it?; *on est* ~ *deux kilomètres de la gare,* we are two kilometres from the station; **2.** (place: 'from', 'off') *boire* ~ *la bouteille,* to drink from the bottle; *prendre sa veste au portemanteau,* to take one's jacket out of the wardrobe; **3.** (time: 'to', 'till', 'at', 'in', 'on') *du matin au soir,* from morning to night; *de dix* ~ *onze heures,* from ten till eleven; ~ *demain!,* till tomorrow!, see you tomorrow!; ~ *deux heures,* at two o'clock; *le 12 au soir,* on the 12th in the evening, on the evening of the 12th; ~ *ce moment-là,* at that moment; *au temps de,* at or in the time of; ~ *temps,* in or on time; *au printemps,* in spring; *au mois de,* in the month of; ~ *l'avenir,* in (the) future; ~ *son arrivée,* on his arrival; **4.** (price, rate, speed, frequency, distribution: 'at', 'by', 'in') ~ *quel prix?,* at what price?; *demain le pain sera* ~ *trois francs,* bread will be three francs tomorrow; *des timbres* ~ *deux francs,* two-franc stamps; ~ *toute vitesse,* at top speed; *rouler* ~ *110 km* ~ *l'heure,* to travel at 110 km an hour; ~ *l'année,* by the year; ~ *la douzaine,* by the dozen; *ils sont sortis* ~ *trois,* the three went out together; **5.** (means, method, manner: 'by', 'on', 'with') ~ *pied,* on foot; ~ *bicyclette,* by bicycle; ~ *la nage,* (by) swimming; *manger* ~ *la fourchette,* to eat with a fork; *marcher* ~ *grands pas,* to stride; *enfoncer* ~ *coups de marteau,* to hammer in, to drive in with a hammer; *il a abîmé la cloison* ~ *coups de pied,* he kicked in the partition; *au moyen de,* by means of; ~ *force de,* by dint of; *au hasard,* at random; ~ *la française,* in the French style; ~ *moi seul,* by myself; *on m'a reçu* ~ *bras ouverts,* I was received with open arms; ~ *peine,* with difficulty, hardly, scarcely; **6.** (method of operation) *une machine* ~ *vapeur,* a steam-engine; *une voiture* ~ *bras,* a hand-cart; **7.** (identification, attribute, qualification: 'with') *l'homme* ~ *la barbe,* the man with the beard; *des gens* ~ *teint foncé,* people with dark skins; *l'employé aux billets,* the ticket-man, the man with the tickets; *une maison* ~ *plusieurs succursales,* a firm with several branches; (theatr.) *une pièce à thèse,* a propaganda play, a play with a message; *du cognac* ~ *trois étoiles,* three-star brandy; **8.** (equipped with) *une chambre* ~ *grand lit,* ~ *deux lits,* a double room, a room with twin beds; *un matelas* ~ *ressorts,* a spring-mattress; *une table* ~ *rallonges,* an extending table; *un fauteuil* ~ *roulettes,* an armchair on castors; **9.** (possession) *c'est* ~ *moi,* ~ *Jean,* it is mine, John's; *un appartement* ~ *moi,* a flat of my own; ~ *qui la faute?,* whose fault is it?; **10.** (purpose, action to be done) *une tasse* ~ *thé,* a tea-cup; *une fourchette* ~ *homard,* a lobster-pick; (*qch.*) ~ *manger,* something to eat; *aider* ~ *faire,* to help to do; *apprendre* ~ *faire,* to learn to do; *beaucoup* ~ *faire,* a lot to do; *une lettre* ~ *écrire,* a letter to write; *des règles* ~ *observer,* rules to be observed; *prêt* ~ *partir,* ready to go; **11.** (direction of thought: 'of', 'on', 'in') *penser* ~, to think of; *réfléchir* ~, to reflect on; *s'intéresser* ~, to be interested in; **12.** (specifying activity, limiting application of adjective) *prendre plaisir* ~ *faire,* to take pleasure in doing; *s'occuper* ~ *faire,* to occupy oneself (in) doing; *réussir* ~ *son travail,* ~ *faire,* to succeed in one's work, in doing; *il est* ~ *travailler,* he is at work, he is busy working; *rester assis* ~ *méditer,* to sit meditating; *c'est difficile* ~ *faire,* it is difficult to do; *long* ~ *venir,* long in coming; *le premier* ~ *le remarquer,* the first to notice it; **13.** (classification, degree) *un homme* ~ *redouter,* a man to be feared; *il est* ~ *plaindre,* he is to be pitied; *laide* ~ *faire peur,* frightfully ugly; *s'ennuyer* ~ *mourir,* to be bored to death; *de l'argent* ~ *n'en savoir que faire,* more money than one knows what to do with; **14.** (conditional) ~ *vrai dire,* to tell the truth, as a matter of fact; ~ *tout prendre,* considering all things, taking it all in all; ~ *l'entendre parler on croirait,* to hear him talk you would think; **15.** (dative, indirect object: 'to', 'from', 'for', 'of') *donner* ~ *qn.,* to give (to) s.o.; *dire* ~ *qn.,* to say to s.o., to tell s.o.; *reconnaissant* ~, grateful to; *prendre, emprunter, ôter, arracher, qch.* ~ *qn.,* to take, borrow, remove, snatch, sth. from s.o.; *ce serait difficile* ~ *un enfant,* it would be difficult for a child; *c'est* ~ *vous de décider,* it is for you to decide; *le commissariat général au tourisme,* the central tourist agency; *c'est très aimable* ~ *vous,* it is very kind of you; **16.** (miscellaneous) ~ *mon avis,* in my opinion; *au voleur!,* stop! thief!; ~ *l'assassin!,* help! murder!; ~ *qui mieux mieux,* to see who could outdo the other; ~ *nous deux!,* come on, let's fight it out!

abaissable [abɛsabl] *adj.* that can be lowered.

abaissant, -e [abɛsɑ̃] *adj.* degrading.

abaisse [abɛs] *s.f.* rolled-out pie crust.

abaisse-langue [abɛslɑ̃g] *s.m.invar.* (surg.) tongue-depressor.

abaissement [abɛsmɑ̃] *s.m.* lowering, letting-down; lessening, reduction, fall, abatement, decrease; (obs.) disgrace, degradation; (geog.) subsidence, dip.

abaisser [abese] *v.t.* to lower, to let or pull down, to bring down; to lessen, to reduce, to abate; (cook.) to roll out; (fig.) to humiliate, to disgrace, to degrade; **s'**~ *v.refl.* to be lowered, to sink, to subside; to decrease, to abate; to slope or slant downwards; to stoop, to lower oneself, to condescend, to cringe, to cheapen oneself; *je ne m'abaisserai pas à me venger,* I will not stoop to revenge.

abaisseur [abɛsœr] *adj., s.m.* (anat.) depressor.

abajoue [abaʒu] *s.f.* (of monkeys, etc.) cheek-pouch.

abandon [abɑ̃dɔ̃] *s.m.* surrender, renunciation; forsaking, desertion; rejection, abandonment, giving-up; forlornness, destitution; carelessness, nonchalance; spontaneity, confidence; *dans un instant d'~*, in an unguarded moment; *à l'~*, neglected, uncared for.

abandonner [abɑ̃dɔne] *v.t.* to surrender, to give up, to hand over, to renounce, to resign, to relinquish; to desert, to forsake, to abandon; to reject; **s'~** *v.refl.* to neglect oneself, to let oneself go; to relax; to give way (*à*, to).

abaque [abak] *s.m.* (arch., math.) abacus.

abasourdir [abazurdir] *v.t.* to deafen, to astound, to dumbfound, to flabbergast.

abasourdissant, -e [abazurdisɑ̃] *adj.* astounding, overwhelming.

abasourdissement [abazurdismɑ̃] *s.m.* astonishment, amazement.

abat [aba] *s.m.* slaughtering, felling, striking-down; (pl.) offal, liver, lights, etc.; *une pluie d'~*, a sudden downpour.

abâtardir [abɑtardir] *v.t.* to debase, to corrupt, to make degenerate; **s'~** *v.refl.* to degenerate.

abâtardissement [abɑtardismɑ̃] *s.m.* degeneracy, debasement, decay.

abat-jour [abaʒur] *s.m.* shade, lamp-shade, reflector; (arch.) skylight.

abat-son [abasɔ̃] *s.m.* sounding-board.

abattage, abatage [abataʒ] *s.m.* felling (of trees); cutting-down, lopping (of branches); slaughtering (of animals); careening (of ships); (mech.) leverage, purchase; *avoir de l'~*, (of an actor) to be a lively performer, to keep the public on its toes.

abattant [abatɑ̃] *s.m.* flap, lid, leaf (of desk, counter, table); tip-up seat.

abattée [abate] *s.f.* (naut.) falling-off (to leeward); (aeron.) nose-dive.

abattement [abatmɑ̃] *s.m.* **1.** exhaustion, prostration, loss of energy; despondency, dejection, despair; **2.** (fin.) amount free of tax; *~ à la base*, tax-free allowance.

abatteur [abatœr] *s.m.* cutter, feller; *~ de besogne*, a great worker, a glutton for work.

abattis [abati] *s.m.* **1.** collection of felled trees, etc.; barricade made of trees, etc.; **2.** (pl.) giblets (of poultry); (*pop.*) arms and legs; *numéroter ses ~*, to make sure one is all in one piece (after an accident); (before a fight) *tu peux numéroter tes ~!*, you'd better watch yourself!

abattoir [abatwar] *s.m.* slaughter-house, abattoir.

abattre [abatr] *v.t.* to beat, knock, throw, pull, blow, or break down; to cut down, to fell (tree); to bring down (opponent); to extract (minerals); to slaughter (animals); to strike down, to assassinate, (persons); (aeron.) to shoot down; *la pluie abat la poussière*, the rain lays the dust; (fig.) to depress, to cast down, to dispirit, to dishearten; (naut.) to fall off (to leeward); *~ un navire en carène*, to careen a ship; *~ de la besogne*, to get through a lot of work; *~ son jeu, ses cartes*, to lay one's cards on the table; **s'~** *v.refl.* to fall down, to collapse; to come down (*sur*, upon), to pounce, to swoop down; to abate, to subside; *un cyclone s'est abattu sur la ville*, a cyclone burst on the town; *le vent s'abat*, the wind is dying down.

abattu, -e [abaty] *adj.* weak; dejected, depressed, cast down, despondent; *à bride ~e*, at breakneck speed.

abat-vent [abavɑ̃] *s.m.* cowl (on chimney); wind-break, weather-shield.

abat-voix [abavwa] *s.m.* sounding-board (over pulpit).

abbatial, -e (**aux**) [abasjal] *adj.* abbatial, pertaining to an abbey, abbot, or abbess.

abbaye [abɛi] *s.f.* abbey, monastery.

abbé [abe] *s.m.* **1.** abbot, head of an abbey; **2.** any ecclesiastic or priest (usually one without a parish); *monsieur l'~*, your reverence; *monsieur l'~ Durand*, Father Durand.

abbesse [abɛs] *s.f.* abbess.

A B C [abese] *s.m.* **1.** spelling book; **2.** rudiments, A B C, (of a subject).

abcès [apsɛ] *s.m.* abscess, gathering; (fig.) dangerous and unhealthy state of affairs.

abcéder [apsede] *v.i.* to form into an abscess, to gather, to come to a head.

abdication [abdikɑsjɔ̃] *s.f.* abdication, renunciation.

abdiquer [abdike] *v.i.* to abdicate, to give up; *~ v.t.* to renounce, to give up, to lay aside.

abdomen [abdɔmɛn] *s.m.* abdomen.

abdominal, -e [abdɔminal] *adj.* abdominal.

abduct-eur, -rice [abdyktœr] *adj.* abducent; **~eur** *s.m.* abductor.

abduction [abdyksjɔ̃] *s.f.* abduction.

abécédaire [ɑbesedɛr] *s.m.* primer.

abée [abe] *s.f.* (mill) sluice, flood-gate.

abeille [abɛj] *s.f.* bee.

aberrance [abɛrɑ̃s] *s.f.* (sci.) aberrance, anomaly.

aberrant, -e [abɛrɑ̃] *adj.* aberrant.

aberration [abɛrɑsjɔ̃] *s.f.* aberration.

aberrer [abere] *v.i.* to blunder, to be mistaken.

abêtir [abetir] *v.t.* to make stupid or dull; **s'~** *v.refl.* to grow stupid or dull.

abêtissant, -e [abetisɑ̃] *adj.* deadening, blunting, which renders stupid or dull.

abêtissement [abetismɑ̃] *s.m.* **1.** rendering stupid or dull; **2.** stupidity, dullness.

abhorrer [abɔre] *v.t.* to abhor, to detest, to loathe, to hate.

abîme [abim] *s.m.* abyss, abysm; chasm, gulf; deep, bottomless pit; mystery, ruin, perdition; unfathomable quantity, utmost degree; *courir à l'~* (or *aux ~s*), to run headlong to perdition; *sur le bord de l'~*, on the brink of ruin; *politique du bord de l'~*, brinkmanship; *un ~ d'ennuis*, a sea of troubles.

abîmé, -e [abime] *adj.* spoiled, damaged; (pop.) injured, disfigured.

abîmer [abime] *v.t.* to damage, to spoil, to make dirty, to ruin, (things); (pop.) to bash in; to hurt; to disfigure, to mark, (persons); **s'~** *v.refl.* **1.** to sink in, to be swallowed up in; (fig.) to be plunged in; **2.** to get spoiled, to get damaged, to get dirty, to decay; *l'avion vint s'~ dans la mer, sur les rochers*, the plane was swallowed up in the sea, came crashing on to the rocks; *s'~ la santé*, to ruin one's health.

ab intestat [abɛ̃tɛsta] *adj.loc.* (law) *héritier ~*, heir-at-law, next of kin; *succession ~*, intestate estate.

abject, -e [abʒɛkt] *adj.* abject, base, vile, despicable, mean.

abjection [abʒɛksjɔ̃] *s.f.* abjection, abjectness, meanness.

abjuration [abʒyrɑsjɔ̃] *s.f.* abjuration, recantation.

abjurer [abʒyre] *v.t.i.* to abjure, to renounce; to recant.

ablatif [ablatif] *s.m.* ablative.

ablation [ablɑsjɔ̃] *s.f.* (surg.) ablation, removal; (geol.) ablation, waste (of glacier or rock).

ablégat [ablega] *s.m.* sub-legate.

ableret [ablərɛ] *s.m.* square net for small fish.

ablette [ablɛt] *s.f.* (ichth.) bleak, ablet.

ablier [ablije] *s.m.* = ABLERET.

ablution [ablysjɔ̃] *s.f.* ablution, washing; *faire ses ~s*, to wash, to have a wash.

abnégation [abnegɑsjɔ̃] *s.f.* abnegation, self-denial, self-sacrifice; *faire ~ de soi-même*, to sacrifice oneself.

aboiement [abwamɑ̃] *s.m.* bark, barking, baying; (*fig., pej.*) baying, yapping, howling.

abois [abwa] *s.m.pl.* barking of dogs (surround-

ing wounded animal); *aux* ~, at bay; (fig.) with one's back to the wall.
abolir [abɔlir] *v.t.* to abolish, to repeal, to annul, to do away with.
abolition [abɔlisjɔ̃] *s.f.* abolition, abolishing, doing away with; repeal; **~nisme** [abɔlisjɔnism] *s.m.* abolitionism; **~niste** [abɔlisjɔnist] *adj., s.m.f.* abolitionist.
abominable [abɔminabl] *adj.* abominable, detestable, loathsome; **~ment** [abɔminabləmɑ̃] *adv.* abominably.
abomination [abɔminɑsjɔ̃] *s.f.* abomination, horror; *avoir qch. en* ~, to abominate sth., to find sth. abominable.
abominer [abɔmine] *v.t.* to abominate, to detest, to loathe.
abondamment [abɔ̃damɑ̃] *adv.* abundantly, plentifully, generously, copiously.
abondance [abɔ̃dɑ̃s] *s.f.* plenty, abundance; affluence, opulence; fluency, eloquence; *parler d'*~, *avec* ~, to speak extempore and eloquently; ~ *de biens ne nuit pas*, you can't have too much of a good thing; *corne d'*~, cornucopia, horn of plenty; *en* ~, in plenty, abundantly.
abondant, -e [abɔ̃dɑ̃] *adj.* abundant, plentiful, thick, rich; (of style) rich, eloquent.
abonder [abɔ̃de] *v.i.* to abound, to be numerous, to be plentiful; *il abonda dans mon sens*, he entirely agreed with me.
abonné, -e [abɔne] *adj.* subscribing; *s.m.f.* subscriber, season-ticket holder.
abonnement [abɔnmɑ̃] *s.m.* subscription, season-ticket; allowance; *prendre un* ~, to take out a subscription or season-ticket.
abonner [abɔne] *v.t.* to take out a subscription (for s.o.); **s'~** *v.refl.* to subscribe (*à*, to).
abord [abɔr] *s.m.* access, approach; air, manner; *d'un* ~ *facile*, easy of access, easy to approach; (pl.) vicinity, outskirts, surroundings; *au premier* ~, *de prime* ~, *dès l'*~, at first sight, immediately; *d'*~, first, firstly, above all; *tout d'*~, first of all, to begin with.
abordable [abɔrdabl] *adj.* accessible, approachable; (fam.) (of price) reasonable, within one's reach.
abordage [abɔrdaʒ] *s.m.* (nav.) boarding (as part of engagement).
aborder [abɔrde] *v.i.* to land, to arrive on land; ~ *v.t.* to board (vessel), to collide with (vessel); to reach (land); to attack; to accost, to address; *il m'a abordé poliment*, he addressed, approached me, politely; (fig.) to approach, to come to grips with, to tackle (a question, etc.).
aborigène [abɔriʒɛn] *adj.* aboriginal, indigenous; ~ *s.m.f.* aboriginal (pl. aborigines).
aborti-f, -ve *adj.* [abɔrtif] abortive.
abot [abo] *s.m.* hobble, fetter.
abouchement [abuʃmɑ̃] *s.m.* **1.** joining, juncture (of pipes, etc.); **2.** (obs.) meeting, contact.
aboucher [abuʃe] *v.t.* **1.** to join (pipes, tubes); **2.** to bring together, to put in contact with; **s'~** *v.refl.* to get in touch, to confer, (*avec*, with).
abouler [abule] *v.t.* (pop.) to fork out, to hand out (money).
aboulie [abuli] *s.f.* aboulia, loss of will-power resulting from nervous disorder.
about [abu] *s.m.* (carp.) tenon; metal collar for fitting needle to syringe.
aboutement [abutmɑ̃] *s.m.* joining end to end; end-to-end joint.
abouter [abute] *v.t.* to join end to end.
aboutir [abutir] *v.i.* **1.** to come to a successful conclusion, to succeed, to materialize; (med.) to come to a head, to burst; *ne pas* ~, to fail, to come to nothing; **2.** ~ *à* or *dans*, to terminate in, to lead (in)to; to abut on; (fig.) to come to, to lead to, to end in; to tend to; *cela n'aboutira à rien*, that will come to nothing, that won't achieve anything.
aboutissant [abutisɑ̃] *s.m.* **1.** *les tenants et les* ~*s*, the ins and outs; **2.** result, outcome.
aboutissement [abutismɑ̃] *s.m.* result, issue, end; (med.) gathering.
aboyer [abwaje] *v.i.* to bark, to bay, to yelp; (fig.) to cry out, to inveigh, (*contre, après*, against); *tous les chiens qui aboient ne mordent pas*, some people's bark is worse than their bite.
aboyeu-r, -se [abwajœr] *s.m.f.* **1.** dog which barks (often without attacking); person who snarls (at people); **2.** busker, hawker.
abracadabrant, -e [abrakadabrɑ̃] *adj.* (fam.) preposterous, extraordinary, incredible.
abrasi-f, -ve [abrasif] *adj.* abrasive.
abrasion [abrazjɔ̃] *s.f.* abrasion.
abrégé [abreʒe] *s.m.* abridgement, summary, abstract, digest, shortened version; *en* ~, in brief, in miniature, in shortened form, in telegraphic style.
abrégement [abrɛʒmɑ̃] *s.m.* abridging, summarizing, shortening.
abréger [abreʒe] *v.t.* to cut short, to curtail, to shorten; to summarize, to abridge; to abbreviate; *abrégez!*, be brief.
abreuvement [abrœvmɑ̃] *s.m.* watering (of animals).
abreuver [abrœve] *v.t.* **1.** to water, to give water to, (animals); (fig.) to overwhelm, to load with; ~ *d'injures*, to shower with abuse; *abreuvé de larmes*, bathed in tears; **2.** (techn.) to soak, to steep; **s'~** *v.refl.* (fam.) to drink to excess; to wallow (*de*, in).
abreuvoir [abrœvwar] *s.m.* trough, horse-pond, watering-place (for animals).
abréviati-f, -ve [abrevjatif] *adj.* serving to abbreviate.
abréviation [abrevjɑsjɔ̃] *s.f.* abbreviating, shortening; abbreviation.
abri [abri] *s.m.* shelter, cover, refuge, screen, shade; shack; dug-out; (fig.) protection, defence, concealment; *à l'*~, under cover, safe; *à l'*~ *de la pluie, du danger*, sheltered from the rain, from danger; *à l'*~ *d'un arbre*, under the shelter of a tree; (fig.) *à l'*~ *du besoin, de tout soupçon*, safe from want, from suspicion; *se mettre à l'*~, to take shelter; *mettre à l'*~, *donner* ~ *à*, to shelter, to protect, to keep safe; ~*-refuge*, air-raid shelter.
abricot [abriko] *s.m.* apricot; **~ier** [abrikɔtje] *s.m.* apricot-tree.
abrité, -e [abrite] *adj.* sheltered, protected from the wind.
abriter [abrite] *v.t.* to shelter, to shield, to cover, to shade, to protect; to take in (refugees, guests); ~ *contre*, to shelter from; **s'~** *v.refl.* to take shelter, to get under cover to take refuge; (fig.) *s'*~ *derrière qn., derrière la loi*, to take refuge behind s.o., in the law.
abrivent [abrivɑ̃] *s.m.* (agric.) wind-break.
abrogati-f, -ve [abrɔgatif] *adj.* abrogative, of abrogative effect; *loi* ~*ve*, law enacted in repeal of a previous law.
abrogation [abrɔgɑsjɔ̃] *s.f.* abrogation, repeal, cancellation, annulment.
abroger [abrɔʒe] *v.t.* to abrogate, to repeal, to cancel, to annul.
abrupt, -e [abrypt] *adj.* abrupt, rugged, steep, craggy; (fig.) blunt, rough, sharp; **~ement** [abryptəmɑ̃] *adv.* abruptly, roughly.
abruti, -e [abryti] *adj.* stupefied, stunned, dazed; (fam.) stupid; *s.m.f.* (fam.) blockhead, oaf.
abrutir [abrytir] *v.t.* to make stupid or brutish; to daze, to tire out; to degrade; ~ *de fatigue*, to tire to death; ~ *de travail*, to overwork; **s'~** *v.refl.* to become stupid or brutish, to sink to the level of a beast.

abrutissant, -e [abrytisɑ̃] *adj.* stupefying, degrading, tiring.

abrutissement [abrytismɑ̃] *s.m.* **1.** (obs.) animal-like existence; **2.** stupefying; reducing to the level of beasts.

a.b.s. [abeɛs] abbrev. *aux bons soins de*, c/o.

abscisse [apsis] *s.f.* (geom.) abscissa.

abscons, -e [apskɔ̃] *adj.* abstruse, obscure.

absence [apsɑ̃s] *s.f.* absence, non-attendance, non-appearance; lack, want; abstraction, absence of mind; *il a des ~s*, he has fits of absent--mindedness.

absent, -e [apsɑ̃] *adj.* absent, missing, out, away (from home); absent-minded; *s.m.f.* absentee; one who is absent or not present.

absentéisme [apsɑ̃teism] *s.m.* absenteeism.

absentéiste [apsɑ̃teist] *s.m.f.* habitual absentee.

(s')absenter [apsɑ̃te] *v.refl.* to absent oneself; to leave home or work (temporarily), to go out, to go away, to disappear.

absidal, -e [apsidal] *adj.* apsidal.

abside [apsid] *s.f.* apse.

absidiole [apsidjɔl] *s.f.* small apse.

absinthe [apsɛ̃t] *s.f.* (bot.) wormwood; absinth (liqueur).

absolu, -e [apsɔly] *adj.* absolute, complete, perfect, pure, ideal, unrestricted; peremptory, despotic, imperious; utter, downright; **~ment** [apsɔlymɑ̃] *adv.* absolutely, at all costs; strictly; arbitrarily, despotically; completely, thoroughly, flatly; *~ment!*, exactly! I quite agree; *~ s.m.* absolute; *dans l'~*, in vacuo, without reference to the circumstances.

absolution [apsɔlysjɔ̃] *s.f.* absolution, remission, forgiveness of sins, pardon.

absolutisme [apsɔlytism] *s.m.* absolutism.

absolutiste [apsɔlytist] *adj., s.m.* absolutist.

absolutoire [apsɔlytwar] *adj.* absolving, giving absolution.

absorbable [apsɔrbabl] *adj.* absorbable.

absorbant, -e [apsɔrbɑ̃] *adj.*; (fig.) absorbing, engrossing; *un travail ~*, work demanding complete concentration; *~ s.m.* absorbent.

absorber [apsɔrbe] *v.t.* to absorb, to imbibe, to suck up; to consume, to eat and drink; (fig.) to use up, to swallow up; to assimilate, to take over (a business); to engross, to absorb the attention of; **s'~** *v.refl.* to be swallowed up, to disappear in; (fig.) *être absorbé dans*, to be engrossed in, to be plunged in.

absorption [apsɔrpsjɔ̃] *s.f.* absorption, ingestion, swallowing, swallowing up; (comm.) take--over.

absorptivité [apsɔrptivite] *s.f.* absorptiveness.

absoudre [apsudr] *v.t.* to absolve, to remit (sins), to give absolution to, to excuse; to discharge, to acquit.

absoute [apsut] *s.f.* (Cath. liturg.) absolution.

(s')abstenir [apstənir] *v.refl.* to abstain, to refrain (*de*, from); to take no action or part; not to vote; *~ de*, to refuse (food, etc.); to go without, to give up; *dans le doute, abstiens-toi*, when in doubt, do nothing; *se sont abstenus...*, the following abstained....

abstention [apstɑ̃sjɔ̃] *s.f.* abstention; **~nisme** [apstɑ̃sjɔnism] *s.m.* refusal to vote; **~niste** [apstɑ̃sjɔnist] *adj.* non-voting; *s.m.f.* non-voter, abstainer.

abstinence [apstinɑ̃s] *s.f.* abstinence, fasting, observance of fast-days.

abstinent, -e [apstinɑ̃] *adj.* abstinent, abstaining.

abstracteur [apstraktœr] *s.m.* (fig.) one given to over-refinement of argument; *~ de quintessence*, a splitter of hairs.

abstracti-f, -ve [apstraktif] *adj.* tending to form abstract ideas.

abstraction [apstraksjɔ̃] *s.f.* abstraction; abstract idea; something unreal; *faire ~ de*, to set aside, to exclude; *~ faite de*, setting aside, leaving aside, excluding.

abstraire [apstrɛr] *v.t.* to abstract, to set aside, to separate, to exclude; **s'~** *v.refl.* to withdraw one's mind, to isolate oneself (mentally), to concentrate.

abstrait, -e [apstrɛ] *adj.* abstract, abstruse; **~ement** [apstrɛtmɑ̃] *adv.* abstractly, in the abstract; *~ s.m.* abstract; *dans l'~*, in the abstract.

abstrus, -e [apstry] *adj.* abstruse.

absurde [apsyrd] *adj.* absurd, incongruous, silly, preposterous, unreasonable; ridiculous; *démonstration par l'~*, 'reductio ad absurdum'; **~ment** [apsyrdəmɑ̃] *adv.* absurdly, unreasonably; *~ s.m.* absurdity, (the) absurd.

absurdité [apsyrdite] *s.f.* absurdity, unreasonableness; nonsense, ridiculous words or acts.

abus [aby] *s.m.* misuse, excessive use (of drink, etc.); abuse (of power, authority); *~ de confiance*, breach of trust; embezzlement, misappropriation; corrupt practice; (law) *appel comme d'~*, application for a writ of error, or of certiorari; (fam.) *il y a de l'~*, that's going too far.

abuser [abyze] *v.t.* to deceive, to mislead; *~ de*, to misuse, to make excessive use of, to use too freely, to take unfair advantage of; to seduce, to lead astray; to deceive, to mislead; *j'abuse de votre bonté*, I am trespassing on your kindness; *si ce n'était ~ de votre obligeance*, if it was not troubling you too much; **s'~** *v.refl.* to deceive oneself, to be deceived, to be mistaken; ⚠ not 'to abuse' in sense 'to revile'.

abusi-f, -ve [abyzif] *adj.* excessive, immoderate; incorrect; **~vement** [abyzivmɑ̃] *adv.* excessively, immoderately; wrongly, incorrectly.

abyssal, -e, (aux) [abisal] *adj.* abysmal, unfathomable, bottomless; (techn.) abyssal (more than 300 fathoms deep).

abysse [abis] *s.m.* abyss; (geog.) abyssal zone.

Abysinnie [abisini] *s.f.* (geog.) Abysinnia.

abyssinien, -ne [abisinjɛ̃], **abyssin, -e** [abisɛ̃] *adj., s.m.f.* Abyssinian.

acabit [akabi] *s.m.* (pej.) quality, nature, stamp; *des gens du même ~*, birds of a feather, people tarred with the same brush; *ces deux livres sont du même ~*, these two books are equally bad; *un gaillard de cet ~*, a fellow of that stamp.

acacia [akasja] *s.m.* (bot.) acacia.

académicien, -ne [akademisjɛ̃] *s.m.f.* academician, member of an, or the, Academy.

académie [akademi] *s.f.* academy; regional university board; *l'Académie*, the French Academy; drawing from the nude; nude model; (fam.) nude body; *elle a une belle ~*, she has a beautiful body.

académique [akademik] *adj.* academic, academical; scholarly, pedantic; **~ment** [akademikmɑ̃] *adv.* academically, in a pedantic manner.

académisme [akademism] *s.m.* conventionalism, lack of originality, adherence to classical convention.

(s')acagnarder [akaɲarde] *v.refl.* (obs.) to lead an idle life.

acajou [akaʒu] *s.m.* mahogany; *noix d'~*, cashew-nut.

acanthe [akɑ̃t] *s.f.* (bot., arch.) acanthus.

acariâtre [akarjɑtr] *adj.* peevish, contrary, cross-grained, sour, quarrelsome, shrewish.

acaule [akol] *adj.* (bot.) acaulous.

accablant, -e [akɑblɑ̃] *adj.* overwhelming, overpowering, crushing, oppressive; (of weather) sultry, sweltering.

accablement [akɑbləmɑ̃] *s.m.* despondency, prostration, dejection, exhaustion.

accabler [akɑble] *v.t.* to overwhelm, to overburden, to weigh down; to overpower, to overcome; to humiliate; to oppress; to depress, to dishearten; *accablé d'affaires*, overburdened with work; ~ *de bienfaits*, to overwhelm with kindness; *ne l'accablez pas!*, don't be too hard on him!

accalmie [akalmi] *s.f.* lull, breathing-space, respite.

accaparement [akaparmɑ̃] *s.m.* cornering, monopolizing; acquisition.

accaparer [akapare] *v.t.* (comm.) to buy up, to corner; to monopolize, to keep for oneself.

accapareu-r, -se [akaparœr] *adj.* tending to monopolize; reluctant to let (s.o.) go; *s.m.f.* one who monopolizes.

accastillage [akastijaʒ] *s.m.* (naut.) upper works of a ship.

accéder [aksede] *v.i.* ~ *à* **1.** to have entry or access to, to reach; (fig.) to arrive at, to achieve; **2.** (obs.) to accede (to treaty, etc.); **3.** to agree to (request, etc.), to subscribe to (agreement, etc.).

accélérat-eur, -rice [akseleratœr] *adj.* accelerating; ~**eur** *s.m.* accelerator.

accélération [akselerɑsjɔ̃] *s.f.* acceleration.

accélérer [akselere] *v.t.i.* to accelerate, to speed up, to hasten; ~ *le pas*, to put on speed, to move or act faster.

accent [aksɑ̃] *s.m.* **1.** accent, stress, pitch, emphasis; **2.** (sign) accent; **3.** tone, sound, voice; *mettre l'~ sur*, to emphasize, to underline, to stress; *prendre, avoir l'~*, to acquire, to have, the right accent.

accentuation [aksɑ̃tɥɑsjɔ̃] *s.f.* **1.** accentuation, stressing; prominence; **2.** accentuation, placing or use of accents.

accentué, -e [aksɑ̃tɥe] *adj.* **1.** accentuated, stressed, emphasized; strongly marked, prominent; **2.** accented, having an accent.

accentuer [aksɑ̃tɥe] *v.t.* **1.** to accentuate, to emphasize, to stress; to heighten, to set off, to underline; to intensify, to increase; ~ *son effort*, to redouble one's efforts; **2.** to put an accent (sign) on; **s'~** *v.refl.* to grow more marked, to become evident.

acceptable [aksɛptabl] *adj.* acceptable, welcome; satisfactory, passable.

acceptant, -e [aksɛptɑ̃] *adj.* accepting; *s.m.f.* acceptor.

acceptation [aksɛptɑsjɔ̃] *s.f.* acceptance.

accepter [aksɛpte] *v.t.* to accept, to receive; to admit, to agree to; to submit to, to bear, to suffer; ~ *de*, to agree to; *il a accepté de venir*, he agreed to come; ~ *que*, to allow; *je n'accepte pas qu'on me parle sur ce ton*, I will not be spoken to like that.

accepteur [aksɛptœr] *adj.*, *s.m.* acceptor.

acception [aksɛpsjɔ̃] *s.f.* acceptation, meaning, sense; *dans toute l'~ du mot*, in the full sense of the word; *sans ~ de*, taking no account of; *sans ~ de personnes*, without favour, without showing personal preference.

accès [aksɛ] *s.m.* **1.** access, approach, admittance, entry, entrance, passage, channel; ~ *interdit*, no entry, no admittance; *d'un ~ facile*, easily approachable, easily accessible; **2.** attack, bout; fit.

accessibilité [aksesibilite] *s.f.* accessibility.

accessible [aksesibl] *adj.* accessible, approachable, available, easily influenced.

accession [aksɛsjɔ̃] *s.f.* **1.** accession; **2.** attainment, achieving; **3.** adherence (to a treaty); **4.** (law) accession, addition, accretion.

accessit [aksesit] *s.m.* honourable mention (in examination, etc.).

accessoire [akseswar] *adj.* accessory, additional, subsidiary, secondary, subordinate; inessential, unimportant; ~**ment** [akseswarmɑ̃] *adv.* in addition, as an extra; ~ *s.m.* accessory; (pl.) stage properties; *~s de toilette*, toiletries, beauty aids.

accessoiriste [akseswarist] *s.m.f.* (theatr., etc.) property-man.

accident [aksidɑ̃] *s.m.* accident, chance, incident; mishap, misfortune, reverse; unevenness, irregularity in structure; *~s de terrain*, broken ground, undulations; (med.) unexpected symptom complication; (mus.) accidental; (lang.) accidence; *par ~*, by accident, accidentally.

accidenté, -e [aksidɑ̃te] *adj.* uneven, broken, diversified, undulating, hilly; (of life, career) eventful, chequered; (fam.) (car) damaged in an accident.

accidentel, -le [aksidɑ̃tɛl] *adj.* accidental, occasional, inessential, unexpected; (mus.) accidental; ~**lement** [aksidɑ̃tɛlmɑ̃] *adv.* accidentally, unexpectedly, by chance.

acclamation [aklamɑsjɔ̃] *s.f.* acclamation, acclaim, cheers, shout, applause; *voté par ~*, carried by acclamation.

acclamer [aklame] *v.t.* to acclaim, to applaud, to greet with cheers.

acclimatable [aklimatabl] *adj.* that can be acclimatized, that can adapt to the climate.

acclimatation [aklimatɑsjɔ̃] *s.f.* acclimatization; *jardin d'~*, zoological garden, zoo.

acclimatement [aklimatmɑ̃] *s.m.* acclimatization; (fig.) adaptation.

acclimater [aklimate] *v.t.* to acclimatize; (fig.) to introduce, to import (custom, etc.); **s'~** *v.refl.* to become acclimatized, to adapt oneself.

accointance [akwɛ̃tɑ̃s] *s.f.* **1.** (obs.) familiarity; **2.** acquaintance, connection; *avoir des ~s*, to have connections, contacts.

accolade [akɔlad] *s.f.* embrace, accolade; *donner, recevoir, l'~*, to dub, to be dubbed, a knight; (print.) brace, bracket; (mus.) accolade.

accolage [akɔlaʒ] *s.m.* (agric.) tying-up (of vines, etc).

accoler [akɔle] *v.t.* **1.** (obs.) to embrace, to hug; **2.** to place side by side, to couple; to tie up (vines); *je n'aime pas voir mon nom accolé au sien*, I don't like to see my name coupled with his.

accommodant, -e [akɔmɔdɑ̃] *adj.* accommodating, obliging, tractable, easy to deal with; *il n'est guère ~*, he won't meet one halfway, he is not very helpful.

accommodation [akɔmɔdɑsjɔ̃] *s.f.* adjustment, adaptation; accommodation, arrangement.

accommodement [akɔmɔdmɑ̃] *s.m.* compromise, conciliation, settlement; *trouver des ~s* to find a compromise, to come to terms.

accommoder [akɔmɔde] *v.t.* to adapt, to adjust, to make suitable; (cook.) to prepare, to dress, to season; (obs.) to conciliate; (obs.) to ridicule (a person); **s'~** *v.refl.* to adapt oneself, to come to terms (with); *s'~ de*, to accept, to make do with, to put up with.

accompagnat-eur, -rice [akɔ̃paɲatœr] *s.m.f.* **1.** (mus.) accompanist; **2.** guide(-companion).

accompagnement [akɔ̃paɲmɑ̃] *s.m.* **1.** accompanying, attendance, escort; **2.** accompaniment, appendage, consequence; (cook.) garnish, dressing; (mus.) accompaniment.

accompagner [akɔ̃paɲe] *v.t.* to accompany, to go with, to escort; (fig.) to go with, to suit, to match; (mus.) to accompany; *tous nos voeux l'accompagnent*, all our wishes go with him; **s'~** *v.refl.* (rare) to keep one another company; to take place at the same time, to go together; *s'~ de*, to be accompanied by, to involve, to have (sth.) as a consequence.

accompli, -e [akɔ̃pli] *adj.* perfect, accomplished, thorough, consummate; completed, finished; *il a vingt ans ~s*, he is over twenty.
accomplir [akɔ̃plir] *v.t.* to achieve, to accomplish, to complete, to finish; to carry out, to fulfil, to put into effect; to obey; **s'~** *v.refl.* to take place, to happen, to be fulfilled.
accomplissement [akɔ̃plismɑ̃] *s.m.* achievement, execution, fulfilment, completion, accomplishment.
accord [akɔr] *s.m.* agreement, harmony, unity, concord; settlement, pact; arrangement, compromise; permission, authorization, consent; (mus.) chord; tuning, pitch; *donner son ~*, to give one's consent; *d'~*, in agreement; (mus.) in tune; *tomber* or *se mettre d'~*, to come to an agreement; *d'~!*, (pop.) *d'acc!*, agreed!, O.K.!; *en ~*, in harmony; **~ailles** [akɔrdɑj] *s.f.pl.* (obs.) betrothal.
accordé, -e [akɔrde] *adj.*, *s.m.f.* betrothed, fiancé(e).
accordéon [akɔrdeɔ̃] *s.m.* accordion.
accordéoniste [akɔrdeɔnist] *s.m.f.* accordion--player.
accorder [akɔrde] *v.t.* **1.** to reconcile, to make agree; (obs.) to conciliate; to harmonize, to match; to unite, to combine; (mus.) to tune; **2.** to admit, to recognize, to confess; **3.** to agree to, to allow, to grant, to confer; to give, to attach; (fig.) *accordez vos flûtes* or *vos violons*, settle your differences; *je vous l'accorde*, I grant you that, I admit it; *on m'a accordé un délai*, I have been allowed some respite; *il n'y accordait aucune importance*, he attached no importance to it; **s'~** *v.refl.* to agree, to be in agreement or harmony, to be reconciled; to permit oneself (sth.).
accordeur [akɔrdœr] *s.m.* **1.** (obs.) conciliator; **2.** (piano, organ) tuner.
accordoir [akɔrdwar] *s.m.* tuning-key.
accore [akɔr] *s.m.* (naut., obs.) prop, stay; *~ adj.* (of coastline) abrupt, sheer.
accort, -e [akɔr] *adj.* **1.** (obs.) clever; **2.** lively, agreeable.
accostable [akɔstabl] *adj.* **1.** (pop.) who can be accosted; **2.** (naut.) (of shore, jetty, etc.) approachable.
accostage [akɔstaʒ] *s.m.* **1.** (fam.) accosting; **2.** (naut.) coming alongside.
accoster [akɔste] *v.t.* **1.** to accost, to speak to (esp. a stranger); **2.** (naut.) to come alongside.
accotement [akɔtmɑ̃] *s.m.* space between highway or wall and ditch; verge, hard-shoulder.
accoter [akɔte] *v.t.* **1.** (obs.) to prop up; **2.** to lean to one side; **s'~** *v.refl.* to lean (*à*, against).
accotoir [akɔtwar] *s.m.* head-rest, arm-rest.
accouchée [akuʃe] *s.f.* woman who has just given birth, mother.
accouchement [akuʃmɑ̃] *s.m.* childbirth, delivery, labour, confinement; *maison d'~*, maternity home.
accoucher [akuʃe] *v.i.* to give birth; *~ de*, to give birth to, to be delivered of; *~ v.t.* to deliver; (fig.) to produce (with much labour); *~ d'un mauvais roman*, to produce a bad novel; (pop.) to make oneself clear, to speak; *alors, tu accouches!*, come on, let's hear it.
accoucheu-r, -se [akuʃœr] *s.m.f.* obstetrician; midwife.
accoudement [akudmɑ̃] *s.m.* leaning or resting one's elbows.
(s')accouder [akude] *v.refl.* to put one's elbows, to rest with one's elbow(s), (*à*, *sur*, on, against).
accoudoir [akudwar] *s.m.* elbow-rest, arm-rest.
accouer [akwe] *v.t.* to tie horses head to tail (by a halter).
accouple [akupl] *s.f.* leash.
accouplement [akupləmɑ̃] *s.m.* **1.** (obs.) pairing; **2.** coupling, connection; copulation, mating; (techn.) *barre d'~*, coupling-rod.
accoupler [akuple] *v.t.* to pair; to couple, to connect; to yoke (oxen to plough); to mate; **s'~** *v.refl.* to copulate, to mate.
accourcir [akursir] *v.t.* (obs.) to shorten (see RACCOURCIR); *~ v.i.* to become shorter.
accourcissement [akursismɑ̃] *s.m.* (obs.) shortening, becoming shorter.
accourir [akurir] *v.i.* to rush up, to rush forward, to run up, to hasten.
accoutrement [akutrəmɑ̃] *s.m.* **1.** (obs.) clothes; **2.** strange or comic get-up.
accoutrer [akutre] *v.t.* **1.** (obs.) to dress; **2.** to dress, to be got up, in ridiculous way.
accoutumance [akutymɑ̃s] *s.f.* adaptation, becoming used or inured to, familiarity; (med.) tolerance, immunization.
accoutumé, -e [akutyme] *adj.* accustomed; usual, customary, habitual; *à l'~e*, as usual.
accoutumer [akutyme] *v.t.* *~ à* to accustom to, to familiarize with, to get (s.o.) used to, to train to; **s'~** *v.refl.* to become accustomed, to get used, (*à*, to).
accouvage [akuvaʒ] *s.m.* (artificial) hatching, incubation (of eggs).
accréditer [akredite] *v.t.* to accredit (an ambassador); to give credibility to, to give currency to; *être accrédité auprès d'une banque*, to have a credit account at a bank; **s'~** *v.refl.* (of rumour, etc.) to spread, to gain credence.
accréditeur [akreditœr] *s.m.* guarantor, surety.
accréditif [akreditif] *s.m.* credit; letter of credit.
accroc [akro] *s.m.* tear, rent; (fig.) blot; snag, hitch.
accrochage [akrɔʃaʒ] *s.m.* hanging up, hooking up, coupling; slight collision (of cars); (mil.) brief engagement, incident; (mining) point of entry of a gallery into a shaft; (fam.) quarrel.
accroche-cœur [akrɔʃkœr] *s.m.* kiss-curl, love-lock.
accroche-plat [akrɔʃpla] *s.m.* plate-hanger.
accrocher [akrɔʃe] *v.t.* to catch on to, to hook on to, to collide with (a vehicle); to hang up; to hook, to catch, to obtain; to attract attention; *~ qn.*, to buttonhole s.o., to delay s.o.; **s'~** *v.refl.* to be hooked on; to hold on, to hold fast; to be attached to; (fam.) *s'~ à qn.*, to cling to s.o., to importune s.o.; (pop.) *tu peux te l'~*, you can whistle for it.
accrocheu-r, -se [akrɔʃœr] *adj.* tenacious; eye--catching; penetrating.
accroire [akrwar] *v.t.* *faire ~ qch.*, to pass sth. off as true; *en faire ~ à qn.*, to deceive, to delude s.o.; *s'en faire ~*, to deceive oneself; *s'en laisser ~*, to let oneself be deceived.
accroissement [akrwasmɑ̃] *s.m.* increase, extension, enlargement, development.
accroître [akrwatr] *v.t.* to augment, to enlarge, to increase, to amplify, to develop, to strengthen; **s'~** *v.refl.* to increase, to grow; (law) to accrue.
accroupi, -e [akrupi] *adj.* squatting, crouching.
(s')accroupir [akrupir] *v.refl.* to squat, to crouch.
accroupissement [akrupismɑ̃] *s.m.* squatting, crouching.
accru [akry] *s.m.* (hort.) sucker.
accrue [akry] *s.f.* **1.** land reclaimed (from water); **2.** extension of forest.
accu [aky] *s.m.* see ACCUMULATEUR.
accueil [akœj] *s.m.* reception, treatment; *faire bon ~ à*, to welcome; *faire mauvais ~ à*, to receive coldly, to cold-shoulder; *centre d'~*, reception centre (for travellers, refugees, etc.).
accueillant, -e [akœjɑ̃] *adj.* welcoming, friendly, hospitable.
accueillir [akœjir] *v.t.* to receive; to welcome, to give hospitality to; to accept (idea, etc.).

accul [aky] *s.m.* (obs.) backwater, blind-alley, corner.
acculer [akyle] *v.t.* to drive into a corner, to corner, to bring to bay; to drive, to force; *je les ai acculés à un aveu*, I forced them into an admission.
accumulateur [akymylatœr] *s.m.* accumulator, battery, (fam. abbrev. *accu*).
accumulation [akymylɑsjɔ̃] *s.f.* accumulation, piling-up; pile, heap, mass; (electr.) accumulation.
accumuler [akymyle] *v.t.* to accumulate, to amass, to heap up, to store, to collect.
accusat-eur, -rice [akyzatœr] *adj.* accusing; *s.m.f.* accuser, indicter, denouncer; *~eur public*, public prosecutor (during the Fr. Revolution).
accusati-f, -ve [akyzatif] *adj.*, *s.m.* accusative; *à l'~f.*, in the accusative.
accusation [akyzɑsjɔ̃] *s.f.* accusation, charge, indictment; prosecution; (law) *acte d'~*, bill of indictment; *chef d'~*, count of indictment; *porter une ~ contre*, to bring a charge against.
accusatoire [akyzatwar] *adj.* accusatory.
accusé, -e [akyze] *s.m.f.* the accused, the defendant; *~ de réception*, acknowledgement (of receipt); *adj.* marked, pronounced.
accuser [akyze] *v.t.* **1.** to accuse, to indict; to blame, to censure, to denounce; to deprecate; (law) to prosecute (in assize court); *~ de*, to charge with, to tax with; **s'~** *v.refl.* to accuse oneself, to blame oneself, to own up (*de*, to); **2.** to indicate, to show, to reveal; to underline, to stress, to accentuate; *le thermomètre accuse 35°*, the thermometer shows 35°; *elle accuse son âge*, she looks her age; *vêtement qui accuse les lignes du corps*, dress which shows off the figure.
acéphale [asefal] *adj.* acephalous.
acerbe [asɛrb] *adj.* sour, sharp; (usu. fig.) bitter, harsh, caustic, sarcastic.
acerbité [asɛrbite] *s.f.* bitterness, harshness.
acéré, -e [asere] *adj.* sharp, cutting, pointed; (fig.) biting, stinging.
acérer [asere] *v.t.* **1.** to face with steel; **2.** to sharpen.
acescence [asesɑ̃s] *s.f.* turning sour, acescency.
acescent, -e [asesɑ̃] *adj.* acescent, turning sour or acid.
acétate [asetat] *s.m.* (chem.) acetate.
acétification [asetifikɑsjɔ̃] *s.f.* acetification.
acétifier [asetifje] *v.t.* to acetify, to turn into vinegar.
acétique [asetik] *adj.* acetic.
acétone [asetɔn] *s.f.* (chem.) acetone.
acétylène [asetilɛn] *s.f.* acetylene.
A.C.F. [aseɛf] abbrev. *Automobile Club de France.*
achalandage [aʃalɑ̃daʒ] *s.m.* custom, clientèle.
achalandé, -e [aʃalɑ̃de] *adj.* well-patronized; well-stocked.
achalander [aʃalɑ̃de] *v.t.* to bring custom to; to supply with goods, to stock.
acharné, -e [aʃarne] *adj.* relentless, unremitting; furious, desperate; *~ à*, eager to, intent on.
acharnement [aʃarnəmɑ̃] *s.m.* fierceness, animosity, obstinacy; *avec ~*, desperately, doggedly.
acharner [aʃarne] *v.t.* **1.** (obs.) to incite (dogs, etc.); **2.** to excite; **s'~** *v.refl.* to persevere, to persist; to go furiously (at sth.); *il s'acharne*, he won't give up; *la malchance s'acharne sur lui*, he is dogged by ill-luck; *s'~ au travail*, to work unremittingly; *s'~ à poursuivre qch.*, to pursue sth. relentlessly.
achat [aʃa] *s.m.* buying; purchase; *faire l'~ de qch.*, to buy sth.; *prix d'~*, purchase price; *pouvoir d'~*, purchasing power.
ache [aʃ] *s.f.* (bot.) wild celery, smallage.
acheminement [aʃminmɑ̃] *s.m.* **1.** forwarding; **2.** way, path, progress.
acheminer [aʃmine] *v.t.* to forward, to send on; (fig.) to help forward; **s'~** *v.refl.* to make one's way, to proceed, (*vers*, towards); (fig.) to advance by degrees, to take a step forward.
acheter [aʃte] *v.t.* to buy, to purchase; (pej.) to buy (votes, etc.); to bribe s.o.; to pay dearly for; **s'~** *v.refl.* to be able to be bought; *la paix ne s'achète pas*, peace cannot be bought.
acheteu-r, -se [aʃtœr] *s.m.f.* purchaser, buyer; *je ne suis pas ~r, ~se*, I'm not in the market.
achevé, -e [aʃve] *adj.* perfect, accomplished, complete; (pej.) arrant, downright.
achèvement [aʃɛvmɑ̃] *s.m.* completion, conclusion.
achever [aʃve] *v.t.* to complete, to finish, to end, to bring to a successful conclusion; to finish off, to kill, to dispatch; to ruin completely; (fam.) to upset, to do for; *voilà qui va l'~*, that will finish him off; *~ de faire*, to finish doing; to end up by doing; to succeed in doing; **s'~** *v.refl.* to draw to an end, to come to an end, to be completed.
achillée [akile] *s.f.* (bot.) Achillea; milfoil, yarrow.
Achille [aʃil] *s.m.* Achilles.
achoppement [aʃɔpmɑ̃] *s.m.* obstacle; *pierre d'~*, stumbling-block.
(**s'**)**achopper** [aʃɔpe] *v.i.* & *refl.* to stumble; to come to grief; *s'~ à*, to bump into, to come up against.
achromatique [akrɔmatik] *adj.* achromatic.
aciculaire [asikylɛr] *adj.* (min., bot.) needle--shaped.
acide [asid] *adj.* acid, sour, sharp; bitter, biting; *~ s.m.* (chem.) acid.
acidifiable [asidifjabl] *adj.* acidifiable.
acidifiant, -e [asidifjɑ̃] *adj.* acidifying.
acidification [asidifikɑsjɔ̃] *s.f.* acidification.
acidifier [asidifje] *v.t.* to acidify; **s'~** *v.refl.* to become sour or acid.
acidimètre [asidimɛtr] *s.m.* acidimeter.
acidimétrie [asidimetri] *s.f.* acidimetry.
acidité [asidite] *s.f.* acidity, sourness; (fig.) bitterness.
acidose [asidoz] *s.f.* acidosis.
acidulé, -e [asidyle] *adj.* acidulated, acidulous; *bonbons ~s*, acid drops.
aciduler [asidyle] *v.t.* to acidulate, to make acid.
acier [asje] *s.m.* steel; *~ doux*, mild steel; *~ fondu*, cast steel; *~ laminé*, rolled steel; *~ inoxydable*, stainless steel; *~ chromé*, chrome steel; (fig.) *d'~*, as hard as steel.
aciérage [asjeraʒ] *s.m.* **1.** (obs.) conversion (of iron) into steel; **2.** steeling, steel-facing, galvanizing.
aciérer [asjere] *v.t.* **1.** to convert (iron) into steel; **2.** to cover with a layer of steel, to steel--face, to galvanize.
aciérie [asjeri] *s.f.* steel-works.
aclinique [aklinik] *adj.* aclinic.
acmé [akme] *s.m.* **1.** (med.) height, crisis (of illness); **2.** acme, apogee.
acné [akne] *s.m.* acne.
acolytat [akɔlita] *s.m.* (eccles.) highest of minor orders.
acolyte [akɔlit] *s.m.* (eccles.) acolyte; (pej.) accomplice.
acompte [akɔ̃t] *s.m.* partial payment in advance, payment on account, deposit; (fam.) foretaste of pleasures to come.
aconit [akɔnit] *s.m.* (bot.) aconite.
aconitine [akɔnitin] *s.f.* (chem.) aconitine.
acoquinement [akɔkinmɑ̃] *s.m.* (pej.) involvement.
(**s'**)**acoquiner** [akɔkine] *v.refl.* (pej.) to take up, to get involved (*avec*, with).
Açores (**Les**) [asɔr] *s.f.pl.* (The) Azores.

à-côté [akote] *s.m.* side-issue; fringe benefit; (fam.) perk.
acotylédone [akɔtiledɔn] *adj.* (bot.) acotyledonous.
à-coup [aku] *s.m.* jerk; *il y a des ~s dans le moteur*, the engine is mis-firing; *par ~s*, by fits and starts, stop-go.
acoustique [akustik] *s.f.* acoustics; *~ adj.* acoustic; *cornet ~*, ear-trumpet.
acquéreur [akerœr] *s.m.* buyer, purchaser.
acquérir [akerir] *v.t.* to acquire, to purchase, to buy; to get, to obtain, to get possession of; **s'~** *v.refl.* to be obtained; to obtain for oneself; *bien mal acquis ne profite jamais*, ill-gotten gains never prosper.
acquêt [akɛ] *s.m.* (law) acquisition; *communauté réduite aux ~s*, marriage settlement in which only later acquisitions are held in common.
acquiescement [akjɛsmɑ̃] *s.m.* acquiescence, consent.
acquiescer [akjese] *v.i.* to acquiesce, to consent, to accept, (*à*, in, to).
acquis [aki] *s.m.* experience, culture, wealth of knowledge, scholarship; *~ adj.* acquired (tastes, characteristics, etc.); *mon soutien vous est ~*, you can count on my support; *je vous suis tout ~*, I am entirely behind you; *il est ~ à notre projet*, he is in favour of our plan.
acquisiti-f, -ve [akizitif] *adj.* acquisitive.
acquisition [akizisjɔ̃] *s.f.* acquisition, purchase.
acquit [aki] *s.m.* receipt; *pour ~*, in full settlement; *par ~ de conscience*, to set one's mind at rest; *par manière d'~*, as a matter of form; *~ à caution*, (customs) bond.
acquittement [akitmɑ̃] *s.m.* **1.** payment (of debt); fulfilment (of obligation); **2.** acquittal.
acquitter [akite] *v.t.* **1.** to acquit, to discharge (a prisoner); to clear (from a debt, an obligation); **2.** to pay (debt, bill, etc.); to receipt (a bill); **s'~** *v.refl.* to pay one's debt(s), to discharge one's obligations; *s'~ de*, to discharge (debts, duties, etc.).
acre [akr] *s.m.* acre.
âcre [ɑkr] *adj.* acrid, sour, sharp; (fig.) painful; bitter.
âcreté [ɑkrəte] *s.f.* acridity, sourness, bitterness.
acrimonie [akrimɔni] *s.f.* acrimony.
acrimonieu-x, -se [akrimɔnjø] *adj.* acrimonious.
acrobate [akrɔbat] *s.m.f.* acrobat; (fig., pej.) expert, virtuoso.
acrobatie [akrɔbasi] *s.f.* acrobatics, stunt; (fig., pej.) virtuosity; *~ aérienne*, aerobatics.
acrobatique [akrɔbatik] *adj.* acrobatic.
acropole [akrɔpɔl] *s.f.* acropolis.
acrostiche [akrɔstiʃ] *s.m.* acrostic.
acrylique [akrilik] *adj.* (chem.) acrylic.
acte [akt] *s.m.* **1.** (law) document, instrument, deed, agreement, contract, certificate; (pl.) proceedings, transactions; *~ de naissance, de mariage, de décès*, birth, marriage, death, certificate; *prendre ~ de*, to register, to take note of; **2.** act, action, deed; writ, resolution, bill, decree; *faire ~ de*, to show, to give proof of; *faire ~ de présence*, to put in an appearance; **3.** (theatr.) act.
act-eur, -rice [aktœr) *s.m.f.* actor, actress, player, artist; protagonist.
acti-f, -ive [aktif] *adj.* active; energetic, busy; able-bodied; *dettes ~ves*, recoverable debts; **~vement** [aktivmɑ̃] *adv.* actively, energetically, briskly; (lang.) transitively; **~f** *s.m.* active (voice); (comm.) assets; credit side of account; (fig.) *avoir à son ~f*, to have to one's credit.
actinie [aktini] *s.f.* Actinia, sea-anemone.
actinique [aktinik] *adj.* actinic.
actinium [aktinjɔm] *s.m.* (chem.) actinium.
actino-mètre [aktinɔmɛtr] *s.m.* actinometer; **~thérapie** [aktinɔterapi] *s.f.* actinotherapy.
action [aksjɔ̃] *s.f.* **1.** act, action, deed; **2.** action, influence, effect; (mech.) movement, operation; **3.** activity, effort; (mil.) battle, encounter; *~ directe*, strike action; *~ catholique, etc.*, Catholic, etc., organization; **4.** lawsuit; *intenter une ~*, to bring a suit against s.o.; **5.** action, plot (of novel, etc.); **6.** share (in joint-stock company); *~ de capital*, preference share; *~ de jouissance*, scrip issue; (fam.) *ses ~s baissent, montent*, his stock is going down, is going up.
actionnaire [aksjɔnɛr] *s.m.f.* shareholder.
actionnement [aksjɔnmɑ̃] *s.m.* setting in motion, operation.
actionner [aksjɔne] *v.t.* **1.** (law) to bring an action against, to sue; **2.** to set in motion, to operate.
activation [aktivɑsjɔ̃] *s.f.* (sci.) activation.
activer [aktive] *v.t.* to quicken, to hasten, to expedite; to stimulate, to encourage; (chem.) to activate; **s'~** *v.refl.* to bustle about, to bestir oneself; (fam.) *allons, activons!*, come on, let's get a move on!
activité [aktivite] *s.f.* activity, energy, dynamism, spirit, vigour; acts, occupations.
actuaire [aktɥɛr] *s.m.f.* actuary.
actualisation [aktɥalizɑsjɔ̃] *s.f.* actualization.
actualiser [aktɥalize] *v.t.* to actualize.
actualité [aktɥalite] *s.f.* actuality; the present, current affairs; *l'~ politique, sportive*, the latest political, sporting, news; *~s*, news (esp. on film or T.V.); *~s télévisées*, T.V. news.
actuel, -le [aktɥɛl] *adj.* actual; present, current, contemporary, up-to-date; *à l'heure ~le*, at the present time; **~lement** [aktyɛlmɑ̃] *adv.* at present, currently; ⚠ not 'actual' as opposed to e.g. 'imaginary'.
acuité [akɥite] *s.f.* acuteness, sharpness, keenness, intensity.
acuminé, -e [akymine] *adj.* (bot.) acuminate.
acupuncture, acuponcture [akypɔ̃ktyr] *s.f.* acupuncture.
acutangle [akytɑ̃gl] *adj.* (geom.) with acute angles, acute-angled.
adage [adaʒ] *s.m.* adage, saying, proverb.
adagio [adadʒjo, adaʒjo) *adv., s.m.* adagio.
adamantin, -e [adamɑ̃tɛ̃] *adj.* adamantine.
adaptable [adaptabl] *adj.* adaptable.
adaptation [adaptɑsjɔ̃] *s.f.* adaptation, modification.
adapter [adapte] *v.t.* to adapt, to fit, to adjust, to modify; **s'~** *v.refl.* to adapt oneself, to acclimatize oneself; to be accommodating.
additi-f, -ve [aditif] *adj.* additive; **~f** *s.m.* additive, supplement.
addition [adisjɔ̃] *s.f.* **1.** addition, admixture; thing added, supplement; **2.** addition, adding-up, sum; **3.** bill (in restaurant).
additionnel, -le [adisjɔnɛl] *adj.* additional.
additionner [adisjɔne] *v.t.* **1.** (obs.) to increase; **2.** to add up; to add in, to add to; *additionné d'eau*, with water added.
adducteur [adyktœr] *adj.* adducent; *~ s.m.* adductor.
adduction [adyksjɔ̃] *s.f.* adduction; (techn.) channelling or piping of water; *~(s) d'eau*, water-supply, piping of water.
adénoïde [adenɔid] *adj.* adenoidal; *végétations ~s*, adenoids.
adent [adɑ̃] *s.m.* (carp.) tongued joint.
adenter [adɑ̃te] *v.t.* (carp.) to make tongued joint.
adepte [adɛpt] *s.m.f.* **1.** (relig.) believer, initiate; **2.** follower (of religion, doctrine).
adhérence [aderɑ̃s] *s.f.* adherence, adhesion, grip, roadholding (of tyres, etc.).
adhérent, -e [aderɑ̃] *adj.* adherent, adhesive; *s.m.f.* supporter, follower, member (of party, etc.).

adhérer [adere] *v.t.* ~ *à*, to adhere to, to stick to, to cling to; (fig.) to agree with (an idea); (international law) to subscribe to, to be a member of (U.N.O., etc.); to join, to be a member of (party, etc.).
adhési-f, -ve [adesif] *adj.* adhesive; **~f** *s.m.* adhesive.
adhésion [adezjɔ̃] *s.f.* (phys.) adherence; (fig.) concurrence, consent; (international law) subscribing to a treaty, etc.; membership (of party, etc.).
ad hoc [adɔk] *adj.* appropriate, specifically intended for use to which it is put; *un instrument* ~, an appropriate tool; (iron.) *c'est l'homme ~!*, he's the right man for the job!
adiante [adjɑ̃t] *s.m.* (bot.) Adiantum, maiden-hair fern.
adieu [adjø] (pl. **-x**) *interj.* farewell!, goodbye!; *dire ~ à qn.*, to take leave of s.o.; *dire ~ à qch.*, to write sth. off; *vous pouvez dire ~ à votre argent*, you can say goodbye to your money; ~ *s.m.* farewell, leave-taking; *faire ses ~x à*, to say goodbye to.
à-Dieu-va(**t**) [adjøva(t)] *interj.* it is in God's hands.
adipeu-x, -se [adipø] *adj.* adipose.
adiposité [adipozite] *s.f.* adiposity.
adjacent, -e [adʒasɑ̃] *adj.* adjacent, contiguous.
adjecti-f, -ve [adʒɛktif] *adj.* adjectival; **~vement** [adʒɛktivmɑ̃] *adv.* adjectivally; **~f** *s.m.* adjective.
adjoindre [adʒwɛ̃dr] *v.t.* to appoint, or add, (s.o. to an existing body); ~ *un bataillon*, to bring in a (new) battalion; **s'~** *v.refl.* to take on as assistant, to enlist, to enrol; *s'~ deux secrétaires*, to take on two (extra) secretaries.
adjoint, -e [adʒwɛ̃] *s.m.f.* assistant, deputy, collaborator; *~s au maire*, mayor's deputies; *directeur-~*, co-director.
adjonction [adʒɔ̃ksjɔ̃] *s.f.* addition.
adjudant [adʒydɑ̃] *s.m.* (mil.) warrant-officer, R.Q.M.S.; *~-chef*, R.S.M.; (*capitaine*) *~-major*, adjutant.
adjudicataire [adʒydikatɛr] *s.m.f.* successful bidder.
adjudicat-eur, -rice [adʒydikatœr] *s.m.f.* awarder of contracts.
adjudication [adʒydikɑsjɔ̃] *s.f.* adjudication; auction-sale.
adjuger [adʒyʒe] *v.t.* to grant, to award; to knock down (at auction); *adjugé!*, gone!; **s'~** *v.refl.* to claim, to take for oneself.
adjuration [adʒyrɑsjɔ̃] *s.f.* (theol.) adjuration; supplication.
adjurer [adʒyre] *v.t.* to adjure, to beseech, to beg, to pray, to entreat.
adjuvant [adʒyvɑ̃] *s.m.* adjuvant, additive; auxiliary, stimulant.
admettre [admɛtr] *v.t.* **1.** to admit, to allow to enter, to let in; *faire ~ qn.*, to introduce s.o. (to a society, etc.); **2.** to acknowledge, to accept, to concede, to admit, to suppose; *faire ~ une idée*, to get an idea accepted, adopted; *j'admets que*, I concede that; *en admettant que*, supposing that; **3.** to allow, to admit of; *il n'admet pas que tu fasses cela*, he won't allow you to do that; *cette règle n'admet aucune exception*, this rule admits of no exceptions.
administrat-eur, -rice [administratœr] *s.m.f.* administrator, manager, manageress, director, governor, trustee; guardian, overseer, executor.
administrati-f, -ve [administratif] *adj.* administrative; **~vement** [administrativmɑ̃] *adv.* administratively.
administration [administrɑsjɔ̃] *s.f.* **1.** administration, management, direction, government; **2.** committee, council, board, organization, (civil) service; *École Nationale d'~*, Civil Service College; **3.** trusteeship, guardianship; *conseil d'~*, governing body, board (of directors).
administrer [administre] *v.t.* **1.** to administer, to manage, to direct, to rule; **2.** to apply, to administer (medicine, sacrament); ~ *qn.*, to administer the last sacrament to s.o.; **3.** to produce legal evidence; **4.** (fam.) to give, to hand out; *sa mère lui a administré une bonne fessée*, his mother gave him a good hiding.
admirable [admirabl] *adj.* admirable, wonderful, marvellous; **~ment** [admirabləmɑ̃] *adv.* admirably, wonderfully, marvellously.
admirat-eur, -rice [admiratœr] *s.m.f.* admirer; ⚠ not 'admirer' in sense 'lover'.
admirati-f, -ve [admiratif] *adj.* admiring, full of admiration; **~vement** *adv.* admiringly, with admiration.
admiration [admirɑsjɔ̃] *s.f.* **1.** (obs.) wonder; **2.** admiration, enthusiasm; *faire l'~ de*, to be admired by; *être en ~ devant*, to regard with admiration; (fam.) to worship.
admirer [admire] *v.t.* **1.** (obs.) to marvel at; **2.** to admire, to enjoy; (iron.) *j'admire votre confiance*, I wish I had your confidence.
admissibilité [admisibilite] *s.f.* admissibility; eligibility.
admissible [admisibl] *adj.* **1.** (obs.) admissible, acceptable; **2.** tolerable, allowable; suitable for admission, who can be admitted, eligible, qualified (esp. to proceed to Part II of examination).
admission [admisjɔ̃] *s.f.* admission, admittance, entry.
admixtion [admikstjɔ̃] *s.f.* admixture.
admonestation [admɔnɛstɑsjɔ̃] *s.f.* admonition, reprimand.
admonester [admɔnɛste] *v.t.* to admonish, to reprimand, to remonstrate with.
admonition [admɔnisjɔ̃] *s.f.* (law) reprimand; (eccles.) admonition; rebuke.
adolescence [adɔlesɑ̃s] *s.f.* adolescence, youth.
adolescent, -e [adɔlesɑ̃] *adj.*, *s.m.f.* adolescent, teen-age(r).
Adonis[1] [adɔnis] *s.m.* Adonis; *un ~*, a handsome young man.
adonis[2] [adɔnis] *s.m.* (bot.) pheasant's eye; (ent.) a kind of butterfly.
(**s'**)**adoniser** [adɔnize] *v.refl.* (obs.) to bedeck oneself.
adonné, -e [adɔne] *adj.* addicted (*à*, to).
(**s'**)**adonner** [adɔne] *v.refl.* to devote, to apply, oneself wholly; to become addicted.
adopter [adɔpte] *v.t.* to adopt, to treat as one's own; to take over, to embrace (idea, etc.); to approve, to pass, to carry (a resolution, etc.).
adopti-f, -ve [adɔptif] *adj.* adoptive, by adoption; *enfant ~f, ~ve*, adopted child.
adoption [adɔpsjɔ̃] *s.f.* adoption; approval, passing (of bill); *d'~*, adopted; *pays d'~*, adopted country.
adorable [adɔrabl] *adj.* adorable, charming, divine; **~ment** [adɔrabləmɑ̃] *adv.* adorably, divinely.
adorat-eur, -rice [adɔratœr] *s.m.f.* worshipper, adorer; admirer, lover.
adoration [adɔrɑsjɔ̃] *s.f.* worship; adoration.
adorer [adɔre] *v.t.* to worship; to adore, to idolize.
ados [ado] *s.m.* (hort.) bank of earth (to protect young plants).
adosser [adose] *v.t.* ~ *à* or *contre*, to place (sth.) with its back to or against; to place back to back; **s'~** *v.refl.* to lean back (*à*, against).
adouber [adube] *v.t.* (obs.) to arm (knight for the ceremony of dubbing); (chess, draughts) to move piece provisionally (the words '*j'adoube*' establishing that the move is not yet definite).
adoucir [adusir] *v.t.* to soften, to smooth, to

soothe; to sweeten; to assuage, to alleviate; **s'~** *v.refl.* to grow mild(er), to soften, to mellow; *le temps s'adoucit*, the weather is getting milder.
adoucissage [adusisaʒ] *s.m.* smoothing, polishing (stone, glass, etc.).
adoucissant, -e [adusisɑ̃] *adj.* soothing, emollient; ~ *s.m.* emollient.
adoucissement [adusismɑ̃] *s.m.* softening (of water); increase (in temperature); (fig.) mitigation, consolation, assuagement.
adoucisseur [adusisœr] *s.m.* water-softener.
adragante [adragɑ̃t] *adj. gomme* ~, (gum-) tragacanth.
adrénaline [adrenalin] *s.f.* adrenalin.
adresse[1] [adrɛs] *s.f.* address, superscription; petition, vote of thanks; *il m'a donné une bonne* ~, he gave me the address of a good (restaurant, supplier, etc.); *à l'~ de*, intended for; *à mon* ~, intended for me.
adresse[2] [adrɛs] *s.f.* dexterity, skill, adroitness; shrewdness, cunning, diplomacy; *jeux d'~*, games of skill; *tour d'~*, trick.
adresser [adrese] *v.t.* to address, to direct (words, question, complaint); to send, to forward; to aim (a blow); ~ *la parole à qn.*, to speak to s.o.; **s'~ à** *v.refl.* to speak to, to apply to, to have recourse to; (fig.) to appeal to; to be addressed, directed at; *s'~ ici*, apply here; *c'est à vous que je m'adresse*, it's you I'm speaking to.
Adriatique [adriatik] *s.f.* (geog.) Adriatic (sea).
adroit, -e [adrwa] *adj.* dexterous, skilful, adroit, handy; shrewd, clever, cunning, artful; **~ement** [adrwatmɑ̃] *adv.* skilfully, adroitly; cunningly, artfully.
adulat-eur, -rice [adylatœr] *s.m.f.* adulator, flatterer, sycophant; *adj.* flattering, sycophantic.
adulation [adylɑsjɔ̃] *s.f.* adulation, flattery, sycophancy.
aduler [adyle] *v.t.* to adulate, to fawn on; to flatter.
adulte [adylt] *adj., s.m.f.* adult, grown-up, mature (person).
adultération [adylterɑsjɔ̃] *s.f.* adulteration, falsification.
adultère [adyltɛr] *adj.* adulterous; ~ *s.m.* adultery; ~ *s.m.f.* adulterer, adulteress.
adultérer [adyltere] *v.t.* to adulterate, to falsify.
adultérin, -e [adylterɛ̃] *adj.* adulterine.
advenir [advənir] *v.i. impers.* to happen, to occur; *advienne que pourra*, come what may.
adventice [advɑ̃tis] *adj.* adventitious, casual, incidental; *plantes ~s*, weeds.
adverbe [advɛrb] *s.m.* adverb.
adverbial, -e [advɛrbjal] *adj.* adverbial; **~ement** [advɛrbjalmɑ̃] *adv.* adverbially.
adversaire [advɛrsɛr] *s.m.* adversary, antagonist, opponent, enemy.
adversati-f, -ve [advɛrsatif] *adj.* (lang.) adversative.
adverse [advɛrs] *adj.* adverse, opposite, contrary, opposing; (law) *la partie* ~, the opposite side.
adversité [advɛrsite] *s.f.* adversity, misfortune.
adynamie [adinami] *s.f.* (med.) adynamia.
A.E. [ae] abbrev. *Affaires Étrangeres* = F.O.
A.E.L.E. [aeɛle] abbrev. *Association Européenne de libre échange*, E.F.T.A.
aérage [aeraʒ] *s.m.*, **aération** [aerɑsjɔ̃] *s.f.* airing, ventilation.
aérateur [aeratœr] *s.m.* ventilator.
aéré, -e [aere] *adj.* well-ventilated, airy.
aérer [aere] *v.t.* to let in air, to ventilate; to air (clothes); **s'~** *v.refl.* (fam.) to take a breather, to take a breath of air.
aérien, -ne [aerjɛ̃] *adj.* **1.** (obs.) airy, ethereal; gaseous; **2.** aerial, air(-), of air, by air, overhead; *voie ~ne à câble*, aerial rope-way; *transports ~s*, air transport; *par voie ~ne*, by air; *circuit* ~, (telephone) circuit carried on overhead wires; ~ *s.m.* aerial.
aérifère [aerifɛr] *adj.* ventilating.
aéro-club [aerɔklœb] *s.m.* flying club, flying school (civil aviation); **~drome** [aerɔdrom] *s.m.* aerodrome; **~dynamique** [aerɔdinamik] *s.f.* aerodynamics; *adj.* aerodynamic, streamlined; **~gare** [aerɔgar] *s.f.* airport reception buildings; air terminal.
aérolit(h)e [aerɔlit] *s.m.* aerolite, aerolith, meteorite.
aéro-modélisme [aerɔmɔdelism] *s.m.* building and/or flying of model aircraft; **~moteur** [aerɔmɔtœr] *s.m.* wind-driven engine; **~naute** [aerɔnot] aeronaut, pilot; **~nautique** [aerɔnotik] *adj.* aeronautic; *s.f.* aeronautics; **~navale** [aerɔnaval] *s.f.* Fleet Air Arm; **~nef** [aerɔnɛf] *s.m.* (obs.) airship; **~plane** [aerɔplan] *s.m.* (obs.) aeroplane; **~port** [aerɔpɔr] *s.m.* airport.
aéroporté, -e [aerɔpɔrte] *adj.* (mil.) airborne.
aérosol [aerɔsɔl] *s.m.* aerosol.
aérostat [aerɔsta] *s.m.* aerostat, balloon; **~ion** [aerɔstɑsjɔ̃] *s.f.* (obs.) aerostation, balloon--navigation; **~ique** [aerɔstatik] *s.f.* aerostatics; *adj.* aerostatic.
aérostier [aerɔstje] *s.m.* balloon-pilot.
aétite [aetit] *s.f.* (min.) aetites.
A.F.A.T. [aɛfate] abbrev. *auxiliaire féminine de l'armée de terre* = W.R.A.C.
affabilité [afabilite] *s.f.* affability, courteousness, courtesy, friendliness.
affable [afabl] *adj.* affable, courteous, gracious; **~ment** [afabləmɑ̃] *adv.* affably, courteously, graciously.
affabulation [afabylɑsjɔ̃] *s.f.* **1.** (obs.) moral (of a fable); **2.** plot (of a novel).
affadir [afadir] *v.t.* to deprive of savour or vigour.
affadissant, -e [afadisɑ̃] *adj.* reducing savour or vigour.
affadissement [afadismɑ̃] *s.m.* loss of savour or vigour.
affaiblir [afɛblir] *v.t.* to weaken, to make feeble, to debilitate; to impair, to diminish; to soften, to alleviate; **s'~** *v.refl.* to grow weaker, to decline, to flag; to abate.
affaiblissant, -e [afɛblisɑ̃] *adj.* weakening, debilitating.
affaiblissement [afɛblismɑ̃] *s.m.* weakening, debilitation; decrease, weakness; decline, decay.
affaire [afɛr] *s.f.* **1.** affair, business, matter; *c'est mon* ~, that's my business; *chacun son* ~, each to his own trade; *j'en fais mon* ~, I will see to it, I will deal with it; *j'ai là votre* ~, I have just the thing for you; (iron.) *je lui ferai son* ~, I will deal with him; (pop.) I will finish him off; *cela fera l'~*, that will do (be suitable); ~ *de cœur*, love affair; ~ *de conscience, de goût, etc.*, a matter or a question of conscience, of taste, etc.; **2.** difficulty, danger, problem; *c'est toute une* ~, it's quite a problem; ~ *d'une seconde, de rien*, a trifling matter; (fam.) *la belle ~!*, what a fuss for nothing!; *se tirer d'~*, to get out of a difficulty; *il est hors d'~*, he is out of danger; **3.** affair, situation, scandal, event; *étouffer une* ~, to hush up a scandal; **4.** (law) case; ~ *civile, criminelle, etc.*, civil, criminal, etc., case; **5.** transaction, speculation, deal, job, bargain; *faire une bonne* ~, to drive a good bargain; (fig.) ~ *d'or*, gold-mine; **6.** (pl.) business, commerce; *il est dans les ~s*, he is in business; *c'est un homme d'~s*, he is a businessman; *les ~s sont les ~s*, business is business; *pour ~s*, on business; *agent, cabinet, d'~s*, stockbroker('s office); **7.** *avoir ~ à*, to have dealings with; *avoir ~ à forte partie*, to be up against strong opposition; (fam.) *vous aurez ~ à moi!*, you will hear from me!; **8.** (pl.)

affairs; *~s publiques, étrangères, indigènes*, public, foreign, native, affairs; *mettre de l'ordre dans ses ~s*, to put one's affairs in order; *être bien, mal, dans ses ~s*, to be in good, in straitened, circumstances; **9.** (pl.) belongings, things; *il ne range jamais ses ~s*, he never puts his things away.

affairé, -e [afere] *adj.* busy, bustling, pretending to be busy.

affairement [afɛrmɑ̃] *s.m.* bustle, appearance of being busy.

(s')affairer [afere] *v.refl.* to bustle about, to appear to be busy.

affairisme [aferism] *s.m.* speculation.

affairiste [aferist] *s.m.* speculator.

affaissé, -e [afese] *adj.* sunk, collapsed, fallen in; (fig.) in low spirits.

affaissement [afɛsmɑ̃] *s.m.* subsidence, collapse; (fig.) weakness, depression.

affaisser [afese] *v.t.* to weigh down, to depress; **s'~** *v.refl.* to sink, to subside, to fall in; to sag, to collapse, to crumple up; (fig.) to decline.

affalé, -e [afale] *adj.* (naut.) adrift on a lee shore; (fig.) sprawling; *il était ~ sur le divan*, he was sprawling on the sofa.

affaler [afale] *v.t.* (naut.) to haul down, in, (rope, etc.); to drive ashore; **s'~** *v.refl.* to be driven ashore; (fig.) to collapse in a heap.

affamé, -e [afame] *adj.* hungry, famished, starving, starved; (fig.) greedy, eager, thirsting, hungering, (*de*, for); *ventre ~ n'a pas d'oreilles*, you can't reason with a starving man.

affamer [afame] *v.t.* to starve.

affameur [afamœr] *s.m.* one who causes starvation or famine.

affectation [afɛktɑsjɔ̃] *s.f.* **1.** appropriation, attribution; **2.** affectation, mannerism, pretension, airs, preciosity, pretence.

affecté, -e [afɛkte] *adj.* affected, studied, feigned, hypocritical.

affecter [afɛkte] *v.t.* **1.** to allot, to appropriate, to appoint to; (mil.) to detail, to post; *des crédits affectés à l'Éducation*, credits allotted to Education; *des trains affectés au service de banlieue*, trains put on to the suburban service; **2.** to affect, to pretend, to feign, to sham; to tend towards; **3.** to affect, to influence, to move, to touch; (math.) to modify; **s'~** *v.refl.* to be affected, to be moved; to grieve; **4.** to be in or to take the form of; *~ une forme pyramidale*, to be in the form of a pyramid.

affecti-f, -ve [afɛktif] *adj.* affective.

affection [afɛksjɔ̃] *s.f.* **1.** affection, fondness, attachment, liking, tenderness, love; *prendre qn. en ~, se prendre d'~ pour qn.*, to take a liking for s.o.; **2.** (med.) affection, disease.

affectionné, -e [afɛksjɔne] *adj.* affectionate, loving (esp. at end of letter).

affectionner [afɛksjɔne] *v.t.* to like, to love, to be fond of, to be partial to, to have a liking for.

affectueu-x, -se [afɛktɥø] *adj.* affectionate, kind, warm-hearted; **~sement** [afɛktɥøzmɑ̃] *adv.* affectionately, kindly.

affenage [afnaʒ] *s.m.* feeding (cattle) with fodder.

afférent, -e [aferɑ̃] *adj.* **1.** (obs.) pertaining to; **2.** (law) accruing to; **3.** (med.) afferent.

affermage [afɛrmaʒ] *s.m.* **1.** leasing, renting (farm property); **2.** renting or buying (advertisement space).

affermer [afɛrme] *v.t.* **1.** to let (farm) on lease; **2.** to lease or sell (advertisement space).

affermir [afɛrmir] *v.t.* to fix, to make firm, to stabilize; to strengthen; (fig.) to fortify, to consolidate, to confirm.

affermissement [afɛrmismɑ̃] *s.m.* (usu. fig.) strengthening, consolidation, confirmation.

affété, -e [afete] *adj.* (obs.) affected.

afféterie [afetri] *s.f.* affectation, preciosity.

affichage [afiʃaʒ] *s.m.* bill-posting, putting up notice, publicizing (by notice or poster); *tableau d'~*, notice-board; score-board.

affiche [afiʃ] *s.f.* poster, bill, placard, notice; *un spectacle qui reste à l'~*, a show which is still running.

afficher [afiʃe] *v.t.* to placard, to stick up bills or posters, or notices; to publish, to proclaim, to announce (by posters, on notice-board or score-board); to make a show of, to parade, to show off; *défense d'~*, stick no bills; *il affiche ses préférences*, he makes it clear which side he's on; **s'~** *v.refl.* to become apparent; to show off, to seek the limelight, to give oneself publicity.

afficheur [afiʃœr] *s.m.* bill-sticker, bill-poster.

affichiste [afiʃist] *s.m.* commercial artist (specializing in posters).

affidé, -e [afide] *adj.* (obs.) trusty; *~ s.m.* (pej.) accomplice, fellow-criminal.

affilage [afilaʒ] *s.m.* sharpening, whetting, honing.

affilé, -e [afile] *adj.* sharp, cutting; (obs.) *avoir la langue ~e*, to have a sharp tongue.

affilée [afile] *adv. d'~*, without interruption, at a stretch.

affiler [afile] *v.t.* to sharpen, to whet, to hone.

affiliation [afiljɑsjɔ̃] *s.f.* affiliation, membership.

affilié, -e [afilje] *adj.* affiliated; *s.m.f.* member.

affilier [afilje] *v.t.* to affiliate; **s'~** *v.refl.* to join, to become affiliated (*à*, to).

affiloir [afilwar] *s.m.* sharpening-machine, whetstone, hone, steel, strop.

affinage [afinaʒ] *s.m.* refinement, purification (of metal, glass); finishing, maturation (of cheese).

affinement [afinmɑ̃] *s.m.* (fig.) refining, maturing.

affiner [afine] *v.t.* to refine, to purify (metal, glass); to finish, to mature (cheese); (fig.) to refine, to make more delicate; **s'~** *v.refl.* (fig.) to become finer, to mature.

affineu-r, -se [afinœr] *s.m.f.* refiner; finisher.

affinité [afinite] *s.f.* affinity, similarity; liking, attraction.

affiquet [afikɛ] *s.m.* **1.** stitch-stop (on knitting--needle); **2.** (usu. pl.) (fam., pej.) trinkets, baubles, frills.

affirmati-f, -ve [afirmatif] *adj.* affirmative; **~ve** *s.f.* affirmative; *répondre par l'~ve*, to reply in the affirmative; **~vement** [afirmativmɑ̃] *adv.* **1.** (obs.) with assurance, affirmatively; **2.** in the affirmative.

affirmation [afirmɑsjɔ̃] *s.f.* affirmation, assertion, statement; (law) statement (of account, etc.); affirmation, manifestation.

affirmer [afirme] *v.t.* to affirm, to assert, to declare, to claim, to certify, to guarantee; to swear (on oath); **s'~** *v.refl.* to become clear, definite.

affixe [afiks] *s.m.* (lang., math.) affix.

affleurement [aflœrmɑ̃] *s.m.* **1.** (techn.) levelling; **2.** (geol.) outcrop; (fig.) appearance, emergence.

affleurer [aflœre] *v.t.* (techn.) to level, to make flush; *~ v.i.* **1.** (obs.) to be level; **2.** (geol.) to crop out, to come to the surface; (fig.) to appear, to emerge.

afflicti-f, -ve [afliktif] *adj.* (law) afflictive, corporal; *peine ~ve*, punishment involving imprisonment or death.

affliction [afliksjɔ̃] *s.f.* (mental) affliction, pain, distress, sorrow.

affligé, -e [afliʒe] *adj.* afflicted, distressed, grieved, sorrowful; *s.m.f.* sorrowing person, one who mourns; *les ~s*, the afflicted, those in distress.

affligeant, -e [afliʒɑ̃] *adj.* distressing, saddening, sad; (fig.) painful, lamentable, pitiful.

affliger [afliʒe] *v.t.* to afflict (mentally), to distress, to grieve, to sadden; (obs.) to mortify; **s'~** *v.refl.* to be sad, to grieve, to be distressed.

afflouer [aflue] *v.t.* to float, to refloat (boat).

affluence [aflyɑ̃s] *s.f.* **1.** (obs.) abundance; **2.** crowd, throng, press; *les heures d'~*, peak hours.

affluent [aflyɑ̃] *s.m.* affluent, tributary.

affluer [aflye] *v.i.* **1.** to run, to flow, to surge; **2.** to arrive in a crowd, in droves, to flock.

afflux [afly] *s.m.* afflux, rush.

affolant, -e [afɔlɑ̃] *adj.* bewildering, upsetting, worrying; (fam.) terrifying, alarming.

affolé, -e [afɔle] *adj.* bewildered, terrified, worried; panic-stricken; *boussole ~e*, compass showing deviations.

affolement [afɔlmɑ̃] *s.m.* **1.** confusion, alarm, excitement, terror, panic; **2.** deviations of compass.

affoler [afɔle] *v.t.* to drive mad, to bewilder, to confuse; to alarm, to excite, to terrify, to make panic-stricken; **s'~** *v.refl.* to lose one's head, to panic, to get excited.

affouage [afwaʒ] *s.m.* right to cut firewood; share of wood cut.

affouillement [afujmɑ̃] *s.m.* undermining, erosion (by water).

affouiller [afuje] *v.t.* (of water) to undermine, to erode.

affourager [afuraʒe] *v.t.* to supply with fodder.

affourcher [afurʃe] *v.t.* (naut.) to moor with two anchors (cables crossed).

affranchi, -e (afrɑ̃ʃi] *adj.* **1.** (of slave) freed, liberated; **2.** emancipated, liberal-minded, free from prejudices; *s.m.f.* (pop.) free-liver, amoral person.

affranchir [afrɑ̃ʃir] *v.t.* **1.** to set free, to free, to liberate; to make politically independent; **2.** (fig.) to deliver, to relieve, to emancipate; **s'~** *v.refl.* to free oneself, to rid oneself (*de*, of); **3.** to frank, to stamp, to prepay (letters).

affranchissement [afrɑ̃ʃismɑ̃] *s.m.* **1.** setting free, liberation, emancipation; **2.** (fig.) deliverance; **3.** prepayment of postage, stamping.

affres [afr] *s.f.pl.* terrors, horrors, pangs; *les ~ de la mort*, death-throes; *les ~ de l'humiliation*, bitter pangs of humiliation.

affrètement [afrɛtmɑ̃] *s.m.* chartering (of cargo-ship).

affréter [afrete] *v.t.* to charter (ship).

affréteur [afretœr] *s.m.* charterer.

affreu-x, -se [afrø] *adj.* frightful, dreadful, horrible, shocking, abominable, atrocious; evil, extremely unpleasant, hateful; ugly, hideous, repulsive, awful; **~sement** [afrøzmɑ̃] *adv.* horribly, dreadfully, abominably; extremely, terribly.

affriander [afrijɑ̃de] *v.t.* to entice, to lure, to tempt; to make attractive.

affriolant, -e [afrijɔlɑ̃] *adj.* alluring, tempting, seductive.

affrioler [afrijɔle] *v.t.* to allure, to tempt, to entice.

affront [afrɔ̃] *s.m.* affront, insult, outrage.

affrontement [afrɔ̃tmɑ̃] *s.m.* **1.** confrontation, meeting, clash; **2.** bringing together.

affronter [afrɔ̃te] *v.t.* **1.** to face, to brave, to confront, to meet boldly; **s'~** *v.refl.* to come face to face, to clash; **2.** to put face to face; to bring together; *~ les lèvres d'une plaie*, to bring together the edges of a wound; (herald.) *animaux affrontés*, beasts affrontee, face to face; ⚠ not 'to affront' in sense 'to insult', 'to outrage'.

affublement [afybləmɑ̃] *s.m.* rig-out, get-up.

affubler [afyble] *v.t.* to dress up, to rig out grotesquely; **s'~** *v.refl.* to dress oneself up grotesquely.

affusion [afyzjɔ̃] *s.f.* affusion.

affût [afy] *s.m.* **1.** gun-carriage; **2.** hide (for hunting); *être* or *se mettre à l'~* (*de*), to be on the look-out (for), to keep one's eyes skinned (for).

affûtage [afytaʒ] *s.m.* **1.** sharpening; **2.** set or chest of workman's tools.

affûter [afyte] *v.t.* to sharpen, to whet, to grind; (sport) to train (race-horse).

affûteu-r [afytœr] *s.m.* tool-grinder, (saw-) setter; **~se** *s.f.* tool-sharpening machine.

affûtiaux [afytjo] *s.m.pl.* (fam.) trinkets, knick-knacks; (pop.) tools.

afghan, -e [afgɑ̃] *adj., s.m.f.* Afghan.

Afghanistan [afganistɑ̃] *s.m.* (geog.) Afghanistan.

afin [afɛ̃] *prep.* *~ de*, in order to, so as to; *~ que*, in order that, so that.

A.F.P. [aɛfpe] abbrev. *Agence France Presse*.

africain, -e [afrikɛ̃] *adj., s.m.f.* African.

africanisation [afrikanizɑsjɔ̃] *s.f.* Africanization.

afrikander [afrikɑ̃dɛr] *s.m.f.* Afrikaaner.

Afrique [afrik] *s.f.* (geog.) Africa.

agaçant, -e [agasɑ̃] *adj.* **1.** (obs.) enticing, provoking; **2.** annoying, irritating.

agace, agasse [agas] *s.f.* (ornith.) magpie.

agacement [agasmɑ̃] *s.m.* irritation, annoyance.

agacer [agase] *v.t.* **1.** (obs.) to torment; **2.** to tease, to provoke, to excite, to allure, to entice; **3.** to annoy, to irritate; to set (teeth) on edge.

agacerie [agasri] *s.f.* (usu. pl.) allurement, flirtation, advances, provocation.

agami [agami] *s.m.* (ornith.) agami, trumpeter.

agape [agap] *s.f.* **1.** (eccles. hist.) communal meal (of early Christians); **2.** (obs.) reunion of old friends; **3.** (pl.) feast, celebration dinner.

agar-agar [agaragar] *s.m.* (bot., pharm.) agar-agar.

agaric [agarik] *s.m.* agaric, mushroom.

agasse see AGACE.

agate [agat] *s.f.* agate.

agave, agavé [agav(e)] *s.m.* (bot.) agave.

age [aʒ] *s.m.* plough-beam.

âge [aʒ] *s.m.* **1.** (span of) life; *être à la fleur de l'~*, to be in the prime of life; *le retour d'~*, the turn of life; (esp.) change of life, menopause; **2.** age, number of years; *quel ~ a-t-il?*, how old is he?; *il est de mon ~*, he is my age; *d'~ moyen*, middle-aged; *~ moyen* (*de*), average age (of); *elle ne paraît, ne porte, pas son ~*, she doesn't look her age; *être d'~ à*, to be old enough to; *~ scolaire*, school age; *~ de raison*, years of discretion; **3.** age, period of life; *un enfant en bas ~*, a baby; *~ tendre*, tender years, infancy; adolescence; *entre deux ~s*, middle-aged; *on apprend à tout ~*, it's never too late to learn; *c'est bien de son ~*, it's what one expects at that age; **4.** old age; *homme d'~*, elderly man; *prendre de l'~*, to grow old; **5.** period, era, epoch, time, century; *le moyen ~*, the Middle Ages; *d'~ en ~*, from generation to generation.

âgé, -e [aʒe] *adj.* **1.** aged, elderly; **2.** old, of age; *~ de dix ans*, ten years old, ten years of age.

agence [aʒɑ̃s] *s.f.* (comm.) agency, office, bureau; branch (of bank); *~ de placement*, employment agency; *~ de voyages*, travel agency; *~ immobilière*, estate agency.

agencement [aʒɑ̃smɑ̃] *s.m.* arrangement, disposition, order; fitting-up, fixtures.

agencer [aʒɑ̃se] *v.t.* to arrange, to dispose, to organize; to fit up.

agenda [aʒɛ̃da] *s.m.* note-book, diary; ⚠ not 'agenda'.

agénésie [aʒenezi] *s.f.* sterility, infertility.

agenouillement [aʒnujmɑ̃] *s.m.* kneeling down, kneeling position.

(**s'**)**agenouiller** [aʒnuje] *v.refl.* to kneel down; (fig.) to bow, to submit, to abase oneself, (*devant*, to, before).

agenouilloir [aʒnujwar] *s.m.* knee-rest (in church pew), hassock, kneeler.
agent[1] [aʒɑ̃] *s.m.* agent; agency, cause.
agent[2] [aʒɑ̃] *s.m.* **1.** (usu. pej.) intermediary, middle man, representative; **2.** (admin., comm.) agent; ~ *d'assurances, immobilier, etc.*, insurance, estate, etc., agent; ~ *de change*, stockbroker; ~ *comptable*, accountant; **3.** policeman.
agglomérat [aglɔmera] *s.m.* (geol.) conglomerate, agglomerate.
agglomération [aglɔmerɑsjɔ̃] *s.f.* **1.** agglomeration; **2.** centre of population, conurbation, built-up area, cluster of dwellings.
aggloméré [aglɔmere] *s.m.* **1.** compressed fuel, briquette; **2.** building block, breeze-block; chipboard.
agglomérer [aglɔmere] *v.t.* to assemble, to collect into a mass; (techn.) to agglomerate, to compress into blocks.
agglutinant, -e [aglytinɑ̃] *adj.* agglutinative.
agglutination [aglytinɑsjɔ̃] *s.f.* agglutination.
agglutiner [aglytine] *v.t.* to agglutinate; **s'~** *v.refl.* to collect in a mass; (fig.) to gather, to assemble.
aggravant, -e [agravɑ̃] *adj.* aggravating, worsening; ⚠ not 'aggravating' in sense 'annoying'.
aggravation [agravɑsjɔ̃] *s.f.* aggravation, worsening.
aggraver [agrave] *v.t.* to aggravate; to make worse, more serious, more dangerous; to increase, to redouble; **s'~** *v.refl.* to get worse; ⚠ not 'to aggravate' in sense 'to annoy'.
agile [aʒil] *adj.* agile, active, nimble, quick; (fig.) quick-witted; **~ment** [aʒilmɑ̃] *adv.* nimbly, quickly.
agilité [aʒilite] *s.f.* agility, nimbleness, quickness.
agio [aʒjɔ] *s.m.* (fin.) agio; charges, commission.
agiotage [aʒjɔtaʒ] *s.m.* (hist.) agiotage, speculation.
agioteur [aʒjɔtœr] *s.m.* (hist.) speculator.
agir [aʒir] *v.i.* **1.** (law) to proceed (*contre*, against), to sue; **2.** to do, to act, to intervene; ~ *pour*, to act for, or on behalf of; ~ *auprès du ministre*, to intervene with the minister; **3.** to behave, to conduct oneself; ~ *mal envers qn.*, to act badly towards s.o., to treat s.o. badly; **4.** to operate, to have an effect or influence (*sur*, on); **5. s'~** (*de*) *v.refl.* to concern, to be about, to be a matter of, to be a question of; *de quoi s'agit-il?*, what is it about?; *il ne s'agit pas de ça*, that is not the question, that is not the point; *il s'agit de sa vie*, his life is at stake; (fam.) *il s'agit que vous le retrouviez*, it is essential that you find it; (obs.) *s'agissant de*, concerning, as regards.
agissant, -e [aʒisɑ̃] *adj.* busy, active, efficient, effective.
agissements [aʒismɑ̃] *s.m.pl.* intrigues, machinations, goings-on.
agitat-eur, -rice [aʒitatœr] *s.m.f.* **1.** agitator; **2. ~eur** *s.m.* stirrer, stirring-rod.
agitation [aʒitɑsjɔ̃] *s.f.* agitation, turbulence, animation; emotion, restlessness, uneasiness, perturbation, excitement; (pol.) agitation, unrest, trouble.
agité, -e [aʒite] *adj.* uneasy, feverish, troubled; (of sea) rough, choppy; restless, never still; (of sleep) disturbed.
agiter [aʒite] *v.t.* to agitate, to shake, to move, to stir, to wave, to wag; to disturb, to trouble, to excite, to worry; to ponder, to discuss (plans, etc.); **s'~** *v.refl.* to fret, to fidget, to be restless; *la mer s'agite*, the sea is getting rough.
agnat [agna] *s.m.* agnate.
agneau [aɲo] *s.m.*, **agnelle** [aɲɛl] *s.f.* lamb; (fig.) gentle creature.
agnelage [aɲlaʒ] *s.m.* lambing; lambing season.
agneler [aɲle] *v.i.* to lamb.
agnelet [aɲlɛ] *s.m.* lambkin, small lamb.
agnelin [aɲlɛ̃] *s.m.* lambskin.
agneline [aɲlin] *s.f.* lambswool.
agnelle see AGNEAU.
agnosticisme [agnɔstisism] *s.m.* agnosticism.
agnostique [agnɔstik] *adj.*, *s.m.f.* agnostic.
agonie [agɔni] *s.f.* the point of death, death-struggles; (fig.) decline, decadence, death-throes; *être à l'~*, to be dying, to be at death's door; ⚠ not 'agony' in sense 'great pain'.
agonir [agɔnir] *v.t.* **1.** to insult, to abuse; **2.** to overwhelm (with ridicule, with ignominy, etc.).
agonisant, -e [agɔnizɑ̃] *adj.*, *s.m.f.* dying (person).
agoniser [agɔnize] *v.i.* to be dying; (fig.) to be in decline, to be in its death-throes.
agoraphobie [agɔrafɔbi] *s.f.* agoraphobia.
agrafage [agrafaʒ] *s.m.* hooking, fastening.
agrafe [agraf] *s.f.* hook, clasp; clip, fastener, paper-clip, staple; (arch.) cramp-iron; ~ *et porte*, hook and eye.
agrafer [agrafe] *v.t.* to hook, to clasp, to fasten; (pop.) to arrest.
agrafeuse [agraføz] *s.f.* stapler (machine).
agraire [agrɛr] *adj.* agrarian.
agrandir [agrɑ̃dir] *v.t.* to enlarge, to extend, to lengthen, to widen; (photo.) to enlarge; to aggrandize, to promote, to develop; to exalt, to dignify; **s'~** *v.refl.* to grow larger; to extend one's estate or business; (fam.) to go up in the world.
agrandissement [agrɑ̃dismɑ̃] *s.m.* enlargement, extension; (photo.) enlargement; aggrandizement, development.
agrandisseur [agrɑ̃disœr] *s.m.* (photo.) enlarger.
agrarien, -ne [agrarjɛ̃] *adj.*, *s.m.f.* agrarian.
agréable [agreabl] *adj.* **1.** pleasing, agreeable, acceptable; (obs.) *avoir pour ~*, to accept, to agree (to); *si cela peut vous être ~*, if that would be agreeable to you, if you would agree to that; **2.** pleasant, graceful, charming, attractive, pleasing, pleasurable, enjoyable, happy; kind; ~ *au goût*, pleasant-tasting, palatable; **~ment** [agreabləmɑ̃] *adv.* pleasantly, agreeably.
agréé [agree] *s.m.* accredited lawyer (at *Tribunal de Commerce*).
agréer [agree] *v.t.* **1.** to accept, to welcome, to receive favourably; (esp. terminating formal letter) *veuillez ~ l'expression de mes sentiments distingués, etc.*, please accept . . ., = yours faithfully; **2.** ~ *à*, to please, to meet with approval (of), to be agreeable (to); *si cela vous agrée*, if it is agreeable to you; *vous agréerait-il de?*, would you consent to?; **3.** (law, comm.) to accredit, to appoint; *fournisseur agréé*, purveyor by appointment.
agrégat [agrega] *s.m.* **1.** (build.) aggregate; (fig.) agglomeration; **2.** aggregate, total.
agrégati-f, -ve [agregatif] *s.m.f.* student preparing for the examination of *agrégation*.
agrégation [agregɑsjɔ̃] *s.f.* **1.** aggregation; **2.** (obs.) admission, incorporation; **3.** admission by examination to title of *agrégé*; the examination or the degree of *agrégation*.
agrégé, -e [agreʒe] *s.m.f.* one holding the degree of *agrégation* (thereby qualified for a post as *professeur de lycée*).
agréger [agreʒe] *v.t.* **1.** to aggregate; **2.** to admit, to receive, to incorporate.
agrément [agremɑ̃] *s.m.* **1.** consent, approval; **2.** pleasantness, charm, grace; (mus.) grace-notes; **3.** pleasure; *arts d'~*, the gentle arts; *voyage d'~*, pleasure trip; ⚠ not 'agreement' in sense 'understanding'.
agrémenter [agremɑ̃te] *v.t.* to ornament, to adorn, to vary, to relieve; (iron.) to punctuate (*de*, with).

agrès [agrɛ] *s.m.pl.* (naut.) rigging, tackle; (sport) gymnastic equipment, apparatus.

agresser [agrese] *v.t.* to attack.

agresseur [agrɛsœr] *s.m.* aggressor.

agressi-f, -ve [agrɛsif] *adj.* aggressive; **~vement** [agrɛsivmɑ̃] *adv.* aggressively.

agression [agrɛsjɔ̃] *s.f.* aggression, unprovoked attack.

agressivité [agresivite] *s.f.* aggressiveness.

agreste [agrɛst] *adj.* (obs. exc. Lit.) rural, rustic.

agricole [agrikɔl] *adj.* agricultural.

agriculteur [agrikyltœr] *s.m.* agriculturalist, farmer, husbandman.

agriculture [agrikyltyr] *s.f.* agriculture, farming, husbandry.

(**s'**)**agriffer** [agrife] *v.refl. s'~ à,* to catch hold of, to claw on to.

agrion [agrijɔ̃] *s.m.* dragon-fly.

agripper [agripe] *v.t.* to clutch, to grab, to seize; **s'~** (*à*) *v.refl.* to clutch, to cling to.

agronom-e [agrɔnɔm] *s.m.* agronomist; **~ie** [agrɔnɔmi] *s.f.* agronomy; **~ique** [agrɔnɔmik] *adj.* agronomic(al).

agrumes [agrym] *s.m.pl.* citrus fruits.

aguerrir [agerir] *v.t.* to inure to war, to season; *troupes aguerries,* seasoned troops; (fig.) to harden; **s'~** *v.refl.* to become inured to war or hardship, to harden oneself.

(**aux**) **aguets** [ozage] *adv. loc.* on the watch, on the look-out.

aguichant, -e [agiʃɑ̃] *adj.* enticing, provocative.

aguicher [agiʃe] *v.t.* to entice, to allure, to tempt, to lead on.

aguicheu-r, -se [agiʃœr] *adj.* tempting; *s.m.f.* tempter, temptress.

ah [ɑ] *interj.* **1.** (expressing pleasure, pain, etc.) *~, que c'est triste!,* how sad!, oh, how sad it is!; **2.** (reinforcing exclamatory phrase) *~! que j'en ai vu de ces spectacles!,* oh, how many of these sights I have seen!; *~! j'y pense,* oh, by the way!, oh, I have just remembered!; **3.** (in exclamatory phrases) *~ ça!,* now then!, come now!, I say!; *~ oui!,* well, yes! of course!; *~ mais!,* really!, and no mistake!; *~ bon!,* all right, then!; *~ s.invar. pousser des ~! et des oh!,* to exclaim with admiration.

ahan [aɑ̃] *s.m.* (obs. exc. Lit.) great effort, groan.

ahaner [aane] *v.i.* (obs.) to make great efforts, to grunt and groan.

ahuri, -e [ayri] *adj.* dumbfounded, bewildered, stupefied; silly; *s.m.f.* idiot.

ahurir [ayrir] *v.t.* to dumbfound, to bewilder, to stupefy, to nonplus.

ahurissant, -e [ayrisɑ̃] *adj.* stupefying; (pop.) staggering, scandalous.

ahurissement [ayrismɑ̃] *s.m.* bewilderment, stupefaction.

aiche see ÈCHE.

aide[1] [ɛd] *s.f.* help, relief, assistance, succour, aid, support; *à l'~!,* help!; *à l'~ de,* with, by means of, with the help of; *apporter son ~ à qn.*; *venir en ~ à qn.,* to come to someone's assistance; *~ sociale,* social assistance.

aide[2] [ɛd] *s.m.f.* aide, assistant; *~ familiale* or *maternelle,* mother's help; (mil.) *~ de camp,* A.D.C.; *~-,* assistant, deputy; *~-chimiste,* assistant chemist; *~-maçon,* bricklayer's mate.

aider [ede] *v.t.* to aid, to help, to assist, to be of assistance or use to; to support, to relieve; *cela m'a beaucoup aidé,* it has been of great assistance to me; *Dieu aidant,* with God's help; *la fatigue aidant, je ne pus dormir,* what with my weariness, I couldn't sleep; *~ à,* (i.) (obs.) to help (person); (ii.) to contribute to, to facilitate, to further; *ces mesures aideront au rétablissement de l'économie,* these measures will contribute to putting the economy on its feet again; **s'~** *v.refl.* to help oneself or each other; *aide-toi, le ciel t'aidera,* heaven helps those who help themselves; *s'~ de,* to make use of, to have recourse to; *j'ai dû m'~ du dictionnaire,* I had to use the dictionary.

aie [aj] *interj.* expressing pain or unpleasant surprise.

aïeul, -e [ajœl] *s.m.f.* (pl. *-s*) (obs.) grandfather, grandmother; **aïeux** [ajø] *s.m.pl.* ancestors, ancestry, forefathers; (fam.) *mes aïeux!,* my goodness!

aigle [ɛgl] *s.m.* **1.** (ornith.) eagle; (fig.) *regard, yeux, d'~,* piercing, penetrating look, eyes; **2.** (fam.) *ce n'est pas un ~,* he is no genius; **3.** (eccles.) lectern; **4.** (paper-making) *papier grand ~,* double-elephant paper; *~ s.f.* **1.** female eagle; **2.** (herald.) eagle; **3.** (mil.) standard; *les ~s romaines,* the Roman eagles.

aiglefin see ÉGLEFIN.

aiglette [ɛglɛt] *s.f.* (herald.) eaglet.

aiglon, -ne [ɛglɔ̃] *s.m.f.* eaglet.

aigre [ɛgr] *adj.* sour, acid, bitter, sharp; shrill, harsh, piercing; biting; (fig.) acrimonious, cutting; **~ment** [ɛgrəmɑ̃] *adv.* shrilly; (fig.) bitterly, acrimoniously.

aigre-doux, -douce [ɛgrədu] *adj.* bitter-sweet; (fig.) *paroles ~-douces,* barbed words, catty remarks.

aigrefin [ɛgrəfɛ̃] *s.m.* sharper, trickster.

aigrelet, -te [ɛgrəlɛ] *adj.* sourish, somewhat sharp or shrill.

aigremoine [ɛgrəmwan] *s.f.* (bot.) agrimony.

aigrette [ɛgrɛt] *s.f.* **1.** (ornith.) egret; **2.** plume, tuft, spray; **3.** (bot.) egret, pappus; **4.** (electr.) aigrette, brush (discharge).

aigretté, -e [ɛgrete] *adj.* crested, tufted, (of owls) horned; (bot.) bearing a pappus.

aigreur [ɛgrœr] *s.f.* sourness, acidity; (fig.) sharpness, bitterness, spite, acrimony; (pl.) acidity (of the stomach).

aigrir [egrir] *v.t.* to turn sour; (fig.) to irritate, to embitter; *~ v.i.* to become acid, to turn sour; **s'~** *v.refl.* to become sour or acid; (fig.) to become bitter.

aig-u, -uë [egy] *adj.* sharp, pointed, sharpened to a point; acute; violent, piercing, shrill; keen, perceptive.

aiguade [ɛgad] *s.f.* place where ship takes on fresh water supplies.

aigue-marine [ɛgmarin] *s.f.* aquamarine.

aiguière [ɛgjɛr] *s.f.* old-fashioned water-jug, ewer.

aiguillage [egɥijaʒ] *s.m.* (rail.) **1.** operation of points; *cabine d'~,* signal-box; *poste d'~,* signal-box; **2.** (fig.) orientation; *mauvais ~,* wrong orientation, taking the wrong direction; **3.** points, switch.

aiguillat [egɥija] *s.m.* (ichth.) spur-dog, spiny dog-fish.

aiguille [egɥij] *s.f.* **1.** needle; *~ à repriser,* darning-needle; *~ à tricoter,* knitting-needle; *~ hypodermique,* hypodermic needle; *de fil en ~,* one thing leading to another; *discuter sur des pointes d'~,* to split hairs; **2.** hand, index, pointer, (of clock, compass, etc.); (obs.) gramophone needle; **3.** (rail.) points; **4.** spire, peak, obelisk; **5.** needle (of coniferous tree).

aiguillée [egɥije] *s.f.* needleful (of thread).

aiguiller [egɥije] *v.t.* **1.** to switch a train by means of points; **2.** (fig.) to direct, to set on a path.

aiguilleter [egɥijte] *v.t.* **1.** (naut.) to tie up, to moor; **2.** to make felt cloth (by sewing tufts into a base).

aiguillette [egɥijɛt] *s.f.* (mil.) shoulder-knot; (naut.) mooring rope; (cook.) thin slice of poultry or steak.

aiguilleur [egɥijœr] *s.m.* (rail.) pointsman.

aiguillier [egɥije] *s.m.* needle-case.
aiguillon [egɥijɔ̃] *s.m.* goad; (of bees, etc.) sting; (of plants) prickle, spine; (fig.) spur, incentive, stimulus.
aiguillonner [egɥijɔne] *v.t.* to goad; (fig.) to stimulate, to spur on.
aiguillot [egɥijo] *s.m.* (naut.) pintle.
aiguisage [eg(ɥ)izaʒ] *s.m.* sharpening, grinding, whetting.
aiguiser [eg(ɥ)ize] *v.t.* to sharpen, to grind, to whet; (fig.) to make keener or sharper, to give sharper point to.
aiguiseur [eg(ɥ)izœr] *s.m.* knife-grinder.
aiguisoir [eg(ɥ)izwar] *s.m.* (tool) sharpener, whetstone.
ail [aj] *s.m.* (pl. rarely *aulx*, now usu. *ails*) garlic; *gousse d'~*, clove of garlic.
ailante [ɛlɑ̃t] *s.m.* (bot.) ailanthus, tree of heaven.
aile [ɛl] *s.f.* wing; (mil.) flank; (of windmill) sweep, sail; *bout d'~*, pinion-feather, (aeron.) wing-tip; *battre d'une ~, ne plus battre que d'une ~*, to be a lame duck, to be in a bad way; *avoir du plomb dans l'~*, (of bird) to have been winged; (fig.) to be undermined; *voler de ses propres ~s*, to stand on one's own feet; *il faut lui rogner les ~s*, we must clip his wings; *sous l'~ de qn.*, under someone's wing; (rugby) *trois-quarts ~*, wing-three-quarter; *~ avant, arrière*, front, rear, wing.
ailé, -e [ele] *adj.* (lit. & fig.) winged.
aileron [ɛlrɔ̃] *s.m.* pinion, wing-tip; fin (of fish); (aeron.) aileron, wing-flap; (arch.) console, ornamental bracket.
ailette [ɛlɛt] *s.f.* (techn.) flange, vane, blade (of fan, turbine, etc.), fin, gill (of radiator); *radiateur à ~s*, winged radiator.
ailier [elje] *s.m.* (football) winger.
aillade [ajad] *s.f.* garlic sauce.
ailleurs [ajœr] *adv.* **1.** elsewhere, somewhere else, anywhere else; *nulle part ~*, nowhere else; *partout ~*, everywhere else; (fig.) *il* (*son esprit*) *est ~*, he is dreaming, he's not with us; *d'~*, from somewhere else; **2.** besides, moreover; also; on the other hand; nevertheless, however, after all, furthermore; *par ~*, otherwise, on the other hand, in other respects.
ailloli [ajɔli] *s.m.* (cook.) garlic mayonnaise.
aimable [ɛmabl] *adj.* **1.** (obs.) lovable; pleasing, lovely; **2.** amiable, affable, courteous, kind; *c'est bien ~ à vous d'être venu*, it's very kind of you to have come; **~ment** [ɛmabləmɑ̃] *adv.* amiably, affably, pleasantly, courteously, kindly.
aimant¹, -e [ɛmɑ̃] *adj.* loving, affectionate.
aimant² [ɛmɑ̃] *s.m.* magnet, lodestone; (fig.) powerful attraction.
aimantation [ɛmɑ̃tɑsjɔ̃] *s.f.* magnetization, magnetizing.
aimanté, -e [ɛmɑ̃te] *adj.* magnetic.
aimanter [ɛmɑ̃te] *v.t.* to magnetize; **s'~** *v.refl.* to become magnetic.
aimer [eme] *v.t.i.* to love, to like, to be fond of; to be in love with, to adore, to worship; to like, to delight in, to take pleasure in; to be partial to; *~* (*à*) *faire*, to like to do, to enjoy doing; *~ mieux, ~ autant*, to prefer, to like better; *j'aimerais mieux mourir*, I would rather die; *qui aime bien châtie bien*, spare the rod and spoil the child; **s'~** *v.refl.* to love, or like, oneself; to love each other, to be in love; (euphem.) to make love; *se faire ~ de qn.*, to endear oneself to s.o.
aine [ɛn] *s.f.* groin.
aîné, -e [ene] *adj., s.m.f.* eldest, first-born, elder, senior; *elle est mon ~e de deux ans*, she is two years my senior, she is two years older than me.
aînesse [enɛs] *s.f.* primogeniture; *droit d'~*, right of the eldest child to succeed.
ainsi [ɛ̃si] *adv., conj.* **1.** so, thus, in this (that) way, like this (that); *~ soit-il*, so be it, (relig.) amen; *s'il en est ~*, if that is the case; *~ dit, ~ fait*, no sooner said than done; *pour ~ dire*, so to speak, so to say, as it were; *et ~ du reste* or *de suite*, and so on, and so forth; **2.** in the same way, likewise; for instance; **3.** so, therefore; *~ donc*, so then; **4.** *~ que*, as well as, even as, just as, so as, as; *~ qu'il a été dit plus haut*, as has been said above.
air¹ [ɛr] *s.m.* air, atmosphere; wind, breeze; sky, heavens; space; *prendre un bol d'~*, to get out in the fresh air; *coup d'~*, chill, cold; *courant d'~*, draught; *donner de l'~*, to air, to aerate; *prendre l'~*, to go for a walk; *vivre de l'~ du temps*, to live on air; *en plein ~*, in the open air; *l'avion a pris l'~*, the plane took off; *armée de l'~*, air force; *hôtesse de l'~*, air hostess; *mal de l'~*, air-sickness; (fig.) *en l'~*, airy, unrealistic; *parler en l'~*, to talk nonsense; *fortune en l'~*, castles in the air, in Spain; *paroles, promesses, en l'~*, idle words, promises; *une tête en l'~*, an idealist, a madman; *je vais envoyer tout cela en l'~*, I'm going to throw it all up; *tout est en l'~ chez nous*, everything is upside down at home; *prendre l'~ du bureau*, to look in at the office; *dans l'~*, in the wind, brewing; *il y a de l'orage dans l'~*, there's a storm, trouble, brewing; *se donner de l'~*, to free oneself from constraint; *mettre un peu d'~ dans un tableau*, to give an impression of space in a picture; *jouer la fille de l'~*, to vanish.
air² [ɛr] *s.m.* look, appearance, bearing, manner, way; air, expression; *avoir grand ~*, to look impressive; *prendre de grands ~s*, to give oneself airs; *avoir l'~ comme il faut*, to look correct; *il a un drôle d'~*, he looks odd; *un ~ de famille*, a family likeness; *votre fils a votre ~*, your son looks like you; *avoir un faux ~ de*, to look something like (but not be so in fact), to give a (false) impression of; *prendre des ~s penchés*, to look thoughtful (often iron.); *avoir l'~*, to look, to seem; *vous avez l'~ triste*, you look sad; *il a l'~ d'une fille*, he looks like a girl; *avoir l'~ de faire*, to seem to be doing; *tu as l'~ de m'en vouloir*, you seem to hold it against me; *n'avoir l'~ de rien*, to seem easy, unimportant (without being so); *il l'a fait sans avoir l'~ de rien*, he did it without apparent effort, without attracting attention.
air³ [ɛr] *s.m.* (mus.) air, aria, song, tune, melody.
airain [ɛrɛ̃] *s.m.* bronze, brass; *d'~*, of bronze, brazen; (fig.) hard, harsh, implacable; *ciel d'~*, leaden sky; *il a un cœur d'~*, he is hard-hearted.
aire [ɛr] *s.f.* **1.** area, space, surface; floor, base; (obs.) threshing-floor; (geol.) basin; (ornith.) eyrie; (aeron.) *~ d'atterrissage*, landing-space, landing-strip; (naut.) *~ du vent*, (compass-) point, quarter; **2.** region, zone, area; *~ linguistique*, linguistic zone.
airelle [ɛrɛl] *s.f.* = MYRTILLE.
ais [ɛ] *s.m.* **1.** (obs.) plank, board; **2.** (bookb.) press-board.
aisance [ɛzɑ̃s] *s.f.* **1.** (pl.) conveniences, amenities; *cabinets d'~s, lieux d'~s*, closet, privy; *fosse d'~s*, cesspool; **2.** competency, easy circumstances, comfort; *vivre dans l'~*, to be comfortably off; **3.** ease, facility, freedom, grace; *avec* (*une parfaite*) *~*, with ease, without difficulty, easily, gracefully.
aise [ɛz] *s.f.* **1.** ease, comfort, convenience; *être à l'~, à son ~* to be at ease, to feel comfortable, to feel free, at home; *mettez-vous à l'~*, make yourself comfortable; *aimer ses ~s*, to like one's comfort; *prendre ses ~s*, to make oneself at home, to spread oneself; *il en prend à son ~*, he takes things easy; *il est à son ~*, he lives comfortably; *mal à l'~, à son ~*, ill at ease, uncomfortable; *mettre qn. à l'~*, to make s.o. welcome, at home,

to put s.o. at ease; *il en parle à son* ~, it's easy for him to talk; *à votre* ~*!*, do as you please!; **2.** (Lit.) joy, pleasure, gratification; ~ *adj.* (Lit.) glad, pleased; *j'en suis bien* ~, I'm glad to hear it.
aisé, -e [eze] *adj.* easy, natural; well-off; **~ment** [ezemɑ̃] *adv.* easily.
aisseau [ɛso] *s.m.* (roofing) shingle.
aisselle [ɛsɛl] *s.f.* **1.** arm-pit; **2.** (bot.) axil.
Aix-la-Chapelle [ɛksla∫apɛl] *s.f.* (geog.) Aix-la--Chapelle, Aachen.
ajointer [aʒwɛ̃te] *v.t.* to join endwise.
ajonc [aʒɔ̃] *s.m.* furze, gorse, whin.
ajour [aʒur] *s.m.* aperture, light (in a wall); (arch., sculpt.) open-work; (embroidery) hemstitch.
ajouré, -e [aʒure] *adj.* pierced, perforated; fretted; hemstitched.
ajourer [aʒure] *v.t.* to pierce, to perforate; to fret; to hemstitch.
ajournement [aʒurnəmɑ̃] *s.m.* adjournment, postponement.
ajourner [aʒurne] *v.t.* to adjourn, to postpone; (mil.) to defer (conscript); to refer (candidate for an examination).
ajout [aʒu], **ajouté** [aʒute] *s.m.* thing added, addition; insertion (in a manuscript).
ajouter [aʒute] *v.t.* to add, to join to; to append, to annex; to go on to say, to say further; *il y ajoute du sien*, he embroiders (on the original story); ~ *foi à*, to believe (in), to give credit to; ~ *à*, to add to, to increase; *cela ajoute à mon plaisir*, it increases my pleasure; **s'~** *v.refl.* to be added to; to make bigger, to aggravate; *les primes s'ajoutent au salaire*, the bonuses increase the wages.
ajustage [aʒystaʒ] *s.m.* adjustment, fitting; join.
ajustement [aʒystəmɑ̃] *s.m.* adjustment, fitting, arranging, fitting together; (fig.) conciliation, settlement; (obs.) dress, attire.
ajuster [aʒyste] *v.t.* **1.** to adjust, to true (up); to aim (a gun), to aim at (a target); (fig.) to arrange, to set up, to organize; (obs.) to dress, to deck out; **2.** to fit, to adapt, to alter; to match, to suit; (obs.) to assemble (parts of machinery); **s'~** *v.refl.* (obs.) to dress oneself; *s'~ à*, to fit, to suit, to match.
ajusteur [aʒystœr] *s.m.* fitter.
ajutage [aʒytaʒ] *s.m.* (mech.) adjutage, nozzle, jet, rose (of hose-pipe).
akène [akɛn] *s.m.* (bot.) achene, seed-pod.
alabastrite [alabastrit] *s.f.* alabaster (gypseous variety).
alacrité [alakrite] *s.f.* alacrity.
alaise, alèse [alɛz] *s.f.* **1.** draw-sheet; **2.** extension-piece (to a panel).
alambic [alɑ̃bik] *s.m.* (chem.) still.
alambiqué, -e [alɑ̃bike] *adj.* over-refined, over--subtle, contorted.
alangui, -e [alɑ̃gi] *adj.* languid, depressed, dispirited.
alanguir [alɑ̃gir] *v.t.* to weaken, to depress; **s'~** *v.refl.* to become depressed, to become dispirited.
alanguissement [alɑ̃gismɑ̃] *s.m.* languor, depression, listlessness.
alarmant, -e [alarmɑ̃] *adj.* alarming, disquieting.
alarme [alarm] *s.f.* alarm, alert, danger-signal; fright, fear, disquiet.
alarmer [alarme] *v.t.* to alarm, to trouble, to frighten; **s'~** *v.refl.* to be alarmed, to take fright.
alarmiste [alarmist] *adj., s.m.f.* alarmist, panic--monger.
alaterne [alatɛrn] *s.m.* (bot.) buckthorn.
albanais, -e [albanɛ] *adj., s.m.f.* Albanian.
Albanie [albani] *s.f.* (geog.) Albania.
albâtre [albɑtr] *s.m.* alabaster; (fig.) *d'~*, dazzlingly white.
albatros [albatros] *s.m.* albatross.
alberge [albɛrʒ] *s.f.* clingstone peach or apricot.
albergier [albɛrʒje] *s.m.* clingstone peach- or apricot-tree.
albinisme [albinism] *s.m.* albinism.
albinos [albinos] *s.m.f.* albino.
albite [albit] *s.f.* (min.) albite, white feldspar.
album [albɔm] *s.m.* album; sketch-book; illustrated brochure.
albumen [albymɛn] *s.m.* albumen.
albumine [albymin] *s.f.* albumin; (fam.) *avoir de l'~*, to suffer from albuminuria.
albuminé, -e [albymine] *adj.* albuminous.
albumineu-x, -se [albyminø] *adj.* albuminous, albuminose.
albumin-oïde [albyminɔid] *adj., s.m.* albuminoid; **~urie** [albyminyri] *s.f.* albuminuria; **~urique** [albyminyrik] *adj.* related to, or suffering from, albuminuria.
alcade [alkad] *s.m.* alcalde.
alcalescence [alkalesɑ̃s] *s.f.* alkalescence.
alcalescent, -e [alkalesɑ̃] *adj.* alkalescent.
alcali [alkali] *s.m.* **1.** (chem.) alkali; (obs.) ~ *volatil*, ammonia; **2.** (comm.) ammonia.
alcalin, -e [alkalɛ̃] *adj.* alkaline; (*médicament*) ~, antacid.
alcalinité [alkalinite] *s.f.* alkalinity.
alcaloïde [alkalɔid] *s.m.* alkaloid.
alcarazas [alkarazɑs] *s.m.* porous jug.
alchimie [al∫imi] *s.f.* (lit. & fig.) alchemy.
alchimique [al∫imik] *adj.* alchemic(al).
alchimiste [al∫imist] *s.m.* alchemist.
alcool [alkɔl] *s.m.* alcohol, spirits; ~ *naturel*, brandy; ~ *industriel*, industrial spirit; ~ *à brûler*, methylated spirit; *lampe à* ~, spirit lamp; **~at** [alkɔla] *s.m.* (pharm.) alcoholate, spirit (of herbs); **~ique** [alkɔlik] *adj., s.m.f.* alcoholic; **~isation** [alkɔlizɑsjɔ̃] *s.f.* **1.** conversion into alcohol; **2.** addition of alcohol (to drinks); preserving (organs, etc.) in alcohol; **~iser** [alkɔlize] *v.t.* **1.** to convert into alcohol; **2.** to add alcohol to; **s'~iser** *v.refl.* (fam.) to drink to excess; to get drunk; **~isme** [alkɔlism] *s.m.* alcoholism.
alcoomètre [alkɔmɛtr] *s.m.* alcoholmeter.
alcoo(l)test [alkɔ(l)tɛst] *s.m.* breathalyser.
alcôve [alkov] *s.f.* alcove, recess (usu. for beds); (fig.) intimacy; *les secrets de l'~*, the secrets of the bedchamber.
alcyon [alsjɔ̃] *s.m.* **1.** (myth.) halcyon; **2.** sea-fan, coral.
aldéhyde [aldeid] *s.f.* (chem.) aldehyde.
aléa [alea] *s.m.* risk, unexpected turn of events, contingency.
aléatoire [aleatwar] *adj.* aleatory, chancy, hazardous, problematic.
alémanique [alemanik] *adj.* Alemannian; relating to German-speaking Switzerland; *la Suisse* ~, German-speaking Switzerland.
alène [alɛn] *s.f.* awl.
alentour [alɑ̃tur] *adv.* around, about; *d'~*, local, in or of the neighbourhood, surrounding.
alentours [alɑ̃tur] *s.m.pl.* surroundings, neighbourhood, vicinity, outskirts; (tapestry) border; (obs.) entourage; (fig.) implications (of a subject).
Alep [alɛp] *s.m.* (geog.) Aleppo.
alépine [alepin] *s.f.* bombasine.
alérion [alerjɔ̃] *s.m.* (herald.) alerion.
alerte [alɛrt] *adj.* **1.** (obs.) vigilant, watchful; **2.** quick, active, nimble.
alerte [alɛrt] *s.f.* alert, alarm; ~ *aérienne*, air--raid warning; *en état d'~*, on call, on stand-by.
alerter [alɛrte] *v.t.* to alert, to give the alarm to.
alésage [alezaʒ] *s.m.* (eng.) reaming, drilling; boring (of cylinders), re-bore.
alèse see ALAISE.
aléser [aleze] *v.t.* to ream, to (re-)bore, to drill.

aléseur [alezœr] *s.m.* mechanic specializing in drilling, etc.
aléseuse [alezøz] *s.f.* drilling- or boring--machine, drill, reamer.
alésoir [alezwar] *s.m.* drill, borer.
aleurone [alørɔn] *s.f.* (biol.) aleurone; proteid grains.
alevin [alvɛ̃] *s.m.* fry (i.e. small fish); **~age** [alvinaʒ] *s.m.* fish-farming; stocking rivers with fish; **~er** [alvine] *v.t.* to (re)stock with fish; **~ier** [alvinje] *s.m.* (fish) hatchery.
Alexandrie [alɛksɑ̃dri] *s.f.* (geog.) Alexandria.
alexandrin, -e [alɛksɑ̃drɛ̃] *adj.* **1.** Alexandrian; **2.** (pros.) alexandrine; ~ *s.m.* (pros.) alexandrine.
alexie [alɛksi] *s.f.* alexia, form of word-blindness.
alezan, -e [alzɑ̃] *adj.*, *s.m.* chestnut (horse).
alfa [alfa] *s.m.* (bot.) alfa, esparto-grass.
alfénide [alfenid] *s.m.* German silver.
algarade [algarad] *s.f.* **1.** (obs.) sudden attack; **2.** altercation, flare-up; *avoir une ~ avec qn.*, to have a row with s.o.
algazelle [algazɛl] *s.f.* white antelope.
algèbre [alʒɛbr] *s.f.* algebra; (fig.) *c'est de l'~ pour moi*, it's all Greek to me.
algébrique [alʒebrik] *adj.* algebraic(al); **~ment** [alʒebrikmɑ̃] *adv.* algebraically.
algébriste [alʒebrist] *s.m.f.* algebr(a)ist.
Alger [alʒe] *s.m.* (geog.) Algiers; (former department of) Alger.
Algérie [alʒeri] *s.f.* (geog.) Algeria.
algérien, -ne [alʒerjɛ̃] *adj.*, *s.m.f.* Algerian.
algérois, -e [alʒerwɑ] *adj.*, *s.m.f.* (inhabitant) of Algiers.
algide [alʒid] *adj.* (med.) algid.
algidité [alʒidite] *s.f.* (med.) algidity.
algorithme [algɔritm] *s.m.* (math.) algorism; algorithm.
algue [alg] *s.f.* seaweed, alga.
alias [aljɑs] *adv.* alias.
alibi [alibi] *s.m.* alibi.
aliboufier [alibufje] *s.m.* (bot.) styrax; gum--tree.
alidade [alidad] *s.f.* alidad(e); index of astrolabe or quadrant.
aliénabilité [aljenabilite] *s.f.* alienability.
aliénable [aljenabl] *adj.* alienable.
aliénataire [aljenatɛr] *s.m.f.* (law) alienee.
aliénat-eur, -rice [aljenatœr] *s.m.f.* (law) alienator.
aliénation [aljenɑsjɔ̃] *s.f.* **1.** (law) alienation, transfer, conveyance of property; (international law) ~ *de territoire*, annexation; **2.** madness, insanity, mental disturbance; **3.** estrangement, hostility; **4.** (fig.) loss.
aliéné, -e [aljene] *adj.*, *s.m.f.* insane, mad, mentally ill (person).
aliéner [aljene] *v.t.* **1.** (law) to alienate, to transfer; (fig.) to lose, to give up; **2.** to estrange, to provoke hostility in; **s'~** *v.refl.* to alienate (e.g. sympathy from oneself).
aliéniste [aljenist] *s.m.f.* alienist.
alifère [alifɛr] *adj.* (of insects) winged.
aliforme [alifɔrm] *adj.* wing-shaped.
alignement [aliɲmɑ̃] *s.m.* lining-up, alignment, line, building-line; straightening; row, line; ~ *monétaire*, fixing rate of exchange; (mil.) *à droite, ~!*, right dress!
aligner [aliɲe] *v.t*, to arrange in a line, to align, to line up, to have lined up, to produce a series of; (mil.) to dress; *les arguments qu'il aligne*, the series of arguments he produces; (pop.) *les ~*, to count out notes, to pay out; **s'~** *v.refl.* to align oneself; to be in line; to square up (for a fight); (pop.) *tu peux toujours t'~*, you haven't a hope (of winning).
aliment [alimɑ̃] *s.m.* aliment, food, foodstuff, nourishment; (pl.) (law) subsistence, maintenance, alimony; (fig.) food, material; **~aire** [alimɑ̃tɛr] *adj.* alimentary, dietetic; *régime ~aire*, diet; (law) *pension ~aire*, alimony, maintenance; **~ation** [alimɑ̃tɑsjɔ̃] *s.f.* supply, provisioning, feeding, nourishment; food supply, provision business; (*magasin d'*)*~ation*, provision shop, grocer's shop; **~er** [alimɑ̃te] *v.t.* to feed; to supply, to provision; (fig.) to sustain, to maintain, to keep alive; **s'~er** *v.refl.* to take food; to be supplied.
alinéa [alinea] *s.m.* indented line; paragraph.
alios [aljos] *s.m.* red sandstone.
aliquante [alikɑ̃t] *adj.f.* (math.) *partie ~*, aliquant part.
aliquote [alikɔt] *adj.f.* (math.) *partie ~*, aliquot part.
alise, alize [aliz] *s.f.* sorb, service-apple.
alisier, alizier [alizje] *s.m.* service tree.
alisme [alism] *s.m.* (bot.) alisma, water--plantain.
aliter [alite] *v.t.* to confine (patient) to bed; *être alité*, to be laid up; **s'~** *v.refl.* to take to one's bed, to be confined to bed.
alitement [alitmɑ̃] *s.m.* confinement to bed.
alizari [alizari] *s.m.* madder; **~ne** [alizarin] *s.f.* alizarin.
alizé [alize] *adj.*, *s.m.* smooth, regular; (*vents*) *~s*, trade winds.
alkékenge [alkekɑ̃ʒ] *s.f.* (bot.) Physalis, winter--cherry, bladder-herb.
alkermès [alkɛrmɛs] *s.m.* alkermes (liqueur).
allaitement [alɛtmɑ̃] *s.m.* suckling, nursing, breast-feeding; ~ *artificiel*, artificial feeding.
allaiter [alete] *v.t.* to suckle, to nurse, to breast--feed.
allant, -e [alɑ̃] *adj.* active, brisk, mobile; ~ *s.m.* go, spirit, heartiness; *avoir de l'~*, to be full of go; (pl.) *les ~s et venants*, passers-by.
alléchant, -e [al(l)eʃɑ̃] *adj.* tempting, appetizing; (fig.) attractive, alluring, enticing.
allèchement [al(l)ɛʃmɑ̃] *s.m.* lure, attraction.
allécher [al(l)eʃe] *v.t.* to attract; (fig.) to tempt, to entice.
allée [ale] *s.f.* **1.** garden path, walk, lane; (obs.) passage; (in town) avenue, tree-lined road; **2.** going; *~s et venues*, comings and goings; ⚠ not 'alley' in sense 'very narrow street'.
allégation [al(l)egɑsjɔ̃] *s.f.* allegation, assertion.
allège [al(l)ɛʒ] *s.f.* **1.** (naut.) lighter, tender; **2.** (arch.) basement (of window).
allégeance [al(l)eʒɑ̃s] *s.f.* allegiance.
allègement [al(l)ɛʒmɑ̃] *s.m.* lightening, relief, alleviation.
alléger [al(l)eʒe] *v.t.* to lighten, to relieve, to alleviate; ⚠ not 'to allege'.
allégorie [al(l)egɔri] *s.f.* allegory.
allégorique [al(l)egɔrik] *adj.* allegoric(al); **~ment** [al(l)egɔrikmɑ̃] *adv.* allegorically.
allègre [al(l)ɛgr] *adj.* sprightly, lively, cheerful, jolly, gay, brisk, carefree; **~ment** [al(l)ɛgrəmɑ̃] *adv.* briskly, cheerfully; (pej.) cheerfully (= carelessly); *il nous a ~ ruinés*, he has cheerfully ruined us.
allégresse [al(l)egrɛs] *s.f.* cheerfulness, gaiety, joy, high spirits.
alléguer [al(l)ege] *v.t.* to quote, to refer to; to allege, to plead, to invoke, to state.
alléluia [al(l)eluja] *s.m.* **1.** alleluia, hallelujah; **2.** (bot.) wood-sorrel.
allemand, -e [almɑ̃] *adj.*, *s.m.f.* German; *querelle d'Allemand*, stupid, unfounded quarrel; *berger ~*, Alsatian dog; ~ *s.m.* German (language); **~e** *s.f.* (mus.) allemande.
Allemagne [almaɲ] *s.f.* (geog.) Germany.
aller [ale] *v.i.* **1.** to go, to move, to travel, to proceed, to get along; ~ *au marché, chez le coiffeur*, to go to market, to the hairdresser's; ~ *à la rencontre de*, to (go and) meet; ~ *en voiture*, to

travel by car; ~ *à pied*, to go on foot, to walk; ~ *à grands pas*, to stride; ~ *son (petit bonhomme de) chemin*, to go one's own way, to mind one's own business; *on va plus vite par le métro*, one gets along quicker on the underground; *va le chercher*, go and look for it; (fig.) *allons au fait!*, let's get down to business; *il est allé jusqu'à lui dire*, he went so far as to say to him, he dared to tell him; *vous y allez un peu fort*, you are rather overdoing it; *y* ~ *de*, to stake, to risk, to lay out, to subscribe (a sum); *j'y vais de 100 frs.*, I will put 100 frs. on it; *cela m'est allé au cœur*, it has moved me deeply; *n'allez pas vous imaginer que*, don't (go and) think that; **2.** (imperative phrases) *vas-y! allez-y! allons-y!*, come on! get moving! let's get on with it!; *allons, du calme!*, come now, don't get excited!; *il n'en saura rien, va!*, after all, he'll never know!; **3.** to be going to, to be about to; *je vais sortir*, I am (just) going out; *je vais rester à la maison*, I am going to stay at home, I shall stop at home; *il va arriver d'un moment à l'autre*, he will be arriving any minute; **4.** to be (in a state of health); *comment allez-vous?*, how are you?; *je vais mieux*, I am better; **5.** to go, to proceed, to happen, to progress, to work, to function; *les affaires vont bien*, things are going well; *ma montre ne va pas bien*, my watch isn't working properly; *le courant fait* ~ *le moteur*, the current works the motor; *sa passion allait jusqu'à la folie*, his passion reached the point of madness; *cela ira tout seul*, it will happen of its own accord, it will see to itself; *il n'en va pas de même de*, it is not the same with, the same thing does not happen with; *cela va sans dire*, it goes without saying, it is understood, it stands to reason; *il y va de ma vie*, my life is at stake; *l'inquiétude allait croissant*, there was increasing anxiety; *son mal va en empirant*, his trouble is getting worse; *laisser* ~ *les affaires*, to let things take their course, to neglect one's affairs; *se laisser* ~, to give up, to lose heart; **6.** to fit, to suit, to go (with); to be all right, to be acceptable; *la clé ne va pas à la serrure*, the key does not fit the lock; *cette robe te va bien*, that dress suits you; *ça me va*, that suits me; *ça va*, that's all right, O.K.; *est-ce que ça va?*, will that be all right?, will it do?, O.K.?; (fam.) *ça va (comme ça)*, that will do, that's enough; **7.** *s'en* ~, to go away, to depart, to go off; to disappear; *allez--vous-en!*, go away!, be off!; *s'en* ~ *au marché*, to be off to the market; *s'en* ~ *de la maison*, to leave the house; *les nuages s'en vont*, the clouds are disappearing; *une chose que je m'en vais vous raconter*, something that I am going to tell you.

aller [ale] *s.m.* outward journey; *un* ~ *(simple) pour Paris*, a single (ticket) for Paris; *un* ~ *et retour*, a return (ticket); **pis-**~ *s.m.invar.* last resort; *au pis-*~, in the last resort, if the worst comes to the worst.

allergie [alɛrʒi] *s.f.* allergy.

allergique [alɛrʒik] *adj.* allergic; (fam.) *il est* ~ *à la musique*, he can't stand music.

alleu see FRANC-ALLEU.

alliacé, -e [aljase] *adj.* alliaceous, of garlic.

alliage [aljaʒ] *s.m.* alloy; (fig.) mixture, admixture.

alliance [aljɑ̃s] *s.f.* **1.** alliance, union, coalition, confederation, league, pact; association, society (e.g. *Alliance Française*); **2.** marriage; wedding--ring; *cousin par* ~, cousin by marriage.

allié, -e [alje] *adj.* allied, united; *s.m.f.* ally, friend, supporter; relation by marriage.

allier [alje] *v.t.* **1.** to alloy; (fig.) to combine, to mix; **2.** to unite, to join together; **s'**~ *à v.refl.* to ally oneself with or to, to make an alliance with, to join with, to mix with, to combine with, to associate with.

alligator [al(l)igatɔr] *s.m.* alligator.

allitération [al(l)iterɑsjɔ̃] *s.f.* alliteration.

allô [alo] *interj.* hello!, hallo! (on telephone only).

allocataire [al(l)ɔkatɛr] *s.m.f.* person in receipt of an allowance or allocation.

allocation [al(l)ɔkɑsjɔ̃] *s.f.* allocation, allowing; allowance, allotment; ~*s familiales*, family allowances.

allocution [al(l)ɔkysjɔ̃] *s.f.* allocution, (short) speech or address by public figure, fireside chat.

allogène [al(l)ɔʒɛn] *adj.* non-indigenous.

allonge [alɔ̃ʒ] *s.f.* **1.** extension, leaf (of table); **2.** meat-hook; **3.** reach (of boxer).

allongé, -e [alɔ̃ʒe] *adj.* elongated, lengthened, stretched; (fig.) slim; *s.m.f.* (pl.) (med.) *les* ~*(e)s*, the bad cases.

allongement [alɔ̃ʒmɑ̃] *s.m.* elongation, lengthening, stretching; protraction.

allonger [alɔ̃ʒe] *v.t.* **1.** to lengthen, to make seem longer; ~ *le pas*, to lengthen one's step, to step out; **2.** to extend, to stretch (out); (cook.) to thin (a sauce); (fam.) to deliver (a blow); (pop.) to knock down; (pop.) to fork out (money); **s'**~ *v.refl.* to grow longer, to lengthen, to extend; to stretch oneself out, to lie down; (pop.) to measure one's length.

allopathe [al(l)ɔpat] *adj.* allopathic; *médecin* ~, allopath.

allopathie [al(l)ɔpati] *s.f.* allopathy.

allotropie [al(l)ɔtrɔpi] *s.f.* allotropy.

allotropique [al(l)ɔtrɔpik] *adj.* allotropic.

allouer [alwe] *v.t.* to allocate, to grant, to award, to attribute, to allow (money, time).

allumage [alymaʒ] *s.m.* lighting, kindling; (car) ignition, sparking, firing; *bougies d'*~, sparking--plugs; *avance à l'*~, pre-ignition; *distributeur d'*~, distributor.

allume-feu [alymfø] *s.m.invar.* firelighter; **~-gaz** [alymgɑz] *s.m.invar.* gas-lighter.

allumer [alyme] *v.t.* to light, to kindle, to set fire to; (fig.) to excite, to fire, to kindle; to light up, to turn on; ~ *une lumière*, to turn on a light; (fam.) ~ *l'électricité*, to turn on the electricity; **s'**~ *v.refl.* to light up, to shine.

allumette [alymɛt] *s.f.* **1.** match, match-stick; ~*s de sûreté*, safety matches; *frotter* or *gratter une* ~, to strike a match; (fig., fam.) *avoir des jambes comme des* ~*s*, to have legs like match-sticks; **2.** (cook.) stick; ~*s au fromage*, cheese-sticks, cheese straws.

allumetti-er, -ère [alymetje] *s.m.f.* match manufacturer; worker in a match factory.

allumeu-r [alymœr] *s.m.* **1.** (obs.) lamplighter; **2.** lighter, ignition device, (car) ignition--system; **~se** [alymøz] *s.f.* (fam.) seductive woman, tart.

allure [alyr] *s.f.* **1.** speed; *rouler à grande, à toute,* ~, to travel at speed, at full speed; **2.** gait, walk, pace, tread, carriage; (of horse) pace; (naut.) tack; **3.** looks, appearance; *avoir de l'*~, to look distinguished; **4.** (usu. pl.) manner, way(s), behaviour, demeanour; **5.** look (of a thing); *elle a une drôle d'*~, *cette maison*, that house looks odd; *cela ne manque pas d'*~, that doesn't look bad.

allusi-f, -ve [al(l)ysif] *adj.* allusive.

allusion [al(l)yzjɔ̃] *s.f.* allusion, hint, reference; *faire* ~ *à*, to allude to, to refer to, to hint at.

alluvial, -e, (aux) [al(l)yvjal] *adj.* alluvial.

alluvion [al(l)yvjɔ̃] *s.f.* **1.** (obs.) = ALLUVIONNEMENT; **2.** (pl.) alluvium, alluvial deposit.

alluvionnement [al(l)yvjɔnmɑ̃] *s.m.* silting-up, deposition of alluvium.

almanach [almana] *s.m.* almanac(k), calendar, annual.

almée [alme] *s.f.* alma(h).

aloès [alɔɛs] *s.m.* aloe(s).

aloi [alwa] *s.m.* degree of fineness, quality; *de bon*

~, good, sound, sterling, deserved; *de mauvais ~*, spurious, doubtful, unworthy.
alopécie [alɔpesi] *s.f.* baldness, alopecia.
alors [alɔr] *adv.* **1.** then, at that time; **2.** in that case, therefore, so; *~?*, what then?; (in reply to an objection) *et ~?*, so what?; (fam.) *non, mais ~!*, now, look here!
alors que [alɔrkə] *conj. loc.* **1.** (obs.) when; **2.** at a time when, while (at the same time), whereas; *alors même que*, even when, even if.
alose [aloz] *s.f.* (ichth.) shad.
alouette [alwɛt] *s.f.* lark, skylark; *~ de mer*, sandpiper; *pied d'~*, (bot.) larkspur.
alourdir [alurdir] *v.t.* to make heavy or heavier; to increase weight; to slow down (pace); (fig.) to dull, to make dull; *la tête alourdie de sommeil*, head heavy with sleep; **s'~** *v.refl.* to get heavy or heavier; to put on weight; to become dull.
alourdissement [alurdismɑ̃] *s.m.* heaviness, increase in weight; slowing down; dullness.
aloyau [alwajo] *s.m.* (cook.) sirloin.
alpaga [alpaga] *s.m.* (zool., text.) alpaca.
alpage [alpaʒ] *s.m.* alpine pasturage; season spent by cattle in this pasturage.
alpe [alp] *s.f.* **1.** alpine pasture; **2.** (geog.) *les Alpes*, the Alps.
alpestre [alpɛstr] *adj.* alpine.
alpha [alfa] *s.m.* alpha; (fig.) *connaître l'~ et l'oméga de*, to know (sth.) from A to Z.
alphabet [alfabɛ] *s.m.* alphabet; spelling-book.
alphabétique [alfabetik] *adj.* alphabetical; **~ment** [alfabetikmɑ̃] *adv.* alphabetically.
alphabétisation [alfabetizɑsjɔ̃] *s.f.* teaching illiterates to read and write; *campagne d'~*, literacy campaign.
alpin, -e [alpɛ̃] *adj.* alpine; **~isme** [alpinism] *s.m.* mountaineering; **~iste** [alpinist] *s.m.f.* mountaineer.
alpiste [alpist] *s.m.* (bot.) canary-grass.
Alsace [alzas] *s.f.* (geog.) Alsace.
alsacien, -ne [alzasjɛ̃] *adj., s.m.f.* Alsatian.
altérabilité [alterabilite] *s.f.* liability to deterioration.
altérable [alterabl] *adj.* liable to deterioration, corruptible; ⚠ not 'alterable' in sense 'can be changed'.
altérant, -e [alterɑ̃] *adj.* causing thirst; (med.) alterative.
altération [alterɑsjɔ̃] *s.f.* **1.** (rare) change, modification; **2.** (mus.) flattening or sharpening (of note); **3.** deterioration, impairment; change (of face); break (of voice); (geol.) weathering; **4.** (comm., law) falsification, adulteration; (fin.) debasement; **5.** (fig.) misrepresentation, distortion, tampering, falsification.
altercation [altɛrkɑsjɔ̃] *s.f.* altercation, wrangling, dispute.
altéré, -e [altere] *adj.* **1.** falsified, adulterated; debased; impaired; (of face) drawn, distorted; (of voice) broken; misrepresented; **2.** thirsty; (fig.) *~ de*, eager for; *~ de sang*, thirsting for blood.
altérer [altere] *v.t.* **1.** to change for the worse, to cause to deteriorate, to damage, to corrupt; to falsify, to adulterate; (fin.) to debase; to misrepresent; to tamper with; to distort; **2.** to make thirsty; **s'~** *v.refl.* to deteriorate, to go bad, to spoil, to decay; to be impaired, to be falsified; ⚠ not 'to alter'.
alternance [altɛrnɑ̃s] *s.f.* alternation, succession, rotation.
alternant, -e [altɛrnɑ̃] *adj.* alternating, rotating.
alternat [altɛrnɑ] *s.m.* alternation; rotation; cycle.
alternateur [altɛrnatœr] *s.m.* (electr.) alternator.
alternati-f, -ve [altɛrnatif] *adj.* alternate, alternating; (electr., of current) alternating; (log., law) alternative; **~vement** [altɛrnativmɑ̃] *adv.* alternately, by turns, successively.
alternative [altɛrnativ] *s.f.* **1.** (pl.) alternation; **2.** *une ~*, a choice of two possibilities; **3.** (anglicism) alternative.
alterne [altɛrn], **alterné, -e** [altɛrne] *adj.* alternate; (agric.) *culture alternée*, rotation of crops.
alterner [altɛrne] *v.i.* to alternate, to succeed each other in turn; *~ v.t.* to rotate (crops).
altesse [altɛs] *s.f.* Highness (title).
althaea [alteɑ] *s.f.* (bot.) Althaea, marsh-mallow.
alti-er, -ère [altje] *adj.* haughty, proud, lofty.
altimètre [altimɛtr] *s.m.* altimeter.
altise [altiz] *s.f.* (ent.) flea-beetle.
altitude [altityd] *s.f.* **1.** (obs.) height; **2.** altitude (above sea level); (esp.) high altitude; *en ~*, at a high altitude; *mal d'~*, altitude sickness.
alto [alto] *s.f.* (mus.) contralto, alto, (voice, singer); *~ s.m.* (mus.) viola.
altruisme [altrɥism] *s.m.* altruism.
altruiste [altrɥist] *adj., s.m.f.* altruist(ic).
aluminate [alyminat] *s.m.* (chem.) aluminate.
alumine [alymin] *s.f.* (chem.) alumina.
alumineu-x, -se [alyminø] *adj.* **1.** (obs.) containing alum; **2.** aluminous.
aluminium [alyminjɔm] *s.m.* aluminium.
alun [alœ̃] *s.m.* (chem.) alum.
alunir [alynir] *v.i.* to land on the moon.
alunissage [alynisaʒ] *s.m.* moon-landing.
alvéolaire [alveɔlɛr] *adj.* alveolar.
alvéole [alveol] *s.m.* alveolus, small cavity; socket (of tooth), cell (of honeycomb).
alvin, -e [alvɛ̃] *adj.* (med.) alvine; *flux ~*, diarrhoea.
alysse [alis], **alysson** [alisɔ̃] *s.m.* (bot.) alyssum.
amabilité [amabilite] *s.f.* amiableness, kindness affability; *veuillez avoir*, or *ayez, l'~ de*, would you be kind enough to?
amadou [amadu] *s.m.* amadou, German tinder; **~vier** [amaduvje] *s.m.* fungus producing *amadou*.
amadouer [amadwe] *v.t.* to coax, to wheedle, to cajole, to flatter, to appease, to calm, to win (s.o.) round, to get round (s.o.); (fam.) to soft-soap.
amaigrir [amegrir] *v.t.* to make thin or lean, to emaciate; (techn.) to reduce thickness (of wood); **s'~** *v.refl.* to get thin(ner), to lose weight.
amaigrissant, -e [amegrisɑ̃] *adj.* thinning, reducing, slimming; *un régime ~*, a slimming diet.
amaigrissement [amegrismɑ̃] *s.m.* thinning, slimming; thinness, emaciation.
amalgamation [amalgamɑsjɔ̃] *s.f.* (chem.) amalgamation.
amalgame [amalgam] *s.m.* **1.** (chem.) amalgam; **2.** (fig.) medley, strange mixture; **3.** (mil., pol.) combination (of different units, viewpoints, etc.).
amalgamer [amalgame] *v.t.* to amalgamate; (fig.) to consolidate, to merge, to combine; **s'~** *v.refl.* to amalgamate, to be amalgamated, to merge.
aman [amɑ̃] *s.m.* (in Islamic countries) reprieve, pardon; *demander l'~*, to surrender, to submit.
amande [amɑ̃d] *s.f.* almond; kernel (of other fruits); *~ mondée*, blanched almond; *en ~*, almond-shaped.
amandier [amɑ̃dje] *s.m.* almond-tree.
amant, -e [amɑ̃] *s.m.f.* **1.** (obs.) sweetheart, suitor; **2.** lover; (pl.) (pair of) lovers; (fig.) devotee.
amarante [amarɑ̃t] *s.f.* (bot.) amaranth, love-lies-bleeding, prince's feather; *~ adj.* amaranthine.

amariner [amarine] *v.t.* **1.** (obs.) to man (ship); **2.** to place a crew on board a prize; to season (sailors); **s'~** *v.refl.* to find one's sea-legs.
amarrage [amaraʒ] *s.m.* (naut.) mooring, berthing; lashing.
amarre [amar] *s.f.* cable, rope, hawser, line; (pl.) moorings.
amarrer [amare] *v.t.* (naut.) to moor, to berth, to tie up; to lash, to fasten, to make fast.
amaryllis [amaril(l)is] *s.f.* amaryllis; ~ (*belle-dame*), belladonna lily.
amas [amɑ] *s.m.* (lit. & fig.) heap, mass, pile, mound, accumulation.
amasser [amɑse] *v.t.* to heap up, to pile up, to amass, to accumulate; to collect, to assemble, to store up; **s'~** *v.refl.* to gather (together), to collect, to assemble.
amateur [amatœr] *s.m.* **1.** amateur, lover, connoisseur, fancier, collector; (fam.) *je ne suis pas ~*, I'm not bidding; **2.** amateur (not professional); (pej.) dilettante; **~isme** [amatœrism] *s.m.* (sport) amateur status; (pej.) unprofessional work.
amatir [amatir] *v.t.* to matt, to give a matt finish to, to dull, to deaden.
amaurose [amɔroz] *s.f.* (med.) amaurosis.
amazone [amazon] *s.f.* Amazon; female rider; riding-habit; *monter en ~*, to ride side-saddle.
ambages [ɑ̃baʒ] *s.f.pl.* ambiguity, circumlocution; *parler sans ~*, to talk straight; *je vous dirai sans ~*, I will tell you in plain English, without beating about the bush.
ambassade [ɑ̃basad] *s.f.* embassy; special mission.
ambassad-eur, -rice [ɑ̃basadœr] *s.m.f.* ambassador, ambassadress; (fig.) envoy, messenger, representative.
ambiance [ɑ̃bjɑ̃s] *s.f.* ambience, atmosphere, climate, surroundings; (fam.) *il y a de l'~ ici*, this place has character, this is a lively spot.
ambiant, -e [ɑ̃bjɑ̃] *adj.* ambient, surrounding.
ambidextre [ɑ̃bidɛkstr] *adj.* ambidextrous.
ambig-u, -uë [ɑ̃bigy] *adj.* ambiguous, vague, unclear; **~ument** [ɑ̃bigymɑ̃] *adv.* ambiguously, vaguely; **~u** *s.m.* hotch-potch.
ambiguïté [ɑ̃bigɥite] *s.f.* ambiguity.
ambitieu-x, -se [ɑ̃bisjø] *adj.* ambitious; (pej.) over-ambitious, pretentious; **~sement** [ɑ̃bisjøzmɑ̃] *adv.* ambitiously.
ambition [ɑ̃bisjɔ̃] *s.f.* ambition; **~ner** [ɑ̃bisjɔne] *v.t.* to aspire to; *~ner de faire*, to have a great desire to do.
ambivalence [ɑ̃bivalɑ̃s] *s.f.* ambivalence.
ambivalent, -e [ɑ̃bivalɑ̃] *adj.* ambivalent.
amble [ɑ̃bl] *s.m.* amble, ambling; *aller l'~*, to amble.
ambler [ɑ̃ble] *v.i.* to amble.
ambleu-r, -se [ɑ̃blœr] *adj.* (of horse) ambling.
amblyopie [ɑ̃bliɔpi] *s.f.* amblyopia.
ambon [ɑ̃bɔ̃] *s.m.* (arch.) ambo.
ambre [ɑ̃br] *s.m.* **1.** ~ *gris*, ambergris; **2.** ~ (*jaune*), amber; *couleur d'~*, amber-coloured.
ambré, -e [ɑ̃bre] *adj.* **1.** perfumed with ambergris; **2.** amber-coloured.
ambrette [ɑ̃brɛt] *s.f.* hibiscus seed.
ambroisie [ɑ̃brwazi] *s.f.* ambrosia.
ambrosien, -ne [ɑ̃brozjɛ̃] *adj.* Ambrosian, relating to St. Ambrose.
ambulance [ɑ̃bylɑ̃s] *s.f.* **1.** (obs.) field-hospital; **2.** ambulance.
ambulanci-er, -ère [ɑ̃bylɑ̃sje] *s.m.f.* **1.** (obs.) stretcher-bearer, medical orderly, nurse; **2.** ambulance-driver.
ambulant, -e [ɑ̃bylɑ̃] *adj.* itinerant, strolling; travelling; walking; *marchand ~*, coster-monger; *courrier ~*, sorter in travelling post-office; *un cadavre ~*, a walking corpse.
ambulatoire [ɑ̃bylatwar] *adj.* ambulatory.
âme [ɑm] *s.f.* **1.** (relig.) soul, spirit; ~ *en peine*, lost soul; *rendre l'~*, to give up the ghost; *être l'~ damnée de qn.*, to be the tool or stooge of s.o.; **2.** mind, heart; *de toute son ~*, with all one's heart; **3.** conscience; *en mon ~ et conscience*, to the best of my knowledge and belief; (iron.) *les bonnes ~s*, the do-gooders; **4.** mind, spirit; *état d'~*, state of mind; **5.** life, spirit; *chanter avec ~*, to sing with spirit; **6.** soul, living person; *une ~ sœur*, a kindred spirit; *il n'y avait ~ qui vive*, there was not a living soul; *une ville de plus de dix mille ~s*, a town of more than 10,000 inhabitants; *mon ~, ma chère ~*, my dear (soul); **7.** soul, essence, life; *l'~ d'un peuple*, the soul of a nation; *l'~ de la conjuration*, the moving-spirit in the plot; **8.** (mus.) sound-post (of violin); bore (of gun); core (of cast); (techn.) main part, centre; (fig.) *l'~ d'une machine*, the hub of a machine.
améliorable [ameljɔrabl] *adj.* capable of being improved.
améliorant, -e [ameljɔrɑ̃] *adj.* (agric.) improving, fertilizing.
amélioration [ameljɔrɑsjɔ̃] *s.f.* improvement, betterment, amelioration; (pl.) repairs, improvements, restoration.
améliorer [ameljɔre] *v.t.* to improve, to make better, to ameliorate, to revise, to correct, to emend; to repair, to restore (a building); to fertilize (land); **s'~** *v.refl.* to improve.
amen [amɛn] *s.m.* amen; *il dit ~ à tout* (*ce qu'on dit, ce qu'on fait*), he agrees to everything (one says or does).
aménagement [amenaʒmɑ̃] *s.m.* **1.** (forestry) management; **2.** fitting-up, arrangement, furnishing, fitting-out; planning; ~ *du territoire*, regional planning.
aménager [amenaʒe] *v.t.* **1.** (forestry) to manage, to regulate (felling, etc.); **2.** to arrange, to fit up, to organize, to furnish.
amendable [amɑ̃dabl] *adj.* amendable.
amende [amɑ̃d] *s.f.* fine, penalty, costs, forfeit; *condamner à une ~*, to fine; *sous peine d'~*, subject to a fine; (fam.) *vous serez mis à l'~*, you'll pay for it; ~ *honorable*, (i.) (obs.) public confession; (ii.) apology.
amendement [amɑ̃dmɑ̃] *s.m.* **1.** (obs.) improvement; **2.** (agric.) enriching, fertilizing, (soil); **3.** (pol.) amendment.
amender [amɑ̃de] *v.t.* **1.** to improve, to correct; **2.** (agric.) to enrich; **3.** (pol.) to amend; **s'~** *v.refl.* to improve.
amène [amɛn] *adj.* (Lit.) amiable, courteous.
amener [amne] *v.t.* **1.** to bring, to lead, to take, to carry; to induce, to cause; to introduce (subject), to bring about; **2.** to pull in, to haul in; (naut.) to lower (sails, flag); **3.** (dice) to throw; **s'~** *v.refl.* (pop.) to turn up, to show up; *amène-toi ici!*, come over here!
aménité [amenite] *s.f.* **1.** (obs.) amenity, charm; **2.** affability, amiability; **3.** (pl.) (iron.) home--truths.
amenuisement [amənɥizmɑ̃] *s.m.* reduction, decrease.
amenuiser [amənɥize] *v.t.* to thin, to make thinner, to whittle away; (fig.) to reduce; **s'~** *v.refl.* to become smaller, to diminish.
am-er, -ère [amɛr] *adj.* (lit. & fig.) bitter, biting, acrid, sharp, galling, sarcastic; **~èrement** [amɛrmɑ̃] *adv.* bitterly.
amer[1] [amɛr] *s.m.* **1.** (obs.) gall; **2.** bitter drink, bitters.
amer[2] [amɛr] *s.m.* (naut.) landmark.
américain, -e [amerikɛ̃] *adj., s.m.f.* American; *vol à l'~e*, confidence trick; (sport) *course à l'~e*, cycle relay-race.
américanis-er [amerikanize] *v.t.* to Americanize; **~ation** [amerikanizɑsjɔ̃] *s.f.* Americaniza-

tion; **~me** [amerikanism] *s.m.* **1.** (obs.) pro--Americanism; **2.** Americanism (expression); **3.** American studies.
Amérique [amerik] *s.f.* (geog.) America; *~ du Nord, du Sud*, North America, South America.
amerlo(t) [amɛrlo], **amerloque** [amɛrlɔk] *s.m.f.* (pop.) American, Yank, Yankee.
amerrir [amerir] *v.i.* (of hydroplane) to land on the sea.
amerrissage [amerisaʒ] *s.m.* landing on the sea.
amertume [amɛrtym] *s.f.* bitter taste; bitterness, sourness; (fig.) melancholy, sadness, gloom.
améthyste [ametist] *s.f.* amethyst.
ameublement [amœbləmɑ̃] *s.m.* furniture, furnishings; *tissus d'~*, furnishing fabrics.
ameublir [amœblir] *v.t.* **1.** (agric.) to break, to dig, to work, to prepare (ground); **2.** (law) to bring (one's realty) to the communal estate.
ameublissement [amœblismɑ̃] *s.m.* **1.** (agric.) breaking or preparing of ground; **2.** (law) marriage agreement bringing personalty to the communal estate.
ameuter [amøte] *v.t.* **1.** to form (hounds) into a pack, to train (young hounds); **2.** to stir up, to collect (a mob), to rouse; *~ contre qn.*, to set on, to mob, s.o.; **s'~** *v.refl.* to riot, to mutiny.
ami, -e [ami] *s.m.f.* friend; (euphem.) lover, mistress; (fig.) supporter, admirer; *chambre d'~(s)*, spare-room, guest-room; *~ de cœur*, bosom friend; *un ~ de la maison*, a family friend; *on connaît ses ~s au besoin*, a friend in need is a friend indeed; (obs.) *hé! l'~!*, (to inferior) I say! you, there!, my good man!; *mon ~(e)*, (between husband and wife) my dear, darling; *bonne ~e*, (fam.) sweetheart; *mes chers ~s*, (form of address) friends, comrades, fellow-workers, etc.; *les ~s du livre*, booklovers, bibliophiles; *en ~*, as a friend; *adj.* friendly, welcoming, familiar, favourable, allied.
amiable [amjabl] *adj.* (law) private, informal; *à l'~*, amicably, privately; *vente à l'~*, sale by private treaty; *régler une affaire à l'~*, to settle out of court; ⚠ not 'amiable' in sense 'well-disposed'.
amiante [amjɑ̃t] *s.m.* asbestos.
amibe [amib] *s.f.* (zool.) amoeba; (fam.) *il a des ~s*, he has caught a bug.
amibien, -ne [amibjɛ̃] *adj.* amoebic.
amical, -e, (aux) [amikal] *adj.* friendly, kind, amicable; *peu ~*, unfriendly; **~ement** [amikalmɑ̃] *adv.* in a friendly way, kindly, amicably; **~e** *s.f.* friendly society, association.
amict [ami] *s.m.* (eccles.) amice.
amide [amid] *s.m.* (chem.) amide.
amidon [amidɔ̃] *s.m.* starch; **~nage** [amidɔnaʒ] *s.m.* starching; **~ner** [amidɔne] *v.t.* to starch; **~nier** [amidɔnje] *s.m.* starch-maker.
amincir [amɛ̃sir] *v.t.* to make thinner; to make (s.o.) look slimmer, to have a slimming effect on; *cette robe l'amincit*, that dress makes her look slimmer; *~ v.i.* (fam.) to get thinner, to get slimmer, to lose weight; *elle a aminci*, she has lost weight; **s'~** *v.refl.* to get thinner.
amincissement [amɛ̃sismɑ̃] *s.m.* thinning, slimming; (fig.) reduction; getting thinner or slimmer.
amiral, (aux) [amiral] *s.m.* admiral; *grand ~*, Admiral of the Fleet; *contre-~*, rear admiral; *vaisseau ~*, flagship; **~e** *s.f.* admiral's wife.
amirauté [amirote] *s.f.* Admiralty; admiral's rank.
amitié [amitje] *s.f.* **1.** friendship, liking, affection; *prendre en ~*, to befriend; *se lier d'~ avec qn.*, to make friends with s.o.; *~ particulière*, (i.) homosexual relationship; (ii.) friendly relations; **2.** favour, kindness; *faites-moi l'~ de*, do me the favour, the kindness, of; **3.** (pl.) greetings, love, kind regards; *faites-lui toutes mes ~s*, give her my love, my very kind regards; (at end of letter) *toutes mes ~s, ~s à tous, meilleures ~s*, kind regards, love (to all).
ammonia-c, -que [amɔnjak] *adj.* ammoniac(al); **~que** *s.f.* ammonia.
ammoniacal, -e, (aux) [amɔnjakal] *adj.* ammoniac(al).
ammonite [amɔnit] *s.f.* ammonite.
ammonium [amɔnjɔm] *s.m.* (chem.) ammonium.
amnésie [amnezi] *s.f.* amnesia.
amnésique [amnezik] *adj., s.m.f.* amnesic; (person) suffering from amnesia.
amnios [amnjos] *s.m.* (obstetrics) amnion; (fam.) water-bag.
amniotique [amnjɔtik] *adj.* amniotic.
amnistie [amnisti] *s.f.* amnesty.
amnistier [amnistje] *v.t.* to grant an amnesty to; (Lit., fig.) to pardon.
amocher [amɔʃe] *v.t.* (pop.) to damage, to beat up; **s'~** *v.refl.* to take a beating, to get hurt.
amodiation [amɔdjɑsjɔ̃] *s.f.* leasing, letting out on lease.
amodier [amɔdje] *v.t.* to let on lease.
amoindrir [amwɛ̃drir] *v.t.* to lessen, to decrease, to diminish, to reduce; **s'~** *v.refl.* to decrease, to diminish.
amoindrissement [amwɛ̃drismɑ̃] *s.m.* lessening, decrease, reduction.
amollir [amɔlir] *v.t.* to soften, to weaken, to melt; (fig.) to enervate, to unnerve, to weaken; **s'~** *v.refl.* to weaken, to become weak.
amollissant, -e [amɔlisɑ̃] *adj.* softening, enervating, weakening.
amollissement [amɔlismɑ̃] *s.m.* (usu. fig.) softening, weakening.
amonceler [amɔ̃sle] *v.t.* to heap up, to pile up, to accumulate, to collect; **s'~** *v.refl.* to pile up, to accumulate, to gather; (of snow) to drift.
amoncellement [amɔ̃sɛlmɑ̃] *s.m.* heap, pile, drift, accumulation; piling up.
amont [amɔ̃] *s.m.* upper reaches (of river); *en ~*, upstream; *vent d'~*, offshore wind.
amoral, -e, (aux) [amɔral] *adj.* amoral; **~isme** [amɔralism] *s.m.* amoralism.
amorçage [amɔrsaʒ] *s.m.* baiting (of hook); priming (of gun, pump, etc.); (electr.) starting, excitation (of dynamo).
amorce [amɔrs] *s.f.* **1.** bait; (fig., obs.) lure, attraction; **2.** primer, cap, detonator, fuse; *sans brûler une ~*, without a shot being fired; **3.** (fig.) beginning, first step (*de*, towards).
amorcer [amɔrse] *v.t.* **1.** to bait (line, hook, trap); (fig., obs.) to allure, to attract; **2.** to prime (gun, pump); **3.** to begin to pierce (hole, opening); **4.** (fig.) to set in motion, to begin, to open (conversation, etc.).
amorphe [amɔrf] *adj.* amorphous; (fig.) limp, listless, inert, without character.
amortir [amɔrtir] *v.t.* **1.** to deaden, to absorb (shock), to break, to cushion; to muffle, to stifle, to lessen (sound); to reduce; (fig.) to calm, to blunt; **2.** (fin.) to amortize, to extinguish (debt); to pay by instalments, to pay off, to redeem; to write off, to allow for depreciation (of material); **s'~** *v.refl.* to be deadened, to be absorbed, to fade away.
amortissable [amɔrtisabl] *adj.* (fin.) redeemable.
amortissement [amɔrtismɑ̃] *s.m.* **1.** deadening, absorbing (shock), breaking (fall), sound--proofing; **2.** (fin.) amortization, redemption; depreciation, writing-off; *caisse* or *fonds d'~*, reserve or sinking fund; **3.** (arch.) finial.
amortisseur [amɔrtisœr] *s.m.* (mech.) shock--absorber.
amour [amur] *s.m.* **1.** love, affection, devotion; passion, adoration; (euphem.) sexual relations;

(pl.) love affairs; *faire l'~*, to make love; **2.** beloved (person); *mon ~*, my love; (fam.) *vous seriez un ~ si vous . . .*, it would be sweet of you if you would . . .; **3.** (myth., art) cupid; *un ~ d'enfant*, a dear little child; (fam.) *un ~ de petit chapeau*, a pretty little hat.

(s')amouracher [amuraʃe] *v.refl. s'~ de*, (pej.) to fall for.

amourette [amurɛt] *s.f.* **1.** passing fancy; **2.** (pop.) lily of the valley; *bois d'~*, mimosa-wood; **3.** (pl.) (cook.) amourettes, calf's marrow.

amoureu-x, -se [amurø] *adj.* loving; love-; (pej.) lascivious, amorous; *~x, ~se de*, in love with, enamoured of; (fig.) keen on, mad about, devoted to; *un regard ~x*, a loving look; *sa vie ~se*, his love-life; *s.m.f.* lover, sweetheart; **~sement** [amurøzmɑ̃] *adv.* lovingly, tenderly; amorously.

amour-propre [amurprɔpr] *s.m.* self-respect, self-esteem, pride.

amovibilité [amɔvibilite] *s.f.* removability (of officials); uncertain tenure of office.

amovible [amɔvibl] *adj.* **1.** removable, liable to be posted elsewhere; (of official) liable to be dismissed; not permanent, liable to be withdrawn or transferred; **2.** removable, detachable; *imperméable à doublure ~*, raincoat with detachable lining.

ampère [ɑ̃pɛr] *s.m.* ampere, amp (fam.); **~-heure** [ɑ̃pɛrœr] *s.m.* ampere-hour; **~mètre** [ɑ̃pɛrmɛtr] *s.m.* ammeter.

amphétamine [ɑ̃fetamin] *s.f.* amphetamine.

amphi [ɑ̃fi] *s.m.* see AMPHITHÉÂTRE 3.

amphibie [ɑ̃fibi] *adj., s.m.* amphibious; amphibian.

amphibiens [ɑ̃fibjɛ̃] *s.m.pl.* amphibians.

amphibologie [ɑ̃fibɔlɔʒi] *s.f.* amphibology, ambiguity.

amphibologique [ɑ̃fibɔlɔʒik] *adj.* amphibological, ambiguous.

amphigouri [ɑ̃figuri] *s.m.* (Lit.) amphigouri, amphigory; tissue of nonsense; **~que** [ɑ̃figurik] *adj.* unintelligible, incomprehensible.

amphioxus [ɑ̃fjɔksys] *s.m.* (ichth.) amphioxus, lancelet.

amphisbène [ɑ̃fisbɛn] *s.m.* (myth., zool.) amphisbaena.

amphithéâtre [ɑ̃fiteɑtr] *s.m.* **1.** amphitheatre; **2.** (theatr.) gallery; **3.** lecture-theatre, lecture-room (fam. abbrev. *amphi*).

Amphitryon [ɑ̃fitrijɔ̃] *s.m.* Amphitryon; *amphitryon*, host, entertainer.

amphore [ɑ̃fɔr] *s.f.* amphora.

ample [ɑ̃pl] *adj.* ample, large, wide, full, broad, loose-fitting; abundant, plentiful, generous; roomy, vast; **~ment** [ɑ̃pləmɑ̃] *adv.* amply, fully, abundantly, widely, more than sufficiently, generously.

amplecti-f, -ve [ɑ̃plɛktif] *adj.* (bot.) amplective.

ampleur [ɑ̃plœr] *s.f.* width, breadth, spaciousness, amplitude (of style), fullness (of dress); abundance, importance, scope, extent.

ampliati-f, -ve [ɑ̃pliatif] *adj.* (law) ampliative, duplicate.

ampliation [ɑ̃pliɑsjɔ̃] *s.f.* certified copy, duplicate; (formula) *pour ~* = this is a true copy.

amplificateur [ɑ̃plifikatœr] *s.m.* **1.** (obs.) person who exaggerates; **2.** (photo.) enlarger; **3.** (electr.) amplifier (fam. abbrev. *ampli*).

amplificat-eur, -rice [ɑ̃plifikatœr] *adj.* amplifying.

amplification [ɑ̃plifikɑsjɔ̃] *s.f.* **1.** (obs.) magnifying; **2.** (photo.) enlarging; (electr.) amplification; **3.** (fig.) amplification, expansion, development (of theme); (pej.) exaggeration.

amplifier [ɑ̃plifje] *v.t.* to enlarge, to amplify, to increase in intensity, to magnify; (pej.) to exaggerate; **s'~** *v.refl.* to grow larger, to increase in volume.

amplitude [ɑ̃plityd] *s.f.* **1.** (obs.) largeness, extent; **2.** (astron., geom., phys.) amplitude.

ampoule [ɑ̃pul] *s.f.* **1.** ampulla; phial, flask; **2.** bulb (of electric light, thermometer, etc.); **3.** blister; *il ne se fait pas d'~s aux mains*, he doesn't overwork.

ampoulé, -e [ɑ̃pule] *adj.* (of style, etc.) bombastic, pompous.

amputation [ɑ̃pytɑsjɔ̃] *s.f.* amputation; (fig.) cutting down, reduction.

amputé, -e [ɑ̃pyte] *s.m.f.* one who has had an amputation, who has lost a limb.

amputer [ɑ̃pyte] *v.t.* to amputate; (fig.) to cut down, to shorten, to reduce.

(s')amuïr [amɥir] *v.refl.* (lang.) to become silent, to become mute, to disappear.

amuïssement [amɥismɑ̃] *s.m.* (lang.) disappearance, becoming silent or mute.

amulette [amylɛt] *s.f.* amulet, charm, talisman.

amure [amyr] *s.f.* (naut.) tack (of sail); clew--line.

amurer [amyre] *v.t.* (naut.) to tack, to brace to windward.

amusant, -e [amyzɑ̃] *adj.* amusing, entertaining, diverting, comic, funny.

amuse-gueule [amyzgœl] *s.m.invar.* (cocktail) snack, savoury; (fig., pop.) preliminaries.

amusement [amyzmɑ̃] *s.m.* **1.** (obs.) diversion, hoax, waste of time; **2.** amusement, entertainment.

amuser [amyze] *v.t.* **1.** (obs. exc. Lit.) to deceive, to mislead, to beguile; **2.** to distract the attention of; *il amusait le caissier pendant qu'on ouvrait le coffre*, he kept the cashier occupied while they broke open the safe; **3.** to amuse, to entertain, to divert, to cause laughter; **s'~** *v.refl.* **1.** to waste one's time on inessentials, to dilly--dally; **2.** to be amused, to enjoy oneself, to have a good time; (pej.) to lead a gay life; *amusez--vous bien!*, have a good time!, enjoy yourselves!; *il s'amuse avec nous*, he's playing with us, he's leading us on.

amusette [amyzɛt] *s.f.* toy, trifle, petty amusement or diversion, pastime.

amuseur [amyzœr] *s.m.* **1.** (obs.) deceiver; **2.** entertainer.

amygdale [ami(g)dal] *s.f.* (anat.) tonsil.

amygdal-ectomie [ami(g)dalɛktɔmi] *s.f.* tonsillectomy; **~ite** [ami(g)dalit] *s.f.* tonsillitis.

amylacé, -e [amilase] *adj.* amylaceous, starchy.

amyle [amil] *s.m.* (chem.) amyl.

amylène [amilɛn] *s.m.* (chem.) amylene.

amylique [amilik] *adj.* (chem.) amylic.

an [ɑ̃] *s.m.* year, twelvemonth; *le jour de l'~*, New Year's Day; *bon ~, mal ~*, taking one year with another, on average; *je m'en moque comme de l'~ quarante*, I don't care a rap.

ana [ana] *s.m.* ana, collection of thoughts and sayings.

anabaptisme [anabatism] *s.m.* anabaptism, doctrine of anabaptists.

anabaptiste [anabatist] *s.m.f.* anabaptist.

anabolisme [anabɔlism] *s.m.* anabolism.

anacardier [anakardje] *s.m.* cashew-nut-tree.

anachorète [anakɔrɛt] *s.m.* anchoret, anchorite, hermit; *mener une vie d'~*, to live as a recluse.

anachronique [anakrɔnik] *adj.* anachronic, anachronistic.

anachronisme [anakrɔnism] *s.m.* anachronism.

anacoluthe [anakɔlyt] *s.f.* (lang.) anacoluthon.

anaconda [anakɔ̃da] *s.m.* (zool.) anaconda.

anacréontique [anakreɔ̃tik] *adj.* anacreontic.

anacrouse [anakruz] *s.f.* (pros., mus.) anacrusis.

anaérobie [anaerobi] *adj.* anaerobian, anaerobic; *~ s.m.* anaerobe.

anaglyphe [anaglif] *s.m.* **1.** anaglyph; **2.** (photo.) stereo-pair.
anagogie [anagɔʒi] *s.f.* (theol.) anagoge.
anagogique [anagɔʒik] *adj.* (theol.) anagogic(al).
anagramme [anagram] *s.f.* anagram.
anal, -e, (aux) [anal] *adj.* anal.
analecta [analɛkta], **analectes** [analɛkt] *s.m.pl.* (Lit.) analects, analecta, gleanings.
analeptique [analɛptik] *adj.* (med.) analeptic, restorative.
analgésie [analʒezi] *s.f.* analgesia.
analgésique [analʒezik] *adj., s.m.* analgesic.
analogie [analɔʒi] *s.f.* analogy.
analogique [analɔʒik] *adj.* analogical.
analogue [analɔg] *adj.* analogous, similar; ~ *s.m.* equivalent.
analphabète [analfabɛt] *adj., s.m.f.* illiterate.
analphabétisme [analfabetism] *s.m.* illiteracy.
analysable [analizabl] *adj.* analysable.
analyse [analiz] *s.f.* **1.** analysis; (lang.) ~ *grammaticale*, parsing; ~ *logique*, analysis; (med.) ~ *du sang, des urines, etc.*, blood, urine, etc., test; *en dernière* ~, after careful consideration, in the last analysis; **2.** psycho-analysis, analysis of motives; *roman d'*~, psychological novel.
analyser [analize] *v.t.* to analyse, to parse, to dissect, to examine; to summarize (book); **s'**~ *v.refl.* to be introspective.
analyste [analist] *s.m.f.* analyst.
analytique [analitik] *s.f.* analytics; ~ *adj.* analytic(al); *géométrie* ~, co-ordinate geometry; ~**ment** [analitikmɑ̃] *adv.* analytically.
anamorphose [anamɔrfoz] *s.f.* anamorphosis.
ananas [anana(s)] *s.m.* pineapple.
anapeste [anapɛst] *s.m.* anapaest.
anaphore [anafɔr] *s.f.* anaphora.
anaplastie [anaplasti] *s.f.* (surg.) anaplasty.
anarchie [anarʃi] *s.f.* anarchy; disorder, confusion.
anarchique [anarʃik] *adj.* anarchic(al); ~**ment** [anarʃikmɑ̃] *adv.* anarchically, in disorderly fashion.
anarchisant, -e [anarʃizɑ̃] *adj.* tending to anarchy; of anarchist sympathies.
anarchisme [anarʃism] *s.m.* anarchism.
anarchiste [anarʃist] *adj., s.m.f.* anarchist.
anastigmat [anastigma] *adj.m.* (photo.) anastigmatic.
anastomose [anastɔmoz] *s.f.* anastomosis.
anastomoser [anastɔmoze] *v.t.* to join by anastomosis; **s'**~ *v.refl.* to anastomose.
anastrophe [anastrɔf] *s.f.* anastrophe.
anathématiser [anatematize] *v.t.* to anathematize; (fig.) to curse, to blame severely.
anathème [anatɛm] *s.m.* **1.** anathema; (fig.) curse; *frapper d'*~, to anathematize, to declare accursed; **2.** anathema, person accursed or excommunicated.
anatife [anatif] *s.m.* (zool.) barnacle.
Anatolie [anatɔli] *s.f.* (geog.) Anatolia.
anatomie [anatɔmi] *s.f.* anatomy; (fam.) *une belle* ~, a good figure.
anatomique [anatɔmik] *adj.* anatomical; ~**ment** [anatɔmikmɑ̃] *adv.* anatomically.
anatomiser [anatɔmize] *v.t.* (obs.) to anatomize, to dissect; (fig.) to analyse.
anatomiste [anatɔmist] *s.m.f.* anatomist; (obs.) analyst.
ancestral, -e, (aux) [ɑ̃sɛstral] *adj.* ancestral.
ancêtre [ɑ̃sɛtr] *s.m.f.* ancestor, ancestress; (fig.) originator, forerunner; (fam.) old man; (pl.) forefathers.
anche [ɑ̃ʃ] *s.f.* (mus.) reed (of clarinet, etc.); reed-pipe (of organ).
anchois [ɑ̃ʃwa] *s.m.* anchovy; *beurre d'*~, anchovy-paste; ~ *de Norvège*, sprat.
ancien, -ne [ɑ̃sjɛ̃] *adj.* **1.** (after the noun) ancient, old, antique, early; *plus* ~, earlier, senior, elder; **2.** (before the noun) former, late, retired, ex-, previous; *l'*~ *ministre*, the former minister, the ex-minister; *un* ~ *élève*, an old boy, a former pupil; *un* ~ *combattant*, an ex-serviceman; ~ *s.m. l'*~, the antique, antiques· senior, elder; *il est mon* ~, he is my senior; *les* ~*s du village*, the village elders; *les* ~*s*, (i.) (hist., Lit.) the Ancients; (ii.) the old (opp. the young).
anciennement [ɑ̃sjɛnmɑ̃] *adv.* formerly, of old, in days gone by (abbrev. *ancienn.*).
ancienneté [ɑ̃sjɛnte] *s.f.* **1.** antiquity, ancientness; *de toute* ~, from time immemorial; **2.** length of service in post, seniority; *à l'*~, by seniority.
ancolie [ɑ̃kɔli] *s.f.* (bot.) columbine.
ancrage [ɑ̃kraʒ) *s.m.* anchorage; (manner of) anchoring.
ancre [ɑ̃kr] *s.f.* **1.** (naut.) anchor; *maîtresse* ~, sheet-anchor; ~ *à jet*, kedge; *jeter, lever, l'*~, to cast, to weigh, anchor; *chasser sur ses* ~*s*, to drag its anchors; (fig.) ~ *de salut*, sheet-anchor; **2.** (building) tie-rod; **3.** (horol.) anchor escapement.
ancrer [ɑ̃kre] *v.t.* **1.** (obs.) to anchor (a ship); **2.** (techn.) to brace, to anchor; **3.** (fig.) to establish, to fix; *idée ancrée*, deep-rooted idea; **s'**~ *v.refl.* to become established, to take root, to dig oneself in.
ancrure [ɑ̃kryr] *s.f.* (techn.) tie-rod.
andain [ɑ̃dɛ̃] *s.m.* (agric.) swath(e).
andalou, -e [ɑ̃dalu] *adj., s.m.f.* Andalusian.
Andalousie [ɑ̃daluzi] *s.f.* (geog.) Andalusia.
Andes [ɑ̃d] *s.f.pl.* (geog.) Andes.
Andorre [ɑ̃dɔr] *s.f.* (geog.) Andorra.
andouille [ɑ̃duj] *s.f.* (cook.) sausage filled with chitterlings; (pop.) imbecile; *faire l'*~, to play the fool; ~**tte** [ɑ̃dujɛt] *s.f.* small chitterling sausage.
andouiller [ɑ̃duje] *s.m.* tine (of antler).
andrinople [ɑ̃drinɔpl] *s.f.* turkey-twill; *rouge d'*~, turkey-red.
androgène [ɑ̃drɔʒɛn] *adj.* androgenous; ~ *s.m.* androgen, male sex hormone.
androgyne [ɑ̃drɔʒin] *adj., s.m.f.* androgynous (person); hermaphrodite.
androïde [ɑ̃drɔid] *s.m.* android.
âne [ɑn] *s.m.* ass, donkey, jackass; (fig.) fool, idiot; *têtu comme un* ~, stubborn as a mule; *le coup de pied de l'*~, final insult; *donner le coup de pied de l'*~ *à qn.*, to kick a man when he's down; *dos d'*~, ridge; *en dos d'*~, (of hill) razor-edged, (of bridge) hump-backed; (ichth.) *tête d'*~, miller's thumb; *un* ~ *bâté*, a hopeless idiot; *bonnet d'*~, dunce's cap; *le pont aux* ~*s*, pons asinorum; *faire l'*~ *pour avoir du son*, to act stupid in order to obtain information.
anéantir [aneɑ̃tir] *v.t.* **1.** to annihilate, to destroy completely, to wipe out, to crush; **2.** (fig.) to paralyse, to prostrate, to exhaust; *aneanti par la terreur*, paralysed with fear; **s'**~ *v.refl.* to come to nothing, to disappear completely; (relig.) to prostrate oneself (before God).
anéantissement [aneɑ̃tismɑ̃] *s.m.* **1.** annihilation, complete destruction; **2.** prostration, exhaustion; self-humiliation.
anecdote [anɛkdɔt] *s.f.* anecdote, (little) story; (art) detail.
anecdotier [anɛkdɔtje] *s.m.* anecdotist.
anecdotique [anɛkdɔtik] *adj.* anecdotal.
anémie [anemi] *s.f.* **1.** (med.) anaemia; **2.** (comm.) crisis, failure.
anémier [anemje] *v.t.* to make anaemic; (fig.) to weaken.
anémique [anemik] *adj., s.m.f.* anaemic; (person) suffering from anaemia.
anémo-graphe [anemɔgraf] *s.m.* anemograph; ~**mètre** [anemɔmɛtr] *s.m.* anemometer.

anémone [anemɔn] *s.f.* **1.** (bot.) anemone; **2.** (zool.) ~ *de mer*, sea anemone.
anencéphale [anɑ̃sefal] *adj.* anencephalous; ~ *s.m.f.* anencephalus.
ânerie [ɑnri] *s.f.* stupidity, gross ignorance; asinine words or behaviour.
anéroïde [anerɔid] *adj.* aneroid.
ânesse [ɑnɛs] *s.f.* she-donkey, she-ass; *lait d'~*, ass's milk.
anesthésie [anɛstezi] *s.f.* anaesthesia.
anesthésier [anɛstezje] *v.t.* to anaesthetize.
anesthésique [anɛstezik] *adj.*, *s.m.* anaesthetic.
anesthésiste [anɛstezist] *s.m.f.* anaesthetist.
anévrisme [anevrism] *s.m.* aneurism, aneurysm.
anfractuosité [ɑ̃fraktɥozite] *s.f.* anfractuosity; (usu. pl.) deep, irregular hollows (in rocks); (med.) anfractuosities (of the brain).
ange [ɑ̃ʒ] *s.m.* **1.** angel; ~ *gardien*, guardian angel; *être le mauvais ~ de qn.*, to be someone's evil genius; *être aux ~s*, to be in the seventh heaven (of delight); *rire aux ~s*, to wear a cherubic smile; (sport) *saut de l'~*, swallow-dive; *cheveux d'~*, tinsel decoration (for Christmas tree); (fam.) *faiseuse d'~s*, abortionist; (fam.) *mon ~*, my sweet; **2.** (ichth.) angel-fish.
angélique [ɑ̃ʒelik] *adj.* angelic.
angélique [ɑ̃ʒelik] *s.f.* (bot., cook.) angelica.
angelot [ɑ̃ʒlo] *s.m.* (art) cherub.
angélus [ɑ̃ʒelys] *s.m.* angelus.
angevin, -e [ɑ̃ʒvɛ̃] *adj.*, *s.m.f.* Angevin; (native or inhabitant) of Angers or Anjou.
angine [ɑ̃ʒin] *s.f.* (med.) quinsy; ~ *rouge*, tonsillitis; ~ *blanche*, diphtheria; ~ *de poitrine*, angina pectoris.
angineu-x, -se [ɑ̃ʒinø] *adj.* anginal.
angiome [ɑ̃ʒjɔm] *s.m.* (med.) angioma.
angiosperme [ɑ̃ʒjɔspɛrm] *adj.* angiospermous; ~ *s.f.* angiosperm.
anglais, -e [ɑ̃glɛ] *adj.*, *s.m.f.* English, British; Englishman; *les Anglais*, the English, the British; ~ *s.m.* English (language); **~e** *s.f.* cursive script; (pl.) ringlets; *filer à l'~e*, to take French leave.
anglaiser [ɑ̃gleze] *v.t.* to nick (horse).
angle [ɑ̃gl] *s.m.* **1.** angle, corner; (fig.) harshness, asperity; *à l'~ de la rue*, at the corner of the street; **2.** (fig.) angle, point of view; *sous cet ~*, from this point of view.
anglet [ɑ̃glɛ] *s.m.* (techn.) channelled groove.
Angleterre [ɑ̃glətɛr] *s.f.* (geog.) England.
anglican, -e [ɑ̃glikɑ̃] *adj.*, *s.m.f.* Anglican; *l'église ~e*, the Church of England.
anglicanisme [ɑ̃glikanism] *s.m.* Anglicanism.
angliciser [ɑ̃glisize] *v.t.* to anglicize.
anglicisme [ɑ̃glisism] *s.m.* (lang.) Anglicism.
angliciste [ɑ̃glisist] *s.m.f.* Anglicist, student of English language and culture.
anglo-mane [ɑ̃glɔman] *s.m.f.* Anglomaniac; **~manie** [ɑ̃glɔmani] *s.f.* Anglomania.
anglo-normand, -e [ɑ̃glɔnɔrmɑ̃] *adj.* *les îles ~-normandes*, the Channel Islands; **~-normand** *s.m.* (lang.) Anglo-Norman.
anglo-phile [ɑ̃glɔfil] *adj.*, *s.m.f.* Anglophile; **~philie** [ɑ̃glɔfili] *s.f.* Anglophilia; **~phobe** [ɑ̃glɔfɔb] *adj.*, *s.m.f.* Anglophobe; **~phobie** [ɑ̃glɔfɔbi] *s.f.* Anglophobia.
anglo-saxon, -ne [ɑ̃glɔsaksɔ̃] *adj.*, *s.m.f.* Anglo--Saxon.
angoissant, -e [ɑ̃gwasɑ̃] *adj.* distressing, alarming, agonizing.
angoisse [ɑ̃gwas] *s.f.* distress, anguish, agony, anxiety.
angoissé, -e [ɑ̃gwase] *adj.* anguished, agonized.
angora [ɑ̃gɔra] *adj.*, *s.m.* angora.
angstrœm [aŋstrœm] *s.m.* (phys.) angström.
anguiforme [ɑ̃gifɔrm] *adj.* anguiform, snake--like.
anguille [ɑ̃gij] *s.f.* eel; ~ *de mer*, conger-eel; ~ *plat-bec* or *de sable*, sand-eel, grig; (cook.) *matelote d'~*, stewed eels; *il glisse comme une ~*, he's as slippery as an eel; *il y a ~ sous roche*, there's something fishy going on.
anguillère [ɑ̃gijɛr] *s.f.* eel-pond.
angulaire [ɑ̃gylɛr] *adj.* angular; (constr. & fig.) *pierre ~*, corner-stone; *dent ~*, eye tooth.
anguleu-x, -se [ɑ̃gylø] *adj.* angular, rugged; rough-hewn; (fig.) awkward, difficult.
angusture [ɑ̃gystyr], **angustura** [ɑ̃gystyra] *s.f.* **1.** (pharm.) angostura bark; **2.** angostura bitters (proprietary name of drink).
anhélation [anelɑsjɔ̃] *s.f.* (med.) anhelation, shortness of breath.
anhéler [anele] *v.i.* to gasp for breath, to have difficulty in breathing.
anhydre [anidr] *adj.* (chem.) anhydrous.
anhydride [anidrid] *s.m.* (chem.) anhydride; *~ide carbonique*, carbon dioxide, carbonic acid gas.
anhydrite [anidrit] *s.f.* (min.) anhydrite.
anicroche [anikrɔʃ] *s.f.* hitch, snag; *se passer sans ~*, to go off without a hitch.
âni-er, -ère [ɑnje] *s.m.f.* donkey-driver.
aniline [anilin] *s.f.* (chem.) aniline.
animal (pl. **aux**) [animal] *s.m.* animal; (fig.) beast, brute, blighter; (fam.) bastard.
animal, -e, (**aux**) [animal] *adj.* animal; (fig.) brutish, bestial.
animalcule [animalkyl] *s.m.* animalcule.
animalier [animalje] *s.m.* (art) animalist, painter of animals.
animalité [animalite] *s.f.* **1.** animality, animal nature; the animal kingdom; **2.** (fig.) the animal or bestial side of man.
animat-eur, -rice [animatœr] *adj.* animating, stimulating; *s.m.f.* (cin.) animator; (radio, TV) M.C., question-master, announcer, presenter, commentator; (comm., pol.) moving spirit.
animation [animɑsjɔ̃] *s.f.* **1.** quickening, bringing to life; (cin.) animation; **2.** animation, liveliness, bustle, vivacity; briskness.
animé, -e [anime] *adj.* **1.** animate, living; **2.** animated, lively, vivacious; busy, brisk; bright; *dessins ~s*, animated cartoons.
animer [anime] *v.t.* **1.** to animate, to give life to, to bring to life, to enliven; **2.** to stimulate, to arouse; to incite; to move, to inspire; **s'~** *v.refl.* to come to life, to become animated, lively, vivacious.
animisme [animism] *s.m.* animism.
animiste [animist] *adj.*, *s.m.f.* animist(ic).
animosité [animozite] *s.f.* animosity.
anion [anjɔ̃] *s.m.* (electr.) anion.
anis [ani(s)] *s.m.* (bot.) anise; aniseed ball; *graine d'~*, aniseed; **~er** [anize] *v.t.* to flavour with aniseed; **~ette** [anizɛt] *s.f.* anisette (liqueur).
anisotrope [anizɔtrɔp] *adj.* anisotropic.
ankylose [ɑ̃kiloz] *s.f.* ankylosis.
ankyloser [ɑ̃kiloze] *v.t.* to ankylose, to make stiff; **s'~** *v.refl.* to ankylose, to become stiff.
annales [anal] *s.f.pl.* annals.
annaliste [analist] *s.m.* annalist.
Annam [anam] *s.m.* (geog.) Annam (now part of Vietnam).
annamite [anamit] *adj.* Annamite, Annamese; ~ *s.m.* (lang.) Annamese.
anneau (pl. **-x**) [ano] *s.m.* ring; link (of chain); ringlet; coil (of snake); (pl.) (gymn.) rings.
année [ane] *s.f.* year; ~ *bissextile*, leap-year; ~ *scolaire*, school or academic year; *~-lumière* (pl. *années-lumière*), light-year; *souhaiter la bonne ~ à qn.*, to wish s.o. a happy New Year.
annelé, -e [anle] *adj.* ringed; (zool.) annulate.
anneler [anle] *v.t.* **1.** to curl (hair); **2.** to ring (bull, etc.).

annexe [anɛks] *adj.* annexed, subsidiary, secondary; *un bâtiment* ~, an annexe, an extension (of a building); ~ *s.f.* **1.** chapel of ease; **2.** annexe; appendix, supplement; enclosure (of document, letter); **3.** (med., biol.) appendage.
annexer [anɛkse] *v.t.* **1.** to append, to enclose, to attach; **2.** to annex; **s'**~ *v.refl.* (fam.) to grab, to appropriate.
annexion [anɛksjɔ̃] *s.f.* annexation.
annihilation [aniilɑsjɔ̃] *s.f.* annihilation; (law) annulment.
annihiler [aniile] *v.t.* to annihilate; (law) to annul; to destroy, to make powerless.
anniversaire [anivɛrsɛr] *adj.*, *s.m.* anniversary, birthday.
annonce [anɔ̃s] *s.f.* **1.** announcement, notice, notification; **2.** advertisement; *petites* ~*s*, classified advertisements, personal or agony column; *insérer une* ~, to advertise (in newspaper); **3.** (cards) call, bid; **4.** (fig.) presage, sign, indication.
annoncer [anɔ̃se] *v.t.* **1.** to announce, to give notice of, to report, to publish; to indicate, to be a sign of; **2.** (cards) to call, to bid; **3.** to announce, to introduce (guest); **4.** to predict, to foretell; **s'**~ *v.refl.* **1.** to announce, to proclaim, oneself; **2.** to promise (well, ill), to augur (well, badly); *s'*~ *bien, mal,* to make a good, bad, start; *cela s'annonce bien,* it looks promising, it promises well.
annonceur [anɔ̃sœr] *s.m.* **1.** advertiser; **2.** (radio, TV) announcer.
annonciat-eur, -rice [anɔ̃sjatœr] *adj.* foreshadowing, presaging; *s.m.f.* one who predicts or announces.
annonciation [anɔ̃sjɑsjɔ̃] *s.f.* (eccles.) Annunciation.
annoncier [anɔ̃sje] *s.m.* advertising manager.
annotat-eur, -rice [anɔtatœr] *s.m.f.* annotator, commentator (of text).
annotation [anɔtɑsjɔ̃] *s.f.* annotation, note.
annoter [anɔte] *v.t.* to annotate.
annuaire [anɥɛr] *s.m.* annual, year-book, directory, almanach; ~ *militaire,* Army list; ~ *des Téléphones,* telephone directory.
annualité [anɥalite] *s.f.* annual character or nature, yearly recurrence.
annuel, -le [anɥɛl] *adj.* annual, yearly; *plante* ~*le,* annual; ~**lement** [anɥɛlmɑ̃] *adv.* annually, yearly; per annum, (so much) a year.
annuité [anɥite] *s.f.* annuity.
annulable [anylabl] *adj.* that can be annulled or rescinded.
annulaire [anylɛr] *adj.* annular; ~ *s.m.* ring--finger.
annulation [anylɑsjɔ̃] *s.f.* annulment; cancellation; (law) quashing (of judgement).
annuler [anyle] *v.t.* (law) to quash, to reverse, to set aside; to annul (marriage); to cancel, to rescind; to call off; to pay off (debt); **s'**~ *v.refl.* to counterbalance, to cancel each other out.
anoblir [anɔblir] *v.t.* to ennoble, to raise to the peerage.
anoblissement [anɔblismɑ̃] *s.m.* ennobling, raising to the peerage; *lettres d'*~, letters patent of nobility.
anode [anɔd] *s.f.* (electr.) anode, positive electrode.
anodin, -e [anɔdɛ̃] *adj.* (fig.) inoffensive, harmless, tame; insignificant; *adj.*, ~ *s.m.* (med.) anodyne.
anomal, -e, (**aux**) [anɔmal] *adj.* (gram.) anomalous.
anomalie [anɔmali] *s.f.* **1.** (lang., astron.) anomaly; **2.** deformity, abnormality, deviation; abnormal behaviour.
ânon [ɑnɔ̃] *s.m.* young donkey.
anone [anɔn] *s.f.* (bot.) Anona; custard-apple.
ânonnement [ɑnɔnmɑ̃] *s.m.* mumbling, mumbled words.
ânonner [ɑnɔne] *v.t.* to stumble through (recitation or reading); ~ *v.i.* to mumble.
anonymat [anɔnima] *s.m.* anonymity; *garder l'*~, to remain anonymous.
anonyme [anɔnim] *adj.* anonymous, nameless, unnamed; *société* ~ (abbrev. *S.A.*), limited company; ~**ment** [anɔnimmɑ̃] *adv.* anonymously.
anophèle [anɔfɛl] *s.m.* anopheles (mosquito).
anorak [anɔrak] *s.m.* anorak.
anordir [anɔrdir] *v.i.* (of wind) to veer or back north.
anorexie [anɔrɛksi] *s.f.* (med.) anorexia.
anormal, -e [anɔrmal] *adj.* abnormal, unnatural, unusual, exceptional, irregular; mentally retarded, backward; unfair, unjust; ~ *s.m.* mental case; ~**ement** [anɔrmalmɑ̃] *adv.* abnormally, unusually.
anosmie [anɔsmi] *s.f.* (med.) anosmia.
anoure [anur] *adj.* (zool.) anourous, anuran, tailless.
anoxémie [anɔksemi] *s.f.* (med.) anoxaemia.
anse [ɑ̃s] *s.f.* **1.** handle (of jug, basket, etc.), ear (of pitcher); (*en*) ~ *de panier,* half-oval; (fig.) *faire danser l'*~ *du panier,* (of servant, employee, etc.) to get pickings, to make a bit on the side; **2.** (geog.) cove, small bay.
ansérine [ɑ̃serin] *s.f.* (bot.) goosefoot.
anspect [ɑ̃spɛk] *s.m.* hand-spike; crow-bar.
antagon-ique [ɑ̃tagɔnik] *adj.* antagonistic; ~**isme** [ɑ̃tagɔnism] *s.m.* antagonism, conflict, opposition; ~**iste** [ɑ̃tagɔnist] *adj.* antagonistic; *s.m.f.* antagonist, opponent, rival.
antalgique [ɑ̃talʒik] *adj.* analgesic, pain-killing.
antan [ɑ̃tɑ̃] *s.m.* (obs.) last year; *d*~, of yore, of times gone by, of yesteryear.
antarctique [ɑ̃tarktik] *adj.* antarctic; *s.m.* (geog.) *l'Antarctique,* the Antarctic, Antarctica.
ante [ɑ̃t] *s.f.* (arch.) anta.
antécédence [ɑ̃tesedɑ̃s] *s.f.* antecedence.
antécédent, -e [ɑ̃tesedɑ̃] *adj.* antecedent; ~ *s.m.* antecedent; (pl.) antecedents, background, history.
antéchrist [ɑ̃tekrist] *s.m.* Antichrist.
antédiluvien, -ne [ɑ̃tedilyvjɛ̃] *adj.* antediluvian; (fam.) very ancient, as old as the hills.
antenais, -e [ɑ̃tnɛ] *adj. agneau, agnelle,* ~(*e*), hogget, teg.
antenne [ɑ̃tɛn] *s.f.* **1.** (naut.) lateen-yard; **2.** (zool.) antenna; (fig.) *avoir des* ~*s,* to be highly percipient; **3.** (radio, TV) aerial; **4.** (mil.) forward post.
anténuptial, -e [ɑ̃tenypsjal] *adj.* pre-marital.
antépénultième [ɑ̃tepenyltjɛm] *adj.* antepenultimate.
antérieur, -e [ɑ̃terjœr] *adj.* anterior, previous, preceding, front, fore-; ~**ement** [ɑ̃terjœrmɑ̃] *adv.* previously, prior (to).
antériorité [ɑ̃terjɔrite] *s.f.* priority, anteriority.
anthère [ɑ̃tɛr] *s.f.* (bot.) anther.
anthéridie [ɑ̃teridi] *s.f.* (bot.) antheridium.
anthérozoïde [ɑ̃terɔzɔid] *s.m.* (bot.) antherozoid.
anthologie [ɑ̃tɔlɔʒi] *s.f.* anthology.
anthozoaires [ɑ̃tɔzɔɛr] *s.m.pl.* (zool.) Anthozoa.
anthracène [ɑ̃trasɛn] *s.m.* (chem.) anthracene.
anthracite [ɑ̃trasit] *s.m.* anthracite; ~ *adj.invar.* (of) dark-grey.
anthrax [ɑ̃traks] *s.m.* (med., obs.) carbuncle; (vet., med.) anthrax.
anthropoïde [ɑ̃trɔpɔid] *adj.*, *s.m.* anthropoid.
anthropo-logie [ɑ̃trɔpɔlɔʒi] *s.f.* anthropology; ~**logique** [ɑ̃trɔpɔlɔʒik] *adj.* anthropological; ~**logue** [ɑ̃trɔpɔlɔg] *s.m.* anthropologist; ~**métrie** [ɑ̃trɔpɔmetri] *s.f.* anthropometry;

~métrique [ɑ̃trɔpɔmetrik] *adj.* anthropometric; **~morphe** [ɑ̃trɔpɔmɔrf] *adj.* anthropomorphous; **~morphisme** [ɑ̃trɔpɔmɔrfism] *s.m.* anthropomorphism; **~phage** [ɑ̃trɔpɔfaʒ] *adj.* anthropophagous, cannibal, cannibalistic; *s.m.f.* cannibal; **~phagie** [ɑ̃trɔpɔfaʒi] *s.f.* anthropophagy, cannibalism.

anti-adhérent, -e [ɑ̃tiaderɑ̃] *adj.* non-stick.

anti-aérien, -ne [ɑ̃tiaerjɛ̃] *adj.* anti-aircraft.

anti-alcoolique [ɑ̃tialkɔlik] *adj.* anti-alcoholic; teetotal; **~atomique** [ɑ̃tiatɔmik] *adj.* anti-nuclear.

anti-aveuglant, -e [ɑ̃tiavœglɑ̃] *adj.* anti-dazzle, anti-glare.

anti-biotique [ɑ̃tibjɔtik] *adj., s.m.* antibiotic; **~brouillard** [ɑ̃tibrujar] *adj., s.m.* (*phare*) *~brouillard,* fog-lamp; **~buée** [ɑ̃tibɥe] *adj.invar. dispositif ~buée,* demister.

anticancéreu-x, -se [ɑ̃tikɑ̃serø] *adj.* anti-cancer; *centre ~x,* cancer research centre.

antichambre [ɑ̃tiʃɑmbr] *s.f.* hall, waiting-room, ante-room; *faire ~,* to be kept waiting; *courir les ~s,* to importune one person after another.

antichar [ɑ̃tiʃar] *adj.* (mil.) anti-tank.

antichrèse [ɑ̃tikrɛz] *s.f.* (law) attachment of income from real estate.

anticipation [ɑ̃tisipɑsjɔ̃] *s.f.* anticipation; foresight; forecast, projection; *par ~,* in advance; *romans d'~,* science fiction.

anticipé, -e [ɑ̃tisipe] *adj.* (in) advance, before the due date; *versement ~,* advance payment.

anticiper [ɑ̃tisipe] *v.t.i.* to anticipate, to do in advance; *~ sur,* to encroach on; *n'anticipons pas!,* let's not get ahead of ourselves.

anticlérical, -e, (**aux**) [ɑ̃tiklerikal] *adj.* anti-clerical.

anticléricalisme [ɑ̃tiklerikalism] *s.m.* anti-clericalism.

anticlinal, -e, (**aux**) [ɑ̃tiklinal] *adj.* anticlinal; *~ s.m.* anticline.

anti-colonialisme [ɑ̃tikɔlɔnjalism] *s.m.* anti-colonialism; **~communisme** [ɑ̃tikɔmynism] *s.m.* anti-communism.

anticonceptionnel, -le [ɑ̃tikɔ̃sɛpsjɔnɛl] *adj.* birth-control, family-planning; contraceptive.

anticonformiste [ɑ̃tikɔ̃fɔrmist] *adj., s.m.f.* anti-conformist, non-conformist.

anticonstitutionnel, -le [ɑ̃tikɔ̃stitysjɔnɛl] *adj.* unconstitutional; **~lement** [ɑ̃tikɔ̃stitysjɔnɛlmɑ̃] *adv.* unconstitutionally.

anti-corps [ɑ̃tikɔr] *s.m.* antibody; **~cyclone** [ɑ̃tisiklon] *s.m.* anticyclone.

anti-date [ɑ̃tidat] *s.f.* antedate; **~dater** [ɑ̃tidate] *v.t.* to antedate.

antidémocratique [ɑ̃tidemɔkratik] *adj.* anti-democratic.

antidérapant, -e [ɑ̃tiderapɑ̃] *adj.* non-skid.

antidétonant, -e [ɑ̃tidetɔnɑ̃] *adj., s.m.* anti-knock (additive).

anti-diphtérique [ɑ̃tidifterik] *adj.* anti-diphtheria; **~dote** [ɑ̃tidɔt] *s.m.* antidote, remedy, (*contre,* to, for, against); **~émétique** [ɑ̃tiemetik] *adj.* anti-emetic.

antienne [ɑ̃tjɛn] *s.f.* anthem, antiphon; (fig.) hobby-horse, theme-song; *chanter toujours la même ~,* to be always harping on the same string, on the same subject.

anti-esclavagiste [ɑ̃tiɛsklavaʒist] *adj.* anti-slavery; **~fasciste** [ɑ̃tifaʃist] *adj.* anti-fascist; **~friction** [ɑ̃tifriksjɔ̃] *s.m.* anti-friction metal; **~gel** [ɑ̃tiʒɛl] *s.m.* anti-freeze; **~gène** [ɑ̃tiʒɛn] *s.m.* antigen.

antigivrant, -e [ɑ̃tiʒivrɑ̃] *adj.* de-icing; *~ s.m.* de-icer.

antigouvernemental, -e, (**aux**) [ɑ̃tiguvɛrnəmɑ̃tal] *adj.* against the government, (in) opposition.

antigrippal, -e [ɑ̃tigripal] *adj.* anti-flu.

anti-halo [ɑ̃tialo] *adj., s.m.* (photo.) anti-halo (backing); **~histaminique** [ɑ̃tiistaminik] *adj., s.m.* antihistamine; **~hygiénique** [ɑ̃tiiʒjenik] *adj.* unhygienic.

antillais, -e [ɑ̃tijɛ] *adj., s.m.f.* West-Indian.

Antilles [ɑ̃tij] *s.f.pl.* (geog.) Antilles, West Indies; *Mer des ~,* Caribbean (sea).

antilope [ɑ̃tilɔp] *s.f.* antelope.

antimatière [ɑ̃timatjɛr] *s.f.* antimatter.

antimigraineu-x, -se [ɑ̃timigrɛnø] *adj.* anti-migraine, anti-headache.

antimilitar-isme [ɑ̃timilitarism] *s.m.* anti-militarism; **~iste** [ɑ̃timilitarist] *adj., s.m.* anti-militarist.

antimite [ɑ̃timit] *adj., s.m.* moth-proof (substance); moth-preventive.

antimoine [ɑ̃timwan] *s.m.* (chem.) antimony.

anti-monarchique [ɑ̃timɔnarʃik] *adj.* anti-monarchic(al).

anti-neutron [ɑ̃tinøtrɔ̃] *s.m.* (phys.) anti-neutron; **~nœud** [ɑ̃tinø] *s.m.* (phys.) antinode.

antinomie [ɑ̃tinɔmi] *s.f.* antinomy, paradox.

antipape [ɑ̃tipap] *s.m.* anti-pope.

antipara-site [ɑ̃tiparasit] *adj.* (radio) anti-interference; **~siter** [ɑ̃tiparasite] *v.t.* (radio) to suppress.

antipath-ie [ɑ̃tipati] *s.f.* antipathy, aversion; **~ique** [ɑ̃tipatik] *adj.* antipathetic, uncongenial, distasteful.

antipersonnel [ɑ̃tipɛrsɔnɛl] *adj.invar.* (mil.) anti-personnel.

anti-phrase [ɑ̃tifrɑz] *s.f.* (lang.) antiphrasis; **~pode** [ɑ̃tipɔd] *s.m.* (geog.) antipode; (fig.) the exact opposite; *aux ~podes,* to or at the ends of the earth, (fig.) far away.

anti-protectionniste [ɑ̃tiprɔtɛksjɔnist] *adj.* anti-protectionist; **~raciste** [ɑ̃tirasist] *adj.* anti-racialist.

antiquaille [ɑ̃tikɑj] *s.f.* (pej.) old junk.

antiquaire [ɑ̃tikɛr] *s.m.* **1.** (obs.) antiquary; **2.** antique-dealer.

antique [ɑ̃tik] *adj.* antique, ancient; old-fashioned, antiquated, out-of-date; *~ s.m.* antiquity, antique art; *~ s.f.* (obs.) antique.

antiquité [ɑ̃tikite] *s.f.* **1.** antiquity, great age; **2.** (classical) antiquity; **3.** (pl.) antiques.

antireligieu-x, -se [ɑ̃tirliʒjø] *adj.* antireligious.

anti-rides [ɑ̃tirid] *adj.invar.* anti-wrinkle; **~rouille** [ɑ̃tiruj] *adj.invar.* anti-rust; **~scorbutique** [ɑ̃tiskɔrbytik] *adj.* antiscorbutic; **~sémite** [ɑ̃tisemit] *adj.* antisemitic; **~sémitisme** [ɑ̃tisemitism] *s.m.* antisemitism; **~sepsie** [ɑ̃tisɛpsi] *s.f.* antisepsis; **~septique** [ɑ̃tisɛptik] *adj., s.m.* antiseptic.

antisocial, -e, (**aux**) [ɑ̃tisɔsjal] *adj.* antisocial; anti-socialist(ic), anti-worker.

anti-sous-marin, -e [ɑ̃tisumarɛ̃] *adj.* (nav.) anti-submarine.

antisporti-f, -ve [ɑ̃tispɔrtif] *adj.* unsporting, unsportsmanlike.

anti-strophe [ɑ̃tistrɔf] *s.f.* antistrophe; **~thèse** [ɑ̃titɛz] *s.f.* antithesis; **~thétique** [ɑ̃titetik] *adj.* antithetic(al); **~toxine** [ɑ̃titɔksin] *s.f.* antitoxin; **~vol** [ɑ̃tivɔl] *s.m.* thief-proof lock, security device, (on car).

antonyme [ɑ̃tɔnim] *s.m.* antonym.

antre [ɑ̃tr] *s.m.* **1.** lair (of wild beasts); (fig.) den; **2.** (anat.) antrum.

anurie [anyri] *s.f.* (med.) anuria.

anus [anys] *s.m.* anus.

Anvers [ɑ̃vɛr(s)] *s.m.* (geog.) Antwerp.

anxiété [ɑ̃ksjete] *s.f.* anxiety, concern.

anxieu-x, -se [ɑ̃ksjø] *adj.* anxious, troubled; *~x de,* anxious to; eager, impatient to; **~sement** [ɑ̃ksjøzmɑ̃] *adv.* anxiously.

aoriste [aɔrist] *s.m.* (lang.) aorist.

aorte [aɔrt] *s.f.* aorta.

aort-ique [aɔrtik] *adj.* aortic; **~ite** [aɔrtit] *s.f.* aortitis, inflammation of the aorta.
août [u] *s.m.* August; (obs.) harvest-time.
aoûtat [auta] *s.m.* harvest-bug.
aoûté, -e [(a)ute] *adj.* ripened by the summer sun.
aoûtien, -ne [ausjɛ̃] *s.m.f.* **1.** person taking holidays in August; **2.** person spending August in the city (esp. Paris).
A.P. [ape] abbrev. *Assistance publique.*
apache [apaʃ] *s.m.* Apache; hooligan, thug.
apaisement [apɛzmɑ̃] *s.m.* appeasement; pacification, quieting, calming; subsiding; alleviation; (pl.) reassurance, assurances.
apaiser [apeze] *v.t.* to placate, to pacify; to appease, to satisfy (hunger); to quench (thirst); to quell, to suppress; to salve (conscience); to alleviate (pain); **s'~** *v.refl.* to be placated, appeased, quenched, etc.; to subside; (fig.) to calm down, to quieten down.
apanage [apanaʒ] *s.m.* appanage; attribute, prerogative, privilege, lot, portion.
aparté [aparte] *s.m.* (theatr.) aside; (fam.) private conversation.
apathie [apati] *s.f.* apathy.
apathique [apatik] *adj.* apathetic, indolent; **~ment** [apatikmɑ̃] *adv.* apathetically.
apatride [apatrid] *s.m.f.* stateless person.
apepsie [apɛpsi] *s.f.* apepsy, dyspepsia.
Apennins [apɛnnɛ̃] *s.m.pl.* (geog.) Apennines.
aperception [apɛrsɛpsjɔ̃] *s.f.* (psychol.) apperception.
apercevable [apɛrsəvabl] *adj.* perceivable, perceptible.
apercevoir [apɛrsəvwar] *v.t.* **1.** to notice, to see briefly; *je n'ai fait que l'~*, I only caught a glimpse of him; **2.** to remark, to observe, to discern, to distinguish, to discover; **s'~** *v.refl.* to realize, to become aware (of); to catch a glimpse of oneself, of each other; to become noticeable; *il s'aperçut que le temps passait*, he realized that time was passing; *il s'aperçut de son erreur*, he realized his mistake; *un détail qui s'aperçoit à peine*, a detail which is hardly noticeable.
aperçu [apɛrsy] *s.m.* **1.** glimpse, fleeting sight; first impression; **2.** rough estimate, rough idea or outline, brief survey, summary.
apériti-f, -ve [aperitif] *adj.* appetizing; **~f** *s.m.* aperitif (pop. abbrev. *apéro*).
apétale [apetal] *adj.* (bot.) apetalous.
à(-)peu(-)près [apøprɛ] *s.m.* **1.** approximation; **2.** (obs.) pun.
apeuré, -e [apœre] *adj.* frightened, timid.
aphas-ie [afazi] *s.f.* aphasia; **~ique** [afazik] *adj., s.m.f.* aphasic, (one) suffering from aphasia.
aphélie [afeli] *s.m.* (astron.) aphelion.
aphérèse [aferɛz] *s.f.* apheresis.
aphidiens [afidjɛ̃], **aphidés** [afide] *s.m.pl.* aphid(e)s, plant-lice, green-fly.
aphone [afɔn] *adj.* aphonous, voiceless.
aphonie [afɔni] *s.f.* aphonia, loss of voice.
aphorisme [afɔrism] *s.m.* aphorism; (pej.) trite remark.
aphrodisiaque [afrɔdizjak] *adj.* aphrodisiac; (myth.) (in honour) of Aphrodite; **~** *s.m.* aphrodisiac.
aphte [aft] *s.m.* (med.) aphtha, thrush.
aphteu-x, -se [aftø] *adj.* (med.) aphthous; (vet.) *fièvre ~se*, foot-and-mouth disease.
aphylle [afil] *adj.* (bot.) aphyllous.
api [api] *s.m.* (bot.) *pomme d'~*, lady-apple.
apicole [apikɔl] *adj.* apiarian.
api-culteur [apikyltœr] *s.m.* apiarist, bee-keeper; **~culture** [apikyltyr] *s.f.* apiculture, bee-keeping; **~dés** [apide] *s.m.pl.* (zool.) Apidae, the bee family.
apiquage [apikaʒ] *s.m.* (naut.) peaking.
apiquer [apike] *v.t.* (naut.) to peak.
apitoiement [apitwamɑ̃] *s.m.* pity, compassion, commiseration.
apitoyer [apitwaje] *v.t.* to touch, to move, to move to pity; **s'~** *v.refl.* to be moved (to pity); to feel pity; *s'~ sur*, to pity, to feel or show compassion for; to commiserate with s.o.
aplanir [aplanir] *v.t.* to smooth or level, to make smooth or even; to plane (wood); (fig.) to smooth down, to remove or iron out (difficulties).
aplanissement [aplanismɑ̃] *s.m.* smoothing; (fig.) ironing-out.
aplat [apla] *s.m.* (paint) flat-wash; (print.) flat-tint.
aplatir [aplatir] *v.t.* to flatten, to level (a surface); (dressm.) to press (seam); to plaster down (hair); to squash, to hammer down; **s'~** *v.refl.* to collapse, to go flat; to be flattened or squashed; (fig.) to humble oneself; (fam.) to fall flat on one's face.
aplatissage [aplatisaʒ] *s.m.* (techn.) rolling (of metal); crushing (of seeds).
aplatissement [aplatismɑ̃] *s.m.* **1.** flattening, levelling; flatness; **2.** (fig.) humiliation; grovelling; servility.
aplatisseur [aplatisœr] *s.m.* **1.** flatter, rolling-mill hand; **2.** seed-crusher (machine).
aplomb [aplɔ̃] *s.m.* **1.** plumb, verticality, uprightness; stability, equilibrium, balance; posture, stance (esp. of horse); **2.** (fig.) (self-) assurance, (self-)confidence; impudence, cheek; *d'~*, (i.) plumb, vertical, true; stable, steady; firmly planted, well-balanced; (ii.) self-assured; (iii.) in good health.
apocalypse [apɔkalips] *s.f.* **1.** (bibl.) apocalypse; revelation; any eschatological work; **2.** Judgement Day; the end of the world.
apocalyptique [apɔkaliptik] *adj.* apocalyptic.
apocope [apɔkɔp] *s.f.* (lang.) apocope.
apocryphe [apɔkrif] *adj.* apocryphal; (fig.) spurious; **~** *s.m.* (pl.) the Apocrypha.
apocynacées [apɔsinase] *s.f.pl.* (bot.) Apocynaceae.
apode [apɔd] *adj.* apodal; **~** *s.m.* apod, apode.
apodictique [apɔdiktik] *adj.* apodictic.
apogamie [apɔgami] *s.f.* (bot.) apogamy.
apogée [apɔʒe] *s.m.* apogee; (fig.) climax, height.
apolitique [apɔlitik] *adj.* non-political.
Apollon [apɔllɔ̃] *s.m.* Apollo.
apologétique [apɔlɔʒetik] *adj.* apologetic; **~** *s.f.* apologetics.
apologie [apɔlɔʒi] *s.f.* apologia, apology, justification, vindication, defence; *faire l'~ de*, to vindicate; *faire l'~ du crime*, to justify the crime; *faire l'~ d'une politique*, to defend a policy; ⚠ not 'apology' in sense 'expressing regret' or 'making polite excuses'.
apologiste [apɔlɔʒist] *s.m.* apologist.
apologue [apɔlɔg] *s.m.* apologue.
apophtegme [apɔftɛgm] *s.m.* apophthegm.
apophyse [apɔfiz] *s.f.* (anat.) apophysis.
apoplectique [apɔplɛktik] *adj.* apoplectic.
apoplexie [apɔplɛksi] *s.f.* apoplexy.
apostasie [apɔstazi] *s.f.* apostasy; renunciation (of vows); (fig.) denial.
apostasier [apɔstazje] *v.i.* to apostatize, to become an apostate.
apostat [apɔsta] *s.m.* apostate.
aposter [apɔste] *v.t.* (obs.) to set or station (s.o. ready to commit a crime).
apostille [apɔstij] *s.f.* marginal note; note o recommendation added to letter or document.
apostiller [apɔstije] *v.t.* to add a (commendatory) note to.
apostolat [apɔstɔla] *s.m.* apostleship, apostolate; (fig.) proselytism; mission, vocation.

apostolique [apɔstɔlik] *adj.* apostolic; **~ment** [apɔstɔlikmɑ̃] *adv.* apostolically.
apostrophe [apɔstrɔf] *s.f.* **1.** (rhet.) apostrophe; **2.** (fam.) invective, abuse; **3.** (gram.) apostrophe.
apostropher [apɔstrɔfe] *v.t.* to apostrophize; to speak rudely to; **s'~** *v.refl.* to exchange insults, to hurl abuse at one another.
apothème [apɔtɛm] *s.m.* (math.) apothem.
apothéose [apɔteoz] *s.f.* **1.** apotheosis, deification; **2.** blaze of glory; glorious fulfilment; **3.** aureole.
apothicaire [apɔtikɛr] *s.m.* (obs.) apothecary; *compte d'~,* (obs.) exorbitant bill, (mod.) rigmarole.
apôtre [apotr] *s.m.* apostle; (fig.) advocate, defender; *faire le bon ~,* to be a wolf in sheep's clothing.
apparaître [aparɛtr] *v.i.* **1.** to appear, to become visible, to come into sight; (fig.) to become evident, to become clear; **2.** to appear, to seem; *cela lui apparut (comme) impossible,* it seemed impossible to him; *il apparaît que,* it is clear, it would seem, that.
apparat [apara] *s.m.* **1.** pomp, pageantry; show, ostentation; **2.** *~ critique,* critical apparatus.
apparaux [aparo] *s.m.pl.* (naut.) gear, tackle; (gymn.) apparatus.
appareil [aparɛj] *s.m.* **1.** (obs. exc. Lit.) display, show, trappings, ceremony; (mod.) *dans le plus simple ~,* naked, with next to nothing on; **2.** organization, system, apparatus; (arch.) bond (-ing), dimensions (of bricks, etc.); *l'~ d'un parti,* party organization; *l'~ digestif,* the digestive system; *~ critique,* critical apparatus; **3.** apparatus, appliance, machine, instrument, equipment; (esp.) telephone, (radio, etc.) set, camera, aircraft; (dentistry) bridge, brace; (med.) splint, plaster; *~s ménagers,* kitchen or household equipment; *~ de prothèse,* artificial limb; (telephone) *qui est à l'~?,* who is speaking?
appareillage [aparɛjaʒ] *s.m.* **1.** (naut.) getting under way, sailing; **2.** equipment, accessories.
appareiller[1] [apareje] *v.t.* to prepare equipment; (naut.) to get ready to sail; (build.) to bond; *~ v.i.* to get under way.
appareiller[2] [apareje] *v.t.* to pair, to match, to mate.
appareilleur [aparɛjœr] *s.m.* foreman mason; fitter.
apparemment [aparamɑ̃] *adv.* **1.** (obs.) in appearance; **2.** apparently.
apparence [aparɑ̃s] *s.f.* **1.** appearance, look, air, aspect; *les différentes ~s de la lune,* the different aspects of the moon; **2.** outward appearance, semblance, exterior, façade; false appearance; probability; *se fier aux ~s,* to judge by appearances; *garder les ~s,* to keep up appearances; *contre toute ~,* contrary to all probability, against all the evidence; **3.** sign, mark, trace, vestige; *ils n'ont plus aucune ~ de liberté,* they have not a shred of liberty left.
apparent, -e [aparɑ̃] *adj.* **1.** apparent, visible, evident, noticeable; **2.** apparent, seeming, ostensible.
apparentement [aparɑ̃tmɑ̃] *s.m.* **1.** marriage into (a family); **2.** (pol.) pre-election coalition.
apparenter [aparɑ̃te] *v.t.* (obs.) to arrange a marriage (*à,* with); **s'~** *à v.refl.* **1.** to marry into; **2.** (pol.) to form a pre-election coalition with; **3.** (fig.) to have much in common with, to be like.
appariement [aparimɑ̃] *s.m.* matching, pairing.
apparier [aparje] *v.t.* to pair, to match, to mate; **s'~** *v.refl.* to mate, to couple.
appariteur [aparitœr] *s.m.* (eccles.) apparitor; porter, bedell; usher.
apparition [aparisjɔ̃] *s.f.* **1.** appearance, arrival; *il n'a fait qu'une courte ~,* he just looked in; **2.** apparition, ghost.
apparoir [aparwar] *v.impers.* (used only in inf. & *il appert*) (law) to appear, to be apparent.
appartement [apartəmɑ̃] *s.m.* flat, suite of rooms; *d'~,* indoor; *plantes, jeux, d'~,* indoor plants, games.
appartenance [apartənɑ̃s] *s.f.* belonging (to), membership (of); (pl.) appurtenances.
appartenir [apartənir] *v.i.* *~ à* **1.** to belong to, to be the property of; to be part of, to be connected with; **2.** to befit, to become; **3.** (impers.) *il appartient à qn. de faire qch.,* it is someone's duty to do sth.; *il lui appartient de ...,* it is up to him to ...; **s'~** *v.refl.* to be one's own master; *je ne m'appartiens plus,* I can't call my soul my own.
appas [apɑ] *s.m.pl.* (obs.) attraction(s); bosom, feminine charms.
appât [apɑ] *s.m.* bait, lure; (fig.) attraction.
appâter [apɑte] *v.t.* **1.** to feed fledgling birds; to fatten poultry; **2.** to lure, to bait, to trap; (fig.) to attract, to entice.
appauvrir [apovrir] *v.t.* to impoverish, to exhaust.
appeau (pl. **-x**) [apo] *s.m.* **1.** bird-call, warbler; **2.** decoy duck; (fig.) lure, bait, trap; *se laisser prendre à l'~,* to take the bait, to fall into the trap.
appel [apɛl] *s.m.* **1.** call, cry, summons; roll-call; (mil.) call-up, (bugle-)call; appeal; (fin.) call for funds; *faire ~ à,* to appeal to, to call for help from; **2.** (law) appeal; *interjeter ~,* to lodge an appeal; *sans ~,* final, irrevocable; irrevocably; *jugement sans ~,* final judgement; **3.** appeal, attraction, pull; **4.** (techn.) *~ d'air,* intake of air, draught, suction.
appelant, -e [aplɑ̃] *adj., s.m.f.* (law) appellant; *~ s.m.* decoy bird.
appelé, -e [aple] *adj., s.m.f.* *~ à,* destined, fated to, called on to; *il y a beaucoup d'~s mais peu d'élus,* many are called but few are chosen; *~ s.m.* conscript.
appeler [aple] *v.t.* **1.** to call, to call for, to summon; (mil.) to call up; **2.** (law) to appeal; *~ d'un jugement,* to appeal against a judgement; *en ~,* to appeal; (fig.) *en ~ à,* to appeal to; **3.** to call, to name, to designate; *~ les choses par leur nom,* to call a spade a spade; **s'~** *v. refl.* to be called, to be known as; *comment s'appelle cette fleur?,* what is the name of this flower?; (fam.) *voilà qui s'appelle parler,* now you are really talking.
appellati-f, -ve [apelatif, apɛllatif] *adj.* appellative.
appellation [apelɑsjɔ̃] *s.f.* naming, name, appellation; (comm.) trade-name; *~ contrôlée,* certified description (of wine).
appendice [apɛ̃dis] *s.m.* appendage, extension; appendix; (anat.) appendix.
appendicectomie [apɛ̃disɛktɔmi] *s.f.* (surg.) appendicectomy, appendectomy.
appendicite [apɛ̃disit] *s.f.* appendicitis.
appendiculaire [apɛ̃dikylɛr] *adj.* appendicular.
appentis [apɑ̃ti] *s.m.* outhouse, lean-to shed; pent-house.
appert [apɛr] see APPAROIR.
appesantir [apzɑ̃tir] *v.t.* **1.** (obs.) to make heavy; **2.** to weigh down, to slow down; to make oppressive, to weigh heavily upon; **s'~** *v.refl.* to become heavy; to become oppressive; *s'~ sur un sujet,* to dwell on a subject.
appesantissement [apzɑ̃tismɑ̃] *s.m.* heaviness, dullness.
appétence [apetɑ̃s] *s.f.* appetence, appetency.
appétissant, -e [apetisɑ̃] *adj.* appetizing, savoury, inviting, tempting; (fig.) desirable, alluring; (fam.) comely.
appétit [apeti] *s.m.* **1.** (pl.) desires, appetites,

urge, instinct; *~s sexuels*, sexual desires, sex--instinct; **2.** (sing.) appetite, hunger; (fig.) desire, thirst, craving, greed, (*de*, for); *mettre en ~*, to make one's mouth water; *bon ~!*, I hope you will enjoy your meal; (fam.) tuck in!; *l'~ vient en mangeant*, the more one has, the more one wants.

applaudir [aplodir] *v.t.i.* to applaud, to cheer, to clap; to acclaim, to approve of; *~ à*, to commend, to approve (of); *s'~ de*, to congratulate oneself on.

applaudissement [aplodismɑ̃] *s.m.* (usu. pl.) applause, clapping, cheering; (fig.) approval, congratulation, commendation.

applaudisseur [aplodisœr] *s.m.* indiscriminate applauder, one who gives sycophantic approval; (theatr.) *~s à gages*, claque.

applicabilité [aplikabilite] *s.f.* applicability.

applicable [aplikabl] *adj.* applicable; appropriate, apposite; due to take effect; (law) chargeable; *~ à dater de*, with effect from; *être ~ à*, to apply to; *cette loi n'est pas ~ aux étrangers*, this law does not apply to foreigners.

applicage [aplikaʒ] *s.m.* (techn.) appliqué; application (of ornaments to pottery, etc.).

applicateur [aplikatœr] *adj., s.m.* **1.** (one) who applies or carries out (a technique, etc.); **2.** (tool) used for application (of sth. to sth.); applicator (tool).

application [aplikɑsjɔ̃] *s.f.* **1.** application, placing in position; (needlew.) appliqué; **2.** application, administration, use (of remedy, law, discovery, etc.); *mettre en ~*, to bring into effect; *mise en ~*, introduction (of law, etc.); **3.** diligence, care, attention, concentration; *travailler avec ~*, to work diligently; ⚠ not 'application' in sense 'request'.

applique [aplik] *s.f.* appliqué; application, applied ornament; (electr.) wall-lamp, wall--fitting, bracket(-lamp), sconce.

appliquer [aplike] *v.t.* **1.** to apply, to place, to stick, to superimpose; (fam.) *~ un baiser, une gifle*, to give a smacking kiss, to land a blow; **2.** to apply, to administer, to use, (treatment, discovery, punishment); (fin.) to appropriate; **3.** *~ son esprit*, to apply one's mind; **s'~** *v.refl.* **1.** to be applied; **2.** to apply (to), to be relevant (to); **3.** to apply oneself, to work diligently; *s'~ à faire*, to take pains to do, to do one's utmost to do.

appoggiature [apɔ(d)ʒjatyr] *s.f.* (mus.) appoggiatura.

appoint [apwɛ̃] *s.m.* **1.** (small) change; balance (of amount due); *faire l'~*, to make up the amount; to pay the exact amount; **2.** (fig.) contribution; *apporter son ~*, to make one's contribution.

appointage [apwɛ̃taʒ] *s.m.* **1.** sewing edge to edge; **2.** sharpening to a point.

appointements [apwɛ̃tmɑ̃] *s.m.pl.* salary (monthly or yearly).

appointer [apwɛ̃te] *v.t.* **1.** to pay a salary to; **2.** to sharpen to a point.

appontage [apɔ̃taʒ] *s.m.* landing on deck (of aircraft-carrier).

appontement [apɔ̃tmɑ̃] *s.m.* landing-stage.

apponter [apɔ̃te] *v.i.* to land on deck (of aircraft-carrier).

apport [apɔr] *s.m.* **1.** (obs.) delivery, supply; **2.** contribution; (fig.) aid, assistance.

apporter [apɔrte] *v.t.* **1.** to bring, to carry; to contribute, to supply; **2.** to bring to bear, to exercise; to show, to evince; *~ du soin à faire son travail*, to take trouble over one's work; *la passion qu'il apportait à tout*, the enthusiasm which he showed in everything; **3.** to cause, to bring about; *les changements qu'a apportés l'automobile*, the changes which the car has brought about.

apposer [apoze] *v.t.* **1.** to put up, to stick up (poster, etc.); to put (in place), to affix; (law) *~ les scellés*, to seal up; *~ sa signature*, to append one's signature, to sign (formally); **2.** (law) to add, to insert (clause).

apposition [apozisjɔ̃] *s.f.* putting up, putting in place, affixing, appending; (law) insertion; (gram.) apposition.

appréciabilité [apresjabilite] *s.f.* appreciability.

appréciable [apresjabl] *adj.* appreciable, noticeable; considerable.

appréciat-eur, -rice [apresjatœr] *s.m.f.* one who appreciates; appraiser, valuer; (fig.) judge.

appréciati-f, -ve [apresjatif] *adj.* denoting value; *état ~f*, valuation.

appréciation [apresjɑsjɔ̃] *s.f.* estimation, evaluation; estimate; judgement; opinion, impression.

apprécier [apresje] *v.t.* **1.** to value, to appraise, to judge; to estimate; **2.** to appreciate, to esteem, to approve of; ⚠ not 'to appreciate' in sense 'to become more valuable'.

appréhender [apreɑ̃de] *v.t.* **1.** (obs.) to understand; **2.** to apprehend, to arrest; **3.** to apprehend, to fear.

appréhensi-f, -ve [apreɑ̃sif] *adj.* apprehensive, fearful.

appréhension [apreɑ̃sjɔ̃] *s.f.* **1.** (obs.) comprehension; **2.** apprehension, arrest; **3.** fear, apprehension.

apprendre [aprɑ̃dr] *v.t.* **1.** to learn (a language, a technique, etc.); *~ à faire qch.*, to learn to do sth.; **2.** to hear (news), to hear about, to be informed of, to learn of; **3.** to teach, to instruct; *~ qch. à qn.*, to teach s.o. sth.; *~ à qn. de faire qch.*, to teach s.o. to do sth.; (fam.) *ça vous apprendra!*, that'll teach you!; **4.** to inform, to advise.

apprenti, -e [aprɑ̃ti] *s.m.f.* apprentice, articled pupil; (fig.) novice; *un ~ maçon*, a builder's apprentice.

apprentissage [aprɑ̃tisaʒ] *s.m.* apprenticeship; noviciate; *mettre en ~ chez*, to apprentice to; *faire son ~*, to be a novice; (fig.) *faire l'~ de*, to take the first steps in; to have the first taste of.

apprêt [aprɛ] *s.m.* **1.** (pl.) preparations; **2.** preparation or finishing (of raw material), priming, dressing, sizing (with glue), etc.; **3.** substance used for finishing, primer, size, starch, etc.; **4.** affectation; *sans ~*, naturally.

apprêtage [aprɛtaʒ] *s.m.* (techn.) preparation, finishing, dressing, priming, etc.

apprêté, -e [aprete] *adj.* studied, affected, unnatural, stiff.

apprêter [aprete] *v.t.* **1.** to get ready, to make ready; to prepare (food); **2.** to dress up, to adorn; **3.** (techn.) to prepare or finish (materials); to prime, to dress, to starch, etc.; **s'~** *v.refl.* **1.** to be imminent, to be brewing; **2.** to get ready (*à*, to); **3.** to dress up.

apprêteur [aprɛtœr] *s.m.* (techn.) sizer, dresser.

apprêteuse [aprɛtøz] *s.f.* hat-trimmer; cutter.

apprivoisable [aprivwazabl] *adj.* tameable.

apprivoisement [aprivwazmɑ̃] *s.m.* taming, domesticating; (fig.) civilizing.

apprivoiser [aprivwaze] *v.t.* to tame; (fig.) to civilize, to domesticate, to make sociable; *s'~ à*, to get used to.

approbat-eur, -rice [aprɔbatœr] *adj.* approving; *s.m.f.* (Lit.) follower, fulsome admirer.

approbati-f, -ve [aprɔbatif] *adj.* approving, approbatory; **~vement** [aprɔbativmɑ̃] *adv.* approvingly.

approbation [aprɔbɑsjɔ̃] *s.f.* approval, consent; approbation, commendation, praise.

approchable [aprɔʃabl] *adj.* accessible; (o, person) approachable.

approchant, -e [aprɔʃɑ̃] *adj.* similar, like, approximate; *qch. d'~*, something similar; *rien d'~*, nothing like it.

approche [aprɔʃ] *s.f.* **1.** approach, approaching, coming, advance; coming or bringing nearer; (print.) (i.) set; (ii.) close-up sign; *l'~ de la nuit*, nightfall; *à mon ~*, at my approach, as I draw near; *à l'~* or *aux ~s de la trentaine*, when nearing thirty, getting on for thirty (years old); *d'~ difficile*, (of person) difficult to approach; *d'une ~ difficile*, (of thing) difficult of access, not easy to set about; *lunette d'~*, spy-glass; *travaux d'~*, approach-works; (fig.) preliminary operations; (mil.) trench-works (preliminary to siege); **2.** (pl.) approaches, surroundings, proximity.

approcher [aprɔʃe] *v.t.* **1.** to bring near, to put close or closer, to bring (sth.) up (*de*, to); *approchez votre chaise*, bring your chair closer; *approchez votre chaise de la table*, bring your chair up to the table; *approchez les deux objets*, put the two objects closer together; **2.** to approach, to come near to (s.o.); (fig.) to approach (with request, etc.); to have a close association with; *ne m'approchez pas*, don't come near me; *c'est un homme qu'on ne peut ~*, he is a quite unapproachable sort of person; *je suis content de l'avoir si bien approché*, I am glad to have had such a close relationship with him; *~ v.i.* to approach, to draw near; *l'hiver approche*, winter is approaching; *~ de*, to approach, to draw near to; (fig.) to approach, to be nearing, to be getting on towards; (fig.) to approach, to be near to, to be something like, to border on; *on approche de Paris*, we are getting near Paris; *il approche de la cinquantaine*, he is getting on for fifty; *cela approche de la vérité*, that is something like the truth; **s'~** *v.refl.* to approach, to come up, to come nearer; *approche-toi*, come nearer, come here; *s'~ de*, to approach, to come up to, to come closer to, to come towards; (fig.) to get near to, to approximate to; *il s'approchait lentement de moi*, he was slowly coming towards me, he was slowly getting closer to me; *s'~ le plus près de la perfection*, to get as near as possible to perfection.

approfondi, -e [aprɔfɔ̃di] *adj.* thorough, full, profound.

approfondir [aprɔfɔ̃dir] *v.t.* to deepen, to make deeper; to examine in depth, to look (more) closely into; **s'~** *v.refl.* to grow deeper.

approfondissement [aprɔfɔ̃dismɑ̃] *s.m.* deepening; (fig.) thorough analysis or study.

appropriation [aprɔprijɑsjɔ̃] *s.f.* appropriation; adaptation; (fin.) embezzlement.

approprié, -e [aprɔprije] *adj.* appropriate, fitting, proper, suitable, relevant.

approprier [aprɔprije] *v.t.* to fit, to adapt, to make suitable; **s'~** *v.refl.* to appropriate (to oneself), to take possession of, to make one's own (legally); to embezzle, to take over (illegally).

approuvé [apruve] *s.m.* endorsement, sanction, countersignature; (at end of document) passed.

approuver [apruve] *v.t.* **1.** to approve of, to agree to, to sanction; to approve formally, to ratify, to confirm; **2.** to approve of, to commend, to praise; to agree with; *~ qn. de faire qch.*, to commend s.o. for doing sth.; *je n'approuve pas qu'il fasse cela*, I am not in favour of his doing that.

approvisionnement [aprɔvizjɔnmɑ̃] *s.m.* **1.** stocking, supplying; (mil., naut.) victualling; **2.** (usu. pl.) stocks, stores, supplies, provisions; raw materials.

approvisionner [aprɔvizjɔne] *v.t.* to stock, to supply (*en*, with); **s'~** *v.refl.* **1.** to lay in a stock; *s'~ de bois pour l'hiver*, to lay in a stock of wood for the winter; **2.** to go shopping; *s'~ chez*, to shop at.

approvisionneu-r, -se [aprɔvizjɔnœr] *s.m.f.* supplier, caterer.

approximati-f, -ve [aprɔksimatif] *adj.* approximate; vague; **~vement** [aprɔksimativmɑ̃] *adv.* approximately, roughly.

approximation [aprɔksimɑsjɔ̃] *s.f.* approximation, rough estimate.

appui [apɥi] *s.m.* support, prop, rest; (build.) shore; (lang., mus.) stress; (fig.) support, assistance, aid; *~ de fenêtre*, window-sill; *barre d'~*, hand-rail; *à hauteur d'~*, breast-, waist-, elbow-high; *prendre ~ sur*, to be supported on; *mur d'~*, retaining wall; *point d'~*, (mech.) fulcrum, pivot; (mil.) base; *à l'~ de*, in support of; (law) *documents à l'~*, supporting documents; (mil.) *~ d'artillerie, d'aviation*, artillery, air, support; *sans ~*, unaided, by oneself.

appui-bras [apɥibra] *s.m.* (car) arm-rest; **~-main** [apɥimɛ̃] *s.m.* hand-rest; (painter's) maulstick; **~-tête** [apɥitɛt] *s.m.* head-rest, antimacassar.

appuyé, -e [apɥije] *adj.* insistent; laboured, overdone.

appuyer [apɥije] *v.t.* **1.** to prop up, to support, to stay, to shore up; **2.** to lean (*sur, contre*, on, against); **3.** (fig.) to support, to back up, to second, to patronize, to recommend; *~ la demande, la candidature, de qn.*, to second or support someone's request or candidature; **4.** to press against; (fig.) *~ le regard sur*, to stare at; *~ v.i.* **1.** to rest on; to be supported by; **2.** *~ sur*, to press; *~ sur le bouton*, to press the button; **3.** (fig.) to stress; to insist upon, to dwell upon; *~ sur un mot, une note*, to emphasize a word, to sustain a note; **4.** to turn; *~ sur la droite*, to turn right; **s'~** *v.refl.* to lean on, to support oneself with; to rely on, to count on; (pop.) *s'~ une corvée*, to land oneself with an unpleasant job.

apraxie [apraksi] *s.f.* (pathol.) apraxia.

âpre [ɑpr] *adj.* **1.** (obs.) rough, uneven; **2.** bitter, biting, keen; (of weather) raw; harsh; tart, sour; (of struggle) hard; **3.** grasping, avid, greedy; *~ au gain*, ruthlessly ambitious; **~ment** [ɑprəmɑ̃] *adv.* bitterly, harshly; keenly, avidly, greedily.

après [aprɛ] *prep.* **1.** (time) after; *~ cela*, next, after that; *~ quoi*, then; *nous allons déjeuner, ~ quoi nous partirons*, we'll have lunch and then we'll leave; *~ avoir mangé*, after eating; *~ coup*, afterwards, later; **2.** (space) behind, after; *courir ~ qn.*, to run after s.o., to chase s.o.; *courir ~ qch.*, to be greedy for sth.; *crier ~ qn.*, to shout abuse at s.o.; *elle est toujours ~ ses enfants*, she is always on at her children; *~ tout*, after all, all things considered; *d'~*, after, in the manner of; in accordance with; according to; *d'~ vous il a tort*, according to you, he is wrong; *~ adv.* **1.** (time) after, afterwards, later; *d'~*, next; *la semaine d'~*, the next week, the week after; *et ~?*, and then what (will you do)?; **2.** (space) behind; *ci-~*, below, further on; *~ que, conj.*, after; *~ qu'il fut parti*, after he had left.

après-demain [aprɛdmɛ̃] *adv.* the day after tomorrow; **~-dîner** [aprɛdine] *s.m.* period after dinner, afternoon, evening; **~-guerre** [aprɛgɛr] *s.m.* period after the *or* a war, post-war years; **~-midi** [aprɛmidi] *s.m.f.invar.* afternoon; **~-rasage** [aprɛrɑzaʒ] *s.m.* after-shave lotion; **~-ski** [aprɛski, apreski] *s.m.invar.* footwear put on after skiing; (fig.) relaxation after skiing.

âpreté [ɑprəte] *s.f.* roughness, harshness; sharpness, bitterness; (fig.) rudeness, severity, keenness.

à-propos [aprɔpo] *s.m.* **1.** appropriateness, aptness, pertinence, relevance; *avoir l'esprit d'~*, to have the knack of saying the right thing; **2.** occasional writing.

apside [apsid] *s.f.* (astron.) apsis.

apte [apt] *adj.* apt, suitable, fit, fitted, qualified;

capable; suited; gifted; (law) entitled; (mil.) ~ *au service armé*, A.1., fit for service.
aptère [aptɛr] *adj.* apterous, wingless.
aptéryx [apteriks] *s.m.* (ornith.) apteryx.
aptitude [aptityd] *s.f.* **1.** (law) capacity; **2.** natural ability, aptitude, tendency; skill, capacity, bent, turn; **3.** professional skill or qualification; efficiency; *certificat d'*~, diploma; (mil.) *brevet d'*~, certificate of efficiency; see C.A.P., C.A.P.E.S.
Apulie [apyli] *s.f.* (geog.) Apulia.
apurement [apyrmɑ̃] *s.m.* (fin.) audit.
apurer [apyre] *v.t.* to audit.
apyre [apir] *adj.* incombustible, fire-proof.
apyrexie [apirɛksi] *s.f.* (med.) apyrexia.
aquafortiste [akwafɔrtist] *s.m.* etcher, aquafortist.
aquaplane [akwaplan] *s.m.* aquaplane.
aquarelle [akwarɛl] *s.f.* water-colour (painting); *peindre à l'*~, to paint in water-colours.
aquarelliste [akwarelist] *s.m.f.* painter in water-colours.
aquarium [akwarjɔm] *s.m.* aquarium.
aquatinte [akwatɛ̃t] *s.f.* aquatint.
aquatique [akwatik] *adj.* aquatic.
aqueduc [akdyk] *s.m.* aqueduct; (anat.) duct.
aqueu-x, -se [akø] *adj.* aqueous, watery.
aqui-cole [akɥikɔl] *adj.* **1.** (obs.) aquatic; **2.** relating to hydroponics; **~culture** [akɥikyltyr] *s.f.* **1.** (rare) fish-farming; **2.** hydroponics.
aquifère [akɥifɛr] *adj.* aquiferous, water-bearing.
aquilin, -e [akilɛ̃] *adj.* aquiline.
aquilon [akilɔ̃] *s.m.* (Lit.) north wind; any strong wind; (fig.) the North.
aquitanien, -ne [akitanjɛ̃] *adj.* Aquitanian.
aquosité [akozite] *s.f.* aqueousness, wateriness.
ara [ara] *s.m.* (ornith.) macaw.
arabe [arab] *adj., s.m.f.* Arabian, Arab; (fam.) *téléphone* ~, bush-telegraph; ~ *s.m.* (lang.) Arabic.
arabesque [arabɛsk] *s.f.* arabesque.
Arabie [arabi] *s.f.* (geog.) Arabia.
arabique [arabik] *adj.* **1.** (obs.) Arabian; **2.** *gomme* ~, gum arabic.
arabisant, -e [arabizɑ̃] *s.m.f.* Arabist, Arabic specialist.
arabisation [arabizɑsjɔ̃] *s.f.* Arabization.
arabiser [arabize] *v.t.* to arabize.
arable [arabl] *adj.* arable.
arachide [araʃid] *s.f.* ground-nut, peanut.
arachnéen, -ne [arakneɛ̃] *adj.* **1.** (zool.) arachnidan, of spiders; **2.** (Lit., fig.) gossamer-like.
arachnoïde [araknɔid] *s.f.* (anat.) arachnoid.
arack, arac [arak] *s.m.* arrack.
aragonite [aragɔnit] *s.f.* (geol.) aragonite.
araignée [areɲe] *s.f.* spider; (naut.) clew-hook, gill-net; (mil.) araignée; (techn.) grapnel, drag; spider-support; *toile d'*~, cobweb, spider's web; ~ *de mer*, spider-crab; (fam.) *avoir une* ~ *au* or *dans le plafond*, to have bats in the belfry, to be mad.
araire [arɛr] *s.m.* swing-plough.
arasement [arɑzmɑ̃] *s.m.* **1.** levelling; **2.** top course of a wall.
araser [arɑze] *v.t.* **1.** to make level or even; **2.** to plane; to make flush; to wear flat.
aratoire [aratwar] *adj.* used in ploughing, ploughing.
araucaria [arokarja] *s.m.* (bot.) araucaria, monkey-puzzle tree.
arbalète [arbalɛt] *s.f.* crossbow; *attelage en* ~, (of horses) unicorn team.
arbalétrier [arbaletrije] *s.m.* **1.** crossbowman; **2.** principal roof beams; **3.** (ornith.) swift.
arbalétrière [arbaletrijɛr] *s.f.* loophole (for firing crossbow).
arbitrage [arbitraʒ] *s.m.* **1.** arbitration, arbitrament; *soumettre un différend à l'*~, to refer a dispute to arbitration; **2.** (fin.) arbitrage; **3.** (sport) refereeing.
arbitraire [arbitrɛr] *adj.* **1.** arbitrary; (pej.) artificial; **2.** capricious, despotic, high-handed; **~ment** [arbitrɛrmɑ̃] *adv.* arbitrarily; despotically; ~ *s.m.* **1.** arbitrariness; **2.** despotism.
arbitral, -e, (aux) [arbitral] *adj.* arbitral; *commission* ~*e*, board of arbitrators; *jugement* ~, *sentence* ~*e*, arbitration award; **~ement** [arbitralmɑ̃] *adv.* by arbitration.
arbitre [arbitr] *s.m.* **1.** arbitrator, mediator, judge; *tiers* ~, umpire; **2.** (sport) umpire, referee; **3.** *libre* ~, free will.
arbitrer [arbitre] *v.t.* **1.** to arbitrate, to mediate, to settle (dispute); **2.** (sport) to umpire, to referee.
arborer [arbɔre] *v.t.* to hoist, to run up, to fly (flags); (fig.) to flaunt, to sport (a colourful tie, etc.).
arborescence [arbɔresɑ̃s] *s.f.* arborescence; (fig.) *les* ~*s du givre*, the tree-like patterns made by the frost.
arborescent, -e [arbɔresɑ̃] *adj.* arborescent; *fougère* ~*e*, tree-fern.
arbori-cole [arbɔrikɔl] *adj.* **1.** tree-dwelling, arboreal; **2.** relating to arboriculture; **~culteur** [arbɔrikyltœr] *s.m.* arboriculturist; **~culture** [arbɔrikyltyr] *s.f.* arboriculture; ~*culture fruitière*, fruit-growing; **~sation** [arbɔrizɑsjɔ̃] *s.f.* arborization, tree-like formation.
arborisé, -e [arbɔrize] *adj.* (min.) arborized, dendritic.
arbouse [arbuz] *s.f.* (bot.) arbutus-berry.
arbousier [arbuzje] *s.m.* (bot.) arbutus (tree).
arbre [arbr] *s.m.* **1.** tree; *entre l'*~ *et l'écorce il ne faut pas mettre le doigt*, no good comes of meddling in family quarrels; *couper l'*~ *pour avoir le fruit*, to kill the goose that lays the golden egg; *les* ~*s cachent la forêt*, you can't see the wood for the trees; **2.** (techn.) arbor, shaft, axle, spindle; ~ *à cames*, camshaft; ~ *de couche*, driving shaft, propeller shaft; ~ *de transmission*, (car) propeller shaft; ~ *coudé*, crank-shaft.
arbrisseau [arbriso] *s.m.* shrub, bush, shrub-like tree.
arbuste [arbyst] *s.m.* shrub, bush.
arbusti-f, -ve [arbystif] *adj.* shrubby, bushy.
arc [ark] *s.m.* **1.** bow; *tir à l'*~, archery; *avoir plusieurs cordes à son* ~, to have more than one string to one's bow; **2.** (math., electr.) arc; **3.** (arch.) arch; ~ *de triomphe*, triumphal arch.
arcade [arkad] *s.f.* (arch.) arcade, arch; arcade, passage (in street); (anat.) *l'*~ *sourcillière*, superciliary arch or ridge.
arcane [arkan] *s.m.* **1.** (alchemy) arcanum; **2.** (pl.) arcana, mysteries, inside secrets.
arcanne [arkan] *s.f.* red ochre, ruddle.
arcanson [arkɑ̃sɔ̃] *s.m.* = COLOPHANE.
arcature [arkatyr] *s.f.* (arch.) arcading.
arc-boutant [arkbutɑ̃] *s.m.* flying buttress; (constr.) stay, spur, bracket, stretcher; (naut.) davit.
arc-bouter [arkbute] *v.t.* to buttress, to shore up, to stay; **s'**~ *v.refl.* to brace oneself.
arc-doubleau [arkdublo] *s.m.* (arch.) groin, rib (of vault), arch-band.
arceau [arso] *s.m.* **1.** (arch.) vault, vaulting; **2.** hoop; **3.** (med.) cradle (for hospital bed).
arc-en-ciel [arkɑ̃sjɛl] *s.m.* (pl. ~*s-en-ciel*) rainbow.
archaïque [arkaik] *adj.* archaic.
archaïsant, -e [arkaizɑ̃] *adj., s.m.f.* (one) using archaic language.
archaïsme [arkaism] *s.m.* archaism.
archal [arʃal] *s.m.* *fil d'*~, brass wire.
archange [arkɑ̃ʒ] *s.m.* archangel.
arche[1] [arʃ] *s.f.* arch, vault.

arche[2] [arʃ] *s.f.* ark; *l'~ d'alliance* or *sainte*, the Ark of the Covenant.
archée [arʃe] *s.f.* (anc. physiol.) principle of life; (alchemy) central fire.
archégone [arkegɔn] *s.m.* (bot.) archegonium.
archéo-logie [arkeɔlɔʒi] *s.f.* archaeology; **~logique** [arkeɔlɔʒik] *adj.* archaeological; **~logue** [arkeɔlɔg] *s.m.f.* archaeologist.
archer [arʃe] *s.m.* archer, bowman; (pl.) (obs.) the watch.
archet [arʃɛ] *s.m.* **1.** (mus.) bow (of violin, etc.); **2.** (techn.) bow; *scie à ~*, bow-saw; **3.** (ent.) membrane used by cicada, etc., to produce chirping sound.
archétype [arketip] *s.m.* archetype.
archevêché [arʃəveʃe] *s.m.* **1.** archbishopric, archdiocese; rank of archbishop; **2.** archbishop's palace.
archevêque [arʃəvɛk] *s.m.* archbishop.
archi- [arʃi] *pref.* intensifying meaning of an *adj.*, e.g.: *~fou*, stark, staring mad; *~bondé*, *~plein*, *~comble*, full to overflowing, packed; *~riche*, stinking rich; *~vieux*, as old as the hills.
archiconfrérie [arʃikɔ̃freri] *s.f.* (eccles.) mother establishment.
archidiacon-at [arʃidjakɔna] *s.m.* archdeaconship; *~é* [arʃidjakɔne] *s.m.* archdeaconry.
archidiacre [arʃidjakr] *s.m.* archdeacon.
archidiocésain, -e [arʃidjɔsezɛ̃] *adj.* archdiocesan.
archidiocèse [arʃidjɔsɛz] *s.m.* archdiocese.
archiduc [arʃidyk] *s.m.* archduke.
archiduchesse [arʃidyʃɛs] *s.f.* archduchess.
archiépiscopal, -e, (**aux**) [arʃiepiskɔpal] *adj.* archiepiscopal.
archiépiscopat [arʃiepiskɔpa] *s.m.* archiepiscopate.
archère [arʃɛr], **archière** [arʃjɛr] *s.f.* loop-hole.
archimandrite [arʃimɑ̃drit] *s.m.* archimandrite.
archipel [arʃipɛl] *s.m.* archipelago.
archiprêtre [arʃiprɛtr] *s.m.* (obs.) arch-priest; (mod.) rural dean.
architecte [arʃitɛkt] *s.m.f.* architect.
architectonique [arʃitɛktɔnik] *adj.* architectonic; *~ s.f.* architectonics.
architectural, -e, (**aux**) [arʃitɛktyral] *adj.* architectural.
architecture [arʃitɛktyr] *s.f.* architecture.
architrave [arʃitrav] *s.f.* architrave.
archives [arʃiv] *s.f.pl.* archives, records; record office.
archiviste [arʃivist] *s.m.f.* archivist, keeper of the archives.
archivolte [arʃivɔlt] *s.f.* (arch.) archivolt.
archonte [arkɔ̃t] *s.m.* (anc. Gr. hist.) archon.
arçon [arsɔ̃] *s.m.* **1.** saddle-bow; *être ferme dans, sur, ses ~s*, to have a good seat; (fig.) to be true to one's principles; *vider les ~s*, to be thrown; (gymn.) *cheval d'~s*, vaulting-horse; **2.** (techn.) bow (for beating wool, etc.); **3.** vine-twig.
arctique [arktik] *adj.* arctic; *s.m.* (geog.) *l'Arctique*, the Arctic.
ardemment [ardamɑ̃] *adv.* ardently, eagerly.
ardent, -e [ardɑ̃] *adj.* burning, fiery, blazing, flaming, glowing, alight; feverish, parching; scorching, boiling; (fig.) ardent, eager, keen, zealous, enthusiastic, passionate, impassioned, lively; *charbons ~s*, live coals; *être sur des charbons ~s*, (fig.) to be on hot bricks; *le mal des ~s*, ergotism, St. Anthony's fire; *un tempérament ~*, a passionate nature.
ardeur [ardœr] *s.f.* heat, warmth; (fig.) ardour; vitality, energy, vigour; eagerness, enthusiasm, fervour.
ardillon [ardijɔ̃] *s.m.* tongue (of buckle); barb (of hook).
ardoise [ardwaz] *s.f.* slate; slate-grey; (fig.) debt, credit; *avoir une ~ chez*, to have credit with, to be able to chalk it up at; *il a des ~s partout*, he has debts everywhere.
ardoisé, -e [ardwaze] *adj.* slate-coloured.
ardoisi-er, -ère [ardwazje] *adj.* slaty; **~er** *s.m.* owner of slate-quarry; slate-worker, slate-quarrier.
ardoisière [ardwazjɛr] *s.f.* slate-quarry.
ardu, -e [ardy] *adj.* (of road, slope) steep, abrupt; (fig.) arduous.
are [ar] *s.m.* (land measure) are (= 100 sq. metres).
arec [arɛk] *s.m.* areca nut, betel-nut.
aréique [areik] *adj.* (geog.) (of region) with no permanent river system.
arénacé, -e [arenase] *adj.* arenaceous.
arène [arɛn] *s.f.* **1.** arena; (fig.) theatre, lists; *descendre dans l'~*, to enter the fray; **2.** bull-ring; **3.** (pl.) amphitheatre.
arénicole [arenikɔl] *adj.* (zool.) arenicolous; *~ s.f.* lobworm, lugworm.
aréolaire [areɔlɛr] *adj.* **1.** (anat.) areolar; **2.** (geol.) *érosion ~*, lateral erosion.
aréole [areɔl] *s.f.* (anat., med.) areola.
aréo-mètre [areɔmɛtr] *s.m.* areometer, hydrometer; **~métrie** [areɔmetri] *s.f.* areometry.
aréopage [areɔpaʒ] *s.m.* (Gr. ant.) Areopagus; distinguished assembly.
arête [arɛt] *s.f.* **1.** fish-bone; **2.** beard (of barley); **3.** line, edge, crest, solid angle of intersection; (arch.) arris, ridge; (geog.) ridge, arête.
aréquier [arekje] *s.m.* areca palm.
arêtier [arɛtje] *s.m.* **1.** hip-roof; **2.** ridge-pole.
argent [arʒɑ̃] *s.m.* **1.** silver; silver coins; *vif ~*, quicksilver (mercury); *d'~*, silver(-coloured), silvery; **2.** money; *payer en ~*, to pay in cash; *jeter son ~ par les fenêtres*, to throw one's money down the drain; *en vouloir, en avoir, pour son ~*, to want, to get, value for one's money; *prendre qch. pour ~ comptant*, to take sth. for granted.
argentan [arʒɑ̃tɑ̃] *s.m.* German silver, nickel silver.
argenté, -e [arʒɑ̃te] *adj.* **1.** silvered, silver-plated; silver(-coloured), silvery; **2.** (fam.) in funds, flush with money.
argenter [arʒɑ̃te] *v.t.* to cover with silver, to plate; to silver.
argenterie [arʒɑ̃tri] *s.f.* silver-plate, plate; table silver.
argentifère [arʒɑ̃tifɛr] *adj.* (min.) argentiferous, silver-bearing.
argentin[1], **-e** [arʒɑ̃tɛ̃] *adj.* **1.** (obs.) silvered; **2.** (fig.) tinkling, silvery.
argentin[2], **-e** [arʒɑ̃tɛ̃] *adj., s.m.f.* Argentinian; *la République ~e*, the Argentine, Argentina.
Argentine [arʒɑ̃tin] *s.f.* (geog.) the Argentine, Argentina.
argenture [arʒɑ̃tyr] *s.f.* silvering; silver-plating.
argilacé, -e [arʒilase] *adj.* argilaceous.
argile [arʒil] *s.f.* clay; *~ à porcelaine*, china clay; *~ réfractaire*, fire-clay.
argileu-x, -se [arʒilø] *adj.* clayey.
argon [argɔ̃] *s.m.* (chem.) argon.
argonaute [argɔnot] *s.m.* **1.** (Gr. myth.) Argonaut; **2.** (zool.) nautilus.
argot [argo] *s.m.* slang.
argotique [argɔtik] *adj.* slang.
argotisme [argɔtism] *s.m.* slang word or expression.
argousin [arguzɛ̃] *s.m.* **1.** (hist.) warder (on galleys); **2.** (obs., pej.) policeman.
arguer [arge] *v.t.* to infer, to argue (*de*, from); *~ de qch.*, to put forward sth. as a reason.
argument [argymɑ̃] *s.m.* **1.** argument, reasoning; **2.** proof, evidence; *tirer ~ de*, to advance as proof; **3.** weapon or means of persuasion; **4.** argument, plot (of book or play).

argumentant, -e [argymɑ̃tɑ̃] *s.m.f.* (law) proponent.
argumentat-eur, -rice [argymɑ̃tatœr] *adj.* argumentative; *s.m.f.* arguer, wrangler.
argumentation [argymɑ̃tɑsjɔ̃] *s.f.* argumentation, argument, reasoning.
argumenter [argymɑ̃te] *v.i.* to argue.
argus [argys] *s.m.* **1.** (zool.) argus; **2.** (Gr. myth.) Argus; (fig.) vigilant person; **3.** (fig.) directory; ~ *de l'automobile*, publication giving prices of second-hand cars; ~ *de la presse*, press-cutting agency.
argutie [argysi] *s.f.* quibble, cavil, hair-splitting.
aria[1] [arja] *s.m.* (fam.) trouble, hitch, bother; *que d'~s!*, what a fuss!
aria[2] [arja] *s.m.* (mus.) aria.
arianisme [arjanism] *s.m.* Arianism.
aride [arid] *adj.* arid, barren, dry, infertile.
aridité [aridite] *s.f.* aridity, barrenness, dryness, infertility.
arien, -ne [arjɛ̃] *adj.* Arian.
ariette [arjɛt] *s.f.* (mus.) arietta.
arille [arij] *s.m.* (bot.) aril.
aristocrate [aristɔkrat] *s.m.f.* aristocrat; (pej. abbrev. *aristo* = nob, bloated aristocrat).
aristocrat-ie [aristɔkrasi] *s.f.* aristocracy; **~ique** [aristɔkratik] *adj.* aristocratic; **~iquement** [aristɔkratikmɑ̃] *adv.* aristocratically.
aristoloche [aristɔlɔʃ] *s.f.* (bot.) Aristolochia, birthwort.
Aristophane [aristɔfan] *s.m.* Aristophanes.
Aristote [aristɔt] *s.m.* Aristotle.
aristotélicien, -ne [aristɔtelisjɛ̃] *adj., s.m.f.* Aristotelian.
aristotélique [aristɔtelik] *adj.* Aristotelian.
aristotélisme [aristɔtelism] *s.m.* Aristotelian philosophy.
arithmétique [aritmetik] *adj.* arithmetical; (fam.) *c'est* ~, that's what it adds up to, it is irrefutable; ~ *s.f.* arithmetic, sums; arithmetic book.
arithmo-graphe [aritmɔgraf] *s.m.* (sci., hist.) arithmograph; **~logie** [aritmɔlɔʒi] *s.f.* arithmology; **~mètre** [aritmɔmɛtr] *s.m.* arithmometer, calculating-machine.
arlequin [arləkɛ̃] *s.m.* **1.** Harlequin; *habit d'~*, motley; **2.** *manteau d'~*, (theatr.) proscenium.
arlequinade [arləkinad] *s.f.* harlequinade; (fig.) buffoonery.
armada [armada] *s.f.* armada.
armagnac [armaɲak] *s.m.* Armagnac (brandy).
armateur [armatœr] *s.m.* ship-owner or captain.
armature [armatyr] *s.f.* **1.** armature, brace, stay, reinforcement, support; frame, framework; **2.** (mus.) key signature.
arme [arm] *s.f.* **1.** arm, weapon; (mil.) *portez ~!*, slope arms!; *place d'~s*, parade-ground; *passer par les ~s*, to shoot (by way of execution); **2.** (pl.) fencing-weapons; *maître d'~s*, fencing-master; *salle d'~s*, fencing school; **3.** arm, branch of service; **4.** (pl.) (herald.) arms.
armé, -e [arme] *adj.* armed; (obs.) armoured; *béton ~*, reinforced concrete; (fig.) ~ *de*, armed with, equipped with.
armée [arme] *s.f.* army, forces; (fig.) crowd, host; *l'Armée de terre, de la mer, de l'air*, land forces, navy, Air Force; *l'Armée du Salut*, the Salvation Army; *l'~ à Bourbaki*, a motley assortment of down-at-heel people, rabble.
armeline [armәlin] *s.f.* ermine.
armement [armәmɑ̃] *s.m.* **1.** arming; loading (of weapon); **2.** arms, equipment; armament (of ship); (pl.) armaments; **3.** (naut.) commissioning, fitting-out; **4.** (comm.) shippers, shipping company.
Arménie [armeni] *s.f.* (geog.) Armenia.
arménien, -ne [armenjɛ̃] *adj., s.m.f.* Armenian.
armer [arme] *v.t.* **1.** to arm, to equip with arms; **2.** to load, to cock, to set; **3.** (techn.) to reinforce, to strengthen; (fig.) to fortify; **4.** (naut.) to equip, to fit out, to commission; **5.** (mus.) to give a key signature to; **s'~** *v.refl.* to arm oneself; (obs.) to take arms; *s'~ de*, to arm oneself with, to equip oneself with, (fig.) to fortify oneself with; *s'~ de tout son courage*, to summon up all one's courage.
armet [armɛ] *s.m.* (medieval) armet.
armillaire [armil(l)ɛr] *adj.* (anc. astron.) armillary.
armille [armij] *s.f.* (anc. astron.) armilla; (ant.) bracelet, armlet; (pl.) (arch.) annulets.
armistice [armistis] *s.m.* armistice.
armoire [armwar] *s.f.* wardrobe, cupboard; (glass-fronted) bookcase; ~ *frigorifique*, ice-chest; ~ *à glace*, mirror-fronted wardrobe; (fig., fam.) (of person) battleship.
armoiries [armwari] *s.f.pl.* arms, armorial bearings.
armoise [armwaz] *s.f.* (bot.) Artemisia, wormwood.
armon [armɔ̃] *s.m.* futchel (of horse-drawn vehicle).
armorial, -e, (aux) [armɔrjal] *adj.* armorial.
armorier [armɔrje] *v.t.* (herald.) to emblazon.
armure [armyr] *s.f.* **1.** armour; (fig.) defence, protection; **2.** armature (of electromagnet); **3.** (mus.) key signature; **4.** (text.) finish, weave.
armurerie [armyrri] *s.f.* armoury; arms-factory; gunsmith's shop.
armurier [armyrje] *s.m.* (mil.) armourer; gunsmith; manufacturer of arms.
arnica [arnika] *s.f.* (bot.) arnica; (pharm.) tincture of arnica.
arobe see ARROBE.
aromate [arɔmat] *s.m.* aromatic (substance).
aromatique [arɔmatik] *adj.* aromatic.
aromatiser [arɔmatize] *v.t.* to perfume.
arôme, arome [arom] *s.m.* aroma, flavour, fragrance.
aronde [arɔ̃d] *s.f.* **1.** (obs.) swallow; **2.** (techn.) *queue d'~*, dovetail; *assembler à queue d'~*, to dovetail.
arpège [arpɛʒ] *s.m.* (mus.) arpeggio.
arpéger [arpeʒe] *v.t.* to play arpeggios; *accord arpégé*, spread or broken chord.
arpent [arpɑ̃] *s.m.* arpent (old land measure = approx. one acre).
arpentage [arpɑ̃taʒ] *s.m.* surveying.
arpenter [arpɑ̃te] *v.t.* to survey, to measure; (fig.) to cover in long strides.
arpenteur [arpɑ̃tœr] *s.m.* surveyor.
arpenteuse [arpɑ̃tøz] *s.f.* (zool.) span-worm, geometer.
arpion [arpjɔ̃] *s.m.* (usu. pl.) (pop.) feet.
arqué, -e [arke] *adj.* bowed; (of eyebrows) arched; *aux jambes ~es*, bow-legged.
arquebuse [arkәbyz] *s.f.* (h)arquebus.
arquebusier [arkәbyzje] *s.m.* (h)arquebusier.
arquer [arke] *v.t.* to bend, to curve, to arch; ~ *v.i.* to bend, to be arched; **s'~** *v.refl.* to bend.
arrachage [araʃaʒ] *s.m.* pulling-up, digging-up (of plants); ~ *des mauvaises herbes*, weeding; (fam.) ~ *d'une dent*, tooth-pulling, extraction.
arrache-clou [araʃklu] *s.m.* claw-hammer, nail-puller.
arrachement [araʃmɑ̃] *s.m.* **1.** pulling-up, uprooting; extraction; **2.** (fig.) heart-break, wrench.
(d')arrache-pied [daraʃpje] *adv. loc.* **1.** without a break; **2.** without faltering, without giving up.
arracher [araʃe] *v.t.* **1.** to uproot, to pull up, to lift (potatoes); **2.** to pull out, to wrench out, to extract, to draw (a cork); to remove, to tear away, to rouse (from sleep); *s'~ les cheveux*,

to tear one's hair, (fig.) to be in desperation; to tear each other's hair out; **3.** to pull away, to snatch, to wrest, to wring, to extort (*à* (of persons), *à* or *de* (of things), from); *un obus lui a arraché le bras*, a shell tore off his arm; ~ *le masque à qn.*, to unmask s.o.; ~ *l'âme à qn.*, to kill s.o., (fig.) to cause s.o. great distress; ~ *de l'argent à un avare*, to squeeze money out of a miser; ~ *des consolations du désastre*, to extract some consolation from the disaster; *s'*~ *qn.*, to vie for someone's favour; *on se l'arrache*, he is all the rage; *s'*~ *à* or *de*, to tear oneself away from.

arrache-racine(**s**) [araʃrasin] *s.m.* grubber.

arracheu-r, -se [araʃœr] *s.m.f.* (person) puller, harvester, (of potatoes, etc.); (obs.) ~*r de dents*, tooth-puller; *mentir comme un* ~*r de dents*, to lie like a trooper; ~**se** *s.f.* potato-lifter (machine), potato-digger (implement).

arrachis [araʃi] *s.m.* **1.** (forestry) clearing; **2.** uprooted trees and brush.

arrachoir [araʃwar] *s.m.* potato-digger (implement).

arraisonnement [arɛzɔnmɑ̃] *s.m.* (naut.) boarding and inspection.

arraisonner [arɛzɔne] *v.t.* (naut.) to board and inspect.

arrangeable [arɑ̃ʒabl] *adj.* **1.** repairable; **2.** negotiable.

arrangeant, -e [arɑ̃ʒɑ̃] *adj.* accommodating, obliging, amenable.

arrangement [arɑ̃ʒmɑ̃] *s.m.* **1.** arrangement, disposition, ordering, organization, classification; (mus.) arrangement; **2.** (pl.) arrangements, preparations; **3.** agreement, settlement, compromise; *faire des* ~*s avec, en venir à des* ~*s avec*, to come to terms with, to settle with.

arranger [arɑ̃ʒe] *v.t.* **1.** to arrange, to put in order, to sort out, to prepare; **2.** to arrange, to organize; **3.** to repair, to overhaul; **4.** to settle, to compromise; **5.** to be suitable; *cela m'arrange*, that suits me; **6.** (fam.) to ill-treat, to beat up; *je l'arrangerai*, I'll fix him; **s'**~ *v.refl.* **1.** to be organized, to be arranged, to fall into place; **2.** to tidy oneself up; **3.** to be repaired, to improve; *cela s'arrangera*, it will sort itself out; **4.** to prepare oneself, to make arrangements (*pour*, to); *arrangez-vous pour que cela ne se sache pas*, see to it that nobody knows about it; **5.** to come to an agreement; **6.** *s'*~ *de qch.*, to put up with sth., to make do with sth.

arrangeur [arɑ̃ʒœr] *s.m.* (mus.) arranger, adapter.

arrenter [arɑ̃te] *v.t.* to rent.

arrérager [areraʒe] *v.i.* to fall into arrears; **s'**~ *v.refl.* to be due.

arrérages [areraʒ] *s.m.pl.* arrears.

arrestation [arɛstɑsjɔ̃] *s.f.* arrest; *en état d'*~, under arrest.

arrêt [arɛ] *s.m.* **1.** stop, stopping, halt, standstill; (techn.) stoppage, blockage; pause, break, cessation (of hostilities); *à l'*~, stopped, at a standstill; *sans* ~, without stopping; *temps d'*~, pause; *marquer un temps d'*~, to pause, to mark time; *chien d'*~, setter, pointer; **2.** stop, stopping-place (of bus, etc.); **3.** (obs.) arrest; (mod.) *mandat d'*~, warrant; *maison d'*~, prison; (mil.) *mettre aux* ~*s*, to put under arrest; **4.** (law) judgement, sentence; (fig.) decree.

arrêté, -e [arete] *adj.* **1.** at a standstill; **2.** decided, fixed, agreed; *avoir des idées* ~*es*, to have fixed ideas; **3.** (fin.) settled, closed; ~ *s.m.* **1.** (fin.) closing, settlement (of account); **2.** decision, order, decree.

arrête-bœuf [arɛtbœf] *s.m.* (bot.) rest-harrow.

arrêter [arete] *v.t.* **1.** to stop, to check, to halt, to stay, to immobilize, to hold up; to hold back, to keep back, to detain, to delay; to pull up (horse); to interrupt, to bring to an end; ~ *de faire*, to stop doing; **2.** to arrest; **3.** (sewing) ~ *un point, un fil*, to make a knot in a thread; **4.** to keep fixed (on), to dwell (on); ~ *ses yeux sur*, to fix one's eyes on; **5.** (obs.) to engage (servant); **6.** to determine, to decide, to fix, to settle; ~ *un marché*, to conclude a bargain, a deal; ~ *v.i.* to stop; **s'**~ *v.refl.* to stop, to halt, to stay; (fig.) *s'*~ *en bon chemin*, to give up in mid-course; *s'*~ *de faire*, to stop doing; *s'*~ *sur*, to fix upon, to fasten on.

arrêtoir [arɛtwar] *s.m.* (mech.) stop, catch.

arrhes [ar] *s.f.pl.* deposit, earnest money, down payment.

arriération [arjerɑsjɔ̃] *s.f.* (psychol.) ~ *mentale*, backwardness.

arrière [arjɛr] *adv.* **1.** (obs.) begone!; **2.** behind, from behind; *vent* ~, following wind; (needlew.) *point* ~, backstitch; (car) *feu* ~, rear light; *siège* ~, back seat; *marche* ~, reverse; *faire marche* ~, to reverse; (fig.) to withdraw, to retreat, to eat one's words; *en* ~, back, backwards; ~ *s.m.* stern (of ship); back (of car); rear; (sport) back; (mil.) (pl.) rear, lines of communication.

arriéré, -e [arjere] *adj.* **1.** in arrears, overdue, owing, outstanding; **2.** retarded, backward, undeveloped; **3.** old-fashioned, out of date; ~ *s.m.* arrears; ~(**e**) *s.m.f.* backward child.

arrière-ban [arjɛrbɑ̃] *s.m.* **1.** general levy; **2.** (fig.) scrapings of the barrel; ~**-bec** [arjɛrbɛk] *s.m.* downstream cutwater (of bridge); ~**-bouche** [arjɛrbuʃ] *s.f.* back of the mouth; ~**-boutique** [arjɛrbutik] *s.f.* back room (behind shop); ~**-corps** [arjɛrkɔr] *s.m.* recessed wing (of building); rear premises; ~**-cour** [arjɛrkur] *s.f.* back-yard; ~**-cuisine** [arjɛrkɥizin] *s.f.* back kitchen, scullery; ~**-faix** [arjɛrfɛ] *s.m.* (med.) afterbirth; ~**-fleur** [arjɛrflœr] *s.f.* second flowering; ~**-fond** [arjɛrfɔ̃] *s.m.* innermost depth, recesses; ~**-garde** [arjɛrgard] *s.f.* **1.** rear-guard; **2.** (fig.) *d'*~*-garde*, behind the times; ~**-goût** [arjɛrgu] *s.m.* after-taste; (fig.) aftermath.

arrière-grand-mère [arjɛrgrɑ̃mɛr] *s.f.* great-grandmother; (similarly with GRAND-PÈRE).

arrière-grand-oncle [arjɛrgrɑ̃tɔ̃kl] *s.m.* great-great-uncle; (similarly with GRAND-TANTE).

arrière-main [arjɛrmɛ̃] *s.f.* **1.** (obs.) back of the hand; **2.** hindquarters (of horse); **3.** (tennis) backhand stroke.

arrière-neveu [arjɛrnvø] *s.m.* great-nephew; (similarly with NIÈCE).

arrière-pays [arjɛrpei] *s.m.* hinterland; ~**-pensée** [arjɛrpɑ̃se] *s.f.* ulterior motive.

arrière-petit-fils [arjɛrpətifis] *s.m.* great-grandson; (similarly with PETITE-FILLE and PETITS-ENFANTS).

arrière-petit-neveu [arjɛrpətinvø] *s.m.* great-great-nephew; (similarly with PETITE-NIÈCE).

arrière-plan [arjɛrplɑ̃] *s.m.* background; *d'*~*-plan*, of secondary importance; ~**-port** [arjɛrpɔr] *s.m.* inner harbour; ~**-saison** [arjɛrsɛzɔ̃] *s.f.* late autumn; end of harvest; (fig.) evening of life; ~**-salle** [arjɛrsal] *s.f.* back-room; ~**-train** [arjɛrtrɛ̃] *s.m.* hindquarters (of animal); (fam.) backside; (obs.) rear (of vehicle).

arriérer [arjere] *v.t.* to delay, to defer, to let fall into arrears; **s'**~ *v.refl.* to fall into arrears, to fall behind.

arrimage [arimaʒ] *s.m.* (naut., aeron.) stowage, stowing, trim.

arrimer [arime] *v.t.* (naut., aeron.) to stow, to trim; to secure (load, etc.).

arrimeur [arimœr] *s.m.* stevedore.

arrivage [arivaʒ] *s.m.* **1.** landing, arrival (of goods); **2.** consignment (of goods); **3.** (fig.) shoal, influx (of people).

arrivant, -e [arivɑ̃] *s.m.f.* arrival (person arriving).
arrivé, -e [arive] *adj.* **1.** *premier, dernier,* ~, first-comer, last-comer; **2.** successful, established.
arrivée [arive] *s.f.* **1.** arrival; **2.** (techn.) intake; **3.** arrival point, arrival lounge, etc.
arriver [arive] *v.i.* **1.** to arrive; to come; ~ *à,* to reach, to achieve; ~ *à ses fins,* to attain one's ends; **2.** to happen, to occur, to take place, to come about; ~ *à qn.,* to happen to s.o.; *cela ne m'est jamais arrivé,* that has never happened to me; *il lui est arrivé un accident,* he's had an accident; *quoi qu'il arrive,* whatever happens; *il arrive qu'il prenne ses repas au restaurant,* he sometimes eats at a restaurant; *il lui arrive de perdre ses lunettes,* he sometimes, frequently, loses his glasses; **3.** to succeed, to do well, to become someone; *il est arrivé par ses propres efforts,* he is a self-made man; **4.** to manage, to find time to, to get round to; ~ *à faire qch.,* to get round to doing sth.; *en* ~ *à,* to come to the point of, to be reduced to; *j'en arrive à me demander,* I am reduced to wondering.
arrivisme [arivism] *s.m.* (unscrupulous) ambition, go-getting.
arriviste [arivist] *s.m.f.* careerist, climber, self--seeker.
arroche [arɔʃ] *s.f.* (bot.) orache; ~ *puante,* stinking goosefoot.
arrogance [arɔgɑ̃s] *s.f.* arrogance, haughtiness.
arrogant, -e [arɔgɑ̃] *adj.* arrogant, haughty, disdainful.
(**s'**)**arroger** [arɔʒe] *v.refl.* to arrogate to oneself, to claim (without justification).
arroi [arwa] *s.m.* (obs.) array, equipage; *être en mauvais* ~, to be in a sorry state.
arrondi, -e [arɔ̃di] *adj.* rounded; plump ~ *s.m.*; **1.** ~ rounded shape; circular portion; **2.** (aeron.) flattening out.
arrondir [arɔ̃dir] *v.t.* **1.** to make round or circular; to hump (back); (fig.) ~ *les angles,* to smooth things out; **2.** (fig.) to round off (an amount); to increase (territory); **s'**~ *v.refl.* to become round.
arrondissage [arɔ̃disaʒ] *s.m.* (techn.) rounding off.
arrondissement [arɔ̃dismɑ̃] *s.m.* **1.** (obs.) rounding off, making round; **2.** (fig.) increase; **3.** arrondissement, ward, borough, administrative division.
arrosage [arozaʒ] *s.m.* watering, sprinkling, spraying, irrigation; (cook.) basting.
arroser [aroze] *v.t.* **1.** to water, to sprinkle, to spray; (fig) to bathe (*de,* in); (cook.) to baste; to wash down (a meal with); (fig., fam.) to bribe; (fam.) to celebrate with drinks; ~ *un repas d'un bon vin,* to wash down a meal with a good wine; ~ *ses galons,* to celebrate one's promotion; **2.** (of river) to water, to flow through.
arroseur [arozœr] *s.m.* sprinkler.
arroseuse [arozøz] *s.f.* water-cart.
arrosoir [arozwar] *s.m.* watering-can.
arrow-root [arorut] *s.m.* arrowroot.
arsenal [arsənal] *s.m.* arsenal; (naval) dockyard; (fig.) armoury; paraphernalia.
arséniate [arsenjat] *s.m.* (chem.) arsen(i)ate.
arsenic [arsənik] *s.m.* (chem.) arsenic.
arsenical, -e, (**aux**) [arsənikal] *adj.* arsenical.
arsénieux [arsenjø] *adj.m.* arsenious.
arséniure [arsenjyr] *s.m.* (chem.) arsenide.
arsin [arsɛ̃] *adj.m.* (forestry) *bois* ~, wood damaged by fire.
arsouille [arsuj] *adj. il a l'air un peu* ~, he looks a bit of a hooligan; ~ *s.f.* (irrespective of sex) hooligan, guttersnipe.
art [ar] *s.m.* art; craft, profession; skill; *avoir l'*~ *de faire qch.,* to have the knack of doing sth.; *les* ~*s,* the arts; ~*s d'agrément,* accomplishments; *beaux* ~*s,* fine arts; ~*s ménagers,* domestic science, home economics; ~*s et métiers,* arts and crafts; *conservatoire des* ~*s et métiers,* institute of engineering.
artefact [artefakt] *s.m.* artefact, artifact.
artel [artɛl] *s.f.* **1.** artel (co-operative in pre--revolutionary Russia); **2.** co-operative (in U.S.S.R.), kolkhoz.
artère [artɛr] *s.f.* **1.** artery; **2.** thoroughfare, arterial road.
artériel, -le [arterjɛl] *adj.* arterial.
artériole [arterjɔl] *s.f.* arteriole, small artery.
artério-sclérose [arterjɔskleroz] *s.f.* arteriosclerosis; ~**tomie** [arterjɔtɔmi] *s.f.* arteriotomy.
artérite [arterit] *s.f.* arteritis.
artésien, -ne [artezjɛ̃] *adj.* artesian.
arthrite [artrit] *s.f.* arthritis.
arthrit-ique [artritik] *adj.* arthritic; ~**isme** [artritism] *s.m.* arthritic condition.
artichaut [artiʃo] *s.m.* (French, globe) artichoke.
artichautière [artiʃotjɛr] *s.f.* **1.** artichoke bed; **2.** (cook.) artichoke-steamer.
article [artikl] *s.m.* **1.** (obs.) (zool.) joint, articulation, segment; **2.** (law, admin.) clause, section, article; **3.** item, point; matter, subject, object; *à l'*~ *de la mort,* on the point of death; **4.** newspaper article; ~ *de fond, de tête,* leading article, editorial; **5.** (comm.) article, commodity, line; (pl.) goods, wares; ~*s de Paris,* fancy goods; *faire l'*~, to boost one's wares; **6.** (lang.) article.
articulaire [artikylɛr] *adj.* articular.
articulation [artikylɑsjɔ̃] *s.f.* **1.** (anat.) articulation, joint, knuckle (of fingers); **2.** (mech.) joint, connection; **3.** (lang.) articulation, pronunciation; **4.** (law) enumeration.
articulé, -e [artikyle] *adj.* articulated, clear, distinct; (mech.) jointed, articulated.
articuler [artikyle] *v.t.* **1.** to articulate, to pronounce; **2.** (law) to enumerate; **3.** (mech.) to joint, to hinge; **s'**~ *v.refl.* to be connected, jointed, hinged; (fig.) to be connected; ~ *v.i.* ~ *bien, mal,* to speak or enunciate clearly, badly.
artifice [artifis] *s.m.* **1.** (obs.) skill; (mod.) stratagem, device, expedient; trick, artifice, ruse; **2.** (mil., nav.) flare, light- or smoke-signal; *feu d'*~, fireworks; (fig.) dazzling display.
artificiel, -le [artifisjɛl] *adj.* artificial; ~**lement** [artifisjɛlmɑ̃] *adv.* artificially.
artificier [artifisje] *s.m.* pyrotechnist.
artificieu-x, -se [artifisjø] *adj.* artful, crafty, cunning; ~**sement** [artifisjøzmɑ̃] *adv.* artfully, craftily, cunningly.
artillerie [artijri] *s.f.* artillery.
artilleur [artijœr] *s.m.* artilleryman, gunner.
artimon [artimɔ̃] *s.m.* (naut.) mizzen (sail); *mât d'*~, mizzen-mast.
artisan [artizɑ̃] *s.m.* artisan, craftsman; (fig.) architect, author, (of sth.).
artisanal, -e, (**aux**) [artizanal] *adj.* at the craft level, not industrialized.
artisanat [artizana] *s.m.* **1.** craft, cottage industry; **2.** artisan class.
artiste [artist] *s.m.* artist; (mus., theatr.) artiste, player, performer; *entrée des* ~*s,* stage--door; ~**ment** [artistəmɑ̃] *adv.* tastefully.
artistique [artistik] *adj.* artistic; ~**ment** [artistikmɑ̃] *adv.* artistically.
artocarpe [artɔkarp] *s.m.* bread-fruit tree.
arum [arɔm] *s.m.* (bot.) arum.
aruspice [aryspis] *s.m.* (Rom. ant.) haruspex.
aryen, -ne [arjɛ̃] *adj., s.m.f.* Aryan.
aryténoïde [aritenɔid] *adj., s.m.* (anat.) arytenoid.
arythmie [aritmi] *s.f.* (med.) arrhythmia, irregularity of pulse.

A.S. [aɛs] abbrev. *Assurances sociales* (= National Insurance).
as [ɑs] *s.m.* **1.** (Rom. coin) as; **2.** (cards, dice) ace; **3.** (fig.) (sport, etc.) ace, star; (fam.) *fichu comme l'~ de pique*, got up fit to kill; (fam.) *être plein aux ~*, to be well-heeled; (fam.) *c'est un ~*, he is a champion.
asbeste [asbɛst] *s.m.* amiant(h)us, asbestos.
ascaride [askarid], **ascaris** [askaris] *s.m.* ascarid, intestinal worm.
ascendance [asɑ̃dɑ̃s] *s.f.* **1.** (astron.) ascent; **2.** ancestry; **3.** (aeron., gliding) *~ thermique*, thermal soaring.
ascendant, -e [asɑ̃dɑ̃] *adj.* ascending; *~ s.m.* **1.** (astron.) ascendant; **2.** ascendancy, influence; *avoir, exercer, de l'~ sur qn.*, to have, to exercise, influence over s.o.; *subir l'~ de qn.*, to come under the influence of s.o.; **3.** (pl.) forebears.
ascenseur [asɑ̃sœr] *s.m.* lift, (U.S.) elevator.
ascension [asɑ̃sjɔ̃] *s.f.* **1.** (astron.) ascension; **2.** (eccles.) Ascension, Ascension Day; **3.** ascent; rise; *faire l'~ d'une montagne*, to climb a mountain.
ascensionnel, -le [asɑ̃sjɔnɛl] *adj.* ascensional; upward (motion); elevating (power); (aeron.) *vitesse ~le*, climbing speed.
ascensionner [asɑ̃sjɔne] *v.i.* to climb (mountains), to make an ascent.
ascensionniste [asɑ̃sjɔnist] *s.m.f.* climber.
ascèse [asɛz] *s.f.* ascesis.
ascète [asɛt] *s.m.f.* ascetic.
ascét-ique [asetik] *adj.* ascetic; **~icisme** [asetisism] *s.m.* asceticism.
ascidie [asidi] *s.f.* **1.** (zool.) ascidian; **2.** (bot.) ascidium.
ascite [asit] *s.f.* (med.) ascites, dropsy.
asclépiade[1] [asklepjad] *s.m.* (pros.) asclepiad; *~ adj.* asclepiadean.
asclépiade[2] [asklepjad] *s.f.* (bot.) milkweed.
ascorbique [askɔrbik] *adj.* ascorbic.
asepsie [asɛpsi] *s.f.* asepsis.
aseptique [asɛptik] *adj.* aseptic.
aseptisation [asɛptizɑsjɔ̃] *s.f.* sterilization.
aseptiser [asɛptize] *v.t.* to render aseptic.
asexué, -e [asɛksɥe] *adj.* asexual.
Asiate [azjat] *s.m.f.* Asian.
asiatique [azjatik] *adj., s.m.f.* Asian, Asiatic.
Asie [azi] *s.f.* (geog.) Asia.
asile [azil] *s.m.* sanctuary, refuge, asylum; home (for aged); (fig.) retreat, shelter; *droit d'~*, right of sanctuary; *sans ~*, homeless; *~ de nuit*, night-shelter, (fam.) doss-house; *~ d'aliénés*, mental hospital.
asinien, -ne [azinjɛ̃] *adj.* (zool.) relating to the ass; (of type of mule) asinine.
asocial, -e [asɔsjal] *adj.* antisocial.
asparagine [asparaʒin] *s.f.* (chem.) asparagine.
aspe [asp], **asple** [aspl] *s.m.* (silk-spinning) winder.
aspect [aspɛ] *s.m.* appearance; aspect, angle, light, point of view; *sous cet ~*, in this light; *sous un ~ nouveau*, from a new angle; *à l'~ de*, at the sight of; *au premier ~*, at first sight.
asperge [aspɛrʒ] *s.f.* (bot.) asparagus; (fig.) tall thin person, bean-pole.
asperger [aspɛrʒe] *v.t.* to sprinkle (*de*, with); (fam.) to spatter (with mud, etc.).
aspergès [aspɛrʒɛs] *s.m.* (eccles.) aspergillum.
aspérité [asperite] *s.f.* unevenness, roughness (of surface); (fig.) harshness.
asperme [aspɛrm] *adj.* (bot.) aspermous, aspermatous.
aspersion [aspɛrsjɔ̃] *s.f.* (eccles.) sprinkling, aspersion (of holy water); ⚠ not 'aspersion' in sense 'calumny'.
aspersoir [aspɛrswar] *s.m.* **1.** (eccles.) aspergillum; **2.** (hort.) fine-spray rose (of watering-can).
asphaltage [asfaltaʒ] *s.m.* asphalting.
asphalte [asfalt] *s.m.* asphalt, bitumen; (fam.) pavement.
asphalter [asfalte] *v.t.* to asphalt.
asphodèle [asfɔdɛl] *s.m.* (bot.) asphodel.
asphyxiant, -e [asfiksjɑ̃] *adj.* asphyxiating, suffocating, choking, stifling; *gaz ~*, poison-gas.
asphyxie [asfiksi] *s.f.* asphyxia, asphyxiation; suffocation; (comm.) strangulation.
asphyxié, -e [asfiksje] *adj.* asphyxiated, suffocated; *s.m.f.* person suffering from asphyxiation.
asphyxier [asfiksje] *v.t.* to asphyxiate, to suffocate; (fig.) to strangle.
aspic[1] [aspik] *s.m.* asp, viper; *langue d'~*, (fig.) backbiter.
aspic[2] [aspik] *s.m.* (bot.) spike lavender.
aspic[3] [aspik] *s.m.* (cook.) aspic.
aspidistra [aspidistra] *s.m.* (bot.) aspidistra.
aspirant, -e [aspirɑ̃] *adj.* (techn.) suction-; *pompe ~e*, suction-pump; *s.m.f.* candidate, aspirant (for post, honours); *~ s.m.* (mil., nav.) cadet, midshipman.
aspirat-eur, -rice [aspiratœr] *adj.* aspiratory; **~eur** *s.m.* (techn.) aspirator, exhaust-fan, dust--extractor; vacuum cleaner.
aspiration [aspirɑsjɔ̃] *s.f.* **1.** aspiration; inhaling; **2.** (techn.) suction; **3.** (fig.) aspiration, yearning.
aspiratoire [aspiratwar] *adj.* aspiratory; inspiratory (breathing).
aspiré, -e [aspire] *adj.* (lang.) aspirated, aspirate.
aspirer [aspire] *v.t.* **1.** to aspirate; to inhale, to breathe in; **2.** to suck up or in; (techn.) to exhaust; **3.** *~ à*, to aspire to, to aim at.
aspirine [aspirin] *s.f.* aspirin.
assa-fœtida [asafetida] *s.f.* (pharm.) asafoetida.
assagir [asaʒir] *v.t.* to make wiser; to calm, to moderate; **s'~** *v.refl.* to become wiser; to sober down, to settle down.
assagissement [asaʒismɑ̃] *s.m.* enlightenment; mellowing, settling down.
assaillant, -e [asajɑ̃] *adj.* attacking, aggressive; *s.m.f.* aggressor, assailant.
assaillir [asajir] *v.t.* to attack, to assault; (fig.) to worry, to harass, to overwhelm.
assainir [asenir] *v.t.* to make healthy or healthier; to drain (swamp); to disinfect (building, wound); (fig.) to purify; (econ.) to stabilize (market, currency).
assainissement [asenismɑ̃] *s.m.* cleansing, draining (of swamp), disinfecting (of building, of wound); (fig.) purification; (econ.) stabilizing (of market, currency).
assainisseur [asenisœr] *s.m.* air-freshener.
assaisonnement [asɛzɔnmɑ̃] *s.m.* (cook.) condiment, seasoning, dressing.
assaisonner [asɛzɔne] *v.t.* (cook.) to season, to flavour, to dress; (fig.) to season, to temper, to give zest to, to enliven; (fam.) *~ qn.*, to tell s.o. off; *il s'est fait ~ par son père*, he got a ticking-off from his father.
assassin, -e [asasɛ̃] *adj.* (jest) provoking; *mouche-~e*, beauty spot (i.e. black patch worn under the eye by ladies); *~ s.m.* assassin, murderer; *à l'~!*, help! murder!; *ce médecin est un ~*, this doctor is a butcher.
assassinat [asasina] *s.m.* murder, assassination.
assassiner [asasine] *v.t.* to murder, to assassinate; (fig., fam.) to demand exorbitant sums in payment; *je ne veux pas vous ~*, I don't want to rob you.
assaut [aso] *s.m.* assault, attack, charge; (fig.) onslaught; *faire ~ d'esprit, d'élégance, etc.*, to compete, to vie, to try to outdo, in wit, in elegance, etc.
asseau [aso] *s.m.* (techn.) sax, zax.
assèchement [asɛʃmɑ̃] *s.m.* draining (of swamp).

assécher [aseʃe] *v.t.* to drain (swamp, tank).
assemblage [asɑ̃blaʒ] *s.m.* assembly, gathering, collection; (techn.) joint.
assemblé [asɑ̃ble] *s.m.* (ballet) assemblé.
assemblée [asɑ̃ble] *s.f.* assembly, audience, congregation; meeting (of a society or institution); parliament.
assembler [asɑ̃ble] *v.t.* to assemble, to gather together, to put together, to collect; (techn.) to assemble, to join, to rivet; **s'~** *v.refl.* to assemble, to meet, to gather, to collect, to congregate; *qui se ressemble s'assemble*, birds of a feather flock together.
assembleu-r, -se [asɑ̃blœr] *s.m.f.* assembler; (print.) gatherer; **~se** *s.f.* (techn.) gathering--machine.
asséner [asene] *v.t.* **1.** ~ *un coup*, to land, to deal, a blow; **2.** (fig.) ~ *une réplique, une plaisanterie*, to make a cutting reply, a devastating joke.
assentiment [asɑ̃timɑ̃] *s.m.* assent, agreement, consent.
asseoir [aswar] *v.t.* to seat, to set, to place; (fig.) to set up, to found, to consolidate, to base; *faire ~ qn.*, to offer s.o. a seat; ~ *un impôt*, to assess a tax; **s'~** *v.refl.* to sit (down), to take a seat; to settle.
assermenté, -e [asɛrmɑ̃te] *adj.* (of persons) sworn, on oath.
assermenter [asɛrmɑ̃te] *v.t.* to swear in, to administer the oath to.
assertion [asɛrsjɔ̃] *s.f.* assertion.
asservir [asɛrvir] *v.t.* to enslave, to subjugate, to dominate; to master, to control (forces of nature, passions, etc.); **s'~** *v.refl.* (techn.) to operate by servo-mechanism; *moteur asservi*, servo-operated motor; *s'~ à*, to be the slave of, to be enslaved by, to submit to.
asservissant, -e [asɛrvisɑ̃] *adj.* enslaving, servile (work, yoke).
asservissement [asɛrvismɑ̃] *s.m.* bondage, subjection, servitude, enslavement; (techn.) remote control, servo-operation.
asservisseu-r, -se [asɛrvisœr] *adj.* enslaving, compelling; **~r** *s.m.* **1.** (obs.) enslaver; **2.** (techn.) actuating device, remote control mechanism, servo-mechanism.
assesseur [asɛsœr] *s.m.* **1.** assistant; **2.** (law) assessor.
assette [asɛt] *s.f.* = ASSEAU.
assez [ase] *adv.* **1.** enough; ~ *grand pour*, big enough to (for); ~ *d'argent pour*, enough money to (for); *en voilà ~!*, that will do!, that's more than enough!; *en avoir ~ de qch.*, to have had enough of sth., to be fed up with sth.; **2.** rather, fairly, passably, quite; *elle est ~ jolie*, she is quite pretty; (fam., intensive) *est-il ~ bête!*, how stupid can you get!
assibilation [asibilɑsjɔ̃] *s.f.* (lang.) assibilation.
assidu, -e [asidy] *adj.* assiduous, conscientious, punctual; full of attentions.
assiduité [asidɥite] *s.f.* assiduity, conscientiousness; attentions.
assidûment [asidymɑ̃] *adv.* assiduously, conscientiously, regularly.
assiégé, -e [asjeʒe] *adj.*, *s.m.f.* besieged, beleaguered, (person); (fig.) pestered (person).
assiégeant, -e [asjeʒɑ̃] *adj.* besieging; *s.m.f.* besieger; *l'~*, the besieging force.
assiéger [asjeʒe] *v.t.* to besiege, to beleaguer, to lay siege to; to surround, to crowd around; (fig.) to pester, to importune, to worry, to torment; (of creditor) to dun.
assiette [asjɛt] *s.f.* **1.** posture; (riding) seat; (naut.) trim; **2.** (fig.) disposition; *ne pas être dans son ~*, to be off colour (physically); **3.** (obs.) position, site; **4.** (law) basis of taxation; **5.** plate, plateful; ~ *creuse* or *à soupe*, soup plate; ~ *plate*, dinner plate; ~ *anglaise*, assorted cold meats; (fig., fam.) *c'est l'~ au beurre*, there are a lot of pickings to be had.
assiettée [asjete] *s.f.* plateful.
assignable [asiɲabl] *adj.* assignable.
assignation [asiɲɑsjɔ̃] *s.f.* **1.** (law) assignment, distribution (of funds, property); **2.** (law) summons, writ.
assigner [asiɲe] *v.t.* **1.** to assign, to allot; **2.** to arrange (appointment), to determine (date); **3.** to attribute; **4.** (law) to summon, to cite.
assimilable [asimilabl] *adj.* assimilable; capable of integration; comparable; (of idea, etc.) possible to assimilate; digestible.
assimilat-eur, -rice [asimilatœr] *adj.* absorptive, assimilatory, digestive; integrating; **~eur** *s.m.* assimilator, integrator.
assimilation [asimilɑsjɔ̃] *s.f.* assimilation, integration; comparison; digestion.
assimilé, -e [asimile] *adj.* assimilated, integrated; digested; ~ *s.m.* civilian attached to fighting unit.
assimiler [asimile] *v.t.* **1.** to assimilate; to liken, to equate, (*à*, to, with); **2.** to digest; **3.** to integrate; **s'~** *v.refl.* to become like, to liken oneself to; (of food, etc.) to be assimilated; to be integrated; *s'~ qch.*, to adopt, to incorporate (sth. foreign).
assis, -e [asi] *adj.* **1.** seated, sitting; *être ~*, to sit, to be sitting, to be seated; *rester ~*, to remain seated; **2.** (fig.) established, stable, firm.
assise [asiz] *s.f.* **1.** (build.) course; layer (of cement); **2.** base, foundation; **3.** (pl.) (geol.) strata.
Assise [asiz] *s.f.* (geog.) Assisi.
assises [asiz] *s.f.pl.* **1.** assizes, assize court; **2.** congress, meeting, assembly.
assistanat [asistana] *s.m.* assistant lectureship.
assistance [asistɑ̃s] *s.f.* **1.** audience, public, company; those present, those standing by; **2.** assistance, aid, help; **3.** (social welfare) relief, assistance; (obs.) ~ *publique*, poor-law relief; (mod.) ~ *sociale*, social security; ~ *judiciaire*, legal aid; *l'Assistance*, child-care institutions.
assistant, -e [asistɑ̃] *s.m.f.* **1.** (pl.) spectators, audience; **2.** assistant, deputy; *~(e) social(e)*, social welfare officer; *maître ~*, assistant lecturer.
assisté, -e [asiste] *adj.*, *s.m.f.* **1.** (obs.) pauper; **2.** (person) receiving social assistance, legal aid, etc.
assister [asiste] *v.i.* ~ *à*, to attend, to be present at; to be a witness of; ~ *v.t.* to assist, to act as assistant to s.o.; (obs.) to relieve, to succour; (rare) to help, to aid.
associati-f, -ve [asɔsjatif] *adj.* associative, operating by association.
association [asɔsjɑsjɔ̃] *s.f.* **1.** associating, association, meeting; **2.** association, society, organization; (comm.) partnership, cartel, consortium, syndicate; ~ *amicale*, friendly society; **3.** (obs.) association football; **4.** (fig.) association, synthesis.
associé, -e [asɔsje] *s.m.f.* associate, partner; *membre ~*, associate member; (law) shareholder.
associer [asɔsje] *v.t.* **1.** to link up, to associate, to connect; to bring together; **2.** to associate (sth. with sth.), to give (s.o.) a share or interest (in sth.); *s'~ qn.*, to take s.o. into partnership, to associate s.o. (in an undertaking); **s'~** *v.refl.* to join, to combine, to ally oneself, to federate; *s'~ à* or *avec qn.*, to join with s.o., to go into partnership with s.o.; *s'~ à qch.*, to join sth., to take part in sth.
assoiffé, -e [aswafe] *adj.* thirsty, athirst; (fig.) eager (*de*, for).
assolement [asɔlmɑ̃] *s.m.* (agric.) rotation of crops.

assoler [asɔle] *v.t.* (agric.) to rotate (crops).
assombrir [asɔ̃brir] *v.t.* to darken, to cloud over; (fig.) to make gloomy, to sadden; **s'~** *v.refl.* to become dark, to cloud over; *le ciel s'assombrit*, the sky clouded over; *son front s'assombrit*, his brow darkened.
assommant, -e [asɔmɑ̃] *adj.* overwhelming; (fig., fam.) boring, tiresome; *elle est ~e*, she is the limit, she is impossible.
assommer [asɔme] *v.t.* **1.** to stun or kill (by a blow on the head); **2.** (obs.) to overwhelm, to confound, (by arguments); **3.** to exhaust (physically); **4.** (fig., fam.) to bore, to exasperate.
assommeur [asɔmœr] *s.m.* slaughterer.
assommoir [asɔmwar] *s.m.* **1.** (obs.) pole-axe; **2.** (obs.) dram-shop, gin-shop.
Assomption [asɔ̃psjɔ̃] *s.f.* (eccles.) (feast of the) Assumption.
assonance [asɔnɑ̃s] *s.f.* assonance.
assonant, -e [asɔnɑ̃] *adj.* assonant.
assorti, -e [asɔrti] *adj.* **1.** matching, in harmony (with); (of couple) matched, well-matched; **2.** (of shop) well-stocked; **3.** (pl.) various, assorted, mixed.
assortiment [asɔrtimɑ̃] *s.m.* **1.** mixture, arrangement, combination; **2.** collection, set; **3.** (comm.) stock, selection; **4.** (cook.) dish of assorted meats, etc.
assortir [asɔrtir] *v.t.* to mix, to blend, to match, to combine; to unite, to bring together; to stock (a shop); **s'~** *v.refl.* to match, to be well-matched, to harmonize, to go well together.
assoupi, -e [asupi] *adj.* **1.** drowsy, dozing; **2.** deadened, diminished; dormant.
assoupir [asupir] *v.t.* to lull to sleep, to make drowsy; (fig.) to deaden, to allay, to appease; **s'~** *v.refl.* to fall asleep, to doze; (fig.) to be assuaged, to be appeased.
assoupissement [asupismɑ̃] *s.m.* drowsiness, somnolence; slothfulness; calming (of sea, etc.); (fig.) appeasement, assuaging.
assouplir [asuplir] *v.t.* to soften, to make flexible or supple; to discipline, to train (child); to make less harsh, to relax (rules, discipline); **s'~** *v.refl.* to become supple; (fig.) to mellow, to unbend.
assouplissement [asuplismɑ̃] *s.m.* softening, relaxing; (fig.) making, or becoming, more amenable.
assourdir [asurdir] *v.t.* to deafen; (fig.) to wear down (with noise); to deaden; to muffle; **s'~** *v.refl.* (lang.) to become unvoiced.
assourdissant, -e [asurdisɑ̃] *adj.* deafening.
assourdissement [asurdismɑ̃] *s.m.* deafening, deadening, muffling; deafening noise; temporary deafness; (lang.) unvoicing.
assouvir [asuvir] *v.t.* to satiate, to satisfy; to gratify (passions); **s'~** *v.refl.* to eat one's fill; to satisfy one's passions; to be satisfied.
assouvissement [asuvismɑ̃] *s.m.* satiating, satisfaction, gratification.
assujetti, -e [asyʒeti] *adj.* subjugated; fixed; *s.m.f.* person liable to tax.
assujettir [asyʒetir] *v.t.* **1.** to subdue, to enslave, to subjugate; to dominate; *~ à*, to make subject to, to subject to; **2.** to fix, to fasten; **s'~** *v.refl.* **1.** to take into one's power; **2.** to subject oneself (*à*, to).
assujettissant, -e [asyʒetisɑ̃] *adj.* binding; demanding, exacting.
assujettissement [asyʒetismɑ̃] *s.m.* subjugation, conquest; servitude, subjection; constraint, obligation.
assumer [asyme] *v.t.* to assume, to take on, to undertake; to endure, to accept (situation, etc.).
assurable [asyrabl] *adj.* insurable.
assurance [asyrɑ̃s] *s.f.* **1.** assurance, (self-) confidence, audacity; **2.** assurance, promise; *veuillez agréer l'~ de mes sentiments distingués, etc.* (at end of letter) yours truly, faithfully, etc.; **3.** surety, security, guarantee, pledge; **4.** (also pl.) insurance, underwriting; *~ contre les accidents, l'incendie*, accident, fire, insurance; *~ sur la vie*, life insurance; *~ automobile, tous risques, au tiers*, motor, comprehensive, third-party, insurance; *~ invalidité-vieillesse*, national insurance; *~s maritimes*, marine insurance; *compagnie d'~s*, insurance company.
assuré, -e [asyre] *adj.* **1.** certain, sure, inevitable; **2.** (of person) assured, confident, bold, firm; **3.** (obs.) safe; *s.m.f.* insured (person), policy-holder.
assurément [asyremɑ̃] *adv.* assuredly, undoubtedly, certainly, for certain, indeed.
assurer [asyre] *v.t.* **1.** to assure, to guarantee, to vouch for, to give one's word (that), to state confidently; *~ qn. de qch.*, to assure s.o. of sth.; *j'en suis assuré*, I am certain of it; **2.** *~ qch. à qn.*, to assure s.o. of sth.; to provide, to secure, sth. for s.o.; **3.** to make secure, to preserve, to protect, to defend; **4.** to make stable, to fix; **5.** to be responsible for, to ensure, to guarantee; to provide for; *~ la marche de qch.*, to be responsible for sth. working; **6.** to insure; **s'~** *v.refl.* **1.** to make sure, to verify; **2.** *s'~ contre*, to defend oneself against, (sth.), to guard against; to insure against; **3.** to settle oneself firmly (in the saddle); **4.** *s'~ (de) qch.*, to make sure of sth., to obtain, to procure, or to win sth.; *s'~ la faveur, la protection, de qn.*, to obtain someone's favour, protection.
assureur [asyrœr] *s.m.* insurer, underwriter; insurance agent.
Assyrie [as(s)iri] *s.f.* (anc. geog.) Assyria.
assyrien, -ne [asirjɛ̃] *adj., s.m.f.* Assyrian.
assyriologie [asirjɔlɔʒi] *s.f.* Assyriology.
astatique [astatik] *adj.* (phys.) astatic.
aster [astɛr] *s.m.* (bot.) Michaelmas daisy, perennial aster; (biol.) aster; ⚠ not other kinds of bot. 'aster'.
astérie [asteri] *s.f.* (zool.) starfish, asteroid.
astérisque [asterisk] *s.m.* asterisk.
astéroïde [asterɔid] *s.m.* (astron.) asteroid.
asthénie [asteni] *s.f.* (med.) asthenia, nervous debility.
asthénique [astenik] *adj.* asthenic.
asthmatique [asmatik] *adj., s.m.f.* asthmatic.
asthme [asm] *s.m.* asthma.
asti [asti] *s.m.* Asti (wine).
asticot [astiko] *s.m.* **1.** maggot; **2.** (fam., fig.) chap.
asticoter [astikɔte] *v.t.* (fam.) to plague, to nag, to worry.
astigmate [astigmat] *adj., s.m.f.* astigmatic.
astigmatisme [astigmatism] *s.m.* astigmatism.
astiquage [astikaʒ] *s.m.* polishing, rubbing-up.
astiquer [astike] *v.t.* to polish, to rub up.
astragale [astragal] *s.m.* **1.** (arch.) astragal; **2.** (anat.) astragalus, ankle-bone; **3.** (bot.) astragalus, tragacanth.
astrakan [astrakɑ̃] *s.m.* astrakhan.
astral, -e, (aux) [astral] *adj.* astral, stellar.
astre [astr] *s.m.* star, heavenly body; (fig.) star, luminary; (poet.) *l'~ du jour, de la nuit*, the sun, the moon.
astreignant, -e [astrɛɲɑ̃] *adj.* restrictive; compelling, exacting.
astreindre [astrɛ̃dr] *v.t.* to compel, to force, to constrain, to oblige; *~ à*, to subject to; **s'~** *v.refl.* to force oneself.
astreinte [astrɛ̃t] *s.f.* compulsion, constraint.
astringence [astrɛ̃ʒɑ̃s] *s.f.* (med.) astringency.
astringent, -e [astrɛ̃ʒɑ̃] *adj., s.m.* astringent.
astro-labe [astrɔlab] *s.m.* astrolabe; **~lâtrie**

[astrɔlɑtri] *s.f.* astrolatry, worship of the stars; **~logie** [astrɔlɔʒi] *s.f.* astrology; **~logique** [astrɔlɔʒik] *adj.* astrological; **~logiquement** [astrɔlɔʒikmɑ̃] *adv.* astrologically; **~logue** [astrɔlɔg] *s.m.f.* astrologer; **~naute** [astrɔnot] *s.m.f.* astronaut, cosmonaut; **~nautique** [astrɔnotik] *s.f.* astronautics, space-travel; **~nef** [astrɔnɛf] *s.f.* space-craft; **~nome** [astrɔnɔm] *s.m.f.* astronomer; **~nomie** [astrɔnɔmi] *s.f.* astronomy; **~nomique** [astrɔnɔmik] *adj.* astronomical; (fig.) astronomic(al), exorbitant; **~nomiquement** [astrɔnɔmikmɑ̃] *adv.* astronomically.

astrophysicien, -ne [astrɔfizisjɛ̃] *s.m.f.* astrophysicist.

astrophysique [astrɔfizik] *s.f.* astrophysics.

astuce [astys] *s.f.* **1.** (obs.) cunning, guile; **2.** gimmick, brain-wave, trick (not pej.); *les ~s du métier*, the tricks of the trade; **3.** (fam.) wisecrack, gag.

astucieu-x, -se [astysjø] *adj.* (obs.) cunning; (mod.) shrewd; **~sement** [astysjøzmɑ̃] *adv.* shrewdly.

asymétrie [asimetri] *s.f.* asymmetry.

asymétrique [asimetrik] *adj.* asymmetrical.

asymptote [asɛ̃ptɔt] *adj.* (math.) asymptotic; ~ *s.f.* asymptote.

asymptotique [asɛ̃ptɔtik] *adj.* (math.) asymptotic.

asynchrone [asɛ̃krɔn] *adj.* asynchronous.

asyndète [asɛ̃dɛt] *s.f.* (lang.) asyndeton.

asystolie [asistɔli] *s.f.* (med.) asystole.

ataraxie [ataraksi] *s.f.* (phil.) ataraxia.

atavique [atavik] *adj.* atavistic.

atavisme [atavism] *s.m.* atavism.

ataxie [ataksi] *s.f.* (med.) ataxia, ataxy; ~ *locomotive*, locomotor ataxy.

ataxique [ataksik] *adj.* ataxic.

atèle [atɛl] *s.m.* (zool.) spider monkey.

atelier [atəlje] *s.m.* **1.** workshop; shop (part of factory); **2.** studio, workroom (of an artist); **3.** followers or pupils of an artist; **4.** (masonic) lodge.

atermoiement [atɛrmwamɑ̃] *s.m.* postponement (of payment of debt); delaying, putting off, procrastination.

atermoyer [atɛrmwaje] *v.t.* (law) to postpone payment; ~ *v.i.* to delay, to hesitate, to procrastinate.

athée [ate] *adj.* atheistic(al); ~ *s.m.f.* atheist.

athéisme [ateism] *s.m.* atheism.

athénée [atene] *s.m.* athenaeum (educational establishment in Switzerland and Belgium).

Athènes [atɛn] *s.f.* (geog.) Athens.

athénien, -ne [atenjɛ̃] *adj.*, *s.m.f.* Athenian.

athermane [atɛrman] *adj.* (phys.) athermanous.

athermique [atɛrmik] *adj.* (phys.) athermic.

athlète [atlɛt] *s.m.f.* athlete.

athlétique [atletik] *adj.* athletic.

athlétisme [atletism] *s.m.* athletics.

Atlante [atlɑ̃t] *s.m.* (myth.) Atlas.

atlantique [atlɑ̃tik] *adj.* (geog.) Atlantic; *l'Atlantique*, *l'océan Atlantique*, the Atlantic (ocean).

atlas [atlɑs] *s.m.* **1.** atlas; **2.** (anat.) uppermost cervical vertebra.

atmosphère [atmɔsfɛr] *s.f.* (lit. & fig.) atmosphere.

atmosphérique [atmɔsferik] *adj.* atmospheric.

atoll [atɔl] *s.m.* atoll.

atome [atom] *s.m.* (lit. & fig.) atom.

atome-gramme [atomgram] *s.m.* (phys.) gram-atom, gramme-atom.

atomicité [atɔmisite] *s.f.* (chem.) atomicity.

atomique [atɔmik] *adj.* atomic, nuclear.

atomisé, -e [atɔmize] *s.m.f.* one subjected to nuclear radiation (by bombing).

atomiser [atɔmize] *v.t.* **1.** to atomize, to vaporize; **2.** to destroy by atom-bomb or with nuclear weapons.

atomiseur [atɔmizœr] *s.m.* atomizer, spray; aerosol.

atomisme [atɔmism] *s.m.* (phil.) atomism.

atomiste [atɔmist] *s.m.f.* **1.** (phil.) atomist; **2.** (or *savant* ~), atomic scientist, atomic physicist.

atomistique [atɔmistik] *adj.* atomistic, atomic; ~ *s.f.* (chem.) atomic theory; (phys.) nuclear physics.

atonal, -e, (als) [atɔnal] *adj.* (mus.) atonal.

atone [atɔn] *adj.* **1.** (med.) atonic; **2.** (fig.) lethargic, lifeless; **3.** (lang.) unstressed.

atonie [atɔni] *s.f.* **1.** (med.) atony; **2.** (fig.) lethargy.

atonique [atɔnik] *adj.* (med.) atonic.

atour [atur] *s.m.* **1.** dress; *dame d'~*, Lady of the Bedchamber; **2.** (pl.) (obs. or iron.) finery; *parée de ses plus beaux ~s*, dressed in all her best finery, dressed to kill.

atout [atu] *s.m.* (cards) trump; (fig.) advantage; *avoir tous les ~s dans son jeu*, to hold all the trump cards, to have all the advantages on one's side.

atoxique [atɔksik] *adj.* atoxic, non-toxic.

atrabile [atrabil] *s.f.* (anc. med.) black bile.

atrabiliaire [atrabiljɛr] *adj.* atrabilious, melancholic, irritable; ~ *s.m.f.* person of moods, of uncertain temper.

âtre [ɑtr] *s.m.* hearth.

atrium [atrijɔm] *s.m.* (Rom. arch.) atrium.

atroce [atrɔs] *adj.* atrocious, dreadful, horrible; unbearable; **~ment** [atrɔsmɑ̃] *adv.* atrociously, dreadfully, horribly.

atrocité [atrɔsite] *s.f.* atrocity, atrociousness.

atrophie [atrɔfi] *s.f.* (med. & fig.) atrophy.

atrophié, -e [atrɔfje] *adj.* (med. & fig.) atrophied, withered.

atrophier [atrɔfje] *v.t.* to cause to wither (by atrophy); **s'~** *v.refl.* to atrophy, to become atrophied, to wither, to waste away.

atropine [atrɔpin] *s.f.* (chem.) atropine.

attabler [atable] *v.t.* to seat at table; **s'~** *v.refl.* to sit down at table.

attachant, -e [ataʃɑ̃] *adj.* (obs.) captivating, enthralling; (mod.) which holds the attention; engaging, attractive.

attache [ataʃ] *s.f.* **1.** attaching, fastening; *à l'~*, tied up; (naut.) *port d'~*, home port; **2.** tie, fastening, bond, cord, strap, leash, hook, clip; **3.** (anat.) joint; *les ~s*, ankles and wrists; *avoir des ~s fines*, to have slender ankles and wrists; **4.** (fig.) attachment; (pl.) ties, links.

attaché, -e [ataʃe] *adj.* fixed, tied, buttoned up; (fig.) inherent (in); devoted (to); *s.m.f.* attaché.

attachement [ataʃmɑ̃] *s.m.* **1.** attachment, affection, ties; **2.** (build.) daily statement (by architect) of work done and materials used.

attacher [ataʃe] *v.t.* to attach, to fasten, to tie, to secure, to tie up; to fasten together; to fix; to bind; (fig.) to endear; to associate, to second (s.o. to a post); to apply, to attribute; ~ *par des épingles*, to pin; ~ *avec une agrafe*, to hook or clip together; ~ *avec une boucle*, to buckle; ~ *avec de la colle*, to glue, to stick; ~ *les yeux sur*, to fix one's gaze on, to stare at; *s'~ qn.*, to gain someone's affection; ~ *à une ambassade*, to attach or second to an embassy; ~ *de l'importance à*, to attach importance to, to consider important; ~ *un sens à une parole*, to attribute a meaning to a word; ~ *v.i.* (cook.) to stick (to bottom of pan); **s'~** *v.refl.* to be attached, to be fastened or fixed; *s'~ à*, (lit. & fig.) to be or to become attached to; (fig.) to go with, to accompany, to be inherent in; to apply oneself to, to concern oneself with; to be determined (to do).

attaquable [atakabl] *adj.* open to attack, vulnerable; questionable, disputable.

attaquant, -e [atakɑ̃] *s.m.f.* attacker; (sport) attacking player.

attaque [atak] *s.f.* attack, assault, onslaught, onrush, fit (of hysteria, etc.); (fam.) *d'~*, fit, in good form.

attaquer [atake] *v.t.* **1.** to attack, to assault, to make an attack on; to tackle (s.o. about sth.); to dispute, to contest; to corrode, to destroy; *~ qn. en justice*, to take s.o. to court; *~ un acte*, to contest a document; **2.** (fig.) to infringe, to violate; to set about, to tackle (a problem); **s'~ à** *v.refl.* to attack; to grapple with.

attardé, -e [atarde] *adj.* **1.** belated; **2.** old-fashioned, behind the times; **3.** retarded, backward.

attarder [atarde] *v.t.* to delay, to keep (s.o.) late; **s'~** *v.refl.* to delay, to linger, to be late, to stay late, to sit up late; to lag behind, to get behind; *s'~ sur*, to dwell on (a subject).

atteindre [atɛ̃dr] *v.t.* **1.** to reach, to overtake, to catch up (with); (fig.) to achieve, to arrive at; *~ à*, to manage to reach, to achieve with difficulty; **2.** to reach, to strike, to hit; **3.** (fig.) to affect, to wound, to touch.

atteint, -e [atɛ̃] *adj.* suffering (from a serious disease); (fam.) touched, cracked.

atteinte [atɛ̃t] *s.f.* **1.** (obs.) blow, stroke; (mod.) injury, damage; attack; *porter ~ à*, to attack, to cast a slur on; **2.** (med.) attack, onset; *une légère ~ de*, a touch of; **3.** reach; *hors d'~*, out of reach.

attelage [atlaʒ] *s.m.* **1.** harnessing, yoking; **2.** harness; (rail.) coupling; **3.** team, yoke, pair (of horses, etc.).

atteler [atle] *v.t.* to harness, to yoke; (fig.) *~ qn. à un travail, une tâche*, to launch s.o. upon a task; **s'~** *à v.refl.* to apply oneself to.

attelle [atɛl] *s.f.* **1.** hame (of horse's collar); **2.** (med.) splint.

attenant, -e [atnɑ̃] *adj.* adjoining, contiguous.

(**en**) **attendant** [ɑ̃natɑ̃dɑ̃] *adv. loc.* meanwhile, for the time being; *en ~ que, en ~ de*, until.

attendre [atɑ̃dr] *v.t.* **1.** to wait for, to await; *attendez-moi sous l'orme*, you may wait until Doomsday; *nous attendons qu'il revienne*, we are waiting for him to return; *attendez de savoir ce qu'il a fait, avant de le condamner*, wait and hear what he's done before you condemn him; *~ v.i.* to wait; *tout vient à point à qui sait ~*, everything comes to him who waits; *faire ~ qn., se faire ~*, to keep s.o. waiting; *se faire ~*, to be a long time coming; *le repas se fait ~*, the meal is a long time coming; **2.** to expect; *~ avec impatience*, to look forward to; **s'~** (*à*) *v.refl.* to expect, to hope for; *il faut s'~ à tout*, you can expect anything; *s'~ à ce que*, to expect; *elle attendait à ce qu'il vînt à Paris*, she was expecting him to come to Paris.

attendrir [atɑ̃drir] *v.t.* to soften, to make tender; to tenderize (meat); (fig.) to affect, to move to pity, to touch, to mollify; **s'~** (*sur*) *v.refl.* to be moved to pity, to pity; (pej.) to become maudlin.

attendrissant, -e [atɑ̃drisɑ̃] *adj.* moving, affecting; touching.

attendrissement [atɑ̃drismɑ̃] *s.m.* compassion, pity, sympathy.

attendrisseur [atɑ̃drisœr] *s.m.* (cook.) meat tenderizer.

attendu, -e [atɑ̃dy] *adj.* expected, awaited; *prep.* considering, given, owing to, in consideration of; *~ que, conj. loc.*, since, seeing that, given that, as; (law) whereas; **~s** *s.m.pl.* (law) reasons adduced (for a judgement).

attentat [atɑ̃ta] *s.m.* outrage, attack, criminal attempt; (law) *~ à la pudeur, aux mœurs*, indecent behaviour, offence against public decency.

attentatoire [atɑ̃tatwar] *adj.* prejudicial (*à*, to).

attente [atɑ̃t] *s.f.* **1.** waiting, wait; *salle d'~*, waiting-room; *passer des heures dans l'~ de*, to spend hours waiting for; **2.** expectation, hope; *dans l'~ de vous lire*, awaiting the favour of a reply; *contre toute ~*, contrary to all expectations.

attenter [atɑ̃te] *v.i.* *~ à*, to make a criminal attempt on; *~ à la vie de qn.*, to make an attempt on someone's life; *~ à ses jours*, to try to kill oneself.

attenti-f, -ve [atɑ̃tif] *adj.* attentive, conscientious; considerate; **~vement** [atɑ̃tivmɑ̃] *adv.* attentively, carefully, with great care.

attention [atɑ̃sjɔ̃] *s.f.* **1.** attention, notice, care; *attirer l'~ de qn. sur qch.*, to draw someone's attention to sth.; *faire ~ à*, to notice, to pay attention to, to be careful with; *faire ~ que, à ce que*, to be careful that; *~!*, look out!, be careful!; **2.** (obs. exc. Lit.) consideration; (mod.) (pl.) attentions, kindness.

attentionné, -e [atɑ̃sjɔne] *adj.* considerate, kind, thoughtful.

attentisme [atɑ̃tism] *s.m.* (pol.) wait-and-see policy, opportunism.

attentiste [atɑ̃tist] *s.m.f.* (pol.) opportunist, one who adopts wait-and-see policy.

atténuant, -e [atenɥɑ̃] *adj.* extenuating.

atténuer [atenɥe] *v.t.* **1.** to make thinner; **2.** to attenuate, to reduce, to relieve (pain); to soften, to moderate, to tone down.

atterrage [ateraʒ] *s.m.* (naut.) landfall.

atterrer [atere] *v.t.* to overwhelm, to crush; to astound.

atterrir [aterir] *v.i.* **1.** (naut.) to sight land, to make a landfall; **2.** to land (also on moon or other planet), to come to earth, to come down.

atterrissage [aterisaʒ] *s.m.* **1.** (naut.) landfall; **2.** landing; (aeron.) *train d'~*, undercarriage.

atterrissement [aterismɑ̃] *s.m.* silt, sand-bank, bar; alluvial deposit.

attestation [atɛstɑsjɔ̃] *s.f.* **1.** affidavit; **2.** certificate; **3.** sign, proof, indication.

attester [atɛste] *v.t.* **1.** to attest, to affirm, to vouch for, to confirm; **2.** to bear witness to, to prove, to demonstrate.

atticisme [at(t)isism] *s.m.* atticism.

attiédir [atjedir] *v.t.* to cool or warm slightly, to make lukewarm; (fig.) to moderate, to cool down, to weaken; **s'~** *v.refl.* (fig.) to become cooler, to moderate, to weaken, to grow lukewarm.

attiédissement [atjedismɑ̃] *s.m.* (fig.) abatement, cooling down.

attifement [atifmɑ̃] *s.m.* (fam.) dolling-up, get-up.

attifer [atife] *v.t.* (fam.) to doll up; **s'~** *v.refl.* to doll oneself up.

attiger [atiʒe] *v.i.* to damage, to hurt; (pop.) to shoot a line, to exaggerate.

attique [atik] *adj.* (Gr. hist.) Attic; *~ s.m.* (arch.) attic (storey).

attirable [atirabl] *adj.* attractable.

attirail (pl. **-ails**) [atiraj] *s.m.* **1.** (obs). equipment, baggage-train; **2.** (fam.) paraphernalia, impedimenta, gear, tackle.

attirance [atirɑ̃s] *s.f.* attraction, power of attraction.

attirant, -e [atirɑ̃] *adj.* attractive, alluring, seductive, enticing.

attirer [atire] *v.t.* (lit. & fig.) to attract, to draw; to seduce, to charm, to lure; to procure, to invite, to cause, to provoke, to bring down; *ses procédés lui attireront des ennuis*, his conduct will cause trouble for him; *~ la colère de qn. sur qn.*, to bring down someone's wrath on s.o.; **s'~** *v.refl.* to be mutually attractive; to incur, to bring upon oneself, to invite.

attisement [atizmɑ̃] *s.m.* (fig.) stirring-up, provoking, (passions).

attiser [atize] *v.t.* to stir up, to revive, (a fire); (fig.) to excite, to inflame, to provoke.

attisoir [atizwar] *s.m.* poker.

attitré, -e [atitre] *adj.* **1.** recognized, accredited; *fournisseur ~ de S.M. la Reine*, by appointment, supplier, to H.M. the Queen; **2.** regular, usual, (supplier).

attitrer [atitre] *v.t.* to recognize, to accredit, to appoint.

attitude [atityd] *s.f.* attitude.

attouchement [atuʃmɑ̃] *s.m.* touch, contact, feel.

attracti-f, -ve [atraktif] *adj.* attractive, magnetic.

attraction [atraksjɔ̃] *s.f.* attraction; (pl.) cabaret (in night-club), floor-show.

attrait [atrɛ] *s.m.* **1.** attraction, charm; **2.** taste, inclination.

attrapade [atrapad] *s.f.*, **attrapage** [atrapaʒ] *s.m.* **1.** (fam.) squabble, tiff; **2.** (fam.) ticking-off.

attrape [atrap] *s.f.* **1.** (obs.) trap, gin; **2.** (fig.) ruse, hoax; **3.** trick; *une boîte de farces et d'~s*, a box of jokes and tricks.

attrape-mouche [atrapmuʃ] *s.m.* (bot.) fly-trap; (ornith.) fly-catcher.

attrape-nigaud [atrapnigo] *s.m.* booby-trap, trap for the gullible, for suckers, etc.

attraper [atrape] *v.t.* **1.** (obs.) to trap; **2.** to catch (person, ball, disease, train, remark); to apprehend; *une maladie qui s'attrape*, an infectious or contagious disease, a disease that is catching; **3.** to catch out, to trick, to surprise; **4.** to reprimand, to scold; **s'~** *v.refl.* to quarrel; **5.** (fam.) to hit (target).

attrayant, -e [atrɛjɑ̃] *adj.* attractive, charming.

attribuable [atribɥabl] *adj.* attributable.

attribuer [atribɥe] *v.t.* to allot, to assign; to confer, to grant; to attribute, to ascribe, to impute; *s'~ qch.*, to claim sth., to take sth. for oneself; *s'~ tout le mérite de qch.*, to take all the credit for sth.

attribut [atriby] *s.m.* attribute.

attributaire [atribytɛr] *s.m.f.* (law) beneficiary.

attributi-f, -ve [atribytif] *adj.* (law) (act, etc.) of assignment; (gram.) predicative.

attribution [atribysjɔ̃] *s.f.* **1.** attribution, grant, award; **2.** (pl.) powers, competence; *cela n'entre pas dans mes ~s*, that is outside my province, I am not competent to deal with that.

attristant, -e [atristɑ̃] *adj.* saddening, grievous, desolating, painful; deplorable.

attrister [atriste] *v.t.* to sadden, to make sad, to grieve, to desolate; *s'~ de*, to be sad, to grieve, about.

attrition [atrisjɔ̃] *s.f.* attrition, abrasion.

attroupement [atrupmɑ̃] *s.m.* crowd, gathering; mob, demonstration; (law) *~ séditieux*, riot.

atypique [atipik] *adj.* atypical.

au, aux [o] see À.

aubade [obad] *s.f.* aubade.

aubaine [obɛn] *s.f.* **1.** (hist.) *droit d'~*, escheat; **2.** windfall, luck, piece of good fortune; bargain.

aube[1] [ob] *s.f.* dawn.

aube[2] [ob] *s.f.* (eccles.) alb.

aube[3] [ob] *s.f.* paddle or blade (of wheel), blade or vane (of turbine, fan).

aubépine [obepin] *s.f.* hawthorn, whitethorn, may.

aubère [obɛr] *adj.*, *s.m.* red roan, flea-bitten (-coloured) (horse).

auberge [obɛrʒ] *s.f.* inn (usu. in the country); *on n'est pas sorti de l'~*, we're not out of the wood yet.

aubergine [obɛrʒin] *s.f.* aubergine, egg-plant; *~ adj.invar.* aubergine (colour).

aubergiste [obɛrʒist] *s.m.* inn-keeper.

aubier [obje] *s.m.* (bot.) alburnum.

aucun, -e [okœ̃] *adj.* any; no, not any; *sans ~e raison*, without any reason, with no reason; *je doute qu'il y ait ~e possibilité de*, I doubt if there is any possibility of; *~ physicien ignore que*, every doctor knows that; *n'avoir ~ talent*, to have no talent, not to have any talent; **~ement** [okynmɑ̃] *adv.* not at all, not in the least, in no way; **~(e)** *pron.* any, any one; none, no one, not one, not any; *il travaille plus qu'~ de ses collègues*, he works harder than any of his colleagues; *je ne connais ~ de ces pays-là*, I know none of those countries; *~ de mes amis n'est venu*, not one of my friends came; (obs.) *d'~s*, some, some people.

audace [odas] *s.f.* audacity, daring, boldness, courage; originality; (pej.) impudence, insolence.

audacieu-x, -se [odasjø] *adj.* **1.** (obs.) audacious, courageous, brave; impudent, insolent; **2.** bold, daring, original, unusual; **~sement** [odasjøzmɑ̃] *adv.* audaciously, boldly.

au-deçà, au-dedans, au-dehors, au-delà, au-dessous, au-dessus, au-devant see under DEÇÀ, etc.

au-delà [odla] *s.m.* eternity, after-life, hereafter.

audibilité [odibilite] *s.f.* audibility.

audible [odibl] *adj.* audible.

audience [odjɑ̃s] *s.f.* **1.** audience, hearing, reception; **2.** (law) sitting, session (of court); ⚠ not 'audience' in theatre, etc.

audiencier [odjɑ̃sje] *s.m.* usher (in law court).

audio-gramme [odjɔgram] *s.m.* audiogram; **~mètre** [odjɔmɛtr] *s.m.* audiometer; **~phone** [odjɔfɔn] *s.m.* hearing-aid.

audio-visuel, -le [odjɔvizɥɛl] *adj.* audio-visual.

audit-eur, -rice [oditœr] *s.m.f.* **1.** listener, member of audience; **2.** one attending a lecture (without being enrolled on the course); **3.** (admin.) treasury clerk.

auditi-f, -ve [oditif] *adj.* auditory.

audition [odisjɔ̃] *s.f.* **1.** hearing, sense of hearing; **2.** (theatr.) performance; audition; **3.** recital.

auditionner [odisjɔne] *v.t.i.* to audition, to give an audition.

auditoire [oditwar] *s.m.* audience, congregation, public.

auditorium [oditɔrjɔm] *s.m.* auditorium; (radio) studio.

auge [oʒ] *s.f.* **1.** feeding or drinking trough; **2.** (bricklayer's) hod; **3.** bucket of water-wheel.

auget [oʒɛ] *s.m.* **1.** little trough, bird-trough; **2.** = AUGE 3; *roue à ~s*, (overshot) water-wheel.

augment [ɔgmɑ̃] *s.m.* (lang.) augment.

augmentable [ɔgmɑ̃tabl] *adj.* which can be augmented.

augmentati-f, -ve [ɔgmɑ̃tatif] *adj.* (lang.) augmentative.

augmentation [ɔgmɑ̃tɑsjɔ̃] *s.f.* increase; increase in salary, rise; supplement (to edition of a book).

augmenter [ɔgmɑ̃te] *v.t.* to increase, to raise (prices, salaries, etc.); *~ qn.*, to give s.o. a rise; *~ v.i.* to increase, to rise; **s'~** *v.refl.* to increase.

augural, -e [ɔgyral] *adj.* (ant.) augural.

augure [ɔgyr] *s.m.* **1.** (ant.) augur; (mod.) prophet, soothsayer; **2.** augury, omen; *de bon ~*, auspicious; *de mauvais ~*, ominous, boding ill.

augurer [ɔgyre] *v.t.* to augur, to predict; (obs.) to conjecture, to surmise; (mod.) *~ une chose d'une autre*, to infer one thing from another.

Auguste [ɔgyst] *s.m.* (Rom. hist.) Augustus.

auguste [ɔgyst] *adj.* august; *~ s.m.* clown, Auguste.

Augustin, -e [ɔgystɛ̃] *s.m.f.* Augustinian, or Austin, friar or nun.

augustinien, -ne [ɔgystinjɛ̃] *adj.* Augustinian.

aujourd'hui [oʒurdɥi] *adv.* **1.** today; *il y a ~ huit, quinze, jours*, a week, a fortnight, ago; *~ en huit, en quinze*, today week, today fortnight;

(pop.) *au jour d'~*, nowadays; **2.** the present day, nowadays, today; *l'Amérique d'~*, present-day America.
aulnaie, aunaie [onɛ] *s.f.* alder plantation.
aulne, aune [on] *s.m.* alder (tree).
aulx [o] obs. pl. of AIL.
aumône [ɔmon] *s.f.* **1.** alms, almsgiving; charity; *demander l'~*, to beg; *être réduit à l'~*, to be reduced to beggary; *faire l'~*, to give alms; **2.** (fig.) favour.
aumônerie [ɔmonri] *s.f.* **1.** chaplaincy; **2.** the body of chaplains to the forces.
aumônier [ɔmonje] *s.m.* chaplain.
aunaie see AULNAIE.
aune[1] [on] *s.f.* ell; (fig.) yard-stick; *mesurer les autres à son ~*, to judge others by oneself.
aune[2] see AULNE.
aunée [one] *s.f.* (bot.) elecampane.
auparavant [oparavɑ̃] *adv.* previously, earlier; first of all.
auprès [oprɛ] *adv.* near by, close by; *~ de*, near, beside, close to, with, to or in the presence of; in the view of, according to; compared with; *ambassadeur ~ de la République française*, ambassador to the French Republic; *il passe pour impoli ~ d'elle*, he is considered rude in her eyes, in her esteem; *être bien ~ de qn.*, to be in someone's good books; *votre mal n'est rien ~ du sien*, your trouble is nothing compared to his.
auquel [okɛl] see LEQUEL.
aura [ɔra] *s.f.* aura.
auréole [ɔreɔl] *s.f.* **1.** aureole, halo, nimbus; **2.** ring (left by stain remover).
auréoler [ɔreɔle] *v.t.* to encircle with an aureole, a halo, a nimbus; (fig.) to glorify, to magnify.
auréomycine [ɔreɔmisin] *s.f.* (med.) aureomycin.
auriculaire [ɔrikylɛr] *adj.* auricular; *témoin ~*, hearsay witness; *~ s.m.* little finger.
auricule [ɔrikyl] *s.f.* auricle.
aurifère [ɔrifɛr] *adj.* auriferous.
aurification [ɔrifikɑsjɔ̃] *s.f.* filling (of tooth) with gold.
aurifier [ɔrifje] *v.t.* to fill (tooth) with gold.
Aurigny [ɔriɲi] *s.m.* (geog.) Alderney.
aurique [ɔrik] *adj.* (naut.) *voile ~*, lug-sail.
aurochs [ɔrɔk(s)] *s.m.* aurochs.
aurore [ɔrɔr] *s.f.* **1.** dawn, daybreak, east; **2.** (fig.) dawn, beginning, morning; **3.** (astron.) *~ boréale, australe*, aurora borealis, australis.
auscultation [ɔskyltɑsjɔ̃] *s.f.* (med.) auscultation.
ausculter [ɔskylte] *v.t.* (med.) to auscult, to auscultate, to sound (with a stethoscope).
auspice [ɔspis] *s.m.* **1.** (Rom. ant.) auspice; **2.** (pl.) omens; *sous de favorables* or *d'heureux ~s*, auspiciously; *sous de fâcheux* or *de tristes ~s*, inauspiciously; **3.** (pl.) patronage; *sous les ~s de qn.*, under the patronage, under the auspices, of s.o.
aussi [osi] *adv.* **1.** also, too, as well; **2.** (comparison) as, so; *il est ~ grand que vous*, he is as tall as you; *~ vite que possible*, as quickly as possible; *je n'ai jamais rien vu d'~ joli*, I have never seen anything so (as) pretty; *~ bien*, as well, equally well; *~ bien que*, as well as, just as much as; **3.** although, however; *~ invraisemblable que cela paraisse*, however unlikely that may seem; *~ conj.* (and) so, therefore, consequently; *les fruits ont augmenté, ~ je n'en ai pris que peu*, fruit has gone up so I have only bought a little.
aussière see HAUSSIÈRE.
aussitôt [osito] *adv.* at once, forthwith, immediately; *~ que*, as soon as; *il le reconnut ~ qu'il le vit*, he recognized him as soon as he saw him; (ellipt.) *~ arrivé, il se coucha*, as soon as he arrived, he went to bed; *~ dit, ~ fait*, no sooner said than done.
austère [ɔstɛr] *adj.* austere, stern; stoical, puritanical, harsh; severe, simple, unadorned; **~ment** [ɔstɛrmɑ̃] *adv.* austerely, sternly, severely.
austérité [ɔsterite] *s.f.* austerity, sternness; severity; (pl.) privations; asceticism.
austral, -e, (als) [ɔstral] *adj.* austral; southern (part of globe); *l'Afrique ~e*, southern Africa; *terres ~es*, south polar regions.
Australasie [ɔstralazi] *s.f.* (geog.) Australasia.
Australie [ɔstrali] *s.f.* (geog.) Australia.
australien, -ne [ɔstraljɛ̃] *adj., s.m.f.* Australian.
australopithèque [ɔstralɔpitɛk] *s.m.* (anthrop.) Australopithecine.
autan [otɑ̃] *s.m.* sirocco.
autant [otɑ̃] *adv.* **1.** as much, so much, as far; as many, so many; *~ que possible*, as much as possible, as far as possible; *il a ~ d'argent, de difficultés, que moi*, he has as much money, as many difficulties, as I do; *je ne croyais pas qu'il avait ~ d'amis*, I didn't think he had so many friends; **2.** the same, as well; *il en fit ~*, he did the same, he did it as well; **3.** *~ . . ., ~ . . .*, just as . . ., so . . .; *~ il est charmant avec elle, ~ il est désagréable avec moi*, he is every bit as charming to her as he is unpleasant to me; **4.** *d'~*, proportionally, by the same amount; *d'~ que*, seeing that; *d'~ plus que*, the more so because.
autel [otɛl] *s.m.* altar; (fig.) religion, church; *maître-~*, high-altar; (fig.) *aller à l'~*, to get married; *conduire, suivre, qn. à l'~*, to marry s.o.; (fig.) *élever des ~s à qn.*, to worship, to idolize, s.o.
auteur [otœr] *s.m.* **1.** author, creator, originator, founder; perpetrator (of crime); **2.** author (of book, etc.); *femme ~*, woman writer; *droit d'~*, copyright; *droits d'~*, royalties.
authenticité [ɔtɑ̃tisite] *s.f.* authenticity.
authentification [ɔtɑ̃tifikɑsjɔ̃] *s.f.* authentication.
authentifier [ɔtɑ̃tifje] *v.t.* to authenticate.
authentique [ɔtɑ̃tik] *adj.* authentic, authenticated; **~ment** [ɔtɑ̃tikmɑ̃] *adv.* authentically.
authentiquer [ɔtɑ̃tike] *v.t.* (obs.) to authenticate.
autisme [ɔtism] *s.m.* autism.
autistique [ɔtistik], **autiste** [ɔtist] *adj.* autistic.
auto [oto] *s.f.* (abbrev. of AUTOMOBILE) car; *~s tamponneuses*, dodgems.
auto-accusation [ɔtɔakyzɑsjɔ̃] *s.f.* self-accusation; **~-allumage** [ɔtɔalymaʒ] *s.m.* (car) spontaneous ignition; pre-ignition; **~-amorçage** [ɔtɔamɔrsaʒ] *s.m.* (mech.) automatic priming; **~berge** [ɔtɔbɛrʒ] *s.f.* car track (on raised river bank); **~biographie** [ɔtɔbjɔgrafi] *s.f.* autobiography; **~biographique** [ɔtɔbjɔgrafik] *adj.* autobiographical; **~bus** [ɔtɔbys] *s.m.* bus; **~car** [ɔtɔkar] *s.m.* coach; **~chenille** [ɔtɔʃnij] *s.f.* tracked vehicle, crawler; **~chrome** [ɔtɔkrom] *adj.* (phot.) colour, autochrome; **~chthone** [ɔtɔktɔn] *adj., s.m.f.* native, indigenous (person); **~clave** [ɔtɔklav] *adj.* self-closing; hermetically sealed; *s.m.* (med.) autoclave; (cook.) pressure-cooker; **~copie** [ɔtɔkɔpi] *s.f.* photo-copying; **~crate** [ɔtɔkrat] *s.m.* autocrat; **~cratie** [ɔtɔkrasi] *s.f.* autocracy; **~cratique** [ɔtɔkratik] *adj.* autocratic; **~critique** [otɔkritik] *s.f.* (pol.) self-accusation, self-criticism; (fam.) *faire son ~critique*, to acknowledge one's mistakes or faults; **~cuiseur** [ɔtɔkɥizœr] *s.m.* pressure-cooker; **~dafé** [ɔtɔdafe] *s.m.* auto-da-fé; **~défense** [otɔdefɑ̃s] *s.f.* self-defence, self-protection; **~destruction** [ɔtɔdɛstryksjɔ̃] *s.f.* self-destruction; **~détermination** [ɔtɔdetɛrminɑsjɔ̃] *s.f.* (pol.) self-determination; **~didacte** [ɔtɔdidakt] *adj., s.m.f.* self-taught (person), autodidact;

~drome [ɔtɔdrom] *s.m.* motor-racing track, circuit; **~-école** [ɔtɔekɔl] *s.f.* driving-school.
auto-excitat-eur, -rice [ɔtɔɛksitatœr] *adj.* (electr.) (of dynamo) self-exciting.
auto-fécondation [ɔtɔfekɔ̃dɑsjɔ̃] *s.f.* self-fertilization; **~financement** [ɔtɔfinɑ̃smɑ̃] *s.m.* self-financing; **~game** [ɔtɔgam] *adj.* autogamous; **~gamie** [ɔtɔgami] *s.f.* autogamy; **~gène** [ɔtɔʒɛn] *adj.* autogenous; *soudure ~gène*, welding; **~gestion** [ɔtɔʒɛstjɔ̃] *s.f.* control (of business) by workers; **~gire** [ɔtɔʒir] *s.m.* autogiro; **~graphe** [ɔtɔgraf] *adj.* autographic, in one's own handwriting; *s.m.* autograph; **~graphie** [ɔtɔgrafi] *s.f.* autography, facsimile reproduction; **~graphier** [ɔtɔgrafje] *v.t.* to autograph; **~graphique** [ɔtɔgrafik] *adj.* autographic, facsimile; **~greffe** [ɔtɔgrɛf] *s.f.* autograft; **~guidage** [ɔtɔgidaʒ] *s.m.* self-steering, homing (device).
autoguidé, -e [ɔtɔgide] (techn.) *adj.* self-steering, homing.
auto-intoxication [ɔtɔɛ̃tɔksikɑsjɔ̃] *s.f.* (med.) auto-intoxication; **~lyse** [ɔtɔliz] *s.f.* autolysis; **~mate** [ɔtɔmat] *s.m.* automaton; **~maticité** [ɔtɔmatisite] *s.f.* automatism; **~mation** [ɔtɔmɑsjɔ̃] *s.f.* automation; **~matique** [ɔtɔmatik] *adj.* automatic; *distributeur ~matique*, slot-machine, vending-machine; **~matiquement** [ɔtɔmatikmɑ̃] *adv.* automatically; **~matisation** [ɔtɔmatizɑsjɔ̃] *s.f.* automation; **~matiser** [ɔtɔmatize] *v.t.* to automate; **~matisme** [ɔtɔmatism] *s.m.* automatism; **~mitrailleuse** [ɔtɔmitrɑjøz] *s.f.* armoured car, machine-gun carrier.
automnal, -e [ɔtɔ(m)nal] *adj.* autumnal.
automne [ɔtɔn] *s.m.* autumn.
automobile [ɔtɔmɔbil] *adj.* **1.** self-propelling, motor-driven; **2.** relating to motor cars; *industrie ~*, *assurances ~s*, car industry, car insurance; *~ s.f.* (motor) car.
automobilisable [ɔtɔmɔbilizabl] *adj.* motor (road), suitable for cars.
automobilisme [ɔtɔmɔbilism] *s.m.* motoring; motor-racing.
automot-eur, -rice [ɔtɔmɔtœr] *adj.* self-propelling, motor-driven; **~eur** *s.m.* motor barge; **~rice** *s.f.* (rail.) diesel (coach).
auto-nome [ɔtɔnɔm] *adj.* autonomous, independent; self-governing; **~nomie** [ɔtɔnɔmi] *s.f.* **1.** autonomy, independence; self-government; **2.** (aeron., naut., etc.) cruising-range; **~plastie** [ɔtɔplasti] *s.f.* autoplasty; **~pompe** [ɔtɔpɔ̃p] *s.f.* fire-engine; **~portrait** [ɔtɔpɔrtrɛ] *s.m.* self-portrait.
autopropulsé, -e [ɔtɔprɔpylse] *adj.* self-propelling, self-steering.
autopropulsion [ɔtɔprɔpylsjɔ̃] *s.f.* self-propulsion, self-steering.
autopsie [ɔtɔpsi] *s.f.* autopsy; (lit. & fig.) post-mortem.
autopsier [ɔtɔpsje] *v.t.* to perform an autopsy or post-mortem on.
auto-punition [ɔtɔpynisjɔ̃] *s.f.* (psychol.) self-punishment; **~rail** [ɔtɔrɑj] *s.m.* railcar, diesel coach; **~réglage** [ɔtɔreglaʒ] *s.m.* self-regulating, self-governing, (actuation of machine); **~régulation** [ɔtɔregylɑsjɔ̃] *s.f.* self-regulation, self-governing (control).
autorisation [ɔtɔrizɑsjɔ̃] *s.f.* permission, consent, sanction, authorization; (written) authority.
autorisé, -e [ɔtɔrize] *adj.* **1.** authoritative, official; **2.** authorized, approved; **3.** permitted, accepted.
autoriser [ɔtɔrize] *v.t.* **1.** *~ qn. à faire qch.*, to authorize, to permit, to empower, to allow, s.o. to do sth.; **2.** *~ qch.*, to sanction, to permit, sth.; **3.** *s'~ de*, to use (sth., s.o.) as a pretext, as justification.

autoritaire [ɔtɔritɛr] *adj.* authoritarian, dictatorial; arbitrary, absolute; masterful, overbearing, imperious.
autoritarisme [ɔtɔritarism] *s.m.* authoritarianism.
autorité [ɔtɔrite] *s.f.* **1.** authority, legal power, sovereignty; *de sa propre ~*, on one's own initiative; *d'~*, arbitrarily; **2.** government, administration; *les ~s*, the authorities; **3.** authoritarian attitude, assurance; **4.** authority, influence.
autoroute [ɔtɔrut] *s.f.* motorway.
autorouti-er, -ère [ɔtɔrutje] *adj.* motorway.
auto-stop [ɔtɔstɔp] *s.m.* hitch-hiking; *faire de l'~*, to hitch-hike.
auto-stoppeu-r, -se [ɔtɔstɔpœr] *s.m.f.* hitch-hiker.
autosuggestion [ɔtɔsygʒɛstjɔ̃] *s.f.* auto-suggestion.
autour[1] [otur] *adv.* around, about; *~ de*, *prep. loc.*, round, around, about; *il a ~ de cinquante ans*, he is about fifty.
autour[2] [otur] *s.m.* (ornith.) goshawk.
autre [otr] *adj.* **1.** other, different, else; changed; *l'~ jour*, the other day; *un ~ jour*, another day, some other day; *~ chose*, something else, something different; *~ part*, elsewhere, somewhere else; *d'~ part*, moreover, besides; *quelqu'un d'~*, someone else; *personne d'~*, nobody else; *rien d'~*, nothing else; *c'est une ~ affaire*, that's something (quite) different; *c'est une ~ paire de manches*, that's a different kettle of fish; *c'est un ~ écrivain*, he is quite a different (and better) sort of author; *elle est tout ~*, she has changed, she is quite different; *c'est tout ~ chose*, that's quite another matter, that's something quite different; *ce n'est pas ~ chose que*, it is nothing but, it is nothing more nor less than; **2.** (emphasizing *pron.*) *nous ~s Français*, we French; *vous ~s hommes êtes seuls coupables*, it is you men who alone are to blame; **3.** another (of the same kind); *c'est un ~ Versailles*, it is another, a second, Versailles; *~ pron.* another person or thing; *d'un bout à l'~*, from one end to the other; *de temps à ~*, from time to time; *à d'~s!*, tell that to the marines!; *j'en ai vu d'~s*, I've seen worse, I'm not surprised; *tout ~*, anybody else; *l'un, l'~, les uns, les ~s*, one another, each other.
autrefois [otrəfwa] *adv.* formerly, in former times, of old; *d'~*, bygone.
autrement [otrəmɑ̃] *adv.* **1.** otherwise, in a different way, differently; *je n'ai pas pu faire ~ que d'y aller*, I couldn't do otherwise than go there; **2.** otherwise, or else; *faites attention, ~ vous tomberez*, take care, otherwise you will fall; **3.** a great deal more; *elle est ~ jolie que sa sœur*, she is a great deal prettier than her sister; *pas ~* not much, not very; *ce n'est pas ~ utile*, it's not very much use.
Autriche [otriʃ] *s.f.* (geog.) Austria.
autrichien, -ne [otriʃjɛ̃] *adj.*, *s.m.f.* Austrian.
autruche [otryʃ] *s.f.* **1.** ostrich; *avoir un estomac d'~*, to have a cast-iron digestion; (fig.) *pratiquer la politique de l'~*, to bury one's head in the sand; **2.** ostrich-skin (used for shoes, etc.).
autruchon [otryʃɔ̃] *s.m.* ostrich-chick.
autrui [otrɥi] *pron.* another, others, other people, one's neighbour(s); *agir pour le compte, au nom, d'~*, to act on behalf of s.o. else.
auvent [ovɑ̃] *s.m.* projecting roof (over door, etc.), shelter; carport.
Auvergne [ɔvɛrɲ] *s.f.* (geog.) Auvergne.
auvergnat, -e [ɔvɛrɲa] *adj.*, *s.m.f.* (native or inhabitant) of (the) Auvergne.
auxiliaire [ɔksiljɛr] *adj.* auxiliary, ancillary; *~ s.m.f.* assistant, deputy; auxiliary; **~ment**

[ɔksiljɛrmɑ̃] *adv.* as an auxiliary, an assistant, a deputy.

avachi, -e [avaʃi] *adj.* **1.** misshapen, baggy; **2.** (of person) dead-beat, flabby.

avachir [avaʃir] *v.t.* **1.** to make shapeless or flabby; **2.** (fig.) to drain of energy; **3. s'~** *v.refl.* to wear out, to become shapeless or flabby; (fam.) (of person) to get fat or flabby; (fig.) to let oneself go.

avachissement [avaʃismɑ̃] *s.m.* flabbiness, limpness; disintegration, collapse.

aval[1] (pl. **-als**) [aval] *s.m.* (comm.) guarantee, endorsement; (fig.) support.

aval[2] [aval] *s.m.* downstream, lower reaches (of river); *en ~ de*, downstream from.

avalanche [avalɑ̃ʃ] *s.f.* avalanche.

avaler [avale] *v.t.* **1.** to swallow, to drink up, to toss off, to gulp down; *il a avalé sa langue*, he kept silent; *~ sa salive*, to bite back one's words; *~ le morceau, la pilule*, to lump it, to take one's medicine; **2.** to hide, to conceal (feelings); to devour (book, etc.); (fig.) to eat alive; to endure; to believe, to swallow; (fam.) *j'ai cru qu'il allait m'~*, he looked as if he could kill me; *une histoire difficile à ~*, an incredible tale, a story which is hard to swallow; *vous avalez n'importe quoi!*, do you believe everything you're told?

avaleur [avalœr] *s.m.* **1.** (obs.) glutton; **2.** *~ de sabres*, sword-swallower.

avaliser [avalize] *v.t.* (comm.) to guarantee, to endorse; (fig.) to support.

avaliseur [avalizœr], **avaliste** [avalist] *s.m.* guarantor, backer.

à-valoir [avalwar] *s.m.* deposit, instalment, payment on account.

avaloir [avalwar], **-e** *s.m.f.* maw, gullet, trap, (of glutton).

avaloire [avalwar] *s.f.* breeching (of horse's harness).

avance [avɑ̃s] *s.f.* **1.** (obs.) projection; **2.** advance, progress; (fig.) *la belle ~!*, where does that get me?; **3.** advance (on s.o.), start, lead; *avoir une heure d'~*, to be an hour early; (techn.) *~ à l'allumage*, pre-ignition; *à l'~*, in advance, ahead of time; *deux heures à l'~*, two hours in advance; *d'~*, in advance; *payer, savoir, d'~*, to pay, to know, in advance; *en ~*, early; *arriver, partir, en ~*, to arrive, to leave, early; **4.** (fin.) advance, subsidy; **5.** (pl.) advances, overtures.

avancé, -e [avɑ̃se] *adj.* advanced, forward, early; precocious; developed; well advanced; (of meat) ripe, high, well-hung, gamey; *une heure~ e*, a late hour; (fig.) *vous voilà bien ~!*, a lot of good that's done you!; *je n'en suis pas plus ~*, that's got me nowhere, I'm no further forward.

avancée [avɑ̃se] *s.f.* **1.** (arch.) projection, overhang, salient; **2.** (mining) heading; **3.** (fishing) hook-end (of line).

avancement [avɑ̃smɑ̃] *s.m.* **1.** advance, forward movement; progress, improvement; **2.** advancement, promotion, preferment; **3.** (law) *~ d'hoirie*, advance on a legacy.

avancer [avɑ̃se] *v.t.* to advance, to bring, push, or put forward; to state, to affirm; to expedite; to advance, to pay (money) in advance; *~ v.i.* to advance, to move forwards, to proceed; to project, to overhang, to overlap; to make progress; to obtain promotion; to grow late; *la nuit avance*, it is getting late; *~ en âge*, to grow old; **s'~** *v.refl.* to advance, to move forward; (fig.) *s'~ trop*, to commit oneself too far.

avanie [avani] *s.f.* insult, humiliation.

avant[1] [avɑ̃] *s.m.* front, front part, prow, bow (of ship); (sport) forward; *à l'~*, in front; *aller de l'~*, (lit. & fig.) to go ahead; *~ adj.invar.* front; *roue, siège, ~*, front wheel, front seat.

avant[2] [avɑ̃] *prep.* **1.** (time) before; *~ peu*, shortly; *~ J.-C.*, B.C.; *~ de* + inf., *~ de partir*, before leaving; *~ que* + subj., *~ qu'il (n')ait fini*, before he has finished; **2.** (space & order) before, in front of; *~ tout*, before everything else, above all; *~ adv.* **1.** (time) before, previously; *la nuit d'~*, the night before; **2.** (space) in front, first; far, deep; *voyez ~*, see above; *bien ~ dans la nuit*, far into the night; *trop ~ dans la forêt*, too deep into the forest; *en ~*, forwards; *regarder en ~*, to look to the future; *mettre qch. en ~*, to put sth. forward; *mettre qn. en ~*, to use s.o. as a shield; *se mettre en ~*, to boast; *en ~ de*, in front of.

avantage [avɑ̃taʒ] *s.m.* advantage, benefit, superiority, privilege; advantage, upper hand; (tennis) (ad)vantage; interest, profit; *remporter un ~*, to get the upper hand, to win; *~ dedans, dehors*, vantage in, out; *~ détruit*, deuce; *avoir ~ à faire qch.*, to be well-advised, to do well, to do sth.

avantageu-x, -se [avɑ̃taʒø] *adj.* advantageous, profitable; (fig.) favourable, flattering; self--satisfied, conceited; *prix ~x*, good price, bargain price; *il a une idée assez ~se de lui-même*, he has a pretty good opinion of himself; **~sement** [avɑ̃taʒøzmɑ̃] *adv.* advantageously, with advantage.

avant-bassin [avɑ̃basɛ̃] *s.m.* outer harbour, outer dock; **~-bec** [avɑ̃bɛk] *s.m.* cutwater (of bridge-pier); **~bras** [avɑ̃bra] *s.m.* fore-arm; **~-centre** [avɑ̃sɑ̃tr] *s.m.* (sport) centre-forward; **~-corps** [avɑ̃kɔr] *s.m.* (arch.) projecting part of building; **~-cour** [avɑ̃kur] *s.f.* forecourt; **~-coureur** [avɑ̃kurœr] *s.m.* forerunner; *adj.m.* portending, foreshadowing.

avant-derni-er, -ère [avɑ̃dɛrnje] *adj.* penultimate, last but one.

avant-garde [avɑ̃gard] *s.f.* (mil.) vanguard, advance guard; (art, etc.) avant-garde; *d'~-garde*, ultra-modern; **~-guerre** [avɑ̃gɛr] *s.m.f.* pre-war period or years; *d'~-guerre*, pre--war; **~-hier** [avɑ̃tjɛr] *adv.* the day before yesterday; **~-main** [avɑ̃mɛ̃] *s.f.* forehand (of horse); **~-mont** [avɑ̃mɔ̃] *s.m.* foothills; **~-port** [avɑ̃pɔr] *s.m.* outer-harbour; **~-poste** [avɑ̃pɔst] *s.m.* (mil.) outpost, advanced post; **~-première** [avɑ̃prəmjɛr] *s.f.* **1.** private view, preview; **2.** review of private viewing; **~--projet** [avɑ̃prɔʒɛ] *s.m.* draft; sketch, plan, model; **~-propos** [avɑ̃prɔpo] *s.m.* foreword, introduction; **~-scène** [avɑ̃sɛn] *s.f.* **1.** (obs.) proscenium; **2.** stage-box; **~-toit** [avɑ̃twa] *s.m.* eaves, overhang; **~-train** [avɑ̃trɛ̃] *s.m.* fore-carriage (of vehicle); forequarters (of horse); **~-veille** [avɑ̃vɛj] *s.f.* the day but one before, two days before.

avare [avar] *s.m.f.* miser; *~ adj.* miserly, niggardly, avaricious, mean; (of soil) unfruitful, infertile; (of light) faint; *~ de*, grudging of, sparing with; **~ment** [avarmɑ̃] *adv.* avariciously, meanly, in a miserly or niggardly fashion.

avarice [avaris] *s.f.* avarice, greed, miserliness, covetousness; stinginess, meanness.

avaricieu-x, -se [avarisjø] *adj.* (obs.) mean, stingy, avaricious; **~x** *s.m.* (jest) Shylock, skinflint.

avarie [avari] *s.f.* damage (in transit by land, sea, air); deterioration.

avarié, -e [avarje] *adj.* (of ship, plane, etc.) damaged; (of goods) damaged, spoilt, rotten.

avarier [avarje] *v.t.* to damage, to spoil; **s'~** *v.refl.* to become damaged, to deteriorate.

avatar [avatar] *s.m.* (Hindu relig.) avatar.

à vau-l'eau [avolo] *adv.* (lit. & fig.) adrift; *s'en aller ~*, (fig.) to lose one's bearings.

Avé, Avé Maria [ave (marja)] *s.m.* Ave, Ave Maria.

avec [avɛk] *prep.* **1.** with, together with; (fam.) ~ *cela*, furthermore; *et* ~ *cela, Madame?*, anything else, Madam?; (pop.) ~ *cela que*, not to mention that; *d'*~, from; *séparer l'ivraie d'*~ *le bon grain*, to separate the wheat from the chaff; *il a divorcé d'*~ *elle*, he is divorced from her; **2.** towards; *se comporter mal* ~ *qn.*, to behave badly towards s.o.; **3.** against, with; *se battre* ~ *qn.*, to fight with or against s.o.; ~ *adv.* (fam.) *tu viens* ~*?*, are you coming with me, us?; *il a pris son parapluie* ~, he took his umbrella with him.
aveline [avlin] *s.f.* cob-nut.
avelinier [avlinje] *s.m.* cob-nut tree.
aven [avɛn] *s.m.* pot-hole.
avenant[1] [avnɑ̃] *s.m.* endorsement (to an insurance policy).
avenant[2], **-e** [avnɑ̃] *adj.* prepossessing, comely, attractive, pleasing; *à l'*~, conformably, suitably; *à l'*~ *de*, in keeping with.
avènement [avɛnmɑ̃] *s.m.* **1.** (eccles.) coming, birth, (of the Messiah); **2.** coming to the throne; **3.** (fig.) coming, establishing.
avenir[1] [avnir] *s.m.* future; prospects; futurity, future generations; *dans un proche* ~, in the near future; *à l'*~, in (the) future, henceforth, from now on; *jeune médecin d'*~, rising young doctor.
avenir[2] [avnir] *s.m.* (law) citation.
avent [avɑ̃] *s.m.* (eccles.) Advent (season).
aventure [avɑ̃tyr] *s.f.* **1.** (obs.) fortune, destiny; (mod.) *diseuse de bonne* ~, fortune-teller; **2.** adventure; love affair; **3.** venture, enterprise, exploit; **4.** chance; *à l'*~, at random, without plan; *par* ~, by chance.
aventuré, -e [avɑ̃tyre] *adj.* adventurous, risky.
aventurer [avɑ̃tyre] *v.t.* to venture, to risk, to hazard, to endanger; **s'**~ *v.refl.* to venture, to take a risk.
aventureu-x, -se [avɑ̃tyrø] *adj.* adventurous, daring; risky, chancy; ~**sement** [avɑ̃tyrøzmɑ̃] *adv.* adventurously, riskily.
aventuri-er, -ère [avɑ̃tyrje] *s.m.f.* **1.** adventurer, explorer; **2.** (pej.) adventurer, adventuress.
aventurine [avɑ̃tyrin] *s.f.* (min.) aventurine.
aventurisme [avɑ̃tyrism] *s.m.* (pol.) foolhardiness.
avenu, -e [avny] *adj.* used only in the phrase *nul(le) et non* ~*(e)*, null and void.
avenue [avny] *s.f.* avenue, drive; (fig.) avenue, gateway, means of access (*de*, to).
avéré, -e [avere] *adj.* authenticated, undeniable.
avérer [avere] *v.t.* (obs.) to aver; **s'**~ *v.refl.* to be confirmed; to turn out to be, to prove to be; *ce raisonnement s'est avéré juste*, this argument proved right.
avers [avɛr] *s.m.* obverse (of coin, etc.).
averse [avɛrs] *s.f.* sudden heavy shower, downpour; (fig.) flood (of tears, etc.).
aversion [avɛrsjɔ̃] *s.f.* aversion, repulsion, repugnance; *avoir de l'*~ *pour* or *contre qn.*, *avoir qn. en* ~, to detest s.o.
averti, -e [avɛrti] *adj.* informed, intelligent; ~ *de qch.*, aware of, informed about, sth.
avertir [avɛrtir] *v.t.* to inform; to warn (*de*, about).
avertissement [avɛrtismɑ̃] *s.m.* warning, advice, caution; (law) notification; admonition; ~ *au lecteur*, preface, foreword.
avertisseu-r, -se [avɛrtisœr] *adj.* warning; ~**r** *s.m.* **1.** (obs.) informer; **2.** alarm, warning-device; (car) horn; ~*r d'incendie*, fire-alarm.
aveu [avø] *s.m.* **1.** admission, avowal, confession; *faire l'*~ *de*, to admit, to confess; *de l'*~ *de*, according to; **2.** (obs.) consent; **3.** *homme sans* ~, vagrant, vagabond.
aveuglant, -e [avœglɑ̃] *adj.* blinding, dazzling; (fig.) obvious.
aveugle [avœgl] *adj., s.m.f.* blind (person); *à l'*~, *en* ~, blindly, thoughtlessly; ~**-né(e)** *adj., s.m.f.* (person) born blind, blind from birth.
aveuglement [avœgləmɑ̃] *s.m.* (obs.) going blind; (mod.) (fig.) blindness, heedlessness, illusion.
aveuglément [avœglemɑ̃] *adv.* (fig.) blindly.
aveugler [avœgle] *v.t.* **1.** to blind, to make blind, to dazzle; (fig.) to delude; **2.** to stop up (flow of water), to block up (window); (naut.) to caulk; **s'**~ *v.refl.* (fig.) to blind oneself, to shut one's eyes (*à*, to); to delude oneself.
aveuglette [avœglɛt] *à l'*~, *adv. loc.*, in the dark, blindly, rashly, at random.
aveulir [avølir] *v.t.* to exhaust, to prostrate, to sap or drain the life from.
aveulissement [avølisəmɑ̃] *s.m.* exhausting, weakening; prostration, lifelessness.
aviat-eur, -rice [avjatœr] *s.m.f.* airman, airwoman, aviator.
aviation [avjɑsjɔ̃] *s.f.* aviation, flying; (mil.) air force; *d'*~, air-, aero-; *ligne d'*~, airline.
avicole [avikɔl] *adj.* relating to aviculture.
avicult-eur, -rice [avikyltœr] *s.m.f.* bird-fancier; poultry farmer.
aviculture [avikyltyr] *s.f.* bird-fancying; poultry farming.
avide [avid] *adj.* greedy, gluttonous; (fig.) thirsting (for); avaricious; ~ *de*, greedy for; eager to; ~ *de sang*, bloodthirsty; ~**ment** [avidmɑ̃] *adv.* greedily, eagerly.
avidité [avidite] *s.f.* greed, covetousness, avidity; eagerness.
avilir [avilir] *v.t.* **1.** to debase, to degrade, to corrupt; to dishonour, to discredit, to disgrace; **2.** (fin.) to depreciate, to debase; **s'**~ *v.refl.* **1.** to become debased, degraded, corrupt; **2.** to lose its value, to be devalued.
avilissant, -e [avilisɑ̃] *adj.* degrading, debasing, humiliating; despicable.
avilissement [avilismɑ̃] *s.m.* **1.** debasement, degradation; **2.** (fin.) depreciation, devaluation.
aviné, -e [avine] *adj.* drunk; smelling of liquor.
aviner [avine] *v.t.* to soak or impregnate with wine.
avion [avjɔ̃] *s.m.* aeroplane, plane, aircraft; flying, aviation; *en* ~, (of travel) by air, in a plane; *par* ~, by air (mail).
aviron [avirɔ̃] *s.m.* oar, sweep, scull; rowing, sculling; *faire de l'*~, to row (as a sport), to be an oarsman.
avis [avi] *s.m.* **1.** opinion, way of thinking, judgement, point of view, impression; *être du même* ~ *que qn.*, to share someone's opinion; *changer d'*~, to change one's mind; *être d'*~ *de faire qch., qu'on fasse qch.*, to have a mind to do sth., to think that sth. should be done; *à mon* ~, in my opinion; *quel est votre* ~*?*, what is your opinion?; **2.** judgement, decision (of body of people); **3.** (obs.) counsel, advice; **4.** notice, warning, information, note, announcement, order, instruction; *jusqu'à nouvel* ~, *sauf* ~ *contraire*, until further notice.
avisé, -e [avize] *adj.* shrewd, wary, clear-sighted, well-advised.
aviser [avize] *v.t.* **1.** (obs.) to perceive, to espy, to notice; **2.** ~ *à*, to think about, to consider; *j'aviserai à ce que je dois faire*, I will consider what to do; **3.** (Lit., admin.) to inform, to advise (in writing), to apprise; **s'**~ *v.refl.* to realize, to discover (that); *s'*~ *de*, (i.) to realize, to discover, to become aware of (sth.); (ii.) to dare or to presume to (do sth.).
aviso [avizo] *s.m.* (nav.) dispatch-boat, corvette.
avitailler [avitɑje] *v.t.* (naut.) to victual, to supply with stores or fuel.
avivage [avivaʒ] *s.m.* (techn.) polishing.

avivement [avivmɑ̃] *s.m.* (med.) keeping a wound open.
aviver [avive] *v.t.* **1.** to revive, to rekindle; to enhance, to heighten (colours); **2.** (fig.) to excite, to irritate, to exacerbate, to rekindle (emotions), to stir up (trouble); **3.** (med.) to keep a wound open; **4.** (carp.) to sharpen the edge(s) of.
avocaillon [avɔkajɔ̃] *s.m.* (fam., pej.) pettifogging lawyer; briefless barrister.
avocasser [avɔkase] *v.i.* (pej.) to pettifog.
avocasserie [avɔkasri] *s.f.* (pej.) pettifogging, chicanery, pettiness.
avocassi-er, -ère [avɔkasje] *adj.* (fam., pej.) relating to lawyers; pettifogging.
avocat[1]**, -e** [avɔka] *s.m.f.* barrister, advocate, counsel; (fig.) champion, defender, advocate, intercessor; ~ *général*, solicitor-general.
avocat[2] [avɔka] *s.m.* (bot.) avocado (pear).
avocatier [avɔkatje] *s.m.* (bot.) avocado pear tree.
avocette [avɔsɛt] *s.f.* (ornith.) avocet.
avoine [avwan] *s.f.* oats; *d'*~, oaten; *farine d'*~, oatmeal; *gruau d'*~, groats; *folle* ~, wild oats.
avoir [avwar] *v.t.* **1.** to have, to possess, to own; to enjoy, to have at one's disposal; *un tiens vaut mieux que deux tu l'auras*, a bird in the hand is worth two in the bush; ~ *la parole*, to have the floor; ~ *tort*, to be wrong; ~ *raison*, to be right; *en* ~ *pour*, to have in return for (money, etc.); to need (time); *en* ~ *pour son argent*, to get one's money's worth; *j'en ai pour 5 minutes*, it will take me 5 minutes; **2.** to obtain, to procure, to get possession of; to buy, to get; to receive; to catch, to hit; to possess (esp. a woman); (fam.) ~ *qn.*, to deceive, to trick, s.o.; *on vous a eu*, you've been had; **3.** to wear, to carry; to contain, to comport; *cela n'a rien d'extraordinaire*, there's nothing unusual about that; **4.** to measure; to be; *ce mur a 2 mètres de haut*, this wall is 2 metres high; ~ *20 ans*, to be 20 (years old); **5.** to feel, to experience; ~ *mal à la tête*, to have a headache; ~ *faim, soif*, to be hungry, thirsty; ~ *besoin de, envie de*, to need, to want; (fam.) *en* ~ *à, contre, après, qn.*, to have it in for s.o.; **6.** to have something wrong; *qu'est-ce qu'il a?*, what's the matter with him?; *qu'est-ce qu'elle a, cette radio?*, what's wrong with this radio?; **7.** (auxiliary) ~ *à faire*, to have to do; *j'ai des lettres à écrire*, I have some letters to write; *j'ai à lui parler*, I want to speak to him; *vous n'avez qu'à tourner le bouton*, you have only to turn the knob; *vous n'aviez qu'à faire attention*, you should have paid attention; **8.** (with p.p. to form compound tenses) *j'ai, j'avais, j'eus, j'aurai, j'aurais, écrit*, I have, had, had, shall have, should have, written; **9.** *il y a*, there is, there are; since, ago; is wrong, is the matter; *il y a du brouillard*, it is foggy; *il y a 2 ans qu'il est parti*, it is 2 years since he left; *il est parti il y a 2 heures*, he left 2 hours ago; *il n'y a pas de quoi* (response to thanks), not at all; *qu'est-ce qu'il y a?*, what is wrong?, what is the matter?
avoir [avwar] *s.m.* **1.** assets, possessions; **2.** (of accounts) credit side; **3.** credit note.
avoisinant, -e [avwazinɑ̃] *adj.* neighbouring, adjoining, nearby.
avoisiner [avwazine] *v.t.* (lit. & fig.) to be near to, to border upon.
avortement [avɔrtmɑ̃] *s.m.* (lit. & fig.) abortion; failure.
avorter [avɔrte] *v.i.* to abort; (agric.) to fail; (techn.) to abort; *faire* ~, to cause (s.o.) to have an abortion, to procure an abortion; *se faire* ~, to have an abortion.
avorteu-r, -se [avɔrtœr] *s.m.f.* abortionist.
avorton [avɔrtɔ̃] *s.m.* abortion, monster, freak.
avouable [avwabl] *adj.* blameless, innocent.
avoué [avwe] *s.m.* attorney, solicitor.
avouer [avwe] *v.t.* **1.** to admit, to grant, to concede, to recognize; to confess (guilt); *il a avoué*, he has confessed; **s'**~ *v.refl.* to confess or admit oneself . . .; *s'*~ *vaincu*, to acknowledge, to concede, defeat; **2.** (obs. exc. Lit.) to acknowledge, to own; **3.** (obs. exc. Lit.) to approve.
avril [avril] *s.m.* April; *poisson d'*~, April fool; *en* ~ *ne te découvre pas d'un fil*, ne'er cast a clout till May is out.
avulsion [avylsjɔ̃] *s.f.* (dentistry) extraction.
avunculaire [avɔ̃kylɛr] *adj.* avuncular.
axe [aks] *s.m.* (lit. & fig.) axis, pivot; (mech.) axle, axle-tree; ~ *coudé*, crankshaft; ~ *moteur*, driving shaft.
axial, -e, (aux) [aksjal] *adj.* axial.
axile [aksil] *adj.* (bot.) axile, axial.
axillaire [aksil(l)ɛr] *adj.* axillary.
axiomatique [aksjɔmatik] *adj.* axiomatic.
axiomatiser [aksjɔmatize] *v.t.* to organize or arrange in symbolic form.
axiome [aksjom] *s.m.* axiom, truism.
axis [aksis] *s.m.* (anat.) axis.
axolotl [aksɔlɔtl] *s.m.* (zool.) axolotl.
axone [aksɔn] *s.m.* (anat.) axon.
axonge [aksɔ̃ʒ] *s.f.* rendered animal fat.
ayant cause [ɛjɑ̃koz] *s.m.* (law) assignee, legatee.
ayant droit [ɛjɑ̃drwa] *s.m.* (law) assignee, claimant.
aye-aye [ajaj] *s.m.* (zool.) aye-aye.
azalée [azale] *s.f.* (bot.) azalea.
azerole [azrɔl] *s.f.* (bot.) azarole, Neapolitan medlar.
azerolier [azrɔlje] *s.m.* azarole tree.
azimut [azimyt] *s.m.* (astron.) azimuth; (fam.) *dans tous les* ~*s*, in all directions.
azimutal, -e, (aux) [azimytal] *adj.* azimuthal.
azimuté, -e [azimyte] *adj.* (fam.) crazy.
azotate [azɔtat] *s.m.* (chem.) nitrate.
azote [azɔt] *s.m.* (chem.) nitrogen.
azoté, -e [azɔte] *adj.* (chem.) nitrogenous, nitrogenized.
azoteu-x, -se [azɔtø] *adj.* (chem.) nitrous.
azotique [azɔtik] *adj.* (chem.) nitric.
azotite [azɔtit] *s.m.* (chem.) nitrite.
azoture [azɔtyr] *s.m.* (chem.) nitride.
aztèque [aztɛk] *adj., s.m.f.* Aztec.
azur [azyr] *s.m.* azure; *pierre d'*~, lapis lazuli.
azuré, -e [azyre] *adj.* azure(-coloured).
azurer [azyre] *v.t.* **1.** to dye or stain azure-coloured; **2.** to whiten (linen with washing blue).
azygos [azigos] *adj., s.f.* (anat.) azygous; azygos (vein).
azyme [azim] *adj.* unleavened; ~ *s.m.* unleavened bread; *la fête des* ~*s*, the feast of the Passover.

B

B, b [be] *s.m.* the letter B, b.
baba [baba] *s.m.* sponge cake; ~ *au rhum*, rum baba; ~ *adj.invar.* (fam.) staggered; *il en est resté* ~, he was struck all of a heap.
Babel [babɛl] *s.f.* *tour de* ~, tower of Babel; (fig.) confusion, uproar, pandemonium.
babeurre [babœr] *s.m.* buttermilk.
babil [babi(l)] *s.m.* (obs.) babble, nonsense; (mod.) chatter, chirping, twittering; babbling (of spring, etc.).
babillage [babijaʒ] *s.m.* prattling, chattering, babbling, tittle-tattle.
babillard, -e [babijar] *adj.* prattling, chattering, garrulous, twittering; *oiseau* ~, sparrow; *s.m.f.* chatterbox; ~**e** *s.f.* (slang) letter.
babiller [babije] *v.i.* to prattle, to chatter, to babble; to chirp, to twitter.
babine [babin] *s.f.* chop (of animal); (fam.) chop, lip (of person); *s'essuyer, se lécher, les* ~*s*, to wipe, to lick, one's chops; *s'en lécher les* ~*s*, to lick one's chops (in anticipation).
babiole [babjɔl] *s.f.* knick-knack; (fig.) trifle.
babiroussa [babirusa] *s.m.* (zool.) babiroussa, Malaysian wild boar.
bâbord [babɔr] *s.m.* (naut.) port; *à* ~, to port; *par* ~, on the port side.
bâbordais [babɔrdɛ] *s.m.* (naut.) man of the port watch.
babouche [babuʃ] *s.f.* babouche, oriental slipper; mule.
babouin [babwɛ̃] *s.m.* baboon.
Babylone [babilɔn] *s.f.* (anc. geog.) Babylon.
babylonien, -ne [babilɔnjɛ̃] *adj.*, *s.m.f.* Babylonian.
bac[1] [bak] *s.m.* **1.** ferry-boat, ferry; **2.** tank, vat, large tub or bowl; ~ *à légumes*, vegetable container, crispator (in refrigerator).
bac[2] [bak] *s.m.* (fam.) abbrev. BACCALAURÉAT.
baccalauréat [bakalɔrea] *s.m.* **1.** examination taken at end of secondary school studies; **2.** school-leaving certificate.
baccara [bakara] *s.m.* baccarat.
bacchanale [bakanal] *s.f.* **1.** (pl.) Bacchanalia; **2.** picture representing Bacchanalia; **3.** (fig., obs.) orgy.
bacchante[1] [bakɑ̃t] *s.f.* **1.** Bacchante; **2.** (fig., obs.) debauched woman.
bacchante[2], **bacante** [bakɑ̃t] *s.f.* (pl.) (pop.) moustache.
baccifère [baksifɛr] *adj.* (bot.) bacciferous, bearing berries.
bacciforme [baksifɔrm] *adj.* bacciform, berry-shaped.
bâchage [bɑʃaʒ] *s.m.* covering with an awning; (hort.) covering with a frame.
bâche [bɑʃ] *s.f.* **1.** (techn.) tank, cistern; **2.** awning, tarpaulin (for cart or van); **3.** (hort.) garden-frame; **4.** (pop.) (bed-)sheet.
bacheli-er, -ère [baʃəlje] *s.m.f.* **1.** holder of *baccalauréat*; **2.** ~**er** *s.m.* (feud.) bachelor, novice at arms; ⚠ not 'bachelor' in sense 'unmarried man'.
bâcher [bɑʃe] *v.t.* to cover with an awning or tarpaulin; *un camion bâché*, a covered van.
bachique [baʃik] *adj.* Bacchic; *chanson* ~, drinking-song.
bachot[1] [baʃo] *s.m.* small ferry-boat, punt.
bachot[2] [baʃo] *s.m.* (fam.) *baccalauréat*; (fam., pej.) *boîte à* ~, crammer's, coaching establishment.
bachotage [baʃɔtaʒ] *s.m.* (fam.) cramming, swotting (for an exam).
bachoter [baʃɔte] *v.i.* (fam.) to cram, to swot (for an exam).
bacillaire [basi(l)lɛr] *adj.* bacillary; ~ *s.m.f.* infectious consumptive (person).
bacille [basil] *s.m.* bacillus.
bacilliforme [basi(l)lifɔrm] *adj.* bacilliform.
bacillose [basi(l)loz] *s.f.* bacillary infection; (med.) tuberculosis.
bâclage [bɑklaʒ] *s.m.* **1.** (obs.) barring (of door, etc.); **2.** scamping, botching, (of work).
bâcle [bɑkl] *s.f.* bar for door or window.
bâcler [bɑkle] *v.t.* **1.** (obs.) to bar (door, etc.); **2.** to scamp, to botch, (work).
bacon [bekɔn] *s.m.* smoked lean bacon; smoked lean pork fillet.
bactéricide [bakterisid] *adj.* bactericide, bactericidal.
bactérie [bakteri] *s.f.* bacterium.
bactérien, -ne [bakterjɛ̃] *adj.* bacterial.
bactério-logie [bakterjɔlɔʒi] *s.f.* bacteriology; ~**logique** [bakterjɔlɔʒik] *adj.* bacteriological; *guerre* ~*logique*, germ warfare; ~**logiste** [bakterjɔlɔʒist] *s.m.f.* bacteriologist; ~**phage** [bakterjɔfaʒ] *s.m.* bacteriophage; ~**statique** [bakterjɔstatik] *adj.* bacteriostatic.
bacul [baky] *s.m.* crupper.
badaud, -e [bado] *adj.* idling, loafing; *s.m.f.* idler, loafer, gaper; (fam.) rubber-neck.
badauderie [badodri] *s.f.* idling, aimless loafing, aimless curiosity.
Bade [bad] *s.f.* (geog.) Baden (former German province).
baderne [badɛrn] *s.f.* (fam.) (*vieille*) ~, old fogy, old fossil; old dug-out.
badiane [badjan] *s.f.* (bot.) star anise.
badigeon [badiʒɔ̃] *s.m.* **1.** distemper, colour-wash; **2.** (arch.) badigeon.
badigeonnage [badiʒɔnaʒ] *s.m.* **1.** distempering, colour-washing; **2.** (med.) painting (with iodine, etc.).
badigeonner [badiʒɔne] *v.t.* **1.** to distemper, to colour-wash; **2.** (med.) to paint (with iodine, etc.); **3.** (arch.) to apply badigeon.
badigeonneur [badiʒɔnœr] *s.m.* **1.** (house-) painter; **2.** (pej.) dauber, poor artist.
badigoinces [badigwɛ̃s] *s.f.pl.* (fam.) lips, chops; *se lécher les* ~, to lick one's chops.
badin, -e [badɛ̃] *adj.* playful, merry, light-hearted, teasing.
badinage [badinaʒ] *s.m.* playfulness, light-heartedness, badinage, banter, teasing.
badine [badin] *s.f.* cane, swagger-stick.
badiner [badine] *v.i.* to play, to jest, to banter, to be light-hearted; *je l'ai dit pour* ~, I said it in fun.
badinerie [badinri] *s.f.* banter, jest, piece of fun.
badminton [badmintɔn] *s.m.* (sport) badminton.
badois, -e [badwa] *adj.*, *s.m.f.* (native or inhabitant) of Baden.
baffe [baf] *s.f.* (pop.) slap, box on the ear.
bafouer [bafwe] *v.t.* to mock, to ridicule, to humiliate; to flout (conventions, etc.).
bafouillage [bafujaʒ] *s.m.* mumbling; (fig.) nonsense.

bafouille [bafuj] *s.f.* (slang) letter.
bafouiller [bafuje] *v.i.* **1.** (fam.) to mumble, to jabber; **2.** (car) to misfire.
bafouilleu-r, -se [bafujœr] *s.m.f.* mumbler.
bâfrer [bɑfre] *v.t.* (pop.) to guzzle, to eat greedily; ~ *v.i.* (pop.) to have a blow-out.
bâfreu-r, -se [bɑfrœr] *s.m.f.* (pop.) glutton, greedy-guts.
bagage [bagaʒ] *s.m.* **1.** luggage, baggage; (usu. pl.) luggage; *plier* ~, to pack up, to go away; ~*s à main*, hand luggage; **2.** (fig.) knowledge, (mental) equipment.
bagarre [bagar] *s.f.* brawl, tumult, squabble, scuffle, riot.
bagarrer [bagare] *v.i.* (pop.) to fight, to struggle; **se** ~ *v.refl.* (fam.) to squabble, to have a punch-up.
bagarreu-r, -se [bagarœr] *s.m.f.* (fam.) rowdy.
bagasse [bagas] *s.f.* bagasse, cane-trash.
bagatelle [bagatɛl] *s.f.* **1.** (obs.) trinket, knick-knack; **2.** (fig.) trifle, futility, frivolity; trifling sum (of money); **3.** love-making.
bagne [baɲ] *s.m.* convict prison; penal servitude; (fig.) hard labour; *quel ~!*, what a hell of a job!
bagnole [baɲɔl] *s.f.* (fam.) (*vieille*) ~, rattletrap, bus, crock; (pop.) car.
bagou(t) [bagu] *s.m.* (fam.) gift of the gab, glibness.
baguage [bagaʒ] *s.m.* (forestry, ornith.) ringing.
bague [bag] *s.f.* (jewellery, ornith.) ring; (techn.) ring, sleeve, collar; band (of cigar, etc.); (arch.) fillet.
baguenaude [bagnod] *s.f.* **1.** (bot.) bladder-nut; **2.** (pop.) ramble, stroll.
baguenauder [bagnode] *v.i.* **1.** (obs.) to fritter away one's time; **2.** (also *se* ~) to ramble, to stroll aimlessly.
baguenaudier [bagnodje] *s.m.* (bot.) bladder-nut tree.
baguer [bage] *v.t.* **1.** to ring (trees, birds); to put rings on (hands); to put a band round (cigar, etc.); **2.** (dressm.) to tack.
baguette [bagɛt] *s.f.* **1.** stick, cane; *mener qn. à la* ~, to rule s.o. with a rod of iron; ~ *magique, des fées*, magic, fairy, wand; (fig.) *d'un coup de* ~, by waving a magic wand; ~ *des sourciers*, dowsing-twig; ~ (*de chef d'orchestre*), (conductor's) baton; ~*s de tambour*, drumsticks; **2.** clock (on sock, stocking); **3.** long stick of bread, French stick.
baguier [bagje] *s.m.* jewel-case; ring-stand.
bah [bɑ] *interj.* expressing lack of interest.
bahut [bay] *s.m.* **1.** chest, trunk; **2.** (Breton) dresser; **3.** (school slang) school.
bai, -e [bɛ] *adj.* (of horse) bay.
baie[1] [bɛ] *s.f.* **1.** (geog.) bay; **2.** (arch.) bay (of window, etc.).
baie[2] [bɛ] *s.f.* (bot.) berry.
baignade [bɛɲad] *s.f.* bathing, bath, bathe; bathing-place.
baigner [beɲe] *v.t.* to bathe, to wash; ~ *v.i.* to be immersed, to soak, to steep; **se** ~ *v.refl.* to bath, to take a bath; to bathe, to go bathing.
baigneu-r, -se [bɛɲœr] *s.m.f.* **1.** (obs.) public bath attendant; **2.** bather; summer visitor; **3.** celluloid baby-doll.
baignoire [bɛɲwar] *s.f.* **1.** bath; **2.** (theatr.) ground-floor box; **3.** (naut.) cockpit (of yacht, of submarine).
bail [baj] (pl. **baux**) *s.m.* (law) lease; (fig., fam.) *c'est un* ~, it's taking ages; *cela fait un* ~ *que je ne vous ai vu*, it's been ages since I saw you; ⚠ not (law) 'bail'.
baille [bɑj] *s.f.* (naut.) tub, bucket; (slang) (i.) water; (ii.) nickname of Naval College.
bâillement [bɑjmɑ̃] *s.m.* yawning, yawn; gap.
bailler [baje] *v.t.* (obs.) to give; (mod. only in phrase) *vous me la baillez bonne* or *belle*, you're having me on.
bâiller [bɑje] *v.i.* to yawn; to gape, to be ajar.
baill-eur, -eresse [bajœr] *s.m.f.* lessor; ~*eur de fonds*, financial backer.
bailli [baji] *s.m.* bailiff.
bâillon [bɑjɔ̃] *s.m.* gag; *mettre un* ~ *à qn.*, to gag s.o., to secure someone's silence.
bâillonner [bɑjɔne] *v.t.* to gag; (fig.) to silence.
bain [bɛ̃] *s.m.* bath; (dyer's) vat; bathing; (public) baths, bathing-place, spa; *salle de* ~(*s*), bathroom; ~*s* (*de mer*), seaside, seaside resort; ~ *de siège*, hip-bath; ~ *turc*, Turkish bath; *maillot de* ~, bathing-costume; (fig.) *envoyer qn. au* ~, to send s.o. packing; (fig.) *être dans le* ~, to be involved (in sth.), to be fully in the know, to be compromised.
bain-marie [bɛ̃mari] *s.m.* (cook.) bain-marie.
baïonnette [bajɔnɛt] *s.f.* bayonet; (electr.) *douille à* ~, bayonet-socket.
baïram [bairam], **beïram** [beiram] *s.m.* Bairam (Islamic festival).
baisemain [bɛzmɛ̃] *s.m.* kissing of hands, homage; *faire le* ~, to kiss (lady's) hand.
baisement [bɛzmɑ̃] *s.m.* (eccles.) kissing of sacred objects.
baiser [beze] *v.t.* to kiss (usu. in phrases e.g. ~ *qn. au front*, ~ *la main de qn.*); ~ *une femme*, (vulg.) to possess a woman; ~ *qch.*, (school, slang) to understand, to get, sth.; *on n'y baise rien*, we don't get it.
baiser (beze] *s.m.* kiss.
baisoter [bɛzɔte] *v.t.* (obs., fam.) to peck, to give repeated little kisses.
baisse [bɛs] *s.f.* fall, decline, reduction, drop; (fin., comm.) *en* ~, falling; *spéculations à la* ~, bear speculations; (fig., fam.) *ses actions sont en* ~, his stock is low.
baisser (bese] *v.t.* to lower, to let down; to bow, to incline, to cast down; to reduce; (naut.) ~ *pavillon*, to strike one's flag; (fig.) ~ *pavillon devant qn.*, to admit defeat; ~ *v.i.* to decline, to go down, to fall, to ebb, to drop; to become weaker; to fall in value, to go down in price; (mus.) to drop in pitch; **se** ~ *v.refl.* to bend down, to stoop.
baissier [besje] *s.m.* (stock exchange) bear.
baissière [bɛsjɛr] *s.f.* depression (in field) where rain-water collects.
bajoue [baʒu] *s.f.* (of animal) chop, chap, cheek; (of person) jowl.
bajoyer [baʒwaje] *s.m.* retaining wall (of river or canal lock).
bakchich [bakʃiʃ] *s.m.* baksheesh.
bakélite [bakelit] *s.f.* bakelite.
bal [bal] *s.m.* ball, dance; dance-hall.
balade [balad] *s.f.* (fam.) stroll, ramble.
balader [balade] *v.t.* (fam.) to drag (s.o.) along; to carry (sth.) around; **se** ~ *v.refl.* to stroll, to ramble aimlessly; to go on a trip.
baladeu-r, -se [baladœr] *adj.* *avoir l'humeur* ~*se*, to like to be on the move, to have itchy feet; (car) *train* ~*r*, gear-change mechanism; ~**se** *s.f.* trailer, hand-barrow; inspection-lamp.
baladin, -e [baladɛ̃] *s.m.f.* (obs.) **1.** strolling player, mummer; **2.** ballet-dancer, ballerina.
balafon [balafɔ̃] *s.m.* balaphon (African mus. instrument).
balafre [balafr] *s.m.* gash, scar (esp. on face).
balafrer [balafre] *v.t.* to gash, to scar (on the face).
balai [balɛ] *s.m.* **1.** broom, sweeping-brush; (aeron.) joystick, control-column; (fig.) *coup de* ~, clean sweep; *manche à* ~, broomstick; (fig.) skeleton; ~ *mécanique*, carpet-sweeper; **2.** train (of hawk); brush (of fox); **3.** (electr.) brush.
balai-brosse [balɛbrɔs] *s.m.* long-handled scrubbing-brush.

balais [balɛ] *adj.m.* balas; *rubis* ~, balas-ruby.
balalaïka [balalaika] *s.f.* balalaika.
balance [balɑ̃s] *s.f.* **1.** balance, scales, weighing--machine; *faire pencher la* ~, to turn the scale; (astron.) Libra, the scales; **2.** balance, equilibrium; *tenir la* ~ *égale entre deux personnes*, to see fair play between two people; *faire pencher la* ~ *d'un côté*, to tip the balance in favour of s.o.
balancé, -e [balɑ̃se] *adj.* (fam.) (of person) well--built.
balancelle [balɑ̃sɛl] *s.f.* (naut.) balancelle.
balancement [balɑ̃smɑ̃] *s.m.* **1.** balancing, oscillation, swaying, swinging to and fro; **2.** (fig.) balance, equilibrium; (art) symmetry.
balancer [balɑ̃se] *v.t.* **1.** to sway, to swing, to rock; **2.** (fam.) to throw (sth.) out or away; to sack (s.o.); **3.** to balance, to poise; (naut.) to trim; (comm., fin.) to balance; **4.** (fig.) to consider, to weigh up; **5.** (fig., obs.) to counterbalance, to compensate; ~ *v.i.* (fig., Lit.) to hesitate; **se** ~ *v.refl.* to sway, to swing, to oscillate; (comm., fin.) to balance; (pop.) *s'en* ~, not to care about, not to give a damn for (sth.).
balancier [balɑ̃sje] *s.m.* **1.** pendulum (of clock); balance wheel (of watch); **2.** (minting) stamping-machine; **3.** (tight-rope walker's) staff; **4.** (zool.) poiser.
balancine [balɑ̃sin] *s.f.* (naut.) garnet (of sail); (aeron.) wing-wheels.
balançoire [balɑ̃swar] *s.f.* swing, see-saw; (fig., obs.) humbug, nonsense.
balane [balan] *s.m.* (conch.) Balanus, acorn--shell, sea-acorn.
balanite [balanit] *s.f.* (med.) balanitis.
balata [balata] *s.m.* balata.
balayage [balɛjaʒ] *s.m.* sweeping; sweep (of beam of light).
balayer [baleje] *v.t.* to sweep, to sweep up or out, to clear away, to clean up; (fig.) to sweep away, to expel; (T.V.) to scan.
balayeu-r, -se [balɛjœr] *s.m.f.* street-sweeper; ~**se** *s.f.* street-sweeping machine.
balayures [balejyr] *s.f.pl.* sweepings.
balbutiant, -e [balbysjɑ̃] *adj.* stammering.
balbutiement [balbysimɑ̃] *s.m.* stammering, stuttering; (fig.) (usu. pl.) teething troubles, early efforts.
balbutier [balbysje] *v.t.i.* to stammer, to stutter.
balbuzard [balbyzar] *s.m.* (ornith.) bald buzzard, sea-eagle.
balcon [balkɔ̃] *s.m.* balcony; (theatr.) dress--circle.
baldaquin [baldakɛ̃] *s.m.* canopy, tester, baldaquin.
bale see BALLE[3].
Bâle [bɑl] *s.f.* (geog.) Basle.
baleine [balɛn] *s.f.* **1.** whale; (fam.) *rire comme une* ~, to laugh like a drain; **2.** whalebone (for corset); rib (of umbrella).
baleiné, -e [balene] *adj.* boned, stiffened (with whalebone).
baleineau (pl. **-x**) [balɛno] *s.m.* whale-calf.
baleini-er, -ère [balenje, balɛnjɛr] *adj.* whaling, whale-; ~**er** *s.m.* (naut.) whaling-ship; whaler; ~**ère** *s.f.* (naut.) whale-boat, whaler.
baleinoptère [balɛnɔptɛr] *s.m.* (zool.) Balaenoptera, rorqual.
balès [balɛs], **balèze** [balɛz] *adj.* (pop.) huge; ~ *s.m.* great hulking brute (of a man).
balèvre [balɛvr] *s.f.* (arch.) lip (of one stone over another).
balisage [balizaʒ] *s.m.* (naut., aeron.) marking with buoys or beacons; signalling, signal--system; course marked with buoys, runway marked with beacons.
balise[1] [baliz] *s.f.* (naut., aeron.) buoy, beacon; radio-beacon.
balise[2] [baliz] *s.f.* (bot.) canna-seed.
baliser [balize] *v.t.* (naut., aeron.) to mark with buoys or beacons; to buoy.
baliseur [balizœr] *s.m.* (naut.) buoy-laying ship.
balisier [balizje] *s.m.* (bot.) canna.
baliste [balist] *s.f.* (ant.) ballista; ~ *s.m.* trigger-fish.
balistique [balistik] *adj.* ballistic; ~ *s.f.* ballistics.
balivage [balivaʒ] *s.m.* (forestry) choosing and marking of staddles.
baliveau [balivo] *s.m.* (forestry) staddle.
baliverne [balivɛrn] *s.f.* (usu. pl.) nonsense, silly remarks.
ballade [balad] *s.f.* ballad; (mus.) ballade.
ballant, -e [balɑ̃] *adj.* swinging, loose, sagging, dangling; ~ *s.m.* sway, rocking motion, instability; (naut.) slack, bight, (of cable).
ballast [balast] *s.m.* (naut., rail.) ballast.
ballastage [balastaʒ] *s.m.* (rail.) ballasting.
ballastière [balastjɛr] *s.f.* quarry (for ballast), ballast-pit, borrow-pit.
balle[1] [bal] *s.f.* **1.** ball; (tennis) *faire des, quelques,* ~*s*, to knock up, to have a knock-up; ~ *de set, de match,* set point, match point; (fig.) *prendre, saisir, la* ~ *au bond,* to seize the opportunity; *renvoyer la* ~, to keep the ball rolling; to give as good as one gets; to pass the buck; **2.** bullet, ball, shot; *tirer à* ~*s*, to fire live ammunition.
balle[2] [bal] *s.f.* **1.** bale, pack; **2.** (fam.) face; **3.** (fam.) franc.
balle[3], **bale** [bal] *s.f.* (agric.) chaff, glume.
baller [bale] *v.i.* **1.** (obs.) to dance; **2.** to hang loose, to swing, to dangle.
ballerine [balrin] *s.f.* ballet-dancer, ballerina; ballerina-shoe.
ballet [balɛ] *s.m.* ballet.
ballon[1] [balɔ̃] *s.m.* **1.** (inflated) ball, football; **2.** balloon; ~ *d'essai*, (fig.) feeler, dummy-run; **3.** (chem.) balloon; brandy-glass.
ballon[2] [balɔ̃] *s.m.* (geog.) name given to peaks in Vosges mountains.
ballonné, -e [balɔne] *adj.* balloon-shaped; (med.) distended; ~ *s.m.* dance step.
ballonnement [balɔnmɑ̃] *s.m.* (med.) distension of the abdomen, tympanites; (of cattle) heaves, hoove.
ballonner [balɔne] *v.t.* to distend, to swell, to blow up.
ballonnet [balɔnɛ] *s.m.* ballonet, small balloon.
ballon-sonde [balɔ̃sɔ̃d] *s.m.* (meteor.) sounding--balloon, sonde-balloon.
ballot [balo] *s.m.* bale, pack, bundle; ~ *adj.* (fam.) stupid, idiotic; ~ *s.m.* idiot.
ballote [balɔt] *s.f.* (bot.) horehound, hoarhound.
ballottage [balɔtaʒ] *s.m.* indecisive result of poll (where a certain majority is required); *scrutin de* ~, second ballot.
ballottement [balɔtmɑ̃] *s.m.* tossing, shaking, swaying, swinging to and fro.
ballotter [balɔte] *v.t.* to toss, to shake, to shake up, to sway; (fig.) *être ballotté entre,* to be torn between; ~ *v.i.* to shake, to be shaken up, to be tossed, to swing to and fro.
balluchon, baluchon [balyʃɔ̃] *s.m.* bundle (esp. in knotted cloth, etc.).
balnéaire [balneɛr] *adj.* bathing; *station* ~, watering-place, seaside resort.
bâlois, -e [bɑlwa] *adj., s.m.f.* (native or inhabitant) of Basle.
balourd, -e [balur] *adj.* dull, heavy, thick--headed, dim-witted, coarse, rough; *s.m.f.* dullard, dim-wit; ~ *s.m.* (mech.) lack of balance, disequilibrium.
balourdise [balurdiz] *s.f.* stupid blunder, idiotic mistake; stupidity, dullness.

Baloutchistan [balutʃistɑ̃] *s.m.* (geog.) Baluchistan.
balsa [balza] *s.m.* balsa (wood).
balsamier [balzamje] *s.m.* = BAUMIER.
balsamine [balzamin] *s.f.* (bot.) balsam.
balsamique [balsamik] *adj.* balsamic, soothing; ~ *s.m.* (pharm.) balsamic.
Baltique [baltik] *s.f.* (geog.) Baltic (sea).
balustrade [balystrad] *s.f.* balustrade.
balustre [balystr] *s.m.* baluster.
balzan [balzɑ̃] *adj.m.* (of horse) with white spots on feet.
balzane [balzan] *s.f.* white spot on foot of horse.
bambin, -e [bɑ̃bɛ̃] *s.m.f.* (fam.) tiny tot, child.
bamboche [bɑ̃bɔʃ] *s.f.* **1.** (obs.) large puppet; **2.** (fam.) spree, binge.
bambocher [bɑ̃bɔʃe] *v.i.* to go on the spree, on the binge, to live it up.
bambocheu-r, -se [bɑ̃bɔʃœr] *s.m.f.* reveller, carouser.
bambou [bɑ̃bu] *s.m.* bamboo; (fam.) *attraper un coup de* ~, to get a touch of the sun, to get sunstroke; (pop.) *avoir le coup de* ~, to go mad; to be worn out.
bamboula [bɑ̃bula] *s.m.* (obs.) tom-tom; ~ *s.f.* African dance; (pop.) *faire la* ~, to go on the binge.
ban[1] [bɑ̃] *s.m.* **1.** (obs.) proclamation; (mod.) banns (of marriage); **2.** drum-beat; clapping, ovation; **3.** (hist.) banishment, exile; *être en rupture de* ~, to be in breach of a restriction order; (fig.) to flout convention; *mettre qn. au* ~ *de la société*, to send s.o. to Coventry; to ostracize s.o. publicly; *le* ~ *et l'arrière-*~, all and sundry.
ban[2] [bɑ̃] *s.m.* (hist.) ban (governor of Croatian province).
banal, -e [banal] *adj.* **1.** (pl. *-aux*) (feud.) banal, communal; **2.** (pl. *-als*) banal, commonplace, trite, petty; ~**ement** [banalmɑ̃] *adv.* in a banal manner, tritely.
banaliser [banalize] *v.t.* to make ordinary, to vulgarize, to cheapen; **se** ~ *v.refl.* to become hackneyed.
banalité [banalite] *s.f.* **1.** (feud.) compulsory use of mill, well, etc.; **2.** banality, commonplace, triviality.
banane [banan] *s.f.* **1.** banana; **2.** (fam.) medal; over-rider (on car-bumper); large helicopter (with two rotors).
bananeraie [bananrɛ] *s.f.* banana-plantation.
bananier [bananjɛ] *s.m.* **1.** banana-tree; **2.** banana boat.
banc [bɑ̃] *s.m.* **1.** bench, form, seat; (techn.) stand, bed; (in parliament) *le* ~ *des ministres*, the front bench; (law) ~ *des accusés*, dock; (eccles.) ~ *d'œuvre*, churchwardens' pew; (techn.) ~ *d'essai*, test-bench; **2.** (sand-, mud-, etc.) bank; reef; (geol.) stratum, layer, bed; shoal (of fish).
bancable, banquable [bɑ̃kabl] *adj.* (fin.) bankable, negotiable.
bancaire [bɑ̃kɛr] *adj.* concerning banking, banking-, bank-.
bancal, -e, (**als**) [bɑ̃kal] *adj.* **1.** (of person) bandy, bandy-legged; **2.** (of furniture, etc.) rickety, wobbly.
banche [bɑ̃ʃ] *s.f.* (build.) form, shutter, (for moulding concrete).
bancher [bɑ̃ʃe] *v.t.* (build.) to mould concrete in forms or shutters.
banco [bɑ̃ko] *adj.* (fin.) banco, bank value; ~ *s.m.* (at baccarat) banco; *faire le* ~, to go banco.
bancroche [bɑ̃krɔʃ] *adj.* (fam., obs.) bandy (-legged).
bandage [bɑ̃daʒ] *s.m.* **1.** (obs.) bandaging; **2.** bandage, dressing; (techn.) steel or rubber tyre (usu. solid); ~ *herniaire*, truss; ~ *plein*, solid tyre; ~ *à talons*, flanged or beaded tyre; **3.** stretching or bending (of bow, etc.); tightening or winding(-up) (of spring, etc.).
bandagiste [bɑ̃daʒist] *s.m.f.* maker of or dealer in bandages, trusses, surgical appliances.
bande[1] [bɑ̃d] *s.f.* band, strap, strip; stripe, border, edging; (radio) (wave-)band; tape (for tape-recorder); (herald.) bend; (billiards) cushion; ~ *de journal*, newspaper-wrapper; (mil.) ~ *molletière*, puttee; *prendre qn., faire qch., par la* ~, to approach s.o., sth., warily.
bande[2] [bɑ̃d] *s.f.* band, gang, set; flight, flock, herd, etc.; *faire* ~ *à part*, to detach themselves, to keep themselves aloof or apart.
bande[3] [bɑ̃d] *s.f.* (naut.) list; *donner de la* ~, to (have a) list.
bandeau [bɑ̃do] *s.m.* **1.** headband; **2.** bandage (over the eyes); **3.** (arch.) platband.
bandelette [bɑ̃dlɛt] *s.f.* narrow band; (archaeol.) fillet; (arch.) bandlet.
bander [bɑ̃de] *v.t.* **1.** to bandage, to bind up, to dress (wound); ~ *les yeux à qn.*, to blindfold s.o.; **2.** to bend, to stretch, (bow, etc.); to tighten, to draw taut, to tense, to wind up.
banderille [bɑ̃drij] *s.f.* banderilla.
banderole [bɑ̃drɔl] *s.f.* pennant, streamer, banderole.
bandit [bɑ̃di] *s.m.* **1.** (obs.) outlaw; **2.** bandit, ruffian, criminal; **3.** (fig., comm.) shark, profiteer.
banditisme [bɑ̃ditism] *s.m.* banditry.
bandoulière [bɑ̃duljɛr] *s.f.* bandoleer, bandolier, shoulder belt; *porter qch. en* ~, to carry sth. slung across the shoulder.
banian [banjɑ̃] *s.m.* **1.** banian; **2.** (bot.) banyan-tree.
banjo [bɑ̃(d)ʒo] *s.m.* banjo.
banlieue [bɑ̃ljø] *s.f.* suburb(s), outskirts of town.
banlieusard, -e [bɑ̃ljøzar] *s.m.f.* (fam.) person living in the suburbs, commuter, suburbanite.
banneret [banrɛ] *s.m.* (feud.) banneret.
banneton [bantɔ̃] *s.m.* wicker basket, creel.
bannette [banɛt] *s.f.* small wicker basket.
banni, -e [bani] *adj.* banished; *s.m.f.* exile.
bannière [banjɛr] *s.f.* banner, flag; *se ranger sous la* ~ *de qn.*, (fig.) to join someone's party, someone's cause; (fig., fam.) *c'est la croix et la* ~ *pour faire qch.*, it's no end of trouble doing sth.; (pop.) *être en* ~, to be in one's shirt-tails, to have one's shirt hanging out.
bannir [banir] *v.t.* to banish, to exile, to expel (from country); to refuse entry (to house); (fig.) to remove; to proscribe, to abolish, to suppress; to refrain from; to abstain from.
bannissement [banismɑ̃] *s.m.* banishment, exile.
banquable see BANCABLE.
banque [bɑ̃k] *s.f.* banking; bank, banking-house; *compte en* ~, bank account; ~ *d'émission*, issuing bank; *billet de* ~, bank-note; ~ *de sang, des yeux, etc.*, blood-bank, eye-bank, etc.; (gambling) *tenir la* ~, to be banker; *faire sauter la* ~, to break the bank.
banquer [bɑ̃ke] *v.i.* (pop.) to pay, to stump up.
banqueroute [bɑ̃krut] *s.f.* (fraudulent) bankruptcy; (fig.) bankruptcy, ruin.
banquerouti-er, -ère [bɑ̃krutje] *s.m.f.* bankrupt.
banquet [bɑ̃kɛ] *s.m.* banquet.
banqueter [bɑ̃kte] *v.i.* **1.** to attend a banquet; **2.** to feast.
banqueteur [bɑ̃ktœr] *s.m.* diner at a banquet.
banquette [bɑ̃kɛt] *s.f.* **1.** (upholstered or cane) seat or stool; seat (in car, train, etc.); (arch.) stone window-seat, coping-stone of retaining wall; (mil.) banquette, fire-step; **2.** footpath, towpath; verge, hard shoulder (of road).
banquier [bɑ̃kje] *s.m.* banker.

banquise [bɑ̃kiz] *s.f.* ice-field, ice-pack, ice-barrier.
bantou, -e [bɑ̃tu] *adj., s.m.f.* Bantu.
baobab [baɔbab] *s.m.* (bot.) baobab (tree).
baptême [batɛm] *s.m.* baptism, christening; naming; *nom de ~*, baptismal or Christian name, first name; *~ de la ligne, du tropique*, crossing the line ceremony.
baptiser [batize] *v.t.* **1.** to christen, to baptize; (fig.) to name, to nickname; **2.** (fam.) to add water to (wine, etc.).
baptismal, -e, (aux) [batismal] *adj.* baptismal; *fonts baptismaux*, font.
baptistaire [batistɛr] *adj.* of baptism; *régistre ~*, register of baptisms.
baptiste [batist] *adj., s.m.* (eccles.) Baptist.
baptistère [batistɛr] *s.m.* baptist(e)ry.
baquet [bakɛ] *s.m.* wooden tub or bucket.
baquetures [baktyr] *s.f.pl.* drippings (of wine from barrel).
bar[1] [bar] *s.m.* (ichth.) bass.
bar[2] [bar] *s.m.* bar, public-house; bar-counter.
bar[3] [bar] *s.m.* (meteor.) bar.
baragouin [baragwɛ̃] *s.m.* gibberish, jabber; double Dutch, jargon, lingo; **~age** [baragwinaʒ] *s.m.* jabbering, gabbling; **~er** [baragwine] *v.t.* to jabber, to gabble; *v.i.* to jabber, to talk double Dutch.
baraque [barak] *s.f.* hut, cabin; booth, stall (at fair, market); hovel, shanty; (pej.) hole; ⚠ not 'barracks'.
baraquement [barakmɑ̃] *s.m.* hutment, shanty-town.
baraquer[1] [barake] *v.t.* (obs.) to lodge in huts.
baraquer[2] [barake] *v.i.* (of camels) to kneel.
baraterie [baratri] *s.f.* (maritime law) barratry.
baratin [baratɛ̃] *s.m.* (pop.) (plausible) story; *faire du ~ à qn.*, to chat s.o. up, to talk s.o. round.
baratiner [baratine] *v.i.* to tell a plausible story; *~ v.t.* to chat up, to talk round.
barattage [barataʒ] *s.m.* churning.
baratte [barat] *s.f.* churn.
baratter [barate] *v.t.* to churn.
barbacane [barbakan] *s.f.* (fort.) barbican, loop-hole; (build.) weep-hole.
Barbade [barbad] *s.f.* (geog.) Barbados.
barbant, -e [barbɑ̃] *adj.* (fam.) boring, deadly dull.
barbare [barbar] *adj.* barbarian; barbarous, uncivilized, barbaric; uncultured, ignorant, uncouth, coarse; inhuman, cruel; *~ s.m.* barbarian.
barbaresque [barbarɛsk] *adj.* Barbaresque, Barbary.
barbarie [barbari] *s.f.* barbarousness, primitiveness, uncivilized state; rudeness, coarseness, roughness; cruelty, barbarity, inhumanity.
barbe[1] [barb] *s.f.* beard; fin (of flat fish); (pl.) rough edges of pages; *faire qch. à la ~ de qn.*, to do sth. to someone's face, under someone's very eyes; (fig., pop.) *la ~!*, that's enough!, shut up!; *quelle ~!*, what a bore!, what a nuisance!
barbe[2] [barb] *s.m.* barb, barbary horse.
barbeau[1] [barbo] *s.m.* (ichth.) barbel; (pop.) ponce.
barbeau[2] [barbo] *s.m.* (bot.) cornflower.
barbecue [barbəkju] *s.m.* barbecue.
barbelé, -e [barbəle] *adj.* barbed, spiked; *fil de fer ~*, barbed wire; **~s** *s.m.pl.* (mil.) barbed wire.
barber [barbe] *v.t.* (pop.) to bore, to be a pain in the neck; **se ~** *v.refl.* to be bored.
barbet [barbɛ] *s.m.* barbet (dog).
barbette [barbɛt] *s.f.* (nun's) wimple; (mil., nav.) barbette; *batterie à ~*, cannon firing over the parapet, from the upper deck.
barbiche [barbiʃ] *s.f.* goatee (beard).
barbier [barbje] *s.m.* (hist.) barber (who shaved).
barbifier [barbifje] *v.t.* (fam.) **1.** to shave; **2.** to bore.
barbille [barbij] *s.f.* rough edge, burr (on coin).
barbillon [barbijɔ̃] *s.m.* **1.** (ichth.) young barbel; **2.** barbule; barbel (of fish); **3.** (vet.) barbles.
barbiturique [barbityrik] *adj., s.m.* (chem.) barbiturate.
barbon [barbɔ̃] *s.m.* (obs.) fogy, greybeard.
barbotage [barbɔtaʒ] *s.m.* **1.** paddling, dabbling; **2.** (chem., techn.) bubbling of gas through liquid.
barboter [barbɔte] *v.i.* **1.** to dabble, to paddle, to splash; **2.** (chem.) (of gas) to bubble (through liquid); *~ v.t.* (pop.) to steal.
barboteu-r, -se [barbɔtœr] *s.m.f.* wader, paddler, dabbler; **~r** *s.m.* (chem.) apparatus for passing gas through liquid; (techn.) tray for washing mineral ores; **~se** *s.f.* (child's) rompers.
barbotière [barbɔtjɛr] *s.f.* duck-pond.
barbotin [barbɔtɛ̃] *s.m.* (naut.) cable-wheel; (mech.) sprocket-wheel.
barbotine [barbɔtin] *s.f.* (pottery) barbotine.
barbouillage [barbujaʒ] *s.m.* daubing, smudging, blurring; smear, smudge; daub; scribble.
barbouiller [barbuje] *v.t.* **1.** to smear, to smudge, to blur; to daub; to scribble on, to cover with scribbling; **2.** to upset (stomach, digestion); *avoir l'estomac* or *le cœur barbouillé*, to have an upset stomach, to feel sick.
barbouilleu-r, -se [barbujœr] *s.m.f.* dauber; scribbler.
barbouze [barbuz] *s.f.* **1.** (pop.) beard; **2.** secret agent, member of secret police.
barbu, -e [barby] *adj.* bearded; *~ s.m.* bearded man.
barbue [barby] *s.f.* (ichth.) brill.
barbule [barbyl] *s.f.* (ornith.) barbule.
barcarolle [barkarɔl] *s.f.* (mus.) barcarol(l)e.
barcasse [barkas] *s.f.* (naut.) lighter, tender.
Barcelone [barsəlɔn] *s.f.* (geog.) Barcelona.
bard [bar] *s.m.* tray, board (with handles for transporting materials, etc.).
barda [barda] *s.m.* (mil., slang) kit, gear.
bardane [bardan] *s.f.* (bot.) burdock.
barde[1] [bard] *s.m.* bard.
barde[2] [bard] *s.f.* **1.** (armour) bard; **2.** (cook.) larding.
barde[3] [bard] *s.f.* *à toute ~*, (fam.) hell for leather.
bardeau[1] (pl. **-x**) [bardo] *s.m.* (build.) shingle.
bardeau[2] (pl. **-x**) [bardo] *s.m.* = BARDOT.
barder [barde] *v.t.* **1.** (armour) to bard; **2.** (cook.) to lard; *~ v.i. impers.* (pop.) to warm up, to take an ugly turn; *ça va ~*, there's trouble brewing.
bardot [bardo] *s.m.* (zool.) hinny.
barême [barɛm] *s.m.* ready-reckoner.
barge [barʒ] *s.f.* **1.** barge; **2.** (ornith.) godwit.
barguigner [bargiɲe] *v.i.* (obs.) to hesitate, to waver, to shilly-shally.
baril [bari(l)] *s.m.* cask, keg, firkin, barrel.
barillet [barijɛ, barilɛ] *s.m.* **1.** small cask, pin; **2.** cylindrical magazine (of revolver); barrel (of clock, watch, etc.); cylinder (of lock).
bariolage [barjɔlaʒ] *s.m.* mixing colours; medley, motley; variegation.
bariolé, -e [barjɔle] *adj.* multi-coloured, variegated.
barioler [barjɔle] *v.t.* to daub with a mixture of colours, to variegate.
bariolure [barjɔlyr] *s.f.* patchwork effect, medley of colours.
barlong, -ue [barlɔ̃] *adj.* (arch.) oblong.

barlotière [barlɔtjɛr] *s.f.* cross-bar (of window--frame).
barmaid [barmɛd] *s.f.* barmaid.
barman [barman] *s.m.* (pl. *~men*, *~mans*) barman.
barnabite [barnabit] *s.m.* Barnabite.
barnache see BERNACHE.
baro-graphe [barɔgraf] *s.m.* (aeron.) barograph, altimeter; **~mètre** [barɔmɛtr] *s.m.* barometer, glass; **~métrique** [barɔmetrik] *adj.* barometric.
baron[1], **-ne** [barɔ̃] *s.m.f.* baron, baroness; ~ *s.m.* (slang) protector, accomplice.
baron[2] [barɔ̃] *s.m.* (cook.) ~ *de bœuf*, baron of beef, ~ *d'agneau*, saddle of lamb.
baronnage [barɔnaʒ] *s.m.* baronage.
baronnet [barɔnɛ] *s.m.* baronet.
baronnie [barɔni] *s.f.* barony.
baroque [barɔk] *adj.*, *s.m.* queer-looking, irregularly-shaped, fantastic; (arch., art, Lit.) baroque.
baroscope [barɔskɔp] *s.m.* baroscope.
baroud [barud] *s.m.* (mil. slang) fighting.
baroudeur [barudœr] *s.m.* (mil. slang) one who likes fighting.
barouf [baruf], **baroufle** [barufl] *s.m.* (pop.) noise, din.
barque [bark] *s.f.* small boat (for rowing, sailing, fishing, etc.); (fig.) *mener la* ~, to be in charge; *bien mener sa* ~, to manage one's affairs well.
barquette [barkɛt] *s.f.* (cook.) pastry-boat.
barrage [baraʒ] *s.m.* blocking, barricading; barrier, barricade; dam, weir.
barre [bar] *s.f.* **1.** bar, rod, rail; (gymn.) ~ *fixe*, horizontal bar; (car) ~ *d'accouplement*, track-rod, tie-rod; *argent en* ~, bar silver; (fig.) *c'est de l'or en* ~, it's as safe as the Bank; (fig.) *un coup de* ~, a shattering blow; *c'est le coup de* ~, it is terribly dear; **2.** (naut.) helm, tiller; *être à la* ~, to be at the helm; (fig.) (also *prendre* or *tenir la* ~) to be in charge; *donner un coup de* ~, to put the helm over, to change course; **3.** bar, barrier, obstacle, (harbour- or river-)bar; bore, tidal wave; surf; ~ *d'appui*, hand-rail, guard-rail; **4.** (pl.) (of horse) bars; **5.** (in writing) line, dash, stroke, cross-stroke; (mus.) bar(-line); (herald.) bar; (fig.) band, stripe, streak; ~ *de soustraction*, minus-sign; **6.** (law) bar (of lawcourt); **7.** *jeu de ~s*, (game) prisoners' base; (fig.) *avoir ~s* or *une ~ sur qn.*, to have the advantage over s.o.
barré, -e [bare] *adj.* **1.** barred, blocked; **2.** struck out; (of cheque) crossed.
barreau (pl. **-x**) [baro] *s.m.* **1.** bar, rod, (of window, prison, cage, chair); rung (of ladder); **2.** (law) bar; *être reçu, admis, se faire inscrire, au* ~, to be called to the bar.
barrement [barmɑ̃] *s.m.* crossing (of cheque).
barrer [bare] *v.t.* **1.** to bar, to block, to obstruct; (fig.) ~ *qn.*, to thwart s.o., to block someone's progress; **2.** (naut.) to steer, to cox; **3.** to cross (a 't', a cheque); to cross out, to strike out; **4.** to make stripes on; **se** ~ *v.refl.* (pop.) to make off.
barrette[1] [barɛt] *s.f.* biretta.
barrette[2] [barɛt] *s.f.* **1.** (jewelled) brooch or bar; medal bar; (electr.) connecting-piece, bus-bar; **2.** hair-slide, hair-grip.
barreu-r, -se [barœr, barœr] *s.m.f.* steersman, cox(-swain); *un quatre sans ~r*, a coxless four.
barricade [barikad] *s.f.* barricade, road-block, barrier; *les ~s*, (fig.) civil war, revolution; *être de l'autre côté de la* ~, to be in the opposite camp.
barricader [barikade] *v.t.* to block (a street) with barricades; to close securely; **se** ~ *v.refl.* to shut oneself up.
barrière [barjɛr] *s.f.* town-gate; gate; barrier.
barrique [barik] *s.f.* hogshead, cask.
barrir [barir] *v.i.* (of elephants) to trumpet.
barrit [bari], **barrissement** [barismɑ̃] *s.m.* trumpeting (of elephants).
barrot [baro] *s.m.* (naut.) cross-beam.
bartavelle [bartavɛl] *s.f.* rock partridge.
baryte [barit] *s.f.* (chem.) baryta, barium oxide.
barytine [baritin] *s.f.* (chem.) barytes, barium sulphate.
baryton [baritɔ̃] *adj.*, *s.m.* baritone.
baryum [barjɔm] *s.m.* (chem.) barium.
bas, -se [bɑ] *adj.* low, lower; lowered; (fig.) humble, mean, vile, abject, base; *être ~ sur pattes*, to have short legs; *soleil* ~, sun low on the horizon; *coup* ~, blow below the belt; *marée ~se*, low tide; *les Pays-Bas*, the Netherlands, (hist.) the Low Countries; *s'en aller l'oreille ~se*, to go away with one's tail between one's legs; *faire main ~se sur qch.*, to steal, to filch, sth.; *avoir la vue ~se*, (lit. & fig.) to be short-sighted; *à voix ~se*, in an undertone; *à ~ prix*, cheaply; *au ~ mot*, to say the least; *de ~se origine, naissance*, low-born, of humble birth; *la Chambre ~se*, the lower House (in parliament).
bas [bɑ] *adv.* low; (fig., fam.) *mettre qn. plus ~ que la terre*, to treat s.o. like dirt; *être* ~, to be very ill, to be in very low spirits; *mettre ~ les armes*, to lay down one's arms; (fig.) to surrender; *mettre* ~, (of animals) to give birth (to), to lamb, etc.; *parler* ~, to lower one's voice; *à ~!*, down with!; *en* ~, below, down below, downstairs.
bas[1] [bɑ] *s.m.* bottom, lower part; (print.) ~ *de casse*, lower case; *au ~ de*, at the bottom of; *les hauts et les* ~, ups and downs.
bas[2] [bɑ] *s.m.* stocking; ~ *de laine*, (fig.) nest--egg; ~ *bleu*, bluestocking.
basalte [bazalt] *s.m.* (geol.) basalt.
basaltique [bazaltik] *adj.* basaltic.
basane [bazan] *s.f.* basan (roughly tanned sheepskin).
basané, -e [bazane] *adj.* tanned, sunburnt.
basaner [bazane] *v.t.* to tan.
bas-côté [bɑkote] *s.m.* **1.** aisle (of church); **2.** path or track (at side of railway or road).
basculant, -e [baskylɑ̃] *adj.* rocking, tilting, tipping; *pont* ~, draw-bridge; (*camion à*) *benne ~e*, tipper(-lorry).
bascule [baskyl] *s.f.* **1.** see-saw, bascule; sway; *cheval à* ~, rocking-horse; *fauteuil à* ~, rocking--chair; *levier à* ~, trip-lever; **2.** weighing machine, scales, (lit. & fig.) balance.
basculer [baskyle] *v.t.i.* to swing, to rock, to see-saw; to sway; to topple (over).
basculeur [baskylœr] *s.m.* (techn.) tip (for tipping wagons); (electr.) trip (switch); (car) dip-switch.
base [bɑz] *s.f.* base, foundation, bottom; (mil., etc.) base; (fig.) basis, fundamental principle; *être à la ~ de qch.*, to be at the bottom of sth.; *salaire de* ~, basic pay.
baselle [bazɛl] *s.f.* (bot.) basella, Malabar nightshade.
baser [bɑze] *v.t.* to base, to ground, to found; *cette prétention n'est basée sur rien*, this claim is without foundation; (mil.) *être basé*, to be based; **se** ~ (*sur*) *v.refl.* to be based on; to take as one's basis, one's grounds.
bas-fond [bɑfɔ̃] *s.m.* **1.** (naut.) shallow; **2.** fen, hollow; **3.** (fig.) (pl.) dregs (of society).
basicité [bɑzisite] *s.f.* (chem.) basicity.
basilaire [bazilɛr] *adj.* (anat.) basilar.
basilic [bazilik] *s.m.* **1.** (bot.) basil; **2.** (myth., zool.) basilisk; (fig., obs.) *regarder qn. avec des yeux de* ~, to look daggers at s.o.
basilical, -e, (aux) [bazilikal] *adj.* (arch.) basilical.
basilique [bazilik] *s.f.* basilica; ~ *adj.* (anat.) (*veine*) ~, basilic vein.

basin [bazɛ̃] *s.m.* (text.) dimity.
basique [bɑsik] *adj.* (chem., min.) basic.
bas-jointé, -e [bɑʒwɛ̃te] *adj.* (of horse) short in the pastern.
basket-ball [baskɛtbol] *s.m.* (usu. abbrev. *basket*) basket-ball.
basketteu-r, -se [baskɛtœr] *s.m.f.* basket-ball player.
basoche [bazoʃ] *s.f.* **1.** (hist.) basoche (body of clerks attached to courts of justice); **2.** legal fraternity.
basque[1] [bask] *adj., s.m.f.* Basque; ~ *s.m.* Basque (language); *tambour de* ~, tambourin(e).
basque[2] [bask] *s.f.* skirt, tail (of clothing); *être toujours pendu aux ~s de qn.*, to be tied to someone's apron-strings.
bas-relief [bɑrəljɛf] *s.m.* (art) bas-relief.
basse[1] [bɑs] *s.f.* (mus.) bass, bass part; bass singer; bass string; ~ *contre*, basso-profundo.
basse[2] [bɑs] *s.f.* (sunken) reef.
basse-cour [bɑskur] *s.f.* farm-yard, poultry-yard; **~-fosse** [bɑsfos] *s.f.* (obs.) deep dungeon, oubliette; *cul-de-~-fosse*, deepest dungeon.
bassement [bɑsmɑ̃] *adv.* basely, meanly, sordidly, vulgarly.
bassesse [bɑsɛs] *s.f.* lowness, baseness, meanness; mean or base act; servility, grovelling.
basset [bɑsɛ] *s.m.* **1.** basset-hound; **2.** (mus.) *cor de* ~, basset-horn.
bassin [bɑsɛ̃] *s.m.* **1.** basin, bowl, tub; bedpan; **2.** pool, pond; **3.** port, pool (e.g. of London); dock; **4.** (river) basin; (geol.) basin; (coal-, etc.) field; **5.** (anat.) pelvis.
bassinant, -e [basinɑ̃] *adj.* (pop.) deadly dull.
bassine [basin] *s.f.* large pan; preserving-pan.
bassiner [basine] *v.t.* **1.** to bathe; **2.** (hort.) to spray; **3.** to air (a bed); **4.** (pop.) to bore, to pester.
bassinet [basinɛ] *s.m.* **1.** pan (of flint-lock); **2.** (armour) basinet; **3.** (renal) pelvis; **4.** (obs.) collection or offertory plate; (fig., fam.) *cracher dans le* ~, to contribute reluctantly; **5.** (bot.) buttercup.
bassinoire [basinwar] *s.f.* **1.** warming-pan; **2.** (pop.) bore, boring person.
bassiste [bɑsist] *s.m.f.* abbrev. CONTRE-BASSISTE.
basson [bɑsɔ̃] *s.m.* bassoon; bassoon-player.
baste[1] [bast] *interj.* bah!, nonsense!
baste[2] [bast] *s.m.* **1.** (cards) basto; **2.** pannier (for pack animal).
bastide [bastid] *s.f.* **1.** (obs.) walled town; **2.** small country house (in Provence).
bastille [bastij] *s.f.* fortress, prison; *la Bastille*, the Bastille.
basting, bastaing [bastɛ̃] *s.m.* (carp.) deal plank.
bastingage [bastɛ̃gaʒ] *s.m.* (naut.) **1.** bulwark; **2.** rails.
bastion [bastjɔ̃] *s.m.* (fort.) bastion; (fig.) bastion, bulwark, stronghold.
bastonnade [bastɔnad] *s.f.* birching, flogging, thrashing; bastinade, bastinado.
bastringue [bastrɛ̃g] *s.f.* **1.** (fam.) low-class hop (dance); **2.** (fam.) tin-pan alley band; (pop.) rumpus, shindy; **3.** (pop.) thing(s), gear, business.
bas-ventre [bɑvɑ̃tr] *s.m.* lower abdomen.
bat see BATTE.
bât [bɑ] *s.m.* pack-saddle; (fig.) *c'est là que le ~ blesse*, that's where the shoe pinches; that's the chink in his armour.
bataclan [bataklɑ̃] *s.m.* (fam.) belongings, kit, gear, paraphernalia; (*et*) *tout le* ~, the whole business, the lot, and all the rest.
bataille [batɑj] *s.f.* battle, fight, engagement; *champ de* ~, battlefield; *cheval de* ~, charger; (fig.) hobby-horse; *plan de* ~, plan of campaign.
batailler [batɑje] *v.i.* to fight, to struggle.
batailleu-r, -se [batɑjœr] *adj.* pugnacious, quarrelsome, argumentative, aggressive, bellicose; *s.m.f.* fighter, aggressive person, controversialist.
bataillon [batajɔ̃] *s.m.* **1.** (mil.) battalion; *chef de* ~, major; **2.** troop, gang, regiment, host, horde.
bâtard, -e [bɑtar] *adj.* **1.** bastard, illegitimate; mongrel; **2.** degenerate, hybrid, inferior; *écriture ~e*, slanting round hand; *s.m.f.* bastard, illegitimate child; mongrel.
batardeau [bɑtardo] *s.m.* embankment, dam.
bâtardise [bɑtardiz] *s.f.* bastardy.
batavique [batavik] *adj.* (phys.) *larmes ~s*, (Prince) Rupert's drops.
batayole [batajɔl] *s.f.* (naut.) stanchion.
bâté see BÂTER.
bateau (pl. **-x**) [bato] *s.m.* boat, ship; any boat-shaped object; *~-citerne*, tanker; (dressm.) *encolure* ~, boat-neck; (fig., fam.) *monter un ~ à qn.*, to play a trick on s.o.; to pull someone's leg.
batelage [batlaʒ] *s.m.* **1.** boatman's dues or wages; **2.** conveyance by boat, lighterage.
bateler [batle] *v.i.* to juggle.
batelet [batlɛ] *s.m.* small boat.
bateleu-r, -se [batlœr] *s.m.f.* (obs.) juggler, conjurer, acrobat.
bateli-er, -ère [batəlje] *s.m.f.* boatman, boatwoman; ferryman.
batellerie [batɛlri] *s.f.* inland water transport; river boats.
bâter [bɑte] *v.t.* to put pack-saddle on; (fig.) *un âne bâté*, a complete ass, an utter fool.
bat-flanc [baflɑ̃] *s.m.invar.* partition in stable or dormitory.
bath [bat] *adj.invar.* (pop.) decent, helpful; super.
bathy-métrie [batimetri] *s.f.* bathymetry; **~scaphe** [batiskaf] *s.m.* bathyscaphe; **~sphère** [batisfɛr] *s.f.* bathysphere.
bâti, -e [bɑti] *adj.* **1.** (of site) built on, built-up; **2.** (of person) built; *un homme bien* ~, a well-built man.
bâti [bɑti] *s.m.* **1.** frame, framework, support; **2.** (sewing) basting.
batifolage [batifɔlaʒ] *s.m.* (fam.) frolic, romp, antics, larking about.
batifoler [batifɔle] *v.i.* (fam.) to frolic, to romp, to lark about.
bâtiment [bɑtimɑ̃] *s.m.* **1.** building trade; construction, building; **2.** (naut.) ship.
bâtir [bɑtir] *v.t.* **1.** to build, to construct, to erect, to raise; **2.** (sewing) to baste.
bâtisse [bɑtis] *s.f.* **1.** shell of building; **2.** large (and usu. ugly) building.
bâtisseu-r, -se [bɑtisœr] *s.m.f.* builder, constructor, developer; (fig., pej.) concocter, dreamer.
batiste [batist] *s.f.* (text.) batiste, cambric.
bâton [bɑtɔ̃] *s.m.* stick, staff, cane, rod, baton, wand; rail (of chair); vertical stroke (in writing); ~ *de vieillesse*, (fig.) prop of old age; ~ *de rouge à lèvres*, lipstick; (fig.) *mettre des ~s dans les roues*, to put a spoke in the wheel; (fig.) *à ~s rompus*, desultorily, in a disconnected fashion; (fig.) *tour de* ~, (illicit) perk, rake-off.
bâtonnat [bɑtɔna] *s.m.* (law) presidency of the bar.
bâtonner [bɑtɔne] *v.t.* to beat with a stick.
bâtonnet [bɑtɔnɛ] *s.m.* small stick, thin rod; rod-bacterium; rod-like cell; rod (of retina).
bâtonnier [bɑtɔnje] *s.m.* (law) president of the bar; leader of the circuit.
batracien [batrasjɛ̃] *s.m.* (zool.) batrachian; (pl.) Batrachia.
battage [bataʒ] *s.m.* beating (of cloth, gold, etc.); (agric.) threshing; (fig., fam.) boosting, vulgar publicity.

battant, -e [batɑ̃] *adj.* beating; (of rain) driving; *porte ~e*, self-closing door; (fig.) *le cœur ~*, tremulously, with one's heart in one's mouth; *tambour ~*, with drums beating; (fig.) smartly, quickly; *tout ~ neuf*, brand-new.

battant [batɑ̃] *s.m.* **1.** clapper (of bell); **2.** door (of double door); leaf, flap, (of table, counter); **3.** (comm.) reserve, margin; **4.** fly (of flag), pennon.

batte, bat [bat] *s.f.* beater; beating (of gold); (sport) bat, mallet.

battée [bate] *s.f.* door lining, jamb lining.

battellement [batɛlmɑ̃] *s.m.* (arch.) eaves.

battement [batmɑ̃] *s.m.* **1.** beating, banging, throbbing, pulsing, flapping, fluttering; beat; blow; (radio) interference; (dancing, fenc.) battement; **2.** interval of time (before next event); *il y a un ~ de vingt minutes*, there are twenty minutes to go (before the departure of the train, etc.); **3.** jamb (of door); catch (to secure shutter).

batterie [batri] *s.f.* **1.** (obs.) fight, exchange of blows; **2.** (artillery, electr.) battery; (fig.) *dresser ses ~s*, to get ready for action; **3.** collection, set, (pop.) set of medals; *~ de cuisine*, set of kitchen utensils; **4.** (mus.) percussion (section of orchestra); arpeggiated; drumming, strumming.

batteur [batœr] *s.m.* **1.** (person) beater, thresher; (fig.) *~ de pavé*, idler, loafer, tramp; **2.** (mus.) percussion-player; **3.** (cook.) beater.

batteuse [batøz] *s.f.* (agric.) threshing--machine; *moissonneuse-~-lieuse*, combine--harvester.

battitures [batityr] *s.f.pl.* scales, dross (from anvil).

battoir [batwar] *s.m.* beater (esp. for laundry); (fig., fam.) big, beefy hand.

battre [batr] *v.t.* **1.** to beat, to strike, to batter, to hammer, to beat up; to beat or knock against, to thrash, to flog; to mark (time, etc.); to mint or coin (money); to churn (butter); to shuffle (cards); (cook.) to whisk, to whip; to fly (flag); *~ comme plâtre*, to beat black and blue; (fig.) *~ un homme à terre*, to hit a man when he is down; (fig.) *~ le fer quand il est chaud*, to strike while the iron is hot; *~ le briquet*, to strike a light; *~ le tambour*, to beat the drum, (fig.) to make a song and dance, a noise, (about sth.); *~ la mesure*, to beat time; *~ les secondes*, to mark the seconds; *~ la retraite*, to beat the retreat (on drums); *~ les buissons*, to beat the bushes (to put up game); *~ la campagne*, to scour the countryside; (fig.) to wander around; *~ le pavé*, to roam the streets; *les vagues battaient les falaises*, the waves beat against the cliffs; *l'ivrogne battait les murs*, the drunken man was bumping against the walls; (mil.) *~ les positions ennemies*, to batter, to bombard, the enemy positions; *~ en brêche*, to batter a breach in, to breach; (fig.) to demolish; **2.** to beat, to defeat, to overcome, to vanquish; *~ v.i.* to beat, to flap, to rattle, to bang; *~ en retraite*, to beat a retreat, to withdraw; *~ des mains*, to clap; *~ des ailes*, to beat or to flap wings; **se** *~ v.refl.* to fight, to struggle.

battu, -e [baty] *adj.* beaten, whipped, thrashed; vanquished, overcome; *avoir les yeux ~s*, to have shadows under the eyes; (fig.) *suivre les chemins ~s*, to keep to well-worn paths.

battue [baty] *s.f.* (shooting) drive, battue, beat.

bau [bo] *s.m.* (naut.) beam.

baudet [bode] *s.m.* **1.** donkey; **2.** sawing-horse, sawyer's trestle.

baudrier [bodrije] *s.m.* baldric(k); shoulder--sash.

baudroie [bodrwa] *s.f.* (ichth.) angler.

baudruche [bodryʃ] *s.f.* gold-beater's skin; (fig.) *c'est une ~*, he is all façade.

bauge [boʒ] *s.f.* **1.** lair (of wild boar); **2.** pigsty; filthy place; **3.** (build.) pisé.

baume [bom] *s.m.* (bot.) balsam, balm.

baumé [bome] *s.m.* (Baumé's) araeometer.

bauquière [bokjɛr] *s.f.* (naut.) clamp.

bauxite [boksit] *s.f.* bauxite.

bavard, -e [bavar] *adj.* talkative, loquacious; (of style) verbose; *s.m.f.* chatterbox, gossip.

bavardage [bavardaʒ] *s.m.* chattering, gossiping; idle talk; verbosity.

bavarder [bavarde] *v.i.* to chatter, to gossip.

bavarois, -e [bavarwa] *adj., s.m.f.* Bavarian.

bavaroise [bavarwaz] *s.f.* (cook.) bavarois.

bave [bav] *s.f.* dribble; slime (left by snail or slug); (fig.) slur, smear.

baver [bave] *v.i.* to dribble, to slobber, to drivel; (of ink, paint, etc.) to run; (fig., pop.) *~ de*, to be wild with (admiration, surprise, etc.); *il en bave*, his eyes are popping out of his head; (fig., pop.) *en ~*, to pay for it; (Lit.) *~ sur*, to smear, to cast aspersions on.

bavette [bavɛt] *s.f.* **1.** child's bib; bib (of apron); **2.** (cook.) lower part of sirloin; **3.** (pop.) *tailler une ~*, to have a little chat.

baveu-x, -se [bavø] *adj.* dribbling, slobbering; (of omelette) runny; (of print) smudged.

Bavière [bavjɛr] *s.f.* (geog.) Bavaria.

bavocher [bavɔʃe] *v.i.* (print.) to blur, to smear.

bavochure [bavɔʃyr] *s.f.* (print.) blur, smear.

bavoir [bavwar] *s.m.* baby's bib.

bavolet [bavɔlɛ] *s.m.* countrywoman's bonnet.

bavure [bavyr] *s.f.* (techn.) burr; (print.) blur; (fig., pop.) *sans ~*, without a hitch, perfectly, faultlessly.

bayadère [bajadɛr] *s.f.* **1.** bayadère; **2.** *tissu ~*, cloth with multi-coloured stripes.

bayart [bajar] *s.m.* = BARD.

bayer [baje] *v.i.* *~ aux corneilles*, to moon, to gaze at nothing.

bazar [bazar] *s.m.* **1.** bazaar; **2.** general store; *de ~*, cheapjack; **3.** messy, untidy house; untidy mess; (pop.) *tout son ~*, all one's stuff.

bazarder [bazarde] *v.t.* (fam.) to flog, to get rid of.

bazooka [bazuka] *s.m.* (mil.) bazooka.

B.C.G. [beseʒe] abbrev. *vaccin Bilié de Calmette et Guérin*, B.C.G. (vaccine).

béant, -e [beɑ̃] *adj.* wide open, open-mouthed; gaping; (of abyss) yawning.

béarnais, -e [bearnɛ] *adj., s.m.f.* (native or inhabitant) of Béarn; *~e s.f.* (cook.) Béarnaise sauce.

béat, -e [bea] *adj.* **1.** blessed, blissful, saintly; **2.** smug, sanctimonious; **~ement** [beatmɑ̃] *adv.* blissfully; smugly, sanctimoniously.

béatification [beatifikɑsjɔ̃] *s.f.* beatification.

béatifier [beatifje] *v.t.* to beatify.

béatifique [beatifik] *adj.* beatific.

béatitude [beatityd] *s.f.* **1.** (eccles.) beatitude, blessedness; **2.** bliss, ecstasy.

beau [bo], **bel** [bɛl] (m. sing. before word beginning with vowel or h-mute), **belle** [bɛl] (f. sing.), (m. pl. **beaux**) *adj.* beautiful, handsome, fair, pretty, superb, splendid, charming; fine, good, admirable, noble; excellent of its kind; big, important, considerable; serious, bad, nasty; *avoir un ~ jeu*, (cards) to have a good hand; *un ~ coup*, (tennis, etc.) a good stroke; (fig.) *l'échapper belle*, to have a close shave; *c'est trop ~ pour être vrai*, it's too good to be true; *ce serait trop ~*, it would be wonderful; *tout nouveau, tout ~*, new brooms sweep clean; (weather) *il fait ~*, it is fine; (fig.) *un ~ jour*, one fine day, one of these days; (sport) *~ joueur*, good sportsman, good loser; *~ parleur*, affected speaker, one who has the gift of the gab; *une belle somme*, a fair amount, a pretty penny; *il y a ~ temps de cela*, that's a long time ago; *une belle* *bronchite*, a nasty attack of bronchitis; *c'est du ~ travail*, now you've made a mess of it; *être dans de ~x draps*, to be in a mess; *en faire, en dire, de belles*, to do or say stupid things; *j'en apprends de belles sur votre compte*, I've heard some nasty things about you; *au ~ milieu*, right in the middle, in the very middle; *avoir ~* (+inf.), to do sth. in vain; *il a ~ parler*, it's no use his talking; (Lit.) *il ferait ~ voir qu'il l'achève*, it would be a miracle if he finished it; *il ferait ~ voir qu'ils agissent sans notre permission*, they had better not act without our permission; *bel et bien*, really and truly; *recommencer de plus belle*, to begin again worse than ever.

beau (pl. **-x**) [bo], **belle** [bɛl] *s.* ~ *s.m.* **1.** beauty, the beautiful, the best; **2.** (obs.) fop; *un vieux ~*, an old dandy; *faire le ~*, (of dog) to sit up and beg; **belle** *s.f.* **1.** beauty, beautiful woman; sweetheart, fiancée; *ma belle*, (affectionate or iron.) my dear; **2.** (sport) deciding game or set.

beaucoup [boku] *adv.* much, very much, highly, considerably; (obs.) very; *~ de*, much, many, a lot of, a great deal of; *de ~*, far, by far, much, a long way; *il est de ~ le plus vieux*, he is much the oldest; *il s'en faut de ~*, it falls far short of it, it is nowhere near it; ~ *pron.* much, many, many people; *il y a ~ à faire*, there is a lot to be done; *~ sont de mon avis*, many people think as I do.

beau-fils [bofis] *s.m.* **1.** son-in-law; **2.** stepson; **~-frère** [bofrɛr] *s.m.* **1.** brother-in-law; **2.** stepbrother; **~-père** [bopɛr] *s.m.* **1.** father-in--law; **2.** stepfather.

beaupré [bopre] *s.m.* (naut.) bowsprit.

beauté [bote] *s.f.* **1.** beauty, handsomeness, fineness, perfection, nobleness; (pl.) beauties, fine points; sights (of a place); (fam.) *faire qch. en ~*, to do sth. superbly well; *être en ~*, to look one's best; (fam.) *se (re)faire une ~*, to do up one's face, one's hair; **2.** beautiful woman.

beaux-arts [bozar] *s.m.pl.* fine arts; *L'École des Beaux-Arts, Les Beaux-Arts*, the School of Fine Art.

beaux-parents [boparɑ̃] *s.m.pl.* parents-in--law.

bébé [bebe] *s.m.* **1.** baby; **2.** child's doll; *faire le ~*, to behave like a baby; ~ *adj.* babyish.

bec [bɛk] *s.m.* **1.** beak, bill (of bird); mouth (of insect, fish, etc., fam. of human being); (fig.) *avoir ~ et ongles*, to have claws, to have teeth; (fig.) *être le ~ dans l'eau*, to be in suspense; *claquer du ~*, to be hungry; *avoir bon ~*, to have a sharp tongue; *une prise de ~*, a set-to, a slanging match, an altercation; *clouer le ~ à qn.*, to shut someone's mouth; **2.** point (of pen); spout (of jug); lip (of pan); mouth-piece (of wind-instrument); (geog.) spit, tongue, (of land); *~ de gaz*, gas jet; (fig.) *tomber sur un ~*, to come up against a snag.

bécane [bekan] *s.f.* (fam.) bike.

bécard, beccard [bekar] *s.m.* (ichth.) houting; pike.

bécarre [bekar] *adj., s.m.* (mus.) natural (sign).

bécasse [bekas] *s.f.* **1.** (ornith.) woodcock; **2.** (fig., fam.) goose, idiot.

bécasseau (pl. **-x**) [bekaso] *s.m.* (ornith.) jack snipe; young woodcock.

bécassine [bekasin] *s.f.* **1.** (ornith.) snipe; **2.** (fig., fam.) silly girl.

bec-croisé [bɛkkrwaze] *s.m.* (ornith.) crossbill; **~-d'âne** [bekdɑn] *s.m.* = BÉDANE; **~-de-cane** [bɛkdəkan] *s.m.* spring-lock; door lever; **~-de-corbeau** [bɛkdəkɔrbo], **~-de-corbin** [bɛkdəkɔrbɛ̃] *s.m.* (mech.) wire nippers, nail--lifter; (med.) curved forceps; **~-de-lièvre** [bɛkdəljɛvr] *s.m.* hare-lip; **~figue** [bɛkfig], **~-fin** [bɛkfɛ̃] *s.m.* (ornith.) warbler.

bêchage [bɛʃaʒ] *s.m.* digging (with spade), digging up.

béchamel [beʃamɛl] *s.f.* (cook.) Béchamel (sauce).

bêche [bɛʃ] *s.f.* spade; (mil.) *~ de crosse*, trail--spade (on gun-carriage).

bêcher [beʃe] *v.t.* to dig (with spade); (fig., fam.) *~ qn.*, to pick on s.o., to pull s.o. to pieces.

bêcheu-r, -se [bɛʃœr] *s.m.f.* digger; (fam.) snob, person who gives himself airs.

bécot [beko] *s.m.* (fam.) peck (kiss).

bécoter [bekɔte] *v.t.* (fam.) to peck (kiss); **se ~** *v.refl.* to bill and coo.

becquée, béquée [beke] *s.f.* beakful; *donner la ~ (à)*, to feed (nestlings); to spoon-feed (child or invalid).

becquet see BÉQUET.

becqueter, béqueter [bɛkte] *v.t.* to peck; (pop.) to eat.

bedaine [bədɛn] *s.f.* (fam.) paunch, fat stomach, corporation.

bédane [bedan] *s.f.* mortise-chisel.

bedeau (pl. **-x**) [bədo] *s.m.* beadle.

bédégar [bedegar] *s.m.* (bot.) bedeguar.

bedon [bədɔ̃] *s.m.* (fam.) = BEDAINE.

bedonner [bədɔne] *v.i.* to acquire a paunch.

bédouin, -e [bedwɛ̃] *adj., s.m.f.* Bedouin.

bée [be] *adj. f. bouche ~*, gaping, open-mouthed; (fig.) *être bouche ~ devant qn.*, to be lost in admiration for s.o.

béer [bee] *v.i.* **1.** to be wide open; **2.** to gape.

beffroi [befrwa] *s.m.* belfry.

bégaiement [begɛmɑ̃] *s.m.* stammer(ing), stutter(ing); childish talk; (fig.) first attempt, hesitant or clumsy attempt; early stages.

bégayant, -e [begɛjɑ̃] *adj.* stammering, stuttering; (fig.) hesitant.

bégayer [begɛje] *v.t.i.* to stammer, to stutter; (fig.) to speak hesitatingly, to express oneself clumsily.

bégonia [begɔnja] *s.f.* (bot.) begonia.

bègue [bɛg] *adj.* stammering, stuttering; ~ *s.m.f.* stammerer, stutterer.

bégueule [begœl] *adj.* prudish, squeamish; ~ *s.f.* prude.

bégueulerie [begœlri] *s.f.* prudery, prudishness.

béguin [begɛ̃] *s.m.* **1.** bonnet worn by beguine; bonnet tied under the chin; baby's bonnet; **2.** (fig., fam.) passion, infatuation, fancy; (pop.) object of infatuation; *avoir le ~ pour qn.*, to have a passion for, to have a crush on, s.o.; *c'est son ~*, she's his flame.

béguinage [beginaʒ] *s.m.* beguinage.

béguine [begin] *s.f.* beguine.

bégum [begɔm] *s.f.* begum.

beige [bɛʒ] *adj., s.m.* beige.

beigne [bɛɲ] *s.f.* (pop.) blow, clout.

beignet [bɛɲɛ] *s.m.* (cook.) fritter.

béjaune, bec-jaune [beʒon] *s.m.* (ornith.) eyas; (fig., obs.) greenhorn, novice.

bel[1] see BEAU *adj.*

bel[2] [bɛl] *s.m.* (phys.) bel.

bélandre [belɑ̃dr] *s.m.* (naut.) bilander.

bêlement [bɛlmɑ̃] *s.m.* (lit. & fig.) bleating, bleat; (fig.) moaning.

bélemnite [belɛmnit] *s.f.* belemnite.

bêler [bele] *v.i.* (lit. & fig.) to bleat.

belette [bəlɛt] *s.f.* weasel.

belge [bɛlʒ] *adj., s.m.f.* Belgian.

belgique [bɛlʒik] *adj.* (anc. hist.) Belgic; ~ *s.f.* (geog.) *la Belgique*, Belgium.

bélier [belje] *s.m.* **1.** ram; **2.** (mil.) battering ram; (techn.) ram; **3.** (astron.) the Ram, Aries.

bélière [beljɛr] *s.f.* **1.** clapper-ring; **2.** sheep--bell; **3.** sword-sling.

bélître [belitr] *s.m.* (obs.) good-for-nothing.

belladone [beladɔn] *s.f.* (bot.) belladonna, deadly nightshade.

bellâtre [bɛlɑtr] *s.m.* lady-killer, fop.
belle *adj., s.f.* see BEAU[1,2].
belle-dame [bɛldam] *s.f.* = BELLADONE.
belle-de-nuit [bɛldənɥi] *s.f.* (bot.) marvel of Peru.
belle-fille [bɛlfij] *s.f.* **1.** daughter-in-law; **2.** stepdaughter.
bellement [bɛlmɑ̃] *adv.* (obs.) gently, nicely; (mod.) well and truly.
belle-mère [bɛlmɛr] *s.f.* **1.** mother-in-law; **2.** stepmother; **~-sœur** [bɛlsœr] *s.f.* **1.** sister-in--law; **2.** stepsister.
belles-lettres [bɛllɛtr] *s.f.pl.* belles-lettres.
bellicisme [belisism] *s.m.* warmongering, bellicosity.
belliciste [belisist] *adj.* warmongering; ~ *s.m.f.* warmonger.
belligérance [beliʒerɑ̃s] *s.f.* belligerence, belligerency.
belligérant, -e [beliʒerɑ̃] *adj., s.m.f.* belligerent.
belliqueu-x, -se [belikø] *adj.* bellicose, warlike, aggressive.
bellot, -te [bɛlo] *adj.* (obs. exc. dial.) nice little, pretty little.
belluaire [belɥɛr] *s.m.* **1.** (obs.) gladiator; **2.** (lion-, etc.) tamer.
belon [bəlɔ̃] *s.m.* Belon oyster.
belote [bəlɔt] *s.f.* belote.
bélouga [beluga], **béluga** [belyga] *s.m.* beluga, white whale.
belvédère [bɛlvedɛr] *s.m.* belvedere; view--point, observation-point.
bémol [bemɔl] *s.m., adj.* (mus.) flat; (fig., fam.) *mettre un* ~, to calm down, to pipe down.
bémoliser [bemɔlize] *v.t.* (mus.) to insert a flat or flats.
bénédicité [benedisite] *s.m.* grace (before meals); benedicite.
bénédictin, -e [benediktɛ̃] *adj., s.m.f.* Benedictine (monk or nun); (fig.) dedicated scholar; **~e** *s.f.* Benedictine (liqueur).
bénédiction [benediksjɔ̃] *s.f.* blessing, benison, benediction.
bénéfice [benefis] *s.m.* **1.** benefit, advantage, favour; *au* ~ *de*, in favour of, for the benefit of; (fig.) *sous* ~ *d'inventaire*, without prejudice; **2.** (hist.) benefice, fief; **3.** (eccles.) benefice, living; **4.** (comm.) profit, gain.
bénéficiaire [benefisjɛr] *s.m.f.* beneficiary; ~ *adj.* (comm.) profit; *marge* ~, profit margin.
bénéficier [benefisje] *v.i.* ~ *de*, to profit from, to benefit from or by; to be granted or allowed (sth.).
bénéficier [benefisje] *s.m.* (eccles.) holder of a living.
bénéfique [benefik] *adj.* **1.** (astrol.) favourable, benefic; **2.** beneficial.
benêt [bənɛ] *adj.* silly, foolish; ~ *s.m.* fool, simpleton.
bénévole [benevɔl] *adj.* **1.** benevolent, willing, gracious; **2.** free, unpaid, honorary; **~ment** [benevɔlmɑ̃] *adv.* **1.** benevolently, willingly, graciously; **2.** gratuitously, voluntarily.
Bengale [bɛ̃gal] *s.m.* (geog.) Bengal.
bengali, -e [bɛ̃gali] *adj., s.m.f.* Bengali; ~ *s.m.* **1.** (lang.) Bengali; **2.** (ornith.) crimson-eared waxwing.
bénignement [beniɲmɑ̃] *adv.* benignly, benignantly.
bénignité [beniɲite] *s.f.* benignity, benignancy.
bénin [benɛ̃], (fem.) **bénigne** [beniɲ] *adj.* benign, benignant, benevolent, mild.
béni-oui-oui [beniwiwi] *s.m.pl.* (fam.) yes-men.
bénir [benir] *v.t.* to bless, to consecrate, to pronounce a blessing; to praise, to thank.
bénit, -e [beni] *adj.* consecrated; *eau* ~*e*, holy water.
bénitier [benitje] *s.m.* **1.** holy water stoup or font; (fig., fam.) *se démener comme un diable dans un* ~, to rush about in a demented way; (pop.) *grenouille de* ~, (woman) bigot; **2.** giant clam.
benjamin, -e [bɛ̃ʒamɛ̃] *s.m.f.* **1.** (obs.) darling, favourite; Benjamin; **2.** youngest member (of family, group, etc.).
benjoin [bɛ̃ʒwɛ̃] *s.m.* (pharm.) benzoin.
benne [bɛn] *s.f.* **1.** skip, truck, scuttle; **2.** tip lorry; **3.** loader (of crane).
Benoît [bənwa] *s.m.* Benedict.
benoît, -e [bənwa] *adj.* (obs.) meek (and mild); sanctimonious; **~ement** [bənwatmɑ̃] *adv.* sanctimoniously.
benoîte [bənwat] *s.f.* (bot.) herb bennet.
benzène [bɛ̃zɛn] *s.m.* (chem.) benzene.
benzénique [bɛ̃zenik] *adj.* (chem.) aromatic.
benzine [bɛ̃zin] *s.f.* (chem.) benzine.
benzoate [bɛ̃zɔat] *s.m.* (chem.) benzoate.
benzoïque [bɛ̃zɔik] *adj.* (chem.) benzoic.
benzol [bɛ̃zɔl] *s.m.* (chem.) benzol(e); **~isme** [bɛ̃zɔlism] *s.m.* (med.) benzolism.
béotien, -ne [beɔsjɛ̃] *adj., s.m.f.* Boeotian; (fig.) dullard, ignoramus, philistine.
béotisme [beɔtism] *s.m.* dullness, stupidity, philistinism.
B.E.P.C. [beepese] abbrev. *Brevet d'études du premier cycle* (school exam).
béquée see BECQUÉE.
béquet, becquet [bekɛ] *s.m.* (print.) slip; slip (attached to proof).
béquillard, -e [bekijar] *s.m.f.* cripple on crutches.
béquille [bekij] *s.f.* (lit. & fig.) crutch, prop; (techn.) jack; stand; door-lever.
béquiller [bekije] *v.i.* (obs.) to walk with crutches; ~ *v.t.* (naut.) to shore up.
ber, bers [bɛr] *s.m.* **1.** (naut.) cradle; **2.** rack (of wagon, etc.).
berbère [bɛrbɛr] *adj., s.m.f.* Berber.
bercail [bɛrkaj] *s.m.* fold, bosom, (of Church, of family).
berce [bɛrs] *s.f.* (bot.) cow-parsnip, hogweed.
berceau (pl. **-x**) [bɛrso] *s.m.* **1.** cot, crib, cradle; infancy, early youth; (techn.) bed, support, mounting; (fig.) birth-place, place of origin; **2.** (arch.) barrel-vault, wagon-vault; **3.** (hort.) arbour, bower.
bercelonnette [bɛrsəlɔnɛt] *s.f.* rocking-cot.
bercement [bɛrsəmɑ̃] *s.m.* rocking.
bercer [bɛrse] *v.t.* to rock, to cradle; (fig.) to lull, to calm, to soothe; to delude, to deceive.
berceu-r, -se [bɛrsœr] *adj.* soothing, lulling.
berceuse [bɛrsøz] *s.f.* **1.** cradle-song, lullaby; **2.** rocking-chair.
béret [berɛ] *s.m.* beret.
bergamasque [bɛrgamask] *s.f.* bergamasque.
bergamote [bɛrgamɔt] *s.f.* **1.** bergamot pear; **2.** bergamot (citrus) fruit.
bergamotier [bɛrgamɔtje] *s.m.* bergamot tree.
berge [bɛrʒ] *s.f.* **1.** bank (of river or canal); **2.** raised pavement, banked edge; **3.** (pop.) year.
berg-er, -ère [bɛrʒe] *s.m.f.* **1.** shepherd, shepherdess; **2.** sheep-dog; *~er allemand*, alsatian (dog); **~ère** *s.f.* wing chair.
bergerie [bɛrʒəri] *s.f.* **1.** sheepfold, sheep-cot, sheep-farm; (fig.) *enfermer le loup dans la* ~, to put the cat among the pigeons; **2.** (Lit. & art) pastoral.
bergeronnette [bɛrʒərɔnɛt], **bergerette** [bɛrʒərɛt] *s.f.* (ornith.) wagtail.
béribéri [beriberi] *s.m.* (pathol.) beriberi.
berkélium [bɛrkeljɔm] *s.m.* (chem.) berkelium.
Berlin [bɛrlɛ̃] *s.m.* (geog.) Berlin.
berline [bɛrlin] *s.f.* berlin, berline; (car) four--door saloon; (mining) trolley, truck.
berlingot [bɛrlɛ̃go] *s.m.* **1.** humbug (sweet); **2.** tetrapak carton (for milk).

berlinois, -e [bɛrlinwa] *adj.* of Berlin; *s.m.f.* Berliner.
berlue [bɛrly] *s.f. avoir la* ~, to see things, to suffer from delusions.
berme [bɛrm] *s.f.* **1.** (fort.) berm; **2.** footpath (along embankment).
Bermudes [bɛrmyd] *s.f.pl.* (geog.) *les* ~, Bermuda, the Bermudas.
bernache [bɛrnaʃ], **barnache** [barnaʃ], **bernacle** [bɛrnakl] *s.f.* **1.** (moll.) barnacle; **2.** (ornith.) barnacle, barnacle-goose.
Bernardin, -e [bɛrnardɛ̃] *s.m.f.* Bernardine monk or nun.
bernard-l'hermite, bernard-l'ermite [bɛrnarlɛrmit] *s.m.* hermit-crab.
berne [bɛrn] *s.f.* **1.** (obs.) tossing in blanket; **2.** *en* ~, (of flag) at half mast.
berner [bɛrne] *v.t.* **1.** (obs.) to toss in a blanket; **2.** (fig.) to make a fool of.
bernicle [bɛrnikl], **bernique** [bɛrnik] *s.f.* limpet.
berthe [bɛrt] *s.f.* **1.** (dressm.) Bertha collar; small cape; **2.** milk-churn.
berthon [bɛrtɔ̃] *s.m.* Berthon-boat, collapsible dinghy.
bertillonage [bɛrtijɔnaʒ] *s.m.* bertillonage (system of identifying criminals).
béryl [beril] *s.m.* beryl.
béryllium [beriljɔm] *s.m.* (chem.) beryllium.
besace [bəzas] *s.f.* beggar's (or pilgrim's) wallet, scrip.
besaiguë [bəzegy], **bisaiguë** [bizegy] *s.f.* twibill, mortising axe; glazier's hammer.
besant [bəzɑ̃] *s.m.* (coin, herald.) bezant.
bésef, bézef [bezɛf] *adv.* (pop.) heaps, loads, a lot.
besicles [bezikl] *s.f.pl.* (old-fashioned) spectacles; (mod., jest) spectacles.
bésigue [bezig] *s.m.* bezique.
besogne [bəzɔɲ] *s.f.* work, labour, task, job; piece of work; *abattre de la* ~, to get through a lot of work; *aller vite en* ~, to be a fast worker; (fig.) to be over-hasty.
besogner [b(ə)zɔɲe] *v.i.* to slog, to slave, to labour.
besogneu-x, -se [b(ə)zɔɲø] *adj., s.m.f.* **1.** (obs.) needy (person); **2.** (person) doing menial job.
besoin [bəzwɛ̃] *s.m.* **1.** need, requirement, necessity; hunger, thirst; *faire ses* ~*s*, to relieve oneself; *avoir* ~ *de*, to need, to need to; *au* ~, in case of necessity, if necessary; **2.** want, privation, poverty.
bessemer [bɛsmɛr] *s.m.* (metall.) Bessemer converter.
bestiaire [bɛstjɛr] *s.m.* **1.** gladiator; **2.** bestiary.
bestial, -e, (aux) [bɛstjal] *adj.* bestial, brutish, beastly.
bestiaux [bɛstjo] *s.m.pl.* cattle, sheep, horses; farm animals.
bestiole [bɛstjɔl] *s.f.* tiny animal, (usu.) insect.
bêta[1] [bɛta] *s.m.* beta; *rayons* ~, beta rays.
bêta[2], **-sse** [bɛta] *adj., s.m.f.* (fam.) silly.
bétail [betaj] *s.m.* (no pl.) cattle, farm animals; *gros* ~, cattle, horses; *petit* ~, sheep, pigs.
bête [bɛt] *s.f.* **1.** beast, animal, creature, insect; ~ *à bon Dieu*, ladybird; *être malade comme une* ~, to be as sick as a dog; (fig.) *chercher la petite* ~, to be finicky, to pick holes (in); ~ *noire*, bête noire, pet aversion; *reprendre du poil de la* ~, to recover, to get back in one's stride; **2.** animal nature, bestiality; **3.** stupid person; *faire la* ~, to behave in a silly way, to act the fool; (affectionately) *grosse* ~*!*, you big so-and-so!
bête [bɛt] *adj.* stupid, foolish, silly; ~ *comme un âne, une oie, un pied*, ~ *à manger du foin*, as stupid as they come; ~ *comme chou*, dead easy; **~ment** [bɛtmɑ̃] *adv.* foolishly, stupidly; *tout* ~*ment*, quite simply.
bétel [betɛl] *s.m.* (bot.) betel.
bêtifiant, -e [betifjɑ̃] *adj.* **1.** (obs.) that makes dull or stupid; **2.** completely silly, full of nothing but drivel.
bêtifier [betifje] *v.t.* to make dull or stupid, to stupefy; ~ *v.i.* to play the fool, to say stupid things.
bêtise [betiz] *s.f.* **1.** foolishness, stupidity, silliness, folly, absurdity; **2.** foolish action or remark, foolery, nonsense, trifle, triviality; **3.** act of folly, blunder.
bétoine [betwan] *s.f.* (bot.) betony.
béton [betɔ̃] *s.m.* concrete; ~ *armé*, reinforced concrete.
bétonnage [betɔnaʒ] *s.m.* concrete work; concreting.
bétonner [betɔne] *v.t.* to concrete, to build with concrete.
bétonnière [betɔnjɛr] *s.f.* concrete-mixer.
bette [bɛt], **blette** [blɛt] *s.f.* (bot.) beet.
betterave [bɛtrav] *s.f.* beetroot; ~ *sucrière*, sugar-beet; ~ *potagère*, edible beetroot; ~ *fourragère*, mangold.
betteravi-er, -ère [bɛtravje] *adj.* beet, sugar-beet; *culture* ~*ère*, cultivation of beet or sugar-beet; *s.m.f.* sugar-beet grower.
beuglant [bøglɑ̃] *s.m.* (pop.) café-concert (end XIX century).
beuglante [bøglɑ̃t] *s.f.* (pop.) blaring song; vociferous protest.
beuglement [bøgləmɑ̃] *s.m.* bellow(ing), low, moo; blare, bawling.
beugler [bøgle] *v.i.* to bellow, to low, to moo; to blare, to bawl, to roar.
beurre [bœr] *s.m.* butter; ~ *noir*, melted, browned butter; (fig., fam.) *œil au* ~ *noir*, black eye; (fig.) *entrer comme dans du* ~, to go in easily, to slice through; (pop.) *c'est du* ~, it's a piece of cake; *mettre du* ~ *dans les épinards*, to go up in the world; *faire son* ~, to make a pile of money; *assiette au* ~, fleshpots, a highly profitable business; *compter pour du* ~, not to count; **~-frais** *adj. invar.* butter-coloured.
beurré [bœre] *s.m.* beurré (pear).
beurrée [bœre] *s.f.* (obs. exc. dial.) slice of bread and butter.
beurrer [bœre] *v.t.* to butter.
beurrerie [bœrri] *s.f.* dairy, creamery; butter-industry.
beurri-er, -ère [bœrje] *s.m.f.* (obs.) one who makes butter; *adj.* butter; *région* ~*ère*, butter-producing area; **~er** *s.m.* butter-dish, receptacle for butter.
beuverie [bœvri], **buverie** [byvri] *s.f.* drinking bout, drunken party.
bévue [bevy] *s.f.* blunder, silly mistake, slip, gaffe, faux pas.
bey [bɛ] *s.m.* bey.
Beyrouth [bɛrut] *s.f.* (geog.) Beirut.
bézef see BÉSEF.
bézoard [bezɔar] *s.m.* bezoar.
B.F. [beɛf] abbrev. *Banque de France*.
biais [bjɛ] *s.m.* **1.** slant, slope, obliquity; (dressm.) cross, bias-binding; *tailler dans le* ~, to cut on the cross; *de* ~, obliquely, aslant, slanting, askew, on the cross; **2.** (fig.) side (of character), slant, angle, way; roundabout way, indirect or devious approach; *par quel* ~ *le prendre?*, in what way should we take, or approach, it?; *prendre le* ~, to take the roundabout way.
biaiser [bjeze] *v.i.* **1.** to slope, to slant, to turn aside, to be on the cross; **2.** (fig.) to hedge, to play for time.
bibelot [biblo] *s.m.* knick-knack, gewgaw, trifle, trinket.
biberon [bibrɔ̃] *s.m.* feeding-bottle.
biberonner [bibrɔne] *v.i.* (fam.) to tipple.

bibi [bibi] *s.m.* **1.** (fam.) woman's small hat; **2.** (pop.) me.

bibine [bibin] *s.f.* (pop.) hogwash; bad beer or wine.

bible [bibl] *s.f.* (lit. & fig.) Bible.

biblio-bus [biblijɔbys] *s.m.* travelling library (vehicle); **~graphe** [biblijɔgraf] *s.m.f.* bibliographer; **~graphie** [biblijɔgrafi] *s.f.* bibliography; **~graphique** [biblijɔgrafik] *adj.* bibliographical; **~manie** [biblijɔmani] *s.f.* bibliomania; **~phile** [biblijɔfil] *s.m.f.* bibliophile; **~thécaire** [biblijɔtekɛr] *s.m.f.* librarian; **~thèque** [biblijɔtɛk] *s.f.* library; book-case, book-shelves; *rat de ~thèque*, book-worm; *~thèque de gare*, station bookstall; (fig., fam.) *c'est une ~thèque vivante* or *ambulante*, he is a walking encyclopaedia.

biblique [biblik] *adj.* biblical.

bicaméralisme, bicamérisme [bikamer(al)ism] *s.m.* (pol.) bicameralism, two-chamber system.

bicarbonate [bikarbɔnat] *s.m.* (chem.) bicarbonate.

bicarré, -e [bikare] *adj.* biquadratic.

bicéphale [bisefal] *adj.* bicephalous.

biceps [bisɛps] *s.m.* (anat.) biceps; brawn, muscle; (fam.) *avoir des ~*, to be brawny or muscular.

biche [biʃ] *s.f.* hind; female deer, doe; (fam.) darling.

bicher [biʃe] *v.i.* **1.** (fam.) to go well; **2.** (pop.) to feel good.

bichette [biʃɛt] *s.f.* little darling.

bichon, -ne [biʃɔ̃] *s.m.f.* **1.** lap-dog; **2.** (fam.) dear, darling.

bichonnage [biʃɔnaʒ] *s.m.* grooming, titivating; cossetting, pampering.

bichonner [biʃɔne] *v.t.* **1.** to groom, to dress up; *se ~*, to titivate oneself, to tidy oneself up; **2.** to cosset, to pamper.

bicolore [bikɔlɔr] *adj.* two-coloured.

bicoque [bikɔk] *s.f.* hovel, shanty.

bicorne [bikɔrn] *adj.* (anat.) bicornuate; *~ s.m.* two-cornered hat, cocked hat.

bicot [biko] *s.m.* **1.** (fam.) young goat, kid; **2.** (fam., pej.) North African.

bicycle [bisikl] *s.m.* (obs.) penny-farthing (bicycle).

bicyclette [bisiklɛt] *s.f.* bicycle.

bidasse [bidas] *s.m.* (pop.) soldier, tommy.

bide [bid] *s.m.* **1.** (pop.) stomach; **2.** (theatr.) *faire un ~*, to be a flop; **3.** (pop.) lie, deception; *c'est du ~*, it's a pack of lies, they're having one on.

bident [bidɑ̃] *s.m.* two-pronged fork.

bidet [bidɛ] *s.m.* **1.** (horse) nag, hack; **2.** bidet.

bidon [bidɔ̃] *s.m.* **1.** can, drum (receptacle); (mil.) water-bottle; **2.** (pop.) stomach; **3.** (pop.) *c'est du ~*, it's all lies; *ce n'est pas du ~*, I'm not bluffing; *~ adj.* feigned, pretended, simulated.

(**se**) **bidonner** [bidɔne] *v.refl.* (pop.) to die of laughter.

bidonville [bidɔ̃vil] *s.m.* shanty town.

bidule [bidyl] *s.m.* (pop.) gadget, what-do-you-call-it.

bief [bjɛf] *s.m.* **1.** stretch, reach, (of water); **2.** mill-race.

bielle [bjɛl] *s.f.* (mech.) connecting-rod; piston-rod; crank; *tête de ~*, crank-head, big-end; (car) *couler, griller, une ~*, to break a big-end.

biellette [bjɛlɛt] *s.f.* (mech.) small connecting-rod.

bien [bjɛ̃] *adv.* **1.** well; correctly; *c'est ~*, that's well done; that's enough; *faire ~*, to do right; *j'ai cru ~ faire de*, I thought I was doing right to; *c'est ~ fait*, it was deserved; *~ fait pour lui*, he was asking for it; **2.** (with adj. or adv.) very, quite; *~ sûr*, quite so; *~ souvent*, very often; *~ avant*, long before; (with verb) a lot, very much; quite; *j'espère ~ vous revoir*, I very much hope to see you again; *je veux ~*, I am quite willing; very well, then; *je voudrais ~*, I would much like (to); **3.** *~ de* (*du, de la, des*) much, many, a lot of; **4.** really, truly; *il part ~ demain?*, is he really leaving tomorrow?; *c'est ~ de lui*, that's just like him; *c'est ~ à moi de*, it's really up to me to; **5.** in any case, no doubt; *nous verrons ~*, well, we shall see; *~ adj.invar.* well; in good health; right, proper; good, comfortable; *tout est ~ qui finit ~*, all's well that ends well; *être ~*, to be comfortable; *être ~ avec qn.*, to be on good terms with s.o.; *un type ~*, a decent fellow; *~ que, conj.* although.

bien [bjɛ̃] *s.m.* **1.** good, benefit, advantage, welfare, good thing; *grand ~ vous fasse*, much good may it do you; *dire du ~, parler en ~, de qn., qch.*, to speak well, favourably, of s.o., sth.; *changer qch. en ~*, to improve sth., to change sth. for the better; *mener une affaire à ~*, to achieve sth., to succeed in sth.; to bring sth. to a successful conclusion; **2.** property, goods, estate, possessions; (comm.) goods, commodities; *~ mal acquis ne profite jamais*, ill-gotten gains never prosper; **3.** goodness, the good, virtue; *un homme de ~*, an honest man; (fam.) *en tout ~, tout honneur*, in good faith, in all innocence.

bien-aimé, -e [bjɛ̃neme] *adj.* well-beloved, favourite; *s.m.f.* lover, mistress, fiancé(e).

bien-dire [bjɛ̃dir] *s.m.* eloquence, elegance of speech.

bien-être [bjɛ̃nɛtr] *s.m.* well-being, happiness, peace, ease, comfort; welfare.

bienfaisance [bjɛ̃fəzɑ̃s] *s.f.* **1.** beneficence, charity, benevolence; **2.** welfare work, relief work, social work; *bureau de ~*, relief committee.

bienfaisant, -e [bjɛ̃fəzɑ̃] *adj.* **1.** (obs.) charitable, benevolent, kind; **2.** salutary, healing, soothing.

bienfait [bjɛ̃fɛ] *s.m.* **1.** (obs.) charity, kindness, generosity; **2.** benefit, advantage; beneficial effect.

bienfait-eur, -rice [bjɛ̃fɛtœr] *s.m.f.* benefactor, benefactress.

bien-fondé [bjɛ̃fɔ̃de] *s.m.* validity; merits, relevance, soundness (of argument, etc.).

bien-fonds [bjɛ̃fɔ̃] *s.m.* real estate.

bienheureu-x, -se [bjɛ̃nœrø] *adj.* blessed, blissful, happy; *s.m.f.* (eccles.) elect; (fig., fam.) *dormir comme un ~x*, to sleep the sleep of the just.

bien-jugé [bjɛ̃ʒyʒe] *s.m.* (law) validity (of judicial decision).

biennal, -e, (**aux**) [bjenal] *adj.* biennial; **~e** *s.f.* biennial exhibition.

bienséance [bjɛ̃seɑ̃s] *s.f.* propriety, decorum, fitness, decency; *les ~s*, the conventions, etiquette, good manners, proper behaviour.

bienséant, -e [bjɛ̃seɑ̃] *adj.* proper, decorous, fit, decent.

bientôt [bjɛ̃to] *adv.* soon, shortly, before long; quickly, easily; *à ~*, see you soon; so long.

bienveillance [bjɛ̃vɛjɑ̃s] *s.f.* benevolence, goodwill; kindness, favour, indulgence.

bienveillant, -e [bjɛ̃vɛjɑ̃] *adj.* (obs. exc. Lit.) benevolent; (mod.) kind, well-disposed, indulgent.

bienvenir [bjɛ̃vnir] *v.i. se faire ~ de qn.*, to get a welcome from s.o.

bienvenu, -e [bjɛ̃vny] *adj.* welcome, opportune; *s.m.f. vous serez toujours le* (*la*) *~(e)*, you will always be welcome.

bienvenue [bjɛ̃vny] *s.f.* welcome; *souhaiter la ~ à qn.*, to bid s.o. welcome.

bière[1] [bjɛr] *s.f.* beer, ale; (fig., fam.) *de la petite ~*, small beer, trifling matters.

bière[2] [bjɛr] *s.f.* coffin, bier.

bièvre [bjɛvr] *s.m.* (obs.) beaver.

biffage [bifaʒ] *s.m.* crossing out, striking out, scratching out, erasure (of word).
biffe [bif] *s.f.* (pop.) infantry.
biffer [bife] *v.t.* to cross out, to scratch out, to strike out.
biffin [bifɛ̃] *s.m.* (slang) **1.** rag-picker; **2.** infantryman.
biffure [bifyr] *s.f.* line (drawn through word or letter to delete it), erasure, cancelling stroke.
bifide [bifid] *adj.* bifid.
bifocal, -e, (aux) [bifɔkal] *adj.* bifocal.
bifteck [biftɛk] *s.m.* beefsteak, steak; (pop.) *gagner son* ~, to earn one's living.
bifurcation [bifyrkɑsjɔ̃] *s.f.* fork, junction, bifurcation.
bifurquer [bifyrke] *v.i.* to fork, to divide, to bifurcate; to branch off; (fig.) to change direction.
bigame [bigam] *adj.* bigamous; ~ *s.m.f.* bigamist.
bigamie [bigami] *s.f.* bigamy.
bigarade [bigarad] *s.f.* Seville or bitter orange.
bigaradier [bigaradje] *s.m.* bitter orange tree.
bigarré, -e [bigare] *adj.* many-coloured, parti-coloured, mottled; (fig.) heterogeneous.
bigarreau [bigaro] *s.m.* white-heart cherry, bigarreau cherry.
bigarrer [bigare] *v.t.* to variegate, to mottle; (fig.) to diversify, to give variety to.
bigarrure [bigaryr] *s.f.* medley, motley; variety, diversity.
bigle [bigl] *adj.* squinting, with a squint.
bigler [bigle] *v.i.* (fam.) to squint; ~ *v.t.* (fam.) to cast side glances at.
bigleu-x, -se [biglø] *adj.* **1.** (fam.) = BIGLE; **2.** (pop.) blind.
bignone [biɲɔn] *s.f.*, **bignonia** [biɲɔnja] *s.m.* (bot.) bignonia.
bigorne [bigɔrn] *s.f.* (techn.) two-beaked anvil; beak-iron.
bigorneau (pl. **-x**) [bigɔrno] *s.m.* periwinkle, winkle.
bigorner [bigɔrne] *v.t.* **1.** to shape on an anvil; **2.** (pop.) to smash up, to bash.
bigot, -e [bigo] *adj.* bigoted; *s.m.f.* bigot.
bigoterie [bigɔtri] *s.f.*, **bigotisme** [bigɔtism] *s.m.* bigotry.
bigoudi [bigudi] *s.m.* hair-curler, hair-roller.
bigre [bigr] *interj.* expressing annoyance (politer form of BOUGRE!); **~ment** [bigrəmɑ̃] *adv.* (fam.) very.
bigue [big] *s.f.* (naut.) derrick.
bihebdomadaire [biɛbdɔmadɛr] *adj.* appearing or taking place twice a week.
bihoreau [biɔro] *s.m.* (ornith.) night-heron.
bijou (pl. **-x**) [biʒu] *s.m.* jewel, gem.
bijouterie [biʒutri] *s.f.* jewellery trade; jeweller's shop; jewellery.
bijouti-er, -ère [biʒutje] *s.m.f.* jeweller.
bikini [bikini] *s.m.* bikini.
bilabiale [bilabjal] *s.f.* (lang.) bilabial.
bilabié, -e [bilabje] *adj.* (bot.) bilabiate.
bilan [bilɑ̃] *s.m.* balance-sheet; (fig.) evaluation, progress-report; *déposer son* ~, to file one's petition in bankruptcy; *faire le* ~ *de la situation*, to take stock of the situation.
bilatéral, -e, (aux) [bilateral] *adj.* bilateral.
bilboquet [bilbɔkɛ] *s.m.* **1.** cup and ball toy; **2.** small doll; **3.** (print.) job work.
bile [bil] *s.f.* (lit. & fig.) bile; *se faire de la* ~, to worry, to get upset.
(se) biler [bile] *v.refl.* (fam.) to get upset, to get in a state.
bileu-x, -se [bilø] *adj.* (fam.) easily upset, given to worrying.
bilharzie [bilarzi] *s.f.* (med.) bilharzia.
biliaire [biljɛr] *adj.* biliary; *vésicule* ~, gall-bladder.
bilieu-x, -se [biljø] *adj.* bilious; choleric, ill-tempered; easily upset.
bilingue [bilɛ̃g] *adj.* bilingual.
bilinguisme [bilɛ̃gɥism] *s.m.* bilingualism.
billard [bijar] *s.m.* billiards; game of billiards; billiard table; billiard room; (fam.) operating table; (fam.) *c'est du* ~, it's dead easy; ~ *japonais, russe, américain*, bar billiards.
bille[1] [bij] *s.f.* **1.** billiard-ball; **2.** marble (toy); (pl.) game of marbles; **3.** (techn.) *roulement à ~s*, ball-bearings; **4.** (pop.) face.
bille[2] [bij] *s.f.* log, billet (of wood).
billet [bijɛ] *s.m.* **1.** note, chit; ~ *doux*, love-letter; **2.** (comm.) note; bank-note; **3.** ticket; ~ *de faveur*, complimentary ticket; **4.** certificate, authorization, permit; ~ *de logement*, billeting order; (fig., fam.) *je vous donne mon* ~ *que*, I promise you that.
billette [bijɛt] *s.f.* (timber, eng., herald., arch.) billet.
billevesée [bijveze] *s.f.* nonsense, silly idea.
billion [biljɔ̃] *s.m.* **1.** billion (a million million); (U.S.) trillion; **2.** (before 1948) a thousand million; (U.S.) billion.
billon [bijɔ̃] *s.m.* **1.** (agric.) ridge; **2.** (obs.) small change.
billonnage [bijɔnaʒ] *s.m.* (agric.) deep ploughing.
billot [bijo] *s.m.* **1.** block of wood, block (esp. of scaffold); **2.** (techn.) bench; (naut.) keel-block; **3.** (agric.) clog, drag.
bilobé, -e [bilɔbe] *adj.* bilobed, bilobate, bilobar.
bimane [biman] *adj.* bimanal, bimanous.
bimbeloterie [bɛ̃blɔtri] *s.f.* manufacture of and trade in knick-knacks; junk, knick-knacks.
bimensuel, -le [bimɑ̃sɥɛl] *adj.* appearing or taking place twice a month.
bimestriel, -le [bimɛstrijɛl] *adj.* bi-monthly.
bimétall-ique [bimetalik] *adj.* bimetallic; **~isme** [bimetalism] *s.m.* bimetallism; **~iste** [bimetalist] *adj., s.m.f.* bimetallist.
bimoteur [bimɔtœr] *adj.* two-engined; ~ *s.m.* twin-engined aircraft.
binage [binaʒ] *s.m.* (agric.) hoeing, second dressing.
binaire [binɛr] *adj.* binary.
binard, binart [binar] *s.m.* two-wheeled trolley (for stone).
biner [bine] *v.t.* (agric.) to hoe, to give second dressing to; ~ *v.i.* (eccles.) to pluralize.
binette [binɛt] *s.f.* (agric.) hoe; (pop.) face.
biniou [binju] *s.m.* Breton bagpipe; (mus. slang) any wind instrument.
binocle [binɔkl] *s.m.* **1.** double telescope; **2.** pince-nez.
binoculaire [binɔkylɛr] *adj.* binocular; ~ *s.f.* field-glasses, binoculars.
binôme [binom] *s.m.* (math.) binomial.
bio-chimie [bjɔʃimi] *s.f.* biochemistry; **~-géographie** [bjɔʒeɔgrafi] *s.f.* biogeography; **~graphe** [bjɔgraf] *s.m.f.* biographer; **~-graphie** [bjɔgrafi] *s.f.* biography; **~graphique** [bjɔgrafik] *adj.* biographical; **~logie** [bjɔlɔʒi] *s.f.* biology; **~logique** [bjɔlɔʒik] *adj.* biological; **~logiste** [bjɔlɔʒist] *s.m.f.* biologist; **~nique** [bjɔnik] *adj.* bionic; *s.f.* bionics; **~physique** [bjɔfisik] *s.f.* biophysics; **~psie** [bjɔpsi] *s.f.* biopsy; **~sphère** [bjɔsfɛr] *s.f.* biosphere; **~synthèse** [bjɔsɛ̃tɛz] *s.f.* biosynthesis; **~-thérapie** [bjɔterapi] *s.f.* biotherapy.
biotite [bjɔtit] *s.f.* biotite.
bioxyde [bi(j)ɔksid] *s.m.* (chem.) dioxide.
bipale [bipal] *adj.* double-bladed (propeller, etc.).
biparti, -e, bipartite [biparti(t)] *adj.* bipartite, two-party.
bipartisme [bipartism] *s.m.* bipartisan government, coalition.

bipartition [bipartisjɔ̃] *s.f.* bipartition.
bipède [bipɛd] *adj., s.m.f.* biped; two-footed, two-legged, (animal).
bipenne [bipɛn] *adj.* dipteral, bipennate; ~ *s.f.* double-edged axe.
bipenné, -e [bipene] *adj.* = BIPENNE.
bipied [bipje] *s.m.* bipod.
biplan [biplɑ̃] *s.m.* (aeron.) biplane.
bipolaire [bipɔlɛr] *adj.* dipolar, dipole, bipolar.
bique [bik] *s.f.* she-goat, nanny-goat; (fam., pej.) *vieille* ~, old crone; *grande* ~, big girl.
biquet, -te [bikɛ] *s.m.f.* kid, young goat; *mon* ~, my child (term of affection).
biquotidien, -ne [bikɔtidjɛ̃] *adj.* twice daily.
birbe [birb] *s.m.* (pop., pej.) old man.
biréacteur [bireaktœr] *s.m.* (aeron.) twin jet.
biréfringence [birefrɛ̃ʒɑ̃s] *s.f.* birefringence.
birème [birɛm] *s.m.* (anc. hist.) bireme.
Birmanie [birmani] *s.f.* (geog.) Burma.
birman, -e [birmɑ̃] *adj., s.m.f.* Burmese.
bis[1]**, -e** [bi] *adj.* greyish-brown; *pain* ~, wholemeal or brown bread.
bis[2] [bis] *adv.* **1.** (mus.) repeat; (theatr., etc.) ~!, encore!; **2.** *12* ~, (house number) 12A.
bisaïeul, -e [bizajœl] *s.m.f.* great-grandfather; great-grandmother.
·**bisaiguë** see BESAIGUË.
bisannuel, -le [bizanɥɛl] *adj.* biennial; ~**le** *s.f.* biennial (plant).
bisbille [bisbij] *s.f.* bickering; fuss about nothing; *être en* ~ *avec qn.*, to be at odds with s.o.
biscaïen [biskajɛ̃] *s.m.* (mil.) biscayan (musket).
Biscaye [biskaj] *s.f.* (geog.) Biscay; *le golfe de* ~, the Bay of Biscay.
biscornu, -e [biskɔrny] *adj.* irregularly shaped, with odd angles; (fig., fam.) distorted, crazy, crack-brained.
biscotte [biskɔt] *s.f.* rusk.
biscuit [biskɥi] *s.m.* **1.** biscuit; sponge-cake; ~*s à la cuiller*, sponge-fingers; (fig., fam.) *s'embarquer sans* ~, to embark on sth. without any preparation or forethought; **2.** biscuit (porcelain); **3.** ~ *de mer*, cuttle-bone.
biscuiter [biskɥite] *v.t.* to re-furnace (china).
biscuiterie [biskɥitri] *s.f.* biscuit making; biscuit factory.
bise[1] [biz] *s.f.* bise, north wind.
bise[2] [biz] *s.f.* (fam.) smacking kiss.
biseau (pl. **-x**) [bizo] *s.m.* **1.** bevel, bezil, basil; chamfer, chamfered edge; **2.** (mortising) chisel; **3.** fipple (of recorder, etc.).
biseauter [bizote] *v.t.* **1.** to bevel, to chamfer; **2.** to mark (playing-cards).
biser[1] [bize] *v.t.* to re-dye.
biser[2] [bize] *v.t.* to give a smacking kiss to.
biser[3] [bize] *v.i.* (of grain) to rust, to darken.
biset [bizɛ] *s.m.* rock-dove, rock-pigeon.
bismuth [bismyt] *s.m.* (chem.) bismuth.
bison, -ne [bizɔ̃] *s.m.f.* (fem. rare) bison.
bisque [bisk] *s.f.* (cook.) bisque.
bisquer [biske] *v.i.* (pop.) to sulk; *faire* ~ *qn.*, to annoy s.o.
bissac [bisak] *s.m.* (obs.) = BESACE.
bissect-eur, -rice [bisɛktœr] *adj.* bisecting; ~**rice** *s.f.* bisector.
bissection [bisɛksjɔ̃] *s.f.* bisection.
bisser [bise] *v.t.* **1.** to encore, to recall; **2.** to repeat, to sing or play again, to give an encore.
bissexte [bisɛkst] *s.m.* 29th February (in leap years).
bissextile [bisɛkstil] *adj. année* ~, leap year.
bissexué, -e [bisɛksɥe] *adj.* bisexual.
bistorte [bistɔrt] *s.f.* (bot.) bistort, snake-weed.
bistouri [bisturi] *s.m.* bistoury, scalpel, lancet; ~ *électrique*, cautery knife.
bistournage [bisturnaʒ] *s.m.* neutering (of male domestic animal).
bistourner [bisturne] *v.t.* **1.** to twist and distort; **2.** to neuter (male domestic animal).
bistre [bistr] *adj.* bistred, tanned, swarthy; ~ *s.m.* bistre, bister.
bistré, -e [bistre] *adj.* = BISTRE.
bistrer [bistre] *v.t.* to turn bistre, to tan.
bistro, bistrot [bistro] *s.m.* (pop.) bistro, French pub; keeper of a *bistro.*
bisulfite [bisylfit] *s.m.* (chem.) bisulphite, acid sulphite.
bisulfure [bisylfyr] *s.m.* (chem.) disulphide, bisulphide.
B.I.T. [beite] abbrev. *Bureau international du travail*, I.L.O.
bitord [bitɔr] *s.m.* (naut.) rope, warp.
bitte [bit] *s.f.* (naut.) bollard, bitt.
bitter [bitɛr] *s.m.* bitters (drink).
bit(t)ure [bityr] *s.f.* **1.** (naut.) range of cable; **2.** (fig., pop.) *prendre une* ~, to have a booze-up; **3.** (fam.) *à toute* ~, hell-for-leather.
bitume [bitym] *s.m.* asphalt; bitumen; (fam.) ground.
bitumer [bityme], **bituminer** [bitymine] *v.t.* to asphalt.
bitumeu-x, -se [bitymø], **bitumineu-x, -se** [bityminø] *adj.* bituminous.
biture see BITTURE.
bivalent, -e [bivalɑ̃] *adj.* bivalent.
bivalve [bivalv] *adj., s.m.* bivalve.
biveau (pl. **-x**) [bivo] *s.m.* bevel-rule, mitre-rule; bevel-square.
bivouac [bivwak] *s.m.* bivouac.
bivouaquer [bivwake] *v.i.* to bivouac.
bizarre [bizar] *adj.* bizarre; strange, odd, peculiar; ~**ment** [bizarmɑ̃] *adv.* oddly, strangely, queerly, abnormally; ~ *s.m.* the unusual, the abnormal.
bizarrerie [bizarri] *s.f.* bizarrerie; oddity, peculiarity, eccentricity.
blackbouler [blakbule] *v.t.* to blackball; to plough (examination candidate), to reject.
black-out [blakawt] *s.m.* black-out.
blafard, -e [blafar] *adj.* pale, pallid, wan, sallow, dull, leaden.
blague [blag] *s.f.* **1.** tobacco-pouch; **2.** tall story, hoax; joke; trick; *sans* ~*!*, you don't say!, I don't believe it!; *prendre tout à la* ~, to treat everything as a joke; *jouer une bonne* or *une sale* ~ *à qn.*, to play a trick or a joke on s.o.; **3.** slip, mistake, faux pas.
blaguer [blage] *v.i.* to joke, to tell stories; ~ *v.t.* (fam.) to pull (someone's) leg.
blagueu-r, -se [blagœr] *adj.* joking, teasing; *s.m.f.* joker.
blair [blɛr] *s.m.* (pop.) nose, face.
blaireau (pl. **-x**) [blɛro] *s.m.* **1.** (zool.) badger; **2.** brush; shaving-brush.
blairer [blere] *v.t.* (pop.) to like; *je ne peux pas le* ~, I can't stand him.
blâmable [blɑmabl] *adj.* blameworthy, to blame (*de*, for).
blâme [blɑm] *s.m.* disapproval, criticism; blame; reprimand, reproof.
blâmer [blɑme] *v.t.* to blame, to criticize, to disapprove of; to reprimand, to censure.
blanc [blɑ̃] *s.m.* **1.** white, whiteness, white paint; *en* ~, white, blank; *à* ~, at white heat; *saigner à* ~, to bleed white; *tirer à* ~, to fire blank; **2.** white meat, white of egg, white wine, white (of eye), etc.; **3.** blank space, gap.
blanc, blanche [blɑ̃, blɑ̃ʃ] *adj.* white, pale, hoar(y), colourless; clean, unsullied, innocent; blank, void, not written on; toneless; (of marriage) unconsummated; *carte blanche*, free hand; *nuit blanche*, sleepless night; *c'est bonnet* ~ *et* ~ *bonnet*, it's six of one and half a dozen of the other; *s.m.f.* white man, white woman.
blanc-bec [blɑ̃bɛk] *s.m.* greenhorn; callow youth.

blanchaille [blɑ̃ʃɑj] *s.f.* (ichth.) whitebait.
blanchâtre [blɑ̃ʃɑtr] *adj.* whitish.
blanche [blɑ̃ʃ] *adj.* see BLANC *adj.*; ~ *s.f.* (mus.) minim; (billiards) white (ball).
blanchet [blɑ̃ʃɛ] *s.m.* **1.** (pharm.) strainer, filter; **2.** (print.) blanket.
blancheur [blɑ̃ʃœr] *s.f.* whiteness, paleness; purity; blankness.
blanchiment [blɑ̃ʃimɑ̃] *s.m.* whitewashing; (text.) bleaching; (hort.) blanching.
blanchir [blɑ̃ʃir] *v.t.* to whiten; (hort., cook.) to blanch; to whitewash, to bleach, to wash; ~ *qn.*, to do someone's laundry; (fig.) to clear, to whitewash s.o.; ~ *v.i.* to pale, to turn pale; (of hair) to grow white.
blanchissage [blɑ̃ʃisaʒ] *s.m.* **1.** washing, laundry, laundering; **2.** (techn.) refining of raw sugar.
blanchissement [blɑ̃ʃismɑ̃] *s.m.* turning white, whitening, (of hair) growing grey or white.
blanchisserie [blɑ̃ʃisri] *s.f.* **1.** bleaching works; **2.** laundry.
blanchisseu-r, -se [blɑ̃ʃisœr] *s.m.f.* laundryman, laundress, washerwoman.
blanc-manger [blɑ̃mɑ̃ʒe] *s.m.* **1.** blancmange; **2.** white-meat jelly.
blanc-seing [blɑ̃sɛ̃] *s.m.* blank cheque, paper signed in blank; (fam.) *donner ~ à qn.*, to give s.o. a free hand or carte blanche.
blandice [blɑ̃dis] *s.f.* blandishment.
blanquette [blɑ̃kɛt] *s.f.* **1.** Limoux sparkling white wine; **2.** (cook.) white-meat stew, blanquette.
blaps [blaps] *s.m.* mealworm beetle.
blasé, -e [blɑze] *adj.* blasé, surfeited; unfeeling, indifferent.
blasement [blɑzmɑ̃] *s.m.* satiety, boredom.
blaser [blɑze] *v.t.* to satiate, to surfeit; **se** ~ *v.refl.* to become blasé.
blason [blɑzɔ̃, blazɔ̃] *s.m.* blazon, escutcheon; blazonry; heraldry; (fig.) *redorer son ~*, to marry a rich commoner.
blasonner [blɑzɔne] *v.t.* to blazon, to emblazon.
blasphémat-eur, -rice [blasfematœr] *s.m.f.* blasphemer.
blasphématoire [blasfematwar] *adj.* blasphemous.
blasphème [blasfɛm] *s.m.* blasphemy; (fig.) outrageous remarks, grossly insulting language (used towards s.o.).
blasphémer [blasfeme] *v.i.* to blaspheme; ~ *v.t.* to blaspheme against; (fig.) to insult, to outrage.
blasto-derme [blastɔdɛrm] *s.m.* blastoderm; **~génèse** [blastɔʒenɛz] *s.f.* blastogenesis; **~mères** [blastɔmɛr] *s.m.pl.* blastomeres; **~mycètes** [blastɔmisɛt] *s.m.pl.* blastomycetes; **~mycose** [blastɔmikoz] *s.f.* blastomycosis.
blastula [blastyla] *s.f.* blastula.
blatérer [blatere] *v.i.* (of camel, ram) to bleat.
blatte [blat] *s.f.* cockroach.
blazer [blɛzœr, blazɛr] *s.m.* blazer (jacket).
blé [ble] *s.m.* **1.** wheat, corn; wheat-grain; ~ *noir*, buckwheat; ~ *cornu*, ergotized rye; (fig.) *manger son ~ en herbe*, to waste one's substance.
bled [blɛd] *s.m.* bush (in Africa); back-of--beyond.
blême [blɛm] *adj.* livid, wan, pale, pallid.
blêmir [blemir] *v.i.* to turn pale.
blende [blɛ̃d] *s.f.* (min.) blende, black-jack.
blennie [bleni] *s.f.* (ichth.) blenny.
blennorragie [blenɔraʒi] *s.f.* gonorrhoea.
blépharite [blefarit] *s.f.* blepharitis.
blèsement [blɛzmɑ̃] *s.m.* lisp, lisping.
bléser [bleze] *v.i.* to lisp.
blessant, -e [blɛsɑ̃] *adj.* offensive, hurtful, unpleasant.
blessé, -e [blese] *adj.* (lit. & fig.) injured, wounded, hurt; *s.m.f.* injured, wounded, person.
blesser [blese] *v.t.* to injure, to wound, to hurt; to offend, to grate on; (obs. exc. Lit.) to offend against, to infringe (conventions); (fig.) to do harm to, to prejudice; ~ *au vif*, to cut to the quick; **se** ~ *v.refl.* to hurt or injure oneself.
blessure [blesyr] *s.f.* injury, wound, hurt; offence.
blet, -te [blɛ] *adj.* (of fruit) over-ripe; (fig.) brownish-red in colour.
blette see BETTE.
blettir [bletir] *v.i.* (of fruit) to become over--ripe.
bleu, -e [blø] *adj.* blue; *colère ~e*, towering rage; *houille ~e*, energy derived from waves or tides; *sang ~*, blue blood, noble descent; *bifteck ~*, underdone steak; *zone ~e*, blue zone (restricted parking); *en devenir* or *en rester* or *en être ~*, to be struck dumb (with surprise, etc.).
bleu [blø] *s.m.* **1.** blue; blue cheese; (pl.) overalls, dungarees, boiler-suit; *gros ~*, cheap red wine; (cook.) *au ~*, cooked in red wine; (obs.) *petit ~*, express letter, telegram; (fig.) *n'y voir que du ~*, to be completely at a loss; **2.** new boy, new recruit, novice; **3.** bruise; *se faire un ~*, to bruise oneself.
bleuâtre [bløɑtr] *adj.* bluish.
bleuet [bløɛ], **bluet** [blyɛ] *s.m.* (bot.) cornflower.
bleuir [bløir] *v.t.* to turn, to make, blue, to give a blue tint to; ~ *v.i.* to turn, to look, blue.
bleuissement [bløismɑ̃] *s.m.* turning blue, making blue.
bleuté, -e [bløte] *adj.* blue-tinted.
blindage [blɛ̃daʒ] *s.m.* **1.** (mil., mining) screening, timbering, sheeting; (electr.) shielding, shrouding; **2.** armour-plating; armour, armour-plate.
blindé, -e [blɛ̃de] *adj.* armoured; (fig., fam.) hardened, immunized; (pop.) drunk; ~ *s.m.* armoured vehicle.
blinder [blɛ̃de] *v.t.* (mil.) to armour; (fig., fam.) to harden.
blizzard [blizar] *s.m.* blizzard.
bloc [blɔk] *s.m.* block; pad (of paper); (fam.) prison; (pol.) bloc, coalition; *tout d'un ~*, all in one piece; *en ~*, all together, in one piece; *à ~*, completely, thoroughly; (fig., fam.) *travailler à ~*, to work like fury.
blocage [blɔkaʒ] *s.m.* **1.** (constr.) rubble, filling; **2.** blocking, jamming on (of brakes); (comm.) freezing (of prices).
blocaille [blɔkɑj] *s.f.* = BLOCAGE 1.
bloc-cylindres [blɔksilɛ̃dr] *s.m.* (engine) cylinder block.
blockhaus [blɔkos] *s.m.* blockhouse.
bloc-moteur [blɔkmɔtœr] *s.m.* engine block.
bloc-notes [blɔknɔt] *s.m.* writing-pad, block.
bloc-système [blɔksistɛm] *s.m.* (rail.) block system.
blocus [blɔkys] *s.m.* **1.** (obs.) = BLOCKHAUS; **2.** blockade.
blond, -e [blɔ̃] *adj.* blond, fair-haired; pale, golden; *s.m.f.* blond.
blondasse [blɔ̃das] *adj.* tow, towy, tow--coloured.
blondeur [blɔ̃dœr] *s.f.* fairness, lightness (of hair, etc.).
blondin[1], **-e** [blɔ̃dɛ̃] *s.m.f.* fair-haired child, youth, or girl.
blondin[2] [blɔ̃dɛ̃] *s.m.* (techn.) cableway.
blondinet, -te [blɔ̃dinɛ] *s.m.f.* fair-haired child.
blondir [blɔ̃dir] *v.i.* to turn blond or golden; ~ *v.t.* (rare) to bleach (hair).
bloquer [blɔke] *v.t.* **1.** to make into a block, to join together; **2.** to blockade; **3.** to block, to jam; to lock (brakes, etc.); (fin.) ~ *le crédit*, to

block or to suspend credit; ~ *un compte*, to freeze an account.

(**se**) **blottir** [blɔtir] *v.refl.* to crouch, to snuggle, to make oneself small, to curl up; to lie low, to hide, to bury oneself.

blouse [bluz] *s.f.* **1.** overall, (peasant's) smock, (white) coat (of doctor, etc.); **2.** lady's blouse.

blouser[1] [bluze] *v.t.* **1.** (obs. billiards) to pocket; **2.** (fig., fam.) to deceive, to lead up the garden path; **se** ~ *v.refl.* to make a mistake.

blouser[2] [bluze] *v.i.* (of shirt at waist) to blouse.

blouson [bluzɔ̃] *s.m.* jacket, windcheater; ~*s noirs*, name applied to delinquent-type youths in the early 1960's.

blue-jean [bludʒin] *s.m.* (pl. ~*-jeans*) jeans.

blues [bluz] *s.m.* (mus.) blues.

bluet see BLEUET.

bluette [blyɛt] *s.f.* **1.** (obs.) glint; **2.** (fig., obs.) literary trifle.

bluff [blœf] *s.m.* bluff, intimidation.

bluffer [blœfe] *v.t.i.* (fam.) to bluff; to be bluffing.

blutage [blytaʒ] *s.m.* bolting, sifting, (of flour).

bluter [blyte] *v.t.* to bolt, to sift, (flour).

blutoir [blytwar] *s.m.* bolter (for flour).

B.M. [beɛm] abbrev. *Beata Maria*, B.V.M.

B.O. [beo] abbrev. *Bulletin Officiel.*

boa [bɔa] *s.m.* **1.** (zool.) boa (constrictor); **2.** (dress) (feather-)boa.

bobard [bɔbar] *s.m.* (fam.) tale, tall story.

bobèche [bɔbɛʃ] *s.f.* **1.** socket or sconce (of candlestick); **2.** (pop.) head.

bobinage [bɔbinaʒ] *s.m.* reeling, winding.

bobine [bɔbin] *s.f.* reel, spool, bobbin; shuttle; (electr.) coil; (pop., pej.) face.

bobiner [bɔbine] *v.t.* to wind (on reel).

bobineu-r, -se [bɔbinœr] *s.m.f.* (person) winder; ~**se** *s.f.* winding-machine, winder.

bobinoir [bɔbinwar] *s.m.* winding-machine, winder.

bobo [bobo] *s.m.* (child. lang.) pain; minor injury, bruise, sore; *avoir* ~, to have a pain; *cela fait* ~, it hurts.

bobsleigh [bɔbslɛg] *s.m.* bobsleigh.

bocage [bɔkaʒ] *s.m.* **1.** (obs. exc. poet.) bosk, small wood; bower; **2.** weald, countryside of fields and woods (esp. *le* ~ *normand*, *le* ~ *vendéen*).

bocag-er, -ère [bɔkaʒe] *adj.* (obs. exc. poet.) bosky, bowery; wooded.

bocal, (pl. **aux**) [bɔkal] *s.m.* jar, bowl (e.g. for goldfish).

bocard [bɔkar] *s.m.* (metall.) crushing-mill, stamping-mill, ore-crusher; ~**age** [bɔkardaʒ] *s.m.* crushing; ~**er** [bɔkarde] *v.t.* to crush.

boche [bɔʃ] *adj.*, *s.m.* (fam., pej.) German, Boche, Hun.

bock [bɔk] *s.m.* **1.** (med.) douche, irrigator; **2.** quarter-litre glass of beer.

boëte, boëtte [bwɛt], **boitte** [bwat] *s.f.* (fishing) bait.

bœuf [bœf] (pl. **-s** [bø]) *s.m.* ox, bullock; (cook.) beef; *mettre la charrue avant les* ~*s*, to put the cart before the horse; ~ *adj. invar.* (fam.) tremendous.

boghei, boguet [bɔgɛ], **buggy** [bœge] *s.m.* buggy.

bogie [bɔʒi], **boggie** [bɔgi] *s.m.* (rail.) bogie, bogey.

bogue [bɔg] *s.f.* chestnut burr.

Bohême, Bohème [bɔɛm] *s.f.* (geog.) Bohemia.

bohème [bɔɛm] *adj.*, *s.m.f.* (fig.) Bohemian.

bohémien, -ne [bɔemjɛ̃] *adj.*, *s.m.f.* **1.** Bohemian; **2.** gipsy, romany.

boire [bwar] *v.t.i.* to drink; to drink to excess; to soak up, to absorb; to swallow; ~ *comme un trou*, to drink like a fish; ~ *à la santé de qn.*, to drink someone's health; (fig.) ~ *un bouillon*, to suffer a reverse of fortune; ~ *du lait, du petit lait*, to be flattered, to swallow flattery; *ce n'est pas la mer à* ~, it's not much to ask; *on ne saurait faire* ~ *un âne qui n'a pas soif*, you can take a horse to water but you can't make it drink; **se** ~ *v.refl.* to be drinkable, to be drunk; *ce vin se boit au dessert*, this wine should be drunk with the dessert.

boire [bwar] *s.m.* drink, drinking; (fam.) *en perdre le* ~ *et le manger*, to be so absorbed or upset that one forgets to eat and drink.

bois [bwa] *s.m.* **1.** wood, timber, firewood; woodcut; wooden portion; (pl.) (mus.) wood-wind instruments; (football) goal-post; antlers, horns; ~ *de lit*, bedstead; *de* or *en* ~, wooden, made of wood; (tennis) *faire un* ~, to hit on the wood; (fig.) *trouver visage de* ~, to find no one at home, to find the door shut; *il fait flèche de tout* ~, everything is grist to his mill; *on verra de quel* ~ *je me chauffe*, you'll see what stuff I'm made of; **2.** wood, grove, copse.

boisage [bwazaʒ] *s.m.* woodwork, panelling, casing; timbering; shoring, propping, (in mines).

boisé, -e [bwaze] *adj.* wooded.

boisement [bwazmɑ̃] *s.m.* afforestation, tree--planting.

boiser [bwaze] *v.t.* **1.** to timber, to panel, to wainscot; **2.** to afforest, to plant with trees.

boiserie [bwazri] *s.f.* woodwork, wainscoting; (pl.) panelling.

boisseau (pl. **-x**) [bwaso] *s.m.* **1.** bushel, bushel-measure; (fig.) *mettre la lumière sous le* ~, to conceal the truth; **2.** (techn.) flue-tile, drain-tile; cock-casing (of tap).

boisselier [bwasəlje] *s.m.* cooper, bushel--maker.

boissellerie [bwasɛlri] *s.f.* making and selling of bushels, cooperage.

boisson [bwasɔ̃] *s.f.* **1.** drink, beverage; liquor, alcoholic drink; *être pris de* ~, to be drunk; **2.** drunkenness, drink, drinking, alcoholism; *s'adonner à la* ~, to take to drink.

boîte [bwat] *s.f.* box, case, caddy, canister, casket, chest, can, tin; boxful, canful; (pop., pej.) hole, job; (slang) = LYCÉE; *mettre en* ~, to box (goods); (fig., fam.) to heckle, to rag; (anat.) ~ *crânienne*, brain-pan; (techn.) ~ *d'essieu*, axle sleeve or bush; ~ *de vitesses*, gear--box; ~ *de nuit*, night-club.

boitement [bwatmɑ̃] *s.m.* limp, limping.

boiter [bwate] *v.i.* to limp, to hobble; (fig.) to be unconvincing.

boiterie [bwatri] *s.f.* lameness, limping.

boiteu-x, -se [bwatø] *adj.* lame, limping, crippled; rickety, unsteady; (fig.) lame, halting, unsound, unconvincing; *s.m.f.* cripple, lame person.

boîtier [bwatje] *s.m.* **1.** case; fitted case (esp. for instruments); **2.** (pol.) proxy.

boitte see BOËTE.

bol[1] [bɔl] *s.m.* bowl, basin, dish; bowlful, basinful; (fig.) *prendre un* ~ *d'air*, to take a breath of air; (pop.) *avoir du* ~, to be lucky; *ne te casse pas le* ~, don't worry your head about it, don't get upset.

bol[2] [bɔl] *s.m.* **1.** (pharm.) bolus; **2.** (med.) ~ *alimentaire*, alimentary bolus, gastric contents.

bolchevik, bolchevique [bɔlʃəvik], **bolcheviste** [bɔlʃəvist] *s.m.f.* (hist.) Bolshevik, Russian communist; (pej.) communist.

bolchevisme [bɔlʃəvism] *s.m.* (hist.) Bolshevism; (pol., obs.) communism.

bolée [bɔle] *s.f.* (dial.) bowlful.

boléro [bɔlero] *s.m.* **1.** (mus.) bolero, Spanish dance; **2.** (dress) bolero (jacket); small round hat.

bolet [bɔlɛ] *s.m.* (bot.) Boletus.

bolide [bɔlid] *s.m.* **1.** (astron.) bolide, meteor,

fire-ball; (fig.) *comme un* ~, at great speed, like a thunderbolt; **2.** fast racing car.

bolier [bɔlje], **boulier** [bulje] *s.m.* bag-net (for inshore fishing).

bolivar [bɔlivar] *s.m.* (hist.) broad-brimmed top-hat; (coin) bolivar.

Bolivie [bɔlivi] *s.f.* (geog.) Bolivia.

bolivien, -ne [bɔlivjɛ̃] *adj., s.m.f.* Bolivian.

bollard [bɔlar] *s.m.* (naut.) bollard.

Bologne [bɔlɔɲ] *s.f.* (geog.) Bologna.

bombance [bɔ̃bɑ̃s] *s.f.* feast, blow-out; *faire* ~, to have a blow-out.

bolonais, -e [bɔlɔnɛ] *adj., s.m.f.* Bolognese.

bombarde [bɔ̃bard] *s.f.* **1.** (mil.) bombard; **2.** (mus.) bombardon (organ-stop).

bombardement [bɔ̃bardəmɑ̃] *s.m.* bombardment, shelling, bombing.

bombarder [bɔ̃barde] *v.t.* **1.** to bombard, to bomb, to shell; (fig.) to bombard, to shower, (*de*, with); **2.** (fig., fam.) to give lightning promotion to (s.o.).

bombardier [bɔ̃bardje] *s.m.* **1.** (mil.) (obs.) bombardier; (⚠ not mod. 'bombardier'); **2.** (aeron.) bomber (plane); bomb-aimer.

bombardon [bɔ̃bardɔ̃] *s.m.* (mus.) bombardon.

bombe [bɔ̃b] *s.f.* **1.** bomb, shell; aerosol; (fig., fam.) *arriver* or *tomber comme une* ~, to come as a bombshell, to be a bolt from the blue; **2.** riding-cap; **3.** spherical container or object; (phys.) ~ *calorimétrique*, bomb calorimeter; ~ *de kirsch*, spherical bottle of kirsch; (cook.) ~ *glacée*, ice-pudding.

bombé, -e [bɔ̃be] *adj.* bulging, convex, rounded, domed; (of road) cambered.

bombement [bɔ̃bmɑ̃] *s.m.* bulge; camber (of road).

bomber [bɔ̃be] *v.t.* to cause to bulge, to fill (sails), to swell; ~ *v.i.* to swell, to bulge, (of sails) to belly.

bombonne see BONBONNE.

bombyx [bɔ̃biks] *s.m.* (ent.) Bombyx (moth of silkworm).

bon, -ne [bɔ̃] *adj.* **1.** good, upright, virtuous, righteous, worthy, honourable; desirable, necessary; profitable, advantageous; sound, valid; *trouver* or *juger* ~ *de*, to think it good, right, advisable, necessary, useful, to; *comme* ~ *vous semble*, as you think fit, as you think best; *à quoi* ~*?*, what's the use?, what's the point?; *c'est* ~ *à savoir*, it is worth knowing; *un* ~ *placement*, a sound investment; ~ *à manger*, good to eat; ~ *en mathématiques*, good at maths; ~ *pour*, good for, suitable for, valid for; **2.** suitable, fit; (mil.) ~ *pour le service*, fit for service, A.1.; ~ *à rien*, good for nothing, useless; **3.** right, correct; *le* ~ *chemin*, the right road; *au* ~ *moment*, at the right time; **4.** ~*!*, good!, right!, well done!; **5.** good, happy, fortunate, pleasant; *bonne année!*, happy New Year!; **6.** good, kind, nice; *il a été très* ~ *pour nous*, he has been very kind to us; *avoir* ~ *cœur*, to be kind-hearted; *avoir qn. à la* ~*ne*, to have a soft spot for s.o.; **7.** good, at least, clear; *trois* ~*s kilomètres*, a good three kilometres; *cela fait une* ~*ne semaine que*, it is at least a week since; *il arriva* ~ *premier*, he came a clear first; *pour de* ~, really, genuinely, for good and all; ~ *adv. sentir* ~, to smell good; *tenir* ~, to stand firm, to hold fast.

bon [bɔ̃] *s.m.* **1.** good, goodness; profit, advantage, good point; *avoir du* ~, to have some advantages; **2.** bond, order, draft; ticket, bill, coupon; ~ *du Trésor*, Treasury bond.

bonace [bɔnas] *s.f.* (at sea) calm (before or after storm).

bonapartisme [bɔnapartism] *s.m.* Bonapartism.

bonapartiste [bɔnapartist] *adj., s.m.f.* Bonapartist.

bonasse [bɔnas] *adj.* wishy-washy, feeble.

bonbon [bɔ̃bɔ̃] *s.m.* sweet, sweetmeat.

bonbonne, bombonne [bɔ̃bɔn] *s.f.* demijohn, carboy.

bonbonnière [bɔ̃bɔnjɛr] *s.f.* **1.** sweet-dish; **2.** prettily furnished little flat.

bon-chrétien [bɔ̃kretjɛ̃] *s.m.* (bot.) bon--chrétien pear.

bond [bɔ̃] *s.m.* bound, leap, spring, jump; rebound, bounce, ricochet; *progresser par* ~*s*, to progress by fits and starts; (fig.) *faire un* ~, to take a big step forward; (fig.) *prendre la balle au* ~, to seize one's chance; (fig.) *faire faux* ~ *à qn.*, to leave s.o. in the lurch.

bonde [bɔ̃d] *s.f.* plug-hole, plug; bung-hole, bung.

bondé, -e [bɔ̃de] *adj.* full, crammed (with people).

bondir [bɔ̃dir] *v.i.* to bound, to leap, to spring, to bounce, to jump; to dash, to dart, to rush; (fig.) ~ *de joie*, to be wild with joy.

bondissant, -e [bɔ̃disɑ̃] *adj.* bounding, gambolling, skipping, leaping.

bondissement [bɔ̃dismɑ̃] *s.m.* bounding, gambolling, skipping, frolicking, leaping.

bondon [bɔ̃dɔ̃] *s.m.* **1.** bung, bung-hole; **2.** small soft cheese.

bondrée [bɔ̃dre] *s.f.* (ornith.) honey-buzzard.

bon enfant [bɔnɑ̃fɑ̃] *adj.invar.* good-natured, simple-hearted.

bonheur [bɔnœr] *s.m.* **1.** luck, good fortune; *porter* ~, to bring good luck; *au petit* ~, at random; *par* ~, luckily, fortunately; **2.** bliss, happiness, contentment.

bonheur-du-jour [bɔnœrdyʒur] *s.m.* (pl. *bonheurs-du-jour*) escritoire.

bonhomie [bɔnɔmi] *s.f.* good nature, kindness, good-heartedness.

bonhomme [bɔnɔm] *s.m.* (pl. *bonshommes*) **1.** (obs.) simple, good-natured man; (mod.) *faux* ~, shifty fellow; **2.** (obs.) simpleton; **3.** (obs.) old man; **4.** man; (fam.) fellow, chap; (to small boy) little lad, sonny; **5.** (roughly executed) human figure; *un* ~ *de neige*, a snowman; **6.** *aller son petit* ~ *de chemin*, to proceed slowly but surely, to go at one's own pace, to do sth. in one's own time; *nom d'un petit* ~*!*, bless my soul!; ~ *adj.invar. des airs* ~, simple, kindly manner.

boni [bɔni] *s.m.* surplus, balance, credit, bonus, profit.

boniche, bonniche [bɔniʃ] *s.f.* (pej.) servant, servant-girl.

bonification [bɔnifikɑsjɔ̃] *s.f.* **1.** improvement, maturing, mellowing; **2.** bonus payment.

bonifier [bɔnifje] *v.t.* **1.** to improve; **2.** to give as a bonus; **se** ~ *v.refl.* to improve; (fig.) to mellow.

boniment [bɔnimɑ̃] *s.m.* claptrap, humbug, smooth talk; (fam.) tale, gossip, story,

bonimenter [bɔnimɑ̃te] *v.i.* to talk smoothly, to boost one's wares.

bonimenteur [bɔnimɑ̃tœr] *s.m.* humbug, gossip, smooth talker.

bonite [bɔnit] *s.f.* (ichth.) bonito.

bonjour [bɔ̃ʒur] *s.m.* good morning, good afternoon, good evening; *bien le* ~, a very good morning to you; *simple comme* ~, as easy as pie.

bon marché [bɔ̃marʃe] *adj.invar.* cheap.

bonne *adj.* see BON *adj.*

bonne [bɔn] *s.f.* (resident) maid, servant; ~ *d'enfant*, nursery maid, nurse; ~ *à tout faire*, general help, maid of all work.

bonne-maman [bɔnmamɑ̃] *s.f.* granny, grandma.

bonnement [bɔnmɑ̃] *adv.* (obs.) simply, straightforwardly; (mod.) *tout* ~, quite simply, honestly, truly.

bonnet [bɔnɛ] *s.m.* **1.** cap; ~ *de nuit*, nightcap; ~ *de police*, forage cap; ~ *d'âne*, dunce's cap;

~ *à poils*, bearskin; (fig.) *triste comme un ~ de nuit*, unutterably dreary; *quel ~ de nuit!*, what a bore!; (fig.) *avoir la tête près du ~*, to be easily roused; *prendre qch. sous son ~*, to do sth. off one's own bat; (fam.) *jeter son ~ par-dessus les moulins*, (of girl) to throw one's cap over the windmill, to throw propriety to the winds; *c'est blanc ~ et ~ blanc*, it's six of one and half a dozen of the other; *opiner du ~*, to nod assent; *un gros ~*, a bigwig, a big noise; **2.** second stomach of ruminant; **3.** cup (of brassière).

bonneteau [bɔnto] *s.m.* three-card trick.

bonneterie [bɔnɛtri] *s.f.* hosiery, knitwear, (manufacture and trade).

bonneteur [bɔntœr] *s.m.* confidence trickster, three-card trickster.

bonneti-er, -ère [bɔntje] *s.m.f.* manufacturer of, or dealer in, hosiery or knitwear.

bonnetière [bɔntjɛr] *s.f.* small cupboard (originally for hats).

bonnette [bɔnɛt] *s.f.* **1.** (fort.) bonnet; **2.** (naut.) studding-sail; **3.** (phys.) light filter; (photo.) auxiliary lens.

bonniche see BONICHE.

bon-papa [bɔ̃papa] *s.m.* grandad, grandpa.

bonsoir [bɔ̃swar] *s.m.* good evening; (fig., fam.) that's that, there's an end of it.

bonté [bɔ̃te] *s.f.* **1.** (obs.) goodness, good quality, (of sth.); **2.** goodness, kindness, benevolence, humaneness, compassion, sympathy; (pl.) act(s) of kindness, kindness, favour; ~ *divine!*, good gracious!; *avoir la ~ de faire qch.*, to be kind enough to do sth.

bonze [bɔ̃z] *s.m.* **1.** bonze, Buddhist priest; (fig., fam.) important, pompous individual; **2.** (pop.) old man; (slang) individual.

bonzerie [bɔ̃zri] *s.f.* bonze monastery.

bookmaker [bukmɛkœr] *s.m.* (abbrev. *book*) bookmaker, bookie.

boom [bum] *s.m.* (comm., fin.) boom.

boomerang [bumrɑ̃g] *s.m.* boomerang.

boqueteau [bɔkto] *s.m.* spinney, clump (of trees).

bora [bɔra] *s.m.* bora (N.E. wind).

borasse [bɔras] *s.m.* (bot.) palmyra palm (tree).

borate [bɔrat] *s.m.* (chem.) borate.

borax [bɔraks] *s.m.* (chem.) borax.

borborygme [bɔrbɔrigm] *s.m.* borborygmus, flatulence; rumbling.

bord [bɔr] *s.m.* **1.** side of ship, (on, over-) board; *jeter par-dessus ~*, to throw overboard; *virer de ~*, to tack, to go about; *à ~*, aboard, on board; *monter à ~*, to go aboard, to board; *hommes du ~*, crew; *journal de ~*, ship's log; *tableau de ~*, dashboard, instrument panel; (fig.) *être du même ~ que qn.*, to be on the same side as s.o.; **2.** edge, border, brim, brink, rim; side, shore, bank; *au ~ de la mer*, at the seaside; *~ à ~*, edge to edge; *chapeau à larges ~s*, broad-brimmed hat; (fig.) *au ~ de*, on the brink of; *au ~ du précipice*, on the brink of disaster.

bordage [bɔrdaʒ] *s.m.* **1.** (naut.) planking, sheathing; **2.** (rare) edging.

bordé [bɔrde] *s.m.* **1.** (naut.) planking, plating; **2.** (dressm.) binding, edging, braid, border.

bordeaux [bɔrdo] *s.m.* Bordeaux wine; ~ *rouge*, red Bordeaux, claret.

bordée [bɔrde] *s.f.* **1.** (naut.) broadside, volley; (fig.) ~ *d'injures*, stream of abuse; **2.** (naut.) board, tack; watch; ~ *de tribord*, starboard watch; **3.** (fig., fam.) pub-crawl.

bordel [bɔrdɛl] *s.m.* brothel; (fig., pop.) chaos, mess.

bordelais, -e [bɔrdəlɛ] *adj.*, *s.m.f.* (native or inhabitant) of Bordeaux.

bordelaise [bɔrdəlɛz] *s.f.* **1.** claret bottle; **2.** claret cask (225 litres).

border [bɔrde] *v.t.* **1.** to border, to fringe, to edge, to form an edge, side, boundary, etc., of, to stand or move along the edge of; *des arbres qui bordaient le chemin*, a line of trees along the side of the road; (naut.) ~ *les côtes*, to sail along the coast; **2.** to edge, to fringe, to trim, to put a border on, to line; (naut.) to haul (sail) taut; (naut.) to plank or plate (ship); *un mouchoir bordé de dentelle*, a handkerchief trimmed with lace; ~ *qn. dans son lit*, to tuck s.o. into bed; ~ *un lit*, to tuck the bedclothes in.

bordereau (pl. **-x**) [bɔrdəro] *s.m.* schedule, list, invoice, memorandum, note.

bordi-er, -ère [bɔrdje] *adj.* (geog.) marginal, epicontinental.

bordure [bɔrdyr] *s.f.* border, edging, edge, trimming; ~ *de chaussée, de pavés*, kerb, kerb-stone; *en ~ de*, at the edge of, alongside.

bore [bɔr] *s.m.* (chem.) boron.

boréal, -e, (aux) [bɔreal] *adj.* northern; (fam.) polar, arctic; *aurore ~e*, aurora borealis.

borgne [bɔrɲ] *adj.* one-eyed; (fig.) disreputable, sleazy; *fenêtre ~*, window with no view.

borique [bɔrik] *adj.* (chem.) boric, boracic.

bornage [bɔrnaʒ] *s.m.* **1.** boundary; demarcation of boundary; **2.** (naut.) inshore sailing.

borne [bɔrn] *s.f.* boundary-stone, milestone, landmark; (pop.) kilometre; (electr.) terminal; (pl.) limits, boundaries, frontiers, bounds; *sans ~s*, boundless; (fig.) *dépasser les ~s*, to go too far.

borné, -e [bɔrne] *adj.* limited, bounded, restricted, narrow(-minded); (fig.) *à l'esprit ~*, narrow-minded, of limited intelligence.

borne-fontaine [bɔrn(ə)fɔ̃tɛn] *s.f.* (ornamental) stand-pipe.

borner [bɔrne] *v.t.* to bound, to limit; to restrict, to confine, to circumscribe; **se ~ à** *v.refl.* to limit or confine oneself to, not to go beyond or further than.

bosco [bɔsko] *s.m.* (naut.) boatswain, bo's'n.

Bosphore [bɔsfɔr] *s.m.* (geog.) Bosphorus (sea).

bosquet [bɔskɛ] *s.m.* clump (of trees), spinney; grove, bower.

bossage [bɔsaʒ] *s.m.* (constr.) bossage, rustic surface.

bosse [bɔs] *s.f.* **1.** bump, lump, swelling, bulge, protuberance; boss, embossment; unevenness; (fig.) *avoir la ~ de qch.*, to have a gift for sth.; **2.** hump; (fig., fam.) *rouler sa ~*, to knock around, to be a rolling stone.

bosselage [bɔslaʒ] *s.m.* repoussé.

bosseler [bɔsle] *v.t.* **1.** to do repoussé work; **2.** to dent, to knock out of shape, to cause to bulge.

bossellement [bɔsɛlmɑ̃] *s.m.* **1.** = BOSSELURE 1; **2.** denting.

bosselure [bɔslyr] *s.f.* **1.** repoussé ornament; **2.** bump, bulge, dent.

bosser [bɔse] *v.t.* (naut.) to stopper; ~ *v.i.* (pop.) to work hard, to slog.

bossette [bɔsɛt] *s.f.* **1.** (harness) boss; blinker; **2.** (on fire-arm) boss, lug.

bosseur [bɔsœr] *s.m.* (pop.) swot.

bossoir [bɔswar] *s.m.* (naut.) **1.** cathead; **2.** davit.

bossu, -e [bɔsy] *adj.* hump-backed, hunch-backed; *s.m.f.* hunchback; (fam.) *rire comme un ~*, to split one's sides (with laughter).

bossuer [bɔsɥe] *v.t.* to dent, to raise a lump on; *ces collines qui bossuent les Landes*, those hills which break up the surface of the Landes.

boston [bɔstɔ̃] *s.m.* Boston (card-game, dance).

bostonner [bɔstɔne] *v.i.* to dance the Boston.

bot, -e [bo] *adj.* *pied ~*, clubfoot; *main ~e*, deformed hand.

botanique [bɔtanik] *adj.* botanical; ~ *s.f.* botany.

botaniste [bɔtanist] *s.m.f.* botanist.

botte[1] [bɔt] *s.f.* truss (of hay); bunch, bundle.

botte[2] [bɔt] *s.f.* boot, rubber boot, thigh-boot, wader, jack-boot, riding-boot; (fam.) *graisser ses ~s*, to prepare to leave; (fig.) *cirer, lécher, les ~s de qn.*, to lick someone's boots; *mettre* or *avoir du foin dans ses ~s*, to make or to have a lot of money; *à propos de ~s*, without reason, pointlessly, for nothing at all.

botte[3] [bɔt] *s.f.* lunge, thrust; (fig.) *porter une ~ à qn.*, to have a dig at s.o., to deal s.o. a nasty blow.

bottelage [bɔtlaʒ] *s.m.* trussing, bundling.

botteler [bɔtle] *v.t.* to truss, to bundle, to bind.

botteleu-r, -se [bɔtlœr] *s.m.f.* trusser, binder; **~se** *s.f.* binder, binding-machine.

botter [bɔte] *v.t.* to supply with boots, to make boots for s.o.; to help s.o. on with his boots; (fam.) to kick; (fig., pop.) *ça me botte*, that's right up my street, that's just my cup of tea.

bottier [bɔtje] *s.m.* bootmaker.

bottillon [bɔtijɔ̃] *s.m.* bootee, short boot.

bottine [bɔtin] *s.f.* half-boot, elastic-sided or buttoned boot.

botulisme [bɔtylism] *s.m.* botulism.

boubou [bubu] *s.m.* boubou, long white robe worn by Muslims in West Africa.

boubouler [bubule] *v.i.* to ululate (of owl uttering its cry).

bouc [buk] *s.m.* **1.** he-goat, billy; *~ émissaire*, scapegoat; **2.** goatee (beard).

boucan[1] [bukɑ̃] *s.m.* barbecued meat; barbecue.

boucan[2] [bukɑ̃] *s.m.* (pop.) row, uproar.

boucanage [bukanaʒ] *s.m.* barbecuing, curing (of meat or fish).

boucaner [bukane] *v.t.* to cure with smoke (meat or fish); to tan; to barbecue; *~ v.i.* to hunt the wild ox.

boucanier [bukanje] *s.m.* buccaneer.

bouchage [buʃaʒ] *s.m.* plugging, stopping, closing-up; corking.

bouche [buʃ] *s.f.* **1.** mouth, lips; *le ~ à ~*, mouth-to-mouth artificial respiration, kiss of life; *faire la petite ~*, to look scornful; *garder qch. pour la bonne ~*, to keep the best for the last; *une fine ~*, a gourmet; **2.** entrance, opening; mouth.

bouché, -e [buʃe] *adj.* stopped-up, blocked; (of weather) cloudy, misty; (of nose) blocked up; (of bottle) corked; (of wine, cider) bottled; (fig.) narrow-minded, obtuse; idiotic, stupid.

bouchée [buʃe] *s.f.* **1.** mouthful; *ne faire qu'une ~ de*, to gobble up; (fig.) to make short work of; *mettre les ~s doubles*, to work twice as fast as usual, to do a double stint; **2.** filled chocolate; **3.** (cook.) *~ à la reine*, patty filled with meat in white sauce.

boucher [buʃe] *v.t.* to close, to stop (up), to plug, to cork, to stopper; to block (up), to obstruct; *se ~ le nez*, to hold one's nose; (fig.) *se ~ les yeux*, to close one's eyes (to sth.); *se ~ les oreilles*, to stop one's ears, to refuse to listen; **se ~** *v.refl.* to get stopped up, to become blocked.

boucher [buʃe] *s.m.* butcher.

bouchère [buʃɛr] *s.f.* butcher's wife; butcher-woman.

boucherie [buʃri] *s.f.* **1.** (obs.) slaughter-house, shambles; (mod.) *animaux de ~*, fat-stock, beef-cattle; **2.** butcher's shop; butcher's trade; (fig.) butchery, shambles, slaughter, massacre.

bouche-trou [buʃtru] *s.m.* (pl. *bouche-trous*) stop-gap.

bouchon [buʃɔ̃] *s.m.* **1.** handful or bunch of straw; bundle, sheaf; (obs.) bush (bunch of straw or foliage serving as inn-sign), inn; (fig., fam.) *mon petit ~*, my little poppet; **2.** cork, stopper, bung, cap, closure; (techn., electr.) plug; obstruction; *~ de circulation*, traffic-jam, bottle-neck; *sentir le ~*, (of wine) to be corked.

bouchonner [buʃɔne] *v.t.* **1.** (obs.) to bundle; **2.** to rub (with a bunch of straw); *~ un cheval*, to rub down a horse; (fig., fam.) to cosset, to spoil (a child).

bouchonnier [buʃɔnje] *s.m.* one who makes or sells corks.

bouchot [buʃo] *s.m.* mussel-bed, mussel-scalp.

bouchot(t)eur [buʃɔtœr] *s.m.* mussel farmer.

bouclage [buklaʒ] *s.m.* **1.** (fam.) putting under lock and key; **2.** (mil.) encirclement; (techn.) enclosing, closing (of circuit, etc.).

boucle [bukl] *s.f.* **1.** buckle, ring, loop; (aeron.) *boucler la ~*, to loop the loop; **2.** lock (of hair), curl, ringlet.

boucler [bukle] *v.t.* **1.** to buckle, to fasten, to close, to close down, to shut up (shop); to ring (bull, etc.); to put in prison; *~ sa valise*, to pack one's bags, to get ready to go; *la ~*, to say nothing, to keep one's mouth shut, to shut up; **2.** to curl, to wave, (hair); **3.** to enclose, to encircle; to complete (a circle); (electr.) to close a circuit; *~ v.i.* (of hair) to curl, to be curly or wavy.

bouclette [buklɛt] *s.f.* small buckle, curl, loop; *laine ~*, bouclé wool.

bouclier [buklije] *s.m.* shield, buckler; armour (of gun); (mining) shield; (of shellfish) shell, carapace; (fig.) *levée de ~s*, demonstration of opposition.

Bouddha [buda] *s.m.* Buddha.

bouddh-isme [budism] *s.m.* Buddhism; **~iste** [budist] *adj., s.m.f.* Buddhist.

bouder [bude] *v.i.* to sulk; *~ v.t.* to ignore, to cold-shoulder, to avoid.

bouderie [budri] *s.f.* sulks, sulking, sulkiness.

boudeu-r, -se [budœr] *adj., s.m.f.* sulky, peevish, cross, (person).

boudeuse [budøz] *s.f.* double back-to-back sofa.

boudin [budɛ̃] *s.m.* (cook.) black pudding, polony; stubby finger; corkscrew curl; flange (of wheel); (arch.) torus; (naut.) fender; *s'en aller en eau de ~*, to fail, to fizzle out; *ressort à ~*, spiral spring.

boudiné, -e [budine] *adj.* **1.** dressed in skin-tight clothes; **2.** sausage-shaped.

boudiner [budine] *v.t.* (text.) to rove, to slub; to twist into a spiral; **se ~** *v.refl.* to cram oneself into tight clothes.

boudineuse [budinøz] *s.f.* (text.) slubbing machine.

boudoir [budwar] *s.m.* boudoir.

boue [bu] *s.f.* mud, clay, dirt, mire; silt, sludge, deposit, sediment; (fig.) filth, gutter; *traîner qn. dans la ~*, to drag someone's name in the mud, to calumniate s.o.

bouée [bwe] *s.f.* buoy; *~ de sauvetage*, lifebuoy; *~-culotte*, breeches-buoy.

boueur [bwœr] *s.m.* dustman, scavenger, street-sweeper.

boueu-x, -se [bwø] *adj.* muddy, miry, foul; (of print) smudged.

bouffant, -e [bufɑ̃] *adj.* puffed, puffy, ballooning; *~ s.m.* (dressm.) puff.

bouffarde [bufard] *s.f.* (fam.) pipe with short stem.

bouffe[1] [buf] *adj.* comic, light (opera); *~ s.m.* buffo.

bouffe[2] [buf], **bouffetance** [buftɑ̃s] *s.f.* (pop.) eating.

bouffée [bufe] *s.f.* puff, whiff; blast, gust; (fig.) flash, spurt, dash; (med.) *~ de chaleur*, hot flush.

bouffer [bufe] *v.i.* to puff, to swell; (pop.) to stuff oneself, to eat; *~ v.t.* to eat; *avoir envie de ~ qn.*, to be furious with s.o.; *se ~ le nez*, to quarrel; *une voiture qui bouffe de l'essence*, a car that eats petrol; *~ du kilomètre*, to do a lot of driving.

bouffi, -e [bufi] *adj.* puffy, swollen; puffed up, bloated, (*de*, with); bombastic.

bouffir [bufir] *v.t.i.* to puff up, to swell, to bloat.

bouffissure [bufisyr] *s.f.* puffiness, swelling, bloated appearance; (fig.) bombast.

bouffon [bufɔ̃] *s.m.* (hist.) clown; court jester; buffoon; laughing-stock, butt; ~, **~ne** *adj.* comic, ludicrous, farcical.

bouffonner [bufɔne] *v.i.* (obs. exc. Lit.) to play the fool.

bouffonnerie [bufɔnri] *s.f.* buffoonery, clowning; ludicrousness.

bougainvillée [bugɛ̃vile] *s.f.*, **bougainvillier** [bugɛ̃vilje] *s.m.* (bot.) bougainvillea.

bouge [buʒ] *s.m.* **1.** bulge, hollow, convexity; **2.** hovel, den, low haunt, low dive.

bougeoir [buʒwar] *s.m.* candlestick (with saucer-shaped base).

bougeotte [buʒɔt] *s.f.* (fam.) *avoir la* ~, to have itchy feet.

bouger [buʒe] *v.i.* to move, to stir, to budge; (fam.) (usu. neg.) to change; (pol.) to be restive; ~ *v.t.* (fam.) to move; **se** ~ *v.refl.* to move, to wake up, to bestir oneself.

bougie [buʒi] *s.f.* **1.** candle; sparking-plug; (med.) probe; **2.** (obs.) unit of candle-power; **3.** (pop.) face.

bougna(t) [buɲa] *s.m.* (pop.) coalman, coal-merchant.

bougon, -ne [bugɔ̃] *adj.* grumbling, grousing; *s.m.f.* grumbler, grouser.

bougonner [bugɔne] *v.i.* to grumble, to grouse, to mumble.

bougran [bugrɑ̃] *s.m.* buckram.

bougre, -sse [bugr] *s.m.f.* (fam.) man, woman, chap, fellow; *un bon* ~, a good sort; ~ *interj.* damn!, hell!; ⚠ not 'bugger' in sense 'sodomite'; milder than Eng. expletive 'bugger!'.

bougrement [bugrəmɑ̃] *adv.* very, extremely, fiendishly.

boui-boui [bwibwi] *s.m.* (fam.) low dive.

bouillabaisse [bujabɛs] *s.f.* (cook.) bouillabaisse.

bouillant, -e [bujɑ̃] *adj.* boiling, scalding; (fig.) hot-headed, fiery; ~ *de colère*, seething with anger.

bouille [buj] *s.f.* **1.** basket for grape harvest; **2.** (fam.) face.

bouilleur [bujœr] *s.m.* **1.** distiller; ~ *de cru*, one who distils from his own produce; **2.** water-space (in boiler).

bouilli [buji] *s.m.* boiled meat.

bouillie [buji] *s.f.* pap, baby-food, porridge, pulp; (viticulture) wash, spray-mixture; *en* ~, cooked to pieces, reduced or crushed to pulp, smashed to pieces; (fig.) ~ *pour les chats*, useless stuff, incomprehensible nonsense.

bouillir [bujir] *v.i.* to boil; *faire* ~, to boil, to sterilize; (fig.) ~ *de colère, etc.*, to seethe with rage, etc.; ~ *v.t.* (fam.) to boil.

bouilloire [bujwar] *s.f.* kettle.

bouillon [bujɔ̃] *s.m.* **1.** bubble, bubbling, ripple; (dressm.) flounce; unsold copies (of publication); *sortir à gros ~s*, to come gushing out; *bouillir à gros ~s*, to boil hard; **2.** broth, stock, soup, stew, beef tea; ~ *de culture*, (biol.) culture medium; (fig.) favourable environment, forcing-bed; *boire un* ~, to swallow water (while swimming); (fig., fam.) to suffer a heavy (financial) loss.

bouillon-blanc [bujɔ̃blɑ̃] *s.m.* (bot.) white mullein.

bouillonnement [bujɔnmɑ̃] *s.m.* boiling, bubbling; (fig.) tumult.

bouillonner [bujɔne] *v.i.* to bubble, to gush out; (fig.) to seethe; *journal qui bouillonne*, paper which doesn't sell; ~ *v.t.* (dressm.) to make flounces, to flounce.

bouillotte [bujɔt] *s.f.* **1.** kettle; **2.** foot-warmer, hot-water bottle.

bouillotter [bujɔte] *v.i.* to simmer, to cook too slowly.

boulaie [bulɛ] *s.f.* birch plantation.

boulange [bulɑ̃ʒ] *s.f.* (fam.) bakery (trade); *bois de* ~, wood for heating oven.

boulang-er, -ère [bulɑ̃ʒe] *s.m.f.* baker, baker's wife.

boulanger [bulɑ̃ʒe] *v.t.* to work flour, to knead.

boulangerie [bulɑ̃ʒri] *s.f.* bakehouse, baker's shop; bakery trade.

boule [bul] *s.f.* ball; (sport) bowl, bowls; (fig., fam.) head; ~ *de neige*, snowball; (fig.) *faire* ~ *de neige*, to snowball; *en* ~, in a ball, rolled up; (fig., fam.) *se mettre en* ~, to lose one's temper; *perdre la* ~, to go off one's head.

bouleau (pl. **-x**) [bulo] *s.m.* birch tree.

boule-de-neige [buldənɛʒ] *s.f.* snowball tree, guelder rose.

boule-dogue [buldɔg] *s.m.* bulldog.

bouler [bule] *v.i.* to roll (like a ball); *envoyer* ~ *qn.*, to send s.o. about his business, to send s.o. packing; ~ *v.t.* to pad horns (of bull).

boulet [bulɛ] *s.m.* **1.** cannon-ball; **2.** shackles; (fig.) *c'est un* ~ *à traîner*, it's a cross to bear; **3.** fetlock; **4.** briquette (of coal).

boulette [bulɛt] *s.f.* pellet, small ball; (cook.) ball, croquette; (fig., fam.) *faire une* ~, to drop a clanger, to make a blunder.

boulevard [bulvar] *s.m.* **1.** boulevard; **2.** (theatr.) light comedy, vaudeville, farce.

boulevardi-er, -ère [bulvardje] *adj.* farcical, witty, satirical; **~er** *s.m.* man about town.

bouleversant, -e [bulvɛrsɑ̃] *adj.* upsetting, distressing, devastating, staggering.

bouleversement [bulvɛrsəmɑ̃] *s.m.* upset, change, commotion, upheaval, confusion, disorder.

bouleverser [bulvɛrse] *v.t.* to overthrow, to overturn, to upset, to throw into disorder, to turn upside down; (fig.) to bring about a complete change in; (fig.) to upset, to shake, to trouble.

boulier[1] see BOLIER.

boulier[2] [bulje] *s.m.* counting frame, abacus.

boulimie [bulimi] *s.f.* (med.) bulimia; (fam.) ravenous hunger.

boulin [bulɛ̃] *s.m.* **1.** (lit.) pigeon-hole; **2.** (constr.) scaffold-support, putlog; putlog-hole.

bouline [bulin] *s.f.* (naut.) bowline.

boulingrin [bulɛ̃grɛ̃] *s.m.* bowling-green.

boulon [bulɔ̃] *s.m.* (techn.) bolt.

boulonner [bulɔne] *v.t.* (techn.) to bolt; ~ *v.i.* (fam.) to work.

boulot, -te [bulo] *adj., s.m.f.* dumpy, stumpy, plump, (person); ~ *s.m.* **1.** (pop.) food; **2.** (fam.) work, job.

boulotter [bulɔte] *v.i.* **1.** (obs.) to jog along; **2.** (fam.) to eat.

boum [bum] *interj.* bang!

boumer [bume] *v.i.* (pop.) to go like a bomb, to be going fine.

bouquet[1] [bukɛ] *s.m.* cluster, clump; bunch, posy, bouquet; (fireworks) gerbe; (of wine) bouquet; (fam.) *c'est le* ~, it's the last straw.

bouquet[2] [bukɛ] *s.m.* **1.** buck-rabbit; **2.** prawn.

bouquetière [buktjɛr] *s.f.* flower-seller.

bouquetin [buktɛ̃] *s.m.* ibex.

bouquin[1] [bukɛ̃] *s.m.* **1.** (obs.) old he-goat; **2.** buck-rabbit, buck-hare.

bouquin[2] [bukɛ̃] *s.m.* old book, book of antiquarian interest; (fam.) book.

bouquiner [bukine] *v.i.* to look for rare books, to collect books; (fam.) to read.

bouquinerie [bukinri] *s.f.* trade in rare or second-hand books.

bouquineu-r, -se [bukinœr] *s.m.f.* collector of rare or second-hand books.

bouquiniste [bukinist] *s.m.f.* dealer in second-hand books.

bourbe [burb] *s.f.* mire, sludge, mud.

bourbeu-x, -se [burbø] *adj.* miry, muddy.
bourbier [burbje] *s.m.* slough, mire; (fig.) quagmire, mess.
bourbillon [burbijɔ̃] *s.m.* (med.) core of boil or abscess.
bourdaine [burdɛn] *s.f.* (bot.) buckthorn.
bourde [burd] *s.f.* **1.** trick, hoax, deception; **2.** blunder, clanger, howler.
bourdon[1] [burdɔ̃] *s.m.* pilgrim's staff.
bourdon[2] [burdɔ̃] *s.m.* **1.** bumble-bee, humble--bee; *faux* ~, drone; (fig., pop.) *avoir le* ~, to be down in the dumps; **2.** (mus.) drone (of bagpipes); bass; bourdon (of organ); **3.** (print.) omission, 'out'.
bourdonnement [burdɔnmɑ̃] *s.m.* humming, buzzing, buzz; (med.) ~ *d'oreilles*, singing in the ears.
bourdonner [burdɔne] *v.i.* to buzz, to hum, to drone; (of ears) to sing.
bourg [bur] *s.m.* market-town.
bourgade [burgad] *s.f.* straggling village.
bourgeois, -e [burʒwa] *s.m.f.* (hist.) burgher; middle-class man or woman; (pop.) *ma* ~*e*, my wife; *adj.* middle-class; (pej.) bourgeois, narrow-minded, vulgar; *petit* ~, lower middle--class; *en* ~, in mufti, in civilian clothes; **~ement** [burʒwazmɑ̃] *adv.* in a comfortable or homely way, unostentatiously; for family or private use; *occuper* ~*ement*, to occupy (rented property) as a private tenant.
bourgeoisie [burʒwazi] *s.f.* middle class.
bourgeon [burʒɔ̃] *s.m.* bud, shoot; (obs.) pimple; ~ *gustatif*, taste-bud.
bourgeonnement [burʒɔnmɑ̃] *s.m.* budding, shooting; breaking out into pimples.
bourgeonner [burʒɔne] *v.i.* **1.** to bud, to shoot; **2.** to come out in pimples.
bourgeron [burʒərɔ̃] *s.m.* (obs.) smock.
bourgmestre [burgmɛstr] *s.m.* burgomaster.
Bourgogne [burgɔɲ] *s.f.* (geog.) Burgundy.
bourgogne [burgɔɲ] *s.m.* Burgundy (wine).
bourguignon, -ne [burgiɲɔ̃] *adj.*, *s.m.f.* Burgundian.
bourlinguer [burlɛ̃ge] *v.i.* (naut.) to be making heavy weather; (fam.) to be always on the move.
bourlingueu-r, -se [burlɛ̃gœr] *s.m.f.* (fam.) globe-trotter, inveterate traveller.
bourrache [buraʃ] *s.f.* (bot.) borage; infusion of borage.
bourrade [burad] *s.f.* shove, nudge, push, dig.
bourrage [buraʒ] *s.m.* stuffing, filling; ~ *de crâne*, brain-washing, cramming.
bourrant, -e [burɑ̃] *adj.* (of food) filling.
bourras [burɑ] *s.m.* (obs.) burlap.
bourrasque [burask] *s.f.* squall, gust.
bourrati-f, -ve [buratif] *adj.* (of food) filling.
bourre[1] [bur] *s.f.* filling, stuffing, hair, flock, bur, floss, padding, plug, wad; (bot.) down, hairs; (pop.) *de première* ~, excellent, first class; (pop.) *à la* ~, late.
bourre[2] [bur] *s.m.* (slang) policeman.
bourreau (pl. **-x**) [buro] *s.m.* executioner, hang-man, headsman; (fig.) tormentor, brute, slave--driver; ~ *des cœurs*, Don Juan; ~ *de travail*, glutton for work.
bourrée [bure] *s.f.* **1.** brushwood; **2.** (danc., mus.) bourrée.
bourrèlement [burɛlmɑ̃] *s.m.* racking pain; (fig.) torment.
bourreler [burle] *v.t.* to rack, to torment, (rare exc. in phr.) *bourrelé de remords*, conscience--stricken.
bourrelet [burlɛ] *s.m.* **1.** (ring-shaped) cushion or pad; roll or fold (of fat); roll (of hair); **2.** draught-excluder.
bourrelier [burəlje] *s.m.* harness-maker.
bourrer [bure] *v.t.* to stuff, to pad, to wad, to cram, to fill full; to cram with food; ~ *le crâne de qn.*, to have s.o. on, to kid s.o., to brainwash s.o.; to cram s.o. (e.g. a pupil); ~ *qn. de coups*, to give s.o. a hiding; (fam.) *se faire* ~ *la gueule*, to take a hiding.
bourrette [burɛt] *s.f.* floss.
bourriche [buriʃ] *s.f.* oblong creel.
bourrichon [buriʃɔ̃] *s.m.* (fam.) head; *se monter le* ~, to work oneself up, to wind oneself up (to do sth.).
bourricot, bourriquot [buriko] *s.m.* foal (of ass); small ass.
bourrique [burik] *s.f.* **1.** she-ass; **2.** (fig., fam.) ass, blockhead; **3.** (pop.) (obs.) policeman; police informer.
bourriquet [burikɛ] *s.m.* **1.** small ass; **2.** (mech.) windlass, winch.
bourru, -e [bury] *adj.* rough; (of wine) young; (fig.) boorish, churlish, surly.
bourse[1] [burs] *s.f.* purse, bag, pouch; scholar-ship, bursary, grant; (anat.) bursa; (pl.) scrotum; *sans* ~ *délier*, without spending any money; *tenir les cordons de la* ~, to hold the purse--strings.
bourse[2] [burs] *s.f.* Stock Exchange, (commodity) exchange; share dealings, speculation; share values; ~ (*de valeurs*), money-market.
bourse-à-pasteur [bursapastœr] *s.f.* (pl. *bourses-à-pasteur*) (bot.) shepherd's purse.
boursicotage [bursikɔtaʒ] *s.m.* dabbling on the Stock Exchange.
boursicoter [bursikɔte] *v.i.* to dabble on the Stock Exchange.
boursicoti-er, -ère [bursikɔtje], **boursicoteu-r, -se** [bursikɔtœr] *s.m.f.* dabbler on the Stock Exchange.
boursi-er[1], **-ère** [bursje] *s.m.f.* scholar, ex-hibitioner, holder of scholarship.
boursi-er[2], **-ère** [bursje] *adj.* Stock Exchange; *s.m.f.* stockbroker, stock-jobber, member of Stock Exchange.
boursouflage [bursuflaʒ], **boursouflement** bursufləmɑ̃] *s.m.* swelling; (fig.) bombast.
boursouflé, -e [bursufle] *adj.* swollen, bloated; (fig.) bombastic, inflated.
boursoufler [bursufle] *v.t.* to cause to swell, to bloat, to puff out.
boursouflure [bursuflyr] *s.f.* swelling, puffiness, bloatedness; (fig.) bombast.
bousculade [buskylad] *s.f.* hustling, jostling; crush (of people).
bousculer [buskyle] *v.t.* to upset, to turn upside down; to jostle, to hustle; to hurry.
bouse [buz] *s.f.* cow-dung.
bouseux [buzø] *s.m.* (fam.) clodhopper, yokel, peasant.
bousier [buzje] *s.m.* dung-beetle.
bousillage [buzijaʒ] *s.m.* (build.) adobe, cob; (fig., fam.) botched work.
bousiller [buzije] *v.t.* **1.** to build with cob; **2.** to botch (work); (fam.) to ruin; (fig., pop.) to do for, to kill.
bousilleu-r, -se [buzijœr] *s.m.f.* botcher.
bousin[1] [buzɛ̃] *s.m.* (techn.) dirt or earth on surface of quarried stone.
bousin[2] [buzɛ̃] *s.m.* **1.** (obs.) = BOUGE; **2.** (fam.) row, uproar.
boussole [busɔl] *s.f.* compass; *perdre la* ~, (fig., fam.) to take leave of one's senses, to have lost one's bearings.
boustifaille [bustifɑj] *s.f.* (pop.) food.
bout [bu] *s.m.* **1.** end, extremity, tip; small piece, fragment, remaining or incomplete portion, fag-end; (fig.) *avoir du mal à joindre les deux* ~*s*, to find it hard to make ends meet; *brûler la chandelle par les deux* ~*s*, to burn the candle at both ends; *on ne sait par quel* ~ *le prendre*, he is not easy to deal with; *tenir le bon* ~, to be on the right track; *un* ~ *de qch.*, an odd bit of sth., sth.

small and incomplete; *faire un ~ de chemin avec qn.*, to go part of the way with s.o.; *un bon ~ de chemin*, a fair distance; **2.** end, limit, furthest point, finish, term; *au ~ du compte*, finally, when all's said and done; *d'un ~ à l'autre*, entirely, thoroughly; (fig.) *à tout ~ de champ*, at every turn, continually; *jusqu'au ~*, completely; *être au ~ de*, to be at the end of; *être à ~ de*, to run out of; *au ~ d'un moment*, after a moment; *être à ~*, to be exhausted; *venir à ~ de qn.*, to get the better of s.o.; *venir à ~ de qch.*, to solve sth., to master sth., to get round (difficulty).

boutade [butad] *s.f.* sally; whim, fancy; *par ~*, capriciously, by fits and starts.

bout-dehors [budəɔr] *s.m.* (naut.) boom.

boute-en-train [butɑ̃trɛ̃] *s.m. invar.* life and soul of the party.

boutefeu (pl. **-x**) [butfø] *s.m.* (obs.) lintstock; (fig.) firebrand, trouble-maker.

bouteille [butɛj] *s.f.* bottle, flask, phial, jar; *aimer la ~*, (fam.) to like one's tipple; *prendre de la ~*, (fig., fam.) to grow old; *c'est la ~ à l'encre*, it's as clear as mud; *~ de Leyde*, Leyden jar.

bouter [bute] *v.t.* (obs.) to chase out.

bouterolle [butrɔl] *s.f.* **1.** chape (of scabbard); **2.** ward (of lock); **3.** (techn.) rivet-set, riveting-die.

boute-selle [butsɛl] *s.m. invar.* (mil. trumpet-call) boot and saddle!; to horse!

boutique [butik] *s.f.* shop, stall, booth, stand; high-class dress shop; (fig., fam.) job, hole; (pop.) *toute la ~*, the whole business.

boutiqui-er, -ère [butikje] *s.m.f.* tradesman, tradeswoman, (also pej.) shopkeeper; *adj.* of a shopkeeper, of shopkeepers; *esprit ~er*, outlook of a small shopkeeper.

boutisse [butis] *s.f.* (constr.) header.

boutoir [butwar] *s.m.* boar's snout; (fig.) *coup de ~*, savage attack, cruel thrust.

bouton [butɔ̃] *s.m.* **1.** bud; **2.** pimple, spot; **3.** button, stud; knob, door-knob; switch; *~s de manchettes*, cuff links.

bouton-d'argent [butɔ̃darʒɑ̃] *s.m.* (pl. *~s-d'argent*) (bot.) fair maid of France.

bouton-d'or [butɔ̃dɔr] *s.m.* (pl. *~s-d'or*) (bot.) buttercup; buttercup colour.

boutonnage [butɔnaʒ] *s.m.* buttoning.

boutonner [butɔne] *v.t.* to button, to button up; **se ~** *v.refl.* to do up one's buttons; *~ v.i.* to bud, to burgeon.

boutonneu-x, -se [butɔnø] *adj.* spotty, pimply.

boutonni-er, -ère [butɔnje] *s.m.f.* button-maker.

boutonnière [butɔnjɛr] *s.f.* **1.** buttonhole; **2.** (surg.) incision; slash, gash.

bouton-pression [butɔ̃presjɔ̃] *s.m.* (pl. *~s-pression*) press-stud.

boutre [butr] *s.m.* (naut.) dhow.

bouturage [butyraʒ] *s.m.* (hort.) propagation by cuttings or slips.

bouture [butyr] *s.f.* (hort.) cutting, slip.

bouturer [butyre] *v.t.* (hort.) to propagate by cuttings or slips; *~ v.i.* (hort.) to send up suckers.

bouverie [buvri] *s.f.* byre, cow-shed.

bouvet [buvɛ] *s.m.* (techn.) grooving-plane, tonguing-plane.

bouvi-er, -ère [buvje] *s.m.f.* ox-drover, cowman, cowherd, cattleman, drover; *~er des Flandres*, breed of sheep-dog.

bouvillon [buvijɔ̃] *s.m.* steer, bullock.

bouvreuil [buvrœj] *s.m.* (ornith.) bullfinch.

bouvril [buvril] *s.m.* ox-pen (in slaughter-house).

bovarysme [bɔvarism] *s.m.* romantic self-deception, bovarism.

bovidés [bɔvide], **bovinés** [bɔvine] *s.m.pl.* (zool.) horned ruminants, Bovidae, bovines.

bovin, -e [bɔvɛ̃] *adj.* cattle, bovine; *~s s.m.pl.* cattle, bovines.

bowling [bɔliŋ] *s.m.* (sport) bowls, bowling; bowling-green.

box [bɔks] *s.m.* (pl. *boxes*) loose-box, stall; cubicle, compartment, section partitioned off.

boxe [bɔks] *s.f.* (sport) boxing.

boxer [bɔkse] *v.i.* (sport) to box; *~ v.t.* (fam.) to box (s.o.), to strike with the fist; (sport) to box against (opponent).

boxeur [bɔksœr] *s.m.* boxer.

boyard [bɔjar] *s.m.* (obs.) boyar; (fig.) nabob.

boyau (pl. **-x**) [bwajo] *s.m.* **1.** gut, bowel, intestine; inner tube (of tyre); **2.** (mil.) zig-zag trench, communication trench; (mining) narrow gallery.

boyauderie [bwajodri] *s.f.* gut-dressing, tripe-dressing.

boyaudi-er, -ère [bwajodje] *s.m.f.* tripe-dresser.

boycottage [bɔjkɔtaʒ] *s.m.* boycott.

boycotter [bɔjkɔte] *v.t.* to boycott.

boy-scout [bɔjskut] *s.m.* (obs.) scout; (fig., fam.) idealist; *de ~*, naïve, innocent.

B.P.F. [bepeɛf] abbrev. *bon pour francs* (=having equivalent cash value).

brabançon, -ne [brabɑ̃sɔ̃] *adj.*, *s.m.f.* Brabantine, Brabanter; *la Brabançonne, s.f.* the Brabançonne (Belgian national anthem).

brabant [brabɑ̃] *s.m.* (agric.) kind of metal-wheeled plough.

bracelet [braslɛ] *s.m.* bracelet, bangle; watch-strap, band, wrist-band.

bracelet-montre [braslɛmɔ̃tr] *s.m.* wrist-watch.

brachial, -e, (aux) [brakjal] *adj.* brachial.

brachycéphale [brakisefal] *adj.* brachycephalic.

braconnage [brakɔnaʒ] *s.m.* poaching.

braconner [brakɔne] *v.i.* to poach, to go poaching; (fig.) *~ sur les terres d'autrui*, to poach on someone's preserves.

braconnier [brakɔnje] *s.m.* poacher.

bractéal, -e, (aux) [brakteal] *adj.* (bot.) bracteal.

bractée [brakte] *s.f.* (bot.) bract.

brader [brade] *v.t.* to sell off as jumble; to flog, to give away.

braderie [bradri] *s.f.* jumble-sale; second-hand clothes shop.

bradycardie [bradikardi] *s.f.* (med.) bradycardia.

bradype [bradip] *s.m.* (zool.) bradypod.

braguette [bragɛt] *s.f.* flies (of trousers).

brahman-e [braman] *s.m.* Brahmin; **~ique** [bramanik] *adj.* Brahminical; **~isme** [bramanism] *s.m.* Brahminism.

brai [brɛ] *s.m.* pitch, tar.

braillard, -e [brɑjar], **brailleur, -se** [brɑjœr] *adj.*, *s.m.f.* (fam.) loud-mouthed (person).

braille [brɑj] *s.m.* Braille.

braillement [brɑjmɑ̃] *s.m.* deafening shout; bawling.

brailler [brɑje] *v.i.* to shout, to bawl, to howl; *~ v.t.* to bawl, to shout.

braiment [brɛmɑ̃] *s.m.* bray, braying.

brain-trust [brɛntrœst] *s.m.* body of government advisers; think-tank.

braire [brɛr] *v.i.* to bray; (fam.) to bawl.

braise [brɛz] *s.f.* **1.** embers; (fig.) *des yeux de ~*, fiery or glowing eyes; **2.** (pop.) brass, cash.

braiser [breze] *v.t.* (cook.) to braise.

braisière [brɛzjɛr] *s.f.* braising-pan.

bramement [brɑmmɑ̃] *s.m.* (of deer) belling; (fig.) howling.

bramer [brɑme] *v.i.* (of deer) to bell; (fig.) to lament; *~ après qch.*, to lament for sth.

bran [brɑ̃] *s.m.* bran; *~ de scie*, sawdust; (dial.) dung.

brancard [brɑ̃kar] *s.m.* **1.** litter, stretcher; **2.** shaft, thill.
brancardier [brɑ̃kardje] *s.m.* stretcher-bearer.
branchage [brɑ̃ʃaʒ] *s.m.* branches, boughs; (pl.) cut branches.
branche [brɑ̃ʃ] *s.f.* branch, bough; subdivision of main body or system; (fig.) branch (of learning), discipline; (arch.) rib; leg (of dividers, etc.); (fam.) *vieille* ~, old chum, my old friend.
branchement [brɑ̃ʃmɑ̃] *s.m.* extension; relief road or channel; subsidiary outlet; tapping; (electr.) lead, branch-circuit, spur.
brancher [brɑ̃ʃe] *v.i.*, **se** ~ *v.refl.* to perch; ~ *v.t.* to branch, to fork; (electr.) to plug in, to wire in, to connect up.
branchette [brɑ̃ʃɛt] *s.f.* twig.
branchial, -e, (aux) [brɑ̃ʃjal] *adj.* branchial.
branchies [brɑ̃ʃi] *s.f.pl.* gills.
branchu, -e [brɑ̃ʃy] *adj.* branchy, branching, with many branches.
brande [brɑ̃d] *s.f.* **1.** heath, heathland; **2.** impregnated faggot, fire-lighter.
Brandebourg [brɑ̃dbur] *s.m.* (geog.) Brandenburg.
brandebourg [brɑ̃dbur] *s.m.* braid, frog (on uniform).
brandiller [brɑ̃dije] *v.t.* (obs.) to swing; ~ *v.i.* to swing to and fro, to dangle.
brandir [brɑ̃dir] *v.t.* to brandish, to flourish.
brandon [brɑ̃dɔ̃] *s.m.* brand, firebrand; (fig.) ~ *de discorde*, firebrand, trouble-maker.
branlant, -e [brɑ̃lɑ̃] *adj.* tottering, shaky.
branle [brɑ̃l] *s.m.* **1.** swing, oscillation, swinging; **2.** impetus, impulse; *donner le* ~ *à une affaire*, to set sth. in motion; *se mettre en* ~, to start moving.
branle-bas [brɑ̃lbɑ] *s.m.invar.* (naut.) clearing (the decks); (fig.) confusion, upheaval.
branlement [brɑ̃lmɑ̃] *s.m.* swinging, shaking, oscillation.
branler [brɑ̃le] *v.t.* (obs.) ~ *la tête*, to nod one's head; ~ *v.i.* to shake, to totter, to be unsteady, to be loose; (fig.) to be unreliable.
braquage [brakaʒ] *s.m.* (car) turning the wheels (by steering); (slang) armed assault, hold-up; *angle de* ~, lock; *rayon de* ~, (radius of) turning circle, lock.
braque [brak] *s.m.* brach (hound); ~ *adj.* harebrained, a little mad.
braquer [brake] *v.t.* to point (gun); to aim, to focus; to fix (eyes upon); (car) to turn, to steer; (pop.) ~ *une banque*, to hold up a bank; *voiture qui braque mal*, car with a poor lock; ~ *qn. contre qch.* or *qn.*, to turn s.o. against sth. or s.o. else; *se* ~ *contre qch.*, to dig one's toes in against sth.
braquet [brakɛ] *s.m.* (bicycle) gears, gear-ratio.
bras [bra] *s.m.* **1.** arm; (fig.) hand; handle; *à bout de* ~, at arm's length; ~ *dessus*, ~ *dessous*, arm in arm; ~ *d'un levier*, arm or handle of a lever; (mech.) ~ *de levier*, leverage; (geog.) ~ *principal*, principal arm or stream (of a river); ~ *de mer*, arm of the sea, narrow strait; ~ *d'un fauteuil*, arm of a chair; *à* ~, by hand, with one's hands; operated by hand; *charrette à* ~, hand-cart; *à tour de* ~, as hard as one can go; *à* ~ *raccourcis*, violently; (fig.) *couper* ~ *et jambes à qn.*, to immobilize, to hamstring, s.o.; *les* ~ *m'en tombent*, I am taken aback; *saisir qn. à* ~*-le-corps*, to seize s.o. round the waist; **2.** arm, power; ~ *séculier*, secular authority; (fig.) ~ *de fer*, iron hand; **3.** workman, hand; (pl.) manpower; *manque de* ~, shortage of labour.
brasage [brɑzaʒ] *s.m.* brazing.
braser [brɑze] *v.t.* to braze, to solder.
brasero [brɑzero] *s.m.* brazier.
brasier [brɑzje] *s.m.* brazier, furnace, inferno; (fig.) hotbed.
brasiller [brazije] *v.i.* **1.** (of sea) to glitter; **2.** (of candle) to gutter.
brassage [brasaʒ] *s.m.* **1.** brewing; (fig.) mixing, mixture; **2.** (naut.) squaring or traversing (of yards).
brassard [brasar] *s.m.* brassard; armlet, arm-band.
brasse [bras] *s.f.* **1.** (naut.) fathom; **2.** breast-stroke; ~ *papillon*, butterfly stroke.
brassée [brase] *s.f.* armful.
brasser [brase] *v.t.* **1.** to mash, to brew; to mix, to stir up, to scatter (leaves); (fam.) to shuffle (cards); **2.** (fig.) to handle or deal with (business, etc.) in a big way; **3.** (naut.) to square or traverse (yards).
brasserie [brasri] *s.f.* brewery, brewing (industry); brasserie, restaurant.
brasseu-r, -se [brasœr] *s.m.f.* **1.** brewer; **2.** ~*r d'affaires*, one in business in a big way, financier, company promoter; **3.** (sport) breast-stroke swimmer.
brassière [brasjɛr] *s.f.* **1.** child's vest; **2.** (pl.) straps (of rucksack, etc.); ⚠ not 'brassière'.
brassin [brasɛ̃] *s.m.* (brewing) mash tun; brew.
brasure [brɑzyr] *s.f.* braze, brazing; hard solder; *souder sans* ~, to weld.
bravache [bravaʃ] *s.m.* bully, blusterer, swaggerer, swashbuckler; ~ *adj.* swashbuckling, blustering.
bravade [bravad] *s.f.* bravado, bluster.
brave [brav] *adj.* **1.** (after the noun) brave, courageous; **2.** (before the noun) good, worthy, decent; *un* ~ *homme*, a decent chap, a good sort; ~**ment** *adv.* bravely, courageously; resolutely; ~ *s.m.* brave man, hero; *mon* ~, my good fellow.
braver [brave] *v.t.* to defy; to brave, to face; to dare.
bravo[1] [bravo] *interj.* bravo!; hear, hear!; ~ *s.m.* cheer, applause.
bravo[2] [bravo] *s.m.* (hist.) bravo, hired assassin.
bravoure [bravur] *s.f.* bravery, gallantry, valour, courage; (mus., art) bravura.
brayer [breje] *s.m.* thong, strap; (mech.) sling, pulley-tackle.
break [brɛk] *s.m.* (obs.) brake, wagonette; (mod.) estate-car, station-wagon.
brebis [brəbi] *s.f.* ewe, sheep; (fig.) faithful member of the flock; (fig.) ~ *galeuse*, black sheep, undesirable element.
brèche[1] [brɛʃ] *s.f.* **1.** opening, gap, hole; breach; clearing (in forest); (fig.) dent; *monter sur la* ~, to step into the breach; (fig.) *être toujours sur la* ~, to be always on the go; *battre en* ~, to batter in, to breach; (fig.) to attack, to undermine, to discredit; **2.** notch, nick (in blade, etc.).
brèche[2] [brɛʃ] *s.f.* (geol.) breccia.
brèche-dent [brɛʃdɑ̃] *adj.* (obs.) gap-toothed.
bréchet [breʃɛ] *s.m.* (ornith.) breastbone.
bredouillant, -e [brədujɑ̃] *adj.* mumbling.
bredouillage [brədujaʒ], **bredouillement** [brədujmɑ̃] *s.m.* mumbling, jabbering, stammering.
bredouille [brəduj] *adj. revenir* ~, to come back empty-handed, with nothing achieved.
bredouiller [brəduje] *v.t.i.* to mumble, to jabber, to stammer, to mutter.
bredouilleu-r, -se [brədujœr] *adj.*, *s.m.f.* stammering, stammerer.
bref[1] [brɛf], fem. **brève** [brɛv] *adj.* short, brief; *soyez* ~, make it short; *en* ~, in short; *d'un ton* ~, in a curt tone; ~ *adv.* briefly, in a word.
bref[2] [brɛf] *s.m.* (papal) brief.
bréhaigne [breɛɲ] *adj.* barren, sterile.
brelan [brəlɑ̃] *s.m.* (cards, dice) pair-royal, three of a kind.
bréler [brele] *v.t.* to rope together, to secure with ropes.
breloque [brəlɔk] *s.f.* **1.** trinket, amulet; **2.**

(mil.) (i.) signal to dismiss; (ii.) mess-call; (fig.) *battre la* ~, to be out of order, to be shaky.
Brême [brɛm] *s.m.* (geog.) Bremen.
brème [brɛm] *s.f.* **1.** (ichth.) bream; **2.** (slang) playing-card.
Brésil [brezil] *s.m.* (geog.) Brazil.
brésil [brezil] *s.m.* Brazil wood.
brésilien, -ne [breziljɛ̃] *adj.*, *s.m.f.* Brazilian.
brésiller[1] [brezije] *v.t.* to dye with Brazil.
brésiller[2] [brezije] *v.t.i.* to pulverize, to crumble.
Bretagne [brətaɲ] *s.f.* (geog.) Brittany; *Grande-*~, Great Britain.
bretelle [brətɛl] *s.f.* strap, sling; (pl.) shoulder--straps; (pl.) braces; (rail.) switch-point; (mil.) link-work; feeder-road, link-road.
breton, -ne [brətɔ̃] *adj.*, *s.m.f.* Breton; ~ *s.m.* Breton (language).
bretonnant, -e [brətɔnɑ̃] *adj.* Breton-speaking, Breton nationalist.
brette [brɛt] *s.f.* **1.** rapier; **2.** mason's tool.
bretter [brete], **bretteler** [brɛtle] *v.t.* (techn.) to tool or tooth (masonry).
bretteur [brɛtœr] *s.m.* (obs.) swashbuckler.
breuvage [brœvaʒ] *s.m.* beverage, draught, potion, drink.
brève [brɛv] *s.f.* (lang.) short vowel, short syllable.
brevet [brəvɛ] *s.m.* certificate, diploma, warrant, (letters) patent; (fig.) guarantee; ~ *d'invention*, patent; ~ *d'apprentissage*, articles, indenture.
brevetable [brəvtabl] *adj.* patentable.
breveté, -e [brəvte] *adj.* patented; qualified, possessing diploma or certificate.
breveter [brəvte] *v.t.* to patent.
bréviaire [brevjɛr] *s.m.* breviary; (fig.) bible, model.
brévité [brevite] *s.f.* (lang.) shortness (of vowel or syllable).
bribe [brib] *s.f.* scrap, bit, crumb, morsel; (pl.) remains, crumbs, fragments, odds and ends, snatches (of conversation); ⚠ not 'bribe'.
bric-à-brac [brikabrak] *s.m.* bric-à-brac, junk; (collection of) curios; junk-shop.
(**de**) **bric et de broc** [dəbrikedbrɔk] *adv.loc.* haphazardly, at random, with odds and ends.
brick [brik] *s.m.* (naut.) brig.
bricolage [brikɔlaʒ] *s.m.* pottering, do-it--yourself; rough repair.
bricole [brikɔl] *s.f.* **1.** breastband (of harness); **2.** (anc. mil.) catapult; **3.** trifle.
bricoler [brikɔle] *v.i.* to do odd jobs, to potter about, to do it yourself; ~ *v.t.* to do a rough repair to, to patch up.
bricoleu-r, -se [brikɔlœr] *s.m.f.* handyman, odd-job man; one who does or likes to do odd jobs.
bride [brid] *s.f.* **1.** bridle, rein, reins; (fig.) *tenir en* ~, to hold in, to restrain; *tenir la* ~ *haute* or *courte*, to ride with a tight rein; (fig.) *tenir la* ~ *haute à qn.*, to keep firm control of s.o.; (fig.) *lâcher la* ~ *à*, to give free rein to; *à* ~ *abattue*, at full speed; *tourner* ~, to turn back; (fig.) to change one's mind; **2.** bonnet string; strap (of brassière, etc.); (dressm.) loop, knot; (surg.) adhesion; (mech.) union.
bridé, -e [bride] *adj.* (of eyes) slanting, slit.
brider [bride] *v.t.* to bridle, to curb; (dressm.) to fasten off; (cook.) to truss; (fig.) to restrain, to hold back.
bridge [bridʒ] *s.m.* **1.** (cards) bridge; **2.** (dentistry) bridge.
bridger [bridʒe] *v.i.* to play bridge.
bridgeu-r, -se [bridʒœr] *s.m.f.* bridge-player.
bridon [bridɔ̃] *s.m.* bridoon, snaffle.
brie [bri] *s.m.* Brie (cheese); (fig., fam.) *quart de* ~, large nose.
brièvement [brijɛvmɑ̃] *adv.* briefly, in short.
brièveté [brijɛvte] *s.f.* brevity, shortness, briefness.
brigade [brigad] *s.f.* brigade, troop; company; squad, gang (of workmen, etc.); *général de* ~, brigadier(-general).
brigadier [brigadje] *s.m.* (obs.) brigadier (-general); (mod.) corporal, bombardier, etc.; headman, foreman, police sergeant; leading--seaman.
brigand [brigɑ̃] *s.m.* brigand, ruffian, armed robber; rascal; (also jest) *petit* ~*!*, little rascal!
brigandage [brigɑ̃daʒ] *s.m.* armed robbery; serious crime.
brigantin [brigɑ̃tɛ̃] *s.m.* (naut.) brigantine.
brigantine [brigɑ̃tin] *s.f.* (naut.) spanker sail, brigantine.
brightisme [brajtism] *s.m.* (med.) Bright's disease.
brigue [brig] *s.f.* intrigue, underhand scheming; (obs.) gang of plotters, cabal.
briguer [brige] *v.t.* (obs.) to seek to obtain by intrigue; (mod.) to seek feverishly, to canvass, to solicit.
brillamment [brijamɑ̃] *adv.* brilliantly.
brillance [brijɑ̃s] *s.f.* (phys., astron.) luminosity; ⚠ not 'brilliance' in other senses.
brillant, -e [brijɑ̃] *adj.* brilliant; shining, shiny, sparkling, bright; *pas* ~, mediocre; ~ *s.m.* **1.** brilliance, lustre, shine; **2.** brilliant (diamond).
brillanter [brijɑ̃te] *v.t.* **1.** to cut a stone into a brilliant; **2.** to make brilliant; to polish (metal), to gloss (thread).
brillantine [brijɑ̃tin] *s.f.* brilliantine.
briller [brije] *v.i.* to shine, to glitter, to sparkle, to gleam, to be brilliant; (fig.) to excel, to shine, to be conspicuous; *tout ce qui brille n'est pas or*, all that glitters is not gold; (fam.) *il ne brille pas par le courage*, he's not noted for his courage; *il brillait par son absence*, he was conspicuous by his absence.
brimade [brimad] *s.f.* ragging (of new boy, etc.); nagging, bullying, persecution.
brimbaler [brɛ̃bale], **bringuebaler** [brɛ̃gbale], **brinquebaler** [brɛ̃kbale] *v.t.* to shake; *v.i.* to sway, to swing; *une vieille auto toute bringuebalante*, an old rattletrap.
brimborion [brɛ̃bɔrjɔ̃] *s.m.* (usu. pl.) baubles, trinkets, trifles.
brimer [brime] *v.t.* to bully, to rag, to harass.
brin [brɛ̃] *s.m.* shoot, sprig; blade (of grass); stick, bit; staple (of rope); *un beau* ~ *de fille*, a fine figure of a girl; *un* ~ *de*, a tiny bit of; *un* ~, *adv.loc.* a bit, a little.
brindille [brɛ̃dij] *s.f.* twig, sprig.
bringue [brɛ̃g] *s.f.* **1.** (pop.) gawky girl; **2.** (pop.) spree.
bringuebaler, brinquebaler see BRIMBALER.
brio [brijo] *s.m.* (mus.) brio; dash, spirit, go.
brioche [brijɔʃ] *s.f.* (cook.) brioche; (fam.) *il a pris de la* ~, he's put on weight, he's getting a tummy.
brique [brik] *s.f.* brick; anything in the shape of a brick; (slang) wad (of banknotes); ~ *de tourbe*, turf; (pop.) *bouffer des* ~*s*, to go hungry.
briquer [brike] *v.t.* **1.** (naut.) to holystone; **2.** to scrub, to scour.
briquet [brikɛ] *s.m.* **1.** (obs.) steel, flint; **2.** (cigarette) lighter; **3.** (zool.) beagle.
briquetage [briktaʒ] *s.m.* **1.** brickwork; simulated brickwork; **2.** briquette making.
briqueter [brikte] *v.t.* **1.** to paint simulated brickwork; **2.** to make into briquettes.
briqueterie [brikt(ə)ri] *s.f.* brickworks, brick-yard.
briquetier [briktje] *s.m.* brick-maker.
briquette [brikɛt] *s.f.* briquette.
bris [bri] *s.m.* (law) breaking; ~ *de clôture*, breaking and entering; (obs.) wreck, wreckage.

brisant, -e [brizɑ̃] *adj.* shattering; *explosif* ∼, high explosive.
brisant [brizɑ̃] *s.m.* submerged rock, reef; (pl.) breakers, waves breaking over reef.
brise [briz] *s.f.* breeze.
brisé, -e [brize] *adj.* broken, cracked; (fig.) worn out; (of door) folding; (arch.) curbed.
brise-bise [brizbiz] *s.m.invar.* casement curtain.
brisées [brize] *s.f.pl.* spoor, track; (fig.) *suivre les* ∼ *de qn.*, to follow in someone's footsteps; *marcher sur les* ∼ *de qn.*, to poach on someone's preserves.
brise-fer [brizfɛr] *s.m.invar.* (of child) holy terror; **∼-glace(s)** [brizglas] *s.m.invar.* starling (on pier of bridge), ice-fender; (naut.) ice--breaker; **∼-jet** [brizʒɛ] *s.m.invar.* anti-splash nozzle; **∼-lames** [brizlam] *s.m.invar.* breakwater.
brisement [brizmɑ̃] *s.m.* breaking.
brise-mottes [brizmɔt] *s.m.invar.* (agric.) clod--crusher, brake-harrow.
briser [brize] *v.t.* to break; to smash, to crush, to snap, to split; (fig.) to exhaust; to interrupt, to break off (conversation); *brisons-là*, let's leave it at that; ∼ *v.i.* (of sea) to break; **se** ∼ *v.refl.* to break, to be broken, to break down.
brise-tout [briztu] *s.m.invar.* bull in a china shop, clumsy person.
briseu-r, -se [brizœr] *s.m.f.* bull in a china shop, one who is always breaking things, destructive person; *∼r d'images*, iconoclast; *∼r de grève*, strike-breaker, blackleg, scab.
brise-vent [brizvɑ̃] *s.m.invar.* windbreak.
brisis [brizi] *s.m.* (constr.) lower slope of roof.
brisque [brisk] *s.f.* **1.** long-service chevron; **2.** (cards) beggar-my-neighbour.
bristol [bristɔl] *s.m.* Bristol-board; visiting--card.
brisure [brizyr] *s.f.* **1.** (herald.) brisure; **2.** crack; **3.** (techn.) break (of hinge).
britannique [britanik] *adj.* British, Britannic; *les Britanniques*, *s.m.pl.* the British.
broc [bro] *s.m.* ewer, pitcher, water-jug.
brocantage [brɔkɑ̃taʒ] *s.m.* (obs.) dealing in second-hand goods.
brocante [brɔkɑ̃t] *s.f.* dealing in second-hand goods, curios, etc.
brocanter [brɔkɑ̃te] *v.t.i.* to deal in, to sell, second-hand goods, curios, etc.
brocanteu-r, -se [brɔkɑ̃tœr] *s.m.f.* dealer in second-hand goods, curios, etc.
brocard[1] [brɔkar] *s.m.* (obs.) taunt, gibe.
brocard[2] [brɔkar] *s.m.* young roe-deer.
brocarder [brɔkarde] *v.t.* (obs. exc. Lit.) to taunt, to gibe.
brocart [brɔkar] *s.m.* brocade.
brocatelle [brɔkatɛl] *s.f.* **1.** (text.) brocatelle; **2.** (geol.) brocatel, clouded marble.
brochage [brɔʃaʒ] *s.m.* **1.** (bookb.) stitching; **2.** (text.) brocading; **3.** (mech.) drifting (of rivet-hole, etc.).
brochant, -e [brɔʃɑ̃] *adj.* (herald.) passing over; (fig.) ∼ *sur le tout*, to crown all.
broche [brɔʃ] *s.f.* **1.** (cook.) spit, skewer; **2.** pin, rod, spindle, spike, needle; (electr.) pin (of plug); **3.** brooch.
brocher [brɔʃe] *v.t.* **1.** to bind in paper-back; **2.** to brocade; **3.** to nail (horsehoe); **4.** (mech.) to ream; to drift (rivet-hole).
brochet [brɔʃɛ] *s.m.* (ichth.) pike.
brocheton [brɔʃtɔ̃] *s.m.* (ichth.) pikelet, pikeen.
brochette [brɔʃɛt] *s.f.* **1.** (cook.) skewer, kebab; **2.** breast-pin (for medal-ribbons).
brocheu-r, -se [brɔʃœr] *s.m.f.* **1.** book-stitcher; **2.** brocade weaver; **∼r** *s.m.* frame for weaving; **∼se** *s.f.* (bookb.) stitching-machine.
brochure [brɔʃyr] *s.f.* **1.** pattern of brocade; **2.** brochure, pamphlet.
brocoli [brɔkɔli] *s.m.* broccoli; cabbage-sprout.
brodequin [brɔdkɛ̃] *s.m.* **1.** (ant.) sock; (fig.) comedy; **2.** boot, half-boot; **3.** (pl.) (torture) boots, bootikin.
broder [brɔde] *v.t.* to embroider; (fig.) to embellish, to exaggerate.
broderie [brɔdri] *s.f.* embroidery, piece of embroidery; (fig.) embellishment, exaggeration, embroidering.
brodeu-r, -se [brɔdœr] *s.m.f.* embroiderer; **∼se** *s.f.* embroidering machine.
broie [brwa] *s.f.* (text.) card.
bromate [brɔmat] *s.m.* bromate.
brome [brom] *s.m.* **1.** (bot.) brome; **2.** (chem.) bromine.
bromhydrique [brɔmidrik] *adj.* (chem.) hydrobromic.
bromique [brɔmik] *adj.* (chem.) bromic.
bromure [brɔmyr] *s.m.* (chem.) bromide.
bronche [brɔ̃ʃ] *s.f.* (anat.) bronchus.
broncher [brɔ̃ʃe] *v.i.* to stumble, to trip; (obs.) to err, to do wrong; (mod.) to flinch, to falter; (fig.) *sans* ∼, without complaint; without turning a hair.
bronchiole [brɔ̃ʃjɔl] *s.f.* (anat.) bronchiole.
bronchique [brɔ̃ʃik] *adj.* bronchial.
bronchite [brɔ̃ʃit] *s.f.* bronchitis.
bronchitique [brɔ̃ʃitik] *adj.* bronchitic.
broncho-pneumonie [brɔ̃kɔpnømɔni] *s.f.* broncho-pneumonia.
bronchoscopie [brɔ̃kɔskɔpi] *s.f.* bronchoscopy.
brontosaure [brɔ̃tɔzɔr] *s.m.* brontosaurus.
bronzage [brɔ̃zaʒ] *s.m.* bronzing (of metal); (sun-)tan, tanning, acquiring sun-tan.
bronze [brɔ̃z] *s.m.* bronze; bronze colour; bronze figure on medal; (fig.) *de* ∼, unfeeling, hard.
bronzer [brɔ̃ze] *v.t.* to bronze, to colour like bronze; to tan, to sunburn; **se** ∼ *v.refl.* to sunbathe, to acquire a tan; (obs.) to become hard.
bronzeur [brɔ̃zœr] *s.m.* bronzer.
bronzier [brɔ̃zje] *s.m.* artist working in bronze, maker of bronzes; bronze founder.
broquette [brɔkɛt] *s.f.* tack (nail).
brossage [brɔsaʒ] *s.m.* brushing.
brosse [brɔs] *s.f.* brush; ∼ *à cheveux*, hairbrush; ∼ *de peintre en bâtiment*, decorator's brush, distemper brush; (*cheveux en*) ∼, crew-cut (hair).
brosser [brɔse] *v.t.* to brush, to paint; (fig.) to depict; (sport) to cut (a ball); (fam.) *se* ∼ *le ventre*, to go hungry.
brosserie [brɔsri] *s.f.* brush-making; brush trade.
brossi-er, -ère [brɔsje] *s.m.f.* brush-maker; worker in brush trade.
brou [bru] *s.m.* walnut-husk; ∼ *de noix*, walnut stain.
brouet [bruɛ] *s.m.* (obs.) thin soup, skilly; ∼ *noir*, Spartan broth.
brouette [bruɛt] *s.f.* wheelbarrow.
brouettée [bruete] *s.f.* barrow-load.
brouetter [bruete] *v.t.* to carry in a (wheel) barrow.
brouhaha [bruaa] *s.m.* (obs.) cheers, applause; (mod.) hullabaloo, hubbub, uproar.
brouillage [brujaʒ] *s.m.* **1.** (mining) fault; **2.** (radio) jamming, interference.
brouillamini [brujamini] *s.m.* (obs.) confusion, muddle.
brouillard [brujar] *s.m.* **1.** fog, mist; (fig.) confusion; (fig.) *être dans le* ∼, to be confused, to be at a loss; **2.** (comm.) day-book.
brouillasse [brujas] *s.f.* drizzle.
brouillasser [brujase] *v.i.* to drizzle.
brouille [bruj] *s.f.* misunderstanding, quarrel, disagreement, coolness.
brouiller [bruje] *v.t.* to mix, to mingle, to muddle, to confuse; to shuffle (cards); to make

indistinct, to blur; (radio) to jam; (fig.) to confuse; to cause misunderstanding (between people), to get (s.o.) into trouble (*avec*, with); *œufs brouillés*, scrambled eggs; *être brouillé avec qn.*, to be on bad terms with s.o.; **se** ~ *v.refl.* to become confused; to cloud over; to quarrel, to disagree.

brouillerie [brujri] *s.f.* tiff.

brouillon[1], **-ne** [brujɔ̃] *adj.* disorderly, bungling; *s.m.f.* muddler, bungler.

brouillon[2] [brujɔ̃] *s.m.* draft, rough draft; *cahier de* ~, rough book.

broussaille [brusɑj] *s.f.* (usu. pl.) brushwood, thicket, undergrowth, brambles, briars; *cheveux en* ~, unkempt hair; *sourcils en* ~, shaggy eyebrows.

broussailleu-x, -se [brusɑjø] *adj.* covered with bushes or scrub; unkempt, bushy, shaggy.

broussard [brusar] *s.m.* (fam.) woodsman, bushwhacker.

brousse [brus] *s.f.* bush, brush, veldt, the wild.

brout [bru] *s.m.* spring growth (of grass).

broutard [brutar] *s.m.* grass-fed calf.

broutement [brutmɑ̃] *s.m.* **1.** grazing; **2.** (mech.) jarring, jumping.

brouter [brute] *v.t.i.* **1.** to graze, to crop, to eat; to browse; **2.** (mech.) to jar, to jump, to chatter.

broutille [brutij] *s.f.* **1.** (obs.) twig; **2.** (fig.) trifle.

broyage [brwajaʒ] *s.m.* crushing, pounding, grinding.

broyer [brwaje] *v.t.* to crush, to pound, to grind; (fig.) ~ *du noir*, to be depressed.

broyeu-r, -se [brwajœr] *adj.* grinding, crushing; *s.m.f.* (person) grinder, crusher; (fig.) ~*r*, ~*se*, *du noir*, one in a state of depression; ~**r** *s.m.* grinding-machine, crusher, shredder.

bru [bry] *s.f.* (obs. exc. dial.) daughter-in-law.

bruant [bryɑ̃] *s.m.* (ornith.) bunting, yellow-hammer.

brucelles [brysɛl] *s.f.pl.* tweezers.

brucellose [bryseloz] *s.f.* brucellosis.

bruche [bryʃ] *s.m.* (ent.) bruchus, weevil.

brucine [brysin] *s.f.* (chem.) brucine.

brugnon [bryɲɔ̃] *s.m.* nectarine.

brugnonier [bryɲɔnje] *s.m.* nectarine tree.

bruine [brɥin] *s.f.* drizzle.

bruiner [brɥine] *v.i.* to drizzle.

bruir [brɥir] *v.t.* (text.) to steam.

bruire [brɥir] *v.i.* **1.** (obs.) to resound; **2.** to rustle, to rumble, to hum, to sound, to splash, to whisper, to hiss.

bruissage [brɥisaʒ] *s.m.* (text.) steaming.

bruissement [brɥismɑ̃] *s.m.* rustling, hissing, splashing, whispering, humming.

bruit [brɥi] *s.m.* **1.** noise, sound; *faire du* ~, to make a noise; (fig.) to create a sensation; *faire grand* ~ *de qch.*, to make much of sth.; *beaucoup de* ~ *pour rien*, much ado about nothing; **2.** rumour, talk, news; **3.** (radio) interference, extraneous noise.

bruitage [brɥitaʒ] *s.m.* (theatr., etc.) sound effects.

bruiteur [brɥitœr] *s.m.* (theatr., etc.) sound-effects man.

brûlage [brylaʒ] *s.m.* burning; singeing (of hair).

brûlant, -e [brylɑ̃] *adj.* burning, hot, boiling, scorching; (fig.) ardent, passionate.

brûlé, -e [bryle] *adj.* **1.** burnt, burnt-out, sunburnt, roasted; (fig.) *une tête brûlée*, a hothead; **2.** (espionage) unmasked, blown; **3.** discredited; ~ *s.m.* burning; *sentir le* ~, to smell of burning; (fig.) to look fishy; to smack of heresy.

brûle-gueule [brylgœl] *s.m.invar.* short pipe, cutty.

brûle-parfum(**s**) [brylparfœ̃] *s.m.invar.* censer.

(**à**) **brûle-pourpoint** [abrylpurpwɛ̃] *adv.loc.* (fig.) point-blank, straight out.

brûler [bryle] *v.t.* to burn, to incinerate, to cremate, to destroy by fire; to singe, to scorch, to scald; to consume (fuel, electricity); to parch; to tan; ~ *une station, un signal, un feu rouge*, to overshoot, to overrun, a station, a signal, a red light; ~ *les étapes*, to scorch, to speed; ~ *la politesse à qn.*, to leave s.o. unceremoniously; ~ *v.i.* to burn, to be on fire, to blaze; to be feverish, to be hot; (fig.) ~ *de*, to be eager to, to be consumed with; ~ *pour qn.*, to be in love with s.o.; **se** ~ *v.refl.* **1.** to incinerate oneself, to have oneself cremated; **2.** *se* ~ *la cervelle*, to blow one's brains out; **3.** to burn, to scald, oneself.

brûleu-r, -se [brylœr] *s.m.f.* (obs.) arsonist; roaster (of coffee, etc.); ~**r** *s.m.* (techn.) burner.

brûlis [bryli] *s.m.* patch of burnt land or forest.

brûloir [brylwar] *s.m.* coffee-roaster (machine).

brûlot [brylo] *s.m.* (naut. obs.) fire-ship; (fig.) *un* ~ *au flanc de*, a thorn in the side of.

brûlure [brylyr] *s.f.* burn, scald, hole made by burning; burning sensation; (hort.) frost-nip.

brumaire [brymɛr] *s.m.* (hist.) Brumaire (second month in Fr. Republican Calendar, October–November).

brumasse [brymas] *s.f.* slight mist, mizzle.

brumasser [brymase] *v.i.* to be slightly misty, to mizzle, to drizzle.

brume [brym] *s.f.* mist, haze, fog; (fig.) vague conception.

brumeu-x, -se [brymø] *adj.* misty, hazy; (fig.) vague.

brun, -e [brœ̃] *adj.* brown, dun; dark; *s.m.f.* dark man, dark woman; ~ *s.m.* brown.

brunâtre [brynɑtr] *adj.* brownish.

brune [bryn] *s.f.* (obs.) dusk, nightfall; (mod.) *à la* ~, at dusk.

brunette [brynɛt] *s.f.* brunette.

bruni [bryni] *s.m.* polished or burnished portion.

brunir [brynir] *v.t.* to brown, to darken; to burnish (metal); to tan; ~ *v.i.* to turn brown, to become tanned.

brunissage [brynisaʒ] *s.m.* burnishing.

brunisseu-r, -se [brynisœr] *s.m.f.* burnisher.

brunissoir [bryniswar] *s.m.* burnishing tool.

brunissure [brynisyr] *s.f.* burnish.

brusque [brysk] *adj.* **1.** gruff, curt, rough; **2.** sudden, short, unexpected; ~**ment** [bryskəmɑ̃] *adv.* **1.** (obs.) curtly, gruffly, rudely; **2.** suddenly, unexpectedly.

brusquer [bryske] *v.t.* **1.** (obs.) to treat roughly; **2.** to be sharp with, to pay little attention to; to hurry, to precipitate.

brusquerie [bryskəri] *s.f.* bluntness, gruffness, rudeness.

brut, -e [bryt] *adj.* **1.** (obs.) primitive; **2.** raw, natural, untreated, unrefined, unpolished; (champagne) extra dry; (fig.) hard (fact), unelaborated (idea); **3.** (comm.) gross, gross weight.

brutal, -e, (**aux**) [brytal] *adj.* **1.** (obs.) brutish, animal; (mod.) *la force* ~*e*, brute force; **2.** brutal, rough, violent, harsh; *s.m.f.* brute; ~**ement** [brytalmɑ̃] *adv.* brutally, roughly, violently; bluntly.

brutaliser [brytalize] *v.t.* to ill-treat, to manhandle.

brutalité [brytalite] *s.f.* brutality, harshness, hardness; brutal treatment, rough treatment.

brute [bryt] *s.f.* **1.** (Lit.) animal, beast; **2.** rough, uneducated person; brute, violent person.

Bruxelles [brysɛl] *s.f.* (geog.) Brussels.

bruyamment [brɥijamɑ̃] *adv.* noisily, loudly.

bruyant, -e [brɥijɑ̃] *adj.* noisy, loud; rowdy.

bruyère [bryjɛr, brɥijɛr] *s.f.* heather, heath; brier-root; brier-pipe; heath-land; (hort.) *terre de* ~, peat-compost.

bryologie [brijɔlɔʒi] *s.f.* bryology.

bryone [brijɔn] *s.f.* (bot.) bryony.
bryophytes [brijɔfit] *s.f.pl.* (bot.) Bryophyta.
bryozoaires [brijɔzɔɛr] *s.m.pl.* (zool.) Bryozoa.
B.S.G.D.G. [beɛsʒedeʒe] abbrev. *Brevet* (= patent) *sans garantie du Gouvernement.*
buanderie [bɥɑ̃dri] *s.f.* wash-house, laundry.
buandi-er, -ère [bɥɑ̃dje] *s.m.f.* launderer, laundress; bleacher.
bubale [bybal] *s.m.* (zool.) hartebeest.
bubon [bybɔ̃] *s.m.* (med.) bubo; **~ique** [bybɔnik] *adj.* bubonic.
buccal, -e, (**aux**) [bykal] *adj.* of the mouth, mouth-, oral.
buccin [byksɛ̃] *s.m.* **1.** (ant., mus.) buccina; **2.** whelk.
buccinateur [byksinatœr] *s.m.* (ant.) buccinator; ~ *adj.m.* (anat.) buccinator (muscle).
bûche [byʃ] *s.f.* log; (fig.) blockhead; ~ *de Noël*, (lit. & cook.) yule-log; (pop.) fall; *ramasser une* ~, to come a cropper.
bûcher [byʃe] *v.t.* to hew, to trim, to chop, to dress (wood or stone); (fam.) to work hard (at), to slog (at).
bûcher [byʃe] *s.m.* **1.** wood-shed; wood-pile; **2.** (funeral) pyre, stake; *brûler au* ~, to burn at the stake.
bûcheron [byʃrɔ̃] *s.m.* woodcutter.
bûchette [byʃɛt] *s.f.* stick, kindling wood.
bûcheu-r, -se [byʃœr] *s.m.f.* plodder, swot, slogger.
bucolique [bykɔlik] *adj.* bucolic, pastoral (esp. poetry); ~ *s.f.* bucolic (poem), eclogue, pastoral.
bucrane [bykran] *s.m.* (arch.) bucrane.
budget [bydʒɛ] *s.m.* budget; estimates.
budgétaire [bydʒetɛr] *adj.* budgetary, fiscal, financial.
buée [bɥe] *s.f.* steam, mist, vapour, condensation.
buffet [byfɛ] *s.m.* **1.** sideboard; buffet, refreshments, supper; ~ *de gare*, station buffet, refreshment room; ~ (*d'orgue*), organ-case; **2.** (pop.) belly.
buffle [byfl] *s.m.* buffalo; buffalo-hide; buff (-leather).
buffleterie [byflətri] *s.f.* buff-leather making; (mil.) leather equipment; harness.
bugle[1] [bygl] *s.m.* (mus.) bugle.
bugle[2] [bygl] *s.m.* (bot.) bugle.
buglosse [byglɔs] *s.f.* (bot.) bugloss.
bugrane [bygran] *s.f.* (bot.) rest-harrow, cammock.
buire [bɥir] *s.f.* (archaeol.) ewer, flagon.
buis [bɥi] *s.m.* box tree; boxwood; ~ *bénit*, palm given on Palm Sunday.
buisson [bɥisɔ̃] *s.m.* thicket; bush; (fig.) *faire* ~ *creux*, to draw a blank.
buisson-ardent [bɥisɔ̃ardɑ̃] *s.m.* (bot.) burning-bush.
buissonneu-x, -se [bɥisɔnø] *adj.* bushy; covered with bushes.
buissonni-er, -ère [bɥisɔnje] *adj.* **1.** (obs.) living in bushes; **2.** *faire l'école ~ère*, to play truant.
bulbe [bylb] *s.m.* (bot., anat.) bulb; onion-shaped dome (of church).
bulbeu-x, -se [bylbø] *adj.* bulbous; onion-shaped.
bulgare [bylgar] *adj., s.m.f.* Bulgarian; ~ *s.m.* Bulgarian (language).
Bulgarie [bylgari] *s.f.* (geog.) Bulgaria.
bullaire [byl(l)ɛr] *s.m.* **1.** bullary; **2.** copyist (of Papal bulls).
bulldozer [buldozœr] *s.m.* bulldozer.
bulle[1] [byl] *s.f.* **1.** bubble; blister; (med.) bulla; **2.** (papal) bull.
bulle[2] [byl] *s.m., adj.* manil(l)a (paper).
bulletin [byltɛ̃] *s.m.* **1.** bulletin, communiqué; (school) report; (press) report, notice; ticket, counterfoil, receipt; ~ *météorologique*, weather forecast; **2.** ballot paper; ~ *nul*, spoiled paper.
bulleu-x, -se [bylø] *adj.* (med.) moist, herpetiform, vesicular.
buna [byna, buna] *s.m.* buna (proprietary name of a synthetic rubber).
bungalow [bœ̃galo] *s.m.* bungalow.
bunker [bunkɛr] *s.m.* (mil.) bunker.
bupreste [byprɛst] *s.m.* Buprestis, golden beetle.
buraliste [byralist] *s.m.f.* tobacconist; sub-postmaster, sub-postmistress.
bure[1] [byr] *s.f.* (text.) russet; monk's habit.
bure[2] [byr] *s.m.* (mining) shaft.
bureau (pl. **-x**) [byro] *s.m.* **1.** writing-table, work-table, desk, bureau; **2.** office, study; office(s); ~ *de poste*, post office; ~ *de tabac*, (state) tobacco shop; ~ *de location*, box-office; **3.** committee, board; officers of a society; commission, sub-committee; ~ *de bienfaisance*, charity organization, relief committee, assistance board.
bureaucrat, -e [byrokrat] *s.m.f.* bureaucrat; (fam., pej.) petty official, jack-in-office; **~ie** [byrokrasi] *s.f.* bureaucracy; **~ique** [byrokratik] *adj.* bureaucratic.
burette [byrɛt] *s.f.* **1.** (eccles.) burette; **2.** cruet (for oil & vinegar); oil-can; **3.** (chem.) burette.
Burgondes [byrgɔ̃d] *s.m.pl.* (hist.) Burgundians.
burgrave [byrgrav] *s.m.* (hist.) burgrave.
burin [byrɛ̃] *s.m.* graver, chisel, cutter; **~age** [byrinaʒ] *s.m.* graving, engraving, chiselling.
buriné, -e [byrine] *adj.* engraved; (fig.) (of features) strong.
buriner [byrine] *v.t.* to grave, to engrave, to cut; to chisel.
burlesque [byrlɛsk] *adj.* burlesque, ludicrous, farcical; *le* (*genre*) ~, burlesque; ~ *s.m.* farce; **~ment** [byrlɛskəmɑ̃] *adv.* ludicrously, farcically.
burnous [byrnus] *s.m.* **1.** burnous; **2.** baby's coat with hood.
buron [byrɔ̃] *s.m.* shepherd's hut.
bus [bys] *s.m.* (fam.) bus.
busard [byzar] *s.m.* (ornith.) harrier.
busc [bysk] *s.m.* bone, steel, (in corset); sill (of lock, dam); shoulder (of rifle-butt).
buse[1] [byz] *s.f.* (ornith.) buzzard; (fig., fam.) blockhead.
buse[2] [byz] *s.f.* pipe; nozzle, tuyère; (car) choke; (mining) ~ (*d'aérage*), air-pipe, air-shaft.
business [biznɛs] *s.m.* (fam.) **1.** mess-up, how d'you do; **2.** thing, gadget.
busqué, -e [byske] *adj.* hooked, hook-.
busquer [byske] *v.t.* to fit with busks, bones, etc., to busk.
buste [byst] *s.m.* bust, head and shoulders; bosom.
bustier [bystje] *s.m.* strapless brassière.
but [by] *s.m.* butt, target; aim, object; (sport) goal, goal-posts; *de ~ en blanc*, out of the blue, point-blank.
butadiène [bytadjɛn] *s.m.* (chem.) butadiene.
butane [bytan] *s.m.* (chem.) butane.
butanier [bytanje] *s.m.* (naut.) butane-carrier.
buté, -e [byte] *adj.* obstinate.
butée [byte] *s.f.* abutment, abutment-pier; (mech.) *palier de* ~, thrust bearing.
butène [bytɛn], **butylène** [bytilɛn] *s.m.* (chem.) butene.
buter [byte] *v.i.* to stumble, (fig.) to come up, (*contre*, against); ~ *v.t.* to prop, to buttress; **se** ~ *v.refl.* to dig one's toes in; *se* ~ *à*, to knock against, to encounter.
buteur [bytœr] *s.m.* (sport) goal-kicker.
butin [bytɛ̃] *s.m.* booty, spoils; loot; profit, result (of research).
butiner [bytine] *v.t.i.* (of bee) to gather pollen; (fig.) to collect (information).

butoir [bytwar] *s.m.* **1.** scraper (for leather); **2.** buffer, (door-)stop; (rail.) buffer(-stop).
butor [bytɔr] *s.m.* (ornith.) bittern; (fig.) churl.
buttage [bytaʒ] *s.m.* (hort.) earthing-up.
butte [byt] *s.f.* **1.** butt, target; (fig.) *être en* ~ *à*, to be a target for, to be exposed to; **2.** mound, knoll, hillock, rise.
butter [byte] *v.t.* **1.** (hort.) to earth up; **2.** (pop.) to kill, to murder.
buttoir [bytwar] *s.m.* ridging plough.
butyle [bytil] *s.m.* (chem.) butyl.
butylène see BUTÈNE.
butylique [bytilik] *adj.* (chem.) butyl-.
butyrate [bytirat] *s.m.* (chem.) butyrate.
butyreu-x, -se [bytirø] *adj.* butyraceous, butyrous; butter-like.
butyrine [bytirin] *s.f.* (chem.) butyrine.
butyrique [bytirik] *adj.* butyric.
butyromètre [bytirɔmɛtr] *s.m.* butyrometer.
buvable [byvabl] *adj.* drinkable, pleasant to drink; (pharm.) to be swallowed with water.
buvard [byvar] *s.m.* writing-pad, blotting-pad; (*papier-*)~, blotting-paper.
buvée [byve] *s.f.* mash (for cattle).
buveti-er, -ère [byvtje] *s.m.f.* bar-keeper.
buvette [byvɛt] *s.f.* bar; (rail.) refreshment room; private bar; pump-room (at spa).
buveu-r, -se [byvœr] *s.m.f.* drinker; habitual drinker.
byssinose [bisinoz] *s.f.* (med.) byssinosis.
byssus [bisys] *s.m.* byssus.
Byzance [bizɑ̃s] *s.f.* (anc. geog.) Byzantium.
byzantin, -e [bizɑ̃tɛ̃] *adj.* Byzantine.

C

C, c [se] *s.m.* the letter C, c.
ça [sa] *dem.pron.* (fam. contraction of *cela*) that, this; (fam., pej.) he, she, they; *c'est* ~, that's right; *comme* ~, in that *or* this way, like that *or* this; *pas de* ~, none of that; *comme ci, comme* ~, (in answer to questions: *comment allez-vous?*, *comment ça va?*) so-so, middling; *qui* ~*?*, *où* ~*?*, who then?, where then?; *c'est toujours* ~, that's something anyhow; *avec* ~*!*, come off it!; ~ *se donne des airs*, she doesn't half put on airs; (in shop) *et avec* ~*?*, anything else?; ~ *y est*, that's it, it's happened, it's done.
çà [sa] *adv.* here; obs. exc. in expression ~ *et là*, here and there.
çà [sa] *interj.* now then!, well now!, come on, then!; ~ *partons!*, well, let's go.
cab [kab] *s.m.* (obs.) hansom (cab).
cabale [kabal] *s.f.* (Jewish theol.) cabbala, cabala; cabal; plot, intrigue.
cabaler [kabale] *v.i.* (obs.) to cabal, to intrigue, to plot.
cabaliste [kabalist] *s.m.f.* (Jewish theol.) cabbalist.
cabalistique [kabalistik] *adj.* **1.** (Jewish theol.) cabbalistic; **2.** (fig.) cabalistic, esoteric, mysterious.
caban [kabɑ̃] *s.m.* pea-jacket, pilot-jacket, reefer (jacket).
cabane [kaban] *s.f.* cabin, shed, hut; (rabbit) hutch; cocoonery (for silkworms).
cabaner [kabane] *v.t.* **1.** to house in huts; to prepare a cocoonery (for silkworms); **2.** (naut.) to capsize.
cabanon [kabanɔ̃] *s.m.* **1.** padded cell, padded room; *bon à mettre au* ~, raving mad; **2.** (in Provence) cottage; beach-hut.
cabaret [kabarɛ] *s.m.* **1.** (rare) tavern, inn, bar; **2.** night-club; **3.** cocktail or drinks cabinet, tantalus.
cabaretier [kabartje] *s.m.* (obs.) inn-keeper, publican.
cabas [kabɑ] *s.m.* chip(-basket), punnet; shopping basket.
cabasset [kabasɛ] *s.m.* (hist.) helmet (16th c.).
cabernet [kabɛrnɛ] *s.m.* cabernet grape.
cabestan [kabɛstɑ̃] *s.m.* capstan, windlass.
cabiai [kabjɛ] *s.m.* (zool.) capybara.
cabillaud [kabijo] *s.m.* fresh cod.
cabillot [kabijo] *s.m.* (naut.) cleat.
cabine [kabin] *s.f.* small room, closet; (naut., aeron.) cabin, berth; car, cage, (of lift); (signal-) box; ~ *téléphonique*, telephone-box, kiosk.
cabinet [kabinɛ] *s.m.* **1.** closet, small room; **2.** study, office; consulting-room; ~ *de lecture*, lending or reference library; **3.** (usu. pl.) lavatory, toilet; **4.** (of doctor, lawyer) practice, business; ~ *d'affaires*, business agency; **5.** (pol.) cabinet, government, ministry; staff, office, of minister; **6.** show-case, display-case, cabinet.
câblage [kɑblaʒ] *s.m.* cable-, wire-making; (electr.) wiring; telegraphing, cabling.
câble [kɑbl] *s.m.* **1.** cable, rope, line, wire, flex, cord; **2.** cable, cablegram.
câblé, -e [kɑble] *adj.* twisted, corded; (text.) spun; (arch.) cabled; ~ *s.m.* cord, sewing-cotton; ~ *six fils*, six-cord(ed) cotton.
câbleau (pl. **-x**), **câblot** [kɑblo] *s.m.* (naut.) painter.
câbler [kɑble] *v.t.* **1.** to twist or lay a cable; **2.** to cable, to send by cable.
câblerie [kɑbləri] *s.f.* cable-works; cable-making.
câblier [kɑblije] *s.m.* **1.** cable-maker; **2.** cable-laying ship.
câblogramme [kɑblɔgram] *s.m.* cablegram, cable.
cabochard, -e [kabɔʃar] *adj.*, *s.m.f.* obstinate, self-willed, pig-headed (person).
caboche [kabɔʃ] *s.f.* **1.** (fam.) head; mind, wits; **2.** hobnail.
cabochon [kabɔʃɔ̃] *s.m.* **1.** cabochon; **2.** stopper (of decanter); **3.** stud; nail with decorated head.
cabosser [kabɔse] *v.t.* to dent, to bash in.
cabot[1] [kabo] *s.m.* **1.** (ichth.) bull-head, miller's thumb; **2.** (fam.) dog; **3.** (fam. mil.) corporal.
cabot[2] [kabo] *adj.*, *s.m.* = CABOTIN.
cabotage [kabɔtaʒ] *s.m.* (naut.) coasting, coastwise trade, cabotage.
caboter [kabɔte] *v.i.* (naut.) to coast.
caboteur [kabɔtœr] *adj.* (naut.) coasting, coastwise; ~ *s.m.* coaster.
cabotin, -e [kabɔtɛ̃] *s.m.f.* (fam., pej.) third-rate actor or actress, ham; poseur, show-off; *adj.* affected, given to showing off.
cabotinage [kabɔtinaʒ] *s.m.* third-rate acting, ham-acting; affectation.
cabotiner [kabɔtine] *v.i.* (fam.) to play to the gallery; to show off.
caboulot [kabulo] *s.m.* (pop.) low dive.
cabré, -e [kɑbre] *adj.* (of horse) rearing, restive; (fig.) aggressive.
cabrer [kɑbre] *v.t.* to cause (horse) to rear; (fig.) to incite, to cause to rebel; (aeron.) to pull up,

to put the nose up; **se** ~ *v.refl.* to rear; (fig.) to rebel, to revolt, to kick against, to protest.
cabri [kabri] *s.m.* **1.** kid, young goat; **2.** (in Africa) goat.
cabriole [kabrijɔl] *s.f.* caper, capriole; somersault; *s'en tirer par une* ~, to wriggle out (of sth.).
cabrioler [kabrijɔle] *v.i.* to cut capers, to perform somersaults; to dance the capriole.
cabriolet [kabrijɔlɛ] *s.m.* **1.** cabriolet, cab; **2.** poke-bonnet.
cabus [kaby] *adj.m.* (of cabbage) with round, firm head.
caca [kaka] *s.m.* (fam. child. lang.) excrement, dirt.
cacaber [kakabe] *v.i.* (of quail or partridge) to call.
cacahouète, cacahouette [kakawɛt], **cacahuète** [kakaɥɛt] *s.f.* ground-nut, peanut.
cacao [kakao] *s.m.* cacao; cocoa.
cacaoyer [kakaɔje], **cacaotier** [kakaɔtje] *s.m.* cacao-tree, cocoa-tree.
cacaoyère [kakaɔjɛr], **cacaotière** [kakaɔtjɛr] *s.f.* cacao-plantation, cocoa-plantation.
cacarder [kakarde] *v.i.* (of goose) to cackle.
cacatoès [kakatɔɛs] *s.m.* cockatoo.
cacatois [kakatwa] *s.m.* (naut.) royal (sail).
cachalot [kaʃalo] *s.m.* cachalot, sperm whale.
cache [kaʃ] *s.f.* **1.** hide, hiding-place; **2.** (photo.) mask.
caché, -e [kaʃe] *adj.* hidden, concealed, secret; furtive, underhand; secluded.
cache-cache [kaʃkaʃ] *s.m.invar.* hide-and-seek.
cache-col [kaʃkɔl] *s.m.invar.* scarf; **~-corset** [kaʃkɔrsɛ] *s.m.invar.* under-bodice; **~-entrée** [kaʃɑ̃tre] *s.m.invar.* escutcheon (of lock).
cachemire [kaʃmir] *s.m.* (text.) cashmere.
Cachemire [kaʃmir] *s.m.* (geog.) Kashmir (Jammu and Kashmir).
cache-misère [kaʃmizɛr] *s.m.invar.* coat or wrap (covering shabbiness underneath); **~-nez** [kaʃne] *s.m.invar.* muffler; **~-pot** [kaʃpo] *s.m.invar.* flower-pot holder; **~-poussière** [kaʃpusjɛr] *s.m.invar.* dust-coat.
cacher [kaʃe] *v.t.* to hide, to conceal, to keep secret; to cover, to veil, to mask; to keep hidden, to disguise, not to show (emotions); **se** ~ *v.refl.* to hide oneself; to conceal from oneself or from each other; to be hidden or concealed; *je ne m'en cache pas*, I make no secret of it; *va te ~!*, get lost!
cache-radiateur [kaʃradjatœr] *s.m.invar.* radiator-grille (in room); **~-sexe** [kaʃsɛks] *s.m.invar.* G-string.
cachet [kaʃɛ] *s.m.* **1.** seal, stamp, signet, signet-ring; (hist.) *lettre de* ~, sealed letter from the king (usu. ordering summary imprisonment or exile); **2.** stamp, mark, seal; rubber-stamp; postmark; trade-mark; **3.** (fig.) style, distinctive character, chic; **4.** charge, fee; token, voucher; *courir le* ~, to advertise for private pupils; **5.** (med.) cachet, capsule.
cachetage [kaʃtaʒ] *s.m.* sealing.
cache-tampon [kaʃtɑ̃pɔ̃] *s.m.invar.* (nursery game) hunt the squirrel.
cacheter [kaʃte] *v.t.* to seal, to seal up; to stamp; *cire* or *pain à* ~, sealing wax; *vin cacheté*, old, vintage wine.
cachette [kaʃɛt] *s.f.* hiding-place; *en* ~, secretly, on the sly, furtively; *en ~ de qn.*, unbeknown to s.o., behind someone's back.
cachexie [kaʃɛksi] *s.f.* (med.) cachexy, cachexia.
cachot [kaʃo] *s.m.* cell, dungeon, prison; solitary confinement.
cachotterie [kaʃɔtri] *s.f.* pretence of secrecy; *faire des ~s*, to make a mystery (of sth. unimportant).
cachotti-er, -ère [kaʃɔtje] *s.m.f.* person who likes to make a mystery about trifles; *adj.* secretive, reticent, close.
cachou [kaʃu] *s.m.* catechu; cachou; ~ *adj. invar.* snuff-coloured.
cachucha [katʃutʃa] *s.f.* cachucha.
cacique [kasik] *s.m.* **1.** cacique, cazique; **2.** candidate placed first in entrance examination (for *l'École Normale Supérieure*).
cacochyme [kakɔʃim] *adj.* (obs. or jest) valetudinarian.
cacodylate [kakɔdilat] *s.m.* (chem.) cacodylate.
caco-graphe [kakɔgraf] *s.m.f.* cacographer; **~graphie** [kakɔgrafi] *s.f.* cacography, faulty spelling, bad writing; **~logie** [kakɔlɔʒi] *s.f.* cacology, incorrect writing; **~phonie** [kakɔfɔni] *s.f.* cacophony; **~phonique** [kakɔfɔnik] *adj.* cacophonous.
cactus [kaktys] *s.m.* cactus.
c.-à-d. [seade] abbrev. *c'est-à-dire*, i.e.
cadastral, -e, (aux) [kadastral] *adj.* cadastral (see CADASTRE).
cadastre [kadastr] *s.m.* official land-register; land-survey.
cadastrer [kadastre] *v.t.* to survey or register land.
cadavéreu-x, -se [kadɑverø] *adj.* cadaverous, ashen, deathly pale.
cadavérique [kadɑverik] *adj.* cadaveric.
cadavre [kadɑvr] *s.m.* corpse, dead body, carcass; (pop.) ~ (*de bouteille*), dead man (i.e. empty bottle).
caddie [kadi] *s.m.* (golf) caddie, caddy.
cade [kad] *s.m.* (bot.) savin(e).
cadeau (pl. **-x**) [kado] *s.m.* **1.** gift, present; **2.** (obs.) entertainment (given to friends).
cadenas [kadna] *s.m.* padlock; **~ser** [kadnase] *v.t.* to padlock.
cadence [kadɑ̃s] *s.f.* cadence, rhythm, time, tempo; (mus.) cadence, cadenza; *en* ~, rhythmically.
cadencé, -e [kadɑ̃se] *adj.* rhythmic(al).
cadencer [kadɑ̃se] *v.t.* to give rhythm to; to follow the rhythm, to regulate (one's step).
cadenette [kadnɛt] *s.f.* (hist.) soldier's side--plait; small plait.
cadet, -te [kadɛ] *adj.* younger, youngest; junior; inferior (in rank); *s.m.f.* junior; least item; (mil.) cadet, (sport) colt, (golf) caddie; *les ~s*, the younger members; (fig.) *c'est le ~ de mes soucis*, it's the least of my worries.
cadi [kadi] *s.m.* cadi.
Cadix [kadis] *s.f.* (geog.) Cadiz.
cadmiage [kadmjaʒ] *s.m.* cadmium-plating.
cadmie [kadmi] *s.f.* furnace-soot.
cadmium [kadmjɔm] *s.m.* (chem.) cadmium.
cadrage [kɑdraʒ] *s.m.* (photo.) centring.
cadran [kadrɑ̃] *s.m.* dial, dial-plate; face (of watch); ~ *solaire*, sundial; *faire le tour du* ~, to come back to where one started from; (fig.) to sleep the clock round.
cadrat [kadra] *s.m.* (print.) quad(rat).
cadratin [kadratɛ̃] *s.m.* (print.) em quad(rat), en quad(rat).
cadrature [kadratyr] *s.f.* train, dial-work, (of watch or clock).
cadre [kɑdr] *s.m.* **1.** frame (of picture, door, bicycle); outline, plan; **2.** crate, container; ~ *de déménagement*, removal crate; ~ *d'emballage*, container (for shipping); **3.** (radio) frame--aerial, loop-aerial; **4.** setting, surroundings; limits, scope, framework, compass; *dans le ~ de*, in the framework of, in the scope of, as part of; **5.** (mil.) *les ~s*, officers and non-commissioned officers; Army, Navy, list; **6.** (comm.) staff, cadre; **7.** (naut.) cot.
cadrer [kɑdre] *v.i.* to agree (with), to tally, to square, to fit, to conform with, to suit; *faire* ~, to square; ~ *v.t.* (cin., photo.) to centre.

cadu-c, -que [kadyk] *adj.* **1.** old, enfeebled, decrepit; outmoded, old-fashioned; (law) lapsed, null, void; **2.** (bot.) deciduous, caducous; **3.** (biol.) *membrane ~que* or *la ~que*, afterbirth.
caducée [kadyse] *s.m.* caduceus.
caducité [kadysite] *s.f.* caducity, decrepitude; lapsing.
cadurcien, -ne [kadyrsjɛ̃] *s.m.f., adj.* (native or inhabitant) of Cahors.
caecal, -e, (aux) [sekal] *adj.* caecal.
caecum [sekɔm] *s.m.* (anat.) caecum, blind gut.
caesium, césium [sezjɔm] *s.m.* (chem.) caesium.
C.A.F., caf [seɑef] abbrev. **1.** (comm.) *coût, assurances, fret*, C.I.F.; **2.** *Caisse d'Allocations familiales*.
cafard[1] [kafar] *s.m.* cockroach, black-beetle; (fig.) hump, blues; *avoir le ~*, to be down in the dumps, to be fed up.
cafard[2], **-e** [kafar] *s.m.f.* humbug, hypocrite; sneak, tell-tale, informer; *adj.* hypocritical.
cafardage [kafardaʒ] *s.m.* sneaking, tale--bearing, informing.
cafarder [kafarde] *v.i.* to sneak, to tell tales, to act as informer.
cafardeu-x, -se [kafardø] *adj.* down in the dumps, fed-up, sunk in gloom.
café [kafe] *s.m.* **1.** coffee; (pop.) *c'est fort de ~*, that's too much, that's a bit thick; **2.** coffee--house, coffee-room, café, bar; *~ adj.* coffee--coloured; **~-concert** [kafekɔ̃sɛr] *s.m.* music--hall, night-club; **~ier** [kafeje] *s.m.* coffee-bush; **~ière** [kafejɛr] *s.f.* coffee-plantation; **~ine** [kafein] *s.f.* caffeine; **~isme** [kafeism] *s.m.* caffe(in)ism.
cafetan, caftan [kaftɑ̃] *s.m.* caftan.
cafeti-er, -ère [kaftje] *s.m.f.* one who keeps a café or bar.
cafetière [kaftjɛr] *s.f.* coffee-pot.
cafouillage [kafujaʒ] *s.m.* (pop.) mess, muddle; (car) misfiring.
cafouiller [kafuje] *v.i.* (pop.) to flounder, to get in a mess; (car) to misfire.
cage [kaʒ] *s.f.* **1.** cage, coop, crate; (sport) goal; (fig.) prison; *en ~*, in prison; **2.** shell, timbering, (of house); case (of clock); casing; well, shaft, (of stairs, lift).
cageot [kaʒo] *s.m.* crate.
cagerotte [kaʒrɔt] *s.f.* cheese(-draining) basket.
cagibi [kaʒibi] *s.m.* cubby-hole, glory-hole.
cagna [kaɲa] *s.f.* (mil. slang) dug-out; hut.
cagnard, -e [kaɲar] *adj.* (obs.) idle.
cagne, khâgne [kaɲ] *s.f.* (slang) (in Fr. schools) highest form on arts side.
cagneu-x, -se [kaɲø] *adj., s.m.f.* knock-kneed (person).
cagneux [kaɲø] *s.m.* (in Fr. schools) pupil in the *cagne*.
cagnotte [kaɲɔt] *s.f.* kitty, pool.
cagot, -e [kago] *s.m.f.* bigot, hypocrite; *adj.* bigoted, hypocritical.
cagoterie [kagɔtri] *s.f.* (obs.) hypocrisy, bigotry.
cagoulard, -e [kagular] *s.m.f.* Cagoulard, French fascist.
cagoule [kagul] *s.f.* cowl, penitent's hood, balaclava helmet.
cahier [kaje] *s.m.* **1.** notebook, exercise book; **2.** (print.) sheet, section; **3.** (hist.) memorandum; (law) *~ des charges*, schedule of conditions; **4.** periodical, proceedings (of learned society).
cahin-caha [kaɛ̃kaa] *adv.* so-so, poorly, middling; precariously; limping along.
cahot [kao] *s.m.* jolt, bump.
cahotant, -e [kaɔtɑ̃] *adj.* (of road) bumpy; (of car, etc.) jolting, bone-shaking.
cahotement [kaɔtmɑ̃] *s.m.* jolting.
cahoter [kaɔte] *v.t.i.* to toss about, to jolt; to be jolted about.
cahute [kayt] *s.f.* hut, hovel, shed.
caïd [kaid] *s.m.* **1.** cadi; **2.** (pop.) gang-leader; chief.
caïeu, cayeu, (pl. **-x**) [kajø] *s.m.* (bot.) adventitious clove.
caillage [kɑjaʒ] *s.m.* curdling.
caillasse [kajas] *s.f.* **1.** (geol.) marl; **2.** (fam.) stones, road metal.
caille [kɑj] *s.f.* quail.
caillé [kɑje] *s.m.* curdled milk, curds.
caillebotis [kɑjbɔti] *s.m.* (naut.) grating; duck--boards, grid.
caillebotte [kɑjbɔt] *s.f.* curds.
caillebotter [kɑjbɔte] *v.t.* (obs.) to curdle.
caille-lait [kɑjlɛ] *s.m. invar.* (bot.) bedstraw.
caillement [kɑjmɑ̃] *s.m.* curdling.
cailler [kɑje] *v.t.* to curdle, to clot, to coagulate.
cailleter [kajte] *v.i.* (obs.) to chatter.
caillette [kajɛt] *s.f.* **1.** fourth stomach of ruminants; **2.** (obs.) flighty woman.
caillot [kajo] *s.m.* clot.
caillou (pl. **-x**) [kaju] *s.m.* flint, pebble, stone, piece of gravel; (pop.) precious stone; bald pate.
cailloutage [kajutaʒ] *s.m.* **1.** metalling (of roads); cobbles; bed of stones; **2.** jasper-ware.
caillouter [kajute] *v.t.* to metal (a road); to gravel, to cover with stones.
caillouteu-x, -se [kajutø] *adj.* stony, full of stones; pebbly, shingly.
cailloutis [kajuti] *s.m.* broken stones, gravel; road metal; shingle; (geol.) *~ glaciaire*, moraine.
caïman [kaimɑ̃] *s.m.* **1.** cayman, alligator; **2.** lecturer at *École Normale Supérieure*.
caïque [kaik] *s.f.* (naut.) caïque.
caire[1] [kɛr] *s.m.* coir, coconut fibre.
(le) Caire [ləkɛr] *s.m.* (geog.) Cairo.
cairn [kɛrn] *s.m.* cairn.
caisse [kɛs] *s.f.* **1.** box, case, packing-case, chest; *~ à eau*, water tank; **2.** case, casing, (of clock, machinery); body (of car); *~ de poulie*, block; *~ du tympan*, antrum (of ear); **3.** (mus.) drum; *grosse ~*, big drum; (lit. & fig.) *battre la grosse ~*, to beat the big drum; **4.** cash-box, till, safe; cash-desk, pay-office, cashier's office; funds, cash; fund; *livre de ~*, cash book; *~ des retraites*, pension fund; *~ d'épargne*, savings bank; *faire sa ~*, to count one's money; *tenir la ~*, to be in charge of the till; *en ~*, in hand.
caisserie [kɛsri] *s.f.* packing-case factory.
caissette [kɛsɛt] *s.f.* small box.
caissi-er, -ère [kesje] *s.m.f.* cashier.
caisson [kɛsɔ̃] *s.m.* **1.** (mil.) caisson; **2.** diving--bell; *maladie des ~s*, decompression sickness, the bends; **3.** (constr.) coffer, caisson, cavity; **4.** (pop.) *se faire sauter le ~*, to blow one's brains out.
cajeput [kaʒpy], **cajeputier** [kaʒpytje] *s.m.* (bot., pharm.) cajuput, cajeput.
cajoler [kaʒɔle] *v.t.* to cajole, to coax, to wheedle; to coddle (child).
cajolerie [kaʒɔlri] *s.f.* cajoling, wheedling, coaxing; flattery.
cajoleu-r, -se [kaʒɔlœr] *s.m.f.* wheedler, flatterer; *adj.* wheedling, coaxing, flattering.
cajou [kaʒu] *s.m.* cashew-nut.
cake [kɛk] *s.m.* fruit-cake.
cal [kal] *s.m.* callosity; callus.
calabrais, -e [kalabrɛ] *adj., s.m.f.* Calabrian.
Calabre [kalɑbr] *s.f.* (geog.) Calabria.
caladion [kaladjɔ̃], **caladium** [kaladjɔm] *s.m.* (bot.) caladium.
calage [kalaʒ] *s.m.* wedging, propping, securing, chocking up; (mech.) adjustment, setting; (car) timing; (aeron.) pitch (of propeller).
calaison [kalɛzɔ̃] *s.m.* (naut.) draught.
calambac [kalɑ̃bak], **calambour** [kalɑ̃bur] *s.m.* aloes wood, eagle-wood.
calame [kalam] *s.m.* (bot.) calamus.

calamine [kalamin] *s.f.* calamine; (car) carbon (deposit).
(se) calaminer [kalamine] *v.refl.* (car) to carbon up.
calamite[1] [kalamit] *s.f.* **1.** (min., paleont.) calamite; **2.** (obs.) liquid amber.
calamite[2] [kalamit] *s.f.* (obs.) lodestone.
calamité [kalamite] *s.f.* calamity, catastrophe, disaster.
calamiteu-x, -se [kalamitø] *adj.* calamitous, catastrophic, disastrous; pitiful, pitiable.
calandrage [kalɑ̃draʒ] *s.m.* mangling, calendering.
calandre[1] [kalɑ̃dr] *s.f.* **1.** calender, mangle, roller; **2.** (car) radiator grille.
calandre[2] [kalɑ̃dr] *s.f.* **1.** (ornith.) calandra, lark; **2.** (ent.) corn-weevil.
calandrer [kalɑ̃dre] *v.t.* to calender, to mangle.
calandreu-r, -se [kalɑ̃drœr] *s.m.f.* calenderer; **~r** *s.m.* roller (of calender).
calanque [kalɑ̃k] *s.f.* cove, creek.
calao [kalao] *s.m.* (ornith.) hornbill.
calcaire [kalkɛr] *s.m.* limestone, chalk; fur (in kettle); ~ *adj.* chalky, limy, calcareous; *eau* ~, hard water.
calcanéum [kalkaneɔm] *s.m.* (anat.) calcaneum; (fam.) heel-bone.
calcédoine [kalsedwan] *s.f.* chalcedony.
calcéolaire [kalseɔlɛr] *s.f.* (bot.) calceolaria.
calcicole [kalsikɔl] *adj.* (bot.) lime-loving.
calcification [kalsifikɑsjɔ̃] *s.f.* calcification, ossification.
calcifié, -e [kalsifje] *adj.* calcified.
calcin [kalsɛ̃] *s.m.* **1.** cullet, crushed glass; **2.** fur, lime deposit, (in boilers).
calcination [kalsinɑsjɔ̃] *s.f.* calcination.
calciner [kalsine] *v.t.* to calcine, to burn to ashes, to a cinder.
calcique [kalsik] *adj.* (chem.) calcic.
calcite [kalsit] *s.f.* (chem.) calcite, calc-spar.
calcium [kalsjɔm] *s.m.* calcium.
calcul[1] [kalkyl] *s.m.* **1.** arithmetic; calculus; *règle à* ~, slide-rule; **2.** calculation, reckoning, estimation; computation; (fig.) plan, scheme.
calcul[2] [kalkyl] *s.m.* (med.) calculus, stone.
calculable [kalkylabl] *adj.* calculable.
calculat-eur, -rice [kalkylatœr] *adj.* good at figures; calculating, shrewd; *s.m.f.* arithmetician, calculator; **~eur** *s.m.* calculator, calculating machine (using punched cards).
calculatrice [kalkylatris] *s.f.* calculating machine, calculator.
calculer [kalkyle] *v.t.i.* to calculate, to reckon, to compute; to count one's pennies; to estimate, to evaluate, to judge; to scheme, to organize, to plan; *machine à* ~, calculating machine.
calculeu-x, -se [kalkylø] *adj.* (med.) calculous.
caldeira [kaldɛra] *s.f.* (geol.) caldera.
cale[1] [kal] *s.f.* **1.** (naut.) hold; (fig.) *être à fond de* ~, to be down and out; **2.** slipway, slip-dock, ramp; ~ *sèche*, dry dock.
cale[2] [kal] *s.f.* wedge, prop, chock, block.
calé, -e [kale] *adj.* **1.** (fam., fig.) well-read, knowledgeable; *il est* ~ *en histoire*, he is good at history; **2.** difficult, tricky.
calebasse [kalbɑs] *s.f.* calabash, gourd.
calebassier [kalbɑsje] *s.m.* calabash-tree; *faux* ~, gourd-tree; ~ *du Sénégal*, baobab.
calèche [kalɛʃ] *s.f.* barouche, calash.
caleçon [kalsɔ̃] *s.m.* pants, underpants, drawers; ~ *de bain*, bathing-trunks.
Calédonie [kaledɔni] *s.f.* Caledonia; *Nouvelle* ~, New Caledonia.
calédonien, -ne [kaledɔnjɛ̃] *adj., s.m.f.* Caledonian.
caléfaction [kalefaksjɔ̃] *s.f.* calefaction.
calembour [kalɑ̃bur] *s.m.* pun.
calembredaine [kalɑ̃brədɛn] *s.f.* absurdity, nonsense.
calendes [kalɑ̃d] *s.f.pl.* calends, kalends; *renvoyer qch. aux* ~ *grecques*, to put sth. off indefinitely, till doomsday.
calendrier [kalɑ̃drije] *s.m.* calendar, almanac; diary, timetable, engagement-book.
cale-pied [kalpje] *s.m.invar.* (bicycle) toe-clip.
calepin [kalpɛ̃] *s.m.* pocket-book, note-book.
caler[1] [kale] *v.t.* (naut.) to lower (sail); ~ *v.i.* (naut.) to draw; (fig.) to yield, to give way.
caler[2] [kale] *v.t.* to wedge, to prop up, to fix, to secure, to stabilize; (techn.) to key, to force or shrink on; to stall; (fig.) *se* ~ *les joues*, to have a good feed; ~ *v.i.* to stall, to jam.
caleter, calter [kalte] *v.i.* (pop.) to hop it quick.
calfat [kalfa] *s.m.* (naut.) caulker; **~age** [kalfataʒ] *s.m.* caulking; **~er** [kalfate] *v.t.* to caulk.
calfeutrage [kalføtraʒ], **calfeutrement** [kalføtrəmɑ̃] *s.m.* sealing up of chinks, draught-proofing.
calfeutrer [kalføtre] *v.t.* to stop up, to seal up, chinks; to make weather-tight; to make draught-proof; **se** ~ *v.refl.* to shut oneself up, to make oneself snug.
calibrage [kalibraʒ] *s.m.* calibration, gauging.
calibre [kalibr] *s.m.* calibre, bore, diameter, size; gauge; (fig.) importance, stature, calibre.
calibrer [kalibre] *v.t.* to calibrate, to gauge, to grade (fruit, etc.).
calibreu-r, -se [kalibrœr] *s.m.f.* calibrating machine, calibrator.
calice [kalis] *s.m.* **1.** chalice, communion-cup; (fig.) ~ *d'amertume, de douleur*, cup of bitterness, of sorrow; *boire le* ~ *jusqu'à la lie*, to drink the cup to the dregs; **2.** (bot.) calyx; (anat.) calix.
calicot [kaliko] *s.m.* **1.** calico; **2.** (fig., obs.) shopman.
calicule [kalikyl] *s.m.* (bot.) calycle.
calier [kalje] *s.m.* (naut.) supercargo.
califat [kalifa] *s.m.* caliphate.
calife [kalif] *s.m.* caliph.
Californie [kalifɔrni] *s.f.* (geog.) California.
californien, -ne [kalifɔrnjɛ̃] *adj., s.m.f.* Californian.
californium [kalifɔrnjɔm] *s.m.* (chem.) californium.
califourchon [kalifurʃɔ̃] *adv.loc. à* ~ astride.
câlin, -e [kɑlɛ̃] *adj.* coaxing, wheedling; winning (ways, etc.); *s.m.f.* wheedler.
câliner [kɑline] *v.t.* to caress, to fondle, to coddle, to pet, to cosset; to coax.
câlinerie [kɑlinri] *s.f.* coaxing, petting, cosseting; caress, caressing.
caliorne [kaljɔrn] *s.f.* (naut.) purchase-tackle, main-tackle.
calleu-x, -se [kalø] *adj.* hardened, horny, callous; (anat.) *corps* ~*x*, corpus callosum.
call-girl [kɔlgœrl] *s.f.* call-girl.
calli-graphe [kal(l)igraf] *s.m.f.* calligrapher; **~graphie** [kal(l)igrafi] *s.f.* calligraphy, penmanship; **~graphier** [kal(l)igrafje] *v.t.i.* to write copper-plate, to engross; **~graphique** [kal(l)igrafik] *adj.* calligraphic(al).
callipyge [kal(l)ipiʒ] *adj.* callipygian, callipygous.
callosité [kalozite] *s.f.* callosity; callus.
calmant, -e [kalmɑ̃] *adj.* calming, soothing; sedative; ~ *s.m.* sedative, anodyne.
calmar [kalmar] *s.m.* (zool.) squid, calamary.
calme [kalm] *s.m.* calm, calmness, quiet, stillness, repose, composure; ~ *plat*, dead calm; *garder son* ~, to keep cool.
calme [kalm] *adj.* calm, quiet, still, smooth, composed, dispassionate; (comm.) quiet, dull, flat; **~ment** *adv.* [kalməmɑ̃] calmly.

calmer [kalme] *v.t.* to calm, to quiet, to still; to pacify, to soothe, to appease, to compose; **se ~** *v.refl.* to become calm or quiet, to calm down, to compose oneself; to be appeased, to be soothed; to abate, to lull, to subside.
calmir [kalmir] *v.i.* (naut.) to become calm.
calomel [kalɔmɛl] *s.m.* calomel.
calomnie [kalɔmni] *s.f.* calumny, slander, defamation.
calomnier [kalɔmnje] *v.t.* to slander, to defame.
calomnieu-x, -se [kalɔmnjø] *adj.* slanderous; **~sement** [kalɔmnjøzmɑ̃] *adv.* slanderously.
calomniat-eur, -rice [kalɔmnjatœr] *adj.* slanderous; *s.m.f.* slanderer.
caloporteur [kalɔpɔrtœr] *adj.m.* coolant.
calorie [kalɔri] *s.f.* calorie, calory.
calori-fère [kalɔrifɛr] *s.m.* central heating (installation); **~fication** [kalɔrifikɑsjɔ̃] *s.f.* calorification; **~fique** [kalɔrifik] *adj.* calorific; **~fuge** [kalɔrifyʒ] *adj.* non-conducting, insulating; *s.m.* non-conductor, insulator; **~fuger** [kalɔrifyʒe] *v.t.* to insulate, to lag; **~mètre** [kalɔrimɛtr] *s.m.* calorimeter; **~métrie** [kalɔrimetri] *s.f.* calorimetry; **~métrique** [kalɔrimetrik] *adj.* calorimetric.
calorique [kalɔrik] *s.m.* (obs.) caloric.
calorisation [kalɔrizɑsjɔ̃] *s.f.* (metall.) calorization, aluminium-plating.
calot[1] [kalo] *s.m.* (mil.) forage-cap.
calot[2] [kalo] *s.m.* **1.** taw (large marble); **2.** (pop.) eye; *rouler des ~s*, to goggle.
calotin [kalɔtɛ̃] *s.m.* (fam., pej.) priest; pro--clerical type.
calotte [kalɔt] *s.f.* **1.** skull-cap; (eccles.) calotte; (pej.) the clergy, priests; **2.** (fig., fam.) box on the ear; **3.** (anat.) upper portion of cranium, brain-pan; **4.** segment of sphere; (arch.) segmental arch, calotte, flattened dome; (geol.) *~ glaciaire*, ice-cap.
calotter [kalɔte] *v.t.* **1.** to box on the ears, to smack; **2.** (pop.) to steal.
calque [kalk] *s.m.* tracing; (fig.) copy, imitation; (lang.) calque; *papier-~*, tracing-paper.
calquer [kalke] *v.t.* to trace; to copy, to imitate; *~ son organisation sur*, to model one's organization on.
calter see CALETER.
calumet [kalymɛ] *s.m.* calumet, American Indian pipe.
calvados [kalvadɔs], **calva** [kalva] *s.m.* calvados.
calvaire [kalvɛr] *s.m.* Calvary; wayside cross; (fig.) martyrdom, tribulation; *le Calvaire*, Calvary.
calville [kalvil] *s.f.* Calville (apple).
calvin-isme [kalvinism] *s.m.* Calvinism; **~iste** [kalvinist] *s.m.f.* Calvinist; *adj.* Calvinist(ic).
calvitie [kalvisi] *s.f.* baldness.
camaïeu (pl. **-x**) [kamajø] *s.m.* **1.** cameo; **2.** camaïeu, monochrome painting.
camail [kamaj] *s.m.* **1.** hooded cape; **2.** (cock's) ruff.
camarade [kamarad] *s.m.f.* friend, comrade; *faire ~*, to cry 'Kamerad', to surrender.
camaraderie [kamaradri] *s.f.* comradeship, friendship, (good) fellowship.
camard, -e [kamar] *adj., s.m.f.* flat-nosed, pug--nosed (person); *la Camarde*, Death.
camarilla [kamarija] *s.f.* camarilla; cabal.
camarin [kamarɛ̃] *s.m.* (ornith.) red-throated diver.
camarine [kamarin] *s.f.* (bot.) crowberry.
cambiste [kɑ̃bist] *s.m.* cambist, exchange--broker.
cambium [kɑ̃bjɔm] *s.m.* (bot.) cambium.
Cambodge [kɑ̃bɔdʒ] *s.m.* (geog.) Cambodia.
cambodgien, -ne [kɑ̃bɔdʒɛ̃] *adj., s.m.f.* Cambodian.
cambouis [kɑ̃bwi] *s.m.* dirty grease.
cambrage [kɑ̃braʒ], **cambrement** [kɑ̃brəmɑ̃] *s.m.* shaping (of wood, cloth, leather, etc.); pressing (of clothes).
cambré, -e [kɑ̃bre] *adj.* arched, (of back) hollow, (of foot) with high instep.
cambrer [kɑ̃bre] *v.t.* to shape, to arch, to curve, to bend; **se ~** *v.refl.* to draw oneself up, to throw one's chest out.
cambrien, -ne [kɑ̃brijɛ̃] *adj., s.m.* (geol.) Cambrian.
cambriolage [kɑ̃brijɔlaʒ] *s.m.* burglary, house--breaking.
cambrioler [kɑ̃brijɔle] *v.t.* to burgle, to break into (house).
cambrioleu-r, -se [kɑ̃brijɔlœr] *s.m.f.* burglar, house-breaker.
cambrure [kɑ̃bryr] *s.f.* bend, curve; arch (of foot, etc.); warping (of wood); (fig.) affectation.
cambuse [kɑ̃byz] *s.f.* **1.** (naut.) steward's stores; **2.** (pop., pej.) doss-house, hovel.
came[1] [kam] *s.f.* (mech.) cam; *arbre à ~s*, camshaft.
came[2] [kam] *s.f.* (slang) cocaine.
camée [kame] *s.m.* cameo.
caméléon [kameleɔ̃] *s.m.* (zool.) chameleon; (fig.) turncoat, fickle person.
camélia [kamelja] *s.m.* (bot.) camellia.
camélidés [kamelide] *s.m.pl.* (zool.) camel family.
cameline [kamlin], **caméline** [kamelin] *s.f.* (bot.) gold of pleasure.
camelot[1] [kamlo] *s.m.* (text.) camlet.
camelot[2] [kamlo] *s.m.* **1.** pedlar, hawker, cheap-jack; newspaper-boy, news-vendor; **2.** *~ du roi*, young Royalist.
camelote [kamlɔt] *s.f.* **1.** trash, trashy goods, cheap goods; worthless material; **2.** (pop.) cocaine.
camembert [kamɑ̃bɛr] *s.m.* Camembert (cheese).
(se) camer [səkame] *v.refl.* (pop.) to take drugs.
caméra [kamera] *s.f.* (cin., T.V.) camera.
camérier [kamerje] *s.m.* (eccles.) chamberlain.
camériste [kamerist] *s.f.* **1.** (hist.) Lady of the Bedchamber; **2.** (fam.) chamber-maid.
camerlingue [kamɛrlɛ̃g] *s.m.* (eccles.) camerlingo.
Cameroun [kamrun] *s.m.* (geog.) Cameroon.
camisole [kamizɔl] *s.f.* (obs.) dressing-jacket; *~ de force*, strait-jacket.
camion [kamjɔ̃] *s.m.* **1.** truck, wagon, lorry; **2.** paint-kettle; **~-citerne** [kamjɔsitɛrn] *s.m.* tanker, tanker-lorry; **~nage** [kamjɔnaʒ] *s.m.* **1.** carting, carriage, road-haulage; **2.** (cost of) carriage; **~ner** [kamjɔne] *v.t.* to haul, to transport by lorry; **~nette** [kamjɔnɛt] *s.f.* van; **~neur** [kamjɔnœr] *s.m.* lorry-driver; haulier.
camomille [kamɔmij] *s.f.* (bot.) camomile.
camouflage [kamuflaʒ] *s.m.* camouflage, disguise.
camoufler [kamufle] *v.t.* to camouflage, to disguise.
camouflet [kamuflɛ] *s.m.* **1.** indignity, affront; **2.** (mil.) camouflet.
camp [kɑ̃] *s.m.* camp; (sport, pol.) side, party; *être en ~ volant*, to camp (in house, hotel, etc.); *lever le ~*, to strike camp; *ficher*, (pop.) *foutre, le ~*, to clear off; *changer de ~*, to change sides; (football) to change ends.
campagnard, -e [kɑ̃paɲar] *adj.* country, rustic, rural; *s.m.f.* countryman, countrywoman.
campagne [kɑ̃paɲ] *s.f.* **1.** country, countryside, open country, fields; *maison de ~*, or *une ~*, house in the country, country cottage; *en pleine ~*, in the open fields; *à la ~*, in the country, to the country; (fig.) *battre la ~*, to wander; **2.** (mil., pol.) campaign, expedition, operation;

(mil.) the field; *faire* ~, to make war, to fight for; (fig.) *se mettre en* ~, to set out on an expedition; *tenue de* ~, battle-dress.
campagnol [kɑ̃paɲɔl] *s.m.* (zool.) field-mouse.
campane [kɑ̃pan] *s.f.* **1.** (obs.) bell (of sheep, cow); **2.** (arch.) bell capital.
campanile [kɑ̃panil] *s.m.* campanile, bell-tower.
campanule [kɑ̃panyl] *s.f.* (bot.) campanula.
campé, -e [kɑ̃pe] *adj.* established, entrenched; *bien* ~, upstanding, sturdy; well executed.
campêche [kɑ̃pɛʃ] *s.m.* campeachy (tree).
campement [kɑ̃pmɑ̃] *s.m.* camping; camp, encampment; (fig.) camping (opp. orderly establishment).
camper [kɑ̃pe] *v.i.* to camp, to camp out, to sleep out; ~ *v.t.* to establish in a camp; to place, to plant, to lay, to fix, to thrust; (fig.) to emphasize; ~ *qn. là*, to leave s.o. standing, to leave s.o. in the lurch; **se** ~ *v.refl.* to stand upright, to plant oneself firmly; to posture, to attitudinize.
campeu-r, -se [kɑ̃pœr] *s.m.f.* camper.
camphre [kɑ̃fr] *s.m.* camphor.
camphré, -e [kɑ̃fre] *adj.* camphorated.
camphrier [kɑ̃frije] *s.m.* camphor-tree.
camping [kɑ̃piŋ] *s.m.* camping; camping-site, holiday camp; *faire du* ~, to go camping.
campos[1] [kɑ̃po] *s.m.* (fam.) break, rest (for students).
campos[2] [kɑ̃pos] *s.m.* Brazilian savannah.
campus [kɑ̃pys] *s.m.* campus.
camus, -e [kamy] *adj.* snub-nosed, flat-nosed; *face* ~*e*, pug-face.
Canada [kanada] *s.m.* (geog.) Canada.
canada [kanada] *s.f.* Canadian rennet (apple).
canadien, -ne [kanadjɛ̃] *adj.*, *s.m.f.* Canadian.
canadienne [kanadjɛn] *s.f.* **1.** Canadian canoe; **2.** sheepskin jacket, lumber-jacket.
canaille [kanɑj] *s.f.* **1.** rabble, mob, the masses; **2.** scoundrel, villain, rascal, blackguard; ~ *adj.* vulgar, coarse, low, offensive.
canaillerie [kanɑjri] *s.f.* vulgarity, coarseness; dishonesty, villainy; dishonest act, dirty trick.
canal (pl. **aux**) [kanal] *s.m.* bed, channel, arm, (of river); canal, waterway; channel (in sea); pipe, tube, duct, groove; (fig.) channel, medium, means.
canalicule [kanalikyl] *s.m.* (anat.) canaliculus.
canal-isable [kanalizabl] *adj.* that can be canalized; ~**isation** [kanalizɑsjɔ̃] *s.f.* canalization, channelling; piping, pipes; ~**iser** [kanalize] *v.t.* to canalize, to channel; to lay down pipes.
cananéen, -ne [kananeɛ̃] *s.m.f.*, *adj.* Canaanite; ~ *s.m.* Canaanite language.
canapé [kanape] *s.m.* **1.** sofa, couch, settee; ~*-lit*, bed-settee; **2.** (cocktail) canapé, savoury.
canard [kanar] *s.m.* **1.** duck; drake; (fam.) *marcher comme un* ~, to waddle; **2.** lump of sugar dipped in brandy or coffee; **3.** rumour, canard; (of newspaper) rag; **4.** discord, harsh sound.
canardeau [kanardo] *s.m* duckling.
canarder [kanarde] *v.t.* to snipe at; ~ *v.i.* **1.** (mus.) to play or sing a false note, to strike a discord; **2.** (naut.) to pitch, to bury her nose.
canardière [kanardjɛr] *s.f.* **1.** duck-pond; duck-shoot; **2.** fowling piece.
canari [kanari] *s.m.* canary; *jaune* ~, canary yellow.
(**les**) **Canaries** [lɛkanari] *s.f.pl.* (geog.) the Canaries, the Canary Islands.
canasson [kanasɔ̃] *s.m.* (pop.) nag, hack.
canasta [kanasta] *s.m.* canasta.
cancan[1] [kɑ̃kɑ̃] *s.m.* tittle-tattle, malicious gossip, scandal-mongering.
cancan[2] [kɑ̃kɑ̃] *s.m.* cancan (dance).
cancaner [kɑ̃kane] *v.i.* **1.** to talk scandal; **2.** (of duck) to quack.
cancani-er, -ère [kɑ̃kanje] *adj.* scandalmongering, gossiping; *s.m.f.* scandalmonger.
cancel [kɑ̃sɛl] *s.m.* enclosure containing the Great Seal.
cancer [kɑ̃sɛr] *s.m.* **1.** (med.) cancer; **2.** (fig.) cancer, canker; **3.** (astron.) Cancer.
cancéreu-x, -se [kɑ̃serø] *adj.* cancerous; *s.m.f.*, *adj.* (one) suffering from cancer.
cancér-igène [kɑ̃seriʒɛn] *adj.* carcinogenic; ~**isation** [kɑ̃serizɑsjɔ̃] *s.f.* canceration; ~**ologie** [kɑ̃serɔlɔʒi] *s.f.* cancerology.
canche [kɑ̃ʃ] *s.f.* (bot.) hair-grass.
cancre [kɑ̃kr] *s.m.* **1.** (obs.) pauper; **2.** dunce, duffer.
cancrelat [kɑ̃krəla] *s.m.* cockroach, black-beetle.
cancroïde [kɑ̃krɔid] *s.m.* (med.) cancroid.
candélabre [kɑ̃delɑbr] *s.m.* candelabrum; (obs.) lamp-post; (arch.) baluster (with candelabrum).
candeur [kɑ̃dœr] *s.f.* innocence, simplicity, ingenuousness, naïveté.
candi [kɑ̃di] *adj.m.* candied; *sucre* ~, sugar-candy; *fruit* ~, candied or crystallized fruit.
candidat, -e [kɑ̃dida] *s.m.f.* candidate.
candidature [kɑ̃didatyr] *s.f.* candidature; *poser sa* ~, to offer oneself as a candidate, to stand for election.
candide [kɑ̃did] *adj.* innocent, simple, ingenuous; sincere, candid; ~**ment** [kɑ̃didmɑ̃] *adv.* ingenuously; candidly.
(**se**) **candir** [kɑ̃dir] *v.refl.* to crystallize; *faire* ~, to candy.
cane [kan] *s.f.* (female) duck.
canepetière [kanpətjɛr] *s.f.* (ornith.) field-duck, little bustard.
canéphore [kanefɔr] *s.f.* (Gr. ant.) canephora.
caner [kane] *v.i.* (fam.) to shirk, to funk, to show the white feather.
caneton [kantɔ̃] *s.m.* duckling, young drake.
canette[1] [kanɛt] *s.f.* (female) duckling; teal.
canette[2], **cannette** [kanɛt] *s.f.* **1.** shuttle (of loom, of sewing machine); **2.** beer-bottle; bottle of beer.
canevas [kanva] *s.m.* **1.** (text.) canvas; **2.** (surv.) skeleton map, triangulation; **3.** (arts) sketch, plan, outline.
canezou [kanzu] *s.m.* (obs.) lace under-bodice.
cange [kɑ̃ʒ] *s.f.* (naut.) cangia.
cangue [kɑ̃g] *s.f.* (hist.) cangue, cang.
caniche [kaniʃ] *s.m.* poodle; *suivre qn. comme un* ~, to dog someone's footsteps.
caniculaire [kanikylɛr] *adj.* canicular, sultry.
canicule [kanikyl] *s.f.* dog-days, heat-wave.
canidés [kanide] *s.m.pl.* (zool.) dog family.
canif [kanif] *s.m.* pen-knife, pocket-knife; (fig., fam.) *donner un coup de* ~ *dans le contrat*, to be unfaithful to one's husband or wife.
canin, -e [kanɛ̃] *adj.* canine; *avoir une faim* ~*e*, to be ravenously hungry.
canine [kanin] *s.f.* canine-tooth, eye-tooth; (of animals) fang, tusk.
canitie [kanisi] *s.f.* (med.) canities, whiteness of hair.
caniveau (pl. **-x**) [kanivo] *s.m.* channel, gutter; kerb.
canna [kana] *s.m.* (bot.) canna.
cannage [kanaʒ] *s.m.* cane-seating (of chairs), wicker-work; cane seat or bottom, wicker-work bottom.
cannaie [kanɛ] *s.f.* cane-field; sugar-cane plantation.
canne [kan] *s.f.* **1.** stem, rod, reed, cane; ~ *à sucre*, sugar-cane; *sucre de* ~, cane sugar; **2.** walking-stick, stick, cane; rod; ~*-épée*, sword-stick; ~*-siège*, shooting-stick; *les* ~*s blanches*,

the blind; *il a l'air d'avoir avalé sa ~*, he is as stiff, straight, as a ramrod; *~ à pêche*, fishing-rod.
canné, -e [kane] *adj.* cane- or rush-bottomed.
canneberge [kanbɛrʒ] *s.f.* cranberry.
cannelé, -e [kanle] *adj.* ribbed, corded, fluted, grooved, channelled.
canneler [kanle] *v.t.* to channel, to flute, to groove.
cannelier [kanəlje] *s.m.* cinnamon (tree).
cannelle[1] [kanɛl] *s.f.* cinnamon (bark); *~ blanche*, canella bark; *pomme ~*, custard-apple.
cannelle[2] [kanɛl] *s.f.* tap, cock, spigot.
cannelloni [kanelɔni] *s.m.* cannelloni.
cannelure [kanlyr] *s.f.* (arch.) flute, fluting, channelling; (bot.) stria, ridge; (mech.) groove, thread (of screw); (geol.) fissure.
canner [kane] *v.t.* to cane(-bottom) a chair.
cannetille [kantij] *s.f.* gold or silver thread (for embroidery).
cannette see CANETTE[2].
canneu-r, -se [kanœr] *s.m.f.* chair-caner, cane-worker.
cannibale [kanibal] *s.m.f.* cannibal; (fig.) savage.
cannibalisme [kanibalism] *s.m.* cannibalism.
canoë [kanɔe] *s.m.* canoe; canoeing.
canoéiste [kanɔeist] *s.m.f.* canoeist.
canon[1] [kanɔ̃] *s.m.* **1.** cannon, gun; *tirer un coup de ~*, *tirer le ~*, to fire a gun; (fam.) *chair à ~*, cannon-fodder; **2.** barrel (of gun); (techn.) tube, cylinder, pipe (of key), nozzle (of watering-can); **3.** (16th c.) trimming for knee-breeches; **4.** (zool.) horse's shank, cannon-bone; **5.** old liquid measure, quartern; (pop.) bottle or glass of wine.
canon[2] [kanɔ̃] *s.m.* **1.** (eccles.) canon; *droit ~*, canon law; **2.** (mus.) canon.
cañon, canyon [kaɲɔ̃] *s.m.* canyon.
canonial, -e, (**aux**) [kanɔnjal] *adj.* canonical; prebendal.
canon-icat [kanɔnika] *s.m.* canonry; **~icité** [kanɔnisite] *s.f.* canonicity, canonical status; **~ique** [kanɔnik] *adj.* canonical; (fam.) *être d'âge ~ique*, to be respectable; **~isation** [kanɔnizɑsjɔ̃] *s.f.* canonization; **~iser** [kanɔnize] *v.t.* to canonize; **~iste** [kanɔnist] *s.m* canonist.
canon-nade [kanɔnad] *s.f.* cannonade, shelling; **~nage** [kanɔnaʒ] *s.m.* gunnery; shelling; **~ner** [kanɔne] *v.t.* to shell, to bombard; **~nière** [kanɔnjɛr] *s.f.* **1.** gun-boat; **2.** (obs.) loop-hole.
canope [kanɔp] *s.m.* (ant.) canopus.
canot [kano] *s.m.* (open) boat, dinghy; *grand ~*, pinnace; *petit ~*, jolly-boat; *~ automobile*, motor boat; *~ de sauvetage*, lifeboat; *~ pneumatique*, inflatable rubber dinghy; ⚠ not 'canoe'; **~age** [kanɔtaʒ] *s.m.* boating, rowing, (dinghy) sailing; **~er** [kanɔte] *v.i.* to go boating or sailing; to scull, to row; **~eur** [kanɔtœr] *s.m.* rower, oarsman; **~ier** [kanɔtje] *s.m.* **1.** oarsman; **2.** straw hat, boater.
cantal [kɑ̃tal] *s.m.* cantal (cheese).
cantaloup [kɑ̃talu] *s.m.* cantaloup melon.
cantate [kɑ̃tat] *s.f.* cantata.
cantatrice [kɑ̃tatris] *s.f.* opera-singer, prima-donna.
canter [kɑ̃tœr] *s.m.* (racing) preliminary canter.
cantharide [kɑ̃tarid] *s.f.* (ent.) cantharis, Spanish fly; (pharm.) *poudre de ~*, cantharides.
cantharidine [kɑ̃taridin] *s.f.* cantharidin.
cantilène [kɑ̃tilɛn] *s.f.* (mus., Lit.) cantilena; melancholy song, lament.
cantilever [kɑ̃tilevœr] *adj.*, *s.m.* cantilever.
cantine [kɑ̃tin] *s.f.* **1.** canteen; **2.** metal trunk; (officer's) uniform-case.
cantini-er, -ère [kɑ̃tinje] *s.m.f.* **1.** (obs.) sutler; **2.** canteen steward(ess).
cantique [kɑ̃tik] *s.m.* hymn, canticle, song; *~ des ~s*, Song of Solomon, Song of Songs.
canton [kɑ̃tɔ̃] *s.m.* canton (in Switzerland); sub-district, section, division, area (of road, railway); (herald.) canton.
cantonade [kɑ̃tɔnad] *s.f.* (theatr.) wings; *parler à la ~*, to speak to s.o. off stage; (fam.) to address the company at large.
cantonal, -e, (**aux**) [kɑ̃tɔnal] *adj.* cantonal; district.
cantonnement [kɑ̃tɔnmɑ̃] *s.m.* **1.** (mil.) cantonment, billets, quarters; **2.** division into sections; section, division; stretch (of water); **3.** (law) limitation (of rights).
cantonner [kɑ̃tɔne] *v.t.* (mil.) to canton, to billet, to quarter; (arch., herald.) to canton; **se ~** *v.refl.* to shut oneself up; (fig.) to bury oneself (*dans*, in (studies, etc.)).
cantonni-er, -ère [kɑ̃tɔnje] *s.m.* roadman; *~er, ~ère adj.* roadman's.
cantonnière [kɑ̃tɔnjɛr] *s.f.* (obs.) bed-curtain; valance.
Cantorbéry [kɑ̃tɔrberi] *s.m.* (geog.) Canterbury.
canulant, -e [kanylɑ̃] *adj.* (pop.) boring, tedious.
canular [kanylar] *s.m.* hoax, practical joke.
canule [kanyl] *s.f.* nozzle; (med.) cannula.
canuler [kanyle] *v.t.* **1.** (pop.) to bore, to plague; **2.** (pop.) to hoax, to play a trick on.
canu-t, -se [kany] *s.m.f.* silk-worker.
canyon see CAÑON.
canzone [kantsɔne] *s.f.* (mus., poet.) canzone.
caouane [kawan] *s.f.* loggerhead (turtle).
caoutchouter [kautʃute] *v.t.* to rubberize, to waterproof.
caoutchouc [kautʃu] *s.m.* rubber; rubber band; waterproof, macintosh; (pl.) rubber boots, overshoes.
caoutchouteu-x, -se [kautʃutø] *adj.* rubbery.
cap [kap] *s.m.* **1.** cape, headland, head, ness; *doubler un ~*, to round a cape; (fig.) *doubler le ~ de la quarantaine*, to turn forty; **2.** (obs.) head; *de pied en ~*, from head to foot, completely; **3.** (naut.) course; *mettre le ~ sur*, to steer for; *changer de ~*, to change course.
(**le**) **Cap** [ləkap] *s.m.* (geog.) Capetown; Cape Province; the Cape; the Cape of Good Hope.
C.A.P. [seape] abbrev. *Certificat d'aptitude professionnelle.*
capable [kapabl] *adj.* **1.** capable, able (*de*, to); likely (to); *~ de tout*, unscrupulous; **2.** qualified, fit, efficient, expert; (law) competent.
capacitaire [kapasitɛr] *s.m.f.* person qualified in (some branches of) law.
capacité [kapasite] *s.f.* **1.** capacity; (naut.) *~ de chargement*, tonnage, bulk, burden; **2.** ability, capability, competence, intellectual powers; (law) capacity, competency.
caparaçon [kaparasɔ̃] *s.m.* caparison; **~ner** [kaparasɔne] *v.t.* to caparison; (fig.) to deck.
cape [kap] *s.f.* **1.** cape, cloak; *roman de ~ et d'épée*, cloak and dagger novel; *rire sous ~*, to laugh in one's sleeve; **2.** (naut. obs.) mainsail; *être à la ~*, to lie to.
capéer, capeyer [kape(j)e] *v.i.* (naut.) to lie to.
capelage [kaplaʒ] *s.m.* (naut.) mast-head rigging.
capelan [kaplɑ̃] *s.m.* (ichth.) cap(e)lin.
capeler [kaple] *v.t.* (naut.) to hitch, to reeve.
capelet [kaplɛ] *s.m.* (vet.) capped hock.
capeline [kaplin] *s.f.* **1.** (obs.) capeline, capelline; **2.** picture hat.
C.A.P.E.S. [kapɛs] abbrev. *Certificat d'aptitude pédagogique à l'enseignement secondaire.*
capésien, -ne [kapesjɛ̃] *s.m.f.* student working for the *C.A.P.E.S.*
capétien, -ne [kapesjɛ̃] *adj.*, *s.m.f.* Capetian.

capeyer see CAPÉER.
capharnaüm [kafarnaɔm] *s.m.* glory-hole, lumber-room, dump.
capillaire [kapil(l)ɛr] *adj.* capillary, hair-like, of or for the hair; ~ *s.m.* **1.** capillary; **2.** (bot.) maidenhair fern; (med.) *sirop de* ~, capillaire.
capillarité [kapilarite] *s.f.* capillarity, capillary attraction.
capilotade [kapilɔtad] *s.f.* *en* ~, reduced to pulp, smashed to pieces; sore all over, all aches and pains.
capiston [kapistɔ̃] *s.m.* (mil. slang) captain.
capitaine [kapitɛn] *s.m.* **1.** (mil.) captain; (air force) flight lieutenant; (nav.) ~ *de corvette*, lieutenant-commander; ~ *de frégate*, commander; ~ *de vaisseau*, captain; ~ *d'armes*, master-at-arms; **2.** (merchant navy) master, skipper; ~ *de port*, harbour-master; ~ *au long cours*, master mariner, master of an ocean-going vessel; **3.** (often pej.) chief, head; leader (of band or gang).
capitainerie [kapitɛnri] *s.f.* harbour-master's office.
capital, -e, (**aux**) [kapital] *adj.* **1.** capital, main, chief, principal, fundamental; **2.** mortal, deadly, death-; *peine* ~*e*, capital punishment; *sentence* ~*e*, death-sentence.
capital (pl. **aux**) [kapital] *s.m.* **1.** main point; **2.** (fin.) capital, principal; (pl.) capital, funds, money (in circulation).
capitale [kapital] *s.f.* **1.** capital (principal town), county town; **2.** capital (letter).
capital-isable [kapitalizabl] *adj.* available for capitalization; **~isation** [kapitalizɑsjɔ̃] *s.f.* capitalization; **~iser** [kapitalize] *v.t.* to capitalize; *v.i.* to accumulate wealth; **~isme** [kapitalism] *s.m.* capitalism; **~iste** [kapitalist] *adj.*, *s.m.f.* capitalist.
capitan [kapitɑ̃] *s.m.* swashbuckler, braggadocio.
capitation [kapitɑsjɔ̃] *s.f.* (hist.) poll-tax.
capité, -e [kapite] *adj.* (bot.) capitate.
capiteu-x, -se [kapitø] *adj.* heady, inebriating.
Capitole [kapitɔl] *s.m.* Capitol (in Rome or Washington).
capitolin, -e [kapitɔlɛ̃] *adj.* Capitoline.
capiton [kapitɔ̃] *s.m.* silk-floss; quilting, tufting; (lit. & fig.) padding.
capitonnage [kapitɔnaʒ] *s.m.* quilting, padding.
capitonner [kapitɔne] *v.t.* to quilt, to pad.
capitulaire [kapitylɛr] *adj.* (eccles.) capitular; ~ *s.m.* capitulary; **~ment** [kapitylɛrmɑ̃] *adv.* capitularly, in chapter.
capitulard, -e [kapitylar] *adj.*, *s.m.f.* defeatist.
capitulation [kapitylɑsjɔ̃] *s.f.* (lit. & fig.) capitulation, surrender, cession; (pl.) (hist.) the Capitulations.
capitule [kapityl] *s.m.* (bot.) capitulum.
capituler [kapityle] *v.i.* to capitulate, to surrender, to yield, to lay down one's arms; (fig.) to give way.
capon, -ne [kapɔ̃] *adj.*, *s.m.f.* coward(ly); ⚠ not 'capon'.
caponnière [kapɔnjɛr] *s.f.* (fort.) caponier.
caporal (pl. **aux**) [kapɔral] *s.m.* **1.** corporal; (air force) leading-aircraftman; **2.** standard tobacco, caporal, shag.
capot[1] [kapo] *s.m.* (naut.) awning; (car) bonnet.
capot[2] [kapo] *s.m.* (obs.) (cards) capot; *adj. invar. être* ~, to have lost all the tricks; (fig., fam.) to be nonplussed, abashed.
capotage [kapɔtaʒ] *s.m.* (of vehicle) **1.** provision of hood; closing by means of hood; **2.** overturning.
capote [kapɔt] *s.f.* **1.** capote; (mil.) greatcoat, trench-coat; **2.** (woman's) bonnet; **3.** hood (of carriage or car); **4.** (vulg.) ~ *anglaise*, condom, French letter.
capoter [kapɔte] *v.t.* to fit (vehicle) with a hood; ~ *v.i.* (of ship or vehicle) to capsize, to overturn.
Capoue [kapu] *s.f.* (geog.) Capua.
câpre [kɑpr] *s.f.* (bot.) caper; ~ *capucine*, nasturtium seed.
capricant, -e [kaprikɑ̃] *adj.* irregular, uneven, jerky; (med.) *pouls* ~, caprizant pulse.
caprice [kapris] *s.f.* whim, fancy, caprice; passing infatuation; (of child) tantrum; (pl.) vagaries, whims; *avoir, faire, des* ~*s*, to be fickle, inconstant, to have sudden fancies, to act on impulse, to be temperamental.
capricieu-x, -se [kaprisjø] *adj.* capricious, whimsical, inconstant; unreliable, moody; irregular, inconsistent; *s.m.f.* unreliable or temperamental person; **~sement** [kaprisjøzmɑ̃] *adv.* capriciously, inconsistently, at a whim.
capricorne [kaprikɔrn] *s.m.* **1.** (astron.) Capricorn; **2.** (ent.) longicorn.
câprier [kɑprije] *s.m.* caper-bush.
caprification [kaprifikɑsjɔ̃] *s.f.* (hort.) caprification.
caprin, -e [kaprɛ̃] *adj.* (zool.) caprine.
capron, caperon [kaprɔ̃] *s.m.* (bot.) hautboy strawberry.
caprylique [kaprilik] *s.m.* (chem.) caproic acid.
capselle [kapsɛl] *s.f.* (bot.) shepherd's purse.
capsulage [kapsylaʒ] *s.m.* crown-capping, sealing (of bottles).
capsulaire [kapsylɛr] *adj.* (bot.) capsular.
capsule [kapsyl] *s.f.* **1.** capsule; (bot.) capsule, seed-case; percussion-cap; crown-cap (of bottle); (astronaut.) ~ *spatiale*, space capsule; **2.** (chem.) evaporating-dish.
capsuler [kapsyle] *v.t.* to cap or seal (bottles).
captage [kaptaʒ] *s.m.* catchment.
captateu-r, -se [kaptatœr] *s.m.f.* (law) inveigler, legacy-hunter.
captation [kaptɑsjɔ̃] *s.f.* (law) inveiglement, undue influence, captation.
captatoire [kaptatwar] *adj.* (law) inveigling.
capter [kapte] *v.t.* **1.** to obtain unfairly; to inveigle, to seduce; to attract, to win; **2.** to tap, to harness, to channel (water); **3.** (radio, electr.) to receive, to intercept.
captieu-x, -se [kapsjø] *adj.* captious, specious, insidious; **~sement** [kapsjøzmɑ̃] *adv.* speciously, insidiously.
capti-f, -ve [kaptif] *adj.*, *s.m.f.* captive, prisoner.
captivant, -e [kaptivɑ̃] *adj.* captivating, fascinating, enthralling; winning, charming.
captiver [kaptive] *v.t.* to captivate, to charm, to fascinate, to enthral; (fig.) to enslave, to subdue, to master; **se** ~ *v.refl.* to be fascinated, enthralled, (*à*, by).
captivité [kaptivite] *s.f.* captivity, bondage, imprisonment.
capture [kaptyr] *s.f.* **1.** capture, seizure, catching; **2.** prize, booty, capture.
capturer [kaptyre] *v.t.* to capture, to seize, to take by force.
capuce [kapys] *s.f.* (monk's) hood, cowl.
capuche [kapuʃ] *s.f.* (woman's) hood; detachable waterproof hood.
capuchon [kapyʃɔ̃] *s.m.* **1.** (garment) hood, cowl; **2.** cap, cover, (chimney) cowl, hood.
capuchonner [kapyʃɔne] *v.t.* to cover with a hood or cowl.
capucin, -e [kapysɛ̃] *s.m.f.* Capuchin friar or nun; ~ *s.m.* capuchin monkey.
capucinade [kapysinad] *s.f.* dull sermon; affected piety.
capucine [kapysin] *s.f.* (bot.) nasturtium.
Cap-vert [kapvɛr] *s.m.* (geog.) *les îles du* ~, Cape Verde islands.

caque [kak] *s.f.* herring-barrel; *serrés comme des harengs en* ~, packed like sardines; *la* ~ *sent toujours le hareng*, what is bred in the bone will come out in the flesh.
caquer [kake] *v.t.* to cure and pack (herrings, etc.) in barrels.
caquet [kakɛ] *s.m.* cackle (of hen); tittle-tattle, gossip, scandal; *rabattre* or *rabaisser le* ~ *à qn.*, to take s.o. down a peg, to shut s.o. up.
caquetage [kaktaʒ] *s.m.* cackling (of hen); chattering, gossiping.
caqueter [kakte] *v.i.* (of hen) to cackle; to talk scandal, to gossip, to chatter away.
car[1] [kar] *conj.* for, because, since, as; *les si et les* ~, the ifs and buts.
car[2] [kar] *s.m.* (motor) coach.
carabe [karab] *s.m.* (ent.) Carabus.
carabin [karabɛ̃] *s.m.* (fam.) medical student.
carabine [karabin] *s.f.* carbine, rifle.
carabiné, -e [karabine] *adj.* (fam.) violent, excessive, strong; *un orage* ~, a violent storm.
carabinier [karabinje] *s.m.* carabineer; (in Italy) policeman; (in Spain) frontier-guard; (fam.) *arriver comme les* ~*s*, to arrive too late.
caracal [karakal] *s.m.* (zool.) caracal.
caraco [karako] *s.m.* (dressm.) smock.
caracoler [karakɔle] *v.i.* **1.** to caracole; **2.** (fam.) to cut capers.
caractère [karaktɛr] *s.m.* **1.** character, temper, disposition, temperament, personality; *avoir (un) bon* ~, to be good-natured; *avoir (un) mauvais* ~, to be ill-natured, surly; **2.** character, characteristic, trait, individuality; **3.** character, letter, symbol, mark, sign, type; ~*s d'imprimerie*, printed letters, print, block capitals; *en gros* ~*s*, *en petits* ~*s*, in big print, in small print; **4.** title, dignity, capacity, quality; **5.** force of character, will-power; *avoir du* ~, to be strong-willed; *sans* ~, spineless; lacking originality, expressionless.
caractériel, -le [karakterjɛl] *adj.* temperamental; *un enfant* ~, a problem child; *s.m.f.* neurotic, psychopath.
caractérisation [karakterizɑsjɔ̃] *s.f.* characterization.
caractérisé, -e [karakterize] *adj.* marked.
caractériser [karakterize] *v.t.* to characterize, to distinguish; to be characteristic of.
caractéristique [karakteristik] *adj., s.f.* characteristic.
caracul [karakyl] *s.m.* caracul, karakul.
carafe [karaf] *s.f.* **1.** decanter, carafe; (fam.) *rester en* ~, to be left out of it, in the cold; (of car) *rester en* ~, to break down; **2.** (pop.) head.
carafon [karafɔ̃] *s.m.* **1.** small decanter, quarter-litre bottle; **2.** (pop.) head.
caraïbe [karaib] *s.m.f., adj.* (ethn., geog.) Carib; Caribbean; *les îles Caraïbes*, the (southern) West Indies, the Leeward and Windward Islands; *la mer des Caraïbes*, the Caribbean (sea).
carambolage [karɑ̃bɔlaʒ] *s.m.* **1.** (billiards) cannon; **2.** (car) pile-up, multiple crash.
caramboler [karɑ̃bɔle] *v.i.* **1.** (billiards) to cannon; **2.** (car) to pile up.
carambouillage [karɑ̃bujaʒ] *s.m.*, **carambouille** [karɑ̃buj] *s.f.* fraudulent conversion; selling stolen goods.
carambouilleur [karɑ̃bujœr] *s.m.* person who deals in stolen goods.
caramel [karamɛl] *s.m.* **1.** caramel, burnt sugar; **2.** (gravy) browning; **3.** caramel, toffee; ~ *adj. invar.* caramel-coloured.
caramélé, -e [karamele] *adj.* caramel-flavoured, like caramel in appearance.
caraméliser [karamelize] *v.t.* to caramelize; to sweeten or colour with caramel; to line a mould with caramel.
carapace [karapas] *s.f.* shell, carapace (of tortoise, etc.); armour (of tank, etc.); (fig.) armour, hide, thick skin.
(**se**) **carapater** [karapate] *v.refl.* (pop.) to take to one's heels.
caraque [karak] *s.f.* (naut.) carrack; *porcelaine* ~, fine Chinese porcelain.
carat [kara] *s.m.* carat.
caravane [karavan] *s.f.* caravan; party, convoy, conducted tour, group; *les chiens aboient, la* ~ *passe*, go your way, let people talk.
caravanier [karavanje] *s.m.* **1.** caravaneer; **2.** caravan-dweller, camper; *chemin* ~, caravan route.
caravansérail [karavɑ̃seraj] *s.m.* caravanserai.
caravelle [karavɛl] *s.f.* (naut. hist.) caravel; (aeron.) name of a French jet aircraft.
carbet [karbɛ] *s.m.* (in the West Indies) communal cabin; communal shed (for fishing nets, etc.).
carbogène [karbɔʒɛn] *s.m.* carbogen.
carbohémoglobine [karbɔemɔglɔbin] *s.f.* carbohaemoglobin.
carbonade see CARBONNADE.
carbonado [karbɔnado] *s.m.* (geol.) carbon diamond, black diamond.
carbonarisme [karbɔnarism] *s.m.* (pol.) carbonarism.
carbonaro [karbɔnaro] *s.m.* (pl. *carbonari*) (pol.) Carbonaro.
carbonate [karbɔnat] *s.m.* (chem.) carbonate.
carbone [karbɔn] *s.m.* **1.** (chem.) carbon; *oxyde de* ~, carbon monoxide; **2.** *papier* ~, carbon paper; ~, (fam.) carbon copy.
carbon-ifère [karbɔnifɛr] *adj., s.m.* carboniferous; **~ique** [karbɔnik] *adj.* (chem.) carbonic; *anhydride* ~*ique*, *gaz* ~*ique*, carbon dioxide; *acide* ~*ique*, carbonic acid; *neige* ~*ique*, dry ice; **~isation** [karbɔnizɑsjɔ̃] *s.f.* carbonization; **~iser** [karbɔnize] *v.t.* to carbonize, to char.
carbonnade, carbonade [karbɔnad] *s.f.* (cook.) grilling meat over charcoal; meat grilled over charcoal.
carborundum [karbɔrɔ̃dɔm] *s.m.* carborundum.
carboxylase [karbɔksilɑz] *s.f.* carboxylase.
carboxyle [karbɔksil] *s.m.* carboxyl.
carburant [karbyrɑ̃] *adj.m.* carburetted; ~ *s.m.* motor-fuel, carburant.
carburateur [karbyratœr] *s.m.* (car) carburettor.
carburation [karbyrɑsjɔ̃] *s.f.* carburation.
carbure [karbyr] *s.m.* carbide.
carburé, -e [karbyre] *adj.* carburetted.
carburéacteur [karbyreaktœr] *s.m.* (aeron.) jet-fuel.
carburer [karbyre] *v.i.* to carburize, to carburate; (pop.) to work, to go well.
carcailler [karkɑje] *v.i.* (of quail) to call.
carcajou [karkaʒu] *s.m.* (zool.) carcajou.
carcan [karkɑ̃] *s.m.* **1.** (hist.) carcan; choker (necklace or scarf); (fig.) yoke, constraint; **2.** (fam.) (horse) nag, jade.
carcasse [karkas] *s.f.* **1.** carcass, carcase, (esp. of poultry); (fam.) body, bones; **2.** framework, frame, skeleton.
carcel [karsɛl] *s.m.* carcel lamp.
carcinogène [karsinɔʒɛn] *adj.* carcinogenic.
carcinologie [karsinɔlɔʒi] *s.f.* **1.** (zool.) carcinology; **2.** = CANCÉROLOGIE.
carcinome [karsinɔm] *s.m.* (med.) carcinoma.
cardage [kardaʒ] *s.m.* (text.) carding.
cardamine [kardamin] *s.f.* (bot.) Cardamine.
cardamome [kardamɔm] *s.m.* (bot.) cardamom.
cardan [kardɑ̃] *s.m.* (mech.) cardan joint, universal joint.
carde [kard] *s.f.* **1.** (bot.) chard; **2.** (text.) card; carding-machine.
cardé, -e [karde] *adj.* (of wool) brushed, carded.

carder [karde] *v.t.* (text.) to card, to brush, to raise; (fig., fam.) ~ *le poil à qn.*, to give s.o. a hiding, to scratch s.o.
cardère [kardɛr] *s.f.* (bot.) teasel.
cardeu-r, -se [kardœr] *s.m.f.* carder; ~**se** *s.f.* carding-machine.
cardia [kardja] *s.f.* (anat.) cardia.
cardialgie [kardjalʒi] *s.f.* cardialgy.
cardiaque [kardjak] *adj.* cardiac; *crise* ~, heart attack; ~ *s.m.f.* cardiac patient, heart case.
cardigan [kardigɑ̃] *s.m.* cardigan.
cardinal (pl. **aux**) [kardinal] *s.m.* **1.** cardinal; **2.** (ornith.) cardinal-bird.
cardinal, -e, (**aux**) [kardinal] *adj.* chief, fundamental, principal, cardinal.
cardinalat [kardinala] *s.m.* cardinalate.
cardinalice [kardinalis] *adj.* of a cardinal, cardinal's.
cardio-gramme [kardjɔgram] *s.m.* cardiogram; ~**graphe** [kardjɔgraf] *s.m.* cardiograph; ~**graphie** [kardjɔgrafi] *s.f.* cardiography; ~**logie** [kardjɔlɔʒi] *s.f.* cardiology; ~**logue** [kardjɔlɔg] *s.m.f.* cardiologist; ~**pathie** [kardjɔpati] *s.f.* cardiopathy; ~**tonique** [kardjɔtɔnik] *adj.* cardiotonic; ~**-vasculaire** [kardjɔvaskylɛr] *adj.* cardiovascular.
cardite [kardit] *s.f.* carditis.
cardon [kardɔ̃] *s.m.* (bot.) cardoon.
carême [karɛm] *s.m.* **1.** Lent; *arriver comme mars en* ~, to happen as sure as fate, without fail; *arriver comme marée en* ~, to come just at the right moment, to be a godsend; **2.** fast, fasting; *faire (son)* ~, to fast, to keep Lent; *face de* ~, thin, pale face.
carême-prenant [karɛmprənɑ̃] *s.m.* **1.** Shrovetide; **2.** mummer; (fig.) s.o. wearing ridiculous or fancy dress.
carénage [karenaʒ] *s.m.* **1.** (naut.) careening, careenage; careening-beach, graving-dock; **2.** streamlining.
carence [karɑ̃s] *s.f.* **1.** deficiency; **2.** remissness, laxity, negligence, neglect.
carène [karɛn] *s.f.* **1.** (naut.) keel; careening; **2.** (bot.) carina.
caréner [karene] *v.t.* **1.** (naut.) to careen; **2.** to streamline.
carentiel, -le [karɑ̃sjɛl] *adj.* (med.) deficiency, arising from deficiency.
caressant, -e [karɛsɑ̃] *adj.* affectionate, loving; soft, gentle, tender; (fig., obs.) ingratiating.
caresse [karɛs] *s.f.* caress, kiss, stroke, pat, touch, embrace; (fig.) smile, endearment; (obs.) flattery, fawning.
caresser [karese] *v.t.* to caress, to fondle, to pat, to stroke, to pass lightly over; (fig., obs.) to flatter, to fawn on, to cajole; ~ *un projet*, to toy with an idea; ~ *des espoirs*, to nurture (vain) hopes.
caret [karɛ] *s.m.* **1.** (zool.) hawksbill turtle; its shell; **2.** (rope-maker's) reel; *fil de* ~, rope yarn.
carex [karɛks] *s.m.* (bot.) Carex.
cargaison [kargɛzɔ̃] *s.f.* cargo, shipload; (fig., fam.) load, pack, collection.
cargo [kargo] *s.m.* cargo ship, freighter; ~ *mixte*, cargo ship taking some passengers; ⚠ not 'cargo'.
cargue [karg] *s.f.* (naut.) brail.
carguer [karge] *v.t.* (naut.) to brail, to haul in.
cari, kari [kari], **curry** [kyri] *s.m.* (cook.) curry; ~ *de volaille*, curried chicken, chicken curry.
cariatide, caryatide [karjatid] *s.f.* (arch.) caryatid.
caribou [karibu] *s.m.* (zool.) caribou.
caricatural, -e, (**aux**) [karikatyral] *adj.* grotesque, ludicrous.
caricature [karikatyr] *s.f.* caricature, cartoon; (fig.) parody; (person) scarecrow, sight, fright.
caricaturer [karikatyre] *v.t.* to caricature, to parody.
caricaturiste [karikatyrist] *s.m.f.* caricaturist, cartoonist.
carie [kari] *s.f.* (of teeth, bones) caries, decay; (bot., agric.) rot; (in timber) ~ *sèche*, dry rot.
carié, -e [karje] *adj.* decayed.
carier [karje] *v.t.* to decay, to cause to decay; to rot.
carillon [karijɔ̃] *s.m.* **1.** bells, peal of bells, change-ringing; carillon; ringing of bells; **2.** (of clock) chime, striking; chimes (door-bell); *horloge à* ~, or *un* ~, striking clock.
carillonner [karijɔne] *v.t.i.* **1.** to chime, to ring the changes, to ring a peal; *fête carillonnée*, festival, feast-day; **2.** to ring (unnecessarily) loudly, to peal (at the door); **3.** to proclaim loudly, to trumpet.
carillonneur [karijɔnœr] *s.m.* bell-ringer, change-ringer.
carlin [karlɛ̃] *s.m.* pug (dog).
carline [karlin] *s.f.* carline (thistle).
carlingue [karlɛ̃g] *s.f.* **1.** (naut.) ke(e)lson; **2.** (aeron.) passenger-cabin.
carl-isme [karlism] *s.m.* (Spanish pol.) Carlism; ~**iste** [karlist] *adj.* Carlist.
carmagnole [karmaɲɔl] *s.f.* **1.** carmagnole (jacket); **2.** carmagnole (revolutionary song and dance).
carme [karm] *s.m.* Carmelite, white friar; ~ *déchaux*, barefooted Carmelite.
carmeline [karməlin] *adj.f.* *laine* ~, vicuña wool.
carmélite [karmelit] *s.f.* Carmelite nun.
carmin [karmɛ̃] *adj.invar.*, *s.m.* carmine.
carminé, -e [karmine] *adj.* carmine.
carnage [karnaʒ] *s.m.* carnage, slaughter, massacre, butchery.
carnassi-er, -ère [karnasje] *adj.* carnivorous, flesh-eating.
carnassier [karnasje] *s.m.* carnivore, flesh-eater; (pl.) Carnivora.
carnassière [karnasjɛr] *s.f.* game-bag.
carnation [karnɑsjɔ̃] *s.f.* complexion; (paint.) flesh-tint; ⚠ not 'carnation' (flower).
carnau see CARNEAU.
carnaval [karnaval] *s.m.* **1.** carnival, Shrovetide; **2.** carnival revels, festivities; **3.** King Carnival; (fig.) scarecrow, guy, fright.
carnavalesque [karnavalɛsk] *adj.* proper to a carnival; carnival-like; (fig.) grotesque.
carne [karn] *s.f.* **1.** bad meat, tough meat, cagmag; **2.** (pop.) (horse) nag, jade; (woman) slut, old cow.
carné, -e [karne] *adj.* **1.** flesh-coloured, flesh-pink; **2.** containing meat, meat-; *régime* ~, meat diet.
carneau, carnau (pl. **-x**) [karno] *s.m.* (boiler) flue.
carnèle [karnɛl] *s.f.* border, rim (of coin).
carnet [karnɛ] *s.m.* pocket-book, notebook; book (of tickets, stamps, etc.); ~ *de bal*, dance-card; ~ *de chèques*, cheque-book.
carnier [karnje] *s.m.* small game-bag.
carnification [karnifikɑsjɔ̃], **carnisation** [karnizɑsjɔ̃] *s.f.* (med.) carnification.
carnivore [karnivɔr] *adj.* carnivorous; ~ *s.m.* carnivore, flesh-eater.
carolingien, -ne [karɔlɛ̃ʒjɛ̃] *adj.*, *s.m.f.* Carolingian, Carlovingian.
carolus [karɔlys] *s.m.* silver and copper coin (issued by Charles VIII).
caronade [karɔnad] *s.f.* (anc. mil.) carronade.
caroncule [karɔ̃kyl] *s.f.* (bot., med.) caruncle; wattle (on turkey, etc.).
carotène [karɔtɛn] *s.m.* carotene.
carotide [karɔtid] *s.f.* carotid (artery).

carotidien, -ne [karɔtidjɛ̃] *adj.* carotid.

carottage [karɔtaʒ] *s.m.* **1.** swindling, cheating; blackmail; **2.** (min.) taking of core sample.

carotte [karɔt] *s.f.* **1.** (bot., hort.) carrot; *les ~s sont cuites*, (fig.) that's cooked his goose, it's all over; **2.** twist of tobacco; tobacconist's sign (in France); **3.** (min.) core sample; **4.** (fig., fam.) swindle; *tirer une ~ à qn.*, to swindle s.o.; **5.** (tennis) drop-shot; ~ *adj.invar.* (of hair) carroty, ginger.

carotter [karɔte] *v.t.* (fam.) to swindle, to blackmail; to wangle.

carotteu-r, -se [karɔtœr], **carotti-er, -ère** [karɔtje] *s.m.f.* swindler, cheat; one who wangles or fiddles (sth.).

carottier [karɔtje] *s.m.* (min.) tool for core-sampling.

caroube [karub] *s.f.* carob-bean, locust-bean.

caroubier [karubje] *s.m.* carob, carob-tree.

(**les**) **Carpathes** [lɛkarpat] *s.m.pl.* (geog.) the Carpathians.

carpe[1] [karp] *s.f.* (ichth.) carp; *faire un saut de ~*, to leap to one's feet (from lying position); *faire des sauts de ~*, to turn somersaults, to jump about; (swimming) to do a jack-knife dive; *bailler comme une ~*, to yawn one's head off; *faire des yeux de ~ à qn.*, to make sheep's eyes at s.o.

carpe[2] [karp] *s.m.* (anat.) carpus.

carpelle [karpɛl] *s.m.* (bot.) carpel.

carpette [karpɛt] *s.f.* rug, mat, bedside rug; (fig.) *s'aplatir comme une ~ devant qn.*, to lick someone's boots; to be a doormat; ⚠ not full-size 'carpet'.

carpien, -ne [karpjɛ̃] *adj.* (anat.) carpal.

carpillon [karpijɔ̃] *s.m.* very small carp; young carp.

carpocapse [karpɔkaps] *s.m.f.* (ent.) Pyralis.

carquois [karkwa] *s.m.* quiver; (fig., obs.) *vider, épuiser, son ~*, to shoot one's bolt; (arch.) *en ~*, quiver-like, fluted.

carrare [karar] *s.m.* Carrara marble.

carre [kar, kɑr] *s.f.* cross-section; edge (of skate or ski).

carré, -e [kare] *adj.* square; square-shouldered, well-built; firm, decided, plain, flat, trenchant, categorical; *mètre ~*, square metre; *être ~ en affaires*, to be straightforward in one's dealings.

carré [kare] *s.m.* **1.** (math., mil.) square quadrangle; **2.** (arch.) landing, stair-head; **3.** (hort.) bed, patch; **4.** ~ *d'agneau*, loin of lamb; **5.** (cook.) cube, dice; **6.** (naut.) ward-room, mess-room; **7.** (cards) four (of a kind).

carreau (pl. **-x**) [karo] *s.m.* **1.** (small) square, lozenge; (pl.) checks; *étoffe à ~x*, checked material; **2.** wall or floor tile; tiled floor; *rester sur le ~*, to be left (for dead) on the spot; to be out of the running; **3.** window-pane; (fam.) eye-glass; **4.** (cards) diamond; *se garder à ~*, to be on one's guard; **5.** (dressm.) goose, pressing-iron; **6.** (mining) ~ *de mine*, pit-head; **7.** (surv.) grid.

carrée [kare] *s.f.* **1.** (obs.) bedstead; **2.** (mus.) breve; **3.** (pop.) bed-sitter, pad.

carrefour [karfur] *s.m.* (lit. & fig.) crossroads; intersection; (in town) square, circus; get-together, meeting (for exchange of ideas), symposium; *être au ~*, (fig.) to be at the parting of the ways.

carrelage [karlaʒ] *s.m.* tiling (of floors, walls); tiled floor.

carreler [karle] *v.t.* to tile (floors, walls); to chequer.

carrelet [karlɛ] *s.m.* **1.** (ichth.) plaice; **2.** square fishing-net; **3.** packing-needle; **4.** (techn.) square file, ruler, etc.; **5.** (pharm.) frame (of swanskin filter).

carreleur [karlœr] *s.m.* tiler (of floors, walls).

carrément [karemɑ̃] *adv.* squarely; (fig.) flatly, frankly, plainly, straight, firmly, categorically.

carrer [kare] *v.t.* to square; to double (one's stake or wager); **se** ~ *v.refl.* (obs.) to strut, to give oneself airs; to settle comfortably (in a chair, etc.); (fig.) to cling obstinately (to hopes, opinions, etc.).

carrick [karik] *s.m.* (obs.) box-coat.

carrier [karje] *s.m.* quarry-owner; quarry-man.

carrière[1] [karjɛr] *s.f.* **1.** career; *la ~*, the diplomatic service; **2.** (obs.) arena, lists; **3.** span, course; **4.** (fig.) play, scope; *donner libre ~ à*, to give free rein to.

carrière[2] [karjɛr] *s.f.* quarry, pit.

carriériste [karjerist] *s.m.f.* careerist.

carriole [karjɔl] *s.f.* cart, trap; jalopy.

carrossable [karɔsabl] *adj.* motor-(road), metalled (road).

carrosse [karɔs] *s.f.* coach, carriage; *avoir, rouler, ~*, to have one's own carriage; to live in style.

carrosser [karɔse] *v.t.* (car) to fit a body (to a chassis).

carrosserie [karɔsri] *s.f.* coach-making; coach-work; (car) body.

carrossier [karɔsje] *s.m.* coach-builder; (car) body-builder.

carrousel [karuzɛl] *s.m.* **1.** carousel, tournament, tattoo; tilting-yard; **2.** roundabout; **3.** (techn.) carousel, rotating conveyor-belt (for luggage at airports, etc.).

carroyage [karwajaʒ] *s.m.* (surv.) squaring (of map); (town-planning) creation of square intersections.

carroyer [karwaje] *v.t.* (surv.) to square (map).

carrure [karyr] *s.f.* breadth of shoulders; breadth, squareness; (fig.) stature, build.

cartable [kartabl] *s.m.* satchel, school-bag.

cartayer [karteje] *v.i.* to drive avoiding ruts, to straddle the ruts (in a road).

carte [kart] *s.f.* **1.** (playing-)card; *jeu de ~s*, pack of cards; *partie de ~s*, game of cards; *battre, mêler, les ~s*, to shuffle or make the cards; *donner les ~s*, to deal the cards, (fig.) *jouer ~s sur table*, to be open, frank, above-board; *tirer les ~s*, to read the cards, to tell fortunes; *connaître le dessous des ~s de qn., d'une affaire*, to be in the know about s.o., sth., to have inside information about s.o., sth.; (fig.) *brouiller les ~s*, to confuse the issue; *il a plus d'une ~ dans son jeu*, he has more than one trick up his sleeve; *château de ~s*, house of cards, (fig.) castle in the air; **2.** pasteboard, card; *donner ~ blanche à qn.*, to give s.o. carte blanche, full power; ~ *de visite*, visiting-card; *~-lettre*, letter-card; ~ *postale*, postcard; ~ *d'identité*, identity-card; ~ *perforée*, punched card; ~ *d'alimentation*, ration-book; (car) ~ *grise*, registration-book; **3.** map, chart; ~ *muette*, outline-map; (fig.) *perdre la ~*, to be at a loss; **4.** ticket; ~ *d'admission, d'entrée*, entry-ticket; ~ *d'abonnement*, season-ticket; **5.** bill of fare, menu; *à la ~*, à la carte, from the menu; ~ *des vins*, wine list.

cartel [kartɛl] *s.m.* **1.** (econ.) cartel; **2.** wall-clock casing; wall-clock; **3.** (duelling) cartel, challenge; **~lisation** [kartelizɑsjɔ̃] *s.f.* (econ.) formation of a cartel.

carter [kartɛr] *s.m.* (mech.) case, casing, housing; (car) (gear-)box, (differential-) housing, (sump-)case.

cartésianisme [kartezjanism] *s.m.* Cartesianism.

cartésien, -ne [kartezjɛ̃] *adj.* Cartesian.

Carthagène [kartaʒɛn] *s.f.* (geog.) Cartagena.

carthaginois, -e [kartaʒinwa] *adj., s.m.f.* Carthaginian.

cartier [kartje] *s.m.* playing-card manufacturer.

cartilage [kartilaʒ] *s.m.* cartilage; gristle.
cartilagineu-x, -se [kartilaʒinø] *adj.* cartilaginous; gristly.
cartisane [kartizan] *s.f.* foil-card (for embroidery).
carto-graphe [kartɔgraf] *s.m.f.* cartographer; **~graphie** [kartɔgrafi] *s.f.* cartography.
cartomancie [kartɔmɑ̃si] *s.f.* fortune-telling by playing-cards, cartomancy.
cartomancien, -ne [kartɔmɑ̃sjɛ̃] *s.m.f.* one who tells fortunes by playing-cards.
carton [kartɔ̃] *s.m.* **1.** cardboard, pasteboard; *~-amiante*, asbestos-board; *~-cuir*, pulp-board; **2.** cardboard box; *~ à chapeaux, à chaussures*, hat-box, shoe-box; **3.** box-file; school-bag; (art) *~ à dessin*, portfolio; **4.** cartoon, sketch, pattern; **5.** (shooting) target; **6.** (geog.) inset map.
cartonnage [kartɔnaʒ] *s.m.* **1.** cardboard manufacture; cardboard goods; packing in cardboard boxes; **2.** (bookb.) boards, cloth-binding.
cartonné, -e [kartɔne] *adj.* (bookb.) in boards, hardback(ed).
cartonner [kartɔne] *v.t.* (bookb.) to stiffen with boards, to bind in boards.
cartonnerie [kartɔnri] *s.f.* cardboard industry; cardboard mill.
cartonneu-x, -se [kartɔnø] *adj.* like cardboard; (of food) dehydrated.
cartonnier [kartɔnje] *s.m.* **1.** cardboard manufacturer; **2.** filing-cabinet.
cartouche[1] [kartuʃ] *s.m.* (arch.) cartouche, scroll.
cartouche[2] [kartuʃ] *s.f.* **1.** cartridge, refill; (mining) shot; **2.** carton (containing packets).
cartoucherie [kartuʃri] *s.f.* cartridge factory; cartridge store.
cartouchière [kartuʃjɛr] *s.f.* cartridge box or bag.
cartulaire [kartylɛr] *s.m.* cartulary.
carvi [karvi] *s.m.* (bot.) caraway; (*graines de*) *~*, caraway seeds.
caryatide see CARIATIDE.
caryocinèse [karjɔsinɛz], **karyokinèse** [karjɔkinɛz] *s.f.* (biol.) kariokinesis.
caryophyllé, -e [karjɔfile] *adj.* (bot.) caryophyllaceous.
caryopse [karjɔps] *s.m.* (bot.) caryopsis.
cas [kɑ] *s.m.* **1.** case, event, circumstance, occasion, eventuality, conjuncture; instance, fact, matter, question, point; *en ~ qu'il vienne, au ~ qu'il vienne*, in case he comes; *au, dans le, pour le, ~ où il viendrait*, in case he comes, should he come; *en tout ~*, in any case, at all events; *en ~ de besoin*, in case of need, if need be, if necessary; *selon le ~*, as the case may be, as required, as appropriate; *le ~ échéant*, if it so happens, if it comes to the point; *en ce ~, en pareil ~*, in such a case, then; *dans ce ~-là*, in that case; *c'est le ~ ou jamais*, it's now or never, now is the right moment; *c'est bien le ~ de le dire*, how right you are, too true; *en-~*, see EN-CAS; *se mettre dans un mauvais ~*, to put oneself in the wrong; **2.** esteem, value; *faire ~ de*, to value, to esteem; *faire grand ~ de qn.* or *qch.*, to consider s.o. or sth. important; *faire peu de ~ de*, to accord little importance to; **3.** (lang.) case.
casani-er, -ère [kazanje] *adj., s.m.f.* home-loving, stay-at-home (person).
casaque [kazak] *s.f.* (obs.) cloak, jacket; jockey's silk shirt; (fig.) *tourner ~*, to change sides, to be a turncoat, to rat.
casaquin [kazakɛ̃] *s.m.* (obs.) woman's jacket; (fig., pop.) *tomber sur le ~ à qn.*, to give s.o. a beating.
casbah [kazba] *s.f.* casbah, kasbah.
cascade [kaskad] *s.f.* waterfall, fall(s), cascade; *~s de rires, d'applaudissements*, peals of laughter, bursts of applause; (electr.) *en ~*, in series.
cascader [kaskade] *v.i.* **1.** (rare) to fall, to cascade; **2.** (pop.) to lead a wild life.
cascadeu-r, -se [kaskadœr] *adj., s.m.f.* loose (man or woman); *s.m.f.* (circus) tumbler, acrobat; (cin.) stunt man, stand-in.
cascatelle [kaskatɛl] *s.f.* small waterfall.
case [kɑz] *s.f.* **1.** (obs.) cabin, hut; native hut; **2.** division, pigeon-hole; square (on chess board); cell (of honeycomb, of brain); box; (fig., pop.) *il lui manque une ~*, he has a screw loose.
caséation [kazeɑsjɔ̃], **caséification** [kazeifikɑsjɔ̃] *s.f.* caseation.
caséeu-x, -se [kazeø] *adj.* caseous.
caséine [kazein] *s.f.* casein.
casemate [kazmat] *s.f.* casemate, bunker.
caser [kɑze] *v.t.* **1.** (obs.) to arrange, to put away, to file; **2.** to find a place for; to find work for; to find a husband for; **se ~** *v.refl.* to settle, to find a place (for oneself).
caseret [kazrɛ] *s.m.*, **caserette** [kazrɛt] *s.f.* mould, form, for cheese.
caserne [kazɛrn] *s.f.* (mil.) barracks; garrison in barracks; (fam.) barrack, tenement.
casernement [kazɛrnəmɑ̃] *s.m.* quartering in barracks; barrack buildings, barracks.
caserner [kazɛrne] *v.t.* to house in barracks.
casernier [kazɛrnje] *s.m.* maintenance officer.
cash [kaʃ] *adv. payer ~*, to pay in cash, on the nail.
casier [kɑzje] *s.m.* **1.** cabinet, rack, set of pigeon-holes, (wine-, etc.) bin; record(s); *~ judiciaire*, police record; **2.** lobster-pot.
casimir [kazimir] *s.m.* (text.) kerseymere.
casino [kazino] *s.m.* casino.
casoar [kazɔar] *s.m.* **1.** (zool.) cassowary; **2.** plume of shako (of Saint-Cyr cadets).
caspien, -ne [kaspjɛ̃] *adj.* (geog.) Caspian; *la (mer) Caspienne*, the Caspian (Sea).
casque [kask] *s.m.* **1.** helmet; helmet-shaped head-dress; hair-drier; *~ colonial*, sun-helmet, topee, pith-helmet; *~ à mèche*, nightcap; *~ téléphonique*, head-phones, head-set; **2.** (zool.) casque, callous or horny protuberance found on head or over beak of certain birds; **3.** (moll.) helmet shell; **4.** (bot.) spur of certain orchids, etc.; **5.** hair; *~ d'or*, blonde heroine (in gangster film); ⚠ not 'cask'.
casqué, -e [kaske] *adj.* helmeted.
casquer [kaske] *v.i.* (pop.) to pay up, to fork out, to stump up.
casquette [kaskɛt] *s.f.* cap.
casquettier [kasketje] *s.m.* cap-maker, cap--seller.
cassable [kɑsabl] *adj.* breakable, fragile.
cassant, -e [kɑsɑ̃] *adj.* **1.** brittle, breakable; **2.** (fig.) abrupt, curt, gruff, short; **3.** (pop.) tiring, wearing.
cassate [kasat] *s.f.* Neapolitan ice-cream, cassata.
cassation [kɑsɑsjɔ̃] *s.f.* **1.** (law) quashing, annulment; (mil.) reducing to lower grade; *Cour de ~*, Supreme Court of Appeal; **2.** (mus.) cassation.
cassave [kasav] *s.f.* cassava bread.
casse [kɑs] *s.f.* **1.** breaking, breakage, damage; (pop.) trouble, violence; *vendre à la ~*, to sell as scrap-metal; **2.** (bot.) cassia; *passe-moi la ~, je te passerai le séné*, one good turn deserves another; **3.** (print.) case; *haut de ~*, upper case; *bas de ~*, lower case; **4.** glass-maker's ladle.
cassé, -e [kɑse] *adj.* broken; (of peas) split; old and bent; (of voice) cracked; (of colours) off-; *blanc ~*, off-white.
casseau (pl. **-x**) [kaso] *s.m.* (print.) half-case, fount-case.
casse-cou [kɑsku] *s.m.invar.* **1.** death-trap; *crier ~ à qn.*, to warn s.o. of danger; **2.** dare-devil.
casse-croûte [kɑskrut] *s.m.invar.* snack.

casse-gueule [kɑsgœl] *s.m.invar.* (fam.) crazy stunt; ~ *adj.* (pop.) risky.
cassement [kɑsmɑ̃] *s.m.* **1.** ~ *de tête*, (fig.) headache; **2.** (slang) breaking-in, burglary.
casse-noisettes [kɑsnwazɛt], **casse-noix** [kɑsnwa] *s.m.invar.* nutcrackers.
casse-pattes [kɑspat] *s.m.invar.* rot-gut.
casse-pieds [kɑspje] *s.m.invar.* (fam.) bore, nuisance.
casse-pierre(s) [kɑspjɛr] *s.m.* **1.** stone-breaker; **2.** (bot.) stonecrop.
casser [kɑse] *v.t.i.* **1.** to break, to crack, to snap, to split, to break down, to chop (wood); to break into, to interrupt; (fig.) ~ *bras et jambes à qn.*, to astound, to disconcert, s.o.; ~ *la croûte*, to have a snack; *on ne fait pas d'omelette sans* ~ *des œufs*, you can't make an omelette without breaking eggs; ~ *la tête à qn.*, to drive s.o. mad; *se* ~ *la tête à qch.*, to slog at, to worry over, sth.; ~ *du sucre sur le dos de qn.*, to speak ill of s.o., to malign s.o.; *se* ~ *le nez à la porte de qn.*, to get no answer, to find the door closed; *se* ~ *le nez*, to fail; ~ *le morceau*, to spill the beans; ~ *sa pipe*, to die; *se* ~ *la figure*, to fall down; to die; ~ *les pieds à qn.*, to pester s.o.; *ça ne casse rien*, (fam.) there's nothing extraordinary about that; *à tout* ~, *adv.* hell for leather, *adj.* stupendous; **2.** (law) to quash, to annul, to reverse; **3.** to demote, to reduce in rank, to dismiss; **se** ~ *v.refl.* (slang) to be off; (fam.) to tire oneself.
casserole [kasrɔl] *s.f.* **1.** saucepan, stewpan; (cook.) casserole; **2.** (fam.) bad piano; **3.** (slang) (cin.) projector.
casse-tête [kɑstɛt] *s.m.invar.* **1.** bludgeon, blunt instrument; **2.** (fig.) headache, puzzle.
cassetin [kastɛ̃] *s.m.* (print.) box.
cassette [kasɛt] *s.f.* **1.** (obs.) casket; privy-purse; (fam.) pin-money; **2.** (tape) cassette.
casseu-r, -se [kɑsœr] *s.m.f.* breaker, smasher; vandal; (slang) burglar; ~*r d'assiettes*, brawler; *adj.* (fam.) given to breaking things.
cassier [kasje] *s.m.* (bot.) cassia bush.
cassine [kasin] *s.f.* (obs.) shooting-box; hut.
cassis[1] [kasis] *s.m.* black currant; black-currant bush; black-currant liqueur, cassis.
cassis[2] [kɑsi(s)] *s.m.* shallow drain across road.
cassitérite [kasiterit] *s.f.* (min.) cassiterite.
cassolette [kasɔlɛt] *s.f.* **1.** cassolette; **2.** (bot.) dame's violet.
casson [kɑsɔ̃] *s.m.* **1.** rough lump sugar; **2.** glass shard.
cassonade [kasɔnad] *s.f.* brown sugar.
cassoulet [kasulɛ] *s.m.* (cook.) cassoulet.
cassure [kɑsyr] *s.f.* break, crack, fracture; (fig.) rupture.
castagnettes [kastaɲɛt] *s.f.pl.* castanets.
caste [kast] *s.f.* caste; (pej.) class; *esprit de* ~, class-consciousness.
castel [kastɛl] *s.m.* small country house.
castillan, -e [kastijɑ̃] *adj., s.m.f.* Castilian.
Castille [kastij] *s.f.* (geog.) Castile.
castine [kastin] *s.f.* limestone flux.
castor [kastɔr] *s.m.* **1.** (zool.) beaver; beaver fur; ~ *du Canada*, musquash; (obs.) beaver hat; **2.** (pl.) amateur builders.
castramétation [kastrametɑsjɔ̃] *s.f.* (ant.) castrametation.
castrat [kastra] *s.m.* (mus. hist.) castrato.
castration [kastrɑsjɔ̃] *s.f.* castration.
castrer [kastre] *v.t.* to castrate.
casuel, -le [kɑzɥɛl] *adj.* chance, accidental, fortuitous, uncertain; ~ *s.m.* perquisites, fringe benefits, casual earnings; (eccles.) (Easter, etc.) offering.
casuiste [kɑzɥist] *s.m.* casuist.
casuistique [kɑzɥistik] *s.f.* casuistry.
catabolisme [katabɔlism] *s.m.* catabolism.
catachrèse [katakrɛz] *s.f.* catachresis.
cataclysme [kataklism] *s.m.* cataclysm, disaster.
catacombe [katakɔ̃b] *s.f.* (usu. pl.) catacomb(s).
catadioptre [katadjɔptr] *s.m.* = CATAPHOTE.
catadioptrique [katadjɔptrik] *s.f.* catadioptrics; ~ *adj.* catadioptric(al).
catafalque [katafalk] *s.m.* catafalque.
cataire [katɛr] *s.f.* (bot.) catmint.
catalan, -e [katalɑ̃] *adj., s.m.f.* Catalan, Catalonian; ~ *s.m.* (lang.) Catalan.
catalectique [katalɛktik] *adj.* catalectic.
catalepsie [katalɛpsi] *s.f.* catalepsy.
cataleptique [katalɛptik] *adj.* cataleptic.
Catalogne [katalɔɲ] *s.f.* (geog.) Catalonia.
catalogue [katalɔg] *s.m.* catalogue, list.
cataloguer [katalɔge] *v.t.* to catalogue, to list, to classify.
catalpa [katalpa] *s.m.* (bot.) catalpa.
catalyse [kataliz] *s.f.* catalysis.
catalys-er [katalize] *v.t.* (lit. & fig.) to act as a catalyst on; ~**eur** [katalizœr] *s.m.* catalyst.
catalytique [katalitik] *adj.* catalytic.
catamaran [katamarɑ̃] *s.m.* **1.** (naut.) catamaran; **2.** (aeron.) seaplane floats.
cataphote [katafɔt] *s.m.* reflector; cat's eye (on road).
cataplasme [kataplasm] *s.m.* poultice; (fig., fam.) stodgy food; wad (of notes or paper).
catapultage [katapyltaʒ] *s.m.* catapulting, launching by catapult.
catapulte [katapylt] *s.f.* **1.** catapult; **2.** (aircraft or rocket) launcher.
catapulter [katapylte] *v.t.* to catapult, to launch by catapult.
cataracte [katarakt] *s.f.* **1.** waterfall, falls, cataract; (fig.) torrents, floods; **2.** (med.) cataract.
catarhiniens [katarinjɛ̃] *s.m.pl.* (zool.) catarrhine primates.
catarrhe [katar] *s.m.* catarrh.
catarrheu-x, -se [katarø] *adj.* catarrhal.
catastrophe [katastrɔf] *s.f.* disaster, catastrophe, calamity.
catastrophé, -e [katastrɔfe] *adj.* (fam.) struck down, overwhelmed, wiped out (by disaster).
catastrophique [katastrɔfik] *adj.* catastrophic, disastrous.
catch [katʃ] *s.m.* catch-as-catch-can; all-in, tag, wrestling.
catcher [katʃe] *v.i.* to play catch-as-catch-can; to go in for all-in wrestling.
catcheu-r, -se [katʃœr] *s.m.f.* wrestler.
catéch-èse [kateʃɛz] *s.f.* catechesis; ~**iser** [kateʃize] *v.t.* **1.** to catechize; **2.** to indoctrinate; ~**isme** [kateʃism] *s.m.* **1.** catechism; **2.** personal belief, faith; ~**iste** [kateʃist] *s.m.* catechist; ~**uménat** [katekymena] *s.m.* catechumenate; ~**umène** [katekymɛn] *s.m.f.* catechumen.
catégorie [kategɔri] *s.f.* category; class, division, set, type.
catégorique [kategɔrik] *adj.* categorical, unequivocal, firm, explicit, definite, clear; ~**ment** [kategɔrikmɑ̃] *adv.* categorically, clearly, explicitly, flatly.
catégorisation [kategɔrizɑsjɔ̃] *s.f.* categorization.
caténaire [katenɛr] *adj., s.f.* catenary.
catgut [katgyt] *s.m.* catgut.
cathédral, -e, (aux) [katedral] *adj.* cathedral.
cathédrale [katedral] *s.f.* cathedral.
catherinette [katrinɛt] *s.f.* unmarried 25-year-old sempstress or milliner.
cathéter [katetɛr] *s.m.* catheter.
cathétérisme [kateterism] *s.m.* catheterizaton, catheterism.
cathode [katɔd] *s.f.* (electr.) cathode.
cathodique [katɔdik] *adj.* (electr.) cathodal, cathodic; *rayons* ~*s*, cathode rays.

cathol-icisme [katɔlisism] *s.m.* Rom. Catholicism; **~icité** [katɔlisite] *s.f.* **1.** conformity with Rom. Catholic doctrine; **2.** the Rom. Catholic world; **~ique** [katɔlik] *adj.* **1.** Rom. Catholic; **2.** orthodox; **3.** (eccles.) universal; *s.m.f.* Rom. Catholic; **~iquement** [katɔlikmɑ̃] *adv.* in conformity with Rom. Catholic doctrine.
catilinaire [katilinɛr] *s.m.* diatribe.
catimini [katimini] *en* ~, *adv.loc.* stealthily, secretly, surreptitiously.
catin [katɛ̃] *s.f.* (obs.) prostitute.
catir [katir] *v.t.* (text.) to lustre or gloss (cloth).
catissage [katisaʒ] *s.m.* (text.) lustring or glossing (of cloth).
catoptrique [katɔptrik] *adj.* catoptric; ~ *s.f.* catoptrics.
Caton [katɔ̃] *s.m.* (Rom. hist.) Cato.
Catulle [katyl] *s.m.* (Rom. Lit.) Catullus.
(**le**) **Caucase** [ləkɔkɑz] *s.m.* (geog.) the Caucasus.
caucasien, -ne [kɔkɑzjɛ̃] *adj., s.m.f.* Caucasian.
cauchemar [kɔʃmar] *s.m.* (lit. & fig.) nightmare; bugbear, horror.
cauchemarder [kɔʃmarde] *v.i.* to suffer from nightmares.
cauchemardesque [kɔʃmardɛsk], **cauchemardeu-x, -se** [kɔʃmardø] *adj.* nightmarish, troubled by nightmares.
caudal, -e, (**aux**) [kodal] *adj.* caudal, tail-(fin, etc.); **~e** *s.f.* caudal fin.
caudataire [kodatɛr] *s.m.* train-bearer; (fig.) lackey, sycophant.
caudillo [kawdijo] *s.m.* (Spanish hist.) caudillo.
caudrette [kodrɛt] *s.f.* crayfish-net.
caulescent, -e [kolɛsɑ̃] *adj.* (bot.) caulescent.
cauri [kori] *s.m.* cowrie, cowry.
causal, -e [kozal] *adj.* (no m. pl.) causal.
causalité [kozalite] *s.f.* causality.
causant, -e [kozɑ̃] *adj.* talkative, loquacious.
causati-f, -ve [kozatif] *adj.* causative.
cause [koz] *s.f.* cause, motive, ground, reason; cause, party, side, interest; case; (law) case, suit, action; trial; (barrister's) brief; *être* ~ *de, que*, to be the cause of, to be the reason for or why; *à* ~ *de*, because of, on account of, owing to; for the sake of; *pour* ~ *de*, for, because of; (obs.) *à* ~ *que*, because; *en tout état de* ~, in any case, however it may be; *sans* ~, without reason; *et pour* ~*!*, and for a very good reason, justifiably; *prendre fait et* ~ *pour qn.*, to side with s.o., to stand up for s.o.; *faire* ~ *commune avec*, to make common cause with; *avoir gain de* ~, to win one's case; to carry one's point, to get one's own way; *la* ~ *est entendue*, the matter is closed; *être en* ~, to be involved, to be under discussion; *mettre qn. en* ~, to cite s.o.; to involve s.o.; *mettre hors de* ~, to clear of suspicion; *parler en connaissance de* ~, to know what one is talking about; to speak with authority; (law) ~ *célèbre*, famous trial, cause célèbre; *affaire en* ~, case before the court; *être chargé d'une* ~, to hold a brief.
causer[1] [koze] *v.t.* to cause, to bring about, to occasion, to give rise to.
causer[2] [koze] *v.i.* to talk (idly), to chat; to gossip; ~ *affaires*, ~ *politique*, to talk shop, to talk politics; *assez causé!*, enough of that!
causerie [kozri] *s.f.* **1.** talk, chat; **2.** informal lecture.
causette [kozɛt] *s.f.* (fam.) *faire la* ~, *faire un brin de* ~, to have a chat.
causeu-r, -se [kozœr] *adj.* talkative; *s.m.f.* talkative person, great talker.
causeuse [kozøz] *s.f.* small settee.
causse [kos] *s.m.* calcareous plateau (in central & southern France).
causticité [kostisite] *s.f.* causticity, caustic quality; (fig.) caustic humour, biting remarks.
caustique [kostik] *adj.* caustic; (fig.) biting, caustic; ~ *s.m.* caustic (substance); ~ *s.f.* (phys.) caustic curve.
cautèle [kotɛl] *s.f.* guile, craft.
cauteleu-x, -se [kotlø] *adj.* (obs.) crafty, guileful; (mod.) hypocritical, cunning.
cautère [kɔtɛr] *s.m.* cautery; *un* ~ *sur une jambe de bois*, a useless remedy.
cautéris-ation [kɔterizɑsjɔ̃] *s.f.* cauterization; **~er** [kɔterize] *v.t.* to cauterize.
caution [kosjɔ̃] *s.f.* **1.** guarantee, pledge, surety, security; bail; *en liberté sous* ~, on bail; *sujet à* ~, untrustworthy, unreliable, unconfirmed; **2.** person giving surety; guarantor; *se porter* ~ *pour qn.*, to go bail for s.o.; to stand surety for s.o.; ⚠ not 'caution' in sense 'prudence', 'wariness'.
cautionnement [kosjɔnmɑ̃] *s.m.* security, bail; deposit.
cautionner [kosjɔne] *v.t.* to stand surety for, to go bail for; to support (a policy, etc.).
cavalcade [kavalkad] *s.f.* cavalcade, procession; (fam.) noisy group, unruly band.
cavalcader [kavalkade] *v.i.* (obs.) to ride in cavalcade; (fam.) to rush about in gangs.
cavalcadour [kavalkadur] *s.m.* (obs.) = Master of the Horse.
cavale [kaval] *s.f.* (poet.) thoroughbred mare.
cavaler [kavale] *v.i.* (pop.) (also *se* ~) to run away, to bolt; ~ *v.t.* (pop.) to bore.
cavalerie [kavalri] *s.f.* cavalry, horse; (obs., fam.) ~ *de S. Georges*, English coins; (comm.) *traite de* ~, accommodation bill.
cavali-er, -ère [kavalje] *s.m.f.* horseman, horsewoman; rider; *adj.* off-hand, cavalier; *piste* ~*ère*, bridle-path; **~er** *s.m.* (mil.) trooper; partner, escort; (chess) knight; (paper size) royal; *faire* ~*er seul*, to play a lone hand; to be the odd man out; **~èrement** [kavaljɛrmɑ̃] *adv.* off-hand, bluntly, in an off-hand or cavalier fashion.
cavatine [kavatin] *s.f.* (mus.) cavatina.
cave [kav] *s.f.* **1.** cellar, wine-cellar, vault; wine kept in the cellar, cellar (of wine); *rat de* ~, (i.) taper, spill; (ii.) exciseman; **2.** cellaret, tantalus; **3.** (gaming) chips, stake.
cave [kav] *s.m.* (pop.) outsider; dupe, sucker.
cave [kav] *adj.* hollow, sunken; *veine* ~, vena cava; *année* ~, *mois* ~, incomplete year, short month.
caveau (pl. **-x**) [kavo] *s.m.* **1.** small cellar; **2.** burial vault, family vault; **3.** underground club.
caveçon [kavsɔ̃] *s.m.* cavesson; (fig., obs.) *donner un coup de* ~ *à qn.*, to take s.o. down a peg.
cavée [kave] *s.f.* sunken lane.
caver [kave] *v.t.* to hollow, to undermine, to erode; **se** ~ *v.refl.* to become hollow or sunken; ~ *v.t.i.* to stake, to wager.
caverne [kavɛrn] *s.f.* **1.** cavern, cave; (fig.) den; **2.** (med.) cavity.
caverneu-x, -se [kavɛrnø] *adj.* cavernous, hollow; sepulchral.
cavernicole [kavɛrnikɔl] *adj.* cave-dwelling; ~ *s.m.* cave-dweller.
cavet [kavɛ] *s.m.* (arch.) cavetto.
caviar [kavjar] *s.m.* caviar; *passer au* ~, to ink out, to censor.
caviarder [kavjarde] *v.t.* to ink out, to censor.
cavicorne [kavikɔrn] *adj.* (zool.) cavicorn; **~s** *s.m.pl.* (zool.) Cavicornia.
caviste [kavist] *s.m.* cellarman.
cavitation [kavitɑsjɔ̃] *s.f.* (phys.) cavitation.
cavité [kavite] *s.f.* cavity, hollow.
C.C. [sese] abbrev. *Corps consulaire.*
C.C.P. [sesepe] abbrev. *compte chèque postal.*
C.D. [sede] abbrev. *Corps diplomatique.*
ce [sə] (**c'** before *e*, **ç'** before *a*) *dem.pron.* **1.** it, that; *c'est lui*, it is he; *ce doit être lui*, it must be he; *ce ne peut être cela*, it can't be that, that can't be

right; *si ce n'est*, unless it is; *fût-ce*, if it were; *est-ce vous?*, is it you?; *qu'est-ce que c'est?*, what is it?; *je sais ce que c'est que travailler*, I know what it is to work; **2.** he, she, they; *c'est une bonne amie*, she is a good friend; *c'est un brave homme*, he is a good man; *ce sont de braves gens*, they are good people; (pop.) *ce n'est pas des amis, c'est des traîtres*, they are not friends, they are traitors; **3.** *c'est toi qui l'as dit*, it was you who said it; *c'est une bonne idée que vous avez là*, that's a good idea of yours; *ce serait une erreur que de faire cela*, it would be a mistake to do that; *s'il est absent, c'est qu'il est malade*, if he's absent, it's because he's ill; *ce n'est pas qu'il ne puisse mieux faire*, not that he can't do better; *ce n'est pas que j'approuve*, not that I approve; **4.** *c'est à lui de jouer*, it's his turn to play; *c'est à vous de le faire*, it's your job to do it; *c'est à pleurer*, it's enough to make one cry; **5.** *ce qui, ce que, ce dont*, what; *dites-moi ce qui vous ennuie*, tell me what's upsetting you; *dites--moi ce que vous désirez*, tell me what you want; *demandez ce dont vous avez besoin*, ask for what you need; *pour ce qui est de*, as for, as far as concerns; *à ce que*, according to what; *en ce que*, in so far as; *ce que c'est beau!*, how beautiful it is!; *ce en quoi*, in what; *ce pour quoi*, for what; **6.** *sur ce*, forthwith, thereupon; *pour ce faire*, to this *or* that end; *ce disant*, (on) saying this; *ce faisant*, on doing this, in so doing.

ce [sə], **cet** [sɛt] (before vowel or h-mute), f. **cette** [sɛt], pl. **ces** [se] *dem.adj.* this, that; these, those; *ce livre-ci(-là)*, this (that) book; *ces livres--ci(-là)*, these (those) books; *ces gens-là*, those people, people like that; *ce jour*, today; *ce soir*, this evening, tonight; *cette nuit*, last night; (fam.) *cette question!, cette idée!*, what a question!, what an idea!

céans [seɑ̃] *adv.* (obs.) in this place; (mod.) only in the phrase *le maître (la maîtresse) de* ~, the master (mistress) of the house.

C.E.C.A. [seesea] abbrev. *Communauté européenne du charbon et de l'acier.*

ceci [səsi] *dem.pron.* this.

cécidie [sesidi] *s.f.* (bot.) gall.

cécité [sesite] *s.f.* blindness; (fig.) inability to see; ~ *verbale*, word-blindness.

cédant, -e [sedɑ̃] *s.m.f.* (law) **1.** grantor; **2.** transferor.

céder [sede] *v.t.* to give up, to resign, to yield, to let have, to part with; to cede, to make over, to transfer; (obs.) *le* ~ *à qn.*, to be inferior to s.o.; (mod.) *il ne lui cède en rien*, he is his equal in every way; ~ *v.i.* to yield, to give in, to give up, to submit, to relent; to give way (under), to break, to collapse; to disappear; ~ *à*, to give in to, to submit to, to defer to, to succumb to.

cédille [sedij] *s.f.* cedilla.

cédrat [sedra] *s.m.* (bot.) citron, cedrate.

cédratier [sedratje] *s.m.* (bot.) citron-tree.

cèdre [sɛdr] *s.m.* (bot.) cedar (tree).

cédule [sedyl] *s.f.* **1.** (before 1949) income-tax return; (mod.) schedule of income-tax: **2.** (law) ~ *de citation*, subpoena.

C.E.E. [seee] abbrev. *Communauté économique européenne*, E.E.C.

C.E.G. [seeʒe] abbrev. *Collège d'enseignement général.*

cégétiste [seʒetist] *s.m.f.* member of the C.G.T. (*Confédération générale du Travail*); ~ *adj.* concerning the C.G.T.

ceindre [sɛ̃dr] *v.t.* (obs. exc. Lit.) to gird on, to gird, to bind, to wreath, to encircle, to surround; *se* ~ *les reins*, to gird up one's loins; *se* ~ *de*, to put on (insignia).

ceinturage [sɛ̃tyraʒ] *s.m.* banding (a shell); ringing (a tree).

ceinture [sɛ̃tyr] *s.f.* **1.** belt, girdle, sash, waistband; waist, middle; (fig.) *se serrer la* ~, to tighten one s belt; ~ *de sauvetage*, life-belt; **2.** circle, enclosure, fence, zone, band; **3.** (rail.) circle, inner circle; ring-road, circular road.

ceinturer [sɛ̃tyre] *v.t.* **1.** to encircle, to girdle, to belt; **2.** to grasp or hold round the waist; (Rugby) to tackle.

ceinturon [sɛ̃tyrɔ̃] *s.m.* (mil.) belt.

cela [s(ə)la] *dem.pron.* that, that thing, it; (fam.) he, she, they; *c'est* ~, that's right, agreed!; *il est comme* ~, he's like that, it's just his way; *comment* ~?, how do you make that out?, what do you mean (by that)?; *c'est* ~ *même*, that's the very thing; *sans* ~, but for that; *comme* ~ *dort, ces enfants*, how these children do sleep; ~ *griffe, les chats*, cats do scratch; (see also ÇA).

céladon [seladɔ̃] *adj.*, *s.m.* pale green, celadon.

célébrant [selebrɑ̃] *s.m.* (eccles.) celebrant; ~ *adj.* officiating.

célébration [selebrɑsjɔ̃] *s.f.* celebration.

célèbre [selɛbr] *adj.* famous, well-known, renowned, illustrious, celebrated.

célébrer [selebre] *v.t.* **1.** to celebrate, to solemnize, to perform, to officiate at; **2.** to celebrate, to commemorate; **3.** to extol, to praise, to sing the praises of.

célébrité [selebrite] *s.f.* fame, renown; celebrity, V.I.P.

celer [s(ə)le] *v.t.* (Lit.) to conceal, to hide, to keep secret.

céléri [sɛlri] *s.m.* celery; celeriac (also ~*-rave*); *un pied de* ~, a head of celery.

célérité [selerite] *s.f.* celerity, speed, swiftness.

célesta [selɛsta] *s.m.* (mus.) celesta.

céleste [selɛst] *adj.* celestial, heavenly, divine; *bleu* ~, sky blue.

célestin [selɛstɛ̃] *s.m.* Celestine (monk).

célibat [seliba] *s.m.* celibacy; chastity; bachelorhood, spinsterhood.

célibataire [selibatɛr] *adj.* unmarried, single, celibate; ~ *s.m.f.* unmarried man or woman, bachelor, spinster, celibate.

celle, celle-ci, celle-là see CELUI.

celléri-er, -ère [selerje] *s.m.f.* (eccles.) cellarer, cellaress.

cellier [selje] *s.m.* still-room, pantry; wine-cellar (not underground).

cellophane [selɔfan] *s.f.* (proprietary name) cellophane.

cellulaire [selylɛr] *adj.* cellular, pertaining to a cell; *régime* ~, solitary confinement; *voiture* ~, prison van.

cellular [selylar] *s.m.* (text.) cellular material.

cellule [selyl] *s.f.* cell; (aeron.) airframe.

cellulite [selylit] *s.f.* (med.) cellulitis.

celluloïd [selylɔid] *s.m.* celluloid.

cellulose [selyloz] *s.f.* cellulose.

cellulosique [selylozik] *adj.* cellulose.

celte [sɛlt] *adj.* Celtic; ~ *s.m.f.* Celt.

celtique [sɛltik] *adj.* Celtic; ~ *s.m.* Celtic (language).

celui [səlɥi], f.sing. **celle** [sɛl], m.pl. **ceux** [sø], f.pl. **celles** [sɛl] *dem.pron.* he, she, that, the one; (pl.) they, those, the ones; *ses opinions n'étaient pas celles de son mari*, her opinions were not those of her husband, *or*, were not her husband's; *celui-ci*, etc., this, this one, this person; the latter; (pl.) these, these ones, these people, these things; *celui-là*, etc., that, that one, that person; the former; (pl.) those, those ones, those people, those things.

cément [semɑ̃] *s.m.* (anat.) cement (of tooth); (metall.) flux, cement, cementation powder.

cémentation [semɑ̃tɑsjɔ̃] *s.f.* (metall.) cementation; case-hardening.

cémenter [semɑ̃te] *v.t.* (metall.) to cement; to case-harden; ⚠ not 'to cement' (with mortar).

cénacle [senakl] *s.m.* **1.** upper room (of Last Supper); **2.** Lit. group, circle or club.

cendre [sɑ̃dr] *s.f.* ash, ashes; cinders; *mercredi des Cendres*, Ash Wednesday.
cendré, -e [sɑ̃dre] *adj.* ash, ash-coloured; *blond* ~, ash-blond.
cendrée [sɑ̃dre] *s.f.* **1.** slag; **2.** (hunt., etc.) dust-shot; **3.** (sport) cinder-track.
cendrer [sɑ̃dre] *v.t.* **1.** to cover with cinders; **2.** to paint ash-grey.
cendreu-x, -se [sɑ̃drø] *adj.* containing ash, mixed with ash; ash-grey, ashen, ashy.
cendrier [sɑ̃drije] *s.m.* **1.** ash-box, ash-pit; **2.** ash-tray.
Cendrillon [sɑ̃drijɔ̃] *s.f.* Cinderella.
cène [sɛn] *s.f.* Last Supper, Lord's Supper, Holy Communion.
cenelle [s(ə)nɛl] *s.f.* (bot.) haw (of whitethorn); holly-berry.
cénobite [senɔbit] *s.m.* coenobite (monk).
cénotaphe [senɔtaf] *s.m.* cenotaph.
cens [sɑ̃s] *s.m.* **1.** (hist.) census; **2.** (hist.) quit--rent; **3.** property-qualification (for franchise).
censé, -e [sɑ̃se] *adj.* presumed, assumed, believed, supposed; *il est* ~ *être à Paris*, he is believed to be in Paris; *nul n'est* ~ *ignorer la loi*, no one is supposed to be ignorant of the law; **~ment** [sɑ̃semɑ̃] *adv.* presumably, supposedly.
censeur [sɑ̃sœr] *s.m.* **1.** (Rom. hist.) censor; **2.** critic, censor; **3.** deputy head (of a *lycée*).
censi-er, -ère [sɑ̃sje] *adj.*, *s.m.f.* (hist.) (person) paying or receiving quit-rent.
censitaire [sɑ̃sitɛr] *s.m.*, *adj.* (person) qualified to vote by payment of property-tax.
censorat [sɑ̃sɔra] *s.m.* (hist.) censorship.
censorial, -e, (aux) [sɑ̃sɔrjal] *adj.* censorial.
censure [sɑ̃syr] *s.f.* **1.** censorship; board of censors; **2.** censure, blame, condemnation.
censurer [sɑ̃syre] *v.t.* **1.** to censure, to blame, to condemn, to criticize; **2.** to censor; to ban.
cent [sɑ̃] *adj.*, *s.m.* (a) hundred; a large number; *pour* ~, per cent; ~ *fois mieux*, far better; *avoir* ~ *fois raison*, to be completely, or abundantly, right; *je vous l'ai dit* ~ *fois*, I have told you again and again; *faire les* ~ *pas*, to walk up and down; *je vous le donne en* ~, you'll never guess.
cent [sɛnt] *s.m.* cent (coin).
centaine [sɑ̃tɛn] *s.f.* a hundred; about a hundred; *par* ~*s*, by the hundred, in large quantities; *une* ~ *de francs*, some hundred francs.
centaure [sɑ̃tɔr] *s.m.* **1.** (myth.) centaur; **2.** expert rider.
centaurée [sɑ̃tɔre] *s.f.* (bot.) centaury.
centenaire [sɑ̃tnɛr] *adj.* a hundred years old; ~ *s.m.f.* centenarian; ~ *s.m.* centenary.
centenier [sɑ̃tənje] *s.m.* centurion.
centennal, -e, (aux) [sɑ̃tenal, sɑ̃tɛnnal] *adj.* (rare) centennial.
centésimal, -e, (aux) [sɑ̃tezimal] *adj.* centesimal.
centiare [sɑ̃tjar] *s.m.* centiare, square metre.
centième [sɑ̃tjɛm] *adj.*, *s.m.* hundredth; ~ *s.f.* hundredth performance (of play, etc.).
centi-grade [sɑ̃tigrad] *adj.* centigrade, divided into 100 degrees; *s.m.* (geom.) 100th part of grade; **~gramme** [sɑ̃tigram] *s.m.* centigram; **~litre** [sɑ̃tilitr] *s.m.* centilitre.
centime [sɑ̃tim] *s.m.* centime; *ne pas avoir un* ~, not to have a penny to one's name; ~ *additionnel*, surtax; *au* ~ *le franc*, at one per cent.
centimètre [sɑ̃timɛtr] *s.m.* centimetre.
centrafricain, -e [sɑ̃trafrikɛ̃] *s.m.f.*, *adj.* (native or inhabitant) of Central African Empire.
centrage [sɑ̃traʒ] *s.m.* centring, aligning.
central, -e, (aux) [sɑ̃tral] *adj.* central, principal; ~ *s.m.* telephone exchange.
centrale [sɑ̃tral] *s.f.* **1.** power-station; **2.** national confederation of trade(s) unions.
centralisat-eur, -rice [sɑ̃tralizatœr] *adj.* centralizing.
centralis-ation [sɑ̃tralizɑsjɔ̃] *s.f.* centralization; **~er** [sɑ̃tralize] *v.t.* to centralize.
centre [sɑ̃tr] *s.m.* centre, central part; middle, midst, main part; seat, focus, focal point.
centrer [sɑ̃tre] *v.t.* to centre; (fig.) *être centré sur*, to revolve round.
centreur [sɑ̃trœr] *s.m.* (mech.) centring mechanism or device.
centri-fugation [sɑ̃trifygɑsjɔ̃] *s.f.* centrifugation; **~fuge** [sɑ̃trifyʒ] *adj.* centrifugal; **~fuger** [sɑ̃trifyʒe] *v.t.* to centrifuge, to separate (by centrifugation).
centrifugeu-r, -se [sɑ̃trifyʒœr] *s.m.f.* centrifuge, centrifugal machine, separator.
centripète [sɑ̃tripɛt] *adj.* centripetal.
centriste [sɑ̃trist] *adj.* (pol.) of the Centre; ~ *s.m.f.* (pol.) moderate.
centrosome [sɑ̃trozɔm] *s.m.* (biol.) centrosome.
centuple [sɑ̃typl] *adj.*, *s.m.* centuple, hundred-fold, (amount).
centupler [sɑ̃typle] *v.t.* to multiply by a hundred, to centuple; ~ *v.i.* to increase a hundredfold.
centurie [sɑ̃tyri] *s.f.* (Rom. hist.) century.
centurion [sɑ̃tyrjɔ̃] *s.m.* (Rom. hist.) centurion.
cénure, cœnure [senyr] *s.m.* (vet.) coenure.
cep [sɛp] *s.m.* **1.** vine-stock, -plant; **2.** (obs.) fetter, shackle; **3.** (agric.) sole (of plough).
cépage [sepaʒ] *s.m.* variety of vine.
cèpe, ceps [sɛp] *s.m.* edible mushroom, boletus.
cépée [sepe] *s.f.* shoots from a tree-stump.
cependant [s(ə)pɑ̃dɑ̃] *adv.*, *conj.* **1.** however, yet, still, nevertheless; **2.** (obs.) meanwhile; ~ *que*, while, whilst.
céphalalgie [sefalalʒi], **céphalée** [sefale] *s.f.* cephalalgia, headache.
céphalique [sefalik] *adj.* cephalic.
céphalopode [sefalɔpɔd] *s.m.* (moll.) cephalopod.
céphalo-rachidien, -ne [sefalɔraʃidjɛ̃] *adj.* cephalorachidian.
céphalothorax [sefalɔtɔraks] *s.m.* cephalothorax.
céphéide [sefeid] *s.f.* (astron.) cepheid.
cérambyx [serɑ̃biks] *s.m.* (ent.) cerambyx.
cérame [seram] *s.m.* terracotta vase; *grès* ~, stoneware.
céram-ique [seramik] *s.f.* ceramics, ceramic; (art of) pottery; *adj.* ceramic, pottery; **~iste** [seramist] *adj.*, *s.m.f.* ceramist.
céraste [serast] *s.m.* (zool.) cerastes, horned viper.
cérat [sera] *s.m.* (pharm.) cerate.
cerbère [sɛrbɛr] *s.m.* (myth. & fig.) Cerberus; watch-dog.
cerce [sɛrs] *s.f.* **1.** sieve-frame; **2.** template.
cerceau (pl. **-x**) [sɛrso] *s.m.* **1.** hoop; **2** rib, support; **3.** pinion-feather.
cerclage [sɛrklaʒ] *s.m.* hooping (of barrels).
cercle [sɛrkl] *s.m.* **1.** circle, ring, hoop; (fig.) sphere, range; *vin en* ~*s*, wine in the wood; **2.** circle, set, club.
cercler [sɛrkle] *v.t.* to hoop, to encircle, to surround, to rim; *lunettes cerclées d'or*, gold--rimmed glasses.
cercopithèque [sɛrkɔpitɛk] *s.m.* (zool.) cercopithecus.
cercueil [sɛrkœj] *s.m.* coffin; (fig.) *descendre au* ~, to die; *être au* ~, to be dead.
céréale [sereal] *s.f.* cereal.
céréali-er, -ère [serealje] *adj.* cereal
cérébelleu-x, -se [serebelø] *adj.* cerebellar, cerebellous.
cérébral, -e, (aux) [serebral] *adj.* cerebral; intellectual; ~ *s.m.* intellectual.
cérébralité [serebralite] *s.f.* intellectuality.
cérébro-spinal, -e, (aux) [serebrɔspinal] *adj.* cerebro-spinal.

cérémonial, -e, (**aux**) [seremɔnjal] *adj.* (obs.) ceremonial; ~ *s.m.* ceremonial, ritual, formalities, etiquette.

cérémonie [seremɔni] *s.f.* ceremony; fuss, ado; *de* ~, state, formal, full-dress; *en* ~, in state; *faire des* ~*s*, to stand upon ceremony, to make a lot of fuss; *voilà bien des* ~*s pour si peu de chose*, what a lot of fuss about nothing; *sans* ~*s*, informal(ly), unceremonious(ly); *sans plus de* ~*s*, without further ado.

cérémoniel, -le [seremɔnjɛl] *adj.* ceremonial.

cérémonieu-x, -se [seremɔnjø] *adj.* ceremonious, formal, unnecessarily fussy; ~**sement** [seremɔnjøzmɑ̃] *adv.* ceremoniously.

cerf [sɛr] *s.m.* stag, deer, red deer, hart; *bois de* ~, stag's horns; *corne de* ~, hartshorn.

cerfeuil [sɛrfœj] *s.m.* (bot.) chervil.

cerf-volant [sɛrvɔlɑ̃] *s.m.* **1.** (toy) kite; **2.** (ent.) stag-beetle.

cerisaie [s(ə)rizɛ] *s.f.* cherry orchard.

cerise [s(ə)riz] *s.f.* cherry; ~ *adj.invar.* cherry--red, cerise.

cerisette [s(ə)rizɛt] *s.f.* **1.** cherry-brandy; **2.** (bot.) bittersweet.

cerisier [s(ə)rizje] *s.m.* cherry-tree; cherry--wood.

cérite [serit] *s.f.* (min.) cerite.

cérite, cérithe [serit] *s.m.* (moll.) cerithium.

cérium [serjɔm] *s.m.* (chem.) cerium.

cerne [sɛrn] *s.m.* ring (round, under, eye); bruising; outlining (of contour).

cerné, -e [sɛrne] *adj.* ringed.

cerneau (pl. **-x**) [sɛrno] *s.m.* green walnut; *vin de* ~, rosé wine to be drunk with walnuts.

cerner [sɛrne] *v.t.* to surround, to encircle; to outline; to ring (a tree).

céroplastique [serɔplastik] *s.f.* ceroplastics, wax modelling.

certain, -e [sɛrtɛ̃] *adj.* **1.** (after noun) certain, sure, determined, fixed, definite; stated; positive, infallible, inevitable; *preuve* ~*e*, definite proof; **2.** (before noun) a certain, some, a certain amount of; *d'un* ~ *âge*, no longer young; *dans* ~*s pays*, in some countries; *il aura besoin d'un* ~ *courage*, he will need a certain amount of courage; ~**s** *pron.pl.* some, some people; ~ *s.m.* (fin.) fixed rate of exchange; ~**ement** [sɛrtɛnmɑ̃] *adv.* certainly, surely, assuredly, infallibly, without doubt.

certes [sɛrt] *adv.* **1.** (obs.) certainly; **2.** however, nevertheless, admittedly.

certificat [sɛrtifika] *s.m.* **1.** certificate, document, testimonial, reference; **2.** certificate, diploma.

certificateur [sɛrtifikatœr] *s.m.* (law) guarantor, attestor.

certification [sɛrtifikɑsjɔ̃] *s.f.* certification, authentication.

certifié, -e [sɛrtifje] *adj., s.m.f.* (one) who holds Teacher's Diploma (C.A.P.E.S.).

certifier [sɛrtifje] *v.t.* to certify, to verify, to attest; to give one's word for.

certitude [sɛrtityd] *s.f.* assurance, confidence; conviction, certitude, certainty.

céruléen, -ne [seryleɛ̃] *adj.* cerulean, caerulean, sky-blue.

cérumen [serymɛn] *s.m.* cerumen, wax (in ear).

cérumineu-x, -se [seryminø] *adj.* ceruminous.

céruse [seryz] *s.f.* ceruse.

cerveau (pl. **-x**) [sɛrvo] *s.m.* brain, brains; intellect, mind; ~ *brûlé*, hothead; *se creuser le* ~, to rack one's brains; *rhume de* ~, cold in the head.

cervelas [sɛrvəla] *s.m.* saveloy, cervelat (sausage).

cervelet [sɛrvəlɛ] *s.m.* (anat.) cerebellum.

cervelle [sɛrvɛl] *s.f.* brain, brains; (cook.) brains; (fig.) brains, intellect, mind, sense; *se brûler, se faire sauter, la* ~, to blow one's brains out; *se creuser la* ~, to rack one's brains; *cela lui trotte dans la* ~, he has it on the brain; *tête sans* ~, brainless person; *une petite* ~, one of little brain.

cervical, -e [sɛrvikal] *adj.* cervical.

cervier see LOUP-CERVIER.

(**le Mont**) **Cervin** [ləmɔ̃sɛrvɛ̃] *s.m.* (geog.) the Matterhorn.

cervoise [sɛrvwaz] *s.f.* (hist.) cervisia, barley--beer.

ces see CE.

C.E.S. [seeɛs] abbrev. *Collège d'enseignement secondaire.*

César [sezar] *s.m.* Caesar.

césarien, -ne [sezarjɛ̃] *adj.* of or belonging to Caesar; (fig.) dictatorial; ~**ne** *s.f.* (surg.) Caesarean section.

césarisme [sezarism] *s.m.* **1.** (hist.) government of Caesars; **2.** (fig.) dictatorship, absolute government.

césium see CAESIUM.

cessant, -e [sɛsɑ̃] *adj. toute(s) chose(s), toute(s) affaire(s), cessante(s)*, leaving aside all other business.

cessation [sɛsɑsjɔ̃] *s.f.* cessation, stoppage, discontinuance.

cesse [sɛs] *s.f.* ceasing, respite; *sans* ~, unceasingly, incessantly, continually; *n'avoir point de* ~ *que*, not to rest until.

cesser [sese] *v.i.* to cease, to stop, to come to an end; *faire* ~, to stop, to put an end to; ~ *v.t.* to stop, to cease, to end, to give up; *cessez vos plaintes*, stop complaining; ~ *tout effort*, to give up all effort; ~ *de faire qch.*, to stop doing sth., to give up doing sth.

cessez-le-feu [seselfø] *s.m.invar.* ceasefire.

cessibilité [sesibilite] *s.f.* transferability.

cessible [sesibl] *adj.* transferable, negotiable.

cession [sɛsjɔ̃] *s.f.* (law) transfer, cession; assignment, surrender (of property); *faire* ~ *de*, to transfer, to surrender, to assign.

cessionnaire [sɛsjɔnɛr] *s.m.f.* transferee, assignee, beneficiary.

c'est-à-dire [sɛtadir] *conj.loc.* that is, that is to say, to wit, namely; ~ *que*, the fact is, this means.

ceste [sɛst] *s.m.* (ant.) cestus.

cestodes [sɛstɔd] *s.m.pl.* (zool.) cestoidea, tape--worms.

césure [sezyr] *s.f.* caesura.

cet see CE.

cétacé, -e [setase] *adj., s.m.* (zool.) cetacean.

cétane [setan] *s.m.* cetane; *indice de* ~, cetane number.

cétérac [seterak] *s.m.* (bot.) ceterach.

cétoine [setwan] *s.f.* (ent.) rose-chafer.

cétone [setɔn] *s.f.* (chem.) ketone.

cette see CE.

ceux see CELUI.

cévenol, -e [sevnɔl] *s.m.f., adj.* (native or inhabitant) of the Cevennes.

Ceylan [sɛlɑ̃] *s.m.* (geog.) Ceylon (Sri Lanka).

C.G.S. [seʒeɛs] abbrev. *centimètre-gramme-seconde*, (phys.) C.G.S., c.g.s.

C.F.D.T. [seɛfdete] abbrev. *Confédération française et démocratique du travail.*

C.F.T.C. [seɛftese] abbrev. *Confédération française des travailleurs chrétiens.*

C.G.A. [seʒeɑ] abbrev. *Confédération générale de l'agriculture.*

C.G.C. [seʒese] abbrev. *Confédération générale des cadres.*

C.G.T. [seʒete] abbrev. **1.** *Confédération générale du travail*, = T.U.C.; **2.** *Compagnie générale transatlantique.*

chabichou [ʃabiʃu] *s.m.* goat's milk cheese.

chabler [ʃable] *v.t.* = GAULER.

chablis[1] [ʃabli] *s.m.* Chablis (wine).
chablis[2] [ʃabli] *adj., s.m.* fallen (wood).
chabot [ʃabo] *s.m.* (ichth.) bullhead.
chabraque, schabraque [ʃabrak] *s.f.* **1.** (anc. mil.) shabrack, saddle-cloth; **2.** (pop.) ugly or stupid woman, prostitute.
chacal [ʃakal] *s.m.* jackal.
chaconne [ʃakɔn] *s.f.* (mus.) chaconne.
chacun, -e [ʃakœ̃] *pron.* each, each one, every one; everybody; ~ *de nous*, each of us; *donner à ~ sa part*, to give each his share; *nous sommes partis ~ de notre côté*, we each went our own way; ~ *pense*, everybody thinks; (obs.) (*tout*) *un* ~, anybody and everybody, all and sundry; (jest) ~ *sa* ~*e*, to every boy a girl.
chadburn [ʃadbœrn] *s.m.* (naut.) engine-room telegraph.
chadouf [ʃaduf] *s.m.* shadoof, shaduf.
chafouin, -e [ʃafwɛ̃] *adj.* foxy(-faced).
chagrin[1] [ʃagrɛ̃] *s.m.* grief, sorrow, affliction; vexation, annoyance, worry; disappointment, chagrin.
chagrin[2] [ʃagrɛ̃] *s.m.* shagreen.
chagrin, -e [ʃagrɛ̃] *adj.* **1.** sorrowful, melancholy, gloomy; **2.** peevish, fretful, morose.
chagriner[1] [ʃagrine] *v.t.* to upset, to distress, to vex.
chagriner[2] [ʃagrine] *v.t.* to shagreen, to grain (leather); *papier chagriné*, granulated, *or* pebbled, paper.
chah [ʃa] *s.m.* = SCHAH.
chahut [ʃay] *s.m.* row, uproar, commotion; (at school) rag, ragging.
chahuter [ʃayte] *v.i.* to cause an uproar, to make a commotion; ~ *v.t.* to rag (a master); to jostle.
chai [ʃɛ] *s.m.* wine and spirit warehouse.
chaînage [ʃɛnaʒ] *s.m.* **1.** (surv.) chain-measuring; **2.** (constr.) strengthening with tie-rods.
chaîne [ʃɛn] *s.f.* **1.** chain; (lit. & fig.) bond, tie, fetter; (naut.) cable, hawse; (car) chains (for use in snow, etc.); (Lit.) penal servitude, being a galley-slave or a convict; (fig.) bondage, servitude, drudgery; **2.** chain, series, succession, train, concatenation; assembly, system; (constr.) tie-iron; stone pier, corner-stone; (T.V.) channel; production line; (text.) warp; *réaction en* ~, chain reaction; ~ *haute fidélité*, hi-fi system; ~ *de montage*, assembly line.
chaîner [ʃene] *v.t.* **1.** (surv.) to chain, to measure by chain; **2.** (constr.) to tie.
chaînette [ʃɛnɛt] *s.f.* **1.** small chain; (needlew.) *point de* ~, chain-stitch; **2.** (geom., etc.) catenary.
chaîneur [ʃɛnœr] *s.m.* surveyor.
chaînier [ʃenje], **chaîniste** [ʃenist] *s.m.* chain-smith.
chaînon [ʃɛnɔ̃] *s.m.* **1.** (lit. & fig.) link (of chain); **2.** short mountain range, part of chain of mountains.
chair [ʃɛr] *s.f.* **1.** flesh; (paint.) flesh tints, nude portions; *en ~ et en os*, in flesh and blood, in person; *être bien en* ~, to be plump, well-covered; ~ *à canon*, cannon fodder; *ni ~ ni poisson*, neither fish nor fowl, of indeterminate character; ~ *de poule*, (fig.) gooseflesh; **2.** flesh, meat (esp. minced); **3.** the flesh, the body; carnal appetite; *l'esprit est prompt, mais la ~ est faible*, the spirit is willing but the flesh is weak; *l'aiguillon de la* ~, the promptings of desire.
chaire [ʃɛr] *s.f.* **1.** throne, seat, (of pontiff); *la ~ apostolique*, the apostolic see; **2.** pulpit; **3.** (professorial) chair.
chaise [ʃɛz] *s.f.* **1.** chair (without arms); (techn.) support, seat, seating, base; ~ *longue*, couch, deck-chair; ~ *percée*, commode; (naut.) *nœud de* ~, bowline hitch; **2.** (obs.) chaise, post-chaise; sedan chair.
chaisière [ʃɛzjɛr] *s.f.* chair-woman (in parks, etc.).
chaland[1] [ʃalɑ̃] *s.m.* barge, lighter.
chaland[2], **-e** [ʃalɑ̃] *s.m.f.* patron, regular customer.
chalaze [kalɑz] *s.f.* (biol.) chalaza.
chalazion [kalazjɔ̃] *s.m.* (med.) chalazion.
chalco-graphie [kalkɔgrafi] *s.f.* chalcography; exhibition of chalcography; ~**pyrite** [kalkɔpirit] *s.f.* (chem.) chalcopyrite, copper pyrites.
chaldéen, -ne [kaldeɛ̃] *adj., s.m.f.* Chaldean.
châle [ʃɑl] *s.f.* shawl.
chalet [ʃalɛ] *s.m.* chalet; country cottage; (obs.) ~ *de nécessité*, public convenience.
chaleur [ʃalœr] *s.f.* **1.** heat, sensation of heat; (of animals) rut, heat; (fig.) warmth, heat, passion, glow, zeal; *en* ~, on heat, in season; **2.** temperature; (pl.) hot weather, heat of the day.
chaleureu-x, -se [ʃalœrø] *adj.* warm, hearty, cordial; ~**sement** [ʃalœrøzmɑ̃] *adv.* warmly, heartily, cordially.
châlit [ʃɑli] *s.m.* bedstead, bed-frame.
challenge [ʃalɑ̃ʒ] *s.m.* (sport) championship, competition.
challengeur [ʃalɑ̃ʒœr] *s.m.* (sport) challenger.
chaloir [ʃalwar] *v.i.impers. peu me chaut, peu m'en chaut*, little do I care.
chaloupe [ʃalup] *s.f.* barge, lighter; launch; ~ *de sauvetage*, ship's lifeboat.
chaloupé, -e [ʃalupe] *adj.* swaying, rocking (dance or gait).
chalouper [ʃalupe] *v.i.* to sway, to rock (in walking, dancing).
chalumeau (pl. **-x**) [ʃalymo] *s.m.* **1.** (drinking) straw; **2.** shepherd's pipe or flute; chalumeau (of clarinet); **3.** blow-pipe; blow-lamp.
chalut [ʃaly] *s.m.* trawl.
chalutage [ʃalytaʒ] *s.m.* trawl-fishing, trawling.
chalutier [ʃalytje] *s.m.* trawler; trawlerman.
chamade [ʃamad] *s.f.* **1.** (obs.) chamade; **2.** *son cœur battait la* ~, his heart was beating wildly.
chamailler (**se**) [ʃamɑje] *v.refl.* to squabble, to wrangle, to bicker.
chamaillerie [ʃamɑjri] *s.f.* (fam.) squabbling, bickering.
chamailleu-r, -se [ʃamɑjœr] *adj., s.m.f.* quarrelsome (person).
chamanisme [ʃamanism] *s.m.* shamanism.
chamarrer [ʃamare] *v.t.* to adorn gaudily, to bedizen, to bedeck; *chamarré de*, bedecked with.
chamarrure [ʃamaryr] *s.f.* (usu. pl.) gaudy ornamentation.
chambard [ʃɑ̃bar], **chambardement** [ʃɑ̃bardəmɑ̃] *s.m.* (fam.) disturbance, upheaval, turning upside down; uproar, commotion.
chambarder [ʃɑ̃barde] *v.t.* to upset, to turn upside down; to smash, to overthrow.
chambellan [ʃɑ̃belɑ̃] *s.m.* chamberlain.
chambertin [ʃɑ̃bɛrtɛ̃] *s.m.* Chambertin (wine).
chambouler [ʃɑ̃bule] *v.t.* (fam.) to turn upside down.
chambranle [ʃɑ̃brɑ̃l] *s.m.* frame (of door, window, chimney-piece).
chambre [ʃɑ̃br] *s.f.* **1.** bedroom; ~ *meublée*, bed-sitting-room; *garder la* ~, to keep to the house, to one's room; *travailler en* ~, to work at home; *faire ~ à part*, to sleep in separate rooms; *femme de* ~, chambermaid, lady's maid; *pot de* ~, chamber pot; *robe de* ~, dressing-gown; **2.** section of court of justice; assembly room, hall; chamber; assembly, parliament; ~ *haute*, ~ *basse*, upper, lower, house; ~ *de commerce, etc.*, chamber of commerce, etc.; **3.** cavity, space, chamber; ~ *à air*, inner tube (of tyre); ~ *d'allumage*, combustion chamber; ~ *de carburation*, carburettor.
chambrée [ʃɑ̃bre] *s.f.* **1.** (mil.) barrack-room, dormitory; **2.** roomful (of sleepers).

chambrer [ʃɑ̃bre] *v.t.* **1.** to confine to one room, to closet; to isolate (esp. for purposes of constraint or persuasion); **2.** to bring (wine) to room temperature.

chambrette [ʃɑ̃brɛt] *s.f.* small bedroom.

chambrière [ʃɑ̃brijɛr] *s.f.* **1.** (obs.) chambermaid; **2.** long-stock whip; **3.** (on cart, etc.) sprag; **4.** wheelwright's stand.

chameau (pl. **-x**) [ʃamo] *s.m.* **1.** camel; **2.** (fig., fam., pej.) pig, cow; beast, brute; **3.** (naut.) caisson, camel.

chamelier [ʃaməlje] *s.m.* cameleer, camel-driver.

chamelle [ʃamɛl] *s.f.* she-camel.

chamito-sémitique [kamitɔsemitik] *adj.* (lang.) Hamito-Semitic.

chamois [ʃamwa] *s.m.* chamois; chamois (-leather); ~ *adj.invar.* buff(-coloured); **~age** [ʃamwazaʒ] *s.m.* chamoising; **~er** [ʃamwaze] *v.t.* to chamoise; **~erie** [ʃamwazri] *s.f.* chamois (-leather) factory or trade.

champ [ʃɑ̃] *s.m.* field, open space, arena; (pl.) country; (techn.) field, range; (fig.) space, opportunity; scope, range; subject, domain; *~ de courses*, race-course; *~ de repos*, garden of rest; *mort au ~ d'honneur*, killed on active service; *~ de foire*, fair-ground; *couper à travers ~s*, to cut across country; *prendre la clef des ~s*, to escape, to run away; *donner la clef des ~s à*, to set free; *prendre du ~*, to take a longer run; (fig.) to take time to consider; *sur-le-~*, at once, immediately; *à tout bout de ~*, over and over again, incessantly; (fig.) *donner libre ~ à*, to give free rein to.

champagne [ʃɑ̃paɲ] *s.m.* champagne (wine).

champagne [ʃɑ̃paɲ] *s.f.* **1.** (geog.) *la Champagne*, Champagne (province); chalk or limestone tract; **2.** *fine ~*, liqueur brandy; **3.** (herald.) base of shield.

champagnis-ation [ʃɑ̃paɲizɑsjɔ̃] *s.f.* processing of champagne; **~er** [ʃɑ̃paɲize] *v.t.* to process champagne; to give a champagne character to.

champenois, -e [ʃɑ̃pənwa] *adj., s.m.f.* (native or inhabitant) of Champagne.

champêtre [ʃɑ̃pɛtr] *adj.* rural, rustic, country; *garde ~*, rural policeman.

champi, champis, -se [ʃɑ̃pi] *adj., s.m.f.* (obs.) foundling.

champignon [ʃɑ̃piɲɔ̃] *s.m.* mushroom; fungus, fungoid growth; mushroom-shaped object; hat- or wig-stand; (car) accelerator pedal; *~ de couche*, cultivated mushroom; *~ vénéneux*, inedible or poisonous mushroom, toadstool; *~ atomique*, mushroom cloud from atomic explosion; (fig.) *pousser comme un ~*, to grow rapidly, to mushroom.

champignonnière [ʃɑ̃piɲɔnjɛr] *s.f.* mushroom farm.

champignonniste [ʃɑ̃piɲɔnist] *s.m.f.* mushroom-grower.

champion, -ne [ʃɑ̃pjɔ̃] *s.m.f.* champion; (fig., fam.) (also *adj.*) outstanding, first-rate, person.

championnat [ʃɑ̃pjɔna] *s.m.* championship.

champlever [ʃɑ̃lve] *v.t.* to chase (plate) for enamelling; *emaux champlevés*, champlevé (enamel).

chançard, -e [ʃɑ̃sar] *adj., s.m.f.* (fam.) lucky (person).

chance [ʃɑ̃s] *s.f.* chance, fortune, (good) luck; risk, hazard; opportunity; (pl.) chances, possibility, probability; *bonne ~!*, good luck!; *pas de ~!*, bad luck!, hard luck!; *courir sa ~*, to take one's chance, to run a risk; *toutes les ~s sont contre lui*, all the odds are against him.

chancelant, -e [ʃɑ̃slɑ̃] *adj.* tottering, unsteady; (fig.) unsettled, irresolute, uncertain, weak.

chanceler [ʃɑ̃sle] *v.i.* to totter, to stagger, to be unsteady; (fig.) to waver, to be uncertain, to be undecided, to hesitate.

chancelier [ʃɑ̃səlje] *s.m.* chancellor.

chancelière [ʃɑ̃səljɛr] *s.f.* foot-muff.

chancellerie [ʃɑ̃sɛlri] *s.f.* chancellor's office, chancery, stamp-office; *style de ~*, legal, diplomatic, language.

chanceu-x, -se [ʃɑ̃sø] *adj.* **1.** (obs.) risky; **2.** lucky.

chanci [ʃɑ̃si] *s.m.* compost heap covered with mushroom spawn.

chancir [ʃɑ̃sir] *v.i.* to go mouldy.

chancre [ʃɑ̃kr] *s.m.* **1.** (bot.) canker; **2.** (med.) rodent ulcer; (venereal) chancre.

chandail [ʃɑ̃daj] *s.m.* pullover, sweater.

chandeleur [ʃɑ̃dlœr] *s.f.* (eccles.) *la Chandeleur*, Candlemas.

chandelier [ʃɑ̃dəlje] *s.m.* **1.** candlestick; **2.** stay, prop; (naut.) stanchion; **3.** (obs.) cicisbeo.

chandelle [ʃɑ̃dɛl] *s.f.* candle, candlelight; *faire des économies de bouts de ~*, to be cheeseparing, to be penny wise and pound foolish; (fig.) *voir trente-six ~s*, to see stars; *devoir une ~ à qn.*, to be under an obligation to s.o., to owe s.o. a debt of gratitude; *le jeu n'en vaut pas la ~*, the game isn't worth the candle; (tennis) *lancer en ~*, to lob (a ball) into the air; (aeron.) *monter en ~*, to rise vertically, to zoom up.

chanfrein[1] [ʃɑ̃frɛ̃] *s.m.* face (of horse, etc.).

chanfrein[2] [ʃɑ̃frɛ̃] *s.m.* (constr.) chamfer.

chanfreiner [ʃɑ̃frene] *v.t.* (constr.) to chamfer.

change [ʃɑ̃ʒ] *s.m.* **1.** exchange; rate of exchange; *lettre de ~*, bill of exchange; *contrôle des ~s*, exchange control; *cote des ~s*, exchange rate; *marché des ~s*, foreign exchange; *agent de ~*, stock-broker, exchange-broker; **2.** switch; *donner le ~ à qn.*, to throw s.o. off the scent; to trick s.o. (by a substitution); *prendre le ~*, to be thrown off the scent, to be hoodwinked.

changeable [ʃɑ̃ʒabl] *adj.* amenable to change, capable of being changed.

changeant, -e [ʃɑ̃ʒɑ̃] *adj.* changeable, variable, fickle, inconsistent; changing; (text.) shot.

changement [ʃɑ̃ʒmɑ̃] *s.m.* change, variation, alteration.

changer [ʃɑ̃ʒe] *v.t.* to change, to exchange; to transform, to alter; to disguise; *~ les draps*, to change the sheets; *~ des francs contre des dollars*, to exchange francs for dollars, to change francs into dollars; *je ne changerais pas avec lui*, I wouldn't swap places with him; *~ qch. de place*, to change the place of sth.; *cela ne changera rien*, that will make no difference; (fam.) *vous n'y changerez rien*, you can't do anything about it; *~ de*, to change, to alter, to vary; *~ de nom*, to change one's name; *~ d'avis*, to change one's mind; (car) *~ de vitesse*, to change gear; ~ *v.i.* to change, to undergo a change; *les choses ont changé*, things have changed; *~ de tout au tout*, to undergo a complete change; **se** ~ *v.refl.* to change (one's clothes).

changeur [ʃɑ̃ʒœr] *s.m.* money-changer.

Changhaï [ʃɑ̃gai] *s.m.* (geog.) Shanghai.

chanlatte [ʃɑ̃lat] *s.f.* (constr.) barge-board, eaves-board.

chanoine [ʃanwan] *s.m.* (eccles.) canon.

chanoinesse [ʃanwanɛs] *s.f.* canoness.

chanson [ʃɑ̃sɔ̃] *s.f.* song; tune, air; ballad, poem; *~s!*, (obs.) fiddlesticks!, rubbish!; *toujours la même ~*, always the same old story; *faire chanter une autre ~ à qn.*, (fig.) to make s.o. sing another tune; *l'air n'est pas la ~*, (fig.) clothes don't make a man.

chansonner [ʃɑ̃sɔne] *v.t.* to lampoon, to take off (in a song).

chansonnette [ʃɑ̃sɔnɛt] *s.f.* (comic) ditty.

chansonnier [ʃɑ̃sɔnje] *s.m.* **1.** song book, collection of ballads; **2.** chansonnier, singer and composer of satirical ditties.

chant[1] [ʃɑ̃] *s.m.* singing; song, tune, melody; chant, chanting; chirping, crowing; poem, canto; *plain* ~, plainsong; ~ *du cygne*, (fig.) swansong; *au* ~ *du coq*, at cockcrow.
chant[2] [ʃɑ̃] *s.m.* (constr.) *mettre de* ~, to place edgewise.
chantage [ʃɑ̃taʒ] *s.m.* blackmail, blackmailing, extortion by threats.
chantant, -e [ʃɑ̃tɑ̃] *adj.* musical, tuneful, melodious; singable; *café* ~, cabaret.
chanteau (pl. **-x**) [ʃɑ̃to] *s.m.* **1.** wedge (of bread); **2.** gusset, gore, (in cloth).
chantepleure [ʃɑ̃tplœr] *s.f.* wine funnel (with holes); spigot; spout and rose of watering-can; weep-hole (in wall).
chanter [ʃɑ̃te] *v.t.i.* **1** to sing, to warble, to carol; to chirrup, to twitter, to crow; (of door) to creak; (of fat) to sizzle; ~ *faux*, ~ *juste*, to sing out of, in, tune; (fig.) *c'est comme si je chantais*, I'm wasting my breath; *si cela vous chante*, if you feel like it; *comme ça vous chante*, as you please; **2.** to chant, to celebrate, to praise, to compose poems; *qu'est-ce que tu nous chantes là?*, what are you on about?; **3.** to resound, to vibrate, to ring (as a string); **4.** to pay up (blackmail money); (pop.) to grass, to squeal; *faire* ~ *qn.*, to blackmail s.o.
chanterelle[1] [ʃɑ̃trɛl] *s.f.* **1.** (mus.) highest--pitched string, chanterelle; (fig.) *appuyer sur la* ~, to stress a point, to rub it in; **2.** decoy-bird, stool-pigeon.
chanterelle[2] [ʃɑ̃trɛl] *s.f.* (bot.) chanterelle.
chanteu-r, -se [ʃɑ̃tœr] *s.m.f.* singer (esp. professional); vocalist; *adj.* singing; *oiseau-*~*r*, song-bird; *maître-*~*r*, blackmailer.
chantier [ʃɑ̃tje] *s.m.* **1.** block, bench; stillage; (naut. constr.) stocks; *mettre en* ~, to lay down (ship); to lay out (piece of work); (fig.) to start, to put in hand; **2.** (obs.) yard, store, stock, depot; (mod.) (building, etc.) site, workings, floor (of foundry); ~ *naval*, naval dockyard; (fam.) *quel* ~*!*, what a mess!
chantignole [ʃɑ̃tiɲɔl] *s.f.* **1.** (constr.) purlin--cleat, bracket; **2.** half-brick.
chantonnement [ʃɑ̃tɔnmɑ̃] *s.m.* humming.
chantonner [ʃɑ̃tɔne] *v.t.i.* to hum.
Chan-Toung [ʃɑ̃tuŋ] *s.m.* (geog.) Shantung.
chantourner [ʃɑ̃turne] *v.t.* to jigsaw.
chantre [ʃɑ̃tr] *s.m.* **1.** (eccles.) chanter, cantor, succentor, choirman; *grand* ~, precentor; **2.** bard, poet.
chanvre [ʃɑ̃vr] *s.m.* hemp; ~ *indien*, Indian hemp, hashish; ~ *du Bengale*, jute; *cravate de* ~, hangman's rope.
chanvri-er, -ère [ʃɑ̃vrije] *s.m.f.* hemp-dresser; *adj.* hemp, hempen.
chaos [kao] *s.m.* chaos, disorder, confusion.
chaotique [kaɔtik] *adj.* chaotic.
chapardage [ʃapardaʒ] *s.m.* (fam.) scrounging, pilfering.
chaparder [ʃaparde] *v.t.* (fam.) to scrounge, to pilfer.
chapardeu-r, -se [ʃapardœr] *adj., s.m.f.* scrounging, pilfering; scrounger, pilferer.
chape [ʃap] *s.f.* **1.** (eccles.) cope; **2.** (techn.) casing, housing, capping; cover or tread (of tyre); (constr.) waterproof layer.
chapeau (pl. **-x**) [ʃapo] *s.m.* hat; cap, bonnet, hood, cover, lid, (of mushroom, of machinery); (hort.) cloche; (print.) heading, subtitle; ~ *haut-de-forme*, top-hat; ~*x bas!*, hats off!; (eccles.) *prendre le* ~, to be made cardinal; (mus.) ~ *chinois*, Chinese bells.
chapeauté, -e [ʃapote] *adj.* hatted, capped.
chapelain [ʃaplɛ̃] *s.m.* chaplain.
chapelet [ʃaplɛ] *s.m.* **1.** rosary, beads, prayer--beads; chaplet, string (of onions, etc.); stick (of bombs); **2.** (arch.) bagnette, baguette.
chapeli-er, -ère [ʃapəlje] *s.m.f.* hat-maker, milliner; *adj.* hat, hat-making.
chapelle [ʃapɛl] *s.f.* **1.** (private) chapel; side--chapel; ~ *ardente*, mortuary chapel; **2.** ornaments and plate for mass; **3.** church music, choir; *maître de* ~, choirmaster; **4.** (fig.) group, brotherhood, chapel; **5.** (constr.) crown, vault.
chapellenie [ʃapɛlni] *s.f.* chaplaincy.
chapellerie [ʃapɛlri] *s.f.* hat-maker's, milliner's, shop; hat-making; hat-factory.
chapelure [ʃaplyr] *s.f.* (cook.) bread-crumbs (browned, for garnish).
chaperon [ʃaprɔ̃] *s.m.* **1.** hood; *le petit* ~ *rouge*, Little Red Riding Hood; **2.** (falconry) hood; **3.** chaperon; **4.** (constr.) coping-stone.
chaperonner [ʃaprɔne] *v.t.* **1.** (constr.) to cope (a wall); **2.** to chaperon.
chapiteau (pl. **-x**) [ʃapito] *s.m.* **1.** (arch.) capital; **2.** hood (over niche, etc.); **3.** circus tent, big top; **4.** (sci.) head (of still).
chapitre [ʃapitr] *s.m.* **1.** chapter (of book); **2.** chapter, subject, head, matter, question; **3.** (eccles.) chapter; chapter-house; (fig.) *avoir voix au* ~, to have a say in the matter.
chapitrer [ʃapitre] *v.t.* **1.** (eccles.) to chapter; **2.** to reprimand, to scold, to take to task.
chapon [ʃapɔ̃] *s.m.* **1.** capon; **2.** garlic-flavoured sippet.
chaponner [ʃapɔne] *v.t.* to caponize.
chapska, schapska [ʃapska] *s.m.* (mil.) Polish cap.
chaptal-isation [ʃaptalizɑsjɔ̃] *s.f.* chaptalization (of wine); ~**iser** [ʃaptalize] *v.t.* to chaptalize.
chaque [ʃak] *adj.* each, every, any; ~ *fois*, each time, every time, whenever; *à* ~ *instant*, every moment, all the time, at any moment.
char [ʃar] *s.m.* cart, wagon; (hist.) chariot; (carnival) float; ~ *funèbre*, hearse; (mil.) ~ *de combat*, *d'assaut*, tank; (fig.) *le* ~ *de l'État*, the ship of state.
charabia [ʃarabja] *s.m.* gibberish.
charade [ʃarad] *s.f.* charade.
charançon [ʃarɑ̃sɔ̃] *s.m.* (ent.) weevil.
charançonné, -e [ʃarɑ̃sɔne] *adj.* weevil-infested.
charbon [ʃarbɔ̃] *s.m.* **1.** coal, piece of coal; smut; ~ (*de bois*), charcoal; charcoal pencil; **2.** (med.) anthrax; **3.** (agric.) smut, black rust.
charbonnage [ʃarbɔnaʒ] *s.m.* coal-mining; (pl.) coal-field; coal-mines, collieries.
charbonner [ʃarbɔne] *v.t.* to blacken (with charcoal); ~ *v.i.* to char, to be burnt black; (naut.) to coal.
charbonnerie [ʃarbɔnri] *s.f.* (Fr. hist.) Carbonarism.
charbonneu-x, -se [ʃarbɔnø] *adj.* **1.** coal-like, coaly; coal-black; **2.** (med.) anthracoid.
charbonni-er, -ère [ʃarbɔnje] *s.m.f.* charcoal--burner; coal-merchant; ~*er est maître chez soi*, every man's home is his castle; *adj.* coal-, coal--mining; ~**er** *s.m.* **1.** (naut.) collier; **2.** (Fr. hist.) = CARBONARO.
charbonnière [ʃarbɔnjɛr] *s.f.* **1.** charcoal kiln; **2.** (ornith.) great-tit; *petite* ~, coal-tit.
charcuter [ʃarkyte] *v.t.* (fam.) to butcher (a patient).
charcuterie [ʃarkytri] *s.f.* **1.** pork-butchery, pork-butcher's shop; **2.** cooked meats, delicatessen; cooked meats shop.
charcuti-er, -ère [ʃarkytje] *s.m.f.* **1.** pork--butcher; **2.** (fam.) butcher (i.e. clumsy surgeon).
chardon [ʃardɔ̃] *s.m.* **1.** (bot.) thistle; **2.** spike (on wall or gate).
chardonneret [ʃardɔnrɛ] *s.m.* (ornith.) goldfinch; ~ *citrinelle*, linnet; ~ *élégant*, siskin.
charentais, -e [ʃarɑ̃tɛ] *adj., s.m.f.* (native or inhabitant) of Charente.
charge [ʃarʒ] *s.f.* **1.** load, burden, weight,

cargo; charge, load; loading (of gun); **2.** burden, care; expense, tax, obligation; *être à ~ à qn.*, to be a burden on s.o.; *être à la ~ de qn.*, to be in someone's care, to be someone's responsibility; *la vie m'est à ~*, my life is a burden to me; *le loyer comprend les ~s*, the rent includes all charges (rates, water, etc.); *à ~ de revanche*, on a reciprocal basis; **3.** function, appointment, post, office; charge, commission, mandate, responsibility; *femme de ~*, housekeeper; **4.** (mil.) attack, charge; (fig.) *revenir à la ~*, to return to the attack; **5.** burlesque, caricature; **6.** accusation, indictment, (incriminating) evidence; **7.** (electr.) charge.

chargé, -e [ʃarʒe] *adj.* **1.** loaded, laden, burdened, (*de*, with); full; heavy; (of letter, etc.) registered; *langue ~e*, furred tongue; **2.** responsible (*de*, for), entrusted (*de*, with); *~ s.m. ~ d'affaires*, chargé d'affaires; (in university) *~ de cours*, reader.

chargement [ʃarʒəmɑ̃] *s.m.* **1.** loading, lading; registration (of letter); **2.** cargo, load, freight, shipment.

charger [ʃarʒe] *v.t.* **1.** to load, to burden; to load, to fill, to charge; **2.** to register (letter); **3.** to instruct, to direct, to commission; *on l'a chargé de prendre la parole*, he has been instructed to act as spokesman; *je vous charge de ce soin*, I leave that to you; *se ~ de*, to undertake (to do), to make sth. one's business; *je me charge de tout*, I'll see to everything; *je me charge de lui*, I undertake to look after him; **4.** (mil.) to charge; **5.** to overdo, to exaggerate, to caricature.

chargeur [ʃarʒœr] *s.m.* **1.** docker, loader; shipper; **2.** loader; charger, stoker (machine).

chariot [ʃarjo] *s.m.* wagon, truck, cart; go-cart; trolley (in shop, at airport, for drinks, etc.); (mech.) truck, carriage, cradle.

charisme [karism] *s.m.* charisma.

charitable [ʃaritabl] *adj.* charitable, kind, benevolent; **~ment** [ʃaritabləmɑ̃] *adv.* charitably, kindly, benevolently.

charité [ʃarite] *s.f.* charity, charitableness, benevolence, kindness; almsgiving, alms, philanthropy; *~ bien ordonnée commence par soi-même*, charity begins at home; *sœurs de la Charité*, Sisters of Mercy.

charivari [ʃarivari] *s.m.* uproar, din; discordant music and catcalls, charivari.

charlatan [ʃarlatɑ̃] *s.m.* quack, mountebank, charlatan; **~erie** [ʃarlatanri] *s.f.* charlatanry; **~esque** [ʃarlatanɛsk] *adj.* charlatanic(al); **~isme** [ʃarlatanism] *s.m.* charlatanism.

charlemagne [ʃarləmaɲ] *faire ~, adv.loc.* to cash in (at cards).

charleston [ʃarlɛstɔn] *s.m.* Charleston (dance).

charlotte [ʃarlɔt] *s.f.* **1.** (cook.) charlotte; **2.** woman's bonnet.

charmant, -e [ʃarmɑ̃] *adj.* charming, delightful, fascinating, attractive.

charme[1] [ʃarm] *s.m.* **1.** (obs. except in certain phrases) spell, magic; amulet; *être sous le ~ de qn.*, to be under the spell of s.o.; *le ~ est rompu*, the spell is broken; *se porter comme un ~*, to be hale and hearty; **2.** charm, attraction, pleasing aspect; charms; beauty; seductive behaviour.

charme[2] [ʃarm] *s.m.* (bot.) hornbeam.

charmer [ʃarme] *v.t.* **1.** (obs. exc. Lit.) to cast a spell on, to bewitch; to charm away (pain, etc.), to soothe, to allay; to beguile; **2.** to charm, to delight, to please, to enchant, to captivate, to attract; *charmé de vous voir*, delighted to see you.

charmeu-r, -se [ʃarmœr] *s.m.f.* **1.** (obs.) sorcerer, magician; *~r de serpent*, snake charmer; **2.** charmer, charming person.

charmille [ʃarmij] *s.f.* hornbeam plantation; hornbeam hedge; bower, arbour.

charnel, -le [ʃarnɛl] *adj.* carnal; (fig.) material; **~lement** [ʃarnɛlmɑ̃] *adv.* carnally; *connaître ~lement*, to have carnal knowledge of, to have had sexual relations with.

charnier [ʃarnje] *s.m.* charnel-house.

charnière [ʃarnjɛr] *s.f.* hinge; (fig.) meeting-point, juncture.

charnu, -e [ʃarny] *adj.* fleshy, plump.

charognard [ʃarɔɲar] *s.m.* (ornith. & fig.) vulture.

charogne [ʃarɔɲ] *s.f.* carrion, carcass; (fig., pej.) (of person) swine.

charpentage [ʃarpɑ̃taʒ] *s.m.* (constr.) carpentry; construction of framework.

charpente [ʃarpɑ̃t] *s.f.* timbers, framework, frame; skeleton; (fig.) structure, construction, plan, outline (of play, book, etc.); *avoir une solide ~*, to be solidly built.

charpent-er [ʃarpɑ̃te] *v.t.* to carpenter; to shape (wood for framework); (fig.) to construct; *pièce bien charpentée*, well-constructed play; **~erie** [ʃarpɑ̃tri] *s.f.* carpentry, timber-work; timber-yard; **~ier** [ʃarpɑ̃tje] *s.m.* carpenter; *~ier (en fer)*, constructional steel-worker.

charpie [ʃarpi] *s.f.* **1.** (med.) lint; **2.** (fig.) *mettre en ~*, to tear to shreds, to cook to pieces.

charrée [ʃare] *s.f.* **1.** (obs.) wood-ash (for laundry); **2.** barilla.

charretée [ʃarte] *s.f.* cartload.

charreti-er, -ère [ʃartje] *s.m.* carter, cart-driver; *jurer comme un ~*, to swear like a trooper; *~ adj.* cart-, suitable for carts; *chemin ~er*, cart-track.

charreton [ʃartɔ̃], **charretin** [ʃartɛ̃] *s.m.* **1.** small cart (without sides), flat cart; **2.** hand-cart.

charrette [ʃarɛt] *s.f.* cart, (in Fr. Revolution) tumbril; *~ à bras*, hand-cart, truck; *être la cinquième roue de la ~*, to be odd man out.

charriage [ʃarjaʒ] *s.m.* **1.** carting, cartage; **2.** (geol.) slide; **3.** (fig., pop.) leg-pulling.

charrier [ʃarje] *v.t.* **1.** to cart, to carry; (of rivers, etc.) to carry along, to sweep along; **2.** (fig., pop.) *~ qn.*, to pull someone's leg; *~ v.i.* to fool, to be kidding.

charroi [ʃarwa] *s.m.* cartage, haulage.

charron [ʃarɔ̃] *s.m.* wheelwright, cartwright; **~nage** [ʃarɔnaʒ] *s.m.* wheelwright's work.

charroyer [ʃarwaje] *v.t.* to cart, to haul.

charruage [ʃarɥaʒ] *s.m.* ploughing.

charrue [ʃary] *s.f.* plough; *~ à avant-train*, wheel-plough; *~ sans avant-train*, swing-plough; (fig.) *mettre la ~ avant* (or *devant*) *les bœufs*, to put the cart before the horse.

charte [ʃart] *s.f.* charter; ancient document; *la Grande Charte* (*d'Angleterre*), Magna Carta; *l'École des Chartes*, the School of Palaeography.

charte-partie [ʃartəparti] *s.f.* (naut.) charter-party.

chart-isme [ʃartism] *s.m.* (hist.) Chartism; **~iste** [ʃartist] *s.m.f.* **1.** (hist.) Chartist; **2.** member of *l'École des Chartes*.

chartreuse [ʃartrøz] *s.f.* **1.** Carthusian monastery; **2.** chartreuse (liqueur); **3.** (obs.) lodge, box.

chartreu-x, -se [ʃartrø] *s.m.f.* Carthusian.

chartrier [ʃartrije] *s.m.* cartulary; charter room; custodian of charters.

chas [ʃa] *s.m.* eye (of needle).

chasse [ʃas] *s.f.* **1.** hunting, shooting, chase; bag; shoot, hunting country; the hunt, the huntsmen and pack; the hunting or shooting season; *~ à courre*, hunting with hounds; *~ au tir*, shooting; *~ au lévrier*, hare-coursing; *~ au faucon*, hawking; *~ au sanglier, au renard, à la perdrix, etc.*, boar-, fox-, hunting, partridge-shooting, etc.; *rendez-vous de ~*, hunting-lodge, shooting-box; *permis de ~*, game licence; *garde-~*, gamekeeper; ~ *sous-marine*, under-water spear fishing; (fig.) *qui va à la ~ perd sa place*, if you leave your place you lose it; **2.** chase, pursuit; ~ *à l'homme*, man-hunt; (mil., nav.) pursuit; *avion de ~*, fighter-plane; **3.** ~ *d'eau*, flush, flushing, (of W.C.); **4.** (techn.) play; **5.** (print.) driving out.

châsse [ʃɑs] *s.f.* **1.** reliquary; **2.** rim, frame (of spectacles); **3.** handle (of lancet); **4.** wheelwright's hammer.

chassé [ʃase] *s.m.* (dancing) chassé.

chasse-clou [ʃasklu] *s.m.* (pl. *~-clous*) punch (for nails, etc.).

chassé-croisé [ʃasekrwaze] *s.m.* **1.** (dancing) chassé-croisé; **2.** (fig.) change round, swapping, general post.

chasselas [ʃasla] *s.m.* chasselas, white dessert grape.

chasse-marée [ʃasmare] *s.m.invar.* three-masted fishing boat; **~-mouches** [ʃasmuʃ] *s.m.invar.* fly-swatter; **~-neige** [ʃasnɛʒ] *s.m.invar.* snow-plough; **~-pierres** [ʃaspjɛr] *s.m.invar.* (rail.) cow-catcher; **~pot** [ʃaspo] *s.m.* Chassepot rifle.

chasser [ʃase] *v.t.* **1.** to hunt, to shoot, to course, to go hunting, shooting, etc.; to drive (before one); to pursue, to follow; **2.** to drive out or away, to expel; to discharge, to sack; (fig.) *un clou chasse un autre*, one thing or person replaces another; *chassez le naturel, il revient toujours*, what is bred in the bone will come out in the flesh; ~ *v.i.* (of clouds, rain, etc.) to drive; (print.) to space out excessively, to over-run; (car) to skid, to lose adhesion; (naut.) ~ *sur ses ancres*, to drag at anchor.

chasseresse [ʃasrɛs] *adj., s.f.* huntress.

chasse-roue [ʃasru] *s.m.* (pl. *chasse-roues*) guard-stone, fender.

chasseu-r, -se [ʃasœr] *s.m.f.* **1.** hunter, huntsman, shot, sportsman; **2.** (obs.) groom; (mod.) page-boy, hotel porter; **3.** (mil.) light-infantryman, rifleman; **4.** (nav.) ~ *de-sous-marins*, submarine chaser; (aeron.) fighter-plane.

chassie [ʃasi] *s.f.* gum (in the eyes).

chassieu-x, -se [ʃasjø] *adj.* (of eye) gummed up; having gummed-up eye(s).

châssis [ʃɑsi] *s.m.* frame (of door, window, etc.); (hort.) frame; (paint.) stretcher; (print.) chase; (photo.) printing frame, slide-holder; (car) body, chassis; (metall.) mould.

chaste [ʃast] *adj.* chaste, pure, innocent; **~ment** [ʃastəmɑ̃] *adv.* chastely, innocently.

chasteté [ʃastəte] *s.f.* chastity, purity, innocence.

chasuble [ʃazybl] *s.f.* chasuble; **~rie** [ʃazybləri] *s.f.* making and selling of vestments and devotional objects.

chat, -te [ʃa] *s.m.f.* cat; *mon ~, ma ~te*, form of endearment; ~ *à neuf queues*, cat-o'-nine-tails; *le Chat botté*, Puss-in-Boots; *avoir un ~ dans la gorge*, to have a frog in one's throat; *à bon ~ bon rat*, tit for tat; *écrire comme un ~*, to write illegibly; *acheter ~ en poche*, to buy a pig in a poke; *appeler un ~ un ~*, to call a spade a spade; *donner sa langue au ~*, to give up (guessing, trying); ~ *échaudé craint l'eau froide*, once bitten twice shy; *ne réveillez pas le ~ qui dort*, let sleeping dogs lie; *quand le ~ n'est pas là les souris dansent*, when the cat's away the mice will play; *il n'y a pas de quoi fouetter un ~*, it is nothing to bother about; *avoir d'autres ~s à fouetter*, to have other fish to fry; *faire une toilette de ~*, to have a lick and a promise; *langue de ~*, finger biscuit, langue de chat; *jouer au ~ perché*, to play tag; *pas un ~ dans les rues*, not a soul in the streets.

châtaigne [ʃɑtɛɲ] *s.f.* **1.** (edible) chestnut; ~ *d'eau*, water-chestnut; ~ *du Brésil*, Brazil-nut; **2.** (pop.) biff, clout.

châtaigneraie [ʃɑtɛɲrɛ] *s.f.* chestnut plantation.

châtaignier [ʃɑteɲe] *s.m.* (bot.) Spanish, *or* sweet, chestnut-tree; chestnut(-wood).

châtain, -e [ʃɑtɛ̃] *adj.* chestnut(-coloured), auburn, with light brown or chestnut-blond hair.

château (pl. **-x**) [ʃɑto] *s.m.* castle, palace, manor, mansion; *~-fort*, stronghold; ~ *d'eau*, water-tower, reservoir; (naut.) ~ *de proue*, forecastle; ~ *d'arrière*, poop (deck); ~ *de cartes*, house of cards; (pop.) abbrev. of *châteaubriant* (steak).

chateaubriand, châteaubriant [ʃɑtobrijɑ̃] *s.m.* (cook.) chateaubriand, fillet steak.

châtelain [ʃɑtlɛ̃] *s.m.* lord of the manor; owner of a château.

châtelaine [ʃɑtlɛn] *s.f.* **1.** lady of the manor; owner of a château; **2.** chatelaine, key-chain.

chat-huant [ʃaɥɑ̃] *s.m.* (ornith.) short- (or long-) -eared owl.

châtier [ʃɑtje] *v.t.* to chastise, to punish, to castigate; (fig.) to correct; (style) to polish, to perfect; *qui aime bien châtie bien*, spare the rod and spoil the child; ~ *la chair*, to mortify the flesh.

chatière [ʃatjɛr] *s.f.* **1.** cat-hole, cat-flap; **2.** cat--trap; **3.** roof-vent, vent.

châtiment [ʃɑtimɑ̃] *s.m.* punishment, chastisement.

chatoiement [ʃatwamɑ̃] *s.m.* iridescence.

chaton[1] [ʃatɔ̃] *s.m.* **1.** kitten; **2.** (bot.) catkin; **3.** fluff (under furniture).

chaton[2] [ʃatɔ̃] *s.m.* bezel, setting (of ring); stone, gem, (in setting).

chatonner [ʃatɔne] *v.i.* to kitten, to have kittens.

chatouille [ʃatuj] *s.f.* (fam.) tickling; *faire des ~s à qn.*, to tickle s.o.

chatouillement [ʃatujmɑ̃] *s.m.* tickling, titillation; tickle (in the throat).

chatouiller [ʃatuje] *v.t.* (lit. & fig.) to tickle, to titillate.

chatouilleu-x, -se [ʃatujø] *adj.* ticklish; touchy, sensitive; *question ~se*, delicate question, sore point.

chatoyant, -e [ʃatwajɑ̃] *adj.* iridescent; (fig.) sparkling, colourful.

chatoyer [ʃatwaje] *v.i.* to be iridescent.

châtré, -e [ʃɑtre] *adj.* castrated, gelded, neutered; spayed; (fig.) expurgated, bowdlerized; ~ *s.m.* = CASTRAT.

châtrer [ʃɑtre] *v.t.* to castrate, to spay, to geld, to neuter, to doctor; (fig.) to expurgate, to bowdlerize; (hort.) to cut back.

chatte [ʃat] *s.f.* see CHAT.

chattemite [ʃatmit] *s.f.* sanctimonious hypocrite.

chatterie [ʃatri] *s.f.* **1.** caress, caressing; winning ways, wheedling; **2.** cake, dainty, sweetmeat.

chatterton [ʃatɛrtɔn] *s.m.* (electr.) insulating tape.

chat-tigre [ʃatigr] *s.m.* tiger-cat.

chaud, -e [ʃo] *adj.* hot, warm; zealous, ardent, animated, heated; warm, passionate; enthusiastic; *pleurer à ~es larmes*, to weep bitterly; *adv. servez ~*, serve hot; **~ement** [ʃodmɑ̃] *adv.* warmly, (fig.) eagerly.

chaud [ʃo] *s.m.* heat, warmth, warmest part; *le ~ du jour*, the heat of the day; *souffler le ~ et le froid*, to blow hot and cold; *prendre un ~ et froid*, to catch a chill; *(se) tenir au ~*, to keep (oneself) warm; *être bien au ~*, to be nice and warm; *avoir ~*, (of person) to be hot, to be warm; *faire ~*, (weather) to be hot; *tout cela ne me fait ni ~ ni froid*, all that leaves me unmoved; *à ~*, white hot; (metall.) heated, hot; (surg.) *opérer à ~*, to operate at the crisis point.

chaude [ʃod] *s.f.* (cook., metall.) heat; (fam.) *faire une ~*, to make the fire blaze up.

chaudeau [ʃodo] *s.m.* caudle.
chaud-froid [ʃofrwa] *s.m.* (cook.) chaudfroid.
chaudière [ʃodjɛr] *s.f.* **1.** (obs.) cauldron; **2.** boiler.
chaudron [ʃodrɔ̃] *s.m.* **1.** cauldron, pan; **2.** (of mus. instrument) tin-can.
chaudronnerie [ʃodrɔnri] *s.f.* (*grosse*) ~, boiler-making; boilers; (*petite*) ~, hollow-ware trade, pots and pans; boiler-works; shop selling hollow-ware.
chaudronni-er, -ère [ʃodrɔnje] *s.m.* boiler--maker, coppersmith, tinsmith; *adj.* boiler--making.
chauffage [ʃofaʒ] *s.m.* **1.** heating, warming; heating apparatus; method of heating; **2.** warming-up, getting up steam.
chauffant, -e [ʃofɑ̃] *adj.* warming, heating; *plaque ~e*, hot plate; *couverture ~e*, electric blanket.
chauffard [ʃofar] *s.m.* road-hog.
chauffe [ʃof] *s.f.* stokehold, stokehole, furnace--room; stoking-up; heating; *surface de ~*, heating surface.
chauffe-bain [ʃofbɛ̃] *s.m.* (pl. *~-bains*) geyser, water-heater, bath-heater; **~-eau** [ʃofo] *s.m invar.* water-heater; **~-pieds** [ʃofpje] *s.m.invar.* foot-warmer; **~-plats** [ʃofpla] *s.m. invar.* hot-plate, dish-warmer.
chauffer [ʃofe] *v.t.* to warm, to heat, to make warm or hot; to stoke up, to fire up (a boiler), to raise steam; (fig., fam.) to urge on, to coach, to cram (pupils); (pop.) to steal, to pinch; ~ *v.i.* to heat, to get hot; to get up steam; (fig., fam.) *ça va ~*, things are warming up, there's trouble brewing; **se ~** *v.refl.* to warm oneself, to get warm; to heat (one's house); *montrer de quel bois on se chauffe*, to show one's mettle, to show what one's made of.
chaufferette [ʃofrɛt] *s.f.* **1.** foot-warmer; **2.** dish-warmer (on table).
chaufferie [ʃofri] *s.f.* stokehold; boiler-room.
chauffeur [ʃofœr] *s.m.* **1.** stoker, fireman; **2.** (car) driver, chauffeur.
chauffeuse [ʃoføz] *s.f.* fireside chair.
chaufour [ʃofur] *s.m.* lime-kiln.
chaufournier [ʃofurnje] *s.m.* lime-burner.
chaul-age [ʃolaʒ] *s.m.* liming, lime-washing; **~er** [ʃole] *v.t.* to lime, to lime-wash, to white-wash; **~euse** [ʃoløz] *s.f.* (agric.) lime-spreader.
chaumage [ʃomaʒ] *s.m.* (agric.) clearing of stubble.
chaume [ʃom] *s.m.* (agric.) stubble, stubble--field; thatch, thatching; *toit de ~*, thatched roof.
chaumer [ʃome] *v.t.* (agric.) to clear of stubble.
chaumière [ʃomjɛr] *s.f.* thatched cottage, cottage.
chaumine [ʃomin] *s.f.* (obs.) small thatched cottage.
chaussant, -e [ʃosɑ̃] *adj.* (comm. of shoes) well-fitting, smart, dressy.
chausse [ʃos] *s.f.* **1.** (pl.) (obs.) hose; *hurler, courir, après les ~s de qn.*, to hound s.o.; *tirer ses ~s*, to take to one's heels; **2.** cloth funnel; **3.** (herald.) chevron.
chaussée [ʃose] *s.f.* **1.** causeway; dike; carriage--way, road, roadway; *rez-de-~*, ground floor; **2.** reef.
chausse-pied [ʃospje] *s.m.* (pl. *chausse-pieds*) shoe-horn.
chausser [ʃose] *v.t.* to put on (one's feet), to wear, (shoes, etc.); to put on (child's, etc.) shoes; to supply shoes to; to wear (shoes, etc., of a certain kind); to take a certain size in shoes; (fam.) to put on, to adjust, (spectacles); to fit tyres to; (hort.) to earth up; *~ des sandales*, to wear sandals; *~ du 40*, to take shoes size 40; *ces souliers chaussent bien*, these make a good pair of shoes.
chausse-trappe [ʃostrap] *s.f.* (pl. *chausse--trappes*) **1** (obs. mil.) caltrop; **2.** trap.
chaussette [ʃosɛt] *s.f.* sock.
chausseur [ʃosœr] *s.m.* bootmaker.
chausson [ʃosɔ̃] *s.m.* **1.** bedroom slipper, carpet slipper; gym-shoe; baby's bootee; **2.** foot boxing; **3.** (cook.) turnover.
chaussure [ʃosyr] *s.f.* footwear; shoe; shoe trade, footwear trade; (fig.) *trouver ~ à son pied*, to find the very thing, to find Mr. or Miss Right.
chaut [ʃo] see CHALOIR.
chauve [ʃov] *adj.* bald, bald-headed; (fig.) bald, bare; ~ *s.m.* bald-headed man.
chauve-souris [ʃovsuri] *s.m.* (pl. *chauves-souris*) (zool.) bat.
chauvin, -e [ʃovɛ̃] *s.m.f.*, *adj.* chauvinist, jingoist(ic).
chauvinisme [ʃovinism] *s.m.* chauvinism, jingoism.
chauvir [ʃovir] *v.i.* (of horses, donkeys, etc.) *~ des oreilles*, to prick up the ears.
chaux [ʃo] *s.f.* lime; *~ vive*, quicklime; *~ éteinte*, slaked lime; *lait de ~*, *blanc de ~*, lime--wash; *bâtir à ~ et à sable*, to build solidly, to build to last; (fig.) *être bâti à ~ et à sable*, to have an iron constitution, to be as strong as a horse.
chavirement [ʃavirmɑ̃] *s.m.* capsizing.
chavirer [ʃavire] *v.t.i.* **1.** (naut.) to capsize, to turn turtle; **2.** to overturn, to upset; (fig.) to sink, to go under; *ses yeux chavirèrent*, he showed the whites of his eyes.
chébec [ʃebɛk] *s.m.* (naut.) xebec.
chèche [ʃɛʃ] *s.m.* long scarf, turban cloth.
chéchia [ʃeʃja] *s.f.* tarboosh, fez.
cheddite [ʃedit] *s.f.* cheddite.
chef [ʃɛf] *s.m.* **1.** head, (herald.) chief; initiative, authority; head, heading, point, (law) count; *de son ~*, on his own initiative; *de son propre ~*, on his own authority; (law) *au premier ~*, on the first, or main, count; (fig.) *il importe au premier ~*, it is vitally important; **2.** chief, leader, head, director, boss; (pop.) champion; *~ de file*, ringleader; *~ de bureau*, chief clerk; *~ d'orchestre*, conductor; *~ de cuisine*, chef, head-cook; *~ de gare*, station-master; *~ de train*, guard; *en ~*, in chief, head, supreme.
chef-d'œuvre [ʃɛdœvr] *s.m.* (pl. *chefs-d'œuvre*) masterpiece.
chefferie [ʃɛfri] *s.f.* area, district, (of authority); area ruled by tribal chief.
chef-lieu [ʃɛfljø] *s.m.* (pl. *chefs-lieux*) head-quarters (of Local Authority); capital, county town.
cheftaine [ʃɛftɛn] *s.f.* (Boy Scouts) cubmistress.
cheik, scheik [ʃɛk] *s.m.* sheikh.
cheiroptères [keirɔptɛr], **chiroptères** [kirɔptɛr] *s.m.pl.* (zool.) Chiroptera.
chelem, schelem [ʃlɛm] *s.m.* (cards) slam.
chélicère [kelisɛr] *s.f.* (zool.) chelicera.
chélidoine [kelidwan] *s.f.* (bot.) celandine.
chelléen, -ne [ʃeleɛ̃] *adj.* (geol.) Chellean.
chemin [ʃ(ə)mɛ̃] *s.m.* **1.** way, path, road; *en ~*, on the way, in progress; *en bon ~*, going on well; *se mettre en ~*, to set out; *passer son ~*, to go one's way; *rebrousser ~*, to retrace one's steps; *ne pas y aller par quatre ~s*, not to beat about the bush, not to do things by halves; *~ faisant*, on the way; *faire une partie du ~*, to make some progress; *faire du ~*, to make good progress; *faire son ~ dans le monde*, to get on in the world; *prendre le ~ des écoliers*, to go the longest way round; *~ de traverse*, cross-country road; *~ de halage*, tow--path; *~ de ronde*, (fort.) round way; *~ d'escalier*, stair-carpet; *~ de table*, (table) runner; **2.** distance; (mech.) travel (of piston); path;

trajectory (of projectile); direction, way or road (*de*, to); *avoir fait la moitié du* ~, to have covered half the distance, to have reached half--way; *quel* ~ *a-t-il pris?*, which way did he go?; *le* ~ *de la gare*, the way to the station; *prendre le* ~ *du bois*, to go in the direction of the wood; (fig.) *le* ~ *de la ruine*, the highroad to ruin.

chemin de fer [ʃ(ə)mɛ̃dfɛr] *s.m.* **1.** railway; **2.** (cards) chemin de fer.

chemineau (pl. **-x**) [ʃ(ə)mino] *s.m.* tramp, (U.S.) hobo.

cheminée [ʃ(ə)mine] *s.f.* **1.** chimney, flue, chimney-stack; (mountaineering) chimney; (naut.) funnel; **2.** fireplace, hearth, mantel-piece; **3.** air-shaft.

cheminement [ʃ(ə)minmɑ̃] *s.m.* **1.** leisurely progress; forward movement; (mil.) approaches; **2.** surveying (with goniometer or plane-table).

cheminer [ʃ(ə)mine] *v.i.* **1.** to progress slowly, with difficulty; to advance; **2.** to survey (see CHEMINEMENT 2).

cheminot [ʃ(ə)mino] *s.m.* railwayman.

chemisage [ʃ(ə)mizaʒ] *s.m.* (constr.) lining, casing.

chemise [ʃ(ə)miz] *s.f.* **1.** shirt; (obs.) shift; *en bras de* ~, in one's shirt sleeves; *changer de qch. comme de* ~, to be constantly changing sth.; **2.** folder, file, cover; **3.** (constr.) lining, coating, casing, revetment.

chemiser [ʃ(ə)mize] *v.t.* (constr.) to line, to coat, to revet.

chemiserie [ʃ(ə)mizri] *s.f.* shirt-making industry; men's outfitters.

chemisette [ʃ(ə)mizɛt] *s.f.* men's short-sleeved shirt; ladies' short-sleeved blouse.

chemisier [ʃ(ə)mizje] *s.m.* **1.** shirt-maker; **2.** (ladies') shirt-blouse; *robe* ~, shirt-waister.

chênaie [ʃɛnɛ] *s.f.* plantation of oak-trees.

chenal (pl. **aux**) [ʃənal] *s.m.* **1.** navigable channel; mill-race; **2.** (geol.) glacial valley.

chenapan [ʃ(ə)napɑ̃] *s.m.* scamp, scoundrel.

chêne [ʃɛn] *s.m.* oak, oak-tree.

chéneau (pl. **-x**) [ʃeno] *s.m.* gutter (on roof).

chêne-liège [ʃɛnljɛʒ] *s.m.* cork-oak.

chenet [ʃ(ə)nɛ] *s.m.* andiron, fire-dog.

chêne-vert [ʃɛnvɛr] *s.m.* holm-oak, evergreen oak.

chènevière [ʃɛnvjɛr] *s.f.* hemp-field.

chènevis [ʃɛnvi] *s.m.* (bot.) hemp-seed.

chenil [ʃ(ə)ni(l)] *s.m.* **1.** (dog) kennel, boarding kennels; **2.** hovel, dirty hole.

chenille [ʃ(ə)nij] *s.f.* (ent.) caterpillar; caterpillar, track, (of vehicle); *véhicules à* ~, tracked vehicles.

chenillé, -e [ʃ(ə)nije] *adj.* (of vehicle) tracked.

chenillette [ʃ(ə)nijɛt] *s.f.* **1.** (bot.) scorpion--grass; **2.** small caterpillar-tractor.

chénopode [kenɔpɔd] *s.m.* (bot.) chenopodium, goosefoot.

chenu, -e [ʃəny] *adj.* **1.** white (with age); **2.** denuded, leafless; **3.** (pop.) first-class.

cheptel [ʃɛptɛl] *s.m.* livestock; farmer's capital; (law) livestock and equipment leased to farmer; ~ *vif*, livestock; ~ *mort*, equipment.

chèque [ʃɛk] *s.m.* cheque; ~ *sans provision*, dud cheque; ~ *barré*, crossed cheque; ~ *en blanc*, blank cheque; ~ *de voyage*, traveller's cheque; *compte* ~ *postal*, = Post Office Giro.

chéquier [ʃekje] *s.m.* cheque-book.

cher, chère [ʃɛr] *adj.* **1.** dear, beloved; cherished, precious; (before the noun) *mon* ~ *ami*, my dear friend; *mon* ~, my dear man; **2.** dear, expensive, costly; ~ *adv.* dear, dearly; *vendre* ~ *sa vie*, to sell one's life dear; *il me le paiera* ~, he shall pay dearly for that; (fig.) *il ne vaut pas* ~, he's not up to much.

chercher [ʃɛrʃe] *v.t.* **1.** to seek, to search (for), to look for; ~ *une aiguille dans une botte de foin*, (fig.) to look for a needle in a haystack; ~ *midi à quatorze heures*, to complicate matters; ~ *la petite bête*, to be finicky; ~ *à*, to try to, to endeavour to, to strive to; *venir, aller, envoyer*, ~, to come and get, to go and get, to fetch, to send for; *venez me* ~ *à huit heures*, call for me at eight o'clock; *allez* ~ *mon parapluie*, go and fetch my umbrella; *j'ai envoyé* ~ *le médecin*, I've sent for the doctor; **2.** to provoke, to go for (s.o.); *si tu me cherches, gare à toi*, if you upset me, you'll be sorry.

chercheu-r, -se [ʃɛrʃœr] *s.m.f.* researcher; ~**r** *s.m.* (opt.) finder, view-finder; (of rocket) probe; ~**r**, ~**se** *adj.* enquiring; (of missile) homing.

chère [ʃɛr] *s.f.* (obs.) cheer, fare; *faire bonne* ~, to eat well.

chèrement [ʃɛrmɑ̃] *adv.* **1.** dearly, lovingly, tenderly; **2.** dearly, expensively, at a high price.

chéri, -e [ʃeri] *adj.* beloved, dear; *s.m.f.* darling.

chérif [ʃerif] *s.m.* sherif, shereef.

chérir [ʃerir] *v.t.* **1.** to cherish, to love dearly, to worship, to adore; **2.** (fig.) to cling to, to be attached to; to keep alive; to nurse (e.g. one's grief).

chérot [ʃero] *adj.m.* (pop.) very expensive.

cherry [ʃeri] *s.m.* cherry-brandy.

cherté [ʃɛrte] *s.f.* high cost, dearness, expensiveness, high price.

chérubin [ʃerybɛ̃] *s.m.* cherub.

chervis [ʃɛrvi] *s.m.* (bot.) skirret, water-parsnip.

chester [ʃɛstɛr] *s.m.* Cheshire cheese.

chéti-f, -ve [ʃetif] *adj.* puny, weakly, frail; (fig.) paltry, worthless; ~**vement** [ʃetivmɑ̃] *adv.* wretchedly, miserably.

chevaine see CHEVESNE.

cheval (pl. **aux**) [ʃ(ə)val] *s.m.* **1.** horse; horse--flesh; riding; *faire du* ~, to ride, to go in for riding; (fig.) ~ *de bataille*, hobby-horse; *monter (à)* ~, to mount one's horse; to ride, to go in for riding; *monter un* ~ *en amazone*, to ride side--saddle; (fig.) *monter sur ses grands chevaux*, to get on one's high horse; ~ *de retour*, old lag; *à* ~, on horseback, astride; (fig.) *être à* ~ *sur*, to be a stickler for; ~ *de bois*, (gymn.) wooden-horse; *chevaux de bois*, (toy) wooden horses; roundabout; ~ *d'arçons*, vaulting-horse; (ichth.) ~ *marin*, sea-horse, hippocampus; **2.** ~*(-vapeur)* (abbrev. *c.v.*), horse-power; *chevaux au frein*, brake horse-power; *une quatre chevaux*, a four--horse-power car.

chevalement [ʃ(ə)valmɑ̃] *s.m.* (constr.) shoring--up.

chevaler [ʃ(ə)vale] *v.t.* (constr.) to shore up.

chevaleresque [ʃ(ə)valrɛsk] *adj.* knightly, chivalrous.

chevalerie [ʃ(ə)valri] *s.f.* chivalry; knighthood.

chevalet [ʃ(ə)valɛ] *s.m.* **1.** easel, saw-horse, bench; **2.** bridge (of stringed instrument).

chevalier [ʃ(ə)valje] *s.m.* **1.** knight; (male) escort; ~ *d'industrie*, adventurer, crook; **2.** (ornith.) sandpiper; ~ *aux pieds roses*, red-shank.

chevalière [ʃ(ə)valjɛr] *s.f.* signet-ring.

chevalin, -e [ʃ(ə)valɛ̃] *adj.* horse-, equine; *boucherie* ~*e*, butcher's selling horse-meat.

cheval-vapeur [ʃ(ə)valvapœr] *s.m.* see CHEVAL 2.

chevauchant, -e [ʃ(ə)voʃɑ̃] *adj.* overlapping.

chevauchée [ʃ(ə)voʃe] *s.f.* **1.** ride (on horseback); **2.** cavalcade.

chevauchement [ʃ(ə)voʃmɑ̃] *s.m.* overlapping.

chevaucher [ʃ(ə)voʃe] *v.t.* to ride (a horse), to bestride, to be seated astride, (sth.); ~ *v.i.* **1.** (obs.) to ride (on horseback); **2.** to overlap.

chevau-légers [ʃ(ə)voleʒe] *s.m.pl.* (obs.) (mil.) light horse.

chevêche [ʃəvɛʃ] *s.f.* (ornith.) little owl.

chevelu, -e [ʃəvly] *adj.* long-haired; hairy,

bearded; (bot.) comose; *le cuir ~*, the scalp; ~ *s.m.* beard (of root).
chevelure [ʃəvlyr] *s.f.* **1.** head of hair, hair; scalp; **2.** tail (of comet).
chevesne, chevaine, chevenne [ʃ(ə)vɛn] *s.m.* (ichth.) chub.
chevet [ʃ(ə)vɛ] *s.m.* **1.** (obs.) bolster; **2.** head of bed; bedside; *table de ~, livre de ~*, bedside table, bedside book; *au ~ de qn.*, at someone's bedside; **3.** (arch.) apse.
chevêtre [ʃ(ə)vɛtr] *s.m.* (carp.) trimmer beam.
cheveu (pl. **-x**) [ʃ(ə)vø] *s.m.* (human) hair; (pop.) hitch, snag, worry; *couper les ~x en quatre*, to split hairs; *sortir en ~x*, to go hatless, bareheaded; *se prendre aux ~x*, to come to blows; *s'arracher les ~x*, to tear one's hair; *c'est à faire dresser les ~x sur la tête*, it's enough to make one's hair stand on end; (fig.) *tiré par les ~x*, far-fetched; *à un ~ près*, within a hair's breadth; *~ d'ange*, fine vermicelli; imitation gossamer (for decoration); (bot.) *~ de Vénus*, maidenhair fern; *~ de la Vierge*, old man's beard; (pop.) *il y a un ~*, there's a hitch, there's a spot of bother.
chevillard [ʃ(ə)vijar] *s.m.* wholesale butcher; meat distributor.
cheville [ʃ(ə)vij] *s.f.* **1.** peg, wooden pin, dowel; (mus.) tuning peg; hook; *viande vendue à la ~*, meat sold wholesale; *~ ouvrière*, pivot, kingpin; (fig.) mainspring; **2.** ankle; *ne pas arriver, venir, à la ~ de qn.*, not to be able to hold a candle to s.o.; **3.** (Lit.) padding; **4.** tine (of antler).
cheviller [ʃ(ə)vije] *v.t.* to peg, to pin, to dowel, to bolt, to rivet; (Lit.) to pad; (fig.) *avoir l'âme chevillée au corps*, to have as many lives as a cat.
cheviotte [ʃəvjɔt] *s.f.* (text.) cheviot.
chèvre [ʃɛvr] *s.f.* **1.** goat, she-goat, nanny-goat; (fig.) *ménager la ~ et le chou*, to sit on the fence; **2.** (techn.) gin, lifting-tackle; *~ s.m.* goat cheese.
chevreau (pl. **-x**) [ʃəvro] *s.m.* **1.** (zool.) kid; **2.** kid (leather).
chèvrefeuille [ʃɛvrəfœj] *s.f.* (bot.) honeysuckle.
chèvre-pied [ʃɛvrəpje] *s.m.* (pl. *chèvre-pieds*) satyr; *~ adj.* goat-footed.
chevreter [ʃəvrəte] **chevretter** [ʃəvrete] *v.i.* (of she-goat) to kid.
chevrette [ʃəvrɛt] *s.f.* **1.** female kid; **2.** kid (leather); **3.** roe, doe; **4.** metal tripod.
chevreuil [ʃəvrœj] *s.m.* roe, roe-deer, roebuck.
chevri-er, -ère [ʃəvrije] *s.m.f.* goatherd; *~***er** *s.m.* white haricot bean.
chevron [ʃəvrɔ̃] *s.m.* **1.** (constr.) rafter; **2.** chevron; (mil.) stripe, long-service stripe; **3.** (text.) twill; **4.** (techn.) *engrenage à ~s*, double helical gear.
chevronné, -e [ʃəvrɔne] *adj.* (herald.) chevronned; (fig.) experienced.
chevrotain [ʃəvrɔtɛ̃] *s.m.* = CHEVROTIN 2.
chevrotant, -e [ʃəvrɔtɑ̃] *adj.* (of voice) tremulous, quavering.
chevrotement [ʃəvrɔtmɑ̃] *s.m.* tremulousness, quavering, (of voice).
chevroter [ʃəvrɔte] *v.i.* **1.** (of goat) to bleat; **2.** to speak or sing in a quavering voice.
chevrotin [ʃəvrɔtɛ̃] *s.m.* **1.** fawn (of the roe); **2.** mouse-deer; **3.** kid (leather).
chevrotine [ʃəvrɔtin] *s.f.* buckshot.
chewing-gum [ʃwiŋgɔm] *s.m.* chewing-gum.
chez [ʃe] *prep.* at or to the house or shop of; with, among; in (the writings of); *passer ~ elle*, to call in at her house; *~ le boulanger*, at the baker's; *~ lui c'est devenu une habitude*, it has become a habit with him; *c'est rare ~ les Esquimaux*, it is rare among Eskimos; *on en trouve des exemples ~ Molière*, one finds examples of it in Molière.
chez-moi [ʃemwa], **chez-soi** [ʃeswa] *s.m.invar.* home.
chiader [ʃjade] *v.t.i.* (slang) to swot (up, for).
chialer [ʃjale] *v.i.* (pop.) to cry, to blubber.
chianti [kjɑ̃ti] *s.m.* chianti.
chiasma [kjasma], **chiasme** [kjasm] *s.m.* (anat.) chiasm, chiasma; (rhet.) chiasmus.
chiasse [ʃjas] *s.f.* **1.** fly-dirt; **2.** (pop.) diarrhœa; (fig.) *avoir la ~*, to be scared.
chibouk, chibouque [ʃibuk] *s.m.* chibouk.
chic [ʃik] *s.m.* **1.** knack, trick, skill; *il a le ~ pour faire cela*, he has the knack of doing that; *peindre de ~*, to paint from the imagination, without a model; **2.** chic, elegance, style; *~ adj. invar.* chic, smart, elegant; (fam.) decent, generous; *c'est un ~ type*, he's a good sort; *~ interj. ~ alors!*, good show!
chicane [ʃikan] *s.f.* **1.** chicane, chicanery; quibble, quibbling, quarrel, squabble; *gens de ~*, pettifogging lawyers; **2.** (mech.) baffle; (sport) chicane, obstacle.
chicaner [ʃikane] *v.t.i.* to quibble, to cavil; to take to law; *~ qch. à qn.*, to quibble with s.o. over sth.; **se ~** *v.refl.* to quarrel.
chicanerie [ʃikanri] *s.f.* chicanery, quibbling.
chicaneu-r, -se [ʃikanœr], **chicani-er, -ère** [ʃikanje] *s.m.f.* quibbler, pettifogger; *adj.* pettifogging, quibbling.
chiche [ʃiʃ] *adj.* (obs.) mean, miserly; (mod.) sparing; *être ~ de ses compliments*, to be sparing with one's compliments; *pois ~*, chick-pea; *~***ment** [ʃiʃmɑ̃] *adv.* meanly; *~ interj.* just you dare!
chichi [ʃiʃi] *s.m.* fuss, ado, to-do; airs and graces, affectation.
chichiteu-x, -se [ʃiʃitø] *adj.* fussy, prissy, affected.
chicon [ʃikɔ̃] *s.m.* (bot.) long-leaved lettuce.
chicorée [ʃikɔre] *s.f.* **1.** (bot.) *~ sauvage*, chicory, succory; *~ cultivée, frisée*, endive; **2.** ground chicory (for use in coffee).
chicot [ʃiko] *s.m.* stump (of tree or tooth).
chicotin [ʃikɔtɛ̃] *s.m.* used only in the phrase *amer comme ~*, as bitter as aloes.
chien, -ne [ʃjɛ̃] *s.m.f.* **1.** dog, bitch, hound; *~ de chasse*, gun-dog; *~ de garde*, watch-dog, house-dog; *~ d'aveugle*, guide-dog; *~ couchant, ~ d'arrêt*, setter; *~ policier*, police-dog; *~ de berger*, sheep-dog; *~ d'appartement*, lap-dog; (fig.) *garder à qn. un ~ de sa chienne*, to bear s.o. a grudge; *se regarder en ~s de faïence*, to look daggers at each other; *arriver comme un ~ dans un jeu de quilles*, to be like a bull in a china-shop; *recevoir qn. comme un ~ dans un jeu de quilles*, to treat s.o. as an unwelcome guest; *vivre comme ~ et chat*, to be like cat and dog; *ne pas attacher ses ~s avec des saucisses*, to be miserly; *faire le ~ couchant*, to cringe, to fawn; *entre ~ et loup*, at dusk; *qui veut noyer son ~ l'accuse de la rage*, give a dog a bad name and hang him; *un ~ peut bien regarder un évêque*, a cat may look at a king; *il n'est pas bon à jeter aux ~s*, he's utterly worthless; *de ~*, wretched, miserable; *un temps de ~*, wretched weather; **2.** (fig.) wretch, cur; *~ de*, beastly, rotten; *~ne de vie!*, rotten life!; *~ de métier*, wretched job; *~ de quartier*, (mil., pop.) dogsbody; **3.** hammer (of gun); **4.** (ichth.) *~ de mer*, dogfish, monkfish, hammerhead; *~ dauphin*, tope; **5.** style, chic, elegance; **6.** (pop.) nap; *piquer un ~*, to have forty winks.
chiendent [ʃjɛ̃dɑ̃] *s.m.* (bot.) couch-grass; (fig.) hitch, snag.
chienlit [ʃjɑ̃li] *s.m.* carnival mask; grotesque disguise.
chien-loup [ʃjɛ̃lu] *s.m.* wolf-hound; Alsatian.
chiennerie [ʃjɛnri] *s.f.* **1.** (obs.) pack of dogs; **2.** stinginess.
chier [ʃje] *v.i.* (vulg.) to shit (vulg.); *tu me fais ~*, you make me sick.
chiffe [ʃif] *s.f.* poor quality cloth; flimsy material; (fig., fam.) person of weak character.

chiffon [ʃifɔ̃] *s.m.* rag; duster; scrap (of paper); (pl.) finery, dress; *parler ~s*, to talk about clothes, about fashion.
chiffonnade [ʃifɔnad] *s.f.* (cook.) chiffonade.
chiffonnage [ʃifɔnaʒ], **chiffonnement** [ʃifɔnmɑ̃] *s.m.* crumpling, rumpling.
chiffonné, -e [ʃifɔne] *adj.* **1.** rumpled, crumpled; **2.** (fig.) (of features, etc.) irregular but pleasing.
chiffonnement see CHIFFONAGE.
chiffonner [ʃifɔne] *v.t.* to crumple (up), to rumple; (fig.) to worry, to vex; **se ~** *v.refl.* to crumple, to crease; **~** *v.i.* to do a bit of dress-making.
chiffonni-er, -ère [ʃifɔnje] *s.m.f.* rag-picker, rag-and-bone dealer; **~er** *s.m.* (furniture) chiffonier.
chiffrage [ʃifraʒ] *s.m.* **1.** ciphering, coding; **2.** pricing, estimating; **3.** (mus.) figuring.
chiffre [ʃifr] *s.m.* **1.** figure, digit, numeral; (mus.) figure; total, number, index; **2.** cipher, code; combination (of lock); **3.** monogram.
chiffrement [ʃifrəmɑ̃] *s.m.* ciphering, coding.
chiffrer [ʃifre] *v.t.i.* **1.** to number, to mark with a number; to value, to estimate, to price, to express in figures; (mus.) to figure (a bass); **2.** to mark with a monogram; **3.** to cipher, to code, to write in code.
chiffreur [ʃifrœr] *s.m.* **1.** cipher-clerk; **2.** calculator.
chignole [ʃiɲɔl] *s.f.* **1.** (fam.) (car) jalopy, banger; **2.** hand or electric drill.
chignon [ʃiɲɔ̃] *s.m.* (hair-style) chignon, roll, bun; *crêper le ~ d'une femme*, to pull a woman's hair; (fig.) (of women) *se crêper le ~*, to have a set-to.
Chili [ʃili] *s.m.* (geog.) Chile.
chilien, -ne [ʃiljɛ̃] *adj.*, *s.m.f.* Chilean.
chimère [ʃimɛr] *s.f.* **1.** (myth., fig.) chimera; delusion, daydream; **2.** (ichth., biol.) chimaera.
chimérique [ʃimerik] *adj.* chimerical; wildly fanciful, visionary.
chimie [ʃimi] *s.f.* chemistry.
chimiothérapie [ʃimjɔterapi] *s.f.* chemotherapy.
chimique [ʃimik] *adj.* chemical; **~ment** [ʃimikmɑ̃] *adv.* chemically.
chimiste [ʃimist] *s.m.f.* chemist; ⚠ not 'chemist' in sense 'pharmacist'.
chimpanzé [ʃɛ̃pɑ̃ze] *s.m.* (zool.) chimpanzee.
chinage [ʃinaʒ] *s.m.* (text.) colouring of warp.
chinchilla [ʃɛ̃ʃila] *s.m.* chinchilla (animal, fur).
Chine [ʃin] *s.f.* (geog.) China; **~** *s.m.* rice--paper.
chine[1] [ʃin] *s.m.* or *f.* porcelain, china.
chine[2] [ʃin] *s.f.* bargain-hunting (in junk-shops).
chiné, -e [ʃine] *adj.* (text.) mottled, clouded, chiné; **~** *s.m.* chiné fabric.
chiner[1] [ʃine] *v.t.* (text.) to mottle, to cloud.
chiner[2] [ʃine] *v.t.* **1.** to look for bargains in junk-shops); **2** to tease.
chineu-r, -se [ʃinœr] *s.m.f.* **1.** bargain-hunter (in junk-shops; **2.** leg-puller, one who teases.
chinois, -e [ʃinwa] *adj.* Chinese, of China; (fig.) outlandish; *s.m.f.* Chinese (man or woman); (fig.) queer customer, very subtle character; **~** *s.m.* **1.** Chinese (language); (fig.) sth. incomprehensible; *c'est du ~*, I can't understand a word of it, it's all Greek to me; **2.** cumquat; **3.** conical strainer.
chinoiserie [ʃinwazri] *s.f.* Chinese knick--knack; (fig.) complication, hair-splitting; *~s administratives*, red tape.
chinook [ʃinuk] *s.m.* (meteor.) chinook.
chintz [ʃints] *s.m.* (text.) chintz.
chinure [ʃinyr] *s.f.* (text.) mottling.
chiot [ʃjo] *s.m.* puppy, cub.
chiottes [ʃjɔt] *s.f.pl.* (pop.) lavatories, latrines.
chiper [ʃipe] *v.t.* (fam.) to steal, to pinch, to nick; (fig.) to catch (a cold).
chipeu-r, -se [ʃipœr] *adj.* (fam.) light-fingered; *s.m.f.* shop-lifter, petty thief.
chipie [ʃipi] *s.f.* shrew, hag.
chipolata [ʃipɔlata] *s.f.* chipolata (sausage).
chipotage [ʃipɔtaʒ] *s.m.* haggling, quibbling.
chipoter [ʃipɔte] *v.i.* **1.** to nibble, to toy with one's food; **2.** to haggle, to quibble; **3.** to fiddle, to trifle, to waste time.
chipoteu-r, -se [ʃipɔtœr] *s.m.f.* haggler, quibbler, trifler.
chips [ʃip(s)] *s.m.pl.* (also *pommes ~*) potato crisps; ⚠ not 'chips'.
chique [ʃik] *s.f.* **1.** quid (of tobacco); (fig., pop.) *couper la ~ à qn.*, to interrupt s.o. rudely; *avaler sa ~*, to die; **2.** (fam.) swelling of cheek; **3.** harvest-bug.
chiqué [ʃike] *s.m.* (fam.) affectation, showing--off; *faire qch. au ~*, to do sth. to show off.
chiquenaude [ʃiknod] *s.f.* fillip, flip, flick.
chiquer [ʃike] *v.t.* to chew (tobacco).
chiqueu-r, -se [ʃikœr] *s.m.f.* person who chews tobacco.
chirographaire [kirɔgrafɛr] *adj.* (of creditor, etc.) unsecured.
chiromancie [kirɔmɑ̃si] *s.f.* chiromancy, palmistry.
chiromancien, -ne [kirɔmɑ̃sjɛ̃] *s.m.f.* chiromancer, palmist.
chiropracteur [kirɔpraktœr] *s.m.* chiropractor.
chiropraxie, chiropractie [kirɔpraksi] *s.f.* chiropractic.
chiroptères see CHEIROPTÈRES.
chirurgical, -e, (aux) [ʃiryrʒikal] *adj.* surgical.
chirurgie [ʃiryrʒi] *s.f.* surgery; ⚠ not 'surgery' in senses 'consulting-room', 'hours of consultation'.
chirurgien [ʃiryrʒɛ̃] *s.m.* surgeon; **~** *dentiste*, dental surgeon.
chistera [(t)ʃistera] *s.f.* or *m.* pelota bat.
chitine [kitin] *s.f.* (zool.) chitin.
chitineu-x, -se [kitinø] *adj.* chitinous.
chiton [kitɔ̃] *s.m.* (Gr. ant.) chiton.
chiure [ʃjyr] *s.f.* fly-speck.
chlamyde [klamid] *s.f.* (Gr. ant.) chlamys.
chlor-al [klɔral] *s.m.* (chem.) chloral; **~amphénicol** [klɔrɑ̃fenikɔl] *s.m.* (chem.) chloramphenicol; **~ate** [klɔrat] *s.m.* chlorate.
chlore [klɔr] *s.m.* chlorine.
chloré, -e [klɔre] *adj.* chlorinated.
chlor-hydrate [klɔridrat] *s.m.* hydrochlorate; **~hydrique** [klɔridrik] *adj.* hydrochloric; **~ique** [klɔrik] *adj.* chloric.
chloro-forme [klɔrɔfɔrm] *s.m.* chloroform; **~former** [klɔrɔfɔrme] *v.t.* to chloroform, to anaesthetize with chloroform; (fig.) to anaesthetize, to lull to sleep; **~formisation** [klɔrɔfɔrmizɑsjɔ̃] *s.f.* chloroforming; **~métrie** [klɔrɔmetri] *s.f.* chlorometry; **~phycées** [klɔrɔfise] *s.f.pl.* (bot.) Chlorophyceae; **~phylle** [klɔrɔfil] *s.f.* chlorophyll.
chlorophyllien, -ne [klɔrɔfiljɛ̃] *adj.* (biol.) chlorophyllian.
chloropicrine [klɔrɔpikrin] *s.f.* (chem.) chloropicrin.
chlorose [klɔroz] *s.f.* (med., bot.) chlorosis.
chlorotique [klɔrɔtik] *adj.* chlorotic.
chlorure [klɔryr] *s.m.* chloride.
chloruré, -e [klɔryre] *adj.* chloridized, containing chloride.
choc [ʃɔk] *s.m.* clash, collision, impact; (lit. & fig.) conflict; (fig.) shock; *premier ~*, brunt; *~ en retour*, recoil, kick; *amortisseur (de ~)*, shock absorber; **~** *adj.invar.* shock.
chocolat [ʃɔkɔla] *s.m.* chocolate; chocolate colour; **~** *adj.invar.* chocolate(-coloured); (fam.) *être ~*, to be done out of sth.
chocolaté, -e [ʃɔkɔlate] *adj.* chocolate-flavoured.

chocolaterie [ʃɔkɔlatri] *s.f.* chocolate factory or manufacture.

chocolati-er, -ère [ʃɔkɔlatje] *s.m.f.* chocolate dealer or manufacturer; *adj.* chocolate; **~ère** *s.f.* chocolate pot.

choéphore [kɔefɔr] *s.f.* (Gr. ant.) choëphoros.

chœur [kœr] *s.m.* **1.** chorus; **2.** choir.

choir [ʃwar] *v.i.* to fall; obs. exc. in phrase *laisser ~ qn.*, to drop s.o.

choisi, -e [ʃwazi] *adj.* chosen; select, choice; selected, carefully chosen.

choisir [ʃwazir] *v.t.* to choose, to select; to pick out, to single out; *il y a de quoi ~*, there is plenty of choice.

choix [ʃwa] *s.m.* choice, selection; option; choosing; *de ~*, choice, picked, selected; *de grand ~*, choicest; *au ~*, at will, as desired; by selection; *avancement au ~*, promotion by selection.

choke-bore [tʃɔkbɔr] *s.m.* choke-bore (of sporting guns).

cholécystite [kɔlesistit] *s.f.* (med.) cholecystitis.

cholédoque [kɔledɔk] *adj.* (anat.) *canal ~*, choledoch.

cholémie [kɔlemi] *s.f.* (med.) cholaemia; cholaemic index.

choléra [kɔlera] *s.m.* cholera; (fig.) pest.

cholériforme [kɔleriform] *adj.* choleriform.

cholér-ine [kɔlerin] *s.f.* (med.) milder form of cholera; **~ique** [kɔlerik] *adj.* (med.) choleraic; ⚠ not 'choleric'.

cholestérine [kɔlɛsterin] *s.f.*, **cholestérol** [kɔlɛsterɔl] *s.m.* cholesterol.

chômage [ʃomaʒ] *s.m.* **1.** (obs.) abstention from work; **2.** unemployment; shut-down (of works); *en ~*, unemployed, out of work, idle; *être au ~*, to be on the dole; *~ partiel*, short-time working; *indemnité de ~*, unemployment benefit.

chômer [ʃome] *v.i.* to be out of work, to be unemployed; (of factory) to shut down; not to work on public holidays; (fig.) to be idle, unused, unoccupied; *laisser ~*, to leave idle.

chômeu-r, -se [ʃomœr] *s.m.f.* unemployed worker.

chondrio-me [kɔ̃drijom] *s.m.* (biol.) chondriome; **~some** [kɔ̃drijozom] *s.m.* (biol.) chondriosome.

chondroblaste [kɔ̃drɔblast] *s.m.* (biol.) chondroblast.

chope [ʃɔp] *s.f.* beer-mug, tankard; mugful of beer.

choper [ʃɔpe] *v.t.* (pop.) to pinch, to steal; to arrest; to catch.

chopine [ʃɔpin] *s.f.* **1.** (obs.) chopin ($=\frac{1}{2}$ litre); **2.** drink (of wine).

chopper [ʃɔpe] *v.i.* to stumble; (fig.) to blunder.

choquant, -e [ʃɔkɑ̃] *adj.* shocking, offensive.

choquer [ʃɔke] *v.t.* **1.** to strike, to collide with; **2.** to shock, to offend, to grate on (the ear).

choral, -e [kɔral] *adj.* (pl. regular or **aux**) choral; *~ s.m.* chorale.

chorale [kɔral] *s.f.* choral society.

chorée [kɔre] *s.f.* (med.) chorea, St. Vitus's dance.

chorège [kɔrɛʒ] *s.m.* (Gr. ant.) choragus.

choré-graphe [kɔregraf] *s.m.f.* choreographer; **~graphie** [kɔregrafi] *s.f.* choreography; **~graphique** [kɔregrafik] *adj.* choreographic.

choréique [kɔreik] *adj.* (med.) choreic.

choreute [kɔrøt] *s.m.* (Gr. ant.) member of chorus.

chorion [kɔrjɔ̃] *s.m.* (anat.) chorion.

choriste [kɔrist] *s.m.f.* chorister, chorus-singer, choral singer.

choroïde [kɔrɔid] *s.f.* (anat.) choroid.

chorus [kɔrys] *s.m.* chorus; *faire ~*, to chime in, to express agreement, to echo (sentiments, etc.); to chorus.

chose [ʃoz] *s.f.* thing, object; event, affair, matter; possession; *les ~s*, facts, reality; *expliquer la ~*, to explain the matter, to explain what it's all about; *être la ~ de qn.*, to be someone's possession, to be just an object to s.o.; *toutes ~s égales d'ailleurs*, other things being equal; *appeler les ~s par leur nom*, to call a spade a spade, to speak plainly; *faire bien les ~s*, to put on a lavish entertainment; *dites-lui bien des ~s de ma part*, give him my kind regards; *autre ~*, something else; *autre ~ est de parler, autre chose d'agir*, it's one thing to talk, another to act; *peu de ~*, nothing much, a trifling matter; *quelque ~*, something; *quelque ~ de bon*, something good; *il y a quelque ~ comme un mois qu'il est parti*, it is about a month since he left; *se croire quelque ~*, to think oneself somebody; *~ s.m., adj.* (pop.) *donnez-moi ce ~*, give me that what-do-you-call--it; *ce monsieur Chose*, this Mr. What's-his-name; (fam.) *se sentir tout ~*, to feel out of sorts.

chott [ʃɔt] *s.m.* (geog.) chott, shott.

chou (pl. **-x**) [ʃu] *s.m.* **1.** cabbage, kale; *~ pommé*, common cabbage; *~ marin*, sea-kale; *~x de Bruxelles*, Brussels sprouts; *~ frisé d'Écosse*, curly kale; *~ rouge*, red cabbage; *feuille de ~*, (fig.) rag (newspaper); *aller planter ses ~x*, to retire to the country; *faire ses ~x gras de*, to feather one's nest with; *ménager la chèvre et le ~*, to bide one's time, to see which way the wind is blowing; *faire ~ blanc*, to draw a blank; *être dans les ~x*, to be in difficulties; *entrer dans le ~ à qn.*, to pitch into s.o.; to collide with s.o.; *bête comme ~*, stupid, simple; **2.** darling, dear, pet; **3.** bow of ribbon; rosette; **4.** choux pastry; puff; *~ adj.invar.* sweet.

chouan [ʃwɑ̃] *s.m.* (Fr. hist.) Chouan, royalist insurgent.

chouannerie [ʃwanri] *s.f.* (Fr. hist.) the Chouan rebellion.

choucas [ʃuka] *s.m.* (ornith.) jackdaw.

chouchou, -te [ʃuʃu] *s.m.f.* (fam.) pet.

chouchouter [ʃuʃute] *v.t.* to pet, to spoil, to pamper.

choucroute [ʃukrut] *s.f.* sauerkraut.

chouette [ʃwɛt] *s.f.* **1.** owl; *~ blanche*, snowy owl; *~ chevêche*, little owl; *~ des bois*, tawny owl; *~ des clochers*, barn-owl; **2.** hag.

chouette [ʃwɛt] *adj., interj.* fine, pretty, super.

chou-fleur [ʃuflœr] *s.m.* (pl. *choux-fleurs*) cauliflower.

chou-navet [ʃunavɛ] *s.m.* (pl. *choux-navets*) (agric.) swede.

chou-palmiste [ʃupalmist] *s.m.* (pl. *choux-palmistes*) cabbage-palm.

chou-rave [ʃurav] *s.m.* (pl. *choux-raves*) kohlrabi.

chow-chow [ʃuʃu, ʃawʃaw] *s.m.* chow, chow--chow (dog.).

choyer [ʃwaje] *v.t.* to coddle, to pamper; (fig.) to nurse, to cultivate.

chrême [krɛm] *s.m.* (eccles.) chrism.

chrestomathie [krɛstɔmati] *s.f.* chrestomathy, anthology.

chrétien, -ne [kretjɛ̃] *adj., s.m.f.* Christian; **~nement** [kretjɛnmɑ̃] *adv.* like a good Christian, as a Christian.

chrétienté [kretjɛ̃te] *s.f.* Christendom; Christianity.

chrisme [krism] *s.m.* (eccles.) chi-rho, chrismon.

christ [krist] *s.m.* **1.** (*le*) *Christ*, Christ; **2.** crucifix.

christiania [kristjanja] *s.m.* (ski-ing) Christiania.

christian-isation [kristjanizɑsjɔ̃] *s.f.* Christianization; **~iser** [kristjanize] *v.t.* to Christianize; **~isme** [kristjanism] *s.m.* Christianity.

christologie [kristɔlɔʒi] *s.f.* Christology.

chromage [kromaʒ] *s.m.* chromium plating, chroming; chromium plate, chrome finish.

chromate [krɔmat] *s.m.* (chem.) chromate.
chromat-ine [krɔmatin] *s.f.* (biol.) chromatin; **~ique** [krɔmatik] *adj.* chromatic; chromosomic; **~isme** [krɔmatism] *s.m.* (opt.) chromatism; (mus.) chromaticism; **~ographie** [krɔmatɔgrafi] *s.f.* chromatography.
chrome [krom] *s.m.* chromium; chrome; *jaune de ~*, chrome yellow; (car) *les ~s*, the chromium parts.
chromer [krome] *v.t.* **1.** to plate with chromium; **2.** to tan (leather with chrome alum), to chrome.
chromique [krɔmik] *adj.* (chem.) chromic.
chromo [krɔmo] *s.m.* (often pej.) lithograph.
chromo-gène [krɔmɔʒɛn] *adj.* chromogenous; **~lithographie** [krɔmɔlitɔgrafi] *s.f.* chromolithography; chromolithograph; **~some** [krɔmozom] *s.m.* chromosome; **~sphère** [krɔmɔsfɛr] *s.f.* (astron.) chromosphere; **~typie** [krɔmɔtipi], **~typographie** [krɔmɔtipɔgrafi] *s.f.* chromotype, chromotypography.
chronaxie [krɔnaksi] *s.f.* (physiol.) chronaxia.
chronicité [krɔnisite] *s.f.* (med.) chronicity.
chronique [krɔnik] *s.f.* chronicle; report, rumour, news; diary.
chronique [krɔnik] *adj.* chronic, persistent; **~ment** [krɔnikmɑ̃] *adv.* chronically.
chroniqueur [krɔnikœr] *s.m.* **1.** chronicler, diarist; **2.** (press) columnist, critic.
chrono-graphe [krɔnɔgraf] *s.m.* chronograph; **~logie** [krɔnɔlɔʒi] *s.f.* chronology; **~logique** [krɔnɔlɔʒik] *adj.* chronological; **~logiquement** *adv.* chronologically, in chronological order; **~métrage** [krɔnɔmetraʒ] *s.m.* chronometry, timing; **~mètre** [krɔnɔmɛtr] *s.m.* chronometer; **~métrer** [krɔnɔmetre] *v.t.* to time (with chronometer, stop-watch); **~métreur** [krɔnɔmetrœr] *s.m.* time-keeper; **~métrie** [krɔnɔmetri] *s.f.* chronometry; **~métrique** [krɔnɔmetrik] *adj.* chronometric(al); **~photographie** [krɔnɔfɔtɔgrafi] *s.f.* (photographic) motion study.
chrysalide [krizalid] *s.f.* (lit. & fig.) chrysalis; (fig.) *sortir de sa ~*, to come out of one's obscurity, or shell.
chrysanthème [krizɑ̃tɛm] *s.m.* (bot.) chrysanthemum.
chryséléphantin, -e [krizelefɑ̃tɛ̃] *adj.* (ant. sculpt.) chryselephantine.
chrysocale [krizɔkal] *s.m.* (metall.) pinchbeck.
chrysolithe [krizɔlit] *s.f.* (min.) chrysolite.
chrysomèle [krizɔmɛl] *s.f.* (ent.) leaf-beetle.
chrysoprase [krizɔprɑz] *s.f.* (min.) chrysoprase.
chuchot-ement [ʃyʃɔtmɑ̃] *s.m.* whispering, whisper; **~er** [ʃyʃɔte] *v.t.i.* to whisper.
chuchoteu-r, -se [ʃyʃɔtœr] *adj.* whispering; *s.m.f.* whisperer.
chuchotis [ʃyʃɔti] *s.m.* (faint) whisper.
chuintant, -e [ʃɥɛ̃tɑ̃] *adj.*, *s.f.* (phon.) hush-sibilant.
chuintement [ʃɥɛ̃tmɑ̃] *s.m.* **1.** whistling, hissing, sizzling sound; **2.** (lang.) see CHUINTER 2.
chuinter [ʃɥɛ̃te] *v.i.* **1.** to hiss, to sizzle; (of owl) to hoot; **2.** (lang.) to sound [s] as [ʃ].
chut [ʃyt] *interj.* Sh!
chute [ʃyt] *s.f.* **1.** fall, falling; descent, slope; waterfall; failure, failing; collapse; drop (in temperature, etc.); *~ d'un toit*, slope of a roof; (theatr.) *~ du rideau*, (final) curtain; *~ du jour*, end of the day, sundown; **2.** (rhet.) end, conclusion; **3.** (dressm.) snippings.
chuter [ʃyte] *v.i.* (theatr.) to be a flop; (cards) to be light, to go down; (pop.) to fall.
chyle [ʃil] *s.m.* (physiol.) chyle.
chylifère [ʃilifɛr] *adj.* chyliferous.
chyme [ʃim] *s.m.* (physiol.) chyme.
Chypre [ʃipr] *s.f.* (geog.) Cyprus.
ci [si] *adv.* (abbrev. of *ici*) here; *~-gît*, here lies; *~-inclus*, *~-joint*, herewith; *~-après*, hereafter, later, below; *~-contre*, opposite; *~-dessous*, below, infra, hereunder; *~-dessus*, above, supra; *~-devant*, former(ly); *de ~, de là, par ~, par là*, here and there, now and then; *~ et ça*, one thing and another, this and that; *comme ~, comme ça*, so-so; -~, this, these; *cet homme-~*, this man; *ces enfants-~*, these children; *celui-, celle-~*, this (one), the latter; *ceux-, celles-~*, these (ones), the latter.
cible [sibl] *s.f.* target; (fig.) butt.
ciboire [sibwar] *s.m.* (eccles.) pyx, ciborium.
ciborium [sibɔrjɔm] *s.m.* (arch.) ciborium.
ciboule [sibul] *s.f.* (bot.) ciboule, Welsh onion.
ciboulette [sibulɛt] *s.f.* (bot.) chive(s).
ciboulot [sibulo] *s.m.* (pop.) head.
cicatrice [sikatris] *s.f.* scar; cicatrice, cicatrix.
cicatriciel, -le [sikatrisjɛl] *adj.* cicatricial.
cicatricule [sikatrikyl] *s.f.* (biol.) cicatricle.
cicatrisant, -e [sikatrizɑ̃] *adj.* healing, cicatrizing; *~ s.m.* cicatrizant.
cicatris-ation [sikatrizɑsjɔ̃] *s.f.* cicatrization, healing, drying, closing, (of wound, etc.); **~er** [sikatrize] *v.t.* to cicatrize, to heal, to close, (wound, etc.); **se ~er** *v.refl.* to heal.
cicéro [sisero] *s.m.* (print.) pica.
Cicéron [siserɔ̃] *s.m.* Cicero.
cicérone [siserɔn] *s.m.* cicerone, guide.
cicéronien, -ne [siserɔnjɛ̃] *adj.* Ciceronian.
cicindèle [sisɛ̃dɛl] *s.f.* (ent.) **1.** (obs.) glow-worm; **2.** (mod.) tiger-beetle.
ciconiidés [sikɔniide] *s.m.pl.* (ornith.) stork family.
cicutaire [sikytɛr] *s.f.* (bot.) water-hemlock.
cicutine [sikytin] *s.f.* (chem.) coniine, conia, conine.
cidre [sidr] *s.m.* cider; *~ bouché*, champagne cider.
cidrerie [sidrəri] *s.f.* cider-mill, cider-factory.
ciel [sjɛl] *s.m.* **1.** (pl. *cieux*) heaven, paradise; God; *le royaume des cieux*, the Kingdom of Heaven; *aide-toi, le ~ t'aidera*, God helps those who help themselves; *~!, O ~!, juste ~!*, (good) heavens!; **2.** (pl. *cieux*) sky, atmosphere, firmament; the heavens; clime; *sous le ~*, on earth; *sous d'autres cieux*, in other climes, in other countries; *à ~ ouvert*, uncovered, open to the sky; (fig.) *tomber du ~*, to arrive like a bolt from the blue, to happen unexpectedly; *avoir l'air de tomber du ~*, to look bewildered; *remuer ~ et terre*, to move heaven and earth, to leave no stone unturned; *être au septième ~*, to be in the seventh heaven; **3.** (pl. *ciels*) (aspect of) sky; (paint.) sky; *ciels nuageux*, cloudy skies; **4.** (pl. *ciels*) canopy, tester (over four-poster bed); (mining) roof (of gallery, etc.).
cierge [sjɛrʒ] *s.m.* **1.** (eccles.) candle, taper; (fig.) *être droit comme un ~*, to be as stiff as a poker; **2.** (bot.) candle-tree; *~ de Notre-Dame*, Aaron's rod; *~ amer* or *laiteux*, spurge.
cigale [sigal] *s.f.* **1.** (ent.) cicada; **2.** *~ de mer*, mantis shrimp; **3.** (naut.) ring (of anchor, etc.).
cigare [sigar] *s.m.* cigar, cheroot.
cigarette [sigarɛt] *s.f.* cigarette.
cigarière [sigarjɛr] *s.f.* (obs.) cigar-maker.
ci-gît [siʒi] see CI.
cigogne [sigɔɲ] *s.f.* **1.** (ornith.) stork; **2.** (mech.) handle, crank.
cigogneau (pl. **-x**) [sigɔɲo] *s.m.* (ornith.) young stork.
ciguë [sigy] *s.f.* (bot., pharm.) hemlock; *petite ~*, fool's parsley.
ci-inclus [siɛ̃kly] see CI.
ci-joint [siʒwɛ̃] see CI.
cil [sil] *s.m.* **1.** eyelash; **2.** (bot., zool.) cilium.
ciliaire [siljɛr] *adj.* ciliary.
cilice [silis] *s.m.* hair-shirt, hair-belt; cilice.
cilié, -e [silje] *adj.* ciliate, ciliated.
cillement [sijmɑ̃] *s.m.* nictitation; blinking.

ciller [sije] *v.t.i.* to nictitate, to blink; *personne n'ose ~ devant lui*, no one dares to bat an eyelid in his presence.
cimaise [simɛz] *s.f.* cyma, wainscoting cap.
cime [sim] *s.f.* top (of tree), summit, peak, (of mountain, etc.); (fig.) height, apogee.
ciment [simɑ̃] *s.m.* cement, concrete, mortar; (fig.) bond; *~ de laitier*, breeze concrete; *~ armé*, reinforced concrete.
cimenter [simɑ̃te] *v.t.* (lit. & fig.) to cement.
cimenterie [simɑ̃tri] *s.f.* cement works; cement industry.
cimentier [simɑ̃tje] *s.m.* cement maker.
cimeterre [simtɛr] *s.m.* scimitar.
cimetière [simtjɛr] *s.m.* cemetery, burial--ground, graveyard, churchyard.
cimier [simje] *s.m.* **1.** (herald.) crest, cimier; **2.** haunch (of venison); topside (of beef).
cinabre [sinabr] *s.m.* cinnabar; vermilion.
cinchonine [sɛ̃kɔnin] *s.f.* (chem.) cinchonine.
cincle [sɛ̃kl] *s.m.* (ornith.) water-ouzel, dipper.
ciné [sine] *s.m.* (pop. abbrev. of *cinéma*) cinema, pictures.
cinéaste [sineast] *s.m.* film-producer, director.
ciné-club [sineklœb] *s.m.* (pl. *ciné-clubs*) film society.
cinéma [sinema] *s.m.* cinema; films, film making; cinema industry; *acteur de ~*, film actor.
cinéma-scope [sinemaskɔp] *s.m.* cinemascope; **~thèque** [sinematɛk] *s.f.* film library.
cinématique [sinematik] *s.f.* kinematics.
cinémato-graphe [sinematɔgraf] *s.m.* **1.** motion picture camera; **2.** (obs.) cinema, films; **~graphie** [sinematɔgrafi] *s.f.* cinematography; **~graphier** [sinematɔgrafje] *v.t.* to film; **~graphique** [sinematɔgrafik] *adj.* cinematographical, film.
cinéphile [sinefil] *s.m.f.* film fan.
cinéraire [sinerɛr] *adj.* cinerary; *~ s.f.* (bot.) cineraria, groundsel.
cinérama [sinerama] *s.m.* cinerama.
ciné-roman [sinerɔmɑ̃] *s.m.* (pl. *ciné-romans*) **1.** (obs.) serial film; **2.** book of a film.
cinétique [sinetik] *adj.* kinetic.
C.I.C.-R. [seiseɛr] abbrev. *Comité international de la croix-rouge*, International Red Cross.
cingalais, -e [sɛ̃gale] *adj., s.m.f.* Cingalese, Sinhalese.
cinglant, -e [sɛ̃glɑ̃] *adj.* (lit. & fig.) cutting, biting, stinging, scathing.
cinglé, -e [sɛ̃gle] *adj.* (fam.) cracked, daft; *s.m.f.* crackpot.
cingler[1] [sɛ̃gle] *v.i.* (naut.) to steer, to sail.
cingler[2] [sɛ̃gle] *v.t.* to lash, to scourge, to whip, to cut; to bite, to go for (s.o.); (carp.) to line out (board, etc.); (metall.) to shingle, to forge.
cinnamome [sin(n)amɔm] *s.m.* (bot.) cinnamon.
cinq [sɛ̃k] *adj., s.m.* five, fifth, five minutes (before or after the hour); *le ~ mai*, the fifth of May; *midi moins ~*, five to twelve; *il était moins ~*, there were only five minutes to go; (fig.) it was touch and go; (fam.) *je lui ai dit les ~ lettres* (euphem. *merde*), I told him to piss off.
cinquantaine [sɛ̃kɑ̃tɛn] *s.f.* fifty, about fifty; fiftieth year (of age).
cinquante [sɛ̃kɑ̃t] *adj.* fifty.
cinquantenaire [sɛ̃kɑ̃tnɛr] *s.m.* fiftieth anniversary; *~ s.m.f.* quinquagenarian.
cinquantième [sɛ̃kɑ̃tjɛm] *adj., s.m.f.* fiftieth.
cinquième [sɛ̃kjɛm] *adj., s.m.f.* fifth; *~ s.m.* fifth floor; **~ment** [sɛ̃kjɛmmɑ̃] *adv.* fifthly.
cintrage [sɛ̃traʒ] *s.m.* arching, curving, bending.
cintre [sɛ̃tr] *s.m.* **1.** arch, vault; **2.** (constr.) centre, cinter; **3.** coat-hanger; *sèche sur ~*, drip--dry.
cintrer [sɛ̃tre] *v.t.* **1.** to curve, to arch; to bend, to camber; **2.** to fit (a garment) to the waist.
cipaye [sipaj] *s.m.* (hist.) sepoy.
cipolin [sipɔlɛ̃] *s.m.* cipolin (marble).
cippe [sip] *s.m.* (archaeol.) cippus.
cirage [siraʒ] *s.m.* **1.** polishing, waxing; **2.** polish; (fig., fam.) *noir comme le ~*, as black as pitch; *être dans le ~*, to be all at sea; (aeron. slang) to be flying blind.
circaète [sirkaɛt] *s.m.* (ornith.) harrier-eagle.
circadien, -ne [sirkadjɛ̃] *adj.* (biol.) circadian.
circon-cire [sirkɔ̃sir] *v.t.* to circumcize; **~cision** [sirkɔ̃sizjɔ̃] *s.f.* circumcision; **~férence** [sirkɔ̃ferɑ̃s] *s.f.* circumference, periphery; **~flexe** [sirkɔ̃flɛks] *adj.* circumflex; **~locution** [sirkɔ̃lɔkysjɔ̃] *s.f.* circumlocution; *parler par ~locutions*, to talk in a roundabout way; *aprés de longues ~locutions*, after much beating about the bush; **~scription** [sirkɔ̃skripsjɔ̃] *s.f.* (admin.) division, district, territory; (parl.) constituency; **~scrire** [sirkɔ̃skrir] *v.t.* to circumscribe, to limit.
circonspect, -e [sirkɔ̃spɛ] *adj.* circumspect, cautious, guarded, diplomatic.
circonspection [sirkɔ̃spɛksjɔ̃] *s.f.* circumspection, caution, cautiousness, discretion.
circonstance [sirkɔ̃stɑ̃s] *s.f.* circumstance, occasion; (pl.) circumstances, situation; *profiter de la ~*, to seize the opportunity; *de ~*, suitable for the occasion; composed or adapted for the occasion; (gram.) adverbial; *à la hauteur des ~*, equal to the occasion.
circonstancié, -e [sirkɔ̃stɑ̃sje] *adj.* full, explicit, detailed.
circonstanciel, -le [sirkɔ̃stɑ̃sjɛl] *adj.* circumstantial; (gram.) adverbial.
circonvallation [sirkɔ̃val(l)ɑsjɔ̃] *s.f.* (fort.) circumvallation.
circonvenir [sirkɔ̃vnir] *v.t.* (fig.) to circumvent, to get round.
circonvoisin, -e [sirkɔ̃vwazɛ̃] *adj.* adjacent, surrounding.
circonvolution [sirkɔ̃vɔlysjɔ̃] *s.f.* circumvolution.
circuit [sirkɥi] *s.m.* **1.** circuit, perimeter; roundabout way; tour; (sport, etc.) round, lap, circuit; *en ~ fermé*, completing the circle, returning to one's starting-point; **2.** (electr.) circuit; *mettre en ~*, to switch on; *couper le ~*, to switch off; *coupe-~*, fuse, cut-out, trip; *court ~*, short circuit; *~ intégré*, integrated circuit; **3.** (comm.) turn-round.
circulaire [sirkylɛr] *adj.* circular; *voyage ~*, round trip; *~ s.f.* circular (letter, memorandum, etc.); **~ment** [sirkylɛrmɑ̃] *adv.* in a circle.
circul-ation [sirkylɑsjɔ̃] *s.f.* **1.** (movement, med., comm.) circulation; **2.** movement of traffic; traffic; **~atoire** [sirkylatwar] *adj.* circulatory, of the circulation; **~er** [sirkyle] *v.i.* to circulate, to flow, to move on; to be current, to be going round; *faire ~er*, to circulate, to spread, to give currency to; to put into circulation; to move on, to get (vehicles, etc.) moving.
circum-duction [sirkɔmdyksjɔ̃] *s.f.* circumgyration; **~lunaire** [sirkɔmlynɛr] *adj.* circumlunar; **~navigation** [sirkɔmnavigasjɔ̃] *s.f.* circumnavigation; **~polaire** [sirkɔmpɔlɛr] *adj.* circumpolar; **~terrestre** [sirkɔmtɛrɛstr] *adj.* round the earth.
cire [sir] *s.f.* **1.** wax, beeswax; ear-wax; wax--polish; *~ à cacheter*, sealing-wax; *cachet de ~*, seal; *bâton de ~*, stick of sealing-wax; **2.** wax figure or object.
ciré, -e [sire] *adj.* waxed, polished; *toile ~e*, oil--cloth, American cloth; *~ s.m.* oilskins.
cirer [sire] *v.t.* to wax, to polish; (fig., fam.) *~ les bottes à qn.*, to lick someone's boots.
cireu-r, -se [sirœr] *s.m.f.* polisher; **~r** *s.m.* shoe-shine boy; **~se** *s.f.* (electr.) floor-polisher.
cireu-x, -se [sirø] *adj.* waxy, waxen.

ciri-er, -ère [sirje] *s.m.f.* wax-chandler, wax-refiner; **~er** *s.m.* (bot.) wax myrtle, candleberry tree; **~ère** *s.f.* worker bee.
ciron [sirɔ̃] *s.m.* (obs.) mite, cheese-mite.
cirque [sirk] *s.m.* **1.** (hist.) arena; **2.** circus; **3.** (geol.) cirque, corrie.
cirrhose [siroz] *s.f.* cirrhosis.
cirripèdes [sir(r)ipɛd] *s.m.pl.* (zool.) Cirripedia, cirripeds.
cirro-cumulus [sir(r)ɔkymylys] *s.m.* (meteor.) cirrocumulus; **~-stratus** [sir(r)ɔstratys] *s.m.* (meteor.) cirrostratus.
cirrus [sir(r)ys] *s.m.* (meteor.) cirrus.
cisaille [sizɑj] *s.f.* **1.** shears; (bolt-, wire-, etc.) cutter; snips; secateurs; **2.** (metal) cuttings, filing, swarf.
cisaillement [sizɑjmɑ̃] *s.m.* cutting; shearing.
cisailler [sizɑje] *v.t.* to cut, to prune; to snip (metal).
cisalpin, -e [sizalpɛ̃] *adj.* cisalpine.
ciseau (pl. **-x**) [sizo] *s.m.* chisel; (pl.) chisels; scissors.
ciseler [sizle] *v.t.* to chase, to chisel, to carve; (fig.) to polish (style, phrase, etc.).
ciselet [sizlɛ] *s.m.* graver, chasing-tool.
ciseleur [sizlœr] *s.m.* chaser, sculptor, carver, (en)graver.
cisellement [sizɛlmɑ̃] *s.m.* thinning out (of bunches of grapes).
ciselure [sizlyr] *s.f.* chasing, carving, embossing.
cisoires [sizwar] *s.f.pl.* bench shears.
ciste[1] [sist] *s.m.* (bot.) cistus, rock-rose.
ciste[2] [sist] *s.f.* (ant.) cist.
cistercien, -ne [sistɛrsjɛ̃] *adj., s.m.* Cistercian.
cistre [sistr] *s.m.* (mus.) zither.
cistude [sistyd] *s.f.* European pond-tortoise.
citadelle [sitadɛl] *s.f.* citadel, fortress, bastion.
citadin, -e [sitadɛ̃] *adj.* urban, town, city; *s.m.f.* townsman, townswoman, city-dweller.
citat-eur, -rice [sitatœr] *adj.* quoting, citing; *s.m.f.* one who quotes.
citation [sitɑsjɔ̃] *s.f.* **1.** (law) summons, subpœna; **2.** quotation; **3.** (mil.) citation, mention.
cité [site] *s.f.* city, town; part of town; *droit de ~*, freedom of the city; (fig.) *avoir droit de ~*, to be accepted; *~ ouvrière*, council estate; *~ universitaire*, (university) halls of residence; *l'île de la Cité*, (in Paris) the île de la Cité; *la Cité de Londres*, the City of London.
cité-dortoir [sitedɔrtwar] *s.m.* dormitory town.
citer [site] *v.t.* **1.** (law) to summons, to subpœna, to call; **2.** to quote, to cite; to draw attention to (as an example); **3.** (mil.) to mention (in despatches).
citerne [sitɛrn] *s.f.* cistern, reservoir, tank; *bateau-~*, *wagon-~*, tanker.
cithare [sitar] *s.f.* (mus.) (hist.) cither(n), cittern; (mod.) zither.
cithariste [sitarist] *s.m.f.* citharist, player of zither, sitar, etc.
citoyen, -ne [sitwajɛ̃] *s.m.f.* citizen(ess), subject; (fam.) type, individual.
citoyenneté [sitwajɛnte] *s.f.* citizenship.
citrate [sitrat] *s.m.* (chem.) citrate.
citrin, -e [sitrɛ̃] *adj.* citrine, lemon, lemon-coloured.
citrique [sitrik] *adj.* citric.
citron [sitrɔ̃] *s.m.* lemon; (pop.) head; ⚠ not 'citron'; *~ adj.invar.* lemon-coloured.
citronnade [sitrɔnad] *s.f.* lemon squash.
citronné, -e [sitrɔne] *adj.* lemon-flavoured; with lemon; lemon-scented.
citronelle [sitrɔnɛl] *s.f.* **1.** lemon balm, southernwood, vervain, wormwood; **2.** lemon-peel liqueur.
citronnier [sitrɔnje] *s.m.* (bot.) lemon-tree.
citrouille [sitruj] *s.f.* pumpkin; (pop.) head.
citrus [sitrys] *s.m.pl.* citrus (trees).
cive [siv] *s.f.* (bot.) chives.
civet [sivɛ] *s.m.* (cook.) jugged hare, rabbit, venison.
civette [sivɛt] *s.f.* **1.** = CIVE; **2.** civet-cat; civet (scent); civet fur.
civière [sivjer] *s.f.* **1.** stretcher; **2.** hand-barrow.
civil, -e [sivil] *adj.* **1.** civil, civic; lay, secular; civil(ian) (opp. mil.); *état ~*, legal status; *officier d'état ~*, registrar (of births, etc.); *le Droit ~*, civil law; *se porter partie ~e*, to bring a civil action; *mariage ~*, civil marriage (at *mairie*); *la vie ~e* (or *le ~*), civilian life; *en ~*, in plain clothes, in mufti; **2.** (obs.) civil, polite; **~ement** [sivilmɑ̃] *adv.* **1.** (law) in a civil court; (admin.) *se marier ~ement*, to be married at the *mairie*; **2.** (Lit.) civilly, politely.
civilisable [sivilizabl] *adj.* civilizable.
civilisat-eur, -rice [sivilizatœr] *adj.* civilizing; *s.m.f.* civilizer.
civilisation [sivilizɑsjɔ̃] *s.f.* civilization.
civilisé, -e [sivilize] *adj., s.m.f.* civilized, cultured, (person).
civiliser [sivilize] *v.t.* to civilize; to reform (someone's) manners; **se ~** *v.refl.* to become civilized; to learn good manners.
civilité [sivilite] *s.f.* civility, courtesy, politeness; (pl.) compliments, kind regards.
civique [sivik] *adj.* civic.
civisme [sivism] *s.m.* good citizenship, sense of civic responsibility; (obs.) patriotism.
clabaud [klabo] *s.m.* hound with long ears which gives tongue frequently.
clabaudage [klabodaʒ] *s.m.* **1.** baying (see CLABAUD); **2.** = CLABAUDERIE.
clabauder [klabode] *v.i.* **1.** to bay; **2.** to grouse, to complain.
clabauderie [klabodri] *s.f.* backbiting, slander; grousing, whining; brawling.
clabaudeu-r, -se [klabodœr] *s.m.f.* backbiter, scandalmonger, brawler, grouser.
claie [klɛ] *s.f.* **1.** (wicker) hurdle; trellis(-work); **2.** screen, riddle.
clair, -e [klɛr] *adj.* light, bright, well-lit; clear, cloudless; (of colours) pale, light; thin, clear; (fig.) clear, plain, obvious, evident, manifest; *bleu ~*, light, pale, blue; *~ adv. parler ~*, to speak clearly; (fig.) to speak plainly, unambiguously; *voir ~*, to see clearly; (fig.) to understand; **~ement** [klɛrmɑ̃] *adv.* clearly, distinctly, plainly.
clair [klɛr] *s.m.* **1.** light; *~ de lune*, moonlight; **2.** (art) (pl.) lights; **3.** *le plus ~ de qch.*, the greater part of sth.; *tirer qch. au ~*, to clarify, to filter, sth.; *en ~*, in clear, not in code; *mettre sabre au ~*, to draw a sword.
claire [klɛr] *s.f.* oyster-park.
clairet, -te [klɛrɛ] *adj.* light, thin; (of wine) light red.
claire-voie [klɛrvwa] *s.f.* trellis, lattice, open-work, grating; (arch.) clerestory; *à ~*, with slits; *caisse à ~*, crate.
clairière [klɛrjɛr] *s.f.* glade, clearing.
clair-obscur [klɛrɔpskyr] *s.m.* (art) chiaroscuro; light and shade, subdued light.
clairon [klɛrɔ̃] *s.m.* bugle, clarion; bugler; clairon stop (of organ).
claironnant, -e [klɛrɔnɑ̃] *adj.* ringing, echoing.
claironner [klɛrɔne] *v.i.* to sound the bugle; *~ v.t.* (fig.) to trumpet, to proclaim.
clairsemé, -e [klɛrsəme] *adj.* scattered, sparse, thin.
clairvoyance [klɛrvwajɑ̃s] *s.f.* clear-sightedness, perspicacity, vision; ⚠ not 'clairvoyance' in sense 'second sight'.
clairvoyant, -e [klɛrvwajɑ̃] *adj.* clear-sighted, perspicacious, shrewd.
clam [klam] *s.m.* clam.
clamecer, clamser [klamse] *v.i.* (pop.) to die.

clamer [klame] *v.t.* to clamour, to shout; to proclaim.
clameur [klamœr] *s.f.* uproar, clamour.
clamp [klɑ̃] *s.m.* (surg.) clamp.
clamser see CLAMECER.
clan [klɑ̃] *s.m.* clan; tribe; set, class, party, clique.
clandestin, -e [klɑ̃dɛstɛ̃] *adj.* clandestine, underhand, surreptitious, secret; **~ement** [klɑ̃dɛstinmɑ̃] *adv.* clandestinely, secretly, surreptitiously.
clandestinité [klɑ̃dɛstinite] *s.f.* secrecy.
clanique [klanik] *adj.* of the clan.
clapet [klapɛ] *s.m.* (hydraul.) flap, flap-valve; (fig., pop.) mouth; *ferme ton ~!*, shut up!; *quel ~!*, what a lot of cackling!
clapier [klapje] *s.m.* rabbit-burrow, warren; (lit. & fig.) rabbit-hutch; (geol.) scree.
clapotage [klapɔtaʒ], **clapotement** [klapɔtmɑ̃] *s.m.* lapping, rippling, ripple.
clapot-er [klapɔte] *v.i.* to lap, to ripple; **~is** [klapɔti] *s.m.* lapping, rippling.
clappement [klapmɑ̃] s.*m.* smacking, clucking, (of tongue).
clapper [klape] *v.i.* to smack, to cluck, (with tongue).
claquage [klakaʒ] *s.m.* strain, pulling (of muscle); pulled muscle.
claquant, -e [klakɑ̃] *adj.* (pop.) exhausting.
claque[1] [klak] *s.f.* **1.** slap, smack; **2.** upper (of shoe); **3.** (theatr.) claque.
claque[2] [klak] *s.m.* opera hat.
claquement [klakmɑ̃] *s.m.* clap(-ping), slap(-ping); crack (of whip); chattering (of teeth).
claquemurer [klakmyre] *v.t.* to place in close confinement; **se~** *v.refl.* to shut oneself away.
claquer [klake] *v.t.* **1.** to crack, to clap, to snap; *il claque des dents*, his teeth are chattering (with fear); (fam.) *~ du bec*, to be hungry; *faire ~ la porte*, to slam the door; **2.** (fig., pop.) to explode, to go bang; (fam.) to die; **3.** to smack, to slap; **4.** (pop.) to waste, to throw away; (fam.) to exhaust; *il s'en fera ~*, he will work (eat, drink, etc.) himself to death; *se ~ un muscle*, to pull a muscle.
claquet [klakɛ] *s.m.* clack-valve, clack.
claqueter [klakte] *v.i.* (of hen) to cackle; (of stork) to clapper.
claquette [klakɛt] *s.f.* rattle, clapper; **~s** *s.f.pl.* tap-dancing.
clarification [klarifikɑsjɔ̃] *s.f.* (lit. & fig.) clarification.
clarifier [klarifje] *v.t.* (lit. & fig.) to clarify; to purify; to refine (sugar).
clarine [klarin] *s.f.* cow or sheep bell.
clarinette [klarinɛt] *s.f.* clarinet.
clarinettiste [klarinetist] *s.m.f.* clarinettist.
clarisse [klaris] *s.f.* (eccles.) Clare, Poor Clare.
clarté [klarte] *s.f.* light, brightness; clearness, limpidity, purity; (fig.) clarity, precision; (obs.) knowledge, understanding.
classe [klɑs] *s.f.* **1.** class, caste, set, rank; (mil.) *hors ~*, of field rank; **2.** class, type, series, sort, category; (biol.) order; *de première ~*, first-class, top-grade, first-rate; **3.** class, form; (mil.) class, entry, year; (pl.) school; lesson, instruction, teaching; *rentrée des ~s*, beginning of school term; *sortie des ~s*, end of school (for the day); *faire la ~*, to teach; (mil.) *faire ses ~s*, to undergo basic training.
classement [klɑsmɑ̃] *s.m.* classification, arrangement, order; filing.
classer [klɑse] *v.t.* to classify, to rank; to arrange, to file; (fam.) *~ qn.*, to sum s.o. up; (fig.) *~ une affaire*, to close a case; **se ~** *v.refl.* to be classed, to be rated.
classeur [klɑsœr] *s.m.* filing cabinet, file.
classicisme [klasisism] *s.m.* classicism.
classificat-eur, -rice [klasifikatœr] *s.m.f.* classifier; *adj. manie ~rice*, mania for classifying.
classification [klasifikɑsjɔ̃] *s.f.* classification, classifying.
classifier [klasifje] *v.t.* to classify.
classique [klasik] *adj.* classic(al); *~ s.m.* classic; classicist; classical music; **~ment** [klasikmɑ̃] *adv.* classically.
clastique [klastik] *adj.* (geol.) clastic; (of anat. model) that can be taken to pieces.
Claude [klod] *s.m.* (Rom. hist.) Claudius.
claudicant, -e [klodikɑ̃] *adj.* lame, halting, limping.
claudication [klodikɑsjɔ̃] *s.f.* lameness, limp.
claudiquer [klodike] *v.i.* to limp.
clause [kloz] *s.f.* (law) clause, provision, article.
claustral, -e, (**aux**) [klostral] *adj.* claustral, cloistral, monastic.
claustration [klostrɑsjɔ̃] *s.f.* claustration, close confinement.
claustrer [klostre] *v.t.* to confine; **se ~** *v.refl.* (fig.) to retire into a shell.
claustrophobie [klostrɔfɔbi] *s.f.* claustrophobia.
clavaire [klavɛr] *s.f.* (bot.) crusted fairy club; coral fungus.
claveau (pl. **-x**) [klavo] *s.m.* (arch.) keystone.
clavecin [klavsɛ̃] *s.m.* harpsichord; **~iste** [klavsinist] *s.m.f.* harpsichordist.
clavelée [klavle] *s.f.* sheep-pox, scab-rot.
clavetage [klavtaʒ] *s.m.* (constr., mech.) keying.
clavette [klavɛt] *s.f.* (mech.) key(-bolt), cotter(-pin), pin.
clavicorde [klavikɔrd] *s.m.* clavichord.
clavicule [klavikyl] *s.f.* clavicle, collar-bone.
clavier [klavje] *s.m.* (mus., typewriter) keyboard; (mus.) compass, register, range; (fig.) gamut.
clayère [klɛjɛr] *s.f.* oyster-park.
claymore [klɛmɔr] *s.f.* claymore.
clayon [klɛjɔ̃] *s.m.* small wicker mat (esp. for draining cheese).
clayon-nage [klɛjɔnaʒ] *s.m.* wattle, wicker-work; wattle fencing; **~ner** [klɛjɔne] *v.t.* to fence or strengthen with wattle or hurdles.
clé [kle] see CLEF.
clearing [kliriŋ] *s.m.* (fin., comm.) clearing.
clebs [klɛps] *s.m.* (pop.) dog.
clef, clé [kle] *s.f.* key; (mus.) key, clef; (techn.) spanner, wrench; (fig.) key, clue; (arch. & fig.) *~ de voûte*, keystone; *fermer à ~*, to lock; *sous ~*, locked up, under lock and key; (fig.) *la ~ des champs*, liberty; *prendre la ~ des champs*, to decamp, to abscond; *mettre la ~ sous la porte*, to do a flit; *~ adj. invar.* key; *industrie ~*, key industry.
clématite [klematit] *s.f.* (bot.) clematis.
clémence [klemɑ̃s] *s.f.* clemency, mercy; (of weather) mildness.
clément, -e [klemɑ̃] *adj.* clement, merciful; mild.
clémentine [klemɑ̃tin] *s.f.* clementine (orange).
clémentinier [klemɑ̃tinje] *s.m.* clementine tree.
clenche [klɑ̃ʃ], **clenchette** [klɑ̃ʃɛt] *s.f.* latch.
Cléopâtre [kleɔpɑtr] *s.f.* (anc. hist.) Cleopatra.
clephte, klephte [klɛft] *s.m.* (Gr. hist.) klepht.
clepsydre [klɛpsidr] *s.f.* (ant.) clepsydra.
cleptomane, cleptomanie see KLEPTOMANE, KLEPTOMANIE.
clerc [klɛr] *s.m.* **1.** clerk (in public admin.), minor official; articled clerk; *faire un pas de ~*, to blunder; **2.** (obs.) scholar; (mod.) intellectual; **3.** clerk.
clergé [klɛrʒe] *s.m.* clergy.
clergie [klɛrʒi] *s.f.* (hist.) *privilège de ~*, benefit of clergy.
clérical, -e, (**aux**) [klerikal] *adj.* clerical; *~ s.m.* clericalist.
cléricalisme [klerikalism] *s.m.* clericalism, sacerdotalism.
cléricature [klerikatyr] *s.f.* priesthood.

clic [klik] *interj.* click.
clichage [kliʃaʒ] *s.m.* stereotyping.
cliché [kliʃe] *s.m.* **1.** (print.) stereotype; **2.** (photo.) negative; *prendre un ~*, to make an exposure, to take a picture; **3.** (Lit.) cliché.
clicher [kliʃe] *v.t.* (print.) to make a stereotype of.
clicherie [kliʃri] *s.f.* stereotyping shop.
clicheur [kliʃœr] *s.m.* stereotyper.
client, -e [klijɑ̃] *s.m.f.* client, customer; patient; regular (customer).
clientèle [klijɑ̃tɛl] *s.f.* clientèle, custom; customers, patrons.
clignement [kliɲmɑ̃] *s.m.* wink, winking, blinking, intermittent flashing.
cligner [kliɲe] *v.t.i.* to wink, to blink; *~ de l'œil*, to wink.
clignotant, -e [kliɲɔtɑ̃] *adj.* winking, blinking, flashing; *~ s.m.* (car) direction indicator, winker; (fig.) warning light, danger signal.
clignotement [kliɲɔtmɑ̃] *s.m.* winking, blinking, flashing.
clignoter [kliɲɔte] *v.t.i.* to wink, to blink; to flash; to twinkle.
climat [klima] *s.m.* climate; (rarely) clime, country; (fig.) climate, ambience.
climatérique [klimaterik] *adj., s.f.* climacteric.
climat-ique [klimatik] *adj.* climatic; *station ~ique*, health resort; **~isation** [klimatizɑsjɔ̃] *s.f.* air-conditioning; **~iser** [klimatize] *v.t.* to air-condition, to equip with air-conditioning; **~iseur** [klimatizœr] *s.m.* air-conditioning apparatus; **~ologie** [klimatɔlɔʒi] *s.f.* climatology; **~-ologique** [klimatɔlɔʒik] *adj.* climatological.
clin d'œil [klɛ̃dœj] *s.m.* wink; *en un ~*, in the twinkling of an eye.
clinfoc [klɛ̃fɔk] *s.m.* (naut.) flying jib.
clinicat [klinika] *s.m.* leadership of a clinical team.
clinicien [klinisjɛ̃] *adj.m., s.m.* clinical (specialist).
clinique [klinik] *adj.* clinical; *~ s.f.* **1.** clinical method; **2.** (private) nursing-home.
clinomètre [klinɔmɛtr] *s.m.* clinometer.
clinquant [klɛ̃kɑ̃] *s.m.* **1.** tinsel; cheap imitation jewellery, etc.; **2.** (fig.) vulgar, ostentatious display; *~(e) adj.* flashy, showy.
clip [klip] *s.m.* clip, brooch.
clipper [klipœr] *s.m.* **1.** (hist., naut.) clipper; **2.** (aeron.) transport plane.
clique [klik] *s.f.* **1.** clique, gang, set; **2.** (mil.) drum and bugle band.
cliques [klik] *s.f.pl. prendre ses ~ et ses claques*, to clear out bag and baggage.
cliquet [klikɛ] *s.m.* (techn.) ratch, ratchet, pawl, click, catch.
cliqueter [klikte] *v.i.* to clink, to jingle, to rattle.
cliquetis [klikti] *s.m.* clinking, jingling, rattling; (fig.) empty verbiage.
cliquette [klikɛt] *s.f.* **1.** (obs.) rattle; **2.** (fishing) sinker.
clisse [klis] *s.f.* wicker mat.
clisser [klise] *v.t.* to protect with wickerwork.
clitoris [klitɔris] *s.m.* (anat.) clitoris.
clivable [klivabl] *adj.* cleavable.
clivage [klivaʒ] *s.m.* cleavage; cleaving; separation into planes or levels; (geol.) *plan de ~*, cleavage plane.
cliver [klive] *v.t.* to cleave; **se ~** *v.refl.* to split, to cleave.
cloaque [klɔak] *s.m.* sewer; (anat.) cloaca.
clochard, -e [klɔʃar] *s.m.f.* tramp, vagrant.
cloche[1] [klɔʃ] *s.f.* bell; bell-jar; dish-cover; (hort.) cloche; (bot.) flower, bell; cloche hat; *paletot ~*, loose coat; *~ à plongeur*, diving-bell; *déménager à la ~ de bois*, to do a moonlight flit; (fam.) *sonner les ~s à qn.*, to tick s.o. off.
cloche[2] [klɔʃ] *s.f., adj.* (pop.) useless, inadequate, (person); (fam.) brigade of tramps.
(**à**) **cloche-pied** [aklɔʃpje] *adv.* hopping; *sauter à ~*, to hop.
clocher [klɔʃe] *s.m.* steeple, bell-tower, belfry; (fig.) parish, village; *rivalités de ~*, local feuds.
clocher [klɔʃe] *v.i.* **1.** (obs.) to limp, to hobble; **2.** to be defective, not to work properly, to present a snag; *il y a qch. qui cloche*, there's something wrong somewhere.
clocheton [klɔʃtɔ̃] *s.m.* bell-turret; (arch.) pinnacle.
clochette [klɔʃɛt] *s.f.* **1.** small bell, hand-bell; **2.** (bot.) bell; *~ des bois*, bluebell; *~ des blés*, bindweed; *~ des murs*, harebell; *~ d'hiver*, snowdrop.
cloison [klwazɔ̃] *s.f.* partition; (naut.) bulkhead; (anat.) partition; (fig.) barrier.
cloisonnage [klwazɔnaʒ] *s.m.* partitioning; partitions.
cloisonné, -e [klwazɔne] *adj.* partitioned; *~ adj.m., s.m.* cloisonné (enamel).
cloisonnement [klwazɔnmɑ̃] *s.m.* partitioning, division.
cloisonner [klwazɔne] *v.t.* to partition.
cloître [klwatr] *s.m.* **1.** cloisters; **2.** cloister, convent, monastery; **3.** (obs.) cathedral close.
cloîtrer [klwatre] *v.t.* **1.** to cloister; to confine, to shut away; **se ~** *v.refl.* to shut oneself away, to live the life of a recluse, to live in an enclosed world.
clone [klɔn] *s.m.* (biol.) clone.
clonique [klɔnik] *adj.* (med.) clonic.
clopin-clopant [klɔpɛ̃klɔpɑ̃] *adv. aller ~*, to limp, to hobble.
clopiner [klɔpine] *v.i.* to limp, to hobble.
cloporte [klɔpɔrt] *s.m.* (ent.) woodlouse.
cloque [klɔk] *s.f.* **1.** blister; **2.** (hort.) rust, peach-leaf curl.
cloqué, -e [klɔke] *adj.* **1.** blistered; **2.** (hort.) curled, suffering from leaf-curl; *~ adj.m., s.m.* (text.) cloqué (material).
cloquer [klɔke] *v.i.* to blister.
clore [klɔr] *v.t.* **1.** (obs. exc. Lit.) to close, to shut; to enclose, to fence; **2.** (fig.) to conclude, to end, to close (meeting, etc.).
clos, -e [klo] *adj.* **1.** closed, enclosed, shut (up); *à huis ~*, behind closed doors, in camera; *à la nuit ~e*, when night has fallen; *avoir la bouche ~e*, to have sealed lips; **2.** concluded, ended, at an end; *l'incident est ~*, the incident is closed.
clos [klo] *s.m.* enclosure, orchard, paddock, vineyard.
closerie [klozri] *s.f.* croft, smallholding.
clôture [klotyr] *s.f.* **1.** enclosure, fence, barrier; **2.** (eccles.) enclosure; **3.** close, closing, end, conclusion.
clôturer [klotyre] *v.t.* **1.** to enclose, to fence; **2.** to end, to conclude, to bring to an end, to to close (an account).
clou [klu] *s.m.* nail, hobnail, brad, tack, stud; (arch.) nailhead; (med.) boil; (fam.) pawnshop; (fam.) old crock (car or bicycle); (fig.) main attraction; (pl.) pedestrian crossing; (cook.) *~ de girofle*, clove; *cela ne vaut pas un ~*, it's worth nothing at all; *mettre au ~*, to pawn; *le ~ du spectacle*, the main attraction of the piece, the hit of the evening.
clouage [kluaʒ] *s.m.* nailing.
clouer [klue] *v.t.* to nail (down), to pin down, to rivet; (fig.) to immobilize, to chain; to transfix; (naut. & fig.) *~ le pavillon*, to nail one's colours to the mast; *être cloué sur place*, to be rooted to the spot; (fam.) *~ le bec à qn.*, to shut s.o. up.
cloutage [klutaʒ] *s.m.* studding.
clouté, -e [klute] *adj.* nailed, studded; *passage ~*, pedestrian crossing.

clouter [klute] *v.t.* to stud; to ornament with nails.
clouterie [klutri] *s.f.* nail-making; nail-factory, nailery.
cloutier [klutje] *s.m.* nail-maker; nail-seller.
clovisse [klɔvis] *s.f.* (moll.) clam.
clown [klun] *s.m.* (circus) clown; buffoon; (fig.) *faire le* ~, to act the buffoon, to clown.
clownerie [klunri] *s.f.* clowning.
clownesque [klunɛsk] *adj.* clown-like.
cloyère [klwajɛr] *s.f.* oyster-basket.
club [klœb] *s.m.* **1.** (hist.) political association; **2.** club, society; **3.** club chair; **4.** golf-club (e.g. niblick).
cluse [klyz] *s.f.* (geol.) cluse, transverse valley (esp. in the Jura mountains).
clystère [klistɛr] *s.m.* (obs.) clyster.
cnémide [knemid] *s.f.* (ant.) greave.
C.N.E.P. [seɛnepe] abbrev. *Comptoir national d'escompte de Paris.*
C.N.P.F. [seɛnpeɛf] abbrev. *Conseil national du patronat français,* = C.B.I.
C.N.R.S. [seɛnɛrɛs] abbrev. *Centre national de la recherche scientifique.*
coaccusé, -e [kɔakyze] *s.m.f.* co-defendant, joint defendant.
coach [kotʃ] *s.m.* (car) two-door saloon.
coacquéreur [kɔakerœr] *s.m.* joint purchaser.
coadjut-eur, -rice [kɔadʒytœr] *s.m.f.* (eccles.) coadjutor, coadjutress, coadjutrix.
coagulable [kɔagylabl] *adj.* coagulable.
coagulation [kɔagylɑsjɔ̃] *s.f.* coagulation.
coaguler [kɔagyle] *v.t.i.* to coagulate, to curdle (milk); **se** ~ *v.refl.* to coagulate, to set; (fig.) to become fixed, to crystallize.
coagulum [kɔagylɔm] *s.m.* coagulum.
coalisé, -e [kɔalize] *adj.* united, combined, allied, in coalition; *s.m.f.* ally, partner in coalition.
(**se**) **coaliser** [kɔalize] *v.refl.* to join or form a coalition; (fig.) to unite, to join together; ~ *v.t.* to unite.
coalition [kɔalisjɔ̃] *s.f.* (pol., fig.) coalition, alliance; (often pej.) union, combination, combining; (obs.) (law) conspiracy.
coaltar [koltar] *s.m.* coal tar.
coassement [kɔasmɑ̃] *s.m.* croaking, croak, (of frog or toad).
coasser [kɔase] *v.i.* (of frog or toad) to croak.
coassocié, -e [kɔasɔsje] *s.m.f.* partner, associate.
coassurance [kɔasyrɑ̃s] *s.f.* co-insurance.
coati [kɔati] *s.m.* (zool.) coati.
coauteur [kɔotœr] *s.m.* joint author; partner in crime.
coaxial, -e, (**aux**) [kɔaksjal] *adj.* coaxial.
cobalt [kɔbalt] *s.m.* (min.) cobalt.
cobaye [kɔbaj] *s.m.* (zool. & fig.) guinea-pig; (fam.) *servir de* ~, to be used as a guinea-pig.
cobéa, cobæa [kɔbea] *s.f.* (bot.) cobaea.
cobelligérant, -e [kɔbeliʒerɑ̃] *adj.* co-belligerent; ~ *s.m.* co-belligerent (state).
Coblence [kɔblɑ̃s] *s.m.* (geog.) Koblenz.
cobra [kɔbra] *s.m.* (zool.) cobra.
coca [kɔka] *s.m.* or *f.* coca (bush); ~ *s.f.* coca (substance); ~ (**-cola**) (proprietary name) coca-cola.
cocagne [kɔkaɲ] *s.f.* Cockaigne; *pays de* ~, (imaginary) land of milk and honey; *mât de* ~, greasy pole.
cocaïne [kɔkain] *s.f.* cocaine.
cocaïnisation [kɔkainizɑsjɔ̃] *s.f.* anaesthesia with cocaine.
cocaïno-mane [kɔkainɔman] *s.m.f.* cocaine addict; ~**manie** [kɔkainɔmani] *s.f.* cocaine addiction.
cocarde [kɔkard] *s.f.* cockade, rosette, badge.
cocardi-er, -ère [kɔkardje] *adj., s.m.f.* chauvinist.
cocasse [kɔkas] *adj.* (fam.) ludicrous, preposterous, absurd.
cocasserie [kɔkasri] *s.f.* ludicrousness, preposterousness, absurdity.
coccinelle [kɔksinɛl] *s.f.* (ent.) ladybird.
coccyx [kɔksis] *s.m.* (anat.) coccyx.
coche[1] [kɔʃ] *s.m.* (hist.) horse-drawn coach; (fig., fam.) *manquer le* ~, to miss the bus.
coche[2] [kɔʃ] *s.f.* notch, cut, nick.
coche[3] [kɔʃ] *s.f.* (obs.) sow.
cochenille [kɔʃnij] *s.f.* **1.** cochineal (insect and substance); **2.** (ent.) aphis, aphid.
cocher [kɔʃe] *s.m.* coachman; ~ (*de fiacre*), cabman.
cocher [kɔʃe] *v.t.* to nick, to notch; to tick (off).
côcher [koʃe] *v.t.* to mount, to tread, (a hen bird).
cochère [kɔʃɛr] *adj.f. porte* ~, carriage entrance, porte cochère.
cochevis [kɔʃvi] *s.m.* (ornith.) crested lark.
Cochinchine [kɔʃɛ̃ʃin] *s.f.* (geog.) Cochin-China (former Fr. colony).
cochléaria [kɔklearja] *s.m.* (bot.) Cochlearia.
cochon [kɔʃɔ̃] *s.m.* pig, hog, swine, porker; pork; ~ *de lait*, sucking-pig; ~ *d'Inde*, guinea-pig; ~ *de mer*, porpoise; (fam.) *ils sont copains comme* ~*s*, they are as thick as thieves; (fig.) *un tour de* ~, a dirty trick.
cochon, -ne [kɔʃɔ̃] *adj.* piggish, swinish, filthy, lewd; *histoire* ~*ne*, dirty story; *s.m.f.* pig, swine, filthy person.
cochonnaille [kɔʃɔnɑj] *s.f.* (fam.) sausages, etc.
cochonner [kɔʃɔne] *v.t.* (fam.) to bungle, to botch, to spoil (work); ~ *v.i.* (rare) to farrow.
cochonnerie [kɔʃɔnri] *s.f.* **1.** dirtiness, filthiness; obscenity, indecency; **2.** sth. dirty or badly made; worthless article, botched job.
cochonnet [kɔʃɔnɛ] *s.m.* **1.** piglet, sucking-pig; **2.** (bowls) jack.
cocker [kɔkɛr] *s.m.* cocker spaniel.
cockpit [kɔkpit] *s.m.* (naut., aeron.) cockpit.
cocktail [kɔktɛl] *s.m.* cocktail; cocktail party; (fig.) mixture.
coco[1] [kɔko] *s.m.* **1.** *noix de* ~, coconut; **2.** liquorice water.
coco[2] [kɔko] *s.m.* **1.** (child. lang.) egg; **2.** term of endearment.
coco[3] [kɔko] *s.m.* (pej.) chap, fellow.
coco[4] [kɔko] *adj., s.m.f.* (pej.) communist, commie.
coco[5] [kɔko] *s.f.* (fam.) cocaine.
cocon [kɔkɔ̃] *s.m.* cocoon.
cocorico [kɔkɔriko] *s.m.* = COQUERICO.
cocotier [kɔkɔtje] *s.m.* coconut palm.
cocotte[1] [kɔkɔt] *s.f.* **1.** (child. lang.) hen; ~ *en papier*, paper folded roughly like a bird; **2.** loose woman, courtesan; **3.** (to a horse) *hue,* ~*!*, gee-up, my beauty!
cocotte[2] [kɔkɔt] *s.f.* cast-iron casserole; ~ *minute* (trade-mark), pressure-cooker.
cocu, -e [kɔky] *adj.* cuckolded, deceived; ~ *s.m.* cuckold.
cocu-age [kɔkɥaʒ] *s.m.* cuckoldry; ~**fier** [kɔkyfje] *v.t.* (pop.) to cuckold.
coda [kɔda] *s.f.* (mus.) coda.
codage [kɔdaʒ] *s.m.* encoding.
code [kɔd] *s.m.* **1.** (law) code, regulation(s); (fam.) *le Code*, the law(s); *dans le* ~, legal; *se tenir dans les marges du* ~, to keep within the law; ~ *de la route*, highway code; *phares en* ~, dipped headlights; *se mettre en* ~, to dip one's headlights; **2.** code, cipher; *mettre en* ~, to encode, to encipher.
codéine [kɔdein] *s.f.* codeine.
codemand-eur, -eresse [kɔdmɑ̃dœr] *s.m.f.* (law) co-plaintiff; co-applicant.
coder [kɔde] *v.t.* to code, to encode.
C.O.D.E.R. [seodeeɛr] abbrev. *Commission de*

développement économique régional, = N.E.D.C. (fam. Neddy).
codétent-eur, -rice [kɔdetɑ̃tœr] *s.m.f.* (law) joint holder.
codétenu, -e [kɔdetny] *s.m.f.* fellow-prisoner.
codex [kɔdɛks] *s.m.* pharmacopoeia, pharmaceutical codex.
codicille [kɔdisil] *s.m.* codicil.
codification [kɔdifikɑsjɔ̃] *s.f.* codification.
codifier [kɔdifje] *v.t.* to codify, to rationalize.
codirect-eur, -rice [kɔdirɛktœr] *s.m.f.* co-director, joint manager(-ess).
coefficient [kɔefisjɑ̃] *s.m.* coefficient; factor.
cœlacanthe [selakɑ̃t] *s.m.* (ichth.) coelacanth.
cœliaque [seljak] *adj.* (anat.) coeliac.
coéquation [kɔekwɑsjɔ̃] *s.f.* proportionment of taxes.
coéquipi-er, -ère [kɔekipje] *s.m.f.* team-mate.
coercibilité [kɔɛrsibilite] *s.f.* (phys.) coercibility, compressibility.
coercible [kɔɛrsibl] *adj.* (phys.) coercible, compressible.
coerciti-f, -ve [kɔɛrsitif] *adj.* coercive.
coercition [kɔɛrsisjɔ̃] *s.f.* coercion, compulsion.
coéternel, -le [kɔetɛrnɛl] *adj.* coeternal.
cœur [kœr] *s.m.* **1.** heart; bosom; stomach; *avoir mal au* ~, to be sick; *avoir des haut-le-*~, to feel sick; (fig.) *soulever le* ~, to disgust, to nauseate; *rester sur le* ~, to rankle; *de bon* ~, *de grand* ~, *de tout* ~, *de gaieté de* ~, heartily, gladly, willingly; *de tout son* ~, with all one's heart; *à* ~ *joie*, to one's heart's content; *en avoir le* ~ *net*, to get to the bottom of sth.; *sans* ~, heartless; *avoir le* ~ *sur la main*, to be open-handed; *faire contre mauvaise fortune bon* ~, to make the best of a bad job; *un grand* ~, *un homme de* ~, a noble heart, a generous person; *ne pas avoir le* ~ *de faire qch.*, to lack the courage to do sth., not to feel like doing sth.; *si le* ~ *vous en dit*, if you feel like it; *à* ~ *ouvert*, frankly; wholeheartedly; *par* ~, by heart, from memory; **2.** central part of sth.; heart (of a lettuce); core (of a fruit); *au* ~ *de l'été*, at the height of summer; *au* ~ *de l'hiver*, in the depths of winter; (cook., etc.) *fait à* ~, done right through; **3.** any heart-shaped object; *en* ~, heart-shaped; **4.** (cards) hearts.
coexistence [kɔɛgzistɑ̃s] *s.f.* coexistence.
coexister [kɔɛgziste] *v.i.* to coexist, to be present, (*avec*, with, at the same time as).
coffin [kɔfɛ̃] *s.m.* whetstone-holder (for scythe); ⚠ not 'coffin'.
coffrage [kɔfraʒ] *s.m.* **1.** (mining, etc.) coffering, timbering, planking, lining, (of gallery, shaft); **2.** (constr.) mould, form, frame, shuttering (for concrete).
coffre [kɔfr] *s.m.* **1.** chest, coffer, box; safe-deposit; (car) boot; **2.** frame, body, case; (naut.) hull; (anat.) (fam.) frame, chest; *avoir du* ~, to be solidly built; *le* ~ *est bon*, he is sound in wind and limb; **3.** (ichth.) coffer-fish.
coffre-fort [kɔfrəfɔr] *s.m.* safe, strong-box.
coffrer [kɔfre] *v.t.* **1.** (fam.) to run in, to imprison; **2.** (constr.) to make frame or shuttering (for concrete).
coffret [kɔfrɛ] *s.m.* casket.
cogérance [kɔʒerɑ̃s] *s.f.* joint management, co-administration.
cogestion [kɔʒɛstjɔ̃] *s.f.* joint administration.
cogitation [kɔʒitɑsjɔ̃] *s.f.* cogitation, (iron.) thinking.
cogiter [kɔʒite] *v.i.* (iron.) to think, to do some thinking.
cognac [kɔɲak] *s.m.* Cognac, brandy.
cognassier [kɔɲasje] *s.m.* (bot.) quince-tree.
cognat [kɔgna] *s.m.* cognate (relative).
cognation [kɔgnɑsjɔ̃] *s.f.* cognation.
cogne [kɔɲ] *s.m.* (pop.) policeman.
cognée [kɔɲe] *s.f.* wood-cutter's axe; (fig.) *jeter le manche après la* ~, to give up, to throw in the sponge.
cognement [kɔɲmɑ̃] *s.m.* knocking (esp. in car engine).
cogner [kɔɲe] *v.t.* **1.** (obs.) to hit, to knock, to bang; *se* ~ *la tête*, to bang one's head; **2.** to hit, to beat, to give a thrashing to; ~ *v.i.* to knock, to tap, to bang; **se** ~ *v.refl. se* ~ *à*, to bump into, to stumble against; (fig.) to run into, to encounter.
cogniti-f, -ve [kɔgnitif] *adj.* cognitive.
cognition [kɔgnisjɔ̃] *s.f.* cognition.
cohabitation [kɔabitɑsjɔ̃] *s.f.* cohabitation.
cohabiter [kɔabite] *v.i.* to cohabit, to live together, to live in the same house.
cohérence [kɔerɑ̃s] *s.f.* coherence, cohesion; consistency.
cohérent, -e [kɔerɑ̃] *adj.* coherent; consistent.
cohéreur [kɔerœr] *s.m.* (electr.) coherer.
cohériti-er, -ère [kɔeritje] *s.m.f.* joint heir(ess).
cohési-f, -ve [kɔezif] *adj.* cohesive.
cohésion [kɔezjɔ̃] *s.f.* cohesion.
cohorte [kɔɔrt] *s.f.* cohort; (fam.) troop, gang, band.
cohue [kɔy] *s.f.* crowd, seething mob; crush, squeeze, press.
coi, -te [kwa] *adj.* (obs.) quiet, silent; (mod.) *se tenir* ~, ~*te*, to say nothing, to keep quiet.
coiffe [kwaf] *s.f.* **1.** head-dress, head-scarf; coif; **2.** hat-lining; **3.** (anat.) caul; **4.** (bot.) calyptra; **5.** (techn.) cap, cover.
coiffé, -e [kwafe] *adj.* wearing a hat or other covering; with tidy hair; *être né* ~, to be born with a caul; (fig.) to be born with a silver spoon in one's mouth.
coiffer [kwafe] *v.t.* **1.** to cover the head with, to wear, (hat, etc.); **2.** to dress someone's hair; *se* ~, to do one's hair; **3.** to cover, to cap; (fig.) to be at the head of; **4.** (obs.) to mislead (s.o.); (mod.) *se* ~ *de*, to be infatuated with; **5.** (racing) to win by a head.
coiffeu-r, -se [kwafœr] *s.m.f.* hairdresser.
coiffeuse [kwaføz] *s.f.* dressing-table.
coiffure [kwafyr] *s.f.* **1.** head-covering, head-gear; **2.** hairdressing, coiffure; **3.** hair-style, hair-do, coiffure.
coin [kwɛ̃] *s.m.* **1.** corner, angle, edge; *regarder du* ~ *de l'œil*, to look sideways at; *jouer aux quatre* ~*s*, to play at puss in the corner; *au* ~ *du feu*, by the fireside; **2.** small space, quiet retreat, (remote) corner, recess, cranny; *les quatre* ~*s du monde*, every quarter of the globe; *connaître une question dans tous les* ~*s*, to know a subject inside out; (fam.) *aller au petit* ~, to go to the toilet; (pop.) *ça vous en bouche un* ~, that surprises you; **2.** wedge; **3.** die, stamp.
coinçage [kwɛ̃saʒ] *s.m.* wedging.
coincement [kwɛ̃smɑ̃] *s.m.* jamming, squeezing.
coincer [kwɛ̃se] *v.t.* to wedge, to jam; (fig.) to corner (s.o.); (fam.) *se faire* ~, to get caught.
coïncidence [kɔɛ̃sidɑ̃s] *s.f.* coincidence; co-inciding; simultaneity.
coïncident, -e [kɔɛ̃sidɑ̃] *adj.* coincident; simultaneous.
coïncider [kɔɛ̃side] *v.i.* to coincide; to be identical, to agree.
coin-coin [kwɛ̃kwɛ̃] *s.m.invar.* quack(-quack).
coïnculpé, -e [kɔɛ̃kylpe] *s.m.f.* co-defendant.
coing [kwɛ̃] *s.m.* (bot.) quince; (fig., fam.) *jaune comme un* ~, sallow.
coït [kɔit] *s.m.* coitus.
coite [kwat] *adj.f.* see COI.
coke [kɔk] *s.m.* coke.
cokéfaction [kɔkefaksjɔ̃] *s.f.* coking.
cokéfier [kɔkefje] *v.t.* to coke.
cokerie [kɔkri] *s.f.* coking-plant.
col [kɔl] *s.m.* **1.** (obs.) neck (of body); (mod.)

narrow portion, neck; **2.** collar; *faux* ~, detachable collar; ~ *rabattu*, turn-down collar; **3.** (geol.) col, pass.

cola [kɔla] *s.m.* = KOLA.

colature [kɔlatyr] *s.f.* filtering; filtrate.

colback [kɔlbak] *s.m.* (hist.) calpac(k), kalpack; (pop.) collar.

col-bleu [kɔlblø] *s.m.* (nav., fam.) bluejacket.

colchique [kɔlʃik] *s.m.* (bot.) colchicum.

colcotar [kɔlkɔtar] *s.m.* (chem.) colcotar.

cold-cream [kɔldkrim] *s.m.* cold cream.

col-de-cygne [kɔldəsiɲ] *s.m.* (pl. *cols-de-cygne*) (techn.) swan-neck (tap, etc.).

colégataire [kɔlegatɛr] *s.m.f.* joint legatee.

coléoptère [kɔleɔptɛr] *s.m.* (ent.) coleopter, beetle; (pl.) Coleoptera.

colère [kɔlɛr] *s.f.* anger, rage; fit of anger, temper, tantrum; (Lit.) wrath; *se mettre en* ~, to get angry.

coléreu-x, -se [kɔlerø] *adj.* irascible, passionate, violent; (fam.) bad-tempered.

colérique [kɔlerik] *adj.* choleric, passionate.

colibri [kɔlibri] *s.m.* (ornith.) colibri, humming-bird.

colicitant, -e [kɔlisitɑ̃] *s.m.f.* (law) joint vendor.

colifichet [kɔlifiʃɛ] *s.m.* bauble, trinket; knick-knack.

colimaçon [kɔlimasɔ̃] *s.m.* snail; *en* ~, spiral, helical.

colin [kɔlɛ̃] *s.m.* **1.** (ichth.) coalfish; (fam.) hake; **2.** (ornith.) Virginian quail.

colin-maillard [kɔlɛ̃majar] *s.m.* blind man's buff.

colin-tampon [kɔlɛ̃tɑ̃pɔ̃] *s.m.* (fam.) *s'en moquer comme de* ~, not to care a hoot.

colique [kɔlik] *s.f.* **1.** (usu. pl.) colic, griping pains; **2.** (sing.) diarrhoea; (fam.) *quelle* ~*!*, (of person) what a bore!; *avoir la* ~, to have diarrhoea, (fig.) to be dead scared.

colis [kɔli] *s.m.* package, parcel, packet.

colite [kɔlit] *s.f.* colitis.

collaborat-eur, -rice [kɔl(l)abɔratœr] *s.m.f.* collaborator, assistant.

collaboration [kɔl(l)abɔrɑsjɔ̃] *s.f.* collaboration.

collaborer [kɔl(l)abɔre] *v.i.* to collaborate (*à*, in; *avec*, with); to work together; to be a collaborator.

collage [kɔlaʒ] *s.m.* **1.** sticking, pasting; paper-hanging; (art) collage; **2.** clarifying (of wine); **3.** (fig., fam.) free love, living together.

collagène [kɔlaʒɛn] *s.m.* collagen.

collant, -e [kɔlɑ̃] *adj.* sticky, adhesive; close-fitting, tight-fitting; (fig., fam.) hard to get rid of, tiresome; ~**s** *s.m.pl.* tights.

collante [kɔlɑ̃t] *s.f.* (slang) summons to exam.

collapsus [kɔl(l)apsys] *s.m.* (med.) collapse (of patient); collapsing (of lung).

collatéral, -e, (aux) [kɔl(l)ateral] *adj.* collateral, parallel; (arch.) *nef* ~*e* (also *s.m.pl. les collatéraux*), (side) aisle; (geog.) *points collatéraux*, intermediate points (of compass); ~**ement** [kɔl(l)ateralmɑ̃] *adv.* collaterally.

collateur [kɔl(l)atœr] *s.m.* (eccles.) advowee.

collation [kɔl(l)ɑsjɔ̃] *s.f.* **1.** conferring (of degrees, honours, etc.); **2.** collation, comparison; **3.** collation, light meal.

collationner [kɔl(l)asjɔne] *v.t.* to collate, to compare; ~ *v.i.* to have a snack.

colle [kɔl] *s.f.* **1.** size, glue, gum, paste; *peinture à la* ~, distemper; **2.** (school slang) (i.) oral exam, viva; (ii.) difficult question, poser; (iii.) detention; **3.** (fig., fam.) s.o. difficult to get rid of, tiresome person.

collecte [kɔl(l)ɛkt] *s.f.* **1.** (liturg.) collect; **2.** collecting, collection (of money, funds, contributions, taxes, etc.).

collecter [kɔl(l)ɛkte] *v.t.* to collect (subscriptions, etc.); to go round collecting.

collect-eur, -rice [kɔl(l)ɛktœr] *s.m.f.* collector (of taxes, contributions, etc.); ~**eur** *s.m.* (electr.) collector, slip-ring, commutator; (car) ~*eur d'echappement*, exhaust manifold; (wireless) ~*eur d'ondes*, aerial, antenna; ⚠ not 'collector' (of e.g. stamps); ~**eur**, ~**rice** *adj.* collecting; *égout* ~*eur*, main sewer.

collecti-f, -ve [kɔl(l)ɛktif] *adj.* collective, joint; ~**f** *s.m.* **1.** (gram.) collective (noun); **2.** (admin.) Finance Act.

collection [kɔl(l)ɛksjɔ̃] *s.f.* collection, set; (med.) gathering (of pus).

collectionner [kɔl(l)ɛksjɔne] *v.t.* to collect (stamps, etc.), to accumulate, to pile up.

collectionneu-r, -se [kɔl(l)ɛksjɔnœr] *s.m.f.* collector.

collectivement [kɔl(l)ɛktivmɑ̃] *adv.* collectively, jointly.

collectiv-iser [kɔl(l)ɛktivize] *v.t.* to collectivize; ~**isme** [kɔl(l)ɛktivism] *s.m.* collectivism; ~**iste** [kɔl(l)ɛktivist] *s.m.f.*, *adj.* collectivist; ~**ité** [kɔl(l)ɛktivite] *s.f.* collectivity, community.

collège [kɔlɛʒ] *s.m.* **1.** college, secondary school; **2.** assembly; ~ *des Cardinaux*, the Sacred College; ~ *électoral*, the electorate.

collégial, -e, (aux) [kɔleʒjal] *adj.* collegiate (pertaining to a Chapter); ~**e** *s.f.* collegiate church.

collégien, -ne [kɔleʒjɛ̃] *s.m.f.* schoolboy, schoolgirl; ~ *s.m.* raw youth.

collègue [kɔl(l)ɛg] *s.m.f.* colleague, partner; (fam.) pal.

coller [kɔle] *v.t.* **1.** to stick, to paste, to glue, to gum; **2.** to apply, to press against; **3.** (pop.) to dump, to stow; **4.** (fam.) to stump, to nonplus; to fail (candidate); to keep (pupil) in; ~ *v.i.* to stick; to fit closely, to cling; (pop.) *ça colle*, that's O.K.; *ça ne colle pas*, it's no go, it doesn't work.

collerette [kɔlrɛt] *s.f.* (obs.) ruched collar; (mod.) collarette; (techn.) collar, flange.

collet [kɔlɛ] *s.m.* **1.** collar; (techn.) collar, flange; (fig.) *une* ~ *monté*, a strait-laced, prudish woman; *prendre qn. au* ~, to arrest s.o.; **2.** (anat., bot., butch.) neck, collar; **3.** snare, noose.

colleter [kɔlte] *v.t.* to take by the scruff of the neck; **se** ~ *v.refl.* to come to blows; (fig.) to come to grips (*avec*, with).

colleteur [kɔltœr] *s.m.* poacher, one who sets snares.

colleu-r, -se [kɔlœr] *s.m.f.* **1.** paper-hanger, bill-sticker; **2.** (school slang) examiner who puts difficult questions; ~**se** *s.f.* sizing machine; splicing machine.

colley [kɔlɛ] *s.m.* collie (dog).

collier [kɔlje] *s.m.* **1.** necklace, chain; **2.** collar, neck-harness, tether; *cheval de* ~, draught horse; *cheval franc du* ~, willing horse; (fig.) *être franc du* ~, to be upright and bold; (fig.) *donner un coup de* ~, to make an effort; ~ *de misère*, drudgery, yoke; **3.** (techn.) ring, collar, flange; **4.** (astron.) astragal.

colliger [kɔl(l)iʒe] *v.t.* (Lit.) to make a collection of.

collimat-eur [kɔl(l)imatœr] *s.m.* (astron.) collimator; ~**ion** (kɔl(l)imɑsjɔ̃] *s.f.* (astron.) collimation.

colline [kɔlin] *s.f.* hill, hillock.

collision [kɔl(l)izjɔ̃] *s.f.* collision, colliding; (fig.) conflict.

collocation [kɔl(l)ɔkɑsjɔ̃] *s.f.* **1.** (law) order of preference (of creditors); **2.** classifying.

collodion [kɔl(l)ɔdjɔ̃] *s.m.* collodion.

colloïdal, -e, (aux) [kɔl(l)ɔidal] *adj.* colloidal.

colloïde [kɔl(l)ɔid] *s.m.* colloid.

colloque [kɔl(l)ɔk] *s.m.* symposium, debate; colloquy, conversation.

colloquer [kɔl(l)ɔke] *v.t.* to place (creditors) in order of preference.

collusion [kɔl(l)yzjɔ̃] *s.f.* collusion.
collusoire [kɔl(l)yzwar] *adj.* collusive.
collutoire [kɔl(l)ytwar] *s.m.* mouth-wash.
collyre [kɔl(l)ir] *s.m.* eye lotion.
colmatage [kɔlmataʒ] *s.m.* (agric.) warping.
colmater [kɔlmate] *v.t.* **1.** (agric.) to warp (land); **2.** to clog, to block, to stop up; **3.** (mil.) to consolidate (position), to close (a gap).
colocase [kɔlɔkɑz] *s.f.* (bot.) Colocasia.
colocataire [kɔlɔkatɛr] *s.m.f.* joint tenant.
Colomb (**Christophe**) [kɔlɔ̃] *s.m.* (Christopher) Columbus.
colombage [kɔlɔ̃baʒ] *s.m.* (constr.) half--timbering.
colombe [kɔlɔ̃b] *s.f.* (ornith.) dove; pigeon; (used also as term of affection).
colombier [kɔlɔ̃bje] *s.m.* **1.** dovecot(e); **2.** colombier (size of paper).
colombin, -e [kɔlɔ̃bɛ̃] *adj.* dove-like; dove--coloured; ~ *s.m.* lead ore; ~**e** *s.f.* pigeon-dung.
colombo-phile [kɔlɔ̃bɔfil] *adj.* pigeon-fancying; *s.m.f.* pigeon-fancier, pigeon-breeder; ~**philie** [kɔlɔ̃bɔfili] *s.f.* pigeon-fancying, pigeon--breeding.
colon [kɔlɔ̃] *s.m.* **1.** tenant-farmer (paying rent in kind), smallholder, husbandman; **2.** colonist, colonizer; colonial; member of colony (of e.g. resident foreigners); child staying at a *colonie de vacances*; **3.** (pop.) (mil. iron.) colonel.
côlon [kolɔ̃] *s.m.* (anat.) colon.
colonel [kɔlɔnɛl] *s.m.* colonel; ~**le** *s.f.* colonel's wife; commandant (of women's corps).
colonial, -e, (**aux**) [kɔlɔnjal] *adj.* colonial; ~ *s.m.* colonial; (mil.) member of colonial forces; ~**e** *s.f.* (mil.) colonial force(s).
colonial-isme [kɔlɔnjalism] *s.m.* colonialism; ~**iste** [kɔlɔnjalist] *adj.*, *s.m.f.* colonialist.
colonie [kɔlɔni] *s.f.* colony, settlement; ~ *pénitentiaire*, reformatory, borstal institution; ~ *de vacances*, children's holiday camp.
colonisat-eur, -rice [kɔlɔnizatœr) *adj.* colonizing; *s.m.f.* colonist, colonizer.
colonis-ation [kɔlɔnizɑsjɔ̃] *s.f.* colonization, colonizing; ~**er** [kɔlɔnize] *v.t.* to colonize.
colonnade [kɔlɔnad] *s.f.* colonnade.
colonne [kɔlɔn] *s.f.* column, pillar.
colonnette [kɔlɔnɛt] *s.f.* small pillar.
colophane [kɔlɔfan] *s.f.* rosin.
coloquinte [kɔlɔkɛ̃t] *s.f.* **1.** (bot.) colocynth; **2.** (pop.) head.
colorant, -e [kɔlɔrɑ̃] *adj.* colouring, tinting; ~ *s.m.* colouring, dye.
coloration [kɔlɔrɑsjɔ̃] *s.f.* coloration, colouring, colour, tint, complexion; (fig.) tone, colouring.
coloré, -e [kɔlɔre] *adj.* **1.** coloured; **2.** (lit. & fig.) vivid, highly coloured; animated, full of expression.
colorer [kɔlɔre] *v.t.* to colour, to stain, to tinge (*de*, with), to tint; (Lit., fig.) to give a favourable aspect to, to varnish, to dress up; **se** ~ *v.refl.* to be tinged (*de*, with).
coloriage [kɔlɔrjaʒ] *s.m.* colouring, tinting.
colorier [kɔlɔrje] *v.t.* to paint, to add colour, to tint.
colorimètre [kɔlɔrimɛtr] *s.m.* colorimeter.
coloris [kɔlɔri] *s.m.* colour, colouring; complexion; (of style) vividness, richness.
coloriste [kɔlɔrist] *s.m.f.* colourist, colourer, painter.
colossal, -e, (**aux**) [kɔlɔsal] *adj.* colossal; ~**ement** [kɔlɔsalmɑ̃] *adv.* colossally, enormously.
colosse [kɔlɔs] *s.m.* colossus, giant.
colostrum [kɔlɔstrɔm] *s.m.* (med.) colostrum.
colportage [kɔlpɔrtaʒ] *s.m.* hawking, peddling; (fig.) spreading, peddling, hawking round, (of gossip, etc.).
colporter [kɔlpɔrte] *v.t.* to hawk, to peddle; (fig.) to spread, to peddle, to circulate, (gossip, etc.).
colporteu-r, -se [kɔlpɔrtœr] *s.m.f.* hawker, pedlar; (fig.) purveyor (of news, gossip, etc.).
colt [kɔlt] *s.m.* Colt (revolver).
coltiner [kɔltine] *v.t.* to carry (loads) on shoulders or head; **se** ~ *v.refl.* (fam.) to carry out, to do, to shoulder, (task).
coltineur [kɔltinœr] *s.m.* (obs.) porter, market--porter.
columbarium [kɔlɔ̃barjɔm] *s.m.* columbarium.
columelle [kɔlymɛl] *s.f.* (conch.) columella.
col-vert [kɔlvɛr] *s.m.* (ornith.) mallard.
colza [kɔlza] *s.m.* (bot.) rape, colza, cole-seed.
coma [kɔma] *s.m.* coma.
comateu-x, -se [kɔmatø] *adj.* comatose.
combat [kɔ̃ba] *s.m.* fight, combat, battle, conflict; struggle, contest.
combati-f, -ve [kɔ̃batif] *adj.* aggressive.
combativité [kɔ̃bativite] *s.f.* aggressiveness.
combattant, -e [kɔ̃batɑ̃] *adj.* fighting; *s.m.f.* fighter, fighting man or woman; combatant; *anciens* ~*s*, ex-servicemen; (ornith.) ruff; ~*s.m.* (ichth.) Siamese fighting fish.
combattre [kɔ̃batr] *v.t.i.* to fight, to combat, to fight against; to contend with, to struggle with or against; to make war.
combe [kɔ̃b] *s.f.* (geog.) coomb, combe, deep valley.
combien [kɔ̃bjɛ̃] *adv.*, *conj.* how much, how, how far, to what extent; ~ *y a-t-il d'ici à la mer?*, how far is it to the sea?; *depuis* ~ *de temps êtes--vous ici?*, how long have you been here?; *si vous saviez* ~ *je l'aime*, if you knew how much I love her; ~ *s.m.invar. le* ~ *êtes-vous?*, which number are you, where do you come (on the list, etc.)?; (fam.) *le* ~ *sommes-nous?*, what is the date?; *tous les* ~ *passe l'autobus?*, how often does the bus go?
combinaison [kɔ̃binɛzɔ̃] *s.f.* **1.** combination, arrangement; composition, mixture; **2.** scheme, plan, device; **3.** (underwear) slip; (men's) overalls, boiler-suit.
combinateur [kɔ̃binatœr] *s.m.* (electr.) selector switch, controller.
combinatoire [kɔ̃binatwar] *adj.* combinatorial, combinative.
combine [kɔ̃bin] *s.f.* (pop.) dodge, trick, fiddle.
combiné, -e [kɔ̃bine] *adj.* combined; ~ *s.m.* **1.** (chem.) compound; **2.** two or more pieces of apparatus in one, e.g. radiogram, telephone receiver, combined rotor and wing aeroplane; **3.** corselet; **4.** (skiing) combined (downhill & slalom) test.
combiner [kɔ̃bine] *v.t.* **1.** to combine, to unite; **2.** to contrive, to scheme; to organize, to plan.
comble [kɔ̃bl] *s.m.* **1.** heaped measure; (fig.) height, utmost degree; *pour* ~ *de malheur*, as a crowning misfortune; *ça, c'est le* ~, that's the last straw; **2.** roof-truss, roofing, roof; *les* ~*s*, the top of the house, the attics; *loger sous les* ~*s*, to live up in the roof, in the attic; *de fond en* ~, from top to bottom, thoroughly.
comble [kɔ̃bl] *adj.* full (to the brim), overflowing; packed (with people).
comblement [kɔ̃bləmɑ̃] *s.m.* filling-up, filling--in.
combler [kɔ̃ble] *v.t.* **1.** to overfill, to heap; to overwhelm, to load, (*de*, with); (fig.) ~ *la mesure*, to go too far, to overstep the mark; **2.** to fill in, to fill up; (fig.) to fill (need, gap); to satisfy in full, to gratify (whim, etc.); ~ *les vœux de qn.*, to meet someone's every wish; *vous me comblez*, you are too kind, you are spoiling me; *je suis comblé*, I have got everything I could desire.
comburant, -e [kɔ̃byrɑ̃] *adj.* combustive; ~ *s.m.* combustible, fuel; oxidant.

combustibilité [kɔ̃bystibilite] *s.f.* combustibility.
combustible [kɔ̃bystibl] *adj.* combustible; ~ *s.m.* fuel.
combustion [kɔ̃bystjɔ̃] *s.f.* combustion.
comédie [kɔmedi] *s.f.* **1.** (obs.) play, drama; (mod.) comedy; **2.** posing, affected behaviour; (in children) tiresome behaviour, showing-off; (fig.) *jouer la* ~, to put on an act.
comédien, -ne [kɔmedjɛ̃] *s.m.f.* actor, actress; comic actor; hypocrite; *adj.* affected, artificial.
comédon [kɔmedɔ̃] *s.m.* (med.) comedo.
comestible [kɔmɛstibl] *adj.* edible; **~s** *s.m.pl.* food(s), provisions.
cométaire [kɔmetɛr] *adj.* (astron.) cometary, cometic.
comète [kɔmɛt] *s.f.* **1.** comet; (herald.) blazing star; **2.** (bookb.) headband.
comices [kɔmis] *s.m.pl.* **1.** (hist.) comitia; **2.** (occasionally sing.) ~ *agricoles*, agricultural show.
comique [kɔmik] *adj.* comic, comical, funny, ludicrous, laughable; ~ *s.m.* **1.** comic actor, comedian, comic; writer of comedy, comic author; **2.** *le* ~, comedy, the comic, the comic part (of), the funny thing (about), the ludicrous; **~ment** [kɔmikmɑ̃] *adv.* comically, ludicrously.
comité [kɔmite] *s.m.* committee, commission; *en petit* ~, among (intimate) friends.
comma [kɔm(m)a] *s.m.* (mus.) comma.
commandant [kɔmɑ̃dɑ̃] *s.m.* (mil.) major; commanding officer; (nav.) commander; (aeron.) ~ *de bord*, captain, pilot; **~, ~e** *adj.* commanding; (fig.) authoritarian.
commande [kɔmɑ̃d] *s.f.* **1.** (comm.) order; *fait sur* ~, made to order; *payable à la* ~, payable on order, cash with order; *de* ~, (obs.) obligatory; (mod.) put on, artificial, insincere; **2.** mooring-cable, lashing; (techn.) control(s), control or regulating mechanism; gear, drive; ~ *à distance*, remote control; (fig.) *prendre les* ~*s*, to take control, to take the wheel; ~ *directe*, direct drive; *de* ~, control (post, lever, etc.).
commandement [kɔmɑ̃dmɑ̃] *s.m.* command, order; (eccles.) commandment; (law) writ; (mil.) command (of unit, etc.).
commander [kɔmɑ̃de] *v.t.* **1.** to command, to order, to direct; ~ *à*, to govern, to control; **2.** (comm.) to order, to bespeak; **3.** (fig.) to compel, to demand; **4.** (fig.) to overlook, to afford (a view); **5.** (techn.) to control, to drive; ~ *v.i.* to be in command, to command.
commanderie [kɔmɑ̃dri] *s.f.* commandery.
commandeur [kɔmɑ̃dœr] *s.m.* commander; Commander (in order of knighthood).
commanditaire [kɔmɑ̃ditɛr] *s.m.f.* sleeping partner; shareholder.
commandite [kɔmɑ̃dit] *s.f.* mixed liability company; partnership.
commandité [kɔmɑ̃dite] *s.m.* active partner.
commanditer [kɔmɑ̃dite] *v.t.* to hold shares in (a company); to finance (s.o.).
commando [kɔmɑ̃do] *s.m.* commando.
comme [kɔm] *adv.* as, like, as well as, such as, so much as, as much as, as it were; how; *tout* ~, just like; as near as makes no difference; (fam.) ~ *tout*, extremely; ~ *il faut*, (*adv.*) properly, suitably, (*adj.*) proper, correct, respectable; *il jette* ~ *une lueur*, it casts a sort of light; ~ *qui dirait*, as it were; ~ *quoi*, to the effect that; ~ *cela*, (in) that way; therefore; ~ *ci*, ~ *ça*, (fam.) so-so; ~ *c'est cher!*, how expensive it is!
comme [kɔm] *conj.* **1.** (time) as, just as, while; *la porte s'est fermée* ~ *je parlais*, the door shut as I was speaking; **2.** (cause) because, since, as; ~ *ils arrivent tout de suite*, as they are coming straight away.
commémoraison [kɔm(m)emɔrɛzɔ̃] *s.f.* (eccles.) commemoration.
commémorati-f, -ve [kɔm(m)emɔratif] *adj.* commemorative.
commémoration [kɔm(m)emɔrɑsjɔ̃] *s.f.* commemoration; remembrance.
commémorer [kɔm(m)emɔre] *v.t.* to commemorate.
commençant, -e [kɔmɑ̃sɑ̃] *s.m.f.* beginner, learner, novice.
commencement [kɔmɑ̃smɑ̃] *s.m.* beginning.
commencer [kɔmɑ̃se] *v.t.* to begin, to start, to commence; ~ *à* or *de faire qch.*, to begin to do sth.; ~ *par faire qch.*, to begin by doing sth.; ~ *v.i.* to begin, to start.
commendataire [kɔmɑ̃datɛr] *adj.* (obs. eccles.) held *in commendam.*
commende [kɔmɑ̃d] *s.f.* (obs. eccles.) commendam.
commensal, -e, (aux) [kɔm(m)ɑ̃sal] *s.m.f.* mess-mate, fellow-guest, (regular) table-companion; (zool.) commensal.
commensalisme [kɔm(m)ɑ̃salism] *s.m.* (zool.) commensalism, commensality.
commensurable [kɔm(m)ɑ̃syrabl] *adj.* commensurable.
comment [kɔmɑ̃] *adv.* how, in what manner; why; (fam.) ~*?*, what?; (fam.) *et* ~*!*, and how!; ~ *s.m.invar.* why, wherefore; *chercher le pourquoi et le* ~ *de qch.*, to want to know the why and the wherefore of sth.
commentaire [kɔm(m)ɑ̃tɛr] *s.m.* commentary, comment(s); (unfavourable) comments, talk, criticism; (fam.) *sans* ~*!*, (often pej.) no further comment required, I need say no more.
commentat-eur, -rice [kɔm(m)ɑ̃tatœr] *s.m.f.* commentator.
commenter [kɔm(m)ɑ̃te] *v.t.* to comment, to comment on, to make a commentary on; (rare) to comment (unfavourably) on, to criticize.
commérage [kɔmeraʒ] *s.m.* (fam.) gossip, tittle-tattle.
commerçant, -e [kɔmɛrsɑ̃] *s.m.f.* dealer, supplier, trader, shop-keeper; *adj.* commercial, mercantile; *une rue* ~*e*, a busy street (with many shops or businesses).
commerce [kɔmɛrs] *s.m.* commerce, trade, business; shop, business; (fig.) commerce, trade, traffic; relations, dealings; ~ *en* or *de gros*, wholesale trade; ~ *de détail*, retail trade.
commercer [kɔmɛrse] *v.i.* to trade, to engage in trade.
commercial, -e, (aux) (kɔmɛrsjal] *adj.* commercial; **~e** *s.f.* van, utility (vehicle); **~ement** [kɔmɛrsjalmɑ̃] *adv.* commercially.
commercialisation [kɔmɛrsjalizɑsjɔ̃] *s.f.* **1.** commercialization; **2.** marketing.
commercialiser [kɔmɛrsjalize] *v.t.* **1.** to commercialize; **2.** to market, to exploit (product).
commère [kɔmɛr] *s.f.* **1.** gossip, crone; **2.** (obs.) fellow-godmother; friend; **3.** (theatr.) commère.
commettage [kɔmɛtaʒ] *s.m.* (naut.) doubling (of cables, etc.).
commettant [kɔmɛtɑ̃] *s.m.* (law) principal.
commettre [kɔmɛtr] *v.t.* **1.** to appoint; to commend to; **2.** to commit (a wrong); **3.** to double (yarns, etc.); **4.** (obs.) to adventure, to endanger; **se** ~ *v.refl.* to compromise oneself.
comminatoire [kɔm(m)inatwar] *adj.* comminatory.
comminuti-f, -ve [kɔm(m)inytif] *adj.* (surg.) comminuting; *fracture* ~*ve*, comminuted fracture.
commis [kɔmi] *s.m.* clerk, employee, shop-assistant; (obs.) ~*-voyageur*, commercial traveller.
commisération [kɔm(m)izerɑsjɔ̃] *s.f.* commiseration.
commissaire [kɔmisɛr] *s.m.* commissary, commissioner; steward (of meeting, etc.); ~ *du bord*, purser; ~ *de police*, police superintendent.

commissaire-priseur [kɔmisɛrprizœr] *s.m.* licensed valuer; auctioneer.
commissariat [kɔmisarja] *s.m.* commissionership, commissioner's office; police station; ~ *maritime*, board of admiralty.
commission [kɔmisjɔ̃] *s.f.* **1.** commission, delegation, charge; **2.** committee, commission; **3.** (comm.) commission, percentage; **4.** (usu. pl.) commission(s), errand(s), shopping.
commissionnaire [kɔmisjɔnɛr] *s.m.* **1.** agent, factor; **2.** errand-boy, commissionaire, porter.
commissionner [kɔmisjɔne] *v.t.* to commission, to empower.
commissoire [kɔmiswar] *adj.* (law) voiding.
commissure [kɔm(m)isyr] *s.f.* (anat.) commisure; (esp.) corner of the mouth.
commode [kɔmɔd] *adj.* **1.** convenient, handy, easy; **2.** accommodating, easy-going; *il n'est pas* ~, he's not easy to deal with.
commode [kɔmɔd] *s.f.* chest of drawers; ⚠ not 'commode'.
commodément [kɔmɔdemɑ̃] *adv.* comfortably, conveniently, at one's ease.
commodité [kɔmɔdite] *s.f.* convenience; (pl.) comforts.
commodore [kɔmɔdɔr] *s.m.* commodore.
commotion [kɔm(m)osjɔ̃] *s.f.* disturbance, shock.
commuable [kɔm(m)ɥabl], **commutable** [kɔm(m)ytabl] *adj.* commutable.
commuer [kɔm(m)ɥe] *v.t.* to commute (a sentence).
commun, -e [kɔmœ̃] *adj.* common, joint; usual, ordinary, common.
commun [kɔmœ̃] *s.m.* **1.** the common, the general; *hors du* ~, out of the ordinary; **2.** the many; *le* ~ *des mortels*, most people, the mass of the people; **3.** (obs.) the common people; **4.** *les* ~*s*, domestic offices.
communal, -e, (aux) [kɔmynal] *adj.* municipal, communal; *école* ~*e*, state (primary) school; *les communaux*, municipally owned land.
communard, -e [kɔmynar] *s.m.f., adj.* (partisan) of the Paris Commune (1871).
communauté [kɔmynote] *s.f.* **1.** community; (eccles.) convent; **2.** (law) joint property; **3.** congeniality, community (of ideas, etc.).
commune [kɔmyn] *s.f.* **1.** town, township, municipality; **2.** *la Chambre des* ~*s*, *les Communes*, the House of Commons; **3.** (Fr. hist.) *La Commune*, the Commune (of Paris, 1871).
communément [kɔmynemɑ̃] *adv.* usually, generally, commonly.
communiant, -e [kɔmynjɑ̃] *s.m.f.* communicant.
communicable [kɔmynikabl] *adj.* communicable.
communicant, -e [kɔmynikɑ̃] *adj.* communicating.
communicat-eur, -rice [kɔmynikatœr] *adj.* connecting.
communicati-f, -ve [kɔmynikatif] *adj.* communicative; (of laugh, etc.) catching.
communication [kɔmynikɑsjɔ̃] *s.f.* communication, relationship; message, news; transmission, communication; access.
communier [kɔmynje] *v.i.* **1.** (eccles.) to communicate, to receive communion; **2.** to be in (spiritual) communion (with); ~ *v.t.* to administer communion to.
communion [kɔmynjɔ̃] *s.f.* communion; (eccles.) communion, (Holy) Communion.
communiqué [kɔmynike] *s.m.* bulletin, communiqué.
communiquer [kɔmynike] *v.t.* to communicate; to pass on, to transmit; ~ *v.i.* to communicate, to be in communication, to be connected.
communisant, -e [kɔmynizɑ̃] *adj.* communist-inspired; *s.m.f.* fellow-traveller.
communisme [kɔmynism] *s.m.* communism.
communiste [kɔmynist] *adj., s.m.f.* communist.
commutable see COMMUABLE.
commutateur [kɔmytatœr] *s.m.* (electr.) switch, change-over switch, circuit-breaker, contact-breaker; commutator.
commutati-f, -ve [kɔmytatif] *adj.* commutative.
commutation [kɔmytɑsjɔ̃] *s.f.* commutation.
compacité [kɔ̃pasite] *s.f.* compactness.
compact, -e [kɔ̃pakt] *adj.* compact, solid, dense, close; massive; (of car) lightweight, compact; *majorité* ~*e*, massive majority.
compactage [kɔ̃paktaʒ] *s.m.* (techn.) compacting.
compagne [kɔ̃paɲ] *s.f.* female friend.
compagnie [kɔ̃paɲi] *s.f.* **1.** company, companionship, fellowship, society; *aller, voyager, de* ~, to go, to travel, together; *tenir* ~ *à qn.*, to keep s.o. company; *fausser* ~ *à qn.*, to give s.o. the slip; *dame (demoiselle) de* ~, paid companion; **2.** (comm.) company, association, society, corporation; (mil.) company; (of animals & birds) covey, flock, etc.
compagnon [kɔ̃paɲɔ̃] *s.m.* **1.** fellow, mate, companion, comrade; **2.** (hist.) journeyman, probationer.
compagnonnage [kɔ̃paɲɔnaʒ] *s.m.* **1.** (hist.) probationary period; **2.** workers' association.
comparable [kɔ̃parabl] *adj.* comparable.
comparaison [kɔ̃parɛzɔ̃] *s.f.* comparison; *en* ~ *de*, in comparison with; *par* ~ *à*, compared to, by comparison with; *sans* ~, indubitably.
comparaître [kɔ̃parɛtr] *v.i.* (law) to appear.
comparant, -e [kɔ̃parɑ̃] *adj., s.m.f.* (law) appearing; person appearing.
comparat-eur, -rice [kɔ̃paratœr] *adj.* given to making comparison(s); ~**eur** *s.m.* comparator.
comparati-f, -ve [kɔ̃paratif] *adj.* comparative; ~**f** *s.m.* (lang.) comparative; *au* ~*f*, in the comparative; ~**vement** [kɔ̃parativmɑ̃] *adv.* comparatively.
comparé, -e [kɔ̃pare] *adj.* (of relig., anat., etc.) comparative.
comparer [kɔ̃pare] *v.t.* to compare.
comparoir [kɔ̃parwar] *v.i.* (law) = COMPARAÎTRE.
comparse [kɔ̃pars] *s.m.f.* (theatr.) super; (fig.) nonentity; *rôle de* ~, walking-on part.
compartiment [kɔ̃partimɑ̃] *s.m.* compartment; division, pigeon-hole; square (on chess-board, etc.); (bookb.) tooling; ~**age** [kɔ̃partimɑ̃taʒ] *s.m.* partitioning; division into compartments or pigeon-holes; pigeon-holing; ~**er** [kɔ̃partimɑ̃te] *v.t.* to partition, to divide into compartments, etc.; (fig.) to classify, to put into categories.
compas [kɔ̃pa] *s.m.* **1.** compasses, pair of compasses; ~ *à pointes sèches*, dividers; ~ *d'épaisseur*, callipers; *avoir le* ~ *dans l'œil*, to have a good eye (for distances, etc.); **2.** (naut.) compass.
compassé, -e [kɔ̃pɑse, kɔ̃pase] *adj.* stilted, stiff, pompous.
compasser [kɔ̃pɑse, kɔ̃pase] *v.t.* to measure with compasses, callipers, etc.; to make exact drawings, to lay out accurately; (fig.) to give (excessively) careful thought to.
compassion [kɔ̃pɑsjɔ̃, kɔ̃pasjɔ̃] *s.f.* compassion.
compatibilité [kɔ̃patibilite] *s.f.* compatibility; consistency.
compatible [kɔ̃patibl] *adj.* compatible; consistent.
compatir [kɔ̃patir] *v.i.* **1.** (obs.) to be compatible; **2.** ~ *à*, to sympathize with, to share (grief, etc.).
compatissant, -e [kɔ̃patisɑ̃] *adj.* compassionate, sympathetic.

compatriote [kɔ̃patrijɔt] *s.m.f.* compatriot; fellow-countryman(woman).
compendieu-x, -se [kɔ̃pɑ̃djø] *adj.* (obs.) compendious, concise; **~sement** [kɔ̃pɑ̃djøzmɑ̃] *adv.* concisely, succinctly.
compendium [kɔ̃pɛ̃djɔm] *s.m.* compendium.
compensat-eur, -rice [kɔ̃pɑ̃satœr] *adj.* compensating, compensatory; compensated; (*pendule*) *~eur*, compensation pendulum.
compensation [kɔ̃pɑ̃sɑsjɔ̃] *s.f.* compensation.
compensatoire [kɔ̃pɑ̃satwar] *adj.* compensatory.
compenser [kɔ̃pɑ̃se] *v.t.* to compensate, to balance, to make up for, to offset; **se ~** *v.refl.* to offset each other, to complement each other.
compérage [kɔ̃peraʒ] *s.m.* (obs.) conspiracy, collusion.
compère [kɔ̃pɛr] *s.m.* **1.** (fam.) friend; **2.** accomplice.
compère-loriot [kɔ̃pɛrlɔrjo] *s.m.* **1.** (med.) sty(e) (on eye); **2.** (ornith.) golden oriole.
compétence [kɔ̃petɑ̃s] *s.f.* **1.** (law) competence, competency; **2.** competence, ability, expertise; (fam.) expert; **3.** sphere, domain, province.
compétent, -e [kɔ̃petɑ̃] *adj.* **1.** (law) competent; **2.** expert.
compétit-eur, -rice [kɔ̃petitœr] *s.m.f.* competitor; rival.
compétiti-f, -ve [kɔ̃petitif] *adj.* (comm.) competitive.
compétition [kɔ̃petisjɔ̃] *s.f.* competition, rivalry; (sport) competition.
compilat-eur, -rice [kɔ̃pilatœr] *s.m.f.* compiler; (pej.) plagiarist.
compilation [kɔ̃pilɑsjɔ̃] *s.f.* compilation; re-hash (of the work of others).
compiler [kɔ̃pile] *v.t.* to compile; to plagiarize.
complainte [kɔ̃plɛ̃t] *s.f.* **1.** (obs.) plaint, lament; **2.** plaintive song.
complaire [kɔ̃plɛr] *v.i.* **~** *à qn.*, to humour s.o., to seek to please s.o.; **se ~** *(à) v.refl.* to delight in, to find pleasure in; *se ~ dans*, to be happy in, to be complacent in (one's illusions, etc.).
complaisamment [kɔ̃plɛzamɑ̃] *adv.* obligingly, kindly, complaisantly; complacently.
complaisance [kɔ̃plɛzɑ̃s] *s.f.* obliging civility, complaisance, kindness; complacency; *par ~*, out of kindness.
complaisant, -e [kɔ̃plɛzɑ̃] *adj.* obliging, helpful, kind, complaisant; complacent; indulgent; (pej.) fawning; self-satisfied; **~** *s.m.* easy-going or indulgent person, (esp.) complaisant husband.
complanter [kɔ̃plɑ̃te] *v.t.* to plant with trees.
complément [kɔ̃plemɑ̃] *s.m.* complement; (gram.) complement, object (of verb).
complémentaire [kɔ̃plemɑ̃tɛr] *adj.* complementary.
compl-et, -ète [kɔ̃plɛ] *adj.* complete, full, whole, entire; utter, perfect, consummate; arrant; *café, thé, ~et*, coffee or tea with rolls and butter, etc.; *au ~et*, with all present; unanimously; (of bus, etc.) full; **~ètement** [kɔ̃plɛtmɑ̃] *adv.* completely, wholly, fully, quite, entirely, thoroughly.
complet [kɔ̃plɛ] *s.m.* suit (of clothes).
complètement *adv.* see COMPLET *adj.*
complètement [kɔ̃plɛtmɑ̃] *s.m.* (rare) completion.
compléter [kɔ̃plete] *v.t.* to complete; to perfect; **se ~** *v.refl.* to complement one another.
compléti-f, -ve [kɔ̃pletif] *adj.* (lang.) adjectival; (*proposition*) *~ve*, adjectival clause.
complexe [kɔ̃plɛks] *adj.* complex, compound; complicated, intricate.
complexe [kɔ̃plɛks] *s.m.* complex.
complexé, -e [kɔ̃plɛkse] *adj.* (fam.) inhibited, having a complex.
complexion [kɔ̃plɛksjɔ̃] *s.f.* **1.** constitution, temperament, nature; **2.** (obs.) humour, complexion.
complexité [kɔ̃plɛksite] *s.f.* complexity, intricacy.
complication [kɔ̃plikɑsjɔ̃] *s.f.* complication, intricacy; (med.) complication.
complice [kɔ̃plis] *adj.* privy (to), abetting; **~** *s.m.f.* accomplice.
complicité [kɔ̃plisite] *s.f.* complicity; aiding and abetting.
complies [kɔ̃pli] *s.f.pl.* (liturg.) compline.
compliment [kɔ̃plimɑ̃] *s.m.* compliment, congratulation(s), kind regards; complimentary speech, poem, etc.; *faire ~ à qn. de* or *sur qch.*, to compliment or congratulate s.o. on sth.; *mes ~s!*, congratulations!; *sans ~*, no flattery; *mes ~s à...*, my compliments, my kind regards, to....
complimenter [kɔ̃plimɑ̃te] *v.t.* to compliment, to congratulate.
complimenteu-r, -se [kɔ̃plimɑ̃tœr] *adj.* flattering, obsequious; *s.m.f.* flatterer.
compliqué, -e [kɔ̃plike] *adj.* complicated, intricate, complex, involved; (fig.) tortuous, devious.
compliquer [kɔ̃plike] *v.t.* to complicate, to entangle; **se ~** *v.refl.* to become complicated; (med.) to get worse; *la maladie se complique*, complications are setting in.
complot [kɔ̃plo] *s.m.* plot, conspiracy.
comploter [kɔ̃plɔte] *v.t.i.* to plot, to conspire, to intrigue.
comploteur [kɔ̃plɔtœr] *s.m.* plotter, conspirator.
componction [kɔ̃pɔ̃ksjɔ̃] *s.f.* compunction; (iron.) *avec ~*, solemnly.
componé, -e [kɔ̃pɔne] *adj.* (herald.) componé, compony.
comporte [kɔ̃pɔrt] *s.f.* wooden tub (for grape harvest).
comportement [kɔ̃pɔrtəmɑ̃] *s.m.* comportment, behaviour.
comporter [kɔ̃pɔrte] *v.t.* to imply, to involve; to comprise; **se ~** *v.refl.* to behave.
composant, -e [kɔ̃pozɑ̃] *adj.* component, composing, constituent; **~** *s.m.* (chem.) component; **~e** *s.f.* (mech., electr.) component (of force, etc., of voltage).
composé, -e [kɔ̃poze] *adj.* compounded, compound, composed; (fig.) stilted; **~** *s.m.* compound.
composées [kɔ̃poze], **composacées** [kɔ̃pozase] *s.f. pl.* (bot.) Compositae.
composer [kɔ̃poze] *v.t.* to compose, to compound, to constitute, to make up; to compose, to write, (mus., essay, etc.); **se ~** *(de) v.refl.* to be composed (of), to consist (of), to comprise; *se ~*, to form, to take shape; (fig.) to calm down, to settle down; **~** *v.i.* to compose, to write an essay, etc.; to come to terms, to settle (e.g. one's differences, or with one's creditors); to compromise, to compound.
composite [kɔ̃pozit] *adj.* composite, heterogeneous; **~** *s.m.* (arch.) composite order.
composit-eur, -rice [kɔ̃pozitœr] *s.m.f.* (mus.) composer; (print.) compositor.
composition [kɔ̃pozisjɔ̃] *s.f.* **1.** composition; (school) test, internal exam; essay; **2.** combination, arrangement; (obs.) settlement, compromise, composition (with creditors, etc.).
compost [kɔ̃pɔst] *s.m.* (agric., hort.) compost.
compostage [kɔ̃pɔstaʒ] *s.m.* punching (of tickets, receipts, etc.), cancelling.
composter[1] [kɔ̃pɔste] *v.t.* (agric., hort.) to compost.
composter[2] [kɔ̃pɔste] *v.t.* **1.** (print.) to assemble (on composing-stick); **2.** to punch, to cancel, (tickets, etc.).
composteur [kɔ̃pɔstœr] *s.m.* **1.** (print.) composing-stick; **2.** cancelling-machine (for tickets, etc.).

compote [kɔ̃pɔt] *s.f.* stewed fruit; (fig., fam.) *en* ~, smashed to a pulp.
compotier [kɔ̃pɔtje] *s.m.* dish for stewed fruit; dishful of stewed fruit.
compound [kɔ̃pund] *adj.invar.* (mech.) compound; (electr.) composite; *moteur* ~, turbo-compound aero engine; ~ *s.f.* compound (steam engine).
compréhensibilité [kɔ̃preɑ̃sibilite] *s.f.* comprehensibility, intelligibility.
compréhensible [kɔ̃preɑ̃sibl] *adj.* comprehensible, intelligible; understandable, natural.
compréhensi-f, -ve [kɔ̃preɑ̃sif] *adj.* comprehensive; understanding, tolerant.
compréhension [kɔ̃preɑ̃sjɔ̃] *s.f.* comprehension; understanding.
comprendre [kɔ̃prɑ̃dr] *v.t.* **1.** to include, to comprise; *tout compris*, inclusive; **2.** to understand, to make out, to realize.
comprenette [kɔ̃prənɛt] *s.f.* (fam.) understanding; *il a la* ~ *un peu dure*, he's a bit slow in the uptake.
compresse [kɔ̃prɛs] *s.f.* bandage, dressing, compress.
compresseur [kɔ̃prɛsœr] *s.m.* compressor; ~ *adj.* compressing.
compressi-f, -ve [kɔ̃prɛsif] *adj.* compressive.
compression [kɔ̃prɛsjɔ̃] *s.f.* **1.** compression; **2.** (obs.) pressure, constraint; (mod.) reduction.
comprimé, -e [kɔ̃prime] *adj.* compressed, pressed; (fig.) repressed; ~ *s.m.* (med.) tablet.
comprimer [kɔ̃prime] *v.t.* to compress, to press, to squeeze; (fig.) to restrain, to check, to repress.
compromettant, -e [kɔ̃prɔmɛtɑ̃] *adj.* compromising, indiscreet; *ce n'est pas* ~, it doesn't commit you to anything.
compromettre [kɔ̃prɔmɛtr] *v.t.* to compromise, to implicate, to endanger, to hazard, to put at risk; ~ *v.i.* to accept arbitration, to compromise.
compromis [kɔ̃prɔmi] *s.m.* compromise.
compromission [kɔ̃prɔmisjɔ̃] *s.f.* compromising; (usu. pej.) compromise.
comptabiliser [kɔ̃tabilize] *v.t.* to enter in the accounts.
comptabilité [kɔ̃tabilite] *s.f.* book-keeping, accountancy; accounting; accounts department; accounting staff; ~ *en partie simple, en partie double*, single, double, entry book-keeping.
comptable [kɔ̃tabl] *s.m.f.* book-keeper, accountant; *expert* ~, chartered accountant; ~ *adj.* accountable, responsible; countable.
comptage [kɔ̃taʒ] *s.m.* reckoning, calculation.
comptant [kɔ̃tɑ̃] *s.m.* ready money, cash; ~ *adj.* (of money) ready; *argent* ~, cash; (fig., fam.) *prendre qch. pour argent* ~, to take sth. for gospel; ~ *adv.* in cash.
compte [kɔ̃t] *s.m.* count, reckoning; amount, quantity, sum; (bank) account; *à bon* ~, cheaply; *de* ~ *à demi*, share and share alike; *à ce* ~*-là*, on that score; if that is the case; *tenir* ~ *de*, to take into account; to pay heed to; *avoir son* ~, to have one's due; (fam.) to have had it; to be drunk; *entrer en ligne de* ~, to come into it, to need to be taken into account; *au bout du* ~, all things considered; *en fin de* ~, at last, finally; *avoir un* ~ *à régler avec qn.*, to have a bone to pick with s.o.; (fig., fam.) *régler son* ~ *à qn.*, to fix s.o.; *trouver son* ~ *à qch.*, to profit from sth., to find sth. to one's advantage; *se rendre* ~ *que*, to realize that; *se rendre* ~ *de*, to understand, to perceive; *un laissé pour* ~, an unclaimed or uncollected article; ~**-rendu** *s.m.* account, report, minute(s), review, critique.
compte-fils [kɔ̃tfil] *s.m.invar.* (embroidery, etc.) mounted magnifying-glass for counting threads.
compte-gouttes [kɔ̃tgut] *s.m.invar.* dropper, pipette, fountain-pen filler; *au* ~, (fig.) parsimoniously, sparingly.
compter [kɔ̃te] *v.t.* **1.** to count, to reckon, to calculate, to number; to count or measure out; *à* ~ *de*, starting from, dating from, with effect from; **2.** to amount to, to include, to comprise; **3.** (Lit.) to esteem, to consider, to deem, to account; **4.** to intend, to hope, to expect; ~ *v.i.* **1.** to count, to calculate; ~ *avec*, to reckon with, to take (sth.) into account; **2.** to rely, to depend (*sur*, on); *j'y compte bien*, I very much hope so; **3.** to count, to be of importance; *cela compte peu*, that is of little consequence; **4.** to be numbered or reckoned (*parmi*, among).
compte-rendu [kɔ̃trɑ̃dy] *s.m.* see COMPTE.
compte-tours [kɔ̃ttur] *s.m.invar.* (revolution) counter, tachometer.
compteur [kɔ̃tœr] *s.m.* **1.** (rare) teller; **2.** meter; ~ *de vitesse*, speedometer.
comptoir [kɔ̃twar] *s.m.* **1.** counter, bar; **2.** (comm., fin.) foreign branch; agency; bank; **3.** cooperative trading agency.
compulser [kɔ̃pylse] *v.t.* to consult, to look through, to examine, (documents, etc.).
compulsi-f, -ve [kɔ̃pylsif] *adj.* (psychol.) compulsive.
compulsion [kɔ̃pylsjɔ̃] *s.f.* (obs.) constraint; (psychol.) compulsion.
comput [kɔ̃pyt] *s.m.* dating (of movable feasts).
computation [kɔ̃pytɑsjɔ̃] *s.f.* computing of time, chronology.
comte [kɔ̃t] *s.m.* count; (in Britain, etc.) earl.
comté [kɔ̃te] *s.m.* **1.** (obs.) earldom; (in Britain, etc.) county, shire; **2.** (or *conté*) a cheese from the Franche-Comté.
comtesse [kɔ̃tɛs] *s.f.* countess.
concassage [kɔ̃kɑsaʒ] *s.m.* crushing, crumbling.
concasser [kɔ̃kɑse] *v.t.* to crush, to crumble.
concasseur [kɔ̃kɑsœr] *s.m.* crushing-mill or roller; *adj.* crushing.
concaténation [kɔ̃katenɑsjɔ̃] *s.f.* concatenation.
concave [kɔ̃kav] *adj.* concave, hollow.
concavité [kɔ̃kavite] *s.f.* concavity, hollowness.
concéder [kɔ̃sede] *v.t.* to grant, to bestow, to allow; (fig.) to concede, to yield, to admit.
concentration [kɔ̃sɑ̃trɑsjɔ̃] *s.f.* concentration; *camp de* ~, concentration camp; ~ *urbaine*, urban agglomeration.
concentré, -e [kɔ̃sɑ̃tre] *adj.* concentrated, condensed; ~ *s.m.* concentrate.
concentrer [kɔ̃sɑ̃tre] *v.t.* to concentrate, to condense; **se** ~ *v.refl.* to concentrate.
concentrique [kɔ̃sɑ̃trik] *adj.* concentric; ~**ment** [kɔ̃sɑ̃trikmɑ̃] *adv.* concentrically.
concept [kɔ̃sɛpt] *s.m.* concept, idea.
conceptacle [kɔ̃sɛptakl] *s.m.* (bot.) conceptacle.
conception [kɔ̃sɛpsjɔ̃] *s.f.* conception; (fig.) idea, understanding, conception.
conceptualisme [kɔ̃sɛptɥalism] *s.m.* conceptualism.
conceptuel, -le [kɔ̃sɛptɥɛl] *adj.* conceptual.
concernant [kɔ̃sɛrnɑ̃] *prep.* concerning, relating to, about, with respect or regard to.
concerner [kɔ̃sɛrne] *v.t.* to concern, to relate to, to affect, to be the concern of; *cela ne vous concerne pas*, that doesn't concern you, that is no business of yours; *en ce qui me concerne*, as far as I am concerned.
concert [kɔ̃sɛr] *s.m.* **1.** (mus.) concert, musical entertainment; music society; **2.** agreement, union, concert; *agir de* ~, to act in concert, in agreement.
concertant, -e [kɔ̃sɛrtɑ̃] *adj.* taking part in a concert; concerted, concertante.
concerter [kɔ̃sɛrte] *v.t.* to arrange, to organize by mutual agreement; ~ *v.i.* to play in concert; **se** ~ *v.refl.* to agree to act together.
concertina [kɔ̃sɛrtina] *s.m.* concertina.
concertino [kɔ̃sɛrtino] *s.m.* (mus.) concertino; solo instruments in a concerto grosso.

concertiste [kɔ̃sɛrtist] *s.m.f.* concert performer.
concerto [kɔ̃sɛrto] *s.m.* concerto.
concessi-f, -ve [kɔ̃sesif] *adj.* (gram.) concessive.
concession [kɔ̃sesjɔ̃] *s.f.* concession; grant or concession (of land, mining rights, etc.); granting, conceding.
concessionnaire [kɔ̃sesjɔnɛr] *s.m.f.* licensee, authorized dealer, concessionnaire; licence-holder, grantee.
concevable [kɔ̃svabl] *adj.* conceivable, comprehensible.
concevoir [kɔ̃s(ə)vwar] *v.t.i.* **1.** to conceive, to become pregnant; **2.** to conceive, to imagine, to form in the mind.
conchoïdal, -e, (aux) [kɔ̃kɔidal] *adj.* conchoidal.
conchoïde [kɔ̃kɔid] *s.f.* (geom.) conchoid.
conchylien, -ne [kɔ̃kiljɛ̃] *adj.* (geol.) conchylaceous.
conchyliologie [kɔ̃kiljɔlɔʒi] *s.f.* conchology.
concierge [kɔ̃sjɛrʒ] *s.m.f.* door-keeper, porter, concierge, caretaker.
conciergerie [kɔ̃sjɛrʒəri] *s.f.* **1.** duties of porter, etc.; caretaker's lodge (in public building); **2.** (hist.) *la Conciergerie*, the Conciergerie (prison in Paris).
concile [kɔ̃sil] *s.m.* (eccles.) council, synod; (pl.) conciliar decrees and records.
conciliable [kɔ̃siljabl] *adj.* reconcilable, compatible.
conciliabule [kɔ̃siljabyl] *s.m.* **1.** (obs.) conventicle; **2.** whispered discussion.
conciliaire [kɔ̃siljɛr] *adj.* conciliar.
conciliant, -e [kɔ̃siljɑ̃] *adj.* conciliatory, conciliating, amenable.
conciliat-eur, -rice [kɔ̃siljatœr] *s.m.f.* arbitrator, mediator; *adj.* reconciling, conciliatory, conciliating.
conciliation [kɔ̃siljɑsjɔ̃] *s.f.* conciliation, arbitration.
concilier [kɔ̃silje] *v.t.* to conciliate, to reconcile; *se ~ qn.*, to win s.o. over, to gain someone's support.
concis, -e [kɔ̃si] *adj.* concise, succinct.
concision [kɔ̃sizjɔ̃] *s.f.* concision, conciseness.
concitoyen, -ne [kɔ̃sitwajɛ̃] *s.m.f.* fellow-countryman or -countrywoman, compatriot, fellow citizen.
conclave [kɔ̃klav] *s.m.* conclave.
concluant, -e [kɔ̃klyɑ̃] *adj.* conclusive, final, decisive, unanswerable.
conclure [kɔ̃klyr] *v.t.i.* **1.** to conclude, to bring to a conclusion, to end, to close; **2.** to infer, to conclude, to assume, to come to the conclusion that; **3.** to be decisive.
conclusion [kɔ̃klyzjɔ̃] *s.f.* **1.** conclusion, end, settlement; **2.** inference, conclusion; **3.** (pl.) (law) arguments.
concombre [kɔ̃kɔ̃br] *s.m.* cucumber.
concomitance [kɔ̃kɔmitɑ̃s] *s.f.* concomitance, concomitancy.
concomitant, -e [kɔ̃kɔmitɑ̃] *adj.* concomitant.
concordance [kɔ̃kɔrdɑ̃s] *s.f.* concordance, agreement, conformity, correspondence; (geol.) parallelism (of strata); (lang.) concord, agreement; *~ des temps*, sequence of tenses.
concordant, -e [kɔ̃kɔrdɑ̃] *adj.* concordant, corroborative.
concordat [kɔ̃kɔrda] *s.m.* **1.** concordat, agreement; **2.** (comm.) composition (with creditors).
concorde [kɔ̃kɔrd] *s.f.* concord, unity, harmony, peace.
concorder [kɔ̃kɔrde] *v.i.* to agree, to concur, to accord.
concourant, -e [kɔ̃kurɑ̃] *adj.* concurring, concurrent, convergent.
concourir [kɔ̃kurir] *v.i.* **1.** to concur; to contribute, to lead, (*à*, to); **2.** (geom.) to meet, to converge; **3.** to compete.
concours [kɔ̃kur] *s.m.* **1.** (obs.) concourse, crowd; **2.** help, assistance, collaboration, co-operation; **3.** competition, contest, competitive examination; *hors-~*, incomparable, supreme; *hors-~*, ineligible, disqualified.
concr-et, -ète [kɔ̃krɛ] *adj.* concrete (opp. abstract); solid (opp. fluid); (fig.) concrete, real, substantial; **~et** *s.m.* *le ~et*, the concrete (opp. abstract); ⚠ not the substance 'concrete'; **~ètement** [kɔ̃krɛtmɑ̃] *adv.* in practice, in fact.
concrétion [kɔ̃kresjɔ̃] *s.f.* concretion; (med.) calculus.
concrétiser [kɔ̃kretize] *v.t.* to concretize, to put into concrete form.
concubin, -e [kɔ̃kybɛ̃] *s.m.f.* lover, concubine.
concubinage [kɔ̃kybinaʒ] *s.m.* concubinage; (pop.) cohabiting, living together.
concupiscence [kɔ̃kypisɑ̃s] *s.f.* concupiscence, sensuality.
concupiscent, -e [kɔ̃kypisɑ̃] *adj.* concupiscent, lustful, lecherous; *~ s.m.* sensualist, lecher.
concurremment [kɔ̃kyramɑ̃] *adv.* **1.** (obs.) in competition; **2.** concurrently, jointly.
concurrence [kɔ̃kyrɑ̃s] *s.f.* **1.** competition, rivalry; *être en ~ avec, faire ~ à*, to compete with, to be in competition with; **2.** concurrence, coincidence; *jusqu'à ~ de*, to the amount of, up to the sum of.
concurrencer [kɔ̃kyrɑ̃se] *v.t.* to compete with, to vie with.
concurrent, -e [kɔ̃kyrɑ̃] *s.m.f.* competitor, rival; candidate; *adj.* concurrent.
concurrentiel, -le [kɔ̃kyrɑ̃sjɛl] *adj.* (econ.) competitive.
concussion [kɔ̃kysjɔ̃] *s.f.* exaction, peculation, embezzlement, extortion; ⚠ not 'concussion'.
concussionnaire [kɔ̃kysjɔnɛr] *adj.* extortive; *s.m.f.* extortioner, embezzler.
condamnable [kɔ̃dɑnabl] *adj.* blameworthy, reprehensible.
condamnation [kɔ̃dɑnɑsjɔ̃] *s.f.* condemnation, conviction, sentence; (fig.) blame, censure.
condamnatoire [kɔ̃dɑnatwar] *adj.* condemnatory.
condamné, -e [kɔ̃dɑne] *s.m.f.* convicted prisoner; *un ~*, a condemned man; *adj.* convicted, sentenced, under sentence; condemned; (of patient) incurable; (of entrance, etc.) blocked up, closed.
condamner [kɔ̃dɑne] *v.t.* to condemn; to convict, to sentence; to forbid or condemn (a practice); (med.) to pronounce (patient) incurable; to block up, to close (entrance, etc.).
condensable [kɔ̃dɑ̃sabl] *adj.* condensable.
condensateur [kɔ̃dɑ̃satœr] *s.m.* (electr., opt.) condenser.
condensation [kɔ̃dɑ̃sɑsjɔ̃] *s.f.* condensation.
condensé, -e [kɔ̃dɑ̃se] *adj.* condensed, concentrated; *~ s.m.* condensation, summary, digest, (of novel, etc.).
condenser [kɔ̃dɑ̃se] *v.t.* to condense; (fig.) to condense, to summarize, to boil down.
condenseur [kɔ̃dɑ̃sœr] *s.m.* (mech., opt.) condenser.
condescendance [kɔ̃desɑ̃dɑ̃s] *s.f.* condescension.
condescendant, -e [kɔ̃desɑ̃dɑ̃] *adj.* condescending, superior.
condescendre [kɔ̃desɑ̃dr] *v.i.* to condescend, to deign, to be kind enough, (*à*, to).
condiment [kɔ̃dimɑ̃] *s.m.* condiment, seasoning; (fig.) stimulus.
condisciple [kɔ̃disipl] *s.m.* schoolfellow, fellow student.
condition [kɔ̃disjɔ̃] *s.f.* **1.** social class, rank, standing; (pl.) circumstances, situation; (obs.) *être de* or *en ~ chez*, to be in domestic service with;

des gens de différentes ~*s*, people in various walks of life; **2.** condition, state, situation; form; *être en* ~, to be in good form, to be in prime condition, to be in training; *mettre en* ~, to train (athlete, etc.); to condition, to work on, (people's minds); **3.** condition, requirement, stipulation, clause (of contract); (pl.) terms; *à* ~, conditionally, provisionally; *à* ~ *de*, provided that; *à* ~ *que*, on condition that, on the understanding that; *sans* ~, unconditional(ly); *sous* ~, conditionally, with reservations.

conditionné, -e [kɔ̃disjɔne] *adj.* conditioned, in (good) condition; (of experiments) controlled; (of foods) processed; *à air* ~, air-conditioned.

conditionnel, -le [kɔ̃disjɔnɛl] *adj.* conditional; ~ *s.m.* (lang.) conditional (tense); ~**lement** [kɔ̃disjɔnɛlmɑ̃] *adv.* conditionally.

conditionnement [kɔ̃disjɔnmɑ̃] *s.m.* conditioning, processing.

conditionner [kɔ̃disjɔne] *v.t.* to condition, to process, to put in good condition; ~ *v.i.* to be a condition of.

conditionneu-r, -se [kɔ̃disjɔnœr] *s.m.f.* processer, packer; ~**r** *s.m.* air conditioner.

condoléances [kɔ̃dɔleɑ̃s] *s.f.pl.* condolences, sympathy.

condominium [kɔ̃dɔminjɔm] *s.m.* condominium.

condor [kɔ̃dɔr] *s.m.* (ornith.) condor.

conductance [kɔ̃dyktɑ̃s] *s.f.* (electr.) conductance.

conduct-eur, -rice [kɔ̃dyktœr] *s.m.f.* guide, leader; director, manager; driver, drover; foreman, clerk of works; (rail.) guard; (print.) machine operator; *adj.* (electr.) conducting; ~**eur** *s.m.* (phys., electr.) conductor.

conductibilité [kɔ̃dyktibilite] *s.f.* conductibility, ability to conduct (heat, current, nervous impulses).

conductible [kɔ̃dyktibl] *adj.* (phys., electr.) conductive.

conduction [kɔ̃dyksjɔ̃] *s.f.* **1.** (phys., etc.) conduction; **2.** (Rom. law) hire, hiring.

conductivité [kɔ̃dyktivite] *s.f.* (electr.) conductivity.

conduire [kɔ̃dɥir] *v.t.* **1.** to conduct, to lead, to take, to bring, to guide; to accompany; to drive; (of road, etc.) to lead; **2.** to conduct, to manage, to superintend, to be in charge of (an operation, etc.); **3.** (phys., electr.) to conduct; **se** ~ *v.refl.* to behave, to conduct oneself.

conduit [kɔ̃dɥi] *s.m.* (constr.) pipe, conduit, drain, culvert; (anat.) passage, duct.

conduite [kɔ̃dɥit] *s.f.* **1.** conducting, leading, guiding, guidance, piloting; accompanying; driving; (of car) ~ *à gauche*, left-hand drive; ~ *intérieure*, saloon, limousine; **2.** directing, control, command, managing; **3.** conduct, behaviour; *n'avoir pas de* ~, to have no manners; (fam.) *s'acheter une* ~, to turn over a new leaf; **4.** pipe, piping; (electr.) wiring, lead.

condyle [kɔ̃dil] *s.m.* (anat.) condyle.

condylien, -ne [kɔ̃diljɛ̃] *adj.* (anat.) condyloid, condylar.

cône [kon] *s.m.* (geom.) cone; (geol.) cone (of volcano); (nav.) warhead (of torpedo); (moll.) cone shell; (bot.) ~ *de pin*, pine-cone; (geom.) *tronc de* ~, ~ *tronqué*, conical frustum, truncated cone; *en* ~, conical, cone-shaped.

confection [kɔ̃fɛksjɔ̃] *s.f.* **1.** (obs.) completion; (mod.) preparation, making, fabrication, cooking; **2.** making of ready-made clothes; *costume de* ~, ready-made costume; *être dans la* ~, to be in the ready-made garment trade; ⚠ not 'confection' in sense 'article of confectionery'.

confectionner [kɔ̃fɛksjɔne] *v.t.* to make, to prepare, to cook; to make up (garment, etc.).

confectionneu-r, -se [kɔ̃fɛksjɔnœr] *s.m.f.* maker, maker-up (esp. of ready-made garments); ⚠ not 'confectioner'.

confédéral, -e, (**aux**) [kɔ̃federal] *adj.* confederal, federal.

confédération [kɔ̃federɑsjɔ̃] *s.f.* confederation, confederacy, federation.

confédéré, -e [kɔ̃federe] *adj.*, *s.m.f.* confederate.

confédérer [kɔ̃federe] *v.t.* to federate, to confederate.

conférence [kɔ̃ferɑ̃s] *s.f.* **1.** conference, discussion, debate; **2.** lecture, lesson; *maître de* ~*s*, (university) lecturer; **3.** conference pear.

conférenc-ier, -ière [kɔ̃ferɑ̃sje] *s.m.f.* lecturer, speaker.

conférer [kɔ̃fere] *v.t.* **1.** to confer, to bestow, to grant; **2.** to compare; ~ *v.i.* to confer; ~ *de*, to discuss.

confesse [kɔ̃fɛs] *s.f.* (eccles.) confession; *aller à* ~, *venir de* ~, to go to, to come from, confession.

confesser [kɔ̃fese] *v.t.* **1.** to confess, to admit, to acknowledge; **2.** (eccles.) to confess, to hear confession of; **3.** to confess (a faith), to proclaim one's belief in; **se** ~ *v.refl.* to confess, to make confession (to priest).

confesseur [kɔ̃fɛsœr] *s.m.* confessor.

confession [kɔ̃fɛsjɔ̃] *s.f.* confession, avowal; (fig., fam.) *on lui donnerait le bon Dieu sans* ~, she looks as if butter wouldn't melt in her mouth.

confessionnal (pl. **-aux**) [kɔ̃fɛsjɔnal] *s.m.* confessional (box).

confessionnel, -le [kɔ̃fɛsjɔnɛl] *adj.* denominational.

confetti [kɔ̃feti] *s.m.* (usu. pl.) confetti.

confiance [kɔ̃fjɑ̃s] *s.f.* **1.** confidence, trust, reliance, assurance; *en toute* ~, with every confidence; *personne de* ~, trustworthy person; *abus de* ~, breach of trust; *acheter qch. de* ~, to buy sth. on trust; **2.** confidence, self-confidence, sense of security.

confiant, -e [kɔ̃fjɑ̃] *adj.* confiding, trusting, trustful; confident, having confidence (in); open-hearted; ~ *en ses amis*, relying on, trusting in, one's friends; ~ *dans le succès*, confident of success.

confidence [kɔ̃fidɑ̃s] *s.f.* confidence, secret; *faire une* ~ *à qn.*, to confide in s.o.; *en* ~, in confidence, confidentially; *mettre qn. dans la* ~, to let s.o. into the secret; ⚠ not 'confidence' in senses 'trust' or 'self-confidence'.

confident, -e [kɔ̃fidɑ̃] *s.m.f.* confidant(e).

confidentiel, -le [kɔ̃fidɑ̃sjɛl] *adj.* confidential, private; ~**lement** [kɔ̃fidɑ̃sjɛlmɑ̃] *adv.* confidentially, in confidence.

confier [kɔ̃fje] *v.t.* **1.** to entrust, to commit, to hand over; ~ *une mission à qn.*, to entrust a mission to s.o., to entrust s.o. with a mission; **2.** to confide, to impart, to disclose, to tell in confidence; ~ *qch. à qn.*, to tell s.o. sth. in confidence; **se** ~ *v.refl. se* ~ *à* or *en*, to trust in, to have confidence in, to rely on; *se* ~ *à qn.*, to confide in s.o., to unbosom oneself to s.o.

configuration [kɔ̃figyrɑsjɔ̃] *s.f.* configuration, conformation.

confiné, -e [kɔ̃fine] *adj.* enclosed; (of atmosphere) stuffy.

confinement [kɔ̃finmɑ̃] *s.m.* confinement, restraint; ⚠ not obstetric 'confinement'.

confiner [kɔ̃fine] *v.i.* to border (*à*, on); ~ *v.t.* to shut up, to confine, to enclose, to limit, to relegate; **se** ~ *v.refl.* to shut oneself up; (fig.) to limit oneself (to).

confins [kɔ̃fɛ̃] *s.m.pl.* confines, borders, limits.

confire [kɔ̃fir] *v.t.* (obs.) to pickle; (mod.) to preserve (fruit) in sugar.

confirmand [kɔ̃firmɑ̃] *s.m.* candidate for confirmation, confirmand.

confirmati-f, -ve [kɔ̃firmatif] *adj.* (law) confirmative, confirmatory.

confirmation [kɔ̃firmɑsjɔ̃] *s.f.* **1.** confirmation, corroboration, ratification; **2.** (eccles.) confirmation.

confirmer [kɔ̃firme] *v.t.* **1.** to confirm, to corroborate, to endorse, to ratify; **2.** to strengthen, to encourage; **3.** (eccles.) to confirm; **se** ~ *v.refl.* to be confirmed, to prove true.

confiscable [kɔ̃fiskabl] *adj.* seizable.

confiscation [kɔ̃fiskɑsjɔ̃] *s.f.* confiscation, seizure.

confiserie [kɔ̃fizri] *s.f.* confectionery; confectionery manufacture or trade.

confiseu-r, -se [kɔ̃fizœr] *s.m.f.* confectioner.

confisquer [kɔ̃fiske] *v.t.* to confiscate, to seize.

confit, -e [kɔ̃fi] *adj.* (of fruit) preserved, candied; (fig.) gentle, soft; (fig.) ~ *dans* or *en*, steeped in, permeated with, eaten up with; ~ *s.m.* conserve (of meat).

confiture [kɔ̃fityr] *s.f.* jam, preserve; ~ *d'oranges*, marmalade.

confiturerie [kɔ̃fityrri] *s.f.* jam manufacture or trade, jam factory.

confitur-ier, -ière [kɔ̃fityrje] *s.m.f.* jam-maker; *adj.* jam; ~**ier** *s.m.* jampot, jam-dish.

conflagration [kɔ̃flagrɑsjɔ̃] *s.f.* conflagration.

conflit [kɔ̃fli] *s.m.* conflict, clash, struggle, encounter.

confluence [kɔ̃flyɑ̃s] *s.f.* confluence.

confluent [kɔ̃flyɑ̃] *s.m.* confluent, junction.

confluer [kɔ̃flye] *v.i.* to join, to meet, to come together; ~ *avec*, (of tributary) to flow into.

confondre [kɔ̃fɔ̃dr] *v.t.* **1.** (obs.) to disconcert; to confound, to overthrow, to thwart; (mod.) to confuse, to astound, to surprise; to defy; to outstrip; *son insolence me confond*, his insolence astounds me; *cela confond l'entendement*, it defies comprehension; ~ *l'imagination*, to outstrip one's imagination; **2.** to confound (s.o., an argument), to prove wrong; **3.** to mix, to mingle; to confuse, to mix up; to have got things mixed up; ~ *des noms*, to get names mixed up; *il est possible que je confonde*, possibly I have got it wrong; **se** ~ *v.refl.* **1.** to become confused, to get mixed up; *se* ~ *en excuses*, to tumble over oneself with apologies; **2.** to mingle, to mix, to unite, to be indistinguishable.

conforme [kɔ̃fɔrm] *adj.* conforming, orthodox; suitable; (of signature, copy, etc.) true; ~ *à*, like, similar to, identical with; suitable to, appropriate to, in conformity or accordance with, consistent with.

conformé, -e [kɔ̃fɔrme] *adj.* formed, shaped, built.

conformément [kɔ̃fɔrmemɑ̃] *adv.* in accordance (*à*, with).

conformer [kɔ̃fɔrme] *v.t.* to conform, to model, to base, to make conform, to adapt, to suit; **se** ~ *v.refl.* to adapt oneself, to conform (*à*, to, with).

conformisme [kɔ̃fɔrmism] *s.m.* **1.** conformity, accordance, affinity; **2.** conforming; (pej.) conformism, acceptance (of convention, etc.); orthodoxy.

conformiste [kɔ̃fɔrmist] *s.m.f.*, *adj.* conformist, traditionalist.

conformité [kɔ̃fɔrmite] *s.f.* conformity, similarity, consistency; (obs.) conforming, acceptance; *en* ~ *avec*, in accordance with.

confort [kɔ̃fɔr] *s.m.* comfort, ease, well-being; amenity, convenience; *pneu* ~, pneumatic (opp. solid) tyre.

confortable [kɔ̃fɔrtabl] *adj.* comfortable, comforting, reassuring; ~**ment** [kɔ̃fɔrtabləmɑ̃] *adv.* comfortably.

confraternel, -le [kɔ̃fratɛrnɛl] *adj.* brotherly, fraternal.

confraternité [kɔ̃fratɛrnite] *s.f.* brotherliness, (good) fellowship.

confrère [kɔ̃frɛr] *s.m.* colleague; fellow-member (of society, etc.); brother.

confrérie [kɔ̃freri] *s.f.* lay community; (obs.) association.

confrontation [kɔ̃frɔ̃tɑsjɔ̃] *s.f.* confrontation; comparison.

confronter [kɔ̃frɔ̃te] *v.t.* to confront; to collate, to compare.

confus, -e [kɔ̃fy] *adj.* **1.** confused, indistinguishable, mixed, jumbled, chaotic; indistinct, vague; *un bruit* ~ *de voix*, a jumble of voices; **2.** ashamed, embarrassed, overwhelmed.

confusément [kɔ̃fyzemɑ̃] *adv.* in a confused way, vaguely, indistinctly.

confusion [kɔ̃fyzjɔ̃] *s.f.* **1.** confusion, disorder, muddle; mistake, misunderstanding; **2.** shame, confusion, embarrassment.

confusionnel, -le [kɔ̃fyzjɔnɛl] *adj.* (psychol.) delusional.

confusionnisme [kɔ̃fyzjɔnism] *s.m.* **1.** confusion (mental state); **2.** (pol.) policy of creating confusion.

conge [kɔ̃ʒ] *s.m.* copper vat (for distilling).

congé [kɔ̃ʒe] *s.m.* **1.** authorization, authority; permission to depart; *donner* ~ *à qn.*, to give s.o. authority or permission; *prendre* ~ *de qn.*, to take one's leave of s.o., to say goodbye to s.o.; **2.** leave of absence; leave, holiday; permission to leave job; *être en* ~, to be on leave, on holiday; *un après-midi de* ~, an afternoon off; *demander son* ~, to ask to be relieved of one's duties, to resign, to give notice; *donner* ~ *d'un mois*, to give a month's notice; **3.** dismissal, discharge; *donner son* ~ *à qn.*, to dismiss s.o.; *donner* ~ *à un locataire*, to give a tenant notice to quit; **4.** (naut.) waybill, clearance; **5.** (arch.) concave moulding.

congédiement [kɔ̃ʒedimɑ̃] *s.m.* dismissal.

congédier [kɔ̃ʒedje] *v.t.* to dismiss, to show out, to send away, to get rid of, to discharge, to sack.

congelable [kɔ̃ʒlabl] *adj.* congealable, that can be frozen.

congélateur [kɔ̃ʒelatœr] *s.m.* (obs.) refrigerator; (mod.) freezer, deep freeze.

congélation [kɔ̃ʒelɑsjɔ̃] *s.f.* congealment, congelation; coagulation; deep freezing.

congeler [kɔ̃ʒle] *v.t.* to congeal, to freeze.

congénère [kɔ̃ʒenɛr] *s.m.f.* congener; ~ *adj.* congeneric, congenerous.

congénital, -e, (aux) [kɔ̃ʒenital] *adj.* congenital; ~**ement** [kɔ̃ʒenitalmɑ̃] *adv.* congenitally.

congère [kɔ̃ʒɛr] *s.f.* snowdrift.

congesti-f, -ve [kɔ̃ʒɛstif] *adj.* congestive.

congestion [kɔ̃ʒɛstjɔ̃] *s.f.* congestion; ~ *cérébrale*, cerebral haemorrhage.

congestionner [kɔ̃ʒɛstjɔne] *v.t.* to congest; (fig.) to block, to jam.

conglomérat [kɔ̃glɔmera] *s.m.* (geol., comm.) conglomerate.

conglomération [kɔ̃glɔmerɑsjɔ̃] *s.f.* conglomeration, accumulation.

conglomérer [kɔ̃glɔmere] *v.t.* to conglomerate.

conglutination [kɔ̃glytinɑsjɔ̃] *s.f.* conglutination, sticking together.

conglutiner [kɔ̃glytine] *v.t.* (obs. exc. Lit.) to stick together; (mod.) to render glutinous.

Congo [kɔ̃go] *s.m.* (geog.) Congo (river).

congratulation [kɔ̃gratylɑsjɔ̃] *s.f.* (jest) congratulation.

congratuler [kɔ̃gratyle] *v.t.* (jest) to congratulate; *se* ~, to exchange compliments.

congre [kɔ̃gr] *s.m.* (ichth.) conger (eel).

congréer [kɔ̃gree] *v.t.* (naut.) to line (rigging, etc.).

congrégation [kɔ̃gregɑsjɔ̃] *s.f.* religious order or community; (at the Vatican) congregation; (fig.) meeting, assembly.

congrégationalisme [kɔ̃gregɑsjɔnalism] *s.m.* Congregationalism.

congrès [kɔ̃grɛ] *s.m.* congress, conference, assembly; (U.S.) Congress.
congressiste [kɔ̃gresist] *s.m.f.* delegate to, member of, a conference.
congru, -e [kɔ̃gry] *adj.* **1.** adequate, proper, fitting; barely sufficient; *portion ~e*, (eccles.) adequate stipend; (fam.) meagre allowance; **2.** (math.) congruent.
congruence [kɔ̃gryɑ̃s] *s.f.* (math.) congruence.
conicine [kɔnisin] *s.f.* = CICUTINE.
conicité [kɔnisite] *s.f.* conicity, conical shape.
conifère [kɔnifɛr] *s.m.* (bot.) conifer.
conique [kɔnik] *adj.* conic, conical, cone-shaped; ~ *s.f.* (geom.) conic section.
conjectural, -e, (**aux**) [kɔ̃ʒɛktyral] *adj.* conjectural; **~ement** [kɔ̃ʒɛktyralmɑ̃] *adv.* by conjecture.
conjecture [kɔ̃ʒɛktyr] *s.f.* conjecture, surmise.
conjecturer [kɔ̃ʒɛktyre] *v.t.* to conjecture, to surmise.
conjoint, -e [kɔ̃ʒwɛ̃] *adj.* conjoined, united, joint; (mus.) conjunct; ~ *s.m.* spouse; *les ~s*, husband and wife; **~ement** [kɔ̃ʒwɛ̃tmɑ̃] *adv.* jointly; in concert.
conjoncteur [kɔ̃ʒɔ̃ktœr] *s.m.* (electr.) automatic make-and-break switch; *~-disjoncteur*, circuit-breaker.
conjoncti-f, -ve [kɔ̃ʒɔ̃ktif] *adj.* (anat., gram.) conjunctive, connective, connecting; (gram.) copulative.
conjonction [kɔ̃ʒɔ̃ksjɔ̃] *s.f.* conjunction, union, connection; (astron., gram.) conjunction.
conjonctive [kɔ̃ʒɔ̃ktiv] *s.f.* (anat.) conjunctiva.
conjonctivite [kɔ̃ʒɔ̃ktivit] *s.f.* (med.) conjunctivitis.
conjoncture [kɔ̃ʒɔ̃ktyr] *s.f.* **1.** conjuncture, contingency, situation, combination of circumstances; **2.** (econ.) projection, forecasting.
conjugable [kɔ̃ʒygabl] *adj.* (gram.) that can be conjugated.
conjugaison [kɔ̃ʒygɛzɔ̃] *s.f.* (gram., biol.) conjugation.
conjugal, -e, (**aux**) [kɔ̃ʒygal] *adj.* conjugal, connubial, matrimonial; **~ement** [kɔ̃ʒygalmɑ̃] *adv.* conjugally.
conjugué, -e [kɔ̃ʒyge] *adj.* joint, combined, paired, inter-connected; (math., biol.) conjugate.
conjuguer [kɔ̃ʒyge] *v.t.* **1.** to combine, to join (together), to couple; **2.** (gram.) to conjugate; **se** ~ *v.refl.* to be conjugated.
conjungo [kɔ̃ʒɔ̃go] *s.m.* (jest) married state.
conjurat-eur, -rice [kɔ̃ʒyratœr] *s.m.f.* **1.** exorcist; **2.** conspirator.
conjuration [kɔ̃ʒyrɑsjɔ̃] *s.f.* **1.** incantation, conjuration, exorcism; **2.** conspiracy, plot.
conjuré, -e [kɔ̃ʒyre] *s.m.f.* conspirator.
conjurer [kɔ̃ʒyre] *v.t.* **1.** to exorcise; to avert; **2.** to entreat, to adjure; **3.** (obs.) to plot; **se** ~ *v.refl.* (lit. & fig.) to conspire.
connaissable [kɔnɛsabl] *adj.* knowable; recognizable (*à*, by).
connaissance [kɔ̃nɛsɑ̃s] *s.f.* **1.** knowledge (that sth. is so); knowing, ascertaining; cognition, cognizance; being aware (of sth.); discernment; *avoir ~ de qch.*, to know sth., to have knowledge of sth., to be aware of sth.; *prendre ~ de*, to make oneself acquainted with, to study, to examine, to go into, to take cognizance of; *à ma ~*, as far as I am aware, to the best of my knowledge; *les ans de ~*, years of discretion; **2.** (often pl.) knowledge (acquired), science, learning, attainments; *toutes les branches de la ~*, every branch of learning; *avoir une ~* or *des ~s d'une langue*, to know a language; *il est sans grandes ~s*, he is a man of no great attainments; **3.** (law) competence, cognizance (of court); (fig.) *en ~ de cause*, with good reason, in full knowledge; **4.** knowing (by recognition), recognizing; acquaintance, familiarity; *faire la ~ de*, *faire ~ avec*, to get to know, to make the acquaintance of; *faire faire ~ à deux personnes*, to introduce two people (to each other); *être en pays de ~*, to be on familiar ground, to know where one is, to be at home; *un visage de ~*, a familiar face; *une ~*, an acquaintance; **5.** consciousness, awareness; *sans ~*, unconscious; *perdre ~*, to lose consciousness, to faint; *avoir toute sa ~*, to be fully aware (of what one is doing).
connaissement [kɔnɛsmɑ̃] *s.m.* (naut.) bill of lading.
connaisseu-r, -se [kɔnɛsœr] *s.m.f.*, *adj.* connoisseur, expert.
connaître [kɔnɛtr] *v.t.* **1.** to know (from learning or examination), to know thoroughly, to be versed in; to understand, to appreciate; ~ *l'allemand, son métier*, to know German, one's trade; ~ *un texte à fond*, to have a thorough knowledge of a text; *vous ne me connaissez pas*, you don't understand me; *se ~*, to know oneself, to be a good judge of oneself; *s'y ~*, to be an expert (*en*, in); **2.** to know, to experience; *il a connu la misère*, he has known hard times; **3.** to know (through familiarity or by recognition); to get to know, to become acquainted with; (bibl.) to have carnal knowledge of (a woman); ~ *une ville*, to know a town; *je ne connais pas cet homme*, I don't know that man; (fig.) *il ne se connaît plus*, he is beside himself (with rage); **4.** to recognize, to admit of, to accept; ~ *qn. à sa voix*, to recognize s.o. by his voice; *sa colère ne connut plus de bornes*, his anger knew no bounds; **5.** (law) ~ *de*, to take cognizance of, to deal with, to be competent (to deal with).
connecter [kɔn(n)ɛkte] *v.t.* (techn.) to connect.
connecteur [kɔn(n)ɛktœr] *s.m.* (techn.) connector, connection.
connecti-f, -ve [kɔn(n)ɛktif] *adj.*, *s.m.* connective (tissue).
connétable [kɔnetabl] *s.m.* (hist.) Constable (of France).
connexe [kɔn(n)ɛks] *adj.* connected, related.
connexion [kɔn(n)ɛksjɔ̃] *s.f.* connection; (electr.) connection, wiring-up.
connexité [kɔn(n)ɛksite] *s.f.* connection.
connivence [kɔn(n)ivɑ̃s] *s.f.* connivance.
connivent, -e [kɔn(n)ivɑ̃] *adj.* (sci.) connivent.
connotation [kɔn(n)ɔtasjɔ̃] *s.f.* connotation.
connoter [kɔn(n)ɔte] *v.t.* to connote.
connu, -e [kɔny] *adj.* known, familiar; well-known, famous.
conoïde [kɔnɔid] *adj.* conoid, pineal; ~ *s.m.* conoid.
conque [kɔ̃k] *s.f.* **1.** conch; **2.** (anat.) concha.
conquérant, -e [kɔ̃kerɑ̃] *adj.* conquering, victorious; (fam.) dashing; ~ *s.m.* conqueror; (fam.) lady-killer.
conquérir [kɔ̃kerir] *v.t.* to conquer, to subjugate, to take by force; to win, to win over; **se** ~ *v.refl.* to be won, to be obtained by effort.
conquêt [kɔ̃kɛ] *s.m.* = ACQUÊT.
conquête [kɔ̃kɛt] *s.f.* conquest.
conquis, -e [kɔ̃ki] *adj.* conquered; won.
conquistador [kɔ̃kistadɔr] *s.m.* (pl. *conquistadores*) (hist.) conquistador.
consacrant, -e [kɔ̃sakrɑ̃] (eccles.) *adj.* consecrating; ~ *s.m.* celebrant.
consacré, -e [kɔ̃sakre] *adj.* consecrated, hallowed; (fig.) accepted, customary, established; *expression ~e*, stock phrase, cliché.
consacrer [kɔ̃sakre] *v.t.* **1.** to consecrate, to sanctify, to hallow; **2.** to devote, to dedicate; **3.** to sanction, to confirm, to perpetuate.
consanguin, -e [kɔ̃sɑ̃gɛ̃] *adj.* consanguineous.
consanguinité [kɔ̃sɑ̃gɥinite] *s.f.* consanguinity.

consciemment [kɔ̃sjamɑ̃] *adv.* consciously, knowingly.
conscience [kɔ̃sjɑ̃s] *s.f.* **1.** consciousness, awareness; *avoir ~ de qch.*, to be conscious of sth., to be aware of sth.; *prendre ~ de qch.*, to become aware of sth., to discover sth.; **2.** conscience; *en ~*, truthfully, conscientiously; *avoir de la ~*, to be conscientious; *par acquit de ~*, for conscience's sake; *objecteur de ~*, conscientious objector.
conscienciеu-x, -se [kɔ̃sjɑ̃sjø] *adj.* conscientious; **~sement** [kɔ̃sjɑ̃sjøzmɑ̃] *adv.* conscientiously.
conscient, -e [kɔ̃sjɑ̃] *adj.* conscious, aware; ~ *s.m.* the conscious mind.
conscription [kɔ̃skripsjɔ̃] *s.f.* conscription.
conscrit [kɔ̃skri] *s.m.* conscript, recruit; (fam.) greenhorn, novice.
consécration [kɔ̃sekrɑsjɔ̃] *s.f.* consecration, dedication; sanction, ratification, confirmation.
consécuti-f, -ve [kɔ̃sekytif] *adj.* consecutive, consequential; *~f à*, resulting from; **~vement** [kɔ̃sekytivmɑ̃] *adv.* consecutively, one after the other.
conseil [kɔ̃sɛj] *s.m.* **1.** advice, counsel; prompting, urging; (obs.) decision, principle; *prendre, demander, ~ à qn.*, to consult s.o., to ask someone's advice; *un homme de bon ~*, a wise counsellor; **2.** adviser, counsellor, consultant; *ingénieur-~*, consultant engineer; **3.** council, board, committee, commission; *Conseil d'État*, Privy Council; *Conseil des ministres*, cabinet, cabinet meeting; (mil.) *~ de révision*, medical board; *~ de discipline*, disciplinary body.
conseiller [kɔ̃seje] *v.t.* to counsel, to advise; to urge, to recommend; ~ *(qch.) à qn.*, to recommend (a course of action) to s.o.; *je vous conseille la prudence*, I urge you to be cautious, I advise caution; *~ à qn. de faire qch.*, to advise, to urge, to recommend, s.o. to do sth.
conseill-er, -ère [kɔ̃seje] *s.m.f.* counsellor, adviser, consultant; councillor.
conseilleu-r, -se [kɔ̃sɛjœr] *s.m.f.* (obs.) councillor; (mod.) adviser; *les ~rs ne sont pas les payeurs*, advice is cheap.
consensuel, -le [kɔ̃sɑ̃sɥɛl] *adj.* (law) consensual.
consensus [kɔ̃sɛ̃sys] *s.m.* consensus.
consentant, -e [kɔ̃sɑ̃tɑ̃] *adj.* consenting.
consentement [kɔ̃sɑ̃tmɑ̃] *s.m.* consent, assent, agreement.
consentir [kɔ̃sɑ̃tir] *v.t.* to consent, to agree; to allow, to grant, to agree to; *qui ne dit mot consent*, silence implies consent; *~ un délai*, to grant, to agree to, a postponement; *~ à*, to agree or consent to, to accept.
conséquemment [kɔ̃sekamɑ̃] *adv.* consequently; (obs.) consequentially.
conséquence [kɔ̃sekɑ̃s] *s.f.* consequence, result; *cela ne tire pas à ~*, that isn't important; *de ~*, important, serious; *sans ~*, unimportant, insignificant; *en ~*, accordingly; *en ~ de*, as a result of; (gram.) *proposition de ~*, consecutive clause.
conséquent, -e [kɔ̃sekɑ̃] *adj.* consistent, logical; (fam.) important; *par ~*, therefore.
conservat-eur, -rice [kɔ̃sɛrvatœr] *adj.* preserving, protecting; (pol.) conservative; *s.m.f.* conservator, guardian, keeper, warden, librarian; conservationist; (pol.) conservative.
conservation [kɔ̃sɛrvɑsjɔ̃] *s.f.* **1.** conservation, preservation; **2.** keepership, librarianship.
conservatisme [kɔ̃sɛrvatism] *s.m.* conservatism, toryism.
conservatoire [kɔ̃sɛrvatwar] *adj.* (law) conservatory, provisional, (order, etc.).
conservatoire [kɔ̃sɛrvatwar] *s.m.* conservatoire, academy, school of music or other arts.
conserve [kɔ̃sɛrv] *s.f.* **1.** (obs.) preserve, conserve; (mod.) tinned, canned, food; *en ~*, tinned; (fig., fam.) *mettre en ~*, to put on ice; *musique en ~*, canned or piped music; **2.** (pl.) dark glasses, tinted spectacles; **3.** (naut.) *naviguer de ~*, to sail in convoy; (fig.) *aller, agir, de ~*, to go or act together.
conserver [kɔ̃sɛrve] *v.t.* to preserve, to keep, to maintain, to retain; **se ~** *v.refl.* to keep (i.e. not go bad), to be preserved, to survive, to last.
conserverie [kɔ̃sɛrvri] *s.f.* canning factory; canning industry.
considérable [kɔ̃siderabl] *adj.* considerable, important; large, extensive; (obs.) eminent, distinguished; **~ment** [kɔ̃siderabləmɑ̃] *adv.* considerably, greatly.
considérant [kɔ̃siderɑ̃] *s.m.* (law) preamble.
considération [kɔ̃siderɑsjɔ̃] *s.f.* **1.** consideration, study, examination, deliberation; observation, reflection; account; *digne de ~*, worth considering, worth studying; *prendre en ~*, to consider, to take into consideration or account; *en ~ de*, in consideration of, in view of, on account of; **2.** consideration, reason, motive, ground; *des ~s d'intérêt*, motives of self-interest; **3.** consideration, respect, esteem; reputation; (ending of formal letter) *veuillez agréer l'assurance de ma ~ distinguée*, = yours faithfully.
considérer [kɔ̃sidere] *v.t.* **1.** to consider, to examine, to study, to contemplate; to regard; *~ comme*, to consider (as being), to regard as, to deem; *~ qn. comme héros*, to consider s.o., to regard s.o. as, a hero; *se ~ responsable*, to hold oneself responsible; **2.** to esteem, to have regard for.
consignataire [kɔ̃siɲatɛr] *s.m.f.* consignee, depositary.
consignation [kɔ̃siɲɑsjɔ̃] *s.f.* consignment, depositing, deposit; leaving (luggage in left-luggage office).
consigne [kɔ̃siɲ] *s.f.* **1.** orders, instructions; **2.** (mil.) confinement to barracks, (school) detention; **3.** cloakroom, left-luggage office; **4.** deposit (charge).
consigner [kɔ̃siɲe] *v.t.* **1.** to consign; to deposit, to leave (in left-luggage office); to invoice sale or return; **2.** to register, to record, to enter; *~ sur un carnet*, to record in a note-book; **3.** (mil.) to confine to barracks; (school) to put in detention, to keep in; **4.** to close, to put out of bounds, to forbid access to; *~ sa porte à qn.*, to refuse s.o. admission.
consistance [kɔ̃sistɑ̃s] *s.f.* consistency, consistence, degree of density (of liquids), stability, firmness; (fig.) firmness, consistency; *sans ~*, unstable, wavering, irresolute.
consistant, -e [kɔ̃sistɑ̃] *adj.* consistent, firm, solid, compact.
consister [kɔ̃siste] *v.i.* *~ en, dans*, to consist of, to be made of; *~ à* (+infin.), to consist in.
consistoire [kɔ̃sistwar] *s.m.* (eccles.) consistory.
consistorial, -e, (aux) [kɔ̃sistɔrjal] *adj.* consistorial; ~ *s.m.* member of a consistory.
consœur [kɔ̃sœr] *s.f.* (often iron.) (female) colleague, fellow member.
consolable [kɔ̃sɔlabl] *adj.* consolable.
consolant, -e [kɔ̃sɔlɑ̃] *adj.* consoling, comforting, cheering.
consolat-eur, -rice [kɔ̃sɔlatœr] *s.m.f.* consoler, comforter; *adj.* consoling, comforting.
consolation [kɔ̃sɔlɑsjɔ̃] *s.f.* consolation, solace, comfort, relief.
console [kɔ̃sɔl] *s.f.* (arch.) console, corbel, bracket; (mus.) console (of organ); console- or bracket-table; (constr.) *grue à ~*, wall-crane.
consoler [kɔ̃sɔle] *v.t.* to console, to comfort, to soothe, to cheer, to alleviate (grief, pain); **se ~** *v.refl.* to be consoled, to get over (sth.); to console each other.
consolidation [kɔ̃sɔlidɑsjɔ̃] *s.f.* consolidation,

stabilization; (med.) knitting (of bones); (fin.) consolidation, funding.
consolidé, -e [kɔ̃sɔlide] *adj.* (fin.) consolidated, funded; **~s** *s.m.pl.* consolidated funds, consols.
consolider [kɔ̃sɔlide] *v.t.* to consolidate, to strengthen, to reinforce; (fin.) to consolidate, to fund.
consommable [kɔ̃sɔmabl] *adj.* consumable, eatable.
consommat-eur, -rice [kɔ̃sɔmatœr] *s.m.f.* **1.** (theol.) consummator; **2.** (econ.) consumer; (in café, etc.) customer.
consommation [kɔ̃sɔmɑsjɔ̃] *s.f.* **1.** consummation; **2.** (econ.) consumption; **3.** (in café, etc.) drink.
consommé, -e [kɔ̃sɔme] *adj.* consummate, accomplished; ~ *s.m.* clear soup, consommé.
consommer [kɔ̃sɔme] *v.t.* **1.** to consummate, to accomplish; **2.** to consume, to use up; ~ *v.i.* to have a drink (in a café, etc.).
consomptible [kɔ̃sɔ̃ptibl] *adj.* (law) consumable.
consompti-f, -ve [kɔ̃sɔ̃ptif] *adj.* consumptive.
consomption [kɔ̃sɔ̃psjɔ̃] *s.f.* **1.** (obs.) consumption, consuming; **2.** consumption (pulmonary tuberculosis).
consonance [kɔ̃sɔnɑ̃s] *s.f.* consonance; (mus.) concord; (fig.) agreement, harmony.
consonant, -e [kɔ̃sɔnɑ̃] *adj.* consonant.
consonantique [kɔ̃sɔnɑ̃tik] *adj.* (phon.) consonantal.
consonantisme [kɔ̃sɔnɑ̃tism] *s.m.* (phon.) consonantal system.
consonne [kɔ̃sɔn] *s.f.* (lang.) consonant (sound and letter).
consort [kɔ̃sɔr] *adj.* (prince) consort; **~s** *s.m.pl.* associates.
consortium [kɔ̃sɔrsjɔm] *s.m.* consortium.
consoude [kɔ̃sud] *s.f.* (bot.) comfrey.
conspirat-eur, -rice [kɔ̃spiratœr] *s.m.f.* conspirator, plotter; *adj.* conspiring, plotting.
conspiration [kɔ̃spirɑsjɔ̃] *s.f.* conspiracy, plot.
conspirer [kɔ̃spire] *v.t.* (obs.) to plot; ~ *v.i.* to conspire, to plot; ~ *à*, to conspire to (cause sth.).
conspuer [kɔ̃spɥe] *v.t.* to hoot, to boo, to shout down.
constable [kɔ̃stabl] *s.m.* in (U.K.) policeman, constable.
constamment [kɔ̃stamɑ̃] *adv.* constantly, for ever.
constance [kɔ̃stɑ̃s] *s.f.* constancy, steadfastness, persistence, application, assiduity.
constant, -e [kɔ̃stɑ̃] *adj.* constant, lasting, sustained, unvarying, permanent; **~e** *s.f.* (math., phys.) constant.
Constantin [kɔ̃stɑ̃tɛ̃] *s.m.* (anc. hist.) Constantine.
constat [kɔ̃sta] *s.m.* sworn written statement, affidavit; account, report.
constatation [kɔ̃statɑsjɔ̃] *s.f.* statement, deposition.
constater [kɔ̃state] *v.t.* to observe, to note, to record; to find out, to discover; to verify, to authenticate.
constellation [kɔ̃stelasjɔ̃] *s.f.* (lit. & fig.) constellation.
constellé, -e [kɔ̃stele] *adj.* starry, spangled.
consteller [kɔ̃stele] *v.t.* to bespangle.
consternation [kɔ̃stɛrnɑsjɔ̃] *s.f.* consternation, dismay.
consterner [kɔ̃stɛrne] *v.t.* to dismay, to alarm; to overwhelm.
constipation [kɔ̃stipɑsjɔ̃] *s.f.* constipation.
constipé, -e [kɔ̃stipe] *adj.* constipated; (fig.) tense, embarrassed; *s.m.f.* one who is constipated.
constiper [kɔ̃stipe] *v.t.* to constipate.
constituant, -e [kɔ̃stitɥɑ̃] *adj.* constituent.
constitué, -e [kɔ̃stitɥe] *adj.* **1.** of (good or bad) constitution or physique; *bien* ~, healthy, having a good constitution; **2.** constitutional, properly constituted.
constituer [kɔ̃stitɥe] *v.t.* **1.** to constitute, to institute, to set up, to found; to appoint, to make; ~ *qn. son héritier*, to make s.o. one's heir; *se* ~ *prisonnier*, to give oneself up; **2.** to constitute, to compose, to form, to amount to, to be.
constituti-f, -ve [kɔ̃stitytif] *adj.* **1.** (law) constitutive, conferring a right; *titres* ~*fs*, title deeds; **2.** constituent.
constitution [kɔ̃stitysjɔ̃] *s.f.* **1.** constitution, structure, composition; (pol.) constitution; **2.** establishing, setting up, creating, institution.
constitutionnaliser [kɔ̃stitysjɔnalize] *v.t.* to constitutionalize, to constitute in due form.
constitutionnalité [kɔ̃stitysjɔnalite] *s.f.* constitutionality.
constitutionnel, -le [kɔ̃stitysjɔnɛl] *adj.* constitutional, of the constitution; **~lement** [kɔ̃stitysjɔnɛlmɑ̃] *adv.* constitutionally.
constricteur [kɔ̃striktœr] *adj.*, *s.m.* **1.** (anat.) (*muscle*) ~, constrictor (muscle); **2.** (zool.) (*boa*) ~, boa constrictor.
constriction [kɔ̃striksjɔ̃] *s.f.* constriction.
construct-eur, -rice [kɔ̃stryktœr] *adj.* building; **~eur** *s.m.* builder, constructor, maker, manufacturer.
construction [kɔ̃stryksjɔ̃] *s.f.* **1.** building, construction, erection; (fig.) construction, composition, arrangement, putting together; construction industry; *matériaux de* ~, building materials; *jeu de* ~, (toy) box of bricks, building set; ~*s aéronautiques*, aircraft construction industry; **2.** building, structure, edifice; **3.** (lang.) construction, structure.
construire [kɔ̃strɥir] *v.t.* to build, to construct, to make; to arrange, to assemble, to compose.
consubstantiation [kɔ̃sypstɑ̃sjɑsjɔ̃] *s.f.* (theol.) consubstantiation, real presence.
consubstantiel, -le [kɔ̃sypstɑ̃sjɛl] *adj.* **1.** (theol.) consubstantial; **2.** co-existent, indivisible.
consul [kɔ̃syl] *s.m.* consul; **~aire** [kɔ̃sylɛr] *adj.* consular; **~at** [kɔ̃syla] *s.m.* (Rom. hist.) consulship; (mod.) consulate.
consultant, -e [kɔ̃syltɑ̃] *adj.* consulting; ~ *s.m.* consultant.
consultati-f, -ve [kɔ̃syltatif] *adj.* consultative.
consultation [kɔ̃syltɑsjɔ̃] *s.f.* **1.** consultation, consulting, sounding (of opinion); meeting of specialists; **2.** advice, (medical or legal) opinion; consultation (given by doctor); *cabinet de* ~, (law) chambers; (med.) consulting-room, surgery; *heures de* ~, consulting-hours, surgery times.
consulte [kɔ̃sylt] *s.f.* assembly.
consulter [kɔ̃sylte] *v.t.* to consult, to refer to; ~ *v.i.* to confer, to deliberate.
consumer [kɔ̃syme] *v.t.* to consume, to destroy, to wear out, to squander; **se** ~ *v.refl.* to wear oneself out.
contact [kɔ̃takt] *s.m.* contact, connection; (electr.) switch, contact; *mettre en* ~, to put in touch (with); *se mettre en* ~ *avec*, to get in touch with, to contact; *mettre le* ~, to switch on; *couper le* ~, to switch off; *clef de* ~, (car) ignition key; *lentilles, verres, de* ~, contact lenses.
contacter [kɔ̃takte] *v.t.* to contact, to get in touch with.
contacteur [kɔ̃taktœr] *s.m.* (electr.) switch, contact.
contage [kɔ̃taʒ] *s.m.* (med.) source of contagion.
contagieu-x, -se [kɔ̃taʒjø] *adj.* (lit. & fig.) contagious, catching.
contagion [kɔ̃taʒjɔ̃] *s.f.* contagion.
contagionner [kɔ̃taʒjɔne] *v.t.* to infect, to transmit a contagious disease to.
contagiosité [kɔ̃taʒjozite] *s.f.* contagiousness.

container [kɔ̃tɛnɛr] *s.m.* (transport) container.
contamination [kɔ̃taminɑsjɔ̃] *s.f.* contamination, pollution.
contaminer [kɔ̃tamine] *v.t.* to contaminate, to pollute.
conte [kɔ̃t] *s.m.* (obs.) record (of facts); (mod.) tale, story; (Lit.) short story; ~ *de fée*, fairy tale.
conté [kɔ̃te] *s.m.* see COMTÉ 2.
contemplat-eur, -rice [kɔ̃tɑ̃platœr] *s.m.f.* contemplator, beholder.
contemplati-f, -ve [kɔ̃tɑ̃platif] *adj., s.m.f.* contemplative.
contemplation [kɔ̃tɑ̃plɑsjɔ̃] *s.f.* contemplation.
contempler [kɔ̃tɑ̃ple] *v.t.* to contemplate, to observe.
contemporain, -e [kɔ̃tɑ̃pɔrɛ̃] *adj.* contemporary; contemporaneous; *s.m.f.* contemporary.
contemporanéité [kɔ̃tɑ̃pɔraneite] *s.f.* contemporaneity, contemporaneousness.
contempt-eur, -rice [kɔ̃tɑ̃ptœr] *s.m.f.* disparager.
contenance [kɔ̃tnɑ̃s] *s.f.* **1.** capacity, contents; extent, area; **2.** countenance, mien, demeanour, composure; *se donner, prendre, une* ~, to put a brave face on things; *perdre* ~, to be put out; *faire bonne* ~, to keep one's composure.
contenant [kɔ̃tnɑ̃] *s.m.* container.
contenir [kɔ̃tnir] *v.t.* **1.** to contain, to hold, to include; **2.** to restrain, to check, to curb, to hold back, to contain; **se** ~ *v.refl.* to contain oneself, to control one's feelings.
content, -e [kɔ̃tɑ̃] *adj.* content, glad, happy, satisfied, pleased, (*de*, with).
contentement [kɔ̃tɑ̃tmɑ̃] *s.m.* content, contentedness, satisfaction, happiness.
contenter [kɔ̃tɑ̃te] *v.t.* to content, to satisfy, to please, to appease; **se** ~ *v.refl.* to be contented, to be satisfied, (*de*, with); to restrict oneself (*de*, to).
contentieu-x, -se [kɔ̃tɑ̃sjø] *adj.* contentious, litigious; ~**x** *s.m.* (law) disputed claims; legal department (of organization).
contenti-f, -ve [kɔ̃tɑ̃tif] *adj.* (surg.) (of bandage, etc.) retentive.
contention[1] [kɔtɑ̃sjɔ̃] *s.f.* (surg.) retention (of fracture, etc.).
contention[2] [kɔ̃tɑ̃sjɔ̃] *s.f.* **1.** contention, strife; **2.** (mental) concentration.
contenu, -e [kɔ̃tny] *adj.* contained; restrained.
contenu [kɔ̃tny] *s.m.* contents.
conter [kɔ̃te] *v.t.* to tell, to relate; to tell a story; to romance; *en* ~ *à qn.*, to lead s.o. up the garden path.
contestable [kɔ̃tɛstabl] *adj.* questionable, disputable.
contestation [kɔ̃tɛstɑsjɔ̃] *s.f.* dispute, conflict, opposition.
conteste [kɔ̃tɛst] *sans* ~ *adv.loc.* undeniably, unquestionably.
contester [kɔ̃tɛste] *v.t.* to question, to contest, to deny; ~ *v.i.* to dispute, to wrangle.
conteu-r, -se [kɔ̃tœr] *s.m.f.* (obs.) narrator; (mod.) short-story writer.
contexte [kɔ̃tɛkst] *s.m.* context.
contexture [kɔ̃tɛkstyr] *s.f.* contexture, texture, structure.
contigu, -ë [kɔ̃tigy] *adj.* contiguous; (fig.) related; ~ *à*, adjoining.
contiguïté [kɔ̃tigɥite] *s.f.* contiguity.
continence [kɔ̃tinɑ̃s] *s.f.* continence, chastity.
continent, -e [kɔ̃tinɑ̃] *adj.* continent, chaste.
continent [kɔ̃tinɑ̃] *s.m.* (geog.) continent.
continental, -e, (aux) [kɔ̃tinɑ̃tal] *adj.* continental.
contingence [kɔ̃tɛ̃ʒɑ̃s] *s.f.* contingency.
contingent, -e [kɔ̃tɛ̃ʒɑ̃] *adj.* contingent; unimportant; ~ *s.m.* contingent, quota, share.
contingentement [kɔ̃tɛ̃ʒɑ̃tmɑ̃] *s.m.* limitation.
contingenter [kɔ̃tɛ̃ʒɑ̃te] *v.t.* to limit, to establish a quota or limit for.
continu, -e [kɔ̃tiny] *adj.* continuous, uninterrupted, unbroken; (electr.) *courant* ~, direct current; (mus.) *basse* ~*e*, ground bass; ~ *s.m.* continuum.
continuation [kɔ̃tinɥɑsjɔ̃] *s.f.* continuation.
continuel, -le [kɔ̃tinɥɛl] *adj.* continual, incessant, unceasing, uninterrupted; ~**lement** [kɔ̃tinɥɛlmɑ̃] *adv.* continually, incessantly, unceasingly.
continuer [kɔ̃tinɥe] *v.t.i* to continue, to go on with, to keep on; to extend; ~ *à* or *de faire qch.*, to keep on, to go on, doing sth.
continuité [kɔ̃tinɥite] *s.f.* continuity.
continûment [kɔ̃tinymɑ̃] *adv.* continuously, without a break.
continuo [kɔ̃tinɥo] *s.m.* (mus.) continuo.
contondant, -e [kɔ̃tɔ̃dɑ̃] *adj.* blunt, contusive.
contorsion [kɔ̃tɔrsjɔ̃] *s.f.* contortion; (pl.) affected behaviour, mannerisms.
(se) contorsionner [kɔ̃tɔrsjɔne] *v.refl.* to contort oneself, to writhe; (fig.) to twist and turn, to make elaborate gestures.
contorsionniste [kɔ̃tɔrsjɔnist] *s.m.f.* contortionist, acrobat.
contour [kɔ̃tur] *s.m.* contour, outline, shape; (of rivers, roads, etc.) winding, loop.
contourné, -e [kɔ̃turne] *adj.* twisting, winding; distorted; (of style) affected; (herald.) contourné.
contourner [kɔ̃turne] *v.t.* **1.** (rare) to sculpt; **2.** to go round, to skirt; (mil.) to outflank; (fig.) to get round (difficulty, law, etc.).
contracepti-f, -ve [kɔ̃trasɛptif] *adj.* contraceptive; ~**f** *s.m.* contraceptive.
contraception [kɔ̃trasɛpsjɔ̃] *s.f.* contraception.
contractant, -e [kɔtraktɑ̃] *adj.* (law) contracting; *s.m.f.* contracting party.
contracté, -e [kɔ̃trakte] *adj.* contracted; (fig., fam.) tense.
contracter[1] [kɔ̃trakte] *v.t.* **1.** to contract, to make a contract of; to undertake, to incur; ~ *un mariage*, to make a contract of marriage; ~ *une assurance*, to take out an insurance policy; ~ *une dette*, to incur a debt; **2.** to contract, to catch, to acquire, (habit, disease, etc.).
contracter[2] [kɔ̃trakte] *v.t.* to contract, to reduce, to constrict, to draw together; (lang.) to contract; *ses traits contractés*, his drawn features; **se** ~ *v.refl.* to contract.
contractile [kɔ̃traktil] *adj.* contractile.
contractilité [kɔ̃traktilite] *s.f.* contractility.
contraction [kɔ̃traksjɔ̃] *s.f.* contraction.
contractuel, -le [kɔ̃traktɥɛl] *adj.* **1.** contractual, stipulated by contract; **2.** (acting as) auxiliary; ~ *s.m.* traffic warden, etc.
contracture [kɔ̃traktyr] *s.f.* (arch., med.) contracture.
contradicteur [kɔ̃tradiktœr] *s.m.* opponent (in debate); (law) opposing counsel; (pl.) opposing parties.
contradiction [kɔ̃tradiksjɔ̃] *s.f.* contradiction, opposition; incompatibility.
contradictoire [kɔ̃tradiktwar] *adj.* contradictory, conflicting, incompatible; (law) *jugement* ~, judgement after both parties have appeared; ~**ment** [kɔ̃tradiktwarmɑ̃] *adv.* contradictorily; (law) both sides having appeared.
contraignable [kɔ̃trɛɲabl] *adj.* constrainable (by process of law).
contraignant, -e [kɔ̃trɛɲɑ̃] *adj.* restraining, constraining.
contraindre [kɔ̃trɛ̃dr] *v.t.* to constrain, to compel, to force, to oblige; to restrain; **se** ~ *v.refl.* to restrain oneself.
contraint, -e [kɔ̃trɛ̃] *adj.* constrained, embarrassed, stiff.

contrainte [kɔ̃trɛ̃t] *s.f.* constraint, restraint, compulsion; (law) ~ *par corps*, imprisonment.
contraire [kɔ̃trɛr] *adj.* contrary, opposite; unfavourable, adverse; ~ *s.m.* contrary, opposite, reverse; *au* ~, on the contrary; *au* ~ *de*, unlike; **~ment** [kɔ̃trɛrmɑ̃] *adv.* contrary; *~ment à*, in contradiction to.
contralto [kɔ̃tralto] *s.m.* contralto.
contrapontiste, contrapuntiste [kɔ̃trapɔ̃tist] *s.m.* (mus.) contrapuntist.
contrapuntique [kɔ̃trapɔ̃tik] *adj.* (mus.) contrapuntal.
contrariant, -e [kɔ̃trarjɑ̃] *adj.* cantankerous, annoying, unpleasant.
contrarié, -e [kɔ̃trarje] *adj.* contested; annoyed, put out, thwarted.
contrarier [kɔ̃trarje] *v.t.* to go counter to, to oppose, to thwart; to upset; to annoy, to vex; to produce a contrast.
contrariété [kɔ̃trarjete] *s.f.* **1.** (obs.) contrariety, contradiction; **2.** annoyance.
contrastant, -e [kɔ̃trastɑ̃] *adj.* contrasting.
contraste [kɔ̃trast] *s.m.* contrast.
contraster [kɔ̃traste] *v.t.* to bring out the contrasts in, to give light and shade to; ~ *v.i.* to contrast (*avec*, with), to be contrasted; *des couleurs qui contrastent entre elles*, colours which set each other off.
contrat [kɔ̃tra] *s.m.* contract, agreement, covenant; deed.
contravention [kɔ̃travɑ̃sjɔ̃] *s.f.* infringement, breach, (of law); misdemeanour; charge, fine; (fam.) parking ticket.
contravis [kɔ̃travi] *s.m.* notification to the contrary; *sauf* ~, unless informed otherwise.
contre [kɔ̃tr] *prep.* **1.** against, contrary to; *nager ~ le courant*, to swim against the current; ~ *toute attente*, contrary to all expectations; **2.** (law, sport) versus; **3.** from; *s'abriter ~ la pluie*, to shelter from the rain; **4.** in exchange for; *donner une chose ~ une autre*, to give one thing in exchange for another; **5.** close to, near to; ~ *adv.* near by, close by; *tout* ~, close by; *ci-*~, opposite; *par* ~, on the contrary, on the other hand; ~ *s.m.* opposite; *le pour et le* ~, the pros and cons; (boxing, fencing) counter; (cards) double.
contre-alizé [kɔ̃tralize] *s.m.* antitrade (wind).
contre-allée [kɔ̃trale] *s.f.* access road (parallel to main road), service road.
contre-amiral [kɔ̃tramiral] *s.m.* (pl. *contre--amiraux*) rear-admiral.
contre-appel [kɔ̃trapɛl] *s.m.* (mil.) second call, check call.
contre-assurance [kɔ̃trasyrɑ̃s] *s.f.* reinsurance.
contre-attaque [kɔ̃tratak] *s.f.* counter-attack.
contre-attaquer [kɔ̃tratake] *v.t.* to counter--attack.
contrebalancer [kɔ̃trəbalɑ̃se] *v.t.* to counterbalance, to compensate; (pop.) *s'en* ~, to disregard, to think nothing of.
contrebande [kɔ̃trəbɑ̃d] *s.f.* smuggling; smuggled goods; *faire la ~ de qch.*, to smuggle sth.
contrebandi-er, -ère [kɔ̃trəbɑ̃dje] *s.m.f.* smuggler.
contrebas [kɔ̃trəbɑ] *en* ~ *adv.loc.* at a lower level.
contrebasse [kɔ̃trəbɑs] *s.f.* (mus.) double-bass; double-bass player.
contrebassiste [kɔ̃trəbɑsist] *s.m.f.* double-bass player.
contrebasson [kɔ̃trəbɑsɔ̃] *s.m.* (mus.) double bassoon.
contrebatterie [kɔ̃trəbatri] *s.f.* (mil.) counter--battery.
contrebuter [kɔ̃trəbyte] *v.t.* to buttress.
contrecarrer [kɔ̃trəkare] *v.t.* to oppose, to thwart.
contrechamp [kɔ̃trəʃɑ̃] *s.m.* (cin.) reverse shot.
contre-chant [kɔ̃trəʃɑ̃] *s.m.* (mus.) counterpoint.
contreclef [kɔ̃trəkle] *s.f.* (arch.) second voussoir.
contrecœur [kɔ̃trəkœr] *à* ~ *adv.loc.* unwillingly, reluctantly.
contrecœur [kɔ̃trəkœr] *s.m.* **1.** fireback; **2.** (rail.) guard-rail.
contrecoup [kɔ̃trəku] *s.m.* **1.** (obs.) repercussion, ricochet; **2.** consequence, repercussion.
contre-courant [kɔ̃trəkurɑ̃] *s.m.* counter--current, undertow.
contre-culture [kɔ̃trəkyltyr] *s.f.* anti-culture.
contredanse [kɔ̃trədɑ̃s] *s.f.* quadrille, country dance.
contre-digue [kɔ̃trədig] *s.f.* second dike.
contredire [kɔ̃trədir] *v.t.* to contradict, to refute, to deny; to disprove.
contredit [kɔ̃trədi] *s.m.* rebuttal; *sauf* ~, subject to correction; *sans* ~, indisputably.
contrée [kɔ̃tre] *s.f.* (obs. exc. dial.) country, land, region.
contre-écrou [kɔ̃trekru] *s.m.* lock-nut.
contre-enquête [kɔ̃trɑ̃kɛt] *s.f.* second inquiry.
contre-épreuve [kɔ̃treprœv] *s.f.* check, cross--check.
contre-espionnage [kɔ̃trɛspjɔnaʒ] *s.m.* counter--espionage.
contre-essai [kɔ̃tresɛ] *s.m.* second test, control test.
contrefaçon [kɔ̃trəfasɔ̃] *s.f.* counterfeiting, imitation; infringement (of copyright); counterfeit; forgery.
contrefacteur [kɔ̃trəfaktœr] *s.m.* counterfeiter, forger.
contrefaire [kɔ̃trəfɛr] *v.t.* **1.** to imitate, to mime, to ape, to parody; **2.** (obs.) to simulate, to feign; (mod.) to counterfeit, to forge; **3.** to disguise; **4.** to deform.
contrefait, -e [kɔ̃trəfɛ] *adj.* deformed.
contre-feu (pl. **-x**) [kɔ̃trəfø] *s.m.* **1.** fireback; **2.** (forest.) counter-fire.
(**se**) **contreficher** [kɔ̃trəfiʃe] *v.refl.* (pop.) *se ~ de qch.*, not to care a damn about sth.
contre-fil, contrefil [kɔ̃trəfil] *s.m.* wrong direction; *à* ~, against the grain.
contre-filet [kɔ̃trəfilɛ] *s.m.* (cook.) hind brisket.
contrefort [kɔ̃trəfɔr] *s.m.* **1.** buttress; stiffening (at back of shoe); **2.** spur (of mountain chain).
(**se**) **contrefoutre** [kɔ̃trəfutr] *v.refl.* vulg. form of (SE) CONTREFICHER.
contre-fugue [kɔ̃trəfyg] *s.f.* counter-fugue.
contre-haut [kɔ̃trəo] *en* ~ *adv.loc.* at a higher level.
contre-indication [kɔ̃trɛ̃dikɑsjɔ̃] *s.f.* (med.) contra-indication.
contre-indiquer [kɔ̃trɛ̃dike] *v.t.* (med.) to contra-indicate; *~-indiqué*, (fam.) inadvisable.
contre-jour [kɔ̃trəʒur] *s.m.* unfavourable light; *à* ~, against the light.
contre-lettre [kɔ̃trəlɛtr] *s.f.* (law) defeasance.
contremaître [kɔ̃trəmɛtr] *s.m.* foreman, overseer.
contremaîtresse [kɔ̃trəmɛtrɛs] *s.f.* forewoman, supervisor.
contremander [kɔ̃trəmɑ̃de] *v.t.* (obs.) to give a countermanding order to (s.o.); (Lit.) to countermand, to cancel.
contre-manifestant, -e [kɔ̃trəmanifɛstɑ̃] *s.m.f.* counter-demonstrator.
contre-manifestation [kɔ̃trəmanifɛstɑsjɔ̃] *s.f.* counter-demonstration.
contre-manifester [kɔ̃trəmanifɛste] *v.i.* to take part in a counter-demonstration.
contremarche [kɔ̃trəmarʃ] *s.f.* **1.** countermarch; **2.** (of stairs) rise, riser.
contremarque [kɔ̃trəmark] *s.f.* **1.** countermark; **2.** (theatr.) ~ (*de sortie*), pass-out ticket.

contre-mesure [kɔ̃trəmzyr] *s.f.* **1.** countermeasure; **2.** (mus.) *à* ~, against the beat.
contre-mine [kɔ̃trəmin] *s.f.* (mil.) countermine.
contre-miner [kɔ̃trəmine] *v.t.* (mil.) to countermine; (fig.) to counter, to undermine.
contre-mur [kɔ̃trəmyr] *s.m.* outer or retaining wall.
contre-offensive [kɔ̃trɔfɑ̃siv] *s.f.* counter-offensive.
contre-ordre see CONTRORDRE.
contrepartie [kɔ̃trəparti] *s.f.* counterpart.
contre-pas [kɔ̃trəpɑ] *s.m.* (mil.) half-step.
contre-passer [kɔ̃trəpɑse] *v.t.* (fin.) to endorse (a bill) back to drawer; (book-keep.) to transfer (items in ledger).
contre-pente, contrepente [kɔ̃trəpɑ̃t] *s.f.* reverse slope.
contre-performance [kɔ̃trəpɛrfɔrmɑ̃s] *s.f.* (sport) poor performance.
contrepèterie [kɔ̃trəpɛtri] *s.f.*, **contrepet** [kɔ̃trəpɛ] *s.m.* spoonerism.
contre-pied [kɔ̃trəpje] *s.m.* **1.** (obs. hunt.) false scent; **2.** contrary, exact opposite; **3.** (sport) *à* ~, on the wrong foot.
contre-placage [kɔ̃trəplakaʒ] *s.m.* plywood manufacture.
contre-plaqué [kɔ̃trəplake] *s.m.* plywood.
contre-plongée [kɔ̃trəplɔ̃ʒe] *s.f.* (cin.) low-angle shot.
contrepoids [kɔ̃trəpwa] *s.m.* counterpoise, counterweight, counterbalance; weight (of clock).
contre-poil [kɔ̃trəpwal] *à* ~ *adv.loc.* the wrong way; (fig., fam.) *prendre qn. à* ~, to rub s.o. up the wrong way.
contrepoint [kɔ̃trəpwɛ̃] *s.m.* (mus.) counterpoint.
contrepoison [kɔ̃trəpwazɔ̃] *s.m.* antidote.
contre-porte [kɔ̃trəpɔrt] *s.f.* screen-door, inner door.
contre-projet, contreprojet [kɔ̃trəprɔʒɛ] *s.m.* alternative scheme, counter-plan.
contre-propagande [kɔ̃trəprɔpagɑ̃d] *s.f.* counter-propaganda.
contreproposition, contre-proposition [kɔ̃trəprɔpozisjɔ̃] *s.f.* opposing motion, counter-proposal.
contrer [kɔ̃tre] *v.i.* (cards) to double; ~ *v.t.* (fam.) to outwit.
contre-rail [kɔ̃trərɑj] *s.m.* (rail.) guard-rail.
contre-révolution [kɔ̃trərevɔlysjɔ̃] *s.f.* counter-revolution; **~naire** [kɔ̃trərevɔlysjɔnɛr] *adj.*, *s.m.* counter-revolutionary.
contrescarpe [kɔ̃trɛskarp] *s.f.* (fort.) counterscarp.
contreseing [kɔ̃trəsɛ̃] *s.m.* countersignature.
contresens [kɔ̃trəsɑ̃s] *s.m.* misconstruction, mistranslation, misinterpretation; wrong side (of cloth); *à* ~, (in) the wrong way, upside down, inside out.
contresigner [kɔ̃trəsiɲe] *v.t.* to countersign.
contre-sujet [kɔ̃trəsyʒɛ] *s.m.* (mus.) second subject.
contre-taille [kɔ̃trətɑj] *s.f.* (comm.) counter-tally; (engr.) cross-hatching.
contretemps [kɔ̃trətɑ̃] *s.m.* **1.** accident, hitch, snag, difficulty; *à* ~, at the wrong moment, inopportunely; **2.** (mus.) syncopation.
contre-terrorisme [kɔ̃trətɛrɔrism] *s.m.* anti-terrorism.
contre-torpilleur [kɔ̃trətɔrpijœr] *s.m.* (nav.) destroyer.
contretype [kɔ̃trətip] *s.m.* (photo.) duplicate.
contre-valeur [kɔ̃trəvalœr] *s.f.* (fin.) value in exchange.
contrevallation [kɔ̃trəval(l)ɑsjɔ̃] *s.f.* (fort.) contravallation.
contrevenant, -e [kɔ̃trəvnɑ̃] *s.m.f.* offender.
contrevenir [kɔ̃trəvnir] *v.i.* ~ *à*, to contravene, to infringe, to offend against.
contrevent [kɔ̃trəvɑ̃] *s.m.* **1.** exterior shutter, storm shutter; **2.** (constr.) brace.
contreventement [kɔ̃trəvɑ̃tmɑ̃] *s.m.* (constr.) brace, crosspiece.
contre-vérité, contrevérité [kɔ̃trəverite] *s.f.* antiphrasis, irony.
contre-visite [kɔ̃trəvizit] *s.f.* second check or inspection; (med.) second opinion.
contre-voie [kɔ̃trəvwa] *à* ~ *adv.loc.* (rail.) in reverse, backwards.
contribuable [kɔ̃tribɥabl] *s.m.f.* ratepayer, taxpayer.
contribuer [kɔ̃tribɥe] *v.i.* to contribute, to co-operate (*à*, in).
contributi-f, -ve [kɔ̃tribytif] *adj.* (law) contributory.
contribution [kɔ̃tribysjɔ̃] *s.f.* contribution, share, subscription; rate, tax; (pl.) tax office, rates office; *mettre à* ~, to place an obligation upon, to call upon, to make use of the services of.
contrister [kɔ̃triste] *v.t.* (Lit.) to sadden.
contrit, -e [kɔ̃tri] *adj.* contrite, penitent.
contrition [kɔ̃trisjɔ̃] *s.f.* contrition.
contrôlable [kɔ̃trolabl] *adj.* verifiable.
contrôle [kɔ̃trol] *s.m.* **1.** check, audit, inspection, verification; **2.** (usu. pl.) roll, list; **3.** hallmark; **4.** audit department or office; **5.** control; ~ *de soi-même*, self-control; ~ *des naissances*, birth control.
contrôler [kɔ̃trole] *v.t.* **1.** to check, to audit, to verify, to inspect; **2.** to hallmark; **3.** to control.
contrôleur [kɔ̃trolœr] *s.m.* **1.** auditor, inspector, controller; **2.** clock, meter, control.
contrordre, contre-ordre [kɔ̃trɔrdr] *s.m.* countermand; *sauf* ~, unless otherwise instructed.
controuvé, -e [kɔ̃truve] *adj.* contrived, fabricated.
controversable [kɔ̃trɔvɛrsabl] *adj.* disputable, controversial.
controverse [kɔ̃trɔvɛrs] *s.f.* controversy.
controversé, -e [kɔ̃trɔvɛrse] *adj.* controversial, debatable.
controverser [kɔ̃trɔvɛrse] *v.t.* to debate; to argue.
controversiste [kɔ̃trɔvɛrsist] *s.m.f.* (eccles.) controversialist.
contumace [kɔ̃tymas] *s.f.* (law) contumacy, non-appearance; *condamné par* ~, sentenced in his absence; ~ *adj.* (or *contumax*) in default.
contus, -e [kɔ̃ty] *adj.* contused, bruised.
contusion [kɔ̃tyzjɔ̃] *s.f.* contusion.
contusionner [kɔ̃tyzjɔne] *v.t.* to contuse, to bruise.
conurbation [kɔnyrbɑsjɔ̃] *s.f.* conurbation.
convaincant, -e [kɔ̃vɛ̃kɑ̃] *adj.* convincing.
convaincre [kɔ̃vɛ̃kr] *v.t.* **1.** to convince, to persuade; **2.** to prove guilty (*de*, of).
convaincu, -e [kɔ̃vɛ̃ky] *adj.* convinced, persuaded.
convalescence [kɔ̃valesɑ̃s] *s.f.* convalescence.
convalescent, -e [kɔ̃valesɑ̃] *adj.*, *s.m.f.* convalescent.
convenable [kɔ̃vnabl] *adj.* **1.** suitable, proper, fit, fitting, appropriate, convenient; **2.** (fam.) adequate, acceptable, fair; **3.** decent, proper; **~ment** [kɔ̃vnabləmɑ̃] *adv.* **1.** (obs.) conveniently, suitably; **2.** (fam.) adequately, fairly; **3.** decently, properly.
convenance [kɔ̃vnɑ̃s] *s.f.* **1.** suitability, fitness; **2.** convenience, taste; **3.** (pl.) propriety, correct conduct; *observer, respecter, les ~s*, to observe the proprieties.
convenir [kɔ̃vnir] *v.i.* **1.** to suit, to be suitable, fitting, right, appropriate (*à qch.*, to or for sth.); **2.** ~ *à qn.*, to suit, to please, s.o.; **3.** *il convient* (*de*

+ inf.; *que* + subj.), it is right, it is fitting, (to, that); **4.** ~ *de*, to admit, to own, to acknowledge; to agree on; **se** ~ *v.refl.* to be suited (to one another).
convent [kɔ̃vɑ̃] *s.m.* Freemasons' lodge meeting; ⚠ not 'convent'.
convention [kɔ̃vɑ̃sjɔ̃] *s.f.* **1.** convention, agreement, contract; **2.** (usu. pl.) conventions; **3.** *de* ~, conventional; **4.** (pol.) convention.
conventionné, -e [kɔ̃vɑ̃sjɔne] *adj.* officially agreed, accepted; *médecin* ~, health service doctor.
conventionnel, -le [kɔ̃vɑ̃sjɔnɛl] *adj.* conventional; ~ *s.m.* (hist.) member of the Convention (1792–95); **~lement** [kɔ̃vɑ̃sjɔnɛlmɑ̃] *adv.* conventionally.
conventionnement [kɔ̃vɑ̃sjɔnmɑ̃] *s.m.* agreement between doctors and government organizations.
conventualité [kɔ̃vɑ̃tɥalite] *s.f.* conventual life.
conventuel, -le [kɔ̃vɑ̃tɥɛl] *adj.* conventual.
convenu, -e [kɔ̃vny] *adj.* agreed, fixed; ~ *s.m.* (pej.) the conventional, banality.
convergence [kɔ̃vɛrʒɑ̃s] *s.f.* convergence.
convergent, -e [kɔ̃vɛrʒɑ̃] *adj.* converging, convergent.
converger [kɔ̃vɛrʒe] *v.i.* to converge; (fig.) to tend to agree, to have the same effect.
convers, -e [kɔ̃vɛr] *adj.* lay; *frère* ~, *sœur* ~*e*, lay brother, sister.
conversation [kɔ̃vɛrsɑsjɔ̃] *s.f.* conversation, talk.
converser [kɔ̃vɛrse] *v.i.* to converse, to talk.
conversion [kɔ̃vɛrsjɔ̃] *s.f.* conversion; (mil. hist.) tactical change of direction.
converti, -e [kɔ̃vɛrti] *adj.* converted; *s.m.f.* convert.
convertibilité [kɔ̃vɛrtibilite] *s.f.* (fin.) convertibility.
convertible [kɔ̃vɛrtibl] *adj.* convertible; ~ *s.m.* aircraft designed for horizontal or vertical flight.
convertir [kɔ̃vɛrtir] *v.t.* to convert; (obs.) to change, to transform; (fin.) to convert, to realize; **se** ~ *v.refl.* to be converted.
convertissable [kɔ̃vɛrtisabl] *adj.* convertible.
convertissage [kɔ̃vɛrtisaʒ] *s.m.* (metall.) converting, conversion (of iron to steel).
convertissement [kɔ̃vɛrtismɑ̃] *s.m.* (fin.) conversion, exchange.
convertisseur [kɔ̃vɛrtisœr] *s.m.* (metall.) converter; (electr.) transformer.
convexe [kɔ̃vɛks] *adj.* convex.
convexité [kɔ̃vɛksite] *s.f.* convexity.
conviction [kɔ̃viksjɔ̃] *s.f.* conviction, certitude; (obs.) convincing proof; *pièce à* ~, exhibit (in criminal case).
convier [kɔ̃vje] *v.t.* to invite, to ask.
convive [kɔ̃viv] *s.m.f.* guest, fellow-guest.
convocable [kɔ̃vɔkabl] *adj.* summonable.
convocation [kɔ̃vɔkɑsjɔ̃] *s.f.* convocation, summons, convening (of a meeting, etc.), notice to appear (for mil. service, examination, etc.).
convoi [kɔ̃vwa] *s.m.* **1.** convoy; **2.** railway train; **3.** funeral cortège.
convoiement [kɔ̃vwamɑ̃], **convoyage** [kɔ̃vwajaʒ] *s.m.* convoying.
convoiter [kɔ̃vwate] *v.t.* to covet.
convoitise [kɔ̃vwatiz] *s.f.* covetousness.
convoler [kɔ̃vɔle] *v.i.* (obs. exc. jest) to marry, to re-marry.
convoluté, -e [kɔ̃vɔlyte] *adj.* (bot.) convoluted.
convolvulacées [kɔ̃vɔlvylase] *s.f.pl.* (bot.) Convolvulaceae.
convolvulus [kɔ̃vɔlvylys] *s.m.* (bot.) convolvulus.
convoquer [kɔ̃vɔke] *v.t.* to summon, to convene, to call.
convoyer [kɔ̃vwaje] *v.t.* to convoy, to escort.
convoyage see CONVOIEMENT.
convoyeur [kɔ̃vwajœr] *s.m.* **1.** convoy or escort ship; **2.** security guard; **3.** conveyor belt.
convulsé, -e [kɔ̃vylse] *adj.* convulsed.
convulser [kɔ̃vylse] *v.t.* to convulse.
convulsi-f, -ve [kɔ̃vylsif] *adj.* convulsive.
convulsion [kɔ̃vylsjɔ̃] *s.f.* convulsion.
convulsionner [kɔ̃vylsjɔne] *v.t.* to convulse.
convulsivement [kɔ̃vylsivmɑ̃] *adv.* convulsively.
cooblige, -e [kɔɔbliʒe] *s.m.f.* (law) co-obligee.
cooccupant, -e [kɔɔkypɑ̃] *s.m.f.* joint occupier.
coolie [kuli] *s.m.* coolie.
coopérat-eur, -rice [kɔɔperatœr] *s.m.f.* **1.** collaborator; **2.** member of a co-operative society.
coopérati-f, -ve [kɔɔperatif] *adj.* co-operative.
coopération [kɔɔperɑsjɔ̃] *s.f.* collaboration, co-operation.
coopératisme [kɔɔperatism] *s.m.* (econ.) co--operative system.
coopérative [kɔɔperativ] *s.f.* co-operative (society).
coopérer [kɔɔpere] *v.i.* to co-operate, to collaborate; ~ *à qch.*, to collaborate in sth.
cooptation [kɔɔptɑsjɔ̃] *s.f.* co-option.
coopter [kɔɔpte] *v.t.* to co-opt.
coordination [kɔɔrdinɑsjɔ̃] *s.f.* co-ordination.
coordonnat-eur, -rice [kɔɔrdɔnatœr], **coordinat-eur, -rice** [kɔɔrdinatœr] *adj., s.m.f.* coordinating; coordinator.
coordonné, -e [kɔɔrdɔne] *adj.* co-ordinated.
coordonnées [kɔɔrdɔne] *s.f.pl.* co-ordinates; (fig., fam.) *donnez-moi vos* ~, give me your name, address, telephone number, etc.
coordonner [kɔɔrdɔne] *v.t.* to co-ordinate.
copahu [kɔpay] *s.m.* copaiba.
copain *s.m.*, **copin, -e** [kɔpɛ̃] *s.m.f.* (fam.) friend, mate, pal.
copal [kɔpal] *s.m.* copal.
copartage [kɔpartaʒ] *s.m.* (law) coparcenary, joint heirship.
copartageant, -e [kɔpartaʒɑ̃] (law) *s.m.f.* coparcener, joint heir; *adj.* joint.
copartager [kɔpartaʒe] *v.t.* (law) to share.
coparticipant, -e [kɔpartisipɑ̃] *s.m.f.* (law) co-partner, sharer; *adj.* participating.
coparticipation [kɔpartisipɑsjɔ̃] *s.f.* (law) co--partnership, participation.
copayer, copaïer [kɔpaje] *s.m.* copaiba tree.
copeau (pl. **-x**) [kɔpo] *s.m.* chip, flake (of wood or metal).
Copenhague [kɔpɛnag] *s.f.* (geog.) Copenhagen.
copépodes [kɔpepɔd] *s.m.pl.* (zool.) Copepoda.
Copernic [kɔpɛrnik] *s.m.* Copernicus.
copiage [kɔpjaʒ] *s.m.* copying, cheating (in examination); servile imitation.
copie [kɔpi] *s.f.* **1.** copy, reproduction, imitation; **2.** (in schools) written work, homework, prep; **3.** (print.) copy, manuscript.
copier [kɔpje] *v.t.* to copy, to reproduce, to imitate; to cheat, to crib.
copieur [kɔpjœr] *s.m.* cheat.
copieu-x, -se [kɔpjø] *adj.* copious, abundant, rich; **~sement** [kɔpjøzmɑ̃] *adv.* copiously.
copilote [kɔpilɔt] *s.m.* co-pilot.
copin, -e see COPAIN.
copiner [kɔpine] *v.i.* (fam.) to chum up.
copinerie [kɔpinri] *s.f.* (fam.) being friends, pals; gang.
copiste [kɔpist] *s.m.f.* **1.** copier, copyist, transcriber; **2.** plagiarist.
coplanaire [kɔplanɛr] *adj.* (geom.) coplanar.
coposséder [kɔpɔsede] *v.t.* to possess or own jointly.
copra(h) [kɔpra] *s.m.* copra.
coproduction [kɔprɔdyksjɔ̃] *s.f.* (cin.) joint production.
copro-lithe [kɔprɔlit] *s.m.* (geol.) coprolite;

~**logie** [kɔprɔlɔʒi] *s.f.* (biol.) coprology; ~**phage** [kɔprɔfaʒ] *adj.* coprophagous.
copropriétaire [kɔprɔprijetɛr] *s.m.f.* joint owner, co-proprietor.
copropriété [kɔprɔprijete] *s.f.* joint ownership.
copte [kɔpt] *s.m.f.* Copt; ~ *adj.*, *s.m.* Coptic.
copulati-f, -ve [kɔpylatif] *adj.* (gram., log.) copulative.
copulation [kɔpylɑsjɔ̃] *s.f.* copulation.
copule [kɔpyl] *s.f.* (lang.) copula.
copyright [kɔpirajt] *s.m.* copyright.
coq [kɔk] *s.m.* **1.** cock (domestic fowl); cock bird (pheasant, etc.); weathercock; ~ *de bruyère*, capercaillie; **2.** (fig.) ladykiller; ~ *du village*, cock of the walk; *être, vivre, comme un* ~ *en pâte*, to be or to live in clover; **3.** ship's cook.
coq-à-l'âne [kɔkalɑn] *s.m.invar.* cock-and-bull story; *passer du coq à l'âne*, to talk nonsense.
coquart [kɔkar] *s.m.* (pop.) black eye.
coque [kɔk] *s.f.* **1.** shell (of nut, etc.); *œuf à la* ~, boiled egg; **2.** (moll.) cockle; **3.** (naut., car, aeron.) hull, body, shell.
coquelet [kɔklɛ] *s.m.* cockerel.
coquelicot [kɔkliko] *s.m.* (bot.) wild poppy.
coqueluche [kɔklyʃ] *s.f.* **1.** whooping cough; **2.** darling, pet.
coquemar [kɔkmar] *s.m.* kettle, pot.
coquerelle [kɔkrɛl] *s.f.* (herald.) three hazel nuts in case.
coquerico [kɔkriko] *s.m.* cock-a-doodle-doo.
coquerie [kɔkri] *s.f.* (naut.) galley, cook-house.
coquet, -te [kɔkɛ] *adj.* flirtatious, coquettish; dressy, dandified; elegant, trim, neat, charming; (fam. of sum of money, etc.) handsome; ~**te** *s.f.* flirt, coquette.
coqueter [kɔkte] *v.i.* to show off, to pose; (obs.) to flirt.
coquetier [kɔktje] *s.m.* **1.** egg-cup; **2.** (obs.) wholesale egg dealer.
coquetière [kɔktjɛr] *s.f.* egg-boiler.
coquettement [kɔkɛtmɑ̃] *adv.* elegantly, neatly, pleasantly.
coquetterie [kɔkɛtri] *s.f.* coquetry; elegance, charm; (pl.) advances.
coquillage [kɔkijaʒ] *s.m.* shellfish, shell.
coquillart [kɔkijar] *s.m.* (min.) shell limestone.
coquille [kɔkij] *s.f.* **1.** shell (of shellfish, nut, egg, etc.); ~ *Saint-Jacques*, scallop; ~ *de noix*, cockle-shell (boat); (fig.) *rentrer dans sa* ~, to go back into one's shell; *sortir de sa* ~, to come out of one's shell; **2.** (print.) misprint.
coquilli-er, -ère [kɔkije] *adj.* (geol.) conchitic, shelly; ~**er** *s.m.* collection of shells.
coquin, -e [kɔkɛ̃] *s.m.f.* (obs.) rogue, knave, slut; (mod.) scamp, rascal; *adj.* (of children) saucy, pert, sly.
coquinerie [kɔkinri] *s.f.* (obs.) knavery, roguishness.
cor[1] [kɔr] *s.m.* **1.** (mus.) ~ *anglais*, cor anglais; ~ *de basset*, basset-horn; ~ (*d'harmonie*), French horn, horn; **2.** tine (of antler).
cor[2] [kɔr] *s.m.* (med.) corn.
coracoïde [kɔrakɔid] *adj.* (anat.) coracoid.
corail (pl. **aux**) [kɔraj] *s.m.* coral; coral (colour).
corailleur [kɔrajœr] *s.m.* coral-fisher; coral--worker.
corallien, -ne [kɔraljɛ̃] *adj.* coral, coralline; ~ *s.m.* (geol.) Corallian.
corallifère [kɔralifɛr] *adj.* coral-bearing.
coralline [kɔralin] *s.f.* coralline (seaweed).
coran [kɔrɑ̃] *s.m.* Koran; (fig.) bedside reading.
coranique [kɔranik] *adj.* Koranic.
corbeau (pl. **-x**) [kɔrbo] *s.m.* **1.** (ornith.) raven, crow; (fig.) miser; (obs.) priest; **2.** (arch.) corbel; **3.** (naut. obs.) grappling-iron.
corbeille [kɔrbɛj] *s.f.* **1.** (light) basket; **2.** (arch.) corbel; **3.** (round or oval) flower-bed; **4.** floor of Stock Exchange; **5.** (theatr.) orchestra stall.
corbillard [kɔrbijar] *s.m.* hearse.
corbillon [kɔrbijɔ̃] *s.m.* small basket.
cordage [kɔrdaʒ] *s.m.* **1.** rope(s), twine, cord, cordage; (naut.) rigging; **2.** (of timber) cord (measure of cut wood); **3.** stringing (of racket).
corde [kɔrd] *s.f.* **1.** twine, rope, string; hangman's rope; ~ *à linge*, clothes-line; *avoir plus d'une* ~ *à son arc*, to have more than one string to one's bow; *se mettre la* ~ *au cou*, (fig.) to put one's head in the noose; *parler de la* ~ *dans la maison d'un pendu*, to drop a brick; ~ *à sauter*, skipping-rope; *saut à la* ~, skipping; *être sur la* ~ *raide*, (fig.) to walk a tightrope; **2.** (mus.) string; (pl.) strings, stringed instruments, (of orchestra); (fig.) *faire vibrer la* ~ *sensible*, to strike home, to touch on the raw; **3.** cord (of wood); **4.** thread (of material); *usé jusqu'à la* ~, (lit. & fig.) threadbare; **5.** (anat.) cord, chord; (fig.) *ce n'est pas dans mes* ~*s*, it's not my line of country.
cordé, -e [kɔrde] *adj.* heart-shaped.
cordeau (pl. **-x**) [kɔrdo] *s.m.* **1.** (hort., constr.) line; (fig.) *au* ~, with precision; **2.** (mining) fuse.
cordée [kɔrde] *s.f.* bundle (secured by rope); party of climbers roped together.
cordeler [kɔrdəle] *v.t.* to twist, to twine.
cordelette [kɔrdəlɛt] *s.f.* string, thread.
cordeli-er, -ère [kɔrdəlje] *s.m.f.* Cordelier, (Franciscan) friar or nun.
cordelière [kɔrdəljɛr] *s.f.* girdle; handle made of rope or string; (arch.) cable moulding.
corder [kɔrde] *v.t.* **1.** to twist, to twine; **2.** to rope; **3.** to cord (wood); **4.** to string (a racket).
corderie [kɔrd(ə)ri] *s.f.* rope manufacture; rope factory.
cordial (pl. **aux**) [kɔrdjal] *s.m.* stimulant, tonic; ~, ~**e** *adj.* stimulating; cordial, hearty, sincere, warm; ~**ement** [kɔrdjalmɑ̃] *adv.* cordially, heartily, sincerely.
cordialité [kɔrdjalite] *s.f.* cordiality, sincerity.
cordier [kɔrdje] *s.m.* rope-maker.
cordiforme [kɔrdifɔrm] *adj.* heart-shaped.
cordillère [kɔrdijɛr] *s.f.* (geog.) cordillera.
cordite [kɔrdit] *s.f.* cordite.
cordon [kɔrdɔ̃] *s.m.* **1.** string, cord; *tenir les* ~*s de la bourse*, to hold the purse-strings; **2.** ribbon or sash (of an order of chivalry); ~*-bleu*, cordon bleu; **3.** (anat.) cord; **4.** cordon, rank, line.
cordonner [kɔrdɔne] *v.t.* to twist, to braid.
cordonnerie [kɔrdɔnri] *s.f.* shoe-making, shoe trade; cobbler's shop.
cordonnet [kɔrdɔnɛ] *s.m.* **1.** twist, thread; **2.** milled edge (of coin).
cordonni-er, -ère [kɔrdɔnje] *s.m.f.* (obs.) shoemaker; (mod.) shoe-repairer, cobbler.
Cordoue [kɔrdu] *s.f.* (geog.) Cordova.
Corée [kɔre] *s.f.* (geog.) Korea.
coréen, -ne [kɔreɛ̃] *adj.*, *s.m.f.* Korean.
coreligionnaire [kɔrəliʒjɔnɛr] *s.m.f.* co--religionist.
coréopsis [kɔreɔpsis] *s.m.* (bot.) coreopsis.
Corfou [kɔrfu] *s.f.* (geog.) Corfu.
coriace [kɔrjas] *adj.* (lit. & fig.) tough, hard.
coriandre [kɔrjɑ̃dr] *s.f.* (bot.) coriander.
coricide [kɔrisid] *s.m.* corn-cure.
corindon [kɔrɛ̃dɔ̃] *s.m.* (min.) corundum.
Corinthe [kɔrɛ̃t] *s.f.* (geog.) Corinth; *raisins de* ~, currants.
corinthien, -ne [kɔrɛ̃tjɛ̃] *adj.*, *s.m.f.* Corinthian.
cormoran [kɔrmɔrɑ̃] *s.m.* (ornith.) cormorant.
cornac [kɔrnak] *s.m.* **1.** mahout; **2.** (fig., fam.) guide, chaperon.
cornage [kɔrnaʒ] *s.m.* **1.** (vet.) roaring; **2.** (med.) death rattle.
cornaline [kɔrnalin] *s.f.* (min.) cornelian, carnelian.
cornard [kɔrnar] *s.m.* (pop.) cuckold.
corne [kɔrn] *s.f.* **1.** horn; ~ *à chaussures*, shoe-

-horn; *prendre le taureau par les ~s*, to take the bull by the horns; **2.** dog-ear (of paper or book).
corné, -e [kɔrne] *adj.* horny, horned.
corned-beef [kɔrndbif] *s.m.* corned beef.
cornée [kɔrne] *s.f.* (anat.) cornea.
cornéen, -ne [kɔrneɛ̃] *adj.* (anat.) corneal; *lentille ~ne*, contact lens.
corneille [kɔrnɛj] *s.f.* (ornith.) crow, rook.
cornélien, -ne [kɔrneljɛ̃] *adj.* of Corneille, in the style of Corneille.
cornement [kɔrnəmɑ̃] *s.m.* ringing, buzzing, (of ears); hooting; roaring (of pipe).
cornemuse [kɔrnəmyz] *s.f.* bagpipe(s).
cornemuseur [kɔrnəmyzœr] *s.m.* bagpipe-player, piper.
corner [kɔrne] *v.t.i.* **1.** to blow or sound a horn, to hoot; **2.** (of ears) to buzz; **3.** (fig., fam.) to trumpet, to din; *~ aux oreilles de qn.*, to din into someone's ears; **4.** to turn down the corner of a page.
cornet [kɔrnɛ] *s.m.* **1.** (obs.) herdsman's horn; **2.** (mus.) *~ à pistons*, cornet; **3.** cornet (of paper, etc.); **4.** (anat.) turbinate bones (of nose); **5.** (pop.) *se mettre qch. dans le ~*, to have a bite to eat.
cornette [kɔrnɛt] *s.f.* **1.** nun's headdress; **2.** (obs. mil.) cavalry standard; (naut.) broad pennant; *~ s.m.* (mil. rank) cornet.
cornettiste [kɔrnetist] *s.m.f.* (mus.) cornet(t)ist.
corniaud [kɔrnjo] *s.m.* **1.** mongrel dog; **2.** (fam.) imbecile.
corniche [kɔrniʃ] *s.f.* (arch.) cornice; corniche (road).
cornichon [kɔrniʃɔ̃] *s.m.* gherkin; (fig., fam.) ninny, ass.
corni-er, -ère [kɔrnje] *adj.* corner-.
cornière [kɔrnjɛr] *s.f.* (constr.) valley; angle-plate, corner-plate.
cornillon [kɔrnijɔ̃] *s.m.* (zool.) horn-core.
cornique [kɔrnik] *adj., s.m.* Cornish.
corniste [kɔrnist] *s.m.f.* horn-player.
Cornouaille [kɔrnwɑj] *s.f.* (geog.) Cornouaille (old district of Brittany); **~s** *s.f.* (geog.) Cornwall.
cornouille [kɔrnuj] *s.f.* dogwood berry.
cornouiller [kɔrnuje] *s.m.* (bot.) dogwood, cornel.
cornu, -e [kɔrny] *adj.* horned; (obs. fig.) preposterous.
cornue [kɔrny] *s.f.* (chem.) retort; (techn.) still.
corollaire [kɔrɔl(l)ɛr] *s.m.* corollary.
corolle [kɔrɔl] *s.f.* (bot.) corolla.
coron [kɔrɔ̃] *s.m.* miners' dwellings.
coronaire [kɔrɔnɛr] *adj.* (anat.) coronary.
coronal, -e, (aux) [kɔrɔnal] *adj.* coronal.
coronarite [kɔrɔnarit] *s.f.* (med.) hardening of the arteries.
coronelle [kɔrɔnɛl] *s.f.* smooth snake.
coroner [kɔrɔnœr] *s.m.* coroner.
coronille [kɔrɔnij] *s.f.* (bot.) crown vetch.
coronographe [kɔrɔnɔgraf] *s.m.* (astron.) coronograph.
corozo [kɔrozo] *s.m.* corozo.
corporal (pl. **aux**) [kɔrpɔral] *s.m.* (eccles.) corporal.
corporati-f, -ve [kɔrpɔratif] *adj.* corporative.
corporation [kɔrpɔrɑsjɔ̃] *s.f.* (hist.) guild, union, craft, trade, profession.
corporatisme [kɔrpɔratism] *s.m.* corporatism.
corporel, -le [kɔrpɔrɛl] *adj.* corporal, bodily, material, physical, corporeal; **~lement** [kɔrpɔrɛlmɑ̃] *adv.* bodily, corporally, materially.
corps [kɔr] *s.m.* **1.** (animal) body, (dead) body, corpse; *~ à ~*, hand-to-hand (fighting), head-on (confrontation, etc.); *à son ~ défendant*, reluctantly, against one's will; *à ~ perdu*, headlong, impetuously; **2.** trunk, torso, body (of garment); **3.** principal or main part (of building, etc.), substance (of letter, etc.); **4.** matter, object; **5.** corps, staff; **6.** body, consistency; (fig.) *donner ~ à* or *du ~ à*, to give substance to; *prendre ~*, to take shape.
corps-mort [kɔrmɔr] *s.m.* (naut.) mooring(s).
corpulence [kɔrpylɑ̃s] *s.f.* corpulence.
corpulent, -e [kɔrpylɑ̃] *adj.* corpulent.
corpus [kɔrpys] *s.m.* (law, Lit.) corpus.
corpusculaire [kɔrpyskylɛr] *adj.* corpuscular.
corpuscule [kɔrpyskyl] *s.m.* corpuscle.
corral [kɔral] *s.m.* corral.
correct, -e [kɔrɛkt] *adj.* **1.** correct, accurate; proper, suitable, right; **2.** (fam.) passable, good enough; **~ement** [kɔrɛktəmɑ̃] *adv.* correctly, properly.
correct-eur, -rice [kɔrɛktœr] *s.m.f.* examiner, marker; (proof) reader; *adj.* correcting, amending.
correcti-f, -ve [kɔrɛktif] *adj.*, **~f** *s.m.* corrective.
correction [kɔrɛksjɔ̃] *s.f.* **1.** correction, correcting; *sauf ~*, subject to correction; **2.** correctness, accuracy, exactitude; **3.** scrupulousness, honesty; **4.** corporal punishment; *maison de ~*, reformatory.
correctionnel, -le [kɔrɛksjɔnɛl] *adj.* (law) petty-sessional; **~le** *s.f.* court of summary jurisdiction.
corrélati-f, -ve [kɔrelatif] *adj.*, **~f** *s.m.* correlative.
corrélation [kɔrelɑsjɔ̃] *s.f.* correlation.
correspondance [kɔrɛspɔ̃dɑ̃s] *s.f.* **1.** correspondence, agreement, harmony; **2.** correspondence, letters; **3.** (transport) connection, connecting flight, etc.
correspondanci-er, -ère [kɔrɛspɔ̃dɑ̃sje] *s.m.f.* correspondence clerk.
correspondant, -e [kɔrɛspɔ̃dɑ̃] *adj.* corresponding, correspondent; *s.m.f.* correspondent.
correspondre [kɔrɛspɔ̃dr] *v.i.* to correspond (*à*, to, *avec*, with).
corrida [kɔrida] *s.f.* corrida, bullfight; (pop.) shambles.
corridor [kɔridɔr] *s.m.* corridor.
corrigé [kɔriʒe] *s.m.* key, model answer.
corriger [kɔriʒe] *v.t.* to correct; (rarely) to punish.
corrigeu-r, -se [kɔriʒœr] *s.m.f.* (print.) type corrector.
corrigible [kɔriʒibl] *adj.* corrigible, rectifiable, open to correction.
corroboration [kɔrɔbɔrɑsjɔ̃] *s.f.* corroboration.
corroborer [kɔrɔbɔre] *v.t.* to corroborate.
corrodant, -e [kɔrɔdɑ̃] *adj.*, *~ s.m.* corrosive.
corroder [kɔrɔde] *v.t.* to corrode.
corroi [kɔrwa] *s.m.* currying (of leather, etc.).
corroierie [kɔrwari] *s.f.* currier's trade or works.
corrompre [kɔrɔ̃pr] *v.t.* to corrupt, to spoil, to make rotten; **se** *~ v.refl.* to rot, to go rotten, to become corrupt.
corrompu, -e [kɔrɔ̃py] *adj.* corrupt, rotten; debased.
corrosi-f, -ve [kɔr(r)ozif] *adj.*, *s.m.* corrosive.
corrosion [kɔr(r)ozjɔ̃] *s.f.* corrosion.
corroyage [kɔrwajaʒ] *s.m.* **1.** currying, dressing, (of leather); **2.** welding (of metal).
corroyer [kɔrwaje] *v.t.* **1.** to curry, to dress, (leather); **2.** to weld (metal); **3.** to plane (wood).
corroyeur [kɔrwajœr] *s.m.* currier.
corrupt-eur, -rice [kɔryptœr] *adj.* corrupting, corruptive; *s.m.f.* corrupter.
corruptible [kɔryptibl] *adj.* corruptible; (of food) perishable.
corruption [kɔrypsjɔ̃] *s.f.* corruption, decay; depravity; corrupt practices.
corsage [kɔrsaʒ] *s.m.* bodice.
corsaire [kɔrsɛr] *s.m.* (hist.) corsair, privateer; (obs. fig.) shark; *pantalon ~*, breeches.

Corse [kɔrs] *s.f.* (geog.) Corsica.
corse [kɔrs] *adj.*, *s.m.f.* Corsican.
corsé, -e [kɔrse] *adj.* (of wine) full-bodied; (of sauce) spicy; (fig.) racy, juicy.
corselet [kɔrsəlɛ] *s.m.* corslet, corselette; (zool.) prothorax.
corser [kɔrse] *v.t.* to fortify (wine, etc.); (fig.) to step up, to add spice to; *se* ~, to get complicated, (of plot, etc.) to thicken.
corset [kɔrsɛ] *s.m.* corset, stays, foundation garment.
corseter [kɔrsəte] *v.t.* to corset; (fig.) to make rigid.
corseti-er, -ère [kɔrsətje] *s.m.f.* corset-maker, corsetière.
corso [kɔrso] *s.m.* parade (of floats at a fête).
cortège [kɔrtɛʒ] *s.m.* retinue; parade, procession, (esp. funeral) cortège.
cortès [kɔrtɛs] *s.f.pl.* Cortes.
cortex [kɔrtɛks] *s.m.* cortex.
cortical, -e, (aux) [kɔrtikal] *adj.* cortical.
cortisone [kɔrtizɔn] *s.f.* cortisone.
corvéable [kɔrveabl] *adj.* liable for corvée.
corvée [kɔrve] *s.f.* (hist.) corvée; (mil.) fatigue; (fig.) *quelle* ~*!*, what a fag!, what a bore!
corvette [kɔrvɛt] *s.f.* (nav.) corvette.
corymbe [kɔrɛ̃b] *s.m.* (bot.) corymb.
coryphée [kɔrife] *s.m.* (ant.) coryphaeus; (fig.) leader.
coryza [kɔriza] *s.m.* (med.) coryza.
cosaque [kɔzak] *s.m.* Cossack; (fam.) ruffian.
cosécante [kɔsekɑ̃t] *s.f.* (math.) cosecant.
cosignataire [kɔsiɲatɛr] *adj.*, *s.m.f.* co-signatory.
cosinus [kɔsinys] *s.m.* (math.) cosine.
cosmétique [kɔsmetik] *adj.*, *s.m.* cosmetic; ~ *s.m.* hair-oil, brilliantine.
cosmétiquer [kɔsmetike] *v.t.* to apply hair-oil, etc., to, to wax (moustache).
cosmétologie [kɔsmetɔlɔʒi] *s.f.* beauty culture.
cosmique [kɔsmik] *adj.* cosmic.
cosmo-drome [kɔsmɔdrom] *s.m.* (in U.S.S.R.) cosmodrome, space-vehicle launching station; **~gonie** [kɔsmɔgɔni] *s.f.* cosmogony; **~gonique** [kɔsmɔgɔnik] *adj.* cosmogonic; **~graphie** [kɔsmɔgrafi] *s.f.* cosmography; **~graphique** [kɔsmɔgrafik] *adj.* cosmographic(al); **~logie** [kɔsmɔlɔʒi] *s.f.* cosmology; **~naute** [kɔsmɔnot] *s.m.f.* cosmonaut, astronaut.
cosmopol-ite [kɔsmɔpɔlit] *adj.*, *s.m.f.* cosmopolitan; **~itisme** [kɔsmɔpɔlitism] *s.m.* cosmopolitanism.
cosmos [kɔsmos] *s.m.* cosmos; (outer) space.
cossard, -e [kɔsar] *adj.*, *s.m.f.* (pop.) bone-idle (person).
cosse[1] [kɔs] *s.f.* **1.** shell, pod; **2.** (electr.) terminal connection, spade or eye terminal.
cosse[2] [kɔs] *s.f.* (pop.) laziness.
cosser [kɔse] *v.t.* (of ram) to butt.
cossu, -e [kɔsy] *adj.* well-to-do, well-off.
costal, -e, (aux) [kɔstal] *adj.* costal.
costaud, costeau [kɔsto] *adj.*, *s.m.* (pop.) hefty, strapping (fellow); solid (thing).
costume [kɔstym] *s.m.* dress, costume; fancy dress; (two- or three-piece) suit.
costumé, -e [kɔstyme] *adj.* in fancy dress; *bal* ~, fancy-dress ball.
costumer [kɔstyme] *v.t.* to dress in fancy dress; **se** ~ *v.refl.* to dress up.
costumi-er, -ère [kɔstymje] *s.m.f.* costumier; (theatr.) wardrobe mistress.
cotangente [kɔtɑ̃ʒɑ̃t] *s.f.* (math.) cotangent.
cotation [kɔtɑsjɔ̃] *s.f.* (Stock Exchange) quotation.
cote [kɔt] *s.f.* **1.** quota, share; ~ *mal taillée*, compromise; **2.** reference, reference number; quotation (on Stock Exchange); number (indicating level on map); ~ *d'alerte*, flood level.
côte [kot] *s.f.* **1.** (anat., bot., arch.) rib; *on lui compterait les* ~*s*, he's nothing but skin and bone; *se tenir les* ~*s*, to split one's sides (laughing); ~ *à* ~, side by side; **2.** hillside, slope; *à mi-*~, halfway up; **3.** coast, (sea)shore; (fig.) *être à la* ~, to be broke, to be on the rocks.
coté, -e [kɔte] *adj.* quoted (on Stock Exchange); rated, appreciated.
côté [kote] *s.m.* (lit. & fig.) side; *à* ~, near, near by, next door; *à* ~ *de*, beside, in comparison with; *de ce* ~*-là*, there, on that side, that way; *de tous* ~*s*, on or from all sides, in every direction; *de* ~, sideways; *de* ~ *et d'autre*, here and there; *du* ~ *de*, in the direction of, near, in the vicinity of; (fig.) *de mon* ~, for my part; (fam.) *de ce* ~, from that quarter; *laisser de* ~, to neglect; *mettre de* ~, to put on one side, to put aside.
coteau (pl. **-x**) [kɔto] *s.m.* hill, hillock.
côtelé, -e [kotle] *adj.* (text.) ribbed.
côtelette [kotlɛt] *s.f.* chop, cutlet; (fam.) rib.
coter [kɔte] *v.t.* **1.** to number, to give a reference number to; **2.** to quote, to price; to rate, to assess, to mark; to mark levels (on a map).
coterie [kɔtri] *s.f.* set, faction, club, coterie; (secret) society.
cothurne [kɔtyrn] *s.m.* (ant.) buskin; (Lit.) tragedy.
cotice [kɔtis] *s.f.* (herald.) cotise.
cotidal, -e, (aux) [kɔtidal] *adj.* (geog.) co-tidal.
côti-er, -ère [kotje] *adj.* coastal, coast-, coastwise, inshore; **~er** *s.m.* (naut.) coaster, coasting vessel.
cotignac [kɔtiɲa(k)] *s.m.* quince or orange jam.
cotillon [kɔtijɔ̃] *s.m.* (obs.) skirt; *courir* or *aimer le* ~, to run after women.
cotisant, -e [kɔtizɑ̃] *adj.* subscribing; *s.m.f.* subscriber.
cotisation [kɔtizɑsjɔ̃] *s.f.* contribution, subscription.
cotiser [kɔtize] *v.i.* (fam.) to subscribe (*pour*, to); **se** ~ *v.refl.* to club together.
coton [kɔtɔ̃] *s.m.* cotton; ~ *hydrophile*, cotton wool; *filer un mauvais* ~, to be in a bad way; (pop.) *c'est* ~, *ce problème*, it's a tricky problem.
cotonnade [kɔtɔnad] *s.f.* cotton cloth.
(se) cotonner [kɔtɔne] *v.refl.* (of cloth) to become fluffy; (of fruit) to have a bloom.
cotonneu-x, -se [kɔtɔnø] *adj.* downy, fluffy; (of clouds) fleecy; (of style) woolly.
cotonni-er, -ère [kɔtɔnje] *adj.* cotton; **~er** *s.m.* (bot.) cotton plant.
coton-poudre [kɔtɔ̃pudr] *s.m.* gun-cotton.
côtoyer [kotwaje] *v.t.* to keep close to, to skirt, to hug; (fig.) to verge on, to keep on the fringe of.
cotre [kɔtr] *s.m.* (naut.) cutter.
cotret [kɔtrɛ] *s.m.* (obs.) bundle of (fire)wood; *sec comme un* ~, as thin as a lath.
cottage [kɔtɛdʒ] *s.m.* small country house.
cotte [kɔt] *s.f.* (obs.) coat; (obs.) petticoat; (mod.) workman's overalls; ~ *de mailles*, coat of mail).
cotutelle [kɔtytɛl] *s.f.* joint guardianship.
cotut-eur, -rice [kɔtytœr] *s.m.f.* joint guardian.
cotyle [kɔtil] *s.f.* (anat.) cotyle.
cotylédon [kɔtiledɔ̃] *s.m.* (bot.) cotyledon.
cotyloïde [kɔtilɔid] *adj.* (anat.) cotyloid.
cou [ku], (obs.) **col** [kɔl] *s.m.* neck; *sauter, se jeter, au* ~ *de qn.*, to make a great fuss of s.o.; *tordre le* ~ *à*, to wring the neck of; *couper le* ~ *à*, to behead; *se rompre* or *se casser le* ~, (fig.) to break one's neck; *prendre ses jambes à son* ~, to take to one's heels; *jusqu'au* ~, (lit. & fig.) up to the neck.
couac [kwak] *s.m.* quack, croak.
couard, -e [kwar] *adj.*, *s.m.f.* (Lit. or dial.) coward(ly).
couardise [kwardiz] *s.f.* (obs.) cowardice.

couchage [kuʃaʒ] *s.m.* **1.** going or putting to bed; billeting (of troops); **2.** bedding.
couchant, -e [kuʃɑ̃] *adj.* setting (of sun); *chien* ~, setter, (fig.) lickspittle; ~ *s.m.* sunset, west.
couche [kuʃ] *s.f.* **1.** (obs.) couch, bed; **2.** baby's napkin, nappy; **3.** (pl.) childbirth; *fausse-*~, miscarriage; **4.** coat, coating, layer; (geol.) layer, stratum; (fig., pop.) *avoir, en tenir, une* ~, to be thick; **5.** compost (heap).
couché, -e [kuʃe] *adj.* **1.** lying, in bed; **2.** slanting, sloping; (of crops) laid; **3.** (of paper) glazed.
coucher [kuʃe] *v.t.* to put to bed; to put up (for the night); to lay, to lay down; ~ *un fusil en joue*, to take aim (with a rifle); ~ *v.i.* to lie (down), to sleep, to stay the night; **se** ~ *v.refl.* to go to bed, to lie down; (of sun, etc.) to set.
coucher [kuʃe] *s.m.* going to bed, bedtime; bed (as opposed to board); ~ *du soleil*, sunset.
coucherie [kuʃri] *s.f.* (pop.) sleeping around.
couchette [kuʃɛt] *s.f.* child's cot; bunk, berth, (rail.) couchette.
coucheu-r, -se [kuʃœr] *s.m.f. mauvais* ~*r*, unpleasant customer.
couchis [kuʃi] *s.m.* (techn.) sub-crust, cushion--course.
couchoir [kuʃwar] *s.m.* (bookbinder's) burnisher.
couci-couça [kusikusa] *adv.loc.* (fam.) so-so.
coucou [kuku] *s.m.* **1.** (ornith.) cuckoo; **2.** cuckoo clock; **3.** (bot.) cowslip; **4.** (obs.) fly (carriage); **5.** (airmen's slang) old crate; ~ *interj.* bo!
coude [kud] *s.m.* **1.** elbow; *lever le* ~, to lift one's elbow (to drink); *huile de* ~, elbow grease; ~ *à* ~, side by side; *se serrer les* ~*s*, (fig.) to stick together; *jouer des* ~*s*, to elbow one's way, (fig.) to push; **2.** bend, turning (in road, etc.).
coudée [kude] *s.f.* (obs. measure) cubit; *avoir les* ~*s franches*, to have elbow room, room to manœuvre; (fig.) *dépasser de cent* ~*s*, to be immeasurably better than.
cou-de-pied [kudpje] *s.m.* (pl. *cous-de-pied*) instep.
couder [kude] *v.t.* to bend.
coudoiement [kudwamɑ̃] *s.m.* contact, proximity.
coudoyer [kudwaje] *v.t.* (obs.) to elbow; (mod.) to brush up against, to be in contact with.
coudraie [kudrɛ] *s.f.* hazel copse.
coudre [kudr] *v.t.i.* to sew, to make (clothes); *machine à* ~, sewing-machine.
coudrier [kudrije] *s.m.* (bot.) hazel.
couenne [kwan] *s.f.* **1.** rind (of pork or bacon), crackling; **2.** (med.) callus; **3.** (pop.) idiot.
couenneu-x, -se [kwanø] *adj.* (med.) callous; *angine* ~*se*, diphtheria.
couette [kwɛt] *s.f.* **1.** feather bed, duvet, continental quilt; **2.** (naut.) keel; **3.** (techn.) sleeve, bearing; **4.** pony-tail (hair-style).
couffe [kuf] *s.f.*, **couffin** [kufɛ̃] *s.m.* basket, holdall.
coufique [kufic] *adj.* Cufic, Kufic.
couguar, cougouar [kugwar] *s.m.* (zool.) puma, cougar.
couic [kwik] *interj.* tweet-tweet.
couillon [kujɔ̃] *s.m.* (pop.) idiot.
couiner [kwine] *v.t.i.* (fam.) to cheep, to twitter.
coulage [kulaʒ] *s.m.* **1.** boiling (of washing); **2.** casting (of statue, etc.); **3.** (fig., fam.) wastage, pilfering.
coulant, -e [kulɑ̃] *adj.* (obs.) sliding, slipping; *nœud* ~, slip-knot; (mod.) (of wine) easy on the palate; (of style) flowing; (fam.) easy-going.
coulant [kulɑ̃] *s.m.* slide, sliding clasp; (hort.) runner (of strawberries, etc.).
coule[1] [kul] *s.f.* (monk's) cowl.
(**à la**) **coule**[2] [alakul] *adv.loc.* (pop.) in the know, wise (to sth.).
coulé [kule] *s.m.* (mus.) slur, slide; (dancing) slide, glide; (billiards, etc.) follow-through.
coulée [kule] *s.f.* casting (of metal); flow, stream (of lava).
couler [kule] *v.i.* **1.** (of liquid) to run, to flow; (of time) to pass; **2.** to leak; **3.** to sink; ~ *v.t.* to boil (washing), to strain (a liquid), to cast (metal); to slip, to glide; to sink (ship, & fig. person); *se la* ~ *douce*, to take things easy; **se** ~ *v.refl.* to slip (noiselessly).
couleur [kulœr] *s.f.* **1.** colour, tint, hue, colouring; **2.** (pl.) favour, livery, colours (of club, etc.), flag; **3.** suit (of cards); **4.** complexion, colour of skin; *haut en* ~, ruddy; **5.** paint, colouring matter; **6.** (fig.) appearance, aspect; political colour; (rare) pretence; *sous* ~ *de*, on the pretence of; (fam.) *en faire voir de toutes les* ~*s à qn.*, to lead s.o. a dance.
couleuvre [kulœvr] *s.f.* ~ (*à collier*), grass snake; ~ *lisse*, smooth snake; (fig.) *avaler des* ~*s*, to swallow insults; to believe anything.
couleuvrine [kulœvrin] *s.f.* (anc. mil.) culverin.
coulis [kuli] *s.m.* (cook.) purée; (constr.) grouting; *vent* ~, draught.
coulissant, -e [kulisɑ̃] *adj.* sliding, gliding.
coulisse [kulis] *s.f.* **1.** groove, furrow, slide; *fenêtre, porte, à* ~, sliding window, door; **2.** (dressm.) hem (through which to pass tape); **3.** (theatr.) wings; (fig.) *se tenir dans la* ~, to stay in the background; *les* ~*s de la politique*, the corridors of power; **4.** (fin.) the outside market; **5.** *faire des yeux en* ~, to cast sidelong glances.
coulisseau (pl. **-x**) [kuliso] *s.m.* (techn.) slide, slide-block, runner.
coulissier [kulisje] *s.m.* (fin.) outside broker.
couloir [kulwar] *s.m.* corridor, passage, gangway; (rail., geog.) corridor; (tennis) tramlines.
coulomb [kulɔ̃] *s.m.* (phys.) coulomb.
coulpe [kulp] *s.f.* (obs.) sin; (mod.) *battre sa* ~, to cry 'peccavi'.
coulure [kulyr] *s.f.* **1.** (hort.) abortion, failure; **2.** (metall.) run-out.
coup [ku] *s.m.* **1.** blow, knock, slap, hit; ~ *de pied*, kick; ~ *de fouet*, lash; ~ *de poing*, (boxing) punch; ~ *bas*, (lit. & fig.) blow below the belt; ~ *de bec*, peck; ~ *de griffe*, scratch; *en venir aux* ~*s*, to come to blows; **2.** shot, report (of firearm); *faire* ~ *double*, (fig.) to kill two birds with one stone; **3.** (fig.) blow, shock; (fig.) *tenir le* ~, to bear up; *sous le* ~ *de*, subject to; **4.** movement, stroke; ~ *d'œil*, glance; ~ *de main*, (mil.) sudden attack, (fig.) helping hand; *donner un* ~ *de main*, to lend a hand; ~ *de téléphone*, telephone call; *à* ~ *de*, with the help of; ~ *de tonnerre*, clap of thunder; ~ *de soleil*, sunstroke; **5.** (dice, etc.) throw, move; **6.** drink, draught; **7.** risky action; ~ *de chance*, stroke of luck; *tenter le* ~, to try one's luck; ~ *de tête*, impulsive action; (pop.) *être dans le* ~, to be in the know; *être auxt cent* ~*s* ,to be mad with worry; *faire les quatre cents* ~*s*, to paint the town red; **8.** time, turn; *du premier* ~, at the first attempt; *du même* ~, at the same time; *sur* ~, repeatedly; *sur le* ~, at once; *après* ~, later; *à* ~ *sûr*, for certain; *tout d'un* ~, *tout à* ~, all at once.
coupable [kupabl] *adj.* guilty; ~ *s.m.f.* guilty person; culprit.
coupage [kupaʒ] *s.m.* (of wines, etc.) mixing, watering.
coupant, -e [kupɑ̃] *adj.* (lit. & fig.) cutting, keen, sharp; ~ *s.m.* (cutting) edge.
coup-de-poing [kudpwɛ̃] *s.m.* (pl. *coups-de-poing*) knuckle-duster; (archaeol.) flint weapon.
coupe[1] [kup] *s.f.* (stemmed) wine glass; (stemmed) dish or bowl (for jam, etc.); (sport, etc.) cup, trophy; *il y a loin de la* ~ *aux lèvres*, there's many a slip 'twixt cup and lip.
coupe[2] [kup] *s.f.* **1.** cut, cutting; felling (of trees); cut (of clothes); haircut; cut, shape, (of face,

etc.); ~ *sombre*, selective felling (of trees), (fig.) serious reduction (in staff, etc.); **2.** (drawing) vertical section; **3.** (cards) cut, cutting; **4.** (fig.) *être, tomber, sous la ~ de qn.*, to be in someone's power.
coupé, -e [kupe] *adj.* cut, loose, broken; (herald.) couped; (arch.) *pan ~*, blunted angle; (sport) *balle ~e*, sliced ball.
coupé [kupe] *s.m.* **1.** (transport) coupé; **2.** (dancing) coupée; **3.** (herald.) coupé.
coupe-circuit [kupsirkɥi] *s.m.invar.* (electr.) circuit-breaker.
coupe-coupe [kupkup] *s.m.invar.* machete.
coupée [kupe] *s.f.* (naut.) port (in ship's side).
coupe-feu [kupfø] *s.m.invar.* fire-break.
coupe-file [kupfil] *s.m.invar.* (priority) pass.
coupe-gorge [kupgɔrʒ] *s.m.invar.* death-trap.
coupe-jarret [kupʒarɛ] *s.m.* (pl. *coupe-jarrets*) (obs. exc. iron.) cutthroat, highwayman.
coupe-légumes [kuplegym] *s.m.invar.* vegetable dicer or chopper.
coupellation [kupelɑsjɔ̃] *s.f.* (techn.) cupellation.
coupelle [kupɛl] *s.f.* (techn.) cupel.
coupe-papier [kuppapje] *s.m.invar.* paper-knife.
couper [kupe] *v.t.i.* **1.** to cut, to cut up, to cut off, to excise; (fig., fam.) *~ l'herbe sous les pieds de qn.*, to cut the ground from under someone's feet; *~ les cheveux en quatre*, to split hairs; **2.** to intersect, to cross; **3.** to take a short cut; **4.** to cut short, to interrupt; to withhold; (pop.) *ça vous la coupe!*, that takes your breath away; **5.** to water (wine), to mix (with another liquid); **6.** (tennis, etc.) to slice; **7.** (cards) to cut; **8.** (fam.) *~ à*, to dodge, to shirk; *~ court à*, to cut off short; **se ~** *v.refl.* to cut oneself; (fig., fam.) to give oneself away.
coupe-racines [kuprasin] *s.m.invar.* (agric.) root-slicer.
couperet [kuprɛ] *s.m.* **1.** cleaver, chopper; **2.** blade of the guillotine, the guillotine; **3.** enameller's chaser.
couperose [kuproz] *s.f.* **1.** (obs.) copperas; **2.** acne.
couperosé, -e [kuproze] *adj.* blotchy.
coupeu-r, -se [kupœr] *s.m.f.* cutter; (fig.) *~r de cheveux en quatre*, hair-splitter.
coupe-vent [kupvɑ̃] *s.m.invar.* wind deflector (on rail. engine).
couplage [kuplaʒ] *s.m.* coupling.
couple [kupl] *s.f.* (hunt.) double leash; (obs.) pair, couple; *~ s.m.* **1.** pair, couple (only of a man & a woman); (mech.) couple; **2.** (naut.) rib.
coupler [kuple] *v.t.* to couple, to link together.
couplet [kuplɛ] *s.m.* verse (of song); (pl.) song.
coupleur [kuplœr] *s.m.* (techn.) coupling.
coupoir [kupwar] *s.m.* cutter (tool).
coupole [kupɔl] *s.f.* cupola, dome; *être reçu sous la Coupole*, to be elected to the *Académie française*.
coupon [kupɔ̃] *s.m.* **1.** remnant (of cloth); **2.** (fin.) coupon, dividend warrant; **3.** ticket.
coupure [kupyr] *s.f.* **1.** cut, gash; cut (in text, etc.); interruption (of supply), power cut; (fig.) breach, break; **2.** press cutting; **3.** banknote (of low value).
cour [kur] *s.f.* **1.** yard, courtyard, court; *la ~ des Miracles*, den of thieves, etc.; **2.** (royal) court; circle (of admirers), followers; *faire la ~ à qn.*, to flatter s.o.; *faire la ~ à une femme*, to woo, to pay court to, a woman; **3.** lawcourt, tribunal; *Cour d'Appel*, Appeal Court; *Cour d'Assises*, Assize Court: *Cour des Comptes*, Audit Department.
courage [kuraʒ] *s.m.* **1.** spirit, enthusiasm; *perdre ~*, to lose heart; **2.** courage, bravery, heroism; *prendre son ~ à deux mains*, to pluck up one's courage; **3.** strength of will, hardness of heart.
courageu-x, -se [kuraʒø] *adj.* brave, courageous; **~sement** [kuraʒøzmɑ̃] *adv.* bravely, courageously.
courailler [kurɑje] *v.i.* (fam.) to live it up.
couramment [kuramɑ̃] *adv.* easily, fluently; ordinarily, usually.
courant, -e [kurɑ̃] *adj.* running, flowing; current, present; usual, common; *le 5 ~*, the 5th inst.
courant [kurɑ̃] *s.m.* **1.** current, stream; electric current; *~ d'air*, draught; **2.** course; *dans le ~ du mois*, during the month; *au ~*, informed; *mettre, tenir, qn. au ~ de qch.*, to inform, to keep s.o. informed, about sth.; *se mettre au ~*, to enquire; *au ~ de la plume*, spontaneously.
courante [kurɑ̃t] *s.f.* **1.** (mus.) courante; **2.** (pop.) diarrhoea.
courbaril [kurbaril] *s.m.* (bot.) courbaril, locust tree.
courbatu, -e [kurbaty] *adj.* tired out, exhausted, aching all over; (of a horse) foundered.
courbature [kurbatyr] *s.f.* extreme tiredness, aching in joints; (of a horse) foundering.
courbaturé, -e [kurbatyre] *adj.* worn out.
courbaturer [kurbatyre] *v.t.* to tire out.
courbe [kurb] *s.f.* curve, bend, turn; chart, graph, diagram; *~ de niveau*, contour line; *~ loxodromique*, loxodrome; *~ adj.* curved.
courbé, -e [kurbe] *adj.* curved, bent.
courber [kurbe] *v.t.i.* to curve, to bend, to bow; **se ~** *v.refl.* to bend, to be bent; to bow (down); (fig.) to submit.
courbette [kurbɛt] *s.f.* curvet; (fig.) self-abasement; *faire des ~s*, to fawn, to cringe.
courbure [kurbyr] *s.f.* curvature.
courcaillet [kurkɑjɛ] *s.m.* cry of the quail; decoy imitating this cry.
courçon, courson [kursɔ̃] *s.m.*, **coursonne** [kursɔn] *s.f.* branch (of fruit tree) cut back.
courette [kurɛt] *s.f.* small courtyard.
coureu-r, -se [kurœr] *s.m.f.* runner, racer; *~r, ~se, de haies*, hurdler; *~r, ~se, cycliste*, racing cyclist; *~r, ~se, automobile*, racing driver; **~r** *s.m.* woman chaser; **~se** *s.f.* loose woman.
courge [kurʒ] *s.f.* pumpkin, marrow, gourd; (pop.) idiot.
courgette [kurʒɛt] *s.f.* courgette.
courir [kurir] *v.i.* **1.** to run, to race, to hurry; *~ après qn.*, to chase s.o.; **2.** to run, to flow, to stream; to spread; **3.** (of time) to pass; *par le temps qui court*, at present; *~ v.t.* to hunt; to run (a race); to seek; to frequent, to haunt; (pop.) to get on (someone's) nerves.
courlis [kurli], **courlieu** [kurljø] *s.m.* (ornith.) curlew.
couronne [kurɔn] *s.f.* **1.** crown, wreath (of flowers, etc.); (fig.) prize; **2.** (sovereign's) crown; (fig.) the crown, sovereignty; *discours de la ~*, speech from the throne; **3.** tonsure; **4.** crown-shaped object, ring; (bot.) corona; (vet.) coronet; crown (of tooth); (mech.) crown (of gear, etc.), ring; (mus.) pause sign; **5.** (astron.) corona.
couronné, -e [kurɔne] *adj.* **1.** (of head, etc.) crowned; **2.** prize-winning; **3.** (vet.) broken-kneed.
couronnement [kurɔnmɑ̃] *s.m.* **1.** coronation, crowning; (fig.) completion, perfection, crowning achievement; (arch.) crowning, coping; **2.** (naut.) taffrail; **3.** (vet.) broken knee.
couronner [kurɔne] *v.t.* **1.** to crown; (fig.) to complete, to perfect; **2.** to reward, to award a prize to; **3.** to wound the knee; **se ~** *v.refl.* to graze one's knees.
courre [kur] *v.t.* (infin. only) to hunt; *chasse à ~*, hunt, hunting.
courrier [kurje] *s.m.* **1.** courier, messenger; **2.** mail, post, correspondence; *par retour du ~*, by return of post.

courriériste [kurjerist] *s.m.f.* columnist, (newspaper) critic.
courroie [kurwɑ] *s.f.* strap, thong, belt; ~ *de transmission*, ~ *sans fin*, conveyor belt; ~ *de ventilateur*, (car) fan-belt.
courroucer [kuruse] *v.t.* to anger, to incense.
courroux [kuru] *s.m.* (Lit.) wrath.
cours [kur] *s.m.* **1.** flow, current, course; ~ *d'eau*, watercourse; *donner libre* ~ *à*, to allow to flow freely, to give free rein to; *au, en,* ~ *de*, in the course of, during; *en* ~, in hand, under way; **2.** currency; (Stock Exchange) price; ~ *légal*, legal tender; *avoir* ~, to be legal tender, (fig.) to be in current use; **3.** course of lessons or lectures, lesson; standard, class; textbook; **5.** walk, mall; **6.** *au long* ~, (naut.) transoceanic.
course [kurs] *s.f.* **1.** run, race; *être à bout de* ~, to be exhausted; (fam.) *être dans la* ~, to be with it; **2.** journey, ride, drive; **3.** (usu. pl.) errands, shopping; **4.** (naut.) privateering; **5.** (techn.) stroke (of piston); ⚠ not 'course'.
coursier[1] [kursje] *s.m.* (Lit.) steed.
coursi-er[2], **-ère** [kursje] *s.m.f.* errand boy or girl, messenger.
coursive [kursiv] *s.f.* (naut.) gangway.
courson, coursonne see COURÇON.
court, -e [kur] *adj.* short, brief, scanty; ~ *adv.* short; *couper* ~ *à*, to cut short; *tout* ~, simply, only, that's all, full stop; *prendre qn. de* ~, to catch s.o. unawares; *à* ~ *de*, short of.
court [kur] *s.m.* tennis-court.
courtage [kurtaʒ] *s.m.* **1.** brokerage; **2.** commission.
courtaud, -e [kurto] *adj.* (of dog or horse) docked; (of person) thickset, dumpy.
courtauder [kurtode] *v.t.* to dock (dog or horse).
court-bouillon [kurbujɔ̃] *s.m.* (cook.) court-bouillon.
court-circuit [kursirkɥi] *s.m.* (electr.) short circuit.
court-circuiter [kursirkɥite] *v.t.* (electr., fig., fam.) to short-circuit.
courtepointe [kurtəpwɛ̃t] *s.f.* quilt.
courti-er, -ère [kurtje] *s.m.f.* broker, agent; ⚠ not 'courtier'.
courtine [kurtin] *s.f.* **1.** four-poster curtain; **2.** portière; **3.** (mil.) curtain wall.
courtisan [kurtizɑ̃] *s.m.* courtier; (fig.) flatterer; ~**e** [kurtizan] *s.f.* courtesan; ~**,** ~**e** *adj.* obsequious, fawning.
courtisanerie [kurtizanri] *s.f.* (obs.) flattery (of the great).
courtiser [kurtize] *v.t.* to pay court to, to flatter; to court, to woo.
court-jointé, -e [kurʒwɛ̃te] *adj.* (pl. *court-jointé(e)s*) (of horse) short in the pastern.
courtois, -e [kurtwa] *adj.* courteous, polite; ~**ement** [kurtwazmɑ̃] *adv.* courteously, politely.
courtoisie [kurtwazi] *s.f.* courtesy, courteousness.
court-vêtu, -e [kurvety] *adj.* (pl. *court-vêtu(e)s*) in short skirt(s).
couru, -e [kury] *adj.* popular, fashionable; (fam.) *c'est* ~, it's a cert.
couscous [kuskus] *s.m.* (cook.) couscous.
couseu-r, -se [kuzœr] *s.m.f.* stitcher, sewer, seamstress.
cousin[1], **-e** [kuzɛ̃] *s.m.f.* cousin; ~*(e) germain(e)*, first cousin; ~*s issus de germains*, second cousins.
cousin[2] [kuzɛ̃] *s.m.* gnat, mosquito.
cousinage [kuzinaʒ] *s.m.* kin, family.
cousiner [kuzine] *v.i.* to hob-nob, to be on familiar terms.
coussin [kusɛ̃] *s.m.* cushion, pillow; padding (of harness, etc.).
coussinet [kusinɛ] *s.m.* **1.** small cushion; **2.** (mech.) bearing; **3.** (rail.) chair.
cousu, -e [kuzy] *adj.* sewn, stitched; (fig.) ~ *de fil blanc*, sticking out a mile; *garder bouche* ~*e*, to keep one's lips sealed; *être tout* ~ *d'or*, to be rolling in money; (fam.) ~ *main*, hand-stitched; (pop.) *c'est du* ~ *main*, it's top quality.
coût [ku] *s.m.* cost, price, charge.
coûtant [kutɑ̃] *adj. prix* ~, cost price.
couteau (pl. **-x**) [kuto] *s.m.* knife; (fig.) *être à* ~*x tirés*, to be at daggers drawn; (fig.) *mettre le* ~ *sur (sous) la gorge à qn.*, to hold a knife to someone's throat; ~ *à papier*, paper-knife; ~ *de vitrier*, glazier's knife.
couteau-scie [kutosi] *s.m.* (pl. *couteaux-scies*) knife with serrated edge, bread knife.
coutelas [kutlɑ] *s.m.* cutlass.
couteli-er, -ère [kutəlje] *s.m.f.* cutler.
coutellerie [kutɛlri] *s.f.* cutlery; cutler's (shop); cutlery trade.
coûter [kute] *v.t.i.* to cost, to be a certain price; (fig.) to be difficult, to cause trouble; to be expensive; ~ *les yeux de la tête*, to cost the earth; (fig.) *cela pourrait vous* ~ *cher*, you could pay dearly for that; *coûte que coûte*, at all costs.
coûteu-x, -se [kutø] *adj.* costly, expensive; ~**sement** [kutøzmɑ̃] *adv.* expensively.
coutil [kuti] *s.m.* (text.) twill, drill.
coutre [kutr] *s.m.* coulter.
coutume [kutym] *s.f.* custom, habit, usual practice; customary law; *une fois n'est pas* ~, this is an exception, not to be repeated; *avoir* ~ *de*, to be in the habit of; *de* ~, usual(ly).
coutumi-er, -ère [kutymje] *adj.* (obs.) accustomed to, in the habit of; (mod.) customary, usual, ordinary; *droit* ~*er*, common law; ~**er** *s.m.* customary, collection of customs.
couture [kutyr] *s.f.* **1.** sewing, needlework; dressmaking; **2.** seam; (fig.) *examiner sur toutes les* ~*s*, to inspect carefully; (fig.) *battre à plate(s)* ~*(s)*, to beat hollow; **3.** long scar.
couturé, -e [kutyre] *adj.* scarred.
couturier [kutyrje] *s.m.* **1.** couturier; **2.** (anat.) sartorius (muscle).
couturière [kutyrjɛr] *s.f.* **1.** needlewoman, dressmaker; **2.** (theatr.) pre-dress rehearsal.
couvain [kuvɛ̃] *s.m.* nest of insect eggs; brood comb (of bees).
couvaison [kuvɛzɔ̃] *s.f.* brooding time, sitting time (of birds on eggs).
couvée [kuve] *s.f.* clutch, brood, hatch; (fig., fam.) brood (of children).
couvent [kuvɑ̃] *s.m.* convent, monastery, nunnery; convent school.
couventine [kuvɑ̃tin] *s.f.* **1.** nun; **2.** convent-schoolgirl.
couver [kuve] *v.t.* **1.** to brood, to sit (on eggs), to hatch; to hatch (plot, etc.), to brew; ~ *une maladie*, to be sickening for sth.; **2.** (fig.) ~ *qn.*, to wrap s.o. up in cotton wool; ~ *des yeux*, to look fondly at, to look longingly at; ~ *v.i.* to smoulder; (fig.) to hatch.
couvercle [kuvɛrkl] *s.m.* lid, cover, cap.
couvert [kuvɛr] *s.m.* **1.** lodging, shelter; **2.** cover, shade, protection; covert; (comm.) security, guarantee; *à* ~, under cover, (comm.) guaranteed; *à* ~ *de*, sheltered from; *sous* ~ *de*, under the pretence of; **3.** cover (table requisites), place setting; *mettre le* ~, to lay the table.
couvert, -e [kuvɛr] *adj.* **1.** covered; *ciel* ~, overcast sky; **2.** dressed, clothed; (esp.) wearing a hat; **3.** veiled, disguised, hidden; *à mots* ~*s*, equivocally, ambiguously; **4.** safeguarded, protected, covered.
couverte [kuvɛrt] *s.f.* glaze (on pottery, etc.).
couverture [kuvɛrtyr] *s.f.* **1.** roof, roofing; **2.** covering, tarpaulin, awning; travelling-rug; blanket; (fig.) *amener, tirer, la* ~ *à soi*, to take the lion's share; **3.** cover (of book), dust-jacket; **4.** (obs.) cover, pretence; **5.** guarantee, surety.

couveuse [kuvøz] *s.f.* **1.** sitting or brooding hen; **2.** incubator.
couvi [kuvi] *adj.m.* (of egg) addled.
couvoir [kuvwar] *s.m.* hatchery.
couvrant, -e [kuvrɑ̃] *adj.* covering (completely), enveloping.
couvre-chef [kuvrəʃɛf] *s.m.* (jest) headgear.
couvre-feu [kuvrəfø] *s.m.* (pl. *couvre-feux*) curfew.
couvre-lit [kuvrəli] *s.m.* (pl. *couvre-lits*) bedspread.
couvre-nuque [kuvrənyk] *s.m.* (pl. *couvre--nuques*) neck-flap (of hat, etc.).
couvre-pied(**s**) [kuvrəpje] *s.m.* (pl. *couvre--pieds*) quilt, counterpane, bedcover.
couvre-plat [kuvrəpla] *s.m.* (pl. *couvre-plats*) dish-cover.
couvreur [kuvrœr] *s.m.* tiler, slater, roofer.
couvrir [kuvrir] *v.t.* **1.** to cover, to cover up, to put a cover on; (fig.) to hide, to conceal; to disguise; ~ *un fauteuil*, to put a cover on an armchair; ~ *une carte*, to cover a (playing-)card; *se* ~ *le visage*, to hide one's face; ~ *ses desseins*, to conceal, to disguise, one's intentions; (fig.) ~ *son jeu*, to play a close game, to hold one's cards close to one's chest; ~ *de*, to cover, to flood, with; to scatter with; (fig.) to load, to overwhelm, with; *couvert de neige*, covered with snow; ~ *d'injures*, to heap insults on; **2.** to cover (a distance); **3.** to cover, to protect, to shield; (fin., comm.) to cover, to meet, (costs, etc.); to guarantee (payment of); to refund; to re--imburse (s.o.); ~ *un emprunt*, to guarantee a loan; *prière de nous* ~ *par chèque*, your remittance will oblige; ~ *les frais de port*, to refund postage, carriage; **4.** (of male animal) to cover (the female); **se** ~ *v.refl.* to become covered, filled, (*de*, with); (of sky) to cloud over; to wrap (oneself) up; (esp.) to put one's hat on; (fig.) to cover oneself (*de*, with, in); to shelter, to take refuge, (*de*, in, behind).
covalence [kɔvalɑ̃s] *s.f.* (sci.) covalence, covalency.
covenant [kɔvnɑ̃] *s.m.* (Scottish hist.) Covenant.
covendeur [kɔvɑ̃dœr] *s.m.* (law) co-vendor.
cow-boy [kawbɔj, kobɔj] *s.m.* cowboy.
coxal, -e, (**aux**) [kɔksal] *adj.* (anat.) coxal.
coxalgie [kɔksalʒi] *s.f.* (med.) coxalgia.
coyau [kɔjo] *s.m.* (techn.) furring (of roof timbers).
coyote [kɔjɔt] *s.m.* (zool.) coyote.
c.q.f.d. [sekyɛfde] abbrev. *ce qu'il fallait démontrer* = Q.E.D.
crabe [krɑb] *s.m.* **1.** crab; (fig.) *panier de* ~*s*, bunch of spiteful people; **2.** caterpillar tractor; **3.** (pop.) idiot.
crabier [krɑbje] *s.m.* (ornith.) squacco (heron).
crac [krak] *interj.* bang!, crack!
crachat [kraʃa] *s.m.* **1.** spit, spittle; (fig.) *se noyer dans un* ~, to give up at the first sign of difficulty; **2.** (fig., fam.) decoration (of an order).
craché, -e [kraʃe] *adj. tout(e)* ~*(e)*, the dead spit of.
crachement [kraʃmɑ̃] *s.m.* spitting; (fig.) sparking, spluttering; crackling (of loudspeaker).
cracher [kraʃe] *v.t.i.* **1.** to spit; to sputter, to crackle; (fig., fam.) ~ *sur qch.*, to scorn sth.; *ne pas* ~ *sur*, to be fond of; **2.** (fig., fam.) to pay, to fork out.
crachin [kraʃɛ̃] *s.m.* drizzle.
crachiner [kraʃine] *v.i.* to drizzle.
crachoir [kraʃwar] *s.m.* spittoon; (fig., fam.) *tenir le* ~, to hold forth; *tenir le* ~ *à qn.*, to listen to s.o. without getting in a word.
crachotement [kraʃɔtmɑ̃] *s.m.* sputtering, spluttering; (radio) crackling.
crachoter [kraʃɔte] *v.i.* to sputter, to splutter; (radio) to crackle.
crack [krak] *s.m.* **1.** (racing) favourite colt or foal; **2.** (fam.) crack, expert.
cracking [krakiŋ] *s.m.* cracking (of petroleum).
Cracovie [krakɔvi] *s.f.* (geog.) Cracow.
craie [krɛ] *s.f.* chalk.
crailler [kraje] *v.i.* (of rook) to caw.
craindre [krɛ̃dr] *v.t.* to fear, to be afraid of; (of perishable goods) to be susceptible of damage by.
crainte [krɛ̃t] *s.f.* fear; *dans la* ~ *de*, ~ *de*, for fear of; *de* ~ *que*, lest, for fear that.
crainti-f, -ve [krɛ̃tif] *adj.* fearful, timorous, nervous; ~**vement** [krɛ̃tivmɑ̃] *adv.* timorously, nervously.
crambe [krɑ̃b], **crambé** [krɑ̃be] *s.m.* (bot.) seakale.
cramer [krame] *v.t.* to singe; ~ *v.i.* (pop.) to go up in smoke.
cramoisi, -e [kramwazi] *adj.* crimson.
crampe [krɑ̃p] *s.f.* cramp.
crampillon [krɑ̃pijɔ̃] *s.m.* (techn.) staple.
crampon [krɑ̃pɔ̃] *s.m.* **1.** crampon; stud (in boot); **2.** (bot.) sucker (of ivy, etc.); (fam.) (of person) limpet, bore; *qu'il est* ~*!*, how he clings!, he sticks like a leech!
cramponnement [krɑ̃pɔnmɑ̃] *s.m.* clinging.
cramponner [krɑ̃pɔne] *v.t.* **1.** (techn.) to cramp; **2.** (fig.) to cling to, to bore; **se** ~ *v.refl.* to cling, to stick, (to).
cramponnet [krɑ̃pɔnɛ] *s.m.* (techn.) staple (of lock).
cran [krɑ̃] *s.m.* **1.** nick, notch; *monter, avancer, baisser, d'un* ~, to go up or down a peg; **2.** catch (of gun); ~ *d'arrêt*, safety-catch; **3.** (fam.) pluck, spirit, guts, cheek.
crâne [krɑn] *s.m.* skull, cranium; head; (fig.) mind, intellect.
crâne [krɑn] *adj.* (obs.) mettlesome, spirited; ~**ment** [krɑnmɑ̃] *adv.* boldly, bravely.
craner [krane] *v.t.* = CRANTER.
crâner [krɑne] *v.i.* (fam.) to swagger, to put on a jaunty air.
crânerie [krɑnri] *s.f.* (obs.) bravado.
crâneu-r, -se [krɑnœr] *s.m.f.* swaggerer, braggart; *adj.* boastful, pretentious.
crânien, -ne [krɑnjɛ̃] *adj.* (anat.) cranial.
craniologie [kranjɔlɔʒi] *s.f.* craniology.
cranter [krɑ̃te] *v.t.* (techn.) to cog (wheel, etc.).
crapaud [krapo] *s.m.* **1.** toad; **2.** flaw (in diamond, etc.); **3.** *fauteuil* ~, low armchair; *piano* ~, baby-grand piano.
crapaudine [krapodin] *s.f.* **1.** toadstone; **2.** (cook.) *à la* ~, split in two and grilled; **3.** (techn.) socket (of hinge), collar; **4.** grating (of drain).
crapouillot [krapujo] *s.m.* trench-mortar (in 1914–18 war).
crapoussin, -e [krapusɛ̃] *s.m.f.* (fam.) runt.
crapule [krapyl] *s.f.* (obs.) debauchery; (obs.) riff-raff; (mod.) blackguard, scoundrel.
crapulerie [krapylri] *s.f.* blackguardly tricks.
crapuleu-x, -se [krapylø] *adj.* (obs.) dissolute; (Lit.) low, dishonest; ~**sement** [krapyløzmɑ̃] *adv.* in a blackguardly way.
craquage [krakaʒ] *s.m.* cracking (of petroleum).
craque [krak] *s.f.* (pop.) whopper, tale, tall story.
craquelage [kraklaʒ] *s.m.* crackling (of porcelain).
craqueler [krakle] *v.t.* to crackle (china, etc.); to fissure (land).
craquelin [kraklɛ̃] *s.m.* cracknel.
craquelure [kraklyr] *s.f.* crackling, crazing, appearance of small cracks.
craquement [krakmɑ̃] *s.m.* crack, cracking, creak, crunch.

craquer [krake] *v.i.* to crack, to crackle, to snap; (fig.) to give way, to break up; *plein à* ~, full to bursting; ~ *v.t.* to crack (petroleum).
craquètement [krakɛtmɑ̃] *s.m.* **1.** (med.) chattering (of teeth); **2.** gabbling (of stork).
craqueter [krakte] *v.i.* **1.** to crackle; **2.** (of stork) to gabble.
crase [krɑz] *s.f.* (lang., med.) crasis.
crasse [kras] *s.f.* filth; dross (of metal); *faire une* ~ *à qn.*, to play a dirty trick on s.o.; ~ *adj.f.* crass.
crasseu-x, -se [krasø] *adj.* filthy, dirty.
crassier [krasje] *s.m.* slag-heap.
crassule [krasyl] *s.f.* (bot.) stonecrop.
cratère [kratɛr] *s.m.* **1.** crater; **2.** (Gr. ant.) crater, mixing-bowl.
cravache [kravaʃ] *s.f.* hunting-crop; horse--whip.
cravacher [kravaʃe] *v.t.* to whip, to horsewhip; to flog (a horse to go faster); (fam.) to race, to speed.
cravate [kravat] *s.f.* tie, necktie; ~ *de chanvre*, hangman's rope.
cravater [kravate] *v.t.* **1.** to put a tie on (s.o.); **2.** to throttle; **3.** (pop.) to stuff full of lies.
crave [krav] *s.m.* (ornith.) chough.
crawl [krol] *s.m.* (swimming) crawl.
crawler [krole] *v.i.* (swimming) to crawl.
crayeu-x, -se [krɛjø] *adj.* chalky; (geol.) cretaceous.
crayon [krɛjɔ̃] *s.m.* **1.** pencil, crayon; ~ *en métal*, propelling pencil; ~ *à bille*, ball point pen; **2.** pencil, stick; ~ *hémostatique*, styptic pencil; ~ *de rouge à lèvres*, lipstick; ~ *à sourcils*, eyebrow pencil; **3.** pencil drawing.
crayonnage [krɛjɔnaʒ] *s.m.* pencil drawing.
crayonner [krɛjɔne] *v.t.* to pencil; to doodle; (fig.) to sketch.
créance [kreɑ̃s] *s.f.* **1.** credence; **2.** credit, belief, (rare except in) *trouver* ~, to be believed; *donner* ~ *à*, to lend credence to; **3.** (law) claim.
créanci-er, -ère [kreɑ̃sje] *s.m.f.* creditor.
créat-eur, -rice [kreatœr] *s.m.f.* creator, inventor, originator, maker, manufacturer; *adj.* creative.
création [kreɑsjɔ̃] *s.f.* creation, making, foundation, production.
créature [kreatyr] *s.f.* **1.** creature; **2.** (fig.) creature, stooge, puppet.
crécelle [kresɛl] *s.f.* rattle; (fig.) chattering; raucous chatterbox; *voix de* ~, corncrake voice.
crécerelle [kresrɛl] *s.f.* (ornith.) kestrel.
crèche [krɛʃ] *s.f.* **1.** (obs.) manger, food trough; **2.** the Manger, crib, crèche; **3.** day-nursery, crèche; **4.** (pop.) room, house.
crécher [kreʃe] *v.i.* (pop.) to live, to doss down.
crédence [kredɑ̃s] *s.f.* credence (table).
crédibilité [kredibilite] *s.f.* credibility.
crédirenti-er, -ère [kredirɑ̃tje] *s.m.f.* annuitant.
crédit [kredi] *s.m.* **1.** (obs.) trust; repute, authority; **2.** (comm., fin.) credit; *à* ~, on credit; **3.** bank; ~ *foncier*, building society; ~ *municipal*, pawnshop.
créditer [kredite] *v.t.* to credit (an account).
crédit-eur, -rice [kreditœr] *s.m.f.* person whose account is credited; *adj.* (of balance, etc.) credit; ⚠ not 'creditor' to whom money is owed.
credo [kredo] *s.m.* creed.
crédule [kredyl] *adj.* credulous; **~ment** [kredylmɑ̃] *adv.* credulously.
crédulité [kredylite] *s.f.* credulity, credulousness.
créer [kree] *v.t.* to create, to make.
crémaillère [kremajɛr] *s.f.* **1.** pot-hook; *pendre la* ~, to hold a house-warming party; **2.** (techn.) toothed rack; notched upright (in adjustable chair, bookshelves, etc.).
crémant [kremɑ̃] *adj.*, *s.m.* slightly sparkling (wine).
crémation [kremɑsjɔ̃] *s.f.* cremation.
crématoire [krematwar] *adj.* crematory; ~ *s.m.* crematorium.
crème [krɛm] *s.f.* (lit. & fig.) cream; custard; ~ *adj. invar.* cream-coloured.
crémer [kreme] *v.i.* to form a cream; *v.t.* to dye cream-coloured.
crémerie [krɛmri] *s.f.* dairy, creamery; café.
crémeu-x, -se [kremø] *adj.* creamy.
crémi-er, -ère [kremje] *s.m.f.* dairyman, dairy-woman.
crémone [kremɔn] *s.f.* window-fastening.
créneau (pl. **-x**) [kreno] *s.m.* crenel, loophole.
crénelage [krɛnlaʒ] *s.m.* milling (on edge of coin).
crénelé, -e [krɛnle] *adj.* crenellated; (bot., zool.) crenate.
créneler [krɛnle] *v.t.* **1.** to crenellate; **2.** to mill (coins); **3.** to cog, to notch.
crénelure [krɛnlyr] *s.f.* crenature.
créner [krene] *v.t.* (print.) to nick (shank of type).
créole [kreɔl] *adj.*, *s.m.f.* Creole.
créosote [kreozɔt] *s.f.* creosote.
crêpage [krɛpaʒ] *s.m.* crimping (of material, hair, etc.); (fam.) ~ *de chignon*, fight between women.
crêpe[1] [krɛp] *s.f.* pancake.
crêpe[2] [krɛp] *s.m.* crêpe (material or rubber); crape, mourning band.
crêpelé, -e [krɛple] *adj.* (of hair) frizzy.
crêpelure [krɛplyr] *s.f.* frizziness (of hair).
crêper [krepe] *v.t.* to frizz, to back-comb, (hair); *se* ~ *le chignon*, (of women) to tear each other's hair out.
crépi [krepi] *s.m.* (build.) roughcast.
crêpi-er, -ère [krepje] *s.m.f.* pancake seller.
crépine [krepin] *s.f.* **1.** passementerie, trimming; **2.** caul (of veal, pork); **3.** strainer (over pipe, etc.).
crépinette [krepinɛt] *s.f.* crépinette, flat sausage.
crépir [krepir] *v.t.* (build.) to roughcast.
crépissage [krepisaʒ] *s.m.* (build.) rough-casting.
crépitation [krepitɑsjɔ̃] *s.f.* crackling; (med.) crepitus.
crépitement [krepitmɑ̃] *s.m.* crackling.
crépiter [krepite] *v.i.* to crackle; (of applause) to ripple.
crépon [krepɔ̃] *s.m.* thick crêpe.
crépu, -e [krepy] *adj.* woolly(-haired).
crépusculaire [krepyskylɛr] *adj.* crepuscular, twilight.
crépuscule [krepyskyl] *s.m.* (obs.) dawn; (mod.) dusk, twilight; (fig.) decline.
crescendo [kreʃɛndo, kreʃɛ̃do] *adv.*, *s.m.invar.* crescendo.
crésol [krezɔl] *s.m.* (chem.) cresol.
cresson [kresɔ̃] *s.m.* cress, watercress.
cressonnette [kresɔnɛt] *s.f.* (bot.) lady's smock, cuckoo flower.
cressonnière [kresɔnjɛr] *s.f.* watercress bed.
Crésus [krezys] *s.m.* Croesus.
crêt [krɛ] *s.m.* ridge, escarpment.
crétacé, -e [kretase] *adj.* cretaceous; (geol.) Cretaceous.
Crète [krɛt] *s.f.* (geog.) Crete.
crête [krɛt] *s.f.* **1.** cock's comb; **2.** crest, peak, (of mountain or wave); top, ridge, (of wall, of roof); watershed; (fig.) peak.
crêté, -e [krete] *adj.* crested.
crête-de-coq [krɛtdəkɔk] *s.f.* (pl. *crêtes-de-coq*) (bot.) cockscomb.
crétin, -e [kretɛ̃] *s.m.f.* cretin, fool; *adj.* cretinous.
crétinerie [kretinri] *s.f.* idiotic action.

crétinisant, -e [kretinizɑ̃] *adj.* stupefying, deadening.
crétiniser [kretinize] *v.t.* to make stupid, to dull the wits of.
crétinisme [kretinism] *s.m.* **1.** (pathol.) cretinism; **2.** idiocy.
crétois, -e [kretwa] *adj., s.m.f.* Cretan.
cretonne [krətɔn] *s.f.* (text.) cretonne.
creusage [krøzaʒ], **creusement** [krøzmɑ̃] *s.m.* digging, deepening, sinking (of a well).
creuser [krøze] *v.t.* **1.** to dig, to excavate, to hollow out; (fig.) *se ~ la tête*, to rack one's brains; *~ l'estomac*, to make hungry; **2.** to deepen, to sink (a well); **3.** (fig.) to study in depth; **se ~** *v.refl.* to become hollow, to become deeper.
creuset [krøzɛ] *s.m.* crucible; (lit. & fig.) melting pot.
creu-x, -se [krø] *adj.* hollow, concave; (fig.) hollow, shallow; *heures ~ses*, spare time, off-peak period; *sonner ~x*, to sound hollow.
creux [krø] *s.m.* hollow, cavity; void; trough (of wave); pit (of stomach); *avoir un ~ dans l'estomac*, to be hungry; *avoir un bon ~*, to have a good deep voice.
crevaison [krəvɛzɔ̃] *s.f.* **1.** burst, puncture; **2.** (fig., pop.) death.
crevant, -e [krəvɑ̃] *adj.* (pop.) killing (=tiring); killing (=funny).
crevard [krəvar] *s.m., adj.* (pop.) very sick (man), (man) on his last legs.
crevasse [krəvas] *s.f.* crevice, fissure, crack, cleft; crevasse; *avoir des ~s aux mains*, to have chapped hands.
crevasser [krəvase] *v.t.* to crack, to fissure; to chap (hands); **se ~** *v.refl.* to crack.
crève [krɛv] *s.f.* (pop.) death; *attraper la ~*, to catch one's death.
crevé, -e [krəve] *adj.* **1.** burst, punctured, torn; (fam.) exhausted; **2.** (of animal, plant) dead; (pop. of person) dead; *~ s.m.* (costume) slash (in sleeves).
crève-cœur [krɛvkœr] *s.m.invar.* heartbreak.
crève-la-faim [krɛvlafɛ̃] *s.m.invar.* starving person.
crever [krəve] *v.i.* **1.** to burst; *~ de*, to be bursting with; **2.** (of plants, animals) to die; (pop. of people) to die; *~ v.t.* **1.** to burst, to split; *~ le cœur à qn.*, to break someone's heart; **2.** *~ les yeux*, to be staring one in the face; **3.** (fig.) to work to death; (fig., fam.) to kill; **se ~** *v.refl.* (fig.) to kill oneself; *se ~ au travail*, to kill oneself with work.
crevette [krəvɛt] *s.f.* shrimp.
crevettier [krəvetje] *s.m.* **1.** shrimping net; **2.** shrimping boat.
C-R.F. [seɛrɛf] abbrev. *Croix-rouge française*, French Red Cross.
cri [kri] *s.m.* cry, shout, yell; outcry; *le dernier ~*, the last word in fashion.
criaillement [kriɑjmɑ̃] *s.m.* bawling, screaming; whining.
criailler [kriɑje] *v.i.* **1.** (of pheasants, etc.) to scream; **2.** to grouse, to whine.
criaillerie [kriɑjri] *s.f.* grousing, whining.
criant, -e [krijɑ̃] *adj.* (fig.) crying, glaring.
criard, -e [krijar] *adj.* whining, screaming, piercing; (of colour) loud, gaudy; (of debts) pressing.
criblage [kriblaʒ] *s.m.* sifting, screening.
crible [kribl] *s.m.* sieve, screen; (fig.) *passer au ~*, to sift out, to screen.
cribler [krible] *v.t.* **1.** to sift, to screen; **2.** to pepper, to riddle; *être criblé*, to be riddled, (pock-)marked, scarred; (fig.) *criblé de dettes*, head over ears in debt.
cribleu-r, -se [kriblœr] *s.m.f.* sifter, screener; *~se s.f.* sifting machine.
criblure [kriblyr] *s.f.* siftings, screenings.
cric [krik] *s.m.* (mech.) jack.
cricket [krikɛt] *s.m.* (sport) cricket.
cricoïde [krikɔid] *adj., s.m.* (anat.) cricoid.
cri-cri [krikri] *s.m.invar.* sound made by cricket; (ent.) cricket.
criée [krije] *s.f.* sale by auction.
crier [krije] *v.t.i.* to cry, to shout, to yell; to creak, to squeak; to complain, to protest, to proclaim; to offer for sale.
crieu-r, -se [krijœr] *s.m.f.* hawker; town crier.
crime [krim] *s.m.* crime, offence.
Crimée [krime] *s.f.* (geog.) Crimea.
criminaliser [kriminalize] *v.t.* (law) to refer (a case) to a criminal court.
criminaliste [kriminalist] *s.m.f.* criminal lawyer.
criminalité [kriminalite] *s.f.* **1.** (rare) criminality; **2.** crime (as general term); criminals.
criminel, -le [kriminɛl] *adj.* criminal; *s.m.f.* criminal, offender, culprit; **~lement** [kriminɛlmɑ̃] *adv.* **1.** criminally; **2.** in a criminal court.
criminologie [kriminɔlɔʒi] *s.f.* criminology.
criminologiste [kriminɔlɔʒist] *s.m.f.* criminologist.
crin [krɛ̃] *s.m.* horsehair; (fig.) *à tous ~s, à tout ~*, out and out, thorough-going; *être comme un ~*, to be irritable; *un ~*, a bad-tempered person.
crincrin [krɛ̃krɛ̃] *s.m.* (fam.) scratchy fiddle.
crinière [krinjɛr] *s.f.* mane (of animal); (fam.) mane, shock of hair.
crinoline [krinɔlin] *s.f.* crinoline.
crique [krik] *s.f.* creek, cove.
criquet [krikɛ] *s.m.* (ent.) cricket, locust.
crise [kriz] *s.f.* crisis; sudden attack, fit.
crispant, -e [krispɑ̃] *adj.* maddening.
crispation [krispɑsjɔ̃] *s.f.* **1.** shrivelling (of surface); **2.** twitch (of muscles); **3.** (fam.) irritation.
crisper [krispe] *v.t.* **1.** to shrivel; **2.** to contract, to draw together; **3.** (fig., fam.) to get on (someone's) nerves.
crispin [krispɛ̃] *s.m.* **1.** (theatr.) manservant, valet (of comedy); **2.** leather gauntlet.
criss [kris] *s.m.* kris.
crissement [krismɑ̃] *s.m.* grating, grinding (of teeth); crunching (of gravel, etc.).
crisser [krise] *v.i.* to grate, to grind.
cristal (pl. **aux**) [kristal] *s.m.* (min.) crystal; *~ d'Islande*, Iceland spar; (pl.) (fam.) washing soda.
cristallerie [kristalri] *s.f.* glass works; glassware.
cristallin, -e [kristalɛ̃] *adj.* crystalline; *~ s.m.* (anat.) crystalline lens.
cristallisable [kristalizabl] *adj.* crystallizable.
cristallisant, -e [kristalizɑ̃] *adj.* crystallizing.
cristallisation [kristalizɑsjɔ̃] *s.f.* crystallization.
cristallisé, -e [kristalize] *adj.* crystallized, candied.
cristalliser [kristalize] *v.t.i.* to crystallize.
cristallisoir [kristalizwar] *s.m.* evaporating dish.
cristallo-génie [kristalɔʒeni] *s.f.* study of crystallization; **~graphie** [kristalɔgrafi] *s.f.* crystallography; **~graphique** [kristalɔgrafik] *adj.* crystallographic.
cristalloïde [kristalɔid] *adj., s.m.* crystalloid.
criste-marine [kristəmarin] *s.f.* = CRITHME.
critère [kritɛr] *s.m.* criterion.
critérium [kriterjɔm] *s.m.* (sport) eliminating heat, qualifying round; (obs.) criterion.
crithme [kritm] *s.m.* (bot.) Crithmum, rock samphire.
criticailler [kritikɑje] *v.i.* (fam.) to carp, to find fault.
criticisme [kritisism] *s.m.* critical philosophy (of Kant).
critiquable [kritikabl] *adj.* open to criticism.

critique [kritik] *adj.* critical.
critique [kritik] *s.f.* criticism; critique, review; ~ *s.m.* critic.
critiquer [kritike] *v.t.* to criticize.
critiqueur [kritikœr] *s.m.* fault-finder.
croassement [krɔasmɑ̃] *s.m.* cawing (of rooks or crows); croaking (of ravens).
croasser [krɔase] *v.i.* to caw, to croak.
croc [kro] *s.m.* **1.** hook; *moustache en* ~, curled-up moustache; **2.** tusk, fang; (fig., fam.) *avoir les* ~*s*, to be hungry.
croc-en-jambe [krɔkɑ̃ʒɑ̃b] *s.m.* (pl. *crocs-en-jambe*) (lit. & fig.) tripping (up).
croche [krɔʃ] *s.f.* (mus.) quaver; *double, triple, quadruple,* ~, semiquaver, demi-semiquaver, semi-demi-semiquaver.
crochet [krɔʃɛ] *s.m.* **1.** hook; (fig.) *vivre aux* ~*s de qn.*, to sponge on s.o.; **2.** crochet hook; crochet (work); **3.** fang (of snakes, etc.); **4.** (print.) brackets; **5.** sharp bend (in road), detour; **6.** (boxing, etc.) hook.
crochetable [krɔʃtabl] *adj.* (of lock) that can be picked.
crocheter [krɔʃte] *v.t.* to pick (a lock), to pick (rags, etc.).
crocheteur [krɔʃtœr] *s.m.* **1.** picklock; **2.** (obs.) porter.
crochu, -e [krɔʃy] *adj.* hooked; *avoir les mains* ~*es*, to be grasping.
crocodile [krɔkɔdil] *s.m.* **1.** (zool.) crocodile; **2.** (rail.) detonator.
crocus [krɔkys] *s.m.* (bot.) crocus.
croire [krwar] *v.t.i.* to believe, to think; *en* ~ *qn.*, to believe what s.o. says; *à l'en* ~, according to him *or* her; *il est à* ~ *que*, it is possible that; ~ *à qch.*, to believe sth. to be true or possible; ~ *en qch.*, to accept sth. (spiritually); ~ *en qn.*, to have faith in s.o.; ~ *en Dieu*, to believe in God.
croisade [krwazad] *s.f.* (hist.) crusade; (fig.) crusade, campaign.
croisé [krwaze] *s.m.* **1.** crusader; **2.** (text.) twill.
croisé, -e [krwaze] *adj.* crossed; (fig.) *rester les bras* ~*s*, to stand idle; (of coat) double-breasted; (of rhyme) alternate; crossbred; (text.) twilled.
croisée [krwaze] *s.f.* **1.** intersection, crossroads; **2.** casement window.
croisement [krwazmɑ̃] *s.m.* crossing; intersection, crossroads; cross-breeding.
croiser [krwaze] *v.t.* **1.** to cross, to lay or put across; **2.** to meet, to pass; **3.** to cross (animals, plants); ~ *v.i.* **1.** to lap over; **2.** (naut.) to cruise; **se** ~ *v.refl.* **1.** to cross, to intersect; **2.** to pass, to meet; **3.** to be crossed with; **4.** to join a crusade.
croisette [krwazɛt] *s.f.* **1.** (herald.) crosslet; **2.** (bot.) crosswort, bedstraw.
croiseur [krwazœr] *s.m.* (nav.) cruiser.
croisière [krwazjɛr] *s.f.* cruise.
croisillon [krwazijɔ̃] *s.m.* **1.** arm of cross; **2.** transept; **3.** crossbar (of window); (pl.) lattice.
croissance [krwasɑ̃s] *s.f.* growth.
croissant [krwasɑ̃] *s.m.* **1.** crescent; **2.** (cook.) croissant.
croissant, -e [krwasɑ̃] *adj.* growing, increasing.
croît [krwa] *s.m.* (agric., law) natural increase in herd or flock.
croître [krwatr] *v.i.* to grow, to increase.
croix [krwa] *s.f.* cross; (fig.) *la* ~ *et la bannière*, an almighty fuss.
cromlech [krɔmlɛk] *s.m.* cromlech (stone circle).
cromorne [krɔmɔrn] *s.m.* (mus.) krummhorn.
croquant [krɔkɑ̃] *s.m.* (pej.) peasant.
croquant, -e [krɔkɑ̃] *adj.* crisp, crunchy.
(**à la**) **croque au sel** [alakrɔkosɛl] *adv.loc.* (cook.) raw, with only salt added.
croque-mitaine [krɔkmitɛn] *s.m.* bogyman, ogre.
croque-monsieur [krɔkməsjø] *s.m.invar.* (cook.) toasted sandwich.
croque-mort [krɔkmɔr] *s.m.* (pl. *croque-morts*) (fam.) undertaker's mute.
croquenot [krɔkno] *s.m.* (pop.) heavy shoe.
croquer [krɔke] *v.t.i.* **1.** to crunch, to scrunch; (obs.) to devour, to eat up; ~ *de l'argent*, to spend freely; ~ *le marmot*, to cool one's heels; **2.** to sketch; *joli, mignon, à* ~, pretty as a picture.
croquet[1] [krɔkɛ] *s.m.* crisp almond biscuit.
croquet[2] [krɔkɛ] *s.m.* (game) croquet.
croquet[3] [krɔkɛ] *s.m.* (dressm., etc.) toothed edging.
croquette [krɔkɛt] *s.f.* (cook.) croquette.
croqueu-r, -se [krɔkœr] *s.m.f.* great eater; (fig., fam.) ~*se de diamants*, (of woman) gold-digger.
croquignole [krɔkiɲɔl] *s.f.* cracknel.
croquignolet, -te [krɔkiɲɔlɛ] *adj.* (fam.) dainty.
croquis [krɔki] *s.m.* sketch, outline.
croskill [krɔskil] *s.m.* (agric.) toothed roller.
crosne [kron] *s.m.* (hort.) Japanese artichoke.
cross-country [krɔskuntri], (fam.) **cross** [krɔs] *s.m.* (sport) cross-country race or racing.
crosse [krɔs] *s.f.* **1.** crosier, crozier; **2.** golf-club, hockey stick, lacrosse stick; **3.** scroll (of violin); **4.** (anat.) arch (of aorta); **5.** knuckle (of beef); **6.** butt (of gun); **7.** (pop.) *chercher des* ~*s à qn.*, to pick a quarrel with s.o.
crossé [krɔse] *adj.m.* (eccles.) crosiered.
crosser [krɔse] *v.t.* **1.** (rare) to hit (with stick, etc.); **2.** (obs.) to bully.
crossette [krɔsɛt] *s.f.* (hort.) layer, slip.
crotale [krɔtal] *s.m.* **1.** (ant.) crotalum, castanet; **2.** rattle-snake.
croton [krɔtɔ̃] *s.m.* (bot.) croton.
crotte [krɔt] *s.f.* **1.** dung; (obs.) mud, dirt; (fam.) ~ *de bique*, something worthless; **2.** ~ *de chocolat*, chocolate drop.
crotter [krɔte] *v.t.* (obs.) to spatter with mud, to make filthy; **se** ~ *v.refl.* to get dirty, to get covered with mud.
crottin [krɔtɛ̃] *s.m.* horse dung.
croulant, -e [krulɑ̃] *adj.* crumbling, ruinous; ~ *s.m.* (pop.) square, fuddy-duddy.
croule [krul] *s.f.* woodcock shooting.
crouler [krule] *v.i.* (lit. & fig.) to collapse, to crumble.
croup [krup] *s.m.* croup.
croupe [krup] *s.f.* **1.** hindquarters, rump; (fam.) behind, buttocks; *monter en* ~, to ride pillion; **2.** knoll.
(**à**) **croupetons** [akruptɔ̃] *adv.* squatting, on one's haunches.
croupi, -e [krupi] *adj.* (of water) stagnant.
croupier [krupje] *s.m.* croupier.
croupière [krupjɛr] *s.f.* **1.** crupper; **2.** (fig.) *tailler des* ~*s à qn.*, to spike someone's guns.
croupion [krupjɔ̃] *s.m.* parson's nose (of cooked fowl); (fam.) rump; (hist.) *le Parlement* ~, the Rump Parliament.
croupir [krupir] *v.i.* **1.** (of persons) to wallow, to rot; **2.** (of water) to stagnate.
croupissant, -e [krupisɑ̃] *adj.* stagnant.
croupon [krupɔ̃] *s.m.* ox-hide.
croustade [krustad] *s.f.* (cook.) croustade.
croustillant, -e [krustijɑ̃] *adj.* crunchy; (fig.) spicy, racy.
croustiller [krustije] *v.i.* to crunch, to be crunchy.
croûte [krut] *s.f.* **1.** crust; (fig., pop.) *casser la* ~, to eat, to have a bite; *gagner sa* ~, to earn one's daily bread; **2.** pastry case; **3.** scab; **4.** daub; **5.** (fig., fam.) old fogey.
croûter [krute] *v.i.* (pop.) to eat.
croûteu-x, -se [krutø] *adj.* scabby.

croûton [krutɔ̃] *s.m.* crust (end) of bread; crouton, sippet; (fig.) fogey.
crown-glass [krawnglas] *s.m.* crown glass.
croyable [krwajabl] *adj.* credible, believable.
croyance [krwajɑ̃s] *s.f.* belief, faith, creed.
croyant, -e [krwajɑ̃] *adj.* religious; *s.m.f.* believer; *les ~s*, the Muslims, the Faithful.
C.R.S. [seɛrɛs] abbrev. *Compagnies républicaines de sécurité*, police riot squads.
cru [kry] *s.m.* **1.** (obs.) local produce; region; **2.** vineyard, vintage; **3.** *de son propre ~*, off one's own bat.
cru, -e [kry] *adj.* raw, uncooked; untreated, unprocessed; crude, rude; *tout ~*, bluntly; *monter à ~*, to ride bareback; *bâtir à ~*, to build without foundations.
cruauté [kryote] *s.f.* cruelty.
cruche [kryʃ] *s.f.* pitcher, jug; (fam.) silly fool.
cruchon [kryʃɔ̃] *s.m.* small jug, cruse.
crucial, -e, (aux) [krysjal] *adj.* **1.** cruciate; **2.** crucial, decisive.
crucifère [krysifɛr] *adj.* cruciferous; *~s s.f.pl.* (bot.) Cruciferae.
crucifié, -e [krysifje] *s.m. le Crucifié*, the Crucified (i.e. Christ); *adj.* crucified; (fig.) tortured.
crucifiement [krysifimɑ̃] *s.m.* crucifixion; (relig.) mortification.
crucifier [krysifje] *v.t.* to crucify; to mortify.
crucifix [krysifi] *s.m.* crucifix.
crucifixion [krysifiksjɔ̃] *s.f.* crucifixion.
cruciforme [krysifɔrm] *adj.* cruciform.
cruciverbiste [krysivɛrbist] *s.m.f.* crossword addict.
crude ammoniac [krudamɔnjak] *s.m.* (agric.) ammonium sulphate (fertilizer).
crudité [krydite] *s.f.* **1.** (rare) rawness; (pl.) raw, uncooked, food; **2.** (fig.) harshness, crudeness.
crue [kry] *s.f.* rise (in level of water), flood.
cruel, -le [kryɛl] *adj.* cruel, bloodthirsty; grievous, painful; **~lement** [kryɛlmɑ̃] *adv.* cruelly; grievously.
cruenté, -e [kryɑ̃te] *adj.* (med., of wound) gory, bloody, raw.
crûment [krymɑ̃] *adv.* crudely, bluntly, harshly.
cruor [kryɔr] *s.m.* (physiol.) coagulated blood.
crural, -e, (aux) [kryral] *adj.* (anat.) crural.
crustacé, -e [krystase] *adj.* (obs.) crustaceous; *~s s.m.pl.* Crustaceae, crustaceans.
cryo-gène [krijɔʒɛn] *adj.* (phys.) cryogenic; *mélange ~gène*, freezing mixture; **~génie** [krijɔʒeni] *s.f.* cryogeny; **~lithe** [krijɔlit] *s.f.* (min.) cryolite; **~métrie** [krijɔmetri] *s.f.* (phys.) cryometry; **~scopie** [krijɔskɔpi] *s.f.* cryoscopy.
crypte [kript] *s.f.* crypt.
cryptocommuniste [kriptɔkɔmynist] *s.m.f.* crypto-Communist.
crypto-game [kriptɔgam] *s.m.* (bot.) cryptogam; *adj.* cryptogamous; **~gamique** [kriptɔgamik] *adj.* cryptogamic; **~gramme** [kriptɔgram] *s.m.* cryptogram; **~graphie** [kriptɔgrafi] *s.f.* cryptography; **~graphique** [kriptɔgrafik] *adj.* cryptographic.
csardas, czardas [ksardɑs, gzardɑs] *s.m.* csardas, czardas.
cténaires [ktenɛr], **cténophores** [ktenɔfɔr] *s.m.pl.* (zool.) Ctenophora.
cubage [kybaʒ] *s.m.* cubing; cubic content, air-space (of room).
cubain, -e [kybɛ̃] *adj., s.m.f.* Cuban.
cubature [kybatyr] *s.f.* (geom.) cubature.
cube [kyb] *s.m.* cube; *~ adj.* cubic.
cubèbe [kybɛb] *s.m.* (bot.) cubeb.
cuber [kybe] *v.t.* to cube; *~ v.i.* to have a cubic volume of; (fig., fam.) to come to a large sum.
cubilot [kybilo] *s.m.* (metall.) cupola.
cubique [kybik] *adj.* cubic; (arith.) *racine ~*, cube root.
cubisme [kybism] *s.m.* cubism.
cubiste [kybist] *adj., s.m.f.* cubist.
cubital, -e, (aux) [kybital] *adj.* cubital.
cubitus [kybitys] *s.m.* (anat.) ulna.
cucul [kyky] *adj.* (fam.) wet, sloppy.
cuculle [kykyl] *s.f.* monk's cowl.
cueillaison [kœjɛzɔ̃] *s.f.* fruit-picking season; (fig.) harvesting, reaping.
cueillette [kœjɛt] *s.f.* picking, gathering, (of fruit); collecting (plants, etc.); collection.
cueilleu-r, -se [kœjœr] *s.m.f.* picker.
cueillir [kœjir] *v.t.* to gather, to pick, to pluck; (fam.) to pick up (s.o.).
cueilloir [kœjwar] *s.m.* fruit-picking tool; fruit basket.
cuesta [kwɛsta] *s.f.* (geog.) cuesta.
cuiller, cuillère [kɥijɛr] *s.f.* spoon, ladle; spoonful.
cuillerée [kɥij(e)re] *s.f.* spoonful.
cuilleron [kɥijrɔ̃] *s.m.* bowl of spoon.
cuir [kɥir] *s.m.* **1.** leather, hide; *~ chevelu*, scalp; *~ à rasoir*, strop; **2.** (fig., fam.) incorrect liaison (in speech).
cuirasse [kɥiras] *s.f.* **1.** (armour & fig.) breast-plate, cuirass; (fig.) *le défaut de la ~*, the chink in the armour; **2.** (naut.) armour-plating; **3.** shell, carapace.
cuirassé, -e [kɥirase] *adj.* armoured, armour-plated; *~ s.m.* battleship.
cuirasser [kɥirase] *v.t.* to armour-plate; **se ~** *v.refl.* (fig.) to protect oneself; to harden one's heart.
cuirassier [kɥirasje] *s.m.* cuirassier.
cuire [kɥir] *v.t.i.* to cook; to bake; (fig.) to swelter; to smart; *les yeux me cuisent*, my eyes are smarting; *en ~ à qn.*, to cause s.o. trouble; *il lui en cuira*, he'll pay for it.
cuisant, -e [kɥizɑ̃] *adj.* searing; excruciating; (fig.) bitter; (dial.) easily cooked.
cuisine [kɥizin] *s.f.* **1.** kitchen; *batterie de ~*, kitchen utensils; **2.** cookery, cooking, cuisine; (fig.) trickery, fiddling; *~ électorale*, gerrymandering; **3.** food; **4.** kitchen staff.
cuisiner [kɥizine] *v.t.i.* to cook; (fig., fam.) to grill.
cuisini-er, -ère [kɥizinje] *s.m.f.* cook.
cuisinière [kɥizinjɛr] *s.f.* cooker, stove, range.
cuissard [kɥisar] *s.m.* (hist.) (armour) cuisse(s).
cuisse [kɥis] *s.f.* thigh; leg (of cooked fowl).
cuisseau (pl. **-x**) [kɥiso] *s.m.* leg of veal.
cuisse-madame [kɥismadam] *s.f.* (hort.) cuisse-madame pear.
cuisson [kɥisɔ̃] *s.m.* cooking; baking; smarting, itching.
cuissot [kɥiso] *s.m.* haunch of venison.
cuistance [kɥistɑ̃s] *s.f.* (pop.) food, cooking.
cuistot [kɥisto] *s.m.* (fam.) cook (in an institution).
cuistre [kɥistr] *s.m.* pedant; *~ adj.* pedantic.
cuistrerie [kɥistrəri] *s.f.* pedantry.
cuit, -e [kɥi] *adj.* cooked; baked; *terre ~e*, terra cotta; (fig.) *être ~*, to be done for; *c'est du tout ~*, it's in the bag.
cuite [kɥit] *s.f.* **1.** baking, firing; **2.** (fam.) *prendre une ~*, to get drunk.
cuivre [kɥivr] *s.m.* copper, brass; *les ~s*, the brasses; (mus.) the brass.
cuivré, -e [kɥivre] *adj.* **1.** copper-coloured; **2.** sonorous.
cuivrer [kɥivre] *v.t.* **1.** (techn.) to copper; **2.** to bronze.
cuivreu-x, -se [kɥivrø] *adj.* (obs.) cupreous; (chem.) cupric.
cuivrique [kɥivrik] *adj.* cupric.
cul [ky] *s.m.* (pop.) **1.** bottom, behind, arse;

bottom (of bottle, etc.); *lécher le* ~ *à qn.*, to lick someone's boots; (vulg.) *en avoir plein le* ~, to be fed up; (pop. mil.) *tirer au* ~, to malinger; *un tire-au-*~, a malingerer; **2.** *faux* ~, (dress) bustle; **3.** (pop.) idiot.
culasse [kylas] *s.f.* breech (of gun); cylinder head, combustion chamber, (of motor).
cul-blanc [kyblɑ̃] *s.m.* (ornith.) wheatear.
culbutage [kylbytaʒ] *s.m.* turning a somersault, overthrowing.
culbute [kylbyt] *s.f.* somersault, fall (head over heels); (fig., fam.) downfall, collapse; *faire la* ~, to come a cropper; (fig., comm.) to make a scoop.
culbuter [kylbyte] *v.i.* to turn a somersault, to turn upside down; ~ *v.t.* to knock down; (fig.) to bring down.
culbuteur [kylbytœr] *s.m.* **1.** tipper, tipping apparatus; **2.** (car) (valve-)rocker; **3.** (electr.) tumbler switch.
cul-de-basse-fosse [kydbɑsfos] *s.m.* (pl. *culs-de--basse-fosse*) dungeon.
cul-de-four [kydfur] *s.m.* (pl. *culs-de-four*) (arch.) half dome, cul de four.
cul-de-jatte [kydʒat] *s.m.f.* (pl. *culs-de-jatte*) legless person, cripple.
cul-de-lampe [kydlɑ̃p] *s.m.* (pl. *culs-de-lampe*) (arch.) cul-de-lampe.
cul-de-sac [kydsak] *s.m.* (pl. *culs-de-sac*) (lit. & fig.) cul-de-sac, blind alley.
culée [kyle] *s.f.* (arch.) pier (of buttress); abutment (of bridge).
culer [kyle] *v.i.* (naut.) to go astern.
culeron [kylrɔ̃] *s.m.* crupper-loop, hindgirth.
culex [kylɛks] *s.m.* gnat.
culière [kyljɛr] *s.f.* crupper.
culinaire [kylinɛr] *adj.* culinary.
culminant, -e [kylminɑ̃] *adj.* (astron.) culminant; culminating, highest, topmost.
culmination [kylminɑsjɔ̃] *s.f.* (astron.) culmination.
culminer [kylmine] *v.i.* (astron.) to culminate; to dominate; to reach the highest point.
culot [kylo] *s.m.* **1.** base, bottom (of lamp, etc.); **2.** residue; dottle (in pipe); **3.** (fig.) youngest child of family; bottom pupil in class or examination; **4.** (fam.) cheek, nerve.
culottage [kylɔtaʒ] *s.m.* blackening, seasoning (of bowl of pipe).
culotte [kylɔt] *s.f.* **1.** knee-breeches, knickerbockers; shorts; bathing trunks; **2.** knickers; **3.** (cook.) rump; **4.** (fig.) *prendre une* ~, to be cleaned out.
culotté, -e [kylɔte] *adj.* **1.** (of pipe) seasoned; **2.** (fam.) cheeky, impudent.
culotter [kylɔte] *v.t.* **1.** to dress in breeches; **2.** to season (a pipe).
culotti-er, -ère [kylɔtje] *s.m.f.* breeches--maker.
culpabilité [kylpabilite] *s.f.* guilt, culpability.
culte [kylt] *s.m.* worship; religious practices, religion, creed; Protestant church service; (fig.) cult, worship, adoration.
cul-terreux [kytɛrø] *s.m.* (pej.) clodhopper, peasant.
cultivable [kyltivabl] *adj.* arable, cultivable.
cultivat-eur, -rice [kyltivatœr] *s.m.f.* farmer, grower, agriculturalist; ~**eur** *s.m.* mechanical cultivator.
cultivé, -e [kyltive] *adj.* **1.** (of land, etc.) cultivated; **2.** cultured.
cultiver [kyltive] *v.t.* to cultivate (land, etc.), to till, to grow; (fig.) to cultivate.
cultuel, -le [kyltɥɛl] *adj.* religious.
cultural, -e, (aux) [kyltyral] *adj.* agricultural; ⚠ not 'cultural'.
culture [kyltyr] *s.f.* **1.** cultivation, tillage, husbandry, farming; **2.** (fig.) culture.
culturel, -le [kyltyrɛl] *adj.* cultural.
cumin [kymɛ̃] *s.m.* (bot.) cumin, cummin, caraway.
cumul [kymyl] *s.m.* plurality (of offices).
cumulard [kymylar] *s.m.* (pej.) pluralist.
cumulati-f, -ve [kymylatif] *adj.* cumulative.
cumuler [kymyle] *v.i.* to hold a plurality (of offices); (law) to cumulate.
cumulo-nimbus [kymylɔnɛ̃bys] *s.m.* (meteor.) cumulonimbus; ~**-stratus** [kymylɔstratys] *s.m.* (meteor.) cumulostratus.
cumulus [kymylys] *s.m.* (meteor.) cumulus.
cunéiforme [kyneifɔrm] *adj.* cuneiform.
cupide [kypid] *adj.* (Lit.) avaricious; ~**ment** [kypidmɑ̃] *adv.* avariciously.
cupidité [kypidite] *s.f.* cupidity, greed.
Cupidon [kypidɔ̃] *s.m.* Cupid.
cuprifère [kyprifɛr] *adj.* cupriferous.
cuprique [kyprik] *adj.* cupric.
cuprite [kyprit] *s.f.* (chem., min.) cuprite.
cupro-ammoniacal, -e, (aux) [kyprɔamɔnjakal] *adj.* (chem.) cuproammoniacal; *liqueur* ~*e*, cuprammonium.
cupro-nickel [kyprɔnikɛl] *s.m.* cupro-nickel.
cupule [kypyl] *s.f.* (bot.) cupule.
curable [kyrabl] *adj.* curable.
curaçao [kyraso] *s.m.* curaçao, curaçoa (liqueur).
curage [kyraʒ] *s.m.* dredging, cleaning out.
curare [kyrar] *s.m.* curare.
curarine [kyrarin] *s.f.* (pharm.) curarine.
curarisant, -e [kyrarizɑ̃] *adj.* curarizant.
curatelle [kyratɛl] *s.f.* (law) curatorship, guardianship.
curat-eur, -rice [kyratœr] *s.m.f.* (law) guardian; (Rom. & Scottish law) curator.
curati-f, -ve [kyratif] *adj.* curative.
curculionidés [kyrkyljɔnide] *s.m.pl.* (ent.) Curculionidae.
curcuma [kyrkyma] *s.m.* (bot.) curcuma.
cure [kyr] *s.f.* **1.** (obs.) care, concern; (mod.) *n'avoir* ~ *de qch.*, not to care about sth.; **2.** cure, course of treatment; **3.** (eccles.) living; priest's house.
curé [kyre] *s.m.* parish priest; (often pej.) priest, parson; ⚠ not 'curate'.
cure-dent [kyrdɑ̃] *s.m.* (pl. *cure-dents*) toothpick.
curée [kyre] *s.f.* **1.** part of stag given to hounds; quarry; **2.** (fig.) scramble, rat race.
cure-ongles [kyrɔ̃gl] *s.m.invar.* nail-file.
cure-pipe [kyrpip] *s.m.* (pl. *cure-pipes*) pipe--cleaner.
curer [kyre] *v.t.* to dredge, to clean out; to pick (teeth); ⚠ not 'to cure'.
curetage [kyrtaʒ] *s.m.* (med.) curettage.
cureter [kyrte] *v.t.* (med.) to curette.
curette [kyrɛt] *s.f.* (med.) curette.
curial, -e, (aux) [kyrjal] *adj.* (of house, etc.) priest's.
curie[1] [kyri] *s.f.* (hist., eccles.) Curia.
curie[2] [kyri] *s.m.* (phys.) curie.
curieu-x, -se [kyrjø] *adj.* **1.** (obs.) interested (*de*, in), a collector (of curios, antiques, etc.); **2.** curious, inquisitive; **3.** curious, unusual, strange; ~**x** *s.m.* **1.** (obs.) collector; **2.** curious or inquisitive person, onlooker; ~**sement** [kyrjøzmɑ̃] *adv.* curiously, strangely.
curiosité [kyrjozite] *s.f.* curiosity.
curiste [kyrist] *s.m.f.* person taking cure (at spa).
curium [kyrjɔm] *s.m.* (chem.) curium.
curling [kœrliŋ] *s.m.* (sport) curling.
curry see CARI.
curseur [kyrsœr] *s.m.* (techn.) cursor, slide, slider, runner, traveller.
cursi-f, -ve [kyrsif] *adj., s.f.* cursive (writing).
curule [kyryl] *adj.* (Rom. hist.) curule.
curviligne [kyrviliɲ] *adj.* curvilinear.
curvimètre [kyrvimɛtr] *s.m.* curvometer.

cuscute [kyskyt] *s.f.* (bot.) dodder.
cuspide [kyspid] *s.f.* (bot.) cusp.
custode [kystɔd] *s.f.* **1.** (eccles.) pyx; **2.** (car) rear side-panel.
cutané, -e [kytane] *adj.* cutaneous.
cuticule [kytikyl] *s.f.* cuticle.
cutine [kytin] *s.f.* (bot.) cutin.
cuti-réaction [kytireaksjɔ̃] *s.f.* (abbrev. *cuti*) (med.) skin test.
cuvage [kyvaʒ] *s.m.*, **cuvaison** [kyvɛzɔ̃] *s.f.* fermenting of wine (in vats).
cuve [kyv] *s.f.* vat, tank; dish.
cuvée [kyve] *s.f.* vatful (of wine); produce of vineyard.
cuvelage [kyvlaʒ], **cuvellement** [kyvɛlmɑ̃] *s.m.* lining (of artesian well); shoring, timbering (of mine).
cuveler [kyvle] *v.t.* to line (a well); to timber (a mine).
cuver [kyve] *v.i.* to ferment; ~ *v.t.* (fig., fam.) ~ *son vin*, to sleep it off.
cuvette [kyvɛt] *s.f.* **1.** basin; **2.** backplate (of watch); **3.** (geol.) basin.
cuvier [kyvje] *s.m.* (obs. exc. dial.) wash-tub, copper.
C.V. [seve] abbrev. *chevaux-vapeur*, h.p.
cyan-amide [sjanamid] *s.f.* (chem.) cyanamide; **~hydrique** [sjanidrik] *adj.* *acide ~hydrique*, hydrogen cyanide; **~ogène** [sjanɔʒɛn] *s.m.* cyanogen; **~ose** [sjanoz] *s.f.* (med.) cyanosis; **~uration** [sjanyrɑsjɔ̃] *s.f.* (gold mining) cyanidation; **~ure** [sjanyr] *s.m.* (chem.) cyanide.
cybernétique [sibɛrnetik] *s.f.* cybernetics.
cycas [sikas] *s.m.* (bot.) cycad.
cyclable [siklabl] *adj.* cycle; *piste ~*, cycle-track.
cyclamen [siklamɛn] *s.m.* (bot.) cyclamen.
cyclane [siklan] *s.m.* (chem.) cyclane.
cycle [sikl] *s.m.* cycle (series or bicycle).
cyclique [siklik] *adj.* cyclic.
cyclisme [siklism] *s.m.* (sport) cycling; cycle-racing.
cycliste [siklist] *adj.* cycle; *s.m.f.* cyclist.
cyclo-cross [siklɔkrɔs] *s.m.* (sport) cyclo-cross.
cycloïdal, -e, (aux) [siklɔidal] *adj.* cycloidal.
cycloïde [siklɔid] *s.f.* cycloid.
cyclomoteur [siklɔmɔtœr] *s.m.* moped.
cyclomotoriste [siklɔmɔtɔrist] *s.m.f.* moped rider.
cyclonal, -e, (aux) [siklɔnal] *adj.* cyclonic.
cyclone [siklon] *s.m.* cyclone; (fig.) whirlwind.
cyclonique [siklɔnik] *adj.* cyclonic.
cyclope [siklɔp] *s.m.* **1.** (Gr. ant.) Cyclops; (fig.) *travail de ~*, titanic task; **2.** (zool.) two-toed anteater; **3.** (crust.) cyclops.
cyclopéen, -ne [siklɔpeɛ̃] *adj.* Cyclopean; (fig.) titanic, enormous.
cyclo-stome [siklɔstɔm] *s.m.* (zool.) cyclostome; **~thymie** [siklɔtimi] *s.f.* (med.) cyclothymia; **~tron** [siklɔtrɔ̃] *s.m.* (phys.) cyclotron.
cygne [siɲ] *s.m.* swan; swansdown.
cylindrage [silɛ̃draʒ] *s.m.* calendering; rolling.
cylindre [silɛ̃dr] *s.m.* cylinder; roller; *bureau à ~*, roll-top desk; (fam.) *une six ~s*, a six-cylinder car.
cylindrée [silɛ̃dre] *s.f.* cubic capacity (of cylinders).
cylindrer [silɛ̃dre] *v.t.* **1.** to make into a cylinder, to roll up; **2.** to calender, to roll.
cylindreu-r, -se [silɛ̃drœr] *s.m.f.* calenderer.
cylindrique [silɛ̃drik] *adj.* cylindrical.
cymbalaire [sɛ̃balɛr] *s.f.* (bot.) ivy-leaved toadflax.
cymbale [sɛ̃bal] *s.f.* (mus.) cymbal.
cymbalier [sɛ̃balje], **cymbaliste** [sɛ̃balist] *s.m.* cymbalist.
cymbalum [sɛ̃balɔm], **czimbalum** [tʃimbalɔm] *s.m.* (mus.) cymbalo, dulcimer.
cyme [sim] *s.f.* (bot.) cyme.
cymrique see KYMRIQUE.
cynips [sinips] *s.m.* (ent.) Cynips, gall-fly.
cynique [sinik] *adj.* cynical; ~ *s.m.* cynic; **~ment** [sinikmɑ̃] *adv.* cynically.
cynisme [sinism] *s.m.* cynicism.
cyno-céphale [sinɔsefal] *s.m.* (zool.) cynocephalus, dog-faced baboon; **~drome** [sinɔdrom] *s.m.* greyhound track or stadium; **~glosse** [sinɔglɔs] *s.f.* (bot.) cynoglossum; **~phile** [sinɔfil] *adj.* fond of dogs; *s.m.f.* dog-lover.
cypéracées [siperase] *s.f.pl.* (bot.) Cyperaceae.
cyprès [siprɛ] *s.m.* (bot.) cypress.
cyprière [siprijɛr] *s.f.* cypress plantation.
cyprin [siprɛ̃] *s.m.* (ichth.) cyprinoid; ~ *doré* goldfish.
cypriote [siprijɔt] *adj.*, *s.m.f.* Cypriot.
cyrillique [siril(l)ik] *adj.* Cyrillic.
cyst-ectomie [sistɛktɔmi] *s.f.* (surg.) cystectomy; **~icerque** [sistisɛrk] *s.m.* (zool.) cysticercus, bladder-worm; **~ique** [sistik] *adj.* cystic; **~ite** [sistit] *s.f.* (med.) cystitis.
cysto-scope [sistɔskɔp] *s.m.* cystoscope; **~scopie** [sistɔskɔpi] *s.f.* cystoscopy; **~stomie** [sistɔstɔmi] *s.f.* (surg.) cystostomy; **~tomie** [sistɔtɔmi] *s.f.* (surg.) cystotomy.
cytise [sitiz] *s.m.* (bot.) laburnum.
cyto-logie [sitɔlɔʒi] *s.f.* cytology; **~lise** [sitɔliz] *s.f.* (biol.) cytolysis; **~plasme** [sitɔplasm] *s.m.* cytoplasm; **~plasmique** [sitɔplasmik] *adj.* cytoplasmic.
czar [tsar, dzar] *s.m.* = TSAR.

D

D, d [de] *s.m.* the letter D, d; (fam.) *système D* see SYSTÈME.
d' see DE.
da [da] *interj.* (obs. or fam.) *oui-~!*, yes, of course!
dacron [dakrɔ̃] *s.m.* (text.) dacron.
dactyle [daktil] *s.m.* (pros.) dactyl.
dactylo [daktilo] *s.f.* typist; **~graphe** [daktilɔgraf] *s.f.* = DACTYLO; **~graphie** [daktilɔgrafi] *s.f.* typewriting, typing; **~graphier** [daktilɔgrafje] *v.t.* to type; **~graphique** [daktilɔgrafik] *adj.* typewriting, typing.
dada [dada] *s.m.* (child.) horse; *à ~*, on horseback; (fig., fam.) hobby-horse, pet subject.
dadais [dadɛ] *s.m.* simpleton, booby.
dadaïsme [dadaism] *s.m.* (art) dadaism.
dague [dag] *s.f.* **1.** dirk; **2.** first growth of antler (of young deer); tusk (of wild boar).
daguerréotype [dagɛreɔtip] *s.m.* (photo.) daguerreotype.
daguet [dagɛ] *s.m.* young deer with first growth of antler.
dahlia [dalja] *s.m.* (bot.) dahlia.
daigner [deɲe] *v.t.* to deign, to condescend, (*à*, to).
daim [dɛ̃] *s.m.* **1.** fallow deer; **2.** suede (leather).
daine [dɛn], **dine** [din] *s.f.* female fallow or red deer, doe.

dais [dɛ] *s.m.* canopy, baldachin, baldaquin; ⚠ not 'dais' in sense 'platform'.
daleau see DALOT.
dallage [dalaʒ] *s.m.* paving with flagstones; pavement of flagstones.
dalle [dal] *s.f* **1.** flagstone, flag; ~ *funèbre*, tombstone; **2.** (slang) throat; *avoir la ~ en pente*, to be fond of a drink; *se rincer la ~*, to drink, to wet one's whistle.
daller [dale] *v.t.* to pave with flagstones, to flag.
dalleur [dalœr] *s.m.* pavior.
dalmate [dalmat] *adj.*, *s.m.f.* Dalmatian.
dalmatique [dalmatik] *s.f.* **1.** (ant.) tunic; **2.** (eccles.) dalmatic (vestment).
dalot, daleau (pl. **-x**) [dalo] *s.m.* (naut.) scupper; (constr.) channel.
daltonien, -ne [daltɔnjɛ̃] *adj.*, *s.m.f.* colour-blind (person).
daltonisme [daltɔnism] *s.m.* daltonism, colour-blindness.
dam [dã] *s.m.* **1.** detriment, harm, disadvantage; *au grand ~ de qn.*, to someone's great disadvantage; **2.** (theol.) damnation.
damage [damaʒ] *s.m.* (constr.) tamping; ⚠ not 'damage'.
Damas [damas] *s.m.* (geog.) Damascus.
damas [dama] *s.m.* **1.** (text.) damask; **2.** (hist.) damask (steel, sword), Damascus steel.
damascène [damasɛn] *adj.*, *s.m.f.* (native or inhabitant) of Damascus.
damasquin-age [damaskinaʒ] *s.m.* damascening; **~er** [damaskine] *v.t.* to damascene.
damasser [damase] *v.t.* (text.) to damask.
dame[1] [dam] *s.f.* **1.** lady; married woman; woman; **2.** (cards, chess) queen; (draughts) king; *jeu de ~s*, game of draughts.
dame[2] [dam] *interj.* of course! to be sure!
dame-d'onze-heures [damdɔ̃zœr] *s.f.* (bot.) star of Bethlehem.
dame-jeanne [damʒɑn] *s.f.* demijohn.
damer [dame] *v.t.* **1.** (draughts) to crown (piece); (chess) to queen (pawn); (fig.) ~ *le pion à qn.*, to outdo or outwit s.o.; **2.** (constr.) to tamp (earth).
damier [damje] *s.m.* draught-board; chequered surface or pattern.
damnable [dɑnabl] *adj.* damnable; deserving condemnation; **~ment** [dɑnabləmã] *adv.* damnably.
damnation [dɑnɑsjɔ̃] *s.f.* damnation.
damné, -e [dɑne] *adj.* damned; (fam.) *être l'âme ~e de qn.*, to belong body and soul to s.o., to be a mere tool in the hands of s.o.; *les ~s*, the damned.
damner [dɑne] *v.t.* to damn.
damoiseau (pl. **-x**) [damwazo] *s.m.* **1.** (hist.) young squire not yet knighted; **2.** (fam.) young gallant, ladies' man.
damoiselle [damwazɛl] *s.f.* (obs.) damozel, damsel.
dancing [dãsiŋ] *s.m.* dance-hall.
dandin [dãdɛ̃] *s.m.* (obs.) clumsy fellow, booby.
dandinement [dãdinmã] *s.m.* waddling; shifting one's weight from one hip to the other.
(**se**) **dandiner** [dãdine] *v. refl.* to waddle; to shift one's weight from one hip to the other.
dandy [dãdi] *s.m.* dandy, fop; **~sme** [dãndism] *s.m.* dandyism, foppishness.
Danemark [danmark] *s.m.* Denmark.
danger [dãʒe] *s.m.* **1.** danger, peril, risk; jeopardy; *être hors de ~*, to be out of danger, to be safe; *signal d'un* or *de ~*, danger signal; *mettre en ~ la réputation de qn.*, to jeopardize someone's reputation. **2.** (fam.) *il n'y a pas de ~ qu'il le fasse*, he's not likely to do it.
dangereu-x, -se [dãʒrø] *adj.* dangerous; **~sement** [dãʒrøzmã] *adv.* dangerously.
danois, -e [danwa] *adj.*, *s.m.f.* Danish; Dane; ~ *s.m.* Great Dane (dog).
dans [dã] *prep.* in, into, inside, within, among, during; *entrer ~ sa chambre*, to go into one's room; *je reviendrai ~ huit jours*, I shall be back in a week; *c'est ~ ses projets*, it is among his projects; *cela lui arriva ~ son enfance*, that happened to him during his childhood; ~ *un court délai*, after a short time, shortly; ~ *le temps*, of old, in olden times; *cela coûtera ~ les trois cents francs*, that will cost in the region of 300 francs.
dansant, -e [dãsã] *adj.* (of music, tune, etc.) dance, good to dance to, lively; when dancing takes place; *soirée ~e*, dance, party with dancing; *thé ~*, tea dance.
danse [dãs] *s.f.* dance, dancing; dance tune; ~ *de St-Guy*, St. Vitus's dance; ~ *macabre*, dance of death; (fig., fam.) *donner une ~ à qn.*, to correct or reprimand s.o.; *entrer en ~*, to begin doing sth., to join in.
danser [dãse] *v.t.i.* to dance; (fig., fam.) *faire ~ les écus*, to spend freely; *ne pas savoir sur quel pied ~*, not to know which way to turn.
danseu-r, -se [dãsœr] *s.m.f.* dancer; professional dancer; ballet dancer; *~r* or *~se de corde*, (tight-)rope dancer.
dantesque [dãtɛsk] *adj.* (Lit.) Dantesque.
Danube [danyb] *s.m.* (geog.) Danube.
danubien, -ne [danybjɛ̃] *adj.*, *s.m.f.* Danubian.
daphné [dafne] *s.m.* (bot.) daphne.
darce see DARSE.
dard [dar] *s.m.* **1.** dart; small harpoon; sting; snake's tongue; **2.** spur (of fruit-tree).
darder [darde] *v.t.* to throw, to hurl; (fig.) ~ *un regard sur qn.*, to dart a look at s.o.
dare-dare [dardar] *adv.* (fam.) in double-quick time, in less than no time, like a shot.
dariole [darjɔl] *s.f.* (cook.) baked custard.
darne [darn] *s.f.* (cook.) steak (of cod, salmon, etc.).
darse, darce [dars] *s.f.* dock (in Mediterranean port).
dartre [dartr] *s.f.* (med.) scaling, scabbing (of skin).
dartreu-x, -se [dartrø] *adj.* scaly, scabby, scurfy.
darwinien, -ne [darwinjɛ̃], **darwiniste** [darwinist] *adj.*, *s.m.f.* Darwinian.
darwinisme [darwinism] *s.m.* Darwinism.
datable [databl] *adj.* datable.
datation [datɑsjɔ̃] *s.f.* dating.
date [dat] *s.f.* date; *prendre ~*, to fix a day; *de longue ~*, (of) long standing; *de fraîche ~*, recent, of recent date; *lettre en ~ du 5 juin*, letter of 5th June, dated 5th June; *être le premier en ~*, to come first, to have priority, (because of seniority).
dater [date] *v.t.i.* to date; *à ~ de*, from, to date from; *cela ne date pas d'hier*, that's nothing new; *cela date dans sa vie*, that marks an epoch in his life.
dateu-r, -se [datœr] *adj.* that marks the date; (*timbre*) *~r*, date-stamp.
datif [datif] *s.m.* (gram.) dative.
datte [dat] *s.f.* (bot.) date.
dattier [datje] *s.m.* (bot.) date-palm.
daube [dob] *s.f.* (cook.) *en ~*, braised, stewed in tightly closed saucepan, e.g. *bœuf en ~*; *servir une ~*, to serve a dish of braised meat.
dauber[1] [dobe] *v.t.i.* (obs.) ~ (*sur*), to rag, to mock, to insult.
dauber[2] [dobe] *v.t.* (cook.) to braise, to stew (meat).
daubière [dobjɛr] *s.f.* stew-pan, covered saucepan.
dauphin[1] [dofɛ̃] *s.m.* (hist.) Dauphin.
dauphin[2] [dofɛ̃] *s.m.* (zool.) dolphin.

dauphine [dofin] *s.f.* (hist.) Dauphiness, wife of Dauphin.
Dauphiné [dofine] *s.m.* (geog.) Dauphiné (Fr. province).
dauphinois, -e [dofinwa] *adj., s.m.f.* (native or inhabitant) of Dauphiné.
daurade, dorade [dɔrad] *s.f.* (ichth.) dorado.
davantage [davɑ̃taʒ] *adv.* **1.** more; *il n'en sait pas ~*, he doesn't know any more about it; *sa sœur est intelligente, mais elle l'est ~*, her sister is clever, but she is more so; **2.** longer; *ne restez pas ~*, don't stay any longer.
davier [davje] *s.m.* (techn.) cramp, clamp; pincers; (surg.) forceps.
D.C.A. [desea] abbrev. *Défense contre avions*, (mil.) A.A., Ack-Ack.
D.D.T. [dedete] abbrev. *Dichloro-diphényl trichloréthane*, D.D.T.
de [də] (**d'** before vowel or h-mute; in combination with arts. *le* and *les* forms **du** and **des** respectively.)
I. *prep.* **1.** (point of departure in space or time, point of origin) from, out of; (written, etc.) by; *venir ~ Paris*, to come from Paris; *du matin au soir*, from morning to night; *~ ce point de vue*, from that point of view; *sortir ~ la maison*, to come out of the house; *c'est ~ mon enfance*, it goes back to my childhood; *être du Périgord*, to come from, to be a native of, the Périgord, *c'est ~ Molière*, it is by Molière; **2.** (cause, reason) because of, for, at, with; *danser ~ joie*, to dance for joy; *punir d'un crime*, to punish for a crime; *étonné ~ qch.*, astonished at sth.; *content ~ qch.*, pleased at or with sth.; *être fâché ~ ce qu'il l'a refusé*, to be upset that he has refused it; **3.** (subject matter) of, about, concerning; *parler ~ roses*, to talk about roses; *histoire ~ revenants*, ghost story; **4.** (possession, belonging) of, from, in, belonging to; forming part of; *la maison de Colette*, Colette's house; *le fond du tiroir*, the bottom of the drawer; *il est ~ nos amis*, he is one of our friends; *le plus grand fleuve du monde*, the largest river in the world; **5.** (composition, contents; completing expressions of quantity) of; *des gants ~ cuir*, leather gloves; *un tas ~ pierres*, a heap of stones; *un verre ~ bière*, a glass of beer; *un demi ~ bière*, a half (litre) of beer; *deux kilos ~ farine*, two kilos of flour; *un million ~ francs*, a million francs; *trop ~ difficultés*, too many difficulties; **6.** (qualifying amounts) *avoir deux mètres ~ long* or *~ longueur*, to be two metres long; *avoir deux kilomètres d'avance*, to have two kilometres start; *âgé ~ 20 ans*, aged 20; *deux fois ~ plus*, twice more; *trois hommes ~ blessés*, three men injured; **7.** (quantifying measurements) *long ~ deux mètres*, two metres long; *plus âgé ~ trois ans*, three years older; **8.** (manner) in, at; *d'une voix basse*, in a low voice; *~ cette façon*, *~ cette manière*, *~ la sorte*, in this way; *d'un seul coup*, at one blow; **9.** (means, agent, instrument) with, by; *toucher du doigt*, to touch with one's finger; *accompagné d'un collègue*, accompanied by a colleague; *être détesté ~ tous*, to be hated by everyone; *encadré ~ fleurs*, framed in flowers; *frappé d'une idée*, struck by an idea; **10.** (type, kind, description, identity; quality, attribute) *la route ~ Paris*, the Paris road, the road to Paris; *la vie ~ province*, provincial life; *un chien ~ race*, a pedigree dog; *un objet ~ valeur*, a valuable object; *un homme d'intelligence*, a man of intelligence; **11.** (as regards, in respect of) *large d'épaules*, broad-shouldered; *haut ~ taille*, tall; *à court d'argent*, short of money; **12.** (subjective; objective) *l'approbation de ses camarades*, the approval of his friends; *l'amour ~ la patrie*, love of one's country; **13.** (in expressions of direction) in, on, from; *~ tous côtés*, *~ toutes parts*, in every direction, on all sides, from all directions; *~ part et d'autre*, here and there, on one side and the other, one way and the other; *d'autre part*, on the other hand; **14.** (during, for the space of) *voyager ~ nuit*, to travel by night; *je n'ai pas dormi ~ la nuit*, I didn't sleep all night; **15.** (in construction with verb) *se souvenir ~*, to remember; *douter ~ qch.*, to doubt sth.; *cesser ~ parler*, to stop talking; *éviter ~ faire qch.*, to avoid doing sth.; (introducing an infin. which is logical subject) *il est impossible ~ l'arrêter*, it is impossible to stop him; *c'est une erreur ~ ne pas l'écouter*, it is a mistake not to listen to him; **16.** (forming historic infin.) *et la vieille ~ crier et ~ hurler*, and the old woman started shouting and screeching.
II. *partitive art.* **1.** (forms *du*, *de l'*, *de la*, *des*) some, some of, any; *prenez du beurre*, take some butter; *acheter des œufs*, to buy (some) eggs; *il mangea du gâteau*, he ate some (of the) cake; *il y a du vin?*, is there any wine?; *il a fait des fautes*, he has made mistakes; *ce ne sont pas là des choses graves*, those are not serious matters; *c'est du propre!*, that's a fine state of affairs!; **2.** (form *de*, in expressions of neg. quantity) no, not any; *il n'a pas d'amis*, he has no friends; *je n'ai plus ~ travail*, I have no more work; *il n'y a pas d'eau*, there isn't any water; **3.** (form *de*, in strict usage, before adj. preceding noun) *boire ~ bon vin*, to drink (some) good wine; *~ petits enfants*, (some) little children.
dé¹ [de] *s.m.* thimble.
dé² [de] *s.m.* die, dice; cube (of stone etc.); (cook.) (small) cube; (fig.) *coup de ~s*, throw of dice, chance; (fig.) *les ~s sont jetés*, the die is cast; (cook.) *carottes en ~s*, diced carrots.
déambulatoire [deɑ̃bylatwar] *s.f.* (arch.) ambulatory.
déambuler [deɑ̃byle] *v.i.* to stroll about, to saunter.
débâcle [debɑkl] *s.f.* débâcle, collapse, breakdown.
débâcler [debɑkle] *v.i.* (of ice) to break up.
débagouler [debagule] *v.i.* (obs. or pop.) to vomit, to spew; *~ v.t.* (fig., fam.) to pour forth, to spew out, (nonsense, etc.).
déballage [debalaʒ] *s.m.* unpacking, (esp.) goods unpacked and displayed for sale; (fig., fam.) complete confession, making a clean breast.
déballer [debale] *v.t.* to unpack; (fig., fam.) to confess fully, to make a clean breast of.
débandade [debɑ̃dad] *s.f.* disbanding, dispersing; stampede, rout; *à la ~*, helter-skelter; in confusion.
débander¹ [debɑ̃de] *v.t.* to unbind, to take the bandage off.
débander² [debɑ̃de] *v.t.* (obs.) to disperse (troops); **se** ~ *v.refl.* to break ranks and scatter.
débaptiser [debatize] *v.t.* to change the name of, to rename.
débarbouillage [debarbujaʒ] *s.m.* washing of the face; hasty wash.
débarbouiller [debarbuje] *v.t.* to wash someone's face; to wash, to clean up (e.g. child); **se** ~ *v.refl.* to wash one's face; (fig., fam.) to get out of a difficulty, to shift for oneself.
débarcadère [debarkadɛr] *s.m.* landing-stage, quay, wharf.
débarder [debarde] *v.t.* **1.** to unload (esp. timber from raft); **2.** (techn.) to transport (felled timber, quarried stone).
débarquement [debarkəmɑ̃] *s.m.* disembarking, landing, disembarkation, unloading.
débardeur [debardœr] *s.m.* docker, stevedore.
débarquer [debarke] *v.t.i.* to land, to disembark, to unship; (fig., fam.) to dismiss; *~ chez qn.*,

(fam.) to arrive as unexpected guest, to descend on s.o.
débarras [debara] *s.m.* **1.** riddance, relief, disembarrassment; **2.** lumber-room.
débarrasser [debarase] *v.t.* to clear, to disencumber; to relieve, to rid, (*de*, of); *~ le chemin*, to clear the road; *vous pouvez ~*, you may clear (the table); *~ qn. de son manteau*, take (and hang up) someone's coat; **se ~** *v.refl.* to get rid, to rid oneself, (*de*, of); *se ~ d'un vêtement*, to take off a garment.
débarrer [debare] *v.t.* (obs.) to unbar.
débat [deba] *s.m.* discussion, debate; argument; (pl.) debate; *~s parlementaires*, parliamentary proceedings.
débâter [debɑte] *v.t.* to unsaddle (a beast of burden).
débâtir [debatir] *v.t.* (dressm.) to untack, to take the tacking threads out of.
débattement [debatmɑ̃] *s.m.* (car) height of ride (clearance between axle and chassis).
débattre [debatr] *v.t.* to debate, to discuss; **se ~** *v.refl.* to resist, to struggle (to free oneself); (fig.) to fight (*contre*, against).
débauche [deboʃ] *s.f.* debauchery, debauch; (fig.) excess, abuse (of sth.); *se livrer à des ~s d'imagination*, to let one's imagination run riot; *une ~ de couleurs*, a riot of colour.
débauché, -e [deboʃe] *adj.* debauched, dissolute; *s.m.f.* profligate, debauchee.
débaucher [deboʃe] *v.t.* **1.** to entice (servant, staff); to incite (workers) to strike; to lay off (workers, owing to shortage of work); **2.** (obs.) to corrupt, to debauch; (fam.) to lead astray.
débet [debɛ] *s.m.* (fin.) debit.
débile [debil] *adj.* weak, sickly, feeble; *~ s.m.f.* (psychol.) *~ (mental)*, mental defective.
débilitant, -e [debilitɑ̃] *adj.* debilitating; (fig.) demoralizing.
débilité [debilite] *s.f.* debility, weakness; (psychol.) mental deficiency.
débiliter [debilite] *v.t.* to debilitate; (fig.) to demoralize.
débillarder [debijarde] *v.t.* (techn.) to cross--cut (timber).
débine [debin] *s.f.* (pop.) poverty; *être dans la ~*, to be hard up; *tomber dans la ~*, to fall on evil days.
débiner [debine] *v.t.* (fam.) to discredit, to denigrate (s.o.); **se ~** *v.refl.* (fam.) to make off, to run away.
débit[1] [debi] *s.m.* **1.** turnover; cutting up (of timber); delivery (in speaking, reciting); flow (of river etc.); output; **2.** retailing; retail shop; *~ de tabac*, tobacconist's; *~ de boissons*, bar, wine-shop.
débit[2] [debi] *s.m.* (book-keep.) debit, debit side.
débitage [debitaʒ] *s.m.* cutting-up (of timber).
débitant, -e [debitɑ̃] *s.m.f.* retailer, shop-keeper.
débiter[1] [debite] *v.t.* to cut up (timber, slate, meat, etc.); to retail; to recite, to reel off, to declaim; to pour out, to cause to flow; to produce, to give out; *le courant débité par la dynamo*, current generated by the dynamo.
débiter[2] [debite] *v.t.* to debit.
débit-eur[1], **-rice** [debitœr] *s.m.f.* debtor; *adj.* debit; *solde ~eur*, debit balance; (cin.) *bobine ~rice*, top spool.
débiteu-r[2], **-se** [debitœr] *s.m.f.* (obs.) fantastic liar, scandalmonger; (obs.) retailer; workman who cuts up (timber, etc.).
déblai [deblɛ] *s.m.* excavating, earth-moving, clearing; *~(s)*, rubbish, debris.
déblaiement [deblɛmɑ̃] *s.m.* clearing (of site, passage).
déblatérer [deblatere] *v.i.* to inveigh (*contre*, against).
déblayer [debleje] *v.t.* to clear (site, etc.), to level (ground); (fig.) *~ le terrain*, to clear the ground.
déblocage [deblɔkaʒ] *s.m.* **1.** freeing, clearing, releasing; **2.** (pop.) talking nonsense.
débloquer [deblɔke] *v.t.* to free, to clear, to release; (print.) to correct (inverted letter), (fin., comm.) to unfreeze; (obs.) to raise blockade or siege of; *~ v.i.* (pop.) to talk nonsense.
débobiner [debɔbine] *v.t.* (techn.) to unwind (coil, etc.).
déboire [debwar] *s.m.* (obs.) unpleasant after--taste; (fig.) (esp. pl.) disappointment, frustration, disillusionment.
déboisement [debwazmɑ̃] *s.m.* clearing (land) of wood or forest, deforestation.
déboiser [debwaze] *v.t.* to clear (land) of wood or forest, to deforest.
déboîtement [debwatmɑ̃] *s.m.* (med.) dislocation, luxation.
déboîter [debwate] *v.t.* (med.) to dislocate, to luxate; to unhinge (door, etc.); to disconnect; *~ v.i.* (mil.) to fall out of line; (of car) to turn off (from a line of vehicles), to filter.
débonder [debɔ̃de] *v.t.* to take the bung or plug out of, to open the sluice of; (fig.) *~ (son cœur)*, *se ~*, to unbosom oneself.
débonnaire [debɔnɛr] *adj.* (obs. exc. Lit.) good--natured, indulgent, easy-going, complaisant; bland, inoffensive; *~***ment** [debɔnɛrmɑ̃] *adv.* (Lit.) blandly, suavely.
débonnaireté [debɔnɛrte] *s.f.* (Lit.) blandness, suavity.
débord [debɔr] *s.m.* (dressm.) binding, piping.
débordant, -e [debɔrdɑ̃] *adj.* (fig.) overflowing; *~ de santé*, bursting with health.
débordement [debɔrdəmɑ̃] *s.m.* overflowing, flooding; (mil.) outflanking, turning or encircling movement; (pl.) excesses, debauchery.
déborder [debɔrde] *v.i.* to overflow; (fig.) *faire ~ qn.*, to drive s.o. to distraction; *~ v.t.* **1.** to overflow; to go or to project beyond; (mil.) to outflank, to turn; **2.** to untuck (bedclothes); (naut.) *~ une embarcation*, to shove off (small boat); **3.** to remove edging or border of.
débosseler [debɔsle] *v.t.* (techn.) to beat out (panel, etc.).
débotté, débotter [debɔte] *s.m.* (obs.) taking--off of boots; (mod.) *au ~*, (immediately) on arriving.
débotter [debɔte] *v.t.* to take off the boots of; **se ~** *v.refl.* to take off one's boots.
débouchage [debuʃaʒ] *s.m.* uncorking.
débouché [debuʃe] *s.m.* issue, mouth (of narrow channel, pass, etc.); junction (of narrow with wider street, etc.); (comm.) outlet, market; (pl.) (fig.) prospects, openings (in career, etc.).
débouchement [debuʃmɑ̃] *s.m.* unblocking (of pipe, conduit, etc.).
déboucher [debuʃe] *v.t.* to unblock (pipe, drain, etc.); to uncork, to open, (bottle); *~ v.i.* to debouch, to open out (*dans*, into).
débouchoir [debuʃwar] *s.m.* (techn.) drain--clearer; (jeweller's) clearing-iron.
déboucler [debukle] *v.t.* **1.** to unbuckle; **2.** to uncurl, to straighten, (hair of); *la pluie l'avait toute débouclée*, the rain had taken all the curl out of her hair.
déboulé [debule] *s.m.* (hunt.) *au ~*, on breaking cover.
débouler [debule] *v.i.* (fam.) to fall head over heels; to tumble, to cascade; *~ l'escalier*, to fall head over heels downstairs.
déboulonnage [debulɔnaʒ], **déboulonnement** [debulɔnmɑ̃] *s.m.* (mech.) unbolting (of assembly).

déboulonner [debulɔne] *v.t.* **1.** (mech.) to unbolt (parts bolted together); **2.** (fig., fam.) to topple, to unseat, to eject.
débouquer [debuke] *v.i.* (naut.) to disembogue, to discharge.
débourbage [deburbaʒ] *s.m.* (mining) washing (of ore).
débourber [deburbe] *v.t.* **1.** to clean (out), to remove mud from, to sluice; to wash (ore); **2.** to pull (vehicle) out of the mud; (fig., obs.) to get (s.o.) out of a mess.
débourbeur [deburbœr] *s.m.* (techn.) washer (device for washing ore, or cleaning mud from roots).
débourrage [deburaʒ] *s.m.* (tanning) unhairing (of hide).
débourrement [deburmɑ̃] *s.m.* opening (of bud).
débourrer [debure] *v.t.* **1.** (tanning) to unhair (hide); **2.** to empty, to knock out (tobacco-pipe); ~ *v.i.* (of bud) to open.
débours [debur] *s.m.* disbursement, money expended, out-of-pocket expenses.
débourser [deburse] *v.t.* to pay out (money), to disburse; *sans ~ un sou*, without spending any money, gratis.
debout [dəbu] *adv.* upright, standing, on end; on one's feet, up (opp. in bed); *mettre qch. ~*, to stand sth. up; *se mettre ~*, to stand up, to get to one's feet; *être ~*, to be up and about, to be up (after illness), to be alive and well, to be still going strong; *tenir ~*, to be sound; (of argument) to hold water; *dormir ~*, to fall asleep on one's feet; *un conte à dormir ~*, a long and boring story; (naut.) *vent ~*, head wind.
débout-é [debute] *s.m.* (law) *jugement de ~é*, dismissal (of case, appeal), nonsuit; **~ement** [debutmɑ̃] *s.m.* dismissal, nonsuit; **~er** [debute] *v.t.* to dismiss (case, appeal), to nonsuit.
déboutonner [debutɔne] *v.t.* to unbutton; *rire à ventre deboutonné*, to laugh fit to burst; **se ~** *v.refl.* to unbutton, to undo, one's clothes; (fig.) to unbosom oneself, to speak one's mind, to keep nothing back.
débraillé, -e [debrɑje] *adj.* untidy, slovenly (in dress), bare-breasted; (fig.) unrestrained, indecent.
(**se**) **débrailler** [debrɑje] *v.refl.* (fam.) to expose one's breasts; (fig.) (of talk, etc.) to become indecent.
débranchement [debrɑ̃ʃmɑ̃] *s.m.* (rail.) shunting; (electr.) disconnecting, switching-off.
débrancher [debrɑ̃ʃe] *v.t.* (rail.) to shunt; (electr.) to disconnect, to switch off.
débrayage [debrɛjɑ̃ʒ] *s.m.* **1.** disengaging, declutching; **2.** going on strike, striking, stoppage (of work).
débrayer [debreje] *v.t.* (mech., techn.) to disengage (moving part(s) from motor); (car) to declutch; ~ *v.i.* (pop.) to down tools, to come out, to go, on strike, to strike.
débridé, -e [debride] *adj.* unrestrained; (fig.) unbridled (imagination, etc.).
débridement [debridmɑ̃] *s.m.* unbridling; (surg.) opening, lancing; (fig.) releasing, letting loose.
débrider [debride] *v.t.* **1.** to unbridle (horse, etc.); (fig.) *sans ~*, continuously, non-stop; **2.** (surg.) to (re-)open, to lance; (cook.) to untruss (fowl).
débris [debri] *s.m.* (usu. pl.) fragments, remains, wreck, wreckage, debris; (pop.) *un vieux ~*, an old fuddy-duddy.
débrochage [debrɔʃaʒ] *s.m.* unstitching (of book).
débrocher [debrɔʃe] *v.t.* (cook.) to take (fowl, joint) off the spit; to unstitch (book).
débrouillage [debrujaʒ] *s.m.* **1.** resourcefulness; **2.** = DÉBROUILLEMENT.
débrouillard, -e [debrujar] *adj.* (fam.) artful, resourceful, cunning; *s.m.f. c'est un ~*, he knows how to shift for himself.
débrouillardise [debrujardiz], **débrouille** [debruj] *s.f.* ability to shift for oneself, resourcefulness.
débrouillement [debrujmɑ̃] *s.m.* disentangling, sorting out, clearing up, finding a way (out).
débrouiller [debruje] *v.t.* to disentangle, to sort out; (fig.) to clear up, to solve; (fam.) *~ qn.*, to show s.o. how to escape, how to manage; *~ un élève*, to teach a pupil the essentials; **se ~** *v.refl.* to find a way (out); (fam.) *il sait se ~*, he knows how to shift for himself.
débroussaillement [debrusɑjmɑ̃] *s.m.* clearing (ground) of undergrowth.
débroussailler [debrusɑje] *v.t.* to clear (ground) of undergrowth; (fig.) *~ une question difficile*, to throw light on a problem.
débuché [debyʃe] *s.m.* (hunt.) breaking cover, starting from cover.
débucher [debyʃe] *v.i.* (hunt.) to break cover; ~ *v.t.* (hunt.) to drive from cover, to raise (game); ~ *s.m.* = DÉBUCHÉ.
débusquer [debyske] *v.t.* (hunt.) to drive from cover; ~ *v.i.* (of game) to break cover.
début [deby] *s.m.* beginning, outset, start; *du ~*, initial, starting; (pl.) beginnings, early days; (theatr.) first appearance, début.
débutant, -e [debytɑ̃] *s.m.f.* beginner; **~e** [debytɑ̃t] *s.f.* débutante.
débuter [debyte] *v.i.* to begin, to start; to make one's début.
deçà [dəsa] *adv., prep.* **1.** (obs.) here, hither; *~, delà, ~ et delà*, here and there, hither and thither; **2.** *en ~ de*, (obs.) *au ~ de*, (on) this side (of); *jambe ~, jambe delà*, astride.
décacheter [dekaʃte] *v.t.* to unseal, to open (letter, etc.).
décadaire [dekadɛr] *adj.* decadal.
décade [dekad] *s.f.* decade; décade (10-day period in Fr. Republican Calendar 1793–1805).
décadence [dekadɑ̃s] *s.f.* decadence, decay, decline.
décadent, -e [dekadɑ̃] *adj.* decadent; ~ *s.m.* decadent.
décadi [dekadi] *s.m.* (hist.) Décadi (10th day of *décade*).
décaèdre [dekaɛdr] *s.m.* decahedron; ~ *adj.* decahedral.
décaféiner [dekafeine] *v.t.* to decaffeinate.
décagonal, -e, (aux) [dekagɔnal] *adj.* decagonal.
décagone [dekagɔn] *s.m.* decagon.
décagramme [dekagram] *s.m.* decagram.
décaissement [dekɛsmɑ̃] *s.m.* disbursement, outlay.
décaisser [dekɛse] *v.t.* to unpack, to unbox, to uncrate; to draw out (sum of money).
décalage [dekalaʒ] *s.m.* unwedging; displacing, displacement; disconnection; break; time lag, difference of time; divergence of views; (electr.) difference of phase.
décalamin-age [dekalaminaʒ] *s.m.* (techn.) decarbonization, decoking; **~er** [dekalamine] *v.t.* (techn.) to decarbonize.
décalcification [dekalsifikɑsjɔ̃] *s.f.* decalcification.
décalcifier [dekalsifje] *v.t.* to decalcify.
décaler [dekale] *v.t.* to unwedge; to displace; to put out of phase or alignment; to change the timing of, to move (times or objects) forward or backward.
décalitre [dekalitr] *s.m.* decalitre.
décalogue [dekalɔg] *s.m.* decalogue.
décalotter [dekaɔte] *v.t.* to take the cap off (sth.), to uncap.

décalquage [dekalkaʒ] *s.m.* transferring, tracing, (of design, etc.).
décalque [dekalk] *s.m.* transfer, trace, (of design, etc.); (fig.) adaptation.
décalquer [dekalke] *v.t.* to transfer, to trace, (design, etc.).
décamètre [dekamɛtr] *s.m.* decametre.
décamper [dekɑ̃pe] *v.i.* to decamp, to disappear; (obs.) to strike camp.
décanat [dekana] *s.m.* (eccles.) deanship, deanery (office).
décaniller [dekanije] *v.i.* (fam.) to decamp, to be off.
décant-age [dekɑ̃taʒ] *s.m.* decanting; **~er** [dekɑ̃te] *v.t.* to decant; (fig.) *~er ses idées*, to turn things over in one's mind; **~eur** [dekɑ̃tœr] *s.m.* (techn.) decanting apparatus.
décap-age [dekapaʒ] *s.m.* cleaning, scouring (of metal surface); **~ant** [dekapɑ̃] *s.m.* chemical or abrasive substance for cleaning metal surface, cleaner, scourer, detergent, solvent, (varnish, etc.) remover, stripper; **~ement** [dekapmɑ̃] *s.m.* = DÉCAPAGE; **~er** [dekape] *v.t.* to clean chemically, to scour, to clean, to strip; **~euse** [dekapøz] *s.f.* (civ. eng.) scraper.
décapitation [dekapitɑsjɔ̃] *s.f.* beheading, decapitation.
décapiter [dekapite] *v.t.* to behead, to decapitate.
décapode [dekapɔd] *s.m., adj.* (zool.) decapod.
décapotable [dekapɔtabl] *adj.* (car) convertible, with sliding roof, with folding hood; *une (voiture) ~*, a convertible.
décapoter [dekapɔte] *v.t.* to put down the hood of, to slide back the roof of, (a car).
décapsuler [dekapsyle] *v.t.* to open (bottle), to remove cap, capsule, crown cork, from.
décapsuleur [dekapsylœr] *s.m.* bottle-opener (esp. for removing crown corks).
décapuchonner [dekapyʃɔne] *v.t.* to take the cap off (fountain-pen, etc.).
décarbur-ation [dekarbyrɑsjɔ̃] *s.f.* (metall.) decarbonization, decarburation, removing carbon or carbon dioxide from; **~er** [decarbyre] *v.t.* (metall., chem.) to decarbonize, to decarburize, to remove carbon or carbon dioxide from.
(**se**) **décarcasser** [dekarkase] *v.refl.* (fam.) to take a lot of trouble, to slave away.
décarreler [dekɑrle] *v.t.* to remove (floor) tiles from.
décartellisation [dekartelizɑsjɔ̃] *s.f.* (econ.) decartel(l)ization.
décasyllabe, décasyllabique [dekasilab, -ik] *adj.* decasyllabic; *~ s.f.* decasyllable.
décatir [dekatir] *v.t.* (text.) to decatise (woollen cloth); **se ~** *v.refl.* (fam.) to age; *être, se sentir, décati*, to be feeling one's age, to be past one's best.
décatissage [dekatisaʒ] *s.m.* (text.) decatising.
décavé, -e [dekave] *adj., s.m.f.* (fam.) ruined, cleaned-out, (gambler).
décaver [dekave] *v.t.* (gambling) to ruin, to clean out; **se ~** *v.refl.* to be cleaned out.
décédé, -e [desede] *adj.* deceased.
décéder [desede] *v.i.* (law, admin.) to decease, to die.
décelable [deslabl] *adj.* detectable, demonstrable.
déceler [desle] *v.t.* to uncover, to reveal; to demonstrate, to betray.
décélération [deselerɑsjɔ̃] *s.f.* deceleration.
décembre [desɑ̃br] *s.m.* December.
décemment [desamɑ̃] *adv.* decently, reasonably, correctly.
décence [desɑ̃s] *s.f.* decency; discretion, tact.
décennal, -e, (**aux**) [desenal] *adj.* decennial.
décennie [deseni] *s.f.* decennium.
décent, -e [desɑ̃] *adj.* decent, respectable, reasonably good.
décentrage [desɑ̃traʒ] *s.m.* (opt.) decentring.
décentralisat-eur, -rice [desɑ̃tralizatœr] *adj.* decentralizing, favouring a policy of decentralization.
décentralisation [desɑ̃tralizɑsjɔ̃] *s.f.* decentralization.
décentraliser [desɑ̃tralize] *v.t.* to decentralize.
décentration [desɑ̃trɑsjɔ̃] *s.f.*, **décentrement** [desɑ̃trəmɑ̃] *s.m.* (opt.) decentration (of lens).
décentrer [desɑ̃tre] *v.t.* (opt.) to decentre.
déception [desɛpsjɔ̃] *s.f.* **1.** disappointment; **2.** (obs.) deception, deceit.
décerner [desɛrne] *v.t.* to award, to confer (prize, honour); (law) *~ un mandat d'arrêt, de dépôt*, to issue a warrant for, to order, the arrest, the imprisonment (of s.o.).
décès [desɛ] *s.m.* decease, death.
décevant, -e [dɛsvɑ̃] *adj.* disappointing; (obs.) deceptive, misleading; seductive.
décevoir [dɛsvwar] *v.t.* to disappoint; (obs.) to deceive.
déchaîné, -e [deʃene] *adj.* let loose, unleashed; out of control.
déchaînement [deʃɛnmɑ̃] *s.m.* unleashing, letting loose; rage, fury.
déchaîner [deʃene] *v.t.* to unleash, to loose, to let loose; to stir up; **se ~** *v.refl.* to break loose, to be unleashed; to fly into a rage (*contre qn.*, with s.o.).
déchant [deʃɑ̃] *s.m.* descant.
déchanter [deʃɑ̃te] *v.i.* (fam.) to change one's tune, to pipe down.
décharge [deʃarʒ] *s.f.* **1.** unloading, dumping; unloading area, dump; *~ **publique***, rubbish tip, refuse dump; **2.** relief, relieving, easing, outlet; (typ.) blotting-sheet; *tuyau de ~*, overflow pipe; (arch.) *voûte, arc, de ~*, relieving arch; **3.** (law) discharge (from obligation, debt, etc.), release, acquittal; *témoin à ~*, witness for the defence; **4.** discharge, volley (from firearms); (electr.) discharge.
déchargement [deʃarʒəmɑ̃] *s.m.* unloading.
déchargeoir [deʃarʒwar] *s.m.* (techn.) overflow pipe.
décharger [deʃarʒe] *v.t.* **1.** to unload (ship, truck, goods, etc.; firearm); **2.** to discharge (waste, excess liquid, electr. current, etc.; firearm); (fam.) *~ sa colère*, to vent one's anger; **3.** (text., of dye) to run. **4.** (fig.) to discharge, to free, (s.o. from obligation, accusation, etc.); *ses employés le déchargent de presque tout*, his employees relieve him of almost all the work; *~ l'accusé*, to clear the accused.
déchargeur [deʃarʒœr] *s.m.* (obs.) stevedore, docker, (market-)porter.
décharné, -e [deʃarne] *adj.* very thin, emaciated, skinny, bony; fleshless; bare and rugged.
décharner [deʃarne] *v.t.* to emaciate, to make thin, to reduce to a skeleton; (obs.) to strip the flesh off.
déchaumage [deʃomaʒ] *s.m.* ploughing in (of stubble).
déchaumer [deʃome] *v.t.* to plough in (stubble).
déchaussage [deʃosaʒ] *s.m.* exposing of roots (of plant).
déchaussé, -e [deʃose] *adj.* barefoot, unshod; (relig.) discalced; (of tooth) gumless; (of plant) with roots exposed; (of wall, etc.) with foundations uncovered.
déchaussement [deʃosmɑ̃] *s.m.* exposure of foundations (of wall); receding of gums.
déchausser [deʃose] *v.t.* **1.** to take off the shoes of; **2.** to uncover the foundations of (wall); to lay bare the roots of (plant); **se ~** *v.refl.* to take off one's shoes; (of tooth) to become exposed at the root.

déchaux [deʃo] *adj.* (relig.) discalced.

dèche [dɛʃ] *s.f.* (pop.) penury, destitution; *être dans la ~, dans une ~ noire*, to be hard up, broke, in very low water.

déchéance [deʃeɑ̃s] *s.f.* **1.** lowering, fall, decay, disgrace; *~ physique*, decline in health; **2.** (law) loss (of right); lapse, forfeiture.

déchet [deʃɛ] *s.m.* (often pl.) waste, débris, scraps; (comm.) loss, deterioration, wastage, deficiency; (fig., of person) wreck, failure.

déchiffrable [deʃifrabl] *adj.* decipherable.

déchiffrage [deʃifraʒ] *s.m.* deciphering; (mus.) sight-reading.

déchiffrement [deʃifrəmɑ̃] *s.m.* deciphering.

déchiffrer [deʃifre] *v.t.* to decipher, to decode; (mus.) to sight-read; (fig.) to uncover (intrigue, etc.), to detect.

déchiffreu-r, -se [deʃifrœr] *s.m.f.* decipherer, decoder.

déchiquetage [deʃiktaʒ] *s.m.* tearing to shreds; slashing.

déchiqueté, -e [deʃikte] *adj.* in shreds, ragged; jagged; (bot.) laciniate.

déchiqueter [deʃikte] *v.t.* to tear to shreds; to slash.

déchiqueture [deʃiktyr] *s.f.* slash, gash, irregular cut; jagged edge.

déchirant, -e [deʃirɑ̃] *adj.* heart-rending, harrowing, agonizing.

déchiré, -e [deʃire] *adj.* torn; heart-broken; divided; *le pays est ~*, the country is torn in two.

déchirement [deʃirmɑ̃] *s.m.* tearing (up); heartbreak; division, separation.

déchirer [deʃire] *v.t.* to tear, to rend; (fig.) to divide; to harrow; to slander.

déchirure [deʃiryr] *s.f.* tear, rent.

déchoir [deʃwar] *v.i.* to come down in the world, to lose caste; to decline; (relig.) to fall from grace.

déchu, -e [deʃy] *adj.* fallen; *~ de*, having forfeited (right, etc.); (relig.) fallen from grace.

décibel [desibɛl] *s.m.* decibel.

décidé, -e [deside] *adj.* decided, settled; determined, resolute; **~ment** [desidemɑ̃] *adv.* decidedly, positively.

décider [deside] *v.t.* **1.** to decide, to determine (*de*, to); to settle (question, etc.); *c'est moi qui décide*, it is I who make the decisions; **2.** *~ qn.*, to persuade s.o., to get s.o. to come to a decision, (*à faire*, to do); **se** *~ v.refl.* to decide, to determine, to make up one's mind, to come to a decision, (*à faire*, to do); *décidez-vous!*, make up your mind!

décigramme [desigram] *s.m.* decigram.

décilitre [desilitr] *s.m.* decilitre.

décimal, -e, (**aux**) [desimal] *adj.* decimal; **~e** *s.f.* decimal.

décimer [desime] *v.t.* (Rom. ant.) to decimate; (mod.) to kill large numbers of, to massacre, to decimate.

décimètre [desimɛtr] *s.m.* decimetre.

décintrage [desɛ̃traʒ], **décintrement** [desɛ̃trəmɑ̃] *s.m.* (build.) decentring, removing centring or truss (from a completed arch).

décintrer [desɛ̃tre] *v.t.* (build.) to decentre, to remove centring (from arch).

décisi-f, -ve [desisif] *adj.* decisive, conclusive, definitive; **~vement** [desisivmɑ̃] *adv.* decisively, definitively.

décision [desizjɔ̃] *s.f.* **1.** decision; **2.** resolution, determination.

décisoire [desizwar] *adj.* (law) decisive, decisory.

déclamat-eur, -rice [deklamatœr] *adj.* (pej.) ranting, bombastic; *s.m.f.* (pej.) ranter; **~eur** *s.m.* (Gr. & Rom. hist.) rhetor, declamator.

déclamation [deklamɑsjɔ̃] *s.f.* **1.** recitation, declamation, rhetoric; **2.** bombast, pompous speech.

déclamatoire [deklamatwar] *adj.* declamatory.

déclamer [deklame] *v.t.* to declaim, to recite; *~ v.i.* to rant, to inveigh (*contre*, against).

déclarati-f, -ve [deklaratif] *adj.* (law) declarative; (gram.) enunciative.

déclaration [deklarɑsjɔ̃] *s.f.* declaration.

déclaratoire [deklaratwar] *adj.* (law) declaratory.

déclaré, -e [deklare] *adj.* self-confessed, declared, open, avowed; *être l'ennemi ~ de qn.*, to be the sworn enemy of s.o.

déclarer [deklare] *v.t.* to declare; *~ son ignorance de qch.*, to proclaim one's ignorance of sth.; *on l'a déclaré coupable*, he was pronounced guilty; **se** *~ v.refl.* to declare oneself; to come to light, to manifest itself; (of fire) to break out.

déclassé, -e [deklase] *adj.* déclassé(e), of lowered social status; downgraded; *s.m.f.* déclassé(e), one who has lost class.

déclassement [deklasmɑ̃] *s.m.* loss of status, demotion.

déclasser [deklase] *v.t.* **1.** to lower the social status of; to downgrade, to demote, to put in a lower class; **2.** to disturb the order of (papers, etc.).

déclenche [deklɑ̃ʃ] *s.f.* (techn.) disconnecting gear, tripping device, trip.

déclenchement [deklɑ̃ʃmɑ̃] *s.m.* setting-off, triggering(-off); releasing, tripping; (fig.) launching, starting, triggering-off.

déclencher [deklɑ̃ʃe] *v.t.* **1.** (techn.) to disengage, to release, to trip; **2.** (techn.) to set (mechanism, etc.) in motion; (fig.) to set off, to trigger (off).

déclencheur [deklɑ̃ʃœr] *s.m.* (techn.) release, trip, disengaging mechanism.

déclic [deklik] *s.m.* **1.** catch, release, pawl, trigger, detent; *chronomètre à ~*, stop-watch; **2.** click (sound).

déclin [deklɛ̃] *s.m.* decline; *~ de la vie, de l'âge*, declining years.

déclinable [deklinabl] *adj.* (gram.) declinable.

déclinaison [deklinɛzɔ̃] *s.f.* (astron., phys.) declination; (gram.) declension.

déclinant, -e [deklinɑ̃] *adj.* declining.

déclinateur [deklinatœr] *s.m.* = DÉCLINATOIRE *s.m.* 2.

déclination [deklinɑsjɔ̃] *s.f.*, **déclinement** [deklinmɑ̃] *s.m.* declining; (obs.) incline.

déclinatoire [deklinatwar] *adj.* declinatory; *~ s.m.* **1.** (law, obs.) declinatory plea; **2.** (surveyor's) compass.

décliner [dekline] *v.t.i.* to decline, to refuse; (of magnetic needle) to deviate, to reflect.

décliquetage [deklikta ʒ] *s.m.* (techn.) disengaging (of gear, etc.).

décliqueter [deklikte] *v.t.* (techn.) to disengage, to disconnect, to declutch.

déclive [dekliv] *adj.* sloping; *~ s.f.* slope; *en ~*, sloping.

déclivité [deklivite] *s.f.* declivity, slope.

déclore [deklɔr] *v.t.* (obs.) to disenclose (field, etc.).

déclouer [deklue] *v.t.* to unnail, to open, (crate, etc.).

décocher [dekɔʃe] *v.t.* to shoot, to let off, to let fly; (fig.) to dart (a glance, etc.).

décoction [dekɔksjɔ̃] *s.f.* decoction; (fig., fam.) *~ de coups*, shower of blows.

décodage [dekɔdaʒ] *s.m.* decoding.

décoder [dekɔde] *v.t.* to decode.

décoffrage [dekɔfraʒ] *s.m.* (constr.) removal of shuttering (from concrete).

décoffrer [dekɔfre] *v.t.* (constr.) to remove shuttering (from concrete).

décoiffement [dekwafmɑ̃], **décoiffage** [dekwafaʒ] *s.m.* disarranging, ruffling, (of hair).

décoiffer [dekwafe] *v.t.* to disarrange, to ruffle, the hair of; (obs.) to remove the hat of, to

uncover (the head of); (techn.) to remove the cap of (sth.).
décoincement [dekwɛ̃smɑ̃], **décoinçage** [dekwɛ̃saʒ] *s.m.* unwedging, freeing, releasing (of sth. jammed), (rail.) unkeying.
décoincer [dekwɛ̃se] *v.t.* (techn.) to unwedge; to free (sth. wedged or jammed).
décolérer [dekɔlere] *v.i.* to calm down (after fit of anger); (esp.) *ne pas* ~, to remain angry, to continue to rage.
décollage [dekɔlaʒ] *s.m.* unsticking; (aeron.) take-off.
décollation [dekɔlɑsjɔ̃] *s.f.* decollation, decapitation.
décollement [dekɔlmɑ̃] *s.m.* unsticking; (med.) detachment (e.g. of retina).
décoller [dekɔle] *v.t.* to unstick, to remove (sth. stuck on); (med.) to become detached; (fig., pop.) ~ *qn.*, to stop clinging to s.o.; *v.i.* to break away (from group, etc.); (of ears) to stand out; (aeron.) to take off; (fam.) to go away; *il ne décolle pas d'ici*, you can't get rid of him.
décolletage [dekɔltaʒ] *s.m.* **1.** (dress) décolletage, low neckline; **2.** (agric.) topping (of root crop); **3.** (techn.) screw-, bolt-, etc., cutting.
décolleté, -e [dekɔlte] *adj.* décolleté(e), low-necked; ~ *s.m.* low neck, décolleté.
décolleter [dekɔlte] *v.t.* **1.** (of cut of dress) to show neck, bosoms, etc.; to cut (a dress) with a low neckline; *se* ~, to wear a low-cut dress; **2.** (agric.) to top (root crop); **3.** (techn.) to cut (screw).
décolleteu-r, -se [dekɔltœr] *s.m.f.* **1.** (techn.) screw-cutter (operative); **2.** **~se** *s.f.* (techn.) screw-cutting machine; (agric.) root-topping machine.
décolonisation [dekɔlɔnizɑsjɔ̃] *s.f.* decolonization.
décoloniser [dekɔlɔnize] *v.t.* to decolonize.
décolorant, -e [dekɔlɔrɑ̃] *adj.* bleaching; ~ *s.m.* bleach, decolorant.
décoloration [dekɔlɔrɑsjɔ̃] *s.f.* fading, bleaching, discoloration.
décoloré, -e [dekɔlɔre] *adj.* faded, washed-out, discoloured, pale; *cheveux* ~*s*, bleached hair.
décolorer [dekɔlɔre] *v.t.* to discolour, to cause to fade, to bleach; **se** ~ *v.refl.* to fade.
décombres [dekɔmbr] *s.m.pl.* ruins, rubble, wreckage (of building).
décommander [dekɔmɑ̃de] *v.t.* to cancel order for (goods); to postpone or cancel (invitation, meal); to put off (guests); **se** ~ *v.refl.* to cancel a rendezvous.
décommettre [dekɔmɛtr] *v.t.* (naut.) to unlay (rope).
décomposable [dekɔ̃pozabl] *adj.* separable, decomposable.
décomposer [dekɔ̃poze] *v.t.* to decompose, to analyse; to discompose; **se** ~ *v.refl.* to decompose, to disintegrate, to rot.
décomposition [dekɔ̃pozisjɔ̃] *s.f.* decomposition.
décompresseur [dekɔ̃prɛsœr] *s.m.* decompressor.
décompression [dekɔ̃prɛsjɔ̃] *s.f.* decompression.
décomprimer [dekɔ̃prime] *v.t.* to decompress.
décompte [dekɔ̃t] *s.m.* **1.** discount, rebate; (fig.) disappointment; **2.** (fin., comm.) breakdown, analysis, detailed account, itemization of charges.
décompter [dekɔ̃te] *v.t.* deduct (rebate); ~ *v.i.* (of clock) to strike amiss.
déconcentration [dekɔsɑ̃trɑsjɔ̃] *s.f.* decentralization, devolution.
déconcertant, -e [dekɔ̃sɛrtɑ̃] *adj.* disconcerting.
déconcerter [dekɔ̃sɛrte] *v.t.* to disconcert.
déconfit, -e [dekɔ̃fi] *adj.* discomfited, abashed; (obs.) defeated (in battle).
déconfiture [dekɔ̃fityr] *s.f.* **1.** (fam.) discomfiture, moral defeat; **2.** (fam.) failure; (law) bankruptcy, insolvency (of private individual).
décongélation [dekɔ̃ʒelasjɔ̃] *s.f.* defrosting, unfreezing.
décongeler [dekɔ̃ʒle] *v.t.* to defrost, to unfreeze, to thaw.
décongestionner [dekɔ̃ʒestjɔne] *v.t.* to relieve of congestion.
déconner [dekɔne] *v.i.* (vulg.) to talk nonsense, to talk a lot of cock.
déconseiller [dekɔ̃seje] *v.t.* to advise against (doing); ~ *à qn. de faire qch.*, to advise s.o. not to do sth.
déconsidération [dekɔ̃siderasjɔ̃] *s.f.* (Lit.) loss of esteem; discredit.
déconsidérer [dekɔ̃sidere] *v.t.* to discredit, to cast a slur on, to tarnish the reputation of; **se** ~ *v.refl.* to be discredited, to forfeit one's reputation.
déconsigner [dekɔ̃siɲe] *v.t.* **1.** to free (from detention, etc.); **2.** to withdraw (luggage) from cloakroom; **3.** to pay the charges on (a package).
décontenancer [dekɔ̃tənɑ̃se] *v.t.* to disconcert, to embarrass, to put out of countenance.
décontracté, -e [dekɔ̃trakte] *adj.* relaxed, free of tension; (fig.) unconcerned.
décontracter [dekɔ̃trakte] *v.t.* to relax; **se** ~ *v.refl.* to relax.
décontraction [dekɔ̃traksjɔ̃] *s.f.* relaxing, relaxation.
déconvenue [dekɔ̃vny] *s.f.* disappointment, discomfiture.
décor [dekɔr] *s.m.* **1.** decoration (of house, etc.); *peintre en* ~, house-painter, decorator; **2.** décor, setting; surroundings, milieu, atmosphere, scene; natural scenery; (theatr.) set, scenery; (fig.) *changement de* ~, altered situation, (abrupt) change of circumstances; (fam.) *entrer dans le* ~, (of car) to run off the road.
décorat-eur, -rice [dekɔratœr] *s.m.f.* **1.** house painter and decorator; interior decorator; **2.** (theatr., etc.) scene-painter, scenery designer.
décorati-f, -ve [dekɔratif] *adj.* decorative.
décoration [dekɔrɑsjɔ̃] *s.f.* **1.** decoration; **2.** decoration, order (conferred as honour).
décorder [dekɔrde] *v.t.* **1.** to untwist or unlay (rope); **2.** to untie, to undo, to open (package).
décoré, -e [dekɔre] *adj.* **1.** decorated, ornamented; **2.** decorated (i.e. wearing or holding a decoration); *un* ~, holder of a decoration, member of an order.
décorer [dekɔre] *v.t.* **1.** to adorn, to decorate, to ornament; **2.** to decorate (s.o., with medal, honour).
décorner [dekɔrne] *v.t.* **1.** to dehorn (cattle); **2.** ~ *une page*, to smooth out a dog-eared page.
décorticage [dekɔrtikaʒ] *s.m.* husking, blanching, decortication.
décortication [dekɔrtikɑsjɔ̃] *s.f.* (bot., surg.) decortication.
décortiquer [dekɔrtike] *v.t.* to decorticate.
décorum [dekɔrɔm] *s.m.* (no pl.) decorum, etiquette; *observer le* ~, to observe the proprieties.
décote [dekɔt] *s.f.* rebate (of rate or tax).
découcher [dekuʃe] *v.i.* to sleep away from home, to spend the night away from home.
découdre [dekudr] *v.t.* **1.** to unstitch, to rip (up, off); **2.** *en* ~, to come to blows.
découler [dekule] *v.t.* **1.** (obs. exc. Lit.) to trickle, to leak; **2.** to follow (as consequence or result).
découpage [dekupaʒ] *s.m.* cutting (up), carving (meat, etc.); cutting out; cut-out (shape, etc.); (art) découpage; (cin.) cutting.

découpé, -e [dekupe] *adj.* cut up, cut out.
découper [dekupe] *v.t.* **1.** to cut up, to carve (joint, etc.); *couteau à* ~, carving knife; **2.** to cut out; **se** ~ *v.refl.* to stand out, to be silhouetted (*sur*, against).
découpeu-r, -se [dekupœr] *s.m.f.* cutter-out; ~**se** [dekupøz] *s.f.* cutting-out machine; fretsaw, band-saw.
découplé, -e [dekuple] *adj.* **1.** (of hounds) uncoupled; **2.** (obs.) lithe; *bien* ~, (of person) well-built, strapping.
découpler [dekuple] *v.t.* to uncouple (hounds).
découpoir [dekupwar] *s.m.* (techn.) cutter, shear.
découpure [dekupyr] *s.f.* **1.** cutting-out; **2.** cut-out (shape, etc.); scallop(s), scalloping; **3.** indentation (of coastline).
décourageant, -e [dekuraʒɑ̃] *adj.* discouraging, disheartening.
découragement [dekuraʒmɑ̃] *s.m.* dejection, despondency, depression.
décourager [dekuraʒe] *v.t.* to dishearten, to discourage; **se** ~ *v.refl.* to lose heart, to become depressed.
découronnement [dekurɔnmɑ̃] *s.m.* (obs.) deposing (of sovereign).
découronner [dekurɔne] *v.t.* **1.** to depose; (fig.) to belittle; **2.** to pollard (tree, etc.).
décours [dekur] *s.m.* **1.** (astron.) wane, waning (of moon); **2.** (med.) *être dans le* ~, (of illness) to be abating.
décousu, -e [dekuzy] *adj.* that has come unstitched; (fig.) disjointed, incoherent.
décousure [dekuzyr] *s.f.* **1.** (obs.) rent in seam (of garment, etc.); **2.** (hunt.) gash inflicted (on dog) by tusk(s) or horn(s).
découvert, -e [dekuvɛr] *adj.* **1.** discovered; **2.** uncovered; open; ~ *s.m.* **1.** (obs.) open country, clearing; **2.** (unsecured) overdraft or credit; (insurance) excess; *à* ~ *adv. loc.* **1.** exposed, in the open; openly, frankly; **2.** (comm.) without security, on credit.
découverte [dekuvɛrt] *s.f.* discovery, finding-out; *aller, partir, à la* ~, to go exploring, to reconnoitre, to go in search (*de*, of).
découvreu-r, -se [dekuvrœr] *s.m.f.* discoverer, inventor.
découvrir [dekuvrir] *v.t.* to discover, to find out, to detect; to uncover, to lay bare, to expose, to reveal; **se** ~ *v.refl.* to take off one's clothes, to take off one's hat; to reveal one's thoughts, to confide (*à qn.*, in s.o); to become visible; to clear (up); *le ciel se découvre*, the weather is clearing up.
décrassage [dekrasaʒ], **décrassement** [dekrasmɑ̃] *s.m.* cleaning, cleansing.
décrasser [dekrase] *v.t.* **1.** to clean, to wash; ~ *du linge*, to soak dirty linen; **2.** (fig.) to lick into shape, to make presentable.
décrément [dekremɑ̃] *s.m.* (sci.) decrement.
décrépir [dekrepir] *v.t.* to strip (wall, etc., of plaster).
décrépit, -e [dekrepi] *adj.* decrepit, feeble (with age).
décrépitation [dekrepitɑsjɔ̃] *s.f.* (sci.) decrepitation.
décrépitude [dekrepityd] *s.f.* decrepitude, decay.
decrescendo [dekreʃɛndo] *adv.*, *s.m.* (mus.) decrescendo; (fig.) *aller* ~, to be waning.
décret [dekrɛ] *s.m.* decree, order, fiat, ordinance.
décrétale [dekretal] *s.f.* (relig. hist.) decretal.
décréter [dekrete] *v.t.* to decree, to order.
décret-loi [dekrɛlwa] *s.m.* government decree (=Eng. Order in Council).
décri [dekri] *s.m.* (obs.) discredit, loss of reputation.
décrier [dekrie] *v.t.* to decry, to disparage.
décrire [dekrir] *v.t.* to describe.
décrochage [dekrɔʃaʒ] *s.m.* **1.** unhooking, taking down; **2.** (mil.) disengagement; (fam.) abandonment, giving up, (of activity).
décrochement [dekrɔʃmɑ̃] *s.m.* being unhooked or disconnected; being out of contact; (geol.) fault.
décrocher [dekrɔʃe] *v.t.* to take off hook, to take down; to unhook, to disconnect, to uncouple; (fig.) to secure for oneself, to succeed in getting, to wangle; ~ (*le récepteur*), to take off, to lift, the (telephone) receiver, to answer (the phone); ~ *une bonne situation*, to land a good job; ~ *v.i.* to lose contact; (fam.) to stop, to give up (an activity).
décrochez-moi-ça [dekrɔʃemwasa] *s.m.invar.* second-hand clothes shop.
décroiser [dekrwaze] *v.t.* to uncross (legs, arms), to untwine.
décroissance [dekrwasɑ̃s] *s.f.* decrease, diminution, decline.
décroissant, -e [dekrwasɑ̃] *adj.* decreasing, diminishing; *classer par ordre* ~, to arrange in descending order.
décroissement [dekrwasmɑ̃] *s.m.* decreasing, declining; waning; ~ *des jours*, drawing in of days.
décroît [dekrwa] *s.m.* (astron.) waning, wane (of moon), esp. last quarter (of moon).
décroître [dekrwatr] *v.i.* to decrease, to diminish, to abate; *les jours décroissent*, the days are getting shorter, are drawing in.
décrottage [dekrɔtaʒ] *s.m.* scraping, removal of mud.
décrotter [dekrɔte] *v.t.* to scrape (shoes, etc.), to remove mud from; (fam.) to lick into shape.
décrottoir [dekrɔtwar] *s.m.* scraper, boot-scraper.
décrue [dekry] *s.f.* decrease; fall (of water-level).
décruer [dekrye], **décruser** [dekryze] *v.t.* (text.) to degum (silk).
décrypter [dekripte] *v.t.* to decipher, to decode (by breaking code).
déçu, -e [desy] *adj.* disappointed.
décuivrage [dekɥivraʒ] *s.m.* (techn.) removal of copper-plating (by electrolysis, etc.).
décuivrer [dekɥivre] *v.t.* (techn.) to remove copper-plating (from a surface).
déculotter [dekylɔte] *v.t.* to take off the trousers of; **se** ~ *v.refl.* (pop.) to take off one's trousers.
décuple [dekypl] *adj.*, *s.m.* decuple, tenfold (amount).
décupler [dekyple] *v.t.i.* to decuple, to increase tenfold.
décussé, -e [dekyse] *adj.* (bot.) decussate.
décuvage [dekyvaʒ] *s.m.* racking, racking off, (of wine).
décuver [dekyve] *v.t.* to rack, to rack off, (wine).
dédaignable [dedɛɲabl] *adj.* (esp. with neg.) contemptible; *pas* ~, not to be despised, not to be underestimated.
dédaigner [dedeɲe] *v.t.* to disdain; to scorn, to consider unworthy of (one's) notice; to pay no heed to; ~ *de répondre*, to scorn to answer.
dédaigneu-x, -se [dedɛɲø] *adj.* disdainful, scornful; haughty, condescending, contemptuous; ~**sement** [dedɛɲøzmɑ̃] *adv.* disdainfully, scornfully, with contempt.
dédain [dedɛ̃] *s.m.* disdain, scorn, contempt.
dédale [dedal] *s.m.* labyrinth, maze.
dédaléen, -ne [dedaleɛ̃] *adj.* (Lit.) Daedalian, Daedalean, labyrinthine.
dedans [dədɑ̃] *adv.* in, inside, within; *mettre* ~, (pop.) to put in prison, to put inside; (fam.) to do (down); *marcher les pieds* ~, to walk with one's toes turned in; *en* ~ (*de*), inside, within; ~ *prep.* (obs.) inside, within; ~ *s.m.* inside; (fig.) inner man; *au* ~ (*de*), within, inside.

dédicace [dedikas] *s.f.* **1.** consecration (of church, etc.); **2.** dedication (of Lit. work to s.o.).
dédicacer [dedikase] *v.t.* to dedicate (book, etc.).
dédicataire [dedikatɛr] *s.m.f.* dedicatee.
dédicatoire [dedikatwar] *adj.* dedicatory.
dédier [dedje] *v.t.* to dedicate, to inscribe; to devote.
dédire [dedir] *v.t.* (obs.) to contradict; **se ~** *v.refl.* to retract (statement, promise, etc.), to go back on one's word, to contradict oneself; (pop.) *cochon qui s'en dédit*, may I die (if I break my word)!
dédit [dedi] *s.m.* (obs.) disavowal; (law) withdrawal; forfeit, compensation; *payer son ~*, to pay up in full.
dédommagement [dedɔmaʒmɑ̃] *s.m.* indemnity, reparation, compensation.
dédommager [dedɔmaʒe] *v.t.* to compensate, to indemnify; to recompense, to repay.
dédorage [dedɔraʒ] *s.m.* (techn.) ungilding.
dédoré, -e [dedɔre] *adj.* that has lost its gilt; (fig.) *aristocratie ~e*, impoverished aristocracy.
dédorer [dedɔre] *v.t.* to ungild; **se ~** *v.refl.* to lose its gilt.
dédouanement [dedwanmɑ̃] *s.m.* customs clearance.
dédouaner [dedwane] *v.t.* to clear (goods) through customs.
dédoublage [dedublaʒ] *s.m.* **1.** removal of lining; **2.** dilution (of alcohol).
dédoublement [dedubləmɑ̃] *s.m.* **1.** (obs.) unfolding; (mod.) removal of lining; division into two; doubling; *~ d'un train*, running of train in two portions; **2.** (psychol.) duality (of personality); two-sidedness, ambivalence, (of character, etc.).
dédoubler [deduble] *v.t.* **1.** (obs.) to unfold; **2.** to remove the lining from; **3.** to divide (regiment, school-class, etc.) into two parts; to run (train, convoy) in two portions; **se ~** *v.refl.* to split (into two); (psychol.) to suffer from split personality.
déducti-f, -ve [dedyktif] *adj.* deductive.
déduction [dedyksjɔ̃] *s.f.* deduction.
déduire [dedɥir] *v.t.* **1.** to deduct; **2.** to deduce, to infer.
déduit [dedɥi] *s.m.* (obs.) dalliance.
déesse [deɛs] *s.f.* goddess.
défaillance [defajɑ̃s] *s.f.* **1.** (obs.) lack, want; **2.** fainting-fit, collapse; **3.** failure; *sans ~*, unfaltering(ly).
défaillant, -e [defajɑ̃] *adj.* **1.** (obs.) lacking, wanting; (of witness) defaulting; **2.** declining, weakening, dying out; faint, fainting.
défaillir [defajir] *v.i.* **1.** (obs.) to be wanting or lacking, to default; **2.** to faint, to collapse; to decline, to diminish; **3.** (Lit.) to fail in one's duty.
défaire [defɛr] *v.t.* **1.** to undo; *~ un mur pierre par pierre*, to take down a wall stone by stone; *~ un contrat*, to break a contract; *~ sa valise, ses bagages*, to unpack (one's suitcase, luggage); *~ la table*, to clear the table; **2.** (obs. exc. Lit.) to rid (*de*, of); (Lit.) to rout, to defeat.
défait, -e [defɛ] *adj.* undone, disarranged; worn out, exhausted; (of face) pale, discomposed; defeated, routed.
défaite [defɛt] *s.f.* defeat.
défaitisme [defɛtism] *s.m.* defeatism.
défalcation [defalkɑsjɔ̃] *s.f.* defalcation.
défalquer [defalke] *v.t.* to defalcate.
défaufiler [defofile] *v.t.* (dressm.) to untack.
défausser [defose] *v.t.* to straighten; **se ~** (*de*) *v.refl.* (cards) to throw away (unimportant cards).
défaut [defo] *s.m.* lack, defect, fault; (esp. law) default; *faire ~*, to be lacking; (phys.) *~ de masse*, mass defect; (fig.) *le ~ de la cuirasse, de l'armure*, the chink in the armour, the weak point, the Achilles' heel; *à ~ de*, in the absence of, for lack of; *sans ~*, faultless.
défaveur [defavœr] *s.f.* disfavour.
défavorable [defavɔrabl] *adj.* unfavourable, adverse; **~ment** [defavɔrabləmɑ̃] *adv.* unfavourably, adversely.
défavoriser [defavɔrize] *v.t.* to put at a disadvantage, to disadvantage.
défécation [defekɑsjɔ̃] *s.f.* defecation.
défecti-f, -ve [defɛktif] *adj.* (gram.) defective.
défection [defɛksjɔ̃] *s.f.* defection, desertion.
défectueu-x, -se [defɛktɥø] *adj.* defective; **~sement** [defɛktɥøzmɑ̃] *adv.* defectively.
défectuosité [defɛktɥozite] *s.f.* defectiveness.
défendable [defɑ̃dabl] *adj.* defensible, tenable.
défend-eur, -eresse [defɑ̃dœr] *s.m.f.* (law) defendant; respondent (in appeal or divorce case).
défendre [defɑ̃dr] *v.t.* **1.** to defend, to shield; *à son corps défendant*, in self-defence; (fig.) reluctantly, under duress; **2.** to forbid, to prohibit; **se ~** *v.refl.* **1.** to defend oneself, to resist; to protect oneself (*de, contre*, from, against); to justify oneself; **2.** to deny oneself (sth.); *se ~ de faire qch.*, not to allow oneself to do sth., to refuse to do sth., to refrain from doing sth.
défenestration [defənɛstrɑsjɔ̃] *s.f.* (hist.) defenestration; (fam.) throwing (sth.) out of the window.
défenestrer [defənɛstre] *v.t.* (fam.) to throw out of the window.
défense [defɑ̃s] *s.f.* **1.** defence; **2.** prohibition; *~ de fumer*, no smoking; **3.** tusk (of elephant, etc.).
défenseur [defɑ̃sœr] *s.m.* **1.** defender; champion (of cause, etc.); **2.** (law) counsel for the defence.
défensi-f, -ve [defɑ̃sif] *adj.* defensive; **~ve** *s.f.* defensive; *être, se tenir, sur la ~ve*, to be, to stand, on the defensive.
déféquer [defeke] *v.t.i.* to defecate.
déférence [deferɑ̃s] *s.f.* deference.
déférant, -e [deferɑ̃] *adj.* deferential; (anat., bot.) deferent.
déférer [defere] *v.t.* **1.** (obs.) to confer; **2.** (law) to bring (case), to send (s.o.) for trial; *~ v.i.* to defer (to s.o., to someone's judgement); ⚠ not 'to defer' in sense 'to postpone'.
déferlage [defɛrlaʒ] *s.m.* (naut.) unfurling (of sail).
déferlant, -e [defɛrlɑ̃] *adj.* (of wave) breaking; spreading.
déferler [defɛrle] *v.t.* to unfurl (sail); *~ v.i.* (of wave) to break.
déferlement [defɛrləmɑ̃] *s.m.* breaking (of wave); (fig.) *un ~ d'enthousiasme*, a surge of enthusiasm.
déferrage [defɛraʒ] *s.m.*, **déferrement** [defɛrmɑ̃] *s.m.*, **déferrure** [defɛryr] *s.f.* unshoeing (of horse, etc.); removal of furniture (of door, etc.); removal of fetters (of prisoner).
déferrer [defɛre] *v.t.* to remove iron furniture or fittings from (door, chest, etc.); to remove fetters from (prisoner); to unshoe (horse, etc.).
défervescence [defɛrvɛsɑ̃s] *s.f.* (chem.) abatement of effervescence; (med.) defervescence, decrease of feverish symptoms.
défet [defɛ] *s.m.* (usu. pl.) (bookb.) waste sheets.
défeuillaison [defœjɛzɔ̃] *s.f.* falling of leaves; defoliation.
défeuiller [defœje] *v.t.* to strip of leaves; to defoliate; *arbre défeuillé*, tree which has lost its leaves; *rose défeuillée*, rose which has lost its petals.
défi [defi] *s.m.* **1.** challenge, gage, gauntlet; dare; *mettre qn. au ~ de faire qch.*, to dare s.o. to do sth.; **2.** defiance (*à*, of).

défiance [defjɑ̃s] *s.f.* distrust; suspicion; ⚠ not 'defiance'.
défiant, -e [defjɑ̃] *adj.* distrustful, suspicious; ⚠ not 'defiant'.
défibrage [defibraʒ] *s.m.* (techn.) pulping, crushing, removal of fibres.
défibrer [defibre] *v.t.* (techn.) to pulp, to crush, to remove fibres from.
défibreu-r, -se [defibrœr] *s.m.f.* crusher (operative); **~se** *s.f.* crusher, shredder, pulper, (machine).
déficeler [defisle] *v.t.* to untie; ~ *un paquet*, to open a parcel.
déficience [defisjɑ̃s] *s.f.* deficiency, inadequacy.
déficient, -e [defisjɑ̃] *adj.* deficient; insufficient.
déficit [defisit] *s.m.* deficit; deficiency; *être en* ~, to show a deficit.
déficitaire [defisitɛr] *adj.* showing a deficit; deficient; *récolte* ~, poor harvest.
défier [defje] *v.t.* to challenge, to defy, to dare; **se** ~ (*de*) *v.refl.* to distrust.
défigurement [defigyrmɑ̃] *s.m.* disfigurement; (fig.) distortion.
défigurer [defigyre] *v.t.* to disfigure; to distort.
défilage [defilaʒ] *s.m.* (papermaking) rag-cutting; (text.) ravelling out.
défilé [defile] *s.m.* **1.** (geog.) defile, gorge; **2.** (mil., etc.) file, march past, fly past; procession, (protest) march.
défilement [defilmɑ̃] *s.m.* (mil.) cover; ⚠ not 'defilement'.
défiler [defile] *v.t.* **1.** to unstring (beads, etc.); **2.** (papermaking) to break in (rags, etc.); (text.) to ravel out; **3.** (mil.) to defilade; **se** ~ *v.refl.* (mil.) to take cover; (fam.) to make oneself scarce; ~ *v.i.* **1.** (mil.) to move in file, to defile; to file (past); **2.** to come one after the other, to come in a procession, to pass in procession; ⚠ not 'to defile' in sense 'to pollute', 'to profane'.
défini, -e [defini] *adj.* definite; defined; precise; (gram.) *article* ~, definite article, *passé* ~, past historic, preterite, past definite; ~ *s.m.* (log.) term.
définir [definir] *v.t.* to define; to describe, to characterize; to determine.
définissable [definisabl] *adj.* definable.
définiti-f, -ve [definitif] *adj.* final, definitive; *en ~ve*, after all, when all's said and done.
définition [definisjɔ̃] *s.f.* definition.
définitivement [definitivmɑ̃] *adv.* finally, definitively.
déflagrant, -e [deflagrɑ̃] *adj.* (techn.) deflagrating.
déflagr-ateur [deflagratœr] *s.m.* (techn.) deflagrator, deflagrating-spoon; **~ation** [deflagrasjɔ̃] *s.f.* (chem.) deflagration; explosion; **~er** [deflagre] *v.i.* (chem., techn.) to deflagrate; to explode.
déflation [deflasjɔ̃] *s.f.* deflation.
déflecteur [deflɛktœr] *s.m.* (naut.) deflector (for determining compass deviation); (techn.) deflector, baffle-plate; (car) wind-deflector, quarter-light.
défleuri, -e [deflœri] *adj.* (Lit.) that has lost its blossom or flowers.
défleurir [deflœrir] *v.i.* to shed its blossom or flowers; ~ *v.t.* to strip of its blossom or flowers.
défloraison [deflɔrɛzɔ̃] *s.f.* (Lit., bot.) shedding of blossom, of flowers.
défloration [deflɔrasjɔ̃] *s.f.* deflowering.
déflorer [deflɔre] *v.t.* **1.** (obs.) to strip the flowers or blossom from; (fig.) to deprive (sth.) of freshness or newness; **2.** to deflower (a virgin), to seduce.
défoliation [defoljasjɔ̃] *s.f.* (bot.) shedding of leaves; defoliation.
défonçage [defɔ̃saʒ], **défoncement** [defɔ̃smɑ̃] *s.m.* **1.** staving in (of cask, etc.); breaking open (of crate, etc.); breaking in (of door, etc.); causing (mattress, etc.) to sag; wearing (of road) into pot-holes; **2.** (agric.) (deep-)-trenching; excavating.
défoncé, -e [defɔ̃se] *adj.* broken, smashed in, worn down; *un sommier* ~, a sagging mattress; *chaussée ~e*, road full of pot-holes.
défoncer [defɔ̃se] *v.t.* **1.** to stave in (cask, etc.); to break open (door, box, etc.); to cause (mattress, etc.) to sag; to wear (road) into pot-holes; **2.** (agric.) to (deep-)trench; to excavate.
défonceuse [defɔ̃søz] *s.f.* (agric.) trench plough.
déformant, -e [defɔrmɑ̃] *adj.* distorting, warping.
déformat-eur, -rice [defɔrmatœr] *adj.* (Lit.) distorting, misrepresenting.
déformation [defɔrmasjɔ̃] *s.f.* distortion, deformation; misrepresentation, travesty; bias, prejudice.
déformer [defɔrme] *v.t.* to distort, to deform, to put out of shape; to misrepresent (fact, etc.); to corrupt; **se** ~ *v.refl.* to lose its shape.
défoulement [defulmɑ̃] *s.m.* (psychol.) release (of tensions, etc.).
(**se**) **défouler** [defule] *v.refl.* (fam.) to let oneself go.
défournage [defurnaʒ], **défournement** [defurnəmɑ̃] *s.m.* unloading (of oven or kiln).
défourner [defurne] *v.t.* to take out (of an oven, a kiln).
défraîchi, -e [defrɛʃi] *adj.* faded, that has lost its freshness; shop-soiled.
(**se**) **défraîchir** [defrɛʃir] *v.refl.* to lose its freshness, to fade, to begin to look shabby.
défrayer [defreje] *v.t.* **1.** to indemnify, to reimburse; **2.** (fig.) ~ *la conversation*, to carry the weight, to be the subject, of the conversation.
défrichage [defriʃaʒ], **défrichement** [defriʃmɑ̃] *s.m.* clearing (of ground).
défricher [defriʃe] *v.t.* to clear (ground); (fig.) to clear up, to unravel, to do the spadework on.
défriper [defripe] *v.t.* to rid (garment) of creases.
défriser [defrize] *v.t.* **1.** to uncurl, to straighten (hair); **2.** (fig., fam.) to put out, to upset; *il y a qch. qui me défrise*, there's something (about it) that bothers me; *ça vous défrise?*, does it worry you?
défroisser [defrwase] *v.t.* to smooth out (sth. crumpled).
défroncer [defrɔ̃se] *v.t.* to unpucker, to undo gathering of.
défroque [defrɔk] *s.f.* cast-off clothing.
défroqué, -e [defrɔke] *adj.* (of monk or nun) having left a religious order; unfrocked; ~ *s.m.* one who has left a religious order or holy orders.
défroquer [defrɔke] *v.t.* to unfrock; **se** ~ *v.refl.*, or ~ *v.i.* to leave a religious order or holy orders.
défruiter [defrɥite] *v.t.* (techn.) to remove the fruity taste (*de*, from).
défunt, -e [defœ̃] *adj.* deceased; (Lit.) defunct, past; *s.m.f.* deceased.
dégagé, -e [degaʒe] *adj.* clear, uncovered; (fig.) free, easy, natural.
dégagement [degaʒmɑ̃] *s.m.* **1.** taking back of, release from, (pledge, promise); taking out of pawn; **2.** freeing, clearing (of obstruction), releasing, undoing, disengagement; **3.** passage(way), space, clearance; **4.** emission, escape, (of steam, etc.).
dégager [degaʒe] *v.t.* **1.** to redeem (article pawned, mortgage); ~ *sa parole*, to go back on one's word; ~ *sa responsabilité*, to decline responsibility; **2.** to free, to release, to clear, to disengage, to separate, to sort out, to remove, to withdraw; to relieve congestion (of highway,

etc.); (football, etc.) to kick clear; *dégagez!*, move on!, clear the way!; **3.** to emit, to give off.
dégaine [degɛn] *s.f.* (fam.) awkward, clumsy gait or manner.
dégainer [degɛne] *v.t.* to draw (sword, revolver, etc.).
déganter [degɑ̃te] *v.t.* to take off the glove(s) of; **se** ~ *v.refl.* to take off one's gloves; *main dégantée*, ungloved hand.
dégarnir [degarnir] *v.t.* to strip, to lay bare, to empty; (mil.) to withdraw forces or garrison from; *ses tempes se dégarnissent*, he is going bald at the temples.
dégât [degɑ] *s.m.* (usu. pl.) damage, havoc; (fam.) *il y a du* ~, there is some damage; (fig.) *limiter les* ~*s*, to avoid the worst.
dégauchir [degoʃir] *v.t.* (techn.) to smooth (stone, timber); to straighten (sth. warped).
dégauchissement [degoʃismɑ̃] *s.m.* (techn.) smoothing (of stone, timber).
dégauchisseuse [degoʃisøz] *s.f.* (techn.) smoothing-mill, smoothing-plane.
dégausser [degose] *v.t.* (phys.) to degauss.
dégazage [degɑzaʒ] *s.m.* degassing, extraction of gas.
dégazonnage [degɑzɔnaʒ], **dégazonnement** [degazɔnmɑ̃] *s.m.* removal of turf.
dégazonner [degɑzɔne] *v.t.* to remove turf from.
dégel [deʒɛl] *s.m.* (lit. & fig.) thaw; thawing.
dégelée [deʒle] *s.f.* hail (of blows, etc.).
dégeler [deʒle] *v.t.i.* to thaw (out); ~ *un compte*, to unfreeze an account.
dégénéré, -e [deʒenere] *adj.*, *s.m.f.* degenerate.
dégénérer [deʒenere] *v.i.* to degenerate.
dégénérescence [deʒenerɛsɑ̃s] *s.f.* degeneration, degeneracy.
dégermer [deʒɛrme] *v.t.* to remove the germ (from barley, etc.).
dégingandé, -e [deʒɛ̃gɑ̃de] *adj.* gangling.
dégivr-age [deʒivraʒ] *s.m.* defrosting, de-icing; ~**er** [deʒivre] *v.t.* to defrost, to de-ice; ~**eur** [deʒivrœr] *s.m.* defroster, de-icer.
déglacer [deglase] *v.t.* **1.** (techn.) to remove the glaze from (paper); **2.** (rare) to remove the ice from.
déglinguer [deglɛ̃ge] *v.t.* (fam.) to break apart, to break to pieces.
déglutir [deglytir] *v.t.i.* to swallow (down).
déglutition [deglytisjɔ̃] *s.f.* (obs.) deglutition, swallowing.
dégobiller [degɔbije] *v.t.i.* (fam.) to spew, to sick up, to throw up.
dégoiser [degwaze] *v.t.i.* (fam., pej.) to spout, to natter (away).
dégommage [degɔmaʒ] *s.m.* degumming, ungumming; (fam.) sacking (from employment).
dégommer [degɔme] *v.t.* to degum, to ungum; (fam.) to sack (from employment), to give the push to.
dégonflage [degɔ̃flaʒ] *s.m.* (fam.) climb-down.
dégonflé, -e [degɔ̃fle] *adj.* **1.** deflated; *pneu* ~, flat tyre; **2.** (fam.) cowardly; *s.m.f.* coward.
dégonflement [degɔ̃fləmɑ̃] *s.m.* **1.** reduction (of swelling); **2.** deflating, deflation.
dégonfler [degɔ̃fle] *v.t.* to reduce (swelling); to let the air out of, to deflate, (tyre, balloon, etc.); **se** ~ *v.refl.* (fam.) to lose courage, to give up.
dégorgeage [degɔrʒaʒ] *s.m.* (text., tanning) fulling, scouring.
dégorgement [degɔrʒəmɑ̃] *s.m.* **1.** disgorging; **2.** outflow, discharge; unstopping, clearing, (of blocked drain, etc.); **3.** (text., tanning) fulling, scouring.
dégorgeoir [degɔrʒwar] *s.m.* **1.** overflow (channel, pipe); **2.** (techn.) apparatus for clearing pipes, etc.; (fishing) disgorger.
dégorger [degɔrʒe] *v.t.* **1.** to disgorge; (of drain, etc.) to discharge; to clear (blocked drain, etc.); **2.** (text., tanning) to full, to scour; ~ *v.i.* to discharge (liquid content), to overflow.
dégoter, dégotter [degɔte] *v.t.* (fam.) to find, to discover, to unearth; *v.i.* (pop.) to cut a (fine, sorry) figure.
dégoulin-ade [degulinad] *s.f.* trickle; ~**ement** [degulinmɑ̃] *s.m.* trickling; ~**er** [deguline] *v.i.* to trickle.
dégoupiller [degupije] *v.t.* to remove the pin from; ~ *une grenade*, to take the pin out of a hand-grenade.
dégourdi, -e [degurdi] *adj.*, *s.m.f.* wide-awake, knowing, resourceful, (person).
dégourdir [degurdir] *v.t.* **1.** to restore feeling, circulation, in (limb, etc.); to take the chill off (water); **2.** (fig.) to make less self-conscious, to sharpen the wits of; **se** ~ *v.refl.* to learn how to shift for oneself.
dégoût [degu] *s.m.* disgust, dislike, loathing, repugnance; *prendre en* ~, to get to hate, to take a dislike to.
dégoûtamment [degutamɑ̃] *adv.* disgustingly.
dégoûtant, -e [degutɑ̃] *adj.* disgusting, filthy; (fam.) vulgar, obscene.
dégoûtation [degutɑsjɔ̃] *s.f.* (fam.) disgust, repugnance; disgusting object or sight, filthiness.
dégoûté, -e [degute] *adj.* **1.** squeamish; finicky; *faire le* ~, to be finicky or difficult, to turn up one's nose (at sth.); **2.** disgusted, nauseated; **3.** ~ *de*, weary of; ~ *de vivre*, tired of life.
dégouter [degute] *v.t.* to nauseate; to disgust, to put (one) off; ~ *qn. de qch.*, to put s.o. off sth; *se* ~ *de*, to get to hate, to take a dislike to.
dégoutter [degute] *v.i.* to drip, to trickle.
dégradant, -e [degradɑ̃] *adj.* degrading.
dégradateur [degradatœr] *s.m.* (photo.) vignetting mask.
dégradation[1] [degradɑsjɔ̃] *s.f.* degradation; deterioration; (geol., phys., etc.) degradation, weathering (of rock).
degradation[2] [degradɑsjɔ̃] *s.f.* shading off (of colours); (photo.) vignetting.
dégrader[1] [degrade] *v.t.* **1.** to dismiss, to demote; (mil.) to cashier, to reduce (officer) to lower rank, to the ranks; **2.** to degrade, to debase; **3.** to wear away, to damage; **se** ~ *v.refl.* to decline, to decrease.
dégrader[2] [degrade] *v.t.* (paint., etc.) to grade, to shade off.
dégrafer [degrafe] *v.t.* to undo, to unhook, (garment, etc.).
dégraissage [degrɛsaʒ] *s.m.* degreasing; skimming; cleaning (of garment, etc.).
dégraisser [degrɛse] *v.t.* to degrease; to skim the fat off; to clean (garment, etc.); to trim (piece of wood).
dégraiss-eur, -euse [degrɛsœr] *s.m.f.* dry--cleaner.
dégras [degra] *s.m.* degras, dubbin (for treating leather).
dégravoiement [degravwamɑ̃] *s.m.* undermining, erosion (by water), washing away.
dégravoyer [degravwaje] *v.t.* (of water) to undermine, to erode, to wash away.
degré [dəgre] *s.m.* **1.** step; **2.** degree, extent, pitch, height, grade; *par* ~*s*, gradually; (obs.) degree, diploma.
dégréer [degree] *v.t.* (naut.) to unrig.
dégressi-f, -ve [degrɛsif] *adj.* degressive.
dégrèvement [degrɛvmɑ̃] *s.m.* relief, rebate, reduction, (of tax, etc.).
dégrever [degrəve] *v.t.* to reduce (tax, etc.); to allow (s.o.) relief (of tax, etc.); to derate (industry, product).
dégringolade [degrɛ̃gɔlad] *s.f.* (lit. & fig.) tumble, collapse, sudden decline.

dégringoler [degrɛ̃gɔle] *v.t.i.* to hurtle down, to fall headlong, to tumble down; (fig.) to collapse.
dégrisement [degrizmɑ̃] *s.m.* sobering (down, up).
dégriser [degrize] *v.t.* to sober (down, up); (fig.) to disillusion.
dégrosser [degrose] *v.t.* to draw (out) (metal).
dégrossir [degrosir] *v.t.* to rough-hew (stone, timber); to rough out (plan, etc.), to sketch out, to make a rough plan of; (fig.) to teach (s.o.) a thing or two, to knock (s.o.) into shape.
dégrossissage [degrosisaʒ], **dégrossissement** [degrosismɑ̃] *s.m.* rough-hewing; roughing out (of plan, etc.); drawing out (of metal).
(**se**) **dégrouiller** [degruje] *v.refl.* (slang) to get a move on, to hurry (up).
déguenillé, -e [degənije] *adj.* dressed in rags, ragged; *s.m.f.* ragamuffin, tatterdemalion.
déguerpir [degɛrpir] *v.t.* (obs. law) to disclaim; ~ *v.i.* to decamp; *faire* ~ *qn.*, to evict s.o.
déguerpissement [degɛrpismɑ̃] *s.m.* (obs. law) disclaimer.
dégueulasse [degœlas] *adj.* (slang) disgusting, dirty, low(-down); ~ *s.m.f.* (slang, of person) filthy beast, skunk.
dégueuler [degœle] *v.t.i.* (slang) to spew, to sick up, to throw up.
déguisé, -e [degize] *adj.* disguised, in disguise.
déguisement [degizmɑ̃] *s.m.* disguising; disguise.
déguiser [degize] *v.t.* to disguise; **se** ~ *v.refl.* to dress up, to disguise oneself (*en*, as).
dégustateur [degystatœr] *s.m.* wine-taster.
dégustation [degystɑsjɔ̃] *s.f.* **1.** wine-tasting; **2.** sampling or partaking of good food or drink.
déguster [degyste] *v.t.* **1.** to taste, to sample, (wine, etc.); **2.** to eat or drink appreciatively, to savour; to sip; **3.** (pop.) ~ (*des coups*), to suffer (blow, setback, etc.).
déhaler [deale] *v.t.* (naut.) to warp (vessel).
déhanché, -e [deɑ̃ʃe] *adj.* gangling, waddling; (vet., of horse) having a dislocated hip, hip-shot.
déhanchement [deɑ̃ʃmɑ̃] *s.m.* waddling gait, waddle; lop-sided stance.
(**se**) **déhancher** [deɑ̃ʃe] *v.refl.* to waddle, to swing one's hips; to stand with one's weight on one hip.
déhiscence [deisɑ̃s] *s.f.* (bot.) dehiscence.
déhiscent, -e [deisɑ̃] *adj.* (bot.) dehiscent.
dehors [dəɔr] *adv.* outside, out of doors, out; ~ *adv.* and *prep.* *au-*~, *au* ~, outside; *de* ~, from outside; *en* ~, outside, outwards; *en* ~ *de*, outside, beyond; ~ *s.m.* (often pl.) outside, exterior; looks, appearance; (skating) outside edge.
déhouiller [deuje] *v.t.* to work out (a seam of coal).
déicide [deisid] *s.m.f.* deicide; ~ *s.m.* deicide (crime).
déification [deifikɑsjɔ̃] *s.f.* deification.
déifier [deifje] *v.t.* to deify.
déisme [deism] *s.m.* deism.
déiste [deist] *s.m.f.* deist; ~ *adj.* deistic(al).
déité [deite] *s.f.* deity, god, goddess.
déjà [deʒa] *adv.* **1.** already, before; *je l'ai* ~ *vu*, I have seen it before; *d'ores et* ~, from now on, from today; **2.** (fam.) anyway, all the same, *ce n'est* ~ *pas si mal*, but it isn't at all bad.
déjanter [deʒɑ̃te] *v.t.* to take off (tyre from rim); *son pneu s'est déjanté*, his tyre has come off.
déjauger [deʒoʒe] *v.i.* (naut., of ship) to ride buoyantly.
déjection [deʒɛksjɔ̃] *s.f.* **1.** (med.) defecation; (pl.) faeces; **2.** (geol.) magma; **3.** (geog.) ~*s*, *cône de* ~, alluvial cone; ⚠ not 'dejection' in sense 'despondency'.
déjeté, -e [deʒte] *adj.* warped, buckled; (fam.) deformed, bent.
déjeter [deʒte] *v.t.* to warp, to bend, to buckle, to deform.
déjeuner [deʒœne] *v.i.* **1.** to breakfast; **2.** to lunch, to have lunch.
déjeuner [deʒœne] *s.m.* **1.** breakfast (also *petit* ~); **2.** lunch, luncheon; **3.** ~ *de soleil*, evanescent colour, passing whim.
déjouer [deʒwe] *v.t.* to foil, to thwart, to defeat; to elude.
déjucher [deʒyʃe] *v.i.* (of hen) to leave perch or roost; ~ *v.t.* to dislodge (hen).
(**se**) **déjuger** [deʒyʒe] *v.refl.* to retract (one's judgement, decision, move at chess), to change one's mind.
delà [dəla] *prep.* and *adv.* (obs.) beyond, across (seas, years); (Lit.) *deçà*, ~, here and there; (mod.) *au-*~, *au* ~, farther; *au* ~ *de*, beyond; *en* ~, farther; *par* ~, *par-*~, beyond, on the farther side (*de*, of).
délabré, -e [delɑbre] *adj.* dilapidated, ruined, in ruins; tattered; (fig., of health, etc.) damaged, ruined.
délabrement [delɑbrəmɑ̃] *s.m.* ruinous state, dilapidation; (fig.) deterioration, ruin.
délabrer [delɑbre] *v.t.* (fig.) to ruin (health, etc.); **se** ~ *v.refl.* to decay; (fig.) to deteriorate.
délacer [delase] *v.t.* to unlace, to undo.
délai [delɛ] *s.m.* **1.** time(-limit); *dans le* ~ *fixé*, within the time allowed; *dans un* ~ *de 30 jours*, within 30 days; **2.** delay, respite; *à bref* ~, soon; *sans* ~, at once; *se donner un* ~ *pour décider*, to give oneself time to reach a decision; **3.** (law) ~ *de préavis*, ~*-congé*, notice (of termination of employment contract).
délainage [delɛnaʒ] *s.m.* (tanning) unhairing (of sheepskins).
délainer [delɛne] *v.t.* (tanning) to unhair (sheepskins).
délaissé, -e [delɛse] *adj.* forsaken; neglected.
délaissement [delɛsmɑ̃] *s.m.* forsaking, being forsaken; (law) renunciation (of heritage, etc.).
délaisser [delɛse] *v.t.* to forsake, to neglect; to give up (activity, etc.); (law) to renounce.
délaiter [delete] *v.t.* (dairying) to work, to dry, (butter).
délaiteuse [delɛtøz] *s.f.* (dairying) butter-drying machine.
délardement [delardəmɑ̃] *s.m.* removal of fat; (cook.) unlarding; (techn.) trimming down, removal of sharp edge (of piece of wood).
délarder [delarde] *v.t.* to remove fat from; (cook.) to unlard; (techn.) to trim down, to remove sharp edge (of piece of wood).
délassant, -e [delɑsɑ̃] *adj.* relaxing, restful, refreshing.
délassement [delɑsmɑ̃] *s.m.* relaxation; recreation.
délasser [delɑse] *v.t.* to rest, to refresh.
délat-eur, -rice [delatœr] *s.m.f.* informer, denouncer.
délation [delɑsjɔ̃] *s.f.* informing, denunciation; delation.
délavage [delavaʒ] *s.m.* washing out (of colours); (text.) steeping.
délavé, -e [delave] *adj.* (of colour) washed-out, wishy-washy; (of ground) sodden.
délaver [delave] *v.t.* **1.** to tone down (colour) with water; **2.** to soak, to saturate.
délayage [delɛjaʒ] *s.m.* **1.** mixing (of powdered substance), thinning down (of sauce, etc.); **2.** (fig.) verbiage, padding, spinning out.
délayement [delejmɑ̃] *s.m.* = DÉLAYAGE 1.
délayer [deleje] *v.t.* **1.** to mix (powdered substance), to thin down (sauce, etc.); **2.** (fig.) to spin out, to pad.

delco [dɛlko] (maker's name) *s.m.* (car) coil ignition system; ignition coil.
délectable [delɛktabl] *adj.* (Lit.) delectable, delicious.
délectation [delɛktɑsjɔ̃] *s.f.* delectation, enjoyment.
délecter [delɛkte] *v.t.* to delight; **se** ~ *v.refl.* to delight, to rejoice (*à, de*, in).
délégant, -e [delegɑ̃] *s.m.f.* (law) assignor.
délégataire [delegatɛr] *s.m.f.* (law) assignee.
délégation [delegɑsjɔ̃] *s.f.* delegation; delegacy; commission; (law) assignment.
délégué, -e [delege] *s.m.f.* delegate, representative, deputy, proxy.
déléguer [delege] *v.t.* to delegate; to assign.
délestage [delɛstaʒ] *s.m.* unloading, unballasting; (electr.) load-shedding.
délester [delɛste] *v.t.* to unload, to unballast; to relieve (s.o.) of a load, to lighten (someone's) burden; (electr.) to shed the load; (fig., iron.) ~ *qn. de qch.*, to steal sth. from s.o.
délétère [deletɛr] *adj.* deleterious, noxious, pernicious.
délibérant, -e [deliberɑ̃] *adj.* (of assembly) deliberative.
délibérati-f, -ve [deliberatif] *adj.* having (right to) vote, deliberative; *avoir voix ~ve*, to have a right to speak and vote.
délibération [deliberɑsjɔ̃] *s.f.* deliberation, discussion, debate; decision.
délibéré, -e [delibere] *adj.* deliberate, considered; *de propos* ~, deliberately, intentionally; ~ *s.m.* (law) deliberation (of tribunal, jury); **~ment** [deliberemɑ̃] *adv.* deliberately; resolutely.
délibérer [delibere] *v.i.* **1.** to confer, to take counsel, to consult (together); **2.** to consider, to reflect; *il a longuement délibéré avant d'accepter*, he thought about it for a long time before he accepted; ~ *de*, to discuss, to debate, (question, etc.).
délicat, -e [delika] *adj.* delicate; sensitive; squeamish, fastidious, hard to please; **~ement** [delikatmɑ̃] *adv.* delicately; finely; gently.
délicatesse [delikatɛs] *s.f.* delicacy; tact, consideration.
délice [delis] *s.m.* delight, joy; *quel ~ de vivre ici!*, how delightful, what a joy, to live here!; (fam.) *ce rôti est un* ~, this joint is delicious; *faire ses ~s de qch.*, to delight, to revel, in doing sth.
délicieu-x, -se [delisjø] *adj.* delicious, delightful, charming; **~sement** [delisjøzmɑ̃] *adv.* deliciously, delightfully.
délictueu-x, -se [deliktɥø] *adj.* illicit, illegal.
délié, -e[1] [delje] *adj.* slender, fine; (fig.) *un esprit* ~, a keen intellect, a quick brain, a subtle mind; ~ *s.m.* (typ., etc.) thin stroke, upstroke (opp. *plein*, downstroke).
délié, -e[2] [delje] *adj.* untied, loosened; nimble, agile; *avoir la langue ~e*, to have a glib tongue; ~ *s.m.* nimbleness, agility.
délier [delje] *v.t.* to untie, to unbind, to loose, to free; *sans bourse* ~, without paying anything, without spending any money; ~ *la langue de qn.*, to loosen someone's tongue, to get s.o. to talk; ~ *de*, to release from (obligation, etc.); *se ~ d'un serment*, to go back on one's word.
délimitation [delimitɑsjɔ̃] *s.f.* delimitation.
délimiter [delimite] *v.t.* to delimit.
délinquance [delɛ̃kɑ̃s] *s.f.* delinquency, criminal offences.
délinquant, -e [delɛ̃kɑ̃] *adj., s.m.f.* delinquent; offender.
déliquescence [delikɛsɑ̃s] *s.f.* **1.** (chem.) deliquescence; **2.** (fig., fam.) decadence, decrepitude.
déliquescent, -e [delikɛsɑ̃] *adj.* **1.** (chem.) deliquescent; **2.** (fig.) decadent; (fam.) decrepit.
délirant, -e [delirɑ̃] *adj.* delirious; (fig.) delirious, extravagant, ecstatic, frenzied, mad.
délire [delir] *s.m.* **1.** (med.) delirium, hallucination(s); (fig.) madness, lunacy, folly; ~ *de grandeur*, megalomania; (fig.) *c'est du* ~, it's sheer madness; **2.** frenzy, ecstasy, delirium.
délirer [delire] *v.i.* **1.** (med.) to be delirious; **2.** to be ecstatic, to rave; ~ *de joie*, to be deliriously happy.
delirium tremens [delirjɔmtremɛ̃s] *s.m.* (med.) delirium tremens, D.T.(s).
délissage [delisaʒ] *s.m.* (papermaking) shredding (of rags).
délisser [delise] *v.t.* (papermaking) to shred (rags).
délit[1] [deli] *s.m.* misdeed, offence; (law) offence, misdemeanour, crime; *être pris en flagrant* ~, to be caught in the act, to be caught red-handed; *être pris en flagrant ~ de qch., de faire qch.*, to be caught doing sth.
délit[2] [deli] *s.m.* **1.** (mason.) false bedding; **2.** (geol.) cleavage, rift (in schist).
délitage [delitaʒ], **délitement** [delitmɑ̃] *s.m.* **1.** supplying (silkworms) with fresh mulberry leaves; **2.** splitting or cleaving (slate, etc.).
délitation [delitɑsjɔ̃] *s.f.* = DÉLITAGE 2.
déliter [delite] *v.t.* **1.** (mason.) to surbed (a stone); **2.** to split or cleave (stone, etc.); **se** ~ *v.refl.* to disintegrate; (fig.) to crumble; (geol.) to exfoliate, to split.
délitescence [delitesɛ̃s] *s.f.* (med.) delitescence.
délivrance [delivrɑ̃s] *s.f.* **1.** liberation, deliverance, release; (fig.) relief; **2.** (med.) delivery; **3.** (comm., law) delivery.
délivre [delivr] *s.m.* (med.) afterbirth, placenta.
délivrer [delivre] *v.t.* to free, to release; to deliver, to hand over; to issue; *le bureau où se délivrent les passeports*, the office where passports are issued.
déloger [delɔʒe] *v.i.* to move, to move house; ~ *v.t.* to turn out, to oust; to dislodge; (hunt.) = DÉBUSQUER.
délot [delo] *s.m.* (techn.) finger-stall.
déloyal, -e, (aux) [delwajal] *adj.* disloyal; false, underhand; (boxing) foul; *coups déloyaux*, hits below the belt; **~ement** [delwajalmɑ̃] *adv.* disloyally, treacherously.
déloyauté [delwajote] *s.f.* disloyalty, treachery, underhandedness.
delta [dɛlta] *s.m.* delta; *avion à ailes* (*en*) ~, delta-winged aircraft.
deltaïque [dɛltaik] *adj.* deltaic.
deltoïde [dɛltoid] *adj.* deltoid; ~ *s.m.* (anat.) deltoid (muscle).
déluge [delyʒ] *s.m.* deluge, flood, downpour; (bibl.) (the) Flood; (fig.) flood, torrent.
déluré, -e [delyre] *adj.* knowing, sharp, wide-awake; (pej.) brazen.
délustrer [delystre] *v.t.* to remove the shine from (worn garment).
démagnétisation [demaɲetizɑsjɔ̃] *s.f.* demagnetization; degaussing.
démagnétiser [demaɲetize] *v.t.* to demagnetize; to degauss.
démago-gie [demagɔʒi] *s.f.* demagogy; **~gique** [demagɔʒik] *adj.* demagogic; **~gue** [demagɔg] *s.m.* demagogue.
démaigrir [demegrir] *v.t.* (techn.) to thin down (plank, etc.).
démaigrissement [demegrismɑ̃] *s.m.* **1.** (techn.) thinning down (of plank, etc.); **2.** (geol.) denudation (of sand beach by currents).
démaillage [demɑjaʒ] *s.m.* laddering; ladder (in stocking, etc.).
démailler [demɑje] *v.t.* to ladder (stocking, etc.); (naut.) to unshackle (chain); **se** ~ *v.refl.* (of stocking, etc.) to ladder.

démailloter [demajɔte] *v.t.* to unwrap, to unswaddle (a baby).
demain [dəmɛ̃] *adv.*, *s.m.* tomorrow; *à* ~, (I'll) see you tomorrow, goodbye till tomorrow; ~ *il fera jour*, it can wait till tomorrow, tomorrow is also a day.
démancher [demɑ̃ʃe] *v.t.* to remove the handle of, to break up, to disjoin; (fam.) *se* ~ *le bras*, to dislocate one's arm; ~ *v.i.* (mus.) to shift (in playing violin, etc.); **se** ~ *v.refl.* (fig.) to go to a great deal of trouble.
demande [dəmɑ̃d] *s.f.* **1.** request, application, petition; asking (for sth.); (comm.) order, inquiry; (econ.) demand (for goods or services); (law) claim, action; *faire une* ~ (*en mariage*), to ask (for someone's) hand in marriage; *alivrison sur* ~, delivery on receipt of order; *la loi de l'offre et de la* ~, the law of supply and demand; ~ *en dommages-intérêts*, claim for damages; ~ *en divorce*, action for divorce; **2.** (obs.) question; (mod.) *leçon par* ~*s et réponses*, learning by question and answer; ⚠ not a peremptory 'demand'.
demander [dəmɑ̃de] *v.t.* **1.** to ask (for), (occasionally) to demand; to apply for; (law) to claim (damages, etc.); to require, to demand, to take (time, etc.); (fam.) to want, to wish; ~ *la permission*, to ask (for) permission; ~ *un médecin*, to ask for a doctor (to be fetched); ~ *la tête d'un coupable*, to ask for the death penalty, to demand the execution of an offender; ~ *à faire qch.*, to ask (to be allowed) to do sth.; ~ *à s'asseoir*, to ask to sit down, to ask for a seat; ~ *qch. à qn.*, to ask s.o. for sth.; *on lui demanda son passeport*, he was asked for his passport; ~ *à qn. de faire qch.*, to ask s.o. to do sth.; *demandez aux enfants de se taire*, ask the children to be quiet; *je demande que vous m'écoutiez*, I ask you to listen to me; *cela demande de la patience*, it demands patience; *le voyage demande deux heures*, the journey takes two hours; (fam.) *voilà ce que je demande*, that's just what I want; *je ne demande pas mieux que de*, I could wish for nothing better than to; **2.** to ask, to inquire (about); ~ *l'heure*, to ask the time; ~ *son chemin à un agent*, to ask a policeman the way; **se** ~ *v.refl.* to wonder.
demand-eur, -eresse [dəmɑ̃dœr] *s.m.f.* **1.** (obs.) petitioner, supplicant; **2.** (law) plaintiff, claimant.
démangeaison [demɑ̃ʒɛzɔ̃] *s.f.* itch, itching.
démanger [demɑ̃ʒe] *v.i.* to itch; *la jambe me démange*, my leg is itching; (fig.) *la langue lui démange*, he is itching to have his say.
démantèlement [demɑ̃tɛlmɑ̃] *s.m.* dismantling, demolishing; (fig.) destruction.
démanteler [demɑ̃tle] *v.t.* to dismantle, to demolish; (fig.) to bring down, to destroy.
démantibuler [demɑ̃tibyle] *v.t.* (fam.) to destroy, to break to pieces, to put out of action.
démaquillant, -e [demakijɑ̃] *adj.* which removes make-up, cleansing; *crême* ~*e*, cleansing cream; ~ *s.m.* make-up remover, cleansing cream.
démaquiller [demakije] *v.t.* to remove make-up of; **se** ~ *v.refl.* to remove one's make-up.
démarcage see DÉMARQUAGE.
démarcation [demarkɑsjɔ̃] *s.f.* demarcation; *ligne de* ~, demarcation line, dividing line, frontier.
démarchage [demarʃaʒ] *s.m.* door-to-door canvassing, selling, etc.
démarche [demarʃ] *s.f.* **1.** carriage, bearing, gait; **2.** approach, request, initiative; démarche; *faire des* ~*s*, to take steps, to make overtures.
démarcheu-r, -se [demarʃœr] *s.m.f.* agent, representative, (commercial) traveller; door-to-door salesman; (fin.) investment clerk.
démarier [demarje] *v.t.* **1.** (obs.) to separate judicially; *se* ~ (of husband, wife) to separate; **2.** (agric.) to thin out (seedlings).
démarquage, démarcage [demarkaʒ] *s.m.* **1.** copying, plagiarizing; copy, plagiarism; **2.** (football, etc.) becoming or being unmarked.
démarque [demark] *s.f.* (comm.) marking-down (of prices).
démarquer [demarke] *v.t.* **1.** to remove brand marks, etc. from; **2.** to copy, to plagiarize; **3.** (comm.) to mark down (goods); **4.** (football, etc.) to cease to mark (player).
démarqueur [demarkœr] *s.m.* plagiarist.
démarrage [demaraʒ] *s.m.* **1.** (naut.) casting-off; **2.** (car) starting (off).
démarrer [demare] *v.t.* **1.** (naut.) to cast off (boat, etc.); **2.** (fam.) to start (job, task); ~ *v.i.* **1.** (naut.) to cast off; **2.** (fig.) ~ *de*, to leave, to give up (project, etc.); **3.** to start off, to get going.
démarreur [demarœr] *s.m.* (car) starter, starter-button.
démasquer [demaske] *v.t.* **1.** to unmask; **2.** (mil.) ~ *une batterie*, to unmask a battery; (fig.) ~ *ses batteries*, to show one's hand.
démasticage [demastikaʒ] *s.m.* (techn.) removal of mastic, cement, stopping.
démastiquer [demastike] *v.t.* (techn.) to remove mastic, cement, stopping, from.
démâtage [demɑtaʒ] *s.m.* (naut.) dismasting.
démâter [demɑte] *v.t.* (naut.) to dismast.
d'emblée see EMBLÉE.
démêlage [demɛlaʒ], **démêlement** [demɛlmɑ̃] *s.m.* disentangling, clearing up, sorting out.
démêlé [demele] *s.m.* wrangle, quarrel, dispute, disagreement; *avoir des* ~*s*, to have a disagreement.
démêler [demele] *v.t.* **1.** to disentangle; to comb out (hair); (fig.) to clear up, to sort out (complication, difficulty); **2.** (Lit.) to discuss, to debate; **se** ~ *v.refl.* (obs.) = (*se*) DÉBROUILLER.
démêloir [demɛlwar] *s.m.* (wide-toothed) comb.
démêlure [demelyr] *s.f.* tuft, tangle, of hair (removed by comb); (pl.) combings.
démembrement [demɑ̃brəmɑ̃] *s.m.* (lit. & fig.) dismemberment.
démembrer [demɑ̃bre] *v.t.* (lit. & fig.) to dismember.
déménagement [demenaʒmɑ̃] *s.m.* removal, moving house; *camion, voiture, de* ~, removal van.
déménager [demenaʒe] *v.t.* to move (furniture to new house); *faire* ~ *qn.*, to turn s.o. out; ~ *v.i.* to move house; (fig., fam.) to have taken leave of one's senses.
déménageur [demenaʒœr] *s.m.* furniture remover.
démence [demɑ̃s] *s.f.* insanity; madness, folly; (med.) dementia; ~ *précoce*, dementia praecox.
(**se**) **démener** [demne] *v.refl.* to struggle; to exert oneself (*pour*, to).
dément, -e [demɑ̃] *adj.* insane, mad, crazy, demented; *s.m.f.* (med.) dement, demented person, mental case; ~, ~*e*, *sénile*, senile person.
démenti [demɑ̃ti] *s.m.* denial; *donner, opposer, un* ~ *à*, to contradict, to belie.
démentiel, -le [demɑ̃sjɛl] *adj.* insane; idiotic, crazy; (med.) of or afflicted with dementia.
démentir [demɑ̃tir] *v.t.* to contradict, to deny; to belie.
(**se**) **démerder** [demɛrde] *v.refl.* (vulg. slang) = (*se*) DÉBROUILLER.
démérite [demerit] *s.m.* (Lit.) fault, demerit.
démériter [demerite] *v.i.* to be blameworthy, to be at fault; ~ *auprès de, aux yeux de, qn.*, (obs.) ~ *de qn.*, to come down in someone's estimation; *en quoi a-t-il démérité?*, what has he done wrong?, in what way is he to blame?

démesure [deməzyr] *s.f.* exaggeration, excess, lack of restraint, immoderate behaviour.
démesuré, -e [deməzyre] *adj.* immense; (fig.) exaggerated, excessive, inordinate; **~ment** [deməzyremɑ̃] *adv.* immensely, excessively, exaggeratedly.
démettre [demɛtr] *v.t.* **1.** to dislocate, to put out; *se ~ le genou*, to put one's knee out; **2.** to dismiss; **se ~** *v.refl.* to resign.
démeubler [demøble] *v.t.* to strip of furniture.
(**au**) **demeurant** [odəmœrɑ̃] *adv.loc.* (Lit.) for the rest, besides, after all.
demeure [dəmœr] *s.f.* **1.** (obs.) delay; (mod.) legal responsibility (for overdue payment, etc.); *mettre un débiteur en ~ (de payer)*, to summon a debtor to pay; *mettre qn. en ~ de faire qch.*, to order or summon s.o. to do sth. (esp. to perform contract); (law) *mise en ~*, summons, order; *à ~*, permanently; **2.** (Lit.) abode, residence; stately house; *dernière ~*, last resting-place, grave.
demeuré, -e [dəmœre] *adj., s.m.f.* mentally retarded (person).
demeurer [dəmœre] *v.i.* **1.** to dwell, to live; **2.** to remain; *en ~ là*, to go no further; *~ d'accord*, to agree.
demi, -e [d(ə)mi] *adj., adv.* half; *un centimètre et ~*, a centimetre and a half; *une heure et ~e*, an hour and a half, half past one; *boîte ~-pleine*, box which is half full; *à ~*, half, by halves; *~ s.m.* **1.** glass of beer (orig. half a litre); **2.** (football, etc.) half; *~-de-mêlée*, scrum-half; *~e s.f.* (the) half-hour; *partir à la ~e*, to leave at the half-hour.
demi-bas [d(ə)mibɑ] *s.m.* sock; (comm.) half-hose.
demi-botte [d(ə)mibɔt] *s.f.* half-boot.
demi-cercle [d(ə)misɛrkl] *s.m.* semicircle.
demi-circulaire [d(ə)misirkylɛr] *adj.* semicircular.
demi-clef [d(ə)mikle] *s.f.* (naut.) half hitch.
demi-colonne [d(ə)mikɔlɔn] *s.f.* (arch.) semi-column.
demi-deuil [d(ə)midœj] *s.m.* half mourning.
demi-dieu (pl. **-x**) [d(ə)midjø] *s.m.* demigod.
demi-douzaine [d(ə)miduzɛn] *s.f.* half (a) dozen.
démieller [demjele] *v.t.* to extract honey from (comb).
demi-fin, -e [d(ə)mifɛ̃] *adj.* medium(-sized); medium fine; (of gold) twelve-carat.
demi-finale [d(ə)mifinal] *s.f.* (sport) semifinal.
demi-fond [d(ə)mifɔ̃] *s.m.* (sport) middle-distance (race, runner, etc.).
demi-frère [d(ə)mifrɛr] *s.m.* half-brother.
demi-gros [d(ə)migro] *s.m.* wholesale dealing (in a small way).
demi-heure [d(ə)mijœr] *s.f.* half-hour, half an hour; *attendez une ~*, wait for half an hour; *toutes les ~s*, every half-hour.
demi-jour [d(ə)miʒur] *s.m.* half-light, twilight.
demi-journée [d(ə)miʒurne] *s.f.* half-day, half a day.
démilitarisation [demilitarizɑsjɔ̃] *s.f.* demilitarization.
démilitariser [demilitarize] *v.t.* to demilitarize.
demi-litre [d(ə)militr] *s.m.* half-litre, half a litre.
demi-longueur [d(ə)milɔ̃gœr] *s.f.* (sport) half a length; *gagner d'une ~*, to win by half a length.
demi-lune [d(ə)milyn] *s.f.* half-moon; (fort.) demilune; *~ adj.* semicircular.
demi-mal [d(ə)mimal] *s.m.* minor mishap; *il n'y a que ~*, it might have been worse.
demi-mesure [d(ə)miməzyr] *s.f.* **1.** half a measure (of grain); **2.** (pl.) (fig.) half-measures; **3.** factory made-to-measure clothing.
demi-mondaine [d(ə)mimɔ̃dɛn] *s.f.* demi-mondaine.
demi-monde [d(ə)mimɔ̃d] *s.m.* demi-monde.
demi-mort, -e [d(ə)mimɔr] *adj.* half-dead; (fig.) dying (e.g. of cold).
demi-mot [d(ə)mimo] *s.m.* euphemism; *à ~ adv.loc.* implied; *comprendre à ~*, to read between the lines, to get the point.
déminage [deminaʒ] *s.m.* clearing of mines, mine-sweeping.
déminer [demine] *v.t.* to clear of mines.
démineur [deminœr] *s.m.* member of mine-clearing squad or minesweeper's crew.
demi-pause [d(ə)mipoz] *s.f.* (mus.) minim rest.
demi-pension [d(ə)mipɑ̃sjɔ̃] *s.f.* demi-pension, part board (in hotel); day-boarding (at school); **~naire** [d(ə)mipɑ̃sjɔnɛr] *s.m.f.* day-boarder.
demi-place [d(ə)miplas] *s.f.* half-fare, half-price (ticket), half.
demi-portion [d(ə)mipɔrsjɔ̃] *s.f.* (fam., pej.) small or insignificant person; half-portion, child's helping (of food).
demi-produit [d(ə)miprɔdɥi] *s.m.* (comm.) semi-finished article.
demi-quart [d(ə)mikar] *s.m.* half a quarter (of a pound); *un ~ de beurre*, 62·5 g butter.
demi-queue [d(ə)mikø] *adj., s.m.invar.* baby grand (piano).
demi-reliure [d(ə)mirəljyr] *s.f.* (bookb.) quarter-binding; *~ à coins*, half-binding.
demi-ronde [d(ə)mirɔ̃d] *s.f.* (techn.) half-round file.
demi-saison [d(ə)misɛzɔ̃] *s.f.* between-season; *manteau de ~*, spring, autumn, coat.
demi-sang [d(ə)misɑ̃] *s.m.invar.* half-bred (horse).
demi-sec [d(ə)misɛk] *adj.* (of wine) medium dry.
demi-sel [d(ə)misɛl] *adj.invar.* slightly salted; *~ s.m.* demi-sel (cheese).
demi-sœur [d(ə)misœr] *s.f.* half-sister.
demi-solde [d(ə)misɔld] *s.f.* half-pay; *~ s.m.* officer on half-pay.
demi-sommeil [d(ə)misɔmɛj] *s.m.* drowsiness, somnolence.
demi-soupir [d(ə)misupir] *s.m.* (mus.) quaver rest.
démission [demisjɔ̃] *s.f.* resignation (of office, etc.); giving-up (of activity, etc.); *donner sa ~*, to hand in one's resignation; *~!*, resign!; **~naire** [demisjɔnɛr] *s.m.f., adj.* (person) who has just resigned; *ministre ~naire*, outgoing minister; **~ner** [demisjɔne] *v.i.* to resign (office, etc.); (fam.) to give up; *~ v.t.* (fam.) to sack.
demi-tarif [d(ə)mitarif] *s.m.* half-price; half-fare; half-rate.
demi-teinte [d(ə)mitɛ̃t] *s.f.* (art) half-tone; (mus.) *chanter en ~*, to sing softly.
demi-tige [d(ə)mitiʒ] *s.f.* half-standard (fruit-tree).
demi-ton [d(ə)mitɔ̃] *s.m.* (mus.) semitone.
demi-tour [d(ə)mitur] *s.m.* about-turn, about-face; (mil.) *~ (à) droite!*, right about turn; *faire ~*, to turn round, to turn back, to retrace one's steps.
démiurge [demjyrʒ] *s.m.* demiurge.
demi-vierge [d(ə)mivjɛrʒ] *s.f.* demi-vierge.
démobilisation [demɔbilizɑsjɔ̃] *s.f.* demobilization.
démobiliser [demɔbilize] *v.t.* to demobilize.
démocrate [demɔkrat] *s.m.f.* democrat; *~ adj.* democratic.
démocrate-chrétien, -ne [demɔkratkretjɛ̃] *s.m.f., adj.* (pol.) Christian Democrat.
démocratie [demɔkrasi] *s.f.* democracy.
démocratique [demɔkratik] *adj.* democratic; **~ment** [demɔkratikmɑ̃] *adv.* democratically.
démocratisation [demɔkratizɑsjɔ̃] *s.f.* democratization.

démodé, -e [demɔde] *adj.* out of fashion, démodé.
(**se**) **démoder** [demɔde] *v.refl.* to go out of fashion.
démographe [demɔgraf] *s.m.f.* demographer.
démographie [demɔgrafi] *s.f.* demography.
démographique [demɔgrafik] *adj.* demographic.
demoiselle [d(ə)mwazɛl] *s.f.* **1.** unmarried woman; (iron. or courteous) young lady; (Lit.) damsel; *rester* ~, to remain single; ~ *d'honneur*, maid of honour, bridesmaid; ~ *de magasin*, (female) shop-assistant; **2.** (ent.) dragonfly; **3.** (zool.) demoiselle (crane); **4.** (techn.) punner; **5.** glove-stretcher.
démolir [demɔlir] *v.t.* (lit. & fig.) to demolish, to destroy; to exhaust, to knock flat; (fam.) ~ *qn.*, to put s.o. hors de combat, to beat s.o. up.
démolissage [demɔlisaʒ] *s.m.* (fig.) pulling to pieces; ruin(ing).
démolisseu-r, -se [demɔlisœr] *s.m.f.* demolition worker, housebreaker; (fig.) demolisher.
démolition [demɔlisjɔ̃] *s.f.* (lit. & fig.) demolition; (pl.) ruins, wreckage (of building).
démon [demɔ̃] *s.m.* demon, devil, fiend; (Gk. myth.) demon, daemon; *le* ~, the Devil; *le* ~ *de midi*, the dangerous age, the seven-year itch.
démone [demɔn] *s.f.* (Lit.) (female) demon.
démonétisation [demɔnetizɑsjɔ̃] *s.f.* (econ.) demonetization; (fig.) discrediting, devaluing.
démonétiser [demɔnetize] *v.t.* (econ.) to demonetize; (fig.) to discredit, to devalue.
démon-iaque [demɔnjak] *adj.* demoniac, possessed; demoniacal, devilish; *s.m.f.* demoniac, one possessed; **~isme** [demɔnism] *s.m.* demonism; **~ologie** [demɔnɔlɔʒi] *s.f.* demonology.
démonstrat-eur, -rice [demɔ̃stratœr] *s.m.f.* demonstrator.
démonstrati-f, -ve [demɔ̃stratif] *adj.* demonstrative; **~f** *s.m.* (gram.) demonstrative.
démonstration [demɔ̃strɑsjɔ̃] *s.f.* demonstration.
démonstrativement [demɔ̃strativmɑ̃] *adv.* demonstratively.
démontable [demɔ̃tabl] *adj.* that can be taken to pieces, in sections, collapsible; *jouet* ~, constructional toy.
démontage [demɔ̃taʒ] *s.m.* dismantling, detaching, taking down, taking to pieces, breaking down (into sections).
démonté, -e [demɔ̃te] *adj.* **1.** unseated, thrown, unhorsed, dismounted; (fig.) taken aback, disconcerted; **2.** (of sea) stormy, tempestuous; **3.** dismantled, taken to pieces.
démonte-pneu [demɔ̃tpnø] *s.m.* tyre-lever.
démonter [demɔ̃te] *v.t.* **1.** to unseat, to throw, to unhorse; (fig.) to take aback, to disconcert; **2.** to dismantle, to take to pieces; to dismount (esp. gun from carriage).
démontrable [demɔ̃trabl] *adj.* demonstrable.
démontrer [demɔ̃tre] *v.t.* to demonstrate, to prove.
démoralisant, -e [demɔralizɑ̃] *adj.* demoralizing.
démoralisat-eur, -rice [demɔralizatœr] *s.m.f.* (Lit.) demoralizer; *adj.* demoralizing.
démoralisation [demɔralizɑsjɔ̃] *s.f.* demoralization.
démoraliser [demɔralize] *v.t.* to demoralize.
démordre [demɔrdr] *v.i.* ~ *de*, (chiefly in neg.) to give up; *ne pas* ~ *de son avis*, to stick to one's opinion; *il n'en démordra pas*, he is very obstinate.
démotique [demɔtik] *adj.* demotic.
démoucheter [demuʃte] *v.t.* (fenc.) to remove button from (foil).
démoulage [demulaʒ] *s.m.* (sculpt., cook., etc.) removal from mould; turning out (of cake, etc.).
démouler [demule] *v.t.* (sculpt., cook., etc.) to remove from mould; to turn out (cake, etc.).
démultiplicateur [demyltiplikatœr] *s.m.*, *adj.* (mech.) reduction (gear).
démultiplication [demyltiplikɑsjɔ̃] *s.f.* (mech.) reduction gearing, gearing down.
démultiplier [demyltiplie] *v.t.* (mech.) to gear down.
démunir [demynir] *v.t.* to divest (*de*, of); *se* ~ *de son argent*, to leave oneself short of money, without means.
démuseler [demyzle] *v.t.* to unmuzzle.
démystification [demistifikasjɔ̃] *s.f.* undeceiving; debunking.
démystifier [demistifje] *v.t.* to demystify, to undeceive: to debunk.
démythifier [demitifje] *v.t.* to demythicize.
dénasalisation [denazalizɑsjɔ̃] *s.f.* (phon.) denasalization.
dénasaliser [denazalize] *v.t.* (phon.) to denasalize.
dénatalité [denatalite] *s.f.* fall in birth-rate.
dénationalisation [denasjɔnalizɑsjɔ̃] *s.f.* denationalization.
dénationaliser [denasjɔnalize] *v.t.* to denationalize.
dénatter [denate] *v.t.* to unplait.
dénaturaliser [denatyralize] *v.t.* to denaturalize, to deprive of naturalization.
dénaturant [denatyrɑ̃] *s.m.* denaturant.
dénaturation [denatyrɑsjɔ̃] *s.f.* denaturation.
dénaturé, -e [denatyre] *adj.* **1.** denatured; **2.** unnatural.
dénaturer [denatyre] *v.t.* (techn.) to denature; (fig.) to distort, to falsify (fact, etc.).
dénazification [denazifikɑsjɔ̃] *s.f.* denazification.
dénazifier [denazifje] *v.t.* to denazify.
dendrite [dɛ̃drit] *s.f.* (min., zool.) dendrite.
dénégation [denegɑsjɔ̃] *s.f.* denial, disclaimer.
dengue [dɛ̃g] *s.f.* dengue(-fever).
déni [deni] *s.m.* (obs.) denial; (mod.) injustice; (law) ~ (*de justice*), denial of justice.
déniaisé, -e [denjeze] *adj.* astute, enlightened.
déniaiser [denjeze] *v.t.* to bring out, to draw out, to enlighten; (fam.) to initiate sexually; **se** ~ *v.refl.* to broaden one's horizon, one's experience.
dénicher [deniʃe] *v.t.* **1.** to take from the nest; **2.** (fig.) to flush out (from hiding); to seek out, to unearth, to discover; ~ *v.i.* to desert the nest; to fly away; (fig., obs.) to depart hurriedly.
dénicheu-r, -se [deniʃœr] *s.m.f.* bird's-nester; one who hunts out or unearths (antiques, etc.), curio-hunter.
denier [dənje] *s.m.* **1.** (Rom. ant.) denarius; **2.** denier (anc. Fr. coin); **3.** (pl.) monies, money, funds; **4.** (text.) denier.
dénier [denje] *v.t.* to deny.
dénigrement [denigrəmɑ̃] *s.m.* denigration; *par* ~, pejoratively.
dénigrer [denigre] *v.t.* to denigrate.
dénitrification [denitrifikɑsjɔ̃] *s.f.* denitrification.
dénitrifier [denitrifje] *v.t.* to denitrify.
dénivelée [denivle] *s.f.* (techn.) difference of level; elevation, depression, (of two features relative to each other).
déniveler [denivle] *v.t.* to make uneven; to diversify the levels of (a piece of ground).
dénivellation [denivɛl(l)ɑsjɔ̃] *s.f.* difference of level, contour, ups and downs.
dénombrement [denɔ̃brəmɑ̃] *s.m.* counting, enumeration; census.
dénombrer [denɔ̃bre] *v.t.* to count, to enumerate.
dénombrable [denɔ̃brabl] *adj.* numerable.
dénominateur [denɔminatœr] *s.m.* (arith.) denominator.

dénominati-f, -ve [denɔminatif] *adj.* (gram.) denominative; **~f** *s.m.* (gram.) denominative.
dénomination [denɔminɑsjɔ̃] *s.f.* denomination, appellation.
dénommer [denɔme] *v.t.* to denominate, to name.
dénoncer [denɔ̃se] *v.t.* **1.** to inform against (person); to expose, to denounce, (injustice, abuse); **2.** to denounce (treaty, etc.).
dénonciat-eur, -rice [denɔ̃sjatœr] *s.m.f.* informer.
dénonciation [denɔ̃sjɑsjɔ̃] *s.f.* **1.** denouncement (of treaty, etc.); **2.** informing, denouncing.
dénotation [denɔtɑsjɔ̃] *s.f.* denoting, denotation.
dénoter [denɔte] *v.t.* to denote.
dénouement, dénoûment [denumɑ̃] *s.m.* dénouement, denouement; (obs.) untying, loosing.
dénouer [denwe] *v.t.* to undo (knot), to untie, to loose; (fig.) to unravel, to clear up.
dénoyauter [denwajote] *v.t.* to stone (fruit).
denrée [dɑ̃re] *s.f.* **1.** (usu. pl.) produce, food, foodstuff; **2.** (fig.) ~ *rare*, rare commodity.
dense [dɑ̃s] *adj.* dense, thick; (phys.) dense; (fig.) condensed, compact; ⚠ not 'dense' in sense 'stupid'.
densimètre [dɑ̃simɛtr] *s.m.* densimeter.
densité [dɑ̃site] *s.f.* density.
dent [dɑ̃] *s.f.* **1.** tooth; ~ *de lait, de remplacement, de sagesse*, milk, second, wisdom, tooth; *manger, rire, à belles ~s*, to eat, to laugh, heartily; (fig.) *déchirer qn. à belles ~s*, to tear s.o. to pieces; *manger du bout des ~s*, to pick at one's food; *armé jusqu'aux ~s*, armed to the teeth; (pop.) *avoir la ~*, to be hungry; *avoir la ~ dure*, to be a severe critic; *avoir les ~s longues*, to be very hungry, (fig.) to be grasping; *avoir, garder, une ~ contre qn.*, to have a grudge against s.o.; *avoir mal aux ~s*, to have toothache; *il claque des ~s*, his teeth are chattering; *coup de ~*, bite; *faire, percer, ses ~s*, to cut one's teeth; *grincer des ~s*, to grind one's teeth; *se laver, se nettoyer, se curer, les ~s*, to clean, to brush, to pick, one's teeth; (lit. & fig.) *montrer les ~s*, to show one's teeth; *prendre le mors aux ~s*, (of horse, etc.) to take the bit between its teeth, to bolt, (fig.) to take the bit between one's teeth; *serrer les ~s*, to clench, to grit, one's teeth; *ne pas desserrer les ~s*, not to utter a word; *être sur les ~s*, to be exhausted, to be worked to death; **2.** (techn., etc.) tooth (of gear-wheel, saw, etc.), prong or tine (of fork, etc.); jagged mountain peak; (pl.) serrations, jagged edge, scalloped edge; *en ~s de scie*, saw-toothed; serrated, indented, jagged; (of knife, etc.) saw-edged.
dentaire[1] [dɑ̃tɛr] *s.f.* (bot.) dentaria, pepper-root, pepperwort, toothwort.
dentaire[2] [dɑ̃tɛr] *adj.* dental.
dental, -e, (aux) [dɑ̃tal] *adj.* (phon.) dental; (obs.) = DENTAIRE[2]; **~e** *s.f.* (phon.) dental.
dent-de-lion [dɑ̃dəljɔ̃] *s.f.* (pl. *dents-de-lion*) dandelion.
dent-de-loup [dɑ̃dlu] *s.f.* (pl. *dents-de-loup*) (mech.) (engaging-) dog, toothed coupling.
denté, -e [dɑ̃te] *adj.* toothed, cogged; (biol.) dentate; *roue ~e*, cog-wheel; *feuille ~e*, dentate, serrated, leaf.
dentée [dɑ̃te] *s.f.* (hunt.) bite, jag.
dentelé, -e [dɑ̃tle] *adj.* indented, dentel(l)ated, jagged; (bot.) dentate; (anat., bot.) serrated.
denteler [dɑ̃tle] *v.t.* to indent, to pink, (edge of sth.).
dentelle [dɑ̃tɛl] *s.f.* lace.
dentelli-er, -ère [dɑ̃təlje] *adj.* lace-; **~ère** *s.f.* lace-maker.
dentelure [dɑ̃tlyr] *s.f.* denticulation, indentation, pinking; (bot.) serration; jagged outline (of coast, mountain range).
denticule [dɑ̃tikyl] *s.m.* denticle; (arch.) dentil.
denticulé, -e [dɑ̃tikyle] *adj.* denticular, denticulate.
dentier [dɑ̃tje] *s.m.* denture.
dentifrice [dɑ̃tifris] *s.m.* dentifrice; ~ *adj. pâte ~*, tooth-paste; *eau ~*, mouth-wash.
dentine [dɑ̃tin] *s.f.* dentine.
dentiste [dɑ̃tist] *s.m.f.* dentist; *chirurgien ~*, dental surgeon.
dentition [dɑ̃tisjɔ̃] *s.f.* dentition.
denture [dɑ̃tyr] *s.f.* **1.** (Lit.) dentition; **2.** (techn.) cogs, teeth; ⚠ not 'denture' in sense 'set of false teeth'.
dénudé, -e [denyde] *adj.* bare, stripped, denuded (of vegetation).
dénuder [denyde] *v.t.* to denude, to lay bare, to strip.
dénué, -e [denɥe] *adj.* **1.** deprived, bereft, (*de*, of); **2.** (Lit.) destitute.
dénuement [denymɑ̃] *s.m.* destitution.
(se) dénuer [denɥe] *v.refl.* to deny oneself; *se ~ de qch.*, to deprive oneself of sth., to go without sth.
dénutrition [denytrisjɔ̃] *s.f.* denutrition.
déodorant see DÉSODORISANT.
déontologie [deɔ̃tɔlɔʒi] *s.f.* deontology.
déontologique [deɔ̃tɔlɔʒik] *adj.* deontological.
dépaillage [depɑjaʒ] *s.m.* removal, wearing--out, of rush-seat (of chair, etc.).
dépailler [depɑje] *v.t.* to remove rush-seat from (chair, etc.); *cette chaise se dépaille*, the (rush-) seat of this chair is wearing out.
dépannage [depanaʒ] *s.m.* repair (of vehicle broken down), running repairs; (fig.) getting (s.o.) out of a difficulty; *voiture de ~*, breakdown vehicle.
dépanner [depane] *v.t.* to repair (car-engine, television, etc.); to bring in (broken-down vehicle); (fam.) to help (s.o.) out.
dépanneur [depanœr] *s.m.* breakdown mechanic.
dépanneuse [depanøz] *s.f.* breakdown vehicle.
dépaqueter [depakte] *v.t.* to undo, to unpack, (a parcel).
déparaffinage [deparafinaʒ] *s.m.* (techn.) extraction of paraffin (from crude oil).
dépareillé, -e [depareje] *adj.* (of set, series) incomplete; odd.
dépareiller [depareje] *v.t.* to break, to spoil, (set, series).
déparer [depare] *v.t.* to spoil the beauty, the look, of; to mar.
déparier see DÉSAPPARIER.
départ[1] [depar] *s.m.* departure; start.
départ[2] [depar] *s.m. faire le ~*, to distinguish (*entre*, between).
départager [departaʒe] *v.t.* **1.** to settle by a casting vote; **2.** to choose between; **3.** (Lit.) to separate.
département [departəmɑ̃] *s.m.* department; (admin.) department, département.
départemental, -e, (aux) [departəmɑ̃tal] *adj.* departmental.
départir [departir] *v.t.* (Lit.) to allot (task), to bestow (favour); *se ~ de*, to depart from (attitude, etc.).
dépassant [depɑsɑ̃] *s.m.* (dressm.) edging.
dépassé, -e [depɑse] *adj.* outstripped, surpassed; outdated; (fig.) *il est complètement ~*, he is not up to it, it is beyond him.
dépassement [depɑsmɑ̃] *s.m.* **1.** overtaking (on road); **2.** (fin.) overspending; **3.** surpassing (oneself).
dépasser [depɑse] *v.t.* **1.** to overtake (esp. on road), to pass, to outstrip; **2.** to exceed, to surpass, to go beyond, to overshoot (destination, etc.); to overstep (rights etc.), to project, beyond; (fig.) to disconcert; *~ qn. de la tête*, to be a head taller than s.o.; (fig.) *~ les bornes*, to

go too far; (fig.) *cela le dépasse*, that's too much for him, that's beyond him; **se** ~ *v.refl.* to surpass oneself.

dépavage [depavaʒ] *s.m.* removal of paving, of cobbles (from road surface).

dépaver [depave] *v.t.* to remove paving, cobbles.

dépaysé, -e [depeize] *adj.* out of one's element, strange, lost.

dépaysement [depeizmɑ̃] *s.m.* change of environment; (obs.) exile.

dépayser [depeize] *v.t.* to make (s.o.) feel out of their element; (obs.) to uproot, to exile.

dépeçage [depəsaʒ], **dépècement** [depɛsmɑ̃] *s.m.* cutting-up, carving up.

dépecer [depəse] *v.t.* (butch.) to joint (carcase); (of animal) to pull (prey) to pieces.

dépeceu-r, -se [depəsœr] *s.m.f.* (butch.) cutter-up.

dépêche [depɛʃ] *s.f.* telegram, wire; dispatch.

dépêcher [depeʃe] *v.t.* to dispatch (message, messenger); **se** ~ *v.refl.* to make haste, to hurry; *dépêchez-vous!*, hurry up!

dépeigné, -e [depeɲe] *adj.* having untidy hair, unkempt.

dépeigner [depeɲe] *v.t.* to ruffle, to untidy, the hair of.

dépeindre [depɛ̃dr] *v.t.* to depict.

dépenaillé, -e [depənɑje] *adj.* tattered, ragged, in rags.

dépendance [depɑ̃dɑ̃s] *s.f.* dependence; dependency; (pl.) appurtenances, outbuildings.

dépendant, -e [depɑ̃dɑ̃] *adj.* dependent; subordinate.

dépendre[1] [depɑ̃dr] *v.i.* to depend (*de*, on); *cela ne dépend pas de vous*, that does not rest with you; *ça dépend*, it (all) depends; *ce parc dépend de la propriété*, this park belongs to (is part of) the property.

dépendre[2] [depɑ̃dr] *v.t.* to take down (sth. hanging).

dépens [depɑ̃] *s.m.pl.* expense; (law) costs; *vivre aux* ~ *d'autrui*, to live at other people's expense.

dépense [depɑ̃s] *s.f.* **1.** expense, expenditure, consumption (of fuel, etc.); cost(s); *faire la* ~ *de qch.*, to spend money on sth., to go to the expense of (buying) sth.; *ne pas regarder à la* ~, not to count the cost, to spare no expense; **2.** store-room, buttery.

dépenser [depɑ̃se] *v.t.* **1.** to spend (money); **2.** to spend, to use up, to consume, to waste, (time, effort, etc.); **se** ~ *v.refl.* to spend oneself, to use up or waste one's energy.

dépensi-er, -ère [depɑ̃sje] *adj.* extravagant, spendthrift; *s.m.f.* **1.** bursar; **2.** spendthrift.

déperdition [depɛrdisjɔ̃] *s.f.* loss, diminution.

dépérir [deperir] *v.i.* to decline, to waste away; (of plant) to wither.

dépérissement [deperismɑ̃] *s.m.* decline; withering; going to ruin.

dépersonnalisation [depɛrsɔnalizɑsjɔ̃] *s.f.* depersonalization.

dépersonnaliser [depɛrsɔnalize] *v.t.* to depersonalize.

dépêtrer [depetre] *v.t.* (obs.) to unhobble (animal); (lit. & fig.) to free (from entanglement), to extricate.

dépeuplé, -e [depœple] *adj.* depopulated; *village* ~, deserted village.

dépeuplement [depœpləmɑ̃] *s.m.* depopulation; thinning (of forest, etc.); depletion (of game, etc.).

dépeupler [depœple] *v.t.* to depopulate; to thin (forest, etc.); to deplete (fish, game, etc.).

déphasage [defɑzaʒ] *s.m.* (phys.) phase deplacement, difference in phase; ~ *en avant*, lead; ~ *en arrière*, lag; (fam., fig.) being out of step.

déphasé, -e [defɑze] *adj.* (phys.) out of phase; (fig.) out of step, disorientated.

déphosphoration [defɔsfɔrɑsjɔ̃] *s.f.* dephosphorization.

déphosphorer [defɔsfɔre] *v.t.* to dephosphorize.

dépiauter [depjote] *v.t.* (fam.) to skin, to flay.

dépicage see DÉPIQUAGE.

dépilage [depilaʒ] *s.m.* (tanning) unhairing (of hide).

dépilation [depilɑsjɔ̃] *s.f.* (med.) falling of hair, hair-loss.

dépilatoire [depilatwar] *adj.*, *s.m.* depilatory.

dépiler[1] [depile] *v.t.* **1.** (med.) to cause the hair to fall; **2.** (tanning) to unhair (hide).

dépiler[2] [depile] *v.t.i.* (mining) to remove roof-supports.

dépiquage, dépicage [depikaʒ] *s.m.* (agric.) threshing, husking (of cereals).

dépiquer[1] [depike] *v.t.* **1.** (dressm.) to unpick, to unstitch; **2.** (hort.) to transplant.

dépiquer[2] [depike] *v.t.* (agric.) to thresh, to husk (cereals).

dépistage [depistaʒ] *s.m.* tracking down; detection.

dépister [depiste] *v.t.* **1.** to track down; to uncover, to detect; **2.** to put off the scent.

dépit [depi] *s.m.* **1.** chagrin, resentment; **2.** *en* ~ *de*, in spite of, despite; *en* ~ *du bon sens*, in a completely wrong way.

dépité, -e [depite] *adj.* vexed, mortified.

dépiter [depite] *v.t.* to disappoint, to vex, to provoke; **se** ~ *v.refl.* to be vexed, to take offence; to be put out (*contre*, by).

déplacé, -e [deplase] *adj.* out of place, displaced; (fig.) out of place, inopportune, in bad taste; *personne* ~*e*, displaced person.

déplacer [deplase] *v.t.* to move, to shift, to displace, to disarrange; to transfer; **se** ~ *v.refl.* to move (from one place to another); to travel.

déplacement [deplasmɑ̃] *s.m.* moving, changing position of (sth.); (med., naut.) displacement; transfer (of s.o.); moving house; travelling.

déplaire [deplɛr] *v.t.* ~ *à*, to displease, to offend, to be distasteful, disagreeable, or repugnant to, to be rejected by, to be unpopular with; *au risque de lui* ~, at the risk of offending him; *elle me déplaît*, I don't like her; (iron.) *ne vous en déplaise*, whatever you may think, whether you like it or not; *n'en déplaise à ces messieurs*, whatever those gentlemen may say, may think.

déplaisant, -e [deplɛzɑ̃] *adj.* unpleasant, unpleasing, displeasing, disagreeable.

déplaisir [deplezir] *s.m.* displeasure, annoyance.

déplantage [deplɑ̃taʒ] *s.m.* (hort.) **1.** lifting (of plants for transplanting); **2.** clearing (bed, etc., of plants).

déplanter [deplɑ̃te] *v.t.* (hort.) **1.** to lift (plants for transplanting); **2.** to clear (bed, etc., of plants).

déplantoir [deplɑ̃twar] *s.m.* (garden) trowel.

déplâtrage [deplɑtraʒ] *s.m.* (build., etc.) stripping of plaster; (surg.) taking (arm, etc.) out of plaster.

déplâtrer [deplɑtre] *v.t.* (build., etc.) to strip of plaster; (surg.) to take (arm, etc.) out of plaster.

dépliage [deplijaʒ], **dépliement** [deplimɑ̃] *s.m.* unfolding, spreading out.

dépliant, -e [deplijɑ̃] *adj.* folding; ~ *s.m.* folder; sheet, map, etc., that folds out of a book.

déplier [deplije] *v.t.* to unfold, to spread out; **se** ~ *v.refl.* to unfold, to open (out).

déplissage [deplisaʒ] *s.m.* ironing out; coming out of pleat.

déplisser [deplise] *v.t.* to iron out; *se* ~, to come out of pleat.

déploiement [deplwamɑ̃] *s.m.* **1.** unfolding, spreading (out); **2.** (mil.) deployment.

déplombage [deplɔ̃baʒ] *s.m.* **1.** unsealing (of meter, etc.); **2.** removal of filling (from tooth).
déplomber [deplɔ̃be] *v.t.* **1.** to unseal (meter, etc.); **2.** to remove filling from (tooth).
déplorable [deplɔrabl] *adj.* deplorable; (obs.) to be pitied, to be mourned; **~ment** [deplɔrabləmɑ̃] *adv.* deplorably.
déplorer [deplɔre] *v.t.* to deplore; (obs.) to grieve over.
déployer [deplwaje] *v.t.* **1.** to unfold, to spread (out); **2.** (mil.) to deploy (troops); *se* **~**, to deploy.
déplumé, -e [deplyme] *adj.* (of bird) moulting, that has moulted; (fam.) losing one's hair, going bald.
(**se**) **déplumer** [deplyme] *v.refl.* (of bird) to moult; (fam.) to grow bald, to lose one's hair.
dépoétiser [depɔetize] *v.t.* to take the poetry out of.
dépoitraillé, -e [depwatrɑje] *adj.* carelessly dressed, with chest or breasts (partly) exposed.
dépolarisant, -e [depɔlarizɑ̃] *adj.* (phys.) depolarizing; **~** *s.m.* depolarizer.
dépolarisation [depɔlarizɑsjɔ̃] *s.f.* depolarization.
dépolariser [depɔlarize] *v.t.* to depolarize.
dépoli, -e [depɔli] *adj.* (of metal, etc.) dull, matt, lustreless; (of glass) ground, frosted.
dépolir [depɔlir] *v.t.* to cause to lose its polish or brilliance; **se ~** *v.refl.* to lose its polish, to become dull.
dépolissage [depɔlisaʒ] *s.m.* (techn.) grinding, frosting (of glass).
dépolitisation [depɔlitizɑsjɔ̃] *s.f.* depoliticization, taking out of the sphere of politics.
dépolitiser [depɔlitize] *v.t.* to depoliticize, to remove from the sphere of politics.
déponent, -e [depɔnɑ̃] *adj.* (gram.) deponent.
dépopulation [depɔpylɑsjɔ̃] *s.f.* depopulation.
déport [depɔr] *s.m.* (Stock Exchange) backwardation.
déportation [depɔrtɑsjɔ̃] *s.f.* **1.** deportation; **2.** internment in a concentration camp.
déporté, -e [depɔrte] *s.m.f.* **1.** deportee; **2.** person interned in a concentration camp (esp. in World War II).
déportement [depɔrtəmɑ̃] *s.m.* **1.** (obs.) deportment; (pl.) misconduct, excesses; **2.** (of vehicle, etc.) being carried off course.
déporter [depɔrte] *v.t.* **1.** to deport; **2.** to carry off course.
déposant, -e [depozɑ̃] *s.m.f.* **1.** depositor; **2.** (law) deponent.
dépose [depoz] *s.f.* taking-down, dismantling.
déposer[1] [depoze] *v.t.* **1.** to put down, to set down, to lay down, to lay aside, to leave; **2.** (of liquid) to leave a deposit; **3.** to deposit (money, etc.); *marque déposée*, registered trade-mark; **~** *v.i.* to give evidence, to depose; **se ~** *v.refl.* (of dust, wine, etc.) to settle.
déposer[2] [depoze] *v.t.* to take down, to dismantle.
dépositaire [depɔzitɛr] *s.m.f.* depositary, trustee; agent, stockist; repository (of secret); **~** *public*, public trustee.
déposition [depɔzisjɔ̃] *s.f.* **1.** deposition, testimony, evidence; **2.** dethronement, deposing, deposition; **3.** (art) **~** *de croix*, deposition.
déposséder [depɔsede] *v.t.* to dispossess.
dépossession [depɔsesjɔ̃] *s.f.* dispossession.
dépôt [depo] *s.m.* **1.** laying, placing, putting, depositing (sth.); **~** *de marques de fabrique*, registration of trade-marks; **2.** (fin.) deposit; (law) lodgement; **3.** repository, warehouse, depot; police cell (esp. in Paris); **4.** (chem., etc.) deposit, sediment; (geol.) deposit.
dépoter [depɔte] *v.t.* **1.** to unpot (plant); **2.** to decant (liquid).
dépotoir [depɔtwar] *s.m.* **1.** night-soil dump; (fig.) sink; (techn.) sludge treatment works; **2.** rubbish-dump; (fig., fam.) junk-room.
dépouille [depuj] *s.f.* **1.** pelt; slough (of snake, etc.); **2. ~** (*mortelle*), (mortal) remains; **3.** (pl.) spoils, booty; *s'arracher les* **~***s d'un mourant*, to fight over the dignities, effects, etc., of s.o. who is dying.
dépouillé, -e [depuje] *adj.* **1.** (of tree) bare (of leaves); **2.** deprived, devoid, (*de*, of); **3.** (of style) severe, plain, matter-of-fact.
dépouillement [depujmɑ̃] *s.m.* **1.** stripping (s.o. of possessions, etc.), deprivation; **2.** minute study (of book, document, etc.); counting of votes.
dépouiller [depuje] *v.t.* **1.** to strip; to skin (animal); **2.** to rob, to strip, (s.o. of possessions); to deprive (*qn. de*, s.o. of); **3.** to study minutely, to analyse, (book, document, etc.); to count votes (after ballot); **4.** to cast, to shed, (fig.) to renounce; **se ~** *v.refl.* to divest oneself (*de*, of).
dépourvu, -e [depurvy] *adj.* devoid (*de*, of), lacking (*de*, in), destitute; *au* **~**, unawares, unexpectedly, without warning.
dépoussiérage [depusjeraʒ] *s.m.* vacuum-cleaning.
dépoussiérer [depusjere] *v.t.* to vacuum-clean.
dépravation [depravɑsjɔ̃] *s.f.* depravity, perversion; (obs.) depravation, debauchery.
dépravé, -e [deprave] *adj.* depraved, perverted.
dépraver [deprave] *v.t.* to deprave, to corrupt.
déprécation [deprekɑsjɔ̃] *s.f.* (liturg.) deprecation.
dépréciat-eur, -rice [depresjatœr] *s.m.f.* detractor.
dépréciati-f, -ve [depresjatif] *adj.* depreciatory.
dépréciation [depresjɑsjɔ̃] *s.f.* depreciation.
déprécier [depresje] *v.t.* **1.** to lower the value of, to spoil; **2.** to underrate, to undervalue; **se ~** *v.refl.* to be self-depreciatory, to underrate one's abilities.
déprédat-eur, -rice [depredatœr] *s.m.f.* depredator.
déprédation [depredɑsjɔ̃] *s.f.* depredation; embezzlement, peculation.
(**se**) **déprendre** [deprɑ̃dr] *v.refl.* *se* **~** *de*, to get free of, to give up, to get out of, (attachment, habit, etc.).
dépressi-f, -ive [depresif] *adj.* depressive.
dépression [deprɛsjɔ̃] *s.f.* depression, hollow.
dépressurisation [depresyrizasjɔ̃] *s.f.* (aeron., astronaut.) depressurization.
déprimant, -e [deprimɑ̃] *adj.* depressing; *climat* **~**, debilitating climate.
déprimer [deprime] *v.t.* to depress, to lower, to cause a depression in.
dépriser [deprize] *v.t.* (Lit.) to undervalue.
dépuceler [depysle] *v.t.* (vulg.) to deflower (a virgin).
depuis [dəpɥi] *prep.* since, from (date), for (past period); **~** *longtemps*, long since, for a long time; **~** *Pâques jusqu'à Noël*, from Easter to Christmas; **~** *le début jusqu'à la fin*, from beginning to end; *on vous cherche* **~** *dix minutes*, we've been looking for you for ten minutes; **~** *adv.* since; **~** *que conj.* **~** *qu'il est parti*, since he left.
dépurati-f, -ve [depyratif] *adj.*, **~f** *s.m.* (med.) depurative.
dépuration [depyrɑsjɔ̃] *s.f.* (med.) depuration.
dépurer [depyre] *v.t.* to depurate.
députation [depytɑsjɔ̃] *s.f.* **1.** deputation; **2.** deputyship (esp. office of *député* in Fr. parliament).
député [depyte] *s.m.* **1.** député, deputy (elected member of Fr. parliament); **2.** delegate, member of deputation.
députer [depyte] *v.t.* to send as delegate, as representative.

der [dɛr] abbrev. *dernière*, last; (pop.) *la ~ des ~s*, the war to end all wars.
déracinement [derasinmɑ̃] *s.m.* uprooting, rooting out; (fig.) eradication.
déraciner [derasine] *v.t.* to uproot, to root out; (fig.) to eradicate.
dérader [derade] *v.i.* (of ship) to be driven out to sea (by storm).
déraillement [derɑjmɑ̃] *s.m.* derailment.
dérailler [derɑje] *v.i.* **1.** to go off the rails; *faire ~*, to derail; **2.** (fig.) to go awry, to go wrong; (fam.) to rave, to wander.
dérailleur [derɑjœr] *s.m.* (of bicycle) derailleur gear(s); (rail.) switch (in shunting-yard).
déraison [derɛzɔ̃] *s.f.* (obs., Lit.) foolishness, unreason.
déraisonnable [derɛzɔnabl] *adj.* unreasonable, irrational; **~ment** [derɛzɔnabləmɑ̃] *adv.* unreasonably, irrationally.
déraisonner [derɛzɔne] *v.i.* to talk irrationally, to wander.
dérangement [derɑ̃ʒmɑ̃] *s.m.* **1.** disarrangement, upset, disturbance; **2.** derangement; indisposition; **3.** *en ~*, out of order.
déranger [derɑ̃ʒe] *v.t.* **1.** to disarrange, to put out of place, to throw into disorder; **2.** to derange (in mind); to upset; to disturb, to inconvenience; **3.** (obs.) to lead astray; **se ~** *v.refl.* to move; to put oneself out (*pour qn.*, for s.o.).
dérapage [derapaʒ] *s.m.* **1.** (naut.) dragging (of anchor); **2.** (car, etc.) skidding, skid.
déraper [derape] *v.i.* **1.** (naut.) (of anchor) to drag; (of ship) to drag the anchor; **2.** (car, etc.) to skid.
déraser [deraze] *v.t.* (techn.) to lower the top of.
dératé [derate] *s.m.* *courir comme un ~*, to run like a hare.
dératisation [deratizɑsjɔ̃] *s.f.* rat disinfestation.
dératiser [deratize] *v.t.* to disinfest, to rid, of rats.
dérayer [dereje] *v.t.i.* to plough the last furrow.
dérayure [derejyr] *s.f.* (agric.) furrow-drain; boundary furrow.
derechef [dərəʃɛf] *adv.* (obs., Lit.) a second time, once more.
déréglé, -e [deregle] *adj.* **1.** out of order, irregular, disturbed; **2.** disorganized, disorderly, immoderate.
dérèglement [derɛgləmɑ̃] *s.m.* **1.** disorder, malfunction, derangement; **2.** (obs.) debauchery, debauch.
dérégler [deregle] *v.t.* **1.** to put out of order, to upset, to disturb; **2.** to corrupt.
dérider [deride] *v.t.* to cheer (s.o.) up; (Lit.) to smooth (*son front*, one's brow); *il est difficile à ~*, it is difficult to cheer him up; **se ~** *v.refl.* to cheer up, to smile; ⚠ not 'to deride'.
dérision [derizjɔ̃] *s.f.* **1.** derision; *tourner en ~*, to ridicule; **2.** sth. ridiculously small; *dix francs! c'est une ~*, ten francs! that's quite ridiculous.
dérisoire [derizwar] *adj.* **1.** (obs.) derisory; derisive, mocking; **2.** ridiculous(-ly small), laughable, tiny, paltry, miserable; contemptible; **~ment** [derizwarmɑ̃] *adv.* (Lit.) ridiculously (small, etc.).
dérivati-f, -ve [derivatif] *adj.*, **~f** *s.m.* derivative.
dérivation[1] [derivɑsjɔ̃] *s.f.* **1.** diversion or diverted portion (of watercourse, etc.); branch, cut (of river, canal, etc.); head race, penstock; (mech.) bypassing, bypass; *conduit de ~*, bypass; *amener en ~*, to bypass; (electr.) shunt; **2.** (lang.) derivation; (math.) derivation (of function); (med.) derivation, counter-irritation.
dérivation[2] [derivɑsjɔ̃] *s.f.* **1.** drifting (off course); (naut.) driftage; (aeron.) drift; **2.** (artill.) deflection.
dérive [deriv] *s.f.* **1.** (naut., aeron.) drift, leeway; *en ~*, adrift; (lit. & fig.) *aller à la ~*, to go adrift, to drift aimlessly; **2.** (naut.) centre-board; fin (of aircraft, rocket); **3.** (artill.) correction (of elevation).
dérivé, -e [derive] *adj.* derived; secondary; *~ s.m.* (lang., sci.) derivative; (math.) derived function or curve.
dérivée [derive] *s.f.* (math.) derivative.
dériver[1] [derive] *v.t.* **1.** to divert (watercourse); **2.** (lang., math.) to derive; *~ v.i.* to derive, to be derived; to originate, to spring, (*de*, from).
dériver[2] [derive] *v.i.* (naut., aeron., & fig.) to drift.
dériver[3] [derive], **dériveter** [derivte] *v.t.* (techn.) to unrivet.
dériveur [derivœr] *s.m.* (naut.) **1.** storm-spanker (sail); **2.** boat with centre-board.
dermatite [dɛrmatit], **dermite** [dɛrmit] *s.f.* dermatitis.
dermato-logie [dɛrmatɔlɔʒi] *s.f.* dermatology; **~logiste** [dɛrmatɔlɔʒist], **~logue** [dɛrmatɔlɔg] *s.m.f.* dermatologist.
derme [dɛrm] *s.m.* (anat.) dermis, derm, derma.
dermique [dɛrmik] *adj.* (anat.) dermal.
dermite see DERMATITE.
dermographie [dɛrmɔgrafi] *s.f.* (pathol.) dermographia, dermographism.
derni-er, -ère [dɛrnje] *adj.* **1.** last, latest; *l'année ~ère*, last year; *ces ~ers temps*, latterly; *le ~er mois de l'année*, the last month of the year; *~ères nouvelles*, latest news; **2.** utmost, extreme; *s.m.f.* last, lowest; youngest (of family); *le ~er des ~ers*, the lowest of the low; *la ~ère des guerres*, the war to end all wars; *ce ~er*, the last-named; *en ~er adv.loc.* last (of all); **~èrement** [dɛrnjɛrmɑ̃] *adv.* recently, lately, of late.
dernier-né [dɛrnjene], **dernière-née** [dɛrnjɛrne] *s.m.f.* (pl. *dernier-nés*, *dernière-nées*) youngest (of family).
dérobade [derɔbad] *s.f.* **1.** (of horse) jibbing, refusing; **2.** shirking, evasion.
dérobé, -e [derɔbe] *adj.* **1.** stolen; **2.** (of door, etc.) hidden, secret; *à la ~e*, covertly, surreptitiously.
dérober [derɔbe] *v.t.* **1.** (Lit.) to steal, to filch; (fig.) to obtain, to extract; *~ un baiser*, to steal a kiss; *~ un secret à qn.*, to worm a secret out of s.o.; **3.** to conceal, to disguise (truth); **4.** (Lit.) to avert (glance, face); **se ~** *v.refl.* to avoid answering, to evade responsibility, to decline to act; to slip away; *se ~ à*, to hide from, to avoid, to evade, to shirk; *se ~ sous*, to slip from under, to give way under; *il sentit ses genoux se ~ sous lui*, he felt his knees give way.
dérochage [derɔʃaʒ] *s.m.* (metall.) pickling, dipping.
dérochement [derɔʃmɑ̃] *s.m.* (techn.) removal of rocks (from river-bed, etc.).
dérocher [derɔʃe] *v.i.* (mountaineering) to fall from a rock face; *~ v.t.* **1.** (metall.) to pickle, to dip; **2.** (techn.) to remove rocks (from river-bed, etc.).
dérogation [derɔgɑsjɔ̃] *s.f.* derogation, breach, (*à*, of, law, etc.).
déroger [derɔʒe] *v.t.* to lower oneself, to lose caste, prestige, etc.; *~ à*, to detract from, to derogate from; to depart, or deviate, from (custom, etc.), to be in breach of (law, etc.).
dérouillée [deruje] *s.f.* (pop.) drubbing.
dérouiller [deruje] *v.t.* **1.** to remove the rust from, to clean; (fig.) *~ sa mémoire*, to refresh one's memory; *se ~ les jambes*, to stretch one's legs; **2.** (pop.) to beat (s.o.) up.
déroulage [derulaʒ] *s.m.* **1.** unrolling; **2.** (techn.) veneer-peeling, wood-peeling.
déroulement [derulmɑ̃] *s.m.* unrolling, unfolding, unwinding, uncurling; passing (of procession, etc.); drifting away (of smoke, etc.);

breaking (of waves); (fig.) unfolding, development, succession, sequence, (of events, plot, etc.).
dérouler [derule] *v.t.* to unroll, to unfold, to unwind, to spread out, to display; **se ~** *v.refl.* (fig.) to unfold, to develop, to take place, to pass off.
dérouleuse [deruløz] *s.f.* (techn.) **1.** reel (for cable, etc.); **2.** veneer-cutting lathe.
déroutant, -e [derutɑ̃] *adj.* disconcerting, baffling.
déroute [derut] *s.f.* rout; *mettre en ~*, to put to rout, to rout, (fig.) to throw into confusion.
déroutement [derutmɑ̃] *s.m.* re-routing (of ship, aircraft).
dérouter [derute] *v.t.* **1.** (obs.) to cause to stray (off one's route); **2.** to re-route (ship, aircraft, etc.); **3.** (fig.) to disconcert, to bewilder.
derrick [dɛrik] *s.m.* derrick (of oil-well).
derrière [dɛrjɛr] *adv., prep.* behind; *sortir de ~ la haie*, to come out from behind the hedge; *pattes de ~*, hind legs; *par ~*, behind, round the back of, from behind; *poignarder qn. par ~*, to stab s.o. in the back; *dire du mal de qn. par ~*, to speak ill of s.o. behind his back; *sens devant ~*, back to front; *~ s.m.* back (opp. front); behind, bottom, backside, buttocks; (pl.) (mil.) rear, rear echelons.
derviche [dɛrviʃ] *s.m.* dervish.
des [de] see DE.
dès [dɛ] *prep.* from (time, place); as soon as; *~ son enfance*, from his childhood (onwards); *vous viendrez me voir ~ mon retour*, come to see me as soon as I return; *~ lors*, from that moment, from that time onwards; *~ que, conj.loc.* as soon as, since.
D.E.S. [deeɛs] abbrev. *Diplôme d'études supérieures.*
désabonnement [dezabɔnmɑ̃] *s.m.* cancellation, non-renewal, (of subscription, season-ticket).
désabonner [dezabɔne] *v.t.* to cancel (subscription); *veuillez me ~*, please cancel my subscription; **se ~** *v.refl.* to cancel, not to renew, (one's subscription, season-ticket).
désabusé, -e [dezabyze] *adj.* disillusioned, disenchanted; (Lit.) disabused, undeceived.
désabusement [dezabyzmɑ̃] *s.m.* (Lit.) disenchantment.
désabuser [dezabyze] *v.t.* (Lit.) to disabuse, to disillusion.
désaccord [dezakɔr] *s.m.* disagreement, variance, conflict; *en ~ avec*, at variance with, at odds with, out of tune with.
désaccordé, -e [dezakɔrde] *adj.* **1.** (Lit.) disharmonious; **2.** (mus.) out of tune.
désaccorder [dezakɔrde] *v.t.* **1.** (Lit.) to bring into disagreement, to disunite; **2.** (mus.) to cause (instrument) to go out of tune; **se ~** *v.refl.* (mus., of instrument) to go out of tune.
désaccoupler [dezakuple] *v.t.* to uncouple.
désaccoutumer [dezakutyme] *v.t.* to cure (s.o.) of the habit (*de*, of); **se ~** *v.refl.* to get out of the habit (*de*, of).
désacraliser [desakralize] *v.t.* to secularize.
désadaptation [dezadaptɑsjɔ̃] *s.f.* loss of adjustment (to society, etc.), becoming maladjusted.
désadapté, -e [dezadapte] *adj.* maladjusted.
désadapter [dezadapte] *v.t.* to cause maladjustment; *se ~ de*, to become maladjusted to.
désaéré, -e [dezaere] *adj.* (techn.) de-aerated.
désaffectation [dezafɛktɑsjɔ̃] *s.f.* (law) disuse; change of use (of building).
désaffecté, -e [dezafɛkte] *adj.* disused; used for other than original purpose, adapted for another use.
désaffecter [dezafɛkte] *v.t.* (law) to change the use of (building).
désaffection [dezafɛksjɔ̃] *s.f.* disaffection, loss of affection.
(se) désaffectionner [dezafɛksjɔne] *v.refl.* (obs.) to lose one's affection (*de*, for).
désagréable [dezagreabl] *adj.* disagreeable, unpleasant, offensive; **~ment** [dezagreabləmɑ̃] *adv.* disagreeably, offensively, unpleasantly.
désagrégation [dezagregasjɔ̃] *s.f.* disintegration, disaggregation.
désagréger [dezagreʒe] *v.t.* to disintegrate, to disaggregate; **se ~** *v.refl.* to disintegrate, to crumble.
désagrément [dezagremɑ̃] *s.m.* unpleasantness, annoyance; ⚠ not 'disagreement'.
désaimanter [dezɛmɑ̃te] *v.t.* to demagnetize.
désaltérant, -e [dezalterɑ̃] *adj.* thirst-quenching.
désaltérer [dezaltere] *v.t.* to quench the thirst of; *~ le malade*, to give the patient a drink; **se ~** *v.refl.* to drink, to quench one's thirst.
désamorçage [dezamɔrsaʒ] *s.m.* removal or absence of charge, priming, fuse, etc., defusing; failure of pump, dynamo, etc.
désamorcer [dezamɔrse] *v.t.* to remove charge, priming, etc., from; to defuse (bomb, etc.); *la pompe est désamorcée*, the pump is not primed.
désapparier [dezaparje], **déparier** [deparje] *v.t.* **1.** to separate (pair of animals); **2.** to break a pair (of objects by removing one).
désappointement [dezapwɛ̃tmɑ̃] *s.m.* disappointment.
désappointer [dezapwɛ̃te] *v.t.* to disappoint.
désapprendre [dezaprɑ̃dr] *v.t.* (Lit.) to forget; *il a désappris le peu d'anglais qu'il savait*, he has forgotten what little English he knew.
désapprobat-eur, -rice [dezaprɔbatœr] *adj.* disapproving.
désapprobation [dezaprɔbɑsjɔ̃] *s.f.* disapproval.
désapprouver [dezapruve] *v.t.* to disapprove of, to condemn.
désapprovisionner [dezaprɔvizjɔne] *v.t.* **1.** to leave without supplies; **2.** to unload (firearm).
désarçonner [dezarsɔne] *v.t.* to unseat (rider); (fig.) to disconcert, to nonplus.
désargenté, -e [dezarʒɑ̃te] *adj.* (fam.) short of cash, hard up.
désargenter [dezarʒɑ̃te] *v.t.* to desilver, to remove silver-plating from; *se ~*, (of cutlery, etc.) to lose its silver-plating (with wear).
désarmant, -e [dezarmɑ̃] *adj.* (fig.) disarming.
désarmement [dezarməmɑ̃] *s.m.* **1.** disarmament; **2.** (naut.) putting out of commission, laying up, (of ship).
désarmer [dezarme] *v.t.* **1.** to disarm; **2.** (naut.) *~ un navire*, to put a ship out of commission; *~ v.i.* to disarm; (fig.) to relax one's hostility.
désarrimage [dezarimaʒ] *s.m.* (naut.) shift(ing) of cargo.
désarrimer [dezarime] *v.t.* (naut.) to shift cargo; *~ v.i.* (of cargo) to shift.
désarroi [dezarwa] *s.m.* confusion, disorder; *être en plein ~, en grand ~*, to be at sixes and sevens.
désarticulation [dezartikylɑsjɔ̃] *s.f.* dislocation
désarticuler [dezartikyle] *v.t.* to dislocate; (surg.) to amputate at the joint.
désassemblage [dezasɑ̃blaʒ] *s.m.* **1.** (techn.) disassembly, stripping down, taking apart, (of machine, etc.); **2.** coming to pieces, falling apart.
désassembler [dezasɑ̃ble] *v.t.* (techn.) to disassemble, to strip down, to take apart, (machine, etc.).
désassimilation [dezasimilɑsjɔ̃] *s.f.* (physiol.) dissimilation, catabolism.
désassorti, -e [dezasɔrti] *adj.* **1.** (of set, series) incomplete; **2.** (of shop) out of stock (of a particular article), short-stocked.

désassortir [dezasɔrtir] *v.t.* **1.** to break up (set, pair, etc.); **2.** to clear (dealer, shop) of stock.
désastre [dezastr] *s.m.* disaster.
désastreu-x, -se [dezastrø] *adj.* disastrous; **~sement** [dezastrøzmɑ̃] *adv.* disastrously.
désavantage [dezavɑ̃taʒ] *s.m.* disadvantage; *voir qn. à son ~*, to see s.o. at a disadvantage.
désavantager [dezavɑ̃taʒe] *v.t.* to put at a disadvantage; to treat unfavourably; to disadvantage.
désavantageu-x, -se [dezavɑ̃taʒø] *adj.* disadvantageous; **~sement** [dezavɑ̃taʒøzmɑ̃] *adv.* disadvantageously.
désaveu [dezavø] *s.m.* disavowal; *~ de paternité*, denial of paternity.
désavouer [dezavwe] *v.t.* to disavow; *~ la paternité d'un enfant*, to deny paternity of a child; *~ un enfant*, to disown a child.
désaxé, -e [dezakse] *adj.* (techn.) offset; (fig.) unbalanced; *s.m.f.* unbalanced person.
désaxer [dezakse] *v.t.* **1.** (techn.) to offset (crankshaft); **2.** (fig.) to unbalance (s.o.).
descellement [desɛlmɑ̃] *s.m.* unsealing; loosening (of mortar, of sth. fixed with mortar).
desceller [desele] *v.t.* **1.** to unseal; **2.** to loosen (mortar); to remove by loosening mortar.
descendance [desɑ̃dɑ̃s] *s.f.* descendants.
descendant, -e [desɑ̃dɑ̃] *adj.* descending, down, downhill; *marée ~e*, ebb-tide; *s.m.f.* descendant.
descenderie [desɑ̃dri] *s.f.* (mining) descending shaft, incline.
descendeu-r, -se [desɑ̃dœr] *s.m.f.* (cycling, skiing) downhill racer.
descendre [desɑ̃dr] *v.i.* to go or come down; to get down; to get out (of train, car, etc.); *~ à terre*, to land (from a ship); to descend; to fall; to sink; *~ à la prochaine*, to get out (of the train) at the next station; *la marée descend*, the tide is going out; *colline qui descend en pente douce*, hill which slopes gently down; *~ v.t.* to go or come down (hill, stairs, etc.); to bring, fetch, get, reach, or take down; (fam.) to knock or shoot down, to fell; (fam.) *je vous descendrai en ville*, I will drop you in town.
descente [desɑ̃t] *s.f.* **1.** going down, coming down, alighting, descent; *~ de police*, police raid; **2.** taking down; *~ de qch. à la cave*, putting sth. in the cellar; **3.** down grade, downward slope; *au bas de la ~*, at the bottom of the hill; **4.** (naut.) companion-ladder, companion-way; (techn.) down-pipe, down-lead, etc.; **5.** *~ de lit*, bedside rug, mat, etc.
descriptible [dɛskriptibl] *adj.* describable.
descripti-f, -ve [dɛskriptif] *adj.* descriptive.
description [dɛskripsjɔ̃] *s.f.* description.
déséchouer [dezeʃwe] *v.t.* (naut.) to refloat.
déségrégation [desegregɑsjɔ̃] *s.f.* desegregation.
désembourber [dezɑ̃burbe] *v.t.* to pull out of the mud.
désemparé, -e [dezɑ̃pare] *adj.* (naut., of ship) disabled; (fig.) at a loss; *être tout ~*, not to know which way to turn.
désemparer [dezɑ̃pare] *v.t.* **1.** (naut.) to disable (ship); **2.** (obs.) to abandon (place); (mod.) *sans ~*, without respite.
désemplir [dezɑ̃plir] *v.t.* (obs.) to empty in part; *la salle se désemplissait peu à peu*, the auditorium gradually became less crowded; *~ v.i. ne pas ~*, to be always full (crowded).
désenchaîner [dezɑ̃ʃene] *v.t.* to unchain, to unshackle.
désenchantement [dezɑ̃ʃɑ̃tmɑ̃] *s.m.* disenchantment; disappointment.
désenchanter [dezɑ̃ʃɑ̃te] *v.t.* to disenchant, to disillusion.
désencombrer [dezɑ̃kɔ̃bre] *v.t.* to disencumber; to clear (of obstruction, rubbish).
désenfiler [dezɑ̃file] *v.t.* to unthread (needle); **se ~** *v.refl.* (of necklace, etc.) to come unstrung.
désenfler [dezɑ̃fle] *v.i.* to become less swollen; (of tyre, swelling) to go down.
désengagement [dezɑ̃gaʒmɑ̃] *s.m.* disengagement.
désengager [dezɑ̃gaʒe] *v.t.* to free (from promise, obligation, etc.); *se ~ d'une obligation*, to withdraw from an obligation.
désengorger [dezɑ̃gɔrʒe] *v.t.* (techn.) to unblock (pipe, etc.).
désengrener [dezɑ̃grəne] *v.t.* (techn.) to disengage, to put out of gear.
désenivrer [dezɑ̃nivre] *v.t.i.* to sober (down, up); to become sober.
désennuyer [dezɑ̃nɥije] *v.t.* to divert, to amuse, to distract; to break the tedium; **se ~** *v.refl.* to relieve one's boredom, to amuse oneself; *pour se ~*, just for fun, in order to pass the time.
désenrayer [dezɑ̃reje] *v.t.* (techn.) to release jammed mechanism (of firearm).
désensabler [dezɑ̃sable] *v.t.* to clear of sand.
désensibilis-ateur [desɑ̃sibilizatœr] *s.m.* (photo.) desensitizer; **~ation** [desɑ̃sibilizɑsjɔ̃] *s.f.* desensitization; **~er** [desɑ̃sibilize] *v.t.* to desensitize.
désensorceler [dezɑ̃sɔrsəle] *v.t.* to remove the spell from, to free (s.o.) from a spell, from an infatuation, to cease to exercise a fascination over.
désentortiller [dezɑ̃tɔrtije] *v.t.* to untwist, to unravel.
désentraver [dezɑ̃trave] *v.t.* to unhobble (horse, etc.); (fig.) to disencumber, to remove impediments.
désenvaser [dezɑ̃vɑze] *v.t.* to dredge (up).
désenverguer see DÉVERGUER.
désépaissir [dezepesir] *v.t.* to thin.
déséquilibre [dezekilibr] *s.m.* disequilibrium, instability.
déséquilibré, -e [dezekilibre] *adj.*, *s.m.f.* unbalanced (person).
déséquilibrer [dezekilibre] *v.t.* to throw off balance; to cause mental instability in (s.o.).
déséquiper [dezekipe] *v.t.* **1.** (naut.) to lay up (ship); **2.** to strip of equipment; **se ~** *v.refl.* to take off one's equipment.
désert, -e [dezɛr] *adj.* uninhabited, deserted, desolate, (of island, etc.) desert; *~ s.m.* desert, wilderness.
déserter [dezɛrte] *v.t.i.* to desert.
déserteur [dezɛrtœr] *s.m.* **1.** deserter (esp. from armed forces); **2.** apostate, renegade.
désertion [dezɛrsjɔ̃] *s.f.* desertion.
désertique [dezɛrtik] *adj.* (geog.) desertic; desert.
désespérance [dezɛsperɑ̃s] *s.f.* (Lit.) despair, hopelessness.
désespérant, -e [dezɛsperɑ̃] *adj.* **1.** (Lit.) heart-breaking; **2.** discouraging, disheartening, depressing.
désespéré, -e [dezɛspere] *adj.* hopeless, despairing; desperate; (fam.) upset, terribly sorry; *s.m.f.* desperate person; **~ment** [dezɛsperemɑ̃] *adv.* despairingly; desperately.
désespérer [dezɛspere] *v.i.* to despair (*de*, of); *~ v.t.* to discourage, to drive to despair; **se ~** *v.refl.* to despair.
désespoir [dezɛspwar] *s.m.* despair, hopelessness, desperation; *être au ~ de* (*ne pas pouvoir faire qch.*), to be desperately sorry (not to be able to do sth.); *en ~ de cause*, in desperation, as a (last) desperate remedy.
déshabillage [dezabijaʒ] *s.m.* undressing.
déshabillé [dezabije] *s.m.* **1.** (obs.) *en déshabillé*, in dishabille, scantily clad; **2.** négligé, house-coat.
déshabiller [dezabije] *v.t.* to undress; (fig.) to

unmask; **se** ~ *v.refl.* to undress; to take off one's (hat and) coat.
déshabituer [dezabitɥe] *v.t.* to cure of an addiction; to make unaccustomed to; **se** ~ *v.refl.* to get out of the habit (*de*, of); *se* ~ *de fumer*, to give up smoking.
désherbage [dezɛrbaʒ] *s.m.* weeding.
désherber [dezɛrbe] *v.t.* to weed.
déshérence [dezerɑ̃s] *s.f.* (law) escheat; *tomber en* ~, to escheat.
déshérité, -e [dezerite] *adj., s.m.f.* **1.** disinherited (person); **2.** under-privileged, unattractive, (person).
déshériter [dezerite] *v.t.* **1.** to disinherit; **2.** to handicap, to disadvantage.
déshonnête [dezɔnɛt] *adj.* improper, indecent, obscene; **~ment** [dezɔnɛtmɑ̃] *adv.* improperly, indecently.
déshonnêteté [dezɔnɛtəte] *s.f.* (obs.) impropriety, indecency.
déshonneur [dezɔnœr] *s.m.* dishonour, disgrace.
déshonorant, -e [dezɔnɔrɑ̃] *adj.* dishonourable, discreditable.
déshonorer [dezɔnɔre] *v.t.* to bring dishonour on, to disgrace; to degrade, to disfigure, (place, building); **se** ~ *v.refl.* to disgrace oneself.
déshuiler [dezɥile] *v.t.* to scour (wool, etc.).
déshydratation [dezidratɑsjɔ̃] *s.f.* dehydration.
déshydraté, -e [dezidrate] *adj.* dehydrated; (fam.) parched with thirst.
déshydrater [dezidrate] *v.t.* to dehydrate.
déshydrogénation [dezidrɔʒenɑsjɔ̃] *s.f.* dehydrogenation, dehydrogenization.
déshydrogéner [dezidrɔʒene] *v.t.* to dehydrogenate, to dehydrogenize.
déshypothéquer [dezipɔteke] *v.t.* to pay off the mortgage on (building, etc.); (law) to disencumber.
désidérabilité [deziderabilite] *s.f.* (econ.) desirability, advantageousness.
desiderata [deziderata] *s.m.pl.* desiderata.
désignati-f, -ve [deziɲatif] *adj.* designating.
désignation [deziɲɑsjɔ̃] *s.f.* designation, description, indication; nomination (of candidate, etc.).
désigner [deziɲe] *v.t.* **1.** to designate; to point out, to mark out; to indicate; to describe; ~ *qn. à* (*l'attention, l'admiration*), to mark s.o. out for (attention, admiration); **2.** to appoint; *président désigné*, president designate.
désiliciage [desilisjaʒ] *s.m.* (techn.) removal of silica (from water).
désillusion [dezilyzjɔ̃] *s.f.* disillusionment.
désillusionner [dezilyzjɔne] *v.t.* to disillusion.
désincarné, -e [dezɛ̃karne] *adj.* disembodied; (fam.) unworldly, other-worldly.
désincrustant, -e [dezɛ̃krystɑ̃] *adj., s.m.* scale-preventive (compound).
désincrustation [dezɛ̃krystɑsjɔ̃] *s.f.* (techn.) scaling (of boiler, etc.).
désincruster [dezɛ̃kryste] *v.t.* (techn.) to scale (boiler, etc.).
désinence [dezinɑ̃s] *s.f.* (gram.) inflexion, termination, ending.
désinentiel, -le [dezinɑ̃sjɛl] *adj.* (lang.) inflexional.
désinfectant, -e [dezɛ̃fɛktɑ̃] *adj.,* ~ *s.m.* disinfectant.
désinfecter [dezɛ̃fɛkte] *v.t.* to disinfect.
désinfection [dezɛ̃fɛksjɔ̃] *s.f.* disinfection.
désintégration [dezɛ̃tegrɑsjɔ̃] *s.f.* **1.** (esp. nuclear phys.) disintegration; **2.** annihilation.
désintégrer [dezɛ̃tegre] *v.t.* to disintegrate; to annihilate, to destroy utterly; **se** ~ *v.refl.* to disintegrate.
désintéressé, -e [dezɛ̃terɛse] *adj.* **1.** disinterested, altruistic, impartial; **2.** (obs.) indifferent, unconcerned, not interested.
désintéressement [dezɛ̃terɛsmɑ̃] *s.m.* **1.** disinterestedness, absence of self-interest; **2.** buying off, buying out, paying off.
désintéresser [dezɛ̃terɛse] *v.t.* to buy off, to buy out, to pay, (claimant, partner, creditor); **se** ~ *v.refl.* to lose interest (*de*, in).
désintérêt [dezɛ̃terɛ] *s.m.* (Lit.) disinterest, indifference.
désintoxication [dezɛ̃tɔksikɑsjɔ̃] *s.f.* detoxication, detoxification; treatment of alcoholism.
désintoxiquer [dezɛ̃tɔksike] *v.t.* to detoxicate, to detoxify; to treat (an alcoholic).
désinvolte [dezɛ̃vɔlt] *adj.* easy, unconstrained; free, forward; *être un peu trop* ~ *avec ses supérieurs*, to be a little too familiar with one's seniors.
désinvolture [dezɛ̃vɔltyr] *s.f.* free and easy manner; excessive familiarity.
désir [dezir] *s.m.* wish, want, desire; lust, (sexual) desire.
désirabilité [dezirabilite] *s.f.* desirability.
désirable [dezirabl] *adj.* desirable.
désirer [dezire] *v.t.* **1.** to want, to wish (for), to long for, to desire; *n'avoir plus rien à* ~, to have everything one wants; *je désire m'entretenir avec vous*, I wish to speak with you; *ce travail laisse beaucoup à* ~, this work leaves much to be desired; **2.** to desire, to lust after, for.
désireu-x, -se [dezirø] *adj.* desirous, anxious, (*de faire qch.*, of doing *or* to do sth.).
désistement [dezistmɑ̃] *s.m.* withdrawal, resignation, standing down.
(**se**) **désister** [deziste] *v.refl.* **1.** (pol.) to withdraw one's candidature; ~ *en faveur de qn.*, to stand down in someone's favour; **2.** (law) ~ *de*, to abandon (lawsuit, etc.); to give up (right, etc.).
désobéir [dezɔbeir] *v.i.* to disobey; to be disobedient; ~ *à qn., à un ordre*, to disobey s.o., an order.
désobéissance [dezɔbeisɑ̃s] *s.f.* disobedience.
désobéissant, -e [dezɔbeisɑ̃] *adj.* (of child) disobedient, unruly.
désobligeance [dezɔbliʒɑ̃s] *s.f.* (Lit.) unhelpfulness, disagreeableness.
désobligeant, -e [dezɔbliʒɑ̃] *adj.* disobliging, disagreeable, unkind; *remarque* ~*e*, hurtful remark.
désobliger [dezɔbliʒe] *v.t.* to disoblige, to displease, to hurt the feelings of, to upset, to offend.
désobstruer [dezɔbstrye] *v.t.* (techn.) to clear of, to free from, obstruction; (med.) to deobstruct.
désodorisant, -e [dezɔdɔrizɑ̃], **déodorant, -e** [deɔdɔrɑ̃] *adj., s.m.* deodorant.
désodoriser [dezɔdɔrize] *v.t.* to deodorize.
désœuvré, -e [dezœvre] *adj.* idle, unemployed, at a loose end; *s.m.f.* idler.
désœuvrement [dezœvrəmɑ̃] *s.m.* inactivity, idleness, lack of occupation.
désolant, -e [dezɔlɑ̃] *adj.* **1.** (Lit.) distressing, grievous; **2.** deplorable, very annoying.
désolation [dezɔlɑsjɔ̃] *s.f.* **1.** (Lit.) devastation, ruin; **2.** desolation, distress, disconsolateness.
désolé, -e [dezɔle] *adj.* **1.** desolate; **2.** disconsolate, inconsolable; **3.** (fam.) extremely sorry.
désoler [dezɔle] *v.t.* **1.** (Lit.) to lay waste, to ravage, to ruin; **2.** to afflict, to distress, to desolate; *elle se désole de ne pouvoir vous aider*, she is very upset that she cannot help you.
(**se**) **désolidariser** [desɔlidarize] *v.refl.* to dissociate oneself (*de, d'avec*, from).
désopilant, -e [dezɔpilɑ̃] *adj.* killingly funny.
désopiler [dezɔpile] *v.t.* **1.** (obs. med.) to deobstruct; ~ *la rate*, to cleanse the spleen; **2.** to convulse with laughter; **se** ~ *v.refl.* to be convulsed with laughter.

désordonné, -e [dezɔrdɔne] *adj.* **1.** (Lit.) disorganized, dissolute, excessive; **2.** disorganized, untidy.
désordre [dezɔrdr] *s.m.* disorder, confusion; (Lit.) dissipation; (pl.) riot, disturbance.
désorganisat-eur, -rice [dezɔrganizatœr] *adj.* disorganizing.
désorganisation [dezɔrganizɑsjɔ̃] *s.f.* disorganization.
désorganiser [dezɔrganize] *v.t.* to disorganize; ~ *les plans de qn.*, to upset someone's plans.
désorientation [dezɔrjɑ̃tɑsjɔ̃] *s.f.* disorientation.
désorienté, -e [dezɔrjɑ̃te] *adj.* disorientated, at a loss, out of one's depth.
désorienter [dezɔrjɑ̃te] *v.t.* to disorientate, to disorient, to disconcert.
désormais [dezɔrmɛ] *adv.* in future, henceforth, henceforward, from now on; thenceforth, thenceforward, from then on, from that time (on).
désorption [desɔrpsjɔ̃] *s.f.* (sci.) desorption.
désossé, -e [dezɔse] *adj.* **1.** (of meat, etc.) boned; **2.** (of person) supple; (fig.) flabby.
désossement [dezɔsmɑ̃] *s.m.* boning, filleting.
désosser [dezɔse] *v.t.* to bone (meat, etc.); to fillet (fish); **se** ~ *v.refl.* (of acrobat, etc.) to perform contortions.
désoxydant, -e [dezɔksidɑ̃] *adj.* deoxidizing; ~ *s.m.* deoxidizer.
désoxyder [dezɔkside] *v.t.* to deoxidize, to remove rust from.
désoxyribonucléique [dezɔksiribɔnykleik] *adj.* (biol.) *acide* ~, deoxyribonucleic acid.
despote [dɛspɔt] *s.m.* despot; ~ *adj.* despotic.
despotique [dɛspɔtik] *adj.* despotic; **~ment** [dɛspɔtikmɑ̃] *adv.* despotically.
despotisme [dɛspɔtism] *s.m.* despotism, tyranny.
desquamation [dɛskwamɑsjɔ̃] *s.f.* (med.) desquamation.
(**se**) **desquamer** [dɛskwame] *v.refl.* (med.) to desquamate.
desquels, desquelles [dekɛl] *rel.pron. pl.* see LEQUEL.
dessabler [desable] *v.t.* = DÉSENSABLER.
dessaisir [desezir] *v.t.* (law) to dispossess, to disseize, (*de*, of); **se** ~ (*de*) *v.refl.* to relinquish, to give up.
dessaisissement [desezismɑ̃] *s.m.* dispossession, relinquishment.
dessaler [desale] *v.t.* **1.** to desalt (fish, ham, etc.); **2.** ~ *qn.*, to teach s.o. a thing or two; *elle est bien dessalée*, she was not born yesterday; ~ *v.i. mettre des harengs à* ~, to leave some herrings to desalt; **se** ~ *v.refl.* to become more worldly-wise.
dessangler [desɑ̃gle] *v.t.* to loosen or take off the girth of (horse, etc.); *le cheval s'est dessanglé*, the horse's girth has come off (*or* come loose).
dessaouler see DESSOÛLER.
desséchant, -e [deseʃɑ̃] *adj.* (lit. & fig.) dry, desiccating, deadening.
dessèchement [desɛʃmɑ̃] *s.m.* drying (up), desiccation, emaciation, dulling (of feelings).
dessécher [deseʃe] *v.t.* to dry (up), to desiccate, to emaciate; to harden, to dull the feelings of; **se** ~ *v.refl.* to dry up, to wither, to waste away.
dessein [desɛ̃] *s.m.* (Lit.) plan, design, intent, aim; *à* ~, on purpose, deliberately; *dans le* ~ *de*, with a view to, with the intention of.
desseller [desele] *v.t.* to unsaddle.
desserrage [desɛraʒ] *s.m.* loosening, unscrewing, unclamping.
desserrer [desere] *v.t.* to undo, to loosen, to unscrew, to open; *ne pas* ~ *les dents*, to say nothing, not to open one's mouth; **se** ~ *v.refl.* to come loose.
dessert [desɛr] *s.m.* dessert.
desserte[1] [desɛrt] *s.f.* **1.** (eccles.) parochial duties; **2.** local rail, bus, etc., service.
desserte[2] [desɛrt] *s.f.* side-table, sideboard.
dessertir [desɛrtir] *v.t.* to remove (gemstone) from its setting.
desservant [desɛrvɑ̃] *s.m.* (eccles.) incumbent.
desservir[1] [desɛrvir] *v.t.* **1.** (eccles.) to serve, to be minister of, (parish, church, etc.); **2.** (rail., bus, etc.) to serve, to provide a service to, (a locality), to call at; **3.** (of door, etc.) to give access to.
desservir[2] [desɛrvir] *v.t.* **1.** to do a disservice to (*qn.*, s.o.); **2.** to clear (*la table*, the table); *vous pouvez* ~, you may clear.
dessiccati-f, -ve [desikatif] *adj.* desiccative; **~f** *s.m.* desiccant.
dessiccation [desikɑsjɔ̃] *s.f.* desiccation, drying, drying out.
dessiller [desije] *v.t.* ~ *les yeux de qn.*, *à qn.*, to open someone's eyes, to undeceive or enlighten s.o.; *alors mes yeux se dessillèrent*, then my eyes were opened.
dessin [desɛ̃] *s.m.* drawing, sketch, design, pattern, outline; ~ *à main levée*, free-hand drawing; ~(*s*) *animé*(*s*), animated cartoon; ~ *humoristique*, *satirique*, cartoon.
dessinat-eur, -rice [desinatœr] *s.m.f.* designer; draughtsman, draughtswoman; artist; *~eur* or *~rice humoristique*, humorous artist, cartoonist.
dessiné, -e [desine] *adj.* drawn; *bande ~e*, strip cartoon.
dessiner [desine] *v.t.* to draw, to sketch; to design; to outline, to trace; **se** ~ *v.refl.* to take shape, to loom.
dessolement [desɔlmɑ̃] *s.m.* (agric.) changing of the rotation of crops.
dessoler[1] [desɔle] *v.t.* to pare the hoof of (horse).
dessoler[2] [desɔle] *v.t.* (agric.) to change the rotation of crops in (area of land).
dessouder [desude] *v.t.* to unsolder; **se** ~ *v.refl.* to become unsoldered.
dessouler, dessoûler, dessaouler [desule] *v.t.i.* (fam.) to sober (up).
dessous [d(ə)su] *adv.*, *prep.* under, underneath, below, beneath; *au-*~, below, lower, downstairs; *au-*~ *de*, under, underneath, below, beneath, lower than, unworthy of, (of price, etc.) below, less than; *être au-*~ *de sa tâche*, not to be equal to one's job; *être au-*~ *de tout*, to be utterly contemptible; *de* ~, from underneath; surreptitiously, furtively; *en* ~, underneath; (fig.) secretly, in an underhand way; *agir en* ~, to behave hypocritically; *par-*~, underneath, under; ~ *s.m.* underside, under-part, bottom, wrong side, lower storey; (pl.) women's underclothes, lingerie; ~ *du pied*, sole of foot; ~ *de table*, secret overpayment in property transaction; *avoir le* ~, to have (*or* get) the worst of it; *être dans le troisième* or *trente-sixième* ~, to be in a desperate situation, in very low water.
dessous-de-bras [d(ə)sudbra] *s.m.invar.* dress-shield.
dessous-de-plat [d(ə)sudpla] *s.m invar.* table-mat.
dessuintage [desɥɛ̃taʒ] *s.m.* (techn.) scouring (of wool, etc.).
dessuinter [desɥɛ̃te] *v.t.* (techn.) to scour (wool, etc.).
dessus [d(ə)sy] *adv.*, *prep.* above, over, on (it), on top; *tu peux mettre la lettre à la poste, le timbre est* ~, you can post the letter, there's a stamp on it; *sens* ~*-dessous*, upside down; *au-*~, above, on (it), on top; *au-*~ *de*, above, higher than, over, beyond; *de* ~, from, from above; *en* ~, above, on top; *tissu écossais en* ~ *et uni en dessous*, material tartan on one (*or* the right) side, plain on the other (*or* the wrong); ~ *s.m.* upper part, upper side, outside, top, cover, upper storey; (fig.)

advantage; *le ~ du panier*, the best, the cream; *avoir le ~*, to have the upper hand, the best of it; *prendre, reprendre, le ~*, to get over (bereavement, illness, etc.).
dessus-de-lit [d(ə)sydli] *s.m.invar.* bedspread.
dessus-de-plat [d(ə)sydpla] *s.m.invar.* dish-cover, lid.
destin [dɛstɛ̃] *s.m.* destiny, fate, doom.
destinataire [dɛstinatɛr] *s.m.f.* consignee, addressee.
destination [dɛstinɑsjɔ̃] *s.f.* destination; *arriver à ~*, to arrive.
destinée [dɛstine] *s.f.* destiny, fate; (Lit.) *finir sa ~*, to die; (Lit.) *unir sa ~ à qn.*, to marry s.o.
destiner [dɛstine] *v.t.* to destine, to intend, (*qn., qch., à*, s.o., sth., for).
destituer [dɛstitɥe] *v.t.* to remove from office, to dismiss.
destitution [dɛstitysjɔ̃] *s.f.* removal from office, dismissal; ⚠ not 'destitution' in sense 'being destitute'.
destrier [dɛstrije] *s.m.* charger (horse).
destroyer [dɛstrwaje, dɛstrɔjœr] *s.m.* (nav.) destroyer (torpedo-boat).
destruct-eur, -rice [dɛstryktœr] *adj.* destructive; *s.m.f.* destroyer, vandal.
destructible [dɛstryktibl] *adj.* destructible.
destructi-f, -ve [dɛstryktif] *adj.* destructive.
destruction [dɛstryksjɔ̃] *s.f.* destruction, devastation, annihilation, ruin.
désu-et, -ète [desɥɛ] *adj.* obsolete, obsolescent; fallen into disuse or desuetude.
désuétude [desɥetyd] *s.f.* desuetude; *tomber en ~*, to fall into disuse or desuetude.
désulfiter [desylfite] *v.t.* to remove sulphite from (wine, etc.).
désulfurer [desylfyre] *v.t.* (sci., techn.) to desulphur, to desulphurize.
désuni, -e [dezyni] *adj.* disunited, separated, estranged; having lost coordination of movement.
désunion [dezynjɔ̃] *s.f.* disunity, disunion, estrangement.
désunir [dezynir] *v.t.* to disunite; *~ une famille, un ménage*, to break up a family, a married couple; **se ~** *v.refl.* (of athlete) to lose one's coordination of movement.
détachable [detaʃabl] *adj.* detachable.
détachage[1] [detaʃaʒ] *s.m.* detaching.
détachage[2] [detaʃaʒ] *s.m.* cleaning, removal of stains from (garment, etc.).
détachant [detaʃɑ̃] *s.m.* stain-remover.
détaché, -e [detaʃe] *adj.* (lit. & fig.) detached; separate(d), loose(d); (mil., etc.) detached, detailed, seconded.
détachement [detaʃmɑ̃] *s.m.* **1.** (lit. & fig.) detachment; **2.** secondment.
détacher[1] [detaʃe] *v.t.* to detach, to unfasten (and remove), (*de*, from); to separate; to (cause to) stand out distinctly; (mil., etc.) to detach, to detail, to second; *ne pouvoir ~ ses yeux de qn., qch.*, to be unable to take one's eyes off s.o., sth.
détacher[2] [detaʃe] *v.t.* to remove stains from, to clean, (garment, etc.).
détacheur [detaʃœr] *s.m.* dry cleaner; *flacon ~*, bottle of stain-remover.
détail [detaj] *s.m.* **1.** retail; *marchand au ~*, retail trader; *magasin de ~*, retail shop; **2.** detail; *faire le ~ d'un compte*, to itemize an account; *en ~*, in detail; *entrer dans le ~*, to go into details; *petit ~*, minor detail.
détaillant, -e [detajɑ̃] *s.m.f.* retailer.
détailler [detaje] *v.t.* **1.** to retail (goods); **2.** (Lit.) to detail, to enumerate, to recount in detail; *récit détaillé*, detailed account.
détaler [detale] *v.i.* (fam.) to decamp, to make off.
détartrage [detartraʒ] *s.m.* scaling (of boiler, of teeth).
détartrant [detartrɑ̃], **détartreur** [detartrœr] *s.m.* scale inhibitor (for use in radiators, etc.).
détaxe [detaks] *s.f.* reduction or removal of tax; refund of tax or duty.
détaxer [detakse] *v.t.* to reduce or abolish the tax on, to decontrol the price of (a commodity).
détecter [detɛkte] *v.t.* to detect.
détect-eur, -rice [detɛktœr] *adj.* detecting, detective; *s.m.f.* detector.
détection [detɛksjɔ̃] *s.f.* detection.
détective [detɛktiv] *s.m.* detective.
déteindre [detɛ̃dr] *v.t.* to cause to fade, to bleach; *~ v.i.* to fade, to run; *~ sur qch.*, (of colour) to run into (e.g. another garment), (fig.) to make a mark on, to influence.
dételage [dɛtlaʒ] *s.m.* unharnessing.
dételer [dɛtle] *v.t.* to unharness; *~ v.i.* (fig.) to ease off, to get out of harness.
détendeur [detɑ̃dœr] *s.m.* (pressure-)reducing valve; compression-type refrigerator.
détendre [detɑ̃dr] *v.t.* to slacken, to loosen, to release; (phys.) *~ un gaz*, to reduce the pressure of a gas; **se ~** *v.refl.* to relax, to unbend; to give, to stretch.
détendu, -e [detɑ̃dy] *adj.* slack; relaxed.
détenir [dɛtnir] *v.t.* **1.** to hold, to be in possession of (sth.); **2.** to detain (s.o.).
détente [detɑ̃t] *s.f.* **1.** trigger; (horol.) detent; (fig.) *dur à la ~*, close-fisted; **2.** expansion (of gas, steam, etc.); **3.** easing, relaxation, détente.
détent-eur, -rice [detɑ̃tœr] *s.m.f.* holder, possessor; *~eur* or *~rice illégal(e)*, receiver (of stolen goods).
détention [detɑ̃sjɔ̃] *s.f.* **1.** holding, possessing; **2.** detention; *~ préventive*, remand in custody.
détenu, -e [dɛtny] *adj.* detained; *s.m.f.* detainee.
détergent, -e [detɛrʒɑ̃] *adj.*, *~ s.m.* detergent.
déterger [detɛrʒe] *v.t.* to cleanse.
détérioration [deterjɔrɑsjɔ̃] *s.f.* deterioration.
détériorer [deterjɔre] *v.t.* to deteriorate, to spoil, to damage; **se ~** *v.refl.* to deteriorate.
déterminable [detɛrminabl] *adj.* determinable.
déterminant, -e [detɛrminɑ̃] *adj.* determining, decisive, determinant; *~ s.m.* determinant.
déterminati-f, -ve [detɛrminatif] *adj.*, **~f** *s.m.* determinative.
détermination [detɛrminɑsjɔ̃] *s.f.* determination; resolve; (math.) solution.
déterminé, -e [detɛrmine] *adj.* determined.
déterminer [detɛrmine] *v.t.* to determine; *ses amis l'ont déterminé à partir*, his friends persuaded him to leave; **se ~** *v.refl.* to decide, to resolve (*à*, to).
déterminisme [detɛrminism] *s.m.* determinism.
déterministe [detɛrminist] *adj.* deterministic; *~ s.m.f.* determinist.
déterrage [detɛraʒ] *s.m.* **1.** (agric.) lifting (of ploughshare); **2.** digging up; (hunt.) digging out, unearthing, (of fox, etc.).
déterré, -e [detere] *s.m.f.* *avoir un air, une mine, une tête, de ~*, to look ghastly, deathly (pale).
déterrement [detɛrmɑ̃] *s.m.* digging up, exhumation, disinterment.
déterrer [detere] *v.t.* to dig up, to unearth; to exhume, to disinter, (corpse).
détersi-f, -ve [detɛrsif] *adj.*, *s.m.f.* detergent, detersive.
détersion [detɛrsjɔ̃] *s.f.* (med.) cleansing; (techn.) detergent action.
détestable [detɛstabl] *adj.* detestable; abominable; **~ment** [detɛstabləmɑ̃] *adv.* detestably, abominably.
détestation [detɛstɑsjɔ̃] *s.f.* detestation, abhorrence.
détester [detɛste] *v.t.* to detest, to hate.
détirer [detire] *v.t.* to stretch (by drawing out).

détireuse [detirøz] *s.f.* (text.) stretcher.
détonant, -e [detɔnɑ̃] *adj.*, ~ *s.m.* explosive.
détonateur [detɔnatœr] *s.m.* detonator.
détonation [detɔnɑsjɔ̃] *s.f.* detonation.
détoner [detɔne] *v.i.* to detonate; *faire* ~, to detonate.
détonner [detɔne] *v.i.* (mus.) to sing or play out of tune; (fig.) to be out of one's element, out of place.
détordre [detɔrdr] *v.t.* to untwist; **se** ~ *v.refl.* to come untwisted.
détors, -e [detɔr] *adj.* untwined, untwisted.
détortiller [detɔrtije] *v.t.* to untwist, to unravel.
détour [detur] *s.m.* detour; deviation, turn, bend; (fig.) subterfuge, circumlocution; *s'expliquer sans* ~, to speak frankly, without beating about the bush.
détourné, -e [deturne] *adj.* roundabout, indirect; *reproche* ~, veiled reproach.
détournement [deturnəmɑ̃] *s.m.* **1.** diversion; **2.** embezzlement, misappropriation (*de fonds*, of funds); **3.** abduction, seduction.
détourner [deturne] *v.t.* **1.** to divert, to turn aside; to lead astray; to distract; to avert (*les yeux*, etc., one's eyes, etc.); **2.** to embezzle, to misappropriate; **se** ~ *v.refl.* to lose one's way; to turn away.
détoxication [detɔksikɑsjɔ̃] *s.f.* detoxication, detoxification.
détracter [detrakte] *v.t.* (Lit.) to denigrate, to belittle, to disparage.
détract-eur, -rice [detraktœr] *s.m.f.* detractor; *adj.* disparaging, depreciatory.
détraction [detraksjɔ̃] *s.f.* (Lit.) detraction, denigration.
détraqué, -e [detrake] *adj.* out of order, broken; (fig., fam.) *santé* ~*e*, impaired health; *avoir le cerveau* ~, to be crazy, deranged; *s.m.f.* crazy person.
détraquement [detrakmɑ̃] *s.m.* breakdown, breaking down.
détraquer [detrake] *v.t.* to put out of order; (fam.) to upset, to unbalance; *le temps se détraque*, the weather is becoming unsettled.
détrempe¹ [detrɑ̃p] *s.f.* distemper, tempera.
détrempe² [detrɑ̃p] *s.f.* (metall.) untempering, annealing.
détremper¹ [detrɑ̃pe] *v.t.* to soak, to dilute.
détremper² [detrɑ̃pe] *v.t.* (metall.) to untemper, to anneal.
détresse [detrɛs] *s.f.* distress; *signal de* ~, distress signal.
détriment [detrimɑ̃] *s.m.* detriment.
détritique [detritik] *adj.* (geol.) detrital.
détritus [detritys] *s.m.* rubbish, refuse; (geol.) detritus, debris.
détroit [detrwa] *s.m.* (geog.) strait, straits.
détromper [detrɔ̃pe] *v.t.* to undeceive; *détrompez-vous!*, don't you believe it!
détrôner [detrone] *v.t.* to dethrone; (fig.) to eclipse, to supersede.
détrousser [detruse] *v.t.* (jest) to hold up, to rob.
détrousseur [detrusœr] *s.m.* (obs.) highwayman.
détruire [detrɥir] *v.t.* to destroy; to kill; **se** ~ *v.refl.* **1.** to do away with oneself, to commit suicide; **2.** to be mutually destructive, to cancel one another out.
dette [dɛt] *s.f.* debt; ~ *publique*, National Debt.
détumescence [detymesɑ̃s] *s.f.* detumescence.
deuil [dœj] *s.m.* mourning; bereavement; *porter le* ~, to wear mourning; (fam.) *faire son* ~ *de qch.*, to write off, to say goodbye to, sth.
deutérium [døterjɔm] *s.m.* (chem.) deuterium.
deutéron [døterɔ̃], **deuton** [døtɔ̃] *s.m.* deuteron.
deux [dø; døz before vowel or h-mute] *adj.* two; second; *c'est à* ~ *pas d'ici, vous y serez en* ~ *secondes*, it's quite close, you'll be there in no time (at all); *Charles* ~, Charles the Second; *le* ~ *mai*, the second of May; *nous sommes le* ~, it's the second (of the month); ~ *s.m.* two; (cards, dice) two, deuce; *tous* (*les*) *deux*, both; *à nous* ~, let's get down to it; (now) let's have it out; *en moins de* ~, in (less than) no time.
(**à**) **deux-deux** [adødø] *adj.loc.* (mus.) (in) two-two time.
deuxième [døzjɛm] *adj.*, *s.m.f.* second (of more than two); *de ses quatre enfants, le* ~ *était le plus robuste*, of his four children, the second was the strongest; *vingt-*~, etc., twenty-second, etc.; ~**ment** [døzjɛmmɑ̃] *adv.* secondly.
deux-pièces [døpjɛs] *s.m.invar.* **1.** woman's two-piece (suit, dress, etc.); bikini; **2.** two-roomed flat.
deux-points [døpwɛ̃] *s.m.invar.* colon (punctuation mark).
deux-ponts [døpɔ̃] *adj.*, *s.m.invar.* double-decker (ship, aircraft).
deux-roues [døru] *s.m.invar.* two-wheeler.
deux-temps [døtɑ̃] *adj.*, *s.m.* two-stroke (engine, etc.).
dévaler [devale] *v.t.i.* to rush down; ~ *v.t.* (obs.) to let down, to lower.
dévaliser [devalize] *v.t.* to rob (person); to burgle (house, etc.).
dévalorisation [devalɔrizɑsjɔ̃] *s.f.* devaluation, depreciation (in value), devalorization.
dévaloriser [devalɔrize] *v.t.* to devalue, to depreciate (in value), to devalorize.
dévaluation [devalɥɑsjɔ̃] *s.f.* devaluation.
dévaluer [devalɥe] *v.t.* to devalue.
devancement [dəvɑ̃smɑ̃] *s.m.* preceding, forestalling, bringing forward (of date); (mil.) ~ *d'appel*, voluntary enlistment in advance of one's call-up date.
devancer [dəvɑ̃se] *v.t.* to outstrip, to surpass; to forestall, to anticipate; (Lit.) ~ *l'aurore, le jour*, to get up before dawn.
devanci-er, -ère [dəvɑ̃sje] *s.m.f.* predecessor.
devant [d(ə)vɑ̃] *prep.*, *adv.* in front (of); before (in space); ahead; *allez* ~, *je vous rejoindrai*, you go on, I'll catch you up; *sens* ~ *derrière*, back to front; *aller au-*~ *de*, to go to meet (s.o.); to court (danger, etc.); to anticipate (someone's wishes, etc.); *ôtez-vous de* ~ *mes yeux*, get out of my sight; *pattes de* ~, forefeet, forelegs; *par-*~, in front; before (magistrate, etc.); ~ *s.m.* front, façade; *prendre le*(*s*) ~(*s*), to forestall (s.o., sth.).
devanture [d(ə)vɑ̃tyr] *s.f.* **1.** shop-front; **2.** shop-window, window display.
dévastat-eur, -rice [devastatœr] *adj.* destructive.
dévastation [devastɑsjɔ̃] *s.f.* devastation, destruction, ruin.
dévaster [devaste] *v.t.* to lay waste, to destroy, to ruin, to devastate.
déveine [devɛn] *s.f.* (fam.) bad luck; *être dans la* ~, to be out of luck, to be having a run of bad luck.
développable [devlɔpabl] *adj.* developable; (geom.) *surface* ~, developable surface.
développante [devlɔpɑ̃t] *s.f.* (geom.) involute.
développée [devlɔpe] *s.f.* (geom.) evolute.
développement [devlɔpmɑ̃] *s.m.* **1.** development, developing; **2.** unwrapping, unfolding, unrolling; extension; **3.** distance covered by bicycle for one turn of pedals.
développer [devlɔpe] *v.t.* to develop; to unwrap, to unfold; **se** ~ *v.refl.* to develop; to spread out; (mil., of troops) to deploy.
devenir [dəvnir] *v.i.* **1.** to become; ~ *fou*, to go mad; *il devient vieux*, he is getting old; *qu'allons-nous* ~?, what will become of us?; *qu'est-ce que vous devenez?*, what have you been doing with yourself?; *qu'est devenu mon chapeau?*, where can my hat have got to?; **2.** (phil.) to evolve.

devenir [dəvnir] *s.m.* (state of) change, evolution; successive developments; *être dans un perpétuel* ~, to be in a constant state of flux.
dévergondage [devɛrgɔ̃daʒ] *s.m.* profligacy; (fig.) extravagance (of thought or its expression).
dévergondé, -e [devɛrgɔ̃de] *adj., s.m.f.* profligate.
(**se**) **dévergonder** [devɛrgɔ̃de] *v.refl.* to become (a) profligate.
déverguer [devɛrge], **désenverguer** [dezɑ̃vɛrge] *v.t.* (naut.) to haul down the yards from.
dévernir [devɛrnir] *v.t.* to strip of varnish.
déverrouillage [devɛrujaʒ] *s.m.* **1.** unbolting (of door); **2.** opening of breech (of firearm).
déverrouiller [devɛruje] *v.t.* **1.** to unbolt (door, etc.); **2.** to open the breech of (firearm).
devers [dəvɛr] *prep.* **1.** (obs.) on the side of, towards; **2.** *par-~ le juge*, before the judge; *avoir qch. par-~ soi*, to have sth. in one's possession, by one.
dévers [devɛr] *s.m.* slant; banking (at bend of road or railway).
déversement [devɛrsəmɑ̃] *s.m.* pouring out (of liquid); (of liquid) discharging, pouring.
déverser [devɛrse] *v.t.* to pour, to pour out, to discharge.
déversoir [devɛrswar] *s.m.* overflow, outlet.
dévêtir [devetir] *v.t.* to undress; *se ~ quand il fait chaud*, to leave off (warm) garment(s) in hot weather.
déviat-eur, -rice [devjatœr] retro-active braking device (on jet aircraft).
déviation [devjɑsjɔ̃] *s.f.* **1.** deviation, deflection; **2.** (traffic) diversion; **~nisme** [devjɑsjɔnism] *s.m.* deviationism; **~niste** [devjɑsjɔnist] *adj., s.m.f.* deviationist.
dévidage [devidaʒ] *s.m.* (text., etc.) winding, reeling, spooling.
dévider [devide] *v.t.* (text., etc.) to wind, to wind off, to unwind; *~ son chapelet*, to tell one's beads (on a rosary); (fig., fam.) *~ son chapelet, son écheveau*, to tell one's whole story, to get it all off one's chest.
dévideu-r, -se [devidœr] *s.m.f.* (text.) reeler, winder.
dévidoir [devidwar] *s.m.* reel, winder; hose-reel.
dévier [devje] *v.i.* to deviate, to swerve; ~ *v.t.* to divert (traffic, etc.).
devin, -eresse [dəvɛ̃, dəvinrɛs] *s.m.f.* diviner, soothsayer; (fig., fam.) *je ne suis pas ~*, I'm not a wizard, I'm not a prophet.
devinable [d(ə)vinabl] *adj.* that can be guessed, predictable, foreseeable.
deviner [d(ə)vine] *v.t.* to guess, to guess right.
devinette [d(ə)vinɛt] *s.f.* riddle, conundrum.
dévirer [devire] *v.t.* (naut.) to wind (capstan, etc.) the opposite way.
devis [d(ə)vi] *s.m.* estimate.
dévisager [devizaʒe] *v.t.* to stare at (s.o.).
devise [d(ə)viz] *s.f.* **1.** device, motto, slogan; **2.** foreign currency.
deviser [dəvize] *v.i.* to chat.
dévissage [devisaʒ] *s.m.* unscrewing.
dévisser [devise] *v.t.* to unscrew; ~ *v.i.* (mountaineering) to fall.
dévitaliser [devitalize] *v.t.* (dentistry) to remove the nerve of (a tooth).
dévoiement [devwamɑ̃] *s.m.* bend, turn (in chimney, etc.).
dévoilement [devwalmɑ̃] *s.m.* unveiling, revealing.
dévoiler [devwale] *v.t.* to unveil, to reveal.
devoir [d(ə)vwar] *v.t.* **1.** to owe; **2.** to have to, to be bound to; *je dois le faire*, I must do it; *que devons-nous faire?*, what ought we to do?; **3.** to be likely to; *vous devez être heureux d'avoir terminé*, you must be glad you have finished; **4.** to intend to; to be supposed to; *il devait venir, mais il est tombé malade*, he was to have come, but he has been taken ill; **5.** *dussé-je tomber raide mort*, even though I were to fall down dead; **6.** *comme il se doit*, rightly, as is proper; (fam.) as was to be expected, as could be foreseen.
devoir [d(ə)vwar] *s.m.* **1.** duty; *se mettre en ~ de faire qch.*, to set about doing sth., to undertake sth.; **2.** (written) homework, prep(aration); **3.** (pl.) respects, devoirs; *présenter ses ~s à qn.*, to pay one's respects (*or* devoirs) to s.o.; *rendre à qn. les derniers ~s*, to pay one's last respects to s.o.
dévoltage [devɔltaʒ] *s.m.* (electr.) stepping down (of current), voltage reduction.
dévolter [devɔlte] *v.t.* (electr.) to step down (current).
dévolu, -e [devɔly] *adj.* escheated; devolved; ~ *s.m. jeter son ~ sur*, to have designs upon.
dévolution [devɔlysjɔ̃] *s.f.* escheat, devolution.
devon [dəvɔ̃] *s.m.* (fish) Devon (bait).
dévonien, -ne [devɔnjɛ̃] *adj.* (geol.) Devonian; ~ *s.m.* Devonian (period, system).
dévorant, -e [devɔrɑ̃] *adj.* (lit. & fig.) voracious, ravenous; consuming, devouring; *un feu ~*, a fire which engulfs everything.
dévorat-eur, -rice [devɔratœr] *adj.* (Lit.) (of passion, etc.) consuming.
dévorer [devɔre] *v.t.* to devour, to eat up, to wolf; to consume, to destroy; *~ des yeux*, to feast one's eyes on; *~ un affront, une injure*, to swallow an insult.
dévot, -e [devo] *adj., s.m.f.* devout, religious, (person); (pej.) bigot(ed); *faux ~*, hypocrite; **~ement** [devɔtmɑ̃] *adv.* (obs.) devoutly.
dévotion [devosjɔ̃] *s.f.* devoutness, piety; devotion; (pl.) prayer, devotions; *être à la ~ de qn.*, to be devoted to s.o.; *faire ses ~s*, to be at one's devotions, at prayer.
dévoué, -e [devwe] *adj.* devoted; *votre (tout) ~, veuillez croire à mes sentiments ~s*, = yours faithfully, sincerely, etc.
dévouement [devumɑ̃] *s.m.* devotion; *~ d'un savant à son œuvre*, dedication of a scholar to his work.
(**se**) **dévouer** [devwe] *v.refl.* to devote oneself, to sacrifice oneself; *elle s'est dévouée pour le soigner*, she has devoted herself to looking after him; *il est toujours prêt à se ~*, he is always ready to put himself out (for others).
dévoyé, -e [devwaje] *adj.* gone astray; *s.m.f.* misguided or delinquent person, bad lot.
dévoyer [devwaje] *v.t.* to lead astray; **se ~** *v.refl.* to go astray, to go wrong.
dextérité [dɛksterite] *s.f.* dexterity.
dextralité [dɛkstralite] *s.f.* dextrality, right-handedness.
dextre [dɛkstr] *s.f.* (obs. exc. jest) right hand.
dextrine [dɛkstrin] *s.f.* (chem.) dextrin.
dextrogyre [dɛkstrɔʒir] *adj.* (chem.) dextrorotatory.
dextrorsum [dɛkstrɔrsɔm] *adj., adv.* (sci.) dextrorse.
dia [dja] *interj.* (to horse) to the left!; (fam.) *l'un tire à hue et l'autre à ~*, they are pulling in opposite directions.
diabète [djabɛt] *s.m.* (med.) diabetes.
diabétique [djabetik] *adj., s.m.f.* diabetic.
diable [djɑbl] *s.m.* **1.** devil; *beauté du ~*, bloom of youth; *il a le ~ au corps*, the devil is in him; he is devil-driven; *faire le ~ à quatre*, to raise Cain; *tirer le ~ par la queue*, to struggle hard for a living; (obs. exc. jest) *que le ~ l'emporte*, devil take him; *c'est (bien) le ~*, it's the (very) devil; *ce n'est pas le ~*, it's not so difficult, it's nothing to worry about; *habiter au ~*, to live a long way away; *faire qch. à la ~*, to do sth. anyhow, in a slipshod way; *un vacarme de tous les ~s*, a hellish row; *être paresseux en ~*, to be as lazy as the devil, extremely lazy; *il est bon ~*, he is a good sort;

pauvre ~!, poor devil!; *~! c'est un peu cher*, good Lord, what a price!; *où ~ est-il caché?*, where the devil is he hiding?; *que ~ fait-elle?*, what the devil is she doing?; **2.** (two-wheeled) barrow; **3.** jack-in-the-box.
diablement [djɑbləmɑ̃] *adv.* (fam.) extremely, very, devilishly.
diablerie [djɑbləri] *s.f.* devilry; devilment.
diablesse [djɑblɛs] *s.f.* she-devil.
diablotin [djɑblɔtɛ̃] *s.m.* **1.** little devil, imp; **2.** (Christmas) cracker.
diabolique [djɑbɔlik] *adj.* diabolical, devilish; **~ment** [djabɔlikmɑ̃] *adv.* diabolically.
diabolo [djabɔlo] *s.m.* (game of) diabolo.
diachronie [djakrɔni] *s.f.* (lang.) diachrony.
diachronique [djakrɔnik] *adj.* (lang.) diachronic.
diaclase [djaklɑz] *s.f.* (geol.) fault.
diaconal, -e, (aux) [djakɔnal] *adj.* diaconal.
diaconesse [djakɔnɛs] *s.f.* deaconess.
diacoustique [djakustik] *s.f.* diacoustics.
diacre [djakr] *s.m.* deacon.
diadème [djadɛm] *s.m.* diadem.
diagnose [djagnoz] *s.f.* diagnosis.
diagnostic [djagnɔstik] *s.m.* (med.) diagnosis; (fig.) forecast, prediction.
diagnostique [djagnɔstik] *adj.* (med.) diagnostic.
diagnostiquer [djagnɔstike] *v.t.* (med.) to diagnose; (fig.) to forecast, to predict.
diagnostiqueur [djagnɔstikœr] *s.m.* diagnostician.
diagonal, -e, (aux) [djagɔnal] *adj.* diagonal; **~e** *s.f.* diagonal; *en ~e*, diagonally; **~ement** [djagɔnalmɑ̃] *adv.* diagonally.
diagramme [djagram] *s.m.* **1.** diagram; **2.** chart, graph.
diagraphe [djagraf] *s.m.* (sci.) diagraph.
dialectal, -e, (aux) [djalɛktal] *adj.* dialectal.
dialecte [djalɛkt] *s.m.* dialect.
dialecticien, -ne [djalɛktisjɛ̃] *s.m.f.* dialectician.
dialectique [djalɛktik] *s.f.* dialectic(s); *~ adj.* dialectic(al).
dialogue [djalɔg] *s.m.* dialogue.
dialoguer [djalɔge] *v.i.* to converse; *~ v.t.* to write dialogue of (radio play, film).
dialoguiste [djalɔgist] *s.m.f.* (cin.) screen-writer.
dialyse [djaliz] *s.f.* (chem., med.) dialysis.
dialyser [djalize] *v.t.* (chem., med.) to dialyse.
dialyseur [djalizœr] *s.m.* dialyser.
diamagnétique [djamaɲetik] *adj.* diamagnetic.
diamagnétisme [djamaɲetism] *s.m.* diamagnetism.
diamant [djamɑ̃] *s.m.* diamond; (techn.) diamond point (glass-cutter).
diamantaire [djamɑ̃tɛr] *adj.* diamond-like; *pierre ~*, sparkling stone; *~ s.m.* jeweller, diamond merchant, diamond-cutter.
diamanté, -e [djamɑ̃te] *adj.* **1.** diamond-studded; **2.** with diamond point.
diamanter [djamɑ̃te] *v.t.* to set or to adorn with diamonds; to cause to sparkle like diamonds.
diamantifère [djamɑ̃tifɛr] *adj.* diamondiferous, diamantiferous.
diamantin, -e [djamɑ̃tɛ̃] *adj.* adamantine.
diamétral, -e, (aux) [djametral] *adj.* diametrical, diametral; **~ement** [djametralmɑ̃] *adv.* diametrically, diametrally.
diamètre [djamɛtr] *s.m.* diameter.
diane [djan] *s.f.* (obs. exc. Lit.) reveille.
Diane [djan] *s.f.* (Rom. myth.) Diana.
diantre [djɑ̃tr] *interj.* (euphem.) = DIABLE; **~ment** [djɑ̃trəmɑ̃] *adv.* (euphem.) = DIABLEMENT.
diapason [djapazɔ̃] *s.m.* (mus.) diapason; tuning-fork, pitch-pipe.
diapédèse [djapedɛz] *s.f.* (med.) diapedesis.
diaphane [djafan] *adj.* diaphanous, translucent; (Lit.) transparent.
diaphanéité [djafaneite] *s.f.* (Lit.) diaphanousness.
diaphorèse [djafɔrɛz] *s.f.* (med.) diaphoresis.
diaphorétique [djafɔretik] *adj.* (med.) diaphoretic.
diaphragmatique [djafragmatik] *adj.* diaphragmatic.
diaphragme [djafragm] *s.m.* diaphragm.
diaphragmer [djafragme] *v.t.* (opt., photo.) to fit with a diaphragm; *~ v.i.* to adjust the aperture (of camera, etc.).
diapositive [djapɔzitiv] *s.f.* (photo.) transparency, slide; (fam. abbrev. *diapo*).
diapré, -e [djapre] *adj.* variegated, diapered.
diaprer [djapre] *v.t.* (Lit.) to variegate, to diaper.
diaprure [djapryr] *s.f.* variegation, diapering.
diarrhée [djare] *s.f.* diarrhoea.
diarrhéique [djareik] *adj.* (med.) diarrhoeal, diarrhoeic.
diastase [djastɑz] *s.f.* (chem.) diastase.
diastasique [djastɑzik] *adj.* (chem.) diastasic, diastatic.
diastole [djastɔl] *s.f.* (physiol.) diastole.
diastolique [djastɔlik] *adj.* (physiol.) diastolic.
diathermane [djatɛrman] *adj.* (phys.) diathermanous, diathermic.
diathermanéité [djatɛrmaneite] *s.f.* (phys.) diathermancy.
diathermie [djatɛrmi] *s.f.* diathermy.
diathèse [djatɛz] *s.f.* (med.) diathesis.
diathésique [djatezik] *adj.* (med.) diathetic.
diatomée [djatɔme] *s.f.* (bot.) diatom.
diatomique [djatɔmik] *adj.* (chem.) diatomic.
diatonique [djatɔnik] *adj.* (mus.) diatonic; **~ment** [djatɔnikmɑ̃] *adv.* diatonically.
diatribe [djatrib] *s.f.* diatribe.
diaule [djol] *s.f.* (Gk. ant.) double flute, diaulos.
diazoïque [diazɔik] *adj.* (chem., of compound) diazo.
dichotomie [dikɔtɔmi] *s.f.* dichotomy.
dichotomique [dikɔtɔmik] *adj.* dichotomic, dichotomous.
dichroïsme [dikrɔism] *s.m.* (phys.) dichroism.
dichromatique [dikrɔmatik] (phys.) dichromatic.
dicline [diklin] *adj.* (bot.) diclinous.
dico [diko] *s.m.* (school slang) abbrev. of DICTIONNAIRE.
dicotylédone [dikɔtiledɔn] *s.f.*, *adj.* (bot.) dicotyledon(ous).
dicrote [dikrɔt] *adj.* (med., of pulse) dicrotic.
dictame [diktam] *s.m.* (bot.) dittany; (fig.) balm, solace.
dictaphone [diktafɔn] *s.m.* dictaphone (proprietary term).
dictat-eur, -rice [diktatœr] *s.m.f.* dictator.
dictatorial, -e, (aux) [diktatɔrjal] *adj.* dictatorial.
dictature [diktatyr] *s.f.* dictatorship.
dictée [dikte] *s.f.* **1.** dictation; *sous la ~*, from dictation; **2.** dictate; *~ du cœur*, dictate(s) of the heart.
dicter [dikte] *v.t.* to dictate.
diction [diksjɔ̃] *s.f.* diction, elocution.
dictionnaire [diksjɔnɛr] *s.m.* dictionary; *traduire à coups de ~*, to translate by looking up every word; *c'est un vrai ~, un ~ vivant*, he is a walking encyclopedia.
dicton [diktɔ̃] *s.m.* proverbial saying, dictum.
didactique [didaktik] *adj.* didactic; **~ment** [didaktikmɑ̃] *adv.* didactically.
didactyle [didaktil] *adj.* (zool.) didactyl.
Didon [didɔ̃] *s.f.* (myth.) Dido.

didyme [didim] *adj.* (bot.) didymous.
dièdre [djɛdr] *s.m.* dihedron; ~ *adj.* dihedral.
diélectrique [djelɛktrik] *adj.*, *s.m.* dielectric.
diérèse [djerɛz] *s.f.* (phon., surg.) diaeresis.
dièse [djɛz] *adj.*, *s.m.* (mus.) sharp.
diesel [djezɛl] *s.m.*, *adj.* diesel (engine, vehicle).
diéser [djeze] *v.t.* (mus.) to sharpen (note).
diète[1] [djɛt] *s.f.* (restricted) diet; starvation diet.
diète[2] [djɛt] *s.f.* (hist.) diet; *la ~ de Worms*, the Diet of Worms.
diéticien, -ne [djetisjɛ̃] *s.m.f.* dietitian, dietician.
diététique [djetetik] *adj.* dietary, dietetic; ~ *s.f.* dietetics.
Dieu, dieu (pl. **-x**) [djø] *s.m.* God, god; *Dieu merci!*, thank heavens!, thank goodness!; *Nom de Dieu!*, *Bon Dieu* (*de bon Dieu*)*!*, profane oaths = Christ almighty!, bloody hell!; *s'il plaît à Dieu*, God willing; *à Dieu ne plaise!*, heaven forbid!; *recevoir le bon Dieu*, to receive the Holy Sacrament; (fig.) *on lui donnerait le bon Dieu sans confession*, (iron., of hypocrite) he looks as if butter wouldn't melt in his mouth.
diffamant, -e [difamɑ̃] *adj.* defamatory.
diffamat-eur, -rice [difamatœr] *s.m.f.* detractor, slanderer; *adj.* defamatory, slanderous.
diffamation [difamɑsjɔ̃] *s.f.* defamation, slander.
diffamer [difame] *v.t.* to defame, to slander.
différé, -e [difere] *adj.* deferred; (radio, T.V., of programme) recorded; *émission en ~*, recorded transmission.
différemment [diferamɑ̃] *adv.* differently.
différence [diferɑ̃s] *s.f.* difference; *à la ~ de*, in contrast with; *à la ~ que*, with the difference that; whereas, while.
différenciat-eur, -rice [diferɑ̃sjatœr] *adj.* differentiating.
différenciation [diferɑ̃sjɑsjɔ̃] *s.f.* differentiation.
différencié, -e [diferɑ̃sje] *adj.* differentiated; (biol., etc.) that has undergone differentiation.
différencier [diferɑ̃sje] *v.t.* to differentiate, to distinguish, (*entre*, between); (math.) to find the differential of; **se** ~ *v.refl.* to be different, to differ, (*de*, from); (biol., etc.) to differentiate.
différend [diferɑ̃] *s.m.* difference, dispute, quarrel.
différent, -e [diferɑ̃] *adj.* **1.** different (*de*, from), unlike, not the same (*de*, as); **2.** (pl., before the noun) different, several, various.
différentiation [diferɑ̃sjɑsjɔ̃] *s.f.* (math.) calculating the differential of a function.
différentiel, -le [diferɑ̃sjɛl] *adj.* differential; ~ *s.m.* (car) differential (gear); **~le** *s.f.* (math.) differential.
différentier [diferɑ̃sje] *v.t.* (math.) = DIFFÉRENCIER.
différer[1] [difere] *v.i.* to differ, to be different, (*de*, from).
différer[2] [difere] *v.t.* to defer, to postpone; to delay; (Lit.) ~ *de faire*, *à faire*, *qch.*, to put off, to delay, doing sth.
difficile [difisil] *adj.* difficult, troublesome; **~ment** [difisilmɑ̃] *adv.* with difficulty.
difficulté [difikylte] *s.f.* difficulty, trouble.
difficultueu-x, -se [difikyltɥø] *adj.* (of person) difficult.
diffluence [diflyɑ̃s] *s.f.* diffluence.
diffluent, -e [diflyɑ̃] *adj.* diffluent.
difforme [difɔrm] *adj.* deformed.
difformité [difɔrmite] *s.f.* deformity.
diffracter [difrakte] *v.t.* (phys.) to diffract.
diffraction [difraksjɔ̃] *s.f.* (phys.) diffraction.
diffus, -e [dify] *adj.* diffuse(d); **~ément** [difyzemɑ̃] *adv.* diffusely, in a long-winded fashion.
diffuser [difyze] *v.t.* to diffuse, to spread widely; to distribute (publication to booksellers, etc.); (radio, TV) to broadcast, to transmit.
diffuseur [difyzœr] *s.m.* **1.** (agric.) extractor (for obtaining juice from sugar-beet); **2.** (techn.) vaporizing-chamber (in carburettor); diffuser (in lighting installation); **3.** broadcaster, disseminator, publisher, distributor.
diffusion [difyzjɔ̃] *s.f.* diffusion, dissemination, spread (of knowledge, etc.); circulation (of publication, etc.); (radio, TV) broadcasting, transmission.
digérer [diʒere] *v.t.* **1.** to digest; (fig.) to digest, to think over, (idea, etc.); ~ *bien*, *mal*, to have a good, a bad, digestion; **2.** (fam.) to swallow (insult, etc.).
digest [dajʒɛst, diʒɛst] *s.m.* digest, résumé, condensed version.
digeste [diʒɛst] *adj.* easily digestible.
digeste [diʒɛst] *s.m.* (Rom. law) digest.
digesteur [diʒɛstœr] *s.m.* (techn.) digester.
digestibilité [diʒɛstibilite] *s.f.* digestibility.
digestible [diʒɛstibl] *adj.* digestible.
digesti-f, -ve [diʒɛstif] *adj.* digestive; taken to aid digestion; *appareil ~f*, digestive system; *tube ~f*, alimentary canal; **~f** *s.m.* liqueur, brandy, etc.
digestion [diʒɛstjɔ̃] *s.f.* digestion.
digital, -e, (**aux**) [diʒital] *adj.* digital; *empreintes ~es*, fingerprints.
digitale [diʒital] *s.f.* (bot.) digitalis, foxglove.
digitaline [diʒitalin] *s.f.* (chem., pharm.) digitalin, digitalis.
digité, -e [diʒite] *adj.* (biol.) digitate.
digitigrade [diʒitigrad] *adj.*, *s.m.* (zool.) digitigrade.
digne [diɲ] *adj.* **1.** worthy, deserving, (*de*, of); **2.** dignified; **~ment** [diɲmɑ̃] *adv.* with dignity; (obs.) suitably, justly.
dignitaire [diɲitɛr] *s.m.* dignitary.
dignité [diɲite] *s.f.* dignity, honour.
digon [digɔ̃] *s.m.* **1.** (naut.) flag-pole, flagstaff; **2.** (fish.) harpoon.
digraphie [digrafi] *s.f.* (book-keep.) double entry.
digression [digrɛsjɔ̃] *s.f.* digression.
digue [dig] *s.f.* dike, dam; (fig.) barrier, obstacle.
diktat [diktat] *s.m.* diktat.
dilapidat-eur, -rice [dilapidatœr] *adj.* squandering, wasteful; *s.m.f.* squanderer, wastrel.
dilapidation [dilapidɑsjɔ̃] *s.f.* squandering (of inheritance, fortune); ⚠ not 'dilapidation' of a building.
dilapider [dilapide] *v.t.* to squander, to fritter away.
dilatabilité [dilatabilite] *s.f.* dilatability.
dilatable [dilatabl] *adj.* dilatable.
dilatant, -e [dilatɑ̃] *adj.* that dilates; ~ *s.m.* (surg.) dilator.
dilatat-eur, -rice [dilatatœr] *adj.* (anat.) dilating; *muscle ~eur*, dilator (muscle).
dilatation [dilatɑsjɔ̃] *s.f.* dilation, dilatation.
dilater [dilate] *v.t.* to dilate, to expand; **se** ~ *v.refl.* to dilate, to expand, to swell.
dilatoire [dilatwar] *adj.* dilatory.
dilatomètre [dilatɔmɛtr] *s.m.* (sci.) dilatometer.
dilection [dilɛksjɔ̃] *s.f.* spiritual love; ~ *du prochain*, love of one's neighbour.
dilettante [diletɑ̃t] *s.m.f.* devotee, dilettante.
dilettantisme [diletɑ̃tism] *s.m.* dilettantism.
diligemment [diliʒamɑ̃] *adv.* diligently.
diligence [diliʒɑ̃s] *s.f.* **1.** (obs.) diligence; **2.** efficiency, keenness; *faire ~*, to be quick (in execution of task, etc.), to hurry; **3.** (hist.) diligence (stage-coach, esp. in France).
diligent, -e [diliʒɑ̃] *adj.* **1.** (obs.) diligent; **2.** efficient, quick, keen.

diluer [dilɥe] *v.t.* to dilute.
dilution [dilysjɔ̃] *s.f.* dilution.
diluvial, -e, (**aux**) [dilyvjal] *adj.* (geol.) diluvial.
diluvien, -ne [dilyvjɛ̃] *adj.* diluvian, diluvial; *pluie ~ne*, torrential rain.
diluvium [dilyvjɔm] *s.m.* (geol.) diluvium, drift.
dimanche [dimɑ̃ʃ] *s.m.* Sunday; (fam.) *du ~*, amateur, inexperienced; *un chauffeur du ~*, a Sunday driver; *un peintre du ~*, an amateur artist.
dîme [dim] *s.f.* **1.** (hist.) tithe; **2.** (U.S. currency) dime.
dimension [dimɑ̃sjɔ̃] *s.f.* dimension.
dîmer [dime] *v.t.* (hist.) to tithe.
diminuendo [diminɥendo, diminɥɛ̃do] *adv.*, *s.m.* (mus.) diminuendo.
diminué, -e [diminɥe] *adj.* diminished, decreased, reduced; weakened (by age, illness, etc.).
diminuer [diminɥe] *v.t.i.* to diminish, to lessen, to abate, to decrease, to reduce; (knitting) to decrease.
diminuti-f, -ve [diminytif] *adj.*, *s.m.* diminutive.
diminution [diminysjɔ̃] *s.f.* diminution, decrease, reduction; (knitting) decreasing.
dimissoire [dimiswar] *s.m.* (eccles.) letters dimissory.
dimorphe [dimɔrf] *adj.* (biol., chem.) dimorphic, dimorphous.
dimorphisme [dimɔrfism] *s.m.* (biol., chem.) dimorphism.
dinanderie [dinɑ̃dri] *s.f.* brassware.
dinandier [dinɑ̃dje] *s.m.* brazier, dealer in brassware.
dinar [dinar] *s.m.* dinar.
dînatoire [dinatwar] *adj. goûter ~*, high tea.
dinde [dɛ̃d] *s.f.* **1.** turkey-hen; (cook.) turkey; **2.** (fig.) stupid girl or woman; *quelle petite ~!*, what a little goose (you are)!
dindon [dɛ̃dɔ̃] *s.m.* **1.** turkey(-cock); **2.** (fig.) *être le ~ de la farce*, to be the victim of deception, to be fooled.
dindonneau (pl. **-x**) [dɛ̃dɔno] *s.m.* turkey-chick, turkey poult.
dîner [dine] *v.i.* to dine; (obs. exc. regional) to have one's (midday) dinner.
dîner [dine] *s.m.* dinner; (obs. exc. regional) (midday) dinner.
dînette [dinɛt] *s.f.* **1.** children's make-believe meal; light, informal meal; **2.** *~ de poupée*, doll's tea-set.
dîneu-r, -se [dinœr] *s.m.f.* diner.
dinghy [dingi] *s.m.* small inflatable life-boat, rubber dinghy.
dingo[1] [dɛ̃go] *s.m.* dingo (Australian dog).
dingo[2] [dɛ̃go] *adj.*, *s.m.f.* (fam.) cracked, crazy, (person).
dingue [dɛ̃g] *adj.*, *s.m.f.* (pop.) = DINGO[2].
dinguer [dɛ̃ge] *v.i.* (fam., after verb) to fall, to be precipitated; *les fruits sont allés ~ sur le trottoir*, the fruit was spilled on the pavement; *envoyer qch ~.*, to fling sth. away; *envoyer qn. ~*, to send s.o. packing.
dinornis [dinɔrnis] *s.m.* (palaeont.) dinornis.
dinosaure [dinozɔr] *s.m.* dinosaur.
dinosauriens [dinɔsɔrjɛ̃] *s.m.pl.* (palaeont.) dinosaurs, Dinosauria.
dinothérium [dinɔterjɔm] *s.m.* (palaeont.) Deinotherium.
diocésain, -e [djɔsezɛ̃] *adj.* diocesan; *~ s.m.* diocesan.
diocèse [djɔsɛz] *s.m.* diocese.
diode [djɔd] *s.f.* (electr.) diode.
dioïque [diɔjik] *adj.* (biol.) dioecious.
dionysiaque [djɔnizjak] *adj.* Dionysiac, Dionysian.
dioptre [djɔptr] *s.m.* (opt.) dioptre.
dioptrie [djɔptri] *s.f.* (opt.) dioptre.
dioptrique [djɔptrik] *adj.* (opt.) dioptric; *~ s.m.* dioptrics.
diorama [djɔrama] *s.m.* diorama.
diorite [djɔrit] *s.f.* (geol.) diorite.
dipétale [dipetal] *adj.* (bot.) dipetalous.
diphasé, -e [difaze] *adj.* (electr.) diphasic, two-phase.
diphthérie [difteri] *s.f.* (med.) diphtheria.
diphthérique [difterik] *adj.* (med.) diphtheric, diphtheritic.
diphtongaison [diftɔ̃gɛzɔ̃] *s.f.* (phon.) diphthongization.
diphtongue [diftɔ̃g] *s.f.* (phon.) diphthong.
diphtonguer [diftɔ̃ge] *v.t.* to diphthongize; **se ~** *v.refl.* to diphthongize.
diplocoque [diplɔkɔk] *s.m.* (biol.) diplococcus.
diplodocus [diplɔdɔkys] *s.m.* (palaeont.) diplodocus.
diploé [diplɔe] *s.m.* (anat.) diploe.
diploïde [diplɔid] *adj.* (biol.) diploid.
diplomate [diplɔmat] *s.m.f.* diplomat, diplomatist; *~ s.m.* (cook.) sponge-fingers with preserved fruits and rum, etc.; *~ adj.* diplomatic.
diplomatie [diplɔmasi] *s.f.* diplomacy; (fig.) discretion, tact.
diplomatique [diplɔmatik] *s.f.* diplomatic(s); *~ adj.* diplomatic; *corps ~*, diplomatic corps; **~ment** [diplɔmatikmɑ̃] *adv.* diplomatically, tactfully, discreetly.
diplôme [diplom] *s.m.* diploma; diploma examination.
diplômé, -e [diplome] *adj.*, *s.m.f.* (person) holding a diploma; qualified or certificated (person); *infirmière ~e*, qualified nurse (=State Registered Nurse).
diplômer [diplome] *v.t.* to confer a diploma on.
diplopie [diplɔpi] *s.f.* (med.) diplopia.
dipolaire [dipɔlɛr] *adj.* (sci.) dipolar.
dipôle [dipol] *s.m.* (sci.) dipole.
dipsacées [dipsase] *s.f.pl.* (bot.) Dipsaceae.
dipsomane [dipsɔman] *s.m.f.*, *adj.* dipsomaniac.
dipsomanie [dipsɔmani] *s.f.* dipsomania.
diptère[1] [diptɛr] *adj.* (arch.) dipteral.
diptère[2] [diptɛr] *s.m.* (ent.) dipteran; (pl.) Diptera; *~ adj.* (ent.) dipterous.
diptyque [diptik] *s.m.* diptych; (fig.) work (of art, etc.) in two parts.
dire [dir] *v.t.* to say, to tell, to speak; *c'est plus facile à ~ qu'à faire*, easier said than done; *il sait ce qu'il dit*, he knows what he is talking about; *à vrai ~*, *à ~ vrai*, to tell the truth; *pour ainsi ~*, so to speak; *ce n'est pas pour ~ ...*, without boasting ...; *pour tout ~*, in a word; (fam.) *ce n'est pas une chose à ~*, it is best not talked about; *cela va sans ~*, of course, naturally; *vouloir ~*, to mean; *qu'est-ce à ~?*, what do you mean by that?; *dites donc, vous là-bas!*, I say (*or* look here), you over there!; *à qui le dites-vous!*, you're telling me!; *cela vous plaît à ~*, it's all very well for you to say that (but I don't agree); *quand je vous le disais!*, didn't I tell you!; I told you so!; *vous m'en direz tant!*, that puts it in a different light!; *qu'en dites-vous?*, what do you think about it?; *on dirait qu'il va pleuvoir*, it looks like rain; *comme qui dirait*, so to say; so to speak; *~ du bien, du mal, de qch.*, to speak well, ill, of sth.; *il est réélu, dit-on*, they say he has been re-elected; *~ qu'il n'a pas encore vingt ans!*, to think that he is not yet twenty!; *qui vous a dit de faire cela?*, who told you to do that?; *~ un poème*, to recite a poem; *son silence dit beaucoup*, his silence speaks volumes; *cela ne me dit rien*, it doesn't appeal to me.
dire [dir] *s.m.* (law, etc.) statement; *aux ~s de* (*qn.*), according to (s.o.).
direct, -e [dirɛkt] *adj.* direct; (rail., of train, carriage) through; *~ s.m.* (radio, TV) live broadcast, transmission; *en ~*, (broadcast) live.

directement [dirɛktəmɑ̃] *adv.* direct, straight, directly; ~ *du producteur au consommateur,* direct from the producer to the consumer; *rentrer* ~ *chez soi,* to go straight home; *cela ne vous concerne pas* ~, that does not directly concern you.

direct-eur, -rice [dirɛktœr] *s.m.f.* director, manager (manageress), editor (of newspaper, etc.), principal; ~*eur,* ~*rice d'école,* headmaster, headmistress, (of primary school); see also DIRECTRICE 2; *adj.* directing, managing, controlling; *principe* ~*eur,* guiding principle.

direction [dirɛksjɔ̃] *s.f.* **1.** direction, management, guidance; directorship, headship (of school, etc.); director(s), directorate, (of organization, etc.); **2.** direction, course, route; destination; (car, etc.) steering; *dans la* or *en* ~ *de,* going to, bound for.

directive [dirɛktiv] *s.f.* (usu. pl.) directive, guide-line.

Directoire [dirɛktwar] *s.m.* (hist.) Directoire (1795–99).

directorat [dirɛktɔra] *s.m.* directorate.

directorial, -e, (**aux**) [dirɛktɔrjal] *adj.* directorial.

directrice [dirɛktris] *s.f.* **1.** see DIRECTEUR; **2.** (geom.) directrix.

dirigeable [diriʒabl] *adj., s.m.* dirigible.

dirigeant, -e [diriʒɑ̃] *adj.* directing, ruling; *s.m.f.* director; (pl.) leaders (of political party, etc.).

dirigé, -e [diriʒe] *adj.* organized; *économie* ~*e,* planned economy.

diriger [diriʒe] *v.t.* to direct; to steer, to drive, (vehicle, etc.), to pilot (aircraft), to conduct (orchestra); **se** ~ *v.refl. se* ~ *vers,* to make for.

dirigisme [diriʒism] *s.m.* dirigism(e), planned economy, (policy of) state control.

dirigiste [diriʒist] *adj.* dirigist(e).

dirimant, -e [dirimɑ̃] *adj.* diriment; (law) *empêchement* ~, diriment impediment.

disaccharide [disakarid] *s.m.* (chem.) disaccharide.

disant see SOI-DISANT.

discal, -e, (**aux**) [diskal] *adj.* of the vertebral discs (*or* vertebrae); (med.) *hernie* ~*e,* slipped disc.

discale [diskal] *s.f.* (comm.) loss of weight (of goods stored or transported in bulk).

discernable [disɛrnabl] *adj.* discernible.

discernement [disɛrnəmɑ̃] *s.m.* discernment, judgement; (Lit.) discrimination.

discerner [disɛrne] *v.t.* **1.** to discern, to make out, to distinguish; to detect, to be aware of; **2.** to differentiate, to make distinctions; to identify, to isolate; ~ *qch. de,* or *d'avec, qch.,* to distinguish, or separate, one thing from another, to make a distinction between one thing and another, to make, or to see, a difference between one thing and another; ~ *le vrai du,* or *d'avec, le faux,* to distinguish the true from the false, to tell right from wrong.

disciple [disipl] *s.m.* disciple.

disciplinable [disiplinabl] *adj.* amenable to discipline.

disciplinaire [disiplinɛr] *adj.* disciplinary; ~ *s.m.* (mil.) soldier in a *compagnie de* DISCIPLINE.

discipline [disiplin] *s.f.* discipline; *conseil de* ~, disciplinary body; (mil.) *compagnie de* ~, (in France) special disciplinary unit (for soldiers guilty of grave offences).

discipliné, -e [disipline] *adj.* (well-)disciplined, amenable, tractable.

discipliner [disipline] *v.t.* to discipline; (fig.) to control (e.g. unruly hair).

discobole [diskɔbɔl] *s.m.* (Gr. ant.) (statue of) discobolus; discus thrower.

discontinu, -e [diskɔ̃tiny] *adj.* discontinuous, intermittent, sporadic; *ligne* ~*e,* dotted, or broken, line (esp. of road-marking).

discontinuation [diskɔ̃tinɥɑsjɔ̃] *s.f.* discontinuance.

discontinuer [diskɔ̃tinɥe] *v.t.* (Lit.) to discontinue; ~ *v.i. sans* ~, without respite, incessantly.

disconvenance [diskɔ̃vnɑ̃s] *s.f.* (Lit.) disparity, incompatibility.

disconvenir [diskɔ̃vnir] *v.i.* to deny; *je n'en disconviens pas,* I do not deny it, I admit it.

discophile [diskɔfil] *adj., s.m.f.* discophil(e).

discophilie [diskɔfili] *s.f.* discography.

discord [diskɔr] *s.m.* (obs.) dispute.

discordance [diskɔrdɑ̃s] *s.f.* **1.** discord(ance); **2.** (geol.) fault.

discordant, -e [diskɔrdɑ̃] *adj.* **1.** discordant; **2.** (geol.) faulted.

discorde [diskɔrd] *s.f.* discord, dissension.

discorder [diskɔrde] *v.i.* (obs.) to disagree; (mus.) to be discordant, to be out of tune.

discothèque [diskɔtɛk] *s.f.* **1.** collection of (gramophone) records; **2.** discothèque, disco.

discoureu-r, -se [diskurœr] *s.m.f.* great talker.

discourir [diskurir] *v.i.* **1.** (obs.) to chat; **2.** to discourse, to expatiate (*sur,* on).

discours [diskur] *s.m.* **1.** (obs.) talk, conversation; **2.** speech, address; discourse; **3.** language; *les parties du* ~, the parts of speech.

discourtois, -e [diskurtwa] *adj.* discourteous; ~**ement** [diskurtwazmɑ̃] *adv.* discourteously.

discrédit [diskredi] *s.m.* discredit, disrepute.

discréditer [diskredite] *v.t.* to discredit, to bring discredit on.

discr-et, -ète [diskrɛ] *adj.* **1.** reserved, circumspect, discreet; **2.** discrete, discontinuous; ~**ètement** [diskrɛtmɑ̃] *adv.* discreetly, unobtrusively.

discrétion [diskresjɔ̃] *s.f.* discretion, circumspection, reserve; *à* ~, at (one's own) discretion; without restriction, as desired, as much as one wants; *être à la* ~ *de qn.,* to be in the power, at the mercy, of s.o.

discrétionnaire [diskresjɔnɛr] *adj.* discretionary.

discriminant, -e [diskriminɑ̃] *adj.* discriminant; ~ *s.m.* (math.) discriminant.

discrimination [diskriminɑsjɔ̃] *s.f.* discrimination.

discriminatoire [diskriminatwar] *adj.* discriminatory, discriminative.

discriminer [diskrimine] *v.t.* (Lit.) to discriminate between, to differentiate.

disculper [diskylpe] *v.t.* to exculpate, to exonerate; **se** ~ *v.refl.* to clear oneself of blame.

discursi-f, -ve [diskyrsif] *adj.* discursive.

discussion [diskysjɔ̃] *s.f.* **1.** discussion, debate; **2.** dispute, disputation, argument.

discutable [diskytabl] *adj.* debatable; questionable.

discutailler [diskytɑje] *v.i.* to altercate, to wrangle.

discuté, -e [diskyte] *adj.* talked-about; controversial.

discuter [diskyte] *v.t.* to discuss, to debate, to question, to argue, to dispute.

disert, -e [dizɛr] *adj.* (Lit.) felicitously eloquent; ~**ement** [dizɛrtəmɑ̃] *adv.* eloquently.

disette [dizɛt] *s.f.* shortage, dearth, want; famine.

diseu-r, -se [dizœr] *s.m.f.* **1.** teller (of fortune, etc.); **2.** (theatr., etc.) diseur, diseuse.

disgrâce [disgrɑs] *s.f.* disgrace, disfavour.

disgracié, -e [disgrasje] *adj.* **1.** (fallen) out of favour; **2.** ill-favoured, unattractive, plain.

disgracier [disgrasje] *v.t.* to treat with disfavour (s.o. previously favoured).

disgracieu-x, -se [disgrasjø] *adj.* ungraceful; awkward, ungainly; unsightly; (of face, etc.)

plain; ~**sement** [disgrasjøzmɑ̃] *adv.* gracelessly, ungracefully.

disjoindre [disʒwɛ̃dr] *v.t.* to disjoin, to disconnect, to take apart, to separate.

disjoint, -e [disʒwɛ̃] *adj.* disconnected, disjointed; (mus.) disjunct.

disjoncteur [disʒɔ̃ktœr] *s.m.* (electr.) cut-out, circuit-breaker, trip.

disjoncti-f, -ve [disʒɔ̃ktif] *adj.* disjunctive.

disjonction [disʒɔ̃ksjɔ̃] *s.f.* disjunction, separation.

dislocation [dislɔkɑsjɔ̃] *s.f.* dislocation; breaking-up, dispersal, (of crowd, procession); dismemberment (of empire, etc.).

disloquer [dislɔke] *v.t.* to dislocate; to disperse (crowd, etc.); to dismember (empire, etc.).

disparaître [disparɛtr] *v.i.* to disappear, to vanish.

disparate [disparat] *adj.* disparate, heterogeneous; dissimilar, (of colours, etc.) discordant; ~ *s.f.* (obs.) disparity; (pl.) disparates.

disparité [disparite] *s.f.* disparity.

disparition [disparisjɔ̃] *s.f.* disappearance.

disparu, -e [dispary] *adj.* **1.** vanished; **2.** (naut., mil., etc.) lost, missing; *s.m.f.* deceased (person); *notre cher* ~, our dear departed.

dispatcher [dispatʃœr, dispatʃɛr] *s.m.* (rail., air) movement controller.

dispatching [dispatʃiŋ] *s.m.* (rail., air) movement control.

dispendieu-x, -se [dispɑ̃djø] *adj.* expensive, costly.

dispensaire [dispɑ̃sɛr] *s.m.* dispensary, clinic.

dispensat-eur, -rice [dispɑ̃satœr] *s.m.f.* dispenser, distributor, (of charity, gifts, etc.); ⚠ not 'dispenser' of medicines, etc.

dispense [dispɑ̃s] *s.f.* exemption, dispensation.

dispenser [dispɑ̃se] *v.t.* **1.** to distribute, to bestow; **2.** ~ *qn. de qch.*, to exempt s.o. from sth. (e.g. tax, obligation); ⚠ not 'to dispense' in sense 'to make up medicine'.

disperser [dispɛrse] *v.t.* to disperse, to scatter; **se** ~ *v.refl.* to disperse, to scatter.

dispersi-f, -ve [dispɛrsif] *adj.* dispersive.

dispersion [dispɛrsjɔ̃] *s.f.* dispersing, dispersal, dispersion.

disponibilité [dispɔnibilite] *s.f.* **1.** disposability, availability; (pl.) disposable assets; **2.** (mil., etc.) being on reserve list.

disponible [dispɔnibl] *adj.* available, at someone's disposal; (mil., etc.) placed on reserve list.

dispos, -e [dispo] *adj.* hale and hearty, in good form.

disposé, -e [dispoze] *adj.* arranged, disposed, prepared; *être bien* (or *mal*) ~ *pour* (or *envers*) *qn.*, to be well (*or* ill) disposed towards s.o.

disposer [dispoze] *v.t.* to arrange, to dispose, to prepare (s.o. for sth.); ~ *de*, to have at one's disposal, to have available; (law) to dispose of (property, possessions) by sale, donation, or will.

dispositif [dispozitif] *s.m.* **1.** (law) purview, enacting terms (of statute); **2.** (mil.) plan; **3.** (techn.) device, mechanism.

disposition [dispozisjɔ̃] *s.f.* **1.** arrangement, lay-out; (pl.) arrangements (for doing sth.); (law) ruling; (pl.) terms (of will); *prendre des ~s pour faire*, to make arrangements to do, for doing; *~s testamentaires*, testamentary dispositions; **2.** disposition, mood, humour; predisposition, propensity; (usu. pl.) tendency, aptitude, (*de*, to, towards, for); **3.** disposal; *avoir à sa* ~, to have at one's disposal, to have available; *se mettre à la* ~ *de qn.*, to put oneself at someone's disposal, to be at someone's service.

disproportion [disprɔpɔrsjɔ̃] *s.f.* disproportion.

disproportionné, -e [disprɔpɔrsjɔne] *adj.* disproportionate, out of proportion.

disputailler [dispytɑje] *v.i.* (obs.) to wrangle endlessly.

dispute [dispyt] *s.f.* dispute, quarrel; (obs.) debate, discussion, disputation.

disputer [dispyte] *v.t.i.* to dispute; ~ *qch. à qn.*, to dispute ownership (or possession) of sth. with s.o.; **se** ~ *v.refl.* to quarrel.

disquaire [diskɛr] *s.m.* dealer in (gramophone) records.

disqualification [diskalifikasjɔ̃] *s.f.* disqualification.

disqualifier [diskalifje] *v.t.* to disqualify.

disque [disk] *s.m.* **1.** disc, disk; **2.** (Gk. ant., sport) discus; **3.** (gramophone) record, disc; (fig., fam.) *changer de* ~, to change the subject.

dissection [disɛksjɔ̃] *s.f.* dissection.

dissemblable [disɑ̃blabl] *adj.* dissimilar, unlike.

dissemblance [disɑ̃blɑ̃s] *s.f.* dissimilarity, difference.

dissémination [diseminɑsjɔ̃] *s.f.* dissemination, scattering, spreading.

disséminer [disemine] *v.t.* to disseminate, to scatter, to spread.

dissension [disɑ̃sjɔ̃] *s.f.* dissension, discord.

dissentiment [disɑ̃timɑ̃] *s.m.* dissent, disagreement.

disséquer [diseke] *v.t.* to dissect.

dissertation [disɛrtɑsjɔ̃] *s.f.* **1.** dissertation; **2.** essay (abbrev. *dissert*).

disserter [disɛrte] *v.i.* to discourse, to speak or write at length (on a subject).

dissidence [disidɑ̃s] *s.f.* dissent, dissidence.

dissident, -e [disidɑ̃] *adj.* dissenting; dissident; *s.m.f.* dissenter; dissident; dissentient.

dissimilation [disimilɑsjɔ̃] *s.f.* (lang.) dissimilation.

dissimilitude [disimilityd] *s.f.* dissimilitude.

dissimulat-eur, -rice [disimylatœr] *s.m.f.* dissembler, dissimulator.

dissimulation [disimylɑsjɔ̃] *s.f.* dissimulation, dissembling.

dissimulé, -e [disimyle] *adj.* **1.** concealed; *bénéfices ~s*, hidden profits; **2.** secretive, underhand.

dissimuler [disimyle] *v.t.* to dissemble, to dissimulate, to conceal, to disguise.

dissipat-eur, -rice [disipatœr] *s.m.f.* spendthrift, squanderer; *adj.* wasteful, ruinously extravagant.

dissipation [disipɑsjɔ̃] *s.f.* (lit. & fig.) dissipation; (in school) idleness, inattention.

dissipé, -e [disipe] *adj.* **1.** (of child, pupil) inattentive; **2.** (Lit.) dissipated.

dissiper [disipe] *v.t.* to dissipate, to disperse, to dispel; to squander, to fritter away; (Lit.) ~ *qn.*, to distract s.o. (from study, etc.).

dissociation [disɔsjɑsjɔ̃] *s.f.* dissociation.

dissocier [disɔsje] *v.t.* to dissociate.

dissolu, -e [disɔly] *adj.* (Lit.) dissolute.

dissolubilité [disɔlybilite] *s.f.* dissolubility, dissolvability.

dissoluble [disɔlybl] *adj.* (chem.) soluble; (of pol. assembly, etc.) dissolvable.

dissolution [disɔlysjɔ̃] *s.f.* dissolution; (Lit.) dissoluteness; (techn.) rubber solution; (chem.) dissolving; solution.

dissolvant, -e [disɔlvɑ̃] *adj.* solvent; (fig.) destructive (of e.g. beliefs); ~ *s.m.* solvent; nail-varnish remover.

dissonance [disɔnɑ̃s] *s.f.* dissonance.

dissonant, -e [disɔnɑ̃] *adj.* dissonant.

dissoner [disɔne] *v.i.* to be dissonant, to jar, (of colours) to clash.

dissoudre [disudr] *v.t.* to dissolve; **se** ~ *v.refl.* to dissolve.

dissuader [disɥade] *v.t.* to dissuade (*de*, from).

dissuasion [disɥazjɔ̃] *s.f.* dissuasion; (mil., pol.) *arme de* ~, deterrent.

dissyllable [disil(l)abl] *adj.* dis(s)yllabic; ~ *s.m.* dis(s)yllable.
dissyllabique [disil(l)abik] *adj.* dis(s)yllabic.
dissymétrie [disimetri] *s.f.* dissymmetry, asymmetry.
dissymétrique [disimetrik] *adj.* dissymmetrical, asymmetrical.
distance [distɑ̃s] *s.f.* distance; remoteness; (fig.) *garder ses ~s*, to keep one's distance; *tenir à ~*, to remain aloof; *tenir qn. à ~*, to keep s.o. at a distance.
distancer [distɑ̃se] *v.t.* **1.** to overtake, to (out)distance; **2.** (racing) to disqualify.
distant, -e [distɑ̃] *adj.* distant; (fig.) reserved, cold, distant.
distendre [distɑ̃dr] *v.t.* to distend.
distension [distɑ̃sjɔ̃] *s.f.* distension.
distillat [distila] *s.m.* distillate.
distillateur [distilatœr] *s.m.* distiller.
distillation [distilɑsjɔ̃] *s.f.* distillation.
distiller [distile] *v.t.i.* to distil.
distillerie [distilri] *s.f.* distillery.
distinct, -e [distɛ̃(kt)] *adj.* distinct, distinguishable, clear; **~ement** [distɛ̃ktəmɑ̃] *adv.* distinctly, clearly.
distincti-f, -ve [distɛ̃ktif] *adj.* distinctive.
distinction [distɛ̃ksjɔ̃] *s.f.* distinction; differentiation.
distinguable [distɛ̃gabl] *adj.* distinguishable, recognizable.
distingué, -e [distɛ̃ge] *adj.* distinguished, eminent; distingué(e); special; (formal and respectful ending to letter) *recevez l'expression de ma considération ~e.*
distinguer [distɛ̃ge] *v.t.* to distinguish, to differentiate, to single out; **se** ~ *v.refl.* (esp.) to distinguish oneself; to be distinguishable, distinct, to be marked out (*de*, from).
distinguo [distɛ̃go] *s.m.* distinguo; (fam.) subtle distinction or nuance (in argument, etc.).
distique [distik] *s.m.* (pros.) distich.
distomatose [distɔmatoz] *s.f.* (med., vet.) distomatosis.
distordre [distɔrdr] *v.t.* to distort.
distorsion [distɔrsjɔ̃] *s.f.* distortion.
distraction [distraksjɔ̃] *s.f.* absent-mindedness, distraction, recreation, amusement; ⚠ not 'distraction' in senses 'perplexity', 'frenzy'.
distraire [distrɛr] *v.t.* to distract (s.o., someone's attention, *de*, from); to entertain, to amuse; to abstract; **se** ~ *v.refl.* to distract oneself, to amuse oneself, to relax; *il a besoin de se ~*, he needs some distraction, he should relax.
distrait, -e [distrɛ] *adj.* absent-minded, inattentive, distrait(e); **~ement** [distrɛtmɑ̃] *adv.* absent-mindedly.
distrayant, -e [distrɛjɑ̃] *adj.* amusing, entertaining, diverting.
distribuer [distribɥe] *v.t.* to distribute, to deal out; to arrange, to classify.
distribut-eur, -rice [distribytœr] *s.m.f.* distributor, retailer; **~eur** *s.m.* (car, etc.) distributor; *~eur automatique*, slot-machine, vending-machine; *~eur d'essence*, petrol-pump.
distributi-f, -ve [distribytif] *adj.* distributive.
distribution [distribysjɔ̃] *s.f.* distribution, supply; arrangement, classification; (post office) delivery (of letters, etc.); (theatr., etc.) casting, cast, (of play, etc.); ~ *des prix*, prize-giving; ~ *des eaux, de l'électricité*, water, electricity, supply.
district [distrik(t)] *s.m.* district.
distyle [distil] *adj.* (arch.) distyle.
dit, -e [di] *adj.* agreed, settled; called, so-called, nicknamed.
dithyrambe [ditirɑ̃b] *s.m.* (Gk. ant.) dithyramb; (Lit.) encomium, panegyric.
dithyrambique [ditirɑ̃bik] *adj.* (Gk. ant.) dithyrambic; (fig. of praise, etc.) fulsome, extravagant.
dito [dito] *adv.* (comm.) ditto, do.
diurèse [djyrɛz] *s.f.* (med.) diuresis.
diurétique [djyretik] *adj., s.m.* diuretic.
diurnal (pl. **aux**) [djyrnal] *s.m.* (relig.) diurnal.
diurne [djyrn] *adj.* diurnal.
diva [diva] *s.f.* (obs.) diva, prima donna.
divagation [divagɑsjɔ̃] *s.f.* divagation, straying, wandering.
divaguer [divage] *v.i.* to divagate, to stray, to wander.
divan [divɑ̃] *s.m.* divan.
dive [div] *adj.* (obs. exc. jest) *la ~ bouteille*, wine.
divergence [divɛrʒɑ̃s] *s.f.* divergence, divergency.
divergent, -e [divɛrʒɑ̃] *adj.* divergent, diverging.
diverger [divɛrʒe] *v.i.* to diverge.
divers, -e [divɛr] *adj.* **1.** diverse; **2.** sundry, several, various, divers; *faits ~*, news-items; **~ement** [divɛrsmɑ̃] *adv.* variously, diversely.
diversifier [divɛrsifje] *v.t.* to diversify, to vary.
diversiforme [divɛrsifɔrm] *adj.* diversiform.
diversion [divɛrsjɔ̃] *s.f.* diversion; *faire ~ à*, to distract from, to take one's mind off.
diversité [divɛrsite] *s.f.* diversity.
diverticule [divɛrtikyl] *s.m.* (anat.) diverticulum.
divertir [divɛrtir] *v.t.* **1.** (obs.) to divert, to embezzle; **2.** to divert, to entertain, to amuse.
divertissant, -e [divɛrtisɑ̃] *adj.* entertaining, amusing, diverting.
divette [divɛt] *s.f.* (obs.) female music-hall or musical comedy singer.
dividende [dividɑ̃d] *s.m.* dividend.
divin, -e [divɛ̃] *adj.* divine, holy, sacred; heavenly, delightful.
divinat-eur, -rice [divinatœr] *s.m.f.* diviner; *adj.* divinatory.
divination [divinɑsjɔ̃] *s.f.* divination; intuition.
divinatoire [divinatwar] *adj.* divinatory, divining; *baguette ~ des sourciers*, divining-rod, dowsing-rod.
divinement [divinmɑ̃] *adv.* divinely.
divinisation [divinizɑsjɔ̃] *s.f.* deification, divinization.
diviniser [divinize] *v.t.* to deify, to divinize.
divinité [divinite] *s.f.* divinity, deity; ⚠ not 'divinity' in sense 'theology'.
divis, -e [divi] *adj.* (law) divided.
diviser [divize] *v.t.* to divide, to separate; **se** ~ *v.refl.* to divide, to be divided.
diviseur [divizœr] *s.m.* (arith.) divisor; *plus grand commun ~*, highest common factor.
divisibilité [divizibilite] *s.f.* divisibility.
divisible [divizibl] *adj.* divisible.
division [divizjɔ̃] *s.f.* division.
divisionnaire [divizjɔnɛr] *adj.* (mil., etc.) divisional; ~ *s.m.* divisional commander.
divisionnisme [divizjɔnism] *s.m.* (paint.) divisionism.
divisionniste [divizjɔnist] *adj., s.m.f.* (paint.) divisionist.
divorce [divɔrs] *s.m.* (lit. & fig.) divorce.
divorcé, -e [divɔrse] *adj.* divorced; *s.m.f.* divorcee, divorcé(e).
divorcer [divɔrse] *v.i.* ~ *(d')avec qn.*, to divorce, to be divorced from, s.o.; (fig.) to break with s.o.
divulgat-eur, -rice [divylgatœr] *s.m.f.* one who divulges or publishes (secret information, news).
divulgation [divylgɑsjɔ̃] *s.f.* divulgence, divulgement, divulgation.
divulguer [divylge] *v.t.* to divulge, to reveal, to make public.
dix [dis; di before consonant; usu. diz before vowel or h-mute] *adj., s.m.* ten, tenth; *ils étaient ~*, there were ten of them; *le ~ janvier*, the tenth

of January; *Charles* ~, Charles the Tenth; (cards) ~ *de carreau*, ten of diamonds.
dix-huit [dizɥit] *adj.*, *s.m.* eighteen(th); **~ième** [dizɥitjɛm] *adj.*, *s.m.f.* eighteenth.
dixième [dizjɛm] *adj.*, *s.m.f.* tenth; **~ment** [dizjɛmmɑ̃] *adv.* tenthly.
dix-neuf [diznœf] *adj.*, *s.m.* nineteen(th).
dix-neuvième [diznœvjɛm] *adj.*, *s.m.f.* nineteenth.
dix-sept [disɛt] *adj.*, *s.m.* seventeen(th); **~ième** [disɛtjɛm] *adj.*, *s.m.f.* seventeenth.
dizain [dizɛ̃] *s.m.* ten-line stanza.
dizaine [dizɛn] *s.f.* ten, about ten; set or series of ten.
djellaba [dʒɛlaba] *s.f.* jellaba.
djinn [dʒin] *s.m.* jinn, djinn.
do [do] *s.m.* (mus.) doh, C.
docile [dɔsil] *adj.* docile, obedient; *cheveux* ~*s*, hair which is easy to manage; **~ment** [dɔsilmɑ̃] *adv.* obediently.
docilité [dɔsilite] *s.f.* docility, obedience.
docimasie [dɔsimazi] *s.f.* (chem.) quantitative analysis of metal ores; (forensic med.) post--mortem, autopsy.
dock [dɔk] *s.m.* (naut., etc.) dock, dockyard.
docker [dɔkɛr] *s.m.* docker.
docte [dɔkt] *adj.* (obs.) learned, erudite; **~ment** [dɔktəmɑ̃] *adv.* (obs. exc. jest) learnedly.
docteur [dɔktœr] *s.m.* doctor; ~ *ès lettres, ès sciences*, doctor of letters, of science; ~ *en droit, en médecine*, doctor of law, of medicine; *il, elle, est* ~, he, she, is a doctor; *le* ~ *Marie Laroche*, Dr. Marie Laroche.
doctoral, -e, (aux) [dɔktɔral] *adj.* doctoral; **~ement** [dɔktɔralmɑ̃] *adv.* (pej.) pompously.
doctorat [dɔktɔra] *s.m.* doctorate, doctor's degree.
doctoresse [dɔktɔrɛs] *s.f.* (obs.) woman doctor (of medicine).
doctrinaire [dɔktrinɛr] *s.m.*, *adj.* doctrinaire.
doctrinal, -e, (aux) [dɔktrinal] *adj.* doctrinal.
doctrine [dɔktrin] *s.f.* doctrine.
document [dɔkymɑ̃] *s.m.* document; deed; instrument.
documentaire [dɔkymɑ̃tɛr] *adj.* documentary; ~ *s.m.* documentary (film).
documenter [dɔkymɑ̃te] *v.t.* to document.
dodécaèdre [dɔdekaɛdr] *s.m.* dodecahedron.
dodécagone [dɔdekagɔn] *s.m.* dodecagon.
dodelinement [dɔdlinmɑ̃] *s.m.* rocking (of body), nodding (of head).
dodeliner [dɔdline] *v.i.* ~ *de la tête*, to nod (one's head in drowsiness); ~ *du corps*, to rock, to sway gently; ~ *v.t.* (obs.) to dandle, to rock, (child).
dodo[1] [dɔdo] *s.m.* (child. lang.) sleep; *faire* ~, to sleep, to go to sleep, (fam.) to go bye-byes.
dodo[2] [dɔdo] *s.m.* = DRONTE.
dodu, -e [dɔdy] *adj.* (fam.) plump.
dogat [dɔga] *s.m.* (hist.) dogate, office of doge.
doge [dɔʒ] *s.m.* (hist.) doge (of Venice or Genoa).
dogma-tique [dɔgmatik] *adj.* dogmatic, dogmatical; **~tiquement** [dɔgmatikmɑ̃] *adv.* dogmatically; **~tiser** [dɔgmatize] *v.i.* to dogmatize; **~tiseur** [dɔgmatizœr] *s.m.* dogmatist; **~tisme** [dɔgmatism] *s.m.* dogmatism.
dogme [dɔgm] *s.m.* dogma.
dogre [dɔgr] *s.m.* (naut.) dogger.
dogue [dɔg] *s.m.* mastiff (or similar breed of dog); (fig.) *être d'une humeur de* ~, to be like a bear with a sore head.
doigt [dwa] *s.m.* finger; (anat., zool.) digit; (fig.) small quantity or distance, finger's breadth, trifle; ~ *de pied*, toe; *boire un* ~ *de cognac*, to drink a finger of brandy; *être à deux* ~*s de* (*la mort*, etc.), to be on the brink of (death, etc.); *être comme les deux* ~*s de la main*, to be hand in glove; *savoir qch. sur le bout du* ~, to have sth. at one's fingertips; *se fourrer le* ~ *dans l'œil*, to be completely mistaken; *mon petit* ~ *me l'a dit*, a little bird told me.
doigté [dwate] *s.m.* **1.** (mus.) fingering; **2.** touch (e.g. of typist, engraver, etc.); **3.** (fig.) tact, skill.
doigter [dwate] *v.t.i.* (mus.) to finger.
doigtier [dwatje] *s.m.* finger-stall.
doit [dwa] *s.m.* (book-keep.) debit.
dol [dɔl] *s.m.* (law) fraud.
doléance [dɔleɑ̃s] *s.f.* complaint, grievance; (pl.) *faire, présenter, ses* ~*s*, to make, to lodge, a complaint.
doleau (pl. **-x**) [dɔlo] *s.m.* (techn.) cleaver for trimming slates.
dolent, -e [dɔlɑ̃] *adj.* complaining, plaintive.
doler [dɔle] *v.t.* (techn.) to trim.
dolichocéphale [dɔlikɔsefal] *adj.* dolichocephalic, dolichocephalous.
doline [dɔlin] *s.f.* (geog.) dolina, doline.
dollar [dɔlar] *s.m.* dollar.
dolman [dɔlmɑ̃] *s.m.* dolman.
dolmen [dɔlmɛn] *s.m.* (archaeol.) dolmen.
doloire [dɔlwar] *s.f.* (techn.) (cooper's) adze.
dolomie [dɔlɔmi], **dolomite** [dɔlɔmit] *s.f.* (min.) dolomite.
Dolomites [dɔlɔmit] *s.f.pl.* (geog.) Dolomites.
dolosi-f, -ve [dɔlɔsif] *adj.* (law) fraudulent.
Dom [dɔ̃] *s.m.* (Cath. & obs. Spanish) Dom.
D.O.M. [deoɛm] abbrev. of Latin *Deo optimo maximo*, to God, the best and greatest.
domaine [dɔmɛn] *s.m.* domain; demesne; estate; *tomber dans le* ~ *public*, to run out of copyright, out of patent.
domanial, -e, (aux) [dɔmanjal] *adj.* **1.** (law) domanial; **2.** *forêts* ~*es*, national forests.
dôme [dom] *s.m.* dome.
domestication [dɔmɛstikɑsjɔ̃] *s.f.* domestication, taming, (of wild animals).
domesticité [dɔmɛstisite] *s.f.* **1.** domestic service; **2.** domestic staff; ⚠ not 'domesticity' in sense 'family life'.
domestique [dɔmɛstik] *adj.* domestic; tame, domesticated; ~ *s.m.f.* domestic servant.
domestiquer [dɔmɛstike] *v.t.* to domesticate, to tame, (wild animal); ⚠ not 'to domesticate' in sense 'to make fond of home life'.
domicile [dɔmisil] *s.m.* domicile; *sans* ~, of no fixed address; ~ *conjugal*, matrimonial home; *travailler à* ~, to work at home; *élire* ~, to take up residence (*à*, at).
domiciliaire [dɔmisiljɛr] *adj.* domiciliary.
domicilier [dɔmisilje] *v.t.* to domicile; *être domicilié*, to be domiciled (*à*, at).
dominance [dɔminɑ̃s] *s.f.* dominance.
dominant, -e [dɔminɑ̃] *adj.* dominant, predominant, ruling, prevailing; **~e** *s.f.* (mus.) dominant.
dominat-eur, -rice [dɔminatœr] *adj.* dominating; *s.m.f.* (Lit.) ruler.
domination [dɔminɑsjɔ̃] *s.f.* domination, dominion; (pl.) (Cath.) dominations.
dominer [dɔmine] *v.t.i.* to dominate (*sur*, over); to predominate.
dominicain[1], **-e** [dɔminikɛ̃] *adj.*, *s.m.f.* Dominican (friar or nun).
dominicain[2], **-e** [dɔminikɛ̃] *adj.*, *s.m.f.* Dominican ((native or inhabitant) of the Dominican Republic).
dominical, -e, (aux) [dɔminikal] *adj.* dominical, Sunday-; *l'oraison* ~*e*, the Lord's Prayer; *promenade* ~*e*, Sunday walk.
dominion [dɔminjɔ̃] *s.m.* (hist.) Dominion (self-governing territory of British Commonwealth).
domino [dɔmino] *s.m.* (costume & game) domino; *jouer aux* ~*s*, to play dominoes.

dominoterie [dɔminɔtri] *s.f.* fancy paper.
dominoti-er, -ère [dɔminɔtje] *s.m.f.* (obs.) fancy-paper maker; (mod.) maker of dominoes.
dommage [dɔmaʒ] *s.m.* **1.** injury, damage; *~s et intérêts, ~s-intérêts*, damages; **2.** pity; *c'est (grand) ~*, it is a (great) pity; *quel ~!*, what a pity!; *~ qu'il soit malade!*, pity he's ill!
dommageable [dɔmaʒabl] *adj.* damaging, prejudicial.
domptable [dɔ̃tabl] *adj.* tameable.
dompter [dɔ̃te] *v.t.* to tame, to subdue, to bring under control.
dompteu-r, -se [dɔ̃tœr] *s.m.f.* (animal-)tamer; *~r de chevaux*, horse-breaker.
don [dɔ̃] *s.m.* **1.** gift, present; **2.** gift, talent.
donataire [dɔnatɛr] *s.m.f.* (law) donee.
donat-eur, -rice [dɔnatœr] *s.m.f.* donor.
donation [dɔnɑsjɔ̃] *s.f.* donation, gift.
donc [dɔ̃k, dɔ̃] *conj.* **1.** so, therefore; **2.** (used to express surprise, or for emphasis) *vous habitez ~ là?*, you live *there*, do you?; *taisez-vous ~!*, *will* you be quiet!
dondon [dɔ̃dɔ̃] *s.f.* (fam.) fat woman.
donjon [dɔ̃ʒɔ̃] *s.m.* keep (of castle), donjon; ⚠ not 'dungeon'.
don Juan, don juan [dɔ̃ʒɥɑ̃] *s.m.* Don Juan; seducer.
donjuanesque [dɔ̃ʒɥanɛsk] *adj.* Don Juanesque.
donnant, -e [dɔnɑ̃] *adj.* (obs.) generous; (mod.) *~, ~*, fair is fair, fair exchanne is no robbery.
donne [dɔn] *s.f.* (cards) deal; *mauvaise ~*, misdeal.
donné, -e [dɔne] *adj.* given; *à une distance ~e*, at a given distance; *étant ~ les circonstances*, considering the circumstances; *~***es** *s.f.pl.* data.
donner [dɔne] *v.t.* to give, to bestow, to grant, to confer, to hand (over); to cause, to produce, to yield (crop), to attribute (quality, etc.); to present (play, film, etc.); (cards) to deal; *quel âge lui donnez-vous?*, how old would you say he is?; *~ à entendre*, to suggest, to give to understand; *~ à rire, à penser*, etc., to make one laugh, think, etc.; *~ à qn. de faire qch.*, to allow s.o. to do sth.; *cela me donne envie de pleurer*, that makes me want to cry; *~ lieu à*, to give rise to, to cause; *~ matière, sujet, à*, to give grounds for; *~ raison, tort, à qn.*, to agree, to disagree, with s.o.; *~ un coup de pied, de poing*, to kick, to punch; (cards) *c'est à vous de ~*, it's your deal; *s'en ~*, to enjoy oneself greatly; *~ v.i.* to knock (*contre*, against; *sur*, on); to (let oneself) fall (*dans, vers*, into) (ambush, trap); (of army, etc.) to go into action, to charge; *~ sur*, (of building, window, etc.) to face, to look, to open, on to; *~ de la tête contre*, to knock one's head against; *le navire alla ~ sur les écueils*, the ship struck the reef; *~ dans le panneau*, to fall into the trap.
donneu-r, -se [dɔnœr] *s.m.f.* giver, donor; (cards) dealer.
don Quichotte [dɔ̃kiʃɔ̃t] *s.m.* Don Quixote.
don-quichottisme [dɔ̃kiʃɔtism] *s.m.* quixotry, quixotism.
dont [dɔ̃] *rel.pron.* (represents sing. or pl. rel. pron. governed by *de*) **1.** (possessive) whose, of whom, of which; *la dame ~ le fils est à l'étranger*, the lady whose son is abroad; *un livre ~ je ne me rappelle plus le nom*, a book the name of which has slipped my memory; **2.** (partitive) of whom, of which, among whom or which, including; *quelques milliers de livres ~ je n'ai gardé que quelques-uns*, some thousands of books of which I have only kept a few; *quelques-uns avaient protesté, ~ son fils*, a few had protested, including his son; **3.** (place) from which, out of which, whence; *la famille ~ il sort*, the family he comes from; *la chambre ~ il est sorti*, the room he came out of; **4.** (concerning) of, about, whom or which; *la personne, la chose, ~ je parle*, the person I am talking about, the matter of which I am speaking; **5.** (rel. pron. complement of verbs constructed with *de*; various Eng. equivalents) *qch. ~ j'ai besoin*, sth. I need, of which I have need; *un événement ~ je ne me souviens guère*, an event (which) I hardly remember; *les élèves ~ il était responsable*, the pupils he was responsible for; *la réponse ~ tout dépend*, the answer on which everything depends; *le système ~ je me sers*, the system I am using; *la petite rente ~ il vivait*, the tiny pension he lived on.
donzelle [dɔ̃zɛl] *s.f.* pretentious young lady.
doper [dɔpe] *v.t.* to dope (esp. horse or athlete); **se** *~ v.refl.* to dope oneself, to take stimulants.
doping [dɔpiŋ] *s.m.* doping, dope.
dorade see DAURADE.
dorage [dɔraʒ] *s.m.* gilding.
doré, -e [dɔre] *adj.* gilt, gilded, golden; *livre ~ sur tranches*, gilt-edged book; *jeunesse ~e*, gilded youth.
dorénavant [dɔrenavɑ̃] *adv.* henceforth, henceforward.
dorer [dɔre] *v.t.* to gild; (cook.) to glaze; (fig.) *~ la pilule*, to sugar the pill (*à qn.*, for s.o.).
doreu-r, -se [dɔrœr] *s.m.f.* gilder.
dorien, -ne [dɔrjɛ̃] *adj., s.m.f.* Dorian, Doric; (mus.) *mode ~*, Dorian mode; *~ s.m.* Doric (dialect).
dorique [dɔrik] *adj.* (lang., arch.) Doric.
d'ores et déjà see DÉJÀ.
doris¹ [dɔris] *s.f.* (moll.) doris, sea lemon.
doris² [dɔris] *s.m.* (naut.) dory.
dorlotement [dɔrlɔtmɑ̃] *s.m.* coddling.
dorloter [dɔrlɔte] *v.t.* to coddle, to pamper; *se ~*, to pamper oneself.
dormant, -e [dɔrmɑ̃] *adj.* **1.** sleeping; (fig. & herald.) dormant; **2.** (of water) stagnant; **3.** (techn.) fixed (not moving or movable), (of window, etc.) that does not open; (naut.) *manœuvres ~es*, standing rigging; *~ s.m.* post (fixed) frame, (of door, casement, etc.).
dormeu-r, -se [dɔrmœr] *s.m.f.* sleeper; *~***r** *s.m.* (fam.) crab; *~***se** *s.f.* stud ear-ring.
dormir [dɔrmir] *v.i.* to sleep, to be asleep; *conte à ~ debout*, boring story, tall story; *~ sur les deux oreilles, à poings fermés, comme une souche, comme un sabot*, to sleep like a log; *il n'est pire eau que l'eau qui dort*, still waters run deep; *ne réveillez pas le chat qui dort*, let sleeping dogs lie.
dormiti-f, -ve [dɔrmitif] *adj.* (obs.) soporific.
dorsal, -e, (aux) [dɔrsal] *adj.* (anat., biol.) dorsal; *~***e** *s.f.* **1.** (lang.) dorsal (sound); **2.** (geog., meteor.) ridge.
dortoir [dɔrtwar] *s.m.* dormitory.
dorure [dɔryr] *s.f.* gilding, gilt; gold braid (on uniform); (cook.) glaze.
doryphore [dɔrifɔr] *s.m.* (ent.) Colorado beetle.
dos [do] *s.m.* back; spine (of book); *faire le gros ~*, (of cat) to arch its back; (lit. & fig.) *tourner le ~ à qn.*, to turn one's back on s.o.; *de ~*, from behind, from the back; (fig.) *se mettre qn. à ~*, to make an enemy of s.o.; *avoir bon ~*, (of person) to have a broad back; (of thing) to be a good excuse; *en avoir plein le ~*, to have had enough of sth.; *courber le ~*, to give in, to submit; *être sur le ~ de qn.*, to be constantly after s.o.
dosable [dozabl] *adj.* measurable, determinable (as to quantity).
dosage [dozaʒ] *s.m.* dosage, proportioning (of ingredients).
dose [doz] *s.f.* dose, proportion (of ingredient), quantity; (fig.) share.
doser [doze] *v.t.* **1.** to quantify a dose of (medicine); **2.** to determine the proportions of ingredients in (medicament); ⚠ not 'to dose' in sense 'to give dose (of medicine) to'.
doseur [dozœr] *s.m.* device for measuring dose, dosimeter.

dossard [dosar] *s.m.* (sport) cloth number worn on back by player or competitor.
dosse [dos] *s.f.* flitch (of timber).
dosseret [dosrɛ] *s.m.* **1.** jamb; **2.** back (of saw).
dossier [dosje] *s.m.* **1.** back (of chair, etc.); **2.** dossier, record; file.
dossière [dosjɛr] *s.f.* **1.** back-band (of harness); **2.** back plate (of armour).
dot [dɔt] *s.f.* dowry, marriage portion.
dotal, -e, (aux) [dɔtal] *adj.* (law) pertaining to a dowry.
dotation [dɔtɑsjɔ̃] *s.f.* **1.** endowment; income (allotted to Head of State, etc. = civil list); **2.** equipping, equipment.
doter [dɔte] *v.t.* **1.** to give dowry to; **2.** to endow; to allot income to (Head of State, etc.); **3.** to equip (hospital, etc.).
douaire [dwɛr] *s.m.* (hist., law) dower.
douairière [dwɛrjɛr] *s.f.* dowager.
douane [dwan] *s.f.* customs, custom-house.
douani-er, -ère [dwanje] *adj.* pertaining to customs; *union ~ère*, customs union; **~er** *s.m.* customs officer.
doublage [dublaʒ] *s.m.* lining; sheathing (of ship); (cin.) dubbing; (text.) doubling; (theatr.) engagement of a stand-in.
double [dubl] *adj.* double; (fig.) *être à ~ face*, to be double-faced; *~ adv. voir ~*, to see double; *~ s.m.* double; *plier en ~*, to fold in two; *les articles que j'ai en ~*, things I have two of; (tennis, etc.) *~ dames*, ladies' doubles; *~ mixte*, mixed doubles.
doublé, -e [duble] *adj.* **1.** doubled; **2.** lined; **3.** (cin.) dubbed; **4.** (fig.) *un menteur ~ d'un lâche*, a liar who is also a coward; *~ s.m.* plated jewellery, etc., plate.
doubleau (pl. **-x**) [dublo] *s.m.* (constr.) beam.
double-crème [dubləkrɛm] *s.m.* cream cheese; ⚠ not 'double cream'.
doublement [dubləmɑ̃] *adv.* doubly, for two reasons.
doublement [dubləmɑ̃] *s.m.* doubling.
doubler [duble] *v.t.* **1.** to double; to fold in two; to repeat; **2.** to line (garment, etc.); **3.** (theatr., cin.) to double (part); to understudy, to stand in for, (actor); to dub; **4.** (car, etc.) to overtake; (naut.) *~ le cap*, to round the cape; *~ v.i.* to double.
doublet [dublɛ] *s.m.* (lang., photo., imitation precious stone) doublet.
doublier [dublije] *s.m.* (agric.) double rack in sheep-fold.
doublon[1] [dublɔ̃] *s.m.* (print.) double.
doublon[2] [dublɔ̃] *s.m.* doubloon (anc. coin).
doublure [dublyr] *s.f.* **1.** lining; **2.** (theatr.) understudy; (cin.) stand-in; stunt man.
douce see DOUX.
douce-amère [dusamɛr] *s.f.* (bot.) woody nightshade, bittersweet.
douceâtre [dusɑtr] *adj.* sweetish, of a sickly sweetness.
doucement [dusmɑ̃] *adv.* **1.** softly, quietly, gently, gradually; **2.** so-so; *comment va le malade? Tout ~, bien ~*, how is the invalid? Only so-so; *~ interj.* gently!, easy!
doucereu-x, -se [dusrø] *adj.* **1.** sickly sweet, sugary; **2.** (of person) smarmy, mealy-mouthed; **~sement** [dusrøzmɑ̃] *adv.* smarmily.
doucet, -te [dusɛ] *adj.* (obs.) gentle, suave; **~te** *s.f.* (bot.) corn salad, lamb's lettuce.
doucettement [dusɛtmɑ̃] *adv.* (fam.) very gently, very quietly.
douceur [dusœr] *s.f.* sweetness, softness, smoothness, gentleness, kindness; (pl.) sweets, sweet things; *en ~*, quietly, softly, gently, cautiously.
douche [duʃ] *s.f.* shower, douche; (fig.) disappointment, damper; (fam.) scolding, dressing-down.
doucher [duʃe] *v.t.* to give shower to, to douche; (fam.) to scold, to dress down; **se ~** *v.refl.* to take a shower, to douche.
doucheu-r, -se [duʃœr] *s.m.f.* shower-bath attendant.
doucine [dusin] *s.f.* (arch.) cyma recta, cyma reversa; (techn.) moulding-plane.
doué, -e [dwe] *adj.* gifted, talented, endowed (*de*, with).
douer [dwe] *v.t.* to endow (with qualities, etc.).
douille [duj] *s.f.* (techn.) socket, sleeve; cartridge; (electr.) lamp-holder.
douillet, -te [dujɛ] *adj.* **1.** soft, yielding, comfortable, cosy; **2.** squeamish, sensitive, delicate, fragile; **~tement** [dujɛtmɑ̃] *adv.* softly, delicately, cosily.
douillette [dujɛt] *s.f.* quilted garment.
douilletterie [dujɛtri] *s.f.* (of person) sensitivity, fragility, squeamishness.
douleur [dulœr] *s.f.* **1.** pain, ache; (pl.) (esp. labour) pains; *être dans les ~s*, to be in labour; **2.** sorrow, grief.
douloureu-x, -se [dulurø] *adj.* painful, sore, tender; grievous, sorrowful, sad; **~sement** [dulurøzmɑ̃] *adv.* painfully, grievously; *gémir ~sement*, to groan with pain; **~se** *s.f.* (fam.) bill to pay.
doum [dum] *s.m.* (bot.) doum-palm.
dourine [durin] *s.f.* (vet.) dourine.
douro [duro] *s.m.* douro, duro (anc. coin).
doute [dut] *s.m.* doubt, uncertainty; *mettre en ~*, to call in question; *cela ne fait aucun ~*, there is no doubt about it; *sans ~*, no doubt, doubtless; *sans aucun ~*, without doubt, certainly.
douter [dute] *v.i.* to doubt; *~ de*, to doubt, to have doubts about (s.o., sth.), to question (sth.); *~ si*, to doubt whether, not to know whether, not to be sure if; *ne ~ de rien*, to be completely self-assured; **se ~** *v.refl.* to suspect (*de qch.*, sth.); *il ne se doute de rien*, he suspects nothing, he has no idea of what is going on.
douteu-r, -se [dutœr] *s.m.f.* doubter.
douteu-x, -se [dutø] *adj.* doubtful, ambiguous, uncertain, dubious, questionable; suspect, suspicious (arousing suspicion).
douvain [duvɛ̃] *s.m.* strip (of oak, etc.) for making stave.
douve[1] [duv] *s.f.* **1.** moat, ditch, trench; (steeplechasing) water-jump; **2.** stave (of cask).
douve[2] [duv] *s.f.* (zool.) flatworm; (vet.) *~ du foie*, liver fluke.
Douvres [duvr] *s.m.* (geog.) Dover.
dou-x, -ce [du] *adj.* sweet, soft, mild, easy, gentle, smooth, dulcet, bland; (of water) fresh, not salt; (of wine) not dry, sweet; *adv.* (fam.) *filer ~x*, to be submissive and obedient; *tout ~x!*, gently!, take it easy!; (fam.) *en ~ce*, unobtrusively, quietly.
douzain [duzɛ̃] *s.m.* twelve-line stanza.
douzaine [duzɛn] *s.f.* dozen; about twelve; *vendus à la ~*, sold by the dozen; *un enfant d'une ~ d'années*, a child of about twelve.
douze [duz] *adj.*, *s.m.* twelve, twelfth.
douzième [duzjɛm] *adj.*, *s.m.f.* twelfth; **~ment** [duzjɛmmɑ̃] *adv.* twelfthly.
doyen, -ne [dwajɛ̃] *s.m.f.* **1.** dean (of chapter, of faculty); doyen (of diplomatic corps), doyenne; **2.** senior (in rank or age), eldest.
doyenné [dwajene] *s.m.* **1.** deanship, deanery; **2.** doyenne pear.
doyenneté [dwajɛnte] *s.f.* (obs.) seniority.
dracéna [drasena] *s.m.* (bot.) dracaena.
drachme [drakm(ə)] *s.f.* **1.** drachm, dram; **2.** drachma.
draconien, -ne [drakɔnjɛ̃] *adj.* Draconian, cruel, strict, rigorous.
drag [drag] *s.m.* **1.** drag-hunt; **2.** drag (carriage).
dragage [dragaʒ] *s.m.* dredging; dragging (of river, etc.).

dragée[1] [draʒe] *s.f.* **1.** sugared almond; (pharm.) sugar-coated pill; *tenir la ~ haute à qn.*, to make s.o. wait a long time, to make s.o. pay dearly, for what he wants; **2.** small shot.
dragée[2] [draʒe] *s.f.* (agric.) crop grown for winter fodder.
dragéifier [draʒeife] *v.t.* to coat (a pill).
drageoir [draʒwar] *s.m.* (obs.) box, etc., for sweets.
drageon [draʒɔ̃] *s.m.* (hort.) sucker.
dragon [dragɔ̃] *s.m.* **1.** dragon; **2.** (mil.) dragoon.
dragonnade [dragɔnad] *s.f.* (hist.) dragonnade.
dragonne [dragɔn] *s.f.* sword-knot; umbrella--cord.
dragonnier [dragɔnje] *s.m.* (bot.) dragon-tree.
drague [drag] *s.f.* drag-net, drag; dredger; (nav.) sweep (for clearing mines).
draguer [drage] *v.t.* **1.** to fish with drag-net (for shell-fish); **2.** to dredge, to drag; (nav.) to sweep (sea for mines); **3.** (fig., fam.) to look for girls to pick up.
dragueur [dragœr] *s.m.* **1.** dredger (boat or man); **2.** mine-sweeper; **3.** (fig., fam.) young man looking for girls to pick up.
draille [drɑj] *s.f.* (naut.) stay.
drain [drɛ̃] *s.m.* land drain; (surg.) drainage tube.
drainage [drɛnaʒ] *s.m.* drainage, draining; tapping (of capital, etc.).
draine, drenne [drɛn] *s.f.* (ornith.) missel--thrush.
drainer [drene] *v.t.* to drain; (lit. & fig.) to drain, or siphon, off.
draisine [drɛzin] *s.f.* (rail.) rail-car (as used for track maintenance).
dramatique [dramatik] *adj.* dramatic; theatrical; **~ment** [dramatikmɑ̃] *adv.* dramatically.
dramatisation [dramatizɑsjɔ̃] *s.f.* dramatization.
dramatiser [dramatize] *v.t.* to dramatize.
dramaturge [dramatyrʒ] *s.m.* dramatist, playwright.
dramaturgie [dramatyrʒi] *s.f.* dramaturgy.
drame [dram] *s.m.* drama; play (usu. serious); (fig.) tragedy, drama.
drap [dra] *s.m.* **1.** (woollen) cloth; **2.** (bed-)-sheet; (fig.) *mettre qn. dans de beaux ~s*, to leave s.o. in a fine mess.
drapé, -e [drape] *adj.* draped, covered with cloth, draped in black (for mourning); *~ s.m.* drape, hang, (of garment).
drapeau (pl. **-x**) [drapo] *s.m.* flag; (regimental, etc.) colour; *être sous les ~x*, to be in the forces, to have joined the colours; *se ranger sous les ~x de*, to join the army of, (fig.) to side with.
drapement [drapmɑ̃] *s.m.* draping.
draper [drape] *v.t.* **1.** (techn.) to tease, to dress, (cloth); **2.** to drape (s.o. or sth.); **se ~** *v.refl.* to drape oneself; (fig.) to attitudinize.
draperie [drapri] *s.f.* **1.** textile mill; textile trade; **2.** drapery.
drapi-er, -ère [drapje] *s.m.f.* textile manufacturer or merchant; draper.
drastique [drastik] *adj.* (med.) *purgatif, remède, ~*, drastic purge, remedy; ⚠ used only in medicine.
drave [drav] *s.f.* (bot.) whitlow grass.
dravidien, -ne [dravidjɛ̃] *adj., s.m.f.* (geog., lang.) Dravidian.
drawback [drobak] *s.m.* (comm.) drawback; ⚠ not 'drawback' in sense 'disadvantage'.
drayage [drɛjaʒ] *s.m.* (tanning) fleshing.
drayer [dreje] *v.t.* (tanning) to flesh.
drayoire [drɛjwar] *s.f.* (tanning) fleshing-iron.
drêche [drɛʃ] *s.f.* (brewing) draff, brewer's grains.
drège[1] [drɛʒ] *s.f.* (fish.) dredge, drag-net.
drège[2] [drɛʒ] *s.f.* (text.) ripple.
drelin [drəlɛ̃] *s.m.* (noise of bell) ting-a-ling, tinkle.
drenne see DRAINE.
Dresde [drɛzd] *s.f.* (geog.) Dresden.
dressage [drɛsaʒ] *s.m.* **1.** setting up, erecting, pitching (of tent, etc.); **2.** training (of animal); breaking in (of horse); (horsemanship) dressage.
dresser [drese] *v.t.* **1.** to set up, to erect; *chien qui dresse les oreilles*, dog which pricks up its ears; *~ une échelle contre un mur*, to lean a ladder against a wall; **2.** to draw up (plan, etc.); **3.** to dress (stone, plank, etc.); **4.** to train (animal).
dresseu-r, -se [drɛsœr] *s.m.f.* animal tamer or trainer; *~r de chiens*, dog-trainer.
dressoir [drɛswar] *s.m.* (furniture) dresser.
dreyfusard [drɛfyzar] *s.m.* (Fr. hist.) supporter of Dreyfus.
dribbler [drible] *v.t.i.* (football, etc.) to dribble.
drift [drift] *s.m.* (geol.) drift.
drill [drij] *s.m.* (zool.) drill.
drille[1] [drij] *s.m.* **1.** (obs.) tramp, vagrant; **2.** *un joyeux ~*, a cheery fellow.
drille[2] [drij] *s.f.* (techn.) drill.
driller [drije] *v.t.* (techn.) to drill.
dring [driŋ] *s.m.* ting-a-ling, tinkle, (esp. of electric bell).
drisse [dris] *s.f.* (naut.) halyard, halliard.
drive [drajv] *s.m.* (tennis) drive.
drogman [drɔgmɑ̃] *s.m.* (obs.) dragoman.
drogue [drɔg] *s.f.* **1.** (obs.) pharmaceutical ingredient; nostrum; **2.** (narcotic) drug.
drogué, -e [drɔge] *s.m.f.* drug addict.
droguer [drɔge] *v.t.* to administer medicine to; **se ~** *v.refl.* **1.** to dose oneself (with medicine); **2.** to take (narcotic) drugs, to drug.
droguerie [drɔgri] *s.f.* chemist's shop.
droguet [drɔgɛ] *s.m.* (text.) **1.** (obs.) drugget; **2.** furnishing brocade.
droguiste [drɔgist] *s.m.f.* druggist, chemist.
droit [drwa] *s.m.* **1.** right; *à bon ~*, rightly, legitimately; *avoir ~ à qch.*, to have a right to sth.; *être en ~ de faire qch.*, to have a right to do sth.; *~s de l'homme*, human rights; *~s de reproduction*, copyright; **2.** due, duty, tax; *~s de douane*, customs duty; *~s d'auteur*, royalties; **3.** law; *faire son ~*, to study law; *de ~*, as of right, by right; *à qui de ~*, to whom it may concern; *responsable en ~*, responsible in law.
droit, -e [drwa] *adj.* straight, direct, upright; right(-hand); (fig.) honest, upright; *rive ~e*, right bank (of river); (geom.) *angle ~*, right angle; *~ adv.* straight; *aller tout ~*, to go straight on (ahead); (fig.) *marcher ~*, to be well-behaved, obedient; **~e** *s.f.* right; right hand; (geom.) straight line; (pol.) right (wing); *tenir, garder, sa ~e*, to keep to the right; **~ement** [drwatmɑ̃] *adv.* rightly, fairly, justly.
droiti-er, -ère [drwatje] *adj., s.m.f.* **1.** right--handed (person); **2.** (pol.) (member of) right wing.
droiture [drwatyr] *s.f.* uprightness, honesty, probity.
drolatique [drɔlatik] *adj.* droll, humorous.
drôle [drol] *adj.* **1.** amusing, funny, comic, droll; **2.** strange, odd; *un ~ d'instrument*, a strange instrument; *la ~ de guerre*, the 'phoney' war (1939–40); *~ s.m.* (obs.) rogue; (in S. of France) youngster, boy; **~ment** [drolmɑ̃] *adv.* strangely, oddly; exceedingly.
drôlerie [drolri] *s.f.* drollery, fun; buffoonery.
drôlesse [drolɛs] *s.f.* (obs.) shameless, contemptible woman, hussy.
dromadaire [drɔmadɛr] *s.m.* (zool.) dromedary.
drome [drom] *s.f.* **1.** (naut.) spare masts, etc.; **2.** (naut.) ship's boats; **3.** main beam (of forge hammer).
dronte [drɔ̃t] *s.m.* (ornith.) dodo.

drop [drɔp], **drop-goal** [drɔpgol] *s.m.* (Rugby football) drop-goal, dropped goal.
droséra [drozera] *s.m.* (bot.) sundew.
drosophile [drozɔfil] *s.f.* (ent.) drosophila, fruit-fly.
drosse [drɔs] *s.f.* (naut.) tiller-rope, rudder-chain.
drosser [drɔse] *v.t.* (naut.) (of current, etc.) to drive (ship) off course.
dru, -e [dry] *adj.* thick, thick-set, bushy; ~ *adv.* hard, fast, thickly; *la pluie tombe* ~, it is raining hard.
druide [drɥid] *s.m.* **druidesse** [drɥidɛs] *s.f.* Druid, Druidess.
druidique [drɥidik] *adj.* Druidic(al).
druidisme [drɥidism] *s.m.* Druidism.
drumlin [drœmlin] *s.m.* (geol.) drum, drumlin.
drupe [dryp] *s.f.* (bot.) drupe.
dryade [drijad] *s.f.* **1.** (myth.) dryad; **2.** (bot.) mountain avens.
du see DE.
dû, due [dy] *adj.* owed, owing, due; (law) *en bonne et due forme*, in due and proper form; ~ *s.m.* due.
dualisme [dɥalism] *s.m.* dualism.
dualiste [dɥalist] *adj., s.m.f.* dualist.
dualité [dɥalite] *s.f.* duality.
dubitati-f, -ve [dybitatif] *adj.* dubitative, hesitant; **~vement** [dybitativmɑ̃] *adv.* in a doubtful tone.
duc [dyk] *s.m.* duke; (ornith.) horned owl; *grand* ~, eagle-owl; *petit* ~, scops (owl).
ducal, -e, (aux) [dykal] *adj.* ducal.
ducat [dyka] *s.m.* ducat (coin).
duché [dyʃe] *s.m.* duchy, dukedom.
duchesse [dyʃɛs] *s.f.* duchess.
ducroire [dykrwar] *s.m.* (comm.) del credere, guarantee commission.
ductile [dyktil] *adj.* ductile.
ductilité [dyktilite] *s.f.* ductility.
duègne [dɥɛɲ] *s.f.* (obs.) duenna.
duel[1] [dɥɛl] *s.m.* duel, duelling.
duel[2] [dɥɛl] *adj., s.m.* (gram.) dual (number).
duelliste [dɥelist] *s.m.* duellist.
duettiste [dɥetist] *s.m.f.* duettist.
duffel-coat [dœfœlkot] *s.m.* duffle-coat, duffel-coat.
dugon [dygɔ̃], **dugong** [dygɔ̃(g)] *s.m.* (zool.) dugong.
duite [dɥit] *s.f.* (text.) weft-yarn.
dulcinée [dylsine] *s.f.* (jest) Dulcinea, inamorata, lady-love.
dulie [dyli] *s.f.* (Cath.) dulia.
dûment [dymɑ̃] *adv.* (law) duly, in due form.
dumping [dœmpiŋ; dœ̃piŋ] *s.m.* (econ.) dumping.
dundee [dœndi] *s.m.* (naut.) ketch.
dune [dyn] *s.f.* dune.
dunette [dynɛt] *s.f.* (naut.) poop(-deck).
Dunkerque [dœ̃kɛrk] *s.m.* (geog.) Dunkirk.
duo [dɥo] *s.m.* duet, duo; (fam.) ~ *d'injures*, exchange of insults.
duodécimal, -e, (aux) [dɥɔdesimal] *adj.* duodecimal.
duodénal, -e, (aux) [dɥɔdenal] *adj.* (anat.) duodenal.
duodénite [dɥɔdenit] *s.f.* (med.) duodenitis.
duodénum [dɥɔdenɔm] *s.m.* (anat.) duodenum.
duodi [dɥɔdi] *s.m.* (hist.) Duodi.
duopole [dɥɔpɔl] *s.m.* (econ.) duopoly.
dupe [dyp] *s.f.* dupe; ~ *adj.* duped, cheated, taken in.
duper [dype] *v.t.* to dupe, to take in, to cheat.
duperie [dypri] *s.f.* dupery, deception.
dupeu-r, -se [dypœr] *s.m.f.* (obs.) duper, trickster.
duplex [dyplɛks] *s.m.* **1.** (teleph.) duplex (system); **2.** maisonette.
duplicata [dyplikata] *s.m.invar.* (law, admin.) exact copy, facsimile.
duplicateur [dyplikatœr] *s.m.* duplicator.
duplication [dyplikɑsjɔ̃] *s.f.* **1.** duplication; **2.** = DUPLEX 1.
duplicité [dyplisite] *s.f.* duplicity, double-dealing.
duquel see LEQUEL.
dur, -e [dyr] *adj.* hard, firm, tough; hardened, hard-hearted, unfeeling, severe, harsh, rough, austere; ~ *adv.* (fam.) hard; ~ *s.m.* **1.** (pop.) tough customer; **2.** *bâtiment en* ~, permanent building; *un verre de* ~, a glass of the hard stuff (brandy); (pop.) *prendre le* ~, to take the train; **~e** *s.f. à la ~e*, the hard way; *coucher sur la ~e*, to sleep rough; *en voir de ~es*, to have a rough time.
durabilité [dyrabilite] *s.f.* durability.
durable [dyrabl] *adj.* durable; **~ment** [dyrabləmɑ̃] *adv.* durably, lastingly.
duralumin [dyralymɛ̃] *s.m.* Duralumin (proprietary name).
duramen [dyramɛn] *s.m.* (bot.) duramen.
durant [dyrɑ̃] *prep.* during; ~ *sa vie*, during his lifetime; while he was (is) alive; *sa vie* ~, for life; as long as he lives (lived); *parler une heure* ~, to talk for an hour; (obs.) ~ *que*, while.
durati-f, -ve [dyratif] *adj.* (gram.) durative.
durcir [dyrsir] *v.t.i.* to harden, to stiffen; to toughen, to get hard.
durcissement [dyrsismɑ̃] *s.m.* hardening.
durée [dyre] *s.f.* duration, continuance; *de longue* ~, lasting; (of gramophone record) long-playing; *bonheur de courte* ~, short-lived happiness.
durement [dyrmɑ̃] *adv.* severely, harshly, rigorously, roughly.
dure-mère [dyrmɛr] *s.f.* (anat.) dura mater.
durer [dyre] *v.i.* to last, to endure, to hold out, to subsist, to continue, to go on and on.
dureté [dyrte] *s.f.* hardness, firmness, toughness, harshness, severity, hard-heartedness; (pl.) (obs.) hard words.
durillon [dyrijɔ̃] *s.m.* (physiol.) callosity, callus, hard skin.
durion [dyrjɔ̃] *s.m.* (bot.) durian.
duumvir [dyɔmvir] *s.m.* (Rom. hist.) duumvir; **~at** [dyɔmvira] *s.m.* duumvirate.
duvet [dyvɛ] *s.m.* **1.** down; **2.** (continental) quilt, duvet.
duveté, -e [dyvte] *adj.* downy, velvety, silky.
(**se**) **duveter** [dyvte] *v.refl.* to become covered with down.
duveteu-x, -se [dyvtø] *adj.* downy, velvety.
dyke [dik; dajk] *s.m.* (geol.) dyke, dike.
dynamique [dinamik] *adj.* dynamic; ~ *s.f.* (sci.) dynamics; **~ment** [dinamikmɑ̃] *adv.* dynamically.
dynamisme [dinamism] *s.m.* dynamism.
dynamiste [dinamist] *s.m.f.* (phil.) dynamist.
dynamitage [dinamitaʒ] *s.m.* dynamiting.
dynamite [dinamit] *s.f.* dynamite.
dynamiter [dinamite] *v.t.* to dynamite, to blow up (with dynamite).
dynamiterie [dinamitri] *s.f.* dynamite factory.
dynamiteu-r, -se [dinamitœr] *s.m.f.* dynamiter.
dynamo [dinamo] *s.f.* dynamo; **~gène** [dinamɔʒɛn], **~génique** [dinamɔʒenik] *adj.* dynamogenous; **~génie** [dinamɔʒeni] *s.f.* dynamogeny; **~mètre** [dinamɔmɛtr] *s.m.* (phys.) dynamometer; **~métrique** [dinamɔmetrik] *adj.* dynamometric(al).
dynaste [dinast] *s.m.* dynast.
dynastie [dinasti] *s.f.* dynasty.
dynastique [dinastik] *adj.* dynastic.
dyne [din] *s.f.* (phys.) dyne.
dysenterie [disɑ̃tri] *s.f.* (med.) dysentery.

dysentérique [disɑ̃terik] *adj.* dysenteric.
dysfonctionnement [disfɔ̃ksjɔnmɑ̃] *s.m.* (med., psychol.) dysfunction.
dyslexie [dislɛksi] *s.f.* (med.) dyslexia.
dyslexique [dislɛksik] *adj.*, *s.m.f.* dyslexic, dyslectic (person).
dysménorrhée [dismenɔre] *s.f.* (med.) dysmenorrhoea.
dyspepsie [dispɛpsi] *s.f.* (med.) dyspepsia.
dyspepsique [dispɛpsik], **dyspeptique** [dispɛptik] *adj.* dyspeptic.
dyspnée [dispne] *s.f.* (med.) dispnoea.
dysprosium [disprozjɔm] *s.m.* (chem.) dysprosium.
dystrophie [distrɔfi] *s.f.* (med.) dystrophy.
dysurie [dizyri] *s.f.* (med.) dysuria.
dytique [ditik] *s.m.* (ent.) Dytiscus, water-beetle.

E

E, e [e, ə] *s.m.* the letter E, e.; abbrev. *Est.*
eau (pl. **-x**) [o] *s.f.* **1.** water; *~ de mer*, sea water; *~ douce*, fresh water; *~ potable*, drinking water; *~ bénite*, holy water; *~ de vaisselle*, dish-water; *cours d'~*, watercourse; *chute d'~*, waterfall; *nappe d'~*, sheet of water; *château d'~*, water tower, reservoir; *jet d'~*, fountain; (fig.) *être comme l'~ et le feu*, to be like oil and water; (fig.) *d'ici là il passera beaucoup d'~ sous les ponts*, a lot may happen between now and then; (fig.) *un coup d'épée dans l'~*, a vain attempt; *mettre de l'~ dans son vin*, (lit.) to water one's wine, (fig.) to come down a peg; *prendre les ~x*, to take the waters; *ville d'~x*, watering place, spa; **2.** stretch of water, sea; (pl.) wash (of a ship); *tomber, se jeter, à l'~*, to drown, (fig.) to take the plunge; *mettre un navire à l'~*, to launch a ship; (naut.) *faire ~*, to spring a leak; (fig.) *naviguer, être, dans les ~x de qn.*, to follow in someone's wake; *il n'est pire ~ que celle qui dort*, still waters run deep; **3.** *~ gazeuse*, *~ de Seltz*, soda water; *~ de Javel*, bleach; **4.** sweat, perspiration, saliva; *être tout en ~*, to be bathed in perspiration; (fig.) *suer sang et ~*, to sweat blood; *faire venir l'~ à la bouche*, to make one's mouth water; **5.** (of diamonds, etc.) water, lustre; (fig.) *de la plus belle ~*, of the first water.
eau-de-vie [odvi] *s.f.* spirit, brandy; liqueur made from various fruits and cereals.
eau-forte [ofɔrt] *s.f.* (chem.) aqua fortis, nitric acid; (art) etching; *graveur à l'~*, etcher.
eaux-vannes [ovan] *s.f.pl.* (techn.) liquid manure, sewage.
ébahir [ebair] *v.t.* to dumbfound, to amaze; **s'~** *v.refl.* to be amazed.
ébahissement [ebaismɑ̃] *s.m.* amazement, wonder.
ébarbage [ebarbaʒ] *s.m.* paring, filing, trimming.
ébarber [ebarbe] *v.t.* to pare, to file, to trim, to remove rough edges from.
ébarbeur [ebarbœr] *s.m.*, **ébarbeuse** [ebarbøz] *s.f.* (techn.) trimming machine.
ébarboir [ebarbwar] *s.m.* (techn.) trimmer, scraper (tool).
ébarbure [ebarbyr] *s.f.* (techn.) trimmings, filings, burr, outer leaves.
ébats [eba] *s.m.pl.* gambol(ling), frolic, revels; *prendre ses ~*, to disport oneself.
(**s'**)**ébattre** [ebatr] *v.refl.* to gambol, to frolic, to sport, to revel.
ébaubi, -e [ebobi] *adj.* (fam.) flabbergasted, amazed.
ébauchage [eboʃaʒ] *s.m.* sketching, outlining, roughing out.
ébauche [eboʃ] *s.f.* rough draft, outline, sketch; (fig.) *~ d'un sourire*, suspicion of a smile.
ébaucher [eboʃe] *v.t.* to rough-hew, to prepare (material); to outline, to sketch, to draft; **s'~** *v.refl.* to take shape, (fig.) to give a semblance of.
ébaucheur [eboʃœr] *s.m.* rough-hewer, rougher-out.
ébauchoir [eboʃwar] *s.m.* roughing chisel, boaster.
ébaudir [ebodir] *v.t.* (obs.) to enliven.
ébavurer [ebavyre] *v.t.* (techn.) to finish, to clean, to ream.
ébénacées [ebenase] *s.f.pl.* (bot.) Ebenaceae.
ébène [ebɛn] *s.f.* ebony; *noir d'~*, jet-black.
ébénier [ebenje] *s.m.* (bot.) ebony (tree); *faux ~*, laburnum.
ébéniste [ebenist] *s.m.* cabinet-maker.
ébénisterie [ebenist(ə)ri] *s.f.* cabinet-making.
éberlué, -e [ebɛrlɥe] *adj.* (fam.) flabbergasted, stunned.
éberluer [ebɛrlɥe] *v.t.* (obs.) to flabbergast, to stun.
éblouir [ebluir] *v.t.* to dazzle, to blind (with light); (fig.) (obs.) to fascinate, (mod.) to impress.
éblouissant, -e [ebluisɑ̃] *adj.* dazzling, blinding.
éblouissement [ebluismɑ̃] *s.m.* dazzling, glare; daze; (fig.) admiration, amazement; *avoir des ~s*, to have fits of giddiness.
ébonite [ebɔnit] *s.f.* ebonite, vulcanite.
éborgnage [ebɔrɲaʒ] *s.m.* (hort.) disbudding.
éborgner [ebɔrɲe] *v.t.* **1.** to make blind in one eye; **2.** (hort.) to disbud.
éboueur [ebwœr] *s.m.* scavenger, dustman.
ébouillanter [ebujɑ̃te] *v.t.* to scald; to blanch (vegetables).
éboulement [ebulmɑ̃] *s.m.* collapse, fall, landslide; débris.
ébouler [ebule] *v.t.* (rare) to knock down, to cause to collapse; *~ v.i.* to collapse, to fall down; **s'~** *v.refl.* to collapse.
éboulis [ebuli] *s.m.* débris, fallen earth; scree.
ébourgeonnage [eburʒɔnaʒ], **ébourgeonnement** [eburʒɔnmɑ̃] *s.m.* (hort.) disbudding.
ébourgeonner [eburʒɔne] *v.t.* (hort.) to disbud.
ébouriffant, -e [eburifɑ̃] *adj.* (fam.) startling, shocking, incredible.
ébouriffé, -e [eburife] *adj.* dishevelled, (of hair) ruffled.
ébouriffer [eburife] *v.t.* **1.** to ruffle (hair of); **2.** (fig., fam.) to shock, to startle.
ébourrer [ebure] *v.t.* (tanning) to unhair (hides).
ébouter [ebute] *v.t.* to cut the end off, to shorten.
ébranchage [ebrɑ̃ʃaʒ], **ébranchement** [ebrɑ̃ʃmɑ̃] *s.m.* lopping (of branch); (hort.) pruning.
ébrancher [ebrɑ̃ʃe] *v.t.* to lop; to prune.
ébranchoir [ebrɑ̃ʃwar] *s.m.* long-handled pruner.
ébranlement [ebrɑ̃lmɑ̃] *s.m.* shaking; (fig.) shakiness, insecurity; shock.
ébranler [ebrɑ̃le] *v.t.* to shake; to loosen; (fig.) to unsettle, to make insecure; **s'~** *v.refl.* to start to move, to set in motion.
ébrasement [ebrɑzmɑ̃] *s.m.* (arch.) splaying, splay (of window opening).

ébraser [ebrɑze] *v.t.* (arch.) to splay.
Èbre [ɛbr] *s.m.* (geog.) Ebro (river).
ébrécher [ebreʃe] *v.t.* to chip, to crack; (fig., fam.) to make a hole in.
ébréchure [ebreʃyr] *s.f.* chip.
ébriété [ebrijete] *s.f.* inebriety, drunkenness.
ébrouement [ebrumɑ̃] *s.m.* snort, snorting, whinnying, (of horse, etc.); flapping (of wings).
(s')ébrouer [ebrue] *v.refl.* **1.** (of horse, etc.) to snort, to whinny; **2.** to shake oneself.
ébruitement [ebrɥitmɑ̃] *s.m.* publishing, spreading (of rumour, etc.).
ébruiter [ebrɥite] *v.t.* to noise abroad, to report, to make known, to divulge.
ébulliomètre [ebyljɔmɛtr], **ébullioscope** [ebyljɔskɔp] *s.m.* ebullioscope.
ébulliométrie [ebyljɔmetri], **ébullioscopie** [ebyljɔskɔpi] *s.f.* ebullioscopy.
ébullition [ebylisjɔ̃] *s.f.* boiling, ebullition; (fig.) *en* ~, in a ferment.
éburné, -e [ebyrne], **éburnéen, -ne** [ebyrneɛ̃] *adj.* ivory-like.
écacher [ekaʃe] *v.t.* (obs.) to squash, to flatten.
écaillage [ekɑjaʒ] *s.m.* scaling (of fish, etc.); opening (of oysters); peeling (of paint, etc.).
écaille [ekɑj] *s.f.* **1.** scale; **2.** flake; **3.** (obs.) shell (of oyster or mussel); **4.** tortoise-shell.
écaillé, -e [ekɑje] *adj.* peeling, flaking.
écailler [ekɑje] *v.t.* **1.** to scale (fish); **2.** to open (oyster); **3.** to peel off (paint); **s'**~ *v.refl.* to peel off, to flake.
écaill-er, -ère [ekɑje] *s.m.f.* oyster seller.
écailleu-x, -se [ekɑjø] *adj.* scaly; (of slate) fissile.
écaillure [ekɑjyr] *s.f.* flake, scale.
écale [ekal] *s.f.* husk, shell.
écaler [ekale] *v.t.* to shell.
écalure [ekalyr] *s.f.* husk (of coffee bean, etc.).
écang [ekɑ̃] *s.m.* (text.) scutcher, scutch blade.
écanguer [ekɑ̃ge] *v.t.* (text.) to scutch (flax, etc.).
écarlate [ekarlat] *adj.*, *s.f.* scarlet.
écarquiller [ekarkije] *v.t.* to open (eyes) wide.
écart[1] [ekar] *s.m.* **1.** distance apart, space, stretch; *faire le grand* ~, to do the splits; *à l'*~, at a distance, on one side; *à l'*~ *de*, at some distance from; (fig.) *tenir qn. à l'*~, to keep s.o. at a distance; **2.** swerve, sidestep; variation, divergence, deviation, departure (from custom, etc.); error; (of horse) *faire un* ~, to shy; **3.** (admin.) isolated hamlet.
écart[2] [ekar] *s.m.* (cards) discard, discarded card; discarding.
écarté, -e [ekarte] *adj.* **1.** isolated, remote; **2.** wide apart.
écartelé, -e [ekartəle] *adj.* (herald.) quartered.
écartèlement [ekartɛlmɑ̃] *s.m.* quartering (torture); (fig.) being torn between two alternatives.
écarteler [ekartəle] *v.t.* to tear to pieces, to quarter; (fig.) to be tugging (at s.o.) in opposite directions.
écartelure [ekartəlyr] *s.f.* (herald.) quartering.
écartement [ekartəmɑ̃] *s.m.* break, parting; space, gap, distance between.
écarter [ekarte] *v.t.* **1.** to separate, to part; to open, to split; **2.** to remove to a distance, to put on one side; to dispel; to repulse; to avert; (fig.) to exclude; **3.** to deviate, to cause to deviate; **4.** (cards) to discard, to throw away; **s'**~ *v.refl.* to part, to disperse; to turn aside, to go astray; (fig.) *s'*~ *de*, to turn aside from, to abandon, to deviate from.
écarteur [ekartœr] *s.m.* **1.** (bullfighting) baiter; **2.** (med.) dilator.
ecce homo [ɛkseɔmo] *s.m.invar.* (art) Ecce Homo.
ecchymose [ekimoz] *s.f.* bruise.
ecclésiastique [eklezjastik] *adj.*, *s.m.* ecclesiastic.
écervelé, -e [esɛrvəle] *adj.* hare-brained, scatter-brained; *s.m.f.* madcap.
échafaud [eʃafo] *s.m.* **1.** (obs.) stage, platform; **2.** gallows, scaffold.
échafaudage [eʃafodaʒ] *s.m.* **1.** scaffolding; **2.** (lit. & fig.) structure (usu. flimsy); **3.** building--up.
échafauder [eʃafode] *v.i.* to erect scaffolding; ~ *v.t.* (fig.) to put together roughly, to string together.
échalas [eʃala] *s.m.* (hort.) stake, post, pole; (fig.) *sec, raide, comme un* ~, as thin as a beanpole.
échalasser [eʃalase] *v.t.* (hort.) to stake.
échalier [eʃalje] *s.m.* stile; hurdle.
échalote [eʃalɔt] *s.f.* shallot.
échancré, -e [eʃɑ̃kre] *adj.* V-shaped; indented, cut away.
échancrer [eʃɑ̃kre] *v.t.* to indent, to cut away, to erode.
échancrure [eʃɑ̃kryr] *s.f.* **1.** indentation; cut--out portion, opening (e.g. of armholes in garment); **2.** cleavage (between woman's breasts).
échange [eʃɑ̃ʒ] *s.m.* exchange; *en* ~, in exchange (*de*, for).
échangeable [eʃɑ̃ʒabl] *adj.* exchangeable.
échanger [eʃɑ̃ʒe] *v.t.* to exchange (*contre*, for).
échangeur [eʃɑ̃ʒœr] *s.m.* **1.** (techn.) heat--exchanger; **2.** (traffic) clover-leaf junction, interchange.
échangiste [eʃɑ̃ʒist] *s.m.f.* exchanger.
échanson [eʃɑ̃sɔ̃] *s.m.* (hist.) cup-bearer; (jest) dispenser of drinks.
échantillon [eʃɑ̃tijɔ̃] *s.m.* sample, specimen, model; (statistics) sample; *bois, brique, d'*~, wood, brick, of regulation pattern.
échantillonnage [eʃɑ̃tijɔnaʒ] *s.m.* (obs.) verification; (mod.) sampling.
échantillonner [eʃɑ̃tijɔne] *v.t.* (obs.) to verify; (mod.) to sample, to take samples of.
échantillonneu-r, -se [eʃɑ̃tijɔnœr] *s.m.f.* one who takes samples.
échappatoire [eʃapatwar] *s.f.* dodge, subterfuge, loophole.
échappé, -e [eʃape] *s.m.f.* (obs.) escapee, fugitive.
échappée [eʃape] *s.f.* **1.** (obs.) escapade; **2.** glimpse, view; (fig.) brief moment; **3.** turning space (for vehicles); headroom (on stairs, etc.); **4.** (cycle racing) break-away.
échappement [eʃapmɑ̃] *s.m.* **1.** (obs.) escape; **2.** (horol.) escapement; **3.** (car, etc.) exhaust.
échapper [eʃape] *v.i.* **1.** (obs.) to escape (from custody); ~ *à* or *de*, to escape from, to get away from; (mod.) ~ *à*, to escape, to slip (away) from, to avoid; not to be noticed by, to escape (one's) notice; *son nom m'échappe*, I don't recollect his name; *tout cela échappe à ma mémoire*, it has all gone from my mind; *rien ne lui échappe*, he doesn't miss a thing; *il lui a échappé que*, it escaped his notice that; **2.** to escape, to slip, to fall; ~ *des mains*, to slip from one's hands; *laisser* ~ *un cri*, to let out a cry; *laisser* ~ *qch.*, to let sth. drop; **3.** to be uttered or done involuntarily (*à qn.*, by s.o.); *des paroles amères lui sont échappées*, bitter words broke from his lips; *il m'est échappé de*, I so far forgot myself as to; ~ *v.t.* (obs.) to escape (from); (mod.) *l'*~ *belle*, to have a narrow escape; **s'**~ *v.refl.* to escape, to slip away, to flow away; to emerge; (obs.) to forget oneself.
écharde [eʃard] *s.f.* splinter, thorn.
échardonner [eʃardɔne] *v.t.* to clear of thistles.
écharnage [eʃarnaʒ] *s.m.* (tanning) fleshing (of hides).
écharner [eʃarne] *v.t.* (tanning) to flesh (hides).

écharnoir [eʃarnwar] *s.m.* (tanning) fleshing knife.
écharpe [eʃarp] *s.f.* **1.** (official) sash; scarf; **2.** (surg.) arm-sling; (techn.) sling; *en* ~, in a sling; aslant, sideways.
écharper [eʃarpe] *v.t.* to slash; to tear limb from limb; to lynch.
échasse [eʃɑs] *s.f.* **1.** stilt; **2.** (ornith.) stilt.
échassier [eʃɑsje] *s.m.* (ornith.) wading bird, wader; (pl.) (obs.) Grallatores.
échaudage [eʃodaʒ] *s.m.* (agric.) shrivelling (of cereals by sun).
échaudé [eʃode] *s.m.* a kind of cake.
échaudé, -e [eʃode] *adj.* **1.** (agric.) shrivelled; **2.** scalded; *chat ~ craint l'eau froide*, once bitten, twice shy.
échauder [eʃode] *v.t.* to scald; (fig.) *se faire* ~, *être échaudé*, to burn one's fingers.
échaudoir [eʃodwar] *s.m.* scalding vat.
échauffant, -e [eʃofɑ̃] *adj.* (of food) heating; binding, causing constipation.
échauffement [eʃofmɑ̃] *s.m.* heating, over-heating; (obs.) mild constipation; (fig.) over--excitement.
échauffer [eʃofe] *v.t.* to heat, to overheat; (fig.) to excite, to rouse; *~ la bile, les oreilles, à qn.*, to annoy s.o.; **s'~** *v.refl.* (obs.) to become heated; (sport) to warm up; (fig.) to become excited.
échauffourée [eʃofure] *s.f.* skirmish, scuffle.
échauguette [eʃoget] *s.f.* (arch.) pepper-pot turret; (fort.) watch-tower.
èche, esche, aiche [ɛʃ] *s.f.* bait (for fishing).
échéance [eʃeɑ̃s] *s.f.* maturity (of bill, etc.), term, completion; *à longue, à courte*, ~, long term, short term.
échéancier [eʃeɑ̃sje] *s.m.* register of bills (receivable or payable).
échéant, e [eʃeɑ̃] *adj.* **1.** maturing, falling due; **2.** arising; *le cas* ~, should the occasion arise, if necessary.
échec [eʃɛk] *s.m.* check, failure; (pl.) chess; set of chessmen; *~ et mat*, checkmate.
échelette [eʃlɛt] *s.f.* **1.** rack (on pack saddle); rail (of cart); **2.** (ornith.) creeper.
échelle [eʃɛl] *s.f.* **1.** ladder; *~ d'incendie*, fire escape; (lit. & fig.) *faire la courte ~ à qn.*, to give s.o. a leg up; (fig.) *après lui, il faut, il n'y a plus qu'à, tirer l'~*, no one can do better than he; (fig.) *monter à l'~*, to rise to the bait; **2.** scale, graduation; level; *carte à grande* ~, large-scale map; *~ mobile*, sliding scale; *à l'~ nationale*, on the national level.
échelon [eʃlɔ̃] *s.m.* rung, step, (of ladder); (fig.) step, grade, rank, echelon.
échelonnement [eʃlɔnmɑ̃] *s.m.* echelonning, spacing out, spreading out, staggering.
échelonner [eʃlɔne] *v.t.* to echelon; to space out.
échenill-age [ɛʃnijaʒ] *s.m.* removal of grubs, caterpillars, etc.; **~er** [ɛʃnije] *v.t.* to rid of grubs, caterpillars, etc.; (fig.) to prune, to cleanse; **~oir** [ɛʃnijwar] *s.m.* long-handled pruner (for removing grubs, etc.).
écheveau (pl. **-x**) [ɛʃvo] *s.m.* skein, hank; (fig.) web, tangled skein.
échevelé, -e [eʃəvle] *adj.* dishevelled; (fig.) wild, frenzied.
écheveler [eʃəvle] *v.t.* to dishevel; to tangle.
échevette [ɛʃvɛt] *s.f.* (text.) lea.
échevin [ɛʃvɛ̃] *s.m.* deputy burgomaster (in Netherlands, Belgium); alderman.
échevinage [ɛʃvinaʒ] *s.m.* office of *échevin*; body of *échevins*.
échidné [ekidne] *s.m.* (zool.) echidna.
échiffre [eʃifr] *s.m.* (constr.) string-wall (of stair-case).
échine[1] [eʃin] *s.f.* spine, backbone; chine (of pork); (fig.) *courber, plier, l'~*, to submit.
échine[2] [eʃin] *s.f.* (arch.) echinus.
échiner [eʃine] *v.t.* (obs.) to break the back of, to kill; **s'~** *v.refl.* to work oneself to death.
échino-cactus [ekinɔkaktys] *s.m.* (bot.) Echino-cactus; **~coque** [ekinɔkɔk] *s.m.* (med.) echino-coccus; **~derme** [ekinɔdɛrm] *s.m.* (zool.) echinoderm; (pl.) Echinodermata.
échiqueté, -e [eʃikte] *adj.* (herald.) chequered.
échiquier [eʃikje] *s.m.* **1.** (lit. & fig.) chessboard; *en* ~, in squares, (herald.) chequered; **2.** Exchequer.
écho [eko] *s.m.* **1.** echo; *à tous les ~s*, in all directions; **2.** rumour; news item; (pl.) gossip column (of newspaper); *se faire l'~ d'un bruit*, to spread a rumour.
échoir [eʃwar] *v.i.* **1.** to fall due; **2.** to befall, to happen.
écholalie [ekɔlali] *s.f.* (psychol.) echolalia.
échoppe[1] [eʃɔp] *s.f.* (obs.) booth, stall.
échoppe[2] [eʃɔp] *s.f.* (techn.) burin, graver.
échopper [eʃɔpe] *v.t.* to engrave, to chisel.
échotier [ekɔtje] *s.m.* gossip writer (in news-paper).
échouage [eʃwaʒ] *s.m.* (naut.) being left high and dry, stranding, grounding.
échouement [eʃumɑ̃] *s.m.* (naut.) grounding, running aground.
échouer [eʃwe] *v.i.* **1.** (naut.) to run aground; (fig.) to come to rest, to land up; **2.** to fail; to come to nothing; ~ *v.t.* to run aground, to beach.
écimage [esimaʒ] *s.m.* polling, pollarding (of trees).
écimer [esime] *v.t.* to poll, to pollard (tree).
éclaboussement [eklabusmɑ̃] *s.m.* splashing, spattering.
éclabousser [eklabuse] *v.t.* to splash, to spatter; (fig.) to smear, to smirch.
éclaboussure [eklabusyr] *s.f.* splash, spatter; (fig.) smear, smirch.
éclair [eklɛr] *s.m.* **1.** lightning, flash of lightning; *avec la rapidité de l'~*, as quick as lightning; *en* ~, in a flash; (fam. in apposition) *visite* ~, lightning visit; *fermeture* ~, zip fastener; *guerre* ~, blitz-krieg; **2.** flash, spark; (fig.) *~ de génie*, flash of genius; **3.** (cook.) éclair.
éclairage [eklɛraʒ] *s.m.* lighting, illumination; light.
éclairant, -e [eklɛrɑ̃] *adj.* lighting, illuminating; (fig.) enlightening.
éclaircie [eklɛrsi] *s.f.* **1.** break (in clouds), bright period; **2.** clearing (in a wood); **3.** (hort.) thinning out (of fruit).
éclaircir [eklɛrsir] *v.t.* **1.** to lighten, to brighten; **2.** to thin (hair, liquids); **3.** to enlighten (s.o.), to throw light on (sth.); **s'~** *v.refl.* **1.** to become clearer, to become brighter; **2.** to become less dense.
éclaircissage [eklɛrsisaʒ] *s.m.* **1.** (rare) glass polishing; **2.** (hort.) thinning out (of fruit).
éclaircissement [eklɛrsismɑ̃] *s.m.* explanation, elucidation.
éclaire [eklɛr] *s.f.* (bot.) celandine.
éclairé, -e [eklere] *adj.* lighted; (fig.) en-lightened.
éclairement [eklɛrmɑ̃] *s.m.* **1.** brightening; (fig.) enlightenment; **2.** (phys.) degree of illumination.
éclairer [eklere] *v.t.* **1.** to give light to, to light (up), to lighten; **2.** to enlighten (s.o.), to shed light on (sth.); **3.** (mil.) to reconnoitre; ~ *v.i.* to give light.
éclaireu-r, -se [eklɛrœr] *s.m.f.* **1.** (mil.) scout; *avion ~r*, reconnaissance plane; **2.** Scout, Guide.
éclairiste [eklɛrist] *s.m.* lighting specialist.
éclampsie [eklɑ̃psi] *s.f.* (med.) eclampsia.
éclanche [eklɑ̃ʃ] *s.f.* (obs.) shoulder of mutton.
éclat [ekla] *s.m.* **1.** splinter, fragment; *en ~s*, in pieces; **2.** crash, clap, peal (of thunder); burst

(of laughter); (fig.) scandal; *rire aux ~s*, to roar with laughter; **3.** brightness, dazzling light; freshness (of colour); brilliance, splendour; *action d'~*, remarkable feat; *coup d'~*, master stroke.

éclatant, -e [eklatɑ̃] *adj.* **1.** piercing, loud; **2.** bright, brilliant, dazzling, radiant; **3.** (fig.) striking; obvious.

éclatement [eklatmɑ̃] *s.m.* bursting, explosion; (of tyre) burst; rupture, breaking up.

éclater [eklate] *v.t.* **1.** (obs.) to break; **2.** (hort.) to divide (a plant); ~ *v.i.* **1.** to burst, to explode; **2.** to break out, to burst out; to show itself, to manifest itself, to become evident; ~ *de rire*, to burst out laughing; **3.** (obs.) to shine, to sparkle.

éclateur [eklatœr] *s.m.* (electr.) spark-gap.

éclectique [eklɛktik] *adj.* eclectic.

éclectisme [eklɛktism] *s.m.* eclecticism.

éclimètre [eklimɛtr] *s.m.* clinometer.

éclipse [eklips] *s.f.* (lit. & fig.) eclipse; (fam.) disappearance; *à ~s*, intermittent; (of light) occulting.

éclipser [eklipse] *v.t.* to eclipse; (fig.) to eclipse, to outdo, to put in the shade; **s'~** *v.refl.* to be eclipsed; (fam.) to disappear.

écliptique [ekliptik] *adj., s.f.* ecliptic.

éclisse [eklis] *s.f.* **1.** wedge (of wood); **2.** (rail.) fishplate; **3.** (med.) splint; **4.** wicker, wicker mat.

éclisser [eklise] *v.t.* **1.** (med.) to splint, to put into splint(s); **2.** (rail.) to assemble (with fishplates).

éclopé, -e [eklɔpe] *adj.* lame, crippled, limping; *s.m.f.* cripple.

éclore [eklɔr] *v.i.* **1.** to hatch (out), to be hatched, to come out of the egg; **2.** (of flower) to open, to bloom; **3.** (fig.) to dawn, to appear.

éclosion [eklozjɔ̃] *s.f.* **1.** hatching (of eggs); **2.** opening (of buds); **3.** (fig.) dawn, appearance, birth.

éclusage [eklyzaʒ] *s.m.* (techn.) taking a boat through a lock.

écluse [eklyz] *s.f.* lock; (fig.) floodgate.

éclusée [eklyze] *s.f.* lockful (of water).

écluser [eklyze] *v.t.* **1.** to build a lock on (river, canal); **2.** to take a boat through a lock; **3.** (pop.) to drink.

éclusi-er, -ère [eklyzje] *s.m.f.* lock-keeper.

écobuage [ekɔbɥaʒ] *s.m.* (agric.) fertilizing by burning stubble.

écobuer [ekɔbɥe] *v.t.* (agric.) to fertilize by burning stubble.

écœurant, -e [ekœrɑ̃] *adj.* (lit. & fig.) sickening, nauseating; pathetic, disheartening.

écœurement [ekœrmɑ̃] *s.m.* (lit. & fig.) sickness, nausea; discouragement.

écœurer [ekœre] *v.t.* (lit. & fig.) to sicken, to nauseate; to discourage, to demoralize.

écoinçon [ekwɛ̃sɔ̃] *s.m.* corner-piece, corner--stone (of wall); *en ~*, (of piece of furniture) corner-(cupboard, chair).

école [ekɔl] *s.f.* **1.** school (esp. primary), college (establishment of higher education); (art, Lit.) school, movement, group; ~ *maternelle*, infant school; *faire ~*, to found a school (of thought, etc.), to attract adherents; (fam.) to become a fashion; **2.** training, drill; schooling, education; (fig.) school (in which one learns by experience); *vaisseau ~*, training ship; *avoir de l'~*, to be well trained; *avoir été à rude ~*, to have learnt the the hard way.

écoli-er, -ère [ekɔlje] *s.m.f.* (obs.) student; (mod.) (primary) schoolboy, schoolgirl, pupil; learner, beginner; *papier ~er*, ruled exercise--paper.

écolog-ie [ekɔlɔʒi] *s.f.* ecology; **~ique** [ekɔlɔʒik] *adj.* ecological; **~iste** [ekɔlɔʒist] *s.m.f.* ecologist.

éconduire [ekɔ̃dɥir] *v.t.* **1.** to dismiss, to turn away; **2.** to show out.

économat [ekɔnɔma] *s.m.* **1.** bursary, bursar's office; **2.** stores (for staff of factory); **3.** cut-price multiple store (= Co-op).

économe [ekɔnɔm] *s.m.* bursar, steward; ~ *adj.* economical, thrifty; (fig.) *être ~ de*, to be sparing with.

économétrie [ekɔnɔmetri] *s.f.* econometrics.

économie [ekɔnɔmi] *s.f.* **1.** economy; (obs.) management; **2.** economy, thrift, saving; (pl.) savings (money); *une ~ de bouts de chandelle*, a cheese-paring policy.

économique [ekɔnɔmik] *adj.* **1.** economic; **2.** economical, cheap; ~ *s.f.* economics; **~ment** [ekɔnɔmikmɑ̃] *adv.* economically; *les ~ment faibles*, those in low income brackets.

économiser [ekɔnɔmize] *v.t.* **1.** to use sparingly, to save; **2.** to save, to put by.

économiseur [ekɔnɔmizœr] *s.m.* (techn.) fuel economiser.

économiste [ekɔnɔmist] *s.m.f.* economist.

écope [ekɔp] *s.f.* (naut.) bailer, scoop.

écoper [ekɔpe] *v.t.* **1.** (naut.) to bail (out); **2.** (obs. exc. pop.) to drink; **3.** (fam.) to catch, to collect; to get caught, to cop it.

écoperche [ekɔpɛrʃ] *s.f.* scaffold pole.

écorçage [ekɔrsaʒ] *s.m.* barking (of tree).

écorce [ekɔrs] *s.f.* bark (of tree); cortex, rind, peel; (geol.) *l'~ terrestre*, the earth's crust; (fig.) appearance, exterior; *il ne faut pas juger de l'arbre par l'~*, one shouldn't judge by appearances.

écorcer [ekɔrse] *v.t.* to bark (tree), to peel, to husk, to decorticate.

écorché [ekɔrʃe] *s.m.* (art) écorché.

écorchement [ekɔrʃəmɑ̃] *s.m.* skinning (of animal), flaying.

écorcher [ekɔrʃe] *v.t.* **1.** to skin (animal), to flay; *il crie avant qu'on l'écorche*, he screams before he's hurt; **2.** to graze (one's knee, etc.); to grate on (the ear); to sting (the throat); **3.** (fig.) to murder (a language); to sting, to fleece, (a customer).

écorcherie [ekɔrʃəri] *s.f.* skinning-room (in abattoir).

écorcheur [ekɔrʃœr] *s.m.* skinner; (fig.) twister, swindler, extortioner.

écorchure [ekɔrʃyr] *s.f.* graze, scratch.

écorner [ekɔrne] *v.t.* **1.** (rare) to poll (cattle); **2.** to chip the corner of; to dog-ear (book); (fig.) to make a hole in.

écornifler [ekɔrnifle] *v.t.* (fam.) to cadge, to scrounge.

écornifleu-r, -se [ekɔrniflœr] *s.m.f.* parasite, scrounger, sponger.

écornure [ekɔrnyr] *s.f.* broken corner, chip.

écossais, -e [ekɔsɛ] *adj.* **1.** Scotch, Scottish; **2.** tartan; *s.m.f.* Scotsman, Scotswoman; ~ *s.m.* **1.** (lang.) Gaelic; **2.** tartan cloth.

Écosse [ekɔs] *s.f.* (geog.) Scotland; *Nouvelle-~*, Nova Scotia.

écosser [ekɔse] *v.t.* to shell, to husk; (pop.) to spend (money), to shell out.

écosystème [ekɔsistɛm] *s.m.* (biol.) ecosystem.

écot[1] [eko] *s.m.* share (of bill), whack.

écot[2] [eko] *s.m.* snag (on tree), stump (left by lopping).

écoté, -e [ekɔte] *adj.* (herald.) lopped.

écoulement [ekulmɑ̃] *s.m.* **1.** flow, flowing; drainage; **2.** passage, movement; **3.** (comm.) outlet.

écouler [ekule] *v.t.* to pass, to dispose of, to sell; **s'~** *v.refl.* to flow, to pass, to disappear.

écourter [ekurte] *v.t.* to shorten; to dock (horse or dog); to curtail, to cut down.

écoute[1] [ekut] *s.f.* (naut.) sheet, rigging.

écoute[2] [ekut] *s.f.* **1.** (obs.) sentinel; (obs.) watch; (mod.) *être aux ~s*, to eavesdrop, (fig.) to be on the watch (*de*, for); (mil.) *poste d'~*, listening-post; **2.** (radio, telephone) listening-

(-in); *être, rester, à l'~*, to be listening-in, to listen; *ne quittez pas l'~*, don't switch off (radio), don't ring off, hold on; **3.** (pl.) ears (of wild boar).

écouter [ekute] *v.t.* to listen (to), to heed; to pay attention (to), to hear; **s'~** *v.refl.* to like the sound of one's own voice; to follow one's own inclination; to be preoccupied with one's health.

écouteu-r, -se [ekutœr] *s.m.f.* (rare) listener; **~r** *s.m.* (telephone) receiver, headphone, earphone.

écoutille [ekutij] *s.f.* (naut.) hatch(way).

écouvillon [ekuvijɔ̃] *s.m.* **1.** baker's long--handled oven-brush; **2.** rifle-cleaning brush; **3.** (med.) swab; **~nage** [ekuvijɔnaʒ] *s.m.* cleaning out (with brush); **~ner** [ekuvijɔne] *v.t.* to clean out (with brush).

écrabouillage [ekrabujaʒ], **écrabouillement** [ekrabujmɑ̃] *s.m.* (fam.) squashing, flattening.

écrabouiller [ekrabuje] *v.t.* (fam.) to squash to pulp, to flatten.

écran [ekrɑ̃] *s.m.* screen, firescreen; *l'~*, the cinema; *porter à l'~*, to screen; *le petit ~*, television, the box.

écrasant, -e [ekrɑzɑ̃] *adj.* (lit. & fig.) crushing, overwhelming.

écrasé, -e [ekrɑze] *adj.* squashed, flattened; (fam.) *les chiens ~s*, small news items (in press).

écrasement [ekrɑzmɑ̃] *s.m.* crushing, squashing.

écraser [ekrɑze] *v.t.* **1.** to crush, to squash; to overwhelm; (fig.) to dominate; to humiliate; **2.** to run over (with a vehicle); *se faire ~*, to get run over.

écraseu-r, -se [ekrɑzœr] *s.m.f.* (fam.) roadhog, bad driver.

écrémage [ekremaʒ] *s.m.* skimming; separating (milk).

écrémer [ekreme] *v.t.* to skim the cream off; (fig.) to cream off, to remove the best parts of; *lait écrémé*, skimmed milk.

écrémeuse [ekremøz] *s.f.* separator.

écrêtement [ekrɛtmɑ̃] *s.m.* levelling.

écrêter [ekrete] *v.t.* (artill.) to raze (fortification); to level (road); (agric.) to remove the tops of.

écrevisse [ekrəvis] *s.f.* **1.** crayfish, crawfish; **2.** blacksmith's tongs.

(**s'**)**écrier** [ekrije] *v.refl.* to cry out, to shout, to exclaim.

écrin [ekrɛ̃] *s.m.* casket, jewel case.

écrire [ekrir] *v.t.* to write, to write down; **s'~** *v.refl.* to be written; to be spelt.

écrit [ekri] *s.m.* writing, anything written, document; written part of exam.; *par ~*, in writing.

écrit, -e [ekri] *adj.* written.

écriteau (pl. **-x**) [ekrito] *s.m.* notice, placard, sign.

écritoire [ekritwar] *s.m.* writing case.

écriture [ekrityr] *s.f.* **1.** writing, handwriting; (Lit.) style; **2.** (pl.) documents, papers, account books; **3.** *l'Écriture*, Holy Writ.

écrivailler [ekrivɑje], **écrivasser** [ekrivase] *v.i.* (pej.) to scribble, to write worthless stuff.

écrivailleu-r, -se [ekrivɑjœr], **écrivassi-er, -ère** [ekrivasje] *s.m.f.* (pej.) scribbler, hack--writer.

écrivain [ekrivɛ̃] *s.m.* writer, author; (obs.) scribe; *~ public*, public letter-writer.

écrivasser see ÉCRIVAILLER.

écrivassi-er, -ère see ÉCRIVAILLEUR.

écrou[1] [ekru] *s.m.* (mech.) nut; *contre-~*, lock--nut; *~ à oreilles*, wing-nut.

écrou[2] [ekru] *s.m.* (law) custody; *levée d'~*, release (from prison).

écrouelles [ekruɛl] *s.f.pl.* (obs.) king's evil, scrofula.

écrouer [ekrue] *v.t.* to take into custody, to imprison.

écrouir [ekruir] *v.t.* (metall.) to hard-hammer, to forge cold.

écrouissage [ekruisaʒ] *s.m.* (metall.) cold forging.

écroulement [ekrulmɑ̃] *s.m.* (lit. & fig.) collapse, fall.

(**s'**)**écrouler** [ekrule] *v.refl.* (lit. & fig.) to collapse, to fall.

écroûter [ekrute] *v.t.* **1.** to remove the crust from; **2.** (agric.) to harrow.

écroûteuse [ekrutøz] *s.f.* (agric.) harrow.

écru, -e [ekry] *adj.* (text.) raw, unbleached, écru; *toile ~e*, holland.

ecthyma [ektima] *s.f.* (med.) ecthyma.

ectoderme [ektɔdɛrm] *s.m.* (biol.) ectoderm.

ectodermique [ektɔdɛrmik] *adj.* (biol.) ectodermal.

ectoplasme [ektɔplasm] *s.m.* ectoplasm.

ectropion [ektrɔpjɔ̃] *s.m.* (med.) ectopy.

écu [eky] *s.m.* **1.** shield; (herald.) escutcheon, arms; **2.** (hist. coin) écu; (obs.) *avoir des ~s*, to have lots of money.

écubier [ekybje] *s.m.* (naut.) hawse-hole.

écueil [ekœj] *s.m.* reef, sandbank; (fig.) hazard, snag.

écuelle [ekɥɛl] *s.f.* bowl, basin; (bot.) *~ d'eau*, pennywort.

écuellée [ekɥele] *s.f.* bowlful.

écuisser [ekɥise] *v.t.* to split a tree trunk (in felling).

éculé, -e [ekyle] *adj.* down-at-heel; (fig.) worn out, threadbare.

écumage [ekymaʒ] *s.m.* skimming.

écumant, -e [ekymɑ̃] *adj.* foaming, frothing; (fig.) foaming at the mouth.

écume [ekym] *s.f.* foam, froth; lather (on animal); (lit. & fig.) scum; *~ de mer*, meerschaum.

écumer [ekyme] *v.i.* (lit. & fig.) to foam, to froth, to seethe; *~ v.t.* to skim; (fig.) to scour (the seas, etc.); to clear out (the best items).

écumeu-r, -se [ekymœr] *s.m.f.* *~r de mer*, pirate; (obs.) *~r, ~se, de marmite*, sponger.

écumeu-x, -se [ekymø] *adj.* frothy, foamy.

écumoire [ekymwar] *s.f.* skimmer.

écurer [ekyre] *v.t.* (obs.) to clean out (a well); to scour (pots and pans).

écureuil [ekyrœj] *s.m.* squirrel.

écurie [ekyri] *s.f.* stable, stabling, mews; racing stable; (motor or cycle) racing team; (fig.) *c'est une vraie ~*, it's a proper pigsty.

écusson [ekysɔ̃] *s.m.* **1.** (herald.) escutcheon, coat of arms; (mil.) regimental badge; **2.** escutcheon (of lock); **3.** (hort.) bud (for grafting); **~nage** [ekysɔnaʒ] *s.m.* (hort.) budding, grafting; **~ner** [ekysɔne] *v.t.* **1.** (hort.) to bud, to graft; **2.** to put a badge or coat of arms on; **~noir** [ekysɔnwar] *s.m.* (hort.) budding-knife.

écuyer [ekɥije] *s.m.* **1.** (obs.) squire; **2.** equerry; **3.** riding master; horseman; circus rider.

écuyère [ekɥijɛr] *s.f.* horsewoman; circus rider.

eczéma [egzema] *s.m.* (med.) eczema.

eczémateu-x, -se [egzematø] *adj.* eczematous.

edelweiss [edɛlvajs] *s.m.* (bot.) edelweiss.

éden [edɛn] *s.m.* (fig.) paradise.

édenté, -e [edɑ̃te] *adj.* toothless; broken-toothed; (zool.) edentate; **~s** *s.m.pl.* (zool.) Edentata.

édenter [edɑ̃te] *v.t.* to break the teeth of (saw, comb, etc.).

E.D.F. [edeɛf] abbrev. *Électricité de France.*

édicter [edikte] *v.t.* to decree, to enact.

édicule [edikyl] *s.m.* **1.** (rare) small temple or chapel; **2.** kiosk, public convenience.

édifiant, -e [edifjɑ̃] *adj.* edifying; (iron.) revealing, illuminating.

édification [edifikasjɔ̃] *s.f.* building, erection, construction; (fig.) edification.
édifice [edifis] *s.m.* (large) building, edifice; creation, fabric.
édifier [edifje] *v.t.* **1.** to erect, to build (on a large scale); **2.** to edify, to inspire.
édile [edil] *s.m.* **1.** (Rom. hist.) aedile; **2.** (iron.) mayor, alderman, councillor, local big-wig.
édilité [edilite] *s.f.* **1.** (Rom. hist.) aedileship; **2.** (rare) public office or officials.
Édimbourg [edɛ̃bur] *s.m.* (geog.) Edinburgh.
édit [edi] *s.m.* (hist.) edict.
éditer [edite] *v.t.* **1.** to edit (a text); **2.** to publish.
édit-eur, -rice [editœr] *s.m.f.* **1.** editor (of text); **2.** publisher.
édition [edisjɔ̃] *s.f.* **1.** editing (of text); (annotated) edition; **2.** edition, issue, impression; ~ *originale*, first edition; **3.** publishing, publication.
éditionner [edisjɔne] *v.t.* to number the copies of an edition.
éditorial (pl. **aux**) [editɔrjal] *s.m.* editorial, leading article.
éditorialiste [editɔrjalist] *s.m.f.* leader-writer.
édredon [edrədɔ̃] *s.m.* eiderdown, quilt.
éducable [edykabl] *adj.* educable; (of animal) that can be trained.
éducat-eur, -rice [edykatœr] *s.m.f.* educator, teacher; *adj.* educational, educative.
éducati-f, -ve [edykatif] *adj.* educative, instructive; educational.
éducation [edykɑsjɔ̃] *s.f.* **1.** education, upbringing; **2.** training; **3.** good manners, breeding.
édulcorer [edylkɔre] *v.t.* to sweeten; (fig.) to water down.
éduquer [edyke] *v.t.* to bring up, to train; *mal éduqué*, ill-bred.
éfaufiler [efofile] *v.t.* to unpick, to unweave.
éfendi see EFFENDI.
effaçable [efasabl] *adj.* effaceable, erasable.
effacé, -e [efase] *adj.* (of colours) shaded, subdued; unobtrusive; withdrawn, retiring, self-effacing.
effacement [efasmɑ̃] *s.m.* effacement, deletion, obliteration; (fig.) self-effacement.
effacer [efase] *v.t.* to efface, to delete, to obliterate, to blot out; to obscure; (fig.) to wipe out, to cancel; to eclipse; (fenc.) to turn sideways (to one's opponent); **s'~** *v.refl.* **1.** to become obliterated, to wear away; to fade; **2.** to stand aside, to keep in the background, to efface oneself; (fenc.) to stand sideways; to move aside.
effaner [efane] *v.t.* (agric.) to remove superfluous leaves from.
effanure [efanyr] *s.f.* (agric.) superfluous leaves.
effarant, -e [efarɑ̃] *adj.* frightening, alarming.
effaré, -e [efare] *adj.* **1.** frightened, alarmed, dismayed; **2.** (herald.) rampant.
effarement [efarmɑ̃] *s.m.* dismay, fright, alarm.
effarer [efare] *v.t.* to scare, to alarm; **s'~** *v.refl.* to take fright.
effarouchement [efaruʃmɑ̃] *s.m.* scaring, startling.
effaroucher [efaruʃe] *v.t.* to startle, to frighten, to scare, to alarm.
effarvatte [efarvat] *s.f.* (ornith.) reed warbler, marsh warbler.
effecteur [efɛktœr] *adj.*, *s.m.* (physiol.) effector.
effecti-f, -ve [efɛktif] *adj.* effective, effectual; **~f** *s.m.* strength, establishment; (pl.) manpower; **~vement** [efɛktivmɑ̃] *adv.* **1.** effectively; **2.** in fact, actually, really.
effectuer [efɛktɥe] *v.t.* to carry out, to accomplish, to execute.
efféminé, -e [efemine] *adj.* effeminate.
efféminer [efemine] *v.t.* to make effeminate; (fig.) to weaken, to emasculate.
effendi, éfendi [efɛ̃di] *s.m.* effendi.
efférent, -e [eferɑ̃] *adj.* (anat.) efferent.
effervescence [efɛrvesɑ̃s] *s.f.* effervescence; (fig.) excitement, ferment.
effervescent, -e [efɛrvesɑ̃] *adj.* effervescent; (fig.) excited, agitated.
effet [efɛ] *s.m.* **1.** effect, result; *mettre à* ~, to put into effect; *prendre* ~, to take effect; *en* ~, in fact; *à cet* ~, to this or that end, for this or that purpose; **2.** impression, effect; *faire* ~, *faire de l'*~, to make an impression; *faire l'*~ *de*, to give the impression of; **3.** ~ *de commerce*, bill; ~*s publics*, government securities; **4.** (pl.) gear, belongings; (rare) goods and chattels.
effeuillage [efœjaʒ] *s.m.* **1.** (hort.) defoliation; **2.** strip-tease.
effeuillaison [efœjɛzɔ̃] *s.f.*, **effeuillement** [efœjmɑ̃] *s.m.* shedding of leaves.
effeuiller [efœje] *v.t.* to defoliate, to strip of leaves; to remove the petals from; **s'~** *v.refl.* to shed leaves.
effeuilleuse [efœjøz] *s.f.* strip-tease artist.
efficace [efikas] *adj.* efficacious; **~ment** [efikasmɑ̃] *adv.* efficaciously, effectively.
efficacité [efikasite] *s.f.* efficacy, efficaciousness, effectiveness.
efficience [efisjɑ̃s] *s.f.* efficiency.
efficient, -e [efisjɑ̃] *adj.* efficient.
effigie [efiʒi] *s.f.* effigy.
effilage [efilaʒ], **effilement** [efilmɑ̃] *s.m.* **1.** fraying, ravelling out (of material); **2.** tapering.
effilé[1], -e [efile] *adj.* tapering, tapered; pointed.
effilé[2] [efile] *s.m.* fringe.
effiler [efile] *v.t.* **1.** to unweave, to unravel, to fray; **2.** to taper; **s'~** *v.refl.* **1.** to become frayed; **2.** to come to a point.
effilochage [efilɔʃaʒ] *s.m.* (text.) ravelling out, teasing out.
effiloche [efilɔʃ] *s.f.* selvage; (pl.) floss silk.
effilocher [efilɔʃe] *v.t.* to ravel out; to shred (rags to pulp); **s'~** *v.refl.* to fray.
effilocheu-r, -se [efilɔʃœr] *s.m.f.* (text.) shoddy-maker; **~se** *s.f.* shredding machine.
effilochure [efilɔʃyr] *s.f.* (text.) shoddy; floss (silk).
efflanqué, -e [eflɑ̃ke] *adj.* emaciated, skeletal, skinny.
effleurage [eflœraʒ] *s.m.* **1.** shaving (of leather); **2.** (med.) light massage.
effleurement [eflœrmɑ̃] *s.m.* touch, stroke, caress; graze.
effleurer [eflœre] *v.t.* **1.** to graze (the skin); **2.** (techn.) to shave (leather); **3.** to touch, to pass lightly over, to stroke; (fig.) to touch upon.
effleurir [eflœrir] *v.i.* to effloresce.
effloraison [eflɔrɛzɔ̃] *s.f.* coming into flower.
efflorescence [eflɔresɑ̃s] *s.f.* efflorescence; (lit. & fig.) flowering; graze (of skin); bloom (on fruit).
efflorescent, -e [eflɔresɑ̃] *adj.* efflorescent, in full flower.
effluent, -e [eflyɑ̃] *adj.*, ~ *s.m.* effluent; ~ *radioactif*, radioactive waste.
effluve [eflyv] *s.m.* effluvium, emanation; (electr.) brush discharge.
effondrement [efɔ̃drəmɑ̃] *s.m.* **1.** collapse, falling in; (geol.) subsidence; (fig.) collapse, ruin, downfall; (fin.) slump; (geol.) *fossé d'*~, rift valley; **2.** (agric.) trenching.
effondrer [efɔ̃dre] *v.t.* **1.** to bring down, to cause to collapse; **2.** (agric.) to trench, to plough deeply; **s'~** *v.refl.* to collapse, to subside; to cave in; (fig.) to collapse, to give up, to come to nothing; to slump.
(s')efforcer [efɔrse] *v.refl.* to strive, to make every effort, to force oneself (*de*, to).
effort [efɔr] *s.m.* **1.** effort, exertion, endeavour; *faire tous ses* ~*s*, to make every effort; *je veux bien*

faire un ~, I'll try (to raise the money, to meet the requirement, etc.); *sans* ~, effortlessly; **2.** (rare) strain, rupture; (mech.) strain, stress.
effraction [efraksjɔ̃] *s.f.* (law) breaking-in; *vol avec* ~, breaking and entering, housebreaking.
effraie [efrɛ] *s.f.* screech owl, barn owl.
effranger [efrɑ̃ʒe] *v.t.* to fray (edges of material); **s'~** *v.refl.* to fray.
effrayant, -e [efrɛjɑ̃] *adj.* frightful, frightening, fearful; (fam.) appalling, dreadful.
effrayé, -e [efreje] *adj.* frightened, afraid.
effrayer [efreje] *v.t.* to frighten, to terrify, to alarm; **s'~** *v.refl.* to be frightened, to be alarmed, to take fright.
effréné, -e [efrene] *adj.* unbridled, wild; frantic, frenzied.
effritement [efritmɑ̃] *s.m.* crumbling; disintegration; impoverishment (of soil); (fig.) gradual depreciation.
effriter [efrite] *v.t.* **1.** to impoverish (soil); **2.** to crumble, to wear away; **s'~** *v.refl.* (lit. & fig.) to crumble, to dwindle away.
effroi [efrwɑ] *s.m.* terror, horror.
effronté, -e [efrɔ̃te] *adj.* shameless, brazen; *s.m.f.* hooligan, hussy; **~ment** [efrɔ̃temɑ̃] *adv.* shamelessly.
effronterie [efrɔ̃tri] *s.f.* effrontery, shamelessness, impudence.
effroyable [efrwajabl] *adj.* frightful, dreadful; (fam.) awful, horrible; **~ment** [efrwajabləmɑ̃] *adv.* awfully, horribly.
effusion [efysjɔ̃] *s.f.* **1.** ~ *de sang*, shedding of blood, bloodshed; **2.** (fig.) effusion.
éfourceau (pl. **-x**) [efurso] *s.m.* two-wheeled cart (for timber).
égaiement [egɛmɑ̃], **égayement** [egɛjmɑ̃] *s.m.* enlivenment; making merry.
(s')égailler [egɑje] *v.refl.* to disperse.
égal, -e, (aux) [egal] *adj.* **1.** equal, equivalent; *toutes choses ~es d'ailleurs*, other things being equal; (sport) *faire jeu* ~, to be well-matched; *traiter d'~ à ~ avec qn.*, to deal with s.o. on an equal footing; *à l'~ de*, as much as; **2.** regular, unchanging; equable; level, even, smooth; **3.** (all) the same; *la chose est ~e*, it's all the same; *être ~ à qn.*, not to matter to s.o.; *cela m'est* ~, it makes no difference to me; *c'est* ~, it's all the same; ~, **~e** *s.m.f.* equal.
égalable [egalabl] *adj.* that can be equalled.
également [egalmɑ̃] *adv.* **1.** equally; **2.** also, likewise.
égaler [egale] *v.t.* **1.** (obs.) to make equal; **2.** to equal, to be equal to; to match.
égalisat-eur, -rice [egalizatœr] *adj.* equalizing, levelling; (sport) *but ~eur*, equalizer.
égalisation [egalizɑsjɔ̃] *s.f.* equalization.
égaliser [egalize] *v.t.* to equalize, to level; to smooth, to make even.
égalit-aire [egalitɛr] *adj.* egalitarian; **~arisme** [egalitarism] *s.m.* egalitarianism; **~ariste** [egalitarist] *s.m.f., adj.* egalitarian.
égalité [egalite] *s.f.* equality; regularity; ~ *d'humeur*, equanimity.
égard [egar] *s.m.* **1.** attention, regard; consideration; *eu ~ à*, considering, in view of; *à l'~ de*, concerning, with regard to; *à cet* ~, in this or that respect; *à tous (les) ~s*, in all respects; **2.** respect; (pl.) attentions, consideration; *par ~ pour*, out of respect for.
égaré, -e [egare] *adj.* wandering, stray, straying; (fig.) distracted, distraught.
égarement [egarmɑ̃] *s.m.* **1.** (obs.) straying; **2.** distraction; (mental) aberration.
égarer [egare] *v.t.* **1.** (lit. & fig.) to mislead, to lead astray; **2.** to mislay; **s'~** *v.refl.* to go astray, to lose one's way, to get lost.
égayant, -e [egɛjɑ̃] *adj.* amusing.
égayement see ÉGAIEMENT.
égayer [egeje] *v.t.* to amuse, to cheer, to enliven; **s'~** *v.refl.* to amuse oneself; *s'~ aux dépens de qn.*, to make fun of s.o.
(la mer) Égée [(lamɛr)eʒe] *s.f.* (geog.) Aegean (sea).
égermer [eʒɛrme] *v.t.* to degerm (barley).
E.G.F. [eʒeɛf] abbrev. *Électricité et Gaz de France.*
égide [eʒid] *s.f.* (Gr. myth.) aegis; (fig.) protection.
églantier [eglɑ̃tje] *s.m.* (bot.) eglantine, sweet-brier.
églantine [eglɑ̃tin] *s.f.* (bot.) wild rose, dog-rose.
églefin, aiglefin [egləfɛ̃] *s.m.* (ichth.) haddock.
Église, église [egliz] *s.f.* Church, church.
églogue [eglɔg] *s.f.* eclogue.
ego [ego] *s.m.* ego.
égo-centrique [egɔsɑ̃trik] *adj.* egocentric, self-centred; **~centrisme** [egɔsɑ̃trism] *s.m.* egocentricity.
égoïne [egɔin] *s.f.* small handsaw, compass saw.
égoïsme [egɔism] *s.m.* egoism, selfishness.
égoïste [egɔist] *adj.* egoistic; ~ *s.m.f.* egoist; **~ment** [egɔistəmɑ̃] *adv.* egoistically, selfishly.
égorger [egɔrʒe] *v.t.* to cut the throat of, to slaughter; (fig.) to fleece.
égorgeu-r, -se [egɔrʒœr] *s.m.f.* cut-throat.
(s')égosiller [egozije] *v.refl.* to shout oneself hoarse; to sing long and loud.
égotisme [egɔtism] *s.m.* egotism.
égotiste [egɔtist] *adj.* egotistic(al); ~*s.m.f.* egotist.
égout [egu] *s.m.* gutter; drain, sewer; *(système du) tout-à-l'~*, main drainage.
égoutier [egutje] *s.m.* sewerman.
égouttage [egutaʒ], **égouttement** [egutmɑ̃] *s.m.* draining, drainage.
égoutter [egute] *v.t.i.* to drain; **s'~** *v.refl.* to drain.
égouttoir [egutwar] *s.m.* drainer; plate-rack.
égoutture [egutyr] *s.f.* drainings, last drops.
égrainer [egrene] *v.t.* = ÉGRENER.
égrappage [egrapaʒ] *s.m.* picking, stripping (of fruit from bunch).
égrapper [egrape] *v.t.* to pick, to strip (fruit from bunch).
égrappoir [egrapwar] *s.m.* machine for stripping fruit.
égratigner [egratiɲe] *v.t.* to scratch; (agric.) to rake over; (fig.) to ruffle.
égratignure [egratiɲyr] *s.f.* scratch; (fig.) pin-prick.
égravillonner [egravijɔne] *v.t.* to clean the roots of a tree (when transplanting).
égrenage [egrənaʒ], **égrènement** [egrɛnmɑ̃] *s.m.* **1.** picking (of fruit); shelling (of peas); telling (of beads); **2.** (fig.) string (of lights, houses, etc.).
égrener [egrəne] *v.t.* to shell (peas, etc.); to pick (fruit); to tell (beads); to offer one by one; **s'~** *v.refl.* **1.** to shed seed, to fall from the stalk; **2.** to be strung out.
égreneuse [egrənøz] *s.f.* machine for husking (maize, etc.).
égrillard, -e [egrijar] *adj.* bawdy, improper.
égrisage [egrizaʒ] *s.m.* polishing (of gems).
égrisé *s.m.*, **égrisée** *s.f.* [egrize] diamond dust, bort.
égriser [egrize] *v.t.* to polish (gems).
égrotant, -e [egrɔtɑ̃] *adj.* (Lit.) sickly.
égrugeage [egryʒaʒ] *s.m.* pulverization.
égrugeoir [egryʒwar] *s.m.* mortar (for kitchen use).
égruger [egryʒe] *v.t.* to pound, to crush, to pulverize.
égueuler [egœle] *v.t.* to chip the rim or spout of; (geol.) *cratère égueulé*, breached crater.
Égypte [eʒipt] *s.f.* (geog.) Egypt.

égyptien, -ne [eʒipsjɛ̃] *adj.*, *s.m.f.* Egyptian; (obs.) gypsy; **~ne** *s.f.* (typ.) clarendon.

égyptologie [eʒiptɔlɔʒi] *s.f.* egyptology.

égyptologue [eʒiptɔlɔg] *s.m.f.* egyptologist.

eh [e] *interj.* ah!, oh!, hey!; ~ *bien!*, well!, now then!

éhonté, -e [eɔ̃te] *adj.* shameless.

eider [ɛdɛr] *s.m.* eider duck.

eidétique [ɛjdetik] *adj.*, *s.m.f.* eidetic.

éjaculation [eʒakylɑsjɔ̃] *s.f.* ejaculation.

éjaculer [eʒakyle] *v.t.* to ejaculate.

éjectable [eʒɛktabl] *adj.* (aeron.) *siège* ~, ejector seat.

éjecter [eʒɛkte] *v.t.* to eject.

éjecteur [eʒɛktœr] *s.m.* ejector.

éjection [eʒɛksjɔ̃] *s.f.* ejection.

élaboration [elabɔrɑsjɔ̃] *s.f.* **1.** assimilation (of food by body); **2.** composition, formulation, elaboration (of plan, etc.).

élaborer [elabɔre] *v.t.* **1.** to develop, to elaborate; **2.** to assimilate; **s'~** *v.refl.* to be developed.

élagage [elagaʒ] *s.m.* pruning (of trees).

élaguer [elage] *v.t.* (lit. & fig.) to prune.

élagueur [elagœr] *s.m.* expert pruner.

élan[1] [elɑ̃] *s.m.* **1.** spring, leap, bound, dash; take-off, run-up (for a jump); ~ *vital*, life force; **2.** (fig.) transport, outburst, surge (of emotion); spirit, warmth, vivacity.

élan[2] [elɑ̃] *s.m.* (zool.) elk, moose.

élancé, -e [elɑ̃se] *adj.* (obs.) lank, thin; (mod.) slender, svelte, slim.

élancement [elɑ̃smɑ̃] *s.m.* **1.** stabbing pain, violent twinge; **2.** (Lit.) mystic ecstasy, yearning.

élancer [elɑ̃se] *v.t.* (obs.) to hurl; (mod.) to lift up; ~ *v.i.* to ache, to hurt; **s'~** *v.refl.* to rush (forward), to leap, to dash; (fig.) to soar.

élargir [elarʒir] *v.t.* **1.** (lit. & fig.) to widen, to broaden, to enlarge; **2.** (law) to set free, to discharge, to release; ~ *v.i.* (fam.) to put on weight; **s'~** *v.refl.* to become wider.

élargissement [elarʒismɑ̃] *s.m.* **1.** widening, broadening, enlarging; **2.** release, discharge.

élasticité [elastisite] *s.f.* elasticity; adaptability, flexibility.

élastique [elastik] *adj.* elastic; flexible; ~ *s.m.* elastic; rubber band.

élastomère [elastɔmɛr] *s.m.* (chem.) elastomer.

élavé, -e [elave] *adj.* washed-out, neutral (esp. of colour of hounds).

Elbe [ɛlb] *s.f.* (geog.) Elba; ~ *s.m.* Elbe (river).

elbeuf [ɛlbœf] *s.m.* (text.) Elbeuf cloth.

Eldorado [ɛldɔrado] *s.m.* Eldorado.

élect-eur, -rice [elɛktœr] *s.m.f.* (hist.) Elector, Electress; (pol.) elector.

électi-f, -ve [elɛktif] *adj.* elective.

élection [elɛksjɔ̃] *s.f.* **1.** (obs.) choice; (law) ~ *de domicile*, choice of residence; (theol.) *le peuple d'~*, the chosen people; **2.** (pol.) election.

électoral, -e, (aux) [elɛktɔral] *adj.* electoral.

électoralisme [elɛktɔralism] *s.m.* vote-catching policies.

électorat [elɛktɔra] *s.m.* electorate.

électricien [elɛktrisjɛ̃] *s.m.* electrician.

électricité [elɛktrisite] *s.f.* electricity.

électrification [elɛktrifikɑsjɔ̃] *s.f.* electrification.

électrifier [elɛktrifje] *v.t.* **1.** to electrify (railways, etc.); **2.** to bring electric power to (village, etc.).

électrique [elɛktrik] *adj.* electric, electrical; **~ment** [elɛktrikmɑ̃] *adv.* electrically, by electricity.

électrisable [elɛktrizabl] *adj.* electrifiable (substance).

électrisant, -e [elɛktrizɑ̃] *adj.* (lit. & fig.) electrifying.

électrisation [elɛktrizɑsjɔ̃] *s.f.* electrification (of substance).

électriser [elɛktrize] *v.t.* (lit. & fig.) to electrify.

électro-aimant [elɛktrɔɛmɑ̃] *s.m.* electromagnet.

électrobiologie [elɛktrɔbjɔlɔʒi] *s.f.* electrobiology.

électrocardio-gramme [elɛktrɔkardjɔgram] *s.m.* (med.) electrocardiogram; **~graphe** [elɛktrɔkardjɔgraf] *s.m.* electrocardiograph; **~graphie** [elɛktrɔkardjɔgrafi] *s.f.* electrocardiography.

électro-chimie [elɛktrɔʃimi] *s.f.* electrochemistry; **~chimique** [elɛktrɔʃimik] *adj.* electrochemical; **~choc** [elɛktrɔʃɔk] *s.m.* (psychiatry) electric-shock treatment; **~cuter** [elɛktrɔkyte] *v.t.* to electrocute; *se faire ~cuter*, to electrocute oneself; **~cution** [elɛktrɔkysjɔ̃] *s.f.* electrocution.

électrode [elɛktrɔd] *s.f.* electrode.

électrodiagnostic [elɛktrɔdjagnɔstik] *s.m.* (med.) electro-diagnosis.

électrodynamique [elɛktrɔdinamik] *s.f.* electrodynamics; ~ *adj.* electrodynamic.

électrodynamomètre [elɛktrɔdinamɔmɛtr] *s.m.* electrodynamometer.

électro-encéphalogramme [elɛktrɔɑ̃sefalɔgram] *s.m.* electroencephalogram.

électro-encéphalographie [elɛktrɔɑ̃sefalɔgrafi] *s.f.* electroencephalography.

électro-gène [elɛktrɔʒɛn] *adj.* **1.** (zool.) producing electricity; **2.** generating; *groupe ~gène*, generating set; **~luminescence** [elɛktrɔlyminesɑ̃s] *s.f.* electroluminescence; **~lyse** [elɛktrɔliz] *s.f.* electrolysis; **~lyser** [elɛktrɔlize] *v.t.* to electrolyse; **~lyseur** [elɛktrɔlizœr] *s.m.* electrolyser; **~lyte** [elɛktrɔlit] *s.m.* electrolyte; **~lytique** [elɛktrɔlitik] *adj.* electrolytic.

électromagnét-ique [elɛktrɔmaɲetik] *adj.* electromagnetic; **~isme** [elɛktrɔmaɲetism] *s.m.* electromagnetism.

électromécan-icien [elɛktrɔmekanisjɛ̃] *s.m.* electrical engineer; **~ique** [elɛktrɔmekanik] *adj.* electromechanical; *s.f.* electromechanics.

électro-ménager [elɛktrɔmenaʒe] *adj.m.* electric (household) appliances; **~métallurgie** [elɛktrɔmetalyrʒi] *s.f.* electrometallurgy; **~mètre** [elɛktrɔmɛtr] *s.m.* electrometer; **~métrie** [elɛktrɔmetri] *s.f.* electrometry.

électromot-eur, -rice [elɛktrɔmɔtœr] *adj.* electromotive; **~eur** *s.m.* electric motor.

électron [elɛktrɔ̃] *s.m.* electron.

électronégati-f, -ve [elɛktrɔnegatif] *adj.* electronegative, carrying a negative charge.

électronicien, -ne [elɛktrɔnisjɛ̃] *s.m.f.* electronics expert.

électronique [elɛktrɔnik] *adj.* electronic; ~ *s.f.* electronics.

électron-volt [elɛktrɔ̃vɔlt] *s.m.* electron-volt.

électrophone [elɛktrɔfɔn] *s.m.* **1.** (obs.) telephone amplifier; **2.** record player.

électrophorèse [elɛktrɔfɔrɛz] *s.f.* electrophoresis.

électropositi-f, -ve [elɛktrɔpozitif] *adj.* electropositive, carrying a positive charge.

électropuncture, électroponcture [elɛktrɔpɔ̃ktyr] *s.f.* (med.) electropuncture.

électro-scope [elɛktrɔskɔp] *s.m.* electroscope; **~statique** [elɛktrɔstatik] *adj.* electrostatic; *s.f.* electrostatics; **~technique** [elɛktrɔtɛknik] *adj.* electrotechnical; *s.f.* electrotechnics; **~thérapie** [elɛktrɔterapi] *s.f.* (med.) electrotherapy, electrotherapeutics; **~thermie** [elɛktrɔtɛrmi] *s.f.* electrothermics; (med.) electrothermy.

électrum [elɛktrɔm] (ant., min.) *s.m.* electrum.

électuaire [elɛktɥɛr] *s.m.* (obs.) electuary.

élégamment [elegamɑ̃] *adv.* elegantly, stylishly.

élégance [elegɑ̃s] *s.f.* elegance, style; good taste.

élégant, -e [elegɑ̃] *adj.* elegant, stylish, distinguished; *s.m.f.* man of fashion, well-dressed woman.

élégiaque [eleʒjak] *adj.* elegiac.
élégie [eleʒi] *s.f.* elegy.
élégir [eleʒir] *v.t.* to plane (wood).
élément [elemɑ̃] *s.m.* **1.** element, constituent, component, part; **2.** (pl.) rudiments; **3.** (pl.) elements (weather); **4.** environment, milieu; *être dans son* ~, to be in one's element, to feel at home.
élémentaire [elemɑ̃tɛr] *adj.* **1.** elemental; **2.** elementary, primary; (fam.) *c'est* ~, it's the least you can do.
éléphant [elefɑ̃] *s.m.* (zool.) elephant; (fig.) a big and clumsy person; *un* ~ *dans un magasin de porcelaine*, a bull in a china shop; **~eau** (pl. **-x**) [elefɑ̃to] *s.m.* elephant calf; **~esque** [elefɑ̃tɛsk] *adj.* (fam.) elephantine; **~iasis** [elefɑ̃tjazis] *s.f.* (med.) elephantiasis.
éléphantin, -e [elefɑ̃tɛ̃] *adj.* (rare) elephantine.
élevage [ɛlvaʒ] *s.m.* rearing, breeding, (of cattle, horses).
élévat-eur, -rice [elevatœr] *adj.* elevating, raising; (anat.) *muscle* ~*eur*, elevator; **~eur** *s.m.* elevator, hoist, lift.
élévation [elevɑsjɔ̃] *s.f.* **1.** raising; (eccles.) elevation; **2.** rise, increase; **3.** (rare) elevation, height, eminence; **4.** (fig.) promotion, accession (to throne); **5.** (fig.) nobility (of mind).
élévatoire [elevatwar] *adj.* (techn.) lifting, hoisting.
élève [elɛv] *s.m.f.* **1.** pupil, disciple; **2.** schoolboy or girl, student; ~ *officier*, officer cadet; **3.** (agric.) home-reared animal; home-produced seedling (tree, plant).
élevé, -e [ɛlve] *adj.* **1.** high, tall; (fig.) noble, lofty; **2.** *bien, mal,* ~, well, badly, brought-up.
élever [ɛlve] *v.t.* **1.** to raise; (fig.) to raise, to increase; **2.** to raise higher, to extend upwards; to erect, to build; **3.** to bring up (child); to rear, to breed (animal); **s'**~ *v.refl.* to rise, to arise; to raise or lift oneself; (fig.) to stand up, to protest, (*contre*, against).
éleveu-r, -se [ɛlvœr] *s.m.f.* breeder; wine producer; **~se** *s.f.* battery, incubator, (for chicks).
elfe [ɛlf] *s.m.* elf.
élider [elide] *v.t.* (lang.) to elide.
Élie [eli] *s.m.* (bibl.) Elijah, Elias.
éligibilité [eliʒibilite] *s.f.* eligibility.
éligible [eliʒibl] *adj.* eligible, qualified, competent.
élimer [elime] *v.t.* to wear through.
éliminat-eur, -rice [eliminatœr] *adj.* eliminating, (of process, etc.) eliminative.
éliminer [elimine] *v.t.* to eliminate.
élingue [elɛ̃g] *s.f.* (naut.) sling.
élinguer [elɛ̃ge] *v.t.* (naut.) to sling.
élire [elir] *v.t.* **1.** (obs.) to choose; **2.** to elect.
élisabéthain, -e [elizabetɛ̃] *adj.* Elizabethan.
Élisée [elize] *s.m.* (bibl.) Elisha.
élision [elizjɔ̃] *s.f.* (lang.) elision.
élite [elit] *s.f.* élite, select few; *les* ~*s*, the élite, the top rank; *d'*~, select, picked, (of regiment, shot, etc.) crack.
élitisme [elitism] *s.m.* elitism.
élixir [eliksir] *s.m.* elixir, cordial.
elle [ɛl] *pers.pron.f.* she, it; her; (pl.) they; them.
ellébore [elebɔr] *s.m.* (bot.) hellebore; ~ *noir*, Helleborus niger, Christmas rose.
ellipse [elips] *s.f.* **1.** (lang.) ellipsis; **2.** (geom.) ellipse.
ellipsoïdal, -e, (aux) [elipsɔidal] *adj.* ellipsoidal.
ellipsoïde [elipsɔid] *s.m.* ellipsoid; ~ *adj.* ellipsoidal.
elliptique [eliptik] *adj.* elliptic(al); **~ment** [eliptikmɑ̃] *adv.* elliptically.
élocution [elɔkysjɔ̃] *s.f.* elocution, speech, diction.
élodée [elɔde] *s.f.* (bot.) Elodea, water-weed.
éloge [elɔʒ] *s.m.* eulogy, encomium; praise.
élogieu-x, -se [elɔʒjø] *adj.* laudatory, eulogistic; **~sement** [elɔʒjøzmɑ̃] *adv.* eulogistically.
éloigné, -e [elwaɲe] *adj.* distant, remote, far; (fig.) ~ *de*, different from, foreign to, far (removed) from.
éloignement [elwaɲmɑ̃] *s.m.* **1.** removal, banishment; **2.** distance, remoteness; separation; **3.** avoidance, keeping away, (*de*, of, from); aversion, antipathy, (*de*, to).
éloigner [elwaɲe] *v.t.* **1.** to remove, to send away, to banish; **2.** to delay, to put off; **3.** to keep (s.o., sth., from); **s'**~ *v.refl.* to go away, to move away, to turn away; (fig.) *s'*~ *de*, to get away from (e.g. subject); to differ from; to become less friendly to.
élongation [elɔ̃gɑsjɔ̃] *s.f.* **1.** (astron.) elongation; **2.** (med.) pulled muscle.
élonger [elɔ̃ʒe] *v.t.* **1.** (obs.) to elongate; **2.** (naut.) to lay out (a cable); **3.** (med.) to strain (a muscle); **4.** (naut.) to come alongside, to skirt (coast, etc.).
éloquemment [elɔkamɑ̃] *adv.* eloquently.
éloquence [elɔkɑ̃s] *s.f.* eloquence.
éloquent, -e [elɔkɑ̃] *adj.* eloquent; that speaks for itself.
élu, -e [ely] *adj.* (eccles.) chosen; *s.m.f.* beloved; elect; elected.
élucidation [elysidɑsjɔ̃] *s.f.* elucidation.
élucider [elyside] *v.t.* to elucidate, to explain.
élucubration [elykybrɑsjɔ̃] *s.f.* (obs.) lucubration, burning the candle at both ends; (mod., pej.) lucubration, elaborate and useless ratiocination.
éluder [elyde] *v.t.* to elude, to evade.
éluvial, -e, (aux) [elyvjal] *adj.* (geol.) eluvial.
éluvion [elyvjɔ̃] *s.f.* (geol.) eluvium.
élyséen, -ne [elizeɛ̃] *adj.* (myth.) Elysian.
élytre [elitr] *s.m.* (ent.) elytron, wing-case.
elzévir [ɛlzevir] *s.m.* (typ.) Elzevir (edition, type).
elzévirien, -ne [ɛlzevirjɛ̃] *adj.* (typ.) Elzevir.
émaciation [emasjɑsjɔ̃] *s.f.* (Lit.) emaciation.
émacié, -e [emasje] *adj.* emaciated.
émacier [emasje] *v.t.* to emaciate.
émail [emaj] *s.m.* (pl. *émaux*) **1.** enamel, enamelled work; enamel of teeth; **2.** (herald.) tincture; (obs.) bright colouring; **3.** glaze.
émaillage [emajaʒ] *s.m.* enamelling.
émailler [emaje] *v.t.* to enamel; to spangle, to speckle, to dot; (fig.) to intersperse, to sprinkle; *une composition émaillée de fautes*, a composition liberally sprinkled with mistakes.
émaillerie [emajri] *s.f.* enamelling.
émailleu-r, -se [emajœr] *s.m.f.* enamellist.
émaillure [emajyr] *s.f.* enamelling, enamel work.
émanation [emanɑsjɔ̃] *s.f.* emanation, efflux.
émancipat-eur, -rice [emɑ̃sipatœr] *adj.* emancipating, liberating; *s.m.f.* emancipator, liberator.
émancipation [emɑ̃sipɑsjɔ̃] *s.f.* emancipation.
émanciper [emɑ̃sipe] *v.t.* to emancipate; **s'**~ *v.refl.* to free oneself, to gain one's freedom; (pej.) to run wild.
émaner [emane] *v.i.* to emanate, to proceed, to arise, to result, (*de*, from).
E.M. [eɛm] abbrev. *État-major.*
émargement [emarʒəmɑ̃] *s.m.* appending of signature or note in the margin; *feuille d'*~, signed record of presence (at a transaction).
émarger [emarʒe] *v.t.* **1.** to write or sign in the margin of; **2.** to draw a salary; **3.** to trim the margin of.
émasculation [emaskylɑsjɔ̃] *s.f.* (lit. & fig.) emasculation; castration.
émasculer [emaskyle] *v.t.* (lit. & fig.) to emasculate; to castrate, to geld.

embâcle [ɑ̃bɑkl] *s.m.* obstruction in a water-course; obstruction caused by ice.
emballage [ɑ̃balaʒ] *s.m.* packing; packing material; (sport) racing cyclist's final sprint.
emballement [ɑ̃balmɑ̃] *s.m.* **1.** over-enthusiasm, craze, being carried away; **2.** (of engine) racing.
emballer [ɑ̃bale] *v.t.* **1.** to pack, to package (goods); **2.** (fam.) to embark; (pop.) to arrest; **3.** to race (an engine); **4.** (fig., fam.) to carry away; **5.** (pop.) to bawl out; **s'~** *v.refl.* (of horse) to bolt; (of engine) to race; (fig.) to be carried away, to go mad.
emballeu-r, -se [ɑ̃balœr] *s.m.f.* packer.
embarbouiller [ɑ̃barbuje] *v.t.* to confuse, to muddle, to befuddle; **s'~** *v.refl.* to become muddled.
embarcadère [ɑ̃barkadɛr] *s.f.* **1.** landing-stage, pier, wharf; **2.** (rail., obs.) platform.
embarcation [ɑ̃barkɑsjɔ̃] *s.f.* small boat, small craft, ship's boat; ⚠ not 'embarkation'.
embardée [ɑ̃barde] *s.f.* (naut.) yaw, lurch; (car) swerve.
embargo [ɑ̃bargo] *s.m.* embargo.
embarquement [ɑ̃barkəmɑ̃] *s.m.* embarkation, boarding; loading, stowage (of goods).
embarquer [ɑ̃barke] *v.t.* to ship, to take or put on board; (fig.) to involve (s.o.), to launch (s.o.); to start (sth.); (fam.) *~ un ami dans un train*, to see a friend on to a train; *~ un malfaiteur*, to arrest a criminal; *~ v.i.* to embark, to go on board; (of sea) to come over the side; **s'~** *v.refl.* (lit. & fig.) to embark.
embarras [ɑ̃bara] *s.m.* **1.** (obs.) obstruction, blockage; *~ de voitures*, traffic jam; (mod.) *~ gastrique*, disorders of the stomach; **2.** obstacle, impediment, hindrance, snag; **3.** (obs. exc. Lit.) complications; **4.** difficulty, trouble(s), difficult or awkward situation; **5.** uncertainty; *avoir l'~ du choix*, to have too many things to choose from; **6.** embarrassment, confusion; *faire de l'~, des ~*, to behave in an affected way, to fuss.
embarrassant, -e [ɑ̃barasɑ̃] *adj.* **1.** embarrassing, awkward, difficult; **2.** cumbersome.
embarrassé, -e [ɑ̃barase] *adj.* **1.** encumbered, hampered; **2.** embarrassed, confused, constrained; **3.** difficult, involved.
embarrasser [ɑ̃barase] *v.t.* **1.** to encumber, to hamper, to obstruct; **2.** to embarrass, to put in a difficult position; **3.** to embarrass, to confuse, to perplex; **s'~** *v.refl.* to be burdened or encumbered (*de*, with); to worry (*de*, about); (lit. & fig.) to get caught up, to get involved, (*dans*, in); to become confused, to feel embarrassed.
embarrer [ɑ̃bare] *v.i.* (techn.) to place a lever under a load; **s'~** *v.refl.* (of horse) to straddle the bar of the stall.
embase [ɑ̃bɑz] *s.f.* (techn.) base.
embasement [ɑ̃bɑzmɑ̃] *s.m.* (constr.) base (of wall, etc.).
embastiller [ɑ̃bastije] *v.t.* (jest) to imprison.
embattage [ɑ̃bataʒ] *s.m.* (techn.) tyring (of cart-wheel).
embattre [ɑ̃batr] *v.t.* (techn.) to tyre (cart-wheel).
embauchage [ɑ̃boʃaʒ] *s.m.* hiring, engaging, taking on, (labour).
embauche [ɑ̃boʃ] *s.f.* job vacancy; employment.
embaucher [ɑ̃boʃe] *v.t.* to hire, to engage, to take on, (labour).
embauchoir [ɑ̃boʃwar] *s.m.* shoe-tree.
embaumement [ɑ̃bommɑ̃] *s.m.* embalming.
embaumer [ɑ̃bome] *v.t.* to embalm; to fill with fragrance; *~ v.i.* to be fragrant, to give off a scent of.
embaumeur [ɑ̃bomœr] *s.m.* embalmer.
embecquer [ɑ̃beke] *v.t.* **1.** (obs.) to feed nestlings; **2.** to gorge (geese, etc.).
embéguiner [ɑ̃begine] *v.t.* **1.** (obs.) to wrap up, to bonnet; **2.** (obs.) to bewitch; **s'~** *v.refl. s'~ de qn.*, to fall for s.o.
embellie [ɑ̃beli] *s.f.* bright period, clear spell, lull (in storm).
embellir [ɑ̃belir] *v.t.* to beautify, to adorn, to embellish; *~ v.i.* to grow prettier.
embellissement [ɑ̃belismɑ̃] *s.m.* beautifying; improvement, embellishment.
emberlificoter [ɑ̃bɛrlifikɔte] *v.t.* (fam.) to entangle; (fig.) to confuse, to diddle; **s'~** *v.refl.* to become entangled.
emberlificoteu-r, -se [ɑ̃bɛrlifikɔtœr] *s.m.f.* duper, diddler, swindler.
embêtant, -e [ɑ̃bɛtɑ̃] *adj.* (fam.) tiresome, annoying, boring.
embêtement [ɑ̃bɛtmɑ̃] *s.m.* (fam.) worry, trouble, bother.
embêter [ɑ̃bɛte] *v.t.* (fam.) to annoy, to worry, to irritate; **s'~** *v.refl.* to be bored.
emblavage [ɑ̃blavaʒ] *s.m.* (agric.) sowing with cereal.
emblaver [ɑ̃blave] *v.t.* (agric.) to sow with cereal.
emblavure [ɑ̃blavyr] *s.f.* (agric.) land sown with cereal.
(d')emblée [dɑ̃ble] *adv.* at once, there and then, right away, without further ado.
emblématique [ɑ̃blematik] *adj.* emblematic(al).
emblème [ɑ̃blɛm] *s.m.* emblem, symbol.
embobeliner [ɑ̃bɔbline] *v.t.* **1.** (obs.) to wrap up; **2.** (fig., fam.) to diddle, to lead up the garden path, to get round (s.o.).
embobiner [ɑ̃bɔbine] *v.t.* **1.** (rare) to reel, to wind; **2.** = EMBOBELINER 2.
emboîtage [ɑ̃bwataʒ] *s.m.* **1.** packing in boxes; **2.** case (for expensive book).
emboîtement [ɑ̃bwatmɑ̃] *s.m.* fitting, joint.
emboîter [ɑ̃bwate] *v.t.* **1.** to fit (*dans*, into), to nest (boxes, etc.); **2.** to case, to encase; **3.** *~ le pas à qn.*, to follow in someone's footsteps, to walk on someone's heels; **s'~** *v.refl.* to fit into each other.
emboîture [ɑ̃bwatyr] *s.f.* fit, joint.
embolie [ɑ̃bɔli] *s.f.* (med.) embolism.
embolisme [ɑ̃bɔlism] *s.m.* intercalary month.
embonpoint [ɑ̃bɔ̃pwɛ̃] *s.m.* (obs.) good health; (mod.) corpulence, embonpoint.
embossage [ɑ̃bɔsaʒ] *s.m.* (naut.) mooring broadside on.
embosser [ɑ̃bɔse] *v.t.* (naut.) to moor broadside on.
embouche [ɑ̃buʃ] *s.f.* fattening of cattle in pastures; rich pasture land.
emboucher [ɑ̃buʃe] *v.t.* to raise (a wind instrument) to one's lips; *~ un cheval*, to put a bit in a horse's mouth; (fig.) *~ la trompette*, to trumpet abroad; *mal embouché(e)*, foul-mouthed.
embouchoir [ɑ̃buʃwar] *s.m.* **1.** mouthpiece (of wind instrument); **2.** band securing barrel of rifle to stock.
embouchure [ɑ̃buʃyr] *s.f.* **1.** mouth (of river, etc.); **2.** bit (of harness); **3.** mouthpiece (of wind instrument).
embouquement [ɑ̃bukmɑ̃] *s.m.* (naut.) entering a canal or a narrow channel.
embouquer [ɑ̃buke] *v.t.i.* (naut.) to enter a canal or a narrow channel.
embourber [ɑ̃burbe] *v.t.* to sink or drive into the mud; **s'~** *v.refl.* to stick in the mud.
embourgeoisement [ɑ̃burʒwazmɑ̃] *s.m.* becoming or making respectable middle-class.
embourgeoiser [ɑ̃burʒwaze] *v.t.* to make middle-class; **s'~** *v.refl.* to become respectable middle-class.
embourrure [ɑ̃buryr] *s.f.* (upholstery) ticking.
embout [ɑ̃bu] *s.m.* ferrule (of stick, umbrella, etc.); end, tip, cap.

embouteillage [ɑ̃butɛjaʒ] *s.m.* **1.** (obs.) bottling; **2.** traffic jam.
embouteiller [ɑ̃buteje] *v.t.* **1.** (obs.) to bottle; **2.** (naut.) to blockade; **3.** to block (road, etc.).
emboutir [ɑ̃butir] *v.t.* **1.** to emboss, to stamp; **2.** to run into (from behind); **3.** (techn.) to tip, to cap.
emboutissage [ɑ̃butisaʒ] *s.m.* embossing, stamping, pressing.
emboutisseur [ɑ̃butisœr] *s.m.* embosser, stamper, presser.
emboutisseuse [ɑ̃butisøz] *s.f.*, **emboutissoir** [ɑ̃butiswar] *s.m.* stamping-press, stamp.
embranchement [ɑ̃brɑ̃ʃmɑ̃] *s.m.* branching, ramification; minor road; (rail.) branch line; junction, fork; (biol.) phylum; (fig.) branch, division.
embrancher [ɑ̃brɑ̃ʃe] *v.t.* to connect (to existing road, line, or channel); **s'~** *v.refl.* (of road, etc.) to branch off (*sur*, from); to form a junction (*sur*, with).
embraquer [ɑ̃brake] *v.t.* (naut.) to haul (a rope) taut.
embrasement [ɑ̃brɑzmɑ̃] *s.m.* **1.** (obs.) fire; **2.** radiance, glow.
embraser [ɑ̃brɑze] *v.t.* **1.** to burn, to set fire to; to scorch; **2.** to illuminate, to set aglow; (fig.) to inflame, to set alight; **s'~** *v.refl.* to blaze, to glow.
embrassade [ɑ̃brasad] *s.f.* embrace.
embrasse [ɑ̃bras] *s.f.* curtain-loop.
embrassement [ɑ̃brasmɑ̃] *s.m.* (Lit.) embrace.
embrasser [ɑ̃brase] *v.t.* **1.** to embrace, to hug, to kiss; (fig.) to embrace, to espouse, to adopt; *qui trop embrasse, mal étreint*, more haste, less speed; **2.** to comprise, to encompass, to include.
embrasseu-r, -se [ɑ̃brasœr] *s.m.f.* inveterate kisser; *adj.* demonstrative.
embrasure [ɑ̃brazyr] *s.f.* embrasure, recess; *~ de la porte*, doorway.
embrayage [ɑ̃brɛjaʒ] *s.m.* (mech.) clutch; letting in of clutch.
embrayer [ɑ̃breje] *v.t.* **1.** to let in the clutch, to get into gear; **2.** (pop.) to re-start work.
embrèvement [ɑ̃brɛvmɑ̃] *s.m.* (carp.) joggle (joint).
embrever [ɑ̃brəve] *v.t.* (carp.) to joggle, to join by a joggle.
embrigadement [ɑ̃brigadmɑ̃] *s.m.* **1.** (obs.) forming a brigade; **2.** recruitment, enlisting (of support).
embrigader [ɑ̃brigade] *v.t.* **1.** (obs.) to form into a brigade; **2.** to merge; (fig.) to regiment.
embringuer [ɑ̃brɛ̃ge] *v.t.* (fam.) to involve (in a shady venture).
embrocation [ɑ̃brɔkɑsjɔ̃] *s.f.* embrocation.
embrochement [ɑ̃brɔʃmɑ̃] *s.m.* putting (meat) on a spit.
embrocher [ɑ̃brɔʃe] *v.t.* **1.** to put on a spit; **2.** (fam.) to run through (with a sword).
embroncher [ɑ̃brɔ̃ʃe] *v.t.* to lay (tiles, etc.) with an overlap.
embrouillage [ɑ̃brujaʒ] *s.m.* (fam.) muddle.
embrouillamini [ɑ̃brujamini] *s.m.* (fam.) muddle, great confusion.
embrouille [ɑ̃bruj] *s.f.* (pop.) misleading; deception.
embrouillé, -e [ɑ̃bruje] *adj.* complicated, intricate, tangled.
embrouillement [ɑ̃brujmɑ̃] *s.m.* entanglement; confusion; intricacy.
embrouiller [ɑ̃bruje] *v.t.* **1.** to entangle; **2.** (fig.) to confuse, to muddle; **s'~** *v.refl.* to become confused or muddled.
embroussaillé, -e [ɑ̃brusɑje] *adj.* (of hair, etc.) tousled, bushy.
embroussailler [ɑ̃brusɑje] *v.t.* to cover with scrub; **s'~** *v.refl.* to become overgrown with scrub.
embrumer [ɑ̃bryme] *v.t.* to cover with mist, to mist over; (fig.) to cloud, to darken.
embrun [ɑ̃brœ̃] *s.m.* (usu. pl.) spray, spindrift.
embryo-génie [ɑ̃brijɔʒeni], **~genèse** [ɑ̃brijɔʒənɛz] *s.f.* embryogeny; **~logie** [ɑ̃brijɔlɔʒi] *s.f.* embryology; **~logique** [ɑ̃brijɔlɔʒik] *adj.* embryological; **~logiste** [ɑ̃brijɔlɔʒist] *s.m.f.* embryologist.
embryon [ɑ̃brijɔ̃] *s.m.* embryo; (fig.) germ.
embryonnaire [ɑ̃brijɔnɛr] *adj.* (lit. & fig.) embryonic; (biol.) embryonal.
embryotomie [ɑ̃brijɔtɔmi] *s.f.* embryotomy.
embu, -e [ɑ̃by] *adj.* (of paintings) dull, faded, flat; ~ *s.m.* flatness, dullness.
embûche [ɑ̃byʃ] *s.f.* (obs.) ambush; (pl.) pitfalls.
embuer [ɑ̃bɥe] *v.t.* to mist (over).
embuscade [ɑ̃byskad] *s.f.* ambush; (fig.) pitfall.
embusquer [ɑ̃byske] *v.t.* **1.** to place in ambush, to position under cover; **2.** (from 1914–18 war) to find a safe job (behind the lines) for; **s'~** *v.refl.* to lie in ambush, to lie in wait.
éméché, -e [emeʃe] *adj.* (fam.) tipsy.
émeraude [ɛmrod] *s.f.* emerald; ~ *adj.invar.* emerald (green).
émergence [emɛrʒɑ̃s] *s.f.* emergence.
émergent, -e [emɛrʒɑ̃] *adj.* emergent, emerging.
émerger [emɛrʒe] *v.i.* to emerge, to come to the surface, to come into view.
émeri [ɛmri] *s.m.* emery; *papier (d')~*, emery paper; *bouchon à l'~*, ground glass stopper; *bouché à l'~*, (fam.) dense, stupid.
émerillon [ɛmrijɔ̃] *s.m.* **1.** (ornith.) merlin; **2.** swivel (hook).
émerillonné, -e [ɛmrijɔne] *adj.* lively, gay.
émeriser [ɛmrize] *v.t.* to coat with emery powder.
émérite [emerit] *adj.* **1.** (obs.) retired, emeritus; **2.** outstanding, highly accomplished.
émersion [emɛrsjɔ̃] *s.f.* (astron.) emersion.
émerveillement [emɛrvɛjmɑ̃] *s.m.* wonder, admiration.
émerveiller [emɛrveje] *v.t.* to astonish, to amaze, to fill with awe; **s'~** *v.refl.* to marvel, to be amazed, to wonder, to be awestruck.
émétique [emetik] *adj.*, *s.m.* emetic.
émett-eur, -rice [emɛtœr] *adj.* **1.** (fin.) issuing; **2.** (radio, etc.) broadcasting; *poste ~eur*, broadcasting station; **~eur** *s.m.* transmitter.
émettre [emɛtr] *v.t.* **1.** to issue, to emit; to draw (a cheque); (eccles.) to take (vows); **2.** (fig.) to express, to give expression to; **3.** (radio, etc.) to transmit, to broadcast.
émeu [emø], **émou** [emu] *s.m.* (ornith.) emu.
émeute [emøt] *s.f.* riot, disturbance.
émeuti-er, -ère [emøtje] *s.m.f.* rioter.
émiettement [emjɛtmɑ̃] *s.m.* crumbling.
émietter [emjete] *v.t.* to crumble; (fig.) to fragment, to disperse; **s'~** *v.refl.* to crumble away.
émigrant, -e [emigrɑ̃] *s.m.f.* emigrant.
émigration [emigrɑsjɔ̃] *s.f.* **1.** emigration; **2.** (zool.) migration.
émigré, -e [emigre] *s.m.f.* (hist., pol.) émigré; refugee.
émigrer [emigre] *v.i.* **1.** to emigrate; **2.** (zool.) to migrate.
émincé [emɛ̃se] *s.m.* (cook.) thin slice, rasher; dish of thin slices of meat in gravy.
émincer [emɛ̃se] *v.t.* to slice thinly.
éminemment [eminamɑ̃] *adv.* eminently, with distinction.
éminence [eminɑ̃s] *s.f.* eminence, height; *son Éminence le cardinal*, his Eminence the Cardinal.

éminent, -e [eminɑ̃] *adj.* eminent, outstanding, distinguished.
émir [emir] *s.m.* emir.
émirat [emira] *s.m.* emirate; (geog.) *Émirats arabes unis*, United Arab Emirates.
émissaire[1] [emisɛr] *s.m.* emissary; *bouc* ~, scapegoat.
émissaire[2] [emisɛr] *adj.* (anat.) *veine* ~, emissary vein; ~ *s.m.* outlet channel from lake.
émissi-f, -ve [emisif] *adj.* emissive.
émission [emisjɔ̃] *s.f.* **1.** emission, production; **2.** issue, issuing; **3.** (radio, etc.) transmission, broadcasting; broadcast, programme.
emmagasinage [ɑ̃magazinaʒ] *s.m.* warehousing, storage.
emmagasiner [ɑ̃magazine] *v.t.* to warehouse, to store; (fig.) to amass.
emmaillotement [ɑ̃majɔtmɑ̃] *s.m.* swaddling, swathing.
emmailloter [ɑ̃majɔte] *v.t.* (obs.) to swaddle (a baby); (mod.) to swathe; (fig.) to envelop.
emmanchement [ɑ̃mɑ̃ʃmɑ̃] *s.m.* fitting of a handle.
emmancher [ɑ̃mɑ̃ʃe] *v.t.* to fit a handle to; (fig., fam.) to start, to set about; **s'**~ *v.refl.* to begin.
emmanchure [ɑ̃mɑ̃ʃyr] *s.f.* armhole (of garment).
emmêlement [ɑ̃mɛlmɑ̃] *s.m.* tangle, mixture, confusion.
emmêler [ɑ̃mele] *v.t.* to tangle, to entangle, to confuse, to muddle up.
emménagement [ɑ̃menaʒmɑ̃] *s.m.* **1.** moving into a new house; **2.** quarters (on a ship).
emménager [ɑ̃menaʒe] *v.i.* to move in (to a new house).
emménagogue [ɑ̃menagɔg] *adj.* (med.) emmenagogic; ~ *s.m.* emmenagogue.
emmener [ɑ̃mne] *v.t.* to take (s.o.) away or out; (mil., sport) to lead.
emment(h)al [emɛ̃tal] *s.m.* Emmenthal (cheese).
emmerdant, -e [ɑ̃mɛrdɑ̃] *adj.* (vulg.) bloody annoying, a bloody nuisance.
emmerdement [ɑ̃mɛrdəmɑ̃] *s.m.* (vulg.) bloody awful trouble; bloody nuisance.
emmerder [ɑ̃mɛrde] *v.t.* (vulg.) **1.** to be a bloody nuisance to, to bore to death; **2.** (expressing contempt) *je les emmerde*, to hell with them!; **s'**~ *v.refl.* to be bored to death.
emmerdeu-r, -se [ɑ̃mɛrdœr] *s.m.f.* (vulg. of person) bloody nuisance.
emmétrope [ɑ̃metrɔp] *adj.* emmetropic; ~ *s.m.f.* emmetrope.
emmétropie [ɑ̃metrɔpi] *s.f.* emmetropia.
emmieller [ɑ̃mjele] *v.t.* **1.** (obs.) to sweeten with honey; (fig.) to sweeten, to sugar, to honey; **2.** (euphem.) = EMMERDER 1.
emmitoufler [ɑ̃mitufle] *v.t.* (fam.) to wrap up, to muffle up; **s'**~ *v.refl.* to swathe oneself.
emmotté, -e [ɑ̃mɔte] *adj.* (agric.) packed in soil.
emmurer [ɑ̃myre] *v.t.* (lit. & fig.) to immure, to wall up.
émoi [emwa] *s.m.* agitation, alarm; unease.
émollient, -e [emɔljɑ̃] *adj.*, ~ *s.m.* emollient.
émolument [emɔlymɑ̃] *s.m.* (obs.) fee; (law) residue (of estate); (pl.) salary.
émonctoire [emɔ̃ktwar] *s.m.* (anat.) emunctory.
émondage [emɔ̃daʒ] *s.m.* pruning, trimming, (of trees).
émonder [emɔ̃de] *v.t.* to prune, to cut out the dead wood from; to clean (grain, etc.).
émondes [emɔ̃d] *s.f.pl.* dead branches.
émondeur [emɔ̃dœr] *s.m.* pruner.
émondoir [emɔ̃dwar] *s.m.* tree-pruner, pruning--hook.
émorfilage [emɔrfilaʒ] *s.m.* (techn.) removing burr or wire-edge from cutting surface.
émorfiler [emɔrfile] *v.t.* (techn.) to remove burr or wire-edge from cutting surface.
émoti-f, -ve [emɔtif] *adj.* emotive, emotional; *s.m.f.* emotional person.
émotion [emosjɔ̃] *s.f.* emotion; (fam.) alarm, fear.
émotionnable [emosjɔnabl] *adj.* emotional, sensitive.
émotionnel, -le [emosjɔnɛl] *adj.* (psychol.) emotional.
émotionner [emosjɔne] *v.t.* (fam.) to move, to touch.
émotivité [emɔtivite] *s.f.* emotional character, sensitivity; emotivity.
émottage [emɔtaʒ], **émottement** [emɔtmɑ̃] *s.m.* (agric.) harrowing and rolling.
émotter [emɔte] *v.t.* (agric.) to break up (soil).
émotteuse [emɔtøz] *s.f.* (agric.) harrow.
émou see ÉMEU.
émouchet [emuʃe] *s.m.* (ornith.) small hawk, kestrel.
émouchette [emuʃɛt] *s.f.* fly-net (for horses).
émouchoir [emuʃwar] *s.m.* fly-whisk.
émoudre [emudr] *v.t.* (obs.) to whet, to grind, to sharpen.
émoulage [emulaʒ] *s.m.* whetting, grinding, sharpening.
émouleur [emulœr] *s.m.* knife-grinder, tool--grinder.
émoulu, -e [emuly] *adj.* **1.** sharp; *se battre à fer* ~, to fight with naked swords; **2.** *frais* ~ (*d'une école*), fresh from, just out of (school).
émousser [emuse] *v.t.* to blunt, to take the edge off; (fig.) to dull, to deaden.
émoustillant, -e [emustijɑ̃] *adj.* stimulating, exciting.
émoustiller [emustije] *v.t.* to stimulate, to enliven.
émouvant, -e [emuvɑ̃] *adj.* moving, touching, affecting.
émouvoir [emuvwar] *v.t.* **1.** (obs.) to move, to set in motion; **2.** (fig.) to move, to touch, to stir, to rouse; **s'**~ *v.refl.* to be touched, to be moved, to be affected; *sans s'*~ *le moins du monde*, without turning a hair.
émpaillage [ɑ̃pɑjaʒ] *s.m.* **1.** taxidermy; **2.** caning (of chairs).
empaillement [ɑ̃pɑjmɑ̃] *s.m.* (agric.) supplying with straw.
empaillé, -e [ɑ̃pɑje] *adj.* stuffed; (fig.) *il a l'air* ~, he looks like a stuffed dummy.
empailler [ɑ̃pɑje] *v.t.* **1.** to stuff (dead animals); to cane (chairs); **2.** to pack in straw; (hort.) to cover with straw.
empailleu-r, -se [ɑ̃pɑjœr] *s.m.f.* **1.** taxidermist; **2.** chair-mender.
empalement [ɑ̃palmɑ̃] *s.m.* impaling.
empaler [ɑ̃pale] *v.t.* to impale; **s'**~ *v.refl.* to become impaled.
empan [ɑ̃pɑ̃] *s.m.* (obs.) span (of hand).
empanaché, -e [ɑ̃panaʃe] *adj.* plumed; crested.
empanner [ɑ̃pane] *v.t.i.* (naut.) to gybe.
empaquetage [ɑ̃paktaʒ] *s.m.* wrapping, packaging.
empaqueter [ɑ̃pakte] *v.t.* to wrap up, to package, to make into a parcel.
empaqueteu-r, -se [ɑ̃paktœr] *s.m.f.* packer.
(s')emparer [ɑ̃pare] *v.refl.* *s'*~ *de*, to seize, to take by force; to take possession of; to snatch; to take hold of, to catch hold of.
empâtement [ɑ̃pɑtmɑ̃] *s.m.* **1.** fattening (of poultry); **2.** puffiness, fleshiness, (of features); **3.** (art) impasto.
empâter [ɑ̃pɑte] *v.t.* **1.** to coat (battery plates); to fur (the tongue); **2.** to fatten (poultry); **s'**~ *v.refl.* to put on flesh.
empattement [ɑ̃patmɑ̃] *s.m.* **1.** (arch.) footing

(of wall); podium; **2.** (print.) serif; **3.** (techn.) base; (car) wheelbase.
empatter [ãpate] *v.t.* to join, to tenon; to support, to fix.
empaumer [ãpome] *v.t.* (fig., fam.) to have in the hollow of one's hand.
empaumure [ãpomyr] *s.f.* **1.** palm (of glove); **2.** palm (of antler).
empêchement [ãpɛʃmã] *s.m.* obstacle, impediment, hindrance, bar; *je m'excuse, j'ai eu un ~*, I'm sorry, I was held up.
empêcher [ãpeʃe] *v.t.* **1.** (obs.) to obstruct, to impede; **2.** to prevent; *cela n'empêche pas que* or *n'empêche que*, nevertheless; **s'~** *v.refl.* to restrain oneself, to stop oneself; (usu. with neg.) *il ne pouvait s'~ de rire*, he couldn't help laughing.
empeigne [ãpɛɲ] *s.f.* upper (of shoe); (pop.) *gueule d'~*, ugly bastard.
empennage [ãpɛnaʒ] *s.m.* **1.** feathering (of arrows); **2.** (aeron.) empennage, stabilizers; fins (of bomb).
empenne [ãpɛn] *s.f.* flight feather (of arrow).
empenner [ãpene] *v.t.* to feather, to flight, (an arrow).
empereur [ãprœr] *s.m.* emperor.
emperler [ãpɛrle] *v.t.* **1.** (rare) to deck with pearls; **2.** (fig.) to bead.
empesage [ãpəzaʒ] *s.m.* starching.
empesé, -e [ãpəze] *adj.* starched; (fig.) starchy, stiff.
empeser [ãpəze] *v.t.* to starch, to stiffen.
empester [ãpɛste] *v.t.* **1.** (rare) to infect with plague; **2.** (fig.) to corrupt, to taint; **3.** to stink out; **4.** to stink; to stink or reek of.
empêtrer [ãpetre] *v.t.* to hamper; (lit. & fig.) to entangle; **s'~** *v.refl.* to become entangled.
emphase [ãfɑz] *s.f.* bombast, pomposity; exaggerated sentiment; ⚠ not 'emphasis'.
emphatique [ãfatik] *adj.* bombastic; (lang.) emphatic; **~ment** [ãfatikmã] *adv.* bombastically.
emphysémateu-x, -se [ãfizematø] *adj.* (med.) emphysematous; *s.m.f.* person affected with emphysema.
emphysème [ãfizɛm] *s.m.* (med.) emphysema.
empiècement [ãpjɛsmã] *s.m.* yoke (of shirt, etc.).
empierrement [ãpjɛrmã] *s.m.* metalling (of road, etc.); bed of metal (for road).
empierrer [ãpjere] *v.t.* to metal (a road); to lay a bed of stones (in a drain).
empiètement [ãpjɛtmã] *s.m.* encroaching, encroachment; infringing; trespass (*sur*, on).
empiéter [ãpjete] *v.i.* (lit. & fig.) *~ sur*, to encroach on, to infringe, to trespass on.
(**s'**)**empiffrer** [ãpifre] *v.refl.* (fam.) to gorge, to stuff oneself.
empilage [ãpilaʒ], **empilement** [ãpilmã] *s.m.* stacking up; stack, pile.
empile [ãpil] *s.f.* (fish.) leader, casting-line.
empiler [ãpile] *v.t.* **1.** to stack up, to pile up; **2.** (fam.) to cheat, to swindle; **s'~** *v.refl.* to pile up.
empileu-r, -se [ãpilœr] *s.m.f.* **1.** stacker; **2.** (pop.) cheat, swindler.
empire [ãpir] *s.m.* **1.** government, sovereignty; sway, dominion, influence; *sous l'~ de*, under the influence of; **2.** (hist., pol.) empire; *Empire*, Empire (of Napoleon I); (of furniture, etc.) *style Empire*, Empire style; *le second Empire*, the Second Empire (of Napoleon III).
empirer [ãpire] *v.i.* to get worse, to worsen, to deteriorate; *~ v.t.* to make worse, to aggravate.
empirique [ãpirik] *adj.* empirical; (obs. med.) empiric; *~ s.m.* (obs. med.) empiric; **~ment** [ãpirikmã] *adv.* empirically.
empirisme [ãpirism] *s.m.* empiricism; (obs.) quackery.
empiriste [ãpirist] *adj.* empirical; *~ s.m.f.* empiricist.
emplacement [ãplasmã] *s.m.* site, location.
emplanture [ãplãtyr] *s.f.* (naut.) step (of a mast); (aeron.) root, socket, (of wing).
emplâtre [ãplɑtr] *s.m.* **1.** plaster, sticking-plaster; patch (for tyre); **2.** (fig., fam.) stodgy food; (pop.) (of person) useless lump; **3.** slap, clout.
emplette [ãplɛt] *s.f.* purchase; *faire ses ~s*, to go shopping.
emplir [ãplir] *v.t.* (obs.) to fill; (mod.) to fill up, to occupy completely; **s'~** *v.refl.* to fill.
emploi [ãplwa] *s.m.* **1.** use, usage; *mode d'~*, directions for use; *~ du temps*, timetable; (fig.) *cela fait double ~*, that is an unnecessary duplication; **2.** (bookkeep.) entry; **3.** employment, occupation; **4.** (theatr.) part, rôle.
employable [ãplwajabl] *adj.* employable, usable.
employé, -e [ãplwaje] *s.m.f.* one in employment (esp. non-manual), white-collar worker, (bank, booking, etc.) clerk, (shop, etc.) assistant; official; *~ d'administration*, government employee, (usu. minor) civil servant.
employer [ãplwaje] *v.t.* **1.** to use, to make use of; **2.** (bookkeep.) to enter; **3.** to employ, to give employment to; **s'~** *v.refl.* to be used; *s'~ à*, to busy oneself with.
empocher [ãpɔʃe] *v.t.* **1.** to receive (money); **2.** (rare) to pocket.
empoignade [ãpwaɲad] *s.f.* quarrel, argument.
empoigne [ãpwaɲ] *s.f.* (obs.) seizing; (mod.) *c'est une vraie foire d'~*, it's just a free-for-all, a rat race.
empoigner [ãpwaɲe] *v.t.* **1.** to seize, to lay hold of, to grasp; **2.** (fig.) to move, to hold spellbound, to enthral; **s'~** *v.refl.* to come to blows.
empointure [ãpwɛ̃tyr] *s.f.* (naut.) peak of square sail.
empois [ãpwa] *s.m.* starch.
empoisonnant, -e [ãpwazɔnã] *adj.* (fam., jest) poisonous, lousy; boring.
empoisonnement [ãpwazɔnmã] *s.m.* poisoning; (obs.) corruption; (fam.) trouble.
empoisonner [ãpwazɔne] *v.t.* **1.** to poison, to add poison to; **2.** to infect, to pollute; (fig.) to corrupt; to mar, to spoil, to make (life) unbearable; **3.** (fam.) to bore, to plague; **s'~** *v.refl.* **1.** to take poison, to poison oneself; **2.** (fam.) to be bored.
empoisonneu-r, -se [ãpwazɔnœr] *s.m.f.* **1.** poisoner; (fam.) bad cook; (fig., Lit.) corrupter; **2.** (fam.) utter bore.
empoisser [ãpwase] *v.t.* to make sticky or tacky.
empoissonnement [ãpwasɔnmã] *s.m.* stocking with fish.
empoissonner [ãpwasɔne] *v.t.* to stock with fish.
emporté, -e [ãpɔrte] *adj.* quick-tempered, fiery.
emportement [ãpɔrtəmã] *s.m.* **1.** (rare) transport, surge; **2.** fit of temper or passion, outburst.
emporte-pièce [ãpɔrtəpjɛs] *s.m.invar.* **1.** (techn.) punch, stamp, cutter (for cutting shapes); **2.** (obs.) biting satire, satirist; *à l'~*, (fig.) biting, cutting.
emporter [ãpɔrte] *v.t.* **1.** to take or carry away, to carry off, to sweep away, to remove; to seize, to snatch; *que le diable l'emporte!*, the devil take him!; *autant en emporte le vent*, gone with the wind; *~ le morceau*, to win the day; *l'~ sur*, to beat, to defeat, to prevail over; **2.** (obs.) to imply, to presuppose; **s'~** *v.refl.* to be carried away, to lose one's temper.
empoté, -e [ãpɔte] *adj.*, *s.m.f.* (fam.) clumsy, awkward (person).
empoter [ãpɔte] *v.t.* to pot (plants, jam).

empourprer [ɑ̃purpre] *v.t.* to stain red or crimson; **s'~** *v.refl.* to turn crimson.
empoussiérer [ɑ̃pusjere] *v.t.* to cover with dust.
empreindre [ɑ̃prɛ̃dr] *v.t.* to imprint, to impress, to stamp; **s'~** *v.refl.* to be stamped (*de*, with).
empreinte [ɑ̃prɛ̃t] *s.f.* impression, stamp; print; *~s digitales*, fingerprints.
empressé, -e [ɑ̃prese] *adj.* attentive, assiduous; eager (*à, de*, to).
empressement [ɑ̃prɛsmɑ̃] *s.m.* eagerness, readiness, enthusiasm.
(**s'**)**empresser** [ɑ̃prese] *v.refl.* to be anxious to please; to show readiness, to be eager; *~ de*, to hasten to (do sth.).
emprésurer [ɑ̃prezyre] *v.t.* to add rennet to (milk).
emprise [ɑ̃priz] *s.f.* **1.** (law) expropriation; **2.** ascendancy, hold, influence.
emprisonnement [ɑ̃prizɔnmɑ̃] *s.m.* imprisonment.
emprisonner [ɑ̃prizɔne] *v.t.* (lit. & fig.) to imprison, to hold captive.
emprunt [ɑ̃prœ̃] *s.m.* borrowing, loan; *d'~*, borrowed; assumed.
emprunté, -e [ɑ̃prœ̃te] *adj.* **1.** borrowed, assumed; **2.** constrained, ill at ease, embarrassed.
emprunter [ɑ̃prœ̃te] *v.t.* to borrow; to take (*à*, from), to assume, to take on.
emprunteu-r, -se [ɑ̃prœ̃tœr] *s.m.f.* borrower.
empuantir [ɑ̃pɥɑ̃tir] *v.t.* to infect, to pollute, to cause to stink.
empyème [ɑ̃pjɛm] *s.m.* (med.) empyema.
empyrée [ɑ̃pire] *s.m.* empyrean.
empyreume [ɑ̃pirøm] *s.m.* (anc. chem.) empyreuma.
ému, -e [emy] *adj.* moved, touched, affected, agitated, excited.
émulation [emylɑsjɔ̃] *s.f.* emulation; rivalry, competition.
émule [emyl] *s.m.f.* (Lit.) emulator, rival.
émulseur [emylsœr] *s.m.* emulsifier.
émulsi-f, -ve [emylsif] *adj.* emulsive.
émulsifiable [emylsifjabl] *adj.* emulsifiable.
émulsine [emylsin] *s.f.* (chem.) emulsin.
émulsion [emylsjɔ̃] *s.f.* emulsion.
émulsionner [emylsjɔne] *v.t.* to emulsify, to emulsionize.
en [ɑ̃] *prep.* **1.** (place) in, at; to, into; *rester ~ France*, to stay in France; *aller ~ France*, to go to France; *mettre ~ prison*, to put in(to) prison; *monter ~ voiture*, to get into a car; *~ tête*, at the head, at the front; *~ avant*, in front, forward; *~ arrière*, behind, backward(s); *de fleur ~ fleur*, from flower to flower; **2.** (time) in, to; *~ (l'an) 1900*, in (the year) 1900; *~ avril*, *~ automne*, in April, in autumn; *~ dix minutes*, in (within) ten minutes; *de temps ~ temps*, from time to time; *de deux heures ~ deux heures*, at two-hourly intervals; **3.** (state) at, in, on, etc.; into; *~ guerre*, at war; *se mettre ~ colère*, to get angry; *~ vacances*, on holiday; *~ réparation*, under repair; *casser ~ mille morceaux*, to break into a thousand fragments; **4.** (form, composition) in, of, from; *tragédie ~ cinq actes*, tragedy in five acts; *fait ~ briques*, made of brick(s); *fait ~ marbre*, made from, out of, marble; **5.** (manner, means) in, by; as, like; *~ hâte*, in haste, in a hurry; *recevoir ~ cadeau*, to receive as a present; *agir ~ fou*, to act like a madman; *vêtu ~ pirate*, dressed as a pirate; *aller ~ auto*, to go by car; **6.** (figurative, and in constr. with verbs, adjs., etc.) *~ fleur(s)*, in flower; *~ deuil*, in mourning; *~ tout*, in all; *~ général*, in general; *~ soi*, in itself, in oneself, by itself; *docteur ~ médecine*, doctor of medicine; *consister ~*, to consist of; *avoir confiance ~*, to have confidence in; *changer ~*, to change into; *être fort ~*, to be strong in; **7.** (with gerund) on, as, while, by; *~ partant*, on leaving, when leaving, as one leaves; *~ attendant*, meanwhile, while waiting, by waiting.
en [ɑ̃] *pron.* (representing thing, statement & sometimes person), *adv.* **1.** (place, origin) thence, from there; *vous allez à Londres, j'en viens*, you're going to London, I've just come from there; **2.** (representing noun governed by *de*) *j'en suis étonné*, I'm surprised at it; *je m'en souviendrai*, I shall remember it; *je vous en prie*, if you please; *qu'en pensez-vous?*, what do you think of it?; *n'en parlons pas*, let's not talk about it; **3.** (with expressions of quantity) *combien de frères avez-vous? J'en ai trois*, how many brothers have you? I have three; **4.** (possessive) *voici la porte mais j'en ai perdu la clef*, here is the door but I have lost the key; *vous trouverez la maison*; *la porte en est peinte en vert*, you will find the house; its door is painted green; **5.** (representing a phrase) *je ne sais pas s'il l'a fait mais il en est capable*, I don't know if he did it but he's capable of doing so; **6.** (partitive) some, any; *je n'ai pas d'argent. En avez-vous?*, I have no money. Have you any?; *avez-vous de l'argent? Oui, j'en ai*, have you any money? Yes, I have (some); **7.** (various verbal phrases) *s'en aller*, to go away; *j'en ai fini avec lui*, I've finished with him; *je m'en remets à vous*, I leave it to you; *je ne vous en veux pas*, I don't hold it against you; *en croire qn.*, to believe s.o.
E.N.A. [enɑ] abbrev. *École nationale d'administration* = Civil Service Staff College.
enamourer [ɑ̃namure], (**s'**)**énamourer** [enamure] *v.refl.* to fall in love (*de*, with).
énanthème [enɑ̃tɛm] *s.m.* (med.) enanthema.
énarthrose [enartroz] *s.f.* (anat.) enarthrosis.
en-avant [ɑ̃navɑ̃] *s.m.invar.* (Rugby football) forward pass, knock-on.
encablure [ɑ̃kablyr] *s.f.* (naut.) cable's length.
encadrement [ɑ̃kɑdrəmɑ̃] *s.m.* framing, frame, framework; border, margin; (mil.) appointment of officers, officering.
encadrer [ɑ̃kɑdre] *v.t.* to frame, to encircle, to surround; (mil.) to bracket (a target); to officer (a unit); **s'~** *v.refl.* to be framed.
encadreur [ɑ̃kɑdrœr] *s.m.* picture-framer.
encager [ɑ̃kaʒe] *v.t.* (lit. & fig.) to cage.
encaissable [ɑ̃kɛsabl] *adj.* (en)cashable, payable.
encaissage [ɑ̃kɛsaʒ] *s.m.* casing, boxing, (of goods).
encaisse [ɑ̃kɛs] *s.f.* cash in hand, cash balance, float; (fin.) *~ métallique*, gold and silver reserves.
encaissé, -e [ɑ̃kese] *adj.* sunken, deeply embanked; enclosed, boxed in.
encaissement [ɑ̃kɛsmɑ̃] *s.m.* **1.** (rare) packing, crating; **2.** (fin.) encashment; **3.** embankment.
encaisser [ɑ̃kese] *v.t.* **1.** (rare) to pack, to crate; **2.** (fin.) to cash, to collect (money); **3.** (fig., fam.) to take, to receive, (blows); to stand, to bear, to stick, to tolerate; **4.** to embank (river, etc.); to trench (ground for a road, etc.).
encaisseur [ɑ̃kɛsœr] *s.m.* collector (of rents, etc.); bank messenger.
encalminé, -e [ɑ̃kalmine] *adj.* (naut.) becalmed.
(**à l'**)**encan** [alɑ̃kɑ̃] *adv.* for sale by auction; (fig.) offered to the highest bidder.
encanaillement [ɑ̃kanɑjmɑ̃] *s.m.* degradation, becoming vulgar.
(**s'**)**encanailler** [ɑ̃kanɑje] *v.refl.* **1.** (obs.) to mix with the riff-raff; **2.** (mod., jest) to go slumming.
encapuchonner [ɑ̃kapyʃɔne] *v.t.* to put a hood or a cowl on; **s'~** *v.refl.* to cover one's head, to muffle up.
encaquement [ɑ̃kakmɑ̃] *s.m.* barrelling (of herrings).
encaquer [ɑ̃kake] *v.t.* to barrel (herrings); (fig., obs.) to pack like sardines.

encart [ɑ̃kar] *s.m.* inset; (bookb.) insert, inset.
encartage [ɑ̃kartaʒ] *s.m.* **1.** (bookb.) insetting; **2.** carding (of buttons, etc.).
encarter [ɑ̃karte] *v.t.* **1.** (bookb.) to inset; **2.** to fix on a card; **3.** to place material between boards (for pressing pleats, etc.).
encarteuse [ɑ̃kartøz] *s.f.* machine for carding (buttons, etc.).
encartonner [ɑ̃kartɔne] *v.t.* = ENCARTER.
en-cas, encas [ɑ̃ka] *s.m.invar.* **1.** (obs.) stand-by; **2.** snack; **3.** en-tout-cas, umbrella-sunshade.
(s')encasteler [ɑ̃kastəle] *v.refl.* (vet.) (of horse) to be hoof-bound.
encastelure [ɑ̃kastəlyr] *s.f.* (vet.) contraction of the hoof.
encastré, -e [ɑ̃kastre] *adj.* (of furniture) built-in, fitted.
encastrement [ɑ̃kastrəmɑ̃] *s.m.* fitting-in; groove.
encastrer [ɑ̃kastre] *v.t.* to build in, to set in, to fit in; ~ *qch. dans le mur,* to build, etc., sth. into the wall; **s'**~ *v.refl.* to be built or set in (*dans qch.,* into sth.).
encaustiquage [ɑ̃kɔstikaʒ] *s.m.* polishing, waxing.
encaustique [ɑ̃kɔstik] *s.f.* **1.** (art) encaustic; **2.** (wax) polish.
encaustiquer [ɑ̃kɔstike] *v.t.* to polish, to wax.
encavement [ɑ̃kavmɑ̃] *s.m.* cellaring (of wine).
encaver [ɑ̃kave] *v.t.* to cellar (wine).
enceindre [ɑ̃sɛ̃dr] *v.t.* to enclose, to surround with walls.
enceinte[1] [ɑ̃sɛ̃t] *s.f.* surrounding wall, fence; barrier ring; enclosure, precincts.
enceinte[2] [ɑ̃sɛ̃t] *adj.f.* pregnant.
encens [ɑ̃sɑ̃] *s.m.* incense; (fig.) fulsome praise.
encensement [ɑ̃sɑ̃smɑ̃] *s.m.* (eccles.) censing; (fig.) bestowing of praise.
encenser [ɑ̃sɑ̃se] *v.t.* to cense; (fig.) to praise excessively, to flatter; (of horse) to move the head up and down.
encenseu-r, -se [ɑ̃sɑ̃sœr] *s.m.f.* **1.** (eccles.) thurifer; **2.** (obs.) flatterer.
encensoir [ɑ̃sɑ̃swar] *s.m.* censer; (fig.) *manier l'*~, *donner des coups d'*~, to pile on the flattery.
encépagement [ɑ̃sepaʒmɑ̃] *s.m.* stock of vines in vineyard.
encéphale [ɑ̃sefal] *s.m.* (anat.) encephalon, brain.
encéphalique [ɑ̃sefalik] *adj.* (anat.) encephalic.
encéphalite [ɑ̃sefalit] *s.f.* (med.) encephalitis.
encéphalo-gramme [ɑ̃sefalɔgram] *s.m.* encephalogram, encephalograph; **~graphie** [ɑ̃sefalɔgrafi] *s.f.* encephalography; **~pathie** [ɑ̃sefalɔpati] *s.f.* encephalopathy.
encerclement [ɑ̃sɛrkləmɑ̃] *s.m.* encircling, encirclement, surrounding.
encercler [ɑ̃sɛrkle] *v.t.* to encircle, to surround.
enchaînement [ɑ̃ʃɛnmɑ̃] *s.m.* concatenation, chain, train, succession, sequence (of events, etc.).
enchaîner [ɑ̃ʃene] *v.t.* **1.** to chain up, to put in chains; (fig.) to tie down, to bind, to captivate; **2.** to link, to connect; (theatr.) to pick up cue (after interruption); (cin.) to fade in; **s'**~ *v.refl.* to be connected, to follow in succession; to hang together.
enchanté, -e [ɑ̃ʃɑ̃te] *adj.* **1.** magic; *la flûte* ~*e,* the Magic Flute (opera); **2.** delighted, very pleased.
enchantement [ɑ̃ʃɑ̃tmɑ̃] *s.m.* **1.** magic, spell; *comme par* ~, as if by magic; **2.** delight.
enchanter [ɑ̃ʃɑ̃te] *v.t.* **1.** to enchant, to bewitch, to charm, to cast a spell on; **2.** to delight.
enchant-eur, -eresse [ɑ̃ʃɑ̃tœr] *s.m.f.* magician, wizard, witch; spell-binder, charmer; *adj.* enchanting, entrancing, delightful.
enchâssement [ɑ̃ʃɑsmɑ̃] *s.m.* mounting, setting (of jewel, etc.).
enchâsser [ɑ̃ʃɑse] *v.t.* **1.** to mount, to set (jewel, etc.); **2.** (eccles.) to enchase, to place in a reliquary.
enchâssure [ɑ̃ʃɑsyr] *s.f.* mounting, setting; casing.
enchatonnement [ɑ̃ʃatɔnmɑ̃] *s.m.* (techn.) mounting (of gem).
enchatonner [ɑ̃ʃatɔne] *v.t.* (techn.) to mount, to set (a gem).
enchausser [ɑ̃ʃose] *v.t.* (hort.) to earth up (for blanching); to put in a clamp.
enchemisage [ɑ̃ʃmizaʒ] *s.m.* (bookb.) putting a dust-jacket on; dust-jacket.
enchemiser [ɑ̃ʃmize] *v.t.* (bookb.) to put a dust-jacket on.
enchère [ɑ̃ʃɛr] *s.f.* bid; *vente aux* ~*s,* auction sale.
enchérir [ɑ̃ʃerir] *v.i.* **1.** to become dearer, to go up in price; **2.** to bid; ~ *sur qn.,* to overbid or outbid s.o.; (fig.) ~ *sur qch.,* to outdo, to go one better than, to improve on, sth.
enchérissement [ɑ̃ʃerismɑ̃] *s.m.* rise in price.
enchérisseur [ɑ̃ʃerisœr] *s.m.* bidder; *le plus offrant (et dernier)* ~, the highest bidder.
enchevalement [ɑ̃ʃvalmɑ̃] *s.m.* (techn.) shoring up, underpinning.
enchevaucher [ɑ̃ʃvoʃe] *v.t.* to lay (tiles, etc.) with an overlap.
enchevauchure [ɑ̃ʃvoʃyr] *s.f.* overlapping (of tiles, etc.).
enchevêtrement [ɑ̃ʃvɛtrəmɑ̃] *s.m.* tangle, confusion.
enchevêtrer [ɑ̃ʃvetre] *v.t.* **1.** (obs.) to halter (a horse); **2.** (constr.) to tie (beams) with a joist; **3.** to mix up, to confuse; **s'**~ *v.refl.* to be muddled, confused.
enchevêtrure [ɑ̃ʃvetryr] *s.f.* (constr.) arrangement of beams to form a shaft.
enchifrené, -e [ɑ̃ʃifrəne] *adj.* sniffling, with a cold in the head, with a blocked nose.
enchifrènement [ɑ̃ʃifrɛnmɑ̃] *s.m.* blockage of nose (by catarrh).
enclave [ɑ̃klav] *s.f.* enclave.
enclavement [ɑ̃klavmɑ̃] *s.m.* being surrounded or enclosed.
enclaver [ɑ̃klave] *v.t.* **1.** to surround, to enclose; **2.** to lock (two things together), to wedge in, to key in.
enclenche [ɑ̃klɑ̃ʃ] *s.f.* (mech.) interlocking part.
enclenchement [ɑ̃klɑ̃ʃmɑ̃] *s.m.* (mech.) interlock.
enclencher [ɑ̃klɑ̃ʃe] *v.t.* (mech.) to lock, to engage; (fig.) *l'affaire est enclenchée,* the matter is closed.
enclin, -e [ɑ̃klɛ̃] *adj.* inclined, prone, apt, given, (*à,* to).
encliquetage [ɑ̃kliktaʒ] *s.m.* (mech.) ratchet, ratchet-wheel.
encliqueter [ɑ̃klikte] *v.t.* (mech.) to stop by operating ratchet.
enclitique [ɑ̃klitik] *s.m.* (phon.) enclitic.
enclore [ɑ̃klɔr] *v.t.* to enclose, to fence (in); to shut in.
enclos [ɑ̃klo] *s.m.* enclosure; paddock; fence.
enclouage [ɑ̃kluaʒ] *s.m.* **1.** (hist.) spiking (of guns); **2.** (surg.) pinning (of bones).
enclouer [ɑ̃klue] *v.t.* **1.** to spike (a gun); **2.** to prick (a horse, when shoeing); **3.** (surg.) to pin (bones).
enclouure [ɑ̃kluyr] *s.f.* (vet.) prick (made when shoeing).
enclume [ɑ̃klym] *s.f.* **1.** anvil, block; (fig.) *remettre sur l'*~, to remodel, to reshape; (fig.) *être entre l'*~ *et le marteau,* to be between the devil and the deep blue sea; **2.** (anat.) incus, anvil (of ear).

encoche [ɑ̃kɔʃ] *s.f.* notch, nick.
encochement [ɑ̃kɔʃmɑ̃], **encochage** [ɑ̃kɔʃaʒ] *s.m.* nicking; nick, notch.
encocher [ɑ̃kɔʃe] *v.t.* to notch, to nick; ~ *une flèche*, to fit an arrow to the bow.
encoignure [ɑ̃kɔɲyr] *s.f.* **1.** angle of wall, corner; **2.** corner cupboard, etc.
encollage [ɑ̃kɔlaʒ] *s.m.* sizing, pasting, gluing.
encoller [ɑ̃kɔle] *v.t.* to paste, to size (paper), to glue (wood).
encolleu-r, -se [ɑ̃kɔlœr] *s.m.f.* sizer; **~se** *s.f.* sizing machine.
encolure [ɑ̃kɔlyr] *s.f.* **1.** neck (of horse); *gagner d'une* ~, to win by a neck; **2.** neck (of garment).
encombrant, -e [ɑ̃kɔ̃brɑ̃] *adj.* cumbersome, bulky; (fig.) inconvenient.
encombre [ɑ̃kɔ̃br] *s.m. sans* ~, without difficulty, without any trouble, without mishap.
encombré, -e [ɑ̃kɔ̃bre] *adj.* overcrowded, overfull; (fig.) crowded, saturated.
encombrement [ɑ̃kɔ̃brəmɑ̃] *s.m.* **1.** congestion, overcrowding; (fig.) saturation; block; traffic jam; obstruction; **2.** space required or taken up (by), clearance (required).
encombrer [ɑ̃kɔ̃bre] *v.t.* to block, to obstruct; to overcrowd, to fill; **s'~** *v.refl.* to burden oneself (*de*, with).
(**à l'**)**encontre** [alɑ̃kɔ̃tr] *adv.* to the contrary, in opposition; ~ **de** *prep.* against, contrary to, in opposition to.
encorbellement [ɑ̃kɔrbɛlmɑ̃] *s.m.* (arch.) corbel, overhang.
encor [ɑ̃kɔr] *adv.* (obs. exc. poetical) = ENCORE.
(**s'**)**encorder** [ɑ̃kɔrde] *v.refl.* (mountaineering) to rope up, to form a rope (with other climbers).
encore [ɑ̃kɔr] *adv.* **1.** still, yet; *pas* ~, not yet, still not; **2.** again, once more; ~ *un(e)*, another; ~ *une fois*, again, once more; *mais* ~*?*, and then?; **3.** more, further; (with comparative) still, even; ~ *pire*, still worse, even worse; **4.** moreover, further, if only; *si* ~ *il voulait m'écouter*, if only he would listen to me; *et* ~*!*, if that!, if then!; *il vous en donnerait trois mille, et* ~*!*, he would give you three thousand for it, if that; **5.** (usu. with inversion of subject and verb) however, all the same; ~ *n'est-il pas certain que*, however, it is not certain that; ~ **que** *conj.* although, notwithstanding that, in spite of the fact that.
encorné, -e [ɑ̃kɔrne] *adj.* **1.** (rare) horned; **2.** (vet.) *javart* ~, swelling under the coronet.
encorner [ɑ̃kɔrne] *v.t.* to gore, to wound with the horns.
encornet [ɑ̃kɔrnɛ] *s.m.* (moll.) squid.
encourageant, -e [ɑ̃kuraʒɑ̃] *adj.* encouraging, heartening.
encouragement [ɑ̃kuraʒmɑ̃] *s.m.* encouragement; incentive; promotion, support; (school) *prix d'*~, prize for meritorious work.
encourager [ɑ̃kuraʒe] *v.t.* to encourage, to inspire; to promote, to support, to sponsor.
encourir [ɑ̃kurir] *v.t.* to incur, to risk, to run the risk of, to bring upon oneself.
encrage [ɑ̃kraʒ] *s.m.* (print.) inking.
encrassement [ɑ̃krasmɑ̃] *s.m.* dirtying, soiling; fouling; choking up, clogging.
encrasser [ɑ̃krase] *v.t.* to dirty, to soil; to foul, to soot up, to choke, to clog; **s'~** *v.refl.* to become fouled, choked, etc.
encre [ɑ̃kr] *s.f.* ink; ~ *de Chine*, Indian ink.
encrer [ɑ̃kre] *v.t.* to ink.
encreur [ɑ̃krœr] *adj.m.* inking.
encrier [ɑ̃krije] *s.m.* inkwell; (print.) ink trough.
encrine [ɑ̃krin] *s.m.* (palaeont.) encrinite.
encroué, -e [ɑ̃krue] *adj.* (of fallen tree) caught in the branches of another tree.
encroûtement [ɑ̃krutmɑ̃] *s.m.* crusting over, crust; (fig.) being hidebound, being in a rut.
encroûter [ɑ̃krute] *v.t.* **1.** to cover with a crust; **2.** to face with mortar; **3.** (fig.) to fossilize; **s'~** *v.refl.* **1.** to become furred or crusted; **2.** (fig.) to become hidebound, to get into a rut.
encuvage [ɑ̃kyvaʒ], **encuvement** [ɑ̃kyvmɑ̃] *s.m.* vatting.
encuver [ɑ̃kyve] *v.t.* to vat.
encyclique [ɑ̃siklik] *s.f.* encyclical.
encyclopéd-ie [ɑ̃siklɔpedi] *s.f.* encyclop(a)edia; **~ique** [ɑ̃siklɔpedik] *adj.* encyclopaedic; **~iste** [ɑ̃siklɔpedist] *s.m.* encyclopaedist.
endémie [ɑ̃demi] *s.f.* endemic, endemic disease.
endémique [ɑ̃demik] *adj.* endemic.
endenté, -e [ɑ̃dɑ̃te] *adj.* with teeth, toothed.
endenter [ɑ̃dɑ̃te] *v.t.* (techn.) **1.** to tooth, to cog; **2.** to dovetail together.
endettement [ɑ̃dɛtmɑ̃] *s.m.* indebtedness, running into debt.
endetter [ɑ̃dete] *v.t.* to involve in debt(s); **s'~** *v.refl.* to run into debt.
endeuiller [ɑ̃dœje] *v.t.* to bereave, to bring great sorrow to; (fig.) to cast a gloom over.
endêver [ɑ̃deve] *v.i.* to get in a rage.
endiablé, -e [ɑ̃djɑble] *adj.* **1.** (obs.) possessed (of the devil), diabolical; **2.** irrepressible, reckless, uncontrollable; (fig.) devilish.
endiabler [ɑ̃djɑble] *v.t.* (obs.) to make diabolical; ~ *v.i.* (obs.) to rage.
endiguement [ɑ̃digmɑ̃] *s.m.* damming up, diking.
endiguer [ɑ̃dige] *v.t.* to dam; (fig.) to hold back, to contain.
(**s'**)**endimancher** [ɑ̃dimɑ̃ʃe] *v.refl.* to dress up (to the nines), to put on one's Sunday best.
endive [ɑ̃div] *s.f.* chicory; endive.
endivisionner [ɑ̃divizjɔne] *v.t.* (mil.) to form into divisions.
endo-carde [ɑ̃dɔkard] *s.m.* (anat.) endocardium; **~cardite** [ɑ̃dɔkardit] *s.f.* (med.) endocarditis; **~carpe** [ɑ̃dɔkarp] *s.m.* (bot.) endocarp; **~crine** *adj.f.* (physiol.) endocrine.
endocrinien, -ne [ɑ̃dɔkrinjɛ̃] *adj.* endocrinal.
endocrinologie [ɑ̃dɔkrinɔlɔʒi] *s.f.* endocrinology.
endoctrinement [ɑ̃dɔktrinmɑ̃] *s.m.* (obs.) instruction; (mod.) indoctrination.
endoctriner [ɑ̃dɔktrine] *v.t.* (obs.) to instruct; (mod.) to indoctrinate.
endo-derme [ɑ̃dɔdɛrm] *s.m.* (biol.) endoderm; **~gamie** [ɑ̃dɔgami] *s.f.* (anthrop.) endogamy; **~gène** [ɑ̃dɔʒɛn] *adj.* (bot., physiol.) endogenous; (geol.) endogenic.
endolorir [ɑ̃dɔlɔrir] *v.t.* to make painful; (rare) to sadden.
endolorissement [ɑ̃dɔlɔrismɑ̃] *s.m.* painfulness, soreness.
endométrite [ɑ̃dɔmetrit] *s.f.* (med.) endometritis.
endommagement [ɑ̃dɔmaʒmɑ̃] *s.m.* damage, harm, impairment.
endommager [ɑ̃dɔmaʒe] *v.t.* to damage, to impair; to spoil.
endoparasite [ɑ̃dɔparazit] *s.m.* (biol.) endoparasite.
endoréique [ɑ̃dɔreik] *adj.* (geol.) boggy, swampy, undrained.
endormant, -e [ɑ̃dɔrmɑ̃] *adj.* (obs.) soporific; (mod.) boring, sleep-inducing.
endormeu-r, -se [ɑ̃dɔrmœr] *s.m.f.* (rare) appeaser, cajoler.
endormi, -e [ɑ̃dɔrmi] *adj.* sleepy, sleeping; (fig.) sluggish, drowsy, inactive; *s.m.f.* (usu. of child) sleepy-head, slowcoach.
endormir [ɑ̃dɔrmir] *v.t.* to put to sleep; to anaesthetize; to hypnotize; (fig.) to bore, to send to sleep; to lull, to calm, to appease; **s'~** *v.refl.* to fall asleep, to go to sleep; (fig.) to become numb, to become inactive.

endormissement [ɑ̃dɔrmismɑ̃] *s.m.* falling asleep.
endos [ɑ̃do] *s.m.* endorsement.
endo-scope [ɑ̃dɔskɔp] *s.m.* (med.) endoscope; **~scopie** [ɑ̃dɔskɔpi] *s.f.* endoscopy.
endosmomètre [ɑ̃dɔsmɔmɛtr] *s.m.* (phys.) endosmometer.
endosmose [ɑ̃dɔsmoz] *s.f.* (phys.) endosmosis.
endossataire [ɑ̃dosatɛr] *s.m.f.* endorsee.
endossement [ɑ̃dosmɑ̃] *s.m.* endorsement.
endosser [ɑ̃dose] *v.t.* **1.** to put on, to don, (a coat, etc.); (fig.) to shoulder (responsibility, etc.), to take responsibility for; **2.** to endorse (cheque, etc.); (bookb.) to back (a book).
endosseur [ɑ̃dosœr] *s.m.* endorser.
endossure [ɑ̃dosyr] *s.f.* (bookb.) backing (of a book).
endothélial, -e, (**aux**) [ɑ̃dɔteljal] *adj.* (anat.) of the endothelium.
endothélium [ɑ̃dɔteljɔm] *s.m.* (anat.) endothelium.
endothermique [ɑ̃dɔtɛrmik] *adj.* (sci.) endothermic.
endotoxine [ɑ̃dɔtɔksin] *s.f.* (physiol.) endotoxin.
endroit [ɑ̃drwa] *s.m.* **1.** place, spot, point; part (of the body); (fam.) *le petit* ~, the toilet (W.C.); *par* ~*s*, in places, here and there; *à l'*~ *de*, towards, with regard to; **2.** right side (of material, etc.).
enduire [ɑ̃dɥir] *v.t.* to coat, to smear, to cover, to plaster.
enduit [ɑ̃dɥi] *s.m.* coat, coating, dressing, coat of plaster.
endurable [ɑ̃dyrabl] *adj.* endurable.
endurance [ɑ̃dyrɑ̃s] *s.f.* endurance, staying--power, stamina, resistance; (car) *épreuve d'*~, reliability test.
endurant, -e [ɑ̃dyrɑ̃] *adj.* (obs.) long-suffering; (mod.) resistant, hardy.
endurci, -e [ɑ̃dyrsi] *adj.* hardened, inured; (fig.) hardened, obdurate, confirmed.
endurcir [ɑ̃dyrsir] *v.t.* **1.** (rare) to make hard or rough; **2.** (lit. & fig.) to harden, to make resistant, to steel; **s'**~ *v.refl.* to become hardened; to steel oneself.
endurcissement [ɑ̃dyrsismɑ̃] *s.m.* **1.** (rare) hardening; **2.** (fig.) hardening, inuring, toughening.
endurer [ɑ̃dyre] *v.t.* to bear, to endure, to suffer; (obs.) to tolerate.
énergétique [enɛrʒetik] *adj.* concerning energy; (of foods) energizing, energy-giving; ⚠ not 'energetic' in sense 'vigorous'.
énergie [enɛrʒi] *s.f.* **1.** energy, strength, vigour, force; **2.** (phys.) energy, power.
énergique [enɛrʒik] *adj.* energetic, active, forceful, vigorous; **~ment** [enɛrʒikmɑ̃] *adv.* energetically, actively, forcefully, vigorously.
énergumène [enɛrgymɛn] *s.m.f.* (obs.) energumen; (mod.) fanatic.
énervant, -e [enɛrvɑ̃] *adj.* **1.** (obs. exc. Lit.) enervating, debilitating; **2.** irritating, exasperating, nerve-racking.
énervation [enɛrvɑsjɔ̃] *s.f.* **1.** (obs.) enervation; **2.** (torture) hamstringing; **3.** (surg.) denervation.
énervé, -e [enɛrve] *adj.* fidgety, on edge, nervous, hysterical.
énervement [enɛrvəmɑ̃] *s.m.* **1.** (obs.) debilitation; **2.** agitation, nerves; irritation, impatience.
énerver [enɛrve] *v.t.* **1.** (obs.) to enervate; **2.** to irritate, to get on the nerves of; **s'**~ *v.refl.* to become irritable, to fidget.
enfaîteau (pl. **-x**) [ɑ̃fɛto] *s.m.* (constr.) ridge-tile.
enfaîtement [ɑ̃fɛtmɑ̃] *s.m.* (constr.) ridging.
enfaîter [ɑ̃fete] *v.t.* (constr.) to ridge.
enfance [ɑ̃fɑ̃s] *s.f.* **1.** (lit. & fig.) infancy; childhood; early stages; **2.** children, the young; **3.** second childhood, dotage.
enfant [ɑ̃fɑ̃] *s.m.f.* **1.** child, infant, boy, girl; ~ *prodige*, infant prodigy; (fam.) *c'est un jeu d'*~, it's child's play; *faire l'*~, to behave childishly; ~ *de chœur*, choirboy, server; **2.** child, offspring, son, daughter; descendant, native (of a country); ~ *trouvé*, foundling; ~ *prodigue*, prodigal son; ~ *adj.* childish, childlike, young.
enfantement [ɑ̃fɑ̃tmɑ̃] *s.m.* (obs.) childbirth; (Lit.) production, bringing forth.
enfanter [ɑ̃fɑ̃te] *v.t.* (lit. & fig.) to give birth to, to be delivered of; to bring forth, to produce.
enfantillage [ɑ̃fɑ̃tijaʒ] *s.m.* childishness, childish behaviour.
enfantin, -e [ɑ̃fɑ̃tɛ̃] *adj.* childish, childlike; (pej.) infantile, puerile.
enfariné, -e [ɑ̃farine] *adj.* white with flour, covered with flour, floured; *venir le bec* ~, *la gueule* ~*e*, to show guileless confidence (like a clown).
enfariner [ɑ̃farine] *v.t.* (obs.) to flour, to whiten with flour.
enfer [ɑ̃fɛr] *s.m.* (lit. & fig.) hell; (myth.) *les* ~*s*, the underworld; *d'*~, infernal, hellish; reckless; *aller un train d'*~, to go hell for leather.
enfermer [ɑ̃fɛrme] *v.t.* **1.** to shut up, to shut in, to confine; to lock up, to put under lock and key; to enclose, to surround; (sport) to hem in, to box in, (an opponent); **2.** (rare) to contain; **s'**~ *v.refl.* to shut oneself up; (fig.) to bury oneself in, to be wrapped up in.
enferrer [ɑ̃fere] *v.t.* (rare) to pierce, to run through (with sword); **s'**~ *v.refl.* to fall on one's opponent's sword; (fig.) to give oneself away, to be hoist with one's own petard.
enfeu [ɑ̃fø] *s.m.* (arch.) recess, niche, (for a tomb).
enfieller [ɑ̃fjele] *v.t.* to embitter.
enfièvrement [ɑ̃fjɛvrəmɑ̃] *s.m.* over-excitement.
enfiévrer [ɑ̃fjevre] *v.t.* (obs.) to make feverish; (mod.) to over-excite, to inflame.
enfilade [ɑ̃filad] *s.f.* **1.** suite, series; endless string, chain; **2.** (mil.) enfilade; *tir d'*~, raking fire.
enfilage [ɑ̃filaʒ] *s.m.* stringing (of beads, etc.).
enfiler [ɑ̃file] *v.t.* **1.** to thread (a needle); to string (beads, etc.); (fam.) *nous ne sommes pas là pour* ~ *des perles*, we're not here just to mess about; **2.** to recite an endless string of; **3.** (fam.) to put on, to slip into; **4.** to make one's way along; **5.** (mil.) to enfilade; **s'**~ *v.refl.* (pop.) (lit. & fig.) to swallow.
enfileu-r, -se [ɑ̃filœr] *s.m.f.* threader, stringer; (fig.) speaker (of great words, etc.).
enfin [ɑ̃fɛ̃] *adv.* **1.** at last, in the end, after all; finally, lastly; **2.** in short, to sum up, that is to say.
enflammé, -e [ɑ̃flame] *adj.* flaming, burning; (med.) inflamed; (fig.) ardent, excited, inflamed.
enflammer [ɑ̃flame] *v.t.* to set fire to, to set alight; to heat, to cause to burn; (med.) to inflame; (fig.) to inflame, to excite; (obs.) to kindle (desires), to fill with passion; **s'**~ *v.refl.* to catch fire; (fig.) to become inflamed.
enflé, -e [ɑ̃fle] *adj.* swollen; (obs. of style) bombastic; *s.m.f.* (fam.) idiot.
enfléchure [ɑ̃fleʃyr] *s.f.* (naut.) ratlines.
enfler [ɑ̃fle] *v.t.* to fill (sails); to swell, to cause to swell; to increase in volume; (fig.) to inflate, to magnify; (obs.) to puff up, to elate; ~ *v.i.* to swell.
enfleurer [ɑ̃flœre] *v.t.* (techn.) to impregnate (oil, etc.) with perfume of flowers.
enflure [ɑ̃flyr] *s.f.* swelling; (fig.) exaggeration; (obs.) bombast.

enfoncé, -e [ɑ̃fɔ̃se] *adj.* sunken, deep-set.
enfoncement [ɑ̃fɔ̃smɑ̃] *s.m.* **1.** driving in, breaking in, breaking through; **2.** hollow; recess, alcove.
enfoncer [ɑ̃fɔ̃se] *v.t.* **1.** to drive in, to push down; to thrust; (fig.) ~ *le clou*, to drive (sth.) home; ~ *qch. dans la tête de qn.*, to get sth. into someone's head; **2.** to stave in, to break down; (fam.) to beat, to overcome; (fig.) ~ *une porte ouverte*, to flog a dead horse; ~ *v.i.* to sink, to go down; **s'~** *v.refl.* (lit. & fig.) to sink; to penetrate (into); (fig.) to be absorbed (in).
enfonceu-r, -se [ɑ̃fɔ̃sœr] *s.m.f.* *~r, ~se, de portes ouvertes*, one who finds difficulties where none exist.
enfonçure [ɑ̃fɔ̃syr] *s.f.* (rare) hole, cavity, hollow.
enfouir [ɑ̃fwir] *v.t.* to bury; to hide; **s'~** *v.refl.* to hide (oneself), (fig.) to bury oneself.
enfouissement [ɑ̃fwismɑ̃] *s.m.* burying, hiding (in the ground); covering with earth.
enfouisseur [ɑ̃fwisœr] *s.m.* (agric.) cultivator (attachment to plough).
enfourchement [ɑ̃furʃəmɑ̃] *s.m.* (arch.) point (of arch); (techn.) tongue-and-groove joint.
enfourcher [ɑ̃furʃe] *v.t.* to bestride, to mount (horse or bicycle); (fig.) ~ *son dada*, to get on to one's hobby horse.
enfourchure [ɑ̃furʃyr] *s.f.* (obs.) fork (of tree, etc.); (mod.) crutch (of trousers).
enfournage [ɑ̃furnaʒ], **enfournement** [ɑ̃furnəmɑ̃] *s.m.* charging (oven or kiln); placing (bread) in oven.
enfourner [ɑ̃furne] *v.t.* **1.** to place in oven or kiln; **2.** (fam.) to gobble down; **3.** (fam.) to put, to load, (into).
enfourneur [ɑ̃furnœr] *s.m.* oven-man, kiln--man.
enfreindre [ɑ̃frɛ̃dr] *v.t.* to infringe, to break.
(s')enfuir [ɑ̃fɥir] *v.refl.* to flee, to run away; to escape; (fig.) to pass, to disappear.
enfumage [ɑ̃fymaʒ] *s.m.* (beekeeping) fumigating, smoking(-out).
enfumer [ɑ̃fyme] *v.t.* to fill with smoke; to fumigate, to smoke (out); (obs.) to blacken with smoke.
enfutailler [ɑ̃fytaje], **enfûter** [ɑ̃fyte] *v.t.* to cask, to barrel.
engagé, -e [ɑ̃gaʒe] *adj.* **1.** (arch.) engaged, embedded; **2.** enlisted; **3.** committed, involved; ~ *s.m.* enlisted man, volunteer.
engageant, -e [ɑ̃gaʒɑ̃] *adj.* attractive, engaging, winning.
engagement [ɑ̃gaʒmɑ̃] *s.m.* **1.** pawning, pledging; pledge; promise, undertaking, obligation, bond; **2.** (mil.) enlistment; (law, comm.) contract; **3.** (mil.) engagement, action; **4.** start of play (in a match); **5.** (sport) entry (to competition, etc.); **6.** (fig.) commitment, involvement.
engager [ɑ̃gaʒe] *v.t.* **1.** to pledge, to pawn; to engage, to promise, to commit; *cela n'engage à rien*, that doesn't commit you to anything; **2.** to enlist, to engage (employee), to take on, to hire; **3.** to insert, to introduce (into); **4.** (fig.) to begin, to undertake; **5.** (sport) to enter (*dans*, for, a race, etc.); **6.** to advise, to exhort, to urge; **7.** to involve; **s'~** *v.refl.* **1.** to promise, to undertake (*à*, to); **2.** to enlist; *s'~ dans*, to enter (competition, etc.); **3.** to take a job (*comme*, as); **4.** to start; **5.** *s'~ dans*, to fit into, to go into; to enter, to turn into (road, etc.); **6.** to become involved.
engainer [ɑ̃gene] *v.t.* to sheathe, to encase.
engazonnement [ɑ̃gɑzɔnmɑ̃] *s.m.* turfing, grassing.
engazonner [ɑ̃gɑzɔne] *v.t.* (obs.) to turf; (mod.) to sow with grass.
engeance [ɑ̃ʒɑ̃s] *s.f.* (pej.) breed, tribe.
engelure [ɑ̃ʒlyr] *s.f.* chilblain.
engendrement [ɑ̃ʒɑ̃drəmɑ̃] *s.m.* engendering, fathering.
engendrer [ɑ̃ʒɑ̃dre] *v.t.* (lit. & fig.) to beget, to engender, to breed, to father.
engerbage [ɑ̃ʒɛrbaʒ] *s.m.* (agric.) sheaving, stacking.
engerber [ɑ̃ʒɛrbe] *v.t.* (agric.) to sheaf, to stack.
engin [ɑ̃ʒɛ̃] *s.m.* device, tackle, gear; missile; *~s de guerre*, weaponry.
englober [ɑ̃glɔbe] *v.t.* to take in, to annex; to include in; to lump together.
engloutir [ɑ̃glutir] *v.t.* **1.** (lit. & fig.) to swallow (up); to bolt (food); to absorb; to engulf, to submerge; **2.** to squander, to dissipate.
engloutissement [ɑ̃glutismɑ̃] *s.m.* swallowing up; engulfing.
engluage [ɑ̃glyaʒ], **engluement** [ɑ̃glymɑ̃] *s.m.* **1.** liming (of birds); **2.** banding, waxing, (of trees).
engluer [ɑ̃glye] *v.t.* **1.** to lime (twigs), to catch (birds) with birdlime; **2.** to band or wax (trees); **s'~** *v.refl.* to stick, to get stuck.
engobage [ɑ̃gɔbaʒ] *s.m.* (pottery) slip-painting.
engobe [ɑ̃gɔb] *s.m.* (pottery) slip.
engober [ɑ̃gɔbe] *v.t.* (pottery) to paint with slip.
engommage [ɑ̃gɔmaʒ] *s.m.* (techn.) sizing, gumming.
engommer [ɑ̃gɔme] *v.t.* (techn.) to size, to gum.
engoncer [ɑ̃gɔ̃se] *v.t.* (of clothes) to fit badly, to give a hunched appearance to.
engorgement [ɑ̃gɔrʒəmɑ̃] *s.m.* obstruction, blockage; (med.) congestion; (econ.) glutting.
engorger [ɑ̃gɔrʒe] *v.t.* to choke, to obstruct; to congest; (econ.) to glut.
engouement [ɑ̃gumɑ̃] *s.m.* **1.** (obs.) blockage; (med.) obstruction; **2.** (fig.) addiction, infatuation, craze.
(s')engouer [ɑ̃gwe] *v.refl.* **1.** (obs.) to choke (while eating); **2.** (fig.) to go mad (about), to become infatuated.
engouffrement [ɑ̃gufrəmɑ̃] *s.m.* engulfing.
engouffrer [ɑ̃gufre] *v.t.* **1.** (fam.) to bolt, to wolf, (food); to devour; **2.** (fig.) to engulf, to swallow up; **s'~** *v.refl.* **1.** to be swallowed up, engulfed; **2.** to rush, to surge; to disappear.
engoulevent [ɑ̃gulvɑ̃] *s.m.* (ornith.) nightjar, goatsucker.
engourdi, -e [ɑ̃gurdi] *adj.* numb(ed), torpid, sluggish.
engourdir [ɑ̃gurdir] *v.t.* to make numb, to numb; to paralyse; to make torpid or sluggish; to dull, to deaden, to blunt; **s'~** *v.refl.* to become numb, (of limbs) to go to sleep; to hibernate.
engourdissement [ɑ̃gurdismɑ̃] *s.m.* numbness, sluggishness; torpor (of hibernation).
engrais [ɑ̃grɛ] *s.m.* **1.** manure, fertilizer, compost; **2.** fattening (of animals); *d'~*, (of beast) for fattening; *mettre à l'~*, to fatten.
engraissement [ɑ̃grɛsmɑ̃] *s.m.* fattening (of livestock).
engraisser [ɑ̃grese] *v.t.* to fatten (animals); to manure (land); ~ *v.i.* to get fatter, to put on weight; **s'~** *v.refl.* (fig.) to grow fat (*de*, on).
engraisseur [ɑ̃grɛsœr] *s.m.* fattener (of livestock).
engrangement [ɑ̃grɑ̃ʒmɑ̃] *s.m.* storing, getting--in, housing, (of corn, etc.).
engranger [ɑ̃grɑ̃ʒe] *v.t.* to bring in, to store, (corn, etc.); (fig.) to garner.
engraver[1] [ɑ̃grave] *v.t.* to notch and fix a strip of lead to (for gutter, etc.).
engraver[2] [ɑ̃grave] *v.t.* (naut.) to strand, to run aground; **s'~** *v.refl.* to ground.
engrêlé, -e [ɑ̃grele] *adj.* (herald.) engrailed.

engrêlure [ãgrelyr] *s.f.* (herald.) engrailed border; purl (of lace).
engrenage [ãgrənaʒ] *s.m.* gear, gearing, cogs; (fig.) meshes, toils, machine, chain of events.
engrènement [ãgrɛnmã] *s.m.* **1.** (mech.) engaging, getting into gear; **2.** filling (mill--hopper) with corn.
engrener [ãgrəne] *v.t.* **1.** (mech.) to engage (clutch), to put into gear; (fig.) to enmesh; **2.** to fill (hopper) with grain, to feed (threshing--machine) with corn.
engreneu-r [ãgrənœr] *s.m.* man in charge of feeding threshing-machine; **~se** *s.f.* mechanical feeder of threshing-machine.
engrenure [ãgrənyr] *s.f.* engaging (of gears); interlocking (of teeth); (anat.) serrated suture.
engrois [ãgrwa] *s.m.* wedge (to secure handle of hammer, etc.).
engrosser [ãgrose] *v.t.* (vulg.) to make pregnant, to put in the family way.
engrumeler [ãgrymle] *v.t.*, **s'~** *v.refl.* to clot, to curdle.
engueulade [ãgœlad] *s.f.*, **engueulement** [ãgœlmã] *s.m.* (pop.) dressing-down, ticking--off.
engueuler [ãgœle] *v.t.* (pop.) to dress down, to tick off, to swear at, to curse; **s'~** *v.refl.* to have a slanging match.
enguirlander [ãgirlãde] *v.t.* **1.** to festoon, to garland; **2.** (fam.) to abuse; to catch.
enhardir [ãardir] *v.t.* to embolden, to make bold(er); **s'~** *v.refl.* to take courage.
enharmonie [ãnarmɔni] *s.f.* (anc. mus.) enharmonic mode; (mod.) enharmonic (change).
enharmonique [ãnarmɔnik] *adj.* (mus.) enharmonic.
enharnacher [ãarnaʃe] *v.t.* to harness; (fig.) to rig out.
enherber [ãnɛrbe] *v.t.* to sow (land) with grass.
énigmatique [enigmatik] *adj.* enigmatic(al).
énigme [enigm] *s.f.* enigma, riddle.
enivrant, -e [ãnivrã] *adj.* (usu. fig.) intoxicating.
enivrement [ãnivrəmã] *s.m.* (obs.) drunkenness; (fig.) intoxication, elation.
enivrer [ãnivre] *v.t.* to intoxicate, to make drunk; to drug; (fig.) to intoxicate, to elate, to enchant; **s'~** *v.refl.* to get drunk; (fig.) to be carried away.
enjambée [ãʒãbe] *s.f.* (lit. & fig.) stride, step.
enjambement [ãʒãbmã] *s.m.* (obs.) encroachment; (pros.) enjambment, enjambement.
enjamber [ãʒãbe] *v.i.* **1.** to encroach, to project; **2.** (pros.) to run on to next line; **~** *v.t.* to stride or step over; to cross, to span; (fig.) to overstep.
enjaveler [ãʒavle] *v.t.* (agric.) to sheaf.
enjeu (pl. **-x**) [ãʒø] *s.m.* stake, wager.
enjoindre [ãʒwɛ̃dr] *v.t.* to enjoin, to prescribe.
enjôler [ãʒole] *v.t.* to coax, to cajole, to wheedle.
enjôleu-r, -se [ãʒolœr] *s.m.f.* coaxer, wheedler; *adj.* coaxing, wheedling, cajoling.
enjolivement [ãʒɔlivmã] *s.m.* embellishment, ornamentation.
enjoliver [ãʒɔlive] *v.t.* to embellish, to ornament, to adorn, to smarten up; (fig.) to embroider.
enjoliveu-r, -se [ãʒɔlivœr] *s.m.f.* embellisher, beautifier; (car) hub-cap, wheel-trim.
enjolivure [ãʒɔlivyr] *s.f.* = ENJOLIVEMENT.
enjoué, -e [ãʒwe] *adj.* lively, bright, jovial, gay, cheerful.
enjouement [ãʒumã] *s.m.* liveliness, cheerfulness, gaiety.
enjuiver [ãʒɥive] *v.t.* to judaize.
enkysté, -e [ãkiste] *adj.* (med.) encysted.
enkystement [ãkistəmã] *s.m.* encystation, encystment.
(s')enkyster [ãkiste] *v.refl.* to encyst.
enlacement [ãlɑsmã] *s.m.* **1.** interlacing, entwining; **2.** embrace.
enlacer [ãlɑse] *v.t.* **1.** to entwine, to interlace; **2.** to embrace.
enlaçure [ãlɑsyr] *s.f.* (techn.) dowelled mortise and tenon joint.
enlaidir [ãledir] *v.t.* to make ugly, to disfigure; **~** *v.i.* to become plain, to lose one's good looks.
enlaidissement [ãledismã] *s.m.* ugliness; disfigurement, loss of good looks.
enlevage [ãlvaʒ] *s.m.* **1.** (techn.) bleaching; **2.** (rowing) final spurt.
enlevé, -e [ãlve] *adj.* dashing, bold, spirited, lively; (rid.) *au trot* **~**, rising in the stirrups.
enlèvement [ãlɛvmã] *s.m.* **1.** removal; abduction, kidnapping; (Lit.) ravishment; **2.** (mil.) storming.
enlever [ãlve] *v.t.* **1.** to remove, to take away; to wipe out; to abduct, to kidnap; to elope with; (lit. & fig.) to carry away, to transport; **2.** (mil.) to take by storm.
enlevure [ãlvyr] *s.f.* relief (in a sculpture).
enliasser [ãljase] *v.t.* to tie in bundles.
enlier [ãlje] *v.t.* (constr.) to bond.
enlisement [ãlizmã] *s.m.* sinking, bogging down.
enliser [ãlize] *v.t.* to sink, to stick (in quicksand, mud, etc.); **s'~** *v.refl.* (fig.) to get bogged down.
enluminer [ãlymine] *v.t.* **1.** to illuminate (a manuscript); **2.** to colour, to light up.
enlumineu-r, -se [ãlyminœr] *s.m.f.* illuminator, miniaturist.
enluminure [ãlyminyr] *s.f.* **1.** illumination, miniature; **2.** high colour (of complexion).
enneigé, -e [ãneʒe] *adj.* snow-covered.
enneigement [ãnɛʒmã] *s.m.* being snow--covered; snow conditions; *bulletin d'~*, snow report.
ennemi, -e [ɛnmi] *s.m.f.* enemy, foe; opponent; *le mieux est l'~ du bien*, let well alone; *adj.* enemy, hostile.
ennoblir [ãnɔblir] *v.t.* to ennoble; to dignify.
ennoblissement [ãnɔblismã] *s.m.* ennobling, ennoblement.
ennuager [ãnɥaʒe] *v.t.* to cloud over, to becloud; **s'~** *v.refl.* to cloud over.
ennui [ãnɥi] *s.m.* **1.** (obs.) sorrow; **2.** annoyance, trouble, worry, difficulty; *quel ~!*, what a nuisance!; **3.** boredom, tedium; **4.** depression, gloom.
ennuyant, -e [ãnɥijã] *adj.* (obs. exc. dial.) annoying.
ennuyé, -e [ãnɥije] *adj.* annoyed, upset, worried.
ennuyer [ãnɥije] *v.t.* **1.** to upset, to worry; to annoy, to disturb; **2.** to bore, to weary; **s'~** *v.refl.* to be bored; (obs. exc. dial.) *s'~ de qn.*, to miss s.o.
ennuyeu-x, -se [ãnɥijø] *adj.* **1.** annoying, worrying, upsetting, tiresome; **2.** boring, tedious.
énoncé [enɔ̃se] *s.m.* **1.** statement; **2.** text, terms, (of a law, etc.).
énoncer [enɔ̃se] *v.t.* to state, to express, to set out; **s'~** *v.refl.* to speak, to express oneself.
énonciati-f, -ve [enɔ̃sjatif] *adj.* enunciative.
énonciation [enɔ̃sjɑsjɔ̃] *s.f.* enunciation, expression, statement.
enorgueillir [ãnɔrgœjir] *v.t.* to elate, to make proud; **s'~** *de v.refl.* to be proud about, to take pride in.
énorme [enɔrm] *adj.* **1.** extraordinary, unheard--of, monstrous; (fam.) outstanding, remarkable; **2.** very large, enormous, huge.
énormément [enɔrmemã] *adv.* enormously, hugely, greatly; a great deal, a great many; **~** *d'argent*, a great deal of money.
énormité [enɔrmite] *s.f.* **1.** (obs.) heinous crime; (mod.) howler, blunder; **2.** enormousness, great size; (fig.) enormity, outrageousness.

énostose [enɔstoz] *s.f.* (med.) enostosis.
énouer [enwe] *v.t.* (text.) to burl.
(s')enquérir [ɑ̃kerir] *v.refl.* to inquire, to make inquiries, to ask (*de*, about).
enquête [ɑ̃kɛt] *s.f.* inquiry, investigation; examination (of witnesses before trial).
enquêter [ɑ̃kete] *v.i.* to inquire, to hold an inquiry.
enquêteu-r, -se [ɑ̃kɛtœr] *s.m.f.* investigator, researcher.
enquiquinant, -e [ɑ̃kikinɑ̃] *adj.* (fam.) infuriating, maddening.
enquiquiner [ɑ̃kikine] *v.t.* (fam.) to annoy, to pester, to plague.
enracinement [ɑ̃rasinmɑ̃] *s.m.* taking root, rooting; (fig.) rootedness.
enraciner [ɑ̃rasine] *v.t.* to root, to dig in; (fig.) to implant; **s'~** *v.refl.* to take root.
enragé, -e [ɑ̃raʒe] *adj.* **1.** furious, beside oneself with rage; (obs.) mad, losing one's reason; **2.** (pathol.) rabid; (fig.) enthusiastic, passionate, out-and-out, inveterate, fanatical, rabid.
enrageant, -e [ɑ̃raʒɑ̃] *adj.* maddening, exasperating.
enrager [ɑ̃raʒe] *v.i.* to be furious, to fume; *faire ~*, to drive mad.
enraiement [ɑ̃rɛmɑ̃], **enrayement** [ɑ̃rɛjmɑ̃] *s.m.* **1.** (obs.) braking (wheels of vehicle); **2.** (fig.) arresting the spread (of disease, etc.).
enrayage [ɑ̃rɛjaʒ] *s.m.* **1.** (obs.) braking (wheels of vehicle); **2.** jamming (of a mechanism).
enrayer[1] [ɑ̃reje] *v.t.* (agric.) to plough the first furrow of (a field).
enrayer[2] [ɑ̃reje] *v.t.* **1.** (obs.) to slow down, to stop, (a vehicle); **2.** to jam (a mechanism); (fig.) to arrest, to check, (progress of disease, etc.); **3.** to fit spokes to; **s'~** *v.refl.* (of gun, etc.) to jam.
enrayure[1] [ɑ̃rejyr] *s.f.* (agric.) first furrow opened by plough.
enrayure[2] [ɑ̃rejyr] *s.f.* spokes (of wheel); wooden beams radiating from a central point.
enrégimenter [ɑ̃reʒimɑ̃te] *v.t.* **1.** (obs.) to assign to a regiment; **2.** to regiment, to enlist.
enregistrable [ɑ̃rʒistrabl] *adj.* recordable.
enregistrement [ɑ̃rʒistrəmɑ̃] *s.m.* **1.** (law) registration, recording, entry; registering (of luggage); noting, recording; **2.** (admin.) registry (office).
enregistrer [ɑ̃rʒistre] *v.t.* **1.** to register; **2.** to record, to note down.
enregistreu-r, -se [ɑ̃rʒistrœr] *adj.* recording; **~r** *s.m.* recording apparatus, recorder.
enrêner [ɑ̃rene] *v.t.* (obs.) to rein.
enrhumé, -e [ɑ̃ryme] *adj. être ~*, to have a cold.
enrhumer [ɑ̃ryme] *v.t.* to give a cold to; **s'~** *v.refl.* to catch a cold.
enrichi, -e [ɑ̃riʃi] *adj.* newly-rich; (of uranium, bread, etc.) enriched.
enrichir [ɑ̃riʃir] *v.t.* to enrich, to make rich; to enrich (uranium, etc.); (fig.) to enrich, to enlarge, to add to; **s'~** *v.refl.* to get rich; (fig.) to be enriched, to be enlarged, to extend.
enrichissant, -e [ɑ̃riʃisɑ̃] *adj.* (fig.) rewarding, profitable.
enrichissement [ɑ̃riʃismɑ̃] *s.m.* (lit. & fig.) enrichment, enriching; acquisition (to collection, etc.), asset.
enrobage [ɑ̃rɔbaʒ], **enrobement** [ɑ̃rɔbmɑ̃] *s.m.* wrapping, coating, covering.
enrober [ɑ̃rɔbe] *v.t.* to wrap, to coat, to cover; (fig.) to gild, to sugar, to wrap up.
enrochement [ɑ̃rɔʃmɑ̃] *s.m.* (constr.) rock fill, rock foundation.
enrocher [ɑ̃rɔʃe] *v.t.* (constr.) to lay a rock foundation for.
enrôlement [ɑ̃rolmɑ̃] *s.m.* enrolment, enlistment, recruitment.
enrôler [ɑ̃role] *v.t.* to enrol, to enlist, to recruit; **s'~** *v.refl.* to enlist.
enroué, -e [ɑ̃rwe] *adj.* hoarse.
enrouement [ɑ̃rumɑ̃] *s.m.* hoarseness, huskiness.
enrouer [ɑ̃rwe] *v.t.* to make hoarse; **s'~** *v.refl.* to become hoarse, to lose one's voice.
enroulement [ɑ̃rulmɑ̃] *s.m.* winding-up, curling-up; (electr.) coil; (arch.) scroll, volute; (hort.) leaf-curl (disease of potatoes).
enrouler [ɑ̃rule] *v.t.* to roll, to roll up; to coil; to wind; **s'~** *v.refl.* to wind, to twine; to wrap oneself (*dans*, in).
enrouleu-r, -se [ɑ̃rulœr] *adj.* winding.
enrubanner [ɑ̃rybane] *v.t.* to adorn with ribbons, to tie up with ribbons.
ensablement [ɑ̃sɑbləmɑ̃] *s.m.* silting-up; sandbank, bar.
ensabler [ɑ̃sɑble] *v.t.* **1.** to cover with sand; **2.** to run aground (in sand); **s'~** *v.refl.* **1.** to silt up; **2.** to stick in sand.
ensachage [ɑ̃saʃaʒ] *s.m.* putting into sacks, bagging.
ensacher [ɑ̃saʃe] *v.t.* to put into sacks, to bag.
ensacheu-r, -se [ɑ̃saʃœr] *s.m.f.* bagger; **~se** *s.f.* bagging machine.
ensanglanter [ɑ̃sɑ̃glɑ̃te] *v.t.* to cover with blood, to make bloody; (poetic) to stain red.
ensauvager [ɑ̃sovaʒe] *v.t.* to make wild.
enseignant, -e [ɑ̃sɛɲɑ̃] *adj.* teaching; *s.m.f.* teacher.
enseigne [ɑ̃sɛɲ] *s.f.* **1.** (obs.) mark, proof; *à bonne ~*, on good authority; (Lit.) *à telle ~ que*, so much so that, to such an extent that; **2.** standard, banner, flag; **3.** (shop, inn, etc.) sign; *à bon vin, point d'~*, good wine needs no bush; (fig.) *être logés à la même ~*, to be in the same boat; **4.** (mil.) ensign; (nav.) sub-lieutenant.
enseignement [ɑ̃sɛɲmɑ̃] *s.m.* **1.** precept, lesson; **2.** instruction, education, teaching; **3.** teaching profession.
enseigner [ɑ̃sɛɲe] *v.t.* to teach; to show, to inform.
ensellé, -e [ɑ̃sele] *adj.* (of horse) saddle-backed, sway-backed.
ensellement [ɑ̃sɛlmɑ̃] *s.m.* (geol.) saddle.
ensellure [ɑ̃selyr] *s.f.* curve of the back, hollow of the back.
ensemble [ɑ̃sɑ̃bl] *adv.* together; at the same time; *être bien ~*, to get on well together; **~** *s.m.* whole, entirety; suite (of furniture); suit (of clothes); (mus.) ensemble; (obs.) cohesion, unity; *dans l'~*, on the whole, taken all round.
ensemencement [ɑ̃smɑ̃smɑ̃] *s.m.* sowing.
ensemencer [ɑ̃smɑ̃se] *v.t.* to sow; to stock (with fish); (biol., med.) to seed (a culture, etc.).
enserrer[1] [ɑ̃sere] *v.t.* to grip tightly, to hold in, to enclose, to encompass.
enserrer[2] [ɑ̃sere] *v.t.* (hort.) to put under glass.
ensevelir [ɑ̃səvlir] *v.t.* to shroud; to bury; (fig.) to swallow up; **s'~** *v.refl.* to become shrouded or buried; (fig.) to bury oneself.
ensevelissement [ɑ̃səvlismɑ̃] *s.m.* shrouding; burial, burying.
ensiforme [ɑ̃sifɔrm] *adj.* (bot.) ensiform.
ensilage [ɑ̃silaʒ] *s.m.* (agric.) ensilage.
ensiler [ɑ̃sile] *v.t.* (agric.) to ensile.
ensoleillé, -e [ɑ̃sɔleje] *adj.* sunny.
ensoleillement [ɑ̃sɔlɛjmɑ̃] *s.m.* hours of sunshine; being in the sun(shine).
ensoleiller [ɑ̃sɔleje] *v.t.* to fill with sunlight; (fig.) to brighten, to light up, to bring happiness to.
ensommeillé, -e [ɑ̃sɔmeje] *adj.* drowsy, half-asleep, somnolent.
ensorcelant, -e [ɑ̃sɔrsəlɑ̃] *adj.* bewitching, spellbinding, enchanting.
ensorceler [ɑ̃sɔrsəle] *v.t.* to bewitch, to cast a spell on; (fig.) to captivate.

ensorceleu-r, -se [ɑ̃sɔrsəlœr] *s.m.f.* enchanter, enchantress; magician, witch.
ensorcellement [ɑ̃sɔrsɛlmɑ̃] *s.m.* spell, enchantment; witchcraft, sorcery; (fig.) charm, fascination.
ensoufrer [ɑ̃sufre] *v.t.* (obs.) to sulphur.
ensouple [ɑ̃supl] *s.f.* (text.) roller (of loom).
ensuite [ɑ̃sɥit] *adv.* later, afterwards, then; next, secondly.
(s')ensuivre [ɑ̃sɥivr] *v.refl.* to follow, to result, to ensue; (impers.) *il s'ensuit que,* it follows that.
entablement [ɑ̃tabləmɑ̃] *s.m.* (arch.) entablature; (constr.) coping; moulding (on furniture.
entabler [ɑ̃table] *v.t.* (techn.) to set (blades of scissors, etc.).
entacher [ɑ̃taʃe] *v.t.* to stain, to blot, to soil; to mar.
entaillage [ɑ̃tɑjaʒ] *s.m.* notching, indenting.
entaille [ɑ̃tɑj] *s.f.* notch; cut, gash.
entailler [ɑ̃tɑje] *v.t.* to notch; to gash, to cut, to slash.
entame [ɑ̃tam] *s.f.* first slice, first cut, (of meat, bread, etc.).
entamer [ɑ̃tame] *v.t.* **1.** to cut, to pierce, to make an incision in, to cut into, to cut a slice or piece from; to start on, to start consuming, to open (bottle of wine, etc.); (fig.) to start (on sth.); **2.** to corrode; (lit. & fig.) to eat into, to make a hole in, to break into; (fig.) to shake, to make an impression on; (obs.) *~ qn.,* to harm someone's reputation.
entartrage [ɑ̃tartraʒ] *s.m.* furring, incrustation, (of boiler, etc.).
entartrer [ɑ̃tartre] *v.t.* to fur, to incrust.
entassement [ɑ̃tɑsmɑ̃] *s.m.* accumulation, heap, pile; crowding, overcrowding.
entasser [ɑ̃tɑse] *v.t.* to heap, to pile up; to accumulate, to amass; to hoard up; to crowd together.
ente [ɑ̃t] *s.f.* (hort.) bud, scion; graft.
entendement [ɑ̃tɑ̃dmɑ̃] *s.m.* understanding.
entendeur [ɑ̃tɑ̃dœr] *s.m.* (obs.) hearer; (mod.) *à bon ~, salut!,* if the cap fits, wear it!
entendre [ɑ̃tɑ̃dr] *v.t.* **1.** to intend, to wish, to mean to (do sth.); *faites comme vous l'entendez,* do as you think best; **2.** to understand, to mean; *~ l'espagnol,* to understand Spanish; *qu'entendez--vous par là?,* what do you mean by that?; *laisser ~, donner à ~,* to insinuate, to hint; *ne pas ~ malice,* to mean no harm; **3.** to hear; to listen to; *~ parler de,* to hear about; to have news of; *~ dire que,* to hear (it said) that; *~ raison,* to listen to reason, to be reasonable; **s'~** *v.refl.* **1.** to be heard, to be understood; *cela s'entend,* that is understood; **2.** *s'~ à,* to be competent at, to be good at, to know how to do; **3.** to understand each other, to agree, to come to an agreement; (fam.) *ils s'entendent comme larrons en foire,* they're as thick as thieves.
entendu, -e [ɑ̃tɑ̃dy] *adj.* **1.** (obs.) capable, competent; (mod.) (of look, air) understanding, knowing; (rare, pej.) *faire l'~,* to look knowing; **2.** understood, agreed; *(c'est) ~!,* agreed!, settled!, done!; *bien ~,* of course, naturally.
enténébrer [ɑ̃tenebre] *v.t.* to envelop in darkness, to plunge into darkness; (lit. & fig.) to darken.
entente [ɑ̃tɑ̃t] *s.f.* **1.** (obs.) understanding, comprehension; (mod.) *à double ~,* with two meanings, ambiguous; **2.** understanding, agreement, alliance, entente.
enter [ɑ̃te] *v.t.* (carp.) to joint, to graft, to assemble by mortises; (hort. & fig.) to graft; (hort.) *~ en œillet,* to bud.
entéralgie [ɑ̃teralʒi] *s.f.* (med.) enteralgia.
entérinement [ɑ̃terinmɑ̃] *s.m.* ratification, confirmation.
entériner [ɑ̃terine] *v.t.* to ratify, to confirm, to validate.
entérique [ɑ̃terik] *adj.* (med.) enteric, intestinal.
entérite [ɑ̃terit] *s.f.* (med.) enteritis.
entérocolite [ɑ̃terɔkɔlit] *s.f.* (med.) enterocolitis.
entérocoque [ɑ̃terɔkɔk] *s.m.* (med.) enterococcus.
enterrage [ɑ̃tɛraʒ] *s.m.* (metall.) bedding.
enterrement [ɑ̃tɛrmɑ̃] *s.m.* burial, interment, funeral; (fig.) end, death.
enterrer [ɑ̃tere] *v.t.* to bury, to inter; to conduct or attend the funeral of; (fig.) to put an end to, to kill; (fig.) *il nous enterrera tous,* he'll outlive us all.
entêtant, -e [ɑ̃tɛtɑ̃] *adj.* (fig.) intoxicating, heady, obsessive.
en-tête [ɑ̃tɛt] *s.m.* heading, superscription; *papier à lettre à ~,* headed notepaper.
entêté, -e [ɑ̃tɛte] *adj.* obstinate, stubborn.
entêtement [ɑ̃tɛtmɑ̃] *s.m.* (obs.) obsession; (mod.) obstinacy, stubbornness.
entêter [ɑ̃tete] *v.t.* **1.** to go to the head of, to intoxicate; **2.** (obs.) to obsess, to infatuate; **s'~** *v.refl.* (obs.) to become infatuated (*de,* with); (mod.) to be obstinate, to dig in one's heels.
enthousiasmant, -e [ɑ̃tuzjasmɑ̃] *adj.* rousing, exciting.
enthousiasme [ɑ̃tuzjasm] *s.m.* enthusiasm, zest, fervour, ecstasy.
enthousiasmer [ɑ̃tuzjasme] *v.t.* to excite, to rouse; **s'~** *v.refl.* to enthuse, to go into ecstasies (*pour qn., qch.,* about, over, s.o., sth.).
enthousiaste [ɑ̃tuzjast] *s.m.f.* enthusiast, fanatic; *~ adj.* enthusiastic.
entiché, -e [ɑ̃tiʃe] *adj.* infatuated, besotted, mad or crazy (*de,* about).
entichement [ɑ̃tiʃmɑ̃] *s.m.* infatuation.
enticher [ɑ̃tiʃe] *v.t.* **1.** (obs.) to bruise, to spoil; **2.** to infatuate; **s'~** *de v.refl.* to be infatuated with, to be crazy about.
enti-er, -ère [ɑ̃tje] *adj.* **1.** whole, complete, entire; intact, integral; unimpaired, perfect; *cheval ~er,* stallion; **2.** (obs. of persons) loyal, true; (mod.) self-willed, obdurate; **~er** *s.m.* whole; integral number; *en (son) ~er,* in its entirety, completely; **~èrement** [ɑ̃tjɛrmɑ̃] *adv.* wholly, entirely, completely, utterly.
entité [ɑ̃tite] *s.f.* entity.
entoilage [ɑ̃twalaʒ] *s.m.* mounting on canvas; stiffening with canvas; canvas mount.
entoiler [ɑ̃twale] *v.t.* to back or stiffen with canvas; to bind with canvas.
entoir [ɑ̃twar] *s.m.* (hort.) grafting-knife.
entôlage [ɑ̃tolaʒ] *s.m.* (pop.) decoying (with intent to rob).
entôler [ɑ̃tole] *v.t.* (of a prostitute) to decoy and rob; (pop.) to fleece.
entomo-logie [ɑ̃tɔmɔlɔʒi] *s.f.* entomology; **~logique** [ɑ̃tɔmɔlɔʒik] *adj.* entomological; **~logiste** [ɑ̃tɔmɔlɔʒist] *s.m.f.* entomologist; **~phage** [ɑ̃tɔmɔfaʒ] *adj.* entomophagous; **~phile** [ɑ̃tɔmɔfil] *adj.* entomophilous.
entonnage [ɑ̃tɔnaʒ] *s.m.,* **entonnaison** [ɑ̃tɔnɛzɔ̃] *s.f.,* **entonnement** [ɑ̃tɔnmɑ̃] *s.m.* barrelling, casking.
entonner[1] [ɑ̃tɔne] *v.t.* **1.** to cask, to barrel; **2.** (fig. rare) to gorge.
entonner[2] [ɑ̃tɔne] *v.t.* to strike up (song, etc.), to intone.
entonnoir [ɑ̃tɔnwar] *s.m.* funnel; (bomb) crater; *en ~,* funnel-shaped.
entorse [ɑ̃tɔrs] *s.f.* sprain, strain; (fig.) twist; *se donner, se faire, une ~ au poignet, etc.,* to sprain one's wrist, etc.; (fig.) *faire une ~ à,* to twist (the meaning of, etc.), to distort; to go beyond, to infringe (the law, etc.).
entortillage [ɑ̃tɔrtijaʒ] *s.m.* (fig.) circumlocution, obscurity.

entortillement [ɑ̃tɔrtijmɑ̃] *s.m.* twisting, twining, entanglement.
entortiller [ɑ̃tɔrtije] *v.t.* **1.** to screw up, to wrap round; **2.** (fig.) to inveigle, to get round (s.o.); **3.** (style) to make involved, to use circumlocutions in; **s'~** *v.refl.* to twine (*autour de*, round).
entour [ɑ̃tur] *s.m.* **1.** *à l'~*, round about; **2.** (pl.) surroundings, environs, approaches.
entourage [ɑ̃turaʒ] *s.m.* **1.** setting; **2.** circle, set, entourage, suite.
entouré, -e [ɑ̃ture] *adj.* sought-after, much--admired; *~ de*, surrounded by.
entourer [ɑ̃ture] *v.t.* to surround, to gather round; to wrap up; (fig.) *~ qn. de soins, d'égards*, to lavish attention on s.o.; **s'~** *de v.refl.* to surround oneself with.
entourloupette [ɑ̃turlupɛt] *s.f.* (fam.) dirty trick.
entournure [ɑ̃turnyr] *s.f.* (dressm.) armhole; (fig.) *être gêné dans les ~s*, to feel awkward, to be in difficulties.
entracte [ɑ̃trakt] *s.m.* interval, interlude.
entraide [ɑ̃trɛd] *s.f.* mutual assistance; *~ sociale*, social assistance.
(**s'**)**entraider** [ɑ̃trede] *v.refl.* to help one another.
entrailles [ɑ̃trɑj] *s.f.pl.* intestines, bowels, entrails, guts; (fig.) bowels, inmost self; compassion; (fig.) *il n'a pas d'~*, he has no feelings.
entrain [ɑ̃trɛ̃] *s.m.* zest, spirit, life, go, vivacity, liveliness.
entraînable [ɑ̃trɛnabl] *adj.* easily led, easily swayed; weak-willed.
entraînant, -e [ɑ̃trɛnɑ̃] *adj.* stirring, rousing.
entraînement [ɑ̃trɛnmɑ̃] *s.m.* **1.** (obs.) chain of events; **2.** (mech.) drive, transmission; (fig.) driving force, impulse, stimulus; (mech.) *arbre d'~*, drive shaft; **3.** (sport) training.
entraîner [ɑ̃trɛne] *v.t.* **1.** to drag, to carry, away; to lead away or off; (fig.) to carry away, to lure away, to lead astray, to drag down; *se laisser ~*, to be led astray; **2.** to cause, to provoke, to result in; *~ qn. à faire qch.*, to cause s.o. to do sth., to lead or inveigle s.o. into doing sth.; **3.** (mech.) to drive, to transmit motion to; **4.** (sport, etc.) to train, to coach (*à*, in; *pour*, for); **s'~** *v.refl.* to train, to train oneself (*à*, in, to).
entraîneur [ɑ̃trɛnœr] *s.m.* (sport) trainer, coach; pace-maker.
entraîneuse [ɑ̃trɛnøz] *s.f.* dance-hostess (in bar, etc.).
entrait [ɑ̃trɛ] *s.m.* (constr.) tie-beam.
entrant, -e [ɑ̃trɑ̃] *adj.* entering; temporary; *s.m.f.* entrant, incomer; *les ~s et les sortants*, those coming and going.
entrave [ɑ̃trav] *s.f.* shackle, fetter, hobble; (fig.) hindrance, impediment.
entravé, -e [ɑ̃trave] *adj.* shackled, fettered; (fig.) impeded, hampered; *jupe ~e*, hobble-skirt.
entraver [ɑ̃trave] *v.t.* to shackle, to fetter, to hobble; (fig.) to hinder, to impede, to thwart, to block, to obstruct.
entre [ɑ̃tr] *prep.* between; among, amongst; in.
entrebâillement [ɑ̃trəbɑjmɑ̃] *s.m.* being ajar, leaving half-open; aperture, crack, chink.
entrebâiller [ɑ̃trəbɑje] *v.t.* to half-open, to open partly, to leave ajar.
entrebâilleur [ɑ̃trəbɑjœr] *s.m.* (security) chain or stop (on door).
entre-bande [ɑ̃trəbɑ̃d] *s.f.* (text.) end-selvedge.
(**s'**)**entrebattre** [ɑ̃trəbatr] *v.refl.* to exchange blows.
entrechat [ɑ̃trəʃa] *s.m.* (danc.) entrechat; (fig.) *faire des ~s*, to leap around, to frisk about.
entrechoquement [ɑ̃trəʃɔkmɑ̃] *s.m.* clash, collision.
entrechoquer [ɑ̃trəʃɔke] *v.t.* to rub together, to cause to clash; **s'~** *v.refl.* to clash, to collide.
entrecôte [ɑ̃trəkot] *s.m.* entrecôte (steak).
entrecoupé, -e [ɑ̃trəkupe] *adj.* interrupted, intermittent, broken.
entrecouper [ɑ̃trəkupe] *v.t.* **1.** (rare) to cut up; **2.** to interrupt, to break into.
entrecroisement [ɑ̃trəkrwazmɑ̃] *s.m.* intersection, interlacing.
entrecroiser [ɑ̃trəkrwaze] *v.t.* to cross, to interlace, to criss-cross; **s'~** *v.refl.* to intersect, to interlock.
entre-deux [ɑ̃trədø] *s.m.invar.* **1.** (obs.) space (between two things); **2.** (fig.) middle ground, middle course; **3.** (dressm.) insertion; **4.** (cook.) middle cut (of fish); **5.** (basket-ball) throw-in (by referee).
entre-deux-guerres [ɑ̃trədøgɛr] *s.m.invar.* (the) inter-war years (1918–1939).
entrée [ɑ̃tre] *s.f.* **1.** entrance, entering, arrival; (theatr.) entrance; (fig.) first appearance, début; joining (a party, etc.); **2.** (comm.) import; *droits d'~*, import duty; **3.** entry, access; admission; entry pass, ticket; **4.** entrance, door, gate; inlet, intake; entrance hall; **5.** beginning; *d'~ en jeu*, from the outset; **6.** (cook.) entrée.
entrefaite [ɑ̃trəfɛt] *s.f.* **1.** (obs.) interval, space of time; **2.** *sur ces ~s*, meanwhile, during this time.
entrefer [ɑ̃trəfɛr] *s.m.* (techn., electr.) clearance, gap.
entrefilet [ɑ̃trəfilɛ] *s.m.* (typ.) paragraph between rules; (in newspaper) paragraph.
entregent [ɑ̃trəʒɑ̃] *s.m.* urbanity, savoir faire, social graces.
entre-jambes [ɑ̃trəʒɑ̃b] *s.m.invar.* (dressm.) gusset; fork (of trousers); (techn.) space enclosed by legs (of table, etc.).
entrelacement [ɑ̃trəlasmɑ̃] *s.m.* interlacing, interweaving; (fig.) network, web.
entrelacer [ɑ̃trəlase] *v.t.* to interlace, to intertwine, to weave; **s'~** *v.refl.* to intertwine.
entrelacs [ɑ̃trəlɑ] *s.m.* tracery, interwoven work.
entrelardé, -e [ɑ̃trəlarde] *adj.* (cook.) larded; (of bacon, etc.) streaky.
entrelarder [ɑ̃trəlarde] *v.t.* (cook.) to lard; (fig.) to interlard.
entre-ligne [ɑ̃trəliɲ] *s.m.* space between lines (of writing).
entremêlement [ɑ̃trəmɛlmɑ̃] *s.m.* (obs.) mixture, jumble.
entremêler [ɑ̃trəmele] *v.t.* to mix, to mingle; *~ de*, to interlard with, to intersperse with.
entremets [ɑ̃trəmɛ] *s.m.* (cook.) sweet course, dessert.
entremetteu-r, -se [ɑ̃trəmɛtœr] *s.m.f.* **1.** (obs.) intermediary; **2.** (pej.) go-between; procurer, procuress.
(**s'**)**entremettre** [ɑ̃trəmɛtr] *v.refl.* to intervene, to interfere; to mediate.
entremise [ɑ̃trəmiz] *s.f.* **1.** intervention; mediation; medium; *par l'~ de*, through the medium, or agency, of; **2.** (nav. arch.) carling.
entre-nerf(s) [ɑ̃trənɛr] *s.m.* (bookb.) space (between bands).
entrepont [ɑ̃trəpɔ̃] *s.m.* (naut.) between-decks; *voyager dans l'~*, to travel steerage.
entreposage [ɑ̃trəpozaʒ] *s.m.* warehousing, storing; putting in bond.
entreposer [ɑ̃trəpoze] *v.t.* to store, to warehouse; to put in bond.
entreposeur [ɑ̃trəpozœr] *s.m.* warehouseman, officer in charge of bonded store.
entrepositaire [ɑ̃trəpozitɛr] *s.m.* depositor (of stored or bonded goods).
entrepôt [ɑ̃trəpo] *s.m.* store, warehouse,

depository; bonded warehouse; entrepôt port; (law) bonding.

entreprenant, -e [ɑ̃trəprənɑ̃] *adj.* enterprising, daring, bold; dashing; fresh (with women).

entreprendre [ɑ̃trəprɑ̃dr] *v.t.* **1.** to undertake, to set about, to begin; to attempt; **2.** (obs.) to attack; **3.** to court (a woman); to take (s.o.) on; to start a discussion with; ~ *v.i.* ~ *sur,* (obs.) to invade, to trespass upon.

entrepreneu-r, -se [ɑ̃trəprənœr] *s.m.f.* contractor, entrepreneur.

entreprise [ɑ̃trəpriz] *s.f.* **1.** undertaking, enterprise, project, operation; **2.** contract; **3.** (comm.) company, business, concern, organization; **4.** (obs. exc. Lit.) attack, infringement; (mod. pl.) seduction.

entrer [ɑ̃tre] *v.i.* to enter, to go or come in; *faire ~ qch.*, to insert sth.; *faire ~ qn.*, to bring or show s.o. in; ~ *dans, à, en,* to go, to come, to get, to walk, etc., into; (fig.) to enter, to take up (profession, etc.), to join, to join in, to take part in, to share; ~ *en,* to begin (an action), to come into, to enter (a state); ~ *en action,* to begin to act, to come into action; ~ *en ébullition,* to begin to boil; ~ *en possession de,* to come into possession of; ~ *en, dans,* to form part of, to enter into; *faire ~ en compte,* to take into consideration; *il n'entre pas dans mes projets de,* it is no part of my plan to; ~ *v.t.* to bring, or take, in.

entre-rail [ɑ̃trərɑj] *s.m.* (rail.) space between rails, gauge.

entresol [ɑ̃trəsɔl] *s.m.* entresol, mezzanine floor.

entretaille [ɑ̃trətɑj] *s.f.* (engr.) fine cut.

(**s'**)**entretailler** [ɑ̃trətɑje] *v.refl.* (of horse) to kick and injure itself.

entre temps [ɑ̃trətɑ̃] *adv.* meanwhile.

entreteneu-r, -se [ɑ̃trətnœr] *s.m.f.* **1.** (obs.) keeper, preserver; **2.** ~**r** *s.m.* lover (of kept woman), one who keeps a mistress.

entretenir [ɑ̃trətnir] *v.t.* **1.** to keep, to maintain; to prolong; to preserve; **2.** to support, to keep (a family, etc.); **3.** (obs.) to converse with; (mod.) ~ *qn. de qch.*, to hold forth to s.o. about sth.; **s'~** *avec v.refl.* to have a conversation with (s.o.).

entretenu, -e [ɑ̃trətny] *adj.* kept, kept up, kept going, maintained, kept in good repair; kept, supported; *femme ~e,* kept woman; (electr.) continuous, undamped.

entretien [ɑ̃trətjɛ̃] *s.m.* **1.** maintenance, upkeep; care, support; **2.** conversation, discussion, interview.

entretoile [ɑ̃trətwal] *s.f.* (dressm.) lace insertion.

entretoise [ɑ̃trətwaz] *s.f.* (constr.) brace, stay; tie-rod, tie-beam; bridging-joist.

entretoisement [ɑ̃trətwazmɑ̃] *s.m.* (constr.) bridging, staying.

entretoiser [ɑ̃trətwaze] *v.t.* (constr.) to brace, to strut, to tie.

(**s'**)**entre-tuer** [ɑ̃trətɥe] *v.refl.* to kill each other, to fight to the death.

entre-voie [ɑ̃trəvwa] *s.f.* (rail.) space between tracks; (in U.K.) six-foot way.

entrevoir [ɑ̃trəvwar] *v.t.* (lit. & fig.) to glimpse, to get a glimpse of; to have an idea of, to foresee.

entrevous [ɑ̃trəvu] *s.m.* (constr.) panel (in wall or partition).

entrevoûter [ɑ̃trəvute] *v.t.* (constr.) to plaster (a panel).

entrevue [ɑ̃trəvy] *s.f.* interview, audience; meeting.

entropie [ɑ̃trɔpi] *s.f.* (sci.) entropy.

entropion [ɑ̃trɔpjɔ̃] *s.m.* (med.) introversion of eyelid.

entrouvert, -e [ɑ̃truvɛr] *adj.* ajar, partly open, half-open.

entrouvrir [ɑ̃truvrir] *v.t.* to part; to open partly, to half-open; **s'~** *v.refl.* to part.

enturbanné, -e [ɑ̃tyrbane] *adj.* turbanned.

enture [ɑ̃tyr] *s.f.* **1.** (hort.) slit (for grafting); **2.** (techn.) peg, dowel; **3.** (constr.) dovetail (joint).

énucléation [enykleɑsjɔ̃] *s.f.* **1.** stoning (of fruit); **2.** (surg.) enucleation.

énucléer [enyklee] *v.t.* **1.** to stone (fruit); **2.** (surg.) to enucleate.

énumérati-f, -ve [enymeratif] *adj.* enumerative.

énumération [enymerɑsjɔ̃] *s.f.* enumeration, listing.

énumérer [enymere] *v.t.* to enumerate, to recite, to detail.

énurésie [enyrezi] *s.f.* (med.) enuresis.

envahir [ɑ̃vair] *v.t.* (lit. & fig.) to invade; to overrun, to spread over; to fill, to overwhelm.

envahissant, -e [ɑ̃vaisɑ̃] *adj.* **1.** (obs.) invading; **2.** (fig.) overwhelming; intrusive, overbearing.

envahissement [ɑ̃vaismɑ̃] *s.m.* **1.** invasion, occupation; **2.** intrusion, encroachment.

envahisseu-r, -se [ɑ̃vaisœr] *s.m.f.* invader; intruder; *adj.* invading.

envasement [ɑ̃vɑzmɑ̃] *s.m.* silting-up.

envaser [ɑ̃vɑze] *v.t.* **1.** to fill with mud; **2.** to sink in mud; **s'~** *v.refl.* **1.** to silt up; **2.** to be stuck in mud.

enveloppant, -e [ɑ̃vlɔpɑ̃] *adj.* enveloping, covering, surrounding; (fig.) engrossing, captivating.

enveloppe [ɑ̃vlɔp] *s.f.* envelope, wrapper, cover; casing, coat, sheath; (fig.) exterior, outward appearance; (obs.) cloak.

enveloppement [ɑ̃vlɔpmɑ̃] *s.m.* (med.) packing, wrapping; (mil.) encircling movement.

envelopper [ɑ̃vlɔpe] *v.t.* to envelop, to wrap up, to pack, to cover, to surround; (fig.) to shroud, to cloak.

envenimé, -e [ɑ̃vnime] *adj.* (fig.) venomous, poisonous; (of wound) infected, festering.

envenimement [ɑ̃vnimmɑ̃] *s.m.* poisoning, infection.

envenimer [ɑ̃vnime] *v.t.* **1.** (obs.) to poison; **2.** (lit. & fig.) to aggravate, to inflame, to cause to fester.

enverguer [ɑ̃vɛrge] *v.t.* (naut.) to set (a sail).

envergure [ɑ̃vɛrgyr] *s.f.* (naut.) spread (of sail); wing-span (of bird or plane); (fig.) breadth, span; *de grande ~,* on a large scale, far-reaching.

envers[1] [ɑ̃vɛr] *prep.* **1.** (obs.) against; ~ *et contre tous,* against all comers, against all odds; **2.** (of feelings, actions) towards, to, with regard to; *bien disposé ~,* well-disposed towards; *faire son devoir ~ qn.*, to do one's duty by s.o.

envers[2] [ɑ̃vɛr] *s.m.* wrong side, back (of material), reverse (of medal or coin); (fig.) reverse, seamy side; *à l'~,* inside out; upside down; topsy-turvy, in disorder; in the wrong direction; (fig.) badly, in the wrong way.

(**à l'**)**envi** [alɑ̃vi] *adv.* trying to outdo one another; emulating one another; *à l'~ de,* in competition with (s.o.); *ils m'attaquaient à l'~ l'un de l'autre,* they vied with one another in their attacks on me.

enviable [ɑ̃vjabl] *adj.* enviable, to be envied.

envider [ɑ̃vide] *v.t.* (text.) to wind (yarn) on a spool.

envie [ɑ̃vi] *s.f.* **1.** envy, covetousness, jealousy; **2.** desire, want, wish, inclination; need; *avoir ~ de,* to want, to desire; *faire ~,* to be tempting, to attract; **3.** birthmark; **4.** (usu. pl.) cuticle.

envier [ɑ̃vje] *v.t.* **1.** to envy, to be envious of, (s.o.); **2.** to covet (sth.).

envieu-x, -se [ɑ̃vjø] *adj.* envious, jealous, covetous; *s.m.f.* jealous person; *faire des ~x,* to arouse jealousy.

enviné, -e [ɑ̃vine] *adj.* (of receptacles) smelling of wine.
environ [ɑ̃virɔ̃] *prep.* near, about, around; *adv.* about, nearly; **~s** *s.m.pl.* vicinity, neighbourhood; *aux ~s*, in the neighbourhood, in the vicinity.
environnant, -e [ɑ̃virɔnɑ̃] *adj.* surrounding.
environnement [ɑ̃virɔnmɑ̃] *s.m.* surroundings, environment; surrounding.
environner [ɑ̃virɔne] *v.t.* to surround, to encompass; to enclose.
envisager [ɑ̃vizaʒe] *v.t.* **1.** (obs.) to look hard at; **2.** to consider, to view, to contemplate; **3.** to envisage, to have in mind; to imagine, to think of; *~ de faire qch.*, to propose, to have it in mind, to do sth.
envoi [ɑ̃vwa] *s.m.* **1.** sending, posting; **2.** parcel, packet; consignment; **3.** (sport) *coup d'~*, kick-off; **4.** (Lit.) envoi.
(s')envoiler [ɑ̃vwale] *v.refl.* (metall.) to warp, to twist.
envol [ɑ̃vɔl] *s.m.* flight; take-off (of aircraft).
envolée [ɑ̃vɔle] *s.f.* (lit. & fig.) flight.
(s')envoler [ɑ̃vɔle] *v.refl.* to take flight, to fly away; (of aircraft) to take off; to blow away, to be blown away; (fig., fam.) to vanish.
envoûtant, -e [ɑ̃vutɑ̃] *adj.* captivating, spell-binding.
envoûtement [ɑ̃vutmɑ̃] *s.m.* spell, charm, enchantment.
envoûter [ɑ̃vute] *v.t.* (lit. & fig.) to cast a spell on, to enchant.
envoyé, -e [ɑ̃vwaje] *s.m.f.* messenger, agent, envoy, delegate; *adj.* sent, dispatched.
envoyer [ɑ̃vwaje] *v.t.* to send, to dispatch, to forward, to transmit; to kick, to hit, (ball, etc.); (fam.) *~ qn. au diable*, to tell s.o. to go to the devil; *~ chercher qn.*, to send for s.o.; (fig., fam.) *~ promener qn.*, to send s.o. about his business; *~ promener qch.*, to give sth. up, to throw sth. over; **s'~** *v.refl.* to send to each other, to exchange; (pop.) to take (for oneself), to take on (a burden, etc.); to eat, to drink.
envoyeu-r, -se [ɑ̃vwajœr] *s.m.f.* sender.
enzootie [ɑ̃zɔɔti] *s.f.* (vet.) enzootic disease.
enzymatique [ɑ̃zimatik] *adj.* enzymatic, enzymic.
enzyme [ɑ̃zim] *s.m.* enzyme.
enzymologie [ɑ̃zimɔlɔʒi] *s.f.* enzymology.
éocène [eɔsɛn] *adj.*, *s.m.* (geol.) Eocene.
éolien, -ne [eɔljɛ̃] *adj.* **1.** (Gr. hist.) Aeolian; **2.** wind-driven; (geol.) wind-induced (erosion, etc.); **~ne** [eɔljɛn] *s.f.* wind-pump, wind-motor.
éolipile [eɔlipil] *s.m.* (phys.) aeolipile.
éon [eɔ̃] *s.m.* aeon, eon.
éosine [eozin] *s.f.* (chem.) eosin.
épacte [epakt] *s.f.* epact.
épagneul, -e [epaɲœl] *s.m.f.* spaniel.
épais, -se [epɛ] *adj.* thick; gross; dense; (fig.) dull, slow-witted; *~ adv.* thickly.
épaisseur [epɛsœr] *s.f.* thickness, density; (fig.) solidity, weight; *un ouvrage qui manque d'~*, a lightweight work.
épaissir [epesir] *v.t.i.* to thicken; to grow stout; **s'~** *v.refl.* to grow thicker, to become denser; to get stouter.
épaississant, -e [epesisɑ̃] *adj.* (techn.) thickening; *~ s.m.* thickener.
épaississement [epesismɑ̃] *s.m.* thickening; growing stouter.
épaississeur [epesisœr] *s.m.* (techn.) thickener.
épamprage [epɑ̃praʒ], **épamprement** [epɑ̃prəmɑ̃] *s.m.* thinning out (of vine leaves).
épamprer [epɑ̃pre] *v.t.* to thin out (vine leaves).
épanchement [epɑ̃ʃmɑ̃] *s.m.* **1.** (obs. exc. Lit.) flow, outflow; **2.** (med.) effusion; (fig.) effusion, outpouring.
épancher [epɑ̃ʃe] *v.t.* **1.** (obs. exc. Lit.) to shed; **2.** (fig.) to pour out, to confide; **s'~** *v.refl.* to pour out, to overflow; to unbosom oneself; (med.) to extravasate.
épandage [epɑ̃daʒ] *s.m.* (agric.) spreading (of manure, etc.); *champ d'~*, sewage farm.
épandeu-r, -se [epɑ̃dœr] *s.m.f.* mechanical spreader (of manure, asphalt).
épandre [epɑ̃dr] *v.t.* to spread, to scatter; (fig.) to shed.
épanneler [epanle] *v.t.* to rough-hew (a block of stone).
épanner [epane] *v.t.* (techn.) to face (a stone).
épanoui, -e [epanwi] *adj.* **1.** (of flower) fully opened, in full bloom; **2.** (of smile, etc.) radiant, joyful; **3.** fully developed, mature.
épanouir [epanwir] *v.t.* **1.** to bring to full bloom; to extend, to stretch out; **2.** (fig.) to light up, to brighten, to rejoice; **3.** to bring to full development; **s'~** *v.refl.* **1.** (of flower) to open; to open out; **2.** (fig.) to brighten, to light up, to become radiant; **3.** to develop, to mature.
épanouissement [epanwismɑ̃] *s.m.* **1.** opening, blooming, (of flowers); fanning out, spreading; **2.** (fig.) lighting-up, brightening; **3.** full development.
épargnant, -e [eparɲɑ̃] *adj.* thrifty, careful; *s.m.f.* saver.
épargne [eparɲ] *s.f.* **1.** thrift, thriftiness, saving, economy; *caisse d'~*, savings bank; **2.** savings.
épargner [eparɲe] *v.t.* **1.** to spare; to reprieve, to pardon; **2.** to save, to use sparingly, to economize on; to put by.
éparpillement [eparpijmɑ̃] *s.m.* scattering, dispersing; diffusion.
éparpiller [eparpije] *v.t.* to scatter, to spread, to disperse; (fig.) to fritter away, to squander.
épars, -e [epar] *adj.* scattered, straggling; (of hair) dishevelled, tousled.
épar(t) [epar] *s.m.* (constr.) tie-beam; cross-bar (of door, etc.), transom; bar (for closing door).
éparvin [eparvɛ̃], **épervin** [epɛrvɛ̃] *s.m.* (vet.) spavin.
épatamment [epatamɑ̃] *adv.* (fam.) splendidly; marvellously, stunningly.
épatant, -e [epatɑ̃] *adj.* (fam.) marvellous, gorgeous, wonderful, stunning.
épate [epat] *s.f.* (fam.) *faire de l'~*, to show off; *le faire à l'~*, to act for effect.
épaté, -e [epate] *adj.* **1.** flat, squat; (of nose) pug; **2.** (fig., fam.) bowled over, astounded.
épatement [epatmɑ̃] *s.m.* **1.** flattening (of nose); **2.** (fig., fam.) astonishment, shock.
épater [epate] *v.t.* **1.** to spread, to flatten; **2.** (obs.) to break the stem of (a glass); **3.** (fig., fam.) to bowl over, to amaze, to shock.
épateu-r, -se [epatœr] *adj.* ostentatious, that tries for effect.
épaulard [epolar] *s.m.* (zool.) killer whale, grampus, orc.
épaule [epol] *s.f.* shoulder; *hausser, lever, les ~s*, to shrug one's shoulders; (fig.) *avoir la tête sur les ~s*, to have a good head on one's shoulders, to know what one is about; (fig.) *donner un coup d'~ à qn.*, to give s.o. a leg-up, a helping hand.
épaulé-jeté [epoleʒ(ə)te] *s.m.* (weightlifting) raising weight to shoulder height and hoisting.
épaulement [epolmɑ̃] *s.m.* **1.** retaining wall; (mil.) breastwork; **2.** shoulder (of hill); (techn.) shoulder.
épauler [epole] *v.t.* **1.** (fig.) to support, to help; **2.** to shoulder (a weapon), to take aim; **3.** (constr.) to retain (with a wall).
épaulette [epolɛt] *s.f.* epaulette; shoulder-strap.
épave [epav] *s.f.* (lit. & fig.) wreck; (law) stray, unclaimed, or ownerless animal or thing; waif.
épeautre [epotr] *s.m.* (agric.) spelt.

épée [epe] *s.f.* **1.** sword; ~ *de salle d'armes*, foil; (fig.) *un coup d'~ dans l'eau*, a vain attempt; *mettre à qn. l'~ dans les reins*, to prod, to press s.o.; **2.** swordsman.
épeiche [epɛʃ] *s.f.* (ornith.) great spotted woodpecker.
épeichette [epɛʃɛt] *s.f.* (ornith.) lesser spotted woodpecker.
épeire [epɛr] *s.f.* garden spider.
épeirogénique [epɛrɔʒenik], **épirogénique** [epirɔʒenik] *adj.* (geol.) epeirogenic.
épéisme [epeism] *s.m.* fencing with swords (not foils).
épéiste [epeist] *s.m.* fencer with sword (not foil).
épeler [eple] *v.t.* to spell; to learn to spell or read; to spell out.
épendyme [epɑ̃dim] *s.m.* (anat.) ependyma.
épenthèse [epɑ̃tɛz] *s.f.* (lang.) epenthesis.
éperdu, -e [epɛrdy] *adj.* distraught, dismayed; bewildered, desperate; ~*(e) de douleur*, mad with pain or grief; ~*(e) de bonheur*, wild with joy; **~ment** [epɛrdymɑ̃] *adv.* desperately, madly, utterly.
éperlan [epɛrlɑ̃] *s.m.* (ichth.) smelt.
éperon [eprɔ̃] *s.m.* **1.** spur; (naut.) beak (of ancient warship); **2.** breakwater, groyne; buttress, fender (of bridge).
éperonner [eprɔne] *v.t.* (lit. & fig.) to spur.
épervier [epɛrvje] *s.m.* **1.** (ornith.) sparrow--hawk; **2.** (fish.) cast-net.
épervière [epɛrvjɛr] *s.f.* (bot.) hawkweed.
épervin see ÉPARVIN.
épeurer [epœre] *v.t.* (obs. exc. Lit.) to frighten.
éphèbe [efɛb] *s.m.* **1.** (Gr. ant.) ephebe; **2.** (pej.) beautiful young man.
éphélide [efelid] *s.f.* freckle.
éphémère [efemɛr] *adj.* ephemeral, transitory; ~ *s.m.* (ent.) mayfly.
éphéméride [efemerid] *s.f.* ephemeris; almanac; tear-off calendar; (pl.) ephemerides, astronomical tables.
Éphèse [efɛz] *s.f.* (anc. geog.) Ephesus.
éphod [efɔd] *s.m.* (Hebrew ant.) ephod.
éphore [efɔr] *s.m.* (Gr. ant.) ephor.
épi [epi] *s.m.* **1.** ear (of corn); spike (of flower); cow-lick (of hair); **2.** (rail.) spur; **3.** (constr.) herring-bone work; finial; **4.** groyne, jetty.
épiage [epjaʒ] *s.m.*, **épiaison** [epjɛzɔ̃] *s.f.* (agric.) earing (of corn).
épiaire [epjɛr] *s.m.* (bot.) marsh woundwort.
épicarpe [epikarp] *s.m.* (bot.) epicarp.
épice [epis] *s.f.* spice; *pain d'~*, = gingerbread.
épicé, -e [epise] *adj.* (lit. & fig.) spicy.
épicéa [episea] *s.m.* (bot.) Norway spruce.
épicène [episɛn] *adj.* (gram.) epicene, of common gender.
épicentre [episɑ̃tr] *s.m.* epicentre.
épicer [epise] *v.t.* to spice, to season; (fig.) to give spice to.
épicerie [episri] *s.f.* **1.** (obs.) spicer's shop; (pl.) spices; **2.** grocery, dry goods; groceries; grocer's (shop).
épici-er, -ère [episje] *s.m.f.* **1.** (obs.) spicer; **2.** grocer; (fig., pej.) philistine; mercenary writer.
épicurien, -ne [epikyrjɛ̃] *adj.* **1.** (phil.) Epicurean; **2.** sybaritic; *s.m.f.* epicure; sybarite.
épicurisme [epikyrism] *s.m.* **1.** (phil.) Epicureanism; **2.** epicurism, hedonism.
épicycle [episikl] *s.m.* epicycle.
épicycloïdal, -e, (**aux**) [episiklɔidal] *adj.* epicycloidal.
épicycloïde [episiklɔid] *s.f.* (geom.) epicycloid.
épidém-icité [epidemisite] *s.f.* (med.) epidemicity; **~ie** [epidemi] *s.f.* epidemic; **~iologie** [epidemjɔlɔʒi] *s.f.* epidemiology; **~ique** [epidemik] *adj.* epidemic; (fig.) catching, infectious.
épiderme [epidɛrm] *s.m.* cuticle, epidermis skin; (fig.) *avoir l'~ chatouilleux*, to be touchy; *chatouiller l'~ de qn.*, to flatter s.o.
épidermique [epidɛrmik] *adj.* epidermal, epidermic, epidermoid; (fig.) skin-deep.
épier[1] [epje] *v.i.* (of corn) to ear.
épier[2] [epje] *v.t.* to watch, to spy upon; to watch for, to wait for, to be on the lookout for.
épierrage [epjɛraʒ], **épierrement** [epjɛrmɑ̃] *s.m.* (agric.) clearing of stones (from winnowed corn).
épierrer [epjere] *v.t.* (agric.) to clear (a field) of stones.
épierreuse [epjɛrøz] *s.f.* (agric.) stone-removing machine.
épieu (pl. **-x**) [epjø] *s.m.* (anc. mil.) pike.
épieu-r, -se [epjœr] *s.m.f.* watcher, spy.
épigastre [epigastr] *s.m.* (anat.) epigastrium.
épigé, -e [epiʒe] *adj.* (bot.) epigeal.
épigénèse [epiʒenɛz] *s.f.* epigenesis.
épigénie [epiʒeni] *s.f.* (min.) pseudomorphism.
épiglotte [epiglɔt] *s.f.* (anat.) epiglottis.
épigrammatique [epigram(m)atik] *adj.* epigrammatic.
épigramme [epigram] *s.f.* **1.** epigram; **2.** (cook.) ~*s d'agneau*, braised lamb-chop or breast of lamb.
épigraphe [epigraf] *s.f.* epigraph, inscription.
épigraph-ie [epigrafi] *s.f.* epigraphy; **~ique** [epigrafik] *adj.* epigraphic; **~iste** [epigrafist] *s.m.f.* epigraphist.
épigyne [epiʒin] *adj.* (bot.) epigynous.
épilation [epilɑsjɔ̃] *s.f.* epilation, depilation.
épilatoire [epilatwar] *adj.* depilatory.
épilepsie [epilɛpsi] *s.f.* epilepsy.
épileptique [epilɛptik] *adj.*, *s.m.f.* epileptic.
épiler [epile] *v.t.* to epilate, to depilate; (techn.) to trim (pewter casting).
épillet [epijɛ] *s.m.* (bot.) spikelet.
épilobe [epilɔb] *s.m.* (bot.) willow-herb.
épilogue [epilɔg] *s.m.* epilogue; (fig.) final outcome (of complicated affair).
épiloguer [epilɔge] *v.t.* (obs.) to censure, to criticize; ~ *v.i.* ~ *sur*, to comment at length on, to cavil about, to go on about.
épinard [epinar] *s.m.* (bot.) spinach; (cook. pl.) spinach.
épinçage [epɛ̃saʒ] *s.m.* = ÉPINCETAGE.
épinceler [epɛ̃sle] *v.t.* = ÉPINCETER 1.
épincer [epɛ̃se] *v.t.* **1.** (hort.) to disbud; **2.** = ÉPINCETER 1.
épincetage [epɛ̃staʒ] *s.m.* (text.) burling (of cloth).
épinceter [epɛ̃ste] *v.t.* **1.** (text.) to burl; **2.** = ÉPINCER 1.
épine [epin] *s.f.* **1.** (obs.) thorn-bush; **2.** thorn, prickle; **3.** ~ *dorsale*, spine, backbone; **4.** spine (of hedgehog, etc.).
épinette [epinɛt] *s.f.* **1.** (mus.) spinet; **2.** (agric.) hen-coop.
épineu-x, -se [epinø] *adj.* thorny, prickly; (fig.) thorny, ticklish, awkward; (of person) prickly.
épine-vinette [epinvinɛt] *s.f.* (bot.) berberis.
épinglage [epɛ̃glaʒ] *s.m.* pinning.
épingle [epɛ̃gl] *s.f.* pin; ~ *de sûreté*, ~ *de nourrice*, ~ *anglaise*, safety pin; ~ *à linge*, clothes peg; *tiré à quatre* ~*s*, spick and span, dressed up to the nines; *tirer son ~ du jeu*, to save one's bacon; *pointe d'~*, pinhead; *monter qch. en ~*, to show sth. off, to make much of sth.
épinglé, -e [epɛ̃gle] *adj.* **1.** pinned; **2.** (text.) ribbed, corded; ~ *s.m.* ribbed material.
épingler [epɛ̃gle] *v.t.* to pin; (fig., fam.) to arrest.
épinglerie [epɛ̃gləri] *s.f.* pin-making; pin trade.
épinglette [epɛ̃glɛt] *s.f.* (anc. mil.) priming--needle.

épingli-er, -ère [epɛ̃glije] *s.m.f.* pin-maker; **~er** *s.m.* pin-box.
épinier [epinje] *s.m.* (hunt.) thorn cover.
épinière [epinjɛr] *adj.f.* *moelle ~*, spinal cord.
épinoche [epinɔʃ] *s.f.* (ichth.) stickleback.
Épiphanie [epifani] *s.f.* (eccles.) Epiphany.
épiphénomène [epifenɔmɛn] *s.m.* (med., phil.) epiphenomenon.
épiphénoménisme [epifenɔmenism] *s.m.* (phil.) epiphenomenalism.
épiphylle [epifil] *adj.* (bot.) epiphyllous; ~ *s.m.* epiphyllum.
épiphyse [epifiz] *s.f.* (anat.) epiphysis.
épiphyte [epifit] *s.m.* (bot.) epiphyte; ~ *adj.* epiphytal, epiphytic.
épiploon [epiplɔɔ̃] *s.m.* (anat.) epiploon.
épique [epik] *adj.* epic.
épirogénique see ÉPEIROGÉNIQUE.
épiscopal, -e, (aux) [episkɔpal] *adj.* episcopal.
épiscopat [episkɔpa] *s.m.* episcopate, episcopacy.
épisode [epizɔd] *s.m.* episode.
épisodique [epizɔdik] *adj.* episodic; **~ment** [epizɔdikmɑ̃] *adv.* episodically.
épisser [epise] *v.t.* (naut.) to splice.
épissoir [episwar] *s.m.* marlinspike, marline-spike.
épissure [episyr] *s.f.* splice.
épistémologie [epistemɔlɔʒi] *s.f.* epistemology.
épistémologique [epistemɔlɔʒik] *adj.* epistemological.
épistolaire [epistɔlɛr] *adj.* epistolary, by correspondence; *échange ~*, exchange of letters; *être en relations ~s avec*, to be in correspondence with.
épistoli-er, -ère [epistɔlje] *s.m.f.* (obs.) author of letters; (iron.) great letter-writer.
épistyle [epistil] *s.m.* (arch.) epistyle.
épitaphe [epitaf] *s.f.* epitaph.
épite [epit] *s.f.* (naut.) treenail.
épithalame [epitalam] *s.m.* epithalamium.
épithélial, -e, (aux) [epiteljal] *adj.* (bot.) epithelial.
épithélioma [epiteljɔma], **épithéliome** [epiteljɔm] *s.m.* (med.) epithelioma.
épithélium [epiteljɔm] *s.m.* (anat.) epithelium.
épithète [epitɛt] *s.f.* (gram.) epithet, attributive adjective; (fig.) epithet, term (of abuse, etc.).
épitoge [epitɔʒ] *s.f.* **1.** (ant.) cope, cloak; **2.** (academic) sash (= Eng. hood).
épitomé [epitɔme] *s.m.* epitome.
épître [epitr] *s.f.* epistle; letter.
épizootie [epizɔɔti] *s.f.* epizootic disease.
épizootique [epizɔɔtik] *adj.* epizootic.
éploré, -e [eplɔre] *adj.* tearful; in tears, weeping.
éployé, -e [eplwaje] *adj.* spread (out), outstretched; (herald.) spread(-eagle).
éployer [eplwaje] *v.t.* (Lit.) to spread (wings).
épluchage [eplyʃaʒ] *s.m.* **1.** peeling, scraping, cleaning, (of vegetables, etc.); **2.** (fig.) detailed examination, combing through.
éplucher [eplyʃe] *v.t.* **1.** to scrape, to peel, to clean, (vegetables, etc.); **2.** (fig.) to examine closely, to comb through, to pick holes in.
éplucheu-r, -se [eplyʃœr] *s.m.f.* **1.** cleaner (of vegetables, etc.); picker (of fabric); *couteau-~r*, potato-peeler; *~r électrique*, electric potato-peeler; **2.** (rare) carping critic.
épluchure [eplyʃyr] *s.f.* peel; (pl.) peelings.
épode [epɔd] *s.f.* epode.
épois [epwa] *s.m.* topmost tine of antler.
épointage [epwɛ̃taʒ] *s.m.* breaking the point of (needle, pencil, etc.).
épointement [epwɛ̃tmɑ̃] *s.m.* bluntness (of a pointed tool).
épointer [epwɛ̃te] *v.t.* to blunt, to break the point of.
éponge [epɔ̃ʒ] *s.f.* sponge; *boire comme une ~*, to drink like a fish; (fig.) *passer l'~ sur*, to wipe out, to say no more about; *tissu ~*, towelling; *serviette ~*, bath towel.
épongeage [epɔ̃ʒaʒ] *s.m.* sponging, wiping with a sponge.
éponger [epɔ̃ʒe] *v.t.* to wipe with a sponge, to mop (up); (fig., fin.) to absorb (surplus, etc.); **s'~** *v.refl.* to wipe one's face, to mop one's brow.
éponte [epɔ̃t] *s.f.* (min.) wall (of lode).
épontille [epɔ̃tij] *s.f.* (naut.) stanchion, shore, prop.
épontiller [epɔ̃tije] *v.t.* (naut.) to shore up, to prop.
éponyme [epɔnim] *adj.* (Gr. ant.) eponymous; ~ *s.m.* eponym.
épopée [epɔpe] *s.f.* epic, epic poem; epos, epopee.
époque [epɔk] *s.f.* age, era, epoch, period, time, date; *faire ~*, to be epoch-making, to make history, to go down in history, to mark an era; (pl.) (obs.) periods, menstruation.
épouillage [epujaʒ] *s.m.* cleansing of vermin, delousing.
épouiller [epuje] *v.t.* to delouse.
(s')époumoner [epumɔne] *v.refl.* to shout at the top of one's voice, to shout oneself hoarse.
épousailles [epuzɑj] *s.f.pl.* (obs.) nuptials, marriage.
épouse [epuz] see ÉPOUX.
épousée [epuze] *s.f.* (obs.) bride.
épouser [epuze] *v.t.* **1.** to marry; (fig.) to espouse (a cause, etc.); **2.** to fit (a shape) exactly, to fit into, to correspond in shape with, to follow the line of; *robe qui épouse les formes du corps*, dress which moulds itself to the body.
épouseur [epuzœr] *s.m.* suitor; marrying man.
époussetage [epustaʒ] *s.m.* dusting.
épousseter [epuste] *v.t.* to dust, to wipe away (dust, etc.).
époussette [epusɛt] *s.f.* dusting brush, feather duster.
époustouflant, -e [epustuflɑ̃] *adj.* (fam.) fabulous, staggering.
époustoufler [epustufle] *v.t.* (fam.) to stagger, to amaze.
époutier [eputje] *v.t.* (text.) to burl, to pick.
épouvantable [epuvɑ̃tabl] *adj.* frightful, frightening; dreadful, awful, horrible, hideous; appalling, terrible; **~ment** [epuvɑ̃tabləmɑ̃] *adv.* frightfully, dreadfully, awfully, horribly, hideously; terribly.
épouvantail [epuvɑ̃taj] *s.m.* (lit. & fig.) scarecrow; bogy.
épouvante [epuvɑ̃t] *s.f.* fright, terror; horror, dread.
épouvantement [epuvɑ̃tmɑ̃] *s.m.* (obs.) terror; terrifying.
épouvanter [epuvɑ̃te] *v.t.* to terrify, to frighten, to scare to death; to appal, to dismay.
épou-x, -se [epu] *s.m.f.* husband, wife, spouse, partner (in marriage); *~x* (pl.), husband and wife, couple.
épreindre [eprɛ̃dr] *v.t.* (obs.) to squeeze, to press.
épreintes [eprɛ̃t] *s.f.pl.* (med.) colic, gripes.
(s')éprendre [eprɑ̃dr] *v.refl.* *s'~ de*, to be taken with; to fall in love with; to become attached or devoted to.
épreuve [eprœv] *s.f.* **1.** ordeal, trial, sorrow, affliction; **2.** test, trial; *faire l'~ de qch.*, to try sth. out; *mettre à l'~*, to put to the test; *à l'~*, sorely tried; *à toute ~*, unflinching, unbreakable; *à l'~ de*, proof against; **3.** examination paper, test; (sport) trial, competition; **4.** (print.) proof; (photo.) print.
épris, -e [epri] *adj.* in love, taken, smitten, (*de*, with); enamoured (*de*, of).
éprouvant, -e [epruvɑ̃] *adj.* trying, testing.

éprouvé, -e [epruve] *adj.* **1.** certain, tested, tried, proven; **2.** stricken, sorely tried.
éprouver [epruve] *v.t.* **1.** to test, to try, to put to the test; to tempt; **2.** to experience, to realize; to feel; to meet with, to undergo.
éprouvette [epruvɛt] *s.f.* test-tube, gauge; (metall.) test-piece.
epsilon [ɛpsilɔn] *s.m.* epsilon.
epsomite [ɛpsɔmit] *s.f.* Epsom salt(s).
épucer [epyse] *v.t.* to rid of fleas.
épuisable [epɥizabl] *adj.* exhaustible.
épuisant, -e [epɥizɑ̃] *adj.* exhausting, tiring.
épuisé, -e [epɥize] *adj.* **1.** worn-out, spent; (of mine, etc.) worked-out; *édition ~e*, out-of-print edition; **2.** exhausted, tired out.
épuisement [epɥizmɑ̃] *s.m.* draining (of liquid); impoverishment (of soil); depletion (of stocks); exhaustion, fatigue, collapse; *~ nerveux*, nervous breakdown.
épuiser [epɥize] *v.t.* **1.** to drain, to run dry; to work out; to impoverish; **2.** to use up, to consume; to sell out (stock); **3.** to wear out, to exhaust, to weaken; **s'~** *v.refl.* to become exhausted, to wear oneself out; to run dry; (of stock, etc.) to run out, to be exhausted.
épuisette [epɥizɛt] *s.f.* **1.** (fish.) landing-net; **2.** (naut.) scoop, bailer.
épulide [epylid], **épulie** [epyli] *s.f.* (med.) epulis, gumboil.
épulpeur [epylpœr] *s.m.* (agric.) pulp separator.
épurateur [epyratœr] *adj.m.* purifying; *~ s.m.* purifying apparatus, purifier, cleanser, separator, scrubber.
épuration [epyrɑsjɔ̃] *s.f.* purification, refining; (fig.) purging; (pol.) purge.
épurati-f, -ve [epyratif], **épuratoire** [epyratwar] *adj.* purifying, refining.
épure [epyr] *s.f.* draft, working drawing.
épuré, -e [epyre] *adj.* purified, refined.
épurement [epyrmɑ̃] *s.m.* purifying, refining.
épurer [epyre] *v.t.* to purify, to refine, to clarify; (fig.) to purge.
épurge [epyrʒ] *s.f.* (bot.) spurge.
équanimité [ekwanimite] *s.f.* (Lit.) equanimity.
équarrir [ekarir] *v.t.* to square, to square off, to cut square; to ream; to cut into squares; to cut up the carcase of (horse, etc.); (fig.) *mal équarri*, badly finished, unpolished.
équarrissage [ekarisaʒ], **équarrissement** [ekarismɑ̃] *s.m.* **1.** squaring; **2.** cutting up (of carcase).
équarrisseur [ekarisœr] *s.m.* knacker.
équarrissoir [ekariswar] *s.m.* **1.** knacker's knife; knacker's yard; **2.** (techn.) reamer.
équateur [ekwatœr] *s.m.* equator; equinoctial line.
Équateur [ekwatœr] *s.m.* (geog.) Ecuador.
équation [ekwɑsjɔ̃] *s.f.* equation.
équatorial, -e, (aux) [ekwatɔrjal] *adj.* equatorial; *~ s.m.* equatorial (telescope).
équerrage [ekɛraʒ] *s.m.* (techn.) squaring, making a right angle; *~ en gras*, making an obtuse angle; *~ en maigre*, making an acute angle.
équerre [ekɛr] *s.f.* square; *~ à dessin*, set-square; *~ en T*, T-square; *fausse ~*, bevel square; *à l'~*, *en ~*, *d'~*, at right angles, forming a right angle; *mettre qch. d'~*, to square sth.
équerrer [ekere] *v.t.* to square, to bevel (timber).
équestre [ekɛstr] *adj.* equestrian.
équeuter [ekøte] *v.t.* to tail (fruit).
équiangle [ekɥiɑ̃gl] *adj.* (geom.) equiangular.
équidés [ekide] *s.m.pl.* (zool.) Equidae.
équidistant, -e [ekɥidistɑ̃] *adj.* equidistant.
équilatéral, -e, (aux) [ekɥilateral] *adj.* (geom.) equilateral; (fam.) *ça m'est ~*, it's all the same to me.
équilibrage [ekilibraʒ] *s.m.* balancing; (techn.) counterbalancing.
équilibrant, -e [ekilibrɑ̃] *adj.* balancing.
équilibration [ekilibrɑsjɔ̃] *s.f.* equilibration.
équilibre [ekilibr] *s.m.* balance, equilibrium; poise, equipoise; stability.
équilibré, -e [ekilibre] *adj.* balanced; stable; (fig.) well-balanced.
équilibrer [ekilibre] *v.t.* to balance, to counterbalance, to equilibrate; **s'~** *v.refl.* to balance each other, to compensate.
équilibreu-r, -se [ekilibrœr] *adj.* balancing; **~r** *s.m.* (aeron.) stabilizer.
équilibriste [ekilibrist] *s.m.f.* equilibrist, acrobat, tightrope walker; (fig.) juggler.
équille [ekij] *s.f.* (ichth.) sand-eel.
équimoléculaire [ekɥimɔlekylɛr] *adj.* (chem.) equimolecular.
équimultiple [ekɥimyltipl] *adj., s.m.* (math.) equimultiple.
équin, -e [ekɛ̃] *adj.* equine; *variole ~e*, horse-pox; *pied ~*, club foot.
équinoxe [ekinɔks] *s.m.* equinox.
équinoxial, -e, (aux) [ekinɔksjal] *adj.* equinoctial.
équipage [ekipaʒ] *s.m.* **1.** (naut., aeron.) crew; **2.** (obs.) outfit, attire; **3.** (obs.) carriage, coach and horses; retinue; **4.** (mil.) (obs.) train; equipment; (mod.) *train des ~s*, army service corps; **5.** (techn.) gear, equipment, apparatus.
équipe [ekip] *s.f.* **1.** gang, shift (of workmen); **2.** (sport) team, side.
équipée [ekipe] *s.f.* escapade, prank, lark.
équipement [ekipmɑ̃] *s.m.* **1.** (naut., mil.) equipment, fitting-out, supplies; **2.** equipment, gear, tackle, kit; **3.** installation, fittings, materials.
équiper [ekipe] *v.t.* to equip, to fit out; to man (a ship); **s'~** *v.refl.* to equip oneself, to fit oneself out; to put on one's equipment.
équipi-er, -ère [ekipje] *s.m.f.* **1.** (obs.) member of gang of workmen; **2.** member of team, player.
équipollence [ekipɔlɑ̃s] *s.f.* equipollence, equipollency.
équipollent, -e [ekipɔlɑ̃] *adj.* equipollent.
équipotentiel, -le [ekɥipɔtɑ̃sjɛl] *adj.* (electr.) equipotential.
équitable [ekitabl] *adj.* fair, just, equitable; **~ment** [ekitabləmɑ̃] *adv.* fairly, justly, equitably.
équitation [ekɥitɑsjɔ̃] *s.f.* riding, horsemanship, equitation.
équité [ekite] *s.f.* equity, fairness, justice.
équivalence [ekivalɑ̃s] *s.f.* equivalence, equivalency.
équivalent, -e [ekivalɑ̃] *adj.* equivalent, of equal value; *~ s.m.* equivalent.
équivaloir [ekivalwar] *v.t.* *~ à*, to be equivalent to; to be the same as, to come to the same as.
équivoque [ekivɔk] *adj.* **1.** equivocal, ambiguous, uncertain; **2.** dubious, suspicious; *~ s.f.* (obs.) pun; (mod.) ambiguity, uncertainty, misunderstanding.
équivoquer [ekivɔke] *v.i.* (Lit.) to equivocate; (obs.) to make puns.
érable [erabl] *s.m.* (bot.) maple (tree).
érablière [erablijɛr] *s.f.* maple plantation.
éradication [eradikɑsjɔ̃] *s.f.* eradication; (med.) removal, excision.
éraflement [erɑfləmɑ̃] *s.m.* scratch, scratching, grazing.
érafler [erɑfle] *v.t.* to scratch, to graze.
éraflure [erɑflyr] *s.f.* scratch, graze.
éraillé, -e [erɑje] *adj.* **1.** (of eyes) bloodshot, red-rimmed; **2.** frayed, scratched; **3.** hoarse, cracked, raucous.

éraillement [erɑjmɑ̃] *s.m.* **1.** (med.) ectropion; **2.** fraying; **3.** hoarseness, cracking, (of voice).
érailler [erɑje] *v.t.* **1.** to fray, to scratch; **2.** to strain (voice); **s'~** *v.refl.* **1.** to fray; **2.** to become hoarse.
éraillure [erɑjyr] *s.f.* **1.** frayed part (of cloth); **2.** scratch.
Érasme [erasm] *s.m.* Erasmus.
erbium [ɛrbjɔm] *s.m.* (chem.) erbium.
erbue [ɛrby] *adj.* = HERBUE.
ère [ɛr] *s.f.* era, epoch, period; *en l'an 1500 de notre ~*, in 1500 A.D.
érect-eur, -rice [erɛktœr] *adj.* erector (muscle).
érectile [erɛktil] *adj.* erectile.
érection [erɛksjɔ̃] *s.f.* erection, construction, setting-up; (physiol.) erection.
éreintage [erɛ̃taʒ] *s.m.* = ÉREINTEMENT 1.
éreintant, -e [erɛ̃tɑ̃] *adj.* exhausting, killing, back-breaking.
éreinté, -e [erɛ̃te] *adj.* exhausted, dead-beat.
éreintement [erɛ̃tmɑ̃] *s.m.* **1.** malicious, merciless criticism, character assassination; **2.** exhaustion.
éreinter [erɛ̃te] *v.t.* **1.** (obs.) to thrash, to kick in the back; **2.** to exhaust, to tire out; **3.** (fig.) to defame, to destroy the reputation of.
éreinteur [erɛ̃tœr] *s.m.* merciless critic.
érémitique [eremitik] *adj.* (Lit.) eremitic; *vie ~*, life of a hermit or recluse.
érepsine [erɛpsin] *s.f.* (chem.) erepsin.
érésipèle see ÉRYSIPÈLE.
éréthisme [eretism] *s.m.* (med. & fig.) erethism.
erg[1] [ɛrg] *s.m.* (geog.) erg (of the Sahara).
erg[2] [ɛrg] *s.m.* (phys.) erg.
ergographe [ɛrgɔgraf] *s.m.* (sci.) ergograph.
ergonomie [ɛrgɔnɔmi] *s.f.* ergonomics.
ergostérol [ɛrgɔsterɔl] *s.m.* ergosterol.
ergot [ɛrgo] *s.m.* **1.** spur (of cock); (zool.) dew--claw; (fig.) *monter, se dresser, sur ses ~s*, to get on one's high horse, to have one's hackles up; **2.** (hort.) stub (on fruit-tree); (techn.) catch, lug, stop, pin; **3.** (agric.) ergot.
ergotage [ɛrgɔtaʒ] *s.m.* = ERGOTERIE.
ergoté, -e [ɛrgɔte] *adj.* **1.** spurred; **2.** (agric.) blighted.
ergoter [ɛrgɔte] *v.i.* to cavil, to quibble.
ergoterie [ɛrgɔtri] *s.f.* cavilling, quibbling.
ergoteu-r, -se [ɛrgɔtœr] *adj.* cavilling; *s.m.f.* quibbler.
ergotine [ɛrgɔtin] *s.f.* (pharm.) ergotin(e).
ergotisme [ɛrgɔtism] *s.m.* (med.) ergotism.
éricacées [ericase] *s.f.pl.* (bot.) Ericaceae.
Érié [erje] *s.m.* (geog.) Erie.
ériger [eriʒe] *v.t.* to erect, to raise, to set up, to establish; (fig.) to raise, to elevate; *s'~ en*, to set oneself up as, to pose as.
érigéron [eriʒerɔ̃] *s.m.* (bot.) Erigeron.
érigne [eriɲ], **érine** [erin] *s.f.* (surg.) tenaculum.
éristale [eristal] *s.m.* (ent.) hover-fly.
éristique [eristik] *adj., s.m.* eristic; *~ s.f.* dialectics.
ermitage [ɛrmitaʒ] *s.m.* hermitage.
ermite [ɛrmit] *s.m.* hermit, eremite.
éroder [erɔde] *v.t.* to erode, to eat away.
érogène [erɔʒɛn], **érotogène** [erɔtɔʒɛn] *adj.* erogenous, erotogenous.
Érôs, Éros [eros] *s.m.* (myth.) Eros.
érosi-f, -ve [erozif] *adj.* erosive.
érosion [erozjɔ̃] *s.f.* erosion, eating away.
érotique [erɔtik] *adj.* erotic; **~ment** [erɔtikmɑ̃] *adv.* erotically.
érotisation [erɔtizɑsjɔ̃] *s.f.* making erotic.
érotiser [erɔtize] *v.t.* **1.** (med.) to stimulate (sexual organs); **2.** to make erotic.
érotisme [erɔtism] *s.m.* erotism, eroticism.
érotomane [erɔtɔman] *adj., s.m.f.* erotomaniac.
érotomanie [erɔtɔmani] *s.f.* erotomania.
errance [ɛrɑ̃s] *s.f.* (Lit.) wandering.
errant, -e [ɛrɑ̃] *adj.* wandering, roving, fugitive; stray, lost.
errata [ɛrata] *s.m.invar.* errata, (pl.).
erratique [ɛratik] *adj.* (geol., med.) erratic.
erratum [ɛratɔm] *s.m.sing.* erratum.
erre [ɛr] *s.f.* (obs.) rate, speed, course; (naut.) way; (pl.) (hunt.) track, spoor.
errements [ɛrmɑ̃] *s.m.pl.* **1.** (obs.) ways, behaviour; **2.** evil ways, bad habits.
errer [ɛre] *v.i.* **1.** (obs. exc. Lit.) to err, to go astray; **2.** to wander, to stray, to roam.
erreur [ɛrœr] *s.f.* error, mistake; *faire ~*, to be mistaken; *~ judiciaire*, miscarriage of justice.
erroné, -e [ɛrɔne] *adj.* erroneous, faulty, misconceived; **~ment** [ɛrɔnemɑ̃] *adv.* erroneously.
ers [ɛr] *s.m.* (bot.) vetch.
ersatz [ɛrzats] *s.m.* ersatz, substitute.
erse[1] [ɛrs] *adj., s.m.* (ethn., lang.) Erse.
erse[2] [ɛrs] *s.f.* (naut.) grummet.
erseau (pl. **-x**) [ɛrso] *s.m.* (naut.) grummet.
érubescence [erybesɑ̃s] *s.f.* (Lit.) erubescence, blushing.
érubescent, -e [erybesɑ̃] *adj.* erubescent, blushing.
éructation [eryktɑsjɔ̃] *s.f.* (Lit.) eructation, belch.
éructer [erykte] *v.i.* (Lit.) to belch; *~ v.t.* (fig.) to pour out a stream of.
érudit, -e [erydi] *adj.* erudite; *s.m.f.* scholar.
érudition [erydisjɔ̃] *s.f.* erudition, scholarship.
érugineu-x, -se [eryʒinø] *adj.* aeruginous.
érupti-f, -ve [eryptif] *adj.* (geol., med.) eruptive.
éruption [erypsjɔ̃] *s.f.* eruption; (fig.) outburst, explosion.
érysipèle [erizipɛl], **érésipèle** [erezipɛl] *s.m.* (med.) erysipelas.
érythème [eritɛm] *s.m.* (med.) erythema.
érythrine [eritrin] *s.f.* **1.** (bot.) erythrina; **2.** (min.) red cobalt.
érythro-blaste [eritrɔblast] *s.m.* (biol.) erythroblast; **~cyte** [eritrɔsit] *s.m.* (biol.) erythrocyte; **~sine** [eritrozin] *s.f.* (chem.) erythrosin(e).
ès [ɛs] *prep.* (contraction of *en les*) in, of; *licencié ~ lettres* = bachelor of arts.
Ésaü [ezay] *s.m.* (bibl.) Esau.
(s')esbigner [ɛsbiɲe] *v.refl.* (pop.) to make off.
esbroufe [ɛsbruf] *s.f.* (fam.) showing off, bluff; *vol à l'~*, picking pockets by jostling the victim.
esbroufer [ɛsbrufe] *v.t.* (fam.) to bluff, to deceive by bluff.
esbroufeu-r, -se [ɛsbrufœr] *s.m.f.* (fam.) show--off, bluffer.
escabeau (pl. **-x**) [ɛskabo] *s.m.* stool; footstool; small pair of steps.
escadre [ɛskadr] *s.f.* (nav.) fleet, squadron; (air force) wing.
escadrille [ɛskadrij] *s.f.* (nav.) flotilla; (air force) squadron.
escadron [ɛskadrɔ̃] *s.m.* (mil., etc.) squadron; (fig.) bevy, swarm.
escalade [ɛskalad] *s.f.* escalade, scaling; climbing (over); (law) breaking-in; (econ.) escalating, escalation.
escalader [ɛskalade] *v.t.* to climb (over), to scale.
escalator [ɛskalatɔr] *s.m.* escalator.
escale [ɛskal] *s.f.* (naut., aeron.) stop, call, port of call; *faire ~ à*, to stop at, to call at.
escalier [ɛskalje] *s.m.* staircase, stairs; *~ roulant, mécanique*, escalator; (fig., fam.) *avoir l'esprit de l'~*, to be slow at repartee.
escalope [ɛskalɔp] *s.f.* (cook.) escalope, scallop.
escamotable [ɛskamɔtabl] *adj.* retractable.
escamotage [ɛskamɔtaʒ] *s.m.* juggling, sleight of hand, legerdemain; spiriting away; ducking, dodging (e.g. an issue); (techn.) retraction; (fig.) juggling.

escamoter [ɛskamɔte] *v.t.* **1.** to conjure away, to spirit away, to cause to disappear (by sleight of hand); to filch, to steal; to hide, to conceal; **2.** (fig.) to get out of, to get round; to dodge, to avoid; **3.** (techn.) to retract.
escamoteu-r, -se [ɛskamɔtœr] *s.m.f.* **1.** juggler, conjurer; **2.** pilferer, pickpocket.
escampette [ɛskɑ̃pɛt] *s.f.* **1.** (obs.) flight; **2.** *prendre la poudre d'~*, to take flight.
escapade [ɛskapad] *s.f.* **1.** (obs.) escape; **2.** escapade, prank.
escape [ɛskap] *s.f.* (arch.) shaft, scape (of column); ⚠ not 'escape'.
escarbille [ɛskarbij] *s.f.* cinder, smut.
escarbot [ɛskarbo] *s.m.* (obs. exc. dial.) cockchafer, dung-beetle, etc.
escarboucle [ɛskarbukl] *s.f.* (obs.) carbuncle (stone); *ses yeux brillaient comme des ~s*, his eyes flashed fire.
escarcelle [ɛskarsɛl] *s.f.* (obs.) money-bag; (iron.) purse.
escargot [ɛskargo] *s.m.* snail.
escargotière [ɛskargɔtjɛr] *s.f.* **1.** snail farm; **2.** dish for serving snails.
escarmouche [ɛskarmuʃ] *s.f.* (lit. & fig.) skirmish.
escarmoucher [ɛskarmuʃe] *v.i.* (obs.) to skirmish.
escarole see SCAROLE.
escarpe[1] [ɛskarp] *s.f.* (fort.) escarp, scarp.
escarpe[2] [ɛskarp] *s.m.* (obs.) assassin, cut-throat.
escarpé, -e [ɛskarpe] *adj.* **1.** steep, precipitous, sheer, abrupt; **2.** (fig.) (of character) difficult.
escarpement [ɛskarpəmɑ̃] *s.m.* escarpment, scarp; sheer drop.
escarpin [ɛskarpɛ̃] *s.m.* pump, dancing shoe, patent-leather shoe.
escarpolette [ɛskarpɔlɛt] *s.f.* (child's) swing; cradle (for working on scaffolding).
escarre[1] [ɛskar] *s.f.* (med.) scar, scab.
escarre[2], **esquarre** [ɛskar] *s.f.* (herald.) L-shaped square.
escarrifier [ɛskarifje] *v.t.* to form a scab.
Escaut [ɛsko] *s.m.* Scheldt (river).
eschatologie [ɛskatɔlɔʒi] *s.f.* eschatology.
eschatologique [ɛskatɔlɔʒik] *adj.* eschatological.
esche see ÈCHE.
Eschyle [ɛʃil] *s.m.* Aeschylus.
escient [esjɑ̃] *s.m.* (obs.) knowledge; (obs.) *à mon ~*, to my (certain) knowledge; (mod.) *à bon ~*, judiciously, with discrimination; *à mauvais ~*, injudiciously, indiscreetly, wrongly.
(s')esclaffer [ɛsklafe] *v.refl.* to roar with laughter, to guffaw.
esclandre [ɛsklɑ̃dr] *s.m.* **1.** (obs.) misadventure; brawl; **2.** scandal, scene, row.
esclavage [ɛsklavaʒ] *s.m.* **1.** slavery, bondage; subjection, servitude; **2.** necklace (reminiscent of slave's chain).
esclavagisme [ɛsklavaʒism] *s.m.* slave system.
esclavagiste [ɛsklavaʒist] *s.m.f.* advocate of slavery; *~ adj.* slave; *les États ~s*, the slave States (in U.S.A.).
esclave [ɛsklav] *s.m.f.* slave; *~ adj.* enslaved, a slave (*de*, to).
esclavon [ɛsklavɔ̃] *s.m.* = SLAVON.
escobar [ɛskɔbar] *s.m.* (obs.) equivocator, pecksniff, hypocrite.
escobarderie [ɛskɔbardri] *s.f.* (obs.) equivocation, hypocrisy.
escogriffe [ɛskɔgrif] *s.m.* lanky, gangling man.
escomptable [ɛskɔ̃tabl] *adj.* (fin.) negotiable, discountable.
escompte [ɛskɔ̃t] *s.m.* discount, rebate; (stock exchange) call for delivery (of securities) before settlement.
escompter [ɛskɔ̃te] *v.t.* to discount; (fig.) to anticipate, to count on.
escompteur [ɛskɔ̃tœr] *s.m.* discount broker.
escopette [ɛskɔpɛt] *s.f.* (anc. mil.) blunderbuss.
escorte [ɛskɔrt] *s.f.* (armed) escort; convoy; retinue, suite.
escorter [ɛskɔrte] *v.t.* to escort, to convoy; to be in attendance on, to accompany.
escorteur [ɛskɔrtœr] *s.m.* (nav.) escort vessel; *~ adj.m.* escorting.
escot [ɛsko] *s.m.* (obs.) serge.
escouade [ɛskwad] *s.f.* gang, group; (mil.) squad, section.
escourgeon [ɛskurʒɔ̃], **écourgeon** [ekurʒɔ̃] *s.m.* (agric.) winter barley.
escrime [ɛskrim] *s.f.* (sport) fencing.
(s')escrimer [ɛskrime] *v.refl.* to defend oneself, to fight; *s'~ à faire qch.*, to struggle to do sth.; (fam.) *s'~ des mâchoires*, to eat heartily.
escrimeu-r, -se [ɛskrimœr] *s.m.f.* fencer.
escroc [ɛskro] *s.m.* swindler, fraud, cheat, scrounger.
escroquer [ɛskrɔke] *v.t.* *~ qn.*, to cheat or swindle s.o.; *~ qch. à qn.*, to cheat s.o. of sth., to trick s.o. out of sth.; to scrounge sth. off s.o.
escroquerie [ɛskrɔkri] *s.f.* swindle, fraud, cheating.
escudo [ɛskydo] *s.m.* escudo.
esculape [ɛskylap] *s.m.* (obs. exc. iron.) famous physician.
esculine [ɛskylin] *s.f.* (chem.) aesculin.
ésérine [ezerin] *s.f.* (pharm.) eserine.
esgourde [ɛsgurd] *s.f.* (pop.) ear.
ésotérique [ezɔterik] *adj.* esoteric.
ésotérisme [ezɔterism] *s.m.* esotericism.
espace [ɛspas] *s.m.* **1.** space, room; *géométrie dans l'~*, solid geometry; **2.** space, void, infinity; (astronaut.) space; *regarder dans l'~*, to gaze into space; **3.** space, distance, interval; **4.** space, period, (of time); *~ s.f.* (typ.) space.
espacé, -e [ɛspase] *adj.* spread out, separated; periodic.
espacement [ɛspasmɑ̃] *s.m.* spacing; periodicity.
espacer [ɛspase] *v.t.* **1.** to leave a space between, to place at intervals, to spread out; **2.** to leave an interval (of time) between; to spread out over a certain time; **s'~** *v.refl.* to become less frequent.
espada [ɛspada] *s.f.* espada, matador.
espadon [ɛspadɔ̃] *s.m.* **1.** (obs.) two-handed sword; **2.** (ichth.) swordfish.
espadrille [ɛspadrij] *s.f.* espadrille, rope-soled canvas shoe.
Espagne [ɛspaɲ] *s.f.* (geog.) Spain.
espagnol, -e [ɛspaɲɔl] *adj.* Spanish; *s.m.f.* Spaniard; *~ s.m.* Spanish language.
espagnolette [ɛspaɲɔlɛt] *s.f.* espagnolette, fastening for French window.
espalier [ɛspalje] *s.m.* (hort.) espalier.
espar [ɛspar] *s.m.* (naut.) spar.
espèce [ɛspɛs] *s.f.* **1.** species, kind, sort, variety, class, race; *l'~ humaine*, the human race; (pej.) *~ d'idiot!*, you bloody fool!; **2.** (law) case in point; *en l'~*, in this case; *un cas d'~*, a special case; **3.** (pl.) specie, coin; *en ~s*, in cash.
espérance [ɛsperɑ̃s] *s.f.* hope, expectation; (pl.) expectations, prospects (esp. of inheritance); promise; *il donne de grandes ~s*, he shows great promise.
espérantiste [ɛsperɑ̃tist] *adj.* Esperanto; *~ s.m.f.* Esperantist.
espéranto [ɛsperɑ̃to] *s.m.* (lang.) Esperanto.
espérer [ɛspere] *v.t.* to hope for, to expect; *j'espère bien!*, I should hope so!; *~ v.i.* to hope, to be hopeful.
espiègle [ɛspjɛgl] *adj.* (usu. of children) mischievous, impish; *~ s.m.f.* imp, little monkey.
espièglerie [ɛspjɛgləri] *s.f.* (usu. of children) impishness, mischievousness; piece of mischief, prank.

espingole [ɛspɛ̃gɔl] *s.f.* (anc. mil.) blunderbuss.
espion, -ne [ɛspjɔ̃] *s.m.f.* spy, secret agent; ~ *s.m.* mirror for spying.
espionnite [ɛspjɔnit] *s.f.* spy-mania.
espionnage [ɛspjɔnaʒ] *s.m.* spying, espionage; secret service.
espionner [ɛspjɔne] *v.t.* to spy upon, to watch; to pry into.
esplanade [ɛsplanad] *s.f.* esplanade, parade, promenade.
espoir [ɛspwar] *s.m.* hope.
esponton [ɛspɔ̃tɔ̃] *s.m.* (anc. mil.) spontoon.
esprit [ɛspri] *s.m.* **1.** (bibl.) spirit, ghost; *le Saint-Esprit, l'Esprit Saint*, the Holy Ghost, the Holy Spirit; *rendre l'~*, to give up the ghost, to die; **2.** vital spirit; *perdre ses ~s*, to be prostrated (by misfortune, etc.); to lose consciousness; **3.** (chem.) spirit(s); *~-de-sel*, spirits of salt, hydrochloric acid; *~-de-bois*, methyl alcohol; *~-de-vin*, ethyl alcohol; **4.** mind, intellect, intelligence, wits; *ça m'est venu à l'~*, it came into my mind; ~ *borné*, limited intelligence, poor intellect; *les grands ~s se rencontrent*, great minds think alike; **5.** character, disposition; mood, humour; *avoir bon ~*, to have an amiable disposition; *avoir ~ à*, to be in the mood to, to feel like, (doing); **6.** feeling, spirit; ~ *d'équipe*, team spirit; **7.** spirit, meaning, essence, genius; *entrer dans l'~ de qch.*, to enter into the spirit of sth.; *se rattacher plutôt à l'~ qu'à la lettre de la loi*, to keep to the spirit rather than the letter of the law; *l'~ de la France*, the French genius; **8.** wit, humour; *mot d'~*, witty remark; ~ *de l'escalier*, rejoinder thought of too late.
esquicher [ɛskiʃe] *v.i.* (dial.) to crush, to squeeze.
esquif [ɛskif] *s.m.* (naut.) skiff.
esquille [ɛskij] *s.f.* splinter (of bone).
esquimau (pl. **-x**), **-de** [ɛskimo] *adj., s.m.f.* eskimo; ~ *s.m.* **1.** choc-ice; **2.** child's woolly suit.
esquintant, -e [ɛskɛ̃tɑ̃] *adj.* (fam.) exhausting.
esquinté, -e [ɛskɛ̃te] *adj.* **1.** ruined; **2.** exhausted.
esquinter [ɛskɛ̃te] *v.t.* **1.** (fam.) to spoil, to damage, to ruin; **2.** to exhaust.
esquisse [ɛskis] *s.f.* sketch, draft, outline, plan; (fig.) beginnings, attempt; *l'~ d'un sourire*, a half smile.
esquisser [ɛskise] *v.t.* to sketch, to draft, to plan, to outline; to begin to make, to make an attempt at.
esquive [ɛskiv] *s.f.* (sport) side-step.
esquiver [ɛskive] *v.t.* (lit. & fig.) to avoid, to evade, to elude, to side-step; **s'~** *v.refl.* to slip away, to make off.
essai [esɛ] *s.m.* **1.** test, trial; assay, assaying (of metal); *vol d'~*, test flight; *à l'~*, on trial, on approval; *mettre à l'~*, to test, to try out; **2.** attempt; **3.** (Rugby football) try; **4.** (Lit.) essay.
essaim [esɛ̃] *s.m.* swarm.
essaimage [esɛmaʒ] *s.m.* swarming, swarming-time.
essaimer [eseme] *v.i.* (of bees) to swarm; to hive off, to disperse; ~ *v.t.* to send out (missionaries, etc.).
essanger [esɑ̃ʒe] *v.t.* to soak (clothes before washing).
essanvage [esɑ̃vaʒ] *s.m.* (agric.) destruction of charlock.
essart [esar] *s.m.* (agric.) cleared land.
essarter [esarte] *v.t.* (agric.) to clear (land).
essayage [esɛjaʒ] *s.m.* trying-on, fitting (of clothes).
essayer [eseje] *v.t.* **1.** to try, to test, to try out; to try on (clothes, etc.); **2.** ~ *qch.*, to try sth.; ~ *de faire*, to try, to attempt, to do; **s'~** *à v.refl.* to try one's hand at, to have a go at.
essayeu-r, -se [esɛjœr] *s.m.f.* fitter (of clothes); **~r** *s.m.* assayer.
essayiste [esejist] *s.m.f.* essayist.
esse[1] [ɛs] *s.f.* **1.** S-hook; **2.** sound-hole, f-hole, of violin, etc.
esse[2] [ɛs] *s.f.* (techn.) linchpin, axle-pin.
essence [esɑ̃s] *s.f.* **1.** (phil.) essence; *par ~*, by its nature, essentially; **2.** essence, perfume, extract, tincture; **3.** petrol; **4.** species (of tree).
essentiel, -le [esɑ̃sjɛl] *adj.* essential, vital; fundamental; ~ *s.m. l'~*, the main point; **~lement** [esɑ̃sjɛlmɑ̃] *adv.* essentially, fundamentally.
esseulé, -e [esœle] *adj.* forlorn, alone.
essieu (pl. **-x**) [esjø] *s.m.* axle, axle-tree.
essor [esɔr] *s.m.* flight, soaring; (fig.) growth, expansion; *prendre son, un, ~*, to take flight, (fig.) to make a good start, to progress, to take off.
essorage [esɔraʒ] *s.m.* drying, wringing, (of clothes).
essorer [esɔre] *v.t.* to wring, to dry, to spin-dry, (clothes); **s'~** *v.refl.* to take flight, to fly up, to soar.
essoreuse [esɔrøz] *s.f.* spin-drier; drying machine.
essoriller [esɔrije] *v.t.* (anc. punishment) to cut off the ears of; to crop the ears of (a dog).
essouchement [esuʃmɑ̃] *s.m.* removal of tree--stumps.
essoucher [esuʃe] *v.t.* to remove tree-stumps.
essoufflement [esufləmɑ̃] *s.m.* shortness of breath, breathlessness, panting.
essouffler [esufle] *v.t.* to wind, to make breathless; **s'~** *v.refl.* to become winded or breathless; (fig.) to run out of inspiration.
essuie-glace [esɥiglas] *s.m.invar.* windscreen--wiper; **~-mains** [esɥimɛ̃] *s.m.invar.* hand--towel, roller-towel; **~-meubles** [esɥimœbl] *s.m.invar.* duster; **~-pieds** [esɥipje] *s.m.invar.* doormat; **~-plume** (pl. *essuie-plume(s)*) [esɥiplym] *s.m.* pen-wiper; **~-verres** *s.m invar.* glass cloth.
essuyage [esɥijaʒ] *s.m.* wiping, drying, dusting.
essuyer [esɥije] *v.t.* **1.** to dry, to wipe (up), to wipe dry, to wipe clean, to wipe away; (fig., fam.) ~ *les plâtres*, to be the first occupant of a new house; **2.** (fig.) to suffer, to endure, to meet with; ~ *un refus*, to meet with a refusal.
essuyeu-r, -se [esɥijœr] *s.m.f.* wiper, drier (of dishes).
est [ɛst] *s.m.* east; *vent (d')~*, east wind; *Est* (in proper names), East; *Berlin Est*, East Berlin; *l'Est*, (i) Eastern France; (ii) Eastern Europe (esp. Communist bloc); *l'Allemagne de l'Est*, East Germany; (iii) (pol.) the East (opp. the West).
estacade [ɛstakad] *s.f.* barricade; boom, breakwater.
estafette [ɛstafɛt] *s.f.* (obs.) messenger; (mod. mil.) courier.
estafier [ɛstafje] *s.m.* (hist.) armed attendant; (pej.) bodyguard.
estafilade [ɛstafilad] *s.f.* **1.** cut, gash; **2.** ladder (in stocking).
estagnon [ɛstaɲɔ̃] *s.m.* (dial.) tin, can, drum (for oil, etc.).
est-allemand, -e [ɛstalmɑ̃] *adj., s.m.f.* East German.
estaminet [ɛstaminɛ] *s.m.* drinking-place, bar; *pilier d'~*, habitual drunkard.
estampage [ɛstɑ̃paʒ] *s.m.* stamping, embossing; (fig., fam.) swindling.
estampe [ɛstɑ̃p] *s.f.* **1.** (techn.) punch, stamp, die; **2.** print, engraving.
estamper [ɛstɑ̃pe] *v.t.* **1.** to stamp, to impress; **2.** (fig., fam.) to cheat, to swindle.
estampeur [ɛstɑ̃pœr] *s.m.* **1.** stamp, die; **2.** engraver; **3.** (fam.) swindler.

estampillage [ɛstɑ̃pijaʒ] *s.m.* stamping, marking, certifying (of goods).
estampille [ɛstɑ̃pij] *s.f.* stamp, mark, trade-mark; postmark; (lit. & fig.) hallmark.
estampiller [ɛstɑ̃pije] *v.t.* to stamp, to mark, to certify (goods).
estampilleuse [ɛstɑ̃pijøz] *s.f.* stamping-machine.
estarie [ɛstari], **starie** [stari] *s.f.* (comm.) *jours d'~*, lay-days (for discharge of cargo).
ester[1] [ɛste] *v.i.* (law) ~ *en justice*, to take legal action.
ester[2] [ɛstɛr] *s.m.* (chem.) ester.
estér-ification [ɛsterifikɑsjɔ̃] *s.f.* esterification; **~ifier** [ɛsterifje] *v.t.* to esterify.
esthète [ɛstɛt] *s.m.f.* (often pej.) aesthete.
esthéticien, -ne [ɛstetisjɛ̃] *s.m.f.* **1.** aesthetician; **2.** beauty specialist.
esthétique [ɛstetik] *s.f.* aesthetics; ~ *adj.* aesthetic; **~ment** [ɛstetikmɑ̃] *adv.* aesthetically.
esthétisme [ɛstetism] *s.m.* aestheticism.
Esthonie see ESTONIE.
estimable [ɛstimabl] *adj.* (obs.) that can be estimated; (mod.) considerable; worthy, estimable; worthy of consideration.
estimateur [ɛstimatœr] *s.m.* (obs.) valuer; (fig.) judge.
estimati-f, -ve [ɛstimatif] *adj.* estimative, estimated.
estimation [ɛstimɑsjɔ̃] *s.f.* **1.** valuation; **2.** estimation, assessment; estimate.
estimatoire [ɛstimatwar] *adj.* estimative.
estime [ɛstim] *s.f.* **1.** (obs.) valuation; **2.** (naut.) reckoning; *à l'~*, dead reckoning; by guesswork; **3.** (obs.) opinion; (mod.) esteem, regard, estimation.
estimer [ɛstime] *v.t.* **1.** to value, to assess the value of; (fig.) to appreciate; **2.** to estimate; **3.** to consider, to believe; **4.** to esteem, to set a high value on, to prize; **s'~** *v.refl.* **1.** to consider oneself, to think oneself; *s'~ satisfait*, to consider oneself satisfied; **2.** to have a good opinion of oneself.
estivage [ɛstivaʒ] *s.m.* (agric.) summering of cattle in mountain pastures.
estival, -e, (aux) [ɛstival] *adj.* summer.
estivant, -e [ɛstivɑ̃] *s.m.f.* summer visitor, holiday-maker.
estivation [ɛstivɑsjɔ̃] *s.f.* (bot., zool.) aestivation.
estive [ɛstiv] *s.f.* (naut.) balanced loading.
estiver [ɛstive] *v.t.* (agric.) to take cattle to summer pastures in mountains; ~ *v.i.* to spend the summer (in a place, resort, etc.).
estoc [ɛstɔk] *s.m.* (obs.) straight sword; (mod.) *frapper d'~ et de taille*, to cut and thrust.
estocade [ɛstɔkad] *s.f.* (obs.) thrust, lunge; (bullfighting) death blow; (fig.) final blow.
estomac [ɛstɔma] *s.m.* stomach; (fig.) pluck, guts.
estomaqué, -e [ɛstɔmake] *adj.* flabbergasted.
estomaquer [ɛstɔmake] *v.t.* (fam.) to shock, to scandalize.
estompage [ɛstɔ̃paʒ], **estompement** [ɛstɔ̃pəmɑ̃] *s.m.* shading-off, softening.
estompe [ɛstɔ̃p] *s.f.* (art) stump; stump drawing.
estompé, -e [ɛstɔ̃pe] *adj.* blurred, imprecise.
estomper [ɛstɔ̃pe] *v.t.* (art) to tone down with a stump; to blur.
Estonie, Esthonie [ɛstɔni] *s.f.* (geog.) Esthonia.
estonien, -ne [ɛstɔnjɛ̃] *adj., s.m.f.* Esthonian.
estoquer [ɛstɔke] *v.t.* (obs.) to lunge; (bullfighting) to wound mortally.
estouffade [ɛstufad], **étouffade** [etufad] *s.f.* (cook.) braised meat.
estourbir [ɛsturbir] *v.t.* (fam.) to kill; (fig.) to flabbergast.
estrade[1] [ɛstrad] *s.f.* (obs.) road; (mod.) *battre l'~*, to go marauding, to roam the streets.
estrade[2] [ɛstrad] *s.f.* platform, dais, rostrum.
estragon [ɛstragɔ̃] *s.m.* (bot.) tarragon.
estramaçon [ɛstramasɔ̃] *s.m.* (hist.) two-edged sword.
estran [ɛstrɑ̃] *s.m.* (geog.) tidal shore, fore-shore.
estrapade [ɛstrapad] *s.f.* **1.** (hist.) strappado; **2.** (gymn.) rope exercises.
estrapader [ɛstrapade] *v.t.* (anc. mil.) to strappado.
estrapader [ɛstrapade] *v.t.* (hist.) to strappado.
estrapasser [ɛstrapɑse] *v.t.* to overtire (horse).
estrope [ɛstrɔp] *s.f.* (naut.) strop.
estropié, -e [ɛstrɔpje] *adj.* crippled, maimed; *s.m.f.* cripple.
estropier [ɛstrɔpje] *v.t.* to cripple, to maim, to disable; (fig.) to murder, to mangle (a language, etc.), to misuse, to mispronounce.
estuaire [ɛstɥɛr] *s.m.* estuary.
estudiantin, -e [ɛstydjɑ̃tɛ̃] *adj.* student.
esturgeon [ɛstyrʒɔ̃] *s.m.* (ichth.) sturgeon.
et [e] *conj.* and; ~ *son frère* ~ *sa sœur*, both his brother and his sister; ~ *les dix francs que je vous ai prêtés?*, and (what about) the ten francs I lent you?
êta [ɛta] *s.m.* eta (Gr. letter).
étable [etabl] *s.f.* cowshed, cow-house; ⚠ not stable for horses.
établer [etable] *v.t.* to house, to bring in, (cattle, etc.); to stable (horses).
établi[1] [etabli] *s.m.* (work-)bench.
établi[2], **-e** [etabli] *adj.* established, solid, firm; in power.
établir [etablir] *v.t.* **1.** to set up, to found, to establish, to settle, to institute; **2.** to demonstrate, to prove, to establish; **s'~** *v.refl.* **1.** to settle down, to take up residence, to set up in business; to become established; **2.** to pose as, to set oneself up as.
établissement [etablismɑ̃] *s.m.* **1.** establishment, foundation; **2.** settlement; **3.** proof, demonstration; **4.** establishment, business; **5.** (hist.) trading-post.
étage [etaʒ] *s.m.* **1.** floor, storey; **2.** stage, tier, step; level (of mine); (geol.) layer; **3.** (obs. exc. Lit.) rank; (mod.) *de bas* ~, lower class, inferior.
étagement [etaʒmɑ̃] *s.m.* terracing, arrangement in tiers.
étager [etaʒe] *v.t.* to arrange in tiers, to terrace.
étagère [etaʒɛr] *s.f.* whatnot; shelf, set of shelves.
étai [etɛ] *s.m.* (naut.) stay; (constr.) prop, strut; (fig.) support.
étaiement see ÉTAYAGE.
étain [etɛ̃] *s.m.* tin, pewter; *papier d'~*, tinfoil, silver paper.
étal [etal] *s.m.* **1.** market stall; **2.** butcher's chopping block; butcher's shop.
étalage [etalaʒ] *s.m.* **1.** display (of goods), shop window, window dressing; **2.** display, show, parade; *faire ~ de*, to show off, to parade.
étalager [etalaʒe] *v.t.* to display, to put on show.
étalagiste [etalaʒist] *s.m.f.* **1.** (obs. exc. law) stall-holder; **2.** window-dresser.
étale [etal] *adj.* smooth, calm; (of ship) hove to; ~ *s.m.* slack water.
étalement [etalmɑ̃] *s.m.* **1.** spreading out; **2.** spreading over a period of time; staggering.
étaler[1] [etale] *v.t.* **1.** to display; to spread (out), to open out; (cards) ~ *son jeu*, to show one's hand; **2.** (fam.) to knock down; **3.** to show, to demonstrate; **4.** (pej.) to show off; **5.** to spread over a period of time, to stagger (holidays, etc.); **s'~** *v.refl.* **1.** to spread, to be spread (out); to be

staggered; **2.** to show off; **3.** (fam.) to sprawl; to fall down.
étaler[2] [etale] *v.t.* (naut.) to heave to; to stem the tide; to weather, to ride out, (storm, etc.).
étaleuse [etaløz] *s.f.* (text.) spreading machine.
étalier [etalje] *s.m.* butcher.
étalinguer [etalɛ̃ge] *v.t.* (naut.) to bend (a cable to an anchor ring), to shackle.
étalingure [etalɛ̃gyr] *s.f.* (naut.) attaching (cable to anchor ring).
étalon[1] [etalɔ̃] *s.m.* stallion; stud-horse.
étalon[2] [etalɔ̃] *s.m.* standard (of weights and measures); (fig.) model, archetype; (fin.) ~ *d'or*, gold standard.
étalonnage [etalɔnaʒ], **étalonnement** [etalɔnmɑ̃] *s.m.* standardization (of weights and measures), calibration (of instruments).
étalonner [etalɔne] *v.t.* to standardize (weights and measures); to calibrate (instruments); to regulate.
étamage [etamaʒ] *s.m.* tinning, tin-plating; silvering (of glass).
étambot [etɑ̃bo] *s.m.* (naut.) stern-post.
étambrai [etɑ̃brɛ] *s.m.* (naut.) partners.
étamer [etame] *v.t.* to tin, to plate, to silver (glass).
étameur [etamœr] *s.m.* tinsmith, silverer (of mirrors).
étamine[1] [etamin] *s.f.* **1.** muslin, butter-muslin; **2.** strainer; (fig., obs.) *passer à l'~*, to sift.
étamine[2] [etamin] *s.f.* (bot.) stamen.
étampage [etɑ̃paʒ] *s.m.* punching of holes in horseshoe.
étampe [etɑ̃p] *s.f.* punch, stamp, die.
étamper [etɑ̃pe] *v.t.* **1.** to punch holes in horseshoe; **2.** to punch, to stamp.
étamperche [etɑ̃pɛrʃ] *s.f.* = ÉCOPERCHE.
étampeur [etɑ̃pœr] *s.m.* (techn.) puncher, stamper.
étampure [etɑ̃pyr] *s.f.* **1.** nail hole (in horseshoe); **2.** splay (of hole in metal plate).
étamure [etamyr] *s.f.* coating (of tin); tinning metal.
étanche [etɑ̃ʃ] *adj.* watertight, impermeable, impervious; ~ *au gaz*, gas-tight; (naut.) *compartiments ~s*, watertight bulkheads; (fig.) *cloison ~*, watertight compartment; *à ~*, watertight.
étanchéité [etɑ̃ʃeite] *s.f.* impermeability, being waterproof, watertight, etc.
étanchement [etɑ̃ʃmɑ̃] *s.m.* (Lit.) stanching (of flow of blood); quenching, slaking, (of thirst).
étancher [etɑ̃ʃe] *v.t.* **1.** to check the flow of, to stanch, to stem; to dry up; to quench; **2.** to make watertight.
étançon [etɑ̃sɔ̃] *s.m.* stanchion, prop.
étançonnement [etɑ̃sɔnmɑ̃] *s.m.* propping, staying, shoring up.
étançonner [etɑ̃sɔne] *v.t.* to prop, to shore up.
étang [etɑ̃] *s.m.* pond, pool, lagoon.
étape [etap] *s.f.* **1.** (obs.) depot, post; **2.** stage, halting place; day's journey; (sport) stage, lap; *faire ~ à*, to stay overnight at; (fig.) *brûler les ~s*, to make rapid progress.
étarquer [etarke] *v.t.* (naut.) to hoist taut (sail).
état [eta] *s.m.* **1.** state, condition; position, situation; *être dans tous ses ~s*, to be very upset; *être en ~ de*, to be in a position to, to be capable of; *en ~*, in (good) condition; *faire ~ de*, to take into account, to refer to; **2.** summary, statement, report, list, return; **3.** (obs.) calling, profession, standing; (mod.) *de son ~*, by trade, by profession; ~ *civil*, status; *officier de l'~ civil*, registrar; *actes de l'~ civil*, certificates of birth, death, etc.; **4.** state, nation; *chef d'~*, head of State; *homme d'~*, statesman.
état-isation [etatizɑsjɔ̃] *s.f.* nationalization (of industry, etc.); **~iser** [etatize] *v.t.* to nationalize, to bring under state control; **~isme** [etatism] *s.m.* state control, state socialism; **~iste** [etatist] *adj.* of state control; *s.m.f.* supporter of state control.
état-major [etamaʒɔr] *s.m.* (mil., etc.) general staff; headquarters staff, administrative staff; leadership; top management.
(**les**) **États-Unis** [lezetazyni] *s.m.pl.* (geog.) the United States (of America).
étau [eto] *s.m.* vice (tool).
étayage [etɛjaʒ], **étayement** [etɛjmɑ̃], **étaiement** [etɛmɑ̃] *s.m.* propping, staying, shoring.
étayer [eteje] *v.t.* to prop, to stay, to shore, to buttress; (fig.) to support, to back up.
été [ete] *s.m.* summer.
éteignoir [etɛɲwar] *s.m.* (candle) snuffer; (fig.) killjoy, damper.
éteindre [etɛ̃dr] *v.t.* to extinguish, to snuff, to turn off, to put out; to quench, to appease; to soften, to dull; **s'~** *v.refl.* (of light, etc.) to go out; (fig.) to disappear, to fade away; to die, to die out.
éteint, -e [etɛ̃] *adj.* extinguished, out, dead; (fig.) pale, lifeless, wan.
étemperche [etɑ̃pɛrʃ] *s.f.* = ÉCOPERCHE.
étendage [etɑ̃daʒ] *s.m.* hanging out to dry; clothes line, drying area.
étendard [etɑ̃dar] *s.m.* standard, flag, colour, colours; (bot.) vexillum.
étendoir [etɑ̃dwar] *s.m.* clothes line, clothes horse; drying area.
étendre [etɑ̃dr] *v.t.* **1.** to stretch (out), to spread (out), to hang out (washing); to lay (down); **2.** to extend, to expand, to enlarge; **s'~** *v.refl.* to stretch, to spread; to lie down; to extend, to increase.
étendu, -e [etɑ̃dy] *adj.* spread, outstretched; wide, extensive, vast.
étendue [etɑ̃dy] *s.f.* extent, expanse; size, length, width; duration, length (of time); (mus.) range; (fig.) scope.
éternel, -le [etɛrnɛl] *adj.* eternal, everlasting; (pej.) endless, everlasting, inevitable, tiresome; ~ *s.m. l'Éternel*, God; **~lement** [etɛrnɛlmɑ̃] *adv.* endlessly, eternally, for ever; (pej.) everlastingly.
éterniser [etɛrnize] *v.t.* **1.** to perpetuate, to immortalize; **2.** to drag out, to go on and on with; **s'~** *v.refl.* **1.** to become immortal; **2.** to drag on, to go on for ever; **3.** (fam.) to stay too long.
éternité [etɛrnite] *s.f.* eternity, endlessness; *de toute ~*, from time immemorial.
éternuement [etɛrnymɑ̃] *s.m.* sneeze.
éternuer [etɛrnɥe] *v.i.* to sneeze.
étésien [etezjɛ̃] *adj.m.* Etesian (wind).
étêtage [etɛtaʒ], **étêtement** [etɛtmɑ̃] *s.m.* pollarding, topping, (of trees).
étêter [etete] *v.t.* **1.** to pollard; **2.** to remove the head of.
éteuf [etœf] *s.m.* (real tennis) ball.
éteule [etœl] *s.f.* (agric.) stubble.
éthane [etan] *s.m.* (chem.) ethane.
éther [etɛr] *s.m.* (Lit., phys., chem.) ether.
éthéré, -e [etere] *adj.* ethereal.
éthér-ification [eterifikɑsjɔ̃] *s.f.* (chem.) etherification; **~ifier** [eterifje] *v.t.* (chem.) to etherify, to convert into ether; **~isation** [eterizɑsjɔ̃] *s.f.* (med.) etherization (of patient); **~iser** [eterize] *v.t.* (med.) to etherize; **~isme** [eterism] *s.m.* (med.) etherism; **~omane** [eterɔman] *adj.* addicted to ether; *s.m.f.* ether addict; **~omanie** [eterɔmani] *s.f.* addiction to ether.
Éthiopie [etjɔpi] *s.f.* (geog.) Ethiopia.
éthiopien, -ne [etjɔpjɛ̃] *adj., s.m.f.* Ethiopian.
éthique [etik] *s.f.* ethics; ~ *adj.* ethical.

ethmoïde [ɛtmɔid] *s.m.* (anat.) ethmoid (bone).
ethnie [ɛtni] *s.f.* ethnic group.
ethnique [ɛtnik] *adj.* ethnic.
ethno-graphe [ɛtnɔgraf] *s.m.f.* ethnographer; **~graphie** [ɛtnɔgrafi] *s.f.* ethnography; **~graphique** [ɛtnɔgrafik] *adj.* ethnographic; **~logie** [ɛtnɔlɔʒi] *s.f.* ethnology; **~logique** [ɛtnɔlɔʒik] *adj.* ethnological; **~logue** [ɛtnɔlɔg] *s.m.f.* ethnologist.
éthologie [etɔlɔʒi] *s.f.* (obs.) ethology; (mod.) study of animal behaviour.
éthologique [etɔlɔʒik] *adj.* ethological.
éthyle [etil] *s.m.* (chem.) ethyl.
éthylène [etilɛn] *s.m.* (chem.) ethylene.
éthylénique [etilenik] *adj.* ethylenic.
éthylique [etilik] *adj.* (chem.) ethyl; ~ *s.m.f.* (med.) alcoholic.
éthylisme [etilism] *s.m.* (med.) alcoholism.
étiage [etjaʒ] *s.m.* lowest water level (of river).
Étienne [etjɛn] *s.m.* Stephen.
étier [etje] *s.m.* small channel (esp. from salt marsh to sea).
étincelant, -e [etɛ̃slɑ̃] *adj.* sparkling, glittering, flashing, scintillating.
étinceler [etɛ̃sle] *v.i.* to sparkle, to glitter, to flash, to scintillate.
étincelle [etɛ̃sɛl] *s.f.* spark, flash, sparkle, twinkle.
étincellement [etɛ̃sɛlmɑ̃] *s.m.* sparkling, flashing, twinkling.
étiolé, -e [etjɔle] *adj.* wilting, faded; (fig.) sickly, weak.
étiolement [etjɔlmɑ̃] *s.m.* wilting, wasting, fading, etiolation; (fig.) impoverishment, decline.
étioler [etjɔle] *v.t.* to cause to wilt or fade; (agric.) to blanch; to weaken, to enfeeble; **s'~** *v.refl.* to fade, to decline, to become atrophied.
étiologie [etjɔlɔʒi] *s.f.* (med.) aetiology, etiology.
étique [etik] *adj.* emaciated, skeletal.
étiquetage [etiktaʒ] *s.m.* labelling, docketing.
étiqueter [etikte] *v.t.* to label, to docket; (fig.) to class.
étiqueteu-r, -se [etiktœr] *s.m.f.* labeller.
étiquette [etikɛt] *s.f.* **1.** label, tag; **2.** etiquette.
étirable [etirabl] *adj.* elastic, ductile.
étirage [etiraʒ] *s.m.* stretching, drawing out, racking; drawing (of metals, wire).
étirement [etirmɑ̃] *s.m.* (geol.) stretching, elongating.
étirer [etire] *v.t.* to stretch, to pull, to draw out; to draw (metals, wire); **s'~** *v.refl.* to stretch (oneself).
étireu-r, -se [etirœr] *s.m.f.* stretcher; drawer (of metals, wire).
étireuse [etirøz] *s.f.* stretching machine; (metall.) draw-bench.
étisie [etizi] *s.f.* (obs. med.) wasting, consumption, decline.
étoc [etɔk] *s.m.* (naut.) dangerous exposed rock pinnacle.
étoffe [etɔf] *s.f.* **1.** cloth, material, fabric, stuff; (fig.) quality; *avoir l'~ d'un héros*, to be the stuff that heroes are made of; *avoir de l'~*, to have a strong personality; **2.** (pl.) (print.) extras, surcharge.
étoffé, -e [etɔfe] *adj.* ample, full-bodied; *voix ~e*, powerful voice.
étoffer [etɔfe] *v.t.* to pad, to stuff, to give more substance to, to give body to; **s'~** *v.refl.* to fill out.
étoile [etwal] *s.f.* (astron., fig., cin., etc.) star; (fig., fam.) *à la belle ~*, in the open air; *en ~*, star-shaped; *~ filante*, shooting star; *~ de mer*, starfish.
étoilé, -e [etwale] *adj.* starry, starlit; starred, studded with stars; star-shaped.
étoilement [etwalmɑ̃] *s.m.* **1.** filling (of sky) with stars; **2.** star-shaped crack, star.
étoiler [etwale] *v.t.* **1.** to stud with stars; **2.** to form a star on; to make a star-shaped crack on.
étole [etɔl] *s.f.* stole.
étonnamment [etɔnamɑ̃] *adv.* surprisingly, amazingly, astonishingly.
étonnant, -e [etɔnɑ̃] *adj.* astonishing, amazing, surprising, wonderful.
étonné, -e [etɔne] *adj.* astonished, amazed, surprised.
étonnement [etɔnmɑ̃] *s.m.* astonishment, amazement, surprise.
étonner [etɔne] *v.t.* (obs.) to overwhelm; (mod.) to surprise, to astonish, to amaze, to astound; **s'~** *v.refl.* **1.** (obs.) to be shaken, to waver; **2.** (obs.) to take fright; **3.** to be astonished, amazed, surprised.
étouffade see ESTOUFFADE.
étouffage [etufaʒ] *s.m.* stifling (of silk-worms or bees).
étouffant, -e [etufɑ̃] *adj.* suffocating, stifling, sultry.
étouffé, -e [etufe] *adj.* suffocated, stifled; (of sound, etc.) subdued, muffled; (of fire) smothered.
étouffe-chrétien [etufkretjɛ̃] *s.m.invar.* (fam.) stodgy food, stodge.
(à l')étouffée [aletufe] *adv.* (cook.) *cuire à l'~*, to braise.
étouffement [etufmɑ̃] *s.m.* suffocation, stifling; choking sensation; (fig.) suppressing, hushing-up.
étouffer [etufe] *v.t.* **1.** to suffocate, to asphyxiate; to stifle; to choke (plant growth); to smother (a fire); to deaden, to muffle (a sound); (fig.) to stifle, to suppress, to hush up, to silence (opposition); **2.** (pop.) to pinch, to steal; ~ *v.i.* to suffocate, to stifle; (fig.) to feel hemmed in; **s'~** *v.refl.* to choke; to be crowded, to be tightly packed.
étouffeur [etufœr] *s.m.* (techn.) damper, suppressor.
étouffoir [etufwar] *s.m.* **1.** charcoal pail; **2.** (mus.) damper.
étoupe [etup] *s.f.* tow, oakum; (techn.) packing, stuffing; *~ de coton*, cotton waste.
étouper [etupe] *v.t.* (naut.) to caulk; (techn.) to pack, to stuff.
étoupille [etupij] *s.f.* (obs. artill.) quick-match; (mod.) fuse (for detonating).
étoupiller [etupije] *v.t.* (obs.) to fit a quick-match to.
étourderie [eturdəri] *s.f.* thoughtless act, blunder, slip; thoughtlessness, inadvertence.
étourdi, -e [eturdi] *adj.* hare-brained, thoughtless, careless, irresponsible; *s.m.f.* scatter-brain; *à l'~e*, thoughtlessly; **~ment** [eturdimɑ̃] *adv.* thoughtlessly, irresponsibly, carelessly.
étourdir [eturdir] *v.t.* to stun, to daze, to stupefy; to go to one's head, to intoxicate; to deafen, to weary; (obs.) to astound; **s'~** *v.refl.* to become dazed, intoxicated.
étourdissant, -e [eturdisɑ̃] *adj.* deafening, stupefying; (fig.) stunning, sensational.
étourdissement [eturdismɑ̃] *s.m.* (fit of) giddiness, dizziness; intoxication, stupefaction.
étourneau (pl. **-x**) [eturno] *s.m.* **1.** (ornith.) starling; **2.** (fig.) scatter-brain, birdbrain.
étrange [etrɑ̃ʒ] *adj.* strange, odd, curious, unusual, abnormal, extraordinary; **~ment** [etrɑ̃ʒmɑ̃] *adv.* strangely, oddly, curiously, unusually, extraordinarily.
étrang-er, -ère [etrɑ̃ʒe] *adj.* **1.** foreign, alien; strange, unfamiliar, unknown; **2.** irrelevant, extraneous; **3.** *être ~er, ~ère, à qch.*, to be ignorant of, to have no knowledge of, no part of,

sth.; *s.m.f.* foreigner, stranger, alien; *à l'~er*, abroad, overseas.

étrangeté [etrɑ̃ʒte] *s.f.* strangeness, oddness, unusualness, foreignness.

étranglé, -e [etrɑ̃gle] *adj.* pinched, restricted, constricted; (med.) (of hernia) strangulated; (of voice) choking.

étranglement [etrɑ̃gləmɑ̃] *s.m.* **1.** (rare) strangling; **2.** (med.) constriction; **3.** narrowing, bottleneck.

étrangler [etrɑ̃gle] *v.t.* to strangle, to throttle, to choke; to constrict; (fig.) to restrict, to suppress; **s'~** *v.refl.* to choke.

étrangleu-r, -se [etrɑ̃glœr] *s.m.f.* strangler; **~r** *s.m.* (car) throttle.

étrangloir [etrɑ̃glwar] *s.m.* (naut.) **1.** brail; **2.** drag (for anchor).

étrave [etrav] *s.f.* (naut.) stem.

être [ɛtr] *v.i.* **1.** to be, to exist; **2.** (with prep. or adv.) *~ à*, to be at (a place); (fig.) *y ~*, to understand; *~ à qn.*, to belong to s.o.; (fig.) to be at someone's disposal; *~ à qch.* or *à faire qch.*, to be occupied with sth. or busy doing sth.; *~ à admirer*, to be admired, to be wondered at; *c'est à prendre ou à laisser*, take it or leave it; *~ de*, to come from; to be part of; *comme si de rien n'était*, nonchalantly, as if nothing was wrong; *en ~ à un certain point*, to have reached a certain point; *ne plus savoir où l'on en est*, to be distraught; *en ~ pour sa peine, son argent*, to have wasted one's time, one's money; *~ en noir*, to be wearing black; *~ pour*, to be in favour of; *~ pour qch. dans*, to have played a part in; to be partly responsible for; *ne pas ~ sans savoir*, to be not unaware of; **3.** to be (joining subject to complement); *c'est mon père*, it is my father; *quelle est son adresse?*, what is his address?; *c'est une sorte de fromage*, it is a kind of cheese; *il est vrai que*, it is true that; **4.** *si ce n'était que*, were it not that; *n'était*, but for, were it not for; *n'eût été*, had it not been for; **5.** (forming passive) to be; *~ aimé*, to be loved; *il fut tué*, he was killed; **6.** (in compound tenses of certain intransitive verbs and of all reflexive verbs) to have; *il est tombé*, he has fallen down; *elle s'était blessée*, she had hurt herself.

être [ɛtr] *s.m.* **1.** existence, being; **2.** being, creature; *les ~s humains*, human beings; *les ~s vivants*, living creatures; **3.** human being, individual, person; *un ~ insupportable*, an intolerable person; **4.** being, nature, essence; *tout son ~*, his whole being.

étrécir [etresir] *v.t.* (obs.) to make narrower; **s'~** *v.refl.* to narrow.

étreindre [etrɛ̃dr] *v.t.* to embrace, to hug, to clasp in one's arms; (fig.) to wring, to torment.

étreinte [etrɛ̃t] *s.f.* embrace, hug, clasp; (lit. & fig.) grip.

étrenne [etrɛn] *s.f.* (often pl.) **1.** New Year's gift; **2.** Christmas box (for tradesmen, etc.); **3.** first use of; *vous en aurez l'~*, you shall be the first to use it.

étrenner [etrene] *v.t.* to be the first to use; to wear for the first time; *~ v.i.* to be the first to suffer.

êtres [ɛtr] *s.m.pl.* (obs.) lay-out (of building); (mod.) *connaître les ~ d'une maison*, to know one's way about, to know the geography of, a house.

étrésillon [etrezijɔ̃] *s.m.* pit-prop, prop, stay, brace.

étrésillonnement [etrezijɔnmɑ̃] *s.m.* propping-up, staying, bracing.

étrésillonner [etrezijɔne] *v.t.* to prop, to shore up, to brace.

étrier [etrije] *s.m.* **1.** stirrup; *avoir le pied à l'~*, to be about to set out, (fig.) to be on the road to success; (fig.) *être ferme sur ses ~s*, to be unshakeable (in one's opinions); *perdre, quitter, vider, les ~s*, (lit. & fig.) to come a cropper; **2.** clamp, clamping-iron; **3.** (surg.) stirrup, leg-rest; calliper-splint; **4.** (anat.) stirrup-bone (in ear), stapes.

étrille [etrij] *s.f.* curry-comb.

étriller [etrije] *v.t.* **1.** to curry, to comb, (a horse); **2.** (fig.) to tear (s.o.) to pieces; **3.** to overcharge.

étripage [etripaʒ] *s.m.* gutting (of fish, etc.), drawing (of birds); disembowelment; (fig., fam.) shambles, massacre.

étriper [etripe] *v.t.* to gut (a fish, etc.), to draw (a bird); to disembowel; **s'~** *v.refl.* (fig., fam.) to tear each other's guts out.

étriqué, -e [etrike] *adj.* (of clothes) skimpy, tight; (lit. & fig.) narrow, cramped.

étriquer [etrike] *v.t.* to skimp, to cramp, to make too tight; to give a pinched appearance to; to shave down.

étrivière [etrivjɛr] *s.f.* stirrup-leather.

étroit, -e [etrwa] *adj.* **1.** narrow; confined, restricted; *à l'~*, cramped; (fig.) in straitened circumstances; **2.** (of relationships, etc.) close, tight; **~ement** [etrwatmɑ̃] *adv.* **1.** narrowly; **2.** tightly, closely; strictly, rigidly.

étroitesse [etrwatɛs] *s.f.* narrowness, confined space, exiguity.

étron [etrɔ̃] *s.m.* dropping, turd (vulg.).

étronçonner [etrɔ̃sɔne] *v.t.* to remove top and branches of (tree).

étrusque [etrysk] *adj., s.m.f.* Etruscan.

étude [etyd] *s.f.* **1.** study; (pl.) studies, education, schooling; **2.** (Lit.) study, essay; survey; (art) sketch; (mus.) étude; **3.** (room) study; office, chambers; practice (of a solicitor).

étudiant, -e [etydjɑ̃] *s.m.f.* (university) student, undergraduate.

étudié, -e [etydje] *adj.* studied, deliberate, affected; *prix très ~s*, keen prices.

étudier [etydje] *v.t.* to study, to read; to consider, to examine; **s'~** *v.refl.* to examine oneself; to survey each other; to take a self-satisfied view of oneself; to strike an attitude (when being observed).

étui [etɥi] *s.m.* case, box, cover; (naut.) sail bag.

étuvage [etyvaʒ] *s.m.* steaming, sterilizing.

étuve [etyv] *s.f.* **1.** sweatroom (in Turkish bath); **2.** drying-oven; steamer, sterilizer.

(à l')étuvée [aletyve] *adv.* = (*à l'*)ÉTOUFFÉE.

étuver [etyve] *v.t.* **1.** (cook.) to steam, to braise; **2.** to sterilize.

étuveu-r, -se [etyvœr] *s.m.f.* steamer, drying-oven.

étymolog-ie [etimɔlɔʒi] *s.f.* etymology; **~ique** [etimɔlɔʒik] *adj.* etymological; **~iquement** [etimɔlɔʒikmɑ̃] *adv.* etymologically; **~iste** [etimɔlɔʒist] *s.m.f.* etymologist.

étymon [etimɔ̃] *s.m.* (lang.) etymon.

E.-U. [ey] abbrev. *États-Unis.*

eucalyptol [økaliptɔl] *s.m.* eucalyptus oil.

eucalyptus [økaliptys] *s.m.* (bot.) eucalyptus.

Eucharistie [økaristi] *s.f.* Eucharist.

eucharistique [økaristik] *adj.* Eucharistic(al).

euclidien, -ne [øklidjɛ̃] *adj.* Euclidean.

eudémis [ødemis] *s.m.* (ent.) vine-moth, leaf-hopper.

eudémonisme [ødemɔnism] *s.m.* (phil.) eudaemonism, eudemonism.

eudiomètre [ødjɔmɛtr] *s.m.* eudiometer.

eudiométr-ie [ødjɔmetri] *s.f.* (phys.) eudiometry; **~ique** [ødjɔmetrik] *adj.* eudiometric(al).

eugénique [øʒenik] *s.f.*, **eugénisme** [øʒenism] *s.m.* eugenics; **eugénique** *adj.* eugenic.

eugéniste [øʒenist] *s.m.f.* eugenist.

euh [ø] *interj.* hm!, er!

eunecte [ønɛkt] *s.m.* (zool.) anaconda.

eunuque [ønyk] *s.m.* eunuch.

eupatoire [øpatwar] *s.f.* (bot.) hemp agrimony.
euphémique [øfemik] *adj.* euphemistic; **~ment** [øfemikmɑ̃] *adv.* euphemistically.
euphémisme [øfemism] *s.m.* euphemism.
euphonie [øfɔni] *s.f.* euphony.
euphonique [øfɔnik] *adj.* euphonic, euphonious; **~ment** [øfɔnikmɑ̃] *adv.* euphonically, euphoniously.
euphorbe [øfɔrb] *s.f.* (bot.) euphorbia, spurge.
euphorbiacées [øfɔrbjase] *s.f.pl.* (bot.) Euphorbiaceae.
euphorie [øfɔri] *s.f.* euphoria.
euphorique [øfɔrik] *adj.* euphoric.
Euphrate [øfrat] *s.m.* Euphrates (river).
euphuisme [øfyism] *s.m.* (Lit. hist.) euphuism.
eurasiatique [ørazjatik] *adj.* (geog.) Eurasian.
eurasien, -ne [ørazjɛ̃] *adj., s.m.f.* (ethn.) Eurasian.
eurêka [øreka] *interj.* eureka!
Europe [ørɔp] *s.f.* (geog.) Europe.
européaniser [ørɔpeanize] *v.t.* to Europeanize.
européanisme [ørɔpeanism] *s.m.* European character; attachment to European culture.
européen, -ne [ørɔpeɛ̃] *adj., s.m.f.* European.
europium [ørɔpjɔm] *s.m.* (chem.) europium.
Eurovision [ørɔvizjɔ̃] *s.f.* (T.V.) Eurovision.
eurythmie [øritmi] *s.f.* harmony.
eurythmique [øritmik] *adj.* eurhythmic.
euscarien, -ne, euskarien, -ne [øskarjɛ̃] *adj., s.m.f.* (ethn.) Euskarian, Basque.
eustache [østaʃ] *s.m.* (obs. fam.) clasp-knife.
eustatique [østatik] *adj.* (geol.) eustatic.
eustatisme [østatism] *s.m.* (geol.) eustasy.
eutectique [øtɛktik] *adj.* (sci.) eutectic.
eutexie [øtɛksi] *s.f.* (sci.) eutexia.
euthanasie [øtanazi] *s.f.* euthanasia.
eux [ø] *pers.pron.m.pl.* **1.** (emphatic) they, them; *si vous acceptez, ~ refuseront*, if you accept, *they* will refuse; **2.** (after prep.) them; *avec ~*, with them; *pour ~*, for them.
E.V. [eve] abbrev. *en ville*.
évacuant, -e [evakɥɑ̃] *adj., s.m.* (med.) evacuant.
évacuat-eur, -rice [evakɥatœr] *adj.* draining; **~eur** *s.m.* overfall (on weir, etc.).
évacuation [evakɥɑsjɔ̃] *s.f.* evacuation; clearing, emptying; draining.
évacué, -e [evakɥe] *adj.* evacuated, emptied; *s.m.f.* evacuee; *les ~s d'une région*, those evacuated from an area.
évacuer [evakɥe] *v.t.* to evacuate; to drain; to abandon (ship).
évadé, -e [evade] *adj.* escaped, on the run; *s.m.f.* escapee.
(**s'**)**évader** [evade] *v.refl.* to escape, to make one's escape, to run away.
évagination [evaʒinɑsjɔ̃] *s.f.* (physiol.) evagination.
évaluable [evalɥabl] *adj.* that can be evaluated, calculable.
évaluation [evalɥɑsjɔ̃] *s.f.* evaluation, assessment; estimate, reckoning.
évaluer [evalɥe] *v.t.* to evaluate, to value; to estimate, to assess.
évanescence [evanesɑ̃s] *s.f.* evanescence.
évanescent, -e [evanesɑ̃] *adj.* evanescent.
évangéliaire [evɑ̃ʒeljɛr] *s.m.* (eccles.) gospel-book.
évangélique [evɑ̃ʒelik] *adj.* evangelic(al); ~ *s.m.f.* Evangelical, Protestant.
évangélisat-eur, -rice [evɑ̃ʒelizatœr] *adj.* evangelizing; *s.m.f.* evangelist, missionary.
évangélisation [evɑ̃ʒelizɑsjɔ̃] *s.f.* evangelization.
évangéliser [evɑ̃ʒelize] *v.t.* to evangelize.
évangélisme [evɑ̃ʒelism] *s.m.* evangelism.
évangéliste [evɑ̃ʒelist] *s.m.* evangelist; missionary.
évangile [evɑ̃ʒil] *s.m.* **1.** Gospel; (the) New Testament; *parole d'~*, gospel truth; **2.** creed, gospel.
évanoui, -e [evanwi] *adj.* **1.** vanished; **2.** unconscious, in a faint.
(**s'**)**évanouir** [evanwir] *v.refl.* **1.** to vanish; **2.** to faint, to lose consciousness.
évanouissement [evanwismɑ̃] *s.m.* **1.** disappearance; **2.** faint, fainting fit.
évaporable [evapɔrabl] *adj.* evaporable, volatile.
évaporateur [evapɔratœr] *s.m.* evaporator.
évaporation [evapɔrɑsjɔ̃] *s.f.* evaporation.
évaporatoire [evapɔratwar] *adj.* (of process, etc.) evaporating, evaporative.
évaporé, -e [evapɔre] *adj., s.m.f.* giddy, irresponsible, flighty (person).
évaporer [evapɔre] *v.t.* (obs.) to evaporate; **s'~** *v.refl.* to evaporate; (fig., fam.) to vanish.
évasé, -e [evɑze] *adj.* funnel-shaped, bell-shaped; flared.
évasement [evɑzmɑ̃] *s.m.* widening, splaying; enlargement; (dressm.) flare.
évaser [evɑze] *v.t.* to widen, to enlarge; **s'~** *v.refl.* to flare, to splay, to spread.
évasi-f, -ve [evazif] *adj.* evasive.
évasion [evazjɔ̃] *s.f.* evasion, escape.
évasivement [evazivmɑ̃] *adv.* evasively.
évêché [eveʃe] *s.m.* **1.** bishopric, diocese, see; **2.** bishop's palace.
évection [evɛksjɔ̃] *s.f.* (astron.) evection.
éveil [evɛj] *s.m.* **1.** alarm, alert; *donner l'~ à*, to put on guard, to alert; *être en ~*, to be on one's guard; **2.** awakening; wakefulness.
éveillé, -e [eveje] *adj.* awake, wide awake, waking; (fig.) lively, sharp, intelligent.
éveiller [eveje] *v.t.* to wake, to awaken; (fig.) to rouse, to stimulate, to excite; **s'~** *v.refl.* to wake up; to be roused, to come to life.
éveilleur [evɛjœr] *s.m.* (fig.) wakener, rouser.
événement [evɛnmɑ̃] *s.m.* **1.** (obs.) issue, result; **2.** event, occurrence.
évent [evɑ̃] *s.m.* **1.** (of whales, etc.) blow-hole; (techn.) vent; **2.** staleness, stale air, stuffy smell; ⚠ not 'event'.
éventail [evɑ̃taj] *s.m.* fan; (fig.) range (of goods), scale (of salaries, etc.); *en ~*, fan-shaped; (arch.) *voûtes en ~*, fan vaulting.
éventailliste [evɑ̃tajist] *s.m.f.* fan-maker; painter of fans.
éventaire [evɑ̃tɛr] *s.m.* **1.** pedlar's tray; **2.** outside display (of goods).
éventé, -e [evɑ̃te] *adj.* **1.** windy, windswept; **2.** (of wine, etc.) stale, flat; **3.** (of secrets, etc.) out, known, discovered; *c'est un truc ~*, it's an old dodge; **4.** (obs.) giddy, flighty.
éventer [evɑ̃te] *v.t.* **1.** to fan; to air; to winnow; **2.** to open up; **3.** to discover; (fig.) ~ *la mèche*, to uncover a secret, to let the cat out of the bag; **4.** (hunt.) to scent; **s'~** *v.refl.* to go stale or flat.
éventration [evɑ̃trɑsjɔ̃] *s.f.* abdominal rupture; disembowelment.
éventrer [evɑ̃tre] *v.t.* to disembowel; to rip open, to break open; to break up (ground).
éventreur [evɑ̃trœr] *s.m.* disemboweller; *Jack l'Éventreur*, Jack the Ripper.
éventualité [evɑ̃tɥalite] *s.f.* eventuality, possibility.
éventuel, -le [evɑ̃tɥɛl] *adj.* possible, probable; eventual, potential; **~lement** [evɑ̃tɥɛlmɑ̃] *adv.* possibly, perhaps, should the occasion arise; ⚠ not 'eventual(ly)' in sense 'final(ly)'.
évêque [evɛk] *s.m.* bishop; *bonnet d'~*, bishop's mitre, (fam.) parson's nose (on chicken); *en bonnet d'~*, mitre-shaped.
(**s'**)**évertuer** [evɛrtɥe] *v.refl.* to make every effort, to strive.
éviction [eviksjɔ̃] *s.f.* eviction.

évidage [evidaʒ], **évidement** [evidmɑ̃] *s.m.* scooping out, hollowing out; thinning (of tree).
évidé, -e [evide] *adj.* scooped out, hollowed out.
évidemment [evidamɑ̃] *adv.* obviously, patently, clearly; of course, certainly.
évidence [evidɑ̃s] *s.f.* obviousness, clearness; obvious fact; *à l'~, de toute ~*, obviously; *être en ~*, to be conspicuous, to be in evidence; *mettre en ~*, to display, to reveal; (fig.) to bring to light, to show up; ⚠ not legal 'evidence'.
évident, -e [evidɑ̃] *adj.* obvious, clear, evident.
évider [evide] *v.t.* to hollow out, to scoop out; to thin (tree).
évidoir [evidwar] *s.m.* (techn.) scooper, gouge.
évidure [evidyr] *s.f.* hollow, cavity.
évier [evje] *s.m.* (kitchen) sink.
évincement [evɛ̃smɑ̃] *s.m.* eviction.
évincer [evɛ̃se] *v.t.* to evict; to force out, to drive out, to oust; to eliminate; ⚠ not 'to evince'.
éviscération [eviserasjɔ̃] *s.f.* disembowelling.
éviscérer [evisere] *v.t.* to disembowel.
évitable [evitabl] *adj.* avoidable.
évitage [evitaʒ] *s.m.* (naut.) turning, swinging (of ship); sea-room.
évitement [evitmɑ̃] *s.m.* **1.** (obs.) avoiding; **2.** (rail.) *gare, voie, d'~*, siding.
éviter [evite] *v.t.* **1.** to avoid, to shun, to evade; *~ qch. à qn.*, to spare s.o. sth.; *~ de faire*, to avoid doing; **2.** (naut.) *~ au vent*, to turn into the wind; *~ à la marée*, to stem the tide.
évocable [evɔkabl] *adj.* that may be evoked; (law) *cause ~*, case that may be summoned (to a higher court).
évocat-eur, -rice [evɔkatœr] *adj.* evocative; reminiscent.
évocation [evɔkɑsjɔ̃] *s.f.* evocation; calling up, conjuring up.
évocatoire [evɔkatwar] *adj.* evocatory.
évolué, -e [evɔlɥe] *adj.* developed, civilized, advanced; cultured, broad-minded.
évoluer [evɔlɥe] *v.i.* **1.** to move, to manœuvre, to move around, to perform evolutions; **2.** to evolve, to progress, to develop.
évoluti-f, -ve [evɔlytif] *adj.* evolutive.
évolution [evɔlysjɔ̃] *s.f.* **1.** manœuvre, movements; **2.** evolution, development, progress; course (of disease); **~nisme** [evɔlysjɔnism] *s.m.* evolutionism; **~niste** [evɔlysjɔnist] *adj.* evolutionary; *s.m.f.* evolutionist.
évoquer [evɔke] *v.t.* **1.** to call up, to conjure up, to evoke; to recall, to remember; to suggest, to describe; to touch on (a matter); **2.** (law) to claim jurisdiction.
évulsion [evylsjɔ̃] *s.f.* (obs.) extraction, evulsion.
exacerbation [ɛgzasɛrbɑsjɔ̃] *s.f.* (lit. & fig.) exacerbation, aggravation.
exacerbé, -e [ɛgzasɛrbe] *adj.* exacerbated; exaggerated.
exacerber [ɛgzasɛrbe] *v.t.* (lit. & fig.) to exacerbate, to intensify.
exact, -e [ɛgzakt] *adj.* **1.** (obs. exc. Lit.) strict, precise, punctilious; **2.** punctual; **3.** exact, correct; **~ement** [ɛgzaktəmɑ̃] *adv.* exactly, precisely; punctually.
exacteur [ɛgzaktœr] *s.m.* (obs.) dun, debt-collector; extortioner.
exaction [ɛgzaksjɔ̃] *s.f.* exaction, extortion.
exactitude [ɛgzaktityd] *s.f.* **1.** (obs. exc. Lit.) punctiliousness, care; **2.** punctuality; **3.** exactness, exactitude, accuracy.
ex aequo [ɛgzeko] *adv.* equal, of equal merit; *premier(s) ~*, equal first, bracketed first.
exagérat-eur, -rice [ɛgzaʒeratœr]; *adj.* exaggerative; *s.m.f.* exaggerator.
exagération [ɛgzaʒerɑsjɔ̃] *s.f.* exaggeration; overstatement.
exagéré, -e [ɛgzaʒere] *adj.* exaggerated, excessive; **~ment** [ɛgzaʒeremɑ̃] *adv.* excessively, unduly, exaggeratedly.
exagérer [ɛgzaʒere] *v.t.* to exaggerate, to overstate, to magnify; to go too far; *s'~ qch.*, to overestimate, to make too much of, sth.
exaltant, -e [ɛgzaltɑ̃] *adj.* exciting, stirring, uplifting.
exaltation [ɛgzaltɑsjɔ̃] *s.f.* **1.** (relig.) exaltation, elevation (of the Cross, etc.); **2.** exalting, extolling, glorifying, glorification; **3.** exaltation, rapture; (med.) intensification (of virulence, etc.).
exalté, -e [ɛgzalte] *adj.* exalted, elated, overexcited; *s.m.f.* fanatic.
exalter [ɛgzalte] *v.t.* **1.** to exalt, to glorify, to extol; **2.** (med.) to increase, to intensify; **3.** to exalt, to elate, to excite; **s'~** *v.refl.* to get excited, to enthuse.
examen [ɛgzamɛ̃] *s.m.* **1.** examination, inspection, survey, study; **2.** (school, etc.) examination.
examinat-eur, -rice [ɛgzaminatœr] *s.m.f.* **1.** (obs.) inspector, observer; **2.** examiner.
examiner [ɛgzamine] *v.t.* to examine; to inspect, to survey, to study, to scrutinize.
exanthémateu-x, -se [ɛgzɑ̃tematø], **exanthématique** [ɛgzɑ̃tematik] *adj.* (med.) exanthematous, eruptive.
exanthème [ɛgzɑ̃tɛm] *s.m.* (med.) exanthema.
exarthrose [ɛgzartroz] *s.f.* (med.) dislocation.
exaspérant, -e [ɛgzasperɑ̃] *adj.* exasperating.
exaspération [ɛgzasperɑsjɔ̃] *s.f.* exasperation; (obs.) aggravation.
exaspérer [ɛgzaspere] *v.t.* to exasperate; to incense, to infuriate; to intensify, to aggravate.
exaucement [ɛgzosmɑ̃] *s.m.* fulfilment, granting (of wish, etc.).
exaucer [ɛgzose] *v.t.* to fulfil, to grant (wishes, etc.).
excavateur [ɛkskavatœr] *s.m.* excavator, mechanical digger.
excavation [ɛkskavɑsjɔ̃] *s.f.* **1.** digging; **2.** excavation, hollow, trench, hole, pit.
excaver [ɛkskave] *v.t.* to excavate, to dig out.
excédant, -e [ɛksedɑ̃] *adj.* excessive; aggravating, tiresome.
excédent [ɛksedɑ̃] *s.m.* excess, surplus; surcharge, excess (payment).
excédentaire [ɛksedɑ̃tɛr] *adj.* excess, surplus.
excéder [ɛksede] *v.t.* **1.** to exceed; **2.** to aggravate, to annoy.
excellemment [ɛksɛlamɑ̃] *adv.* excellently, extremely well.
excellence [ɛksɛlɑ̃s] *s.f.* **1.** excellence; *par ~*, pre-eminently, particularly; **2.** (title) *Son Excellence*, His Excellency.
excellent, -e [ɛksɛlɑ̃] *adj.* excellent.
exceller [ɛksɛle] *v.i.* to excel (*dans*, in; *à faire*, in doing).
excentration [ɛksɑ̃trɑsjɔ̃] *s.f.* (techn.) offsetting, throwing off centre.
excentrer [ɛksɑ̃tre] *v.t.* (techn.) to offset, to throw off centre.
excentricité [ɛksɑ̃trisite] *s.f.* eccentricity, oddity; (of suburb, etc.) remoteness, being on the outskirts.
excentrique [ɛksɑ̃trik] *adj.* eccentric, odd; (of suburb, etc.) on the outskirts, remote, peripheral; **~ment** [ɛksɑ̃trikmɑ̃] *adv.* out of centre; excentrically.
excentrique [ɛksɑ̃trik] *s.m.* (techn.) excentric.
excepté [ɛksɛpte] *prep.* except, apart from; *~ que*, except (for the fact) that.
excepté, -e [ɛksɛpte] *adj.* excepted, excluded, not including.
excepter [ɛksɛpte] *v.t.* to except, to exclude, to leave out, to make an exception of.
exception [ɛksɛpsjɔ̃] *s.f.* **1.** exception; *d'~*,

exceptional; *à l'~ de*, with the exception of, except; **2.** (law) bar, demurrer.
exceptionnel, -le [ɛksɛpsjɔnɛl] *adj.* exceptional; **~lement** [ɛksɛpsjɔnɛlmɑ̃] *adv.* exceptionally, as an exception.
excès [ɛksɛ] *s.m.* **1.** excess; *avec ~, à l'~, jusqu'à l'~*, excessively, to excess; **2.** (pl.) excesses, intemperate behaviour.
excessi-f, -ve [ɛksesif] *adj.* excessive, immoderate; **~vement** [ɛksesivmɑ̃] *adv.* excessively, immoderately, extremely.
exciper [ɛksipe] *v.i.* (law) to plead, to allege; *~ de sa bonne foi*, to plead one's good faith; *~ d'un contrat*, to rely on a contract.
excipient [ɛksipjɑ̃] *s.m.* (pharm.) excipient.
excise [ɛksiz] *s.m.* (Eng. admin.) excise duty.
exciser [ɛksize] *v.t.* to excise, to cut out.
excision [ɛksizjɔ̃] *s.f.* excision.
excitabilité [ɛksitabilite] *s.f.* (biol.) excitability.
excitable [ɛksitabl] *adj.* excitable.
excitant, -e [ɛksitɑ̃] *adj.* exciting, stimulating; *~ s.m.* excitant, stimulant.
excitat-eur, -rice [ɛksitatœr] *s.m.f.* agitator, fomenter; **~eur** *s.m.* (electr.) exciter, discharger; **~rice** *s.f.* (electr.) exciter dynamo.
excitation [ɛksitɑsjɔ̃] *s.f.* **1.** incitement, provocation, stimulation; **2.** excitement; **3.** (phys.) excitation.
excité, -e [ɛksite] *adj.* (over-)excited, elated, heated; *s.m.f.* fanatic, hothead.
exciter [ɛksite] *v.t.* to excite; to provoke, to arouse, to stimulate, to incite; to animate, to inflame, to irritate.
exclamati-f, -ve [ɛksklamatif] *adj.* exclamatory.
exclamation [ɛksklamɑsjɔ̃] *s.f.* exclamation; *point d'~*, exclamation mark.
(s')exclamer [ɛksklame] *v.refl.* to exclaim.
exclu, -e [ɛkskly] *adj.* excluded, rejected, barred; *jusqu'au 15 ~*, up to, but not including, the 15th.
exclure [ɛksklyr] *v.t.* to exclude, to reject, to bar; **s'~** *v.refl.* to be mutually exclusive.
exclusi-f, -ve [ɛksklyzif] *adj.* exclusive; sole (right, etc.); self-opinionated; *~f de*, which excludes, is exclusive of.
exclusion [ɛksklyzjɔ̃] *s.f.* exclusion, rejection, barring; *à l'~ de*, excluding.
exclusive [ɛksklyziv] *s.f.* veto.
exclusivement [ɛksklyzivmɑ̃] *adv.* exclusively, solely.
exclusivisme [ɛksklyzivism] *s.m.* exclusivism.
exclusivité [ɛksklyzivite] *s.f.* **1.** (obs.) exclusiveness; **2.** exclusive right, monopoly; *en ~*, exclusively, solely; **3.** (cin.) exclusive feature, exclusive showing.
excommunication [ɛkskɔmynikɑsjɔ̃] *s.f.* excommunication; (fig.) banning.
excommunier [ɛkskɔmynje] *v.t.* to excommunicate; (fig.) to ban.
excoriation [ɛkskɔrjɑsjɔ̃] *s.f.* excoriation, grazing.
excorier [ɛkskɔrje] *v.t.* to excoriate, to graze, to scratch.
excrément [ɛkskremɑ̃] *s.m.* (obs.) excretion; (fig.) off-scouring, scum; (mod.) excrement, excreta, dung.
excrémenteu-x, -se [ɛkskremɑ̃tø], **excrémentiel, -le** [ɛkskremɑ̃sjɛl] *adj.* excremental.
excréter [ɛkskrete] *v.t.* to excrete.
excrét-eur, -rice [ɛkskretœr], **excrétoire** [ɛkskretwar] *adj.* excretive, excretory.
excrétion [ɛkskresjɔ̃] *s.f.* excretion; (pl.) excreta.
excroissance [ɛkskrwasɑ̃s] *s.f.* (lit. & fig.) excrescence.
excursion [ɛkskyrsjɔ̃] *s.f.* excursion, trip, tour.
excursionner [ɛkskyrsjɔne] *v.i.* to go on an excursion, to tour.
excursionniste [ɛkskyrsjɔnist] *s.m.f.* tourist, tripper.
excusable [ɛkskyzabl] *adj.* excusable, pardonable.
excuse [ɛkskyz] *s.f.* excuse; (pl.) apology, apologies.
excuser [ɛkskyze] *v.t.* to excuse, to forgive; to exempt; **s'~** *v.refl.* to apologize; *s'~ de faire qch.*, to apologize for doing sth., (obs.) to decline to do sth.
exeat [ɛgzeat] *s.m.invar.* exeat.
exécrable [ɛgzekrabl] *adj.* execrable, detestable, disgusting, abominable; **~ment** [ɛgzekrabləmɑ̃] *adv.* execrably, detestably, abominably.
exécration [ɛgzekrɑsjɔ̃] *s.f.* execration; *avoir en ~*, to execrate.
exécrer [ɛgzekre] *v.t.* to execrate, to detest.
exécutable [ɛgzekytabl] *adj.* practicable, feasible.
exécutant, -e [ɛgzekytɑ̃] *s.m.f.* **1.** agent; **2.** (mus., etc.) performer.
exécuter [ɛgzekyte] *v.t.* **1.** to execute, to implement, to carry out; (law) to implement, to put into effect; **2.** (mus., etc.) to execute, to perform; **3.** to execute, to put to death; (fig.) to kill; **s'~** *v.refl.* to bring oneself to do (sth. unpleasant).
exécut-eur, -rice [ɛgzekytœr] *s.m.f.* **1.** executor, executrix; **2.** executioner.
exécuti-f, -ve [ɛgzekytif] *adj.* executive; **~f** *s.m.* (pol. admin.) executive.
exécution [ɛgzekysjɔ̃] *s.f.* **1.** implementation, carrying out, fulfilment; *mettre à ~*, to put into effect, to carry out; **2.** (law) distraint; **3.** performance; **4.** execution, death penalty.
exécutoire [ɛgzekytwar] *adj.* (law) enforceable, executory.
exégèse [ɛgzeʒɛs] *s.f.* exegesis.
exégète [ɛgzeʒɛt] *s.m.* exegetist, exegete.
exégétique [ɛgzeʒetik] *adj.* exegetic(al).
exemplaire [ɛgzɑ̃plɛr] *adj.* exemplary; *~ s.m.* **1.** (obs.) model, pattern; **2.** copy (of book, etc.); sample, specimen; **~ment** [ɛgzɑ̃plɛrmɑ̃] *adv.* in an exemplary fashion.
exemplarité [ɛgzɑ̃plarite] *s.f.* exemplariness.
exemple [ɛgzɑ̃pl] *s.m.* example; model; specimen; *à l'~ de*, in imitation of, like; *par ~*, for example; *par ~!*, for goodness' sake!
exemplifier [ɛgzɑ̃plifje] *v.t.* to exemplify.
exempt, -e [ɛgzɑ̃] *adj.* exempt, free; *~ de*, exempt from, excused (from); free of, free from; *~ de port*, carriage, or post, free; *~ d'erreurs*, free from mistakes; *~ s.m.* one exempted or excused; (obs. mil.) exempt; (obs. police) runner.
exempter [ɛgzɑ̃te] *v.t.* to exempt, to free, to excuse, (*de*, from); to preserve (*de*, from, against); **s'~** *v.refl.* to get out (of doing sth.).
exemption [ɛgzɑ̃psjɔ̃] *s.f.* exemption, being exempt.
exequatur [ɛgzekwatyr] *s.m.invar.* (law) exequatur.
exerçant, -e [ɛgzɛrsɑ̃] *adj.* (med., etc.) practising.
exercé, -e [ɛgzɛrse] *adj.* practised, experienced.
exercer [ɛgzɛrse] *v.t.* **1.** to exercise, to train, to drill; **2.** to exert, to exercise, to make use of; **3.** to practise (profession, etc.); **s'~** *v.refl.* **1.** to practise, to train (oneself); **2.** to manifest itself; to be exerted, to be applied.
exercice [ɛgzɛrsis] *s.m.* **1.** (physical) exercise, training, practice; **2.** (school) exercise; (pl.) book of exercises; **3.** exercise, use, (of power, etc.); **4.** (comm.) financial year; **5.** inspection (for tax liability); **6.** practice (of a profession); *en ~*, practising, active, in service.
exerciseur [ɛgzɛrsizœr] *s.m.* (gymn.) exercising apparatus.
exérèse [ɛgzerɛz] *s.f.* (surg.) removal, excision.
exergue [ɛgzɛrg] *s.m.* exergue.
exfoliation [ɛksfɔljɑsjɔ̃] *s.f.* exfoliation.

exfolier [ɛksfɔlje] *v.t.* (rare) to exfoliate; **s'~** *v.refl.* to exfoliate.
exhalaison [ɛgzalɛzɔ̃] *s.f.* exhalation.
exhalation [ɛgzalɑsjɔ̃] *s.f.* exhaling, exhalation.
exhaler [ɛgzale] *v.t.* to exhale, to emit, to breathe out; (fig.) to show, to express.
exhaure [ɛgzɔr] *s.f.* (techn.) pumping out (of a pit, etc.); pumping-installation.
exhaussement [ɛgzosmɑ̃] *s.m.* raising to a higher level, elevating.
exhausser [ɛgzose] *v.t.* to raise to a higher level, to elevate, to make higher; (fig.) to exalt.
exhausteur [ɛgzostœr] *s.m.* (techn.) suction pipe.
exhausti-f, -ve [ɛgzostif] *adj.* exhaustive.
exhaustion [ɛgzostjɔ̃] *s.f.* exhaustion, pumping out; ⚠ not 'exhaustion' in sense 'fatigue'.
exhaustivement [ɛgzostivmɑ̃] *adv.* exhaustively.
exhérédation [ɛgzeredɑsjɔ̃] *s.f.* (law) disinheritance.
exhéréder [ɛgzerede] *v.t.* (law) to disinherit.
exhiber [ɛgzibe] *v.t.* to show, to produce, (documents); to exhibit, to put on show; to make a show of, to show off.
exhibition [ɛgzibisjɔ̃] *s.f.* **1.** production (of documents); **2.** exhibition, show; **3.** (pej.) exhibition, showing off; indecent spectacle.
exhibitionnisme [ɛgzibisjɔnism] *s.m.* exhibitionism.
exhibitionniste [ɛgzibisjɔnist] *s.m.f.* exhibitionist.
exhilarant, -e [ɛgzilarɑ̃] *adj.* (obs.) exhilarant, mirth-provoking.
exhortation [ɛgzɔrtɑsjɔ̃] *s.f.* exhortation.
exhorter [ɛgzɔrte] *v.t.* to exhort, to urge.
exhumation [ɛgzymɑsjɔ̃] *s.f.* exhumation, disinterment; (archaeol.) excavation; unearthing.
exhumer [ɛgzyme] *v.t.* to exhume, to disinter; to dig up, to unearth.
exigeant, -e [ɛgziʒɑ̃] *adj.* exacting, demanding, strict.
exigence [ɛgziʒɑ̃s] *s.f.* **1.** (obs.) exigence, exigency; **2.** demand, claim; **3.** demanding nature.
exiger [ɛgziʒe] *v.t.* **1.** to demand, to claim; **2.** to necessitate, to require.
exigibilité [ɛgziʒibilite] *s.f.* liability to be demanded.
exigible [ɛgziʒibl] *adj.* exigible.
exigu, -ë [ɛgzigy] *adj.* exiguous, inadequate, narrow.
exiguïté [ɛgzigɥite] *s.f.* exiguity, exiguousness, slenderness (of resources, etc.).
exil [ɛgzil] *s.m.* exile, banishment.
exilé, -e [ɛgzile] *adj.* exiled, banished; (fig.) buried; *s.m.f.* exile.
exiler [ɛgzile] *v.t.* to exile, to banish; **s'~** *v.refl.* to go into (voluntary) exile; to live far from home.
exinscrit, -e [ɛksɛ̃skri] *adj.* (math.) escribed.
existant, -e [ɛgzistɑ̃] *adj.* **1.** existing, living; **2.** present, current; ~ *s.m.* (comm.) stock in hand.
existence [ɛgzistɑ̃s] *s.f.* existence, being; life, life style; (comm.) stock in hand.
existentialisme [ɛgzistɑ̃sjalism] *s.m.* existentialism.
existentialiste [ɛgzistɑ̃sjalist] *adj.*, *s.m.f.* existentialist.
existentiel, -le [ɛgzistɑ̃sjɛl] *adj.* existential.
exister [ɛgziste] *v.i.* to exist, to be, to live, to be in existence; to be extant, to be valid; (impers.) *il existe*, there is, there are.
exit [ɛgzit] *s.m.* (theatr.) exit; ⚠ not 'exit' in sense 'way out'.
ex-libris [ɛkslibris] *s.m.invar.* ex-libris, book-plate.
exocet [ɛgzɔsɛ] *s.m.* (ichth.) flying-fish.
exode [ɛgzɔd] *s.m.* (bibl.) Exodus; exodus, flight; ~ *des cerveaux*, brain drain; ~ *rural*, drift from the countryside.
exogamie [ɛgzɔgami] *s.f.* exogamy.
exogène [ɛgzɔʒɛn] *adj.* exogenous.
exondation [ɛgzɔ̃dɑsjɔ̃] *s.f.*, **exondement** [ɛgzɔ̃dmɑ̃] *s.m.* subsidence of flood water.
(s')exonder [ɛgzɔ̃de] *v.refl.* to emerge (from below flood water).
exonération [ɛgzɔnerɑsjɔ̃] *s.f.* exoneration; exemption.
exonérer [ɛgzɔnere] *v.t.* to exonerate; to exempt.
exophtalmie [ɛgzɔftalmi] *s.f.* (med.) exophthalmus, exophthalmos.
exophtalmique [ɛgzɔftalmik] *adj.* (med.) exophthalmic.
exorbitant, -e [ɛgzɔrbitɑ̃] *adj.* exorbitant.
exorbité, -e [ɛgzɔrbite] *adj.* (of eyes) protruding, bulging.
exorcisation [ɛgzɔrsizɑsjɔ̃] *s.f.* exorcising, exorcisation.
exorciser [ɛgzɔrsize] *v.t.* to exorcise.
exorciseur [ɛgzɔrsizœr] *s.m.* exorcist.
exorcisme [ɛgzɔrsism] *s.m.* exorcism.
exorciste [ɛgzɔrsist] *s.m.* exorcist.
exorde [ɛgzɔrd] *s.m.* exordium.
exoréique [ɛgzɔreik] *adj.* (geog.) draining to the sea.
exosmose [ɛgzɔsmoz] *s.f.* (phys.) exosmosis.
exostose [ɛgzɔstoz] *s.f.* (med., biol.) exostosis.
exotérique [ɛgzɔterik] *adj.* exoteric.
exothermique [ɛgzɔtɛrmik] *adj.* exothermal, exothermic.
exotique [ɛgzɔtik] *adj.* exotic.
exotisme [ɛgzɔtism] *s.m.* exoticism.
expansibilité [ɛkspɑ̃sibilite] *s.f.* (phys.) expansibility.
expansible [ɛkspɑ̃sibl] *adj.* expansible.
expansi-f, -ve [ɛkspɑ̃sif] *adj.* expansive; demonstrative, communicative.
expansion [ɛkspɑ̃sjɔ̃] *s.f.* **1.** expansion; **2.** expansiveness, demonstrativeness.
expansionniste [ɛkspɑ̃sjɔnist] *adj.*, *s.m.f.* expansionist.
expansivité [ɛkspɑ̃sivite] *s.f.* expansiveness, expansivity.
expatriation [ɛkspatrijɑsjɔ̃] *s.f.* expatriation.
expatrié, -e [ɛkspatrije] *adj.*, *s.m.f.* expatriate, expatriated (person).
expatrier [ɛkspatrije] *v.t.* to banish; to send (employee, funds) overseas; **s'~** *v.refl.* to emigrate.
expectant, -e [ɛkspɛktɑ̃] *adj.* expectant.
expectative [ɛkspɛktativ] *s.f.* expectation, expectancy; *être, rester, dans l'~*, to be waiting, to wait and see.
expectorant, -e [ɛkspɛktɔrɑ̃] *adj.* expectorant; ~ *s.m.* expectorant.
expectoration [ɛkspɛktɔrɑsjɔ̃] *s.f.* expectoration.
expectorer [ɛkspɛktɔre] *v.t.* to expectorate.
expédient, -e [ɛkspedjɑ̃] *adj.* expedient; ~ *s.m.* expedient, resort.
expédier [ɛkspedje] *v.t.* **1.** (obs. exc. admin.) to expedite; **2.** to rush through, to toss off, to give summary attention to; **3.** (law) to engross; **4.** to send, to dispatch; (fig.) to kill.
expédit-eur, -rice [ɛkspeditœr] *s.m.f.* sender.
expéditi-f, -ve [ɛkspeditif] *adj.* expeditious, prompt, speedy.
expédition [ɛkspedisjɔ̃] *s.f.* **1.** expedition; **2.** (law) transcript, copy; **3.** sending, dispatching; consignment (of goods).
expéditionnaire [ɛkspedisjɔnɛr] *adj.* expeditionary; ~ *s.m.* dispatch clerk; copying clerk.
expéditivement [ɛkspeditivmɑ̃] *adv.* expeditiously.
expérience [ɛksperjɑ̃s] *s.f.* **1.** experience; *faire l'~ de*, to experience; **2.** experiment.

expérimental, -e, (**aux**) [ɛksperimɑ̃tal] *adj.* experimental; **~ement** [ɛksperimɑ̃talmɑ̃] *adv.* experimentally, by experiment.
expérimentat-eur, -rice [ɛksperimɑ̃tatœr] *s.m.f.* experimenter; experimentalist.
expérimentation [ɛksperimɑ̃tɑsjɔ̃] *s.f.* experimentation.
expérimenté, -e [ɛksperimɑ̃te] *adj.* experienced, skilled.
expérimenter [ɛksperimɑ̃te] *v.t.* **1.** to experience; **2.** to experiment (with), to try out.
expert, -e [ɛkspɛr] *adj.* expert, experienced, skilled; *s.m.f.* expert, authority; **~ement** [ɛkspɛrtəmɑ̃] *adv.* expertly.
expertise [ɛkspɛrtiz] *s.f.* **1.** expert survey and report; **2.** expertise.
expertiser [ɛkspɛrtize] *v.t.* to make an expert valuation, or survey, of.
expiable [ɛkspjabl] *adj.* expiable.
expiat-eur, -rice [ɛkspjatœr] *adj.* expiatory.
expiation [ɛkspjɑsjɔ̃] *s.f.* expiation, atonement.
expiatoire [ɛkspjatwar] *adj.* expiatory.
expier [ɛkspje] *v.t.* to expiate, to atone for; (fig.) to pay for.
expirant, -e [ɛkspirɑ̃] *adj.* dying, expiring.
expirateur [ɛkspiratœr] *adj.m.* expiratory; **~** *s.m.* expiratory muscle.
expiration [ɛkspirɑsjɔ̃] *s.f.* **1.** expiration; **2.** (fig.) expiry, termination.
expirer [ɛkspire] *v.t.* to expire, to breathe out; **~** *v.i.* to expire, to die; to cease to be valid.
expléti-f, -ve [ɛkspletif] *adj.* (gram.) expletive.
explicable [ɛksplikabl] *adj.* explicable, explainable.
explicati-f, -ve [ɛksplikatif] *adj.* explanatory.
explication [ɛksplikɑsjɔ̃] *s.f.* explanation; showdown; critical commentary (on text); construing (of Gr. or Latin text); *avoir une ~ avec qn.*, to have it out with s.o.
explicite [ɛksplisit] *adj.* explicit; definite, clearly stated; **~ment** [ɛksplisitmɑ̃] *adv.* explicitly.
expliciter [ɛksplisite] *v.t.* to state clearly.
expliquer [ɛksplike] *v.t.* **1.** to explain; to expound; **2.** to explain, to account for; **s'~** *v.refl.* **1.** to explain oneself, to express oneself; **2.** to have a discussion; (pop.) to fight it out; **3.** to understand; *je m'explique mal pourquoi*, I find it hard to understand why; **4.** to be explained, to be understood.
exploit [ɛksplwa] *s.m.* **1.** exploit, feat, achievement; **2.** (law) *~ d'huissier*, writ.
exploitable [ɛksplwatabl] *adj.* **1.** (law) distrainable; **2.** (of mine, land, etc.) workable (at a profit); (economically) viable; **3.** (fig. of person) easily exploited.
exploitant, -e [ɛksplwatɑ̃] *adj.* **1.** (law) writ-serving; **2.** operating, managing; *s.m.f.* owner-operator; (small) farmer; cinema owner.
exploitation [ɛksplwatɑsjɔ̃] *s.f.* **1.** exploitation, working, running, operating; **2.** undertaking; farm, factory, etc.; **3.** exploitation, taking unfair advantage of.
exploité, -e [ɛksplwate] *adj.* **1.** (of land, mine, etc.) worked, in use or operation; **2.** exploited; *s.m.f.* exploited person.
exploiter [ɛksplwate] *v.t.* **1.** to operate, to work, to run, to put to use; **2.** to exploit, to take advantage of.
exploiteu-r, -se [ɛksplwatœr] *s.m.f.* **1.** operator; **2.** (pej.) exploiter, oppressor.
explorat-eur, -rice [ɛksplɔratœr] *s.m.f.* explorer; **~eur** *s.m.* (med.) probe, trocar.
exploration [ɛksplɔrɑsjɔ̃] *s.f.* **1.** exploration, discovery; **2.** study; examination.
exploratoire [ɛksplɔratwar] *adj.* exploratory.
explorer [ɛksplɔre] *v.t.* **1.** to explore; **2.** to study; to examine.
exploser [ɛksploze] *v.i.* (lit. & fig.) to explode.
exploseur [ɛksplozœr] *s.m.* electric detonator.
explosible [ɛksplozibl] *adj.* explosive.
explosi-f, -ve [ɛksplozif] *adj.* (lit. & fig.) explosive; **~f** *s.m.* explosive.
explosion [ɛksplozjɔ̃] *s.f.* (lit. & fig.) explosion; outburst.
exponentiel, -le [ɛkspɔnɑ̃sjɛl] *adj.* exponential.
exportable [ɛkspɔrtabl] *adj.* exportable.
exportat-eur, -rice [ɛkspɔrtatœr] *s.m.f.* exporter; *adj.* exporting.
exportation [ɛkspɔrtɑsjɔ̃] *s.f.* exporting, exportation; export.
exporter [ɛkspɔrte] *v.t.* to export.
exposant, -e [ɛkspozɑ̃] *s.m.f.* **1.** (obs. law) petitioner; **2.** exhibitor; **~** *s.m.* (math.) exponent.
exposé [ɛkspoze] *s.m.* statement, account, report, summary.
exposer [ɛkspoze] *v.t.* **1.** to exhibit, to display, to show; **2.** to state, to report on, to summarize; **3.** to expose; to put in danger, to risk; to abandon (infant, etc.); to expose (film); *~ à*, to expose to, to lay open to, to subject to; **s'~** *v.refl.* to expose oneself, to put oneself in a vulnerable position, to compromise oneself; *s'~ à*, to expose oneself to, to risk.
exposition [ɛkspozisjɔ̃] *s.f.* **1.** show, exhibition, display; **2.** exposition, explanation, statement; (mus.) exposition; **3.** exposure; (law) abandonment (of infant, etc.); **4.** aspect, situation, (of building).
expr-ès, -esse [ɛksprɛs] *adj.* (law) specific, strict; **~ès** *adj.invar.* (of letter, etc.) express; **~ès** *s.m.* messenger; express message.
exprès [ɛksprɛ] *adv.* on purpose, specially; *un fait ~*, an unwelcome coincidence.
express [ɛksprɛs] *adj., s.m.invar.* express (train).
expressément [ɛksprɛsemɑ̃] *adv.* **1.** expressly, strictly; **2.** specially.
expressi-f, -ve [ɛkspresif] *adj.* expressive.
expression [ɛksprɛsjɔ̃] *s.f.* expression; expressiveness; phrase, form of words, term.
expressionnisme [ɛksprɛsjɔnism] *s.m.* expressionism.
expressionniste [ɛksprɛsjɔnist] *adj., s.m.f.* expressionist.
expressivement [ɛkspresivmɑ̃] *adv.* expressively.
expressivité [ɛkspresivite] *s.f.* expressivity.
exprimable [ɛksprimabl] *adj.* expressible.
exprimer [ɛksprime] *v.t.* **1.** to express, to convey, to show; **2.** (techn.) to squeeze (out); **s'~** *v.refl.* to express oneself; to be expressed.
expropriant, -e [ɛksprɔprijɑ̃] *adj.* expropriating; *s.m.f.* expropriator.
expropriation [ɛksprɔprijɑsjɔ̃] *s.f.* expropriation.
exproprier [ɛksprɔprije] *v.t.* to expropriate.
expulsé, -e [ɛkspylse] *adj.* expelled, evicted; *s.m.f.* expellee, ejected or evicted person.
expulser [ɛkspylse] *v.t.* to expel, to banish; to eject, to evict; to evacuate (from the body).
expulsion [ɛkspylsjɔ̃] *s.f.* expulsion, banishment, exile; ejection, eviction; (med.) evacuation.
expurgation [ɛkspyrgɑsjɔ̃] *s.f.* (obs.) purging; (mod.) expurgation, bowdlerizing.
expurgatoire [ɛkspyrgatwar] *adj.* expurgatory.
expurger [ɛkspyrʒe] *v.t.* (obs.) to purge; (mod.) to expurgate.
exquis, -e [ɛkski] *adj.* exquisite, delicate, delightful; *douleur ~e*, sharp, localized pain.
exquisément [ɛkskizemɑ̃] *adv.* exquisitely, delicately, delightfully.
exquisité [ɛkskizite] *s.f.* exquisiteness.
exsangue [ɛksɑ̃g] *adj.* bloodless, anaemic, pale; (fig.) lifeless.
exsanguino-transfusion [ɛksɑ̃ginɔtrɑ̃sfyzjɔ̃] *s.f.* (med.) replacement of blood.

exsudat [ɛksyda] *s.m.* (med.) exudate.
exsudation [ɛksydɑsjɔ̃] *s.f.* (med.) exudation.
exsuder [ɛksyde] *v.t.i.* to exude.
extase [ɛkstɑz] *s.f.* ecstasy, rapture; *être en* ~ *devant qn.*, to go into ecstasies about s.o.
extasié, -e [ɛkstɑzje] *adj.* in raptures, entranced.
(**s'**)**extasier** [ɛkstɑzje] *v.refl.* to go into ecstasies (*sur*, about), to be enraptured.
extatique [ɛkstatik] *adj.* ecstatic, rapturous.
extemporané, -e [ɛkstɑ̃pɔrane] *adj.* extemporaneous.
extenseur [ɛkstɑ̃sœr] *adj., s.m.* extensor (muscle); chest expander.
extensibilité [ɛkstɑ̃sibilite] *s.f.* extensibility.
extensible [ɛkstɑ̃sibl] *adj.* extensile, extensible, elastic.
extensi-f, -ve [ɛkstɑ̃sif] *adj.* extensive; (sci.) tensile.
extension [ɛkstɑ̃sjɔ̃] *s.f.* extension, stretching; expansion, enlargement.
extensomètre [ɛkstɑ̃sɔmɛtr] *s.m.* extensometer.
exténuant, -e [ɛkstenɥɑ̃] *adj.* exhausting; ⚠ not 'extenuating'.
exténuation [ɛkstenɥɑsjɔ̃] *s.f.* exhaustion; ⚠ not 'extenuation'.
exténuer [ɛkstenɥe] *v.t.* **1.** (obs.) to emaciate, to weaken; (fig.) to soften; **2.** to exhaust; **s'**~ *v.refl.* to wear oneself out; ⚠ not 'to extenuate' in sense 'to palliate'.
extérieur, -e [ɛksterjœr] *adj.* exterior, external; outward, foreign; ~**ement** [ɛksterjœrmɑ̃] *adv.* externally, outwardly; on the outside; superficially, on the surface.
extérieur [ɛksterjœr] *s.m.* exterior, outside; foreign countries; (obs. exc. Lit.) appearance; *à l'*~, outside; *de l'*~, from outside; from abroad; (fig.) objectively; (cin.) *en* ~, on location.
extériorisation [ɛksterjɔrizɑsjɔ̃] *s.f.* exteriorization.
extérioriser [ɛksterjɔrize] *v.t.* to exteriorize.
extériorité [ɛksterjɔrite] *s.f.* exteriority.
exterminat-eur, -rice [ɛkstɛrminatœr] *adj.* exterminating, destroying; *s.m.f.* exterminator, destroyer.
extermination [ɛkstɛrminɑsjɔ̃] *s.f.* extermination.
exterminer [ɛkstɛrmine] *v.t.* to exterminate, to destroy; (fig., fam.) *s'*~ *à*, to kill oneself with.
externat [ɛkstɛrna] *s.m.* **1.** day school, day-school system; **2.** non-resident medical student(s).
externe [ɛkstɛrn] *adj.* external; ~ *s.m.f.* **1.** day-boy or day-girl; **2.** non-resident medical student.
exterritorialité [ɛkstɛritɔrjalite] *s.f.* extraterritoriality, exterritoriality.
extinct-eur, -rice [ɛkstɛ̃ktœr] *adj.* extinguishing; ~**eur** *s.m.* (fire) extinguisher.
extinction [ɛkstɛ̃ksjɔ̃] *s.f.* **1.** extinguishing, putting out; ~ *des feux*, lights out; **2.** extinction, disappearance; ~ *de voix*, loss of voice; **3.** abolition (of law, custom, etc.); termination (of contract); paying off (of debt).
extinguible [ɛkstɛ̃gibl] *adj.* extinguishable, quenchable.
extirpable [ɛkstirpabl] *adj.* eradicable.
extirpateur [ɛkstirpatœr] *s.m.* (agric.) mechanical weeder.
extirpation [ɛkstirpɑsjɔ̃] *s.f.* extirpation, eradication, uprooting.
extirper [ɛkstirpe] *v.t.* to extirpate, to eradicate; (fig., fam.) to dig out; **s'**~ *v.refl.* to extract oneself.
extorquer [ɛkstɔrke] *v.t.* to extort.
extorqueu-r, -se [ɛkstɔrkœr] *s.m.f.* extortioner.
extorsion [ɛkstɔrsjɔ̃] *s.f.* extortion.
extra [ɛkstra] *s.m.invar.* extra; treat; temporary domestic help; ~ *adj.invar.* extra-special, specially good, first class.
extra-courant [ɛkstrakurɑ̃] *s.m.* (electr.) extra-current, self-induction current.
extracteur [ɛkstraktœr] *s.m.* extractor.
extractible [ɛkstraktibl] *adj.* extractable.
extracti-f, -ve [ɛkstraktif] *adj.* (techn.) extractive.
extraction [ɛkstraksjɔ̃] *s.f.* **1.** extraction, removal; **2.** (obs.) descent; (mod.) *être de haute, de basse*, ~, to be of noble, of humble, birth.
extrader [ɛkstrade] *v.t.* to extradite.
extradition [ɛkstradisjɔ̃] *s.f.* extradition.
extrados [ɛkstrado] *s.m.* **1.** (arch.) extrados; **2.** (aeron.) outer surface (of wing).
extra-dry [ɛkstradraj] *adj.* (of champagne) extra dry.
extra-fin, -e [ɛkstrafɛ̃] *adj.* superfine; of the highest quality.
extra-fort, -e [ɛkstrafɔr] *adj.* extra-strong; ~ *s.m.* (dressm.) binding.
extragalactique [ɛkstragalaktik] *adj.* (astron.) extragalactic.
extraire [ɛkstrɛr] *v.t.* to extract, to remove; to draw, pull, or dig out; to make extracts (from a book, etc.); to summarize.
extrait [ɛkstrɛ] *s.m.* **1.** extract, essence; **2.** extract, passage, abstract, quotation; **3.** certified copy, certificate; ~ *de naissance*, birth certificate.
extrajudiciaire [ɛkstraʒydisjɛr] *adj.* extrajudicial.
extra-légal, -e, (**aux**) [ɛkstralegal] *adj.* illegal, outside the law.
extra-lucide [ɛkstralysid] *adj.* clairvoyant.
extra-muros [ɛkstramyros] *adj., adv.* suburban; outside the town.
extraordinaire [ɛkstraɔrdinɛr] *adj.* extraordinary, unusual, uncommon; astonishing, surprising; odd, strange; remarkable, unusually good, large, etc.; ~**ment** [ɛkstraɔrdinɛrmɑ̃] *adv.* **1.** unusually; **2.** by some extraordinary occurrence; **3.** extraordinarily, oddly, remarkably.
extra-parlementaire [ɛkstraparləmɑ̃tɛr] *adj.* extra-parliamentary.
extrapolation [ɛkstrapɔlɑsjɔ̃] *s.f.* extrapolation.
extrapoler [ɛkstrapɔle] *v.i.* to extrapolate.
extra-sensible [ɛkstrasɑ̃sibl] *adj.* that cannot be perceived by the senses.
extra-sensoriel, -le [ɛkstrasɑ̃sɔrjɛl] *adj.* extrasensory.
extra-territorialité [ɛkstratɛritɔrjalite] *s.f.* extraterritoriality.
extra-utérin, -e [ɛkstrayterɛ̃] *adj.* extra-uterine.
extravagance [ɛkstravagɑ̃s] *s.f.* extravagance; outrageousness; foolish talk, folly; nonsense.
extravagant, -e [ɛkstravagɑ̃] *adj.* extravagant, outrageous, wild, foolish; *s.m.f.* eccentric, crank.
extravaguer [ɛkstravage] *v.i.* (obs. exc. iron.) to think, talk, or act wildly, to rave.
extravasation [ɛkstravɑzɑsjɔ̃] *s.f.* (med.) extravasation.
(**s'**)**extravaser** [ɛkstravɑze] *v.refl.* (med.) to extravasate.
extraverti, -e [ɛkstravɛrti] *adj., s.m.f.* extrovert(ed).
extrême [ɛkstrɛm] *adj.* extreme, farthest, utmost; *Extrême-Orient*, Far East; ~ *droite*, ~ *gauche*, (pol.) far right, far left; ~ *s.m.* extreme, extreme limit; *à l'*~, in the extreme; ~**ment** [ɛkstrɛmmɑ̃] *adv.* extremely.
extrême-onction [ɛkstrɛmɔ̃ksjɔ̃] *s.f.* (eccles.) extreme unction.
extrême-oriental, -e, (**aux**) [ɛkstrɛmɔrjɑ̃tal] *adj.* Far-Eastern.
extrémisme [ɛkstremism] *s.m.* extremism.
extrémiste [ɛkstremist] *adj., s.m.f.* extremist.

extrémité [ɛkstremite] *s.f.* **1.** extremity, end, furthest point; (pl.) extremities (hands and feet); **2.** final point, verge of death; **3.** extremity; violent action; extreme measure.
extremum [ɛkstremɔm] *s.m.* (sci.) extremum.
extrinsèque [ɛkstrɛ̃sɛk] *adj.* extrinsic.
extroverti, -e [ɛkstrɔvɛrti] = EXTRAVERTI.
extrusion [ɛkstryzjɔ̃] *s.f.* (techn.) extrusion.
exubérance [ɛgzyberɑ̃s] *s.f.* **1.** abundance, profusion; **2.** exuberance.
exubérant, -e [ɛgzyberɑ̃] *adj.* **1.** luxuriant, abundant, profuse; **2.** exuberant.
exulcérer [ɛgzylsere] *v.t.* (med.) to ulcerate.
exultation [ɛgzyltɑsjɔ̃] *s.f.* exultation.
exulter [ɛgzylte] *v.i.* to exult, to be exultant, to rejoice greatly.
exutoire [ɛgzytwar] *s.m.* **1.** (obs. med.) exutory; **2.** outlet.
ex-voto [ɛksvɔto] *s.m.invar.* ex voto.
eyra [ɛra] *s.m.* (zool.) eyra.

F

F, f [ɛf] *s.m.* the letter F, f; abbrev. *franc(s)*; (mus.) *forte, fa*; abbrev. parts of verb *foutre*; *il s'en f...* for *il s'en fout.*
fa [fɑ, fa] *s.m.* (mus.) fah, fa, F.
fable [fɑbl] *s.f.* **1.** fable, allegory; **2.** fable, invention, fiction, figment; **3.** (obs.) story, narrative element, subject matter; **4.** laughing-stock.
fabliau (pl. **-x**) [fablijo] *s.m.* fabliau.
fablier [fɑblije] *s.m.* book of fables.
fabricant, -e [fabrikɑ̃] *s.m.f.* manufacturer, maker.
fabricat-eur, -rice [fabrikatœr] *s.m.f.* (obs.) maker, creator; *le ~eur souverain*, the Creator; (mod. pej.) fabricator, forger; *~eur de fausse monnaie*, coiner, counterfeiter; *~eur de faux papiers*, forger.
fabrication [fabrikɑsjɔ̃] *s.f.* **1.** manufacture, fabrication, making; (pej.) producing (sth.) mechanically; *défaut de ~*, fault in manufacture; *est-ce une robe de votre ~?*, is it a dress you made yourself?; **2.** (pej.) fabrication, forging, counterfeiting.
fabricien [fabrisjɛ̃] *s.m.* churchwarden, master of the fabric.
fabrique [fabrik] *s.f.* **1.** (obs.) making, manufacture, make, brand; (fig.) *c'est de sa ~*, it's his own invention, it's something he has made up himself; *ce drap est de bonne ~*, this is a good make of cloth; (mod.) *marque de ~*, trade-mark; **2.** factory, works, mill; *prix de ~*, factory price, manufacturer's price, price ex works; **3.** fabric (of building), structure; architectural element (in a painting); (eccles.) *la ~*, or *le conseil de ~*, church council, vestry, section of chapter concerned with finances; ⚠ not 'fabric' in sense 'textile material'.
fabriquer [fabrike] *v.t.* **1.** to manufacture, to fabricate, to make; (fam.) to do; *qu'est-ce qu'il fabrique là?*, what's he up to now?; **2.** to fabricate, to forge, to counterfeit; to invent, to devise; to create artificially.
fabulat-eur, -rice [fabylatœr] *s.m.f.* (psychol.) fantasist.
fabulation [fabylasjɔ̃] *s.f.* (psychol.) fantasizing.
fabuler [fabyle] *v.i.* to fantasize.
fabuleu-x, -se [fabylø] *adj.* fabulous, fabled; fantastic, incredible; fictitious; **~sement** [fabyløzmɑ̃] *adv.* fantastically, incredibly.
fabuliste [fabylist] *s.m.* fabulist.
façade [fasad] *s.f.* front, frontage, façade, face; (fig.) appearance, pretence, show, façade; (pop.) *se refaire la ~*, to make oneself up.
face [fas] *s.f.* **1.** face; (fig.) *cracher à la ~ de qn.*, to spit in someone's face; *perdre la ~*, to lose face; *sauver la ~*, to save one's face, to keep up appearances; *~ à ~*, face to face; **2.** front, face, front surface or aspect, part facing forwards; (of coin) heads; *faire ~ à*, to face, to front on; (fig.) to face up to, to cope with; *~ à*, facing, in front of; *en ~*, in the face; opposite, facing; *regarder qn. en ~*, to look s.o. straight in the eyes; *la maison d'en ~*, the house opposite; *en ~ de*, facing, opposite; in (the) face of; *de ~*, front, from the front, facing forward; *vue de ~*, front view; (theatr.) *loge de ~*, box facing the stage; (rail.) *coin ~*, corner-seat facing the engine; **3.** surface, face, side; (fig.) aspect, appearance, side; *~ inférieure*, under-surface; *~s d'un prisme*, sides of a prism; *considérer qch. sous toutes ses ~s*, to consider sth. from every angle, from all its aspects; *changer la ~ de qch.*, to change the appearance of sth.; *il ne donne qu'une ~ de la chose*, he only presents one side of the case.
face-à-main [fasamɛ̃] *s.m.* (pl. *faces-à-main*) lorgnette.
facétie [fasesi] *s.f.* joke, buffoonery, jest; facetiousness.
facétieu-x, -se [fasesjø] *adj.* facetious, jocular.
facette [fasɛt] *s.f.* facet; *à ~s*, faceted, cut in facets, (fig.) of many aspects, with many facets, multifarious; (zool.) *œil à ~s*, compound eye.
facetter [fasɛte] *v.t.* to facet (diamond, etc.).
fâché, -e [fɑʃe] *adj.* sorry, upset, put out; angry, offended, vexed, (*contre*, with; *de*, about, over); on bad terms, fallen out, (*avec*, *contre*, with); *vous n'êtes pas ~(s)?*, you're not angry, are you?; *ils sont ~s*, they have had a quarrel.
fâcher [fɑʃe] *v.t.* to upset, to anger, to offend, to displease, to make angry, to vex; (obs.) to grieve, to pain; **se ~** *v.refl.* to get angry, to take offence, to lose one's temper; to fall out, to quarrel.
fâcherie [fɑʃri] *s.f.* (obs.) vexation; (mod.) quarrel, disagreement, coolness of relations.
fâcheu-x, -se [fɑʃø] *adj.* (obs.) painful; (mod.) disagreeable, tiresome, annoying, irritating, vexatious, awkward, unfortunate; regrettable, deplorable; *s.m.f.* tiresome or irritating person, bore; **~sement** [fɑʃøzmɑ̃] *adv.* annoyingly, unfortunately, regrettably.
facial, -e, (als or **aux)** [fasjal] *adj.* facial.
facies, faciès [fasjɛs] *s.m.* facies, facial appearance, general aspect.
facile [fasil] *adj.* easy, facile; natural, fluent, flowing, ready, quick; easy-going, tolerant, good-natured, compliant; (of woman) of easy virtue; **~ment** [fasilmɑ̃] easily, without difficulty or effort, readily; lightly, for little reason.
facilité [fasilite] *s.f.* facility, ease, aptitude; fluency; talent, skill, ability; opportunity, possibility; pliancy, complaisance; indulgence, tolerance, good nature.
faciliter [fasilite] *v.t.* to facilitate, to make easy or possible.

façon [fasɔ̃] *s.f.* **1.** making, fashioning, making-up (of suit, etc.), composition, work, workmanship; fashion, style, cut; (agric.) dressing; *un poème de ma ~*, a poem of my own composition; *payer la ~ d'un habit*, to pay for having a costume made up; *tailleur à ~*, jobbing tailor; *cuir ~ porc*, imitation pigskin; **2.** manner, mode, way; sort; *la ~ dont on fait qch.*, the way one does sth.; *c'est une ~ de parler*, it's a manner of speaking (not to be taken too literally); *de cette ~*, in this way, thus, so; *de ~ à, de ~ que*, so that, in such a way that; *à la ~ de*, in the style or manner of; *à sa ~*, as one likes, in one's own way; *en aucune ~*, not at all, by no means; *une ~ de secrétaire*, a secretary of sorts; **3.** (obs.) appearance; (mod.) (pl.) manner(s), behaviour; ceremony, fuss; *ses ~s me déplaisent*, I don't like his manner, his way of behaving; *faire des ~s*, to stand on ceremony, to make a lot of fuss (about sth.); *sans ~*, simply, without more ado; simple; abrupt, without manners; abruptness; *un dîner sans ~*, a simple little dinner.

faconde [fakɔ̃d] *s.f.* (Lit., often pej.) fluency, flow of words, loquacity.

façonnage [fasɔnaʒ], **façonnement** [fasɔnmɑ̃] *s.m.* making, fashioning, shaping; turning (on lathe); dressing (of soil, of timber).

façonné [fasɔne] *s.m.* (text.) figured stuff.

façonner [fasɔne] *v.t.* to make, to work, to make up, to fashion, to shape, to mould; to train, to educate; to modify; to turn (on lathe); (agric.) to dress.

façonni-er, -ère [fasɔnje] *adj., s.m.f.* **1.** ceremonious, fussy (person); **2.** jobbing (tailor, etc.); (person) working at home.

fac-similé [faksimile] *s.m.* facsimile.

factage [faktaʒ] *s.m.* carriage, delivery (of goods, letters, etc.); delivery charge, transport (costs).

facteur [faktœr] *s.m.* **1.** maker (of organs or pianos); **2.** (obs.) factor, auctioneer (at *Les Halles*), agent, middleman; **3.** postman; porter, carrier; **4.** (math.) factor, coefficient; (fig.) factor, element; *~ de sûreté*, safety factor, coefficient of safety; *le ~ humain*, the human element.

factice [faktis] *adj.* factitious, artificial, imitation, dummy; (fig.) forced, feigned, false; *bouteille ~*, dummy bottle; **~ment** [faktismɑ̃] *adv.* artificially.

factieu-x, -se [faksjø] *adj.* factious, seditious; *s.m.f.* factious person, trouble-maker, sedition-monger.

faction [faksjɔ̃] *s.f.* **1.** (pol., etc.) faction; **2.** (mil.) sentry-duty, guard; (fig.) observation, watching, watch, long wait; *être en* or *de ~*, to be a sentry, to be on sentry-go, to be on the watch; to be waiting; *poster un homme, un soldat, en ~*, to post a sentry, to put a guard or watch.

factionnaire [faksjɔnɛr] *s.m.* (mil.) sentry.

factorage [faktɔraʒ] *s.m.* (comm.) factorage.

factorerie [faktɔrri] *s.f.* trading-station, agency, factory (in colonies).

factoriel, -le [faktɔrjɛl] *adj.* factorial; **~le** *s.f.* (math.) factorial.

factotum [faktɔtɔm] *s.m.* factotum, jack-of-all-trades.

factuel, -le [faktɥɛl] *adj.* factual.

factum [faktɔm] *s.m.* factum, statement, memorial, treatise; controversial or scurrilous pamphlet.

facturation [faktyrasjɔ̃] *s.f.* (comm.) invoicing; invoicing office.

facture[1] [faktyr] *s.f.* making, composition, rendering, execution; style, technique; making or building (of mus. instruments).

facture[2] [faktyr] *s.f.* (comm.) bill, invoice; *prix de ~*, invoice price; *~ simulée*, pro-forma invoice.

facturer [faktyre] *v.t.* to invoice.

facturi-er, -ère [faktyrje] *s.m.f.* invoice clerk; **~er** *s.m.* sales book.

facule [fakyl] *s.f.* (astron.) facula.

facultati-f, -ve [fakyltatif] *adj.* optional, facultative; *arrêt ~f*, request stop (for bus, etc.); **~vement** [fakyltativmɑ̃] *adv.* optionally, at discretion.

faculté [fakylte] *s.f.* **1.** option, choice, liberty, freedom, right; *~ de rachat*, option to repurchase; **2.** (mental, etc.) faculty; capacity, aptitude; (pl.) (obs.) means, resources; *une grande ~ de travail*, a great capacity for work; *dépenser au delà de ses ~s*, to spend beyond one's means; **3.** (university, etc.) faculty; (fam.) *la Faculté*, the medical faculty, doctors, my medical advisers.

fadaise [fadɛz] *s.f.* silly remark, weak joke; pointless or boring detail.

fadasse [fadas] *adj.* (fam.) insipid, sickly, dreary.

fade [fad] *adj.* insipid, tasteless; dreary, flat, stale, conventional.

fadé, -e [fade] *adj.* (pop., iron.) good of its kind.

fadement [fadmɑ̃] *adv.* drearily, in an unexciting way.

fadeur [fadœr] *s.f.* insipidity, lack of taste or flavour; dreariness, uneventfulness, dullness, staleness; dull or conventional phrase.

fading [fɑdiŋ, fɛdiŋ] *s.m.* (radio) fading.

fafiot [fafjo] *s.m.* (pop.) banknote; (pl.) money.

fagot [fago] *s.m.* faggot, bundle of sticks or firewood; *il y a ~ et ~*, people, things, are not all alike; *vin de derrière les ~s*, wine from under the counter, from one's private store, wine kept for a special occasion; *sentir le ~*, to smack of heresy.

fagotage [fagɔtaʒ] *s.m.* **1.** (obs.) muddle, botched work; **2.** get-up, manner of dressing.

fagoter [fagɔte] *v.t.* **1.** (obs.) to bundle, to faggot; **2.** to make a mess or muddle of; to dress, to get up (esp. in a ridiculous way); *être mal fagoté*, to look a fright.

fagotin [fagɔtɛ̃] *s.m.* kindling.

faiblard, -e [fɛblar] *adj.* (fam.) rather weak, a bit off colour.

faible [fɛbl] *adj.* **1.** weak, feeble, delicate, fragile, puny; enfeebled, debilitated, powerless, impotent, spineless; pusillanimous, cowardly; lethargic; easy-going, weak-willed, weak-kneed, compliant; *avoir les jambes ~s*, to feel unsteady on one's legs, weak at the knees; *le sexe ~*, the weaker sex; *être un peu ~ en math.*, to be rather weak or backward in maths; *les économiquement ~s*, the poor; *le côté, le point, la partie, ~*, the weak point; **2.** uncertain, wavering, ineffective; **3.** small, low, slight, light, dim, poor, insufficient, inadequate; *~ quantité*, small quantity; *un lac à ~ profondeur*, a shallow lake; *brise ~*, light breeze; *jour ~*, dim or poor light; *~ d'esprit*, mentally retarded, dim-witted; *~ s.m.* **1.** weak or defenceless person, weakling; weak-minded or mentally retarded person; **2.** (obs.) weak point, weakness, fault, defect; (mod.) weakness, taste (*pour*, for); **~ment** [fɛbləmɑ̃] *adv.* feebly, weakly, with difficulty; slightly; faintly, dimly.

faiblesse [fɛblɛs] *s.f.* **1.** weakness, feebleness, debility, exhaustion, collapse; *tomber en ~*, to faint, to collapse; **2.** weakness, cowardliness, indecision; **3.** weakness, defect; **4.** smallness, weakness; insufficiency, inadequacy; *~ du nombre*, smallness of number; *~ de ressources*, inadequacy of resources.

faiblir [fɛblir] *v.i.* to become weak, to weaken; to relent, to slacken, to flag; to abate, to give way, to yield.

faïence [fajɑ̃s] *s.f.* faience, earthenware, crockery.

faïencé, -e [fajɑ̃se] *adj.* given an earthenware finish or effect.
faïencerie [fajɑ̃sri] *s.f.* crockery, earthenware, pottery; manufacture of earthenware; pottery works or trade.
faïenci-er, -ère [fajɑ̃sje] *s.m.f.* manufacturer of or dealer in pottery, etc.
faignant see FEIGNANT; and = FAINÉANT.
faille [faj] *s.f.* (geol.) fault, fissure; (fig.) fault, defect.
failli, -e [faji] *s.m.f., adj.* bankrupt.
faillibilité [fajibilite] *s.f.* fallibility.
faillible [fajibl] *adj.* fallible.
faillir [fajir] *v.i.* **1.** to fail, to fall short of, to miss, to be deficient; ~ *à son devoir*, to fail in one's duty; **2.** to err, to be at fault, to be mistaken, to do wrong, to sin; **3.** to be on the point of, to have nearly; *j'ai failli l'oublier*, I nearly forgot it; *il a failli tomber*, he very nearly fell.
faillite [fajit] *s.f.* failure; bankruptcy; *faire* ~, to fail, to break; to go bankrupt, to be insolvent.
faim [fɛ̃] *s.f.* hunger, famine, starvation; (fig.) appetite, desire, thirst; *avoir* ~, to be hungry; *avoir une* ~ *de loup*, to be ravenously hungry; *mourir de* ~, to starve to death; *réduire par la* ~, to starve out; *avoir* ~ *de gloire*, to thirst for fame; *la* ~ *chasse le loup du bois*, necessity knows no laws.
faîne [fɛn] *s.f.* beech-nut.
fainéant, -e [fɛneɑ̃] *adj.* idle, sluggish, lazy; *s.m.f.* idler, sluggard, good-for-nothing, lazybones, loafer; *faire le* ~, to idle.
fainéanter [fɛneɑ̃te] *v.i.* to idle, to be lazy, to loaf.
fainéantise [fɛneɑ̃tiz] *s.f.* idleness, laziness, slothfulness, loafing.
faire [fɛr] *v.t.* **1.** to make, to build, to construct, to compose, to set up, to establish; ~ *sa fortune*, to make one's fortune; ~ *une institution*, to establish an institution; **2.** to make, to create, to produce; to defecate; ~ *des petits*, to produce young; ~ *un enfant*, to have a baby; (pop.) to father a child; *il lui a fait un enfant*, he has put her in the family way; *le bébé fait ses dents*, the baby is getting some teeth; **3.** to get, to procure; to take on supplies of; ~ *des bénéfices*, to make profits; ~ *de l'essence*, to get petrol, to fill up with petrol; **4.** to make, to form, to compose, to constitute, to be, to equal, to be equivalent to; *deux et deux font quatre*, two and two make four; ~ *un bon mari*, to make a good husband; *chose qui fait obstacle*, thing which forms an obstacle; **5.** to make, to do, to perform, to execute, to practise, to play, to operate, to deal in, to sell; ~ *un mouvement*, to make a movement; ~ *des études*, to study; ~ *le ménage*, to do the housework; ~ *ses ongles*, to do one's nails; ~ *un pas*, to take a step; ~ *la musique*, to make or play music; ~ *du tennis*, to play tennis; *faites-vous le vêtement d'enfant?*, do you sell children's wear?; *faites-vous le blé?*, do you grow wheat?; **6.** to make, to change, to transform, to do (sth. with sth.); ~ *un drame de qch.*, to make a drama out of sth.; *nous en ferons un médecin*, we are going to make a doctor out of him; ~ *de patience vertu*, to make a virtue of patience; *qu'est-ce que j'ai fait de mes lunettes?*, what have I done with my glasses?; **7.** to do, to act, to behave; to serve (as); ~ *bien*, to do well (to do sth.); *il ferait mieux de*, he would do better to; *il ne fit que rire*, he merely laughed; *faites comme chez vous*, make yourself at home; (fam.) *le* ~ *au bluff*, to bluff it out; *en* ~ *à sa tête*, to do what one pleases, to follow one's whim; *cela fera bien comme table*, this will do well as a table; **8.** *j'ai à* ~ *avec lui*, I have business to do with him; *je n'ai rien à* ~ *avec lui*, I don't want to have anything to do with him; *si fait*, yes, indeed, that is so; **9.** to affect, to alter, to matter; *qu'est-ce que cela fait?*, what difference does it make?; *cela ne fera rien à l'affaire*, it won't alter things at all; *cela ne fait rien*, it doesn't matter; **10.** to act (a part), to act as, to put on an appearance of, to seem, to look, to produce an effect of; ~ *Harpagon*, to play Harpagon, to act the part of Harpagon; ~ *le malin*, to put on a sly air; *un vieillard qui fait le jeune homme*, an old man who carries on like a young one; ~ *le brave*, to pretend to be brave; *elle fait vieux*, or *vieille*, she looks old; *appartement qui fait riche*, flat which gives an impression of wealth; **11.** to make, to cause, to occasion; ~ *du bruit*, to make a noise; ~ *des inconvénients*, to cause inconvenience; (with infin.) (i.) to make (s.o. do sth.), to cause (sth. to happen); *ça l'a fait pleurer*, it made her weep; ~ *changer qn. d'avis* to make s.o. change their mind; ~ *tomber qch.*, to cause sth. to fall, to knock sth. over; ~ *venir qn.*, to send for s.o.; (ii.) to have sth. done; ~ *réparer ses chaussures*, to have one's shoes mended; ~ *construire une maison à*, or *par*, *un architecte*, to have a house built by an architect; **12.** to have (an illness, etc.); *j'ai fait une grippe*, I have had influenza; **13.** (impers.) to be (of weather, general conditions); *il fait beau*, it is fine; *il a fait de la neige*, it has been snowing; *il fait bon chasser au bois*, it is pleasant to go hunting in the woods; **14.** (repetition of sense of previous verb) *il court mieux que je ne fais*, he runs better than I do; *il le regarda comme il l'aurait fait pour un cheval*, he looked at him as he would have done a horse; **se** ~ *v.refl.* **1.** to develop, to form, to become, to get; to grow, to mature; *cela se fait rare*, it is becoming rare; *il se fait tard*, it is getting late; *se* ~ *à*, to get used to; (fam.) *s'en* ~, to get upset, to worry; *ne t'en fais pas*, don't get worked up; *il ne s'en fait pas, celui-là*, that chap doesn't care a damn; **2.** to be made, to be done; to happen; *le pain se fait de farine*, bread is made from flour; *cela ne se fait pas*, it's not done, it's bad manners; *comment se fait-il que?*, how does it come about that?
faire [fɛr] *s.m.* doing, making, execution; make; workmanship, technique; action.
faire-part [fɛrpar] *s.m.invar.* note or card announcing birth, bereavement, etc.; invitation (to wedding, etc.).
faisable [fəzabl] *adj.* feasible, practicable, possible.
faisan, -e [fəzɑ̃] *s.m.f.* (ornith.) pheasant.
faisandé, -e [fəzɑ̃de] *adj.* (of meat) high, gamy.
faisandeau [fəzɑ̃do], **faisanneau** [fəzano], (pl. **-x**) *s.m.* young pheasant.
faisander [fəzɑ̃de] *v.t.* to hang (game, etc.).
faisanderie [fəzɑ̃dri] *s.f.* rearing of pheasants.
faisandier [fəzɑ̃dje] *s.m.* pheasant-breeder.
faisceau (pl. **-x**) [fɛso] *s.m.* bundle, bunch, fascicle; cluster, nest; beam or pencil (of light, of rays, etc.); (anat.) fasciculus; (mil.) pile of arms; (fig.) bunch, collection; (mil.) *formez les* ~*x!*, pile arms!; (astronaut.) ~ *inverse*, back beam; (phys.) ~ *herzien*, herzian wave.
faiseu-r, -se [fəzœr] *s.m.f.* **1.** maker, constructor, builder; doer, performer; ~*r de ponts*, bridge--builder; *une robe de chez le bon* ~*r*, a dress made by a first-class dressmaker; ~*r d'affaires*, company promoter, financier; ~*r de miracles*, miracle-worker; ~*r de tours*, practical joker, mountebank; ~*r d'embarras*, awkward customer, nuisance; *un grand* ~*r de mots-croisés*, a crossword addict; *une* ~*se d'anges*, an abortionist.
faisselle [fɛsɛl] *s.f.* cheese-vat.
fait, -e [fɛ] *adj.* made, done, shaped; suited, intended; grown, grown up, fully developed, ripe, matured, seasoned; fixed, settled; (fam.)

caught; *habits tout ~s*, or *le tout ~*, ready-made clothes; *aussitôt dit, aussitôt ~*, no sooner said than done; *c'est bien ~*, that is as it should be, it serves them right; *esprit bien ~*, good or intelligent man, sound intellect; *jambe bien ~e*, well shaped leg; *un homme ~*, a grown man; *un fromage ~*, a matured cheese; *prix ~*, set price, fixed price; *c'est une affaire ~e*, it's settled; *comme vous voilà ~!*, what a state you are in!, you do look a sight!; *~s comme des rats*, caught like rats in a trap; *c'en est fait de*, that is the end of, it is all up with.

fait [fɛ] *s.m.* **1.** act, action, deed, feat; (fig.) characteristic, quality, strong point; *par son ~*, by his action, through his fault; *les ~s et les gestes de qn.*, someone's actions or movements; *hauts ~s*, deeds of prowess; *~ d'armes*, feat of arms; *voie de ~*, blows, physical violence; *la générosité n'est pas son ~*, generosity is not one of his qualities, is not his strong point; *dire son ~ à qn.*, to tell s.o. a few home truths; **2.** fact, event; *un résumé des ~s*, a summary of the facts; *rapporter un ~*, to record an event; *~s divers*, news in brief, small news items; *du ~ de, du ~ que*, as a consequence of; **3.** fact (opp. fiction, falsehood), reality; *c'est un ~*, it is a fact, it is certain, it is true; *erreur de ~*, factual error, error of substance; *gouvernement de ~*, de facto government; *par le ~, de ~, en ~*, in fact, indeed, actually, in reality, in truth; *tout à ~*, completely, quite, entirely; *point de ~*, question of fact; **4.** matter, question, subject, matter in hand; essential part, crux; *aller, venir, au ~*, to come to the point, to get down to the question; *au ~!*, come to the point!, let's get down to things!; *au ~*, by the way, in this connection; *mettre qn. au ~*, to put s.o. in the picture; *être au ~ de*, to be fully informed about; *de ce ~*, consequently, it follows (that); *en ~ de*, as regards, concerning, in the matter of.

faîtage [fɛtaʒ] *s.m.* ridge (of roof); ridge-tiling, ridge-sheathing; (Lit.) roof.

faîte [fɛt] *s.m.* top, zenith, summit, ridge; (fig.) pinnacle, zenith, summit.

faîteau (pl. **-x**) [fɛto] *s.m.* finial, ornamental ridge-tile.

faîtière [fɛtjɛr] *s.f.* **1.** ridge-tile; **2.** skylight; *~ adj.* ridge, of the ridge.

fait-tout [fɛtu] *s.m.invar.*, **faitout** [fɛtu] *s.m.* stew-pan.

faix [fɛ] *s.m.* **1.** burden, load, weight, encumbrance; **2.** builder's rubbish; **3.** (med.) contents of womb.

fakir, faquir [fakir] *s.m.* fakir.

falaise [falɛz] *s.f.* cliff.

falbala [falbala] *s.m.* furbelow; (pl.) trimmings, finery.

fallacieu-x, -se [falasjø] *adj.* fallacious, deceptive, misleading; *argument ~x*, specious argument.

falloir [falwar] *v.impers.* **1.** to be wanting, to be lacking; to be required, to be necessary; to be suitable; *il lui faut un pardessus*, he needs an overcoat; *combien vous faut-il?*, how much do you require?, how much are you short of?; *il faut un prétexte*, we need some pretext; *prenez tout ce qu'il vous faut*, take all you want; *il m'a fallu dix heures pour le faire*, it took me ten hours to do it; *voilà l'homme qu'il faut*, he is the right man (for the job), he is just the man we want; *il fallait les horreurs de la guerre pour*, it needed the horrors of war to; *comme il faut*, proper(ly), suitable, well-bred, respectable, lady-like, gentlemanly; **s'en ~** *v.refl. impers.* to be lacking, wanting, short; to miss; *il s'en faut de cinq mille francs*, it is five thousand francs short; *il s'en faut d'un seul point qu'il n'ait été admissible*, he missed passing by only one mark; *il ne s'en fallut que d'un moment qu'il ne l'eût attrapé*, he only missed him by a moment, another moment and he would have caught him; *il s'en faut de beaucoup, il s'en faut bien*, far from it; *tant s'en faut*, in no way, on the contrary; *il s'en faut de peu, peu s'en faut*, very nearly, just about; *peu s'en fallut qu'il ne perdît sa place*, he very nearly lost his place; *il est perdu, ou peu s'en faut*, he is just about ruined; **2.** to be necessary, to be compulsory or obligatory, must, have to, ought, should; to be necessarily so; *il faut partir*, we must go; *il faut dire que*, one is bound to say that; *il m'a fallu y renoncer*, I have had to give it up; *il ne faut pas faire cela*, one ought not to do that; *il fallait le dire*, you should have said so, you ought to have spoken up; *il fallait voir ça*, you ought to have seen it, it was an incredible sight; *il faut que tu te sois trompé*, you must have made a mistake; *il faut qu'il soit bête*, he really must be a fool.

falot [falo] *s.m.* **1.** lantern, lamp; **2.** (mil. slang) court-martial.

falsificat-eur, -rice [falsifikatœr] *s.m.f.* falsifier, forger, debaser, adulterator.

falsification [falsifikɑsjɔ̃] *s.f.* falsification, adulteration, forging, forgery, faking, tampering; plagiarism.

falsifier [falsifje] *v.t.* to falsify, to forge, to tamper with, to adulterate; to travesty.

falun [falœ̃] *s.m.* (geol.) shell-marl; **~er** [falyne] *v.t.* (agric.) to dress with shell-marl; **~ière** [falynjɛr] *s.f.* shell-marl pit.

famé [fame] *adj. bien ~*, reputable, of good repute; *mal ~*, disreputable, shady.

famélique [famelik] *adj.* starving, famished, hungry.

fameu-x, -se [famø] *adj.* famous, renowned, celebrated, well-known, memorable, remarkable; notorious; first-rate, excellent; (iron.) famous, everlasting; *un ~x repas*, a first-rate meal; *pas ~x*, nothing very special, mediocre; *vous et vos ~x principes*, you and your precious principles; **~sement** [famøzmɑ̃] *adv.* remarkably, extremely.

familial, -e, (aux) [familjal] *adj.* of the family or home; *allocations ~es*, family allowances.

familiariser [familjarize] *v.t.* to familiarize, to accustom; **se ~** *v.refl.* **1.** to become familiar, to get on familiar terms; (of animals) to become tame; **2.** to get used, accustomed, (*avec*, to), to familiarize oneself (*avec*, with).

familiarité [familjarite] *s.f.* **1.** familiarity, intimacy, familiar terms, intimate relationship, close acquaintance; **2.** familiarity, offhanded tone, impudence; (pl.) liberties; *prendre des ~s avec qn.*, to be over-familiar, to take liberties, with s.o.

familier [familje] *s.m.* familiar friend, one of the family, intimate friend; familiar spirit.

famili-er, -ère [familje] *adj.* **1.** familiar, intimate, of the family; (of manner, etc.) easy, relaxed; (pej.) over-familiar; **2.** familiar, well--acquainted, well-known; (of expressions, etc.) colloquial; integrated, assimilated; **~èrement** [familjɛrmɑ̃] *adv.* familiarly, freely, easily.

famille [famij] *s.f.* family, relatives, parentage, kin, kindred, race, group, clan; *avoir de la ~*, to have children; *en ~*, at home; *avoir un air de ~*, to have a family likeness; *affaires de ~*, family matters, private affairs, domestic concerns; *fils de ~*, young man of good family; *nom de ~*, family name, surname; *soutien de ~*, bread-winner.

famine [famin] *s.f.* famine, hunger, starvation; scarcity, dearth; (fig.) *crier ~*, to moan about one's poverty; *salaire de ~*, wages below subsistence level, starvation wage.

fan [fan] *s.m.* fan, devotee, supporter, ardent enthusiast.

fana [fana] *adj.* (fam. abbrev. *fanatique*) fanatical, enthusiastic, keen.

fanage [fanaʒ] *s.m.* turning, tedding, (of hay).

fanal (pl. **aux**) [fanal] *s.m.* lantern, lamp, signal light, (navigation, etc.) light, beacon light.

fanatique [fanatik] *adj.* fanatical, zealous; enthusiastic, devoted, ardent, fervent, keen; ~ *de*, devoted to, keenly interested in, mad on; ~ *s.m.f.* fanatic, zealot; devotee, enthusiast, ardent admirer; **~ment** [fanatikmɑ̃] *adv.* fanatically.

fanatiser [fanatize] *v.t.* to fanaticize, to make a fanatic of.

fanatisme [fanatism] *s.m.* fanaticism.

fanchon [fɑ̃ʃɔ̃] *s.f.* kerchief, head-scarf.

fandango [fɑ̃dɑ̃go] *s.m.* fandango.

fane [fan] *s.f.* turnip-tops, carrot-tops, etc.

fané, -e [fane] *adj.* withered, wilted, faded; (of colour) pale, pastel.

faner [fane] *v.t.* **1.** to turn, to ted, (hay); to wither, to cause to fade or wilt; to tarnish, to take the colour from; ~ *v.i.* (Lit.) to fade, to wither; **se** ~ *v. refl.* to fade, to wither, to wilt.

faneu-r, -se [fanœr] *s.m.f.* haymaker; **~se** *s.f.* tedding-machine.

fanfare [fɑ̃far] *s.f.* fanfare, flourish (of trumpets, etc.); brass band, martial music; (fig.) flourish, ostentation; clamour; *réveil en* ~, rude awakening; (bookb.) *reliure à* ~, fanfare binding.

fanfaron, -ne [fɑ̃farɔ̃] *adj.* boasting, swaggering; *s.m.f.* boaster, braggart, blusterer; *faire le* ~, to swagger.

fanfaronnade [fɑ̃farɔnad] *s.f.* boasting, bragging, swaggering; boast.

fanfaronner [fɑ̃farɔne] *v.i.* (obs.) to swagger, to boast.

fanfreluche [fɑ̃frəlyʃ] *s.f.* bauble, trinket, frill.

fange [fɑ̃ʒ] *s.f.* mud, mire, dirt, filth; (fig.) foulness, filth, squalor.

fangeu-x, -se [fɑ̃ʒø] *adj.* muddy, miry, murky, filthy.

fanion [fanjɔ̃] *s.m.* small flag, fanion, emblem, colour(s) (of organization, etc.).

fanon [fanɔ̃] *s.m.* **1.** (eccles.) fanon, maniple; pendant or lappet (of mitre); **2.** (naut.) hanging fold, goose-wing (of brailed sail); **3.** dewlap (of ox), wattle (of turkey, etc.); **4.** whalebone, baleen.

fantaisie [fɑ̃tezi] *s.f.* **1.** fancy, imagination; (mus.) fantasia, selection; illusion; *se mettre dans la* ~ *que*, to fancy or imagine that, to get it into one's head that; *bijoux de* ~, fancy jewellery; *uniforme de* ~, non-regulation uniform; **2.** fancy, whim, caprice; extravagant idea; vagary, folly, madness, lunacy; *à sa* ~, as one pleases; *agir selon sa* ~, to indulge one's whims, to do as the fancy takes one; **3.** imagination, inventiveness; *plein de* ~, imaginative; *manquer de* ~, to be unimaginative, to be dull or dreary.

fantaisiste [fɑ̃tezist] *s.m.f.* whimsical or unconventional person; variety artiste; ~ *adj.* **1.** whimsical, fanciful, freakish, off-beat; **2.** fanciful, imaginary, not based on fact.

fantasia [fɑ̃tazja] *s.f.* fantasia, Arab display of horsemanship.

fantasmagorie [fɑ̃tasmagɔri] *s.f.* phantasmagoria, weird spectacle.

fantasmagorique [fɑ̃tasmagɔrik] *adj.* phantasmagoric, fantastic, weird.

fantasme [fɑ̃tasm] *s.m.* (psychol.) phantasm, hallucination.

fantasque [fɑ̃task] *adj.* fanciful, whimsical, capricious, odd, temperamental; fantastic.

fantassin [fɑ̃tasɛ̃] *s.m.* foot-soldier, infantryman.

fantastique [fɑ̃tastik] *adj.* fantastic, fanciful, unbelievable, incredible; ~ *s.m. le* ~, the fantastic, the incredible; **~ment** [fɑ̃tastikmɑ̃] *adv.* fantastically.

fantoche [fɑ̃tɔʃ] *s.m.* marionette; (fig.) unreliable person, turncoat, time-server.

fantomatique [fɑ̃tɔmatik] *adj.* spectral, ghostly, ghost-like.

fantôme [fɑ̃tom] *s.m.* phantom, ghost, spectre, apparition, vision; (fig.) ghost, pale imitation; chimera; *le train* ~, the ghost train; *un gouvernement* ~, a non-existent government.

fanton see FENTON.

faon [fɑ̃] *s.m.* (zool.) fawn.

faquin [fakɛ̃] *s.m.* rogue, low fellow.

farad [farad] *s.m.* (phys.) farad.

faramineu-x, -se [faraminø] *adj.* (fam.) fantastic.

farandole [farɑ̃dɔl] *s.f.* farandole (dance).

faraud, -e [faro] *adj.*, *s.m.f.* vain, affected, proud, (person); *faire le* ~, to boast, to pretend to be smart.

farce[1] [fars] *s.f.* (cook.) forcemeat, stuffing.

farce[2] [fars] *s.f.* farce; trick, joke, prank; joke item, novelty (as sold in shop); *faire des ~s à qn.*, to play tricks or jokes on s.o.; *~s et attrapes*, jokes and tricks; ~ *adj.* funny, comic.

farceu-r, -se [farsœr] *s.m.f.* joker, humorist; humbug, practical joker; *adj.* fond of playing tricks.

farcin [farsɛ̃] *s.m.* (vet.) farcy.

farcir [farsir] *v.t.* (cook.) to stuff; (fig.) to stuff, to cram, to fill, to lard; **se** ~ *v.refl.* (pop.) *se* ~ *de qch.*, to give or allow oneself sth.; *il faut se le* ~, we shall have to put up with him, with it.

fard [far] *s.m.* make-up, paint, rouge; (fig.) pretence, disguise, deception; (fig.) *sans* ~, straightforward, frank, natural; (fam.) *piquer un* ~, to blush.

farde [fard] *s. f.* bale (of coffee weighing 185 kg).

fardé, -e [farde] *adj.* made-up, painted, powdered.

fardeau (pl. **-x**) [fardo] *s.m.* burden, load, weight.

farder[1] [farde] *v.t.* to make up, to paint or powder (the face); (fig.) to disguise, to conceal; (comm.) to put the best items at the top of the basket; **se** ~ *v.refl.* to make (oneself) up.

farder[2] [farde] *v.i.* (obs.) to weigh heavy, to bear down; (mod.) to sink, to settle; (naut.) (of sails) to fill, to set.

fardier [fardje] *s.m.* truck, trolley.

farfadet [farfadɛ] *s.m.* hobgoblin, elf, sprite,

farfouiller [farfuje] *v.i.* to rummage, to rummage about.

fargues [farg] *s.f.pl.* (naut.) gunwales.

faribole [faribɔl] *s.f.* nonsense, idle talk.

farinacé, -e [farinase] *adj.* farinaceous.

farine [farin] *s.f.* flour, meal; (fig.) kind, sort; *fleur de* ~, fine flour; (fig.) *ce sont des gens de la même* ~, they are birds of a feather, they are two of a kind.

fariner [farine] *v.t.* to flour; ~ *v.i.* to acquire a floury appearance.

farineu-x, -se [farinø] *adj.* farinaceous, floury; covered with flour or white dust; **~x** *s.m.* cereal, farinaceous substance.

farlouse [farluz] *s.f.* (ornith.) meadow pipit, titlark.

farniente [farnjɛnte, farnjɑ̃t] *s.m.* far niente, idleness.

farouche [faruʃ] *adj.* **1.** wild, savage, fierce; grim, sullen; **2.** shy, timid, coy, unsociable; **~ment** [faruʃmɑ̃] *adv.* fiercely, savagely.

farrago [farago] *s.m.* (agric.) mixed corn (for feeding).

fart [far(t)] *s.m.* wax (for skis); **~er** [farte] *v.i.* to wax (skis).

fasce [fas] *s.f.* (herald.) fesse.

fascé, -e [fase] *adj.* (herald.) in fess.

fascicule [fasikyl] *s.m.* section, part, (of publication); folder, fascicle; annexed instructions.

fasciculé, -e [fasikyle] *adj.* (bot.) fasciculate; (arch.) fascicular.
fascié, -e [fasje] *adj.* (zool.) fasciated, banded, striped.
fascinant, -e [fasinɑ̃] *adj.* fascinating, enchanting, compelling.
fascinat-eur, -rice [fasinatœr] *adj.* = FASCINANT; *s.m.f.* charmer.
fascination [fasinɑsjɔ̃] *s.f.* fascination, charm; bewitching.
fascine [fasin] *s.f.* fascine, faggot.
fasciner[1] [fasine] *v.t.* (constr., etc.) to use fascines or brushwood.
fasciner[2] [fasine] *v.t.* to fascinate, to charm, to bewitch, to captivate, to seduce.
fascisme [fasism, faʃism] *s.m.* Fascism.
fasciste [fasist, faʃist] *adj.*, *s.m.f.* Fascist.
faséole [fazeɔl] *s.f.* = FÉVEROLE.
faséyer, faseiller [fazeje] *v.i.* (of sail) to shiver, to shake.
faste [fast] *s.m.* pomp, splendour, magnificence; display, ostentation.
faste [fast] *adj.* auspicious, favourable, lucky.
fastes [fast] *s.m.pl.* annals, records.
fastidieu-x, -se [fastidjø] *adj.* tedious, irksome, dull, boring, tiresome; **~sement** [fastidjøzmɑ̃] *adv.* tediously; ⚠ not 'fastidious'.
fastigié, -e [fastiʒje] *adj.* (bot.) fastigiate.
fastueu-x, -se [fastɥø] *adj.* magnificent, sumptuous, gorgeous, ostentatious; **~sement** [fastɥøzmɑ̃] *adv.* sumptuously.
fat [fa(t)] *adj.* conceited, affected, foppish, ridiculous; ~ *s.m.* fop, conceited ass.
fatal, -e, (**als**) [fatal] *adj.* **1.** fatal, deadly, mortal, disastrous, dire; **2.** fated, destined, inevitable, inescapable, irresistible; *c'est* ~, it is fated to be, it is bound to happen, there's no escaping it; *femme* ~*e*, siren; **~ement** [fatalmɑ̃] *adv.* inevitably, necessarily.
fatal-isme [fatalism] *s.m.* fatalism; **~iste** [fatalist] *s.m.f.* fatalist; *adj.* fatalistic.
fatalité [fatalite] *s.f.* **1.** fate, destiny, fatality, fatefulness; inevitability, necessity; **2.** mischance, misadventure; ⚠ not 'fatality' in sense 'fatal accident'.
fatidique [fatidik] *adj.* prophetic; fateful.
fatigant, -e [fatigɑ̃] *adj.* fatiguing, tiring; tiresome, wearisome, irksome.
fatigue [fatig] *s.f.* fatigue, tiredness, weariness, lassitude, weakness; hardship, strain(s), stress; (techn.) fatigue; *mort, brisé, recru, de* ~, dog-tired, dead beat.
fatigué, -e [fatige] *adj.* **1.** tired, fatigued; weary, fed up; exhausted, worn out; out of order; (fam.) off one's head; **2.** worn-out, shabby, showing signs of wear.
fatiguer [fatige] *v.t.* to tire, to weary, to wear out, to exhaust; to overstrain; to fatigue, to worry, to exasperate, to pester, to importune; to toss or mix (salad); (agric.) to work (the land); ~ *v.i.* to tire oneself, to labour, to be under strain or stress; **se** ~ *v.refl.* to tire oneself, to wear oneself out; to become tired; to make vain efforts; *ne vous fatiguez pas à mentir*, no need to make up any stories, it's pointless to lie; *se* ~ *de*, to be or to get tired of, to be weary of, to have had enough of.
fatras [fatra] *s.m.* lumber, rubbish; (fig.) jumble, medley, hotchpotch, confused mass.
fatuité [fatɥite] *s.f.* conceit, self-complacency, pretensions.
fauber(**t**) [fobɛr] *s.m.* (naut.) mop, swab.
faubourg [fobur] *s.m.* suburb, outskirts; working-class quarter.
faubourien, -ne [foburjɛ̃] *adj.* suburban; working-class; *s.m.f.* inhabitant of suburb or working-class quarter.
faucard [fokar] *s.m.* river-scythe.
faucarder [fokarde] *v.t.* to clean out weeds (from pond, etc.).
fauchage [foʃaʒ] *s.m.* mowing; (mil.) sweeping fire.
fauchaison [foʃɛzɔ̃] *s.f.* mowing, reaping; mowing time.
fauche [foʃ] *s.f.* **1.** (obs.) = FAUCHAISON; **2.** (fam.) being broke; stolen goods.
fauché, -e [foʃe] *adj.* **1.** mown; **2.** (fam.) broke.
faucher [foʃe] *v.t.* **1.** to mow, to cut, to reap, to scythe, to mow or cut down; **2.** (fam.) to steal, to pinch; ~ *v.i.* (mil.) to sweep (ground with fire); (of horse) to swing leg out sideways.
fauchet [foʃɛ] *s.m.* hay-rake.
faucheu-r, -se [foʃœr] *s.m.f.* mower, reaper, haymaker; **~se** *s.f.* mowing-machine, reaper; (Lit., fig.) *la* ~*se*, Death.
faucheur [foʃœr], **faucheux** [foʃø] *s.m.* (ent.) crane-fly, daddy-long-legs.
faucille [fosij] *s.f.* sickle, reaping-hook.
faucon [fokɔ̃] *s.m.* falcon, hawk; *chasser au* ~, to hawk.
fauconneau (pl. **-x**) [fokɔno] *s.m.* eyas, young hawk; (anc. artill.) falconet.
fauconnerie [fokɔnri] *s.f.* falconry, hawking; falcon-house, hawk-house.
fauconnier [fokɔnje] *s.m.* falconer, hawker.
faufil [fofil] *s.m.* tacking or basting thread; **~age** [fofilaʒ] (dressm.) tacking, basting; **~er** [fofile] *v.t.* (dressm.) to tack, to baste; (fig.) to slip (sth.) in; **se ~er** *v.refl.* to slip in or through, to creep, to edge, to twist; to insinuate oneself; **~ure** [fofilyr] *s.f.* **1.** = FAUFILAGE; **2.** sewing with large stitches.
faune[1] [fon] *s.m.* (myth.) faun.
faune[2] [fon] *s.f.* fauna.
faunesque [fonɛsk] *adj.* faun-like.
faunesse [fonɛs] *s.f.* (myth.) female faun.
faussaire [fosɛr] *s.m.f.* forger, counterfeiter.
faussement [fosmɑ̃] *adv.* falsely, untruly, erroneously, wrongfully.
fausser [fose] *v.t.* **1.** to falsify, to pervert, to alter, to distort, to get wrong; to put out of true, to bend, to warp; to force, to strain; *une roue faussée*, a wheel out of true; ~ *une serrure*, to force a lock; **2.** to lack, to fail to keep, to abandon; ~ *politesse à qn.*, to be lacking in politeness towards s.o.; ~ *parole à qn.*, to break one's word to s.o.; ~ *compagnie à qn.*, to part company with s.o.; **se** ~ *v.refl.* (of voice) to break, to crack, to tremble.
fausset[1] [fosɛ] *s.m.* falsetto, head voice.
fausset[2] [fosɛ] *s.m.* spigot, tap.
fausseté [foste] *s.f.* falsity, falseness; falsehood, lie.
faute [fot] *s.f.* **1.** lack, need, want, scarcity, dearth; *faire* ~, to be lacking, to be short; *se faire* ~ *de*, to refrain from; *ne pas se faire* ~ *de*, not to fail to, not to hesitate to; ~ *de*, for want of, for lack of; ~ *de mieux*, for want of something better; ~ *d'avoir*, without having; *sans* ~, without fail; **2.** fault, offence, crime, transgression, misdeed, misdemeanour, wrongful conduct; *punition d'une* ~, punishment for a crime; ~ *civile*, civil offence; **3.** fault, error, mistake; *c'est ma* ~, it is my fault, I am to blame; ~ *d'inattention*, slip, careless mistake; ~ *d'impression*, misprint; *c'est par la* ~ *de son mari*, it is all her husband's fault, it's all because of her husband.
fauter [fote] *v.i.* (fam.) (of woman) to get into trouble.
fauteuil [fotœj] *s.m.* arm-chair, easy chair; (Academician's or chairman's) chair; ~ *roulant*, wheel-chair; (fam., fig.) *arriver dans un* ~, to win at a canter.
faut-eur, -rice [fotœr] *s.m.f.* favourer, supporter, abetter; fomenter.

fauti-f, -ve [fotif] *adj.* **1.** at fault, faulty, erroneous, incorrect, containing errors; **2.** guilty, at fault, in the wrong; **~vement** [fotivmɑ̃] *adv.* incorrectly, wrongly, erroneously.
fauve [fov] *adj.* **1.** fawn(-coloured), fallow, tawny, buff; (of smell) musky; **2.** wild, savage; ~ *s.m.* fawn colour; wild beast; *les Fauves*, name given to school of Fr. painters about 1900.
fauvette [fovɛt] *s.f.* (ornith.) warbler; ~ *riveraine*, reed-warbler; ~ *à tête noire*, blackcap warbler.
fau-x, -sse [fo] *adj.* **1.** false, untrue, wrong, incorrect; *~x rapport*, false report; *faire ~sse route*, to take the wrong road, to go astray; *~x pas*, false step, blunder; *idées ~sses*, wrong ideas; **~x** *adv.* wrong; *chanter ~*, to sing out of tune; *sonner ~*, to ring false; *à ~x*, wrongly, incorrectly, out of true; not well-founded; *porter à ~x*, to be out of plumb, to be incorrectly positioned, (fig.) to be unsoundly based, to be wide of the mark.
faux[1] [fo] *s.m.* (the) false, falsehood, untruth; forging, imitation; (law) *s'inscrire en ~ contre qch.*, to indict sth. as false, to deny sth., to dispute the validity of sth.
faux[2] [fo] *s.f.* scythe; (anat.) falx.
faux-filet [fofilɛ] *s.m.* sirloin; **~-fuyant** [fofɥijɑ̃] *s.m.* (obs.) by-way, forest path; (mod.) evasion, subterfuge, pretence, pretext, excuse; **~-monnayeur** [fomɔnɛjœr] *s.m.* coiner, counterfeiter.
faverole see FÉVEROLE.
faveur [favœr] *s.f.* **1.** favour, kindness, special treatment, indulgence; *faites-moi la ~ de*, be so kind as to; *traitement de ~*, favourable or favoured treatment; *billet de ~*, complimentary ticket; **2.** favour, approval, support; reason, grounds; advantage; *il doit cela à la ~ du ministre*, he owes it to ministerial favour; *en ~ de*, for, in favour of; in view of, by reason of; *parler en ~ de qch.*, to speak for, in favour of, sth.; *en ~ de sa belle conduite*, in view of his good record; *une décision en ma ~*, a decision in my favour; *à la ~ de*, by means of, with the help of, thanks to; **3.** favour, fashion, vogue, popularity; *être en ~*, to be in favour, to be fashionable, to be in vogue; **4.** favour, ribbon.
favorable [favɔrabl] *adj.* favourable, propitious; favourably inclined, sympathetic; **~ment** [favɔrabləmɑ̃] *adv.* favourably.
favori, -te [favɔri] *adj.*, *s.m.f.* favourite; **~s** *s.m.pl.* (side-)whiskers.
favoriser [favɔrize] *v.t.* to favour, to encourage, to promote, to facilitate.
favoritisme [favɔritism] *s.m.* favouritism.
fayot [fajo] *s.m.* haricot bean; (mil. slang) (pej.) re-engaged N.C.O.; keen soldier.
féal, -e, (**aux**) [feal] *adj.* trusty, faithful; ~ *s.m.* trusty friend.
fébrifuge [febrifyʒ] *adj.*, *s.m.* febrifuge.
fébrile [febril] *adj.* febrile, (lit. & fig.) feverish; **~ment** [febrilmɑ̃] *adv.* feverishly.
fécal, -e, (**aux**) [fekal] *adj.* faecal.
fèces [fɛs] *s.f.pl.* (chem.) sediment, precipitate; (physiol.) faeces, excrement, excreta.
fécond, -e [fekɔ̃] *adj.* fecund, prolific, fertile, fruitful, rich; life-giving.
fécondant, -e [fekɔ̃dɑ̃] *adj.* fecundating, fertilizing; life-giving.
fécond-ation [fekɔ̃dɑsjɔ̃] *s.f.* fecundation, fertilization, impregnation; **~er** [fekɔ̃de] *v.t.* to fecundate, to fertilize, to impregnate, to make fertile; **~ité** [fekɔ̃dite] *s.f.* fecundity, fruitfulness, fertility, fertileness; abundance.
fécule [fekyl] *s.f.* fecula, starch.
féculence [fekylɑ̃s] *s.f.* feculence, starchiness; turbidity.
féculent, -e [fekylɑ̃] *adj.* feculent, starchy, containing starch; turbid; ~ *s.m.* starchy substance.
féculer [fekyle] *v.t.* to extract starch from.
féculerie [fekylri] *s.f.* starch manufacture; starch works.
fédéral, -e, (**aux**) [federal] *adj.* federal.
fédéral-iser [federalize] *v.t.* to federalize; **~isme** [federalism] *s.m.* federalism; **~iste** [federalist] *adj.*, *s.m.f.* federalist.
fédérati-f, -ve [federatif] *adj.* federative, federal.
fédération [federɑsjɔ̃] *s.f.* federation, confederation, association, league; ~ *ouvrière*, trade union.
fédéré, -e [federe] *adj.*, (pol.) federate; ~ *s.m.* (Fr. hist.) Federate (of 1792, 1815, and esp. 1871).
fédérer [federe] *v.t.* to federate; **se ~** *v.refl.* to federate.
fée [fe] *s.f.* fairy; *conte de ~s*, fairy-tale, fairy story, tale of enchantment; *travail de ~*, delicate piece of work; *avoir des doigts de ~*, to have deft fingers; ~ *adj.invar.* fairy-tale, enchanted.
feed-back [fidbak] *s.m.* (techn.) feedback.
feeder [fidœr] *s.m.* (techn.) feed-pipe, supply pipe.
féerie [fe(e)ri] *s.f.* **1.** (obs.) faerie, world of fairies; **2.** fairy-land, enchantment; **3.** magic or dazzling spectacle; (theatr.) fairy-play, pantomime with fairies, etc.
féerique [fe(e)rik] *adj.* fairy, fairy-tale, fairy-like, enchanting.
feignant, -e, faignant, -e [fɛɲɑ̃] *adj.* (pop.) lazybones, loafer, idler, good-for-nothing.
feindre [fɛ̃dr] *v.t.i.* to feign, to sham, to pretend, to simulate; to dissemble; (obs.) to make up, to imagine; ~ *de*, to pretend to, to make a pretence of; ~ *d'être malade*, to feign illness.
feint, -e [fɛ̃] *adj.* feigned, false, sham, simulated, dummy.
feinte [fɛ̃t] *s.f.* feint, sham, dissimulation, pretence, artifice, make-believe; (obs.) fiction, figment.
feinter [fɛ̃te] *v.i.* (sport) to feint, to make a feint; ~ *v.t.* to make a feint against (s.o.), to dodge, to trick.
feintise [fɛ̃tiz] *s.f.* (obs.) feinting, dodging.
feld-maréchal (pl. **aux**) [fɛldmareʃal] *s.m.* Field Marshal.
feldspath [fɛldspat] *s.m.* (min.) fel(d)spar; **~ique** [fɛldspatik] *adj.* feldspathic.
fêlé, -e [fele] *adj.* cracked; (fig.) cracked, crazy.
fêler [fele] *v.t.* to crack.
félibre [felibr] *s.m.* writer employing the *langue d'oc*.
félibrige [felibriʒ] *s.m.* association of *félibres*.
félicitation [felisitɑsjɔ̃] *s.f.* (usu. pl.) congratulations, felicitations, compliments, praise.
félicité [felisite] *s.f.* felicity, bliss, happiness, joy.
féliciter [felisite] *v.t.* to congratulate, to compliment, to praise; **se ~** *v.refl.* to congratulate oneself, to rejoice, to be pleased or satisfied.
félidés [felide] *s.m.pl.* (zool.) Felidae.
félin, -e [felɛ̃] *adj.*, *s.m.* feline.
fellah [fela, fɛlla] *s.m.* fellah.
félon, -ne [felɔ̃] *adj.* (feud.) felon, felonious; *s.m.f.* felon.
félonie [felɔni] *s.f.* felony, treason.
felouque [f(ə)luk] *s.f.* (naut.) felucca.
fêlure [felyr] *s.f.* crack; (fig.) rift.
femelle [fəmɛl] *s.f.* (zool.) female; (pop., pej.) woman, female; ~ *adj.* (zool., techn.) female.
féminin, -e [feminɛ̃] *adj.* feminine, female, womanish; ~ *s.m.* (gram.) feminine (gender).
fémin-iser [feminize] *v.t.* to feminize, to give a feminine character or appearance to; (biol.) to induce female characteristics in; (gram.) to put in the feminine gender; **~isme** [feminism]

s.m. feminism; ~**iste** [feminist] *adj.*, *s.m.f.* feminist; ~**ité** [feminite] *s.f.* feminineness, femininity, femineity.

femme [fam] *s.f.* **1.** woman (opp. man or girl), female; woman or women (in general); (obs.) *bonne* ~, simple soul, countrywoman; *jeune* ~, young (married) woman; *une maîtresse* ~, a strong-minded, energetic woman; ~ *publique*, prostitute; ~ *de chambre*, lady's maid, chamber--maid; ~ *de charge*, housekeeper; ~ *de ménage*, charwoman, domestic help; (adj.) *elle est très* ~, she is very feminine, very much a woman; *elle se fait* ~, she is growing up into a woman; *une* ~ *auteur*, a female author, authoress; **2.** wife; *prendre* ~, to take a wife, to get married; *prendre pour* ~, to marry, to take as one's wife.

femmelette [famlɛt] *s.f.* **1.** weak, timid woman; **2.** (of man) weakling.

fémoral, -e, (**aux**) [femɔral] *adj.* (anat.) femoral.

fémur [femyr] *s.m.* (anat.) femur.

fenaison [fənɛzɔ̃] *s.f.* haymaking, hay-harvest.

fendage [fɑ̃daʒ] *s.m.* splitting, cleaving.

fendant [fɑ̃dɑ̃] *s.m.* **1.** (obs.) (fenc.) cut; **2.** *faire le* ~, to swagger, to show off, to bluster.

fendeur [fɑ̃dœr] *s.m.* splitter, cleaver.

fendillement [fɑ̃dijmɑ̃] *s.m.* (surface) cracking, crackling, crazing.

fendiller [fɑ̃dije] *v.t.* to crack, to split; **se** ~ *v.refl.* to crack, to chap.

fendoir [fɑ̃dwar] *s.m.* cleaver, chopper.

fendre [fɑ̃dr] *v.t.* to split, to cleave, to slit, to rend, to rip up, to sliver; (fig.) to rend; *cela fend le cœur*, it's heart-rending; ~ *la foule*, to force or elbow a way through the crowd; **se** ~ *v.refl.* **1.** to split, to crack, to be rent asunder; to chap; **2.** (fenc.) to lunge; **3.** (fam.) to pay (money), to fork out.

fenestration [f(ə)nɛstrɑsjɔ̃] *s.f.* window--opening.

fenêtrage [f(ə)nɛtraʒ] *s.m.* (arch.) windows; fenestration.

fenêtre [f(ə)nɛtr] *s.f.* window, casement; opening, aperture, cut-away portion; window (in envelope); blank space (to be filled in on document); (anat.) fenestra (of tympanum); ~ *à guillotine*, sash-window; ~ *en saillie*, bow or bay window; ~ *en ogive*, lancet window; *jeter l'argent par les* ~*s*, to throw one's money away.

fenêtrer [f(ə)netre] *v.t.* to put windows in, to cut openings in.

fenil [fəni(l)] *s.m.* hay-loft.

fenouil [fənuj] *s.m.* (bot.) fennel.

fente [fɑ̃t] *s.f.* **1.** split, crack, slit, chink, cleft, fissure, slot, gap, cranny, crevice, interstice; rip; vent (in jacket); **2.** (fenc.) lunge.

fenton, fanton [fɑ̃tɔ̃] *s.m.* iron cramp, iron tie.

féodal, -e, (**aux**) [feɔdal] *adj.* feudal; ~ *s.m.* feudal lord.

féodalisme [feɔdalism] *s.m.* feudal character.

féodalité [feɔdalite] *s.f.* feudality, feudalism, feudal system; (fig.) (econ., fin.) empire.

fer [fɛr] *s.m.* **1.** (min., chem.) iron; ~ *de fonte*, cast iron; ~ *forgé*, wrought iron; ~ *en plaques*, boiler-plate; *fil de* ~, wire; *chemin de* ~, railway; *de* ~, iron, of iron; (fig.) cast-iron, of steel, inflexible; *une main de* ~, a mailed fist; *une santé de* ~, a cast-iron constitution; **2.** iron (or steel) portion of sth.; tip, point, blade, cutting edge; ~ *de gaffe*, boat-hook; ~ *de flèche*, arrowhead; ~ *de lance*, lance-head, (lit. & fig.) spearhead; *en* ~ *de lance*, lancet-headed, pointed; (bot.) lanceolate; **3.** object made of iron (esp. tools, etc.); sword; (pl.) (obstetric) forceps; ~ *à T*, T-iron; ~ (*à repasser*), iron, smoothing-iron; ~ *à friser*, curling-tongs; ~ (*à cheval*), horseshoe; ~ *à marquer*, branding-iron; ~*s de relieur*, book-binder's tools; *croiser le* ~ *avec qn.*, to cross swords with s.o.; *tomber les quatre* ~*s en l'air*, (of horse) to fall on its back; (of person) to go sprawling; **4.** (pl.) irons; (lit. & fig.) chains, bonds, fetters; *mettre un prisonnier aux* ~*s*, to put a prisoner in irons or chains; (fig.) *être dans les* ~*s*, to be in bondage.

fer-blanc [fɛrblɑ̃] *s.m.* tin, tin-plate.

ferblanterie [fɛrblɑ̃tri] *s.f.* tinware, tin trade.

ferblantier [fɛrblɑ̃tje] *s.m.* tinsmith, tinman, tinker.

férial, -e, (**aux**) [ferjal] *adj.* ferial.

férie [feri] *s.f.* (Rom. ant.) feria, holiday; (eccles.) weekday.

férié, -e [ferje] *adj. jour* ~, holiday, public holiday, bank holiday; (eccles.) holy day, feast-day.

férir [ferir] *v.t.* to strike, to smite; *sans coup* ~, without striking a blow, without encountering resistance; (see also FÉRU).

ferler [fɛrle] *v.t.* to furl (a sail).

fermage [fɛrmaʒ] *s.m.* tenant-farming; farm--rent.

fermail (pl. **aux**) [fɛrmaj] *s.m.* clasp.

fermant, -e [fɛrmɑ̃] *adj.* closing; that can be closed or locked; *à jour* ~, at the close of day; *arriver à portes* ~*es*, to arrive as the gates are closing.

ferme [fɛrm] *adj.* firm, solid, steady, fast, fixed; resolute, steadfast, constant; ~ *de pied*, unflinchingly, resolutely; *achat* ~, firm offer to buy; *terre* ~, terra firma, land, shore, continent; ~ *adv.* fast, firmly, stoutly; *tenir* ~, to stand or hold fast, not to give way; to hold one's own.

ferme[1] [fɛrm] *s.f.* **1.** farm-lease; *prendre à* ~, to rent, to take a lease of, (farmland); *donner à* ~, to rent out (land); to farm out (right to collect fees, etc.); **2.** (Fr. hist.) farming (of taxes), tax-farming; **3.** farm, farmhouse.

ferme[2] [fɛrm] *s.f.* (arch.) roof-timbers; (theatr.) set piece.

fermement [fɛrməmɑ̃] *adv.* firmly, steadily, steadfastly; *croire* ~ *qch.*, to be firmly convinced of sth.

ferment [fɛrmɑ̃] *s.m.* ferment, leaven; enzyme, catalyst; (fig.) one who stirs up (hatred, etc.); ~**ation** [fɛrmɑ̃tɑsjɔ̃] *s.f.* fermentation; (fig.) ferment, unrest; ~**er** [fɛrmɑ̃te] *v.i.* to ferment, to work, to rise; (fig.) to be in turmoil, to seethe.

fermer [fɛrme] *v.t.* **1.** to close, to shut up; (pop.) to shut (s.o.) up; to lock; to clench (fist); ~ *les yeux*, to close one's eyes; ~ *la main*, to close or clench one's hand; ~ *la bouche*, to shut one's mouth, to shut up; ~ *à clef*, to lock; ~ *au verrou*, to bolt; **2.** to close, to turn off, to shut or switch off (taps, gas, etc.); (electr.) to close (a circuit); to obstruct, to bar, to enclose; ~ *l'électricité*, to switch off the electricity; ~ *un chemin*, to close a road; *un chemin fermé par un arbre abattu*, a road obstructed by a fallen tree; *un champ fermé par des haies*, a field enclosed by hedges; **3.** to close, to bring to an end, to round off; ~ *la discussion*, to close the debate; ~ *la marche*, to bring up the rear; ~ *v.i.* to close, to shut; *on ferme le lundi*, we close on Mondays; **se** ~ *v.refl.* to close, to shut; to be closed; (of dress) to fasten, to do up.

fermeté [fɛrməte] *s.f.* firmness, solidity, hardness; steadfastness, steadiness, stability; soundness; ~ *d'âme*, fortitude; ~ *de caractère*, strength of character.

fermette [fɛrmɛt] *s.f.* small farm or country property.

fermeture [fɛrmətyr] *s.f.* shutting, closing; close, end; fastening, shutter, stopper.

fermi-er, -ère [fɛrmje] *s.m.f.* farmer, farmer's wife; tenant farmer; *beurre* ~*er*, farmhouse butter.

fermoir [fɛrmwar] *s.m.* clasp, snap, hook, closure.
féroce [ferɔs] *adj.* ferocious, fierce, savage, wild, cruel; *appétit* ~, ravenous appetite; **~ment** [ferɔsmɑ̃] *adv.* ferociously, savagely.
férocité [ferɔsite] *s.f.* ferocity, ferociousness, savageness, savagery, cruelty.
Féroé [ferɔe] *les îles* ~, the Faroe Islands, the Faroes.
ferrage [fɛraʒ] *s.m.* **1.** shoeing (of horse); tiring, rimming, (of wheel); **2.** door-fittings.
ferraillage [fɛrɑjaʒ] *s.m.* (constr.) steelwork (for reinforced concrete).
ferraille [fɛrɑj] *s.f.* scrap-iron, old iron; piece of scrap-iron; (fig.) scrap; small change; (*tas de*) ~, scrap-heap; *bruit de* ~, clanking noise.
ferraillement [fɛrɑjmɑ̃] *s.m.* **1.** clashing of swords, fighting with swords; **2.** clanking, rattling.
ferrailler [fɛrɑje] *v.i.* **1.** to clash swords; **2.** to clank, to rattle.
ferrailleur [fɛrɑjœr] *s.m.* **1.** (pej.) swashbuckler; **2.** scrap-iron dealer.
ferrate [fɛrat] *s.m.* (chem.) ferrate.
ferré, -e [fɛre] *adj.* bound or tipped with iron; (of horse) shod; (of boots, etc.) hobnailed; (fig.) knowledgeable, well up, strong, (in sth.); *chemin* ~, metalled road; *voie ~e*, railway, permanent way; *il n'est pas très ~ en géographie*, he is not very well up in geography, geography is not his strong point.
ferrement [fɛrmɑ̃] *s.m.* **1.** shoeing (of horse); putting (of convict) in irons; **2.** metal fittings.
ferrer [fɛre] *v.t.* to bind or fit with iron; to shoe (horse); to tip (a stick, etc.); to tag (a lace); to hobnail (boots, etc.); ~ *un poisson*, to strike a fish.
ferret [fɛrɛ] *s.m.* **1.** tag, tab; **2.** (min.) ~ *d'Espagne*, haematite; ⚠ not 'ferret'.
ferreur [fɛrœr] *s.m.* farrier, shoeing-smith, coach-smith.
ferreux [fɛrø] *adj.m.* (chem.) ferrous.
ferricyanure [fɛrisjanyr] *s.m.* (chem.) ferricyanide.
ferrique [fɛrik] *adj.* (chem.) ferric.
ferrite [fɛrit] *s.f.* (chem.) ferrite.
ferrocyanure [fɛrɔsjanyr] *s.m.* (chem.) ferrocyanide.
ferronnerie [fɛrɔnri] *s.f.* iron foundry; ironwork; steelwork (of building).
ferronnier [fɛrɔnje] *s.m.* iron-founder, iron-worker, blacksmith.
ferronnière [fɛrɔnjɛr] *s.f.* ferron(n)ière (ornament).
ferrotypie [fɛrɔtipi] *s.f.* (photo.) ferrotype.
ferroviaire [fɛrɔvjɛr] *adj.* railway, rail.
ferrugineu-x, -se [fɛryʒinø] *adj.* ferruginous, chalybeate.
ferrure [fɛryr] *s.f.* **1.** shoeing, shoes, (of horse); **2.** metal fittings.
ferry-boat [fɛrebot] *s.m.* ferry, ferry-boat (esp. for cars, trains).
fertile [fɛrtil] *adj.* fertile, productive, fruitful, prolific.
fertilisation [fɛrtilizɑsjɔ̃] *s.f.* fertilization.
fertiliser [fɛrtilize] *v.t.* to fertilize.
fertilité [fɛrtilite] *s.f.* fertility, fruitfulness, richness; (fig.) abundance, resourcefulness.
féru, -e [fery] *adj.* (*p.p.* of *férir*) struck, smitten, taken, infatuated, (*de*, with); ~ *d'amour*, enamoured.
férule [feryl] *s.f.* **1.** (bot.) ferula, giant fennel; **2.** (in school) cane, ruler (as used for punishment); (fig.) authority, domination, sway; *être sous la ~ de qn.*, to be under someone's thumb or authority.
fervemment [fɛrvamɑ̃] *adv.* fervently.
fervent, -e [fɛrvɑ̃] *adj.* fervent, ardent, earnest.
ferveur [fɛrvœr] *s.f.* fervour, fervency, devotion, earnestness.
fesse [fɛs] *s.f.* buttock; (pl.) buttocks, bottom; (pop.) women, sex; (fam.) *donner sur les ~s à un enfant*, to give a child a spanking; *botter les ~s de qn.*, to kick s.o. up the backside; *poser ses ~s*, to sit down; *montrer ses ~s*, to appear semi-nude (in a show); (fig.) *serrer les ~s*, *avoir chaud aux ~s*, to be scared; (pop.) *histoire de ~s*, a spot of sex.
fessée [fese] *s.f.* spanking, smacking (on the bottom).
fesse-mathieu [fɛsmatjø] *s.m.* (pl. *fesse-mathieux*) (obs.) moneylender; miser, skinflint.
fesser [fese] *v.t.* to spank, to smack (on the bottom).
fessi-er, -ère [fesje] *adj.* (anat.) gluteal; **~er** *s.m.* (anat.) gluteal muscle; (fam.) bottom, bum.
fessu, -e [fesy] *adj.* having a big bottom.
festin [fɛstɛ̃] *s.m.* feast, banquet, rich repast.
festival [fɛstival] *s.m.* festival; (fig.) feast, treat.
festivité [fɛstivite] *s.f.* (usu. pl.) festivities, junketings.
feston [fɛstɔ̃] *s.m.* festoon, garland; (arch.) festoon; (needlew.) scallop; *faire des ~s*, to scallop; *point de* ~, button-hole stitch.
festonner [fɛstɔne] *v.t.* to festoon, to garland; (needlew.) to scallop.
festoyer [fɛstwaje] *v.t.i.* to feast, to entertain, to make good cheer.
fêtard [fɛtar] *s.m.* (fam.) party-goer, one who is always for having a good time.
fête [fɛt] *s.f.* **1.** feast, festival, (saint's, etc.) day; holiday; anniversary, birthday; (eccles.) *~s mobiles*, movable feasts; *la ~ des Morts*, All Souls Day; *dimanches et ~s*, Sundays and holidays; *la ~ Nationale*, the National Holiday (14 July); *~ des Mères*, Mothers' Day; *souhaiter à qn. sa* ~, to wish s.o. a happy birthday, or name-day; **2.** festivity, celebration, rejoicing, treat; ~ *de la moisson*, harvest festival; ~ *de famille*, family celebration; *faire la* ~, to revel, to give oneself over to pleasure; *faire ~ à qn.*, to give s.o. a great welcome; *se faire une ~ de qch.*, to look forward to sth.; *en* ~, in festive or holiday mood; *être à la* ~, to be in the seventh heaven, to be enjoying oneself hugely; *ne pas être à la* ~, to be out of it, to be out in the cold; *ce n'est pas tous les jours* ~, you can't have fun all the time; **3.** entertainment, fête, party.
Fête-Dieu [fɛtdjø] *s.f.* (pl. *Fêtes-Dieu*) (eccles.) Corpus Christi.
fêter [fete] *v.t.* **1.** to keep as a holiday, to observe, to celebrate; **2.** to welcome, to entertain, to treat, to feast, to make much of.
fétiche [fetiʃ] *s.m.* (lit. & fig.) fetish.
fétichisme [fetiʃism] *s.m.* fetishism; (fig.) adulation.
fétichiste [fetiʃist] *s.m.f.* fetishist; ~ *adj.* fetishist(ic).
fétide [fetid] *adj.* fetid, stinking, putrid, offensive, foul, disgusting.
fétidité [fetidite] *s.f.* fetidness.
fétu [fety] *s.m.* piece or wisp of straw, straw.
fétuque [fetyk] *s.f.* (bot.) fescue-grass.
feu (pl. **-x**) [fø] *s.m.* **1.** fire, flame, combustion, burning, firing; heat, inflammation; hearth, home; light (for lighting cigarettes, etc.); (fig.) heat, ardour, passion, flame; (fig., fam.) rush-hour, very busy time; *allumer, faire, du* ~ or *un* ~, to light or make a fire; *faire* ~, to strike sparks; *faire ~ de tout bois*, to put everything to good use; *faire du ~ de* or *avec qch.*, to burn sth.; *mettre le ~ à*, to set fire to; *au ~!*, fire!; *le ~ est à la maison*, the house is on fire; *en* ~, burning, alight, on fire, in flames; *cuire à grand, à petit,* ~, to cook on a high, on a low, flame; *premier* ~, first firing (of pot, etc.); *coup de* ~, browning (under grill, etc.); *coin du* ~, fireside, chimney-

-corner; *avez-vous du ~?*, have you a light?; **2.** fire (from firearms); (pop.) revolver, pistol; action (in battle); *arme à ~*, firearm; *coup de ~*, shot; *recevoir un coup de ~*, to be shot; *recevoir des coups de ~*, to be shot at; *puissance de ~*, fire-power; *faire ~*, to fire; *faire ~ sur*, to fire at or on; *faire long ~*, (lit. & fig.) to hang fire, to misfire; *~ roulant*, running fire; *aller au ~*, to go into action, to come under fire; *~ d'artifice*, firework; **3.** light, signal light, traffic light, light from lighthouse; (theatr.) *~x de la rampe*, footlights; *~x de position*, (naut.) riding-lights; (car) side-lights; *~x de route*, (naut.) navigation lights; (car) headlights; *~ rouge*, traffic light, red light; (fig.) *donner le ~ vert à*, to give the green light, the go-ahead, to; *~ à éclipse*, occulting light (from lighthouse).

feu, -e [fø] *adj.* (invar. before art. or poss.) late, deceased; *~ ma tante, ma ~e tante*, my late aunt.

feudataire [fødatɛr] *s.m.f.* feudatory, vassal.

feuillage [fœjaʒ] *s.m.* foliage, leaves.

feuillaison [fœjɛzɔ̃] *s.f.* foliation.

feuillard [fœjar] *s.m.* **1.** hoop-wood; **2.** hoop-iron.

feuille [fœj] *s.f.* **1.** leaf; (Lit.) petal; *trembler comme une ~*, to tremble like an aspen leaf; **2.** sheet (of paper), thin sheet (of cardboard, metal, wood, etc.), foil; leaf or page (of book); newspaper, journal, periodical; leaflet, folder, chart, document, voucher; *~ volante*, loose leaf; (fig.) *lire sous les ~s*, to read between the lines; *~s de carton*, cardboard sheets; *~ de paye*, pay-slip; *~ de température*, temperature chart; *~ de présence*, attendance register, time-sheet; *~ d'impôt*, tax form; *~ de chou*, (of newspaper) rag; (pop.) ear; (pop.) *dur de la ~*, hard of hearing.

feuillé, -e [fœje] *adj.* in leaf.

feuillée [fœje] *s.f.* **1.** foliage; bower, arbour; *sous la ~*, under the greenwood tree; **2.** (mil.) *les ~s*, the latrines.

feuille-morte [fœjmɔrt] *adj.invar.* of colour of dead leaves, russet.

feuiller [fœje] *v.i.* to put forth leaves; *~ v.t.* (carp.) to rabbet, to groove.

feuilleret [fœjrɛ] *s.m.* (carp.) rabbet-plane, grooving-plane.

feuillet [fœjɛ] *s.m.* **1.** leaf (of book); thin sheet of wood; **2.** third stomach of ruminant; **3.** (biol.) parablast.

feuilletage [fœjtaʒ] *s.m.* (cook.) making flaky or puff pastry; flaky pastry.

feuilleté, -e [fœjte] *adj.* foliated, laminated; (geol.) lamellar; *pâte ~e*, puff pastry.

feuilleter [fœjte] *v.t.* **1.** to turn over the leaves (of a book, etc.), to thumb, to peruse; **2.** (cook.) to make puff pastry.

feuilleton [fœjtɔ̃] *s.m.* (newspaper) article, regular feature; instalment of serial; (TV, etc.) serial, series; *roman ~*, serialized novel, romance; **~niste** [fœjtɔnist] *s.m.f.* feature-writer, writer of serial novels.

feuillette [fœjɛt] *s.f.* cask (capacity 100–140 litres according to region).

feuillu, -e [fœjy] *adj.* leafy, leafed.

feuillure [fœjyr] *s.f.* (carp.) groove, rabbet.

feulement [følmɑ̃] *s.m.* roar (of tiger).

feuler [føle] *v.i.* (of tiger) to roar, (of cat) to growl.

feutrage [føtraʒ] *s.m.* felting.

feutre [føtr] *s.m.* felt, felt-cloth; felt hat.

feutrer [føtre] *v.t.i.* to felt, to pad, to mat; (fig.) to muffle, to deaden.

fève [fɛv] *s.f.* bean, broad bean.

féverole [fɛvrɔl], **faverole** [favrɔl] *s.f.* horse-bean, field bean.

févier [fevje] *s.m.* (bot.) horned acacia, gleditschia.

février [fevrije] *s.m.* February.

fez [fɛz] *s.m.* fez.

F.F.I. [ɛfɛfi] *s.m.* letters denoting member of *Forces Françaises de l'Intérieur* (1940–44).

F.F.L. [ɛfɛfɛl] abbrev. *Forces Françaises Libres.*

fi [fi] *interj.* expressing disapproval, scorn, disgust; fie; *faire ~ de*, to scorn, to think nothing of.

fiacre [fjakr] *s.m.* hackney carriage, cab.

fiançailles [fjɑ̃sɑj] *s.f.pl.* betrothal, engagement.

fiancé, -e [fjɑ̃se] *adj.* betrothed, engaged; *s.m.f.* fiancé(e), boy-friend, girl-friend; *les deux ~s*, the engaged couple.

fiancer [fjɑ̃se] *v.t.* to betroth, to engage; **se ~** *v.refl.* to get engaged.

fiasco [fjasko] *s.m.* failure; fiasco, disaster; *faire ~*, to fail, to come to grief.

fiasque [fjask] *s.f.* flask, bottle.

fibre [fibr] *s.f.* fibre; thread, filament; (fig.) feeling, sensibility; *avoir la ~ sensible*, to be susceptible, sensitive; *faire jouer la ~ patriotique*, to play on feelings of patriotism.

fibreu-x, -se [fibrø] *adj.* fibrous.

fibrillation [fibril(l)asjɔ̃] *s.f.* (pathol.) fibrillation (of heart muscle).

fibrille [fibril] *s.f.* small fibre, thread; fibril, fibrilla.

fibrine [fibrin] *s.f.* (chem.) fibrin.

fibrome [fibrom] *s.m.* (med.) fibrous tumour, fibroma.

fibule [fibyl] *s.f.* fibula, clasp.

fic [fik] *s.m.* (vet.) wart, fig (on horse).

ficaire [fikɛr] *s.f.* (bot.) lesser celandine, pilewort.

ficelage [fislaʒ] *s.m.* tying up; string wrapping.

ficelé, -e [fisle] *adj.* tied up, done up, bound; (fam.) dressed, done up.

ficeler [fisle] *v.t.* to tie up, to do up, to bind; (fam.) to dress.

ficelle [fisɛl] *s.f.* string, twine, thread; (fig.) trick, dodge; *~s d'une marionnette*, strings operating a marionette; (fig.) *c'est lui qui tire les ~s*, it is he who pulls the strings, who can work the oracle; *les ~s du métier*, the tricks of the trade.

fiche [fiʃ] *s.f.* **1.** (techn.) pin, peg, picket; (electr.) plug, key, jack; **2.** slip (of paper), card, ticket, tag, label; form.

ficher [fiʃe] *v.t.* **1.** (p.p. *fiché*) (obs.) to drive in, to fix; **se ~** *v.refl.* to lodge, to become fixed; **2.** (p.p. *fichu*) (milder and fam. equivalent of *foutre*) to do, to give, to put, to throw, to leave; *qu'est-ce que tu fiches là?*, what are you up to now?; *fiche-moi la paix*, leave me alone; *~ qn. à la porte*, to throw s.o. out; *~ le camp*, to be off, to hop it, to decamp, to vanish; *~ qn. dedans*, to deceive s.o., to lead s.o. up the garden path; **se ~** *v.refl.* to throw oneself; *se ~ de*, to make fun of, to mock; not to care about, to think nothing of; *il s'est fichu de moi*, he laughed at me; *je m'en fiche*, I couldn't care less, it doesn't worry me, to hell with it.

fichier [fiʃje] *s.m.* card index, file; filing cabinet.

fichiste [fiʃist] *s.m.* card-indexer, filing-clerk, one who collects slips.

fichoir [fiʃwar] *s.m.* peg, clothes-peg.

fichtre [fiʃtr] *interj.* expressing surprise, admiration, vexation.

fichtrement [fiʃtrəmɑ̃] *adv.* (fam.) extremely, awfully.

fichu [fiʃy] *s.m.* headscarf, fichu.

fichu, -e [fiʃy] *adj.* **1.** (fam.) bad, nasty, unpleasant; **2.** done for, finished, worn out, dead; *mes chaussures sont ~es*, my shoes have had it; **3.** dressed, turned out; built; **4.** *être ~ de*, to be capable of, to be quite up to.

ficti-f, -ve [fiktif] *adj.* fictitious, imaginary, sham; (econ.) *valeur ~ve*, nominal value.

fiction [fiksjɔ̃] *s.f.* fiction, invention, fabrication, figment.
fictivement [fiktivmɑ̃] *adv.* fictitiously.
fidéicommis [fideikɔmi] *s.m.* (law) trust.
fidéicommissaire [fideikɔmisɛr] *s.m.* (law) trustee.
fidéjusseur [fideʒysœr] *s.m.* (law) surety.
fidéjussion [fideʒysjɔ̃] *s.f.* (law) security.
fidèle [fidɛl] *adj.* faithful, true, loyal, constant, trusty, trustworthy; accurate, exact; *être ~ à*, to be faithful or loyal to, to hold (fast) to, to adhere to, to stick to; *~ s.m.f.* loyal supporter, or customer, faithful adherent, faithful, or trusted, friend; trustworthy person; (eccles.) *les ~s*, the faithful, the congregation; **~ment** [fidɛlmɑ̃] *adv.* faithfully, loyally; exactly, truly.
fidélité [fidelite] *s.f.* fidelity, faithfulness, loyalty, devotion, trustiness, constancy; adherence (to cause, etc.); accuracy (of translation, memory, etc.).
F.I.D.E.S. [ɛfideɛs] abbrev. *Fonds d'investissement pour le développement économique et social.*
Fidji [fidʒi] *s.m.* (geog.) Fiji.
fiduciaire [fidysjɛr] *adj.*, *s.m.* (law, econ.) fiduciary; trustee; **~ment** [fidysjɛrmɑ̃] *adv.* (law) in trust.
fief [fjɛf] *s.m.* (feud.) fief, feoff, fee, feu; (fig.) private domain; (pol.) *~ électoral*, safe seat.
fieffé, -e [fjefe] *adj.* (pej.) utter, arrant, downright.
fiel [fjɛl] *s.m.* gall; (lit. & fig.) bile; (fig.) spleen, spite, malice, rancour, venom.
fielleu-x, -se [fjɛlø] *adj.* (fig.) bitter, venomous.
fiente [fjɑ̃t] *s.f.* dung, droppings.
fienter [fjɑ̃te] *v.i.* to deposit droppings.
(**se**) **fier** [fje] *v.refl. se ~ à*, to trust, to put one's trust in.
fi-er, -ère [fjɛr] *adj.* **1.** (obs.) fierce, cruel, wild; **2.** proud, haughty, arrogant, superior; (Lit.) dignified, noble; **3.** proud (*de*, of, with); **4.** (preceding noun; usu. iron.) fine, famous, rare; *un ~er imbécile*, a prize fool; **~èrement** [fjɛrmɑ̃] *adv.* **1.** haughtily; **2.** proudly, with dignity; **3.** (obs.) extremely.
fiérot, -te [fjero] *adj.* pretentious, stuck-up; taking childish pride or pleasure (*de*, in).
fierté [fjɛrte] *s.f.* **1.** (obs.) fierceness; bravery; **2.** pride, haughtiness, arrogance; **3.** pride, satisfaction.
fièvre [fjɛvr] *s.f.* (med.) fever, high temperature; (fig.) fever, heat, passion, excitement, animation; *discuter avec ~*, to discuss heatedly, to have an animated discussion.
fiévreu-x, -se [fjevrø] *adj.* (med.) feverish, febrile, having a fever; (fig.) feverish, restless, anxious; *la salle des ~x*, the fever ward (of hospital); **~sement** [fjevrøzmɑ̃] *adv.* (fig.) feverishly, restlessly.
fifille [fifij] *s.f.* (term of endearment) little girl, small daughter; *~ à son papa*, daddy's little girl.
fifre [fifr] *s.m.* (mus.) fife, pipe; fife-player.
figaro [figaro] *s.m.* (fam.) barber.
figement [fiʒmɑ̃] *s.m.* coagulation, congealing, clotting.
figer [fiʒe] *v.t.* **1.** to coagulate, to cause to clot; (fig.) to curdle (the blood); **se** *~ v.refl.* to coagulate, to clot, to curdle, to get thick, to solidify; **2.** to fix, to immobilize; **se** *~ v.refl.* to become fixed, to be rooted, to be firmly established, to be immovable or unchangeable.
fignolage [fiɲɔlaʒ] *s.m.* finishing (of a product) with minute care.
fignoler [fiɲɔle] *v.t.* to finish with minute care.
figue [fig] *s.f.* (bot.) fig; *~ de Barbarie*, prickly pear; (fig.) *d'un air moitié ~ moitié raisin*, half in jest, half in earnest.
figuier [figje] *s.m.* (bot.) fig-tree; *~ de Barbarie*, prickly pear, opuntia.
figurant, -e [figyrɑ̃] *s.m.f.* **1.** (obs.) figurant(e) (in ballet); **2.** (theatr., etc.) one playing minor role or walking-on part; one appearing in crowd scene, super; *jouer un rôle de ~*, to have a walk-on part; (fig.) to be standing in the wings, to be taking no active part.
figurati-f, -ve [figyratif] *adj.* figurative, emblematic; representative, depictive, pictorial.
figuration [figyrɑsjɔ̃] *s.f.* figuration, depiction, presentation; (ballet) figurants, corps-de-ballet; (theatr., etc.) crowd, walkers-on, supers; walk-on, or non-speaking, part.
figurativement [figyrativmɑ̃] *adv.* figuratively, symbolically.
figure [figyr] *s.f.* **1.** form, shape, image, diagram, (geom.) figure, representation, symbol; appearance; (danc.) steps, figure; (sculpt., etc.) figure; *une ~ de proue*, (lit. & fig.) a figure-head; *faire ~*, to cut a figure, to play an important role, to be a public figure; *faire ~ de*, to appear, to pass as, to present an image of; **2.** (human) face; (fig.) expression, appearance; *faire triste ~*, to look miserable, to cut a sorry figure, to be woefully inadequate; **3.** figure (of speech), metaphor, trope, rhetorical figure.
figuré, -e [figyre] *adj.* **1.** illustrated, represented, shown, indicated, marked (in drawing, etc.); (arch.) figured, decorated with figures; **2.** figurative, metaphorical; (of style) full of images, florid, ornate; *au (sens) ~*, or *~ment* (*adv.*), figuratively, metaphorically, in a figurative or metaphorical sense.
figurer [figyre] *v.t.* to represent, to draw, to depict, to carve, to sculpt; (obs.) to present, to express, to symbolize; **se** *~ v.refl.* to imagine; *~ v.i.* to appear, to be present, to figure, to take part (in); (theatr., etc.) to appear in a minor role, to appear in the crowd, as a super; (fig.) to play a minor role.
figurine [figyrin] *s.f.* figurine (statue), small figure.
fil [fil] *s.m.* **1.** thread, yarn, filament, fibre; wire; (fig.) thread, connection; *~ de lin*, (linen) thread; (fig.) *cousu de ~ blanc*, transparent, obvious; (fig.) *donner du ~ à retordre à qn.*, to cause s.o. trouble; *~ de canne à pêche*, fishing-line; *~ de fer*, wire; (fig.) *perdre le ~ de sa pensée*, to lose the thread of one's thought; *démêler les ~s de*, to unravel; *~ d'Ariane*, *~ conducteur*, guide-rope, guide-line; *~ d'araignée*, spider's web; *~ de la vierge*, gossamer; *~ à plomb*, plumb-line; *télégraphie sans ~s*, (wireless) telegraphy; (telephone) *être au bout du ~*, to be on the line, to be speaking; **2.** grain (of wood); *couper dans le ~*, to cut with the grain; **3.** (obs.) course (of river, etc.); (mod.) *au ~ de l'eau*, downstream, with the stream; *au ~ des jours*, as the days go by; **4.** edge (of blade, etc.); *passer au ~ de l'épée*, to put to the sword.
filable [filabl] *adj.* that can be spun.
filage [filaʒ] *s.m.* spinning.
filaire [filɛr] *s.f.* (zool.) filaria.
filament [filamɑ̃] *s.m.* filament, thread, string; thin wire; (electr.) filament; fibre (in meat).
filamenteu-x, -se [filamɑ̃tø] *adj.* fibrous; (of meat) stringy.
filandière [filɑ̃djɛr] *s.f.* spinner; (myth.) *les sœurs ~s*, the Fates.
filandre [filɑ̃dr] *s.f.* **1.** = FILAMENT (in meat); **2.** gossamer.
filandreu-x, -se [filɑ̃drø] *adj.* stringy, fibrous, tough; (fig.) involved, confused.
filant, -e [filɑ̃] *adj.* viscous, viscid; *pouls ~*, feeble pulse.
filasse [filas] *s.f.* tow, textile fibre; *cheveux de ~*, flaxen hair.
filateur [filatœr] *s.m.* spinner; owner of spinning-mill.

filature [filatyr] *s.f.* **1.** spinning-mill; spinning; **2.** following, shadowing; *prendre en* ~, to shadow, to follow.

fil-de-fériste [fildəferist] *s.m.f.* trapeze artist, performer on the high wire.

file [fil] *s.f.* row, file, line, procession, queue; (mil.) file; *à la* ~, one after another, in succession, in procession; *deux heures à la* ~, for two hours on end; *chef de* ~, top man, leader; *prendre la* ~, to join the queue.

filé [file] *s.m.* **1.** cotton yarn; **2.** metal thread (woven into textile).

filer [file] *v.t.* **1.** to spin; (naut.) to pay out (cable); (fig.) to spin out, to prolong, to sustain (note); (naut.) ~ *20 nœuds*, to do 20 knots; (cards) ~ *une carte*, to palm off a card; (obs.) ~ (*une carte*), to discard; (mod.) ~ *ses cartes*, to play out one's cards slowly; ~ *doux*, to be submissive, to say yes sir, no sir; **2.** to follow, to shadow; **3.** (pop.) to give, to hand or deal out; ~ *v.i.* **1.** to flow, to run, to flow along, to move swiftly and smoothly; to rush, to dash; to flow away, to pass swiftly (away); (of mesh) to run, to ladder; (naut. of cable) to run out; to become viscous; *étoile filante*, shooting star; (naut.) *laisser* ~ *un câble*, to pay out a cable; ~ *à toute vitesse*, to dash away at high speed; **2.** (fam.) to be off, to disappear; ~ *à l'anglaise*, to take French leave, to slip away; *l'argent lui file entre les doigts*, money slips through his fingers.

filet[1] [filɛ] *s.m.* net, network, netting; luggage-net or -rack; (pl. fig.) snare; *rideaux en* ~, net curtains; *faire tomber dans ses* ~*s*, to ensnare.

filet[2] [filɛ] *s.m.* fillet (of beef, etc., or fish).

filet[3] [filɛ] *s.m.* **1.** (anat.) fr(a)enum; (bot.) filament; thread (of screw); (arch.) fillet; (print.) rule; (rid.) snaffle; **2.** trickle, drop, wisp.

filetage [filtaʒ] *s.m.* thread, threading (of screws), screw-cutting.

fileter [filte] *v.t.* to cut the thread of (screw, etc.); to draw (wire).

fileu-r, -se [filœr] *s.m.f.* spinner, spinning operative; owner of spinning-mill.

filial, -e, (**aux**) [filjal] *adj.* filial; ~**ement** [filjalmɑ̃] *adv.* filially.

filiale [filjal] *s.f.* (comm.) subsidiary or affiliated company, provincial branch.

filiation [filjɑsjɔ̃] *s.f.* filiation, affiliation; direct descent; (fig.) relationship, connection.

filière [filjɛr] *s.f.* (techn.) die, die-plate; tap (for cutting screws); *travailler un métal à la* ~, to draw out metal (into wire); (fig.) *passer par la* ~, to make one's way up the ladder; to go through all the necessary channels, or procedures.

filiforme [filifɔrm] *adj.* filiform, threadlike.

filigrane [filigran] *s.m.* **1.** filigree; **2.** watermark (of paper).

filigraner [filigrane] *v.t.* **1.** to filigree, to make in filigree; **2.** to watermark (paper).

filin [filɛ̃] *s.m.* (naut.) rope, line.

filipendule [filipɑ̃dyl] *s.f.* (bot.) dropwort, spiraea.

fille [fij] *s.f.* **1.** daughter, female descendant; *petite-*~, grand-daughter; **2.** girl; spinster, maid; female employee; prostitute; *petite* ~, (little) girl, child; *elle est toujours petite* ~, she is still a child; *jeune* ~, girl (of marriageable age); *rester* ~, to remain single; *vieille* ~, spinster, old maid; ~ *de chambre*, chamber-maid; ~ *d'honneur*, maid of honour; ~ *de joie*, ~ *des rues*, ~ *publique*, prostitute.

fillette [fijɛt] *s.f.* **1.** little girl; teenager; *rayon* ~*s*, junior miss department (in store); **2.** (pop.) half-bottle of wine.

filleul, -e [fijœl] *s.m.f.* godson, god-daughter, godchild; adopted godson, protégé.

film [film] *s.m.* film.

filmage [filmaʒ] *s.m.* filming.

filmer [filme] *v.t.* **1.** to film; **2.** (techn.) to coat with film.

filmique [filmik] *adj.* of films, of the cinema.

filon [filɔ̃] *s.m.* vein, lode, seam (of metal), reef (of gold); (fig.) source of profits, bit of luck; windfall; cushy job; *il a trouvé le* ~, he has struck gold, he has got himself a nice job.

filoselle [filozɛl] *s.f.* (text.) filoselle, floss silk.

filou (pl. **-s**) [filu] *s.m.* pickpocket, thief, sharper, cheat, swindler.

filouter [filute] *v.t.* to steal, to pinch, to swindle, to cheat; ~ *qn.*, to pick someone's pocket, to swindle s.o.; *il m'a filouté 20 francs*, he has done me out of 20 francs.

filouterie [filutri] *s.f.* pocket-picking, swindling.

fils [fis] *s.m.* **1.** son, male child, male descendant; (fig.) product; ~ *de famille*, young man of a good family; ~ *à papa*, young man who owes his position to his father; *il est bien le* ~ *de son père*, he is a chip off the old block; *être le* ~ *de son travail*, to have made one's way in the world; **2.** young man, lad; *bonjour*, ~*!*, hullo, young man!

filtrage [filtraʒ] *s.m.* filtering, straining, filtration; checking, editing, censoring (of news).

filtrat [filtra] *s.m.* (chem.) filtrate.

filtration [filtrɑsjɔ̃] *s.f.* filtration, filtering.

filtre [filtr] *s.m.* filter, strainer.

filtre-presse [filtrəprɛs] *s.m.* (techn.) filter-press.

filtrer [filtre] *v.t.* to filter, to strain; ~ *v.i.* to filter, to seep.

fin [fɛ̃] *s.f.* end, close, termination, conclusion; death; aim, object, purpose; *toucher à sa* ~, to be coming to an end, to be near one's end; *arriver à ses* ~*s*, to gain one's end, to achieve one's objectives; *à quelle* ~*?*, to what purpose?; *à la* ~, in the end; finally, at last, after all; *à la* ~ *des* ~*s*, in the final outcome, in the upshot; *en* ~ *de compte*, when all is said and done; *sans* ~, endless(ly), perpetually; *prendre, tirer, à sa* ~, to come to an end; *mettre* ~ *à*, to stop, to put an end to; *à toute* ~, for all purposes; *mener à bonne* ~, to bring to a successful conclusion, to make a success of; *la* ~ *justifie les moyens*, the end justifies the means; (law) ~ *de non-recevoir*, refusal; demurrer, estoppel.

fin, -e [fɛ̃] *adj.* **1.** (obs.) farthest, final, last; *le* ~ *mot*, the final, or key, word, the real motive; (mod.) *au* ~ *fond de*, right at the back of, right at the end, or bottom, of; **2.** fine, refined, delicate; precious; nice; slender, thin, tenuous, minute; subtle, keen, acute, sharp; *pierres* ~*es*, precious stones, gems; ~*es herbes*, savoury herbs; *des traits* ~*s*, delicate features; ~*e* (*champagne*), brandy; *une* ~*e*, a (glass of) brandy; *taille* ~*e*, slender waist; *pluie* ~*e*, fine, persistent rain; *avoir l'oreille* ~*e*, to have a sharp ear; *avoir le nez* ~, to have a good nose (for sth.), (fig.) to be quick to detect (sth.), to have a flair (for sth.); *un* ~ *connaisseur*, a real connoisseur; *une* ~*e lame*, a good swordsman; *une* ~*e mouche*, a sharp customer; *le* ~ *du* ~, the quintessence, the ultimate refinement; *jouer au plus* ~, to finesse, to play a very subtle game.

final, -e (pl. **-s**) [final] *adj.* final, last, ultimate; (gram., phil.) final; *point* ~, full stop; *mettre le point* ~ *à*, to bring (sth.) to a conclusion, to round off (debate, etc.); ~**ement** [finalmɑ̃] *adv.* finally, lastly, in conclusion, in the last analysis, when all is said and done.

finale [final] *s.f.* **1.** final syllable, ending (of word); (mus.) keynote, tonic; **2.** (sport) final.

finale [final] *s.m.* (mus.) finale; final movement.

finaliste [finalist] *s.m.f.* (sport) finalist.

finalité [finalite] *s.f.* finality.

finance [finɑ̃s] *s.f.* **1.** (obs.) (ready) money,

cash; (mod.) *moyennant* ~, for payment, for a consideration; **2.** finance; (pl.) finances, funds; Treasury, Exchequer.
financement [finɑ̃smɑ̃] *s.m.* financing.
financer [finɑ̃se] *v.i.* to pay, to fork out; ~ *v.t.* **1.** (obs.) to pay (a sum) cash down; **2.** to finance, to back.
financi-er, -ère [finɑ̃sje] *adj.* financial, fiscal, money, banking; *le marché* ~*er*, the money market; ~**er** *s.m.* financier, rich man; ~**èrement** [finɑ̃sjɛrmɑ̃] *adv.* financially.
finasser [finase] *v.i.* to finesse, to indulge in sharp practice.
finasserie [finasri] *s.f.* (pej.) finesse, trickery, subterfuge, cunning.
finaud, -e [fino] *adj., s.m.f.* sly or cunning (person).
finement [finmɑ̃] *adv.* finely, delicately, subtly; minutely; skilfully, shrewdly.
fines [fin] *s.f.pl.* filler (for compacting concrete, etc.).
finesse [finɛs] *s.f.* **1.** (obs.) fineness (of thread, etc.); (mod., pl.) finer points, subtleties, niceties; **2.** fineness (of perception, etc.), delicacy; keenness, sharpness, acuteness; perspicacity, penetration, subtlety; ~ *de touche*, delicacy of touch; *les* ~*s de la langue*, the niceties of the language.
finette [finɛt] *s.f.* (text.) flannelette (with brushed underside).
fini, -e [fini] *adj.* **1.** finished, ended, completed, perfected; executed; settled, concluded; (fig., usu. pej.) complete, thorough, consummate; *vêtement bien* ~, well-finished garment; *menteur* ~, out-and-out liar; **2.** (phil., math.) finite; ~ *s.m.* **1.** (excellence of) finish, careful execution; **2.** (phil.) *le* ~, the finite.
finir [finir] *v.t.* to finish, to end, to cease, to stop, to put a stop or end to; to complete, to conclude; ~ *sa vie*, to end one's days; *finissez ces querelles!*, stop this quarrelling!; ~ *de faire qch.*, to stop doing sth.; ~ *v.i.* to finish, to end, to come to an end, to cease, to stop; to turn out; *tout est bien qui finit bien*, all's well that ends well; *il finira mal*, he will come to a bad end; ~ *par faire qch.*, to end in, or by, doing sth.; to do sth. in the end; *ils ont fini par accepter*, they finally agreed; *en* ~, to put an end (to sth.); *il faut en* ~, we must stop it, we must finish with it, we must put an end to it; *n'en* ~ *plus, pas*, to be endless, interminable; *des discours qui ne finissaient plus*, interminable speeches; *un chemin qui ne finit pas*, a road without end, a long, long road; *en* ~ *avec qch.*, to have done with sth., to settle sth.; *en* ~ *avec qn.*, to finish, to break off relations, with s.o.
finish [finiʃ] *s.m.* **1.** (boxing) *match au* ~, fight to the finish; **2.** (sport) staying-power.
finissage [finisaʒ] *s.m.* finishing, finish; completion.
finisseu-r, -se [finisœr] *s.m.f.* (techn.) finisher, polisher; (sport) finisher.
finition [finisjɔ̃] *s.f.* finishing, finish; (pl.) finishing touches.
finlandais, -e [fɛ̃lɑ̃dɛ] *adj.* Finnish; *s.m.f.* Finn.
Finlande [fɛ̃lɑ̃d] *s.f.* (geog.) Finland.
finnois, -e [finwa] *adj.* Finnish; ~ *s.m.* Finnish (language).
fiole [fjɔl] *s.f.* phial, flask, small bottle; (fam.) face, head; *tu veux te payer ma* ~, you want to make a fool of me.
fion [fjɔ̃] *s.m.* (pop.) finish, final touch; *donner un coup de* ~, to give the finishing touch, to smarten up.
fioriture [fjɔrityr] *s.f.* (mus.) flourish, ornament; (often pej.) superfluous ornament.
firmament [firmamɑ̃] *s.m.* firmament.
firman [firmɑ̃] *s.m.* (hist.) firman.
firme [firm] *s.f.* (comm.) firm.
fisc [fisk] *s.m.* the Treasury, the Exchequer; tax department, Inland Revenue.
fiscal, -e, (aux) [fiskal] *adj.* fiscal, tax, taxation; *fraude* ~*e*, tax evasion; *politique* ~*e*, taxation policy; ~**ement** [fiskalmɑ̃] *adv.* fiscally.
fiscaliser [fiskalize] *v.t.* to tax, to subject to tax.
fiscalité [fiskalite] *s.f.* tax system; taxation laws.
fissible [fisibl] *adj.* (phys.) fissionable.
fissile [fisil] *adj.* fissile.
fission [fisjɔ̃] *s.f.* (phys.) fission.
fissipare [fisipar] *adj.* (biol.) fissiparous.
fissuration [fisyrɑsjɔ̃] *s.f.* fissuring, cracking.
fissure [fisyr] *s.f.* fissure, cleft, crevice, slit, crack; (fig.) crack, dent, breach.
fissurer [fisyre] *v.t.* to fissure, to crack, to cleave, to split; **se** ~ *v.refl.* to split, to crack.
fiston [fistɔ̃] *s.m.* (pop.) sonny, my boy, lad.
fistulaire [fistylɛr] *adj.* fistular, fistulous.
fistule [fistyl] *s.f.* fistula.
fistuleu-x, -se [fistylø] *adj.* (med.) fistulous.
fistuline [fistylin] *s.f.* (bot.) beefsteak fungus.
five o'clock [fajvɔklɔk] *s.m.* (obs.) afternoon tea.
fixage [fiksaʒ] *s.m.* (photo., techn.) fixing (of colours, etc.).
fixat-eur, -rice [fiksatœr] *adj.* (rare) fixing, fixative; ~**eur** *s.m.* (techn.) fixing-bath; fixer, fixative.
fixatif [fiksatif] *s.m.* (techn.) fixative.
fixation [fiksɑsjɔ̃] *s.f.* **1.** (sci.) fixation; **2.** settling; **3.** (psychol.) fixation; **4.** determining, fixing (of date, etc.).
fixe [fiks] *adj.* fixed, immovable; unchanging, invariable, permanent; settled, predetermined, appointed, regular; *avoir la vue, le regard*, ~, *avoir les yeux* ~*s*, to stare (fixedly), to stare into space; (mil.) ~*!*, eyes front!; (meteor.) *beau* ~, set fair; ~ *s.m.* fixed salary.
fixé, -e [fikse] *adj.* fixed, settled, stated; (psychol.) fixated.
fixe-chaussette [fiksəʃosɛt] *s.m.* (pl. *fixe-chaussettes*) sock-suspender, garter.
fixement [fiksəmɑ̃] *adv.* fixedly, steadfastly; (of gaze) intently.
fixer [fikse] *v.t.* **1.** to fix, to attach firmly; to settle (s.o.); ~ *les yeux, les regards, sur*, to stare at; ~ *son attention sur*, to give all one's attention to; **2.** to fix, to make permanent, to consolidate; ~ *qn. sur qch.*, to explain sth. clearly to s.o., to put s.o. in the picture about sth.; **3.** to determine, to lay down (rule, etc.); to arrange (date, etc.); to prescribe; **se** ~ *v.refl.* to settle, to establish oneself.
fixisme [fiksism] *s.m.* (sci. hist.) creationism.
fixiste [fiksist] *adj.* (sci. hist.) creationist.
fixité [fiksite] *s.f.* fixity, fixedness, stability; steadiness, intentness (of gaze).
fjord, fiord [fjɔr] *s.m.* fjord, fiord.
flac [flak] *interj.* splash!, plop!
flaccidité [flaksidite] *s.f.* flaccidity.
flache [flaʃ] *s.f.* **1.** wane, flaw, (in wood); **2.** puddle, pothole, (in road).
flacon [flakɔ̃] *s.m.* flask, phial, small bottle.
flaconnage [flakɔnaʒ] *s.m.*, **flaconnerie** [flakɔnri] *s.f.* bottle-making; bottles.
flaconnier [flakɔnje] *s.m.* bottle-maker; bottle-case.
flafla [flafla] *s.m.* (fam.) show, ostentation, hoo-ha; *faire du* ~, to show off, to make a fuss.
flagellant [flaʒɛlɑ̃] *s.m.* (relig. hist.) flagellant.
flagellation [flaʒɛlɑsjɔ̃] *s.f.* flagellation, scourging, flogging.
flagelle [flaʒɛl], **flagellum** [flaʒɛlɔm] *s.m.* (biol.) flagellum.
flagellé, -e [flaʒele] *adj.* (biol.) flagellate.
flageller [flaʒele] *v.t.* to flagellate, to scourge, to flog.
flageoler [flaʒɔle] *v.i.* to tremble, to shake; ~ *sur ses jambes*, to be shaky on one's legs.

flageolet[1] [flaʒɔlɛ] *s.m.* (mus.) flageolet; an organ stop.

flageolet[2] [flaʒɔlɛ] *s.m.* (small) kidney-bean, flageolet.

flagorner [flagɔrne] *v.t.* to fawn upon, to flatter.

flagornerie [flagɔrnəri] *s.f.* base flattery, fawning.

flagorneu-r, -se [flagɔrnœr] *s.m.f.* sycophant, fawner, flatterer, toady; *adj.* sycophantic, fawning.

flagrant, -e [flagrɑ̃] *adj.* flagrant, glaring; *en ~ délit*, in flagrante delicto, in the very act.

flair [flɛr] *s.m.* (of dog) scent, nose; (fig.) flair, perspicacity.

flairer [flere] *v.t.* (of dog) to scent, to smell; to smell out; (fig.) to detect, to suspect.

flamand, -e [flamɑ̃] *adj.* Flemish, of Flanders; *s.m.f.* Fleming; *~ s.m.* Flemish (language).

flamant [flamɑ̃] *s.m.* (ornith.) flamingo.

flambage [flɑ̃baʒ] *s.m.* **1.** singeing (of fowl, etc.); **2.** (techn.) buckling.

flambant, -e [flɑ̃bɑ̃] *adj.* flaming, blazing; (*tout*) *~ neuf*, brand new.

flambart, flambard [flɑ̃bar] *s.m.* **1.** burning (piece of) coal; **2.** (fig., fam.) (obs.) gay dog; (mod.) *faire le ~*, to show off.

flambe [flɑ̃b] *s.f.* **1.** kris; **2.** (bot.) iris.

flambé, -e [flɑ̃be] *adj.* **1.** (cook.) flambé; **2.** (fig., fam.) ruined, done for.

flambeau (pl. **-x**) [flɑ̃bo] *s.m.* **1.** flambeau, torch; *aux ~x*, (by) torchlight; **2.** (fig.) flame, light; **3.** candlestick, candelabra.

flambement [flɑ̃bəmɑ̃] *s.m.* = FLAMBAGE 2.

flamber [flɑ̃be] *v.i.* to blaze, to flame, to go up in flames; (fig.) to burn, to be on fire; *~ v.t.* to singe (hair, etc.); to sterilize (needle in flame); (obs., fam.) to ruin, to cheat; to gamble away.

flamberge [flɑ̃bɛrʒ] *s.f. mettre ~ au vent*, to draw the sword; (fig.) to enter the fray.

flambeur [flɑ̃bœr] *s.m.* (slang) gambler.

flamboiement [flɑ̃bwamɑ̃] *s.m.* blazing, blaze, flaring up.

flamboyant, -e [flɑ̃bwajɑ̃] *adj.* blazing, flaming; (arch.) flamboyant; *~ s.m.* (bot.) flame-tree.

flamboyer [flɑ̃bwaje] *v.i.* to flame, to blaze, to flash, to flare.

flamenco [flamɛnko] *adj., s.m.* flamenco.

flamine [flamin] *s.m.* (Rom. ant.) flamen.

flamingant, -e [flamɛ̃gɑ̃] *adj.* Flemish-speaking; *s.m.f.* Flemish nationalist.

flamme [flam] *s.f.* **1.** flame; (fig.) fire, ardour, passion, desire; (eccles.) *les ~s*, hell-fire; *en ~s*, in flames, ablaze; (fig.) *jeter, lancer, feu et ~s*, to breathe fire, to fly into a rage; (techn.) *passer à la ~*, to singe; **2.** (mil., naut.) pennon, pennant, streamer; **3.** (vet.) fleam.

flammèche [flamɛʃ] *s.f.* spark, flake of fire.

flammerole [flamrɔl] *s.f.* (obs. exc. dial.) ignis fatuus, will-o'-the-wisp.

flan [flɑ̃] *s.m.* **1.** (cook.) baked custard; custard tart; **2.** (coin.) blank, coin-plate; **3.** (print.) flong; **4.** (pop.) *en être, en rester, comme deux ronds de ~*, to be flabbergasted; (pop.) *c'est du ~*, it's a load of nonsense; *à la ~*, useless(ly), worthless(ly).

flanc [flɑ̃] *s.m.* flank, side, (of animal, person, army, ship, etc.); *être sur le ~*, to be laid up (in bed); *mettre sur le ~*, to exhaust; (pop.) *tirer au ~*, to swing the lead; *un tire-au-~*, lead-swinger; (obs. exc. Lit.) bosom, womb; *l'enfant qu'elle porte dans ses ~s*, the child she carries in her womb; *à ~ de*, on the side of; *à ~ de coteau*, on the hillside; *prêter le ~*, (mil.) to expose one's flank; (fig.) to lay oneself open (to criticism, etc.).

flancher [flɑ̃ʃe] *v.i.* (fam.) to give way, to waver, to weaken, to give up.

flanchet [flɑ̃ʃɛ] *s.m.* flank (of beef).

flanconade [flɑ̃kɔnad] *s.f.* (fenc.) flanconade.

Flandre(s) [flɑ̃dr] *s.f.* (geog.) Flanders.

flandrin [flɑ̃drɛ̃] *s.m.* (usu. *grand ~*) lanky fellow, gawky man.

flanelle [flanɛl] *s.f.* (text.) flannel; (fam.) *avoir les jambes en ~*, to be weak at the knees.

flâner [flɑne] *v.i.* to loiter, to saunter, to stroll, to dawdle.

flânerie [flɑnri] *s.f.* loitering, idling, sauntering; stroll.

flâneu-r, -se [flɑnœr] *s.m.f.* idler, loafer, saunterer; *adj.* of an idle disposition.

flanquer[1] [flɑ̃ke] *v.t.* to flank.

flanquer[2] [flɑ̃ke] *v.t.* (fam.) to fling, to throw, to pitch; *~ un coup à qn.*, to fetch s.o. a blow; *~ qn. à la porte*, to kick s.o. out, to send s.o. packing; *~ la frousse à qn.*, to give s.o. a scare; **se** *~ v.refl. se ~ par terre*, to come a cropper.

flapi, -e [flapi] *adj.* (fam.) knocked up, exhausted, fagged out.

flaque [flak] *s.f.* puddle, small pool.

flash [flaʃ] *s.m.* (photo.) flash(light); (cin.) short scene; news flash.

flasque [flask] *adj.* flaccid, flabby, slack, limp.

flasque[1] [flask] *s.f.* (obs.) powder-horn; (mod.) small, flat flask.

flasque[2] [flask] *s.f.* (techn.) support, side plates; *~ s.m.* cheek (of gun carriage); whelp (of capstan); (car) wheel disc.

flatter [flate] *v.t.* **1.** to flatter, to compliment; **2.** (obs.) to deceive, to delude; (mod.) *~ qn. de* (*l'espoir de*) *qch.*, to hold out to s.o. the hope of sth.; **3.** to stroke (animal); **4.** to delight, to please, to gratify; *être flatté de*, to be gratified by; **5.** to encourage, to pander to; *~ les goûts de qn.*, to pander to someone's tastes; **se** *~ v.refl.* to persuade oneself, to imagine; *se ~ de gagner*, to persuade oneself that one will win; *se ~ de son bel esprit*, to pride oneself on one's wit; to have a good opinion of oneself.

flatterie [flatri] *s.f.* flattery, excessive compliments, blandishment(s).

flatteu-r, -se [flatœr] *s.m.f.* flatterer; *adj.* flattering, complimentary, gratifying; over--optimistic; **~sement** [flatøzmɑ̃] *adv.* flatteringly.

flatulence [flatylɑ̃s] *s.f.* flatulence.

flatulent, -e [flatylɑ̃] *adj.* flatulent.

flatuosité [flatɥozite] *s.f.* flatulence.

flavescent, -e [flavesɑ̃] *adj.* flavescent, yellowish.

fléau (pl. **-x**) [fleo] *s.m.* **1.** (agric.) flail; **2.** beam (of balance); **3.** (fig.) scourge, calamity, plague; curse, menace.

fléchage [fleʃaʒ] *s.m.* marking (of route) with arrows; route marked with arrows.

flèche[1] [flɛʃ] *s.f.* **1.** arrow, dart; (fig.) shaft, barb (of criticism, etc.); *monter en ~*, (lit. & fig.) to spiral, to rocket; *il fait ~ de tout bois*, all is grist to his mill; *la ~ du Parthe*, Parthian shot; **2.** spire (of church, etc.); (agric.) leader, main shoot; pole (of mast); beam (of plough); jib (of crane); *chevaux attelés en ~*, horses harnessed one behind the other; (fig.) *se trouver en ~*, to be out on a limb; **3.** (arch.) rise (of arch); (artill.) highest point of trajectory; **4.** direction--indicator, arrow; (car) trafficator.

flèche[2] [flɛʃ] *s.f.* flitch (of bacon).

flécher [fleʃe] *v.t.* to mark (route) with arrows.

fléchette [fleʃɛt] *s.f.* dart; *jeu de ~s*, darts (game).

fléchir [fleʃir] *v.t.* to bend, to flex; (fig.) to move, to appease, to touch; *~ le genou*, (lit. & fig.) to bow the knee; *~ v.i.* to bend, to give way, to weaken, to fall off, to sag; (of prices) to fall.

fléchissement [fleʃismɑ̃] *s.m.* bending, giving way; fall (in prices).

fléchisseur [fleʃisœr] *adj., s.m.* flexor (muscle).

flegmatique [flɛgmatik] *adj., s.m.f.* phlegmatic, imperturbable (person); **~ment** [flɛgmatikmɑ̃] *adv.* phlegmatically, imperturbably.
flegme [flɛgm] *s.m.* (med.) phlegm; (fig.) coolness, imperturbability.
flein [flɛ̃] *s.m.* punnet, chip basket.
flémard, flemmard, -e [flemar] *adj.* (fam.) idle, lazy; *s.m.f.* idler, slacker.
flemmarder [flemarde] *v.i.* (fam.) to be lazy, to do nothing.
flemme [flɛm] *s.f.* (fam.) laziness; *avoir la ~*, to be disinclined to work; *tirer sa ~*, to be idle, lazy.
fléole, phléole [fleɔl] *s.f.* (bot.) cat's-tail grass, timothy-grass.
flet [flɛ] *s.m.* (ichth.) flounder.
flétan [fletɑ̃] *s.m.* (ichth.) halibut.
flétri, -e [fletri] *adj.* withered, wilted, wrinkled.
flétrir[1] [fletrir] *v.t.* to wither, to cause to wilt; **se ~** *v.refl.* to wither, to wilt.
flétrir[2] [fletrir] *v.t.* (hist.) to brand (a criminal); (fig.) to brand, to stigmatize, to condemn.
flétrissement [fletrismɑ̃] *s.m.* (agric.) withering, blight.
flétrissure [fletrisyr] *s.f.* **1.** withering, fading; **2.** (Lit.) brand, stigma.
fleur [flœr] *s.f.* **1.** flower, bloom, blossom; *en ~*, in flower, in bloom; *à ~s*, flowered; *~ de lis*, fleur-de-lis, heraldic lily; (fig.) *couvrir qn. de ~s*, *jeter des ~s à qn.*, to praise s.o. profusely; *une vie semée de ~s*, an easy life; *la petite ~ bleue*, romantic sentimentality; *être ~ bleue*, to be sentimental; (fam.) *comme une ~*, easily, without any trouble; **2.** (obs. exc. Lit.) *la ~ de qch.*, the best of sth.; (mod.) *à la, dans la, ~ de*, in the prime of, at the height of; *la (fine) ~ de la société*, the cream of society; (fam.) *la ~ des pois*, the height of fashion; *~ de farine*, cornflour; **3.** *à ~ de*, on a level with, on the surface of; *yeux à ~ de tête*, prominent eyes, goggle eyes; *sensibilité à ~ de peau*, hypersensitivity.
fleurage [flœraʒ] *s.m.* **1.** floral pattern (on carpet, etc.); **2.** fine bran (for dusting bread before baking).
fleuraison [flørɛzɔ̃] *s.f.* = FLORAISON.
fleurdelisé, -e [flœrdəlize] *adj.* decorated with fleur-de-lis.
fleurer [flœre] *v.i.* to be fragrant, to exhale an odour; *~ la menthe*, to smell of mint.
fleuret [flœrɛ] *s.m.* **1.** (fenc.) foil; *~ démoucheté*, foil with the button off; **2.** (techn.) bit (of drill, etc.).
fleurette [flœrɛt] *s.f.* (obs.) floweret; (fig.) *conter ~ à une femme*, to flirt with a woman.
fleuri, -e [flœri] *adj.* **1.** flowering (tree, shrub); flowery, full of flowers, covered in flowers; *la saison ~e*, spring; *Pâques ~es*, Palm Sunday; **2.** (of cloth, etc.) flowered, flower-patterned; (fig.) (of complexion) florid; (of style) ornate.
fleurir [flœrir] *v.i.* to flower, to blossom; (fig.) to flourish; *~ v.t.* to adorn, to deck, with flowers, to pin a flower on (s.o.).
fleurissant, -e [flœrisɑ̃] *adj.* flowering, blossoming, blooming.
fleuriste [flœrist] *s.m.f.* florist, flower-seller; (obs.) lover of flowers; *~ adj.* flower-; *jardin ~*, flower-garden.
fleuron [flœrɔ̃] *s.m.* **1.** fleuron, flower-shaped ornament; *c'est le plus beau ~ de sa couronne*, (lit. & fig.) it's the brightest jewel in his crown; **2.** (bot.) floret.
fleuronné, -e [flœrɔne] *adj.* **1.** decorated with fleurons; **2.** (bot.) having florets.
fleuve [flœv] *s.m.* large river; river flowing into the sea; (fig.) river (of blood); flood, stream; *roman ~*, saga, novel covering several generations.
flexibilité [flɛksibilite] *s.f.* flexibility.
flexible [flɛksibl] *adj.* flexible, pliable; (fig.) accommodating, adaptable.
flexion [flɛksjɔ̃] *s.f.* flexion, bending; (gram.) inflexion.
flexionnel, -le [flɛksjɔnɛl] *adj.* (gram.) inflexional.
flexueu-x, -se [flɛksɥø] *adj.* flexuous, winding.
flexuosité [flɛksɥozite] *s.f.* flexuosity.
flibuste [flibyst] *s.f.* (obs.) filibustering, buccaneering.
flibuster [flibyste] *v.i.* to filibuster, to buccaneer; *~ v.t.* (fam.) to steal.
flibustier [flibystje] *s.m.* freebooter, buccaneer, pirate; crook, swindler.
flic [flik] *s.m.* (pop.) policeman; *les ~s*, the police.
flic flac [flikflak] *interj.* (fam.) flap!, splash!
flingot [flɛ̃go], **flingue** [flɛ̃g] *s.m.* (pop.) gun.
flinguer [flɛ̃ge] *v.t.* (pop.) to shoot at (s.o.).
flint-glass [flintglas], **flint** [flint] *s.m.* (techn.) flint glass.
flirt [flœrt] *s.m.* flirtation; flirt, boy-friend.
flirter [flœrte] *v.i.* to flirt.
flirteu-r, -se [flœrtœr] *adj.* flirtatious; *s.m.f.* flirt.
floc [flɔk] *interj.* plop!; *~ s.m.* splash.
floche [flɔʃ] *adj. soie ~*, floss silk.
floche [flɔʃ] *s.f.* tuft, puff, wreath (of smoke, etc.).
flocon [flɔkɔ̃] *s.m.* **1.** tuft, flock (of wool, etc.); **2.** (snow-)flake; wisp (of cloud, etc.); flake (as in corn-flakes); *~s d'avoine*, porridge oats.
floconneu-x, -se [flɔkɔnø] *adj.* fleecy, fluffy.
floculation [flɔkylɑsjɔ̃] *s.f.* (chem.) flocculation.
floculer [flɔkyle] *v.i.* (chem.) to flocculate.
flonflon [flɔ̃flɔ̃] *s.m.* fol-de-rol; strains of noisy popular music.
flopée [flɔpe] *s.f.* (pop.) large quantity, mass, crowd.
floraison [flɔrɛzɔ̃] *s.f.* blossoming, flowering, florescence; flowering season.
floral, -e, (aux) [flɔral] *adj.* floral, flower; *exposition ~e*, flower-show; *jeux floraux de Toulouse*, literary competition held annually in Toulouse.
floralies [flɔrali] *s.f.pl.* flower-show.
flore [flɔr] *s.f.* flora.
floréal [flɔreal] *s.m.* (hist.) Floreal (eighth month in Fr. Republican Calendar, April–May).
florence [flɔrɑ̃s] *s.m.* **1.** (text.) sarsenet; **2.** silkworm gut (used in angling).
florentin, -e [flɔrɑ̃tɛ̃] *adj., s.m.f.* Florentine, (native or inhabitant) of Florence.
florès [flɔrɛs] *s.m. faire ~*, to be highly successful; to be in vogue, to be all the fashion.
floriculture [flɔrikyltyr] *s.f.* floriculture, flower-growing.
florifère [flɔrifɛr] *adj.* floriferous, flower--bearing.
florilège [flɔrilɛʒ] *s.m.* florilegium, anthology.
florin [flɔrɛ̃] *s.m.* florin.
florissant, -e [flɔrisɑ̃] *adj.* flourishing, prosperous, thriving; *avoir une mine ~e*, to be the picture of health.
flosculeu-x, -se [flɔskylø] *adj.* (bot.) floscular, flosculous.
flot [flo] *s.m.* (pl.) waves, billows, (Lit.) the sea; (sing.) flood, torrent, stream; flood tide; (fig.) cascade, flood, torrent, river, stream; *à ~*, afloat, floating; *mettre à ~*, (lit. & fig.) to launch; *remettre à ~*, (fig.) to restore; *être à ~*, (fig.) to be holding one's own; *à ~s*, in abundance, in plenty, in torrents.
flottable [flɔtabl] *adj.* **1.** navigable (for floating timber); **2.** buoyant.
flottage [flɔtaʒ] *s.m.* floating of wood, rafting.

flottaison [flɔtɛzɔ̃] *s.f.* flotation; (naut.) *ligne de* ~, water-line, plimsoll line.
flottant, -e [flɔtɑ̃] *adj.* floating, flowing, waving; (fig.) irresolute, wavering, unsettled, undecided; *dette* ~*e*, floating debt.
flottard [flɔtar] *s.m.* (slang) naval cadet; ~, ~**e** *adj.* (fam.) watery, too liquid.
flottation [flɔtasjɔ̃] *s.f.* (mining, glass-making) flotation.
flotte [flɔt] *s.f.* **1.** fleet, navy; ~ *de commerce*, merchant fleet; **2.** float (on fishing line); **3.** (fam.) rain, water; *il tombe de la* ~, it's pouring with rain.
flottement [flɔtmɑ̃] *s.m.* undulation; (fin.) movement, floating (of exchange rates, etc.); (fig.) wavering, hesitation.
flotter [flɔte] *v.i.* to float; to wave (in the wind); to hang loosely; (fig.) to wander; to waver; ~ *v.t.* to float (timber).
flotteur [flɔtœr] *s.m.* float; ball (of cistern).
flotille [flɔtij] *s.f.* flotilla.
flou, -e [flu] *adj.* soft, blurred, dim; vague, imprecise; loose-fitting; (of hair) fluffy.
flouer [flue] *v.t.* (obs., fam.) to cheat, to diddle.
flouve [fluv] *s.f.* (bot.) sweet (vernal) grass.
fluage [flyaʒ] *s.m.* (techn.) creep (of metal).
fluate [flyat] *s.m.* (chem.) (obs.) fluoride; (mod.) fluorine.
fluctuant, -e [flyktɥɑ̃] *adj.* fluctuating, varying, unstable.
fluctuation [flyktɥɑsjɔ̃] *s.f.* fluctuation.
fluctuer [flyktɥe] *v.i.* **1.** (rare) to float; **2.** to vary, to fluctuate.
fluer [flye] *v.i.* to flow; (med.) to run, to bleed.
fluet, -te [flyɛ] *adj.* thin, spare, slender, slim; *voix* ~*te*, piping voice.
fluide [flɥid] *adj.* fluid; (obs.) liquid; ~ *s.m.* fluid, flux, emanation.
fluidifier [flɥidifje] *v.t.* to fluidify.
fluidité [flɥidite] *s.f.* fluidity.
fluor [flyɔr] *s.m.* (chem.) fluorine; (min.) fluorspar.
fluorescence [flyɔresɑ̃s] *s.f.* fluorescence.
fluorescent, -e [flyɔresɑ̃] *adj.* fluorescent.
fluorhydrique [flyɔridrik] *adj.* (chem.) hydrofluoric.
fluorine [flyɔrin] *s.f.* (min.) native fluoride of calcium, fluorspar, fluorite; ⚠ not 'fluorine'.
fluorure [flyɔryr] *s.m.* (chem.) fluoride.
flush [flœʃ] *s.m.* (cards) flush; *quinte* ~, straight flush.
flûte [flyt] *s.f.* **1.** (mus.) flute, flautist; **2.** long thin stick of bread; **3.** (tall) champagne-glass; **4.** (pl., fam.) legs; *se tirer des* ~*s*, to run, to take to one's heels; ~ *interj.* = ZUT.
flûté, -e [flyte] *adj.* (of sound) flute-like, (of voice) piping.
flûteau [flyto], **flutiau** [flytjo] (pl. **-x**) *s.m.* **1.** whistle, pipe; child's toy whistle; **2.** (bot.) water plantain.
flûtiste [flytist] *s.m.f.* flautist, flute-player.
fluvial, -e, (**aux**) [flyvjal] *adj.* fluvial, river-.
fluviatile [flyvjatil] *adj.* fluviatile, river.
fluvio-glaciaire [flyvjɔglasjɛr] *adj.* (geol.) fluvio-glacial; ~**mètre** [flyvjɔmɛtr] *s.m.* fluviometer; ~**métrique** [flyvjɔmetrik] *adj.* fluviometric.
flux [fly] *s.m.* (obs.) flow; (med.) flux, flow; (sci.) flux; (incoming) tide; (fig.) abundance, flood, torrent; (fig.) ~ *et reflux*, ebb and flow, changing tide, (of opinion, etc.).
fluxion [flyksjɔ̃] *s.f.* **1.** (med.) inflammation, fluxion; gumboil, swollen face; ~ *de poitrine*, inflammation of the lungs, pneumonia; **2.** (math.) fluxion.
F.M.I. [ɛfɛmi] abbrev. *Fonds monétaire international*, I.M.F.
F.N.E.F. [ɛfɛneœf] abbrev. *Fédération nationale des Étudiants de France* = N.U.S.
F.N.S.A. [ɛfɛnɛsɑ] abbrev. *Fédération nationale des syndicats agricoles* = U.A.A.W.
F.O. [ɛfo] abbrev. *Force ouvrière* (a trade-union confederation).
foc [fɔk] *s.m.* (naut.) jib; *grand* ~, main jib, boom jib; *petit* ~, fore-topmast staysail; *clin* ~ flying jib; ~ *d'artimon*, mizzen staysail.
focal, -e, (**aux**) [fɔkal] *adj.* (opt., math.) focal; ~**e** *s.f.* (geom.) focal distance or length.
focaliser [fɔkalize] *v.t.* to focalize.
fœhn [føn] *s.m.* föhn (wind).
foène, foëne [fwɛn] *s.f.* (fish.) fish-gig, eel--spear.
fœtal, -e, (**aux**) [fetal] *adj.* foetal.
fœtus [fetys] *s.m.* foetus.
fofolle see FOU-FOU.
foi [fwa] *s.f.* **1.** faith, pledge, promise; *violer sa* ~, to break one's word; (obs.) *jurer sa* ~, to swear on oath; *par ma* ~, *sur ma* ~, ~ *d'honnête homme*, on my honour; (mod.) *ma* ~, certainly, in fact; *ma* ~ *oui!*, indeed, yes!; *sous la* ~ *du serment*, on oath; *sur la* ~ *de*, on the evidence of; *croire qch. sur la* ~ *de qn.*, to believe sth. on the word of s.o.; *faire* ~, to bear witness, to be evidence; (law) *en* ~ *de quoi*, in testimony whereof; **2.** (opt., naut.) zero alignment; **3.** (obs.) loyalty; (mod.) *bonne* ~, good faith, honesty, sincerity; *mauvaise* ~, dishonesty, insincerity; **4.** belief; confidence; *digne de* ~, reliable, worthy of belief; *avoir* ~ *en qn.*, to have confidence in s.o.; **5.** (relig.) faith, belief; religion, creed; *acte de* ~, act of faith; *profession de* ~, profession of faith; ~ *du charbonnier*, unquestioning, simple faith; *n'avoir ni* ~ *ni loi*, to fear neither God nor man.
foie [fwa] *s.m.* liver; *huile de* ~ *de morue*, cod liver oil; *pâté de* ~, liver pâté; (fig., fam.) *avoir les jambes en pâté de* ~, to be weak at the knees; *se ronger, se manger, les* ~*s*, to worry; (pop.) *avoir les* ~*s*, to be scared.
foin [fwɛ̃] *s.m.* hay; (pl.) mowing grass; (fig.) *quand il n'y a plus de* ~ *dans le râtelier*, when the money runs out; *être bête à manger du* ~, to be an ass, to be a complete idiot; *faire les* ~*s*, to make hay; *rhume des* ~*s*, hay fever; ~ *d'artichaut*, choke of artichoke; (pop.) *faire du* ~, to make a din, to make a scene, to kick up a fuss.
foin [fwɛ̃] *interj.* (obs.) ~ *de!*, away with!
foirade [fwarad] *s.f.* (fam.) flop, disaster.
foirail [fwaraj] *s.m.* (dial.) fair-ground.
foire[1] [fwar] *s.f.* fair, market; trade fair; (fig., fam.) bear-garden; *champ de* ~, fair-ground; *s'entendre comme larrons en* ~, to be as thick as thieves; ~ *d'empoigne*, free for all; (pop.) *faire la* ~, to go on the spree.
foire[2] [fwar] *s.f.* (vulg.) diarrhoea.
foirer [fware] *v.i.* **1.** (vulg.) to have diarrhoea; **2.** to fail (to operate); *écrou qui foire*, screw that won't bite; *fusée qui foire*, rocket which hangs fire; **3.** (fam.) to flop, to be a failure.
foireu-x, -se [fwarø] *adj., s.m.f.* **1.** (vulg.) (person) suffering from diarrhoea; (fig., fam.) nervous, cowardly, (person); **2.** (fam.) (person, thing) that is a failure.
fois [fwa] *s.f.* **1.** time, occasion; *une* ~, once; *encore une* ~, once again; *une bonne* ~, *une* ~ *pour toutes*, once and for all; *plus d'une* ~, more than once, often; *une* ~, *deux* ~, *trois* ~, (at auction) going, going, gone; *une* ~ *par mois*, once a month; (pop.) *des* ~, sometimes; *par deux, trois* (etc.) ~, twice, three times, etc.; *y regarder à deux* ~, to take a second look at sth.; *à la* ~, at the same time, both; *il est à la* ~ *aimable et sévère*, he is both kind and strict; *ne parlez pas tous à la* ~, don't all speak at the same time; *il y avait une* ~, once upon a time, there was

(fairy-story opening); *une* ~ (*que*), once; *une* ~ *qu'il a commencé, il ne saura plus s'arrêter*, once he's started, he won't know when to stop; *une* ~ *parti, il ne reviendra plus*, once he's gone, he won't come back; (pop.) *des* ~ *que* (with conditional), in case; *je vais le chercher, des* ~ *qu'il aurait eu un accident*, I'm going to look for him, in case he's had an accident; *non, mais des* ~*!*, well, now, look here!; **2.** (pl.) times (in multiplication); *trois* ~, three times, thrice; *deux* ~ *quatre*, twice four; (fig.) *merci mille* ~, thank you so much; *vous avez mille* ~ *raison*, you are abundantly right; *c'est trois* ~ *rien*, it's nothing at all.

foison [fwazɔ̃] *s.f.* (obs.) plenty, abundance; (mod.) *à* ~, in plenty, in abundance; *il y a des fleurs à* ~, there are plenty of flowers.

foisonnant, -e [fwazɔnɑ̃] *adj.* abundant, plentiful; increasing, growing.

foisonnement [fwazɔnmɑ̃] *s.m.* abundance, swarm; swelling, expansion, proliferation.

foisonner [fwazɔne] *v.i.* **1.** to abound, to swarm, to proliferate; to be plentiful; ~ *en, de*, to abound in, to swarm with; **2.** to swell, to increase in size; (fig.) to develop.

fol see FOU *adj.*

folasse [fɔlas] *adj.f.* (fam. pej.) unbalanced, crazy.

folâtre [fɔlɑtr] *adj.* playful, frolicsome, lively, gay.

folâtrer [fɔlɑtre] *v.i.* to play, to frolic, to frisk.

foliacé, -e [fɔljase] *adj.* foliaceous, leaflike.

foliaire [fɔljɛr] *adj.* (bot.) foliar.

foliation [fɔljɑsjɔ̃] *s.f.* (bot.) foliation.

folichon, -ne [fɔliʃɔ̃] *adj.* light-hearted, gay, amusing; (usu. in neg.) *ma vie n'est pas exactement* ~*ne*, my life isn't exactly fun.

folichonner [fɔliʃɔne] *v.i.* (obs.) to lark (about), to frolic.

folie [fɔli] *s.f.* **1.** madness; craziness; irrational behaviour; blind passion; ~ *des grandeurs*, megalomania; ~ *de la persécution*, persecution mania; *c'est une* ~ *de faire cela*, it's mad to do that; *vous n'aurez pas la* ~ *de faire cela*, you won't be crazy enough to do that; *à la* ~, madly, passionately; **2.** folly, piece of folly; extravagance; *dire des* ~*s*, to talk nonsense; **3.** folly (extravagant piece of architecture, esp. in country).

folié, -e [fɔlje] *adj.* (bot.) foliate.

folio [fɔljo] *s.m.* folio; (print.) page number, folio.

foliole [fɔljɔl] *s.f.* (bot.) foliole, leaflet.

foliotage [fɔljɔtaʒ] *s.m.* foliation, pagination.

folioter [fɔljɔte] *v.t.* to foliate, to paginate.

folioteuse [fɔljɔtøz] *s.f.* paginating machine.

folklore [fɔlklɔr] *s.m.* folklore.

folklorique [fɔlklɔrik] *adj.* traditional; (fam.) olde worlde, quaint.

folle¹ see FOU *adj., s.m.f.*

folle² [fɔl] *s.f.* (fish.) square large-meshed net.

follement [fɔlmɑ̃] *adv.* madly, extravagantly, foolishly.

follet, -te [fɔlɛ] *adj.* **1.** (obs. exc. dial.) wanton; **2.** lively, merry; *esprit* ~, goblin, sprite; *poil* ~, downy hair, fluff; *feu* ~, ignis fatuus, will-o'--the-wisp; (fig.) *c'est un vrai feu* ~, he's always on the move, he comes and goes, you can't pin him down.

folliculaire [fɔlikylɛr] *s.m.* (pej.) pamphleteer, hack journalist.

follicule [fɔlikyl] *s.m.* (bot., anat.) follicle.

fomentat-eur, -rice [fɔmɑ̃tatœr] *s.m.f.* agitator, stirrer-up (of trouble, etc.).

fomentation [fɔmɑ̃tɑsjɔ̃] *s.f.* (med.) fomentation; (fig.) instigation (to revolt, etc.).

fomenter [fɔmɑ̃te] *v.t.* (med.) to foment; (fig.) to excite, to stir up, to rouse, to foment.

fonçage [fɔ̃saʒ] *s.m.* **1.** bottoming (of cask); **2.** boring or sinking (of well); **3.** plain-colour sizing (of wallpaper).

foncé, -e [fɔ̃se] *adj.* (of colours) deep, dark; *vert* ~, dark green.

foncer [fɔ̃se] *v.t.* **1.** to bottom (cask, etc.); (cook.) to line (tin, etc.); **2.** to darken, to deepen, (a colour); ~ *v.i.* to rush, to dash, to charge; (fam.) ~ *dans le brouillard*, to press on regardless.

fonci-er, -ère [fɔ̃sje] *adj.* **1.** landed, land-; based on or derived from land; *propriété* ~*ère*, landed property; *propriétaire* ~*er*, landowner, ground landlord; *crédit* ~*er*, loan bank (granting loans on land); *impôt* ~*er*, land tax; **2.** (fig.) fundamental, basic; *qualités* ~*ères*, fundamental qualities; ~**èrement** [fɔ̃sjɛrmɑ̃] *adv.* fundamentally, basically, thoroughly.

fonction [fɔ̃ksjɔ̃] *s.f.* function, duty, office, rôle; position, profession; (math.) function; *faire* ~ *de*, to act as, to fulfil the duties of; *entrer en* ~, to take office, to begin one's duties; *se démettre de ses* ~*s*, to resign from office; *en* ~, in office; *la* ~ *publique*, the civil service; *en* ~ *de*, in relation to, according to; *être* ~ *de*, to vary with, to depend on, to be conditional on; (math., phys.) to be a function of.

fonctionnaire [fɔ̃ksjɔnɛr] *s.m.f.* official, civil servant.

fonctionnariser [fɔ̃ksjɔnarize] *v.t.* to assimilate to the civil service, to make bureaucratic; to tie up in red tape.

fonctionnarisme [fɔ̃ksjɔnarism] *s.m.* (pej.) bureaucracy, red tape.

fonctionnel, -le [fɔ̃ksjɔnɛl] *adj.* functional; ~**lement** [fɔ̃ksjɔnɛlmɑ̃] *adv.* functionally.

fonctionnement [fɔ̃ksjɔnmɑ̃] *s.m.* working, operation, running.

fonctionner [fɔ̃ksjɔne] *v.i.* to work, to operate, to function.

fond [fɔ̃] *s.m.* **1.** bottom, base; (mining) face; *mineur de* ~, underground worker; **2.** bed (of sea, river, etc.); depth; *assez de* ~ *pour plonger*, deep enough for diving; **3.** furthest part, depth, back; crown (of hat); seat (of trousers); pit (of stomach); (fig.) depths (of sorrow, despair, etc.); *au* ~ *de la salle*, at the back of the room; *au* ~ *des bois*, in the depths of the woods; *du* ~ *du cœur*, from the bottom of one's heart; **4.** (lit. & fig.) background; *bruit de* ~, background noise; ~ *de teint*, foundation cream; **5.** foundation, basis; fund (of knowledge, etc.); substance (opp. form); (fig.) root (of problem); *au* ~, (fam.) *dans le* ~, basically, in reality, in fact; *à* ~, in depth, in detail; *respirer à* ~, to breathe deeply; *à* ~ *de train*, at full speed; *de* ~, fundamental, serious; *article de* ~, leading article (in newspaper); *ouvrage de* ~, standard work; *faire* ~ *sur*, to rely on; (sport) *avoir du* ~, to have staying-power; *courses de* (*grand*) ~, long-distance races.

fondamental, -e [fɔ̃damɑ̃tal] *adj.* fundamental; ~**ement** [fɔ̃damɑ̃talmɑ̃] *adv.* fundamentally.

fondant, -e [fɔ̃dɑ̃] *adj.* melting, juicy, luscious, that melts in the mouth; ~ *s.m.* **1.** (med., chem.) solvent, flux; **2.** fondant, sweetmeat.

fondat-eur, -rice [fɔ̃datœr] *s.m.f.* founder, foundress.

fondation [fɔ̃dɑsjɔ̃] *s.f.* **1.** (usu. pl.) (constr.) foundations; **2.** founding, foundation, endowment.

fondé, -e [fɔ̃de] *adj.* founded, well-founded, justified; *être* ~ *à faire qch.*, to have good grounds for doing sth.

fondé de pouvoir [fɔ̃dedpuvwar] *s.m.* (law, comm.) agent (holding power of attorney, or authorized to sign), proxy.

fondement [fɔ̃dmɑ̃] *s.m.* **1.** (usu. pl.) (obs. constr.) foundations; (mod. fig.) foundations, basis; **2.** grounds, basis, justification; *rumeur sans* ~, baseless rumour; **3.** (fam.) behind, bottom.

fonder [fɔ̃de] *v.t.* **1.** (rare) to place on a foundation of; **2.** to found, to establish, to institute, to set up, to endow; **3.** ~ *qch. sur*, to base sth. on; ~ *des espoirs en qn.*, to place great hopes in s.o.; **4.** to justify; *se* ~ *sur*, to rely on (argument, etc.), to take as authority.

fonderie [fɔ̃dri] *s.f.* foundry; smelting, casting; wrought-iron work.

fondeur [fɔ̃dœr] *s.m.* iron-master, founder, smelter.

fondeuse [fɔ̃døz] *s.f.* (metall.) casting machine.

fondis see FONTIS.

fondoir [fɔ̃dwar] *s.m.* melting-house (in abattoir).

fondre [fɔ̃dr] *v.t.* (lit. & fig.) to melt, to soften; to smelt, to cast, to found (bell); (fig.) to merge, to blend (colours); ~ *v.i.* to melt, to dissolve; to lose weight; ~ *sur*, to pounce upon; **se** ~ *v.refl.* (lit. & fig.) to melt; to merge, to fuse.

fondrière [fɔ̃drijɛr] *s.f.* pot-hole, rut (in road); muddy place, bog.

fonds [fɔ̃] *s.m.* **1.** estate, property; ~ *de commerce*, business; **2.** capital (opp. interest); funds, finances; ~ *publics*, Government stock; ~ *consolidés*, consols; *prêter à* ~ *perdu*, to lend without security; *mise de* ~, putting up capital, investment; ~ *de roulement*, working capital; *Fonds monétaire international*, International Monetary Fund; **3.** (pl.) funds, means, resources; *être en* ~, to be in funds, to have money; **4.** (fig.) fund, stock; heritage.

fondu, -e [fɔ̃dy] *adj.* melted, molten, cast; (of colours) blended; ~ *s.m.* (cin.) *ouverture en* ~, fade-in, fading-in; *fermeture en* ~, fade-out, fading-out; ~ *enchaîné*, cross fade.

fondue [fɔ̃dy] *s.f.* (cook.) fondue.

fongible [fɔ̃ʒibl] *adj.* (law) fungible.

fongicide [fɔ̃ʒisid] *adj.* fungicidal.

fongiforme [fɔ̃ʒifɔrm] *adj.* fungiform.

fongosité [fɔ̃gozite] *s.f.* (med.) fungosity, fungus.

fongueu-x, -se [fɔ̃gø] *adj.* (med.) fungous.

fongus [fɔ̃gys] *s.m.* (bot., med.) fungus.

fontaine [fɔ̃tɛn] *s.f.* **1.** spring, well; (fig.) source; **2.** fountain; **3.** water-container or -filter (with tap).

fontainier [fɔ̃tenje] *s.m.* **1.** well-borer; **2.** turncock (water board official); **3.** maker of domestic water-filters.

fontanelle [fɔ̃tanɛl] *s.f.* (anat.) fontanelle.

fonte[1] [fɔ̃t] *s.f.* **1.** melting, thaw, thawing; *la* ~ *des neiges*, thaw; **2.** smelting, casting; cast-iron, pig-iron; **3.** (print.) fount.

fonte[2] [fɔ̃t] *s.f.* (usu. pl.) saddle-holster.

fontis [fɔ̃ti], **fondis** [fɔ̃di] *s.m.* (techn.) subsidence.

fonts [fɔ̃] *s.m.pl.* font; *tenir un enfant sur les* ~ *baptismaux*, to stand godparent to a child.

foot [fut] *s.m.* (fam.) soccer.

football [futbol] *s.m.* football (game).

footing [futiŋ] *s.m.* walking (for exercise); *faire du* ~, to take a constitutional.

for [fɔr] *s.m.* (Lit.) *le* ~ *intérieur*, one's conscience; *dans, en, son* ~ *intérieur*, in one's heart of hearts.

forage [fɔraʒ] *s.m.* boring, drilling.

forain, -e [fɔrɛ̃] *adj.* **1.** (obs.) outside, foreign; (mod.) (naut.) *rade* ~*e*, open roadstead; **2.** itinerant; *marchand* ~, hawker, pedlar; stall-keeper (at fair); *fête* ~*e*, fair.

foraminé, -e [fɔramine] *adj.* foraminate, perforated.

foraminifères [fɔraminifɛr] *s.m.pl.* (zool.) Foraminifera.

forban [fɔrbɑ̃] *s.m.* pirate; unscrupulous rogue, shark.

forçage [fɔrsaʒ] *s.m.* **1.** (hunt.) bringing to bay; **2.** (hort.) forcing.

forçat [fɔrsa] *s.m.* (hist.) galley-slave; (mod.) convict; (fig.) slave, drudge; *travail de* ~, drudgery.

force [fɔrs] *s.f.* **1.** (often pl.) strength, vigour, energy, power, ability; *avoir de la* ~, to be strong; *épreuve de* ~, trial of strength; ~ *de volonté*, will-power; *ne pas avoir la* ~ *de marcher*, not to be strong enough to walk; *ménager ses* ~*s*, to conserve one's energy; *de toutes ses* ~*s*, with all one's might; *ce travail est au-dessus de ses* ~*s*, this work is too much for him; *faire* ~, to strain, to go hard (at sth.); *faire* ~ *de rames*, to row hard; *en* ~, hard, vigorously; *dans la* ~ *de l'âge*, at the height of one's powers; **2.** power, force; intensity, strength; (mech.) force; (pl.) forces; ~ *motrice*, driving power; *la* ~ *d'un argument*, the force of an argument; *la* ~ *d'un acide*, the strength of an acid; *dans toute la* ~ *du mot*, in the full meaning of the word; *la* ~ *armée*, the military power; *la* ~ *publique*, the police force; *être là en* ~, to be present in strength; *avec* ~, vigorously, forcefully, in strong terms; (mil.) ~ *de frappe*, striking force; ~*s navales*, naval forces; **3.** force, superior force, compulsion; *céder à la* ~, to yield to force; *par la* ~ *de l'habitude*, by force of habit; *la* ~ *des choses*, the force of circumstances; *par la* ~ *des choses*, of necessity; ~ *est de*, there is no choice but to; ~ *lui fut d'admettre son erreur*, he was compelled to admit his mistake; *de, par*, ~, by force; *à toute* ~, at all costs, come what may; *à* ~, (fam.) by sheer effort; (obs.) copiously, in plenty; *à* ~ *de*, by means of, by dint of; ~ *adv.* (obs. exc. Lit.) much, a lot of, many, copious, numerous; *avec* ~ *poignées de main*, with much hand-shaking.

forcé, -e [fɔrse] *adj.* **1.** forced, compulsory, inevitable; *travaux* ~*s*, hard labour; (fam.) *c'est* ~, it's inevitable; **2.** affected, artificial; unnatural, forced.

forcement [fɔrsəmɑ̃] *s.m.* forcing (open).

forcément [fɔrsemɑ̃] *adv.* necessarily; inevitably.

forcené, -e [fɔrsəne] *adj.* (obs.) mad; furious, frantic; *s.m.f.* madman, madwoman.

forceps [fɔrsɛps] *s.m.* (surg.) forceps.

forcer [fɔrse] *v.t.* **1.** to force, to break open (door, etc.); **2.** to force, to oblige, to compel (s.o.); ~ *à* or *de*, to force to, to oblige to; ~ *la main à qn.*, to force someone's hand; **3.** to force (s.o., sth.), to do violence to; (hort.) to force; (fig.) to stretch, to abuse; ~ *v.i.* **1.** (naut.) ~ *de voiles, de rames*, to put on speed; *la brise force*, the wind is strengthening; **2.** (cards) to raise; (sport) to make an effort, to stretch oneself; **se** ~ *v.refl.* to force oneself, to compel oneself.

forcerie [fɔrsəri] *s.f.* (hort.) forcing-house.

forces [fɔrs] *s.f.pl.* (techn.) shears.

forcing [fɔrsiŋ] *s.m.* (sport) pressure.

forcir [fɔrsir] *v.i.* to put on weight; to grow stronger.

forclore [fɔrklɔr] *v.t.* (law) to foreclose; *se laisser* ~, to forfeit (a right).

forclusion [fɔrklyzjɔ̃] *s.f.* (law) foreclosure.

forer [fɔre] *v.t.* to bore, to drill, to pierce.

foresti-er, -ère [fɔrɛstje] *adj.* forest, relating to forests; *garde* ~*er*, forester, keeper; ~**er** *s.m.* forester.

foret [fɔrɛ] *s.m.* drill, borer.

forêt [fɔrɛ] *s.f.* (lit. & fig.) forest; (fig.) *les arbres cachent la* ~, you can't see the wood for the trees; *la Forêt-Noire*, the Black Forest.

foreur [fɔrœr] *s.m.* driller, borer.

foreuse [fɔrøz] *s.f.* machine-drill, rock-drill.

forfaire [fɔrfɛr] *v.i.* (obs. exc. Lit.) to be false to, to fail (in); ~ *v.t.* (obs.) to forfeit.

forfait[1] [fɔrfɛ] *s.m.* serious crime.

forfait[2] [fɔrfɛ] *s.m.* (fixed-price) contract; *travail à* ~, contract work.

forfait[3] [fɔrfɛ] *s.m.* fine, forfeit (esp. for scratching horse from race); *déclarer* ~, to scratch, to withdraw (from a competition); (racing) *déclarer* ~ *pour un cheval*, to scratch a horse.
forfaitaire [fɔrfɛtɛr] *adj.* contractual, by contract; *prix* ~, contracted price.
forfaiture [fɔrfetyr] *s.f.* **1.** (feud.) felony; disloyalty; **2.** misuse or abuse of authority (by civil servant), breach of trust.
forfanterie [fɔrfɑ̃tri] *s.f.* bragging, boasting, boast.
forficule [fɔrfikyl] *s.f.* (ent.) earwig.
forge [fɔrʒ] *s.f.* forge, smithy; iron-works; *maître de* ~*s*, ironmaster.
forgé, -e [fɔrʒe] *adj.* forged; *fer* ~, wrought iron; (fig.) fabricated; ⚠ see FORGER 2.
forgeage [fɔrʒaʒ] *s.m.* forging.
forger [fɔrʒe] *v.t.* **1.** (metall.) to forge, to work; (fig.) *c'est en forgeant qu'on devient forgeron*, practice makes perfect; (fig.) ~ *les fers, les chaînes, de qn.*, to enslave s.o.; **2.** to invent, to fabricate, to coin (a word), to make up; ⚠ not 'to forge' money or signature.
forgeron [fɔrʒərɔ̃] *s.m.* blacksmith.
forgeu-r [fɔrʒœr] *s.m.* (techn. & fig.) (metal-) forger; ~**r**, ~**se** *s.m.f.* fabricator, inventor; ⚠ not 'forger' of money or signature.
forjeter [fɔrʒəte] *v.t.* to build (sth.) as a projection; ~ *v.i.* to jut out, to be out of line.
forlancer [fɔrlɑ̃se] *v.t.* (hunt.) to start (quarry).
forligner [fɔrliɲe] *v.i.* **1.** (obs.) to disgrace one's ancestors; **2.** to demean oneself, to lose caste.
formage [fɔrmaʒ] *s.m.* (techn.) shaping, moulding.
formaldéhyde [fɔrmaldeid] *s.m.* (chem.) formaldehyde.
formalisation [fɔrmalizɑsjɔ̃] *s.f.* formalization.
formaliser [fɔrmalize] *v.t.* to formalize; **se** ~ *v.refl.* to take offence, to take exception (*de*, to).
formalisme [fɔrmalism] *s.m.* formalism.
formaliste [fɔrmalist] *adj.* formalistic; ~ *s.m.f.* formalist, stickler for etiquette.
formalité [fɔrmalite] *s.f.* formality; *sans autre* ~, without further ado; *ce n'est qu'une simple* ~ it's merely a matter of form.
formant [fɔrmɑ̃] *s.m.* (lang.) formant.
format [fɔrma] *s.m.* format.
format-eur, -rice [fɔrmatœr] *adj.* formative; ~**eur** *s.m.* creator, fashioner.
formati-f, -ve [fɔrmatif] *adj.* formative.
formation [fɔrmɑsjɔ̃] *s.f.* **1.** formation, forming, creation; **2.** (mil., etc.) formation, unit; **3.** education, training.
forme [fɔrm] *s.f.* **1.** form, shape; *sans* ~, shapeless; *prendre* ~, to take shape; *en* ~ *de*, in the shape of; *sous la* ~ *de*, in the disguise of; *sous* ~ *de*, as, in the form of; **2.** (human) figure; (pl.) curves; (fam.) *prendre des* ~*s*, to get fat; **3.** form, state; kind, variety, type; **4.** etiquette, usage, form; (pl.) manners; *dans les* ~*s*, formally, with due ceremony; *sans autre* ~ *de procès*, unceremoniously; *pour la* ~, for the sake of form; **5.** form, condition, state, (of horse, sportsman, etc.); *en* ~, in form; *en pleine* ~, in good form; **6.** (techn.) mould, form; last (for shoes); block (for hats); *chapeau haut de* ~, top hat; **7.** (naut.) dock; **8.** bed of sand or gravel (for laying paving); **9.** (vet.) ring-bone; **10.** form (of hare).
formé, -e [fɔrme] *adj.* formed, fully developed; assembled, made up.
formel, -le [fɔrmɛl] *adj.* formal, precise; express, explicit; ~**lement** [fɔrmɛlmɑ̃] *adv.* expressly, explicitly, strictly; formally.
former [fɔrme] *v.t.* **1.** (relig.) to create, to make; **2.** to imagine, to conceive; **3.** to form, to collect, to establish, to set up; **4.** to form, to fashion, to shape; **5.** to train, to develop, to educate; **6.** to form, to constitute, to make up, to make; **se** ~ *v.refl.* to be formed, to take shape; to develop, to educate or train oneself.
formiate [fɔrmjat] *s.m.* (chem.) formate.
formicant, -e [fɔrmikɑ̃] *adj.* (of pulse) weak and rapid.
formication [fɔrmikɑsjɔ̃] *s.f.* (med.) formication.
formidable [fɔrmidabl] *adj.* **1.** (rare) formidable, dreadful; **2.** extraordinary, amazing; (fam.) tremendous, marvellous; ~**ment** [fɔrmidabləmɑ̃] *adv.* **1.** (rare) formidably; **2.** extremely, tremendously.
formique [fɔrmik] *adj.* (chem.) formic.
formulable [fɔrmylabl] *adj.* that can be formulated; *désir difficilement* ~, wish difficult to put into words.
formulaire [fɔrmylɛr] *s.m.* **1.** formulary; **2.** printed form.
formulation [fɔrmylɑsjɔ̃] *s.f.* formulation.
formule [fɔrmyl] *s.f.* **1.** (chem., etc.) formula; **2.** form of words; phrase, expression; ~ *de politesse*, polite form of words; **3.** printed form.
formuler [fɔrmyle] *v.t.* to draw up (according to a formula), to make up (prescription); to formulate, to express clearly; to put into words.
fornication [fɔrnikɑsjɔ̃] *s.f.* fornication.
forniquer [fɔrnike] *v.i.* to fornicate.
fors [fɔr] *prep.* (obs.) except, but, save.
fort, -e [fɔr] *adj.* **1.** strong, powerful, robust, vigorous; ~ *comme un Turc*, ~ *comme un bœuf*, as strong as a horse, as an ox; *recourir à la manière* ~*e*, to have recourse to violence; **2.** large; *femme* ~*e*, stout woman; **3.** able, clever, good (*en*, at); *être* ~ *en math.*, to be good at maths; *être* ~ *en gueule*, to be a great talker; **4.** strong, resistant, hard-wearing; fortified; (fig.) strong, courageous; *les esprits* ~*s*, unbelievers, free thinkers; **5.** strong, active, energetic; *un vent* ~, a strong wind; (before the noun) extraordinary, abnormal; intense; (fam.) exaggerated; ~*es chutes de neige*, unusually heavy falls of snow; *une* ~*e somme*, a very large sum; *accent* ~, strong, marked, accent; *odeur* ~*e*, powerful smell or scent; *avoir une* ~*e envie de*, to have a great desire to; *c'est un peu* ~, it's a bit thick; *ce qu'il y a de plus* ~, *c'est que*, the worst (or best) of it is that; **6.** powerful, effective; influential; *être* ~ *de*, to rely on, to take strength from; *se porter* ~ *pour qn.*, to act as guarantor for s.o.; *se faire* ~ *de*, to be confident of one's ability to; *c'est plus* ~ *que moi*, I can't help it.
fort [fɔr] *s.m.* **1.** strong point, strength; *le* ~ *et le faible d'une affaire*, the pros and cons of an affair; (iron.) *la générosité n'est pas son* ~, generosity is not his strong point; *l'histoire n'est pas mon* ~, I'm not very good at history; **2.** heart, depth; *au* ~ *de l'hiver*, in the depth of winter; *au plus* ~ *de la bataille*, at the height of the battle; **3.** strong man; influential person; *les* ~*s des Halles*, market porters; **4.** fort, fortress, stronghold.
fort [fɔr] *adv.* **1.** hard, violently; loud; fast; *frapper* ~, to hit hard; *tousser* ~, to cough violently; *cœur qui bat* ~, heart which beats fast; *crier* ~, to shout loud; *vent qui souffle* ~, wind which blows hard; *sentir* ~, to smell strongly; (fig.) *y aller* ~, to go too far; **2.** very much, extremely, very; *il me déplaît* ~, I dislike him very much; *j'en doute* ~, I very much doubt it; *avoir* ~ *à faire*, to have a lot to do; ~ *petit*, very small; ~ *bien*, very well.
forte [fɔrte] *adv.*, *s.m.* (mus.) forte.
fortement [fɔrtəmɑ̃] *adv.* strongly, vigorously; intensely; very much, greatly.
forteresse [fɔrtərɛs] *s.f.* (lit. & fig.) fortress, stronghold.

fortifiant, -e [fɔrtifjɑ̃] *adj.* strengthening, fortifying, invigorating, bracing; ~ *s.m.* tonic.
fortification [fɔrtifikɑsjɔ̃] *s.f.* fortification.
fortifier [fɔrtifje] *v.t.* to strengthen, to invigorate, to brace; to surround with fortifications, to fortify; (fig.) to increase, to strengthen, to corroborate; **se** ~ *v.refl.* to grow stronger; (fig.) to entrench oneself.
fortin [fɔrtɛ̃] *s.m.* small fort.
fortissimo [fɔrtisimo] *adv.*, *s.m.* fortissimo.
fortrait, -e [fɔrtrɛ] *adj.* (of horses) foundered.
fortraiture [fɔrtretyr] *s.f.* (obs.) (of horses) over-fatigue.
fortuit, -e [fɔrtɥi] *adj.* fortuitous, casual, accidental; **~ement** [fɔrtɥitmɑ̃] *adv.* fortuitously, casually, accidentally.
fortune [fɔrtyn] *s.f.* **1.** fortune, chance, luck, fate; *bonne* ~, good luck; *faire contre mauvaise* ~ *bon cœur*, to make the best of things, to put a brave face on things; *inviter qn. à la* ~ *du pot*, to invite s.o. to take pot luck; *de* ~, makeshift; (naut.) *voile de* ~, cross-jack sail; *mât de* ~, jury mast; **2.** fortunes, career, success; position; **3.** wealth, means, prosperity; *posséder de la* ~, to be well off; *faire* ~, to make a fortune, to get rich, to succeed.
fortuné, -e [fɔrtyne] *adj.* **1.** (obs. exc. Lit.) fortunate, lucky, happy; **2.** rich, wealthy.
forum [fɔrɔm] *s.m.* forum.
forure [fɔryr] *s.f.* (techn.) drill-hole, pipe (of key).
fosse [fos] *s.f.* **1.** pit, hole in the ground, trench; (mining) pit; (car) inspection-pit; dungeon; ~ *aux ours*, bearpit; ~ *aux lions*, lions' den; ~ *à fumier*, midden pit; ~ *d'aisances*, cesspit; ~ *septique*, septic tank; ~ *mobile*, portable latrine; **2.** grave, tomb; ~ *commune*, common grave, pauper's grave; *creuser sa* ~, (fig.) to dig one's own grave; **3.** (geol.) ~ *d'effondrement*, rift valley; **4.** (anat.) fossa.
fossé [fose] *s.m.* ditch, trench, drain, moat, fosse; (fig.) rift, gulf; *sauter le* ~, (fig.) to take the plunge, to cross the Rubicon; *au bout du* ~ *la culbute!*, a short life and a merry one!
fossette [fosɛt] *s.f.* dimple; *jouer à la* ~, to play marbles.
fossile [fosil] *s.m.*, *adj.* fossil; ~ *adj.* (fig., fam.) antediluvian; ~ *s.m.* (fig.) *vieux* ~, old fossil.
fossilifère [fosilifɛr] *adj.* fossiliferous.
fossilisation [fosilizɑsjɔ̃] *s.f.* fossilization.
fossilisé, -e [fosilize] *adj.* fossilized; (fig.) antiquated.
fossiliser [fosilize] *v.t.* to fossilize; (fig.) to make antiquated; **se** ~ *v.refl.* to become fossilized.
fossoir [foswar] *s.m.* (agric.) vineyard hoe.
fossoyer [foswaje] *v.t.* to ditch; to dig (a grave).
fossoyeur [foswajœr] *s.m.* grave-digger; (fig.) destroyer.
fou [fu], **fol** [fɔl] (before m. sing. noun beginning with vowel or h-mute) *adj.m.*, **folle** [fɔl] *adj.f.* **1.** (mental condition) mad, insane, mentally deranged; (of character or behaviour) mad, crazy, distracted; wild, insane; ~ *à lier*, raving mad; *son insolence me rend* ~, his insolence is driving me mad; ~ *de joie*, mad with joy; ~ *de colère*, wild with anger; ~ *d'amour*, madly in love; *être* ~ *de musique*, to be mad about music; *tu es* ~ *d'avoir fait ça*, you are crazy to have done that; (fam.) *il n'est pas* ~, he is all there; ~ *rire*, hysterical laughter; **2.** senseless, ridiculous, irrational; *un fol espoir*, a foolish hope; *idée folle*, crazy idea; **3.** (after noun) irregular, abnormal; huge, extraordinary; *moteur* ~, racing engine; *boussole folle*, deviating compass; *il y avait un monde* ~, there was an incredible crowd; *succès* ~, unbelievable success; *mettre un temps* ~ *à faire qch.*, to take ages to do sth.; *dépenser un argent* ~, to spend huge sums of money.
fou, folle [fu, fɔl] *s.m.f.* madman, madwoman, lunatic; madcap, scatterbrain; *maison de* ~*s*, (obs.) lunatic asylum; (mod. fig.) madhouse; *faire le* ~, to play the fool; *plus on est de* ~*s, plus on rit*, the more the merrier; ~ *s.m.* **1.** jester; **2.** (chess) bishop; **3.** (ornith.) gannet.
fouace [fwas], **fougasse** [fugas] *s.f.* girdle-cake.
fouaille [fwɑj] *s.f.* (hunt.) parts of boar given to hounds.
fouailler [fwɑje] *v.t.* (obs.) to lash, to whip repeatedly; (fig.) to lash, to torment.
foucade [fukad] *s.f.* (obs.) whim, fad, impulse.
foudre[1] [fudr] *s.f.* lightning, thunderbolt; (pl.) condemnation; *coup de* ~, (fig.) (obs.) shattering blow, thunderbolt; (mod.) love at first sight; *les* ~*s du Vatican*, the thunderings of the Vatican; ~ *s.m.* (iron.) *un* ~ *de guerre*, a great general.
foudre[2] [fudr] *s.m.* **1.** large cask, tun; **2.** (techn.) housing for blower (fan).
foudroiement [fudrwamɑ̃] *s.m.* striking down (by lightning); being struck by lightning; (fig.) being thunderstruck, struck down.
foudroyant, -e [fudrwajɑ̃] *adj.* crushing, overwhelming; rapid, very fast, lightning.
foudroyer [fudrwaje] *v.t.* to strike by lightning; to electrocute; to strike down, to crush, to destroy; (fig.) to overwhelm; *être foudroyé*, to be struck by lightning; (fig.) to be shattered, to be thunderstruck; ~ *qn. du regard*, to crush s.o. with a look.
fouet [fwɛ] *s.m.* **1.** whip, birch; birching, whipping, beating; *donner un coup de* ~ *à*, to whip, to lash; *donner le* ~ *à*, to whip, to beat; (artill.) *tir de plein* ~, direct fire; *frapper la balle de plein* ~, to hit the ball cleanly; *coup de* ~, (fig.) stimulus, spur; **2.** light cord, whipcord, whipping, lashing; **3.** (med.) tearing a muscle; **4.** (cook.) whisk, beater; **5.** tip (of bird's wing or tail).
fouettard, -e [fwɛtar] *adj.* *père* ~, *mère* ~*e*, bogyman.
fouetté, -e [fwete] *adj.* (of cream) whipped; ~ *s.m.* (danc.) fouetté.
fouettement [fwɛtmɑ̃] *s.m.* whipping, beating; lashing.
fouetter [fwete] *v.t.* to whip, to lash, to beat; to whisk, to whip up (eggs, cream, etc.); (fig.) to stimulate, to excite; *la pluie fouettait les vitres*, the rain was lashing against the windows; (fig.) *il n'y a pas de quoi* ~ *un chat*, there's nothing to make a fuss about; *avoir d'autres chats à* ~, to have other fish to fry; ~ *v.i.* to lash, to whip; (pop.) to stink; (pop.) to be scared.
fou-fou [fufu], **fofolle** [fɔfɔl] *adj.* slightly mad, dotty.
fougasse[1] [fugas] *s.f.* (mil.) fougasse, small mine.
fougasse[2] see FOUACE.
fouger [fuʒe] *v.i.* (of boar) to root.
fougeraie [fuʒrɛ] *s.f.* fern-brake, patch of ferns.
fougère [fuʒɛr] *s.f.* (bot.) fern, bracken.
fougerole [fuʒrɔl] *s.f.* (bot.) small fern.
fougue[1] [fug] *s.f.* impetuosity, fire, spirit, passion.
fougue[2] [fug] *s.f.* (naut.) mizzen topmast.
fougueu-x, -se [fugø] *adj.* impetuous, ardent, spirited; (of horse) mettlesome; **~sement** [fugøzmɑ̃] *adv.* impetuously.
fouille [fuj] *s.f.* **1.** digging, excavation; (pl.) (archaeol.) excavations, dig; **2.** search, searching (of person, luggage, etc.).
fouillé, -e [fuje] *adj.* detailed, elaborately worked; *étude* ~*e*, study in depth.
fouiller [fuje] *v.t.* **1.** to dig, to excavate; (art) to undercut; **2.** to examine, to search thoroughly, to go through, to inspect, to ransack; (fig.) ~ *un problème*, to go into a problem in detail; ~ *v.i.* (of animals) to root; to rummage, to burrow; ~ *dans un tiroir*, to rummage in a drawer; ~ *dans*

les poches, to go through one's pockets; ~ *dans ses souvenirs*, to delve into one's memories; **se** ~ *v.refl.* to go through one's pockets; (fam.) *il peut se* ~*!*, he's got a hope!
fouilleu-r, -se [fujœr] *s.m.f.* searcher, researcher; rummager; ~**se** *s.f.* **1.** woman police searcher; **2.** (agric.) subsoil plough.
fouillis [fuji] *s.m.* (lit. & fig.) medley, litter, confusion, mess, jumble.
fouinard, -e [fwinar] *adj.* (fam.) inquisitive, nosey; *s.m.f.* nosey-parker, snooper.
fouine [fwin] *s.f.* (zool.) marten, beech-marten; (fam.) *à figure de* ~, sharp-nosed, ferret-faced.
fouiner [fwine] *v.i.* (fam.) to pry, to nose about, to nose round, to poke one's nose (*dans*, into).
fouineu-r, -se [fwinœr] *adj.*, *s.m.f.* = FOUINARD.
fouir [fwir] *v.t.* (esp. of animals) to dig, to burrow.
fouisseu-r, -se [fwisœr] *adj.* (of animal) burrowing; ~**r** *s.m.* burrower.
foulage [fulaʒ] *s.m.* treading (of grapes); fulling (of cloth); (print.) impression; *trop de* ~, over-impression.
foulant, -e [fulɑ̃] *adj.* **1.** pressing down, forcing; *pompe* ~*e*, force pump; **2.** (pop.) (usu. neg.) tiring; *ce n'est pas bien* ~, it's not exactly hard work.
foulard [fular] *s.m.* **1.** silk scarf, headscarf; **2.** (text.) foulard.
foule [ful] *s.f.* crowd, multitude, mass; *il y a* ~, it's very crowded; *la* ~, the common herd, the masses; *une* ~ *de*, a crowd of, a mass of, a heap of, a quantity of; *en* ~, in crowds, in numbers, in plenty.
foulée [fule] *s.f.* (hunt.) track, spoor; stride (of horse, athlete); (lit. & fig.) *dans la* ~, in one's stride.
fouler [fule] *v.t.* **1.** to full (cloth); to press; to tread (grapes); (cook.) to knead; to tread on; ~ *le sol de la patrie*, to set foot on one's native soil; ~ *aux pieds*, to trample on, (fig.) to scorn, to suppress; **2.** to sprain; *se* ~ *la cheville*, to sprain one's ankle; (fig. fam.) *se* ~ *la rate*, to strain oneself; *ne pas se* ~, not to over-exert oneself.
foulerie [fulri] *s.f.* fulling-mill, fulling-machine.
fouleu-r, -se [fulœr] *s.m.f.* fuller.
fouloir [fulwar] *s.m.* fulling-machine; wine press; dentist's filling tool.
foulon [fulɔ̃] *s.m.* (obs.) fuller; (mod.) *terre à* ~, fuller's earth; (*moulin à*) ~, fulling-mill.
foulque [fulk] *s.f.* (ornith.) coot.
foulure [fulyr] *s.f.* sprain, strain.
four [fur] *s.m.* (baker's) oven, oven (of cooker); (techn.) kiln, furnace; (fig.) *on ne peut être à la fois au* ~ *et au moulin*, you can't be in two places at once; *noir comme dans un* ~, pitch black; *petits* ~*s*, small fancy cakes, petits fours; (fig.) *faire un* ~, to be a flop, to fail.
fourbe [furb] *adj.* sly, crafty, untrustworthy; ~ *s.m.* knave, rogue, cheat.
fourberie [furbəri] *s.f.* cheating, imposture, deceit, knavery.
fourbi [furbi] *s.m.* **1.** (pop.) complicated affair, dubious transaction; **2.** (fam.) (soldier's) kit; gear, belongings; collection of rubbish; gadget, thing.
fourbir [furbir] *v.t.* to furbish, to polish, to rub up, (metal).
fourbissage [furbisaʒ] *s.m.* furbishing.
fourbu, -e [furby] *adj.* (of animal) foundered, over-fatigued; (of person) exhausted.
fourbure [furbyr] *s.f.* (vet.) foundering, founder.
fourche [furʃ] *s.f.* (agric.) fork, pitchfork; (bicycle) fork; crutch, fork (of trousers); fork (of tree).
fourchée [furʃe] *s.f.* forkful (of hay, etc.).
fourcher [furʃe] *v.i.* (obs.) to fork; (mod.) *la langue lui a fourché*, he made a slip of the tongue; ~ *v.t.* to fork (hay, etc.).
fourchet [furʃɛ] *s.m.* (vet.) foot-rot.
fourchette [furʃɛt] *s.f.* **1.** (table-)fork; *la* ~ *du père Adam*, one's fingers; *avoir un joli*, *un bon*, *coup de* ~, to be a good trencherman; **2.** beam-support (of balance); (car) gear-selector fork; frog (of horse's hoof); (artill.) bracket (in ranging); (econ., statistics) bracket; (cards) tenace.
fourchon [furʃɔ̃] *s.m.* prong, tine, (of fork).
fourchu, -e [furʃy] *adj.* forked; *pied* ~, cloven hoof, cloven foot.
fourgon[1] [furgɔ̃] *s.m.* wagon, baggage or ammunition wagon; delivery van, van; (rail.) luggage van; ~ *funéraire*, motor hearse.
fourgon[2] [furgɔ̃] *s.m.* oven rake, poker.
fourgonner [furgɔne] *v.t.* to poke, to stir (a fire); (fig.) to poke, to rummage, (*dans*, in).
fourguer [furge] *v.t.* (pop.) to sell, to flog (stolen goods); (fam.) to sell, to palm off, (bad goods).
fourme [furm] *s.f.* type of cheese (from Auvergne).
fourmi [furmi] *s.f.* (ent.) ant; *avoir des* ~*s dans les jambes*, to have pins and needles in one's legs.
fourmilier [furmilje] *s.m.* (zool.) ant-bear, ant-eater; (ornith.) ant-bird.
fourmilière [furmiljɛr] *s.f.* ant-hill; (fig.) swarm, seething mass.
fourmi-lion, fourmilion [furmiljɔ̃] *s.m.* (ent.) ant-lion.
fourmillant, -e [furmijɑ̃] *adj.* seething, swarming; prickling.
fourmillement [furmijmɑ̃] *s.m.* **1.** swarming; **2.** pins and needles, tingling, prickling.
fourmiller [furmije] *v.i.* **1.** to swarm, to seethe, (*de*, with); **2.** to tingle.
fournaise [furnɛz] *s.f.* (lit. & fig.) furnace.
fourneau (pl. **-x**) [furno] *s.m.* furnace; stove, (kitchen) range, cooker; bowl (of pipe); ~ *à gaz*, gas cooker, gas stove; ~ *à alcool*, spirit stove; *haut* ~, blast furnace; ~ *de mine*, (mil.) mine chamber; (mining) blast-hole, shot-hole.
fournée [furne] *s.f.* baking, batch (of loaves); (fig.) batch, bevy, contingent.
fourni, -e [furni] *adj.* well-supplied, well stocked; (of beard, etc.) thick, bushy.
fournil [furni] *s.m.* bakehouse.
fourniment [furnimɑ̃] *s.m.* (mil.) equipment; (fam.) outfit, paraphernalia.
fournir [furnir] *v.t.* to supply, to produce, to give, to make; to supply (provisions, etc.) to; ~ *des renseignements*, to supply information; ~ *les pièces nécessaires*, to produce the necessary documents; ~ *un effort considérable*, to make a great effort; (sport) ~ *un jeu remarquable*, to put up a remarkable performance; ~ *une famille*, to supply a family (with groceries, etc.); ~ *à qch.*, to supply the whole or part of sth.; ~ *aux dépenses*, to defray the expenses, to contribute to the expenses; ~ *qch. à qn.*, to supply, to provide, s.o. with sth.; ~ *qch. de qch.*, to supply, to provide, to equip, to furnish, to stock, sth. with sth.; ~ *un restaurant de vins*, to supply a restaurant with wines; ~ *qn. de qch.*, or more usu. *en qch.*, to supply, to provide, s.o. with sth.; *notre voisin nous fournit de*, *en*, *poisson*, our neighbour keeps us supplied with fish.
fournissement [furnismɑ̃] *s.m.* (fin.) contribution in shares (to a company), backing; (law) *compte de* ~, repartition account.
fournisseu-r, -se [furnisœr] *s.m.f.* supplier, purveyor, tradesman.
fourniture [furnityr] *s.f.* providing, supplying; supply, supplies; (dressm.) trimmings, materials; ~*s de bureau*, office equipment; (cook.) seasoning (for salad); ⚠ not 'furniture'.

fourrage [furaʒ] *s.m.* fodder, feed.
fourrager [furaʒe] *v.i.* to forage, to rummage; ~ *v.t.* to rumple, to scatter, to disarrange.
fourrag-er, -ère [furaʒe] *adj.* for use as fodder; *betterave ~ère*, beet grown for fodder.
fourragère [furaʒɛr] *s.f.* **1.** field of fodder; **2.** cart (for hay, etc.); **3.** lanyard worn by certain French regiments.
fourré [fure] *s.m.* thicket.
fourré, -e [fure] *adj.* **1.** fur-lined; furry; thickly-wooded; (cook.) stuffed; **2.** (fig.) *paix ~e*, hollow peace, phoney peace; *coup ~*, (fencing) exchange blow, (fig.) underhand trick; *monnaie ~e*, plated coin.
fourreau (pl. **-x**) [furo] *s.m.* sheath, case, scabbard, cover; sheath dress.
fourrer [fure] *v.t.* **1.** (obs.) to line or cover; (mod.) to line with fur; **2.** to thrust, to push; to cram, to stuff; *~ son nez dans les affaires de qn.*, to poke one's nose into someone's business; *se ~ le doigt dans l'œil*, to be mistaken; *~ des objets dans un sac*, to cram things into a bag; *~ qch. dans la tête de qn.*, to hammer sth. into someone's head; **se ~** *v.refl.* to hide; to become involved (in); (fig.) *ne plus savoir où se ~*, to be overcome with confusion.
fourre-tout [furtu] *s.m.invar.* **1.** lumber-room; **2.** holdall.
fourreur [furœr] *s.m.* furrier.
fourrier [furje] *s.m.* (mil.) quartermaster sergeant; (nav.) writer; (fig.) precursor, forerunner; ⚠ not 'furrier'.
fourrière [furjɛr] *s.f.* pound (for animals, cars); *mettre en* or *à la ~*, to impound, to tow away (car).
fourrure [furyr] *s.f.* **1.** fur, fur coat; animal's coat; (herald.) vair, ermine, etc.; **2.** (techn.) lining, filling, block, plug.
fourvoyer [furvwaje] *v.t.* to mislead, to lead astray; **se ~** *v.refl.* to stray, to go astray; to be completely mistaken.
foutaise [futɛz] *s.f.* rubbish, nonsense, trifle.
foutoir [futwar] *s.m.* (vulg.) shambles, mess.
foutral, -e, (aux) [futral] *adj.* (pop.) extraordinary.
foutraque [futrak] *adj., s.m.f.* (fam.) crazy, mad, (person).
foutre [futr] *v.t.* (pop., = FICHER) **1.** to do; to make a difference, to matter; *il ne fout rien de la journée*, he does damn all the whole day; *qu'est-ce que ça fout?*, so what?, what the hell?; **2.** to deliver (a blow); *tais-toi ou je te fous une gifle*, shut up, or I'll bash you; **3.** to put, to throw; *~ qn. à la porte*, to sling s.o. out; *~ en l'air*, to chuck in the air, to chuck up; **4.** *~ le camp*, to decamp, to scram; *ça la fout mal*, that's no good, it won't do, it's no go; it's a bloody nuisance, a damned shame; **se ~** *v.refl. se ~ de*, to make fun of, to think nothing of; *vous vous foutez de nous*, you're having us on, you're trying to make us look silly; *il s'en fout complètement*, he couldn't care less.
foutriquet [futrikɛ] *s.m.* (pej. of person) drip, little squit.
foutu, -e [futy] *adj.* **1.** (before noun) bad, rotten, wretched; *il est dans un ~ état*, he's in a dreadful state; **2.** (after noun) ruined, spoiled; *la sauce est ~e*, the sauce is ruined; **3.** *mal ~*, out of sorts; badly dressed; **4.** capable; *il n'est même pas ~ de faire ça*, he can't even do that; *il est ~ d'arriver en retard*, he's sure to be late.
fox-hound [fɔksawnd] *s.m.* foxhound.
fox-terrier [fɔkstɛrje], **fox** [fɔks] *s.m.* fox-terrier; ⚠ not 'fox'.
fox-trot [fɔkstrɔt] *s.m.* foxtrot (dance).
foyer [fwaje] *s.m.* **1.** hearth, hearthstone; grate, fire, fireside; (techn.) fire-box, furnace; (fig.) focus, source, centre, seat; *~ d'incendie*, seat of a fire; *~ d'épidémie*, source of an epidemic; **2.** home, family, family life; club (for soldiers, etc.); students' union; *fonder un ~*, to set up home; *rentrer dans ses ~s*, to go back home; **3.** (theatr.) foyer.
frac [frak] *s.m.* frock coat, dress coat, morning coat.
fracas [fraka] *s.m.* crash, din, uproar, fracas, tumult; (fig.) fuss.
fracassant, -e [frakasɑ] *adj.* (of noise) shattering; (fig.) sensational, startling.
fracasser [frakase] *v.t.* to break to pieces, to shatter, to smash; **se ~** *v.refl.* to break in pieces, to shatter.
fraction [fraksjɔ̃] *s.f.* (obs.) breaking; (mod.) fraction, portion.
fractionnaire [fraksjɔnɛr] *adj.* fractional, fractionary; (comm.) *livre ~*, separate ledger (for special transactions).
fractionnel, -le [fraksjɔnɛl] *adj.* divisive.
fractionnement [fraksjɔnmɑ̃] *s.m.* dividing into fractions; segmentation; (chem.) fractionation.
fractionner [fraksjɔne] *v.t.* to divide into fractions, to break up; (chem.) to fractionate; **se ~** *v.refl.* to divide, to break up.
fracture [fraktyr] *s.f.* (obs.) breaking, rupture; (surg., geol.) fracture.
fracturer [fraktyre] *v.t.* **1.** (surg.) to fracture; **2.** to break open, to smash.
fragile [fraʒil] *adj.* fragile, brittle; delicate, weak; unstable; precarious; **~ment** [fraʒilmɑ̃] *adv.* delicately; precariously.
fragilité [fraʒilite] *s.f.* fragility, brittleness; weakness, frailty, delicateness; instability, inconstancy.
fragment [fragmɑ̃] *s.m.* fragment, piece, scrap; remnant; extract.
fragmentaire [fragmɑ̃tɛr] *adj.* fragmentary; **~ment** [fragmɑ̃tɛrmɑ̃] *adv.* in fragmentary or incomplete form.
fragmentation [fragmɑ̃tɑsjɔ̃] *s.f.* division into fragments, fragmentation.
fragmenter [fragmɑ̃te] *v.t.* to fragment.
fragon [fragɔ̃] *s.m.* (bot.) knee-holly, butcher's broom.
fragrance [fragrɑ̃s] *s.f.* fragrance.
frai[1] [frɛ] *s.m.* **1.** spawning, spawn; spawning season; **2.** fry (of fish).
frai[2] [frɛ] *s.m.* wear, abrasion, (of coin).
fraîche [frɛʃ] *adj.f.* see FRAIS *adj.*
fraîchement [frɛʃmɑ̃] *adv.* **1.** newly, recently; **2.** (fig.) coolly, coldly; **3.** freshly, coolly; (fam.) *comment ça va? ~!*, how are you? Not so hot.
fraîcheur [frɛʃœr] *s.f.* coolness, chilliness; freshness, bloom; purity, naturalness.
fraîchin [frɛʃɛ̃] *s.m.* smell of fresh fish, smell of the sea.
fraîchir [frɛʃir] *v.i.* (of wind) to freshen; (of temperature) to get colder.
frairie [freri] *s.f.* (obs.) merry-making, feast.
frais, fraîche [frɛ, frɛʃ] *adj.* **1.** cool, fresh; (fig.) cool, distant; *servir ~*, serve cool; **2.** new, recent; *de fraîche date*, recent; *~ émoulu du lycée*, fresh from school; **3.** fresh (opp. stale, dried, preserved), (of eggs) new-laid; (of paint, etc.) wet; **4.** (of persons) fresh, blooming, youthful; (of things) neat, clean; (fig.) pure, undefiled; *avoir le teint ~*, to have a healthy colour; (fam. iron.) *nous voilà ~!*, now we're in a jam!; *être ~ et dispos*, to be ready and willing; *~ adv.* **1.** cool; *il fait ~ ce matin*, it is cool this morning; **2.** recently; *~ paru*, newly appeared; *foin ~ coupé*, newly cut hay.
frais[1] [frɛ] *s.m.* cool, coolness, cool place; *prendre le ~*, to take the air, to breathe fresh air; *tenir au ~*, to keep in a cool place.
frais[2] [frɛ] *s.m.pl.* expenses, expenditure, charges; (law) costs; (comm.) overheads,

operating costs; (fig.) trouble, effort, pains; *à grands ~*, at great expense, (fig.) with a lot of trouble; *à peu de ~*, at little cost, (fig.) easily; *aux ~ de qn.*, at someone's expense; *aux ~ de la princesse*, free; *se mettre en ~*, to involve oneself in expense, (fig.) to go to a lot of trouble; *faire les ~*, to stand the cost, (fig.) to go to the trouble; to pay for; *faire ses ~*, to get one's expenses paid, (fig.) to be repaid for one's trouble; *en être pour ses ~*, to lose one's money, (fig.) to waste one's time; *sur de nouveaux ~*, all over again.
fraisage [frɛzaʒ] *s.m.* (techn.) milling, drilling, countersinking.
fraise[1] [frɛz] *s.f.* strawberry; strawberry-mark.
fraise[2] [frɛz] *s.f.* **1.** mesentery (of animal); (cook.) *~ de veau*, dish made of membrane of calf's intestine; **2.** wattle (of turkey); **3.** (costume) ruff, ruffle.
fraise[3] [frɛz] *s.f.* (techn.) milling-tool, countersink(-bit), fraise.
fraiser[1] [freze] *v.t.* (obs.) to shell (beans, etc.); to knead (dough).
fraiser[2] [freze] *v.t.* (obs.) to fold into a ruff.
fraiser[3] [freze] *v.t.* (techn.) to mill, to drill, to countersink.
fraiseraie [frɛzrɛ], **fraisière** [frɛzjɛr] *s.f.* strawberry bed.
fraiseuse [frɛzøz] *s.f.* (techn.) drilling or countersinking machine.
fraisier [frezje] *s.m.* (bot.) strawberry plant.
fraisil [frezi] *s.m.* charcoal dust, coal dross.
fraisure [frezyr] *s.f.* (techn.) countersunk hole, countersink.
framboise [frɑ̃bwaz] *s.f.* raspberry.
framboiser [frɑ̃bwaze] *v.t.* to flavour with raspberry.
framboisier [frɑ̃bwazje] *s.m.* (bot.) raspberry cane.
franc [frɑ̃] *s.m.* franc.
franc, franche [frɑ̃, frɑ̃ʃ] *adj.* **1.** (obs.) free (not enslaved); (mod.) free, unhindered, unfettered; *avoir ses coudées ~hes*, to have a free hand, to have elbow room; *~ du collier*, sincere; *~he lippée*, free meal; (sport) *coup ~*, free kick; (naut.) *barre ~he*, hand steering, tiller; *pompe ~he*, dry pump; **2.** free, exempt; *port ~*, free port; *~ de port*, carriage free; **3.** frank, open, honest, sincere; *jouer ~ jeu*, to put one's cards on the table, to act above board; *~he hostilité*, open hostility; **4.** simple, pure; *couleur ~he*, simple colour; *terre ~he*, good ground; (of tree) *~ de pied*, ungrafted; **5.** (before noun) genuine, arrant, downright; *c'est une ~he canaille*, he's a downright scoundrel; **6.** (law) *huit jours ~s*, eight full days; *~ adv.* frankly; *à parler ~*, to speak plainly.
franc, franque [frɑ̃, frɑ̃k] *adj.* Frankish; *s.m.f.* Frank.
français, -e [frɑ̃sɛ] *adj.* French; *s.m.f.* Frenchman, Frenchwoman; *~ s.m* French (language); (fam.) *en bon ~*, in plain terms; *à la ~e*, in the French way.
franc-alleu [frɑ̃kalø] *s.m.* (pl. *francs-alleux*) (feud.) freehold.
franc-bord [frɑ̃bɔr] *s.m.* **1.** strip of public land along river or canal; **2.** (naut.) freeboard.
franc-bourgeois [frɑ̃burʒwa] *s.m.* (hist.) freeman.
franc-comtois, -e [frɑ̃kɔ̃twa] *adj., s.m.f.* (native or inhabitant) of the Franche-Comté.
France [frɑ̃s] *s.f.* (geog.) France.
Francfort [frɑ̃kfɔr] *s.f.* (geog.) Frankfurt.
franchement [frɑ̃ʃmɑ̃] *adv.* frankly, openly, honestly; plainly, candidly, unreservedly; really, completely; *c'était ~ idiot*, it was completely stupid; *~ interj.* honestly!
franchir [frɑ̃ʃir] *v.t.* **1.** (obs.) to free; (mod.) *~ une pompe*, to free a pump; **2.** to jump over, to climb over, to clear; (fig.) to overcome (obstacles); *~ le Rubicon*, to cross the Rubicon; **3.** to pass (a limit), to go beyond, to overstep; to cover (space or time), to span.
franchise [frɑ̃ʃiz] *s.f.* **1.** freedom (of city, etc.); exemption, immunity (from tax, etc.); *en ~*, duty free; *~ postale*, exemption from postage (=O.H.M.S.); *~ de bagages*, free baggage-allowance; **2.** frankness, sincerity, openness, candour; *en toute ~*, in all honesty, to be frank; ⚠ not 'franchise' in senses 'right to vote' or 'agency' (for goods).
franchissable [frɑ̃ʃisabl] *adj.* passable, negotiable.
franchissement [frɑ̃ʃismɑ̃] *s.m.* clearing, crossing, passing.
francique [frɑ̃sik] *s.m.* Frankish (language).
francisation [frɑ̃sizɑsjɔ̃] *s.f.* **1.** gallicizing (of word, etc.); **2.** (naut.) registration as French.
franciscain, -e [frɑ̃siskɛ̃] *adj., s.m.f.* Franciscan (friar or nun).
franciser [frɑ̃size] *v.t.* **1.** to gallicize; **2.** (naut.) to register as French.
francisque [frɑ̃sisk] *s.f.* battle-axe.
francium [frɑ̃sjɔm] *s.m.* (chem.) francium.
franc-jeu [frɑ̃ʒø] *s.m.* fair play.
franc-maçon [frɑ̃masɔ̃] *s.m.* Freemason.
franc-maçonnerie [frɑ̃masɔnri] *s.f.* Freemasonry; (fig.) freemasonry.
franco [frɑ̃ko] *adv.* free of charge, post paid, post free; (pop.) *vas-y ~*, go ahead.
franco-canadien, -ne [frɑ̃kɔkanadjɛ̃] *adj., s.m.f.* French Canadian.
francolin [frɑ̃kɔlɛ̃] *s.m.* (ornith.) francolin.
francophile [frɑ̃kɔfil] *adj., s.m.f.* francophil(e).
francophobe [frɑ̃kɔfɔb] *adj., s.m.f.* francophobe.
francophone [frɑ̃kɔfɔn] *adj., s.m.f.* French-speaking (person).
franc-parler [frɑ̃parle] *s.m.* outspokenness; *avoir son ~*, to speak one's mind.
franc-tireur [frɑ̃tirœr] *s.m.* irregular (soldier), guerrilla, partisan; (fig.) independent, free lance.
frange [frɑ̃ʒ] *s.f.* fringe; (fig.) borderline.
frangeant [frɑ̃ʒɑ̃] *adj.m.* (geog.) (of reef) fringing.
franger [frɑ̃ʒe] *v.t.* to fringe.
frangin, -e [frɑ̃ʒɛ̃] *s.m.f.* (pop.) brother, sister; *~e s.f.* (slang) woman.
frangipane [frɑ̃ʒipan] *s.f.* **1.** frangipani (perfume); **2.** almond-flavoured cream(-cake).
frangipanier [frɑ̃ʒipanje] *s.m.* (bot.) frangipani.
franglais [frɑ̃glɛ] *s.m.* (lang.) franglais, French corrupted by indiscriminate use of anglicisms.
franquette [frɑ̃kɛt] *s.f.* *à la bonne ~*, simply, without ceremony.
frappage [frapaʒ] *s.m.* striking, stamping; coining (of money).
frappant, -e [frapɑ̃] *adj.* striking, impressive.
frappe[1] [frap] *s.f.* striking, minting, (of coins); (typing) touch; (sport) hit, kick; *faute de ~*, typing error; (mil.) *force de ~*, strike force, striking power.
frappe[2], **frape** [frap] *s.f.* (pop.) scoundrel.
frappé, -e [frape] *adj.* struck, surprised, impressed; (of liquids) iced; coined, stamped.
frappe-devant [frapdəvɑ̃] *s.m.invar.* sledge-hammer.
frappement [frapmɑ̃] *s.m.* striking, beating, beat.
frapper [frape] *v.t.* to strike, to hit, to tap, to beat, to slap; to afflict; to impress, to surprise, to overcome; to emboss (cloth or paper); to stamp (coins); to ice (wine, coffee, etc.); *~ d'une punition*, to inflict a punishment on; *~ d'une amende*, to impose a fine on; *~ de mutisme*, to strike dumb; *~ des mains*, to clap one's hands;

~ *v.i.* to knock, to tap; ~ *à la porte*, to knock on the door; *entrez sans* ~, walk straight in; **se** ~ *v.refl. se* ~ *la poitrine*, to beat one's breast, (fig.) to worry, to fuss; (fam.) *ne te frappe pas!*, don't panic!; *sans se* ~, calmly.

frappeu-r, -se [frapœr] *s.m.f.* beater; embosser, stamper.

frasque [frask] *s.f.* prank, folly, piece of extravagance; *des ~s de jeunesse*, youthful escapades.

frater [fratɛr] *s.m.* (obs.) barber's or surgeon's assistant; lay brother.

fraternel, -le [fratɛrnɛl] *adj.* fraternal, brotherly; **~lement** [fratɛrnɛlmɑ̃] *adv.* fraternally.

fraternisation [fratɛrnizɑsjɔ̃] *s.f.* fraternization.

fraterniser [fratɛrnize] *v.i.* to fraternize.

fraternité [fratɛrnite] *s.f.* fraternity, brotherhood; brotherly love.

fratricide [fratrisid] *s.m.f.* fratricide (person); ~ *s.m.* fratricide (crime); ~ *adj.* fratricidal.

fraude [frod] *s.f.* fraud, deceit, cheating; *en* ~, fraudulently; (fig.) secretly, furtively; *faire passer en* ~, to smuggle.

frauder [frode] *v.t.* to defraud; ~ *v.i.* to smuggle, to cheat.

fraudeu-r, -se [frodœr] *s.m.f.* defrauder, cheat, swindler; smuggler; *adj.*, fraudulent.

frauduleu-x, -se [frodylø] *adj.* fraudulent; **~sement** [frodyløzmɑ̃] *adv.* fraudulently, by fraud.

fraxinelle [fraksinɛl] *s.f.* (bot.) dittany.

frayer [freje] *v.t.* **1.** to trace out, to mark out, to open out, to beat (path, track); (fig.) to prepare; ~ *la voie à qn.*, to pave the way for s.o.; **2.** (of deer) to fray, to rub; (vet.) to gall; **se** ~ *v.refl. se* ~ *un passage*, to clear a way for oneself; ~ *v.i.* **1.** (of fish) to spawn; **2.** to associate, to go around, (with s.o.); *il frayait peu avec ses collègues*, he did not have much to do with his colleagues.

frayère [frɛjɛr] *s.f.* spawning-ground.

frayeur [frɛjœr] *s.f.* fright, fear, terror.

fredaine [frədɛn] *s.f.* prank, escapade; *faire des ~s*, to sow one's wild oats.

fredon [frədɔ̃] *s.m.* (obs.) trill, humming.

fredonnement [frədɔnmɑ̃] *s.m.* humming (of tune).

fredonner [frədɔne] *v.t.* to hum (tune).

freezer [frizœr] *s.m.* freezing-compartment (of refrigerator).

frégate [fregat] *s.f.* frigate; (ornith.) frigate-bird.

frein [frɛ̃] *s.m.* **1.** (obs.) bit (of bridle); (mod. fig.) *ronger son* ~, to champ at the bit; **2.** (fig.) curb, restraint; *sans* ~, unbridled, unrestrained; **3.** (mech.) brake; ~ *à main*, hand-brake; ~ *à pédale*, foot-brake; *serrer, mettre, le* ~, to brake, to apply the brake; *donner un (brusque) coup de* ~, to brake suddenly, to pull up short; (fig.) *donner un coup de* ~ *à qn.*, to pull s.o. up; **4.** (anat.) fraenum, frenum.

freinage [frɛnaʒ] *s.m.* braking.

freiner [frene] *v.i.* to brake, to apply the brake(s); ~ *v.t.* to hold back; (fig.) to impede, to check.

freinte [frɛ̃t] *s.f.* (comm.) loss of weight or volume during manufacture or transit.

frelatage [frəlataʒ] *s.m.* adulteration.

frelaté, -e [frəlate] *adj.* adulterated, doctored, (of wine) watered; (fig.) watered-down, artificial.

frelater [frəlate] *v.t.* to adulterate, to doctor (food, drink).

frêle [frɛl] *adj.* fragile, delicate, frail.

frelon [frəlɔ̃] *s.m.* (ent.) hornet; (obs. fig.) drone, parasite.

freluche [frəlyʃ] *s.f.* tuft of silk, tassel.

freluquet [frəlykɛ] *s.m.* coxcomb, conceited young puppy, whipper-snapper.

frémir [fremir] *v.i.* to rustle, to quiver; (cook.) to simmer; to tremble, to quake, to shudder; *c'est à faire* ~, it gives one the shivers.

frémissant, -e [fremisɑ̃] *adj.* quivering, trembling.

frémissement [fremismɑ̃] *s.m.* rustling (of leaves), sighing (of wind); quivering; simmering (of water); trembling, shuddering; tremor.

frênaie [frɛnɛ] *s.f.* ash-grove, ash plantation.

frêne [frɛn] *s.m.* (bot.) ash (tree).

frénésie [frenezi] *s.f.* **1.** (anc. med.) madness, frenzy; **2.** frenzy, rage, excitement; *avec* ~, frantically.

frénétique [frenetik] *adj.* frantic, frenzied; **~ment** [frenetikmɑ̃] *adv.* frantically.

fréquemment [frekamɑ̃] *adv.* frequently, often.

fréquence [frekɑ̃s] *s.f.* frequency; (electr.) frequency.

fréquencemètre [frekɑ̃smɛtr] *s.m.* (phys.) frequency meter.

fréquent, -e [frekɑ̃] *adj.* frequent; (of pulse) rapid; repeated; usual; *j'en fais un* ~ *usage*, I often use it.

fréquentable [frekɑ̃tabl] *adj.* worth knowing, pleasant to be with; *un individu peu* ~, a socially unacceptable person.

fréquentati-f, -ve [frekɑ̃tatif] *adj.* (gram.) frequentative.

fréquentation [frekɑ̃tɑsjɔ̃] *s.f.* company, relationship, association; *de mauvaises ~s*, bad company; ~ *de*, frequenting, associating with, going about with, living with; paying frequent visits to; (obs.) regular use or practice of; *la* ~ *des comédiennes*, associating with actresses; *la* ~ *des animaux*, living with animals; *la* ~ *des musées*, frequent visits to museums.

fréquenté, -e [frekɑ̃te] *adj.* frequented; *rue ~e*, busy street; *hôtel bien* ~, hotel with a respectable clientele; *endroit mal* ~, place of doubtful repute.

fréquenter [frekɑ̃te] *v.t.* to frequent, to visit (place) frequently; to associate with, to visit, to see a lot of, (a person); ~ *v.i.* (obs.) to be a frequent visitor.

frère [frɛr] *s.m.* **1.** brother; (eccles.) brother, friar, monk; fellow Christian; friend, companion; *~s jumeaux*, twin brothers; *~s siamois*, Siamese twins; *il lui ressemble comme un* ~, he is very like him; ~ *d'armes*, brother in arms; *faux* ~, traitor, faithless friend; *vieux* ~, old pal; **2.** (fig.) twin, double; *j'ai vu le* ~ *de votre vase chez l'antiquaire*, I saw the twin of your vase in the antique shop.

frérot [frero] *s.m.* (fam.) little brother.

fresque [frɛsk] *s.f.* (art) fresco; (fig. of Lit. work) vast picture, broad canvas.

fresquiste [frɛskist] *s.m.f.* fresco painter.

fressure [fresyr] *s.f.* pluck, fry, (of meat).

fret [frɛ] *s.m.* freightage, freight, chartering; freight, cargo, load.

fréter [frete] *v.t.* to charter; to freight out; to hire (vehicle).

fréteur [fretœr] *s.m.* freighter, charterer, shipowner.

frétillant, -e [fretijɑ̃] *adj.* wriggling; lively, frisky.

frétillement [fretijmɑ̃] *s.m.* wriggling, frisking; wagging (of tail).

frétiller [fretije] *v.i.* to wriggle, (of tail) to wag; to get excited, to fidget.

fretin [frətɛ̃] *s.m.* fry, young fish; (fig.) *menu* ~, small fry.

frette[1] [frɛt] *s.f.* iron band, hoop.

frette[2] [frɛt] *s.f.* (arch., herald.) fret.

fretté, -e [frete] *adj.* (herald.) fretty.

fretter [frete] *v.t.* to hoop, to bind with iron.

freudien, -ne [frødjɛ̃] *adj.* Freudian.

freudisme [frødism] *s.m.* Freudianism.

freux [frø] *s.m.* (ornith.) rook.

friabilité [frijabilite] *s.f.* friability.

friable [frijabl] *adj.* friable, crumbly.
friand, -e [frijɑ̃] *adj.* **1.** fond (*de*, of), greedy (*de*, for); *être ~ de miel*, to be fond of honey; *être ~ de compliments*, to be avid for praise; **2.** (obs.) dainty, appetizing; *~ s.m.* meat pasty; small almond cake.
friandise [frijɑ̃diz] *s.f.* **1.** (obs.) greediness, love of good food; **2.** sweet, dainty, titbit.
Fribourg [fribur] *s.f.* (geog.) **1.** Freiburg (in West Germany); **2.** Fribourg (in Switzerland).
fric [frik] *s.m.* (pop.) money.
fricandeau (pl. **-x**) [frikɑ̃do] *s.m.* (cook.) fricandeau, braised veal.
fricassée [frikase] *s.f.* (cook.) fricassée; (fig.) *~ de museaux*, hugs and kisses.
fricasser [frikase] *v.t.* (cook.) to fricassée; (fig.) to squander.
fricative [frikativ] *adj.*, *s.f.* (lang.) fricative.
fric-frac [frikfrak] *s.m.* (pl. *fric-frac(s)*) (pop.) burglary, breaking and entering.
friche [friʃ] *s.f.* fallow, fallow land, uncultivated or waste land; *en ~*, uncultivated, fallow; (fig.) undeveloped, unexploited, unused.
frichti [friʃti] *s.m.* (pop.) food, grub.
fricot [friko] *s.m.* (fam.) stew, food; *faire le ~*, to do the cooking.
fricotage [frikɔtaʒ] *s.m.* (fam.) underhand dealings, cooking (of accounts, etc.).
fricoter [frikɔte] *v.t.* (fam.) to cook; (fig.) to cook up, to plot; *~ v.i.* to be engaged in underhand dealings.
fricoteu-r, -se [frikɔtœr] *s.m.f.* (fam.) one engaged in underhand dealings.
friction [friksjɔ̃] *s.f.* (lit. & fig.) friction; rubbing, chafing; massage.
frictionnel, -le [friksjɔnɛl] *adj.* frictional.
frictionner [friksjɔne] *v.t.* to rub, to massage.
frigidaire [friʒidɛr] *s.m.* (proprietary name) Frigidaire; refrigerator; (fig. fam.) *mettre au ~*, to put on ice.
frigide [friʒid] *adj.* frigid.
frigidité [friʒidite] *s.f.* frigidity, coldness.
frigo [frigo] *s.m.* (fam.) **1.** frozen meat; **2.** fridge; refrigerator, cold store.
frigorie [frigɔri] *s.f.* (sci.) negative calorie.
frigorifier [frigɔrifje] *v.t.* to refrigerate, to freeze; (fam.) *je suis frigorifié*, I'm frozen stiff.
frigorifique [frigɔrifik] *adj.* frigorific, refrigerating, freezing; *chambre ~*, cold chamber; *wagon ~*, refrigerated truck.
frigoriste [frigɔrist] *s.m.* refrigeration engineer.
frileu-x, -se [frilø] *adj.* chilly, sensitive to cold; *être ~x, ~se*, to feel the cold.
frimaire [frimɛr] *s.m.* (hist.) Frimaire (third month in Fr. Republican Calendar, November–December).
frimas [frimɑ] *s.m.* rime, (hoar-)frost.
frime [frim] *s.f.* **1.** (fam.) sham, make-believe, pretence; *c'est de la ~*, it's all bunkum; *faire qch. pour la ~*, to do sth. for the sake of appearances; **2.** (slang) face, expression.
frimousse [frimus] *s.f.* (fam.) little face (of child or girl).
fringale [frɛ̃gal] *s.f.* pang of hunger; (fig.) burning desire; *avoir la ~ de*, to hanker after.
fringant, -e [frɛ̃gɑ̃] *adj.* brisk, lively, smart, dashing, dapper; (of horse) frisky, mettlesome.
fringuer [frɛ̃ge] *v.i.* (obs.) to frisk about, to prance; *~ v.t.* to dress (s.o.); (pop.) to dress well; *être bien fringué*, to be dressed up.
fringues [frɛ̃g] *s.f.pl.* (pop.) clothes.
friper [fripe] *v.t.* to rumple, to crumple, to crease; (fig.) *une figure fripée*, a worn, wrinkled face.
friperie [fripri] *s.f.* second-hand clothes; old--clothes business or shop; ⚠ not 'frippery'.
fripi-er, -ère [fripje] *s.m.f.* second-hand clothes dealer.
fripon, -ne [fripɔ̃] *s.m.f.* (obs.) rogue, cheat; (mod., fam. of child) wretch, rascal; *adj.* roguish, mischievous.
friponner [fripɔne] *v.t.* (obs.) to cheat, to rob.
friponnerie [fripɔnri] *s.f.* (obs.) roguery, knavery, robbery; knavish trick.
fripouille [fripuj] *s.f.* (obs.) rabble, riff-raff; (fam.) swindler, blackguard, bad lot.
friquet [frikɛ] *s.m.* (ornith.) tree-sparrow.
frire [frir] *v.t.i.* to fry; *faire ~*, to fry; *poêle à ~*, frying pan; *pâte à ~*, batter; (fam.) *être frit*, to be done for.
frisage [frizaʒ] *s.m.* curling, waving.
frisant, -e [frizɑ̃] *adj.* (of light) oblique.
frise [friz] *s.f.* frieze, border.
Frise [friz] *s.f.* (geog.) Friesland.
frisé, -e [frize] *adj.* curled, curly, curly-headed; *chou ~*, savoy cabbage; *velours ~*, uncut velvet.
friser [frize] *v.t.i.* to curl, to wave; to graze, to brush; (fig.) to be near to, to border on; *~ la cinquantaine*, to be getting on for fifty; *~ l'impertinence*, to border on impertinence.
frisette [frizɛt] *s.f.* small curl, ringlet.
frisolée [frizɔle] *s.f.* (agric.) potato-leaf curl.
frison[1] [frizɔ̃] *s.m.* small curl; shaving of wood or paper.
frison[2]**, -ne** [frizɔ̃] *adj.*, *s.m.f.* Friesian, (native or inhabitant) of Friesland; *vache ~ne*, Friesian (cow).
frisottant, -e [frizɔtɑ̃], **frisotté, -e** [frizɔte] *adj.* in tight curls.
frisotter [frizɔte] *v.t.* to curl tightly, to crimp; *~ v.i.* to be in tight curls.
frisquet, -te [friskɛ] *adj.* chill, chilly; *~ s.m.* chilliness; *il fait ~ ce matin*, it's a bit chilly this morning.
frisson [frisɔ̃] *s.m.* shiver, shudder; quiver, thrill.
frissonnant, -e [frisɔnɑ̃] *adj.* shivering, shuddering, shaking, quivering.
frissonnement [frisɔnmɑ̃] *s.m.* slight shiver, shudder; quivering.
frissonner [frisɔne] *v.i.* to shiver (*de*, with), to shudder; to quiver, to tremble.
frisure [frizyr] *s.f.* curling, curls; curliness; curl, ringlet; *tenir la ~*, to keep the curl.
frit, -e [fri] *adj.* (p.p. of *frire*) fried; **~es** *s.f.pl.* fried potatoes, chips.
friterie [fritri] *s.f.* frying-room (in canning factory); fish-and-chip stall.
friteuse [fritøz] *s.f.* (cook.) deep fryer, chip pan.
fritillaire [fritilɛr] *s.f.* (bot.) fritillary.
frittage [fritaʒ] *s.m.* (techn.) fritting.
fritte [frit] *s.f.* (glass-making) frit.
fritter [frite] *v.t.* (techn.) to frit.
friture [frityr] *s.f.* frying; fried food; fried fish; oil or fat for frying; (radio) crackling, sizzling.
frivole [frivɔl] *adj.* frivolous, futile, flimsy, trifling; **~ment** [frivɔlmɑ̃] *adv.* frivolously.
frivolité [frivɔlite] *s.f.* **1.** frivolity, frivolousness; trifle; (pl.) fancy goods; **2.** tatting.
froc [frɔk] *s.m.* **1.** cowl, hood, frock (of monk); *jeter le ~ aux orties*, to unfrock oneself; **2.** (pop.) trousers.
frocard [frɔkar] *s.m.* (obs.) monk.
froid [frwa] *s.m.* cold, chill, cold weather; (fig.) coldness, chill; *il fait ~*, it is cold; *avoir ~*, to be cold; *avoir ~ aux pieds*, to have cold feet; (fig.) *n'avoir pas ~ aux yeux*, to be resolute, firm; *prendre, attraper, ~*, to catch cold; *cela ne me fait ni chaud ni ~*, it doesn't bother me one way or the other; *être en ~ avec*, to be on bad terms with.
froid, -e [frwa] *adj.* cold, icy, chill; (fig.) calm, dispassionate; frigid; cool, reserved, distant; dull, uninspiring; *à ~*, cold, in the cold state, when cold; (fig.) without emotion, cold; (metall.) *tôle laminée à ~*, cold-rolled sheet; *démarrer à ~*, to start (car engine) from cold;

il parlait à ~ de son crime, he spoke of his crime without emotion; *colère à ~*, cold anger; *prendre, cueillir, son adversaire à ~*, to catch an opponent unawares; **~ement** [frwadmɑ̃] *adv.* (lit. & fig.) coldly, coolly; in cold blood, dispassionately, unemotionally.

froideur [frwadœr] *s.f.* (obs.) cold; (fig.) coolness, frigidity; distance, lack of warmth.

froidure [frwadyr] *s.f.* (obs.) coldness (of weather); (med.) frostbite.

froissable [frwasabl] *adj.* easily crumpled, liable to crease.

froissement [frwasmɑ̃] *s.m.* rumpling, crumpling, creasing; (fig.) friction, conflict; ruffling, giving, or taking, offence.

froisser [frwase] *v.t.* to rumple, to crumple, to crease; to bruise; (fig.) to offend, to ruffle, to hurt the feelings of, to annoy, to vex; **se ~** *v.refl.* to crease, to become creased; (fig.) to take offence.

frôlement [frolmɑ̃] *s.m.* grazing, light contact, brushing against; rustling.

frôler [frole] *v.t.* to graze, to brush against, to touch lightly; (fig.) to come close to.

frôleu-r, [frolœr] *s.m.* sexual pervert; **~se** [froløz] *s.f.* coquette.

fromage [frɔmaʒ] *s.m.* cheese; (meat) brawn; (fig.) *un bon ~*, a cushy job.

fromag-er, -ère [frɔmaʒe] *adj.* cheese, pertaining to cheese-making; *industrie ~ère*, cheese industry.

fromager [frɔmaʒe] *s.m.* **1.** cheese-maker; **2.** (bot.) silk cotton tree.

fromagerie [frɔmaʒri] *s.f.* cheese factory; manufacture, or selling, of cheeses.

fromegi, fromgi [frɔmʒi], **frometon, fromton** [frɔmtɔ̃] *s.m.* (pop.) cheese.

froment [frɔmɑ̃] *s.m.* wheat; oatmeal (colour); *de ~*, wheaten, of wheat.

fromental [frɔmɑ̃tal] *s.m.* (bot.) oat-grass (for fodder).

fronce [frɔ̃s] *s.f.* gather, crease; *jupe à ~s*, gathered skirt.

froncement [frɔ̃smɑ̃] *s.m.* gathering, puckering; *~ de sourcils*, knitting of the brows, frown.

froncer [frɔ̃se] *v.t.* to gather, to pucker, to wrinkle; *~ les sourcils*, to knit one's brows, to frown; *~ les lèvres*, to purse one's lips.

froncis [frɔ̃si] *s.m.* (dressm.) gathering.

frondaison [frɔ̃dɛzɔ̃] *s.f.* leafing, coming into leaf; foliage.

fronde[1] [frɔ̃d] *s.f.* sling, catapult; (Fr. hist.) *la Fronde*, the Fronde.

fronde[2] [frɔ̃d] *s.f.* (bot.) frond.

fronder [frɔ̃de] *v.i.* **1.** (obs.) to fling a stone (with a catapult); **2.** (hist.) to be a member of the Fronde; *~ v.t.* to criticize, to attack, to find fault with.

frondeu-r, -se [frɔ̃dœr] *s.m.f.* **1.** (mil. hist.) slinger; **2.** (hist.) member of the Fronde; **3.** fault-finder, critic (esp. of authority, etc.); *adj.* censorious, insubordinate, critical.

front [frɔ̃] *s.m.* **1.** forehead, brow; head, forepart; *courber le ~*, to submit; *relever le ~*, to rebel; *le ~ haut*, proudly; **2.** (obs.) manner, attitude; (mod.) effrontery; **3.** frontage, façade (of building); (mil.) front, front line; *faire ~ à*, to stand up to; (pol.) front, group, block; (techn.) face; (meteor.) front; *de ~*, in the face; abreast; (fig.) simultaneously; *attaquer de ~*, (fig.) to run slap into, to confront.

frontail (pl. **aux**) [frɔ̃taj] *s.m.* forehead-strap (of harness), head-piece (of horse's armour).

frontal, -e, (**aux**) [frɔ̃tal] *adj.* frontal; *~ s.m.* = FRONTAIL.

frontali-er, -ère [frɔ̃talje] *s.m.f.* inhabitant of a frontier zone; *adj.* border, frontier.

frontalité [frɔ̃talite] *s.f.* (arch., art) frontality.

fronteau (pl. **-x**) [frɔ̃to] *s.m.* headband, frontlet; (arch.) small pediment.

frontière [frɔ̃tjɛr] *s.f.* frontier, border, boundary; (fig.) limit.

frontignan [frɔ̃tiɲɑ̃] *s.m.* Frontignan (wine).

frontispice [frɔ̃tispis] *s.m.* frontispiece; (obs. arch.) main façade.

fronton [frɔ̃tɔ̃] *s.m.* (arch.) fronton, pediment; wall (for pelota game); pelota court.

frottage [frɔtaʒ] *s.m.* rubbing, polishing, waxing.

frottée [frɔte] *s.f.* **1.** (pop.) hiding, thrashing; **2.** piece of bread rubbed with garlic.

frottement [frɔtmɑ̃] *s.m.* rubbing; friction, chafing, contact; (fig.) difficulty, snag, clash.

frotter [frɔte] *v.t.* **1.** to rub; to polish, to scrape; (fig.) to put in contact with; *se ~ les mains*, to rub one's hands; (fig.) *être frotté de*, to have a smattering of; **2.** to thrash, to beat; *~ v.i.* to rub, to stick; **se ~** *v.refl.* to rub oneself; (fig.) *se ~ de*, to learn a smattering of; *se ~ à qn.*, to attack s.o., to provoke s.o.; *ne vous y frottez pas*, don't get involved; *qui s'y frotte, s'y pique*, you'll burn your fingers.

frotteu-r, -se [frɔtœr] *s.m.f.* **1.** floor-polisher; (techn.) friction piece; **2.** (pop.) = FRÔLEU-R, -SE.

frottis [frɔti] *s.m.* thin wash of colour; (biol.) smear.

frottoir [frɔtwar] *s.m.* rubber, polisher, brush; striking surface (for matches); (electr.) brush.

frouer [frue] *v.i.* to pipe (as a decoy, in bird-catching).

frou-frou, froufrou [frufru] *s.m.* rustle, rustling.

froufrouter [frufrute] *v.i.* to rustle.

froussard, -e [frusar] *adj.* (pop.) cowardly; *s.m.f.* funk, coward.

frousse [frus] *s.f.* (pop.) fright, fear; *avoir la ~*, to have the wind up.

fructidor [fryktidɔr] *s.m.* (hist.) Fructidor (12th month in Fr. Republican Calendar, August–September).

fructifère [fryktifɛr] *adj.* fructiferous, fruit-bearing.

fructification [fryktifikɑsjɔ̃] *s.f.* fructification.

fructifier [fryktifje] *v.i.* to fructify, to fruit; (lit. & fig.) to bear fruit; (fig.) to be profitable.

fructose [fryktoz] *s.m.* fructose.

fructueu-x, -se [fryktɥø] *adj.* fruitful, profitable, lucrative; **~sement** [fryktɥøzmɑ̃] *adv.* fruitfully, profitably.

frugal, -e, (**aux**) [frygal] *adj.* frugal; **~ement** [frygalmɑ̃] *adv.* frugally.

frugalité [frygalite] *s.f.* frugality.

frugivore [fryʒivɔr] *adj.* frugivorous, fruit-eating.

fruit[1] [frɥi] *s.m.* **1.** (pl.) produce, fruits; *~s de mer*, sea-food; (bot.) fruit; *le ~ défendu*, the forbidden fruit; (fig.) *~ sec*, failure; **2.** (fig.) fruit, advantage, profit; outcome, issue; *avec ~*, profitably; *sans ~*, fruitlessly.

fruit[2] [frɥi] *s.m.* (constr.) batter (of wall, etc.); *avoir du ~*, to batter.

fruité, -e [frɥite] *adj.* fruity.

fruiterie [frɥitri] *s.f.* fruit shop, greengrocer's shop; fruit-store.

fruiti-er[1], **-ère**[1] [frɥitje] *adj.* fruit-bearing, fruit; *arbre ~er*, fruit tree; *s.m.f.* fruiterer, greengrocer; **~er** *s.m.* orchard; fruit-store; fruit-rack.

fruiti-er[2] [frɥitje] *s.m.* (in Jura, Savoie, etc.) cheese manufacturer, cheese-maker; **~ère**[2] [frɥitjɛr] *s.f.* cheese-making co-operative.

frusques [frysk] *s.f.pl.* (pop.) clothes, rags.

fruste [fryst] *adj.* (of medals, etc.) worn, defaced; (lit. & fig.) unpolished, rough, primitive; *le ~*, primitive or rough character.

frustration [frystrɑsjɔ̃] *s.f.* frustration.

frustrer [frystre] *v.t.* **1.** to defraud, to deprive; **2.** to frustrate, to disappoint.
frutescent, -e [frytesɑ̃] *adj.* (bot.) frutescent.
fuchsia [fyʃja] *s.m.* (bot.) fuchsia.
fuchsine [fyksin] *s.f.* (chem.) fuchsine.
fucus [fykys] *s.m.* (bot.) fucus, sea-wrack.
fuégien, -ne [fɥeʒjɛ̃] *adj., s.m.f.* (native or inhabitant) of Terra del Fuego, Fuegian.
fuel-oil [fylɔjl], **fuel** [fjul] *s.m.* fuel oil.
fugace [fygas] *adj.* (obs.) fugitive; (fig.) fleeting, transient; *mémoire* ~, unreliable memory.
fugiti-f, -ve [fyʒitif] *adj.* fugitive, runaway; fleeting, transient; *s.m.f.* fugitive, runaway; **~vement** [fyʒitivmɑ̃] *adv.* briefly, fleetingly.
fugue [fyg] *s.f.* **1.** (mus.) fugue; **2.** flight, escape, running away; *faire une* ~, to run away from home.
fugué, -e [fyge] *adj.* (mus.) fugal.
fugueu-r, -se [fygœr] *s.m.f., adj.* (esp. child) who runs away from home.
fuie [fɥi] *s.f.* dovecote.
fuir [fɥir] *v.i.* **1.** to flee, to run away, to take flight; (of time) to fly, to vanish; *faire* ~, to put to flight; **2.** to leak; ~ *v.t.* to flee from, to run away from; to avoid, to shun; **se** ~ *v.refl.* to avoid each other; to try to escape from oneself.
fuite [fɥit] *s.f.* **1.** (of persons) flight, running away, escape; evasion (of responsibility, etc.); *prendre la* ~, to take flight; *mettre en* ~, to put to flight; (law) *délit de* ~, failure to stop after an accident; **2.** (of things) disappearance, passing, flight; **3.** (lit. & fig.) leak.
fulgurant, -e [fylgyrɑ̃] *adj.* flashing; blinding, dazzling; (of pain) stabbing; (fig.) rapid, lightning.
fulguration [fylgyrɑsjɔ̃] *s.f.* (meteor.) lightning; (metall.) flashing; (med.) fulguration, electrotherapy; (fig.) sudden flash.
fulgurer [fylgyre] *v.i.* to flash.
fuligineu-x, -se [fyliʒinø] *adj.* fuliginous, sooty; (fig.) murky, obscure.
fulmicoton, fulmi-coton [fylmikɔtɔ̃] *s.m.* gun-cotton.
fulminant, -e [fylminɑ̃] *adj.* fulminating, thundering; (lit. & fig.) explosive; (fig.) threatening.
fulminate [fylminat] *s.m.* (chem.) fulminate.
fulmination [fylminɑsjɔ̃] *s.f.* (eccles. law) fulmination.
fulminatoire [fylminatwar] *adj.* fulminatory.
fulminer [fylmine] *v.t.i.* to fulminate; (fig.) to threaten, to thunder, to storm.
fulminique [fylminik] *adj.* (chem.) fulminic.
fumable [fymabl] *adj.* smokeable.
fumage [fymaʒ] *s.m.* **1.** (agric.) manuring; **2.** (cook.) smoking, curing, (of ham, etc.).
fumaison [fymɛzɔ̃] *s.f.* = FUMAGE 1 & 2.
fumant, -e [fymɑ̃] *adj.* smoking, steaming; (fig.) fuming, seething; (fam.) *un coup* ~, a clever trick; *c'est* ~*!*, it's great!
fumé [fyme] *s.m.* (engr.) smoke proof.
fumé, -e [fyme] *adj.* smoked; *verres* ~*s*, dark glasses (spectacles).
fume-cigare [fymsigar] *s.m.invar.* cigar-holder; **~-cigarette** [fymsigarɛt] *s.m.invar.* cigarette-holder.
fumée [fyme] *s.f.* smoke; steam, vapour; (pl.) fumes; *il n'y a pas de* ~ *sans feu*, there's no smoke without fire; (fig.) *s'en aller en* ~, to go up in smoke.
fumer [fyme] *v.i.* to smoke, to steam; (fig.) to fume, to rage; *v.t.* **1.** to cure, to smoke, (ham, etc.); to smoke (pipe, etc.); **2.** (agric.) to manure.
fumerie [fymri] *s.f.* habit of smoking; ~ *(d'opium)*, opium den.
fumerolle [fymrɔl] *s.f.* (geol.) fumarole.
fumeron [fymrɔ̃] *s.m.* **1.** smoky bit of charcoal; **2.** small portable lamp; **3.** (pl.) (pop.) legs.
fumet [fymɛ] *s.m.* **1.** smell (of food cooking), aroma; bouquet (of wine); scent (of game); **2.** sauce with truffles and mushrooms.
fumeterre [fymtɛr] *s.f.* (bot.) fumitory.
fumeu-r, -se [fymœr] *s.m.f.* smoker.
fumeu-x, -se [fymø] *adj.* smoky, smoking; misty; (fig.) hazy, confused, vague.
fumier [fymje] *s.m.* dung, manure; dunghill, manure heap.
fumigateur [fymigatœr] *s.m.* fumigator.
fumigation [fymigɑsjɔ̃] *s.f.* fumigation; (med.) inhalation.
fumigatoire [fymigatwar] *adj.* fumigating.
fumigène [fymiʒɛn] *adj.* smoke-producing; *grenade* ~, smoke-grenade; ~ *s.m.* smoke-bomb.
fumiger [fymiʒe] *v.t.* to fumigate.
fumiste [fymist] *s.m.* installer of fireplaces, heating engineer; (fig.) practical joker, humbug, fraud.
fumisterie [fymistəri] *s.f.* installation of fireplaces, of boilers; (fig.) foolery, humbug, farce.
fumivore [fymivɔr] *adj.* smoke-consuming; ~ *s.m.* smoke-absorber.
fumoir [fymwar] *s.m.* smoke-house (for curing); smoking-room.
fumure [fymyr] *s.f.* (agric.) manuring.
funambule [fynɑ̃byl] *s.m.f.* funambulist, rope-walker.
funambulesque [fynɑ̃bylɛsk] *adj.* funambulatory; grotesque, bizarre.
funèbre [fynɛbr] *adj.* (of ceremony, etc.) funeral; (fig.) funereal, mournful; *service des pompes* ~*s*, undertaker's business.
funérailles [fynerɑj] *s.f.pl.* funeral, obsequies.
funéraire [fynerɛr] *adj.* funeral; *dalle, pierre,* ~, tombstone.
funeste [fynɛst] *adj.* fatal, mortal, deadly; disastrous, catastrophic.
funiculaire [fynikylɛr] *s.m.* funicular, cable railway.
funicule [fynikyl] *s.m.* (bot.) funiculus.
funin [fynɛ̃] *s.m.* (naut.) untarred rope.
fur [fyr] *s.m. au* ~ *et à mesure*, gradually, in succession, as soon (as), in proportion (to); as fast (as), progressively; *au* ~ *et à mesure de vos besoins*, according to your needs; *au* ~ *et à mesure qu'on avance*, as one proceeds.
furax [fyraks] *adj.invar.* (fam.) furious.
furet [fyrɛ] *s.m.* **1.** (zool.) ferret; (phys.) rabbit (device for taking radiation samples from a nuclear reactor); (fig.) Paul Pry, ferret; **2.** (game) hunt the slipper.
furetage [fyrtaʒ] *s.m.* ferreting; (fig.) prying, rummaging.
fureter [fyrte] *v.i.* to ferret, to hunt with a ferret; (fig.) to rummage, to pry, to nose about.
fureteu-r, -se [fyrtœr] *s.m.f.* ferreter; (fig.) rummager, Nosey Parker; *adj.* prying, nosey.
fureur [fyrœr] *s.f.* fury, rage, madness, passion, frenzy, craze; *entrer en* ~, to fly into a rage; *faire* ~, to be all the rage.
furfuracé, -e [fyrfyrase] *adj.* (med.) furfuraceous.
furibond, -e [fyribɔ̃] *adj.* furious, furious-looking, raging, frenzied.
furie [fyri] *s.f.* (myth.) Fury; (fig.) termagant; fury, rage.
furieu-x, -se [fyrjø] *adj.* furious, raging, wild; mad; *s.m.f.* madman, madwoman; **~sement** [fyrjøzmɑ̃] *adv.* furiously, madly; tremendously, with a vengeance.
furole [fyrɔl] *s.f.* (obs. exc. dial.) will-o'-the-wisp.
furoncle [fyrɔ̃kl] *s.m.* (med.) furuncle, boil.
furonculeu-x, -se [fyrɔ̃kylø] *adj.* (med.) furunculous; suffering from boils.

furonculose [fyrɔ̃kyloz] *s.f.* furunculosis.
furti-f, -ve [fyrtif] *adj.* furtive, stealthy, secret; **~vement** [fyrtivmɑ̃] *adv.* furtively, stealthily.
fusain [fyzɛ̃] *s.m.* **1.** (bot.) spindle-tree; **2.** charcoal (for drawing); charcoal drawing.
fusant, -e [fyzɑ̃] *adj.* (of explosive) fusing; (artill.) *obus ~*, time shell.
fuscine [fysin] *s.f.* (Rom. ant.) trident.
fuseau (pl. **-x**) [fyzo] *s.m.* spindle, bobbin; (techn.) spindle, axle, stave, leaf (of pinion); (aeron.) pod (housing engine, etc.); (geog.) *~ horaire*, time belt, time zone; *pantalon ~*, tapered trousers, ski pants; *jambes en ~*, spindle-shanks.
fusée [fyze] *s.f.* **1.** (obs.) spindleful; (mod.) tang (of rapier blade); (mech.) spindle (of axle); fusée (chain) of watch; **2.** rocket; (mil.) *~ éclairante*, or *de signalisation*, flare; *~ à parachute*, parachute flare; *~ de rire*, ripple of laughter; **3.** (mus.) run.
fusel [fyzɛl] *s.m.* (chem.) (*huile de*) *~*, fusel oil.
fuselage [fyzlaʒ] *s.m.* (aeron.) fuselage, body, frame.
fuselé, -e [fyzle] *adj.* spindle-shaped, slender, tapering.
fuseler [fyzle] *v.t.* to taper.
fuser [fyze] *v.i.* **1.** to fuse, to melt; to burn slowly; **2.** to spread, to break out, to gush out.
fusette [fyzɛt] *s.f.* small tubular cotton-reel.
fusibilité [fyzibilite] *s.f.* fusibility.
fusible [fyzibl] *adj.* fusible; *~ s.m.* fuse-wire.
fusiforme [fyzifɔrm] *adj.* fusiform, spindle--shaped.
fusil [fyzi] *s.m.* **1.** (obs.) steel (of tinder box); (mod.) gas lighter; steel (for sharpening knives); *pierre à ~*, flint; **2.** gun, rifle; *coup de ~*, shot; (fig.) *changer son ~ d'épaule*, to change one's opinions; (fam.) *coup de ~*, overcharging (in hotel, etc.); (pop.) *n'avoir rien dans le ~*, to be famished; (of person) *un excellent ~*, an excellent shot.
fusilier [fyzilje] *s.m.* fusilier; *~ marin*, = marine.
fusillade [fyzijad] *s.f.* fusillade, volley of shots, firing, shooting.
fusiller [fyzije] *v.t.* to shoot (down), to execute (by firing squad); (fig. fam.) to shoot (with camera); (pop.) to ruin.
fusilleur [fyzijœr] *s.m.* member, or commander, of a firing squad.
fusil-mitrailleur [fyzimitrɑjœr] *s.m.* automatic rifle, light machine-gun.
fusion [fyzjɔ̃] *s.f.* fusion, melting, blending; (fig.) union, merger.
fusionnement [fyzjɔnmɑ̃] *s.m.* amalgamating, amalgamation, merging.
fusionner [fyzjɔne] *v.t.i.* to amalgamate, to blend, to unite, to merge.
fustanelle [fystanɛl] *s.f.* fustanella, kilt.
fustigation [fystigɑsjɔ̃] *s.f.* (Lit.) whipping, flogging, beating.
fustiger [fystiʒe] *v.t.* (Lit.) to whip, to flog, to beat; (fig.) to castigate.
fût [fy] *s.m.* stock (of gun); shaft (of column); bole (of tree); cask (of wine).
futaie [fytɛ] *s.f.* forest (of established trees); *haute ~*, full-grown trees.
futaille [fytɑj] *s.f.* cask, barrel; (collectively) casks.
futaine [fytɛn] *s.f.* (text.) fustian.
futé, -e [fyte] *adj.* sharp, cunning, sly; *c'est une petite ~e*, she's as cunning as a fox.
futée [fyte] *s.f.* (techn.) filling, stopping, mastic.
futile [fytil] *adj.* futile, frivolous, trifling; **~ment** [fytilmɑ̃] *adv.* futilely, frivolously.
futilité [fytilite] *s.f.* futility, frivolity; trifle.
futur, -e [fytyr] *adj.* future; *~ s.m.* future; (gram.) future tense; **~(e)** *s.m.f.* future husband, future wife, fiancé(e).
futurisme [fytyrism] *s.m.* futurism.
futuriste [fytyrist] *s.m.f.* futurist.
fuyant, -e [fɥijɑ̃] *adj.* flying, fleeing; fleeting, ephemeral; fading, vanishing, diminishing; *yeux ~s*, shifty eyes.
fuyard, -e [fɥijar] *adj., s.m.f.* fugitive, runaway.

G

G, g [ʒɛ] *s.m.* the letter G, g; abbrev. *gramme*; (mus.) g.
gabardine [gabardin] *s.f.* (text.) gabardine; gabardine raincoat.
gabare [gabar] *s.f.* (naut.) **1.** lighter, barge, flat; **2.** drag-net.
gabarier [gabarje] *s.m.* lighterman.
gabarier [gabarje] *v.t.* to mould, to form, to construct or cut out from a template.
gabarit [gabari] *s.m.* model, mould, shape, form; template, jig; gauge.
gabegie [gabʒi] *s.f.* muddle, disorder, mess, waste (due to negligence).
gabelle [gabɛl] *s.f.* salt-tax; excise.
gabelou [gablu] *s.m.* (hist.) collector of *gabelle*; (mod. pej.) customs officer, exciseman.
gabier [gabje] *s.m.* (naut.) topman; able seaman.
gabion [gabjɔ̃] *s.m.* gabion, rough wicker basket; **~nage** [gabjɔnaʒ] *s.m.* (fort.) gabionage; **~ner** [gabjɔne] *v.t.* (fort.) to gabion.
gable, gâble [gɑbl] (arch.) gable, gable end.
Gabon [gabɔ̃] *s.m.* (geog.) Gaboon.
gâchage [gɑʃaʒ] *s.m.* wasting, spoiling; mixing (of plaster).
gâche[1] [gɑʃ] *s.f.* striking-plate (of lock).
gâche[2] [gɑʃ] *s.f.* (plasterer's) trowel; (cook's) spatula.
gâcher [gɑʃe] *v.t.* to mix (mortar, plaster, etc.); (fig.) to spoil, to waste, to make a mess of; *~ le métier*, to sell under price, to be too generous.
gâchette [gɑʃɛt] *s.f.* **1.** follower, spring-catch, (of lock); **2.** safety-catch; trigger.
gâcheur [gɑʃœr] *s.m.* bricklayer's or plasterer's labourer.
gâcheu-r, -se [gɑʃœr] *s.m.f.* bungler, waster; **~se** *s.f.* (pop.) spoil-sport.
gâchis [gɑʃi] *s.m.* wet mortar; mire, slush; (fig.) muddle, mess, waste.
gade [gad] *s.m.* (ichth.) gadoid, fish of the cod family.
gadget [gadʒɛt] *s.m.* gadget, novelty.
gadin [gadɛ̃] *s.m.* (fam.) fall; *ramasser un ~*, to fall, to come down, to take a tumble.
gadoue [gadu] *s.f.* sewage, night-soil; (fig.) dirt, mire, slush.
gaélique [gaelik] *adj., s.m.* Gaelic.
gaffe [gaf] *s.f.* **1.** (naut.) boat-hook, gaff; **2.** gaffe, blunder, faux pas; **3.** (pop.) *faire ~*, to take care, to mind out.
gaffer [gafe] *v.t.* to hook, to gaff; *~ v.i.* **1.** to make a gaffe or blunder; **2.** (pop.) to watch out, to pay attention.
gaffeu-r, -se [gafœr] *s.m.f.* blunderer, idiot; *adj.* blundering, idiotic.

gag [gag] *s.m.* (cin., etc.) gag.
gaga [gaga] *adj.* doddering, senile; weak in the head; ~ *s.m.f.* senile person.
gage [gaʒ] *s.m.* **1.** pledge, deposit, security, surety, bond, guarantee; stake; (at games) forfeit; token, proof, promise; *prêteur sur ~s*, pawnbroker; *mettre en ~*, to pawn, to pledge; *en ~ d'amitié*, as a token of friendship; **2.** (pl.) wages, hire; (pej.) *à ~s*, hired; *être aux ~s de qn.*, to be hired by s.o., to be in someone's pay.
gager [gaʒe] *v.t.* **1.** to wager, to bet; **2.** to guarantee, to pledge, to secure (loan, etc.); *emprunt gagé*, secured loan, loan against security; **3.** (obs.) to pay (wages to), to hire.
gageure [gaʒyr] *s.f.* wager, bet; (fig.) challenge; *soutenir une ~*, to take up a wager, (fig.) to accept a challenge.
gagiste [gaʒist] *s.m.* (law) (*créancier*) ~, secured creditor.
gagnant, -e [gaɲɑ̃] *s.m.f.* winner; *adj.* winning.
gagne-pain [gaɲpɛ̃] *s.m.invar.* livelihood.
gagne-petit [gaɲpəti] *s.m.invar.* one in business in a very small way.
gagner [gaɲe] *v.t.* **1.** to gain, to earn, to win, to get, to acquire; to defeat, to gain on, to overtake; ~ *gros*, to make big profits; ~ *bien*, or *bien ~*, to earn plenty of money; ~ *le gros lot*, to win the jackpot, to scoop the pool; ~ *sur qn.*, to defeat s.o., to get the better of s.o.; ~ *sur qch.*, to encroach on sth.; ~ *à qch.*, to gain or profit by sth.; ~ *du terrain sur*, to gain ground on, to catch up with, to encroach on; ~ *à être*, to gain from being; ~ *en*, to gain or increase in; ~ *qn.*, to defeat s.o.; ~ *qn. à qch.*, to win over s.o. to sth.; ~ *qn. de vitesse*, to outrun s.o.; (fig.) to outmanœuvre s.o.; *se laisser ~ par qch.*, to give in to sth.; **2.** to arrive at, to reach; (fig.) to overcome, to overtake; to infect; to spread; ~ *sa place*, to reach one's seat; (naut.) ~ *le large*, to reach the open sea; *le sommeil le gagne*, he is getting sleepy; *sa joie nous gagnait*, her joy was infectious; *l'incendie gagne*, the fire is spreading.
gagneu-r, -se [gaɲœr] *s.m.f.* winner.
gai, -e [ge] *adj.* gay, bright, lively, cheerful, merry; amusing, funny, exciting; (obs.) ribald, spicy; *ce n'est pas ~*, it's dreary, it's boring, it is not amusing; *être un peu ~*, to be merry, to be a bit tipsy; *des propos un peu ~s*, some rather ribald remarks.
gaïac [gajak] *s.m.* (bot.) guaiacum, guaiac; lignum vitae.
gaiement, gaîment [gemɑ̃] *adv.* gaily, merrily, brightly, cheerfully.
gaieté, gaîté [gete] *s.f.* gaiety, liveliness, merriness, cheerfulness, brightness; humour, amusing nature, wittiness, fun, amusement; *de ~ de cœur*, lightly, on impulse.
gaillard, -e [gajar] *adj.* vigorous, hearty, healthy, fit, in good trim, robust; lively, in good form; (obs.) jolly, full of fun; (mod.) ribald, spicy, naughty, coarse; *frais et ~*, hale and hearty; *humeur ~e*, jolly disposition; *tenir des propos ~s*, to make naughty remarks; *s.m.f.* healthy and vigorous man, jolly fellow; (fam.) fellow, chap; bold woman, hussy, wench; ~ *s.m.* (naut.) **1.** (obs.) quarter-deck; (mod.) poop; **2.** ~ (*d'avant*), forecastle; **~e** *s.f.* **1.** galliard (dance); **2.** (typ.) 8-point type, brevier; **~ement** [gajardəmɑ̃] *adv.* cheerfully, jovially, merrily; heartily, boldly, briskly; freely.
gaillardise [gajardiz] *s.f.* (obs.) gaiety, jollity; (mod.) naughty remark or story, broad joke.
gaillet [gajɛ] *s.m.* (bot.) bedstraw, cheese-rennet.
gaillet-erie [gajtri, gajɛtri] *s.f.* (coal) slack; **~in** [gajtɛ̃] *s.m.* small coal, nuts.
gaillette [gajɛt] *s.f.* medium-sized coal, cobs.
gain [gɛ̃] *s.m.* **1.** gaining, winning, success; *chances égales de ~ et de perte*, equal chances of winning or losing, of success or failure; *avoir* or *obtenir ~ de cause*, to be successful, to win one's case; *donner ~ de cause à qn.*, to decide in someone's favour; **2.** gain, profit, advantage, saving; earnings, winnings; *compensation des ~s et des pertes*, balancing of profit and loss; *un ~ de temps*, a saving of time; *se retirer sur son ~*, to collect one's winnings or profit, to stop while the going is good.
gainage [gɛnaʒ] *s.m.* sheathing, casing.
gaine [gɛn] *s.f.* sheath, case, cover, sleeve, housing; container (attached to parachute); corset; (bot.) ocrea; (arch.) terminal; (naut.) tabling (of sail); (mining) ~ *d'aérage*, ventilation-shaft.
gainer [gɛne] *v.t.* to sheathe, to case; (naut.) to table (a sail); to fit tightly on.
gainerie [gɛnri] *s.f.* sheath-making, case-making.
gainier [gɛnje] *s.m.* sheath- or case-maker.
gaîté see GAIETÉ.
gal [gal] *s.m.* (phys.) gal.
gala [gala] *s.m.* gala, festive occasion; *habits de ~*, gala dress, full dress.
galact-agogue [galaktagɔg] *adj.*, *s.m.* galactagogue; **~ique** [galaktik] *adj.* (astron.) galactic; **~omètre** [galaktɔmɛtr] *s.m.* lactometer; **~ophore** [galaktɔfɔr] *adj.* (physiol.) galactophorous; **~ose** [galaktoz] *s.f.* (chem.) galactose.
galamment [galamɑ̃] *adv.* politely, courteously, tactfully, like a gentleman, showing attentions (esp. to ladies), gallantly; ⚠ not 'gallantly' in sense 'courageously'.
galandage [galɑ̃daʒ] *s.m.* brick partition.
galant, -e [galɑ̃] *adj.* gallant, attentive (to ladies), amorous, amorously inclined; courteous, polite, polished; (of behaviour) handsome, gentlemanly; elegant, dashing; *un ~ homme*, a gentleman; *une femme ~e*, a woman of easy virtue; ⚠ not 'gallant' in sense 'courageous'; ~ *s.m.* (obs.) seducer, lady-killer, womanizer, gay spark, ladies' man, gallant; *vert ~*, (obs.) forest highwayman, (mod.) woman-chaser.
galanterie [galɑ̃tri] *s.f.* **1.** (obs.) elegance; **2.** courtesy, politeness, gallantry, attentiveness (to ladies), flirting; **3.** love affair, intrigue; pretty speech; billet doux; ⚠ not 'gallantry' in sense 'bravery'.
galantine [galɑ̃tin] *s.f.* (cook.) galantine.
galapiat [galapja] *s.m.* (fam.) scamp.
galaxie [galaksi] *s.f.* (astron.) Milky Way, galaxy.
galbe [galb] *s.m.* outline, contour, sweep, curve; (arch.) entasis; (fig.) elegance, dash, style, line.
galbé, -e [galbe] *adj.* (slightly) curved, rounded; well-proportioned, of graceful shape.
galber [galbe] *v.t.* to round, to impart a gentle curve to.
gale [gal] *s.f.* itch; scab; mange; (bot.) scurf; (fig., of person) pest; ⚠ not 'gale'.
galéasse, galéace [galeas] *s.f.* (hist.) Venetian galley, galliass.
galéjade [galeʒad] *s.f.* (Provençal dial.) tall story.
galène [galɛn] *s.f.* galena, lead ore, lead glance; (radio) *poste à ~*, crystal set.
galén-ique [galenik] *adj.* (med. hist.) galenic; **~isme** [galenism] *s.m.* galenism.
galère [galɛr] *s.f.* **1.** galley; *qu'allait-il faire dans cette ~?*, why did he have to get involved in that business?; *vogue la ~!*, let her rip!; come what may!; here goes!; **2.** (pl.) galleys, hard labour, penal servitude, chain-gang.
galerie [galri] *s.f.* gallery, corridor, passage, hall; (art, etc.) gallery; (pl.) department store;

(spectators') gallery; (theatr.) gallery, circle, balcony; (fig.) the audience, the gallery; (mining) gallery, road, level; (car) roof-rack; kerb (of hearth); *amuser la* ~, to play to the gallery.

galérien [galerjɛ̃] *s.m.* galley-slave; (fig.) *mener une vie de* ~, to live a dog's life.

galet [galɛ] *s.m.* **1.** pebble; (pl.) shingle; *plage de* ~*s*, shingle beach; **2.** (mech.) roller, castor, slide.

galetas [galta] *s.m.* garret, attic; hovel.

galette [galɛt] *s.f.* flat cake, pancake; (naut.) ship's biscuit; (pop.) money.

galetteu-x, -se [galɛtø] *adj.* (pop.) rich.

galeu-x, -se [galø] *adj.* mangy, scabby, with the itch; (bot.) scurfy; (fig.) *brebis* ~*se*, black sheep; *s.m.f.* (fig.) leper.

galgal [galgal] *s.m.* (archaeol.) tumulus, cairn.

galhauban [galobɑ̃] *s.m.* (naut.) backstay.

galibot [galibo] *s.m.* (mining) pit-boy.

Galice [galis] *s.f.* (geog.) Galicia (in Spain).

Galicie [galisi] *s.f.* (geog.) Galicia (in Central Europe).

galicien, -ne [galisjɛ̃] *adj.*, *s.m.f.* Galician (of *Galice* or *Galicie*).

Galilée [galile] **1.** *s.f.* (geog.) Galilee; **2.** *s.m.* Galileo.

galiléen, -ne [galileɛ̃] *adj.*, *s.m.f.* Galilean.

galimafrée [galimafre] *s.f.* hotchpotch, hash, unappetizing dish; (fig.) gallimaufry.

galimatias [galimatja] *s.m.* galimatias, gibberish.

galion [galjɔ̃] *s.m.* (hist.) galleon.

galiote [galjɔt] *s.f.* (naut.) **1.** (ant.) gal(l)iot, small galley; (mod.) coaster, Dutch fishing-vessel with sails; **2.** bar for securing hatch-covers.

galipette [galipɛt] *s.m.* (fam.) caper, gambol, frolic.

galipot [galipo] *s.m.* galipot, white resin; (naut.) mastic paint; ~**er** [galipɔte] *v.t.* (naut.) to treat with mastic paint.

galle [gal] *s.f.* (bot.) gall, gallnut; ~ *de chêne*, oak-apple, oak-gall; *noix de* ~*s*, nut-galls.

gallérie [galeri] *s.f.* (ent.) bee-moth.

Galles [gal] *s.f.* (geog.) Wales; *le pays de* ~, Wales; *la* ~ *du Nord*, North Wales; *la Nouvelle-*~ *du Sud*, New South Wales.

gallican, -e [galikɑ̃] *adj.*, *s.m.f.* Gallican.

gallicanisme [galikanism] *s.m.* Gallicanism.

gallicisme [galisism] *s.m.* Gallicism.

gallinacé, -e [galinase] *adj.* gallinaceous; ~**s** *s.m.pl.* Galliformes.

gallique[1] [galik] *adj.* Gallic, of the Gauls.

gallique[2] [galik] *adj.* (chem.) gallic.

gallium [galjɔm] *s.m.* (chem.) gallium.

gallois, -e [galwa] *adj.* Welsh, of Wales; *s.m.f.* Welshman, Welshwoman.

gallomanie [galɔmani] *s.f.* gallomania.

gallon [galɔ̃] *s.m.* gallon (=4·54 litres).

gallo-romain, -e [galɔrɔmɛ̃] *adj.*, *s.m.f.* Gallo-Roman.

gallo-roman [galɔrɔmɑ̃] *s.m.* (lang.) Gallo-Roman.

gallup [galœp] *s.m.* Gallup poll, opinion poll.

galoche [galɔʃ] *s.f.* **1.** clog; *menton en* ~, nutcracker chin; **2.** (naut.) open snatch-block.

galon [galɔ̃] *s.m.* galloon, lace, braid; (mil., nav.) stripe, pip, badge of rank, insignia; *avoir ses* ~*s*, to get one's stripes; *prendre du* ~, to get promotion; ~**ner** [galɔne] *v.t.* to trim with braid; (mil.) (fam.) *un galonné*, an officer or N.C.O.

galop [galo] *s.m.* gallop, galloping; (dance) gallop; *petit* ~, canter; *grand* ~, full gallop; *un temps de* ~, a short gallop; (fig.) ~ *d'essai*, trial run; *au* ~, at the gallop, in a great hurry; *au* ~*!*, gallop!, at the double!

galopade [galɔpad] *s.f.* gallop, galloping; (fig.) rush; *à la* ~, hastily, in a rush.

galoper [galɔpe] *v.i.* to gallop, to run quickly, to scurry along; ~ *v.t.* to gallop (a horse).

galopeu-r, -se [galɔpœr] *s.m.f.* (of horse) galloper.

galopin [galɔpɛ̃] *s.m.* errand-boy; (fam.) street-urchin, young rascal.

galoubet [galubɛ] *s.m.* three-hole flute, tabor pipe.

galuchat [galyʃa] *s.m.* sharkskin or dogfish-skin prepared for cases, sheaths, etc.

galurin [galyrɛ̃], **galure** [galyr] *s.m.* (pop.) hat.

galvan-ique [galvanik] *adj.* galvanic; ~**isation** (galvanizasjɔ̃] *s.f.* galvanization, galvanizing; electroplating; (med.) electric-shock treatment; ~**iser** [galvanize] *v.t.* to galvanize; to electroplate; (med.) to give electric-shock treatment to; (fig.) to galvanize, to electrify; ~**isme** [galvanism] *s.m.* galvanism.

galvano [galvano] *s.m.* abbrev. *galvanotype*; ~**métre** [galvanɔmɛtr] *s.m.* galvanometer; ~**plastie** [galvanɔplasti] *s.f.* galvanoplasty, electro-deposition; electroplating; (print.). electrotype; ~**plastique** [galvanɔplastik] *adj.* galvanoplastic; ~**type** [galvanɔtip] *s.m.* (print.) electrotype; ~**typie** [galvanɔtipi] *s.f.* (print.) electrotyping.

galvauder [galvode] *v.t.* (obs.) to spoil, to botch; (mod.) to disgrace, to smirch, to sully; to debase; ~ *v.i.* to idle; **se** ~ *v.refl.* to degrade oneself.

galvaudeu-x, -se [galvodø] *s.m.f.* tramp, vagabond, layabout.

gambade [gɑ̃bad] *s.f.* gambol, caper.

gambader [gɑ̃bade] *v.i.* to gambol, to caper, to dance around.

gambe [gɑ̃b] *s.f.* **1.** (naut.) (pl.) shrouds; **2.** (mus.) *viole de* ~, viola da gamba.

gambette [gɑ̃bɛt] *s.f.* or *m.* (ornith.) redshank, sandpiper; (pop.) leg.

Gambie [gɑ̃bi] *s.f.* (geog.) Gambia.

gambiller [gɑ̃bije] *v.i.* (fam.) (obs.) to kick one's legs, to fidget; (pop.) to dance about.

gambit [gɑ̃bi] *s.m.* (chess) gambit.

gamelle [gamɛl] *s.f.* (mil., nav.) dixie; mess-tin; (officers') mess; (pop.) *ramasser une* ~, to come a cropper.

gamète [gamɛt] *s.m.* (biol.) gamete.

gamin, -e [gamɛ̃] *s.m.f.* (obs.) errand-boy, boy (assistant); street-urchin; (mod.) mischievous boy or girl, young rogue, scamp; (fam.) child, kid; (pop.) young son or daughter; *adj.* mischievous, roguish, sly, pert, saucy.

gaminerie [gaminri] *s.f.* childish prank, antics.

gamme [gam] *s.f.* **1.** (mus.) scale; gamut; **2.** range, scale, gradation, series; gamut.

gamo-pétale [gamɔpetal] *adj.* (bot.) gamopetalous; ~**sépale** [gamɔsepal] *adj.* (bot.) gamosepalous.

ganache [ganaʃ] *s.f.* **1.** lower jaw (of horse); (pop.) jaw or head (of person); **2.** (fam.) blockhead, incompetent; ~ *adj.* stupid, incompetent.

Gand [gɑ̃] *s.m.* (geog.) Ghent.

gandin [gɑ̃dɛ̃] *s.m.* fop, dandy.

gang [gɑ̃g] *s.m.* gang (of criminals).

ganga [gɑ̃ga] *s.m.* (ornith.) sand-grouse.

Gange [gɑ̃ʒ] *s.m.* (geog.) Ganges (river).

ganglion [gɑ̃gliɔ̃] *s.m.* ganglion; (pl.) (fam.) adenoids; ~**naire** [gɑ̃gliɔnɛr] *adj.* ganglionated, ganglionic.

gangrène [gɑ̃grɛn] *s.f.* (pathol.) gangrene, necrosis; (fig.) canker, corruption.

gangrener [gɑ̃grəne] *v.t.* to gangrene; (fig.) to corrupt, to poison; **se** ~ *v.refl.* to mortify, to gangrene, to become gangrened.

gangréneu-x, -se [gɑ̃grenø] *adj.* gangrenous, gangrened.

gangster [gɑ̃gstɛr] *s.m.* gangster; hooligan.

gangstérisme [gɑ̃gsterism] *s.m.* gangsterism; hooliganism.
gangue [gɑ̃g] *s.f.* (min.) gangue; (fig.) matrix, covering, wrapping.
ganse [gɑ̃s] *s.f.* cord, braid, plait, twist, band, edging; loop (of diamonds).
ganser [gɑ̃se] *v.t.* to braid, to trim with silk cord or edging.
gant [gɑ̃] *s.m.* glove, gauntlet; (fig.) challenge; *souple comme un* ~, pliable, easily managed; *retourner qn. comme un* ~, to make s.o. completely change their opinion; *aller comme un* ~, to fit like a glove; (fam.) *prendre* or *mettre des* ~*s*, to act circumspectly; *il n'a pris des* ~*s pour le lui dire*, he told him so in no uncertain fashion; *se donner les* ~*s de qch.*, to take the credit for sth.; *se donner les* ~*s de faire qch.*, to boast of doing sth.; (fig.) *jeter le* ~, to throw down the gauntlet; *ramasser* or *relever le* ~, to take up the challenge.
gantelée [gɑ̃tle] *s.f.* (bot.) foxglove, columbine, throatwort.
gantelet [gɑ̃tle] *s.m.* gauntlet.
ganter [gɑ̃te] *v.t.* to glove, to put gloves on; (fig.) to fit, or to suit, perfectly; *une main gantée de blanc*, a white-gloved hand; ~ *du sept*, to take sevens in gloves; **se** ~ *v.refl.* to put on one's gloves.
ganterie [gɑ̃tri] *s.f.* glove-making; glove trade; glove shop.
ganti-er, -ère [gɑ̃tje] *s.m.f.* glover.
garage [garaʒ] *s.m.* **1.** garage; shed; ~ *d'avions*, aircraft shed or hangar; ~ *de canots*, boat-house; **2.** (rail.) shunting; (car) parking; (rail.) *voie de* ~, siding.
garagiste [garaʒist] *s.m.f.* garage proprietor.
garance [garɑ̃s] *s.f.* (bot.) madder; madder red.
garant, -e [garɑ̃] *s.m.f.* guarantor, surety; *être* or *se porter* ~ *de*, to guarantee, to be responsible for, to vouch for, to answer for, to go bail for; ~ *s.m.* guarantee, security, surety, pledge; authority.
garantie [garɑ̃ti] *s.f.* guarantee; warranty, surety, pledge, assurance; indemnification; insurance; underwriting; *prendre des* ~*s contre*, to insure against.
garantir [garɑ̃tir] *v.t.* **1.** to guarantee, to vouch for, to answer for, to be responsible for; to assure; **2.** to insure, to secure; **3.** to shelter, to protect.
garbure [garbyr] *s.f.* (cook.) soup of cabbage, bacon, goose-meat, etc.
garce [gars] *s.f.* (vulg.) prostitute, bitch.
garcette [garsɛt] *s.f.* (obs.) cat-o'-nine-tails; (mod.) rope's end.
garçon [garsɔ̃] *s.m.* **1.** boy, lad, young man; fellow; *petit* ~, small boy (up to 12); *jeune* ~, youth; *bon* ~, amiable fellow, good chap; **2.** bachelor, single man; **3.** (obs.) boy, lad, servant, assistant; ~ *d'écurie*, stable-lad, groom; ~ *de ferme*, farm-hand; ~ *de cabine*, steward; **4.** ~ (*de café, de restaurant, d'hôtel*), waiter.
garçonne [garsɔn] *s.f.* bachelor girl, emancipated young woman.
garçonnet [garsɔnɛ] *s.m.* little boy.
garçonni-er, -ère [garsɔnje] *adj.* bachelor, mannish.
garçonnière [garsɔnjɛr] *s.f.* bachelor flat.
garde[1] [gard] *s.f.* **1.** guarding, watching; guard, watch, guardianship, custody, keeping; ~ *à vue*, police custody; *chien de* ~, watch-dog; *être de* ~, to be on guard, on the watch, to be on duty; *médecin de* ~, doctor on call; (mil.) *officier de* ~, officer of the watch, duty officer; *monter la* ~, to mount guard; **2.** guard, watch, care; *faire bonne* ~, to keep a good watch; *être en* ~, to be on (one's) guard, to be on the watch, to beware; *prendre* ~, to be careful, to watch out; *prendre* ~ *à*, to mind, to beware of, to be careful of, to look out for; *prendre* ~ *à faire*, to be careful to do; *prendre* ~ *de faire*, to beware of doing, to be careful not to do; to avoid doing; *avoir* ~ *de faire*, to have no intention of doing; to be far from doing; **3.** (mil.) guard; guard-room; ~ *d'honneur*, guard of honour; (fig.) *la Vieille Garde*, the Old Guard; **4.** guard, protector, hilt; ward (of lock); (bookb.) end-paper, fly-leaf.
garde[2] [gard] *s.m.* **1.** warden, guardian, keeper, warder, watchman, attendant; guardsman, guard; ~ *du corps*, bodyguard; ~ *forestier*, forester, ranger, keeper; ~ *s.f.* nurse.
gardé, -e [garde] *adj.* guarded, protected, reserved, private.
garde-à-vous [gardavu] *s.m.* (mil.) (position of) attention; *se mettre au* ~, to come to attention; (fig.) to stiffen, to become tense.
garde-barrière [gard(ə)barjɛr] *s.m.f.* level-crossing keeper; **~-bébé** [gard(ə)bebe] *s.m.* (pl. *garde-bébés*) baby-sitter; **~-bœuf** [gardəbœf] *s.m.* (pl. *garde-bœuf(s)*) (ornith.) cattle egret; **~-boue** [gardəbu] *s.m.invar.* mudguard, splash-board; **~-chasse** [gardəʃas] *s.m.* (pl. *garde-chasse(s)*) gamekeeper; **~-chiourme** [gardəʃjurm] *s.m.* (pl. *garde(s)-chiourme(s)*) (obs.) warder of chain-gang; (mod. fig.) slave-driver; **~-corps** [gardəkɔr] *s.m.invar.* railing, rail, guard-rail, handrail, parapet; (naut.) lifeline, man-rope; **~-côte** [gardəkot] *s.m.* (pl. *garde-côte(s)*) coastguard; coastguard or fisheries protection vessel; **~-feu** [gardəfø] *s.m.invar.* fire-guard; **~-fou** [gardəfu] *s.m.* (pl. *garde-fous*) = GARDE-CORPS; **~-frein** [gardəfrɛ̃] *s.m.* (pl. *gardes-frein(s)*) (rail.) brakesman; **~-magasin** [gardmagazɛ̃] *s.m.* (pl. *gardes-magasin(s)*) warehouseman, storeman; (mil.) storekeeper, quartermaster sergeant; **~-malade** [gard(ə)malad] *s.m.f.* nurse; **~-manger** [gardmɑ̃ʒe] *s.m.invar.* larder; food-safe; **~-meuble** [gardəmœbl] *s.m.* (pl. *garde-meubles*) furniture repository; **~-nappe** [gardənap] *s.m.* (pl. *garde-nappe(s)*) table-mat, coaster.
gardénia [gardenja] *s.m.* (bot.) gardenia.
garde-pêche [gardəpɛʃ] *s.m.invar.* **1.** water-bailiff; **2.** fisheries protection vessel; **~-port** [gardəpɔr] *s.m.* (pl. *garde-port(s)*) wharf-master.
garder [garde] *v.t.* **1.** to guard, to watch, to look after, to keep; to keep to; ~ *à vue*, to keep an eye on; ~ *la chambre*, to keep to one's room; **2.** to guard, to protect, to preserve, to keep, to store, to retain; ~ *un secret*, to keep a secret; ~ *son chapeau*, to keep one's hat on; ~ *tout en soi-même*, to be very secretive; **3.** to keep, to maintain; ~ *le silence*, to keep silent, to say nothing; ~ *les yeux baissés*, to keep one's eyes on the ground, not to look up; ~ *rancune*, to harbour a grudge; **4.** to keep, to put aside; (fig.) ~ *une dent contre qn.*, to have a grudge against s.o.; ~ *une poire pour la soif*, to put sth. aside for a rainy day; **5.** to keep, to observe, (rule, distance, etc.); **se** ~ *v.refl.* (obs.) to guard oneself; (mod.) to keep (i.e. not to go bad); *se* ~ *de*, to beware of, to refrain from, to be careful not to, to avoid; *je m'en garderai bien*, I certainly won't, that's the last thing I would do, I would never think of it.
garderie [gardəri] *s.f.* **1.** (forester's) beat; **2.** day nursery.
garde-robe [gardərɔb] *s.f.* (pl. *garde-robes*) wardrobe (furniture or clothes); (obs.) closet, W.C.
gardeu-r, -se [gardœr] *s.m.f.* keeper, herd; ~*se d'oies*, goose-girl.
garde-voie [gardəvwa] *s.m.* (pl. *gardes-voie(s)*) (rail.) lengthman; soldier guarding railway line; **~-vue** [gardəvy] *s.m.invar.* eye-shade, eye-shield.
gardien, -ne [gardjɛ̃] *s.m.f.* guardian, warden,

keeper, protector; warder, wardress; caretaker; door-keeper; watchman; ~ *de but*, goalkeeper; ~ *judiciaire*, bailiff's man; ~ *de la paix*, policeman; *ange* ~, guardian angel.
gardiennage [gardjɛnaʒ] *s.m.* guardianship; wardenship; guarding, watching, surveillance; (port) conservancy.
gardon [gardɔ̃] *s.m.* (ichth.), roach; *frais comme un* ~, fit as a fiddle.
gare [gar, gɑr] *s.f.* (rail., coach, etc.) station; (on river) lay-by, basin; ~ *terminus*, terminus; ~ *aérienne*, air terminal; *chef de* ~, station-master; (of train) *entrer, être, en* ~, to arrive, to be in; (pop.) *à la* ~*!*, buzz off!
gare [gar] *interj.* look out!, mind your backs!; *sans crier* ~, without a word of warning; ~ *à*, look out for, watch out for; ~ *à la tête*, mind your head; ~ *à la peinture*, wet paint; ~ *à toi, si*, woe betide you, if.
garenne [garɛn] *s.f.* **1.** (rabbit-)warren; *un (lapin de)* ~, a wild rabbit; **2.** fishing-preserve.
garer [gare] *v.t.* to put in a safe place; to garage; to shunt; to dock; to park; **se** ~ *v.refl.* to get out of the way, to pull to one side, to shunt into a siding; (fam.) to park (one's car); *se* ~ *de*, to take cover from, to keep clear of.
Gargantua [gargɑ̃tɥa] *s.m.* Gargantua, glutton.
gargantuesque [gargɑ̃tɥɛsk] *adj.* Gargantuan.
(**se**) **gargariser** [gargarize] *v.refl.* to gargle; (fig.) *se* ~ *de*, to delight in, to relish.
gargarisme [gargarism] *s.m.* gargle, mouthwash; gargling.
gargote [gargɔt] *s.f.* (pej.) cheap and nasty eating-place.
gargoti-er, -ère [gargɔtje] *s.m.f.* one who runs a *gargote*.
gargouille [garguj] *s.f.* (arch.) gargoyle, water--spout; downpipe, rain-water gutter.
gargouillement [gargujmɑ̃] *s.m.* gurgling; rumbling (in the stomach).
gargouiller [garguje] *v.i.* to gurgle; (of stomach) to rumble.
gargouillis [garguji] *s.m.* = GARGOUILLEMENT.
gargoulette [gargulɛt] *s.f.* porous water-jug, water-cooler.
gargousse [gargus] *s.f.* (artill.) cartridge, charge.
garnement [garnəmɑ̃] *s.m.* scapegrace, good--for-nothing; unruly child, young hooligan.
garni [garni] *s.m.* furnished house or room.
garni, -e [garni] *adj.* furnished, supplied, provided, (*de*, with); (cook.) garnished, with trimmings, with vegetables.
garnir [garnir] *v.t.* **1.** to protect, to lag (pipes, etc.), (naut.) to serve or whip (a rope); **2.** to provide, to equip, to fit out or up; to stock, to furnish; to fill; to cover (*de*, with); **se** ~ *v.refl.* to fill, to fill up; **3.** to trim, to line; to garnish; to adorn, to decorate.
garnison [garnizɔ̃] *s.f.* garrison.
garnissage [garnisaʒ] *s.m.* (techn.) packing, stuffing, padding, lagging; (text.) napping, teazling, raising, (of cloth); decoration (of china).
garnisseu-r, -se [garnisœr] *s.m.f.* (techn.) packer.
garniture [garnityr] *s.f.* **1.** (techn.) covering, protection; packing, stuffing, filling, lagging; lining; (print.) furniture; ~ *de frein*, brake--lining; **2.** decoration, ornament(s), trimmings, garnishing(s); ~ *de cheminée*, (set of) mantel-piece ornaments; **3.** furniture, furnishings, fittings, requisites; (naut.) rigging; set; ~ *de foyer*, set of fire-irons
garou[1] [garu] *s.m.* = LOUP-GAROU.
garou[2] [garu] *s.m.* (bot.) spurge-flax, garou--bush; (pharm.) garou bark.
garrigue [garig] *s.f.* arid scrub-land.
garrot[1] [garo] *s.m.* withers (of horse).
garrot[2] [garo] *s.m.* **1.** tourniquet, garrot, racking-stick; tongue (of frame-saw); **2.** garrotte (instrument of torture).
garrotte [garɔt] *s.f.* (obs.) = GARROT[2] 2.
garrotter [garɔte] *v.t.* to bind or tie down, to pinion; to garrotte; (fig.) to hamstring.
gars [gɑ] *s.m.* young fellow, boy, lad; fellow, chap.
Gascogne [gaskɔɲ] *s.f.* (geog.) Gascony; *le Golfe de* ~, the Bay of Biscay.
gascon, -ne [gaskɔ̃] *adj., s.m.f.* Gascon, (native) of Gascony; (fig.) boaster, braggart.
gasconnade [gaskɔnad] *s.f.* boasting, bragging; tall story.
gas-oil [gɑzɔjl] *s.m.* gas oil, diesel fuel.
gaspillage [gaspijaʒ] *s.m.* wasting, squandering.
gaspiller [gaspije] *v.t.* to waste, to squander.
gaspilleu-r, -se [gaspijœr] *adj.* wasting, wasteful; *s.m.f.* squanderer, spendthrift, waster.
gastéropode [gasterɔpɔd] *s.m.* (zool.) gastropod.
gastr-algie [gastralʒi] *s.f.* (med.) gastralgia; ~**algique** [gastralʒik] *adj.* gastralgic; ~**-ectomie** [gastrɛktɔmi] *s.f.* (surg.) gastrectomy; ~**ique** [gastrik] *adj.* gastric; *s.m.f.* one with gastric trouble; ~**ite** [gastrit] *s.f.* (med.) gastritis.
gastro-entérite [gastrɔɑ̃terit] *s.f.* (med.) gastro--enteritis; ~**-entérologie** [gastrɔɑ̃terɔlɔʒi] *s.f.* gastro-enterology; ~**-entérologue** [gastrɔ-ɑ̃terɔlɔg] *s.m.f.* gastro-enterologist.
gastro-intestinal, -e [gastrɔɛ̃tɛstinal] *adj.* gastro--intestinal.
gastro-nome [gastrɔnɔm] *s.m.* gastronome, epicure; ~**nomie** [gastrɔnɔmi] *s.f.* gastronomy; ~**nomique** [gastrɔnɔmik] *adj.* gastronomic(al); ~**scope** [gastrɔskɔp] *s.m.* (med.) gastroscope; ~**tomie** [gastrɔtɔmi] *s.f.* (surg.) gastrotomy.
gastrula [gastryla] *s.f.* (zool.) gastrula.
gâté, -e [gɑte] *adj.* rotten, decayed, bad; (lit. & fig.) spoilt, spoiled.
gâteau (pl. **-x**) [gɑto] *s.m.* cake, gâteau, tart, dessert pastry; disc, round piece; (fig., fam.) profit, spoils; ~ *de cire* or *de miel*, honeycomb; (fam.) *c'est du* ~, it's a piece of cake, it's money for jam.
gâter [gɑte] *v.t.* (obs.) to damage, to dirty, to soil; (mod.) to spoil, to injure, to do harm to, to impair, to ruin; to corrupt, to cause to go bad; to diminish, to detract from; to spoil (a child), to pamper; *ce qui ne gâte rien*, which is all to the good; **se** ~ *v.refl.* to spoil, to go bad, to rot, to deteriorate, to become worse; to go wrong; *le temps se gâte*, the weather is breaking up.
gâterie [gɑtri] *s.f.* spoiling, pampering; (pl.) treats, goodies.
gâte-sauce [gɑtsos] *s.m.invar.* (obs.) bad cook; (mod.) kitchen-boy.
gâteu-x, -se [gɑtø] *adj.* senile, imbecile, doting; *s.m.f.* dotard.
gâtine [gɑtin] *s.f.* marshy ground.
gâtisme [gɑtism] *s.m.* dotage, senility.
gatte [gat] *s.f.* (naut.) manger.
gattilier [gatilje] *s.m.* (bot.) Agnus castus.
gauche [goʃ] *adj.* **1.** left, left-hand; *mariage de la main* ~, unlawful union; (fig.) *se lever du pied* ~, to get out of bed on the wrong side, to be in a bad temper; **2.** gauche, awkward, clumsy; warped, crooked, out of true; ~ *s.f.* left, left hand, left side; (pol.) Left; *à ma* ~, on or to my left; *tournez à* ~, turn left; *tenir la* ~, to keep to the left; (pol.) *les* ~*s* (*s.m.pl.*) the parties of the Left; *être à* ~, to be left-wing; (fig.) *mettre de l'argent à* ~, to tuck money away; *passer l'arme à* ~, to die; *jusqu'à la* ~, completely, up to the hilt; ~**ment** [goʃmɑ̃] *adv.* awkwardly, clumsily.

gauch-er, -ère [goʃe] *adj., s.m.f.* left-handed (person).
gaucherie [goʃri] *s.f.* awkwardness, clumsiness; clumsy gesture, stupid mistake.
gauchir [goʃir] *v.i.* to warp, to twist, to get out of shape, to become distorted; (obs.) to deviate, to turn aside, to dodge; ~ *v.t.* to twist, to distort, to put out of shape; (aeron.) to bank; (fig.) to distort, to falsify.
gauchisant, -e [goʃizɑ̃] *adj.* (pol.) with leftist tendencies.
gauchisme [goʃism] *s.m.* (pol.) leftism.
gauchissement [goʃismɑ̃] *s.m.* warping, buckling, distortion; (aeron.) banking.
gauchiste [goʃist] *adj., s.m.f.* (pol.) leftist.
gaude [god] *s.f.* (bot.) dyer's weed; weld.
gaudriole [godrijɔl] *s.f.* **1.** (fam.) broad joke, dirty story; **2.** sexual intercourse.
gaufrage [gofraʒ] *s.m.* goffering, crimping, fluting; embossing.
gaufre [gofr] *s.m.* **1.** (cook.) waffle, wafer; **2.** honeycomb.
gaufrer [gofre] *v.t.* to goffer, to crimp; to emboss; *fer à* ~, goffering-iron.
gaufrette [gofrɛt] *s.f.* (cook.) wafer.
gaufreu-r, -se [gofrœr] *s.m.f.* gofferer, crimper; embosser; **~se** *s.f.* crimping- or embossing--machine.
gaufrier [gofrie] *s.m.* waffle-iron.
gaufroir [gofrwar] *s.m.* goffering- or crimping--iron.
gaufrure [gofryr] *s.f.* goffering; embossing; embossed design.
gaulage [golaʒ] *s.m.* beating (of trees); knocking down (of fruit).
gaule [gol] *s.f.* pole; rod, fishing-rod; switch.
Gaule [gol] *s.f.* (Rom. hist.) Gaul.
gauleiter [gawlɑjtɛr] *s.m.* (Nazi) Gauleiter.
gauler [gole] *v.t.* to beat (trees), to knock down (fruit, etc.) with a pole.
gaullisme [golism] *s.m.* (pol.) Gaullism.
gaulliste [golist] *adj., s.m.f.* Gaullist.
gaulois, -e [golwa] *adj.* **1.** Gallic, Gaulish, of Gaul; **2.** (of humour, etc.) Gallic, broad; ~ *s.m.* Gaulish (language); **~e** *s.f.* Gauloise, Fr. cigarette.
gauloiserie [golwazri] *s.f.* broad joke, dirty story; broadness, licentiousness.
gaupe [gop] *s.f.* (pop.) slut, prostitute.
gauss [gos] *s.m.* (phys.) gauss.
(se) gausser [gose] *v.refl.* **1.** (Lit.) *se ~ de*, to make fun of, to deride, to jeer at; **2.** to be joking, to speak mockingly, to laugh.
gavage [gavaʒ] *s.m.* cramming (of poultry); (med.) force-feeding.
gave [gav] *s.m.* (in the Pyrenees) torrent, river.
gaver [gave] *v.t.* (lit. & fig.) to cram, to stuff; to force-feed; (aeron.) to supercharge (engine); (fig.) *être gavé de*, to be surfeited with; **se** ~ *v.refl.* to stuff or gorge oneself.
gaveu-r, -se [gavœr] *s.m.f.* (poultry) crammer; **~r** *s.m.* (techn.) supercharger; **~se** *s.f.* (poultry) cramming-apparatus.
gavial [gavjal] *s.m.* (zool.) gavial, gharial.
gavotte [gavɔt] *s.f.* (mus., danc.) gavotte.
gavroche [gavrɔʃ] *s.m.* street arab, urchin.
gaz [gɑz] *s.m.invar.* **1.** (chem.) gas; (pl.) intestinal gases, flatulence, wind; ~ *des marais* or *des houillères*, marsh gas, methane, fire-damp; (mil.) ~ *de combat*, poison gas; *chambre à* ~, gas--chamber; **2.** gas (as fuel, etc.); gaslight; gas supply; gas undertaking; ~ *de houille*, coal-gas; ~ *de pétrole*, natural gas; *compteur à* ~, gas--meter; *réchaud à* ~, gas-ring; *employé du* ~, gasman, gas-board official; (fig., pop.) *il y a de l'eau dans le* ~, there's trouble brewing; **3.** (internal combustion engine) gas, mixture; (pl.) gas, throttle; ~ *d'échappement*, exhaust (gas); *pédale des* ~, accelerator (pedal); *à pleins* ~, at full throttle, flat out.
gaze [gɑz] *s.f.* gauze.
gazé, -e [gɑze] *adj.* gassed; *s.m.f.* one suffering from effects of poison gas.
gazéifier [gɑzeifje] *v.t.* to gasify, to convert into gas; to aerate (mineral water, etc.).
gazelle [gazɛl] *s.f.* (zool.) gazelle.
gazer[1] [gɑze] *v.t.* (obs.) to veil, to conceal.
gazer[2] [gɑze] *v.t.* to gas (with poison gas); (text.) to gas; *v.i.* (fam.) to go at top speed, at full throttle, to step on the gas; (fig.) to go (properly), to work.
gazeti-er, -ère [gaztje] *s.m.f.* (obs.) gazetteer.
gazette [gazɛt] *s.f.* gazette, newspaper; retailing of news; newsmonger.
gazeu-x, -se [gɑzø] *adj.* gaseous, gassy; aerated, effervescent, fizzy; (med.) *gangrène ~se*, gas gangrene.
gazi-er, -ère [gɑzje] *adj.* gas; **~er** *s.m.* gas--worker, gasman, gas-board official.
gazo-duc [gɑzɔdyk] *s.m.* gas pipeline, gas--main; **~gène** [gɑzɔʒɛn] *s.m.* **1.** (obs.) seltzogene, soda-water maker; **2.** gas-producer, gas--generator; *gaz de ~gène*, producer-gas; **~line** [gɑzɔlin] *s.f.* gasoline, gasolene; **~mètre** [gɑzɔmɛtr] *s.m.* gas meter; gasometer, gas--holder.
gazon [gɑzɔ̃] *s.m.* grass, sod, turf; lawn, grass--plot.
gazonnant, -e [gɑzɔnɑ̃] *adj.* turfy, giving the effect of a lawn.
gazonné, -e [gɑzɔne] *adj.* grassy.
gazonner [gɑzɔne] *v.t.* to turf; **se** ~ *v.refl.* to become covered with grass.
gazonneu-x, -se [gɑzɔnø] *adj.* grassy.
gazouillant, -e [gazujɑ̃] *adj.* warbling, chirping, babbling.
gazouillement [gazujmɑ̃] *s.m.* warbling, twittering, chirping, babbling, prattling.
gazouiller [gazuje] *v.i.* to warble, to chirp, to twitter; to babble, to prattle.
gazouillis [gazuji] *s.m.* = GAZOUILLEMENT.
G.D.F. [ʒedeɛf] abbrev. *Gaz de France.*
geai [ʒɛ] *s.m.* (ornith.) jay; *le ~ paré des plumes du paon*, the jackdaw in borrowed plumes.
géant, -e [ʒeɑ̃] *s.m.f.* giant, giantess, collossus; *à pas de* ~, with giant strides; *adj.* gigantic, giantlike.
gecko [ʒeko] *s.m.* (zool.) gecko.
géhenne [ʒeɛn] *s.f.* Gehenna, hell; (fig.) torment, misery.
geignard, -e [ʒɛɲar] *adj.* whining, complaining, moaning; *s.m.f.* whiner.
geignement [ʒɛɲmɑ̃] *s.m.* whining, moan, groan, complaining.
geindre [ʒɛ̃dr] *v.i.* to moan, to whine; to complain, to grouse.
geindre [ʒɛ̃dr] *s.m.* = GINDRE.
geisha, ghesha [gɛʃa] *s.f.* geisha.
gel [ʒɛl] *s.m.* frost, freezing; (phys.) gel; (econ.) ~ *des credits*, credit-squeeze.
gélatine [ʒelatin] *s.f.* gelatine.
gélatineu-x, -se [ʒelatinø] *adj.* gelatinous.
gelé, -e [ʒ(ə)le] *adj.* frozen, freezing, icy cold; (econ.) (of assets, etc.) frozen.
gelée [ʒ(ə)le] *s.f.* **1.** frost; **2.** (cook.) jelly.
geler [ʒ(ə)le] *v.t.i.* to freeze, to be bitterly cold, to congeal; **se** ~ *v.refl.* to freeze, to get frozen.
géli-f, -ve [ʒelif] *adj.* frost-cleft, frost-riven.
gélifier [ʒelifje] *v.t.* (chem.) to cause to gel; **se** ~ *v.refl.* to gel.
gélinotte [ʒelinɔt] *s.f.* (ornith.) hazel-grouse.
gélivure [ʒelivyr] *s.f.* frost-crack.
gélose [ʒeloz] *s.f.* (chem.) gelose.
gelure [ʒ(ə)lyr] *s.f.* (med.) frost-bite.
gémeaux [ʒemo] *s.m.pl.* (astron.) Gemini, the Twins.

gémination [ʒeminɑsjɔ̃] *s.f.* (biol., lang.) gemination; (rhet.) repetition.
géminé, -e [ʒemine] *adj.* geminate, double, in pairs, twin.
gémir [ʒemir] *v.i.* to groan, to moan, to whine, to bewail, to complain, to lament; to creak.
gémissant, -e [ʒɛmisɑ̃] *adj.* groaning, moaning, complaining, lamenting; mournful.
gémissement [ʒemismɑ̃] *s.m.* groan, moan, groaning, moaning; creaking; (fig.) wail, complaint, lament; protest.
gemmage [ʒɛmaʒ] *s.m.* tapping pine-trees to get resin.
gemmation [ʒɛmɑsjɔ̃] *s.f.* budding, gemmation.
gemme [ʒɛm] *s.f.* **1.** gem, precious stone; **2.** pine-resin; ~ *adj. sel* ~, rock-salt.
gemmé, -e [ʒeme] *adj.* adorned with gems; (bot.) gemmate.
gemmer [ʒeme] *v.t.* to tap (pine-trees for resin); ~ *v.i.* to bud, to gemmate.
gemmifère [ʒɛmifɛr] *adj.* (min.) gemmiferous; (bot.) budding; (forestry) producing resin.
gemmule [ʒɛmyl] *s.f.* (bot.) plumule.
gênant, -e [ʒɛnɑ̃] *adj.* troublesome, in the way, inconvenient, a nuisance, embarrassing, awkward, annoying, irksome.
gencive [ʒɑ̃siv] *s.f.* gum (of the teeth); (pl.) (pop.) jaw, teeth.
gendarme [ʒɑ̃darm] *s.m.* **1.** (obs.) man-at-arms, soldier; (mod.) gendarme, member of police militia; (fig.) martinet, virago; *le* ~, the police, the forces of law and order; (fam.) *faire le* ~, to discipline, to police, to lay down the law; *chapeau de* ~, paper hat; **2.** (pop.) red herring; kind of hard, flat sausage; **3.** flaw, spot, (in diamond); **4.** local name for various fish, birds, insects, and plants.
(**se**) **gendarmer** [ʒɑ̃darme] *v.refl.* (fig.) to be up in arms, to flare up, to speak angrily.
gendarmerie [ʒɑ̃darməri] *s.f.* **1.** (obs.) heavy cavalry; lifeguards; **2.** gendarmerie, police militia; station or barracks of *gendarmerie*.
gendre [ʒɑ̃dr] *s.m.* son-in-law; ⚠ not 'gender'.
gêne [ʒɛn] *s.f.* **1.** (obs.) torture, torment; **2.** trouble, difficulty, discomfort, inconvenience, awkwardness; embarrassment, confusion; disturbance, nuisance, bother; *sans* ~, unconstrained, uninhibited, free and easy, offhand; **3.** financial embarrassment, poverty, penury, want; *être dans la* ~, to be in need, to be in straitened circumstances.
gêné, -e [ʒene] *adj.* uncomfortable, awkward, inconvenienced, hampered, encumbered; embarrassed, self-conscious, constrained, upset, disturbed; in straitened circumstances.
généalog-ie [ʒenealɔʒi] *s.f.* genealogy, pedigree, descent; **~ique** [ʒenealɔʒik] *adj.* genealogical; *arbre ~ique*, family tree; **~iquement** [ʒenealɔʒikmɑ̃] *adv.* genealogically; **~iste** [ʒenealɔʒist] *s.m.* genealogist.
génépi [ʒenepi] *s.m.* **1.** (bot.) wormwood, Alpine mugwort; **2.** absinthe.
gêner [ʒene] *v.t.* **1.** (obs.) to torture, to torment; **2.** to inconvenience, to hamper, to constrain, to make uncomfortable, to encumber, to cramp, to impede; to cause trouble or awkwardness (to), to bother, to be a nuisance (to); **3.** to embarrass, to disturb, to upset; **4.** to cause financial embarrassment (to); **se** ~ *v.refl.* to put oneself out, to put oneself to trouble or inconvenience, to squeeze up (on seat); to feel awkwardness or constraint; *ne pas se* ~, not to hesitate (*de*, to); (iron.) to make oneself at home.
général, -e, (aux) [ʒeneral] *adj.* **1.** general (opp. particular); *en* ~, treated as a whole, in universal terms; (mil.) *quartier* ~, general headquarters; (theatr.) *répétition ~e*, dress-rehearsal; **2.** general, common, widespread, usual, ordinary; collective; *en* ~, in general, generally speaking, on the whole, commonly, usually; ~ *s.m.* (mil.) general; (Air Force) Air (Vice-) Marshal; (eccles.) general; **~e** *s.f.* **1.** general's wife; **2.** (eccles.) general, abbess.
généralat [ʒenerala] *s.m.* generalship (office, not strategy).
généralement [ʒeneralmɑ̃] *adv.* generally, usually, in general, in a general sense; ~ *admis*, current, commonly accepted.
généralisable [ʒeneralizabl] *adj.* capable of general application.
généralisat-eur, -rice [ʒeneralizatœr] *adj.* generalizing.
généralisation [ʒeneralizɑsjɔ̃] *s.f.* generalization.
généraliser [ʒeneralize] *v.t.* **1.** to apply (sth.) generally, to make universal; **2.** to generalize; **se** ~ *v.refl.* to be applied generally, to become universal; to become generalized, to become general or widespread.
généralissime [ʒeneralisim] *s.m.* generalissimo.
généralité [ʒeneralite] *s.f.* **1.** generality; (pej.) generalization, vague statement; **2.** (obs.) generality, entire body or population; (mod.) majority.
générat-eur, -rice [ʒeneratœr] *adj.* generating, generative; (fig.) productive, conducive (*de*, of, to); (*machine*) **~rice**, generator; **~eur** *s.m.* generator, producer.
génération [ʒenerɑsjɔ̃] *s.f.* generation, procreation; (fig.) production; generation (age group); descent.
généreu-x, -se [ʒenerø] *adj.* generous, noble; bountiful, generous, abundant, plentiful, fertile, liberal, open-handed, unstinted; warm-hearted; of ample proportions; courageous; *un don ~x*, a handsome gift; *un sol ~x*, a fertile soil, a rich or fruitful country; *être d'un sang ~x*, to be of noble birth, to have a noble nature, to have innate courage; *une poitrine ~se*, an ample bosom; **~sement** [ʒenerøzmɑ̃] *adv.* generously, nobly, liberally, munificently, without stint; courageously.
générique [ʒenerik] *adj.* generic; ~ *s.m.* (cin.) credit titles.
générosité [ʒenerozite] *s.f.* generosity, magnanimity, bounteousness, liberality; nobility of character; act of generosity; (pl.) generous gifts, benefactions; *sans* ~, ungenerously, meanly.
Gênes [ʒɛn] *s.f.* (geog.) Genoa.
genèse [ʒənɛz] *s.f.* Genesis; origin, birth, formation.
génésique [ʒenezik] *adj.* (of instinct, etc.) genetic.
genet [ʒ(ə)nɛ] *s.m.* jennet (Spanish horse).
genêt [ʒ(ə)nɛ] *s.m.* (bot.) broom, genista; ~ *épineux*, gorse, furze.
généticien, -ne [ʒenetisjɛ̃] *s.m.f.* geneticist.
génétique [ʒenetik] *adj.* genetic; ~ *s.f.* genetics; **~ment** [ʒenetikmɑ̃] *adv.* genetically.
genette [ʒənɛt] *s.f.* (zool.) genet, civet-cat.
gêneu-r, -se [ʒɛnœr] *s.m.f.* intruder, bore, killjoy; tiresome person, nuisance, obstacle.
Genève [ʒ(ə)nɛv] *s.f.* (geog.) Geneva.
genevois, -e [ʒənvwa] *adj., s.m.f.* Genevese, Genevan, (native or inhabitant) of Geneva.
genévrier [ʒənevrije] *s.m.* (bot.) juniper-tree, juniper.
génial, -e, (aux) [ʒenjal] *adj.* of genius, inspired, brilliant; *œuvre ~e*, work of genius; *idée ~e*, brilliant idea; **~ement** [ʒenjalmɑ̃] *adv.* with genius, brilliantly; ⚠ not 'genial', 'genially'.
génie [ʒeni] *s.m.* **1.** genius, spirit, (guardian) angel; ~ *tutélaire*, tutelary deity; *mauvais* ~,

evil genius; **2.** genius, spirit, essence; characteristic, disposition; gift; *le ~ des Français*, the genius of the French, the essence or spirit of France; *avoir le ~ de*, to have a gift or genius for; **3.** genius (attribute or person); *avoir du ~*, to have genius; *un homme de ~*, a man of genius, a genius; *c'est un ~*, he is a genius; **4.** engineering; engineers; *~ maritime*, naval engineering; corps of naval constructors; (mil.) *le (corps du) ~*, = the (Corps of) Royal Engineers.

genièvre [ʒənjɛvr] *s.m.* **1.** juniper, juniper-tree; **2.** Hollands (gin), geneva.

génisse [ʒenis] *s.f.* heifer.

génital, -e, (aux) [ʒenital] *adj.* genital.

génit-eur, -rice [ʒenitœr] *s.m.f.* (jest) sire, begetter, parent; **~eur** *s.m.* animal kept for breeding.

génitif [ʒenitif] *s.m.* (gram.) genitive.

génito-urinaire [ʒenitɔyrinɛr] *adj.* (anat.) genito-urinary, urino-genital.

génocide [ʒenɔsid] *s.m.* genocide.

génois, -e [ʒenwa] *adj., s.m.f.* Genoese, (native or inhabitant) of Genoa; **~e** *s.f.* **1.** Genoese sponge, Genoa cake; **2.** Provençal frieze of superimposed tiles.

génotype [ʒenɔtip] *s.m.* (biol.) genotype.

genou (pl. **-x**) [ʒ(ə)nu] *s.m.* knee; (mech.) elbow-joint, ball-and-socket joint; (nav. arch.) knee, futtock; *à ~x*, kneeling, on one's knees, (fig.) on bended knee; *à ~x!*, kneel down!, down on your knees!; *se mettre à ~x*, to kneel (down); *tomber aux ~x de qn.*, to fall at someone's feet, to prostrate oneself before s.o.; *faire du ~ à une femme*, to play knees with a woman.

genouillère [ʒ(ə)nujɛr] *s.f.* knee-pad, shin-guard, pad; knee-piece (of armour); kneecap; (techn.) knuckle-joint, elbow-joint.

genre [ʒɑ̃r] *s.m.* **1.** race; genus, kind; (art, etc.) genre; *le ~ humain*, the human race, mankind; *peinture de ~*, genre painting; **2.** sort, kind, class, order, description; way, manner, style; *de ce ~*, of this kind; *en tout ~*, *en tous ~s*, of every kind, of all descriptions; *en* or *dans son ~*, in his way; *unique en son ~*, unique of its kind; *~ de vie*, way of life; *~ bohème*, bohemian way of life; *avoir un mauvais ~*, to behave rudely or awkwardly; *avoir bon ~*, to be well brought-up, to be elegant or distinguished; *faire* or *se donner du ~*, to pose; *ce n'est pas mon ~*, it's not my sort of thing, it's not my cup of tea; **3.** (gram.) gender.

gens [ʒɑ̃] *s.m.* or *f.pl.* (agreements, including those of adjectives following, are masculine; but if an adjective immediately preceding *gens* has a distinctive feminine form, this adjective, and any other preceding adjective, must be in feminine; e.g.: *tous ces braves gens, gens honnêtes et bons*; but *toutes ces bonnes gens, toutes ces bonnes gens sont ennuyeux*); people, persons; people (opp. things or animals); men; (obs.) servants; *la plupart des ~*, most people; (fam.) *un tas de ~*, a crowd of people; *jeunes ~*, young people; *~ et bêtes*, people and animals, man and beast; *~ de loi*, lawyers, legal men; *~ d'affaires*, businessmen; (see also GENT).

gent [ʒɑ̃] *s.f.* (pl. *gens*) race, tribe, people, nation; *droit des gens*, law of nations; (poet.) *la ~ ailée*, the winged tribe.

gentiane [ʒɑ̃sjan] *s.f.* (bot.) gentian.

gentil, -le [ʒɑ̃ti] *adj.* (obs.) noble; (mod.) gentle, nice, pleasant, amiable, kind, pretty, agreeable; (of children) good; considerable; *une ~le somme*, a tidy sum.

gentil [ʒɑ̃ti] *s.m.* gentile.

gentilhomme [ʒɑ̃tijɔm] *s.m.* (pl. *gentilshommes*) nobleman, gentleman.

gentilhommière [ʒɑ̃tijɔmjɛr] *s.f.* gentleman's country seat, small manor.

gentillesse [ʒɑ̃tijɛs] *s.f.* **1.** prettiness; **2.** (obs.) piece of wit; (iron.) nasty remark, insult; **3.** kindness, amiability; kind act, kindness, attention, act of thoughtfulness.

gentillet, -te [ʒɑ̃tijɛ] *adj.* rather pretty, pretty little; (pej.) quite nice.

gentiment [ʒɑ̃timɑ̃] *adv.* gently, prettily, gracefully, amiably, kindly, pleasantly, nicely.

gentleman [dʒɛntləman] *s.m.* gentleman; (racing) gentleman rider.

génuflexion [ʒenyflɛksjɔ̃] *s.f.* genuflexion, kneeling.

géocentrique [ʒeɔsɑ̃trik] *adj.* geocentric.

géode [ʒeɔd] *s.f.* (geol., mining) geode.

géo-désie [ʒeɔdezi] *s.f.* geodesy, surveying; **~désique** [ʒeɔdezik] *adj.* geodesic, geodetic; **~dynamique** [ʒeɔdinamik] *adj.* geodynamic(al); **~graphe** [ʒeɔgraf] *s.m.f.* geographer; *ingénieur ~graphe*, surveyor; **~graphie** [ʒeɔgrafi] *s.f.* geography; **~graphique** [ʒeɔgrafik] *adj.* geographic(al); **~iquement** [ʒeɔgrafikmɑ̃] *adv.* geographically.

géoïde [ʒeɔid] *s.m.* (sci.) geoid.

geôle [ʒol] *s.f.* gaol, jail, prison.

geôli-er, -ère [ʒolje] *s.m.f.* gaoler, jailer.

géo-logie [ʒeɔlɔʒi] *s.f.* geology; **~logique** [ʒeɔlɔʒik] *adj.* geological; **~logiquement** [ʒeɔlɔʒikmɑ̃] *adv.* geologically; **~logue** [ʒeɔlɔg] *s.m.* geologist; **~magnétique** [ʒeɔmaɲetik] *adj.* geomagnetic; **~mancie** [ʒeɔmɑ̃si] *s.f.* geomancy.

géométral, -e, (aux) [ʒeɔmetral] *adj.* (of projection, elevation) flat, geometrical (not perspective); *(plan) ~*, flat projection.

géo-mètre [ʒeɔmɛtr] *s.m.* geometrician; geometer; *(arpenteur) ~mètre*, surveyor; **~métrique** [ʒeɔmetrik] *adj.* geometric(al); *exactitude, précision, rigueur, ~métrique*, mathematical exactitude; **~métriquement** [ʒeɔmetrikmɑ̃] *adv.* geometrically; with mathematical exactitude, with scientific precision; **~morphologie** [ʒeɔmɔrfɔlɔʒi] *s.f.* geomorphology; **~physique** [ʒeɔfizik] *adj.* geophysical; *s.f.* geophysics; **~politique** [ʒeɔpɔlitik] *adj.* geopolitical; *s.f.* geopolitics.

Géorgie [ʒeɔrʒi] *s.f.* (geog.) Georgia (in Russia; in U.S.A.).

géorgien, -ne [ʒeɔrʒjɛ̃] *adj., s.m.f.* Georgian.

géorgique [ʒeɔrʒik] *adj.* (Lit. hist.) bucolic.

géosynclinal (pl. **aux**) [ʒeɔsɛ̃klinal] *s.m.* (geol.) geosyncline.

géo-thermie [ʒeɔtɛrmi] *s.f.* geothermy, study of the earth's internal heat; **~thermique** [ʒeɔtɛrmik] *adj.* geothermal; **~tropisme** [ʒeɔtrɔpism] *s.m.* (biol.) geotropism.

gérance [ʒerɑ̃s] *s.f.* management, administration, conduct; managership, editorship.

géraniées [ʒeranje], **géraniacées** [ʒeranjase] *s.f.pl.* (bot.) Geraniaceae.

géranium [ʒeranjɔm] *s.m.* (bot.) geranium; pelargonium.

gérant, -e [ʒerɑ̃] *s.m.f.* manager, manageress, managing director; administrator; editor.

gerbage [ʒɛrbaʒ] *s.m.* (agric.) binding (of sheaves), sheaving, stooking.

gerbe [ʒɛrb] *s.f.* (agric.) sheaf, stook; bunch or spray (of flowers); (poetry) anthology; jet, spout, column, spray, (of water, etc.); shower (of sparks); (artill.) cone of fire; (fireworks) gerbe.

gerbée [ʒɛrbe] *s.f.* (agric.) fodder-straw.

gerber [ʒɛrbe] *v.t.* **1.** (agric.) to bind (sheaves), to sheave; **2.** (techn.) to stack (casks, etc.).

gerbeu-r, -se [ʒɛrbœr] *s.m.f.* binder, stacker; **~se** *s.f.* stacking-machine.

gerbier [ʒɛrbje] *s.m.* (agric.) stack (of corn-sheaves).

gerbière [ʒɛrbjɛr] *s.f.* (agric.) harvest-wain.

gerbille [ʒɛrbij] *s.f.* (zool.) gerbil.

gerboise [ʒɛrbwaz] *s.f.* (zool.) jerboa.
gerce [ʒɛrs] *s.f.* **1.** (ent.) clothes-moth; bookworm; **2.** crack (in wood).
gercer [ʒɛrse] *v.t.* to crack; ~ *v.i.* to crack, to become cracked; **se** ~ *v.refl.* to crack, to become chapped.
gerçure [ʒɛrsyr] *s.f.* chap, crack.
gérer [ʒere] *v.t.* to manage, to conduct, to administer, to carry on.
gerfaut [ʒɛrfo] *s.m.* (ornith.) gerfalcon.
gériatrie [ʒerjatri] *s.f.* geriatrics.
gériatrique [ʒerjatrik] *adj.* geriatric.
germain[1], **-e** [ʒɛrmɛ̃] *adj.* german, of the first degree (of relationship), closely related; *frère* ~, full brother, brother german, (opp. half-brother); *cousin* ~, first cousin; *cousin issu du* ~, second cousin; *s.m.f.* member of immediate family, close relative.
germain[2], **-e** [ʒɛrmɛ̃] *adj., s.m.f.* (ethn., hist.) Germanic; German.
germandrée [ʒɛrmɑ̃dre] *s.f.* (bot.) germander.
Germanie [ʒɛrmani] *s.f.* (hist.) Germania.
germanique [ʒɛrmanik] *adj., s.m.f.* (ethn., lang.) Germanic, German.
germanisant, -e [ʒɛrmanizɑ̃] *adj.* Germanizing; *s.m.f.* Germanophile.
german-isation [ʒɛrmanizɑsjɔ̃] *s.f.* Germanization; **~iser** [ʒɛrmanize] *v.t.* to Germanize; **~isme** [ʒɛrmanism] *s.m.* (lang.) Germanism; **~iste** [ʒɛrmanist] *s.m.f.* Germanist, German scholar.
germanium [ʒɛrmanjɔm] *s.m.* (chem.) germanium.
germano-phile [ʒɛrmanɔfil] *adj., s.m.f.* Germanophile; **~phobe** [ʒɛrmanɔfɔb] *adj., s.m.f.* Germanophobe.
germe [ʒɛrm] *s.m.* germ, seed; sprout; (fig.) germ, origin, source.
germen [ʒɛrmɛn] *s.m.* (bot.) germen.
germer [ʒɛrme] *v.i.* to germinate, to sprout, to shoot; (fig.) to spring up, to germinate, to form.
germicide [ʒɛrmisid] *adj.* germicidal.
germinal [ʒɛrminal] *s.m.* (hist.) Germinal (7th month in Fr. Republican calendar, March–April).
germinal, -e, (**aux**) [ʒɛrminal] *adj.* (biol.) germinal.
germinati-f, -ve [ʒɛrminatif] *adj.* germinal, germinative.
germination [ʒɛrminɑsjɔ̃] *s.f.* germination.
germoir [ʒɛrmwar] *s.m.* malt-house; seed-tray, seed-bed.
gérondif [ʒerɔ̃dif] *s.m.* gerund.
géronte [ʒerɔ̃t] *s.m.* old fool.
géronto-cratie [ʒerɔ̃tɔkrasi] *s.f.* gerontocracy; **~logie** [ʒerɔ̃tɔlɔʒi] *s.f.* gerontology.
gerzeau (pl. **-x**) [ʒɛrzo] *s.m.* (bot.) corn-cockle.
gésier [ʒesje] *s.m.* gizzard; (pop.) stomach.
gésir [ʒezir] *v.i.* *ci-gît*, here lies (buried); *c'est là que gît le lièvre*, that's the point, that's the crux of the matter.
gesse [ʒɛs] *s.f.* (bot.) vetch; everlasting pea.
gestapo [gɛstapo] *s.f.* (German hist.) Gestapo.
gestation [ʒɛstɑsjɔ̃] *s.f.* gestation.
geste[1] [ʒɛst] *s.m.* **1.** gesture, motion, movement; *faire des ~s*, to gesticulate; *un ~ de la tête*, a movement of the head; *précision des ~s*, precision of movement; (fig.) *avoir le ~ large*, to be generous, open-handed; **2.** act, action (see also GESTE *s.f.*).
geste[2] [ʒɛst] *s.f.* **1.** (obs.) (Lit., hist.) heroic deed, exploit; heroic story, geste; **2.** (pl.) *les faits et ~s* (*de qn.*), (someone's) conduct or behaviour; *rendre compte de ses faits et ~s*, to give an account of one's behaviour or movements (esp. to police).
gesticulation [ʒɛstikylɑsjɔ̃] *s.f.* gesticulation, gesticulating.
gesticuler [ʒɛstikyle] *v.i.* to gesticulate.
gestion [ʒɛstjɔ̃] *s.f.* management, administration, conduct (of business, etc.); acting as agent, administratorship.
gestionnaire [ʒɛstjɔnɛr] *adj.* managing; ~ *s.m.f.* manager, manageress, administrator; *administrateur* ~, administrator; officer or official in charge (esp. of mil. store or mess).
gestuel, -le [ʒɛstɥɛl] *adj.* gestural.
getter [gɛtɛr] *s.m.* (phys.) getter.
geyser [ʒɛzɛr] *s.m.* geyser; column of water; ⚠ not 'geyser' for heating water.
Ghana [gana] *s.m.* (geog.) Ghana.
ghanéen, -ne [ganeɛ̃] *adj., s.m.f.* Ghanaian.
ghesha see GEISHA.
ghetto [gɛto, geto] *s.m.* (lit. & fig.) ghetto.
gibbeu-x, -se [ʒibø] *adj.* gibbous, hump-backed.
gibbon [ʒibɔ̃] *s.m.* (zool.) gibbon.
gibbosité [ʒibozite] *s.f.* gibbosity, hump.
gibecière [ʒibsjɛr] *s.f.* game-bag, pouch, satchel.
gibelin [ʒiblɛ̃] *s.m.* (hist.) Ghibelline.
gibelotte [ʒiblɔt] *s.f.* fricassée (usu. of rabbit or hare) in white wine.
giberne [ʒibɛrn] *s.f.* cartridge-case or -pouch; (fig.) *avoir le bâton de maréchal dans sa* ~, to carry a field marshal's baton in one's knapsack.
gibet [ʒibɛ] *s.m.* gibbet, gallows.
gibier [ʒibje] *s.m.* game; ~ *à plumes*, wildfowl, game-birds; ~ *à poil*, venison, rabbits, hares, game-animals; (fig.) ~ *de potence*, gallows bird.
giboulée [ʒibule] *s.f.* sudden storm, or shower of rain, hail, etc.
giboyeu-x, -se [ʒibwajø] *adj.* abounding in game.
gibus [ʒibys] *s.m.* (*chapeau*) ~, opera hat.
giclée [ʒikle] *s.f.* jet, spurt, (of water, etc.).
gicler [ʒikle] *v.i.* to splash; to spurt out, to squirt.
gicleur [ʒiklœr] *s.m.* nozzle; jet (of carburettor).
gifle [ʒifl] *s.f.* slap; box on the ear; (lit. & fig.) slap in the face; (fam.) *c'est une tête à ~s*, he's so stupid, or obstinate, you could hit him.
gifler [ʒifle] *v.t.* to slap, to smack; (fig.) to wound; *giflé par la pluie*, lashed by rain.
gigantesque [ʒigɑ̃tɛsk] *adj.* gigantic, colossal, tremendous; **~ment** [ʒigɑ̃tɛskmɑ̃] *adv.* gigantically.
gigantisme [ʒigɑ̃tism] *s.m.* gigantism.
gigogne [ʒigɔɲ] *s.f.* (pantomime character) *la mère* ~, the old woman who lived in a shoe; *une mère* ~, a woman with many children; *table* ~, nest of tables; (nav.) *vaisseau* ~, mother-ship; *fusée* ~, multi-stage rocket.
gigolo [ʒigɔlo] *s.m.* ladies' man, fancy man, kept man, gigolo.
gigot [ʒigo] *s.m.* leg of mutton or lamb; hind leg (of horse); (fam.) leg or thigh (of person); *manche à* ~, leg-of-mutton holder (for carving); (hist.) *manches à* ~, leg-of-mutton sleeves.
gigoter [ʒigɔte] *v.i.* to jig about, to kick (with one's legs); to twitch.
gigue [ʒig] *s.f.* **1.** haunch (of venison); (fam.) leg; (pop.) *une grande* ~, a tall, lanky girl; **2.** (dance) jig; *danser la* ~, to dance a jig, to jig about.
gilet [ʒilɛ] *s.m.* **1.** waistcoat; cardigan, jersey, sweater, pullover; ~ *d'escrime*, fencing-jacket; ~ *de sauvetage*, life-jacket; ~ *de force*, strait-jacket; ~ *croisé*, double-breasted waistcoat; ~ *droit*, single-breasted waistcoat; **2.** vest (undergarment).
gilde *s.f.* see GUILDE.
gileti-er, -ère [ʒiltje] *s.m.f.* waistcoat-maker.
gille [ʒil] *s.m.* fool, simpleton, clown.
gimblette [ʒɛ̃blɛt] *s.f.* (cook.) jumbal, jumble, ring-biscuit.
gindre [ʒɛ̃dr] *s.m.* baker's man.
gingembre [ʒɛ̃ʒɑ̃mbr] *s.m.* ginger.

gingival, -e, (**aux**) [ʒɛ̃ʒival] *adj.* (anat.) gingival.
gingivite [ʒɛ̃ʒivit] *s.f.* gingivitis, inflammation of the gums.
ginguet, -te [ʒɛ̃gɛ] *adj., s.m.* thin, acid, (wine).
ginkgo [ʒɛ̃ko] *s.m.* (bot.) ginkgo (tree).
(**à**) **giorno** [adʒɔrno, aʒjɔrno] *adv.* brilliantly (lit), as light as day.
girafe [ʒiraf] *s.f.* (zool.) giraffe.
girandole [ʒirɑ̃dɔl] *s.f.* **1.** chandelier; festoons of lights; (fireworks) girandole; **2.** cluster or spray (of flowers, diamonds, rockets, water-jets).
girasol [ʒirasɔl] *s.f.* girasol(e), fire-opal.
giration [ʒirɑsjɔ̃] *s.f.* gyration; (naut.) *cercle de ~*, turning-circle.
giratoire [ʒiratwar] *adj.* gyratory; *sens ~*, (traffic) roundabout.
giraumon(t) [ʒiromɔ̃] *s.m.* (bot.) pumpkin.
giravion [ʒiravjɔ̃] *s.m.* (aeron.) gyroplane.
girie [ʒiri] *s.f.* (fam.) fuss (about nothing).
girofle [ʒirɔfl] *s.m.* (bot.) clove; *clou de ~*, (a) clove.
giroflée [ʒirɔfle] *s.f.* (bot.) stock, wall-flower; (fam.) *~ à cinq feuilles*, slap in the face.
giroflier [ʒirɔflije] *s.m.* (bot.) clove-tree.
girolle [ʒirɔl] *s.f.* (bot.) chanterelle (mushroom), edible agaric.
giron [ʒirɔ̃] *s.m.* **1.** lap; (fig.) bosom; **2.** (herald.) gyron, giron; **3.** (techn.) tread (of step).
girond, -e [ʒirɔ̃] *adj.* (pop.) shapely, comely; plump.
Gironde [ʒirɔ̃d] *s.f.* **1.** (geog.) Gironde (estuary); **2.** (Fr. hist.) Girondist party, Gironde.
girondin, -e [ʒirɔ̃dɛ̃] *adj.* (geog.) of the Gironde; (hist.) Girondist; *~ s.m.* (hist.) Girondist, Girondin.
gironné [ʒirɔne] *adj.* (herald.) gyronny; (of steps) winding.
girouette [ʒirwɛt] *s.f.* vane, weather-cock; (fig.) time-server, turncoat.
gisant, -e [ʒisɑ̃] *adj.* lying, recumbent; *~ s.m.* recumbent effigy.
gisement [ʒismɑ̃] *s.m.* (geol., min.) deposit, bed, stratum, layer, ore body; (naut.) bearing, lie (of coast, etc.).
gît [ʒi] see GÉSIR.
gitan, -e [ʒitɑ̃] *s.m.f., adj.* gipsy; *~***e** *s.f.* gitane (proprietary name of Fr. cigarette).
gîte [ʒit] *s.m.* **1.** home, lodging, shelter, quarters, refuge; form (of a hare); **2.** (geol.) layer, bed, deposit, stratum; **3.** (butch.) *~ à la noix*, silverside (of beef); **4.** *~ s.f.* (naut.) heeling, heel, list; site of wreck.
gîter [ʒite] *v.i.* to lodge, to sleep, to take shelter; (of hare, etc.) to couch; (naut.) to list, to heel; *~ v.t.* (obs.) to lodge, to provide with lodging or shelter; **se** *~ v.refl.* to lodge, to sleep, to shelter.
givrage [ʒivraʒ] *s.m.* (aeron.) icing.
givre [givr] *s.m.* rime, (white) frost, hoar-frost; white crystalline deposit.
givré, -e [ʒivre] *adj.* frosted, frost-covered.
givrer [ʒivre] *v.t.* to cover with frost; **se** *~ v.refl.* to ice up.
glabelle [glabɛl] *s.f.* (anat.) glabella.
glabre [glɑbr] *adj.* glabrous, smooth-skinned; clean-shaven.
glaçage [glasaʒ] *s.m.* glazing (of materials, paper, etc.).
glaçant, -e [glasɑ̃] *adj.* (lit. & fig.) freezing, chilly, icy.
glace [glas] *s.f.* **1.** ice; ice(-cream), iced drink; (pl.) ice (e.g. in Arctic); (fig.) chilliness, iciness (of social atmosphere, etc.); *mer de ~*, glacier; *navire pris dans les ~s*, ship held fast in the ice; *~s flottantes*, ice-floes, drift-ice; *~ de fond*, ground ice; *~ à la vanille*, vanilla ice; (fig.) *rompre la ~*, to break the ice; **2.** glass, window-glass, glass panel (on door, partition); (in car, etc.) window; **3.** mirror; **4.** (cook.) glaze, glazing; **5.** flaw (in gem).
glacé, -e [glase] *adj.* frozen, iced; icy, glacial, very cold, chilled; (fig.) chilly, icy; (cook.) glazed, glacé; (of paper, materials, etc.) glazed, glossy; *fruits ~s*, candied or crystallized fruit; *gants en chevreau ~*, glacé kid gloves.
glacer [glase] *v.t.* **1.** to freeze; to ice, to chill, to make very cold; to congeal; (fig.) to chill, to cool, to damp, to freeze, to petrify; *cela me glace le sang*, it makes my blood run cold; *cela me glace le cœur*, it sends a chill down my spine; *quand l'âge nous glace*, when age cools our passions; *se ~*, to freeze, to ice over; **2.** to glaze, to gloss (paper, materials, etc.); to scumble (a painting); (cook.) to glaze, to frost, to ice.
glacerie [glasir] *s.f.* mirror- and glass-making.
glaceur [glasœr] *s.m.* glazer.
glaceu-x, -se [glasø] *adj.* (of gem) flawed.
glaciaire [glasjɛr] *adj.* (geol.) glacial; *période ~*, ice-age, glacial epoch.
glacial, -e (pl. **-s**, or **aux**) [glasjal] *adj.* (lit. & fig.) glacial, icy, frozen, freezing; *vent ~*, biting wind; *accueil ~*, chilly reception.
glaciation [glasjɑsjɔ̃] *s.f.* turning to ice; (geol.) glaciation.
glacier [glasje] *s.m.* **1.** glacier; **2.** (obs.) maker of mirrors or plate-glass; **3.** ice-cream maker or vendor.
glacière [glasjɛr] *s.f.* **1.** (lit. & fig.) ice-house; **2.** ice-box, refrigerator.
glacio-logie [glasjɔlɔʒi] *s.f.* glaciology; **~logue** [glasjɔlɔg] *s.m.f.* glaciologist.
glacis[1] [glasi] *s.m.* (fort.) glacis; (arch.) weathering.
glacis[2] [glasi] *s.m.* (art) scumble, glaze.
glaçon [glasɔ̃] *s.m.* block of ice; ice-cube; (fig., fam.) cold fish, frigid person.
glaçure [glasyr] *s.f.* glazing.
gladiateur [gladjatœr] *s.m.* gladiator.
glaïeul [glajœl] *s.m.* (bot.) gladiolus.
glaire [glɛr] *s.f.* white of egg, glair; (med.) glair, mucus.
glairer [glere] *v.t.* (bookb.) to glair.
glaireu-x, -se [glɛrø] *adj.* glairy, glaireous.
glaise [glɛz] *s.f.* clay, marl, potter's earth, loam; *terre ~*, potter's clay.
glaiser [gleze] *v.t.* to marl; to line with clay, to puddle.
glaiseu-x, -se [glɛzø] *adj.* clayey, loamy; **~x** *s.m.* (pej.) peasant, clodhopper.
glaisière [glɛzjɛr] *s.f.* marl-pit, clay-pit.
glaive [glɛv] *s.m.* **1.** (ant.) two-edged sword; **2.** (Lit.) sword, blade; (fig.) sword, act of war; power; *le ~ de la loi*, the strong arm of the law.
glanage [glanaʒ] *s.m.* gleaning.
gland [glɑ̃] *s.m.* **1.** acorn; **2.** tassel; **3.** (anat.) glans; ⚠ not 'gland'.
glande [glɑ̃d] *s.f.* (anat.) gland.
glandée [glɑ̃de] *s.f.* crop of acorns.
glandulaire [glɑ̃dylɛr], **glanduleu-x, -se** [glɑ̃dylø] *adj.* glandular.
glandule [glɑ̃dyl] *s.f.* (anat.) glandule.
glane [glan] *s.f.* gleaning; small sheaf, handful of ears of corn; *~ d'oignons*, rope of onions.
glaner [glane] *v.t.* (lit. & fig.) to glean.
glaneu-r, -se [glanœr] *s.m.f.* gleaner.
glanure [glanyr] *s.f.* gleanings; short memorandum on scientific point.
glapir [glapir] *v.i.* (of animals) to yelp, to yap, to squeak; (of persons) to yelp, to screech, to scream, to shrill.
glapissant, -e [glapisɑ̃] *adj.* yelping, barking.
glapissement [glapismɑ̃] *s.m.* yelping, barking, squeaking.
glas [glɑ] *s.m.* knell, passing bell, tolling; *sonner le ~*, to toll the knell; (fig.) to sound the knell, to mark the end, (of sth.).

glass [glas] *s.m.* (slang) glass (of sth. to drink).
glaucome [glokom] *s.m.* (pathol.) glaucoma.
glauque [glok] *adj.* glaucous, pale sea-green.
glèbe [glɛb] *s.f.* glebe land, ground, soil; clod, sod; (feud.) *attaché à la* ~, attached to the soil.
gléchome, glécome [glekom] *s.m.* (bot.) ground ivy.
glène [glɛn] *s.f.* (anat.) glene, socket; (naut.) coil.
gléner [glene] *v.t.* (naut.) to coil.
glénoïde [glenɔid] *adj., s.f.,* **glénoïdal, -e, (aux)** [glenɔidal] *adj.* glenoid.
glissade [glisad] *s.f.* slide, sliding; slip; (danc.) glissade, glide; (mountaineering) *descendre en* ~, to glissade; (aeron.) ~ *sur l'aile*, side-slip; ~ *sur la queue*, tail-dive; *faire une* ~, to slide, to slip.
glissant, -e [glisɑ̃] *adj.* slippery; (fig.) ticklish, hazardous; (fig.) *terrain* ~, slippery ground.
glissage [glisaʒ] *s.m.* sliding down (of cut timber in the mountains).
glissé [glise] *s.m.* (danc.) slide, glissade, glide.
glissement [glismɑ̃] *s.m.* slipping, sliding, gliding motion or noise; (mech.) sliding surface; (fig.) slide, swing, gradual evolution; (geol.) slip; ~ *de terrain*, landslip.
glisser [glise] *v.i.* to slide, to slip; to glide; to skid; (fig.) to slip, to move imperceptibly; to pass over things lightly; to have little effect; (fig.) ~ *sur une mauvaise pente*, to be on a slippery slope; (fam.) *se laisser* ~, to die; *n'insistons pas, glissons*, don't let's make a fuss about it, let it pass; *un être sur qui tout glisse*, a person who is little affected by anything; ~ *sur*, to glide over, to touch lightly, (fig.) to pass over (sth.) quickly, to skim over, to pay little attention to; ~ *v.t.* to slip (in), to insert; *tâche de lui* ~ *cela*, try and slip him a word about this; ~ *un mot à l'oreille de qn.*, to drop a word to s.o., to whisper to s.o.; **se** ~ *v.refl.* (lit. & fig.) to slip, to creep; *il s'est glissé quelques fautes dans ce livre*, some errors have crept into this book.
glissière [glisjɛr] *s.f.* groove, slide; slide-bar, guide-rod; (rowing) *siège à* ~, sliding seat.
glissoir [gliswar] *s.m.* guide-block (for chain); slide-way, shoot, (for sliding timber down mountain).
glissoire [gliswar] *s.f.* slide (stretch of ice made into a slide).
global, -e, (aux) [glɔbal] *adj.* total, entire, whole, aggregate; *somme* ~*e*, lump sum, total; ~**ement** [glɔbalmɑ̃] *adv.* in aggregate, in total, taken as a whole.
globe [glɔb] *s.m.* globe, sphere, orb; glass cover, glass case; *le* ~ (*terrestre*), the world, the earth; *un* ~ *terrestre*, a globe (representing the earth); ~ *électrique*, electric-light globe; *pendule sous* ~, clock under a glass case; (fig.) *mettre sous* ~, to keep in a glass case, to shield from all harm.
globe-trotter [glɔbtrɔtœr] *s.m.* globe-trotter, world traveller.
globulaire [glɔbylɛr] *adj.* globular.
globule [glɔbyl] *s.m.* globule.
globuleu-x, -se [glɔbylø] *adj.* globular.
gloire [glwar] *s.f.* glory, fame, renown; honour, reputation; pride, boast; famous person, celebrity; cloud of glory; *à la* ~ *de*, to the glory of, in honour of; *s'attribuer la* ~ *de*, to take the credit for; *se faire* ~ *de*, to glory in, to boast of, to take pride in; *rendre* ~ *à*, to give glory to (God); to honour, to glorify; (fig.) *rendre* ~ *à la vérité*, to honour or respect the truth.
glomérule [glɔmeryl] *s.m.* (bot.) glomerule.
gloria [glɔrja] *s.m.* **1.** (liturg.) Gloria; **2.** (obs., fam.) coffee with brandy.
gloriette [glɔrjɛt] *s.f.* **1.** summer-house, pavilion; **2.** elaborate aviary.
glorieu-x, -se [glɔrjø] *adj.* **1.** glorious, famous, renowned, celebrated, illustrious, covered with glory; **2.** proud, boastful, overweening, presumptuous, vain; *faire le* ~*x*, to boast, to brag, to swagger; **3.** (theol.) elect; *les* ~*x*, the elect; ~**sement** [glɔrjøzmɑ̃] *adv.* gloriously, splendidly.
glorification [glɔrifikasjɔ̃] *s.f.* glorification.
glorifier [glɔrifje] *v.t.* to glorify, to honour, to praise, to magnify, to exalt; to enhance; **se** ~ *v.refl.* to boast (*de*, of), to glory (*de*, in).
gloriole [glɔrjɔl] *s.f.* vainglory, vanity, petty pride, conceit.
glose [gloz] *s.f.* **1.** comment, gloss, explanatory note; **2.** hostile comment, criticism.
gloser [gloze] *v.t.* **1.** to comment on, to expound, to explain, to make a gloss on; **2.** (obs.) to find fault with, to criticize; ~ *v.i.* to get involved in endless discussion; ~ *sur tout*, to comment on everything in the greatest detail.
glossaire [glɔsɛr] *s.m.* glossary, dictionary.
glossateur [glɔsatœr] *s.m.* commentator.
glossine [glɔsin] *s.f.* (ent.) Glossina, tsetse-fly.
glottal, -e, (aux) [glɔtal] *adj.* glottal.
glotte [glɔt] *s.f.* (anat.) glottis.
glouglou [gluglu] *s.m.* gurgling, gurgle; gobbling (of turkeys).
glouglouter [gluglute] *v.i.* (of turkeys) to gobble.
gloussement [glusmɑ̃] *s.m.* clucking, cluck; chuckle.
glousser [gluse] *v.i.* to cluck; to chuckle.
glouteron [glutrɔ̃] *s.m.* (bot.) burdock, burr.
glouton, -ne [glutɔ̃] *adj.* gluttonous, greedy; *s.m.f.* glutton; (zool.) wolverine; ~**nement** [glutɔnmɑ̃] *adv.* gluttonously, ravenously, greedily.
gloutonnerie [glutɔnri] *s.f.* gluttony, greediness; (fig.) appetite, avidity.
glu [gly] *s.f.* birdlime, glue; (fig.) *il est collant comme la* ~, he sticks to you like a leech.
gluant, -e [glyɑ̃] *adj.* sticky, slimy, gluey, adhesive.
gluau (pl. **-x**) [glyo] *s.m.* lime-twig (for catching birds).
glucinium [glysinjɔm] *s.m.* (chem.) beryllium, glucin(i)um.
glucomètre [glykɔmɛtr] *s.m.* (brewing) saccharometer.
glucose [glykoz] *s.m.* glucose.
glucoside [glykozid] *s.m.* (chem.) glucoside.
glui [glɥi] *s.m.* rye-straw, thatching-straw.
glume [glym] *s.m.* (bot.) glume; husk, chaff.
glumelle [glymɛl] *s.f.* (bot.) glumella, palea.
gluten [glytɛn] *s.m.* gluten.
glutineu-x, -se [glytinø] *adj.* glutinous, viscous.
glyc-émie [glisemi] *s.f.* (physiol.) glycaemia; ~**éride** [gliserid] *s.f.* (chem.) glyceride; ~**érine** [gliserin] *s.f.* (chem.) glycerine; ~**ériner** [gliserine] *v.t.* to treat with glycerine; ~**érol** [gliserɔl] *s.m.* (chem.) = GLYCÉRINE; ~**ine** [glisin] *s.f.* (bot.) wistaria, wisteria.
glyco-colle [glikɔkɔl] *s.m.* (chem.) glycocol; ~**gène** [glikɔʒɛn] *s.m.* (chem.) glycogen; ~**génèse** [glikɔʒenɛz] *s.f.* (physiol.) glycogenesis.
glycol [glikɔl] *s.m.* (chem.) glycol.
glycosurie [glikɔsyri] *s.f.* (pathol.) glycosuria.
glyphe [glif] *s.m.* glyph.
glyptique [gliptik] *s.f.* glyptics.
glypto-don [gliptɔdɔ̃] *s.m.* (palaeont.) glyptodon; ~**graphie** [gliptɔgrafi] *s.f.* glyptography; ~**thèque** [gliptɔtɛk] *s.f.* collection of carved gems, cameos, etc.
gnaf, gniaf [ɲaf] *s.m.* (pop.) cobbler.
gnian-gnian, gnangnan [ɲɑ̃ɲɑ̃] *adj.* (fam.) flabby, soft, always whining; *s.m.f.* wet, namby--pamby.
gneiss [gnɛs] *s.m.* (geol.) gneiss.
gneisseu-x, -se [gnɛsø] *adj.* (geol.) gneissic.

gneissique [gnɛsik] *adj.* = GNEISSEUX.
gnète [gnɛt] *s.f.* (bot.) Gnetum.
gnognot(**t**)**e** [ɲɔɲɔt] *s.f.* (fam.) rubbish, worthless stuff.
gnome [gnom] *s.m.* gnome.
gnomique [gnɔmik] *adj.* gnomic, sententious.
gnomon [gnɔmɔ̃] *s.m.* gnomon, pin or triangular plate of sundial; **~ique** [gnɔmɔnik] *adj.* gnomonic; *s.f.* gnomonics, art of making sundials.
gnose [gnoz] *s.f.* **1.** gnosis; **2.** gnosticism.
Gnosse [gnɔs] *s.m.* (anc. geog.) Knossos.
gnosticisme [gnɔstisism] *s.m.* gnosticism.
gnon [ɲɔ̃] *s.m.* (pop.) blow, clout.
gnou [gnu] *s.m.* (zool.) gnu.
(**tout de**) **go** [tudəgo] *adv.loc.* at once, straight away; without ceremony, without more ado.
goal [gol] *s.m.* (football, etc.); **1.** (obs.) goal; **2.** goalkeeper.
gobelet [gɔblɛ] *s.m.* goblet, tumbler, mug, cup; thimble (as used in sleight-of-hand); dice-box, dice-shaker.
gobeleterie [gɔblɛtri] *s.f.* making of goblets, etc.
gobeletier [gɔblɛtje] *s.m.* maker of goblets, etc.
gobelin [gɔblɛ̃] *s.m.* Gobelin (tapestry).
gobe-mouche(**s**) [gɔbmuʃ] *s.m.* **1.** (ornith.) flycatcher; **2.** (fig.) simpleton.
gober [gɔbe] *v.t.* to gobble up, to swallow; (fam.) to eat; (pop.) to catch, to arrest, to nab; (fig., fam.) to swallow, to lap up (sth. incredible); to esteem, to appreciate; **se** ~ *v.refl.* to have a high opinion of oneself.
(**se**) **goberger** [gɔbɛrʒe] *v.refl.* to take one's ease, to indulge oneself, to do oneself well.
gobeu-r, -se [gɔbœr] *s.m.f.* (fig., fam.) simpleton, one who will swallow anything.
gobichonner [gɔbiʃɔne] *v.i.* (fam.) to feast, to have a good time.
gobie [gɔbi] *s.m.* (ichth.) goby.
godage [gɔdaʒ] *s.m.* creasing, bagginess, (of clothes).
godasse [gɔdas] *s.f.* (pop.) shoe, boot.
godelureau (pl. **-x**) [gɔdlyro] *s.m.* dandy.
goder [gɔde], **godailler** [gɔdaje] *v.i.* (of clothes) to hang badly, to be baggy.
godet [gɔdɛ] *s.m.* mug, cup (without handle), cup-shaped receptacle; (pop.) glass, tumbler; bucket (of dredger, etc.); (dressm.) gore, flare, godet.
godiche [gɔdiʃ] *adj.*, *s.m.f.* awkward, silly, (person).
godille [gɔdij] *s.f.* (naut.) scull; stern-oar; (ski-ing) wedelling; *avancer à la* ~, to scull.
godiller [gɔdije] *v.i.* to scull; (ski-ing) to wedel.
godillot [gɔdijo] *s.m.* kind of army boot; (pop.) large, heavy shoe.
godiveau (pl. **-x**) [gɔdivo] *s.m.* (cook.) forcemeat balls.
godron [gɔdrɔ̃] *s.m.* gadroon; goffered pleat, goffer; **~ner** [gɔdrɔne] *v.t.* to gadroon, to goffer.
goéland [gɔelɑ̃] *s.m.* (ornith.) sea-gull.
goélette [gɔelɛt] *s.f.* (naut.) schooner; (*voile*) ~, trysail.
goémon [gɔemɔ̃] *s.m.* (bot.) wrack, seaweed; seaweed used as fertilizer.
gogo [gɔgo] *s.m.* (fam.) credulous person.
(**à**) **gogo** [agɔgo] *adv.* (fam.) in plenty, enough and to spare; *avoir tout à* ~, to have bags of everything.
goguenard, -e [gɔgnar] *adj.* mocking, bantering, chaffing, ironical.
goguenardise [gɔgnardiz] *s.f.* mocking, banter, chaff.
goguenot [gɔgno] *s.m.* chamber-pot; (pl.) (also vulg. *gogues*) latrines.
goguette [gɔgɛt] *s.f.* (fam.) *en* ~, in festive mood, merry.
goinfre [gwɛ̃fr] *s.m.* glutton; *adj.* gluttonous, greedy.
goinfrer [gwɛ̃fre] *v.i.* or **se** ~ *v.refl.* to stuff, to guzzle.
goinfrerie [gwɛ̃frəri] *s.f.* gluttony, guzzling.
goitre [gwatr] *s.m.* (pathol.) goitre.
goitreu-x, -se [gwatrø] *adj.* goitred, goitrous.
golden [gɔldɛn] *s.f.invar.* Golden Delicious apple.
golf [gɔlf] *s.m.* golf; ~ *miniature*, miniature golf; *culotte de* ~, plus-fours.
golfe [gɔlf] *s.m.* gulf, bay.
golfeu-r, -se [gɔlfœr] *s.m.f.* golfer.
gommage [gɔmaʒ] *s.m.* gumming.
gomme [gɔm] *s.f.* **1.** gum; ~ *arabique*, or *d'Arabie*, or *du Sénégal*, gum arabic; ~ *gutte*, gamboge; ~ *à mâcher*, chewing-gum; (pop.) *un type à la* ~, a useless chap; (pop.) *mettre* (*toute*) *la* ~, to step on the gas (when driving); **2.** (pathol.) gumma; (hort.) gum, gummosis; **3.** (india)rubber, eraser.
gommer [gɔme] *v.t.* **1.** to gum; **2.** to mix with gum; **3.** to rub out, to erase.
gommeu-x, -se [gɔmø] *adj.* gummy, sticky; producing gum; **~x** *s.m.*, *adj.* fop(pish).
gommier [gɔmje] *s.m.* (bot.) gum-tree, gum acacia, eucalyptus.
gommose [gɔmoz] *s.f.* (hort.) gum, gummosis.
gonade [gɔnad] *s.f.* (biol.) gonad.
gonadotrope [gɔnadɔtrɔp] *adj.* (biol.) gonadotrop(h)ic.
gond [gɔ̃] *s.m.* hinge; (fig.) *jeter* or *mettre qn. hors des*, or *de ses*, *~s*, to exasperate or enrage s.o.; *sortir de ses ~s*, to become enraged, to fly off the handle.
gondolage [gɔ̃dɔlaʒ] *s.m.* warping.
gondolant, -e [gɔdɔlɑ̃] *adj.* (pop.) side-splitting.
gondole [gɔ̃dɔl] *s.f.* gondola.
gondolement [gɔ̃dɔlmɑ̃] *s.m.* = GONDOLAGE.
gondoler [gɔ̃dɔle] *v.i.* **1.** (naut.) to pitch; **2.** to warp, to buckle; (pop.) to laugh fit to burst.
gondoli-er, -ère [gɔ̃dɔlje] *s.m.f.* gondolier.
gonflable [gɔ̃flabl] *adj.* inflatable.
gonflé, -e [gɔ̃fle] *adj.* swollen, inflated; bursting, eaten up, consumed, (with pride, etc.); (fam.) *être ~ à bloc*, to be all keyed up, to be ready for anything; (pop.) *il est vraiment ~*, he's got plenty of guts, he's got a nerve.
gonflement [gɔ̃fləmɑ̃] *s.m.* swelling, inflation, distension; blowing up, pumping up (of tyres); (fig.) inflation.
gonfler [gɔ̃fle] *v.t.* to inflate, to blow or pump up, to distend, to swell; (fig.) to fill; to inflate, to magnify; ~ *v.i.* to swell, to expand; (of dough, etc.) to rise; **se** ~ *v.refl.* to swell, to swell up, to become swollen or inflated.
gong [gɔ̃(g)] *s.m.* gong.
gonio-mètre [gɔnjɔmɛtr] *s.m.* goniometer; **~métrie** [gɔnjɔmetri] *s.f.* goniometry; **~-métrique** [gɔnjɔmetrik] *adj.* goniometric(al).
gono-coque [gɔnɔkɔk] *s.m.* gonococcus; **~rrhée** [gɔnɔre] *s.f.* (pathol.) gonorrhoea.
gonze [gɔ̃z] *s.m.* (slang) man, chap.
gonzesse [gɔ̃zɛs] *s.f.* (vulg.) woman, tart.
gord [gɔr] *s.m.* fishing weir; kiddle.
gordien [gɔrdjɛ̃] *adj.m.* *nœud* ~, Gordian knot.
goret [gɔrɛ] *s.m.* **1.** young pig, pig; (fam.) (addressing child) dirty little pig; **2.** (naut.) hog, scrubbing-broom.
gorge [gɔrʒ] *s.f.* **1.** neck; throat; bosom, breast, breasts, bust; *mal de* ~, sore throat, throat infection; *prendre qn. à la* ~, to suffocate s.o., to have s.o. by the throat, to threaten violence to s.o.; ~ *serrée par l'angoisse*, voice choking with anguish; *crier à pleine* ~, to shout at the top of one's voice; *avaler à pleine* ~, to gulp down; *rire à* ~ *déployée*, to laugh heartily, to roar with laughter; *voix de* ~, deep or guttural voice; (fig.)

faire rentrer à qn. ses mots dans la ~, to make s.o. eat his words; *faire des ~s chaudes de qch.*, to gloat over sth.; *rendre* ~, to regurgitate; to disgorge; to make restitution (of ill-gotten gains, etc.); **2.** gorge, ravine, defile, narrow pass; (fort.) gorge; (techn.) groove, channel, notch; score (in pulley-block); ⚠ not 'gorge' in sense 'contents of stomach or crop'.
gorge-de-pigeon [gɔrʒdəpiʒɔ̃] *adj.invar.* dove--coloured.
gorgée [gɔrʒe] *s.f.* draught, gulp, mouthful; *boire à petites ~s*, to sip.
gorger [gɔrʒe] *v.t.* to gorge, to cram, to glut, to saturate, to fill to bursting; to soak, to saturate, to impregnate.
gorgerette [gɔrʒərɛt] *s.f.* lady's ruffle, gorget.
gorgerin [gɔrʒərɛ̃] *s.m.* **1.** (armour) gorget, neckpiece; **2.** (arch.) gorgerin, gorge, quirk.
gorgone [gɔrgɔn] *s.f.* (myth.) gorgon; (arch.) gorgon's head motif, gorgoneion; (zool.) = GORGONIE.
gorgonie [gɔrgɔni] *s.f.* (zool.) gorgonia, sea-fan.
gorille [gɔrij] *s.m.* (zool.) gorilla.
gosier [gozje] *s.m.* throat, gullet; windpipe; *s'humecter le* ~, to wet one's whistle; *s'éclaircir le* ~, to clear one's throat; *coup de* ~, shout, bellow; *chanter à plein* ~, to sing at the top of one's voice.
gosse [gɔs] *s.m.f.* child, boy, girl; ~ *adj.* young; *encore tout* ~, still a child.
gothique [gɔtik] *adj.* Gothic; ~ *s.m.* (arch., lang.) Gothic; ~ *s.f.* (print.) Gothic type.
goton [gɔtɔ̃] *s.f.* (obs.) country wench; prostitute.
gouache [gwaʃ] *s.f.* (paint.) gouache.
gouaille [gwɑj] *s.f.* mocking, making fun (of things).
gouailler [gwɑje] *v.t.* (obs.) to jeer rudely at (s.o.); ~ *v.i.* to speak mockingly.
gouaillerie [gwɑjri] *s.f.* spirit of mockery.
gouailleu-r, -se [gwɑjœr] *adj.* mocking.
goualante [gwalɑ̃t] *s.f.* (fam.) popular ballad.
goualeuse [gwaløz] *s.f.* (fam.) street-singer.
gouape [gwap] *s.f.* (pop.) hooligan.
goudron [gudrɔ̃] *s.m.* tar; **~nage** [gudrɔnaʒ] *s.m.* tarring; **~ner** [gudrɔne] *v.t.* to tar; *toile goudronnée*, tarpaulin; *papier goudronné*, tar-lined paper; **~neur** [gudrɔnœr] *s.m.* tar-sprayer (workman).
goudronneu-x, -se [gudrɔnø] *adj.* tarry; **~se** *s.f.* tar-sprayer (machine).
gouffre [gufr] *s.m.* gulf, abyss, chasm, pit; whirlpool, vortex; (geol.) swallow-hole, pot--hole; (fig.) abyss, precipice, bottomless pit; *être au bord du* ~, to be on the edge of the precipice; *ce procès est un* ~, this lawsuit is swallowing up endless sums of money.
gouge [guʒ] *s.f.* (techn.) gouge.
gouine [gwin] *s.f.* **1.** (obs.) prostitute; **2.** female homosexual.
goujat [guʒa] *s.m.* **1.** (obs.) camp-follower; **2.** (obs.) yokel, country bumpkin; (mod.) lout, boor.
goujaterie [guʒatri] *s.f.* boorishness.
goujon[1] [guʒɔ̃] *s.m.* **1.** (techn.) gudgeon(-pin), pin, pintle, stud, stud-bolt, dowel; **2.** sculptor's hollow chisel.
goujon[2] [guʒɔ̃] *s.m.* (ichth.) gudgeon.
goule [gul] *s.f.* ghoul.
goulée [gule] *s.f.* gulp, big mouthful.
goulet [gulɛ] *s.m.* narrow pass (in mountains); (naut.) narrows, narrow channel.
goulot [gulo] *s.m.* neck (of bottle, etc.).
goulu, -e [guly] *adj.* greedy, voracious, gluttonous; ~ *s.m.f.* glutton; **~e** *s.f.* (pop.) big--mouthed woman.
goulûment [gulymɑ̃] *adv.* greedily, voraciously, gluttonously.
goum [gum] *s.m.* (mil.) native contingent in Algeria; **~ier** [gumje] *s.m.* cavalryman of a *goum*.
goupil [gupi] *s.m.* (obs.) fox.
goupille [gupij] *s.f.* (techn.) pin, split-pin, cotter(-pin).
goupiller [gupije] *v.t.* (techn.) to pin, to key; (fam.) to fix, to arrange, to wangle.
goupillon [gupijɔ̃] *s.m.* **1.** (eccles.) aspergillum, holy-water sprinkler; (fig.) the Church; **2.** bottle-brush, flue-brush, etc.
gour [gur] *s.m.pl.* eroded hillsides (in Sahara).
goura [gura] *s.m.* (ornith.) goura.
gourance [gurɑ̃s] *s.f.* (pop.) being mistaken; mistake.
gourbi [gurbi] *s.m.* Arab hut; trench-shelter; hovel.
gourd, -e [gur] *adj.* numbed, numb, swollen.
gourde [gurd] *s.f.* **1.** (bot.) gourd, calabash; **2.** wicker bottle, travelling-flask; (fig.) silly or clumsy person.
gourdin [gurdɛ̃] *s.m.* cudgel, thick stick.
(**se**) **gourer** [gure] *v.refl.* (pop.) to make a mistake, to be taken in.
gourgandine [gurgɑ̃din] *s.f.* loose woman.
gourmand, -e [gurmɑ̃] *adj.* **1.** (obs.) greedy, eating excessively; (mod.) fond of good cooking, particular about one's food; ~ *de*, fond of, greedy for; **2.** (hort.) *branche ~e*, sucker; ~ *s.m.* gourmand, epicure, gastronome.
gourmander [gurmɑ̃de] *v.t.* **1.** (obs.) to treat roughly; (fig.) to master, to restrain; **2.** to rebuke harshly, to give a severe reprimand to.
gourmandise [gurmɑ̃diz] *s.f.* **1.** greediness, over-fondness for eating; **2.** (pl.) delicacies, dishes for the epicure.
gourme [gurm] *s.f.* (med.) impetigo; (vet.) strangles; (fig.) *jeter sa* ~, to sow one's wild oats.
gourmé, -e [gurme] *adj.* stiff, formal, starched, (of manner) stuck-up.
gourmet [gurmɛ] *s.m.* gourmet, epicure, gastronome, connoisseur of fine food.
gourmette [gurmɛt] *s.f.* **1.** (harness) curb chain, curb; **2.** watch-chain, chain bracelet.
gournable [gurnabl] *s.f.* (nav. arch.) tree-nail.
gourou [guru] *s.m.* guru.
gousse [gus] *s.f.* pod, shell, husk; clove (of garlic).
gousset [gusɛ] *s.m.* **1.** (obs.) armpit; purse (in form of fob-pocket); (fig.) *il a le ~ bien rempli*, his pocket is well-lined; **2.** fob (pocket); (dressm.) gusset; **3.** (techn.) (shoulder-)bracket, stay, gusset.
goût [gu] *s.m.* **1.** taste, flavour, savour, bouquet; (sense of) taste; ~ *de moisi*, musty taste; ~ *relevé*, well-flavoured; *relever le ~ de qch.*, to give sth. a flavour or relish, to season sth.; *manquer de* ~, to be tasteless; **2.** taste, liking, inclination, appetite; *avoir du ~ pour qch.*, to have a taste or liking for sth., to be fond of sth.; *n'avoir ~ à rien*, to have no appetite for anything; (fig.) *faire passer à qn. le ~ du pain*, to do away with s.o.; to deprive s.o. of the will to live; **3.** (good) taste, discernment; *le (bon)* ~, good taste; *habillée avec* ~, tastefully dressed; *de mauvais* ~, in bad taste; **4.** taste, preference, fashion, style; *le ~ du jour*, contemporary taste, current or prevailing fashion; *à chacun son* ~, tastes differ, there's no accounting for tastes; *dans le ~ moderne*, in contemporary style, in modern taste.
goûter [gute] *v.t.* to taste, to try, to savour, to appreciate, to relish, to enjoy; ~ *à*, to taste, to have a taste of, to take a bite or sip of; *il a à peine goûté à ce plat*, he scarcely took a mouthful of this dish; ~ *de*, to taste (for the first time); (fig.) to experience; ~ *v.i.* to have (afternoon) tea, to have an afternoon snack.
goûter [gute] *s.m.* (afternoon) tea, afternoon snack; *l'heure du* ~, tea-time.
goutte [gut] *s.f.* **1.** drop (of liquid); drop, small mouthful or nip, (of spirits); (pharm.) (pl.)

drops; (jewellery) drop, pendant; (arch.) gutta; *tomber ~ à ~*, to drip; *suer à grosses ~s*, to sweat profusely; (fam.) *avoir la ~ au nez*, to have a runny nose; (fig.) *ne pas avoir une ~ de sang dans les veines*, to be utterly lacking in vigour or in character; *se ressembler comme deux ~s d'eau*, to be as like as two peas; *boire la ~*, to have a nip; (fig.) *je n'y vois ~*, I can't see anything, I can make nothing of it; **2.** (pathol.) gout.

gouttelette [gutlɛt] *s.f.* small drop, droplet.

goutter [gute] *v.i.* to drip; to leak.

goutteu-x, -se [gutø] *adj.*, *s.m.f.* (pathol.) gouty (toe, joint, etc.); (person) suffering from gout.

gouttière [gutjɛr] *s.f.* (roof-)gutter, guttering; spout, rain-pipe; (surg.) splint; (anat.) groove (in bone); ⚠ not 'gutter' in street.

gouvernable [guvɛrnabl] *adj.* governable; manageable.

gouvernail [guvɛrnaj] *s.m.* rudder; (lit. & fig.) helm; (naut.) *la roue du ~*, the wheel; (aeron. & submarine) *~ d'altitude, de profondeur*, horizontal rudder, elevator, elevating plane; (fig.) *tenir le ~*, to be at the helm, to be in control.

gouvernant, -e [guvɛrnɑ̃] *adj.* governing, ruling, in power; **~s** *s.m.pl. les ~s*, the rulers, the government.

gouvernante [guvɛrnɑ̃t] *s.f.* **1.** governess; **2.** housekeeper.

gouverne [guvɛrn] *s.f.* guidance, direction, line of conduct; (naut.) steering; (aeron.) controls; *je vous confie cela pour votre ~*, I tell you this for information, for your guidance.

gouvernement [guvɛrnəmɑ̃] *s.m.* governing; government.

gouvernemental, -e, (aux) [guvɛrnəmɑ̃tal] *adj.* governmental, of the government.

gouverner [guvɛrne] *v.t.* to steer, to direct, to control, to govern, to manage; *~ v.i.* (naut.) to steer, to answer the helm, to swing, to be driven (by current, tide, etc.); **se ~** *v.refl.* to govern oneself, to be self-governing.

gouverneur [guvɛrnœr] *s.m.* **1.** governor; **2.** tutor, preceptor.

goyave [gɔjav] *s.f.* (bot.) guava.

goyavier [gɔjavje] *s.m.* (bot.) guava-tree.

G.Q.G. [ʒekyʒe] abbrev. *Grand Quartier-général*, Supreme H.Q.

grabat [graba] *s.m.* wretched bed; (obs.) *être sur le ~*, to be on one's sick-bed.

grabuge [grabyʒ] *s.m.* (fam.) squabble, row, brawl, fighting.

grâce [grɑs] *s.f.* **1.** grace, act of grace, favour, graciousness; *trouver ~ devant qn.*, to find favour with s.o., to receive favourable treatment from s.o.; *rentrer en ~*, to reingratiate oneself, to get back into favour; *de ~*, (obs.) graciously; (mod.) I beg you, don't mention it; **2.** grace, pardon, respite, remission; *crier ~*, to cry mercy, to beg for mercy; *faire ~*, to pardon, to excuse, to remit, to let off; *faire ~ à qn. d'une dette*, to forgive s.o. a debt, to let s.o. off a debt; *coup de ~*, finishing blow, coup de grâce, quietus; **3.** thanks, thanksgiving; (pl.) grace (after meal); *action de ~s*, thanksgiving; *~ à*, thanks to, owing to; **4.** grace, gracefulness, charm; (myth.) *les Grâces*, the Graces; *de bonne ~*, with good grace, willingly; *de mauvaise ~*, ungraciously, unwillingly; *il aurait mauvaise ~ à se plaindre*, he would be churlish to complain, he is in no position to complain.

gracier [grasje] *v.t.* (law) to pardon, to reprieve.

gracieusement [grasjøzmɑ̃] *adv.* **1.** graciously, kindly, gratuitously, by grace; **2.** gracefully, with grace.

gracieuseté [grasjøzte] *s.f.* **1.** graciousness, kindness, affability; kind or gracious act; **2.** (obs.) gratuity.

gracieu-x, -se [grasjø] *adj.* **1.** gracious, gratuitous, courteous; *à titre ~x*, as a favour, gratis, free of charge, (of copy, ticket, etc.) complimentary; **2.** graceful, pleasing.

gracile [grasil] *adj.* slender, delicate, slim.

gracilité [grasilite] *s.f.* slenderness, delicacy, slimness.

Gracques [grak] *s.m.pl.* (Rom. hist.) *les ~*, the Gracchi.

gradation [gradɑsjɔ̃] *s.f.* gradation, stage, gradual process; *par ~*, gradually; *par une ~ insensible*, imperceptibly.

grade [grad] *s.m.* rank, grade, position; (university) degree; (geom.) grade; *avancer* or *monter en ~*, to be promoted; (fam.) *(en) prendre qch. pour son ~*, to be severely reprimanded; *en avoir pour son ~*, to get full measure.

gradé [grade] *s.m.* (mil.) non-commissioned officer.

gradin [gradɛ̃] *s.m.* step, ledge, shelf, bench, tier; (mining) stope.

graduation [gradɥɑsjɔ̃] *s.f.* graduating, graduation; ⚠ not 'graduation' in academic sense.

gradué, -e [gradɥe] *adj.* graduated; progressive, gradual.

graduel, -le [gradɥɛl] *adj.* gradual, progressive; *~ s.m.* (liturg.) gradual; **~lement** [gradɥɛlmɑ̃] *adv.* gradually, by degrees.

graduer [gradɥe] *v.t.* to graduate, to grade, to calibrate; ⚠ not 'to graduate' in academic sense.

graillement [grɑjmɑ̃] *s.m.* huskiness, hoarseness.

grailler [grɑje] *v.i.* **1.** to croak; **2.** (hunt.) to sound the horn to recall the hounds.

graillon[1] [grɑjɔ̃] *s.m.* fried fat; smell of burnt fat; greasy cooking.

graillon[2] [grɑjɔ̃] *s.m.* (pop.) phlegm, gob.

graillonner[1] [grɑjɔne] *v.i.* to smell of burnt fat.

graillonner[2] [grɑjɔne] *v.i.* (fam.) to hawk up phlegm, to hawk; to croak.

grain [grɛ̃] *s.m.* **1.** grain, seed, fruit, berry; bead; (pharm.) small pill, pellet; (fig.) essence, substance; *~ de blé*, grain of corn; *alcool de ~s*, grain spirit; *semer le ~*, to sow the seed; *~ de raisin, de groseille*, grape, currant; *~ de poivre*, peppercorn; *~ de café*, coffee-bean; *~ d'orge*, barleycorn; (med.) stye; (techn.) cleat, wedge; diamond-point chisel; *~ de beauté*, beauty-spot; *~ de chapelet*, bead of a rosary; (fig.) *le ~ d'une chose*, the substance, the essence, of a thing; *réduire en ~s*, to granulate; (fam.) *mettre* or *mêler son ~ de sel*, to interfere, to poke one's nose in, to shove one's oar in; **2.** grain, speck, particle, atom; grain (weight = 0·065 g); (fig.) touch, hint; *pas un ~ de bon sens*, not a grain, not an atom, of sense; *un ~ de malice*, a hint of malice; *avoir un (petit) ~*, to be a bit touched; **3.** grain, texture; *à gros ~s*, coarse-grained; *à petits ~s*, fine-grained; *à ~s serrés*, close-textured; **4.** squall, shower, sudden storm; *veiller au ~*, to watch out for squalls, (fig.) to keep a weather-eye out.

graine [grɛn] *s.f.* seed; egg, graine, (of silkworm); *~s d'épinards*, bullion (of epaulets); *~ de paradis*, cardamom; *monter en ~*, to run to seed; (fig.) to be getting on (in age), to be turning into an old maid; *en tirer la ~*, to learn a lesson, to draw a conclusion, (from sth.); *mauvaise ~*, a bad lot; *c'est ~ de voyou*, he's a real hooligan.

grainer [grene] *v.t.* = GRENER *v.t.*

graineterie [grɛntri] *s.f.* seed-trade; seed-merchant's shop.

graineti-er, -ère [grɛntje] *s.m.f.* seed-merchant; corn-chandler.

graini-er, -ère [grenje] *s.m.f.* seedsman, seedswoman; **~er** *s.m.* seed-store.

graissage [grɛsaʒ] *s.m.* greasing, oiling, lubrication; *huile de ~*, lubricating oil.

graisse [grɛs] *s.f.* **1.** fat, grease; ~ *de laine*, lanolin; ~ *de porc*, lard; ~*s végétales*, vegetable fats; *prendre de la* ~, to put on fat; **2.** grease, (lubricating) oil; **3.** ropiness (of wine).

graisser [grese] *v.t.* to grease, to oil, to lubricate; to dirty, to smear; (fig., fam.) ~ *la patte à qn.*, to grease someone's palm; ~ *v.i.* (of wine) to become ropy.

graisseur [grɛsœr] *s.m.* lubricator; greaser, oiler; ~ *adj.m.* lubricating.

graisseu-x, -se [grɛsø] *adj.* greasy, fatty.

gramen [gramɛn] *s.m.* (bot.) grass.

graminacées [graminase] *s.f.pl.* (bot.) Gramineae.

graminée [gramine] *adj.*, *s.f.* graminaceous (plant).

grammaire [gram(m)ɛr] *s.f.* grammar.

grammairien, -ne [gram(m)ɛrjɛ̃] *s.m.f.* grammarian.

grammatical, -e, (**aux**) [gram(m)atikal] *adj.* grammatical; ~**ement** [gram(m)atikalmɑ̃] *adv.* grammatically.

gramme [gram] *s.m.* gram, gramme (=15·432 Troy grains); (fig.) grain, ounce; *pas un* ~ *de bon sens*, not an ounce of sense.

gramophone [gramɔfɔn] *s.m.* (obs.) gramophone, phonograph.

grand, -e [grɑ̃] *adj.* **1.** tall, big, grown-up, adult; *un homme* ~ *et maigre*, a tall, thin man; *quand tu seras* ~, when you grow up; *je suis assez grand pour*, I am old enough to; *les* ~*es personnes*, adults, grown-ups; **2.** great, large, big; grand; ~*e hauteur*, great height; *il n'y a pas* ~ *monde dans la salle*, there are not many people in the hall; *marcher à* ~*s pas*, to take big steps, to stride; ~ *ouvert*, wide open; *laver à* ~*e eau*, to wash with plenty of water, to sluice down; *au* ~ *jour*, in broad daylight; ~ *prêtre*, high priest; *le* ~ *monde*, high society; *Grand Hôtel*, Grand Hotel; (obs.) *un* ~, a great personage, a noble lord, a grandee; *faire* ~, to do things on a big scale; *voir* ~, to have a broad vision, to take a broad view; *en* ~, on a large scale, full-size, life-size; **3.** *grand-* or *grand'* with fem. nouns; ~*-rue*, ~*'rue*, high street, main street; ~*-route*, main road; ~*-messe*, high mass; *avoir* ~*-faim*, ~*-soif*, ~*-peur*, to be very hungry, very thirsty, very much afraid; *à* ~*-peine*, with great difficulty; ~ *adv. en* ~, on a large scale; full size; *voir* ~, to take a broad view, to visualize (sth.) on a large scale; *faire* ~, to act in a big way, to do things on a large scale; ~ *s.m.* (obs.) grandee, noble; (mod.) great person; (at school) bigger or older boy; *les* ~*s*, the great, the powerful; the senior pupils.

grand-angulaire [grɑ̃tɑ̃gylɛr] *adj.*, *s.m.* (photo.) wide-angle (lens).

grand-chose [grɑ̃ʃoz] *s.invar.* (used only in neg. context) *pas* ~, nothing much, not much, very little; *pas* ~ *en sortira*, nothing much will come of it; *cela ne vaut pas* ~, it is of no great value; *sans que cela fasse* ~, without it making much difference; *un* or *une pas* ~, a person of no account, a nonentity.

grand-croix [grɑ̃krwa] *s.f.invar.* Grand Cross (of order); ~ *s.m.invar.* Knight Grand Cross.

grand-duc [grɑ̃dyk] *s.m.* **1.** grand duke; **2.** (ornith.) eagle-owl, horned owl.

grand-ducal, -e, (**aux**) [grɑ̃dykal] *adj.* grand-ducal.

grand-duché [grɑ̃dyʃe] *s.m.* Grand Duchy.

Grande-Bretagne [grɑ̃dbrətaɲ] *s.f.* (geog.) Great Britain.

grande-duchesse [grɑ̃ddyʃɛs] *s.f.* Grand Duchess.

grandelet, -te [grɑ̃dlɛ], **grandet, -te** [grɑ̃dɛ] *adj.* (fam.) getting tall, growing up.

grandement [grɑ̃dmɑ̃] *adv.* greatly, largely, highly, vastly; grandly, lavishly, handsomely; *il est* ~ *temps de partir*, it is high time to go; *faire* ~ *les choses*, to treat guests, etc., handsomely, lavishly, to do things on a grand scale.

grandeur [grɑ̃dœr] *s.f.* size, bulk, magnitude, extent, length, breadth, tallness, height; greatness, dignity, grandeur, nobleness; (title) *sa* ~, his Lordship; ~ *d'âme*, magnanimity; (*de*) ~ *naturelle* or ~ *nature*, life-size; *par ordre de* ~, according to size; *regarder qn. du haut de sa* ~, to look down on s.o.

grandiloquence [grɑ̃dilɔkɑ̃s] *s.f.* grandiloquence.

grandiloquent, -e [grɑ̃dilɔkɑ̃] *adj.* grandiloquent, pompous, bombastic.

grandiose [grɑ̃djoz] *adj.* grandiose, grand.

grandir [grɑ̃dir] *v.i.* to grow, to grow up, to grow big, to grow tall; to increase, to rise; ~ *v.t.* to make greater or taller, to increase; (fig.) to exalt, to ennoble, to magnify; **se** ~ *v.refl.* to make oneself bigger or taller.

grandissant, -e [grɑ̃disɑ̃] *adj.* growing, increasing.

grandissement [grɑ̃dismɑ̃] *s.m.* (obs.) increase; growing, increasing; magnifying.

grandissime [grɑ̃disim] *adj.* (fam.) very great, tremendous.

grand-livre [grɑ̃livr] *s.m.* (book-keep.) ledger.

grand-mère [grɑ̃mɛr] *s.f.* grandmother, granny; old woman.

grand-oncle [grɑ̃tɔ̃kl] *s.m.* great-uncle.

(**à**) **grand-peine** [agrɑ̃pɛn] see GRAND 3.

grand-père [grɑ̃pɛr] *s.m.* grandfather; old man.

grands-parents [grɑ̃parɑ̃] *s.m.pl.* grandparents.

grand-tante [grɑ̃tɑ̃t] *s.f.* great-aunt.

grange [grɑ̃ʒ] *s.f.* barn; ⚠ not 'grange'.

granit(**e**) [granit] *s.m.* granite; (fig.) *cœur de* ~, heart of stone.

granité, -e [granite] *adj.* granité, grained; ~ *s.m.* (text.) pebble-weave.

graniter [granite] *v.t.* to give a rough or pebble-like surface to.

graniteu-x, -se [granitø] *adj.* (min.) containing granite, granitic.

granit-ique [granitik] *adj.* granitic, of granite; (fig.) rock-like; ~**oïde** [granitɔid] *adj.* granitoid.

granivore [granivɔr] *adj.* granivorous.

granul-aire [granylɛr] *adj.* granular; ~**ation** [granylɑsjɔ̃] *s.f.* granulation.

granule [granyl] *s.m.* granule.

granuler [granyle] *v.t.* to granulate.

granuleu-x, -se [granylø] *adj.* granulous, granulose, granular.

graphie [grafi] *s.f.* writing, system of writing, script.

graphique [grafik] *adj.* graphic; ~ *s.m.* (sci.) graph, diagram, trace, chart, table, graphic; ~ *s.f.* graphics; ~**ment** [grafikmɑ̃] *adv.* graphically, by means of diagram or writing.

graphisme [grafism] *s.m.* writing, handwriting.

graphitage [grafitaʒ] *s.m.* lubrication with graphite.

graphite [grafit] *s.m.* graphite, blacklead, plumbago.

graphiter [grafite] *v.t.* to lubricate with graphite; to mix with graphite.

graphiteu-x, -se [grafitø] *adj.* graphitic, plumbaginous.

grapho-logie [grafɔlɔʒi] *s.f.* graphology; ~**logique** [grafɔlɔʒik] *adj.* graphological; ~**logue** [grafɔlɔg] *s.m.f.* graphologist; ~**mètre** [grafɔmɛtr] *s.m.* graphometer, alidade.

grappe [grap] *s.f.* bunch, cluster; ~ *de raisin*, bunch of grapes.

grappillage [grapijaʒ] *s.m.* vine-gleaning; (fig.) petty pilfering.

grappiller [grapije] *v.i.* to glean (in vineyard);

(fig.) to make a bit on the side, to pilfer; ~ *v.t.* to glean, to gather at random; (fig.) to pick up (by chance), to glean (information, etc.).

grappilleu-r, -se [grapijœr] *s.m.f.* gleaner; pilferer.

grappillon [grapijɔ̃] *s.m.* small bunch of grapes.

grappin [grapɛ̃] *s.m.* grapnel, grappling-iron, hook; (fig.) *mettre le ~ sur,* to hook, to clutch, to get hold of, (fig.) to get one's claws into.

gras, -se [grɑ] *adj.* **1.** fat, fatty, containing fat or grease, greasy, oily; stout, plump, fattened; with meat or gravy; (obs.) vulgar; *le ~,* the fat (of a piece of meat); *matière ~se,* fat, fatty substance; *acide ~,* fatty acid; *crème ~se,* cream containing oil or grease (for dry skins); *des mains ~ses,* greasy hands; *chapon ~,* plump capon; *choux ~,* cabbage in gravy or fat; (fig., fam.) *faire ses choux ~,* to make a nice profit; (eccles.) *jours ~,* meat-days; *faire ~,* to eat meat (opp. fasting or eating fish); *Mardi-Gras,* Shrove Tuesday; (obs.) *propos ~,* vulgar remarks, dirty talk; **2.** greasy, slippery; thick, heavy; fleshy, juicy, succulent; rich, abundant, lush; (of wine) ropy; *voix ~se,* thick or fruity voice; *caractères ~,* thick letters, heavy or bold type; (bot.) *plantes ~ses,* thick-leaved plants, succulents; *~ses pâturages,* lush pastures; *~ses récompenses,* rich rewards; *faire (la) ~se matinée,* to have a lie-in; ~ *adv.* (pop.) *il n'y a pas ~ à manger,* there's not much to eat; ~ *s.m.* fat, fat part; *le ~ de la jambe,* the fleshy part of the leg.

gras-double [grɑdubl] *s.m.* (cook.) tripe.

grassement [grɑsmɑ̃] *adv.* plentifully, liberally, generously, abundantly; handsomely, heartily.

grasset [grɑsɛ] *s.m.* stifle (of horse).

grasseyement [grasɛjmɑ̃] *s.m.* speaking with a guttural voice; sounding one's R's gutturally.

grasseyer [graseje] *v.i.* to speak with a guttural voice; to sound one's R's gutturally (opp. roll one's R's).

grassouillet, -te [grasujɛ] *adj.* chubby, plump.

grateron, gratteron [gratrɔ̃] *s.m.* (bot.) goose-grass, cleavers, woodruff.

graticul-ation [gratikylɑsjɔ̃] *s.f.* graticulation; **~er** [gratikyle] *v.t.* to divide drawing into squares (in order to reduce or increase scale).

gratification [gratifikɑsjɔ̃] *s.f.* gratuity, present, tip, reward, bonus, extra pay; ⚠ not 'gratification'.

gratifier [gratifje] *v.t.* ~ *qn. de qch.,* to bestow or confer sth. on s.o.; (often iron.) to favour s.o. with sth., to reward s.o. with sth., to attribute or impute sth. to s.o.; ⚠ not 'to gratify'.

gratin [gratɛ̃] *s.m.* (cook.) **1.** (obs.) burnt food scraped from side of pan; **2.** (mod.) bread-crumbs, grated cheese, etc. (used as covering for dishes to be browned under the grill); coating of bread-crumbs and grated cheese; dish so prepared; (fig.) the upper crust, the cream (of society); *chou-fleur au ~,* cauliflower cheese.

gratiné, -e [gratine] *adj.* (cook.) bread-crumbed, cooked *au gratin;* (fig., fam.) fantastic, outrageous.

gratiner [gratine] (cook.) *v.i.* (obs.) to catch, to stick (to the sides of the pan); ~ *v.t.* to cook in bread-crumbs, to prepare *au gratin.*

gratiole [grasjɔl] *s.f.* (bot.) hyssop; hedge-hyssop.

gratis [gratis] *adv.* free, without charge, gratuitously, gratis.

gratitude [gratityd] *s.f.* gratitude, thankfulness.

grattage [grataʒ] *s.m.* scratching, scraping; scratching out, erasing.

gratte [grat] *s.f.* **1.** scraper, hoe; **2.** (fam.) profit on the side, fiddle; *faire de la ~,* to work a fiddle; **3.** (med.) mange, itch; **~-ciel** [gratsjɛl] *s.m.invar.* skyscraper; **~-cul** [gratky] *s.m.* (pl. *gratte-culs*) (rose-)hip; **~-dos** [gratdo] *s.m.invar.* back-scratcher; **~ment** [gratmɑ̃] *s.f.* (fam.) back-scratcher; **~ment** [gratmɑ̃] *s.m.* scratching.

grattelle [gratɛl] *s.f.* (fam.) itch.

grattement [gratmɑ̃] *s.m.* scratching.

gratte-papier [gratpapje] *s.m.* (pl. *gratte--papier(s)*) (pej.) pen-pusher, quill-driver, clerk, (literary) hack.

gratter [grate] *v.t.* **1.** to scratch, to scrape; to cause to itch; to scratch out, to erase, to scrape off; to make a profit, to get sth. (out of sth.); *une plume qui gratte,* a scratchy pen; ~ *le papier,* to drive a quill, to do clerking; ~ *la terre,* to scratch the ground, to dig over lightly; to till the soil; *se ~ la jambe,* to scratch one's leg; (fig.) ~ *une vieille plaie,* to open an old wound; *ça me gratte terriblement,* I've got a terrible itch; (fig.) ~ *qn. là où ça le démange,* to play on someone's weakness; (fig.) ~ *le fond du tiroir,* to scrape the bottom of the barrel; ~ *un mot,* to scratch out, to erase, a word; *il n'y a pas grand-chose à ~,* there's not much to be got out of it, not much in the way of pickings; ~ *sur tout,* to make a bit on everything; **2.** (fam.) (esp. sport) to overtake, to pass; ~ *v.i.* **1.** ~ *à la porte,* to scratch on the door; ~ *du violon,* to scrape away on the violin; **2.** (pop.) to work.

grattoir [gratwar] *s.m.* scraper, shoe-scraper; (techn.) shave-hook; scraper-eraser, erasing--knife.

gratuit, -e [gratɥi] *adj.* gratuitous, free, free of charge; *école ~e,* non-fee-paying school; **2.** arbitrary, unfounded, (of assumption, etc.) gratuitous, unjustified, unprovoked.

gratuité [gratɥite] *s.f.* gratuitousness, arbitrary nature, absence of motive or justification; ⚠ not 'gratuity'.

gratuitement [gratɥitmɑ̃] *adv.* **1.** gratuitously, gratis, free, for nothing, out of kindness; **2.** arbitrarily; without cause or provocation, for no good reason, wantonly, mindlessly.

grau [gro] *s.m.* (in south of France) channel connecting salt lake or river with the sea.

gravatier [gravatje] *s.m.* one who removes rubble or builder's rubbish.

gravats [grava] *s.m.pl.* **1.** screenings (in plaster--work); **2.** rubble, builder's rubbish.

grave [grav] *adj.* **1.** (fig.) grave, serious, dignified, solemn; severe; weighty, important, momentous; *~s sanctions,* severe punishment, strict sanctions; *blessé ~,* gravely wounded; *de ~s raisons,* weighty or important reasons; **2.** heavy; (of voice, etc.) deep, bass; (mus.) *le ~,* the bass register; (lang.) *accent ~,* grave accent.

gravé, -e [grave] *adj.* engraved, carved; pitted, pock-marked.

graveleu-x, -se [gravlø] *adj.* sandy, gritty; (med.) suffering from gravel; (fig.) dirty, lewd, obscene.

gravelle [gravɛl] *s.f.* (pathol.) gravel.

gravelure [gravlyr] *s.f.* obscenity, lewdness, filthy talk, dirty story.

gravement [gravmɑ̃] *adv.* gravely, seriously, solemnly; deeply, severely; dangerously, grievously; ~ *blessé,* seriously injured.

graver [grave] *v.t.* to engrave, to score; to impress, to imprint; (fig.) to mark; ~ *à l'eau forte,* to etch; ~ *au burin,* to engrave; ~ *en creux,* to sink; ~ *en relief,* to emboss; ~ *qch. dans la mémoire de qn.,* to impress sth. on someone's mind; *cela reste gravé dans ma mémoire,* it remains deeply engraved in my memory; *un visage gravé par la souffrance,* a face deeply marked by suffering.

graves [grav] *s.f.pl.* (in Bordeaux region) sandy and stony ground; ~ *s.m.* Graves (wine).

graveur [gravœr] *s.m.* engraver, etcher; die--sinker.
gravide [gravid] *adj.* gravid, pregnant.
gravidéviation [gravidevjɑsjɔ̃] *s.f.* (space travel) swing-by.
gravier [gravje] *s.m.* gravel, grit; (med.) gravel.
gravillon [gravijɔ̃] *s.m.* (also pl.) grit, fine gravel; **~nage** [gravijɔnaʒ] *s.m.* gritting (of roads); **~neuse** [gravijɔnøz] *s.f.* gritting-lorry.
gravimétrie [gravimetri] *s.f.* gravimetry.
gravir [gravir] *v.t.* (also *~ à*, *~ sur*) to climb, to clamber up, to scale, to ascend.
gravitation [gravitɑsjɔ̃] *s.f.* gravitation, gravitational pull.
gravité [gravite] *s.f.* **1.** gravity, seriousness, solemnity, sedateness; **2.** gravity, weight, importance, severity, seriousness, grievousness; **3.** (phys.) gravity.
graviter [gravite] *v.i.* to gravitate; *~ autour de*, to revolve round; (fig.) to flutter or hang around (s.o.).
gravois [gravwa] *s.m.pl.* = GRAVATS.
gravure [gravyr] *s.f.* engraving, print; illustration, reproduction; carving; *~ sur bois*, woodcut; *~ au trait*, line-engraving; *(~ à l')eau forte*, etching.
gré [gre] *s.m.* will, pleasure, inclination, liking, taste, whim, fancy; consent, agreement; gratitude; *à votre ~!*, as you please!; *est-ce à votre ~?*, is this to your liking?; *rien n'était à son ~*, nothing suited him, nothing was to his taste; *à son ~ tout était médiocre*, according to him everything was second-rate; *bon ~ mal ~*, or *de ~ ou de force*, willy-nilly; *de plein ~*, willingly, of one's own free will; *contre son ~*, unwillingly, reluctantly, against the grain, by compulsion; *prendre en ~*, to take a liking to, to regard favourably; *de bon ~*, of one's own accord; *de mauvais ~*, grudgingly, with an ill grace; *vendre de ~ à ~*, to sell by private treaty (opp. by auction); *je lui en sais (bon) ~*, I feel grateful to him; *sachons lui ~ de cela*, let us count that to his credit; *savoir mauvais ~ à qn. de*, to take it ill that s.o. should; to resent s.o. doing; *au ~ des circonstances*, as circumstances permit; *au ~ des flots*, at the mercy of the waves.
grèbe [grɛb] *s.m.* (ornith.) grebe.
grébiche [grebiʃ], **grébige** [grebiʒ], **gribiche** [gribiʃ] *s.f.* **1.** (print.) file number (of manuscript); **2.** loose-leaf binder; **3.** metal edging (on leather-goods, etc.).
grec, -que [grɛk] *adj.* Greek, Grecian; *s.m.f.* Greek; Grecian, Greek scholar; *~ s.m.* Greek (language); see also GRECQUE.
Grèce [grɛs] *s.f.* (geog.) Greece.
gréciser [gresize] *v.t.* to hellenize.
gréco-latin, -e [grekɔlatɛ̃] *adj.* Graeco-Latin.
gréco-romain, -e [grekɔrɔmɛ̃] *adj.* Graeco--Roman.
grecque [grɛk] *s.f.* **1.** bookbinder's saw; **2.** Greek key-pattern (motif); **3.** see GREC.
gredin, -e [grədɛ̃] *s.m.f.* scoundrel, rogue, rascal.
gredinerie [grədinri] *s.f.* (obs.) villainy, knavery.
gréement [gremɑ̃] *s.m.* (naut.) rigging.
gréer [gree] *v.t.* (naut.) to rig.
greffage [grɛfaʒ] *s.m.* grafting (of trees, vines, etc.).
greffe[1] [grɛf] *s.m.* record-office, registry; registrar's office.
greffe[2] [grɛf] *s.f.* (hort.) graft, grafting; graft, bud, shoot, scion; (surg.) graft.
greffer [grefe] *v.t.* to graft; **se ~** *v.refl.* to be grafted; (fig.) to become grafted.
greffier [grɛfje] *s.m.* clerk of the court; registrar; recorder; *~-municipal*, Town Clerk.
greffoir [grɛfwar] *s.m.* grafting-knife.
greffon [grɛfɔ̃] *s.m.* (hort.) graft, bud, shoot, slip; (surg.) graft.
grégaire [gregɛr] *adj.* gregarious; *esprit ~*, herd instinct.
grège [grɛʒ] *adj.* (of silk) raw.
grégeois [greʒwa] *adj.m*, *feu ~*, Greek fire.
grégorien, -ne [gregɔrjɛ̃] *adj.* Gregorian; *chant ~*, Gregorian chant, plainchant.
grègues [grɛg] *s.f.pl.* (obs.) breeches; (obs.) *tirer ses ~*, to take to one's heels.
grêle[1] [grɛl] *adj.* slender, delicate, slim; thin; (of sound) piping, shrill; *intestin ~*, or *le ~*, small intestine.
grêle[2] [grɛl] *s.f.* hail, hailstorm; (fig.) hail, volley.
grêler [grele] *v.i.* to hail; *~ v.t.* to hail upon; *être grêlé*, to be damaged or devastated by hail.
grelin [grəlɛ̃] *s.m.* (naut.) hawser, small cable, warp.
grêlon [grɛlɔ̃] *s.m.* hailstone.
grelot [grəlo] *s.m.* small bell (esp. round neck of animal); (fig.) *attacher le ~*, to make a cautious sounding, to take the initiative (in a dangerous enterprise), to bell the cat; to sound the alarm; (pop.) *avoir les ~s*, to be dead scared.
grelottement [grəlɔtmɑ̃] *s.m.* **1.** shivering; **2.** tinkling.
grelotter [grəlɔte] *v.i.* **1.** to shiver with cold, to shake till one's teeth chatter; **2.** to tinkle.
greluchon [grəlyʃɔ̃] *s.m.* (obs.) lover.
grémil [gremil] *s.m.* (bot.) gromwell.
grémille [grəmij] *s.f.* (ichth.) ruff.
grenache [grənaʃ] *s.m.* a kind of vine (in Languedoc and Roussillon); wine made from this.
grenade [grənad] *s.f.* **1.** (bot.) pomegranate; **2.** (mil.) grenade.
Grenade [grənad] *s.f.* (geog.) **1.** Granada (in Spain); **2.** Grenada (in West Indies).
grenadeur [grənadœr] *s.m.* (mil.) grenade--thrower.
grenadier [grənadje] *s.m.* **1.** (bot.) pomegranate--tree; **2.** (mil.) grenadier; (fig.) tall fellow; masculine woman; *c'est un ~*, he's a great big chap, a real guardsman.
grenadière [grənadjɛr] *s.f.* grenade-pouch.
grenadille [grənadij] *s.f.* (bot.) granadilla.
grenadin, -e [grənadɛ̃] *adj.*, *s.m.f.* (native or inhabitant) of Granada or Grenada; *~ s.m.* **1.** (cook.) grenadine (glazed veal or poultry fillets); **2.** (ornith.) African finch; **3.** (bot.) a kind of carnation; **~e** *s.f.* **1.** (text.) grenadine; **2.** pomegranate syrup.
grenaillage [grənɑjaʒ] *s.m.* (techn.) shot--blasting.
grenaille [grənɑj] *s.f.* **1.** shot (as in cartridge); granulated metal; *~ de plomb*, lead-shot; **2.** refuse grain, tailings.
grenailler [grənɑje] *v.t.* to granulate, or to make shot from, metal.
grenaison [grənɛzɔ̃] *s.f.* (agric.) seeding; formation of seed.
grenat [grəna] *s.m.* garnet; *~ adj.invar.* garnet--red, claret(-coloured).
grené, -e [grəne] *adj.* stippled; *~ s.m.* stipple, stippling.
greneler [grənle] *v.t.* to grain (leather, paper, etc.).
grener [grəne] *v.i.* (agric.) to seed, to form seed; *~ v.t.* (techn.) to granulate, to grain.
grènetis [grɛnti] *s.m.* milling, milled edge, (of coins).
grenier [grənje] *s.m.* loft, store-house, granary; garret, attic, lumber-room; *~s d'abondance*, public granary; *fouiller une maison de la cave jusqu'au ~*, to search a house from top to bottom.
grenouille [grənuj] *s.f.* frog; (fig., fam.) money--box (=china pig); *manger la ~*, to make off with the funds.

grenouillère [grənujɛr] *s.f.* marsh-land; frog-pond.
grenouillet [grənujɛ] *s.m.* **1.** (bot.) Solomon's seal; **2.** = GRENOUILLETTE 1.
grenouillette [grənujɛt] *s.f.* **1.** (bot.) water crowfoot; **2.** (pathol.) ranula, tumour of the tongue.
grenu, -e [grəny] *adj.* **1.** (bot.) full of seed or grain; **2.** grained, showing the grain; (geol.) granular, granular-textured.
grenure [grənyr] *s.f.* stippling, stipple; (of leather) grain, graining.
grès [grɛ] *s.m.* **1.** sandstone, gritstone; ~ *à meule,* millstone grit; ~ *vert,* greensand; **2.** stoneware, earthenware; *pot de* ~, earthenware or stone pot.
grésage [grezaʒ] *s.m.* (techn.) sanding, polishing, buffing (on wheel).
gréser [greze] *v.t.* (techn.) to sand, to buff.
gréseu-x, -se [grezø] *adj.* gritty, sandy.
grésil [grezi(l)] *s.m.* sleet, small hail; **~lement** [grezijmɑ̃] *s.m.* crackling; pattering (as of sleet); sizzling; **~ler** [grezije] *v.i.* **1.** to sleet; **2.** to crackle, to sputter.
grève [grɛv] *s.f.* **1.** strand, shore, beach; *la Grève, la place de Grève,* square in Paris where executions took place; *pendaison en Grève,* public hanging; **2.** strike (of labour); *faire* or *se mettre en* ~, to strike, to go on strike; *être en* ~, to be on strike; ~ *perlée,* go-slow; ~ *tournante,* staggered strike; ~ *de sympathie,* strike in sympathy; ~ *de lait,* strike of milkmen; ~ *de la faim,* hunger-strike.
grever [grəve] *v.t.* to burden; (law) to encumber, to entail.
gréviste [grevist] *s.m.f.* striker.
gribouillage [gribujaʒ] *s.m.* scrawl, scribble.
gribouille [gribuj] *s.m.* booby, fool.
gribouiller [gribuje] *v.t.i.* to scrawl, to scribble.
gribouilleu-r, -se [gribujœr] *s.m.f.* scrawler, scribbler.
gribouillis [gribuji] *s.m.* scrawl, scribble, scribbling.
grief [griɛf] *s.m.* **1.** (obs.) damage, injury; **2.** grievance, wrong, injury; complaint, ground for complaint; (law) statement of grounds (for bringing action, etc.); *avoir des ~s contre qn.,* to have a grievance, or grounds for complaint, against s.o.; *exposer* or *formuler ses ~s,* to complain, to protest, to lodge a complaint; *faire* ~ *de qch. à qn.,* to blame or reproach s.o. for sth., to bear s.o. a grudge for sth.; (law) *~s d'accusation,* grounds for prosecution; ⚠ not 'grief'.
grièvement [griɛvmɑ̃] *adv.* grievously, severely, sorely.
griffade [grifad] *s.f.* scratch, clawing.
griffe [grif] *s.f.* **1.** claw; talon; (pl.) (fig.) clutches; *coup de* ~, scratch; (fig.) vicious attack; *tomber sous la* ~ *de,* to fall into the clutches of; **2.** signature, stamp, facsimile signature; (fig.) mark, stamp; **3.** (agric.) root (of asparagus); offset tuber (of anemones, etc.); **4.** (techn.) claw, clip, clamp; grip, handle.
griffer [grife] *v.t.* to scratch, to claw.
griffon [grifɔ̃] *s.m.* **1.** (myth., herald.) griffin, griffon, gryphon; **2.** griffon (dog); **3.** (obs.) tap of a fountain; (mod.) place where spring appears.
griffon-nage [grifɔnaʒ] *s.m.* scrawl; **~nement** [grifɔnmɑ̃] *s.m.* (sculpt.) maquette, clay or wax mould; **~ner** [grifɔne] *v.t.i.* to scrawl, to scribble.
griffonneu-r, -se [grifɔnœr] *s.m.f.* scribbler.
griffu, -e [grify] *adj.* armed with claws or talons; (fig.) clawing, greedy, cruel, vicious.
griffure [grifyr] *s.f.* scratch.
grigne [griɲ] *s.f.* pucker; slit (in breadcrust).
grigner [griɲe] *v.i.* (sewing, dressm.) to pucker, to wrinkle, to be uneven.
grignon [griɲɔ̃] *s.m.* **1.** crust end of French loaf; **2.** (agric.) olive-oil cake.
grignotement [griɲɔtmɑ̃] *s.m.* gnawing, sound of gnawing; nibbling.
grignoter [griɲɔte] *v.t.* to nibble, to gnaw; to peck at; (fig.) to erode, to wear down; to acquire, to get a bit of; *il n'y a rien à* ~ *dans cette affaire,* there are no pickings there; ~ *v.i.* to take a nibble, to have just a taste.
grignoteu-r, -se [griɲɔtœr] *adj.* nibbling; *s.m.f.* nibbler; **~se** *s.f.* (techn.) cutter, jigsaw.
grignotis [griɲɔti] *s.m.* (engr.) dotting.
grigou [grigu] *s.m.* (fam.) skinflint, miser.
grigri see GRISGRIS.
gril [gri(l)] *s.m.* gridiron, grill; toaster; grating (on sluice); (theatr.) flies; (fig.) *être sur le* ~, to be on tenterhooks.
grillade [grijad] *s.f.* grilling; grilled meat.
grillage[1] [grijaʒ] *s.m.* grilling, toasting.
grillage[2] [grijaʒ] *s.m.* grating; lattice, lattice-work; fence of wire-netting.
grillager [grijaʒe] *v.t.* to fit with wire-netting or lattice.
grillageur [grijaʒœr] *s.m.* erector of wire-fencing or lattice-work.
grille [grij] *s.f.* iron bars, wrought-iron gate, iron railings; lattice, trellis, grille; grating, screen, netting; fire-bars; fire-grate; (electr.) grid; cipher stencil; *être sous les ~s,* to be behind bars, in prison.
grille-pain [grijpɛ̃] *s.m.invar.* toaster.
griller[1] [grije] *v.t.* to grill, to roast, to toast, to scorch, to burn, to blast, to shrivel; (electr.) to burn out (resistance, etc.); (fam.) to smoke (cigarette); (fig.) to fail to stop (at stopping-place, etc.); (fam.) to outstrip, to supplant (rival); ~ *v.i.* to grill, to roast, to scorch; (fig.) to be burning, to be itching, to be longing, to be impatient, (to do sth.).
griller[2] [grije] *v.t.* to rail in, to enclose with wire fence; to bar (window), to fit a grating or lattice to; (obs.) to put behind bars.
grillon [grijɔ̃] *s.m.* (ent.) cricket.
grimaçant, -e [grimasɑ̃] *adj.* grinning, grimacing, distorted.
grimace [grimas] *s.f.* **1.** grimace, grin, face; crease (in a garment); ~ *de douleur,* wince of pain; *faire la* ~, to make a face, to make a wry face, to grimace, to pout; (fig.) to show disquiet or reluctance; **2.** (obs.) pretence, hypocrisy; (mod.) (pl.) affected behaviour, airs, pretensions; smirking, mincing; **3.** grotesque face (carved on misericord, etc.).
grimacer [grimase] *v.i.* to make faces, to grimace, to grin; (of garment) to crease.
grimaci-er, -ère [grimasje] *adj.* grimacing; mincing, simpering; affected, hypocritical; *s.m.f.* affected person; humbug, hypocrite.
grimage [grimaʒ] *s.m.* (theatr.) make-up.
grimaud [grimo] *s.m.* (obs.) **1.** dunce; **2.** boorish or pedantic person; third-rate writer.
grime [grim] *s.m.* (theatr.) silly old man; actor playing such a part; ⚠ not 'grime'.
grimer [grime] *v.t.* (theatr.) **1.** (obs.) to make up (an actor) as an old man; **2.** (mod.) to make up; **se** ~ *v.refl.* to make (oneself) up.
grimoire [grimwar] *s.m.* book of spells; (fig.) obscure or unintelligible work, gibberish; illegible or unintelligible document.
grimpant, -e [grɛ̃pɑ̃] *adj.* (of plants) climbing, creeping; *rosier* ~, climbing rose; *plante ~e,* creeper; ~ *s.m.* (pop.) trousers.
grimper [grɛ̃pe] *v.i.* to climb, to go up, to rise, to creep up; ~ *à un mât, à une corde,* to climb a mast, a rope; ~ *à une échelle,* to climb up a ladder; ~ *à* or *sur un arbre,* to climb a tree; ~ *à travers les roches,* to climb over the rocks; *la route grimpe dur,* the road rises sharply; ~ *au*

pouvoir, to rise to power; *les prix ont grimpé*, prices have soared; ~ *v.t.* to climb, to go up, to mount; ~ *une montagne*, to climb a mountain; ~ *l'escalier*, to go up the stairs; ~ *s.m.* (gymn.) rope--climbing.

grimpereau (pl. **-x**) [grɛ̃pro] *s.m.* (ornith.) tree-creeper.

grimpeu-r, -se [grɛ̃pœr] *adj.* climbing; scansorial; *s.m.f.* climber; ~**rs** *s.m.pl.* (zool.) climbers.

grincement [grɛ̃smɑ̃] *s.m.* grating, grinding, grating sound, squeak, gnashing (of teeth).

grincer [grɛ̃se] *v.i.* to grind, to grate, to creak, to squeak; ~ *des dents*, to grind or gnash one's teeth; *faire* ~ *des dents à qn.*, to set someone's teeth on edge.

grincheu-x, -se [grɛ̃ʃø] *adj.* grumpy, surly, crabbed, peevish; *s.m.f.* grumbler.

gringalet [grɛ̃galɛ] *adj.*, *s.m.f.* puny, undersized, (person).

griot [grijo] *s.m.* seconds (of meal or flour).

griot, -te [grijo] *s.m.f.* (ethn.) Griot.

griotte [grijot] *s.f.* **1.** (bot.) morello cherry; **2.** a kind of marble with red and brown spots.

grippage [gripaʒ] *s.m.* (mech.) seizing(-up), binding, jamming, (of piston, etc.).

grippe [grip] *s.f.* **1.** influenza, flu; **2.** dislike; *prendre qn.*, *qch.*, *en* ~, to take a dislike to s.o., sth.

grippé, -e [gripe] *adj.* **1.** ill with influenza; **2.** (of face in painful illness) pinched, drawn.

grippement [gripmɑ̃] *s.m.* **1.** = GRIPPAGE; **2.** (med.) pinched, drawn features.

gripper [gripe] *v.t.* (obs.) to pounce upon; (mod.) (mech.) to (cause to) jam; ~ *v.i.*, or **se** ~ *v.refl.* to seize (up), to bind, to jam; (of material) to wrinkle, to crumple, to shrink.

grippe-sou [gripsu] *s.m.* skinflint, money--grubber, miser.

gris, -e [gri] *adj.* grey, grey-haired; (fig.) grey, dull, colourless, shadowy; tipsy; *papier* ~, brown paper; *vin* ~, rosé wine; *faire* ~*e mine à qn.*, to give s.o. black looks, to give s.o. a cool reception; ~ *s.m.* grey, grey horse; shag tobacco.

grisaille [grizɑj] *s.f.* (art) grisaille; piece in grisaille; (fig.) grisaille effect, greyness, gloom, absence of colour or life.

grisailler [grizɑje] *v.t.* to paint in grisaille; ~ *v.i.* to turn grey.

grisâtre [grizɑtr] *adj.* greyish.

grisbi [grizbi] *s.m.* (slang) money.

grisé [grize] *s.m.* (engr.) grey shading (obtained by hatching, etc.).

griser [grize] *v.t.* to intoxicate, to make drunk, to befuddle; (fig.) to intoxicate, to stimulate, to carry away; *se laisser* ~ *par le succès*, to allow success to go to one's head; **se** ~ *v.refl.* to become intoxicated; (fig.) to be carried away.

griserie [grizri] *s.f.* tipsiness; (fig.) intoxication, exaltation.

griset [grizɛ] *s.m.* **1.** (ornith.) young sparrow; **2.** (ichth.) a kind of small shark.

grisette [grizɛt] *s.f.* (obs.) shop-girl (of easy virtue).

grisgris, grigri [grigri] *s.m.* greegree, ju-ju; charm or fetish.

grison, -ne [grizɔ̃] *adj.*, *s.m.f.* **1.** (obs.) (one who is) going grey; **2.** (geog.) (inhabitant) of the Swiss canton of Grisons.

grisonnant, -e [grizɔnɑ̃] *adj.* going grey, greying; grizzled.

grisonner [grizɔne] *v.i.* to turn grey, to grow grey.

grisou [grizu] *s.m.* firedamp; *coup de* ~, explosion of fire-damp.

grive [griv] *s.f.* (ornith.) thrush; ~ *commune* or *musicienne*, song-thrush; ~ *litorne*, fieldfare; ~ *mauvis*, redwing; *soûl comme une* ~, drunk as a lord.

grivelé, -e [grivle] *adj.* speckled, dappled.

griveler [grivle] *v.i.* (obs.) to make illicit profits, to pilfer.

grivèlerie [grivɛlri] *s.f.* pilfering, bilking, going off without paying (from restaurant, etc.).

griveton [grivtɔ̃] *s.m.* (pop.) soldier.

grivois, -e [grivwa] *adj.* broad, licentious, loose, dirty, spicy; ~ *s.m.* **1.** (obs.) mercenary; **2.** licentious or dirty-minded fellow.

grivoiserie [grivwazri] *s.f.* licentiousness; dirty story or talk.

Groenland [grɔɛnlɑ̃d] *s.m.* (geog.) Greenland.

groenlandais, -e [grɔɛnlɑ̃dɛ] *adj.* of Greenland; *s.m.f.* Greenlander.

grizzli, grizzly [grizli] *s.m.* grizzly (bear).

grog [grɔg] *s.m.* grog, toddy.

grognard [grɔɲar] *adj.* (obs.) grumbling; ~ *s.m.* veteran (esp. of Napoleonic wars).

grognasse [grɔɲas] *s.f.* (pop.) ugly old woman, old hag.

grogne [grɔɲ] *s.f.* (fam.) grouse; grousing, moaning.

grognement [grɔɲmɑ̃] *s.m.* grunt, grunting, growl, growling, snarling; (fig.) grumbling, grousing.

grogner [grɔɲe] *v.i.* to grunt, to growl, to snarl; (fig.) to grumble, to grouse.

grogneu-r, -se [grɔɲœr] *adj.* grumbling, discontented.

grognon, -ne [grɔɲɔ̃] *adj.* (often invar. in fem.) grumbling, complaining, sullen; *une femme* ~(*ne*), a woman who is always complaining; ~ *s.m.* grumbler.

grognonner [grɔɲɔne] *v.i.* to grunt; to grumble, to mutter.

groin [grwɛ̃] *s.m.* snout (of pig); bestial face; ⚠ not 'groin'.

groisil [grwazi(l)] *s.m.* (glass-making) cullet.

grole, grolle [grɔl] *s.f.* **1.** (ornith.) rook; **2.** (pop.) shoe.

grommeler [grɔmle] *v.t.i.* to mutter, to grumble, to grunt.

grommellement [grɔmɛlmɑ̃] *s.m.* grumbling, muttering; grunt, grunting.

grondant, -e [grɔ̃dɑ̃] *adj.* roaring, growling; rumbling; (fig.) hostile, threatening.

grondement [grɔ̃dmɑ̃] *s.m.* roar, roaring, growl, growling, snarling; rumbling.

gronder [grɔ̃de] *v.i.* to roar, to growl, to snarl; to rumble, to thunder; (fig.) to rumble threateningly, to be threatening; ~ *v.t.* to scold, to reprimand; to chide (gently).

gronderie [grɔ̃dri] *s.f.* reprimand, scolding, chiding.

grondeu-r, -se [grɔ̃dœr] *adj.* scolding, grumbling, grousing, nagging; rumbling, thundering, booming; ~**r** *s.m.* (obs.) grumbler.

grondin [grɔ̃dɛ̃] *s.m.* (ichth.) gurnard, red gurnet.

groom [grum] *s.m.* (obs.) groom; (mod.) page, page-boy, buttons, bell-hop.

gros, -se [gro] *adj.* large, big, stout, bulky, great, considerable, thick, swollen; fat, corpulent, stout, obese, gross; heavy; coarse, broad; loud, plain; ~ *bétail*, cattle, bovines; ~*se caisse*, big drum; (eng.) ~ *travaux*, major works; ~ *appetit*, hearty appetite; *avoir le ventre* ~, to have a swollen stomach; *avoir le cœur* ~, to be heavy--hearted, to be deeply affected; *en avoir* ~ *sur le cœur*, to have had as much as one can bear; *une* ~*se femme*, a stout woman; (obs.) *une femme* ~*se*, a pregnant woman; *de* ~ *mots*, high words, strong language; ~*se plaisanterie*, coarse joke; ~ *drap*, coarse thick cloth; *un* ~ *bourgeois*, a wealthy or substantial citizen; *une* ~*se somme*, a considerable sum of money; *de* ~ *souliers*, heavy shoes; *un* ~ *rhume*, a severe cold; ~*se fièvre*, high fever; *mer* ~*se*, heavy sea; rough or high seas; (naut.) ~ *de l'eau*, high water; ~ *temps*, foul or heavy weather; *une ~se voix*, a loud voice; *c'est de l'esprit* ~, it's witty, but not very subtle; *le ~ bon sens*, plain common sense; *jouer ~ (jeu)*, to play for high stakes; ~ *adv. risquer* ~, to take big risks; *gagner* ~, to be earning good profits; *il y a ~ à parier que*, the odds are that, it is a safe bet that; *en* ~, large, on a large scale, in quantity, wholesale; (fig.) in general; *écrit en* ~, written large, in large letters.

gros, -se [gro] *s.m.f.* big person, man or woman; rich or influential person; *les* ~, the great, the high-ups; ~ *s.m.* main part, larger or largest part, bulk, majority; essence, essential part; (fig.) height, depth; wholesale (trade); *le ~ des troupes*, the main body of troops; *le ~ de l'affaire*, the essence of the matter; *le ~ de l'hiver*, the depths of winter; *commerce de* ~, wholesale business.

gros-bec [grobɛk] *s.m.* (ornith.) hawfinch, grosbeak.

groseille [grozɛj] *s.f.* (bot.) red currant; bright red (colour); ~ *noire*, blackcurrant; ~ *à maquereau*, gooseberry.

groseillier [grozɛje] *s.m.* (bot.) currant-bush; ~ *à maquereau*, gooseberry-bush.

gros-grain [grogrɛ̃] *s.m.* grosgrain, petersham.

gros-porteur [groportœr] *s.m.* (aeron.) wide--body aircraft, jumbo jet.

grosse [gros] *s.f.* **1.** large writing, round hand; (law) engrossing, engrossment; engrossed document; *écrire en* ~, to write large or round hand; (law) to engross; **2.** gross, twelve dozen.

grosserie [grosri] *s.f.* **1.** ironmongery; **2.** silver plate; **3.** (obs.) wholesale trade.

grossesse [grosɛs] *s.f.* pregnancy; *robe de* ~, maternity dress.

grosseur [grosœr] *s.f.* **1.** size, bulk, thickness, stoutness, fatness; **2.** tumour, swelling.

grossi-er, -ère [grosje] *adj.* coarse, thick, rough; gross, vulgar; homely, plain, common; clumsy, rough, rude, blunt, uncouth; unmannerly; (Lit.) sensual, of the flesh; *mœurs ~ères*, vulgar or uncouth behaviour; *d'un air ~er*, rudely; *sur un ton ~er*, in an uncivil manner, bluntly; **~èrement** [grosjɛrmɑ̃] *adv.* roughly, grossly, coarsely, rudely.

grossièreté [grosjɛrte] *s.f.* roughness, plainness, coarseness, grossness; vulgarity; rudeness; rude word, coarse expression.

grossir [grosir] *v.t.* to make bigger, to enlarge, to increase, to augment; to magnify, to intensify, to exaggerate; to make look fatter; ~ *v.i.* to grow bigger or fatter, to increase, to expand; **se** ~ *v.refl.* to grow bigger, to increase, to augment.

grossissant, -e [grosisɑ̃] *adj.* increasing, magnifying; *verre* ~, magnifying glass.

grossissement [grosismɑ̃] *s.m.* increase, swelling out; magnifying, magnification, amplification; enlargement; exaggeration.

grossiste [grosist] *s.m.f.* wholesaler.

grosso-modo [grɔsɔmɔdo] *adv. loc.* roughly, at a rough estimate.

grossoyer [groswaje] *v.t.* (law) to engross.

grotesque [grɔtɛsk] *adj.* grotesque, ludicrous; ~ *s.m.* the grotesque; (art, arch.) grotesque ornamentation; grotesque figure, caricature, figure of fun; **~ment** [grɔtɛskmɑ̃] *adv.* grotesquely, ludicrously, absurdly.

grotte [grɔt] *s.f.* cave, cavern.

grouillant, -e [grujɑ̃] *adj.* swarming, crawling, alive, wriggling, seething, teeming, (*de*, with).

grouillement [grujmɑ̃] *s.m.* swarming, crawling, wriggling; swarming mass.

grouiller [gruje] *v.i.* to swarm, to crawl, to stir, to be alive, to teem, to be overrun (*de*, with); (fig.) to abound; **se** ~ *v.refl.* (obs.) to move; (mod., pop.) to hurry up, to get a move on.

groupe [grup] *s.m.* group, bunch, clump, cluster; team, pool; association, circle, coterie; set; (mil.) unit; (air force) group; (bot., zool.) division; *travail en* ~, team work, working as a team; ~ *de dactylos*, typing pool; (electr.) ~ *électrogène*, generator set.

groupement [grupmɑ̃] *s.m.* grouping, forming into groups, arrangement; coupling, connecting; group, association, bloc.

grouper [grupe] *v.t.* to group, to put or group together, to arrange (in groups); to gather, to collect; **se** ~ *v.refl.* to form a group or groups, to assemble, to collect, to gather.

gruau (pl. **-x**) [gryo] *s.m.* **1.** (finest) wheaten flour; **2.** oatmeal, groats; **3.** grist.

grue [gry] *s.f.* (ornith.) crane; (mech.) crane; (pop.) prostitute; (fig.) *faire le pied de* ~, to kick one's heels, to hang about.

gruger [gryʒe] *v.t.* to crunch, to eat up, to devour; (fig.) to cheat, to rob.

grume [grym] *s.f.* **1.** bark (left on felled trees); undressed timber; *en* ~, in the log, unbarked, rough; **2.** grape.

grumeau (pl. **-x**) [grymo] *s.m.* clot, lump; *en ~x*, clotted.

grumeler [grymle] *v.t.* to form clots on; **se** ~ *v.refl.* to clot.

grumeleu-x, -se [grymlø] *adj.* clotted, grumous, rough.

grumelure [grymlyr] *s.f.* (metall.) cavity (in casting).

grutier [grytje] *s.m.* crane-driver.

gruyère [gryjɛr] *s.m.* Gruyère (cheese).

guai(s) [gɛ] *adj.m.* (of herring) shotten.

guanaco [gwanako] *s.m.* (zool.) guanaco, wild llama.

guano [gwano] *s.m.* guano; fish-manure.

Guatémala [gwatemala] *s.m.* (geog.) Guatemala.

guatémalien, -ne [gwatemaljɛ̃], **guatémaltèque** [gwatemaltɛk] *adj., s.m.f.* Guatemalan.

gué [ge] *s.m.* ford; *passer à* ~, to ford.

gué [ge] *interj.* joyful refrain in popular song, e.g. heigh-ho!

guéable [geabl] *adj.* fordable.

guèbre [gɛbr] *s.m.f.* Guebre, Zoroastrian.

guède [gɛd] *s.f.* woad, dyer's woad, pastel.

guéer [gee] *v.t.* to ford.

guelfe [gɛlf] *s.m.f.* Guelph.

guelte [gɛlt] *s.f.* percentage on sales, commission.

guenille [gənij] *s.f.* (pl.) tattered garment, rags; *én ~s*, in rags; (sing.) (fig.) worthless object; (of person) wreck.

guenon [gənɔ̃] *s.f.* **1.** (obs.) long-tailed monkey; **2.** (mod.) female monkey; (fig.) ugly woman.

guépard [gepar] *s.m.* (zool.) cheetah.

guêpe [gɛp] *s.f.* (ent.) wasp.

guêpier [gɛpje] *s.m.* **1.** wasps' nest, (lit. & fig.) hornets' nest; **2.** (ornith.) bee-eater.

guère [gɛr] *adv.* not very, not much, very little, not many, hardly any, only (a) little, only (a) few, but few, but little; not very often, hardly ever, not long; hardly, scarcely; *il n'y a ~ deux heures que*, it is just about two hours since; *ce n'est ~ difficile*, it is not very difficult; *vous exagérez, guère*, you are exaggerating, very little; *il n'a ~ d'amis*, he has hardly any friends; *il ne parla* ~, he spoke but little; *elle ne sort* ~, she hardly ever goes out; *cela ne durera* ~, it won't last long; *elle n'a ~ plus de trente ans*, she is scarcely more than thirty; *il n'y a ~ que vous qui puisse m'aider*, you are just about the only person who can help me.

guéret [gerɛ] *s.m.* fallow (land).

guéri, -e [geri] *adj.* cured, recovered, well again.

guéridon [geridɔ̃] *s.m.* occasional table, stand, guéridon.
guérilla [gerija] *s.f.* guerrilla warfare; band of guerrillas.
guérir [gerir] *v.t.* to cure, to heal, to restore to health; (fig.) to help to recover, to remedy, to rid, to free; *il faut le ~ de cette obsession*, we must cure him, we must help him to get rid, of this obsession; ~ *v.i.* to be cured, to recover, to get better; (fig.) *douleur qui ne guérit pas*, inconsolable grief; ~ *de*, to recover from, to get over; **se** ~ *v.refl.* to recover, to get better; (fig.) to get rid, to cure oneself, (*de*, of).
guérison [gerizɔ̃] *s.f.* recovery, cure, healing.
guérissable [gerisabl] *adj.* curable.
guérisseu-r, -se [gerisœr] *s.m.f.* healer, curer; (pej.) quack.
guérite [gerit] *s.f.* sentry-box, box, cabin (for signalman, night-watchman, crane-driver, etc.).
Guernesey [gɛrnəze] *s.m.* (geog.) Guernsey.
guerre [gɛr] *s.f.* **1.** war, hostilities, warfare; state of war; *la Guerre*, War Ministry, War Office; ~ *éclair*, lightning campaign, blitzkrieg; *grande* ~, large-scale warfare; *petite* ~, minor operations, guerrilla warfare; skirmishing; sham warfare, phoney war; ~ *froide*, cold war; *faire la ~ à* or *contre*, to make war on, to wage war against; *faire la ~ avec qn.*, to serve with or under s.o. in the war; *de* ~, war, warlike; *correspondant de* ~, war correspondent; *faits de* ~, acts of war, warlike acts; *en* ~, at war, in a state of hostility; *se mettre en* ~, to go to war; (fig.) *à la ~ comme à la* ~, we must put up with it, that's how it is, one must take the rough with the smooth; **2.** fight, strife, combat, hostility, quarrel, feud; *faire la ~ à qn. sur qch.*, to fight s.o., to have a quarrel with s.o., over sth.; to keep on at s.o. about sth.; ~ *ouverte*, open hostility; ~ *à mort*, deadly feud; *être sur le pied de ~ avec qn.*, to be at daggers drawn with s.o.; (fig.) *de ~ lasse*, from sheer weariness, for the sake of peace and quiet; *la bonne* ~, fair dealing, fair play; *de bonne* ~, honestly, straightforwardly.
guerri-er, -ère [gɛrje] *adj.* warlike, war, martial, bellicose; *s.m.f.* warrior, soldier.
guerroyer [gɛrwaje] *v.i.* to wage war; ~ *contre*, to wage war against, (fig.) to wage war on, to combat; ~ *v.t.* (obs.) to make war against.
guet [gɛ] *s.m.* watch, watching; night-patrol; *faire le* ~, to keep watch, to be on the watch; to mount guard; *avoir l'œil au* ~, to keep a sharp look-out; *l'oreille au* ~, listening intently; *crier au* ~, to call the watch, to turn out the guard; *mot du* ~, watchword, password.
guet-apens [gɛtapɑ̃] *s.m.* **1.** ambush, trap, snare; treacherous attack; *tomber dans un* ~, to fall into an ambush or a trap, to be treacherously attacked; **2.** ambushing, lying in wait; (law) *par* ~, with felonious intent; *de* ~, with premeditation.
guêtre [gɛtr] *s.m.* gaiter, legging.
guetter [gete] *v.t.* to watch or wait for, to be on the look-out for, to lie in wait for; to be waiting to pounce on; to keep an eye on.
guetteur [gɛtœr] *s.m.* watchman, watch, observer; sentry, look-out man; operator of coastguard signals.
gueulante [gœlɑ̃t] *s.f.* howl of protest, roar of applause.
gueulard, -e [gœlar] *adj., s.m.f.* loud-mouthed (person); ~ *s.m.* **1.** throat (of blast furnace); fire-door (of locomotive, etc.); **2.** (naut.) loud-hailer.
gueule [gœl] *s.f.* **1.** (of animals) mouth, jaws; (fig.) *se jeter* or *se précipiter dans la ~ du loup*, to rush into the lion's jaws; **2.** (fam.) (of persons) mouth, throat, face; appearance; (pop.) *vas-tu fermer ta* ~, just shut up; *ta* ~*!*, shut up!, pipe down!, shut your trap!; *un fort en ~, une grande* ~, a loud-mouthed person, one who is always shouting his head off; *pousser un coup de* ~, to shout or sing loudly; *s'en mettre plein la* ~, to stuff oneself full; *avoir la ~ de bois*, to have a hangover, to have a mouth like a limekiln; *une fine* ~, a gourmet; *avoir une sale* ~, to look unpleasant; *une ~ d'enterrement*, a long face. *faire la* ~, to pull a long face; *avoir la ~ enfarinée*, to be mealy-mouthed; *casser la ~ de qn.*, to bash someone's face in; *se faire casser la* ~, to get hurt, to come a cropper; (mil.) *une ~ cassée*, a soldier wounded in the face; *ce chapeau a une drôle de* ~, that hat looks funny; *avoir de la* ~, to look striking; **3.** opening, aperture, mouth (of pot, etc.); throat (of blast-furnace); muzzle (of gun).
gueule-de-loup [gœldəlu] *s.f.* (pl. *gueules-de-loup*) **1.** (bot.) snapdragon; **2.** chimney-cowl; **3.** (arch.) cyma, ogee moulding, dado, doucine.
gueulement [gœlmɑ̃] *s.m.* (fam.) shout, cry, howl.
gueuler [gœle] (fam.) *v.i.* to shout, to bellow, to bawl, to sing at the top of one's voice; to complain loudly, to protest, to be in an uproar about; ~ *v.t.* to bawl, to shout (an order, etc.).
gueules [gœl] *s.m.* (herald.) gules.
gueuleton [gœltɔ̃] *s.m.* (fam.) feast, good tuck-in, blow-out; ~**ner** [gœltɔne] *v.i.* to tuck in, to feast.
gueuse [gøz] *s.f.* (metall.) pig-iron; (pig-)-mould.
gueuser [gøze] *v.i.* to beg, to go begging; ~**ie** [gøzri] *s.f.* (obs.) beggary, mendicity; vileness, filth.
gueu-x, -se [gø] *s.m.f.* beggar, pauper; (obs.) rogue; (fam.) prostitute.
gui[1] [gi] *s.m.* (bot.) mistletoe.
gui[2] [gi] *s.m.* (naut.) boom.
guibole, guibolle [gibɔl] *s.f.* (pop.) leg.
guibre [gibr] *s.f.* (naut.) cutwater.
guiche [giʃ] *s.f.* **1.** shield strap; **2.** (pl.) side-curls, kiss-curls.
guichet [giʃɛ] *s.m.* wicket-gate, small window in a door; ticket-window or office, booking office, box-office, counter (in post-office, bank, etc.), (cashier's) desk.
guichetier [giʃtje] *s.m.* booking-clerk, cashier, counter-hand.
guidage [gidaʒ] *s.m.* guiding, guidance, centring; (aeron.) homing (by beacon, etc.), control; (techn.) guides, guide-bars.
guide[1] [gid] *s.m.* **1.** guide, leader, director, pilot; **2.** guide(book), handbook; **3.** (techn.) guide, guide-bar.
guide[2] [gid] *s.f.* (girl) Guide; (pl.) reins; *conduire à grandes ~s*, to drive at full tilt; (fig.) *mener la vie à grandes ~s*, (obs.) to waste one's substance, to ruin one's health; (mod.) to spend lavishly.
guide-âne [gidɑn] *s.m.* (pl. *guide-âne(s)*) handbook.
guideau (pl. **-x**) [gido] *s.m.* **1.** (hydr.) guide-vane; **2.** (fishing) kiddle.
guider [gide] *v.t.* to guide, to lead, to direct, to steer, to control; to advise; **se** ~ *v.refl.* to find one's way, to take one's bearings, to guide or direct oneself.
guidon [gidɔ̃] *s.m.* handlebar (of cycle); (mil.) guidon, pennant; (naut.) pennant; sight (of firearm).
guiderope [gidrɔp] *s.m.* (ballooning) trail-rope.
guignard [giɲar] *s.m.* (ornith.) dotterel.
guigne[1] [giɲ] *s.f.* heart-cherry; *se soucier de qn., de qch., comme d'une* ~, to care little or nothing for s.o., for sth.
guigne[2] [giɲ] *s.f.* (fam.) bad luck.
guigner [giɲe] *v.t.* to peep at, to spy on; to covet, to have an eye on.

guignol [giɲɔl] *s.m.* **1.** glove puppet; (fig.) ridiculous figure; (pop.) policeman; **2.** puppet-show, Punch-and-Judy show.
guignolet [giɲɔlɛ] *s.m.* a cherry liqueur.
guignon [giɲɔ̃] *s.m.* (fam.) bad luck.
guilde, gilde [gild] *s.f.* (medieval) guild; (mod.) trade association.
guillaume [gijom] *s.m.* rabbet-plane; (plasterer's) scraping-hook.
guilledou [gijdu] *s.m.* (fam.) *courir le ~*, to be after the girls, to go womanizing.
guillemet [gijmɛ] *s.m.* inverted comma, quotation mark; *entre ~s*, in inverted commas, quoted; **~er** [gijmete] *v.t.* to put in inverted commas.
guillemot [gijmo] *s.m.* (ornith.) guillemot.
guilleret, -te [gijrɛ] *adj.* sprightly, brisk, merry, lively; (of joke) broad.
guillochage [gijɔʃaʒ] *s.m.* (metalwork) engine-turning, chasing.
guilloche [gijɔʃ] *s.m.* (metalwork) chaser.
guilloch-er [gijɔʃe] *v.t.* (metalwork) to engine-turn, to chase, to guilloche; **~is** [gijɔʃi] *s.m.* guilloche; guilloche pattern; **~ure** [gijɔʃyr] *s.f.* guilloche work, chequering.
guillotine [gijɔtin] *s.f.* guillotine; *fenêtre à ~*, sash-window; ⚠ not 'guillotine' (paper trimmer).
guillotin-er [gijɔtine] *v.t.* to guillotine, to behead; **~eur** [gijɔtinœr] *s.m.* guillotiner.
guimauve [gimov] *s.f.* marshmallow (flower), marshmallow (sweet); (fig.) *une sentimentalité de ~* or *à la ~*, sickly sentiment.
guimbarde [gɛ̃bard] *s.f.* **1.** Jew's harp; third-rate guitar; **2.** (techn.) router-plane, grooving-plane; **3.** (obs.) long covered carriage; (mod.) old car, old crock, boneshaker, rattletrap.
guimpe [gɛ̃p] *s.f.* chemisette, inset; (nun's) wimple.
guindage [gɛ̃daʒ] *s.m.* (naut.) hoisting.
guindant [gɛ̃dɑ̃] *s.m.* (naut.) hoist (of sail); drop (of flag); hounding (of mast).
guindé, -e [gɛ̃de] *adj.* stiff, formal, stuck up; strained, stilted, affected, unnatural.
guindeau (pl. **-x**) [gɛ̃do] *s.m.* (naut.) windlass, winch.
guinder [gɛ̃de] *v.t.* to hoist, to hoist up; to strain, to force, to make affected or unnatural; **se ~** *v.refl.* to become affected or formal; to be stilted.
guinderesse [gɛ̃drɛs] *s.f.* (naut.) mast-rope, top-tackle pennant.
guinée [gine] *s.f.* **1.** guinea; **2.** cotton cloth for export to West Africa.
Guinée [gine] *s.f.* (geog.) Guinea; *la Nouvelle ~*, New Guinea.
guinéen, -ne [gineɛ̃] *adj.*, *s.m.f.* Guinean.
guingan [gɛ̃gɑ̃] *s.m.* (text.) gingham.
guingois [gɛ̃gwa] *s.m. de ~*, (fam.) across, obliquely; (fig.) awry, askew, wrong; *tout va de ~*, everything is going wrong.
guinguette [gɛ̃gɛt] *s.f.* country or riverside public house (esp. with garden).
guip-age [gipaʒ] *s.m.* (techn.) winding, taping, wrapping, lapping, covering; (electr.) insulation (of wire); **~er** [gipe] *v.t.* (techn.) to wind, to lap, to tape, to wrap; to produce a lace pattern (on vellum); (electr.) to insulate (wire); **~on** [gipɔ̃] *s.m.* (naut.) mop, tar-mop or -brush; **~ure** [gipyr] *s.f.* guipure; (fig.) lace-work, lace pattern.
guirlande [girlɑ̃d] *s.f.* garland, wreath, cluster; (naut.) breast-hook, fore-hook.
guise [giz] *s.f.* way, manner, guise, wise; humour, fancy, choice; *à votre ~*, as you like; *faire* or *agir à sa ~*, to do as one likes, to have one's own way; *il n'en fait qu'à sa ~*, he won't listen to advice, he does it the way he wants; *en ~ de*, by way of, instead of; ⚠ not 'guise' in senses 'appearance', 'costume'.
guitare [gitar] *s.f.* guitar.
guitariste [gitarist] *s.m.f.* guitarist, guitar-player.
guitoune [gitun] *s.f.* (mil. slang) dug-out, tent.
guivre [givr] *s.f.* serpent; (herald.) wyvern.
gummifère [gɔmifɛr] *adj.* gummiferous, gum-bearing.
gustati-f, -ve [gystatif] *adj.* gustatory.
gustation [gystɑsjɔ̃] *s.f.* tasting, gustation.
gutta-percha [gytapɛrka] *s.f.* gutta-percha.
guttural, -e, (**aux**) [gytyral] *adj.* guttural, throaty; (lang.) *consonne ~e* (or **~e** *s.f.*) guttural.
Guyane [gɥijan] *s.f.* (geog.) Guyana.
gymn-ase [ʒimnɑz] *s.m.* gymnasium; (in Germany and Switzerland) secondary grammar school; **~aste** [ʒimnast] *s.m.f.* gymnast; **~astique** [ʒimnastik] *s.f.* gymnastics; **~** *adj.* gymnastic; **~ique** [ʒimnik] *s.f.* gymnastics; *adj.* (ant.) gymnic.
gymnosperme [ʒimnɔspɛrm] *adj.* (bot.) gymnospermous; **~** *s.f.* gymnosperm.
gymnote [ʒimnɔt] *s.m.* (ichth.) gymnotus, electric eel.
gynandre [ʒinɑ̃dr] *adj.* (bot.) gynandrous.
gynécée [ʒinese] *s.f.* (ant.) gynaeceum; (bot.) gynoecium.
gynéco-logie [ʒinekɔlɔʒi] *s.f.* gynaecology; **~logique** [ʒinekɔlɔʒik] *adj.* gynaecological; **~logue** [ʒinekɔlɔg] *s.m.f.* gynaecologist.
gypaète [ʒipaɛt] *s.m.* (ornith.) bearded vulture.
gypse [ʒips] *s.m.* (geol.) gypsum; plaster of Paris.
gypseu-x, -se [ʒipsø] *adj.* gypseous.
gypsophile [ʒipsɔfil] *s.f.* (bot.) gypsophila.
gyro-compas [ʒirɔkɔ̃pa] *s.m.* gyrocompass, gyroscopic compass; **~mètre** [ʒirɔmɛtr] *s.m.* gyrometer; **~pilote** [ʒirɔpilɔt] *s.m.* automatic pilot; **~scope** [ʒirɔskɔp] *s.m.* gyroscope; **~scopique** [ʒirɔskɔpik] *adj.* gyroscopic; **~stat** [ʒirɔsta] *s.m.* gyrostat.

H

Where the initial H is aspirated the headword is preceded by an apostrophe, e.g. **'hacher.**

H, h [aʃ] *s.m.* or *f.* the letter H, h; abbrev. *hydrogène, hecto-* (as in metric system), *heure.*
'ha [ɑ, hɑ] *interj.* **1.** *ha, ha!*, ha, ha!; **2.** expression of surprise or pain.
habile [abil] *adj.* able, clever, adroit, skilful, expert; cunning; (law) qualified, competent; **~ment** [abilmɑ̃] *adv.* ably, cleverly, adroitly, skilfully, expertly.
habileté [abilte] *s.f.* skill, skilfulness, expertness, cleverness, talent; ability; capacity.
habilitation [abilitɑsjɔ̃] *s.f.* (law) qualification, enabling.
habilité [abilite] *s.f.* (law) competency, qualification; capacity.
habiliter [abilite] *v.t.* (law) to render competent, to qualify.
habillage [abijaʒ] *s.m.* dressing, preparation, cleansing, trimming, pruning; assembling, putting together; packing, wrapping, framing.
habillé, -e [abije] *adj.* dressed, fully or properly dressed; smart, elegant, dressy; *trop ~*, over dressed (for the occasion); *~ de blanc*, dressed in white, wearing white; *~e en homme*, dressed as a man, wearing man's clothes; *une robe ~e*, a smart dress, a party frock.
habillement [abijmɑ̃] *s.m.* **1.** dressing, clothing, fitting-out (with clothes, uniform); *magasin d'~*, outfitters, dress-shop; **2.** dress, clothes, costume.
habiller [abije] *v.t.* to dress, to supply (with clothing, uniform), to fit out; to cover, to wrap up; to trim, to prune, to prepare; (of clothes) to fit, to look well on; (fam.) to slander; *~ qn. de laine*, to dress s.o. in wool; *~ qn. en soldat*, to dress s.o. up as a soldier; *~ une bouteille*, to affix (labels, capsule, etc.) to a bottle; *~ une gravure*, to add titling to a print; *cette robe vous habille bien*, that dress looks well on you; **s'~** *v.refl.* to dress, to put on clothes, to dress up, to put on formal clothes; to have one's clothes made (*chez*, at); *comment t'habilles-tu?*, what are you going to wear?; *faut-il s'~?*, do we have to dress up?, must one wear evening dress?
habilleu-r, -se [abijœr] *s.m.f.* **1.** dresser (of skins), cleaner (of fish); **2.** (theatr., etc.) dresser.
habit [abi] *s.m.* **1.** dress, costume, coat; robe, attire, garb, uniform, habit; (pl.) clothes; *~ de cour*, court dress; *~ de cheval*, riding-habit; *~ de magistrat*, magistrate's robe; (fig.) *prendre l'~*, to become a priest, or monk or nun; *marchand d'~s*, old-clothes man; **2.** (full) evening dress, tails; *venir en ~*, to arrive in full evening dress.
habitabilité [abitabilite] *s.f.* **1.** habitability; **2.** (of car, lift, etc.) carrying capacity (in numbers of persons).
habitable [abitabl] *adj.* habitable, inhabitable, fit to live in.
habitacle [abitakl] *s.m.* (poet.) abode; (aeron.) cockpit; (naut.) binnacle.
habitant, -e [abitɑ̃] *s.m.f.* inhabitant, occupier; local population; (pl.) inhabitants, population; (poet.) denizens; *l'~ d'une maison*, the occupier of a house; *loger chez l'~*, to lodge with a local family; *recensement des ~s*, population census.
habitat [abita] *s.m.* habitat, environment.
habitation [abitɑsjɔ̃] *s.f.* **1.** housing; (law) cohabitation; occupancy (of house, etc.); inhabiting; *conditions d'~*, housing conditions; **2.** house, flat, etc., dwelling, residence, accommodation, lodging, abode; *changer d'~*, to move house.
habité, -e [abite] *adj.* inhabited.
habiter [abite] *v.i.* to live; *~ à la campagne, en France*, to live in the country, in France; *~ chez des amis*, to live with friends; *~ avec qn.*, to live with s.o. (esp. as man and wife); *~ v.t.* to live in, to inhabit, to occupy; *~ la campagne, Paris*, to live in the country, in Paris.
habitude [abityd] *s.f.* **1.** habit, custom, practice, usage; *d'~*, usually, normally, ordinarily; *par ~*, by force of habit; (*comme*) *à son ~*, *selon* or *suivant son ~*, as was his wont, as he usually did; *avoir ~ de*, to be in the habit of, to be accustomed to; *les ~s de l'endroit*, the local customs; **2.** familiarity, use, practice, skill, knack; *avoir l'~ du malheur*, to be inured to misfortune; *avoir l'~ des enfants*, to be used to children; *c'est une question d'~*, it's a matter of getting used to it; it's a question of practice; *l'~ du métier*, professional skill or expertise; *je n'ai pas l'~ de cette voiture*, I haven't learnt to manage this car.
habitué, -e [abitɥe] *s.m.f.* habitué, regular customer.
habituel, -le [abitɥɛl] *adj.* habitual, customary, usual, wonted; **~lement** [abitɥɛlmɑ̃] *adv.* usually, generally, normally, most often.
habituer [abitɥe] *v.t.* to habituate, to accustom, to make familiar, to inure; *être habitué à*, to be in the habit of, to be accustomed to; **s'~** *v.refl.* to get accustomed, to accustom oneself, to get used (*à*, to), to become familiar (*à*, with).
'hâblerie [ɑbləri] *s.f.* boasting, bragging.
'hâbleu-r, -se [ɑblœr] *adj.* boastful, boasting, bragging; *s.m.f.* boaster, braggart.
'hachage [aʃaʒ] *s.m.* chopping, cutting.
'hache [aʃ] *s.f.* axe; *~ à main*, hatchet; *~ de bûcheron*, felling-axe; *~ d'armes*, battle-axe; (fig.) *fait* or *taillé à coups de ~*, rough-hewn, rugged, in rough and ready fashion; *porter la ~ dans*, to wield the axe in, to make sweeping reforms or economies in, (an organization, etc.); *enterrer la ~ de guerre*, to bury the hatchet; *périr sous la ~*, to die on the scaffold.
'haché, -e [aʃe] *adj.* minced; (fig.) jerky, staccato, in short sentences; *~ s.m.* mince.
'hache-légumes [aʃlegym] *s.m.* vegetable shredder; **~ment** [aʃmɑ̃] *s.m.* = 'HACHAGE; **~-paille** [aʃpɑj] *s.m.* chaff-cutter.
'hacher [aʃe] *v.t.* to chop, to hack, to mince, to hash, to cut up, to cut to pieces; to make a mess of; to trim, to shave down (a plank); (drawing) to cross-hatch, to hachure; (fig.) to interrupt, to punctuate (speech, etc.); *~ menu*, to chop fine; (fig.) *~ menu comme chair à pâté*, to make mincemeat of; *se faire ~*, (mil.) to be cut to pieces, to be mown down; (fig.) to go through fire and water (for s.o.), to suffer any fate (rather than).
'hachereau (pl. **-x**) [aʃro] *s.m.* hatchet.
'hachette [aʃɛt] *s.f.* hatchet.
'hachis [aʃi] *s.m.* hash, mincemeat, forcemeat.
'hachish [aʃiʃ] *s.m.* = 'HASCHISCH.
'hachoir [aʃwar] *s.m.* **1.** chopping-knife, cleaver, mincer; **2.** chopping-board.
'hachure [aʃyr] *s.f.* (drawing) cross-hatching,

hachure, shading; (metalwork) scoring; streak, stripe.
'hachurer [aʃyre] *v.t.* (drawing) to cross-hatch, to hachure, to shade; (metalwork) to score, to stripe.
'haddock [adɔk] *s.m.* haddock.
'hadji [adʒi] *s.m.* hadji.
'hagard, -e [agar] *adj.* haggard, wild-looking.
hagio-graphe [aʒjɔgraf] *adj.* hagiographic; *s.m.f.* hagiographer; **~graphie** [aʒjɔgrafi] *s.f.* hagiography; **~graphique** [aʒjɔgrafik] *adj.* hagiographic.
'haie [ɛ] *s.f.* **1.** hedge; hedgerow, fence, hurdle; line, row, hedge, (of people lining route); *~ vive*, quickset hedge; *faire, former, la ~*, to stand in a line; *entourer d'une ~*, to hedge in, to fence in; **2.** beam (of plough).
'haillon [ɑjɔ̃] *s.m.* rag, tatter; *en ~s*, or *vêtu, couvert de, ~s*, in rags (and tatters), ragged, tattered.
'haillonneu-x, -se [ɑjɔnø] *adj.* tattered, in rags.
'haine [ɛn] *s.f.* hatred, hate, abhorrence; *en ~ de, par ~ de*, out of hatred of, through aversion to.
'haineu-x, -se [ɛnø] *adj.* malevolent, vindictive, full of hate; inspired by hatred; **~sement** [ɛnøzmɑ̃] *adv.* malevolently, vindictively, out of hate; ⚠ not 'hateful(ly)' in sense 'odious(ly)'.
'haïr [air] *v.t.* to hate, to loathe.
'haire [ɛr] *s.f.* hair shirt; (text.) haircloth, rough sackcloth.
'haïssable [aisabl] *adj.* heinous, odious, hateful, detestable.
Haïti [aiti] *s.m.* (geog.) Haiti.
haïtien, -ne [aisjɛ̃] *adj., s.m.f.* Haitian, of Haiti.
'halage [alaʒ] *s.m.* towage, towing, hauling; (*chemin de*) ~, towpath.
'halbran [albrɑ̃] *s.m.* young wild duck.
'hâle [ɑl] *s.m.* sunburn; (obs.) weather which dries and withers plants.
'hâlé, -e [ɑle] *adj.* sunburnt, tanned, swarthy; (obs.) dried-up, withered, blasted.
haleine [alɛn] *s.f.* breath, wind; *hors d'~*, winded, out of breath; *perdre ~*, to get out of breath; *courir à perdre ~*, to run till one is out of breath; *reprendre ~*, to get one's breath, to draw breath; (fig.) to have a rest, to take a breather; *l'~ courte*, shortness of breath; *avoir l'~ courte*, to be short of breath, to be short-winded; (fig.) *un travail de longue ~*, a lengthy, or long-term, operation; *d'une* (*seule*) ~, in one breath, at one go; *tenir qn. en ~*, to keep s.o. awake, or on his toes; to keep s.o. in suspense.
halener [alne] *v.t.* (hunt.) to scent.
'haler [ale] *v.t.* to haul, to tow.
'hâler [ɑle] *v.t.* to burn, to tan; (obs.) to dry up, to wither.
'haletant, -e [altɑ̃] *adj.* out of breath, winded, breathless, panting.
'halètement [alɛtmɑ̃] *s.m.* panting, puffing, gasping.
'haleter [alte] *v.i.* to pant, to gasp for breath, to puff; (fig.) to hold one's breath, to be in suspense.
'haleur [alœr] *s.m.* hauler, boat-tower.
halitueu-x, -se [alitɥø] *adj.* moist, clammy, halituous.
'hall [ol] *s.m.* entrance hall (of large building); (in factory, etc.) *~ d'assemblage*, assembly shop.
'hallage [alaʒ] *s.m.* market dues.
hallali [alali] *s.m.* (stag-hunt.) halloo, tally-ho; death of the stag.
'halle [al] *s.f.* market hall, market; *langage des ~s*, billingsgate.
'hallebarde [albard] *s.f.* (hist.) halberd; *il tombe des ~s*, it's raining cats and dogs.
'hallebardier [albardje] *s.m.* (hist.) halberdier.
'hallier [alje] *s.m.* thicket.
hallucinant, -e [al(l)ysinɑ̃] *adj.* (med.) hallucinating, producing hallucinations; (fig.) deceptive, evocative, haunting.
hallucination [al(l)ysinɑsjɔ̃] *s.f.* hallucination delusion.
halluciné, -e [al(l)ysine] *adj., s.m.f.* (person) suffering from hallucinations.
hallucinogène [al(l)ysinɔʒɛn] *adj.* hallucinogenic.
'halo [alo] *s.m.* halo.
'halogène [alɔʒɛn] *adj.* (chem.) halogenous.
'haloïde [alɔid] *s.m., adj.* (chem.) haloid.
'hâloir [ɑlwar] *s.m.* drying-room for hemp.
'halte [alt] *s.f.* halt, halting-place; *faire ~*, to stop, to make a halt, to halt; *~! ~ là!*, stop! halt!
haltère [altɛr] *s.m.* dumb-bell.
'hamac [amak] *s.m.* hammock.
hamadryade [amadrijad] *s.f.* (myth.) hamadryad, wood-nymph.
hamadryas [amadrijɑs] *s.m.* (zool.) hamadryad, Abyssinian baboon.
hamamélis [amamelis] *s.m.* (bot.) witch-hazel.
'Hambourg [ɑ̃bur] *s.m.* (geog.) Hamburg.
'hambourgeois, -e [ɑ̃burʒwa] *adj., s.m.f.* (native or inhabitant) of Hamburg, Hamburger.
'hameau (pl. **-x**) [amo] *s.m.* hamlet.
hameçon [amsɔ̃] *s.m.* hook, fish-hook; (fig.) bait; *mordre à l'~*, to take the bait.
'hampe[1] [ɑ̃p] *s.f.* pole (of flag), flagstaff; shaft (of spear, etc.); (zool.) shaft (of feather); (arch.) shaft (of column); (bot.) stem; (bot., ent., arch.) scape; downstroke (in writing).
'hampe[2] [ɑ̃p] *s.f.* (hunt.) breast (of stag); (butch.) thin flank of beef.
'hamster [amstɛr] *s.m.* (zool.) hamster.
'han [ɑ̃, hɑ̃] *s.m.* han (guttural grunt uttered when striking a heavy blow).
'hanap [anap] *s.m.* (hist.) hanap, goblet, tankard.
'hanche [ɑ̃ʃ] *s.f.* hip; (of horses, etc.) haunch, (pl.) hindquarters; (naut.) quarter (of ship); *les poings sur les ~s*, hands on hips, arms akimbo.
'handicap [ɑ̃dikap] *s.m.* handicap; **~er** [ɑ̃dikape] *v.t.* to handicap; **~eur** [ɑ̃dikapœr] *s.m.* handicapper.
'handicapé, -e [ɑ̃dikape] *adj., s.m.f.* handicapped (person).
'hangar [ɑ̃gar] *s.m.* shed, outhouse, lean-to, shanty; (aeron.) hangar.
'hanneton [antɔ̃] *s.m.* (ent.) cockchafer, may-bug; *~ des roses* or *des jardins*, rose-beetle, rose-chafer; *étourdi comme un ~*, as mad as a hatter; (fig., fam.) *qui n'est pas piqué des ~s*, in full force, the genuine article; *un petit froid qui n'est pas piqué des ~s*, a real touch of cold; **~nage** [antɔnaʒ] *s.m.* (agric.) clearing (an area) of cockchafers; **~ner** [antɔne] *v.t.* (agric.) to clear of cockchafers.
'Hanovre [anɔvr] *s.m.* (geog.) Hanover.
'hanovrien, -ne [anɔvrjɛ̃] *adj., s.m.f.* Hanoverian.
'hanse [ɑ̃s] *s.f.* (hist.) Hanse; *la Hanse*, the Hanse Towns, the Hanseatic League.
'hanséatique [ɑ̃seatik] *adj.* Hanseatic.
'hanté, -e [ɑ̃te] *adj.* haunted.
'hanter [ɑ̃te] *v.t.* (lit.) to haunt; to frequent, to keep company with, to hang around, (people or places); (fig.) to haunt, to obsess.
'hantise [ɑ̃tiz] *s.f.* **1.** obsession, preoccupation, (*de*, with); **2.** (obs.) frequenting, associating with (people).
haploïde [aplɔid] *adj.* (biol.) haploid.
'happe [ap] *s.f.* cramp, cramp-iron; (on cart) clout (of axle).
'happement [apmɑ̃] *s.m.* **1.** catching, snapping up; **2.** adhering, sticking.
'happer [ape] *v.t.* to catch, to seize, to snap up; *être happé par un train*, to be caught (and hit) by a train.

'haquenée [akne] *s.f.* hack; (obs.), quiet riding-horse for ladies.
'haquet [akɛ] *s.m.* dray.
'harangue [arɑ̃g] *s.f.* speech, harangue, address, oration.
'haranguer [arɑ̃ge] *v.t.* to harangue, to address, to deliver a harangue.
'harangueu-r, -se [arɑ̃gœr] *s.m.f.* (obs.) orator, tub-thumper; (Lit.) one who makes interminable speeches.
'haras [arɑ] *s.m.* (horse-breeding) stud, stud-farm.
'harrassant, -e [arasɑ̃] *adj.* tiring, fatiguing.
'harasse [aras] *s.f.* open-sided crate (for glass-ware, etc.), skip.
'harassement [arasmɑ̃] *s.m.* wearying; fatigue, exhaustion.
'harasser [arase] *v.t.* (obs. exc. in p.p.) *être harassé de travail*, to be worn out with work.
'harcelant, -e [arsəlɑ̃] *adj.* harassing, tormenting, worrying, nagging; (of work, etc.) urgent; (of creditors) persistent.
'harcèlement [arsɛlmɑ̃] *s.m.* worrying, harassing, tormenting, badgering.
'harceler [arsəle] *v.t.* to harass, to torment, to harry, to badger, to pursue, to nag at.
'harde [ard] *s.f.* **1.** herd (of deer), flock; **2.** (hunt.) leash.
'harder [arde] *v.t.* (hunt.) to leash, to couple, (hounds).
'hardes [ard] *s.f.pl.* **1.** (obs.) (law) clothing, personal effects; **2.** (pej.) old clothes, rags.
'hardi, -e [ardi] *adj.* bold; audacious, rash; enterprising, determined, courageous; daring, impudent, risqué; *~!*, well done!, keep going!; **~ment** [ardimɑ̃] *adv.* boldly, fearlessly, recklessly; impudently; ⚠ not 'hardy'.
'hardiesse [ardjɛs] *s.f.* boldness, daring, fearlessness, intrepidity; hardihood, impudence, rashness, freedom, licence.
'harem [arɛm] *s.m.* harem.
'hareng [arɑ̃] *s.m.* herring; *~ doux*, kipper; *~ saur*, (lit.) red-herring; *serrés comme des ~s*, packed like sardines; **~aison** [arɑ̃gɛzɔ̃] *s.f.* herring-fishing; herring-season; **~ère** [arɑ̃ʒɛr] *s.f.* fish-woman, (lit. & fig.) fishwife; **~uet** [arɑ̃gɛ] *s.m.* sprat; **~uier** [arɑ̃gje], **~ueux** [arɑ̃gø] *s.m.* herring-boat.
'hargne [arɲ] *s.f.* peevishness, grumpiness, bad temper, spitefulness.
'hargneu-x, -se [arɲø] *adj.* peevish, bad-tempered, cantankerous, spiteful.
'haricot [ariko] *s.m.* **1.** bean, kidney bean, haricot bean; *~s blancs*, haricot beans; *~s grimpants*, runner beans; *~s verts*, French beans; **2.** (cook) *~ de mouton*, mutton stew.
'haridelle [aridɛl] *s.f.* worn-out old horse, nag.
harmonica [armɔnika] *s.m.* harmonica; *~ à bouche*, mouth-organ.
harmonie [armɔni] *s.f.* harmony; (fig.) concord, harmony, peace; harmoniousness, regularity, balance, unity; accordance, conformity; *être en ~ avec*, to be in keeping with, to be in accordance or conformity with; *~ d'un visage*, regularity of features; *~ d'une composition*, balance of a composition.
harmonieu-x, -se [armɔnjø] *adj.* harmonious, melodious, harmonizing; coherent, balanced, well-ordered; **~sement** [armɔnjøzmɑ̃] *adv.* harmoniously, in harmony; peaceably, in a balanced or orderly way.
harmonique [armɔnik] *adj.* harmonic; *~ s.m.* or *f.* harmonic, overtone; **~ment** [armɔnikmɑ̃] *adv.* harmonically.
harmonisation [armɔnizɑsjɔ̃] *s.f.* harmonization, harmonizing.
harmoniser [armɔnize] *v.t.* to harmonize; to match, to balance, to co-ordinate; to conciliate; **s'~** *v.refl.* to harmonize, to be in accordance or agreement, to match.
harmoniste [armɔnist] *s.m.* (mus.) harmonist.
harmonium [armɔnjɔm] *s.m.* harmonium.
'harnachement [arnaʃmɑ̃] *s.m.* harness, saddlery; equipment; trappings; (fig.) cumbersome equipment.
'harnacher [arnaʃe] *v.t.* to harness; to equip, to rig out; **se ~** *v.refl.* (of soldier, etc.) to put on one's equipment.
'harnais [arnɛ] *s.m.* harness, trappings; armour, equipment; harness or mounting (of loom); (mech.) *~ d'engrenages*, train of gears; (fig.) *blanchi sous le ~* or *harnois*, grown grey in the service.
'haro [aro] *s.m.* hue and cry; *crier ~ sur qn.*, to denounce s.o.
harpagon [arpagɔ̃] *s.m.* miser, skinflint.
'harpail *s.m.*, **'harpaille** *s.f.* [arpaj] herd of young hinds and deer.
'harpaye [arpɛj] *s.f.* (ornith.) moor-buzzard, marsh-harrier.
'harpe[1] [arp] *s.f.* harp; (moll.) harp-shell.
'harpe[2] [arp] *s.f.* **1.** toothing (in masonry); **2.** hook (implement).
'harpie [arpi] *s.f.* harpy; (fig.) shrew; (ornith.) harpy-eagle.
'harpiste [arpist] *s.m.f.* harpist.
'harpon [arpɔ̃] *s.m.* harpoon; spear; grappling-iron; (techn.) cramp-iron; **~nage** [arpɔnaʒ], **~nement** [arpɔnmɑ̃] *s.m.* harpooning; **~ner** [arpɔne] *v.t.* to harpoon; (fig.) to catch hold of, to lay hands on; **~neur** [arpɔnœr] *s.m.* harpooner.
'hart [ar] *s.f.* **1.** withe, binder for faggots; **2.** rope, halter; *mériter la ~*, to deserve hanging.
'hasard [azar] *s.m.* **1.** chance, luck, accident, coincidence; *jeu de ~*, game of chance; *coup de ~*, chance occurrence, stroke of fortune, piece of luck, fluke; *par un coup de ~*, by mere chance, as luck would have it; *par ~*, by accident, by chance; *par un pur ~*, by pure accident; *au ~*, at random, haphazard, at a guess, blindly; **2.** risk, danger, hazard; *au ~ de*, at the risk of; *à tout ~*, (obs.) at all events, come what may; (mod.) as a measure of precaution, for all eventualities, to be on the safe side, just in case.
'hasardé, -e [azarde] *adj.* hazardous, risky, rash.
'hasarder [azarde] *v.t.* to hazard, to risk, to venture, to stake; **se ~** *v.refl.* (obs.) to endanger oneself; (mod.) to venture.
'hasardeu-x, -se [azardø] *adj.* (obs.) foolhardy; (mod.) dangerous, unsafe, risky, hazardous, perilous.
'haschisch, 'haschich [aʃiʃ] *s.m.* hashish.
'hase [ɑz] *s.f.* doe-hare, doe-rabbit.
hast(**e**) [ast] *s.m.* (obs.) spear, lance, javelin; *arme d'~*, long-shafted weapon.
'hasté, -e [aste] *adj.* (bot.) lance-shaped.
'hâte [ɑt] *s.f.* haste, hurry, speed; precipitation, impatience; *à la ~*, in a hurry, hurriedly, hastily; *en ~*, speedily, promptly; *avoir ~*, to be in a hurry (*de*, to); *mettre de la ~ à, mettre peu de ~ à*, to be in a hurry to, to be in no hurry to; *la ~ d'en avoir terminé*, impatience to get it over, to get it done.
'hâter [ɑte] *v.t.* to hasten, to hurry (on), to advance, to put forward, to accelerate, to expedite; (hort.) to force; *~ le pas*, to quicken one's step, to hurry up; **se ~** *v.refl.* to hurry, to hasten, to make haste (*de*, to), to lose no time (*de*, in).
'hâtier [ɑtje] *s.m.*(cook.) spit-rack.
'hâti-f, -ve [ɑtif] *adj.* precocious, forward, early, premature; hasty, in too much of a hurry; **~vement** [ɑtivmɑ̃] *adv.* hastily, hurriedly.

'hauban [obɑ̃] *s.m.* (naut.) shroud; **~age** [obanaʒ] *s.m.* (aeron.) staying, bracing; **~er** [obane] *v.t.* to stay, to brace.

'haubert [obɛr] *s.m.* hauberk; coat of mail.

'hausse [os] *s.f.* **1.** raiser, heightener, prop, block; (hydr. eng.) flash-board, shutter; **2.** rise, rising, increase (esp. of prices, etc.); *en ~*, rising, increasing; (fig.) improving, looking up; (stock exchange) *jouer à la ~*, to speculate on a rise; **3.** back-sight (of rifle).

'hausse-col [oskɔl] *s.m.* (pl. *hausse-cols*) (armour) gorget, neck-piece.

'haussement [osmɑ̃] *s.m.* raising, lifting; *~ d'épaules*, shrug of the shoulders.

'hausser [ose] *v.t.* to raise, to make higher (*de*, by), to lift; *~ les épaules*, to shrug (one's shoulders); *~ v.i.* (obs.) to rise, to increase, to go up; **se ~** *v.refl.* to raise oneself, to rise; *se ~ sur la pointe des pieds*, to stand on tiptoe.

'haussier [osje] *s.m.* (stock exchange) bull, speculator on a rise.

'haussière, aussière [osjɛr] *s.f.* hawser.

'haut, -e [o] *adj.* high, lofty, tall, raised; high-class; high in price; superior; upper, higher; elevated, upright, erect, uplifted, upraised; eminent, grand; loud; remote (in time); *jeter les ~s cris*, to raise an outcry, to complain loudly; *être ~ en couleur*, to have a high colour, a florid complexion; *~s faits*, great deeds; (fig.) *de ~e volée*, in the top class; *prendre des airs trop ~s*, to be superior; *le ~ style*, elevated style; *~e mer*, high seas, open sea; *en ~e mer*, out to sea, on the high seas; *vaisseau de ~e mer*, sea-going vessel; *la main ~e*, with hand upraised (as though to strike); (fig.) *avoir la ~e main dans qch.*, to be the main instigator of sth., to be the person behind sth.; *exécuteur des ~es œuvres*, executioner; *la ~e ville*, the upper part of the town; *le ~ Niger*, the upper Niger; *le Très-Haut*, the Most High; *de ~e taille*, tall; *avoir le verbe ~*, to talk very loud; to be peremptory or arrogant in speech; *à ~e voix*, aloud; *à voix ~e*, in a loud or high voice; *viande de ~ goût*, highly-seasoned meat; *dans la plus ~e antiquité*, in very ancient times; *~ adv.* high, highly, aloft, up, at a high price, aloud; back (in time); *~ le pied*, unencumbered, unladen, (of horse, etc.) unmounted, (of rail. engine) light; *~ les mains!*, hands up!; *~ la main*, (lit.) with hand upraised, (fig.) lightly, easily, coolly; *l'emporter ~ la main*, to carry it off lightly; *personnes ~ placées*, highly-placed persons, high-up people; *parlez plus ~*, speak louder, speak up; *plus ~*, above (in text); *remonter plus ~*, to go further back (in time); *lire, penser, plus ~*, to read, to think, aloud; *rêver tout ~*, to talk in one's sleep; *condamner ~ et ferme*, to condemn utterly, out of hand; *en ~*, above, up, upstairs, at or to the top; *regarder en ~*, to look up; *d'en ~*, from above, from on high; *voir qch. de ~*, to see sth. from on top; *voir les choses de ~*, to take a detached or broad view of things; *le prendre de ~*, to be arrogant; *de ~ en bas*, from top to bottom; (fig.) haughtily, disdainfully; *par en ~*, round the top, by the upper route; upwards; *~ s.m.* **1.** height; *avoir cent mètres de ~*, to be a hundred metres high; *voler à mille mètres de ~*, to fly at a height of a thousand metres; *tomber de son ~*, to fall down flat, (fig.) to have a nasty surprise, to be knocked flat; **2.** top, upper part; (on packing case, etc.) top, this side up; (mus.) high notes; (pl.) (naut.) upper works, topsides; (geog.) uplands, heights; *des ~s et des bas*, ups and downs; *du ~ en bas*, from top to bottom.

'hautain, -ne [otɛ̃] *adj.* haughty, proud, arrogant, condescending.

'hautbois [obwɑ] *s.m.* oboe; oboe-player, oboist.

'hautboïste [obɔist] *s.m.f.* oboist.

'haut-de-chausse(s) [odʃos] *s.m.* (obs.) breeches.

'haut-de-forme [odfɔrm] *s.m.* (pl. *hauts-de-forme*) top hat.

'haute-contre [otkɔ̃tr] *adj.*, *s.m.* (pl. *hautes-contre*) (mus.) counter-tenor (singer); *s.f.* counter-tenor (voice).

'haute-fidélité [otfidelite] *adj.invar.* high-fidelity (sound equipment).

'haute-forme [otfɔrm] *s.m.* = HAUT-DE-FORME.

'hautement [otmɑ̃] *adv.* **1.** (obs.) aloud; loudly, boldly; **2.** highly.

'hautesse [otɛs] *s.f.* Highness (as title).

'hauteur [otœr] *s.f.* height, altitude, elevation, hill, loftiness, haughtiness; *~s*, heights, uplands; *à la ~ de*, on a level with, equal or up to; (naut.) in the same latitude as, off (a particular point of the coast); *il n'est pas à la ~*, he is not up to it, he is unequal to the task.

'haut-fond [ofɔ̃] *s.m.* (naut.) shoal, submerged peak.

'haut-le-cœur [olkœr] *s.m.invar.* heave (of stomach), retching, nausea.

'haut-le-corps [olkɔr] *s.m.invar.* start, bound, sudden leap.

'haut-parleur [oparlœr] *s.m.* (pl. *haut-parleurs*) loudspeaker.

'haut-relief [orəljɛf] *s.m.* (art) high relief.

'hauturi-er, -ère [otyrje] *adj.* (naut.) of the high seas; *pilote ~er*, deep-sea pilot.

'havage [avaʒ] *s.m.* (mining) undercutting.

'havanais, -e [avanɛ] *adj.*, *s.m.f.* (native) of Havana; *~ s.m.* a small dog.

'havane [avan] *s.m.* Havana cigar or tobacco; *la Havane*, Havana; *~ adj.* cigar-coloured; light brown.

'hâve [ɑv] *adj.* emaciated, wan, pale.

'haveneau (pl. **-x**) [avno] *s.m.* (fish.) purse-net.

'haver [ave] *v.t.* (mining) to undercut.

'havre [ɑvr] *s.m.* haven, harbour, port.

'havresac [avrəsak] *s.m.* knapsack, haversack, pack, tool-bag.

(**La**) **Haye** [laɛ] *s.f.* (geog.) The Hague.

'hayon [ajɔ̃] *s.m.* rear door (of van, estate-car, etc.).

'hé [e, he] *interj.* hi, there!, hullo!, I say; *~ oui!*, oh, yes!; *~! ~!*, well! well!

'heaume [om] *s.m.* helm, helmet.

hebdomadaire [ɛbdɔmadɛr] *adj.*, *s.m.* weekly (publication); **~ment** [ɛbdɔmadɛrmɑ̃] *adv.* weekly, each week, once a week.

hébergement [ebɛrʒəmɑ̃] *s.m.* lodging, sheltering.

héberger [ebɛrʒe] *v.t.* to lodge, to harbour, to entertain, to give shelter or asylum to.

hébété, -e [ebete] *adj.* dazed, stupefied, bewildered.

hébètement [ebɛtmɑ̃] *s.m.* stupefaction, bewilderment.

hébéter [ebete] *v.t.* to dull, to stupefy, to daze.

hébétude [ebetyd] *s.f.* dullness, stupidity, (med.) hebetude.

hébraïque [ebraik] *adj.* Hebraic, Hebrew.

hébraïsme [ebraism] *s.m.* Hebraism.

hébreu (pl. **-x**) [ebrø] *adj.m.*, *s.m.* Hebrew; Hebrew language; (fam.) *c'est de l'~*, it's all Greek to me.

hécatombe [ekatɔ̃b] *s.f.* hecatomb; massacre, slaughter.

hectare [ɛktar] *s.m.* hectare (=2·471 acres).

hectique [ɛktik] *adj.* (med.) hectic.

hectisie [ɛktizi] *s.f.* = ÉTISIE.

hecto [ɛkto] *s.m.* abbrev. *hectogramme*, *hectolitre*; **~gramme** [ɛktɔgram] *s.m.* hectogram; **~litre** [ɛktɔlitr] *s.m.* hectolitre; **~mètre** [ɛktɔmɛtr] *s.m.* hectometre; **~watt** [ɛktɔwat] *s.m.* hectowatt.

hédonisme [edɔnism] *s.m.* (phil.) Hedonism.

hédoniste [edɔnist] *s.m.f.*, *adj.* hedonist(ic).

hégélianisme [egeljanism] *s.m.* (phil.) Hegelianism.
hégélien, -ne [egeljɛ̃] *adj.* Hegelian.
hégémonie [eʒemɔni] *s.f.* hegemony, domination, supremacy, supreme power.
hégire [eʒir] *s.f.* Hegira.
'hein [ɛ̃, hɛ̃] *interj.* what?, eh?; *fiche-moi la paix,* ~*!*, clear off, will you!
hélas [elɑs] *interj.* alas.
'héler [ele] *v.t.* to hail, to call, to speak (a ship).
héli-anthe [eljɑ̃t] *s.m.* (bot.) helianthus, sunflower; **~anthème** [eljɑ̃tɛm] *s.m.* (bot.) Helianthemum, rock-rose; **~aque** [eljak] *adj.* (astron.) heliacal.
hélice [elis] *s.f.* **1.** helix, spiral; *en* ~, spiral, winding, corkscrew; **2.** (mech.) propeller, screw, air-screw.
hélicoïdal, -e, (aux) [elikɔidal] *adj.* helicoidal, spiral.
hélicoïde [elikɔid] *s.m.* helicoid.
hélicon [elikɔ̃] *s.m.* (mus.) helicon (kind of horn).
hélicoptère [elikɔptɛr] *s.m.* helicopter.
héligare [eligar] *s.f.* helicopter station.
hélio-centrique [eljɔsɑ̃trik] *adj.* heliocentric; **~chromie** [eljɔkrɔmi] *s.f.* heliochromy, colour photography; **~graphe** [eljɔgraf] *s.m.* **1.** heliograph; **2.** (phys.) = HÉLIOSTAT; **~graphie** [eljɔgrafi] *s.f.* heliography; (astron.) description of sun; (techn.) process engraving, photogravure; **~graveur** [eljɔgravœr] *s.m.* photogravure worker, process engraver; **~gravure** [eljɔgravyr] *s.f.* heliogravure, photogravure; **~mètre** [eljɔmɛtr] *s.m.* heliometer; **~stat** [eljɔsta] *s.m.* heliostat, heliograph; **~thérapie** [eljɔterapi] *s.f.* (med.) heliotherapy, sunlight or ultraviolet ray treatment; **~trope** [eljɔtrɔp] *s.m.* **1.** (bot.) heliotrope; **2.** (min.) bloodstone; **~tropisme** [eljɔtrɔpism] *s.m.* heliotropism.
héliport [elipɔr] *s.m.* heliport, helidrome, helicopter station.
heliporté, -e [elipɔrte] *adj.* helicopter-borne.
héli-station [elistɑsjɔ̃] *s.f.* helicopter station; **~surface** [elisyrfas] *s.f.* (temporary) helicopter landing-place.
hélium [eljɔm] *s.m.* (chem.) helium.
hélix [eliks] *s.m.* (anat., arch., zool.) helix.
hellène [elɛn] *adj.* Hellenic; *s.m.f.* Hellene.
hellénique [elenik] *adj.* Hellenic.
hellénisant, -e [ɛlenizɑ̃] *adj.* Hellenizing, speaking Hellenic Greek; *s.m.f.* Hellenist.
hellénisation [elenizɑsjɔ̃] *s.f.* hellenization.
hellénisme [elenism] *s.m.* Hellenism.
helléniste [elenist] *s.m.f.* Hellenist.
hellénistique [ɛlenistik] *adj.* Hellenistic.
helminthe [ɛlmɛ̃t] *s.m.* (zool., med.) helminth.
helvète [ɛlvɛt] *adj.* (hist.) Helvetian; *les Helvètes,* the Helvetii.
helvétique [ɛlvetik] *adj.* Swiss.
'hem [ɛm, hɛm] *interj.* hem!, ahem!, m-m!, noise of clearing the throat.
hématie [emati] *s.f.* red blood corpuscle.
hématite [ematit] *s.f.* (min.) haematite.
hémato-logie [ematɔlɔʒi] *s.f.* haematology; **~logique** [ematɔlɔʒik] *adj.* haematological; **~logiste** [ematɔlɔʒist], **~logue** [ematɔlɔg] *s.m.f.* haematologist.
hématose [ematoz] *s.f.* (physiol.) haematosis, conversion of venous blood into arterial blood.
hématurie [ematyri] *s.f.* (med.) haematuria.
hémérocalle [emerɔkal] *s.f.* (bot.) hemerocallis, day lily.
hémi-cycle [emisikl] *s.m.* hemicycle, semicircle; **~one** [emjɔn] *s.m.* (zool.) Asian wild ass, kiang, dziggetai; **~plégie** [emipleʒi] *s.f.* (pathol.) hemiplegia; **~ptère** [emiptɛr] (ent.) *adj.* hemipteral, hemipterous; *s.m.pl.* Hemiptera; **~sphère** [emisfɛr] *s.m.* hemisphere; **~-sphérique** [emisferik] *adj.* hemispherical; domed, (of screw, etc.) round-head; **~stiche** [emistiʃ] (pros.) hemistich.
hémo-globine [emɔglɔbin] *s.f.* haemoglobin; **~phile** [emɔfil] *adj., s.m.f.* haemophiliac; **~philie** [emɔfili] *s.f.* haemophilia; **~ptysie** [emɔptizi] *s.f.* (pathol.) haemoptysis, spitting of blood; **~rragie** [emɔraʒi] *s.f.* haemorrhage; (fig.) blood-letting; **~rragique** [emɔraʒik] *adj.* haemorrhagic; **~rroïde** [emɔrɔid] *s.f.* (usu. pl.) haemorrhoids, piles; **~stase** [emɔstɑz], **~stasie** [emɔstazi] *s.f.* (pathol.) haemostasia; **~statique** [emɔstatik] *adj., s.m.* haemostatic.
hendécagone [ɑ̃dekagɔn] *s.m.* hendecagon.
'henné [ene] *s.m.* henna.
'hennir [enir] *v.i.* to neigh, to whinny.
'hennissement [enismɑ̃] *s.m.* neighing, neigh.
henry [ɑ̃ri] *s.m.* (electr.) henry.
'hep [ɛp, hɛp] *interj.* hi!, I say!
hépatique [epatik] *adj.* hepatic, of the liver; ~ *s.m.f.* (one) suffering from a liver complaint; ~ *s.f.* (bot.) hepatica, liverwort.
hépatite [epatit] *s.f.* **1.** (pathol.) hepatitis; **2.** (min.) hepatite.
heptacorde [ɛptakɔrd] *s.m.* heptachord.
heptaèdre [ɛptaɛdr] *s.m.* heptahedron.
heptagonal, -e, (aux) [ɛptagɔnal] *adj.* heptagonal.
heptagone [ɛptagɔn] *s.m.* heptagon.
heptamètre [ɛptamɛtr] *s.m.* (pros.) heptameter.
héraldique [eraldik] *adj.* heraldic; ~ *s.f.* heraldry.
'héraut [ero] *s.m.* herald; (poet.) harbinger.
herbacé, -e [ɛrbase] *adj.* herbaceous.
herbage [ɛrbaʒ] *s.m.* **1.** grass, herbage; **2.** pasture.
herbag-er, -ère [ɛrbaʒe] *s.m.f.* grazier.
herbager [ɛrbaʒe] *v.t.* to graze, to pasture.
herbe [ɛrb] *s.f.* **1.** herb, plant; *mauvaise* ~, weed; *fines* ~*s*, herbs used for flavouring (e.g. parsley, chives, tarragon, chervil); ~*s potagères*, pot--herbs; **2.** grass; *en* ~, green, (of corn) unripe, in the blade; (fig.) budding, embryo; *déjeuner sur l'*~, to picnic; (bot.) *l'*~ *de la Saint-Jean*, St. John's wort, hypericum; (fig.) *avoir toutes les* ~*s de la Saint-Jean*, to be ready for any eventuality.
herbette [ɛrbɛt] *s.f.* short grass, turf, greensward.
herbeu-x, -se [ɛrbø] *adj.* grassy, grass-grown.
herbicide [ɛrbisid] *adj.* herbicidal; ~ *s.m.* herbicide, weed-killer.
herbier [ɛrbje] *s.m.* herbal; herbarium.
herbivore [ɛrbivɔr] *adj.* herbivorous; ~ *s.m.* herbivore.
herborisat-eur, -rice [ɛrbɔrizatœr] *s.m.f.* herborizer, botanizer.
herborisation [ɛrbɔrizɑsjɔ̃] *s.f.* herborizing, botanizing; plant-gathering expedition.
herborisé, -e [ɛrbɔrize] *adj.* (min.) arborized, dendritic.
herboriser [ɛrbɔrize] *v.i.* to herborize, to botanize.
herboriste [ɛrbɔrist] *s.m.f.* herbalist.
herboristerie [ɛrbɔristəri] *s.f.* herbalist's shop; herbalist trade.
herbu, -e [ɛrby] *adj.* grassy, lush; **~e** *s.f.* light pasture-land.
'hercher [ɛrʃe] *v.t.* (mining) to haul (coal, ore).
'hercheu-r, -se [ɛrʃœr] *s.m.f.* (mining) haulage--man, etc., putter.
hercule [ɛrkyl] *s.m.* Hercules, strong man; (myth.) *Hercule*, Hercules.
herculéen, -ne [ɛrkyleɛ̃] *adj.* Herculean.
'hère [ɛr] *s.m.* **1.** (obs.) wretch; (mod.) *pauvre* ~, miserable wretch, down-and-out, drop-out; **2.** young stag.
héréditaire [ereditɛr] *adj.* hereditary; **~ment**

[ereditɛrmɑ̃] *adv.* hereditarily, by inheritance, by heredity.
hérédité [eredite] *s.f.* heredity, hereditary transmission, inheritance.
hérésie [erezi] *s.f.* heresy.
hérétique [eretik] *adj.* heretical; ~ *s.m.f.* heretic.
'hérissé, -e [erise] *adj.* bristling, (of hair) standing on end; prickly, spiny; (fig.) prickly, bad-tempered, sensitive; bristling (*de*, with).
'hérissement [erismɑ̃] *s.m.* (lit. & fig.) bristling.
'hérisser [erise] *v.t.* to bristle, to erect (feathers, etc.), to ruffle, to make (hair, etc.) stand on end; to be sharp or spiky with; to equip with spikes; ~ *qch. de*, to make sth. bristle with, (fig.) to lard or pepper sth. with; ~ *qn.*, to make s.o. bristle; *clous qui hérissent une planche*, nails standing up on a board like spikes; *cela me hérisse*, it makes me bristle, it gets my back up, it makes my hackles rise; **se** ~ *v.refl.* to bristle, (of hair, etc.) to stand on end; (fig.) to bristle, to get one's back up; *se* ~ *de*, to bristle with.
'hérisson [erisɔ̃] *s.m.* hedgehog; (zool.) sea-urchin; (ichth.) porcupine-fish; (bot.) a kind of mushroom; (techn.) grapnel; row of spikes or broken glass set on a wall; portable barbed-wire obstacle; bottle-drainer; (agric.) spiked roller; (mil.) hedgehog, position armed for all-round defence; (fig.) bristly or difficult person.
héritage [eritaʒ] *s.m.* inheritance, heritage, patrimony; tradition.
hériter [erite] *v.t.* to inherit; ~ *de qn.*, to inherit someone's estate, to be someone's heir.
hériti-er, -ère [eritje] *s.m.f.* heir, heiress.
hermaphrodisme [ɛrmafrɔdism] *s.m.* hermaphroditism.
hermaphrodite [ɛrmafrɔdit] *s.m., adj.* hermaphrodite.
hermès [ɛrmɛs] *s.m.* Hermes; (art) head of Hermes, herm.
hermétique [ɛrmetik] *adj.* **1.** (obs.) hermetic, relating to alchemy; **2.** tightly closed, hermetically sealed, airtight, watertight; **~ment** [ɛrmetikmɑ̃] *adv.* hermetically, tightly, closely.
hermine [ɛrmin] *s.f.* (zool.) ermine, ermine fur; (herald.) ermine.
herminette, [ɛrminɛt] *s.f.* (carp.) adze.
'herniaire [ɛrnjɛr] *adj.* hernial; *bandage* ~, truss; ~ *s.f.* (bot.) rupturewort.
'hernie [ɛrni] *s.f.* (pathol.) hernia, rupture; protrusion, bulge, (on tyre).
héroï-comique [erɔikɔmik] *adj.* heroi-comic, mock-heroic.
héroïne [erɔin] *s.f.* **1.** heroine, heroic woman; **2.** (chem.) heroin.
héroïque [erɔik] *adj.* heroic, fearless, stoical; epic; **~ment** [erɔikmɑ̃] *adv.* heroically, stoically.
héroïsme [erɔism] *s.m.* heroism.
'héron [erɔ̃] *s.m.* (ornith.) heron; **~neau** (pl. **-x**) [erɔno] *s.m.* young heron; **~nière** [erɔnjɛr] heronry.
'héros [ero] *s.m.* hero.
herpès [ɛrpɛs] *s.m.* (pathol.) herpes.
herpétique [ɛrpetik] *adj.* (med.) herpetic.
herpétologie, erpétologie [ɛrpetɔlɔʒi] *s.f.* (zool.) herpetology.
'hersage [ɛrsaʒ] *s.m.* (agric.) harrowing.
'herse [ɛrs] *s.f.* **1.** (agric.) harrow; **2.** (fort.) herse, portcullis; **3.** (theatr.) stage lights, battens.
'herser [ɛrse] *v.t.* (agric.) to harrow.
'herseu-r, -se [ɛrsœr] *adj.* harrow; *s.m.f.* harrower; *rouleau* **~r**, harrow-roller; **~se** *s.f.* mechanical harrow.
hertz [ɛrts] *s.m.* (electr.) hertz.
hertzien, -ne [ɛrtzjɛ̃] *adj.* (electr.) Hertzian.
hésitant, -e [ezitɑ̃] *adj.* hesitating, wavering, undecided; faltering.
hésitation [ezitɑsjɔ̃] *s.f.* hesitation, uncertainty; faltering, delaying (tactics), shilly-shallying.
hésiter [ezite] *v.i.* to hesitate, to be uncertain or undecided, to waver, to falter; to delay; to hesitate for words, to stammer; ~ *à*, to hesitate to, to be reluctant to; *il n'y a pas à* ~, this is no time for hesitation, you must make up your mind quickly, we must get on with it.
'hessois, -e [ɛswa] *adj., s.m.f.* (geog.) Hessian.
hétaïre [etair] *s.f.* hetaera, hetaira.
hétéro-clite [eterɔklit] *adj.* heteroclite, mixed, varied, incongruous; strange, peculiar, unusual; **~doxe** [eterɔdɔks] *adj.* heterodox, unorthodox; **~doxie** [eterɔdɔksi] *s.f.* heterodoxy; **~dyne** [eterɔdin] *s.f., adj.* (radio) heterodyne; **~gène** [eterɔʒɛn] *adj.* heterogeneous, mixed, incongruous; **~généité** [eterɔʒeneite] *s.f.* heterogeneousness, heterogeneity; **~morphe** [eterɔmɔrf] *adj.* (sci.) heteromorphic; **~plastie** [eterɔplasti] *s.f.* (surg.) heteroplasty, grafting of tissue; **~plastique** [eterɔplastik] *adj.* heteroplastic; **~sexualité** [eterɔsɛksɥalite] *s.f.* heterosexuality.
hétérosexuel, -le [eterɔsɛksɥɛl] *adj.* heterosexual.
'hêtraie [ɛtrɛ] *s.f.* beech-groove, beech-plantation.
'hêtre [ɛtr] *s.m.* beech(-tree).
'heu [ø] *interj.* m-m!, well!, er!
heur [œr] *s.m.* good fortune; *avoir l'~ de*, to have the good fortune to, to be so fortunate as to, to have the pleasure of.
heure [œr] *s.f.* **1.** hour; time by the clock, o'clock; *quelle ~ est-il?*, what is the time?; *à quelle ~?*, at what time?; *une* ~, one hour; one o'clock; *une ~ et demie*, an hour and a half; half past one; *à deux ~s*, at two (o'clock); *cent kilomètres à l'~*, a hundred kilometres an hour; *être payé à l'~*, to be paid by the hour; *trois fois l'~*, three times an hour; ~ *locale*, local time; ~ *de bord*, ship's time; *une ~ de chemin de fer*, an hour's journey by train; *d'~ en ~*, every hour, hourly; *d'une ~ à l'autre*, within an hour; from one moment to the next; **2.** time, hour, time of day; appointed time, right time (for sth.); *à cette ~, à l'~ qu'il est*, at this time, at the present time; *à toute ~*, at any time; *à toutes ~s*, at all hours; *mettre sa montre à l'~*, to set one's watch, to put one's watch right; *arriver à l'~*, to arrive on time, at the right time, punctually; *arriver après l'~*, to arrive late; *de bonne ~*, early; *tout à l'~*, (i.) just now, a moment ago; (ii.) presently, soon, in a moment; *l'~ du dîner*, dinner-time; *l'~ de pointe*, the rush-hour; *à la première ~*, very early; at the earliest possible moment, as soon as possible; *de première ~*, original, initial; *à la bonne ~!*, good!, marvellous!, well done!; **3.** (pl.) (eccles.) prayer-book, service-book, book of hours.
heureu-x, -se [œrø] *adj.* **1.** happy, pleased, content; flourishing, prosperous; **2.** happy, lucky, fortunate, favourable; **3.** successful, that turns out well; felicitous; *s.m.f.* fortunate or lucky person; *faire un ~x*, to make s.o. happy; **~sement** [œrøzmɑ̃] *adv.* **1.** (obs.) happily, in happiness; **2.** fortunately, favourably, advantageously; **3.** successfully.
'heurt [œr] *s.m.* knock, shock, bump, collision, clash; bruise.
'heurté, -e [œrte] *adj.* harsh, abrupt, rough, jerky, uneven; with excessive contrasts.
'heurter [œrte] *v.t.* to bump into, to knock against, to collide with; to bump, to knock; (fig.) to shock, to offend; to come into opposition or conflict with, to jar against, to conflict or clash with; ~ *sa tête contre* or *à un mur*, to knock one's head against a wall; ~ *qn. de front*, to come

into direct opposition with s.o., to have a confrontation with s.o.; ~ *v.i.* **1.** (obs.) ~ *contre*, to bump or knock into, to stumble over; to strike; **2.** ~ *à*, to knock on (door, etc.); **se** ~ *v.refl.* to bump into one another, to collide; (fig.) to come into conflict; to contrast strongly; *se* ~ *contre*, to bump into; (fig.) *se* ~ *à*, to come up against, to encounter (difficulty, etc.).

'heurtoir [œrtwar] *s.m.* knocker; (techn.) catch, stop, buffer.

hexaèdre [ɛkzaɛdr] *adj.* hexahedral; ~ *s.m.* hexahedron.

hexagonal, -e, (**aux**) [ɛkzagɔnal] *adj.* hexagonal.

hexagone [ɛkzagɔn] *s.m.* hexagon.

hexamètre [ɛkzamɛtr] *s.m.* hexameter.

hiatus [jatys] *s.m.* hiatus.

hibernal, -e, (**aux**) [ibɛrnal] *adj.* wintry, hibernal.

hibernant, -e [ibɛrnɑ̃] *adj.* (zool.) hibernating.

hibernation [ibɛrnɑsjɔ̃] *s.f.* (zool.) hibernation.

hiberner [ibɛrne] *v.i.* to hibernate.

'hibou (pl. **-x**) [ibu] *s.m.* owl.

'hic [ik] *s.m.* (fam.) *voilà le* ~, that's the difficulty, there's the rub.

'hideur [idœr] *s.f.* hideousness; (fig.) repulsiveness; hideous sight.

'hideu-x, -se [idø] *adj.* hideous, repulsive; **~sement** [idøzmɑ̃] *adv.* hideously.

'hie [i] *s.f.* paving-rammer or beetle; pile-driver.

hièble [jɛbl] *s.f.* (bot.) dwarf elder, danewort.

hiémal, -e, (**aux**) (jemal) *adj.* winter, wintry.

hier [jɛr] *adv., s.m.* yesterday; (fig.) *ne dater que d'*~, to be of recent origin; *il n'est pas né d'*~, he wasn't born yesterday, he knows a thing or two.

'hiér-archie [jerarʃi] *s.f.* hierarchy; **~archique** [jerarʃik] *adj.* hierarchical; **~archiquement** [jerarʃikmɑ̃] *adv.* hierarchically; **~atique** [jeratik] *adj.* hieratic; **~atiquement** [jeratikmɑ̃] *adv.* hieratically.

hiéro-glyphe [jerɔglif] *s.m.* hieroglyph, hieroglyphic; **~glyphique** [jerɔglifik] *adj.* hieroglyphic; **~phante** [jerɔfɑ̃t] *s.m.* (ant.) hierophant, (fig.) high priest, expounder (of doctrine, etc.).

'highlander [ajlɑ̃dœr] *s.m.* (Scottish) Highlander.

'hi-han [iɑ̃] *s.m.* hee-haw; bray; *pousser des* ~*s*, to bray.

hilarant, -e [ilarɑ̃] *adj.* **1.** exhilarating; (chem.) *gaz* ~, laughing-gas; **2.** amusing, comic, mirth-provoking.

hilare [ilar] *adj.* hilarious, laughing, cheerful.

hilarité [ilarite] *s.f.* hilarity, loud laughter mirth, cheerfulness.

hile [il] *s.m.* (anat., bot.) hilum.

Himalaya [imalaja] *s.m.* (geog.) Himalaya; *les monts* ~, the Himalayas.

himalayen, -ne [imalajɛ̃] *adj.* (geog.) Himalayan; (fig.) vast, very high.

hindi [indi] *s.m.* (lang.) Hindi.

hindou, -e [ɛ̃du] *adj., s.m.f.* Hindu, Indian.

Hindoustan [ɛ̃dustɑ̃] *s.m.* (geog.) Hindustan.

hindoustani [ɛ̃dustani] *s.m.* (lang.) Hindustani.

hippique [ipik] *adj.* of horses, horse-, relating to horses; *concours* ~, horse-show.

hippisme [ipism] *s.m.* horse-racing; horse-riding, equitation.

hippo-campe [ipɔkɑ̃p] *s.m.* (myth.) hippocampus; (ichth.) hippocampus, sea-horse; **~cratique** [ipɔkratik] *adj.* (med.) Hippocratic; **~drome** [ipɔdrom] *s.m.* (ant.) hippodrome, circus; (mod.) race-course; **~griffe** [ipɔgrif] *s.m.* (myth.) hippogriff; **~mobile** [ipɔmɔbil] *adj.* horse-drawn; **~phagique** [ipɔfaʒik] *adj.* *boucherie ~phagique*, horse-butcher's; **~potame** [ipɔpɔtam] *s.m.* (zool.) hippopotamus.

hirondelle [irɔ̃dɛl] *s.f.* (ornith.) swallow; martin; ~ *des fenêtres*, house martin; ~ *de mer*, tern; ~ *de rivage*, sand martin; *une* ~ *ne fait pas le printemps*, one swallow does not make a summer.

hirsute [irsyt] *adj.* hirsute, shaggy, hairy, unkempt.

hispanique [ispanik] *adj.* Hispanic, Spanish.

hispanisme [ispanism] *s.m.* (lang.) Hispanicism, Spanish idiom.

hispano-américain, -e [ispanɔ-amerikɛ̃] *adj., s.m.f.* Hispano-American, Spanish American.

hispide [ispid] *adj.* (bot.) hispid, bristly.

'hisser [ise] *v.t.* to hoist, to haul up, to run up (a flag); **se** ~ *v.refl.* to raise oneself, to hoist oneself.

histamine [istamin] *s.f.* (biol.) histamine.

histogénèse [istɔʒenɛz] *s.f.* **1.** (physiol.) histogenesis; **2.** (med.) histogeny.

histogénie [istɔʒeni] *s.f.* = HISTOGÉNÈSE 2.

histoire [istwar] *s.f.* **1.** history; history book; **2.** story, tale, account, narrative; story, fiction, untruth, fib; ~ *naturelle*, natural history; *écrire sa propre* ~, to write one's life-story; *c'est toujours la même* ~, it's always the same old story; *ce sont des* ~*s, tout cela*, it's all a pack of lies; **3.** event, business, affair, matter; *il m'est arrivé une drôle d'*~, a funny thing happened to me; *une sale* ~, an unpleasant business; *l'*~ *des diamants*, the affair of the diamonds; *c'est* (*toute*) *une* ~, it is a long story, it is a lengthy or tiresome business; (fam.) *qu'est-ce que c'est que cette* ~*-là?*, what's all that about?; (fam.) ~ *de*, for, in order to; ~ *de rire*, just for fun, for a laugh; **4.** fuss, bother, trouble; *avoir des* ~*s avec qn.*, to have a row with s.o.; *allons, pas d'*~*s!*, don't let's have any nonsense!

histo-logie [istɔlɔʒi] *s.f.* histology; **~logique** [istɔlɔʒik] *adj.* histological; **~lyse** [istɔliz] *s.f.* histolysis.

historicité [istɔrisite] *s.f.* historicity, authenticity.

historié, -e [istɔrje] *adj.* historiated, illuminated, storied.

historien, -ne [istɔrjɛ̃] *s.m.f.* historian.

historier [istɔrje] *v.t.* to historiate, to decorate with figures, to embellish.

historiette [istɔrjɛt] *s.f.* short tale or story, anecdote.

historiographe [istɔrjɔgraf] *s.m.* historiographer.

historique [istɔrik] *adj.* historic, historical; real; ~ *s.m.* historical record, historical account; **~ment** [istɔrikmɑ̃] *adv.* historically.

histrion [istrjɔ̃] *s.m.* mountebank, clown; (pej.) comic (actor).

hitlérien, -ne [itlerjɛ̃] *adj.* Hitlerite.

hitlérisme [itlerism] *s.m.* Hitlerism.

hiver [ivɛr] *s.m.* winter.

hivernage [ivɛrnaʒ] *s.m.* **1.** wintering (of cattle, etc.); (naut.) laying up for the winter; winter harbour; (agric.) winter ploughing; winter fodder; **2.** hibernation, anaesthesia (of plants, silkworm eggs); **3.** rainy season (in tropics).

hivernal, -e, (**aux**) [ivɛrnal] *adj.* wintry, hibernal, winter.

hivernant, -e [ivɛrnɑ̃] *s.m.f.* winter (holiday) visitor.

hiverner [ivɛrne] *v.t.i.* to winter; (agric.) to plough for the winter.

H.L.M. [aʃɛlɛm] *s.m.* abbrev. *habitation à loyer modéré*, low-cost (esp. council) housing.

'hobby [ɔbi] *s.m.* hobby, pastime.

'hobereau (pl. **-x**) [ɔbro] *s.m.* **1.** (ornith.) hobby; **2.** (pej.) country squire.

'hocco [ɔko] *s.m.* (ornith.) hocco, curassow.

'hochement [ɔʃmɑ̃] *s.m.* ~ *de tête*, tossing or shaking of the head; nod.

'hochequeue [ɔʃkø] *s.m.* (ornith.) wagtail.

'hocher [ɔʃe] *v.t.* (obs.) to wag; (mod.) ~ *la tête*, to shake one's head; to nod (one's head).

'hochet [ɔʃɛ] *s.m.* child's rattle; (fig.) toy, bauble.
'hockey [ɔkɛ] *s.m.* hockey; ~ *sur glace*, ice hockey.
'hockeyeu-r, -se [ɔkejœr] *s.m.f.* hockey-player.
hoir [war] *s.m.* heir.
hoirie [wari] *s.f.* inheritance; (law) *avance* or *avancement d'*~, settlement of portion by anticipation.
holà [ɔla, hɔla] *interj.* hallo!, hi there! stop!, not so fast!; ~ *s.m. mettre le* ~ *à*, to intervene in, to check, to stop.
'holding [ɔldiŋ] *s.m.* (fin.) holding company.
'hold-up [ɔldœp] *s.m.invar.* hold-up (of bank, etc.).
'hollandais, -e [ɔlɑ̃dɛ] *adj.* Dutch; *sauce* ~*e*, hollandaise sauce; *s.m.f.* Dutchman, Dutchwoman; ~ *s.m.* Dutch (language).
'hollande [ɔlɑ̃d] *s.m.* Dutch cheese; Dutch china.
'hollande [ɔlɑ̃d] *s.f.* **1.** (text.) holland; **2.** a kind of potato; **3.** (geog.) *la Hollande*, Holland.
holocauste [ɔlɔkost] *s.m.* holocaust, burnt offering, sacrifice; sacrificial victim.
holothurie [ɔlɔtyri] *s.f.* (zool.) holothurian.
'homard [ɔmar] *s.m.* lobster.
hombre [ɔ̃br] *s.m.* ombre (card-game).
homélie [ɔmeli] *s.f.* homily; (pej.) tedious sermon, lecture.
homéo-pathe [ɔmeɔpat] *s.m.f.* homoeopath; **~pathie** [ɔmeɔpati] *s.f.* homoeopathy; **~-pathique** [ɔmeɔpatik] *adj.* homoeopathic.
homérique [ɔmerik] *adj.* Homeric.
homicide [ɔmisid] *s.m.f.* (Lit.) homicide, murderer, murderess; ~ *s.m.* homicide, murder; ~ *adj.* homicidal, murderous, murdering.
hominidé [ɔminide] *s.m.* (zool.) hominid.
hommage [ɔmaʒ] *s.m.* homage, respect; tribute, credit, token of esteem; (pl.) respects, compliments; *rendre* ~ *à*, to render homage to, to do homage to, to pay tribute to, to give credit to; *faire* ~ *de qch. à qn.*, to offer sth. to s.o. as a token of esteem; ~ *de l'auteur*, with the author's compliments; *présenter ses* ~*s à*, to pay one's respects to.
hommasse [ɔmas] *adj.* (of woman) mannish.
homme [ɔm] *s.m.* **1.** (opp. God or animal) man, mankind, human being; *tous les* ~*s*, all men, all mankind; *les caractères de l'*~, the characteristics of man; *digne du nom d'*~, worthy of the name of man; **2.** (individual) man; *agir comme un seul* ~, to act as one (man); *trois* ~*s sont morts*, three men died; **3.** (type of) man; *un* ~ *de peu*, a worthless or insignificant man; *être* ~ *à*, to be capable of; *être l'*~ *à*, to be the sort of man to; **4.** (opp. woman, coward, or boy); *se montrer un* ~, to show oneself a man; *l'âge d'*~, manhood, man's estate; **5.** (subordinate of master, lord, employer, (ship's) captain, officer, etc.) man, servant, vassal, hand; (pl.) crew, other ranks; (naut.) *les* ~*s* (*d'équipe*), the crew, the hands, the ship's company; *le caporal et ses* ~*s*, the corporal and his men.
homme-grenouille [ɔmgrənuj] *s.m.* frogman; **~-orchestre** [ɔmɔrkɛstr] *s.m.* one-man band; **~-sandwich** [ɔmsɑ̃dwitʃ] *s.m.* sandwich-man.
homo-centrique [ɔmɔsɑ̃trik] *adj.* homocentric; **~gène** [ɔmɔʒɛn] *adj.* homogeneous; **~-généisation** [ɔmɔʒeneizasjɔ̃] *s.f.* homogenization; **~généiser** [ɔmɔʒeneize], **~généifier** [ɔmɔʒeneifje] *v.t.* to homogenize; **~généité** [ɔmɔʒeneite] *s.f.* homogeneity, homogeneousness; **~graphe** [ɔmɔgraf] *s.m.* (lang.) homograph; **~greffe** [ɔmɔgrɛf] *s.f.* (biol.) homograft; **~logation** [ɔmɔlɔgasjɔ̃] *s.f.* homologation, confirmation, ratification; **~logue** [ɔmɔlɔg] *adj.* homologous, equivalent; *s.m.* homologue; **~loguer** [ɔmɔlɔge] *v.t.* to homologate, to confirm, to ratify; to grant probate; **~nyme** [ɔmɔnim] (lang.) *adj.* (i.) homonymous, having the same name; (ii.) = HOMOPHONE *adj.*; *s.m.* homonym, person or place of the same name; **~nymie** [ɔmɔnimi] *s.f.* homonymy; **~phone** [ɔmɔfɔn] *adj.* (phon.) homophonous, having the same sound; *s.m.* homophone; **~phonie** [ɔmɔfɔni] *s.f.* homophony; **~sexualité** [ɔmɔsɛksɥalite] *s.f.* homosexuality.
homosexuel, -le [ɔmosɛksɥɛl] *adj.*, *s.m.f.* homosexual.
homuncule, homoncule [ɔmɔ̃kyl] *s.m.* homunculus, dwarf.
'hongre [ɔ̃gr] *adj.* gelded; ~ *s.m.* gelding.
'hongrer [ɔ̃gre] *v.t.* to geld.
'Hongrie [ɔ̃gri] *s.f.* (geog.) Hungary.
'hongrois, -e [ɔ̃grwɑ] *adj.*, *s.m.f.* Hungarian.
honnête [ɔnɛt] *adj.* **1.** honest, upright; honourable; trustworthy, faithful; decent, respectable, virtuous; *un* ~ *homme*, or *un homme* ~, an honest man, an honourable man; **2.** reasonable, satisfactory, acceptable; *faire un repas* ~, to have a decent or satisfactory meal; **3.** well-bred, courteous, polite, civil, well-mannered; (obs.) *un* ~ *homme*, a gentleman; *vous êtes trop* ~, you are too kind, that is most civil of you; **~ment** [ɔnɛtmɑ̃] *adv.* **1.** honestly, honourably, faithfully; frankly; **2.** reasonably, satisfactorily; **3.** courteously, civilly, politely.
honnêteté [ɔnɛtəte] *s.f.* **1.** honesty, uprightness, probity, integrity, good faith, trustworthiness; decency, seemliness, virtue; **2.** courtesy, civility, politeness; act of politeness, attention, obligingness.
honneur [ɔnœr] *s.m.* **1.** honour, virtue; (pl.) honours, privileges; respects, compliments; (cards) honours; *un point d'*~, a point of honour; *se faire un point d'*~ *de*, to be scrupulous about; *affaire d'*~, affair of honour; duel; (*je le jure*) *sur l'*~, (I swear) on my honour; **2.** honour, glory, esteem, credit; *en* ~, honoured, respected; in fashion; *mourir au champ d'*~, to die on the field of battle; *à vous l'*~*!*, your turn to begin!; *sauf votre* ~, with all due respect; *c'est lui faire trop d'*~, that is giving him too much credit, that is over-rating him; *à tout seigneur tout* ~, to every man his due; *en l'*~ *de*, in honour of, to celebrate; (fam.) *en quel* ~ *tout cela?*, for whose benefit is all this?, what's all this in aid of?; (at wedding) *garçon d'*~, *demoiselle d'*~, best man, bridesmaid; *escalier d'*~, grand staircase; *prix d'*~, top prize, supreme award; *faire* ~ *à*, to honour, to respect, to do honour to, to be a credit to; *se faire* ~ *de*, to be proud of, to glory in; ~*s militaires*, military honours, salute of guns; (mil. etc.) *faire les* ~*s*, to present arms, to pay compliments; (naut.) *faire* ~ *à une terre*, or *ranger une terre à l'*~, to pass very close to land.
'honnir [ɔnir] *v.t.* to brand, to disgrace, to cover with shame; *honni soit qui mal y pense*, evil be to him who evil thinks.
honorabilité [ɔnɔrabilite] *s.f.* honourableness, respectability.
honorable [ɔnɔrabl] *adj.* honourable, respectable, creditable; **~ment** [ɔnɔrabləmɑ̃] *adv.* honourably, respectably, creditably.
honoraire [ɔnɔrɛr] *adj.* honorary; **~s** *s.m.pl.* honorarium, fee, fees, emoluments, stipend.
honorer [ɔnɔre] *v.t.* to honour, to pay honour to, to do credit to, to be an honour to; *s'*~ *de*, to be proud of, to be proud to.
honorifique [ɔnɔrifik] *adj.* honorary, honorific; *à titre* ~, honorary, honoris causa.
'honte [ɔ̃t] *s.f.* shame, disgrace, humiliation; confusion, embarrassment; *c'est une* ~, it is disgraceful, it is a scandal; *fausse* ~, self-consciousness, bashfulness; *avoir* ~, to be ashamed (*de*, of, to); *avoir toute* ~ *bue*, to have

become utterly shameless; *faire ~ à*, to shame, to disgrace.
'honteu-x, -se [ɔ̃tø] *adj.* shameful, disgraceful, disreputable; ashamed, abashed, looking foolish; *un pauvre ~x*, a poor man, ashamed to beg; *un communiste ~x*, a crypto-communist; **~sement** [ɔ̃tøzmɑ̃] *adv.* shamefully, disgracefully, in disgrace, with ignominy.
hôpital (pl. **aux**) [ɔpital] *s.m.* hospital.
hoplite [ɔplit] *s.m.* (Gr. ant.) hoplite.
'hoquet [ɔkɛ] *s.m.* hiccup; (fig.) snag.
horaire [ɔrɛr] *adj.* horary, relating to hours; ~ *s.m.* time-table.
'horde [ɔrd] *s.f.* horde, rabble.
'horion [ɔrjɔ̃] *s.m.* (usu. pl.) blow(s).
horizon [ɔrizɔ̃] *s.m.* horizon, skyline, level; (fig.) outlook.
horizontal, -e, (**aux**) [ɔrizɔ̃tal] *adj.* horizontal; **~ement** [ɔrizɔ̃talmɑ̃] *adv.* horizontally.
horloge [ɔrlɔʒ] *s.f.* clock (usu. on public building); *une régularité d'~*, clockwork regularity.
horlog-er, -ère [ɔrlɔʒe] *adj.* clock and watch making; **~er** *s.m.* clockmaker, watchmaker.
horlogerie [ɔrlɔʒri] *s.f.* horology, clock and watch making; clockmaker's shop; *pièces d'~*, clock or watch parts.
hormis [ɔrmi] *prep.* except, but, save, with the exception of.
hormonal, -e, (**aux**) [ɔrmɔnal] *adj.* hormonal, hormonic.
hormone [ɔrmɔn] *s.f.* (biol.) hormone.
hormonothérapie [ɔrmɔnɔterapi] *s.f.* hormone treatment.
horodateur [ɔrɔdatœr] *s.m.* time-and-date stamping machine.
horoscope [ɔrɔskɔp] *s.m.* horoscope.
horreur [ɔrœr] *s.f.* **1.** horror, revulsion, repugnance, disgust, abhorrence, detestation; *avoir ~ de*, to have a horror of, to abhor, to detest, to abominate; to be averse to; *faire ~*, to horrify, to disgust; **2.** horror, horrible deed, atrocity; horrible sight, monstrosity; (pl.) horrible words, evil stories; *commettre des ~s*, to commit atrocities; (fam.) *quelle ~!*, what a ghastly sight!; *il a dit des ~s à ton sujet*, he has been saying dreadful things about you.
horrible [ɔribl] *adj.* horrible, hideous, dreadful, awful, shocking, frightful; **~ment** [ɔribləmɑ̃] *adv.* horribly, dreadfully, awfully, shockingly, frightfully.
horrifiant, -e [ɔrifjɑ̃] *adj.* horrifying, shocking.
horrifier [ɔrifje] *v.t.* to horrify.
horrifique [ɔrifik] *adj.* (jest) horrid.
horripilant, -e [ɔripilɑ̃] *adj.* annoying, irritating.
horripilation [ɔripilɑsjɔ̃] *s.f.* horripilation, goose-flesh; (fig.) irritation, revulsion.
horripiler [ɔripile] *v.t.* (lit. & fig.) to make (someone's) hair stand on end; (fig.) to irritate, to exasperate.
'hors [ɔr] *adv.* out, outside; ~ *prep.* out of, outside, without, beside, save, except; ~ *de*, out of, beyond; ~ *d'ici!*, away with you!; ~ *de là*, beyond that, otherwise, without it; ~ *de chez soi*, away from home; *être ~ de soi*, to be beside oneself; ~ *d'affaire, de danger*, out of danger; ~ *de combat*, out of action, disabled; ~ *d'haleine*, out of breath, breathless; ~ *ligne*, out of the ordinary, uncommon; unrivalled, matchless, incomparable; ~ *de prix*, fantastically dear; ~ *de service*, retired (from service), out of service, out of action, not working; unfit for service or use; **~-bord** [ɔrbɔr] *s.m.invar.* boat with outboard motor; **~-concours** [ɔrkɔ̃kur] *s.m.invar., adj.* (one who is) disqualified, ineligible; unmatched; **~-d'œuvre** [ɔrdœvr] *s.m.invar.* **1.** (arch.) annexe, outwork; (fig.) extraneous or irrelevant matter; **2.** (cook.) hors d'œuvre, starter.
'hors-jeu [ɔrʒø] *s.m.invar.* (sport) offside; **~-la-loi** [ɔrlalwa] *s.m.invar.* outlaw; **~-texte** [ɔrtɛkst] *s.m.invar.* (bookb.) inset (plate, etc.).
hortensia [ɔrtɑ̃sja] *s.m.* (bot.) hydrangea.
horti-cole [ɔrtikɔl] *adj.* horticultural; **~culteur** [ɔrtikyltœr] *s.m.* horticulturist, gardener; **~-culture** [ɔrtikyltyr] *s.f.* horticulture, gardening.
hosanna [ɔzan(n)a] *s.m.* hosanna; (fig.) song of praise.
hospice [ɔspis] *s.m.* hospice (in monastery); home (for old people).
hospitali-er, -ère [ɔspitalje] *adj.* **1.** hospital, relating to hospitals; **2.** hospitable; **~er** *s.m.* hospitaller.
hospitalisation [ɔspitalizɑsjɔ̃] *s.f.* hospitalization, admission to hospital.
hospitaliser [ɔspitalize] *v.t.* to hospitalize, to send or admit to hospital.
hospitalité [ɔspitalite] *s.f.* hospitality, hospitableness; shelter, lodging.
hostellerie [ɔstɛlri] *s.f.* smart country hotel.
hostie [ɔsti] *s.f.* host, (consecrated) wafer; (obs.) victim, offering.
hostile [ɔstil] *adj.* hostile, unfriendly, inimical; **~ment** [ɔstilmɑ̃] *adv.* in a hostile manner.
hostilité [ɔstilite] *s.f.* hostility (*contre*, to), animosity, ill will, opposition; act of warfare.
'hot [ɔt] *adj., s.m.* hot (music).
hôte, hôtesse [ot, otɛs] *s.m.f.* **1.** host, hostess; **2.** host, landlord, innkeeper, proprietress (of inn, etc.); *table d'~*, table d'hôte or fixed menu; **3.** (*hôtesse* not used in these senses) guest, visitor; inhabitant, (poet.) denizen.
hôtel [otɛl] *s.m.* **1.** hotel; ~ *meublé*, hotel providing room but not main meals; *maître d'~*, head-waiter; **2.** (in towns) large house, mansion; *maître d'~*, butler, major-domo; **3.** public building; ~ *des Postes*, General Post Office; ~ *de Ville*, Town Hall; ~ *des Ventes*, auction mart.
hôteli-er, -ère [otəlje] *s.m.f.* hotel-keeper, hotelier, inn-keeper, landlord, landlady; *adj.* hotel-, pertaining to hotels and hotel-keeping; **~er** *s.m.* (eccles.) hosteller.
hôtellerie [otɛlri] *s.f.* **1.** (obs.) hostelry, inn; (eccles.) guest-house; **2.** = HOSTELLERIE.
'hotte [ɔt] *s.f.* basket carried on back, dosser; chimney-hood (over cooker, etc.).
'hottentot, -e [ɔtɑ̃to] *adj., s.m.f.* Hottentot.
'hou [u] *interj.* boo!
'houache [waʃ], **'houaiche** [wɛʃ] *s.f.* wake (of a ship).
'houblon [ublɔ̃] *s.m.* (bot.) hop.
'houblonni-er, -ère [ublɔnje] *adj.* hop-producing; **~er** *s.m.* hop-grower.
'houblonnière [ublɔnjɛr] *s.f.* hop-field.
'houe [u] *s.f.* hoe.
'houer [we] *v.t.* to hoe.
'houille [uj] *s.f.* coal, pit-coal; ~ *blanche*, hydro-electric power; ~ *verte*, power from waves or tides.
'houill-er, -ère [uje] *adj.* coal; *terrain ~er*, coal-field.
'houillère [ujɛr] *s.f.* colliery, coal-mine.
'houle [ul] *s.f.* swell, surge, billows; (fig.) billowing, rolling contours.
'houlette [ulɛt] *s.f.* **1.** (shepherd's) crook; (eccles.) crozier; **2.** (hort.) trowel, spud.
'houleu-x, -se [ulø] *adj.* swelling, rough, rolling; (fig.) stormy.
'houp [up, hup] *interj.* off!, get going!
'houppe [up] *s.f.* tuft, crest, top-knot, puff; ~ *à poudre*, powder-puff.
'houppelande [uplɑ̃d] *s.f.* (obs.) overcoat, greatcoat, surcoat.
'houpper [upe] *v.t.* to tuft, to comb (wool, silk, etc.).
'houppette [upɛt] *s.f.* small tuft; powder-puff.

'hourd [ur] *s.m.* (ant.) palisade; spectators' stand (at tournament).
'hourdage [urdaʒ] *s.m.* rough-walling; lath-and--plaster work.
'hourder [urde] *v.t.* **1.** to palisade; **2.** to rough--wall.
hourdis [urdi] *s.m.* (constr.) rough-walling (in stud-work).
'houri [uri] *s.f.* houri.
'hourra [ura, hura] *s.m.* hurrah, cheer.
'hourvari [urvari] *s.m.* **1.** (hunt.) cry to call back the hounds; **2.** (fam.) tumult, uproar.
'housard [uzar] *s.m.* (obs.) = 'HUSSARD.
'houseau (pl. **-x**) [uzo] *s.m.* legging, gaiter, spatterdash.
'houspiller [uspije] *v.t.* to knock about, to maltreat; to attack (verbally), to abuse.
'housse [us] *s.f.* loose cover, dust-cover, dust--sheet, (protective) bag; horse-cloth, saddle--cloth.
'houssine [usin] *s.f.* switch, rod, carpet-beater.
'houssiner [usine] *v.t.* to beat (carpets, etc.).
'houssoir [uswar] *s.m.* whisk, feather-duster.
'houx [u] *s.m.* holly, holly-tree, holly-bush.
'hoyau (pl. **-x**) [wajo] *s.m.* mattock.
'hublot [yblo] *s.m.* port-hole, scuttle; window (in aircraft).
'huche [yʃ] *s.f.* chest, bin.
'huchet [yʃɛ] *s.m.* call-horn, hunting-horn.
'hue [y, hy] *interj.* gee up!, get on!; (fig.) *tirer à ~ et à dia*, to be pulling in different directions.
'huée [ɥe] *s.f.* **1.** (hunt.) halloo; **2.** boo, catcall, jeer.
'huer [ɥe] *v.t.* **1.** (hunt.) to halloo, to hunt with halloos; **2.** to boo, to jeer at, to greet with derision; ~ *v.i.* (of owl) to hoot.
'huguenot, -e [ygno] *s.m.f., adj.* Huguenot; **~e** *s.f.* low cooking-stove; pipkin.
hui [ɥi] *adv.* (obs.) today, this day.
huilage [ɥilaʒ] *s.m.* oiling; coating with oil, steeping in oil.
huile [ɥil] *s.f.* **1.** oil, grease; oil-paint, oils; (fig.) midnight oil, great labour; *~ de table*, *~ comestible*, salad oil; *~ de graissage*, or *à graisser*, lubricating oil or grease; *~ à brûler*, *~ lampante*, lamp-oil; (fig.) *~ solaire*, sun-tan oil; *jeter de l'~ sur le feu*, to add fuel to the flames; *mer d'~*, dead calm sea, (fig.) mill-pond; *tache d'~*, grease-spot; (fig.) insidious penetration or progress; *faire tache d'~*, to spread insidiously, to snowball; **2.** (pop.) high-up (person); (pl.) authorities
huiler [ɥile] *v.t.* to oil, to cover with oil, to anoint; to grease; to put oil to (salad, etc.).
huilerie [ɥilri] *s.f.* oil-works; oil business, oil trade; (obs.) oil-mill.
huileu-x, -se [ɥilø] *adj.* oily, greasy, viscous; (fig.) oily, unctuous.
huilier [ɥilje] *s.m.* **1.** oilman; **2.** oil-and-vinegar cruet.
huili-er, -ère [ɥilje] *adj.* oil.
huis [ɥi] *s.m.* (obs.) door; (mod.) *à ~ clos*, with closed doors, in private, privately; *demander le ~ clos*, to demand the exclusion of the public.
huisserie [ɥisri] *s.f.* door-frame, window-frame.
huissier [ɥisje] *s.m.* usher, sheriff's officer, bailiff, tipstaff; process-server; beadle, door--keeper.
'huit [ɥi(t)] *adj., s.m.* eight, the eighth (of the month); *~ jours*, eight days, a week; *de demain en ~*, tomorrow week; *il y a ~ jours*, a week ago, it is a week (*que*, since); *il y a eu ~ jours mardi*, a week ago last Tuesday; **~ain** [ɥitɛ̃] *s.m.* stanza of eight lines; **~aine** [ɥitɛn] *s.f.* **1.** eight (of a kind), set of eight; **2.** eight days, week; **~ième** [ɥitjɛm] *adj., s.m.* eighth; (school) eighth form; **~ièmement** [ɥitjɛmmɑ̃] *adv.* eighthly.
huître [ɥitr] *s.f.* oyster; (fig., fam.) fool.
huîtri-er, -ère [ɥitrije] *adj.* relating to oysters, oyster-; **~ère** *s.f.* oyster-bed.
'hulotte [ylɔt] *s.f.* wood-owl, tawny owl.
hululement [ylylmɑ̃] *s.m.* (of owls) ululation, hooting.
hululer [ylyle] *v.i.* (of owls) to ululate, to hoot.
humain, -e [ymɛ̃] *adj.* **1.** human; *respect ~*, fear of public opinion; **2.** humane; ~ *s.m.* human being, human; (pl.) mankind; **~ement** [ymɛnmɑ̃] *adv.* humanly; humanely, mercifully.
humaniser [ymanize] *v.t.* to render human; to humanize; to civilize; to render humane, kind; **s'~** *v.refl.* to become more tractable, to mellow, to become more sociable.
humanisme [ymanism] *s.m.* humanism, study of the humanities.
humaniste [ymanist] *s.m.* humanist, classical scholar; ~ *adj.* humanist.
humanitaire [ymanitɛr] *adj.* humanitarian, philanthropic.
humanité [ymanite] *s.f.* **1.** humanity, human nature; mankind; mercy, humanity, humaneness; **2.** (pl.) humanities.
humble [œ̃bl] *adj.* humble, modest, obscure; meek; **~ment** [œ̃bləmɑ̃] *adv.* humbly, respectfully, modestly.
humectage [ymɛktaʒ] *s.m.* moistening, wetting, damping.
humecter [ymɛkte] *v.t.* to moisten, to wet, to damp; (fam.) *s'~ le gosier*, to wet one's whistle.
'humer [yme] *v.t.* **1.** (obs.) to imbibe, to inhale, to drink in; **2.** to sniff (at), to smell.
huméral, -e, (**aux**) [ymeral] *adj.* (anat.) humeral.
humérus [ymerys] *s.m.* (anat.) humerus.
humeur [ymœr] *s.f.* **1.** (med.) (obs.) humour, (mod.) fluid; **2.** humour, temper, mood, inclination; disposition, temperament, character; *être en ~ de*, to be in the mood to or for; *être d'~ à*, to be disposed or inclined to; **3.** ill temper, petulance; whim, impulse; *avec ~*, petulantly, peevishly; *mouvement d'~*, fit of temper; sudden whim; ⚠ very rarely = HUMOUR.
humide [ymid] *adj.* humid, damp, wet, moist, watery, tearful.
humidi-fication [ymidifikɑsjɔ̃] *s.f.* damping, moistening, humidification, humification; **~fier** [ymidifje] *v.t.* to wet, to moisten, to damp, to humidify; **~té** [ymidite] *s.f.* humidity, moisture, damp.
humiliant, -e [ymiljɑ̃] *adj.* humiliating, mortifying, humbling, degrading.
humil-iation [ymiljɑsjɔ̃] *s.f.* humiliation, humbling, mortification, degradation; shame; **~ier** [ymilje] *v.t.* **1.** (obs.) to prostrate, to bring low; **2.** to humiliate, to abase, to crush, to degrade; **s'~ier** *v.refl.* to humble oneself; to prostrate oneself; to debase oneself; *s'~ier jusqu'à*, to stoop to; **~ité** [ymilite] *s.f.* humility, humbleness, modesty; lowliness, humble position.
humoral, -e, (**aux**) [ymɔral] *adj.* (med.) humoral.
humoriste [ymɔrist] *s.m.f.* humorist; ~ *adj.* humorous, witty.
humoristique [ymɔristik] *adj.* humoristic, humorous, witty.
humour [ymur] *s.m.* humour; *avoir de l'~*, to be humorous, to have a sense of humour.
humus [ymys] *s.m.* humus, vegetable mould.
'Hun [œ̃] *s.m.* (hist.) Hun.
'hune [yn] *s.f.* (naut.) top; *grand'~*, main-top; *mât de ~*, topmast; (nav.) *~ de direction de tir*, fire-control top.
'hunier [ynje] *s.m.* (naut.) topsail; *grand ~*, main topsail; *petit ~*, fore topsail.
'huppe [yp] *s.f.* **1.** tuft (of feathers); **2.** (ornith.) hoopoe.

'huppé, -e [ype] *adj.* tufted, crested; (fig. & fam.) high up, high-ranking.
'hure [yr] *s.f.* (cook.) head of boar, jowl of salmon, etc.; brawn.
'hurlement [yrləmɑ̃] *s.m.* howling, howl, yelling, yell, roaring, roar, shrieking, shriek; *pousser des ~s de rage*, to howl with rage.
'hurler [yrle] *v.t.i.* to howl, to yell, to shriek, to roar; (fig.) (of colours) to shout, to clash; *~ avec les loups*, to conform, to follow the crowd.
'hurleu-r, -se [yrlœr] *s.m.f.* howler; *adj.* howling, yelling; (zool.) *singe ~r*, howler monkey.
hurluberlu [yrlybɛrly] *s.m.* harum-scarum; scatter-brained or happy-go-lucky person.
'huron, -ne [yrɔ̃] *s.m.f., adj.* **1.** (obs.) boor(ish); **2.** (ethn., lang.) Huron.
'hussard [ysar] *s.m.* hussar.
'hussarde [ysard] *s.f.* hussarde (dance); (fig.) *à la ~*, brutally, unceremoniously, in cavalier fashion.
'hussite [ysit] *s.m.* Hussite.
'hutte [yt] *s.f.* hut, log hut, cabin, hovel.
hyacinthe [jasɛ̃t] *s.f.* **1.** (gem) hyacinth, jacinth; **2.** (bot.) (obs.) = JACINTHE.
hyalin, -e [jalɛ̃] *adj.* (min.) hyaline; *quartz ~*, rock-crystal.
hyaloïde [jalɔid] *adj.* hyaloid, vitriform.
hybridation [ibridɑsjɔ̃] *s.f.* hybridization, crossing, cross-breeding.
hybride [ibrid] *adj., s.m.* hybrid, mongrel.
hybrid-er [ibride] *v.t.* to hybridize, to cross; **~isme** [ibridism] *s.m.* (biol.) hybridism; **~ité** [ibridite] *s.f.* hybridity, hybrid character.
hydne [idn] *s.m.* (bot.) a kind of mushroom.
hydrargyre [idrarʒir] *s.m.* (chem.) hydrargyrum, mercury.
hydrargyrisme [idrarʒirism] *s.m.* (med.) hydrargyrism, mercury poisoning.
hydratation [idratɑsjɔ̃] *s.f.* (chem., med.) hydration.
hydrate [idrat] *s.m.* hydrate; hydroxide; *~ de chaux, de calcium*, calcium hydrate, calcium hydroxide; *~ de potasse*, caustic potash; *~ de carbone*, carbohydrate.
hydrater [idrate] *v.t.* to hydrate; **s'~** *v.refl.* to hydrate, to become hydrated.
hydraulicien [idrolisjɛ̃] *s.m.* hydraulic engineer.
hydraulique [idrolik] *s.f.* hydraulics; *~ adj.* hydraulic.
hydravion [idravjɔ̃] *s.m.* seaplane.
hydrazine [idrazin] *s.f.* (chem.) hydrazine.
hydre [idr] *s.f.* (myth., zool.) hydra; (fig.) monster.
hydrémie [idremi] *s.f.* (med.) hydraemia.
hydro-base [idrɔbɑz] *s.f.* seaplane base; **~carbonate** [idrɔkarbɔnat] *s.m.* (chem.) hydrogen carbonate; **~carbure** [idrɔkarbyr] *s.m.* (chem.) hydrocarbon; **~cèle** [idrɔsɛl] *s.f.* (pathol.) hydrocele; **~céphale** [idrɔsefal] *adj., s.m.f.* hydrocephalic, hydrocephalous, (person); **~céphalie** [idrɔsefɑli] *s.f.* (pathol.) hydrocephalus, hydrocephaly; **~cotyle** [idrɔkɔtil] *s.f.* (bot.) Hydrocotyle, pennywort; **~craquage** [idrɔkrakaʒ] *s.m.* (chem. eng.) hydrocracking; **~craqueur** [idrɔkrakœr] hydrocracker; **~dynamique** [idrɔdinamik] *adj.* hydrodynamic; *s.f.* hydrodynamics; **~électrique** [idrɔelɛktrik] *s.f.* hydroelectric; **~-fuge** [idrɔfyʒ] *adj.* waterproof, damp-proof, rainproof; (constr.) *couche ~fuge*, damp course; **~fuger** [idrɔfyʒe] *v.t.* to waterproof, to damp-proof; **~foil** [idrɔfɔil] *s.m.* hydrofoil; **~génation** [idrɔʒenɑsjɔ̃] *s.f.* (chem., techn.) hydrogenation; **~gène** [idrɔʒɛn] *s.m.* (chem.) hydrogen; **~géner** [idrɔʒene] *v.t.* to hydrogenate; **~graphe** [idrɔgraf] *s.m.f.* hydrographer; **~graphie** [idrɔgrafi] *s.f.* hydrography; **~-graphique** [idrɔgrafik] *adj.* hydrographic; **~logie** [idrɔlɔʒi] *s.f.* hydrology; **~logique** [idrɔlɔʒik] *adj.* hydrological; **~logiste** [idrɔlɔʒist], **~logue** [idrɔlɔg] *s.m.f.* hydrologist; **~lyse** [idrɔliz] *s.f.* (chem.) hydrolysis; **~lyser** [idrɔlize] *v.t.* to hydrolyse; **~mètre** [idrɔmɛtr] **1.** *s.m.* hydrometer, pressure-gauge, depth-gauge; **2.** *s.f.* (zool.) water-spider; **~métrie** [idrɔmetri] *s.f.* hydrometry; **~métrique** [idrɔmetrik] *adj.* hydrometric; **~phile** [idrɔfil] *adj.* hydrophilic, absorbent; **~phobe** [idrɔfɔb] *adj., s.m.f.* hydrophobic (person); **~phobie** [idrɔfɔbi] *s.f.* (med.) hydrophobia, rabies; **~pique** [idrɔpik] *adj., s.m.f.* hydropic, dropsical, (person) suffering from dropsy; **~pisie** [idrɔpizi] *s.f.* (med.) hydropsy, dropsy; **~pneumatique** [idrɔpnømatik] *adj.* hydropneumatic; **~quinone** [idrɔkinɔn] *s.f.* (chem.) hydroquinone, quinol; **~soluble** [idrɔsɔlybl] *adj.* (sci.) water-soluble; **~sphère** [idrɔsfɛr] *s.f.* (geog.) hydrosphere; **~statique** [idrɔstatik] *adj.* hydrostatic; *s.f.* hydrostatics; **~thérapie** [idrɔterapi] *s.f.* (med.) hydrotherapy, hydrotherapeutics, water cure; **~xyde** [idrɔksid] *s.m.* (chem.) hydroxide; **~xyle** [idrɔksil] *s.m.* (chem.) hydroxyl; **~zoaires** [idrɔzɔɛr] *s.m.pl.* (zool.) Hydrozoa.
hydrure [idryr] *s.m.* (chem.) hydride.
hyène [iɛn] *s.f.* (zool.) hyena, hyaena.
hygiène [iʒjɛ̃n] *s.f.* hygiene, sanitation; *~ publique*, Public Health.
hygiénique [iʒjenik] *adj.* hygienic, healthy, sanitary; *papier ~*, toilet-paper; *serviette ~*, sanitary towel; *promenade ~*, constitutional (walk); **~ment** [iʒjenikmɑ̃] *adv.* hygienically.
hygiéniste [iʒjenist] *s.m.f.* hygienist, health expert, public health specialist.
hygro-mètre [igrɔmɛtr] *s.m.* hygrometer; **~métrie** [igrɔmetri] *s.f.* hygrometry; **~-métrique** [igrɔmetrik] *adj.* hygrometric(al); **~scope** [igrɔskɔp] *s.m.* hygroscope; **~scopie** [igrɔskɔpi] *s.f.* = HYGROMÉTRIE; **~scopique** [igrɔskɔpik] *adj.* hydroscopic(al).
hymen [imɛn] *s.m.* **1.** (Lit.) marriage; **2.** (anat.) hymen, maidenhead.
hyménée [imene] *s.m.* = HYMEN 1.
hyménoptère [imenɔptɛr] *s.m.* (ent.) hymenopteran, hymenopter.
hymne [imn] *s.m.* hymn, anthem; song of praise; *~ s.m.* or *f.* (eccles.) hymn.
hyoïde [jɔid] *adj., s.m.* (anat.) hyoid.
hypallage [ipalaʒ] *s.f.* (rhet.) hypallage.
hyper-acidité [ipɛrasidite] *s.f.* (med.) hyperacidity; **~bate** [ipɛrbat] *s.f.* (rhet.) hyperbation, inversion; **~bole** [ipɛrbɔl] *s.f.* hyperbole exaggeration; (geom.) hyperbola; **~bolique** [ipɛrbɔlik] *adj.* hyperbolic(al), exaggerated; (math.) hyperbolic; **~boliquement** *adv.* hyperbolically; exaggeratedly; **~boloïde** [ipɛrbɔlɔid] *adj., s.m.* (geom.) hyperboloid.
hyperboréen, -ne [ipɛrbɔreɛ̃] *adj.* (Lit.) hyperborean, northern, arctic.
hyper-critique [ipɛrkritik] *s.m.* hypercritic, severe critic; *s.f.* hypercriticism, harsh criticism; *adj.* hypercritical; **~émotivité** [ipɛremɔtivite] *s.f.* (psychol.) hypersensitivity, over-emotionalism; **~espace** [ipɛrɛspas] *s.m.* (geom.) hyperspace; **~esthésie** [ipɛrɛstezi] *s.f.* (med.) hyperaesthesia.
hyperfocal, -e [ipɛrfɔkal] *adj.* (photo.) hyperfocal.
hyper-fréquence [ipɛrfrekɑ̃s] *s.f.* (radio) ultra-high frequency, microwave; **~glycémie** [ipɛrglisemi] *s.f.* (med.) hyperglycaemia; **~golique** [ipɛrgɔlik] *adj.* hypergolic; **~marché** [ipɛrmarʃe] *s.m.* hypermarket; **~métrope** [ipɛrmetrɔp] *adj., s.m.f.* hypermetropic, long-sighted, (person) **~métropie** [ipɛrmetrɔpi]

s.f. hypermetropia, hyperopia, long-sightedness; **~sensibilité** [ipɛrsɑ̃sibilite] *s.f.* hypersensitiveness, hypersensitivity; **~-sensible** [ipɛrsɑ̃sibl] *adj., s.m.f.* hypersensitive, over-sensitive, (person); **~sonique** [ipɛrsɔnik] *adj.* hypersonic.
hypertendu, -e [ipɛrtɑ̃dy] *s.m.f., adj.* (med.) (one) suffering from hypertension.
hyper-tension [ipɛrtɑ̃sjɔ̃] *s.f.* (med.) hypertension, high blood-pressure; **~thermie** [ipɛrtɛrmi] *s.f.* (med.) hyperthermia; **~thyroïdie** [ipɛrtirɔidi] *s.f.* (med.) hyperthyroidism; **~tonie** [ipɛrtɔni] *s.f.* (med.) hypertension.
hyper-trophie [ipɛrtrɔfi] *s.f.* hypertrophy, over-enlargement, over-nourishment; **~-trophié, -e** [ipɛrtrɔfje] *adj.* hypertrophied, over-enlarged; **~trophier** [ipɛrtrɔfje] *v.t.* to cause hypertrophy; **s'~trophier** *v.refl.* to become hypertrophied; **~trophique** [ipɛrtrɔfik] *adj.* hypertrophic.
hypn-agogique [ipnagɔʒik] *adj.* hypnagogic, sleep-inducing; *hallucination ~agogique*, hallucination induced by sleep or fatigue; **~ose** [ipnoz] *s.f.* hypnosis; **~otique** [ipnɔtik] *adj.* hypnotic, soporific, sleep-inducing; *s.m.f.* person susceptible to hypnosis; *s.m.* hypnotic drug, etc.; **~otiser** [ipnɔtize] *v.t.* to hypnotize; **s'~otiser** *v.refl.* to be hypnotized or fascinated; **~otiseur** [ipnɔtizœr] *s.m.* hypnotizer; **~-otisme** [ipnɔtism] *s.m.* hypnotism.
hypo-condre [ipɔkɔ̃dr] *s.m.* **1.** (anat.) hypochondrium; **2.** hypochondriac; **~condriaque** [ipɔkɔ̃drijak] *adj., s.m.f.* hypochondriac(al); **~crisie** [ipɔkrisi] *s.f.* hypocrisy, deception; **~crite** [ipɔkrit] *adj.* hypocritical; *s.m.f.* hypocrite; **~critement** [ipɔkritmɑ̃] *adv.* hypocritically; **~derme** [ipɔdɛrm] *s.m.* (bot., etc.) hypoderm, hypoderma, hypodermis; **~-dermique** [ipɔdɛrmik] *adj.* hypodermic; **~-gastre** [ipɔgastr] *s.m.* (anat.) hypogastrium; **~gastrique** [ipɔgastrik] *adj.* hypogastric; **~gée** [ipɔʒe] *s.m.* (archaeol.) hypogeum; *adj.* (bot.) hypogean; **~glosse** [ipɔglɔs] *adj.* (anat.) hypoglossal; **~glycémie** [ipɔglisemi] *s.f.* (med.) hypoglycaemia; **~gyne** [ipɔʒin] *adj.* (bot.) hypogynous; **~phosphate** [ipɔfɔsfat] *s.m.* (chem.) hypophosphate; **~phosphite** [ipɔfɔsfit] *s.m.* (chem.) hypophosphite.
hypophosphoreu-x, -se [ipɔfɔsfɔrø] *adj.* (chem.) hypophosphorous.
hypo-phosphorique [ipɔfɔsfɔrik] *adj.* (chem.) hypophosphoric; **~physe** [ipɔfiz] *s.f.* hypophysis, pituitary body; **~stase** [ipɔstaz] *s.f.* (med., theol., phil., lang.) hypostasis; **~-statique** [ipɔstatik] *adj.* hypostatic; **~style** [ipɔstil] *adj.* (arch.) hypostyle; **~sulfate** [ipɔsylfat] *s.m.* (chem.) dithionate; **~sulfite** [ipɔsylfit] *s.m.* (chem.) hyposulphite, thiosulphate; **~tension** [ipɔtɑ̃sjɔ̃] *s.f.* (med.) hypotension, low blood-pressure; **~ténuse** [ipɔtenyz] *s.f.* hypotenuse; **~thalamus** [ipɔtalamys] *s.m.* (anat.) hypothalamus; **~-thécable** [ipɔtekabl] *adj.* mortgageable; **~-thécaire** [ipɔtekɛr] *adj.* relating to mortgage, on mortgage, mortgage; *créancier ~thécaire*, mortgagee; *débiteur ~thécaire*, mortgagor; **~thécairement** [ipɔtekɛrmɑ̃] *adv.* by mortgage; **~thénar** [ipɔtenar] *s.m.* (anat.) hypothenar; **~thèque** [ipɔtɛk] *s.f.* mortgage; (fig.) obstacle; *grevé d'une ~thèque*, mortgaged; **~théquer** [ipɔteke] *v.t.* to mortgage, to lodge as security; **~thermie** [ipɔtɛrmi] *s.f.* (med.) hypothermia; **~thèse** [ipɔtɛz] *s.f.* hypothesis, assumption, supposition, theory; **~thétique** [ipɔtetik] *adj.* hypothetical; **~thétiquement** [ipɔtetikmɑ̃] *adv.* hypothetically; **~typose** [ipɔtipoz] *s.f.* (rhet.) hypotyposis.
hypso-mètre [ipsɔmɛtr] *s.m.* hypsometer; **~métrie** [ipsɔmetri] *s.f.* hypsometry; **~-métrique** [ipsɔmetrik] *adj.* hypsometric.
hysope [izɔp] *s.f.* (bot.) hyssop.
hystérectomie [isterɛktɔmi] *s.f.* (surg.) hysterectomy.
hystérèse [isterɛz], **hystérésis** [isterezis] *s.f.* (phys.) hysteresis.
hystérie [isteri] *s.f.* (pathol.) hysteria; (fig.) madness, hysteria.
hystérique [isterik] *adj.* (med.) hysteric(al); (fig.) hysterical, crazy.
hystérotomie [isterɔtɔmi] *s.f.* (surg.) hysterotomy, Caesarian section.

I

I, i [i] *s.m.* the letter I, i; *~ grec*, (letter) Y, y; *mettre les points sur les i*, to dot one's i's; to leave nothing unexplained; to be very precise.
ïambe [iɑ̃b] *s.m.* iambus; iambic verse or poem; satirical poem.
ïambique [iɑ̃bik] *adj.* iambic.
ibère [ibɛr] *adj., s.m.f.* (ethn.) Iberian.
ibérique [iberik] *adj.* (geog.) Iberian.
ibis [ibis] *s.m.* (ornith.) ibis.
iceberg [ajsbɛrg; isbɛrg] *s.m.* iceberg.
icefield [ajsfild] *s.m.* ice-field.
icelui, icelle (pl. **iceux, icelles**) [islɥi, isɛl; isø, isɛl] *pron., adj.* (obs. exc. law) this, these, the said, the aforesaid.
ichneumon [iknømɔ̃] *s.m.* **1.** (zool.) ichneumon; **2.** (ent.) ichneumon (fly).
ichor [ikɔr] *s.m.* **1.** (med.) ichor, matter; **2.** (geol.) ichor.
ichoreu-x, -se [ikɔrø] *adj.* (med.) ichorous.
ichtyo-logie [iktjɔlɔʒi] *s.f.* ichthyology; **~-logique** [iktjɔlɔʒik] *adj.* ichthyological; **~-logiste** [iktjɔlɔʒist] *s.m.f.* ichthyologist; **~phage** [iktjɔfaʒ] *adj.* ichthyophagous; *s.m.f.* ichthyophagist; **~phagie** [iktjɔfaʒi] *s.f.* ichthyophagy; **~saure** [iktjɔsɔr] *s.m.* (palaeont.) ichthyosaurus.
ici [isi] *adv.* here, in this place, at this point; hither; now, this time; *~-bas*, here, in this world (opp. in heaven), here below; *c'est ~*, this is the place; here we are; *d'~*, hence, from here; of or from these parts, hereabouts; *les gens d'~*, the local inhabitants; *je ne suis pas d'~*, I am a stranger here; *d'~ à ce que*, by the time that; *d'~ demain*, by tomorrow; *d'~ le treize*, between now and the thirteenth; *d'~ (à) trois jours*, within three days; *d'~ peu*, soon, before long; *d'~ là*, in the meantime, by that time; till this point is reached; *~ et là, d'~ de là*, here and there, hither and thither; *jusqu'~*, hitherto, till now, as yet, up to this time; *par ~*, this way, through here; *~ près*, close by, hard by, near by; (fam.) *vous voyez ça d'~*, you can just picture it.
icône [ikon] *s.f.* icon.
icono-claste [ikɔnɔklast] *s.m.* iconoclast; *adj.* iconoclastic; **~graphie** [ikɔnɔgrafi] *s.f.* icono-

graphy; **~lâtre** [ikɔnɔlɑtr] *s.m.f.* iconolater; **~latrie** [ikɔnɔlɑtri] *s.f.* iconolatry; **~logie** [ikɔnɔlɔʒi] *s.f.* iconology; **~scope** [ikɔnɔskɔp] *s.m.* iconoscope (electron camera).

icosaèdre [ikɔzaɛdr] *s.m.* icosahedron.

ictère [iktɛr] *s.m.* (pathol.) icterus, jaundice.

idéal, -e, (**aux**) [ideal] *adj.* ideal, unreal, imaginary; perfect; ~ *s.m.* (pl. **als** or **aux**) ideal; **~ement** [idealmɑ̃] *adv.* ideally; perfectly.

idéalisat-eur, -rice [idealizatœr] *adj.* idealizing.

idéal-isation [idealizɑsjɔ̃] *s.f.* idealization, idealizing; **~iser** [idealize] *v.t.* to idealize; **~isme** [idealism] *s.m.* idealism; **~iste** [idealist] *adj.* idealistic; *s.m.f.* idealist; **~ité** [idealite] *s.f.* ideality.

idée [ide] *s.f.* idea, notion, conception; purpose, intention, plan; mind; (fam.) faint touch, suspicion, (of sth.); ~ *lumineuse*, bright idea; ~ *fixe*, obsession; ~*s reçues*, conventional opinions, prejudices; *changer d'~*, to change or to alter one's mind; *se mettre dans l'~ que*, to take it into one's head that; *faire à son ~*, to do as one fancies; *j'ai ~ que*, it seems to me that, I rather think that; *j'ai dans l'~ que*, it is in my mind that, I can't help thinking that; *on n'a pas ~ de cela*, you can't imagine it, you can't think what it was like; *il m'est venu à l'~*, it occurred to me; *se faire des ~s*; to imagine things; *avoir une haute ~ de*, to esteem highly; *en ~* in imagination.

idéel, -le [ideɛl] *adj.* (phil.) ideal, conceptual; ⚠ not 'ideal' in sense 'perfect'.

idem [idɛm] *adv.* idem, ditto.

identifiable [idɑ̃tifjabl] *adj.* identifiable.

identification [idɑ̃tifikɑsjɔ̃] *s.f.* identification.

identifier [idɑ̃tifje] *v.t.* to identify; **s'~** *v.refl.* to identify oneself.

identique [idɑ̃tik] *adj.* identical (*à*, with), the same, the very same; **~ment** [idɑ̃tikmɑ̃] *adv.* identically.

identité [idɑ̃tite] *s.f.* identity; sameness, identicalness; *pièce d'~*, identification paper(s), proof of identity; *carte d'~*, identity card; ~ *judiciaire*, or *le Bureau d'~*, Criminal Records Office.

idéo-gramme [ideɔgram] *s.m.* (lang.) ideogram, ideograph; **~graphie** [ideɔgrafi] *s.f.* ideography; **~graphique** [ideɔgrafik] *adj.* ideographical; **~logie** [ideɔlɔʒi] *s.f.* ideology; **~logique** [ideɔlɔʒik] *adj.* ideological; **~logue** [ideɔlɔg] *s.m.* ideologist.

ides [id] *s.f.pl.* (Rom. ant.) ides.

idiomatique [idjɔmatik] *adj.* idiomatic.

idiome [idjom] *s.m.* language, dialect; idiom; ⚠ not 'idiom' in sense 'idiomatic expression'.

idiosyncrasie [idjɔsɛ̃krazi] *s.f.* idiosyncrasy.

idiot, -e [idjo] *adj.* idiotic, senseless; (med.) idiot, imbecile; *s.m.f.* idiot, imbecile; **~ement** [idjɔtmɑ̃] *adv.* senselessly.

idiotie [idjɔsi] *s.f.* **1.** idiocy, imbecility, mental deficiency; **2.** senseless action, act of stupidity; stupid thing to say; (fam.) silly piece of writing, piece of nonsense.

idiotisme [idjɔtism] *s.m.* idiom, idiomatic expression.

idoine [idwan] *adj.* (obs.) proper, suitable; (mod.) *voilà l'homme ~*, he's just the man.

idolâtre [idɔlɑtr] *adj.* idolatrous, idolizing; *s.m.f.* idolater, idolatress.

idolâtrer [idɔlɑtre] *v.t.* to idolize, to worship, to adore.

idolâtrie [idɔlɑtri] *s.f.* idolatry; (fig.) *il l'aime à l'~*, he idolizes her.

idolâtrique [idɔlɑtrik] *adj.* idolatrous.

idole [idɔl] *s.f.* idol; *faire son ~ de*, to idolize, to make a god of; *être l'~ de*, to be worshipped by, to be idolized by.

idylle [idil] *s.f.* idyll.

idyllique [idilik] *adj.* idyllic.

Iéna [jena] *s.* (geog.) Jena.

if [if] *s.m.* (bot.) yew, yew-tree.

igloo, iglou [iglu] *s.m.* igloo.

igname [iɲam] *s.f.* (bot.) yam.

ignare [iɲar] *adj.* ignorant, illiterate, uneducated.

igné, -e [igne] *adj.* igneous.

ignifugation [ignifygɑsjɔ̃] *s.f.*; **ignifugeage** [ignifyʒaʒ] *s.m.* fireproofing.

igni-fuge [ignifyʒ] *adj.* fireproof(ed), fire--resistant; **~fuger** [ignifyʒe] *v.t.* to fireproof.

ignition [ignisjɔ̃] *s.f.* ignition; *entrer en ~*, to ignite; *mettre en ~*, to ignite.

ignoble [iɲɔbl] *adj.* ignoble, vile, base, mean, revolting, filthy; **~ment** [iɲɔbləmɑ̃] *adv.* revoltingly.

ignominie [iɲɔmini] *s.f.* ignominy, shame, baseness; disgraceful deed.

ignominieu-x, -se [iɲɔminjø] *adj.* shameful, ignominious; **~sement** [iɲɔminjøzmɑ̃] *adv.* shamefully.

ignorance [iɲɔrɑ̃s] *s.f.* ignorance; *être dans l'~ de*, to be ignorant of, to be unaware of.

ignorant, -e [iɲɔrɑ̃] *adj.* ignorant, uneducated; untrained, inexperienced; ~ *en histoire*, having no knowledge of history; ~ *de*, ignorant of, unaware of, not knowing; *s.m.f.* ignorant or uneducated person; *faire l'~*, to feign ignorance (of sth.).

ignoré, -e [iɲɔre] *adj.* unknown, concealed, secluded.

ignorer [iɲɔre] *v.t.* **1.** not to know, to be unaware of, to have no knowledge or experience of; to fail to recognize; ~ *que*, not to know that, to be unaware that; *ne pas ~ que*, to be well aware that; **2.** to ignore (s.o.), to snub; **s'~** *v.refl.* to be unaware of one's own nature; *c'est un criminel qui s'ignore*, he is a criminal without knowing it.

iguane [igɥan] *s.m.* (zool.) iguana.

iguanodon [igɥanɔdɔ̃] *s.m.* (zool.) iguanodon.

il [il] *pron.m.* (pl. **ils**) he, it; there; (pl.) they; ~ *est malade*, he is ill; *où est mon portefeuille? il a disparu*, where is my wallet? it has disappeared; ~*s sont là*, they are there; ~ *pleut*, it is raining; *il y a*, there is, there are; (as anticipatory subject) *il en arrive de toutes sortes*, all kinds turn up; *il en sortit un petit lapin*, out came a little rabbit.

île [il] *s.f.* island; isle; *l'~ de France*, Mauritius; *l'Île-de-France*, the Île-de-France (Fr. province); *les Îles*, the West Indies; the Antilles; *les ~s sous le Vent*, the Leeward Islands; *les ~s du Vent*, the Windward Islands; *les ~s Britanniques*, the British Isles.

iléon [ileɔ̃] *s.m.* (anat.) ileum.

iléus [ileys] *s.m.* (pathol.) occlusion of the intestine, ileus.

Iliade [iljad] *s.f.* (Gr. Lit.) Iliad.

iliaque [iljak] *adj.* (anat.) iliac.

ilion [iljɔ̃], **ilium** [iljɔm] *s.m.* (anat.) ilium.

illégal, -e, (**aux**) [ilegal] *adj.* illegal, unlawful; **~ement** [ilegalmɑ̃] *adv.* illegally.

illégalité [ilegalite] *s.f.* illegality; illegal act.

illégitime [ileʒitim] *adj.* illegitimate; unlawful, unjust, spurious; **~ment** [ileʒitimmɑ̃] *adv.* ilegitimately, unlawfully.

illégitimité [ileʒitimite] *s.f.* illegitimacy.

illettré, -e [iletre] *adj.* illiterate, ignorant.

illicite [ilisit] *adj.* illicit, unlawful; **~ment** [ilisitmɑ̃] *adv.* illicitly, unlawfully.

illico [iliko] *adv.* (fam.) at once, forthwith, there and then.

illimité, -e [ilimite] *adj.* unlimited, boundless, unbounded; indefinite; ~ *s.m.* infinite.

illisibilité [ilizibilite] *s.f.* illegibility.

illisible [ilizibl] *adj.* illegible; unreadable; **~ment** [iliziblәmɑ̃] *adv.* illegibly.

illogique [ilɔʒik] *adj.* illogical; **~ment** [ilɔʒikmɑ̃] *adv.* illogically.

illogisme [ilɔʒism] *s.m.* illogicalness, illogicality.

illumination [ilyminɑsjɔ̃] *s.f.* **1.** (fig.) illumination, inspiration; **2.** illumination, lighting; (pl.) illuminations, lights.

illuminé, -e [ilymine] *adj.* illuminated, lit; (fig.) enlightened; *s.m.f.* (relig.) visionary; illuminato.

illuminer [ilymine] *v.t.* to illuminate, to light up; to illumine, to enlighten; ⚠ not 'to illuminate' a manuscript, etc.

illusion [ilyzjɔ̃] *s.f.* **1.** illusion, mirage, vision, deception; ~ *d'optique*, optical illusion; (fig.) erroneous view; *donner l'~ de*, to give an illusion of; **2.** delusion, hallucination, illusion, empty dream; *avoir* or *se faire des ~s*, to delude oneself, to labour under a delusion; *chercher à faire ~*, to seek to deceive or to impress; *faire ~ à qn.*, to delude s.o.

illusionner [ilyzjɔne] *v.t.* (rare) to delude; **s'~** *v.refl.* to delude oneself.

illusionniste [ilyzjɔnist] *s.m.f.* illusionist, conjurer.

illusoire [ilyzwar] *adj.* illusory, illusive, delusive, fallacious, deceptive; **~ment** [ilyzwarmɑ̃] *adv.* illusively, deceptively.

illustrateur [ilystratœr] *s.m.* illustrator, draughtsman.

illustration [ilystrɑsjɔ̃] *s.f.* **1.** (obs.) making illustrious, shedding lustre (*de*, on); (mod.) celebrity, illustrious person; **2.** illustration.

illustre [ilystr] *adj.* illustrious, famous, renowned.

illustrer [ilystre] *v.t.* **1.** (obs.) to make famous; **s'~** *v.refl.* to become famous, to make a name for oneself; **2.** to illustrate (by an example), to make clear; **3.** to illustrate (book, etc.).

illustrissime [ilystrisim] *adj.* most illustrious.

illuvial, -e, (aux) [ilyvjal] *adj.* alluvial.

illuviation [ilyvjɑsjɔ̃] *s.f.* alluvial deposition, formation of alluvium.

illuvion [ilyvjɔ̃], **illuvium** [ilyvjɔm] *s.m.* alluvion, alluvium, alluvial deposit.

îlot [ilo] *s.m.* **1.** islet, small island; (anat.) islet (in pancreas); (fig.) island, small isolated area; *des ~s de resistance*, pockets of resistance; **2.** small block of houses (in town).

ilote [ilɔt] *s.m.* helot; (fig.) serf, drudge.

ilotisme [ilɔtism] *s.m.* helotism; (fig.) serfdom.

image [imaʒ] *s.f.* image, likeness, reflection, picture, effigy, print; semblance; mental picture, idea, impression; (rhet.) metaphor, simile, comparison; (pl.) imagery; *livre d'~s*, picture-book; *sage comme une ~*, as quiet as a mouse.

imagé, -e [imaʒe] *adj.* full of images, imaged, figurative, picturesque.

imagerie [imaʒri] *s.f.* **1.** coloured prints; making or selling of coloured prints; **2.** pictures, illustrations (in a particular style); imagery.

imagi-er, -ère [imaʒje] *s.m.f.* **1.** sculptor or painter (esp. in medieval art); **2.** artist, illustrator, picture-dealer; *adj.* relating to pictures or illustration.

imaginable [imaʒinabl] *adj.* imaginable, conceivable.

imaginaire [imaʒinɛr] *adj.* imaginary, fantastic, unreal, fancied; *un malade ~*, a hypochondriac; ~ *s.m. l'~*, the imaginary, the unreal.

imaginati-f, -ve [imaʒinatif] *adj.* full of imagination, imaginative; **~ve** *s.f.* imagination.

imagination [imaʒinɑsjɔ̃] *s.f.* **1.** imagination; **2.** fancy, delusion; *c'est une pure ~*, it's sheer fabrication, it is entirely imaginary.

imaginé, -e [imaʒine] *adj.* imagined, invented, fabricated.

imaginer [imaʒine] *v.t.* to imagine, to conceive, to fancy, to picture, to think up, to invent, to contrive, to surmise; **s'~** *v.refl.* to believe, to imagine, to fancy, to surmise, to persuade oneself, to get into one's head.

imam [imam], **iman** [imɑ̃] *s.m.* imam.

imbattable [ɛ̃batabl] *adj.* unbeatable; matchless.

imbécile [ɛ̃besil] *adj.* imbecile, foolish; ~ *s.m.f.* imbecile, idiot, fool; **~ment** [ɛ̃besilmɑ̃] *adv.* foolishly.

imbécillité [ɛ̃besilite] *s.f.* imbecility, idiocy, foolishness, foolish act or talk.

imberbe [ɛ̃bɛrb] *adj.* beardless.

imbiber [ɛ̃bibe] *v.t.* to soak, to imbue, to wet, to impregnate; **s'~** *v.refl.* to absorb, to soak up, to become soaked or impregnated; (fam.) *s'~ de vin*, to drink wine to excess.

imbibition [ɛ̃bibisjɔ̃] *s.f.* imbibition, soaking, absorption, impregnation.

imbrication [ɛ̃brikasjɔ̃] *s.f.* imbrication, overlapping.

imbriqué, -e [ɛ̃brike] *adj.* imbricated, overlapping, covered with overlapping tiles, etc.; (fig.) closely linked.

imbriquer [ɛ̃brike] *v.t.* to imbricate, to lay tiles, etc., overlapping, to overlap; **s'~** *v.refl.* to overlap.

imbroglio [ɛ̃brɔljo] *s.m.* imbroglio.

imbu, -e [ɛ̃by] *adj.* imbued, soaked, steeped (*de*, with, in).

imbuvable [ɛ̃byvabl] *adj.* undrinkable; (fig., fam.) intolerable.

imitable [imitabl] *adj.* imitable.

imitat-eur, -rice [imitatœr] *adj.* imitative; ~ *s.m.f.* imitator; (theatr.) mimic, impersonator.

imitati-f, -ve [imitatif] *adj.* imitative.

imitation [imitɑsjɔ̃] *s.f.* imitation, copy, mimicry; *à l'~ de*, in imitation of, modelled on.

imiter [imite] *v.t.* to imitate, to copy, to mimic, to be like, to look like; to counterfeit.

immaculé, -e [imakyle] *adj.* immaculate, spotless.

immanence [immanɑ̃s] *s.f.* immanence.

immanent, -e [imanɑ̃] *adj.* immanent.

immangeable [ɛ̃mɑ̃ʒabl] *adj.* uneatable.

immanquable [ɛ̃mɑ̃kabl] *adj.* certain, infallible, sure; **~ment** [ɛ̃mɑ̃kabləmɑ̃] *adv.* infallibly, unfailingly.

immarcescible [imarsesibl] *adj.* incorruptible, unfading, evergreen.

immatérialité [imaterjalite] *s.f.* immateriality.

immatériel, -le [imaterjɛl] *adj.* immaterial, insubstantial, not consisting of matter, ethereal; ⚠ not 'immaterial' in sense 'unimportant'.

immatriculation [imatrikylɑsjɔ̃] *s.f.* matriculation, registration, enrolling; *carte d'~*, membership card, registration card; (car) *plaque d'~*, number-plate.

immatriculer [imatrikyle] *v.t.* to matriculate, to register, to enrol; *se faire ~*, to register, to enrol, to put one's name down.

immature [imatyr] *adj.* immature.

immaturité [imatyrite] *s.f.* immaturity.

immédiat, -e [imedja] *adj.* immediate, instantaneous; ~ *s.m.* (the) present; *dans l'~*, for the moment; **~ement** [imedjatmɑ̃] *adv.* immediately, at once.

immémorial, -e, (aux) [imemɔrjal] *adj.* immemorial; *de temps ~*, from time immemorial.

immense [imɑ̃s] *adj.* immense, huge, immeasurable, vast, boundless.

immensément [imɑ̃semɑ̃] *adv.* immensely, vastly, hugely.

immensité [imɑ̃site] *s.f.* immensity, vastness, infinity, boundlessness, hugeness.

immensurable [imɑ̃syrabl] *adj.* immensurable, immeasurable.

immerger [imɛrʒɛ] *v.t.* to immerse, to submerge; **s'∼** *v.refl.* (of submarine) to submerge.
immérité, -e [imerite] *adj.* undeserved, unjust, unmerited.
immersion [imɛrsjɔ̃] *s.f.* immersion; submergence, submersion, submerging, (of submarine); (astron.) occultation; (opt.) *objectif à ∼*, immersion objective.
immettable [ɛ̃mɛtabl] *adj.* (of garment) unwearable.
immeuble [imœbl] *adj.* fixed, (of estate) real; immovable; ∼ *s.m.* real estate, property (in land or buildings); building, block of flats.
immigrant, -e [imigrɑ̃] *s.m.f., adj.* immigrant.
immigration [imigrɑsjɔ̃] *s.f.* immigration.
immigré, -e [imigre] *adj., s.m.f.* immigrant; settler.
immigrer [imigre] *v.i.* to immigrate, to settle.
imminence [iminɑ̃s] *s.f.* imminence.
imminent, -e [iminɑ̃] *adj.* imminent, impending.
(s')immiscer [imise] *v.refl.* to meddle, to interfere, to intervene, to intrude.
immixtion [imikstjɔ̃] *s.f.* interfering, meddling, intervention.
immobile [imɔbil] *adj.* immobile, motionless, immovable; (fig.) unmoved; rigid, unshakable.
immobili-er, -ère [imɔbilje] *adj.* (law) real, immovable; relating to property, buildings or real estate; *biens ∼ers*, or *l'∼er*, real estate, realty, property (in buildings or land); *vente ∼ère*, sale of property; *héritier ∼er*, heir to real estate; *société ∼ère*, property company; *agence ∼ère*, estate agency.
immobilisation [imɔbilizɑsjɔ̃] *s.f.* immobilization, stop, tying up, fastening; (pl.) fixed assets.
immobiliser [imɔbilize] *v.t.* to immobilize, to stop, to tie up, to fasten; to convert into real estate; **s'∼** *v.refl.* to stop, to come to a stop, to stand still or motionless.
immobilisme [imɔbilism] *s.m.* opposition to change or progress.
immobilité [imɔbilite] *s.f.* immobility, fixedness, inactivity, supineness, stillness.
immodération [imɔderɑsjɔ̃] *s.f.* immoderation.
immodéré, -e [imɔdere] *adj.* immoderate, excessive; **∼ment** [imɔderemɑ̃] *adv.* excessively.
immodeste [imɔdɛst] *adj.* (obs.) immodest, indecent.
immodestie [imɔdɛsti] *s.f.* (obs.) immodesty.
immolation [imɔlɑsjɔ̃] *s.f.* immolation, sacrifice.
immoler [imɔle] *v.t.* to immolate, to sacrifice, to kill; **s'∼** *v.refl.* to sacrifice oneself, to give one's life.
immonde [imɔ̃d] *adj.* filthy, unclean, foul, disgusting, ignoble, vile.
immondice [imɔ̃dis] *s.f.* (obs.) something dirty or impure; (mod.) (pl.) dirt, filth, refuse.
immoral, -e, (aux) [imɔral] *adj.* immoral; **∼ement** [imɔralmɑ̃] *adv.* immorally.
immoralisme [imɔralism] *s.m.* (phil.) immoralism.
immoraliste [imɔralist] *s.m.f.* (phil.) adherent of immoralism.
immoralité [imɔralite] *s.f.* immorality.
immortaliser [imɔrtalize] *v.t.* to immortalize, to perpetuate the memory of.
immortalité [imɔrtalite] *s.f.* immortality.
immortel, -le [imɔrtɛl] *adj.* immortal, everlasting; ∼ *s.m.* Academician (member of *l'Académie française*).
immortelle [imɔrtɛl] *s.f.* (bot.) everlasting flower, immortelle.
immotivé, -e [imɔtive] *adj.* motiveless, groundless, mindless.
immuabilité [imɥabilite] *s.f.* = IMMUTABILITÉ.
immuable [imɥabl] *adj.* immutable, immovable steadfast, unvarying; **∼ment** [imɥabləmɑ̃] *adv.* immutably, unalterably.
immuniser [imynize] *v.t.* to immunize, to inoculate.
immunité [imynite] *s.f.* immunity, exemption.
immunologie [imynɔlɔʒi] *s.f.* immunology.
immutabilité [imytabilite] *s.f.* immutability.
impact [ɛ̃pakt] *s.m.* impact, collision.
impaction [ɛ̃paksjɔ̃] *s.f.* (med.) impaction.
impair, -e [ɛ̃pɛr] *adj.* (arith.) odd, uneven; (anat.) single, singular.
impair [ɛ̃pɛr] *s.m.* blunder, gaffe; *faire un ∼*, to make a blunder, to drop a brick.
impalpable [ɛ̃palpabl] *adj.* impalpable, intangible.
impardonnable [ɛ̃pardɔnabl] *adj.* unpardonable, unforgivable.
imparfait, -e [ɛ̃parfɛ] *adj.* imperfect, incomplete, defective; ∼ *s.m.* (gram.) imperfect (tense); **∼ement** [ɛ̃parfɛtmɑ̃] *adv.* imperfectly, incompletely, not entirely.
imparité [ɛ̃parite] *s.f.* imparity, oddness; disparity, inequality.
impartageable [ɛ̃partaʒabl] *adj.* indivisible.
impartial, -e, (aux) [ɛ̃parsjal] *adj.* impartial, unprejudiced, unbiased; **∼ement** [ɛ̃parsjalmɑ̃] *adv.* impartially.
impartialité [ɛ̃parsjalite] *s.f.* impartiality.
impartir [ɛ̃partir] *v.t.* (law) to grant, to allow; to impart (gift, etc.); ⚠ not 'to impart' information, etc.
impasse [ɛ̃pas] *s.f.* blind alley, dead end, cul-de-sac; (fig.) impasse, deadlock, dilemma; (at cards) *faire une ∼*, to finesse; ∼ *budgétaire*, deficit that must be met by borrowing.
impassibilité [ɛ̃pasibilite] *s.f.* impassibility, impassiveness.
impassible [ɛ̃pasibl] *adj.* impassible, impassive; unmoved, unperturbed, unconcerned; unimpressionable.
impatiemment [ɛ̃pasjamɑ̃] *adv.* impatiently.
impatience [ɛ̃pasjɑ̃s] *s.f.* impatience, restlessness, longing; (pl.) show or gesture of impatience, fidgets; *avoir des ∼s dans les jambes*, to have the fidgets.
impatient, -e [ɛ̃pasjɑ̃] *adj.* impatient, restless, fidgety, anxious, eager.
impatientant, -e [ɛ̃pasjɑ̃tɑ̃] *adj.* provoking, tiresome, irksome.
impatienter [ɛ̃pasjɑ̃te] *v.t.* to make impatient, to make (s.o.) lose patience, to provoke, to exasperate; **s'∼** *v.refl.* to show impatience, to be impatient; *s'∼ contre qn.*, to lose patience with s.o.; *s'∼ de qch.*, to get impatient or fed up, with sth.; *s'∼ de faire qch.*, to be impatient to do sth.
impatroniser [ɛ̃patrɔnize] *v.t.* to put in authority or possession; **s'∼** *v.refl.* to assume authority, to impose oneself.
impayable [ɛ̃pɛjabl] *adj.* invaluable, priceless, exceedingly funny.
impayé, -e [ɛ̃peje] *adj.* unpaid; *les ∼s*, unpaid bills, etc.
impeccabilité [ɛ̃pekabilite] *s.f.* impeccability, unimpeachableness.
impeccable [ɛ̃pekabl] *adj.* impeccable, unerring; perfectly correct, faultless, unimpeachable; (fam.) perfect; **∼ment** [ɛ̃pekabləmɑ̃] *adv.* impeccably, faultlessly.
impédance [ɛ̃pedɑ̃s] *s.f.* (electr.) impedance.
impedimenta [ɛ̃pidmɛ̃ta] *s.m.pl.* impedimenta.
impénétrabilité [ɛ̃penetrabilite] *s.f.* impenetrability, imperviousness.
impénétrable [ɛ̃penetrabl] *adj.* impenetrable, impervious, inscrutable.
impénitence [ɛ̃penitɑ̃s] *s.f.* impenitence; *mourir dans l'∼ finale*, to die impenitent.

impénitent, -e [ɛ̃pinitɑ̃] *adj.* impenitent, incorrigible.
impensable [ɛ̃pɑ̃sabl] *adj.* inconceivable, incredible.
impense [ɛ̃pɑ̃s] *s.f.* expense (for repairs and improvements to an estate).
impérati-f, -ve [ɛ̃peratif] *adj.* imperative, commanding, peremptory, imperious; **~f** *s.m.* (gram., phil.) imperative; **~vement** [ɛ̃perativmɑ̃] *adv.* imperatively.
impératrice [ɛ̃peratris] *s.f.* empress.
imperceptibilité [ɛ̃pɛrsɛptibilite] *s.f.* imperceptibility.
imperceptible [ɛ̃pɛrsɛptibl] *adj.* imperceptible, indistinguishable, insignificant; **~ment** [ɛ̃pɛrsɛptibləmɑ̃] *adv.* imperceptibly.
imperdable [ɛ̃pɛrdabl] *adj.* that cannot be lost.
imperfectible [ɛ̃pɛrfɛktibl] *adj.* imperfectible.
imperfection [ɛ̃pɛrfɛksjɔ̃] *s.f.* imperfection, imperfectness; defect, blemish.
impérial, -e, (**aux**) [ɛ̃perjal] *adj.* imperial; **~ement** [ɛ̃perjalmɑ̃] *adv.* imperially.
impériale [ɛ̃perjal] *s.f.* **1.** (of coach, bus, etc.) top, roof, outside; **2.** (at cards) all-fours; **3.** imperial (beard).
impérialisme [ɛ̃perjalism] *s.m.* imperialism.
impérialiste [ɛ̃perjalist] *adj., s.m.f.* imperialist.
impérieu-x, -se [ɛ̃perjø] *adj.* imperious, domineering, overbearing; **~sement** [ɛ̃perjøzmɑ̃] *adv.* imperiously.
impérissable [ɛ̃perisabl] *adj.* imperishable, everlasting.
impéritie [ɛ̃perisi] *s.f.* incapacity, inefficiency.
imperméabiliser [ɛ̃pɛrmeabilize] *v.t.* to make waterproof.
imperméabilité [ɛ̃pɛrmeabilite] *s.f.* impermeability, imperviousness.
imperméable [ɛ̃pɛrmeabl] *adj.* impermeable, impervious, waterproof, water-repellent, watertight, airtight; **~** *s.m.* raincoat, mackintosh, waterproof.
impersonnalité [ɛ̃pɛrsɔnalite] *s.f.* impersonality, impersonal quality.
impersonnel, -le [ɛ̃pɛrsɔnɛl] *adj.* impersonal; **~lement** [ɛ̃pɛrsɔnɛlmɑ̃] *adv.* impersonally.
impertinemment [ɛ̃pɛrtinamɑ̃] *adv.* impertinently, insolently; (obs.) inappropriately, foolishly.
impertinence [ɛ̃pɛrtinɑ̃s] *s.f.* **1.** (obs.) irrelevance, inappropriateness; foolishness; **2.** impertinence, rudeness, insolence; piece of impertinence, rude remark.
impertinent, -e [ɛ̃pɛrtinɑ̃] *adj.* **1.** (obs.) irrelevant, out of place; foolish; **2.** impertinent, rude, insolent, cheeky.
imperturbabilité [ɛ̃pɛrtyrbabilite] *s.f.* imperturbability.
imperturbable [ɛ̃pɛrtyrbabl] *adj.* imperturbable; **~ment** [ɛpɛrtyrbabləmɑ̃] *adv.* imperturbably.
impétigo [ɛ̃petigo] *s.m.* (med.) impetigo.
impétrant, -e [ɛ̃petrɑ̃] *s.m.f.* recipient (of diploma, etc.); (law) grantee.
impétrer [ɛ̃petre] *v.t.* (law) to obtain (authority).
impétueu-x, -se [ɛ̃petɥø] *adj.* impetuous, hot-headed, impulsive; **~sement** [ɛ̃petɥøzmɑ̃] *adv.* impetuously.
impétuosité [ɛ̃petɥozite] *s.f.* impetuosity, impulsiveness.
impie [ɛ̃pi] *adj.* impious, godless, ungodly; **~** *s.m.f.* impious person, blasphemer; atheist, non-believer.
impieté [ɛ̃piete] *s.f.* impiety, ungodliness; act of impiety, blasphemy.
impitoyable [ɛ̃pitwajabl] *adj.* pitiless, unpitying, ruthless, relentless, unmerciful, hard-hearted, inexorable; **~ment** [ɛ̃pitwajabləmɑ̃] *adv.* pitilessly, ruthlessly, inexorably.
implacabilité [ɛ̃plakabilite] *s.f.* implacability.
implacable [ɛ̃plakabl] *adj.* implacable, irreconcilable, relentless, inexorable; **~ment** [ɛ̃plakabləmɑ̃] *adv.* implacably.
implant [ɛ̃plɑ̃] *s.m.* (med.) implant, graft.
implantation [ɛ̃plɑ̃tɑsjɔ̃] *s.f.* **1.** (med.) implantation; **2.** introduction, settling, establishing, (of new population, industries, etc.); laying-out (of building-site, etc.).
implanter [ɛ̃plɑ̃te] *v.t.* **1.** to plant, to fix; **2.** to implant, to establish, to introduce; **s'~** *v.refl.* to implant itself, to take root, to be fixed, to be introduced.
implexe [ɛ̃plɛks] *adj.* (obs.) intricate.
implication [ɛ̃plikɑsjɔ̃] *s.f.* implication, involvement.
implicite [ɛ̃plisit] *adj.* implicit, implied; **~ment** [ɛ̃plisitmɑ̃] *adv.* implicitly.
impliquer [ɛ̃plike] *v.t.* to implicate, to involve, to imply.
imploration [ɛ̃plɔrɑsjɔ̃] *s.f.* imploration, imploring, supplication.
implorer [ɛ̃plɔre] *v.t.* to implore, to beseech, to crave, to beg.
impoli, -e [ɛ̃pɔli] *adj.* uncivil, rude, discourteous, impolite; (obs.) uncivilized, uncouth; *s.m.f.* uncivil person; **~ment** [ɛ̃pɔlimɑ̃] *adv.* uncivilly, rudely.
impolitesse [ɛ̃pɔlitɛs] *s.f.* incivility, rudeness, impoliteness, piece of rudeness; *faire une ~*, to behave rudely.
impolitique [ɛ̃pɔlitik] *adj.* impolitic, unwise.
impondérabilité [ɛ̃pɔ̃derabilite] *s.f.* imponderability.
impondérable [ɛ̃pɔ̃derabl] *adj.* imponderable; **~** *s.m.* (pl.) imponderables.
impopulaire [ɛ̃pɔpylɛr] *adj.* unpopular.
impopularité [ɛ̃pɔpylarite] *s.f.* unpopularity.
importable[1] [ɛ̃pɔrtabl] *adj.* (of goods) that can be imported.
importable[2] [ɛ̃pɔrtabl] *adj.* (of garment) unwearable.
importance [ɛ̃pɔrtɑ̃s] *s.f.* importance, moment, worth, value, consequence; influence, prestige, high position, authority, credit; *avoir de l'~*, to be of importance or of moment; *attacher de l'~ à*, to consider important, to attach importance to; *c'est de peu d'~*, it's of little importance; *sans ~*, of no moment, of no consequence, of no importance, unimportant; *d'~*, (*adj. loc.*) important, of some consequence, (*adv. loc.*) soundly, thoroughly; *rosser qn. d'~*, to give s.o. a sound thrashing.
important, -e [ɛ̃pɔrtɑ̃] *adj.* important, momentous, of consequence, weighty, considerable; chief, essential; *peu ~*, unimportant; *une somme ~e*, a considerable sum; **~** *s.m.* important point, main thing, essential; self-important person; *l'~ est de*, the main thing is to; *faire l'~*, to put on airs, to pretend to be somebody.
importat-eur, -rice [ɛ̃pɔrtatœr] *s.m.f.* importer; *adj.* importing.
importation [ɛ̃pɔrtɑsjɑ̃] *s.f.* importation, importing; introduction; import.
importer[1] [ɛ̃pɔrte] *v.t.* to import; (fig.) to introduce, to bring in.
importer[2] [ɛ̃pɔrte] *v.t.i.* (used only in infin. and 3rd pers.) to be of importance or consequence, to matter, to mean; *qu'importe?*, what does it matter?, what difference does it make?; (*il*) *n'importe*, it doesn't matter, it makes no difference; *peu importe*, it doesn't much matter, it makes little difference; *peu m'importe que*, I don't mind if; *cela m'importe peu*, it doesn't mean much to me, it makes little difference to me; *que m'importent de telles choses?*, what do such things

matter to me?, what do I care about such things?; *n'importe qui*, anyone; *n'importe quoi*, anything, something or other; *n'importe quel*, any; *n'importe lequel*, any, either, it doesn't matter which; *n'importe où*, anywhere; *n'importe comment*, anyhow, somehow; *n'importe quand*, at any time.

import–export [ɛ̃pɔrɛkspɔr] *s.m.* import and export (business).

importun, -e [ɛ̃pɔrtœ̃] *adj.* importunate, tiresome, troublesome; ill-timed, unwelcome, obtrusive; *s.m.f.* intruder, bore, tiresome person.

importunément [ɛ̃pɔrtynemɑ̃] *adv.* importunately, obtrusively.

importuner [ɛ̃pɔrtyne] *v.t.* to importune, to annoy, to pester, to harass, to trouble, to inconvenience, to molest, to intrude on.

importunité [ɛ̃pɔrtynite] *s.f.* importunity, importuning, pestering; tiresomeness, disagreeableness; discomfort; *obtenir qch. de qn. à force d'~*, to pester s.o. into giving sth.

imposable [ɛ̃pozabl] *adj.* taxable.

imposant, -e [ɛ̃pozɑ̃] *adj.* imposing, impressive, commanding.

imposé, -e [ɛ̃poze] *adj.* **1.** prescribed, laid down; **2.** liable to tax; *s.m.f.* taxpayer, ratepayer.

imposer [ɛ̃poze] *v.t.* **1.** (obs.) to impute, to ascribe (sth. evil), (*à*, to); **2.** *~ à qn.*, to impose on s.o., to deceive s.o.; **3.** to exact (payment, etc.); *~ à qn.*, to exact payment from s.o., to make s.o. liable to tax; *~ qch.*, to tax sth., to put a tax on sth.; **4.** to impose, to prescribe, to lay down, to enforce, to force (sth. on s.o.), to force acceptance (of sth.); to inflict; **5.** (obs.) *~ à*, (mod.) *en ~ à*, to impose on, to impress; **6.** (print.) to impose; (eccles.) to lay on hands; **s'~** *v.refl.* to impose or lay (sth.) on oneself; to assert oneself; to compel recognition; to be indispensable; *s'~ un devoir*, to lay a duty on oneself; *s'~ pour chef*, to get oneself recognized as leader; *la solution qui s'impose*, the only possible solution.

imposition [ɛ̃pozisjɔ̃] *s.f.* imposition; laying on (of hands); inflicting, infliction; tax, assessment; (print.) imposition; ⚠ not school 'imposition'.

impossibilité [ɛ̃pɔsibilite] *s.f.* impossibility; *de toute ~*, utterly impossible; *être, se trouver, dans l'~ de faire qch.*, to find it impossible to do sth.

impossible [ɛ̃pɔsibl] *adj.* impossible, out of the question; impracticable, not feasible; fantastic, fabulous; (fam.) absurd, unlikely, improbable; *~!*, impossible!, it can't be so!, I don't believe it!; *~ s.m.* (the) impossible; *je ferai l'~ pour*, I will make every effort to, I will do everything I possibly can to; *si, par ~*, if, against all probability; if, by any remote chance.

imposte [ɛ̃pɔst] *s.f.* (arch.) impost, fanlight, transom-light.

imposteur [ɛ̃pɔstœr] *s.m.* impostor, cheat, swindler, charlatan.

imposture [ɛ̃pɔstyr] *s.f.* imposture, deception, deceit, cheat, lie, swindle.

impôt [ɛ̃po] *s.m.* tax, duty, impost, taxation, rate; obligation; *~ sur le revenu*, income-tax; *frapper d'un ~*, to tax; *l'assiette de l'~*, the basis of taxation.

impotence [ɛ̃pɔtɑ̃s] *s.f.* impotence, impotency.

impotent, -e [ɛ̃pɔtɑ̃] *adj.* impotent, crippled; powerless; *être ~ d'un bras*, to have lost the use of an arm; *s.m.f.* cripple, invalid; ⚠ not sexually 'impotent'.

impraticabilité [ɛ̃pratikabilite] *s.f.* impracticability.

impraticable [ɛ̃pratikabl] *adj.* impracticable; (of road, etc.) impassable; not feasible, impossible to achieve.

imprécation [ɛ̃prekasjɔ̃] *s.f.* imprecation, curse, denunciation.

imprécatoire [ɛ̃prekatwar] *adj.* imprecatory.

imprécis, -e [ɛ̃presi] *adj.* imprecise, inaccurate, vague, blurred.

imprécision [ɛ̃presizjɔ̃] *s.f.* lack of precision, vagueness, inaccuracy.

imprégnation [ɛ̃preɲasjɔ̃] *s.f.* impregnation; (fig.) assimilation.

imprégner [ɛ̃preɲe] *v.t.* to impregnate, to saturate; **s'~** *v.refl.* to be impregnated or saturated; (fig.) to become imbued with.

imprenable [ɛ̃prənabl] *adj.* impregnable, inexpugnable, unassailable; protected.

imprésario, impresario [ɛ̃presarjo] *s.m.* impresario, manager.

imprescriptibilité [ɛ̃prɛskriptibilite] *s.f.* (law) imprescriptibility.

imprescriptible [ɛ̃preskriptibl] *adj.* (law) imprescriptible, indefeasible.

impression [ɛ̃presjɔ̃] *s.f.* impression; impress, impressing, stamping; printing, print, issue, edition; (paint.) priming; *être à l'~*, to be printing, to have gone to press; *faute d'~*, misprint; *faire ~*, to be impressive, to make or leave an impression; *avoir l'~ de*, to have an impression or feeling of; *avoir l'~ que*, to have the impression that, to feel that; *donner l'~*, or *une ~, de*, to give an impression of, to produce an effect or illusion of.

impressionnabilité [ɛ̃presjɔnabilite] *s.f.* impressionability, excitableness; (photo.) sensitivity.

impressionnable [ɛ̃presjɔnabl] *adj.* impressionable, sensitive, excitable.

impressionnant, -e [ɛ̃presjɔnɑ̃] *adj.* impressive, sensational, striking, moving.

impressionner [ɛ̃presjɔne] *v.t.* to impress, to make an impression on; to move, to affect; to act on (the retina); (photo.) to produce an image (on film, etc.).

impressionnisme [ɛ̃presjɔnism] *s.m.* impressionism.

impressionniste [ɛ̃presjɔnist] *s.m.f.* impressionist; *~ adj.* impressionist; impressionistic.

imprévisibilité [ɛ̃previzibilite] *s.f.* unforeseeableness.

imprévisible [ɛ̃previzibl] *adj.* unforeseeable.

imprévision [ɛ̃previzjɔ̃] *s.f.* want of foresight.

imprévoyance [ɛ̃prevwajɑ̃s] *s.f.* improvidence, carelessness, want of foresight.

imprévoyant, -e [ɛ̃prevwajɑ̃] *adj.* improvident, lacking in foresight.

imprévu, -e [ɛ̃prevy] *adj.* unforeseen, unexpected; *~ s.m.* the unforeseen; *en cas d'~*, for contingencies; in an emergency; *sauf ~*, barring accidents; unless something unforeseen should occur.

imprimable [ɛ̃mprimabl] *adj.* printable, worthy of publication.

imprimatur [ɛ̃primatyr] *s.m.invar.* imprimatur.

imprimé, -e [ɛ̃prime] *adj.* printed; *~ s.m.* print, printed letters or book; item of printed matter; (pl.) printed matter, books.

imprimer [ɛ̃prime] *v.t.* to impress, to imprint, to communicate, to impart, to instil; to stamp; to print, to have printed, to get into print, to publish; (paint.) to prime; *~ un mouvement à*, to give motion to, to set in motion; *se faire ~*, to have one's work published.

imprimerie [ɛ̃primri] *s.f.* art of printing, printing; printing office or house, press; *caractère d'~*, type.

imprimeur [ɛ̃primœr] *s.m.* printer.

improbabilité [ɛ̃prɔbabilite] *s.f.* improbability, unlikelihood.

improbable [ɛ̃prɔbabl] *adj.* improbable, unlikely.

improbat-eur, -rice [ɛ̃prɔbatœr] *adj.* disapprobatory, disapproving.

improbation [ɛ̃prɔbɑsjɔ̃] *s.f.* disapproval, disapprobation.
improbité [ɛ̃prɔbite] *s.f.* improbity, dishonesty.
improducti-f, -ve [ɛ̃prɔdyktif] *adj.* unproductive.
impromptu [ɛ̃prɔ̃pty] *s.m.* impromptu; *en* ~, on impulse, on the spur of the moment; ~ *adv.*, *adj.invar.* impromptu, without preparation, extempore, unpremeditated(ly), sudden(ly).
imprononçable [ɛ̃prɔnɔ̃sabl] *adj.* unpronounceable.
impropre [ɛ̃prɔpr] *adj.* unfit, unsuitable (*à*, for), inappropriate; inaccurate, wrong; improper; **~ment** [ɛ̃prɔprəmɑ̃] *adv.* incorrectly, inaccurately; ⚠ not 'improper' in sense 'indecent'.
impropriété [ɛ̃prɔpriete] *s.f.* unfitness, inappropriateness; inaccuracy, incorrectness; ⚠ see IMPROPRE.
improvisat-eur, -rice [ɛ̃prɔvizatœr] *s.m.f.* improviser, extemporizer.
improvisation [ɛ̃prɔvizɑsjɔ̃] *s.f.* improvisation; (mus.) improvisation, extemporization.
improviser [ɛ̃prɔvize] *v.t.* **1.** to improvise, to extemporize, to do or say (sth.) on the spur of the moment; ~ *un discours*, to speak extempore; ~ *un pique-nique*, to arrange a hasty picnic; ~ *à l'orgue*, to improvise, to extemporize, on the organ; **2.** to put (s.o.) in a job extempore; *on l'improvisa maître d'hôtel*, he was appointed extempore butler.
(**à l'**)**improviste** [alɛ̃prɔvist] *adv.loc.* all of a sudden, unexpectedly; extempore; *prendre qn. à l'*~, to take s.o. unawares or by surprise; *survenir à l'*~, to turn up unexpectedly, to happen out of the blue.
imprudemment [ɛ̃prydamɑ̃] *adv.* imprudently, incautiously, indiscreetly.
imprudence [ɛ̃prydɑ̃s] *s.f.* imprudence, heedlessness, rashness, unwisdom, indiscretion; imprudent act or speech; *commettre une* ~, to be guilty of an indiscretion; *faire des* ~*s*, to act imprudently or rashly.
imprudent, -e [ɛ̃prydɑ̃] *adj.* imprudent, heedless, incautious, rash, foolhardy, daring; unwise, indiscreet.
impubère [ɛ̃pybɛr] *adj.* (law) under the age of puberty.
impubliable [ɛ̃pybliabl] *adj.* unpublishable.
impudemment [ɛ̃pydamɑ̃] *adv.* impudently, shamelessly.
impudence [ɛ̃pydɑ̃s] *s.f.* impudence, shamelessness, effrontery, brazenness, cheek.
impudent, -e [ɛ̃pydɑ̃] *adj.* impudent, shameless, brazen, cheeky.
impudeur [ɛ̃pydœr] *s.f.* immodesty, indecency, impudicity; impudence.
impudicité [ɛ̃pydisite] *s.f.* impudicity, unchastity, lewdness; indecent act, lewd behaviour, obscenity of speech.
impudique [ɛ̃pydik] *adj.* immodest, unchaste, lewd, indecent, obscene; **~ment** [ɛ̃pydikmɑ̃] unchastely, immodestly, lewdly, obscenely.
impuissance [ɛ̃pɥisɑ̃s] *s.f.* powerlessness, impotence, inability, incapacity; (pathol.) impotence.
impuissant, -e [ɛ̃pɥisɑ̃] *adj.* powerless, unable, ineffectual; ~ *à*, incapable of; ~ *s.m.*, *adj.* impotent (man).
impulsi-f, -ve [ɛ̃pylsif] *adj.* (obs.) impellent; (mod.) impulsive; *s.m.f.* impulsive person; **~vement** [ɛ̃pylsivmɑ̃] *adv.* impulsively.
impulsion [ɛ̃pylsjɔ̃] *s.f.* impulsion, impulse, impetus, spur; compulsion, urge.
impulsivité [ɛ̃pylsivite] *s.f.* impulsiveness.
impunément [ɛ̃pynemɑ̃] *adv.* with impunity, without risk, without suffering disadvantage.
impuni, -e [ɛ̃pyni] *adj.* unpunished; *laisser un affront* ~, to put up with an insult.
impunité [ɛ̃pynite] *s.f.* impunity.
impur, -e [ɛ̃pyr] *adj.* impure, foul, unclean, unchaste, lewd; adulterated; **~ement** [ɛ̃pyrmɑ̃] *adv.* impurely.
impureté [ɛ̃pyrte] *s.f.* impurity, obscenity; corruption; (pl.) impurities (in water, etc.).
imputable [ɛ̃pytabl] *adj.* imputable, attributable; chargeable (*sur*, to, on).
imputation [ɛ̃pytɑsjɔ̃] *s.f.* **1.** imputation, accusation, charge; **2.** charge, charging (of expenses, etc.); appropriation (of moneys to a debt).
imputer [ɛ̃pyte] *v.t.* **1.** to impute, to attribute, to ascribe; ~ *un crime à qn.*, to impute a crime to s.o., to accuse s.o. of a crime; ~ *qch. à négligence*, to attribute sth. to carelessness; *on ne peut en* ~ *la faute à personne*, one cannot put the blame for it on anyone; **2.** to charge (a sum to an account); to assign (moneys to a debt).
inabordable [inabɔrdabl] *adj.* inaccessible, unapproachable, unassailable; (of price) prohibitive.
inabrité, -e [inabrite] *adj.* unsheltered.
inabrogeable [inabrɔʒabl] *adj.* not repealable.
inaccentué, -e [inaksɑ̃tɥe] *adj.* (lang.) unaccented, unstressed.
inacceptable [inaksɛptabl] *adj.* unacceptable.
inaccessibilité [inaksesibilite] *s.f.* inaccessibility.
inaccessible [inaksesibl] *adj.* inaccessible, unattainable, unapproachable; (fig.) insensible, unmoved.
inaccomplissement [inakɔ̃plismɑ̃] *s.m.* non-fulfilment, non-accomplishment.
inaccordable [inakɔrdabl] *adj.* not allowable, ungrantable, inadmissible.
inaccoutumé, -e [inakutyme] *adj.* unaccustomed, unwonted, unusual.
inachevé, -e [inaʃve] *adj.* unfinished, incomplete.
inachèvement [inaʃɛvmɑ̃] *s.m.* incompletion, incompleteness, unfinished state.
inacti-f, -ve [inaktif] *adj.* inactive, inert, sluggish, unemployed.
inactinique [inaktinik] *adj.* (phys.) inactinic; (photo.) *éclairage* ~, safe light.
inaction [inaksjɔ̃] *s.f.* inaction, inertness, sluggishness, idleness; *rester dans l'*~, to remain inactive.
inactivité [inaktivite] *s.f.* inactivity, inaction; *être dans l'*~, to be unemployed.
inadaptation [inadaptɑsjɔ̃] *s.f.* (psychol.) maladjustment.
inadapté, -e [inadapte] *adj.* unsuited; (psychol.) maladjusted; *les* ~*s*, social misfits.
inadéquat, -e [inadekwa] *adj.* inadequate.
inadmissibilité [inadmisibilite] *s.f.* inadmissibility.
inadmissible [inadmisibl] *adj.* inadmissible, unacceptable, intolerable, unthinkable.
inadvertance [inadvɛrtɑ̃s] *s.f.* inadvertence, oversight; *par* ~, inadvertently, by an oversight.
inaliénabilité [inaljenabilite] *s.f.* inalienability.
inaliénable [inaljenabl] *adj.* inalienable, untransferable.
inalliable [inaljabl] *adj.* (of metals) that cannot be alloyed; (fig.) incompatible.
inaltérabilité [inalterabilite] *s.f.* inalterability, immutability.
inaltérable [inalterabl] *adj.* inalterable, unchangeable, immutable, unchanging; that cannot be spoilt or worn out; *matière* ~ *à la chaleur*, substance not affected by heat.
inamical, -e, (**aux**) [inamikal] *adj.* unfriendly, hostile.
inamovibilité [inamɔvibilite] *s.f.* irremovability, permanency.

inamovible [inamɔvibl] *adj.* irremovable, permanent, for life.
inanimé, -e [inanime] *adj.* inanimate, lifeless, inert.
inanité [inanite] *s.f.* inanity, emptiness, nothingness, vanity, futility.
inanition [inanisjɔ̃] *s.f.* inanition, starvation; *tomber d'*~, to faint for want of food; to be madly hungry.
inapaisable [inapɛzabl] *adj.* unappeasable, that cannot be relieved, unquenchable.
inapaisé, -e [inapeze] *adj.* unappeased, unquenched, unassuaged, unpacified.
inaperçu, -e [inapɛrsy] *adj.* unperceived, unseen, unnoticed, unheeded.
inappétence [inapetɑ̃s] *s.f.* inappetence, want of appetite; listlessness, indifference.
inapplicable [inaplikabl] *adj.* inapplicable, irrelevant.
inapplication [inaplikɑsjɔ̃] *s.f.* **1.** lack of application, inattention; **2.** non-application (of a law, etc.).
inappliqué, -e [inaplike] *adj.* **1.** inattentive, lacking in application; **2.** not applied.
inappréciable [inapresjabl] *adj.* **1.** inestimable, invaluable; **2.** imperceptible.
inapprivoisable [inaprivwazabl] *adj.* untamable.
inapprivoisé, -e [inaprivwaze] *adj.* untamed.
inapte [inapt] *adj.* inapt, without aptitude, unfit (*à*, for); unsuited; ~ *s.m.f.* handicapped person.
inaptitude [inaptityd] *s.f.* inaptitude, incapacity, unfitness.
inarrangeable [inarɑ̃ʒabl] *adj.* unarrangeable, (of dispute) that cannot be settled.
inarticulé, -e [inartikyle] *adj.* inarticulate.
inassimilable [inasimilabl] *adj.* not assimilable.
inassouvi, -e [inasuvi] *adj.* unsatiated, unsatisfied, unquenched, ungratified.
inattaquable [inatakabl] *adj.* unassailable, inexpugnable; (fig.) unimpeachable, irreproachable, unquestionable.
inattendu, -e [inatɑ̃dy] *adj.* unexpected, unlooked for, unforeseen.
inattenti-f, -ve [inatɑ̃tif] *adj.* inattentive; unmindful, heedless, (*à*, of).
inattention [inatɑ̃sjɔ̃] *s.f.* inattention, carelessness, heedlessness, inadvertency.
inaudible [inodibl] *adj.* inaudible; not worth listening to.
inaugural, -e, (**aux**) [inogyral] *adj.* inaugural, opening.
inauguration [inogyrɑsjɔ̃] *s.f.* inauguration, opening, ushering-in; unveiling (of plaque, etc.).
inaugurer [inogyre] *v.t.* to inaugurate, to open, to unveil, to institute, to usher in; to mark the beginning of.
inauthenticité [inotɑ̃tisite] *s.f.* want of authenticity.
inauthentique [inotɑ̃tik] *adj.* not authentic, not genuine.
inavouable [inavwabl] *adj.* unavowable, shameful.
inca [ɛ̃ka] *adj.invar.*, *s.* (hist.) Inca.
incalculable [ɛ̃kalkylabl] *adj.* incalculable, countless.
incandescence [ɛ̃kɑ̃dɛsɑ̃s] *s.f.* incandescence.
incandescent, -e [ɛ̃kɑ̃dɛsɑ̃] *adj.* incandescent, white-hot.
incantation [ɛ̃kɑ̃tɑsjɔ̃] *s.f.* incantation; spell.
incapable [ɛ̃kapabl] *adj.* incapable, unable, unfit; unqualified, not qualified, disqualified, incompetent; ~ *s.m.f.* disqualified or unfit person.
incapacité [ɛ̃kapasite] *s.f.* incapacity, incapability, inability, unfitness; (law) disqualification, incompetence; *frapper d'*~, to incapacitate.
incarcération [ɛ̃karserɑsjɔ̃] *s.f.* incarceration.
incarcérer [ɛ̃karsere] *v.t.* to incarcerate, to imprison.
incarnadin, -e [ɛ̃karnadɛ̃] *adj.* incarnadine, flesh-coloured.
incarnat, -e [ɛ̃karna] *adj.* incarnadine, rose-red; *trèfle* ~, crimson clover; ~ *s.m.* flesh-colour, crimson.
incarnation [ɛ̃karnɑsjɔ̃] *s.f.* incarnation; (fig.) embodiment, incarnation.
incarner [ɛ̃karne] *v.t.* to incarnate; to embody in flesh; (fig.) to be the embodiment of; (theatr.) to play the part of; **s'**~ *v.refl.* to be incarnated; to be made flesh.
incartade [ɛ̃kartad] *s.f.* **1.** rude outburst; **2.** sudden swerve (of horse); (fig.) indiscretion, kicking over the traces.
incassable [ɛ̃kɑsabl] *adj.* unbreakable.
incendiaire [ɛ̃sɑ̃djɛr] *adj.* incendiary; (fig.) inflammatory, provocative, that inflames desire.
incendie [ɛ̃sɑ̃di] *s.m.* fire, conflagration, blaze, burning light; (fig.) upheaval, war.
incendier [ɛ̃sɑ̃dje] *v.t.* to set fire to, to burn down; (fig.) to inflame, to excite; (pop.) to heap abuse on.
incertain, -e [ɛ̃sɛrtɛ̃] *adj.* uncertain, questionable, undecided, unsettled, dubious, doubtful, wavering; indistinct, vague, faint.
incertitude [ɛ̃sɛrtityd] *s.f.* uncertainty, doubt, incertitude, suspense; indecision, hesitation.
incessamment [ɛ̃sɛsamɑ̃] *adv.* at once, directly; incessantly, unceasingly.
incessant, -e [ɛ̃sɛsɑ̃] *adj.* incessant, ceaseless, unceasing, continual, repeated.
incessibilité [ɛ̃sesibilite] *s.f.* inalienability.
incessible [ɛ̃sesibl] *adj.* not transferable, inalienable.
inceste [ɛ̃sɛst] *s.m.* incest, incestuous passion.
incestueu-x, -se [ɛ̃sɛstɥø] *adj.*, *s.m.f.* incestuous (person).
inchangé, -e [ɛ̃ʃɑ̃ʒe] *adj.* unchanged.
inchauffable [ɛ̃ʃofabl] *adj.* impossible or difficult to heat.
inchavirable [ɛ̃ʃavirabl] *adj.* uncapsizable.
inchoati-f, -ve [ɛ̃kɔatif] *adj.* (gram.) inceptive, inchoative.
incidemment [ɛ̃sidamɑ̃] *adv.* incidentally, casually.
incidence [ɛ̃sidɑ̃s] *s.f.* incidence; effect, influence.
incident, -e [ɛ̃sidɑ̃] *adj.* incidental, fortuitous, casual; (phys.) (of light, etc.) incident, falling on; ~**e** *s.f.* (gram.) parenthetical clause, parenthesis.
incident [ɛ̃sidɑ̃] *s.m.* incident, occurrence, event; episode; subordinate action; point of law; objection.
incinérateur [ɛ̃sineratœr] *s.m.* incinerator.
incinération [ɛ̃sinerɑsjɔ̃] *s.f.* incineration, cremation.
incinérer [ɛ̃sinere] *v.t.* to incinerate, to cremate.
incirconcis [ɛ̃sirkɔ̃si] *adj.*, *s.m.* uncircumcised (person); (obs., fig.) sinner.
incise [ɛ̃siz] *s.f.* (gram.) interpolated clause, parenthetical phrase.
incisé, -e [ɛ̃size] *adj.* (bot.) incised.
inciser [ɛ̃size] *v.t.* to make an incision in, to incise, to gash, to tap.
incisi-f, -ve [ɛ̃sizif] *adj.* incisive, sharp, cutting; (*dent*) ~*ve*, incisor (tooth).
incision [ɛ̃sizjɔ̃] *s.f.* incision, cut, gash, notch.
incitat-eur, -rice [ɛ̃sitatœr] *s.m.f.* inciter, instigator.
incitation [ɛ̃sitɑsjɔ̃] *s.f.* incitation, incitement, incentive.

inciter [ɛ̃site] *v.t.* to incite, to urge, to stir up; to instigate.
incivil, -e [ɛ̃sivil] *adj.* uncivil, rude, discourteous.
incivilisable [ɛ̃sivilizabl] *adj.* uncivilizable.
incivilité [ɛ̃sivilite] *s.f.* incivility, rudeness, discourtesy; rude remark; *commettre une* ~, to behave rudely.
incivique [ɛ̃sivik] *adj.* unpatriotic.
inclassable [ɛ̃klɑsabl] *adj.* unclassifiable, nondescript.
inclémence [ɛ̃klemɑ̃s] *s.f.* inclemency.
inclément, -e [ɛ̃klemɑ̃] *adj.* inclement, harsh.
inclinaison [ɛ̃klinɛzɔ̃] *s.f.* inclination, incline, gradient, slope; tilt, (naut.) list; inclining, leaning; dip, dipping; bow, bowing.
inclination [ɛ̃klinɑsjɔ̃] *s.f.* **1.** inclination, tendency; **2.** bow, nod.
incliner [ɛ̃kline] *v.t.* to incline, to slant, to slope, to tip, to bow; (fig.) to incline, to influence; ~ *v.i.* (obs.) to slope away; (mod.) ~ *à*, to be inclined to; **s'~** *v.refl.* to bend, to slant, to slope, to bow, to give way.
inclure [ɛ̃klyr] *v.t.* to include, to enclose.
inclus, -e [ɛ̃kly] *adj.* enclosed, included; *ci-~*, enclosed (herewith).
inclusi-f, -ve [ɛ̃klyzif] *adj.* inclusive.
inclusion [ɛ̃klyzjɔ̃] *s.f.* inclusion, enclosing.
inclusivement [ɛ̃klyzivmɑ̃] *adv.* inclusively; *du vendredi au mardi* ~, from Friday to Tuesday inclusive; *jusqu'au 20* ~, up to and including the 20th.
incoercible [ɛ̃kɔɛrsibl] *adj.* incoercible, irrepressible.
incognito [ɛ̃nkɔɲito] *adv., s.m.* incognito.
incohérence [ɛ̃kɔerɑ̃s] *s.f.* incoherence, incoherency.
incohérent, -e [ɛ̃kɔerɑ̃] *adj.* incoherent, rambling, disjointed; inconsistent.
incollable [ɛ̃kɔlabl] *adj.* (fam.) (of candidate) who cannot be stumped or failed, who knows all the answers.
incolore [ɛ̃kɔlɔr] *adj.* colourless; (fig.) lifeless; *un sourire* ~, a wan smile.
incomber [ɛ̃kɔ̃be] *v.t.* to be incumbent (*à*, on); *les devoirs qui vous incombent*, the duties which fall on you; *c'est à vous qu'il incombe de faire une démarche*, the onus of making a move lies on you, it is up to you to make a move.
incombustibilité [ɛ̃kɔ̃bystibilite] *s.f.* incombustibility.
incombustible [ɛ̃kɔ̃bystibl] *adj.* incombustible, fireproof.
incommensurabilité [ɛ̃kɔmɑ̃syrabilite] *s.f.* incommensurability.
incommensurable [ɛ̃kɔmɑ̃syrabl] *adj.* incommensurable, immeasurable, boundless, enormous; ~ *s.m. l'~*, the infinite; **~ment** [ɛ̃kɔmɑ̃syrablamɑ̃] *adv.* enormously, infinitely.
incommodant, -e [ɛ̃kɔmɔdɑ̃] *adj.* annoying, troublesome, inconvenient.
incommode [ɛ̃kɔmɔd] *adj.* inconvenient, incommodious, troublesome, tiresome, disagreeable; uncomfortable, unhandy.
incommodément [ɛ̃kɔmɔdemɑ̃] *adv.* uncomfortably.
incommoder [ɛ̃kɔmɔde] *v.t.* to incommode, to inconvenience, to disagree with, to annoy, to trouble, to disturb, to upset; (obs.) *être incommodé*, to be indisposed.
incommodité [ɛ̃kɔmɔdite] *s.f.* inconvenience, trouble, discomfort, uncomfortableness; (obs.) indisposition.
incommunicable [ɛ̃kɔmynikabl] *adj.* **1.** incommunicable, that cannot be communicated or expressed, not transmittable; **2.** with no communication.
incommutabilité [ɛ̃kɔmytabilite] *s.f.* (law) indefeasibility.
incommutable [ɛ̃kɔmytabl] *adj.* (law) inalienable.
incomparable [ɛ̃kɔ̃parabl] *adj.* incomparable, matchless, unequalled; **~ment** [ɛ̃kɔ̃parabləmɑ̃] *adv.* incomparably.
incompatibilité [ɛ̃kɔ̃patibilite] *s.f.* incompatibility.
incompatible [ɛ̃kɔ̃patibl] *adj.* incompatible, contradictory.
incompétence [ɛ̃kɔ̃petɑ̃s] *s.f.* incompetence, incompetency.
incompétent, -e [ɛ̃kɔ̃petɑ̃] *adj.* incompetent, not qualified, unqualified.
incompl-et, -ète [ɛ̃kɔ̃plɛ] *adj.* incomplete, imperfect; **~ètement** [ɛ̃kɔ̃plɛtmɑ̃] *adv.* incompletely, imperfectly.
incompréhensibilité [ɛ̃kɔ̃preɑ̃sibilite] *s.f.* incomprehensibility.
incompréhensible [ɛ̃kɔ̃preɑ̃sibl] *adj.* incomprehensible, unintelligible, inconceivable.
incompréhensi-f, -ve [ɛ̃kɔ̃preɑ̃sif] *adj.* uncomprehending, lacking in understanding.
incompréhension [ɛ̃kɔ̃preɑ̃sjɔ̃] *s.f.* incomprehension, lack of understanding, obtuseness; misunderstanding.
incompressibilité [ɛ̃kɔ̃prɛsibilite] *s.f.* incompressibility.
incompressible [ɛ̃kɔ̃prɛsibl] *adj.* incompressible; irreducible.
incompris, -e [ɛ̃kɔ̃pri] *adj.* not understood, unappreciated; *s.m.f.* misunderstood person.
inconcevable [ɛ̃kɔ̃svabl] *adj.* inconceivable, unimaginable; incredible; **~ment** [ɛ̃kɔ̃svabləmɑ̃] *adv.* inconceivably.
inconciliable [ɛ̃kɔ̃siljabl] *adj.* irreconcilable, incompatible.
inconditionnel, -le [ɛ̃kɔ̃disjɔnɛl] *adj.* unconditional; unquestioning (obedience, etc.); **~lement** [ɛ̃kɔ̃disjɔnɛlmɑ̃] *adv.* unconditionally.
inconduite [ɛ̃kɔ̃dɥit] *s.f.* misconduct, immoral behaviour.
inconfort [ɛ̃kɔ̃fɔr] *s.m.* lack of comfort.
inconfortable [ɛ̃kɔ̃fɔrtabl] *adj.* uncomfortable; (fig.) disquieting; **~ment** [ɛ̃kɔ̃fɔrtɑbləmɑ̃] *adv.* uncomfortably.
incongru, -e [ɛ̃kɔ̃gry] *adj.* unsuitable, inappropriate, out of place; unseemly; with no manners.
incongruité [ɛ̃kɔ̃grɥite] *s.f.* unsuitability, inappropriateness; unseemliness, impropriety; unseemly remarks or behaviour.
inconnaissable [ɛ̃kɔnɛsabl] *adj.* unknowable; ~ *s.m. l'~*, the unknowable.
inconnu, -e [ɛ̃kɔny] *adj.* unknown, unfamiliar; obscure; (math.) (*quantité*) *~e*, unknown (quantity); (fig.) *être en pays* ~, to be in unfamiliar surroundings; to be at sea; *s.m.f.* unknown person, stranger; nobody; (law) *porter plainte contre* ~, to bring an action against person or persons unknown; ~ *s.m. l'~*, the unknown.
inconsciemment [ɛ̃kɔ̃sjamɑ̃] *adv.* unconsciously, unknowingly, unwittingly; thoughtlessly.
inconscience [ɛ̃kɔ̃sjɑ̃s] *s.f.* unconsciousness, unawareness, ignorance; thoughtlessness.
inconscient, -e [ɛ̃kɔ̃sjɑ̃] *adj.* unconscious, not conscious; unaware, ignorant; oblivious; ~ *s.m.* (psychol.) (the) unconscious.
inconséquence [ɛ̃kɔ̃sekɑ̃s] *s.f.* inconsequence, inconsistency; irresponsibility, thoughtless act or words.
inconséquent, -e [ɛ̃kɔ̃sekɑ̃] *adj.* inconsequential, inconsistent; irresponsible.
inconsidéré, -e [ɛ̃kɔ̃sidere] *adj.* unconsidered, thoughtless, without due reflection; ⚠ not 'inconsiderate' of people's feelings; **~ment** [ɛ̃kɔ̃sideremɑ̃] *adv.* thoughtlessly.

inconsistance [ɛ̃kɔ̃sistɑ̃s] *s.f.* inconsistency.
inconsistant, -e [ɛ̃kɔ̃sistɑ̃] *adj.* **1.** inconsistent, fickle; **2.** (of substances) loose, soft, lacking in consistency.
inconsolable [ɛ̃kɔ̃sɔlabl] *adj.* disconsolate, inconsolable.
inconsolé, -e [ɛ̃kɔ̃sɔle] *adj.* unconsoled, uncomforted.
inconstance [ɛ̃kɔ̃stɑ̃s] *s.f.* inconstancy, fickleness, changeableness.
inconstant, -e [ɛ̃kɔ̃stɑ̃] *adj.* inconstant, fluctuating, changeable, fickle, unsteady.
inconstatable [ɛ̃kɔstatabl] *adj.* inverifiable, indeterminable.
inconstitutionnalité [ɛ̃kɔ̃stitysjɔnalite] *s.f.* unconstitutionality.
inconstitutionnel, -le [ɛ̃kɔ̃stitysjɔnɛl] *adj.* unconstitutional; **~lement** [ɛ̃kɔ̃stitysjɔnɛlmɑ̃] *adv.* unconstitutionally.
inconstructible [ɛ̃kɔ̃stryktibl] *adj.* (of land) not suitable for building, not to be built over.
incontestable [ɛ̃kɔ̃tɛstabl] *adj.* incontestable, indisputable, unquestionable; **~ment** [ɛ̃kɔ̃tɛstabləmɑ̃] *adv.* incontestably, indisputably, unquestionably.
incontesté, -e [ɛ̃kɔ̃tɛste] *adj.* uncontested, unquestioned, undisputed.
incontinence [ɛ̃kɔ̃tinɑ̃s] *s.f.* incontinence, lack of restraint.
incontinent, -e [ɛ̃kɔ̃tinɑ̃] *adj.* incontinent; ~ *adv.* (obs.) forthwith.
incontrôlable [ɛ̃kɔ̃trolabl] *adj.* that cannot be verified or checked.
incontrôlé, -e [ɛ̃kɔ̃trole] *adj.* unchecked.
inconvenance [ɛ̃kɔ̃vnɑ̃s] *s.f.* impropriety, unseemliness; breach of good manners.
inconvenant, -e [ɛ̃kɔ̃vnɑ̃] *adj.* improper, unseemly, ill-mannered; indecent.
inconvénient [ɛ̃kɔ̃venjɑ̃] *s.m.* inconvenience, disadvantage, drawback, objection.
inconvertible [ɛ̃kɔ̃vɛrtibl] *adj.* **1.** (of paper-money) inconvertible; **2.** (obs.) (also *inconvertissable*) beyond hope of conversion.
incoordination [ɛ̃kɔɔrdinɑsjɔ̃] *s.f.* inco-ordination, lack of co-ordination; (med.) ataxia.
incorporation [ɛ̃kɔrpɔrɑsjɔ̃] *s.f.* incorporation; (mil.) enrolment, taking on strength.
incorporel, -le [ɛ̃kɔrpɔrɛl] *adj.* incorporeal.
incorporer [ɛ̃kɔrpɔre] *v.t.* to incorporate (*à*, with), to insert, to combine, to fuse, to mix; (mil.) to enrol; to embody; **s'~** *v.refl.* to get oneself incorporated.
incorrect, -e [ɛ̃kɔrɛkt] *adj.* incorrect, inaccurate, faulty; improper, rude, vulgar; **~ement** [ɛ̃kɔrɛktəmɑ̃] *adv.* incorrectly, inaccurately, wrongly.
incorrection [ɛ̃kɔrɛksjɔ̃] *s.f.* incorrectness, inaccuracy; breach of manners.
incorrigible [ɛ̃kɔriʒibl] *adj.* incorrigible, irreclaimable, hopeless, confirmed.
incorruptibilité [ɛ̃kɔryptibilite] *s.f.* incorruptibility.
incorruptible [ɛ̃kɔryptibl] *adj.* incorruptible.
incrédibilité [ɛ̃kredibilite] *s.f.* incredibility.
incrédule [ɛ̃kredyl] *adj.* incredulous, unbelieving; ~ *s.m.f.* unbeliever, free thinker.
incrédulité [ɛ̃kredylite] *s.f.* incredulity, unbelief.
incriminable [ɛ̃kriminabl] *adj.* **1.** (obs.) liable to prosecution, indictable; **2.** (Lit.) reprehensible.
incrimination [ɛ̃kriminɑsjɔ̃] *s.f.* incrimination, charge.
incriminer [ɛ̃krimine] *v.t.* to incriminate, to impeach, to charge (*de*, with), to indict.
incroyable [ɛ̃krwajabl] *adj.* incredible, past belief; unheard of; fantastic; ~ *s.m.* fop (under the French Directory), incroyable; **~ment** [ɛ̃krwajabləmɑ̃] *adv.* incredibly.
incroyance [ɛ̃krwajɑ̃s] *s.f.* unbelief.
incroyant, -e [ɛ̃krwajɑ̃] *adj.* unbelieving, irreligious; *s.m.f.* unbeliever.
incrustation [ɛ̃krystɑsjɔ̃] *s.f.* incrustation; inlaid work, inlaying.
incruster [ɛ̃kryst] *v.t.* to incrust; to inlay; to overlay, to cover; *un radiateur incrusté de tartre*, a furred-up radiator; **s'~** *v.refl.* to become incrusted or embedded; to be covered with a layer (of); to adhere (to); (fig.) to establish oneself permanently; to become engrained; *s'~ chez qn.*, to settle in on s.o. (and refuse to go).
incrusteu-r, -se [ɛ̃krystœr] *s.m.f.* inlayer.
incubateur [ɛ̃kybatœr] *s.m.* incubator.
incubation [ɛ̃kybɑsjɔ̃] *s.f.* incubation; (lit. & fig.) hatching.
incube [ɛ̃kyb] *s.m.* incubus.
incuber [ɛ̃kybe] *v.t.* to incubate.
inculpable [ɛ̃kylpabl] *adj.* chargeable, indictable.
inculpation [ɛ̃kylpɑsjɔ̃] *s.f.* inculpation, charge.
inculpé, -e [ɛ̃kylpe] *adj.* accused, charged; *s.m.f.* accused, defendant.
inculper [ɛ̃kylpe] *v.t.* to inculpate, to charge (*de*, with), to indict.
inculquer [ɛ̃kylke] *v.t.* to inculcate, to teach, to instil.
inculte [ɛ̃kylt] *adj.* uncultivated, untilled; (fig.) unkempt, neglected, rough, uncultured.
incultivable [ɛ̃kyltivabl] *adj.* (agric.) uncultivatable.
inculture [ɛ̃kyltyr] *s.f.* lack of culture.
incurable [ɛ̃kyrabl] *adj.* incurable; hopeless; **~ment** [ɛ̃kyrabləmɑ̃] *adv.* incurably.
incurie [ɛ̃kyri] *s.f.* carelessness, negligence, lack of interest.
incuriosité [ɛ̃kyrjozite] *s.f.* incuriosity, lack of curiosity.
incursion [ɛ̃kyrsjɔ̃] *s.f.* incursion, inroad, raid.
incurvation [ɛ̃kyrvɑsjɔ̃] *s.f.* incurvation, curvature.
incurvé, -e [ɛ̃kyrve] *adj.* curved, bent.
incurver [ɛ̃kyrve] *v.t.* to curve inward, to bend, to incurvate; **s'~** *v.refl.* to curve inward.
incuse [ɛ̃kyz] *adj.*, *s.f.* incuse (medal).
inde [ɛ̃d] *s.m.* indigo (dye).
Inde [ɛ̃d] *s.f.* (geog.) (also pl.) India; *la Mer des ~s*, the Indian Ocean; *les ~s occidentales, orientales*, the West, East, Indies.
indébrouillable [ɛ̃debrujabl] *adj.* inextricable; inexplicable.
indécemment [ɛ̃desamɑ̃] *adv.* indecently, improperly.
indécence [ɛ̃desɑ̃s] *s.f.* indecency, impropriety, obscenity; indecent act or speech.
indécent, -e [ɛ̃desɑ̃] *adj.* indecent, immodest, unseemly, improper, obscene.
indéchiffrable [ɛ̃deʃifrabl] *adj.* undecipherable, illegible; (fig.) unintelligible, incomprehensible, inexplicable.
indéchirable [ɛ̃deʃirabl] *adj.* untearable.
indécis, -e [ɛ̃desi] *adj.* uncertain, irresolute, wavering; indistinct, blurred, doubtful, vague.
indécision [ɛ̃desizjɔ̃] *s.f.* indecision, irresoluteness; doubt.
indéclinable [ɛ̃deklinabl] *adj.* indeclinable.
indécomposable [ɛ̃dekɔ̃pozabl] *adj.* irresolvable; not decomposable; that cannot be broken down into components.
indécrochable [ɛ̃dekrɔʃabl] *adj.* undetachable; (fig.) unattainable.
indécrottable [ɛ̃dekrɔtabl] *adj.* that is impossible to clean; (fig.) incorrigible.
indéfectible [ɛ̃defɛktibl] *adj.* indefectible, unfailing; **~ment** [ɛ̃defɛktibləmɑ̃] *adv.* indefectibly, unfailingly.
indéfendable [ɛ̃defɑ̃dabl] *adj.* indefensible, untenable.

indéfini, -e [ɛ̃defini] *adj.* indefinite, unlimited, undefined, undetermined; *passé* ~, perfect tense; **~ment** [ɛ̃definimɑ̃] *adv.* indefinitely.
indéfinissable [ɛ̃definisabl] *adj.* undefinable, indefinable, indeterminable.
indéformable [ɛ̃defɔrmabl] *adj.* that will not lose its shape, crease-resisting.
indéfrisable [ɛ̃defrizabl] *s.f.* (obs.) (hairdressing) permanent wave.
indélébile [ɛ̃delebil] *adj.* indelible, ineffaceable.
indélibéré, -e [ɛ̃delibere] *adj.* not deliberate, unpremeditated.
indélicat, -e [ɛ̃delika] *adj.* indelicate; unscrupulous; **~ement** [ɛ̃delikatmɑ̃] *adv.* indelicately, unscrupulously.
indélicatesse [ɛ̃delikatɛs] *s.f.* indelicacy; indelicate act; unscrupulous act.
indemne [ɛ̃dɛmn] *adj.* uninjured, unscathed, unharmed, safe and sound.
indemnisation [ɛ̃dɛmnizɑsjɔ̃] *s.f.* indemnification.
indemniser [ɛ̃dɛmnize] *v.t.* to indemnify, to compensate; to make good; (law) to recoup.
indemnité [ɛ̃dɛmnite] *s.f.* indemnity; compensation; expenses, allowance; ~ *de route*, travelling expenses; ~ *de chômage*, unemployment benefit.
indémontable [ɛ̃demɔ̃tabl] *adj.* that cannot be taken to pieces.
indémontrable [ɛ̃demɔ̃trabl] *adj.* undemonstrable.
indéniable [ɛ̃denjabl] *adj.* undeniable, unquestionable, evident; **~ment** [ɛ̃denjabləmɑ̃] *adv.* undeniably.
indentation [ɛ̃dɑ̃tɑsjɔ̃] *s.f.* indentation.
indépassable [ɛ̃depɑsabl] *adj.* not to be exceeded.
indépendamment [ɛ̃depɑ̃damɑ̃] *adv.* independently; ~ *de*, beside, in addition to.
indépendance [ɛ̃depɑ̃dɑ̃s] *s.f.* independence.
indépendant, -e [ɛ̃depɑ̃dɑ̃] *adj.* independent; unconnected (*de*, with); (of flat, etc.) self--contained.
indéracinable [ɛ̃derasinabl] *adj.* ineradicable.
indéréglable [ɛ̃dereglabl] *adj.* that cannot get out of order, foolproof.
indescriptible [ɛ̃dɛskriptibl] *adj.* indescribable.
indésirable [ɛ̃dezirabl] *adj.*, *s.m.f.* undesirable (person).
indestructibilité [ɛ̃dɛstryktibilite] *s.f.* indestructibility.
indestructible [ɛ̃dɛstryktibl] *adj.* indestructible.
indéterminable [ɛ̃detɛrminabl] *adj.* indeterminable, indefinable.
indétermination [ɛ̃detɛrminɑsjɔ̃] *s.f.* indetermination; indefiniteness; irresolution.
indéterminé, -e [ɛ̃detɛrmine] *adj.* indeterminate, vague, unascertained; irresolute, undecided.
index [ɛ̃dɛks] *s.m.* **1.** index finger, forefinger; **2.** index; *l'Index*, (Cath. church) Index; *être à l'*~, to be banned; *mettre à l'*~, to ban, to boycott.
indexer [ɛ̃dɛkse] *v.t.* (econ.) to peg, to index, (prices, etc.).
indicat-eur, -rice [ɛ̃dikatœr] *adj.* indicatory, indicating, warning; *poteau* ~*eur*, signpost; *lampe* ~*rice*, warning-light; **~eur** *s.m.* **1.** (abbrev. *indic*) informer; **2.** guide, directory; timetable; indicator; ~*eur de direction*, direction-finder.
indicati-f, -ve [ɛ̃dikatif] *adj.* indicative; **~f** *s.m.* (gram.) indicative (mood); ~*f* (*d'appel*), call--sign; code-letter; signature-tune; (radio) station-signal.
indication [ɛ̃dikasjɔ̃] *s.f.* indication, information, instruction, direction, sign, token, symptom; hint, pointer.
indice [ɛ̃dis] *s.m.* sign, indication, token, mark, symptom; (math., econ.) index, ratio; rating; ~ *d'octane*, octane rating; (astronaut. eng.) ~ *de construction*, structural ratio.
indicible [ɛ̃disibl] *adj.* unspeakable, ineffable, indescribable, unutterable; **~ment** [ɛ̃disibləmɑ̃] *adv.* unspeakably, indescribably.
indiction [ɛ̃diksjɔ̃] *s.f.* (*relig.*) indiction.
indien, -ne [ɛ̃djɛ̃] *adj.*, *s.m.f.* Indian.
indienne [ɛ̃djɛn] *s.f.* printed cotton, printed calico.
indifféremment [ɛ̃diferamɑ̃] *adv.* indifferently, with indifference, coolly; equally, alike, impartially, without discrimination; ⚠ not 'indifferently' in sense 'not very'.
indifférence [ɛ̃diferɑ̃s] *s.f.* indifference, unconcern.
indifférencié, -e [ɛ̃diferɑ̃sje] *adj.* undifferentiated.
indifférent, -e [ɛ̃diferɑ̃] *adj.* indifferent, unconcerned; immaterial, unimportant, of no concern or interest, all the same; *cela m'est* ~, it is a matter of indifference to me, it's all the same to me; *il est* ~ *de faire ceci ou cela*, it makes no difference whether you do this or that.
indifférer [ɛ̃difere] *v.t.* (fam.) to be of no interest to; *cela m'indiffère*, that leaves me cold; *vos avis m'indiffèrent*, I don't care what you think.
indigénat [ɛ̃diʒena] *s.m.* native population; native administration.
indigence [ɛ̃diʒɑ̃s] *s.f.* indigence, need, want; (lit. & fig.) poverty.
indigène [ɛ̃diʒɛn] *adj.* native, indigenous; *s.m.f.* native.
indigent, -e [ɛ̃diʒɑ̃] *adj.* indigent, poor, needy, destitute; (fig.) sparse, scanty, limited; *s.m.f.* destitute person, pauper.
indigeste [ɛ̃diʒɛst] *adj.* indigestible; (fig.) undigested, confused, ill-arranged, half-baked, indigestible.
indigestion [ɛ̃diʒɛstjɔ̃] *s.f.* indigestion; (fig.) *avoir une* ~ *de qch.*, to be fed up with sth., to have had more than enough of sth.
indignation [ɛ̃diɲɑsjɔ̃] *s.f.* indignation.
indigne [ɛ̃diɲ] *adj.* **1.** (obs.) humble, unworthy; **2.** undeserving, unworthy; shameful, despicable; ~ *de*, unworthy or undeserving of; (law) debarred from; **~ment** [ɛ̃diɲmɑ̃] *adv.* unworthily; shamefully.
indigné, -e [ɛ̃diɲe] *adj.* indignant.
indigner [ɛ̃diɲe] *v.t.* to arouse the indignation of, to make (s.o.) indignant; **s'~** *v.refl.* to be or to become indignant.
indignité [ɛ̃diɲite] *s.f.* unworthiness; vileness, baseness; indignity, outrage; (law) disqualification.
indigo [ɛ̃digo] *s.m.* indigo (plant, dye).
indigoterie [ɛ̃digɔtri] *s.f.* indigo works; indigo plantation.
indigotier [ɛ̃digɔtje] *s.m.* **1.** (bot.) indigo-plant; **2.** indigo manufacturer or worker.
indiquer [ɛ̃dike] *v.t.* to indicate, to mark, to point out, to show, to explain; to indicate, to call for; to sketch, to outline, to indicate roughly; to appoint, to name, to fix, (day, etc.); ~ *du doigt*, to point to; (fig.) *c'est le moyen indiqué*, it is the appropriate method; *ce n'est guère indiqué*, it is not really what is called for; *à l'endroit indiqué*, at the appointed place.
indirect, -e [ɛ̃dirɛkt] *adj.* indirect; oblique, roundabout, back-handed; underhand; *témoignage* ~, circumstantial evidence; *renseignement* ~, second-hand information; (law) *ligne* ~*e*, collateral descent; **~ement** [ɛ̃dirɛktəmɑ̃] *adv.* indirectly.
indiscernable [ɛ̃disɛrnabl] *adj.* indiscernible, indistinguishable.
indisciplinable [ɛ̃disiplinabl] *adj.* not disciplinable, intractable, unruly.

indiscipline [ɛ̃disiplin] *s.f.* indiscipline, insubordination.
indiscipliné, -e [ɛ̃disipline] *adj.* undisciplined, unruly, insubordinate.
indiscr-et, -ète [ɛ̃diskrɛ] *adj.* **1.** (obs.) indiscreet, thoughtless, imprudent; **2.** indiscreet, tactless, tiresome, awkward, pushing; **3.** indiscreet, over-talkative, unable to keep a secret; **~ètement** [ɛ̃diskrɛtmɑ̃] *adv.* **1.** (obs.) thoughtlessly; **2.** indiscreetly.
indiscrétion [ɛ̃diskresjɔ̃] *s.f.* indiscretion, indiscreetness, imprudence; tactlessness.
indiscutable [ɛ̃diskytabl] *adj.* indisputable, incontestable, unquestionable; **~ment** [ɛ̃diskytabləmɑ̃] *adv.* indisputably.
indiscuté, -e [ɛ̃diskyte] *adj.* undisputed.
indispensable [ɛ̃dispɑ̃sabl] *adj.* indispensable, essential; ~ *s.m.* what is (strictly) necessary, the essential(s); **~ment** [ɛ̃dispɑ̃sabləmɑ̃] *adv.* indispensably.
indisponible [ɛ̃dispɔnibl] *adj.* not available, unavailable; (law) entailed, inalienable.
indisposé, -e [ɛ̃dispoze] *adj.* indisposed, unwell.
indisposer [ɛ̃dispoze] *v.t.* to make unwell; to antagonize, to alienate, (s.o.).
indisposition [ɛ̃dispozisjɔ̃] *s.f.* indisposition, slight ailment; (euphem.) monthly period.
indissolubilité [ɛ̃disɔlybilite] *s.f.* indissolubility.
indissoluble [ɛ̃disɔlybl] *adj.* indissoluble; **~ment** [ɛ̃disɔlybləmɑ̃] *adv.* indissolubly.
indistinct, -e [ɛ̃distɛ̃(kt)] *adj.* indistinct; **~ement** [ɛ̃distɛ̃ktəmɑ̃] *adv.* indistinctly; without discrimination, impartially.
individu [ɛ̃dividy] *s.m.* individual, person; (often pej.) fellow, chap, type, character; *un ~ louche*, a suspicious character.
individualiser [ɛ̃dividɥalize] *v.t.* to individualize, to particularize; **s'~** *v.refl.* to assume an individuality, to take on individual characteristics.
individualisme [ɛ̃dividɥalism] *s.m.* individualism.
individualiste [ɛ̃dividɥalist] *adj., s.m.f.* individualist(ic).
individualité [ɛ̃dividɥalite] *s.f.* individuality; individual, personality.
individuel, -le [ɛ̃dividɥɛl] *adj.* individual, personal; **~lement** [ɛ̃dividɥɛlmɑ̃] *adv.* individually, separately.
indivis, -e [ɛ̃divi] *adj.* undivided; *par ~*, jointly.
indivisibilité [ɛ̃divizibilite] *s.f.* indivisibility.
indivisible [ɛ̃divizibl] *adj.* indivisible; inseparable.
indivision [ɛ̃divizjɔ̃] *s.f.* wholeness; joint ownership.
in-dix-huit [indizɥit] *adj. invar.* decimo-octavo, 18mo.
Indo-chine, Indochine [ɛ̃dɔʃin] *s.f.* (geog.) Indo-China.
indo-chinois, -e [ɛ̃dɔʃinwa] *adj., s.m.f.* Indo-Chinese.
indocile [ɛ̃dɔsil] *adj.* intractable, unmanageable, disobedient, unruly, recalcitrant.
indocilité [ɛ̃dɔsilite] *s.f.* intractability.
indo-européen, -ne [ɛ̃dɔœrɔpeɛ̃] *adj., s.m.f.* (ethn., lang.) Indo-European.
indole [ɛ̃dɔl] *s.m.* (chem.) indole.
indolemment [ɛ̃dɔlamɑ̃] *adv.* indolently.
indolence [ɛ̃dɔlɑ̃s] *s.f.* indolence, listlessness, apathy, sluggishness, indifference.
indolent, -e [ɛ̃dɔlɑ̃] *adj.* indolent, sluggish, indifferent, apathetic.
indolore [ɛ̃dɔlɔr] *adj.* painless.
indomptable [ɛ̃dɔ̃tabl] *adj.* indomitable, untameable, uncontrollable, unmanageable, ungovernable.
indompté, -e [ɛ̃dɔ̃te] *adj.* untamed, wild, uncontrolled, unbroken, unsubdued.
Indonésie [ɛ̃dɔnezi] *s.f.* (geog.) Indonesia.
indonésien, -ne [ɛ̃dɔnezjɛ̃] *adj., s.m.f.* Indonesian.
indou, -e [ɛ̃du] *adj., s.m.f.* = HINDOU.
in-douze [induz] *adj.invar.* duodecimo, 12mo.
indu, -e [ɛ̃dy] *adj.* **1.** undue, excessive, unreasonable; against the regulations; abnormal; unseasonable, inappropriate; *à une heure ~e*, at an inappropriate moment; *rentrer à des heures ~es*, to come home at an unearthly hour, at all times of the day and night; **2.** unwarranted; (of money) not owed, not due; ~ *s.m.* sum of money not due.
indubitable [ɛ̃dybitabl] *adj.* indubitable, unquestionable, beyond doubt; **~ment** [ɛ̃dybitabləmɑ̃] *adv.* indubitably, unquestionably.
induct-eur, -rice [ɛ̃dyktœr] *adj.* inductive, inducing; **~eur** *s.m.* inductor.
inducti-f, -ve [ɛ̃dyktif] *adj.* inductive.
induction [ɛ̃dyksjɔ̃] *s.f.* induction; inference; (electr.) induction; *bobine d'~*, induction coil.
induire [ɛ̃dɥir] *v.t.* **1.** to induce, to lead, to tempt; (phys.) to induce; *~ en erreur*, to mislead, to delude, to lead into temptation; **2.** to infer, to reason by induction.
induit, -e [ɛ̃dɥi] *adj.* (electr.) (of current, charge) induced, (of circuit, winding) secondary; ~ *s.m.* armature (of dynamo).
indulgence [ɛ̃dylʒɑ̃s] *s.f.* indulgence, leniency; (eccles.) indulgence.
indulgent, -e [ɛ̃dylʒɑ̃] *adj.* indulgent, lenient, forbearing.
indûment [ɛ̃dymɑ̃] *adv.* unduly; improperly, wrongly, illicitly.
induration [ɛ̃dyrɑsjɔ̃] *s.f.* (med.) induration.
indurer [ɛ̃dyre] *v.t.* (med.) to indurate.
industrial-isation [ɛ̃dystrijalizɑsjɔ̃] *s.f.* industrialization; **~iser** [ɛ̃dystrijalize] *v.t.* to industrialize, to run on industrial lines; **~isme** [ɛ̃dystrijalism] *s.m.* industrialism.
industrie [ɛ̃dystri] *s.f.* **1.** (obs.) industry, skill, ingenuity; (pej.) *vivre d'~*, to live by one's wits; *chevalier d'~*, swindler; **2.** (obs.) craft, trade, work; **3.** industry, trade, manufacture, business; *l'~ mécanique*, engineering (industry); *~s des bâtiments*, building trades; *~ du spectacle*, entertainment industry, show business.
industriel, -le [ɛ̃dystrijɛl] *adj.* industrial, large-scale; ~ *s.m.* manufacture; **~lement** [ɛ̃dustrijɛlmɑ̃] *adv.* industrially; on an industrial scale, by industrial methods.
industrieu-x, -se [ɛ̃dystrijø] (obs.) **1.** industrious, skilful, ingenious; **2.** industrial.
inébranlable [inebrɑ̃labl] *adj.* immovable, unshakeable, firm, steady, constant; **~ment** [inebrɑ̃labləmɑ̃] *adv.* unshakeably.
inéchangeable [ineʃɑ̃ʒabl] *adv.* not exchangeable.
inécouté, -e [inekute] *adj.* unheard, ignored.
inédit, -e [inedi] *adj.* unpublished; unknown; ~ *s.m.* unpublished work; novelty.
inéducable [inedykabl] *adj.* ineducable.
ineffable [inefabl] *adj.* ineffable, unutterable, exquisite, unspeakable; **~ment** [inefabləmɑ̃] *adv.* ineffably, unspeakably.
ineffaçable [inefasabl] *adj.* indelible, ineradicable, ineffaceable; **~ment** [inefasabləmɑ̃] indelibly.
inefficace [inefikas] *adj.* inefficacious, ineffectual, ineffective; **~ment** [inefikasmɑ̃] *adv.* ineffectually.
inefficacité [inefikasite] *s.f.* inefficacy, ineffectiveness, inefficiency.
inégal, -e, (aux) [inegal] *adj.* **1.** unequal; **2.** uneven, rough; irregular; inequable.

inégalable [inegalabl] *adj.* incomparable, matchless.
inégalé, -e [inegale] *adj.* unequalled, unmatched.
inégalement [inegalmɑ̃] *adv.* unequally, unevenly.
inégalité [inegalite] *s.f.* **1.** inequality, disparity; **2.** unevenness, irregularity, roughness; capriciousness.
inélastique [inelastik] *adj.* inelastic.
inélégamment [inelegamɑ̃] *adv.* inelegantly.
inélégance [inelegɑ̃s] *s.f.* inelegance.
inélégant, -e [inelegɑ̃] *adj.* inelegant, vulgar.
inéligibilité [inelizibilite] *s.f.* ineligibility.
inéligible [inelizibl] *adj.* ineligible.
inéluctable [inelyktabl] *adj.* ineluctable, unavoidable, inevitable; ~ *s.m.* *l'*~, the inevitable; **~ment** [inelyktabləmɑ̃] *adv.* unavoidably.
inemployé, -e [inɑ̃plwaje] *adj.* not in use; vacant, unutilized; unused; unemployed; ⚠ not usu. 'unemployed' of persons.
inénarrable [inenarabl] *adj.* (obs.) unspeakable, indescribable; (mod.) too funny for words.
inepte [inɛpt] *adj.* inept, silly, absurd.
ineptie [inɛpsi] *s.f.* ineptitude, ineptness; piece of nonsense.
inépuisable [inepɥizabl] *adj.* inexhaustible, unfailing, never-ending; tireless; **~ment** [inepɥizabləmɑ̃] *adv.* inexhaustibly, endlessly.
inerme [inɛrm] *adj.* (bot.) thornless, inerm.
inerte [inɛrt] *adj.* inert; inactive, motionless; unresponsive.
inertie [inɛrsi] *s.f.* inertia; inertness, inactivity, sluggishness, apathy; passive resistance.
inescomptable [inɛskɔ̃tabl] *adj.* (fin.) undiscountable.
inespéré, -e [inɛspere] *adj.* unhoped for; unlooked for.
inesthétique [inɛstetik] *adj.* unaesthetic, ugly.
inestimable [inɛstimabl] *adj.* inestimable, priceless, invaluable.
inévitable [inevitabl] *adj.* inevitable, unavoidable; **~ment** [inevitabləmɑ̃] *adv.* inevitably, unavoidably.
inexact, -e [inɛgzakt] *adj.* inexact, inaccurate, wrong, unreliable; unpunctual; **~ement** [inɛgzaktəmɑ̃] *adv.* inaccurately, incorrectly; unpunctually.
inexactitude [inɛgzaktityd] *s.f.* inexactitude, inexactness, inaccuracy; unpunctuality.
inexcusable [inɛkskyzabl] *adj.* inexcusable, unwarrantable, unpardonable.
inexécutable [inɛgzekytabl] *adj.* incapable of execution, impracticable.
inexécuté, -e [inɛgzekyte] *adj.* unexecuted, not carried out.
inexécution [inɛgzekysjɔ̃] *s.f.* non-fulfilment, non-performance.
inexercé, -e [inɛgzɛrse] *adj.* untrained, unpractised.
inexigible [inɛgzizibl] *adj.* not demandable, not due.
inexistant, -e [inɛgzistɑ̃] *adj.* non-existent, zero; (fam.) insignificant, valueless.
inexorable [inɛgzɔrabl] *adj.* inexorable, unrelenting, inflexible, pitiless; **~ment** [inɛgzɔrabləmɑ̃] *adv.* inexorably.
inexpérience [inɛksperjɑ̃s] *s.f.* inexperience.
inexpérimenté, -e [inɛksperimɑ̃te] *adj.* inexperienced; untried.
inexpiable [inɛkspjabl] *adj.* inexpiable; (obs.) relentless.
inexplicable [inɛksplikabl] *adj.* inexplicable, unaccountable; **~ment** [inɛksplikabləmɑ̃] *adv.* inexplicably.
inexpliqué, -e [inɛksplike] *adj.* unexplained, unaccounted for; ~ *s.m.* (sth.) inexplicable.
inexploitable [inɛksplwatabl] *adj.* unworkable, uncultivable.
inexploité, -e [inɛksplwate] *adj.* unworked, uncultivated, undeveloped.
inexploré, -e [inɛksplɔre] *adj.* unexplored.
inexplosible [inɛksplozibl] *adj.* non-explosive.
inexpressi-f, -ve [inɛksprɛsif] *adj.* inexpressive; expressionless.
inexprimable [inɛksprimabl] *adj.* inexpressible, beyond words, unutterable; ~ *s.m.* (sth.) inexpressible.
inexprimé, -e [inɛksprime] *adj.* unexpressed, unvoiced.
inexpugnable [inɛkspygnabl] *adj.* inexpugnable, impregnable.
inextensible [inɛkstɑ̃sibl] *adj.* inextensible, unstretchable.
inextinguible [inɛkstɛ̃gibl] *adj.* inextinguishable, unquenchable; irrepressible, uncontrollable.
inextricable [inɛkstrikabl] *adj.* inextricable, entangled; (fig.) involved; **~ment** [inɛkstrikabləmɑ̃] *adv.* inextricably.
infaillibilité [ɛ̃fajibilite] *s.f.* infallibility.
infaillible [ɛ̃fajibl] *adj.* infallible; (obs.) certain, sure; **~ment** [ɛ̃fajibləmɑ̃] *adv.* infallibly, surely.
infaisable [ɛ̃fɛzabl] *adj.* unfeasible, impossible, impracticable.
infamant, -e [ɛ̃famɑ̃] *adj.* infamous, degrading, ignominious.
infâme [ɛ̃fɑm] *adj.* **1.** (obs.) vile, base; infamous, degrading, ignominious, shameful; **2.** (mod.) detestable, odious; repulsive, filthy, squalid.
infamie [ɛ̃fami] *s.f.* **1.** infamy, dishonour, disgrace; vileness; ignominy; **2.** slander, calumny.
infant, -e [ɛ̃fɑ̃] *s.m.f.* infante, infanta.
infanterie [ɛ̃fɑ̃tri] *s.f.* infantry; ~ *de marine*, marines, marine light infantry; ~ *portée*, lorry-borne troops; ~ *de l'air* or *aéroportée*, airborne troops.
infanticide [ɛ̃fɑ̃tisid] *s.m.f.* infanticide, child-murderer, -murderess.
infantile [ɛ̃fɑ̃til] *adj.* infantile, child-, childish.
infarctus [ɛ̃farktys] *s.m.* (med.) infarct, infarction.
infatigable [ɛ̃fatigabl] *adj.* indefatigable; **~ment** [ɛ̃fatigabləmɑ̃] *adv.* indefatigably.
infatuation [ɛ̃fatɥɑsjɔ̃] *s.f.* **1.** (obs.) infatuation; **2.** (mod.) self-conceit.
infatué, -e [ɛ̃fatɥe] *adj.* **1.** (obs.) infatuated; **2.** (mod.) conceited, self-satisfied, vain.
infatuer [ɛ̃fatɥe] *v.t.* to infatuate; **s'~** *v.refl.* **1.** (obs.) to be infatuated; **2.** (mod.) to be infatuated with oneself, to be thoroughly conceited, to be consumed with one's own importance.
infécond, -e [ɛ̃fekɔ̃] *adj.* unfruitful, barren, sterile.
infécondité [ɛ̃fekɔ̃dite] *s.f.* unfruitfulness, barrenness, sterility.
infect, -e [ɛ̃fɛkt] *adj.* foul, stinking, infected, filthy, disgusting, revolting; vile.
infectant, -e [ɛ̃fɛktɑ̃] *adj.* (med.) infectious, causing infection.
infecter [ɛ̃fɛkte] *v.t.* to infect, to taint, to pollute, to corrupt, to contaminate, to cause to stink, to make (a place) reek; **s'~** *v.refl.* to become infected, to turn septic.
infectieu-x, -se [ɛ̃fɛksjø] *adj.* infectious, contagious.
infection [ɛ̃fɛksjɔ̃] *s.f.* infection, contagion, corruption; stench.
inféodation [ɛ̃feɔdɑsjɔ̃] *s.f.* infeudation, enfeoffment; (fig.) subjection.
inféoder [ɛ̃feɔde] *v.t.* to enfeoff; **s'~** (*à*) *v.refl.* to give oneself (to); to attach oneself (to).
infère [ɛ̃fɛr] *adj.* (bot.) inferior.
inférence [ɛ̃ferɑ̃s] *s.f.* inference.
inférer [ɛ̃fere] *v.t.* to infer.

inférieur, -e [ɛ̃ferjœr] *adj.* inferior, lower, under; below, nether, subordinate; ~ *s.m.* inferior, subordinate.
infériorité [ɛ̃ferjɔrite] *s.f.* inferiority; disadvantage, handicap.
infernal, -e, (aux) [ɛ̃fɛrnal] *adj.* infernal, hellish; diabolical; terrible, unbearable.
infertile [ɛ̃fɛrtil] *adj.* infertile, barren.
infertilité [ɛ̃fɛrtilite] *s.f.* infertility; barrenness, aridity.
infestation [ɛ̃fɛstɑsjɔ̃] *s.f.* **1.** (obs.) infesting, overrunning; **2.** (mod.) infestation.
infester [ɛ̃fɛste] *v.t.* to infest, to overrun.
infeutrable [ɛ̃føtrabl] *adj.* (of material) non-felting.
infidèle [ɛ̃fidɛl] *adj.* unfaithful, faithless, false, disloyal; inaccurate; unbelieving; ~ *s.m.f.* infidel, unbeliever; **~ment** [ɛ̃fidɛlmɑ̃] *adv.* unfaithfully, inaccurately.
infidélité [ɛ̃fidelite] *s.f.* infidelity, unfaithfulness, faithlessness; inaccuracy; *faire des ~s à*, to be unfaithful to; ~ *à la parole donnée*, breaking one's word.
infiltration [ɛ̃filtrɑsjɔ̃] *s.f.* infiltration.
(s')infiltrer [sɛ̃filtre] *v.refl.* to infiltrate, to filter, to percolate; (fig.) to spread, to creep.
infime [ɛ̃fim] *adj.* lowest; tiny, infinitesimal.
infini, -e [ɛ̃fini] *adj.* infinite, boundless, endless, numberless; ~ *s.m.* infinite, infinity, infinite expanse; *à l'~*, to infinity, endlessly, ad infinitum; **~ment** [ɛ̃finimɑ̃] *adv.* infinitely, boundlessly; extremely, exceedingly; *l'~ment grand*, the infinite; *le calcul des ~ment petits*, infinitesimal calculus; *un homme d'~ment d'esprit*, an extremely witty man.
infinité [ɛ̃finite] *s.f.* infinity, infiniteness, boundlessness; infinitude; very large number, whole mass (of).
infinitésimal, -e, (aux) [ɛ̃finitezimal] *adj.* infinitesimal.
infiniti-f, -ve [ɛ̃finitif] *adj., s.m.* (gram.) infinitive; *(proposition) ~ve*, infinitive clause.
infirmati-f, -ve [ɛ̃firmatif] *adj.* invalidating, annulling.
infirmation [ɛ̃firmɑ̃sjɔ̃] *s.f.* invalidation, annulment, quashing.
infirme [ɛ̃firm] *adj.* infirm, crippled, disabled; ~ *s.m.f.* cripple, disabled person, invalid.
infirmer [ɛ̃firme] *v.t.* to invalidate, to nullify; to weaken, to quash.
infirmerie [ɛ̃firməri] *s.f.* infirmary, sick-room.
infirmi-er, -ère [ɛ̃firmje] *s.m.f.* hospital attendant, nurse; (mil.) medical orderly, stretcher-bearer.
infirmité [ɛ̃firmite] *s.f.* infirmity, weakness, failing, chronic disease.
inflammabilité [ɛ̃flamabilite] *s.f.* inflammability.
inflammable [ɛ̃flamabl] *adj.* inflammable.
inflammation [ɛ̃flamɑsjɔ̃] *s.f.* **1.** inflammation; **2.** combustion.
inflammatoire [ɛ̃flamatwar] *adj.* inflammatory.
inflation [ɛ̃flɑsjɔ̃] *s.f.* inflation.
inflationniste [ɛ̃flɑsjɔnist] *s.m.f.* inflationist; ~ *adj.* inflationist; inflationary.
infléchi, -e [ɛ̃fleʃi] *adj.* bent inwards; inflected.
infléchir [ɛ̃fleʃir] *v.t.* to inflect, to bend; (fig.) to divert, to modify; **s'~** *v.refl.* to bend; to deviate.
inflexibilité [ɛ̃flɛksibilite] *s.f.* inflexibility.
inflexible [ɛ̃flɛksibl] *adj.* inflexible, unbending, unyielding; **~ment** [ɛ̃flɛxibləmɑ̃] *adv.* inflexibly.
inflexion [ɛ̃flɛksjɔ̃] *s.f.* inflexion, bend, bending, modulation.
infliger [ɛ̃fliʒe] *v.t.* to inflict, to impose.
inflorescence [ɛ̃flɔresɑ̃s] *s.f.* inflorescence.
influençable [ɛ̃flɥɑ̃sabl] *adj.* easily influenced.
influence [ɛ̃flɥɑ̃s] *s.f.* influence, authority, weight, power, sway, action; prestige.
influencer [ɛ̃flɥɑ̃se] *v.t.* to influence, to put pressure on, to sway; to react on.
influent, -e [ɛ̃flɥɑ̃] *adj.* influential.
influenza [ɛ̃flɥɛnza] *s.f.* (obs.) influenza.
influer [ɛ̃flɥe] *v.i.* ~ *sur*, to influence, to affect, to have an influence or effect on.
influx [ɛ̃fly] *s.m.* influx.
in-folio [infɔljo] *s.m., adj.invar.* folio.
informat-eur, -rice [ɛ̃fɔrmatœr] *s.m.f.* informant.
information [ɛ̃fɔrmɑsjɔ̃] *s.f.* **1.** inquiry, investigation; acquiring of information; (law) preliminary investigation; *prendre des ~s, aller aux ~s*, to make inquiries; *être en voyage d'~*, to be on a journey of investigation, to be on a fact-finding mission; *ouvrir une ~*, to institute legal investigations; **2.** information, piece of information, knowledge; (pl.) news, information, data; informing, supplying information; *bulletin d'~s*, news bulletin; ⚠ not 'information' as in 'laying information against'.
informe [ɛ̃fɔrm] *adj.* shapeless, formless, misshapen; imperfect.
informé, -e [ɛ̃fɔrme] *adj.* well-informed; ~ *s.m.* (law) inquiry; *jusqu'à plus ample ~*, until further inquiry has been made.
informer [ɛ̃fɔrme] *v.t.* **1.** to inform, to mould, to give form or meaning to; **2.** to inform, to notify, to advise, to enlighten; *être informé de*, to be informed of or about, to be aware or cognizant of; ~ *v.i.* (law) **1.** ~ *sur*, to investigate; **2.** ~ *contre*, to inform, to lay information against (s.o.); **s'~** *v.refl.* to inquire, to make inquiries, to ask.
infortune [ɛ̃fɔrtyn] *s.f.* misfortune, adversity, calamity.
infortuné, -e [ɛ̃fɔrtyne] *adj.* unfortunate, ill-fated.
infraction [ɛ̃fraksjɔ̃] *s.f.* infraction, infringement, breach; offence, crime; *commettre une ~*, to commit an offence, to be in breach of the law.
infranchissable [ɛ̃frɑ̃ʃisabl] *adj.* impassable, insurmountable.
infra-rouge [ɛ̃fraruʒ] *adj., s.m.* infra-red; **~-son** [ɛ̃frasɔ̃] *s.m.* (phys.) infrasonic vibration; **~structure** [ɛ̃frastryktyr] *s.f.* infrastructure, sub-structure, understructure, under-frame; earthworks; bed (of road, etc.); (aeron.) ground installations.
infréquentable [ɛ̃frekɑ̃tabl] *adj.* with whom one cannot associate.
infroissable [ɛ̃frwasabl] *adj.* (text.) uncreasable, uncrushable; crease-resisting.
infructueu-x, -se [ɛ̃fryktɥø] *adj.* vain, unfruitful, fruitless, unavailing, unsuccessful.
infumable [ɛ̃fymabl] *adj.* unsmokable.
infus, -e [ɛ̃fy] *adj.* inborn, innate, intuitive.
infuser [ɛ̃fyze] to infuse; to steep, to macerate; ~ *v.i.* to infuse; *laisser ~ le thé*, to let the tea draw.
infusible [ɛ̃fyzibl] *adj.* infusible.
infusion [ɛ̃fyzjɔ̃] *s.f.* infusion.
ingambe [ɛ̃gɑ̃b] *adj.* having the use of one's legs, active, mobile.
(s')ingénier [sɛ̃ʒenje] *v.refl.* to tax one's ingenuity, to make every use of one's wits, to strain and strive.
ingéniérie [ɛ̃ʒenieri] *s.f.* engineering.
ingénieur [ɛ̃ʒenjœr] *s.m.* engineer; ~ *chimiste*, chemical engineer; ~ *des constructions navales*, naval architect.
ingénieu-x, -se [ɛ̃ʒenjø] *adj.* ingenious, clever, resourceful; **~sement** [ɛ̃ʒenjøzmɑ̃] *adv.* ingeniously.
ingéniosité [ɛ̃ʒenjozite] *s.f.* ingenuity, ingeniousness, cleverness.
ingénu, -e [ɛ̃ʒeny] *adj.* ingenuous, candid,

guileless, unsophisticated, artless; **~e** *s.f.* (theatr.) ingénue.
ingénuité [ɛ̃ʒenɥite] *s.f.* ingenuousness, candour, frankness, openness, artlessness; ⚠ not 'ingenuity'.
ingénument [ɛ̃ʒenymɑ̃] *adv.* ingenuously, candidly, artlessly.
ingérence [ɛ̃ʒerɑ̃s] *s.f.* meddling, interference.
ingérer [ɛ̃ʒere] *v.t.* to ingest; **s'~** *v.refl.* to interfere, to meddle (*dans*, with).
ingestion [ɛ̃ʒɛstjɔ̃] *s.f.* ingestion.
ingouvernable [ɛ̃guvɛrnabl] *adj.* ungovernable, unruly.
ingrat, -e [ɛ̃gra] *adj.* ungrateful, unthankful; thankless; unprofitable; unpromising, sterile, unpleasant, unattractive, graceless; *l'âge ~*, the awkward age; *s.m.f.* ungrateful person, ingrate.
ingratitude [ɛ̃gratityd] *s.f.* ingratitude, ungratefulness, thanklessness; unprofitableness.
ingrédient [ɛ̃gredjɑ̃] *s.m.* ingredient, constituent.
inguérissable [ɛ̃gerisabl] *adj.* incurable.
inguinal, -e, (aux) [ɛ̃gɥinal] *adj.* (anat.) inguinal.
ingurgiter [ɛ̃gyrʒite] *v.t.* to ingurgitate, to swallow.
inhabile [inabil] *adj.* unskilful, unskilled, inexpert; (law) unqualified, disqualified, incompetent; **~ment** [inabilmɑ̃] *adv.* unskilfully, awkwardly.
inhabileté [inabilte] *s.f.* unskilfulness; awkwardness.
inhabilité [inabilite] *s.f.* (law) incompetency, disability.
inhabitable [inabitabl] *adj.* uninhabitable, lacking every comfort.
inhabité, -e [inabite] *adj.* uninhabited, empty; ⚠ not 'inhabited'.
inhabituel, -le [inabitɥɛl] *adj.* unusual, abnormal.
inhalateur [inalatœr] *s.m.* inhaler.
inhalation [inalɑsjɔ̃] *s.f.* inhalation, inhaling.
inhaler [inale] *v.t.* to inhale.
inharmonieu-x, -se [inarmɔnjø] *adj.* inharmonious, discordant.
inhérence [inerɑ̃s] *s.f.* inherence.
inhérent, -e [inerɑ̃] *adj.* inherent.
inhibé, -e [inibe] *adj., s.m.f.* inhibited (person).
inhiber [inibe] *v.t.* (law) to prohibit; (psychol.) to inhibit.
inhibit-eur, -rice [inibitœr] *adj.* inhibitory, inhibiting; **~eur** *s.m.* (chem., biol.) inhibitor.
inhibition [inibisjɔ̃] *s.f.* (law) prohibition; (psychol.) inhibition.
inhospitali-er, -ère [inɔspitalje] *adj.* inhospitable, forbidding, unfriendly.
inhumain, -e [inymɛ̃] *adj.* inhuman, cruel, unfeeling; terrible; *une (femme) ~e*, a cruel woman (who rejects one's advances); **~ement** [inymɛnmɑ̃] *adv.* inhumanely.
inhumanité [inymanite] *s.f.* inhumanity, cruelty.
inhumation [inymɑsjɔ̃] *s.f.* burial, inhumation, interment.
inhumer [inyme] *v.t.* to bury, to inhume, to inter.
inimaginable [inimaʒinabl] *adj.* unimaginable, inconceivable.
inimitable [inimitabl] *adj.* inimitable.
inimitié [inimitje] *s.f.* enmity, feud, hatred, aversion; *avoir de l'~ pour*, to bear enmity towards, to have an aversion to.
ininflammable [inɛ̃flamabl] *adj.* non-inflammable.
inintelligemment [inɛ̃teliʒamɑ̃] *adv.* unintelligently.
inintelligence [inɛ̃teliʒɑ̃s] *s.f.* lack of intelligence, obtuseness.
inintelligent, -e [inɛ̃teliʒɑ̃] *adj.* unintelligent, obtuse.
inintelligible [inɛ̃teliʒibl] *adj.* unintelligible; **~ment** [inɛ̃teliʒibləmɑ̃] *adv.* unintelligibly.
ininterrompu, -e [inɛ̃tɛrɔ̃py] *adj.* uninterrupted, unbroken, continuous.
inique [inik] *adj.* iniquitous; **~ment** [inikmɑ̃] *adv.* iniquitously, unjustly.
iniquité [inikite] *s.f.* **1.** iniquity, sin; **2.** inequity, injustice; act of injustice.
initial, -e, (aux) [inisjal] *adj.* initial; **~e** *s.f.* initial, initial letter; **~ement** [inisjalmɑ̃] *adv.* initially.
initiat-eur, -rice [inisjatœr] *s.m.f.* initiator; *adj.* initiatory.
initiation [inisjɑsjɔ̃] *s.f.* initiation (*à*, into).
initiative [inisjativ] *s.f.* initiative.
initié, -e [inisje] *adj.* initiated, in the secret; *s.m.f.* initiate; *les ~s*, the initiated.
initier [inisje] *v.t.* to initiate, to teach, to admit; **s'~** *v.refl.* to initiate oneself, to make oneself acquainted (*à*, with); ⚠ not 'to initiate' in sense 'to begin'.
injecté, -e [ɛ̃ʒɛkte] *adj.* bloodshot; injected.
injecter [ɛ̃ʒɛkte] *v.t.* to inject.
inject-eur, -rice [ɛ̃ʒɛktœr] *adj.* injecting; **~eur** *s.m.* (techn.) injector.
injection [ɛ̃ʒɛksjɔ̃] *s.f.* injection.
injonction [ɛ̃ʒɔ̃ksjɔ̃] *s.f.* (law) injunction, order.
injouable [ɛ̃ʒuabl] *adj.* unplayable, unactable.
injure [ɛ̃ʒyr] *s.f.* wrong, injury, (Lit.) damage; affront, outrage; insult, insulting words, slander, abuse; *faire ~ à qn.*, to outrage, to insult, s.o.; ⚠ not physical 'injury'.
injurier [ɛ̃ʒyrje] *v.t.* to abuse, to insult; ⚠ see INJURE.
injurieu-x, -se [ɛ̃ʒyriø] *adj.* injurious, insulting, abusive; (obs.) unjust.
injuste [ɛ̃ʒyst] *adj.* unjust, unfair, wrong, undeserved, unequal; (obs.) unjustified; *le juste et l'~*, right and wrong; **~ment** [ɛ̃ʒystəmɑ̃] *adv.* unjustly, wrongly.
injustice [ɛ̃ʒystis] *s.f.* injustice, wrong, act of injustice.
injustifiable [ɛ̃ʒystifjabl] *adj.* unjustifiable, unwarrantable.
injustifié, -e [ɛ̃ʒystifje] *adj.* unjustified, unwarranted.
inlassable [ɛ̃lɑsabl] *adj.* untiring, indefatigable.
inné, -e [ine] *adj.* innate, inborn.
innéité [ineite] *s.f.* innateness.
innervation [inɛrvɑsjɔ̃] *s.f.* innervation.
innerver [inɛrve] *v.t.* to innervate.
innocemment [inɔsamɑ̃] *adv.* innocently.
innocence [inɔsɑ̃s] *s.f.* innocence, guiltlessness; artlessness, purity, simplicity.
innocent, -e [inɔsɑ̃] *adj.* **1.** innocent, guiltless, harmless, inoffensive; pure; **2.** innocent, guileless, naïve, simple-minded, silly; *s.m.f.* simple-minded person, idiot.
innocenter [inɔsɑ̃te] *v.t.* to declare innocent, to find not guilty, to acquit; to hold (s.o.) innocent.
innocuité [inɔkɥite] *s.f.* innocuousness, harmlessness.
innombrable [inɔ̃brabl] *adj.* innumerable, numberless; (Lit.) having many facets.
innomé, -e [inɔme] *adj.* = INNOMMÉ.
innominé, -e [inɔmine] *adj.* (obs.) (anat., of bone, artery) innominate.
innommable [inɔmabl] unspeakable; unnameable.
innommé, -e [inɔme] *adj.* nameless, unnamed; innominate.
innovat-eur, -rice [inɔvatœr] *s.m.f.* innovator; *adj.* innovating.
innovation [inɔvɑsjɔ̃] *s.f.* innovation.
innover [inɔve] *v.t.* to make changes in, to

bring a new or unfamiliar element to; ~ *une mode*, to change a fashion, to bring in a new fashion; ~ *v.i.* to innovate, to make changes or innovations.

inobservance [inɔpsɛrvɑ̃s] *s.f.* non-observance, neglect.

inobservation [inɔpsɛrvɑsjɔ̃] *s.f.* non-observance, non-execution, non-compliance.

inobservé, -e [inɔpsɛrve] *adj.* unnoticed, unobserved.

inoccupation [inɔkypɑsjɔ̃] *s.f.* inoccupation.

inoccupé, -e [inɔkype] *adj.* unoccupied, idle, unemployed; empty, vacant.

in-octavo [inɔktavo] *s.m., adj.invar.* octavo, 8vo.

inoculable [inɔkylabl] *adj.* inoculable.

inoculation [inɔkylɑsjɔ̃] *s.f.* inoculation.

inoculer [inɔkyle] *v.t.* **1.** to inject; (lit. & fig.) to infect; ~ *une maladie à qn.*, to infect s.o. with a disease; **2.** to inoculate; ~ *la fièvre typhoïde à qn.*, to inoculate s.o. against typhoid; ~ *un vaccin à qn.*, to vaccinate s.o.; **s'~** *v.refl.* to innoculate oneself against.

inodore [inɔdɔr] *adj.* odourless, scentless, free from smell.

inoffensi-f, -ve [inɔfɑ̃sif] *adj.* inoffensive, harmless.

inondation [inɔ̃dɑsjɔ̃] *s.f.* inundation, deluge, flood, overflow; (fig.) invasion, influx.

inondé, -e [inɔ̃de] *adj.* flooded, inundated, drowned, waterlogged; suffering from floods; *s.m.f.* flood victim.

inonder [inɔ̃de] *v.t.* to inundate, to flood, to deluge, to overflow; to drench; (fig.) to invade, to fill, to cover.

inopérable [inɔperabl] *adj.* inoperable.

inopérant, -e [inɔperɑ̃] *adj.* inoperative, ineffective.

inopiné, -e [inɔpine] *adj.* unexpected, sudden; **~ment** [inɔpinemɑ̃] *adv.* unexpectedly, suddenly, unawares.

inopportun, -e [inɔpɔrtœ̃] *adj.* inopportune, ill-timed.

inopportunité [inɔpɔrtynite] *s.f.* inopportuneness, unseasonableness.

inorganique [inɔrganik] *adj.* inorganic.

inorganisé, -e [inɔrganize] *adj.* **1.** (sci.) unorganized, inorganic; **2.** (of labour) non-union.

inoubliable [inublijabl] *adj.* unforgettable.

inouï, -e [inwi] *adj.* unheard of, unprecedented; extraordinary.

inox [inɔks] abbrev. *inoxydable.*

inoxydable [inɔksidabl] *adj.* inoxidizable; rustless, rust-proof; ~ *s.m.* stainless steel, non-corroding metal.

in petto [inpeto] *adv.* inwardly.

inqualifiable [ɛ̃kalifjabl] *adj.* unspeakable, beyond words.

inquart [ɛ̃kar] *s.m.*, **inquartation** [ɛ̃kartɑsjɔ̃], **quartation** [kartɑsjɔ̃] *s.f.* (techn.) quartation.

in-quarto [inkwarto] *s.m., adj.invar.* quarto, 4to.

inqui-et, -ète [ɛ̃kjɛ] *adj.* uneasy, disquieted, anxious, restless, fidgety.

inquiétant, -e [ɛ̃kjetɑ̃] *adj.* disquieting, disturbing, upsetting, alarming.

inquiéter [ɛ̃kjete] *v.t.* to disquiet, to alarm, to make uneasy, to trouble, to worry, to upset; **s'~** *v.refl.* to become alarmed or uneasy, to worry, to be worried.

inquiétude [ɛ̃kjetyd] *s.f.* disquiet, anxiety, uneasiness, concern; restlessness; (obs.) unrest; *donner de l'~*, to cause anxiety; *être dans l'~*, to be anxious or uneasy; *soyez sans ~*, don't worry.

inquisit-eur, -rice [ɛ̃kizitœr] *adj.* inquisitorial; **~eur** *s.m.* inquisitor.

inquisition [ɛ̃kizisjɔ̃] *s.f.* inquisition.

inquisitorial, -e, (aux) [ɛ̃kizitɔrjal] *adj.* inquisitorial.

insaisissable [ɛ̃sezisabl] *adj.* **1.** unseizable, not distrainable; **2.** imperceptible, indiscernible; elusive, fleeting.

insalubre [ɛ̃salybr] *adj.* insalubrious, unhealthy, insanitary, dangerous to health.

insalubrité [ɛ̃salybrite] *s.f.* insalubrity, unhealthiness.

insanité [ɛ̃sanite] *s.f.* insanity, madness; nonsense, foolish action or words.

insatiabilité [ɛ̃sasjabilite] *s.f.* insatiability.

insatiable [ɛ̃sasjabl] *adj.* insatiable, unquenchable; **~ment** [ɛ̃sasjabləmɑ̃] *adv.* insatiably.

insatisfaction [ɛ̃satisfaksjɔ̃] *s.f.* dissatisfaction.

insatisfait, -e [ɛ̃satisfɛ] *adj.* dissatisfied, unsatisfied.

inscription [ɛ̃skripsjɔ̃] *s.f.* **1.** inscription, writing, legend, notice; **2.** inscribing, enrolling, enrolment, entering, entry, matriculation, registration, registry, record; putting down (of question on order paper); (nav.) conscription; *prendre ses ~s*, to enter oneself, to enrol, to matriculate; (law) ~ *de* or *en faux*, plea of forgery.

inscrire [ɛ̃skrir] *v.t.* **1.** to inscribe, to engrave; **2.** to inscribe, to write, to put down, to enter, to register, to enrol; **s'~** *v.refl.* to enter (oneself); *s'~ à*, to put one's name down for, to enrol in, to join; (law) *s'~ en faux contre qch.*, to deny sth., to dispute the validity of sth.

inscrit, -e [ɛ̃skri] *adj.* inscribed, registered, on the register, member (of a party, etc.), enrolled.

insecte [ɛ̃sɛkt] *s.m.* insect.

insecticide [ɛ̃sɛktisid] *adj., s.m.* insecticide.

insectivore [ɛ̃sɛktivɔr] *adj.* insectivorous; ~ *s.m.* insectivore.

insécurité [ɛ̃sekyrite] *s.f.* insecurity.

in-seize [insɛz] *adj.invar.* sixteen-mo, 16mo.

insémin-ation [ɛ̃seminɑsjɔ̃] *s.f.* insemination; **~er** [ɛ̃semine] *v.t.* to inseminate.

insensé, -e [ɛ̃sɑ̃se] *adj.* insane, senseless, mad, absurd, extravagant.

insensibil-isation [ɛ̃sɑ̃sibilizɑsjɔ̃] *s.f.* anaesthetization; **~iser** [ɛ̃sɑ̃sibilize] *v.t.* to anaesthetize; **~ité** [ɛ̃sɑ̃sibilite] *s.f.* insensibility, unconsciousness; insensitivity, absence of feeling, analgesia; (fig.) indifference, apathy, coldness, frigidity, calm, impassibility, detachment.

insensible [ɛ̃sɑ̃sibl] *adj.* insensible; unconscious, lifeless; (lit. & fig.) insensitive; (fig.) unfeeling, indifferent, apathetic, cold, frigid, calm, impassible, detached; **~ment** [ɛ̃sɑ̃sibləmɑ̃] *adv.* insensibly, imperceptibly, gradually, by degrees.

inséparable [ɛ̃separabl] *adj.* inseparable; *ce sont deux ~s*, they are always together; **~ment** [ɛ̃separabləmɑ̃] *adv.* inseparably, indissolubly.

insérer [ɛ̃sere] *v.t.* to insert, to put in, to attach (note, etc.); to graft, to implant; **s'~** *v.refl.* to attach itself, to become attached or grafted.

insermenté [ɛ̃sɛrmɑ̃te] *adj.m.* (of priest) non-juring, recusant.

insertion [ɛ̃sɛrsjɔ̃] *s.f.* insertion.

insidieu-x, -se [ɛ̃sidjø] *adj.* insidious; **~sement** [ɛ̃sidjøzmɑ̃] *adv.* insidiously.

insigne [ɛ̃siɲ] *adj.* signal, remarkable; (pej.) glaring.

insigne [ɛ̃siɲ] *s.m.* badge, token; (pl.) insignia; emblem, mark, sign, symbol.

insignifiance [ɛ̃siɲifjɑ̃s] *s.f.* insignificance, unimportance, mediocrity.

insignifiant, -e [ɛ̃siɲifjɑ̃] *adj.* insignificant, unimportant, trivial, negligible.

insinuant, -e [ɛ̃sinɥɑ̃] *adj.* insinuating, ingratiating.

insinuation [ɛ̃sinɥɑsjɔ̃] *s.f.* **1.** (obs.) introduction; **2.** insinuation, innuendo.

insinuer [ɛ̃sinɥe] *v.t.* to insinuate; to hint at, to suggest; **s'~** *v.refl.* (obs.) to penetrate; (mod.) to steal, to worm one's way, (into).

insipide [ɛ̃sipid] *adj.* insipid, tasteless; dull, flat, tame.
insipidité [ɛ̃sipidite] *s.f.* insipidity, tastelessness, flatness, dullness.
insistance [ɛ̃sistɑ̃s] *s.f.* insistence, persistence; *avec* ~, earnestly, insistently; (lang.) *accent d'*~, emphasis, stress.
insister [ɛ̃siste] *v.i.* to insist, to be insistent; to persist, to persevere; ~ *sur*, to insist on, to emphasize, to lay stress on; ~ *auprès de qn.*, to be insistent with s.o., to press s.o.; ~ *auprès de qn. sur la nécessité de*, to urge on s.o. the necessity of; ~ *pour faire qch.*, to insist on doing sth.
insociabilité [ɛ̃sɔsjabilite] *s.f.* unsociableness.
insociable [ɛ̃sɔsjabl] *adj.* unsociable.
insolation [ɛ̃sɔlasjɔ̃] *s.f.* insolation, sunstroke.
insolemment [ɛ̃sɔlamɑ̃] *adv.* insolently, impudently.
insolence [ɛ̃sɔlɑ̃s] *s.f.* insolence, impertinence; arrogance.
insolent, -e [ɛ̃sɔlɑ̃] *adj.* insolent, rude, impertinent; arrogant; unheard of, extraordinary.
insolite [ɛ̃sɔlit] *adj.* unusual, unwonted, out of the ordinary, eccentric.
insolubilité [ɛ̃sɔlybilite] *s.f.* insolubility.
insoluble [ɛ̃sɔlybl] *adj.* (chem.) insoluble; unsolvable.
insolvabilité [ɛ̃sɔlvabilite] *s.f.* insolvency.
insolvable [ɛ̃sɔlvabl] *adj.* insolvent.
insomnie [ɛ̃sɔmni] *s.f.* sleeplessness, insomnia.
insondable [ɛ̃sɔ̃dabl] *adj.* unfathomable.
insonore [ɛ̃sɔnɔr] *adj.* **1.** soundless, silent; (phon.) unvoiced; **2.** sound-proof(ed).
insonoris-ation [ɛ̃sɔnɔrizɑsjɔ̃] *s.f.* sound-proofing; ~**er** [ɛ̃sɔnɔrize] *v.t.* to sound-proof, to silence, to deaden or remove sound.
insouciance [ɛ̃susjɑ̃s] *s.f.* carelessness, heedlessness, unconcern, thoughtlessness.
insouciant, -e [ɛ̃susjɑ̃] *adj.* careless, carefree, happy-go-lucky; heedless; indifferent (*de*, to).
insoucieu-x, -se [ɛ̃susjø] *adj.* careless, heedless; free from care.
insoumis, -e [ɛ̃sumi] *adj.* refractory, unsubdued, unruly; ~ *s.m.* (mil.) defaulter.
insoumission [ɛ̃sumisjɔ̃] *s.f.* insubordination.
insoupçonnable [ɛ̃supsɔnabl] *adj.* above suspicion.
insoupçonné, -e [ɛ̃supsɔne] *adj.* unsuspected.
insoutenable [ɛ̃sutnabl] *adj.* indefensible, untenable; unbearable.
inspecter [ɛ̃spɛkte] *v.t.* to inspect, to survey, to examine.
inspect-eur, -rice [ɛ̃spɛktœr] *s.m.f.* inspector, surveyor, superintendent.
inspection [ɛ̃spɛksjɔ̃] *s.f.* inspection, survey; inspectorship.
inspirant, -e [ɛ̃spirɑ̃] *adj.* inspiring.
inspirat-eur, -rice [ɛ̃spiratœr] *s.m.f.* inspirer; *adj.* inspiring; (anat.) inspiratory.
inspiration [ɛ̃spirɑsjɔ̃] *s.f.* inspiration; (physiol.) inhaling, inspiration.
inspiré, -e [ɛ̃spire] *adj.*, *s.m.f.* inspired (person), mystic.
inspirer [ɛ̃spire] *v.t.* to inspire; (fam.) to interest, to attract; to suggest, to instigate; (physiol.) to inhale, to inspire; **s'**~ *v.refl. s'*~ *de*, to be inspired by, to draw inspiration from, to be suggested by, to be derived from.
instabilité [ɛ̃stabilite] *s.f.* instability, want of stability; changeableness, unsteadiness, uncertainty.
instable [ɛ̃stabl] *adj.* unstable, unsteady; unreliable; ~ *s.m.f.* (emotionally) unstable person.
installation [ɛ̃stalɑsjɔ̃] *s.f.* **1.** installation, installing; settling in, establishment; fitting up, equipping, fixing (up); **2.** installation(s), arrangements, equipment.
installer [ɛ̃stale] *v.t.* **1.** to instal, to establish, to settle in, to lodge; **2.** to arrange, to fix (up), to fit up, to equip; **s'**~ *v.refl.* to settle (down), to establish oneself, to take up one's abode.
instamment [ɛ̃stamɑ̃] *adv.* urgently, insistently, earnestly.
instance [ɛ̃stɑ̃s] *s.f.* **1.** insistence, urgency, earnestness; entreaty; **2.** lawsuit, legal proceedings; court; *introduire une* ~, to institute an action or proceedings; *en* ~, in process, in progress, before the court; *tribunal de première* ~, court of first instance, lower court; *jugement en première* ~, judgement in the lower court; ~ *supérieure*, higher court; **3.** authority; ⚠ not 'instance' in sense 'example'.
instant, -e [ɛ̃stɑ̃] *adj.* instant, urgent, pressing, eager; imminent.
instant [ɛ̃stɑ̃] *s.m.* instant, moment; *à l'*~, (i.) in a moment, straight away; (ii.) just now, a moment ago; *dans un* ~, in a few moments; *en un* ~, in a moment, in a flash; *à tout* or *à chaque* ~, every moment, all the time; *d'un* ~ *à l'autre*, any moment; *un* ~*!*, just a moment!, stop!; *pour l'*~, for the moment, for the time being; *par* ~*s*, at moments, at times.
instantané, -e [ɛ̃stɑ̃tane] *adj.* instantaneous; ~ *s.m.* (photo.) snapshot.
instantanéité [ɛ̃stɑ̃taneite] *s.f.* instantaneousness.
instantanément [ɛ̃stɑ̃tanemɑ̃] *adv.* instantaneously, in an instant.
(**à l'**)**instar** (**de**) [alɛ̃stardə] *prep. loc.* like, in imitation of, after, after the fashion of, modelled on.
instauration [ɛ̃stɔrɑsjɔ̃] *s.f.* establishment, founding.
instaurer [ɛ̃store] *v.t.* to establish, to found.
instigat-eur, -rice [ɛ̃stigatœr] *s.m.f.* instigator, inciter.
instigation [ɛ̃stigɑsjɔ̃] *s.f.* instigation, suggestion; *à l'*~ *de*, at the instigation of, on the advice or at the suggestion of, under pressure from.
instillation [ɛ̃stilɑsjɔ̃] *s.f.* instillation.
instiller [ɛ̃stile] *v.t.* to instil.
instinct [ɛ̃stɛ̃] *s.m.* instinct; *d'*~, *par* ~, instinctively.
instincti-f, -ve [ɛ̃stɛ̃ktif] *adj.* instinctive; impulsive, spontaneous; ~**vement** [ɛ̃stɛ̃ktivmɑ̃] *adv.* instinctively.
instinctuel, -le [ɛ̃stɛ̃ktɥɛl] *adj.* (psychol.) instinctual.
instituer [ɛ̃stitɥe] *v.t.* to institute, to establish, to found; to appoint.
institut [ɛ̃stity] *s.m.* institute, institution; (relig.) order, rule; *l'Institut* (*de France*), the Institute (composed of the five Academies).
institut-eur, -rice [ɛ̃stitytœr] *s.m.f.* teacher, schoolmaster; (primary) schoolmistress; tutor, governess.
institution [ɛ̃stitysjɔ̃] *s.f.* **1.** institution, foundation, establishment; (law) appointment; *usages d'*~, man-made customs; **2.** (obs.) education; (mod.) private school, college, etc.
instructeur [ɛ̃stryktœr] *adj.* instructing; *juge* ~, examining magistrate; ~ *s.m.* instructor.
instructi-f, -ve [ɛ̃stryktif] *adj.* instructive.
instruction [ɛ̃stryksjɔ̃] *s.f.* **1.** instruction, tuition, education, training, teaching; knowledge, learning; *avoir de l'*~, to be well educated; **2.** direction, instructions, orders; **3.** (law) examination, inquiry; *juge d'*~, examining magistrate, police magistrate.
instruire [ɛ̃strɥir] *v.t.* **1.** to instruct, to teach, to educate, to train; to inform; **2.** (law) to examine, to investigate; **s'**~ *v.refl.* **1.** to learn, to acquire knowledge, to acquire some education; **2.** to inquire.
instruit, -e [ɛ̃strɥi] *adj.* well educated, learned, well informed; ~ *de*, aware of, acquainted with.

instrument [ɛ̃strymɑ̃] *s.m.* instrument, implement, tool; agent; deed, treaty, document.
instrumentaire [ɛ̃strymɑ̃tɛr] *adj.* (law) *témoin* ~, witness to a deed or legal instrument.
instrumental, -e, (**aux**) [ɛ̃strymɑ̃tal] *adj.* instrumental.
instrumentation [ɛ̃strymɑ̃tɑsjɔ̃] *s.f.* (mus.) instrumentation.
instrumenter [ɛ̃strymɑ̃te] *v.t.* (mus.) to instrument, to orchestrate; ~ *v.i.* (law) to instrument, to draw up instruments, deeds; to proceed.
instrumentiste [ɛ̃strymɑ̃tist] *s.m.f.* instrumentalist.
insu [ɛ̃sy] *s.m. à l'*~ *de qn.*, unknown to s.o., without s.o. knowing; *à mon* ~, unknown to me, without my knowledge, without my being aware of it.
insubmersible [ɛ̃sybmɛrsibl] *adj.* unsinkable, insubmersible.
insubordination [ɛ̃sybɔrdinɑsjɔ̃] *s.f.* insubordination.
insubordonné, -e [ɛ̃sybɔrdɔne] *adj.* insubordinate.
insuccès [ɛ̃syksɛ] *s.m.* failure, lack of success.
insuffisamment [ɛ̃syfizamɑ̃] *adv.* insufficiently.
insuffisance [ɛ̃syfizɑ̃s] *s.f.* insufficiency, lack, shortage, deficiency; incompetence, incapacity, inefficiency.
insuffisant, -e [ɛ̃syfizɑ̃] *adj.* insufficient, deficient, inadequate; incompetent, incapable.
insufflation [ɛ̃syflɑsjɔ̃] *s.f.* insufflation.
insuffler [ɛ̃syfle] *v.t.* to insufflate, to breathe, to inspire.
insulaire [ɛ̃sylɛr] *adj.* insular, of an island or islands; ~ *s.m.f.* islander.
insularité [ɛ̃sylarite] *s.f.* insularity.
insuline [ɛ̃sylin] *s.f.* insulin.
insultant, -e [ɛ̃syltɑ̃] *adj.* insulting, offensive.
insulte [ɛ̃sylt] *s.f.* insult, affront, indignity.
insulter [ɛ̃sylte] *v.t.* to insult, to affront; ~ *à*, to be insulting to, to abuse, to jeer at; to be an insult or affront to.
insulteur [ɛ̃syltœr] *s.m.* insulter.
insupportable [ɛ̃sypɔrtabl] *adj.* insupportable, insufferable, unbearable; ~**ment** [ɛ̃sypɔrtabləmɑ̃] *adv.* insufferably, unbearably.
insurgé, -e [ɛ̃syrʒe] *s.m.f., adj.* insurgent.
(s')insurger [ɛ̃syrʒe] *v.refl.* to rebel, to revolt, to rise in insurrection.
insurmontable [ɛ̃syrmɔ̃tabl] *adj.* insurmountable, insuperable, unconquerable.
insurpassable [ɛ̃syrpɑsabl] *adj.* unsurpassable.
insurrection [ɛ̃syrɛksjɔ̃] *s.f.* insurrection, rising, revolt, mutiny.
insurrectionnel, -le [ɛ̃syrɛksjɔnɛl] *adj.* insurrectional, of insurrection, of revolt.
intact, -e [ɛ̃takt] *adj.* intact, untouched, entire, unblemished, whole, inviolate.
intaille [ɛ̃tɑj] *s.f.* intaglio.
intangibilité [ɛ̃tɑ̃ʒibilite] *s.f.* intangibility.
intangible [ɛ̃tɑ̃ʒibl] *adj.* intangible.
intarissable [ɛ̃tarisabl] *adj.* inexhaustible, unfailing, never-ending; ~**ment** [ɛ̃tarisabləmɑ̃] *adv.* inexhaustibly, endlessly.
intégrable [ɛ̃tegrabl] *adj.* (math.) integrable.
intégral, -e, (**aux**) [ɛ̃tegral] *adj.* integral, whole, complete, entire; ~**e** *s.f.* (math.) integral; ~**ement** [ɛ̃tegralmɑ̃] *adv.* integrally, wholly in full, complete(ly), in its entirety.
intégralité [ɛ̃tegralite] *s.f.* integrality, wholeness, completeness, entirety; *dans son* ~, in full, in its entirety.
intégrant, -e [ɛ̃tegrɑ̃] *adj.* integrant, integral; *faire partie* ~*e de*, to be an integral part of.
intégration [ɛ̃tegrɑsjɔ̃] *s.f.* integration; (econ.) vertical concentration.
intègre [ɛ̃tɛgr] *adj.* upright, honest.
intégrer [ɛ̃tegre] *v.t.* to integrate, to incorporate, to assimilate; ~ *v.i.* (slang) to gain entry (to one of the *grandes Écoles*); (electr.) *circuit intégré*, integrated circuit; **s'**~ *v.refl.* to become integrated or assimilated.
intégrité [ɛ̃tegrite] *s.f.* integrity, honesty, probity, uprightness; soundness, entireness.
intellect [ɛ̃telɛkt] *s.m.* intellect, understanding.
intellectuel, -le [ɛ̃telɛktɥɛl] *adj.* intellectual; ~ *s.m.f.* intellectual, brain-worker, professional person; ~**lement** [ɛ̃telɛktɥɛlmɑ̃] *adv.* intellectually.
intelligemment [ɛ̃teliʒamɑ̃] *adv.* intelligently.
intelligence [ɛ̃teliʒɑ̃s] *s.f.* **1.** intelligence, intellect, brain-power; (of person) brain, intellect; understanding, comprehension, grasp, feeling (*de*, for); **2.** (esp. secret) understanding, agreement, relations, communication, correspondence; complicity, collusion; *être d'*~ *avec qn.*, to have an understanding with s.o., to be in collusion or in league with s.o.; *entretenir des* ~*s avec l'ennemi*, to have dealings with, to be in secret communication with, the enemy; *avoir des* ~*s* (*avec*), to have contacts (with); *vivre en bonne* ~, to live on good terms; *vivre en parfaite* ~, to live in perfect harmony; ⚠ not 'intelligence' in sense 'information'.
intelligent, -e [ɛ̃teliʒɑ̃] *adj.* intelligent, quick, clever, shrewd.
intelligentsia, intelligentzia [ɛ̃teligɛn(t)sja] *s.f.* intelligentsia, intellectuals.
intelligibilité [ɛ̃teliʒibilite] *s.f.* intelligibility.
intelligible [ɛ̃teliʒibl] *adj.* intelligible, distinct, clear; *parler à haute et* ~ *voix*, to speak loud and clear; ~**ment** [ɛ̃teliʒibləmɑ̃] *adv.* intelligibly, distinctly.
intempérance [ɛ̃tɑ̃perɑ̃s] *s.f.* intemperance, excess, gluttony, drunkenness.
intempérant, -e [ɛ̃tɑ̃perɑ̃] *adj.* intemperate, excessive, self-indulgent.
intempérie [ɛ̃tɑ̃peri] *s.f.* **1.** (obs.) intemperateness (of climate), bad weather conditions; **2.** (usu. pl.) inclemency, rigours, (of climate).
intempesti-f, -ve [ɛ̃tɑ̃pɛstif] *adj.* unseasonable, out of place, ill-timed.
intenable [ɛ̃tnabl] *adj.* **1.** untenable; **2.** intolerable.
intendance [ɛ̃tɑ̃dɑ̃s] *s.f.* management, direction, administration, intendancy; (mil.) commissariat.
intendant, -e [ɛ̃tɑ̃dɑ̃] *s.m.f.* intendant, manager, steward, bailiff, bursar, commissioner, comptroller; (mil.) commissariat officer.
intense [ɛ̃tɑ̃s] *adj.* intense, extreme, vehement, excessive.
intensément [ɛ̃tɑ̃semɑ̃] *adv.* intensely, with intensity.
intensi-f, -ve [ɛ̃tɑ̃sif] *adj.* intensive; ~**vement** [ɛ̃tɑ̃sivmɑ̃] *adv.* intensively.
intensification [ɛ̃tɑ̃sifikɑsjɔ̃] *s.f.* intensifying, intensification.
intensifier [ɛ̃tɑ̃sifje] *v.t.* to intensify; **s'**~ *v.refl.* to intensify, to increase.
intensité [ɛ̃tɑ̃site] *s.f.* intensity, violence, severity, depth, strength, capacity; (electr.) ~ *de chargement*, rate of charge; (phon.) *accent d'*~, stress.
intenter [ɛ̃tɑ̃te] *v.t.* (law) to bring (an action).
intention [ɛ̃tɑ̃sjɔ̃] *s.f.* intention, intent, purpose, design; *à l'*~ *de*, for, in honour of; *dans l'*~ *de*, with a view to, with the intention of; *dans les meilleures* ~*s*, with the best of intentions; *avoir l'*~ *de*, to intend to.
intentionné, -e [ɛ̃tɑ̃sjɔne] *adj. bien* ~, well-intentioned, well-disposed, well-meaning; *mal* ~, ill-disposed, malevolent.
intentionnel, -le [ɛ̃tɑ̃sjɔnɛl] *adj.* intentional; wilful, deliberate; ~**lement** [ɛ̃tɑ̃sjɔnɛlmɑ̃] *adv.*

intentionally, on purpose, deliberately, wilfully; (obs.) *coupable ~lement*, guilty by intention.

interaction [ɛ̃tɛraksjɔ̃] *s.f.* interaction.

intercal-aire [ɛ̃tɛrkalɛr] *adj.* intercalary, interpolated; **~ation** [ɛ̃tɛrkalɑsjɔ̃] *s.f.* intercalation, insertion; **~er** [ɛ̃tɛrkale] *v.t.* to intercalate, to insert, to interpose, to introduce.

intercéder [ɛ̃tɛrsede] *v.i.* to intercede.

intercept-er [ɛ̃tɛrsɛpte] *v.t.* to intercept; **~eur** [ɛ̃tɛrsɛptœr] *s.m.* (aeron.) interceptor fighter; **~ion** [ɛ̃tɛrsɛpsjɔ̃] *s.f.* interception, intercepting.

intercesseur [ɛ̃tɛrsesœr] *s.m.* intercessor, interceder, mediator.

intercession [ɛ̃tɛrsesjɔ̃] *s.f.* intercession, mediation.

interchangeabilité [ɛ̃tɛrʃɑ̃ʒabilite] *s.f.* interchangeability.

interchangeable [ɛ̃tɛrʃɑ̃ʒabl] *adj.* interchangeable.

interclasse [ɛ̃tɛrklɑs] *s.m.* (at school) short break between classes.

intercommunication [ɛ̃tɛrkɔmynikɑsjɔ̃] *s.f.* intercommunication.

interconnexion [ɛ̃tɛrkɔnɛksjɔ̃] *s.f.* (electr.) linking-up (of power-station) on grid.

intercontinental, -e, (**aux**) [ɛ̃tɛrkɔ̃tinɑ̃tal] *adj.* intercontinental.

intercostal, -e, (**aux**) [ɛ̃tɛrkɔstal] *adj.* (anat.) intercostal.

intercourse [ɛ̃tɛrkurs] *s.f.* (maritime law) mutual right of access to ports; ⚠ not social or sexual 'intercourse'.

interdépartemental, -e, (**aux**) [ɛ̃tɛrdɛpartəmɑ̃tal] *adj.* interdepartmental.

interdépendance [ɛ̃tɛrdepɑ̃dɑ̃s] *s.f.* interdependence.

interdépendant, -e [ɛ̃tɛrdepɑ̃dɑ̃] *adj.* interdependent.

interdiction [ɛ̃tɛrdiksjɔ̃] *s.f.* interdiction, prohibition, ban; deprivation (of rights); *frapper d'~*, to prohibit, to ban, to lay under an interdict.

interdire [ɛ̃tɛrdir] *v.t.* to interdict, to prohibit, to ban, to refuse, to forbid, to suspend, to prevent; (obs.) to confound, to nonplus, to disconcert.

interdit [ɛ̃tɛrdi] *s.m.* interdict, ban, prohibition.

interdit, -e [ɛ̃tɛrdi] *adj.* **1.** interdicted, banned, forbidden; *~ de séjour*, prohibited from residence (in a particular locality); **2.** confounded, disconcerted, nonplussed, open-mouthed; *s.m.f.* prohibited person.

intéressant, -e [ɛ̃terɛsɑ̃] *adj.* interesting; worthy of attention, consideration, sympathy, etc.; (of price, proposition, etc.) attractive.

intéressé, -e [ɛ̃terese] *adj.* **1.** interested, concerned, having an interest (in); *les parties ~es*, or *les ~s*, the interested parties, those concerned; **2.** self-seeking, selfish, motivated by self-interest; calculated, with ulterior motives.

intéressement [ɛ̃terɛsmɑ̃] *s.m.* (comm., fin.) profit-sharing (scheme).

intéresser [ɛ̃terese] *v.t.* to interest, to be of interest to; to concern, to affect; *~ qn. à qch.*, to interest s.o. in sth.; to give s.o. a share or participation in sth.; *être intéressé aux bénéfices*, to have a share in the profits; *~ les employés dans une affaire*, to give the employees a financial stake in an enterprise; **s'~** *v.refl.* to be interested, to take an interest, (*à*, in).

intérêt [ɛ̃terɛ] *s.m.* **1.** interest, attention; importance; *sans ~*, uninteresting, unimportant; (rail.) *ligne d'~ local*, branch line; **2.** (fin.) (often pl.) interest, dividend; **3.** interest(s) (esp. financial), profit, advantage, share; cause; self-interest; *avoir des ~s dans une compagnie*, to be financially interested in a company; *trouver son ~ à faire qch.*, to consider it advantageous to do sth.; *il a ~ à faire qch.*, it is in his interest to do sth.; *épouser les ~s de qn.*, to espouse someone's cause; *agir par ~*, to act out of self-interest; *parler sans ~*, to speak disinterestedly; (law) *dommages et ~s*, or *dommages-~s*, damages.

interférence [ɛ̃tɛrferɑ̃s] *s.f.* (phys.) interference; conflict, confusion.

interférer [ɛ̃tɛrfere] *v.i.* (phys.) to interfere; (fig.) to conflict.

interféromètre [ɛ̃tɛrferɔmɛtr] *s.m.* (phys.) interferometer.

interfolier [ɛ̃tɛrfɔlje] *v.t.* to interleave (a book, etc.).

intérieur, -e [ɛ̃terjœr] *adj.* interior, inner, internal, inward, inside; inland; home, domestic; **~ement** [ɛ̃terjœrmɑ̃] *adv.* inwardly, internally, inside.

intérieur [ɛ̃terjœr] *s.m.* inside, interior, inner part; home, home life, domestic comforts; country (opp. foreign countries); *à l'~*, inside, on the inside, indoors, within, inside the country, at home (opp. abroad); *à l'~ de*, inside; *une femme d'~*, a domesticated woman; *à l'~ et à l'extérieur*, inside and out, at home and abroad; *ennemis de l'~*, enemies inside the country; *le Ministère de l'Intérieur*, the Home Office.

intérim [ɛ̃terim] *s.m.* interim; office as deputy; *assurer* or *faire l'~ de qn.*, to deputize for s.o.; *par ~*, interim, ad interim, provisionally, as deputy; *commander par ~*, to hold temporary command.

intérimaire [ɛ̃terimɛr] *adj.* temporary, interim, acting, deputy; *~ s.m.f.* deputy, locum, temporary holder of office.

intérioriser [ɛ̃terjɔrize] *v.t.* (psychol.) to interiorize.

interjection [ɛ̃tɛrʒɛksjɔ̃] *s.f.* interjection; (law) lodging (of an appeal).

interjeter [ɛ̃tɛrʒəte] *v.t.* (law) to lodge (an appeal).

interligne [ɛ̃tɛrliɲ] *s.m.* space between two lines, spacing; interlining; (mus.) space (between staves); *~ s.f.* (print.) lead, space between lines.

interligner [ɛ̃tɛrliɲe] *v.t.* to interline, to write between lines; (print.) to space out, to lead.

interlinéaire [ɛ̃tɛrlineɛr] *adj.* interlinear.

interlocut-eur, -rice [ɛ̃tɛrlɔkytœr] *s.m.f.* interlocutor, questioner, speaker; contact, one with whom one can talk business.

interlocutoire [ɛ̃tɛrlɔkytwar] *adj.* interlocutory; (*jugement*) *~*, interlocutory judgement or decree, provisional order.

interlope [ɛ̃tɛrlɔp] *adj.* **1.** illicit; **2.** shady, dubious; *~ s.m.* (obs.) (of ship) smuggler, blockade-runner.

interloquer [ɛ̃tɛrlɔke] *v.t.* **1.** (law) to subject to an interlocutory decree; **2.** to nonplus, to disconcert.

intermède [ɛ̃tɛrmɛd] *s.m.* interlude, interval.

intermédiaire [ɛ̃tɛrmedjɛr] *adj.* intermediate, intermediary, intervening, interposed; *~ s.m.f.* intermediary, middle-man, agent, medium, go-between; *par l'~ de*, through the medium of; *sans ~*, directly.

interminable [ɛ̃tɛrminabl] *adj.* interminable, endless, never-ending; **~ment** [ɛ̃tɛrminabləmɑ̃] *adv.* endlessly, interminably.

intermittence [ɛ̃tɛrmitɑ̃s] *s.f.* intermission, intermittence; *par ~*, intermittently.

intermittent, -e [ɛ̃tɛrmitɑ̃] *adj.* intermittent, irregular, (of labour) casual.

internat [ɛ̃tɛrna] *s.m.* **1.** boarding-school; being a boarder; **2.** service as junior hospital doctor; qualifying exam for hospital service.

international, -e, (**aux**) [ɛ̃tɛrnasjɔnal] *adj.* international.

internationalisme [ɛ̃tɛrnasjɔnalism] *s.m.* internationalism.
interne [ɛ̃tɛrn] *adj.* internal, inward, interior; ~ *s.m.f.* **1.** boarder (esp. at school); **2.** junior hospital doctor, house-surgeon.
interné, -e [ɛ̃tɛrne] *adj., s.m.f.* (person) under confinement (esp. in mental institution).
internement [ɛ̃tɛrnəmɑ̃] *s.m.* internment; confinement (of mental case).
interner [ɛ̃tɛrne] *v.t.* to intern; to confine (in a mental institution).
interparlementaire [ɛ̃tɛrparləmɑ̃tɛr] *adj.* interparliamentary.
interpellat-eur, -rice [ɛ̃tɛrpelatœr] *s.m.f.* interpellator, questioner.
interpellation [ɛ̃tɛrpelɑsjɔ̃] *s.f.* interpellation; (in parliament) question; challenge, sharp words.
interpeller [ɛ̃tɛrpele] *v.t.* to interpellate, to question; to speak sharply to, to make rude remarks to; **s'~** *v.refl.* to exchange words.
interphone [ɛ̃tɛrfɔn] *s.m.* internal telephone system, interphone, intercom.
interpolation [ɛ̃tɛrpɔlɑsjɔ̃] *s.f.* interpolation.
interpoler [ɛ̃tɛrpɔle] *v.t.* to interpolate.
interposé, -e [ɛ̃tɛrpoze] *adj.* (law) *personne ~e*, third party, nominee (as cover for real beneficiary).
interposer [ɛ̃tɛrpoze] *v.t.* to interpose; **s'~** *v.refl.* to intervene.
interposition [ɛ̃tɛrposizjɔ̃] *s.f.* interposition, intervention.
interprétariat [ɛ̃tɛrprɛtarja] *s.m.* interpretership, interpreting.
interprétation [ɛ̃tɛrpretɑsjɔ̃] *s.f.* interpretation, construction.
interprète [ɛ̃tɛrprɛt] *s.m.f.* interpreter, spokesman.
interpréter [ɛ̃tɛrprete] to interpret, to explain.
interrègne [ɛ̃tɛrrɛɲ] *s.m.* interregnum.
interrogat-eur, -rice [ɛ̃terɔgatœr] *adj.* interrogative, questioning, searching; *s.m.f.* interrogator, questioner, examiner.
interrogati-f, -ve [ɛ̃terɔgatif] *adj.* interrogative, questioning; (law) interrogatory.
interrogation [ɛ̃terɔgɑsjɔ̃] *s.f.* interrogation, questioning; question, series of questions; *point d'~*, (lit. & fig.) question-mark.
interrogativement [ɛ̃terɔgativmɑ̃] *adv.* interrogatively, questioningly.
interrogatoire [ɛ̃terɔgatwar] *s.m.* examination, interrogatory, interrogation.
interroger [ɛ̃terɔʒe] *v.t.* to interrogate, to examine, to cross-examine, to question; to consult, to sound; ~ *qn. du regard*, to look inquiringly at s.o., to give s.o. a questioning look.
interrompre [ɛ̃terɔ̃pr] *v.t.* to interrupt; to stop, to suspend, to cut off, to break in upon; **s'~** *v.refl.* to break off, to stop.
interrupt-eur, -rice [ɛ̃teryptœr] *s.m.f.* interrupter; **~eur** *s.m.* (electr.) switch, contact-breaker, cut-out; *adj.* interrupting.
interruption [ɛ̃terypsjɔ̃] *s.f.* interruption.
intersection [ɛ̃tɛrsɛksjɔ̃] *s.f.* intersection.
interstellaire [ɛ̃tɛrstɛlɛr] *adj.* interstellar.
interstice [ɛ̃tɛrstis] *s.m.* interstice, chink, crevice.
interstitiel, -le [ɛ̃tɛrstisjɛl] *adj.* interstitial.
intertropical, -e, (aux) [ɛ̃tɛrtrɔpikal] *adj.* intertropical.
interurbain, -e [ɛ̃tɛryrbɛ̃] *adj.* interurban, inter-city; (of telephone lines) trunk; ~ *s.m.* (teleph.) trunk, long-distance, system or line.
intervalle [ɛ̃tɛrval] *s.m.* interval; distance, gap, space; interval or period of time; *par ~s*, every now and then, at intervals; *dans l'~*, in the meantime, between now and then.
intervenant, -e [ɛ̃tɛrvənɑ̃] *adj.* intervening; *s.m.f.* intervening party.
intervenir [ɛ̃tɛrvənir] *v.i.* to intervene; to be involved; **2.** to occur, to arise, to be effected; *un accord est intervenu*, an agreement has been reached.
intervention [ɛ̃tɛrvɑ̃sjɔ̃] *s.f.* intervention, involvement; ~ *chirurgicale*, operation; **~niste** [ɛ̃tɛrvɑ̃sjɔnist] *adj., s.m.f.* (pol.) interventionist.
interversion [ɛ̃tɛrvɛrsjɔ̃] *s.f.* inversion, reversal, transposition, change of order.
intervertir [ɛ̃tɛrvɛrtir] *v.t.* to invert, to change the order of, to reverse, to transpose.
interview [ɛ̃tɛrvju] *s.f.* interview; **~er** [ɛ̃tɛrvjuve] *v.t.* to interview; **~er** [ɛ̃tɛrvjuvœr] *s.m.* interviewer.
intestat [ɛ̃tɛsta] *s.m., adj.invar.* intestate.
intestin [ɛ̃tɛstɛ̃] *s.m.* intestine, bowel, gut; ~ *grêle*, small intestine.
intestin, -e [ɛ̃tɛstɛ̃] *adj.* internal, domestic, civil.
intestinal, -e, (aux) [ɛ̃tɛstinal] *adj.* intestinal.
intimation [ɛ̃timɑsjɔ̃] *s.f.* (law) notice (of appeal).
intime [ɛ̃tim] *adj.* intimate, inmost, deep, secret, confidential, private; ~ *s.m.f.* close friend.
intimé, -e [ɛ̃time] *s.m.f., adj.* (law) defendant, respondent.
intimement [ɛ̃timəmɑ̃] *adv.* intimately, privately, deeply, closely.
intimer [ɛ̃time] *v.t.* (law) **1.** to summons; **2.** to give notice of.
intimidant, -e [ɛ̃timidɑ̃] *adj.* intimidating.
intimidation [ɛ̃timidɑsjɔ̃] *s.f.* intimidation, threatening behaviour; threats, bluff.
intimider [ɛ̃timide] *v.t.* to intimidate; to scare, to terrorize; to browbeat; *se laisser ~*, to be easily intimidated.
intimité [ɛ̃timite] *s.f.* inward parts, depth; intimacy, close connection; privacy; private life; cosiness; *dans l'~*, in the home, privately, in private, informally, in a simple way; *le mariage aura lieu dans la plus stricte ~*, the wedding will be a very quiet one.
intitulé, -e [ɛ̃tityle] *s.m.* title
intituler [ɛ̃tityle] *v.t.* to entitle, to name; **s'~** *v.refl.* to call oneself; to be entitled.
intolérable [ɛ̃tɔlerabl] *adj.* intolerable, unbearable.
intolérance [ɛ̃tɔlerɑ̃s] *s.f.* intolerance; (med.) inability to tolerate (drug, etc.), allergy.
intolérant, -e [ɛ̃tɔlerɑ̃] *adj.* intolerant, narrow-minded.
intonation [ɛ̃tɔnɑsjɔ̃] *s.f.* intonation, accent, inflexion.
intouchable [ɛ̃tuʃabl] *adj.* (obs.) intangible; (mod.) not to be touched; (fig.) untouchable, sacrosanct; ~ *s.m.f.* (an) untouchable, outcast.
intoxication [ɛ̃tɔksikɑsjɔ̃] *s.f.* intoxication, poisoning; (fig.) indoctrination; ⚠ not 'intoxication' in sense 'drunkenness'.
intoxiquer [ɛ̃tɔksike] *v.t.* to intoxicate, to poison; (fig.) to indoctrinate; **s'~** *v.refl.* to poison oneself.
intrados [ɛ̃trado] *s.m.* (arch.) intrados, soffit, inner surface; (aeron.) under-surface of wing.
intraduisible [ɛ̃tradɥizibl] *adj.* untranslatable.
intraitable [ɛ̃trɛtabl] *adj.* unmanageable, intractable, headstrong, unruly, unyielding.
intra-muros [ɛ̃tramyros] *adv. loc.* within the walls, within the town.
intransigeance [ɛ̃trɑ̃ziʒɑ̃s] *s.f.* intransigence, uncompromising attitude.
intransigeant, -e [ɛ̃trɑ̃ziʒɑ̃] *adj.* intransigent, uncompromising, intolerant; *s.m.f.* intransigent, die-hard.
intransiti-f, -ve [ɛ̃trɑ̃zitif] *adj.* (gram.) intransitive; **~vement** [ɛ̃trɑ̃zitivmɑ̃] *adv.* intransitively.

intransportable [ɛ̃trɑ̃spɔrtabl] *adj.* untransportable, too ill to be moved.
intra-utérin, -e [ɛ̃trayterɛ̃] *adj.* intra-uterine.
intraveineu-x, -se [ɛ̃travɛnø] *adj.* intravenous.
in-trente-deux [intrɑ̃tdø] *adj., s.invar.* trigesimo-secundo, 32mo.
intrépide [ɛ̃trepid] *adj.* intrepid, dauntless, fearless, undaunted; **~ment** [ɛ̃trepidmɑ̃] *adv.* fearlessly, dauntlessly.
intrépidité [ɛ̃trepidite] *s.f.* intrepidity, fearlessness.
intrigant, -e [ɛ̃trigɑ̃] *s.m.f.* schemer, intriguer; *adj.* intriguing, scheming.
intrigue [ɛ̃trig] *s.f.* **1.** intrigue, plot, scheme; love-affair; **2.** (of play, etc.) plot, action, story.
intriguer [ɛ̃trige] *v.t.* to intrigue, to interest, to arouse the curiosity of; ~ *v.i.* to intrigue, to scheme, to have recourse to intrigue, to pull strings.
intrinsèque [ɛ̃trɛ̃sɛk] *adj.* intrinsic; **~ment** [ɛ̃trɛ̃sɛkmɑ̃] *adv.* intrinsically.
introduct-eur, -rice [ɛ̃trɔdyktœr] *s.m.f.* introducer, initiator, promoter.
introducti-f, -ve [ɛ̃trɔdyktif] *adj.* introductive; (law) introductory.
introduction [ɛ̃trɔdyksjɔ̃] *s.f.* introduction; introducing, showing in; insertion.
introduire [ɛ̃trɔdɥir] *v.t.* to introduce, to show in, to usher in; to insert, to put in, to bring in; **s'~** *v.refl.* to be introduced; *s'~ dans*, to get into, to enter, to make or worm one's way into.
introït [ɛ̃trɔit] *s.m.* introit.
intronisation [ɛ̃trɔnizɑsjɔ̃] *s.f.* enthroning, enthronement.
introniser [ɛ̃trɔnize] *v.t.* to enthrone.
introspecti-f, -ve [ɛ̃trɔspɛktif] *adj.* introspective.
introspection [ɛ̃trɔspɛksjɔ̃] *s.f.* introspection.
introuvable [ɛ̃truvabl] *adj.* not to be found, hard to find; rare.
introversion [ɛ̃trɔvɛrsjɔ̃] *s.f.* (psychol.) introversion.
introverti, -e [ɛ̃trɔvɛrti] *adj.* introverted; *s.m.f.* (psychol.) introvert.
intrus, -e [ɛ̃try] *adj.* intruding; *s.m.f.* intruder, interloper, unwelcome visitor.
intrusion [ɛ̃tryzjɔ̃] *s.f.* intrusion, intruding.
intuiti-f, -ve [ɛ̃tɥitif] *adj.* intuitive.
intuition [ɛ̃tɥisjɔ̃] *s.f.* intuition.
intuitivement [ɛ̃tɥitivmɑ̃] *adv.* intuitively.
intumescence [ɛ̃tymesɑ̃s] *s.f.* intumescence, swelling.
intumescent, -e [ɛ̃tymesɑ̃] *adj.* intumescent, swelling up.
inule [inyl] *s.f.* (bot.) Inula, elecampane.
inusable [inyzabl] *adj.* everlasting, that will never wear out.
inusité [inyzite] *adj.* unusual, not in use, rare.
inutile [inytil] *adj.* useless, of no use, unnecessary, needless, vain, no good; worthless; ~ *de vous dire que*, needless to say; I need not say that; **~ment** [inytilmɑ̃] *adv.* uselessly, to no purpose.
inutilisé, -e [inytilize] *adj.* not utilized, unused, unemployed.
inutilité [inytilite] *s.f.* uselessness, futility, unprofitableness; pointless remark.
invaincu, -e [ɛ̃vɛ̃ky] *adj.* unvanquished, unconquered.
invalidation [ɛ̃validɑsjɔ̃] *s.f.* invalidation.
invalide [ɛ̃valid] *adj.* invalid, infirm, disabled, unfit for work; (obs.) invalid, not valid; ~ *s.m.f.* invalid, cripple, disabled person or soldier.
invalider [ɛ̃valide] *v.t.* to invalidate; (law) to nullify.
invalidité [ɛ̃validite] *s.f.* invalidity; infirmity, disablement, unfitness for work.
invariabilité [ɛ̃varjabilite] *s.f.* invariability.
invariable [ɛ̃varjabl] *adj.* invariable, unchanging, fixed; **~ment** [ɛ̃varjabləmɑ̃] *adv.* invariably.
invariant, -e [ɛ̃varjɑ̃] *adj.* invariant, constant; ~ *s.m.* constant.
invasion [ɛ̃vɑzjɔ̃] *s.f.* invasion, invading, inroad, irruption; encroachment.
invective [ɛ̃vɛktiv] *s.f.* invective, abuse.
invectiver [ɛ̃vɛktive] *v.i.* to inveigh (against), to fulminate; ~ *v.t.* to abuse, to insult.
invendable [ɛ̃vɑ̃dabl] *adj.* unsaleable.
invendu, -e [ɛ̃vɑ̃dy] *adj.* unsold; **~s** *s.m.pl.* unsold copies.
inventaire [ɛ̃vɑ̃tɛr] *s.m.* inventory, stock-taking, survey, review; stock, stock-list, schedule; *sous bénéfice d'~*, (law) without liability for debts beyond the assets of the estate; (fig.) with reservations, conditionally, subject to verification.
inventer [ɛ̃vɑ̃te] *v.t.* to invent, to discover; to think up, to imagine; to fabricate, to make up.
invent-eur, -rice [ɛ̃vɑ̃tœr] *s.m.f.* inventor, discoverer, creator; (law) finder.
inventi-f, -ve [ɛ̃vɑ̃tif] *adj.* inventive.
invention [ɛ̃vɑ̃sjɔ̃] *s.f.* invention, discovery, creation; invention, fabrication; inventive ability, imagination; (law) finding.
inventorier [ɛ̃vɑ̃tɔrje] *v.t.* to inventory, to draw up an inventory of, to catalogue, to list, to schedule.
invérifiable [ɛ̃verifjabl] *adj.* unverifiable.
inversable [ɛ̃vɛrsabl] *adj.* that cannot be upset.
inverse [ɛ̃vɛrs] *adj.* inverse, opposite, contrary; (math.) *nombres ~s*, inverse numbers, reciprocals; *raison ~*, inverse proportion, inverse ratio; ~ *s.m.* opposite, contrary, reverse; *à l'~*, quite the reverse; *à l'~ de*, contrary to; **~ment** [ɛ̃vɛrsmɑ̃] *adv.* inversely.
invers-er [ɛ̃vɛrse] *v.t.* to reverse, to invert; **~eur** [ɛ̃vɛrsœr] *s.m.* reversing mechanism; (electr.) reversing switch, change-over switch; **~ion** [ɛ̃vɛrsjɔ̃] *s.f.* inversion, reversal, reversing, transposition.
invertébré, -e [ɛ̃vɛrtebre] *adj., s.m.* invertebrate.
invertir [ɛ̃vɛrtir] *v.t.* to invert, to reverse, to transpose.
investigat-eur, -rice [ɛ̃vɛstigatœr] *adj.* investigating, investigatory, inquiring, searching; *s.m.f.* investigator.
investigation [ɛ̃vɛstigɑsjɔ̃] *s.f.* investigation, research, inquiry, scrutiny.
invest-ir [ɛ̃vɛstir] *v.t.* **1.** to invest, to besiege; **2.** to invest (funds, etc.); **3.** *~ir qn. de*, to invest s.o. with (powers, office, etc.), to confer honour on s.o.; to bestow sth. on s.o.; **~issement** [ɛ̃vɛstismɑ̃] *s.m.* **1.** investing, besieging, siege, blockade; **2.** investment, investing (of funds, etc.); **~iture** [ɛ̃vɛstityr] *s.f.* investiture; (pol.) nomination (of candidate).
invétéré, -e [ɛ̃vetere] *adj.* inveterate, confirmed, hardened; ingrained, deep-seated.
invincibilité [ɛ̃vɛ̃sibilite] *s.f.* invincibleness, invincibility.
invincible [ɛ̃vɛ̃sibl] *adj.* invincible; unconquerable, insurmountable, irresistible; **~ment** [ɛ̃vɛ̃sibləmɑ̃] *adv.* invincibly, unsurmountably.
inviolabilité [ɛ̃vjɔlabilite] *s.f.* inviolability; immunity (from prosecution).
inviolable [ɛ̃vjɔlabl] *adj.* inviolable; immune (from prosecution); **~ment** [ɛ̃vjɔlabləmɑ̃] *adv.* inviolably.
invisibilité [ɛ̃vizibilite] *s.f.* invisibility.
invisible [ɛ̃vizibl] *adj.* invisible; **~ment** [ɛ̃viziblәmɑ̃] *adv.* invisibly.
invitant, -e [ɛ̃vitɑ̃] *adj.* inviting, attractive; (acting as) host.
invitation [ɛ̃vitɑsjɔ̃] *s.f.* invitation.
invite [ɛ̃vit] *s.f.* **1.** (obs.) (at cards) lead, call; **2.** invitation, inducement.

invité, -e [ɛ̃vite] *s.m.f.* guest.
inviter [ɛ̃vite] *v.t.* to invite, to beg, to request; to urge, to incite, to induce, to tempt.
invivable [ɛ̃vivabl] *adj.* **1.** *une existence* ~, an impossible existence, a life hardly worth living; **2.** (of person) impossible (to live with).
invocation [ɛ̃vɔkɑsjɔ̃] *s.f.* invocation; protection (of saint, etc.).
invocatoire [ɛ̃vɔkatwar] *adj.* invocatory.
involontaire [ɛ̃vɔlɔ̃tɛr] *adj.* involuntary, unintentional; unwilling; **~ment** [ɛ̃vɔlɔ̃tɛrmɑ̃] *adv.* involuntarily, unwillingly, without intending or wishing.
involucré, -e [ɛ̃vɔlykre] *adj.* (bot.) involucrate.
involuté, -e [ɛ̃vɔlytɛ] *adj.* (bot.) involute(d).
involution [ɛ̃vɔlysjɔ̃] *s.f.* involution.
invoquer [ɛ̃vɔke] *v.t.* to invoke, to appeal to, to implore, to call for.
invraisemblable [ɛ̃vrɛsɑ̃blabl] *adj.* unlikely, improbable, unbelievable, incredible, astonishing; **~ment** [ɛ̃vrɛsɑ̃blabləmɑ̃] *adv.* improbably, astonishingly.
invraisemblance [ɛ̃vrɛsɑ̃blɑ̃s] *s.f.* unlikelihood, improbability.
invulnérabilité [ɛ̃vylnerabilite] *s.f.* invulnerability, immunity.
invulnérable [ɛ̃vylnerabl] *adj.* invulnerable, immune, proof (*à*, against).
iode [jɔd] *s.m.* iodine.
ioder [jɔde] *v.t.* to iodize.
iodhydrique [jɔdidrik] *adj.* (chem.) hydriodic.
iodler see JODLER.
iodoforme [jɔdɔfɔrm] *s.m.* iodoform.
iodure [jɔdyr] *s.m.* (chem.) iodide.
ioduré, -e [jɔdyre] *adj.* iodized.
ion [jɔ̃] *s.m.* ion.
ionien, -ne [jɔnjɛ̃] *adj., s.m.f.* Ionian.
ionique[1] [jɔnik] *adj.* (arch.) Ionic.
ionique[2] [jɔnik] *adj.* (sci.) ionic.
ion-isation [jɔnizɑsjɔ̃] *s.f.* (sci.) ionization; **~one** [jɔnɔn] *s.f.* (chem.) ionone; **~osphère** [jɔnɔsfɛr] *s.f.* ionosphere.
iota [jɔta] *s.m.* iota; (fig.) jot, iota, tittle; *sans changer un* ~, to the very letter, without departing by a hair's breadth.
iotacisme [jɔtasism] *s.m.* iotacism.
iouler [jule] *v.i.* = JODLER.
ipéca [ipeka] *s.m.* (pharm.) ipecacuanha.
Irak [irak] *s.m.* (geog.) Iraq.
irakien, -ne [irakjɛ̃] *adj., s.m.f.* Iraqui.
Iran [irɑ̃] *s.m.* (geog.) Iran.
iranien, -ne [iranjɛ̃] *adj., s.m.f.* Iranian.
Iraouaddi, Irouaddy [irawadi] *s.m.* (geog.) Irrawaddy (river).
irascibilité [irasibilite] *s.f.* irascibility.
irascible [irasibl] *adj.* irascible.
ire [ir] *s.f.* (obs.) wrath, anger, ire.
iridectomie [iridɛktɔmi] *s.f.* (surg.) iridectomy.
iridées [iride] *s.f.pl.* (bot.) Iridaceae.
iridescent, -e [iridesɑ̃] *adj.* iridescent.
iridium [iridjɔm] *s.m.* (chem.) iridium.
iris [iris] *s.m.* **1.** (bot.) iris, flag, orris; (anat., photo.) iris; **2.** (obs.) rainbow; (mod.) rainbow effect, prismatic halo.
irisation [irizɑsjɔ̃] *s.f.* iridescence.
irisé, -e [irize] *adj.* iridescent, rainbow-coloured.
iriser [irize] *v.t.* to give the colours of the rainbow to; **s'~** *v.refl.* to become iridescent.
irlandais, -e [irlɑ̃dɛ] *adj.* Irish; *s.m.f.* Irishman, Irishwoman; ~ *s.m.* Irish (language).
Irlande [irlɑ̃d] *s.f.* (geog.) Ireland.
ironie [irɔni] *s.f.* irony.
ironique [irɔnik] *adj.* ironic(al); **~ment** [irɔnikmɑ̃] *adv.* ironically.
ironiser [irɔnize] *v.i.* to speak ironically or mockingly.
ironiste [irɔnist] *s.m.f.* ironist.
iroquois, -e [irɔkwa] *adj., s.m.f.* Iroquois.
irrachetable [iraʃtabl] *adj.* irredeemable.
irradiation [iradjɑsjɔ̃] *s.f.* irradiation, radiation; (photo.) halation; X-ray treatment.
irradier [iradje] *v.i.* to radiate; *v.t.* to irradiate.
irraisonné, -e [irɛzɔne] *adj.* unreasoning, irrational, spontaneous.
irrationalité [irasjɔnalite] *s.f.* irrationality.
irrationnel, -le [irasjɔnɛl] *adj.* irrational.
irréalisable [irealizabl] *adj.* unrealizable, unattainable.
irréalisme [irealism] *s.m.* lack of realism, unrealistic quality.
irréalité [irealite] *s.f.* unreality.
irrecevabilité [irsəvabilite] *s.f.* inadmissibility.
irrecevable [irsəvabl] *adj.* inadmissible, that cannot be accepted.
irréconciliable [irekɔ̃siljabl] *adj.* irreconcilable.
irrécouvrable [irekuvrabl] *adj.* irrecoverable.
irrécupérable [irekyperabl] *adj.* not repairable; (of person) incapable of reintegration.
irrécusable [irekyzabl] *adj.* irrecusable, unexceptionable; indisputable.
irrédent-isme [iredɑ̃tism] *s.m.* irredentism; **~iste** [iredɑ̃tist] *adj., s.m.f.* irredentist.
irréductibilité [iredyktibilite] *s.f.* irreducibility.
irréductible [iredyktibl] *adj.* irreducible; unshakeable, indomitable.
irréel, -le [ireɛl] *adj.* unreal.
irréfléchi, -e [irefleʃi] *adj.* thoughtless, inconsiderate, unguarded, irresponsible.
irréflexion [ireflɛksjɔ̃] *s.f.* thoughtlessness.
irréfragable [irefragabl] *adj.* irrefragable; irrefutable.
irréfutable [irefytabl] *adj.* irrefutable; **~ment** [irefytabləmɑ̃] *adv.* irrefutably.
irrégularité [iregylarite] *s.f.* irregularity, unevenness.
irréguli-er, -ère [iregylje] *adj.* irregular, erratic, disordered, illegal; **~èrement** [iregyljɛrmɑ̃] *adv.* irregularly; illegally.
irréligieu-x, -se [ireliʒjø] *adj.* irreligious.
irréligion [ireliʒjɔ̃] *s.f.* irreligion, irreligiousness.
irrémédiable [iremedjabl] *adj.* irremediable, irretrievable, irreparable; **~ment** [iremedjabləmɑ̃] *adv.* irremediably, irretrievably, irreparably.
irrémissible [iremisibl] *adj.* irremissible, unpardonable.
irréparable [ireparabl] *adj.* irreparable, irretrievable; **~ment** [ireparabləmɑ̃] *adv.* irreparably, irretrievably.
irrépréhensible [irepreɑ̃sibl] *adj.* irreprehensible, unimpeachable.
irrépressible [irepresibl] *adj.* irrepressible.
irréprochable [ireprɔʃabl] *adj.* irreproachable, unexceptionable; **~ment** [ireprɔʃabləmɑ̃] *adv.* irreproachably.
irrésistible [irezistibl] *adj.* irrestible, conclusive; **~ment** [irezistibləmɑ̃] *adv.* irresistibly.
irrésolu, -e [irezɔly] *adj.* irresolute, wavering; unresolved, unsolved.
irrésolution [irezɔlysjɔ̃] *s.f.* irresolution, indecision.
irrespect [irɛspɛ] *s.m.* disrespect, lack of respect.
irrespectueu-x, -se [irɛspɛktɥø] *adj.* disrespectful; **~sement** [irɛspɛktɥøzmɑ̃] *adv.* disrespectfully.
irrespirable [irɛspirabl] *adj.* unbreathable.
irresponsabilité [irɛspɔ̃sabilite] *s.f.* irresponsibility.
irresponsable [irɛspɔ̃sabl] *adj.* irresponsible, not responsible.
irrétrécissable [iretresisabl] *adj.* unshrinkable.
irrévérence [ireverɑ̃s] *s.f.* irreverence, lack of respect, impertinence.

irrévérencieu-x, -se [ireverɑ̃sjø] *adj.* irreverent, disrespectful; **~sement** [ireverɑ̃sjøzmɑ̃] *adv.* irreverently, disrespectfully.
irreversible [irevɛrsibl] *adj.* irreversible; (techn.) non-reversing.
irrévocable [irevɔkabl] *adj.* irrevocable, binding; **~ment** [irevɔkabləmɑ̃] *adv.* irrevocably.
irrigable [irigabl] *adj.* irrigable.
irrigateur [irigatœr] *s.m.* irrigator, device for watering.
irrigation [irigɑsjɔ̃] *s.f.* irrigation.
irriguer [irige] *v.t.* to irrigate.
irritabilité [iritabilite] *s.f.* irritability, irritableness, touchiness; sensitiveness.
irritable [iritabl] *adj.* irritable, touchy, sensitive.
irritant, -e [iritɑ̃] *adj.* irritating, provoking; ~ *s.m.* irritant.
irritation [iritɑsjɔ̃] *s.f.* irritation, inflammation; (sci.) excitation.
irriter [irite] *v.t.* to irritate, to annoy, to vex, to provoke, to anger; to inflame; to excite; **s'~** *v.refl.* to become angry, to show irritation, to lose one's temper; to become irritated or enflamed.
irruption [irypsjɔ̃] *s.f.* inrush; invasion, raid, incursion; *faire ~* (*dans*), to rush or burst into, to invade.
isabelle [izabɛl] *adj. invar.*, *s.m.* light-bay (horse).
isard [izar] *s.m.* (zool.) izard, chamois of the Pyrenees.
isatis [izatis] *s.m.* (zool.) isatis, blue fox, arctic fox.
isba [isba] *s.f.* isba.
ischémie [iskemi] *s.f.* ischaemia.
ischiatique [iskjatik] *adj.* (anat.) ischiatic, sciatic.
ischion [iskjɔ̃] *s.m.* (anat.) ischium.
isiaque [izjak] *adj.* pertaining to goddess Isis.
islam [islam] *s.m.* Islam; **~ique** [islamik] *adj.* Islamic; **~iser** [islamize] *v.t.* to Islamize, to convert to Islam; **~isme** [islamism] *s.m.* Islamism, Muhammadanism.
islandais, -e [islɑ̃dɛ] *adj.* Icelandic; *s.m.f.* Icelander.
Islande [islɑ̃d] *s.f.* (geog.) Iceland.
isobare [izɔbar] *adj.* isobaric, isobarometric; ~ *s.f.* isobar.
isocèle [izɔsɛl] *adj.* isosceles.
isochromatique [izɔkrɔmatik] *adj.* isochromatic.
isochrone [izɔkrɔn] *adj.* isochronal, isochronous.
isocline [izɔklin] *adj.* (geol.) isoclinal.
isodynamique [izɔdinamik] *adj.* isodynamic.
iso-game [izɔgam] *adj.* (biol.) isogamic; **~gamie** [izɔgami] *s.f.* (biol.) isogamy.
isogone [izɔgɔn] *adj.* isogonic, isogonal.
isolable [izɔlabl] *adj.* (chem.) isolable; (electr.) insulatable.
isolant, -e [izɔlɑ̃] *adj.* insulating; isolating; ~ *s.m.* insulator, insulating material.
isolateur [izɔlatœr] *s.m.* insulator.
isolation [izɔlɑsjɔ̃] *s.f.* insulation, (sound-, etc.) proofing; ⚠ not 'isolation'; **~nisme** [izɔlɑsjɔnism] *s.m.* (pol.) isolationism; **~niste** [izɔlɑsjɔnist] *adj.*, *s.m.f.* (pol.) isolationist.
isolé, -e [izɔle] *adj.* isolated, detached, lonely, solitary; removed from its context; (electr.) insulated.
isolement [izɔlmɑ̃] *s.m.* isolation; (electr.) insulation.
isolément [izɔlemɑ̃] *adv.* separately; in isolation.
isoler [izɔle] *v.t.* to isolate, to detach, to separate, to segregate; to consider (sth.) in isolation; (electr.) to insulate; **s'~** *v.refl.* to isolate or detach oneself, to live in isolation.
isoloir [izɔlwar] *s.m.* polling booth.
isomère [izɔmɛr] *adj.* (bot.) isomerous; (chem.) isomeric; ~ *s.m.* (chem.) isomer.
isométrique [izɔmetrik] *adj.* isometric.
isomorphe [izɔmɔrf] *adj.* isomorphous, isomorphic.
isotherme [izɔtɛrm] *adj.* isothermal; ~ *s.f.* isotherm.
isotonique [izɔtɔnik] *adj.* (sci.) isotonic.
isotope [izɔtɔp] *adj.* isotopic; ~ *s.m.* isotope.
isotrope [izɔtrɔp] *adj.* isotropic.
Israël [israɛl] *s.m.* Israel.
israélien, -ne [israeljɛ̃] *adj.*, *s.m.f.* Israeli.
israélite [izraelit] *adj.*, *s.m.f.* Israelite.
issant, -e [isɑ̃] *adj.* (herald.) issuant.
issu, -e [isy] *adj.* born, descended, sprung (*de*, from, of); *cousin ~ de germain*, second cousin.
issue [isy] *s.f.* **1.** (obs.) issuing, emerging; (mod.) way out, exit; (fig.) way out, way of escape; *rue, voie, sans ~*, no through road, no thoroughfare; **2.** end, conclusion, result; **3.** (pl.) bran; **4.** (pl.) offal; ⚠ not 'issue' of a publication, nor (pol., etc.) 'issue'.
isthme [ism] *s.m.* isthmus.
isthmique [ismik] *adj.* isthmic.
italianiser [italjanize] *v.t.* to Italianize.
Italie [itali] *s.f.* (geog.) Italy.
italien, -ne [italjɛ̃] *adj.*, *s.m.f.* Italian.
italique [italik] *adj.* italic; ~ *s.m.* italic (type, letter); *mettre en ~*, to italicize.
item [itɛm] *adv.* item, likewise, also.
itérati-f, -ve [iteratif] *adj.* iterative; (gram.) frequentative, iterative; repeated; **~vement** [iterativmɑ̃] *adv.* repeatedly, reiteratively.
itinéraire [itinerɛr] *adj.* itinerary, concerning roads; ~ *s.m.* itinerary, route, guide-book, road-book.
itinérant, -e [itinerɑ̃] *adj.* travelling; (while) moving; *ambassadeur ~*, roving ambassador.
itou [itu] *adv.* also, likewise; (fam.) *et moi ~*, and I, too.
iule [jyl] *s.m.* (zool.) millipede; (bot.) catkin.
I.U.T. [iyte] abbrev. *Institut Universitaire de Technologie.*
ivoire [ivwar] *s.m.* ivory; dentine; ivory (figure, etc.).
ivoirerie [ivwarri] *s.f.* ivory-carving; ivory figures, etc.
ivoirier [ivwarje] *s.m.* ivory-carver.
ivoirin, -e [ivwarɛ̃] *adj.* ivory, shining like ivory.
ivraie [ivrɛ] *s.f.* (bot.) darnel, rye-grass, tare; (fig.) *séparer l'~ d'avec le bon grain*, to separate the wheat from the tares.
ivre [ivr] *adj.* drunk, intoxicated, inebriated; (fig.) intoxicated, beside oneself, mad; *~ de sang*, thirsting for blood, drunk with blood.
ivresse [ivrɛs] *s.f.* drunkenness, inebriation; (lit. & fig.) intoxication; (fig.) ecstasy, rapture, exaltation, frenzy.
ivrogne [ivrɔɲ] *s.m.* drunkard.
ivrognerie [ivrɔɲəri] *s.f.* (habitual) drunkenness, alcoholism, dipsomania.
ivrognesse [ivrɔɲɛs] *s.f.* drunken woman.
ixia [iksja] *s.f.* (bot.) ixia.

J

J, j [ʒi] *s.m.* the letter J, j; *j'* see JE.
jabiru [ʒabiry] *s.m.* (ornith.) jabiru (stork).
jable [ʒabl] *s.m.* (techn.) stave-groove; grooved stave-ends.
jaborandi [ʒabɔrɑ̃di] *s.m.* (bot.) jaborandi.
jabot [ʒabo] *s.m.* **1.** crop (of bird); **2.** (dressm.) frill, ruff, jabot.
jaboter [ʒabɔte] *v.i.* **1.** (obs.) to gobble (noise made by turkey); **2.** (fam.) to chatter away.
jaboteu-r, -se [ʒabɔtœr] *s.m.f.* chatterer, chatterbox.
J.A.C. [ʒiase] abbrev. *Jeunesse agricole chrétienne.*
jacasse [ʒakas] *s.f.* **1.** magpie; **2.** (woman) chatterbox.
jacasser [ʒakase] *v.i.* (of magpies and persons) to chatter, to cackle, to jabber away.
jacasserie [ʒakasri] *s.f.* chattering.
jacée [ʒase] *s.f.* (bot.) knapweed; ~ *des blés*, cornflower.
jacent, -e [ʒasɑ̃] *adj.* (law) in abeyance.
jachère [ʒaʃɛr] *s.f.* fallow, fallow ground; *laisser une parcelle en* ~, to let a plot lie fallow.
jacinthe [ʒasɛ̃t] *s.f.* (bot.) hyacinth; ~ *des prés*, bluebell; ⚠ not the gem 'jacinth'.
jaciste [ʒasist] *adj.*, *s.m.f.* (member) of *J.A.C.*
jack [(d)ʒak] *s.m.* jack (in knitting-machine); (electr., etc.) jack(-plug).
jacobée [ʒakɔbe] *s.f.* (bot.) ragwort.
jacobin, -e [ʒakɔbɛ̃] *s.m.f.* **1.** (obs.) Dominican; **2.** (Fr. hist.) Jacobin; (mod.) extreme republican.
jacobinisme [ʒakɔbinism] *s.m.* Jacobinism.
jaconas [ʒakɔnɑ] *s.m.* (text.) jaconet.
jacquard [ʒakar] *s.m.* jacquard loom; jacquard cloth; patterned jumper, jersey, etc.; ~ *adj.m.* jacquard; patterned.
jacquemart see JAQUEMART.
jacquerie [ʒakri] *s.f.* Jacquerie, rising of peasantry, esp. that of 1357–8.
Jacques [ʒɑk] *s.m.* James, Jim; ~ *Bonhomme*, symbolic name for the French peasant; *maître* ~, Jack of all trades; *faire le* ~, to play the fool.
jacquet [ʒakɛ] *s.m.* backgammon.
jacquot, jaco(t) [ʒako] *s.m.* Polly, Poll (name for parrot).
jactance [ʒaktɑ̃s] *s.f.* **1.** arrogance, conceit; **2.** (pop.) chattering, gossiping.
jaculatoire [ʒakylatwar] *adj.* (eccles.) ejaculatory (prayer).
jade [ʒad] *s.m.* jade (semi-precious stone).
jadis [ʒadis; ʒɑdis] *adv.* in the old days, once upon a time, formerly; *au temps* ~, in the good old days, in days of old, of yore.
jaguar [ʒagwar] *s.m.* (zool.) jaguar.
jaillir [ʒajir] *v.i.* to spout, to gush (out), to burst forth, to spurt out, to spring up, to stick out, to splash; to flash; *faire* ~ *une étincelle*, to strike a spark.
jaillissant, -e [ʒajisɑ̃] *adj.* (lit. & fig.) gushing.
jaillissement [ʒalismɑ̃] *s.m.* gushing, spouting, splashing, etc.; see JAILLIR.
jaïnisme [ʒainism] *s.m.* (relig.) Jainism.
jais [ʒɛ] *s.m.* (min.) jet; *noir comme le* ~, jet-black.
jalap [ʒalap] *s.m.* (pharm.) jalap.
jale [ʒal] *s.f.* large bowl or tub.
jalon [ʒalɔ̃] *s.m.* surveying staff, stake, pole, landmark, beacon; (fig.) *poser* or *planter les* ~*s de*, to prepare the ground for, to plan, to map out.
jalonnement [ʒalɔnmɑ̃] *s.m.* staking-out, marking-out.
jalonner [ʒalɔne] *v.t.i.* to mark out, to stake out, to peg out (a claim); to place landmarks; (fig.) to mark, to indicate; ~ *la route pour*, to show the way to, to blaze the trail for.
jalonneur [ʒalɔnœr] *s.m.* marker.
jalousement [ʒaluzmɑ̃] *adv.* jealously.
jalouser [ʒaluze] *v.t.* to be jealous of, to envy; **se** ~ *v.refl.* to envy each other.
jalousie [ʒaluzi] *s.f.* **1.** jealousy; envy; *donner de la* ~ *à qn.*, to make s.o. jealous; **2.** Venetian blind, jalousie, shutter; **3.** (bot.) sweet-william.
jalou-x, -se [ʒalu] *adj.* jealous; envious; anxious, watchful; ~*x de plaire*, anxious to please; ~*x de son origine*, proud of one's extraction; ~*x de ses privilèges*, jealous of one's privileges; *s.m.f.* jealous person, envious person; *faire des* ~*x*, to excite envy.
Jamaïque [ʒamaik] *s.f.* (geog.) Jamaica.
jamaïquain, -ne [ʒamaikɛ̃] *adj.*, *s.m.f.* Jamaican.
jamais [ʒamɛ] *adv.* **1.** ever, at any time; *as-tu* ~ *fait du ski?*, have you ever done any skiing?; *sans* ~ *se taire*, without ever stopping talking; *à* or *pour* ~, for ever; *à tout* ~, for ever and ever; **2.** (with *ne* expressed or understood) never, not ever; *il ne l'a* ~ *vue*, he never saw her; ~ *je n'y retournerai*, I shall not ever go back there; ~ *le lundi*, never on Mondays; ~ *plus*, never again; ~ *de la vie!*, never!, out of the question!; *c'est le cas ou* ~, it's now or never; *mieux vaut tard que* ~, better late than never.
jambage [ʒɑ̃baʒ] *s.m.* **1.** (writing) down-stroke; **2.** (arch.) jamb, side-post, cheek (of fire-place).
jambe [ʒɑ̃b] *s.f.* leg, shank, stem (of a glass); (car) stay-rod, torque-rod; *j'ai les* ~*s comme du coton*, my legs are shaky, I feel unsteady on my feet; *en avoir plein les* ~*s*, to be tired out, to be dead on one's feet; ~ *de force*, prop, stay; *jouer des* ~*s*, *prendre ses* ~*s à son cou*, to take to one's heels; *être dans les* ~*s de qn.*, to be under someone's feet; *traiter qn. par-dessous la* ~, to treat s.o. with scorn or offhandedly; *tirer dans les* ~*s à qn.*, to fire at someone's legs; (fig.) to hit s.o. below the belt, to play a dirty trick on s.o.; *à toutes* ~*s*, at top speed; *cela me fait une belle* ~, thank you for nothing.
jambé, -e [ʒɑ̃be] *adj. bien* ~, with well-shaped legs.
jambière [ʒɑ̃bjɛr] *s.f.* legging, shin-guard; (armour) greave.
jambon [ʒɑ̃bɔ̃] *s.m.* ham; (fig., pop.) thigh.
jambonneau (pl. **-x**) [ʒɑ̃bɔno] *s.m.* shoulder (of pork); small ham.
janissaire [ʒanisɛr] *s.m.* janissary.
jansénisme [ʒɑ̃senism] *s.m.* Jansenism.
janséniste [ʒɑ̃senist] *adj.*, *s.m.f.* Jansenist.
jante [ʒɑ̃t] *s.f.* rim (of a wheel), felloe, felly; *frein sur* ~, rim-brake.
janvier [ʒɑ̃vje] *s.m.* January.
Japon [ʒapɔ̃] *s.m.* (geog.) Japan.
japon [ʒapɔ̃] *s.m.* Japan paper; Japanese porcelain.
japonais, -e [ʒapɔnɛ] *adj.*, *s.m.f.* Japanese.
japonaiserie [ʒapɔnɛzri], **japonerie** [ʒapɔnri] *s.f.* Japanese curio.
jappement [ʒapmɑ̃] *s.m.* yelping, yapping.
japper [ʒape] *v.i.* to yelp, to yap.

jaquemart, jacquemart [ʒakmar] *s.m.* Jack-of-the-clock, jack, (a figure of a man which strikes the bell of a clock).
jaquette [ʒakɛt] *s.f.* (man's) morning-coat; (woman's) coat or jacket (of two-piece costume); (of book) jacket, dust-cover; *complet* ~, morning suit; ⚠ not e.g. sports 'jacket'.
jaquier [ʒakje] *s.m.* (bot.) breadfruit tree.
jar see JARS[2].
jard [ʒar] *s.m.* river-gravel.
jarde [ʒard] *s.f.* (vet.) bone spavin.
jardin [ʒardɛ̃] *s.m.* garden; fertile region; ~ *potager*, kitchen-garden; ~ *des plantes*, botanical garden; herbarium; ~ *d'acclimatation*, zoological gardens, zoo; ~ *d'enfants*, kindergarten, nursery-school; ~ *de curé*, (approx.) old-fashioned cottage garden; (fig.) *jeter une pierre dans le* ~ *de qn.*, to make a sly attack on s.o.
jardinage[1] [ʒardinaʒ] *s.m.* gardening; (forestry) management.
jardinage[2] [ʒardinaʒ] *s.m.* flaw (in diamond).
jardiner [ʒardine] *v.i.* to garden; ~ *v.t.* to manage (forest).
jardinet [ʒardinɛ] *s.m.* very small garden.
jardineu-x, -se [ʒardinø] *adj.* (of precious stones) flawed.
jardini-er, -ère [ʒardinje] *s.m.f.* gardener; ~*er*, ~*ère*, *fleuriste*, flower-grower; ~*er maraîcher*, market-gardener; ~*ère d'enfants*, kindergarten teacher; *adj.* garden; ~**ère** *s.f.* **1.** (obs.) market cart; **2.** flower-stand (or similar display-stand outside shop); window-box; **3.** (cook.) dish of cooked mixed vegetables (esp. carrots and peas); **4.** (ent.) ground-beetle.
jardiniste [ʒardinist] *s.m.f.* landscape-gardener, garden designer.
jardon [ʒardɔ̃] *s.m.* = JARDE.
jargon[1] [ʒargɔ̃] *s.m.* jargon; lingo, gibberish, technical language, cant, slang; debased, barbarous, or unintelligible language.
jargon[2] [ʒargɔ̃] *s.m.* **1.** (min.) jargon, jargoon; **2.** kind of zircon.
jargonner [ʒargɔne] *v.i.* to talk in jargon or technical language, to talk gibberish; (of geese) to cackle.
jarosse [ʒarɔs], **jarousse** [ʒarus] *s.f.* (bot.) vetch.
jarre [ʒar] *s.f.* jar, earthenware vessel, large basin, vat.
jarre [ʒar] *s.m.* kemp (coarse hair in wool or fur).
jarret [ʒarɛ] *s.m.* ham, hock, hough, hamstring; (cook.) knuckle (of veal); shin or leg (of beef); (arch.) unevenness, break of outline (in curve, etc.); (plumbing) elbow, elbow-joint; *couper le* ~ *à*, to hamstring; *avoir du* ~, to be a good walker.
jarreté, -e [ʒarte] *adj.* (vet.) *bien* ~, close-hocked; (arch.) bulging, protruding.
jarretelle [ʒartɛl] *s.f.* stocking suspender.
jarreter [ʒarte] *v.i.* (arch.) to form a bulge, to show an uneven curve.
jarretière [ʒartjɛr] *s.f.* garter; (naut.) gasket.
jars[1] [ʒar] *s.m.* gander.
jars[2], **jar** [ʒar] *s.m.* (thieves', etc.) slang; *il entend le* ~, he speaks the same language, he knows the form.
jas [ʒɑ] *s.m.* (naut.) stock (of anchor).
jaser [ʒɑze] *v.i.* to chatter, to gossip, to prattle away; to talk, to make critical comment; to tell tales, to give the game away, to talk; *on jase sur vous*, people are talking about you; *cela fait* ~, it causes comment; *interroger qn. pour le faire* ~, to interrogate s.o. to make him talk; *n'allez pas* ~, don't go and give the game away.
jaseran [ʒazrɑ̃], **jaseron** [ʒazrɔ̃] *s.m.* fine gold chain (for locket, etc.).
jaseu-r, -se [ʒɑzœr] *s.m.f.* chatterer, chatterbox, gossip; *adj.* chattering, babbling; ~**r** *s.m.* (ornith.) waxwing.
jasmin [ʒasmɛ̃] *s.m.* (bot.) jasmine, jessamine.
jaspe [ʒasp] *s.m.* jasper.
jasper [ʒaspe] *v.t.* to marble; to vein; to sprinkle; to mottle; (bookb.) *jaspé sur tranche*, sprinkled, with marbled edges.
jaspiner [ʒaspine] *v.i.* (colloq.) to chat, to talk.
jaspure [ʒaspyr] *s.f.* marbling, sprinkling, veins, variegating.
jatte [ʒat] *s.f.* bowl; platter, porringer, basin; (also *jattée*) bowlful.
jauge [ʒoʒ] *s.f.* gauge, gauging-rod, dip-stick, calliper-gauge, callipers; capacity, standard of capacity; (hosiery) gauge; (naut.) tonnage, burthen; (hort.) trench for heeling-in saplings or seedlings; ~ *à huile*, oil-gauge; (naut.) ~ *officielle*, registered tonnage.
jaugeage [ʒoʒaʒ] *s.m.* gauging, measurement; fee for gauging.
jauger [ʒoʒe] *v.t.* to gauge, to measure the capacity of; (fig.) to size up, to estimate, to gauge; ~ *v.i.* **1.** to hold, to have a capacity of; (naut.) to be of (so many tons) burthen or register; *un verre qui jaugeait une demi-bouteille*, a glass holding half-a-bottle; **2.** (naut.) to draw; *une péniche jaugeant un mètre*, a barge with a draught of one metre.
jaugeur [ʒoʒœr] *s.m.* gauger; gauge, measure.
jaumière [ʒomjɛr] *s.f.* (naut.) rudder-hole; *trou de* ~, helm-port.
jaunâtre [ʒonɑtr] *adj.* yellowish.
jaune [ʒon] *adj.* yellow; *toile* ~, unbleached calico; *souliers* ~*s*, light brown shoes; ~ *s.m.* **1.** yellow; yolk (of egg); **2.** non-striker, black-leg; non-unionist; ~ *adv. rire* ~, to give a sickly smile.
jaunet, -te [ʒonɛ] *adj.* slightly yellow; ~ *s.m.* **1.** yellow pond-lily; **2.** (fam.) gold coin.
jaunir [ʒonir] *v.t.* to make yellow, to paint or dye yellow; ~ *v.i.* to grow or turn yellow.
jaunissant, -e [ʒonisɑ̃] *adj.* turning yellow; ripening, golden.
jaunisse [ʒonis] *s.f.* (pathol.) jaundice; (agric.) yellows (disease).
jaunissement [ʒonismɑ̃] *s.m.* yellowing, turning yellow; giving a yellow colour to.
Java [ʒava] *s.f.* (geog.) Java.
java [ʒava] *s.f.* Java (dance).
javanais, -e [ʒavane] *adj.*, *s.m.f.* Javan, Javanese.
javart [ʒavar] *s.m.* (vet.) quittor, ulcer on pastern.
javeau (pl. **-x**) [ʒavo] *s.m.* sandbank.
javel [ʒavɛl] *s.f.* (also *eau de* ~) bleaching liquid, bleach.
javelage [ʒavlaʒ] *s.m.* laying in swaths or loose sheaves.
javeler [ʒavle] *v.t.* to lay in swaths or loose sheaves; *v.i.* to ripen (in the sheaf).
javelle [ʒavɛl] *s.f.* swath, loose sheaf; handful, bundle (of faggots, poles, etc.).
javelot [ʒavlo] *s.m.*, **javeline** [ʒavlin] *s.f.* javelin.
jazz [dʒɑz] *s.m.* **1.** (obs.) jazz-band; **2.** jazz (music).
je, j' [ʒə] *pers. pron.* I; (phil.) *le* ~, the ego.
jeannette [ʒanɛt] *s.f.* **1.** small gold cross (hung at the neck, once worn by peasant girls); **2.** sleeve-board (for ironing).
J.-C. [ʒise] abbrev. *Jésus-Christ*; *44 avant* ~, 44 B.C.
J.E.C. [ʒiese] abbrev. *Jeunesse étudiante chrétienne.*
jéciste [ʒesist] *adj.*, *s.m.f.* (member) of *J.E.C.*
jectisses [ʒɛktis], **jetisses** [ʒətis] *adj.f.pl. terres* ~, made earth, loose soil; *pierres* ~, building-stones, movable by hand.
jeep [(d)ʒip] *s.m.* jeep.

je-m'en-fichisme [ʒmɑ̃fiʃism] (fam.), **je-m'en--foutisme** [ʒmɑ̃futism] (vulg.) *s.m.* complete indifference, cynical non-involvement, couldn't--care-less attitude; hence **je-m'en-fichiste, -foutiste,** *adj., s.m.f.*

jenny [ʒɛni] *s.f.* (spinning-)jenny.

jérémiade [ʒeremjad] *s.f.* (fam.) lamentations, doleful tale, moaning, whining.

jerricane, jerrycan [(d)ʒerikan] *s.m.* jerrycan.

Jersey [ʒɛrze] *s.m.* (geog.) Jersey.

jersey [ʒɛrze] *s.m.* jersey (garment), jumper; jersey (material); *point de* ~, stocking-stitch.

jersiais, -e [ʒɛrzjɛ] *adj.* (geog., agric.) Jersey.

jésuite [ʒezɥit] *s.m.* Jesuit; (pej.) hypocrite; ~ *adj.* Jesuitical; (pej.) hypocritical.

jésuitique [ʒezɥitik] *adj.* (pej.) Jesuitical; **~ment** [ʒezɥitikmɑ̃] *adv.* Jesuitically, hypocritically.

jésuitisme [ʒezɥitism] *s.m.* (pej.) Jesuitism, hypocrisy.

Jésus [ʒezy] *s.m.* Jesus; picture or figure of Jesus.

jésus [ʒezy] *adj., s.m.* **1.** a size of paper (56 × 76 cm); *petit* ~, paper size 56 × 72 cm; **2.** a lovable child; *mon* ~, my dear little one.

jet¹ [ʒɛ] *s.m.* throw, throwing; cast, casting; jet, gush, spurt; shoot, sprout (of plants); ray, stream; toss, tossing; nozzle, spout; (build.) drip-moulding, weather-board; sketch; ~ *d'eau,* fountain; *d'un seul* ~, at one stroke, with a single effort; (fam.) *à* ~ *continu,* in a never--ending stream; *c'est un premier* ~, that is a first sketch; *à un* ~ *de pierre,* at a stone's throw.

jet² [dʒɛt] *s.m.* jet (aircraft).

jeté [ʒəte] *s.m.* (dance) jeté.

jetée [ʒəte] *s.f.* jetty, mole, pier.

jeter [ʒəte] *v.t.* **1.** to throw; to throw away, out, or down; to drop; to shed (load, tears); to cast, to fling, to hurl, to dash, to toss, to pitch; to emit, to shoot; to sow (discord, etc.); to utter; ~ *l'ancre,* to cast anchor; ~ *les yeux sur,* to cast one's eyes on; to select (a person); ~ *un cri,* to utter a cry; ~ *des vapeurs,* to emit, to belch, smoke and steam; ~ *un soupir,* to heave a sigh; (pop.) *s'en* ~ *un verre,* to have a drink; (pop.) *en* ~, to sparkle, to look splendid; ~ *son bonnet par-dessus les moulins,* to throw off all restraint, to lose all sense of modesty; (slang) *n'en jetez plus, la cour est pleine!,* don't go on, that will do!; come off it!; (fig.) ~ *sa gourme,* to sow one's wild oats; ~ *de l'huile sur le feu,* to add fuel to the flame; ~ *son argent par les fenêtres,* to play ducks and drakes with one's money; ~ *des racines,* to strike root; *le sort en est jeté,* the die is cast; ~ *les fondations de,* to lay the foundation of; ~ *un coup d'œil à,* to cast an eye over, to glance at, to look at; **2.** (med.) to discharge; ~ *du pus,* to run, to suppurate; **se** ~ *v.refl.* to throw oneself, to fling oneself, to fall, to pounce, to rush; *se* ~ *à corps perdu,* to rush headlong, to plunge; (of rivers, etc.) to flow, to empty, (*dans,* into).

jeton [ʒtɔ̃, ʒətɔ̃] *s.m.* mark, counter, tally, token; ~ *de téléphone,* counter for use in call-box; (pop.) *c'est un faux* ~, he is false, he's a hypocrite; (pop.) *avoir les* ~*s,* to be afraid.

jeu (pl. **-x**) [ʒø] *s.m.* **1.** game, play, sport, pastime, amusement, frolic; trick; freak, sport; stake (gambling); playing, acting; execution; *c'est le* ~, that's the game, those are the rules; (fam.) *ce n'est pas de* ~, that's against the rules, that's not allowed, it's unfair; *jouer le* ~, to play the game, to conform; *par* ~, for fun, for amusement, for sport; *faire un* ~ *de,* to do (sth.) for amusement, to make a sport of; to make light of, to triumph over; ~ *de la nature,* freak (of nature), sport; (theatr.) ~ *de scène,* (stage) effect; *vieux* ~, old-fashioned (stuff), old hat; ~*x du souvenir,* tricks of the memory; *en* ~, at stake, at risk, involved; *mettre en* ~, to start, to bring into play, to bring to bear; to involve or employ (resources, etc.); to stake, to risk; *ne me mettez pas en* ~, do not mix me up in it; ~ *de mains,* sparring, horse-play, rough stuff; *avoir du* ~, to get good cards; *avoir beau, mauvais,* ~, to have a good, poor, hand; *avoir du bonheur au* ~, to be lucky at cards; (fig.) *cacher son* ~, to play a cunning game; *jouer gros* ~, to play for high stakes, to play high; (fig.) to risk much; *entrer en* ~, to open play; (fig.) to enter into (a discussion, etc.), to be involved; *des facteurs qui entrent en* ~, relevant factors; *entrer dans le* ~, to take part, to join in (sth.); *entrer dans le* ~ *de qn.,* to co-operate or go along with s.o.; *faire le* ~ *de qn.,* to play someone's game, to play into someone's hands; *faire bonne mine à mauvais* ~, to make the best of a bad job; to put a good face on the matter; *se piquer au* ~, to stick to, to become passionately keen on, (game, enterprise, etc.); *beau* ~ *beau retour,* one good turn deserves another; *maison de* ~, gambling-house; *faites vos* ~*x,* make your stakes; *jeux de société,* indoor games, round games, party games; *un* ~ *brillant,* brilliant playing or acting; *un* ~ *net,* neat execution; ~ *de physionomie,* facial play, changing expressions; ~ *de mots,* pun; ~ *d'esprit,* witticism; *cela passe le* ~, that is beyond a joke; *le* ~ *n'en vaut pas la chandelle,* the game is not worth the candle; **2.** set, suit, pack (of cards); ~ *de clefs, d'avirons, d'aiguilles,* set of spanners, oars, needles; ~*x d'orgue,* organ-stops; *un* ~ *de quilles,* a set of ninepins; ~ *d'échecs,* (i.) chess-board; (ii.) set of chess-men; (iii.) chess game; **3.** (mech.) play, looseness; *la direction a du* ~, there is some play in the steering; *corriger le* ~, to take up the play, to take up the slack.

jeudi [ʒødi] *s.m.* Thursday; ~ *saint,* Maundy Thursday; *semaine des quatre* ~*s,* month of Sundays; never.

(**à**) **jeun** [aʒœ̃] *adv.* fasting, on an empty stomach; before meals.

jeune [ʒœn] *adj.* **1.** young, youthful; immature; (fam.) green; *un homme* ~, a man still young; *un* ~ *homme,* a young man; *un très* ~ *homme,* a youth; *un visage* ~, a young, youthful, face; *dans mon* ~ *temps,* in my youth; *son essai est un peu* ~, his essay is rather immature; *vous êtes bien* ~, *mon ami,* you are very green, my friend; *un* ~ *vin,* young, immature wine; **2.** younger, junior; *mon* ~ *fils,* my younger son; *Dupont* ~, Dupont junior; (theatr.) *jouer les* ~*s premiers,* to act the lovers' parts; to play the juvenile lead; *adv. s'habiller* ~, to dress like a young person; ~ *s.m.f.* young person, youth, adolescent; *les* ~*s,* young people, the young, youth.

jeûne [ʒøn] *s.m.* fast, fasting, abstinence; (fig.) deprivation.

jeûner [ʒøne] *v.i.* to fast, to go without food or a meal.

jeunesse [ʒœnɛs] *s.f.* **1.** youth, youthful days; youthfulness, youthful appearance or attitude; *dans sa* ~, in his youth, in his young days, when young; *dans sa première* ~, in his early youth; *elle n'est plus de la première* ~, she is no longer young; *de* ~, *dès sa* ~, from early youth, from youth onwards; *il faut que* ~ *se passe,* youth will be served; boys will be boys; **2.** youth, young people; (pl.) youth organization; (obs.) young girl or woman; *la* ~ *du village,* the youth of the village; (hist.) *les* ~*s hitlériennes,* the Hitler youth organization; *enseigner la* ~, to teach young people.

jeunet, -te [ʒœnɛ] *adj.* (fam.) very young.

jeûneu-r, -se [ʒønœr] *s.m.f.* one who fasts, faster.

jeunot [ʒœno] *s.m.* (fam.) young man.

jiu-jitsu [ʒiyʒitsy] *s.m.* ju-jitsu, jiu-jitsu.

J.O. [ʒio] abbrev. *Journal Officiel*; *Jeux Olympiques.*
joaillerie [ʒɔɑjri] *s.f.* **1.** jewellery, jewelry, gems, jewels; **2.** jewellery trade; jeweller's workshop.
joailli-er, -ère [ʒɔɑje] *s.m.f.* jeweller.
job[1] [ʒɔb] *s.m.* (slang) *monter le ~ à qn.*, to deceive s.o., to take s.o. in; *se monter le ~*, (i.) to delude oneself; (ii.) to work oneself up.
job[2] [dʒɔb] *s.m.* (casual) job.
jobard, -e [ʒɔbar] *adj.* silly; *s.m.f.* fool, simpleton.
jobarderie [ʒɔbardri], **jobardise** [ʒɔbardiz] *s.f.* gullibility, credulity.
J.O.C. [ʒiose] abbrev. *Jeunesse Ouvrière Chrétienne.*
jocasse [ʒɔkɑs] *s.f.* (ornith., fam.) missel-thrush.
jociste [ʒɔsist] *adj.*, *s.m.f.* (member) of *J.O.C.*
jockey [ʒɔke] *s.m.* **1.** (obs.) postilion, outrider; **2.** jockey.
jocrisse [ʒɔkris] *s.m.* fool, simpleton.
jodler [ʒɔdle], **iodler** [jɔdle] *v.t.i.* to yodel.
joie [ʒwɑ] *s.f.* joy, joyfulness, gladness, delight; pleasure, enjoyment; *pleurer de ~*, to weep for joy; *faire la ~ de qn.*, to please, to give pleasure to, s.o.; *se faire une ~ de*, to take delight in; to look forward to; *renoncer aux ~s de ce monde*, to renounce the pleasures of this world; *un rabat-~*, a kill-joy, a wet blanket; *fille de ~*, prostitute.
joindre [ʒwɛ̃dr] *v.t.* to join, to unite, to put or bring together, to connect, to link; to enclose (with letter), to add, to annex; to combine (*à*, with); to touch, to meet, to make contact with, to catch up with; (fig.) *~ les deux bouts*, to make (both) ends meet (financially); *~ les mains*, to clasp one's hands; *~ les pieds*, to put one's feet together; *isthme joignant deux continents*, isthmus linking two continents; *joignez cette pièce au dossier*, add this paper to the file; *une photo jointe à une lettre*, a photo enclosed with, or attached to, a letter; *~ l'utile à l'agréable*, to combine business with pleasure; *notre maison joint la leur*, our house adjoins theirs; *je n'ai pas pu le ~*, I couldn't get hold of him; *~ v.i.* to meet, to join; *les deux planches ne joignent pas tout à fait*, the two boards don't quite meet; **se** *~ v.refl. se ~ à*, to join with, to mix with, to combine with; to meet, to join, to join in; to be added to; *mon mari se joint à moi pour envoyer*, my husband joins with me in sending; *se ~ à ses amis*, to join or meet one's friends; *se ~ à la conversation*, to join in the conversation.
joint [ʒwɛ̃] *adj.* joined, united, connected, combined, close together; additional, added, attached, enclosed; *pieds ~s*, feet close together; *mains ~es*, hands clasped; *efforts ~s*, combined efforts; *avantages ~s*, additional advantages; *ci-~*, herewith, enclosed herewith, annexed; *vous trouverez ci-~*, please find enclosed or attached; *~ à cela que*, added to which, besides which.
joint [ʒwɛ̃] *s.m.* (anat.) joint, articulation; (techn.) joint coupling, seam, bond, weld; gasket; gland, seal; (build.) jointing; (geol.) joint, line of jointing; (fam.) *trouver le ~*, to hit on the best way of tackling something, to find the answer.
jointé, -e [ʒwɛ̃te] *adj.* (vet.) jointed; *court-~*, short-jointed; *long-~*, long-jointed.
jointi-f, -ve [ʒwɛ̃tif] *adj.* (of slats, boards, etc.) close together, touching, joining; *~***ve** *s.f.* partition of plain boards (not tongued and grooved).
jointoiement [ʒwɛ̃twamɑ̃] *s.m.* (mason.) pointing, grouting (of walls).
jointoyer [ʒwɛ̃twaje] *v.t.* (techn.) to point, to grout.
jointoyeur [ʒwɛ̃twajœr] *s.m.* (techn.) workman employed in pointing.
jointure [ʒwɛ̃tyr] *s.f.* join, joint; (anat.) joint, articulation.
joker [ʒɔkɛr] *s.m.* (cards) joker.
joli, -e [ʒɔli] *adj.* pretty, pleasing, handsome, nice; amusing; considerable, pretty good, (colloq.) tidy; (iron.) fine, nice; *une ~e figure*, a pretty face; *un ~ garçon*, a handsome boy; *une ~e voix*, a pleasing voice; *le plus ~ de l'histoire, c'est que*, the funny thing about it is; *dans un ~ pétrin*, in a fine pickle; *c'est du ~*, this is a nice state of affairs; *une ~e somme*, a tidy sum; *de ~s bénéfices*, fat profits; *~***ment** [ʒɔlimɑ̃] *adv.* prettily, nicely; enormously, tremendously, very much; (iron.) nicely, well and truly; *un compliment ~ment tourné*, a nicely turned compliment; *vous voilà ~ment arrangé*, you do look a sight; *on vous a ~ment trompé*, you have been well and truly had; *il est ~ment riche*, he is enormously rich; *vous vous êtes ~ment trompé*, you are very much mistaken, you have made a big mistake.
joliesse [ʒɔljɛs] *s.f.* (Lit.) prettiness, delicacy.
jonc [ʒɔ̃] *s.m.* **1.** (bot.) rush; *panier de ~*, rush basket; **2.** *~ (d'Inde)*, rattan, cane; cane (stick); **3.** plain ring.
joncacées [ʒɔ̃kase] *s.f.pl.* (bot.) rushes.
joncer [ʒɔ̃se] *v.t.* to rush-bottom (a chair).
jonchaie [ʒɔ̃ʃɛ], **joncheraie** [ʒɔ̃ʃrɛ], **jonchère** [ʒɔ̃ʃɛr] *s.f.* bed or clump of rushes.
jonchée[1] [ʒɔ̃ʃe] *s.f.* **1.** scattering, strewing, of flowers; **2.** heap (of things) on the ground.
jonchée[2] [ʒɔ̃ʃe] *s.f.* **1.** (obs.) rush basket for straining curds; **2.** cream cheese (made in rush basket).
joncher [ʒɔ̃ʃe] *v.t.* to scatter, to strew, to litter; *les feuilles mortes jonchent le sol*, the ground is strewn, littered, with dead leaves.
jonchets [ʒɔ̃ʃɛ] *s.m.pl.* spillikins.
joncier [ʒɔ̃sie] *s.m.* (bot.) Spanish broom.
jonction [ʒɔ̃ksjɔ̃] *s.f.* junction; joining, meeting; *point de ~*, meeting-point, junction; *opérer une ~*, to effect a junction.
jongler [ʒɔ̃gle] *v.i.* to juggle; to play sleight-of--hand tricks; (fig.) *~ avec*, to juggle with, to manipulate; *~ avec les difficultés*, to make light of the difficulties.
jonglerie [ʒɔ̃glǝri] *s.f.* **1.** juggling, sleight-of--hand; **2.** (fig.) juggling, manipulation, tricks.
jongleu-r, -se [ʒɔ̃glœr] *s.m.f.* **1.** (hist.) minstrel, jongleur; **2.** mountebank; **3.** juggler.
jonque [ʒɔ̃k] *s.f.* (Chinese) junk.
jonquille [ʒɔ̃kij] *s.f.* (bot.) jonquil; *~ adj.* jonquil colour, pale yellow.
Jordanie [ʒɔrdani] *s.f.* (geog.) Jordan (country).
jordanien, -ne [ʒɔrdanjɛ̃] *adj.*, *s.m.f.* (native or inhabitant) of Jordan, Jordanian.
joseph [ʒozef] *adj. papier ~*, filter paper.
jottereaux [ʒɔtro] *s.m.pl.* (naut.) cheeks.
jouable [ʒwabl] *adj.* (theatr.) playable.
jouailler [ʒwaje] *v.i.* (fam.) **1.** to play for low stakes; **2.** to play (mus. instrument) indifferently or without feeling.
joubarbe [ʒubarb] *s.f.* (bot.) houseleek.
joue [ʒu] *s.f.* (anat.) cheek; (techn.) cheek (of pulley-block); cheek or wing (of armchair); (pl.) (naut.) bows; *embrasser sur la ~*, to kiss on the cheek; *coucher* or *mettre un fusil en ~*, to aim a rifle, to bring a rifle to the aim; *coucher* or *mettre qch. en ~*, to aim at sth.
jouée [ʒwe] *s.f.* (arch.) reveal (of doorway, recess).
jouer [ʒwe] *v.i.* to play, to toy, to fiddle, to trifle, to take risks, to gamble, to speculate; *~ avec sa santé*, to risk one's health; *~ à*, to play (a game); to play at being (sth.); *~ aux cartes*, to play cards; *~ aux courses*, to play the horses; *~ à la marchande*, to play shops; *~ au grand savant*, to pretend to be very learned; *~ sur*, to bank on, to gamble on, to speculate on; *~ sur la paresse d'autrui*, to bank on other people's laziness; *~ sur les mots*, to play on words; *~ de*, to make use of, to make play with, to perform

with; to play (mus. instrument); ~ *des coudes*, to use one's elbows, to elbow one's way; ~ *du piano*, to play the piano; **2.** to work, to act, to operate, to be operative; to be involved; *faire ~ la clef dans la serrure*, to turn the key in the lock; *faire ~ les pompes*, to operate the pumps; *la question d'intérêt ne joue pas entre eux*, questions of self-interest are not involved in their relationship; **3.** to move, to have (a certain amount of) play, to fit loosely, (of wood, etc.) to shrink, to warp; ~ *sur son ancre*, to swing at anchor; *boiserie qui joue*, woodwork which has shrunk or warped; ~ *v.t.* to play, to act, to impersonate, to pretend to be, to give an impression of, to look like (without being); to stake, to risk; ~ *un jeu, une balle, une carte, un rôle*, to play a game, a ball, a card, a part; ~ *de la musique*, to play music; ~ *une pièce*, to act a play; *faire ~ une pièce*, to perform or present a play; *qu'est-ce qu'on joue au cinéma?*, what's on at the cinema?; ~ *un tour*, to play a trick; (fam.) ~ *la surprise*, to feign surprise; *du zinc jouant le bronze*, zinc made to look like bronze; ~ *gros jeu*, to play for high stakes; ~ *sa réputation*, to risk one's reputation; **se** ~ *v.refl.* **1.** (obs.) to play, to frolic; **2.** to disdain, to make fun of, to make light of; *en se jouant*, with the greatest of ease.

jouet [ʒwɛ] *s.m.* toy, plaything; (fig.) victim, laughing-stock; *le ~ d'une illusion*, the victim of a deception; *le ~ de toute la ville*, the laughing-stock of the whole town; *être le ~ des événements*, to be overtaken by events.

joueu-r, -se [ʒwœr] *s.m.f.* player; performer; gambler; *~r, ~se, de flûte*, flute-player, flautist; *un beau ~r*, a good sportsman; *adj.* keen on sport.

joufflu, -e [ʒufly] *adj.* (fam.) chubby, chubby-cheeked, plump-faced.

joug [ʒu] *s.m.* yoke; (fig.) yoke, domination; (techn.) beam (of a balance).

jouir [ʒwir] *v.i.* to experience pleasure or enjoyment, to enjoy oneself; *ils ne vivent que pour ~*, they live only for pleasure; *ça l'a fait ~*, (i.) he greatly enjoyed it; (ii.) (iron.) it really hurt him; ~ *de*, (i.) to enjoy, to take pleasure in; ~ *d'un bon dîner*, to enjoy a good dinner; (ii.) to enjoy (use or possession of); ~ *d'une bonne santé*, to enjoy good health; ~ *d'un privilège*, to enjoy a privilege, to have an exclusive right.

jouissance [ʒwisɑ̃s] *s.f.* **1.** enjoyment, pleasure, joy, delight; *trouver une ~ à faire*, to take pleasure in doing, to enjoy doing; **2.** enjoyment, possession, use; right (to interest, dividends, etc.); (law) usufruct; *entrer en ~ d'une propriété*, to enter into possession of a property; *la ~ d'un jardin*, the use of a garden, the right to use a garden; *maison à vendre avec ~ immédiate*, house for sale with vacant possession; ~ *de passage*, right of way, way-leave; (fin.) *date de ~*, date from which interest is payable.

jouissant, -e [ʒwisɑ̃] *adj.* **1.** (obs.) in possession, enjoying a right (*de*, to); **2.** (pop.) enjoyable.

jouisseu-r, -se [ʒwisœr] *s.m.f.* sensualist, sybarite.

joujou (pl. **-x**) [ʒuʒu] *s.m.* toy or plaything.

jour [ʒur] *s.m.* **1.** light, daylight; *le point du ~*, break of day, dawn; *en plein ~*, in broad daylight; *contre le ~*, against the light; *il fait ~*, it is light, it is getting light; *donner ~ à*, to give birth to; *mettre à ~*, to publish, to expose, to divulge; to bring up to date; *être en ~*, to be visible; *sous un ~ favorable*, in a favourable light; *être comme le ~ et la nuit*, to be totally different, to be as different as chalk from cheese; **2.** window, opening, aperture, open-work; *percer un ~ dans une muraille*, to make a window-opening in a wall; *faire des ~s à un mouchoir*, to trim a handkerchief in open-work; *à ~*, open, in open-work, pierced, that can be seen through; *clôture à ~*, open fence; *cloison à ~*, open-work or pierced panelling; (fig.) *percer à ~*, to see through (a stratagem, etc.); *se faire ~*, (i.) to become apparent, to emerge; (ii.) to clear a space (for oneself), to make one's way (through a crowd, etc.); **3.** day (opp. night), daytime; *les ~s raccourcissent*, the days are getting shorter; *service de ~*, day service; *le ~ ils ne se voient guère*; they are not often to be seen in the daytime; **4.** day (period of time, 24 hours), day (of an event, etc.), date; *ce ~-là*, (on) that day; *durer deux ~s*, to last two days; *huit ~s*, a week; *quinze ~s*, a fortnight; ~ *ouvrable*, working day; ~ *de pluie*, rainy day; *quel ~ sommes-nous?*, what is the date?; *le ~ de l'An*, New Year's Day; *tous les ~s*, every day; *de tous les ~s*, ordinary, everyday; *un ~ j'y parviendrai*, one day, one of these days, I'll get round to it; *de ~ en ~*, day by day, gradually, as each day passes; *d'un ~ à l'autre*, from day to day, any day now; all the time; *du ~ au lendemain*, from one day to the next, instantly, (fig.) overnight; *du ~*, of today, today's, for today; *œufs du ~*, new-laid eggs; *les nouvelles du ~*, the day's news; *15 francs par ~*, 15 francs per day; *vivre au ~ le jour*, to live from day to day or from hand to mouth; *le travail avance au ~ le ~*, the work progresses steadily; **5.** (particular or appointed) day; *le ~ du scrutin*, the day of the election, voting day; *le jeudi, c'est mon ~*, Thursday is the day I receive visitors; Thursday is my day off; **6.** day, period, epoch; *le héros du ~*, the hero of the day; *la mode du ~*, the current fashion; **7.** day (of life); *finir ses ~s en paix*, to end one's days in peace; *dans ses derniers ~s*, in his latter days, in his old age.

Jourdain [ʒurdɛ̃] *s.m.* (geog.) (river) Jordan.

journal (pl. **aux**) [ʒurnal] *s.m.* **1.** journal, diary; (comm.) journal, day-book; (naut.) ~ *de bord*, log-book; **2.** newspaper, paper; (radio, TV) news.

journali-er, -ère [ʒurnalje] *adj.* daily, everyday; (obs.) transient, changeable; *s.m.f.* day-labourer, agricultural worker.

journalisme [ʒurnalism] *s.m.* journalism.

journaliste [ʒurnalist] *s.m.f.* journalist.

journée [ʒurne] *s.f.* **1.** day; daytime; *passer ses ~s à dormir*, to spend one's days sleeping; *travailler toute la ~*, to work the whole day long; (fam.) *toute la sainte ~*, the whole blessed day; *travailler à la ~*, to work by the day; (fam.) *à petites ~s*, little by little, by easy stages; *travailler pendant la ~*, to work during the daytime; **2.** daily wage, day's wages; day's work; *il a fait une bonne ~*, he has done a good day's work; *la ~ de huit heures*, the eight-hour day; *aller en ~*, to work by the day, to do daywork; *homme de ~*, day-labourer; *femme de ~*, charwoman; daily woman; *c'est à une ~ d'ici*, it is a day's journey from here; **3.** historic day, contest, battle; *les ~s de septembre 1939*, the days of September 1939; *gagner la ~*, to carry, win, the day.

journellement [ʒurnɛlmɑ̃] *adv.* every day, daily; *le docteur fait sa visite ~*, the doctor visits daily; *cela se voit ~*, it is a thing one sees daily, it is an everyday occurrence.

joute [ʒut] *s.f.* joust, tilt, tilting-match; (fig.) contest.

jouter [ʒute] *v.i.* to joust, to tilt; (fig.) to contest, to contend.

jouteur [ʒutœr] *s.m.* jouster; (fig.) antagonist, opponent.

jouvence [ʒuvɑ̃s] *s.f.* youthfulness, youth.

jouvenceau (pl. **-x**) [ʒuvɑ̃so] *s.m.* (fam.) youth, lad, young fellow.

jouvencelle [ʒuvɑ̃sɛl] *s.f.* (fam., often iron.) lass, girl, maiden, damsel.

jovial, -e, (**aux**) [ʒɔvjal] *adj.* jovial, convivial, jolly, merry; **~ement** [ʒɔvjalmɑ̃] *adv.* jovially, convivially.
jovialité [ʒɔvjalite] *s.f.* joviality, conviviality, jollity.
joyau (pl. **-x**) [ʒwajo] *s.m.* (lit. & fig.) jewel.
joyeusement [ʒwajɔ̃zmɑ̃] *adv.* joyfully, joyously, gladly.
joyeuseté [ʒwajøzte] *s.f.* jest, joke, prank.
joyeu-x, -se [ʒwajø] *adj.* joyful, joyous, happy, merry, delighted, glad, jolly; *il était tout ~x de vous voir,* he was delighted to see you; *mener ~se vie,* to live a gay life, a life of pleasure; **~x** *s.m.* (hist.) soldier serving in the *Bataillons d'Afrique,* or '*bat' d'Af*' (punishment regiment in Fr. N. Africa).
jubé [ʒybe] *s.m.* (arch.) rood-loft, rood-screen.
jubilaire [ʒybilɛr] *adj.* (of year, etc.) jubilee, of the jubilee; (of person) who has reached his fiftieth year of service.
jubilant, -e [ʒybilɑ̃] *adj.* jubilant.
jubilation [ʒybilɑsjɔ̃] *s.f.* jubilation, rejoicing.
jubilé [ʒybile] *s.m.* (eccles.) jubilee; (mod.) jubilee, fiftieth anniversary, fifty years of service, golden wedding.
jubiler [ʒybile] *v.i.* (fam.) to rejoice, to be jubilant.
juchée [ʒyʃe] *s.f.* pheasant's perch or roost.
jucher [ʒyʃe] *v.i.* to roost, to go to roost; (fam.) to live on a high storey; to perch oneself up; ~ *v.t.* to perch; **se ~** *v.refl.* to perch, to perch oneself.
juchoir [ʒyʃwar] *s.m.* roost, perch, roosting-place.
judaïque [ʒydaik] *adj.* Judaic, Judaical, Jewish.
judaïser [ʒydaize] *v.i.* to follow Jewish customs.
judaïsme [ʒydaism] *s.m.* Judaism.
judas [ʒydɑ] *s.m.* **1.** Judas, traitor; betrayer; **2.** judas, peep-hole.
judicature [ʒydikatyr] *s.f.* judicature.
judiciaire [ʒydisjɛr] *adj.* judicial, forensic, legal; *nouvelles ~s,* law reports; *casier ~,* criminal record; *police ~,* C.I.D.; *vente ~,* sale by order of the Court; (obs.) *combat ~,* trial by combat; *poursuites ~s,* legal proceedings; **~ment** [ʒydisjɛrmɑ̃] *adv.* in legal form, by order of the court.
judicieu-x, -se [ʒydisjø] *adj.* judicious, sensible, discerning, wise, discreet; **~sement** [ʒydisjøzmɑ̃] *adv.* judiciously, sensibly, wisely.
jugal, -e, (**aux**) [ʒygal] *adj.* (anat.) jugal; *os ~,* cheek-bone.
juge [ʒyʒ] *s.m.* judge; magistrate, justice; arbiter, umpire, referee; *~ de paix,* justice of the peace, magistrate; *~ consulaire,* judge for commercial cases; *~ d'instruction,* examining magistrate, police magistrate; *être ~ et partie,* to be judge of one's own cause; (sport) *~ de touche,* touch-judge.
jugé, juger [ʒyʒe] *s.m. au ~,* at a guess, roughly; *tirer au ~,* to fire blind, to fire at a venture
jugeable [ʒyʒabl] *adj.* that can be brought to court, that can be decided in a court of law.
jugement [ʒyʒmɑ̃] *s.m.* **1.** (law) judgement, sentence, decision, award; *prononcer le ~,* to pass sentence; *rendre un ~,* to pass a sentence, to deliver judgement, to make a decision or award; *mettre* or *faire passer en ~,* to bring to trial; *passer en ~,* to be brought for trial, to stand one's trial; *poursuivre en ~,* to take to court, to take legal proceedings against; *~ provisoire,* decree nisi; *~ définitif,* decree absolute; **2.** judgement, opinion, estimation; *émettre* or *exprimer* or *porter ~ sur,* to pass judgement on, to express an opinion on; *~ préconçu,* preconceived opinion; **3.** judgement, discernment, discrimination; *avoir du ~,* to have good judgement; *manquer de ~,* to be lacking in judgement, to lack discernment; *erreur de ~,* error of judgement.
jugeote [ʒyʒɔt] *s.f.* (fam.) judgement, good sense.
juger [ʒyʒe] *v.t.* **1.** to judge, to try; to pass sentence or judgement on; to adjudicate, to decide; to form an opinion about, to make a judgement of, to criticize, to censure; *~ un accusé,* to try a prisoner; *~ un différend,* to decide a dispute; *~ un ouvrage,* to judge a work, to form an opinion of a work, to make a critical review of a work, to criticize a work; *mal ~,* to be mistaken in one's judgement; **2.** to judge, to consider, to think, to find, to deem; *~ nécessaire,* to consider necessary; *si vous le jugez bon,* if you think right; *~ de,* to judge of, to imagine; *jugez de ma surprise,* imagine my surprise; *~ s.m.* see JUGÉ.
jugulaire [ʒygylɛr] *adj.* (anat.) jugular; *~ s.f.* (anat.) jugular vein; (mil.) chin-strap.
juguler [ʒygyle] *v.t.* **1.** (obs.) to strangle, to seize or cut the throat of; **2.** to arrest the progress of, (fig.) to throttle, to thwart, to frustrate.
jui-f, -ve [ʒɥif] *adj.* Jewish; *s.m.f.* Jew, Jewess.
juillet [ʒɥije] *s.m.* July.
juin [ʒɥɛ̃] *s.m.* June.
juiverie [ʒɥivri] *s.f.* **1.** (hist.) ghetto; **2.** (pej.) the Jews.
jujube [ʒyʒyb] *s.m.* **1.** (bot.) jujube (fruit); **2.** (pharm.) jujube (lozenge).
jujubier [ʒyʒybje] *s.m.* (bot.) jujube-tree.
juke-box [(d)ʒykbɔks] *s.m.* juke-box.
julep [ʒylɛp] *s.m.* (pharm.) julep.
Jules [ʒyl] *s.m.* **1.** (pop.) chamber-pot, jerry; **2.** (pop.) criminal; (pop.) lover, boy-friend, husband; *c'est mon ~,* that's the man I'm after; *c'est son ~,* it's her boy-friend.
julien, -ne [ʒyljɛ̃] *adj.* Julian; *calendrier ~,* Julian calendar.
julienne [ʒyljɛn] *s.f.* **1.** (bot.) rocket; **2.** (cook.) julienne (vegetables cut in small pieces, for soup).
jumeau (pl. **-x**) [ʒymo] *fem.* **jumelle** *adj.* twin, twin-born; double, alike; *cerises jumelles,* double cherries; *s.m.f.* twin; see also JUMELLES *s.f.pl.*
jumelage [ʒymlaʒ] *s.f.* coupling, pairing; twinning (of towns).
jumelé, -e [ʒymle] *adj.* coupled, paired, in pairs, twin, (of towns) twinned; (bot.) geminate; (techn.) reinforced, double, consisting of two parallel members, strengthened with side-pieces.
jumeler [ʒymle] *v.t.* to double, to pair, to couple, to link; (techn.) to reinforce with side-pieces, etc.
jumelles [ʒymɛl] *s.f.pl.* **1.** twin sisters; **2.** opera-glasses, binoculars, field-glasses; **3.** (techn.) cheeks, side-pieces; **4.** (herald.) gemel.
jument [ʒymɑ̃] *s.f.* mare.
jumping [dʒœmpiŋ] *s.m.* (riding) jumping.
jungle [ʒɔ̃gl] *s.f.* jungle.
junte [ʒœ̃t] *s.f.* junta.
jupe [ʒyp] *s.f.* skirt; (techn.) skirt (of piston); *pendu aux ~s de sa mère,* tied to his mother's apron-strings.
jupe-culotte [ʒypkylɔt] *s.f.* divided skirt.
jupette [ʒypɛt] *s.f.* very short skirt.
jupon [ʒypɔ̃] *s.m.* petticoat, underskirt; (fam.) woman, girl, a bit of skirt.
jurande [ʒyrɑ̃d] *s.f.* (obs.) wardenship of a guild.
jurassien, -ne [ʒyrasjɛ̃] *adj., s.m.f.* Jurassian, (native) of the Jura.
jurassique [ʒyrasik] *adj.* (geol.) Jurassic.
jurat [ʒyra] *s.m.* (obs.) jurat, municipal officer in south of France before the Revolution.
juratoire [ʒyratwar] *adj.* (law) juratory; *caution ~,* guarantee given on oath.
juré, -e [ʒyre] *adj.* sworn; who has taken an

oath; *ennemis ~s*, sworn enemies; *s.m.f.* juryman, juror.
jurement [ʒyrmɑ̃] *s.m.* oath, swearing.
jurer [ʒyre] *v.t.* **1.** to swear, to state, (something) on oath, to take an oath, to vow, to promise; **2.** to swear, to blaspheme; *~ comme un charretier*, to swear like a trooper; **3.** to clash, to jar, to be out of keeping (*avec*, with); **4.** *il ne faut ~ de rien*, you never can tell.
jureur [ʒyrœr] *s.m.* **1.** (eccles. hist.) juror; **2.** swearer, blasphemer.
juridiction [ʒyridiksjɔ̃] *s.f.* jurisdiction.
juridictionnel, -le [ʒyridiksjɔnɛl] *adj.* jurisdictional.
juridique [ʒyridik] *adj.* judicial, legal, juridical; **~ment** [ʒyridikmɑ̃] *adv.* juridically, judicially, legally.
jurisconsulte [ʒyriskɔ̃sylt] *s.m.* jurist, lawyer, jurisconsult.
jurisprudence [ʒyrisprydɑ̃s] *s.f.* **1.** jurisprudence; **2.** case-law; **3.** legal precedents.
juriste [ʒyrist] *s.m.* jurist.
juron [ʒyrɔ̃] *s.m.* oath, swear-word; *lâcher un ~*, to let out an oath, to swear.
jury [ʒyri] *s.m.* jury; selectors, examiners, adjudicators; *chef du ~*, foreman of the jury; *dresser la liste du ~*, to empanel a jury; *~ d'examen*, board of examiners.
jus [ʒy] *s.m.* **1.** juice; gravy; (fam.) *le ~ de la treille*, wine; (fig.) *laisser qn. cuire* or *mijoter dans son ~*, to let s.o. stew in his own juice; **2.** (pop.) coffee; water; *balancer qn. au ~*, to throw s.o. in the water; (mil. slang) *soldat de premier ~*, = lance-corporal; **3.** (pop.) (electr.) current; *mettre le ~*, to switch on; *court-~*, short circuit; **4.** (pop.) *ça vaut le ~*, that's worth while.
jusant [ʒyzɑ̃] *s.m.* ebb-tide.
jusée [ʒyze] *s.f.* tan-liquor.
jusqu'au-boutisme [ʒyskobutism] *s.m.* extremism, policy of going the whole hog.
jusque [ʒysk] *prep.* till, until, to; up to, as far as; even, down to, to the point of; *jusqu'au dernier moment*, till, up to, the last moment; *jusqu'au 30 novembre*, until, up to, the 30th November; *jusqu'alors*, till then, up to that time; *jusqu'ici*, till now, up to this point, as far as here; *~-là*, till then, up to that point, as far as that; *jusqu'à quand?*, till when?, how long?; *jusqu'au moment où*, until, until the time when, until such time as; *jusqu'à la poste*, as far as the post office; *jusqu'au bout*, to the end, thoroughly; *jusqu'où?*, where?, to what point?, how far?; *jusqu'au cou*, up to the neck; *aller jusqu'à faire qch.*, to go as far as, to go to the point of, doing sth.; *il en vient ~ de Paris*, people come from as far away as Paris; *il y a des hommes et jusqu'à des femmes qui*, there are men and even women who; *il a vendu jusqu'aux vêtements qu'il portait*, he sold everything, down to the very clothes he was wearing; (conj. loc.) *jusqu'à ce que*, (obs.) *jusqu'à tant que*, until.
jusques [ʒysk] *prep.* (obs., exc. poet.) = JUSQUE.
jusquiame [ʒyskjam] *s.f.* (bot.) henbane.
jussion [ʒysjɔ̃] *s.f.* (anc. law) Royal command.
justaucorps [ʒystokɔr] *s.m.* (hist.) jerkin, close-fitting body-garment.
juste [ʒyst] *adj.* **1.** just, equitable, right, righteous, fair, legitimate; *~ récompense*, just reward; **2.** just, accurate, exact, true, sound, correct; *c'est ~*, that's right, quite so; *avoir l'oreille ~*, to have a good ear; *le total est ~*, the sum is accurate, or correct; *cette pendule est ~*, this clock is right; **3.** tight, narrow; barely enough; *des souliers trop ~s*, shoes which are too small; *100 francs, c'est bien ~*, 100 frs., that's barely enough; (fam.) *ça a été ~*, it was a near thing; it was cutting it fine; *au plus ~*, at the lowest; *comme de ~*, of course; *je ne puis le dire au ~*, I cannot tell exactly; *c'est ~*, that's right; *~ ciel!*, *~s cieux!*, heavens!; *~ adv. ~ en cet endroit*, just at that spot; *il est ~ trois heures*, it's just three o'clock; *j'ai passé tout ~*, I just managed to pass.
justement [ʒystəmɑ̃] *adv.* **1.** justly, equitably, fairly, rightly; **2.** just, exactly, precisely; indeed, quite so; *voilà ~ ce que j'attendais*, this is just what I was expecting; *~ ce soir-là il était sorti*, it so happened that on that particular evening he was not at home.
justesse [ʒystɛs] *s.f.* justness, accuracy, exactness, precision, correctness, propriety; *de ~*, by a hairbreadth, just in time.
justice [ʒystis] *s.f.* justice; fairness, equitableness, righteousness, impartiality; courts of justice; jurisdiction; *Palais de Justice*, Law Courts; *~ de paix*, magistrates' court; *aller en ~*, to go to law; *appeler qn. en ~*, to take s.o. to court; *citer qn. en ~*, to sue s.o.; *faire* or *rendre ~ à*, to do justice to, to accord just treatment to; *rendre la ~*, to administer justice; *faire ~ de*, to refute, to make short work of; *faire ~ à qn.*, to treat s.o. as they deserve; *se faire ~ à soi-même*, to take the law into one's own hands; *réclamer ~*, or *demander ~*, to seek redress; ⚠ not 'justice' = 'magistrate', 'judge'.
justiciable [ʒystisjabl] *adj.* justiciable, within the jurisdiction (*de*, of), amenable (*de*, to); *~ des tribunaux français*, within the jurisdiction of, amenable to the jurisdiction of, the French courts; *une maladie ~ d'un traitement*, an illness amenable to treatment.
justicier [ʒystisje] *s.m.* justiciary, administrator of justice; one who redresses wrong.
justifiable [ʒystifjabl] *adj.* justifiable, warrantable, understandable.
justifiant, -e [ʒystifjɑ̃] *adj.* (theol.) justifying.
justificat-eur, -rice [ʒystifikatœr] *adj.* justificatory; **~eur** *s.m.* (print.) justifier.
justificati-f, -ve [ʒystifikatif] *adj.* justificative, supporting; *document* or *mémoire ~f*, *pièce ~ve*, document in proof, supporting document, voucher; *exemplaire ~f*, voucher copy.
justification [ʒystifikɑsjɔ̃] *s.f.* justification, vindication; proof; (print.) adjustment of line, justification.
justifier [ʒystifje] *v.t.* to justify, to manifest, to prove, to give proof of, to clear, to vindicate, to legitimate, to make good; (print.) to adjust or justify (lines); (law) *~ de*, to give proof of.
jute [ʒyt] *s.m.* jute.
juter [ʒyte] *v.i.* to be juicy, to produce juice.
juteu-x, -se [ʒytø] *adj.* juicy; **~x** *s.m.* (mil. slang) warrant officer, C.S.M., R.S.M.
juvénile [ʒyvenil] *adj.* juvenile, youthful.
juvénilité [ʒyvenilite] *s.f.* (Lit.) juvenility, youthfulness.
juxtalinéaire [ʒykstalineɛr] *adj.* juxtalinear, line for line.
juxtaposable [ʒykstapozabl] *adj.* that can be placed side by side; *mobilier à éléments ~s*, unit furniture.
juxtaposer [ʒykstapoze] *v.t.* to juxtapose.
juxtaposition [ʒykstapozisjɔ̃] *s.f.* juxtaposition; (techn.) *par simple ~*, butt-jointed.

K

K, k [kɑ] *s.m.* the letter K, k.
kabyle [kabil] *adj., s.m.f.* Kabyle, Berber.
kafkaïen, -ne [kafkajɛ̃] *adj.* Kafkaesque, reminiscent of Kafka.
kaïnite [kainit] *s.f.* (chem.) kainit(e).
kakatoès [kakatɔɛs] *s.m.* = CACATOÈS.
kaki[1] [kaki] *s.m.* (bot.) Japanese persimmon kaki (fruit).
kaki[2] [kaki] *adj.invar., s.m.* khaki.
kaléidoscope [kaleidɔskɔp] *s.m.* kaleidoscope.
kali [kali] *s.m.* (bot.) saltwort.
kamichi [kamiʃi] *s.m.* (ornith.) horned screamer.
kan, khan [kɑ̃] *s.m.* khan, caravanserai.
kangourou [kɑ̃guru] *s.m.* (zool.) kangaroo.
kantien, -ne [kɑ̃tjɛ̃] *adj.* Kantian.
kantisme [kɑ̃tism] *s.m.* Kantianism, Kantian philosophy.
kaolin [kaɔlɛ̃] *s.m.* kaolin; **~isation** [kaɔlinizɑsjɔ̃] *s.f.* kaolinization.
kapok [kapɔk] *s.m.* kapok.
kappa [kapa] *s.m.* kappa (Gr. letter).
karakul [karakyl] *s.m.* = CARACUL.
kari see CARI.
karting [kartiŋ] *s.m.* go-kart racing.
kascher [kaʃɛr] *adj.invar.* kosher.
kayac, kayak [kajak] *s.m.* kayak (canoe).
képi [kepi] *s.m.* kepi, cap.
kératine [keratin] *s.f.* keratin.
kératite [keratit] *s.f.* (med.) keratitis, inflammation of the cornea.
kératoplastie [keratɔplasti] *s.f.* (surg.) keratoplasty, corneal graft.
kératose [keratoz] *s.f.* (pathol.) thickening of the cornea.
kermès [kɛrmɛs] *s.m.* (ent.) kermes.
kermesse [kɛrmɛs] *s.f.* kermis, fair.
kérosène [kerozɛn] *s.m.* paraffin, kerosene.
ketch [kɛtʃ] *s.m.* (naut.) ketch.
ketchup [kɛtʃœp] *s.m.* ketchup.
ketmie [kɛtmi] *s.f.* (bot.) ketmia.
khamsin [kamsin] *s.m.* khamsin (wind).
khan [kɑ̃] *s.m.* **1.** (hist.) Khan (Mongol or Tartar prince); **2.** see KAN.
khanat [kana] *s.m.* khanate.
khédivat [kediva] *s.m.* khedivate.
khédive [kediv] *s.m.* Khedive.
khédival, -e, (aux) [kedival] *adj.* khedival.
kibboutz [kibuts] *s.m.* kibbutz.
kidnappage [kidnapaʒ] *s.m.* kidnapping.
kidnapper [kidnape] *v.t.* to kidnap.
kidnappeu-r, -se [kidnapœr] *s.m.f.* kidnapper.
kief[1] [kjɛf] *s.m.* (in Turkey) kef; state of bliss.
kief[2] [kjɛf], **kif** [kif] *s.m.* kef, mixture of tobacco and hemp.
kif-kif [kifkif] *adv.loc.* (pop.) *c'est ~*, it's six of one and half a dozen of the other; it's much of a muchness; it comes to the same.
kilo [kilo] *s.m.* abbrev. of KILOGRAMME.
kilo-cycle [kilɔsikl] *s.m.* (electr.) kilocycle; **~gramme** [kilɔgram] *s.m.* kilogram(me); **~grammètre** [kilɔgramɛtr] *s.m.* (mech.) kilogrammetre; **~métrage** [kilɔmetraʒ] *s.m.* measuring in kilometres; distance in kilometres; **~mètre** [kilɔmɛtr] *s.m.* kilometre; **~métrer** [kilɔmetre] *v.t.* to mark off in kilometres, to erect kilometre stones; to measure in kilometres; **~métrique** [kilɔmetrik] *adj.* kilometric, kilometre; *bornes ~métriques*, kilometre stones; **~tonne** [kilɔtɔn] *s.f.* kiloton; **~volt** [kilɔvɔlt] *s.m.* (electr.) kilovolt; **~watt** [kilɔwat] *s.m.* (electr.) kilowatt.
kilowatt-heure [kilɔwatœr] *s.m.* (electr.) kilowatt-hour, unit.
kimono [kimɔno] *s.m.* kimono; *robe ~*, dress with kimono sleeves.
kinescope [kinɛskɔp] *s.m.* recording TV pictures on film.
kinesthésie [kinɛstezi] *s.f.* (psychol.) kinaesthesia.
King-Charles [kiŋʃarl] *s.m.* King Charles spaniel.
kinkajou, kincajou [kɛ̃kaʒu] *s.m.* (zool.) kinkajou.
kiosque [kjɔsk] *s.m.* **1.** kiosk; summer-house, small pavilion, shelter; *~ à musique*, band-stand; **2.** kiosk or stall (selling newspapers, flowers, etc.); **3.** (naut.) *~ de timonerie*, wheel-house; *~ de navigation*, chart-room; (of submarine) superstructure, conning-tower; (electr.) *~ de transformation*, transformer box.
klaxon [klaksɔn] *s.m.* klaxon, hooter, (car) horn; **~ner** [klaksɔne] *v.i.* to hoot, to sound one's horn.
klephte see CLEPHTE.
klepto-mane, cleptomane [klɛptɔman] *adj., s.m.f.* kleptomaniac; **~manie, cleptomanie** [klɛptɔmani] *s.f.* kleptomania.
klystron [klistrɔ̃] *s.m.* (phys.) klystron.
knock-out [nɔkawt] *s.m.* knock-out (abbrev. *K.-O.*); *mettre qn. ~*, to knock s.o. out; *être ~*, to be knocked out.
knout [knut] *s.m.* knout.
koala [kɔala] *s.m.* (zool.) koala, koala bear.
kobold [kɔbɔld] *s.m.* kobold.
kohl, kohol [kol] *s.m.* kohl.
kola [kɔla] *s.m.* (bot.) cola, kola; *noix de ~*, cola-nut.
kopeck [kɔpɛk] *s.m.* copeck, kopeck.
korrigan, -e [kɔrigɑ̃] *s.m.f.* korrigan, leprechaun, sprite.
koumis, koumys [kumis] *s.m.* koumiss, kumiss.
krach [krak] *s.m.* financial crash.
kraft [kraft] *s.m.* kraft (paper).
krypton [kriptɔ̃] *s.m.* (chem.) krypton.
ksar [ksar] *s.m.* (pl. *ksour*) (in N. Africa) ksar, fortified place.
kugelhof, kouglof [kuglɔf] *s.m.* kugelhopf, an Alsatian cake.
kummel [kymɛl] *s.m.* kümmel (liqueur).
kurde [kyrd] *adj.* Kurdish, of Kurdistan; *s.m.f.* Kurd.
kwas, kvas [kvɑs] *s.m.* kvass (Russian rye-beer).
kymrique [kimrik], **cymrique** [simrik] *adj., s.m.f.* Cymric.
kyrie [kirie] *s.m.* kyrie, kyrie eleison.
kyrielle [kirjɛl] *s.f.* litany; (fam.) long string of words.
kyste [kist] *s.m.* (pathol.) cyst.
kystique [kistik] *adj.* cystic.

L

L, l [ɛl] *s.m.* the letter L, l; *l.* abbrev. *litre, livre* (=500 g); *L. ès L.* abbrev. *Licencié ès Lettres.*
l' see LE.
la [la] *def. art., pron.* see LE.
la [la] *s.m.* (mus.) lah, A; (fig.) *donner le ~*, to set the fashion.
là [la] *adv.* **1.** there, thither, here; in, at home, present; *qui va ~?*, who goes there?; *n'allez pas ~*, don't go there; *je reste ~*, I am stopping here, I stop at that point; *par ~*, that (this) way, along there (here); *ôte-toi de ~!*, get out of here!, go away!; *d'ici ~ c'est sept bons kilomètres*, it is a good seven kilometres from here, *or* away; *~ où*, where, wherever; *~ où la route bifurque*, where the road forks; *~-bas*, down there, over there; (fig.) *en être ~*, to have reached that point, to be in that position, to have got to that state; *Monsieur est-il ~?*, is the gentleman at home?; *les faits sont ~*, the facts are there (to be seen); (fam.) *il est un peu ~*, he is all there, he is something important; **2.** then, at that moment, at that point; *~, il interrompit son discours*, at that point he interrupted his remarks; *d'ici ~*, between now and then, by that time; **3.** that, those; it, them; *qu'entendez-vous par ~?*, what do you mean by that?; *c'est ~ la raison*, that is the reason; *ce sont ~ mes parents*, those are my parents; *~-dedans*, in it, inside; *~-dessus*, on it, above, on top; thereupon; *~-haut*, up there, (fig.) in heaven; *en ce moment-~*, at that moment; *ces hommes-~*, those men; *celle-~*, that, that one, that woman; *~ interj.* well, come, gently; *~! ~!*, come now!; *hé ~!*, gently!, come, come!
label [labɛl] *s.m.* trade-mark, guarantee, etc., label; ⚠ not 'label' in sense 'description'.
labelle [labɛl] *s.m.* (bot.) labellum.
labeur [labœr] *s.m.* labour, work, toil, pains; (print.) book-work, long numbers.
labiacées [labjase] *s.f.pl.* = LABIÉES.
labial, -e, (**aux**) [labjal] *adj.* labial; **~e** *s.f.* (phon.) labial.
labié, -e [labje] *adj.* (bot.) labiate; **~es** *s.f.pl.* (bot.) labiates, Labiatae.
labile [labil] *adj.* labile; unstable, liable to fail.
laborantin, -e [labɔrɑ̃tɛ̃] *s.m.f.* laboratory assistant.
laboratoire [labɔratwar] *s.m.* laboratory.
laborieu-x, -se [labɔrjø] *adj.* **1.** laborious; hard-working, industrious; labouring, working; *les classes ~ses*, the working classes; **2.** laborious, toilsome, arduous, requiring hard work; laboured, forced; *une vie ~se*, a life of toil; *style ~x*, laboured style; **~sement** [labɔrjøzmɑ̃] *adv.* laboriously, with difficulty, painfully.
labour [labur] *s.m.* tillage, ploughing; ploughed land; *bœufs de ~*, plough-oxen; ⚠ not 'labour'.
labourable [laburabl] *adj.* fit for tillage; arable.
labourage [laburaʒ] *s.m.* ploughing; dressing (of vines); working on the land.
labourer [labure] *v.t.* to plough, to dig; to dress (vines); (fig.) to cut, to rip up; (naut.) to drag; *~ le fond*, to graze the bottom.
laboureur [laburœr] *s.m.* ploughman; (obs.) husbandman; ⚠ not 'labourer'.
labrador [labradɔr] *s.m.* **1.** (min.) Labrador felspar; **2.** Labrador (dog).
labre [labr] *s.m.* **1.** (ent.) upper lip; **2.** (ichth.) rock-fish.
labyrinthe [labirɛ̃t] *s.m.* **1.** labyrinth, maze; **2.** (anat.) labyrinth.
labyrinthodon [labirɛ̃tɔdɔ̃] *s.m.* (palaeont.) labyrinthodon.
lac [lak] *s.m.* lake; (fig., fam.) *être* or *tomber dans le ~*, to be a failure, a flop.
laçage [lɑsaʒ], **lacement** [lɑsmɑ̃] *s.m.* lacing.
laccase [lakaz] *s.f.* (chem.) laccin.
lacé [lɑse] *s.m.* lace-glass.
lacédémonien, -ne [lasedemɔnjɛ̃] *adj., s.m.f.* Lacedaemonian.
lacer [lɑse] *v.t.* to lace; to interlace; (naut.) to fasten (sails) together.
lacération [laserɑsjɔ̃] *s.f.* laceration, tearing up.
lacérer [lasere] *v.t.* to lacerate, to tear up.
lacertiens [lasɛrtjɛ̃], **lacertiliens** [lasɛrtiljɛ̃] *s.m.pl.* (zool.) lacertians, Lacertilia.
lacet [lɑsɛ] *s.m.* lace; braid; bowstring; snare; sharp bend; (fig.) snare, toils; *route en ~s*, zigzag road; road with numerous sharp bends; *ferrer un ~*, to tag a lace; *mouvement de ~*, rocking.
laceu-r, -se [lɑsœr] *s.m.f.* net-maker.
lâchage [lɑʃaʒ] *s.m.* letting go; (fam.) abandoning, giving the slip (to), dropping.
lâche [lɑʃ] *adj.* **1.** loose, slack; **2.** cowardly, slothful, mean-spirited, dastardly, base; *~ s.m.* coward, sluggard; **~ment** [lɑʃmɑ̃] *adv.* in a cowardly or dastardly fashion; idly.
lâché, -e [lɑʃe] *adj.* hastily or carelessly executed.
lâcher [lɑʃe] *v.t.* to loosen, to slacken, to relax, to loose, to loose one's hold of, to let slip, to let go, to release, to liberate; *~ sa proie*, to let one's prey escape; *~ un coup de fusil*, to let off a shot, to fire; (fam.) *~ ses alliés*, to abandon one's allies; *~ une sottise*, to blurt out a foolish remark; *~ prise*, to let go; *~ pied*, to give ground, to flee; *elle l'a lâché*, she has thrown him over; *vous n'allez pas nous ~?*, you won't leave us in the lurch?
lâcher [lɑʃe] *s.m.* release, releasing, (of pigeons, balloons).
lâcheté [lɑʃte] *s.f.* cowardice, faint-heartedness; meanness, baseness; *une ~*, an act of cowardice, etc.
lâcheu-r, -se [lɑʃœr] *s.m.f.* (fam.) turncoat; shirker; one who abandons his friends.
lacinié, -e [lasinje] *adj.* (bot.) laciniate, jagged.
lacis [lɑsi] *s.m.* network; (anat.) plexus.
laconique [lakɔnik] *adj.* laconic, concise; **~ment** [lakɔnikmɑ̃] *adv.* laconically.
laconisme [lakɔnism] *s.m.* conciseness, brevity.
lacryma-christi [lakrima kristi] *s.m.* lachryma Christi (wine).
lacrymal, -e, (**aux**) [lakrimal] *adj.* (anat.) lachrymal.
lacrymatoire [lakrimatwɑr] *s.m., adj.* lachrymatory.
lacrymogène [lakrimɔʒɛn] *adj.* tear-producing; *gaz ~*, tear-gas.
lacs [lɑ] *s.m.pl.* noose, snare; toils; cord; *~ d'amour*, lover's knot.
lactaire [laktɛr] *adj.* lactary, lacteous; *~ s.m.* (bot.) kind of mushroom.
lactate [laktat] *s.m.* (chem.) lactate.
lactation [laktɑsjɔ̃] *s.f.* lactation.
lacté, -e [lakte] *adj.* milky, lacteous; *diète ~e*, milk diet; (astron.) *la voie ~e*, the Milky Way.
lactescence [laktesɑ̃s] *s.f.* lactescence, milkiness.

lactescent, -e [laktesɑ̃] *adj.* lactescent, milky.
lactifère [laktifɛr] *adj.* lactiferous, milk-bearing, (of duct, etc.) lacteal.
lactique [laktik] *adj.* lactic.
lactomètre [laktɔmɛtr] *s.m.* lactometer.
lactose [laktoz] *s.f.* lactose.
lacunaire [lakynɛr] *adj.* = LACUNEUX.
lacune [lakyn] *s.f.* lacuna; gap, hiatus, missing link, blank, omission, deficiency; *combler une* ~, to fill a blank or gap; to meet a want.
lacuneu-x, -se [lakynø] *adj.* lacunar(y), with gaps, incomplete, defective.
lacustre [lakystr] *adj.* lacustrine, lacustrian, living in or beside lakes; *village* ~, lake village.
ladanum [ladanɔm] *s.m.* ladanum, gum-resin.
ladre [lɑdr] *adj.* (obs.) leprous; (vet.) measled; (fig.) insensitive, hard-hearted; ~ *s.m.f.* leper; (fig.) miser, skinflint; ~ *s.m.* (vet.) *taches de* ~, bare patches of skin.
ladrerie [lɑdrəri] *s.f.* leprosy; (vet.) measles; (fig.) meanness, miserliness.
lagon [lagɔ̃] *s.m.* lagoon; salt-water pool.
lagopède [lagɔpɛd] *s.m.* (ornith.) lagopode, ptarmigan.
laguis [lagis] *s.m.* (naut.) running bowline.
lagune [lagyn] *s.f.* lagoon.
lai [lɛ] *s.m.* lay (poem).
lai, -e [lɛ] *adj.* lay; *s.m.f.* lay brother, lay sister.
laïc [laik] *s.m.* layman.
laiche [lɛʃ] *s.f.* (bot.) sedge.
laïcisation [laisizɑsjɔ̃] *s.f.* secularization.
laïciser [laisize] *v.t.* to laicize, to secularize.
laïcité [laisite] *s.f.* secularity, undenominationalism.
laid, -e [lɛ] *adj.* ugly, ill-favoured, plain, unattractive, disgusting, repellent; base, evil, (child. lang.) naughty; ~ *s.m.* ugliness; ~**ement** [lɛdmɑ̃] *adv.* in an ugly way, unattractively.
laideron [lɛdrɔ̃] *s.m.* unattractive girl; ~ (f. ~**ne**) *adj.* unattractive, plain.
laideur [lɛdœr] *s.f.* ugliness, plainness; unsightliness, deformity; unseemliness, repulsiveness, baseness, shabbiness, (of conduct); evil deed, squalid action.
laie [lɛ] *s.f.* **1.** wild sow; **2.** (forest.) service-path; **3.** (mus.) wind-chest (of organ); **4.** (techn.) stone-cutter's hammer.
lainage [lɛnaʒ] *s.m.* woollen goods; fleece, wool; woollens; teaseling.
laine [lɛn] *s.f.* wool; woolly hair; fibre; (bot.) down; *bêtes à* ~, sheep; ~ *filée*, worsted; ~ *à quatre fils*, four-ply wool; *pure* ~, all wool; ~ *de bois*, wood wool, wood-fibre; ~ *de verre*, glass-fibre; *se laisser manger la* ~ *sur le dos*, to let oneself be exploited or cheated.
lainer [lene] *v.t.* to tease, to teasel, to raise (cloth); ~ *s.m.* pile, texture, nap.
lainerie [lɛnri] *s.f.* manufacture of wool, woollen trade; wholesale wool-dealers; woollen goods.
laineu-r, -se [lɛnœr] *s.m.f.* woollen-worker; ~**se** *s.f.* napping machine; gig(-mill).
laineu-x, -se [lɛnø] *adj.* **1.** woolly, fleecy; **2.** (bot.) downy.
laini-er, -ère [lɛnje] *adj.* of wool, woollen; *s.m.f.* woollen-worker; wool-merchant.
laïque [laik] *adj.* lay, secular, (of school) undenominational; ~ *s.m.f.* layman, laywoman; (pl.) (also *f.sing.*) laity.
lais [lɛ] **1.** (geog.) alluvium, silt; **2.** (forest.) staddle; **3.** (pl.) (law) foreshore.
laisse [lɛs] *s.f.* **1.** leash, lead, strings; **2.** (geog.) tide-mark.
laissées [lese] *s.f.pl.* (hunt.) droppings.
laissé-pour-compte [lesepurkɔ̃t] *s.m.* (pl. *laissés-pour-compte*) article left on the dealer's hands, return.
laisser [lese] *v.t.* to leave, to quit; to give up; to let alone; to leave behind; to leave off; to discard; to abandon; to forget; to entrust; to bequeath; to allow, to permit; *laissez donc!*, leave off!, don't bother; ~ *aller*, to let go, to neglect; ~ *à désirer*, to leave room for improvement; *c'est à prendre ou à* ~, you may take it or leave it; it's a case of Hobson's choice; ~ *là*, to leave in the lurch; *il est pauvre, mais il ne laisse pas d'être honnête homme*, he is poor, but nevertheless honest; ~ *tomber*, to let fall, to drop; to utter negligently (words); (slang) to drop (a person); to chuck up (a thing); ~ *faire*, to let things drift; to refrain from interference; *laissez-moi la paix*, let me alone; ~ *à l'abandon*, to leave, or to let lie about, in disorder; to neglect completely; **se** ~ *v.refl.* to let oneself; *se* ~ *aller*; to let oneself go; to let oneself be disheartened, to be careless, to get into slovenly ways, to let things drift; *se* ~ *aller à faire qch.*, to drift into doing sth., to get involved in doing sth., to go as far as to do sth.; *se* ~ *éblouir*, to let oneself be dazzled; *je me suis laissé dire que*, I have been given to understand that; *se* ~ *faire*, to put up no resistance.
laisser aller [leseale] *s.m.invar.* taking things easy, easy-going attitude; lack of constraint; slackness; indifference, neglect, carelessness, listlessness.
laisser faire [lesefɛr] *s.m.invar.* policy of non-intervention or inaction.
laisser-passer, laissez-passer [lesepɑse] *s.m. invar.* pass, permit; (customs) transire, clearance.
lait [lɛ] *s.m.* **1.** milk; *frère de* ~, foster-brother; *battre le* ~, to churn; *petit* ~, or ~ *clair*, whey; ~ *coupé*, milk and water; ~ *de poule*, egg flip, milk with sugar and yolk of egg; *au* ~, made with milk; (fig.) *sucer avec le* ~, to be brought up to (hold an opinion, etc.); **2.** liquid resembling milk; white of egg; ~ *d'amandes*, milk of almonds; ~ *de chaux*, white lime; (fig.) *boire du* ~, to experience keen satisfaction; to find something intensely gratifying; *il monte comme une soupe au* ~, he flares up easily; *vache à* ~, (lit. & fig.) milch cow.
laitage [lɛtaʒ] *s.m.* milk foods; milk diet.
laitance [lɛtɑ̃s], **laite** [lɛt] *s.f.* milt, soft roe.
laité, -e [lete] *adj.* soft-roed.
laiterie [lɛtri] *s.f.* dairy; dairy-farming; dairy industry.
laiteron [lɛtrɔ̃] *s.m.* (bot.) sow-thistle; hare's-lettuce.
laiteu-x, -se [lɛtø] *adj.* milky, lacteal; milk-white.
laiti-er, -ère [letje, lɛtje] *s.m.f.* milkman, dairyman; milkmaid, dairymaid; *adj.* milk, dairy; producing milk; *vache* ~*ère*, milch cow; ~**er** *s.m.* (metall.) slag, dross.
laiton [lɛtɔ̃] *s.m.* (metall.) brass.
laitonner [lɛtɔne] *v.t.* **1.** to stiffen with brass wire; **2.** to plate with brass.
laitue [lety] *s.f.* (bot.) lettuce; ~ *romaine*, cos lettuce; ~ *pommée*, cabbage lettuce; ~ *d'âne*, wild teasel; ~ *de chien*, dandelion.
laïus [lajys] *s.m.* (fam.) speech, lecture, holding forth; ~**ser** [lajyse] *v.i.* to hold forth.
laize [lɛz] *s.f.* width (of material, sail-cloth, paper).
lakiste [lakist] *s.m.* (Eng. Lit.) Lake Poet.
lama [lama] *s.m.* **1.** (zool.) llama; **2.** (Tibetan) Lama.
lamaïsme [lamaism] *s.m.* lamaism.
lamaïste [lamaist] *s.m.f.*, *adj.* lamaist.
lamanage [lamanɑʒ] *s.m.* (naut.) piloting, pilotage; harbour-pilotage.
lamaneur [lamanœr] *s.m.* (naut.) pilot; harbour-pilot.
lamantin [lamɑ̃tɛ̃] *s.m.* (zool.) sea-cow, manatee.

lamarckien, -ne [lamarkjɛ̃] *adj.* (biol.) Lamarckian.
lamarckisme [lamarkism] *s.m.* (biol.) Lamarckism, Lamarckianism.
lamaserie [lamazri] *s.f.* lamasery.
lambda [lɑ̃bda] *s.m.* (Gr. letter) lambda.
lambdacisme [lɑ̃bdasism] *s.m.* lambdacism; lallation.
lambeau (pl. **-x**) [lɑ̃bo] *s.m.* rag, tatter, strip, shred; piece, part, fragment; remains, remnant; scrap, bit, morsel; *en ~x*, in rags and tatters; *mettre en ~x*, to tear to shreds.
lambel [lɑ̃bel] *s.m.* (herald.) label.
lambic(k) [lɑ̃bik] *s.m.* lambick (Belgian beer).
lambin, -e [lɑ̃bɛ̃] *s.m.f.* dawdler, loiterer, slow-coach; *adj.* dawdling, loitering, slothful, slow.
lambiner [lɑ̃bine] *v.i.* to dawdle, to loiter; to trifle, to waste time; to dilly-dally.
lambourde [lɑ̃burd] *s.f.* **1.** (carp.) joist; wall-plate; **2.** (agric.) fruit-bearing spur.
lambre [lɑ̃br] *s.m.* (zool.) spider-crab.
lambrequin [lɑ̃brəkɛ̃] *s.m.* **1.** (arch.) lambrequin, scallop, festoon; **2.** (herald.) lambrequin, mantle; **3.** valance, fringe.
lambris [lɑ̃bri] *s.m.* panelling, wainscot, lining; (arch.) roof, ceiling; (poet.) rich adornment; *~ d'appui*, dado.
lambrissage [lɑ̃brisɑʒ] *s.m.* wainscoting, panelling, lining.
lambrisser [lɑ̃brise] *v.t.* to wainscot, to panel, to line.
lambruche [lɑ̃bryʃ], **lambrusque** [lɑ̃brysk] *s.f.* wild vine.
lame [lam] *s.f.* **1.** (metall.) plate, sheet; foil; wire; (techn.) plate, leaf, lamina; blade; sword; swordsman; *une fine ~*, a first-rate swordsman or fencer; *visage en ~ de couteau*, hatchet-face; **2.** wave, billow; (fig.) sudden surge.
lamé, -e [lame] *adj.* spangled, lamé; *~ s.m.* lamé (material).
lamellaire [lamelɛr] *adj.* lamellar.
lamelle [lamɛl] *s.f.* lamella, thin plate; strip; slide (for microscope).
lamellé, -e [lamele], **lamelleu-x, -se** [lamelø] *adj.* lamellate, lamellated, foliated, fissile, flaky.
lamelli-branche [lamelibrɑ̃ʃ] *s.m.* (mollusc.) lamellibranch, bivalve; **~corne** [lamelikɔrn] *s.m.* (ent.) lamellicorn; **~forme** [lamelifɔrm] *adj.* lamelliform, lamellar; **~rostre** [lamelirɔstr] *s.m.* (ornith.) lamelliroster.
lamentable [lamɑ̃tabl] *adj.* lamentable, deplorable, pitiable, pitiful; sorry; **~ment** [lamɑ̃tabləmɑ̃] *adv.* lamentably, deplorably, pitifully, woefully.
lamentation [lamɑ̃tɑsjɔ̃] *s.f.* lamentation, lament, lamenting; wailing, wail, whine.
(**se**) **lamenter** [lamɑ̃te] *v.refl.* to lament (*sur*, for, over), to bewail, to moan.
lamie [lami] *s.f.* **1.** (myth.) lamia; **2.** (ichth.) lamia, lamna, white shark.
lamier [lamje] *s.m.* (bot.) dead-nettle.
laminage [laminaʒ] *s.m.* lamination, laminating, rolling; drawing (of synthetic yarn).
laminaire [laminɛr] *s.f.* (bot.) laminaria, sea-girdle; *~ adj.* (min., phys.) laminar.
laminer [lamine] *v.t.* to laminate, to roll, to flatten.
lamineur [laminœr] *s.m.* roller, flatter; *adj.* rolling, roller.
lamineu-x, -se [laminø] *adj.* laminose.
laminoir [laminwar] *s.m.* rolling-mill, flatting-mill; roller; (papermaking) rolling-press; calendering machine, plate-glazing machine; (fig.) *passer au ~*, to go through the mill, to take a hammering.
lampadaire [lɑ̃padɛr] *s.m.* candelabrum, lamp-stand; lamp-post.
lampant, -e [lɑ̃pɑ̃] *adj.* (of mineral oil) refined for use in lamps; *huile ~e*, lamp oil.
lampas[1] [lɑ̃pɑ(s)] *s.m.* **1.** (obs.) throat; *s'arroser le ~*, to wet one's whistle; **2.** (vet.) lampas.
lampas[2] [lɑ̃pɑ(s)] *s.m.* (text.) lampas.
lampassé, -e [lɑ̃pɑse] *adj.* (herald.) langued.
lampe [lɑ̃p] *s.f.* lamp; (radio) valve; *~ à alcool*, spirit-lamp or -stove; *~ à souder*, blow-lamp, (mil. slang) sub-machine-gun.
lampée [lɑ̃pe] *s.f.* large gulp (of drink), swill, swig.
lamper [lɑ̃pe] *v.t.* to gulp down, to toss off, to swig.
lampion [lɑ̃pjɔ̃] *s.m.* lampion; Chinese lantern.
lampiste [lɑ̃pist] *s.m.f.* **1.** (obs.) lamp-maker; **2.** (rail.) lamp-man; one in charge of lighting; (fig.) general dogsbody.
lampisterie [lɑ̃pistəri] *s.f.* **1.** (obs.) lamp-manufacture, lamp-trade; **2.** (rail.) lamp-room.
lampourde [lɑ̃purd] *s.f.* (bot.) bur-weed.
lamprillon [lɑ̃prijɔ̃] *s.m.* (ichth.) small lamprey.
lamproie [lɑ̃prwa] *s.f.* (ichth.) lamprey; *~ fluviale*, lampern, river lamprey.
lampyre [lɑ̃pir] *s.m.* (ent.) glow-worm, Lampyris.
lançage [lɑ̃saʒ] *s.m.* = LANCEMENT.
lance [lɑ̃s] *s.f.* **1.** lance, spear; lancer; (fig.) *rompre une ~ avec* or *contre qn.*, to break a lance, to try a fall, with s.o., to have a set-to with s.o.; *rompre une ~ pour qn.*, to stand up for s.o.; *fer de ~*, (lit. & fig.) spear-head; lance-head ornament; **2.** jet, nozzle.
lancé, -e [lɑ̃se] *adj.* received (in good society), popular.
lance-bombes [lɑ̃sbɔ̃b] *s.m.invar.* **1.** (mil.) (obs.) mortar; **2.** (aeron.) bomb-release gear.
lancée [lɑ̃se] *s.f.* **1.** impetus, momentum; (fig.) *continuer sur sa ~*, to maintain momentum, to keep up the pace; **2.** (med.) (pl.) shooting pains.
lance-flammes [lɑ̃sflɑm] *s.m.invar.* flame-thrower, flame-gun; **~-fusées** [lɑ̃sfyze] *s.m.invar.* rocket-launcher; **~-grenades** [lɑ̃sgrənad] *s.m.invar.* grenade-launcher.
lancement [lɑ̃smɑ̃] *s.m.* throwing, flinging, hurling, casting, cast; launching; starting, start; (comm.) promotion (by advertising, etc.).
lance-missiles [lɑ̃smisil] *s.m.invar.* missile-launcher.
lancéolé, -e [lɑ̃seɔle] *adj.* lanceolate, spear-shaped.
lance-pierre(s) [lɑ̃spjɛr] *s.m.invar.* catapult.
lancer [lɑ̃se] *v.t.* to throw, to fling, to hurl, to cast, to dart, to toss; to shoot forth; to emit; to issue (warrant, etc.); to launch; to promote (product, etc.); to put in motion, to let loose, to let fly; (hunt.) to start (stag, etc.); *~ son cheval*, to set one's horse (at sth.); *~ un coup*, to deal a blow; *~ un regard*, to throw a glance; **se ~** *v.refl.* (lit. & fig.) to rush, to hurl or throw oneself; to become known (in society); ⚠ not usu. 'to lance' in sense 'to pierce'.
lancer [lɑ̃se] *s.m.* throw, throwing, cast; cast of fishing-line; *pêche au ~*, rod-fishing; (hunt.) starting (of stag, etc.); ⚠ not 'lancer'.
lance-roquettes [lɑ̃srɔkɛt] *s.m.invar.* (portable) rocket-launcher, bazooka; **~-torpilles** [lɑ̃stɔrpij] *s.m.invar.* torpedo-tube.
lancette [lɑ̃sɛt] *s.f.* (surg.) lancet; (arch.) *ogive à ~*, lancet arch; *gothique à ~s*, lancet-head Gothic (=Early English).
lanceu-r, -se [lɑ̃sœr] *s.m.f.* person who starts or launches undertakings; promoter; (athletics) thrower (of discus, etc.); (astronaut.) launcher.
lancier [lɑ̃sje] *s.m.* (mil.) lancer; (danc.) (*quadrille des*) *~s*, lancers.
lancinant, -e [lɑ̃sinɑ̃] *adj.* (of pain) lancinating, shooting, throbbing; (fig.) tormenting, nagging; *douleur ~e*, shooting pain, twinges of pain.

lanciner [lɑ̃sine] *v.i.* (of pain) to shoot, to throb; ~ *v.t.* (fig.) to torment.
lançon [lɑ̃sɔ̃] *s.m.* (ichth.) sand-eel, sand-lance, grig.
landais, -e [lɑ̃dɛ] *adj., s.m.f.* belonging to Les Landes, (inhabitant) of the Landes.
landau [lɑ̃do] *s.m.* **1.** landau; **2.** kind of pram.
landaulet [lɑ̃dolɛ] *s.m.* landaulet(te).
lande [lɑ̃d] *s.f.* heath, moor, wasteland; (pl.) dunes; barren tracts; *Les Landes,* the Landes (in S.W. France).
landgrave [lɑ̃dgrav] *s.m.* landgrave.
landgraviat [lɑ̃dgravja] *s.m.* landgraviate.
landier [lɑ̃dje] *s.m.* andiron, fire-dog.
laneret [lanrɛ] *s.m.* (ornith.) lanneret.
langage [lɑ̃gaʒ] *s.m.* language, tongue; speech, dialect; diction; talk, words; style; expression; tone; *changer de langage,* to change one's tone; *beau* ~, fine talk.
lange [lɑ̃ʒ] *s.m.* swaddling-clothes; (fig.) *dans les* ~*s,* in infancy, in the early stages.
langer [lɑ̃ʒe] *v.t.* to swaddle.
langoureu-x, -se [lɑ̃gurø] *adj.* languishing; pining; languid, yearning, longing, sentimental; ~**sement** [lɑ̃gurøzmɑ̃] *adv.* languorously, languidly, longingly.
langouste [lɑ̃gust] *s.f.* (crust.) spiny lobster; rock lobster, crayfish.
langoustier [lɑ̃gustje] *s.m.* **1.** lobster-net (also *langoustière s.f.*); **2.** lobster-boat.
langoustine [lɑ̃gustin] *s.m.* (crust.) Norway lobster.
langue [lɑ̃g] *s.f.* **1.** tongue; *tirer la* ~ *à qn.,* to put out one's tongue at s.o.; (fig.) *tirer la* ~, to be thirsty; to be in need, to be unsatisfied; *avaler sa* ~, to hold one's tongue; *se mordre la* ~, to bite off one's tongue, to regret what one has said; to stop short; *sur le bout de la* ~, on the tip of one's tongue; *donner sa* ~ *au chat,* or *jeter sa* ~ *aux chiens,* to give up (guessing riddle, etc.); *une mauvaise* ~, a slanderer, a backbiter; *coup de* ~, cutting remark, cruel witticism; *la* ~ *lui a fourché,* he made a slip of the tongue; *avoir la* ~ *trop longue,* to be unable to keep a secret; *ne pas avoir sa* ~ *dans sa poche,* never to be at a loss for words; **2.** tongue-shaped object, tongue, strip, neck (of land); ~*-d'agneau,* (bot.) plantain; ~*-de-bœuf,* (i.) (bot.) arum lily; a kind of mushroom; (ii.) a mason's tool; ~*-de-chat,* langue-de-chat, finger-biscuit; **3.** language, tongue; style; mode of expression, speech; ~ *vivante,* living language, modern language; ~ *verte,* slang; ~ *mère,* primitive language, language from which another is derived; ~ *maternelle,* mother tongue, native language.
Languedoc [lɑ̃gdɔk] *s.m.* (geog.) Languedoc.
languedocien, -ne [lɑ̃gdɔsjɛ̃] *adj., s.m.f.* (native or inhabitant) of Languedoc.
languette [lɑ̃gɛt] *s.f.* small tongue; tongue-shaped object; needle (of a balance); tongue (of a musical instrument); stem (of a key); partition (in a chimney); (naut.) wedge; (techn.) flat key; feather.
langueur [lɑ̃gœr] *s.f.* languor; languidness; listlessness.
languide [lɑ̃gid] *adj.* (Lit.) languid.
languier [lɑ̃gje] *s.m.* smoked hog's tongue.
languir [lɑ̃gir] *v.i.* to languish; to waste away; to wither; to long; to pine; to droop; to flag; to drag; ~ *d'amour,* to pine away for love; ~ *après,* to long for (sth.); *faire* ~, to weary; (in south of France) **se** ~ *v.refl.* to languish.
languissamment [lɑ̃gisamɑ̃] *adv.* languidly; feebly, weakly; languishingly; apathetically; listlessly; wearily.
languissant, -e [lɑ̃gisɑ̃] *adj.* languishing, languid, languorous; drooping, flagging; spiritless, listless, apathetic.
lanice [lanis] *adj.* (techn.) *bourre* ~, wool flocks.
lanier [lanje] *s.m.* (ornith.) lanner.
lanière [lanjɛr] *s.f.* thong; lash; strap.
lanifère [lanifɛr], **lanigère** [laniʒɛr] *adj.* laniferous, lanigerous, wool-bearing.
lanlaire [lɑ̃lɛr] (fam.) used only in phrases: *va te faire* ~*!,* clear out!, scram!, go to hell!, get lost!; *envoyer faire* ~, to tell (s.o.) to clear out, etc.
lanoline [lanɔlin] *s.f.* lanolin.
lansquenet [lɑ̃skənɛ] *s.m.* lansquenet.
lantanier [lɑ̃tanje], **lantana** [lɑ̃tana] *s.m.* (bot.) Lantana.
lanterne [lɑ̃tɛrn] *s.f.* lantern; lamp; street-lamp; (arch.) lantern tower; (mech.) lantern-wheel, trundle; ~ *sourde,* dark lantern; ~*s que tout cela,* that's all rubbish; (in Fr. Revolution) *à la* ~*!,* lynch him!, string him up to the lamp-post!; *prendre des vessies pour des* ~*s,* to believe the moon is made of green cheese; *oublier d'allumer* or *d'éclairer sa* ~, to forget the most important piece of information, to fail to make oneself clear; ~ *vénitienne,* Chinese lantern.
lanterneau (pl. **-x**) [lɑ̃tɛrno], **lanternon** [lɑ̃tɛrnɔ̃] *s.m.* (arch.) lantern-light; skylight.
lanterner [lɑ̃tɛrne] *v.i.* to dally, to trifle, to dawdle; to fritter one's time away; *faire* ~ *qn.,* to keep s.o. waiting; ~ *v.t.* to keep (s.o.) waiting, to put (s.o.) off with empty promises, on flimsy pretexts.
lanternier [lɑ̃tɛrnje] *s.m.* **1.** lamp-lighter; **2.** (fam.) frequenter of brothels.
lanthane [lɑ̃tan] *s.m.* (chem.) lanthanum.
lanugineu-x, -se [lanyʒinø] *adj.* woolly; downy, lanuginous.
lapalissade [lapalisad] *s.f.* obvious truth, truism, ridiculous platitude.
laparotomie [laparɔtɔmi] *s.f.* (surg.) laparotomy.
lapement [lapmɑ̃] *s.m.* lapping.
laper [lape] *v.t.* to lap; to lap up; to lick up.
lapereau (pl. **-x**) [lapro] *s.m.* young rabbit.
lapicide [lapisid] ~ *s.m.* (archaeol.) stone-engraver, lapicide.
lapidaire [lapidɛr] *adj.* (of style) lapidary, terse, concise; ~ *s.m.* lapidary; lapidary's wheel.
lapidation [lapidɑsjɔ̃] *s.f.* stoning.
lapider [lapide] *v.t.* to stone; to stone to death; (fig.) to abuse, to vilify.
lapidification [lapidifikɑsjɔ̃] *s.f.* (geol.) lapidification, petrifaction.
lapidifier [lapidifje] *v.t.* (geol.) to lapidify, to petrify.
lapilli [lapili] *s.m.pl.* (geol.) lapilli.
lapin, -e [lapɛ̃] *s.m.f.* rabbit; (fig.) fellow, chap; non-paying passenger or parcel; ~ *de garenne,* wild rabbit; ~ *de chou,* tame rabbit; *courir comme un* ~, to run like a hare; ~ *du Brésil,* guinea-pig; *c'est un fameux* ~, he's a good chap, a stout lad; *une mère* ~*e,* a woman who is always having children; *pattes de* ~, short whiskers; *voyager en* ~, to sit beside the driver, to travel without paying; *poser un* ~ *à qn.,* to fail to turn up (at a rendezvous), to stand s.o. up.
lapiner [lapine] *v.i.* (of doe-rabbits) to litter.
lapinière [lapinjɛr] *s.f.* rabbit-farm; rabbit-hutch.
lapis, lapis-lazuli [lapis (lazyli)] *s.m.* (min.) lapis lazuli.
lapon, -e [lapɔ̃] *adj., s.m.f.* Lapp; Laplander.
Laponie [lapɔni] *s.f.* (geog.) Lapland.
laps [laps] *s.m.* lapse or space (of time).
laps, -e [laps] *adj.* (relig.) lapsed, relapsed.
lapsus [lapsys] *s.m.* lapse, slip, error, mistake; ~ *calami,* slip of the pen; ~ *linguae,* slip of the tongue.
laptot [lapto] *s.m.* Senegalese soldier.

laquage [lakaʒ] *s.m.* lacquering.
laquais [lakɛ] *s.m.* lackey; flunkey; footman; servant; *âme de* ~, servile nature.
laque [lak] *s.f.* lacquer, lac, (also *s.m.*) shellac; ~ *s.m.* lacquer; lacquer-work.
laquer [lake] *v.t.* to lacquer, to japan, to varnish, to paint.
laqueur [lakœr] *s.m.* lacquer-worker.
laraire [larɛr] *s.m.* (Rom. ant.) shrine of the lares.
larbin [larbɛ̃] *s.m.* (fam.) flunkey.
larcin [larsɛ̃] *s.m.* larceny, petty theft, pilfering; stolen article; plagiarism.
lard [lar] *s.m.* pork fat, fat pork, fat or streaky bacon; blubber; (fam.) fat (on person); *tranche de* ~, slice of bacon; *omelette au* ~, bacon omelette; *pierre de* ~, steatite talc (used by tailors); *se faire du* ~, to put on fat (esp. through idleness); (pop., pej.) *tête de* ~, fat slob; *un gros* ~, a big, fat man; ⚠ not 'lard' in form of cooking-fat.
larder [larde] (cook.) to lard; (build.) to stud (a beam for plastering); to stab or pierce repeatedly; (fig.) to interlard, to intersperse, (*de*, with); (cook.) *aiguille à* ~, larding-needle.
lardoire [lardwar] *s.f.* **1.** larding-needle; **2.** (constr.) metal foot (on stake); **3.** (fam.) pointed weapon.
lardon [lardɔ̃] *s.m.* **1.** (cook.) strip of bacon for larding, lardon; piece of browned fat bacon (as accompaniment); **2.** (techn.) metal plug (to seal crack); **3.** (fig.) jibe, taunt; **4.** (pop.) small child, kid.
lardonner [lardɔne] *v.t.* (cook.) to cut in strips (for larding).
lare [lar] *s.m.* (Rom. ant.) lar, household god; ~*s*, household gods; home; *les dieux* ~*s*, the household gods, the lares.
larenier [larnje] *s.m.* = LARMIER.
large [larʒ] *adj.* broad, wide, extensive, ample; big; generous, liberal; lax, loose, free, easy, unscrupulous; abundant, large, copious; grand, bold; *portes* ~*s ouvertes*, wide-open doors; *conscience* ~, accommodating conscience; ~ *de deux mètres*, two metres wide; ~ *adv.* boldly, broadly, freely, roughly; wide; *habiller* ~, to dress in loose-fitting clothes; *voir* ~, to take a broad view; *peindre* ~, to paint boldly; *mesurer* ~, to measure roughly; (of horse) *aller* ~, to run wide; *il n'en mène pas* ~, he is making a poor showing; ~ *s.m.* breadth, width; (naut.) open sea, the offing; *courir au* ~, to run for the offing; *passer au* ~, to sheer off, to give a wide berth to; *prendre le* ~, to put to sea; *vent du* ~, sea-breeze; *au* ~, (i.) (interj.) keep off!; (ii.) spaciously, comfortably; at one's ease; *en long et en* ~, in both length and breadth; *marcher* or *aller de long en* ~, to go, or pace, to and fro, or up and down; (fig.) *prendre le* ~, to run away; ~**ment** [larʒəmɑ̃] *adv.* largely, widely, amply, abundantly, copiously; generously, liberally; boldly, in the grand manner; broadly, roughly.
largesse [larʒɛs] *s.f.* liberality, bounty, munificence, money bestowed; (arch.) largesse.
largeur [larʒœr] *s.f.* breadth, width; (rail.) gauge; ~ *d'idées*, broadness of mind; *dans les grandes* ~*s*, on a large scale; in grand style; with a vengeance; completely.
larghetto [largeto] *adv., s.m.* (mus.) larghetto.
largo [largo] *adv., s.m.* (mus.) largo.
largue [larg] *adj.* (naut.) (of wind) large, on the quarter, abaft the beam; (of cable) slack; (naut.) *courir* ~, to run large, to run off the wind.
larguer [large] *v.t.* **1.** (naut.) to slacken or to cast off (cable); **2.** (aeron.) to drop (parachutes, bombs).
larigot [larigo] *s.m.* flageolet, rustic pipe; larigot (stop of organ).
larme [larm] *s.f.* tear; drop; *être en* ~*s*, to be in tears; *fondre en* ~*s*, to melt or burst into tears; *pleurer à chaudes* ~*s*, to cry one's eyes out; to weep copiously; *être touché aux* ~*s*, to be moved to tears; *verser des* ~*s*, to shed tears; *avoir la* ~ *à l'œil*, to be moved; to have tears in one's eyes; to be in a sentimental mood; *avec des* ~*s dans la voix*, in a tremulous voice; tremulously; *rire aux* ~*s*, to cry with laughing, to laugh till the tears come; *avoir le don des* ~*s*, to be able to cry at will; (chem.) ~*s bataviques*, Prince Rupert's drops; *une* ~ *de vin*, a drop of wine.
larmier [larmje] *s.m.* **1.** (arch.) drip, larmier, corona; **2.** (anat.) angle of eye nearest to nose; tear-bag (of deer); eye-vein (of horse).
larmoiement [larmwamɑ̃] *s.m.* watering or running of the eyes; (fig.) whining, whimpering, snivelling.
larmoyant, -e [larmwajɑ̃] *adj.* watering (of the eyes); weeping, tearful, in tears, lachrymose; (fig.) sentimental and pathetic, maudlin.
larmoyer [larmwaje] *v.i.* (of eyes) to water; to weep, to shed tears, to cry, to whimper, to snivel.
larron [larɔ̃] *s.m.* thief, robber, pilferer; (print.) bite, blank space (due to faulty printing), dog's ear; *s'entendre comme* ~*s en foire*, to be as thick as thieves; *quand les* ~*s se battent, les larcins se découvrent*, when thieves fall out honest folks come by their own; *le mauvais* ~, the impenitent thief; *l'occasion fait le* ~, opportunity makes the thief; ~ *d'eau*, take-off channel (for water).
larvaire [larvɛr] *adj.* larval; (fig.) embryonic.
larve [larv] *s.f.* (zool.) larva, grub; (ant.) spectre, ghost.
larvé, -e [larve] *adj.* (med.) larvated, masked.
laryngé, -e [larɛ̃ʒe], **laryngien, -ne** [larɛ̃ʒjɛ̃] *adj.* (anat.) laryngeal.
laryng-ite [larɛ̃ʒit] *s.f.* (med.) laryngitis; ~**ologie** [larɛ̃gɔlɔʒi] *s.f.* laryngology; ~**ologue** [larɛ̃gɔlɔg], ~**ologiste** [larɛ̃gɔlɔʒist] *s.m.f.* laryngologist; ~**oscope** [larɛ̃gɔskɔp] *s.m.* laryngoscope; ~**oscopie** [larɛ̃gɔskɔpi] *s.f.* laryngoscopy; ~**otomie** [larɛ̃gɔtɔmi] *s.f.* (surg.) laryngotomy.
larynx [larɛ̃ks] *s.m.* (anat.) larynx.
las [lɑs] *interj.* alas!
las, -se [lɑ, lɑs] *adj.* tired, weary; ~ *de*, tired of, sick of; bored, disgusted, fed up, with; *de guerre* ~*se*, for the sake of peace and quiet.
lasagne [lazaɲ] *s.f.* (cook.) lasagne (pl.).
lascar [laskar] *s.m.* (fam.) **1.** tough character; **2.** artful rogue; ⚠ not 'Lascar'.
lasci-f, -ve [lasif] *adj.* lascivious, lustful; ~**vement** [lasivmɑ̃] *adv.* lasciviously.
lascivité [lasivite] *s.f.* lasciviousness, lust.
laser [lazɛr] *s.m* (phys.) laser.
lassant, -e [lɑsɑ̃] *adj.* tiring, fatiguing; tedious, boring.
lasser [lɑse] *v.t.* to tire, to fatigue, to weary; to bore; **se** ~ *v.refl.* to get tired, to grow weary.
lassis [lɑsi] *s.m.* silk-floss.
lassitude [lɑsityd] *s.f.* lassitude, fatigue, weariness; languor; (fig.) boredom; weariness.
lasso [laso] *s.m.* lasso, lariat.
lasting [lastiŋ] *s.m.* lasting (woollen cloth).
latence [latɑ̃s] *s.f.* latency, pause in development; *temps de* ~, time-lag.
latent, -e [latɑ̃] *adj.* latent; hidden, concealed; dormant, secret; not visible; not apparent.
latéral, -e, (**aux**) [lateral] *adj.* lateral; side; ~**ement** [lateralmɑ̃] *adv.* laterally, sideways, at or on the side, from the side.
latérite [laterit] *s.f.* (min.) laterite.
latex [latɛks] *s.m.* (bot.) latex; sap.
laticifère [latisifɛr] *adj.* (bot.) laticiferous, latex-producing.

latifolié, -e [latifɔlje] *adj.* (bot.) latifoliate; broad-leaved.

latifundia [latifɔ̃dja] *s.m.pl.* latifundia; large private estates.

latin, -e [latɛ̃] *adj.*, *s.m.f.* Latin; Roman; of Latium; ~ *de cuisine*, dog Latin; *y perdre son* ~, to rack one's brain in vain; to be unable to make head or tail of it; *être au bout de son* ~, to be at one's wit's end; (naut.) *voile* ~*e*, lateen sail.

latin-isation [latinizɑsjɔ̃] *s.f.* Latinization; **~iser** [latinize] *v.t.* **1.** to Latinize; ~ *v.i.* (obs.) to affect Latin speech; **2.** (eccles.) to practise Rom. Catholic liturgy in Orthodox countries; **~isme** [latinism] *s.m.* Latinism; Latin idiom or expression; **~iste** [latinist] *s.m.f.* Latinist, Latin scholar or student; **~ité** [latinite] *s.f.* Latinity; Rom. world, Rom. civilization.

latino-américain, -e [latinɔamerikɛ̃] *adj.* Latin American.

latitude [latityd] *s.f.* latitude; climate; space, room; (fig.) latitude; freedom, tolerance, scope.

latitudinaire [latitydinɛr] *adj.*, *s.m.* (theol.) latitudinarian.

latomie [latɔmi] *s.f.* (ant.) quarry used as prison.

latrines [latrin] *s.f.pl.* latrines.

latrodecte [latrɔdɛkt] *s.m.* (ent.) poisonous spider.

lattage [lataʒ] *s.m.* lathing; lath-work.

latte [lat] *s.f.* **1.** lath; **2.** (obs.) straight cavalry sword.

latter [late] *v.t.* to lath.

lattis [lati] *s.m.* lath-work, lathing.

Latvie [latvi] *s.f.* (geog.) Latvia.

latvien, -ne [latvjɛ̃] *adj.*, *s.m.f.* Latvian.

laudanum [lodanɔm] *s.m.* laudanum.

laudati-f, -ve [lodatif] *adj.* laudatory.

laudes [lod] *s.f.pl.* (eccles.) lauds.

lauracées [lɔrase] *s.f.pl.* (bot.) Lauraceae.

lauré, -e [lɔre] *adj.* (numismatics) crowned with laurel.

lauréat, -e [lɔrea] *adj.*, *s.m.f.* laureate; prize--winner.

lauréole [lɔreɔl] *s.f.* (bot.) daphne.

laurier [lɔrje] *s.m.* (bot.) laurel; (fig.) honour; glory; *se reposer sur ses* ~*s*, to rest on one's laurels; *se couvrir de* ~*s*, to cover oneself with glory; *flétrir ses* ~*s*, to sully one's honour; ~*-cerise*, cherry-laurel; ~*-rose*, oleander; ~*-sauce*, bay--tree; ~*-tin*, laurustinus.

lavable [lavabl] *adj.* washable.

lavabo [lavabo] *s.m.* **1.** (eccles.) lavabo; linen towel; **2.** wash-basin; wash-stand; euphem. for lavatory, W.C.

lavage [lavaʒ] *s.m.* washing; (med.) irrigation.

lavallière [lavaljɛr] *s.f.* large floppy bow-tie.

lavande [lavɑ̃d] *s.f.* (bot.) lavender.

lavanderie [lavɑ̃dri] *s.f.* wash-house; washing--place.

lavandière [lavɑ̃djɛr] *s.f.* **1.** washer-woman; **2.** (ornith.) wagtail.

lavaret [lavarɛ] *s.m.* (ichth.) Coregonus, fresh-water herring.

lavasse [lavas] *s.f.* **1.** (obs.) sudden downpour; **2.** dish-water (referring to over-thin soup, weak coffee, etc.).

lave [lav] *s.f.* lava.

lavé, -e [lave] *adj.* washed; (of colours) pale, faint, light.

lave-glace [lavglas] *s.m.* (pl. *lave-glaces*) (car) screen-washer.

lave-mains [lavmɛ̃] *s.m.invar.* (obs.) wash--basin, wash-hand-basin.

lavement [lavmɑ̃] *s.m.* (med.) enema.

laver [lave] *v.t.* to wash; to cleanse; to wash away; to bathe; (fig.) to absolve, to purify; to clear; to expiate; (paint.) to colour-wash; (pop.) to sell off cheap (to get money), to flog; ~ *la tête à qn.*, to give s.o. a severe reprimand; **se** ~ *v.refl.* to wash oneself, to have a wash; (fig.) to justify oneself, to clear oneself; *se* ~ *la figure*, to wash one's face; *se* ~ *de*, to clear oneself of, to expiate; *s'en* ~ *les mains*, to wash one's hands of it.

laverie [lavri] *s.f.* **1.** (techn.) washery; **2.** ~ *automatique*, launderette.

lavette [lavɛt] *s.f.* dish-cloth; pot-scourer; (fam.) flabby individual; (pop.) tongue.

laveu-r, -se [lavœr] *s.m.f.* washer; washer-woman; scourer; ~*se de vaisselle*, scullery-maid, dish-washer; **~se** *s.f.* washing-machine.

lavis [lavi] *s.m.* (paint.) colour-wash; *dessin au* ~, Indian-ink sketch; wash drawing.

lavoir [lavwar] *s.m.* washing-place; wash-house; (techn.) washing-trough; washery.

lavure [lavyr] *s.f.* (lit. & fig.) dish-water (see LAVASSE 2); (metall.) washing, scouring; (pl.) sweepings, washings.

laxati-f, -ve [laksatif] *adj.*, *s.m.* laxative.

laxité [laksite] *s.f.* laxity, laxness; looseness; slackness.

laye [lɛ] *s.f.* = LAIE 3.

layer [leje] *v.t.* to cut (a path); to blaze (trees); to tool (stone).

layetier [lɛjtje] *s.m.* box-maker; case-maker; ~*-emballeur*, packing-case maker.

layette [lɛjɛt] *s.f.* **1.** baby-linen, layette; **2.** small case (esp. for documents).

layon [lɛjɔ̃] *s.m.* (hunt.) narrow track or path in coverts.

lazaret [lazarɛ] *s.m.* lazaretto, lazaret; isolation hospital.

lazariste [lazarist] *s.m.* (eccles.) Lazarist.

lazulite [lazylit] *s.m.* = LAPIS(-LAZULI).

lazzi [lazi] *s.m.pl.* gibes, witty sarcasms.

le [lə], **la** [la] (contracted to **l'** before vowel or h-mute), pl. **les** [le] **1.** *def. art.* the; a; *savoir la réponse*, to know the answer; *2 francs la douzaine*, 2 francs a dozen; *le(s) samedi(s)*, on Saturdays; *le samedi, 2 mars*, (on) Saturday, 2nd March; *la chambre 17*, room 17; *à la page 20*, on page 20; *la France*, France; *la justice*, justice; *le russe*, Russian (language); *je préfère la bière*, I prefer beer; *se laver les mains*, to wash one's hands; *se serrer la main*, to shake hands, to shake each other by the hand; **2.** *pron.* him, her, it, them; so; *je le crois*, I believe him, it; I think so; *évitez de le faire*, avoid doing it; *c'est vrai, je le sais*, it is true, I know; *il est très intelligent sans le paraître*, he is very clever without appearing to be so.

lé [le] *s.m.* breadth, width, (of material); width of towpath; towpath, towage-way.

lèche [lɛʃ] *s.f.* (pop.) *faire de la* ~ *à qn.*, to suck up to s.o., to lick someone's boots.

léché, -e [leʃe] *adj.* licked; (fig.) over-polished, over-refined; *c'est un ours mal* ~, he wants licking into shape; *une image* ~*e*, an over-finished picture.

lèchefrite [lɛʃfrit] *s.f.* (cook.) dripping-pan.

lèchement [lɛʃmɑ̃] *s.m.* licking, lick.

lécher [leʃe] *v.t.* to lick, to lick off, to lap; (fig.) to labour, to overdo, to over-polish; *s'en* ~ *les doigts*, to smack one's lips; (fig.) ~ *les bottes de qn.*, to lick someone's boots, to fawn on s.o.

lécheu-r, -se [leʃœr] *s.m.f.* gormandizer, glutton; (fig.) flatterer, parasite, toady.

lèche-vitrines [lɛʃvitrin] *s.m.* window-shopping.

lécithine [lesitin] *s.f.* (biol.) lecithin.

leçon [l(ə)sɔ̃] *s.f.* **1.** lesson; (pl.) private lessons, private tuition; lecture; reading (of text); ~ *de choses*, object lesson; **2.** lesson, instruction(s), precept, warning, moral; *faire la* ~ *à qn.*, to tell s.o. what to do, to dictate to s.o.; *que cela vous serve de* ~, let that be a lesson, or warning, to you.

lect-eur, -rice [lɛktœr] *s.m.f.* reader; lector;

proof-reader; (in German university) lecturer; (in Fr. university or school) foreign language assistant; (cin.) *~eur de sons*, sound-reproducing unit (of projector).

lecture [lɛktyr] *s.f.* reading; proof-correcting; ⚠ not 'lecture'.

légal, -e, (**aux**) [legal] *adj.* legal, lawful, legitimate; of the law, legal, forensic; required by law; *médecine ~e*, forensic medicine; *moyens légaux*, the law, legal proceedings; **~ement** [legalmɑ̃] *adv.* legally, lawfully.

légal-isation [legalizɑsjɔ̃] *s.f.* legalization; authentication, certification; **~iser** [legalize] *v.t.* to legalize; to authenticate, to certify, to confirm; **~ité** [legalite] *s.f.* legality, lawfulness; *rester dans la ~ité*, to keep within the law.

légat [lega] *s.m.* legate.

légataire [legatɛr] *s.m.f.* legatee; *~ universel*, residuary legatee.

légation [legɑsjɔ̃] *s.f.* (diplom.) legation; (eccles.) legateship.

legato [legato] *adv.* (mus.) legato.

lège [lɛʒ] *adj.* (naut.) light; in ballast.

légendaire [leʒɑ̃dɛr] *adj.* legendary; fabulous.

légende [leʒɑ̃d] *s.f.* **1.** legend, myth; story, fable; record, narrative; **2.** key; reference; explanation; **3.** inscription, motto.

lég-er, -ère [leʒe] *adj.* light; slight, trifling; loose; airy; nimble, agile, swift, fleet; gentle, soft; slender, small, moderate, unimportant; light-armed; unencumbered; buoyant; clear; flimsy, delicate; superficial, fickle, inconsiderate, thoughtless, wanton; *à la ~ère*, inconsiderately, thoughtlessly, carelessly, wantonly, unwisely; *d'un cœur ~er*, with a clear conscience; *avoir la main ~ère*, to rule with a light hand; *avoir la tête ~ère*, to be hare-brained; *~er à la course*, nimble- or swift-footed; (fig.) *avoir le pied ~er*, to be always on the move; **~èrement** [leʒɛrmɑ̃] *adv.* lightly, thinly, loosely; slightly; softly, delicately; nimbly; thoughtlessly, inconsiderately, wantonly; cursorily.

légèreté [leʒɛrte] *s.f.* lightness; nimbleness; swiftness; slightness; buoyancy; levity; airiness, fickleness; thoughtlessness, inconsiderateness, imprudence, carelessness; facility, ease; (obs.) trivial mistake.

leggings [legiŋs], **leggins** [legins] *s.m.* or *f.pl.* leggings.

légiférer [leʒifere] *v.i.* to legislate; to make laws, to lay down rules.

légion [leʒjɔ̃] *s.f.* (ant.) legion; host, multitude; *Légion d'honneur*, Legion of Honour; *Légion (étrangère)*, Foreign Legion.

légionnaire [leʒjɔnɛr] *s.m.* legionary; soldier of *Légion étrangère*; member of *Légion d'honneur*.

législat-eur, -rice [leʒislatœr] *s.m.f.* legislator; lawgiver; *adj.* legislating, law-giving, law-making.

législati-f, -ve [leʒislatif] *adj.* legislative; having the effect of law.

législation [leʒislɑsjɔ̃] *s.f.* legislation; body of laws.

législature [leʒislatyr] *s.f.* legislature; time of office of a legislative body.

légiste [leʒist] *s.m.f.* legist; jurist, legal expert; *médecin ~*, expert in forensic medicine.

légitimation [leʒitimɑsjɔ̃] *s.f.* legitimation; legal recognition, legitimization.

légitime [leʒitim] *adj.* legitimate; born in wedlock; lawful, rightful; justifiable, allowable; *~ s.f.* (pop.) wife; **~ment** [leʒitimmɑ̃] *adv.* legitimately, lawfully, legally; rightfully; justifiably.

légitimer [leʒitime] *v.t.* to legitimize; to legitimate; to recognize; to justify; to serve as justification for.

légitimiste [leʒitimist] *s.m., adj.* (Fr. pol.) legitimist.

légitimité [leʒitimite] *s.f.* legitimacy; legitimateness, lawfulness, justifiability.

legs [lɛ, lɛg] *s.m.* legacy, bequest; *faire un ~*, to leave a legacy.

léguer [lege] *v.t.* to bequeath, to leave (in one's will); to transmit, to hand down; **se ~** *v.refl.* to be handed down.

légume [legym] *s.m.* vegetable; (bot.) pod, pulse, leguminous plant; *~ s.f.* (pop.) *une grosse ~*, an important person, a big shot.

légumi-er, -ère [legymje] *adj.* vegetable; **~er** *s.m.* vegetable-dish.

légumine [legymin] *s.f.* (chem.) legumin.

légumineu-x, -se [legyminø] *adj.* (bot.) leguminous; **~ses** *s.f.pl.* (bot.) leguminous plants.

leitmotiv [lajtmɔtif] *s.m.* (mus.) leitmotiv; (fig.) catch-phrase.

lemme [lɛm] *s.m.* (math., log.) lemma.

lemming [lemiŋ] *s.m.* (zool.) lemming.

lemnacées [lɛmnase] *s.f.pl.* (bot.) Lemnaceae.

lemniscate [lɛmniskat] *s.f.* (math.) lemniscate.

lémures [lemyr] *s.m.pl.* (Rom. ant.) lemures; ghosts.

lémuriens [lemyrjɛ̃] *s.m.pl.* (zool.) Lemuridae.

lendemain [lɑ̃dmɛ̃] *s.m.* next day, following day, day after; period following; (fig.) consequence, sequel; *remettre au ~*, to put off till tomorrow; *le plus beau ~ ne nous rend pas la veille*, what's past is gone for ever; *il n'y a pas de bonne fête sans ~*, all good things must come to an end; *penser au ~*, to think of the morrow; *une chose décidée du jour au ~*, a matter settled somewhat hastily; *au ~ de la guerre*, in the period after the war; *le ~ de*, the day after; *le ~ matin*, the next morning; *cette affaire a eu d'heureux ~s*, this affair had a happy sequel.

lendit [lɑ̃di] *s.m.* (Fr. hist.) lendit; fair at Saint-Denis.

lénifier [lenifje] *v.t.* to soothe, to mitigate, to assuage.

lénin-isme [leninism] *s.m.* Leninism; **~iste** [leninist] *adj.* Leninist.

léniti-f, -ve [lenitif] *adj.* lenitive; emollient; (fig.) soothing, palliative.

lent, -e [lɑ̃] *adj.* slow, tardy; remiss, backward; dull, sluggish; indolent; (med.) low; *d'esprit ~*, slow in the uptake; *avoir la parole ~e*, to be slow of speech; **~ement** [lɑ̃tmɑ̃] *adv.* slowly, sluggishly.

lente [lɑ̃t] *s.f.* nit.

lenteur [lɑ̃tœr] *s.f.* slowness; dullness; sluggishness; indolence; delay; procrastination; dilatoriness.

lenticelle [lɑ̃tisɛl] *s.f.* (bot.) lenticel.

lenticulaire [lɑ̃tikylɛr], **lenticulé, -e** [lɑ̃tikyle] *adj.* lenticular.

lenticule [lɑ̃tikyl] *s.f.* (bot.) Lemna, duckweed.

lentigo [lɑ̃tigo] *s.m.* (med.) lentigo.

lentille [lɑ̃tij] *s.f.* **1.** lentil; *~ d'eau*, duckweed; (colloq.) *plat de ~s*, (Esau's) mess of pottage; **2.** (opt.) lens; magnifying-glass; *~ (cornéenne)*, contact lens; **3.** (med.) lentigo.

lentillon [lɑ̃tijɔ̃] *s.m.* red lentil.

lentisque [lɑ̃tisk] *s.m.* (bot.) lentisk, mastic-tree.

lento [lɛntɔ] *adv.* (mus.) lento.

léonin, -e [leɔnɛ̃] *adj.* leonine; lion-like; *partage ~*, lion's share.

léonure [leɔnyr] *s.m.* (bot.) motherwort.

léopard [leɔpar] *s.m.* (zool.) leopard; (herald.) leopard, lion passant guardant as in arms of England.

léopardé, -e [leɔparde] *adj.* (herald.) passant.

lépido-dendron [lepidɔdɛ̃drɔ̃] *s.m.* (palaeont.) lepidodendrum; **~lithe** [lepidɔlit] *s.m.* (min.) lepidolite; **~ptère** [lepidɔptɛr] *s.m.* (ent.)

lepidopteran, (pl.) Lepidoptera; *adj.* lepidopterous; **~sirène** [lepidɔsirɛn] *s.m.* (ichth.) Lepidosiren.
lépiote [lepjɔt] *s.f.* (bot.) kind of mushroom.
lépisme [lepism] *s.m.* (ent.) Lepisma; silver fish.
lèpre [lɛpr] *s.f.* leprosy.
lépreu-x, -se [leprø] *s.m.f.* leper; *adj.* leprous; (fig.) peeling, flaking.
léproserie [leprozri] *s.f.* leper-house, leper hospital.
lepte [lɛpt] *s.m.* (ent.) leptus; ~ *automnal*, harvest-bug.
leptospirose [lɛptɔspiroz] *s.f.* (pathol.) leptospirosis.
lepture [lɛptyr] *s.f.* (ent.) Leptora.
lequel [ləkɛl], **laquelle** [lakɛl], **lesquels, lesquelles** [lekɛl] (in combination with *à*, *de*, gives forms *auquel*, *duquel*, *auxquels*, *desquels*, *auxquelles*, *desquelles*); **1.** *rel. pron.* which, who, whom; **2.** *int. pron.* which?, which one(s)?, who?, whom?
lérot [lero] *s.m.* (zool.) garden dormouse.
les [le] *art.*, *pron.* see LE.
lès [lɛ], **lez** [le] *prep.* near (in place-names).
lesbien, -ne [lɛsbjɛ̃] *adj.* (geog.) Lesbian, of Lesbos; **~ne** *adj.f.*, *s.f.* lesbian, homosexual (woman).
lèse [lɛz] *~-majesté*, *s.f.* lese-majesty; *~-humanité*; *s.f.* treason against society.
léser [leze] *v.t.* to wrong, to injure.
lésine [lezin] *s.f.* stinginess, niggardliness, meanness; parsimony; close-fistedness.
lésiner [lezine] *v.t.* to be stingy, mean, niggardly, parsimonious; to haggle; to chaffer; to pinch and scrape.
lésineu-r, -se [lezinœr] *adj.* (obs.) miserly; *s.m.f.* miser.
lésion [lezjɔ̃] *s.f.* lesion, injury, hurt; (law) breaking (of a contract); wrong, damage.
lessivage [lesivaʒ] *s.m.* washing, cleaning out.
lessive [lesiv] *s.f.* **1.** (chem.) lixivium; lye; soda, sodium carbonate, washing-powder, detergent; **2.** washing, wash; (articles for) laundry.
lessiver [lesive] *v.t.* **1.** (obs.) to wash in soda; to lixiviate, to leach; **2.** to wash in detergent; **3.** (fig., pop.) to clean (s.o.) out (at gambling); to eliminate (a competitor); *être lessivé*, to be completely exhausted.
lessiveuse [lesivøz] *s.f.* wash-boiler, copper, washing-machine.
lest [lɛst] *s.m.* ballast; (naut.) *être sur son ~*, to be in ballast; *jeter du ~*, to throw out ballast; (fig.) to give up one thing for the sake of another that is better or more urgent; to come down a peg or two.
lestage [lɛstaʒ] *s.m.* ballasting.
leste [lɛst] *adj.* lively, brisk, alert, agile, nimble, light-footed, smart; quick; skilful; free, saucy, improper; **~ment** [lɛstəmɑ̃] *adv.* briskly, nimbly, smartly, quickly; skilfully.
lester [lɛste] *v.t.* (naut.) to ballast; to fill, to load; **se** ~ *v.refl.* (fam.) to have a good meal, to fill oneself up.
léthargie [letarʒi] *s.f.* lethargy.
léthargique [letarʒik] *adj.* lethargic.
lette [lɛt], **letton, -(n)e** [lɛtɔ̃] *adj.*, *s.m.f.* = LATVIEN.
Lettonie [lɛtɔni] *s.f.* (geog.) = LATVIE.
lettre [lɛtr] *s.f.* **1.** letter, character, type; ~ *majuscule*, capital letter; ~ *initiale*, initial (letter); *~s d'imprimerie*, printed characters, print; *en toutes ~s*, in full, in words (opp. in figures); (fig.) clearly, spelt out; **2.** the letter, the literal sense; the words of the text, the actual text; inscription (on engraving); *la ~ et l'esprit*, the letter and the spirit; *la ~ de la loi*, the letter of the law; *à la ~* or *au pied de la ~*, literally, to the letter, in the literal, or strict, sense; word for word; ~ *morte*, (fig.) dead letter, law no longer observed; *avant la ~*, (of engraving) print taken before inscription inserted; (fig.) premature, before completion; **3.** letter, note, epistle; ~ *recommandée*, registered letter; ~ *de change*, bill of exchange; ~ *de crédit*, letter of credit; *~s patentes*, letters patent; ~ *de grâce*, reprieve; *~s de noblesse*, patents of nobility; ~ *de voiture*, way-bill; (naut.) ~ *de mer*, clearance certificate, ship's papers; **4.** (pl.) letters, literature; arts (opp. sciences), humanities; *homme de ~s*, writer, literary man; *licence ès ~s*, arts degree; *~s modernes*, modern language and literature.
lettré, -e [letre] *adj.* learned; literate; literary; *s.m.f.* literary man or woman, scholar, cultivated person.
lettrine [letrin] *s.f.* (print.) reference letter; heading.
leu [lø] *s.m.* (obs.) wolf; (mod.) used only in phrase *à la queue ~ ~*, in single file, one after another, in Indian file.
leucanie [løkani] *s.f.* (ent.) leucania.
leucémie [løsemi] *s.f.* leukaemia.
leucite [løsit] *s.f.* (min.) leucite; ~ *s.f.* (bot.) leucoplast.
leuco-cyte [løkɔsit] *s.m.* (biol.) leucocyte, white corpuscle; **~ma, ~me** [løkɔm(a)] *s.m.* (med.) leucoma, albugo; **~pénie** [løkɔpeni] *s.f.* (med.) leucopenia, deficiency of white corpuscles; **~rrhée** [løkɔre] *s.f.* (med.) leucorrhoea.
leude [lød] *s.m.* (hist.) liege lord; great vassal.
leur [lœr] *poss. adj.* their; *donnez-le-~*, give it to them; *ne ~ faites pas de mal*, don't harm them; *le* or *la ~*, *les ~s*, (*poss. pron.*) theirs, their own; *les pauvres ont leurs peines, les riches ont aussi les ~s*, poor people have their troubles, but rich people have also theirs; ~ *s.m. les ~s*, their relations, friends, allies; *il n'est pas des ~s*, he is not one of them.
leur [lœr] *pers. pron.* to them, them; *il ~ a dit*, he said to them, he told them; *cela ne ~ plaira guère*, that won't please them very much.
leurre [lœr] *s.m.* lure, decoy; bait; (fig.) bait, allurement, enticement; delusion; *c'était un ~*, it was a delusion.
leurrer [lœre] *v.t.* to draw to a lure; (fig.) to entice; to allure; to decoy; **se** ~ *v.refl.* to delude oneself.
levage [ləvaʒ] *s.m.* **1.** raising, lifting; *appareils de ~*, hoisting or lifting devices, cranes, jacks, etc.; **2.** rising (of yeast); blistering (of paint).
levain [ləvɛ̃] *s.m.* (lit. & fig.) leaven.
levant [ləvɑ̃] *s.m.* East; Levant; rising sun; ~ *adj.m.* rising.
levantin, -e [ləvɑ̃tɛ̃] *adj.*, *s.m.f.* Levantine.
lève [lɛv] *s.f.* mallet, mall.
levé, -e [l(ə)ve] *adj.* raised, hoisted, lifted, erect; *au pied ~*, at a moment's notice, unawares, unexpectedly; *tête ~e*, with head erect; fearlessly; *à main ~e*, freehand (drawing); ~ *s.m.* **1.** (mus.) up beat; **2.** plan, survey.
levée [ləve] *s.f.* raising; removal; abandoning; levy; rising; collection, gathering, gathering up or in, clearing (of letter-box); crop; harvest; (cards) trick; (naut.) weighing (of anchor); (eng.) embankment, dyke, levee, sea-wall, causeway; breaking-up; breaking (of seals); adjournment (of meeting); (law) rising (of court); taking up; exercising (of option); (mil.) recruitment, enlistment, levying.
lever [l(ə)ve] *v.t.* to lift, to lift up, to raise, to elevate, to hoist, to set up, to take up, to heave up; to haul up, to weigh (anchor); to levy, to gather, to call up, to collect; to break up, to close; to abolish; to remove (a difficulty, etc.); to clear; (print.) to compose; (hunt.) to start; ~ *l'ancre*, to weigh anchor; ~ *une armée*, to

levy troops, or an army; ~ *la main sur qn.*, to raise one's hand against s.o., to threaten to hit s.o.; ~ *les épaules*, to shrug one's shoulders; ~ *la boîte aux lettres*, to clear the letter-box; ~ *le camp*, to break up, or strike, camp; ~ *le masque*, to throw off the mask; (fig.) ~ *le pied*, to abscond with the cash-box; ~ *la séance*, to close or adjourn the meeting; to end the sitting; ~ *un lièvre*, (lit. & fig.) to start a hare; (fig.) to bring up (an awkward question); ~ *un plan*, to make a survey, to draw a plan; (slang) ~ *une femme*, to 'pick up' a woman; *poudre à faire* ~ *la pâte*, baking-powder; ~ *v.i.* to rise, to come or get up; to spring up, to grow; **se** ~ *v.refl.* to rise, to get up, to stand up, to spring up, to get out of bed, to be raised, to be collected, to be levied; *à qui se lève matin, Dieu prête la main*, the early bird catches the worm; *le soleil se lève*, the sun is rising; *se* ~ *de table*, to leave the (dinner) table; *le vent se lève*, the wind is getting up.

lever [l(ə)ve] *s.m.* getting up; rising; levee; *le* ~ *du soleil*, sunrise; (theatr.) ~ *de rideau*, curtain-raiser; ~ *du rideau*, (rise of) curtain.

levier [ləvje] *s.m.* (mech.) lever; crowbar; hand-spike; (fig.) lever, motive, driving force; *faire* ~, to lever, to exert leverage; (lit. & fig.) ~ *de commande*, control, control-lever; *être aux* ~*s de commande*, to be at the controls, to be in control; ~ *des vitesses*, gear-lever.

lévigation [levigɑsjɔ̃] *s.f.* levigation.

léviger [levige] *v.t.* to levigate; to grind fine.

lévitation [levitɑsjɔ̃] *s.f.* levitation.

lévite [levit] *s.m.* Levite; ~ *s.f.* surcoat, long coat.

lévogyre [levɔʒir] *adj.* (chem.) laevorotatory.

levraut [ləvro] *s.m.* leveret.

lèvre [lɛvr] *s.f.* lip; (pl.) lips (of wound), (anat.) labia; *du bout des* ~*s*, in a forced manner, half-heartedly; *sur le bord des* ~*s*, on the tip of the tongue; *avoir le cœur sur les* ~*s*, to wear one's heart on one's sleeve; *ne pas desserrer les* ~*s*, not to open one's mouth.

levrette [ləvrɛt] *s.f.* greyhound bitch; Italian greyhound; ⚠ not 'leveret'.

lévrier [levrije] *s.m.* greyhound, harrier.

levron, -ne [ləvrɔ̃] *s.m.f.* greyhound or harrier pup.

lévulose [levyloz] *s.f.* (chem.) laevulose, levulose; fruit-sugar.

levure [l(ə)vyr] *s.f.* yeast, barm, leaven.

levurier [l(ə)vyrje] *s.m.* yeast-maker; yeast-merchant.

lexical, -e, (**aux**) [lɛksikal] *adj.* (lang.) lexical.

lexico-graphe [lɛksikɔgraf] *s.m.f.* lexicographer; ~**graphie** [lɛksikɔgrafi] *s.f.* lexicography; ~**graphique** [lɛksikɔgrafik] *adj.* lexicographical; ~**logie** [lɛksikɔlɔʒi] *s.f.* lexicology; ~**logique** [lɛksikɔlɔʒik] *adj.* lexical; ~**logue** [lɛksikɔlɔg] *s.m.f.* lexicologist.

lexique [lɛksik] *s.m.* lexicon; concise dictionary; glossary, vocabulary, list of technical terms.

lez see LÈS.

lézard [lezar] *s.m.* lizard; *faire le* ~, to bask in the sun; ~ *d'eau*, newt.

lézarde [lezard] *s.f.* **1.** crevice, crack, chink; **2.** gold or silver braid.

lézardé, -e [lezarde] *adj.* cracked, full of cracks, crannied.

lézarder[1] [lezarde] *v.t.* to crack, to make cracks in; **se** ~ *v.refl.* to become cracked, to crack.

lézarder[2] [lezarde] *v.i.* (fam.) to laze or bask in the sun.

liage [ljaʒ] *s.m.* binding, fastening.

liais [ljɛ] *s.m.* (geol.) lias, freestone; *pierre de* ~, Portland stone.

liaison [ljɛzɔ̃] *s.f.* joining, junction, joint; binding together; union, unity; connection; coherence; tie, bond; intimate relationship, love affair; (mil.) liaison; (build.) mortar, pointing; bond; (cook.) thickening; (mus.) slur, tie, bind, ligature; liaison (between words); (writing) stroke; *officier de* ~, liaison officer; *rompre une* ~, to break off an attachment or love affair; *en* ~ *avec*, jointly with.

liaisonner [ljɛzɔne] *v.t.* (build.) to point, to grout; to bond.

liane [ljan] *s.f.* (bot.) liana; tropical creeper.

liant, -e [ljɑ̃] *adj.* sociable, engaging, affable, friendly, pliant, yielding, supple; soft; flexible; pliable; compliant, gentle, courteous; ~ *s.m.* pliancy; suppleness; flexibility, elasticity; compliance; gentleness; affability; (techn.) cementing agent, binder.

liard [ljar] *s.m.* (obs.) coin worth a quarter of a sou; (fig.) farthing, rap; *n'avoir pas un* ~, to be completely broke.

liarder [ljarde] *v.i.* to be a skinflint.

lias [ljɑs] *s.m.* (geol.) lias.

liasique [ljɑzik] *adj.* (geol.) liassic.

liasse [ljas] *s.f.* bundle; file (of papers), wad (of notes).

libage [libaʒ] *s.m.* (build.) ashlar; rough stone.

Liban [libɑ̃] *s.m.* (geog.) Lebanon.

libanais, -e [libanɛ] *adj., s.m.f.* Lebanese.

libation [libɑsjɔ̃] *s.f.* (ant.) libation; (jest) drinking, potation.

libelle [libɛl] *s.m.* lampoon.

libellé [libele] *s.m.* (of document, letter) wording, terms, contents; drawing-up, writing.

libeller [libele] *v.t.* to draw up, to write; to word, to formulate; ~ *un chèque*, to write, to draw, a cheque.

libelliste [libelist] *s.m.* (rare) lampoonist.

libellule [libelyl] *s.f.* (ent.) dragonfly.

liber [libɛr] *s.m.* (bot.) liber; bast.

libera [libera] *s.m.* (liturg.) prayer for the dead.

libérable [liberabl] *adj.* that can be freed (esp. from mil. service).

libéral, -e, (**aux**) [liberal] *adj.* liberal; ample; free, generous; open-handed; (of opinions, etc.) liberal, broadminded; (of knowledge, etc.) wide; ~ *s.m.* (Eng. pol.) Liberal; ~**ement** [liberalmɑ̃] *adv.* liberally, generous, open-handedly.

libéral-isation [liberalizɑsjɔ̃] *s.f.* liberalization; ~**iser** [liberalize] *v.t.* to liberalize, to free from restrictions; ~**isme** [liberalism] *s.m.* liberalism (esp. opp. socialism, authoritarianism, intolerance); tolerance, broadmindedness; ~**ité** [liberalite] *s.f.* liberality, generosity, act of liberality; donation.

libérat-eur, -rice [liberatœr] *s.m.f.* liberator; deliverer; rescuer; *adj.* liberating, releasing, freeing.

libération [liberɑsjɔ̃] *s.f.* liberation; deliverance, rescue; setting free; exemption, release; discharge; ~ *conditionnelle*, release (of prisoner) on parole.

libératoire [liberatwar] *adj.* liberating; freeing; clearing from debt; discharging financial obligation.

libéré, -e [libere] *adj.* freed, liberated, released, discharged; *forçat* ~, released convict; *action* ~*e*, paid-up share.

libérer [libere] *v.t.* to liberate, to free; to discharge, to release; to clear; to pay off, to redeem, (debt); **se** ~ *v.refl.* to free oneself, to arrange to be available, to rid oneself (*de*, of), to clear oneself of debt; to be discharged.

Libéria [liberja] *s.m.* (geog.) Liberia.

libérien[1], **-ne** [liberjɛ̃] *adj., s.m.f.* Liberian.

libérien[2], **-ne** [liberjɛ̃] *adj.* (bot.) liberian, of the liber or bast.

libertaire [libɛrtɛr] *s.m.f., adj.* libertarian; anarchist(ic).

liberté [libɛrte] *s.f.* liberty, freedom; independence; ease; licence; franchise; privilege; boldness; *en* ~, free, freely, at liberty; *mettre* or *remettre en* ~, to free, to set at liberty, to liberate; *mettre en* ~ *provisoire*, to discharge conditionally; ~ *d'esprit*, ease of mind; freedom from prejudice; *prendre la* ~ *de faire*, to take the liberty of doing, to presume to do; *prendre des* ~*s*, to take liberties, to be unduly familiar.

liberticide [libɛrtisid] *adj.*, *s.m.f.* (Lit.) liberticide.

libertin, -e [libɛrtɛ̃] *s.m.f.* **1.** libertine, rake; **2.** free thinker; *adj.* **1.** libertine, licentious; **2.** free-thinking.

libertinage [libɛrtinaʒ] **1.** *s.m.* dissoluteness, licentiousness; **2.** (obs.) free-thinking.

libidineu-x, -se [libidinø] *adj.* libidinous, lascivious, lustful.

libido [libido] *s.f.* desire (esp. sexual); (psychol.) libido.

libouret [liburɛ] *s.m.* (fish.) mackerel-line.

libraire [librɛr] *s.m.f.* bookseller; ~ *éditeur*, bookseller and publisher; ⚠ not 'librarian'.

librairie [librɛri] *s.f.* book trade; bookshop; (obs.) library.

libration [librasjɔ̃] *s.f.* (astron.) libration.

libre [libr] *adj.* free; at liberty; exempt; disengaged; unoccupied; clear; unemployed; unattached; (of schools) private, independent; (of official paper) unstamped; (of verse) irregular; frank; open; broad; ~ *à vous de*, you are quite free to; it's up to you to; you may if you like; ~ *de tout lien*, quite free, disengaged, quite at liberty; *avoir le champ* ~, to have free scope; *à l'air* ~, in the open (air); *avoir l'esprit* ~, to be free of cares; *des propos un peu* ~*s*, rather risqué remarks; ~ *arbitre*, free will; ~ *penseu-r, -se*, free thinker; free-thinking; ~ *passage*, right of way, free passage; ~**ment** [librəmɑ̃] *adv.* freely, independently; boldly, familiarly; *en user* ~*ment*, to make free use of.

libre-échange [libreʃɑ̃z] *s.m.* free trade.

libre-service [librəsɛrvis] *s.m.invar.* self-service; self-service shop, supermarket.

librettiste [libretist] *s.m.f.* librettist.

libretto [libreto] *s.m.* libretto.

Libye [libi] *s.f.* (geog.) Libya.

libyen, -ne [libjɛ̃] *adj.*, *s.m.f.* Libyan.

lice [lis] *s.f.* **1.** lists; (fig.) arena, field of action; (lit. & fig.) *entrer dans la* ~, to enter the lists; **2.** paddock, enclosure, wooden fence; **3.** (hunt.) bitch hound; **4.** (or *lisse*) (weaving) warp; ⚠ not 'lice'.

licence [lisɑ̃s] *s.f.* **1.** licence; leave, permission; liberty; (obs.) licence, licentiousness; **2.** degree, diploma, licence.

licencié, -e [lisɑ̃sje] *s.m.f.* holder of degree, diploma, licence, etc., graduate; *adj.* holding degree, etc., licensed.

licenciement [lisɑ̃simɑ̃] *s.m.* disbanding; breaking-up; dismissal.

licencier [lisɑ̃sje] *v.t.* to disband; to break up; to dismiss, to discharge.

licencieu-x, -se [lisɑ̃sjø] *adj.* licentious, dissolute, ribald.

lichen [likɛn] *s.m.* (bot.) lichen.

licher [liʃe] *v.t.* (pop.) to drink.

licier, lissier [lisje] *s.m.* warp-weaver.

licitation [lisitɑsjɔ̃] *s.f.* (law) sale by auction.

licite [lisit] *adj.* licit, lawful, allowable; ~**ment** [lisitmɑ̃] *adv.* licitly.

liciter [lisite] *v.t.* (law) to sell by auction.

licorne [likɔrn] *s.f.* unicorn; ~ *de mer*, narwhal.

licou [liku], **licol** [likɔl] *s.m.* halter.

licteur [liktœr] *s.m.* (Rom. ant.) lictor.

lido [lido] *s.m.* (geog.) lagoon.

lie [li] *s.f.* (lit. & fig.) dregs; lees; grounds; scum; *boire le calice jusqu'à la* ~, to drink the cup to the very dregs; ~ **de vin** *adj.invar.* purplish-red, wine-coloured.

liège [liɛʒ] *s.m.* cork; (bot.) *chêne-*~, cork-oak.

liégeois, -e [ljeʒwa] *adj.*, *s.m.f.* (native or inhabitant) of Liège.

lien [ljɛ̃] *s.m.* bond, tie; band, strap, cord, string; ligament, ligature; link, chain; fetter, shackle; ⚠ not 'lien'.

lier [lje] *v.t.* to bind, to tie, to tie up; to fasten; to connect, to link up; to bind down; to enter into, to engage in; (cook.) to thicken; (mus.) to slur; *ils sont très liés*, they are intimate friends, they are thick as thieves; ~ *connaissance avec*, to strike an acquaintance with; ~ *conversation*, to enter into conversation; (fig.) *avoir les mains liées*, to have one's hands tied; **se** ~ *v.refl.* (fig.) to bind oneself; to form a connection (*avec*, with); to associate oneself (*avec*, with); *se* ~ *d'amitié avec*, to become friends with.

lierre [ljɛr] *s.m.* (bot.) ivy.

liesse [ljɛs] *s.f.* merriment, rejoicing (esp. public, mass); *en* ~, in joyful or festive mood, in a state of rejoicing.

lieu (pl. **-x**) [ljø] *s.m.* place, spot, scene; ground; reason, occasion; position, place; family, extraction; source, authority; dwelling-place; stead, lieu; (pl.) (i.) premises; (ii.) privy; *au* ~ *de*, instead of; in lieu of; *au* ~ *que*, whereas; *avoir* ~, to take place, to happen; *avoir tout* ~ *de*, to have every reason to; *donner* ~ *à*, to give rise to; *tenir* ~ *de*, to take the place of, to serve as; *en haut* ~, in high quarters; *en* ~ *sûr*, in a place of safety; *en dernier* ~, lastly; *en premier* ~, in the first place; *en quelque* ~ *que*, wherever; *en tout* ~, everywhere; *mauvais* ~, house of ill fame; *n'avoir ni feu ni* ~, to be homeless; *au* ~ *et place de*, or *en son* ~ *et place*, as a substitute for; *en temps et* ~, at the right time; ~ *commun*, commonplace, platitude, trite saying; *être sur les* ~*x*, to be on the spot; *aller aux* ~*x*, to go to the W.C.

lieue [ljø] *s.f.* league; ~ *kilométrique* = 4 km (2½ miles); ~ *marine* = 5½ km (3 miles); *cela se sent à une* ~, you can smell it a mile away; *être à cent* ~*s de penser que*, to be very far from thinking that.

lieu-r, -se [ljœr] *s.m.f.* binder; trusser; ~**se** *s.f.* binder (machine).

lieutenance [ljœtnɑ̃s] *s.f.* lieutenancy.

lieutenant [ljœtnɑ̃] *s.m.* lieutenant; (fig.) lieutenant, deputy; ~*-colonel*, lieutenant-colonel; (nav.) ~ *de vaisseau*, lieutenant-commander; ~ (*d'un navire de commerce*) second mate; ~ *de port*, deputy harbour-master.

lieutenante [ljœtnɑ̃t] *s.f.* lieutenant (in women's services).

lièvre [ljɛvr] *s.m.* (zool.) hare; (lit. & fig.) *lever un* ~, to start a hare; *avoir une mémoire de* ~, to have a memory like a sieve; *courir le même* ~, to be after the same thing; *pour faire un civet, prenez un* ~, first catch your hare, then cook it; *c'est là que gît le* ~, that's the point, that's where the trouble lies; *il ne faut pas courir deux* ~*s à la fois*, you must not have too many irons in the fire.

liftier [liftje] *s.m.* lift-man, lift-boy.

ligament [ligamɑ̃] *s.m.* (anat.) ligament.

ligamenteu-x, -se [ligamɑ̃tø] *adj.* ligamental.

ligature [ligatyr] *s.f.* ligature; binding, bandage, splice; (mus.) slur, tie.

ligaturer [ligatyre] *v.t.* to ligature, to bind, to splice, to tie.

lige [liʒ] *adj.* (feudal) liege.

lignage [liɲaʒ] *s.m.* **1.** lineage; race; family, descent; **2.** (print.) linage.

lignard [liɲar] *s.m.* **1.** (obs.) soldier of the line; **2.** journalist paid by the line.

ligne [liɲ] *s.f.* line; row, rank; formation; outline; fishing-line; (naut.) twine; (geog.)

equator, line; *passer la* ~, to cross the line; (rail., bus, etc.) line, service; *grande* ~, main line; *en* ~, in a row; *en première* ~, in the forefront, of primary importance; ~ *de sonde*, lead-line; *faire entrer en* ~ *de compte*, to take into account; *hors* ~, beyond comparison; *en* ~*!*, fall in!; *aller à la* ~, to begin a new paragraph; *garder la* ~, to keep slim; *troupes de* ~, troops of the line; *vaisseaux en* ~, ships in line abreast; ~ *d'arrivée*, winning-post; (sport) ~ *de touche*, touch-line; ~ *de flottaison*, water-line; *pêcher à la* ~, to angle; *en droite* ~, straight, straight across, directly.

lignée [liɲe] *s.f.* **1.** line, race; **2.** offspring, descendants.

ligner [liɲe] *v.t.* to line, to mark lines on.

lignerolle [liɲrɔl] *s.f.* (naut.) thin twine.

ligneul [liɲœl] *s.m.* wax-thread, wax end, shoemaker's end.

ligneu-x, -se [liɲø] *adj.* (bot.) woody; ligneous.

lignicole [liɲikɔl] *adj.* (zool.) living in wood.

lignification [liɲifikɑsjɔ̃] *s.f.* (bot.) lignification.

(**se**) **lignifier** [liɲifje] *v.refl.* (bot.) to lignify.

lignine [liɲin] *s.f.* (bot.) lignin.

lignite [liɲit] *s.m.* lignite, fossil wood.

lignomètre [liɲɔmɛtr] *s.m.* (print.) line-rule, line-measurer.

ligotage [ligɔtaʒ] *s.m.* binding, tying-up.

ligoter [ligɔte] *v.t.* to bind, to tie up.

ligroïne [ligrɔin] *s.f.* (chem.) ligroin, petroleum ether.

ligue [lig] *s.f.* league; confederation; association; coalition.

liguer [lige] *v.t.* to unite; to band together; *ligué avec*, leagued with; **se** ~ *v.refl.* to form a league, to league together.

ligueu-r, -se [ligœr] *s.m.f.* member of a league; (Fr. hist.) member of the *Sainte Ligue*.

ligule [ligyl] *s.f.* (bot., ent.) ligula, ligule.

ligulé, -e [ligyle] *adj.* (bot.) ligulated.

liguliflore [ligyliflɔr] *adj.* with ligulated flowers.

Ligurie [ligyri] *s.f.* (geog.) Liguria.

ligurien, -ne [ligyrjɛ̃] *adj.*, *s.m.f.* Ligurian.

lilas [lilɑ] *s.m.* (bot.) lilac; lilac colour; ~ *adj. invar.* lilac.

liliacées [liljase] *s.f.pl.* (bot.) Liliaceae.

lilial, -e [liljal] *adj.* like a lily, lily-white.

lilliputien, -ne [lilipysjɛ̃] *adj.* Lilliputian, tiny, midget.

limace [limas] *s.f.* (zool.) slug; (fig.) snail, sluggard; (pop.) shirt.

limaçon [limasɔ̃] *s.m.* (zool.) snail; (mech.) screw; (anat.) cochlea; *escalier en* ~, spiral staircase.

limage [limaʒ] *s.m.* (techn.) filing.

limaille [limɑj] *s.f.* filings.

liman [limɑ̃] *s.m.* lagoon (near the Black Sea).

limande [limɑ̃d] *s.f.* (ichth.) dab; (naut.) parcelling; (carp.) graving-piece.

limbaire [lɛ̃bɛr] *adj.* (bot.) limbate.

limbe [lɛ̃b] *s.m.* (math.) limb, rim, edge, border; halo; (bot.) edge, limb, blade, lamina; ⚠ not 'limb' of body.

limbes [lɛ̃b] *s.m.pl.* (theol. & fig.) limbo.

lime[1] [lim] *s.f.* **1.** (techn.) file; **2.** (mollusc.) lima; ⚠ not substance 'lime'.

lime[2] [lim] *s.f.* (bot.) lime, lime-tree (citrus).

limer [lime] *v.t.* to file; (fig.) to polish, to perfect; to cause to fray.

limette [limɛt] *s.f.* (bot.) sweet lime.

limettier [limetje] *s.m.* sweet lime tree.

limeu-r, -se [limœr] *s.m.f.* filer, polisher; ~**se** *s.f.* filing-machine, shaping-machine.

limier [limje] *s.m.* bloodhound; (fig.) detective; sleuth.

liminaire [liminɛr] *adj.* preliminary; introductory; prefatory; (psychol.) liminal.

liminal, -e (**aux**) [liminal] *adj.* (psychol.) liminal.

limitati-f, -ve [limitatif] *adj.* limitative, limiting, restrictive, specifying.

limitation [limitɑsjɔ̃] *s.f.* limitation; restriction; ⚠ not 'limitation' in sense 'shortcoming'.

limite [limit] *s.f.* bound, bounds, border, boundary; extent; (pl.) limitations; *dans une certaine* ~, within certain limits, to a certain extent; *sans* ~*s*, boundless, unbridled; *angle* ~, (opt.) critical angle; (mil.) limiting angle (of fire); *cas* ~, borderline case; (math.) *valeur* ~, ultimate or limiting value; *vitesse* ~, maximum velocity.

limité, -e [limite] *adj.* limited, restricted, bounded, with limited resources.

limiter [limite] *v.t.* to limit, to restrict; to restrain; to set bounds or limits to; **se** ~ *v.refl.* to be limited (*à*, to); to limit oneself, to set oneself limits.

limitrophe [limitrɔf] *adj.* limitrophe, bordering upon; adjacent to; living on the frontier; having a common frontier.

limnée [limne] *s.f.* (mollusc.) Limnaea.

limoger [limɔʒe] *v.t.* (fam.) to relieve (a general) of his command; to remove (a high official) from his post; to retire compulsorily.

limon[1] [limɔ̃] *s.m.* mud, slime, sediment, ooze, alluvium; (fig.) clay (of which God formed man), mould, temper.

limon[2] [limɔ̃] *s.m.* lime (fruit).

limon[3] [limɔ̃] *s.m.* (techn.) **1.** shaft, thill; **2.** (constr.) notch-board (of stairs).

limonade [limɔnad] *s.f.* **1.** (obs.) lemonade, lemon squash; **2.** (fizzy) lemonade, mineral, pop; **3.** supply or service of drinks (in café).

limonadi-er, -ère [limɔnadje] *s.m.f.* **1.** manufacturer of lemonade (see LIMONADE 2); **2.** café-keeper.

limonage [limɔnaʒ] *s.m.* (agric.) mud-manuring.

limoneu-x, -se [limɔnø] *adj.* muddy, slimy; alluvial.

limonier[1] [limɔnje] *s.m.* lime-tree (citrus).

limonier[2] [limɔnje] *s.m.* shaft-horse, thiller.

limonière [limɔnjɛr] *s.f.* shafts (of carriage, etc.).

limonite [limɔnit] *s.f.* (min.) limonite.

limoselle [limɔzɛl] *s.f.* (bot.) mudwort.

Limousin [limuzɛ̃] *s.m.* (geog.) Limousin.

limousin, -e [limuzɛ̃] *adj.*, *s.m.* (native or inhabitant) of Limoges, of Limousin; ~ *s.m.* rough-waller; ~**e** *s.f.* **1.** limousine; **2.** shepherd's cloak.

limousinage [limusinaʒ] *s.m.* (build.) rough--walling, ashlar-work.

limousiner [limuzine] *v.t.* to rough-wall.

limpide [lɛ̃pid] *adj.* limpid; clear, pure; (fig.) lucid.

limpidité [lɛ̃pidite] *s.f.* limpidness; clearness; (fig.) lucidity.

limule [limyl] *s.m.* (zool.) king-crab.

lin [lɛ̃] *s.m.* (bot.) flax; (text.) linen.

linacées [linase] *s.f.pl.* (bot.) Linaceae.

linaigrette [linɛgrɛt] *s.f.* (bot.) cotton-grass.

linaire [linɛr] *s.f.* (bot.) toad-flax; flax-weed.

linceul [lɛ̃sœl] *s.m.* shroud, winding-sheet.

lincoir, linsoir [lɛ̃swar] *s.f.* (carp.) trimming--joist.

linéaire [lineɛr] *adj.* linear; long and narrow; (fig.) having length but no breadth.

linéal, -e, (**aux**) [lineal] *adj.* linear, lineal.

linéament [lineamɑ̃] *s.m.* lineament; feature; line, outline; main features.

linette [linɛt] *s.f.* flax-seed; linseed.

linge [lɛ̃ʒ] *s.m.* linen; ~ *de table*, table-linen; ~ *d'autel*, altar-cloth; ~ *de corps*, underlinen, underwear; *sac à* ~ (*sale*), linen-bag; *changer de* ~, to change one's underclothes.

lingère [lɛ̃ʒɛr] *s.f.* sewing-maid.
lingerie [lɛ̃ʒri] *s.f.* **1.** linen trade; linen manufacture; **2.** ironing-room, sewing-room; **3.** lingerie, underwear (usu. women's).
lingot [lɛ̃go] *s.m.* **1.** ingot; ~ *d'or*, gold bar or ingot; *or en* ~*s*, gold bullion; **2.** (print.) slug.
lingotière [lɛ̃gɔtjɛr] *s.f.* ingot-mould.
lingual, -e, (**aux**) [lɛ̃gwal] *adj.* lingual.
linguet [lɛ̃gɛ] *s.m.* (mech.) pawl, catch.
linguiforme [lɛ̃gɥifɔrm] *adj.* tongue-shaped; linguiform.
linguiste [lɛ̃gɥist] *s.m.f.* linguist.
linguistique [lɛ̃gɥistik] *s.f.* linguistics; philology; ~ *adj.* linguistic; **~ment** [lɛ̃gɥistikmɑ̃] *adv.* linguistically.
lini-er, -ère [linje] *adj.* linen; *industrie* ~*ère*, linen trade; **~ère** *s.f.* field of flax.
liniment [linimɑ̃] *s.m.* liniment; embrocation.
links [links] *s.m.* (golf) links.
linnéen, -ne [lineɛ̃] *adj.* (sci.) Linnaean.
linoléum [linɔleɔm] *s.m.* linoleum, oil-cloth, floor-cloth, lino.
linon [linɔ̃] *s.m.* (text.) lawn.
linotte [linɔt] *s.f.* (ornith.) linnet; (fig.) *avoir une tête de* ~ to be hare-brained or flighty.
linotype [linɔtip] *s.f.* (print.) linotype (machine).
linotypie [linɔtipi] *s.f.* linotype.
linotypiste [linɔtipist] *s.m.f.* linotype operator.
linsang [lɛ̃sɑ̃g] *s.m.* (zool.) linsang.
linsoir see LINÇOIR.
linteau (pl. **-x**) [lɛ̃to] *s.m.* lintel.
lion [ljɔ̃] *s.m.* lion; (fig.) (social) lion; lion-hearted man; (astrol.) Leo; *la part du* ~, the lion's share; (zool.) ~ *de mer*, sea-lion; (geog.) *le golfe du Lion*, the Gulf of Lions.
lionceau (pl. **-x**) [ljɔ̃so] *s.m.* lion cub.
lionne [ljɔn] *s.f.* lioness; (fig., obs.) fashionable woman.
lipase [lipɑz] *s.f.* (chem.) lipase.
lipides [lipid] *s.m.pl.* (chem.) lipoids.
lipoïde [lipɔid] *adj.* fatty, fat-like.
lipome [lipom] *s.m.* (med.) lipoma, adipoma; fatty tumour.
lipothymie [lipɔtimi] *s.f.* (med.) lipothymia.
lippe [lip] *s.f.* thick under-lip; *faire la* ~, to pout.
lippée [lipe] *s.f.* (obs.) mouthful; good meal.
lippu, -e [lipy] *adj.* thick-lipped.
liquation [likwasjɔ̃] *s.f.* (metall.) liquation.
liquéfaction [likefaksjɔ̃] *s.f.* liquefaction.
liquéfiable [likefjabl] *adj.* liquefiable.
liquéfiant, -e [likefjɑ̃] *adj.* liquefying.
liquéfier [likefje] *v.t.* to liquefy; **se** ~ *v.refl.* to liquefy; (fig.) to collapse, to be prostrated.
liquette [likɛt] *s.f.* (pop.) shirt.
liqueur [likœr] *s.f.* liquid, liquor, (chem.) solution; liqueur; (chem.) ~ *titrée*, standard solution; *vin de* ~, dessert wine.
liquidambar [likidɑ̃bar] *s.m.* (bot.) liquidambar.
liquidat-eur, -rice [likidatœr] *s.m.f.* (law) liquidator.
liquidati-f, -ve [likidatif] *adj.* of liquidation; *acte* ~*f*, winding-up order.
liquidation [likidɑsjɔ̃] *s.f.* (law) liquidation; clearance sale; settling up; winding up; (fig.) clearing up; ~ *judiciaire*, voluntary liquidation.
liquide [likid] *adj.* liquid; smooth, clear; (of money) ready, available; *argent* ~, ready money, cash; ~ *s.m.* liquid, fluid; liquor; ~ *s.f.* (phon.) liquid.
liquider [likide] *v.t.* to liquidate, to settle; to wind up; to sell off; (fig.) to liquidate, to make an end of, to wipe out.
liquidité [likidite] *s.f.* fluidity, liquidity; (fin.) liquidity, liquid assets.
liquoreu-x, -se [likɔrø] *adj.* (of wine) sweet, liqueur-like.
liquoriste [likɔrist] *s.m.* dealer in spirits; manufacturer of liqueurs.
lire [lir] *s.f.* lira.
lire [lir] *v.t.* to read, to read out, to read off; *cela se lit sur son visage*, you can see that in his face; *dans l'espoir* or *l'attente de vous* ~, hoping to hear from you; awaiting your reply.
lis, lys [lis] *s.m.* (bot.) lily; *teint de* ~, lily-white; *fleurs de* ~, (herald.) fleur-de-lis.
Lisbonne [lisbɔn] *s.f.* (geog.) Lisbon.
lisbonnin, -e [lisbɔnɛ̃] *adj.*, *s.m.f.* (native or inhabitant) of Lisbon.
lise [liz] *s.f.* quicksands.
lisérage [lizeraʒ] *s.m.* (sewing) piping, edging, cording, binding.
liséré [lizere], **liseré** [lizre] *s.m.* piping; cording; welting; binding; narrow border.
lisérer [lizere], **liserer** [lizre] *v.t.* to bind, to pipe.
liseron [lizrɔ̃] *s.m.* (bot.) bindweed, convolvulus.
liseu-r, -se [lizœr] *s.m.f.* reader, great reader.
liseuse [lizœz] *s.f.* **1.** paper-knife cum book--marker; **2.** book-cover; **3.** bed-jacket.
lisibilité [lizibilite] *s.f.* legibility.
lisible [lizibl] *adj.* legible; readable; **~ment** [lizibləmɑ̃] *adv.* legibly.
lisière [lizjɛr] *s.f.* border, selvage; (text.) list; edge (of a forest); **~s** *s.f.pl.* leading-strings; *être toujours tenu en* ~*s*, to be always tied to one's mother's apron-strings; (fig.) to be hamstrung.
lissage [lisaʒ] *s.m.* **1.** smoothing; glossing; glazing; **2.** (weaving) warping.
lisse [lis] *adj.* smooth; glossy; polished.
lisse[1] [lis] *s.f.* (naut.) **1.** ribband (of hull); **2.** (=LICE 2), rail; ~*s de couronnement*, taffrail; handrail.
lisse[2] [lis] *s.f.* warp (=LICE 4).
lisse[3] [lis] *s.f.* (techn.) smoothing-tool, smoother.
lissé, -e [lise] *adj.* smooth; glossy; polished; sleek; *amandes* ~*es*, sugared almonds; ~ *s.m.* (cook.) a certain point reached when boiling sugar.
lisser[1] [lise] *v.t.* to smooth; to glaze; to polish.
lisser[2] [lise] *v.t.* (naut.) to fit with rails.
lisseu-r, -se [lisœr] *s.m.f.* polisher; **~se**, *s.f.* polishing-machine; rolling-machine
lissier see LICIER.
lissoir [liswar] *s.m.* polishing-tool; burnisher; glazing-machine; (roadmaking) hot-rolling machine.
liste [list] *s.f.* list; roll, register, catalogue; *grossir la* ~, to swell the numbers; (admin.) ~ *civile*, civil list.
listel [listɛl] *s.m.* (pl. ~*s* or *listeaux*) listel, fillet; moulding; small rail; edge, rim, (of coin); (herald.) scroll.
lit [li] *s.m.* bed; (river-)bed; layer, stratum; (fig.) marriage; (naut.) ~ *du vent*, the wind's eye; ~ *de la marée*, tideway; ~ *d'enfant*, cot; *bois de* ~, bedstead; ~ *de fer*, iron bedstead; *descente de* ~, bedside rug; *ruelle d'un* ~, space beside a bed; ~ *à colonnes*, four-poster (bed); ~ *de douleur*, bed of sickness; *prendre le* ~, to go to bed (because sick), to take to one's bed; *sauter à bas du* ~, to jump out of bed; *chambre à deux* ~*s*, double bedroom, bedroom with twin beds; *chambre à grand lit*, bedroom with double bed; *ne faire qu'un* ~, to sleep together; *faire* ~ *à part*, not to sleep together; ~ *de parade*, bed of State; (anc. law) ~ *de justice*, bed of justice; *comme on fait son* ~ *on se couche*, as you make your bed, so you must lie on it; *enfant du premier* ~, child by the first marriage; ~ *clos*, cupboard--bed.
litanie [litani] *s.f.* (fig.) litany, rigmarole, long recital (of woes, etc.); (pl.) (eccles.) litany.
litchi [litʃi], **letchi** [lɛtʃi] *s.m.* (bot.) litchi, lychee.

liteau (pl. **-x**) [lito] *s.m.* **1.** stripe (in linen); **2.** (carp.) wooden bracket.
litée [lite] *s.f.* lair, haunt; litter.
liter [lite] *v.t.* to place in layers; to pack fish between layers of salt.
literie [litri] *s.f.* bed and bedding; bedding, bedclothes.
litham [litam] *s.m.* Turkish veil.
litharge [litarʒ] *s.f.* (chem.) litharge.
lithiase [litiɑz] *s.f.* (med.) formation of stone (in kidney, etc.).
lithine [litin] *s.f.* (chem.) oxide of lithium.
lithiné, -e [litine] *s.m., adj.* (tablet) containing oxide of lithium.
lithinifère [litinifɛr] *adj.* containing or made from lithium.
lithium [litjɔm] *s.m.* (chem.) lithium.
litho [lito] *s.f.* abbrev. *lithographie.*
litho-dome [litɔdɔm] *s.m.* (mollusc.) Saxicava; **~graphie** [litɔgrafi] *s.f.* lithography; lithograph; **~graphier** [litɔgrafje] *v.t.* to lithograph, to reproduce in lithograph; **~graphique** [litɔgrafik] *adj.* lithographic(al); **~logie** [litɔlɔʒi] *s.f.* lithology, petrography; **~logique** [litɔlɔʒik] *adj.* lithological; **~phage** [litɔfaʒ] *adj., s.m.* lithophagous, rock-boring (creature); **~phanie** [litɔfani] *s.f.* lithophane porcelain; **~phyte** [litɔfit] *s.m.* (bot.) lithophyte; **~sphère** [litɔsfɛr] *s.f.* (geol.) lithosphere; **~tomie** [litɔtɔmi] *s.f.* (surg.) lithotomy; **~tritie** [litɔtrisi] *s.f.* (surg.) lithotrity; **~typographie** [litɔtipɔgrafi] *s.f.* lithograph printing.
Lit(h)uanie [litɥani] *s.f.* (geog.) Lithuania.
lit(h)uanien, -ne [litɥanjɛ̃] *adj., s.m.f.* Lithuanian.
litière [litjɛr] *s.f.* stable-litter; litter, palanquin; (fig.) *faire ~ de qch.*, to despise, to neglect, to discard, (scruples, etc.).
litige [litiʒ] *s.m.* litigation; lawsuit; strife; *en ~*, at issue, disputed, under litigation.
litigieu-x, -se [litiʒjø] *adj.* **1.** = *en litige*; **2.** (obs.) litigious.
litispendance [litispɑ̃dɑ̃s] *s.f.* pending judgement; pendency.
litorne [litɔrn] *s.f.* (ornith.) fieldfare.
litote [litɔt] *s.f.* (rhet.) litotes.
litre [litr] *s.m.* litre.
litron [litrɔ̃] *s.m.* **1.** (obs.) ancient measure ($\frac{1}{16}$ bushel); **2.** (pop.) litre of wine.
littéraire [literɛr] *adj.* literary; *~ s.m.* literary person, expert in literature; teacher of literature; **~ment** [literɛrmɑ̃] *adv.* from a literary point of view.
littéral, -e, (aux) [literal] *adj.* **1.** literal; **2.** written; in letters (opp. figures); **~ement** [literalmɑ̃] *adv.* literally, word for word.
littérateur [literatœr] *s.m.* man of letters; one devoted to the humanities.
littérature [literatyr] *s.f.* literature; knowledge of literature.
littoral, -e, (aux) [litɔral] *adj.* littoral; coastal; *~ s.m.* coast; coastline; sea-shore; seaboard.
littorine [litɔrin] *s.f.* (zool.) Littorina.
Lituanie, lituanien see LITHUANIE, LITHUANIEN.
liturgie [lityrʒi] *s.f.* liturgy; ritual.
liturgique [lityrʒik] *adj.* liturgical.
liturgiste [lityrʒist] *s.m.* liturgist.
liure [liyr] *s.f.* roping, lashing; (naut.) gammoning, frapping.
livarde [livard] *s.f.* (naut.) sprit; *voile à ~*, sprit-sail.
livarot [livaro] *s.m.* Livarot cheese.
livèche [livɛʃ] *s.f.* (bot.) lovage.
livet [livɛ] *s.m.* (naut., constr.) bridge-line.
livide [livid] *adj.* livid; ashen, ghastly pale; ⚠ not 'livid' with anger.
lividité [lividite] *s.f.* (med.) lividness, deathly pallor.
livie [livi] *s.f.* (ent.) marsh-fly.
living(-room) [liviŋ(rum)] *s.m.* living-room.
Livourne [livurn] *s.m.* (geog.) Leghorn.
livrable [livrabl] *adj.* ready for delivery; that can be delivered.
livraison [livrɛzɔ̃] *s.f.* **1.** delivery; *voiture de ~*, delivery-van; **2.** (book) volume, part, number, issue.
livre [livr] *s.m.* book; work; register; book trade; *~ de bord* or *journal de bord*, log-book; *~ de comptes*, account-book; *grand-~*, ledger; *Grand-Livre (de la Dette Publique)*, Register of the National Debt; *~ d'heures*, prayer-book, book of hours; *~ de loch*, ship's log; log-book; *traduire à ~ ouvert*, to translate at sight; *placer sur le Grand ~*, to invest in public funds; *publier* or *faire paraître un ~*, to publish a book; *~ épuisé*, book out of print; (comm.) *tenue de(s) ~s*, book-keeping.
livre [livr] *s.f.* **1.** livre (an old Fr. money of account); **2.** (obs.) franc; *avoir cent mille ~s de rente*, to have an income of 100,000 francs; **3.** pound sterling; **4.** half a kilogram, 500 g.
livrée [livre] *s.f.* livery, uniform; (hunt.) coat, plumage; (fig.) outward signs; colours.
livrer [livre] *v.t.* to deliver; to hand over; to surrender; to give up, to betray; to abandon; to entrust, to confide; *~ bataille*, to offer or give battle; **se ~** *v.refl.* to surrender, to give oneself up; to give oneself over (*à*, to); to give way (*à*, to); to devote one's attention (*à*, to); (of struggle, etc.) to take place, to be in progress.
livresque [livrɛsk] *adj.* bookish; learnt from books.
livret [livrɛ] *s.m.* small book; booklet; libretto, book of words; catalogue; guide; handbook; bank-book; memorandum-book; record book; licence; *~ de Caisse d'Épargne*, Savings Bank depositor's book.
livreu-r, -se [livrœr] *s.m.f.* deliverer; messenger; *adj.* delivery; *garçon ~r*, delivery boy.
lixiviation [liksivjɑsjɔ̃] *s.f.* (chem.) lixiviation.
llanos [ljanos] *s.m.pl.* (geog.) llano, savannah.
Lloyd [lɔjd] *s.m.* Lloyd's underwriters.
lobe [lɔb] *s.m.* (anat., bot.) lobe; (arch.) cusp, foil.
lobé, -e [lɔbe] *adj.* lobed, lobate.
lobectomie [lɔbɛktɔmi] *s.f.* (surg.) lobectomy.
lobélie [lɔbeli] *s.f.* (bot.) lobelia.
lober [lɔbe] *v.i.* (tennis) to lob, to play a lob; *~ v.t.* (football, etc.) to lob the ball past (one's opponent).
lobotomie [lɔbɔtɔmi] *s.f.* (surg.) lobotomy.
lobulaire [lɔbylɛr] *adj.*, **lobulé, -e** [lɔbyle] lobular.
lobule [lobyl] *s.m.* lobelet, lobule.
lobuleu-x, -se [lɔbylø] *adj.* lobular.
local, -e, (aux) [lɔkal] *adj.* local; *~ s.m.* **1.** location, situation; **2.** premises, building, quarters; **~ement** [lɔkalmɑ̃] *adv.* locally, in a particular spot.
localisation [lɔkalizɑsjɔ̃] *s.f.* localization, localizing, placing (of e.g. event).
localisé, -e [lɔkalize] *adj.* localized, located; (fig.) concentrated, restricted.
localiser [lɔkalize] *v.t.* **1.** to localize, to locate, to place; **2.** to localize, to restrict, to circumscribe; **se ~** *v.refl.* to be localized or restricted.
localité [lɔkalite] *s.f.* place, spot; locality; (obs.) local circumstance or characteristic.
locataire [lɔkatɛr] *s.m.f.* tenant, lodger; lessee; householder.
locati-f, -ve [lɔkatif] *adj.* pertaining to tenancy; *valeur ~ve*, letting value, rent; *réparations ~ves*, repairs for which the tenant is liable.
locati-f, -ve [lɔkatif] *adj., s.m.* (gram.) locative (case).
location [lɔkɑsjɔ̃] *s.f.* **1.** letting, letting-out, hiring(-out), renting (to tenant); **2.** renting,

hiring; tenancy; booking, reservation (of seats, etc.); *donner en* ~, to let out; *prendre en* ~, to hire; to rent; to book (seats); *agent de* ~, house-agent; (theatr.) *bureau de* ~, box-office; ⚠ not 'location' in any sense relating to 'place'.

loch [lɔk] *s.m.* (naut.) log; *filer le* ~, to heave the log; *ligne de* ~, log-line; *table de* ~, log-board.

loche [lɔʃ] *s.f.* **1.** (ichth.) loach; **2.** (zool.) slug.

locher [lɔʃe] *v.t.* to shake (tree to make fruit fall).

lock-out [lɔkawt] *s.m.* lock-out (by employers).

locomobile [lɔkɔmɔbil] *adj.* movable, locomotive, portable; ~ *s.f.* locomotive, traction-engine, portable engine.

locomot-eur, -rice [lɔkɔmɔtœr] *adj.* locomotor.

locomoti-f, -ve [lɔkɔmɔtif] *adj.* locomotive; of locomotion; locomotory.

locomotion [lɔkɔmɔsjɔ̃] *s.f.* locomotion, moving, travelling.

locomotive [lɔkɔmɔtiv] *s.f.* locomotive (engine); (fig.) (of horse) fast runner; (fam.) *fumer comme une* ~, to smoke like a chimney.

locomotrice [lɔkɔmɔtris] *s.f.* (rail.) locomotive, engine (usu. smaller than a *locomotive*).

locotracteur [lɔkɔtraktœr] *s.m.* (rail.) light engine, shunting-engine.

loculaire [lɔkylɛr], **loculé, -e** [lɔkyle] *adj.* (zool., bot.) locular.

locuste [lɔkyst] *s.f.* (ent.) locust.

locution [lɔkysjɔ̃] *s.f.* locution, style of speech, idiom, word or phrase, expression.

loden [lɔdɛn] *s.m.* loden (waterproof and wind-proof woollen material).

lods [lo] *s.m.pl.* (obs.) only used in: *lods et ventes* (feud. law), lord's due.

lœss [løs] *s.m.* (geol.) loess.

lof [lɔf] *s.m.* (naut.) luff; windward; *virer* ~ *pour* ~, to veer, to tack; *aller au* ~, to luff; ~ *de grand'voile*, weather tack of the mainsail; *lever les* ~*s*, to raise tacks and sheets.

lofer [lɔfe] *v.i.* (naut.) to luff.

logarithme [lɔgaritm] *s.m.* (math.) logarithm, log.

logarithmique [lɔgaritmik] *adj.* logarithmic.

loge [lɔʒ] *s.f.* cell, den, hut, woodman's cabin; (pig-)sty; (theatr.) (i.) box; (ii.) dressing-room; (fig.) *être aux premières* ~*s*, to have a front-row seat, to have an excellent view; (Freemasonry) lodge; porter's room; keeper's lodge (at gates of park); ⚠ not 'lodge' in sense 'small country house'.

logeable [lɔʒabl] *adj.* fit to live in, habitable.

logement [lɔʒmɑ̃] *s.m.* **1.** lodgings, quarters, accommodation, rooms; **2.** lodging, placing, quartering; billeting; **3.** (techn.) housing, seating, recess, groove; ~ *de clef*, key-way, cotter slot, ~ *de vis*, screw-hole.

loger [lɔʒe] *v.i.* to lodge, to live, to be quartered, to put up, to stay; ~ *v.t.* to lodge, to house, to accommodate, to take in, to quarter; to place, to plant, to embed; ~ *une balle dans la cible*, to put a bullet in the target; **se** ~ *v.refl.* to lodge, to become fixed or embedded.

logeu-r, -se [lɔʒœr] *s.m.f.* lodging-house keeper, landlord, landlady.

logicien, -ne [lɔʒisjɛ̃] *s.m.f.* logician.

logique [lɔʒik] *s.f.* logic, logicality; ~ *adj.* logical; (fam.) reasonable, understandable; ~**ment** [lɔʒikmɑ̃] *adv.* logically, if considered reasonably.

logis [lɔʒi] *s.m.* home, dwelling, abode, house, lodging; (fig.) *la folle du* ~, fancy, imagination; *maréchal des* ~, sergeant; (arch.) *corps de* ~, main part of a building (opp. wings).

logistique [lɔʒistik] *s.f.* (math., mil.) logistics; ~ *adj.* logistic.

logo-graphe [lɔgɔgraf] *s.m.* (Gr. ant.) logographer; ~**griphe** [lɔgɔgrif] *s.m.* logogriph, word-puzzle; ~**machie** [lɔgɔmaʃi] *s.f.* logomachy, battle of words; verbiage.

logos [lɔgos] *s.m.* Logos; (theol.) the Word.

loi [lwa] *s.f.* law, the law, rule, statute, decree, act, enactment; sway; command; *avoir force de* ~, to be law; to have the force of law; *faire* ~, to be law; *faire des* ~*s*, to make, or enact, laws; *faire la* ~ *à qn.*, to dictate to s.o., to lay down the law to s.o., to browbeat s.o.; *selon les* ~*s*, in accordance with law, legal(ly); *tomber sous le coup de la* ~, to come under the law; *homme de* ~, lawyer, law-officer; *hors la* ~, outlawed, outlaw; *mettre hors la* ~, to outlaw; *se faire une* ~ *de*, to make a point or rule of; *les* ~*s du mouvement*, the laws of motion; *les* ~*s de la grammaire*, the rules of grammar; *nécessité n'a pas de* ~, necessity knows no law; *n'avoir ni foi ni* ~, to be without honour or honesty; *projet de* ~, (parliament) bill, draft bill.

loi-cadre [lwakɑdr] *s.f.* outline law (to be completed by decrees).

loin [lwɛ̃] *adv.* far, far off, away, a long way off; *au* ~, far away, in the distance; *bien* ~, very far, a long way off; *bien* ~ *de me plaindre, je veux* ..., far be it from me to complain, but I intend ...; *de* ~, from afar; from a distance; *être parent de* ~, to be a distant relation; *il y a* ~ *de*, it is a long way to; (fig.) it is a far cry from; (fig.) *je vous vois venir de* ~, I can see what you are aiming at; *il revient de* ~, he has had a narrow escape; he has come back from death's door; *a beau mentir qui vient de* ~, travellers tell fine tales; *de* ~ *en* ~, at long intervals; ~ *de là*, on the contrary, quite the opposite; *vous êtes* ~ *de compte!*, you are out in your reckoning; ~ *des yeux*, ~ *du cœur*, out of sight, out of mind; *du plus* ~, or *d'aussi* ~, *que je me souvienne*, as far back as I can remember; *voir* ~, to be far-sighted; *aller* ~, to go far; (fig.) *vous allez trop* ~*!*, this is beyond a joke; you are going too far!, you exaggerate, you are laying it on a bit thick; *plus* ~, further on, later, below (in text); *aller plus* ~, (lit. & fig.) to go further; *j'irai plus* ~, I would even say; *ce garçon ira* ~, this young man has a future before him, or will go far; ~ *de moi une pareille pensée!*, far be it from me to have such a thought!; *cela remonte* ~, that's long past; that dates far back; that can be traced far back; that began long ago.

lointain, -e [lwɛ̃tɛ̃] *adj.* remote, distant, far off; ~ *s.m.* distance; background; *dans le* ~, in the distance, far off.

loir [lwar] *s.m.* (zool.) dormouse; *dormir comme un* ~, to sleep like a log.

loisible [lwazibl] *adj.* permissible, licit, allowable; *il vous est* ~ *de partir quand vous voudrez*, you have a perfect right to leave when you choose.

loisir [lwazir] *s.m.* leisure, freedom, time (to do sth.); (pl.) leisure, spare time; leisure occupation; *à* ~, at leisure, at (one's) convenience; to one's heart's content; free, unoccupied.

lolo [lolo] *s.m.* (child. lang.) milk.

lombago [lɔ̃bago] *s.m.* = LUMBAGO.

lombaire [lɔ̃bɛr] *adj.* (anat.) lumbar, of the loins.

lombard, -e [lɔ̃bar] *adj.*, *s.m.f.* Lombard.

Lombardie [lɔmbardi] *s.f.* (geog.) Lombardy.

lombes [lɔ̃b] *s.m.pl.* (anat.) loins.

lombric [lɔ̃brik] *s.m.* (zool.) earthworm.

londonien, -ne [lɔ̃dɔnjɛ̃] *adj.* of London; *s.m.f.* Londoner.

Londres [lɔ̃dr] *s.f.* (geog.) London.

londrès [lɔ̃drɛs] *s.m.* Havana cigar (originally made for Londoners).

long, -ue [lɔ̃] *adj.* long, lengthy; ~ *s.m.* length; *le* ~ *de*, along; *tout le* ~ *du jour*, the whole day long; *au* ~ *de*, alongside of; in the course of, during; *tout au* ~, all along; at length; in full; *à la* ~*ue*, in the long run; after a time; *trois mètres* *de* ~, three metres long; *de* ~ *en large*, to and fro; up and down; *de* ~*ue main*, a long time in advance; slowly and carefully prepared; of long standing; ~ *travail*, slow work; *être* ~ *à faire*, to be a long time, to be slow, doing; *étendu tout de son* ~ or *de tout son* ~, lying at full length; *avoir la vue* ~*ue*, to be far-sighted; *avoir la mine* ~*ue*, to look gloomy, to pull a long face; *sauce trop* ~*ue*, too thin or watery sauce; *en* ~, lengthwise; *scier en* ~, to saw along the grain, to rip; *tirer de* ~, to protract, to spin out; *vous avez eu la langue trop* ~*ue*, you have been talking too much; your tongue has been running too fast; you said too much; *il a le bras* ~, he has a long arm, is very influential, can make his power felt; *capitaine au* ~ *cours*, ocean- or sea-going captain; *de* ~*s mois*, many months; ~ *adv.* much; *cela en dit* ~, that is very significant, it speaks volumes; *en savoir* ~, to know all about it; *vouloir en apprendre plus* ~, to want to hear more about it; *habillée* ~, wearing a long dress.

longanimité [lɔ̃ganimite] *s.f.* patience, forbearance, long-suffering.

long-courrier [lɔ̃kurje] *adj.m.* ocean-going, long-distance, long-haul; *s.m.* ocean-going ship; long-distance or intercontinental aircraft.

longe[1] [lɔ̃ʒ] *s.f.* tether, thong, leading-rein.

longe[2] [lɔ̃ʒ] *s.f.* loin (of veal or venison).

longer [lɔ̃ʒe] *v.t.* to go or lie along; to skirt.

longeron [lɔ̃ʒrɔ̃] *s.m.* longitudinal bearer, stringer; side-member; sole-bar, longeron.

longévité [lɔ̃ʒevite] *s.f.* longevity.

longicorne [lɔ̃ʒikɔrn] *adj.* (zool.) longicorn, longhorn beetle.

longitude [lɔ̃ʒityd] *s.f.* longitude; *Bureau des Longitudes*, Central Astronomical Office.

longitudinal, -e, (**aux**) [lɔ̃ʒitydinal] *adj.* longitudinal; ~**ement** [lɔ̃ʒitydinalmɑ̃] *adv.* longitudinally, lengthwise.

long-jointé, -e [lɔ̃ʒwɛ̃te] *adj.* long in the pastern, long-legged.

longrine [lɔ̃grin] *s.f.* railway sleeper.

longtemps [lɔ̃tɑ̃] *adv.* long, (for) a long time, a long while; *depuis* ~, long ago, long since; for a long time past; *c'est fini depuis* ~, it has been finished a long time; *il a mis* ~ *à trouver*, he was a long time finding out; *avant* ~, before long; *aussi* ~ *que*, as long as; *je n'attendrai pas plus* ~, I shall not wait any longer.

longue [lɔ̃g] *adj.* see LONG; ~ *s.f.* long syllable; (mus.) long note; *à la* ~, in the long run.

longuement [lɔ̃gmɑ̃] *adv.* long, at length, lengthily; *plus* ~, at greater length, more fully; *moins* ~, more briefly.

longuet, -te [lɔ̃gɛ] *adj.* rather too long, longish; ~ *s.m.* bread-stick.

longueur [lɔ̃gœr] *s.f.* length; duration; slowness; prolixity; lengthy (and boring) passage; *en* ~, lengthwise; *traîner en* ~, to drag on; *tirer en* ~, to drag out, to protract; *gagner par trois* ~*s*, to win by three lengths; *de six mètres de* ~, or *d'une* ~ *de six m.*, six metres in length, or six m. long; *à* ~ *de*, during the whole of, throughout.

longue-vue [lɔ̃gvy] *s.f.* telescope; spyglass.

looch [lɔk] *s.m.* (pharm.) emollient, soothing syrup.

looping [lupiŋ] *s.m.* (aeron.) looping (the loop).

lopin [lɔpɛ̃] *s.m.* bit, portion, patch (usually of ground), small field; ~ *de terre*, patch of ground.

loquace [lɔkas] *adj.* loquacious, talkative.

loquacité [lɔkasite] *s.f.* loquacity, loquaciousness, talkativeness.

loque [lɔk] *s.f.* rag; (fig.) (of person) derelict, wreck; *en* ~*s*, in rags, tattered.

loquet [lɔkɛ] *s.m.* latch; ⚠ not 'locket'.

loqueteau (pl. **-x**) [lɔkto] *s.m.* small latch, catch.

loqueteu-x, -se [lɔktø] *adj.* ragged, in rags, tattered.

loran [lɔrɑ̃] *s.m.* (techn.) loran (navigation system).

lord [lɔr] *s.m.* lord.

lord-maire [lɔr(d)mɛr] *s.m.* Lord Mayor.

lordose [lɔrdoz] *s.f.* (pathol.) lordosis.

lorette [lɔrɛt] *s.f.* (obs.) woman of easy virtue.

lorgner [lɔrɲe] *v.t.* to stare at, to spy on, to scrutinize (esp. through opera-glasses, etc.); to make eyes at; (fig.) to have one's eyes on, to covet.

lorgnette [lɔrɲɛt] *s.f.* opera-glasses; field-glasses; ⚠ not 'lorgnette'.

lorgnon [lɔrɲɔ̃] *s.m.* eye-glasses (without side-pieces), pince-nez, lorgnette.

lori [lɔri] *s.m.* (ornith.) lory.

loriot [lɔrjo] *s.m.* (ornith.) oriole.

loris [lɔris] *s.m.* (zool.) loris.

lorrain, -e [lɔrɛ̃] *adj.*, *s.m.f.* (native or inhabitant) of Lorraine.

Lorraine [lɔrɛn] *s.f.* (geog.) Lorraine.

lorry [lɔri] *s.m.* (rail.) platelayers' trolley.

lors [lɔr] *adv.* then; *dès* ~, thenceforth, from that time; *depuis* ~, since then, thenceforth; ~ *même que*, even though; ~ *de*, at the time of; *pour* ~, in that case, then, so.

lorsque [lɔrsk(ə)] *conj.* (*lors* and *que* may be separated) when, at the time or moment when; ~ *vous viendrez*, when you come; *lors donc qu'il arriva*, so, when he arrived.

losange [lɔzɑ̃ʒ] *s.m.* lozenge, rhomb, diamond figure; *en* ~, diamond-shaped, lozenge-shaped; ⚠ not pharm. 'lozenge'.

losangé, -e [lɔzɑ̃ʒe] *adj.* with diamond pattern, with lozenge motif; (herald.) lozengy.

lot [lo] *s.m.* lot, portion, batch; share; fate; prize; *gagner le gros* ~, to win the big prize (in a lottery); (fig.) to carry the day, to be very lucky or successful; *tirage à* ~*s*, draw (for prize, or of numbers of shares to be redeemed); *le* ~ *qui lui est échu*, the portion that has fallen to his share; *le* ~ *commun*, the common fate, the human lot; ⚠ not 'lot' in sense 'large quantity', or as in 'drawing lots'.

loterie [lɔtri] *s.f.* lottery, raffle, draw.

loti, -e [lɔti] *adj.* provided for, favoured; *bien* ~, favoured, well provided for; *mal* ~, not favoured, in an unhappy situation.

lotier [lɔtje] *s.m.* (bot.) bird's-foot trefoil; melilot.

lotion [losjɔ̃] *s.f.* **1.** (obs.) washing, bathing; **2.** lotion.

lotionner [losjɔne] *v.t.* to wash, to bathe; to apply lotion to.

lotir [lɔtir] *v.t.* **1.** to divide into lots, to divide up, to parcel out; to sell in lots, *terrains à* ~, land for sale in lots; **2.** to allot, to allocate, to provide with; *être loti d'une maison*, to be provided with a house, to have a house allocated to one.

lotissement [lɔtismɑ̃] *s.m.* **1.** allotting, allotment, apportioning; **2.** plot, the ground allotted, lot.

loto [lɔto] *s.m.* lotto, bingo; *avoir des yeux en boules de* ~, to be goggle-eyed.

lotte [lɔt] *s.f.* (ichth.) **1.** (freshwater fish) burbot, eel-pout; **2.** (sea fish) conger (eel).

lotus [lɔtys] *s.m.* (bot.) lotus.

louable[1] [lwabl] *adj.* praiseworthy, commendable, laudable.

louable[2] [lwabl] *adj.* lettable; *appartement difficilement* ~, flat not easy to let.

louage [lwaʒ] *s.m.* **1.** (obs.) letting; taking on lease; rent; **2.** renting, hiring, chartering.

louange [lwɑ̃ʒ] *s.f.* praise, commendation; compliment, eulogy; flattery, adulation; honour, glory; *c'est à sa* ~, it is to his credit; *à la* ~ *de*, in praise of, to the glory of, in honour of.

louanger [lwɑ̃ʒe] *v.t.* (Lit.) to extol, to sing the praises of, to overwhelm with compliments.

louangeu-r, -se [lwɑ̃ʒœr] *adj.* laudatory, eulogistic; *s.m.f.* flatterer.
louche [luʃ] *adj.* **1.** (obs.) squinting, squint-eyed; **2.** murky, cloudy; (fig.) dubious, equivocal, suspicious, shady, fishy, cock-eyed.
louche [luʃ] *s.f.* soup-ladle; (techn.) reamer, countersink bit.
loucher [luʃe] *v.i.* to squint; (fig.) ~ *sur*, to covet, to have an eye on; *faire ~ qn. de jalousie*, to make s.o. green with envy.
loucherie [luʃri] *s.f.* strabismus, squint.
louchet [luʃɛ] *s.m.* spade.
loucheu-r, -se [luʃœr] *s.m.f.* squinter, squint-eyed person.
louer[1] [lwe] *v.t.* to praise, to laud, to bestow praise on, to commend; to extol, to eulogize; *se ~ de*, to congratulate oneself on; to be fortunate in, to be completely satisfied with.
louer[2] [lwe] *v.t.* **1.** to let out, to let, to hire out; to let on lease; **2.** to rent, to hire, to reserve, to book, (seat, etc.).
loueu-r, -se [lwœr] *s.m.f.* hirer, renter (out), letter.
loufiat [lufja] *s.m.* (pop.) waiter.
loufoque [lufɔk] *adj.* (pop.) mad, crazy.
loufoquerie [lufɔkri] *s.f.* craziness; act of lunacy.
lougre [lugr] *s.m.* (naut.) lugger.
louis [lwi] *s.m.* (hist.) louis (gold coin); (mod.) 20 francs.
louise-bonne [lwizbɔn] *s.f.* Louise-bonne pear.
loulou [lulu] *s.m.* **1.** Pomeranian (dog); **2.** (fam.) term of endearment.
loup [lu] *s.m.*, **1.** wolf (fem. *louve*, see LOUVE 1); (techn.) defect, misfit, flaw, error, gap; *aller à pas de ~*, to walk or tread stealthily; *avoir une faim de ~*, to be ravenously hungry; *il fait un froid de ~*, it is bitterly cold; *avoir vu le ~*, to know a thing or two, to have lost one's virginity; *connu comme le ~ blanc*, well known to everybody; *vieux ~ de mer*, old salt; old sea-dog; *enfermer le ~ dans la bergerie*, to shut up the wolf in the sheep-fold; to set the fox to keep the geese; *tenir le ~ par les oreilles*, to have the wolf by the ears, to be in a fix; *il faut hurler avec les ~s*, when we are in Rome, we must do as Rome does; *les ~s ne se mangent pas entre eux*, there is honour among thieves; dog doesn't eat dog; *se jeter dans la gueule du ~*, to rush into the lion's mouth; *quand on parle du ~ on en voit la queue*, talk of the Devil and he is sure to appear; *entre chien et ~*, at dusk; in the twilight; *tête de ~*, Turk's head (long-handled feather duster); *saut de ~*, sunk fence, ha-ha; *mon ~*, term of affection; *crier au ~*, to cry wolf; **2.** velvet mask; **3.** (ichth.) sea-perch, sea-dace.
loup-cervier [luservje] *s.m.* (zool.) lynx.
loupe [lup] *s.f.* **1.** magnifying glass, lens; *vu à la ~*, magnified; *regarder à la ~*, to scrutinize closely; **2.** (pathol.) wen, tumour; excrescence, nodosity, gnarl, (on wood).
louper [lupe] *v.t.* (fam.) **1.** to bungle, to make a mess of, to do badly; (theatr.) to fluff (part), to miss (cue); **2.** to miss (train, opportunity, etc.).
loup-garou [lugaru] *s.m.* werewolf; (fig.) surly fellow, recluse.
loupiot, -te [lupjo] *s.m.f.* (fam.) child.
loupiote [lupjɔt] *s.f.* (fam.) small lamp, light.
lourd, -e [lur] *adj.* heavy, weighty, loaded (*de*, with); (fig.) dull, thick, clumsy, gross, oppressive, close; drowsy; *peser ~*, to be or weigh heavy, to lie heavy; to be of great importance; *avoir l'esprit ~*, to be slow-witted, not to be very bright; *avoir la main ~e*, to be heavy-handed; *le temps est ~*, the weather is sultry; *avoir la tête ~e*, to feel heavy, drowsy, to have a headache; *une ~e faute*, a grave mistake; (fam.) *il n'en sait pas ~*, he doesn't know much about it; **~ement** [lurdəmɑ̃] *adv.* heavily; clumsily, awkwardly.
lourdaud, -e [lurdo] *adj.*, *s.m.f.* heavy, clumsy, awkward (person).
lourde [lurd] *s.f.* (pop.) door.
lourdeur [lurdœr] *s.f.* heaviness; dullness, tediousness; clumsiness.
loure [lur] *s.f.* (mus.) **1.** loure, kind of bagpipe; **2.** a dance played on the loure.
lourer [lure] *v.t.* (mus.) to play (tied notes) with slight accent on each.
loustic [lustik] *s.m.* licensed jester, facetious person, wag, wit, joker; (fam., pej.) fellow, chap.
loutre [lutr] *s.f.* (zool.) otter; otter-fur, otter-skin.
louve [luv] *s.f.* **1.** she-wolf; **2.** (techn.) clips; lewis; sling; claw; (hoisting) scissors; **3.** (fish.) hoop-net.
louvet, -te [luvɛ] *adj.* (of horses) wolf-coloured.
louveteau (pl. **-x**) [luvto] *s.m.* wolf-cub.
louveter [luvte] *v.i.* (of she-wolves) to whelp.
louveterie [luvtri, luvɛtri] *s.f.* wolf-hunting.
louvetier [luvtje] *s.m.* master of the wolf-hounds.
louvoiement [luvwamɑ̃] *s.m.* (naut.) tacking; (fig.) manœuvre.
louvoyer [luvwaje] *v.i.* **1.** (naut.) to tack, to tack about; *~ au plus près*, to beat to windward; **2.** (fig.) to manœuvre, to scheme.
lovelace [lɔvlas] *s.m.* (Lit.) seducer.
lover [lɔve] *v.t.* (naut.) to coil (rope); **se ~** *v.refl.* (of snake, etc.) to coil up, to coil itself.
loxodrom-ie [lɔksɔdrɔmi] *s.f.* (naut.) loxodromic curve, rhumb-line; loxodromics; **~ique** [lɔksɔdrɔmik] *adj.* (naut.) loxodromic.
loyal, -e, (aux) [lwajal] *adj.* **1.** honest, fair, straightforward; sincere, genuine, accurate; *jeu ~*, fair play; (comm.) *qualité ~e*, genuine quality; *bon et ~ inventaire*, true and accurate inventory; **2.** loyal, trustworthy; **~ement** [lwajalmɑ̃] *adv.* **1.** honestly, fairly, sincerely; **2.** loyally.
loyalisme [lwajalism] *s.m.* loyalism; (fig.) devotion, loyalty.
loyaliste [lwajalist] *adj.*, *s.m.f.* loyalist.
loyauté [lwajote] *s.f.* honesty, fairness, sincerity, genuineness; (esp. conjugal) fidelity; ⚠ not usu. 'loyalty' to a cause, a leader, etc.; see LOYALISME.
loyer [lwaje] *s.m.* rent, hire, wages; (fig.) reward; *donner à ~*, to let; (law) *le ~ de l'argent*, the rate of interest.
lubie [lybi] *s.f.* whim, fad, fancy; *il lui prend des ~s*, he gets ideas into his head.
lubricité [lybrisite] *s.f.* lubricity, lewdness.
lubrifiant, -e [lybrifjɑ̃] *adj.* lubricant, lubricating; *~ s.m.* lubricant.
lubrifi-cation [lybrifikɑsjɔ̃] *s.f.* lubrication; **~er** [lybrifje] *v.t.* to lubricate.
lubrique [lybrik] *adj.* lubricious, lewd, lecherous.
lucane [lykan] *s.m.* (ent.) stag-beetle.
lucarne [lykarn] *s.f.* skylight; dormer-window; garret-window; small window or peep-hole (in door).
lucide [lysid] *adj.* lucid, clear, clear-sighted, perspicacious; sane; **~ment** [lysidmɑ̃] *adv.* lucidly, clearly; ⚠ not 'lucid' in senses 'transparent', 'brilliant'.
lucidité [lysidite] *s.f.* lucidity; sanity, period of lucidity.
luciole [lysjɔl] *s.f.* (ent.) firefly.
lucrati-f, -ve [lykratif] *adj.* lucrative, profitable; **~vement** [lykrativmɑ̃] *adv.* lucratively, profitably.
lucre [lykr] *s.m.* **1.** (obs.) profit, gain; **2.** (pej.) lucre.
ludion [lydjɔ̃] *s.m.* ludion, Cartesian diver (toy).
luette [lɥɛt] *s.f.* (anat.) uvula.

lueur [lɥœr] *s.f.* glimmer, gleam, glint, faint light; (fig.) gleam, ray.
luge [lyʒ] *s.f.* luge, toboggan.
luger [lyʒe] *v.i.* to luge, to toboggan.
lugeu-r, -se [lyʒœr] *s.m.f.* tobogganer.
lugubre [lygybr] *adj.* lugubrious, dismal, gloomy; ominous; **~ment** [lygybrəmɑ̃] *adv.* gloomily.
lui [lɥi] *pers. pron.* him, her, it; to or at him, her, it; he, it; *je ~ ai dit,* I said to him, I told him; *c'est ~,* it's he; *je suis plus vieux que ~,* I am older than he; *sans ~,* without him.
luire [lɥir] *v.i.* to shine, to gleam, to glitter, to glisten; to dawn, to appear.
luisant, -e [lɥizɑ̃] *adj.* shining; shiny, glossy, bright; *ver ~,* glow-worm; *~ s.m.* shine, sheen.
lumachelle [lymaʃɛl] *s.f.* shell-marble.
lumbago [lɔ̃bago] *s.m.* lumbago.
lumen [lymɛn] *s.m.* lumen, unit of light.
lumière [lymjɛr] *s.f.* **1.** light; daylight, day; luminary, lamp, candle; (fig.) enlightenment, knowledge, intelligence, intellect; civilization; (paint.) light; *couper la ~,* to turn out the lights, to black out; *à la ~,* by artificial light; *voir la ~* or *le jour,* to be born; *mettre en ~,* to bring to light, to elucidate, to throw light on; to stress; *avoir des ~s sur,* to have information about; **2.** opening, hole, orifice; (techn.) port (of valve).
lumignon [lymiɲɔ̃] *s.m.* snuff (of candle), candle-end, guttering candle; lamp giving faint light.
luminaire [lyminɛr] *s.m.* lights, lighting, lighting arrangements.
luminescence [luminesɑ̃s] *s.f.* (phys.) luminescence.
luminescent, -e [lyminesɑ̃] *adj.* luminescent.
lumineu-x, -se [lyminø] *adj.* luminous, bright, shining; (fig.) clear; (fam.) *idée ~se,* brilliant idea; **~sement** [lyminøzmɑ̃] *adv.* brightly, with complete clarity.
luminosité [lyminozite] *s.f.* luminosity, brilliance.
lunaire [lynɛr] *adj.* lunar, moonlike; (fig.) fanciful.
lunaire [lynɛr] *s.f.* (bot.) lunary, moonwort.
lunaison [lynɛzɔ̃] *s.f.* lunation; lunar month.
lunatique [lynatik] *adj., s.m.f.* whimsical, capricious, eccentric person; ⚠ usu. 'lunatic' only in sense 'affected by the phases of the moon'.
lunch [lœntʃ, lœ̃ʃ] *s.m.* light lunch, buffet or fork lunch; *~ de mariage,* wedding breakfast.
lundi [lœ̃di] *s.m.* Monday.
lune [lyn] *s.f.* moon; satellite (of planet); (fig.) the impossible; *pleine ~,* full moon; *nouvelle ~,* new moon; (fig.) *vieilles ~s,* old days, times past; *~ rousse,* April moon, time of late frosts; *~ de miel,* honeymoon; *clair de ~,* moonlight, moonshine; *visage en pleine ~,* moon face; (fig.) *être dans la ~,* to be absent-minded or a day-dreamer; *faire un trou à la ~,* to shoot the moon, to run from one's creditors; *demander la ~,* to demand the impossible; to cry for the moon; *avoir des ~s,* to have whims; (bot.) *~ d'eau,* white water-lily.
luné, -e [lyne] *adj. bien ~,* in a good temper, well-disposed; *mal ~,* in a bad temper.
luneti-er, -ère [lyntje] *s.m.f.,* **lunettier** [lynetje] *s.m.* spectacle-maker or seller, optician.
lunette [lynɛt] *s.f.* **1.** telescope, spyglass; *~ d'approche,* telescope; **2.** (pl.) glasses, spectacles, goggles; **3.** (arch.) lunette; (car) rear window; **4.** lavatory pan, lavatory seat; **5.** aperture of guillotine; **6.** rim of watch (holding glass).
lunetté, -e [lynete] *adj.* wearing spectacles; *~ d'écailles,* with tortoise-shell spectacles.
lunetterie [lynɛtri] *s.f.* spectacle trade, spectacle-making.
lunettier see LUNETIER.
lunisolaire [lynisɔlɛr] *adj.* lunisolar.
lunule [lynyl] *s.f.* lunula; (geom.) lune, crescent-shaped figure; (liturg.) lunette.
lupanar [lypanar] *s.m.* (Lit.) brothel.
lupercales [lypɛrkal] *s.f.pl.* (Rom. ant.) Lupercalia.
lupin [lypɛ̃] *s.m.* (bot.) lupin.
lupinelle [lypinɛl] *s.f.* (bot.) sainfoin, trefoil.
lupulin [lypylɛ̃] *s.m.* (brewing) lupulin.
lupuline [lypylin] *s.f.* (bot.) hop-trefoil.
lupus [lypys] *s.m.* (pathol.) lupus.
lurette [lyrɛt] *s.f.* (fam.) only used in: *il y a belle ~ que,* it's a long time since.
luron, -ne [lyrɔ̃] *s.m.f.* strapping man or girl; *~ s.m.* stout lad; *joyeux ~,* gay dog.
lusin, luzin [lyzɛ̃] *s.m.* (naut.) marline.
Lusitanie [lyzitani] *s.f.* (anc. geog.) Lusitania.
lusitanien, -ne [lyzitanjɛ̃], **lusitain, -e** [lyzitɛ̃] *adj., s.m.f.* (anc. geog.) Lusitanian.
lustrage [lystraʒ] *s.m.* (text.) glossing.
lustral, -e, (aux) [lystral] *adj.* lustral.
lustration [lystrɑsjɔ̃] *s.f.* lustration; (liturg.) aspersion.
lustre[1] [lystr] *s.m.* **1.** gloss, lustre, brilliance; (fig.) glamour; **2.** chandelier, lustre, hanging lamp, lamp fitment.
lustre[2] [lystr] *s.m.* lustrum, period of five years.
lustrer [lystre] *v.t.* to gloss, to glaze, to give a gloss to, to make shiny.
lustrerie [lystrəri] *s.f.* manufacture or selling of lamp fitments, chandeliers, etc.
lustrine [lystrin] *s.f.* (text.) lustre; lustrine.
lut [lyt] *s.m.* (chem.) lute, luting.
lutéine [lytein] *s.f.* (biol.) lutein.
luter [lyte] *v.t.* (techn.) to lute.
luth [lyt] *s.m.* (mus.) lute.
luthéranisme [lyteranism] *s.m.* Lutheranism.
lutherie [lytri] *s.f.* making or selling of stringed instruments.
luthérien, -ne [lyterjɛ̃] *adj., s.m.f.* Lutheran.
luthier [lytje] *s.m.* maker of violins (and other stringed instruments).
lutin [lytɛ̃] *s.m.* elf, goblin, sprite, leprechaun; (of child) imp.
lutin, -e [lytɛ̃] *adj.* lively, sharp, sly.
lutiner [lytine] *v.t.* to tease; to be over-familiar with, to get fresh with.
lutrin [lytrɛ̃] *s.m.* lectern; choir singing-desk.
lutte [lyt] *s.f.* wrestling; struggle, contest, strife, conflict; battle; *de haute ~,* by sheer force; with all the authority at one's command.
lutter [lyte] *v.i.* to wrestle; to grapple (*avec,* with), to struggle, to battle (*contre,* against), to fight; to strive; to contend, to compete.
lutteu-r, -se [lytœr] *s.m.f.* wrestler; (fig.) fighter; determined upholder (of cause, etc.).
lux [lyks] *s.m.* (phys.) lux, unit of light.
luxation [lyksɑsjɔ̃] *s.f.* luxation, dislocation.
luxe [lyks] *s.m.* **1.** luxury; richness, sumptuousness, magnificence; *vivre dans le ~,* to live in luxury; *s'offrir un ~,* to allow oneself a luxury; *de ~,* luxury, de luxe, richly furnished, equipped, etc., lavishly got up; *édition de ~,* library edition; (fam.) *poule de ~,* high-class prostitute; **2.** luxuriance, profusion, abundance.
Luxembourg [lyksɑ̃bur] *s.m.* **1.** (geog.) Luxemburg; Luxembourg; **2.** *le* (*Palais du*) *~,* the Luxembourg (in Paris).
luxembourgeois, -e [lyksɑ̃burʒwa] *adj., s.m.f.* (native or inhabitant) of Luxemburg; Luxemburger.
luxer [lykse] *v.t.* to luxate, to dislocate.
luxueu-x, -se [lyksɥø] *adj.* luxurious, sumptuous, magnificent, costly, rich; **~sement** [lyksɥøzmɑ̃] *adv.* luxuriously, sumptuously.
luxure [lyksyr] *s.f.* lust, lewdness; debauchery; ⚠ not 'luxury'.

luxuriance [lyksyrjɑ̃s] *s.f.* luxuriance, exuberance, profusion.
luxuriant, -e [lyksyrjɑ̃] *adj.* luxuriant, exuberant, abundant.
luxurieu-x, -se [lyksyrjø] *adj.* lustful, lewd; ⚠ see LUXURE.
luzerne [lyzɛrn] *s.f.* (bot.) lucern, lucerne.
luzernière [lyzɛrnjɛr] *s.f.* field of lucerne.
luzule [lyzyl] *s.f.* (bot.) wood rush, Luzula.
lycanthrope [likɑ̃trɔp] *s.m.* lycanthrope.
lycanthropie [likɑ̃trɔpi] *s.f.* lycanthropy.
lycée [lise] *s.m.* State secondary school in France; (period of) secondary education.
lycéen, -ne [liseɛ̃] *s.m.f.* pupil at a *lycée*.
lychnis [liknis] *s.m.* (bot.) lychnis, campion, ragged robin.
lycopode [likɔpɔd] *s.m.* (bot.) lycopod, lycopodium.
lyddite [lidit] *s.f.* (chem.) lyddite.
lydien, -ne [lidjɛ̃] *adj., s.m.f.* Lydian.
lymphatique [lɛ̃fatik] *adj.* lymphatic.
lymphatisme [lɛ̃fatism] *s.m.* lymphatism.
lymphe [lɛ̃f] *s.f.* lymph.
lymphocyte [lɛ̃fɔsit] *s.m.* (biol.) lymphocyte.
lymphoïde [lɛ̃fɔid] *adj.* (biol.) lymphoid.
lynchage [lɛ̃ʃaʒ] *s.m.* lynching.
lyncher [lɛ̃ʃe] *v.t.* to lynch.
lynx [lɛ̃ks] *s.m.* (zool.) lynx; (fig.) *il a des yeux de ~*, he is lynx-eyed, or sharp-sighted.
Lyon [ljɔ̃] *s.m.* (geog.) Lyons.
lyonnais, -e [ljɔnɛ] *adj., s.m.f.* (native or inhabitant) of Lyons.
lyre [lir] *s.f.* lyre; (fig.) poetic talent, poetry; (astron.) Lyra; (fam.) *toute la ~*, the whole range, the whole lot; (*oiseau-*)~, lyre-bird.
lyrique [lirik] *adj.* **1.** lyric, lyrical; (fig.) lyrical, enthusiastic; **2.** set to music, sung; *drame ~*, opera, etc.; *comédie ~*, comic opera, operetta; **~ment** [lirikmɑ̃] *adv.* lyrically.
lyrisme [lirism] *s.m.* lyricism; (fig.) poetic enthusiasm.
lys see LIS.
lysimaque [lizimak] *s.f.* (bot.) yellow loose-strife, Lysimachia.
lysine [lizin] *s.f.* (chem.) lysin.

M

M, m [ɛm] *s.m.* the letter M, m; *M.*, *MM.*, abbrev. *Monsieur*, *messieurs*; *m.*, abbrev. *mètre*, *million*, *milli-*, (chem.) *méta-*.
m' see ME.
ma see MON.
maboul, -e [mabul] *adj.* (pop.) mad.
macabre [makabr] *adj.* macabre; gruesome, deathly, ghastly; *danse ~*, dance of death.
macache [makaʃ] *adv.* (pop.) not at all, nothing at all, nothing doing; *~ les permissions!*, not a hope of any leave!
macadam [makadam] *s.m.* macadam, macadamized road; **~isage** [makadamizaʒ] *s.m.* macadamization, macadamizing; **~iser** [makadamize] *v.t.* to macadamize.
macaque [makak] *s.m.* (zool.) macaque; (fig.) ugly old man.
macareux [makarø] *s.m.* (ornith.) puffin, Labrador auk.
macaron [makarɔ̃] *s.m.* **1.** macaroon; (fam.) rosette; round decorative motif; **2.** coil of hair over ears.
macaroni [makarɔni] *s.m.* macaroni; (pop., pej.) (*un*) *Macaroni*, (an) Italian.
macaronique [makarɔnik] *adj.* macaronic.
macassar [makasar] *s.m.* **1.** Macassar oil; **2.** Macassar wood (a kind of ebony).
macchabée [makabe], **macchab** [makab] *s.m.* (slang) dead body, corpse.
macédoine, Macédoine [masedwan] *s.f.* (cook.) fruit or vegetable salad; (geog.) Macedonia.
macédonien, -ne [masedɔnjɛ̃] *adj., s.m.f.* Macedonian.
macérat-eur, -rice [maseratœr] *adj.* macerating; **~eur** *s.m.* macerator, receptacle for maceration.
macération [maserɑsjɔ̃] *s.f.* maceration, soaking, steeping; liquid resulting from maceration, decoction; (fig.) mortification (of the flesh).
macérer [masere] *v.t.* to macerate, to soak, to steep; *~ (dans une marinade)*, to marinate; (fig.) to mortify (the flesh, oneself); *vous m'avez laissé ~ dans mon ignorance*, you have left me to stew in my ignorance.
maceron [masrɔ̃] *s.m.* (bot.) alexanders, horse-parsley.
macfarlane [makfarlan] *s.m.* Inverness cape.
Mach [mak] *s.m.* (phys.) Mach, mach number; *voler à ~ 2*, to fly at Mach 2, at twice the speed of sound.
machaon [makaɔ̃] *s.m.* (ent.) machaon, swallow-tail (butterfly).
mâche [mɑʃ] *s.f.* (bot.) corn-salad, lamb's-lettuce.
mâchefer [mɑʃfɛr] *s.m.* slag, dross (of iron), clinkers, cinders, scoria.
mâchement [mɑʃmɑ̃] *s.m.* chewing, munching, mastication, grinding action.
mâcher [mɑʃe] *v.t.* **1.** to chew, to masticate, to munch; to bite, to bite at, to tear; to grind, to mince, to reduce to a pulp; (fig.) to chew over; to champ (the bit); to mumble (one's words); (obs.) to eat gluttonously; **2.** (fig.) to cut out, to prepare; to explain; **3.** (fig.) to mince (matters or words); *ne pas ~ ses mots*, not to mince matters, or words; *ne pas ~ ce qu'on pense*, to speak one's mind, to make no bones about it; *~ à vide*, to move one's jaws up and down, to chew the air; (fig.) to live on hope, to delude oneself with false expectations; *on lui avait mâché toute sa besogne*, the work was all cut and dried for him.
machette [maʃɛt] *s.f.* machete, matchet.
mâcheu-r, -se [mɑʃœr] *s.m.f.* (obs.) chewer, muncher.
machiavél-ique [makjavelik] *adj.* Machiavellian; cunning, politically astute; **~isme** [makjavelism] *s.m.* Machiavellianism; cunning, artifice, astute political manœuvre.
mâchicoulis [mɑʃikuli] *s.m.* (fort.) machicolations.
machin [maʃɛ̃] *s.m.* what's-his-name, whatsit, thingummy, thing; gadget; *qu'est-ce que c'est que ce ~-là?*, what's that gadget.
machinal, -e, (aux) [maʃinal] *adj.* mechanical, automatic, instinctive; **~ement** [maʃinalmɑ̃] *adv.* mechanically, automatically, instinctively.
machination [maʃinɑsjɔ̃] *s.f.* machination, plot, scheming, scheme, intrigue.
machine [maʃin] *s.f.* machine, engine, loco-

motive, implement, piece of machinery; (pl.) machinery; mechanism, apparatus; (electr.) dynamo; appliance, contrivance, system; organism; (obs.) machination, plot, intrigue, scheme; ~ *à battre*, threshing-machine; ~*-outil*, machine-tool; ~ *pneumatique*, air-pump; (industry) ~*-transfert*, (automatic) transfer machine; ~ *à calculer*, calculator, calculating machine; ~ *à signaux*, machine providing data or calculations (e.g. computer); *faire* ~ *arrière*, to reverse the engine; *c'est une simple* ~, he is a mere machine; *la* ~ *animale*, the animal system; (fig.) *la* ~ *ronde*, the earth, the globe; *chambre des* ~*s*, engine-room; ~*s agricoles*, agricultural implements.

machiner [maʃine] *v.t.* to machinate, to plot, to plan, to contrive; (theatr.) to set up scenery, to arrange a scene.

machinerie [maʃinri] *s.f.* machinery; machine- or engine-room; ⚠ not 'machinery' in sense of means or mechanism (by which sth. is carried out).

machinisme [maʃinism] *s.m.* mechanism, machinery; mechanization.

machiniste [maʃinist] *s.m.f.* machinist; driver; engineer; (theatr.) stage-carpenter, scene--shifter; effects man (slang abbrev. *machino*).

machmètre [makmɛtr] *s.m.* (aviat.) Mach--meter.

mâchoire [mɑʃwar] *s.f.* jaw, jawbone; jaws, grip (of vice or chuck); mandible; (fig.) blockhead, dolt; *jouer* or *travailler des* ~*s*, to eat; ~ *de frein*, brake-block.

mâchonnement [mɑʃɔnmɑ̃] *s.m.* chewing, munching; mumbling.

mâchonner [mɑʃɔne] *v.t.* to chew slowly or with difficulty, to munch; to mumble.

mâchure [mɑʃyr] *s.f.* defect, flaw (in nap or pile of material); bruise (in fruit).

mâchurer [mɑʃyre] *v.t.* **1.** to daub, to smear, to smudge, to blot, to blacken; to spoil; **2.** to bruise, to dent.

macis [masi] *s.m.* mace (of nutmeg).

macle [makl] *s.f.* **1.** (chem.) macle, twin crystal; **2.** (herald.) mascle; **3.** = MACRE.

maclé, -e [makle] *adj.* (chem.) macled, twinned (of crystals).

macler [makle] *v.t.* (glass-making) to mix or stir (melted glass).

mâcon [mɑkɔ̃] *s.m.* Mâcon wine.

maçon [masɔ̃] *s.m.* mason, bricklayer, builder; (*franc-*)~, Freemason; ~, ~**ne** *adj.* (zool.) mason (of certain bees, ants, etc.).

maçon-nage [masɔnaʒ] *s.m.* mason's work, stonework, masonry; ~**ner** [masɔne] *v.t.* to build; to wall up, to brick, to plaster up, to stop up; to block up; to line with masonry or brick; ~**nerie** [masɔnri] *s.f.* masonry, stonework, brickwork; (*franc-*)*maçonnerie*, Freemasonry; ~**nique** [masɔnik] *adj.* Masonic.

macramé [makrame] *s.m.* macramé, macramé work.

macre [makr] *s.f.* (bot.) water-caltrop, water--chestnut.

macreuse [makrøz] *s.f.* **1.** (ornith.) scoter, widgeon; **2.** (butch.) part of shoulder of beef.

macrobiotique [makrɔbjɔtik] *adj.* macrobiotic.

macro-céphale [makrɔsefal] *adj.* macrocephalic; ~**cosme** [makrɔkɔsm] *s.m.* macrocosm; ~**molécule** [makrɔmɔlekyl] *s.f.* (chem.) macromolecule; ~**pode** [makrɔpɔd] *adj.* (zool., bot.) macropodous, macropodal; *s.m.* macropod; ~**scélide** [makrɔselid] *s.m.* (zool.) elephant--shrew; ~**scopique** [makrɔskɔpik] *adj.* macroscopic; ~**spore** [makrɔspɔr] *s.f.* (bot.) macrospore.

macroures [makrur] *s.m.pl.* (zool.) Macrura.

maculage [makylaʒ] *s.m.*, **maculation** [makylɑsjɔ̃] *s.f.* maculation, spotting, staining, blotting.

maculature [makylatyr] *s.f.* (print.) maculature, waste proof-sheet; protective sheet, wrapping-paper; stamping (e.g. with receipt stamp).

macule [makyl] *s.f.* stain, spot, blemish, blot, blur; macula, sun-spot; (print.) mackle, cover--sheet.

maculer [makyle] *v.t.* to maculate; to blot, to spot, to stain, to smudge, to blur, to mackle.

Madame [madam] *s.f.* (pl. *mesdames*) Madam, ma'am, wife; Mrs., mistress; lady, my lady; your or her ladyship; (Fr. hist.) *Madame*, wife of *Monsieur*; ~ *la duchesse*, your or her grace; ~ *votre mère*, your mother; ~ *est servie*, lunch, dinner, is ready, or served, madam; *faire la* ~, to give oneself airs; *jouer à la* ~, to play the fine lady.

madapolam [madapɔlam] *s.m.* (text.) madapollam.

madécasse [madekas] *adj.*, *s.m.f.* = MALGACHE.

madeleine [madlɛn] *s.f.* **1.** kind of sponge-cake; **2.** early pear, plum, peach; **3.** (fam.) magdalen, repentant prostitute; *pleurer comme une Madeleine*, to weep copious tears.

mademoiselle [madmwazɛl] *s.f.* (pl. *mesdemoiselles*) Miss, miss; this, or the, young lady; (Fr. hist.) *Mademoiselle*, daughter of *Monsieur*; ~ *désire-t-elle attendre?*, would you care to wait, Miss?; ~ *votre sœur*, your sister.

Madère [madɛr] *s.f.* (geog.) Madeira; ~ *s.m.* Madeira (wine).

madérien, -ne [maderjɛ̃], **madérois, -e** [maderwa] *adj.*, *s.m.f.* Madeiran.

madone [madɔn] *s.f.* madonna.

madrague [madrag] *s.f.* (fish.) crawl, tunny--net, kettle-net.

madras [madrɑ] *s.m.* (text.) madras; bandanna, headscarf or handkerchief of madras (cotton).

madré, -e [madre] *adj.* **1.** cunning, crafty, sly, sharp; **2.** (techn.) speckled, spotted, mottled.

madrépor-e [madrepɔr] *s.m.* (zool.) madrepore; ~**ique** [madrepɔrik], ~**ien,** ~**ienne** [madrepɔrjɛ̃] *adj.* (zool.) madreporic.

madrier [madrije] *s.m.* thick plank, joist, beam.

madrigal (pl. **aux**) [madrigal] *s.m.* madrigal, (poetic) epigram, elaborately turned compliment, pretty speech.

madrilène [madrilɛn] *adj.*, *s.m.f.* Madrileno, (native or inhabitant) of Madrid.

maestria [maɛstrija] *s.f.* mastery; dash; *avec* ~, in a masterly manner, brilliantly, with dash.

maestro [maɛstro] *s.m.* (mus.) maestro.

maffia, mafia [mafja] *s.f.* mafia, secret society.

mafflu, -e [mafly] *adj.* (fam.) chubby, chubby--faced.

magasin [magazɛ̃] *s.m.* shop, store; emporium, warehouse, store-room, depot; stock; magazine; *marchandises en* ~, goods in stock; *mettre en* ~, to warehouse, to store.

magasinage [magazinaʒ] *s.m.* warehousing; storage, storing, lying in store; warehouse-rent; *droits de* ~, warehouse-dues, storage charges.

magasinier [magazinje] *s.m.* warehouse-man, warehouse-keeper, storeman, store-keeper.

magazine [magazin] *s.m.* magazine.

magdalénien, -ne [magdalenjɛ̃] *adj.* (archaeol.) Magdalenian.

mage [maʒ] *s.m.* magus, magician; *les rois* ~*s*, the Magi, the three wise men from the East.

magenta [maʒɛ̃ta] *adj.*, *s.m.* magenta (colour).

magicien, -ne [maʒisjɛ̃] *s.m.f.* magician, enchanter, necromancer, sorcerer, sorceress, wizard, witch; (fig.) transformer.

magie [maʒi] *s.f.* magic; enchantment, charm; ~ *noire*, black art, black magic, witchcraft.

magique [maʒik] *adj.* magic, magical; (fig.) enchanting, wonderful, astonishing, mysterious; supernatural; **~ment** [maʒikmɑ̃] *adv.* magically.
magister [maʒistɛr] *s.m.* village schoolmaster, dominie; (fig.) pedant.
magistère [maʒistɛr] *s.m.* grand-mastership (of an order); (fig.) absolute authority; (chem.) sovereign remedy.
magistral, -e, (**aux**) [maʒistral] *adj.* magistral, of masters, of a master; authoritative, dictatorial; principal, sovereign; clever, brilliant, masterly, first class; (slang) smashing; *ligne ~e*, principal outline; *remède ~*, sovereign remedy; *parler d'un ton ~*, to speak in an authoritative tone; **~ement** [maʒistralmɑ̃] *adv.* in a masterly fashion, brilliantly; with authority.
magistrat [maʒistra] *s.m.* magistrate, judge, justice; civic officer.
magistrature [maʒistratyr] *s.f.* magistracy, magistrature, bench; (pl.) (obs.) civil service, public servants, administrators; *~ assise*, the judges, the bench; *~ debout*, body of public prosecutors; *entrer dans la ~*, to become a judge or public prosecutor.
magma [magma] *s.m.* magma.
magnanarelle [maɲanarɛl] *s.f.* silkworm breeder, woman who tends silkworms.
magnanerie [maɲanri] *s.f.* silkworm nursery; silkworm breeding, sericulture.
magnani-er, -ère [maɲanje] *s.m.f.* silkworm breeder.
magnanime [maɲanim] *adj.* magnanimous, generous, high-souled, noble-minded; **~ment** [maɲanimmɑ̃] *adv.* magnanimously.
magnanimité [maɲanimite] *s.f.* magnanimity.
magnat [magna] *s.m.* magnate.
(**se**) **magner** [maɲe] *v.refl.* (slang) to hurry, to get a move on.
magnésie [maɲezi] *s.f.* (chem.) magnesia; *sulfate de ~*, Epsom salts.
magnésien, -ne [maɲezjɛ̃] *adj.* (chem.) magnesian.
magnésite [maɲezit] *s.f.* (min.) magnesite.
magnésium [maɲeziɔm] *s.m.* (chem.) magnesium.
magnétique [maɲetik] *adj.* magnetic; mesmeric, hypnotic; (fig.) attractive, compelling; *bande ~*, magnetic tape; **~ment** [maɲetikmɑ̃] *adv.* magnetically, by magnetism.
magnétis-ation [maɲetizɑsjɔ̃] *s.f.* magnetization, mesmerization; **~er** [maɲetize] *v.t.* to magnetize; to mesmerize, to hypnotize, to fascinate; **~eur** [maɲetizœr] *s.m.* mesmerizer, mesmerist, hypnotist.
magnétisme [maɲetism] *s.m.* (phys.) magnetism; mesmerism, hypnotism; (fig.) charm, fascination, attraction.
magnétite [maɲetit] *s.f.* (min.) magnetite.
magnéto [maɲeto] *s.m.* (electr.) magneto.
magnéto-mètre [maɲetɔmɛtr] *s.m.* (phys.) magnetometer; **~phone** [maɲetɔfɔn] *s.m.* tape-recorder.
magnétron [maɲetrɔ̃] *s.m.* (phys.) magnetron.
magnificat [magnifikat] *s.m.* Magnificat.
magnificence [maɲifisɑ̃s] *s.f.* magnificence, splendour, luxury, lavishness, grandeur, pomp, stateliness; generosity; richness.
magnifier [maɲifje] *v.t.* to magnify; to praise, to extol, to exalt, to laud, to glorify, to celebrate, to aggrandize, to embellish.
magnifique [maɲifik] *adj.* magnificent, splendid, grand, stately, sumptuous; munificent, generous, liberal; pompous, lavish, ostentatious; lofty, sublime, noble, brilliant, fine; *il fait un temps ~*, it is glorious weather; **~ment** [maɲifikmɑ̃] *adv.* magnificently.
magnitude [magnityd] *s.f.* magnitude; size.
magnolia [magnolja], **magnolier** [magnolje] *s.m.* magnolia, magnolia tree.
magot[1] [mago] *s.m.* **1.** (zool.) Barbary ape, macaque; **2.** grotesque (china) figure; ugly man; ⚠ not 'maggot'.
magot[2] [mago] *s.m.* (fam.) hoard (of money), savings, money put by, pile.
mahaleb [maalɛb] *s.m.* (bot.) mahaleb, wild cherry tree.
maharajah [maaraʒa] *s.m.* maharaja(h).
mahatma [maatma] *s.m.* mahatma.
mahdi [mɑdi] *s.m.* Mahdi.
mahdiste [mɑdist] *s.m.* Mahdist.
mahométan, -e [maɔmetɑ̃] *adj., s.m.f.* Muhammadan.
mahométisme [maɔmetism] *s.m.* Muhammadanism.
mahonie [maɔni] *s.f.*, **mahonia** [maɔnja] *s.m.* (bot.) mahonia.
mahout [mau] *s.m.* mahout, elephant-driver.
mai [mɛ] *s.m.* May; maypole; *le premier ~*, Mayday; (bot.) *bois de ~*, hawthorn, may; *lis de ~*, May-lily, lily-of-the-valley; *planter le ~*, to set up the maypole.
maie [mɛ] *s.f.* kneading-trough; bread-bin.
maïeur [maiœr] *s.m.* (obs.) mayor.
maigre [mɛgr] *adj.* lean, thin, spare, gaunt; skinny, scraggy, lanky; poor, mediocre, sorry, scanty, meagre, slim; barren; (arch.) slender; (of coal) close-burning; (fam.) *~ échine*, scrawny fellow; *~ comme un chat de gouttière, un hareng, un clou*, thin as a lath, as a post; nothing but skin and bone; *viande ~*, lean meat; *jour ~*, fast-day, day of abstinence; *faire ~*, to fast, to abstain from meat; *soupe ~*, vegetable soup; *repas ~*, fish meal, meal without meat, scanty meal; *fromage ~*, cheese with low fat content; *~ chère*, poor fare; *faire ~ chère*, to fare badly, to have a meagre diet; *un sol ~*, barren soil; *une ~ réception*, a cold reception; *colonne ~*, slender column; *imprimer en ~*, to print in plain (not bold) type; *~ eau*, shallow water; *~ s.m.* lean; diet without meat; shallow(s), shallow part (of river, etc.); *donnez-moi du ~*, give me some of the lean; **~ment** [mɛgrəmɑ̃] *adv.* meagrely, sparely, sparsely, poorly, sparingly.
maigrelet, -te [mɛgrəlɛ], **maigrichon, -ne** [mɛgriʃɔ̃], **maigriot, -te** [mɛgrijo] *adj.* thin, over-thin, on the thin side, lean, spare.
maigreur [mɛgrœr] *s.f.* leanness, thinness, spareness, emaciation; meagreness, poorness, scantiness, barrenness; (arch.) slenderness.
maigrir [mɛgrir] *v.i.* to grow lean, to get thin, to waste away; *~ v.t.* to make thin, to give a slim appearance to.
mail [maj] *s.m.* **1.** (obs.) mallet, mall, pall-mall (implement, game); **2.** promenade, mall, avenue, sheltered walk.
mail-coach [mɛlkotʃ] *s.m.* four-in-hand coach.
maille[1] [mɑj] *s.f.* **1.** stitch; knot; mesh; ring, link (of chain or chain-mail); *~ tombée*, dropped stitch; *cotte de ~s*, coat of mail; **2.** speck, speckle, spot (on bird's wing); web (in the eye).
maille[2] [mɑj] *s.f.* maille (old copper coin); (fig.) farthing, penny, etc.; *n'avoir ni sou ni ~*, not to have a penny to one's name, to be as poor as a church mouse; *avoir ~ à partir avec qn.*, to have a quarrel with s.o., to have a bone to pick with s.o.
maillé, -e [mɑje] *adj.* stitched; mailed; reticulated, linked, netted; speckled; *fer ~*, wire netting.
mailler [mɑje] *v.t.* to make network, to reticulate, to link; to lace (a studding sail); to mail, to arm with mail; *~ v.i.* (of vines) to bud; to grow speckled; to get enmeshed, to get caught in the net.
maillet [majɛ] *s.m.* mallet.

mailloche [majɔʃ] *s.f.* big mallet, beetle, maul; bass-drum stick.

maillon [mɑjɔ̃] *s.m.* shackle, ring, link (of chain).

maillot [majo] *s.m.* swaddling band, swaddling clothes, long clothes; (fig.) infancy; vest, jersey; tights (of dancer, acrobat, etc.); ~ *de bain*, bathing-costume; *enfant au* ~, infant in arms.

maillotin [majɔtɛ̃] *s.m.* **1.** olive-press; **2.** (mil.) war-hammer; *les* ~*s*, rebel inhabitants of Paris under Charles VI.

maillure [majyr] *s.f.* **1.** = MAILLE[1] 2; **2.** blemish (on wood).

main [mɛ̃] *s.f.* hand, fist; handwriting; lead, trick, deal, (at cards); hook, grip, holder, handle; hand-shovel, scoop; quire (of paper); body, texture, (of material or paper); authority, power, help; (bot.) tendril; ~ *de fer*, handhold, hanger (of spring); *à deux* ~*s*, *des deux* ~*s*, with both hands, for two hands, two-handed; (fig.) eagerly; (mus.) *à quatre* ~*s*, duet for piano; *à la* ~, in one's hand, or hands; by hand; to hand, handy; *à la portée de la* ~, within reach; *à* ~ *armée*, by main force; *à pleines* or *belles* ~*s*, by handfuls, lavishly, liberally, plentifully; *un homme à toute* ~, a handy man, a handyman, one prepared to do anything; *avoir une belle* ~, to write a good hand; *avoir la* ~, to have the lead, to deal, to play first, (at cards); *avoir les* ~*s liées*, to have one's hands tied, to be unable to do anything; *avoir la* ~ *légère*, to be skilful, to have a light touch; *il n'y va pas de* ~ *morte*, he does not do things by halves; *de toute* ~, from anyone, anyhow; *battre des* ~*s*, to clap, to applaud; *coup de* ~, (i.) skill, knack; (ii.) help; (iii.) unexpected attack; *le coup de* ~ *pour*, the knack of (doing), skill at; *de la* ~ *à la bouche se perd souvent la soupe*, there's many a slip 'twixt the cup and the lip; *de la* ~ *à la* ~, direct from one person to another, handed direct; *de longue* ~, of long standing; long since, long ago; (fam.) *donner la* ~, to consent, to give in; *donner la* ~ *à*, to offer one's hand to, to take (someone's) hand, to shake hands with; to give help, or show favour, to; *se donner la* ~, to shake hands, to join hands, to make contact, to effect a junction; *lever la* ~, to raise one's hand, to take one's oath, to swear; *lever la* ~ *sur*, to raise one's hand against; *en* ~, in hand, at one's disposal, under control; *prendre en* ~, to take in hand, to undertake; *en* ~*s propres*, into one's own hands, personally; *en venir aux* ~*s*, to come to blows, to close (with), to come to close quarters; *entre les* ~*s de*, in(to) the hands of, in the power of; *faire* ~ *basse sur*, to lay hold of, to steal; *frapper dans la* ~, to strike a bargain; *fait (à la)* ~, hand-made, made by hand; *l'argent lui fond dans la* ~, money slips through his fingers; *avoir la* ~ *heureuse* or *bonne*, to be lucky, to be a lucky person; *il en a les* ~*s nettes*, he is clear of all guilt, or responsibility, for it; *haut la* ~, with a high hand, with authority; easily, hands down; *mener un cheval haut la* ~, to hold a tight rein; *avoir la haute* ~ *sur*, to command, to be in control of; *haut les* ~*s!*, *les* ~*s en l'air!*, hands up!; *à bas les* ~*s!*, hands off!; *j'en mettrai ma* ~ *au feu*, I would stake my life on it; ~ *chaude*, (party game) hot cockles; *mettre la dernière* ~ *à*, to put the finishing touch to; *mettre la* ~ *à*, to set one's hand to; *mettre la* ~ *à la plume*, to put pen to paper; *mettre la* ~ *à la pâte*, to put one's shoulder to the wheel; *mettre la* ~ *sur*, to lay hands on, to take possession of, (fam.) to collar; *passer la* ~, to pass (the deal), (fig., fam.) to stand aside, to give up, to give s.o. else a chance; *passer la* ~ *dans le dos à qn.*, to flatter s.o., (fam.) to butter s.o. up; *perdre la* ~, to lose one's skill, to forget the knack; *porter la* ~ *sur*, to lay (violent) hands on; *prendre qn. la* ~ *dans le sac*, to catch s.o. red-handed; *savoir de bonne* ~, to have it on good authority, from a reliable source; *se faire la* ~, to get one's hand in; to try one's hand; *serrer la* ~ *à*, to shake hands with, to clasp (someone's) hand; *sous la* ~, at hand, ready to hand, on the spot; *tomber sous la* ~, to come to hand; *sous la* ~ *de*, in the power of, under the thumb of; *sous* ~, underhand, secretly, clandestinely; ~ *sur* ~, hand over hand; *tendre la* ~, to hold out one's hand; to lend a helping hand; to make an offer of conciliation; to beg; *les* ~*s m'en tombent*, I am astounded; *tour de* ~, sleight-of-hand, dexterity, knack; ~ *courante*, (i.) (comm.) rough book, counter cash-book, day-book; (ii.) or ~ *coulante*, hand-rail; *en un tour de* ~, in the twinkling of an eye; *allons, la* ~ *et que ce soit fini!*, now, let's shake hands, and not a word more about it!

main-d'œuvre [mɛ̃dœvr] *s.f.* (pl. *mains-d'œuvre*) work, workmanship, labour, manpower, labour-force; labour costs.

main-forte [mɛ̃fɔrt] *s.f.invar.* help, assistance; *prêter* ~, to lend assistance.

mainlevée [mɛ̃lve] *s.f.* (law) withdrawal, replevin.

mainmise [mɛ̃miz] *s.f.* (law) seizure, distraint; annexation; (fig.) dominion.

mainmortable [mɛ̃mɔrtabl] *adj.* subject to mortmain; inalienable.

mainmorte [mɛ̃mɔrt] *s.f.* (law) mortmain.

maint, -e [mɛ̃] *adj.* many a, many; *à* ~*es reprises*, again and again.

maintenance [mɛ̃tnɑ̃s] *s.f.* **1.** (obs.) maintaining, upholding; **2.** maintenance (of vehicles, buildings, etc.), repairs; keeping up to strength, replenishment of stock; ⚠ not 'maintenance' in sense 'paying living expenses'.

maintenant [mɛ̃tnɑ̃] *adv.* now, at present, at this time, nowadays; next; *dès* ~, henceforth, henceforward, from now on.

maintenir [mɛ̃tnir] *v.t.* to uphold, to sustain; to defend; to support; to hold to (opinion, etc.); to keep, to keep together; to keep in order; to maintain, to keep up; to hold fast, to hold down; to enforce; to preserve; ~ *le bon ordre*, to maintain order; ~ *sa position*, to hold one's own; **se** ~ *v.refl.* to keep up, to remain; to be kept up, to be sustained; to last, to subsist, to continue; to hold out, to stand one's ground, to maintain one's position; to remain in force; *se* ~ *en bonne santé*, to keep in good health; *les prix se maintiennent*, prices remain steady, or firm; ⚠ not 'to maintain' in sense 'to pay living expenses of'.

maintien [mɛ̃tjɛ̃] *s.m.* maintenance, preservation, keeping up; carriage, deportment, bearing, attitude, demeanour, behaviour; (mil.) retention (with the colours).

maire [mɛr] *s.m.* mayor; (hist.) ~ *du palais*, Mayor of the Palace, chief officer of state under Merovingian kings; *adjoint du* ~, deputy mayor; (fam.) *être passé devant le* ~, to be legally married.

mairesse [mɛrɛs] *s.f.* **1.** (fam.) mayoress, wife of the mayor; **2.** (obs.) (lady) mayor.

mairie [meri] *s.f.* **1.** mayoralty, office of mayor; **2.** town hall, local administration offices, municipal offices.

mais [mɛ] *adv.* more; *je n'en peux* ~, I cannot help it, I can do no more, I am exhausted, I am at the end of my tether; ~ *conj.* but, yet, all the same; why; ~ *encore*, but yet; ~ *non*, indeed not; no, indeed; no, of course; ~ *oui*, ~ *si*, but of course; yes, indeed; *eh!* ~, why!; (pop.) *je vais te fermer le bec, ah!* ~, I'll shut your trap for you, just see if I don't!

maïs [mais] *s.m.* (bot.) maize, Indian corn; (U.S.) corn; *farine de* ~, cornflour.

maison [mɛzɔ̃] *s.f.* house, residence; home;

household, family; establishment, firm, agency; shop, warehouse, premises; ~ *d'arrêt* or *de force*, gaol, prison; ~ *de chasse*, hunting-box, shooting--lodge; ~ *de commerce*, firm; ~ *de commission*, commission agency; ~ *garnie* or *meublée*, furnished house, furnished rooms; ~ *de jeu*, gaming-house, gambling-house; ~ *religieuse*, convent, religious house; ~ *de retraite*, old people's home; ~ *du roi*, the king's household, household troops; ~ *rustique*, country cottage; ~ *de santé*, asylum, nursing-home; ~ *de ville*, town hall; *état* or *train de* ~, establishment, style of living; *à la* ~, at home, indoors; *de* ~, domestic; *en* ~, in (domestic) service; *faire sa* ~, to set up house; *garder la* ~, to stay at home, to remain indoors, to mind the house; *tenir* ~, to keep house; *tenir la* ~, to run the house; *Petites Maisons*, former Paris lunatic asylum; *être de la* ~, to be one of the family; *les* ~*s empêchent de voir la ville*, you cannot see the wood for the trees; *avoir* ~ *ouverte*, to keep open house; ~ *close* or *de tolérance*, licensed brothel; ~ *de correction*, reformatory; ~ *de garde*, (i.) porter's lodge; (ii.) watchman's cottage; *il est de bonne* ~, he comes from a good family; *une tarte* ~, a home-made flan; (*plat*) ~, (dish which is) a speciality of the establishment; (pop.) *quelque chose de* ~, something really special.

maisonnée [mɛzɔne] *s.f.* whole house, household, family.

maisonnette [mezɔnɛt] *s.f.* small house, cottage, lodge.

maistrance [mɛstrɑ̃s] *s.f.* (nav.) body of petty officers.

maître [mɛtr] *s.m.*, **maîtresse** [mɛtrɛs] *s.f.* master, mistress; ruler, lord; owner, proprietor, landlord; instructor, teacher, tutor; governor, director; chief, head; (law) Mr. (as title of barristers, etc.); (naut.) boatswain, second mate; *premier* ~, chief petty officer; *second* or *quartier* ~, second-class petty officer; *être passé* ~ *en*, to have obtained the degree of master in; (fig.) to be proficient, skilled, a past master, in; ~ *d'armes*, fencing-master; ~ *de chapelle*, precentor, choirmaster; ~, *maîtresse*, (*d'école*), (school)master, (school)mistress; (naut.) ~ *d'équipage*, boatswain; ~ *d'étude*, usher, junior master; ~ *de forges*, ironmaster; ~ *d'hotel*, steward, butler, major-domo; head-waiter; *sauce* (*à la*) ~ *d'hôtel*, sauce of melted butter, parsley, and lemon juice; ~ *Jacques*, Jack-of-all--trades, factotum; ~ *de maison*, master of the house; host; *être* ~ *de*, to have under control, to control, to command; *n'être plus* ~ *de*, to have lost control of; *être* ~ *de soi* or *être son* ~, to be one's own master, to be free and independent, to be master of one's fate; *être* ~ *de soi*, to be in control of oneself, to be calm; *un mouvement dont il ne fut pas* ~, an impulse which he could not check; *je le laisse* ~ *de faire ce qu'il voudra*, I leave him free to do as he likes; *se trouver* ~ *d'un secret*, to be in possession of a secret; *entretenir une maîtresse*, to keep a mistress; *faire le* ~, to lord it, to behave in a high and mighty fashion; *frapper en* ~, to knock hard; *trouver son* ~, to meet one's match; *se rendre* ~ *de*, to master, to win over, to control, to get under control, to quell, to restrain; *tel* ~, *tel valet*, like master, like man; ~ *des hautes œuvres*, executioner, hangman; ~ *de conférences*, senior lecturer; ~ *d'œuvre*, foreman; director of studies; *voiture de* ~, owner-driven car; *adj.* chief, main, principal, high, master, capable, grand; key, governing, essential; complete, out-and-out, utter, arrant; *la maîtrese poutre*, the main beam; *l'idée maîtresse de l'œuvre*, the essential idea of the work; *le but* ~, the principal object; *le* ~*-autel*, the high altar; *une maîtresse femme*, a capable woman; *un* ~ *fripon*, an utter scoundrel; (mech.) *une cheville-maîtresse*, a king-pin.

maîtrisable [mɛtrizabl] *adj.* governable, controllable.

maîtrise [mɛtriz] *s.f.* **1.** mastership, authority; degree or post of *maître*; choirmastership; masterly quality; mastery, control; ~ *de conférences*, senior lectureship; ~ *de soi-même*, self-control; **2.** choir school; choir.

maîtriser [mɛtrize] *v.t* to master, to govern, to rule, to control; to subdue, to overcome, to overpower, to keep down, to get the better of; **se** ~ *v.refl.* to control oneself.

maïzéna [maizena] *s.f.* maizena (a proprietary brand of cornflour).

majesté [maʒɛste] *s.f.* majesty, dignity, stateliness, grandeur; *Sa* ~ *Très Chrétienne*, His most Christian Majesty, the king of France; *Sa* ~ *Catholique*, the king of Spain.

majestueu-x, -se [maʒɛstɥø] *adj.* majestic, stately, imposing; ~**sement** [maʒɛstɥøzmɑ̃] *adv.* majestically.

majeur, -e [maʒœr] *adj.* major, greater; superior, main, chief, principal, most important; (law) of age; major; (mus.) major; (at cards) major; *la* ~*e partie*, the greater part, the bulk; *en* ~*e partie*, for the most part; *force* ~*e*, superior force, absolute necessity, act of God; *des raisons* ~*es*, imperative reasons; *pour raison* ~*e*, unavoidably, owing to circumstances beyond one's control; *un peuple* ~, a nation fit to govern itself; (naut.) *les mâts* ~*s*, the main masts; (mus.) *tierce* ~*e*, major third; (geog.) *le lac Majeur*, Lake Maggiore; ~ *s.m.* **1.** (law) major, male of full age; **2.** the middle finger; **3.** (mus.) major (key); ~**e** *s.f.* (logic) major premiss.

majolique [maʒɔlik], **maïolique** [majɔlik] *s.f.* majolica, earthenware from Majorca.

major [maʒɔr] *s.m.* (mil.) major; commander; army doctor, surgeon-major; top candidate in competitive examination; *état-*~, general staff, staff, staff-officers, headquarters; ~ *général*, chief of staff (at army headquarters); *tambour-*~, drum-major.

majorat [maʒɔra] *s.m.* (law) majorat; right of primogeniture; entailed estate.

majoration [maʒɔrɑsjɔ̃] *s.f.* over-estimation; increase in price, additional charge, surcharge; supplementary allowance.

majordome [maʒɔrdɔm] *s.m.* major-domo; Master of the (Royal) Household.

majorer [maʒɔre] *v.t.* to over-estimate, to over--value; to increase (price), to make an additional charge; ~ *une facture de 10%*, to add 10% to the invoice price, to add a 10% surcharge.

majorette [maʒɔrɛt] *s.f.* majorette (girl drum--major).

majoritaire [maʒɔritɛr] *adj.* majority, by a majority (vote, system of voting); (business) holding the majority of shares; ~ *s.m.* member of a majority; (pl.) the majority.

majorité [maʒɔrite] *s.f.* **1.** majority; coming of age, full age; *atteindre sa* ~, to come of age; **2.** majority; *en* ~, for the most part; *être en* ~ or *avoir la* ~, to be in the majority; *à la* ~ *de deux voix*, by a majority of two; **3.** (nav.) staff of admiral superintendent of dockyard.

Majorque [majɔrk] *s.f.* (geog.) Majorca.

majorquin, -e [majɔrkɛ̃] *adj.*, *s.m.f.* Majorcan.

majuscule [maʒyskyl] *adj.* capital, large; ~ *s.f.* capital letter.

maki [maki] *s.m.* (zool.) lemur.

mal (pl. **maux**) [mal, mo] *s.m.* evil, ill, wrong, mischief, sin; ache, pain, harm, hurt, sore, soreness, sickness, ailment; hardship, suffering, misfortune, grief, trouble, toil, difficulty, inconvenience, dislike, repugnance; *avoir* ~ *à*, to have a pain in; *j'ai ~ à la tête*, I have a headache, my head aches; *j'ai ~ au pied*, my foot hurts, my foot is sore; *j'ai le ~ de mer*, I feel sea-sick; *j'ai ~ au cœur*, I feel sick; *j'ai le ~ du pays*, I am homesick; *~ d'enfant*, pains of childbirth, labour; (obs.) *haut ~*, epilepsy; *il a eu plus de peur que de ~*, he was more frightened than hurt; *il n'y a que demi ~*, no great harm done; *s'en tirer sans aucun ~*, to escape unharmed, unscathed; *induire à ~*, to lead into evil; *faire ~*, to hurt; to ache; to cause pain; *vous me faites ~*, you are hurting me; *cela fait ~*, it hurts; *faire le ~*, to do evil, to sin; *le bien et le ~*, right and wrong, good and evil; *faire du ~ à*, to injure, to harm, to wrong, to do evil to; *prendre (du) ~*, to catch (one's death of) cold, to catch an illness, to make oneself ill; *dire du ~ de*, to speak ill of, to slander; *avoir du ~ à faire*, to have difficulty in doing; *donner du ~*, to give trouble, to cause trouble; to be difficult (to achieve); *se donner beaucoup de ~*, or *un ~ de chien*, or *un ~ de tous les diables*, to take pains, to try hard, to strive, to leave no stone unturned, to take a great deal of trouble; *mettre à ~*, (i.) to beat severely; (ii.) to ruin; (iii.) to seduce; *prendre* or *tourner en ~*, to take amiss, to put a bad interpretation on, to distort the meaning of; *vouloir du ~ à*, to wish harm to; *raconter ses maux*, to tell one's troubles; *quel ~ y a-t-il à cela?*, or *quel ~ voyez-vous à cela?*, what harm is there in that?; *chacun sent bien son ~*, nobody knows where the shoe pinches as well as he who wears it; *aux grands maux les grands remèdes*, desperate cases call for desperate remedies.

mal [mal] *adv.* wrong, not right, amiss, badly, incorrectly, not properly, not sufficiently; uncomfortably; at variance, on bad terms; out of favour, in disgrace; ugly, plain; badly-off; *prendre ~ un propos*, to take offence at a remark; *cela va ~*, things are going badly; *ce chapeau vous va ~*, this hat does not suit you; *un écrou ~ serré*, a bolt not properly secured; *de ~ en pis*, from bad to worse; *tant bien que ~*, fairly well, after a fashion; *bien ou ~, on y parviendra*, we shall manage somehow or other; *aller*, or *se porter*, *~*, to be ill; *être au plus ~*, to be critically ill, to be at death's door; *être ~ avec*, to be on bad terms with; *être ~ vu de*, to be in bad odour with; *être ~ dans ses affaires*, to be in a bad way, to be in low water; *~ à propos*, out of place, at an inconvenient time; *cela tombe ~*, it is unfortunate, it comes at the wrong moment; *~ gérer*, to mismanage; *n'être pas ~*, to be not bad-looking; *se trouver ~*, to faint, to feel faint; *trouver ~*, to find amiss; *tourner ~*, to go to the bad; to go wrong, to turn out badly; *~ lui en prit*, it turned out badly for him, misfortune befell him; *pas ~ de*, quite a number of, quite a lot of, not a few; *vous vous y prenez ~*, you are setting about it the wrong way.

mal, -e [mal] *adj.* bad, fatal; *bon gré, ~ gré*, willing or not, willy-nilly; *bon an, ~ an*, one year with another; year in, year out.

malabar, -e [malabar] *adj.* of Malabar; *~ s.m.* (slang) a strong, hefty fellow.

malachite [malakit] *s.f.* (min.) malachite.

malacologie [malakɔlɔʒi] *s.f.* (zool.) malacology, study of molluscs.

malade [malad] *adj.* sick, ill, poorly, unwell; sickly, ailing, infirm, diseased, unhealthy; upset; affected, attacked, disordered, out of order; in a bad way or plight; *avoir une jambe ~*, to have a bad leg; *avoir une dent ~*, to have an aching tooth; *la vigne est ~*, the vine is diseased; *avoir l'esprit ~*, to be sick in mind; *ce livre est bien ~*, that book is in a bad condition, in a poor state; *j'en suis ~*, it has upset me, it is making me ill; *~ s.m.f.* sick person, invalid, patient, sufferer; *soigner un ~*, to nurse a sick person, or patient; *faire le ~*, to feign illness; (mil.) *se faire porter ~*, to report sick.

maladie [maladi] *s.f.* illness, sickness, malady; disease, complaint, ailment, disorder; distemper; passion, mania; *faire une ~*, to have an illness; *la ~ de la vigne*, phylloxera; *la ~ des chiens*, distemper; *avoir la ~ des vieux meubles*, to have a passion for old furniture; (fam.) *en faire une ~*, to get very upset (about it).

maladi-f, -ve [maladif] *adj.* sickly, ailing, unhealthy, delicate, frail; (fig.) morbid, pathological; **~vement** [maladivmɑ̃] *adv.* unhealthily, morbidly.

maladrerie [maladrəri] *s.f.* (obs.) leper-hospital, lazar-house.

maladresse [maladrɛs] *s.f.* awkwardness, lack of skill, clumsiness; blunder; tactless behaviour or speech.

maladroit, -e [maladrwa] *adj.* awkward, unskilful, clumsy, bungling; (fig.) stupid, foolish, tactless, blundering; **~ement** [maladrwatmɑ̃] *adv.* clumsily, awkwardly, unskilfully; (fig.) foolishly, stupidly, tactlessly.

malaga [malaga] *s.m.* Malaga (wine, grapes).

malaire [malɛr] *adj.* (anat.) malar, of the cheek.

malais, -e [malɛ] *adj.* Malay.

malaise [malɛz] *s.m.* uncomfortableness, discomfort; indisposition; (fig.) uneasiness, unrest; (obs.) straitened circumstances, hard times; *avoir un ~*, to feel unwell, or indisposed.

malaisé, -e [maleze] *adj.* hard, difficult, rough, trying, troublesome, arduous; **~ment** [malezemɑ̃] *adv.* with difficulty.

Malaisie [malɛzi] *s.f.* (geog.) **1.** Malaya; **2.** Malaysia.

malandre [malɑ̃dr] *s.f.* **1.** (vet.) mallenders; **2.** rotten portion or knot (in wood).

malandreu-x, -se [malɑ̃drø] *adj.* (vet.) suffering from mallenders.

malandrin [malɑ̃drɛ̃] *s.m.* (disbanded mercenary turned) robber, highwayman, bandit.

malappris, -e [malapri] *adj.* ill-bred, uncouth, ill-mannered, unmannerly, uncivil; *s.m.f.* ill-bred person, lout.

malard, malart [malar] *s.m.* (ornith.) mallard, wild drake.

malaria [malarja] *s.f.* malaria.

malavisé, -e [malavize] *adj.* ill-advised, imprudent, rash, unwise, ill-judged, injudicious; *s.m.f.* imprudent person.

malaxage [malaksaʒ] *s.m.* malaxation, mixing, kneading; massage.

malaxer [malakse] *v.t.* to malaxate, to mix, to knead; to massage.

malaxeur [malaksœr] *s.m.* mixer, mixing-machine; kneader; *~ adj.m.* kneading, mixing.

Malaysia [malɛsja] *s.f.* (geog.) = MALAISIE 2.

malchance, malechance [malʃɑ̃s] *s.f.* ill-luck, bad luck, mishap, mischance, misfortune.

malchanceu-x, -se [malʃɑ̃sø] *adj.* unlucky, unfortunate.

malcommode [malkɔmɔd] *adj.* inconvenient; impractical.

maldisant, -e [maldizɑ̃] *adj.* = MÉDISANT.

maldonne [maldɔn] *s.f.* misdeal; (fig.) mistake, misunderstanding; *faire ~*, to misdeal.

mâle [mɑl] *s.m.* male; he, cock (bird), buck (rabbit), dog (fox, etc.), bull (elephant, etc.), tom(-cat); he-man; *~ adj.* masculine, male, manly, virile.

malédiction [malediksjɔ̃] *s.f.* malediction, curse, execration; *donner sa ~ à*, to curse.

maléfice [malefis] *s.m.* spell; witchcraft, sorcery.

maléfique [malefik] *adj.* maleficent, malevolent, baleful, evil; *né sous une étoile ~*, born under an unlucky star.

malencontre [malɑ̃kɔ̃tr] *s.f.* (fam.) mischance, mishap, untoward accident.

malencontreu-x, -se [malɑ̃kɔ̃trø] *adj.* unlucky, unfortunate, untoward, inopportune; **~sement** [malɑ̃kɔ̃trøzmɑ̃] *adv.* unfortunately, inopportunely.

mal-en-point [malɑ̃pwɛ̃] *adv.loc.* in a bad way. in a sorry plight.

malentendu [malɑ̃tɑ̃dy] *s.m.* misunderstanding, mistake, misapprehension.

malfaçon [malfasɔ̃] *s.f.* bad work; defect in work; bungled or badly-done work.

malfaisance [malfəzɑ̃s] *s.f.* evil-doing, wrongdoing, evil action or influence, maleficence.

malfaisant, -e [malfəzɑ̃] *adj.* maleficent, mischievous, malicious, evil-minded, ill--intentioned; injurious, noxious, hurtful.

malfait-eur, -rice [malfɛtœr] *s.m.f.* scoundrel, criminal, felon, offender, malefactor, evil-doer.

malfamé, -e [malfame] *adj.* ill-famed, disreputable, notorious.

malformation [malfɔrmɑsjɔ̃] *s.f.* malformation.

malgache [malgaʃ] *adj.*, *s.m.f.* Malagasy, (native or inhabitant) of Madagascar.

malgracieu-x, -se [malgrasjø] *adj.* uncivil, rude, ungracious; **~sement** [malgrasjøzmɑ̃] *adv.* ungraciously, uncivilly, rudely.

malgré [malgre] *prep.* in spite of, despite; notwithstanding; *~ tout*, for all that, in spite of everything, whatever may happen, nevertheless; *il l'a fait ~ moi*, he did it in spite of me, *or* against my will; *~ le mauvais temps*, notwithstanding the bad weather; *~ tout son talent il était peu connu*, with all his gifts he was little known; *~ que*, in spite of the fact that, although, notwithstanding that; *~ que j'en aie*, in spite of myself, however reluctant I may be.

malhabile [malabil] *adj.* unskilful, awkward, clumsy, inexperienced; **~ment** [malabilmɑ̃] *adv.* awkwardly, clumsily.

malheur [malœr] *s.m.* unhappiness; misfortune, ill luck, mischance, mishap, calamity, disaster, accident; woe, misery, adversity, poverty; disgrace; *à quelque chose ~ est bon*, it is an ill wind that blows nobody any good; *c'est dans le ~ qu'on connaît ses vrais amis*, a friend in need is a friend indeed; *avoir (bien) du ~*, to suffer (much); *les ~s du temps*, these troubled times; *~ aux vaincus!*, woe betide the losers!; *faire le ~ de*, to bring misfortune on, to be the misfortune of, to be a sore trial to; *tout n'est qu'heur et ~ dans ce monde*, that's the way of the world; *jouer de ~*, to be unlucky, to have a run of bad luck; *par ~*, unhappily, unfortunately, as (ill) luck would have it; *oiseau de ~*, bird of ill omen; *pour comble* or *surcroît de ~*, to crown all, as the crowning misfortune; *pour mon ~*, unfortunately for me, to my cost; *quel ~!*, how unfortunate!, what a pity!; *un ~ ne vient jamais seul*, misfortunes never come singly, it never rains but it pours; *porter ~*, to bring bad luck; *il vous arrivera un ~*, you will come to grief, you are courting disaster; *faire un ~*, to do something desperate or violent; to cause an accident; to do (oneself or s.o.) mischief.

malheureu-x, -se [malœrø] *adj.* unfortunate, unlucky, ill-starred, unsuccessful, disastrous, fatal, ill-omened, untoward; ill-judged; unpleasant, disagreeable; unhappy, miserable, wretched, sorry, paltry; beggarly, poor; a pity; *être ~x comme les pierres*, to be utterly wretched, to be absolutely penniless; *avoir la main ~se*, to be unlucky, never to have any luck; to be always breaking things; *des temps ~x*, unhappy, *or* troubled, times; *pour un ~x billet de cent francs*, for the sake of a miserable hundred-franc note; *le voilà enfin, et ce n'est pas ~x!*, there he is at last, and about time too!; *c'est ~x, mais*, it is a pity, but; (pop.) *si c'est pas ~x, de voir une chose pareille*, isn't it shocking to see something like that?; *~x!*, (you) wretch!, (you) madman!, what do you mean by it?, you naughty child!; *il est né sous une ~se étoile*, he was born under an unlucky star; *les ~x*, the unfortunate, the poor; **~sement** [malœrøzmɑ̃] *adv.* unhappily, unfortunately, unluckily; badly, miserably, wretchedly.

malhonnête [malɔnɛt] *adj.* **1.** dishonest, fraudulent; **2.** rude, uncivil, impolite, unmannerly; **3.** indecent, improper; **~ment** [malɔnɛtmɑ̃] *adv.* dishonestly.

malhonnêteté [malɔnɛtte] *s.f.* **1.** dishonesty, piece of dishonesty, lack of integrity; **2.** rudeness, incivility; **3.** impropriety, indecency.

malice [malis] *s.f.* malice; maliciousness, spite, spitefulness; mischief, mischievousness; harm; roguishness, archness, slyness; prank, trick; sly dig, pointed remark; *boîte à ~*, jack-in-the--box; *sac à ~*, (conjurer's) bag of tricks; *faire des ~s à*, to play tricks on; *entendre ~ à qch.*, to find a sly meaning in sth.; *ne pas y entendre ~*, to do a thing in all innocence, to mean no harm by; *une ~ cousue de fil blanc*, a transparent stratagem; ⚠ not 'malice' as in legal 'malice prepense'.

malicieu-x, -se [malisjø] *adj.* malicious (⚠ see MALICE); mocking, sly, roguish, mischievous (person), naughty; **~sement** [malisjøzmɑ̃] *adv.* maliciously, slily, mockingly.

malien, -ne [maljɛ̃] *adj.* (geog.) of Mali.

malignité [maliɲite] *s.f.* malignity, malignancy; spite, malice.

malin [malɛ̃], (fem.) **maligne** [maliɲ] *adj.* malicious, malign, malignant, mischievous; evil, ill; sly, cunning, artful, sharp, shrewd, clever, smart, knowing; difficult; satirical; roguish, saucy; *fièvre maligne*, malignant fever; *c'est ~!*, that's well done!; *ce n'est pas ~ d'avoir fait cela*, it was not very clever to do that; *bien ~ qui trouvera*, it will take a clever person to find it, to find the answer; *c'est un ~*, he's a sly customer, a cunning fellow; there are no flies on him; *faire le ~*, to try to be smart, to try to be too clever, to show off; *le ~*, the devil, the evil one.

Malines [malin] *s.f.* **1.** (geog.) Malines, Mechlin; **2.** Mechlin lace.

malingre [malɛ̃gr] *adj.* sickly, ailing, weakly, puny; ⚠ not 'malingering'.

malinois, -e [malinwa] *adj.*, *s.m.f.* (native or inhabitant) of Malines (Mechlin); ~ *s.m.* Belgian sheep-dog.

malintentionné, -e [malɛ̃tɑ̃sjɔne] *adj.* evil--minded, ill-disposed, ill-intentioned.

malique [malik] *adj.* (chem.) malic.

mal-jugé [malʒyʒe] *s.m.* miscarriage of justice.

malle [mal] *s.f.* trunk; pedlar's pack; boot (of car); mail-coach; mail service; *faire, défaire, sa ~*, to pack, to unpack.

malléabilité [malleabilite] *s.f.* malleability; (fig.) pliability.

malléable [malleabl] *adj.* malleable; (fig.) supple, docile, compliant, tractable.

malléolaire [malleɔlɛr] *adj.* (anat.) malleolar.

malléole [malleɔl] *s.f.* (anat.) malleolus, ankle--bone.

mallette [malɛt] *s.f.* **1.** small trunk, attaché case, case, box; **2.** (bot.) shepherd's purse.

malmener [malməne] *v.t.* to maltreat, to mishandle, to handle or use roughly; to give a rough time to, to knock about, to abuse.

malnutrition [malnytrisjɔ̃] *s.f.* malnutrition, under-nourishment.

malodorant, -e [malɔdɔrɑ̃] *adj.* malodorous, evil-smelling, stinking, fetid.

malotru, -e [malotry] *adj.* rough, rude, uncivil, ill-bred; coarse, uncouth; ~ *s.m.* ruffian, boor, lout.

malouin, -e [malwɛ̃] *s.m.f.*, *adj.* (native or inhabitant) of Saint-Malo.
malpighie [malpigi] *s.f.* (bot.) malpighia.
malpropre [malprɔpr] *adj.* unclean, dirty, filthy, untidy, unsavoury; indecent; unfit, ill-fitting; dishonest; **~ment** [malprɔprəmɑ̃] *adv.* dirtily, nastily, badly, fraudulently, in a dishonest manner.
malpropreté [malprɔprəte] *s.f.* dirtiness, uncleanness, nastiness, slovenliness, filth; indecency; dishonesty.
malsain, -e [malsɛ̃] *adj.* unhealthy; unwholesome, injurious, dangerous; (fig.) immoral, corrupting, demoralizing, pernicious, unnatural, morbid.
malséance [malseɑ̃s] *s.f.* unseemliness, impropriety.
malséant, -e [malseɑ̃] *adj.* unseemly, unbecoming, unsuitable; improper, indecorous.
malsonnant, -e [malsɔnɑ̃] *adj.* objectionable, offensive, scandalous, obnoxious.
malt [malt] *s.m.* malt.
maltage [maltaʒ] *s.m.* malting.
maltais, -e [maltɛ] *adj.*, *s.m.f.* Maltese.
maltase [maltɑz] *s.f.* (chem.) maltase.
Malte [malt] *s.f.* (geog.) Malta.
malté, -e [malte] *adj.* malted.
malter [malte] *v.t.* to malt.
malterie [maltəri] *s.f.* malt-house, maltings; malting industry.
malteur [maltœr] *s.m.* maltman, maltster.
malthusianisme [maltyzjanism] *s.m.* Malthusianism.
malthusien, -ne [maltyzjɛ̃] *adj.*, *s.m.f.* Malthusian.
maltose [maltoz] *s.f.* (chem.) maltose.
maltôte [maltot] *s.f.* (obs.) (Fr. hist.) tax levied in 1292, etc., for the wars in Flanders; exaction, extortion; tax-collecting; tax-gatherers.
maltraiter [maltrɛte] *v.t.* to maltreat, to ill-treat, to ill-use, to give rough treatment to; to vilify, to injure, to wrong, to damage, to abuse.
malvacées [malvase] *s.f.pl.* (bot.) Malvaceae.
malveillamment [malvɛjamɑ̃] *adv.* malevolently, spitefully, maliciously, with ill will.
malveillance [malvɛjɑ̃s] *s.f.* malevolence, ill-will; spite, malice.
malveillant, -e [malvɛjɑ̃] *adj.* malevolent, ill-disposed, evil-minded, malicious; spiteful.
malvenu, -e [malvəny] *adj.* **1.** unjustified, without justification, ill-advised, unwarranted, ill-founded; *être ~ à se plaindre*, to have no grounds for complaint, to be ill-advised to complain; **2.** stunted, retarded.
malversation [malvɛrsɑsjɔ̃] *s.f.* malversation, peculation, embezzlement, breach of trust, corruption.
malvoisie [malvwazi] *s.m.* malmsey wine.
maman [mamɑ̃] *s.f.* mother, mamma, mummy, mum, ma.
mamelle [mamɛl] *s.f.* breast; (of animals) udder, dug; (fig.) bosom; heart; mother's milk; (pop., pej.) big breast; (bot.) *herbe aux ~s*, nipplewort; *enfant à la ~*, child at the breast, infant; *porter un cœur sous la ~*, to be warm-hearted.
mamelon [mamlɔ̃] *s.m.* nipple, teat, pap; dug; (fig.) rounded hill, knoll, hummock, hillock, mound, pap.
mamelonné, -e [mamlɔne] *adj.* mamillate(d); covered with rounded protuberances or hillocks.
mamelu, -e [mamly] *adj.* (pop.) full-breasted, big-bosomed.
mameluk, mamelouk [mamluk] *s.m.* (hist.) Mameluke.
m'amie [mami] *s.f.* (archaic abbrev. of *ma amie*) my love, my darling.
mammaire [mamɛr] *adj.* mammary.
mammalogie [mamalɔʒi] *s.f.* (zool.) mammalogy, study of mammals.
mammifère [mamifɛr] *adj.* mammalian; ~ *s.m.* mammal.
mammite [mamit] *s.f.* (pathol.) mastitis.
mammouth [mamut] *s.m.* mammoth.
mamours [mamur] *s.m.pl.* show of affection; *faire des mamours à*, to caress; (fig.) to have a love affair with, to be on very affectionate terms with.
mam'selle, mam'zelle [mamzɛl] *s.f.* (pop. abbrev. of *mademoiselle*) Miss, miss.
man [mɑ̃] *s.m.* (ent.) larva of cockchafer, grub.
manade [manad] *s.f.* (Provençal dial.) herd of bulls or horses.
management [manaʒmɑ̃] *s.m.* management, direction.
manager [manadʒɛr] *s.m.* (sport, entertainment) manager.
manant [manɑ̃] *s.m.* (feud. law) peasant, villager; villein, serf; (pej.) peasant, rustic, clodhopper, bumpkin, clown.
mancelle [mɑ̃sɛl] *s.f.* tug, thill-tug, (of harness).
mancenille [mɑ̃snij] *s.f.* (bot.) manchineel.
mancenillier [mɑ̃snilje] *s.m.* (bot.) manchineel-tree.
manche [mɑ̃ʃ] *s.m.* handle, holder, haft, helve; stick, stock, shaft, pole, rod; neck (of violin, etc.); tail (of plough); loom (of oar); knuckle-bone (of meat); *~ à balai*, broomstick; (aeron.) joystick, steering-control; *~ à gigot*, bone-holder (for carving mutton); *~ de gigot*, knuckle-bone of leg of mutton; *jeter le ~ après la cognée*, to throw the helve after the hatchet, to give up in despair; *branler au* or *dans le ~*, to waver, to hesitate, to be shaky, to be unsafe, to be in a parlous state; to totter; *se mettre du côté du ~*, to side with the strongest, or with the party in power.
manche [mɑ̃ʃ] *s.f.* sleeve; flexible pipe, hose; neck (of balloon); strait, channel; rubber, game, heat; *avoir qn. dans sa ~*, to have s.o. in one's pocket, to have someone's services at one's command; *tirer la ~ à qn.*, to buttonhole s.o., to pluck s.o. by the sleeve; *avoir la ~ large*, to be easy-going, or broad-minded; *on ne se mouche plus sur sa ~*, the world has grown wiser; *c'est une autre paire de ~s*, that is quite another pair of shoes, that is quite another matter, or a different proposition; *~ à ~*, even (at play), neck-and-neck; *j'ai gagné la première ~*, I have won the first round, rubber, game, heat, leg; *retrousser ses ~s*, to roll up one's sleeves, (fig.) to get down to work; *~ à gigot*, leg-of-mutton sleeve; *~ à vent*, (i.) (aeron.) wind-sock; (ii.) (naut.) ventilator, air-shaft; *la Manche*, the (English) Channel; name of a (Fr.) department.
mancheron [mɑ̃ʃrɔ̃] *s.m.* **1.** handle (of plough); **2.** short sleeve; upper part of sleeve.
manchette [mɑ̃ʃɛt] *s.f.* **1.** cuff, wristband, ruffle, gauntlet (of glove); (boxing) jab to the chin; (fig.) handcuff; **2.** (print.) side-note, marginal note; headline (in newspaper).
manchon [mɑ̃ʃɔ̃] *s.m.* muff; (techn.) casing; jacket, sleeve, grip; *~ d'accouplement*, coupler, coupling; gas-mantle; *chien de ~*, lap-dog.
manchot, -e [mɑ̃ʃo] *adj.*, *s.m.f.* one-handed or one-armed (person); (fam.) clumsy, unhandy (person); *il n'est pas ~*, he is clever with his hands, (fig.) he is all there; *~ s.m.* (ornith.) penguin.
mancipation [mɑ̃sipɑsjɔ̃] *s.f.* (Rom. law) mancipation.
mandant, -e [mɑ̃dɑ̃] *s.m.f.* mandator, one giving a mandate; elector.
mandarin, -e [mɑ̃darɛ̃] *adj.*, *s.m.f.* **1.** mandarin;

(fig.) member of intellectual elite; **2.** (*canard*) ~, mandarin-duck.
mandarinat [mɑ̃darina] *s.m.* mandarinate; intellectual and administrative hierarchy; system of competitive examinations (establishing this hierarchy).
mandarine [mɑ̃darin] *s.f.* mandarin orange; tangerine.
mandarinier [mɑ̃darinje] *s.m.* (bot.) mandarin orange tree.
mandat [mɑ̃da] *s.m.* mandate, authority; commission, charge; warrant, writ; draft, cheque, money order, (fin.) order; ~ *d'arrêt* or *d'amener*, warrant for arrest; ~ *de comparution*, summons to appear; ~ *de dépôt*, commitment, committal-order; ~ *de perquisition*, search-warrant; ~ *de poste* or ~*-postal*, money order, postal order; *s'acquitter d'un* ~, to carry out one's orders, or duty, to discharge an obligation; ⚠ not 'order' in sense 'injunction' or 'command'.
mandataire [mɑ̃datɛr] *s.m.* mandatory; proxy, attorney, representative, agent.
mandater [mɑ̃date] *v.t.* **1.** to pay by money or postal order; to make out an order for payment; **2.** to give a mandate to, to empower, to entrust, to authorize, to employ as agent; to elect.
mandchou, -e [mɑ̃tʃu] *adj., s.m.f.* Manchu, Manchurian.
Mandchourie [mɑ̃tʃuri] *s.f.* (geog.) Manchuria.
mandement [mɑ̃dmɑ̃] *s.m.* mandate, mandamus; charge (of a bishop).
mander [mɑ̃de] *v.t.* **1.** to send word or instructions; to give orders; to send (information) in writing; *on mande de*, it is reported from; *on nous mande que*, we have word that, we have received a report that; ~ *des nouvelles*, to send news, to write with news; **2.** to summon; *on a mandé le médecin*, they have sent for the doctor.
mandibulaire [mɑ̃dibylɛr] *adj.* (anat.) mandibular.
mandibule [mɑ̃dibyl] *s.f.* mandible, jaw.
mandoline [mɑ̃dɔlin] *s.f.* mandolin(e).
mandore [mɑ̃dɔr] *s.f.* (mus.) mandora, mandore.
mandragore [mɑ̃dragɔr] *s.f.* (bot.) mandragora, mandrake.
mandrill [mɑ̃drij] *s.m.* (zool.) mandrill.
mandrin [mɑ̃drɛ̃] *s.m.* **1.** (techn.) mandrel, chuck, drift, punch, strike, former; **2.** ruffian, bandit.
manducation [mɑ̃dykɑsjɔ̃] *s.f.* manducation, eating, chewing, mastication.
manécanterie [manekɑ̃tri] *s.f.* parish choir-school.
manège [manɛʒ] *s.m.* **1.** manège; training of horses; riding, riding-school; **2.** roundabout, merry-go-round; horse-mill; **3.** (fig.) trick, play, ploy, manœuvre, intrigue, stratagem.
mânes [mɑn] *s.m.pl.* manes, ghosts, spirits, shades.
maneton [mantɔ̃] *s.m.* **1.** crank-handle; **2.** crank-pin.
manette [manɛt] *s.f.* hand-lever, control lever, grip, small handle, key; (naut.) spoke (of steering-wheel).
mangan-ate [mɑ̃ganat] *s.m.* (chem.) manganate; ~**èse** [mɑ̃ganɛs] *s.m.* (chem.) manganese; ~**eux** [mɑ̃ganø] *adj.* (chem.) manganous; ~**ique** [mɑ̃ganik] *adj.* (chem.) manganic; ~**ite** [mɑ̃ganit] *s.f.* (chem.) manganite.
mangeable [mɑ̃ʒabl] *adj.* edible, eatable.
mangeaille [mɑ̃ʒɑj] *s.f.* food (for animals), feed; (fam., pej.) food, grub.
mangeant, -e [mɑ̃ʒɑ̃] *adj. être bien* ~*(e)*, to be a hearty eater.
mangeoire [mɑ̃ʒwar] *s.f.* manger, crib, trough.
mangeotter [mɑ̃ʒɔte] *v.t.* to eat little of, to peck at.
manger [mɑ̃ʒe] *v.t.* to eat, to eat up, to eat away; to devour, to consume; to take, to absorb; to corrode, to destroy, to ruin; to run through (money, etc.); to spend, to squander; to chew, to gnaw, to bite; to clip; ~ *à sa faim*, to eat one's fill; *mangé des vers, des mites*, worm-eaten, moth-eaten; *mangé de rouille*, rusted away, eaten away by rust; *mangé d'herbes*, overgrown with weeds; *un visage mangé d'une barbe grise*, a face concealed, or swallowed up, by a grey beard; *les gros poissons mangent les petits*, might overcomes right; ~ *son blé en herbe*, to anticipate one's income; ~ *son pain blanc le premier*, to have one's best time first; ~ *la consigne*, to break bounds, to disobey orders; ~ *son bien*, to squander one's fortune; *salle à* ~, dining-room; *ce poêle mange beaucoup de charbon*, this stove consumes a lot of coal; ~ *ses mots*, to mumble, to speak indistinctly, to clip, or swallow, one's words; ~ *de la vache enragée*, to have a hard time, to have a rough time of it; ~ *un morceau*, to have a snack; (fig.) ~ *le morceau*, to let on, to reveal the secret, to turn informer, (slang) to blow the gaff, to grass; *donner à* ~ *à*, to feed, to give s.o. sth. to eat; ~ *du bout des dents* or *comme un oiseau*, to nibble, to pick at one's food; *on mange bien ici*, the food is good here; (pop.) *se* ~ *les sangs*, to be sick with worry; **se** ~ *v.refl.* to be eaten; to devour each other; (gram.) to be elided; ~ *s.m.* eating, food; dish; *il en perd le boire et le* ~, it takes away his appetite.
mangerie [mɑ̃ʒri] *s.f.* (fam.) gorging, guzzling, stuffing oneself with food.
mange-tout, mangetout [mɑ̃ʒtu] *s.m.invar.* **1.** (bot.) bean or pea, the pod of which is also edible; *pois* ~, sugar-peas; **2.** spendthrift, prodigal, squanderer.
mangeu-r, -se [mɑ̃ʒœr] *s.m.f.* eater; waster, spendthrift; ~*r de petits enfants*, boaster, braggart; ~*r de livres*, bookworm.
mangeure [mɑ̃ʒyr] *s.f.* (rare) part eaten or nibbled away.
manglier [mɑ̃glje] *s.m.* (bot.) mangrove.
mangoustan [mɑ̃gustɑ̃] *s.m.* (bot.) mangosteen.
mangouste [mɑ̃gust] *s.f.* **1.** (zool.) ichneumon, mongoose; **2.** (bot.) mangosteen.
mangrove [mɑ̃grɔv] *s.f.* mangrove swamp.
mangue [mɑ̃g] *s.f.* (bot.) mango.
manguier [mɑ̃gje] *s.m.* (bot.) mango-tree.
maniabilité [manjabilite] *s.f.* suppleness, pliability; manageableness, manœuvrability, handiness, ease of handling, tractability.
maniable [manjabl] *adj.* easy to handle, easily handled, supple, pliable, manageable, ductile, tractable, workable, handy.
maniaco-dépressi-f, -ve [manjakɔdeprɛsif] *adj., s.m.f.* (psychol.) manic-depressive.
maniaque [manjak] *adj.* maniac, mad, lunatic, eccentric, faddy, crotchety; ~ *s.m.f.* maniac, crank, eccentric; ⚠ the sense 'mentally deranged' is obsolescent. The modern meaning is rather 'obsessed with fads, habits, special interests, etc.'.
manichéen, -ne [maniʃeɛ̃] *adj., s.m.f.* Manich(a)ean.
manichéisme [maniʃeism] *s.m.* Manich(a)eism.
manichordion [manikɔrdjɔ̃], **manicorde** [manikɔrd] *s.m.* (mus.) manichord; clavichord.
manicle [manikl], **manique** [manik] *s.f.* **1.** protective gauntlet or sleeve; **2.** handle (of tool).
manicure [manikyr] *s.m.f.* = MANUCURE.
manie [mani] *s.f.* mania, obsession; passion, rage; whim, fancy, fad, craze, eccentricity, little habit; hobby; ⚠ see MANIAQUE.
maniement [manimɑ̃] *s.m.* **1.** handling, fingering, touching; management, use, conduct; handling (of money); **2.** (butch.) certain parts

of an animal from which its fatness can be judged by handling.

manier [manje] *v.t.* to handle, to touch, to finger; to use, to wield, to ply, to work; to manage, to control, to manœuvre; *il manie bien la langue*, he expresses himself well; ~ *s.m.* touch, feel; *au* ~, by feel, by the touch.

manière [manjɛr] *s.f.* manner, way, method, fashion, style; sort, kind; affectation, mannerism; (pl.) manners, affected behaviour; *chacun à sa* ~, everyone does things in his own way; *faire à sa* ~, to do things in one's own way, to act as one thinks best; *de la même* ~, in the same way; *à la* ~ *de*, like, in the style of, after the manner of; *de la bonne* ~, in the right way, handsomely; *de* ~ *ou d'autre*, somehow or other; *en quelque* ~, in a way, to some extent; *de toute* ~, in any case; (fam., iron.) *de la belle* ~, good and proper, soundly; *c'est sa* ~ *d'être*, that is what he is like, that is the sort of man he is; ~ *de voir*, view, viewpoint, opinion; *faire des* ~*s*, to behave in an affected way, to affect reluctance; *ne pas faire de* ~*s pour accepter*, to accept straight away, not to have to be asked twice; *de* ~ *à*, so as to; *de* ~ *que* or *de* ~ *à ce que*, so that, in such a way that.

maniéré, -e [manjere] *adj.* affected, unnatural, artificial, forced, mannered, mincing.

maniérisme [manjerism] *s.m.* mannerism, affectation.

maniériste [manjerist] *adj.*, *s.m.f.* mannerist(ic).

manieu-r, -se [manjœr] *s.m.f.* handler; manager, controller, manipulator; (often pej.) ~*r d'argent*, financier.

manifestant, -e [manifɛstɑ̃] *s.m.f.* demonstrator, one taking part in a demonstration.

manifestation [manifɛstɑsjɔ̃] *s.f.* **1.** manifestation, demonstration, public expression of feeling, etc.; (med.) manifestation, symptom; **2.** (theol.) revelation.

manifeste [manifɛst] *adj.* manifest, evident, obvious, clear, plain, palpable; **~ment** [manifɛstəmɑ̃] *adv.* manifestly, evidently, obviously, plainly, visibly.

manifeste [manifɛst] *s.m.* manifesto, declaration, proclamation; (naut.) manifest; (aeron.) passenger-list.

manifester [manifɛste] *v.t.* to manifest, to make known, to make clear, to reveal, to show, to exhibit, to evince, to give an indication of, to evidence; **se** ~ *v.refl.* to show oneself or itself, to manifest itself, to appear, to be revealed, to be made manifest; ~ *v.i.* to demonstrate, to take part in a demonstration.

manifold [manifɔld] *s.m.* **1.** (techn.) manifold; **2.** (comm.) duplicate book (for orders, etc.).

manigance [manigɑ̃s] *s.f.* (fam.) manœuvre, underhand practices, wire-pulling, petty intrigue.

manigancer [manigɑ̃se] *v.t.* (fam.) to intrigue, to get (sth.) done by intrigue or wire-pulling.

manille[1] [manij] *s.f.* manille (kind of card-game); master card at manille.

manille[2] [manij] *s.m.* Manila (cigar).

manille[3] [manij] *s.f.* anklet, ring; shackle.

maniller [manije] *v.t.* (naut.) to shackle.

manillon [manijɔ̃] *s.m.* (cards) each of four aces in manille.

manioc [manjɔk] *s.m.* (bot.) manioc, cassava.

manipulat-eur, -rice [manipylatœr] *s.m.f.* manipulator, operator; **~eur** *s.m.* morse-key.

manipulation [manipylɑsjɔ̃] *s.f.* manipulation, handling; (fig.) intrigue; ~*s électorales*, gerrymandering.

manipule [manipyl] *s.m.* (Rom. ant., Cath.) maniple.

manipuler [manipyle] *v.t.* to manipulate, to work, to operate, to handle.

manique see MANICLE.

manitou (pl. **-s**) [manitu] *s.m.* manitou, god of certain North American Indians; (fig.) *grand* ~, big boss, big noise, someone high up.

manivelle [manivɛl] *s.f.* handle; crank, starting-handle.

manne[1] [man] *s.f.* manna; (fig.) manna from heaven; substance exuding from certain trees.

manne[2] [man] *s.f.* hamper, basket; ~ *d'enfant*, wicker cradle.

mannequin[1] [mankɛ̃] *s.m.* wicker-basket (used by market-gardeners).

mannequin[2] [mankɛ̃] *s.m.* **1.** manikin; lay figure, dressmaker's dummy, dummy or model (in shop); scarecrow; (lit. & fig.) puppet, automaton; **2.** (male or female) mannequin or fashion model.

mannite [manit] *s.f.* (chem.) mannite.

manœuvrabilité [manœvrabilite] *s.f.* manœuvrability, handling qualities.

manœuvrable [manœvrabl] *adj.* manœuvrable, easy to handle.

manœuvre[1] [manœvr] *s.f.* action, working; handling, manipulation, managing, control, driving, manœuvring; (mil., nav.) drill, drilling, manœuvre, movement; (rail.) shunting, marshalling; (fig.) contrivance, trick, stratagem, move; (pl.) rigging, ropes; *grandes* ~*s*, field or large-scale manœuvres; (naut.) *maître de* ~, boatswain; ~*s dormantes*, standing rigging; *faire une fausse* ~, to make a false move, or a wrong decision.

manœuvre[2] [manœvr] *s.m.* labourer, manual or unskilled labourer; (fig.) hack; *travail de* ~, manual or unskilled labour; (fig.) hack-work.

manœuvrer [manœvre] *v.t.i.* to work, to manœuvre, to manipulate, to handle, to manage; to work the ship, to steer; to drill; (rail.) to shunt, to marshal; *faire* ~ *des soldats*, to drill soldiers, to manœuvre; to contrive, to scheme; *il a bien manœuvré dans cette affaire*, he managed that affair cleverly.

manœuvri-er [manœvrje] *s.m.* (naut., mil.) able, capable, competent seaman, officer, etc.; (fig.) clever tactician; **~er, ~ère** *adj.* manœuvring, skilled in manœuvre, well-trained.

manoir [manwar] *s.m.* manor, manor-house, country house.

manomètre [manɔmɛtr] *s.m.* manometer, pressure-gauge.

manométrique [manɔmetrik] *adj.* manometric, manometrical.

manoque [manɔk] *s.f.* **1.** (naut.) hank (of rope); **2.** hand (of tobacco leaves).

manouvri-er, -ère [manuvrje] *s.m.f.* worker, labourer.

manquant, -e [mɑ̃kɑ̃] *adj.* missing, absent, lacking, wanting; short; *s.m.f.* defaulter, absentee; missing object.

manque [mɑ̃k] *s.m.* want, lack, need, deficiency, incompleteness; shortcoming, failure, defect, breach; miss; dropped stitch; (rid.) stumble; (fam.) ~ *de pot*, bad luck; ~ *de parole*, breach of faith, breaking one's word; ~ *à gagner*, missed opportunity or profit; (*par*) ~ *de*, for want of; ~ *de touche* or *à toucher*, miss (at billiards); ~ *s.f.* *à la* ~, = MANQUÉ.

manqué, -e [mɑ̃ke] *adj.* defective, imperfect; unsuccessful, miscarried, abortive, that hasn't come off; lost, spoiled, missed, to no purpose, would-be, failed, manqué; having missed one's vocation as; *c'est un cuisinier* ~, he would have made a good cook; *c'est un garçon* ~, she should have been a boy; she is a real tomboy.

manquement [mɑ̃kmɑ̃] *s.m.* omission, oversight, slip; lack, shortcoming, failure, failure to observe (decencies, etc.), want; failing, fault; miss, missing; breach; lapse; dereliction.

manquer [mɑ̃ke] *v.i.* to miss, to fail, to go

wrong; to be wanting, to be lacking, to be deficient, to be missing; to give way, to slip; to miss fire; to be short, to disappoint, to fail to come up to expectations; to be insolvent, to go bankrupt; to miscarry; ~ *à qn.*, to be missed by s.o., to be lacking in respect towards s.o.; ~ *à qch.*, to fail in sth., to fail to observe, or to carry out, sth.; ~ *de*, to lack, to be lacking in, to want, to be short of, to be deficient in; ~ *de* (or *à*) *faire qch.*, to fail to do sth.; ~ (*de*) *faire qch.*, to very nearly do sth.; *un fusil qui manque*, a gun that misses fire; *il a manqué de tomber*, he nearly fell; *il manque de tout*, he is destitute; *il ne manque de rien*, he lacks nothing; *il ne manquait plus que cela*, that is the last straw, that crowns all; *il manque deux personnes*, there are two people missing; *je n'y manquerai pas*, I will not fail, I won't forget; *cela ne pouvait* ~ *d'arriver*, it was bound to happen; *l'affaire a manqué*, the affair has fallen through; *l'argent lui manque*, he is short of money; *le cœur lui manque*, his heart fails him; *le pied m'a manqué*, my foot slipped; ~ *à sa parole*, to break one's word; ~ *à son devoir*, to fail in one's duty; *vous me manquez*, I miss you; ~ *v.t.* to miss, to lose, to let slip, to spoil, to make a failure of; to be absent from, to fail to attend; ~ *son coup*, to miss one's aim, (fig.) to fail; ~ *son train*, to miss one's train.

mansarde [mɑ̃sard] *s.f.* **1.** mansard (roof); **2.** garret, attic, lodging under the roof.

mansardé, -e [mɑ̃sarde] *adj.* with attics, with a sloping roof or ceiling; (of roof) sloping; *étage* ~, attic storey.

manse [mɑ̃s] *s.m.* small country estate, small manor; ⚠ not 'manse'.

mansion [mɑ̃sjɔ̃] *s.f.* **1.** (Rom. ant.) halting-place; **2.** (medieval theatr.) mansion; ⚠ not 'mansion' in sense 'large house'.

mansuétude [mɑ̃sɥetyd] *s.f.* mansuetude, gentleness, forbearance.

mante [mɑ̃t] *s.f.* **1.** mantle; **2.** (ent.) mantis; ~ *religieuse*, praying mantis.

manteau (pl. **-x**) [mɑ̃to] *s.m.* cloak, mantle, coat, great-coat; (of animals) back, mantle (referring to distinguishing colour); mantel, mantelpiece; (herald.) mantling; (fig.) mask, pretence; *sous le* ~, sub rosa, clandestinely; *sous le* ~ *de*, under cloak, or pretence, of; ~ *de cheminée*, mantelpiece, chimney-piece; (theatr.) *le manteau d'Arlequin*, the proscenium arch.

mantelé, -e [mɑ̃tle] *adj.* mantled; (of crows) hooded.

mantelet [mɑ̃tlɛ] *s.m.* short coat or cloak; tippet, mantlet; (carriage-) apron; (fort.) mantlet; (naut.) port-lid, deadlight.

mantelure [mɑ̃tlyr] *s.f.* = MANTEAU (referring to animals).

mantille [mɑ̃tij] *s.f.* mantilla.

mantisse [mɑ̃tis] *s.f.* (math.) mantissa.

manucure [manykyr] *s.m.f.* manicurist.

manucurer [manykyre] *v.t.* (fam.) to manicure.

manuel, -le [manɥɛl] *adj.* manual; by hand, with the hands; *s.m.f.* practical type (of person), one good with his hands (rather than intellectual); ~ *s.m.* manual, handbook, text-book; **~lement** [manɥɛlmɑ̃] *adv.* manually, by hand.

manufacturable [manyfaktyrabl] *adj.* manufacturable.

manufacture [manyfaktyr] *s.f.* manufacture, making, fabrication; factory, mill, works.

manufacturer [manyfaktyre] *v.t.* to manufacture, to make, to fabricate, to process.

manufacturi-er, -ère [manyfaktyrje] *adj.* manufacturing; *s.m.f.* manufacturer.

manumission [manymisjɔ̃] *s.f.* (Rom. & feud. law) manumission, freeing (of slaves).

manuscrit, -e [manyskri] *adj.* manuscript, in manuscript, written by hand; ~ *s.m.* manuscript; (print.) copy.

manutention [manytɑ̃sjɔ̃] *s.f.* administration, management; handling (of goods, etc.); store, store-keeping; army bake-house; **~naire** [manytɑ̃sjɔnɛr] *s.m.* store-keeper; handler (of goods); **~ner** [manytɑ̃sjɔne] *v.t.* to handle or store goods.

maori, -e [maɔri] *adj.* Maori.

maous, -se [maus] *adj.* **1.** (pop.) big, hefty; **2.** (obs.) magnificent.

mappemonde [mapmɔ̃d] *s.f.* map of the world; globe, sphere; planisphere; ~ *céleste*, map of the heavens.

maquereau[1] (pl. **-x**) [makro] *s.m.* (ichth.) mackerel.

maquereau[2] (pl. **-x**) [makro] *s.m.* pimp, pander, procurer; **maquerelle** [makrɛl] *s.f.* procuress; brothel-keeper.

maquette [makɛt] *s.f.* small rough model, mock-up, maquette, miniature model, scale-model, demonstration model; rough sketch, sketch (of scenery, for large picture); (print.) layout, dummy.

maquignon [makiɲɔ̃] *s.m.* horse-dealer, horse-jobber; (fig., pej.) jobber, go-between, shady dealer; **~nage** [makiɲɔnaʒ] *s.m.* horse-dealing, horse-coping, horse-faking; (fig.) horse-trading, shady dealing, sharp practice; **~ner** [makiɲɔne] *v.t.* to fake up (a horse); (fig.) to engage in sharp practice.

maquillage [makijaʒ] *s.m.* make-up, making-up; (fig.) disguising (defects, etc.) with paint, painting-over.

maquiller [makije] *v.t.* to make up; (fig.) to fake, to disguise, to falsify.

maquilleu-r, -se [makijœr] *s.m.f.* (theatr.) maker-up, make-up man or woman.

maquis [maki] *s.m.* scrub, bush, bush-covered heath, jungle, maquis; hide-out; resistance movement; *prendre le* ~, to take to the bush, to go into hiding.

maquisard [makizar] *s.m.* resistance fighter, member of resistance movement.

marabout [marabu] *s.m.* **1.** marabout; marabout shrine; **2.** big-bellied kettle or coffee-pot; **3.** marabou-stork; marabou-feathers; **4.** (mil.) bell-tent.

maraîch-er, -ère [marɛʃe] *adj.* market-gardening; *s.m.f.* market-gardener.

marais [marɛ] *s.m.* marsh, swamp, fen, bog, moor, (lit. & fig.) morass; market-garden; ~ *salant*, salt-marsh; *dessécher un* ~, to drain a marsh; *le Marais*, (i.) an old district of Paris; (ii.) (hist.) moderate group in Fr. Revolution.

marante [marɑ̃t] *s.f.* (bot.) maranta.

marasme [marasm] *s.m.* marasmus, consumption; atrophy, emaciation; (fig.) stagnation, depression; *dans le* ~, in a state of stagnation, depressed.

marasque [marask] *s.f.* (bot.) marasca cherry.

marasquin [maraskɛ̃] *s.m.* maraschino.

marathon [maratɔ̃] *s.m.* (lit. & fig.) marathon-race, marathon; **~ien** [maratɔnjɛ̃] *s.m.* marathon runner.

marâtre [marɑtr] *s.f.* stepmother, unkind, harsh mother; *être* ~ *pour*, to treat harshly or unkindly.

maraud, -e [maro] *s.m.f.* (obs.) rogue, knave, rascal, scoundrel; (fem.) jade, hussy.

maraudage [marodaʒ] *s.m.* marauding, plundering, pilfering.

maraude [marod] *s.f.* marauding, plundering, looting, pilfering; (of taxis) *en* ~, driving slowly looking for fares, 'crawling'.

marauder [marode] *v.i.* to maraud, to go marauding, to pilfer; (of taxis) to 'crawl'.

maraudeu-r, -se [marodœr] *s.m.f.* plunderer, marauder, pilferer; (of taxis) = EN MARAUDE.

maravédis [maravedi] *s.m.* maravedi (old Spanish copper coin); (fam.) *pas un* ~, not a penny (left).

marbre [marbr] *s.m.* marble; marble slab, marble top; marble-work; marble statue; (print.) imposing-stone; (bookbind.) marbling; (fig.) *être froid comme du* ~, to be hard-hearted, impassive; *demeurer comme un* ~, to remain stock-still, motionless; (naut.) ~ *du gouvernail*, barrel of the steering-wheel; (print.) *sur le* ~, in type, ready for the press; (journalism) *avoir du* ~ or *rester sur le* ~, (of article) to be set up in type but held over for later publication.

marbré, -e [marbre] *adj.* marbled, veined, mottled.

marbrer [marbre] *v.t.* to marble, to vein, to mottle; to make blotchy.

marbrerie [marbrəri] *s.f.* marble-cutting, marble-work; marble-mason's yard.

marbreu-r, -se [marbrœr] *s.m.f.* paper--marbler.

marbrier [marbrije] *s.m.* marble-cutter, marble--polisher; marble-dealer; marble-grainer; ~, **marbrière** *adj.* marble.

marbrière [marbrijɛr] *s.f.* marble-quarry.

marbrure [marbryr] *s.f.* marbling, marble--graining; mottling; blotchiness.

marc[1] [mar] *s.m.* residuum, residue (of fruit, etc., after pressing), marc; grounds, dregs; ~ *de raisin*, skins of grapes (after pressing); ~ *de café*, coffee-grounds.

marc[2] [mar] *s.m.* mark (i. old weight = 8 *onces*; ii. gold or silver coin of that weight); (law) *au* ~ *le franc*, pro rata, at so much in the pound.

marcassin [markasɛ̃] *s.m.* young wild boar.

marcassite [markasit] *s.f.* (min.) marcasite.

marceline [marsəlin] *s.f.* (min., text.) marceline.

marcescence [marsɛssɑ̃s] *s.f.* (bot.) marcescence, withering.

marcescent, -e [marsɛssɑ̃] *adj.* (bot.) marcescent, withering.

marchand, -e [marʃɑ̃] *s.m.f.* merchant, dealer, trader; shop-keeper, shopman, tradesman, store-keeper; salesman; buyer, customer; (auctions) bidder; ~ *d'habits*, old-clothes dealer; ~*e à la toilette*, wardrobe dealer; ~*e d'amour* or *de plaisir*, prostitute; ~ *de biens*, (real) estate agent; (pej.) ~ *de canons*, armament dealer; ~ *de tabac*, tobacconist; ~ *forain*, stall--keeper (at fair, etc.), hawker; ~ *en gros*, wholesale dealer, merchant, wholesaler; ~ *au détail*, retail dealer, retailer; ~(*e*) *des quatre saisons*, costermonger, barrow-boy; (pej.) ~ *de soupe*, (i.) proprietor of cheap and nasty restaurant; (ii.) (fig.) headmaster of private school run for profit; *trouver* ~, to find a purchaser or a bidder; *y a-t-il* ~?, is there a bidder?, any bids?; *n'est pas* ~ *qui toujours gagne*, you can't win all the time.

marchand, -e [marʃɑ̃] *adj.* merchantable, marketable, saleable, vendible; mercantile, trade, trading, merchant, commercial; good for trade, fit for trade; (of river) navigable; wholesale; *galerie* ~*e*, shopping arcade; *marine* ~*e*, merchant service, mercantile marine; *vaisseau, navire*, ~, merchantman, cargo ship; *place* ~*e*, good trading position; *prix* ~, trade price, wholesale price; *valeur* ~*e*, market value, commercial value.

marchandage [marʃɑ̃daʒ] *s.m.* bargaining; haggling; (fig., pej.) horse-trading; sub--contracting of labour, sweated labour.

marchander [marʃɑ̃de] *v.t.* to bargain for; to haggle over or about; to stand bargaining over; to beat down; (law) to close a deal; (fig.) to spare, to grudge; to sub-contract for labour; ~ *sur le prix*, to haggle over the price; *ne pas* ~ *sa peine*, not to grudge one's trouble; to spare no pains, to go to all lengths; *ne pas* ~ *sa vie*, to hold one's life of little account; ~ *les éloges*, to give grudging praise to, to praise with reluctance; ~ *les consciences*, to bribe, to make a tempting offer; ~ *v.i.* to haggle, to chaffer, to bargain; (fig.) to hesitate, to be irresolute, to boggle (*à*, at); *sans* ~, without hesitating, without making any bones about it; *il n'y a pas à* ~, it's either the one or the other, you can take it or leave it.

marchandeu-r, -se [marʃɑ̃dœr] *s.m.f.* bargainer, haggler; sub-contractor of labour.

marchandise [marʃɑ̃diz] *s.f.* merchandise, goods, wares, commodity; article; *faire valoir sa* ~, to push one's goods; to show off one's goods; (fig.) to put oneself in a favourable light; *tromper sur la* ~, to sell faked or adulterated goods, to cheat; *faire métier et* ~ *d'une chose*, to trade in a commodity; (fig.) to be used to, to be in the habit of doing, sth.

marchant, -e [marʃɑ̃] *adj.* walking, moving, on the move, proceeding; *aile* ~*e*, (mil.) leading wing; (fig.) active element (of party, etc.).

marche[1] [marʃ] *s.f.* walk, walking; gait; march, distance, journey; marching; progress, advance; rate (of progress), speed (of movement); procession; sequence; course; movement, working (of machines); operation, functioning; sailing, steaming (of ships), running (of trains, etc.); move (at chess); conduct, way of proceeding, process; spoor (of deer); (mus.) march; ~ *d'harmonie*, harmonic progression; *fermer la* ~, to close the procession, to bring up the rear; *ouvrir la* ~, to lead the way; *être construit pour la* ~, to be built for speed; *avoir la* ~ *sur*, to outsail, (fig.) to outstrip; *gagner une* ~ *sur*, to steal a march on; *en* ~, on the march, on the move, in motion, in progress, going, working, functioning; *mettre en* ~, to set going, to start up, to start working; *se mettre en* ~, to start out, to start, to move off, to set off; ~ *funèbre*, dead march; *la* ~ *de la civilisation*, the progress of civilization; *mise en* ~, starting (of machine, etc.), running (of a service); *une* ~ *de deux heures*, a two hours' walk; *c'est à deux heures de* ~, it is two hours' walk from here; *gêner la* ~ *de*, to impede the progress of; *voici la* ~ *à suivre*, this is the course to follow, this is the way to set about it; *suivre la* ~ *de la maladie*, to observe the course of the illness; ~ *arrière*, reverse, reversing, backing, backward motion, reverse gear.

marche[2] [marʃ] *s.f.* stair, step, tread (of stair); treadle (of lathe); pedal (of organ); handle (of hurdy-gurdy); (fig.) *être sur les* ~*s du trône*, to be the next heir to the throne, (fig.) to be the likely successor.

marche[3] [marʃ] *s.f.* march, border-district, frontier.

marché [marʃe] *s.m.* market; market-place; mart, emporium, fair; commercial outlet, sale--point; dealing, buying; bargain, purchase; price, rate; state of the market; agreement, contract, treaty; *faire son* ~, to go to the market; *le cours du* ~, the market price; ~ *encombré*, overstocked market, glut; ~ *aux fleurs*, flower market; *bon, meilleur*, ~, cheap, cheaper; *à bon* ~, cheap, cheaply; *le bon* ~, the cheapness, the low price; *faire* or *conclure un* ~, to strike a bargain, to make a deal; *faire un* ~ *avantageux*, to make a good bargain; ~ *au comptant*, cash transaction; ~ *à terme*, for future settlement, for settlement on a specified date, time contract; ~ *noir*, black market; *le Marché commun*, the Common Market; ~ *de fournitures*, supply contract; ~ *à* *forfait*, contract with penalty clause; (fig.) *être quitte à bon* ~, to come off better than one expected, to get off lightly; *avoir bon* ~ *de*, to make short work of, to get the better of easily; *je lui ai mis le* ~ *dans la main*, I told him he could take it or leave it, he has got to say yes or no; *être en* ~ *avec*, to be negotiating with; *c'est* ~ *fait!*, done!, it's a deal!; *on ne revient pas sur un* ~, a bargain's a bargain; *le* ~ *est nul*, the deal is off, no sale, nothing doing!; *un article qui n'a pas de* ~, an article for which there is no sale; *faire bon* ~ *de*, to hold cheap, to think little of; *il ne sera pas quitte à si bon* ~, he will not get off so easily; *un* ~ *d'or*, a great bargain; *on n'a jamais bon* ~ *de mauvaise marchandise*, a bad article is dear at any price; *par-dessus le* ~, into the bargain, besides that.

marchepied [marʃəpje] *s.m.* step, stair; folding stairway; footboard, running-board; pair of steps; (naut.) foot-rope; footpath (along canal, etc., opposite towpath); (fig.) stepping-stone.

marcher [marʃe] *v.i.* to walk, to go on foot; to step, to tread; to go, to move, to travel, to march; (of machine) to work, to operate, to function; (of ships) to sail, to run, to ply; to advance, to proceed, to go on; to succeed; to move on, to progress; to behave; *cette montre ne marche plus*, this watch has stopped, this watch won't go; *faire* ~, to set going, to start working, to make (to) work, to operate, to run; (slang) to humbug, to fool; *il veut vous faire* ~, he is pulling your leg, he is having you on; ~ *à grands pas*, to stride along; ~ *à l'ennemi*, to march against the enemy; ~ *avec*, to walk with; (fig.) to go along with, to agree with; ~ *dans l'eau*, to wade; ~ *dans une histoire*, to be taken in by a story; ~ *dans la combine*, to fall in with the scheme, to join in the plot; ~ *ensemble*, to go together; ~ *à pas de loup*, to walk stealthily, to creep; ~ *à quatre pattes*, to go on all fours; ~ *sur la pointe des pieds*, to walk on tiptoe; ~ *à pas comptés*, to walk with measured tread; ~ *à reculons*, to walk backwards, to retreat, to retrogress; ~ *sur qn.*, to advance (aggressively) towards s.o.; ~ *sur ses principes*, to ride rough-shod over one's principles; ~ *à tâtons*, to grope one's way; ~ *droit*, to walk straight, (fig.) to behave properly; *il marchera*, he will do what he is told; *(est-ce que) ça marche?*, how are you doing?, things going all right?; *ce procédé a marché*, this method was successful; ~ *sur les pas de* or *sur les traces de qn.*, to follow in someone's footsteps, to follow someone's example; ~ *sur les pieds de qn.*, to tread on someone's toes, to treat s.o. in cavalier fashion; ~ *s.m.* walk, gait, step, pace, tread; walking, ground (on which one walks).

marcheu-r, -se [marʃœr] *adj.* walking; *s.m.f.* pedestrian, walker; (fam., pej.) *un vieux* ~*r*, an old rake.

marcottage [markɔtaʒ] *s.m.* (hort.) layering.

marcotte [markɔt] *s.f.* (hort.) layer, runner.

marcotter [markɔte] *v.t.* (hort.) to layer.

mardi [mardi] *s.m.* Tuesday; ~ *gras*, Shrove Tuesday.

mare [mar] *s.f.* pool, pond.

marécage [marekaʒ] *s.m.* marsh, bog, fen, swamp, morass.

marécageu-x, -se [marekaʒø] *adj.* marshy, swampy, boggy.

maréchal (pl. **aux**) [mareʃal] *s.m.* **1.** farrier; **2.** (mil.) marshal, field marshal; ~ *ferrant*, farrier, shoeing-smith; ~ *de France*, field marshal; ~ *des logis*, non-commissioned officer (in cavalry or artillery, equivalent to 'sergeant').

maréchalat [mareʃala] *s.m.* marshalship, post of marshal.

maréchale [mareʃal] *s.f.* **1.** field marshal's wife; **2.** forge coal.

maréchalerie [mareʃaləri] *s.f.* farriery; farrier's shop.

maréchaussée [mareʃose] *s.f.* (hist.) marshalsea; constabulary, mounted police; (iron.) police.

marée [mare] *s.f.* tide, flood; fresh sea-fish; ~ *morte*, neap tide; *grande* ~, spring tide; ~ *montante, descendante*, rising, ebbing, tide; *prendre la* ~, to take advantage of the tide, to sail on the tide; (fig.) *aller contre vents et* ~*s*, to pursue one's own course in face of all opposition; *marchand de* ~, fishmonger; *la* ~ *est abondante*, there is plenty of fish in; *arriver comme* ~ *en carême*, to arrive most opportunely; *la* ~ *n'attend personne*, time and tide wait for no man; *ce qui vient de flot s'en retourne de* ~, easy come, easy go; *train de* ~, fish train.

marégraphe [maregraf], **maréographe** [mareɔgraf], **maréomètre** [mareɔmɛtr] *s.m.* marigraph, tide-gauge.

marelle [marɛl] *s.f.* hopscotch.

marémot-eur, -rice [maremɔtœr] *adj.* (esp. of power, power-stations) generated, operated, by the tides.

marengo [marɛ̃go] *s.m.invar.* speckled cloth; pepper-and-salt (colour); *poulet (à la)* ~, chicken cooked with mushrooms and tomatoes.

mareyage [marɛjaʒ] *s.m.* fish trade.

mareyeu-r, -se [marɛjœr] *s.m.f.* fish-dealer, fish-wholesaler.

margarine [margarin] *s.f.* margarine.

margay [margɛ] *s.m.* (zool.) margay, tiger-cat.

marge [marʒ] *s.f.* margin (of paper, books, etc.); border, edge; (fig.) latitude, scope, room, time; *en* ~, in the margin, marginal, on the fringe; *en* ~ *de*, on the fringe of, arising out of, as a footnote to; *nous avons de la* ~, we have means, or time, enough to spare, we have sufficient latitude.

margelle [marʒɛl] *s.f.* kerb, kerbstone; curb, lip (round pond or well).

marger [marʒe] *v.t.* (print.) to feed in paper (to the machine); (typing) to set the margin.

margeu-r, -se [marʒœr] *s.m.f.* (print.) layer-on (operative or machine); ~**r** *s.m.* margin-set (of typewriter).

marginal, -e, (aux) [marʒinal] *adj.* marginal.

marginer [marʒine] *v.t.* to write in the margin of, to make marginal notes in.

margis [marʒi] *s.m* mil. slang abbrev. *maréchal des logis*.

margoter [margɔte] *v.i.* (of quail) to cry.

margotin [margɔtɛ̃] *s.m.* small bundle of kindling.

margouillis [marguji] *s.m.* mud, mess, filth.

margoulette [margulɛt] *s.f.* (pop.) mouth, jaw; *casser la* ~ *à qn.*, to bash someone's face in.

margoulin [margulɛ̃] *s.m.* small speculator; small and unscrupulous businessman.

margrave [margrav] *s.m.* margrave; ~ *s.f.* margravine.

margraviat [margravja] *s.m.* margraviate.

marguerite [margərit] *s.f.* (bot.) daisy, marguerite, ox-eye daisy; (obs.) pearl; (naut.) messenger-chain, deck-tackle; (leather-work) graining-board; *jeter des* ~*s aux pourceaux*, to cast pearls before swine; **Marguerite** *s.f.* (proper name) Margaret.

marguillerie [margijri] *s.f.* churchwardenship.

marguillier [margije] *s.m.* churchwarden.

mari [mari] *s.m.* husband, spouse.

mariable [marjabl] *adj.* marriageable, of marriageable age.

mariage [marjaʒ] *s.m.* marriage, matrimony, wedlock, married state; match; wedding, nuptial ceremony; union; (fig.) joining, uniting, blending; (naut.) marrying (of two ropes); ~ *d'inclination*, love-match; ~ *de convenance* or *de raison*, marriage of convenience; *acte de* ~, marriage certificate; *contrat de* ~, marriage settlement; *messe de* ~, nuptial mass; *né hors du* ~, born out of wedlock; *prendre en* ~, to take to wife; *promettre* ~ *à*, to promise to marry; *demande en* ~, proposal of marriage.

marial, -e [marjal] *adj.* (eccles.) of the Virgin (Mary); Marian.

marié, -e [marje] *adj.* married; (fig.) matched, blended; ~ *s.m.* bridegroom, married man; **~e** *s.f.* bride, married woman; *se plaindre que la ~e est trop belle*, to complain of a good bargain, to consider it too much of a good thing; *les nouveaux ~s*, the bride and bridegroom, the newly-weds.

marier [marje] *v.t.* to marry (see ⚠ below), to join in marriage, to give in marriage; (fig.) to match, to join, to blend, to unite, to mingle; (naut.) to marry (ropes); *il a marié sa fille à un marquis*, he married his daughter to a marquis; ~ *des couleurs*, to match colours; (hort.) ~ *deux variétés de roses*, to cross two kinds of roses; **se** ~ *v.refl.* to marry (see ⚠ below), to get married; (fig.) to match, to blend, to go, to harmonize, to combine (*avec*, with); ⚠ *marier* is 'to marry', as performed by the priest or registrar, or in the sense of 'marrying one's daughter to s.o.'; *se marier* is 'to get married' (*avec qn.*, to s.o.).

marie-salope [marisalɔp] *s.f.* **1.** (naut.) dredger; mud-barge, mud-lighter; **2.** (pop.) slut, prostitute.

marieu-r, -se [marjœr] *s.m.f.* match-maker.

marigot [marigo] *s.m.* marigot, side channel of a tropical river.

marihuana [marihuana], **marijuana** [mariʒɥana] *s.f.* marijuana.

marin, -e [marɛ̃] *adj.* marine; off-shore; nautical, seagoing, seafaring; found in the sea; seaworthy, with good sea-keeping qualities; sailor('s); *col* ~, sailor collar; (*costume*) ~, child's sailor-suit; *avoir le pied* ~, to have good sea-legs; ~ *s.m.* seaman, sailor, seafarer, mariner; ~ *d'eau douce*, freshwater sailor, land-lubber; (mil.) *fusilier* ~, marine.

marinade [marinad] *s.f.* (cook.) marinade, pickle, brine; marinated meat or fish.

marinage [marinaʒ] *s.m.* marinating, pickling, sousing.

marine[1] [marin] *s.f.* (obs.) sea, sea-water; (mod.) service at sea, naval service; seamanship; naval administration; Admiralty; navy, fleet, naval forces; shipping, ships; smell or taste of the sea; (paint.) seascape, sea-piece; *officier de* ~, naval officer; ~ *marchande*, merchant service, mercantile marine; ~ *de guerre*, navy, = Royal Navy; *sentir la* ~, to smell of the sea; ~ *adj.invar.* (*bleu*) ~, navy blue.

marine[2] [marin] *s.m.* marine (British or American soldier).

mariner [marine] *v.t.* to cure, to pickle, to preserve; to souse, to marinate; ~ *v.i.* to be in pickle, or in a marinade; to be pickled, or preserved, or marinated; (fig.) to languish, to rot.

maringouin [marɛ̃gwɛ̃] *s.m.* mosquito.

marini-er, -ère [marinje] *adj.* marine; *officier ~er*, petty officer; (cook.) *moules ~ère*, mussels cooked in onion sauce; **~er** *s.m.* bargee, lighterman, waterman, boatman; (obs.) seaman, sailor.

mariol, mariolle [marjɔl] *adj.* (pop.) clever, self-important; *faire le ~le*, to show off.

mariolâtrie [marjɔlatri] *s.f.* Mariolatry.

marionnette [marjɔnɛt] *s.f.* marionette, (lit. & fig.) puppet; (techn.) ninepin-block; (pl.) marionette or puppet show

marionnettiste [marjɔnetist] *s.m.f.* one who gives a marionette or puppet show.

mariste [marist] *s.m.f.* (Rom. Cath.) Marist.

marital, -e, (aux) [marital] *adj.* marital; (law) *autorisation ~e*, husband's consent; **~ement** [maritalmɑ̃] *adv.* maritally, matrimonially; as husband and wife; (obs.) as a husband.

maritime [maritim] *adj.* maritime, sea; by sea; sea-going; nautical, naval; *législation* ~, maritime law, navigation laws; *ville* ~, seaside town; *gare* ~, harbour station; *assurance* ~, marine insurance; *agent* ~, shipping agent.

maritorne [maritɔrn] *s.f.* slattern, slut, wench, maid-of-all-work.

marivaud-age [marivodaʒ] *s.m.* affected style after the manner of Marivaux; **~er** [marivode] *v.i.* to imitate the style of Marivaux; to make pretty speeches; to flirt.

marjolaine [marʒɔlɛn] *s.f.* (bot.) sweet marjoram.

mark [mark] *s.m.* mark (German monetary unit).

marli [marli] *s.m.* raised rim of a plate.

marlou [marlu] *s.m.* (slang) pimp, procurer.

marmaille [marmɑj] *s.f.* brats, a lot of noisy brats.

marmelade [marməlad] *s.f.* compote, jam, jelly, marmalade; (fig.) mess; *viande en* ~, meat cooked to a jelly; (fig.) *avoir la figure en* ~, to have one's face smashed to pulp.

marmenteau (pl. **-x**) [marmɑ̃to] *adj.*, *s.m.* ornamental growing timber on an estate, not to be cut by lessees.

marmitage [marmitaʒ] *s.m.* bombarding (by heavy artillery).

marmite [marmit] *s.f.* boiler; pan, saucepan, pot, stew-pot; potful; digester; (fig.) heavy artillery shell; (techn.) ~ *de Papin*, Papin's digester; (fig.) *faire bouillir la* ~, to keep the pot boiling; *écumer la* ~, to skim the pot, (fig.) to sponge; *écumeur de* ~, sponger, parasite; *renverser la* ~, to give up entertaining; *nez en pied de* ~, bulbous nose; (geol.) ~ *de géants*, huge hollow in rocks, worn away by water, pot-hole.

marmitée [marmite] *s.f.* potful.

marmiter [marmite] *v.t.* to bombard with heavy artillery.

marmiton [marmitɔ̃] *s.m.* scullion, scullery-boy; pastry-cook's errand-boy.

marmonnement [marmɔnmɑ̃] *s.m.* mumbling, muttering.

marmonner [marmɔne] *v.i.* to mutter, to mumble, to murmur.

marmoréen, -ne [marmɔreɛ̃] *adj.* marmoreal, marmorean, marble-like, as marble; (fig.) icy, frigid.

marmorisation [marmɔrizɑsjɔ̃] *s.f.* (geol.) marmorization.

marmot [marmo] *s.m.* (fam.) child, brat; (obs.) grotesque figure (esp. as door-knocker); (fig.) *croquer le* ~, to dance attendance, to kick, or to cool, one's heels.

marmotte [marmɔt] *s.f.* **1.** (zool.) marmot; *dormir comme une* ~, to sleep like a top; **2.** woman's head-scarf; **3.** box of samples; **4.** (bot.) kind of plum.

marmottement [marmɔtmɑ̃] *s.m.* murmuring, muttering, mumbling.

marmotter [marmɔte] *v.t.* to mutter, to mumble, to murmur.

marmotteu-r, -se [marmɔtœr] *s.m.f.* mumbler, mutterer.

marmottier [marmɔtje] *s.m.* (bot.) kind of plum-tree.

marmouset [marmuzɛ] *s.m.* **1.** grotesque

figure (esp. as decorative motif); **2.** urchin, small boy, whipper-snapper; ⚠ not 'marmoset'.

marnage [marnaʒ] *s.m.* (agric.) marling, claying.

marne [marn] *s.f.* marl.

marner[1] [marne] *v.t.* (agric.) to marl; (pop.) to work hard.

marner[2] [marne] *v.i.* (of tide) to rise above the normal level.

marneur [marnœr] *s.m.* marler, marl-digger.

marneu-x, -se [marnø] *adj.* marly.

marnière [marnjɛr] *s.f.* marl-pit.

Maroc [marɔk] *s.m.* (geog.) Morocco.

marocain, -e [marɔkɛ̃] *adj., s.m.f.* Moroccan, (native or inhabitant) of Morocco; ~ *s.m.* (text.) marocain.

marolles [marɔl] *s.m.* cheese made at Maroilles.

maronite [marɔnit] *adj., s.m.f.* Maronite.

maronner [marɔne] *v.i.* (fam.) to grumble, to growl, to curse.

maroquin [marɔkɛ̃] *s.m.* **1.** morocco (leather); roan; *papier* ~, morocco-paper; **2.** (ministerial) portfolio, ministerial post.

maroquinage [marɔkinaʒ] *s.m.* preparation of morocco leather.

maroquiner [marɔkine] *v.t.* to morocco, to give a morocco finish to.

maroquinerie [marɔkinri] *s.f.* morocco-leather dressing; morocco-leather factory; morocco--leather trade or shop.

maroquinier [marɔkinje] *s.m.* morocco-leather dresser, tanner, leather-goods maker, leather--goods dealer.

marotique [marɔtik] *adj.* Marotic, in the manner of Marot.

marotte [marɔt] *s.f.* fool's bauble; (fig.) fancy, whim, hobby, mania; (millinery, hairdressing) dummy, head, model; *chacun a sa* ~, everyone has his fads.

marouette[1] [marwɛt], **maroute** [marut] *s.f.* (bot.) stinking camomile, dog-fennel.

marouette[2] [marwɛt] *s.f.* (ornith.) water-rail.

marouflage [maruflaʒ] *s.m.* (paint.) lining, pasting, backing.

maroufle[1] [marufl] *s.m.* bumpkin, boor, rustic; rascal, scoundrel.

maroufle[2] [marufl] *s.f.* painter's glue, lining--paste.

maroufler [marufle] *v.t.* (paint.) to line, to paste, to back.

maroute see MAROUETTE[1].

marquage [markaʒ] *s.m.* marking, branding.

marquant, -e [markɑ̃] *adj.* of note, notable, conspicuous, striking, remarkable; significant, memorable; *personnage* ~, person of note, (fam.) big shot; *cartes* ~*es*, cards that count.

marque [mark] *s.f.* mark, imprint, stamp; trade-mark; cipher, private mark; label; brand, branding-iron; print, trace, (of footsteps); testimony, proof, token; counter (at play); (sport) score; scar, pit (on the skin); note, distinction; (naut., car manufacture) marque; *la* ~ *d'une charge*, the badge of office; *un homme de* ~, a man of note, a distinguished man; *produits de* ~, branded goods; *liqueurs de* ~, liqueurs of superior quality; ~ *de fabrique*, trade--mark; (naut.) *lettre de* ~, letter of marque; ⚠ not 'mark' in senses 'target', (examination, etc.) 'mark', or 'level'.

marqué, -e [marke] *adj.* marked, stamped, branded; lined, scarred; evident, conspicuous, obvious; decided, fixed, determined; appointed; *être* ~, to be lined or wrinkled, to look old; to be branded; (fig.) to be marked out, to be labelled, to be designated, to be a marked man; *le moment* ~, the appointed time; *il est né* ~, he was born with a birth-mark; ~ *de l'A*, first-class, A1; ~ *de la petite vérole*, pitted with smallpox; *une tendance très* ~*e*, a pronounced tendency.

marquer [marke] *v.t.* to mark, to mark out, to leave a mark on; to stamp; to brand, to stigmatize; to indicate, to show, to betoken, to denote, to portray, to express; to record, to register; to show off, to emphasize; to appoint; to state, to tell, to let know, to inform, to mention; to show marks of, to bear the stamps of; to testify to; to characterize, to distinguish; to score, to mark or note down; ~ *par écrit*, to inform in writing; *je lui ai marqué que*, I notified him that; ~ *sa reconnaissance*, to show one's gratitude; ~ *un point*, to score a point, to score, to make a point; ~ *le coup*, to underline, to emphasize, to celebrate the occasion, to react, to register (a reaction); ~ *le pas*, (lit. & fig.) to mark time; ~ *le pas* or *le rythme*, to beat in time (with the rhythm); *cet acteur marque la passion sans l'outrer*, this actor portrays feeling without overdoing it; *l'horloge marque l'heure*, the clock indicates, or tells, the time; *le thermomètre marque 30°*, the thermometer registers, or stands at, 30°; *cela marque l'adolescence*, that is a mark of adolescence, it is a characteristic of adolescence; ~ *v.i.* to make one's mark; to be remarked, to be remarkable, to attract notice, to be conspicuous, to be evident, to stand out, to make an impression; to be significant; (fam.) *cela marquerait trop*, that would be too noticeable, that would attract too much attention; ~ *mal*, to make a bad impression.

marqueté, -e [markəte] *adj.* **1.** speckled; **2.** inlaid.

marqueterie [markɛtri] *s.f.* marquetry, inlaid work, inlaying; (fig.) patchwork, miscellany, mosaic.

marqueteur [markətœr] *s.m.* inlayer, worker in marquetry.

marqueu-r, -se [markœr] *s.m.f.* marker; scorer, tally-keeper; ~**se** *s.f.* stamping- or marking-machine.

marquis [marki] *s.m.* **1.** (obs.) marcher, one who guarded a march; **2.** marquis, marquess; (fig.) elegant man; (pej.) fop.

marquisat [markiza] *s.m.* marquisate.

marquise [markiz] *s.f.* **1.** marchioness; **2.** canopy, awning; covered porch, glass roof; **3.** marquise ring; **4.** kind of pear.

marquoir [markwar] *s.m.* **1.** marker; **2.** (needlew.) sampler.

marraine [marɛn] *s.f.* godmother; sponsor, one who names and launches a ship; ~ (*de guerre*), one who 'adopts' a soldier (and sends food--parcels, etc.).

marrant, -e [marɑ̃] *adj.* (slang) **1.** amusing; **2.** strange, queer, boring; (fam.) the limit.

marre [mar] *adv. j'en ai* ~, I am fed up with it, I have had enough of it; *c'est* ~, (pop.) that's enough; (slang) that's the lot!, that's it!

(**se**) **marrer** [mare] *v.refl.* to enjoy oneself immensely, to split one's sides laughing.

marri, -e [mari] *adj.* sorry, grieved, contrite, repentant.

marron[1] [marɔ̃] *s.m.* chestnut, Spanish chestnut; (firework) cracker, maroon; tally, check; chestnut colour; (pop.) blow or slap (on the head); ~ *d'Inde*, horse-chestnut; *tirer les* ~*s du feu*, to serve as catspaw; ~ *adj.invar.* reddish--brown, maroon; (fig., pop.) caught, tricked, swindled.

marron[2], **-ne** [marɔ̃] *adj.* fugitive, runaway; (of animals) gone wild; (comm.) unlicensed, pirate, pirated, unofficial; clandestine; spurious, sham; *nègre* ~, runaway slave; *médecin* ~, unqualified doctor.

marronner [marɔne] *v.i.* to be a runaway slave.

marronnier [marɔnje] *s.m.* **1.** Spanish-chestnut tree; **2.** ~ (*d'Inde*), horse-chestnut tree.
marrube [maryb] *s.m.* (bot.) horehound.
Mars [mars] *s.m.* (myth., astron.) Mars; (fig.) war; *champ de* ~, parade ground, large open space.
mars [mars] *s.m.* March; (pl.) spring corn; *arriver comme* ~ *en carême*, to be sure to happen.
marsault, marseau (pl. **-x**) [marso] *s.m.* (bot.) sallow, marsh-willow.
marseillais, -e [marsɛjɛ] *adj., s.m.f.* Marseillais, (native or inhabitant) of Marseilles; *la Marseillaise*, the Marseillaise (Fr. national anthem).
marsouin [marswɛ̃] *s.m.* **1.** porpoise, sea-hog; **2.** soldier or N.C.O. of (former Fr.) colonial infantry.
marsupial, -e, (**aux**) [marsypjal] *adj., s.m.* (zool.) marsupial; marsupials.
martagon [martagɔ̃] *s.m.* (bot.) martagon, Turk's cap.
marte see MARTRE.
marteau (pl. **-x**) [marto] *s.m.* hammer; (ichth.) hammer-head shark; door-knocker; striker (of gong, clock, etc.); (auctioneer's) hammer, gavel; (anat.) malleus; ~ *à deux mains* or *de forge*, sledge-hammer; *enfoncer un clou avec un* ~ or *à coups de* ~, to hammer in a nail; *aplatir à coups de* ~, to hammer out; *travailler au* ~, to hammer, to hand-forge; (fam.) *avoir un coup de* ~, or *être* ~, to be mad, to be not all there; *être entre le* ~ *et l'enclume*, to be between the devil and the deep (blue) sea; *il vaut mieux être* ~ *qu'enclume*, better to be biter than bit.
marteau-pilon [martopilɔ̃] *s.m.* (pl. *marteaux-pilons*) power-hammer, forge-press.
martel [martɛl] *s.m.* (obs.) hammer; *avoir* or *se mettre* ~ *en tête*, to be very uneasy, to be worried.
martelage [martəlaʒ] *s.m.* hammering; marking (of trees).
martelé, -e [martəle] *adj.* hammered; (fig.) hammered out, (of music) thumped out.
martèlement, martellement [martɛlmɑ̃] *s.m.* **1.** hammering noise, noise of hammer-blows; **2.** hammer-like rhythm.
marteler [martəle] *v.t.* to hammer, to forge; to mark (trees); (fig.) to torment; to accentuate (a syllable).
martelet [martəlɛ] *s.m.* small hammer.
marteleur [martəlœr] *s.m.* hammerer; hammer-man; hammersmith.
martellerie [martɛlri] *s.f.* forging-shop.
martial, -e, (aux) [marsjal] *adj.* martial, war-like; military, soldierly; (chem.) chalybeate, containing iron; *cour* ~*e*, court-martial; (med.) *carence* ~*e*, iron deficiency; ~**ement** [marsjalmɑ̃] *adv.* martially, in a soldierly manner.
martien, -ne [marsjɛ̃] *adj.* of or from Mars; *s.m.f.* Martian.
martinet[1] [martinɛ] *s.m.* (ornith.) swift.
martinet[2] [martinɛ] *s.m.* **1.** drop-hammer; **2.** tawse, cat-o'-nine-tails, lash.
martingale [martɛ̃gal] *s.f.* **1.** martingale; **2.** (dressm.) half-belt.
martin-pêcheur [martɛ̃pɛʃœr] *s.m.* (ornith.) kingfisher.
martre [martr], **marte** [mart] *s.f.* (zool.) marten; ~ *blanche*, ermine; ~ *zibeline*, sable; *fourrure de* ~, sable; (fig.) *prendre* ~ *pour renard*, to be misled by a resemblance.
martyr, -e [martir] *adj.* martyred; *s.m.f.* martyr.
martyre [martir] *s.m.* martyrdom; (fig.) agonies, tortures, great physical or moral suffering.
martyriser [martirize] *v.t.* to martyr, to make into a martyr; (fig.) to torment, to persecute, to torture.
martyrium [martirjɔm] *s.m.* shrine of a martyr.
marxien, -ne [marksjɛ̃] *adj.* Marxian.
marxisme [marksism] *s.m.* Marxism.
marxiste [marksist] *adj., s.m.f.* Marxist.
maryland [marilɑ̃d] *s.m.* Maryland (Virginia) tobacco.
mas [mɑ, mɑs] *s.m.* (in S. of France) farm, (farm-)house.
mascarade [maskarad] *s.f.* masquerade, masked procession; (fig.) masquerade, disguise, pretence, hypocrisy.
mascaret [maskarɛ] *s.m.* bore, eagre (at mouth of river).
mascaron [maskarɔ̃] *s.m.* (arch.) mascaron; grotesque figure.
mascotte [maskɔt] *s.f.* mascot, lucky charm.
masculin, -e [maskylɛ̃] *adj.* masculine, male, manly; (gram.) masculine; *métier* ~, man's trade or job; ~ *s.m.* masculine (gender); *au* ~, in the masculine.
masculiniser [maskylinize] *v.t.* to make masculine, to give a mannish appearance to; (biol.) to induce male characteristics.
masculinité [maskylinite] *s.f.* masculinity, masculineness.
maser [mazɛr] *s.m.* (phys.) maser.
masque [mask] *s.m.* mask; (fig.) cloak, disguise, pretence; masquerader, masker, mummer; (fenc.) face-guard; cast, death-mask; (mil.) screen; (fig.) face, countenance, expression, physiognomy; (arch.) mascaron; ~ *à gaz*, gas-mask, respirator; ~ *mortuaire* or *funéraire*, death-mask; ~ *facial*, face-mask (beauty treatment); *lever* or *jeter le* ~, to unmask (oneself); to throw off the mask, to abandon pretence; *arracher le* ~ *à*, to unmask; *prendre le* ~ *de la vertu*, to assume a cloak of virtue.
masqué, -e [maske] *adj.* masked; disguised; hidden, concealed; *bal* ~, masked ball, masquerade, fancy-dress ball; *virage* ~, blind corner, concealed turning; (mil.) *tir* ~, indirect fire, fire from a concealed position.
masquer [maske] *v.t.* to mask; to cloak, to disguise; to camouflage; to conceal, to hide, to screen; (naut.) to take aback (sails); ~ *les feux* or *les lumières*, to cover or obscure lights; **se** ~ *v.refl.* to mask oneself, to put on a mask; to be disguised; to hide oneself; to be concealed, masked, screened.
massacrante [masakrɑ̃t] *adj.f.* (fam.) *humeur* ~, vile temper; *de* ~ *humeur*, in a vile temper.
massacre [masakr] *s.m.* massacre, butchery, slaughter, certain death, wholesale destruction; (fig.) havoc; waste, squandering; spoiling; smashing, mangling, hacking to bits, murdering (of piece of music, etc.); disaster, horrible mess; (herald., hunt.) head (of stag); *jeu de* ~, Aunt Sally (game).
massacrer [masakre] *v.t.* to massacre, to slaughter, to murder, to butcher; to mangle, to destroy; to waste, to squander; to smash, to hack about or to bits, to make a mess of, to spoil, to bungle; (theatr.) ~ *son rôle*, to murder one's part; ~ *la langue*, to murder the language.
massacreu-r, -se [masakrœr] *s.m.f.* slaughterer, slayer, butcher; bungler; (fig.) murderer.
massage [masaʒ] *s.m.* massage.
massaliote [masaljɔt] *adj., s.m.f.* (person) from or of Massilia (anc. Marseilles).
masse[1] [mas] *s.f.* mass, large quantity or number, heap, lump; bulk, aggregate; main body; mob; capital, stock, common fund; deduction or retention (from pay); stakes (at play); ~ *d'eau*, volume of water (flowing); large sheet of water; *en* ~, mass, in a mass, en masse, in a body, in the mass, in full force, in great numbers or quantity, in bulk; *les* ~*s*, the masses, the people; (comm.) large quantity (usu. 12 gross); (sculpture) *tailler dans la* ~,

to cut from the block; (mil.) ~ *de manœuvre*, main striking force, strategic reserve; (phys.) mass; (electr.) earth; *faire* ~ or *mettre à la* ~, to earth, to make an earth connection.
masse[2] [mas] *s.f.* mace; sledge-hammer; rammer; ~ *d'armes*, mace; (fig., fam.) *coup de* ~, great shock, blow, body-blow; sheer murder (referring to prices, etc.); (bot.) ~ *d'eau*, reed-mace, cat's tail.
massé [mase] *s.m.* (billiards) massé, push-stroke.
masselotte [maslɔt] *s.f.* (techn.) deadhead (of casting); ball or striker operating inertial mechanism.
massepain [maspɛ̃] *s.m.* marzipan, almond-paste confectionery.
masser[1] [mase] *v.t.* to massage.
masser[2] [mase] *v.t.* to mass, to group together, to pile up; (billiards) to strike with a push-stroke; **se** ~ *v.refl.* to mass, to group together, to crowd together, to collect.
masséter [masetɛr] *s.m.* (anat.) masseter.
massette[1] [masɛt] *s.f.* (bot.) reed-mace, cat's-tail, bulrush.
massette[2] [masɛt] *s.f.* sledge-hammer; two-handed hammer; mace.
masseu-r, -se [masœr] *s.m.f.* masseur, masseuse.
massicot [masiko] *s.m.* **1.** (metall.) massicot, yellow oxide of lead; **2.** guillotine (for cutting paper, etc.).
massier[1] [masje] *s.m.* mace-bearer.
massi-er[2]**, -ère** [masje] *s.m.f.* student-treasurer (of an art studio).
massi-f, -ve [masif] *adj.* massive, bulky, solid, substantial; heavy, solidly-built, on a massive scale; *argent* ~*f*, solid silver; *ventes* ~*ves*, heavy sales; *défections* ~*ves*, desertions on a large scale; ~**f** *s.m.* group, clump, cluster, (of trees, flowers), flower-bed; thicket, grove; (arch.) solid mass, block (of masonry), wall, pier, pile; mountain mass; ~**vement** [masivmɑ̃] *adv.* massively, heavily, solidly, on a large scale, in large doses.
massiquot [masiko] *s.m.* = MASSICOT 2.
massique [masik] *adj.* (phys.) of mass, by unit of mass.
massue [masy] *s.f.* **1.** club, bludgeon; *coup de* ~, knock-out blow; (fig.) calamity, catastrophe; *la nouvelle fut un coup de* ~, the news stunned him; *prendre une* ~ *pour écraser une fourmi* or *une mouche*, to use a sledge-hammer to crack a nut; *arguments* ~*s*, crushing arguments; **2.** (bot., ent.) knob-shaped tip of fungi or antennae.
mastic [mastik] *s.m.* mastic (resin); putty; filling, stopping; cement; (bot.) mastic, species of thyme; (print.) accidental transposition of matter; ~ *adj.* mastic- or putty-coloured.
masticage [mastikaʒ] *s.m.* cementing, puttying, stopping, filling.
masticat-eur, -rice [mastikatœr] *adj.* masticatory, masticating; ~**eur** *s.m.* (*appareil*) ~*eur*, masticating- or mincing-machine.
mastication [mastikɑsjɔ̃] *s.f.* mastication, masticating, chewing.
masticatoire [mastikatwar] *adj.*, *s.m.* masticatory.
mastiff [mastif] *s.m.* mastiff.
mastiquer[1] [mastike] *v.t.* to cement, to putty, to fill, to stop.
mastiquer[2] [mastike] *v.t.i.* to masticate, to chew.
mastoc [mastɔk] *adj.invar.* heavy, heavily-built, clumsy, large and ugly.
mastodonte [mastɔdɔ̃t] *s.m.* (zool.) mastodon.
mastoïde [mastɔid] *adj.* (anat.) mastoid; (pathol.) *apophyse* ~, mastoid process, mastoid.
mastoïdien, -ne [mastɔidjɛ̃] *adj.* (anat.) mastoid.
mastoïdite [mastɔidit] *s.f.* (med.) inflammation of the mastoid, mastoiditis.
mastroquet [mastrɔkɛ] *s.m.* (fam.) keeper of a pub, publican; wine-shop, pub.
masturbation [mastyrbɑsjɔ̃] *s.f.* masturbation.
(**se**) **masturber** [mastyrbe] *v.refl.* to masturbate.
m'as-tu vu [matyvy] *s.m.invar.* vain person, lover of publicity, one who loves to show off.
masure [mazyr] *s.f.* hovel, shanty, shack, tumbledown dwelling.
mat [mat] *adj.invar.*, *s.m.* (chess) mate(d); *échec et* ~, checkmate; *faire* (*échec et*) ~, to checkmate, to mate.
mat, -e [mat] *adj.* matt, mat, dull, lustreless unpolished; dead, dull-sounding, flat, insipid; heavy; *coloris* ~, drab or dull colour; *teint* ~, dull or pasty complexion; *or* ~, unpolished gold; *son* ~, dull or muffled sound.
mât [mɑ] *s.m.* mast, pole; (*bout de*) ~, spar; *le grand* ~, the mainmast; ~ *de fortune*, jury-mast; ~ *de pavillon*, flag-mast, flagstaff; ~ *d'artimon*, mizen-mast; ~ *de beaupré*, bowsprit; ~ *de misaine*, foremast; ~ *de hune*, topmast; ~ *de charge*, derrick; *aller à* ~ *et à corde*, to go under bare poles; (rail.) ~ *de sémaphore*, signal-post; *abaisser un* ~, to strike a mast; ~ *de cocagne*, greasy pole.
matador [matadɔr] *s.m.* matador; (slang) important person, magnate; (cards) principal cards at *hombre* and *quadrille*.
matage [mataʒ] *s.m.* **1.** matting (of gilt, etc.); **2.** caulking (of seams, joints).
mâtage [mɑtaʒ] *s.m.* masting, fitting of masts.
matamore [matamɔr] *s.m.* braggart, boaster; *faire le* ~, to boast.
match [matʃ] *s.m.* match (in sport); (fam.) contest; ~ *d'aviron*, boat-race; ~ *nul*, draw; ⚠ not any of the other meanings of 'match'.
maté [mate] *s.m.* (bot.) maté; maté tea.
matelas [matla] *s.m.* mattress; cushion, pad, padding, squab; (fam.) wad (of banknotes); ~ *à air*, air-bed, inflatable mattress; ~ *à eau*, water-bed; *toile à* ~, ticking; (fig., fam.) *il a le* ~, he is rolling in money, he has a well-lined purse.
matelassé, -e [matlase] *adj.* upholstered, stuffed, padded, quilted.
matelasser [matlase] *v.t.* to stuff, to pad, to upholster, to quilt, to line with quilting; to cover up, to wrap up.
matelassi-er, -ère [matlasje] *s.m.f.* mattress-maker, remaker of mattresses.
matelassure [matlasyr] *s.f.* padding, wadding, stuffing, padded lining.
matelot [matlo] *s.m.* sailor, seaman; shipmate, mariner, messmate; consort ship; child's sailor-suit.
matelotage [matlɔtaʒ] *s.m.* seamanship; seaman's wages, pay.
matelote [matlɔt] *s.f.* **1.** (rare) seaman's wife; **2.** matelote, fish cooked with wine and onions; **3.** hornpipe; *à la* ~, seamanlike, sailor fashion.
mater[1] [mate] *v.t.* (chess) to mate, to checkmate; (fig.) to tame, to subdue, to repress, to thwart.
mater[2] [mate], **matir** [matir] *v.t.* **1.** to matt, to give a matt finish to, to etch (glass); **2.** to caulk (seams, joints).
mâter [mɑte] *v.t.* (naut.) to mast, to fit with masts; *machine à* ~, masting-crane, heavy crane.
mâtereau (pl. **-x**) [mɑtro] *s.m.* (naut.) small mast; spar, pole.
matérial-isation [materjalizɑsjɔ̃] *s.f.* materialization, materializing, causing to materialize; ~**iser** [materjalize] *v.t.* to materialize, to cause to materialize, to give material form to; to symbolize; **se** ~**iser** *v.refl.* to materialize, to become visible or real; ~**isme** [materjalism] *s.m.* materialism; ~**iste** [materjalist] *s.m.f.*, *adj.* materialist; materialistic; ~**ité** [materjalite] *s.f.* materiality, material character; reality.

matériau (pl. **-x**) [materjo] *s.m.* (more usu. pl.) material, materials.

matériel, -le [materjɛl] *adj.* material, heavy, physical, of the body, dull; sensuous, sensual; essential, vital, necessary; palpable, sizable; *impossibilité ~le*, physical impossibility; *erreur ~le*, sizable error; *besoins ~s*, bodily needs; (fam.) *la ~le*, one's daily needs, the necessities of life; ~ *s.m.* **1.** that which is material, or concerned with the matter, the material; matter; **2.** material, stores; stock-in-trade, working-stock; plant; rolling-stock; implements, apparatus; furniture, fittings, equipment, requisites; **~lement** [materjɛlmɑ̃] *adv.* materially; positively, to all intents and purposes, in fact; sensually, physically.

maternel, -le [matɛrnɛl] *adj.* maternal, motherly, of one's mother, of mothers; *langue ~le*, mother-tongue; *parents ~s*, relations on the mother's side; **~le** *s.f.* infants' school, crèche, kindergarten; **~lement** [matɛrnɛlmɑ̃] *adv.* maternally, in a motherly manner.

maternité [matɛrnite] *s.f.* maternity, motherhood, pregnancy, childbirth; maternity hospital or home; *service de ~*, maternity ward or section; (art) picture of mother and child.

math, maths [mat] *s.f.pl.* maths (abbrev. of *mathématiques*).

mathématicien, -ne [matematisjɛ̃] *s.m.f.* mathematician.

mathématique [matematik] *adj.* mathematical; ~ *s.f.* (usu. pl.) mathematics; **~ment** [matematikmɑ̃] *adv.* mathematically; rigorously; (fig.) *cela devait ~ment arriver*, it was mathematically certain to happen.

matheu-x, -se [matø] *s.m.f.* **1.** mathematics student or pupil; **2.** student good at mathematics.

matière [matjɛr] *s.f.* matter; material, substance; (fig.) subject-matter, topic, theme, subject; cause, reason, motive, grounds; contents; point, question; (law) *la ~ d'un crime*, the gravamen of a charge; *~s grasses*, fat (as a constituent of food), fat content; *~ grise*, (anat. & fig.) grey matter, bràin; *~ d'honneur*, point of honour, question of honour; *~ à réflexions*, food for thought; *il n'y a pas ~ à rire*, there's nothing to laugh about, it is no joking matter; *en ~ de*, in matters of, as regards, concerning; *entrer en ~*, to broach the subject, to begin; *~ première*, raw material; *~s d'or et d'argent*, bullion; *~ médicale*, materia medica; *~ à procès* or *à poursuite*, grounds for litigation; (iron.) *s'élever au-dessus de la ~*, to soar above material things, to rise superior to material considerations; *~ imposable*, taxable article.

matin [matɛ̃] *s.m.* morning, forenoon; dawn; (fig.) prime, youth; *un beau ~*, one fine morning; *un de ces quatre ~s*, one of these (fine) days; *être du ~*, to be up (and doing) early; *de bon* or *de grand ~*, early in the morning; *petit ~*, (crack of) dawn, break of day; *il était grand ~*, it was early in the day; *du ~ au soir*, from morning to night, all day long; (fig.) all the time, without ever stopping; *heure du ~, heure du gain*, the early bird catches the worm; ~ *adv.* early, early in the morning; *se lever ~*, to get up early; *ce n'est pas tout de se lever ~, il faut arriver à l'heure*, it is one thing to hurry and another to succeed.

mâtin [mɑtɛ̃] *s.m.* mastiff; large watch-dog; (fig.) ugly brute; ~, **~e** *s.m.f.* spiteful or ill-behaved person; ~ *interj.* expressing surprise.

matinal, -e, (aux) [matinal] *adj.* morning; early, early rising; matutinal; *une personne ~e*, an early riser; *à une heure ~e*, at an early hour, early in the morning; *comme vous êtes ~ aujourd'hui!*, you are up early this morning!

mâtiné, -e [mɑtine] *adj.* (of dogs) crossed, mongrel; (fig.) mongrel, mixed, mingled (*de*, with).

matinée [matine] *s.f.* **1.** morning, forenoon; *dormir* or *faire la grasse ~*, to lie abed late, to have a long lie; **2.** morning's work; (theatr., etc.) afternoon performance; afternoon gathering; **3.** (obs.) house-coat.

mâtiner [mɑtine] *v.t.* to cross, to cross-breed; to cover (of dogs).

matines [matin] *s.f.pl.* matins, mattins.

matineu-x, -se [matinø] *adj.* early, early rising; *être ~x, ~se*, to be an early riser.

matini-er, -ère [matinje] *adj.* (obs.) *l'étoile ~ère*, the morning star.

matir see MATER[2].

matité [matite] *s.f.* deadness, dullness, matt effect, drabness; heaviness.

matoir [matwar] *s.m.* tool for deadening metals.

matois, -e [matwɑ] *adj.* cunning, sly, artful, crafty; *s.m.f.* cunning person, sly fellow; *c'est un fin ~*, he's a very slippery customer.

matoiserie [matwazri] *s.f.* cunning, slyness, artfulness, (an) artful dodge.

matou [matu] *s.m.* tom-cat.

matraquage [matrakaʒ] *s.f.* clubbing, coshing.

matraque [matrak] *s.f.* club, truncheon, cosh.

matraquer [matrake] *v.t.* to club, to bludgeon, to cosh; (fig.) to clobber.

matras [matra] *s.m.* **1.** bolt (from crossbow); **2.** (chem.) matrass.

matriarcal, -e, (aux) [matriarkal] *adj.* matriarchal.

matriarcat [matriarka] *s.m.* matriarchy, matriarchate.

matriçage [matrisaʒ] *s.m.* (techn.) forging, pressing, die-stamping.

matricaire [matrikɛr] *s.f.* (bot.) Matricaria, feverfew, wild camomile.

matrice [matris] *s.f.* **1.** (anat.) matrix, womb; **2.** tax register; **3.** (techn.) mould, block, die; **4.** (math.) matrix.

matricer [matrise] *v.t.* (techn.) to forge, to press, to mould, to stamp.

matricide [matrisid] *adj.* matricidal; *s.m.f.* matricidal person, matricide; ~ *s.m.* matricide (the crime).

matriciel, -le [matrisjɛl] *adj.* pertaining to the tax register; for tax purposes.

matricule [matrikyl] *s.f.* register, roll, rolls, list of members; registration, enrolment, certification; *numéro ~* (or ~ *s.m.*) registration number, administrative or regimental number; ~ *adj.* matriculation.

matriculer [matrikyle] *v.t.* to register, to enter in the register, to enrol; to grant a certificate (of registration) to; to mark or stamp with a registration number; ⚠ not 'to matriculate'.

matrimonial, -e, (aux) [matrimɔnjal] *adj.* matrimonial; **~ement** [matrimɔnjalmɑ̃] *adv.* matrimonially; *joindre ~ement*, to join in marriage.

matrone [matrɔn] *s.f.* matron, matronly figure; fat and vulgar woman; (obs.) midwife; back-street abortionist; ⚠ not '(hospital or school) matron'.

matte [mat] *s.f.* (metall.) matte.

matthiole [matjɔl] *s.f.* (bot.) Matthiola.

maturation [matyrɑsjɔ̃] *s.f.* maturation, maturing, ripening; (med.) suppuration.

mature [matyr] *adj.* mature, fully grown.

mâture [mɑtyr] *s.f.* masting, masts, spars; masting timber; method of masting; mast-shed.

maturément [matyremɑ̃] *adv.* after full consideration.

maturité [matyrite] *s.f.* maturity, ripeness, mellowness, state of full development; mature

age, prime; completion; circumspection, mature judgment; ~ *précoce*, precocity, precociousness, early maturity; ~ *tardive*, late or retarded development; *avec* ~, maturely, after mature, or careful, consideration; *venir à* ~, to ripen; to come to maturity.
matutinal, -e, (aux) [matytinal] *adj.* matutinal.
maubèche [mobɛʃ] *s.f.* (ornith.) sandpiper.
maudire [modir] *v.t.* to curse, to call down curses upon, to execrate, to anathematize; to express hatred or detestation of; ~ *du haut de la chaire*, to curse with bell, book and candle.
maudissable [modisabl] *adj.* execrable, detestable.
maudit, -e [modi] *adj.* cursed, accursed; horrible, detestable, abominable, wretched; damnable, confounded; *~e soit l'espérance!*, to hell with hope!; ~ *soit le coquin!*, damn his eyes!; ~ *s.m. le Maudit*, the Devil; *les ~s*, the accursed, the damned, those rejected by society.
maugré [mogre] *prep.* old form of MALGRÉ.
maugréer [mogree] *v.i.* to grumble, to fume, to curse and swear, to grouse.
maure, more [mɔr] *adj.* Moorish; ~ *s.m.* Moor.
maurelle [mɔrɛl] *s.f.* (bot.) dyer's croton.
mauresque, moresque [mɔrɛsk] *adj.* Moorish, Moresque; ~ *s.f.* Moorish woman.
mauser [mozɛr] *s.m.* Mauser, make of rifle or pistol.
mausolée [mozɔle] *s.m.* mausoleum.
maussade [mosad] *adj.* sulky, sullen, glum, cross, disgruntled; disagreeable, unpleasant; dull, tedious, depressing; **~ment** [mosadmɑ̃] *adv.* disagreeably, sullenly, grumpily.
maussaderie [mosadri] *s.f.* crossness, sullenness, sulkiness, grumpiness.
mauvais, -e [mɔvɛ, movɛ] *adj.* bad, ill, evil; wicked, evil-minded, ill-natured, vicious, naughty; mischievous, injurious, hurtful; wrong, incorrect, amiss; foul, unpleasant; sinister, unlucky, unpropitious; contrary, adverse; wretched, sorry, cheap, poor; nasty; (print.) battered; hard, difficult; defective, (of doctrine, etc.) unsound; *avoir l'air* ~, to look evil, vicious, or nasty; *un rire* ~, a nasty laugh; *bête ~e*, vicious animal; ~ *ange* or *génie*, evil genius; *femme de ~e vie*, loose woman, prostitute; (law) ~ *procès*, difficult case; ~ *métier*, unprofitable occupation or business; *~e mesure*, short measure or weight; *né sous une ~e étoile*, born under an unlucky star; *la ~e direction*, the wrong direction; *rire au* ~ *endroit*, to laugh in the wrong place; ~ *calcul*, erroneous calculation; *passer un* ~ *quart d'heure*, to have a bad quarter of an hour, to have an unpleasant time; *avoir ~e mine*, to look ill; ~ *jours*, hard times; *il est très ~e langue*, he has a sharp tongue; ~ *sujet*, black sheep, rogue, bad lad; *~e tête*, hot-headed individual; *il fait* ~, the weather is bad; *trouver* ~ *que*, to take it amiss that; *trouver* ~ *qu'il fasse cela*, to disapprove of his doing it; *prendre en ~e part*, to take in bad part; *mer ~e*, rough sea; *pas* ~, not bad, pretty good; *~e herbe*, weed; *il la trouve ~e*, he is disgusted, he doesn't think it funny; ~ *s.m.* bad, wrong; *discerner le bon du* ~, to distinguish good from bad, or right from wrong; *il faut prendre le bon avec le* ~, you must take the rough with the smooth, you must take things as they come; ~ *adv. sentir* ~, to smell bad; *il fait* ~ *d'être pauvre*, it is a wretched thing to be poor.
mauvaiseté [mɔvɛzte, movɛzte] *s.f.* naughtiness; ill-nature, viciousness.
mauve [mov] *s.f.* (bot.) mallow; (ornith.) gull, sea-mew; ~ *s.m.* mauve (colour); ~ *adj.* mauve.
mauvéine [movein] *s.f.* (chem.) mauve aniline dye.
mauviette [movjɛt] *s.f.* (fam.) thin, frail person; *quelle ~!*, what a slip of a girl!
mauvis [movi] *s.m.* (ornith.) redwing; (poet.) mavis.
maxillaire [maksilɛr] *adj.* maxillary; ~ *s.m.* maxilla, jaw(-bone).
maxima [maksima] *adj., s.m.pl.* see MAXIMUM.
maximal, -e, (aux) [maksimal] *adj.* maximal.
maximaliste [maksimalist] *s.m.* maximalist.
maxime [maksim] *s.f.* maxim, saying; *tenir* or *avoir pour* ~, to hold as a maxim.
maximum (pl. *maximums, maxima*; also *adj.f. maxima*) [maksimɔm] *s.m.* maximum, the most, the height, highest point, maximum level or price, maximum effort, one's best, maximum penalty; *au* ~, at the most, at the highest point; *pression* ~ or *maxima*, maximum pressure; *prix ~s* or *maxima*, maximum prices; (law) *avoir le* ~, to receive the maximum sentence; *faire rendre son* ~ *à un coureur*, to extend a runner; *thermomètre à maxima*, maximum thermometer.
maya [maja] *s.m.f.* Maya(n); *adj.* Mayan; ~ *s.m.* Maya (language).
maye [mɛ] *s.f.* stone trough into which oil pours from the press.
mayonnaise [majɔnɛz] *adj.* with or in mayonnaise; ~ *s.f.* mayonnaise.
mazagran [mazagrɑ̃] *s.m.* coffee served in a glass; coffee watered down.
mazarinade [mazarinad] *s.f.* (hist.) libel written against Mazarin in the wars of the Fronde.
mazdéisme [mazdeism] *s.m.* Mazdaism, Zoroastrianism.
mazéage [mazeaʒ] *s.m.* (metall.) first operation in refining cast iron.
mazer [maze] *v.t.* (metall.) to refine cast iron.
mazette [mazɛt] *s.f.* small and wretched horse; (fig.) bad performer at game, duffer; weakling; ~ *interj.* expressing surprise.
mazout [mazut] *s.m.* heavy oil, fuel oil.
mazouter [mazute] *v.i.* to take on fuel oil, to oil.
mazurka [mazyrka] *s.f.* mazurka.
me [mə] (**m'** before vowel or h-mute) *pers. pron.* me, to me, for me; myself, to myself, for myself; ~ *voici*, here I am.
mea-culpa [meakylpa] *s.m. dire* or *faire son* ~, to cry peccavi; to plead guilty, to repent.
méandre [meɑ̃dr] *s.m.* meander, meandering, winding, sinuosity.
méandrine [meɑ̃drin] *s.f.* (zool.) coral of genus Maeandra.
méat [mea] *s.m.* (anat., bot.) meatus, duct, passage, orifice.
mec [mɛk] *s.m.* **1.** (slang) energetic man, keen type; **2.** (pop.) bloke.
mécanicien, -ne [mekanisjɛ̃] *s.m.f.* specialist in mechanics, mechanics expert; mechanical engineer, mechanic, engineer (mechanic); (nav.) artificer; driver, engine-man, engine driver; *ouvrier* ~, mechanic; *~-dentiste*, dental mechanic; *adj.* mechanical, mechanized, mechanically-minded.
mécanique [mekanik] *adj.* mechanic, of mechanics, mechanical; mechanized; machine-made, made by machinery; (fig.) mechanical, automatic; (phil.) mechanistic; ~ *s.f.* mechanics, mechanism, machinery, movement (of clock, etc.), action; machine, piece of machinery; (fam.) complicated piece of machinery; mechanical skill; *fait à la* ~, machine-made; (fam.) *ennuis ~s*, engine-trouble; *la* ~ *céleste*, the structure of the heavens; ~ *appliquée*, applied mechanics; **~ment** [mekanikmɑ̃] *adv.* mechanically, like a machine, automatically.
mécanis-ation [mekanizɑsjɔ̃] *s.f.* mechanization; **~er** [mekanize] *v.t.* to mechanize, to

render mechanical, to turn into a machine; *~er les hommes*, to turn men into machines.

mécanisme [mekanism] *s.m.* mechanism, machinery, works; appliance, device; mechanics, working, technique; operation; process; mechanical skill; (phil.) mechanism, mechanistic theory.

mécaniste [mekanist] *adj.* (phil.) mechanistic.

mécano [mekano] *s.m.* (fam.) mechanic.

mécano-graphie [mekanɔgrafi] *s.f.* use of calculating, accounting, etc., machines, computerization; **~graphique** [mekanɔgrafik] *adj.* (of accounting, etc.) by machine; *machine ~graphique*, computer; **~thérapie** [mekanɔterapi] *s.f.* (med.) mechanotherapy.

mécène [mesɛn] *s.m.* Maecenas, patron of the arts.

méchage [meʃaʒ] *s.m.* **1.** fumigating (of cask); **2.** (surg.) tenting or draining (of wound, etc.).

méchamment [meʃamɑ̃] *adv.* wickedly; spitefully, maliciously, ill-naturedly, cruelly; mischievously.

méchanceté [meʃɑ̃ste] *s.f.* wickedness; spite, spitefulness, malice, maliciousness; spiteful or unkind act or word; perverseness, mischievousness, naughtiness.

méchant, -e [meʃɑ̃] *adj.* wicked, evil, bad; ill-natured, spiteful, malicious; naughty, mischievous; wretched, worthless; sorry, paltry, poor; unpleasant, disagreeable; (of animal) vicious, dangerous; (fam.) extraordinary, terrific; *un ~ poète*, a sorry poet; *une ~e affaire*, an unpleasant affair, a nasty business; *il n'est pas ~*, he means no harm; *il n'est pas si ~ qu'il en a l'air*, his bark is worse than his bite; (fam.) *pas ~*, harmless, (lit. & fig.) tame; *il n'est nul si ~ qu'il ne trouve pas sa ~e*, every Jack has his Jill; *s.m.f.* wicked person, evil-doer, reprobate; (pl.) the wicked; *faire le ~*, to turn nasty, to be awkward, to be truculent, to give trouble.

mèche[1] [mɛʃ] *s.f.* wick; tinder, match, touch, fuse; whiplash; lock (of hair); tuft, tassel; gimlet, corkscrew, bit, drill; (surg.) tent; (mech.) barrel or drum (of winch, capstan, etc.); *~ anglaise*, centre-bit; *découvrir* or *éventer la ~*, (mil.) to discover the enemy's mine by means of a counter-mine; (fig.) to uncover a plot; (fam.) *vendre la ~*, to let the cat out of the bag.

mèche[2] [mɛʃ] *s.f.invar. être de ~ avec*, to be hand in glove with; (fam.) *il n'y a pas ~*, it is impossible, it's no go, nothing doing.

mécher [meʃe] *v.t.* **1.** to fumigate (a cask); **2.** (surg.) to tent or drain (a wound).

mécheu-x, -se [meʃø] *adj.* forming a cord (of raw wool).

mécompte [mekɔ̃t] *s.m.* miscalculation, miscount; mistake, error; mistaken judgment; unfounded hope, disappointment, disillusionment.

méconium [mekɔnjɔm] *s.m.* (med.) meconium.

méconnaissable [mekɔnɛsabl] *adj.* unrecognizable, hardly recognizable, altered beyond recognition.

méconnaissance [mekɔnɛsɑ̃s] *s.f.* failure to recognize, failure to understand or appreciate, lack of appreciation, misunderstanding, misjudgment.

méconnaître [mekɔnɛtr] *v.t.* not to recognize, not to know again, to fail to recognize; to disown, to deny, to refuse to admit or accept; to disregard, to ignore; to misunderstand, to fail to understand or appreciate; to misjudge; **se ~** *v.refl.* to misjudge oneself or one's position; to have a mutual misunderstanding.

méconnu, -e [mekɔny] *adj.* misunderstood, misjudged, not appreciated; unrecognized.

mécontent, -e [mekɔ̃tɑ̃] *adj.* displeased, dissatisfied, discontented, annoyed (*de*, with); *vous êtes ~ de tout*, nothing ever pleases you; *s.m.f.* malcontent, dissatisfied person.

mécontentement [mekɔ̃tɑ̃tmɑ̃] *s.m.* displeasure, dissatisfaction; discontent; *donner du ~ à qn.*, to give s.o. grounds for dissatisfaction or complaint.

mécontenter [mekɔ̃tɑ̃te] *v.t.* to displease, to dissatisfy, to annoy, to upset.

mécréant, -e [mekreɑ̃] *adj.* unbelieving, irreligious, sceptical; *s.m.f.* unbeliever, non-believer, infidel; ⚠ not 'miscreant'.

médaille [medaj] *s.f.* medal, medal ribbon, etc.; (arch.) medallion; metal badge or token, official badge; (bot.) honesty; *~ d'honneur*, prize medal; *le revers de la ~*, the reverse of the medal, (fig.) the other side of the picture; *tourner la ~*, to look at the other side; *la ~ est renversée*, the tables are turned.

médaillé, -e [medaje] *adj.* medalled, with a medal, wearing medals, holding a medal; *s.m.f.* medallist, holder of a medal, prizewinner.

médailler [medaje] *v.t.* to award a medal to, to confer a medal on.

médailleur [medajœr] *s.m.* medal-engraver; die-sinker.

médaillier [medaje] *s.m.* cabinet or collection of medals.

médailliste [medajist] *s.m.* collector of medals; medal-engraver.

médaillon [medajɔ̃] *s.m.* medallion; locket; (journalism, etc.) inset portrait; pat (of butter).

médecin [medsɛ̃] *s.m.* doctor, physician, medical attendant, medical adviser; medical man; (fig.) healer; *femme ~*, woman doctor; *~ (généraliste)*, general practitioner; *~ consultant*, consulting physician, consultant, *~ chirurgien*, surgeon; *~ militaire*, (army) medical officer; *~ sanitaire* or *du service de la santé*, medical officer (of health), health, officer; (fig.) *~ de l'âme*, father-confessor; *il est abandonné des ~s*, the doctors have given him up; *le temps est un grand ~*, time cures all ills, time is the great healer.

médecine [medsin] *s.f.* medicine, dose of medicine, physic; medical science; the Faculty; remedy, draught, purge; *étudiant(e) en ~*, medical student; *faire sa ~*, to study medicine; *~ légale*, forensic medicine, medical jurisprudence; *~ de cheval*, drastic remedy, extra large dose; *~ opératoire*, surgery; (fig.) *avaler sa ~*, to make the best of it, to take one's punishment.

média [medja] *s.m.* (advertising, etc.) medium; (pl.) media (radio, TV, press).

médian, -e [medjɑ̃] *adj.* median, mesial, middle, in the middle, centre; **~e** *s.f.* (geom.) median.

médianoche [medjanɔʃ] *s.m.* midnight supper (after fast).

médiante [medjɑ̃t] *s.f.* (mus.) mediant.

médiastin [medjastɛ̃] *s.m.* (anat.) mediastinum.

médiat, -e [medja] *adj.* mediate.

médiat-eur, -rice [medjatœr] *s.m.f.* mediator, intermediary; *adj.* mediating, mediatory.

médiation [medjɑsjɔ̃] *s.f.* mediation, acting as intermediary.

médiatiser [medjatize] *v.t.* to mediatize.

médical, -e, (aux) [medikal] *adj.* medical; *matière ~e*, materia medica; *corps ~*, the medical faculty; **~ement** [medikalmɑ̃] *adv.* medically.

médicament [medikamɑ̃] *s.m.* medicament, medicine, remedy; **~er** [medikamɑ̃te] *v.t.* to medicate, to doctor.

médicamenteu-x, -se [medikamɑ̃tø] *adj.* medicinal, having medicinal or therapeutic qualities.

médicastre [medikastr] *s.m.* quack (doctor).

médication [medikɑsjɔ̃] *s.f.* medication; medical treatment (of disease).

médicinal, -e [medisinal] *adj.* medicinal.
medicine-ball [medisinbol] *s.m.* (sport) medicine ball.
médico-légal, -e, (aux) [medikolegal] *adj.* medico-legal, forensic; *institut* ~, morgue.
médiéval, -e, (aux) [medjeval] *adj.* medieval.
médiév-isme [medjevism] *s.m.* medievalism; **~iste** [medjevist] *s.m.f.* medievalist.
médiocre [medjɔkr] *adj.* mediocre, middling; moderate, passable; indifferent; ~ *s.m.* mediocrity; **~ment** [medjɔkrəmɑ̃] *adv.* middlingly, moderately, tolerably, passably; indifferently; poorly; hardly, barely.
médiocrité [medjɔkrite] *s.f.* mediocrity; lack of distinction, lack of talent; limited outlook, banality; moderation, restraint; *une* ~, a mediocrity, a nobody; *vivre dans la* ~, to lead an undistinguished existence; to live in humble circumstances.
médique [medik] *adj.* Median, of the Medes.
médire [medir] *v.i.* to speak ill; ~ *de* or *sur*, to speak ill of, to slander, to traduce, to denigrate, to vilify; *personne qui aime à* ~, backbiter, scandalmonger.
médisance [medizɑ̃s] *s.f.* slander, slandering, defamation; scandal, backbiting; piece of scandal, malicious gossip.
médisant, -e [medizɑ̃] *adj.* slanderous, scandalous; *s.m.f.* slanderer, scandalmonger.
méditati-f, -ve [meditatif] *adj.* meditative, contemplative, pensive, given to meditation, reflective.
méditation [meditɑsjɔ̃] *s.f.* meditation, cogitation, reflection.
méditer [medite] *v.t.* to meditate, to meditate upon, to think over, to consider; to contemplate, to plan, to project; ~ *la ruine de*, to plot the destruction of; ~ *v.i.* to meditate, to contemplate; *passer sa vie à* ~, to spend one's life in meditation.
méditerrané, -e [mediterane] *adj.* midland, inland, land-locked; *une mer ~e*, an inland sea; *la (mer) Méditerranée*, the Mediterranean Sea.
méditerranéen, -ne [mediteraneɛ̃] *adj.* Mediterranean.
médium [medjɔm] *s.m.* (paint., spiritualism) medium; (mus.) middle register; (log.) middle term; ⚠ not 'means' or 'intermediary'; nor in sense of e.g. advertising 'medium' (but see MÉDIA).
médius [medjys] *s.m.* middle finger.
médoc [medɔk] *s.m.* Médoc (wine).
médullaire [medyllɛr] *adj.* (anat.) medullary.
médulleu-x, -se [medyllø] *adj.* medullary, containing marrow or pith.
méduse [medyz] *s.f.* (zool.) medusa, jelly-fish; *Méduse*, (myth.) Medusa.
méduser [medyze] *v.t.* (fam.) to petrify, to stupefy, to astound, to dumbfound.
meeting [mitiŋ, metɛ̃g] *s.m.* meeting, gathering; ⚠ not in sense 'encounter'.
méfait [mefɛ] *s.m.* misdeed, misdoing, crime; damage, harm.
méfiance [mefjɑ̃s] *s.f.* mistrust, distrust; suspicion; caution.
méfiant, -e [mefjɑ̃] *adj.* mistrustful, distrustful; suspicious; cautious, apprehensive.
(**se**) **méfier** [mefje] *v.refl.* to be suspicious, to be on one's guard; ~ *de*, to mistrust, to distrust, to suspect, to be suspicious of; to mind, to look out for, to beware of, to be on one's guard against; *il ne se méfie de rien*, he does not suspect anything, he is quite unsuspecting.
mégacycle [megasikl] *s.m.* = MÉGAHERTZ.
mégahertz [megaɛrts] *s.m.* (radio, TV) megahertz, megacycle.
mégalith-e [megalit] *s.m.* megalith; **~ique** [megalitik] *adj.* megalithic.
mégalomane [megalɔman] *adj.*, *s.m f.* megalomaniac.
mégalomanie [megalɔmani] *s.f.* megalomania.
mégaphone [megafɔn] *s.m.* megaphone, speaking-trumpet.
mégaptère [megaptɛr] *s.m.* (zool.) hump-backed whale.
mégarde [megard] *s.f.* inadvertence, inadvertency, inattention, carelessness; *par* ~, inadvertently, unawares, through carelessness, accidently.
mégathérium [megaterjɔm] *s.m.* (zool.) megatherium.
mégatonne [megatɔn] *s.f.* megaton(ne) (explosive effect equivalent to 1 million tons T.N.T.).
mégère [meʒɛr] *s.f.* (fig.) shrew, vixen, termagant; *La Mégère apprivoisée*, the Taming of the Shrew.
mégir [meʒir], **mégisser** [meʒise] *v.t.* to dress (leather).
mégis [meʒi] *s.m.* bath for dressing skins; *veau* ~, dressed calf(-leather).
mégisserie [meʒisri] *s.f.* tawing, leather-dressing.
mégissier [meʒisje] *s.m.* tawer, leather-dresser.
mégohm [megom] *s.m.* (electr.) megohm.
mégot [mego] *s.m.* (slang) cigar-stump, cigarette-end.
mégoter [megɔte] *v.t.* (fam.) to be stingy, to niggle, to haggle.
méhari [meari] *s.m.* kind of dromedary, racing-camel.
méhariste [mearist] *s.m.* soldier mounted on a *méhari*; racing-camel driver.
meilleur, -e [mɛjœr] *adj.* (comparative of *bon*) better, preferable, superior; *de ~e heure*, earlier; *de ~e qualité*, of superior quality; (*à*) ~ *marché*, cheaper; *il fait* ~, the weather is better; *il fait* ~ *ici*, it is pleasanter, milder, more comfortable, here; *le* ~ (superlative of *bon*), best, the best; *mon* ~ *ami*, my best friend; ~ *s.m.* the best, the best thing, the cream, the élite, the best part of; *boire du* ~, to drink the best wine; *du* ~ *de mon cœur*, with all my heart; *donner le* ~ *de soi-même*, to give of one's best.
méiose [mejoz] *s.f.* (biol.) meiosis.
meistre, mestre [mɛstr] *s.m.* (naut.) mainmast.
méjuger [meʒyʒe] *v.t.* to misjudge, to underestimate; **se** ~ *v.refl.* to underestimate one's own qualities.
mélampyre [melɑ̃pir] *s.m.* (bot.) cow-wheat.
mélancolie [melɑ̃kɔli] *s.f.* melancholy, sadness, gloom, dejection, depression; melancholy thoughts; (med.) melancholia; *ne pas engendrer la* ~, to be always bright and gay.
mélancolique [melɑ̃kɔlik] *adj.* melancholy, dismal, sad, gloomy, mournful, dejected, depressed; subject to melancholy or depression; **~ment** [melɑ̃kɔlikmɑ̃] *adv.* melancholically, mournfully, gloomily.
Mélanésie [melanezi] *s.f.* (geog.) Melanesia.
mélanésien, -ne [melanezjɛ̃] *adj.*, *s.m.f.* Melanesian.
mélange [melɑ̃ʒ] *s.m.* mixture, mixing, mingling; blending, fusion, medley, assortment, jumble; crossing, intermixture; alloy, alloying, amalgamation; admixture, added element, modifying feature; mash (for brewing); (pl.) miscellaneous works, miscellany, miscellanea; jumble; *sans* ~, unmixed, unblended; (fig.) pure, unalloyed, unadulterated; *un mal sans* ~ *de bien*, an unmitigated evil; *sa vertu ne montre aucun* ~ *de faiblesse*, his courage is unalloyed by weakness.
mélangé, -e [melɑ̃ʒe] *adj.* mixed, blended; motley, heterogeneous; forming a mixture.
mélanger [melɑ̃ʒe] *v.t.* to mix, to mingle, to blend, to cross, to intermix; to mix together, to

mix up, to jumble, to shuffle; to produce an assortment of.

mélangeu-r, -se [melɑ̃ʒœr] *s.m.f.* mixer, mixing-machine, blender; *robinet ~r*, mixer tap.

mélanose [melanoz] *s.f.* (med.) melanosis.

mélasse [melas] *s.f.* molasses, treacle; (fam.) thick fog, mud; mess, mix-up; *être dans la ~*, to be in a fix; *quelle ~!*, what a mess!

mêlé, -e [mɛle] *adj.* mixed, blended, mingled; tangled, involved (*à*, with); miscellaneous, assorted, varied; *sang ~*, mixed blood.

mêlée [mɛle] *s.f.* scrimmage, mêlée, tussle, conflict, fray, hand-to-hand fight, free fight, scuffle; altercation, squabble, quarrel; confusion, confused mixture; (Rugby football) scrum, scrummage; *~ ouverte fermée*, loose, tight scrum.

mêler [mɛle] *v.t.* to mix, to mingle, to blend, to cross; to mix up, to jumble, to entangle, to implicate, to involve (*à*, in); to shuffle (cards); *~ les fils*, to cross the threads, to get the wires crossed; *~ à*, to add to, to mix with, to mingle with; *~ avec*, to mix with, to combine; *~ de*, to add to, to adulterate with; *~ des détails pittoresques à un récit*, to embroider a story with picturesque details; *~ la danse avec la musique*, to combine dancing and music; *~ d'eau son vin*, to water one's wine; **se** *~ v.refl.* to mix, to be mixed, to mingle; *se ~ à* or *avec*, to join (up) with, to combine with, to unite with, to associate oneself with; to mingle with; to be, or to become, involved in, to take part in; *se ~ de*, to involve oneself in, to have, or to take, a hand in, to meddle or interfere in; to take it into one's head to; *ne pas se ~ de*, to keep away or aloof from, to take no part in, not to dabble in; *leurs sanglots se mêlaient à leurs prières*, their tears mingled with their prayers; *il se mêle du dépit à sa colère*, there is an element of spite in his anger; *il s'est mêlé à une rixe*, he got involved in a scuffle; *se ~ de politique*, to take up politics; *se ~ de ses affaires*, to mind one's own business, to be concerned with one's own affairs; *de quoi vous mêlez-vous?*, what business is that of yours?; *l'orgueil s'en mêle*, pride is involved; *lorsqu'il se mêle de travailler, il réussit bien*, when he makes up his mind to work, he makes a success of it; *ne vous en mêlez pas*, keep away from it, leave it alone, have nothing to do with it.

mélèze [melɛz] *s.m.* (bot.) larch, European larch.

mélia [melja] *s.m.* (bot.) Melia.

mélilot [melilo] *s.m.* (bot.) melilot, sweet-clover.

méli-mélo [melimelo] *s.m.* (fam.) medley, jumble.

mélinite [melinit] *s.f.* melinite.

mélique [melik] *s.f.* (bot.) melic-grass.

mélisse [melis] *s.f.* (bot.) balm, balm-mint; *eau de ~*, extract of balm, melissa cordial.

mélitte [melit] *s.f.* (bot.) Melittis, bastard balm.

mellifère [mɛllifɛr] *adj.* melliferous.

mellification [mɛllifikɑsjɔ̃] *s.f.* mellification, honey-making.

melliflue [mɛllifly] *adj.* mellifluous; (fig., obs.) honeyed, soft; (pej.) sugared, cloying.

mellite [mɛllit] *s.m.* (med.) medicament prepared with honey.

mélo [melo] *s.m.* (fam.) abbrev. of MÉLODRAME; *un film qui tourne au ~*, a film which tends to the melodramatic.

mélodie [melɔdi] *s.f.* melody, tune, song; melodiousness, melodic character.

mélodieu-x, -se [melɔdjø] *adj.* melodious; musical, sweet, harmonious, tuneful; **~sement** [melɔdjøzmɑ̃] *adv.* melodiously, harmoniously.

mélodique [melɔdik] *adj.* (mus.) melodic.

mélodiste [melɔdist] *s.m.f.* melodist.

mélodramatique [melɔdramatik] *adj.* melodramatic.

mélodrame [melɔdram] *s.m.* melodrama (abbrev. *mélo*).

méloé [meloe] *s.m.* (ent.) Meloe, may-beetle, oil-beetle.

mélomane [melɔman] *adj., s.m.f.* melomaniac, music-mad (person).

mélomanie [melɔmani] *s.f.* melomania.

melon [məlɔ̃] *s.m.* **1.** (bot.) melon; **2.** (*chapeau*) *~*, bowler-hat; **3.** (slang) first-year cadet at Saint-Cyr; **4.** (pop., pej.) Arab.

melongène [məlɔ̃ʒɛn] *s.f.* = AUBERGINE.

melonné, -e [məlɔne] *adj.* melon-shaped; *~e s.f.* variety of pumpkin.

melonnière [məlɔnjɛr] *s.f.* melon-bed.

mélopée [melɔpe] *s.f.* **1.** (mus. hist.) melopoeia, recitative chant; **2.** recitative, monotonous chant.

mélophage [melɔfaʒ] *s.m.* (ent.) sheep-tick.

membrane [mɑ̃bran] *s.f.* (anat.) membrane; film; *~ vibrante*, diaphragm (of telephone, loudspeaker, etc.); *~ interdigitale*, web (of bird's foot).

membraneu-x, -se [mɑ̃branø] *adj.* membran(e)ous.

membre [mɑ̃br] *s.m.* member; limb; constituent part; portion (of line of verse); (arch.) member, part of structure, decorative feature; (math.) side (of equation); (naut.) rib-timber, part of frame; *~ (viril)*, membrum virile, member, penis; *un ~ de la famille*, one of the family; (fam.) *se saigner aux quatre ~s*, to work oneself to the bone.

membré, -e [mɑ̃bre] *adj.* limbed; (herald.) membered; *être bien ~*, to be well-built.

membru, -e [mɑ̃bry] *adj.* strong-limbed, large-limbed.

membrure [mɑ̃bryr] *s.f.* limbs, frame; (naut.) ribs, timbers; (carp.) panel-frame.

même [mɛm] *adj.* same, like, equal; self-same, very same; self; even; *la ~ chose*, the same thing; *de ~ espèce*, of like kind, similar; *de ~ valeur*, of equal value; *le jour ~*, the very same day; *les enfants ~s*, the children themselves, even the children; *lui-~*, himself; *d'elle-~*, of her own accord, by itself; *c'est cela ~*, it is the very thing, that is just the point; *Marie? c'est la bonté ~*, Mary? she is kindness itself; *~ pron.* same, the same, the same person or thing; *ce sont toujours les ~s qui se font tuer*, it is always the same people who get killed; *cela revient au ~*, that comes to the same thing; *~ adv.* even, also, likewise; in fact, indeed; *ici ~*, in this very place; *je le pense, ~ je le crois*, I think, indeed I believe so; *à ~*, on a level with, directly on, or from; *coucher à ~ le sol*, to lie on the bare ground; *boire à ~ le goulot*, to drink from the bottle; *à ~ de faire*, in a position to do, equal to doing; *il n'est pas à ~ de faire le voyage*, he is not up to the journey, he is not fit to travel; *mettre qn. à ~ de*, to enable s.o. to, to put s.o. in a position to; *de ~*, likewise, the same, in the same way; *il en est de ~ des autres*, it is the same with the others, so it is with the others; *faites de ~*, do the same, do likewise; *de ~ que*, just as, as well as, in the same way as; *quand ~ il me l'aurait dit*, even if he had told me; *tout de ~*, all the same, however; **~ment** [mɛmmɑ̃] *adv.* (obs.) likewise, in the same way.

mémento [memɛ̃to] *s.m.* memento, reminder; memorial picture; (liturgy) memento (prayer); (obs.) memorandum, aide-mémoire.

mémère [memɛr], **mémé** [meme] *s.f.* (pop.) **1.** granny, gran; **2.** (fig.) old woman, granny.

mémoire [memwar] *s.f.* memory, power of memory; recollection, remembrance; commemoration; fame; (techn.) storage of information (in computer), memory-bank; *à la ~ de*, in memory of; *avoir beaucoup, peu, de* ~, to have a good, a bad, memory; *une* ~ *de lièvre*, a memory like a sieve; *lacune* or *trou de* ~, gap in one's recollection; *garder la* ~ *de*, to keep sth. in mind; *de* ~ *d'homme*, in living memory; *je n'en ai pas la moindre* ~, I haven't the faintest recollection of it; *cela m'est sorti de* ~, it slipped my memory, it went out of my head, I completely forgot about it; *une* ~ *fidèle*, a retentive memory; *se mettre qch. en* ~, to commit sth. to memory; *se remettre qch. en* ~, to refresh one's memory of sth.; *rappeler qch. à la* ~ *de qn.*, to remind s.o. of sth.; *si j'ai bonne* ~, if I remember rightly; *jouer de* ~, to play from memory; *conserver qch. dans la* ~, to bear sth. in mind; *pour* ~, as a reminder, for information.

mémoire [memwar] *s.m.* memorandum; petition; bill, statement of account; report, treatise, thesis, dissertation; memorial; (pl.) memoirs; transactions (of a learned society); *dresser un* ~, to draw up an account; ~ *acquitté*, receipted bill; ~ *d'apothicaire*, exorbitant bill.

mémorable [memɔrabl] *adj.* memorable, noteworthy, remarkable; **~ment** [memɔrabləmɑ̃] *adv.* memorably.

mémorandum [memɔrɑ̃dɔm] *s.m.* memorandum, note, memo; written order (to contractor); memorandum-book.

mémorial (pl. **aux**) [memɔrjal] *s.m.* memorial; book of notes, rough-book; memoirs.

mémorialiste [memɔrjalist] *s.m.f.* memorialist, writer of memoirs.

mémorisation [memɔrizɑsjɔ̃] *s.f.* memorization; storing in memory (in computer).

mémoriser [memɔrize] *v.t.* to memorize; to store in memory (in computer).

menaçant, -e [mənasɑ̃] *adj.* threatening, menacing.

menace [mənas] *s.f.* menace, threat; intimidation; *~s en l'air*, idle threats; *lourd de ~s*, ominous.

menacer [mənase] *v.t.* to threaten (*de*, with), to (seek to) intimidate; to hang over; to menace, to be threatening; to forbode, to portend, to presage; to be impending; *son discours menace d'être long*, his speech threatens to be lengthy, *or* looks like being a long one; *des orages qui menaçaient*, threatening clouds; ~ *ruine*, or ~ *de tomber*, to totter, to be on the point of collapse; ~ *du poing*, to shake one's fist at.

ménade [menad] *s.f.* maenad, Bacchante.

ménage [menaʒ] *s.m.* housekeeping, domestic duties, housewifery; household, domestic arrangements, house, family; household goods, set of furniture; married couple, couple, man and wife; housework; management, administration; good management, thrift, saving, economy; *elle entend bien le* ~, she is a good housewife; *se mettre en* ~, to set up house, to marry, to live together as man and wife; *faux* ~, couple living together; *faire bon* ~, to get on well together; *faire le* ~, to do the housework; to do the cleaning; *femme de* ~, charwoman; *jeune* ~, young couple; *pain de* ~, home-made bread; ~ *de garçon*, bachelor establishment; ~ *à trois*, three-cornered establishment, the eternal triangle.

ménagement [menaʒmɑ̃] *s.m.* regard, consideration; tenderness; circumspection, discretion; caution, care; (obs.) management, administration; *sans ~(s)*, bluntly, unsparingly; *expliquer la chose sans ~s*, to put the matter quite plainly.

ménager [menaʒe] *v.t.* to husband, to be sparing of, to use economically, to save, to economize (on); to take care of, to be careful of, to treat with caution, to treat kindly or tactfully, to spare the feelings of, to treat with respect, to take care not to offend, to humour; to reserve; to procure, to provide; to contrive, to manage; to arrange, to make, to prepare, to bring about; ~ *ses forces*, to spare one's strength; ~ *ses ressources*, to husband one's resources; ~ *ses sous*, to make one's money go a long way, to count one's pennies; ~ *une agréable surprise à*, to prepare a pleasant surprise for; ~ *l'étoffe*, to make the most of a piece of material; ~ *un escalier dans une maison*, to build a staircase into a house; ~ *une ouverture dans le mur*, to make an opening in the wall; ~ *des effets de scène*, to contrive stage effects; ~ *ses paroles*, to speak little, to be sparing of words; ~ *la chèvre et le chou*, to run with the hare and hunt with the hounds; **se** ~ *v.refl.* to take care of oneself, to spare oneself; to arrange for oneself; to behave with circumspection; to have regard for one another's feelings; to keep on mutual good terms.

ménag-er, -ère [menaʒe] *adj.* domestic, household, connected with housekeeping or the household, relating to household management or domestic science, housewifely; economical, managing well, careful, thrifty, sparing (*de*, with); *eaux ~ères*, domestic waste water, slops; *appareils ~ers*, household or kitchen equipment; *arts ~ers*, (manufacture and supply of) household equipment; *le Salon des arts ~ers* = Ideal Home Exhibition; *enseignement ~er*, (instruction in, or course of) domestic science; **~er** *s.m.* (obs.) manager, administrator; **~ère** *s.f.* **1.** housewife, housekeeper; **2.** canteen of cutlery.

ménagerie [menaʒri] *s.f.* menagerie.

mendélien, -ne [mɛ̃deljɛ̃] *adj.* (biol.) Mendelian.

mendélisme [mɛ̃delism] *s.m.* (biol.) Mendelism.

mendiant, -e [mɑ̃djɑ̃] *adj.* mendicant, begging; *s.m.f.* beggar, mendicant; *les quatre ~s*, (i.) the four orders of mendicant friars; (ii.) dessert of hazel-nuts, almonds, figs and raisins.

mendicité [mɑ̃disite] *s.f.* beggary, mendicity, begging.

mendier [mɑ̃dje] *v.i.* to beg, to be a beggar; ~ *v.t.* to beg (for); to solicit, to canvass; ~ *sa vie*, to live by begging; ~ *des voix* or *des suffrages*, to canvass votes.

mendigot, -e [mɑ̃digo] *s.m.f.* (pop.) beggar.

mendigoter [mɑ̃digɔte] *v.t.i.* (pop.) to beg.

mendole [mɑ̃dol] *s.f.* (ichth.) mendole, cackerel.

meneau (pl. **-x**) [məno] *s.m.* (arch.) mullion.

menées [məne] *s.f.pl.* intrigues, machinations.

mener [məne] *v.t.* to guide, to conduct, to take, to lead, to be at the head or front of; to be the leader, to be leading or winning; (lit. & fig.) to be the way (to); to drive, to steer; to bring, to convey, to carry; to manage, to control, to direct, to run, to administer, to govern, to carry on; to draw, to trace, to introduce; *on ne le mène pas comme on veut*, he won't be driven; *mené par sa femme*, hen-pecked; *il mène tout*, he rules the roost, he orders everyone about; ~ *à bonne fin*, to carry out, to see (sth.) through, to bring to a successful conclusion; *cela ne vous mènera pas loin*, that won't get you very far; *le journalisme mène à tout*, journalism is the gateway to everything; ~ *bien sa barque*, to manage one's affairs well; ~ *grand train*, to cut a dash; ~ *rudement*, to treat badly; ~ *la vie dure à qn.*, to lead s.o. a hard life; ~ *à la baguette*, to rule with a high hand; ~ *grand deuil de qch.*, to regret sth. bitterly.

ménestrel [menɛstrɛl] *s.m.* minstrel.

ménétrier [menetrije] *s.m.* fiddler, village musician.

meneu-r, -se [mənœr] *s.m.f.* conductor, leader; keeper, minder; ring-leader; (pej.) agitator; transporter, carrier; *~r de jeu*, compère.

menhir [menir] *s.m.* (archaeol.) menhir.

menin, -e [mənɛ̃] *s.m.f.* (hist.) young nobleman or noblewoman chosen as attendant to Spanish

princely family; ~ *s.m.* young man of good birth attendant on the Dauphin.
méninge [menɛ̃ʒ] *s.f.* (anat.) meninx; (pl.) meninges, (fam.) brain.
méningite [menɛ̃ʒit] *s.f.* (med.) meningitis.
ménisque [menisk] *s.m.* (opt.) meniscus; (anat.) disc, cartilage; crescent-shaped ornament.
ménologe [menɔlɔʒ] *s.m.* menology, martyrology.
ménopause [menɔpoz] *s.f.* (physiol.) menopause.
menotte [mənɔt] *s.f.* (fam.) little hand, tiny hand (of children); (pl.) handcuffs, manacles.
mense [mɑ̃s] *s.f.* (eccles.) income, revenue, stipend.
mensonge [mɑ̃sɔ̃ʒ] *s.m.* lie, lying, falsehood, untruth, untruthfulness; (fig.) fiction, fable; error, fallacy, unreality; illusion, delusion; *faire* or *dire un* ~, to tell a lie; *débiter des* ~*s*, to tell lies; *l'habitude du* ~, mendacity, (habitual) untruthfulness; ~ *officieux*, white lie; *vivre dans le* ~, to live in a world of unreality; *la poésie vit de* ~*s*, poetry is all fiction; *tout n'est que* ~, all is vanity; (proverb) *songes*, ~*s*, dreams are an illusion.
mensong-er, -ère [mɑ̃sɔ̃ʒe] *adj.* lying, untrue, deceitful; false, vain, illusory; **~èrement** [mɑ̃sɔ̃ʒɛrmɑ̃] *adv.* mendaciously, deceitfully.
menstruation [mɑ̃stryɑsjɔ̃] *s.f.* (physiol.) menstruation.
menstruel, -le [mɑ̃stryɛl] *adj.* (physiol.) menstrual.
menstrues [mɑ̃stry] *s.f.pl.* (physiol.) menstruation, menstrual flow.
mensualité [mɑ̃sɥalite] *s.f.* monthly payment; monthly allowance; monthly instalment; *payer par* ~*s*, to pay by monthly instalments.
mensuel, -le [mɑ̃sɥɛl] *adj.* monthly; **~lement** [mɑ̃sɥɛlmɑ̃] *adv.* monthly, per month, by the month.
mensuration [mɑ̃syrɑsjɔ̃] *s.f.* mensuration, measurement.
mental, -e, (aux) [mɑ̃tal] *adj.* mental; *calcul* ~, mental arithmetic; *aliénation* ~*e*, insanity; *médecine* ~*e*, psychiatry; **~ement** [mɑ̃talmɑ̃] *adv.* mentally, in the mind, in one's mind, inwardly.
mentalité [mɑ̃talite] *s.f.* mentality, (mental) outlook, attitude; (fam.) bad joke.
menterie [mɑ̃tri] *s.f.* (fam.) story, fib, falsehood.
menteu-r, -se [mɑ̃tœr] *s.m.f.* liar, story-teller, fibber; *adj.* lying, false, deceptive, deceitful.
menthe [mɑ̃t] *s.f.* (bot.) mint; peppermint; ~ *poivrée* or *anglaise*, peppermint; ~ *verte*, spearmint; ~ *aquatique*, watermint; ~ *coq*, tansy; ~ *pouliot*, pennyroyal; ~ *de chat*, catmint; *pastilles de* ~, peppermint drops, peppermints; *crème de* ~, crème de menthe, peppermint-flavoured cordial.
menthol [mɛ̃tɔl] *s.m.* (chem.) menthol.
mentholé, -e [mɛ̃tɔle] *adj.* (chem.) mentholated, containing menthol.
mention [mɑ̃sjɔ̃] *s.f.* mention; note, instruction, indication, endorsement; (in examination) grade, credit or distinction; *faire* ~ *de*, to mention; *la lettre est revenue avec* ~ '*décédé*', the letter was returned marked 'deceased'; (in examination) *être reçu sans* ~, to achieve a bare pass; *être reçu avec* ~ (*bien*), to pass with credit (distinction).
mentionner [mɑ̃sjɔne] *v.t.* to mention, to make mention of; to name; *mentionné ci-dessus*, above-mentioned; *ne faire que* ~ *qch.*, simply to refer to sth. (without giving further details).
mentir [mɑ̃tir] *v.i.* to lie, to tell a lie, an untruth; ~ *à qn.*, to lie to s.o., to deceive s.o.; ~ *à qch.*, to belie, to deny, to fail to live up to, sth.; *faire* ~ *qn.*, to make a liar of s.o., to falsify someone's prediction; *faire* ~ *qch.*, to belie sth.; ~ *à sa réputation*, to belie one's reputation; ~ *à sa promesse*, not to live up to one's promise; *faire* ~ *le proverbe*, to belie the proverb; *à ne point* ~, to tell the truth, to be frank; *il en a menti*, he was not telling the truth.
menton [mɑ̃tɔ̃] *s.m.* chin; ~ *avancé, fuyant*, protruding, receding, chin; *double* ~, double chin; ~ *en galoche*, turned-up chin.
mentonnet [mɑ̃tɔnɛ] *s.m.* (mech.) catch, stop, lug.
mentonnière [mɑ̃tɔnjɛr] *s.f.* chin-band; chin-piece (of helmet); chin-rest (of violin); chin-strap; chin-bandage.
mentor [mɛ̃tɔr] *s.m.* mentor, guide, tutor.
menu, -e [məny] *adj.* tiny, small, slim, thin, fine; minute, exact; minor, lesser, petty, trifling; common; ~*s frais*, small expenses, sundry outgoings; ~*e monnaie*, small change; ~*s propos*, small talk; ~*s détails*, minute details, full particulars; ~ *plomb*, small shot; ~ *gibier*, small game; *le* ~ *peuple*, the lower classes, the common people; ~ *adv.* small, fine, minutely; *hacher* ~, to chop small or fine, to mince; *écrire* ~, to write small; *il pleuvait dru et* ~, the rain came down in a steady drizzle.
menu [məny] *s.m.* small details, detailed list, particulars; menu, bill of fare; *par le* ~, in detail, in great detail, at great length, with every particular.
menuet [mənɥɛ] *s.m.* minuet.
menuise [mənɥiz] *s.f.* **1.** small shot; **2.** twigs, faggots.
menuiser [mənɥize] *v.t.* to cut down, to plane down (wood to size); to do carpenter's or joiner's work.
menuiserie [mənɥizri] *s.f.* carpentry, woodwork, joinery, joiner's work; ~ *d'art*, cabinet-making; ~ *métallique*, metal windows, door-frames, etc.
menuisier [mənɥizje] *s.m.* joiner, carpenter; ~ *de bâtiment*, builder's carpenter, house-carpenter; ~ *en meubles, en sièges*, furniture-maker, chair-maker; ~ *d'art*, cabinet-maker.
ménure [menyr] *s.f.* (ornith.) lyre-bird.
menu-vair [mənyvɛr] *s.m.* miniver, minever.
ményanthe [menjɑ̃t] *s.m.* (bot.) marsh trefoil, buckbean.
méphistophélique [mefistɔfelik] *adj.* Mephistophelian.
méphitique [mefitik] *adj.* mephitic.
méphitisme [mefitism] *s.m.* mephitis, pollution.
méplat, -e [mepla] *adj.* (obs.) flat in shape, flattened; (art.) *lignes* ~*es*, lines forming the transition from one plane to another; ~ *s.m.* any one of the planes which together form the surface of a body; plane surface, flat surface.
(**se**) **méprendre** [meprɑ̃dr] *v.refl.* to make a mistake, to be mistaken; *vous vous méprenez*, you are mistaken, you have misunderstood it; ~ *à* or *sur*, to be mistaken about, to misjudge, to misapprehend; *il se méprenait au sens de mes paroles*, he mistook my meaning; *c'est à ne pas s'y* ~, there is no mistaking it, there can be no mistake about it; *c'est son père à s'y* ~, he is the very image of his father; *imiter à s'y* ~, to give a lifelike imitation of.
mépris [mepri] *s.m.* contempt, scorn, disregard, disparagement, disrespect; (pl.) contemptuous treatment, sneers, disparaging remarks; *avoir du* ~ *pour*, to despise; *au* ~ *de*, in defiance of, in contempt of; *la familiarité engendre le* ~, familiarity breeds contempt.
méprisable [meprizabl] *adj.* contemptible, despicable.
méprisant, -e [meprizɑ̃] *adj.* contemptuous, scornful.

méprise [mepriz] *s.f.* mistake, oversight, error, misunderstanding; *faire une lourde* ~, to make a bad mistake; *par* ~, by mistake, in error.

mépriser [meprize] *v.t.* to scorn, to despise; to make light of, to belittle, to slight, to disregard.

mer [mɛr] *s.f.* sea; deep, main, ocean; tide; (fig.) a vast quantity or expanse of; *à la* ~, in the sea, overboard; *un homme à la* ~, a man overboard; (fig.) a wreck, a drifter; *en* ~, in the sea, off-shore; *sur* ~, on the sea, afloat; *grosse* or *mauvaise* ~, heavy sea, rough sea; ~ *fermée* or *intérieure*, inland sea; *en pleine* or *en haute* ~, in the open sea, out at sea, on the high seas; *la* ~ *est haute, basse*, it is high, low, tide; *grandes* ~*s*, spring-tides; *bains de* ~, sea-bathing; seaside resort; *le bord de la* ~, the seaside; *un coup de* ~, a heavy sea; *homme* (pl. *gens*) *de* ~, sailor, seafarer, seafaring man; *loup de* ~, old salt; *avoir le mal de* ~, to be seasick; *mettre à la* ~, to put to sea; to launch, to lower (a boat); *prendre la* ~, to go to sea, to put out to sea; *tenir la* ~, to be seaworthy; to keep to seaward; (fig.) to rule the waves; *ce n'est pas la* ~ *à boire*, it is no great task, it is not as hard as all that; *porter de l'eau à la* ~, to carry coals to Newcastle; *une* ~ *de sable*, a sea of sand, a vast expanse of desert.

mercanti [mɛrkɑ̃ti] *s.m.* **1.** bazaar-keeper, bazaar merchant; **2.** dishonest shopkeeper, profiteer, (fam.) shark.

mercantile [mɛrkɑ̃til] *adj.* mercantile, commercial; profiteering, money-grubbing; *système* ~, mercantilism.

mercantilisme [mɛrkɑ̃tilism] *s.m.* mercantilism; (pej.) commercialism, profiteering.

mercenaire [mɛrsənɛr] *adj.* mercenary, venal, paid, hired; ~ *s.m.f.* hired soldier, mercenary; hired man or woman, one who is paid (to do the job); *travailler comme un* ~, to slave away, to work like a navvy.

mercerie [mɛrsri] *s.f.* mercery, haberdashery.

merci [mɛrsi] *s.f.* mercy, discretion, will, pleasure, pity; *crier* or *implorer* ~, to cry (for) mercy; *sans* ~, merciless, pitiless; *être à la* ~ *de*, to be at the mercy of, to be exposed to the risk of, to be vulnerable to; ~ *s.m., interj.* thanks, thank you, no thank you; *Dieu* ~, thank God; *grand* ~, or *mille* ~*s*, many thanks; ~ *d'être venu*, thank you for coming; (often iron.) ~ *du compliment!*, thanks for the compliment!

merci-er, -ère [mɛrsje] *s.m.f.* haberdasher, mercer; ⚠ not 'mercer' in sense of dealer in silk.

mercredi [mɛrkrədi] *s.m.* Wednesday; *le* ~ *des cendres*, Ash Wednesday.

mercure [mɛrkyr] *s.m.* mercury, quicksilver; (Rom. myth., astron.) *Mercure*, Mercury.

mercureux [mɛrkyrø] *adj.m.* (chem.) mercurous.

mercuriale[1] [mɛrkyrjal] *s.f.* market prices, current prices (of commodities).

mercuriale[2] [mɛrkyrjal] *s.f.* rebuke, reprimand; (obs.) judicial assembly held every Wednesday in Paris; speech made on this occasion.

mercuriale[3] [mɛrkyrjal] *s.f.* (bot.) mercury; ~ *vivace*, dog's mercury.

mercuriel, -le [mɛrkyrjɛl] *adj.* mercurial; ⚠ not 'mercurial' in fig. sense 'lively', 'volatile'.

mercurique [mɛrkyrik] *adj.m.* mercuric.

merde [mɛrd] (vulg.) *s.f.* excrement; shit, turd; ~ *interj.* **1.** expression of anger, scorn, impatience; **2.** expression of admiration or astonishment.

merdeu-x, -se [mɛrdø] *adj.* (vulg.) covered with excrement, shitty, filthy; (*bâton*) ~, revolting individual; urchin, gutter-snipe.

merdier [mɛrdje] *s.m.* (fig.) mess, muddle.

mère [mɛr] *s.f.* mother; dam (of animals); Mother Superior; (fig.) parent, cause, source, reason, root; the chief, the head; matrix, mould; *notre* ~ *commune*, mother earth; *notre première* ~, Eve; ~ *patrie*, mother country; *belle-*~, step-mother, mother-in-law; *la Grèce,* ~ *des arts*, Greece, cradle of the arts; ~ *nourrice*, foster-mother; ~ *de vinaigre*, mother (produced by fermentation of vinegar); (*la petite*) ~, (pop. equivalent of *madame*) mum, ma, missis; ~ *adj.* mother; first, chief, principal; *la reine* ~, the queen mother; *langue* ~, mother tongue; *l'idée* ~, the main or basic idea; *maison* ~, (comm.) parent establishment; (eccles.) mother house.

mère [mɛr] *adj. f.* pure, fine; ~ *goutte*, wine which flows before grapes are pressed; ~ *laine*, fine lamb's-wool.

mergule [mɛrgyl] *s.m.* (ornith.) merganser, goosander.

méridien, -ne [meridjɛ̃] *adj.* meridian, meridional; at noon, midday, noon-day; *hauteur* ~*ne*, meridian altitude; *lunette* ~*ne*, transit instrument; *chaleur* ~*ne*, noon-day heat; ~ *s.m.* meridian; ~**ne** *s.f.* **1.** meridian line; **2.** siesta, nap; *faire la* ~*ne*, to take an afternoon nap; **3.** kind of sofa.

méridional, -e, (**aux**) [meridjɔnal] *adj.* meridional, southern, south; *la pointe* ~*e de*, the southernmost point of; ~ *s.m.* southerner, inhabitant of the south (esp. of France).

meringue [mərɛ̃g] *s.f.* meringue.

meringuer [mərɛ̃ge] *v.t.* (cook.) to give a covering of meringue to.

mérinos [merinos] *s.m.* merino sheep; merino wool; merino (material); *bélier* ~, merino ram; (pop.) *laisser pisser les* ~, to let things take their course.

merise [məriz] *s.f.* (bot.) wild cherry.

merisier [mərizje] *s.m.* wild-cherry tree.

méritant, -e [meritɑ̃] *adj.* meritorious, deserving, (often iron.) worthy.

mérite [merit] *s.m.* merit, worth; virtue; desert, due; talent, ability, capacity, attainments, excellence; *être traité selon ses* ~*s*, to be treated according to one's deserts; *cela a au moins le* ~ *d'être clair*, it has at least the virtue of being clear; *se donner le* ~ *de qch.*, to take credit for having done sth.; *se faire un* ~ *de*, to glory in.

mériter [merite] *v.t.* to merit, to deserve; to earn, to gain; to entitle to; to need, to require; to prove worthy or deserving, to deserve well (*de*, of); *cela ne mérite pas qu'on en parle*, that is not worth mentioning; *voilà ce qui lui a mérité cet honneur*, that is what earned him this distinction; *cette nouvelle mérite confirmation*, that news requires confirmation; ~ *d'être récompensé*, to deserve to be rewarded; *bien* ~ *de sa patrie*, to deserve well of one's country.

méritoire [meritwar] *adj.* meritorious, deserving.

merl see MAËRL.

merlan [mɛrlɑ̃] *s.m.* (ichth.) whiting; (pop.) hairdresser, barber; *faire des yeux de* ~ *frit*, to gaze comically heavenwards, to express mock astonishment.

merle [mɛrl] *s.m.* (ornith.) blackbird; (fam.) fellow; *un vilain* ~, or (iron.) *un beau* ~, a nasty type; *un* ~ *blanc*, rara avis, rare specimen, something that one would rarely or never come across.

merlette [mɛrlɛt] *s.f.* hen blackbird; (herald.) martlet.

merlin[1] [mɛrlɛ̃] *s.m.* pole-axe, axe; cleaver, chopper.

merlin[2] [mɛrlɛ̃] *s.m.* (naut.) marline.

merlon [mɛrlɔ̃] *s.m.* (fort.) merlon.

merluche [mɛrlyʃ] *s.f.*, **merlus** [mɛrly] *s.m.* (ichth.) hake, stockfish.

mérou [meru] *s.m.* (ichth.) grouper.

mérovingien, -ne [merɔvɛ̃ʒjɛ̃] *adj.* Merovingian.

mèrrain, mairain [mɛrɛ̃] *s.m.* stave-wood,

cask-wood (for cooperage); beam (of deer's antlers).

merveille [mɛrvɛj] *s.f.* wonder, marvel, miracle, prodigy; *faire ~*, to do wonderfully or remarkably well; *faire des ~s*, to do wonders, to perform miracles; *dire ~ de*, to speak highly of; *c'est ~ que*, it is a wonder that, it is remarkable that; *tomber à ~*, to be most welcome, to come at a very good time; *à ~*, admirably, wonderfully well, famously, marvellously; *je me porte à ~*, I am in splendid health, I am very fit.

merveilleu-x, -se [mɛrvɛjø] *adj.* wonderful, amazing, marvellous; excellent, superior, first--rate; strange, miraculous, supernatural; **~x** *s.m.* the wonderful, the marvellous, the wonderful part or thing; the supernatural; **~x, ~se** *s.m.f.* ultra-fashionable person (of the *Directoire* period); **~sement** [mɛrvɛjøzmɑ̃] *adv.* wonderfully, marvellously, splendidly.

mérycisme [merisism] *s.m.* (med.) merycism.

mes see MON.

mésaise [mezɛz] *s.m.* (obs.) malaise, discomfort, uneasiness; financial embarrassment.

mésalliance [mezaljɑ̃s] *s.f.* misalliance, bad match.

(se) mésallier [mezallje] *v.refl.* to make a bad match, to marry beneath one.

mésange [mezɑ̃ʒ] *s.f.* (ornith.) titmouse, tomtit, tit.

mésangette [mezɑ̃ʒɛt] *s.f.* bird-trap.

mésaventure [mezavɑ̃tyr] *s.f.* mischance, misadventure, misfortune, mishap.

mescaline [mɛskalin] *s.f.* mescalin(e).

mesdames [mɛdam], **mesdemoiselles** [mɛdmwazɛl] *s.f.pl.* pl. of MADAME, MADEMOISELLE.

mésentente [mezɑ̃tɑ̃t] *s.f.* misunderstanding, disagreement.

mésentère [mezɑ̃tɛr] *s.m.* (anat.) mesentery.

mésentérique [mezɑ̃terik] *adj.* (anat.) mesenteric.

mésestime [mezɛstim] *s.f.* low esteem, lack of esteem or respect, poor opinion.

mésestimer [mezɛstime] *v.t.* to hold in little esteem, to have little respect for, to think little of; to under-rate, to undervalue, to underestimate; to misjudge.

mésintelligence [mezɛ̃tɛliʒɑ̃s] *s.f.* misunderstanding, disagreement, discord, bad relations; *en ~ avec*, on bad terms with, at variance with.

mesmérien, -ne [mɛzmerjɛ̃] *adj.* mesmeric; relating to Mesmer or mesmerism.

mesmérisme [mɛzmerism] *s.m.* mesmerism.

méso- [mezɔ] *pref.* meso-; **~carpe** [mezɔkarp] *s.m.* (bot.) mesocarp; **~derme** [mezɔdɛrm] *s.m.* (anat.) mesoderm; **~lithique** [mezɔlitik] *adj.* mesolithic; *s.m.* mesolithic period, Middle Stone Age.

méson [mezɔ̃] *s.m.* (phys.) meson.

mésophyte [mezɔfit] *s.m.* (bot.) mesophyte.

Mésopotamie [mezɔpɔtami] *s.f.* (geog.) Mesopotamia.

mésopotamien, -ne [mezɔpɔtamjɛ̃] *adj.* Mesopotamian.

méso-sphère [mezɔsfɛr] *s.f.* (meteor.) mesosphere; **~thorax** [mezɔtɔraks] *s.m.* (anat., zool.) mesothorax; **~zoïque** [mezɔzɔik] *adj.* (geol.) mesozoic.

mesquin, -e [mɛskɛ̃] *adj.* shabby; paltry, poor, cheap, pitiful; mean, stingy, niggardly; illiberal, narrow; *une chambre ~e*, a shabby room; *des idées ~es*, narrow views; *être ~*, to be mean or stingy; **~ement** [mɛskinmɑ̃] *adv.* shabbily, meanly; stingily.

mesquinerie [mɛskinri] *s.f.* meanness, shabbiness, poorness; stinginess; shabby trick, mean act.

mess [mɛs] *s.m.* (officers' or NCOs') mess; messing; mess-staff.

message [mesaʒ] *s.m.* message; official communication; (advertising) short film, spot.

messag-er, -ère [mesaʒe] *s.m.f.* messenger, carrier, bearer (of tidings), harbinger, herald, forerunner, precursor; *le ~er des dieux*, Mercury, the messenger of the gods; *l'Aurore, ~ère du jour*, Aurora, harbinger of day.

messagerie [mesaʒri] *s.f.* carriage (of letters, parcels, passengers); (pl.) messenger service; transport undertaking; dispatch of goods (by passenger-train, mail-boat, etc.), parcel service; *~s maritimes*, shipping line.

messe [mɛs] *s.f.* mass; *~ basse*, low mass; *grand' ~*, high mass; *~ des morts*, requiem mass; *livre de ~*, prayer-book, missal.

messeoir [meswar] *v.i.impers.* to be unseemly or unbecoming; to ill become; to be unfitting; not to suit.

messer [mesɛr] *s.m.* (obs.) master; *~ gaster*, the stomach.

messianique [mesjanik] *adj.* Messianic.

messidor [mesidɔr] *s.m.* Messidor (10th month in Fr. Republican Calendar, June to July).

Messie [mesi] *s.m.* Messiah; *attendre qn. comme le ~*, to await s.o. with great expectations or great hopes.

messier [mesje] *s.m.* keeper (of fields and vineyards), crop-watcher.

messieurs [mesjø] pl. of MONSIEUR.

messire [mesir] *s.m.* sir, sire, master, (also used as form of address to priests, lawyers, doctors, etc.).

mestre, meistre [mɛstr] *s.m.* **1.** (obs. mil.) *~ de camp*, colonel, commanding officer, commandant; **2.** (naut.) mainmast; *voile de ~*, mainsail.

mesurable [məzyrabl] *adj.* measurable.

mesurage [məzyraʒ] *s.m.* measurement, measuring.

mesure [məzyr] *s.f.* measure, gauge, standard; measurement, size, extent, bounds, dimension, capacity, limit, compass; calculation, reckoning; moderation, restraint, propriety; prudence, precaution; (mus.) bar; time; (pros.) metre; (fenc.) distance; *faire bonne ~*, to give good measure; *à la ~*, by measure, on draught; (mus.) *~ à trois temps*, triple time; *battre la ~*, to beat time; *en ~*, in time; *aller en ~*, to keep time; *à ~*, in proportion, little by little, successively; *à ~ que*, in proportion as, according as, at the same time as; *à ~ que l'un avançait, l'autre reculait*, as fast as one advanced, the other retreated; *dans une certaine ~*, to a certain extent; *dans la ~ de*, within the bounds or limits of; *dans la ~ du possible*, so far as is possible; *en ~ de faire*, in a position to do, able to do, having the power to do; *fait sur ~*, made to measure; *dépasser la ~*, to overstep the bounds, to exaggerate, to overdo it; *garder la ~*, to keep within bounds, to exercise restraint; *outre ~*, beyond all bounds, excessively; *combler la ~*, to go to extremes; *prendre des ~s*, to take action, to take measures or steps, to make provision, to make arrangements; *donner sa ~*, to show one's capabilities; *sans ~*, unbounded, unrestrained, unbridled; *ne point garder de ~ avec*, not to spare someone's feelings; *se mettre en ~ de*, to get ready to, to prepare to.

mesuré, -e [məzyre] *adj.* measured, regular, proportioned; temperate, moderate, restrained; cautious, circumspect, guarded, prudent; *il est très ~ dans ses discours*, he is very guarded in what he says.

mesurer [məzyre] *v.t.* to measure; to measure off or out, to ration; to judge, to estimate, to gauge; to temper, to restrain; to proportion, to calculate; to compare, to consider; to weigh, to weigh up, to examine; (pros.) to scan; *il mesure chaque parole*, he weighs every word; *~ qn. des* *yeux*, to eye s.o., to weigh s.o. up; ~ *qch. à* or *sur qch.*, to measure sth. by sth.; to match or proportion sth. to sth.; to make sth. fit sth.; *il faut* ~ *son travail aux résultats*, one must judge one's work by the results; ~ *sa dépense sur son profit*, to keep one's expenses in line with one's profits; ~ *le châtiment à l'offense*, to make the punishment fit the crime; ~ *qch. à qn.*, to measure sth. out to s.o. (esp. grudgingly); *on me mesure le chauffage*, my heating is rationed; **se** ~ *v.refl.* to be measured, to be proportioned; *se* ~ *avec*, to measure oneself against, to try one's strength against, to pit oneself against; *se* ~ *des yeux*, to eye one another.

mesureur [məzyrœr] *s.m.* measurer; meter.

mésuser [mezyze] *v.t.* ~ *de*, to misuse, to abuse.

méta [meta] *s.m.* meta (brand name of solid fuel based on metaldehyde).

métabolisme [metabɔlism] *s.m.* (biol.) metabolism.

métacarpe [metakarp] *s.m.* (anat.) metacarpus.

métacarpien, -ne [metakarpjɛ̃] *adj.* (anat.) metacarpal.

métacentre [metasɑ̃tr] *s.m.* (phys., naut., aeron.) metacentre.

métairie [metɛri] *s.f.* farm held on *métayage* basis; small farm, dairy farm.

métal (pl. **aux**) [metal] *s.m.* metal, steel; bullion, specie; (fig.) mettle; ~ *anglais*, gun-metal; Britannia metal; ~ *blanc*, German silver, white metal; (fig.) *il était de pur* ~, he was completely trustworthy, he was one of the best.

métaldéhyde [metaldeid] *s.m.* or *f.* (chem.) metaldehyde.

métal-lifère [metallifɛr] *adj.* metalliferous, containing metal; **~lique** [metallik] *adj.* metallic, in metal, bullion; **~lisation** [metallizɑsjɔ̃] *s.f.* metallization, converting into metal, plating with metal; **~liser** [metallize] *v.t.* to metallize, to give a metal finish to, to plate (with metal).

métallo [metallo] *s.m.* abbrev. of MÉTALLURGISTE.

métallo-chromie [metallɔkrɔmi] *s.f.* metallochromy; **~graphie** [metallɔgrafi] *s.f.* metallography; **~graphique** [metallɔgrafik] *adj.* metallographic.

métalloïde [metallɔid] *adj.* metalloid.

métallurg-ie [metallyrʒi] *s.f.* metallurgy, metallurgical processes; metal industry, (esp.) iron- or steel-works; **~ique** [metallyrʒik] *adj.* metallurgical; *industries ~iques*, metal (esp. iron & steel) industries; **~iste** [metallyrʒist] *s.m.* metallurgist; worker in metal industry, (esp.) steel-worker.

métamère [metamɛr] *adj.* metameric; ~ *s.m.* (zool.) metamere.

métamérie [metameri] *s.f.* (chem.) metamerism.

métamorph-ique [metamɔrfik] *adj.* (geol.) metamorphic; **~isme** [metamɔrfism] *s.m.* (geol.) metamorphism; **~osable** [metamɔrfozabl] *adj.* metamorphosable; **~ose** [metamorfoz] *s.f.* metamorphosis; **~oser** [metamɔrfoze] *v.t.* to metamorphose, to change, to transform.

métaphor-e [metafɔr] *s.f.* (rhet.) metaphor, figure of speech, image; **~ique** [metafɔrik] *adj.* metaphoric, metaphorical, figurative; **~iquement** [metafɔrikmɑ̃] *adv.* metaphorically, figuratively.

métaphosph-ate [metafɔsfat] *s.m.* (chem.) metaphosphate; **~orique** [metafɔsfɔrik] *adj.* (chem.) metaphosphoric.

métaphysicien, -ne [metafizisjɛ̃] *s.m.f.* metaphysician.

métaphysique [metafizik] *s.f.* (phil.) metaphysics; abstraction; ~ *adj.* metaphysical; **~ment** [metafizikmɑ̃] *adv.* metaphysically.

métastase [metastɑz] *s.f.* (med., rhet.) metastasis.

métatarse [metatars] *s.m.* (anat.) metatarsus.

métatarsien, -ne [metatarsjɛ̃] *adj.*, ~ *s.m.* (anat.) metatarsal.

métathèse [metatɛz] *s.f.* metathesis.

métathorax [metatɔraks] *s.m.* (ent.) metathorax.

métayage [metɛjaʒ] *s.m.* metayage, system by which a farm crop is shared between landlord and tenant.

métay-er, -ère [metɛje] *s.m.f.* metayer, farmer holding land on *métayage* system; small farmer; smallholder.

métazoaire [metazɔɛr] *s.m.* (zool.) metazoon.

méteil [metɛj] *s.m.* (agric.) maslin (mixture of wheat and rye).

métempsycose [metɑ̃psikoz] *s.f.* metempsychosis.

météo [meteo] abbrev. *météorologie, météorologique.*

météor-e [meteɔr] *s.m.* meteor; any atmospheric phenomenon; (fig.) meteoric event or personage, nine-days wonder; **~ique** [meteɔrik] *adj.* meteoric; **~iser** [meteɔrize] *v.t.* (med.) to distend with flatulence; **~isme** [meteɔrism] *s.m.*, **~isation** [meteɔrizɑsjɔ̃] *s.f.* (med.) meteorism, flatulence; **~ite** [meteɔrit] *s.f.* meteorite; **~ologie** [meteɔrɔlɔʒi] *s.f.* meteorology; weather bureau; weather forecasting; **~ologique** [meteɔrɔlɔʒik] *adj.* meteorological; *bulletin ~ologique*, weather report; **~ologiste** [meteɔrɔlɔʒist], **~ologue** [meteɔrɔlɔg] *s.m.f.* meteorologist, (weather) forecaster.

métèque [metɛk] *s.m.* (Gr. ant.) stranger living in Athens; (mod., pej.) resident alien.

méthane [metan] *s.m.* (chem.) methane, natural gas.

méthanier [metanje] *s.m.* (naut.) methane-carrier, transporter of liquid gas.

méthode [metɔd] *s.f.* method, system, way, procedure, custom, habit; rudiments, primer; *avec* ~, methodically; ~ *de piano*, pianoforte tutor.

méthodique [metɔdik] *adj.* methodical, systematic; **~ment** [metɔdikmɑ̃] *adv.* methodically, systematically.

méthodisme [metɔdism] *s.m.* Methodism.

méthodiste [metɔdist] *adj.*, *s.m.f.* Methodist.

méthodologie [metɔdɔlɔʒi] *s.f.* methodology.

méthyl-e [metil] *s.m.* (chem.) methyl; **~ène** [metilɛn] *s.m.* (chem.) methylene; **~ique** [metilik] *adj.* (chem.) methylic.

méticuleu-x, -se [metikylø] *adj.* meticulous, punctilious, scrupulously careful; **~sement** [metikyløzmɑ̃] *adv.* meticulously, scrupulously.

méticulosité [metikylozite] *s.f.* meticulousness, scrupulousness.

métier [metje] *s.m.* **1.** trade, craft; business, profession, calling; employment, occupation, work; *faire* or *exercer un* ~, to follow a trade; *faire le* ~ *de*, to take up the profession of; *faire* ~ *de*, to make a trade or business of; to trade or deal in; *de* ~, of the trade, trade, technical, professional, expert; *homme* (pl. *gens*) *de* ~, craftsman, professional, expert; *termes de* ~, technical or trade terms; *armée de* ~, professional army; *corps de* ~, guild, corporation; *être du* ~, to be in the trade; *arts et ~s*, arts and crafts; *le* ~ *des armes*, the military profession; *de son* ~, by trade, by profession; (fam.) *faites votre* ~*!*, mind your own business!; *ce n'est pas de mon* ~, it is not in my line; *chacun son* ~ *et les vaches seront bien gardées*, everyone to his trade; **2.** loom, (embroidery, lace-making) frame; ~ *à bas*, stocking-frame; ~ *à main*, hand-loom; ~ *mécanique*, power-loom; ~ *à tapisserie*, tapestry-frame or -loom; ~ *à broder*, embroidery frame; *mettre sur le* ~, to undertake (a piece of work); *avoir plusieurs* *ouvrages sur le* ~, to have several works on hand, to have several irons in the fire.

métis, -se [metis] *adj.* mixed, half-bred, half-caste, mongrel, cross-bred, hybrid; (text.) (*tissu*) ~, mixture; *s.m.f.* half-breed, half-caste, mongrel, cross-breed, hybrid.

métissage [metisaʒ] *s.m.* cross-breeding, hybridization.

métisser [metise] *v.t.* to cross, to hybridize.

métonymie [metɔnimi] *s.f.* metonymy.

métope [metɔp] *s.f.* (arch.) metope.

métrage [metraʒ] *s.m.* measurement, length (esp. of material or cinema film); (cin.) *un long* ~, a full-length film; *un court* ~, a short.

mètre [mɛtr] *s.m.* **1.** metre (=1·093633 English yards); metre rule, measure; ~ *carré* (abbrev. m^2), square metre; ~ *cube* (abbrev. m^3), cubic metre; ~ *à ruban*, (metallic) tape-measure; **2.** (pros.) metre; metrical foot.

métr-é [metre] *s.m.* measurement in metres; **~er** [metre] *v.t.* to measure (by the metre), to survey; **~eur** [metrœr] *s.m.* measurer, surveyor, appraiser; *~eur vérificateur*, quantity surveyor.

métrique [metrik] *adj.* **1.** metric; **2.** (pros.) metrical; ~ *s.f.* versification, prosody; scansion.

métro [metro] abbrev. MÉTROPOLITAIN *s.m.* 2.

métrolog-ie [metrɔlɔʒi] *s.f.* metrology; **~ique** [metrɔlɔʒik] *adj.* metrological.

métronome [metrɔnɔm] *s.m.* (mus.) metronome.

métropole [metrɔpɔl] *s.f.* mother country; metropolis, capital; metropolitan see.

métropolitain, -e [metrɔpɔlitɛ̃] *adj.* metropolitan; archiepiscopal; *église* ~*e*, mother-church; ~ *s.m.* **1.** archbishop, metropolitan; **2.** metropolitan railway, (Paris) metro, underground.

métropolite [metrɔpɔlit] *s.m.* (Gr. church) metropolitan.

mets [mɛ] *s.m.* dish, article of prepared food.

mettable [mɛtabl] *adj.* wearable, fit to wear.

metteur [mɛtœr] *s.m.* (rarely **metteuse** *s.f.*) ~ *en œuvre*, one who puts a plan into action, one who sets up the necessary machinery; setter, mounter (of jewellery, instruments, etc.); (fig.) promoter; (print.) ~ *en pages*, maker-up; ~ *au point*, (i.) (sculpt.) rough-hewer; (ii.) setter, tuner (of mechanism); (theatr.) ~ *en scène*, producer; (radio & TV) ~ *en ondes*, producer; (rail.) ~ *de rails*, plate-layer.

mettre [mɛtr] *v.t.* to put, to set, to lay, to place; to put in, to fit, to introduce; to put on, to wear; to bring; to employ; to contribute, to expend; to put or write down; to turn on; to suppose, to imagine; ~ *sa robe*, to put on one's dress; ~ *cent francs à un chapeau*, to spend a hundred francs on a hat; *je ne peux pas y* ~ *tant que cela*, I can't afford as much as that; *il met son orgueil dans la réussite*, he stakes his pride on succeeding; ~ *dans le blanc*, to hit the bull, to score a bull's-eye; *il me met dans toutes ses affaires*, he tells me all his business, he lets me into all his secrets; *mettez du soin dans tout ce que vous faites*, be careful in all that you do; *j'ai mis une heure à y aller*, it took me an hour to get there; ~ *en bouteille*, to bottle; ~ *en état*, to get ready; ~ *en feu* or *en flammes*, to burn, to set fire to; ~ *en mouvement*, to start, to set going; ~ *qn. en retard*, to make s.o. late; ~ *en vente*, to put up for sale; ~ *en bouillon*, to make into a stew; ~ *en ordre*, to set in order, to arrange; *mettons que vous ayez raison*, (let us) suppose you are right, granted that you are right; *mettez que je n'ai rien dit*, I take that back, I withdraw that remark; ~ *bas*, to put or take down; (of animals) to give birth, to drop; ~ *le contact*, to turn on the switch, to switch on; ~ *le chauffage*, to turn the heating on; ~ *le couvert*, to lay the table; (sport) ~ *un coup à*, to score against; *ils leur ont mis 5 coups à 0*, they scored 5–0 against them; ~ *à l'envers* or *sens dessus dessous*, to turn upside down; ~ *le feu à*, to set fire to; ~ *fin à*, to stop, to put an end to; ~ *un manche à un balai*, to fix a handle to a broom; ~ *une pendule à l'heure*, to set a clock; ~ *le siège à*, to lay siege to; ~ *le verrou*, to bolt, to shoot the bolt; (boxing) *mettre knock-out*, to knock out; ~ *une terre en blé*, to sow a field with corn; ~ *la main à la pâte*, to put one's shoulder to the wheel; ~ *la main sur*, to arrest, to lay hands on; ~ *la dernière main à*, to put the finishing touches to; ~ *la main à la plume*, to take up one's pen; ~ *un vaisseau à la mer*, to launch a ship; ~ *de côté*, to put on one side, to save; ~ *en pièces*, to break, to crush; ~ *à sec*, to dry up, to empty; ~ *à l'épreuve*, to prove, to put to the test; ~ *à même de*, to enable, to put (s.o.) in a position to; *y* ~ *du sien*, to make a contribution (to an undertaking), to pull one's weight; ~ *qn. au pied du mur*, to corner s.o.; ~ *des paroles en musique*, to set words to music; ~ *la charrue devant les bœufs*, to put the cart before the horse; ~ *par écrit*, to set down in writing; ~ *à l'amende*, to fine; ~ *dehors*, to throw out (of doors); ~ *qn. au fait*, to put s.o. in the picture; ~ *au jour*, (i.) to give birth to; (ii.) to publish; (mil.) ~ *aux arrêts*, to put under arrest; (fig.) ~ *sur la paille*, to ruin; *mettez cela dans votre poche, et votre mouchoir par-dessus*, put that in your pipe and smoke it; (slang) ~ *les bouts* or *les bâtons*, to be off, to get a move on; *alors, on les met?*, come on, let's get moving!; **se** ~ *v.refl.* to put or place oneself; to sit down; to lie down; to stand; to dress, to put on; *se* ~ *à*, to begin (to), to set about; to take to, to apply oneself to, to turn one's thoughts to; to go, to get, to get in; to spread; to set in, to break out; *l'épouvante s'est mis partout*, terror spread on all sides; *le temps se met à la pluie*, it is turning to rain, rain is on the way; *il s'est mis au beau*, it has turned out fine; *se* ~ *à table*, to sit down to table; (slang) to confess, to own up; *se* ~ *à travailler*, to begin work; *il faut s'y* ~, we must get down to work; *se* ~ *au pas*, (i.) to fall into step; (ii.) to slow down to a walk; *se* ~ *au régime*, to go on a diet; *se* ~ *en colère*, to get angry; *se* ~ *à son aise*, to take one's ease, to make oneself comfortable; *se* ~ *bien*, to dress well; *se* ~ *en frais*, to put oneself to expense; *se* ~ *en marche*, to start, to start moving, to set off; *se* ~ *en tête*, to take it into one's head; *se* ~ *à tout*, to turn one's hand to anything; *se* ~ *à la fenêtre*, to stand by the window; *se* ~ *bien avec*, to get on good terms with; *se* ~ *mal avec*, to fall out with; *se* ~ *dans le commerce*, to go into business; *se* ~ *du fard*, to make up; *se* ~ *en route*, to set off; *se* ~ *sur son quant-à-soi*, to keep one's distance.

meublant, -e [mœblɑ̃] *adj.* suitable as furnishing or furniture, giving a furnished effect, filling; *meubles* ~*s*, movables, furniture.

meuble [mœbl] *adj.* movable, loose; (of property) personal; (of securities, etc.) transferable; *sol* ~, light or friable soil; *le* ~ or *biens* ~*s*, personal property, estate, possessions, chattels, movables; ~ *s.m.* piece of furniture; suite of furniture; (obs.) utensil; *être dans ses* ~*s*, to have one's own furniture (in one's flat, etc.); *se mettre dans ses* ~*s*, to set up house, to furnish a house of one's own.

meublé, -e [mœble] *adj.* furnished; (fig.) stocked, supplied; ~ *s.m.* furnished apartment.

meubler [mœble] *v.t.* to furnish; to form the furniture of; to give a furnished effect to; to stock, to store, to fill, to garnish (*de*, with); *une seule chaise meublait la pièce*, one chair was the only furniture in the room; *un tissu qui meuble bien*, a material very suitable for furnishing; ~ *sa*

mémoire, to stock one's memory; *avoir la bouche bien meublée*, to have a fine set of teeth.
meuglement [møgləmɑ̃] *s.m.* = BEUGLEMENT.
meugler [møgle] *v.i.* = BEUGLER.
meule[1] [mœl] *s.f.* **1.** millstone, grindstone; **2.** large round cheese.
meule[2] [mœl] *s.f.* stack, rick (of hay, etc.), pile; (hort.) hotbed; ~ *à champignons*, mushroom-bed.
meuler [møle] *v.t.* to grind, to grind down.
meulier [mølje] *s.m.* millstone-maker.
meuli-er, -ère [mølje] *adj.* pertaining to millstone or grindstone; *pierre ~ère*, millstone, millstone grit; **~ère** *s.f.* millstone quarry.
meulon [mølɔ̃] *s.m.* haycock, small stack.
meunerie [mønri] *s.f.* milling; milling trade, millers.
meuni-er, -ère [mønje] *s.m.f.* miller; miller's wife, mistress of a mill; (ornith.) *mésange ~ère*, blue tit.
meurt-de-faim [mœrdəfɛ̃] *s.m.invar.* starveling, starving wretch.
meurtre [mœrtr] *s.m.* murder, voluntary homicide or manslaughter; (fig.) crime.
meurtri-er, -ère [mœrtrije] *adj.* murderous, sanguinary, deadly; *arme ~ère*, murder weapon; *s.m.f.* murderer, murderess; **~ère** *s.f.* (fort.) loophole.
meurtrir [mœrtrir] *v.t.* **1.** (obs.) to murder; **2.** to bruise, to make black and blue; to injure, to batter; *tout meurtri*, covered with bruises, black and blue; *visage meurtri de fatigue*, face lined with fatigue; *cœur meurtri*, broken heart.
meurtrissure [mœrtrisyr] *s.f.* bruise, bruising, contusion, lesion, damage.
meute [møt] *s.f.* pack (of hounds); (fig.) ringleaders; ~ *de créanciers*, pursuing band of creditors; *chef de ~*, leader of the pack, whipper-in.
mévente [mevɑ̃t] *s.f.* **1.** (obs.) sale at a loss, unfavourable sale; **2.** slump, falling-off of sales.
mexicain, -e [mɛksikɛ̃] *adj.*, *s.m.f.* Mexican.
Mexique [mɛksik] *s.m.* (geog.) Mexico.
mezzanine [mɛdzanin] *s.f.* (arch.) mezzanine, mezzanine storey, mezzanine window.
mezzo-soprano [mɛdzosɔprano] *s.m.* mezzo-soprano; ~ *s.f.* mezzo-soprano (singer) (abbrev. *mezzo*).
mezzo-tinto [mɛdzotinto] *s.m.* mezzotint.
mi [mi] *s.m.* (mus.) me, E.
mi [mi] *pref.invar.* half, demi, semi, mid, in the middle, half way between, partly; *une étoffe ~-laine, ~-coton*, a material half-wool, half-cotton; *la ~-août*, the middle of August; *à ~-chemin*, half-way; *à ~-corps*, to the waist; *à ~-côte*, half-way up the hill; *à ~-jambe*, half-way up the leg; *~-parti*, equally divided; composed of two dissimilar halves.
miaou [mjau] *s.m.* (onom.) miaow, mew.
miasmatique [mjasmatik] *adj.* miasmatic, miasmal.
miasme [mjasm] *s.m.* miasma.
miaulement [mjolmɑ̃] *s.m.* mewing, mew; whining or whistling noise.
miauler [mjole] *v.i.* (onom.) to mew; to caterwaul, to whine.
mi-bas [mibɑ] *s.m.* (usu. pl.) knee-stockings.
mica [mika] *s.m.* mica; mica window.
micacé, -e [mikase] *adj.* micaceous.
mi-carême [mikarɛm] *s.f.* mid-Lent.
micaschiste [mikaʃist] *s.m.* mica-schist, mica-slate.
miche [miʃ] *s.f.* loaf, round loaf.
Michel-Ange [mikɛlɑ̃ʒ] *s.m.* Michelangelo.
micheline [miʃlin] *s.f.* railcar (on pneumatic tyres).
mic-mac [mikmak] *s.m.* trick, scheme, intrigue, machination, put-up job.
micocoulier [mikɔkulje] *s.m.* (bot.) nettle-tree.
micro [mikro] abbrev. *microphone* = mike.
micro-ampère [mikrɔɑ̃pɛr] *s.m.* microampère; **~analyse** [mikrɔanaliz] *s.f.* micro-analysis; **~balance** [mikrɔbalɑ̃s] *s.f.* micrometer balance.
microbe [mikrɔb] *s.m.* microbe, germ, bacillus, virus; (fig. of person or child) little fellow.
microbicide [mikrɔbisid] *adj.* microbicidal, germicidal; ~ *s.m.* germicide.
microbien, -ne [mikrɔbjɛ̃] *adj.* microbial, microbic, of microbic origin.
micro-biologie [mikrɔbiɔlɔʒi] *s.f.* microbiology; **~bus** [mikrɔbys] *s.m.* small bus, mini-bus; **~céphale** [mikrɔsefal] *adj.*, *s.m.f.* microcephalous (person or creature); **~climat** [mikrɔklima] *s.m.* microclimate; **~cosme** [mikrɔkɔsm] *s.m.* microcosm; **~farad** [mikrɔfarad] *s.m.* (electr.) microfarad; **~fiche** [mikrɔfiʃ] *s.f.* microfiche; **~film** [mikrɔfilm] *s.m.* microfilm; **~filmer** [mikrɔfilme] *v.t.* to microfilm; **~graphie** [mikrɔgrafi] *s.f.* micrography.
microhm [mikrom] *s.m.* (electr.) microhm.
micro-mètre [mikrɔmɛtr] *s.m.* micrometer; **~métrie** [mikrɔmetri] *s.f.* micrometry.
micron [mikrɔ̃] *s.m.* micron (millionth of a metre).
micro-organisme [mikrɔɔrganism] *s.m.* micro-organism.
micro-phone [mikrɔfɔn] *s.m.* microphone; **~plaquette** [mikrɔplakɛt] *s.f.* (electr.) *~-plaquette de silicium*, silicon chip; **~processeur** [mikrɔprɔsesœr] *s.m.* (electr.) microprocessor; **~scope** [mikrɔskɔp] *s.m.* microscope; **~-scopique** [mikrɔskɔpik] *adj.* microscopic; (fig.) minute, extremely small; **~sillon** [mikrɔsijɔ̃] *s.m.* microgroove; long-playing record; **~-thermie** [mikrɔtɛrmi] *s.f.* therm, millionth of a THERMIE; **~tome** [mikrɔtɔm] *s.m.* microtome.
miction [miksjɔ̃] *s.f.* urination, micturition, making water.
midi [midi] *s.m.* noon, midday, twelve o'clock, noontide; south, south aspect, facing south; *le Midi*, the South (of France); *en plein ~*, facing south; in broad daylight, (fig.) in the full light of day; *le ~ de la vie*, the prime of life; *il a sonné ~*, or *~ a sonné*, it has struck twelve; (pop.) *c'est ~ (sonné)*, nothing doing; *chercher ~ à quatorze heures*, to make difficulties where there are none, to make an unnecessary fuss.
midinette [midinɛt] *s.f.* office girl, shop-girl, girl working in fashion shop or couture house (esp. in Paris).
midshipman [mitʃipman], **midship** [mitʃip] *s.m.* (pl. *midshipmen, midships*) (nav.) (British) midshipman; (Fr.) sub-lieutenant.
mie[1] [mi] *s.f.* crumb (opp. crust); *pain de ~*, bread without crusts (for sandwich-making); (pop., pej.) *à la pain de ~*, worthless; (obs.) *ne . . . ~*; not at all.
mie[2] [mi] *s.f.* (obs. or Lit.) dearest; loved one; *ma ~*, my darling, my love.
miel [mjɛl] *s.m.* honey; (fig., often pej.) sweetness, charm; *rayon de ~*, honeycomb; *être tout ~ (et) tout sucre*, to be all sugar and honey, to be all sweetness; *lune de ~*, honeymoon; (obs.) *mouche à ~*, honey-bee.
miellé, -e [mjɛle] *adj.* honeyed; honey-sweet.
mielleu-x, -se [mjɛlø] *adj.* honey, honey-like; (fig.) honeyed, sugared, unctuous, hypocritical; **~sement** [mjɛløzmɑ̃] *adv.* blandly, with honeyed words, unctuously.
mien, -ne [mjɛ̃] *poss. adj.* & *pron.* mine, my own, of mine; *ce livre est ~*, this book is mine; *un ~ livre*, a book of mine, a book of my own; *laisse ta voiture, la ~ne a plus de place*, don't take your car, mine has more room; *vos idées sont les ~nes*, your ideas are the same as mine; *des protestations que je fais ~nes*, remarks with which I associate

myself; *le* ~, my property, my own work; *la distinction du tien et du* ~, the distinction between mine and thine; *j'y ai mis du* ~, I have made a real effort; *les* ~*s*, my family, my friends, my people, my supporters.

miette [mjɛt] *s.f.* small crumb, tiny piece, least bit, particle; *mettre* or *réduire en* ~*s*, to break to pieces, to break into fragments, to smash to atoms or smithereens; (fig., fam.) *ne pas en perdre une* ~, to miss nothing.

mieux [mjø] *adv.* better, more; (superlative) *le* ~, best, the best; *il écrit* ~ *que je ne pensais*, he writes better than I thought; *rien de* ~, nothing better; *de* ~ *en* ~, better and better; *tant* ~*!*, so much the better!, good! I am glad to hear it; *le* ~ *du monde*, perfectly; *la femme le* ~ *habillée de Paris*, the best-dressed woman in Paris; *pouvez--vous faire* ~ *que ça?*, can you better that?; *il vaut* ~ *les surveiller*, you must keep a closer watch on them; *aller* ~, to be better, to be in better health; *pour ne pas dire* ~ or ~ *dire*, to say the least of it; *j'aimerais* ~, I would prefer, I would rather; *je ne demande pas* ~, nothing would please me better; *qui* ~ *est*, what is better, better still; *on y sera* ~, we shall be more comfortable, or better off, there; *elle est* ~ *qu'indolente, elle est paresseuse*, she is more than indolent, she is idle; *ce qu'il y a de* ~ *dans ce spectacle*, the best feature of this play; *c'est on ne peut* ~, it couldn't be better, it is going perfectly; *à qui* ~ ~, in competition, in emulation of one another, to see who can win; *une maison tout ce qu'il y a de* ~, an absolutely first-rate house; *au* ~, at best; *en mettant les choses au* ~, putting things in their most favourable light; *au* ~ *de vos intérêts*, in your best interests.

mieux [mjø] *s.m.* best, the best, the best way, the best thing; something better; *j'espérais* ~ *de lui*, I expected better of him; *il a changé en* ~, he has changed for the better; *faute de* ~, for want, or lack, of something better; *faire de son* ~, to do one's best (*pour*, to); *le* ~ *est de*, it is best to, it would be the best thing to; *de mon* ~, as best I can; *j'ai fait de mon* ~, I have done my best; *le* ~ *est l'ennemi du bien*, leave well alone; *il y a du* ~, things are getting better, some progress has been made.

mieux-être [mjøzɛtr] *s.m.* improved state; betterment.

mièvre [mjɛvr] *adj.* **1.** (obs.) mischievous, sharp; **2.** affected, prim, genteel, fragile.

mièvrerie [mjɛvrəri] *s.f.* **1.** (obs.) roguishness; **2.** primness, affectation, preciosity.

mi-fin, -e [mifɛ̃] *adj.* medium-sized, middle grade.

mignard, -e [miɲar] *adj.* **1.** (obs.) dainty, caressing; **2.** (pej.) affected, precious, pretty--pretty; **3.** of delicate shape or appearance, small and graceful.

mignardise [miɲardiz] *s.f.* **1.** delicate charm; **2.** affectation, prettiness (of style); **3.** (bot.) garden-pink.

mignon, -ne [miɲɔ̃] *adj.* **1.** small and graceful, delicate, pretty little, sweet; *péché* ~, foible, besetting sin; *filet* ~, small steak (cut from best part of fillet); **2.** (fam.) kind, easy-going; *sois* ~*ne, aide-moi à*, be an angel and help me to; ~ *s.m.* **1.** what is dainty or delicate; **2.** favourite; **3.** (print.) minion; ~(**ne**) *s.m.f.* darling, pet; ~**ne** *s.f.* (hort.) a kind of pear.

mignonnette [miɲɔnɛt] *s.f.* **1.** mignonette lace; **2.** ground pepper; **3.** fine gravel; **4.** (bot.) a variety of pink (⚠ not Eng. 'mignonette').

mignoter [miɲɔte] *v.t.* to fondle, to caress, to make much of; **se** ~ *v.refl.* to make an elaborate toilet, to spruce oneself up, to titivate.

migraine [migrɛn] *s.f.* migraine, sick headache.

migraineu-x, -se [migrɛnø] *adj.* causing a headache; of migraine; subject to migraine; *des accès* ~*x*, attacks of migraine.

migrant, -e [migrɑ̃] *adj., s.m.f.* migrant.

migrat-eur, -rice [migratœr] *adj.* migrant, migrating, migratory; *s.m.f.* migrating or migratory bird.

migration [migrɑsjɔ̃] *s.f.* migration; (theol.) transmigration (of the soul).

migratoire [migratwar] *adj.* migratory.

mijaurée [miʒore] *s.f.* affected or pretentious woman, prudish person; *faire la* ~, to be affected, prudish, or stuck-up, to be all affectation.

mijoter [miʒɔte] *v.t.i.* to simmer, to stew gently, to cook slowly; *faire* ~, to allow to simmer; (fig.) to plot, to devise, to hatch.

mikado [mikado] *s.m.* mikado.

mil[1] [mil] *s.m.* (gymn.) Indian club.

mil[2] [mij, mil] *s.m.* (bot.) = MILLET 1.

mil [mil] *adj.* see MILLE *adj.*

milan [milɑ̃] *s.m.* (ornith.) kite; ~ *blanc*, buzzard.

mildiou [mildju] *s.m.* mildew; (agric.) rust.

mildiousé, -e [mildjuze] *adj.* mildewed.

mile [majl] *s.m.* mile.

miliaire [miljɛr] *adj.* miliary; ~ *s.f.* (med.) miliary fever, miliaria.

milice [milis] *s.f.* **1.** (obs.) art of war; **2.** (obs.) army, (fig.) host; **3.** militia; police force (organized on military lines, or in a para-military role).

milicien [milisjɛ̃] *s.m.* militiaman.

milieu (pl. **-x**) [miljø] *s.m.* middle, middle point, centre, midst, medium, heart; circle, environment, ambiance, surroundings; society, milieu, sphere; mean, something half-way; *au* ~ *de*, in the middle of, in the midst of; among; *au* ~ *de sa carrière*, in mid-career; (naut.) *au* ~ *du navire*, amidships; *au beau* or *en plein* ~, right in the middle; *juste* ~, golden mean; *il n'y a pas de* ~, there is no middle course, it must be the one or the other; *tenir le* ~ *entre*, to be half-way between, to be the happy medium between; *le doigt du* ~, the middle finger; *un* ~ *de table*, a centre-piece (as table decoration); *les* ~*x littéraires*, literary circles; *l'Empire du Milieu*, the Middle Kingdom (i.e. China); *le Milieu*, the criminal classes (known to the police, esp. thieves and those living on immoral earnings).

militaire [militɛr] *adj.* military; army; of the army, in the armed forces, service; of war; martial; *marine* ~, navy; *aviation* ~, air force; *faire son service* ~, to do one's military service; to serve in the army; *heure* ~, sharp, punctually; ~ *s.m.* **1.** soldier, military man; **2.** the military; military life; ~**ment** [militɛrmɑ̃] *adv.* militarily, in a military manner, like a military operation, with military precision or discipline; with troops, using military force; *saluer* ~*ment*, to give a military salute; *occuper* ~*ment*, to occupy with troops.

militant, -e [militɑ̃] *adj., s.m.f.* militant; serving; *les* ~*s du parti*, the rank and file militants of the party, the party-workers.

militarisation [militarizɑsjɔ̃] *s.f.* militarization.

militariser [militarize] *v.t.* to militarize.

militarisme [militarism] *s.m.* **1.** militarism, bellicosity, warlike dispotion; **2.** military regime.

militariste [militarist] *adj., s.m.* militarist.

militer [milite] *v.i.* **1.** to militate; **2.** to fight (without violence, for or against a cause); to be a fighter or militant.

mille [mil] *adj., s.m.invar.* (in dates, also **mil**) thousand, a thousand; (fig.) countless, innumerable; *l'an* ~, the year 1000; *l'an mil huit cents*, the year 1800; ~ *fois merci*, ~ *remercie-*

ments, very many thanks, a thousand thanks; *mettre dans le* ~, to score 1000, to hit the bull's--eye, to score a win, to come out top; (fam.) *en plein dans le* ~!, a bull's-eye!, spot on!; (*tapisserie à*) ~ *fleurs*, XVth century tapestry with elaborate floral background; *avoir* or *gagner des* ~ *et des cents*, to have piles of money, to rake in the money; *je vous le donne en* ~, I give you any number of guesses, you'll never guess it; *un* ~ *de briques*, a thousand(-lot) of bricks.
mille [mil] *s.m.* mile (=1609 metres); ~ *marin* or *romain*, nautical mile (=1852 metres).
mille-feuille [milfœj] *s.f.* (pl. *mille-feuilles*) **1.** (bot.) milfoil, yarrow; **2.** mille-feuille pastry.
millénaire [millenɛr] *adj.* millenary, a thousand years old, dating back a thousand years; ~ *s.m.* millenary; millennium.
millenium [millenjɔm] *s.m.* millennium.
mille-pattes [milpat] *s.m.invar.* (ent.) millepede; centipede.
mille-pertuis [milpɛrtɥi] *s.m.* (bot.) St. John's wort.
millépore [millepɔr] *s.m.* millepore (coral).
mille-raies [milrɛ] *s.m.* (text.) (*velours*) ~, needlecord.
millésime [millezim] *s.m.* millesimal, the thousand digit (in a figure); date (on coins, etc.).
millet [mijɛ] *s.m.* **1.** (bot.) canary-seed; millet, millet-grass; **2.** (med.) miliary eruption.
milliaire [miljɛr] *adj.* miliary, marking a mile; *pierre* ~, milestone; ~ *s.m.* milestone.
milliard [miljar] *s.m.* 1000 millions, milliard.
milliardaire [miljardɛr] *adj.*, *s.m.f.* (multi-) millionaire.
milliasse [miljas] *s.f.* (obs.) thousands, swarms.
millième [miljɛm] *adj.*, *s.m.* thousandth, one thousandth part.
millier [milje] *s.m.* thousand, about a thousand, large number; *par* ~*s*, in thousands.
milligramme [milligram] *s.m.* milligram (= 0·0154 grain).
millilitre [millilitr] *s.m.* millilitre; the thousandth part of a litre.
millimètre [millimɛtr] *s.m.* millimetre; the thousandth part of a metre.
millimétré, -e [millimetre] *adj.* divided into millimetres, ruled in millimetres.
millimicron [millimikrɔ̃] *s.m.* millimicron.
million [miljɔ̃] *s.m.* million, vast number; *être riche à* ~*s*, to be a millionaire.
millionième [miljɔnjɛm] *adj.*, *s.m.* millionth.
millionnaire [miljɔnɛr] *adj.*, *s.m.f.* millionaire.
millithermie [millitɛrmi] *s.f.* 1000 therms (=thousandth part of a THERMIE).
milord [milɔr] *s.m.* **1.** lord; wealthy foreigner; **2.** four-wheeled carriage, phaeton.
milouin [milwɛ̃] *s.m.* (ornith.) pochard.
mime [mim] *s.m.* mime; miming; mimic.
mimer [mime] *v.t.* to mimic; to mime.
mimétique [mimetik] *adj.* (zool.) mimetic.
mimétisme [mimetism] *s.m.* (biol.) mimesis, mimicry.
mimi [mimi] *s.m.* **1.** (child's lang.) pussy; **2.** kiss; **3.** (fam.) darling, pet.
mimique [mimik] *adj.* mimic, miming; ~ *s.f.* miming, sign-language, dumb-show.
mimodrame [mimodram] *s.m.* mimodrama, (performance in) mime.
mimographe [mimograf] (obs.) *s.m.f.* writer or composer of mime.
mimosa [mimoza] *s.m.* (bot.) mimosa.
minable [minabl] *adj.* **1.** pitiable, pitiful; **2.** shabby, down-at-heel, dilapidated, seedy, lamentable, wretched.
minaret [minarɛ] *s.m.* minaret.
minauder [minode] *v.i.* to simper, to smirk, to court attention.
minauderie [minodri] *s.f.* simpering, airs, affected ways.
minaudi-er, -ère [minodje] *adj.* simpering, affected.
mince [mɛ̃s] *adj.* thin, slim, slender, slight, spare; insignificant, inconsiderable, scanty, feeble, insubstantial; ~ *interj.* (pop.) ~*!* or ~ *alors!*, expressing surprise, admiration or annoyance.
minceur [mɛ̃sœr] *s.f.* thinness, slenderness, slimness; scantiness.
mine[1] [min] *s.f.* look, appearance, face, expression, mien, countenance, bearing; *avoir bonne* ~, *mauvaise* ~, to look well, unwell; *avoir une* ~ *de déterré*, to look like a corpse; *tu en as une* ~*!*, you look terrible!; *avoir la* ~ *de*, to look like, to look as if; *vous avez la* ~ *d'avoir mal dormi*, you look as if you hadn't slept well; *avoir* or *porter une* ~ *de fripon*, to have a rascally appearance; *avoir la* ~ *allongée*, to have a long face, to look gloomy; *faire une* ~ *de dix pieds de long*, to pull a very long face; *faire triste* ~, to look disappointed; *faire* ~ *de*, to make a show of, to pretend to, to make as if to, to make signs (to s.o.) to; *il fit* ~ *de sortir*, he made as if to go out; *il me fit* ~ *de sortir*, he signalled me to go out; *faire des* ~*s*, to put on airs, to show off; *faire bonne* ~ *à*, to be pleasant to, to behave cheerfully towards or in face of; *faire grise* ~, to look sour; *de bonne* ~, attractive, pleasant-looking, of prepossessing appearance; *de mauvaise* ~, unprepossessing, of unpleasant appearance; *ça ne paie pas de* ~, it looks most unattractive; (pop.) ~ *de rien*, casually, as though nothing had happened.
mine[2] [min] *s.f.* **1.** ore; ~ *de fer*, iron ore; ~ *de plomb*, black lead, graphite, plumbago; **2.** lead (of a pencil); **3.** mine, pit; (pl.) mining; (fig.) mine, storehouse, fertile source (of information, etc.); ~ *de cuivre*, copper-mine; *exploitation des* ~*s*, mining; *puits de* ~, pit-shaft; *une* ~ *de science*, a storehouse of knowledge; **4.** (explosive) mine; tunnel or hole dug for a mine; *creuser une* ~, to lay a mine (in the ground); (nav.) *poser* or *mouiller une* ~, to lay a mine (in water); *dragueur de* ~*s*, mine-sweeper; *coup de* ~, explosion of a mine; blasting.
mine[3] [min] *s.f.* mine (old Fr. measure of corn).
miner [mine] *v.t.* to mine; (lit. & fig.) to undermine, to sap, to wear away, to consume; to prey upon.
minerai [minrɛ] *s.m.* ore.
minéral, -e, (aux) [mineral] *adj.*, ~ *s.m.* mineral.
minéralier [mineralje] *s.m.* (naut.) ore-carrier.
minéralisat-eur, -rice [mineralizatœr] *adj.* mineralizing.
minéralis-ation [mineralizɑsjɔ̃] *s.f.* mineralization; ~**er** [mineralize] *v.t.* to mineralize.
minéralog-ie [mineralɔʒi] *s.f.* mineralogy; ~**ique** [mineralɔʒik] *adj.* mineralogical; ~**iste** [mineralɔʒist] *s.m.f.* mineralogist.
Minerve [minɛrv] *s.f.* (Rom. myth.) Minerva.
minerve [minɛrv] *s.f.* (print.) Minerva machine, Minerva press.
minerviste [minɛrvist] *s.m.f.* Minerva-press operator.
minestrone [minɛstrɔn] *s.m.* minestrone (soup).
minet, -te [minɛ] *s.m.f.* **1.** cat, pussy, puss; **2.** darling, pet; ~ *s.m.* elegant young man; ~**te** *s.f.* (bot.) hop-trefoil.
mineur [minœr] *s.m.* miner, pitman, collier; (mil.) sapper.
mineur, -e [minœr] *adj.* lesser, minor; under age; (mus.) *mode* ~, minor mode; *tierce* ~*e*, minor third; *l'Asie* ~*e*, Asia Minor; ~ *s.m.* (mus.) minor (key); ~**e** *s.f.* (logic) minor term, minor premiss.
miniature [minjatyr] *s.f.* miniature, small-

-scale model; ornamental initial letter in manuscript; *en* ~, miniature, in miniature, on a small scale, tiny.
miniaturé, -e [minjatyre] *adj.* illustrated with miniatures; painted in miniature.
miniaturis-ation [minjatyrizasjɔ̃] *s.f.* (techn.) miniaturization; **~er** [minjatyrize] *v.t.* (techn.) to miniaturize, to manufacture on a minute scale.
miniaturisé, -e [minjatyrize] *adj.* (electr.) *circuit* ~, miniaturized circuit.
miniaturiste [minjatyrist] *s.m.f.* miniature-painter, miniaturist.
mini-er, -ère [minje] *adj.* mining; ore-bearing; **~ère** *s.f.* opencast mine.
minima [minima] *adj.f., s.m.pl.* see MINIMUM.
(**à**) **minima** [aminima] *adv.loc.* (law) *appel à* ~, appeal against leniency of sentence.
minimal, -e, (**aux**) [minimal] *adj.* minimal, minimum.
minime [minim] *adj.* minimal, very small, trifling, trivial, minute; ~ *s.m.* minim; (pl.) (sport) colts (14–16 years).
minimiser [minimize] *v.t.* to minimize, to reduce or keep to a minimum.
minimum [minimɔm] *s.m.* (pl. *minimums* or *minima*) minimum, lowest point or value; *au* ~, at or to the minimum, at least; *dans le* ~ *de temps*, in the shortest possible time; ~ *de vitesse*, minimum, or lowest permissible, speed; ~ *adj.* (f. & pl. also *minima*) minimum, minimal; *prix* ~, reserve price (at auction); *pertes* ~*s* or *minima*, minimal losses.
ministère [ministɛr] *s.m.* ministry; ministry building; (government) department; (ministerial) office, function, duties; government; services, agency, medium; ~ *des Affaires Étrangères*, Foreign Office; ~ *de l'Intérieur*, Home Office; ~ *public*, (department of) Director of Public Prosecutions; *former un* ~, to form a government; *par* ~ *de*, through the agency of; *offrir son* ~, to offer one's services.
ministériel, -le [ministerjɛl] *adj.* ministerial, government, official, pro-government; (law) *les* ~*s*, the law officers.
ministrable [ministrabl] *adj.* in the running for a ministerial appointment.
ministre [ministr] *s.m.* minister, minister of state; agent, instrument; clergyman; *premier* ~, prime minister, premier; ~ *de l'Intérieur*, Home Secretary; ~ *de la Marine*, First Lord of the Admiralty; ~ *des Finances*, Chancellor of the Exchequer; *papier* ~, official stationery.
minium [minjɔm] *s.m.* minium, red lead.
minoen, -ne [minɔɛ̃] *adj.* (Gr. ant.) Minoan.
minois [minwa] *s.m.* pretty face.
minoritaire [minɔritɛr] *adj., s.m.f.* minority.
minorité [minɔrite] *s.f.* **1.** minority; *en* ~, in a minority; **2.** (law) minority, infancy.
minorquin, -e [minɔrkɛ̃] *adj., s.m.f.* Minorcan; (native or inhabitant) of Minorca.
minoterie [minɔtri] *s.f.* flour-milling; flour-mill.
minotier [minɔtje] *s.m.* flour-miller; owner of a flour-mill.
minou [minu] *s.m.* = MINET 1.
minuit [minɥi] *s.m.invar.* midnight, twelve o'clock at night.
minuscule [minyskyl] *adj.* small, diminutive, tiny, miniature, minute, minuscule; ~ *s.f.* minuscule, small letter, (print.) lower case.
minus (**habens**) [minys (abɛ̃s)] *s.m.invar.* mental defective.
minutage [minytaʒ] *s.m.* strictly-timed programme, programme timed to the minute.
minutaire [minytɛr] *adj.* (law) in the form of a minute; in the original document, in the record.
minute [minyt] *s.f.* **1.** minute (sixtieth part of an hour or of a degree); (fig.) instant, very short time; *je reviens dans une* or *la* ~, I will be back in a moment; ~*!*, one minute!, half a moment!; *à la* ~, instant, while you wait; *la* ~ *de vérité*, the moment of truth; **2.** minute, original document, record, memorandum; **3.** small writing, small hand.
minuter [minyte] *v.t.* **1.** to record, (law) to enter (a judgement); **2.** (obs.) to propose, to meditate (doing); **3.** to time (a programme, etc.) to the minute.
minuterie [minytri] *s.f.* **1.** (horol.) minute-train; **2.** (electr.) delay-switch (for switching off lights on stairs, etc.).
minutie [minysi] *s.f.* **1.** minutia (pl. minutiae), minute detail, trifle; **2.** extreme care, meticulousness, minute attention to detail; *avec* ~, minutely, in minute detail, with great precision.
minutieu-x, -se [minysjø] *adj.* meticulous, minute, accurate, particular, close, thorough, scrupulous; **~sement** [minysjøzmɑ̃] *adv.* minutely, meticulously, thoroughly, scrupulously.
miocène [miɔsɛn] *adj.* (geol.) Miocene.
mioche [mjɔʃ] *s.m.f.* (fam.) kid, brat, urchin.
mi-parti, -e [miparti] *adj.* see MI *pref.*
mirabelle [mirabɛl] *s.f.* (bot.) mirabelle plum.
miracle [mirakl] *s.m.* miracle, wonder, marvel, prodigy; miracle play; *opérer des* ~*s*, to work miracles; *à* ~, marvellously well; *par* ~, by a miracle, miraculously, for a wonder; *crier au* ~, to extol, to praise to the skies; to declare to be a miracle; *faiseur de* ~*s*, miracle-worker; *c'est* ~ *qu'il réussisse*, it would be a miracle if he succeeded.
miraculé, -e [mirakyle] *adj.* cured by a miracle; the subject of a miracle.
miraculeu-x, -se [mirakylø] *adj.* miraculous, wonderful, marvellous; **~sement** [mirakyløzmɑ̃] *adv.* miraculously, wonderfully.
mirador [miradɔr] *s.m.* **1.** mirador, belvedere; **2.** (mil.) observation-post, watch-tower (esp. in prison-camp).
mirage [miraʒ] *s.m.* **1.** mirage; (fig.) illusion, chimera; **2.** candling (of eggs).
mire [mir] *s.f.* sight, aim; land-surveyor's pole, levelling-rod; test-card (on TV); *ligne de* ~, line of sight, sighting-line; *point de* ~, aim, mark; object in view, (fig.) object of attention, cynosure of all eyes; *prendre sa* ~, to take aim.
mirer [mire] *v.t.* to look at, to aim at; (fam.) to have one's eye on; to mirror; ~ *des œufs*, to candle eggs; **se** ~ *v.refl.* to look at one's reflection, to be reflected.
mirette [mirɛt] *s.f.* (fam.) eye.
mirifique [mirifik] *adj.* (iron.) marvellous, wonderful.
mirliflore [mirliflɔr] *s.m.* dandy.
mirliton [mirlitɔ̃] *s.m.* reed-pipe; *vers de* ~, doggerel.
mirmidon see MYRMIDON.
mirobolant, -e [mirɔbɔlɑ̃] *adj.* (fam.) wonderful, astounding, prodigious.
miroir [mirwar] *s.m.* mirror, looking-glass; (fig.) mirror, reflection; *œufs au* ~, eggs fried in butter; ~ *ardent*, burning-glass; ~ *à alouettes*, revolving mirror used to catch larks; (fig.) decoy, lure, specious attraction.
miroitant, -e [mirwatɑ̃] *adj.* glistening, glittering, flashing, sparkling, shining, shimmering.
miroité, -e [mirwate] *adj.* (of horse's coat) dappled.
miroitement [mirwatmɑ̃] *s.m.* flash, flashing, glistening, glitter, reflection of light.
miroiter [mirwate] *v.i.* to flash, to glisten, to glitter, to sparkle, to glint, to reflect light; *faire* ~ *qch. aux yeux de qn.*, to dazzle s.o. with the prospect of sth.

miroiterie [mirwatri] *s.f.* mirror-making; mirror trade.
miroitier [mirwatje] *s.m.* cutter, silverer, mounter, of mirrors.
miroton [mirɔtɔ̃], **mironton** [mirɔ̃tɔ̃] *s.m.* (cook.) hash, stew.
mis, -e [mi] *p.p.* of METTRE.
misaine [mizɛn] *s.f.* foremast; *voile de* ~, foresail; ⚠ not 'mizen'.
misanthrope [mizɑ̃trɔp] *adj.* misanthropic; ~ *s.m.f.* misanthrope, misanthropist.
misanthrop-ie [mizɑ̃trɔpi] *s.f.* misanthropy; ~**ique** [mizɑ̃trɔpik] *adj.* misanthropic.
miscellanées [misɛllane] *s.f.pl.* miscellanea.
miscible [misibl] *adj.* miscible, mixable.
mise [miz] *s.f.* putting, setting, laying; stake, staking, betting, bid; outlay; dress, manner or style of dressing; *de* ~, in fashion, being worn, suitable, presentable; in circulation; ~ *négligée*, careless way of dressing, slovenly appearance; ~ *en accusation*, indictment; ~ *en action*, bringing into use, bringing out, realization; ~ *en cause*, implication, involvement; ~ *en court-circuit*, short-circuiting; ~ *en demeure*, demand, summons, formal notice; ~ *à l'eau* or *à flot*, launching; ~ *en état*, putting in order; ~ *à exécution*, carrying--out, realization; ~ *de fonds*, outlay, investment, disbursement, putting-up of money; ~ *à jour*, putting in order or up to date; ~ *au jour*, bringing to light, revealing; ~ *en liberté*, release, discharge; ~ *en marche*, starting, setting in motion; starter (on car); ~ *au monde*, giving birth to; bringing forth; producing; ~ *à nu*, laying bare, exposing (thoughts, etc.); ~ *en œuvre*, bringing into use or application; (radio, TV, etc.) ~ *en ondes*, production; (print.) ~ *en pages*, making-up, page-setting; ~ *à pied*, dismissal; ~ *sur pied*, raising, establishing setting-up, restoring; ~ *en place*, placing, setting, laying; ~ *en plis*, (of hair) setting; ~ *au point*, focusing; (fig.) clarification, explanation; (mech.) regulating, tuning; ~ *à la poste*, posting; ~ *en pratique*, application, putting into practice or action, carrying out; ~ *à prix*, (i.) setting a price on; (ii.) estimating; (iii.) (at auction) upset price; ~ *en relief*, emphasizing, underlining; ~ *en retraite*, pensioning-off, retiring; (theatr.) ~ *en scène*, staging, production, getting-up; ~ *en train*, starting, launching; (print.) making ready; ~ *en valeur*, development, exploitation, improvement; ~ *en vigueur*, enforcement; ~ *en vente*, putting up for sale; ~ *bas*, (of animals) bringing forth, dropping.
miser [mize] *v.t.i.* to stake, to bet, to bid; (fig.) to speculate, to count, (*sur*, on); ~ *sur les deux tableaux*, to run with the hare and hunt with the hounds, to try to have it both ways, to hedge one's bets.
misérable [mizerabl] *adj.* miserable, pitiful, wretched, sorry, worthless, insufficient; mean, despicable, contemptible; poverty-stricken; villainous; *une existence* ~, a wretched life; *un salaire* ~, insufficient wages, starvation wages; ~ *s.m.f.* wretch; (obs.) villain; ~**ment** [mizerabləmɑ̃] *adv.* wretchedly, miserably, pitifully.
misère [mizɛr] *s.f.* misery, extreme poverty, destitution, want; wretchedness, sad or wretched state of affairs; distress, trouble, affliction, ill, woe, misfortune, worry; meanness, pettiness; trifle, mere nothing; *petites* ~*s*, little worries, minor afflictions; *cent francs! une* ~*!*, a hundred francs! a mere nothing!; *crier* ~, (i.) to complain of one's poverty or one's afflictions; (ii.) to indicate poverty (of the owner); *des vêtements qui crient* ~, shabby clothes; *manger le pain de* ~, to eat the bread of affliction; *parer à la* ~, to keep the wolf from the door.
miserere, miséréré [mizerere] *s.m.* (liturg.) miserere.
miséreu-x, -se [mizerø] *adj., s.m.f.* destitute (person).
miséricorde [mizerikɔrd] *s.f.* mercy, pity; *demander* ~, to beg, to cry, for mercy; *faire* ~, to show mercy; *à tout péché* ~, no sin but should find mercy; ~*!*, mercy on us!, God help us!; (naut.) *ancre de* ~, sheet-anchor.
miséricordieu-x, -se [mizerikɔrdjø] *adj.* merciful, compassionate.
misogyne [mizɔʒin] *adj.* misogynous; ~ *s.m.* misogynist, woman-hater.
misogynie [mizɔʒini] *s.f.* misogyny.
missel [misɛl] *s.m.* missal.
missile [misil] *s.m.* guided missile.
mission [misjɔ̃] *s.f.* mission, commission, function, responsibility, business, errand; (diplomatic) mission; (eccles.) mission, mission station, missionary work or field; *quelle est votre* ~*?*, what is your errand?; *en* ~, on a (special) mission; (mil.) on detached duty; *sans* ~, without authority; *avoir* ~ *de*, to have the responsibility of.
missionnaire [misjɔnɛr] *adj., s.m.f.* missionary; (law) *lettre* ~, letter missive.
missive [misiv] *adj., s.f.* missive.
mistelle [mistɛl] *s.f.* mistelle (must of which the fermentation has been stopped).
mistoufle [mistufl] *s.f.* **1.** (fam.) dirty trick; **2.** (pop.) poverty.
mistral [mistral] *s.m.* mistral (wind).
mitaine [mitɛn] *s.f.* **1.** mitten; (fig.) *je n'ai pas pris de* ~*s pour*, I made no bones about; **2.** (fam.) *miton* ~, innocuous and worthless medicament; eyewash.
mite [mit] *s.f.* mite, weevil, (clothes-)moth; *mangé des* ~*s*, moth-eaten; (fig., fam.) *avoir la* ~ *à l'œil*, to have one's eyes gummed up with sleep.
mité, -e [mite] *adj.* moth-eaten; (fig., fam.) shabby, seedy.
miteu-x, -se [mitø] *adj.* wretched, shabby; *s.m.f.* shabby or down-at-heel individual.
mithridatisation [mitridatizɑsjɔ̃] *s.f.*, **mithridatisme** [mitridatism] *s.m.* gradual immunization against poison, mithridatism.
mithridatiser [mitridatize] *v.t.* to immunize against poison.
mitigation [mitigɑsjɔ̃] *s.f.* mitigation.
mitigé, -e [mitiʒe] *adj.* mitigated, alleviated; modified.
mitiger [mitiʒe] *v.t.* to mitigate, to moderate, to alleviate, to reduce the severity of.
miton [mitɔ̃] *s.m.* see MITAINE 2.
mitonner [mitɔne] *v.t.i.* to simmer gently; to nurse, to brew up, to prepare quietly, (a project); to coddle, to be very attentive to; **se** ~ *v.refl.* to pamper oneself.
mitose [mitoz] *s.f.* (biol.) mitosis.
mitoyen, -ne [mitwajɛ̃] *adj.* party, partition, middle; *mur* ~, party-wall; *cloison* ~*ne*, partition wall.
mitoyenneté [mitwajɛnte] *s.f.* joint ownership, party right, party property.
mitraillade [mitrɑjad] *s.f.* volley of grape-shot; (burst of) machine-gun fire.
mitraille [mitrɑj] *s.f.* mitraille, grape-shot, canister-shot; shell-fire; scrap-iron; (fam.) coppers, small change.
mitrailler [mitrɑje] *v.i.* to fire grape-shot; ~ *v.t.* to machine-gun; (fig.) to bombard, to photograph (a celebrity) repeatedly from all angles.
mitraillette [mitrɑjɛt] *s.f.* sub-machine-gun, tommy-gun.
mitrailleur [mitrɑjœr] *s.m.* machine-gunner.
mitrailleuse [mitrɑjøz] *s.f.* machine-gun; (obs.) mitrailleuse.

mitral, -e, (aux) [mitral] *adj.* mitral, mitre-shaped; ~**e** *s.f.* mitral valve (of the heart).
mitre [mitr] *s.f.* mitre; cowl (on chimney).
mitré, -e [mitre] *adj.* mitred.
mitron [mitrɔ̃] *s.m.* baker's boy, apprentice baker.
(**à**) **mi-voix** [amivwɑ] *adv.loc.* under one's breath; in an undertone, in a low voice.
mixer, mixeur [miksœr] *s.m.* (cook.) mixer.
mixte [mikst] *adj.* mixed; composite, combined.
mixtion [mikstjɔ̃] *s.f.* mixing, compounding; mixture.
mixture [mikstyr] *s.f.* mixture, compound; (fig.) mélange.
M.K.S.(A.) [ɛmkaɛs(a)] (phys.) M.K.S.(A.) system of units indicated by initial letters of *mètre, kilogramme, seconde,* (*ampère*).
Mlle, MM., Mme abbrevs. MADEMOISELLE, MESSIEURS, MADAME.
mnémonique [mnemɔnik] *adj.* mnemonic.
mnémotechnique [mnemɔtɛknik] *adj.* mnemotechnic.
mobile [mɔbil] *adj.* mobile, movable, moving, detachable, loose, floating; changeable, changing, unsteady, inconstant, fickle, capricious; lively, vivacious; *un visage* ~, a face full of expression; ~ *s.m.* **1.** moving body; **2.** mover, motive power, prime mover, originator; motive, spring, incentive, incitement; **3.** (hist.) soldier of *garde mobile* (of 1870); **4.** (art) mobile.
mobili-er, -ère [mɔbilje] *adj.* movable; of personal property; *biens* ~*ers,* personal estate, chattels; *vente* ~*ère,* sale of furniture; *valeurs* ~*ères,* transferable securities; *crédit* ~*er,* loan on personal security; ~**er** *s.m.* furniture, movables; suite (of furniture); ~*er de salon,* drawing-room suite.
mobilisable [mɔbilizabl] *adj.* mobilizable, available.
mobilisation [mɔbilizɑsjɔ̃] *s.f.* mobilization; (fin.) liquidation.
mobiliser [mɔbilize] *v.t.* to mobilize, to call up; to call upon, to call into play; *un mobilisé,* a soldier who has been called up.
mobilité [mɔbilite] *s.f.* mobility, movability; (fig.) instability, fluctuation, changeableness; liveliness.
moblot [mɔblo] *s.m.* (fam.) = MOBILE *s.m.* 3.
mocassin [mɔkasɛ̃] *s.m.* moccasin; casual (shoe).
moche [mɔʃ] *adj.* (fam.) ugly, rotten, lousy.
mocheté [mɔʃte] *s.f.* (fam.) ugly woman.
modal, -e, (aux) [mɔdal] *adj.* modal; ~**e** *s.f.* (log.) modal proposition.
modalité [mɔdalite] *s.f.* modality, nature, form; (pl.) manner, ways and means; (mus.) form of scale; ~*s de paiement,* method of payment; (fin.) ~*s d'une émission,* terms and conditions of an issue; ~*s d'application d'une loi,* manner in which the law shall apply; (gram.) *adverbe de* ~, adverb qualifying the sentence as a whole.
mode [mɔd] *s.m.* mode, way, method; (gram.) mood, mode; (log., mus.) mode; ~ *de vie,* way of life; ~ *d'emploi,* directions for use.
mode [mɔd] *s.f.* fashion, mode, way, manner, style, custom; fashion trade, fashion dressmaking; (pl.) fashions, fashionable clothes, millinery; (*de*) ~, fashionable; *des teintes* ~, fashionable shades; *à la* ~, in fashion, into fashion, fashionable; cooked according to a local recipe, e.g. *tripes à la* ~ (*de Caen*); *cette année c'est très à la* ~, it is very fashionable this year; *c'est revenu à la* ~, it has come back into fashion; *à la* ~ *de,* in the manner of, in the . . . style; *c'est passé de* ~, it has gone out of fashion; *de* ~, fashion, fashionable, in fashion; *gravures de* ~, fashion-plates; *être de* ~, to be fashionable; *magasin de* ~*s,* milliner's shop.
modelage [mɔdlaʒ] *s.m.* modelling; model.
modèle [mɔdɛl] *s.m.* model; pattern, design, specimen, sample; type; ~ *de broderie,* sampler; *les différents* ~*s d'organisation,* the different types of organization; ~ *déposé,* patent, patented; ~ *d'écriture,* handwriting copy, calligraphy; *grand* ~, large size; ~ *de vertu,* paragon of virtue; ~ *adj.* model, exemplary.
modelé [mɔdle] *s.m.* relief, representation of relief (on map), modelling, model.
modeler [mɔdle] *v.t.* to model, to make a model or pattern of, to fashion, to shape; *se* ~ *sur,* to take for one's model, to conform to.
modeleu-r, -se [mɔdlœr] *s.m.f.* modeller; (techn.) pattern-maker.
modéliste [mɔdelist] *s.m.f.* dress-designer; (dressm., techn.) pattern-maker.
modénature [mɔdenatyr] *s.f.* (arch.) profile of cornice.
modérantisme [mɔderɑ̃tism] *s.m.* (hist.) moderantism.
modérat-eur, -rice [mɔderatœr] *adj.* moderating, restraining; *s.m.f.* moderator; ~**eur** *s.m.* regulator, damper, restrainer.
modération [mɔderɑsjɔ̃] *s.f.* moderation, restraint, mitigation, moderating, reducing; moderateness.
modéré, -e [mɔdere] *adj.* moderate, reasonable, temperate, restrained, subdued, (mus.) moderato; ~**ment** [mɔderemɑ̃] *adv.* moderately, in moderation.
modérer [mɔdere] *v.t.* to moderate, to mitigate, to restrain, to curb, to check, to reduce, to abate; to regulate; **se** ~ *v.refl.* to restrain oneself, to control oneself.
moderne [mɔdɛrn] *adj.* modern, up-to-date; (iron.) new-fangled; *à la* ~, in the modern style; ~ *s.m.* modern style; *meublé en* ~, furnished in the modern idiom; ~**s** *s.m.pl.* the moderns, modern authors.
modernisation [mɔdɛrnizɑsjɔ̃] *s.f.* modernization.
moderniser [mɔdɛrnize] *v.t.* to modernize.
modernisme [mɔdɛrnism] *s.m.* modernism.
modernité [mɔdɛrnite] *s.f.* modernity, modernness.
modeste [mɔdɛst] *adj.* modest, unassuming, quiet, unpretentious; humble; of limited means; moderate, restrained; limited; ~**ment** [mɔdɛstəmɑ̃] modestly; moderately.
modestie [mɔdɛsti] *s.f.* modesty, simplicity, unpretentiousness; moderation, restraint.
modicité [mɔdisite] *s.f.* smallness, lowness (of price), slenderness (of means), limited range.
modifiable [mɔdifjabl] *adj.* modifiable, subject to change, liable to be influenced.
modificat-eur, -rice [mɔdifikatœr] *adj.* modificatory, modifying; ~**eur** *s.m.* modifier, transformer.
modificati-f, -ve [mɔdifikatif] *adj.* (gram.) modifying.
modification [mɔdifikɑsjɔ̃] *s.f.* modification, alteration, amendment; restriction; variation, another form.
modifier [mɔdifje] *v.t.* to modify, to alter; to tone down; (gram.) to modify, to qualify; **se** ~ *v.refl.* to change, to alter.
modillon [mɔdijɔ̃] *s.m.* (arch.) modillion.
modique [mɔdik] *adj.* small, moderate, modest; ~**ment** [mɔdikmɑ̃] *adv.* moderately, modestly.
modiste [mɔdist] *s.m.f.* milliner, modiste; ⚠ not 'dressmaker'.
modulation [mɔdylɑsjɔ̃] *s.f.* modulation, inflexion (of voice); (mus.) modulation, transition; (radio) ~ *de fréquence,* frequency modulation.
module [mɔdyl] *s.m.* module, standard, standard unit of measure; (math., phys.) modulus; *cigare de gros* ~, king-size cigar.
moduler [mɔdyle] *v.t.i.* to modulate; to pass

from key to key; (radio) *à fréquence modulée*, frequency-modulated.

moelle [mwal] *s.f.* marrow, (anat.) medulla; (bot.) pith; (fig.) pith, gist, substance; (anat.) *~ allongée*, medulla oblongata; *~ épinière*, spinal cord; *os à ~*, marrow-bone; (bot.) *courge à ~*, vegetable marrow; *pourri jusqu'aux ~s*, rotten to the core.

moelleu-x, -se [mwalø] *adj.* marrowy, pithy; mellow, smooth, bland, soft, springy, elastic, rich, comfortable; **~x** *s.m.* mellowness, springiness, elasticity, softness; **~sement** [mwaløzmɑ̃] *adv.* softly, luxuriously.

moellon [mwalɔ̃] *s.m.* quarry-stone, ashlar, rubble, roughstone.

mœurs [mœr(s)] *s.f.pl.* manners, habits, customs, ways; morals; (animal) behaviour; *certificat de bonnes vie et ~*, certificate of good conduct; *sans ~*, unprincipled; *avoir de bonnes ~*, to be an upright person; *de ~ faciles*, of easy virtue; *cela n'est plus dans nos ~*, that is no longer the custom; *autre temps, autre ~*, manners change with the times; *quelles ~!*, what manners!, what a way to behave!

mofette [mɔfɛt] *s.f.* **1.** choke-damp, noxious fumes; **2.** = MOUFFETTE.

mogol [mɔgɔl] *s.m.* Mogul.

mohair [mɔɛr] *s.m.* mohair.

moi [mwa] *pers. pron.* me, to me; I, for my part, personally; *à ~!*, help!; *c'est à ~*, it is mine, it belongs to me; it is my turn; *un ami à ~*, a friend of my own; *il n'aime que ~*, he loves only me; *écrivez-moi*, write to me; *~, je crois que*, personally I think that; *~ qui vous parle, j'ai vu*, I myself have seen; *~-même*, myself; *~ aussi*, I too, me too; *ni ~ non plus*, neither do I, nor I; *de vous à ~*, between you and me; *~ s.m.* ego, self; *le culte du ~*, egoism.

moie see MOYE.

moignon [mwaɲɔ̃] *s.m.* (biol.) stump, vestigial limb.

moindre [mwɛ̃dr] *adj.* less, lesser, smaller, minor, lower, inferior, of less importance; *le ~*, the least, the smallest, the slightest; *une question de ~ importance*, a question of minor importance; *sans le ~ doute*, without the slightest doubt; *certains savants, et non des ~s*, certain scientists, and not the least important ones; **~ment** [mwɛ̃drəmɑ̃] *adv. pas le ~ment*, not in the least.

moine [mwan] *s.m.* monk, friar; bed-warmer, warming-pan; (print.) friar; (ornith.) puffin; (zool.) monk-seal; *l'habit ne fait pas le ~*, the cowl does not make the monk; *gras comme un ~*, fat as a pig.

moineau (pl. **-x**) [mwano] *s.m.* sparrow; *têtes de ~*, nuts (of coal); *tirer* or *brûler sa poudre aux ~x*, to waste powder and shot; (fig.) *un sale* or *vilain ~*, a nasty-looking type.

moinerie [mwanri] *s.f.* monks (collectively); monastic life; monastery, convent, friary.

moins [mwɛ̃] *adv., s.m.* less; fewer; not so, not so much, not so many; (math.) minus, minus sign; *le ~*, least, the least; *il travaille ~ que moi*, he works less than I, he does not work so much as I; *elle travaille le ~*, she works least; *il a ~ de travail*, he has less work, he has not so much work; *il a ~ d'amis*, he has fewer friends, he has not so many friends; *en ~ d'une demi-heure*, in less than half-an-hour; *à ~ de*, for less than, unless, without, except by, except in the case of, barring, failing; *à ~ d'être payé, je ne le fais pas*, unless I am paid, I shall not do it; *à ~ d'accidents*, barring accidents; *à ~ d'avis contraire*, failing notice to the contrary; *à ~ que*, unless; *au ~*, at least; *il a au ~ cinq voitures*, he has at least five cars; *de ~*, less; too little; *ça coûte dix francs de ~ que l'autre*, it costs ten francs less than the other one; *vous avez payé dix francs de ~*, you have paid ten francs too little; *de ~ en ~*, less and less; *du ~*, at any rate, at least; *du ~ personne n'a été blessé*, at any rate no one was hurt; *pour le ~*, to say the least; at (the) least; *ni plus ni ~*, neither more nor less; *non ~ que*, as well as, no less than, quite as much as; *pas le ~ du monde*, not in the least; *rien ~ que*, anything but, nothing less than; *tout au ~, à tout le ~*, at the very least; *midi ~ le quart*, quarter to twelve; *elle n'est rien ~ que jolie*, she is anything but pretty; *il ne s'agit de rien ~ que sa fortune*, nothing less than his fortune is at stake; *il n'est pas ~ vrai que*, it is nevertheless true that; *on ne peut ~*, as little as possible, the least possible; *10 ~ 5*, 10 minus 5; *~ 3 degrés*, minus 3 degrees, 3 degrees below zero.

moins-perçu [mwɛ̃pɛrsy] *s.m.* (law, fin.) under-drawing, credit.

moins-value [mwɛ̃valy] *s.f.* decline in value, depreciation, falling-off.

moirage [mwaraʒ] *s.m.* watering (of silk).

moire [mwar] *s.f.* watered or shot silk; watered effect, shot-silk effect.

moiré [mware] *adj.* watered, moiré; *~ s.m.* shot-silk effect; *~ métallique*, crystal tin-plate.

moirer [mware] *v.t.* to give a watered or moiré effect to, to moiré.

mois [mwɑ] *s.m.* month; monthly allowance or pay; *payé au ~*, paid by the month; *au ~ de*, in the month of; *par ~*, monthly; a month; *tous les 36 du ~*, once in a blue moon; *toucher son ~*, to draw one's salary.

moise [mwaz] *s.f.* (techn.) cross-piece, tie, tie-beam, tie-piece, brace.

moïse [mɔiz] *s.m.* bassinet, wicker-cradle.

moisi, -e [mwazi] *adj.* mouldy, musty, mildewed; *~ s.m.* mould, mustiness; *ça sent le ~*, it smells mouldy or musty.

moisir [mwazir] *v.t.i.* to grow mouldy or musty, to become mildewed; (fig.) to stagnate, to vegetate, to rot away, to waste one's time; to make mouldy, to mildew; *je ne vais pas ~ ici*, I am not going to waste my time here, I have no intention of mouldering in this place.

moisissure [mwazisyr] *s.f.* mouldiness, mustiness, mould, mildew; mouldy part; (fig.) rottenness, corruption.

moissine [mwasin] *s.f.* vine-branch with grapes attached (for preserving).

moisson [mwasɔ̃] *s.f.* harvest, crop; harvest-time; *faire* or *rentrer la ~*, to harvest, to gather in the harvest.

moissonnage [mwasɔnaʒ] *s.m.* (method of) harvesting.

moissonner [mwasɔne] *v.t.* to harvest, to reap, to gather in the harvest; to sweep away, to devastate; *~ un champ*, to reap a field; *qui sème le vent moissonne la tempête*, he who sows the wind reaps the whirlwind; *la guerre a moissonné les jeunes*, the war carried off the young men; *la tempête a tout moissonné*, the storm destroyed all the crops.

moissonneu-r, -se [mwasɔnœr] *adj.* harvesting; *s.m.f.* harvester, reaper, harvest-worker; **~se** *s.f.* reaping-machine, reaper, harvester; *~se-batteuse-lieuse*, combine harvester.

moite [mwat] *adj.* moist, clammy, damp.

moiteur [mwatœr] *s.f.* moisture, humidity, dampness, sweating.

moitié [mwatje] *s.f.* half; (fam.) wife, better half; moiety; *à ~*, half, by halves, partly; *il ne fait rien à ~*, he does nothing by halves, he never takes half-measures; *plus grand de ~*, half as large again; *réduire de ~*, to reduce by half; *partager par ~*, to halve, to divide in half; *~-~*, half-and-half, so so, yes and no, not very; *se mettre de ~ avec*, to go halves with; *à ~ prix*, for or at half-price; *à ~ chemin*, half-way; *à ~ fait qui commence bien*, well begun is half done.

moitir [mwatir] *v.t.* to moisten.
moka [mɔka] *s.m.* **1.** mocha (coffee); **2.** mocha cake.
mol, -le [mɔl] *adj.* see MOU *adj.*
molaire [mɔlɛr] *adj.* (phys.) molar; ~ *s.f.* molar (tooth).
molasse, mollasse [mɔlas] *s.f.* (geol.) molasse; ⚠ not 'molasses'.
mole [mɔl] *s.f.* (sci.) mole.
môle [mol] *s.m.* pier, mole; ⚠ not the animal 'mole'.
môle [mol] *s.f.* (ichth.) sunfish.
moléculaire [mɔlekylɛr] *adj.* molecular.
molécule [mɔlekyl] *s.f.* molecule.
molène [mɔlɛn] *s.f.* (bot.) mullein.
moleskine [mɔlɛskin] *s.f.* American cloth, imitation leather; ⚠ not 'moleskin'.
molestation [mɔlɛstɑsjɔ̃] *s.f.* molestation.
molester [mɔlɛste] *v.t.* to molest, to annoy, to handle roughly.
moletage [mɔltaʒ] *s.m.* (techn.) milling, knurling.
moleter [mɔlte] *v.t.* (techn.) to mill, to knurl.
molette [mɔlɛt] *s.f.* **1.** muller (for mixing and grinding colours); **2.** rowel (of spur); **3.** (techn.) serrated wheel, knurled wheel, marking-wheel; milling-tool; *clé à* ~, adjustable spanner; ~ *à briquet*, flint-wheel (on lighter).
mollah [mɔla] *s.m.* mullah.
mollasse [mɔlas] *adj.* flabby; (fig.) apathetic, spineless, lazy; ~ *s.f.* see MOLASSE.
mollement [mɔlmɑ̃] *adv.* softly, loosely; indolently, apathetically, slackly, tamely, effeminately, feebly.
mollesse [mɔlɛs] *s.f.* softness, flabbiness, laxity, slackness, indolence, tameness, effeminacy; *vivre dans la* ~, to live a life of ease and luxury.
mollet [mɔlɛ] *s.m.* calf (of the leg).
mollet, -te [mɔlɛ] *adj.* soft, softish, light; *œuf* ~, soft-boiled egg.
molletière [mɔltjɛr] *s.f.* legging, puttee.
molleton [mɔltɔ̃] *s.m.* brushed wool or cotton; ~ *de laine*, flannel.
molletonner [mɔltɔne] *v.t.* to line or pad with flannel, etc.
mollir [mɔlir] *v.i.* to soften, to become soft; to slacken; (fam.) to hesitate, to weaken; *le vent mollit*, the wind is dying down; *sentir ses jambes* ~ *de fatigue*, to feel one's legs giving way with fatigue; ~ *v.t.* **1.** (obs.) to soften; **2.** (naut.) to slacken off (a cable).
mollusque [mɔlysk] *s.m.* mollusc; (fam.) flabby or spineless individual.
molosse [mɔlɔs] *s.m.* mastiff, watch-dog, large dog.
molybdène [mɔlibdɛn] *s.m.* molybdenum.
môme [mom] *s.m.f.* (fam.) kid, brat, urchin; (pop.) girl.
moment [mɔmɑ̃] *s.m.* moment, instant; short time; the present time; the right time; (mech.) moment; *en* or *à ce* ~, just now, at present, at the moment; *les puissants du* ~, those in power at the moment; *un éclat d'un* ~, momentary brilliance; *j'étais occupé à ce moment-là*, I was busy at the time, at that moment; *dans un* ~, *un petit* ~, *un* ~*!*, half a moment!, a moment!, in a moment!; *ce n'est pas le* ~, it is not the right time; *c'est le bon* ~, it is the right moment, now is the time; *dans un mauvais* ~, at a bad time, at an awkward moment; *à tout* ~, every moment, at any moment; *à tous* ~*s*, at every turn, constantly; *au* ~ *de*, on the point of, just when, just as; *au* ~ *de sortir nous*, just as we were going out, we; *au* ~ *où*, *au* ~ *que*, just when, just as, the instant that; *jusqu'au* ~ *où*, until, till such time as; *par* ~*s*, at times, now and then; *de* ~ *en* ~, *d'un* ~ *à l'autre*, any moment, (at) any time, from one moment to the next; *à mes* ~*s perdus*, in my spare time, whenever I have time; *du* ~ *que*, (i.) from the moment when; from the moment that; (ii.) since, seeing that; *du* ~ *qu'il refuse, il n'y a rien à faire*, since he refuses, there is nothing to be done; *abuser de vos* ~*s*, to trespass on your time; ⚠ not 'moment' in the sense of 'importance'.
momentané, -e [mɔmɑ̃tane] *adj.* momentary, temporary, transitory; ~**ment** [mɔmɑ̃tanemɑ̃] *adv.* momentarily, for a moment, temporarily, for the time being.
momerie [momri] *s.f.* **1.** mummery, parody; **2.** hypocritical pretence, mumbo-jumbo.
momie [mɔmi] *s.f.* **1.** mummy; (fig., fam.) a bag of skin and bones, old fossil, death's-head; **2.** bituminous preparation used in embalming.
momification [mɔmifikɑsjɔ̃] *s.f.* **1.** mummification; **2.** (pathol.) desiccation (of the tissues).
momifier [mɔmifje] *v.t.* **1.** to mummify; **2.** (fig.) to atrophy.
mon [mɔ̃] (also used instead of *ma* before vowel or h-mute), (fem.) **ma** [ma], (pl.) **mes** [mɛ] *poss. adj.* my.
monacal, -e, (aux) [mɔnakal] *adj.* monac(h)al, monastic, monkish.
monachisme [mɔnaʃism] *s.m.* monachism, monasticism, monastic life; monastic institution.
monaco [mɔnako] *s.m.* (pop.) cash, money.
monade [mɔnad] *s.f.* monad.
monarch-ie [mɔnarʃi] *s.f.* monarchy; ~**ique** [mɔnarʃik] *adj.* monarchical, monarchic; ~**iste** [mɔnarʃist] *adj.*, *s.m.f.* monarchist.
monarque [mɔnark] *s.m.* monarch, sovereign, ruler.
monastère [mɔnastɛr] *s.m.* monastery, convent.
monastique [mɔnastik] *adj.* monastic, monachal; monkish.
monaural, -e, (aux) [mɔnɔral] *adj.* = MONOPHONIQUE 2.
monceau (pl. **-x**) [mɔ̃so] *s.m.* heap, pile, stack, mass.
mondain, -e [mɔ̃dɛ̃] *adj.* worldly, worldly-minded; (of man, woman, life, gathering, etc.) mundane, earthly, secular; society; *auteur* ~, writer dealing with high society life; *s.m.f.* man or woman in society, man about town, social figure; ⚠ not 'mundane' in senses 'dull', 'routine'.
mondanité [mɔ̃danite] *s.f.* worldliness, mundanity, mundaneness; ~*s*, social life, social events, social gossip column.
monde [mɔ̃d] *s.m.* world, sphere, universe; mankind, people; society, company, milieu; lot of people, crowd; (obs.) servants, domestic staff; *le* ~ *entier*, the whole world; *être au* ~, to be in the land of the living; *être seul au* ~, to be alone in the world; *il n'est plus de ce* ~, he is no longer alive; *venir au* ~, to be born; *mettre au* ~, to give birth to; *l'homme le plus fier du* ~, the proudest man in the world, the proudest man alive; *au bout du* ~, at the other end of the world; *de par le* ~, over the whole world, roaming the world; *si vous en tirez dix francs, c'est tout le bout du* ~, if you get ten francs out of it, it is the most you can expect; *ce grand magasin est un* ~, this large store is a world in itself; *se moquer du* ~, to take people for a pack of fools, to act impudently; to be joking; *il s'en est fait un* ~, he has made a whole business out of it; *rien au* ~, nothing in the world, nothing at all; *pour rien au* ~, not on any account; *l'autre* ~, the next or the other world; *c'est vieux comme le* ~, it is as old as the hills; *on ne peut contenter tout le* ~ *et son père*, you cannot satisfy everyone; *il y a beaucoup de* ~, there is a lot of people, there is a crowd; it is crowded; *tout le* ~, everybody, everyone, everyone else; *il n'y a pas grand* ~, there are not many people (present); *le grand* ~, high society, the

best people, the fashionable world, the upper crust; *un homme du* ~, a gentleman, a society man, a man about town; *une femme du* ~, a society woman, a lady; *le petit* ~, (i.) the young people, the children; (ii.) people of modest origin, small fry; *il n'est pas de notre* ~, he does not move in the same circles as we do; *connaître son* ~, (i.) to know whom one has to deal with; to know one's customers; (ii.) to know how to behave; *savoir son* ~, to move in polite circles.
monde [mɔ̃d] *adj.* (obs.) clean.
monder [mɔ̃de] *v.t.* to cleanse; to husk, to shell, to hull; to blanch (almonds).
mondial, -e, (**aux**) [mɔ̃djal] *adj.* world, world-wide; ~**ement** [mɔ̃djalmɑ̃] *adv.* on a world-wide scale, throughout the world, universally.
mondialisation [mɔ̃djalizɑsjɔ̃] *s.f.* becoming world-wide, distribution throughout the world.
mondovision [mɔ̃dɔvizjɔ̃] *s.f.* world-wide TV transmission (by satellite).
monégasque [mɔnegask] *adj., s.m.f.* Monegasque, (native or inhabitant) of Monaco.
monel [mɔnɛl] *s.m.* monel (an alloy of nickel, copper, etc.).
monère [mɔnɛr] *s.f.* (biol.) moneron (pl. monera).
monétaire [mɔnetɛr] *adj.* monetary, money, currency.
monétisation [mɔnetizɑsjɔ̃] *s.f.* monetization.
monétiser [mɔnetize] *v.t.* to monetize.
mongol, -e [mɔ̃gɔl] *adj., s.m.f.* Mongol, Mongolian.
mongolien, -ne [mɔ̃gɔljɛ̃] *adj.* **1.** (obs.) (geog.) Mongolian; **2.** (med.) mongol, mongoloid.
mongolique [mɔ̃gɔlik] *adj.* Mongolian.
mongolisme [mɔ̃gɔlism] *s.m.* (med.) mongolism.
monisme [mɔnism] *s.m.* (phil.) monism.
monit-eur, -rice [mɔnitœr] *s.m.f.* monitor; adviser, guide, instructor.
monition [mɔnisjɔ̃] *s.f.* monition.
monitoire [mɔnitwar] *adj.* monitory; ~ *s.m.* monitory (letter).
monitor [mɔnitɔr] *s.m.* (nav.) monitor.
monnaie [mɔnɛ] *s.f.* coin, money, change; mint; currency; *pièce de* ~, coin; *ne pas avoir de* ~, to have no change; *faites-moi la* ~ *de cent francs*, give me change for a hundred francs; *papier-*~, paper money; ~ *légale*, legal tender; (*Hôtel de*) *la Monnaie*, Mint; *payer en* ~ *de singe*, to defraud (one's creditors); *fausse* ~, counterfeit coin; (fig.) *il lui a rendu la* ~ *de sa pièce*, he paid him back in his own coin; (fig.) *c'est* ~ *courante*, it is common currency; it is a common occurrence; (bot.) ~ *du pape*, honesty, moneywort.
monnayage [mɔnɛjaʒ] *s.m.* coining, coinage, minting.
monnayer [mɔneje] *v.t.* to coin, to mint; (fig.) to exploit, to sell, to market, to cash in on (one's talent, etc.).
monnayeur [mɔnɛjœr] *s.m.* coiner; minter; *faux* ~, counterfeiter.
mono- [mɔnɔ] *pref.* mono-, single; ~**atomique** [mɔnɔatɔmik] *adj.* (chem.) monatomic; ~**basique** [mɔnɔbɑzik] *adj.* (chem.) monobasic; ~**bloc** [mɔnɔblɔk] *adj.invar.* cast in a single block; *s.m.* engine cast in a single block; ~**caméralisme** [mɔnɔkameralism], ~**camérisme** [mɔnɔkamerism] *s.m.* single-chamber constitution; ~**chrome** [mɔnɔkrom] *adj.* monochrome.
monocle [mɔnɔkl] *s.m.* monocle, eyeglass.
mono-coque [mɔnɔkɔk] *adj., s.m.* (car body) welded in a single piece, monoshell; ~**corde** [mɔnɔkɔrd] *s.m.* (mus.) monochord; *adj.* (fig.) monotonous, tedious; ~**cotylédone** [mɔnɔkɔtiledɔn] *adj.* (bot.) monocotyledonous; *s.f.* monocotyledon.
monoculaire [mɔnɔkylɛr] *adj.* monocular.
monodie [mɔnɔdi] *s.f.* monody; unaccompanied solo.
mono-game [mɔnɔgam] *adj.* monogamous; ~**gamie** [mɔnɔgami] *s.f.* monogamy; ~**gamique** [mɔnɔgamik] *adj.* monogamous; ~**gramme** [mɔnɔgram] *s.m.* monogram; ~**graphie** [mɔnɔgrafi] *s.f.* monograph.
monoïque [mɔnɔik] *adj.* (bot.) monoecious.
mono-lingue [mɔnɔlɛ̃g] *adj.* monolingual; ~**lithe** [mɔnɔlit] *adj.* monolithic; *s.m.* monolith; ~**logue** [mɔnɔlɔg] *s.m.* monologue, soliloquy; ~**loguer** [mɔnɔlɔge] *v.i.* to soliloquize, to talk to oneself; ~**mane** [mɔnɔman], ~**maniaque** [mɔnɔmanjak] *adj., s.m.f.* monomaniac; ~**manie** [mɔnɔmani] *s.f.* monomania, obsession.
monôme [mɔnom] *s.m.* (alg.) monomial; (fam.) students' rag procession (in single file).
mono-mètre [mɔnɔmɛtr] *adj.* monometric; ~**moteur** [mɔnɔmɔtœr] *adj., s.m.* single-engined (aircraft); ~**nucléaire** [mɔnɔnykleɛr] *adj.* (bot.) mononuclear, uninuclear.
monophasé, -e [mɔnɔfaze] *adj.* (electr.) monophase, single-phase.
mono-phonique [mɔnɔfɔnik] *adj.* **1.** (mus.) monophonic (opp. polyphonic); **2.** (radio, etc.) monophonic (opp. stereophonic), in monophone; ~**place** [mɔnɔplas] *adj., s.m.* single-seater; ~**pole** [mɔnɔpɔl] *s.m.* monopoly, exclusive possession; ~**polisation** [mɔnɔpɔlizɑsjɔ̃] *s.f.* monopolization; ~**poliser** [mɔnɔpɔlize] *v.t.* to monopolize, to have the monopoly of.
monoptère [mɔnɔptɛr] *adj.* (arch.) monopteral.
mono-rail [mɔnɔrɑj] *adj., s.m.* monorail; ~**sépale** [mɔnɔsepal] *adj.* (bot.) monosepalous; ~**sperme** [mɔnɔspɛrm] *adj.* (bot.) monospermous; ~**syllabe** [mɔnɔsillab] *adj.* monosyllabic; *s.m.* monosyllable; ~**syllabique** [mɔnɔsillabik] *adj.* monosyllabic; ~**théique** [mɔnɔteik] *adj.* monotheistic; ~**théisme** [mɔnɔteism] *s.m.* monotheism; ~**théiste** [mɔnɔteist] *adj.* monotheistic; *s.m.f.* monotheist; ~**tone** [mɔnɔtɔn] *adj.* monotonous, wearisome, humdrum; ~**tonie** [mɔnɔtɔni] *s.f.* monotony, monotonousness, sameness; ~**trème** [mɔnɔtrɛm] *adj., s.m.* (zool.) monotreme; ~**type** [mɔnɔtip] *adj.* **1.** (bot.) monotypic(al); **2.** (of yacht) one-design; *s.f.* (print.) Monotype (machine) proprietary name.
monovalent, -e [mɔnɔvalɑ̃] *adj.* (chem.) monovalent, univalent.
Monseigneur [mɔ̃sɛɲœr] *s.m.* (pl. *messeigneurs, nosseigneurs*) My Lord, Your Lordship, Your Grace, Lord, His Grace; ~ *s.m.* (pl. *monseigneurs*) = PINCE-MONSEIGNEUR.
Monsieur [məsjø] *s.m.* (pl. *messieurs*) gentleman; M., Mr.; sir; the master (of the house), the gentleman, the husband; (hist.) eldest brother of the King of France; *cher* ~, dear sir; *Messieurs*, Gentlemen, Messrs.; ~ *le Maire*, Mr. Mayor, Your Worship; *un vilain* ~, a nasty individual, a bad lot.
monstre [mɔ̃str] *s.m.* monster; monstrosity; ~ *adj.* huge, colossal, monster; *un succès* ~, a huge success.
monstrueu-x, -se [mɔ̃stryø] *adj.* monstrous, huge, grotesque; outrageous, atrocious; ~**sement** [mɔ̃stryøzmɑ̃] *adv.* monstrously, outrageously.
monstruosité [mɔ̃stryozite] *s.f.* monstrosity, deformity; monstrousness.
mont [mɔ̃] *s.m.* mountain, mount; *les Monts*, the Alps; *par* ~*s et par vaux*, up hill and down dale; *promettre* ~*s et merveilles*, to promise the earth; ~*-de-piété*, official pawnbroking establishment; *mettre au* ~*-de-piété*, to pawn.
montage [mɔ̃taʒ] *s.m.* **1.** carrying up, taking up, lifting; **2.** mount; mounting, setting; fixing up,

fitting up, assembling; (electr.) connecting up, wiring up; (photo., cin.) montage.

montagnard, -e [mɔ̃taɲar] *adj.* mountain, highland; *s.m.f.* mountaineer; one who lives in the mountains, highlander; (Fr. hist.) member of *la Montagne*.

montagne [mɔ̃taɲ] *s.f.* mountain, mountains; (fig.) pile, large amount, mountain; *passer ses vacances à la* ~, to spend one's holidays in the mountains; (fig.) *se faire une* ~ or *des* ~*s*, to make a mountain out of a molehill, to make heavy weather (of sth.); (fig.) *soulever des* ~*s*, to move mountains; (Fr. hist.) *la Montagne*, an ultra--revolutionary party; ~*s russes*, switchback, scenic railway.

montagneu-x, -se [mɔ̃taɲø] *adj.* mountainous, hilly; mountain.

montaison [mɔ̃tɛzɔ̃] *s.f.* migration (of salmon) up rivers.

montanisme [mɔ̃tanism] *s.m.* (relig. hist.) montanism.

montant, -e [mɔ̃tɑ̃] *adj.* ascending, rising, uphill, going uphill or upstream; vertical, up(-); *chemin* ~, uphill road; *train* ~, up train; *bateau* ~, boat going upstream; (techn.) *joint* ~, vertical joint; *course* ~*e*, up-stroke (of piston); *robe* ~*e*, high-necked dress; *col* ~, stand-up collar; *marée* ~*e*, rising tide, flood tide.

montant [mɔ̃tɑ̃] *s.m.* **1.** upright, vertical portion or member, post (of gate, etc.); (naut.) stanchion; **2.** total, amount; **3.** pronounced flavour, piquancy; appeal, attraction.

monte [mɔ̃t] *s.f.* **1.** serving, covering, (of animals); **2.** riding; way of riding.

monté, -e [mɔ̃te] *adj.* **1.** mounted (on horseback); **2.** (fig.) *collet* ~, affected, strait-laced; **3.** *être* ~ *contre qn.*, to be angry with s.o.

monte-charge [mɔ̃tʃarʒ] *s.m. invar.* lift, hoist, elevator, service-lift.

montée [mɔ̃te] *s.f.* slope, rise, ascent, climb; (arch.) height; going up, rising, ascending, boiling up.

monte-plats [mɔ̃tplɑ] *s.m. invar.* service-lift.

monter [mɔ̃te] *v.i.* to go up, to come up, to ascend, to climb, to mount; to rise, to slope up(wards); to grow; to rise (in the world, etc.), to obtain promotion, to be on the up-grade; to amount (*à*, to); to boil up, to become angry or heated; ~ *à sa chambre, à Paris*, to go up to one's room, to Paris; ~ *à bicyclette*, to ride a bicycle; ~ *à cheval*, to ride, to mount; ~ *à l'assaut de*, to storm; ~ *à* or *sur un arbre*, to climb a tree; ~ *dans un train*, to get into a train, to take a train; ~ *en haut* (*de*), to go up, to ascend; ~ *à bord*, to go on board, to embark; ~ *sur un vaisseau*, to go aboard a ship; ~ *sur le trône*, to ascend the throne; *le chemin monte*, the road goes uphill; *la marée monte*, the tide is coming in; *les frais montent*, costs are mounting; *les larmes lui montaient aux yeux*, tears came into her eyes; *ce vin monte à la tête*, this wine goes to one's head; *le total monte, se monte, à*, the total comes to; *une vedette qui monte*, an up-and-coming star; *le ton monte*, the atmosphere (of the discussion, etc.) is becoming heated; *faire* ~ *qn.*, to provoke or enrage s.o.; ~ *v.t.* to go up, to ascend, to climb, to mount; to mount or ride (a horse); to raise, to take up, to bring up, to carry up; to turn up (gas, etc.); to wind up (watch, etc.); to set or mount (jewellery, etc.); to set up, to fix up, to arrange, to hatch (plot, etc.); to stock (*en*, with); to make up (a dress); (electr.) to connect up, to wire up; (of stallions, etc.) to cover, to mount, to serve; ~ *une machine*, to set up or assemble a machine; ~ *un complot*, to hatch a plot; ~ *un coup*, to plan a crime, etc.; (fam.) ~ *le coup à qn.*, to take s.o. in; ~ *la tête à qn.*, to incite s.o. (*contre*, against); **se** ~ *v.refl.* **1.** to provide oneself (*en*, with); **2.** to amount (*à*, to); **3.** to get excited or angry; *se* ~ *la tête*, to get over-excited, to get ideas into one's head.

monte-sacs [mɔ̃tsak] *s.m. invar.* sack-hoist.

monteu-r, -se [mɔ̃tœr] *s.m.f.* setter, mounter, fitter, assembler.

montgolfière [mɔ̃gɔlfjɛr] *s.f.* hot-air balloon.

monticule [mɔ̃tikyl] *s.m.* hillock, knoll, mound, hummock.

montjoie [mɔ̃ʒwa] *s.m.* (obs.) cairn, heap of stones.

montmorency [mɔ̃mɔrɑ̃si] *s.f.* a variety of cherry.

montoir [mɔ̃twar] *s.m.* **1.** horse-block, mounting--block; **2.** (techn.) assembling-tool.

montrable [mɔ̃trabl] *adj.* presentable.

montre[1] [mɔ̃tr] *s.f.* watch; ~*-bracelet*, wrist--watch; ~ *à répétition*, repeater.

montre[2] [mɔ̃tr] *s.f.* show, display; shop-window, show-window, show-case; (pottery) sample firing; *en* ~, in the window, on display; (fig.) *faire* ~ *de*, to display, to show off; *pour la* ~, for show, for appearances.

montrer [mɔ̃tre] *v.t.* to show, to display, to point out, to indicate, to present, to exhibit, to manifest, to evince, to betray, to reveal; to teach; to demonstrate, to prove; ~ *à qn. à faire*, to show s.o. how to do; ~ *la corde*, to be thread-bare; ~ *le chemin*, to show the way, (fig.) to set an example; ~ *au doigt*, to point at; ~ *du sang-froid*, to show presence of mind; ~ *qu'on a raison*, to prove that one is right; ~ *les dents*, (lit. & fig.) to show one's teeth; **se** ~ *v.refl.* to show one-self, to appear; to prove to be, to turn out.

montreu-r, -se [mɔ̃trœr] *s.m.f.* exhibitor, showman; ~*r d'ours*, bear-leader.

montueu-x, -se [mɔ̃tɥø] *adj.* steep, hilly, mountainous.

monture [mɔ̃tyr] *s.f.* **1.** mount, steed; *qui veut aller loin, ménage sa* ~, slow and steady wins the race; **2.** setting, mounting, frame; rims or frame (of spectacles); stock (of gun).

monument [mɔnymɑ̃] *s.m.* monument; public or historic building, building of architectural interest, archaeological remains; memorial; (fam.) enormous object; (fig.) work of great and lasting importance.

monumental, -e, (aux) [mɔnymɑ̃tal] *adj.* monumental, grand, imposing, huge, prodi-gious.

moque [mɔk] *s.f.* (naut.) heart, dead-eye.

(se) moquer [mɔke] *v.refl.* to laugh (*de*, at), to make fun (of), to jeer; to be joking; not to care; *se* ~ *de*, to laugh or jeer at, to make fun of, to mock, to ridicule; to make light of; to care nothing for; to belittle, to scorn; *je m'en moque pas mal, je m'en moque comme de l'an quarante*, I couldn't care less, it doesn't bother me; *vous vous moquez!*, you must be joking!; *se* ~ *du monde*, to be joking, to be deceiving people; *se* ~ *des gens*, to behave out-rageously; *on se moque de lui*, he is being laughed at, he is being made a fool of; *la pelle se moque du fourgon*, the pot is calling the kettle black; *se faire* ~ *de soi*, to make oneself an object of ridicule.

moquerie [mɔkri] *s.f.* mockery, absurdity, farce; jeer, scoff, derision, ridicule.

moquette [mɔkɛt] *s.f.* **1.** moquette; **2.** fitted carpet.

moqueu-r, -se [mɔkœr] *adj.* mocking, scoffing, jeering, joking, jesting, teasing; *s.m.f.* mocker, scoffer, derider, wag; ~**r** *s.m.* (ornith.) mocking--bird.

moraille [mɔrɑj] *s.f.* (farriery) barnacles (for restive horses); (vet.) ring (for leading bulls); (pl.) (techn.) glassmaker's tongs.

moraillon [mɔrɑjɔ̃] *s.m.* hasp (of lock).

moraine [mɔrɛn] *s.f.* moraine.

moral, -e, (**aux**) [mɔral] *adj.* moral, ethical, relating to morals or customs; of good morals, righteous, upright; spiritual, intellectual; *un conte ~*, a story with a moral; *~ s.m.* nature, moral disposition; morale; *le ~ de l'homme*, human nature; *au ~*, in the moral or spiritual sphere; *son ~ était bas*, his morale was low, he was in low spirits.
morale [mɔral] *s.f.* ethics, moral science, morality, morals; moral (of story, event, etc.); *il m'a fait* (*de*) *la ~*, he has been lecturing me; *la ~ de cette histoire c'est que*, the moral of all this is; *la ~ chrétienne*, Christian ethics; ⚠ not 'morale'; see MORAL *s.m.*
moralement [mɔralmɑ̃] *adv.* morally, spiritually; in a moral fashion; *se conduire ~*, to behave in an upright way.
moralisant, -e [mɔralizɑ̃] *adj.* moralizing.
moralisat-eur, -rice [mɔralizatœr] *adj.* edifying, improving, uplifting, elevating; moralizing; *s.m.f.* moralizer.
moralisation [mɔralizɑsjɔ̃] *s.f.* moralization, raising moral standard.
moraliser [mɔralize] *v.t.* to lecture, to sermonize, to admonish; *~ v.i.* to moralize.
moraliste [mɔralist] *adj.* moralizing; *~ s.m.f.* moralist, moral philosopher.
moralité [mɔralite] *s.f.* morality, morals, moral sense, moral value, good conduct, integrity; moral reflection; morality play.
morasse [mɔras] *s.f.* (print.) final proof of a newspaper; ⚠ not 'morass'.
moratoire [mɔratwar] *adj.* moratory; *~ s.m.* = MORATORIUM.
moratorium [mɔratɔrjɔm] *s.m.* moratorium.
morbide [mɔrbid] *adj.* morbid, unhealthy.
morbidesse [mɔrbidɛs] *s.f.* (art) morbidezza, delicacy of flesh tints; languid grace.
morbidité [mɔrbidite] *s.f.* morbidness, morbidity.
morbleu [mɔrblø] *interj.* (obs.) expressing indignation, e.g. by Jove!
morceau (pl. **-x**) [mɔrso] *s.m.* piece, morsel, bit, snack, fragment; *manger un ~*, to have a bite of food, to have a snack; (fig.) *manger le ~*, to give the show away; *un fin ~, un ~ délicat*, a titbit; *~x choisis*, selection, selected extracts; *un bon ~ de*, a nice piece of, a sizeable chunk of; *un beau ~ de femme*, a pretty woman; *~ de terre*, parcel of land; *emporter le ~*, to win, to be the winner or gainer; *mettre en ~x*, to break to pieces.
morceler [mɔrsəle] *v.t.* to parcel out, to break up, to cut up, to divide (into portions).
morcellement [mɔrsɛlmɑ̃] *s.m.* breaking-up, division; (fig.) dissipation (of forces, etc.).
mordache [mɔrdaʃ] *s.f.* **1.** box-clamps, vice-clamps; **2.** jaws (of pincers, etc.).
mordacité [mɔrdasite] *s.f.* **1.** corrosiveness; **2.** mordancy, causticity (of criticism, etc.).
mordant, -e [mɔrdɑ̃] *adj.* mordant, caustic, biting, corrosive, pungent, cutting; *~ s.m.* **1.** corrosiveness; bite, cutting effect; mordant; **2.** (mus.) mordent.
mordicant, -e [mɔrdikɑ̃] *adj.* corrosive, mordant, caustic.
mordicus [mɔrdikys] *adv.* doggedly, tenaciously, tooth and nail.
mordillage [mɔrdijaʒ] *s.m.* nibbling.
mordiller [mɔrdije] *v.t.* to nibble.
mordoré, -e [mɔrdɔre] *adj.* mordoré, bronze; *~ s.m.* mordoré shade.
mordorer [mɔrdɔre] *v.t.* to give a mordoré or bronze shade to.
mordre [mɔrdr] *v.t.* to bite, to bite at or into; to cut into; to gnaw, (fig.) to eat into; to corrode, to etch; *~ à*, to bite at or into, to take a bite out of; (fig.) to get one's teeth into, to make good progress with; *l'inquiétude lui mord le cœur*, anxiety is eating into his heart; *~ à l'hameçon*, to nibble at the bait; *il mord au latin*, he is getting on well with his Latin; *se ~ la langue*, to bite one's tongue; (fig.) to repent; *il s'en mord la langue*, he is cursing himself for having spoken.
mordu, -e [mɔrdy] *adj.* **1.** (lit. & fig.) bitten (*de*, with); **2.** in love; mad, crazy, (*de*, about); *c'est un ~ du football*, he is football-mad.
more, moresque see MAURE, MAURESQUE.
mor-eau (pl. **-x**), **-elle** [mɔro] *adj., s.m.f.* jet--black (horse).
morelle [mɔrɛl] *s.f.* (bot.) morel, nightshade.
morfil [mɔrfil] *s.m.* wire-edge, burr, scarf (on edge of tool after sharpening).
(**se**) **morfondre** [mɔrfɔ̃dr] *v.refl.* to get bored or fed up, to languish, to mope.
morfondu, -e [mɔrfɔ̃dy] *adj.* **1.** chilled, soaked (to the skin); **2.** disappointed, downcast.
morganatique [mɔrganatik] *adj.* morganatic; **~ment** [mɔrganatikmɑ̃] *adv.* morganatically.
morgeline [mɔrʒəlin] *s.f.* (bot.) chickweed.
morgue[1] [mɔrg] *s.f.* haughtiness, arrogance.
morgue[2] [mɔrg] *s.f.* morgue, mortuary.
moribond, -e [mɔribɔ̃] *adj.* moribund, dying, at the point of death.
moricaud, -e [mɔriko] *s.m.f.* dark-skinned, (pej.) coloured person.
morigéner [mɔriʒene] *v.t.* **1.** (obs.) to bring up, to teach manners to; **2.** to rebuke, to lecture, to give (s.o.) a good talking to.
morille [mɔrij] *s.f.* (bot.) morel (mushroom).
morillon [mɔrijɔ̃] *s.m.* **1.** black grape; **2.** tufted duck; **3.** (pl.) small rough emeralds.
morio [mɔrjo] *s.m.* (ent.) Camberwell Beauty (butterfly).
morion [mɔrjɔ̃] *s.m.* (hist.) morion.
mormon, -e [mɔrmɔ̃] *adj., s.m.f.* Mormon.
mormonisme [mɔrmɔnism] *s.m.* Mormonism.
morne [mɔrn] *adj.* gloomy, bleak, dismal; dejected, dull, dreary, cheerless.
morne [mɔrn] *s.m.* (in West Indies) bluff, hillock.
morné, -e [mɔrne] *adj.* (herald.) blunted; disarmed.
mornifle [mɔrnifl] *s.f.* (fam.) slap in the face.
morose [mɔroz] *adj.* morose, sullen, sour-faced, moody, peevish, gloomy.
morosité [mɔrozite] *s.f.* moroseness, sullenness, moodiness, gloominess.
morphème [mɔrfɛm] *s.m.* (lang.) morpheme.
morphin-e [mɔrfin] *s.f.* morphia, morphine; **~isme** [mɔrfinism] *s.m.* morphinism, addiction to morphine; **~omane** [mɔrfinɔman] *adj., s.m.f.* morphinomaniac, (person) addicted to morphine; **~omanie** [mɔrfinɔmani] *s.f.* morphinomania, morphine addiction.
morpholog-ie [mɔrfɔlɔʒi] *s.f.* (biol., lang.) morphology; **~ique** [mɔrfɔlɔʒik] *adj.* morphological.
morpion [mɔrpjɔ̃] *s.m.* **1.** (vulg.) crab(-louse); **2.** (pop.) kid, brat; **3.** game similar to noughts and crosses.
mors [mɔr] *s.m.* bit (of bridle); jaw (of vice, pincers, etc.); (bookb.) joint; *prendre le ~ aux dents*, to bolt, to run away; (fig.) to take the bit between one's teeth, to go full tilt (at a job, etc.).
morse[1] [mɔrs] *s.m.* walrus, morse.
morse[2] [mɔrs] *adj., s.m.* (radio telegraphy) Morse.
morsure [mɔrsyr] *s.f.* bite, biting; sting; etching.
mort [mɔr] *s.f.* death, decease; poison; (fig.) end; *à ~*, to the death, fatal(ly), deadly, mortal(ly); *combattre à ~*, to fight to the death; *guerre à ~*, war to the knife; *blessé à ~*, mortally wounded, fatally injured; *ennemis à ~*, deadly or mortal enemies; *à ~ le tyran!*, death to the tyrant!; *de ~*, death, deathly, deathlike; *lit de ~*,

deathbed; *silence de ~*, deathly silence; *être à l'article de la ~*, to be at the point of death; *faire une bonne ~*, to die in the faith; *mourir de sa belle ~*, to die a natural death, to die in one's bed; *mettre à ~*, to put to death; *se donner la ~*, to commit suicide; *il avait la ~ dans l'âme*, he was sick at heart, the iron had entered into his soul; *souffrir mille ~s*, to die a thousand deaths, to suffer agonies; *à la vie, à la ~!*, for ever, till death us do part, in life and in death; *~ aux rats*, rat-poison; *~ aux mouches*, fly-killer; *c'est la ~ du commerce*, it is killing business, it is fatal to business.

mort, -e [mɔr] *adj.* dead; lifeless, inanimate, numb, inert; benumbed, insensible, hardened (*à*, to, against); obsolete, past, extinct; dull, lustreless; (sport) *ballon ~*, dead ball, ball out of play; *balle ~e*, spent bullet; *eaux ~es*, stagnant water; *langue ~e*, dead language; (naut.) *œuvres ~es*, dead works, upper works; (paint.) *nature ~e*, still life; (mech.) *point ~*, dead centre, dead point; neutral gear; *yeux ~s*, lifeless gaze; *il n'y va pas de main ~e*, he does not do things by halves, he strikes hard; *~e la bête, ~ le venin*, dead men tell no tales; *~e saison*, slack time, dead season; *s.m.f.* dead person, deceased, corpse, defunct; fatal casualty; (at games) dummy; *jour* or *fête des ~s*, All Souls' Day; *office des ~s*, burial service; *faire le ~*, to sham dead; (fig.) to keep quiet, to lie low.

mortadelle [mɔrtadɛl] *s.f.* Bologna sausage, mortadella, polony.

mortais-age [mɔrtɛzaʒ] *s.m.* mortising; mortise; **~e** [mɔrtɛz] *s.f.* mortise; keyway; **~er** [mɔrtɛze] *v.t.* to mortise; **~euse** [mɔrtɛzøz] *s.f.* mortising-machine.

mortalité [mɔrtalite] *s.f.* **1.** mortality; **2.** death rate.

morte-eau [mɔrto] *s.f.* (pl. *mortes-eaux*) neap-tide.

mortel, -le [mɔrtɛl] *adj.* mortal, deadly, deathly, fatal; *coup ~*, fatal blow, death-blow; *dépouille ~le*, mortal remains; *haine ~le*, deadly, implacable hatred; *maladie ~le*, fatal illness; *silence ~*, deathly hush; *attendre deux ~les heures*, to wait for two solid hours; *s.m.f.* mortal; *le commun des ~s*, the common herd, ordinary people; **~lement** [mɔrtɛlmɑ̃] *adv.* mortally, fatally, deadly.

mort-gage [mɔrgaʒ] *s.m.* (law) mortgage (of chattels); ⚠ not 'mortgage' (of house).

mortier [mɔrtje] *s.m.* (vessel) mortar; (mil.) mortar; (build.) mortar, cement; mortier (cap worn by Fr. magistrates, etc.).

mortifiant, -e [mɔrtifjɑ̃] *adj.* mortifying; humiliating.

mortification [mɔrtifikɑsjɔ̃] *s.f.* mortification; humiliation; (med.) necrosis, gangrene.

mortifier [mɔrtifje] *v.t.* to mortify; (cook.) to hang (game).

mortinatalité [mɔrtinatalite] *s.f.* ratio of still to live births.

mort-né, -e [mɔrne] *adj.* stillborn, born dead; (fig.) abortive.

mortuaire [mɔrtɥɛr] *adj.* funerary, mortuary, pertaining to burial or funerals; *domicile ~*, house of the deceased; *drap ~*, pall; *masque ~*, death-mask; *registre ~*, register of deaths.

morue [mɔry] *s.f.* cod, codfish; *huile de foie de ~*, cod-liver oil.

morutier [mɔrytje] *s.m.* cod-fishing boat; cod-fisherman.

morve [mɔrv] *s.f.* (vet.) glanders; nasal mucus.

morveu-x, -se [mɔrvø] *adj.* glandered; snotty; *qui se sent ~x se mouche*, if the cap fits, wear it; *s.m.f.* (fam.) brat, urchin, young puppy, snotty-nose.

mosaïque [mɔzaik] *s.f.* mosaic, mosaic work, inlay, inlaid leather, inlaid floor, tessellated pavement; (fig.) mosaic, miscellany, intricate pattern.

mosaïque [mɔzaik] *adj.* Mosaic, of Moses.

mosaïsme [mɔzaism] *s.m.* Mosaism.

mosaïste [mɔzaist] *s.m.f.* worker in mosaic, mosaicist.

Moscou [mɔsku] *s.m.* (geog.) Moscow.

moscouade [mɔskwad] *s.f.* muscovado (unrefined sugar).

moscoutaire [mɔskutɛr] *s.m.f.* (pej.) communist who takes his orders from Moscow.

moscovite [mɔskɔvit] *adj.*, *s.m.f.* Muscovite.

mosquée [mɔske] *s.f.* mosque.

mot [mo] *s.m.* word; saying, expression; short letter, note; answer, key, (to problem, etc.); *~ à* or *pour ~*, word for word, literally, verbatim; *bon ~*, witticism, joke, pun; *gros ~*, rude word, obscenity; *~s-croisés*, crosswords, crossword-puzzle(s); *au bas ~*, at the least; at the lowest estimate; *comprendre à demi-~*, to take the hint, to tumble to it; *ignorer le premier ~ de*, not to know the first thing about; *~ d'ordre*, watchword, order; *~ de passe*, password; *avoir toujours le ~ pour rire*, to be always ready with a joke; *faire des ~s*, to make jokes, to make clever remarks; *dire deux ~s à*, to have a word with; *envoyez-moi un ~*, drop me a line; *c'est là mon dernier ~*, that is my lowest price, that is my last word; *je l'ai pris au ~*, I took him at his word; *tranchons le ~!*, to put it plainly; *il ne mâche pas ses ~s*, he does not mince matters, he says what he means; *qui ne dit ~ consent*, silence gives consent; *donner le ~ à qn.*, to give s.o. their cue; to tip s.o. off; *ils s'étaient donné le ~*, they had passed the word round; they had fixed it all beforehand; *n'en soufflez pas ~!*, don't breathe a word!; *en peu de* or *en quelques ~s*, in a few words, briefly, in a nutshell; *en deux ~s comme en cent*, to cut a long story short; *elle veut dire son ~*, she will have her say; *ils ont eu des ~s ensemble*, they have had words (i.e. have quarrelled); *voilà le fin ~ de l'affaire!*, so that's the answer!, that's what is at the bottom of it!; *le ~ de l'énigme*, the key to the riddle; *je lui en toucherai un ~*, I will mention it to him.

motard [mɔtar] *s.m.* (fam.) motor-cyclist (esp. police or mil.).

motel [mɔtɛl] *s.m.* motel.

motet [mɔtɛ] *s.m.* (mus.) motet.

mot-eur, -rice [mɔtœr] *adj.* propelling, motive, moving, driving; *l'appareil ~eur*, the (driving or propelling) machinery, the engine(s); *force ~rice*, motive power; *arbre ~eur*, driving-shaft, main-shaft; *essieu ~eur*, driving axle, live axle; (anat.) *muscle ~eur*, motor; **~eur** *s.m.* motor, engine, motive power, propeller; *~eur à explosion*, internal combustion engine; *~eur à deux temps*, two-stroke engine; *~eur à vapeur*, steam-engine; *mû par ~eur*, power-driven; **~rice** *s.f.* electric locomotive, motor-carriage (of tram or multiple-unit train).

motif [mɔtif] *s.m.* motive, incentive; cause, reason, ground, explanation; (mus., etc.) motif, theme; pattern, design; *pour quel ~?*, on what ground?; *sans ~*, without motive, motiveless, groundless, gratuitous (insult, etc.); *pour le bon ~*, for good reasons; (fam.) with honourable intentions.

motilité [mɔtilite] *s.f.* motility.

motion [mosjɔ̃] *s.f.* **1.** motion, moving, movement; **2.** motion, proposal.

motivation [mɔtivɑsjɔ̃] *s.f.* motivation.

motiver [mɔtive] *v.t.* to give the reason for, to establish the motives for; to be the reason or motive for; to justify, to warrant; *décision motivée*, reasoned or justified decision; *refus non motivé*, unwarranted refusal.

moto [mɔtɔ] *s.f.* abbrev. of *motocyclette*; **~cross** [mɔtɔkrɔs] *s.m.* cross-country motor-cycle racing.

moto-culteur [mɔtɔkyltœr] *s.m.* mechanical cultivator, rotavator; **~culture** [mɔtɔkyltyr] *s.f.* mechanized agriculture; **~cycle** [mɔtɔsikl] *s.m.* mechanically-propelled two-wheeled vehicle; **~cyclette** [mɔtɔsiklɛt] *s.f.* motor cycle, motor bike (over 125cc.); **~cycliste** [mɔtɔsiklist] *s.m.f.* motor-cyclist; **~godille** [mɔtɔgɔdij] *s.f.* outboard-motor; **~nautisme** [mɔtɔnotism] *s.m.* motor-boating; **~pompe** [mɔtɔpɔ̃p] *s.f.* motor-pump; **~propulseur** [mɔtɔprɔpylsœr] *adj.* propelling, driving.

motoris-ation [mɔtɔrizɑsjɔ̃] *s.f.* motorization, mechanization; **~er** [mɔtɔrize] *v.t.* to motorize, to mechanize; *être motorisé,* (mil.) to be motorized; (fam.) to have a car, to be mobile.

motorship [mɔtɔrʃip] *s.m.* motor-ship (opp. steamship).

mots-croisiste [mokrwazist] *s.m.f.* crossword fan.

motte [mɔt] *s.f.* lump, clod, ball of earth (esp. round tree-roots); mound; *~ à brûler,* peat, turf; briquette (of dried tan, etc.); *~ de gazon,* sod, piece of turf; *~ de beurre,* pat or roll of butter.

mottereau (pl. **-x**) [mɔtro] *s.m.* (ornith.) sand-martin.

motteux [mɔtø] *s.m.* (ornith.) wheatear.

motus [motys] *interj.* hush!, not a word (about it)!

mou [mu], **mol** [mɔl] (before m.sing.noun beginning with vowel or h-mute) *adj.m.*, **molle** [mɔl] *adj.f.* soft, yielding, slack, lacking in vigour, loose, flaccid, lax, indolent; mild, gentle; effeminate; *temps ~,* close or muggy weather; *~ adv.* softly, gently, quietly; *vas-y ~!,* take it gently!; *~ s.m.* **1.** (fam.) weakling; **2.** soft, slackness; *le ~ et le dur,* the soft and the hard; **3.** slack, slackness; *avoir du ~,* to be slack, to be insufficiently taut or twisted; (naut.) *donner du ~ à,* to slacken (a cable).

mou [mu] *s.m.* lights; lungs (of sheep, bullocks, etc.); (pop.) *bourrer le ~ à qn.,* to stuff someone's head full (of ideas); to delude; *rentrer dans le ~ de qn.,* to bash s.o.

mouchage [muʃaʒ] *s.m.* blowing one's nose.

mouchard [muʃar] *s.m.* spy, police-spy, informer. nark, stool-pigeon; sneak, tell-tale; (techn.) concealed instrument for checking speed (of trains, lorries, etc.), tell-tale; (mil.) observation-plane, spy-plane; **~age** [muʃardaʒ] *s.m.* spying, informing; sneaking; **~er** [muʃarde] *v.t.i.* to spy on, to inform against; to be an informer or sneak.

mouche [muʃ] *s.f.* fly; spot, speck, stain; patch; beauty-spot; (fish.) fly; (fenc.) button (on foil); small beard; bull's-eye (of target); spy, informer; *c'est une fine ~,* he is a sly one; *faire ~,* to hit the bull's-eye; *prendre la ~,* to fly into a temper, to take offence; *quelle ~ vous pique?,* what's the matter with you?, what is upsetting you?; *pattes de ~,* illegible scrawl; *chiures de ~,* fly-spots; *couvert de chiures de ~,* fly-blown; *~ à viande,* blow-fly; *~ bleue,* bluebottle (fly); *~ à miel,* honey-bee; *~ d'Espagne,* Spanish fly, cantharides; *c'est la ~ du coche,* he is a regular busybody, he shoves his nose into everything; *on prend plus de ~s avec du miel qu'avec du vinaigre,* gently does the trick; *on aurait entendu voler une ~,* you could have heard a pin drop; *faire d'une ~ un éléphant,* to make a mountain out of a mole-hill; (naut.) (i.) passenger steamer (on Seine); (ii.) advice-boat.

moucher [muʃe] *v.t.* to wipe the nose of; to snuff (candle, etc.); (fam.) to put (s.o.) in his place, to tell (s.o.) off; *~ du sang,* to bleed from the nose; **se ~** *v.refl.* to blow one's nose; *il ne se mouche pas du pied* or *du coude,* he does things in grand style; he thinks a lot of himself; he won't play second fiddle.

moucherolle [muʃrɔl] *s.m.* (ornith.) flycatcher.

moucheron [muʃrɔ̃] *s.m.* midge, gnat.

moucheté, -e [muʃte] *adj.* spotted, speckled, flecked; *chat ~,* tabby cat; (fenc.) *fleuret ~,* capped foil.

moucheter [muʃte] *v.t.* to spot, to speckle, to fleck; (fenc.) to button (foil).

mouchette [muʃɛt] *s.f.* **1.** (arch.) listel, beading; **2.** (pl.) candle-snuffers.

moucheture [muʃtyr] *s.f.* spot, speckle, fleck; spotting.

mouchoir [muʃwar] *s.m.* handkerchief; scarf; *~ de tête,* head-scarf; (sport) *arriver dans un ~,* to come in in a bunch.

mouchure [muʃyr] *s.f.* nasal mucus; (candle-) snuff.

moudre [mudr] *v.t.* to grind, to mill; (fam.) to bash; (fig.) to grind out (a tune).

moue [mu] *s.f.* pouting, pout; *faire la ~,* to pout, to look sulky.

mouette [mwɛt] *s.f.* (ornith.) sea-gull, sea-mew.

mouffette [mufɛt] *s.f.* (zool.) skunk.

moufle [mufl] *s.f.* **1.** mitten, glove; **2.** tackle--block, pulley-block.

moufle [mufl] *s.m.* **1.** (chem.) muffle; **2.** (techn.) oven (for firing china).

mouflet, -te [muflɛ] *s.m.f.* small child.

mouflon [muflɔ̃] *s.m.* moufflon, wild sheep.

mouillage [mujaʒ] *s.m.* **1.** watering, soaking, steeping, mixing with water, watering-down; **2.** (naut.) anchoring; anchorage; (nav.) laying (of mines); *être au ~,* to lie at anchor.

mouillant, -e [mujɑ̃] *adj.* wetting; *~ s.m.* wetting agent.

mouillé, -e [muje] *adj.* moist, damp, wet, soaked; (naut.) at anchor; (lang.) palatalized; (weather) *il fait ~,* it is wet, it is rainy; *sentir le ~,* to smell damp; *yeux ~s,* eyes full of tears; *voix ~e,* voice full of emotion; *~ jusqu'aux os,* drenched to the skin.

mouillement [mujmɑ̃] *s.m.* wetting, moistening; (lang.) palatalization.

mouiller [muje] *v.t.i.* to soak, to water, to wet, to moisten, to damp; to mix with water, to add liquid to, to dilute; (naut.) to anchor; (nav.) to lay (a mine); (lang.) to palatalize; (pop.) to wet oneself (in fear); **se ~** *v.refl.* to get wet, to become wet, to fill with water; (fam.) to get into an awkward situation, to run risks; *ses yeux se mouillèrent,* her eyes filled with tears.

mouillette [mujɛt] *s.f.* sippet, finger of bread (for dipping).

mouilleur [mujœr] *s.m.* damper, sponge-pot (for wetting stamps, etc.); (naut.) tumbler (for holding anchor); (nav.) *~ (de mines),* minelayer.

mouilloir [mujwar] *s.m.* sprinkler, water-pot (for damping-down clothes or keeping fingers moist).

mouillure [mujyr] *s.f.* wetting, wet, dampness; damp-mark; (lang.) palatalization.

mouise [mwiz] *s.f.* (pop.) poverty; *être dans la ~,* to be hard up.

moujik [muʒik] *s.m.* moujik.

moukère [mukɛr] *s.f.* (slang) woman.

moulage [mulaʒ] *s.m.* **1.** casting, moulding, founding; cast, mould; **2.** grinding.

moule [mul] *s.m.* mould, form, cast, matrix; *faire un ~,* to take a cast(ing); (fig.) *le ~ en est perdu,* they don't make them like that any more; *fait au ~,* beautifully proportioned or moulded; *jeté dans le même ~,* cast in the same mould, exactly alike.

moule [mul] *s.f.* mussel; (pop.) fool, flabby individual.

moulé, -e [mule] *adj.* cast, moulded, made in a

mould; well-formed; close-fitting; *pain ~*, tin--loaf; *lettres ~es,* print, block letters; *écriture ~e*, copperplate writing.

mouler [mule] *v.t.* to cast, to make a cast of, to mould, to found; to shape, to form; to show the shape of, to follow the curves of; *une robe qui moule la taille*, a dress that shows off the figure, a closely-fitting dress; (fig.) *~ ses actions sur une loi*, to make one's actions conform to a law; *~ sur*, to adapt or conform to; *~ une lettre*, to shape a letter perfectly; *se ~ sur*, to model oneself on, to take as a model.

mouleur [mulœr] *s.m.* moulder.

moulière [muljɛr] *s.f.* mussel-bed.

moulin [mulɛ̃] *s.m.* mill; crusher, grinder; (fam.) engine (of car or plane); *~ à café*, coffee-mill, coffee-grinder; (slang) machine-gun; *~ à vent*, windmill; *~ à paroles*, chatterbox; *~ à prières*, prayer-wheel; *faire venir l'eau au ~*, to bring grist to the mill; (fig.) *se battre contre des ~s à vent*, to tilt at windmills; *jeter son bonnet par-dessus les ~s*, to throw off all restraint, not to care what people think.

moulinage [mulinaʒ] *s.m.* **1.** grinding, milling; **2.** (text.) throwing (of silk).

mouliner [muline] *v.t.* **1.** (obs.) (of worm) to eat into (wood); **2.** to grind, to mill; **3.** (text.) to throw (silk).

moulinet [mulinɛ] *s.m.* winch; small mill or grinder; cylinder, drum; turnstile; (fenc.) flourish; *faire des ~s, des deux bras*, to wave one's arms around.

moulinette [mulinɛt] *s.f.* (cook.) moulinette.

moulineu-r, -se [mulinœr], **moulini-er, -ère** [mulinje] *s.m.f.* silk-thrower.

moult [mult] *adv.* (obs.) much, very.

moulu, -e [muly] *adj.* ground, powdered; (fig.) tired, worn out; *or ~*, ground gold (for gilding), ormolu.

moulure [mulyr] *s.f.* (arch., join.) moulding.

moulurer [mulyre] *v.t.* (arch., join.) to decorate with moulding, to cut a moulding on; *machine, rabot, à ~*, moulding-machine, moulding-plane; *panneau mouluré*, moulded panel.

mourant, -e [murɑ̃] *adj.* dying, expiring; (fig.) faltering, languishing, fading, very pale; (fam.) deadly boring; screamingly funny; *s.m.f.* dying person.

mourir [murir] *v.i.* to die, to expire, to breathe one's last; to perish, to die away; (of fire, light) to go out; (of voice, sound) to die out, to die away; *bien ~*, to die bravely, to die in the faith; *~ à la peine*, to die in harness; *~ à la tâche*, to kill oneself with work; *il mourra dans la peau d'un ivrogne*, he is an incurable drunkard; *~ au monde*, to renounce the world; *s'ennuyer à ~*, to be bored to death; *être las à ~ de*, to be utterly sick of; *à ~ de rire*, too funny for words, killing; *~ de faim*, to starve, to starve to death, (fam.) to be starving; (fig.) *~ d'envie de*, to be dying to, to be longing to; *faire ~*, to kill, to put to death; (lit. & fig.) to be the death of; *faire ~ à petit feu*, to kill by inches, to put to death slowly and painfully; *faire ~ qn. de chagrin*, to break someone's heart; **se ~** *v.refl.* to be dying; to die away, to fade (out or away); *le jour se meurt*, the day is dying, the light is fading.

mouron [murɔ̃] *s.m.* (bot.) chickweed; pimpernel; groundsel.

mourre [mur] *s.f.* mor(r)a (game).

mousquet [muskɛ] *s.m.* musket.

mousquetade [muskətad] *s.f.* volley of musket shots.

mousquetaire [muskətɛr] *s.m.* musketeer.

mousqueton [muskətɔ̃] *s.m.* **1.** musketoon, blunderbuss; **2.** carbine; **3.** snap-buckle.

moussaillon [musajɔ̃] *s.m.* young cabin-boy.

moussant, -e [musɑ̃] *adj.* foaming, frothing, forming a lather; *crème à raser ~e*, lather shaving-cream.

mousse [mus] *s.m.* young sailor (under 16 years old), ship's boy, cabin-boy.

mousse [mus] *s.f.* **1.** (bot.) moss; *couvert de ~*, moss-grown, mossy; (proverb) *pierre qui roule n'amasse pas ~*, a rolling stone gathers no moss; **2.** froth, scum, foam, lather; effervescence; (cook.) mousse; (fam.) *se faire de la ~*, to fret, to worry, to get into a state.

mousse [mus] *adj.* blunt, not sharp.

mousseline [muslin] *s.f.* muslin; *verre ~*, fine glass, muslin-glass; (cook.) *pommes ~*, creamed potatoes; *~ de soie*, chiffon.

mousser [muse] *v.i.* to froth, to foam; (of wine) to sparkle; (fig.) *faire ~*, to praise, to vaunt, to puff up; to provoke (to anger).

mousseron [musrɔ̃] *s.m.* (bot.) button-mushroom.

mousseu-x, -se [musø] *adj.* **1.** foaming, frothy; (of wines) sparkling; **2.** moss, mossy; covered with down or fine hair; *rose ~se*, moss-rose; **~x** *s.m.* sparkling wine (not champagne).

mousson [musɔ̃] *s.f.* monsoon.

moussu, -e [musy] *adj.* mossy, moss-grown.

moustache [mustaʃ] *s.f.* moustache; (of cats, etc.) whiskers.

moustachu, -e [mustaʃy] *adj.* moustached, with a thick moustache.

moustérien, -ne [musterjɛ̃] *adj.* (archaeol.) Mousterian.

moustiquaire [mustikɛr] *s.f.* mosquito-net.

moustique [mustik] *s.m.* mosquito, gnat; (fig., fam.) midget.

moût [mu] *s.m.* must (unfermented wine); wort (of beer).

moutard [mutar] *s.m.* (pop.) urchin, small boy; (pl.) kids.

moutarde [mutard] *s.f.* mustard; mustard colour; (fam.) *la ~ lui monte au nez*, he is getting really angry, he is losing patience; *c'est comme de la ~ après dîner*, it is too late (to be of any use).

moutardier [mutardje] *s.m.* mustard-pot; mustard-maker; (fam.) *il se croit le premier ~ du pape*, he thinks no end of himself.

moutier, moustier [mutje] *s.m.* (obs.) monastery.

mouton [mutɔ̃] *s.m.* sheep, wether; mutton; (fig.) lamb; stool-pigeon, informer; small fluffy cloud; (pl.) white horses (on waves); (techn.) rammer, monkey, beetle, drop--hammer, head of pile-driver; *doux comme un ~*, gentle as a lamb; (fig.) *un ~ à cinq pattes*, a rarity, an impossibility; (fig.) *revenons à nos ~s*, to return to the subject; *faire le ~*, to act as a decoy; *~, ~ne* *adj.* sheep-like, ovine, docile.

moutonnant, -e [mutɔnɑ̃] *adj.* foaming, beginning to foam.

moutonné, -e [mutɔne] *adj.* **1.** curly, frizzy (of hair); **2.** (of sky) full of small fluffy clouds; **3.** (geol.) glaciated.

moutonnement [mutɔnmɑ̃] *s.m.* billowing, foaming (of sea).

moutonner [mutɔne] *v.i.* to billow, to foam, to break into foam or white horses; to present a frothy or fleecy appearance.

moutonnerie [mutɔnri] *s.f.* sheep-like stupidity.

moutonneu-x, -se [mutɔnø] *adj.* billowy, foam--crested.

moutonni-er, -ère [mutɔnje] *adj.* sheep-like, sheepish.

mouture [mutyr] *s.f.* grinding; grist; mixture of rye, wheat and barley; (obs.) milling-dues; (fig., pej.) re-hash; (fig.) *tirer d'un sac deux ~s*, to make a double profit (on sth.).

mouvance [muvɑ̃s] *s.f.* tenure.

mouvant, -e [muvɑ̃] *adj.* moving, shifting, fluid,

ever-changing, unstable; (fig.) fickle; (herald.) issuant; *sables ~s*, quicksands.

mouvement [muvmɑ̃] *s.m.* movement, motion, move; gesture; mobility; impulse, emotion; transfer (of personnel, etc.); change, modification, trend; undulation, curve, contour; agitation, disturbance; sensation; (horol.) works, movement; (mus.) (i.) time, tempo; (ii.) movement; *sans ~*, lifeless, limp, inanimate; *en ~*, in motion, on the move, moving, active, bustling about; *mettre en ~*, to start, to set going, to put in motion; *se mettre en ~*, to start; to move, to set off; to bestir oneself; *faire un ~*, to make a move, to move; *cet enfant, c'est le ~ perpétuel*, that child is never still; *un ~ d'air*, a puff of wind, an atmospheric disturbance; *un ~ de population*, a population change; *le ~ des naissances*, the trend in the birth-rate; *les ~s du terrain*, the undulations of the ground; *le doux ~ d'un dossier*, the gentle curve of a chair-back; *~ d'humeur*, outburst of temper; *~ de répulsion*, wave of repulsion; *~ de surprise*, start of surprise; *bon ~*, kind thought, kindly impulse; *c'est le premier ~ qui est le bon*, first thoughts are best; *les ~s de l'âme*, the emotions, the passions; *faire une chose de son propre ~*, to do something of one's own accord; *être dans le ~*, to be up to date, to be abreast of the times.

mouvementé, -e [muvmɑ̃te] *adj.* animated, agitated, bustling; varied, chequered; full of incident or variety; (of ground) broken, undulating.

mouvementer [muvmɑ̃te] *v.t.* to enliven, to give animation to.

mouvoir [muvwar] *v.t.* to move, to start; to prompt; to drive, to propel, to actuate; *mû par la vapeur*, driven by steam; *mû par la pitié*, prompted by compassion; **se** *~ v.refl.* to be in motion, to move, to stir.

moye, moie [mwa] *s.f.* soft vein (in stone).

moyen, -ne [mwajɛ̃] *adj.* mean, middle, intermediate; middle-sized, medium, moderate; average; *le Moyen-Orient*, the Middle East; (lang.) *le français ~*, Middle French; *le ~ âge*, the Middle Ages; *une femme d'âge ~*, a middle-aged woman; *~ terme*, middle course, (log.) middle term; (math.) *terme ~*, middle term, mean; *prix ~*, medium, or moderate, price; *un élève ~ en mathématiques*, a pupil who is average in mathematics; *cours ~*, intermediate course; *le Français ~*, the average Frenchman; *température ~ne annuelle*, mean annual temperature.

moyen [mwajɛ̃] *s.m.* means, way, manner, medium; device; plant; (fig.) machinery; ability; possibility; (pl.) means, resources; power, abilities; scope, range, (of ability); faculties; (law) grounds; *au ~ de*, by means of; *par tous les ~s*, by all manner of means, in every way possible; at all costs; *trouver (le) ~ de*, to find a way to; *il n'y a pas ~!*, it can't be done!, it's impossible!; *par ses propres* or *seuls ~s*, by one's own resources, under its own steam; *dans mes ~s*, within my scope or capabilities; *au-delà de ses ~s*, beyond one's means; *je n'en ai pas les ~s*, I can't afford it; *avoir largement les ~s de*, to have ample resources to, to be well able to; *être en possession de tous ses ~s*, to be in full possession of one's faculties; (law) *~s de défense*, grounds for defence.

moyen âge, moyen-âge [mwajɛnaʒ] *s.m.* Middle Ages; ⚠ not 'middle age'.

moyenâgeu-x, -se [mwajɛnɑʒø] *adj.* medieval, of the Middle Ages.

moyennant [mwajɛnɑ̃] *prep.* by means of; in consideration of; on condition of, in return, or exchange, for; on payment of; by buying or obtaining; *~ un billet*, on purchase of a ticket; *~ quoi*, by means of which.

moyenne [mwajɛn] *s.f.* average, mean, medium; *en ~*, on (the) average; *plus accommodant que la ~ des patrons*, more helpful than most employers.

moyennement [mwajɛnmɑ̃] *adv.* moderately; on average, averagely; middling, fairly well.

moyette [mwajɛt] *s.f.* shock (of corn, etc.), stook.

moyeu (pl. **-x**) [mwajø] *s.m.* **1.** nave, hub, boss, (of a wheel, etc.); **2.** yolk; **3.** preserved plum.

M.R.P. [ɛmɛrpe] abbrev. *Mouvement républicain populaire.*

mû, mue [my] *p.p.* of MOUVOIR.

muance [mɥɑ̃s] *s.f.* (anc. mus.) changing a note, mutation; (obs.) breaking of the voice.

mucilage [mysilaʒ] *s.m.* mucilage.

mucosité [mykozite] *s.f.* mucus, mucosity.

mucron [mykrɔ̃] *s.m.* (bot.) mucro.

mucus [mykys] *s.m.* mucus.

mue [my] *s.f.* **1.** moulting, moulting season; **2.** breaking (of voice); **3.** coop (for hens, etc.).

mue [my] *adj.f. rage ~*, mute rabies (of dogs).

muer [mɥe] *v.i.* to moult; to slough or shed skin, horns, etc.; **2.** (of voice) to break; **3.** to change; **se** *~ v.refl.* to change, to be transformed (*en*, into).

muet, -te [mɥɛ] *adj.* dumb, mute; speechless, voiceless; unspoken; silent; (lang.) unvoiced; *h-muet*, h-mute; *sourd-~*, deaf and dumb; *scène ~te* or *jeu ~*, dumb show; (theatr.) *rôle ~*, non-speaking part; *le cinéma ~*, the silent screen; *s.m.f.* dumb person, mute; **~te** *s.f.* mute letter.

muette [mɥɛt] *s.f.* hunting-lodge.

mufle [myfl] *s.m.* snout, muzzle; (fig.) unpleasant, coarse individual, boor; (bot.) *~ de veau*, snapdragon; *~ adj.* coarse.

muflerie [myflәri] *s.f.* coarseness, beastliness.

muflier [myflje] *s.m.* (bot.) snapdragon, antirrhinum.

muge [myʒ], **mulet** [mylɛ] *s.m.* (ichth.) mullet.

mugir [myʒir] *v.i.* to bellow, to low; (fig.) to roar, to howl.

mugissement [myʒismɑ̃] *s.m.* bellowing, lowing, roaring, roar.

muguet [mygɛ] *s.m.* **1.** (bot.) lily of the valley; **2.** (obs.) dandy; **3.** (med.) thrush.

mugueter [mygte] *v.t.i.* to pay court to; to play the gallant.

muid [mɥi] *s.m.* hogshead.

mulard, -e [mylar] *s.m.f.* hybrid duck.

mulassi-er, -ère [mylasje] *adj.* pertaining to or producing mules.

mulâtre, -sse [mylɑtr, mylɑtrɛs] *adj., s.m.f.* mulatto, half-caste.

mule[1] [myl] *s.f.* mule, she-mule.

mule[2] [myl] *s.f.* slipper, mule.

mulet[1] [mylɛ] *s.m.* mule, he-mule.

mulet[2] see MUGE.

muleti-er, -ère [myltje] *s.m.f.* muleteer; *adj.* mule, suitable for mules; *piste ~ère*, mule-track.

mulot [mylo] *s.m.* (zool.) field-mouse.

multi-colore [myltikɔlɔr] *adj.* multicolour, multicoloured; **~filaire** [myltifilɛr] *adj.* formed of several wires or threads; (of aerial, etc.) multi-wire; **~flore** [myltiflɔr] *adj.* multiflorous; **~forme** [myltifɔrm] *adj.* multiform; (fig.) many-sided, many-headed.

multilobé, -e [myltilɔbe] *adj.* (biol.) multilobate, multilobar.

multi-millionnaire [myltimiljɔnɛr], **multi-milliardaire** [myltimiljardɛr] *adj., s.m.f.* multimillionaire; **~pare** [myltipar] *adj.* (biol.) multiparous; (woman) who has had several children; **~place** [myltiplas] *adj., s.m.* (aeron.) multi-seater (plane).

multiple [myltipl] *adj., s.m.* multiple, manifold;

(math.) multiple; *plus petit commun* ~, least common multiple.
multiplex [myltiplɛks] *adj.*, *s.m.* (telegraphy) multiplex.
multipliable [myltiplijabl] *adj.* multipliable.
multiplicande [myltiplikɑ̃d] *s.m.* multiplicand.
multiplicat-eur, -rice [myltiplikatœr] *adj.* multiplying; ~**eur** *s.m.* multiplier.
multiplicati-f, -ve [myltiplikatif] *adj.* multiplicative, multiplying; *signe* ~*f*, multiplication sign.
multi-plication [myltiplikɑsjɔ̃] *s.f.* **1.** multiplication; proliferation; **2.** (mech.) gear-ratio, gear; ~**plicité** [myltiplisite] *s.f.* multiplicity, great number, wide variety; ~**plier** [myltiplije] *v.t.i.* to multiply; to proliferate; to repeat; ~*plier des offres*, to make repeated offers; **se** ~**plier** *v.refl.* to multiply; to reproduce; (fig.) to be everywhere; to be doing a number of things at once.
multi-polaire [myltipɔlɛr] *adj.* (electr., biol.) multipolar; ~**tube** [myltityb] *adj.* (mil.) multi-tube; multi-barrelled (rocket-launcher); ~**tubulaire** [myltitybylɛr] *adj.* multi-tubular.
multitude [myltityd] *s.f.* multitude, crowd, large number, mass; majority.
munichois, -e [mynikwa] *adj.* of Munich; *s.m.f.* native or inhabitant of Munich; (hist., pej.) appeaser.
municipal, -e, (aux) [mynisipal] *adj.* municipal, town; *conseil* ~, town or city council; *garde* ~, soldier of the municipal guard.
municipalité [mynisipalite] *s.f.* municipality; seat of local government; town council; town hall.
munificence [mynifisɑ̃s] *s.f.* munificence, bounteousness, generosity.
munificent, -e [mynifisɑ̃] *adj.* munificent, generous, bountiful, bounteous.
munir [mynir] *v.t.* **1.** (mil.) to provision (army, stronghold), to arm; **2.** to provide, to supply, to equip, to fit, (*de*, with); *se* ~ *de*, to provide, to fit, to arm, to furnish, oneself with; *se* ~ *de patience*, to possess one's soul in patience, to have patience.
munition [mynisjɔ̃] *s.f.* **1.** provisions, supplies, stores; means of subsistence; (jest) ~*s de bouche*, food; (mil.) *pain de* ~, bread ration; ration bread; **2.** (pl.) munitions, ammunition.
munitionnaire [mynisjɔnɛr] *s.m.* **1.** commissary, official of commissariat; **2.** supplier of munitions.
muntjac [mœ̃tʒak] *s.m.* (zool.) muntjak.
muqueu-x, -se [mykø] *adj.* mucous; ~**se** *s.f.* mucous membrane.
mur [myr] *s.m.* wall; ~ *d'appui*, parapet; ~ *de clôture* or *d'enceinte*, surrounding wall, perimeter wall; ~ *de soutènement*, retaining wall; ~ *mitoyen*, party wall; (aeron.) ~ *sonique* or *du son*, sound-barrier; ~ *de chaleur*, heat-barrier; *entre quatre* ~*s*, (i.) (lit.) in bare walls (i.e. house with no furniture); (ii.) (fig.) shut in, imprisoned; (fig.) *sauter le* ~, to break out (of an institution, etc.); (fig.) *donner de la tête contre un* ~, to beat one's head against a brick wall; (fig.) *être au pied du* ~, to have one's back to the wall, to be in a tight corner; *mettre qn. au pied du* ~, to drive s.o. into a corner, to insist on a straight answer from s.o.
mûr, -e [myr] *adj.* ripe, matured; (fig.) mature, no longer young, middle-aged; (pop.) drunk; *être* ~ *pour*, to be fit or ready for; *âge* ~, maturity, mature age; *esprit* ~, mature or serious mind; *après* ~*e délibération*, after careful consideration; *étoffe trop* ~*e*, worn-out material.
murage [myraʒ] *s.m.* walling, walling-up.
muraille [myrɑj] *s.f.* wall, partition; rampart; (naut.) side (of ship); *la grande* ~ (*de Chine*), the Great Wall of China.
mural, -e, (aux) [myral] *adj.* mural, wall; *carte* ~*e*, wall-map; *plantes* ~*es*, wall-growing plants.
mûre [myr] *s.f.* (bot.) mulberry; ~ (*sauvage*), blackberry.
mûrement [myrmɑ̃] *adv.* thoroughly, deeply, profoundly, carefully, maturely.
murène [myrɛn] *s.f.* (ichth.) Muraena, moray eel, sea-lamprey.
murer [myre] *v.t.* to wall, to wall up, to wall in, to brick up; to immure; (fig.) to confine, to enclose; **se** ~ *v.refl.* to shut oneself up.
murex [myrɛks] *s.m.* (moll.) murex.
muriate [myrjat] *s.m.* (chem.) muriate.
muriatique [myrjatik] *adj.* (chem.) muriatic, hydrochloric.
mûrier [myrje] *s.m.* (bot.) mulberry-tree; mulberry-bush; ~ (*sauvage*), blackberry-bush.
mûrir [myrir] *v.t.i.* to ripen, to mature; to come to maturity, to develop.
mûrissage [myrisaʒ], **mûrissement** [myrismɑ̃] *s.m.* maturing, maturation.
mûrissant, -e [myrisɑ̃] *adj.* ripening, maturing; (fig.) no longer young.
mûrisserie [myrisri] *s.f.* ripening shed (for e.g. imported bananas).
murmurant, -e [myrmyrɑ̃] *adj.* murmuring, babbling.
murmure [myrmyr] *s.m.* murmur, hum, babbling, whispering.
murmurer [myrmyre] *v.t.i.* to murmur, to whisper, to mutter; to complain.
mûron [myrɔ̃] *s.m.* blackberry.
musaraigne [myzarɛɲ] *s.f.* (zool.) shrew-mouse.
musard, -e [myzar] *adj.* idling, loitering, musing; *s.m.f.* idler, loiterer.
musarder [myzarde] *v.i.* to loiter, to idle.
musarderie [myzardəri], **musardise** [myzardiz] *s.f.* loitering, idling; idle disposition.
musc [mysk] *s.m.* musk.
muscade [myskad] *s.f.* **1.** nutmeg; *rose* ~, musk-rose; **2.** small cork ball used in thimble-riggers' vanishing trick; *passez* ~*!*, hey presto, it's gone!
muscadet [myskadɛ] *s.m.* muscatel wine, muscadet (wine); muscat(el) grape.
muscadier [myskadje] *s.m.* (bot.) nutmeg-tree.
muscadin [myskadɛ̃] *s.m.* fop, dandy.
muscardin [myskardɛ̃] *s.m.* (zool.) small dormouse.
muscardine [myskardin] *s.f.* muscardine (disease of silkworms).
muscat [myska] *s.m.* muscat grape; muscatel wine.
muscidées [myside] *s.f.pl.* (ent.) Muscidae.
muscle [myskl] *s.m.* muscle; *avoir des* ~*s* or *du* ~, to be robust or muscular; *être tout en* ~*s*, to be all muscles, to have no spare fat; *sans* ~*s*, flabby.
musclé, -e [myskle] *adj.* muscular, robust; (fig.) energetic.
muscler [myskle] *v.t.* to develop the muscles of.
musculaire [myskylɛr] *adj.* muscular, muscle; *tissu* ~, muscle tissue.
musculature [myskylatyr] *s.f.* musculature, muscle structure.
musculeu-x, -se [myskylø] *adj.* muscular, having well-developed muscles.
muse [myz] *s.f.* muse, poetic inspiration.
museau (pl. **-x**) [myzo] *s.m.* muzzle, snout; (fig.) face; (pop.) *fricassée de* ~*x*, kissing.
musée [myze] *s.m.* museum, art gallery or collection.
museler [myzle] *v.t.* to muzzle; (fig.) to silence, to muzzle, to clamp down on.
muselet [myzlɛ] *s.m.* wiring (of cork of champagne bottle).
muselière [myzəljɛr] *s.f.* muzzle.

musellement [myzɛlmɑ̃] *s.m.* muzzling; silencing.
muser [myze] *v.i.* to idle, to dawdle, to fritter away time.
muserolle [myzrɔl] *s.f.* (harness) nose-band.
musette [myzɛt] *s.f.* **1.** bag-pipe, musette; (*bal*) ~, popular dance-hall; *valse* ~, dance-hall waltz; **2.** haversack, satchel; horse's nose-bag; (fig.) *ne pas être dans une* ~, to be the reverse of small, of ordinary; to be sizeable or significant; *c'est un accomplissement qui n'est pas dans une* ~, it is no mean achievement.
muséum [myzeɔm] *s.m.* museum (of science or natural history).
musical, -e, (**aux**) [myzikal] *adj.* musical, relating to music; harmonious, melodious; *l'art* ~, the art of music; *une voix* ~*e*, a melodious voice; ~**ement** [myzikalmɑ̃] *adv.* musically, harmoniously; ⚠ not 'musical' in senses 'fond of music', 'skilled in music'.
musicalité [myzikalite] *s.f.* musical quality.
music-hall [myzikol] *s.m.* music-hall.
musicien, -ne [myzisjɛ̃] *adj.* musical; *s.m.f.* musician, bandsman, member of a band or orchestra.
musico-graphe [myzikɔgraf] *s.m.f.* musicographer, one who writes about music, historian of music; ~**logie** [myzikɔlɔʒi] *s.f.* musicology, science of music; ~**logue** [myzikɔlɔg] *s.m.f.* musicologist.
musique [myzik] *s.f.* music; band, orchestra; (obs.) concert; *la* ~ *du régiment*, the regimental band; ~ *de chambre*, chamber music; ~ *enregistrée*, music on records; *boîte à* ~, musical box; *instrument de* ~, musical instrument; *mettre en* ~, to set to music; *travailler en* ~, to work to (the sound of) music; *faire de la* ~, to make music, to play music; to go in for music; (fig.) *changer de* ~, to change the subject; (fig.) *connaître la* ~, to know how to set about (sth.), to know the form; *réglé comme du papier à* ~, regular as clockwork; (fam.) *il en a fait une* ~, he made a great fuss.
musiquer [myzike] *v.t.i.* to make music; to set to music.
musiquette [myzikɛt] *s.f.* light music, music of no great difficulty or value.
musoir [myzwar] *s.m.* (naut.) pier-head, jetty-head.
musqué, -e [myske] *adj.* perfumed with musk, musk; (fig.) affected; *bœuf* ~, musk-ox; *rat* ~, musk-rat.
(**se**) **musser** [myse] *v.refl.* (obs.) to hide.
mussi-f, -ve [mysif] *adj.* (chem.) mosaic; *or* ~*f*, mosaic gold, ormolu; disulphide of tin.
mussitation [mysitɑsjɔ̃] *s.f.* (med.) mussitation, movement of lips without emission of sound.
mustang [mystɑ̃] *s.m.* mustang.
mustélidés [mystelide] *s.m.pl.* (zool.) Mustelidae.
musulman, -e [myzylmɑ̃] *adj., s.m.f.* Muslim.
mutabilité [mytabilite] *s.f.* mutability, changeableness.
mutable [mytabl] *adj.* mutable.
mutage [mytaʒ] *s.m.* mutage (checking fermentation of wine).
mutant, -e [mytɑ̃] *adj., s.m.f.* (biol.) mutant.
mutation [mytɑsjɔ̃] *s.f.* mutation, change; transfer (between jobs, teams, etc.); (law) transfer, conveyance; (mus.) *jeux de* ~, mutation stops (of an organ).
muter [myte] *v.t.* **1.** to check the fermentation (of grapes); **2.** to transfer (to another post); ~ *v.i.* (biol.) to mutate.
mutilat-eur, -rice [mytilatœr] *s.m.f.* mutilator, defacer.
mutilation [mytilɑsjɔ̃] *s.f.* mutilation, maiming, mangling, defacement.
mutilé, -e [mytile] *adj., s.m.f.* mutilated (person), disabled (soldier, etc.), (one) who has lost a limb or limbs; ~(*e*) *du bras*, having lost an arm.
mutiler [mytile] *v.t.* to mutilate, to maim, to disable, to deface, to damage; (fig.) to distort; to censor or make cuts in (a text, etc.).
mutin, -e [mytɛ̃] *adj.* **1.** mutinous, insubordinate, refractory; **2.** pert, sly; *s.m.f.* mutineer.
mutiné, -e [mytine] *adj.* mutinying; *s.m.f.* mutineer.
mutiner [mytine] *v.t.* (obs.) to excite to rebellion; **se** ~ *v.refl.* to rebel, to mutiny.
mutinerie [mytinri] *s.f.* **1.** mutiny, riot; **2.** roguishness.
mutisme [mytism] *s.m.* dumbness, muteness, silence; *s'enfermer dans le* ~, to maintain a stubborn silence.
mutité [mytite] *s.f.* dumbness; (med.) mutism.
mutualité [mytɥalite] *s.f.* mutuality, reciprocity; mutual insurance.
mutuel, -le [mytɥɛl] *adj.* mutual, reciprocal; *société de secours* ~, friendly society, mutual benefit society; ~**le** *s.f.* mutual insurance society; ~**lement** [mytɥɛlmɑ̃] *adv.* mutually, reciprocally.
mutule [mytyl] *s.f.* (arch.) mutule.
mycélium [miseljɔm] *s.m.* (bot.) mycelium.
myco-logie [mikɔlɔʒi] *s.f.* (bot.) mycology; ~**rhizes** [mikɔriz] *s.m.pl.* (bot.) mycorrhizae.
mycose [mikoz] *s.f.* (pathol.) mycosis.
myéline [mjelin] *s.f.* (anat.) myelin.
myélite [mielit] *s.f.* (pathol.) myelitis.
myologie [miɔlɔʒi] *s.f.* myology.
myope [mjɔp] *adj., s.m.f.* myopic, (lit. & fig.) short-sighted, (person).
myopie [mjɔpi] *s.f.* myopia, short-sightedness.
myosotis [mjɔzɔtis] *s.m.* (bot.) Myosotis, forget-me-not.
myriade [mirjad] *s.f.* myriad, large number, swarm.
myriapode [mirjapɔd] *s.m.* (zool.) myriapod.
myrmidon, mirmidon [mirmidɔ̃] *s.m.* myrmidon; (fam.) small insignificant individual.
myrobolan [mirɔbɔlɑ̃] *s.m.* (bot.) myrobalan.
myrrhe [mir] *s.f.* (bot.) myrrh.
myrtacées [mirtase] *s.f.pl.* (bot.) Myrtaceae.
myrte [mirt] *s.m.* (bot.) myrtle.
myrtille [mirtil] *s.f.* (bot.) bilberry, whortleberry.
mystère [mistɛr] *s.m.* mystery, secret; miracle play, mystery; secret cult.
mystérieu-x, -se [misterjø] *adj.* mysterious, enigmatic, secret; ~**sement** [misterjøzmɑ̃] *adv.* mysteriously.
mysticisme [mistisism] *s.m.* mysticism.
mysticité [mistisite] *s.f.* mysticalness, mysticism; ardent faith.
mystificat-eur, -rice [mistifikatœr] *adj.* mystifying, deluding; *s.m.f.* mystifier, hoaxer, trickster.
mystification [mistifikɑsjɔ̃] *s.f.* mystification, hoax, practical joke.
mystifier [mistifje] *v.t.* to mystify, to hoax, to trick, to delude.
mystique [mistik] *adj., s.m.f.* mystical; mystic; ~ *s.f.* mystique; mystical theology; ~**ment** [mistikmɑ̃] *adv.* mystically.
mythe [mit] *s.m.* myth, legend, fable; fiction.
mythique [mitik] *adj.* mythical.
mythologie [mitɔlɔʒi] *s.f.* mythology.
mythologique [mitɔlɔʒik] *adj.* mythological.
mythologue [mitɔlɔg] *s.m.f.* mythologist.
mytiliculture [mitilikyltyr] *s.f.* mussel breeding.
myxœdème [miksedɛm] *s.m.* myxoedema.
myxomatose [miksɔmatoz] *s.f.* myxomatosis.
myxomycètes [miksɔmisɛt] *s.m.pl.* (bot.) myxomycetes.

N

N, n *s.m.* the letter N, n; abbrev. *nord, nom.*
n' see NE.
na [na] *interj.* (child.) there; there it is; there you are!; so there!; I don't care.
nabab [nabab] *s.m.* **1.** (hist.) nabob; nawab; **2.** (obs.) nabob; (mod.) rich person living life of luxury.
nabot, -e [nabo] *adj.* dwarfish; *s.m.f.* dwarf.
nacarat [nakara] *adj.* (of) nacarat (colour); ~ *s.m.* nacarat.
nacelle [nasɛl] *s.f.* **1.** skiff, wherry, cockle, cockle-shell, cockle boat; **2.** (aeron.) nacelle; car, gondola, (of balloon or airship).
nacre [nakr] *s.f.* nacre, mother-of-pearl.
nacré, -e [nakre] *adj.* nacreous, nacrous, pearly.
nacrer [nakre] *v.t.* to give a pearly gloss to.
nadir [nadir] *s.m.* (astron.) nadir.
naevus [nevys] *s.m.* (pl. *naevi*) naevus, birth-mark.
nage [naʒ] *s.f.* **1.** swimming; swimming stroke; ~ *libre*, free style; *à la* ~, by swimming; *se jeter à la* ~, to jump into the water; *traverser, passer, à la* ~, to swim across, over; **2.** (naut.) rowing, paddling, sculling; rowlock; *banc de* ~, thwart; *chef de* ~, stroke, stroke-oar; *donner la* ~, to give the stroke, to row stroke; **3.** sweat, perspiration; *être tout en* ~, to be bathed in sweat, to be drenched with perspiration.
nagée [naʒe] *s.f.* stroke (in swimming), length of stroke.
nageoire [naʒwar] *s.f.* fin (of fish), flipper (of seal, etc.).
nager [naʒe] *v.i.* **1.** to swim, to float, to be buoyed up; ~ *entre deux eaux*, to swim under water; **2.** (naut.) to row, to pull; **3.** ~ *dans*, to swim, to float, to be immersed, in; (fig.) to welter in, to be rolling in; ~ *dans l'opulence*, to be rolling in riches; ~ *dans la joie*, to be overjoyed; **4.** (slang) *il sait* ~, he knows what's what; *il nage*, he is at sea.
nageu-r, -se [naʒœr] *s.m.f.* **1.** swimmer; (fig.) sly customer; **2.** (naut.) oarsman; *adj.* swimming, natatorial.
naguère [nagɛr] *adv.* but lately, not long ago, formerly, recently.
naïade [najad] *s.f.* **1.** (myth.) naiad, water-nymph; **2.** (bot.) naiad.
naï-f, -ve [naif] *adj.* artless, naïve, unaffected, candid; (pej.) credulous, unsuspecting, silly, green; *s.m.f.* naïve, credulous person, simpleton.
nain, -e [nɛ̃] *s.m.f.* dwarf; (card-game) ~ *jaune*, Pope Joan; *adj.* dwarf, dwarfish; puny; *arbre* ~, dwarf tree.
naissain [nɛsɛ̃] *s.m.* spawn of shellfish, spat.
naissance [nɛsɑ̃s] *s.f.* birth, extraction, descent, lineage, rise, springing up, beginning, root, dawn; (arch.) spring, spandrel, (of arch or vault); *de* ~, from one's birth; by birth; *sourd de* ~, born deaf; *anniversaire de* ~, *jour de* ~, birthday; *lieu de* ~, birthplace; *donner* ~ *à*, to give birth to; *donner* ~ *à qch.*, to give rise to sth.; *point de* ~, point of origin; *prendre* ~, to take its rise, to originate (in); *de haute* ~, high-born; *de basse* ~, low-born; *seconde* ~, conversion, turning to God; *la* ~ *du jour*, day-break; *ce fleuve, à sa* ~, this river, at its source; *à la* ~ *des cheveux*, at the line where the hair begins.
naissant, -e [nɛsɑ̃] *adj.* new-born, incipient, nascent, just beginning to grow, springing up, rising, dawning, budding; (chem.) nascent.
naître [nɛtr] *v.i.* (very irreg.: *je naquis, né, naissant*) to be born (*de*, of); to come into the world, to spring into existence; to spring (from), to begin, to appear (on the scene); to arise (from), to originate (in), to spring up; to bud; *il naquit à Londres*, he was born in London; *encore à* ~, unborn; *faire* ~, to give birth to; to cause to grow, to bring forth; to raise, to give rise to, to call into existence, to start, to suggest; *faire* ~ *des soupçons*, to give rise to suspicion; *avoir vu* ~ *qn.*, (i.) to have known s.o. from infancy; (ii.) to be someone's birthplace; *qui vient de* ~, new-born; ~ *à la politique*, to make one's début in politics.
naïvement [naivmɑ̃] *adv.* naïvely, artlessly, candidly, ingenuously, innocently; credulously.
naïveté [naivte] *s.f.* artlessness, ingenuousness, candour, innocence, naïvety, naïveté; (pej.) silliness; *dire des* ~*s*, to say silly, childish things; to make a foolish remark.
naja [naʒa] *s.m.* (zool.) Naja, cobra.
Namibie [namibi] *s.f.* (geog.) Namibia.
nana [nana] *s.f.* (pop.) mistress; woman.
nanan [nanɑ̃] *s.m.* (child. lang.) goodies, sweets, something very pleasant, lollipop.
nandou [nɑ̃du] *s.m.* (ornith.) nandu, rhea, South American ostrich.
nanisme [nanism] *s.m.* dwarfishness.
nankin [nɑ̃kɛ̃] *s.m.* (text.) nankeen; *pantalon de* ~, nankeens (pl.); ~ *adj.* light yellow, pale buff.
nansouk, nanzouk [nɑ̃zuk] *s.m.* (text.) nainsook.
nanti, -e [nɑ̃ti] *adj.* rich, well-to-do.
nantir [nɑ̃tir] *v.t.* to give security to, to give as a pledge; to provide (*de*, with); *être nanti de*, to be provided with, to be in possession of (guarantee, certificate, etc.); **se** ~ *v.refl.* to provide oneself (*de*, with); to take possession; (fig.) to feather one's nest.
nantissement [nɑ̃tismɑ̃] *s.m.* pledge, security, mortgage, collateral; *donner en* ~, to give as a pledge or security.
napalm [napalm] *s.m.* napalm.
napel [napɛl] *s.m.* (bot.) wolfsbane, aconite, monkshood; nightshade.
naphtalène [naftalɛn] *s.m.* (chem.) naphthalene.
naphtaline [naftalin] *s.f.* (chem.) commercial naphthalene.
naphte [naft] *s.m.* (chem.) naphtha.
naphtol [naftɔl] *s.m.* (pharm.) naphthol.
napoléon [napɔleɔ̃] *s.m.* (hist.) napoleon (gold coin of 20 francs).
napoléonien, -ne [napɔleɔnjɛ̃] *adj.* Napoleonic, Napoleon's; Napoleonistic.
napolitain, -e [napɔlitɛ̃] *adj., s.m.f.* Neapolitan.
nappage [napaʒ] *s.m.* napery, table-linen sold by length; (cook.) couverture.
nappe [nap] *s.f.* table-cloth, cloth; ~ *d'autel*, communion-cloth; ~ (*d'eau*), sheet (of water); underground water level, (geog.) water-table; (fish.) net; (geom.) nappe; *mettre la* ~, to lay the cloth; *ôter la* ~, to remove the cloth; *éclair en* ~, sheet-lightning.
napper [nape] *v.t.* to cover with a table-cloth; (cook.) to cover (with sauce, jam, etc.).
napperon [naprɔ̃] *s.m.* table-mat; doily; ~ *individuel*, place mat.
narcéine [narsein] *s.f.* (chem.) narceine.

narcisse [narsis *s.m.* (bot.)] narcissus, daffodil, (fig.) narcissistic, self-worshipping man.
narcissisme [narsisism] *s.m.* narcissism.
narcose [narkoz] *s.f.* (med.) narcosis.
narcotique [narkɔtik] *adj.*, *s.m.* narcotic, soporific.
nard [nar] *s.m.* nard, spikenard; ~ *sauvage*, asarabacca.
narghileh, narguilé [nargile] *s.m.* narghile, hookah.
narguer [narge] *v.t.* to beard, to defy, to snap one's fingers at, to laugh to scorn.
narine [narin] *s.f.* nostril.
narquois, -e [narkwa] *adj.* cunning, sneering, sly, mocking, jeering; **~ement** [narkwazmɑ̃] *adv.* jeeringly, mockingly, slyly.
narrat-eur, -rice [naratœr] *s.m.f.* narrator, story-teller, relater.
narrati-f, -ve [naratif] *adj.* narrative.
narration [narɑsjɔ̃] *s.f.* narration, narrative, story, relation, tale, reproduction (of story, as school exercise).
narré [nare] *s.m.* narrative, account.
narrer [nare] *v.t.* to narrate, to relate, to tell, to recount.
narthex [nartɛks] *s.m.* (arch.) narthex.
narval [narval] *s.m.* (zool.) narwhal, sea-unicorn.
nasal, -e, (aux) [nazal] *adj.* nasal; ~ *s.m.* (anc. armour) nasel, nasal; ~e *s.f.* (phon.) nasal.
nasalisation [nazalizɑsjɔ̃] *s.f.* nasalization.
nasaliser [nazalizə] *v.t.* to nasalize.
nasalité [nazalite] *s.f.* nasality.
nasarde [nazard] *s.f.* rap on the nose; (fig.) taunt, scoff, snub, rebuff.
naseau (pl. **-x**) [nazo] *s.m.* nostril (of animal); *fendeur de ~x*, braggart, bully.
nasillard, -e [nazijar] *adj.* nasal, snuffling.
nasillement [nazijmɑ̃] *s.m.* **1.** snuffling, speaking with a nasal sound; **2.** quacking (of duck).
nasiller [nazije] *v.t.* **1.** to speak or intone through the nose, to make nasal sounds; to snuffle; **2.** (of duck) to quack; **3.** (of boar) to root; (of dog) to follow scent.
nasilleu-r, -se [nazijœr] *s.m.f.* snuffler, one who speaks through the nose.
nasique [nazik] *s.m.* (zool.) proboscis monkey.
nasse [nas] *s.f.* bow-net, weel, eel-basket, lobster-basket; net (for catching small birds).
natal, -e [natal] *adj.* natal, native, birth-; *ciel ~*, native clime; *langue ~e*, mother-tongue; *lieu ~*, birthplace; *ma terre ~e*, my native land, my country.
nataliste [natalist] *adj.* (of propaganda, etc.) aimed at increasing birth-rate.
natalité [natalite] *s.f.* natality; birth-rate; *centre de ~*, maternity centre.
natation [natɑsjɔ̃] *s.f.* swimming, natation.
natatoire [natatwar] *adj.* natatory, swimming.
nati-f, -ve [natif] *adj.* native, inborn.
nation [nɑsjɔ̃] *s.f.* nation, people, race; *les Nations Unies*, the United Nations.
national, -e, (aux) [nasjɔnal] *adj.* national; native; **nationaux** [nasjɔno] *s.m.pl.* nationals, fellow-countrymen.
nationalisation [nasjɔnalizɑsjɔ̃] *s.f.* nationalization.
nationaliser [nasjɔnalize] *v.t.* to nationalize.
nationalisme [nasjɔnalism] *s.m.* nationalism.
nationaliste [nasjɔnalist] *s.m.f.*, *adj.* nationalist.
nationalité [nasjɔnalite] *s.f.* nationality; *acte de ~* (*de navire*), ship's certificate.
national-socialisme [nasjɔnalsɔsjalism] *s.m.* National Socialism.
national-socialiste [nasjɔnalsɔsjalist] *adj.*, *s.m.f.* National Socialist.
nativement [nativmɑ̃] *adv.* innately, as an inborn characteristic; originally.
nativité [nativite] *s.f.* Nativity; (astrol.) horoscope.
natron [natrɔ̃], **natrum** [natrɔm] *s.m.* (chem.) natron, soda.
natte [nat] *s.f.* **1.** plait, tress, plaited tress; **2.** mat, matting, rush mat, straw mat.
natté [nate] *s.m.* **1.** (text.) material woven in checks; **2.** plaited loaf.
natter [nate] *v.t.* to plait, to braid, to mat, to twist; (obs.) to cover with mats.
natti-er, -ère [natje] *s.m.f.* mat-maker, mat-seller.
naturalisation [natyralizɑsjɔ̃] *s.f.* naturalization.
naturaliser [natyralize] *v.t.* **1.** to naturalize; *se faire ~*, to obtain letters of naturalization; **2.** to acclimatize; to introduce (an art, etc., into a country); **3.** to stuff (a dead animal).
naturalisme [natyralism] *s.m.* naturalism.
naturaliste [natyralist] *s.m.f.* **1.** naturalist; **2.** taxidermist; ~ *adj.* naturalist, naturalistic.
nature [natyr] *s.f.* nature, kind, sort, essence, constitution, temper, disposition; *d'après ~*, from life; *de sa ~*, by nature, in its nature; *de ~ à*, calculated to, of a kind to; *payer en ~*, to pay in kind; *contre ~*, monstrous, unnatural; *état de ~*, natural state; state of nature; ~ *morte*, still life; *grandeur ~*, life-size; ~ *adj.* plain, unadorned, natural, unadulterated; *café ~*, black coffee.
naturel, -le [natyrɛl] *adj.* natural, native, innate, inborn, artless, genuine, ingenuous, free, genial, congenial, easy; *grandeur ~le*, life-size; *loi ~le*, law of nature; *fils ~*, illegitimate son; **~lement** [natyrɛlmɑ̃] *adv.* naturally; by nature; artlessly, candidly; as a matter of course; (*interj.*) of course!
naturel [natyrɛl] *s.m.* naturalness, simplicity, native ease, genuineness, native disposition, natural characteristic; native (of a country, etc.); *au ~*, to the life; plain; *d'un bon ~*, good-natured; *d'un mauvais ~*, ill-natured; *un heureux ~*, a happy disposition; *chassez le ~, il revient au galop*, what is bred in the bone will not go out of the flesh.
naturisme [natyrism] *s.m.* naturism.
naturiste [natyrist] *adj.*, *s.m.f.* naturist, nudist.
naucore [nokɔr] *s.f.* (ent.) kind of aquatic hemipter.
naufrage [nofraʒ] *s.m.* shipwreck, wreck; (fig.) ruin, total destruction; *faire ~*, to be shipwrecked.
naufragé, -e [nofraʒe] *adj.* shipwrecked, wrecked; *s.m.f.* shipwrecked person; shipwrecked sailor, castaway.
naufrager [nofraʒe] *v.i.* to be shipwrecked.
naufrageur [nofraʒœr] *s.m.* wrecker.
naumachie [nomaʃi] *s.f.* (ant.) naumachia, mock sea-fight.
nauséabond, -e [nozeabɔ̃] *adj.* nauseous, nauseating, stinking; (fig.) loathsome.
nausée [noze] *s.f.* nausea; seasickness, retching; (fig.) disgust; *cela vous donne la ~*, or *des ~s*, it makes one sick.
nauséeu-x, -se [nozeø] *adj.* nauseous, causing retching.
nautile [notil] *s.m.* **1.** (zool.) nautilus; **2.** vase made from a shell on a jewelled stem.
nautique [notik] *adj.* nautical; *l'art ~*, seamanship; *carte ~*, sea-chart; *sports ~s*, aquatic sports.
nautoni-er, -ère [notɔnje] *s.m.f.* (poet.) mariner, pilot, boatman, boatwoman; *le ~er des sombres bords* or *des enfers*, the grim ferryman of Hell (Charon).
navaja [navaʒa] *s.f.* navaja, Spanish cutlass.
naval, -e [naval] *adj.* naval, sea-, nautical, maritime.

navarin [navarɛ̃] *s.m.* (cook.) mutton stew with potatoes, turnips, etc.

navet [navɛ] *s.m.* turnip; (fig., pej.) tripe, worthless piece of work; *chou-~*, swede; *il a du sang de ~*, he is spineless.

navette[1] [navɛt] *s.f.* **1.** shuttle; *point de ~*, lock-stitch; *faire la ~ entre*, to go backwards and forwards between, to provide a regular service to and from, to operate a shuttle service between; **2.** incense-box.

navette[2] [navɛt] *s.f.* (bot.) rape.

navicert [navisɛr] *s.m.* (nav., comm.) navicert.

naviculaire [navikylɛr] *adj.* navicular.

navicule [navikyl] *s.f.* (bot.) kind of seaweed.

navigabilité [navigabilite] *s.f.* navigability; seaworthiness.

navigable [navigabl] *adj.* navigable, affording passage for ships; open.

navigant, -e [navigɑ̃] *adj.* (naut.) navigating, sailing, sea-going; (aeron.) (of personnel) flying.

navigateur [navigatœr] *s.m.* **1.** (Lit.) navigator, mariner; (naut.) sailor, deck-hand; **2.** (naut., aeron.) navigator; ~ *adj.* (fem. *navigatrice*) navigating, seafaring.

navigation [navigɑsjɔ̃] *s.f.* navigation, sailing, shipping, voyage.

naviguer [navige] *v.i.* to navigate, to sail, to voyage, to row, to go over; (fig., fam.) to be much on the move; (fig.) *ici il nous faut ~ avec prudence*, here we must tread lightly.

navire [navir] *s.m.* ship; vessel, boat; *~ de guerre*, warship, man-of-war; *~ marchand*, merchantman; *~ de charge*, cargo-boat, freighter; *~-citerne*, tanker; *les ~s*, shipping (collectively).

navrant, -e [navrɑ̃] *adj.* distressing, heart-rending, harrowing, causing great grief.

navré, -e [navre] *adj.* distressed, broken-hearted; (fam.) *je suis ~ de vous avoir fait attendre*, I am awfully sorry to have kept you waiting.

navrer [navre] *v.t.* **1.** (obs.) to wound; **2.** to distress, to cause grief to, to upset.

nazi, -e [nazi] *adj., s.m.f.* Nazi.

nazisme [nazism] *s.m.* Naz(i)ism.

N.D. [ɛnde] abbrev. *Notre-Dame.*

ne [nə] (**n'** before vowel or h-mute) *adv.* **1.** as negative standing alone: not; *je ne sais*, I don't know; **2.** as part of compound negative: *il ~ va pas*, he's not going; *je n'ai pas d'argent*, I have no money, I haven't any money; *nous ~ sortons jamais*, we never go out, we don't ever go out; *il n'a ni frères ni sœurs*, he has neither brothers nor sisters; *je ~ travaille plus*, I no longer work, I don't work any more, I don't work now; *mon frère ~ boit pas non plus*, my brother doesn't drink either, nor does my brother drink; *aucun invité n'est arrivé*, no guest came; *il n'a que ses économies*, he's only got his savings, he has nothing but his savings; **3.** without negative force in Eng. (with certain verbs and conjunctions, and in clauses dependent on comparatives): *je crains qu'il ~ soit mort*, I am afraid he is dead; *à moins qu'on n'y arrive trop tard*, unless we get there too late; *il est plus riche qu'on ~ pense*, he is richer than people think.

né, -e [ne] *adj.* born, descended; produced, foaled; *~ poète*, a poet born; *il est ~ français*, he is French by birth; *Mme Lenoir, née Dupré*, Mrs. Lenoir, née Dupré; *un ennemi-~ de*, a natural enemy of; *bien ~*, of good birth, of good family; well constituted, well balanced, noble, generous, brave; *mort-~*, stillborn; *nouveau-~*, new-born; *premier-~*, first-born.

néanmoins [neɑ̃mwɛ̃] *adv.* however, nevertheless, notwithstanding, yet, for all that, still.

néant [neɑ̃] *s.m.* nothingness, naught, nonentity, vacancy, worthlessness, emptiness; annihilation, nothing, nil; *réduire à ~*, to reduce to nothing; to knock to pieces, to annihilate, to set at naught; *un homme de ~*, a man of no significance, a nonentity; *tirer du ~*, to bring from obscurity; *le témoignage de notre ~*, the token of our nothingness; *le ~ des grandeurs*, the worthlessness of glory.

nébuleuse [nebyløz] *s.f.* (astron.) nebula; (fig.) formless mass.

nébuleu-x, -se [nebylø] *adj.* **1.** nebulous; **2.** hazy, vague, obscure; **~sement** [nebyløzmɑ̃] *adv.* in a vague manner.

nébulosité [nebylozite] *s.f.* **1.** nebulosity; **2.** haziness, obscurity, vagueness.

nécessaire [nesesɛr] *adj.* necessary, indispensable, requisite; unavoidable, needful; *~ à* (or *pour*), necessary to; *il est ~ que vous fassiez cela*, it is necessary that you should do that, it is necessary for you to do that; *se rendre ~*, to make oneself indispensable, or necessary; *il n'y a pas d'homme ~*, nobody is indispensable; *rendre ~s des mesures énergiques*, to call for strong measures; **~ment** [nesesɛrmɑ̃] *adv.* necessarily, fatally, inevitably, of course, unavoidably.

nécessaire [nesesɛr] *s.m.* **1.** necessaries, what is necessary; *il manque même du ~*, he lacks or wants the first necessaries of life; *se refuser le ~*, to deny oneself necessaries; *faire le ~*, (i.) to do what is needed; (ii.) to be a busybody, to fuss around; **2.** *~ de couture*, work-box; *~ de réparations*, repair-outfit; *~ de toilette*, dressing-case.

nécessitant, -e [neseutɑ̃] *adj.* (theol.) *grâce ~e*, necessitating grace.

nécessité [nesesite] *s.f.* necessity; necessariness, exigency; need, want, pinch; *faire de ~ vertu*, to make a virtue of necessity; *être* (or *se trouver*) *dans la ~ de faire*, to be under the necessity of doing; *de toute ~*, necessarily; unavoidably, of necessity; *c'est une ~ que de*, it is necessary to (infin.); *~ fait loi*, necessity knows no law; *denrées de première ~*, essential foodstuffs, staple commodities.

nécessiter [nesesite] *v.t.* to necessitate, to render or make necessary; to compel, to force, to imply, to oblige.

nécessiteu-x, -se [nesesitø] *adj., s.m.f.* necessitous, needy, poor, (person).

nécro-loge [nekrɔlɔʒ] *s.m.* necrology, obituary list, death-roll; **~logie** [nekrɔlɔʒi] *s.f.* necrology, obituary notice, deaths column (in newspaper); **~logue** [nekrɔlɔg] *s.m.* necrologist.

nécromancie [nekrɔmɑ̃si] *s.f.* necromancy.

nécromancien, -ne [nekrɔmɑ̃sjɛ̃] *s.m.f.* necromancer.

nécro-phage [nekrɔfaʒ] *adj.* necrophagous; **~phore** [nekrɔfɔr] *s.m.* (ent.) necrophore, scavenger-beetle, carrion-beetle; **~pole** [nekrɔpɔl] *s.f.* necropolis, city of the dead.

nécropsie [nekrɔpsi] *s.f.* (obs.) autopsy.

nécrose [nekroz] *s.f.* (pathol.) necrosis (of bone); (bot.) canker.

nécroser [nekroze] *v.t.* (med.) to cause to necrose; (bot.) to canker; **se ~** *v.refl.* to become necrosed or cankered.

nectaire [nɛktɛr] *s.m.* (bot.) nectary.

nectar [nɛktar] *s.m.* (lit. & myth.) nectar.

néerlandais, -e [neɛrlɑ̃dɛ] *adj.* Netherlandish, Dutch; *s.m.f.* Netherlander, Dutchman, Dutchwoman.

nef [nɛf] *s.f.* **1.** (obs.) ship, vessel; **2.** nave (of church); *~ latérale*, aisle.

néfaste [nefast] *adj.* unlucky, inauspicious, ill-fated, evil, baneful, harmful.

nèfle [nɛfl] *s.f.* (bot.) medlar; (slang) *des ~s!*, nothing doing!

néflier [neflije] *s.m.* (bot.) medlar-tree.

négat-eur, -rice [negatœr] *adj.* denying; *s.m.f.* denier.

négati-f, -ve [negatif] *adj.* negative; **~f** *s.m.* (photo.) negative; **~ve** *s.f.* negative, denial, refusal; *se tenir sur la ~ve*, to persist in refusal;

dans la ~*ve*, if not, if the answer is no; ~**vement** [negativmɑ̃] *adv.* negatively, in the negative.

négation [negɑsjɔ̃] *s.f.* negation, denial; *répondre par une* ~, to answer in the negative.

négativité [negativite] *s.f.* **1.** (electr.) negativity; **2.** negative character or attitude.

négaton [negatɔ̃] *s.m.* (phys.) negatron, negative electron.

négligé [negliʒe] *s.m.* **1.** négligé; loose garment; déshabillé, undress; **2.** carelessness, negligence, freedom from restraint or artificiality; ~, ~**e** *adj.* neglected, unadorned, unstudied, careless, slovenly, loose, etc.

négligeable [negliʒabl] *adj.* negligible, unimportant, not to be taken into account, that may be omitted, or neglected; *quantité* ~, negligible quantity, (person) of no importance.

négligemment [negliʒamɑ̃] *adv.* carelessly, negligently, neglectfully, remissly, in a slovenly manner.

négligence [negliʒɑ̃s] *s.f.* neglect, negligence, remissness; instance of neglect, shortcoming, mistake, oversight, inaccuracy; carelessness, slovenliness; *par ma* ~, through my neglect; *il y a en cela de la* ~ *de votre part*, you have been careless in this matter.

négligent, -e [negliʒɑ̃] *adj.* neglectful, negligent, careless, casual, remiss, inaccurate.

négliger [negliʒe] *v.t.* to neglect, to omit, to be careless of, to leave out, to overlook, to slight, to disregard, to pay insufficient attention to; **se** ~ *v.refl.* to neglect oneself, to be careless of one's appearance; *ils se sont longtemps négligés* (*mutuellement*), they have long neglected each other.

négoce [negɔs] *s.m.* (obs.) trade, dealings, business.

négociabilité [negɔsjabilite] *s.f.* negotiability.

négociable [negɔsjabl] *adj.* negotiable, convertible into cash or notes.

négociant, -e [negɔsjɑ̃] *s.m.f.* merchant, trader, businessman, wholesaler; ~ *en vins*, wine-merchant.

négociat-eur, -rice [negɔsjatœr] *s.m.f.* negotiator, mediator, transactor.

négociation [negɔsjɑsjɔ̃] *s.f.* negotiation, transaction, mediation, palaver; compromise, discussion (in order to bring about an arrangement); business; *engager des* ~*s*, to enter into negotiations.

négocier [negɔsje] *v.t.i.* to negotiate, to trade; to discuss.

nègre [nɛgr], (fem.) **négresse** [negrɛs] *adj.* Negro, black; dark-brown (colour); *s.m.f.* Negro, Negress, black man or woman; ~ *s.m.* (fig.) ghost writer, hack; *petit* ~, (lang.) (i.) trading French (equivalent pidgin Eng.); (ii.) bad French.

négrier [negrije] *s.m.* slave-ship; slave-trader; *capitaine* ~, captain of a slave-ship.

négrillon, -ne [negrijɔ̃] *s.m.f.* black child; dark-skinned child.

négritude [negrityd] *s.f.* (Lit., pol.) consciousness of being African or black; African-ness.

négroïde [negrɔid] *adj.* Negroid.

neige [nɛʒ] *s.f.* **1.** snow; **2.** (fig.) whiteness; *d'un blanc de* ~, of a snowy whiteness; snow-white; *une boule de* ~, a snowball; *il était tombé beaucoup de* ~, it had snowed very hard; *faire boule de* ~, to increase rapidly, (fam.) to snowball; *où sont les* ~*s d'antan?*, where are the snows of yester-year?; *perce-*~, snowdrop; (cook.) *œufs à la* ~, floating islands; *œufs battus en* ~, eggs whipped to a froth; *bloqué par les* ~*s*, snowbound.

neiger [nɛʒe] *v.i.* to snow; (fig.) *il a neigé sur sa tête*, his head is white with age; (fig.) *il neigeait des pétales*, the ground was sprinkled with petals, there was a shower of petals.

neigeu-x, -se [nɛʒø] *adj.* snowy, snow-covered, snow-white.

nélombo, nelumbo [nelɔ̃bo] *s.m.* (bot.) nelumbo.

nématode [nematɔd] *s.m.* (zool.) nematode; ~ *de la betterave*, beetroot-worm.

nématoïde [nematɔid] *adj.* thread-shaped, nematoid, nematode.

ne m'oubliez pas [nəmublijepɑ] *s.m.* (bot.) forget-me-not.

nénais, nénet [nenɛ], **néné** [nene] *s.m.* (usu. pl.) (slang) breasts.

nénies [neni] *s.f.pl.* (Gr. & Rom. ant.) funeral songs.

nenni [nani, neni] *adv.* (obs. & dial.) nay, no, not at all.

nénuphar [nenyfar] *s.m.* (bot.) nenuphar, water-lily.

néo-celtique [neɔsɛltik] *adj.* neo-Celtic; ~**-classicisme** [neɔklasisism] *s.m.* neo-classicism; ~**-classique** [neɔklasik] *adj.* neo-classical; ~**-colonialisme** [neɔkɔlɔnjalism] *s.m.* neo-colonialism; ~**-colonialiste** [neɔkɔlɔnjalist] *adj.* neo-colonialist.

néocomien, -ne [neɔkɔmjɛ̃] *adj.*, *s.m.* (geol.) Neocomian.

néo-grec, -que [neɔgrɛk] *adj.* neo-Greek, modern Greek.

néo-impressionnisme [neɔɛ̃presjɔnism] *s.m.* post-impressionism; ~**lithique** [neɔlitik] *adj.* neolithic; ~**logisme** [neɔlɔʒism] *s.m.* neologism.

néon [neɔ̃] *s.m.* neon; *tube au* ~, neon tube.

néo-phyte [neɔfit] *s.m.f.* neophyte; (fig.) beginner, tyro, novice; ~**plasme** [neɔplasm] *s.m.*, ~**plasie** [neɔplazi] *s.f.* (med.) neoplasm.

néo-platonicien, -ne [neɔplatɔnisjɛ̃] *adj.* neo-Platonic; *s.m.f.* neo-Platonist.

néo-platonisme [neɔplatɔnism] *s.m.* neo-Platonism.

néoténie [neɔteni] *s.f.* (biol.) neoteny.

néo-zélandais, -e [neɔzelɑ̃dɛ] *adj.*, *s.m.f.* (native or inhabitant) of New Zealand, New Zealander.

néozoïque [neɔzɔik] *adj.* (geol.) neozoic.

Népal [nepal] *s.m.* (geog.) Nepal.

népalais, -e [nepalɛ] *adj.*, *s.m.f.* Nepalese.

nèpe [nɛp] *s.f.* (ent.) water-scorpion.

népenthès [nepɛ̃tɛs] *s.m.* **1.** (bot.) Nepenthes, pitcher-plant; **2.** (ant.) nepenthes, nepenthe (drug capable of banishing grief or trouble).

néphrétique [nefretik] *adj.* nephritic.

néphrite [nefrit] *s.f.* **1.** (pathol.) nephritis; **2.** (min.) nephrite, jade.

néphrologie [nefrɔlɔʒi] *s.f.* nephrology.

népotisme [nepɔtism] *s.m.* nepotism.

néréide [nereid] *s.f.* (myth., zool.) nereid.

nerf [nɛr] *s.m.* **1.** nerve; **2.** sinew, tendon; **3.** (fig.) vigour, strength, stamina, energy; ~ *de bœuf*, lash, scourge; *vous me portez sur les* ~*s*, you get on my nerves; *cela vous met les* ~*s à vif*, it frays the nerves; *avoir une attaque de* ~*s*, to have a fit of hysterics; *l'argent, c'est le* ~ *de la guerre*, money is the sinews of war; *manquer de* ~, to lack energy; (fam.) *avoir les* ~*s en pelote*, to have one's nerves all on edge.

nérine [nerin] *s.f.* (bot.) nerine, Guernsey lily.

néroli [nerɔli] *s.m.* neroli, essential oil distilled from bitter-orange flowers.

néronien, -ne [nerɔnjɛ̃] *adj.* Neronian; cruel, wanton.

nerprun [nɛrprœ̃] *s.m.* (bot.) buckthorn.

nervation [nɛrvɑsjɔ̃] *s.f.* nervation, neuration.

nerveu-x, -se [nɛrvø] *adj.* nervous; irritable, excitable; sinewy, nervy, wiry, strong; (of style) terse, vigorous, nervous; ~**sement** [nɛrvøzmɑ̃] *adv.* nervously, impatiently, irritably; energetically, vigorously.

nervin [nɛrvɛ̃] *adj.*, *s.m.* nervine.

nervosité [nɛrvozite] *s.f.* nervousness, state of nerves.
nervure [nɛrvyr] *s.f.* (biol.) nervure; (arch.) rib, fillet; (bookb.) rib, band; (techn.) flange, rib, fin; (needlew.) piping, braiding.
nestorianisme [nɛstɔrjanism] *s.m.* Nestorianism.
nestorien, -ne [nɛstɔrjɛ̃] *adj., s.m.* (eccles. hist.) Nestorian.
net, -te [nɛt] *adj.* clean, neat, clear, tidy, sharp, distinct, free, plain, frank, point-blank, empty, blameless; (of price) net; (lit. & fig.) *avoir les mains ~tes*, to have clean hands; *avoir l'esprit ~*, to be clear-headed; *j'en aurai le cœur ~*, I am resolved to know the truth about it; *faire maison ~te* or *faire place ~te*, to clear one's house (of unpleasant people); to make a clean sweep (of); *bénéfice ~*, net profit; *mettre au ~*, to make a fair copy of; *~ adv.* flatly, plainly, point-blank; *refuser ~*, to refuse point-blank, to decline flatly; **~tement** [nɛtmɑ̃] *adv.* neatly, cleanly, clearly, sharply, purely, frankly, flatly, point-blank.
netteté [nɛtte] *s.f.* neatness, cleanness, cleanliness, clearness, distinctness, sharpness, plainness, tidiness.
nettoiement [nɛtwamɑ̃], **nettoyage** [nɛtwajaʒ] *s.m.* cleaning, cleansing, clearing, scouring, sweeping, wiping, dry-cleaning; *appareil de ~ par le vide*, vacuum cleaner (= ASPIRATEUR).
nettoyer [nɛtwaje] *v.t.* to clean, to cleanse, to clear, to scour, to sweep, to wipe; (pop.) to eliminate, to liquidate, to kill; *donner un vêtement à ~*, to send a garment to be dry-cleaned; (games) *~ le tapis*, to sweep the board; *se ~ les mains*, to wash one's hands; *se ~*, to wash and dry oneself; (fam.) *se faire ~*, to be cleaned out, stripped of one's money.
nettoyeu-r, -se [nɛtwajœr] *s.m.f.* cleaner.
neuf [nœf] *adj., s.m.* nine; ninth; *deux ~*, two nines; *Louis neuf*, Louis the Ninth; *un ~ de carreau*, a nine of diamonds.
neu-f, -ve [nœf] *adj.* **1.** new, fresh; *battant ~f*, brand-new; *remettre à ~f*, to do up like new; **2.** (fig.) raw, inexperienced, innocent, green, fresh; **~f** *s.m.* what is new; novelty; *elle ne veut porter que du ~f*, she will wear nothing but new clothes; *quoi de ~f?*, what's the news?
neufchâtel [nøʃɑtɛl] *s.m.* Neufchâtel cheese.
neume [nøm] *s.m.* neum(e) (group of notes sung to single syllable in plainsong).
neural, -e, (aux) [nøral] *adj.* (anat.) neural.
neur-asthénie [nørasteni] *s.f.* neurasthenia; **~asthénique** [nørastenik] *adj., s.m.f.* neurasthenic (person).
neuro-chirurgie [nørɔʃiryrʒi] *s.f.* neurosurgery; **~logie** [nørɔlɔʒi] *s.f.* neurology; **~logue** [nørɔlɔg], **~logiste** [nørɔlɔʒist] *s.m.f.* neurologist, nerve-specialist.
neurone [nørɔn] *s.m.* (biol.) neuron(e).
neustrien, -ne [nøstrjɛ̃] *adj.* (hist.) Neustrian.
neutralisant, -e [nøtralizɑ̃] *adj.* neutralizing.
neutral-isation [nøtralizɑsjɔ̃] *s.f.* neutralization; **~iser** [nøtralize] *v.t.* to neutralize; **~isme** [nøtralism] *s.m.* neutralism; **~iste** [nøtralist] *adj., s.m.f.* neutralist; **~ité** [nøtralite] *s.f.* neutrality.
neutre [nøtr] *adj.* neutral, neuter; (bot., ent.) neuter, asexual; *rester ~*, to remain neutral; *de teinte ~*, neutral-tinted; *~ s.m.* neuter.
neutrino [nøtrino] *s.m.* (phys.) neutrino.
neutron [nøtrɔ̃] *s.m.* (phys.) neutron.
neuvaine [nœvɛn] *s.f.* (Cath. liturgy) novena, neuvaine, prayers for nine days.
neuvième [nœvjɛm] *adj., s.m.* ninth, ninth (part), ninth (regiment); *~ s.f.* (mus.) ninth; **~ment** [nœvjɛmmɑ̃] *adv.* ninthly.
névé [neve] *s.m.* glacier-snow, névé.
neveu (pl. **-x**) [nəvø] *s.m.* **1.** (obs.) grandson, descendant; **2.** nephew; *petit-~*, great-nephew; *~ à la mode de Bretagne*, first cousin once removed; see NIÈCE.
névr-algie [nevralʒi] *s.f.* neuralgia; **~algique** [nevralʒik] *adj.* neuralgic; **~axe** [nevraks] *s.m.* (anat.) neural axis; **~ite** [nevrit] *s.f.* neuritis.
névro-pathe [nevrɔpat] *adj.* neuropathic; *s.m.f.* neuropath; **~pathie** [nevrɔpati] *s.f.* neuropathy; **~ptères** [nevrɔptɛr] *s.m.pl.* (ent.) Neuroptera.
névrose [nevroz] *s.f.* (pathol.) neurosis.
névrosé, -e [nevroze] *adj., s.m.f.* neurotic.
névro-tique [nevrɔtik] *adj.* neurotic; **~tomie** [nevrɔtɔmi] *s.f.* (surg.) neurotomy.
newtonien, -ne [njutɔnjɛ̃] *adj., s.m.f.* Newtonian.
new-yorkais, -e [njujɔrkɛ] *adj., s.m.f.* (native or inhabitant) of New York, New Yorker.
nez [ne] *s.m.* **1.** nose, nostrils; **2.** nose, smell; (of dogs) scent, nose; **3.** (arch.) nosing; **4.** (naut.) nose, bow, head; *il saigne du ~*, his nose is bleeding; *~ à ~*, face to face; *~ en pied de marmite*, pug-nose (with thick turned-up end); *au ~ et à la barbe de qn.*, under someone's very nose; (fig.) *se casser le ~*, to be disappointed, to find nobody at home; to be frustrated; (fig.) *donner sur le ~*, to mortify, to humiliate, to scold; *il fait un ~!* or *un ~ d'une aune!*, he pulls a long face, he looks foolish; (fig.) *il a fait un pied de ~*, he cocked a snook, he mocked (at); *il en fit un ~*, he looked down his nose, he pulled a face, (at it); *à vue de ~*, by rule of thumb; *il ne montre jamais son ~ au bureau*, he never appears in the office; *il met son ~ partout*, or *il fourre le ~ partout*, he pokes his nose into everything; *cela lui pend au ~*, the same is in store for him, he has got it coming to him; *il m'a ri au ~*, he laughed in my face; *on voulait lui tirer les vers du ~*, they wished to pump him; *marcher le ~ au vent*, to walk with one's nose in the air; *il me regarda sous le ~*, he stared me in the face; *il me l'a jeté au ~*, he cast it in my teeth; *mettre le ~ dessus*, to guess right, to discover or nose out the important (hidden) point; *je lui fermai la porte au ~*, I shut the door in his face; *elle le mène par le bout du ~*, she leads him by the nose, she knows how to manage him; *donner du ~ en terre*, to fall on one's face; to fail; to come a nasty cropper; *avoir le ~ fin* or *avoir du ~*, to have a good nose; to be far-sighted, sagacious, perspicacious; *qui coupe son ~ dégarnit son visage*, it is an ill bird that fouls its own nest; *si vous crachez en l'air, cela vous retombera sur le ~*, curses come home to roost; *parler du ~*, to speak through one's nose; (fam.) *se manger le ~*, to quarrel bitterly, to fight; *se piquer le ~*, to booze, to be a confirmed drinker; (aeron.) *piquer du ~*, to nosedive.
N.F. [ɛnɛf] abbrev. *norme française*.
ni [ni] *conj.* (*ne* is expressed or implied) nor, or; neither, either; *~ moi (non plus)*, nor do I, nor I either; *il ne boit ~ ne mange*, he neither drinks nor eats; *sans chapeau ~ pardessus*, without hat or coat; *~ elle ~ son frère ne sortent jamais*, neither she nor her brother ever go out; ⚠ not 'nor' at the beginning of a clause, as in 'nor will my mother be there'; see NE and NON.
niable [njabl] *adj. pas ~*, undeniable.
niais, -e [njɛ] *adj.* silly, foolish; *s.m.f.* simpleton; *faire le ~*, to pretend to know nothing; **~ement** [njɛzmɑ̃] *adv.* foolishly, in a silly manner.
niaiserie [njɛzri] *s.f.* silliness, foolishness; nonsense, foolery, trifle.
nicaise [nikez] *s.m.* = NICODÈME.
niche [niʃ] *s.f.* **1.** niche, recess, alcove, retreat; **2.** (dog-)kennel; **3.** trick, prank; *il m'a fait une ~*, he played a trick upon me.
nichée [niʃe] *s.f.* nest, nestlings, brood; numerous offspring.
nicher [niʃe] *v.i.* to nestle, to build a nest; (fig.)

to lodge; ~ *v.t.* (fig.) to nestle, to place, to settle, to thrust; **se** ~ *v.refl.* to nestle, to place oneself, to ensconce oneself, to lie, to lodge or hide oneself; *où la vertu va-t-elle se ~!*, in what strange places is virtue to be found!
nichet [niʃɛ] *s.m.* nest-egg.
nichoir [niʃwar] *s.m.* breeding-cage.
nichons [niʃɔ̃] *s.m.pl.* (vulg.) breasts, tits.
nickel [nikɛl] *s.m.* nickel; ~ *adj.* (pop.) first-rate.
nickelage [niklaʒ] *s.m.* nickelling, nickel-plating.
nickelé, -e [nikle] *adj.* nickelled, nickel-plated; (fig., fam.) *avoir les pieds ~s*, to be thoroughly idle.
nickeler [nikle] *v.t.* to nickel, to coat with nickel.
nickélifère [nikelifɛr] *adj.* nickeliferous.
nicodème [nikɔdɛm] *s.m.* (fam.) fool, simpleton.
niçois, -e [niswa] *adj., s.m.f.* (native or inhabitant) of Nice.
nicotine [nikɔtin] *s.f.* (chem.) nicotine.
nictation [niktɑsjɔ̃], **nictitation** [niktitɑsjɔ̃] *s.f.* nictation, nictitation.
nictitant, -e [niktitɑ̃] *adj.* nictitating; *paupière ~e*, nictitating eyelid, membrane.
nid [ni] *s.m.* nest; hole; berth, den, retreat, post; *petit à petit l'oiseau fait son ~*, little strokes fell great oaks; *~ à rats*, rat-hole; *à chaque oiseau son ~ est beau*, home is home, be it never so homely; *revenir au ~*, to come home; *trouver la pie au ~*, to make a lucky discovery, to strike lucky.
nidification [nidifikɑsjɔ̃] *s.f.* nidification, nest-building.
nidifier [nidifje] *v.i.* to nidificate, to build a nest.
nièce [njɛs] *s.f.* niece; *~ à la mode de Bretagne*, first cousin once removed; *petite-~*, great-niece.
niellage [njɛlaʒ] *s.m.* niello-work.
nielle[1] [njɛl] *s.m.* niello, niello-work.
nielle[2] [njɛl] *s.f.* **1.** (bot.) ear-cockles, corn-cockle; **2.** (agric.) purples, smut; black rust.
nieller[1] [njele] *v.t.* (agric.) to smut, to blight.
nieller[2] [njele] *v.t.* to niello, to inlay with niello.
nielleur [njɛlœr] *s.m.* niellist, niello-worker.
niellure[1] [njelyr] *s.f.* (agric.) smut, blight.
niellure[2] [njelyr] *s.f.* niello work.
nième [njɛm] *adj.* (math.) nth; *la ~ puissance*, the power of n; (fig.) *pour la ~ fois*, for the umpteenth time.
nier [nje] *v.t.* to deny, to disown; *cela ne peut se ~*, it is undeniable; *~ une dette*, to repudiate a debt.
nigaud, -e [nigo] *adj.* silly, foolish; *s.m.f.* **1.** simpleton, block-head; **2.** (ornith.) green cormorant, booby.
nigauderie [nigodri] *s.f.* silliness, foolishness, foolery.
nigelle [niʒɛl] *s.f.* (bot.) nigella, love-in-the-mist.
Niger [niʒɛr] *s.m.* (geog.) Niger.
nigérian, -e [niʒerjɑ̃] *adj., s.m.f.* Nigerian.
Nigérie [niʒeri] *s.f.* (geog.) Nigeria.
nigérien, -ne [niʒerjɛ̃] *adj., s.m.f.* (native or inhabitant) of (the Republic of) Niger.
nihil-isme [niilism] *s.m.* nihilism; **~iste** [niilist] *adj., s.m.f.* nihilist.
Nil [nil] *s.m.* (geog.) Nile.
nilgaut [nilgo] *s.m.* (zool.) nilgai, nylghau.
nille [nij] *s.f.* (techn.) collar, freely-revolving ring on handle of crank.
nilotique [nilɔtik] *adj.* Nilotic.
nimbe [nɛ̃b] *s.m.* glory, halo, nimbus.
nimber [nɛ̃be] *v.t.* to give a halo to; (fig.) to suffuse, to tinge.
nimbus [nɛ̃bys] *s.m.* nimbus, rain-cloud.
nippe [nip] *s.f.* (usu. pl.) clothes, togs; (pop.) old clothes, rags.
nipper [nipe] *v.t.* (fam.) to provide with clothes, to rig out; **se** ~ *v.refl.* to buy new clothes.
nippon, -e [nipɔ̃] *adj., s.m.f.* Nipponese, Japanese.
nique [nik] *s.f.* sign of mockery; *faire la ~ à*, to mock, to make a derisive gesture at.
niquedouille [nikduj] (obs.) *s.m.* fool, simpleton.
nitescence [nitesɑ̃s] *s.f.* light, radiance.
nitouche [sɛ̃tnituʃ] see SAINTE NITOUCHE.
nitrate [nitrat] *s.m.* nitrate.
nitraté, -e [nitrate] *adj.* nitrated.
nitre [nitr] *s.m.* nitre, saltpetre.
nitré, -e [nitre] *adj.* nitrated.
nitreu-x, -se [nitrø] *adj.* nitrous.
nitrière [nitrjɛr] *s.f.* nitre-bed, saltpetre-bed.
nitrification [nitrifikɑsjɔ̃] *s.f.* nitrification.
nitrifier [nitrifje] *v.t.*, **se** ~ *v.refl.* to nitrify.
nitrique [nitrik] *adj.* nitric.
nitrite [nitrit] *s.m.* nitrite.
nitro-benzène [nitrɔbɛ̃zɛn], **~benzine** [nitrɔbɛ̃zin] *s.f.* (chem.) nitrobenzene; **~glycérine** [nitrɔgliserin] *s.f.* (chem.) nitroglycerine; **~toluène** [nitrɔtɔlɥɛn] *s.f.* (chem.) nitrotoluene.
nivéal, -e, (aux) [niveal] *adj.* winter-flowering.
niveau (pl. **-x**) [nivo] *s.m.* level; *être de ~ avec*, or *au ~ de*, to be level with, to be equal to; *~ d'eau*, water-level; *~ des eaux*, water-mark; *~ de maçon* or *à plomb*, plumb-level; *~ à bulle d'air*, spirit-level; *~ d'essence*, petrol-gauge; *il est au ~ des plus grands peintres*, he is on a par with the best painters.
nivelage [nivlaʒ] *s.m.* levelling.
niveler [nivle] *v.t.* to level, to make equal, to make even; to survey (ground); **se** ~ *v.refl.* to be levelled; to settle.
niveleu-r, -se [nivlœr] *s.m.f.* leveller; *adj.* levelling; **~se** *s.f.* grader (machine).
nivellement [nivɛlmɑ̃] *s.m.* levelling; surveying.
nivéole [niveɔl] *s.f.* (bot.) snowflake.
nivernais, -e [nivɛrnɛ] *adj., s.m.f.* (native or inhabitant) of Nevers.
nivôse [nivoz] *s.m.* (hist.) Nivose (fourth month in Fr. Republican Calendar, December–January).
nixe [niks] *s.f.* (myth.) nixie, water-elf.
nizeré [nizre] *s.m.* essence of white roses.
nobiliaire [nɔbiljɛr] *adj.* noble, of the nobility; *~ s.m.* register of noble families, peerage (book).
noble [nɔbl] *adj.* noble, high, lofty, noble-minded, elevated; of noble birth or descent; *~ s.m.f.* noble, nobleman, noblewoman; *~ s.m.* (hist.) noble (gold coin); *~ à la rose*, rose noble; **~ment** [nɔbləmɑ̃] *adv.* nobly, honourably, as befits a gentleman, with dignity.
noblesse [nɔblɛs] *s.f.* **1.** nobility, noblesse; *petite ~*, gentry; *~ oblige*, rights imply duties, noblesse oblige; **2.** nobleness.
nobliau (pl. **-x**) [nɔblijo] *s.m.* lordling, petty nobleman.
noce [nɔs] *s.f.* **1.** (sing. or pl.) wedding, nuptials, wedding-feast; **2.** (sing.) drinking-bout, revelry, orgy; dissipation; *gâteau de ~s*, wedding-cake; *il n'avait jamais été à pareille ~*, he had never had such a time of it; *il l'avait epousée en secondes ~s*, she was his second wife; *~s d'argent*, silver wedding; *n'être pas à la ~*, to have a bad time of it; *faire la ~*, to go on the spree, to live a dissipated life.
noceu-r, -se [nɔsœr] *s.m.f.* reveller, rake, gay dog, libertine, debauchee, fast or dissipated woman.
nocher [nɔʃe] *s.m.* (poet.) mariner, pilot; *le ~ des Enfers*, Charon, Hell's ferryman.
noci-f, -ve [nɔsif] *adj.* noxious, poisonous, harmful, unwholesome.
nocivité [nɔsivite] *s.f.* noxiousness.
noctambule [nɔktɑ̃byl] *adj.* night-walking, noctambulant; *~ s.m.f.* noctambulist, somnambulist; night prowler, fly-by-night.

noctambulisme [nɔktɑ̃bylism] *s.m.* noctambulism, somnambulism; given to nocturnal activity.
noctiluque [nɔktilyk] *s.m.* (zool.) Noctiluca.
noctuelle [nɔktɥɛl] *s.f.* (ent.) little owl, owl--moth.
noctule [nɔktyl] *s.f.* (zool.) noctule (bat).
nocturne [nɔktyrn] *adj.* nocturnal, of night, by night, nightly, night-; ~ *s.m.* (zool.) nocturnal bird; (mus.) nocturne; (Cath. liturg.) nocturn.
nodal, -e, (**aux**) [nɔdal] *adj.* nodal; (*ligne*) ~*e*, nodal line.
nodosité [nɔdozite] *s.f.* nodosity, node, knot.
nodule [nɔdyl] *s.m.* nodule.
noduleu-x, -se [nɔdylø] *adj.* nodulous, nodular.
nodus [nɔdys] *s.m.* (med.) node.
Noël [nɔɛl] *s.m.f.* Christmas; Yule; Nowel; Christmas carol, Christmas hymn; *joyeux ~!*, Happy Christmas!; *à* (*la*) ~, at Christmas; *voici* (*la*) ~ *qui arrive*, Christmas is coming; *bûche de* ~, Yule log; *fêtes de* ~, Christmas holidays; *la veillée de* ~, Christmas Eve; *le* (*petit*) *noël*, Christmas gift.
nœud [nø] *s.m* **1.** knot, bow, tie; *faire un* ~, to tie a knot or a bow; *trancher le* ~ *gordien*, to cut the Gordian knot; ~ *d'ajust*, carrick bend; ~ *d'anguille*, running bowline; ~ *de bouline*, outside clinch; ~ *coulant*, slip-knot; ~ *d'écoute*, sheet--knot; clew; ~ *de fouet*, rolling hitch; ~ *de grappin*, fisherman's bend; ~ *de hauban*, French shroud-knot; ~ *d'orin*, buoy-rope knot; ~ *plat*, reef-knot, square knot; ~ *de ride*, Matthew Walker knot; ~ *de trésillon*, marlin-spike hitch; **2.** (naut.) knot; *le navire file dix ~s*, the ship is doing ten knots; **3.** (in wood, etc.) knot, joint; (fig.) knotty point, difficulty, rub; main point; **4.** tie, bond, fetters, knot; **5.** nodal point; ~ *ferroviaire*, railway-junction; ~ *de communications*, centre of communications; **6.** (slang) *filer son* ~, (i.) to be off; (ii.) to die, to peg out.
noir, -e [nwar] *adj.* black; Negro; swarthy, sable, dark, smutty, coal-black; (fig.) dirty, dark, gloomy, dismal, wicked, base; (slang) drunk; *pain* ~, black bread, rye-bread; *café* ~, black coffee (without milk); *il fait* ~ *comme dans un four*, it is pitch-dark; *il voit tout en* ~, he is gloomy, he sees everything in a bad light, he looks on the dark side; *viandes ~es*, brown meat (game); *c'est ma bête ~e*, I hate the sight of him; it is one of my pet aversions; *un froid* ~, bitter cold; a black frost; *gravure à la manière ~e*, mezzotint; *il est dans ses humeurs ~es*, he is in a melancholy mood; ~ *de coups*, all black and blue; *un point* ~, a dark spot, a cloud; *une ~e ingratitude*, base ingratitude; *une action ~e*, a black deed; *faire une peinture bien ~e de la situation*, to give a gloomy view of the case.
noir [nwar] *s.m.* black; Negro; black (apparel), mourning; (fig.) gloom, spleen, the blues; *~-animal*, bone-black; ~ *de fumée*, lamp-black; smut; ~ *d'ivoire*, ivory black; *être en* ~, to be dressed in black, to wear black; *broyer du* ~, to have the blues, to be gloomy, to be in the dumps; *mettre dans le* ~, to hit the bull's-eye; *deux ~s ne font pas un blanc*, two wrongs do not make a right; *prendre le* ~, to go into mourning.
noirâtre [nwarɑtr] *adj.* blackish.
noiraud, -e [nwaro] *adj.* swarthy, swarthy--looking, black, dark-skinned; *s.m.f.* dark--skinned person.
noirceur [nwarsœr] *s.f.* blackness, darkness; (fig.) gloominess, wickedness, baseness, heinousness, atrocity, base trick or act, slander.
noircir [nwarsir] *v.t.* to blacken, to black; (fig.) to blacken, to slander, to defame; **se** ~ *v.refl.* to blacken oneself; to slander each other; to turn black, to become dark or overcast.
noircissement [nwarsismɑ̃] *s.m.* blackening, blacking, darkening.
noircisseu-r, -se [nwarsisœr] *s.m.f.* blackener; (fam.) *~r de papier*, scribbler.
noircissure [nwarsisyr] *s.f.* black spot, smudge, darkening.
noire [nwar] *s.f.* (mus.) crotchet.
noise [nwaz] *s.f.* quarrel (obs. except in *chercher* ~ *à*, to pick a quarrel with).
noiseraie [nwazrɛ] *s.f.* grove of walnut- or nut--trees.
noisetier [nwaztje] *s.m.* (bot.) hazel-tree, nut--tree.
noisette [nwazɛt] *s.f.* hazel-nut; ~ *adj.* hazel (-coloured).
noix [nwa] *s.f.* walnut, nut; *coquille de* ~, nutshell; (fig.) small light vessel; ~ *du genou*, knee-cap; ~ *de moulin*, cogwheel, cone; (carp.) rule--joint; ~ *d'Amérique* or *du Brésil*, Brazil nut; ~ *de coco*, coconut; ~ *de galle*, gall-nut; (slang) *à la* ~, worthless; *boniments à la* ~, empty talk, nonsense, eyewash.
noli me tangere [nɔlimetɑ̃ʒere] *s.m.* **1.** (bot.) touch-me-not; **2.** (anc. med.) lupus.
nolis [nɔli] *s.m.* (naut.) freight.
nolisement [nɔlizmɑ̃] *s.m.* chartering, freighting.
noliser [nɔlize] *v.t.* to charter, to freight.
nom [nɔ̃] *s.m.* **1.** name, surname; ~ *de famille*, surname, family name; ~ *de baptême*, *petit* ~, Christian name; *petit* ~ *d'amitié* pet name; ~ *de jeune fille*, ~ *de demoiselle*, maiden name; ~ *déposé*, registered (trade) name; ~ *de guerre*, pseudonym, assumed name, alias; ~ *de plume*, pen-name; ~ *propre*, proper name; ~ *de théâtre*, stage name; ~ *marchand*, trade-name; *avoir* ~, to be called; *porter le* ~ *de*, *le prénom de*, to be called after, to be named; *porter un beau* ~, to bear a great name; *sans* ~, nameless; *de* ~, by name, nominally; *au* ~ *de*, in the name of, for the sake of, on behalf of; *appeler les choses par leur* ~, to call a spade a spade; **2.** reputation, fame, title; *se faire un* ~, to win a name for oneself; *il n'était roi que de* ~, he was king only in name; **3.** (gram.) noun; ~ *commun*, common noun; ~ *propre*, proper noun, proper name; ~ *de nombre*, numeral noun; **4.** used to form mild expletives, as in ~ *de* ~*!*, ~ *d'un petit bonhomme!*, *d'un chien!*, *d'une pipe!*, *d'un tonnerre!*, and, more profanely, in ~ *de Dieu!*
nomade [nɔmad] *adj.* nomad, nomadic, wandering, migrating; ~ *s.m.f.* nomad.
nomadisme [nɔmadism] *s.m.* nomadism.
nombrable [nɔ̃brabl] *adj.* numerable, countable.
nombre [nɔ̃br] *s.m.* **1.** number; ~ *entier*, whole number, integer; ~ *d'or*, golden number; ~ *cardinal*, cardinal number; ~ *ordinal*, ordinal number; ~ *pair*, even number; ~ *impair*, odd number; **2.** number(s), quantity; *au* ~ *de*, to the number of; *bon* ~ *de gens*, a great many people; *en* ~, in great numbers; *être en* ~ *suffisant*, to form a quorum; *pour faire* ~, to make up a number; *être au* ~ *des élus*, to be numbered with the elect; *dans le* ~, among the number; *tout fait* ~, every little helps; *sans* ~, countless, innumerable; **3.** (Lit.) harmony, cadence; **4.** (gram.) number; *le* ~ *pluriel*, the plural number.
nombrer [nɔ̃bre] *v.t.* (obs. exc. Lit.) to number, to count.
nombreu-x, -se [nɔ̃brø] *adj.* numerous, large, many; multifarious, manifold; (Lit.) harmonious; *réunion peu ~se*, small party; *pendant de ~ses générations*, for many generations; *une prose ~se*, a rhythmic or harmonious prose.
nombril [nɔ̃bri] *s.m.* navel; (fig.) centre; (bot.) eye; (fam.) *se prendre pour le* ~ *du monde*, to think oneself highly important.
nome [nɔm] *s.m.* nome (province of (i.) anc. Egypt; (ii.) mod. Greece).
nomenclat-eur, -rice [nɔmɑ̃klatyr] *adj.* nomenclative; *s.m.f.* nomenclator.

nomenclature [nɔmɑ̃klatyr] *s.f.* **1.** nomenclature; **2.** (comm.) list, catalogue; *prix de* ~, list price.

nominal, -e, (aux) [nɔminal] *adj.* nominal, of names; *faire l'appel* ~, to call the roll; *appel* ~, roll-call; (fin.) *valeur* ~*e*, face value; ~ *s.m.* pronoun; **~ement** [nɔminalmɑ̃] *adv.* by name; nominally, in name only, not effectively.

nominal-isme [nɔminalism] *s.m.* nominalism; **~iste** [nɔminalist] *adj.* nominalistic, nominalist.

nominati-f, -ve [nɔminatif] *adj.* nominative; (of shares) registered, personal; *état* ~*f*, nominal roll; **~f** *s.m.* (gram.) nominative, nominative case.

nomination [nɔminɑsjɔ̃] *s.f.* nomination, appointment.

nominativement [nɔminativmɑ̃] *adv.* by name.

nommé, -e [nɔme] *adj.* **1.** named; *un* ~ *Smith*, one Smith; *le* ~ *Smith*, the man named Smith, the said Smith; *ah! il est bien* ~, he deserves his name!; **2.** appointed, designate, elect; *à point* ~, in the nick of time; at just the right time; *à jour* ~, on the appointed day.

nommément [nɔmemɑ̃] *adv.* namely, particularly, especially, by name.

nommer [nɔme] *v.t.* **1.** to name, to call, to nickname, to mention; *sans* ~ *personne*, without mentioning any names, naming no names; **2.** to appoint, to nominate; to designate, to elect; *faire nommer qn. à*, to obtain someone's appointment to; **se** ~ *v.refl.* **1.** to be named or called; **2.** to give one's name, to introduce oneself.

non [nɔ̃] *adv.* no, not; ~ *pas*, no, not so; ~ *point!*, by no means!; ~ *pas que* (with subj.), not that; ~ *plus*, either; *ni moi* ~ *plus*, nor I either; ~ *plus que*, no more than; *que* ~*!*, no indeed, dear me, no!, certainly not!; *jurer que* ~, to swear that it is not so; (used in the same way as *n'est-ce pas*) *vous ne parlerez pas,* ~*?*, you won't speak, will you?; *il a fait cela?* ~*?*, he has done it!, is it true?, is it possible?; ~ *s.m.invar. un* ~, a no, a negative answer or vote; *les* ~ *l'emportent*, the noes have it.

non-activité [nɔnaktivite] *s.f.* non-activity; suspension (from job).

nonagénaire [nɔnaʒenɛr] *adj., s.m.f.* nonagenarian.

non-agression [nɔnagrɛsjɔ̃] *s.f.* non-aggression; **~-alignement** [nɔnaliɲmɑ̃] *s.m.* (pol.) non-alignment.

nonante [nɔnɑ̃t] *adj.* (in Switzerland, in Belgium) ninety.

non-assistance [nɔnasistɑ̃s] *s.f.* (law) failure to assist (police or person in danger); **~-belligérance** [nɔ̃beliʒerɑ̃s] *s.f.* non-belligerency.

nonce [nɔ̃s] *s.m.* nuncio.

nonchalamment [nɔ̃ʃalamɑ̃] *adv.* nonchalantly; lazily, carelessly, heedlessly.

nonchalance [nɔ̃ʃalɑ̃s] *s.f.*, **nonchaloir** [nɔ̃ʃalwar) *s.m.* nonchalance, listlessness, laziness, carelessness, heedlessness.

nonchalant, -e [nɔ̃ʃalɑ̃] *adj.* lazy, listless, careless, heedless, supine, sluggish.

nonciature [nɔ̃sjatyr] *s.f.* nunciature; nuncio's residence.

non-combattant, -e [nɔ̃kɔ̃batɑ̃] *adj., s.m.* (mil.) non-combatant; *les* ~*s d'une armée*, the non-combat elements in an army.

non-comparution [nɔ̃kɔ̃parysjɔ̃] *s.f.* (law) non-appearance, failure to appear (in court); **~-conformisme** [nɔ̃kɔ̃fɔrmism] *s.m.* nonconformism, nonconformity; **~-conformiste** [nɔ̃kɔ̃fɔrmist] *adj., s.m.f.* nonconformist; **~-conformité** [nɔ̃kɔ̃fɔrmite] *s.f.* nonconformity, failure to conform.

none [nɔn] *s.f.* (Cath. liturg.) nones (ninth hour); (pl.) (Rom. calendar) nones.

non-engagé, -e [nɔnɑ̃gaʒe] *adj., s.m.f.* (pol.) uncommitted (person or nation).

non-être [nɔnɛtr] *s.m.* (phil.) non-existence, nonentity; **~-exécution** [nɔnɛgsekysjɔ̃] *s.f.* (law) non-fulfilment (of contract, etc.).

nonidi [nɔnidi] *s.m.* (hist.) nonidi (ninth day of *décade* in Fr. Republican Calendar).

non-intervention [nɔnɛ̃tɛrvɑ̃sjɔ̃] *s.f.* non-intervention; **~-interventionniste** [nɔnɛ̃tɛrvɑ̃sjɔnist] *adj., s.m.f.* non-interventionist; **~-lieu** [nɔ̃ljø] *s.m.* (law) no grounds for prosecution, no true bill; *ordonnance de* ~*-lieu*, nonsuit; *rendre un* ~*-lieu*, to dismiss the case; *bénéficier d'un* ~*-lieu*, to be discharged; **~-moi** [nɔ̃mwa] *s.m.* (phil.) non-ego.

nonnette [nɔnɛt] *s.f.* **1.** (ornith.) tit; **2.** small round gingerbread cake.

nonobstant [nɔnɔbstɑ̃] *prep.* notwithstanding, in spite of; ~ *adv.* notwithstanding.

nonpareil, -le [nɔ̃parɛj] *adj.* matchless, peerless, unequalled, nonpareil; **~le** *s.f.* **1.** nonpareil (very small article, tiny sweets); **2.** (print.) nonpareil; **3.** (bot., hort.) nonesuch; nonsuch apple.

non-recevoir [nɔ̃rsəvwar] *s.m.* see FIN *s.f.*

non-sens [nɔ̃sɑ̃s] *s.m.invar.* nonsense, absurdity.

non-valeur [nɔvalœr] *s.f.* non-productive land or property; (fin.) bad debt; useless person or thing.

nopal [nɔpal] *s.m.* (bot.) nopal, cochineal fig.

nord [nɔr] *s.m.* north; northern countries, etc., North; (department of France) Nord; *faire le* ~, to steer northwards; *au* ~, *vers le* ~, northwards, to, in, at, the north; *du* ~, northern, northerly, from the north; ~*-est*, north-east, north-easter (wind); ~*-ouest*, north-west, north-wester (wind); (fig.) *perdre le* ~, to lose one's bearings; *ne pas perdre le* ~, to keep one's wits about one; ~ *adj.invar.* northern, north; northerly; *pôle* ~, North Pole.

nord-africain, -e [nɔrafrikɛ̃] *adj., s.m.f.* North African.

nord-américain, -e [nɔramerikɛ̃] *adj., s.m.f.* North American.

nord-coréen, -ne [nɔrkɔreɛ̃] *adj., s.m.f.* North Korean.

nordique [nɔrdik] *adj.* Nordic, Scandinavian.

nordir [nɔrdir] *v.i.* to veer to the north.

noria [nɔrja] *s.f.* noria, bucket elevator, bucket conveyor.

normal, -e, (aux) [nɔrmal] *adj.* **1.** normal, regular, standard, average; *poids* ~, standard weight; *école* ~*e*, teachers' training college; **2.** (geom.) perpendicular; **~e** *s.f.* **1.** normality, (the) normal, usual state, average quantity; **2.** abbrev. of *École Normale Supérieure*, highest French teachers' training college; **3.** (geom.) perpendicular line; **~ement** [nɔrmalmɑ̃] *adv.* normally.

normalien, -ne [nɔrmaljɛ̃] *s.m.f.* **1.** pupil of an *école normale*; **2.** pupil or ex-pupil of *École Normale Supérieure*.

normaliser [nɔrmalize] *v.t.* to standardize.

normand, -e [nɔrmɑ̃] *s.m.f.* **1.** Norman, native or inhabitant of Normandy; **2.** (hist.) Northman, Viking, native or inhabitant of Scandinavia; *adj.* **1.** Norman; **2.** (hist.) of Scandinavia; **3.** (fig.) crafty, sly, ambiguous, evasive; *à* ~, ~ *et demi*, set a thief to catch a thief; *réponse de Normand*, evasive, cunning answer; ⚠ not (arch.) 'Norman'.

Normandie [nɔrmɑ̃di] *s.f.* (geog.) Normandy.

norme [nɔrm] *s.f.* norm, rule, pattern, standard, type.

norois, -e, norrois, -e [nɔrwɑ] *adj.* Norse; of the Northmen; ~ *s.m.* Norse (language).

norois, noroît [nɔrwa] *s.m.* north-west wind, north-wester, nor'-wester.

Norvège [nɔrvɛʒ] *s.f.* (geog.) Norway.

norvégien, -ne [nɔrveʒjɛ̃] *adj., s.m.f.* Norwegian, (native or inhabitant) of Norway; ~ *s.m.* Norwegian (language).

nos see NOTRE.

nostalgie [nɔstalʒi] *s.f.* nostalgia, home-sickness.

nostalgique [nɔstalʒik] *adj.* nostalgic.

nota [nɔta] *s.m.* (pl. *nota*) marginal note; ~ *bene* (abbrev. *N.B.*), nota bene, N.B.

notabilité [nɔtabilite] *s.f.* **1.** notableness, notability; **2.** notable person; (fam.) V.I.P., big shot.

notable [nɔtabl] *adj.* notable, important; ~ *s.m.f.* notable person, worthy, eminent man or woman; **~ment** [nɔtabləmɑ̃] *adv.* much, appreciably, considerably, notably.

notaire [nɔtɛr] *s.m.* notary, notary-public, solicitor; **~sse** *s.f.* wife of a *notaire*.

notamment [nɔtamɑ̃] *adv.* especially, particularly, among others.

notarial, -e, (aux) [nɔtarjal] *adj.* notarial.

notariat [nɔtarja] *s.m.* function, profession, of a notary.

notarié, -e [nɔtarje] *adj.* executed and authenticated by a notary.

notation [nɔtɑsjɔ̃] *s.f.* notation; noting, recording; note, observation.

note [nɔt] *s.f.* **1.** note, mark, remark, observation, notice or mention (in a newspaper or review), minute; *prendre ~ de*, to note down; **2.** bill, account; ~ *d'hôtel*, hotel bill; **3.** (mus.) note; *fausse ~*, wrong note; (fig.) discordance; *donner la ~*, to strike the note, (fig.) to lead the fashion; *être bien dans la ~*, to do the right thing in the right place; to harmonize; ⚠ not 'note' in sense of a short letter.

noter [nɔte] *v.t.* to note, to note down, to make a memorandum of, to keep a record of; to observe, to notice; to mark, to give marks to; (mus.) to set to music; *personne bien notée*, person of good repute; *il est mal noté*, he has a black mark against his name.

notice [nɔtis] *s.f.* notice, review, brief introduction (to book), account, list; ~ *biographique*, biographical notice or sketch; ~ *explicative*, explanatory note.

notification [nɔtifikɑsjɔ̃] *s.f.* notification, notice.

notifier [nɔtifje] *v.t.* to notify.

notion [nɔsjɔ̃] *s.f.* notion, idea, element, knowledge.

notoire [nɔtwar] *adj.* notorious, manifest (injustice, etc.), publicly known; **~ment** [nɔtwarmɑ̃] *adv.* notoriously; manifestly, to public knowledge.

notoriété [nɔtɔrjete] *s.f.* notoriety, notoriousness; *il est de ~ publique que*, it is notorious that; it is well known that; (law) *acte de ~*, attested certificate (of identity, death, etc.).

notre [nɔtr], (pl.) **nos** [no] *poss.adj.* our, our own.

nôtre [notr] *poss.pron.* ours, our own; *le ~, la ~, les ~s*, our, our own, ours; ~ *s.m. le ~*, our property; our part; *il faut y mettre du ~*, we must do something to help; (pl.) *les ~s*, our relations; our compatriots; our friends; our fellow-partisans; our side; *serez-vous des ~s?*, will you join us?

Notre-Dame [nɔtrədam] *s.f.* **1.** Our Lady; **2.** Notre-Dame (cathedral of Paris).

notule [nɔtyl] *s.f.* short note or annotation.

nouage [nuaʒ] *s.m.* knotting, tying, joining.

nouaison [nwɛzɔ̃] *s.f.* (agric., hort.) setting (of fruit).

nouba [nuba] *s.f.* (hist.) military music of the Fr. North-African troops; (fig.) *faire la ~*, to go on the spree; to paint the town red.

noue [nu] *s.f.* **1.** (agric.) meadow pasture; **2.** gutter, gutter-lead; valley (in roof).

noué, -e [nue] *adj.* **1.** knotted; (sewing) *point ~*, lock-stitch; **2.** (pathol.) rickety.

nouer [nue] *v.t.* to knot, to tie (up); (fig.) ~ *une intrigue*, to scheme, to plot; ~ *des relations*, to form an acquaintance, or friendship; **se ~** *v.refl.* to be tied; to form knots; (of fruit) to set; (pathol.) to grow rickety; (of joints) to knot.

noueu-x, -se [nuø] *adj.* knotty, knotted, nodose, gnarled.

nougat [nuga] *s.m.* nougat; (pl.) (pop.) feet.

nouille [nuj] *s.f.* **1.** (pl.) nouilles, noodles; ribbon vermicelli; **2.** (sing.) (fig., fam.) silly and spineless person.

noumène [numɛn] *s.m.* (phil.) noumenon (pl. noumena).

nounou [nunu] *s.f.* (child. lang.) nanny.

nourrain [nurɛ̃] *s.m.* young fish, fry.

nourrice [nuris] *s.f.* **1.** nurse, wet-nurse; *en ~*, (of baby) at nurse, out at nurse; **2.** (techn.) reserve tank, feed-tank, feed-pump.

nourrici-er, -ère [nurisje] *adj.* nutritive, nourishing; *père ~er*, foster-father.

nourrir [nurir] *v.t.* to nourish, to feed, to provide a living (for), to nurture, to keep, to maintain, to foster, to suckle, to board (as pupils); (fig.) to foment, to encourage, to entertain, to provide; (mil.) *feu nourri*, brisk steady fire; *dix francs par jour et nourri*, ten francs a day and meals; ~ *un espoir*, to entertain hopes; ~ *v.i.* to be nourishing; **se ~** *v.refl.* to feed, to live, (*de*, on); to maintain oneself, to thrive.

nourrissage [nurisaʒ] *s.m.* rearing and feeding (of cattle).

nourrissant, -e [nurisɑ̃] *adj.* nutritive, nourishing, nutritious.

nourisseur [nurisœr] *s.m.* **1.** cattle-breeder, grazier, raiser of fat-stock; dairy-farmer; **2.** feed-bin.

nourrisson [nurisɔ̃] *s.m.* nursling, suckling, unweaned child; foster-child.

nourriture [nurityr] *s.f.* nourishment, food, diet, keep, maintenance; (obs.) breast-feeding.

nous [nu] *pers.pron.* we; us, to us; each other; ~ *voici*, here we are; ~ ~ *convenons*, we suit each other; *à ~*, ours, our own, our turn; *à ~ deux*, let's have a go at it; *~-mêmes*, ourselves.

nouure [nuyr] *s.f.* (pathol.) rickets; (bot.) setting (of fruit).

nouveau (pl. **-x**) [nuvo], **nouvel** [nuvɛl] (before vowel or h-mute), (fem.) **nouvelle** [nuvɛl] *adj.* new, fresh, novel, additional, recent, new-fangled; *le nouvel an*, the New Year; ~ *adv.* new, newly; *les ~x mariés*, the newly married couple; *un ~ venu*, a newcomer; *à ~*, anew, afresh, again; *de ~*, anew, again, over again, once more; *quoi de ~?*, what news?; ~ *s.m.* novelty, new thing, new man, new pupil; *tout ~ tout beau*, a new broom sweeps clean; all that is new is fair; **nouvellement** [nuvɛlmɑ̃] *adv.* newly, recently, lately.

nouveau-né, -e [nuvone] *s.m.f.* new-born child; *une fille ~e*, a baby daughter.

nouveauté [nuvote] *s.f.* novelty, newness, change, innovation; new thing, latest fashion, new idea, new experience, new publication, new play, etc.; early fruit or vegetable; linen-drapery; *magasin de ~s*, linen-draper's shop; draper's; *haute ~*, latest fashion.

nouvelle [nuvɛl] *s.f.* **1.** news, tidings, fresh information, intelligence; (relig.) *la bonne ~*, the gospel tidings; *vous m'en direz des ~s!*, you will be surprised at it!; you will be highly pleased with it!; *donnez-moi de vos ~s*, let me hear from you; **2.** short story; ⚠ not 'novel'.

Nouvelle-Écosse [nuvɛlekɔs] *s.f.* (geog.) Nova Scotia.
Nouvelle-Orléans [nuvɛlɔrleɑ̃] *s.f.* (geog.) New Orleans.
Nouvelle-Zélande [nuvɛlzelɑ̃d] *s.f.* (geog.) New Zealand.
nouvelliste [nuvɛlist] *s.m.f.* **1.** (obs.) purveyor of news; **2.** writer of short stories.
nova [nɔva] *s.f.* (pl. *novae*) (astron.) nova.
novat-eur, -rice [nɔvatœr] *s.m.f.* innovator; *adj.* innovating, innovatory.
novembre [nɔvɑ̃br] *s.m.* November.
novice [nɔvis] *s.m.f.* **1.** novice, probationer; neophyte; **2.** (fig.) apprentice, new hand, greenhorn; ~ *adj.* raw, inexperienced.
noviciat [nɔvisja] *s.m.* **1.** novitiate, time of probation; **2.** novices' quarters; **3.** (fig.) apprenticeship.
noyade [nwajad] *s.f.* drowning, death by drowning.
noyau (pl. **-x**) [nwajo] *s.m.* **1.** stone; *fruits à* ~, stone-fruit; *il faut casser le* ~ *pour avoir l'amande*, he must crack the nut that would have the kernel; **2.** nucleus, central part, (city) centre, origin, core; (arch.) central column, newel (of stairs).
noyé, -e [nwaje] *adj.* drowned, flooded, deluged, bathed; *des yeux* ~*s de larmes*, eyes swimming in tears; *s.m.f.* drowned person.
noyer [nwaje] *v.t.* to drown, to flood, to immerse, to drench, to scuttle (ship), to dilute; (fig.) to lose (*dans*, in), to forget (in), to overwhelm; ~ *son chagrin dans le vin*, to drown one's sorrows in wine; ~ *sa pensée dans le verbiage*, to water down or dilute one's thought in a torrent of words; (fig.) ~ *le poisson*, to confuse issues (purposely); **se** ~ *v.refl.* to be drowning, to drown oneself; (fig.) to wallow, to lose oneself, to go to ruin.
noyer [nwaje] *s.m.* (bot.) walnut-tree, walnut-wood.
N.S.J.-C. [ɛnɛsjise] abbrev. *Notre Seigneur Jésus-Christ.*
nu, -e [ny] *adj.* naked, stark naked, bare, uncovered, undressed; plain, unadorned; *bras* ~*s*, with bare arms; *jambes* ~*es*, ~*-jambes*, bare-legged; ~*-pieds, pieds* ~*s*, barefoot(ed); ~*-tête, tête* ~*e*, bare-headed; ~*e propriété*, bare ownership; property without the usufruct; *à* ~, bare, laid bare; (fig.) openly, frankly; *monter à* ~, to ride bareback.
nu [ny] *s.m.* (paint.) nude, naked figure.
nuage [nɥaʒ] *s.m.* cloud, mist, (fig.) shadow, gloom, quarrel, threat to happiness or good accord; *il est toujours dans les* ~*s*, he is always in the clouds, or absent-minded.
nuageu-x, -se [nɥaʒø] *adj.* cloudy, clouded; (fig.) vague, obscure, hazy.
nuance [nɥɑ̃s] *s.f.* **1.** shade, hue, tint, nuance; (mus.) modification of time and expression; **2.** difference, distinction, gradation; *oh! il y a une* ~*!*, oh! but that is different!; observe the shades of meaning; *observer les* ~*s*, to mark the shades; to render the shades of expression; *une* ~ *de mépris*, a touch, or shade, of contempt.
nuancer [nɥɑ̃se] *v.t.* to shade, to tint, to tinge; to vary, to variegate, to moderate (tone, etc.).
nubien, -ne [nybjɛ̃] *adj., s.m.f.* Nubian.
nubile [nybil] *adj.* nubile, marriageable.
nubilité [nybilite] *s.f.* nubility, marriageableness.
nucléaire [nykleɛr] *adj.* (biol., phys.) nuclear; atomic.
nucléique [nykleik] *adj.* (biol., chem.) nucleic.
nucléon [nykleɔ̃] *s.m.* (phys.) nucleon.
nucléole [nykleɔl] *s.m.* (biol.) nucleolus.
nudisme [nydism] *s.m.* nudism.
nudiste [nydist] *adj. s.m.f.* nudist.
nudité [nydite] *s.f.* nakedness, nudity; (fig.) bareness, nakedness, blatancy; (pl.) naked figures, nudes.
nue [ny] *s.f.* cloud, sky; *tomber des* ~*s*, to be astounded, to be thunderstruck; to be taken aback; *porter aux* ~*s*, to praise or extol to the skies; (fig.) *se perdre dans les* ~*s*, to be lost in the clouds.
nuée [nɥe] *s.f.* rain-cloud, storm-cloud, storm, heavy shower; **2.** swarm, host, multitude; flight (of birds).
nuer [nɥe] *v.t.* to shade, to shade off, to graduate, to match.
nuire [nɥir] *v.i.* to harm, to injure, to hurt, to wrong, to be harmful, injurious, hurtful, noxious; ~ *à*, to hurt, to wrong, to spoil, to be prejudicial to, to hinder, to be in the way of; *ne* ~ *en rien*, to do no harm at all; **se** ~ *v.refl.* to harm oneself or each other; *se* ~ *l'un (à) l'autre*, to harm each other; *ce qui nuit à l'un sert l'autre*, one man's meat is another man's poison.
nuisible [nɥizibl] *adj.* harmful, hurtful, injurious, noxious, detrimental; **~ment** [nɥiziblәmɑ̃] *adv.* injuriously, harmfully.
nuit [nɥi] *s.f.* night, night-time; darkness, dark; *il (se) fait* ~, it is night, it is getting dark; *de* ~, by night, at night, nightly; *toute la* ~, all night long; *je n'ai pas dormi de la nuit*, I have not slept all night; *la* ~ *des temps*, time immemorial; ~ *blanche*, sleepless night; *à la* ~ *tombante*, at nightfall; ~ *close*, ~ *noire*, night, pitch-dark; *la* ~, at night; *faire une bonne* ~, to have a good night's rest; *passer la* ~, to spend the night; to sit up all night; *la* ~ *porte conseil*, sleep on it; seek advice of your pillow; time will show a plan; *la* ~*, tous les chats sont gris*, all cats are grey in the dark; *bonne* ~, good night; *chemise de* ~, nightgown; *vase de* ~, chamber-pot, chamber; *c'est le jour et la* ~, it's quite different, one is the reverse of the other; *il ne passera pas la* ~, he will be dead before morning.
nuitamment [nɥitamɑ̃] *adv.* nightly, by night, in the night.
nuitée [nɥite] *s.f.* night, the space of one night; night (spent in hotel, etc.).
nul, -le [nyl] *adj.* **1.** no, not one, not any; **2.** null, ineffectual, ignorant, of no worth, nil; ~ *et non avenu*, null and void; *c'est un coup* ~, that stroke does not count; *partie* ~*le, match* ~, drawn game or match; *il est* ~, he is a nonentity; *pron.* no one, nobody; ~ *n'est prophète en son pays*, no man is a prophet in his own country; **~lement** [nylmɑ̃] *adv.* in no way, by no means, not at all, in nowise.
nullard, -e [nylar] *adj.* (fam.) no good at all.
nullité [nylite] *s.f.* **1.** nullity; **2.** incapacity, invalidity, worthlessness, non-existence, nonentity, cipher, nobody.
nûment, nuement [nymɑ̃] *adv.* frankly, openly, plainly.
numéraire [nymerɛr] *adj.* legal (of money values); ~ *s.m.* specie, hard cash, coin.
numéral, -e, (aux) [nymeral] *adj.* numeral.
numérateur [nymeratœr] *s.m.* numerator.
numération [nymerɑsjɔ̃] *s.f.* numeration, numeral notation; counting.
numérique [nymerik] *adj.* numerical.
numériquement [nymerikmɑ̃] *adv.* numerically.
numéro [nymero] *s.m.* **1.** number, size, sort; (fam.) (of person) character; *être du bon* ~, to be of good quality; *c'est mon* ~ *deux*, it is my second-best (hat, etc.); *tirer un mauvais* ~, to be unlucky; *quel* ~*!*, what a type!; **2.** ticket (in lottery, etc.); **3.** copy, issue; number; **4.** turn, stunt.

numérotage [nymerɔtaʒ] *s.m.*, **numérotation** [nymerɔtɑsjɔ̃] *s.f.* numbering, paging (of book).
numéroter [nymerɔte] *v.t.* to number; to page; (fig., fam.) to tick off (list of sth.); **se** ~ *v.refl.* (mil.) to number off.
numéroteur [nymerɔtœr] *s.m.* numberer, numbering-machine, paging-machine.
numide [nymid] *s.m.f.*, *adj.* Numidian.
numismate [nymismat] *s.m.f.* numismatist.
numismatique [nymismatik] *s.f.* numismatics; ~ *adj.* numismatic.
nummulaire [nymylɛr] *adj.* nummulary; ~ *s.f.* (bot.) moneywort.
nummulite [nymylit] *s.f.* (fossil) nummulite.
nuptial, -e, (**aux**) [nypsjal] *adj.* nuptial, wedding-; *anneau*~, wedding-ring; *bénédiction*~*e*, marriage service.
nuptialité [nypsjalite] *s.f.* marriage-rate; study of marriage- and divorce-rate.
nuque [nyk] *s.f.* nape (of the neck).
nutriti-f, -ve [nytritif] *adj.* nutritive, nutritious, nourishing.
nutrition [nytrisjɔ̃] *s.f.* nutrition.
nyctalope [niktalɔp] *adj.* nyctalopic.
nyctalopie [niktalɔpi] *s.f.* nyctalopia, night--sight.
nymphal, -e, (**aux**) [nɛ̃fal] *adj.* (zool.) nymphal.
nymphe [nɛ̃f] *s.f.* nymph; (ent.) nymph, pupa, chrysalis.
nymphéa [nɛ̃fea] *s.m.* (bot.) Nymphaea, water--lily, nenuphar.
nymphéacées [nɛ̃fease] *s.f.pl.* (bot.) Nymphaeaceae.
nymphée [nɛ̃fe] *s.m.* nymphaeum, grotto, marble fountain.
nymphomane [nɛ̃fɔman] *adj.*, *s.f.* nymphomaniac.
nymphomanie [nɛ̃fɔmani] *s.f.* nymphomania.
nystagmus [nistagmys] *s.m.* nystagmus.

O

O, o [o] *s.m.* the letter O, o.
ô [o] *interj.* O!, Oh!
oasien, -ne [ɔazjɛ̃] *adj.*, *s.m.f.* (inhabitant) of an oasis.
oasis [ɔazis] *s.f.* or *m.* (lit. & fig.) oasis.
obédience [ɔbedjɑ̃s] *s.f.* obedience; *lettre d'*~, teaching-certificate (granted by religious superior to member of a teaching order).
obéir [ɔbeir] *v.i.* to obey, to be obedient (*à*, to); to yield (to), to comply (with); to be pliant, to bend; *se faire* ~ *de*, to get obedience from; ~ *au mors, à la barre*, to answer the bit, the helm.
obéissance [ɔbeisɑ̃s] *s.f.* obedience; dutifulness; allegiance; dominion, authority; pliancy; *par* ~ *à*, in obedience to; *jurer* ~ *à*, to swear allegiance to; *sous l'*~ *de*, under the authority of; ⚠ not 'obeisance'.
obéissant, -e [ɔbeisɑ̃] *adj.* obedient, dutiful, pliant, docile; *peu* ~, disobedient; *votre fils* ~, your dutiful son; *nature* ~*e*, pliable disposition.
obélisque [ɔbelisk] *s.m.* obelisk.
obérer [ɔbere] *v.t.* to involve in debt, to burden; *être fort obéré*, to be heavily in debt; **s'**~ *v.refl.* to involve oneself in debt, to run into debt.
obèse [ɔbɛz] *adj.* corpulent, fat, stout, obese.
obésité [ɔbezite] *s.f.* corpulence, obesity.
obier [ɔbje] *s.m.* (bot.) guelder-rose.
obit [ɔbit] *s.m.* (Cath. liturg.) obit, memorial service.
obituaire [ɔbitɥɛr] *adj.* (eccles.) obituary; ~ *s.m.* obituary list, register of deaths.
objecter [ɔbʒɛkte] *v.t.* to object (*que*, that); to put forward as an objection, to use as a pretext or excuse; *on lui objecta sa jeunesse*, they objected to him on account of his youth.
objecteur [ɔbʒɛktœr] *s.m.* objector; ~ *de conscience*, conscientious objector.
objecti-f, -ve [ɔbʒɛktif] *adj.* objective; ~**f** *s.m.* objective, object, aim, target; (opt.) object--glass, objective; (photo.) lens; ~**vement** [ɔbʒɛktivmɑ̃] *adv.* objectively.
objection [ɔbʒɛksjɔ̃] *s.f.* objection; *faire des* ~*s à*, to raise objections to, to object to; *aller au--devant d'une* ~, to meet an objection; *je n'y vois pas d'*~, I see no objection (to that); (fam.) I am agreeable.
objectiver [ɔbʒɛktive] *v.t.* **1.** to objectify; **2.** to express, to exteriorize, (ideas, feelings, etc.).
objectivisme [ɔbʒɛktivism] *s.m.* objectivism.
objectivité [ɔbʒɛktivite] *s.f.* objectivity, objectiveness.
objet [ɔbʒɛ] *s.m.* **1.** object, thing, article, matter, subject; *grandir les* ~*s*, to magnify things; ~*s de première nécessité*, articles of everyday use; *un* ~ *d'art*, a work of art; ~ *de risée*, laughing-stock; **2.** (phil.) object; **3.** object, purpose, aim, end; subject, subject-matter, theme; *sans* ~, without an object; *il avait pour* ~, his object was; he aimed at; *ces choses ont toutes le même* ~, these things all aim at the same object; *faire l'*~ *d'un entretien*, to form the subject of a conversation; **4.** (gram.) object, complement.
objurgations [ɔbʒyrgɑsjɔ̃] *s.f.pl.* remonstrances, objurgations.
oblat [ɔbla] *s.m.* oblate.
oblation [ɔblɑsjɔ̃] *s.f.* oblation, offering.
obligataire [ɔbligatɛr] *s.m.f.* (law, fin.) bond--holder, debenture-holder.
obligation [ɔbligɑsjɔ̃] *s.f.* **1.** obligation, bounden duty; *c'est une* ~ *pour vous de le faire*, it is your bounden duty to do it; *avoir des* ~*s à*, to be under an obligation to; to be beholden to; *je vous en aurai une grande* ~, I shall be greatly obliged to you; *malgré les* ~*s que je vous ai*, much as I am obliged to you; *remplir ses* ~*s*, to fulfil one's obligations; **2.** (law) recognizance, obligation, bond; *souscrire une* ~ *en due forme*, to enter into recognizances; **3.** (fin.) bond, debenture, preference share.
obligatoire [ɔbligatwar] *adj.* compulsory, binding, incumbent, obligatory; (fam.) inevitable; *acte* ~, act of obligation; ~**ment** [ɔbligatwarmɑ̃] *adv.* compulsorily; (fam.) inevitably.
obligé, -e [ɔbliʒe] *adj.* **1.** obliged, bound; *vous y êtes* ~, you are bound to do it; *je suis son* ~, I am in his debt; **2.** necessary, indispensable; inevitable; **3.** grateful, obliged, beholden; *être bien* ~ *à qn. de qch.*, to be greatly obliged to s.o. for sth.
obligé, -e [ɔbliʒe] *s.m.f.* obligee, debtor, one under an obligation, one under the necessity (of doing sth.); *un de vos* ~*s*, a person you have obliged, one who is under an obligation to you.
obligeamment [ɔbliʒamɑ̃] *adv.* obligingly, kindly, courteously.
obligeance [ɔbliʒɑ̃s] *s.f.* obligingness, kindness;

d'une extrême ~, most obliging; *ayez l'~ de*, be so kind as to, be good enough to.
obligeant, -e [ɔbliʒɑ̃] *adj.* obliging, kind (*pour*, to); *paroles ~es*, kind words.
obliger [ɔbliʒe] *v.t.* **1.** to oblige (*à*, *de*, to), to compel, to bind, to call upon; *votre devoir vous y oblige*, you are in duty bound to do it; *votre intérêt vous y oblige*, it is in your interest to do so; **2.** to oblige, to please, to gratify, to do a service to; *vous m'obligerez en faisant cela immédiatement*, you will oblige me by doing that immediately.
oblique [ɔblik] *adj.* oblique, slanting; (fig.) indirect, underhand, oblique; (gram.) oblique; *conduite ~*, crooked behaviour; double-dealing; **~ment** [ɔblikmɑ̃] *adv.* obliquely, slantwise; (fig.) indirectly, in an underhand way.
obliquer [ɔblike] *v.i.* to turn, to move in an oblique direction, to change one's direction or opinion; *~ à droite*, to bear to the right, to turn or swerve to the right.
obliquité [ɔblikɥite] *s.f.* obliquity, obliqueness, slant; (fig.) insincerity, crookedness.
oblitération [ɔbliterɑsjɔ̃] *s.f.* obliteration; cancellation (of stamps, etc.); *cachet d'~*, postmark.
oblitérer [ɔblitere] *v.t.* to obliterate, to destroy, to wipe out, to cancel (stamps, etc.); **s'~** *v.refl.* to become obliterated, to disappear.
oblong, -ue [ɔblɔ̃] *adj.* oblong.
obnubiler [ɔbnybile] *v.t.* (fig.) to cloud, to obscure.
obole [ɔbɔl] *s.f.* obol, obole, obolus; (fig.) farthing, mite, small gift or contribution; *l'~ de la veuve*, the widow's mite; *n'avoir pas une ~*, not to have a penny to one's name; *je n'en donnerais pas une ~*, I would not give a straw for it; *je vous apporte mon ~*, here is my small contribution.
obscène [ɔpsɛn] *adj.* lewd, obscene, filthy; ⚠ not 'obscene' in sense of 'offensive to the senses'.
obscénité [ɔpsenite] *s.f.* obscenity, obsceneness, lewdness, lubricity, filthy talk or remark.
obscur, -e [ɔpskyr] *adj.* dark, dim, dingy, gloomy; (fig.) obscure, abstruse, not clear; hidden, unnoticed, humble, doubtful; *faire ~*, to be dark; to grow dark; *naissance ~e*, humble birth; *clair-~*, chiaroscuro, light and shade.
obscurantisme [ɔpskyrɑ̃tism] *s.m.* obscurantism.
obscurantiste [ɔpskyrɑ̃tist] *adj.*, *s.m.f.* obscurant, obscurantist.
obscurcir [ɔpskyrsir] *v.t.* to obscure, to cloud, to darken, to dim; *le chagrin a obscurci sa raison*, sorrow has clouded (or dimmed) his mind; **s'~** *v.refl.* to grow dark, obscure, or dim, to cloud (over).
obscurcissement [ɔpskyrsismɑ̃] *s.m.* dimming, darkening, obscuration.
obscurément [ɔpskyremɑ̃] *adv.* dimly, darkly, obscurely, vaguely; humbly.
obscurité [ɔpskyrite] *s.f.* darkness, obscurity, gloom; dimness; (fig.) obscurity, unintelligibility, humbleness; *dans une complète ~*, in utter darkness; *dans l'~*, in the dark; *vivre dans l'~*, to live in obscurity; *l'~ de sa naissance*, the humbleness of his birth; *un discours rempli d'~s*, an unintelligible speech.
obsécration [ɔpsekrɑsjɔ̃] *s.f.* obsecration.
obsédé, -e [ɔpsede] *s.m.f.* one suffering from an obsession.
obséder [ɔpsede] *v.t.* to beset, to haunt; to obsess, to torment; to pester, to importune, to prey upon; *obsédé par*, obsessed by.
obsèques [ɔpsɛk] *s.f.pl.* obsequies, funeral.
obséquieu-x, -se [ɔpsekjø] *adj.* obsequious, fawning; **~sement** [ɔpsekjøzmɑ̃] *adv.* obsequiously.
obséquiosité [ɔpsekjozite] *s.f.* obsequiousness.
observable [ɔpsɛrvabl] *adj.* observable.
observance [ɔpsɛrvɑ̃s] *s.f.* observance, rule; keeping or performance of a law, custom, duty, or ritual.
observat-eur, -rice [ɔpsɛrvatœr] *s.m.f.* observer, watcher, spy, spectator; looker-on; *adj.* observant, observing; heedful, attentive; *peu ~eur*, unobservant.
observation [ɔpsɛrvɑsjɔ̃] *s.f.* observation, look-out; observance; (naut.) sight, watch; objection, remark, notice, hint, slight reproof; *faire une ~*, to make an observation, to observe; (astron.) to take an observation; *faire une ~ à*, to reprimand slightly, to admonish, to give a warning to; *assez d'~s!*, that will do!; (mil.) *corps d'~*, reconnaissance corps; *être en ~*, (i.) to be on the look-out; (ii.) to be placed under observation.
observatoire [ɔpsɛrvatwar] *s.m.* observatory.
observer [ɔpsɛrve] *v.t.* **1.** to observe, to examine, to watch, to look at; to remark, to notice, to perceive; *je lui ai fait ~ que*, I pointed out to him that; I reminded him that; **2.** to comply with; to fulfil; to obey, to keep, to maintain; *~ le silence*, to keep silent; **s'~** *v.refl.* to be on one's guard, to behave cautiously; to observe each other; to be observed, to occur; *cela s'observe fréquemment*, that occurs frequently; one often sees it.
obsession [ɔpsesjɔ̃] *s.f.* obsession; possession; importunity; *je ne puis me délivrer de cette ~*, I cannot rid myself of this obsession.
obsidienne [ɔpsidjɛn] *s.f.* (geol.) obsidian.
obsidional, -e, (aux) [ɔpsidjɔnal] *adj.* pertaining to a siege; *fièvre ~e*, siege mentality; (psychol.) *délire ~*, persecution mania.
obsolète [ɔpsɔlɛt] *adj.* obsolete.
obstacle [ɔpstakl] *s.m.* obstacle, hindrance, obstruction, impediment; bar; *mettre* or *faire ~ à*, to hinder; to stand in the way of; *course d'~s*, obstacle race.
obstétrical, -e, (aux) [ɔpstetrikal] *adj.* obstetric(al).
obstétrique [ɔpstetrik] *adj.* obstetric(al); *~ s.f.* obstetrics.
obstination [ɔpstinɑsjɔ̃] *s.f.* obstinacy, stubbornness, persistency, self-will, wilfulness.
obstiné, -e [ɔpstine] *adj.* obstinate, stubborn, self-willed, wilful, persistent, unremitting; **~ment** [ɔpstinemɑ̃] *adv.* obstinately, stubbornly, persistently.
(s')obstiner [ɔpstine] *v.refl.* to be obstinate, to persist; *il s'obstine à penser que*, he persists in thinking that; *il s'obstine dans son silence*, he remains obstinately silent.
obstructi-f, -ve [ɔpstryktif] *adj.* obstructive; (med.) obstruent.
obstruction [ɔpstryksjɔ̃] *s.f.* obstruction, obstructive tactics, stoppage, blocking.
obstructionnisme [ɔpstryksjɔnism] *s.m.* obstructionism.
obstructionniste [ɔpstryksjɔnist] *adj.* obstructive; *~ s.m.f.* obstructionist.
obstruer [ɔpstrɥe] *v.t.* to obstruct, to stop up, to block up, to choke, to be in the way of.
obtempérer [ɔptɑ̃pere] *v.t.* to obey, to submit (*à*, to), to comply (*à*, with); *~ à un ordre*, to obey an order.
obtenir [ɔptənir] *v.t.* to obtain, to get, to secure, to gain, to procure, to come by, to achieve; *faire ~ à qn.*, to get, to procure, for s.o.
obtention [ɔptɑ̃sjɔ̃] *s.f.* obtainment, obtaining.
obturat-eur, -rice [ɔptyratœr] *adj.* stopping, closing; **~eur** *s.m.* (anat.) obturator; (photo.) shutter; (techn.) stop-valve, stop-cock; throttle, choke; seal; puncture stop; breech-plug; *~eur de joint*, gasket, seal.

obturation [ɔptyrɑsjɔ̃] *s.f.* obturation, stopping--up, shutting; (dentistry) stopping, filling.
obturer [ɔptyre] *v.t.* to obturate, to stop up; to stop, to fill, (a tooth); to close, to seal.
obtus, -e [ɔpty] *adj.* obtuse, dull, blunt; *à angle* ~, obtuse-angled; *d'esprit* ~, slow-witted, dull-minded, stupid, obtuse.
obus [oby] *s.m.* shell; ~ *à balles*, shrapnel-shell.
obusier [ɔbyzje] *s.m.* howitzer, field howitzer.
obvenir [ɔbvənir] *v.i.* (law) to escheat, to revert by escheat.
obvers, obverse [ɔbvɛr] *s.m.* obverse, face, (of coin).
obvier [ɔbvje] *v.t.* ~ *à*, to obviate, to prevent; ~ *à un inconvénient*, to eliminate a drawback.
oc [ɔk] *adv.* (obs.) yes; *langue d'*~, the dialect (spoken south of the Loire in the Middle Ages) in which this affirmative adv. was used; langue d'oc.
ocarina [ɔkarina] *s.m.* (mus.) ocarina.
occase [ɔkɑz] *s.f.* (pop.) occasion, opportunity.
occasion [ɔkazjɔ̃] *s.f.* occasion, opportunity, suitable juncture; (good) bargain; cause, reason, motive; *à l'*~, if need be, eventually, (up)on occasion; *à l'*~ *de*, with regard to, as a result of, in celebration of; *d'*~, second-hand; *en toute* ~, on all occasions, at all times; whenever need arises; *dans quelle* ~*?*, in what circumstances?; *être l'*~ *de*, to bring about, to cause; *dans les grandes* ~*s*, on special occasions; *profiter d'une* ~, to improve the opportunity, to get a bargain; *saisir l'*~ *aux cheveux*, to seize the opportunity.
occasionnel, -le [ɔkazjɔnɛl] *adj.* occasional; chance, providing cause or opportunity (*de*, for); ~**lement** [ɔkazjɔnɛlmɑ̃] *adv.* occasionally, accidentally, by chance.
occasionner [ɔkazjɔne] *v.t.* to occasion, to cause, to bring about.
occident [ɔksidɑ̃] *s.m.* Occident, West; *d'*~, Western, Occidental.
occidental, -e, (aux) [ɔksidɑ̃tal] *adj.* Occidental, Western, west; *s.m.f.* Occidental.
occidentalisation [ɔksidɑ̃talizɑsjɔ̃] *s.f.* westernization.
occidentaliser [ɔksidɑ̃talize] *v.t.* to westernize; **s'**~ *v.refl.* to become westernized.
occipital, -e, (aux) [ɔksipital] *adj.* (anat.) occipital.
occiput [ɔksipyt] *s.m.* (anat.) occiput.
occire [ɔksir] *v.t.* to kill, to slay.
occlure [ɔklyr] *v.t.* (med., surg.) to occlude, to stop up.
occlusi-f, -ve [ɔklyzif] *adj.*, ~**ve** *s.f.* (phon.) occlusive.
occlusion [ɔklyzjɔ̃] *s.f.* occlusion, shutting up, shutting off, complete closure.
occultation [ɔkyltɑsjɔ̃] *s.f.* **1.** (astron.) occultation; **2.** occulting (of lighthouse beam, etc.).
occulte [ɔkylt] *adj.* occult, hidden, secret, esoteric, recondite.
occultisme [ɔkyltism] *s.m.* occultism, science of occult things.
occupant, -e [ɔkypɑ̃] *adj.* **1.** occupying; engrossing; **2.** (law) in charge, (of solicitor in case) acting; *s.m.f.* occupier, occupant; *le droit du premier* ~, the rights of the first settler or occupier; ~ *s.m.* (mil.) occupying forces.
occupation [ɔkypɑsjɔ̃] *s.f.* **1.** occupation, pursuit; employment, business, work; *être sans* ~, (i.) to have nothing to do; (ii.) to be unemployed; **2.** (law) occupancy; **3.** (mil.) occupation, taking possession of or holding a country or district.
occupé, -e [ɔkype] *adj.* occupied, busy, engaged, preoccupied, engrossed (*de*, with); (of seat, etc.) taken.
occuper [ɔkype] *v.t.* to occupy, to take up, to employ; to engross, to preoccupy; to take possession of (a country, town, etc.); to reside in; **s'**~ *v.refl.* to be busy, to trouble (oneself); *s'*~ *de*, to see to, to attend to, to concern oneself with, to be concerned with or engaged on, to turn one's mind to, to engage in, to spend one's time (doing); (obs.) *s'*~ *à*, to be engaged in, to be busy with, to put in time (doing), to apply oneself to.
occurrence [ɔkyrɑ̃s] *s.f.* occurrence, happening, event; *en l'*~, in this case.
occurrent, -e [ɔkyrɑ̃] *adj.* (eccles.) occurrent.
O.C.D.E. [osedee] abbrev. *Organisation de coopération et de développement économiques*, O.E.C.D.
océan [ɔseɑ̃] *s.m.* ocean; (fig.) oceans, immense expanse or quantity.
océanide [ɔseanid] *s.f.* (myth.) oceanid, sea nymph.
Océanie [ɔseani] *s.f.* (geog.) Oceania.
océanien, -ne [ɔseanjɛ̃] *adj.*, *s.m.f.* Oceanian, South Sea Island(er).
océanique [ɔseanik] *adj.* oceanic.
océano-graphe [ɔseanɔgraf] *s.m.f.* oceanographer; ~**graphie** [ɔseanɔgrafi] *s.f.* oceanography; ~**graphique** [ɔseanɔgrafik] *adj.* oceanographic.
ocelle [ɔsɛl] *s.m.* (zool.) ocellus.
ocellé, -e [ɔsele] *adj.* ocellated, ocellate.
ocelot [ɔslo] *s.m.* (zool.) ocelot; ocelot (fur).
ocre [ɔkr] *s.f.* (min.) ochre; ochre (pigment); ~ *s.m., adj.invar.* ochre (colour); ochre(-coloured).
ocreu-x, -se [ɔkrø] *adj.* ochreous, ochrous, ochry.
octaèdre [ɔktaɛdr] *s.m.* (geom.) octahedron.
octaédrique [ɔktaedrik] *adj.* octahedral.
octane [ɔktan] *s.m.* (chem.) octane.
octant [ɔktɑ̃] *s.m.* (geom., techn.) octant; (naut.) octant (instrument).
octante [ɔktɑ̃t] *adj.* (in Switzerland) eighty.
octave [ɔktav] *s.f.* **1.** (mus.) octave, octave interval; octave-flute, piccolo; **2.** (Cath. church) octave.
octavier [ɔktavje] *v.t.i.* (mus.) to play an octave higher.
octavin [ɔktavɛ̃] *s.m.* (mus.) octave-flute, piccolo.
octidi [ɔktidi] *s.m.* (hist.) Octidi (eighth day of *décade* in Fr. Republican Calendar).
octobre [ɔktɔbr] *s.m.* October.
octogénaire [ɔktɔʒenɛr] *adj.*, *s.m.f.* octogenarian.
octogonal, -e, (aux) [ɔktɔgɔnal] *adj.* octagonal.
octogone [ɔktɔgɔn] *s.m.* (geom.) octagon; ~ *adj.* octagonal.
octosyllabe [ɔktɔsil(l)ab], **octosyllabique** [ɔktɔsil(l)abik] *adj.* octosyllabic.
octroi [ɔktrwa] *s.m.* **1.** grant, concession, privilege, granting of concession; **2.** town-due, toll, city-toll, duty; **3.** toll-house, toll-office.
octroyer [ɔktrwaje] *v.t.* to grant; to concede; **s'**~ *v.refl.* to allow oneself.
octuor [ɔktɥɔr] *s.m.* (mus.) octet.
octuple [ɔktypl] *adj.* octuple, eightfold.
octupler [ɔktyple] *v.t.* to multiply by eight.
oculaire [ɔkylɛr] *adj.* ocular; eye-; *témoin* ~, eye-witness; ~ *s.m.* eyeglass, eyepiece, ocular.
oculariste [ɔkylarist] *s.m.f.* ocularist; maker of artificial eyes.
oculiste [ɔkylist] *s.m.f.* oculist, ophthalmic surgeon.
odalisque [ɔdalisk] *s.f.* odalisque.
ode [ɔd] *s.f.* ode.
odelette [ɔdlɛt] *s.f.* little ode.
odéon [ɔdeɔ̃] *s.m.* **1.** (Gr. ant.) odeum; **2.** Odéon (name of a theatre in Paris).
odeur [ɔdœr] *s.f.* odour; smell; scent; perfume; fragrance; (fig.) repute; *il n'est pas en* ~ *de sainteté auprès de son curé*, he is not in his curé's

good graces; he does not stand very high in the opinion of his curé.
odieu-x, -se [ɔdjø] *adj.* odious, hateful; invidious; **~x** *s.m.* odium, odiousness; **~sement** [ɔdjøzmɑ̃] *adv.* odiously, hatefully, invidiously.
odomètre [ɔdɔmɛtr] *s.m.* odometer.
odontalgie [ɔdɔ̃talʒi] *s.f.* toothache.
odontologie [ɔdɔ̃tɔlɔʒi] *s.f.* odontology, dentistry.
odorant, -e [ɔdɔrɑ̃] *adj.* odorous, fragrant, scented, sweet-scented, sweet-smelling, sweet.
odorat [ɔdɔra] *s.m.* smell, sense of smell.
odoriférant, -e [ɔdɔriferɑ̃] *adj.* odoriferous, scented, sweet-smelling.
odyssée [ɔdise] *s.f.* odyssey, narrative of adventures; eventful travels, series of wanderings.
O.E.C.E. [oesee] abbrev. *Organisation européenne de coopération économique*, E.E.C. (formerly O.E.E.C.).
œcolog-ie [ekɔlɔʒi] *s.f.* ecology; **~ique** [ekɔlɔʒik] *adj.* ecological.
œcumén-ique [ekymenik] *adj.* ecumenical; **~isme** [ekymenism] *s.m.* ecumenism, ecumenicalism.
œdémateu-x, -se [edematø] *adj.* (med.) oedematous.
œdème [edɛm] *s.m.* (med.) oedema.
œdicnème [ediknɛm] *s.m.* (ornith.) great plover.
Œdipe [edip] *s.m.* Oedipus; (psychol.) *complexe d'~*, Oedipus complex
œil [œj] (pl. **yeux** [jø]) *s.m.* eye; sight; spy-hole (in door), hole (in cheese, bread, etc.), eyelet; (hort.) eye; lustre (of gems); bubble, speck; face (of letters); *~ électrique*, photo-electric cell; *~-de-bœuf*, (i.) bull's-eye; (ii.) oval window; *~-de-chat*, cat's-eye (stone); (naut.) *~-de-pie*, eyelet (in sail); *avoir des yeux d'aigle*, to be eagle-eyed; *clin d'~*, wink, twinkling of an eye; *coup d'~*, glance; peep; survey; view; *au premier coup d'~*, at first sight, at a glance; *à vue d'~*, visibly, apace; *avoir l'~*, to be wide awake, to be on one's guard; *risquer un ~*, to peep out; (pop.) *à l'~*, on tick; gratis; without paying; on the free list; *avoir qn. à l'~*, *avoir l'~ sur qn.*, to have one's eye on s.o., to keep a close watch on s.o.; *avoir l'~ à*, to mind; (fam.) *avoir de l'~*, to have a good eye (for choosing sth.); *s'en battre l'~*, not to care a rap for it; *donner dans l'~ à qn.*, to dazzle s.o., to take someone's fancy; *faire de l'~ à*, to ogle, to make eyes at; *se fourrer le doigt dans l'~*, to be quite out; to deceive oneself blindly; to be grossly mistaken; *voir d'un bon ~*, to look favourably upon; *mauvais ~*, evil eye; *avoir le mauvais ~*, to bring bad luck; *avoir le compas dans l'~*, to be good at judging distances, etc.; *ouvrez l'~, et le bon!*, look out!; *un ~ au beurre noir, un ~ poché*, a black eye; *à l'~ nu*, with the naked eye; *tourner de l'~*, (i.) to be seasick; to be sick; to faint; (ii.) to die; *~ de perdrix*, (i.) corn between the toes; soft corn; (ii.) kind of huckaback material, diaper; *entre quatre (z')yeux*, privately, between you and me and the gatepost; *par-dessus les yeux*, over head and ears; *pour ses beaux yeux*, gratuitously, for love; *il n'a pas froid aux yeux*, he is plucky; he is not a coward; he is not short of cheek; *fermer les yeux sur*, to shut one's eyes to; to wink at; to tolerate; to connive at; *faire les yeux doux à*, to look lovingly at, to ogle, to gloat over; to give the glad eye to; *à mes yeux*, to my mind; *ouvrir de grands yeux*, to stand staring, to look astonished; to stare in astonishment; *tout voir par ses propres yeux*, to keep a personal check on everything; *il n'a d'yeux que pour elle*, he has eyes only for her; *je l'ai regardé dans le blanc des yeux*, I looked him full in the face; *cela saute aux yeux*, that is obvious; that's as clear as noonday; *jeter les yeux sur*, to cast one's eyes on; to have a look at; (fig.) to select; *faire des yeux furieux*, to cast furious looks (*à*, upon); *cela coûte les yeux de la tête*, it costs a mint of money; *elle n'a pas les yeux dans sa poche*, she is wide awake, clear-sighted, observant; *je suis tout yeux*, I am all eyes, expectant, keenly attentive; *couver des yeux*, to look covetously, greedily, or passionately at; *voir avec les yeux de la foi*, believe blindly; *je l'ai vu de mes yeux*, I have seen it with my own eyes; *voir tout par les yeux de qn.*, to see everything through someone's eyes; *loin des yeux, loin du cœur*, out of sight, out of mind; *en mettre plein les yeux à qn.*, to try to deceive s.o.; *yeux bridés*, slit eyes, slanting eyes.
œillade [œjad] *s.f.* glance, sly look, wink, ogle, leer.
œillère [œjɛr] *s.f.* **1.** (*dent*) ~, eye-tooth; **2.** blinker; eye-flap; (fig.) *avoir des ~s*, to be narrow-minded or prejudiced; **3.** eye-bath.
œillet [œjɛ] *s.m.* **1.** eyelet, eyelet-hole; **2.** (bot.) pink, carnation; *~ de poète*, sweet-william; *~ d'Inde*, African marigold; *~ des prés*, ragged robin.
œilleton [œjtɔ̃] *s.m.* **1.** (hort.) sucker, offshoot; layer; eye-bud; **2.** eyepiece (of telescope, etc.); **~nage** [œjtɔnaʒ] *s.m.* (hort.) layering; de-budding; **~ner** [œjtɔne] *v.t.* (hort.) to layer; to de-bud.
œillette [œjɛt] *s.f.* (bot.) oil-poppy, white poppy; opium-poppy; *huile d'~*, poppy-seed oil.
œnanthe [enɑ̃t] *s.f.* (bot.) Oenanthe.
œno-logie [enɔlɔʒi] *s.f.* oenology; science of wine-making; **~métrie** [enɔmetri] *s.f.* oenometry, measurement of alcohol content of wine.
œsophage [ezɔfaʒ] *s.m.* (anat.) oesophagus, gullet.
œsophagien, -ne [ezɔfaʒjɛ̃] *adj.* oesophageal, pertaining to the oesophagus.
œsophagite [ezɔfaʒit] *s.f.* (pathol.) oesophagitis, inflammation of the oesophagus.
œstral, -e, (aux) [ɛstral] *adj.* (zool.) oestrous.
œstre [ɛstr] *s.m.* (ent.) gadfly, bot-fly.
œstrogène [ɛstrɔʒɛn] *s.m.* (biol.) oestrogen.
œstrus [ɛstrys] *s.m.* (physiol.) oestrus (cycle); rut.
œuf [œf] (pl. **-s** [ø]) *s.m.* egg; (of fish) roe, spawn; egg-shaped object; *~ du jour*, new-laid egg; *~s en poudre*, dried eggs; *~ à la coque*, (soft-)boiled egg; *~s dur*, hard-boiled eggs; *~ poché*, poached egg; *~s brouillés*, scrambled eggs; *~ de Pâques*, Easter egg; Easter gift; *~ clair*, wind-egg; *blanc d'~*, white of egg; *jaune d'~*, egg-yolk; (proverb) *qui vole un ~ vole un bœuf*, he who steals an ounce will steal a pound; *marcher sur des ~s*, to walk or skate on thin ice; *tondre un ~*, to skin a flint; *mettre tous ses ~s dans le même panier*, to have or put all one's eggs in one basket; *plein comme un ~*, chock-full.
œufrier [œfrije] *s.m.* egg-boiler; egg-stand.
œuvé, -e [œve] *adj.* (of fish) hard-roed.
œuvre [œvr] *s.f.* **1.** work, labour; *à l'~!*, to work!; *se mettre à l'~*, to set to work; *faire ~ de*, to behave as; *faire ~ d'ami*, to act or behave as a friend; **2.** piece of work; production of the mind; *fils de ses ~s*, self-made man; *à l'~ on connaît l'artisan* (or *l'ouvrier*), a man is known by what he does, the workman is known by his work; *les plus belles ~s de Chopin*, Chopin's finest compositions; *être à l'~*, to be busy with or engaged on something; **3.** moral deed, act of charity; *~s pies*, acts of piety; **4.** charitable society, social work; charity committee; **5.** fabric, revenue, plate, (of a church); *banc d'~*, churchwardens' pew; **6.** (jewellery) mounting, setting; *mettre en ~*, to work up; to set (a jewel); (fig.) to carry out (an idea); to set going; *mettre*

tout en ~, to leave no stone unturned; **7.** (naut.) ~*s mortes*, topsides, upper works; (naut.) ~*s vives*, bottom, quick works; ~ *s.m.* **1.** the complete works of a great author, painter, musician, etc.; *tout l'*~ *de Chopin*, the whole of Chopin's compositions or works; **2.** (arch.) *le gros* ~, the foundations, the main structure; *escalier dans* ~, inside staircase; *hors d'*~, projecting, separate, from the main structure; *à pied d'*~, at hand, on site; *reprendre en sous-*~, to underpin; **3.** (alchemy) *le grand* ~, the search for the philosophers' stone.

œuvrer [œvre] *v.i.* to work or to devote oneself to a cause.

offensant, -e [ɔfɑ̃sɑ̃] *adj.* offensive, insulting.

offense [ɔfɑ̃s] *s.f.* **1.** offence, abuse, insult; **2.** transgression, offence, trespass, wrong; *pardonnez-nous nos* ~*s*, forgive us our trespasses.

offensé, -e [ɔfɑ̃se] *adj.* offended; *s.m.f.* offended party, injured party.

offenser [ɔfɑ̃se] *v.t.* **1.** to offend, to shock, to injure; to give offence to; to be offensive to, to be injurious or detrimental to; *soit dit sans vouloir vous* ~, no offence meant; no offence, I hope; *il n'y a que la vérité qui offense*, the greater the truth, the greater the libel; **2.** to offend against, to sin against, to trespass against, to transgress; **s'**~ *v.refl.* to take offence, to be offended (*de*, with); to take exception, to be angry.

offenseur [ɔfɑ̃sœr] *s.m.* offender, one who causes offence; attacker; ⚠ not 'offender' in sense 'criminal'.

offensi-f, -ve [ɔfɑ̃sif] *adj.* offensive, aggressive, attacking; ~**ve** *s.f.* offensive; *prendre l'*~*ve*, to take the offensive; to attack.

offert, -e [ɔfɛr] *p.p.* of OFFRIR.

offerte [ɔfɛrt], **offertoire** [ɔfɛrtwar] *s.f.* offertory.

office[1] [ɔfis] *s.m.* **1.** divine service; mass; *l'*~ *des morts*, burial service, office for the dead, prayers for the dead; **2.** office, post, duty, functions, turn; agency; department; board; *d'*~, (i.) in virtue of one's office; (ii.) officially; (iii.) of one's own accord; *faire* ~ *de*, to serve as, to act as; *bons* ~*s*, good turn, service, good offices; *exercer un* ~, to hold an office.

office[2] [ɔfis] *s.f.* or *m.* pantry, offices; (fig.) servants' hall or room, servants' quarters, the servants collectively; *ragots d'*~, servants' gossip.

official [ɔfisjal] *s.m.* official (presiding officer of an ecclesiastical court); ~**ité** [ɔfisjalite] *s.f.* officiality, ecclesiastical court.

officiant, -e [ɔfisjɑ̃] *adj.* officiating; *s.m.f.* officiating priest or nun.

officiel, -le [ɔfisjɛl] *adj.* official, officially confirmed, authorized; *la nouvelle a été* ~*le vers minuit*, the news was confirmed about midnight; (fam.) ~*!*, definite!, absolutely certain!; (pej.) *la version* ~*le de l'incident*, the official (but not necessarily true) version of the incident; ~ *s.m.* **1.** official; **2.** *l'Officiel* (=*le Journal* ~), official record of laws, government business, etc.; ~**lement** [ɔfisjɛlmɑ̃] *adv.* officially, formally.

officier [ofisje] *v.i.* (eccles.) to officiate.

officier [ofisje] *s.m.* officer; *être* ~, to be an officer; (mil.) ~ *général*, general officer; ~ *supérieur*, field officer; ~ *de compagnie* or *de corps*, company officer; ~ *d'ordonnance*, orderly officer; *sous-*~, non-commissioned officer; (hist.) ~ *de bouche, du gobelet*, officer of the Household; (naut.) ~ *de port*, harbour-master; ~ *de marine*, naval officer; ~ *général*, flag-officer; ~ *de quart*, officer of the watch; ~ *de santé*, surgeon (who has not taken all examinations); ~ *d'état civil* registrar (of births, deaths, etc.).

officieu-x, -se [ɔfisjø] *adj.* **1.** unofficial, semi--official, informal; **2.** obliging, officious, meddlesome; ~**sement** [ɔfisjøzmɑ̃] *adv.* **1.** informally; **2.** officiously.

officinal, -e, (**aux**) [ɔfisinal] *adj.* officinal, used in medicine.

officine [ɔfisin] *s.f.* **1.** laboratory; **2.** (fig.) a place where mysterious (political or other) things are concocted; (fam.) den, hotbed.

offrande [ɔfrɑ̃d] *s.f.* offering, oblation; present.

offrant [ɔfrɑ̃] *s.m.* bidder; *au plus* ~, to the highest bidder.

offre [ɔfr] *s.f.* offer, tender; *faire une* ~ *de*, to make an offer or tender of; *l'*~ *et la demande*, supply and demand.

offrir [ɔfrir] *v.t.* **1.** to offer, to present, to hold out, to proffer; *ceci n'offre pas de difficultés*, this presents no difficulties; **2.** to afford, to provide, to exhibit, to expose to view; *cette campagne offre des aspects agréables*, this countryside presents pleasant aspects; **3.** to bid; **s'**~ *v.refl.* to propose oneself, to present itself, to offer; *le premier chemin qui s'offre*, the first path you come to; *jamais pareille occasion ne s'offrira*, you will never have such an opportunity again.

offset [ɔfsɛt] *s.m., adj.invar.* (print.) offset.

offusquer [ɔfyske] *v.t.* **1.** (obs.) to cloud, to obscure; to dazzle, to prevent from seeing; *les larmes m'offusquaient la vue*, tears clouded my vision, I couldn't see for weeping; **2.** to offend, to cause offence to; **s'**~ *v.refl.* to be offended or shocked, to take exception, to take offence.

ogival, -e, (**aux**) [ɔʒival] *adj.* (arch.) ogival, Gothic.

ogive [ɔʒiv] *s.f.* **1.** (arch.) ogive, diagonal groin or rib of vault; Gothic arch; *en* ~, shaped as a pointed arch; ogival; **2.** (mil.) cap (of shell); nose-cone (of rocket).

ogre [ɔgr] *s.m.* ogre; man-eating giant; (fig.) blusterer, brute; *manger comme un* ~, to eat like a wolf; ~**sse** [ɔgrɛs] *s.f.* ogress.

oh [o] *interj.* oh!, o!, ho!, indeed!

ohé [ɔe] *interj.* halloo!, hi!, I say!; (naut.) ahoy!; ~ *du canot!*, *du navire!*, boat ahoy!, ship ahoy!

ohm [om] *s.m.* ohm, unit of electrical resistance; ~**mètre** [ommɛtr] *s.m.* ohmmeter.

oïdium [ɔidjɔm] *s.m.* oidium, vine-mildew.

oie [wa] *s.f.* goose; (fig.) goose, silly girl; (mil.) *pas de l'*~, goose-step; *patte d'*~, (bot.) goose--foot; (fig.) (i.) crow's foot (wrinkle), (ii.) crossing, intersection.

oignon [ɔɲɔ̃] *s.m.* **1.** onion; (bot.) bulb, bulbous root; *en rang d'*~*s*, in a row; (fig., fam.) *aux petits* ~*s*, perfect, just the job; *occupe-toi de tes* ~*s*, mind your own business; **2.** bunion; **3.** large watch, turnip.

oignonière [ɔɲɔnjɛr] *s.f.* onion-bed.

oïl [ɔjl] *adv. langue d'*~, the old French language spoken north of the Loire; langue d'oïl.

oindre [wɛ̃dr] *v.t. irreg.* to anoint, to impregnate, to imbue; *oignez vilain, il vous poindra*, save a thief from the gallows, and he will be the first to cut your throat.

oint, -e [wɛ̃] *adj.*, ~ *s.m.* anointed.

oiseau (pl. **-x**) [wazo] *s.m.* **1.** bird; fowl; hawk; *à vol d'*~, as the crow flies; *comme l'*~ *sur la branche*, temporarily, in an unsettled way, always on the move; ~*x de passage*, migratory birds, birds of passage; *l'*~ *de Junon*, Juno's bird (the peacock); *l'*~ *de Minerve*, the owl; ~*-mouche*, humming bird; ~*x de basse-cour*, fowls, poultry; *un* ~ *de mauvais augure*, a bird of ill omen, a bearer of bad news; *vilain* ~, *celui qui salit son nid!*, it's an ill bird that fouls its own nest; **2.** (mason.) hod; (carp.) trestle, support; **3.** (fig., pej.) fellow, bird, customer; *un drôle d'*~, a queer customer.

oiseler [wazle] *v.i.* to trap birds; ~ *v.t.* to train (a hawk).

oiselet [wazlɛ] *s.m.* little bird.
oiseleur [wazlœr] *s.m.* fowler, bird-catcher.
oiseli-er, -ère [wazlje] *s.m.f.* bird-breeder, bird-dealer, bird-seller.
oiselle [wazɛl] *s.f.* **1.** (poet.) female bird; **2.** (fam.) silly girl.
oisellerie [wazɛlri] *s.f.* **1.** (obs.) aviary; **2.** bird--shop; bird-trade.
oiseu-x, -se [wazø] *adj.* idle; useless, vain, trifling; *paroles ~ses*, idle words, empty talk.
oisi-f, -ve [wazif] *adj.* idle, unoccupied, unemployed; useless, lying idle; *s.m.f.* idler; one who does not need to work.
oisillon [wazijɔ̃] *s.m.* little bird, young bird, fledg(e)ling.
oisivement [wazivmɑ̃] *adv.* idly, without doing any work.
oisiveté [wazivte] *s.f.* idleness; leisure hours, vacant hours; *un jour d'~*, a day of leisure, a holiday; *l'~ est mère de tous les vices*, idleness is the root of all evil, Satan finds some mischief still for idle hands to do.
oison [wazɔ̃] *s.m.* gosling; (fig.) goose, someone easily led or taken in.
O.I.T. [oite] abbrev. *Organisation international du travail*, I.L.O.
okapi [ɔkapi] *s.m.* (zool.) okapi.
oléacées [ɔlease] *s.f.pl.* (bot.) Oleaceae.
oléagineu-x, -se [ɔleaʒinø] *adj.* oleaginous, oily.
oléandre [ɔleɑ̃dr] *s.m.* (bot.) oleander.
oléate [ɔleat] *s.m.* (chem.) oleate.
olécrane, olécrâne [ɔlekrɑn] *s.m.* (anat.) olecranon.
oléfine [ɔlefin] *s.m.* (chem.) olefin(e).
oléiculture [ɔleikyltyr] *s.f.* olive-growing.
oléine [ɔlein] *s.f.* (chem.) olein.
oléique [ɔleik] *adj.* oleic.
oléo-duc [ɔleɔdyk] *s.m.* (oil) pipeline; **~mètre** [ɔleɔmɛtr] *s.m.* (techn.) oleometer.
olfacti-f, -ve [ɔlfaktif] *adj.* olfactory, olfactive.
olfaction [ɔlfaksjɔ̃] *s.f.* olfaction, smelling, sense of smell.
olibrius [ɔlibrijys] *s.m.* braggart; swaggerer; queer and obtrusive fellow.
olifant [ɔlifɑ̃] *s.m.* Roland's horn, horn of ivory.
oligarch-ie [ɔligarʃi] *s.f.* oligarchy; **~ique** [ɔligarʃik] *adj.* oligarchic(al).
oligarque [ɔligark] *s.m.* oligarch.
olim [ɔlim] *s.m.* (hist.) registers of Paris Parliament 1254–1318.
olivaie [ɔlivɛ], **oliveraie** [ɔlivrɛ] *s.f.* olive--plantation or -grove.
olivaison [ɔlivɛzɔ̃] *s.f.* olive season, olive--gathering.
olivâtre [ɔlivɑtr] *adj.* olive-coloured, olive--green, sallow.
olive [ɔliv] *s.f.* **1.** olive; olive-shaped thing (esp. knob, switch); **2.** (arch.) olive-moulding, olive-head; ~ *adj.invar.* olive(-green).
olivette [ɔlivɛt] *s.f.* **1.** olive-grove or -plantation; **2.** a kind of grape; **3.** (pl.) olivettes (dance after the olive-gathering).
olivier [ɔlivje] *s.m.* (bot.) olive-tree, olive; olive--wood; *le mont des Oliviers*, the Mount of Olives; (fig.) *tendre la branche d'~*, to hold out the olive--branch; to make overtures for reconciliation.
olivine [ɔlivin] *s.f.* olivine (a precious stone, a kind of chrysoprase).
olla-podrida [ɔjapɔdrida] *s.f.* (fig.) hotchpotch, salmagundi, medley.
olographe [ɔlɔgraf] *adj.* (law) holograph.
olympiade [ɔlɛ̃pjad] *s.f.* **1.** Olympiad; **2.** Olympic games.
olympien, -ne [ɔlɛ̃pjɛ̃] *adj.* Olympian.
olympique [ɔlɛ̃pik] *adj.* Olympic; *jeux ~s*, Olympic games.
ombelle [ɔ̃bɛl] *s.f.* (bot.) umbel.
ombellé, -e [ɔ̃bele] *adj.* (bot.) umbellate, umbellar.
ombellifère [ɔ̃belifɛr] *adj.* (bot.) umbelliferous; **~s** *s.f.pl.* Umbelliferae.
ombelliforme [ɔ̃belifɔrm] *adj.* umbelliform.
ombellule [ɔ̃belyl] *s.f.* (bot.) umbellule.
ombilic [ɔ̃bilik] *s.m.* **1.** navel; umbilicus; (bot.) hilum; **2.** (geom.) umbilicus, point of surface through which all the lines of curvature pass; (fig.) focal point.
ombilical, -e, (aux) [ɔ̃bilikal] *adj.* umbilical; umbilicate.
ombiliqué, -e [ɔ̃bilike] *adj.* umbilicate, navel--shaped.
omble(-chevalier) [ɔ̃bl(ʃəvalje)] *s.m* (ichth.) char, hill-trout; grayling; umber.
ombrage [ɔ̃braʒ] *s.m.* **1.** shade; (poet.) shade, umbrage; *les verts ~s*, the verdant shades; **2.** (fig.) umbrage, sense of slight; *faire, porter ~ à*, to give umbrage (or offence) to.
ombragé, -e [ɔ̃braʒe] *adj.* shaded, shady, leafy.
ombrager [ɔ̃braʒe] *v.t.* to shade; to cover, to shelter; to conceal, to hide, to adorn.
ombrageu-x, -se [ɔ̃braʒø] *adj.* suspicious, distrustful, easily offended or frightened; (of horses) nervous, shy, skittish.
ombre[1] [ɔ̃br] *s.f.* **1.** shade, shadow; *les ~s du soir*, the shades of night; *c'est l'~ au tableau*, it is the dark side of the picture; *il a peur de son ~*, he is afraid of his own shadow; *il n'y a pas l'~ d'un doute*, there is not a shadow of doubt; *il n'est plus que l'~ de lui-même*, he is but the shadow of his former self; **2.** spirit, ghost; **3.** obscurity, darkness, dark, gloom; *il vaut autant laisser cela dans l'~*, it would be just as well to take no notice of that; (fam.) *mettre un homme à l'~*, to put a man into prison; **4.** (fig.) protection, shelter, cover; **5.** (min.) umber.
ombre[2] [ɔbr] *s.m.* (ichth.) grayling, umber; *~-chevalier* = OMBLE-CHEVALIER.
ombrelle [ɔ̃brɛl] *s.f.* parasol, sunshade; ⚠ not 'umbrella'.
ombrer [ɔ̃bre] *v.t.* to shade, to darken parts of a drawing, to give effects of light and shade.
ombreu-x, -se [ɔ̃brø] *adj.* shady, shaded, shadowy; (poet.) umbrageous.
ombrien, -ne [ɔ̃brijɛ̃] *adj., s.m.f.* Umbrian.
ombrine [ɔ̃brin] *s.m.* (ichth.) a Mediterranean fish.
oméga [ɔmega] *s.m.* omega.
omelette [ɔmlɛt] *s.f.* omelette, omelet; ~ *aux fines herbes*, omelette flavoured with herbs.
omettre [ɔmɛtr] *v.t.* to omit; to leave out, to pass over; *une lettre omise*, a letter left out; *j'ai omis de l'avertir*, I omitted, or neglected, to warn him.
omission [ɔmisjɔ̃] *s.f.* omission, oversight; *sauf erreur ou ~*, errors and omissions excepted.
omnibus [ɔmnibys] *s.m.* omnibus, bus; ~ *adj.* **1.** slow; *train ~*, slow train; **2.** general, of all work; (electr.) *barre ~*, busbar.
omnidirectionnel, -le [ɔmnidirɛksjɔnɛl] *adj.* (radio, radar) omnidirectional (aerial, beam, etc.).
omnipotence [ɔmnipɔtɑ̃s] *s.f.* omnipotence.
omnipotent, -e [ɔmnipɔtɑ̃] *adj.* omnipotent.
omnipraticien, -ne [ɔmnipratisjɛ̃] *s.m.f.* (med.) general practitioner.
omniprésence [ɔmniprezɑ̃s] *s.f.* omnipresence.
omniprésent, -e [ɔmniprezɑ̃] *adj.* omnipresent.
omniscience [ɔmnisjɑ̃s] *s.f.* omniscience.
omnium [ɔmnjɔm] *s.m.* **1.** (fin.) company transacting various kinds of business; **2.** (sport) all comers', or open, race; (cycling) track--event combining several races.
omnivore [ɔmnivɔr] *adj.* omnivorous.
omoplate [ɔmɔplat] *s.f.* shoulder-blade, scapula.

O.M.S. [oɛmɛs] abbrev. *Organisation mondiale de la santé*, W.H.O.
on [ɔ̃] *ind. pron.* one, we, people (pl.); a woman, a man, you; they; somebody, someone, (often construed with a passive verb in English); ~ *doit aimer son pays*, one is bound to love one's country, we ought to love our country; ~ *dit*, they say, it is said, people say; ~ *me dit que*, they tell me that; I am told that; I hear that; *quand* ~ *est jeune*, when one (or a man) is young; ~ *pardonne tant que l'*~ *aime*, we forgive as long as we love; ~ *ferme!*, closing time!; ~ *bâtit un pont superbe*, they are building a magnificent bridge; ~ *vous appelle*, somebody is calling you; ~ *y va*, coming!; ~ *demande*, wanted (in small advertisements, etc.); ~ *s'imagine que*, people think that; ~ *assure que*, it is stated that; ~ *croirait que*, one would think that; ~ *sonne*, there's a ring; ~ *frappe*, there's a knock at the door; ~ *n'en sait rien*, nobody knows; *un* ~*-dit*, a rumour, a piece of hearsay.
onagre [ɔnagr] *s.m.* (zool.) onager, wild ass.
onagre [ɔnagr] *s.f.* (bot.) evening primrose.
onanisme [ɔnanism] *s.m.* onanism, masturbation.
once[1] [ɔ̃s] *s.f.* (weight) ounce; (fig.) trace, very small quantity; *il n'a pas une* ~ *de vanité*, he has not a trace of vanity.
once[2] [ɔ̃s] *s.f.* (zool.) ounce, snow-leopard.
oncial, -e, (aux) [ɔ̃sjal] *adj., s.f.* uncial.
oncle [ɔ̃kl] *s.m.* uncle.
oncques, onc [ɔ̃k] *adv.* (obs.) ever, never.
onction [ɔ̃ksjɔ̃] *s.f.* unction; anointing; (fig.) unctuousness, soothing, flattering eloquence or persuasiveness, mellifluous eloquence; (eccles.) *l'extrême* ~, supreme unction.
onctueu-x, -se [ɔ̃ktɥø] *adj.* unctuous, oily; (fig.) unctuous, mellifluous, smooth; soothing; (pej.) oily; ~**sement** [ɔ̃ktɥøzmɑ̃] *adv.* unctuously, soothingly.
onctuosité [ɔ̃ktɥozite] *s.f.* unctuousness, oiliness.
onde [ɔ̃d] *s.f.* **1.** wave; undulation; corrugation; water, the sea; (pl., fig.) waves; ~ *électrique*, electric wave; *longueur d'*~*s*, wavelength; *l'*~ *amère*, the briny wave; *l'*~ *noire*, the Stygian lake.
ondé, -e [ɔ̃de] *adj.* undulated, wavy, waved; watered (as silk, moire, etc.); grained (as wood).
ondée [ɔ̃de] *s.f.* (short but heavy) shower.
ondin, -e [ɔ̃dɛ̃] *s.m.f.* water-sprite, undine.
on-dit [ɔ̃di] *s.m.invar.* see ON.
ondoiement [ɔ̃dwamɑ̃] *s.m.* **1.** undulatory motion; waving; undulation; **2.** private baptism.
ondoyer [ɔ̃dwaje] *v.i.* to undulate, to wave, to meander; ~ *v.t.* to baptize privately.
ondulation [ɔ̃dylɑsjɔ̃] *s.f.* undulation, waving, flowing; (of hair) waving; (~) *permanente*, permanent waving.
ondulatoire [ɔ̃dylatwar] *adj.* undulatory; wavy.
onduler [ɔ̃dyle] *v.t.i.* to undulate, to wave, to flow gently, to ripple; ~ *v.t.* to wave; *tôle ondulée*, corrugated iron; *chaussée ondulée*, road with uneven surface.
onduleu-x, -se [ɔ̃dylø] *adj.* undulating, waving, wavy.
onéreu-x, -se [ɔnerø] *adj.* onerous; (fig.) burdensome, heavy, expensive; *à titre* ~*x*, burdened with certain conditions, subject to certain payments.
ongle [ɔ̃gl] *s.m.* **1.** nail (of human fingers or toes); *brosse à* ~*s*, nail-brush; (fig.) *il a de l'esprit jusqu'au bout des* ~*s*, he is witty to his fingertips; he is extremely witty; *payer rubis sur l'*~, to pay cash, to pay on the nail, to pay readily enough; *avoir les* ~*s en deuil*, to have dirty finger-nails; ~ *incarné*, in-growing nail; **2.** (animal's) claw, hoof; (bird's) talon, claw; (fig.) *il a bec et* ~*s*, he will fight tooth and nail.
onglé, -e [ɔ̃gle] *adj.* armed with claws or talons.
onglée [ɔ̃gle] *s.f.* painful numbness of the finger-tips (from cold); *j'ai l'*~, my fingers are aching and quite numb.
onglet [ɔ̃glɛ] *s.m.* (bookb., print.) guard, stub; two-page cancel; slip of paper or cardboard; (techn.) notch; mitre; *tailler à* ~, to mitre.
onglette [ɔ̃glɛt] *s.f.* flat graver.
onglier [ɔ̃glije] *s.m.* manicure-case, manicure-set.
onglon [ɔ̃glɔ̃] *s.m.* each division of hoof or foot (of artiodactyls and elephants).
onguent [ɔ̃gɑ̃] *s.m.* ointment, unguent, salve; *de l'*~ *miton mitaine*, eyewash; *dans les petits pots les bons* ~*s*, small parcels hold fine wares.
onguicule [ɔ̃g(ɥ)ikyl] *s.m.* small nail or claw.
onguiculé, -e [ɔ̃g(ɥ)ikyle] *adj.* unguicular, unguiculate.
onguiforme [ɔ̃g(ɥ)ifɔrm] *adj.* unguiform.
ongulé, -e [ɔ̃gyle] *adj.* ungulate.
oniro-logie [ɔnirɔlɔʒi] *s.f.* oneirology, interpretation of dreams; ~**logue** [ɔnirɔlɔg] *s.m.* oneirologist; ~**mancie** [ɔnirɔmɑ̃si] *s.f.* oneiromancy, divination by dreams.
onomastique [ɔnɔmastik] *adj.* onomastic, pertaining to proper names.
onomatopée [ɔnɔmatɔpe] *s.f.* onomatopoeia, onomatopoeic word.
onomatopéique [ɔnɔmatɔpeik] *adj.* onomatopoeic.
onto-génèse [ɔ̃tɔʒenɛz], ~**génie** [ɔ̃tɔʒeni] *s.f.* ontogenesis; ~**logie** [ɔ̃tɔlɔʒi] *s.f.* ontology; ~**logique** [ɔ̃tɔlɔʒik] *adj.* ontological.
O.N.U. [ɔny, ɔɛny] abbrev. *Organisation des Nations Unies*, U.N.O.
onyx [ɔniks] *s.m.* onyx.
onze [ɔ̃z] *adj., s.m.* eleven; eleventh.
onzième [ɔ̃zjɛm] *adj.* eleventh; ~ *s.m.* eleventh (part).
oolithe [ɔɔlit] *s.m.* (geol.) oolite, roe-stone.
oolithique [ɔɔlitik] *adj.* oolitic.
oosphère [ɔɔsfɛr] *s.f.* (bot.) oosphere.
opacité [ɔpasite] *s.f.* opacity, opaqueness; denseness, absence of clarity.
opale [ɔpal] *s.f.* opal.
opalescence [ɔpalesɑ̃s] *s.f.* opalescence.
opalescent, -e [ɔpalesɑ̃] *adj.* opalescent.
opalin, -e [ɔpalɛ̃] *adj.* opaline; ~**e** *s.f.* opaline, milk-glass.
opaque [ɔpak] *adj.* opaque; (fig.) not lucid, dark, obscure.
ope [ɔp] *s.f.* or *m.* (constr.) hole for scaffolding or joist.
O.P.E.P. [opeepe] abbrev. *Organisation des pays producteurs de pétrole*, O.P.E.C.
opéra [ɔpera] *s.m.* **1.** opera; opera-house; **2.** purple-red colour.
opérable [ɔperabl] *adj.* (med.) operable.
opérant, -e [ɔperɑ̃] *adj.* operative, effective.
opérat-eur, -rice [ɔperatœr] *s.m.f.* operator; ~**eur** *s.m.* (mech.) working part (of machine).
opération [operɑsjɔ̃] *s.f.* operation; working; performance; process; *salle d'*~, operating-theatre; *une* ~ *commerciale*, a business transaction; (mil.) *le théâtre des* ~*s*, the theatre of operations; (fam.) *par l'*~ *du Saint-Esprit*, of itself, miraculously.
opérationnel, -le [ɔperɑsjɔnɛl] *adj.* operational, for operations.
opératoire [ɔperatwar] *adj.* of surgical operations, operative; *médecine* ~, surgery.
operculaire [ɔpɛrkylɛr] *adj.* opercular, operculate.
opercule [ɔpɛrkyl] *s.m.* (biol.) operculum; (techn.) lid, closure.

operculé, -e [ɔpɛrkyle] *adj.* operculate, operculated.
opéré, -e [ɔpere] *adj.* **1.** under surgical treatment; **2.** carried out, (of order) executed, (of transaction) completed; *s.m.f.* patient undergoing surgical treatment.
opérer [ɔpere] *v.t.* to operate; to work, to work out, to effect, to bring about; to operate upon; *se faire* ~, to undergo an operation; ~ *qn.*, to operate on s.o.; ~ *un œil de la cataracte*, to operate on an eye for cataract; ~ *des merveilles*, to work wonders; ~ *v.i.* to be effective; *le remède opère*, the remedy is acting, or is having the desired effect; **s'**~ *v.refl.* to be effected; to be operative; to take place, to come about.
opérette [ɔperɛt] *s.f.* operetta, musical comedy.
ophicléide [ɔfikleid] *s.m.* (mus.) ophicleide.
ophidien, -ne [ɔfidjɛ̃] *adj.* ophidian, snake-like; ~**s** *s.m.pl.* Ophidia.
ophioglosse [ɔfjɔglɔs] *s.f.* (bot.) adder's-tongue, ophioglossum.
ophiolâtrie [ɔfjɔlɑtri] *s.f.* serpent-worship.
ophiologie [ɔfjɔlɔʒi] *s.f.* ophiology.
ophite [ɔfit] *s.m.* (min.) ophite, serpentine marble.
ophrys [ɔfris] *s.f.* (bot.) Ophrys, orchid.
ophtalmie [ɔftalmi] *s.f.* (pathol.) ophthalmia.
ophtalmique [ɔftalmik] *adj.* ophthalmic.
ophtalmo-logie [ɔftalmɔlɔʒi] *s.f.* ophthalmology; ~**logique** [ɔftalmɔlɔʒik] *adj.* ophthalmological; ~**logiste** [ɔftalmɔlɔʒist], ~**logue** [ɔftalmɔlɔg] *s.m.f.* ophthalmologist, oculist; ~**scope** [ɔftalmɔskɔp] *s.m.* ophthalmoscope.
opiacé, -e [ɔpjase] *adj.* (pharm.) opiate.
opiacer [ɔpjase] *v.t.* (pharm.) to opiate.
opiat [ɔpja] *s.m.* (pharm.) opiate.
opimes [ɔpim] *adj.f.pl.* **1.** (Rom. hist.) *dépouilles* ~, spolia opima; **2.** (fam.) rich profit.
opiner [ɔpine] *v.i.* to opine, to be of opinion, to give one's opinion; ~ *à*, to agree to; ~ *pour*, to decide in favour of, to decide on; (fam.) ~ *du bonnet*, to nod assent.
opiniâtre [ɔpinjɑtr] *adj.* opinionated; obstinate, stubborn; unyielding, steady, persevering; ~**ment** [ɔpinjɑtrəmɑ̃] *adv.* obstinately, stubbornly.
(s')opiniâtrer [ɔpinjɑtre] *v.refl.* to be obstinate; *s'*~ *dans*, to persist in, to cling obstinately to.
opiniâtreté [ɔpinjɑtrəte] *s.f.* obstinancy, stubbornness, self-will, resolution, steadiness, obduracy.
opinion [ɔpinjɔ̃] *s.f.* opinion, belief, judgement; public opinion; *c'est affaire d'*~, it's a matter of opinion; *se faire une* ~, to form an opinion; *il a trop bonne* ~ *de lui-même*, he has too high an opinion of himself; *l'*~ *publique*, public opinion; *avoir le courage de son* ~, to have the courage of one's convictions; *braver l'*~, to defy or scorn public opinion.
opiomane [ɔpjɔman] *s.m.f.* opium addict.
opium [ɔpjɔm] *s.m.* opium.
oponce [ɔpɔ̃s], **opuntia** [ɔpɔ̃sja] *s.m.* (bot.) prickly pear, opuntia.
opopanax [ɔpɔpanaks] *s.m.* opopanax.
opossum [ɔpɔsɔm] *s.m.* (zool.) opossum; opossum fur.
opotherapie [ɔpoterapi] *s.f.* treatment by means of extracts of an organ or organs.
opportun, -e [ɔpɔrtœ̃] *adj.* opportune, timely, well-timed, seasonable, favourable, expedient, convenient; *en temps* ~, opportunely, timely, seasonably; *au moment* ~, at the right moment.
opportunément [ɔpɔrtynemɑ̃] *adv.* opportunely, timely, seasonably, in good time, at the right moment.
opportun-isme [ɔpɔrtynism] *s.m.* opportunism; ~**iste** [ɔpɔrtynist] *adj.*, *s.m.f.* opportunist; ~**ité** [ɔpɔrtynite] *s.f.* opportuneness, timeliness, expediency; ⚠ not 'opportunity'.
opposabilité [ɔpozabilite] *s.f.* opposability.
opposable [ɔpozabl] *adj.* opposable.
opposant, -e [ɔpozɑ̃] *adj.* opposing, adverse; *s.m.f.* opponent, adversary; ~ *s.m.* (anat.) opponens (muscle).
oppose, -e [ɔpoze] *adj.* opposite; opposed; adverse, hostile; facing, face to face; back to back; ~ *s.m.* opposite, contrary, reverse; *à l'*~ *de*, contrary to, (as) opposed to; *c'est tout l'*~*!*, it's quite the reverse!
opposer [ɔpoze] *v.t.* to oppose; to place opposite (*à*, to); to compare or contrast (*à*, with), to plead (*que*, that); to stand in the way of; **s'**~ *v.refl.* to be opposed, to oppose, to resist, to object (*à*, to), to set oneself (*à*, against), to stand in the way (*à*, of); *je m'y oppose*, I am against this; I won't have it; I strongly object to this.
opposite [ɔpozit] *s.m.* opposite, reverse; *à l'*~ *de*, opposite, facing.
opposition [ɔpozisjɔ̃] *s.f.* opposition, antagonism, resistance, hindrance, stop; antithesis, contrast; (law) garnishment; opposition; caveat; (pol.) the party in opposition, the opposition; *les bancs de l'*~, the opposition benches; *mettre* ~ *sur le salaire de qn.*, to lodge an objection to someone's wages; *je n'y mets aucune* ~, I offer no opposition to it; *sans* ~, nem. con.; *à l'*~ *de*, as opposed to; (fin.) *frapper d'*~, to stop payment (of cheques, etc.).
oppositionnel, -le [ɔpɔzisjɔnɛl] *adj.* (pol.) of the opposition, in opposition; *s.m.f.* opposition, member of the opposition.
oppressant, -e [ɔpresɑ̃] *adj.* oppressive; (fig.) depressing, overwhelming.
oppressé, -e [ɔprese] *adj.* breathless, short of breath, having difficulty in breathing.
oppresser [ɔprese] *v.t.* to cause difficulty in breathing, to cause a feeling of constriction; (fig.) to oppress, to lie heavy on; ⚠ not 'to oppress' in pol. sense.
oppresseur [ɔpresœr] *s.m.* oppressor, tyrant.
oppressi-f, -ve [ɔpresif] *adj.* oppressive.
oppression [ɔpresjɔ̃] *s.f.* **1.** oppression, tyranny; **2.** difficulty in breathing; (lit. & fig.) feeling of constriction or oppression.
opprimé, -e [ɔprime] *adj.*, *s.m.f.* oppressed.
opprimer [ɔprime] *v.t.* to oppress, to crush down, to govern tyrannically, to keep down by force.
opprobre [ɔprɔbr] *s.m.* opprobrium, shame, disgrace, obloquy.
optati-f, -ve [ɔptatif] *adj.*, *s.m.* (lang.) optative.
opter [ɔpte] *v.i.* to choose (*entre*, between); ~ *pour*, to choose, to vote for, to decide in favour of.
opticien [ɔptisjɛn] *s.m.* optician.
optimal, -e, (aux) [ɔptimal] *adj.* optimal, optimum.
optim-isation [ɔptimizɑsjɔ̃] *s.f.* optimization; ~**iser** [ɔptimize] *v.t.* to optimize; ~**isme** [ɔptimism] *s.m.* optimism; ~**iste** [ɔptimist] *adj.* optimist; ~**um** [ɔptimɔm] *adj.*, *s.m.* (pl. *optimums* or *optima*) optimum.
option [ɔpsjɔ̃] *s.f.* option, choice, choosing.
optique [ɔptik] *s.f.* (sci.) optics; aspect, perspective; ~ *adj.* optical; optic; *le nerf* ~, the optic nerve.
optomètre [ɔptɔmetr] *s.m.* (opt.) optometer.
optométrie [ɔptɔmetri] *s.f.* optometry.
opulence [ɔpylɑ̃s] *s.f.* opulence, wealth, affluence; (fig.) amplitude, richness.
opulent, -e [ɔpylɑ̃] *adj.* opulent, wealthy, rich, affluent; (fig.) buxom, (of contours, etc.) ample.
opuntia see OPONCE.

opuscule [ɔpyskyl] *s.m.* opuscule, opusculum.
or [ɔr] *conj.* now; but; well; ~ *ça*, now then; ~ *donc*, well, then.
or [ɔr] *s.m.* gold; gold ornament; gold money; gold colour; ~ *vierge*, native gold; ~ *en barre*, gold in bar; *lingot d'*~, gold-ingot; ~ *en feuille*, gold-leaf; ~ *filé*, spun gold; *d'or, en* ~, gold, of gold; (fig.) golden; *une montre en* ~, or *d'*~, a gold watch; *il a un cœur d'*~, he has a heart of gold; *au poids de l'*~, for its weight in gold; (fig.) very dear; *parler d'*~, to speak like an angel; to give capital advice; *être tout cousu d'*~, to be made of money; *rouler sur l'*~, to be rolling in money; *c'est un marché d'*~, it is an excellent bargain, it is a very profitable business; (proverb) *le silence est d'*~, silence is golden; *tout ce qui brille n'est pas* ~, all is not gold that glitters; *vaisselle d'*~, gold plate; *c'est de l'*~ *en barre*, (i.) she, or he, is pure gold; (ii.) it's as safe as the Bank of England; *on n'en peut avoir ni pour* ~ *ni pour argent*, it cannot be had for love or money; *noces d'*~, golden wedding; *on lui a fait un pont d'*~, he was offered splendid terms, it was made well worth his while; ~ *adj.invar.* gold, golden.
oracle [ɔrɑkl] *s.m.* oracle.
orage [ɔraʒ] *s.m.* thunderstorm, storm, tempest; *le temps est à l'*~, the weather is stormy; *il va faire de l'*~, there's going to be a storm; there's a storm brewing; *laisser passer l'*~, to let the storm blow over.
orageu-x, -se [ɔraʒø] *adj.* stormy, tempestuous; (fig.) noisy, riotous; **~sement** [ɔraʒøzmɑ̃] *adv.* stormily.
oraison [ɔrɛzɔ̃] *s.f.* **1.** (obs.) oration, speech; ~ *funèbre*, funeral oration; (obs.) *les parties de l'*~, the parts of speech; **2.** orison, prayer; *faire* ~, to say prayers; *l'*~ *dominicale*, the Lord's Prayer.
oral, -e, (aux) [ɔral] *adj.* oral, verbal, by word of mouth; **~ement** [ɔralmɑ̃] *adv.* orally.
orange [ɔrɑ̃ʒ] *s.f.* orange; ~ *sanguine*, blood--orange; ~ *adj.invar.* orange-coloured, orange.
orangé, -e [ɔrɑ̃ʒe] *adj.* orange-coloured, orange; ~ *s.m.* orange (colour).
orangeade [ɔrɑ̃ʒad] *s.f.* orangeade, orange--juice.
orangeat [ɔrɑ̃ʒa] *s.m.* candied orange-peel.
oranger [ɔrɑ̃ʒe] *s.m.* orange-tree; *fleur d'*~, orange-blossom.
orangerie [ɔrɑ̃ʒri] *s.f.* **1.** orangery; **2.** orange--grove, orange plantation.
orangette [ɔrɑ̃ʒɛt] *s.f.* orange-berry (the orange gathered before maturity and used in confectionery, or crystallized).
orang-outan(g) [ɔrɑ̃gutɑ̃] *s.m.* (zool.) orang--utan, orang-outang.
orat-eur, -rice [ɔratœr] *s.m.f.* orator, speaker; spokesman; mouthpiece (of a body of people), pleader; *n'être pas ~eur*, to be no great speaker.
oratoire [ɔratwar] *adj.* oratorical, of public speaking; *art* ~, the art of public speaking, oratory.
oratoire [ɔratwar] *s.m.* oratory, private chapel.
oratorien [ɔratɔrjɛ̃] *s.m.* (Cath.) Oratorian.
oratorio [ɔratɔrjo] *s.m.* (mus.) oratorio.
orbe [ɔrb] *s.m.* orb, orbit; sphere, globe; ~ *adj.* **1.** (arch.) (of wall, etc.) blind; **2.** (med.) bruise, contusion.
orbiculaire [ɔrbikylɛr] *adj.* (anat.) orbicular; ~ *s.m.* orbicular muscle.
orbitaire [ɔrbitɛr] *adj.* (anat.) orbital.
orbital, -e, (aux) [ɔrbital] *adj.* (astron.) orbital.
orbite [ɔrbit] *s.f.* **1.** (astron., astronaut., pol.) orbit; (fig.) sphere of influence; (astronaut.) ~ *d'attente*, parking orbit; **2.** (anat.) orbit, socket (of the eye).
orcanète, orcanette [ɔrkanɛt] *s.f.* (bot.) alkanet.
orchestral, -e, (aux) [ɔrkɛstral] *adj.* orchestral.
orchestration [ɔrkɛstrɑsjɔ̃] *s.f.* (mus.) orchestration, scoring.
orchestre [ɔrkɛstr] *s.m.* **1.** orchestra, band; the musicians; *chef d'*~, conductor, band-master, leader of the band; **2.** orchestra stalls (in theatre or concert-hall).
orchestrer [ɔrkɛstre] *v.t.* (mus.) to orchestrate, to arrange or score for orchestral performance.
orchidacées [ɔrkidase] *s.f.pl.* (bot.) Orchidaceae.
orchidée [ɔrkide] *s.f.* (bot.) orchid.
orchis [ɔrkis] *s.m.* (bot.) orchis.
orchite [ɔrkit] *s.f.* (pathol.) orchitis, inflammation of the testicles.
ord, -e [ɔr] *adj.* (obs.) dirty, foul, nasty.
ordalie [ɔrdali] *s.f.* ordeal (old form of trial in Middle Ages).
ordinaire [ɔrdinɛr] *adj.* ordinary, common, usual, customary, average, everyday; *médecin* ~ *du roi*, physician in ordinary to the king; ~ *s.m.* ordinary; custom, wont, usual practice; set or usual meal, daily fare; (mil.) mess, messing; *au-dessus de l'*~, above average, out of the ordinary; *peu* ~, unusual, uncommon; *je sortirai sans chapeau, comme à mon* ~, I shall go out without a hat, as I usually do; *d'*~, usual(ly), generally; *comme à l'*~, as usual; **~ment** [ɔrdinɛrmɑ̃] *adv.* ordinarily, commonly, usually, generally.
ordinal, -e, (aux) [ɔrdinal] *adj.* ordinal; ~ *s.m.* (eccles.) ordinal.
ordinand [ɔrdinɑ̃] *s.m.* candidate for holy orders, ordinand.
ordinant [ɔrdinɑ̃] *s.m.* ordaining bishop.
ordinateur [ɔrdinatœr] *s.m.* **1.** computer, calculating-machine; **2.** (eccles.) ordaining bishop, etc.
ordination [ɔrdinɑsjɔ̃] *s.f.* **1.** ordination; **2.** computing, computer operations.
ordo [ɔrdo] *s.m.* ordo, church calendar.
ordonnance [ɔrdɔnɑ̃s] *s.f.* **1.** order, array, disposition; **2.** ordering; regulation; (law) (judge's) ruling or order; *prendre une* ~, to make an official order; *rendre une* ~, to make a judicial order; ~ *de police*, police regulation; **3.** (admin.) statute; *prendre une* ~, to issue an order; **4.** (med.) prescription; *préparer une* ~, to dispense a prescription; **5.** (mil.) orderly, batman; *officier d'*~, orderly officer, duty officer.
ordonnancement [ɔrdɔnɑ̃smɑ̃] *s.m.* **1.** (admin.) order for reimbursement; **2.** (comm.) execution of order.
ordonnancer [ɔrdɔnɑ̃se] *v.t.* **1.** to pass (an account) for payment, to sanction (expenditure); **2.** (obs.) = ORDONNER 4.
ordonnat-eur, -rice [ɔrdɔnatœr] *s.m.f.* manager, director, ruler, master of the ceremonies; person authorized to pass accounts; *commissaire ~eur*, pay commissioner, auditor, inspector (of accounts); *~eur des cérémonies*, master of ceremonies.
ordonné, -e [ɔrdɔne] *adj.* well-regulated, ordered; orderly, methodical, well behaved.
ordonnée [ɔrdɔne] *s.f.* (geom.) ordinate.
ordonner [ɔrdɔne] *v.t.* **1.** to order, to set in order, to dispose, to array; *il a bien ordonné sa vie*, he has managed his life well; **2.** to enjoin, to order, to direct, to provide; **3.** to ordain (a priest); **4.** (med.) to prescribe.
ordre [ɔrdr] *s.m.* **1.** order; disposition, array; (mil.) line, order; sequence; *avec* ~, in good order; methodically; *avoir de l'*~, to be orderly; *mettre en* ~ *ses idées*, to organize one's thinking; *dans un* ~ *parfait*, in perfect order; in apple-pie order; *rentrer dans l'*~, to be quiet again; *faire*

rentrer dans l'~, to put to rights; to restore peace and order; *j'y mettrai bon ~*, I'll see to that; I'll set that straight; I'll put a stop to that; *numéro d'~*, reference number; **2.** command, behest, order, direction; writ, order, regulation, mandate; rule, duty; *par ~*, (i.) by order; on duty; (ii.) in regular order, each in his turn; *~ du jour*, order of the day; resolution; programme, agenda; (pol.) *passer à l'~ du jour*, to proceed to the business of the day, to set aside a motion; *à l'~!, à l'~!*, order! order!; *rappeler à l'~*, to call to order; *mot d'~*, password; *jusqu'à nouvel ~*, until further orders; until one hears to the contrary; *d'~ et pour compte de*, by order and on account of; *en sous-~*, subordinate, subordinately, under another; *mettre* or *citer à l'~ du jour de l'armée*, to proclaim to the army; to mention in general orders; *billet à ~*, promissory note; **3.** (biol.) (natural) order (group below class, and above family); class, tribe, corporation, category; (religious, etc.) order; fraternity; (arch.) order; *entrer dans les ~s*, to take (holy) orders; *de premier ~*, of the highest order; first-class; (fam.) A1.

ordure [ɔrdyr] *s.f.* ordure, dung, excrement; household refuse, filth; (fig.) obscenity, foul language, ribaldry; *boîte à ~s*, dustbin; *jeter aux ~s*, to throw into the dustbin; *déposer des ~s*, to tip rubbish.

orduri-er, -ère [ɔrdyrje] *adj.* filthy, ribald, foul, obscene.

oréade [ɔread] *s.f.* (myth.) oread, mountain-nymph.

orée [ɔre] *s.f.* edge, border, (esp. of wood, forest, etc.).

oreillard, -e [ɔrɛjar] *adj.* lop-eared; *~ s.m.* **1.** (zool.) long-eared bat; **2.** wing (of armchair).

oreille [ɔrɛj] *s.f.* ear; hearing; dog's-ear (in a book); ear-flap (of a cap); flange; wing (of wing-nut, of armchair); fluke (of an anchor); breast, mould-board, (of a plough); ear-shaped appendage or thing; (bot.) *~ d'ours*, auricula, bear's ear; *avoir l'~ dure*, to be hard of hearing; *avoir de l'~*, to have a good ear (for music); *aux longues ~s*, long-eared; *avoir mal à l'~*, to have earache; *prêter l'~ à*, to listen to, to lend an ear to, to attend to; *faire la sourde ~*, to turn a deaf ear; *dormir sur les deux ~s*, to sleep quietly, or soundly; to have an easy mind; *de toutes ses ~s*, with all one's ears; *dire un mot à l'~ de qn.*, to whisper a word in someone's ear; *se faire tirer l'~*, to be most unwilling, to hang back, to need pressing; (fig.) *montrer le bout de l'~*, to show oneself as one is; to show the cloven hoof; *il n'entend pas de cette ~-là*, he is deaf on that side; *il ne l'entend pas de cette ~-là*, he won't have it; *il se retira l'~ basse*, he went away crestfallen, or with his tail between his legs, or looking sheepish; *j'ai les ~s rebattues de cela*, I am sick of hearing that; *il n'écoute que d'une ~*, he pays very little attention to what is being said; *ne venez pas ainsi me corner aux ~s* do not come and din it into my ears like that; *par-dessus les ~s*, (fig.) up to the ears; *autant lui en pend à l'~*, he has got the same coming to him; *les ~s ont dû vous corner* (or *tinter*), your ears must have been burning; *je lui frotterai les ~s*, I will twist his tail (or pull his ears) for him; (fig.) *échauffer les ~s à qn.*, to irritate s.o.; *dresser l'~*, to prick one's ears; (fig.) to smell a rat; *fendre l'~ à*, (mil.) to pension off, to cashier; to dismiss from service; to sack.

oreiller [ɔreje] *s.m.* pillow; *taie d'~*, pillow-case; pillow-slip.

oreillette [ɔrɛjɛt] *s.f.* **1.** ear-flap (of a cap); **2.** (anat.) auricle.

oreillons [ɔrɛjɔ̃] *s.m.pl.* (pathol.) mumps.

orémus [ɔremys] *s.m.* (fam., obs.) prayer.

ores [ɔr] *adv. d'~ et déjà*, from this moment; henceforth, thenceforth.

orfèvre [ɔrfɛvr] *s.m.* goldsmith, silversmith; (fig.) *être ~ en la matière*, to be an expert; *vous êtes ~, M. Josse*, you are in the trade, my dear sir; that is not disinterested advice.

orfévré, -e [ɔrfevre] *adj.* wrought by a gold- or silversmith.

orfèvrerie [ɔrfɛvrəri] *s.f.* **1.** gold- or silversmith's art, trade, or work; **2.** gold or silver plate or jewellery.

orfraie [ɔrfrɛ] *s.f.* (ornith.) osprey.

orfroi [ɔrfrwɑ] *s.m.* orphrey, orfray.

organdi [ɔrgɑ̃di] *s.m.* organdie.

organe [ɔrgan] *s.m.* **1.** (bodily) organ; *aucun des ~s essentiels*, no vital part; *l'~ de la parole*, the organs of speech; **2.** voice; *un bel ~*, a good voice; **3.** spokesman, agent, agency, mouthpiece (of a body of people); means, organ, medium of communication; newspaper, etc., representing party, etc.; **4.** mechanism; ⚠ not (mus.) 'organ'.

organeau (pl. **-x**) [ɔrgano] *s.m.* (naut.) anchor-ring, mooring-ring.

organique [ɔrganik] *adj.* organic, of the bodily organs, vital; (pathol., chem.) organic; **~ment** [ɔrganikmɑ̃] *adv.* organically.

organisable [ɔrganizabl] *adj.* organizable.

organisat-eur, -rice [ɔrganizatœr] *s.m.f.* organizer, steward; *adj.* organizing.

organisation [ɔrganizɑsjɔ̃] *s.f.* organization, formation, arrangement, structure, constitution; nature, disposition; being, individual; organized body, system, or society; *chargé de l'~ des secours*, entrusted with making arrangements for relief.

organisé, -e [ɔrganize] *adj.* **1.** organic, possessing organs; **2.** organized; systematically arranged; methodical; constituted; *bien ~*, well-organized, well-ordered.

organiser [ɔrganize] *v.t.* to organize, to get up, to form, to draw up, to arrange, to settle; **s'~** *v.refl.* to become organized; to get into working order.

organisme [ɔrganism] *s.m.* organism, system, constitution, arrangement; institution.

organiste [ɔrganist] *s.m.f.* organist.

organsin [ɔrgɑ̃sɛ̃] *s.m.* organzine.

orgasme [ɔrgasm] *s.m.* orgasm.

orge [ɔrʒ] *s.f.* barley; (*orge* is *masc.* in: *~ mondé*, husked, or hulled barley; scotch barley; and *~ perlé*, pearl barley); *faire ses ~s*, to mow barley; (fig.) to feather one's nest; *sucre d'~*, barley-sugar, rock (sweet).

orgeat [ɔrʒa] *s.m.* orgeat (a sweet drink made of barley or almonds, sugar, and orange-flower water).

orgelet [ɔrʒəlɛ] *s.m.* stye (on the eye).

orgiaque [ɔrʒjak] *adj.* orgiastic.

orgie [ɔrʒi] *s.f.* orgy; drinking-bout, revelry, debauchery; (fig.) riot, wealth, extravagance; excess; *une ~ de fleurs*, a profusion of flowers.

orgue [ɔrg] *s.m.* (but usu. *fem.* in the plural) **1.** organ; *jeu d'~*, organ-stop; *buffet d'~*, organ-case; *~ de Barbarie*, street-organ, barrel-organ; *~ à pédales*, pedal-organ; (mus.) *point d'~*, 𝄐, pause; (fig.) full stop; **2.** (geol.) *~s basaltiques*, basalt columns; **3.** (zool.) tubipore.

orgueil [ɔrgœj] *s.m.* pride, arrogance; *avec ~*, proudly; haughtily; *faire l'~ de*, to be the pride of; *nous devrions mettre notre ~ à*, it should be our pride to.

orgueilleu-x, -se [ɔrgœjø] *adj.* proud; haughty, arrogant; **~sement** [ɔrgœjøzmɑ̃] *adv.* proudly; haughtily, arrogantly.

oriel [ɔrjɛl] *s.m.* oriel window.

orient [ɔrjɑ̃] *s.m.* **1.** the East, the Orient; *de l'~*, eastern, of the east; *en ~*, in the East; *l'Extrême-Orient*, the Far East; *le Proche-Orient*, the Near

East; *le Moyen-Orient*, the Middle East; *le Grand--Orient*, the Grand Lodge (of Freemasons); **2.** water, orient, lustre, (of pearls).

oriental, -e, (aux) [ɔrjɑ̃tal] *adj.* oriental, eastern, easterly; *à l'~e*, in the oriental fashion; **Oriental, -e** *s.m.f.* Oriental; Oriental woman.

oriental-isme [ɔrjɑ̃talism] *s.m.* orientalism; **~iste** [ɔrjɑ̃talist] *adj., s.m.f.* orientalist.

orientation [ɔrjɑ̃tɑsjɔ̃] *s.f.* **1.** orientation, finding the cardinal points; guidance (in career, etc.); direction of policy; positioning (of aerial); (nav.) training (of gun); **2.** position, bearings; direction, aspect (of building); *sens de l'~*, sense of direction; **3.** (naut.) trimming (of sails, yards).

orienté, -e [ɔrjɑ̃te] *adj.* orientated; (fig.) tendentious; *~ à*, facing.

orientement [ɔrjɑ̃tmɑ̃] *s.m.* (naut.) trim (of sails).

orienter [ɔrjɑ̃te] *v.t.* to orientate, to set (a map); to set or direct (an aerial); (fig.) to direct; to trim (a sail, a yard); **s'~** *v.refl.* to orientate oneself, to find out in what direction the east is; to ascertain one's position; to take one's bearings; (fig.) to see what one is about.

orifice [ɔrifis] *s.m.* orifice, opening, aperture, hole, mouth; nozzle (of hose, atomizer, pipe, etc.); port (of valve).

oriflamme [ɔriflɑm] *s.f.* oriflamme.

origan [ɔrigɑ̃] *s.m.* (bot.) wild marjoram, origan, origanum.

originaire [ɔriʒinɛr] *adj.* **1.** *~ de*, coming originally from; native of; *vous n'êtes pas ~ de ce pays*, you are not a native of this country; **2.** original, first, primitive, innate; **~ment** [ɔriʒinɛrmɑ̃] *adv.* originally.

original, -e, (aux) [ɔriʒinal] *adj.* **1.** original, model, primitive, first; innate, initial, earliest; **2.** original, novel in character, not imitative; **3.** strange, queer, singular, peculiar, eccentric, quaint; *s.m.f.* eccentric, original, or odd person; **~ement** [ɔriʒinalmɑ̃] *adv.* originally.

original (pl. **aux**) [ɔriʒinal] *s.m.* original, original version, text, etc.; *une copie conforme à l'~*, a copy which agrees with the original.

originalité [ɔriʒinalite] *s.f.* **1.** originality; novel feature; eccentricity, oddness, oddity, quaintness, singularity.

origine [ɔriʒin] *s.f.* origin, source, starting-point, (math.) zero point, beginning, derivation, extraction; descent, birth, breed; *dès l'~*, from the very beginning; *à l'~*, originally; *avoir son ~ dans, tirer son ~ de*, to come from, to be derived from, to originate in or from, to spring from; *d'~ illustre*, of illustrious descent; *d'~ française*, of French extraction or birth; made in France, of French origin; *emballage d'~*, original packing.

originel, -le [ɔriʒinɛl] *adj.* original; **~lement** [ɔriʒinɛlmɑ̃] *adv.* originally, in the beginning.

orignac [ɔriɲak], **orignal** (pl. **aux**) [ɔriɲal] *s.m.* (zool.) Canadian elk.

orin [ɔrɛ̃] *s.m.* (naut.) buoy-rope (of an anchor).

oripeau (pl. **-x**) [ɔripo] *s.m.* **1.** Dutch leaf, Dutch gold, foil, tinsel; **2.** gaudy clothes, tinselled or faded finery; showy rags; tawdry ornaments, tawdry style, anything showy but worthless.

O.R.L. [oɛrɛl] abbrev. *oto-rhino-laryngologiste*, E.N.T. (ear, nose, throat).

orle [ɔrl] *s.m.* (arch., herald.) orle.

orléanais, -e [ɔrleanɛ] *adj., s.m.f.* (native or inhabitant) of Orleans; *~ s.m.* Orleanais (old French province).

orléaniste [ɔrleanist] *adj., s.m.f.* (hist.) Orleanist, (supporter) of the Orleans princes (as claimants to the French throne).

ormaie [ɔrmɛ], **ormoie** [ɔrmwa] *s.f.* elm--grove, elm-plantation.

orme [ɔrm] *s.m.* (bot.) elm; *~ tilleul*, broad--leaved elm; *~ de montagne*, wych-elm; *attendez--moi sous l'~!*, you may wait until Doomsday.

ormeau (pl. **-x**) [ɔrmo] *s.m.* **1.** (bot.) young elm, elm; **2.** (zool.) sea-ear, ormer, haliotis.

ormille [ɔrmij] *s.f.* very young elm, elm sapling; plantation of young elms.

orne[1] [ɔrn] *s.m.* (bot.) flowering ash.

orne[2] [ɔrn] *s.m.* (forest.) *faire ~*, to cut down a swathe or straight line of trees.

ornemaniste [ɔrnəmanist] *s.m.f.* ornamentalist.

ornement [ɔrnəmɑ̃] *s.m.* ornament, adornment, decorative feature; knick-knack, embroidery; tracery, moulding; (eccles.) vestment; (mus.) ornament, grace-notes; *d'~*, ornamental, decorative; *sans ~*, unadorned.

ornemental, -e, (aux) [ɔrnəmɑ̃tal] *adj.* ornamental, decorative.

ornementation [ɔrnəmɑ̃tɑsjɔ̃] *s.f.* ornamentation, adornment, decoration.

ornementer [ɔrnəmɑ̃te] *v.t.* to ornament, to decorate, to adorn, to beautify.

orner [ɔrne] *v.t.* to adorn, to ornament, to decorate; (fig.) to grace, to embellish; *~ de fleurs*, to decorate with flowers; *style orné*, ornate style.

ornière [ɔrnjɛr] *s.f.* rut; (fig.) beaten track, old way, groove, path.

ornitho-gale [ɔrnitɔgal] *s.m.* (bot.) star of Bethlehem, Ornithogalum; **~logie** [ɔrnitɔlɔʒi] *s.f.* ornithology; **~logiste** [ɔrnitɔlɔʒist]; **~logue** [ɔrnitɔlɔg] *s.m.f.* ornithologist; **~rhynque** [ɔrnitɔrɛ̃k] *s.m.* (zool.) ornithorhynchus, duck-billed platypus.

orobanche [ɔrɔbɑ̃ʃ] *s.f.* (bot.) broomrape.

orobe [ɔrɔb] *s.m.* (bot.) bitter vetch; black pea.

orographie [ɔrɔgrafi] *s.f.* orography, oreography.

orographique [ɔrɔgrafik] *adj.* orographic(al).

oronge [ɔrɔ̃ʒ] *s.f.* (bot.) orange-milk mushroom; imperial mushroom; orange agaric; *fausse ~*, toadstool, fly-agaric.

orpailleur [ɔrpɑjœr] *s.m* gold-washer, gold--seeker, gold-finder.

Orphée [ɔrfe] *s.m.* (myth.) Orpheus.

orphelin, -e [ɔrfəlɛ̃] *adj., s.m.f.* orphan; *enfant ~ de père*, fatherless child.

orphelinat [ɔrfəlina] *s.m.* orphanage, school for orphans.

orphéon [ɔrfeɔ̃] *s.m.* orphéon, choral society; brass band.

orphéoniste [ɔrfeɔnist] *s.m.f.* member of a choral society or brass band.

orphie [ɔrfi] *s.f.* (ichth.) garfish, sea-pike, sea--needle, horn-fish.

orphique [ɔrfik] *adj.* Orphic, Orphean.

orpiment [ɔrpimɑ̃] *s.m.* orpiment.

orpin [ɔrpɛ̃] *s.m.* **1.** (bót.) stonecrop; **2.** (min.) orpiment.

orque [ɔrk] *s.f.* (zool.) grampus, orc.

orseille [ɔrsɛj] *s.f.* **1.** (bot.) orchil; **2.** red dye extracted from orchil.

orteil [ɔrtɛj] *s.m.* toe; *le gros ~*, the big toe.

O.R.T.F. [oɛrteɛf] abbrev. *Office de la radio--diffusion et télévision française*, French broadcasting authority.

orthodoxe [ɔrtɔdɔks] *adj.* orthodox; (fig.) correct, approved, conventional; *l'Église ~*, the Orthodox Church.

orthodoxie [ɔrtɔdɔksi] *s.f.* orthodoxy, soundness (of opinion), correctness.

orthogonal, -e, (aux) [ɔrtɔgɔnal] *adj.* orthogonal.

orthographe [ɔrtɔgraf] *s.f.* orthography, spelling; *faute d'~*, spelling mistake; mis-spelling, wrong or bad spelling, mis-spelt word; *savoir l'~*, to know how to spell; to spell correctly; *il a une ~ déplorable*, his spelling is shocking.

orthographie [ɔrtɔgrafi] *s.f.* orthography, elevation plan, section; (geom.) orthogonal or orthographic projection.
orthographier [ɔrtɔgrafje] *v.t.* to spell (correctly); **s'~** *v.refl.* to be spelt.
orthographique [ɔrtɔgrafik] *adj.* orthographic(al).
orthopéd-ie [ɔrtɔpedi] *s.f.* orthopaedics; **~ique** [ɔrtɔpedik] *adj.* orthopaedic; **~iste** [ɔrtɔpedist] *s.m.f.* orthopaedist; seller or manufacturer of orthopaedic equipment.
orthoptère [ɔrtɔptɛr] *adj.* (ent.) orthopterous; ~ *s.m.* orthopteran; (pl.) Orthoptera.
ortie [ɔrti] *s.f.* (bot.) nettle; stinging nettle; ~ *blanche*, dead-nettle; *jeter le froc aux ~s*, (of monks) to unfrock oneself.
ortolan [ɔrtɔlɑ̃] *s.m.* (ornith.) ortolan.
orvale [ɔrval] *s.f.* (bot.) clary.
orvet [ɔrvɛ] *s.m.* (zool.) slow-worm, blindworm.
orviétan [ɔrvjetɑ̃] *s.m.* orvietan, Venice treacle; (fig.) quack medicine; *marchand d'~*, quack, charlatan.
oryx [ɔriks] *s.m.* (zool.) oryx.
os [ɔs; *pl.* ɔ] *s.m.* bone; *il ne fera pas de vieux ~*, he'll never make old bones; he will not live long; *n'avoir que les ~ et le peau*, to be nothing but skin and bone; *trempé jusqu'aux ~*, drenched to the skin; *les ~ lui percent la peau*, his bones stick out.
oscillateur [ɔsilatœr] *s.m.* (phys.) oscillator.
oscillation [ɔsilɑsjɔ̃] *s.f.* oscillation, vibration, swing, sweep; (fig.) fluctuation, wavering.
oscillatoire [ɔsilatwar] *adj.* oscillatory.
osciller [ɔsile] *v.i.* to oscillate, to vibrate, to swing, to rock, to sweep; to fluctuate, to waver, to hesitate.
oscillo-gramme [ɔsilɔgram] *s.m.* oscillogram; **~graphe** [ɔsilɔgraf] *s.m.* **1.** (naut.) wheel-pendulum; **2.** (electr.) oscillograph, oscilloscope; *~graphe cathodique*, cathode-ray tube; **~mètre** [ɔsilɔmɛtr] *s.m.* **1.** (electr.) = OSCILLOGRAPHE; **2.** (med.) oscillometer.
osculat-eur, -rice [ɔskylatœr] *adj.* (geom.) osculatory.
osculation [ɔskylɑsjɔ̃] *s.f.* (geom.) osculation; ⚠ not 'osculation' in sense 'kissing'.
osé, -e [oze] *adj.* bold, daring; venturesome, hazardous; risqué; *être assez ~ pour*, to be bold enough to; *une entreprise ~e*, a daring venture; a risky undertaking.
oseille [ozɛj] *s.f.* (bot.) sorrel; (pop.) money; *sel d'~*, oxalic acid, salts of sorrel; (pop.) *la faire à l'~ à qn.*, to deceive s.o.
oser [oze] *v.t.* to dare, to venture, to attempt; to be daring, to be bold enough to; to presume; *si j'ose le dire*, if I may venture to say so; *il n'oserait pas!*, he would not dare!
oseraie [ozrɛ] *s.f.* osier-bed.
osier [ozje] *s.m.* osier, water-willow; wicker, withy, basket-work; *panier d'~*, wicker basket; *fauteuil en ~*, basket-chair.
osmium [ɔsmjɔm] *s.m.* (chem.) osmium.
osmonde [ɔsmɔ̃d] *s.f.* (bot.) osmund, osmund royal, royal fern, flowering fern.
osmose [ɔsmoz] *s.f.* osmosis; (fig.) interpenetration, intermingling.
osmotique [ɔsmɔtik] *adj.* osmotic.
ossature [ɔsatyr] *s.f.* osseous frame; bony structure; skeleton; (fig.) framework, frame, build, structure.
osséine [ɔsein] *s.f.* (chem.) ossein.
osselet [ɔslɛ] *s.m.* **1.** ossicle, small bone; **2.** knuckle-bone; *jouer aux ~s*, to play knuckle-bones; **3.** (vet.) osselet.
ossements [ɔsmɑ̃] *s.m.pl.* bones (of dead bodies).
osseu-x, -se [ɔsø] *adj.* osseous, bony.
ossianique [ɔsjanik] *adj.* Ossianic; of Ossian.
ossification [ɔsifikɑsjɔ̃] *s.f.* ossification.
(s')ossifier *v.refl.* to ossify, to turn into bony tissue.
ossu, -e [ɔsy] *adj.* bony; big-boned.
ossuaire [ɔsɥɛr] *s.m.* ossuary, charnel-house.
ostéine [ɔstein] *s.f.* = OSSÉINE.
ostéite [ɔsteit] *s.f.* (pathol.) osteitis; inflammation of the osseous substance.
ostensible [ɔstɑ̃sibl] *adj.* apparent, open, patent; **~ment** [ɔstɑ̃sibləmɑ̃] *adv.* openly.
ostensoir [ɔstɑ̃swar] *s.m.* (Cath.) monstrance; ostensory.
ostentation [ɔstɑ̃tɑsjɔ̃] *s.f.* ostentation, show, vain display; *par ~*, for show, for effect; *faire ~ de* or *mettre de l'~ dans*, to make a show of.
ostéo-arthrite [ɔsteɔartrit] *s.f.* (med.) osteoarthritis; **~blaste** [ɔsteɔblast] *s.m.* (biol.) osteoblast; **~génie** [ɔsteɔʒeni], **~génèse** [ɔsteɔʒenɛz] *s.f.* **1.** (biol.) osteogenesis, formation of bone; **2.** ossification; **~logie** [ɔsteɔlɔʒi] *s.f.* osteology; **~malacie** [ɔsteɔmalasi] *s.f.* (med.) osteomalacia, softening of the bones; **~myélite** [ɔsteɔmjelit] *s.f.* (med.) osteomyelitis; **~plastie** [ɔsteɔplasti] *s.f.* osteoplasty, bone surgery; **~sarcome** [ɔsteɔsarkɔm] *s.m.* (med.) osteosarcoma, bone tumour; **~tomie** [ɔsteɔtɔmi] (surg.) osteotomy.
ostracé, -e [ɔstrase] *adj.* oyster-like, shell-like.
ostracisme [ɔstrasism] *s.m.* ostracism; *frapper d'~*, to ostracize.
ostréicole [ɔstreikɔl] *adj.* pertaining to oyster-breeding.
ostréicult-eur, -rice [ɔstreikyltœr] *s.m.f.* oyster-farmer, oyster-breeder.
ostréiculture [ɔstreikyltyr] *s.f.* oyster-culture, oyster-breeding.
ostrogoth, -e [ɔstrogɔt] *s.m.f.* Ostrogoth; (fig.) rude uncivilized person, rough fellow.
otage [ɔtaʒ] *s.m.* hostage.
otalgie [ɔtalʒi] *s.f.* earache.
O.T.A.N. [ɔtan] abbrev. *Organisation du traité de l'Atlantique Nord*, N.A.T.O.
otarie [ɔtari] *s.f.* (zool.) otary, eared seal, sea-lion.
ôter [ote] *v.t.* to take away; to remove; to take off, to take, to snatch; to strip off, to take off, to pull off (one's clothes); to cut off; to take away, to deprive of; to relieve, or to rid of; *ôtez votre manteau*, take off your coat; *on lui a ôté son emploi*, he has been dismissed; *ôtez-lui cette idée de la tête*, get this nonsense out of his head; *de six ôtez deux*, take (or subtract) two from six; *ôtez-moi cette incertitude*, relieve me of this doubt; *il me l'a ôté des mains*, he snatched it out of my hands; *on lui a ôté tout espoir*, he has been deprived of all hope; they did not give him the least hope; **s'~** *v.refl.* **1.** to remove oneself; (fam.) *ôte-toi de là, que je m'y mette*, you get out and let me in; make room for your betters; **2.** to rid oneself of; *je ne puis m'~ cela de la tête*, I cannot get it out of my mind.
otite [ɔtit] *s.f.* (pathol.) otitis, inflammation of the ear.
oto-rhino-laryngologiste [ɔtɔrinɔlarɛ̃gɔlɔʒist], **oto-rhino** [ɔtɔrino] *s.m.f.* ear, nose, and throat specialist.
ottoman, -e [ɔtɔmɑ̃] *adj.*, *s.m.f.* Ottoman; **~e** *s.f.* ottoman, divan.
ou [u] *conj.* or, either, else, otherwise; *~ bien*, or else, or otherwise; *ce sera lui ~ moi*, it will be either he or I.
où [u] *adv.* where, whither; at which, in which, from which, to which; when; that; *d'~*, whence, from which; where . . . from; how; *~ allez-vous?*, where are you going?; *~ allons-nous si la hausse continue?*, where shall we be if prices go on rising?; *~ as-tu pris cela?*, where did you get that from?; *le jour ~*, the day when, on which; *la boîte ~ je l'ai mis*, the box in which I put it;

d'~ venez-vous?, where do you come from?; *~ en êtes-vous de cette affaire?*, how are you getting on with that business?; *d'~ vient la nouvelle?*, where does this news come from?; *voilà par ~ j'ai passé*, (i.) that's the way I came; (ii.) that's what I have had to endure; *au prix ~ est le beurre*, at the present price of butter; *dans le cas ~*, in case; *c'est là ~ je voulais en venir*, that's what I was driving at; *d'~ vient que?*, how is it that?; *par ~?*, which way?; *~ que vous alliez*, wherever you may go.

O.U.A. [oya] abbrev. *Organisation de l'unité africaine*, O.A.U.

ouaille [wɑj] *s.f.* sheep, ewe; (pl.) (fig.) flock, faithful congregation.

ouais [wɛ] *interj.* **1.** (obs.) expression of surprise; **2.** (iron.) yes! oh, yes!

ouate [wat] *s.f.* cotton wool; cotton padding; wadding; (fig.) softness, whiteness; *~ hydrophile*, absorbent cotton wool.

ouaté, -e [wate] *adj.* padded, wadded; (fig.) (of footsteps, etc.) soft, silent.

ouater [wate] *v.t.* to wad, to pad, to line with wadding.

oubli [ubli] *s.m.* forgetting, forgetfulness; oblivion, oversight, inadvertence, neglect, omission, slip, breach; pardon, forgiveness, forgiving; *par ~*, by an oversight; *mettre en ~*, to forget; *~ de soi-même*, abnegation, forgetfulness of self; *tomber dans l'~*, to fall into oblivion; *l'~ de ses devoirs*, neglect of one's duty; *réparer un ~*, to redeem an act of neglect; to repair an oversight.

oublie [ubli] *s.f.* wafer (biscuit).

oublier [ublije] *v.t.* to forget, to overlook, to neglect, to omit; *faisant ~ jusqu'au nom*, causing the very name to be forgotten; *oubliant toute décence*, disregarding all considerations of decency; *oublier le passé*, to let bygones be bygones; *j'ai oublié mon parapluie chez vous*, I left my umbrella at your house; **s'~** *v.refl.* **1.** to neglect one's own interests; to be unselfish, forgetful of self; (iron.) *il ne s'est pas oublié*, he saw to it that he got a good share; **2.** to forget oneself, to act unbecomingly; **3.** to be (easily) forgotten.

oubliette [ublijɛt] *s.f.* usu. *pl.* oubliette (secret dungeon); (fig.) *mettre aux ~s*, to consign to oblivion.

oublieu-x, -se [ublijø] *adj.* forgetful, thoughtless, unmindful.

ouche [uʃ] *s.f.* small vegetable-garden or orchard.

oued [wɛd] *s.m.* (Arabic *pl. ouadi*) North African river-bed or ravine; wadi.

ouest [wɛst] *s.m., adj.invar.* west; western; *vent d'~*, west wind, westerly wind; *la côte ~*, the west(ern) coast; *à l'~*, to or in the west; west, westward, westerly; *vers l'~*, westward; (pol.) *l'Ouest*, the West.

ouest-allemand, -e [wɛstalmɑ̃] *adj., s.m.f.* West German.

ouf [uf] *interj.* (i.) of relief; (ii.) of sudden pain or feeling of choking.

Ouganda [ugɑ̃da] *s.m.* (geog.) Uganda.

oui [wi] *adv., s.m.invar.* yes, yea, ay; an affirmative answer or vote; so?, indeed?, eh?; *~ vraiment!*, yes indeed!; *que ~!*, yes, to be sure!; *dire ~*, to say yes (esp. to proposal of marriage); *dire que ~*, to say that it is so; *ne dire ni ~ ni non*, to give no positive answer; not to say either yes or no; *pour un ~, pour un non*, for the least thing; *~ da!*, yes, to be sure!; *vous irez, ~?*, you will go, won't you?

ouï-dire [widir] *s.m.invar.* hearsay, rumour; *par ~*, by hearsay, according to rumour.

ouïe [wi] *s.f.* **1.** hearing; *avoir l'~ fine*, to be sharp of hearing; **2.** sound-hole (of musical instrument); (pl.) gills (of fish).

ouiller [uje] *v.t.* to ullage (a cask).

ouïr [wir] *v.t.* (obs.) to hear; *j'ai ouï (dire)*, I have heard it said.

ouistiti [wistiti] *s.m.* (zool.) marmoset.

oukase see UKASE.

ouragan [uragɑ̃] *s.m.* hurricane, (fig.) explosion (of temper); *un ~ politique*, a political storm; *arriver comme un ~*, to arrive like a whirlwind.

Oural [ural] *s.m.* (geog.) Ural (river); *les Monts ~s*, the Ural Mountains.

ourdir [urdir] *v.t.* to warp; to plait (straw); (fig.) to plot, to contrive, to brew, to hatch, to form, to frame; *~ une toile*, to warp a cloth; *~ un complot*, to hatch a plot; *~ la perte de*, to plot the downfall or destruction of.

ourdissage [urdisaʒ] *s.m.* warping.

ourdisseu-r, -se [urdisœr] *s.m.f.* warper.

ourdissoir [urdiswar] *s.m.* warp-beam; warping-mill; warping-frame.

ourdu [urdu] *s.m., adj.invar.* Urdu.

ourler [urle] *v.t.* (dressm.) to hem; to make a lap-joint; (fig.) to border; *~ à jour*, to hemstitch.

ourlet [urlɛ] *s.m* (dressm.) hem; lap-joint; (fig.) border; *~ à jour*, open hem, hemstitching; *faire un ~*, to make a hem.

ours [urs] *s.m.* bear, he-bear; (fig.) unsociable, disagreeable (or ill-bred) man; *~ blanc*, polar bear; *~ gris*, grizzly bear; (fig.) *c'est un ~ mal léché*, he is an ill-licked cub, or a rough, rude fellow; *c'est le pavé de l'~*, it was well meant, but disastrous; save me from my friends; *il ne faut pas vendre la peau de l'~ avant de l'avoir tué*, don't count your chickens before they are hatched; *~ adj.invar.* rough, coarse.

ourse [urs] *s.f.* she-bear; (astron.) Ursa; *la Grande ~*, the Great Bear, Ursa Major.

oursin [ursɛ̃] *s.m.* (zool.) sea-urchin, sea-hedgehog.

ourson [ursɔ̃] *s.m.* **1.** bear-cub; **2.** small American bear; **3.** (mil.) bearskin.

oust, ouste [ust] *interj.* away with you!, off you go!

outarde [utard] *s.f.* (ornith.) bustard.

outardeau (pl. **-x**) [utardo] *s.m.* young bustard.

outil [uti] *s.m.* tool; implement, instrument; (slang) *va donc eh! ~!*, get away with you, you old fool.

outillage [utijaʒ] *s.m.* **1.** stock or set of tools or implements; tools, implements, machinery, gear, plant; **2.** making or supplying of tools or plant, tooling-up; **3.** equipment, resources; *~ national*, national communications network.

outiller [utije] *v.t.* to supply, furnish, or stock with tools or instruments; to equip; *mal outillé*, badly supplied with tools; badly equipped.

outrage [utraʒ] *s.m.* insult, outrage, abuse, offence, injury, ravages; *faire ~ à*, to outrage, to commit an outrage on, to commit an offence against, to offend (public decency, etc.); *l'~ des ans*, the ravages of time.

outrageant, -e [utraʒɑ̃] *adj.* outrageous, insulting.

outrager [utraʒe] *v.t.* to outrage, to insult, to abuse, to offend against; to shock.

outrageu-x, -se [utraʒø] *adj.* outrageous, offensive; **~sement** [utraʒøzmɑ̃] *adv.* outrageously; excessively.

outrance [utrɑ̃s] *s.f.* excess; *à ~, à toute ~*, to excess, beyond all measure, out-and-out, to the utmost, to a finish; desperately, furiously, unsparingly, unmercifully, to the bitter end; *se battre à ~*, to fight to the death; *guerre à ~*, war to the knife.

outranci-er, -ère [utrɑ̃sje] *adj.* carrying things to extremes or to excess; extreme, excessive, exaggerated.

outre [utr] *s.f.* leather bottle, goatskin bottle; *plein comme une ~*, tight as a drum.

outre [utr] *prep., adv.* **1.** beyond, farther, further; **2.** besides, in addition to; *passer* ~, to go beyond, to go further, to go on, to pass on, to proceed; (fig.) to take no notice; *~-mer*, overseas; *d'~-tombe*, from beyond the tomb; posthumous; *en* ~, besides, moreover; ~ *que*, besides, notwithstanding that, apart from the fact that.

outré, -e [utre] *adj.* **1.** exaggerated, carried to excess, excessive, far-fetched, overdone, extravagant; **2.** out of patience, beside oneself, scandalized, indignant, much upset (*de*, by, at).

outrecuidance [utrəkɥidɑ̃s] *s.f.* overweening conceit, vanity, presumption, audacity, arrogance; (fam.) cheek.

outrecuidant, -e [utrəkɥidɑ̃] *adj.* overweening, presumptuous, impertinent, cheeky.

outremer [utrəmɛr] *s.m.* ultramarine, lapis lazuli; *bleu d'~*, ultramarine blue; ~ *adj. invar.* ultramarine.

outrepasser [utrəpase] *v.t.* to overstep, to transgress; to go beyond, to exceed; ~ *ses pouvoirs*, to exceed one's powers.

outrer [utre] *v.t.* **1.** to overdo, to carry too far, to overstrain, to exaggerate; **2.** to exasperate, to incense.

outsider [awtsajdœr, utsidɛr] *s.m.* (sport) outsider; (fig.) doubtful candidate.

ouvert, -e [uvɛr] *adj.* open; unfortified; unprotected, unsheltered; free; (fig.) open-hearted, frank, sincere, ready, free; *à bras ~s*, cordially, heartily; with open arms; *à bureau* ~, on presentation, on the nail; *à ciel* ~, open, in the open; *grand* ~, wide open; *traduire à livre* ~, to translate at sight; *en guerre ~e*, at war; *port* ~, open harbour; *en pays* ~, in open country; *la politique de la porte ~e*, the open-door policy; *à cœur* ~, unreservedly, open-heartedly; *opération à cœur* ~, open-heart surgery; *un esprit* ~, an open-minded person; *un compte* ~, a running account; **~ement** [uvɛrtəmɑ̃] *adv.* openly, frankly.

ouverture [uvɛrtyr] *s.f.* **1.** opening, aperture, orifice, mouth, inlet, gap, hole, passage; **2.** beginning, opening, commencement; opening move or gambit; (mus.) overture; *l'~ de la chasse*, the opening of the shooting season; **3.** being open; *heures d'~*, opening hours, business hours, visiting hours; **4.** (pl.) overtures, proposal, opening of negotiations; **5.** (arch.) opening, span, width of door, window, etc.; *d'une grande ~ d'esprit*, with great width of vision, of great broadness of mind; ~ *de cœur*, warm-heartedness; ~ *d'une succession*, proving of a will; time when an inheritance can be acquired or received.

ouvrable [uvrabl] *adj.* working; *jours ~s*, workdays, working days; *heures ~s*, hours of business.

ouvrage [uvraʒ] *s.m.* work, piece of work; workmanship, handiwork; performance; fortification; ~ *d'art*, engineering work, outwork, bridge, tunnel, etc.; (⚠ not 'work of art'); *avoir du cœur à l'~*, to work with a will; *n'avoir pas d'~*, *être sans* ~, to be out of employment (or work), to be unemployed; *se mettre à l'~*, to set to work; *laisser l'~*, to leave off working; (fam.) to knock off work; (fort.) *~s extérieurs*, outworks; ~ *à l'aiguille*, needlework; *panier à* ~, work-basket; *c'est le meilleur ~ que vous ayez fait*, it is the best work you have written.

ouvragé, -e [uvraʒe] *adj.* wrought, figured.

ouvrager [uvraʒe] *v.t.* to work, to figure; to decorate, to chisel, to finish; to embellish.

ouvraison [uvrɛzɔ̃] *s.f.* working (of raw silk).

ouvrant, -e [uvrɑ̃] *adj.* opening; *à jour* ~, at dawn, at day-break; *à portes ~es*, on the opening of the gates; ~ *s.m.* part of a door, cupboard, case, etc., which swings open; leaf.

ouvré, -e [uvre] *adj.* wrought; worked with embroidery or lace; diapered.

ouvre-boîte(**s**) [uvrəbwat] *s.m.* tin-opener; **~-bouteille**(**s**) [uvrəbutɛj] *s.m.* bottle-opener; **~-gant**(**s**) [uvrəgɑ̃] *s.m.* glove-stretcher.

ouvrer [uvre] *v.i.* to work; ~ *v.t.* to work, to chisel, to chase; to work (with a needle), to embroider.

ouvreu-r, -se [uvrœr] *s.m.f.* opener, one who makes opening move, bid, etc.; **~se** *s.f.* (theatr., cin.) box-opener, usherette.

ouvri-er, -ère [uvrije] *s.m.f.* workman, artisan, operative, worker; craftsman, journeyman; hand; maker; *premier ~er*, foreman; *~er, ~ère, à la journée*, day-worker; *~er agricole*, agricultural labourer; *mauvais ~er n'a jamais de bons outils*, a bad workman always blames his tools; *adj.* working, labouring, operative; of working men, of work-people; trade-; *la classe ~ère*, the working class; *jour ~er*, working day; *la question ~ère*, the labour question; (fig.) *la cheville ~ère*, the mainspring; the working part; *habitations ~ères*, workmen's dwellings.

ouvrir [uvrir] *v.t.i.* to open, to open up, to unclose, to unlock, to set open, to break open, to throw open; to spread, to unfold; to uncork; to sharpen; to begin, to start; to propose, to broach; ~ *de grands yeux*, to stare; *ouvrez l'œil, et le bon!*, look out!; ~ *une boutique, un commerce*, to open a shop, a business; ~ *le feu*, to open fire, to begin shooting; ~ *de belles perspectives*, to open up good prospects; ~ *le débat*, to open the debate, or the case; (electr.) to open, to break (the circuit); *les magasins n'ouvrent pas le lundi*, the shops don't open on Monday; *ce salon ouvre sur la pelouse*, this drawing-room opens on to the lawn; *la séance est ouverte*, the session is opened; *on devrait lui ~ les yeux*, somebody ought to enlighten him; ~ *une souscription*, to start a subscription list; ~ *un compte à qn.*, to open an account with or for s.o.; ~ *l'appetit*, to sharpen the appetite; *s'~ un passage*, to make or force one's way; **s'~** *v.refl.* to be opened, to open; to expand; (fig.) to open oneself, to open one's mind; to unbosom oneself; to disclose one's intentions.

ouvroir [uvrwar] *s.m.* work-room (in convent, etc.); charity needlework establishment.

ovaire [ɔvɛr] *s.m.* (anat., bot.) ovary.

ovale [ɔval] *adj., s.m.* oval; *en* ~, oval, elliptical.

ovalisation [ɔvalizɑsjɔ̃] *s.f.* (techn.) ovalization, wearing out of round (of cylinders, bearings, etc.).

ovalisé, -e [ɔvalize] *s.f.* (techn.) ovalized, worn out of round.

ovarien, -ne [ɔvarjɛ̃] *adj.* ovarian.

ovation [ɔvɑsjɔ̃] *s.f.* ovation, enthusiastic reception; *faire une ~ à*, to give an ovation to, to acclaim.

ove [ɔv] *s.m.* (arch.) ovum.

ové, -e [ɔve] *adj.* ovate.

ovibos [ɔvibos] *s.m.* (zool.) ovibovine, musk-ox.

oviducte [ɔvidykt] *s.m.* (anat.) oviduct.

ovin, -e [ɔvɛ̃] *adj.* ovine; *bétail ~, bêtes ~es, les ~s*, sheep.

ovipare [ɔvipar] *adj.* oviparous.

ovoïde [ɔvɔid] *adj.* ovoid.

ovulaire [ɔvylɛr] *adj.* ovular.

ovulation [ɔvylɑsjɔ̃] *s.f.* ovulation.

ovule [ɔvyl] *s.m.* ovule.

oxalate [ɔksalat] *s.m.* (chem.) oxalate.

oxalide [ɔksalid] *s.f.* (bot.) Oxalis, wood-sorrel.

oxalique [ɔksalik] *adj.* (chem.) oxalic.

oxhydrique [ɔksidrik] *adj.* oxyhydrogen (for or of blowpipes).

oxyacétylénique [ɔksiasetilenik] *adj.* (techn.) oxyacetylene.

oxycarboné, -e [ɔksikarbɔne] *adj.* (med.) suffering from carbon monoxide poisoning.
oxycoupage [ɔksikupaʒ] *s.m.* (techn.) cutting with oxyacetylene or oxyhydrogen apparatus.
oxycrat [ɔksikra] *s.m.* (ant.) oxycrate, mixture of vinegar and water.
oxydable [ɔksidabl] *adj.* (chem.) oxidizable, liable to rust.
oxydation [ɔksidɑsjɔ̃] *s.f.* (chem.) oxidation, oxidization.
oxyde [ɔksid] *s.m.* (chem.) oxide; ~ *de carbone*, carbon monoxide.
oxyder [ɔkside] *v.t.* to oxidize; **s'~** *v.refl.* to become oxidized, to rust.
oxy-génation [ɔksiʒenɑsjɔ̃] *s.f.* oxygenation; **~gène** [ɔksiʒɛn] *s.m.* oxygen.
oxygéné, -e [ɔksiʒene] *adj.* oxygenated; (fam.) (of hair) bleached; *eau* ~, peroxide of hydrogen.
oxygéner [ɔksiʒene] *v.t.* to oxygenate, to oxygenize; to peroxide (hair).
oxymel [ɔksimɛl] *s.m.* oxymel, mixture of vinegar, honey, and water.
oxyton [ɔksitɔ̃] *s.m.* (lang.) oxytone.
oxyure [ɔksjyr] *s.f.* (zool.) worm, nematode.
ozone [ozɔn] *s.m.* ozone.
ozoné, -e [ozɔne] *adj.* ozonized.
ozonis-er [ozɔnize] *v.t.* to ozonize; **~eur** [ozɔnizœr] *s.m.* ozonizer.

P

P, p [pe] *s.m.* the letter P, p; abbrev. *page*; (mus.) *piano* (opp. *forte*); *P*, (eccles.) *Père*.
pacage [pakaʒ] *s.m.* pasturage, pasture, pasture-land.
pacager [pakaʒe] *v.t.i.* to pasture, to graze.
pacha [paʃa] *s.m.* pasha.
pachyderme [paʃidɛrm, pakidɛrm] *adj.* (zool.) pachydermatous; ~ *s.m.* pachyderm; (pl.) Pachydermata.
pacificat-eur, -rice [pasifikatœr] *s.m.f.* pacifier, peace-maker; *adj.* pacifying, peace-making.
pacification [pasifikɑsjɔ̃] *s.f.* pacification, peace-making, appeasement.
pacifier [pasifje] *v.t.* to pacify, to calm, to appease.
pacifique [pasifik] *adj.* pacific, peaceful, peaceable, conciliatory, quiet, gentle, mild; *l'Océan Pacifique*, the Pacific Ocean; *d'humeur* ~, in peaceful mood, of a peaceful disposition; **~ment** [pasifikmɑ̃] *adv.* peacefully, in peace, quietly, peaceably.
pacifisme [pasifism] *s.m.* pacificism.
pacifiste [pasifist] *adj.*, *s.m.f.* pacifist, (advocate) of peace.
pack [pak] *s.m.* **1.** (naut.) ice-pack, pack-ice; **2.** (Rugby football) pack, forwards.
pacotille [pakɔtij] *s.f.* small stock of goods; cheap wares, job lot, shoddy goods; pedlar's pack or bale.
pacquage [pakaʒ] *s.m.* packing (of fish).
pacquer [pake] *v.t.* to pack (fish).
pacte [pakt] *s.m.* pact, compact, contract, covenant, agreement, treaty; (fig.) bargain; (comm.) ~ *social*, articles of association; ~ *de famille*, family settlement; (hist.) *le* ~ *de famille*, the Family Compact; *faire un* ~ *avec*, to enter into an agreement with; *il a un* ~ *avec le diable*, he has made a bargain with the devil.
pactiser [paktize] *v.i.* to make an agreement, to come to terms, to treat, (*avec*, with); (fig.) to compound, to compromise, (*avec*, with).
pactole [paktɔl] *s.m.* source of wealth; (fig.) eldorado, gold-mine.
paddock [padɔk] *s.m.* paddock, enclosure; (pop.) bed.
padou [padu] *s.m.* (text.) ferret, tape.
padouan, -e [paduɑ̃] *adj.*, *s.m.f.* Paduan.
pæan see PÉAN.
paf [paf] *adj.invar.* (fam.) drunk; *interj.* ~*!*, bang!, pop!
pagaie [pagɛ] *s.f.* paddle (for canoe, etc.).
pagaïe, pagaille, pagaye [pagaj] *s.f.* (fam.) **1.** *en* ~, in great quantity; **2.** disorder; *en* ~, in disorder, higgledy-piggledy, all over the place.
paganisme [paganism] *s.m.* paganism, heathenism.
pagayer [pagɛje] *v.i.* to paddle.
pagayeu-r, -se [pagɛjœr] *s.m.f.* paddler (of canoe).
page¹ [paʒ] *s.f.* page; *à la* ~ *20*, on page 20; *mettre en* ~*s*, to make up (newspaper, etc.); *mise en* ~, making-up; (fam.) *être à la* ~, to be in the know; to be up to date or in the fashion.
page² [paʒ] *s.m.* (hist.) page; *effronté comme un* ~, bold as brass; *être hors de* ~, to be one's own master (to have served one's time as a page); ⚠ not 'page-boy' at an hotel.
page³ [paʒ], **pageot** [paʒo] *s.m.* (pop.) bed.
pagination [paʒinɑsjɔ̃] *s.f.* pagination, paging.
paginer [paʒine] *v.t.* to paginate, to page.
pagne [paɲ] *s.m.* loincloth.
(se) pagnoter [paɲɔte] *v.refl.* (pop.) to go to bed.
pagode [pagɔd] *s.f.* pagoda (temple).
paie [pɛ] *s.f.* pay, wages.
paiement [pɛmɑ̃] *s.m.* payment, remuneration; (fig.) recompense, reward.
païen, -ne [pajɛ̃] *adj.* pagan, heathen; *s.m.f.* pagan, heathen, infidel.
paierie [peri] *s.f.* treasury, pay-office.
paillage [pɑjaʒ] *s.m.* (hort.) mulching.
paillard, -e [pajar] *adj.* lewd, lecherous; *s.m.f* lewd person.
paillardise [pajardiz] *s.f.* lewdness, lechery, debauchery; lewd word or story.
paillasse¹ [pɑjas; pajas] *s.f.* straw mattress, palliasse, pallet; (pop.) *crever la* ~ *à qn.*, to slit s.o. open, to run s.o. through; **2.** (pop.) prostitute; **3.** draining-board (part of sink unit).
paillasse² [pajas] *s.m.* clown; (fig.) mountebank, turncoat.
paillasson [pɑjasɔ̃; pajasɔ̃] *s.m.* **1.** (agric.) straw matting; **2.** doormat; (fig.) sycophant; (fig.) *mettre la clé sous le* ~, to flit, to abscond; **3.** straw for hat-making; straw hats.
paille [pɑj] *s.f.* **1.** straw, chaff; (fig.) trifle; ~ *de fer*, steel wool, metal turnings; (fig.) *un feu de* ~, a short-lived blaze, brush fire; *mettre qn. sur la* ~, to reduce s.o. to beggary; *il mourra sur la* ~, he will die in the gutter; *tirer à la courte* ~, to draw lots; *homme de* ~, man of straw, man who lends his name to some shady transaction, agent, tool; *des gants* ~, straw-coloured gloves; **2.** flaw, mote; *voir la* ~ *dans l'œil de son prochain*, to see the mote in one's neighbour's eye.
paillé, -e [pɑje] *adj.* **1.** straw-coloured; **2.** flawed; **3.** (of chair) straw-bottomed.
pailler [pɑje] *s.m.* straw-stack, straw-yard; straw-barn.
pailler [pɑje] *v.t.* **1.** to straw-bottom (chair); **2.**

to wrap in straw; to cover with straw mats; **3.** (hort.) to mulch.

paillet [paje] *adj.m.* (of red wine) pale; ~ *s.m.* **1.** (naut.) collision-mat, fender; **2.** (techn.) spring (portion of flat door-bolt).

pailleté, -e [pajte] *adj.* spangled, bespangled; adorned with sequins.

pailleter [pajte] *v.t.* to spangle, to adorn with sequins.

paillette [pajɛt] *s.f.* **1.** spangle, sequin; **2.** grain (of gold-dust); **3.** flake (of mica); *savon en ~s*, soap-flakes; **4.** flaw; **5.** = PAILLET 2.

pailleu-x, -se [pajø] *adj.* **1.** (metall.) flawy, flawed; **2.** (agric.) (of manure) strawy.

paillis [paji] *s.m.* (hort.) mulch, straw matting.

paillon [pajɔ̃] *s.m.* **1.** straw wrapping (for bottles); **2.** bunch of straw used for straining; **3.** (jeweller's) foil; **4.** link of small chain.

paillot [pajo] *s.m.* small palliasse or straw mattress.

pain [pɛ̃] *s.m.* **1.** bread, loaf, loaf of bread; (fig.) living, life; *petit ~*, roll; *se vendre comme des petits ~s*, to sell like hot cakes; *~ bis*, brown bread; *~ rassis*, stale bread; *~ de munition*, regulation or ration bread; *~ à cacheter*, stick of sealing-wax; *faire son ~*, to bake, to make bread; *gagner son ~*, to earn one's living; *~ d'épice*, gingerbread; *~ de beurre*, pat of butter; *~ de sucre*, sugar-loaf; *~ de savon*, cake of soap; (relig.) *~ azyme*, unleavened bread; *~ bénit*, consecrated bread; *c'est ~ bénit!*, it serves him right!; *manger son ~ blanc le premier*, to have an easy start, to have beginner's luck; (pop.) *perdre le goût du ~*, to die; *ôter* or *faire passer le goût du ~ à qn.*, to kill s.o., to do s.o. in; *avoir du ~ sur la planche*, to have plenty on hand; to have one's work cut out; *long comme un jour sans ~*, interminable, never-ending; *je ne mange pas de ce ~-là*, I don't go in for that sort of thing; **2.** blow, slap, clout; *coller un ~ à qn.*, to hit s.o., to fetch s.o. a clout.

pair [pɛr] *s.m.* peer, equal; (fin.) par; (of bird) mate; *de ~*, on a par, on an equal footing; *aller de ~ avec*, to rank with; *marcher de ~ avec*, to keep pace with; *hors (de) ~*, peerless, unequalled, unrivalled; *être avec qn.* or *traiter qn. de ~ à compagnon*, to be on familiar terms with s.o.; *au ~*, au pair, (work) in exchange for board and lodging.

pair, -e [pɛr] *adj.* (of numbers) even.

paire [pɛr] *s.f.* pair, couple, brace; (pej.) *les deux font la ~*, they make a fine pair.

pairesse [pɛrɛs] *s.f.* peeress.

pairie [peri] *s.f.* peerage.

pairle [pɛrl] *s.m.* (herald.) pall.

paisible [pɛzibl] *adj.* peaceful, peaceable, quiet, placid; **~ment** [pɛzibləmɑ̃] *adv.* peacefully, peaceably, calmly, placidly.

paître [pɛtr] *v.t.i.* to graze, to graze on, to feed on, to crop, to pasture, to feed; (fam.) *envoyer ~ qn.*, to tell s.o. to be off, to send s.o. about his business.

paix [pɛ] *s.f.* peace, quiet, calm; peace (treaty or settlement), peace (opp. war); *~!*, be quiet!, shut up!, that will do!; *faire la ~*, to make peace; *faire sa ~ avec*, to make one's peace with; *en ~*, at peace, in peace, peacefully; *laissez-le en ~*, (or, slang) *fichez-lui la ~*, leave him alone, let him alone; *juge de ~*, police-court magistrate; *~ fourrée*, hollow or sham peace.

Pakistan [pakistɑ̃] *s.m.* (geog.) Pakistan.

pakistanais, -e [pakistanɛ] *adj.*, *s.m.f.* Pakistani.

pal [pal] *s.m.* **1.** pale, stake; impalement (medieval torture); **2.** (herald.) pale.

palabre [palabr] *s.f.* palaver; (fig.) interminable discussion.

palabrer [palabre] *v.i.* to palaver; (fig.) to have a lengthy discussion.

palace [palas] *s.m.* luxury hotel; (fam.) *mener la vie de ~*, to live in great luxury.

paladin [paladɛ̃] *s.m.* paladin, champion.

palais[1] [palɛ] *s.m.* palace; *Palais (de Justice)*, Law Courts; *terme de Palais*, legal or forensic term; *style de Palais*, legal jargon.

palais[2] [palɛ] *s.m.* palate, roof (of the mouth); (fig.) taste, sense of taste; *voile du ~*, soft palate, velum.

palan [palɑ̃] *s.m.* lifting-tackle; pulley-block.

palanche [palɑ̃ʃ] *s.f.* yoke (for carrying two pails, etc.).

palançon [palɑ̃sɔ̃] *s.m.* lath, stake, (in mud wall).

palangre [palɑ̃gr] *s.f.* trawl-line.

palanque [palɑ̃k] *s.f.* timber stockade.

palanquer [palɑ̃ke] *v.i.* (naut.) to use block and tackle; *~ v.t.* (mil.) to fortify with a stockade.

palanquin [palɑ̃kɛ̃] *s.m.* palanquin, palankeen.

palastre [palastr] *s.m.* lock-plate, back-plate (of lock); *serrure à ~*, rim-lock.

palatal, -e, (aux) [palatal] *adj.* (phon.) palatal; (anat.) palatal, palatine; *~e s.f.* (phon.) palatal.

palatin,[1] **-e** [palatɛ̃] *adj.* Palatine; of the palace.

palatin,[2] **-e** [palatɛ̃] *adj.* (anat.) palatal, palatine, of the palate.

palatinat [palatina] *s.m.* palatinate.

palatine [palatin] *s.f.* (hist.) fur tippet (made fashionable by Princess Palatine, 1676).

pale[1] [pal] *s.f.* blade (of an oar); float, paddle-board; sluice; (aeron.) *~ d'hélice*, blade (of propeller).

pale[2] [pal] *s.f.* (Cath. liturg.) pall (for covering chalice).

pâle [pɑl] *adj.* pale, pallid, wan, ghastly; (fig.) colourless, tame; *~ comme un linge*, as pale as death, as white as a sheet; *bleu ~*, pale blue; *un style bien ~*, a tame, or a colourless, style; (mil. slang) *se faire porter ~*, to report sick.

pale-ale [pɛlɛl] *s.m.* pale ale.

palée [pale] *s.f.* row of stakes or pales, piles, piling.

palefrenier [palfrənje] *s.m.* groom, stable-man, ostler.

palefroi [palfrwa] *s.m.* palfrey.

palémon [palemɔ̃] *s.m.* (crust.) palaemon (prawn).

paléo-graphe [paleɔgraf] *s.m.f.* palaeographer; **~graphie** [paleɔgrafi] *s.f.* palaeography; **~graphique** [paleɔgrafik] *adj.* palaeographic; **~lithique** [paleɔlitik] *adj.* palaeolithic; *s.m.* palaeolithic period, Early Stone Age.

paléontolog-ie [paleɔ̃tɔlɔʒi] *s.f.* palaeontology; **~iste** [paleɔ̃tɔlɔʒist], **~ue** [paleɔ̃tɔlɔg] *s.m.f.* palaeontologist.

paléozoïque [paleɔzɔik] *adj.* palaeozoic.

paleron [palrɔ̃] *s.m.* (butch.) shoulder-blade, chuck, blade-bone.

palestinien, -ne [palɛstinijɛ̃] *adj.*, *s.m.f.* Palestinian.

palestre [palɛstr] *s.f.* (Gr. ant.) palaestra,

palet [palɛ] *s.m.* quoit; *jouer au ~*, to play quoits.

paletot [palto] *s.m.* overcoat.

palette [palɛt] *s.f.* **1.** pallet; wooden racket, battledore; beater (used in washing); (mil.) marker (used in target practice); **2.** (techn.) vane, blade (of turbine, etc.); pallet (of watch mechanism); pallet (used with fork-lift trucks); **3.** (cook.) shoulder of mutton or pork; **4.** (paint.) palette.

palétuvier [paletyvje] *s.m.* (bot.) mangrove-tree.

pâleur [pɑlœr] *s.f.* pallor, wanness, pallidness.

pali [pali] *s.m.* Pali (language).

pâlichon, -ne [paliʃɔ̃] *adj.* (fam.) rather pale.

palier [palje] *s.m.* **1.** landing, stairhead; (fig.) level, stage, pause, period of stability; *par ~s*,

in stages, progressively; *un ~ dans la hausse des prix*, a pause in the rise of prices; *en ~*, (of speed, flight, etc.) on the level, level, horizontal; **2.** (mech.) bearing; *~ de butée*, thrust-bearing.
palière [paljɛr] *adj.f.* top, level with the landing; *marche ~*, top step; *porte ~*, door opening on to the landing.
palimpseste [palɛ̃psɛst] *s.m.* palimpsest.
palindrome [palɛ̃drɔm] *adj., s.m.* palindrome (sentence or word).
palingénésie [palɛ̃ʒenezi] *s.f.* palingenesis, revival.
palinodie [palinɔdi] *s.f.* palinode, recantation.
pâlir [pɑlir] *v.t.i.* to give a pale colour to; to turn or grow pale; to wane; to pale, to grow dim, to be on the wane; *~ sur ses livres*, to pore over one's books; *son étoile pâlit*, his star is on the wane.
palis [pali] *s.m.* stake, pale; paling; picket-fence; staked enclosure.
palissade [palisad] *s.f.* palisade, paling, hoarding; trees or shrubs cut to form hedge.
palissader [palisade] *v.t.* to palisade, to fence, to rail in, to stockade; to protect with a hedge or row of trees.
palissage [palisaʒ] *s.m.* (hort.) nailing up, training, paling.
palissandre [palisɑ̃dr] *s.m.* (bot.) rosewood, jacaranda; violet wood.
pâlissant, -e [pɑlisɑ̃] *adj.* turning pale, fading, waning.
palisser [palise] *v.t.* to nail up, to train (vine, espalier, etc.).
palisson [palisɔ̃] *s.m.* (furrier's) softening iron.
palladium[1] [paladjɔm] *s.m.* (Gr. ant.) palladium, statue of Pallas; (fig.) safeguard, talisman.
palladium[2] [paladjɔm] *s.m.* (chem.) palladium.
palliati-f, -ve [paljatif] *adj.*, **~f** *s.m.* palliative.
pallier [palje] *v.t.* to palliate, to mitigate, to alleviate; to cover up, to conceal.
palmaire [palmɛr] *adj.* (anat.) palmar; of or in the palm of the hand.
palmarès [palmarɛs] *s.m.* prize-list, list of honours; hit-parade, top-of-the-pops.
palme [palm] *s.f.* palm-branch; palm-tree; (fig.) success, victory, the palm; *remporter la ~*, to be the victor, to bear the palm; *la ~ du martyre*, the crown of martyrdom; *les ~s (académiques)*, decoration for services to education.
palmé, -e [palme] *adj.* **1.** (bot.) palmate; **2.** (ornith.) web-footed.
palmeraie [palmərɛ] *s.f.* palm-grove, plantation of palm-trees.
palmette [palmɛt] *s.f.* **1.** (arch.) palm-leaf moulding, palmette; **2.** (hort.) fan-shaped espalier.
palmier [palmje] *s.m.* palm-tree; (cook.) puff-pastry cake in shape of palm-leaf.
palmipède [palmipɛd] *adj., s.m.* (ornith.) palmiped, web-footed (bird).
palmiste [palmist] *s.m.* **1.** (bot.) cabbage-tree, cabbage-palm, palmetto; **2.** (zool.) *rat ~*, palm-squirrel; (ent.) *ver ~*, palm-weevil.
palmite [palmit] *s.f.* pith of palm-tree.
palmure [palmyr] *s.f.* (ornith.) web (of palmipeds).
palois, -e [palwa] *adj., s.m.f.* (native or inhabitant) of Pau (France).
palombe [palɔ̃b] *s.f.* ring-dove, wood-pigeon.
palonnier [palɔnje] *s.m.* swingle-bar (of horse-carriage); (aeron.) rudder-bar; (car) compensator-bar (in brake-linkage).
palot [palo] *s.m.* spade used for turf-cutting or for digging worms, etc., from the sand.
pâlot, -te [pɑlo] *adj.* rather pale.
palourde [palurd] *s.f.* (mollusc.) clam.
palpable [palpabl] *adj.* palpable, tangible; obvious.
palpation [palpɑsjɔ̃] *s.f.* (med.) palpation.
palpe [palp] *s.f.* palp, feeler (of insects, etc.).
palpébral, -e, (**aux**) [palpebral] *adj.* (anat.) palpebral, pertaining to the eyelids.
palper [palpe] *v.t.* (med.) to palpate; to handle, to finger; (fam.) to pocket, to receive (money).
palpeur [palpœr] *s.m.* (techn.) feeler-gauge.
palpitant, -e [palpitɑ̃] *adj.* **1.** palpitating, throbbing; **2.** exciting, thrilling; *~ s.m.* (pop.) heart.
palpitation [palpitɑsjɔ̃] *s.f.* palpitation, throb, throbbing; alternating movement; (astron.) pulsation.
palpiter [palpite] *v.i.* to palpitate, to throb; (astron.) to pulsate; (fig.) to be thrilled.
palplanche [palplɑ̃ʃ] *s.f.* pile, coffer-dam plank, sheeting-pile.
palsambleu [palsɑ̃blø] *interj.* (obs.) expletive equivalent to ''s blood!'.
paltoquet [paltɔkɛ] *s.m.* **1.** (obs., fam.) lout, churl, bumpkin; **2.** (mod.) insignificant and bumptious individual.
paluche [palyʃ] *s.f.* (pop.) hand.
palud(e) [palyd], **palus** [paly] *s.m.* **1.** (obs.) marsh; **2.** (in Bordeaux region) former salt-marsh planted with vines.
paludéen, -ne [palydeɛ̃] *adj.* marshy, marsh-, paludal, malarial; *fièvre ~ne*, marsh fever, malaria; *s.m.f.* one suffering from malaria.
paludier [palydje] *s.m.* worker in salt-marsh.
paludisme [palydism] *s.m.* malaria, marsh fever.
palustre [palystr] *adj.* **1.** paludal; **2.** (med.) *fièvre ~*, malaria.
pâmer *v.i.*, **se pâmer** *v.refl.* [pɑme] to swoon, to faint away; to be enraptured; *se ~ d'admiration*, to be overcome with admiration; *se ~ de rire*, to nearly die with laughing; *c'est à ~ de rire!*, it's enough to make one die with laughing.
pâmoison [pɑmwazɔ̃] *s.f.* swoon, fainting-fit; *tomber en ~*, to fall into a swoon, to faint away.
pampa [pɑ̃pa] *s.f.* pampas (pl.).
pamphlet [pɑ̃flɛ] *s.m.* lampoon, satirical or scurrilous pamphlet; ⚠ not an informative leaflet.
pamphlétaire [pɑ̃fletɛr] *s.m.f.* pamphleteer; ⚠ see PAMPHLET.
pampille [pɑ̃pij] *s.f.* drop (of pendant, etc.); small tassel.
pamplemousse [pɑ̃pləmus] *s.m.* grapefruit; shaddock, pomelo.
pampre [pɑ̃pr] *s.m.* vine-branch; (arch.) vine-branch ornament; (poet.) vine, grape, wine; vine-covered arbour.
pan [pɑ̃] *s.m.* **1.** piece or panel (of material), flap, free end, skirt, tail (of shirt); *s'attacher au pan de l'habit de qn.*, to cling to someone's coat-tails; **2.** section, surface, face, side; *un ~ de mur*, a wall-surface; *les ~s d'un prisme*, the faces of a prism; *un écrou à six ~s*, a hexagonal nut; *à ~s coupés*, with the corners cut off.
pan [pɑ̃] *interj.* bang!
panacée [panase] *s.f.* panacea.
panache [panaʃ] *s.m.* tuft, plume; top; triangular part of pendentive of an arch; (fig.) panache, flourish, dash; *avoir du ~*, to look dashing; *y mettre du ~*, to do (sth.) with a flourish.
panaché, -e [panaʃe] *adj.* variegated, streaked, mixed; *un (demi) ~*, a lemonade shandy.
panacher [panaʃe] *v.t.* **1.** to plume; **2.** to streak, to variegate, to mix, to arrange (e.g. black and white) alternately.
panachure [panaʃyr] *s.f.* streak, variegation, stripe.

panade [panad] *s.f.* panada, bread soup; (fam.) *être* or *tomber dans la* ~, to be hard up, to fall on hard times.
panafricain, -e [panafrikɛ̃] *adj.* pan-African.
panafricanisme [panafrikanism] *s.m.* pan-Africanism.
panais [panɛ] *s.m.* parsnip.
panama [panama] *s.m.* panama (hat).
panaméricain, -e [panamerikɛ̃] *adj.* pan-American.
panaméricanisme [panamerikanism] *s.m.* pan-Americanism.
panamien, -ne [panamjɛ̃], **panaméen, -ne** [panameɛ̃] *adj., s.m.f.* Panamanian, (native or inhabitant) of Panama.
panarabisme [panarabism] *s.m.* pan-Arabism.
panard [panar] *s.m.* (pop.) foot.
panard, -e [panar] *adj.* (of horses) with out-turned feet.
panaris [panari] *s.m.* (pathol.) whitlow.
panca, panka [pɑ̃ka], **punka** [pɔ̃ka] *s.m.* punkah (fan).
pancarte [pɑ̃kart] *s.f.* placard, bill, show-card.
panchromatique [pɑ̃krɔmatik] *adj.* (abbrev. *panchro*) panchromatic.
pancrace [pɑ̃kras] *s.m.* (Gr. ant.) pancratium (wrestling and boxing contest).
pancréas [pɑ̃kreɑs] (anat.) *s.m.* pancreas.
pancréatique [pɑ̃kreatik] *adj.* pancreatic.
panda [pɑ̃da] *s.m.* (zool.) panda.
pandanus [pɑ̃danys] *s.m.* (bot.) pandanus (tree).
pandectes [pɑ̃dɛkt] *s.f.pl.* pandects.
pandémonium [pɑ̃demɔnjɔm] *s.m.* pandemonium, utter confusion; (fig.) den of vice; ⚠ not 'pandemonium' in sense 'loud noise'.
pandit [pɑ̃di(t)] *s.m.* pundit, learned Hindu.
pandore [pɑ̃dɔr] *s.m.* (obs., fam.) policeman.
pandour [pɑ̃dur] *s.m.* (hist.) pandour; free-booter, rapacious soldier; brute.
pané, -e [pane] *adj.* (cook.) fried in breadcrumbs.
panégyrique [paneʒirik] *s.m.* panegyric, eulogy.
panégyriste [paneʒirist] *s.m.f.* panegyrist; (often iron.) eulogist.
paner [pane] *v.t.* (cook.) to turn in breadcrumbs.
panerée [panre] *s.f.* basketful.
paneterie [pantri] *s.f.* bread store, bread pantry.
panetier [pantje] *s.m.* (hist.) pantler.
panetière [pantjɛr] *s.f.* **1.** shepherd's scrip; **2.** bread bin.
paneton [pantɔ̃] *s.m.* wicker mould for a loaf of bread.
pangermanisme [pɑ̃ʒɛrmanism] *s.m.* pan-Germanism.
pangolin [pɑ̃gɔlɛ̃] *s.m.* (zool.) scaly ant-eater, pangolin.
panic [panik] *s.m.* (bot.) panic-grass, millet.
panicaut [paniko] *s.m.* (bot.) Eryngium.
panicule [panikyl] *s.m.* (bot.) panicle.
paniculé, -e [panikyle] *adj.* paniculate.
panier [panje] *s.m.* basket, hamper, wicker basket; pannier (for beast of burden); hoop petticoat, pannier; (sport) *balle au* ~, basket-ball; ~ *à salade*, salad-net, salad-basket; (fam.) prison van, Black Maria; (fig.) ~ *percé*, spend-thrift; *faire danser l'anse du* ~, to make something on the side (when shopping or marketing); *le dessus du* ~, the pick of the basket; ~ *à ouvrage*, work-basket; ~ *à papier*, waste-paper basket.
panière [panjɛr] *s.f.* large basket.
panifiable [panifjabl] *adj.* (of cereals) suitable for making bread.
panification [panifikɑsjɔ̃] *s.f.* panification, bread-making.
panifier [panifje] *v.t.* to make into bread.
paniquard [panikar] *s.m.* one who panics, panic-stricken man.
panique [panik] *adj.* panic; ~ *s.f.* panic, wild stampede.
panka see PANCA.
panne[1] [pan] *s.f.* **1.** (text.) plush; (herald.) pean; **2.** fat (of pig).
panne[2] [pan] *s.f.* **1.** (naut.) *mettre en* ~, to bring to, to heave to; (pop.) *être dans la* ~, to be hard up; **2.** (mech.) breakdown, failure, standstill; ~ *du moteur*, engine-failure; ~ *d'électricité*, electricity failure, loss of current, black-out; (car) ~ *d'allumage*, ignition trouble; *en* ~, broken down, at a standstill; *rester* or *tomber en* ~, to break down; *être en* ~, to have broken down, to be unable to go on; (fam.) *être en* ~ *de qch.*, to be short of sth.
panne[3] [pan] *s.f.* **1.** (build.) purlin (of roof); **2.** (techn.) pane (of hammer); flat end of pickaxe.
panné, -e [pane] *adj.* hard-up, penniless, in Queer Street.
panneau (pl. **-x**) [pano] *s.m.* **1.** snare, net (for game); *tomber* or *donner dans le* ~, to fall into the trap; **2.** panel, section; (pl.) panelling; face (of dressed stone); facet (of jewel); ~ *de contrôle*, control-panel; **3.** board, notice-board, sign-board, sign, notice, signal; hoarding; ~*-réclame*, advertisement hoarding.
panneton [pantɔ̃] *s.m.* bit (of key); window-catch.
panonceau (pl. **-x**) [panɔ̃so] *s.m.* escutcheon; sign in form of escutcheon.
panoplie [panɔpli] *s.f.* panoply; trophy of arms; collection of weapons; (fireman's, nurse's, etc.) outfit (for a child).
panoptique [panɔptik] *s.m.* panopticon (prison).
panorama [panɔrama] *s.m.* panorama; wide-ranging survey.
panoramique [panɔramik] *adj.* panoramic; ~ *s.m.* (cin., TV) panning.
pansage [pɑ̃saʒ] *s.m.* grooming (of a horse).
panse [pɑ̃s] *s.f.* **1.** (zool.) rumen, paunch; (fam.) belly, paunch, pot-belly, fat stomach; **2.** bulge, rounded portion, belly; brim or sound-bow (of bell); body or oval portion (of a letter); (fig.) *il n'a pas fait la* ~ *d'un a*, he hasn't done a stroke (of work).
pansement [pɑ̃smɑ̃] *s.m.* dressing (of or for a wound).
panser [pɑ̃se] *v.t.* to dress (a wound); to groom (a horse).
pansu, -e [pɑ̃sy] *adj.* pot-bellied; bulging, fat, rounded.
pantalon [pɑ̃talɔ̃] *s.m.* **1.** trousers, pair of trousers, (U.S.) pants; **2.** (obs., usu. pl.) knickers, drawers.
pantalonnade [pɑ̃talɔnad] *s.f.* pantaloonery, buffoonery; (fig.) sham, false demonstration (of devotion, etc.).
pante [pɑ̃t] *s.m.* **1.** (obs. slang) mug; **2.** (pop.) bloke, chap.
pantelant, -e [pɑ̃tlɑ̃] *adj.* panting, gasping, palpitating, quivering.
panteler [pɑ̃tle] *v.i.* to pant, to gasp, to quiver, to palpitate.
pantenne, pantène [pɑ̃tɛn] *s.f.* draw-net; (naut.) *en* ~, in disorder.
panthéisme [pɑ̃teism] *s.m.* pantheism.
panthéiste [pɑ̃teist] *adj.* pantheistic(al); ~ *s.m.f.* pantheist.
panthéon [pɑ̃teɔ̃] *s.m.* pantheon.
panthère [pɑ̃tɛr] *s.f.* panther.
pantière [pɑ̃tjɛr] *s.f.* draw-net (for catching birds); game-net.
pantin [pɑ̃tɛ̃] *s.m.* puppet, jumping-jack; (fig.) mere puppet.
pantographe [pɑ̃tɔgraf] *s.m.* pantograph.
pantois, -e [pɑ̃twa] *adj.* **1.** (obs.) panting; **2.** astounded, nonplussed, aghast, amazed.
pantomime [pɑ̃tɔmim] *s.f.* pantomime, dumb show; affected behaviour.
pantouflard [pɑ̃tuflar] *s.m.* (fam.) stay-at-home,

one who likes his comforts, one who sticks to his little ways.
pantoufle [pɑ̃tufl] *s.f.* slipper; *en ~s*, in one's slippers; (fig.) at one's ease, free and easy.
pantoufler [pɑ̃tufle] *v.i.* **1.** (obs.) to chat in a free and easy manner; **2.** to buy oneself out of State service.
panure [panyr] *s.f.* breadcrumbs (as used in cooking).
paon [pɑ̃] *s.m.* **1.** (ornith.) peacock, peafowl; *se parer des plumes du ~*, to deck oneself in borrowed plumes; **2.** (ent.) peacock butterfly; emperor moth.
paonne [pan] *s.f.* peahen.
papa [papa] *s.m.* father, daddy, dad, papa; *bon ~*, grandpa, grandad; *à la ~*, familiarly, good-naturedly, in a leisurely way; (pej.) *de ~*, old-fashioned, out of date.
papal, -e, (aux) [papal] *adj.* papal.
papauté [papote] *s.f.* papacy.
papaye [papaj] *s.f.* papaw, papaya.
papayer [papaje] *s.m.* (bot.) papaw-tree.
pape [pap] *s.m.* pope.
papegai [papgɛ] *s.m.* popinjay.
papelard [paplar] *s.m.* (fam.) paper, piece of paper.
papelard, -e [paplar] *adj.* hypocritical, sanctimonious; *s.m.f.* hypocrite.
papelardise [paplardiz] *s.f.* hypocrisy.
paperasse [papras] *s.f.* old paper, waste paper, old document.
paperasserie [paprasri] *s.f.* pile of old papers, endless forms, etc., (to fill in), (slang) bumf; (fig.) red tape.
paperassi-er, -ère [paprasje] *adj., s.m.f.* (one who is) fond of keeping files, of sending out forms, of red tape; (slang) bumf-merchant.
papesse [papɛs] *s.f.* female pope; *la ~ Jeanne*, Pope Joan.
papeterie [pap(e)tri] *s.f.* **1.** paper-factory, paper-mill; **2.** paper-making; paper trade; **3.** stationer's shop.
papeti-er, -ère [paptje] *s.m.f.* **1.** stationer; **2.** paper-maker.
papier [papje] *s.m.* paper, piece of paper; document; (comm., fin.) bill; *~ buvard*, blotting-paper; *~ à calquer*, tracing-paper; *~ d'emballage*, wrapping-paper; *~ gris*, brown paper; *~ à lettres*, notepaper; *~-monnaie*, paper money; *~ de verre* (or *verré* or *-émeri*), glass-paper, sand-paper, emery-paper; *~ de soie*, tissue paper; *~ de tournesol*, litmus paper; *~ carbone* or (obs.) *au charbon*, carbon-paper; *~ hygiénique* or *de cabinets* or (vulg.) *cul*, toilet-paper, bumf; *~ d'étain*, tin-foil; *~ journal*, newspaper, newsprint; *~ ministre*, official foolscap; *~ timbré*, (official) stamped paper; *~ peint* or *à tapisser* or *-tenture*, wallpaper; (fig.) *sur le ~*, on paper, in theory; *vos ~s sont en ordre?*, are your (identity) papers in order?; *~ à courte échéance*, short-dated bill; *~ sur Londres*, bill on London; *être dans les petits ~s de qn.*, to be in someone's good books; *rayez cela de vos ~s*, leave that out of your reckoning; do not count on that!
papilionacé, -e [papiljɔnase] *adj.* (bot.) papilionaceous; **~es** *s.f.pl.* Papilionaceae.
papillaire [papilɛr] *adj.* papillary.
papille [papij] *s.f.* (anat., bot.) papilla.
papillon [papijɔ̃] *s.m.* **1.** butterfly; (fig.) *~s noirs*, blues, gloomy thoughts; *~ de nuit*, moth; *nœud ~*, bow, bow-tie; **2.** (mech.) wing-nut; butterfly-valve, (disc-type) throttle; *bec ~*, fish-tail burner.
papillonnage [papijɔnaʒ], **papillonnement** [papijɔnmɑ̃] *s.m.* flitting about.
papillonner [papijɔne] *v.i.* **1.** to flutter; **2** (fig.) to flutter about, to flit (from one person or thing to another); to mess around.
papillotage [papijɔtaʒ] *s.m.* blinking (of the eyes); dazzle; (print.) slurring.
papillote [papijɔt] *s.f.* **1.** (obs.) spangle; **2.** curl-paper; **3.** sweet-wrapper; **4.** (cook.) buttered paper; **5.** screwed-up paper; *tu peux en faire des ~s*, it's only fit for the waste-paper basket.
papilloter [papijɔte] *v.t.* (obs.) to adorn with spangles; *~ v.i.* **1.** (of eyes) to blink, to be dazzled; **2.** to sparkle.
papisme [papism] *s.m.* popery, papism.
papiste [papist] *s.m.f.* papist.
papotage [papɔtaʒ] *s.m.* prattle, gossip; chatter, small talk, tittle-tattle.
papoter [papɔte] *v.i.* to prattle, to chatter.
papou, -e [papu] *adj., s.m.f.* Papuan.
Papouasie [papwazi] *s.f.* (geog.) Papua (New Guinea).
papule [papyl] *s.f.* papula, papule, pimple.
papuleu-x, -se [papylø] *adj.* papulous, pimply.
papyrus [papirys] *s.m.* (bot.) papyrus; (ant.) papyrus manuscript; papyrus motif.
pâque [pɑk] *s.f.* Passover; see PÂQUES.
paquebot [pakbo] *s.m.* liner, steamer; (hist.) packet-boat, mail-boat.
pâquerette [pɑkrɛt] *s.f.* daisy.
Pâques [pɑk] *s.m.* Easter; *jour de ~*, Easter day; *~ s.f.pl. joyeuses ~*, Happy Easter; *~ fleuries*, Palm Sunday; *faire ses ~*, to take communion at Easter; *à ~ prochain*, next Easter; *fleur de ~*, pasque-flower.
paquet [pakɛ] *s.m.* packet, parcel, bundle; lump, mass; (print.) slip; (Rugby football) pack; *embarquer un ~ de mer*, to ship a heavy sea; *faire ses ~s*, to pack up, to be off; *donner son ~ à qn.*, to give s.o. the sack; to give s.o. a piece of one's mind, to let s.o. have it; *recevoir son ~*, to get the sack, to get told off; *risquer le ~*, to chance it.
paquetage [paktaʒ] *s.m.* (mil.) kit.
par [par] *prep.* by, by means of, through, from, across, per, for every; for the sake of; *couper ~ morceaux*, to cut into pieces; *tant ~ tête*, so much per head, so much a head; *cinq francs ~ personne*, five francs a person; five francs each; *voyager ~ mer*, to travel by sea; *se promener ~ la ville*, to walk about the town; *~ monts et ~ vaux*, over hill and dale; *tomber ~ terre*, to fall on or to the ground; *tenir ~ la main*, to hold by the hand; *~ curiosité*, out of curiosity; *~ pitié!*, for pity's sake!; *regarder ~ la fenêtre*, to look out of the window; *page ~ page*, page after page; *commencer ~ dire*, to begin by saying; *de ~ le roi*, in the king's name; *je l'ai fait ~ moi-même*, I did it on my own; *~ temps de neige*, in snowy weather; *~ un jour d'été*, on a summer's day; *~ ailleurs*, in other respects, besides; *~-ci ~-là*, here and there, hither and thither, now and then; *~ delà*, beyond; *~ derrière*, from behind; *~-dessus*, over (the top of); *~ devant*, before, forwards; *~ trop*, far too much.
para [para] abbrev. *parachutiste*.
parabole [parabɔl] *s.f.* **1.** parable, allegory; **2.** (geom.) parabola.
parabolique [parabɔlik] *adj.* parabolic; **~ment** [parabɔlikmɑ̃] *adv.* parabolically, describing a parabola.
paraboloïde [parabɔlɔid] *s.m.* (geom.) paraboloid.
parachèvement [paraʃɛvmɑ̃] *s.m.* finishing, completion, bringing to perfection.
parachever [paraʃve] *v.t.* to finish, to complete, to bring to perfection.
parachut-age [paraʃytaʒ] *s.m.* parachuting, parachute landing, parachute drop (of supplies); **~er** [paraʃyte] *v.t.* to parachute, to drop by parachute; (fam.) to pitchfork (s.o. into an unpleasant job); **~isme** [paraʃytism] *s.m.* parachuting, parachute-dropping; **~iste** [para-

ʃytist] *adj.* parachute; *s.m.f.* (abbrev. *para*) parachutist, (pl.) parachute troops.

parade [parad] *s.f.* parade, show, display, pageant, state; (fenc.) parrying, parry, defence; (fig.) repartee; (rid.) checking or pulling-up of horse (as part of display); *faire ~ de*, to display, to show off (sth.); *de ~*, parade, for special occasions, for show; *habits de ~*, full-dress clothes; *il n'est pas heureux à la ~*, he is a bad hand at repartee.

parader [parade] *v.i.* to show off; *faire ~ un cheval*, to show off the paces of a horse.

paradigme [paradigm] *s.m.* paradigm, model.

paradis [paradi] *s.m.* paradise; (theatr.) gallery; (hort.) apple-stock used for grafting on; bird of paradise; *le ~ terrestre*, the Garden of Eden.

paradisiaque [paradizjak] *adj.* paradisiac, of or in paradise.

paradisier [paradizje] *s.m.* bird of paradise.

parados [parado] *s.m.* (fort.) parados.

paradoxal, -e, (aux) [paradɔksal] *adj.* paradoxical; **~ement** [paradɔxalmɑ̃] *adv.* paradoxically.

paradoxe [paradɔks] *s.m.* paradox.

parafe, paraphe [paraf] *s.m.* paraph, flourish (after one's signature); initials (by way of signature); *mettre son ~ au bas d'un acte*, to initial a document.

parafer, parapher [parafe] *v.t.* to paraph, to sign with a flourish, to initial.

paraffine [parafin] *s.f.* paraffin, paraffin wax; *huile de ~*, medicinal paraffin; ⚠ not 'paraffin' as used for burning.

paraffiner [parafine] *v.t.* to cover with paraffin wax.

parafoudre [parafudr] *s.m.* lightning-arrester (protecting electr. installation).

parage [paraʒ] *s.m.* **1.** (usu. pl.) quarter, locality, parts, place; **2.** extraction, descent, quality; *une dame de haut ~*, a lady of high degree, a lady of quality; **3.** (butch.) trimming (of meat); **4.** (viticulture) preparing of ground before winter.

paragraphe [paragraf] *s.m.* paragraph.

paragrêle [paragrɛl] *adj.*, *s.m.* (contrivance) for converting hail into rain.

paraître [parɛtr] *v.i.* to appear, to come in sight, to show oneself, or itself; to become visible; to seem, to look like; to come out, to be published; to cut a figure, to make a show; *il paraît cinquante ans*, he looks fifty; *elle a quarante ans, mais ne les paraît pas*, she is forty but she does not look her age; *cela paraît satisfaisant*, this seems quite all right; *chercher à ~*, to try to cut a figure; *à ce qu'il paraît*, as it would seem; *sans qu'il y paraisse*, (i.) although it does not look like it; (ii.) without its being seen; *il y paraît*, it's easy to see; *il n'y paraît pas*, one would not have thought it; there are no signs of it; *il paraît qu'il est venu*, they say that he came; *il paraîtrait qu'il est mort*, it is rumoured that he is dead; *vient de ~*, just published, just out; *faire ~*, to show, to give evidence of; to publish.

parallactique [paralaktik] *adj.* (astron.) parallactic.

parallaxe [paralaks] *s.f.* (astron.) parallax.

parallèle [paralɛl] *adj.* parallel; (fin.) *taux de change ~*, unofficial rate of exchange; *~ s.f.* parallel; *~ s.m.* (astron., geog.) parallel, (fig.) parallel, simile, comparison; *mettre en ~ avec*, to draw a parallel between; *montage en ~*, multiple connection, wiring in parallel; **~ment** [paralɛlmɑ̃] *adv.* parallel, in a parallel direction, (*à*, to, with); together, in conjunction, at the same time.

parallélépipède [paralelepipɛd], **parallélipipède** [paralelipipɛd] *s.m.* parallelepiped.

parallélisme [paralelism] *s.m.* parallelism.

parallélogramme [paralelɔgram] *s.m.* parallelogram.

paralogisme [paralɔʒism] *s.m.* paralogism.

paralysant, -e [paralizɑ̃] *adj.* paralysing.

paralyser [paralize] *v.t.* to paralyse, to render powerless.

paralysie [paralizi] *s.f.* paralysis, palsy; *attaque de ~*, paralytic stroke.

paralytique [paralitik] *adj.* paralysed, palsied, paralytic; *~ s.m.f.* paralytic.

paramètre [paramɛtr] *s.m.* parameter.

paramilitaire [paramilitɛr] *adj.* paramilitary.

parangon [parɑ̃gɔ̃] *s.m.* paragon, model of excellence; flawless diamond, pearl, etc.; (print.) double pica; *mettre en ~*, to compare; *marbre ~*, black marble.

parangonner [parɑ̃gɔne] *v.t.* (print.) to adjust, to range.

paranoïa [paranɔja] *s.f.* paranoia.

paranoïde [paranɔid] *adj.* paranoid.

paranoïaque [paranɔjak] *adj.*, *s.m.f.* paranoiac.

parapet [parapɛ] *s.m.* parapet, breastwork.

paraphe, parapher see PARAFE, PARAFER.

paraphernal, -e, (aux) [parafɛrnal] *adj.* (law) paraphernal; *biens paraphernaux*, paraphernalia, wife's property (other than the dowry).

paraphrase [parafrɑz] *s.f.* paraphrase, lengthy commentary.

paraphraser [parafrɑze] *v.t.* to paraphrase; to amplify, to expand, to add to (statement, etc.).

paraphrastique [parafrɑstik] *adj.* paraphrastic, paraphrased, not literal.

paraplégie [parapleʒi] *s.f.* paraplegia.

parapluie [paraplɥi] *s.m.* umbrella.

parasitaire [parazitɛr] *adj.* parasitical.

parasite [parazit] *s.m.* parasite; (pl.) (radio, TV) interference; *~ adj.* parasitic, parasitical.

parasiter [parasite] *v.t.* to be a parasite of; (fig.) to sponge on; (radio) to cause interference.

parasitique [parazitik] *adj.* parasitic(al).

parasitisme [parazitism] *s.m.* parasitism; (fig.) parasitical life, sponging.

parasitologie [parasitɔlɔʒi] *s.f.* parasitology.

parasol [parasɔl] *s.m.* parasol.

paratonnerre [paratɔnɛr] *s.m.* lightning--conductor, lightning-rod.

paravent [paravɑ̃] *s.m.* screen, folding screen.

parbleu [parblø] *interj.* (expressing agreement, reinforcement) indeed, to be sure; why, of course!

parc [park] *s.m.* park; parking-place; enclosure; depot; fold, sheepfold, pen, cattle-run, paddock; vivarium, oyster-bed or -park; fleet (of buses; taxis, etc.); total number or stock (of vehicles, aircraft, etc.); pleasure grounds, ground, (artill.) park; *~ zoologique*, wild-life park.

parcage [parkaʒ] *s.m.* folding (of sheep); penning (of cattle); laying down (of oysters); (rare) parking, parking-place.

parcellaire [parselɛr] *adj.* by small portions, in detail.

parcelle [parsɛl] *s.f.* part, particle; portion, parcel, patch, (of land).

parce que [parsəkə] *conj. loc.* because.

parchemin [parʃəmɛ̃] *s.m.* parchment; document; (fig.) title of nobility.

parcheminé, -e [parʃəmine] *adj.* parchment--like, (fig.) wrinkled.

parcheminer [parʃmine] *v.t.* to give a parchment finish to; **se ~** *v.refl.* to become wrinkled, to shrivel up.

parchemini-er, -ère [parʃminje] *s.m.f.* parchment-maker.

parcimonie [parsimɔni] *s.f.* parsimony, stinginess.

parcimonieu-x, -se [parsimɔnjø] *adj.* parsimonious, stingy; ~**sement** [parsimɔnjøzmɑ̃] *adv.* parsimoniously, grudgingly.

parcmètre [parkmɛtr], **parcomètre** [parkɔmɛtr] *s.m.* parking-meter.

parcourir [parkurir] *v.t.* to travel over or through, to traverse, to cover (a distance), to run about, to scour, to wander over; (fig.) to survey, to run over; ~ *des yeux*, to survey, to glance over; ~ *un livre*, to run through, to read cursorily, to peruse, a book.

parcours [parkur] *s.m.* course, run, length of run (of piping, wiring, etc.); travel (of piston); distance, line, journey, way, route; course (of river); (obs.) *droit de* ~, grazing rights; (rail.) *libre* ~, running rights; *effectuer le* ~, to cover the distance, to make the journey; *le* ~ *d'un autobus*, the bus-route; *payer le* ~, to pay the fare.

pardessus [pardəsy] *s.m.* overcoat, greatcoat.

pardi [pardi], **pardieu** [pardjø] *interj.* = PARBLEU.

pardon [pardɔ̃] *s.m.* pardon, forgiveness, condonation; (in Brittany) pilgrimage; *je vous demande* ~, I beg your pardon; excuse me; ~*!*, I beg your pardon!; stop!, now look here!, I say!; ~**s** *s.m.pl.* (eccles.) indulgences.

pardonnable [pardɔnabl] *adj.* pardonable, excusable.

pardonner [pardɔne] *v.t.* to pardon, to forgive, to condone, to excuse, to overlook; to spare; *pardonnez-moi cette irruption*, forgive me for intruding; *une erreur qui ne pardonne pas*, an irreparable mistake.

paré, -e [pare] *adj.* **1.** adorned, trimmed, dressed(-up); (law) *titre* ~, title in due form; **2.** ready, prepared (*contre*, for), fortified; (naut.) ready, clear.

pare-balles [parbal] *s.m.invar.* bullet-proof shield; ~**-boue** [parbu] *s.m.invar.* **1.** (obs.) mudguard; **2.** mud-flap; ~**-brise** [parbriz] *s.m.invar.* windscreen; ~**-chocs** [parʃɔk] *s.m.invar.* (car) bumper; ~**-étincelles** [paretɛ̃sɛl] *s.m.invar.* fire-screen; spark-arrester; ~**-feu** [parfø] *s.m.invar.* fire-break (in woodland); ~**-fumée** [parfyme] *s.m.invar.* smoke-shield, smoke-extractor.

parégorique [paregɔrik] *adj., s.m.* paregoric.

pareil, -le [parɛj] *adj.* like, alike, similar, such, like that, identical, same; *dire une chose* ~*le!*, to say such a thing!; *une méchanceté sans* ~*le*, an unheard-of wickedness; *il n'a pas son* ~ *pour*, he has not his equal for, there is nobody like him for, (fam.) he is the one for; ~ *s.m.* equal, match; ~**le** *s.f.* the like, tit for tat; *lui rendre la* ~*le*, to give tit for tat, to do the same to him, to repay him in the same coin; ~**lement** [parɛjmɑ̃] *adv.* similarly, in like manner, likewise, too.

parélie see PARHÉLIE.

parement [parmɑ̃] *s.m.* **1.** altar-cloth; **2.** (dressm.) facing; (build.) face of stone wall or of stone in wall, top surface of paving-stone.

parementer [parmɑ̃te] *v.t.* (build.) to face.

parenchyme [parɑ̃ʃim] *s.m.* (bot., anat.) parenchyma.

parent, -e [parɑ̃] *s.m.f.* relative, relation, kinsman; *c'est un* ~ *du côté maternal*, he is a relation on the mother's side; *proche* ~, near relative; ~**s** *s.m.pl.* parents (father and mother), relatives, relations, kindred, family; ~, ~**e** *adj.* related.

parenté [parɑ̃te] *s.f.* relationship, consanguinity; kinship; kindred, relatives, kith and kin; (fig.) affinity.

parenthèse [parɑ̃tɛz] *s.f.* parenthesis; (fig.) interlude; *entre* ~*s*, in parenthesis; *par* ~, *entre* ~*s*, by the way.

parer[1] [pare] *v.t.* to adorn, to dress, to attire, to set off, to embellish, to trim; to prepare, to fit out, to arrange; ~ *qn. de*, to attribute (a quality, etc.) to s.o.; **se** ~ *v.refl.* to adorn oneself, to dress up; *se* ~ *de*, to dress up in, to deck oneself out in, to borrow (finery), to attribute (a quality) to oneself.

parer[2] [pare] *v.t.* to parry, to ward off, to fend off, to avoid, to keep clear of; ~ *à*, to avert, to guard against, to prepare against, to provide for, to ward off, to meet (danger, eventuality, etc.).

pare-soleil [parsɔlɛj] *s.m.invar.* (car) sun-visor.

paresse [parɛs] *s.f.* laziness, sloth, idleness, sluggishness, indolence; dullness; (med.) atony.

paresser [parese] *v.i.* to idle, to fritter away one's time, to do nothing, to laze about.

paresseu-x, -se [parɛsø] *adj.* lazy, idle, slothful, sluggish, indolent, slow; *s.m.f.* idler, sluggard, lazy person; ~**x** *s.m.* (zool.) ai, three-toed sloth; ~**sement** [parɛsøzmɑ̃] *adv.* idly, sluggishly; slowly, in leisurely fashion

pareu-r, -se [parœr] *s.m.f.* (indust.) finisher; ~**se** *s.f.* (text.) sizing-machine.

parfaire [parfɛr] *v.t.* to complete, to finish, to perfect; to make up (a sum of money).

parfait, -e [parfɛ] *adj.* perfect, finished, complete, faultless, accomplished; (fam.) capital, excellent, first-rate; ~ *s.m.* perfection; (gram.) perfect tense, past tense; *plus que* ~, pluperfect; ~**ement** [parfɛtmɑ̃] *adv.* perfectly, completely, thoroughly, quite; ~*ement!*, exactly!, quite so!, I quite agree.

parfilage [parfilaʒ] *s.m.* unravelling, unweaving.

parfiler [parfile] *v.t.* to unravel, to unweave.

parfois [parfwa] *adv.* sometimes, occasionally, now and then.

parfum [parfœ̃] *s.m.* perfume, scent, fragrance, odour, flavour; bouquet (of wine).

parfumer [parfyme] *v.t.* to perfume, to scent, (cook.) to flavour; **se** ~ *v.refl.* to use scent.

parfumerie [parfymri] *s.f.* perfumery (trade or shop); perfume factory; perfumes.

parfumeu-r, -se [parfymœr] *s.m.f.* perfumer.

parhélie, parélie [pareli] *s.m.* (astron.) parhelion.

pari [pari] *s.m.* bet, wager, stake; *faire un* ~, to lay a bet; *tenir, accepter un* ~, to take a bet; ~*-mutuel*(*urbain*), pari-mutuel, totalizator betting.

paria [parja] *s.m.* pariah, outcast.

pariade [parjad] *s.f.* pairing, mating-time, (of birds).

parian [parjɑ̃] *s.m.* Parian (porcelain).

parier [parje] *v.t.* **1.** (obs.) to pair, to mate; **2.** to bet, to wager, to stake; *il y a gros à* ~ *que*, the odds are that; ~ *à coup sûr*, to bet on a certainty; ~ *pour* or *sur qn.*, to back s.o.

pariétaire [parjetɛr] *s.f.* (bot.) pellitory.

pariétal, -e, (**aux**) [parjetal] *adj.* (anat., bot.) parietal; ~ *s.m.* parietal bone.

parieu-r, -se [parjœr] *s.m.f.* wagerer, better, punter, betting man or woman.

parigot, -e [parigo] *adj., s.m.f.* (fam.) Parisian.

parisette [parizɛt] *s.f.* (bot.) herb Paris, true love.

parisianisme [parizjanism] *s.m.* Parisian customs, Parisian idiom.

parisien, -ne [parizjɛ̃] *adj., s.m.f.* Parisian.

paritaire [paritɛr] *adj.* (of conferences, etc.) where both sides have equal representation; *commission* ~, joint commission; *réunion* ~, round-table conference.

parité [parite] *s.f.* parity, equality; (math.) evenness (opp. oddness).

parjure [parʒyr] *s.m.* perjury; ~ *s.m.f.* perjurer; ~ *adj.* perjured, false.

(**se**) **parjurer** [parʒyre] *v.refl.* to perjure oneself, to commit perjury.

parking [parkiŋ] *s.m.* parking; parking-place, car-park.

parlant, -e [parlɑ̃] *adj.* speaking, talking; (fig.) eloquent, lifelike, expressive; *un portrait ~*, a speaking likeness; (herald.) allusive, canting; *film ~*, sound (opp. silent) film; *preuve ~e*, eloquent proof.

parlé, -e [parle] *adj.* spoken, colloquial; (radio) *journal ~*, news.

parlement [parləmɑ̃] *s.m.* **1.** (Fr. hist.) Parlement (high judicial court); **2.** parliament.

parlementaire[1] [parləmɑ̃tɛr] *adj.* **1.** (hist.) of the *Parlement*; **2.** parliamentary, of Parliament; *~ s.m* (Fr.) deputy; Member of Parliament; parliamentarian.

parlementaire[2] [parləmɑ̃tɛr] *adj. drapeau ~*, flag of truce; *~ s.m.* bearer of flag or offer of truce, one sent to parley.

parlementarisme [parləmɑ̃tarism] *s.m.* parliamentary system, parliamentary government.

parlementer [parləmɑ̃te] *v.i.* to parley, to negotiate.

parler [parle] *v.t.i.* to speak, to talk, to converse; to treat, to mention; to express oneself; *sans ~ de*, not to mention; to say nothing of; besides; *trouver à qui ~*, to find someone to talk to, to find one's match; *faire ~ de soi*, to be much talked about, to get oneself a name; to get a bad name; *j'entends beaucoup ~ de lui*, I hear a lot about him; *il sait ce que ~ veut dire*, he understands what is meant; he can take a hint; he knows what's what; *~ du nez*, to speak through one's nose; *~ d'abondance*, to speak extempore; *~ d'or*, to speak wisely; *~ en l'air*, to talk at random; *~ haut*, to speak loud; to speak firmly; *~ au cœur*, to move the heart; *~ à son bonnet*, to talk to oneself; *cela ne vaut pas la peine d'en ~*, it is not worth mentioning; don't mention it; *parlez-moi de cela!*, now, that's something!; *vous en parlez bien à votre aise!*, it's easy for you to say so; *~ trois langues*, to speak three languages; *~ affaires*, to talk business, to talk shop; (proverb) *trop ~ nuit*, least said, soonest mended; (slang) *tu parles!*, you're telling me!, you can say that again!; **se ~** *v.refl.* to speak to each other; to be spoken.

parler [parle] *s.m.* speech, utterance, way of speaking or pronouncing; parlance; *avoir son franc-~*, to be able to speak one's mind.

parleu-r, -se [parlœr] *s.m.f.* speaker, talker; (radio) announcer; *beau ~r*, (obs.) eloquent speaker; (mod.) great talker.

parloir [parlwar] *s.m.* parlour; visiting-room (in school, prison, etc.).

parlote, parlotte [parlɔt] *s.f.* (fam.) **1.** debating session (for barristers in training); **2.** idle chatter; gossip-shop.

parmélie [parmeli] *s.f.* (bot.) Parmelia, yellow wall-lichen.

parmesan, -e [parməzɑ̃] *adj., s.m.f.* Parmesan; *~ s.m.* Parmesan (cheese).

parmi [parmi] *prep.* among, from among, amongst, amid, amidst.

parnasse [parnas] *s.m.* Parnassus, poetry, anthology of Parnassian verse; *le Parnasse*, the Parnassian School (of Fr. poets).

parnassien, -ne [parnasjɛ̃] *adj.* Parnassian.

parodie [parɔdi] *s.f.* parody, travesty, skit.

parodier [parɔdje] *v.t.* to parody, to mimic, to burlesque.

parodiste [parɔdist] *s.m.f.* parodist.

paroi [parwa] *s.f.* wall, partition, side, face, facing, inner surface (of pipe, vase, etc.); (anat.) coat, wall.

paroir [parwar] *s.m.* paring-knife.

paroisse [parwas] *s.f.* parish; parish church; parishioners.

paroissial, -e, (aux) [parwasjal] *adj.* parochial, parish.

paroissien, -ne [parwasjɛ̃] *s.m.f.* parishioner; (fam.) *c'est un drôle de ~!*, he is a queer fellow!; *~ s.m.* prayer-book.

parole [parɔl] *s.f.* speech, utterance, voice, tone; language; word; sentence, saying; word of honour; (pl.) (theatr.) lyrics; *avoir la ~*, to have leave to speak; *porter la ~*, to act as spokesman (*pour*, for); *prendre la ~*, to speak; *demander la ~*, to ask leave to speak; *la ~ est à lui*, it is his turn to speak; *couper la ~ à qn.*, to cut s.o. short; to interrupt s.o.; *perdre la ~*, to lose (the use of) one's tongue; *retrouver la ~*, to find one's tongue (again); *reprendre la ~*, to resume speaking; *donner sa ~, engager sa ~*, to pledge one's word; *c'est un homme de ~*, he is a man of his word; *manquer de ~, manquer à sa ~*, to break one's word; *tenir sa ~*, to keep one's word; *rendre sa ~ à qn.*, to release s.o. from his promise; *reprendre sa ~*, to retract one's promise; *prisonnier sur ~*, prisoner on parole; (cards) *~!*, pass!, no bid!; *ma ~!*, upon my word!

paroli [parɔli] *s.m.* paroli, double stake; *faire ~*, to double.

paroli-er, -ère [parɔlje] *s.m.f.* librettist, writer of lyrics.

paronomase [parɔnɔmɑz] *s.f.* (rhet.) word--play, paronomasia.

paronymie [parɔnimi] *s.f.* paronymy.

parotide [parɔtid] *s.f., adj.* (anat.) parotid (gland).

parotidien, -ne [parɔtidjɛ̃] *adj.* parotid.

paroxysme [parɔksism] *s.m.* paroxysm.

parpaillot, -e [parpajo] *s.m.f.* Huguenot, protestant; (fam.) unbeliever (in the Roman Catholic faith).

parpaing [parpɛ̃] *s.m.* (build.) parpen-stone, perpend-stone, through-stone, bond-stone; breeze-block, cement block.

parquer [parke] *v.t.* to pen, to pen up; to fold (sheep); to bed (oysters); to enclose, to imprison; to park (car); **se ~** *v.refl.* to park.

parquet [parkɛ] *s.m.* **1.** floor, flooring, parquet floor; **2.** (law) Public Prosecutor's department; **3.** (stock exchange) dealing floor.

parquetage [parkətaʒ] *s.m.* parquet flooring, parquetry; laying of parquet floors.

parqueterie [parkətri] *s.f.* making or laying of parquet floors.

parrain [parɛ̃] *s.m.* godfather, sponsor; introducer.

parrainage [parɛnaʒ] *s.m.* sponsorship.

parrainer [parene] *v.t.* to sponsor.

parricide [parisid] *s.m.* **1.** parricide (murder); **2.** *s.m.f.* parricide (murderer); *~ adj.* parricidal.

parsec [parsɛk] *s.m.* (astron.) parsec.

parsemer [parsəme] *v.t.* to strew, to sprinkle, to dot, to stud, to spangle; to be strewn on.

parsi, -e [parsi] *s.m.f., adj.* Parsee.

part[1] [par] *s.m.* (obs.) parturition; (law) infant.

part[2] [par] *s.f.* share, part, portion; side; *avoir ~ à*, to share in; to partake of; *prendre ~ à*, to have a hand in, to take part in, to participate in, to be a party to; to sympathize with; *prendre qn. à ~*, to take s.o. aside; *mettre qn. de ~*, to give s.o. a share; *prendre en bonne ~*, to take in good part; *prendre en mauvaise ~*, to take amiss; *faire la ~ à qn.*, to allot s.o. a share; *faire la ~ de*, to make allowance for; *faire la ~ du feu*, to make a fire--break; (fig.) to cut one's losses; *faire ~ de qch. à qn.*, to inform s.o. of sth.; see FAIRE-PART; *à ~*, aside, apart (from), out of the ordinary; *à ~ soi*, inwardly; *de ~ en ~*, through and through; *de ~ et d'autre*, on both sides; *d'une ~*, on the one hand; *d'autre ~*, on the other hand; besides; *de toutes ~s*, on all sides; *de la ~ de qn.*, in someone's name, on someone's part, from s.o.; *nulle ~*, nowhere; *quelque ~*, somewhere; *je le tiens de bonne ~*, I have it on good authority.

partage [partaʒ] *s.m.* sharing, dividing, division,

dealing out, apportionment, partition; share, lot, portion; *être le ~ de*, to be the lot of; *il eut en ~ la force et la bonté*, strength and goodness fell to his lot; *ligne de ~ des eaux*, dividing ridge, watershed.

partagé, -e [partaʒe] *adj.* portioned, divided; *les avis sont ~s à ce sujet*, opinions are divided on this point; *amour ~*, requited love, reciprocal affection.

partageable [partaʒabl] *adj.* divisible into shares.

partager [partaʒe] *v.t.* to divide, to share out, to portion, to parcel, to distribute, to deal out; to share, to partake of, to participate in, to go shares in; to gift, to endow; *la nature l'a bien mal partagé*, nature has treated him badly; *il est joliment bien partagé!*, his bread is well buttered; the fates have been most kind to him; *~ la poire en deux*, to split the difference; *~ l'opinion de qn.*, to be of the same opinion as s.o.; **se ~** *v.refl.* to divide, to be divided; to branch, to fork.

partageu-x, -se [partaʒø] *s.m.f.* (obs.) sharer, communist.

partance [partɑ̃s] *s.f.* readiness to sail or to depart; *en ~*, ready to sail; sailing, leaving, taking off, (*pour*, for).

partant [partɑ̃] *conj.* (obs.) consequently, therefore, thus.

partant, -e [partɑ̃] *s.m.f.* leaver; (racing) starter.

partenaire [partənɛr] *s.m.f.* partner, associate.

parterre [partɛr] *s.m.* flower-bed, flower-garden, parterre; (theatr.) stalls; (fig.) audience.

parthénogénèse [partenoʒenɛz] *s.f.* parthenogenesis.

parti [parti] *s.m.* **1.** party, side, cause; match; *le ~*, the socialist party; *se ranger du ~ de qn.*, to join someone's side; *épouser un bon ~*, to make a good match, to make an advantageous marriage; **2.** decision, course; *hésiter entre deux ~s*, to hesitate between two courses; *prendre ~*, to take a decision, to make one's choice, to make up one's mind; *prendre son ~ de qch.*, to reconcile oneself to sth.; *prendre le ~ de faire qch.*, to decide to do sth.; *~ pris*, foregone conclusion; set purpose; prepossession, prejudice; *de ~ pris*, partial, with one's mind already made up; **3.** (obs.) wages, reward; (mod.) outcome, profit, advantage; *prendre le ~ des armes*, to turn soldier; *faire mauvais ~ à qn.*, to treat s.o. badly or roughly; *tirer ~ de*, to profit from, to exploit; *tirer bon ~ de*, to turn to good account.

parti, -e [parti] *adj.* **1.** divided, parted; parti-coloured; (herald.) party; **2.** departed, absent, gone; (fam.) drunk.

partiaire [parsjɛr] *adj. colon ~*, share-cropper.

partial, -e, (aux) [parsjal] *adj.* partial (*pour*, to); biased, unfair; **~ement** [parsjalmɑ̃] *adv.* with partiality or bias.

partialité [parsjalite] *s.f.* partiality, bias.

participant, -e [partisipɑ̃] *s.m.f.* participant, sharer; participator; *adj.* participating, contributing, concerned.

participation [partisipɑsjɔ̃] *s.f. ~ à*, participation in, partaking of; share or interest in; having knowledge of, being privy to.

participe [partisip] *s.m.* (gram.) participle.

participer [partisipe] *v.i. ~ à*, to participate in, to take part in, to partake of; to have a share or interest in; to be a party to, to have knowledge of.

participial, -e, (aux) [partisipjal] *adj.* (gram.) participial; **~e** *s.f.* participial phrase.

particulariser [partikylarize] *v.t.* to particularize, to give in exact detail, to specify.

particularisme [partikylarism] *s.m.* (theol.) particularism; (pol.) regionalism.

particularité [partikylarite] *s.f.* peculiarity, special quality or circumstance; characteristic, particularity, particular.

particule [partikyl] *s.f.* **1.** particle; **2.** *~ nobiliaire*, the word *de*, *du*, *de la*, or *des* preceding one's name (a mark of nobility); **3.** (gram.) particle.

particuli-er, -ère [partikylje] *adj.* particular, peculiar, specific, special, circumstantial; private, personal, intimate; **~er** *s.m.* private person, civilian; individual, fellow; *en ~er*, apart, separately, privately; in particular, specially; **~èrement** [partikyljɛrmɑ̃] *adv.* particularly, in particular, especially, peculiarly, chiefly; apart, singly, in detail; ⚠ not 'particular' in sense 'fussy'.

partie [parti] *s.f.* part, portion; match, game; party, gathering, excursion, amusement; line of business, profession, special pursuit; (comm.) lot, goods; litigant, party; (mus.) part; (pl.) (vulg.) private parts; *être juge et ~*, to be one's own judge; *prendre à ~*, (law), to sue; (fam.) to take to task, to attack; (law) *se porter ~ civile*, to bring a civil action against; *avoir affaire à forte ~*, to have a powerful opponent; (comm.) *livre en double ~*, double-entry ledger; *avoir ~ liée avec*, to be jointly liable with, to share risks and profits with; *la ~ est perdue!*, it's all up!; *la ~ est remise, c'est ~ remise*, the pleasure is only deferred; (sport) *~ nulle*, drawn game; *la ~ n'est pas égale*, it's not an equal match; *perdre la ~*, to lose the game; *voulez-vous être de la ~?*, will you join us?; *faire ~ de*, to belong to; to form part of; to be a member of; *faire une ~ de*, to play a game of; *~ de plaisir*, pleasure trip; *~ de campagne*, excursion to the country; *en ~*, partly, in part; *~ carrée*, party of four (two men and two women).

partiel, -le [parsjɛl] *adj.* partial, incomplete, in parts; *éclipse ~le*, partial eclipse; **~lement** [parsjɛlmɑ̃] *adv.* partially, in part(s), by instalments.

partir [partir] *v.i.* to start, to set out, to leave, to go, to be off, to depart; (of birds) to spring up; (of firearms) to go off; to pop; to dart; to come, to originate (*de*, from); *à ~ de*, from, reckoning from; *son abonnement part du 20*, his subscription starts on the 20th; *en partant de*, starting from (principle, etc.); *faire ~*, to send off, to dispatch; to fire or let off (gun, etc.); to wipe off (a stain); *~ d'un grand éclat de rire*, to burst out laughing; *un mot qui part du cœur*, a word which comes from the heart; *cela part d'un bon cœur*, that shows a kind heart.

partir [partir] *v.t.* (obs.) to divide; (mod.) *avoir maille à ~ avec*, to have a bone to pick with.

partisan [partizɑ̃] *s.m.* partisan, follower, supporter, upholder, advocate, believer (*de*, in); *je suis assez ~ de*, I am rather in favour of; **~, ~e** *adj.* party, partisan, factional.

partiti-f, -ve [partitif] *adj.* partitive.

partition [partisjɔ̃] *s.f.* partition, division; (mus.) score; musical composition; (herald.) quarter, quartering; ⚠ not a partition wall.

partouse, partouze [partuz] *s.f.* (pop.) orgy.

partout [partu] *adv.* everywhere; *~ où*, wherever, wheresoever, whenever; *~ ailleurs*, everywhere else, in any other place; *un peu ~*, all over, all over the place; (tennis) *deux jeux ~*, two games all.

parturition [partyrisjɔ̃] *s.f.* parturition.

parure [paryr] *s.f.* attire, dress, ornament, head-dress; finery; set (of undergarments); paring, parings, (of skins, etc.); trimmings (of meat); *~ de diamants*, set of diamond jewellery.

parution [parysjɔ̃] *s.f.* publication, issuing; *dès la ~ de ce livre*, as soon as this book is out.

parvenir [parvənir] *v.i.* to arrive; *~ à*, to reach,

to arrive at, to get to (somewhere), to gain access to, to attain; to obtain; to succeed in (achieving sth.); to rise to; *faire ~ une lettre à*, to forward a letter to; *~ à faire*, to succeed in doing, to manage to do.

parvenu, -e [parvəny] *s.m.f.* (pej.) upstart, parvenu.

parvis [parvi] *s.m.* parvis, precinct, square in front of church.

pas [pɑ] *s.m.* step; pace; tread, gait, stride; spacing (between posts); pitch (of screw or propeller); progress; footprint, trace; passage, mountain pass, strait; (fig.) difficulty, obstacle; *porter ses ~ vers*, to turn one's steps towards; *presser le ~*, to quicken one's pace, to hurry up; *~ à ~*, step by step; *au ~*, at a walking pace; in time; *à ~ comptés*, with measured steps; *à grands ~, à ~ de géant*, with long strides, with giant strides; at a great pace; *à ~ lents*, at a slow pace; slowly; *emboîter le ~ à qn., marcher sur les ~ de qn.*, to follow in someone's footsteps, to follow someone's example, to follow on someone's heels; (fig.) *à ~ de loup*, stealthily; with stealthy steps; *~ accéléré*, quick step; *au ~ (de) gymnastique* or *de course* or *de charge*, at the double; *faux ~*, false step, trip, stumble; (fig.) slip, fault, mistake; *se tirer d'un mauvais ~*, to get out of a scrape; *sauter* or *franchir le ~*, to take a resolution, to take the plunge; *marquer le ~*, to mark time; (fig.) to wait; *faire les cent ~*, to pace to and fro; to do sentry-go; *mettre qn. au ~*, to discipline s.o., to bring s.o. into line; *se mettre au ~*, to get into step; *attention, il y a un ~*, take care, there's one step; *le ~ de la porte*, the threshold; (comm.) *~ de porte*, goodwill; *j'y vais de ce ~*, I am going there directly; *prendre le ~ sur qn.*, to take precedence over s.o., to have a lead over s.o.; *retourner* or *revenir sur ses ~*, to retrace one's steps; *~ de clerc*, blunder; *vis à ~ à gauche*, screw with left-hand thread.

pas [pɑ] *adv.* no, not, not any; *~ du tout*, not at all; *presque ~*, hardly, scarcely any; *~?* (fam. abbrev. of *n'est-ce pas?*); *tu m'en apporteras un, pas?*, you will bring me one, won't you?; see also NE.

pascal, -e, (aux) [paskal] *adj.* paschal, of the Jewish Passover; of Easter.

passable [pɑsabl] *adj.* passable, tolerable, middling, decent, fairly good, that will pass muster; indifferent; *santé ~*, indifferent health; **~ment** [pɑsabləmɑ̃] *adv.* passably, tolerably; somewhat; *~ment de*, a certain amount of.

passacaille [pasakɑj] *s.f.* (mus., danc.) passacaglia.

passade [pɑsad] *s.f.* **1.** (rid.) passade; **2.** brief love affair; passing fancy.

passage [pɑsaʒ] *s.m.* passing; passage, corridor; way, thoroughfare, lane; crossing; passage-money; transition; passage (in book, etc.); (rail.) *~ à niveau*, level crossing; *guetter au ~*, to lie in wait for; *barrer le ~*, to bar the way; *s'ouvrir un ~*, to make or force one's way through; *oiseaux de ~*, birds of passage; migratory birds; *je suis de ~*, I am only passing through; *droit(s) de ~*, right of way; toll, dues; *~ souterrain*, subway, underpass; *~ interdit*, no entry.

passag-er, -ère [pɑsaʒe] *adj.* passing, transient, transitory, migratory, short-lived; *rue ~ère*, busy street; *s.m.f.* passenger; **~èrement** [pasaʒɛrmɑ̃] *adv.* momentarily, fleetingly.

passant, -e [pɑsɑ̃] *adj.* much-frequented, busy; *en ~*, by the way; cursorily; (chess) en passant; (herald.) passant; *s.m.f.* passer-by; *~ s.m.* keeper (part of strap).

passation [pɑsasjɔ̃] *s.f.* drawing-up (of a title-deed, contract, etc.).

passavant [pɑsavɑ̃] *s.m.* (naut.) gangway; (customs) pass, permit.

passe [pɑs] *s.f.* **1.** pass, passing, passage; putting through; turn (of rope over pulley); (sport) *faire une ~*, to pass, to make a pass; *mot de ~*, password; *maison de ~*, brothel, hotel catering for prostitutes, house of assignation; *~ d'armes*, passage of arms, lively argument; **2.** pass, passage, channel; **3.** position, situation; (obs.) *être en ~*, to be in a winning position; (mod.) *être en ~ de*, to be in a position to, to be about to; *être en mauvaise ~*, to be going through a bad period; **4.** extra; (print.) overplus; (roulette) passe; brim (of lady's hat); *~ de caisse*, allowance to cashier for errors; *de ~*, extra, over; *exemplaires de ~*, surplus copies, over copies.

passé, -e [pɑse] *adj.* past, gone, over, dead, vanished; faded, withered; *la semaine ~e*, last week; *il est dix heures ~es*, it's past ten; *il a trente ans ~s*, he is over thirty; *~ prep.* after, past, after passing; *~ une heure*, after one o'clock; *~ la ferme*, after passing the farm; *~ s.m.* past, time past, things past; (gram.) past tense; *comme par le ~*, as before.

passe-boule(s) [pɑsbul] *s.m.* passe-boule(s) (game resembling Aunt Sally).

passe-droit [pɑsdrwa] *s.m.* (pl. *~-droits*) **1.** illicit favour; **2.** (obs.) injustice.

passée [pɑse] *s.f.* flight (of woodcock, etc.); (hunt.) trace, spoor, slot.

passe-lacet [pɑslasɛ] *s.m.* (pl. *~-lacets*) bodkin.

passement [pɑsmɑ̃] *s.m.* braid, trimming.

passementer [pɑsmɑ̃te] *v.t.* to braid, to trim.

passementerie [pɑsmɑ̃tri] *s.f.* braid, trimmings, passementerie; manufacture of or trade in braid, etc.

passementi-er, -ère [pɑsmɑ̃tje] *s.m.f., adj.* (maker or seller) of braid, trimmings, etc.

passe-montagne [pɑsmɔ̃taɲ] *s.m.* (pl. *~-montagnes*) balaclava helmet.

passe-partout [pɑspartu] *s.m.invar.* **1.** latch-key, master-key; (fig.) open sesame, key, passport; **2.** cross-cut saw; compass-saw; **3.** (photo., print.) passe-partout frame or block; **4.** sth. that is suitable anywhere; *une tenue ~*, a costume for all occasions.

passe-plat [pɑspla] *s.m.* (pl. *~-plats*) serving-hatch.

passepoil [pɑspwal] *s.m.* (dressm.) piping, edging.

passeport [pɑspɔr] *s.m.* passport; (fig.) recommendation.

passer [pɑse] *v.i.* to pass, to pass by, to pass through or along, to pass over or across, to go, to go past, to move on; to turn, to change, to be transferred (to another post, etc.); to disappear, to fade; to cease; to pass away, to die; to be considered; to pass, to be acceptable; to be in circulation, to be current, (of film, etc.) to be on; to change over (*à*, to); *~ avant*, to have precedence over; *~ chez qn.*, to call on s.o., to drop in on s.o.; *il est passé par le pont*, he went across the bridge; *en ~ par là*, to submit to it, to put up with it, to have to go through it; *tout le monde y passe*, everyone has to go through it, it happens to all of us, no one is spared it; *~ sur*, to cross, to run over; (fig.) to pass over; *le camion lui a passé sur les jambes*, the lorry ran over his legs; *~ pour*, to be considered, to pass for, to be said to be; *~ outre*, to pass on, to go on, to proceed, to take no notice; *cela m'a passé de l'esprit*, it passed out of my mind, it has slipped my memory; *cela fait ~ une heure ou deux*, that whiles away an hour or two; *cela m'a fait ~ mon rhume*, that has cured my cold; *cela peut ~*, that will do, that will pass; (law) *l'affaire passera en janvier*, the case will come up in January; *ce film a passé la semaine dernière*, that film was on last week; *~ v.t.* (auxil. *avoir*) to pass, to cross; to undergo; to sit (an exam); to overlook, to omit, to pass over, to forgive; to sift, to sieve, to strain; to put; to put on (film, tape, etc., on machine); to slip on (garment); to place (order); to spend (time); to satisfy (desire); to vent (anger); to engage (gear); to enter (an item under an account heading); to draw up (document); ~ *une rivière*, to cross a river; ~ *à la nage*, to swim across; ~ *à gué*, to ford; *passez-moi le beurre*, pass me the butter; ~ *une épreuve*, to sit an exam, to submit to a test; *faire* ~ *un examen à qn.*, to examine s.o., to put s.o. in for an exam; ~ *un mot*, to omit a word; *passez-moi le mot*, if you will pardon the expression; (cards) *je passe*, pass, no bid; ~ *une sauce*, to strain a sauce; ~ *une bande*, to put a tape on (the machine); ~ *son pantalon*, to slip one's trousers on; ~ *une commande*, to place an order; ~ *son temps à faire*, to spend one's time doing; ~ *un mauvais quart d'heure*, to have an unpleasant experience; ~ *son envie*, to satisfy or gratify one's desire; ~ *son colère sur*, to vent one's anger on; (car) ~ *la seconde*, to engage second gear; (comm.) ~ *un article en compte* or *sur le compte*, to enter an item in the accounts; (law) ~ *un accord*, to draw up an agreement; (fam.) ~ *un coup de fil à qn.*, to ring s.o. up, to give s.o. a ring; **se** ~ *v.refl.* to happen, to take place; (of time) to be spent; to pass, to finish, to be over; *que se passe-t-il?*, what's going on?; *l'action se passe en 24 heures*, the action takes place within 24 hours; *la moitié de sa vie se passe en sommeil*, he spends half his life asleep; *attendons que la crise se passe*, let us wait until the crisis is over; *se* ~ *de*, to do without, to dispense with, not to need; *se* ~ *de tabac*, to go without, to give up, smoking; (iron.) *je me passerais bien volontiers de cette corvée*, I wouldn't mind being relieved of that nasty job.

passerage [pɑsraʒ] *s.f.* (bot.) pepperwort.

passereau (pl. **-x**) [pɑsro] *s.m.* (ornith.) sparrow.

passerelle [pɑsrɛl] *s.f.* foot-bridge; (naut.) bridge; gangway.

passe-temps [pɑstɑ̃] *s.m.invar.* pastime, diversion, hobby.

passeu-r, -se [pɑsœr] *s.m.f.* ferryman, ferry-woman.

passible [pasibl] *adj.* (theol.) passible; liable (*de*, to).

passi-f, -ve [pasif] *adj.* **1.** passive, not active; **2.** on the debit side; *dettes* ~*ves*, liabilities; (gram.) passive.

passif [pasif] *s.m.* debts, liabilities; (gram.) passive.

passiflore [pasiflɔr] *s.f.* (bot.) passion-flower.

passion [pɑsjɔ̃] *s.f.* passion, agony; deep or strong emotion; fondness, craze, love; the object of one's passion; *avoir la* ~ *du tennis*, to have a craze for tennis; *souffrir mort et* ~, to suffer excruciating pains.

passionnant, -e [pɑsjɔnɑ̃] *adj.* thrilling, exciting.

passionné, -e [pɑsjɔne] *adj.* passionate, doting (*pour*, on), passionately fond (*de*, of); impassioned; ~**ment** [pɑsjɔnemɑ̃] *adv.* passionately, ardently, vehemently.

passionnel, -le [pɑsjɔnɛl] *adj.* of the passions; caused by love or passion.

passionner [pɑsjɔne] *v.t.* to impassion; to interest powerfully, to move with passion; **se** ~ *v.refl.* *se* ~ *pour*, to be passionately fond (of); to be deeply interested (in); to give way to passion (for).

passivement [pasivmɑ̃] *adv.* passively.

passivité [pasivite] *s.f.* passivity, passiveness, passive attitude; inertia.

passoire [pɑswar] *s.f.* colander, strainer.

pastel[1] [pastɛl] *s.m.* pastel; pastel colour(s); pastel-drawing.

pastel[2] [pastɛl] *s.m.* (bot.) woad.

pastelliste [pastelist] *s.m.f.* pastellist.

pastèque [pastɛk] *s.f.* (bot.) water-melon.

pasteur [pastœr] *s.m.* shepherd; pastor, clergyman, (Protestant) minister; *le Bon Pasteur*, the Good Shepherd.

pasteurisation [pastœrizɑsjɔ̃] *s.f.* pasteurization (of milk, etc.).

pasteuriser [pastœrize] *v.t.* to pasteurize (milk, etc.).

pastiche [pastiʃ] *s.m.* pastiche, pasticcio, imitation, parody.

pasticher [pastiʃe] *v.t.* to imitate, to make a pastiche of, to parody.

pasticheu-r, -se [pastiʃœr] *s.m.f.* imitator, author of a pastiche.

pastille [pastij] *s.f.* pastille, lozenge, drop.

pastoral, -e, (**aux**) [pastɔral] *adj.* pastoral; ~**e** *s.f.* pastoral (play, poem, or piece of music).

pastorat [pastɔra] *s.m.* pastorate, pastorship.

pastourelle [pasturɛl] *s.f.* **1.** (mus.) pastoral; **2.** a kind of dance.

pat [pat] *adj.*, *s.m.* (chess) stalemate(d); *faire* ~, to stalemate.

patache [pataʃ] *s.f.* **1.** (hist., naut.) revenue-cutter; **2.** ancient stage-coach; (fam.) rickety old car.

patachon [pataʃɔ̃] *s.m.* *mener une vie de* ~, to live a wild life, to flit from one pleasure to the next.

patagon, -ne [patagɔ̃] *adj.*, *s.m.f.* Patagonian.

Patagonie [patagɔni] *s.f.* (geog.) Patagonia.

patapouf [patapuf] *s.m.* podgy person or child; ~ *interj.* bang!, crash!

pataquès [patakɛs] *s.m.* fault in speaking (e.g. sounding a *t* for an *s* or vice versa); dreadful slip; mistake, howler.

patate [patat] *s.f.* batata, sweet potato; (fam.) potato; stupid person; *en avoir gros sur la* ~, to be heavy at heart.

patati, patata [patati, patata] onom. phrase applied to endless talk or gossiping.

patatras [patatra] *interj.* bang!, crash!

pataud, -e [pato] *adj.* clumsy, awkward; *s.m.f.* awkward child or person; ~ *s.m.* puppy with large paws.

patauger [patoʒe] *v.i.* to flounder, to splash, to wade, to paddle (in the mud); (fig.) ~ *dans*, to flounder about in, to become entangled in; to make a mess of.

patchouli [patʃuli] *s.m.* (bot.) patchouli; (perfume) patchouli.

pâte [pɑt] *s.f.* dough, batter; paste; pastry; pulp; (fig.) constitution, temper; ~ *brisée*, short pastry; ~ *feuilletée*, puff pastry, flaky pastry; ~ *dentifrice*, toothpaste; ~*s d'Italie* or *alimentaires*, Italian paste, pasta, (macaroni, noodles, etc.); (fig.) *mettre la main à la* ~, to put one's shoulder to the wheel, to set one's hand to the work; *vivre comme un coq en* ~, to live in clover; *c'est une bonne* ~, he is a good sort.

pâté [pɑte] *s.m.* **1.** pie, pasty, patty; pâté; ~ *de maisons*, block (of buildings); *cela s'enlève* or *se vend comme des petits* ~*s*, it sells like hot cakes; **2.** blot (of ink); *faire un* ~ (*sur son papier*), to make a blot (on one's paper).

pâtée [pɑte] *s.f.* bran-mash, mess (for dogs, etc.), paste (for fattening poultry).

patelin, -e [patlɛ̃] *adj.* wheedling, crafty, sly, artfully meek; *un air* ~, an oily manner; ~ *s.m.* **1.** wheedler, flatterer; **2.** (fam.) small place, village; birthplace, home town; 'the old home'.

patelinage [patlinaʒ] *s.m.* wheedling; flattering ways.

patelle [patɛl] *s.f.* **1.** (anat.) patella; **2.** (zool.) limpet.

patène [patɛn] *s.f.* paten.

patenôtre [patnotr] *s.f.* **1.** (obs.) Lord's

prayer; (mod., iron.) prayer, paternoster; **2.** unintelligible muttering.
patent, -e [patɑ̃] *adj.* patent, obvious; *lettres ~es,* letters patent.
patentable [patɑ̃tabl] *adj.* liable to pay a licence-fee; that requires a licence.
patente [patɑ̃t] *s.f.* patent, letters patent, trade-licence; professional tax; (naut.) bill of health; *~ nette,* clean bill of health.
patenté, -e [patɑ̃te] *adj.* licensed, patented, patent.
patenter [patɑ̃te] *v.t.* to license; *faire ~ une invention,* to patent an invention; to obtain a patent for an invention.
pater [pɑtɛr] *s.m.* **1.** paternoster; great bead (of a chaplet); **2.** (fam.) father, dad.
patère [patɛr] *s.f.* coat-peg, hat-peg.
paternalisme [patɛrnalism] *s.m.* paternalism.
paternaliste [patɛrnalist] *adj.* paternalistic.
paterne [patɛrn] *adj.* hypocritical, mawkish, mealy-mouthed; patronizing.
paternel, -le [patɛrnɛl] *adj.* paternal, fatherly, on the father's side; *~ s.m.* (fam.) father; *voilà le* or *mon ~,* here comes the old man; **~lement** [patɛrnɛlmɑ̃] *adv.* paternally, in a fatherly manner.
paternité [patɛrnite] *s.f.* paternity, fatherhood; (fig.) authorship.
pâteu-x, -se [pɑtø] *adj.* pasty, clammy, doughy, sticky, viscous; (of fruit) woolly; (of voice) thick; (of style) heavy, cumbrous.
pathétique [patetik] *adj.* pathetic, moving, touching; *~ s.m.* pathos; **~ment** [patetikmɑ̃] *adv.* pathetically.
patho-gène [patɔʒɛn] *adj.* pathogenic, pathogenous; **~logie** [patɔlɔʒi] *s.f.* pathology; **~logique** [patɔlɔʒik] *adj.* pathological; **~logiquement** [patɔlɔʒikmɑ̃] *adv.* pathologically; **~logiste** [patɔlɔʒist] *s.m.f.* pathologist.
pathos [patos] *s.m.* affected or misplaced pathos; bathos, bombast, rant; ⚠ not 'pathos' in sense of what is genuinely pathetic.
patibulaire [patibylɛr] *adj.* of the gallows; fit or destined for the gallows; *fourches ~s,* the gallows; *une mine ~,* a criminal appearance.
patiemment [pasjamɑ̃] *adv.* patiently.
patience [pasjɑ̃s] *s.f.* patience, forbearance, endurance, fortitude; puzzle; game of patience; *je suis à bout de ~,* I am out of patience, my patience is exhausted; *prenez ~,* be patient; have patience; *exercer la ~ de qn.,* to try someone's patience; *~!,* wait a bit!, have patience!; *en ~,* patiently.
patient, -e [pasjɑ̃] *adj.* patient, forbearing, enduring; *s.m.f.* **1.** (med.) patient; **2.** sufferer, victim (of torture).
patienter [pasjɑ̃te] *v.i.* to have patience, to be patient.
patin [patɛ̃] *s.m.* **1.** skate; *~s à roulettes,* roller-skates; **2.** (techn.) foot, runner, skid; brake-shoe, brake-block; pad, plate.
patinage[1] [patinaʒ] *s.m.* **1.** skating; **2.** skidding, slipping.
patinage[2] [patinaʒ] *s.m.* application of patina.
patine [patin] *s.f.* patina.
patiner[1] [patine] *v.i.* **1.** to skate; **2.** to skid, to slip.
patiner[2] [patine] *v.t.* to apply (artificial) patina to.
patinette [patinɛt] *s.f.* (child's) scooter.
patineu-r, -se [patinœr] *s.m.f.* skater.
patinoire [patinwar] *s.f.* skating-rink.
pâtir [pɑtir] *v.i.* to suffer.
pâtis [pɑti] *s.m.* pasture-ground, common.
pâtisserie [pɑtisri] *s.f.* **1.** pastry; pastry-making; cake-shop, confectioner's, tea-rooms; confectionery trade; **2.** stucco-work (on ceilings).
pâtissi-er, -ère [pɑtisje] *s.m.f.* **1.** pastry-cook, confectioner; **2.** proprietor of a *pâtisserie.*
pâtissoire [pɑtiswar] *s.f.* pastry-board.
patoche [patɔʃ] *s.f.* (fam.) hand, paw.
patois [patwɑ] *s.m.* patois, dialect; jargon.
patoiser [patwaze] *v.i.* to speak patois.
pâton [pɑtɔ̃] *s.m.* paste, bolus, (for fattening poultry).
patouiller [patuje] *v.i.* to dabble, to splash about; *~ v.t.* to handle roughly, to paw about.
patraque [patrak] (fam.) *s.f.* worn-out or badly-made machine, clock, etc.; worn-out, sickly person; *~ adj.* worn-out; sickly, seedy, poorly; *se sentir ~,* to feel poorly, to feel out of sorts.
pâtre [pɑtr] *s.m.* shepherd, herdsman.
patriarcal, -e, (**aux**) [patriarkal] *adj.* patriarchal.
patriarcat [patriarka] *s.m.* patriarchate.
patriarche [patriarʃ] *s.m.* patriarch.
patrice [patris] *s.m.* (Rom. hist.) patrician.
patriciat [patrisja] *s.m.* patriciate.
patricien, -ne [patrisjɛ̃] *s.m.f.* (Rom. hist.) patrician; (Lit.) aristocrat; *adj.* aristocratic, patrician.
patrie [patri] *s.f.* fatherland, native country, country, birthplace, home.
patrimoine [patrimwan] *s.m.* patrimony, inheritance, heritage.
patrimonial, -e, (**aux**) [patrimɔnjal] *adj.* patrimonial.
patriotard, -e [patrijɔtar] *s.m.f., adj.* chauvinist.
patriote [patrijɔt] *s.m.f.* patriot; *~ adj.* patriotic.
patriotique [patrijɔtik] *adj.* patriotic; **~ment** [patrijɔtikmɑ̃] *adv.* patriotically, as a patriot.
patriotisme [patrijɔtism] *s.m.* patriotism.
patristique [patristik] *adj.* patristic; *~ s.f.* patristics, patrology, (study of the life and writings of the Fathers of the Church).
patrologie [patrɔlɔʒi] *s.f.* **1.** patrology (collection of patristic writings); **2.** = PATRISTIQUE *s.f.*
patron[1]**, -ne** [patrɔ̃] *s.m.f.* patron, patron saint; employer, (fam.) boss, head, guv'nor, principal, proprietor, manager, manageress, proprietress; skipper, master of a vessel, coxswain; (fam.) *demandez ça à la ~ne,* ask my wife; ask the missis.
patron[2] [patrɔ̃] *s.m.* pattern, model; stencil, template; standard.
patronage [patrɔnaʒ] *s.m.* **1.** patronage, support, sponsorship; **2.** advowson; **3.** youth club; (relig.) youth fellowship.
patronal, -e, (**aux**) [patrɔnal] *adj.* patronal; *fête ~e,* patron saint's day; **2.** employer's, of employers; *cotisation ~e,* employer's contribution.
patronat [patrɔna] *s.m. le ~,* the employers.
patronne [patrɔn] *s.f.* see PATRON[1].
patronner[1] [patrɔne] *v.t.* to patronize, to sponsor, to protect.
patronner[2] [patrɔne] *v.t.* **1.** (dressm.) to cut out from a pattern; **2.** to stencil.
patronnesse [patrɔnɛs] *adj., s.f.* (that is a) patroness, patron.
patronymique [patrɔnimik] *adj.* patronymic.
patrouille [patruj] *s.f.* (mil.) patrol.
patrouiller [patruje] *v.i.* **1.** to patrol; **2.** = PATOUILLER *v.i.*
patte [pat] *s.f.* paw (of animals), foot (of birds), leg (of insects); (fig.) clutches, claws; (fam.) human hand, paw, human foot; fluke (of an anchor), strap, band, flap, tab; end (of braces); bracket, holdfast, hook, cramp, foot (of a spoke); (fig.) *~s de mouche,* scrawl; hooks and hangers; ill-formed, minute writing; *coup de ~,* scratch, claw, pat, slap; (fig.) sly dig; *faire ~ de velours,*

(of cat) to draw in its claws; (fig.) to cajole, to flatter, to show the velvet glove, to be all smiles; *montrer ~ blanche*, to say the password, to show one's credentials; *~s de lapin*, very short whiskers; (fam.) sideboards; *marcher à quatre ~s*, to go on all fours; *mille ~s*, centipede; *graisser la ~ à qn.*, to bribe s.o., to grease someone's palm; (*à*) *bas les ~s!*, hands off!; none of your games!, *tomber sous la ~ de qn.*, to fall into someone's clutches; (slang) *se tirer des ~s*, to take oneself off, to make oneself scarce; to flee, to escape, to run away; *~ de lièvre*, powder-puff.

patte-d'oie [patdwa] *s.f.* (pl. *pattes-d'oie*) road-junction (with several forks); **2.** crow's-foot (wrinkle); **3.** (naut.) mooring-bridle; **4.** (bot.) goosefoot, Chenopodium.

pattemouille [patmuj] *s.f.* damp cloth (for ironing).

pattu, -e [paty] *adj.* large-pawed, broad-footed; (of pigeons) feather-legged.

pâturable [pɑtyrabl] *adj.* pasturable, suitable for grazing.

pâturage [pɑtyraʒ] *s.m.* pasture, pasture-ground, pasturage, grazing-land.

pâture [pɑtyr] *s.f.* food for animals, fodder; pasture, pasturage; *servir de ~ à*, to become the prey of; *droit de vaine ~*, common grazing rights.

pâturer [pɑtyre] *v.t.i.* to pasture, to graze, to feed, to feed on.

pâturin [pɑtyrɛ̃] *s.m.* (bot.) meadow-grass.

paturon [patyrɔ̃] *s.m.* pastern (of a horse).

paulinien, -ne [polinjɛ̃] *adj.* (eccles.) Pauline.

paulownia [polɔnja] *s.m.* (bot.) paulownia (tree).

paume [pom] *s.f.* **1.** palm (of the hand); **2.** (real) tennis, tennis-court.

paumelle [pomɛl] *s.f.* **1.** (bot.) two-rowed barley; **2.** hinge; French-window handle; **3.** protective gauntlet; **4.** (tanning) graining-board.

paumé, -e [pome] *adj.* (pop.) wretched; (fam.) lost.

paumer [pome] *v.t.* to smack, to slap; (slang) to lay hold of, to scrounge; (pop.) to lose; *se faire ~*, to get nabbed, caught; **se ~** *v.refl.* to get lost.

paupérisation [poperizɑsjɔ̃] *s.f.* pauperization, debasement of living standards.

paupérisme [poperism] *s.m.* pauperism, poverty.

paupière [popjɛr] *s.f.* eyelid; (fig.) *ouvrir la ~*, to wake up; *fermer la ~*, to go to sleep.

pause [poz] *s.f.* pause, stop; rest-period, (meal-) break; (football) half-time; (mus.) bar rest, semibreve rest; *demi-~*, minim rest.

pauser [poze] *v.i.* to pause.

pauvre [povr] *adj.* poor, needy, necessitous, indigent, unfortunate, destitute; wretched, sorry, paltry, pitiful, mean; barren, sterile; dear; *le ~ homme!*, poor devil!; *~ d'esprit*, dull-witted, not very bright; *~ en esprit*, poor in spirit; *un sol ~*, a barren soil; *mon ~ ami*, my dear friend; *un ~ sire*, a poor wretch, a wretched fellow; *~ s.m.* (see PAUVRESSE *s.f.*) poor person, pauper; *un ~ honteux*, a poor man who is ashamed to beg; **~ment** [povrəmɑ̃] *adv.* poorly, wretchedly, shabbily; in poor circumstances.

pauvresse [povrɛs] *s.f.* extremely poor woman, beggar-woman, woman in rags.

pauvret, -te [povrɛ] *adj.* poor, shabby; *s.m.f.* poor little thing, poor creature.

pauvreté [povrəte] *s.f.* poverty, indigence; wretchedness; barrenness; penury, dearth; poorness; sorry thing, stupid saying; *~ n'est pas vice*, poverty is no crime; *dire des ~s*, to deal in platitudes.

pavage [pavaʒ] *s.m.* paving; pavement.

pavane [pavan] *s.f.* pavane (dance).

(**se**) **pavaner** [pavane] *v.refl.* to strut, to flaunt; to show off, to sit in state.

pavé [pave] *s.m.* paving-stone, paving, cobbles; pavement; (fig.) street; *se trouver sur le ~*, to be out of work, to be without a home, to be utterly destitute; *tenir le haut du ~*, to take precedence, to hold the first rank; *battre le ~*, to roam the streets; *brûler le ~*, to tear along; *tâter le ~*, to proceed cautiously; *le ~ du roi*, the king's highway.

pavement [pavmɑ̃] *s.m.* paving; pavement.

paver [pave] *v.t.* to pave; *pavé de bonnes intentions*, paved with good intentions.

paveur [pavœr] *s.m.* pavior, paviour, paver.

pavie [pavi] *s.f.* (bot.) clingstone peach.

pavillon [pavijɔ̃] *s.m.* **1.** pavilion, tent, summer-house, lodge, box, detached house, wing of a house, outhouse; **2.** bell (of trumpet, etc.); horn (of siren, loudspeaker, etc.); ear- or mouth-piece (of telephone); **3.** flag, colours; *amener le ~*, to haul down the colours; (fig.) *baisser ~*, to yield, to surrender, to give in; *~ de complaisance*, flag of convenience.

pavois [pavwa] *s.m.* (hist.) pavis(e); (naut.) bulwark, armour; flags arranged for dressing ship; (fig.) *élever sur le ~*, to laud to the skies.

pavoiser [pavwaze] *v.t.* to deck, to dress with flags.

pavot [pavo] *s.m.* (bot.) poppy.

payable [pɛjabl] *adj.* payable, due.

payant, -e [pɛjɑ̃] *adj.* paying; paid for; which must be paid for; *billet ~*, bought (opp. complimentary) ticket; *école ~e*, fee-paying school; *spectacle ~*, show where there is a charge for admission; *s.m.f.* payer.

paye [pɛj] *s.f.* = PAIE.

payement [pɛjmɑ̃] *s.m.* = PAIEMENT.

payer [peje] *v.t.* to pay, to pay for, to pay off; to pay down, to pay away; to repay; to discharge; to reward; to atone for; *~ un dîner à qn.*, to stand s.o. a dinner; *~ d'audace* or *d'effronterie*, to brazen it out; to put a bold face on it; *~ comptant*, to pay cash down, to pay cash; *~ qn. sur la caisse*, to pay s.o. out of the till, from the funds; *~ de sa personne*, to exert oneself, to expose oneself; *je leur ai laissé la note à ~*, I left them to foot the bill; *je suis payé pour le savoir*, I know it to my cost; *~ les violons*, to pay the piper; *~ son écot*, to pay one's share; *se faire ~*, to obtain or to enforce payment; *~ de retour*, to pay back; *il me le paiera!*, I will make him pay for this; **se ~** *v.refl.* to be paid; to treat oneself to; *se ~ un bon dîner*, to treat oneself to a good dinner; *se ~ la tête de qn.*, to make fun of s.o., to take a rise out of s.o.; *se ~ de mots*, to be put off with empty promises.

payeu-r, -se [pɛjœr] *s.m.f.* payer; paymaster.

pays [pei] *s.m.* country, land, region, district; home, birthplace, fatherland; nation; (fam., fem. *payse*) fellow-countryman, -countrywoman, compatriot; *vin du ~*, local wine; *avoir le mal du ~*, to be homesick; *voir du ~*, to travel; *se trouver en ~ de connaissance*, to be among friends; to know one's ground; *~ perdu*, out-of-the-way place; *être bien de son ~*, (i.) to be a simpleton; (ii.) to have all the characteristics of one's race; *tiens! voilà une ~e!*, hallo! here is a girl from my country (or village).

paysage [peizaʒ] *s.m.* landscape, scenery; landscape painting; (Lit.) description of landscape.

paysagiste [peizaʒist] *s.m.* landscape painter; *jardinier ~*, landscape gardener.

paysan, -ne [peizɑ̃] *s.m.f.* peasant, farmer, rustic, countryman, countrywoman; *les ~s*, the peasantry, the farmers; *adj.* rustic, country-.

paysannerie [peizanri] *s.f.* rusticity; peasantry; pastoral play or novel.

payse [peiz] *s.f.* see PAYS.

P.C. [pese] abbrev. **1.** *Parti Communiste*; **2.** (mil.) *poste de commandement.*
péage [peaʒ] *s.m.* toll; toll-house.
péag-er, -ère [peaʒe] *s.m.f.* toll-gatherer, toll--collector.
péan [peɑ̃] *s.m.* paean, song of praise or triumph.
peau (pl. **-x**) [po] *s.f.* skin; hide; peel, rind; coating; leather; *risquer sa ~*, to risk one's skin, or one's life; *vendre cher sa ~*, to sell one's life dearly; *faire ~ neuve*, to turn over a new leaf; to turn one's coat; *sur la ~*, or *à même la ~*, next to one's skin; *il mourra dans la ~ d'un imbécile*, he will be a fool as long as he lives; *n'avoir que les os et la ~*, to be as thin as a lath; to be nothing but skin and bone; *il a juré d'avoir sa ~*, he swore he would do for him, he has sworn to kill him; (slang) *avoir la ~ trop courte*, to be lazy; *avoir qn. dans la ~*, to be violently in love with s.o.; (pop.) *~ de balle!*, nothing doing!
peaucier [posje] *adj.*, *s.m.* (anat.) cutaneous (muscle).
peaufiner [pofine] *v.t.* to polish with chamois leather; (fig.) to polish (a piece of work).
peau-rouge [poruʒ] *s.m.f.* Red Indian, red-skin.
peausserie [posri] *s.f.* leather-dressing, fur--trade, skin-trade; dressed skin.
peaussier [posje] *s.m.* skin-dresser, leather--dealer, fellmonger.
pec [pɛk] *adj. m.* (of herring) newly-salted.
pécaïre [pekair] *interj.* (in South of France) expression (often iron.) of regret.
pécari [pekari] *s.m.* (zool.) peccary, Mexican hog.
peccable [pekabl] *adj.* peccable, liable to sin.
peccadille [pekadij] *s.f.* pecadillo.
pechblende [pɛʃblɛ̃d] *s.m.* (min.) pitchblende (an ore of uranium).
pêche[1] [pɛʃ] *s.f.* (bot.) peach; peach-colour; (pop.) blow.
pêche[2] [pɛʃ] *s.f.* fishing, angling; *~ à la ligne*, angling; *canne à ~*, fishing-rod; *aller à la ~*, to go fishing; *vendre sa ~*, to sell one's catch; *articles de ~*, fishing-tackle; *grande ~*, deep-sea fishing; *~ à la dérive*, drift-nct fishing.
péché [peʃe] *s.m.* sin, transgression, trespass, offence; *~ mignon*, besetting sin, foible; *à tout ~ miséricorde*, forgive and forget; we must not desire the death of the sinner.
pécher [peʃe] *v.i.* to sin, to transgress; to be at fault, to be deficient; *ce raisonnement pèche par la base*, this reasoning is fundamentally false; *ce n'est pas par là qu'il pèche*, that is not his failing; *~ contre les convenances*, to offend against decency.
pêcher [pɛʃe] *s.m.* (bot.) peach-tree.
pêcher [pɛʃe] *v.t.i.* to fish, to angle; to fish up; to fish for, to drag out; (fig.) to get hold of; *où avez-vous pêché cela?*, where did you get hold of that?; **se ~** *v.refl.* to be fished, to be found.
pécheresse [peʃrɛs] *s.f.* see PÉCHEUR.
pêcherie [pɛʃri] *s.f.* fishery, fishing-ground, fisheries.
péch-eur, -eresse [peʃœr] *s.m.f.* sinner.
pêcheu-r, -se [pɛʃœr] *s.m.f.* fisher, angler, fisherman, fisherwoman; *~r, ~se, à la ligne*, angler.
pécore [pekɔr] *s.f.* **1.** (obs.) animal, beast; **2.** silly, pretentious woman; *~ s.m.f.* (pop.) rustic, peasant.
pecque [pɛk] *s.f.* (obs.) = PÉCORE 2.
pectine [pɛktin] *s.f.* pectin.
pectiné, -e [pɛktine] *adj.* (anat.) pectinate, comb-shaped.
pectoral, -e, (aux) [pɛktɔral] *adj.* pectoral, of or for the chest; *pastilles ~es*, cough lozenges; *~ s.m.* pectoral, breastplate.
péculat [pekyla] *s.m.* peculation, embezzlement.
pécule [pekyl] *s.m.* savings, hoard; earnings (of prisoner, etc.); (mil.) gratuity.
pécuniaire [pekynjɛr] *adj.* pecuniary, financial; *peine ~*, fine.
pédago-gie [pedagɔʒi] *s.f.* pedagogy, pedagogics; teaching method; teaching ability; **~gique** [pedagɔʒik] *adj.* pedagogic(al); **~gue** [pedagɔg] *s.m.f.* pedagogue, schoolmaster, teacher.
pédale [pedal] *s.f.* pedal; (mus.) pedal-note; (pop.) pederast.
pédaler [pedale] *v.i.* to pedal; (fig.) to cycle; (pop.) to run, to move fast.
pédalier [pedalje] *s.m.* (mus.) pedal-board (of organ); (cycle) crank-gear.
pédant, -e [pedɑ̃] *adj.* pedantic, priggish; *s.m.f.* pedant, prig.
pédanterie [pedɑ̃tri] *s.f.* (Lit.) pedantry.
pédantesque [pedɑ̃tɛsk] *adj.* pedantic.
pédantisme [pedɑ̃tism] *s.m.* pedantry.
pédéraste [pederast] *s.m.* pederast.
pédérastie [pederasti] *s.f.* pederasty.
pédestre [pedɛstr] *adj.* pedestrian, foot-; walking; **~ment** [pedɛstrəmɑ̃] *adv.* on foot.
pédiatre [pedjatr] *s.m.* paediatrician.
pédiatrie [pedjatri] *s.f.* paediatrics.
pédicelle [pedisɛl] *s.m.* (bot., zool.) pedicel, pedicle.
pédiculaire [pedikylɛr] *adj.* pedicular, lousy, louse-infested; *~ s.f.* (bot.) lousewort.
pédicule [pedikyl] *s.m.* (bot., zool.) pedicle, peduncle.
pédiculé, -e [pedikyle] *adj.* pedunculate, pedicellate.
pédicure [pedikyr] *s.m.f.* chiropodist, pedicure.
pédieu-x, -se [pedjø] *adj.* pertaining to the foot.
pedigree [pedigri] *s.m.* pedigree.
pédimane [pediman] *adj.* (zool.) having an opposable big toe.
pédonculaire [pedɔ̃kylɛr] *adj.* (bot.) peduncular.
pédoncule [pedɔ̃kyl] *s.m.* (bot.) peduncle, stalk; (anat.) appendix of the brain.
pédonculé, -e [pedɔ̃kyle] *adj.* pedunculate.
pègre [pɛgr] *s.f.* criminal class.
peignage [pɛɲaʒ] *s.m.* combing; wool-combing.
peigne [pɛɲ] *s.m.* **1.** comb; card (for wool); *se donner un coup de ~*, to have a quick comb; (fig.) *passer au ~ fin*, to go through with a fine-tooth comb, to examine minutely; **2.** (zool.) pecten, scallop.
peigné, -e [peɲe] *adj.* (of wool) combed, brushed; *~ s.m.* brushed wool; worsted yarn.
peignée [peɲe] *s.f.* **1.** cardful (of wool); **2.** (slang) thrashing.
peigner [pɛɲe] *v.t.* to comb; to card (wool, etc.); (fig.) to groom, to tend; (slang) to thrash; *un jardin bien peigné*, a well-kept garden; **se ~** *v.refl.* to comb one's hair.
peigneu-r, -se [pɛɲœr] *s.m.f.* comber, wool--comber; **~se** *s.f.* carding-machine.
peignoir [pɛɲwar] *s.m.* wrapper, dressing-gown; bath robe, bathing-wrap; house-coat.
peille [pɛj] *s.f.* rags (for paper-making).
peindre [pɛ̃dr] *v.t.* to paint; to stain; to make up (face); to portray, to describe, to depict, to express; *se faire ~*, to sit for one's portrait; *la terreur se peint* (or *est peinte*) *sur son visage*, terror is written on his face.
peinard, -e [pɛnar] *adj.* (slang) quiet; *se tenir ~*, to lie quiet.
peine [pɛn] *s.f.* punishment, penalty; pain, grief, sorrow, affliction, misery, anxiety; labour, effort, trouble, pains, toil; difficulty, ado; *à ~*, hardly, scarcely; *c'est à ~ si je le connais*, I hardly know him; *à grand ~*, with much difficulty; *cela fait ~*, it hurts one to see that; *ce n'est pas la ~*, it's not worth while; don't bother about it; *être en ~ de*, to be concerned with; to be anxious to;

en être pour sa ~, to have had one's trouble for nothing; *être dans la* ~, to be in trouble; to be afflicted; *faire de la* ~ *à qn.*, to pain s.o.; *il a de la* ~ *à marcher*, he walks with difficulty; he is scarcely able to walk; *sous* ~ *de*, at the risk of, under penalty of; *sous* ~ *de mort*, on (or under) pain of death; *mourir à la* ~, to die in harness; to work oneself to death; *se donner de la* ~, to take pains; *prenez la* ~ *de vous asseoir*, pray take a seat; *toute* ~ *mérite salaire*, the labourer is worthy of his hire; ⚠ not physical 'pain'.

peiné, -e [pene] *adj.* pained, afflicted, grieved; (of style) laboured.

peiner [pene] *v.t.* to pain, to grieve, to make uneasy, to fatigue; ~ *v.i.* to labour hard, to toil.

peint, -e [pɛ̃] *adj.* painted, coloured; *papier* ~, wallpaper; *une femme très* ~*e*, a very much made--up woman.

peintre [pɛ̃tr] *s.m.* painter; (fig.) depicter, describer; ~ *en bâtiments*, house-painter; ~ *d'enseignes*, sign-painter.

peinture [pɛ̃tyr] *s.f.* painting; paint; picture; (fig.) description, depiction, portrayal, picture; ~ *à l'huile*, oil-painting; ~ *à l'aquarelle*, water--colour; ~ *au pistolet*, spray-painting; (fam.) *je ne peux pas le voir en* ~*!*, I can't bear the sight of him.

peinturer [pɛ̃tyre] *v.t.* to paint badly, to daub.

peinturlurer [pɛ̃tyrlyre] *v.t.* (fam.) to paint in crude colours, to daub; **se** ~ *v.refl.* to make oneself up badly, to make a mess of one's face.

péjorati-f, -ve [peʒɔratif] *adj.* pejorative, disparaging, depreciatory; ~**vement** [peʒɔrativmɑ̃] *adv.* in a disparaging manner, in a depreciatory sense.

pékan [pekɑ̃] *s.m.* (zool.) pekan, Canadian marten; pekan-fur.

Pékin [pekɛ̃] *s.m.* (geog.) Peking, Pekin.

pékin [pekɛ̃] *s.m.* **1.** pekin (Chinese patterned silk); **2.** (also *péquin*) (mil., pej.) civilian, civilians; civilian dress, mufti.

pékinois, -e [pekinwa] *adj.*, *s.m.f.* (native or inhabitant) of Peking, Pekin(g)ese; ~ *s.m.* (i.) Pekinese dialect; (ii.) Pekinese (dog).

pelade [pəlad] *s.f.* alopecia.

pelage [pəlaʒ] *s.m.* **1.** coat, fur, hair, (of animal); **2.** removal of hair from skin.

pélagien, -ne [pelaʒjɛ̃] *adj.* **1.** (theol.) Pelagian; **2.** pelagian, pelagic, of the open sea.

pélagique [pelaʒik] *adj.* pelagic, of the open sea.

pelard [pəlar] *adj.*, *s.m.* barked (wood).

pélargonium [pelargɔnjɔm] *s.m.* (bot.) pelargonium, geranium.

pélasgien, -ne [pelaʒjɛ̃] *adj.* (Gr. ant.) Pelasgic, Pelasgian.

pelé, -e [pəle] *adj.* bald, bald-headed; naked, bare; peeled; threadbare, shabby; (fam.) *il n'y avait que quatre* ~*s et un tondu*, there were only two men and a boy.

pêle-mêle [pɛlmɛl] *s.m.* jumble, pell-mell, medley, disorder; *adv.* pell-mell, helter-skelter, promiscuously, in disorder or confusion.

peler [pəle] *v.t.i.* to skin, to peel, to peel off, to pare, to pare off, to strip of hair; **se** ~ *v.refl.* to peel, to peel off, to come off.

pèlerin, -e [pɛlrɛ̃] *s.m.f.* pilgrim; traveller; (zool.) basking shark; (*faucon*) ~, peregrine falcon.

pèlerinage [pɛlrinaʒ] *s.m.* pilgrimage; place of pilgrimage; *aller en* ~, *faire un* ~, to go on a pilgrimage.

pèlerine [pɛlrin] *s.f.* pelerine, tippet, cape.

pélican [pelikɑ̃] *s.m.* (ornith.) pelican.

pelisse [pəlis] *s.f.* pelisse, greatcoat, fur-lined coat or cloak.

pellagre [pɛlagr] *s.f.* (med.) pellagra.

pelle [pɛl] *s.f.* shovel, spade, scoop; blade (of an oar); ~ *mécanique*, grab, mechanical shovel; (slang) *ramasser une* ~, to come a cropper; to fall (from one's bicycle, horse, etc.); *remuer à la* ~, to shovel; (fig.) *remuer l'argent à la* ~, to have heaps of money; to be rolling in riches.

pelletée [pɛlte] *s.f.* shovelful.

pelleter [pɛlte] *v.t.* to shovel.

pelleterie [pɛltri] *s.f.* peltry, furriery; skins; fur-trade.

pelleteur [pɛltœr] *s.m.* shoveller; mechanical shovel.

pelleti-er, -ère [pɛltje] *s.m.f.* furrier.

pellicule [pelikyl] *s.f.* **1.** pellicle; scurf, dandruff; **2.** film (e.g. of oil on water); (photo.) film.

pelliculeu-x, -se [pelikylø] *adj.* scurfy.

pellucide [pelysid] *adj.* pellucid.

péloponnésien, -ne [pelɔpɔnezjɛ̃] *adj.*, *s.m.f.* Peloponnesian.

pelotage [plɔtaʒ] *s.m.* **1.** winding (of wool) into balls; **2.** (fam.) caressing, cuddling, fondling.

pelote [plɔt] *s.f.* **1.** ball (esp. of wool, etc.); (fig.) mass, pile; ~ *de neige*, snowball; *faire sa* ~, to make one's pile; **2.** pincushion; surgical pad; **3.** pelota, Basque tennis; pelota ball; **4.** (mil. slang) punishment drill; defaulters' squad.

peloter [plɔte] *v.t.* **1.** to wind or roll into a ball; **2.** to caress, to fondle; (fig.) to flatter.

peloton [plɔtɔ̃] *s.m.* ball; group, knot, cluster; (mil.) platoon, half-company, troop, squad, detachment; (racing) main body of runners, the bunch.

pelotonner [plɔtɔne] *v.t.* to wind into balls; **se** ~ *v.refl.* to roll oneself up, to curl oneself up, to huddle up, to huddle, to cluster, to bunch.

pelouse [pəluz] *s.f.* lawn, grass plot, greensward; (racing) enclosure.

peluche [plyʃ] *s.f.* (text.) plush, shag.

peluché, -e, pelucheu-x, -se, [plyʃe, plyʃø] *adj.* shaggy, plushy, fluffy.

pelucher [plyʃe] *v.i.* to fluff up, to become fluffy (with wear).

pelure [pəlyr] *s.f.* rind, peel, paring; (jest) clothes, coat; *papier* ~, India paper.

pelvien, -ne [pɛlvjɛ̃] *adj.* (anat.) pelvic.

pelvis [pɛlvis] *s.m.* (anat.) pelvis.

pemmican [pɛmikɑ̃] *s.m.* pemmican.

pénal, -e, (aux) [penal] *adj.* penal; ~**ement** [penalmɑ̃] *adv.* in penal law.

pénalisation [penalizɑsjɔ̃] *s.f.* (sport) penalty, penalization.

pénaliser [penalize] *v.t.* to penalize, to award a penalty against; *être pénalisé*, to be penalized; to be fined.

pénalité [penalite] *s.f.* **1.** (law) awarding of punishment or fine; penal system; **2.** penalty, fine; **3.** (sport) penalty; (Rugby football) *coup de pied de* ~, penalty kick.

penalty [penalti] *s.m.* (football) foul (incurring a penalty free kick).

pénates [penat] *s.m.pl.* (Rom. myth.) penates; (fig.) home, fireside.

penaud, -e [pəno] *adj.* abashed, crestfallen, sheepish, embarrassed.

penchant [pɑ̃ʃɑ̃] *s.m.* declivity, slope, slant; (fig.) tendency, bent, inclination, taste, propensity; fondness; decline, decay; brink (of disaster, etc.); *suivre ses* ~*s* (or *son* ~), to follow one's bent.

pencher [pɑ̃ʃe] *v.i.* to incline, to bend, to stoop, to droop, to be bent; to lean; to lean over, to slope; (fig.) to be inclined; *faire* ~ *la balance*, (lit. & fig.) to tip the balance; (fig.) ~ *vers*, to incline towards; ~ *v.t.* to incline, to tip; ~ *une carafe*, to tip up a carafe (to pour sth. out); **se** ~ *v.refl.* to bend, to lean, to lean over, to stoop; (fig.) *se* ~ *sur*, to apply oneself to, to concern oneself with.

pendable [pɑ̃dabl] *adj.* deserving hanging,

abominable; *cas* ~, (obs.) hanging matter; (mod.) wrong action, punishable offence; *tour* ~, dirty trick.
pendaison [pɑ̃dɛzɔ̃] *s.f.* **1.** hanging (on the gallows); hanging oneself; **2.** hanging-up (of picture, etc.).
pendant, -e [pɑ̃dɑ̃] *adj.* hanging, drooping, pendent; (fig.) pending, undecided.
pendant [pɑ̃dɑ̃] *s.m.* **1.** pendant; frog (of a sword-belt); anything hanging by way of ornament; ear-drop; drop (of chandelier); **2.** counterpart, match; *faire* ~, to match.
pendant [pɑ̃dɑ̃] *prep.* during; ~ *que*, while.
pendard, -e [pɑ̃dar] *s.m.f.* (fam.) rascal, rogue; ~**e** *s.f.* jade, hussy.
pendeloque [pɑ̃dlɔk] *s.f.* pendant, drop, hanging ornament.
pendentif [pɑ̃dɑ̃tif] *s.m.* **1.** (arch.) pendentive; **2.** pendant.
penderie [pɑ̃dɑri] *s.f.* hanging wardrobe; cloak-room.
pendiller [pɑ̃dije] *v.i.* to dangle.
pendre [pɑ̃dr] *v.t.i.* to hang, to hang up, to hang on the gallows, to suspend; to hang down, to dangle, to be hanging, to be pending, to be suspended, to droop, to sag; *il a dit pis que* ~ *de vous*, he said everything that was bad of you; (fam.) *cela lui pend au nez*, he has got it coming to him; *je veux bien être pendu si*, I'll be hanged if; *être pendu à*, to be clinging to, to be hanging on (someone's words, etc.); *se* ~ *à*, to cling to, to refuse to leave; *il se pend à notre sonnette*, he is ringing our bell all day long.
pendu, -e [pɑ̃dy] *adj.* hung, hanging, suspended; hanged; *avoir la langue bien* ~*e*, to be a great talker; *s.m.f.* hanged man or woman.
pendule [pɑ̃dyl] *s.m.* pendulum.
pendule [pɑ̃dyl] *s.f.* clock, time-piece.
pêne [pɛn] *s.m.* bolt (of a lock).
pénétrabilité [penetrabilite] *s.f.* penetrability.
pénétrable [penetrabl] *adj.* penetrable; (fig.) distinguishable, intelligible.
pénétrant, -e [penetrɑ̃] *adj.* penetrative, penetrating, piercing; shrewd, keen, acute, searching, sagacious; *un froid* ~, piercing cold; *un esprit* ~, a penetrating mind, a keen intelligence.
pénétration [penetrɑsjɔ̃] *s.f.* penetration; acuteness, shrewdness, perspicacity.
pénétré, -e [penetre] *adj.* ~ *de*, impregnated with, imbued with, full of; convinced of; ~ *de son importance*, full of his own importance.
pénétrer [penetre] *v.t.i.* to penetrate, to pierce, to go through; to pervade, to imbue; to search, to fathom, to understand, to divine, to see through, to unravel; **se** ~ *v.refl.* to combine, to interpenetrate; to convince oneself (*de*, of), to be penetrated, impregnated, or filled, (*de*, with).
pénible [penibl] *adj.* painful, laborious, troublesome, uneasy, hard, difficult, toilsome; distressing; ~**ment** [peniblǝmɑ̃] *adv.* painfully, laboriously, distressingly; with difficulty, only just.
péniche [peniʃ] *s.f.* (naut.) pinnace, shallop, pram; barge, lighter; (mil.) ~ *de débarquement*, landing-craft.
pénil [penil] *s.m.* (anat.) pubes, mons Veneris.
péninsulaire [penɛ̃sylɛr] *adj.* peninsular.
péninsule [penɛ̃syl] *s.f.* peninsula.
pénis [penis] *s.m.* (anat.) penis.
pénitence [penitɑs] *s.f.* penitence, penance; punishment; penalty (in games); *faire* ~, to do penance; *mettre en* ~, to punish, to put in the corner.
pénitencier [penitɑ̃sje] *s.m.* penitentiary, reformatory, penal establishment.
pénitent, -e [penitɑ̃] *adj.* penitent, repentant, contrite; *s.m.f.* penitent.
pénitentiaire [penitɑ̃sjɛr] *adj.* penitentiary.
pénitenti-aux, -elles [penitɑ̃sjo] *adj. pl.* (eccles.) penitential, of penitence or penance.
penne [pɛn] *s.f.* **1.** feather (of tail or wing), quill-feather; **2.** (naut.) peak (of lateen yard).
penné, -e [pɛne] *adj.* (bot.) pinnate.
pennon [pɛnɔ̃] *s.m.* pennon.
pénombre [penɔ̃br] *s.f.* penumbra, dim or subdued light.
penon [pǝnɔ̃] *s.m.* (naut.) dog-vane.
pensant, -e [pɑ̃sɑ̃] *adj.* thinking; *bien* ~, having the right ideas, who thinks the same way as we do, conformist, orthodox, pro-establishment.
pensée [pɑ̃se] *s.f.* thought, thinking, mind, intention, meaning, opinion, conception, idea; maxim, sentence; (bot.) pansy, heartsease; *rendre sa* ~, to express one's thoughts; *parler contre sa* ~, to say the opposite of what one is thinking; *il me vient dans la* ~ *que*, it comes into my mind that; *entrer dans la* ~ *de qn.*, to understand what is in someone's mind, to follow someone's train of thought; *lire dans la* ~ *de qn.*, to read someone's thoughts.
penser [pɑ̃se] *v.t.i.* to think, to cogitate, to reflect, to consider, to think out, to conceive; to be near, to be on the point (of doing), to expect (to do); *cela donne à* ~, that gives food for reflection, or for thought; *je ne sais que* ~ *de cela*, I do not know what to think of that; *il pense comme moi*, he agrees with me; *dire sa façon de* ~ *à qn.*, to give s.o. a piece of one's mind; ~ *à qch.*, to think of sth.; *à quoi pensez-vous?*, what are you thinking of?; *sans y* ~, unintentionally; *faites-moi* ~ *à*, remind me to (do sth.); *pensez à votre santé*, take care of your health; *vous n'y pensez pas!*, surely you don't mean it!; *pensez donc!*, just think of it!; *il a pensé mourir*, he nearly died; *je pense le voir demain*, I expect to see him tomorrow.
penser [pɑ̃se] *s.m.* (Lit.) thought, thinking, train of thought.
penseu-r, -se [pɑ̃sœr] *s.m.f.* thinker; *adj.* thinking, thoughtful.
pensi-f, -ve [pɑ̃sif] *adj.* pensive, thoughtful.
pension [pɑ̃sjɔ̃] *s.f.* pension, allowance, annuity; board, board and lodging; boarding-house; boarding-school; ~ *de famille*, family boarding-house; *prendre en* ~, to receive as boarder (or paying guest); *mettre en* ~, to send to boarding-school; ~ *viagère*, life annuity.
pensionnaire [pɑ̃sjɔnɛr] *s.m.f.* boarder; paying guest; schoolboy, schoolgirl at boarding-school; (obs.) pensioner; *prendre des* ~*s*, to take in boarders; to receive paying guests.
pensionnat [pɑ̃sjɔna] *s.m.* boarding-school.
pensionner [pɑ̃sjɔne] *v.t.* to pension, to grant an allowance to.
pensivement [pɑ̃sivmɑ̃] *adv.* pensively.
pensum [pɛ̃sɔm] *s.m.* imposition, extra work (at school).
pentaèdre [pɛ̃taɛdr] *s.m.* pentahedron; ~ *adj.* pentahedral.
pentagonal, -e, (aux) [pɛ̃tagɔnal] *adj.* pentagonal.
pentagone [pɛ̃tagɔn] *s.m.* pentagon.
pentamètre [pɛ̃tamɛtre] *s.m.* (pros.) pentameter.
pentathlon [pɛ̃tatlɔ̃] *s.m.* pentathlon.
pentatonique [pɛ̃tatɔnik] *adj.* (mus.) pentatonic.
pente [pɑ̃t] *s.f.* declivity, slope, descent; ascent; angle; pitch (of roof); side, wall, (of tent); valance (of bed); incline, gradient; downward course; (fig.) bent, propensity; *en* ~, sloping, shelving; *suivre sa* ~, to follow one's bent or inclinations; *s'engager sur une* ~ *dangereuse*, to embark on a dangerous course.
Pentecôte [pɑ̃tkot] *s.f.* Whitsuntide, Pentecost.

pentstémon [pɛ̃tstemɔ̃] *s.m.* (bot.) pentstemon.
penthode, pentode [pɛ̃tɔd] *s.f.* (phys.) pentode.
penture [pɑ̃tyr] *s.f.* strap-hinge; iron brace.
pénultième [penyltjɛm] *adj.* last but one, penultimate; ~ *s.f.* penultimate syllable.
pénurie [penyri] *s.f.* scarcity, dearth, want, penury.
péon [peɔ̃] *s.m.* peon.
pépé [pepe] *s.m.* (child. lang.) grandpa.
pépée [pepe] *s.f.* **1.** (child. lang.) doll; **2.** (pop.) woman, girl.
pépère [pepɛr] *s.m.* **1.** (child. lang.) grandpa; **2.** big, easy-going person or child; ~ *adj.* (pop.) big; nice, quiet; *une vie* ~, a nice quiet life.
pépètes [pepɛt] *s.f.pl.* (pop.) money.
pépie [pepi] *s.f.* pip (disease of fowls); (fam.) *avoir la* ~, to be tremendously thirsty.
pépiement [pepimɑ̃] *s.m.* chirping, chirp.
pépier [pepje] *v.i.* to chirp.
pépin [pepɛ̃] *s.m.* **1.** pip, stone; **2.** (obs.) *avoir un* ~ *pour qn.*, to be in love with s.o.; **3.** hitch, difficulty, complication; **4.** (fam.) umbrella.
pépinière [pepinjɛr] *s.f.* nursery (for young trees), seed-bed; (fig.) nursery, breeding-ground.
pépiniériste [pepinjerist] *s.m.* nurseryman.
pépite [pepit] *s.f.* nugget.
peplum [peplɔm] *s.m.* peplum.
pepsine [pɛpsin] *s.f.* pepsin.
peptique [pɛptik] *adj.* peptic, digestive.
peptone [pɛptɔn] *s.f.* peptone.
perçage [pɛrsaʒ] *s.m.* piercing, boring; broaching (of cask).
percale [pɛrkal] *s.f.* cambric, cambric muslin, percale.
percaline [pɛrkalin] *s.f.* (text.) percaline.
perçant, -e [pɛrsɑ̃] *adj.* piercing, sharp, keen, shrill, acute; penetrating; *froid* ~, piercing cold; *vue* ~*e*, keen sight; *cris* ~*s*, shrill cries.
perce [pɛrs] *s.f.* piercer, borer; hole (in flute, etc.); *mettre en* ~, to broach (cask of wine), to tap (cask).
percé, -e [pɛrse] *adj.* pierced, bored, perforated, in holes, out at elbows; opened, tapped; (fig.) stricken, afflicted; (fig.) ~ *à jour*, seen through; *panier* ~, spendthrift; *des bas* ~*s*, stockings with holes in them; *chaise* ~*e*, commode.
percée [pɛrse] *s.f.* opening, vista, glade; (mil., sport) breakthrough.
percement [pɛrsmɑ̃] *s.m.* piercing, boring, perforation, opening, cutting (of canal, etc.).
perce-muraille [pɛrsəmyrɑj] *s.f.* (pl. ~-*murailles*) (bot.) pellitory-of-the-wall; **~-neige** [pɛrsənɛʒ] *s.m.invar.* (bot.) snowdrop; **~-oreille** [pɛrsɔrɛj] *s.m.* (pl. ~-*oreilles*) (ent.) earwig; **~-pierre** [pɛrsəpjɛr] *s.f.* (pl. ~-*pierres*) (bot.) **1.** samphire; **2.** meadow-saxifrage.
percept-eur, -rice [pɛrsɛptœr] *adj.* perceiving, perceptive, of perception; *organes* ~*eurs*, organs of perception; **~eur** *s.m.* collector, tax-collector.
perceptibilité [pɛrsɛptibilite] *s.f.* perceptibility, audibility.
perceptible [pɛrsɛptibl] *adj.* perceptible, audible; (of tax, etc.) collectable; **~ment** [pɛrsɛptibləmɑ̃] *adv.* perceptibly.
percepti-f, -ve [pɛrsɛptif] *adj.* perceptive, perceptional.
perception [pɛrsɛpsjɔ̃] *s.f.* **1.** perception, faculty of perception; **2.** collection, gathering, levying, (of taxes, etc.); collectorship; collector's office.
percer [pɛrse] *v.t.* to pierce, to bore, to drill, to perforate, to make a hole in or through; to lance (a boil); to broach, to tap; to open, to make an opening in, to make a way through, to break through; to come or go through, to soak through; to unravel, to uncover, to see into, to see through; ~ *un mur*, to bore through a wall, to make a hole or opening in a wall; ~ *un coffre-fort*, to break a safe; ~ *un tonneau*, to broach a cask; ~ *une porte*, to make a doorway (in a wall); ~ *un tunnel*, to bore a tunnel; ~ *la foule*, to make one's way through the crowd; *les os lui percent la peau*, his bones stick out; ~ *de part en part*, to go right through; ~ *à jour*, to see through (stratagem, etc.); ~ *un complot*, to uncover a plot; ~ *l'avenir*, to see into the future; ~ *v.i.* to come through, to break through; (of boil) to burst; to emerge, to come to light, to appear; to come to fame, to make a reputation; *le soleil perce*, the sun is breaking through; *rien n'a percé de cette entrevue*, nothing emerged from this interview; *un auteur qui commence à* ~, an author who is beginning to become known.
perceu-r, -se [pɛrsœr] *s.m.f.* borer, driller; **~se** *s.f.* boring-machine, drill.
percevable [pɛrsəvabl] *adj.* collectable; perceivable.
percevoir [pɛrsəvwar] *v.t.* **1.** to perceive; **2.** to collect (taxes); ~ *un droit*, to charge a fee.
perche¹ [pɛrʃ] *s.f.* (ichth.) perch.
perche² [pɛrʃ] *s.f.* perch, pole, rod; old land measure; *saut à la* ~, pole-vaulting; (fig.) *tendre la* ~ *à qn.*, to hold out a helping hand to s.o.
percher [pɛrʃe] *v.i.*, **se** ~ *v.refl.* to perch, to roost; (fam.) *où perchez-vous?*, where are you staying?; where do you hang out?
percheron, -ne [pɛrʃərɔ̃] *adj.*, *s.m.f.* (native or inhabitant) of the Perche; horse or mare (from the Perche); percheron.
percheu-r, -se [pɛrʃœr] *adj.* perching; roosting.
perchiste [pɛrʃist] *s.m.f.* **1.** pole-vaulter; **2.** (cin., TV) perchman, boom operator (holding boom with microphone).
perchlorate [pɛrklɔrat] *s.m.* (chem.) perchlorate.
perchlorique [pɛrklɔrik] *adj.* perchloric.
perchlorure [pɛrklɔryr] *s.m.* perchloride.
perchoir [pɛrʃwar] *s.m.* roost, perch, stand.
perclus, -e [pɛrkly] *adj.* crippled, impotent, disabled, paralysed.
perçoir [pɛrswar] *s.m.* piercer (to tap casks, etc.), fret; borer, awl, gimlet, auger.
percolateur [pɛrkɔlatœr] *s.m.* percolator.
percussion [pɛrkysjɔ̃] *s.f.* percussion, impact.
percussionniste [pɛrkysjɔnist] *s.m.f.* (mus.) percussion-player.
percutant, -e [pɛrkytɑ̃] *adj.* percussive, producing percussion; (fig.) causing shock, shattering, brutal; *fusée* ~*e*, percussion-fuse.
percuter [pɛrkyte] *v.t.* to percuss, to strike, to crash into or against; (of car) ~ *un arbre*, to crash into a tree; ~ *v.i.* to hit (and explode); to crash; *les obus percutaient contre le mur*, the shells were hitting the wall; *la voiture a percuté contre un camion*, the car crashed into a lorry, was in collision with a lorry.
percuteur [pɛrkytœr] *s.m.* striker (of gun hammer), striker-pin.
perdant, -e [pɛrdɑ̃] *adj.* losing; *s.m.f.* loser; ~ *s.m.* (naut.) ebb-tide.
perdition [pɛrdisjɔ̃] *s.f.* perdition, destruction, wreck; *navire en* ~, ship in distress; sinking ship.
perdre [pɛrdr] *v.t.* **1.** to lose, to be deprived of; to waste; ~ *du poids*, to lose weight, to get thinner; ~ *l'esprit*, to go out of one's mind; ~ *la tête*, to lose one's head, to take leave of one's senses; ~ *le nord* or *la carte*, to lose one's bearings, to become confused; ~ *de vue*, to lose sight of, to forget; (naut.) ~ *la terre*, to lose sight of land; ~ *le fil*, to lose the thread, to forget what one was going to say; *ne* ~ *aucune occasion de*, to miss no opportunity to; ~ *son temps*, to waste one's time; **2.** (obs.) to kill; to destroy, to ruin, to be the ruin of; to destroy the reputation of; to corrupt, to lead (s.o.) the wrong way; *ce qui perdit Fouquet*, the cause of Fouquet's downfall; (mod.)

notre guide nous a perdus, our guide has taken us the wrong way; ~ *v.i.* to lose, to be a loser, to deteriorate, to fall behind, to fall, to fail; (naut.) to ebb; to lose way, to stick fast; **se** ~ *v.refl.* to lose one's way, to get lost; to disappear; to vanish; to blend; to spoil, to be wasted, disused; to ruin oneself, to be ruined, to destroy oneself; *cet usage se perd*, this custom is falling into disuse; *je m'y perds*, I cannot make head or tail of it; it beats me; I am bewildered; (naut.) *se* ~ *corps et biens*, to founder with all hands.

perdreau (pl. **-x**) [pɛrdro] *s.m.* (ornith.) young partridge; (cook.) partridge.

perdrix [pɛrdri] *s.f.* (ornith.) partridge; ~ *rouge*, red-legged partridge.

perdu, -e [pɛrdy] *adj.* lost, ruined, undone, dead, destroyed, doomed, spoiled, wasted; invisible; forlorn, stray; *à corps* ~, headlong, desperately; *à vos moments* ~*s*, in your spare time; *crier, courir, comme un* ~, to shout, to run, like mad; *sentinelle* ~*e*, advanced sentry; *pour un de* ~ *dix de retrouvés*, there's as good fish in the sea as ever came out of it; *salle des pas* ~*s*, outer hall, waiting-hall; *placer de l'argent à fonds* ~, to sink one's money in an annuity; *pays* ~, out-of-the-way place.

père [pɛr] *s.m.* father, sire, parent; (pl.) forefathers; (fam.) old fellow, old chap; creator, inventor; ~ *nourricier*, foster-father; *Dumas* ~, the older Dumas, Dumas senior; (of priest) *le Père Gaucher*, Father Gaucher; *le* ~ *Smith*, old Smith; *on ne peut contenter tout le monde et son* ~, one cannot please all the world and his wife.

pérégrination [peregrinɑsjɔ̃] *s.f.* peregrination, wandering.

péremption [perɑ̃psjɔ̃] *s.f.* (law) nonsuit; limitation.

péremptoire [perɑ̃ptwar] *adj.* that precludes all debate; decisive; peremptory; *d'un ton* ~, peremptorily; ~**ment** [perɑ̃ptwarmɑ̃] *adv.* peremptorily.

pérennité [perenite] *s.f.* perenniality, everlastingness.

péréquation [perekwɑsjɔ̃] *s.f.* equal distribution; equalization, standardization; making proportionate.

perfectibilité [pɛrfɛktibilite] *s.f.* perfectibility.

perfectible [pɛrfɛktibl] *adj.* perfectible.

perfection [pɛrfɛksjɔ̃] *s.f.* perfection, completeness; completion; *à la* ~, to perfection; ~*s*, qualities, virtues.

perfectionnement [pɛrfɛksjɔnmɑ̃] *s.m.* improvement; finishing, perfecting; further training.

perfectionner [pɛrfɛksjɔne] *v.t.* to bring to perfection, to perfect, to improve, to improve upon; **se** ~ *v.refl.* to improve oneself, to improve; *se* ~ *dans*, to improve one's knowledge of or one's skill in.

perfide [pɛrfid] *adj.* perfidious, treacherous, false; ~ *s.m.f.* traitor, traitress; ~**ment** [pɛrfidmɑ̃] *adv.* falsely, treacherously, perfidiously.

perfidie [pɛrfidi] *s.f.* perfidy, treachery, act of perfidy, deception.

perfolié, -e [pɛrfɔlje] *adj.* (bot.) perfoliate.

perforant, -e [pɛrfɔrɑ̃] *adj.* perforating, perforative, boring, penetrating; *obus* ~, armour-piercing shell.

perforat-eur, -rice [pɛrfɔratœr] *adj.* perforative; ~**eur** *s.m.* drill, punch; ~**rice** *s.f.* perforating-machine, drilling-machine, rock-drill.

perforation [pɛrfɔrɑsjɔ̃] *s.f.* perforation.

perforer [pɛrfɔre] *v.t.* to perforate, to bore, to drill, to punch; *carte perforée*, punched card.

perforeuse [pɛrfɔrøz] *s.f.* perforator (machine); ~ *à percussion*, percussion-drill.

performance [pɛrfɔrmɑ̃s] *s.f.* performance (of race-horse, etc.).

pergola [pɛrgɔla] *s.f.* pergola.

péri [peri] *s.m.f.* peri, fairy, genius.

périanthe [perjɑ̃t] *s.m.* (bot.) perianth.

péricarde [perikard] *s.m.* (anat.) pericardium.

péricarpe [perikarp] *s.m.* (bot.) pericarp, seed-vessel.

péricliter [periklite] *v.i.* to be in jeopardy, to threaten to fall, to be in danger, to be in a bad way; *faire* ~, to jeopardize, to endanger.

péridot [perido] *s.m.* (min.) peridot, chrysolite.

périgée [periʒe] *s.m.* (astron.) perigee.

périgourdin, -e [perigurdɛ̃] *adj., s.m.f.* (native or inhabitant) of Perigord.

périhélie [perieli] *s.m.* (astron.) perihelion.

péril [peril] *s.m.* peril, danger, hazard, jeopardy, risk; *être en* ~ *de*, to be in danger of; *mettre en* ~, to put in jeopardy, to endanger; *au* ~ *de sa vie*, at his peril, at the risk of his life; *il n'y a pas* ~ *en la demeure*, there is no need to hurry.

périlleu-x, -se [perijø] *adj.* perilous, hazardous, risky; ~**sement** [perijøzmɑ̃] *adv.* perilously.

périmé, -e [perime] *adj.* lapsed, expired, out-of-date.

(**se**) **périmer** [perime] *v.refl.* to be barred by limitation, to pass out of date, to lapse.

périmètre [perimɛtr] *s.m.* perimeter, measurement round; area, sphere (of influence, etc.).

périnéal, -e, (**aux**) [perineal] *adj.* (anat.) perineal.

périnée [perine] *s.m.* (anat.) perineum.

période [perjɔd] *s.f.* period, cycle; (gram., mus.) period; (phys.) ~ *radioactive*, (radioactive) half-life.

périodicité [perjɔdisite] *s.f.* periodicity.

périodique [perjɔdik] *adj.* periodic, periodical; (arith.) recurring; circulating; ~ *s.m.* periodical, newspaper, magazine, etc.; ~**ment** [perjɔdikmɑ̃] *adv.* periodically.

péri-oste [perjɔst] *s.m.* (anat.) periosteum; ~**ostite** [perjɔstit] *s.f.* (pathol.) periostitis.

péripatéticien, -ne [peripatetisjɛ̃] *adj., s.m.f.* peripatetic; ~**ne** *s.f.* (fam.) street-walker, prostitute.

péri-patétique [peripatetik] *adj.* (phil.) peripatetic; ~**patétisme** [peripatetism] *s.m.* (phil.) peripateticism; ~**pétie** [peripesi] *s.f.* peripeteia, sudden change of fortune; (pl.) vicissitudes, ups and downs; ~**phérie** [periferi] *s.f.* periphery, circumference, girth; outskirts, outlying parts; ~**phérique** [periferik] *adj.* peripheral, outlying, on the outskirts, forming an outer ring; *boulevard* ~*phérique*, outer boulevard; (*route*) ~*phérique*, ring-road; ~**phrase** [perifrɑz] *s.f.* periphrasis, circumlocution; ~**ptère** [peripter] *adj.* (arch.) peripteral; *s.m.* peripter.

périr [perir] *v.i.* (auxiliary *avoir*) to perish, to die, to be wrecked, ruined, lost; to be destroyed; (law) to lapse; *faire* ~, to put to death; ~ *de froid*, to perish with cold; ~ *d'ennui* or *s'ennuyer à* ~, to be bored to death.

péri-scope [periskɔp] *s.m.* periscope; ~**scopique** [periskɔpik] *adj.* periscopic; ~**sperme** [perispɛrm] *s.m.* (bot.) perisperm.

périssable [perisabl] *adj.* perishable; (fig.) fleeting, transitory; *denrées* ~*s*, perishable foodstuffs.

périssoire [periswar] *s.f.* kind of canoe.

péri-staltique [peristaltik] *adj.* (physiol.) peristaltic; ~**stome** [peristɔm] *s.m.* (bot., zool.) peristome; ~**style** [peristil] *s.m.* (arch.) peristyle; ~**toine** [peritwan] *s.m.* (anat.) peritoneum; ~**tonite** [peritɔnit] *s.f.* (pathol.) peritonitis.

perle [pɛrl] *s.f.* pearl, bead; (fig.) cream, best, jewel; (iron.) howler; ~ *fine*, real pearl; *c'est la* ~ *des maris*, he is the best of husbands.

perlé, -e [pɛrle] *adj.* **1.** adorned with pearls; **2.** pearl-shaped, pearly; *orge* ~, pearl-barley; **3.**

exquisitely done, rendered to perfection, perfect; cunningly executed; *grève ~e*, go-slow strike, work-to-rule.

perler [pɛrle] *v.t.* to bead, to adorn with pearls; to pearl (barley); to husk (rice); to finish to perfection, to execute brilliantly, to do meticulously; ~ *v.i.* to pearl, to form in beads, to stand out in drops, to drop, to glisten; *la sueur lui perlait au front*, sweat stood in drops on his forehead.

perli-er, -ère [pɛrlje] *adj.* pearl-bearing, pearl, of pearls; *huître ~ère*, pearl oyster.

perlimpinpin [pɛrlɛ̃pɛ̃pɛ̃] *s.m. poudre de ~*, quack powder, charlatan's nostrum.

perlot [pɛrlo] *s.m.* (pop.) tobacco.

permalloy [pɛrmelɔj; pɛrmalwa] *s.m.* permalloy (alloy of iron and nickel).

permanence [pɛrmanɑ̃s] *s.f.* permanence, permanency; service or staff functioning continuously; institution always open; ~ *de police*, police-station open day and night; ~ *nocturne*, all-night service; *en ~*, permanently, holding permanent sittings.

permanent, -e [pɛrmanɑ̃] *adj.* permanent, standing, continuous; *armée ~e*, standing army; ~ *s.m.* permanent member, official, (of party, etc.); **~e** *s.f.* (hairdressing) permanent wave.

permanganate [pɛrmɑ̃ganat] *s.m.* (chem.) permanganate.

perme [pɛrm] *s.f.* (abbrev. of *permission*) (mil. slang) leave, furlough.

perméabilité [pɛrmeabilite] *s.f.* permeability.

perméable [pɛrmeabl] *adj.* permeable, pervious; (fig.) susceptible.

permettre [pɛrmɛtr] *v.t.* to allow, to permit, to let, to authorize; to suffer, to put up with; to enable, to afford room for or the possibility of; to allow of, to admit of; *permettez!*, allow me!; wait a bit!; *permettez-moi de*, allow me to; **se ~** *v.refl.* to indulge in, to allow oneself; to be suffered or tolerated; *il se permet bien des choses*, he takes a good many liberties, he takes a lot on himself.

permis [pɛrmi] *s.m.* permit, licence, (customs) clearance, pass, permission; ~ *de chasse*, shooting--licence; ~ *de conduire*, driving-licence, driving--test.

permissi-f, -ve [pɛrmisif] *adj.* permissive.

permission [pɛrmisjɔ̃] *s.f.* permission, leave; leave of absence; leave-pass.

permissionnaire [pɛrmisjɔnɛr] *s.m.f.* soldier on leave.

permutable [pɛrmytabl] *adj.* that can be changed round; (math.) permutable.

permutant, -e [pɛrmytɑ̃] *s.m.f.* permuter; one who exchanges (job, etc.).

permutation [pɛrmytɑsjɔ̃] *s.f.* change (of job, etc.); (math.) permutation.

permuter [pɛrmyte] *v.i.* to permute, to exchange one's post or function with another.

pernicieu-x, -se [pɛrnisjø] *adj.* pernicious, hurtful, noxious, injurious; nefarious; **~sement** [pɛrnisjøzmɑ̃] *adv.* perniciously.

péroné [perɔne] *s.m.* (anat.) fibula.

péroniste [perɔnist] *adj., s.m.f.* Peronist, (supporter) of President Peron.

péronnelle [perɔnɛl] *s.f.* silly girl.

péroraison [perɔrɛzɔ̃] *s.f.* peroration.

pérorer [perɔre] *v.i.* to perorate, to expatiate, to hold forth, to make a pompous speech.

pérot [pero] *s.m.* sapling (left after two thinnings--out of growing trees).

Pérou [peru] *s.m.* (geog.) Peru.

peroxyde [perɔksid] *s.m.* (chem.) peroxide.

perpendiculaire [pɛrpɑ̃dikylɛr] *adj.* perpendicular, vertical, straight up and down, directly overhead, at right angles (*à*, to); ~ *s.f.* perpendicular; *abaisser une ~*, to drop a perpendicular; **~ment** [pɛrpɑ̃dikylɛrmɑ̃] *adv.* perpendicularly, vertically, at right angles (*à*, to).

(**à**) **perpète, perpette** [apɛrpɛt] *adv.loc.* (pop.) for ever.

perpétration [pɛrpetrɑsjɔ̃] *s.f.* perpetration, committing.

perprétrer [pɛrpetre] *v.t.* to perpetrate, to commit.

perpétuation [pɛrpetɥɑsjɔ̃] *s.f.* perpetuation.

perpétuel, -le [pɛrpetɥɛl] *adj.* perpetual, permanent; for life, life-; endless; *commentaire ~*, running commentary; **~lement** [pɛrpetɥɛlmɑ̃] *adv.* perpetually, endlessly, everlastingly.

perpétuer [pɛrpetɥe] *v.t.* to perpetuate; **se ~** *v.refl.* to endure; to become established.

perpétuité [pɛrpetɥite] *s.f.* perpetuity; *à ~*, for ever; for life; *travaux forcés à ~*, penal servitude for life.

perplexe [pɛrplɛks] *adj.* perplexed, irresolute, puzzled, confused.

perplexité [pɛrplɛksite] *s.f.* perplexity, bewilderment.

perquisition [pɛrkizisjɔ̃] *s.f.* investigation, search; *lancer un mandat de ~*, to issue a search--warrant.

perquisitionner [pɛrkizisjɔne] *v.i.* to search, to make a search; ~ *dans un appartement*, to search a flat.

perré [pɛre] *s.m.* dry-stone facing (to an embankment).

perrière [pɛrjɛr] *s.f.* (obs.) (artill.) swivel-gun, perrier.

perron [pɛrɔ̃] *s.m.* perron; flight of stone steps leading up to door.

perroquet [pɛrɔkɛ] *s.m.* **1.** parrot; *répéter comme un ~*, to repeat parrot-fashion; **2.** (naut.) topgallant sail; *grand ~*, main topgallant sail; *petit ~*, fore topgallant sail; ~ *volant*, royal sail; **3.** (fam.) glass of absinthe.

perruche [pɛryʃ] *s.f.* **1.** hen-parrot; **2.** parakeet; **3.** (naut.) mizen topgallant sail.

perruque [pɛryk] *s.f.* wig, periwig, peruke; (fig.) *vieille ~, tête à ~*, very old-fashioned person, old fogy.

perruqui-er, -ère [pɛrykje] *s.m.f.* wig-maker, peruke-maker, hairdresser.

pers [pɛr] *adj.m.* bluish-green, perse; *la déesse aux yeux ~*, Minerva.

persan, -e [pɛrsɑ̃] *adj., s.m.f.* Persian (Iranian).

Perse [pɛrs] *s.f.* (geog.) Persia (Iran).

perse [pɛrs] *adj., s.m.f.* (anc. hist.) Persian; ~ *s.f.* (text.) chintz.

persécuter [pɛrsekyte] *v.t.* to persecute, to harass, to pester, not to leave in peace, to torment; to importune, to annoy; to bore; to dun.

persécut-eur, -rice [pɛrsekytœr] *s.m.f.* persecutor, tormentor.

persécution [pɛrsekysjɔ̃] *s.f.* persecution, annoyance, tormenting; (psychol.) *folie* or *manie de la ~*, persecution mania.

persévérance [pɛrseverɑ̃s] *s.f.* perseverance, steadiness, persistence, constancy.

persévérant, -e [pɛrseverɑ̃] *adj.* persevering, persistent, steady, steadfast.

persévérer [pɛrsevere] *v.i.* to persevere, to persist, to hold on, to continue steadfastly.

persicaire [pɛrsikɛr] *s.f.* (bot.) persicaria, peachwort.

persienne [pɛrsjɛn] *s.f.* shutter (usu. slatted, folding back outside window).

persiflage [pɛrsiflaʒ] *s.m.* mocking, mockery, banter, chaff, persiflage.

persifler [pɛrsifle] *v.t.* to mock, to chaff.

persifleu-r, -se [pɛrsiflœr] *adj., s.m.f.* (one) given to mockery, chaff, etc.

persil [pɛrsi] *s.m.* (bot.) parsley.

persillade [pɛrsijad] *s.f.* (cook.) seasoning made

of oil, vinegar, and chopped parsley; cold beef served with *persillade*.
persillé, -e [pɛrsije] *adj.* (of cheese) green--spotted; (of meat) spotted with fat.
persique [pɛrsik] *adj.* (anc. hist.) Persian; (geog.) *le golfe Persique*, the Persian Gulf.
persistance [pɛrsistɑ̃s] *s.f.* persistence, persistency; persisting.
persistant, -e [pɛrsistɑ̃] *adj.* persistent, persisting, lasting.
persister [pɛrsiste] *v.i.* to persist, to hold out, to maintain one's opinion, to continue; to last.
personnage [pɛrsɔnaʒ] *s.m.* personage, person, somebody famous or important; character, figure, individual, fellow; (theatr.) *les ~s*, the characters or dramatis personae; *un grossier ~*, an ill-mannered fellow.
personnaliser [pɛrsɔnalize] *v.t.* **1.** (obs.) to personify (an abstraction); **2.** to personalize; to give a personal touch to.
personnalité [pɛrsɔnalite] *s.f.* personality, individuality, personal character; personal remark; personage, important person; (obs.) egoism.
personne[1] [pɛrsɔn] *s.f.* person, one's person, individual, body, external appearance; (gram.) person; *payer de sa ~*, not to spare oneself; *c'est la bonté en ~*, she is kindness itself; *j'irai en ~*, I will go in person; *il soigne sa petite ~*, he looks after number one; *jeune ~*, young girl, young lady; *sans acception de ~*, without distinction of persons; *erreur sur la ~*, mistaken identity; (comm. law) *~ morale*, group collectivity, corporation, legal entity.
personne[2] [pɛrsɔn] *indef.pron.m.sing.* anyone, anybody; no one, nobody; *~ n'est parfait*, nobody is perfect; *je doute que ~ vienne*, I doubt whether anybody will come; *je n'ai trouvé ~*, I found nobody at home; nobody was there.
personnel, -le [pɛrsɔnɛl] *adj.* personal; *~ s.m.* staff, personnel, work-people, workers; those engaged in an occupation; *le ~ politique*, those in politics; **~lement** [pɛrsɔnɛlmɑ̃] *adv.* personally, in person.
personnification [pɛrsɔnifikasjɔ̃] *s.f.* personification.
personnifier [pɛrsɔnifje] *v.t.* to personify.
perspecti-f, -ve [pɛrspɛktif] *adj.* perspective; **~ve** *s.f.* perspective, view, vista, prospect; aspect; viewpoint; expectation; *en ~ve*, in the distance; in view, in prospect; *sous une ~ve différente*, from a different aspect; *dans une ~ve marxiste*, from a Marxist viewpoint.
perspicace [pɛrspikas] *adj.* perspicacious, shrewd, penetrating.
perspicacité [pɛrspikasite] *s.f.* perspicacity, shrewdness.
perspiration [pɛrspirɑsjɔ̃] *s.f.* (med.) insensible perspiration; ⚠ not visible 'perspiration'.
persuader [pɛrsɥade] *v.t.* to persuade, to induce, to convince, to satisfy; **se** *~ v.refl.* to persuade oneself, to be persuaded, to imagine, to get into one's mind, to be convinced.
persuasi-f, -ve [pɛrsɥazif] *adj.* persuasive, convincing.
persuasion [pɛrsɥazjɔ̃] *s.f.* persuasion, conviction, belief; persuading, persuasiveness.
persuasivement [pɛrsɥazivmɑ̃] *adv.* persuasively, convincingly.
persulfate [pɛrsylfat] *s.m.* (chem.) persulphate.
perte [pɛrt] *s.f.* loss, privation, ruin, fall, wreck; waste; perdition; leak, escape; (med.) flooding; *à ~ de vue*, as far as the eye can reach; *à ~*, at a loss; *être en ~*, to be a loser; *en pure ~*, uselessly, to no purpose; *à ~ d'haleine*, out of breath; *profits et ~s*, profit and loss; *~ sèche*, dead loss.
pertinacité [pɛrtinasite] *s.f.* pertinacity.
pertinemment [pɛrtinamɑ̃] *adv.* pertinently, appositely; for certain; *savoir ~*, to know for a fact.
pertinence [pɛrtinɑ̃s] *s.f.* pertinence, pertinency, relevance.
pertinent, -e [pɛrtinɑ̃] *adj.* pertinent, relevant.
pertuis [pɛrtɥi] *s.m.* opening, sluice, hole; (geog.) straits, narrows; pass (in the Jura).
pertuisane [pɛrtɥizan] *s.f.* (archaeol.) partisan, halberd.
perturbat-eur, -rice [pɛrtyrbatœr] *s.m.f.* disturber, perturber, agitator; *adj.* disturbing.
perturbation [pɛrtyrbɑsjɔ̃] *s.f.* disturbance, perturbation, upheaval, upset.
perturber [pɛrtyrbe] *v.t.* to disturb, to perturb.
péruvien, -ne [peryvjɛ̃] *adj., s.m.f.* Peruvian.
pervenche [pɛrvɑ̃ʃ] *s.f.* (bot.) periwinkle; *~ adj.* periwinkle blue; (of eyes) forget-me-not blue.
pervers, -e [pɛrvɛr] *adj.* perverse, wayward, persisting in evil or in error, depraved, wicked; *s.m.f.* pervert, anti-social type; ⚠ not 'perverse' in sense 'awkward', 'difficult', 'contrary'.
perversion [pɛrvɛrsjɔ̃] *s.f.* perversion.
perversité [pɛrvɛrsite] *s.f.* perversity, depravity, perverseness; ⚠ see PERVERS.
pervertir [pɛrvɛrtir] *v.t.* to pervert, to lead astray, to corrupt, to deprave; **se** *~ v.refl.* to get corrupted, to be perverted, to become warped.
pervertissement [pɛrvɛrtismɑ̃] *s.m.* perverting.
pervertisseu-r, -se [pɛrvɛrtisœr] *adj.* perverting, corrupting; *s.m.f.* corrupter, perverter.
pesade [pəzad] *s.f.* (rid.) rearing.
pesage [pəzaʒ] *s.m.* **1.** weighing; **2.** (racing) weigh-in; weighing room or paddock.
pesamment [pəzamɑ̃] *adv.* heavily; (fig.) ponderously, clumsily.
pesant, -e [pəzɑ̃] *adj.* heavy, weighty; ponderous, clumsy, burdensome, sluggish, slow; *~ s.m.* weight; *il vaut son ~ d'or*, he is worth his weight in gold.
pesanteur [pəzɑ̃tœr] *s.f.* weight, heaviness, dullness, sluggishness, ponderousness; (phys.) gravity, gravitation; *lois de la ~*, laws of gravity.
pèse-acide [pɛzasid] *s.m.* (pl. *pèse-acides*) acidimeter.
pèse-alcool [pɛzalkɔl] *s.m.* (pl. *pèse-alcools*) alcoholometer.
pesée [pəze] *s.f.* **1.** weighing; amount weighed at one time; **2.** pressure, force, leverage.
pèse-lettre [pɛzlɛtr] *s.m.* (pl. *pèse-lettres*) letter--balance.
pèse-liqueur [pɛzlikœr] *s.m.* (pl. *pèse-liqueurs*) = PÈSE-ALCOOL.
peser [pəze] *v.t.i.* to weigh; (fig.) to estimate, to ponder, to weigh; to exert pressure, weight, leverage or force; (fig.) to apply pressure (*sur*, to); to press (*sur*, on or against); to be heavy, to lie heavy (*à*, on), to be a burden (*à*, to); to lay stress, to dwell.
pesette [pəzɛt] *s.f.* assay-scales.
peseu-r, -se [pəzœr] *s.m.f.* weigher, weighman.
peson [pəzɔ̃] *s.m.* spring-balance; steelyard.
pessaire [pesɛr] *s.m.* pessary.
pesse [pɛs] *s.f.* (bot.) mare's-tail.
pessimisme [pesimism] *s.m.* pessimism.
pessimiste [pesimist] *s.m.f.* pessimist; *~ adj.* pessimistic.
peste [pɛst] *s.f.* pestilence, plague, scourge; (fig.) pest, torment, nuisance, bore; *~ noire*, Black Death; *la ~ soit de!*, a plague upon!; *~!*, expression of astonishment.
pester [pɛste] *v.i.* to curse and swear, to storm, to fulminate, to grumble.
pesticide [pɛstisid] *s.m.* (agric.) pesticide.
pestiféré, -e [pɛstifere] *adj.* plague-stricken; pestiferous; *s.m.f.* person infected with the plague.

pestilence [pɛstilɑ̃s] *s.f.* pestilence, plague; putrid smell.
pestilentiel, -le [pɛstilɑ̃sjɛl] *adj.* pestilential, stinking.
pet [pɛ] *s.m.* **1.** (vulg.) fart; **2.** *ça ne vaut pas un* ~ (*de lapin*), it isn't worth a tinker's curse, it is of no account; **3.** (vulg.) scandal, outrage; *il va y avoir du* ~, it will cause a row, or make a stink; *porter* ~, to make a complaint or row, to bring an action; ~*!*, watch out!
pétale [petal] *s.m.* petal.
pétant, -e [petɑ̃] *adj.* (of time) exactly, sharp; *à dix heures* ~*es*, at ten o'clock sharp.
pétarade [petarad] *s.f.* series of explosions, fusillade, crackle, backfiring.
pétard [petar] *s.m.* **1.** explosive charge, blast; (rail.) detonator, fog-signal; fire-cracker, thunderflash; (fig.) bombshell, sensational piece of news; **2.** (fam.) noise, row, fuss; *il va y avoir du* ~, there is going to be a row; *être en* ~, to be in a temper; **3.** (pop.) (i.) revolver; (ii.) bottom, backside.
pétaudière [petodjɛr] *s.f.* disorderly, noisy assembly; bear garden; bedlam broken loose.
pet-de-nonne [pɛdnɔn] *s.m.* (pl. *pets-de-nonne*) (cook.) fritter.
pet-en-l'air [pɛtɑ̃lɛr] *s.m.invar.* short indoor jacket.
péter [pete] *v.i.* **1.** (vulg.) to fart; *envoyer* ~ *qn.*, to send s.o. about their business; (fig.) ~ *le feu*, to be a fire-eater, to be bursting with energy; *ça va* ~ *le feu*, there's going to be the hell of a row; **2.** to explode, to burst; (lit. & fig.) to go off, to blow up.
pètesec, pète-sec [pɛtsɛk] *s.m.* martinet.
péteu-x, -se [petø] *s.m.f.* (fam.) coward.
pétillant, -e [petijɑ̃] *adj.* crackling; (lit. & fig.) sparkling.
pétillement [petijmɑ̃] *s.m.* crackling; sparkling; sparkle, liveliness.
pétiller [petije] *v.i.* to crackle, to sparkle, to bubble; ~ *d'impatience*, to boil with impatience, to be all eagerness; *ce livre pétille d'esprit*, this book sparkles with wit.
pétiole [pesjɔl] *s.m.* (bot.) petiole.
pétiolé, -é [pesjɔle] *adj.* (bot.) petiolate.
petiot, -e [pətjo] *adj.* (fam.) little, tiny; *s.m.f.* little child.
petit, -e [pəti] *adj.* small, little, diminutive, tiny, wee, short, young, junior; lesser, minor; unimportant, petty, slight, trifling; low, shabby, mean, humble; *être aux* ~*s soins pour qn.*, to be all attention to s.o.; *un* ~ *esprit*, a narrow-minded person; *avoir une* ~*e santé*, to be in poor health; *le* ~ *peuple*, the common people; *se faire* ~ *devant qn.*, to humble oneself in front of s.o.; *se faire tout* ~, to make oneself inconspicuous, to cower; ~*e-fille*, granddaughter; ~*-fils*, grandson; ~(*e*)*-cousin*(*e*), second cousin; ~*-gris*, miniver, Siberian squirrel; ~*-lait*, whey; ~*-maître*, dandy, fop, beau; ~*-neveu*, great-nephew; ~*e-nièce*, great-niece; ~*s-enfants*, grandchildren; *s.m.f.* little boy, little girl, child; *les* ~*s*, the children, the young (of animals), (at school) the juniors; *les* ~*s de ce monde*, the poor, the humble; *faire des* ~*s*, to bring forth young ones, to multiply; to breed; ~ *adv.* ~ *à* ~, little by little, by degrees; *en* ~, on a small scale; ~**ement** [pətitmɑ̃] *adv.* in small quantity, to a limited extent, poorly; meanly, stingily.
petit-bourgeois [pətiburʒwa], **petite-bourgeoise** [pətitburʒwaz] *adj.*, *s.m.f.* lower-middle-class (person); (person) having narrow outlook.
petite-bourgeoisie [pətitburʒwazi] *s.f.* lower-middle-class.
petitesse [pətitɛs] *s.f.* **1.** smallness, littleness, shortness; insignificance; **2.** meanness, piece of meanness; ~ *d'esprit*, narrowness of mind, narrow-mindedness.
pétition [petisjɔ̃] *s.f.* petition, request; ~ *de principe*, petitio principii; begging the question.
pétitionnaire [petisjɔnɛr] *s.m.f.* (law) petitioner.
pétitoire [petitwar] *s.m.* claim of ownership.
peton [pətɔ̃] *s.m.* (fam.) tiny foot.
pétoncle [petɔ̃kl] *s.m.* (zool.) scallop, shellfish.
pétré, -e [petre] *adj.* (geog.) stony; *Arabie* ~*e*, Arabia Petraea.
pétrel [petrɛl] *s.m.* (ornith.) petrel, storm(y) petrel.
pétreu-x, -se [petrø] *adj.* petrous, stone-like.
pétri, -e [petri] *adj.* kneaded; (fig.) ~ *de*, full of, imbued with, steeped in.
pétrifiant, -e [petrifjɑ̃] *adj.* petrifying.
pétrification [petrifikasjɑ̃] *s.f.* petrifaction.
pétrifier [petrifje] *v.t.* to petrify, to turn into stone, to immobilize; **se** ~ *v.refl.* to petrify; (fig.) to become fixed.
pétrin [petrɛ̃] *s.m.* kneading-trough; (fig.) tight corner, mess, fix; *il s'est mis dans le* ~, he has got himself into a mess.
pétrir [petrir] *v.t.* to knead; (fig.) to form, to mould.
pétrissage [petrisaʒ] *s.m.* kneading; massage; shaping, moulding.
pétrisseu-r, -se [petrisœr] *s.m.f.* kneader; ~**se** *s.f.* kneading-machine, dough-mixer.
pétrochimique [petrɔʃimik], **pétrolochimique** [petrɔlɔʃimik] *adj.* petrochemical.
pétrole [petrɔl] *s.m.* petroleum, (crude) oil; paraffin oil, paraffin; ⚠ not 'petrol'.
pétrolette [petrɔlɛt] *s.f.* **1.** (obs.) small car; **2.** small motor cycle, moped.
pétroleuse [petrɔløz] *s.f.* (hist.) female incendiary (during *Commune*).
pétroli-er, -ère [petrɔlje] *adj.* oil, petroleum, of the oil industry; oil-producing; *géologue* ~*er*, oil-company geologist; *pays* ~*er*, oil-producing country; ~**er** *s.m.* **1.** oil-tanker; **2.** oil-magnate, oil-man.
pétrolifère [petrɔlifɛr] *adj.* petroliferous, oil-bearing.
P. et T. [peete] abbrev. *Postes et Télécommunications.*
pétulance [petylɑ̃s] *s.f.* petulance, petulancy; liveliness, irrepressibility.
pétulant, -e [petylɑ̃] *adj.* lively, exuberant, irrepressible.
pétunia [petynja] *s.m.* (bot.) petunia.
peu [pø] *adv.* little, not much; few, not many; not very; *à* ~ *près, à* ~ *de chose près*, about; nearly; *d'ici* ~, *sous* ~, in a few days; shortly; before long; *depuis* ~, lately; not long ago; recently; a little while ago; ~ *à* ~, by degrees; little by little; ~ *de chose*, not much, nothing much, a trifling matter, of little account; *c'est* ~ (*que*) *de parler*, talking is not enough; *quelque* ~, somewhat; *tant soit* ~, ever so little; *pour* ~ *que vous hésitiez*, if you so much as hesitate, if you hesitate but a fraction, or but for a moment; *si* ~ *que*, however, how . . . soever; *si* ~ *que rien*, a mere nothing; *très* ~, *fort* ~, *bien* ~, very little; ~ *aimable*, not very amiable; ~ *de livres*, few books; *parler* ~, to speak little; ~ *ou prou*, little or much; *vivre de* ~, to live on next to nothing; *un homme de* ~, a common sort of man; *se contenter de* ~, to be content with little; ~ *s.m.* little, bit, few; *attendez un* ~, wait a bit; *encore un* ~, a little longer; a little more; *pour un* ~ *il eût pleuré*, he was very near to tears; (iron.) *excusez du* ~, how modest!; *un petit* ~, a little bit, a little while; *un* ~ *mieux*, a little better; *le* ~ *qu'il sait*, the little he knows.
peuh [pø] *interj.* expressing scorn or indifference.

peulven [pølvɛn] *s.m.* = MENHIR.
peuplade [pœplad] *s.f.* tribe, clan, horde, colony, people.
peuple [pœpl] *s.m.* people, nation, tribe, race; population, common people, crowd, lower classes; working classes; *le bas* ~, the rabble, the mob; *un grand concours de* ~, a great crowd; ~ *adj.* vulgar, common, plebeian.
peuplement [pœpləmɑ̃] *s.m.* peopling; population; stocking (of a poultry-yard, pond, etc.).
peupler [pœple] *v.t.* **1.** to people, to populate, to fill, to stock (*de*, with); **2.** to people, to inhabit; **se** ~ *v.refl.* to be populated, to fill, to be filled.
peuplier [pœplje] *s.m.* (bot.) poplar.
peur [pœr] *s.f.* fear, fright, dread, terror; *avoir* ~, to be afraid; *avoir grand'*~, to be in great fear, to be very much afraid; *à faire* ~, frightful, frightfully; *faire* ~ *à qn.*, to frighten s.o.; *mourir de* ~, to die of fright, to be frightened to death; *en être quitte pour la* ~, to come off with nothing worse than a fright; *avoir* ~ *de son ombre*, to be afraid of one's shadow, to be afraid of everything; *avoir plus de* ~ *que de mal*, to be more frightened than hurt; *de* ~ *de*, for fear of; *de* ~ *que*, lest, for fear that; *sans* ~, fearless, fearlessly.
peureu-x, -se [pœrø] *adj.* fearful, timorous, timid, shy, easily frightened; *s.m.f.* coward; **~sement** [pœrøzmɑ̃] *adv.* fearfully, timorously, in a cowardly way, timidly.
peut-être [pøtɛtr] *adv.* maybe, perhaps, perchance, possibly; ~ *que*, *conj.loc.* perhaps, it may be that.
pèze [pɛz] *s.m.* (slang) money
P.G.C.D. [peʒesede] abbrev. *plus grand commun diviseur*, highest common factor, H.C.F.
pH [peaʃ] abbrev. *potentiel d'Hydrogène*, pH.
phacochère [fakɔʃɛr] *s.m.* (zool.) wart-hog.
phaéton [faetɔ̃] *s.m.* **1.** (iron.) driver, coachman; **2.** phaeton.
phagocyte [fagɔsit] *s.m.* phagocyte.
phagocytose [fagɔsitoz] *s.f.* phagocytosis.
phalange [falɑ̃ʒ] *s.f.* **1.** phalanx; army, host; **2.** (anat.) phalanx, bone of finger or toe.
phalanger [falɑ̃ʒe] *s.m.* (zool.) phalanger.
phalène [falɛn] *s.f.* (ent.) phalaena, moth.
phallique [falik] *adj.* phallic.
phallus [falys] *s.m.* phallus.
phanérogame [fanerɔgam] *adj.* (bot.) phanerogamous; ~ *s.f.* phanerogamous plant, phanerogam.
phantasme [fɑ̃tasm] *s.m.* = FANTASME.
pharamineu-x, -se [faraminø] *adj.* (fam.) stupendous, amazing, astounding; immense.
pharaon [faraɔ̃] *s.m.* **1.** Pharaoh; **2.** faro (card-game).
pharaonien, -ne [faraɔnjɛ̃], **pharaonique** [faraɔnik] *adj.* Pharaonic, of the Pharaohs.
phare [far] *s.m.* lighthouse; beacon, radio-beacon; (car) headlight; searchlight; (naut.) mast.
pharillon [farijɔ̃] *s.m.* light used for night-fishing.
pharisaïque [farizaik] *adj.* Pharisaic, Pharisaical, hypocritical.
pharisaïsme [farizaism] *s.m.* Pharisaism, hypocrisy.
pharisien, -ne [farizjɛ̃] *s.m.f.* Pharisee; self-righteous person.
pharmaceutique [farmasøtik] *adj.* pharmaceutical; ~ *s.f.* pharmaceutics.
pharmacie [farmasi] *s.f.* pharmacy, dispensing; pharmaceutics; chemist's shop; dispensary; medicine-chest; medicines, drugs.
pharmacien, -ne [farmasjɛ̃] *s.m.f.* chemist, pharmacist.
pharmaco-logie [farmakɔlɔʒi] *s.f.* pharmacology; **~logique** [farmakɔlɔʒik] *adv.* pharmacological; **~copée** [farmakɔpe] *s.f.* pharmacopoeia.
pharyngien, -ne [farɛ̃ʒjɛ̃] *adj.* pharyngeal.
pharyngite [farɛ̃ʒit] *s.f.* pharyngitis.
pharynx [farɛ̃ks] *s.m.* pharynx.
phase [fɑz] *s.f.* phase (of moon or planet); phase, aspect, stage, period, turn.
phénicien, -ne [fenisjɛ̃] *adj.*, *s.m.f.* Phoenician.
phenicoptère [fenikɔptɛr] *s.m.* (ornith.) flamingo.
phénique [fenik] *adj.* (chem.) *acide* ~, carbolic acid, phenol.
phénix [feniks] *s.m.* (myth.) phoenix; (fig.) phoenix; paragon; wonderful person.
phénol [fenɔl] *s.m.* (chem.) phenol, carbolic acid.
phénoménal, -e, (**aux**) [fenɔmenal] *adj.* phenomenal; (fig.) prodigious, remarkable; **~ement** [fenɔmenalmɑ̃] *adv.* phenomenally, amazingly, remarkably.
phénomène [fenɔmɛn] *s.m.* phenomenon; (fig.) wonder, prodigy, wonderful person or event; (fam.) eccentric, queer customer.
philanthrop-e [filɑ̃trɔp] *s.m.f.* philanthropist; **~ie** [filɑ̃trɔpi] *s.f.* philanthropy; **~ique** [filɑ̃trɔpik] *adj.* philanthropic(al).
philatél-ie [filateli] *s.f.* philately, stamp-collecting; **~ique** [filatelik] *adj.* philatelic; **~iste** [filatelist] *s.m.f.* philatelist, stamp-collector.
philharmon-ie [filarmɔni] *s.f.* **1.** (obs.) love of music; **2.** local music society; **~ique** [filarmɔnik] *adj.* **1.** (obs.) fond of music; **2.** philharmonic (referring to (i.) large orchestra, (ii.) local musical society or activities).
philippine [filipin] *s.f.* philippina; double almond.
philippique [filipik] *s.f.* Philippic; (fig.) bitter invective.
philistin, -e [filistɛ̃] *s.m.f.* Philistine.
philolog-ie [filɔlɔʒi] *s.f.* philology; **~ique** [filɔlɔʒik] *adj.* philological; **~iquement** [filɔlɔʒikmɑ̃] *adv.* philologically; **~ue** [filɔlɔg] *s.m.f.* philologist.
philosoph-ale [filɔsɔfal] *adj.f.* *pierre ~ale*, (alchemy) philosophers' stone; **~e** [filɔsɔf] *s.m.f.* philosopher, sage; *adj.* philosophical; **~er** [filɔsɔfe] *v.i.* to philosophize; to reason; **~ie** [filɔsɔfi] *s.f.* philosophy; wisdom, resignation; *classe de ~ie*, philosophy class (top class in *lycée* or *collège*); *avec ~ie*, philosophically, with resignation; **~ique** [filɔsɔfik] *adj.* philosophical; **~iquement** [filɔsɔfikmɑ̃] *adv.* philosophically, calmly, with resignation.
philtre [filtr] *s.m.* philtre, love-potion.
phlébite [flebit] *s.f.* (pathol.) phlebitis.
phlébotomie [flebɔtɔmi] *s.f.* phlebotomy.
phlogistique [flɔʒistik] *s.m.* (sci. hist.) phlogiston.
phlox [flɔks] *s.m.* (bot.) phlox.
phobie [fɔbi] *s.f.* phobia.
phobique [fɔbik] *adj.*, *s.m.f.* phobic; (person) subject to phobia.
phœnix [feniks] *s.m.* (bot.) phoenix (palm-tree).
pholade [fɔlad] *s.f.* (moll.) Pholas, stone-borer.
phone [fɔn] *s.m.* (phys.) phon.
phonème [fɔnɛm] *s.m.* (phon.) phoneme.
phonétique [fɔnetik] *adj.* phonetic; *s.f.* phonetics; **~ment** [fɔnetikmɑ̃] *adv.* phonetically.
phonie [fɔni] *s.f.* abbrev. RADIOPHONIE.
phonique [fɔnik] *adj.* phonic, sound, audio-, audible; *signal* ~, sound or audible signal.
phono [fɔno] *s.m.* abbrev. *phonographe* or *électrophone*.
phonographe [fɔnɔgraf) *s.m.* phonograph, gramophone.
phonographique [fɔnɔgrafik] *adj.* phonographic; for gramophone, on record.

phonologie [fɔnɔlɔʒi] *s.f.* phonology.
phonothèque [fɔnɔtɛk] *s.f.* record library; sound archives.
phoque [fɔk] *s.m.* (zool.) seal
phormium [fɔrmjɔm], **phormion** [fɔrmjɔ̃] *s.m.* (bot.) phormium, New Zealand flax.
phosphatage [fɔsfataʒ] *s.m.* (agric.) spreading of phosphate (as fertilizer).
phosphate [fɔsfat] *s.m.* (chem.) phosphate.
phosphaté, -e [fɔsfate] *adj.* treated with phosphate, phosphatic.
phosphater [fɔsfate] *v.t.* (agric.) to spread phosphate, to use phosphate fertilizer, on (field, etc.).
phosphène [fɔsfɛn] *s.m.* phosphene.
phosphine [fɔsfin] *s.f.* (chem.) phosphine.
phosphite [fɔsfit] *s.m.* (chem.) phosphite.
phosphore [fɔsfɔr] *s.m.* (chem.) phosphorus.
phosphoré, -e [fɔsfɔre] *adj.* phosphorated.
phosphorescence [fɔsfɔresɑ̃s] *s.f.* phosphorescence.
phosphorescent, -e [fɔsfɔresɑ̃] *adj.* phosphorescent.
phosphoreux [fɔsfɔrø] *adj.m.* (chem.) phosphorous; *bronze* ~, phosphor bronze.
phosphorique [fɔsfɔrik] *adj.* (chem.) phosphoric.
phosphorite [fɔsfɔrit] *s.f.* phosphorite, apatite.
phosphure [fɔsfyr] *s.m.* (chem.) phosphide, phosphuretted . . .; ~ *d'hydrogène*, phosphine.
phot [fɔt] *s.m.* (phys.) phot.
photo [fɔto] *s.f.* (abbrev. of *photographie*) photo; snapshot; portrait; *prendre en* ~, to photograph.
photochim-ie [fɔtɔʃimi] *s.f.* photochemistry; **~ique** [fɔtɔʃimik] *adj.* photochemical.
photocop-ie [fɔtɔkɔpi] *s.f.* photocopy; **~ier** [fɔtɔkɔpje] *v.t.* to photocopy.
photoélectricité [fɔtɔelɛktrisite] *s.f.* (phys.) photoelectricity.
photoélectrique [fɔtɔelɛktrik] *adj.* photoelectric.
photo-finish [fɔtɔfiniʃ] *s.m.* (racing) photo finish; photo-finish camera.
photogén-ie [fɔtɔʒeni] *s.f.* **1.** (obs.) generation of light; **2.** (cin., etc.) photogenic quality; **~ique** [fɔtɔʒenik] *adj.* photogenic.
photogrammétrie [fɔtɔgrametri] *s.f.* photogrammetry; photographic surveying.
photograph-e [fɔtɔgraf] *s.m.f.* photographer; photographic dealer; **~ie** [fɔtɔgrafi] *s.f.* photography; photograph; **~ier** [fɔtɔgrafje] *v.t.* to photograph, to take a photograph of; *se faire ~ier*, to have one's picture taken; **~ique** [fɔtɔgrafik] *adj.* photographic; *appareil ~ique*, camera; *reconnaissance ~ique*, photo-reconnaissance; **~iquement** [fɔtɔgrafikmɑ̃] *adv.* photographically, by photography.
photogravure [fɔtɔgravyr] *s.f.* photo-engraving, photogravure.
photolithographie [fɔtɔlitɔgrafi] *s.f.* photolithography.
photomètre [fɔtɔmɛtr] *s.m.* photometer.
photométrie [fɔtɔmetri] *s.f.* photometry.
photosphère [fɔtɔsfɛr] *s.f.* (astron.) photosphere.
photostat [fɔtɔsta] *s.m.* photostat.
photosynthèse [fɔtɔsɛ̃tez] *s.f.* (sci.) photosynthesis.
phototropisme [fɔtɔtrɔpism] *s.m.* (biol.) phototropism.
phototypie [fɔtɔtipi] *s.f.* collotype.
phrase [frɑz] *s.f.* phrase, sentence; *sans* ~, straight out, plainly; (gram.) *membre de* ~, clause, phrase; *faire des ~s*, to speak in flowery language.
phrasé [frɑze] *s.m.* (mus.) phrasing.
phraséologie [frɑzeɔlɔʒi] *s.f.* phraseology; (iron.) fine phrases, empty verbiage.
phraser [frɑze] *v.t.i.* to phrase, to mark the phrases of, to articulate in phrases; ~ *un compliment*, to turn a compliment.
phraseu-r, -se [frɑzœr] *s.m.f.* one who makes pretty speeches.
phrénologie [frenɔlɔʒi] *s.f.* phrenology.
phrygane [frigan] *s.f.* (ent.) caddis-fly.
phrygien, -ne [friʒjɛ̃] *adj., s.m.f.* Phrygian; (Fr. hist.) *bonnet* ~, Phrygian cap.
phtisie [ftizi] *s.f.* (pathol.) phthisis, consumption, pulmonary tuberculosis.
phtisique [ftizik] *adj., s.m.f.* phthisical, tubercular, consumptive, (person).
phylactère [filaktɛr] *s.m.* phylactery; (ant.) amulet, charm.
phylloxéra [filɔksera] *s.m.* (ent.) phylloxera.
physalis [fizalis] *s.m.* (bot.) Physalis, winter--cherry.
physicien, -ne [fizisjɛ̃] *s.m.f.* physicist; ⚠ not 'physician'.
physiolog-ie [fizjɔlɔʒi] *s.f.* physiology; **~ique** [fizjɔlɔʒik] *adj.* physiological; **~iquement** [fizjɔlɔʒikmɑ̃] *adv.* physiologically; **~iste** [fizjɔlɔʒist] *s.m.f.* physiologist.
physionom-ie [fizjɔnɔmi] *s.f.* physiognomy, countenance, appearance, look, characteristic features; face; **~iste** [fizjɔnɔmist] *s.m.f.* (obs.) physiognomist; *adj., s.m.f.* (person) good at recognizing faces.
physiothérapie [fizjɔterapi] *s.f.* physiotherapy.
physique [fizik] *adj.* physical, material, bodily; real; ~ *s.f.* physics; ~ *s.m.* constitution, body, physique; physical appearance; **~ment** [fizikmɑ̃] *adv.* physically, bodily, materially.
phytotron [fitɔtrɔ̃] *s.m.* (bot.) phytotron.
pi [pi] *s.m.* (math.) pi, π.
piaf [pjaf] *s.m.* (pop.) sparrow.
piaffement [pjafmɑ̃] *s.m.* (of horse) pawing the ground; (fig.) fidgeting.
piaffer [pjafe] *v.i.* (of horse) to paw the ground; (fig.) to stamp one's feet or tap one's foot (with impatience).
piaffeu-r, -se [pjafœr] *adj.* restive, impatient.
piaillard, -e [pjɑjar] *adj.* squeaking, bawling, squalling.
piailler [pjɑje] *v.i.* to chirp shrilly, to squeak; to bawl, to squall.
piaillerie [pjɑjri] *s.f.* shrill chirping; bawling, squalling.
piailleu-r, -se [pjɑjœr] *adj., s.m.f.* bawling, squalling (child); squeaking (bird).
piane-piane [pjanpjan] *adv.* (pop.) softly, softly.
pianiste [pjanist] *s.m.f.* pianist.
piano [pjano] *s.m.* piano; ~ *droit*, upright piano; ~ *à queue*, grand piano; ~ *crapaud*, baby grand; ~ *mécanique*, player-piano; piano organ; *toucher du* ~, to play the piano.
piano [pjano] *adv.* (mus.) piano; softly, not loud; gently; (fam.) *allez-y ~!*, play it cool!
pianoter [pjanɔte] *v.i.* to strum, to play (piano) badly; to drum (with one's fingers).
piastre [pjastr] *s.f.* piastre (coin).
piaulement [pjolmɑ̃] *s.m.* peeping, puling (of chickens, etc.); whining (of child).
piauler [pjole] *v.i.* (of chicks) to peep, to pule; (of child) to whine, to whimper.
(**à**) **pible** [apibl] *adv.loc.* (naut.) *mât à* ~, pole--mast.
pic[1] [pik] *s.m.* (ornith.) woodpecker; *pic-vert, pivert*, green woodpecker.
pic[2] [pik] *s.m.* pick, pickaxe; (at piquet) pique.
pic[3] [pik] *s.m.* peak, summit; *à* ~, precipitous, vertical(ly), sheer; (fig., fam.) just at the right moment, in the nick of time; (naut.) *couler à* ~, to sink like a stone.
picador [pikadɔr] *s.m.* picador.
picaillons [pikajɔ̃] *s.m.pl.* (pop.) money.
picard, -e [pikar] *adj., s.m.f.* Picard, (native or inhabitant) of Picardy.

Picardie [pikardi] *s.f.* (geog.) Picardy.
picaresque [pikarɛsk] *adj.* picaresque.
pichenette [piʃnɛt] *s.f.* fillip, flick (of the finger).
pichet [piʃɛ] *s.m.* jug, pitcher, mug.
picholine [piʃɔlin] *s.f.* picholine (olive).
pick-up [pikœp] *s.m.invar.* **1.** (techn.) pick-up, playing-head; **2.** gramophone, record-player; **3.** pick-up (van or truck); **4.** (agric.) pick-up baler.
picorée [pikɔre] *s.f.* (of birds) *aller à la* ~, to go in search of food, to peck around.
picorer [pikɔre] *v.t.i.* to peck around, to pick up (food).
picot [piko] *s.m.* **1.** edging, purl (of lace), picot; **2.** small splinter (of wood); **3.** fine straw for hat-making; **4.** (fish.) net for catching flat-fish.
picoté, -e [pikɔte] *adj.* marked; pitted, pocked, dotted, spotted; pricked.
picotement [pikɔtmɑ̃] *s.m.* pricking (sensation), pins and needles.
picoter [pikɔte] *v.t.* to prick; to peck; to tease, to sting, to irritate.
picotin [pikɔtɛ̃] *s.m.* peck of oats; feed of corn.
picrate [pikrat] *s.m.* (chem.) picrate.
picrique [pikrik] *adj.* (chem.) picric.
pictural, -e, (**aux**) [piktyral] *adj.* pictorial, graphic.
pic-vert [pivɛr] *s.m.* see PIC[1].
pie [pi] *s.f.* magpie, pie; (fig.) chatterbox; *une femme bavarde comme une* ~, a woman who talks nineteen to the dozen; *trouver la* ~ *au nid*, to make a profitable discovery; ~ *adj.invar.* (of horse, etc.) piebald.
pie [pi] *adj.f.* pious; *œuvre* ~, charitable deed, good work.
pièce [pjɛs] *s.f.* piece, fragment, part, length, portion, bit, single item or article; document, paper, instrument; gun; coin; play; trick; room, apartment; joint (of meat), dish; cask; *mettre, tailler, en* ~*s*, to break to pieces, to cut to pieces, to rout; *de* ~*s et de morceaux*, of odds and ends; of shreds and patches; ~ *à* ~, bit by bit, piecemeal; *coûter 10 francs* (*la*) ~, to cost 10 francs each; *vendre à la* ~, to sell singly; *faire* ~ *à*, (obs.) to play a trick on; (mod.) to resist, to defy; *vin en* ~, wine in the cask, or in the wood; ~ *d'eau*, sheet of water, ornamental lake; *de toutes* ~*s*, entirely, wholly, at all points; *tout d'une* ~, all of a piece; in a single motion; (fig.) blunt, straightforward; *donner la* ~ *à*, to tip; *travailler aux* ~*s*, to work by the job, to do piece-work, to be paid by the piece; (fig.) *rendre à qn. la monnaie de sa* ~, to pay s.o. back (for an injury); ~*s de rechange*, spare parts; ~ *de théâtre*, play; *un deux* ~*s cuisine*, a two-room flat with kitchen.
piécette [pjesɛt] *s.f.* small coin.
pied [pje] *s.m.* foot; leg; stalk, plant; head (of celery); *à* ~, on foot, foot-; dismounted; *coup de* ~, kick; *à* ~ *d'œuvre*, near at hand; (build.) on site; *à* ~*s joints*, with feet together; *à* ~ *sec*, dry-shod, on dry land; *au petit* ~, on a small scale; *au* ~ *levé*, without a moment's notice; *au* ~ *de la lettre*, literally; *de* ~ *en cap*, from top to toe; *de* ~ *ferme*, unflinchingly; *doigt de* ~, toe; *portrait en* ~, full-length likeness; *machine, train, haut le* ~, light engine, empty train; *cheval haut le* ~, unmounted horse; *sur* ~, on foot; on one's feet; well again; alive, awake, up and about; *sur le* ~ *de*, on the footing of, at the rate of; *être sur un* ~ *d'égalité avec*, to be on an equal footing with; *être sur un bon* ~ *avec*, to be on good terms with; *de plain-*~, on the same level or footing; on level or equal terms (*avec*, with); *sur le* ~ *de paix*, on a peace footing; *sur ce* ~*-là*, on that footing; at that rate; *sur la pointe du* ~, or *des* ~*s*, on tiptoe; *avoir* ~, to be in one's depth; *avoir le* ~ *marin*, to have one's sea-legs, to be a good sailor; *avoir bon* ~ *bon œil*, to be hale and hearty; *faire le* ~ *de grue*, to dance attendance; *frapper du* ~, to stamp; *tenir* ~, to stand one's ground, to hold firm; *tenir* ~ *à qn.*, to stand up to s.o.; *lâcher* ~, to give way, to run away; (fig.) *lever le* ~, to take to one's heels, to abscond, to decamp; to run away with the till; (fig.) *marcher sur les* ~*s de qn.*, to tread on someone's toes; *partir du* ~ *gauche*, to make a good start, to start off on the right foot; *se lever du* ~ *gauche*, to get out of bed on the wrong side; *mettre* ~ *à terre*, to dismount; to alight; *je ne mettrai plus les* ~*s chez lui*, I will never again set foot in his house; *mettre les* ~*s dans le plat*, to put one's foot in it; to make a blunder; *mettre à* ~, to unseat; (fig.) to dismiss, to discharge, to suspend; *faire un* ~ *de nez*, to make a long nose (at); to cock a snook; *perdre* ~, to get out of one's depth, to lose one's foothold; (fig.) to be out of one's depth, to be in deep water; *prendre* ~, to find oneself on firm ground; (fig.) to establish oneself firmly, to gain a footing; ~ *à* ~, step by step, inch by inch; *couper l'herbe sous les* ~*s à qn.*, to cut the ground from under someone's feet, to forestall s.o.; *sécher sur* ~, to wither away, to languish; *aller* ~*s nus*, to go barefoot; *ne savoir sur quel* ~ *danser*, not to know which way to turn; *mettre qn. au* ~ *du mur*, to corner s.o., to drive s.o. into a corner; ~*-bot* (*s.m.*), club-footed man; club-foot; ~ *à coulisse*, sliding callipers; ~ *à repasser*, sleeve-board (for ironing); *partir du bon* ~, to put one's best foot foremost; *faire des* ~*s et des mains*, to move heaven and earth; to do one's utmost; *le* ~ *m'a manqué*, my foot slipped; *travailler d'arrache-*~, to work unremittingly, strenuously; ~*s et poings liés*, tied hand and foot; *il ne se mouche pas du* ~, he thinks a lot of himself; he acts big; he is no fool.
pied-à-terre [pjetatɛr] *s.m.invar.* pied-à-terre, temporary lodging, small flat.
pied-d'alouette [pjedalwɛt] *s.m.* (pl. ~*s-d'alouette*) (bot.) larkspur.
pied-de-biche [pjedbiʃ] *s.m.* **1.** (pl. ~*s-de-biche*) type of chair- or table-leg; **2.** knocker, bell-pull (orig. hind's foot); **3.** (techn.) nail-puller, nail-bar; presser-foot (of sewing-machine).
pied-de-chèvre [pjedʃɛvr] *s.m.* (pl. ~*s-de-chèvre*) footing (of heavy sheers).
pied-de-loup [pjedlu] *s.m.* (pl. ~*s-de-loup*) (bot.) lycopod, club-moss.
pied-de-veau [pjedvo] *s.m.* (pl. ~*s-de-veau*) (bot.) lords-and-ladies, cuckoo-pint.
pied-droit, piédroit [pjedrwa] *s.m.* (pl. ~*s-droits, piédroits*) (arch.) piedroit.
piédestal (pl. **aux**) [pjedɛstal] *s.m.* pedestal.
pied-noir [pjenwar] *s.m.* Frenchman born in Algeria.
piédouche [pjeduʃ] *s.m.* piedouche, small pedestal.
piège [pjɛʒ] *s.m.* trap; snare; *prendre au* ~, to trap, to ensnare, to catch in a trap; *donner dans le* ~, to be caught in a trap; *tendre un* ~, to set a trap.
piégeage [pjeʒaʒ] *s.m.* setting traps, trapping.
piéger [pjeʒe] **1.** (hunt.) to trap; **2.** (mil.) to booby-trap (a mine, etc.).
piégeur [pjeʒœr] *s.m.* trapper.
pie-grièche [pigriɛʃ] *s.f.* shrike; (fig.) shrew.
pie-mère [pimɛr] *s.f.* (anat.) pia mater.
Piémont [pjemɔ̃] *s.m.* (geog.) Piedmont.
piémontais, -e [pjemɔ̃tɛ] *adj., s.m.f.* Piedmontese.
piéride [pjerid] *s.f.* (ent.) Pieris, cabbage white butterfly.
pierraille [pjɛrɑj] *s.f.* small stones, broken stones, rubble, ballast, road-metal, rocky, stony soil.

pierre [pjɛr] *s.f.* stone, flint, rock, grit; ~ *à aiguiser*, whetstone; ~ *calcaire*, limestone; ~ *de taille*, freestone; ~ *infernale*, silver nitrate; ~ *philosophale*, philosophers' stone; ~ *à plâtre*, gypsum; ~ *de touche*, touchstone; ~ *précieuse*, precious stone, gem; *jeter la* ~ *à qn.*, to accuse s.o., to condemn or revile s.o.; *une* ~ *dans mon jardin!*, that's aimed at me!; that's a dig at me!; ~ *d'achoppement*, stumbling-block; ~ *angulaire*, corner-stone; (proverb) ~ *qui roule n'amasse pas mousse*, a rolling stone gathers no moss; *malheureux comme les* ~*s des champs*, acutely unhappy; as wretched as can be; *faire d'une* ~ *deux coups*, to kill two birds with one stone; *maladie de la* ~, calculus stone; *poser la première* ~, to lay the foundation-stone.
pierrée [pjɛre] *s.f.* drystone conduit.
pierreries [pjɛrri] *s.f.pl.* gems, precious stones.
pierreu-x, -se [pjɛrø] *adj.* stony, flinty, gritty; (pathol.) calculous; ~**se** *s.f.* (obs.) prostitute.
pierrier [pjɛrje] *s.m.* **1.** swivel-gun; **2.** (obs.) gun for firing stones.
pierrot [pjɛro] *s.m.* **1.** pierrot, clown; **2.** house--sparrow.
piétaille [pjetɑj] *s.f.* (jest) infantry, those on foot, pedestrians; children, juniors.
piété [pjete] *s.f.* piety; godliness; ~ *filiale*, filial devotion.
piéter [pjete] *v.i.* (obs.) to walk; (mod.) (of hunted birds) to run (opp. fly); **se** ~ *v.refl.* to plant one's feet firmly; (fig.) to stand up (against sth.).
piétinement [pjetinmɑ̃] *s.m.* trampling, stamping, tramping, (of feet); (lit. & fig.) marking time.
piétiner [pjetine] *v.t.i.* to trample, to stamp, to stamp on, to tramp; (lit. & fig.) to trample on; to mark time.
piétisme [pjetism] *s.m.* pietism.
piétiste [pjetist] *s.m.f.* pietist.
piéton [pjetɔ̃] *s.m.* pedestrian, walker, one on foot; ~, ~**ne** *adj.* foot-, for pedestrians; *sentier* ~, footpath; *porte* ~*ne*, entry for pedestrians.
piètre [pjɛtr] *adj.* paltry, sorry, shabby, wretched.
pieu[1] (pl. **-x**) [pjø] *s.m.* stake, post, pale; pile.
pieu[2] [pjø] *s.m.* (pop.) bed; *au* ~*!*, to bed!
pieusement [pjøzmɑ̃] *adv.* piously, devoutly, reverently.
pieuvre [pjøvr] *s.f.* octopus, devil-fish; (fig., of person) blood-sucker.
pieu-x, -se [pjø] *adj.* pious, devout, devoted.
piézo-électricité [pjezɔelɛktrisite] *s.f.* piezo--electricity; ~**-électrique** [pjezɔelɛktrik] *adj.* piezo-electric; ~**mètre** [pjezɔmɛtr] *s.m.* (phys.) piezometer.
pif [pif] *s.m.* (pop.) big nose, nose.
pif [pif] *interj.* (usu. ~ *paf!*) bang!, crash!, smack!
pifomètre [pifɔmɛtr] *s.m.* (fam.) common sense, guesswork; *au* ~, at a guess, by guess, (fig.) by ear.
pige[1] [piʒ] *s.f.* **1.** measuring-rod, measure, standard; **2.** (print.) take, amount of copy to be set up in given time; (journalism) rate of payment per line; **3.** (pop.) year.
pige[2] [piʒ] *s.f. faire la* ~ *à qn.*, to outdo s.o.
pigeon, -ne [piʒɔ̃] *s.m.f.* **1.** pigeon, dove; ~ *ramier*, wood-pigeon; ~ *voyageur*, carrier-pigeon, homing-pigeon; **2.** (fig., fam.) dupe, victim, mug; *plumer le* ~, to pluck a pigeon (i.e. take money off s.o. inexperienced); (build.) lump of prepared plaster; piece of stone in lime.
pigeonneau (pl. **-x**) [piʒɔno] *s.m.* young pigeon.
pigeonner [piʒɔne] *v.t.* **1.** (fam.) to dupe, to swindle, to take money off; **2.** (build.) to plaster.
pigeonnier [piʒɔnje] *s.m.* dovecot; (fig.) small upstairs room or flat.
piger[1] [piʒe] *v.t.* to measure.
piger[2] [piʒe] *v.t.* (obs.) to catch, to get hold of; (mod.) to understand, to grasp, catch, or get (meaning).
pigiste [piʒist] *s.m.* freelance journalist.
pigment [pigmɑ̃] *s.m.* pigment.
pigmentaire [pigmɑ̃tɛr] *adj.* pigmentary, pigmental.
pigmentation [pigmɑ̃tɑsjɔ̃] *s.f.* pigmentation.
pigmenter [pigmɑ̃te] *v.t.* to colour with pigment.
pigne [piɲ] *s.f.* pine-cone; pine-kernel.
pignocher [piɲɔʃe] *v.i.* **1.** to eat very little, to take only a nibble (*dans*, at); **2.** to paint badly, with too tiny strokes.
pignon[1] [piɲɔ̃] *s.m.* gable, gable-end; (fig.) *avoir* ~ *sur rue*, (obs.) to have a house looking onto the street; (mod.) to have a flourishing shop on a good site.
pignon[2] [piɲɔ̃] *s.m.* (mech.) pinion, gear-wheel, cog-wheel, chain-wheel, sprocket.
pignon[3] [piɲɔ̃] *s.m.* kernel of fir-cone, pine--kernel; *pin* ~, stone-pine, umbrella-pine.
pignoratif [piɲɔratif] *adj.m.* (law) pignorative; *contrat* ~, contract of sale with option to re-purchase.
pignouf [piɲuf] *s.m.* (pop.) coarse, badly brought-up person.
pilaf [pilaf], **pilau** [pilo] *s.m.* (cook.) pilaf(f).
pilaire [pilɛr] *adj.* = PILEUX.
pilastre [pilsatr] *s.m.* pilaster.
pile[1] [pil] *s.f.* **1.** pile, heap; **2.** pier (of bridge), mole (of masonry); **3.** (electr.) battery, cell, pile; (nuclear phys.) pile, reactor.
pile[2] [pil] *s.f.* **1.** (fam.) hail of blows; crushing defeat; **2.** (papermaking) stamping-trough.
pile[3] [pil] *s.f.* reverse of coin, tails, (opp. *face*); ~ *ou face?*, heads or tails?; (herald.) pile.
piler [pile] *v.t.* to pound, to crush; (fig.) to thrash, to rain blows on; (sport) *se faire* ~, to get a thrashing.
pilet [pilɛ] *s.m.* (ornith.) pintail duck.
pileur [pilœr] *s.m.* pounder, beater, crusher.
pileu-x, -se [pilø] *adj.* pilose, pilous, hairy.
pilier [pilje] *s.m.* pillar, post, column; (Rugby football) prop(-forward); (fig.) support, pillar, prop; frequenter; *c'est un* ~ *de cabaret*, he spends all his time in the pub.
pilifère [pilifɛr] *adj.* (bot.) piliferous.
pillage [pijaʒ] *s.m.* pillage, looting, plunder; spoil; *mettre au* ~, to plunder, to loot, to rob; *maison où tout est au* ~, house where pilfering is rife.
pillard, -e [pijar] *s.m.f.* pillager, plunderer, looter; *adj.* pillaging, plundering, looting, pilfering.
piller [pije] *v.t.* to pillage, to plunder, to loot, to ransack, to pilfer, to steal, to rob, to steal from; (fig.) to steal, to plagiarize.
pilon [pilɔ̃] *s.m.* **1.** pestle; beetle, stamp, crusher, rammer; *mettre au* ~, to destroy, to pulp (books, etc.); **2.** drumstick (of cooked fowl); **3.** artificial (wooden) leg.
pilonnage [pilɔnaʒ] *s.m.* pounding, ramming.
pilonner [pilɔne] *v.t.* to pound, to ram, to crush, to mill.
pilori [pilɔri] *s.m.* pillory; *mettre au* ~, (lit. & fig.) to pillory.
piloselle [pilozɛl] *s.f.* (bot.) mouse-ear hawkweed.
pilot [pilo] *s.m.* **1.** pile, stake; **2.** rags (used for making paper); ⚠ not 'pilot'.
pilotage[1] [pilɔtaʒ] *s.m.* pile-driving.
pilotage[2] [pilɔtaʒ] *s.m.* piloting, pilotage; steering; (space navigation) altitude control.
pilote [pilɔt] *s.m.* **1.** pilot; (fig.) guide; **2.** pilot--fish.
piloter[1] [pilɔte] *v.t.* to drive piles into.

piloter[2] [pilɔte] *v.t.* to pilot, to steer, to guide, to act as guide to.
pilotin [pilɔtɛ̃] *s.m.* (merchant navy) apprentice officer.
pilotis [pilɔti] *s.m.* piles, piling.
pilou [pilu] *s.m.* thick flannelette.
pilulaire [pilylɛr] *adj.* pilular; ~ *s.m.* tube for giving pills to horses, cattle, etc.
pilule [pilyl] *s.f.* pill; (fig.) *quelle ~!*, what a horrible thing to have to put up with!; (pop.) *il a pris la ~*, he took a good thrashing.
pimbêche [pɛ̃bɛʃ] *adj., s.f.* superior and disagreeable (woman).
piment [pimɑ̃] *s.m.* pimento, capsicum, red pepper; (fig.) spice, piquancy.
pimenter [pimɑ̃te] *v.t.* to flavour with pimento, to spice; (fig.) to give piquancy to.
pimpant, -e [pɛ̃pɑ̃] *adj.* sprightly and smart, spruce, trim, spick and span.
pimprenelle [pɛ̃prənɛl] *s.f.* (bot.) burnet; ⚠ not 'pimpernel'.
pin [pɛ̃] *s.m.* pine (tree), Scotch fir; ~ *pignon*, stone-pine; *pomme de ~*, pine-cone.
pinacle [pinakl] *s.m.* pinnacle, ridge-ornament; (fig.) top of the tree, height of power or fame; *porter qn. au ~*, to exalt s.o. to the skies.
pinacothèque [pinakɔtɛk] *s.f.* picture-gallery.
pinard [pinar] *s.m.* (pop.) wine.
pinasse [pinas] *s.f.* pinnace.
pinastre [pinastr] *s.m.* (bot.) pinaster, cluster pine.
pinçage [pɛ̃saʒ] *s.m.* pinching; nipping off (of buds, etc.).
pinçard, -e [pɛ̃sar] *adj.* (of horse) wearing the shoe at the toe.
pince [pɛ̃s] *s.f.* pinch, pinching; hold, grip; pincers, nippers, pliers, forceps, tongs, tweezers, gripper, clip; point or toe (of horse's hoof or shoe); incisor tooth (of herbivore); claw (of lobster); crowbar, lever; (dressm.) dart; (pop.) hand; (pl.) legs; ~ *coupante*, cutting-pliers; ~ *à glace*, ice-tongs; ~ *à linge*, clothes-peg; ~ *ronde*, round-nosed pliers; ~ *à sucre*, sugar-tongs; *~-monseigneur*, jemmy.
pincé, -e [pɛ̃se] *adj.* affected, prim, stiff, pursed, pinched; *lèvres ~es*, thin lips; pursed mouth.
pinceau (pl. **-x**) [pɛ̃so] *s.m.* brush, paint-brush; pencil; style of painting; pencil of light; tuft of hairs; (pop.) foot; *coup de ~*, stroke, brush-stroke.
pincée [pɛ̃se] *s.f.* pinch (of snuff, etc.).
pincelier [pɛ̃slje] *s.m.* dip-cup (for painting).
pincement [pɛ̃smɑ̃] *s.m.* **1.** (obs.) gnawing (of jealousy, etc.); (mod.) nip, pinch, twinge; **2.** (mus.) plucking (of strings); (hort.) nipping, pinching-out (of tree-buds).
pince-nez [pɛ̃sne] *s.m.invar*, pince-nez.
pincer [pɛ̃se] *v.t.* to pinch, to compress, to draw tight, to squeeze, to grip; to nip, to nip off, to clip; (dressm.) to take in; (mus.) to pluck (strings); to catch; (mus.) ~ *sur* or *de*, to play or pluck at (harp, etc.); ~ *de*, to take a pinch of; *il en a pincé*, he has had a bite of it; *se faire ~*, to get caught; to get found out; *en ~ pour qn.*, to be in love with s.o.; ~ *v.i.* (fam.) *ça pince (dur) ce matin*, it's bitterly cold this morning.
pince-sans-rire [pɛ̃ssɑ̃rir] *s.m.* one given to dry jokes, dead-pan humorist; ~ *adj.invar.* dry, dead-pan.
pincette(s) [pɛ̃sɛt] *s.f.* (*pl.*) tongs; (fig.) *il n'est pas à prendre avec des ~s*, I shouldn't touch him with a pair of tongs, I shouldn't go near him.
pinçon [pɛ̃sɔ̃] *s.m.* pinch; mark left by a pinch.
pindarique [pɛ̃darik] *adj.* Pindaric.
pinéal, -e, (aux) [pineal] *adj.* (anat.) pineal.
pineau [pino] *s.m.* a kind of brandy.
pinède [pinɛd], **pineraie** [pinrɛ] *s.f.* pine grove, pine or fir plantation.
pingouin [pɛ̃gwɛ̃] *s.m.* (ornith.) penguin, puffin, guillemot, auk.
ping-pong [piŋpɔ̃g] *s.m.* table-tennis, ping-pong; table-tennis table or set.
pingre [pɛ̃gr] *adj.* miserly; *s.m.f.* miser.
pingrerie [pɛ̃grəri] *s.f.* stinginess, meanness.
pinière [pinjɛr] *s.f.* = PINÈDE.
pinne [pin], **pinne marine** [pinmarin] *s.f.* (zool.) Pinna, wing-shell.
pinné, -e [pine] *adj.* (bot.) pinnate.
pinnule [pinyl] *s.f.* pinnule, sight-vane, (in sextant, etc.).
pinson [pɛ̃sɔ̃] *s.m.* (ornith.) finch, chaffinch; *gai comme un ~*, merry as a lark, happy as a sandpiper.
pintade [pɛ̃tad] *s.f.* (ornith.) guinea-fowl, guinea-hen.
pintadeau (pl. **-x**) [pɛ̃tado] *s.m.* guinea-chick.
pinte [pɛ̃t] *s.f.* pint; pint-pot; pint-measure; *se payer une ~ de bon sang*, to have a good time, to enjoy oneself.
pinter [pɛ̃te] *v.i.* (pop.) to drink a lot, to booze; *v.t.* (pop.) to drink.
pin up [pinœp] *s.f.invar.* pin-up (picture); pin-up girl.
piochage [pjɔʃaʒ] *s.m.* digging with a pick; (fig.) hard work, slogging, swotting.
pioche [pjɔʃ] *s.f.* pick-axe, pick, mattock; *une tête de ~*, an obstinate person.
piocher [pjɔʃe] *v.t.i.* to dig with a pick; (fig.) to work hard (at), to slog away, to study hard, to swot (at); ~ *dans le tas*, to dig into the pile; ~ *sa géométrie*, to swot away at one's geometry.
piocheu-r, -se [pjɔʃœr] *s.m.f.* digger, labourer, navvy; (agric.) scarifier; (fig.) hard worker, swot.
piolet [pjɔlɛ] *s.m.* piolet, ice-axe.
pion [pjɔ̃] *s.m.* **1.** (obs.) infantryman; (mod., pej.) junior master, auxiliary teacher; pedantic intellectual; **2.** (chess) pawn; (draughts, etc.) piece; (fig.) *damer le ~ à qn.*, to outwit or outdo s.o.
pioncer [pjɔ̃se] *v.i.* (pop.) to sleep.
pionni-er, -ère [pjɔnje] *s.m.f.* (mil. & fig.) pioneer.
pioupiou [pjupju] *s.m.* (fam.) young soldier.
pipa [pipa] *s.m.* (zool.) pipa, Surinam toad.
pipe [pip] *s.f.* **1.** (obs.) pipe, cask, (measure for wine, etc.); **2.** (tobacco-)pipe; (pop.) cigarette; pipe, tube; *fumer la ~*, to smoke a pipe; *fourneau de ~*, bowl of a pipe; *tuyau de ~*, pipe-stem; (pop.) *par tête de ~*, per head, per person.
pipeau (pl. **-x**) [pipo] *s.m.* **1.** reed-pipe; bird-call; **2.** lime-twigs, snare (for birds).
pipée[1] [pipe] *s.f.* bird-catching (by decoy); *prendre à la ~*, to catch birds with a bird-call; to decoy.
pipée[2] [pipe] *s.f.* pipeful.
pipelet, -te [piplɛ] *s.m.f.* (pop.) concierge.
pipe-line [pajplajn; piplin] *s.m.* pipeline.
piper [pipe] *v.t.* to catch (birds with a bird-call), to decoy, to deceive, to beguile; to cheat; to load (dice), to mark, to prepare, (cards); (fig.) *les dés sont pipés*, the dice are loaded, the game has been rigged, it has been fixed.
piperie [pipri] *s.f.* (obs.) trickery, cheating; (mod.) deception, beguilement.
pipette [pipɛt] *s.f.* (chem.) pipette.
pipi[1] [pipi] *s.m.* (child. lang.) wee-wee, piddle.
pipi[2] [pipi], **pipit** [pipit], **pitpit** [pitpit] *s.m.* (ornith.) pipit, titlark.
pipi-er, -ère [pipje] *s.m.f.* pipe-maker; *adj.* pipe, pipe-making.
pipistrelle [pipistrɛl] *s.f.* (zool.) pipistrelle, common bat.
pipo [pipo] *s.m.* (slang) **1.** the *École* POLYTECHNIQUE; **2.** = POLYTECHNICIEN.
piquage [pikaʒ] *s.m.* stitching.
piquant, -e [pikɑ̃] *adj.* prickling, prickly,

stinging, sharp, pungent, piercing, biting; (fig.) piquant, pointed, lively, stimulating, spicy, witty; *un froid* ~, biting cold; *des mots* ~*s*, pungent words.

piquant [pikɑ̃] *s.m.* prickle, thorn, sting, stinging-nettle; quill (of porcupine); (fig.) piquancy, pungency, zest, point.

pique[1] [pik] *s.f.* pike; pike-thrust; ~ *s.m.* (cards) spade(s).

pique[2] [pik] *s.f.* **1.** (obs.) pique, ill-humour; **2.** cutting remark.

piqué [pike] *s.m.* **1.** piqué (material), quilting; **2.** piqué (dance movement); **3.** (aeron.) vertical dive; *bombardement en* ~, dive-bombing.

piqué, -e [pike] *adj.* pricked, stitched, quilted; (cook.) larded; studded, pitted, spotted; (mus.) staccato; (of wine) sour; (fig., fam.) cracked, crazy, mad; ~ *des vers*, worm-eaten.

pique-assiette [pikasjɛt] *s.m.invar.* sponger, parasite.

pique-bœuf [pikbœf] *s.m.* (pl. ~*-bœufs*) (ornith.) ox-pecker.

pique-feu [pikfø] *s.m.invar.* poker, fire-rake.

pique-nique [piknik] *s.m.* (pl. ~*-niques*) picnic; *faire un* ~, to have a picnic.

pique-niquer [piknike] *v.i.* to picnic.

pique-niqueu-r, -se [piknikœr] *s.m.f.* picnicker.

pique-notes [piknɔt] *s.m.invar.* bill-file.

piquer [pike] *v.t.* to prick, to goad, to spur; to sting; to stick or insert (sth. into sth.), to inject (s.o. with serum, etc.); (cook.) to lard; to pin; to stitch; to make holes in, to puncture; to spot, to speckle; to sting, to cause smarting or tingling in; to prickle; to offend, to provoke, to arouse, to irritate; to strike; (pop.) to steal, to pinch; to catch, to arrest; to do (sth.) suddenly, to have a sudden attack of; *on lui a piqué le bras droit*, he was injected in the right arm; *être piqué de taches de rousseur*, to be covered in freckles; *les vers ont piqué ce meuble*, the worm has got into this piece of furniture; *la fumée leur piquait les yeux*, the smoke was making their eyes smart; *il a piqué une rage de dents*, he had a sudden attack of violent toothache; ~ *une tête*, to dive head first, to rush headlong; ~ *v.i.* to gallop off, to rush away; to plunge down, to fall headlong; (aeron.) to make a vertical dive, to nosedive; (naut.) ~ *de l'avant*, to go down by the bows; **se** ~ *v.refl.* to be pricked, stung, etc.; to inject oneself; to become spotted or speckled; to become worm- or moth-eaten; (of wine) to turn sour; (fig.) to be offended or piqued; *se* ~ *de*, to pride oneself on, to pretend to (sth.).

piquet [pikɛ] *s.m.* **1.** stake, peg, post; **2.** (mil., etc.) picket; ~ *d'incendie*, fire-fighting detachment; *être de* ~, to be on picket duty; ~ *de grève*, strike picket; (school) *être au* ~, to be stood in the corner; **3.** piquet (card-game).

piquetage [piktaʒ] *s.m.* marking with stakes or pegs.

piqueter [pikte] *v.t.* to mark with stakes or pegs; to dot.

piquette[1] [pikɛt] *s.f.* inferior or acid wine; (fig.) *ce n'était pas de la* ~, it was no trifling matter.

piquette[2] [pikɛt] *s.f.* running the gauntlet; (pop.) hail of blows; crushing defeat.

piqueu-r, -se [pikœr] *s.m.f.* **1.** stud-groom; huntsman; **2.** stitcher; **3.** foreman; **4.** pickman (miner); chipper, scaler (using a pneumatic hammer); *adj.* (of insects) stinging.

piqueux [pikø] *s.m.* = PIQUEUR 1 .

piquier [pikje] *s.m.* pikeman.

piquoir [pikwar] *s.m.* (art, techn.) pricker.

piqûre [pikyr] *s.f.* prick, pricking, sting, bite; puncture; worm-hole; spot (of mould, rust, etc.); stitching, quilting, stitched seam; (med.) injection.

piranha [pirana], **piraya** [piraja] *s.m.* (ichth.) piranha.

pirate [pirat] *s.m.* pirate; (fig.) dishonest speculator; shark.

pirater [pirate] *v.i.* to practise piracy.

piraterie [piratri] *s.f.* piracy, act of piracy; (fig.) dishonest speculation.

piraya see PIRANHA.

pire [pir] *adj.* worse; *le remède est* ~ *que le mal*, the remedy is worse than the disease; *le, la, les* ~(*s*), the worst; *les* ~*s dangers*, the worst dangers; *les* ~*s calomnies*, the basest slanders; ~ *s.m.* the worst; *le* ~ *est que*, the worst thing is that; *s'attendre au* ~, to expect the worst.

piriforme [pirifɔrm] *adj.* pear-shaped.

pirogue [pirɔg] *s.f.* (naut.) piragua, pirogue, dug-out, canoe.

pirouette [pirwɛt] *s.f.* **1.** (obs.) top, whirligig; **2.** pirouette; (fig.) sudden change (of opinion, etc.), volte-face; evasiveness; *répondre par des* ~*s*, to laugh off an awkward question.

pirouetter [pirwɛte] *v.i.* to pirouette, to whirl about.

pis [pi] *s.m.* udder.

pis [pi] *adv.* worse; *aller de mal en* ~, to go from bad to worse; *qui* ~ *est*, what is worse; *de* ~ *en* ~, worse and worse; ~ *s.m.* the worst, the worst thing; *le* ~ *qui puisse arriver*, the worst thing that can happen; *tant* ~*!*, what a pity!, it can't be helped, that's that!; so much the worse!; *au* ~ *aller*, if the worst comes to the worst, taking the most unfavourable view.

pis-aller [pizale] *s.m.* last resort, makeshift.

piscicult-eur, -rice [pisikyltœr] *s.m.f.* pisciculturist, fish-breeder.

pisciculture [pisikyltyr] *s.f.* pisciculture, fish--breeding.

piscine [pisin] *s.f.* **1.** piscina; **2.** bathing-pool, swimming bath.

pisé [pize] *s.m.* (mason.) pisé, cob.

pissaladière [pisaladjɛr] *s.f.* (cook.) pissaladière, pizza.

pisse [pis] *s.f.* (vulg.) piss.

pisse-froid [pisfrwa] *s.m.* (fam.) (of person) cold fish.

pissement [pismɑ̃] *s.m.* (vulg.) pissing); ~ *de sang*, passing blood.

pissenlit [pisɑ̃li] *s.m.* (bot.) dandelion.

pisser [pise] *v.i.* (vulg.) to piss; *il pleut comme une vache qui pisse*, it's pissing with rain; *il y a de quoi* ~, it makes you die laughing; ~ *v.t.* to pass with one's water; (fig.) to pour out in large quantities; ~ *du sang*, to pass blood; *son nez pisse le sang*, blood is pouring out of his nose.

pisseu-x, -se [pisø] *adj.* stained with urine; (fig.) faded yellow.

pissoir [piswar] *s.m.* urinal.

pissotière [pisɔtjɛr] *s.f.* (fam.) public urinal.

pistache [pistaʃ] *s.f.* pistachio (nut); ~ *adj. invar.* pistachio-green.

pistard [pistar] *s.m.* (cycle racing) track rider.

pistachier [pistaʃje] *s.m.* (bot.) pistachio tree.

piste [pist] *s.f.* track, trail, trace; scent; piste, race-course, ring; dance-floor; (aeron.) runway; *être sur la* ~ *de*, to be after; to be on the trail of; *suivre à la* ~, to follow in the track of, to track.

pistil [pistil] *s.m.* (bot.) pistil.

pistole [pistɔl] *s.f.* **1.** (hist.) pistole; **2.** (obs.) separate ward in prison, in which the prisoners may buy their food.

pistolet [pistɔlɛ] *s.m.* **1.** pistol; spray-gun (for painting); **2.** (bread) roll; French curve (drawing aid); (naut.) davit; bed-bottle; **3.** (pop.) peculiar individual.

pistolet-mitrailleur [pistɔlɛmitrajœr] *s.m.* light sub-machine-gun.

piston [pistɔ̃] *s.m.* **1.** piston; sucker; plunger,

ram; *coup de* ~, stroke of the piston; *course du* ~, travel of the piston; *segment de* ~, piston-ring; *tige de* ~, piston-rod; *fusil à* ~, percussion-gun; **2.** (mus.) valve (of brass wind instrument); cornet; **3.** (fig.) recommendation, influential support, protection, special backing; *avoir du* ~, to be able to pull strings, to have backing, to have friends at court.

pistonner [pistɔne] *v.t.* to recommend, to protect, to support, to back, to push.

pitance [pitɑ̃s] *s.f.* pittance, daily allowance of food.

pitchpin [pitʃpɛ̃] *s.m.* (bot.) pitch-pine.

pite [pit] *s.f.* (bot.) kind of agave; coir.

piteu-x, -se [pitø] *adj.* piteous, pitiable, paltry, sorry, disgraceful; **~sement** [pitøzmɑ̃] *adv.* piteously, woefully, miserably.

pithécanthrope [pitekɑ̃trɔp] *s.m.* pithecanthrope.

pitié [pitje] *s.f.* pity, compassion; (condescending) pity, sorry sight, lamentable state of affairs; *~!*, mercy!; *par* ~, for pity's sake; *c'est* ~, it is sad, it is a sorry state of affairs; *avoir ~ de*, to take pity on; *prendre qn. en* ~, to have pity on s.o.; *quelle ~!*, what a pity!, what a pitiful state of affairs!; *c'est à faire* ~, it is sad, it is pitiful or lamentable; *un sourire de* ~, a pitying smile.

piton [pitɔ̃] *s.m.* (techn.) eye, screw-ring; (mountaineering) piton; (isolated) mountain-peak

pitoyable [pitwajabl] *adj.* pitiable, pitiful, merciful; paltry, wretched, poor; **~ment** [pitwajabləmɑ̃] *adv.* wretchedly, pitifully.

pitpit see PIPI[2].

pitre [pitr] *s.m.* clown, buffoon.

pitrerie [pitrəri] *s.f.* buffoonery, clowning.

pittoresque [pitɔrɛsk] *adj.* picturesque, vivid, graphic, pictorial; ~ *s.m.* picturesque, picturesqueness, vividness, graphic quality; **~ment** [pitɔrɛskəmɑ̃] *adv.* picturesquely, quaintly.

pituitaire [pitɥitɛr] *adj.* pituitary.

pivert [pivɛr] *s.m.* see PIC[1].

pivoine [pivwan] *s.f.* (bot.) peony.

pivot [pivo] *s.m.* pivot, hinge; (fig.) pivot, main point or part, key man, leading spirit.

pivotant, -e [pivɔtɑ̃] *adj.* **1.** revolving, pivoting, swivelling; **2.** (bot.) tap-rooted; *racine ~e*, tap-root.

pivoter [pivɔte] *v.i.* to pivot, to revolve, to swing round, to hinge; (bot.) to put down tap-roots.

P.J. [peʒi] abbrev. (fam.) *Police judiciaire.*

placage [plakaʒ] *s.m.* veneering, plating, covering, facing; (fig.) later addition.

placard [plakar] *s.m.* **1.** placard, poster, bill, advertisement; (print.) galley-proof; lampoon; **2.** cupboard (esp. built-in); panel (of door).

placarder [plakarde] *v.t.* to post, to stick, to stick up (bills, etc.); (print.) to pull galley-proofs; to cover with placards.

place [plas] *s.f.* place, spot, room, seat, space, stand, (taxi-)rank, square, market-place; (comm.) mart, market, exchange; charge, office, function; situation; rank; (mil.) place, fortress, stronghold, parade ground; *à sa* ~, or *en* ~, in its place; *à votre* ~, if I were you; *mettre en* ~, to arrange, to put straight; *faire ~ à*, to make room for; to give way to; *faire la* ~, to canvass for orders; *entrer en* ~, to get a situation; *prenez* ~, sit down, take a seat; *quitter la* ~, to give up one's place; to leave; *retenir une* ~, to book, to reserve, a seat; *tenir la ~ de*, to stand instead of; to do instead of; to take the place of; *se tenir à sa* ~, to know one's place; *sur* ~, on the spot; *demeurer sur* ~, to remain still; *les ~s s'il vous plaît!*, fares, please!; *~ entière*, full fare, full price; (fig.) *remettre qn. à sa* ~, to put s.o. in his place, to tell s.o. a few home truths.

placé, -e [plase] *adj.* placed, having secured a place, situated; *être bien ~ pour*, to be in a good position to; *jouer un cheval gagnant et* ~, to back a horse both ways.

placement [plasmɑ̃] *s.m.* placing; investing, investment; *bureau de* ~, employment agency, appointments board.

placenta [plasɛ̃ta] *s.m.* placenta.

placentaire [plasɛ̃tɛr] *adj.* placental.

placer [plase] *v.t.* to place, to locate, to put, to set, to lay, to invest (money); to place in employment; to sell, to dispose of; to find room for; *bien ~ sa confiance*, to bestow one's confidence wisely; (boxing) *~ un gauche*, to land a left; **se ~** *v.refl.* to place or put oneself, to take one's place; to be placed; to obtain employment, to get a job; *le fauteuil se place là*, the armchair goes there.

placer [plasɛr] *s.m.* placer, diggings.

placet [plasɛ] *s.m.* placet, petition.

placeu-r, -se [plasœr] *s.m.f.* (techn.) fitter, erector; (theatr.) usherette; employment agent.

placide [plasid] *adj.* placid, calm, serene, unruffled, good-tempered; **~ment** [plasidmɑ̃] *adv.* calmly, placidly.

placidité [plasidite] *s.f.* placidity, placidness, calm.

placi-er, -ère [plasje] *s.m.f.* placer, letting-agent (for market-stalls); agent, commercial traveller.

plafond [plafɔ̃] *s.m.* **1.** ceiling, roof; (cloud) cover; (fig.) ceiling, upper limit, maximum; *prix* ~, maximum price; **2.** flat bottom, bed, horizontal surface; floor (of valley); under-surface.

plafonnage [plafɔnaʒ] *s.m.* ceiling-work.

plafonnement [plafɔnmɑ̃] *s.m.* attainment of maximum or ceiling.

plafonner [plafɔne] *v.t.* to put a ceiling in a room; *cette pièce n'est pas plafonnée*, this room has no ceiling; ~ *v.i.* (aeron.) to fly at maximum height; (fig.) to reach a ceiling or maximum, to reach the limit.

plafonneur [plafɔnœr] *s.m.* plasterer, ceiling-maker.

plafonnier [plafɔnje] *s.m.* ceiling light, pendant; (car) interior light.

plage [plaʒ] *s.f.* beach, sea-shore; seaside resort; band (on gramophone record), track (on magnetic tape); (photo.) area, portion of surface, (of negative); raised deck or platform.

plagiaire [plaʒjɛr] *s.m.f.* plagiarist.

plagiat [plaʒja] *s.m.* plagiarism.

plagier [plaʒje] *v.t.* to plagiarize; (fig.) to counterfeit.

plagiste [plaʒist] *s.m.f.* beach-attendant; letter of bathing-huts, etc.

plaid[1] [plɛ] *s.m.* **1.** (law) court sitting; **2.** (law) trial, case; (fig.) dispute, argument.

plaid[2] [plɛd] *s.m.* **1.** (Scottish) plaid; **2.** (obs.) travelling-cloak; (mod.) travelling-rug.

plaidant, -e [plɛdɑ̃] *adj.* (law) pleading; *les parties ~es*, the litigants.

plaider [plɛde] *v.t.* (law) to plead or defend (a case); to plead or make a plea of (insanity, etc.); to plead or enter a plea of (guilty or not guilty); (fig.) *~ la cause de qn.*, to plead someone's case; *~ la folie*, to plead insanity; *~ coupable*, to plead guilty; ~ *v.i.* **1.** (law) to plead, to argue a case, to make submissions; **2.** (law) to defend, to act for the defence; *~ pour son client*, to defend one's client; (fig.) *~ pour* or *en faveur de*, to make a plea for; to justify, to speak in favour of; **3.** to go to law.

plaideu-r, -se [plɛdœr], **plaidant, -e** [plɛdɑ̃] *s.m.f.* litigant, party to a suit.

plaidoirie [plɛdwari] *s.f.* pleading; speech by counsel; (fig.) reasoned plea in justification.

plaidoyer [plɛdwaje] *s.m.* speech (for the defence), address; (fig.) defence, justification, impassioned plea.

plaie [plɛ] *s.f.* wound, sore; (fig.) hurt, evil, plague; *panser une ~*, to dress a wound; *ne rêver que ~s et bosses*, to be bent on violence; to court danger; (fig.) *mettre le doigt sur la ~*, to put one's finger on the spot; *les ~s d'Égypte*, the plagues of Egypt.

plaignant, -e [plɛɲɑ̃] *s.m.f.* plaintiff, prosecutor, complainant; *adj.* complaining, litigant.

plain [plɛ̃] *adj.* (obs.) exc. in *loc.*; *de ~-pied*, on a level, on the same floor; on a footing of equality; smoothly, easily; *~ s.m.* (naut.) high water.

plain-chant [plɛ̃ʃɑ̃] *s.m.* plainsong, plainchant.

plaindre [plɛ̃dr] *v.t.* **1.** to pity, to feel compassion for, to commiserate; *elle est à ~*, she is to be pitied; **2.** to grudge, to be sparing of; *~ sa peine*, to grudge one's trouble; **se ~** *v.refl.* to complain, to lament, to moan, to grumble, to groan; to lodge a complaint.

plaine [plɛn] *s.f.* plain, field, level ground.

plainte [plɛ̃t] *s.f.* complaint, plaint, lamentation; wail, wailing, groan, moan; *porter ~*, *déposer une ~*, *contre*, to lodge a complaint against, to bring an action against.

plainti-f, -ve [plɛ̃tif] *adj.* plaintive, wailing, mournful, querulous; **~vement** [plɛ̃tivmɑ̃] *adv.* plaintively, querulously.

plaire [plɛr] *v.t.i.* to please, to give pleasure; to be liked, to find favour, to be acceptable; *~ à*, to please, to be pleasing to, to be agreeable or pleasant to; to be liked by; *le spectacle a plu*, the play had a favourable reception; *ne jamais parler de soi, c'est tout l'art de plaire*, the secret of being popular is never to talk about oneself; *cela vous plaît?*, do you like it?; *cela ne plaît à personne*, that pleases nobody, no one likes that; *s'il vous plaît*, please, if you please; *comme il vous plaira*, as you like, just as you please; *vous plaît-il de faire cela?*, would you like to do that?; *plaît-il?*, I beg your pardon (didn't hear); *plût à Dieu que*, would to God that; *à Dieu ne plaise que*, God forbid that; **se ~** *v.refl.* to be pleased with oneself, to be self-satisfied; to like one another, to be in love; to be happy, to enjoy oneself; to flourish; *se ~ à*, to take pleasure or delight in, to delight to; *se ~ avec qn.*, to be happy in someone's company.

plaisamment [plɛsamɑ̃] *adv.* pleasantly, agreeably, humorously, comically, ridiculously, ludicrously.

plaisance [plɛzɑ̃s] *s.f.* pleasance, pleasure (obs. except in the phrase *de ~*); *bateau de ~*, pleasure-boat, yacht; *maison de ~*, country-seat; *port de ~*, yacht-harbour, marina.

plaisancier [plɛzɑ̃sje] *s.m.* yachtsman, canoeist, etc.

plaisant, -e [plɛzɑ̃] *adj.* pleasant, pleasing, nice, agreeable; comical, funny, humorous, ridiculous, ludicrous; *~ s.m.* **1.** jester, joker, wag; *mauvais ~*, feeble humorist, practical joker, one who makes jokes in bad taste; **2.** comical side, humour, laughable part, fun; *le ~ de l'aventure*, the funny part of it.

plaisanter [plɛzɑ̃te] *v.i.* to joke, to make jokes, to exchange jokes, to jest, to speak in jest, not to be serious; to trifle; *vous plaisantez?*, are you joking?; you're not serious?; *il ne plaisante pas*, he takes everything seriously; he is very much in earnest; he is not to be trifled with; *on ne plaisante pas avec ces choses-là*, one mustn't take that sort of thing lightly; *~ v.t.* to tease, to chaff.

plaisanterie [plɛzɑ̃tri] *s.f.* joke, jest, facetiousness, humour, witticism; practical joke; trifling, derision, mockery; *faire des ~s*, to crack jokes; *tourner tout en ~*, to make fun of everything; *entendre la ~*, to know how to take a joke; *cela passe la ~*, that is beyond a joke; *~ à part*, joking apart; seriously; *par ~*, by way of a joke; *quelle ~!*, what a mockery!; that's going too far!

plaisantin [plɛzɑ̃tɛ̃] *s.m.* (pej.) joker, leg-puller; one who takes nothing seriously.

plaisir [plezir] *s.m.* **1.** pleasure, delight, gratification; diversion, amusement, pastime; consent, agreeableness, agreement, kindness; *à ~*, wantonly, plentifully, without restriction; *au ~ (de vous revoir)!*, good-bye!, hope we shall meet again soon; *avoir du ~ à*, to take pleasure in, to be pleased to; *trouver*, or *prendre du ~ à*, to delight in; *cela me fait ~*, that gives me pleasure; that's a pleasure to me; *faites-moi le ~ de*, do me the favour of; *pour vous faire ~*, to please you; *à son bon ~*, at his own sweet will; *régime du bon ~*, absolute monarchy; *menus ~s*, entertainments, amusements; **2.** a kind of wafer, rolled in the shape of a cone.

plan [plɑ̃] *s.m.* **1.** plane; (fig.) sphere, point of view; *~ incliné*, inclined plane; *~ focal*, focal plane; (cin. etc.) *gros ~*, or *~ rapproché*, close-up; *sur le ~ économique*, in the economic field, from the economic angle; **2.** plan, map, drawing, diagram, draught; **3.** design, plan, scheme, project; **4.** plane, ground, distance; (theatr.) division of stage; *au premier ~*, in the foreground, to the fore; down stage; *au second ~*, in the middle distance; *upstage*; *à l'arrière-~*, in the background; upstage; *reléguer au second ~*, *à l'arrière-~*, to put in the background; *laisser en ~*, to leave unfinished; to give (a person) the slip, to leave in the lurch.

plan, -e [plɑ̃] *adj.* level, even, flat, plane; *surface ~e*, plane surface.

planage [planaʒ] *s.m.* (techn.) planing.

planaire [planɛr] *s.f.* (zool.) planarian (worm).

planche [plɑ̃ʃ] *s.f.* board, plank, shelf; (engr.) plate, illustration; (pl.) (theatr.) boards, stage, theatrical profession; (hort.) bed; (swimming) *faire la ~*, to float on one's back; *~ de salut*, sheet-anchor; (car, aeron.) *~ de tablier*, or *de bord*, dashboard, fascia-board, instrument-panel; *maigre comme une ~*, thin as a rake; (fig.) *avoir du travail sur la ~*, to have work on hand; *monter sur les ~s*, to tread the boards, to become an actor or actress.

planchéiage [plɑ̃ʃejaʒ] *s.m.* boarding, flooring.

planchéier [plɑ̃ʃeje] *v.t.* to board, to floor, to plank.

plancher [plɑ̃ʃe] *s.m.* floor, flooring; (obs.) ceiling; (fig.) *le ~ des vaches*, dry land; *vider* or *débarrasser le ~*, to clear out, to be chased off; (car) *mettre le pied au ~*, to put one's foot hard down (on the accelerator).

planchette [plɑ̃ʃɛt] *s.f.* small board; plane-table (for surveying).

plançon [plɑ̃sɔ̃] *s.m.* **1.** (hort.) shoot (used as a cutting); sapling; **2.** plank timber.

plan-concave [plɑ̃kɔ̃kav] *adj.* (opt.) plano-concave; **~-convexe** [plɑ̃kɔ̃vɛks] *adj.* (opt.) plano-convex.

plancton [plɑ̃ktɔ̃] *s.m.* (biol.) plankton.

plane [plan] *s.f.* spoke-shave; drawing-knife, cutting-tool; paring-knife; ⚠ not 'plane'.

plané, -e [plane] *adj.* (aeron.) gliding; *vol ~*, glide, gliding (with engines off); (of birds) soaring; (fig., fam.) *faire un vol ~*, to fall, to tumble.

planer[1] [plane] *v.t.* to plane, to pare off, to smooth, to make even.

planer[2] [plane] *v.i.* to soar, to hover; (fig.) to look down; (fig.) *~ sur*, (i.) to survey; (ii.) to hover over, to threaten; *~ au-dessus des difficultés*, to rise superior to difficulties; (aeron.) to glide; (of birds) to soar.

planétaire [planetɛr] *adj.* planetary.

planétarium [planetarjɔm] *s.m.* planetarium; orrery.
planète [planɛt] *s.f.* planet.
planeur [planœr] *s.m.* (aeron.) glider.
planeu-r, -se [planœr] *s.m.f.* planer, finisher; **~se** *s.f.* planing-machine.
planification [planifikɑsjɔ̃] *s.f.* (pol., econ.) planning.
planificat-eur, -rice [planifikatœr] *s.m.f.* planner; *adj.* planning.
planifier [planifje] *v.t.* (pol., econ.) to plan.
planisme [planism] *s.m.* (pol.) planning.
planisphère [planisfɛr] *s.m.* planisphere.
planning [planiŋ] *s.m.* plan, programme; planning, programming; ~ *familial*, family planning.
planque [plɑ̃k] *s.f.* (pop.) hide, hide-out; (fig.) safe place; quiet job.
planquer [plɑ̃ke] *v.t.* (pop.) to hide, to tuck away; **se** ~ *v.refl.* to hide oneself away (from danger), to find a safe place.
plant [plɑ̃] *s.m.* plant, slip, sapling; bed, plantation; seedlings.
plantage [plɑ̃taʒ] *s.m.* **1.** planting, plantation; **2.** (naut.) rack for twisting ropes.
plantain [plɑ̃tɛ̃] *s.m.* (bot.) plantain.
plantaire [plɑ̃tɛr] *adj.* (anat.) plantar, of the sole of the foot.
plantation [plɑ̃tɑsjɔ̃] *s.f.* **1.** planting, erection (of posts, stage scenery, etc.); **2.** plantation.
plante [plɑ̃t] *s.f.* **1.** plant; *Jardin des Plantes*, Botanic Gardens; *~s grasses*, succulents; **2.** (anat.) sole (of the foot).
planter [plɑ̃te] *v.t.* to plant; to set, to fix, to drive in; to set up, to station; ~ *un clou*, to drive in a nail; *il m'a planté là*, he has given me the slip; he left me in the lurch; *un garçon bien planté*, a well-built fellow; a sturdy lad; **se** ~ *v.refl.* to station oneself, to plant oneself, to stand, to place oneself; to be planted, to be positioned.
planteur [plɑ̃tœr] *s.m.* planter; owner of a plantation.
planteuse [plɑ̃tøz] *s.f.* (agric.) potato-planter (machine).
plantigrade [plɑ̃tigrad] *adj.*, *s.m.* (zool.) plantigrade.
plantoir [plɑ̃twar] *s.m.* dibber; planting-tool, setting-stick.
planton [plɑ̃tɔ̃] *s.m.* (mil.) orderly; *être de* ~, to be on orderly duty.
plantule [plɑ̃tyl] *s.f.* (bot.) embryo of a plant.
plantureu-x, -se [plɑ̃tyrø] *adj.* abundant, copious, plentiful, luxuriant; fertile; fleshy, buxom; **~sement** [plɑ̃tyrøzmɑ̃] *adv.* abundantly, copiously, plentifully, luxuriantly.
plaquage [plakaʒ] *s.m.* **1.** (Rugby football) tackle, tackling; **2.** (pop.) abandoning.
plaque [plak] *s.f.* plate, slab, sheet; grid, lid, cover; veneer; plaque, badge, star; (photo.) plate; mark, stain; ~ *de blindage*, armour-plate; shield; revetment; ~ *de cheminée*, chimney-back, register; ~ *d'égout*, manhole-cover; ~ *de propreté*, finger-plate (on door); ~ *de chocolat*, bar of chocolate; (rail.) ~ *tournante*, turntable; (fig.) focal point; ~ *d'accumulateur*, (accumulator) plate or electrode; (car) ~ *matricule* or *d'immatriculation* or *de police*, number-plate.
plaqué [plake] *s.m.* plated metal, plate; (mus.) sustained chord.
plaqueminier [plakminje] *s.m.* (bot.) ebony-tree, persimmon-tree.
plaquer [plake] *v.t.* to plate; to veneer; to overlay; to press flat, to plaster down; (mus.) to strike (and hold a chord); (Rugby football) to tackle; to push, to press; (pop.) to abandon, to give up, to cast off, to jilt, to leave (wife, etc.); *se* ~ *contre le mur, au sol*, to flatten oneself against the wall, on the ground; *elle a plaqué son mari*, she has left her husband; *tout* ~, to give up everything, to chuck it all up.
plaquette [plakɛt] *s.f.* booklet; thin book; small plaque (esp. as souvenir); (physiol.) ~ *sanguine*, blood platelet, haematoblast.
plaqueu-r, -se [plakœr] *s.m.f.* plater; veneerer.
plasma [plasma] *s.m.* (physiol., phys.) plasma.
plastic [plastik] *s.m.* plastic explosive.
plasticage, plastiquage [plastikaʒ] *s.m.* blowing-up with plastic explosive.
plasticité [plastisite] *s.f.* plasticity.
plastifiant [plastifjɑ̃] *s.m.* (chem., techn.) plasticizer.
plastifier [plastifje] *v.t.* to plasticize; to coat with plastic; *fils plastifiés*, plastic-covered wire.
plastiquage see PLASTICAGE.
plastique [plastik] *adj.* plastic; beautifully modelled, well-rounded; ~ *s.f.* plastic art, art of modelling; ~ *s.m.* plastic (substance).
plastiquer [plastike] *v.t.* to blow up with plastic explosive.
plastron [plastrɔ̃] *s.m.* breastplate, body-shield, (fenc.) plastron; front (of shirt, etc.); (mil.) squad of men representing enemy on manœuvres; ~ *de chemise*, shirt-front, starched shirt.
plastronner [plastrɔne] *v.t.* to protect with a breastplate, etc.; (fig.) to shield, to protect; ~ *v.i.* to throw out one's chest; (fig.) to pose, to show off.
plat [pla] *s.m.* dish; course; pan (of scales); collection-plate; flat part, blade (of oar, etc.); *~s*, (bookb.) sides; *mettre les petits ~s dans les grands*, to make great preparations; to kill the fatted calf; *mettre les pieds dans le* ~, to put one's foot in it; *il nous a servi un* ~ *de sa façon*, he played us one of his tricks; ~ *allant au feu*, fireproof dish; (fam.) *faire tout un* ~ *de qch.*, to make a song and dance about sth.
plat, -e [pla] *adj.* flat, level, smooth; plain; (fig.) bald, dull, insipid, undistinguished; *calme* ~, (of sea) dead calm, (fig.) doldrums; *cheveux ~s*, straight hair; *eau ~e*, still (not fizzy) water; *il est très* ~ *devant ses supérieurs*, he is very obsequious to his superiors; *à* ~, flat, (of tyre) deflated, (of battery) run-down; (fig.) *être à* ~, to be depressed; (lit. & fig.) *tomber à* ~, to fall flat, to be a complete failure, a flop; *à* ~ *ventre*, flat on one's stomach; (fig.) *se mettre à* ~ *ventre devant*, to cringe or crawl before.
platane [platan] *s.m.* (bot.) plane-tree.
plat-bord [plabɔr] *s.m.* (naut.) gunwale.
plateau (pl. **-x**) [plato] *s.m.* tray, salver; scale (of balance); table-land, plateau; platform, stage, (cin., TV) set; turntable (of record-player; ~ *à fromages*, cheese-board; *les hauts ~x*, the uplands.
plate-bande [platbɑ̃d] *s.f.* flower-bed; (arch.) lintel; *marcher sur les plates-bandes de qn.*, to trespass on someone's preserves.
platée [plate] *s.f.* **1.** dishful; **2.** (arch.) foundations.
plateforme [platfɔrm] *s.f.* platform; (rail.) road-bed; ~ *électorale*, electoral platform.
platelage [platlaʒ] *s.m.* planking, flooring, decking; (naut.) (armour) plating.
plate-longe [platlɔ̃ʒ] *s.f.* (harness) kicking-strap.
platement [platmɑ̃] *adv.* dully, prosaically, baldly, plainly.
platine[1] [platin] *s.m.* (chem.) platinum; ~ *adj.* platinum (colour).
platine[2] [platin] *s.f.* **1.** lock-plate (of firearm); plate (of lock); stage-plate (of microscope); plate (of clock or watch); platen (of printing-press or typewriter); **2.** (pop.) gift of the gab; patter, sales-talk.
platiné, -e [platine] *adj.* **1.** platinum-tipped; **2.**

bleached platinum-colour; *blonde ~e*, platinum blonde.

platiner [platine] *v.t.* to platinize, to plate with platinum.

platitude [platityd] *s.f.* platitude, dullness, banality; (rare) flatness; (obs.) abjectness, servility.

Platon [platɔ̃] *s.m.* Plato.

platonicien [platonisjɛ̃] *adj.* (phil.) Platonic.

platonique [platɔnik] *adj.* **1.** (phil., obs.) Platonic; **2.** (fig.) (of attachment, etc.) Platonic; theoretical, academic.

platonisme [platɔnism] *s.m.* Platonism.

plâtrage [plɑtraʒ] *s.m.* plastering, plaster-work; clearing (of wine with gypsum); (med.) administration of antacid.

plâtras [plɑtra] *s.m.* old plaster, rubbish, rubble; heavy lump; *avoir un ~ sur l'estomac*, to have an overloaded stomach.

plâtre [plɑtr] *s.m.* gypsum; plaster; plaster cast, plaster figure; *~ fin*, plaster of Paris; *essuyer les ~s*, to live in a newly-built (damp) house; *battre qn. comme ~*, to pound s.o. to a jelly.

plâtrer [plɑtre] *v.t.* to plaster; to set (fracture, etc.) in plaster; (agric.) to treat (field) with gypsum; (fam.) **se** ~ *v.refl.* to paint one's face.

plâtrerie [plɑtrəri] *s.f.* plaster works; plaster-work.

plâtreu-x, -se [plɑtrø] *adj.* chalky, plastery, of the consistency of plaster; plastered.

plâtrier [plɑtrje] *s.m.* plasterer.

plâtrière [plɑtrjɛr] *s.f.* gypsum quarry; plaster-kiln.

plausibilité [plozibilite] *s.f.* plausibility, credibility.

plausible [plosibl] *adj.* plausible; **~ment** [plozibləmɑ̃] *adv.* plausibly.

plèbe [plɛb] *s.f.* **1.** (Rom. ant.) plebs; **2.** (obs., pej.) populace, lower orders.

plébéien, -ne [plebejɛ̃] *adj., s.m.f.* plebeian.

plébiscitaire [plebissitɛr] *adj.* plebiscitary; *par voie ~*, by plebiscite.

plébiscite [plebissit] *s.m.* plebiscite, referendum.

plectre [plɛktr] *s.m.* (mus.) plectrum.

pléiade [plejad] *s.f.* (astron., Lit.) Pleiad; (astron.) *la Pléiade*, the Pleiades; (fig.) constellation, galaxy (of talent, etc.).

plein, -e [plɛ̃] *adj.* full (*de*, of), filled (*de*, with), replete, whole, fraught, solid, complete, thorough, copious; *à ~*, *en ~*, fully, entirely; right in the middle of; *à ~es mains*, freely, liberally, abundantly; *à ~es voiles*, in full sail; all sails set; *en ~ air*, out of doors, in the open air; *jeux de ~ air*, outdoor games; *en ~ jour*, in broad daylight; *en ~ hiver*, in the depth of winter; *en ~e mer*, on the open sea; *en ~ midi*, (i.) at noon, in the heat of the day; (ii.) facing full south; *en ~ champ*, in the open fields; *en ~e classe*, before the whole class; *un jour ~*, a whole day; *~e lune*, full moon; *~e mer*, high tide; *la mer est ~e*, it is high tide; *vache ~e*, cow in calf; *~ de son sujet*, engrossed with one's subject; *~ de soi-même*, conceited; *~ d'inquiétude*, full of anxiety; *en ~e lumière*, in full light; *de son ~ gré*, of one's own free will; *~ de vin*, or *~*, (fam.) drunk, full up; *en bois ~*, in solid wood; *roue ~e*, solid wheel; *donner ~s pouvoirs*, to give full powers; *avoir le cœur ~*, to have one's heart full, to be sad, to be full of grief; ~ *adv.* (naut.) *porter ~*, to keep the sails full; *tout ~*, (i.) quite full; (ii.) very, very much, very many; *avoir tout ~ d'amis*, to have many friends; *avoir de l'argent ~ ses poches*, to have plenty of money; *il en a ~ la bouche*, he is full of it, he talks of nothing else, he is brimming over with it; **~ement** [plɛnmɑ̃] *adv.* fully, entirely, thoroughly, completely.

plein [plɛ̃] *s.m.* full part, plenum, full quantity, full extent, height (of season, power, etc.); solid part, middle; (writing) thick stroke; (naut.) full tide, high tide; *battre son ~*, to be in full swing; (car) *faire le ~*, to fill up (with petrol).

plein-emploi [plɛnɑ̃plwa] *s.m.* (econ.) full employment.

plein-vent [plɛ̃vɑ̃] *s.m.* hardy or isolated fruit-tree.

pléni-er, -ère [plenje] *adj.* plenary.

plénipotentiaire [plenipɔtɑ̃sjɛr] *adj., s.m.* plenipotentiary.

plénitude [plenityd] *s.f.* plenitude, fullness, completeness; ampleness, profusion.

pléonasme [pleɔnasm] *s.m.* pleonasm.

pléonastique [pleɔnastik] *adj.* pleonastic.

pléthore [pletɔr] *s.f.* plethora; abundance, excess.

pléthorique [pletɔrik] *adj.* plethoric; overloaded, superabundant, excessive.

pleur [plœr] *s.m.* tear; *verser, répandre des ~s*, to shed tears.

pleural, -e, (aux) [plœral] *adj.* (anat.) pleural.

pleurard, -e [plœrar] *adj.* whimpering, whining, tearful; *s.m.f.* whimperer.

pleurer [plœre] *v.i.* to weep, to cry, to shed tears; (of eyes) to water; (of vines, etc.) to bleed; (Lit.) to make a mournful sound; (fig.) to mourn, to be afflicted; *~ à chaudes larmes*, to weep bitter tears; *~ comme une Madeleine*, to cry one's eyes out; *~ comme un veau*, to blubber; *~ de joie*, to weep for joy; *~ de rire*, to laugh until one cries; *~ sur*, to weep over, to mourn, to bewail; *aller ~ dans le gilet de qn.*, to weep on someone's shoulder; *~ après la lune*, to cry for the moon; *consoler ceux qui pleurent*, to comfort those that mourn, or the afflicted; *l'oignon fait ~*, onions make your eyes water; ~ *v.t.* to weep for, to mourn (for), to lament, to bewail; *mourir sans être pleuré*, to die unmourned.

pleurésie [plœrezi] *s.f.* (pathol.) pleurisy.

pleurétique [plœretik] *adj.* pleuritic, suffering from pleurisy.

pleureu-r, -se [plœrœr] *s.m.f.* weeper, whimperer, mourner; *adj.* weeping, whimpering; *saule ~r*, weeping willow.

pleurnicher [plœrniʃe] *v.i.* to whimper, to whine, to snivel.

pleurnichement [plœrniʃmɑ̃] *s.m.*, **pleurnicherie** [plœrniʃri] *s.f.* whimpering, whining, snivelling.

pleurnicheu-r, -se [plœrniʃœr] *s.m.f.* whimperer, sniveller; *adj.* snivelling, whining.

pleurodynie [plœrodini] *s.f.* (pathol.) pleurodynia.

pleutre [pløtr] *s.m.* dastard, coward, contemptible wretch; ~ *adj.* cowardly.

pleutrerie [pløtrəri] *s.f.* cowardice, act of cowardice.

pleuvasser [pløvase], **pleuviner** [pløvine], **pluviner** [plyvine] *v.i.* to drizzle, to be showery.

pleuvoir [plœvwar] *v.impers.* to rain; to pour, to shower down; (fig.) to come thick, to fall, to come abundantly; *il pleut à verse*, or *à seaux*, it is pouring (down), it is raining buckets; *il pleut des hallebardes*, it is raining cats and dogs; *comme s'il en pleuvait*, freely, in quantities, easily; *les coups pleuvaient*, there was a hail of blows, blows came thick and fast.

plèvre [plɛvr] *s.f.* (anat.) pleura.

plexus [plɛksys] *s.m.* (anat.) plexus.

pli [pli] *s.m.* fold, crease, tuck, pleat; rumple; wrinkle, inequality, difficulty; envelope, letter, message; habit, bend, turn, routine; *cela ne fera pas un ~*, there will not be the slightest difficulty about that; *il a pris un mauvais ~*, he has contracted bad habits, or a bad habit; *un faux ~*, a crease, a false pleat; *sous ce ~*, enclosed;

herewith; *un ~ de terrain*, an undulation of the ground; *un ~ au front*, a wrinkle on the forehead; (hairdressing) *mise en ~s*, set.
pliable [pliabl] *adj.* pliable, flexible.
pliage [pliaʒ] *s.m.* folding.
pliant, -e [pliɑ̃] *adj.* flexible, supple, pliant; folding; ~ *s.m.* folding chair, camp-stool, folding seat, deck-chair.
plie [pli] *s.f.* (ichth.) plaice.
plier [plie] *v.t.* to fold, to fold up, to bend; (fig.) to curb, to bring under; ~ *bagage*, to decamp; to be off, bag and baggage; to clear out; ~ *les genoux*, to kneel; to bend the knee; ~ *v.i.* to bend, to give; to submit, to yield, to give way (*sous*, to); to be weighed down (*sous*, by); **se** ~ *v.refl.* to submit (*à*, to), to yield (to), to comply (with); to be folded, to be bent.
plieu-r, -se [pliœr] *s.m.f.* folder; **~se** *s.f.* folding-machine.
plinthe [plɛ̃t] *s.f.* plinth.
pliocène [pliɔsɛn] *adj.*, *s.m.* Pliocene.
plioir [plijwar] *s.m.* **1.** paper-knife; folder; **2.** fishing-reel.
plique [plik] *s.f.* (pathol.) plica.
plissage [plisaʒ] *s.m.* plaiting, pleating, tucking; crinkling (of paper).
plissé, -e [plise] *adj.* pleated; wrinkled; ~ *s.m.* pleat, pleating.
plissement [plismɑ̃] *s.m.* folding, pleating; (geol.) corrugation, folding.
plisser [plise] *v.t.* to plait, to fold, to pleat, to tuck, to kilt, to crease, to crumple; (geol.) to corrugate; ~ *v.i.* to wrinkle, to pucker, to crease.
plisseu-r, -se [plisœr] *s.m.f.* pleater; **~se** *s.f.* pleating-machine.
pliure [pliyr] *s.f.* folding; fold.
ploc [plɔk] *interj.* plop!
ploiement [plwamɑ̃] *s.m.* bending, folding; (mil.) re-forming into marching order.
plomb [plɔ̃] *s.m.* lead; shot; plumb-line; plummet; sink; lead seal; (electr.) fuse; (fig.) ballast, weight; *dormir d'un sommeil de ~*, to sleep heavily, soundly, like a log; (fig.) *avoir du ~ dans l'aile*, to be winged, to be crippled, to be in a bad way; *saumon de ~*, pig-lead; ~ *de chasse*, shot; *il lui faudrait un peu de ~ dans la tête*, he wants a little ballast, he is much too flighty; *fil à ~*, plumb-line, plummet; (build.) *les ~s*, lead-work, (window-)leads; *mine de ~*, plumbago, blacklead; *à ~*, perpendicularly; right, just in time, opportunely; *en ~*, leaden.
plombage [plɔ̃baʒ] *s.m.* **1.** leading; sealing with lead seal; **2.** stopping (of tooth); (fam.) stopping, dental amalgam.
plombagine [plɔ̃baʒin] *s.f.* plumbago, black-lead.
plombé, -e [plɔ̃be] *adj.* (of sticks, etc.) loaded; (of teeth) stopped; sealed; leaden-hued, livid.
plomber [plɔ̃be] *v.t.* **1.** to load, to cover with lead; to glaze with lead; **2.** to seal, to stamp with lead; **3.** to stop (a tooth); **4.** to plumb; ~ *un mur*, to plumb a wall; **se** ~ *v.refl.* to take on a leaden hue, to become livid.
plomberie [plɔ̃bri] *s.f.* plumbing, lead-work; lead works.
plombier [plɔ̃bje] *s.m.* plumber.
plombifère [plɔ̃bifɛr] *adj.* plumbiferous; *glaçure ~*, lead-glaze.
plongeant, -e [plɔ̃ʒɑ̃] *adj.* plunging; diving; downward; (mil.) *tir ~*, plunging fire; *décolleté ~*, plunging neckline.
plongée [plɔ̃ʒe] *s.f.* dive, diving, immersion, submersion (of submarine); (fort.) glacis; (geol.) dip or incline (in ocean bed).
plongement [plɔ̃ʒmɑ̃] *s.m.* plunging, dipping. immersion.
plongeoir [plɔ̃ʒwar] *s.m.* diving-board.
plongeon [plɔ̃ʒɔ̃] *s.m.* **1.** dive, diving, plunge; (fam.) deep bow; *faire un ~*, to dive, (lit. & fig.) to plunge; (fam.) *faire le ~*, to incur heavy losses, to get into deep water financially; **2.** (ornith.) diver, loon.
plonger [plɔ̃ʒe] *v.t.* to plunge, to dip, to immerse; to thrust; ~ *le regard* or *les yeux dans*, to gaze or peer into; *être plongé dans son travail*, to be immersed or absorbed in one's work; *plongé dans ses méditations*, sunk in meditation; ~ *v.i.* to sink, to dive, to plunge, (of submarine) to submerge; to fall (*dans*, into); to be immersed; to dip, to hang down; to look down; (naut., of ship) to pitch violently, to bury her nose in the seas; *point de vue d'où le regard plonge*, viewpoint from which one can look down; **se** ~ *v.refl.* (lit. & fig.) to immerse oneself.
plongeu-r, -se [plɔ̃ʒœr] *s.m.f.* **1.** diver; dipper, vatman; **2.** dish-washer, scullery-boy (in hotels, etc.); **~r** *s.m.* (ornith.) diver.
plot [plo] *s.m.* (electr.) contact, point; stud, press-button switch.
plouf [pluf] *interj.* plop!
ploutocrat-e [plutɔkrat] *s.m.* plutocrat; **~ie** [plutɔkrasi] *s.f.* plutocracy; **~ique** [plutɔkratik] *adj.* plutocratic.
ployer [plwaje] *v.t.i.* to bend, to bow, to fold, to fold up; (fig.) to curb, to submit, to give way; ~ *sous le faix*, to give way under the burden; **se** ~ *v.refl.* to yield, to submit, to give way; to be folded.
pluches [plyʃ] *s.f.pl.* (mil. slang or fam.) potato-peeling, spud-bashing.
pluie [plɥi] *s.f.* rain; shower, downpour; abundance; *jour de ~*, rainy day; *le temps est à la ~*, it looks like rain; *ennuyeux comme la ~*, as dull as ditch-water; *après la ~ le beau temps*, every cloud has a silver lining; *une ~ de coups*, a hail of blows; *faire la ~ et le beau temps*, to rule the roost; to be all-powerful; *parler de la ~ et du beau temps*, to talk of this and that.
plumage [plymaʒ] *s.m.* plumage, feathers.
plumard [plymar] *s.m.* (pop.) bed.
plumasserie [plymasri] *s.f.* feather trade.
plumassi-er, -ère [plymasje] *s.m.f.*, *adj.* plumassier, feather-dresser, feather-dealer.
plume [plym] *s.f.* feather, plume, quill; pen; (fig.) style of writing; ~ *d'oie*, goose-quill; *lit de ~(s)*, feather bed; *tenir la ~*, to write; to act as secretary, to do the writing; *prendre la ~*, to write, to put pen to paper; *dessin à la ~*, pen-and-ink sketch; *guerre de ~*, paper war; *il y a laissé des ~s*, it cost him something, he didn't get off lightly; *écrire au courant de la ~*, to write spontaneously; *trait de ~*, dash, stroke, of the pen.
plumeau (pl. **-x**) [plymo] *s.m.* feather duster; tuft of feathers or hair.
plumer [plyme] *v.t.* to pluck (bird, etc.); (fig.) to pluck, to fleece; (rowing) to feather; **se** ~ *v.refl.* (pop.) to go to bed.
plumet [plymɛ] *s.m.* plume, plume of feathers.
plumetis [plymti] *s.m.* (embroidery) feather-stitch, satin-stitch; *brodé au ~*, feather-stitched.
plumeu-x, -se [plymø] *adj.* feathery, plumose.
plumier [plymje] *s.m.* pencil-box.
plumitif [plymitif] *s.m.* (pej.) bureaucrat.
plumule [plymyl] *s.f.* (bot., zool.) plumule.
(**la**) **plupart** [laplypar] *s.f.* most, the greatest part, the majority, most people; *la ~ du temps*, mostly, generally; *la ~ des gens disent*, most people say; *pour la ~*, mostly.
plural-e, (**aux**) [plyral] *adj.* plural.
pluralité [plyralite] *s.f.* plurality, multiplicity; (obs.) majority.
pluriel, -le [plyrjɛl] *adj.*, ~ *s.m.* plural.
plus [ply(s)] *adv.* more, most, further, farther, longer, any more, any longer; the more; (~

marks the comparative in French; with def. art. it marks the superlative; ~ *cher*, dearer; *le ~ long*, the longest, etc.); plus, besides; *ne ... ~*, no more, no longer, not now, not again, never again, never more; *au ~*, *tout au ~*, at most, at the utmost; *d'autant ~*, the more so, all the more; *bien ~*, much more, more than that; *de ~*, moreover, besides; *de ~ en ~*, more and more; *de ~ en ~ mal*, worse and worse; *en ~*, in addition (to), besides, more, over, extra; *le ~*, the most; *~ malheureux que*, more unhappy than; *je n'ai ~ que cela*, I have nothing left but that; *ni ~ ni moins*, neither more nor less; *~ ou moins*, more or less; *qui ~ est*, what is more; *sans ~*, without any more; only; *sans ~ tarder*, without further delay; *tant et ~*, abundantly; enough and to spare; *il n'est ~ temps*, it is too late; *~ tard*, later; later on; *il n'est ~*, he is dead; *~ on est de fous, ~ on rit*, the more the merrier; *~ le jour est long, ~ la nuit est courte*, the longer the day, the shorter the night; *il n'en peut ~*, he is exhausted, he is tired out; *je n'ai ~ qu'à vous remercier*, it only remains for me to thank you; *deux fois ~ grand*, twice as large; *six fois ~*, six times more; *~ tôt*, earlier, sooner; (see PLUTÔT); *~ s.m.* the most, the maximum; *les gens qui ont rendu le ~ de services*, the people who have helped most.

plusieurs [plyzjœr] *adj., pron. pl.* several, many, some, a number (of), some people, a number of people; *une ou ~ personnes*, one or more people.

plus-que-parfait [plyskəparfɛ] *s.m.* (pl. *plus-que-parfaits*) (gram.) pluperfect.

plus-value [plyvaly] *s.f.* increase in value, betterment, appreciation; increment; (budgetary) surplus; additional or contingency payments (on building contract).

plutonien, -ne [plytɔnjɛ̃] *adj.* Plutonian; plutonic.

plutonium [plytɔnjɔm] *s.m.* (chem.) plutonium.

plutôt [plyto] *adv.* rather, sooner, preferably; somewhat; *~ que*, rather than, before; *~ souffrir que mourir*, better to suffer than to die; *voyez ~*, see for yourself.

pluvial, -e, (aux) [plyvjal] *adj.* rain-, of rain; *eau ~e*, rain-water; *ruissellement ~*, patter of rain.

pluvier [plyvje] *s.m.* (ornith.) plover.

pluvieu-x, -se [plyvjø] *adj.* rainy, wet.

pluviner see PLEUVINER.

pluviomètre [plyvjɔmɛtr] *s.m.* pluviometer, rain-gauge.

pluviôse [plyvjoz] *s.m.* (hist.) Pluviose (fifth month in Fr. Republican Calendar, January–February).

pluviosité [plyvjozite] *s.f.* (meteor.) rainfall, precipitation.

P.M. [peɛm] abbrev. **1.** p.m. (opp. a.m.); **2.** *pistolet-mitrailleur*; *préparation militaire*.

P.M.U. [peɛmy] *s.m.* abbrev. *pari mutuel urbain*.

pneu [pnø] *s.m.* **1.** tyre; **2.** express letter (by pneumatic tube).

pneumatique [pnømatik] *adj.* pneumatic, inflatable; *~ s.f.* pneumatics; *~ s.m.*; **1.** tyre; **2.** = PNEU 2.

pneumatologie [pnømatɔlɔʒi] *s.f.* pneumatology.

pneumon-ie [pnømɔni] *s.f.* pneumonia; **~ique** [pnømɔnik] *adj.* (med.) pneumonic; *s.m.f.* person suffering from pneumonia.

pochade [pɔʃad] *s.f.* (paint.) rough sketch; (theatr., etc.) sketch, amusing short piece.

pochard, -e [pɔʃar] *s.m.f.* (fam.) drunkard; **se ~er** *v.refl.* (fam.) to get drunk.

poche [pɔʃ] *s.f.* **1.** pocket; *argent de ~*, pocket-money; *dictionnaire de ~*, pocket-dictionary; (cook.) *~ à douille*, forcing-bag; *~ de gaz*, gas-pocket; *elle n'a pas les yeux dans sa ~*, she's got eyes in her head; *connaître comme sa ~*, to know like the palm of one's hand; *mettre qch. dans ses ~s*, to pocket or appropriate sth.; *mettez ça dans votre ~ et votre mouchoir par-dessus*, you may put that in your pipe and smoke it; *mettre qn. dans sa poche*, to be too good for s.o., to twist s.o. round one's little finger; *fouiller dans ses ~s*, to search one's pockets; (pop.) *c'est dans la poche*, it's in the bag, it's all tied up; **2.** pouch, bag, sack; crop (of bird); *acheter chat en ~*, to buy a pig in a poke.

poché, -e [pɔʃe] *adj.* **1.** poached; **2.** bruised; *un œil ~*, a black eye; *aux yeux ~s*, with bags under the eyes.

pocher [pɔʃe] *v.t.* **1.** to poach; (fig.) to execute roughly, to make a rough drawing; **2.** to bruise; *~ l'œil à qn.*, to give s.o. a black eye.

pochetée [pɔʃte] *s.f.* **1.** (obs.) pocketful; **2.** (pop.) fool, idiot.

pochette [pɔʃɛt] *s.f.* **1.** small pocket; small packet or pouch, document wallet, (pencil, etc.) case; **2.** fancy pocket handkerchief; **3.** (obs.) small violin.

pocheuse [pɔʃøz] *s.f.* (cook.) egg-poacher.

pochoir [pɔʃwar] *s.m.* stencil-plate.

podestat [pɔdɛsta] *s.m.* podesta.

podomètre [pɔdɔmɛtr] *s.m.* pedometer.

poêle[1] [pwɑl] *s.m.* pall; (obs.) canopy (held over bridal pair at Catholic marriage service).

poêle[2]**, poële** [pwɑl] *s.m.* stove.

poêle[3] [pwɑl] *s.f.* (cook.) shallow pan; *~ (à frire)*, frying-pan; *passer* or *sauter à la ~*, to fry; (fig.) *tenir la queue de la ~*, to be running the show, to be the one who gives the orders; *sauter de la ~ dans la braise*, to jump out of the frying-pan into the fire.

poêlée [pwɑle] *s.f.* panful.

poêlon [pwɑlɔ̃] *s.m.* small pot or saucepan; pipkin.

poème [pɔɛm] *s.m.* poem.

poésie [pɔezi] *s.f.* poetry; poesy; piece of poetry.

poète [pɔɛt] *s.m.* poet (man or woman).

poétereau (pl. **-x**) [pɔetro] *s.m.* wretched poet, poetaster.

poétesse [pɔetɛs] *s.f.* (usu. pej.) poetess.

poétique [pɔetik] *adj.* poetical, poetic; (fig.) lyrical, imaginative, of poetic beauty; *l'art ~*, the art of poetry; *~ s.f.* poetics; theory or critique of poetry; **~ment** [pɔetikmɑ̃] *adv.* poetically, as poetry.

poétiser [pɔetize] *v.t.* to make poetry out of, to poeticize; (fig.) to idealize, to romanticize.

pognon [pɔɲɔ̃] *s.m.* (pop.) money.

pogrom, pogrome [pɔgrɔm] *s.m.* pogrom.

poids [pwa] *s.m.* weight, heaviness; (phys.) gravity; burden, (fig.) importance, consequence, purport, weight; *~ brut*, gross weight; *~ net*, net weight; *~ lourd*, heavy lorry; (boxing) heavy-weight; *~ mort*, dead weight; (fig.) useless burden, passenger; *~ plume*, (boxing) feather-weight; (fig.) lightweight, person of no consequence; *~ utile*, useful weight, carrying capacity; *faire le ~*, to be of the right weight; *ne pas faire le ~*, to be underweight; (fig.) to be unequal (to one's job, etc.); (fam.) *avoid deux ~ et deux mesures*, to have double standards; *un homme de ~*, a man of importance; *vendre au ~*, to sell by weight; *vendre au ~ de l'or*, to sell at an extortionate price; *son opinion est d'un grand ~*, his opinion carries much weight.

poignant, -e [pwaɲɑ̃] *adj.* poignant.

poignard [pwaɲar] *s.m.* poniard, dagger, dirk; *frapper qn. d'un coup de ~*, to stab s.o.; (fig.) to cut s.o. to the quick.

poignarder [pwaɲarde] *v.t.* to stab; (fig.) to cut to the quick, to wound deeply.

poigne [pwaɲ] *s.f.* grip, grasp; (fig.) strong will, energy; *à* or *de ~*, strong, energetic, masterful, authoritarian; *avoir de la ~*, to exercise firm control.

poignée [pwaɲe] *s.f.* handful; handle, hilt (of a

sword), holder; (fig.) small number, handful; *à ~s*, by handfuls; *~ de main*, handshake.

poignet [pwaɲɛ] *s.m.* wrist; wristband, cuff; (fig.) *à la force du ~*, by one's own efforts, by sheer hard work.

poil [pwal] *s.m.* (of persons) hair (on body or face), bristle (on chin, etc.), beard; (of animals) hair, fur, coat, skin; colour; (of materials) nap, pile; (of brush) hair, bristle; (of plants) fibre, down, pubescence; capillary (root); (fig.) kind, complexion; hair's breadth; *à ~*, naked, (rid.) bareback; (fig.) *au ~*, perfect, just right, exactly; (fam.) *ne pas avoir un ~ sur le caillou*, to be completely bald; *avoir un ~ dans la main*, to be bone idle; (fig.) *de tout ~*, or *de tous ~s*, of every complexion; *ça a changé de ~*, it has taken a turn for the better; *à un ~ près*, by a hair's breadth; *il s'en est fallu d'un ~*, it was a very close shave; (fig.) *reprendre du ~ de la bête*, to have another go to refuse to be defeated; *être de bon ~*, to be in a, good mood, in good form.

(**se**) **poiler** [pwale] *v.refl.* (pop.) to roar with laughter.

poilu, -e [pwaly] *adj.* hairy, shaggy; (bot.) pilose; *~ s.m.* soldier (esp. of 1914–18 war).

poinçon [pwɛ̃sɔ̃] *s.m.* punch, awl, piercer, pricker, (engraver's) point; die, stamp; punch-hole, punch-mark, stamp; (build.) king-post.

poinçonnage [pwɛ̃sɔnaʒ], **poinçonnement** [pwɛ̃sɔnmɑ̃] *s.m.* stamping, punching, perforating.

poinçonner [pwɛ̃sɔne] *v.t.* to stamp, to punch.

poinçonneuse [pwɛ̃sɔnøz] *s.f.* punching-machine, punch.

poindre [pwɛ̃dr] *v.i.* to appear, to come up, to break, to dawn; *~ v.t.* **1.** (obs.) to sting; **2.** (fig.) to maltreat, to cause suffering to.

poing [pwɛ̃] *s.m.* fist; *un revolver au ~*, holding a revolver; *coup de ~*, blow with the fist, punch; *pieds et ~s liés*, bound hand and foot; *serrer les ~s*, to clench one's fists; *coup-de-~ américain*, knuckle-duster; *dormir à ~s fermés*, to sleep soundly, or like a top.

point [pwɛ̃] *s.m.* point, dot, speck; stitch; stop, full stop; score, mark; condition, state; position, bearings, situation; (fig.) respect, matter; *deux ~s*, colon; *~-virgule*, semicolon; *~ d'interrogation*, question mark; *~ d'exclamation*, exclamation mark; *mettre les ~s sur les i*, to dot the i's, to insist (on a point); *à ~*, just in time; at the right moment; (cook.) (of grilled steak) medium, (of roasted meat) done to a turn; (of fruit) ripe; *à ~ nommé*, at just the right moment, on the dot, just in time, just when wanted; *à quel ~?*, to what extent?, how far?; *au ~ où nous en sommes*, as matters stand; *mettre au ~*, to focus, to put in focus or perspective, to make clear, to perfect, to put in working order, to tune (engine), to bring to a state of readiness; *au dernier ~*, in the highest degree; *de ~ en ~*, minutely, to the letter, in every particular; *de tous ~s*, in every respect; *en tout ~*, absolutely; *être sur le ~ de*, to be about to, to be just going to, to be on the point or verge of, to be ready to; *à tel ~ que*, to such a degree that, so much so that; *jusqu'à un certain ~*, to a certain extent; *~ de chaînette*, chain-stitch; *~ de chausson*, herring-bone stitch; *~ de croix*, cross-stitch; *~ de côté*, hem-stitch; *un ~ fait à temps*, a stitch in time; *avoir un ~ de côté*, to have a stitch in one's side; *~ d'appui*, base of operations, support, fulcrum, leverage; *~ d'arrêt*, stopping-place; *~ d'ébullition*, boiling-point; *~ de départ*, starting-point; *~ de fuite*, vanishing-point; *~ de fusion*, fusing-point; melting-point; *~ d'ignition*, flash-point; *au ~ du jour*, at dawn, at daybreak; *~ de jonction*, meeting-point; (artill.) *~ de mire*, sighting-mark; (fam.) aim, target, object; *~ mort*, (phys.) static equilibrium; (car) neutral (gear); (mus.) *~ d'orgue*, pause; *~ de repère*, sighting-mark, guide mark, reference point, (lit. & fig.) landmark; *~ de vue*, point of view, opinion; viewpoint; *à ce ~ de vue*, in that light; *un beau ~ de vue*, a fine view; *les ~s cardinaux*, the cardinal points; *faire le ~*, (naut. & fig.) to ascertain one's position, to take one's bearings, to take stock of (situation, etc.), (journalism) to give a round-up (of information); (obs.) *en bon ~*, in good form, in good condition; *mal en ~*, in a bad way; *compter les ~s*, to keep the score; *marquer un ~*, to score a point or an advantage; (boxing) *être vainqueur aux ~s*, to be the winner on points; *il vous rendrait des ~s*, he is more than a match for you; he can give you points (and a beating); *un ~ noir à l'horizon*, breakers ahead, a black cloud on the horizon; *un ~ c'est tout*, there's an end to it.

point [pwɛ̃] *adv.* no, not, not at all, not any, none, no such thing; *je n'en veux ~*, I won't have any, I won't have anything to do with it.

pointage [pwɛ̃taʒ] *s.m.* **1.** pointing, aiming, levelling; **2.** checking, ticking off, marking off.

pointe [pwɛ̃t] *s.f.* point, head, tip, top; nail, tack; cape, ness, foreland; peak, pinnacle; leading position; forward thrust, lunge; (mil.) spearhead, forward reconnaissance; nose-cone (of rocket); (fig.) pungency, sharpness, flavour, zest; witticism; touch; *pousser une ~*, to make an advance; *pousser sa ~*, to press one's point; (fencing) *coup de ~*, lunge; *à la ~ du jour*, at the break of day; *heure de ~*, peak hour, rush hour; *industrie de ~*, advanced or leading industry; (fig.) *à la ~ de l'épée*, forcibly; by main force, by storm; *une ~ d'ironie*, a touch of irony; *sur la ~ des pieds*, on tiptoe; (danc.) *faire des ~s*, to dance on tips of toes; *lancer des ~s à qn.*, to tease s.o., to make pointed remarks to s.o.

pointeau (pl. **-x**) [pwɛ̃to] *s.m.* **1.** needle, spindle, (of carburettor, tap, etc.); **2.** checker (in factory).

pointer[1] [pwɛ̃te] *v.t.* **1.** to dot; to mark, to mark out, to mark off, to tick off, to number off; to check; (mus.) to dot (a note); (print.) to register (sheets); (naut.) *~ la carte*, to prick the chart (establishing position); **2.** to aim, to lay, to train (gun, telescope, etc.); **se ~** *v.refl.* (pop.) to appear, to pop up.

pointer[2] [pwɛ̃te] *v.t.* **1.** to thrust, to stab, to prick; to prick up (ears); **2.** to sharpen, to put a point on; *~ v.i.* to appear, to spring up, to sprout; to push out, to push on; to stand out, to stick up.

pointer [pwɛ̃tœr] *s.m.* pointer (dog).

pointeu-r, -se [pwɛ̃tœr] *s.m.f.* **1.** checker; marker, scorer; (mil.) gun-layer; **2.** pointer, sharpener, (of tools, etc.).

pointillage [pwɛ̃tijaʒ] *s.m.* (paint.) stippling, pointillage.

pointillé, -e [pwɛ̃tije] *adj.* dotted; *ligne ~e*, dotted line; *~ s.m.* dotted line; perforation (formed by dotted line); pointillé (painting, etc.).

pointiller [pwɛ̃tije] *v.t.* to stipple; to paint or draw by means of dots; *~ v.i.* (obs.) to argue every little point.

pointilleu-x, -se [pwɛ̃tijø] *adj.* captious, carping; particular, fastidious.

pointillisme [pwɛ̃tijism] *s.m.* (paint.) pointillism.

pointilliste [pwɛ̃tijist] *adj.*, *s.m.f.* pointillist (painter).

pointu, -e [pwɛ̃ty] *adj.* pointed, sharp, angular, acute, peaked; shrill, harsh; (fig.) sharp, disagreeable, touchy; *~ adv.* pointedly.

pointure [pwɛ̃tyr] *s.f.* **1.** (of shoes, gloves, etc.) size; **2.** (print.) point.

poire [pwar] *s.f.* **1.** pear; pear-shaped object;

bulb (on syringe, motor-horn, etc.); (electr.) pear-switch; ~ *d'angoisse*, metal gag; *garder une ~ pour la soif*, to put sth. aside for a rainy day; **2.** (pop.) face; (fam.) fool, simpleton, mug, sap.

poiré [pware] *s.m.* perry.

poireau (pl. **-x**) [pwaro], **porreau** (pl. **-x**) [pɔro] *s.m.* **1.** leek; (fam.) s.o. who is waiting; *faire le ~, rester planté comme un ~*, to be kept waiting, to cool one's heels; **2.** wart.

poireauter [pwarote], **poiroter** [pwarɔte] *v.i.* = *faire le* POIREAU.

poirée [pware] *s.f.* white beet.

poirier [pwarje] *s.m.* pear-tree; pear-wood.

pois [pwa] *s.m.* **1.** (bot.) pea (pl. peas and (obs.) pease); *petits ~*, green peas; ~ *cassés*, split peas; ~ *chiches*, chick peas; ~ *de senteur*, sweet peas; (fam.) *la fleur des ~*, fashionable, elegant person; the cream of society; **2.** wart; **3.** spot, dot, polka dot; *cravate à ~*, spotted tie; *robe à ~*, polka-dot dress.

poison [pwazɔ̃] *s.m.* poison, venom.

poissard, -e [pwasar] *adj.* vulgar, low; **~e** *s.f.* fishwife, vulgar loud-voiced woman.

poisse [pwas] *s.f.* **1.** (obs.) poverty, (financial) embarrassment; **2.** bad luck; *quelle ~!*, what bad luck!, what a nuisance!

poisser [pwase] *v.t.* to pitch, to wax; to make sticky; (pop.) to catch, to arrest; *se ~ les mains*, to get one's hands sticky or dirty; (pop.) *se faire ~*, to get nabbed; ~ *v.i.* to be sticky.

poisseu-x, -se [pwasø] *adj.* sticky; messy, dirty.

poisson [pwasɔ̃] *s.m.* fish; (astron.) *les Poissons*, Pisces; ~ *d'avril*, April fool, April fool hoax; ~ *de rivière*, freshwater fish; ~ *rouge*, goldfish; *ni chair ni ~*, neither fish, flesh, nor good red herring; *être comme un ~ dans l'eau*, to be in one's element.

poisson-épée [pwasɔ̃epe] *s.m.* swordfish.

poissonnerie [pwasɔnri] *s.f.* fish-market, fishmonger's shop; dealing in fish and other sea food.

poissonneu-x, -se [pwasɔnø] *adj.* abounding in fish.

poissonni-er, -ère [pwasɔnje] *s.m.f.* fishmonger; **~er** *s.m.* (naut.) lugger buying fish from fishing-boats; **~ère** *s.f.* fish-kettle.

poisson-lune [pwasɔ̃lyn] *s.m.* moonfish, opah.

poisson-scie [pwasɔ̃si] *s.m.* sawfish.

poitevin, -e [pwatvɛ̃] *s.m.f.*, *adj.* (native or inhabitant) of Poitou or Poitiers; ~ *s.m.* Poitevin (dialect).

poitrail (pl. **-s**) [pwatraj] *s.m.* **1.** breast, chest (of horse, etc.; iron. of person); breastplate, breast-strap (of harness); **2.** (build.) breast-summer, bressummer.

poitrinaire [pwatrinɛr] *adj.*, *s.m.f.* consumptive.

poitrine [pwatrin] *s.f.* chest; breast, breasts, bosom; lungs; (butch.) breast, brisket (of beef); (obs.) consumption, tuberculosis; *à pleine ~*, at the top of one's voice; *respirer à pleine ~*, to inhale deeply; (fig.) *se frapper la ~*, to put the blame on oneself.

poivrade [pwavrad] *s.f.* poivrade (sauce); *à la ~*, dressed with pepper and salt.

poivre [pwavr] *s.m.* pepper; (lit. & fig.) piquancy, spice, spiciness; *grain de ~*, peppercorn; ~ *et sel*, pepper and salt (colour, mixture), grizzled, iron grey, (hair).

poivrer [pwavre] *v.t.* to pepper, to add pepper to; **se ~** *v.refl.* (fam.) to get drunk.

poivrier [pwavrie] *s.m.* **1.** (bot.) pepper plant; **2.** pepper-pot.

poivrière [pwavriɛr] *s.f.* **1.** pepper plantation; **2.** pepper-pot; **3.** (arch.) corner-turret.

poivron [pwavrɔ̃] *s.m.* capsicum.

poivrot, -e [pwavro] *s.m.f.* (pop.) drunkard.

poix [pwa] *s.f.* pitch; shoemaker's wax; *enduire de ~*, to pitch; *~-résine*, resin.

poker [pɔkɛr] *s.m.* poker (card-game); *partie de ~*, game of poker; (fig.) tough bargaining; ~ *d'as*, poker-dice.

polacre [pɔlakr] *s.f.* (naut.) polacre, polacca.

polaire [pɔlɛr] *adj.* (geog., astron., math., electr.) polar, pole-; ~ *s.f.* (math.) polar.

polaque [pɔlak] *s.m.* **1.** (hist.) Polish cavalryman (18th c.); **2.** (pop., pej.) Pole, Polack.

polarimètre [pɔlarimɛtr] *s.m.* polarimeter.

polarisant, -e [pɔlarizɑ̃] *adj.* (phys.) polarizing.

polaris-ation [pɔlarizɑsjɔ̃] *s.f.* polarization; (fig.) polarization, concentration, focusing; **~cope** [pɔlariskɔp] *s.m.* polariscope; **~er** [pɔlarize] *v.t.* (phys.) to polarize; (fig.) to polarize, to focus; **~eur** [pɔlarizœr] *adj.* polarizing; *s.m.* polarizer.

polarité [pɔlarite] *s.f.* (phys., biol.) polarity; (fig.) opposed qualities, diametrical opposition.

polder [pɔldɛr] *s.m.* polder.

pôle [pol] *s.m*, (geog., astron., electr., math.) pole.

polémarque [pɔlemark] *s.m.* (Gr. ant.) polemarch.

polémique [pɔlemik] *s.f.* controversy, polemic; polemics; ~ *adj.* polemic, polemical, controversial.

polémiquer [pɔlemike] *v.i.* to engage in controversy; ~ *contre qn.*, to dispute with s.o.

polémiste [pɔlemist] *s.m.f.* polemist, controversialist.

polenta [pɔlɛnta] *s.f.* polenta, Italian semolina.

poli, -e [pɔli] *adj.* **1.** polished, glossy, smooth; (fig.) elegant, civilized; **2.** polite; civil; ~ *s.m.* polish, finish; **~ment** [pɔlimɑ̃] *adv.* politely, civilly.

police[1] [pɔlis] *s.f.* police, police force; policing; police regulations; *bonnet de ~*, forage cap; *agent de ~*, policeman; constable, inspector; ~ *judiciaire*, detective force = C.I.D.; (mil.) *salle de ~*, guard-room; *tribunal de simple ~*, police court; *faire la ~*, to maintain order.

police[2] [pɔlis] *s.f.* (insurance) policy.

policer [pɔlise] *v.t.* (obs.) **1.** to regulate, to control; **2.** to civilize, to refine.

polichinelle [pɔliʃinɛl] *s.m.* Punch, punchinello; puppet; jumping-jack; (fig.) buffoon, clown; comic (and ugly) person, figure of fun; irresponsible person; *secret de ~*, open secret; *faire le ~*, to act the buffoon; *mener une vie de ~*, to act irresponsibly, to live a disordered life.

polici-er, -ère [pɔlisje] *adj.* police, of the police; (fig.) relating to crime, mystery; *régime ~er*, police state; *roman ~er*, crime or detective story, thriller; **~er** *s.m.* policeman, police inspector, officer, etc.

poliomyélite [pɔljɔmjelit], **polio** [pɔljo] *s.f.* poliomyelitis, infantile paralysis.

poliomyélitique [pɔljɔmjelitik] *adj.*, *s.m.f.* poliomyelitic.

polir [pɔlir] *v.t.* to polish; to civilize, to refine, to give a finish to.

polissage [pɔlisaʒ] *s.m.* polishing.

polisseu-r, -se [pɔlisœr] *s.m.f.* polisher.

polissoir [pɔliswar] *s.m.* polisher (implement or machine); (archaeol.) polishing-stone (used for polishing flints).

polissoire [pɔliswar] *s.f.* **1.** knife-polisher (machine); polishing-brush (for shoes); **2.** (pin manufacture) polishing-shop.

polisson, -ne [pɔlisɔ̃] *adj.* dirty, lewd; *s.m.f.* (obs.) guttersnipe, street urchin; (mod.) naughty child; depraved character.

polissonner [pɔlisɔne] *v.i.* **1.** (of child) to be naughty; **2.** (obs.) to joke; to act or speak lewdly.

polissonnerie [pɔlisɔnri] *s.f.* **1.** (of child) naughtiness; **2.** (obs.) joking; (mod.) dirty talk, lewd behaviour; (pl.) obscenities.

politesse [pɔlitɛs] *s.f.* politeness, good breeding, civility; act of civility, kindness; *brûler la ~ à qn.*, to leave s.o. abruptly, without saying good-bye.
politicard [pɔlitikar] *s.m.* (pej.) politician (out to feather own nest).
politicien, -ne [pɔlitisjɛ̃] *s.m.f.* politician; *adj.* of a politician.
politique [pɔlitik] *s.f.* politics; policy; (*homme*) ~ *s.m.* politician.
politique [pɔlitik] *adj.* political; politically-minded; politic, prudent, shrewd, (fig.) diplomatic; **~ment** [pɔlitikmɑ̃] *adv.* politically; shrewdly, (fig.) diplomatically.
politiquer [pɔlitike] *v.i.* (fam.) to talk politics.
politiser [pɔlitize] *v.t.* to make political, to give a political character or aspect to.
politologie [pɔlitɔlɔʒi], **politicologie** [pɔlitikɔlɔʒi] *s.f.* political science, science of politics.
polka [pɔlka] *s.f.* polka (dance).
pollen [pɔl(l)ɛn] *s.m.* pollen.
pollicitation [pɔl(l)isitɑsjɔ̃] *s.f.* (law) pollicitation, tentative offer, provisional undertaking.
pollinique [pɔl(l)inik] *adj.* (bot.) pollinic.
pollinisation [pɔl(l)inizɑsjɔ̃] *s.f.* (bot.) pollination.
polluer [pɔl(l)ɥe] *v.t.* to pollute.
pollution [pɔl(l)ysjɔ̃] *s.f.* pollution; (obs.) profanation, desecration; (med.) *~s nocturnes*, night emission (of semen).
polo [pɔlo] *s.m.* **1.** polo; **2.** (obs.) (woman's) round knitted cap; **3.** open-necked sports shirt; ⚠ not 'polo-neck'.
polochon [pɔlɔʃɔ̃] *s.m.* (pop.) bolster.
Pologne [pɔlɔɲ] *s.f.* (geog.) Poland.
polonais, -e [pɔlɔnɛ] *adj.* Polish; *s.m.f.* Pole, Polish man or woman; ~ *s.m.* Polish (language); (fam.) *soûl comme un ~*, drunk as a lord.
polonaise [pɔlɔnɛz] *s.f.* **1.** (mus., danc.) polonaise; **2.** meringue fruit-cake flavoured with kirsch.
polonium [pɔlɔnjɔm] *s.f.* (phys.) polonium.
poltron, -ne [pɔltrɔ̃] *adj.* coward, chicken-hearted, cowardly; *s.m.f.* coward, poltroon.
poltronnerie [pɔltrɔnri] *s.f.* cowardice, poltroonery.
poly-acide [pɔliasid] *adj.*, *s.m.* (chem.) polyacid; **~amide** [pɔliamid] *s.f.* (chem.) polyamide.
polyandr-e [pɔljɑ̃dr] *adj.* (anthrop., bot.) polyandrous; **~ie** [pɔliɑ̃dri] *s.f.* (anthrop.) polyandry; (bot.) Polyandria.
polychrom-e [pɔlikrom] *adj.* polychrome, in colour, decorated in colours; **~ie** [pɔlikrɔmi] *s.f.* polychromy, decoration in colours; colour photography
polyclinique [pɔliklinik] *s.f.* polyclinic, non-specialist clinic.
polycop-ie [pɔlikɔpi] *s.f.* duplicating, copying, (by stencil, etc.), cyclostyling; **~ié** [pɔlikɔpje] *s.m.* duplicated copy, cyclostyle text (esp. of university lectures); **~ier** [pɔlikɔpje] *v.t.* to duplicate, to cyclostyle, etc.
polyculture [pɔlikyltyr] *s.f.* mixed farming.
polyèdr-e [pɔliɛdr] *s.m.* polyhedron.
polyédrique [pɔliedrik] *adj.* polyhedral.
polyester [pɔliɛstɛr] *s.m.* (chem.) polyester.
polyéthylène [pɔlietilɛn], **polythène** [pɔlitɛn] *s.m.* (chem.) polyethylene, polythene.
polygam-e [pɔligam] *adj.* polygamous; **~ie** [pɔligami] *s.f.* polygamy.
polyglotte [pɔliglɔt] *adj.*, *s.m.f.* polyglot.
polygonal, -e, (aux) [pɔligɔnal] *adj.* polygonal.
polygone [pɔligɔn] *s.m.* polygon.
polygraphe [pɔligraf] *s.m.* polygraph, versatile author.
polymèr-e [pɔlimɛr] *adj.* (chem.) polymeric; **~e** *s.m.* polymer; **~ie** [pɔlimeri] *s.f.* (chem., biol.) polymerism; **~isation** [pɔlimerizɑsjɔ̃] *s.f.* polymerization; **~iser** [pɔlimerize] *v.t.* to polymerize.
polymorph-e [pɔlimɔrf] *adj.* (chem., biol.) polymorphous, polymorphic; **~ie** [pɔlimɔrfi] *s.f.*, **~isme** [pɔlimɔrfism] *s.m.* (chem., biol.) polymorphism.
Polynésie [pɔlinezi] *s.f.* (geog.) Polynesia.
polynésien, -ne [pɔlinezjɛ̃] *adj.*, *s.m.f.* Polynesian.
polynôme [pɔlinom] *s.m.* (alg.) polynomial, polynome.
polype [pɔlip] *s.m.* (zool.) polyp; (pathol.) polyp, polypus.
polypétale [pɔlipetal] *adj.* (bot.) polypetalous.
polypeu-x, -se [pɔlipø] *adj.* (med.) polypous.
polyphon-ie [pɔlifɔni] *s.f.* (mus.) polyphony; **~ique** [pɔlifɔnik] *adj.* polyphonic.
polypier [pɔlipje] *s.m.* (zool.) polypary.
polypode [pɔlipɔd] *s.m.* (bot.) Polypodium, polypody.
polysyllabe [pɔlisil(l)ab] *adj.* polysyllabic; ~ *s.m.* polysyllable.
polysyllabique [pɔlisil(l)abik] *adj.* polysyllabic.
polytechnicien [pɔlitɛknisjɛ̃] *s.m.* pupil or former pupil of *École polytechnique*.
polytechnique [pɔlitɛknik] *adj.* polytechnic; ~ *s.f. la Polytechnique = l'École polytechnique* (in Paris).
polythé-isme [pɔliteism] *s.m.* polytheism; **~iste** [pɔliteist] *adj.*, *s.m.f.* polytheistic; polytheist.
polythène [pɔlitɛn] *s.m.* see POLYÉTHYLÈNE.
polyvalent, -e [pɔlivalɑ̃] *adj.* polyvalent, multivalent, having many functions; ~ *s.m.* general factotum.
pommade [pɔmad] *s.f.* pomade, ointment; (fig.) *passer de la ~ à qn.*, to flatter s.o., to butter s.o. up.
pommader [pɔmade] *v.t.* to pomade, to apply ointment to.
pomme [pɔm] *s.f.* apple; pippin; apple-shaped fruit; ~ (*de terre*), potato; knob (on walking-stick, furniture, etc.); heart (of lettuce, etc.); (pine-, etc.) cone; rose (of watering-can); ~ *d'amour*, tomato, love-apple; *~s frites*, fried potatoes, chips; *~s chips*, potato crisps; (anat.) ~ *d'Adam*, Adam's apple; (fig.) ~ *de discorde*, bone of contention, apple of discord; (fam.) *aux ~s*, first-rate.
pommé, -e [pɔme] *adj.* grown to a round head; rounded; (fig.) complete, utter, out and out, consummate.
pommeau (pl. **-x**) [pɔmo] *s.m.* pommel; knob; butt (of pistol).
pomme de terre [pɔmdətɛr] *s.f.* see POMME.
pommelé, -e [pɔmle] *adj.* dappled, dappled with clouds; *ciel ~*, dappled sky, mackerel sky.
(**se**) **pommeler** [pɔmle] *v.refl.* **1.** to become dappled; **2.** (of lettuce, etc.) to form a heart.
pommelle [pɔmɛl] *s.f.* grating, drain-cover.
pommer [pɔme] *v.i.* = SE POMMELER 2.
pommeraie [pɔmrɛ] *s.f.* apple-orchard.
pommette [pɔmɛt] *s.f.* **1.** ball-ornament; butt (of pistol); **2.** cheek-bone; *aux ~s rouges*, apple-cheeked.
pommier [pɔmje] *s.m.* (bot.) apple-tree.
pomologie [pɔmɔlɔʒi] *s.f.* pomology.
pompe[1] [pɔ̃p] *s.f.* pomp, state, ceremony; (pl., Lit.) vanities; *~s funèbres*, funeral (ceremony); undertaking; undertaker's, funeral director's; *en grande ~*, in state.
pompe[2] [pɔ̃p] *s.f.* pump, pumping-machine; ~ *à incendie*, fire-engine; ~ *à air, à pneu*, air-pump, tyre pump; ~ *foulante*, force-pump; ~ *aspirante et (re)foulante*, lift- and force-pump; ~ *à bière*, beer-engine; ~ *alimentaire*, feed-pump.
pomper [pɔ̃pe] *v.t.* to pump; to suck up, to

absorb, to drain away; (fig.) to pump (for information); to exhaust.

pompette [pɔ̃pɛt] *adj.* (pop.) tipsy.

pompeu-r, -se [pɔ̃pœr] *s.m.f.* pump-operator.

pompeu-x, -se [pɔpø] *adj.* pompous, stately, grand, high-flown, over-done, emphasized; **~sement** [pɔ̃pøzmɑ̃] *adv.* pompously; emphatically, with emphasis.

pompier [pɔ̃pje] *s.m.* **1.** fireman, member of fire brigade; **2.** = POMPEUR.

pompi-er, -ère [pɔ̃pje] *adj.* pretentious, over-done, pompous; *s.m.f.* (tailoring) alteration hand.

pompiste [pɔ̃pist] *s.m.f.* **1.** (garage) pump-attendant; **2.** pump-operator, pumping engineer.

pompon [pɔ̃pɔ̃] *s.m.* pompon, top-knot, tuft, tassel; (often iron.) *avoir le ~*, to be the winner; (obs.) *avoir son ~*, to be tipsy.

pomponner [pɔ̃pɔne] *v.t.* to deck out, to adorn, to dress (oneself) with great care.

ponant [pɔnɑ̃] *s.m.* west.

ponçage [pɔ̃saʒ] *s.m.* pumicing, rubbing-down, sandpapering; pouncing (of drawings).

ponce [pɔ̃s] *s.f.* pumice; (drawing) pounce; *pierre ~*, pumice-stone.

ponceau[1] (pl. **-x**) [pɔ̃so] *s.m.* small bridge; culvert.

ponceau[2] (pl. **-x**) [pɔ̃so] *s.m.* corn-poppy; *~ adj. invar.* flame-coloured, poppy-red.

Ponce-Pilate [pɔ̃spilat] *s.m.* Pontius Pilate.

poncer [pɔ̃se] *v.t.* to pumice, to sandpaper; (drawing) to pounce.

poncho [pɔ̃tʃo] *s.m.* poncho.

poncif [pɔ̃sif] *s.m.* pattern (for pounced drawing); (Lit., art., etc.) unoriginal, conventional piece of work.

ponction [pɔ̃ksjɔ̃] *s.f.* **1.** (surg.) puncture, tapping; **2.** deduction (of tax, commission, etc.).

ponctionner [pɔksjɔne] *v.t.* **1.** (surg.) to puncture, to tap; **2.** to deduct (tax, etc.).

ponctualité [pɔ̃ktɥalite] *s.f.* punctuality; punctiliousness, exactitude.

ponctuation [pɔ̃ktɥɑsjɔ̃] *s.f.* punctuation, pointing.

ponctuel, -le [pɔ̃ktɥɛl] *adj.* **1.** punctual, exact; **2.** pin-point (of light-beam); *lampe ~le*, lamp giving pin-hole beam; **~lement** [pɔ̃ktɥɛlmɑ̃] *adv.* punctually.

ponctuer [pɔ̃ktɥe] *v.t.* to punctuate, to point; to dot, to mark, to spot.

pondérable [pɔ̃derabl] *adj.* ponderable, of measurable weight.

pondérat-eur, -rice [pɔ̃deratœr] *adj.* balancing, moderating.

pondération [pɔ̃derɑsjɔ̃] *s.f.* ponderation; balance, equilibrium, moderation; (econ.) weighting.

pondéré, -e [pɔ̃dere] *adj.* balanced, well-poised, calm; (econ., of index, etc.) weighted.

pondérer [pɔ̃dere] *v.t.* to balance, to bring into equilibrium; (econ.) to weight.

pondéreu-x, -se [pɔ̃derø] *adj.* weighty, heavy; **-x** *s.m.pl.* heavy goods.

pondeur [pɔ̃dœr] *s.m.* (pej.) prolific author.

pondeuse [pɔ̃døz] *s.f.* good layer (of eggs); prolific mother.

pondoir [pɔ̃dwar] *s.m.* laying-place; laying-basket.

pondre [pɔ̃dr] *v.t.i.* to lay eggs, to lay; (pop., pej.) to give birth to (child); (fig.) to produce (a novel, etc.).

poney [pɔne] *s.m.* pony.

pongiste [pɔ̃ʒist] *s.m.f.* table-tennis player.

pont [pɔ̃] *s.m.* **1.** bridge; (mech.) live axle, axle, drive; (electr.) bridge, bridge connector; (dressm.) flap (of trousers); bending (of card to cheat opponent); extra holiday taken between official ones; (fig.) bridge, link; *~ tournant*, swing bridge; *~ suspendu*, suspension bridge; *~ roulant*, gantry crane; *les Ponts et Chaussées*, highways department, civil engineer's department; (mil.) *tête de ~*, bridgehead; *~ aérien*, airlift; (geom.) *~ aux ânes*, pons asinorum, (fig.) something everyone knows; *~ avant*, front axle, front drive; *~ arrière*, rear axle, rear-axle assembly; *~ flottant*, floating axle; (electr.) *~ d'éclatage*, spark-gap; *faire le ~*, to take an extra holiday between two official ones; (fig.) *brûler* or *rompre ses ~s*, to burn one's bridges; (fig.) *faire un ~*, to provide a link; *faire un ~ d'or à qn.*, to give s.o. a financial inducement to accept a job; *il est solide comme le Pont-Neuf*, he is as fit as a fiddle, he is still going strong; **2.** (naut.) deck; *~ d'envol*, flight-deck; *faux-~*, orlop deck; ⚠ not (naut.) 'bridge'.

ponte[1] [pɔ̃t] *s.m.* punter (at baccarat, etc.); (fam.) important person.

ponte[2] [pɔ̃t] *s.f.* **1.** laying, clutch, sitting, (of eggs); **2.** ovulation.

ponté, -e [pɔ̃te] *adj.* (naut.) decked.

ponter [pɔ̃te] *v.t.* **1.** to bridge; **2.** (naut.) to deck; **3.** to stake (at cards, etc.); *~ v.i.* to punt (at baccarat, etc.).

pontet [pɔ̃tɛ] *s.m.* trigger-guard.

pontier [pɔ̃tje] *s.m.* **1.** bridge-keeper (of swing bridge, etc.); **2.** gantry-crane operator.

pontife [pɔ̃tif] *s.m.* pontiff; (fig.) self-important person.

pontifical, -e, (**aux**) [pɔ̃tifikal] *adj.* pontifical, papal; *~ s.m.* pontifical; (pl.) pontificals.

pontificat [pɔ̃tifika] *s.m.* pontificate, papacy.

pontifier [pɔ̃tifje] *v.i.* (usu. fig.) to pontificate, to lay down the law.

pont-levis [pɔ̃ləvi] *s.m.* drawbridge.

ponton [pɔ̃tɔ̃] *s.m.* pontoon, floating jetty; hulk; *~-grue*, floating crane.

pontonnier [pɔ̃tɔnje] *s.m.* **1.** soldier in bridge-building section of Engineers; **2.** = PONTIER 1.

pool [pul] *s.m.* pool, common marketing arrangements; *le ~ du charbon et de l'acier*, the coal and steel pool.

pope [pɔp] *s.m.* pope (parish priest of Orthodox church in Russia).

popeline [pɔplin] *s.f.* poplin.

poplité, -e [pɔplite] *adj.* (anat.) popliteal.

popote [pɔpɔt] *s.f.* (fam.) cooking, food, eating; (mil.) mess; *~ adj.invar.* (fam.) stay-at-home, homely.

populace [pɔpylas] *s.f.* populace, mob, rabble.

populaci-er, -ère [pɔpylasje] *adj.* low, vulgar, plebeian, mob-.

populage [pɔpylaʒ] *s.m.* (bot.) marsh marigold.

populaire [pɔpylɛr] *adj.* **1.** popular; of the people; **2.** vulgar, common; **~ment** [pɔpylɛrmɑ̃] *adv.* in the manner of the people; *s'exprimer ~ment*, to use the popular idiom.

populariser [pɔpylarize] *v.t.* to popularize; to make popular.

popularité [pɔpylarite] *s.f.* popularity.

population [pɔpylɑsjɔ̃] *s.f.* population.

populeu-x, -se [pɔpylø] *adj.* populous, densely populated.

populo [pɔpylo] *s.m.* (fam.) the common people, rabble; crowd.

poquet [pɔkɛ] *s.m.* (agric.) seed-hole, seed-pocket.

porc [pɔr] *s.m.* hog, pig, swine; pork; pigskin; (fig., of person) pig, swine.

porcelaine [pɔrslɛn] *s.f.* **1.** porcelain, china, chinaware; **2.** cowrie(-shell).

porcelaini-er, -ère [pɔrslɛnje] *adj.* porcelain; **~er** *s.m.* porcelain or china manufacturer or dealer.

porcelet [pɔrslɛ] *s.m.* young pig, piglet.

porc-épic [pɔrkepik] *s.m.* (zool.) porcupine; (fig.) prickly person, one easily irritated.
porche [pɔrʃ] *s.m.* porch, portal; hall, vestibule.
porch-er, -ère [pɔrʃe] *s.m.f.* swine-herd.
porcherie [pɔrʃri] *s.f.* (lit. & fig.) pigsty; piggery.
porcin, -e [pɔrsɛ̃] *adj.* porcine; pig, pig-like; *industrie ~e*, pig-breeding; *peste ~e*, swine-fever; ~ *s.m.* pig, boar.
pore [pɔr] *s.m.* pore.
poreu-x, -se [pɔrø] *adj.* porous.
porion [pɔrjɔ̃] *s.m.* (mining, oil) overman.
porno-graphe [pɔrnɔgraf] *adj.* pornographic, of pornography; *s.m.f.* pornographer; **~-graphie** [pɔrnɔgrafi] *s.f.* pornography; **~-graphique** [pɔrnɔgrafik] *adj.* pornographic.
porosité [pɔrozite] *s.f.* porosity.
porphyre [pɔrfir] *s.m.* porphyry.
porque [pɔrk] *s.f.* (naut.) riders.
porreau see POIREAU.
port[1] [pɔr] *s.m.* harbour, haven, port, seaport town; mountain pass (in Pyrenees); (fig.) haven, refuge, shelter; *arriver à bon ~*, to arrive safely; (fig.) *mener à bon ~*, to bring to a successful conclusion; (fig.) *faire naufrage au ~*, to be lost at the eleventh hour; to fall at the last fence; *~ de guerre*, naval base; *~ marchand*, commercial port.
port[2] [pɔr] *s.m.* **1.** bearing, gait, mien, presence; **2.** carrying, carriage; carriage charge, delivery fee, cost of transport, postage; (naut.) burden; wearing; bearing (title, etc.); *franco* or *franc de ~*, *~ payé*, carriage paid, post free; *se mettre au ~ d'armes*, to shoulder arms; (mus.) *~ de voix*, glide, portamento.
portable [pɔrtabl] *adj.* portable; wearable; (law) *dette ~*, debt payable at address of payee.
portage [pɔrtaʒ] *s.m.* carriage, porterage, transport, conveyance; carriage by porters; portage.
portail [pɔrtaj] *s.m.* portal, gateway, main door.
portant, -e [pɔrtɑ̃] *adj.* bearing, carrying; in health; *bien ~*, in good health; *mal ~*, in bad health, unwell; *à bout ~*, close; at point-blank range; (fig.) point-blank; to one's face.
portant [pɔrtɑ̃] *s.m.* (electr.) armature, keeper (of magnet); (naut.) outrigger; (theatr.) framework supporting scenery or lighting, batten; (arch.) supporter, upright.
portati-f, -ve [pɔrtatif] *adj.* portable; (mus.) portative; *glaces ~ves*, ices to be taken away.
porte [pɔrt] *s.f.* door, doorway, gate, gateway, entrance; gorge, defile; (hist.) Porte; eye (for a hook); (skiing) gate, pair of flags; *mettre à la ~* to turn out; *être aux ~s du tombeau*, to be at death's door; *fermer* (or *refuser*) *sa ~ à qn.*, not to be at home to s.o.; to forbid s.o. the house; (fig.) *frapper à toutes les ~s*, to leave no stone unturned; (fig.) *mettre la clef sous la ~*, to abscond; *prendre la ~*, to slip away, to go out; *à ~s ouvrantes*, when the doors open; *~ à deux battants*, folding doors; *~ cochère*, carriage entrance; *~ à coulisse*, sliding door; *~ d'entrée*, entrance-door, main door, front door; *de ~ en ~*, from house to house; *faire du ~ à ~*, to be a door-to-door salesman; (fig.) *entrer par la grande ~*, to take a short cut to a top job; *entrer par la petite ~*, to start at the bottom of the ladder; *se ménager* or *se réserver une ~ de sortie*, to keep open a line of retreat; *c'est la ~ ouverte à*, it is an open invitation, an encouragement, to; (fig.) *il faut qu'une ~ soit ouverte ou fermée*, it must be either one thing or the other.
porte [pɔrt] *adj.f.* (anat.) *veine ~*, portal vein.
porté, -e [pɔrte] *adj.* inclined, disposed, prone, (*à*, to); *être ~ sur*, to be given to, to have a weakness for; (fam.) *être porté sur la chose*, to be keen on sex.
porte-aiguille [pɔrteguij] *s.m.invar.* (surg.) needle-holder; **~-aiguilles** [pɔrteguij] *s.m. invar.* needle-case; **~-allumettes** [pɔrtalymɛt] *s.m.invar.* match-holder; **~-amarre** [pɔrtamar] *s.m.invar.* life-saving rocket apparatus; **~-avions** [pɔrtavjɔ̃] *s.m.invar.* aircraft-carrier; **~-bagages** [pɔrtbagaʒ] *s.m.invar.* luggage-rack (on car), carrier (on bicycle, etc.); **~-baïonnette** [pɔrtbajɔnɛt] *s.m.invar.* bayonet-frog; **~-balais** [pɔrtbalɛ] *s.m.invar.* (electr.) brush-holder; **~-billets** [pɔrtbije] *s.m.invar.* note-case; **~-bonheur** [pɔrtbɔnœr] *s.m.invar.* lucky charm, amulet, mascot; **~-bouteilles** [pɔrtbutɛj] *s.m. invar.* bottle-rack, wine-rack; bottle-drainer; **~-cartes** [pɔrtəkart] *s.m.invar.* **1.** card-case; **2.** map-holder; **~-chapeaux** [pɔrtʃapo] *s.m. invar.* hat-rack, hat-stand; **~-cigares** [pɔrtsigar] *s.m.invar.* cigar-case; **~-cigarettes** [pɔrtsigarɛt] *s.m.invar.* cigarette-case; **~-clefs, ~-clés** [pɔrtəkle] *s.m.invar.* **1.** (obs.) turnkey; **2.** key-ring, key-holder; **~-copie** [pɔrtkɔpi] *s.m. invar.* (print., typewriting) copy-holder; **~-couteau** [pɔrtkuto] *s.m.* (pl. *~-couteau(x)*) knife-rest; **~-crayon** [pɔrtkrɛjɔ̃] *s.m.* (pl. *~-crayon(s)*) pencil-holder, portcrayon; **~-croix** [pɔrtkrwa] *s.m.invar.* cross-bearer; **~-documents** [pɔrtdɔkymɑ̃] *s.m.invar.* document-case, document wallet; **~-drapeau** [pɔrtdrapo] *s.m.* (pl. *~-drapeau(x)*) (mil.) colour-bearer, ensign; (lit. & fig.) standard-bearer.
portée [pɔrte] *s.f.* **1.** (of animals) brood, litter, farrow, etc.; **2.** (naut.) burden, load, cargo; capacity; **3.** (build., etc.) load (on joist, etc.); bearer; span; (mus.) stave; **4.** range, reach; (fig.) scope, capacity; force, effect, implication (of words, etc.); *à ~*, within reach; (mil.) *à ~ de tir*, within range; *à (la) ~ de*, within reach of, within range of; (fig.) accessible to, within the capability of.
porte-enseigne [pɔrtɑ̃sɛɲ] *s.m.invar.* = PORTE-DRAPEAU; **~faix** [pɔrtəfɛ] *s.m.invar.* porter, street-porter; docker, stevedore.
porte-fenêtre [pɔrtfənɛtr] *s.f.* French window.
portefeuille [pɔrtəfœj] *s.m.* **1.** (obs.) portfolio, folder, document-wallet; brief-case, satchel; (mod.) portfolio (symbol of ministerial responsibilities); portfolio (of investments); *ministre sans ~*, minister without portfolio; *faire un lit en ~*, to make an apple-pie bed; **2.** note-case, wallet.
porte-greffe [pɔrtəgrɛf] *s.m.* (pl. *~-greffe(s)*) (hort.) stock; **~-jarretelles** [pɔrtʒartɛl] *s.m. invar.* suspender-belt; **~-jupe** [pɔrtəʒyp] *s.m. invar.* skirt-hanger; **~-lames** [pɔrtəlam] *s.m. invar.* (techn.) blade-holder; **~-malheur** [pɔrtmalœr] *s.m.invar.* bringer of bad luck, bird of ill omen.
portemanteau (pl. **-x**) [pɔrtmɑ̃to] *s.m.* **1.** (obs.) portmanteau, wardrobe-trunk; **2.** coat-rack, (hat-and-)coat-stand; **3.** (naut.) davit.
porte-menu [pɔrtməny] *s.m.invar.* menu-holder; **~-mine** [pɔrtəmin] *s.m.* (pl. *~-mine(s)*) propelling pencil; **~-monnaie** [pɔrtmɔnɛ] *s.m. invar.* purse; **~-musique** [pɔrtmyzik] *s.m.invar.* music-case; **~-objet** [pɔrtɔbʒɛ] *s.m.* (pl. *~-objet(s)*) (in microscope) (i.) object-slide; (ii.) stage; **~-outil** [pɔrtuti] *s.m.* (pl. *~-outil(s)*) tool-holder (in machine-tool); **~-parapluies** [pɔrtparaplɥi] *s.m.invar.* umbrella-stand; **~-parole** [pɔrtparɔl] *s.m.invar.* spokesman, mouthpiece; **~-plume** [pɔrtəplym] *s.m.invar.* penholder; (obs.) *~-plume réservoir*, fountain pen.
porter [pɔrte] *v.t.* to bear, to support; to carry, to take, to convey, to bring; to wear, to have on; to hold, to have, to carry; to induce, to incline; *portez armes!*, shoulder arms!; *~ les armes*, to bear arms, to serve as a soldier; *~ bonheur*, to bring luck; *~ les cheveux longs*, to wear one's hair long; *~ le deuil de*, to be in mourning for; ~

envie à, to envy; ~ *des fruits*, to bear fruit; *vous portez tout à l'extrême*, you always carry things to extremes; ~ *intérêt*, (i.) to yield interest; (ii.) to show interest or solicitude; ~ *un jugement sur*, to pass judgement upon; ~ *la main sur qn.*, to strike s.o.; ~ *malheur*, to bring bad luck; ~ *qn. aux nues*, to praise s.o. to the skies; ~ *la parole*, to be the spokesman; ~ *préjudice à*, to be prejudicial to, to be injurious to; ~ *ses pas vers*, to bend one's steps towards; *il en portera la peine*, he will suffer for it; ~ *ses regards sur*, to look towards, to glance at, to glance over; (fig.) ~ *la robe*, to be a magistrate; (fig.) ~ *la soutane*, to be a priest; ~ *la santé de qn.*, to drink someone's health; ~ *témoignage*, to bear witness; ~ *la tête haute*, to carry one's head high; ~ *un toast à*, to drink a toast to; *il porte bien le vin*, he can carry his liquor; ~ *sur le registre*, to enter on the register; ~ *v.i.* **1.** to reach, to carry; (of gun) to have a (long, short) range; to strike; to fall; (fig.) to strike home, to have an effect, to register; to relate (*sur*, to); *une voix qui porte*, a voice that carries; *ce canon porte loin, à 4 km*, this gun has a long range, a range of 4 km; *sa tête porta sur un tabouret, contre le mur*, his head hit a stool, he fell with his head against the wall; *l'accent porte sur la dernière syllabe*, the stress falls on the last syllable; *des mots qui portent*, words which strike home; *vos observations ont porté*, your remarks have registered; *cela porte plus sur la forme que la matière*, that relates more to the form than the content; **2.** to bear, to rest, to be supported, (*sur*, by, on); ~ *à faux*, to be out of plumb; **se** ~ *v.refl.* **1.** to be (well, ill, etc.); *il se porte à merveille*, he is in remarkably good health; **2.** to be carried, to be worn; *les jupes se portent plus courtes*, skirts are being worn shorter; **3.** to move, to go; to be directed; *se* ~ *à la rencontre de*, to advance to meet; *se* ~ *à des extrémités*, to go to extremes; *des regards se portaient sur nous*, glances were being shot in our direction; **4.** to offer oneself as, to present oneself as; to stand (surety, as candidate, etc.); to appear; *se* ~ *candidat*, to present oneself or to stand as a candidate; *se* ~ *garant*, to stand surety; (law) *se* ~ *partie civile*, to claim damages.

porter [pɔrtɛr] *s.m.* porter (beer).

porte-savon [pɔrtsavɔ̃] *s.m.* (pl. ~*-savon(s)*) soap-dish, soap-holder.

porte-serviettes [pɔrtsɛrvjɛt] *s.m.invar.* towel-rail.

porteu-r, -se [pɔrtœr] *s.m.f.* carrier, porter, bearer; holder; *titres au* ~*r*, bonds payable to bearer; bearer securities; *cheval* ~*r*, near-side horse; *chaise à* ~*rs*, sedan-chair; *adj.* carrying, carrier; (radio) *onde* ~*se*, carrier-wave.

porte-voix [pɔrtəvwɑ] *s.m.invar.* megaphone, speaking-trumpet; (naut.) loud hailer.

porti-er, -ère [pɔrtje] *s.m.f.* porter, door-keeper, janitor.

portière [pɔrtjɛr] *s.f.* **1.** door-curtain; **2.** door (of car, railway-carriage, etc.).

portière [pɔrtjɛr] *adj.f.* (of cows, etc.) of an age to bear young.

portillon [pɔrtijɔ̃] *s.m.* small gate, side gate, postern, barrier; *ses mots se bousculent au* ~, he can't get his words out.

portion [pɔrsjɔ̃] *s.f.* portion, part, share, lot; helping (of food).

portique [pɔrtik] *s.m.* **1.** portico, porch; *le Portique*, the Stoics; Stoic philosophy; **2.** cross-beam, cross-bar; gantry; ~ *roulant, grue à* ~, gantry-crane.

portland [pɔrtlɑ̃] *s.m.* Portland cement.

porto [pɔrto] *s.m.* port (wine).

portrait [pɔrtrɛ] *s.m.* portrait, likeness, picture; (fig.) description, image, semblance; (pop.) face; *cet enfant est le* ~ *de son père*, that child is the very image of his father; (pop.) *abîmer le* ~ *à qn.*, to disfigure s.o.

portrait-iste [pɔrtretist] *s.m.f.* portrait-painter; ~**urer** [pɔrtretyre] *v.t.* to paint the portrait of; (fig.) to depict, to describe.

port-salut [pɔrsaly] *s.m.* Port Salut cheese.

portugais, -e [pɔrtygɛ] *adj., s.m.f.* Portuguese; ~**e** *s.f.* Portuguese oyster.

Portugal [pɔrtygal] *s.m.* (geog.) Portugal.

pose [poz] *s.f.* **1.** placing, laying, fixing, fitting; **2.** attitude; posture; pose; sitting (for portrait, etc.); **3.** showing off; affectation; posing; **4.** (photo.) exposure; time-exposure; *temps de* ~, (correct) exposure, exposure-time; (fam.) *le faire à la* ~, to show off, to bluff.

posé, -e [poze] *adj.* staid, sober, steady, sedate.

posément [pozemɑ̃] *adv.* calmly, deliberately, without hurry.

poser [poze] *v.t.* to place, to lay down, to set, to put; to post up, to apply; to post (sentries); to state, to admit, to declare; to ask (a question); to pose or present (a problem); (arith.) to put down (a number); (techn.) to fit, to fix up, to hang, to affix; (mus.) ~ *bien sa voix*, to pitch one's voice correctly; ~ *v.i.* **1.** to rest, to be supported; **2.** to pose; (fam.) ~ *à*, to pose as; **se** ~ *v.refl.* **1.** to perch; (of aircraft) to land; **2.** *se* ~ *en, comme*, to pose as; **3.** to be placed or put; **4.** (of problem, etc.) to present itself.

poseu-r, -se [pozœr] *s.m.f.* **1.** (techn.) layer, setter, etc.; **2.** poseur, affected person.

positi-f, -ve [pozitif] *adj.* positive, affirmative, certain, actual; matter-of-fact, practical, realist; (electr.) positive; (math.) *nombre* ~*f*, positive number; ~**vement** [pɔzitivmɑ̃] *adv.* positively, definitely.

positif [pozitif] *s.m.* positive, reality; (gram., photo.) positive; (mus.) choir organ.

position [pozisjɔ̃] *s.f.* position, situation, station; attitude, posture, stance; balance (of account); status; standing; case; circumstances; *il est en* ~ *de*, he is in a position to; he is able to; *être dans une bonne* ~, to be well off; *perdre sa* ~, to lose one's employment; to lose one's rank or social status; *feuille de* ~, balance-sheet; (fam.) *être dans une* ~ *intéressante*, to be pregnant.

positiv-isme [pozitivism] *s.m.* (phil.) positivism; ~**iste** [pozitivist] *adj., s.m.f.* positivist; ~**ité** [pozitivite] *s.f.* (phil., electr.) positivity.

positon [pozitɔ̃] *s.m.* (phys.) positron.

possédant, -e [pɔsedɑ̃] *adj.* propertied, property-owning; *s.m.f.* (pl.) *les* ~*s*, the propertied class, property-owners, (fam.) the haves.

possédé, -e [pɔsede] *adj.* possessed (esp. by evil spirit); infatuated; *s.m.f.* mad person, maniac, one possessed.

posséder [pɔsede] *v.t.* to possess, to own, to have; to enjoy, to be master of, to know thoroughly, to dominate; (pop.) to deceive, to 'have'; *être possédé d'une idée*, to be possessed by (or with) an idea; *l'ambition le possède*, he is eaten up with ambition; *l'ambition qu'il possède*, the ambition he is possessed of; ~ *une femme*, to possess, (pop.) to have, a woman; ~ *son sujet*, to have a thorough command of one's subject; **se** ~ *v.refl.* to restrain oneself, to be master of one's passions; *il ne se possède pas de joie*, he is beside himself with joy.

possesseur [pɔsɛsœr] *s.m.* possessor, owner, holder, occupier, one able to enjoy (sth.), repository (of secret, truth).

possessi-f, -ve [pɔsɛsif] *adj.* possessive; ~**f** *s.m.* (gram.) possessive case.

possession [pɔsɛsjɔ̃] *s.f.* **1.** possession, ownership; (pl.) possessions; possession (by evil spirit); *mettre qn. en* ~ *de*, to give s.o. possession of, to invest s.o. with (an office).

possessoire [pɔsɛswar] *adj.* (law) possessory; ~ *s.m.* right of possession.
possibilité [pɔsibilite] *s.f.* possibility, eventuality; feasibility; (pl.) means, capacity; *payer selon ses ~s*, to pay according to one's means; *les ~s de la salle*, the capacity of the hall.
possible [pɔsibl] *adj.* possible; *c'est bien ~*, that may be; *pas ~!*, you don't say so!, no, really?; *le plus ~*, as much as possible; *le plus tôt ~*, as soon as possible; *dans la mesure du ~*, as far as is possible; *le moins ~*, the least possible; as few . . . as possible; as little as can be; *vous est-il ~ de venir?*, can you possibly come?; ~ *s.m.* possible, possibility, what is possible; *au ~*, extremely; *je ferai tout mon ~*, I will do my best.
postage [pɔstaʒ] *s.m.* posting, mailing; dispatch by mail-boat.
postal, -e, (**aux**) [pɔstal] *adj.* postal; *carte ~e*, postcard; *colis ~*, postal packet, parcel post.
postcombustion [pɔstkɔ̃bystjɔ̃] *s.f.* (aeron.) after-burning.
postdater [pɔstdate] *v.t.* to post-date.
poste [pɔst] *s.f.* post, (relay) post, post office, mail, postal service; ~ *aérienne*, air mail; *maître de ~*, postmaster; *courir la ~*, to go post-haste; (hist.) *chaise de ~*, post-chaise; *mettre une lettre à la ~*, to post a letter; *bureau de ~*, post office; *Postes et Télécommunications* (formerly *Postes, Télégraphes et Téléphones*), the Post Office; *timbre-~*, (postage) stamp.
poste [pɔst] *s.m.* post, station, employment, place, position, appointment, berth, office; (naut.) quarters; (mil., police) guardroom, guard-post; police station, police-post; (radio, TV) set, station; *à ~ fixe*, permanently; ~ *d'incendie*, fire station; *être conduit au ~*, to be arrested; to be taken to the police station; (radio) ~ *émetteur*, transmitter, transmitting station.
poster[1] [pɔste] *v.t.* to station, to post, to position; **se** ~ *v.refl.* to take up a position.
poster[2] [pɔste] *v.t.* to send by post, to post.
postérieur, -e [pɔsterjœr] *adj.* posterior, later, subsequent; back, hind; ~ *s.m.* bottom, behind, backside; **~ement** [pɔsterjœrmɑ̃] *adv.* later, subsequently, afterwards.
postériorité [pɔsterjɔrite] *s.f.* posteriority.
postérité [pɔsterite] *s.f.* posterity; descendants, issue.
posthume [pɔstym] *adj.* posthumous.
postiche [pɔstiʃ] *adj.* superadded; false, artificial, sham; ~ *s.m.* false hair, hair-piece.
posti-er, -ère [pɔstje] *s.m.f.* postman, postwoman, post-office employee.
postillon [pɔstijɔ̃] *s.m.* postilion, post-boy; (fam.) *envoyer des ~s* or *postillonner*, to splutter a spray of saliva while talking.
postillonner [pɔstijɔne] *v.i.* see POSTILLON.
postscolaire [pɔstskɔlɛr] *adj.* after leaving school; *enseignement ~*, further education, further studies.
post-scriptum [pɔstskriptɔm] *s.m.invar.* postscript.
postulant, -e [pɔstylɑ̃] *s.m.f.* applicant, postulant, candidate.
postulat [pɔstyla] *s.m.* postulate.
postuler [pɔstyle] *v.t.* to apply for (a post); to postulate; ~ *v.i.* (law) to act (for a client), to conduct a suit.
posture [pɔstyr] *s.f.* posture, attitude; situation; *être en bonne ~ pour*, to be in a fair way to; *être en mauvaise ~*, to be in a bad way; to be in an awkward position.
pot [po] *s.m.* pot, jug, tankard, can, jar, vessel, crucible; *un ~ à eau*, a water-jug; (fig.) *mettre la poule au ~*, to have a good meal, to eat fowl (once a week); ~ *de chambre*, chamber-pot, chamber; (car) ~ *d'échappement*, silencer; (fig.) ~ *de vin*, bribe; *payer les ~s cassés*, to stand the racket, to pay the damage, to face the music; (fig.) *tourner autour du ~*, to beat about the bush; *sourd comme un ~*, as deaf as a post; (fig.) *découvrir le ~ aux roses*, to discover the ugly truth; (fig.) *c'est le ~ de terre contre le ~ de fer*, it's an unequal struggle; *à la fortune du ~*, pot luck; (fig.) *faire le ~ à deux anses*, to have a lady on each arm; (fig.) ~ *au noir*, a hopeless muddle, a murky business; (fig.) *faire bouillir le ~*, to keep the pot boiling; *il n'y a si vilain ~ qui ne trouve son couvercle*, every Jack must have his Jill.
potable [pɔtabl] *adj.* potable, drinkable; (fig.) tolerable; *eau ~*, drinking water.
potache [pɔtaʃ] *s.m.* (fam.) schoolboy.
potage [pɔtaʒ] *s.m.* soup; (fig.) *pour tout ~*, all told.
potager [pɔtaʒe] *s.m.* vegetable or kitchen garden.
potag-er, -ère [pɔtaʒe] *adj.* (of herbs, etc.) culinary, comestible, used in cooking.
potamot [pɔtamo], **potamogéton** [pɔtamɔʒetɔ̃] *s.m.* (bot.) pond-weed.
potard [pɔtar] *s.m.* (fam.) chemist, druggist.
potasse [pɔtas] *s.f.* potash.
potasser [pɔtase] *v.t.* (fam.) to study hard, to swot, (at).
potassique [pɔtasik] *adj.* potassic.
potassium [pɔtasjɔm] *s.m.* (chem.) potassium.
pot-au-feu [pɔtofø] *s.m.* beef stew with vegetables; stewing-steak; ~ *adj.invar.* stay-at-home.
pote [pɔt] *s.m.* (pop.) friend, pal, mate.
poteau (pl. **-x**) [pɔto] *s.m.* **1.** post, stake; starting-post; ~ *télégraphique*, telegraph-pole; **2.** (pop.) = POTE.
potée [pɔte] *s.f.* **1.** jugful, potful; (fig.) large quantity; **2.** stew of boiled beef or pork and vegetables; **3.** (techn.) powder, solution, preparation, (for industrial use, esp. polishing); (metall.) luting loam.
potelé, -e [pɔtle] *adj.* plump, chubby.
potence [pɔtɑ̃s] *s.f.* gallows, gibbet; bracket, cross-piece, T-piece; *en ~*, T-shaped; *gibier de ~*, gaolbird, gallows-bird.
potentat [pɔtɑ̃ta] *s.m.* potentate; (fig.) powerful figure, tyrant.
potentialité [pɔtɑ̃sjalite] *s.f.* potentiality, possibility.
potentiel, -le [pɔtɑ̃sjɛl] *adj.* potential; ~ *s.m.* potential, potentialities; **~lement** [pɔtɑ̃sjɛlmɑ̃] *adv.* potentially.
potentille [pɔtɑ̃tij] *s.f.* (bot.) potentilla, cinquefoil.
potentiomètre [pɔtɑ̃sjɔmɛtr] *s.m.* (electr.) potentiometer.
poterie [pɔtri] *s.f.* pottery, earthenware; (domestic) hollow-ware; pottery works; ~ *de cuivre*, copperware.
poterne [pɔtɛrn] *s.f.* postern, postern-gate.
potiche [pɔtiʃ] *s.f.* **1.** Chinese or Japanese porcelain vase; **2.** (fig.) figure-head (person).
potier [pɔtje] *s.m.* potter; manufacturer of earthenware; seller of earthenware.
potin [pɔtɛ̃] *s.m.* **1.** (usu. pl.) gossip, scandal; **2.** row, noise, rumpus.
potiner [pɔtine] *v.i.* to gossip.
potini-er, -ère [pɔtinje] *adj.*, *s.m.f.* (person) given to gossip or scandal-mongering.
potinière [pɔtinjɛr] *s.f.* gossip-shop.
potion [pɔsjɔ̃] *s.f.* potion, draught.
potiron [pɔtirɔ̃] *s.m.* (bot.) pumpkin.
pot-pourri [popuri] *s.m.* **1.** (cook.) hot-pot; **2.** hotchpotch, medley.
potron-jaquet [pɔtrɔ̃ʒakɛ], **potron-minet** [pɔtrɔ̃minɛ] *s.m.* dawn; *dès ~*, at peep of day.
pou (pl. **-x**) [pu] *s.m.* louse; *laid comme un ~*, as ugly as sin; (fig.) *chercher des ~x à qn.*, or *dans la tête de qn.*, to pick a quarrel with s.o.; *chercher des*

~x parmi la paille, to look for a needle in a haystack.

pouacre [pwakr] *adj., s.m.f.* filthy, repulsive, hideous (person).

pouah [pwa] *interj.* expressing disgust or scorn.

poubelle [pubɛl] *s.f.* dustbin, refuse-bin; (fig.) *jeter à la ~*, to throw out, to consign to the waste-paper basket.

pouce [pus] *s.m.* thumb; big toe; inch; *mettre les ~s*, to give in; to throw up the sponge; *manger sur le ~*, to take a snack; (pop.) *et le ~!*, and a good bit more!; *se tourner les ~s*, to twiddle one's thumbs, to sit idle; *donner un coup de ~ à qn.*, to help s.o. on; *donner le coup de ~*, to put the finishing touches.

poucier [pusje] *s.m.* **1.** thumb-stall; **2.** thumb-piece (of door-latch).

pou-de-soie, pou(l)t-de-soie [pudəswa] *s.m.* (text.) paduasoy.

pouding see PUDDING.

poudingue [pudɛ̃g] *s.m.* (geol.) pudding-stone.

poudre [pudr] *s.f.* powder, dust; gunpowder; *sucre en ~*, granulated sugar; *~ de riz*, rice-powder, face-powder; *~ de perlimpinpin*, nostrum; quack powder; *coton-~*, gun-cotton; *soute aux ~s*, powder-magazine; *~ aux yeux*, bluff, eyewash; *jeter de la ~ aux yeux*, to bluff, to blind (s.o.) to the facts, to throw dust in (someone's) eyes; *mettre le feu aux ~s*, (fig.) to ignite the powder barrel, to set the place on fire; (fig.) *ça sent la ~*, it is a tense or highly-charged situation; *il n'a pas inventé la ~*, he is not very bright; *tirer sa ~ aux moineaux*, to waste powder and shot; *réduire en ~*, to grind, to pulverize.

poudrer [pudre] *v.t.* to powder, to sprinkle with powder or dust, to dust, to cover with dust; **se ~** *v.refl.* to powder oneself, to use powder.

poudrerie [pudrəri] *s.f.* gunpowder-works.

poudrette [pudrɛt] *s.f.* dried night-soil; rubber waste (ground up for recycling).

poudreuse [pudrøz] *s.f.* sugar-sifter; (agric.) powder-sprinkler.

poudreu-x, -se [pudrø] *adj.* dusty, powdery; *neige ~se*, powder snow.

poudrier [pudrije] *s.m.* powder-box.

poudrière [pudrijɛr] *s.f.* (lit. & fig.) powder-magazine.

poudroiement [pudrwamɑ̃] *s.m.* clouds of dust, dusty haze.

poudroyer [pudrwaje] *v.i.* to throw up clouds of dust, to show a dusty haze.

pouf [puf] *interj.* (noise of falling) plump!, bump!, plop!; (child. lang.) *faire ~*, to fall down.

pouf [puf] *s.m.* **1.** pouffe; **2.** pad, bustle (in dress).

pouffer [pufe] *v.i.* *~ de rire*, to burst out laughing; to guffaw.

pouf(f)iasse [pufjas] *s.f.* (vulg.) prostitute; slut.

pouillard [pujar] *s.m.* young partridge; young pheasant.

pouillerie [pujri] *s.f.* squalor.

pouilles [puj] *s.f.pl.* *chanter ~ à qn.*, to jeer at s.o., to make offensive remarks to s.o.

pouilleu-x, -se [pujø] *adj., s.m.f.* lousy, filthy, wretched (person); *adj.* (geog.) dry, barren.

pouillot [pujo] *s.m.* (ornith.) willow warbler.

poulailler [pulɑje] *s.m.* **1.** hen-house, hen-roost, fowl-house; **2.** (fig., theatr.) gallery, 'gods'.

poulain [pulɛ̃] *s.m.* **1.** foal, colt; (fig.) student, beginner, up-and-coming writer, etc.; (sport) colt, promising young player; **2.** skid (for unloading casks, etc.); **3.** (naut.) fender, collision-mat.

poulaine [pulɛn] *s.f.* **1.** (naut.) prow, head; latrine, 'heads'; **2.** medieval fashion for shoes; *souliers à la ~*, long-pointed shoes.

poularde [pulard] *s.f.* fattened pullet.

poule [pul] *s.f.* **1.** hen; fowl; (fam.) girl of loose morals, tart, mistress; (fam.) girl, woman; *~ d'eau*, moorhen; *la ~ aux œufs d'or*, the goose that lays the golden eggs; (fig.) *~ mouillée*, timid, cowardly person; *chair de ~*, goose-flesh; *ça me donne la chair de ~*, it gives me the creeps; **2.** (billiards, cards, etc.) pool, kitty; (sport) competition, tournament, pool.

poulet [pulɛ] *s.m.* **1.** chicken; fowl; *~ de grain*, corn-fed chicken; **2.** (obs.) love-letter, short note; **3.** (fam.) policeman.

poulette [pulɛt] *s.f.* pullet; (fam.) girl, young woman; *sauce ~*, a kind of white sauce.

pouliche [puliʃ] *s.f.* filly.

poulie [puli] *s.f.* pulley; block.

pouliner [puline] *v.i.* (of mares) to foal.

poulinière [pulinjɛr] *adj.f., s.f.* brood-(mare).

pouliot [puljo] *s.m.* (bot.) pennyroyal.

poulot, -te [pulo] *s.m.f.* (fam.) term of affection to a child.

poulpe [pulp] *s.m.* (zool.) octopus.

pouls [pu] *s.m.* pulse; *tâter le ~ de*, to take the pulse of, (fig.) to check the state of, to test; (fig.) *se tâter le ~*, to think carefully (before acting).

poumon [pumɔ̃] *s.m.* lung; *~ d'acier*, iron lung; *à pleins ~s*, (of breathing) deeply; at the top of one's voice.

poupard [pupar] *s.m.* chubby baby; (obs.) baby doll.

poupe [pup] *s.f.* (naut.) stern, poop; *avoir le vent en ~*, to sail before the wind; (fig.) to be in luck's way; to be in favour.

poupée [pupe] *s.f.* **1.** doll; figure, (shooting) figure-target; pretty, empty-headed woman; young woman; girl; bandaged finger; **2.** headstock (of lathe).

poupin, -e [pupɛ̃] *adj.* doll-like.

poupon [pupɔ̃] *s.m.* infant, baby, small child.

pouponnière [pupɔnjɛr] *s.f.* day-nursery, crêche.

pour [pur] *prep.* **1.** for, for the sake of; in favour of, pro, on the side of; *faites-le ~ moi*, do it for me, for my sake; *je suis ~*, I am in favour; *il n'est pas ~ eux*, he is not on their side; **2.** for, in exchange for; instead of; as; *en avoir ~ son argent*, to get one's money's worth; *œil ~ œil*, an eye for an eye; *je l'ai eu ~ rien*, I got it for nothing; *~ si peu*, for so little, for so small a thing; *~ toute réponse il me tourna le dos*, his only reply was to turn his back on me; *il l'a pris ~ un imbécile*, he took him for a fool; *je la prendrai ~ femme*, I shall take her as my wife; *avoir ~ résultat*, to have as a result; **3.** as for, as to, as far as (sth. or s.o.) is concerned; *~ moi, je crois*, personally, I think; *~ ce qui est de cela*, as far as that is concerned; **4.** for, intended for, to, so as to, in order to; for (the possibility that); *c'est ~ son bien*, it is for his own good; *trop jeune ~ le savoir*, too young to know it; *jouer ~ la galerie*, to play to the gallery; *~ rire*, for fun, for a joke; *~ ainsi dire*, so to speak, as it were; *~ ne pas le rencontrer*, so as not to meet him; *~ de vrai* or *de bon*, genuine, the real thing; **5.** for, to, towards; *partir ~ l'Orient*, to set off for the East; **6.** for, for the reason that, through, because of; by reason or nature of; *~ avoir perdu son passeport il dut attendre une semaine*, through having lost his passport he had to wait a week; *et ~ cause*, and with good reason; *il l'épousa ~ ses beaux yeux*, he married her for her looks; **7.** seeing that, although, in spite of the fact that; *~ avoir passé deux ans en France, il ne parle pas couramment*, although, seeing that, he has spent two years in France, he doesn't speak fluently; **8.** for, as though; *laissé ~ mort*, left for dead; **9.** *~ que, conj.*, so that, in order that; for . . . to; *je te le dis ~ que tu puisses le savoir*, I am telling it you so that you should know; *c'est trop difficile ~ qu'on le comprenne*, it is too difficult for people to grasp; **10.** *~ intelligents que soient les hommes*, however intelligent mankind may be; *~ peu que*, if ever, if . . . so much as; *~ peu que vous hésitiez*, if you hesitate but for a moment, if you so much as hesitate; ~ *s.m.* good point, advantage; *le ~ et le contre*, the pros and cons.

pourboire [purbwar] *s.m.* tip; gratuity.

pourceau (pl. **-x**) [purso] *s.m.* (lit. & fig.) hog, pig, swine; *~ de mer*, porpoise.

pourcentage [pursɑ̃taʒ] *s.m.* percentage.

pourchasser [purʃase] *v.t.* to pursue, to chase after.

pourfendeur [purfɑ̃dœr] *s.m.* killer, one who commits acts of violence.

pourfendre [purfɑ̃dr] *v.t.* **1.** (obs.) to cleave asunder; **2.** to do violence to, to smash up.

pourlécher [purleʃe] *v.t.* to lick all over; **se ~** *v.refl.* to lick one's lips.

pourparler [purparle] *s.m.* (usu. pl.) parley, negotiations; (diplomatic) conversations.

pourpier [purpje] *s.m.* (bot.) purslane.

pourpoint [purpwɛ̃] *s.m.* doublet.

pourpre [purpr] *s.f.* deep red; (fig.) purple, sovereign dignity; (herald.) purpure; (pathol.) purpura, purples; (moll.) murex.

pourpre [purpr] *adj.* deep red, purple-red, crimson, scarlet, ruby; ⚠ not 'purple' as a shade of blue or violet.

pourpré, -e [purpre] *adj.* = POURPRE *adj.*

pourquoi [purkwa] *conj.*, *adv.* why; what for; for what reason; *voilà ~*, that's why; *~ pas?*, why not?; ~ *s.m.* the reason why; the why and the wherefore.

pourri, -e [puri] *adj.* rotten, decayed, putrid, dank; *être ~ de préjugés*, to be steeped in prejudice.

pourrir [purir] *v.i.* to rot, to decay, to putrefy, to become rotten, to go bad; (fig.) to deteriorate, to rot away; ~ *v.t.* to rot, to corrupt, to spoil, to ruin; to infect (with gangrene); **se ~** *v.refl.* to deteriorate.

pourrissement [purismɑ̃] *s.m.* deterioration, worsening.

pourriture [purityr] *s.f.* rottenness, rot, putrefaction, decay, corruption; utterly corrupt person; *~ d'hôpital*, gangrene.

poursuite [pursɥit] *s.f.* pursuit, chase; tracking (of criminal, of space-ship); (law) (often pl.), suit, proceedings, legal action.

poursuivant, -e [pursɥivɑ̃] *s.m.f.* **1.** applicant; suitor, prosecutor, plaintiff; **2.** pursuer.

poursuivre [pursɥivr] *v.t.* to pursue, to follow, to chase, to seek; to harry, to persecute; never to leave alone; to sue, to prosecute, to proceed against; *~ son chemin*, to go one's way; *~ son discours*, to proceed with one's speech; *~ en justice*, to prosecute, to sue, to take proceedings against; *~ au civil*, to take a civil action against.

pourtant [purtɑ̃] *adv.* however, yet, still, all the same.

pourtour [purtur] *s.m.* circumference, periphery; outer edge.

pourvoi [purvwa] *s.m.* (law) appeal.

pourvoir [purvwar] *v.i.* *~ à*, to provide for, to make provision for, to see to, to supply, to fill (vacancy, need, etc.); *~ aux besoins de qn.*, to supply someone's needs; ~ *v.t.* to provide, to supply, to equip; to provide for; *~ qn. d'un emploi*, to provide s.o. with a job; *~ une place de munitions*, to supply a fortress with munitions; *~ son fils*, to provide for one's son; *être pourvu de*, to be supplied, provided, or equipped with, to be in possession of; **se ~** *v.refl.* to supply oneself (*de*, with); (law) to appeal, to lodge an appeal.

pourvoyeu-r, -se [purvwajœr] *s.m.f.* provider, purveyor; caterer, contractor; **~r** *s.m.* (mil.) gun-server.

pourvu que [purvykə] *conj.loc.* provided, provided that, as long as.

poussah [pusa] *s.m.* (toy) tumbler, skipjack; (fig.) fat little man.

pousse [pus] *s.f.* shoot, sprout; growth; (vet.) heaves, broken wind; over-fermentation (of wine).

pousse-café [puskafe] *s.m.invar.* liqueur taken with coffee; **~-cailloux** [puskaju] *s.m.invar.* (obs.) (mil. slang) infantryman, foot-slogger.

poussée [puse] *s.f.* push, pushing, shove, thrust; pressure.

pousse(-pousse) [pus(pus)] *s.m.invar.* rickshaw.

pousser [puse] *v.t.* **1.** to push, to shove, to impel, to propel, to drive on; to advance, to further, to promote; to compel, to urge, to incite, to provoke; *~ une porte*, to push open a door; *quelque diable me pousse*, some devil is driving me on; *~ qn. à bout*, to exasperate s.o.; *~ qch. trop loin*, to carry sth. too far; *~ une discussion*, to promote a discussion; *~ une enquête*, to pursue an inquiry; *~ qn. à faire qch.*, to incite s.o. to do sth.; **2.** to utter; *~ un cri*, to utter a cry; *~ un soupir*, to heave a sigh; *~ un hurlement*, to let out a yell; ~ *v.i.* **1.** to push, to press, to put on pressure; to push on; *~ de toutes ses forces*, to push with all one's might; *les conditions poussent à une hausse des prix*, conditions are forcing prices upwards; *~ plus loin*, to push on further; **2.** to grow, to shoot, to spring up; to appear; (of wine) to ferment; *un désert où rien ne pousse*, a desert where nothing grows; *l'herbe avait poussé partout*, grass had sprung up everywhere; *une dent pousse*, there is a tooth coming through; **se ~** *v.refl.* to push oneself forward, to make one's way (in society, etc.).

poussier [pusje] *s.m.* coal-dust.

poussière [pusjɛr] *s.f.* dust, powder; great number or diversity; (fam.) trifle.

poussiéreu-x, -se *adj.* dusty.

poussi-f, -ve [pusif] *adj.* wheezy, short of breath; (vet.) broken-winded.

poussin [pusɛ̃] *s.m.* chick, chicken.

poussinière [pusinjɛr] *s.f.* chicken-coop; incubator.

poussoir [puswar] *s.m.* (push-)button, bell-push.

poutre [putr] *s.f.* beam; girder.

poutrelle [putrɛl] *s.f.* small beam.

pouvoir [puvwar] *v.t.* **1.** to be able, to have (the) power; *je peux le porter*, I can carry it; *je le peux*, I can (do it); *il a pu le sauver*, he was able to save it; *il est on ne peut plus serviable*; he is as obliging as could be; **2.** to be allowed (can, may); *on ne peut pas l'abandonner*, you can't abandon him; *tu pourras sortir plus tard*, you may go out later; **3.** *il a pu le faire*, he may have, could have, done it; *il aurait pu y être*, he could have, might have, been there; **4.** (expressing wish) *puisse le ciel te protéger!*, may heaven protect you!; **se ~** *v.refl.* to be possible; *il se peut que*, it is possible that, it may be that.

pouvoir [puvwar] *s.m.* power, might, force, ability, capacity, authority, right; government, command, authorities; (law) power of attorney; *je ferai tout ce qui est en mon ~*, I will do my utmost; *arriver au ~*, to come into power; to achieve power.

pouzzolane [pudzɔlan] *s.f.* pozzolana.

P.P. [pepe] abbrev. *port payé*.

P.P.C.M. [pepeseɛm] abbrev. (math.) *plus petit commun multiple*, L.C.M.

pragmat-ique [pragmatik] *adj.* pragmatic(al); **~isme** [pragmatism] *s.m.* pragmatism.

prairial [prɛrjal] *s.m.* (hist.) Prairial (ninth month in Fr. Republican Calendar, May–June).

prairie [prɛri] *s.f.* meadow, grassland, pasture; (geog.) *les Prairies*, the Prairies (of North America); ⚠ not 'prairie' except as prop. geog. name.

praline [pralin] *s.f.* burnt almond, praline.

praliné [praline] *s.m.* chocolate almonds, praline paste.

prame [pram] *s.f.* (naut.) pram, flat-bottomed boat.

praticabilité [pratikabilite] *s.f.* practicability.

praticable [pratikabl] *adj.* practicable, viable, usable; (theatr.) *porte* ~, door that can be used; ~ *s.m.* (theatr.) framework (for scenery, lighting).

praticien, -ne [pratisjɛ̃] *s.m.f.* **1.** practitioner (opp. theorist); **2.** (sculpt.) sculptor's assistant, rougher-out.

pratiquant, -e [pratikɑ̃] *adj.* (of Christian, etc.) practising, churchgoing; *s.m.f.* churchgoer.

pratique [pratik] *s.f.* **1.** practice, execution, dealing, way of doing things, knack; observance, experience, performance; habit, routine; frequenting, association (*de*, with); (naut.) pratique; *avoir la libre* ~, to be free of quarantine; *donner libre* ~, to admit to pratique; *mettre en* ~, to put into practice; to carry out; *terme de* ~, legal term; *en* ~, by rule of thumb; **2.** practice, custom; customer; *avoir beaucoup de* ~*s*, to have many customers; to do good business; **3.** whistle (as used by Punch-and-Judy man, etc., to distort voice).

pratique [pratik] *adj.* practical, matter-of-fact; convenient, practicable, feasible; experienced, skilful; ~**ment** [pratikmɑ̃] *adv.* practically, in practice, in fact, virtually.

pratiquer [pratike] *v.t.* to practise, to carry out, to exercise; to frequent, to visit frequently; to associate with; to make (opening, hole, etc.); to open (road, etc.); (mining) to pierce (gallery, etc.); to execute; ~ *une opération*, to perform an operation; **se** ~ *v.refl.* to be done, to be customary, to be practised.

pré [pre] *s.m.* meadow, pasture; (fig.) *aller sur le* ~, to fight a duel.

préalable [prealabl] *adj.* previous, preliminary; *au* ~, first; previously; before going any further; ~**ment** [prealabləmɑ̃] *adv.* first, previously.

préambule [preɑ̃byl] *s.m.* preamble; prelude.

préau (pl. **-x**) [preo] *s.m.* courtyard, covered playground.

préavis [preavi] *s.m.* forewarning.

prébende [prebɑ̃d] *s.f.* prebend.

prébendier [prebɑ̃dje] *s.m.* prebendary.

précaire [prekɛr] *adj.* precarious, uncertain; ~**ment** [prekɛrmɑ̃] *adv.* precariously.

précarité [prekarite] *s.f.* precariousness.

précaution [prekosjɔ̃] *s.f.* precaution, foresight, caution, prudence, care, wariness; *prendre des* or *ses* ~*s*, to take precautions; to play for safety; *user de* ~*s*, to proceed warily, to behave cautiously; *par* ~, as a precaution.

précautionner [prekosjɔne] *v.t.* to forewarn, to caution; **se** ~ *v.refl.* to take precautions, to guard (*contre*, against); *se* ~ *de*, to provide oneself with (sth. in advance).

précautionneu-x, -se [prekosjɔnø] *adj.* wary, cautious.

précédemment [presedamɑ̃] *adv.* previously, before.

précédent, -e [presedɑ̃] *adj.* previous, preceding, precedent, former; ~ *s.m.* precedent, previous case taken as example or justification; *sans* ~, unprecedented, unexampled.

précéder [presede] *v.t.* to precede, to happen before, to go before; to go in front of; to take precedence of; *les mots qui précèdent*, the words that precede (this sentence); *ce qui précède*, the foregoing.

préceinte [presɛ̃t] *s.f.* (naut.) wale (of ship).

précepte [presɛpt] *s.m.* precept.

précept-eur, -rice [presɛptœr] *s.m.f.* tutor; teacher; ~**rice** *s.f.* governess.

préceptorat [presɛptɔra] *s.m.* tutorship, preceptorship.

précession [presesjɔ̃] *s.f.* (astron.) precession; ~ *des équinoxes*, precession of the equinoxes.

prêche [prɛʃ] *s.m.* sermon, preaching; (fam.) lecture.

prêcher [preʃe] *v.t.i.* to preach, to preach upon; to sermonize; to preach to; ~ *l'Évangile*, to preach the gospel; ~ *d'exemple*, to practise what one preaches; ~ *pour son saint*, to have an eye to one's own interest; ~ *dans le désert*, to preach in the wilderness, to talk to deaf ears; ~ *les infidèles*, to preach to the heathen.

prêcheu-r, -se [prɛʃœr] *adj.* preaching; (fig.) given to preaching (at people); *les frères* ~*rs*, the Dominicans; *s.m.f.* (obs.) preacher.

prêchi-prêcha [prɛʃiprɛʃa] *s.m.* (fam.) rambling-on, drivel; sermonizing.

précieu-x, -se [presjø] *adj.* **1.** precious, valuable, costly, rare, esteemed; *pierres* ~*ses*, precious stones, gems; **2.** precious, affected, over-elaborate, over-refined; ~**x** *s.m.* preciosity, affectedness, affected style; ~**se** *s.f.* (17th cent.) *une Précieuse*, a Précieuse, a woman of affected literary tastes and conversational style; ~**sement** [presjøzmɑ̃] *adv.* **1.** preciously, with great care; *garder* ~*sement*, to treasure up; **2.** in an affected or precious way.

préciosité [presjozite] *s.f.* preciosity, affectedness, affectation.

précipice [presipis] *s.m.* precipice, abyss, chasm, deep gorge; (fig.) ruin, disaster.

précipitamment [presipitamɑ̃] *adv.* hastily, precipitately, rashly, headlong.

précipitant [presipitɑ̃] *s.m.* (chem.) precipitant.

précipitation [presipitɑsjɔ̃] *s.f.* precipitation, haste, hurry, precipitancy; (chem.) precipitation; *avec trop de* ~, over-hastily.

précipité [presipite] *s.m.* (chem.) precipitate.

précipité, -e [presipite] *adj.* precipitate, precipitated, hurried, hasty, sudden, headlong; *départ* ~, hurried departure; *course* ~*e*, headlong flight; *à pas* ~*s*, with hurried steps.

précipiter [presipite] *v.t.* **1.** to precipitate, to hurl, to fling, to throw or dash down, to plunge; **2.** to hasten, to hurry, to urge, to quicken; ~ *ses pas*, to hurry along; *il ne faut rien* ~, never do things in a hurry; **3.** (chem.) to precipitate, to form a precipitate; **se** ~ *v.refl.* **1.** to throw oneself headlong; to rush down; **2.** to rush on, to hasten, to hurry, to accelerate; to be precipitate.

préciput [presipy] *s.m.* (law) preference legacy.

précis, -e [presi] *adj.* precise, accurate, exact, fixed, formal, concise, terse; ~ *s.m.* summary, précis; compendium, manual; ~**ément** [presizemɑ̃] *adv.* precisely, exactly, accurately; just so, (just) as it happens; *c'est* ~*ément mon jour de repos*, it is, as it happens, my day off.

préciser [presize] *v.t.* to state precisely, to specify, to define; to be explicit.

précision [presizjɔ̃] *s.f.* precision, preciseness, accuracy; *demander des* ~*s*, to ask for further details, for full particulars.

précité, -e [presite] *adj.* aforementioned, above-mentioned, aforesaid.

précoce [prekɔs] *adj.* precocious, early; forward; premature; *fruits* ~*s*, early fruit; *mort* ~, premature death; *esprit* ~, precocious mind, precociousness; ~**ment** [prekɔsmɑ̃] *adv.* precociously, prematurely, (too) early.

précocité [prekɔsite] *s.f.* precociousness, precocity, earliness, forwardness.

précolombien, -ne [prekɔlɔ̃bjɛ̃] *adj.* pre-Columbian.

précombustion [prekɔ̃bystjɔ̃] *s.f.* precombustion.
précompte [prekɔ̃t] *s.m.* previous deduction (from account or remuneration).
préconception [prekɔ̃sɛpsjɔ̃] *s.f.* preconception.
préconçu, -e [prekɔ̃sy] *adj.* preconceived.
préconisation [prekɔnizɑsjɔ̃] *s.f.* preconization, commendation.
préconiser [prekɔnize] *v.t.* **1.** (eccles.) to preconize, to commend; **2.** to praise, to extol, to advocate, to recommend.
précontraint, -e [prekɔ̃trɛ̃] *adj.*, *s.m.* pre-stressed (concrete).
précontrainte [prekɔ̃trɛ̃t] *s.f.* pre-stressing.
précurseur [prekyrsœr] *s.m.* forerunner, harbinger, precursor; ~ *adj.m.* precursory, premonitory; (mil.) *détachement* ~, advance party.
prédat-eur, -rice [predatœr] *s.m.f.* **1.** (obs.) pillager, looter; **2.** (zool.) predator; ~ *adj.* predatory.
prédécesseur [predesɛsœr] *s.m.* predecessor, ancestor, precursor.
prédestination [predɛstinɑsjɔ̃] *s.f.* predestination.
prédestiné, -e [predɛstine] *adj.* predestined; predetermined; reserved, prepared, (*à*, for), elect; *s.m.f.* one of the elect or predestined.
prédestiner [predɛstine] *v.t.* to predestinate, to foredoom; to predetermine, to preordain, to predestine.
prédétermin-ation [predetɛrminɑsjɔ̃] *s.f.* predetermination; **~er** [predetɛrmine] *v.t.* to predetermine; **~ism** [predetɛrminism] *s.m.* predeterminism.
prédicant [predikɑ̃] *s.m.* preacher; Protestant clergyman; ~ *adj.* given to moralizing.
prédicat [predika] *s.m.* (gram., logic) predicate.
prédicat-eur, -rice [predikatœr] *s.m.f.* preacher, religious orator; predicant.
prédication [predikɑsjɔ̃] *s.f.* preaching; sermon.
prédiction [prediksjɔ̃] *s.f.* prediction, foretelling, prophecy.
prédigéré, -e [prediʒere] *adj.* (of milk, etc.) pre-digested.
prédilection [predilɛksjɔ̃] *s.f.* predilection, preference, partiality; foible, weakness; *avoir une* ~ *pour*, to be partial to; *mes livres de* ~, my favourite books.
prédire [predir] *v.t.* to predict, to foretell, to prophesy; *je vous l'avais prédit*, I told you it would happen, I warned you.
prédisposer [predispoze] *v.t.* to predispose, to influence, to prejudice; ~ *à*, to predispose to, to incline (s.o.) to; *être prédisposé à*, to be predisposed or inclined to, to have a tendency to, to be in the right frame of mind for.
prédisposition [predispozisjɔ̃] *s.f.* predisposition, propensity, tendency; bias.
prédominance [predɔminɑ̃s] *s.f.* predominance, ascendancy.
prédominant, -e [predɔminɑ̃] *adj.* predominant, prevalent, prevailing.
prédominer [predɔmine] *v.i.* to predominate, to prevail (over).
préemballé, -e [preɑ̃bale] *adj.* pre-packed.
prééminence [preeminɑ̃s] *s.f.* pre-eminence, precedence.
prééminent, -e [preeminɑ̃] *adj.* pre-eminent.
préemption [preɑ̃psjɔ̃] *s.f.* pre-emption.
préencollé, -e [preɑ̃kɔle] *adj.* (of wallpaper, etc.) pre-pasted.
préenquête [preɑ̃kɛt] *s.f.* pre-testing (of TV commercial on sample public).
préétabli, -e [preetabli] *adj.* pre-established; pre-arranged.
préexistant, -e [preɛgzistɑ̃] *adj.* pre-existent, pre-existing.
préexistence [preɛgzistɑ̃s] *s.f.* pre-existence.
préexister [preɛgziste] *v.i.* to pre-exist.
préfabrication [prefabrikɑsjɔ̃] *s.f.* prefabrication.
préfabriqué, -e [prefabrike] *adj.* prefabricated.
préface [prefas] *s.f.* preface, introduction (to book).
préfacer [prefase] *v.t.* to preface.
préfacier [prefasje] *s.m* author of preface.
préfectoral, -e, (aux) [prefektɔral] *adj.* prefectorial, prefectoral, pertaining to a French *préfet.*
préfecture [prefɛktyr] *s.f.* prefecture; place of residence of a *préfet*, county town; ~ *de police*, police headquarters (in Paris); ~ *maritime*, naval port; centre of administration of maritime district.
préférable [preferabl] *adj.* preferable, better; **~ment** [preferabləmɑ̃] *adv.* preferably, in preference.
préféré, -e [prefere] *adj.*, *s.m.f.* favourite, preferred (person or thing).
préférence [preferɑ̃s] *s.f.* preference; preferential position or treatment; *de* ~, preferably; *par* ~ *à*, in preference to.
préférer [prefere] *v.t.* to prefer, to value higher, to put (sth.) above (sth.); *je préfère rester ici*, I prefer to, I would rather, stay here; *il préfère sa tranquillité à tout*, he puts his peace and quiet before everything else.
préfet [prefɛ] *s.m.* prefect, head, chief administrator of a district or county (in France); ~ *des études*, vice-principal in a school; director of studies; ~ *maritime*, chief administrator of maritime district; ~ *de police* (in Paris), head of Paris police, prefect of police.
préfète [prefɛt] *s.f.* wife of a *préfet.*
préfix, -e [prefiks] *adj.* (law) predetermined, (of day, etc.) appointed; stipulated.
préfixe [prefiks] *s.m.* (gram.) prefix.
préfixer [prefikse] *v.t.* to prefix.
prégnant, -e [preɲɑ̃] *adj.* (phil., lang.) pregnant; ⚠ not 'pregnant' in physiol. sense.
préhenseur [preɑ̃sœr] *adj.m.*, **préhensile** [preɑ̃sil] *adj.* (zool.) prehensile.
préhension [preɑ̃sjɔ̃] *s.f.* prehension.
préhistoire [preistwar] *s.f.* prehistory.
préhistorien, -ne [preistɔrjɛ̃] *s.m.f.* prehistorian.
préhistorique [preistɔrik] *adj.* prehistoric, primeval; (fig.) ancient, very old-fashioned.
préjudice [preʒydis] *s.m.* damage, detriment, wrong, hurt, harm, injury, prejudice; *porter* ~ *à qn.*, to wrong s.o.; *le* ~ *qu'on lui a causé*, the harm which has been done to him; *sans* ~ *de mes droits*, without prejudice to my claims; ⚠ not 'prejudice' in sense 'bias' or 'preconceived idea'.
préjudiciable [preʒydisjabl] *adj.* detrimental, prejudicial, injurious.
préjudiciel, -le [preʒydisjɛl] *adj.* (law) interlocutory.
préjudicier [preʒudisje] *v.i.* to be prejudicial, to be detrimental; ~ *à*, to harm, to hurt, to injure, (cause, etc.).
préjugé [preʒyʒe] *s.m.* presumption, prejudice, bias, preconceived idea, prepossession; (law) precedent.
préjuger [preʒyʒe] *v.t.* (more usu. ~ *de*) to prejudge.
prélart [prelar] *s.m.* (naut.) tarpaulin.
(se) prélasser [prelɑse] *v.refl.* to take one's ease, to lounge, to loll, to relax.
prelat [prela] *s.m.* prelate.
prélature [prelatyr] *s.f.* prelature; prelates collectively.
prèle, prêle, presle [prɛl] *s.f.* (bot.) horsetail.
prélegs [prelɛ] *s.m.* preferential legacy.
prélèvement [prelɛvmɑ̃] *s.m.* previous deduction; the substance or sum taken or deducted;

taking (of sample, etc.); sample; ~ *de sang*, (taking of) blood-sample.

prélever [prelve] *v.t.* to deduct previously, to take first, to reserve, to levy, to take (sample); ~ *sur*, to make a deduction from.

préliminaire [preliminɛr] *adj.* preliminary, introductory; **~s** *s.m.pl.* preliminaries.

prélude [prelyd] *s.m.* (mus. & fig.) prelude.

préluder [prelyde] *v.i.* (mus.) to begin (with a prelude); to tune up (with a prelude); ~ *par*, to begin with (song, etc.), to sing (song, etc.) as a prelude; ~ *v.t.* ~ *à*, to lead up to, to be an introduction to or preparation for, to precede, to be a prelude to.

prématuré, -e [prematyre] *adj.* premature; untimely; *s.m.f.* premature child; **~ment** [prematyremɑ̃] *adv.* prematurely.

préméditation [premeditɑsjɔ̃] *s.f.* premeditation; (law) malice prepense; *avec* ~, wilfully, deliberately; with malice aforethought.

prémédité, -e [premedite] *adj.* premeditated, deliberate.

préméditer [premedite] *v.t.* to premeditate, to plan; ~ *de faire*, to plan to do.

prémices [premis] *s.f.pl.* first-fruits; (fig.) beginning, first results, early promise.

premi-er, -ère [prəmje] *adj.* first, former (of two), foremost, best; prime, primary; primeval, early; original; leading, principal; (math.) prime; *nombres ~ers entre eux*, numbers prime to each other; *au ~er abord*, at first sight; *en ~er lieu*, in the first place, first; *matières ~ères*, raw materials; *de ~ère main*, first-hand; *~er-né(e)*, first-born; *le ~er venu*, the first comer; anyone; the man in the street; **~r** *s.m.* first floor; premier, prime minister; (theatr.) male lead; *en ~er*, senior, leading; **~èrement** [prəmjɛrmɑ̃] *adv.* first(ly), in the first place.

première [prəmjɛr] *s.f.* **1.** first race, etc.; (school) top class, fifth form; first-class (compartment, cabin, etc.); (theatr.) first night, première; (school) *entrer en* ~, to move up into the fifth form; *voyager en* ~, to travel first-class; *prendre des ~s*, to take first-class tickets; *de ~!*, first-class!, first rate!; **2.** (shoemaking) insole; **3.** (in dressm. establishment) forewoman; skilled couturière.

prémilitaire [premilitɛr] *adj.* premilitary.

prémisse [premis] *s.f.* (log.) premiss; (fig.) starting-point.

prémolaire [premɔlɛr] *s.f.* premolar (tooth).

prémonition [premɔnisjɔ̃] *s.f.* premonition, presentiment.

prémonitoire [premɔnitwar] *adj.* premonitory.

prémunir [premynir] *v.t.* to caution, to forewarn, to put (s.o.) on his guard; **se** ~ *v.refl.* to arm oneself, to provide (*contre*, against).

prenant, -e [prənɑ̃] *adj.* taking, receiving; prehensile; (fig.) captivating, fascinating; *queue ~e*, prehensile tail; *partie ~e*, payee.

prendre [prɑ̃dr] *v.t.* to take, to take up, to grasp, to lay hold of, to seize, to snatch; to apprehend, to catch; to fetch, to collect; to receive, to accept; to deal with; to manage; to adopt, to contract (a habit, etc.); to put on, to wear; to choose, to appoint, to name (a day); to charge (money); ~ *qch. à qn., à un tas, sur la table, dans sa poche*, to take sth. from s.o., from a pile, off the table, out of one's pocket; ~ *d'assaut*, to take by storm; *à tout* ~, on the whole; *autant de pris sur l'ennemi*, so much to the good; ~ *les armes*, to take up arms; ~ *la balle au bond*, to take the ball on the rebound; to seize the opportunity; *bien lui a pris de*, he was lucky to; ~ *garde*, to take care, to mind, to beware, to be on one's guard; ~ *place*, to take a seat; to take place, to happen; ~ *soin de*, to look after; ~ *pied*, to get a footing; *que je vous y prenne!*, let me catch you at it!; *qu'est-ce qui vous prend?*, what's the matter with you?, what has come over you?; *mal vous en prendra*, you'll be sorry; *je sors d'en* ~, I've been had that way once; *prenez-le comme vous voudrez*, you can take it as you like; *c'est à ~ ou à laisser*, there it is, take it or leave it; *le ~ de haut*, to be haughty, to get on one's high horse; ~ *son parti de quelque chose*, to make the best of something; ~ *son parti*, to make up one's mind; ~ *parti pour qn.*, to side with s.o.; *prenez que je n'aie rien dit*, let's suppose I said nothing; ~ *par le plus court*, to go the shortest way; ~ *naissance*, to take its rise, to begin, to start; ~ *le change*, to be thrown off the scent, to be taken in; *je viendrai vous ~ chez vous*, I will come and collect you from your house; (slang) *qu'est-ce qu'il va ~?*, he'll get it hot!; *prenez patience*, have patience; ~ *en mauvaise part*, to take amiss; ~ *en main*, to take in hand, to undertake, to manage; ~ *qn. par son faible*, to get round s.o.; ~ *qn. au mot*, to take s.o. at his word; *l'envie l'a pris de*, he took it into his head to, he was seized with a desire to; *je le prends pour ami*, (i.) I take him for a friend; (ii.) I consider him a friend; *pour qui me prenez-vous?*, what do you take me for?; *pris de vin*, tipsy; *être pris de vertige*, to have an attack of giddiness; ~ *v.i.* to thicken, to freeze over; to stick; (of fire) to catch; (of vaccination, etc.) to take; (of fashion) to catch on; to be believed; (of idea, etc.) to work; to go off in a direction, (of path, etc.) to begin, to turn off; *cette mode n'a jamais pris*, this fashion never caught on; *ça ne prend pas*, it doesn't work, it won't do, it won't wash; *au coin du bois prenez à gauche* or *sur la gauche*, at the corner of the wood turn left; *juste avant la poste un petit sentier prend à gauche*, just before the post office a little path goes off to the left; **se** ~ *v.refl.* to be held, to be caught, to take oneself, to be taken; to harden, to freeze over; (of food in saucepan) to catch; to start; to take (to); to take an interest (*à*, in); *se ~ par la main* to take oneself in hand; *se ~ par les cheveux*, to grab each other's hair; *se ~ pour un génie*, to think oneself a genius; *elle se prit à tousser*, she started to cough; *s'en ~ à qn.*, to be angry with s.o., to blame s.o., to attack s.o.; *se ~ d'amitié pour qn.*, to take a liking to s.o.; *savoir s'y* ~, to know how to set about it, how to deal with it.

preneu-r, -se [prənœr] *s.m.f.* taker; buyer, payee; lessee; purchaser.

prénom [prenɔ̃] *s.m.* Christian name, first name, forename.

prénommé, -e [prenɔme] *adj.* above-named, aforementioned.

préoccupant, -e [preɔkypɑ̃] *adj.* disquieting.

préoccupation [preɔkypɑsjɔ̃] *s.f.* preoccupation, anxiety, care; absorption, engrossment; obsession.

préoccupé, -e [preɔkype] *adj.* preoccupied, anxious, thoughtful, absorbed, engrossed (*de*, in).

préoccuper [preɔkype] *v.t.* to engross, to trouble, to cause anxiety to, to preoccupy; **se** ~ *v.refl.* to be concerned or worried (*de*, about).

préparat-eur, -rice [preparatœr] *s.m.f.* preparer, assistant.

préparatif [preparatif] *s.m.* (usu. pl.) preparations.

préparation [preparɑsjɔ̃] *s.f.* preparation, preparing; ~ *militaire*, pre-service training; *sans* ~, extempore.

préparatoire [preparatwar] *adj.* preparatory.

préparer [prepare] *v.t.* to prepare, to make ready, to arrange; **se** ~ *v.refl.* to prepare oneself, to get ready; to be imminent; *un orage se prépare*, there is a storm brewing; *il se prépare qch.*, there is something afoot.

prépayer [prepeje] *v.t.* to prepay.
prépondérance [prepɔ̃derɑ̃s] *s.f.* preponderance.
prépondérant, -e [prepɔ̃derɑ̃] *adj.* preponderant, dominant, leading; *jouer un rôle ~*, to play a leading part; *voix ~e*, casting vote.
préposé, -e [prepoze] *s.m.f.* **1.** person in charge; officer, clerk, attendant, etc.; *la ~e du vestiaire*, the cloakroom attendant; **2.** postman, postwoman.
préposer [prepoze] *v.t.* to set over; to put in charge (*à*, of); to appoint.
prépositi-f, -ve [prepozitif] *adj.* (gram.) prepositive, prepositional.
préposition [prepozisjɔ̃] *s.f.* (gram.) preposition.
prépuce [prepys] *s.m.* (anat.) prepuce, foreskin.
préraphaélite [prerafaelit] *adj.*, *s.m.* Pre-Raphaelite.
prérogative [prerɔgativ] *s.f.* prerogative, privilege.
près [prɛ] *adv.* near, by, hard by, close, close by; nearly, on the point of; *à beaucoup ~*, by far, by a long way; *ce n'est pas à beaucoup ~ la somme nécessaire*, it is nowhere near the sum required; *il se rappelait, à un liard ~, le prix*, he remembered the price to a penny; *à cela ~*, except for that, except on this point; *à peu de chose ~*, nearly; to within a trifle; about; *à peu ~*, nearly, nearly so, almost; pretty much; *c'est à peu ~ la même chose*, it is much the same thing; *au plus ~*, (naut.) close to the wind; *de ~*, close, near, intimately; (fig.) *ne pas y regarder de si ~*, not to be too particular; *rasé de ~*, clean-shaven; *serrer de ~*, to be hard upon, to press hard; to be very pressing; *tout ~*, close by, quite near; **~ de,** *prep. loc.* near (to), close; beside; in the vicinity of; nearly; on the verge of, about to; *~ d'ici*, near here; (naut.) *naviguer ~ du vent*, to sail close to the wind; *il est ~ de trois heures*, it is nearly three; *~ de pleurer*, on the verge of tears.
présage [prezaʒ] *s.m.* presage, omen; foreboding.
présager [prezaʒe] *v.t.* to presage, to forbode; to foretell.
pré-salé [presale] *s.m.* salt-marsh sheep or mutton.
presbyte [prɛsbit] *adj.*, *s.m.f.* presbyopic (person).
presbytéral, -e, (aux) [prɛsbiteral] *adj.* priestly, of priests.
presbytère [prɛsbitɛr] *s.m.* (Cath.) presbytery, priest's house.
presbytérianisme [prɛsbiterjanism] *s.m.* Presbyterianism.
presbytérien, -ne [prɛsbiterjɛ̃] *adj.*, *s.m.f.* Presbyterian.
presbytie [prɛsbiti] *s.f.* presbyopia.
prescience [presjɑ̃s] *s.f.* prescience, foreknowledge, foresight.
préscolaire [preskɔlɛr] *adj.* pre-school.
prescriptible [prɛskriptibl] *adj.* (law) prescriptible.
prescription [prɛskripsjɔ̃] *s.f.* prescription; instruction; regulation; (law) prescription, limitation.
prescrire [prɛskrir] *v.t.* to prescribe, to ordain, to lay down, to stipulate; (law) to bar; *chèque prescrit*, out-of-date cheque; **se ~** *v.refl.* to be prescribed; to become out of date, (law) to be lost by limitation.
préséance [prezeɑ̃s] *s.f.* precedence; *avoir la ~ sur*, to take precedence of.
présélection [preselɛksjɔ̃] *s.f.* preselection; *bouton de ~*, preselector button; **~ner** [preselɛksjɔne] *v.t.* to preselect.
présence [prezɑ̃s] *s.f.* presence, attendance; *faire acte de ~*, to put in an appearance; *jeton de ~*, director's attendance fee; *en ~*, face to face, facing each other; in each other's presence; *en ~ de*, in the presence of, in face of; in view of; *~ d'esprit*, presence of mind; wits; consciousness.
présent[1] [prezɑ̃] *s.m.* gift, present; *faire ~ de*, to give as a present; to give, to make a present of, to present (sth.).
présent[2] [prezɑ̃] *s.m.* present time, present; (gram.) present tense; *vivre dans le ~*, to live in the present; *au ~*, in the present tense.
présent, -e [prezɑ̃] *adj.* present, actual, current; attentive, attending; this; *dans le cas ~*, in the present case; *être ~ en pensée*, to be present in thought; (law, comm.) *par les ~es (lettres)*, by these present letters, by these presents; *du mois ~*, of this month; *à ~*, at present, now, today; *dès à ~*, from this moment; *jusqu'à ~*, till now; *pour le ~*, for the time being; *à ~ que*, now that; **~ement** [prezɑ̃tmɑ̃] *adv.* at the moment, now.
présentable [prezɑ̃tabl] *adj.* presentable, fit to be seen, suitable for presentation.
présentat-eur, -rice [prezɑ̃tatœr] *s.m.f.* **1.** (fin.) presenter (of bill, etc.); **2.** (eccles.) presenter (of living); presenter, introducer, (of exhibition, programme, show, etc.); *~eur, ~rice, de disques*, disc-jockey.
présentation [prezɑ̃tasjɔ̃] *s.f.* presentation, introduction; (comm.) *payable à ~*, payable at sight, on presentation.
présenter [prezɑ̃te] *v.t.* to present, to offer, to hold out, to introduce, to show, to exhibit, to bring forward; to deliver; **se ~** *v.refl.* to present oneself, to introduce oneself; to turn up; to report (oneself); to offer oneself; to make a (good, bad, etc.) impression; to arise, to occur, to appear; (law) to appear; *se ~ chez son ami*, to turn up at one's friend's house; *il se présente bien*, he makes a good impression, he has a good presence; *une difficulté s'est présentée*, a difficulty has arisen.
présentoir [prezɑ̃twar] *s.m.* display-shelf, slab (on which goods are set out).
présérie [preseri] *s.f.* (industry) pilot run (before mass-production).
préservat-eur, -rice [prezɛrvatœr] *adj.* preservative.
préservati-f, -ve [prezɛrvatif] *adj.*, *s.m.* preservative; **~f** *s.m.* protection; condom.
préservation [prezɛrvɑsjɔ̃] *s.f.* preservation, protection, safeguarding.
préserver [prezɛrve] *v.t.* to preserve, to keep from harm, to protect, to safeguard, to save, to defend; *que le ciel m'en préserve!*, heaven forbid!; *Dieu vous préserve de ce malheur!*, may God preserve you from this misfortune!; ⚠ not 'to preserve' e.g. fruit.
présidence [prezidɑ̃s] *s.f.* presidency, chairmanship; presidential palace, president's office.
président [prezidɑ̃] *s.m.* president, chairman, presiding judge; *~ du conseil*, prime minister, premier.
présidente [prezidɑ̃t] *s.f.* **1.** president's wife; **2.** (woman) chairman.
présidentiel, -le [prezidɑ̃sjɛl] *adj.* presidential.
présider [prezide] *v.t.i.* to be president or chairman, to preside, to take the chair; to be president or chairman of, to preside over, to chair; *~ une assemblée*, to be president of an assembly; *~ un débat*, to chair a debate; *~ à*, (i.) (obs.) to preside at, to take the chair at; (ii.) to direct, to supervise, to be in charge of; to govern; *~ aux préparatifs*, to be in charge of the arrangements; *des règles qui président qch.*, rules which govern sth.
presle see PRÈLE.
présompti-f, -ve [prezɔ̃ptif] *adj.* presumptive, apparent; *héritier ~f*, heir apparent.
présomption [prezɔ̃psjɔ̃] *s.f.* **1.** presumption,

supposition; **2.** conceit, conceitedness, presumptuousness.

présomptueu-x, -se [prezɔ̃ptɥø] *adj.* presumptuous, conceited, presuming; **~sement** [prezɔ̃ptɥøzmɑ̃] *adv.* presumptuously.

presque [prɛsk] *adv.* almost, nearly, all but; ~ *jamais*, hardly ever; ~ *pas*, scarcely; hardly, scarcely any; ~ *toujours*, almost always; ~ *personne*, hardly anybody, almost no one; *il n'y en a* ~ *plus*, there is hardly any left.

presqu'île [prɛskil] *s.f.* peninsula.

pressage [prɛsaʒ] *s.m.* pressing.

pressant, -e [prɛsɑ̃] *adj.* pressing, earnest, vehement, importunate, insistent; urgent; *affaires* ~*es*, urgent matters.

presse [prɛs] *s.f.* **1.** crowd, throng; **2.** press; printing-press; (the) press, newspapers; *mettre sous* ~, to put into press; ~ *à copier*, copying-machine (or -press); *il a une mauvaise* ~, he gets a bad press; (fig.) he has got a bad reputation; **3.** pressure, congestion; *aux moments de* ~, at busy or peak times.

pressé, -e [prese] *adj.* **1.** pressed, squeezed; *citron* ~, lemon squash; **2.** hurried, in a hurry, pressed, under pressure; **3.** pressing, urgent, vital; *aller au plus* ~, to deal with the most urgent aspect.

presse-bouton [prɛsbutɔ̃] *adj.invar. guerre* ~, press-button warfare.

presse-citron [prɛssitrɔ̃] *s.m.invar.* lemon-squeezer; (fig.) *on lui a fait le coup du* ~, they got every ounce of work out of him.

presse-étoupe [prɛsetup] *s.m.invar.* (techn.) pressure-seal, steam-gland.

pressée [prese] *s.f.* (agric.) pressing (of fruit, etc.).

pressentiment [presɑ̃timɑ̃] *s.m.* presentiment, foreboding, intuition, misgiving.

pressentir [presɑ̃tir] *v.t.* **1.** to have a presentiment of, to have some idea of; to guess, to feel (something) coming; **2.** to sound, to ascertain the opinion of.

presse-papiers [prɛspapje] *s.m.invar.* paper-weight.

presse-purée [prɛspyre] *s.m.invar.* potato-masher; sieve.

presser [prese] *v.t.* to press, to squeeze, to crush, to jam; to hurry, to hasten, to urge, to urge on, to importune, to harass; ~ *une orange*, to squeeze an orange; ~ *le pas*, to quicken one's step; ~ *qn. de faire qch.*, to press or urge s.o. to do sth., to insist on s.o. doing sth.; ~ *v.i.* to be urgent or pressing, to admit of no delay; *l'affaire presse beaucoup*, the matter is very urgent; *rien ne presse*, *ça ne presse pas*, there's no hurry; **se** ~ *v.refl.* **1.** to crowd, to throng; **2.** to make haste, to hurry up; to hasten (*de faire*, to do); *sans se* ~, without hurrying, deliberately, calmly, taking one's time.

pressing [presiŋ] *s.m.* steam-pressing, dry-cleaners.

pression [prɛsjɔ̃] *s.f.* pressure, steam-pressure; (dressm.) press-stud (also *un* (*bouton-*)~); ~ *atmosphérique*, atmospheric pressure; *exercer une* ~ *sur qn.*, to bring pressure to bear on s.o.; *faire* ~ *sur qn.*, to press s.o. (to agree); *bière* (*à la*) ~, draught beer; *un* ~, a glass of draught beer.

pressoir [prɛswar] *s.m.* press, wine-press, cider-press; press-house.

pressurage [presyraʒ] *s.m.* pressing; squeezing.

pressurer [presyre] *v.t.* **1.** to press, to squeeze; **2.** (fig.) to oppress, to grind, to extort from, to overtax, to exhaust.

pressureu-r, -se [presyrœr] *s.m.f.* press-operator.

pressuris-ation [presyrizɑsjɔ̃] *s.f.* (aeron.) pressurization; **~er** [presyrize] *v.t.* (aeron.) to pressurize.

prestance [prɛstɑ̃s] *s.f.* commanding appearance, bearing, carriage, presence.

prestant [prɛstɑ̃] *s.m.* (mus.) prestant, principal, (organ stop).

prestation [prɛstɑsjɔ̃] *s.f.* tax consisting either of money or of labour on the public roads; (mil.) allowance (in kind); ~ *de serment*, taking an oath.

preste [prɛst] *adj.* agile, nimble, quick; **~ment** [prɛstəmɑ̃] *adv.* nimbly, quickly.

prestesse [prɛstɛs] *s.f.* agility, nimbleness, quickness.

prestidigitat-eur, -rice [prɛstidiʒitatœr] *s.m.f.* conjurer, juggler.

prestidigitation [prɛstidiʒitɑsjɔ̃] *s.f.* conjuring, legerdemain; sleight-of-hand; *tour* or *truc de* ~, conjuring trick.

prestige [prɛstiʒ] *s.m.* **1.** (obs.) trick, illusion; **2.** prestige, distinction, glamour.

prestigieu-x, -se [prɛstiʒjø] *adj.* fascinating; impressive; conferring prestige, prestigious.

presto [prɛsto] *adv.* (mus.) presto; (fam.) quick, sharp.

présumer [prezyme] *v.t.* to presume, to suppose; to point to (conclusion, etc.); ~ *sur*, to presume upon; to overestimate; *trop* ~ *sur soi*, to be presumptuous.

présupposer [presypoze] *v.t.* to presuppose.

présupposition [presypozisjɔ̃] *s.f.* presupposition.

présure [prezyr] *s.f.* rennet.

prêt [prɛ] *s.m.* loan; advance; (mil.) subsistence allowance.

prêt, -e [prɛ] ready, prepared; disposed; in readiness, at hand; ~ *à*, ready to or for, prepared or disposed to; (obs.) about to; ~ *pour*, ready for or to; (obs.) ~ *de*, on the point of.

prétantaine see PRÉTENTAINE.

prêt-à-porter [prɛtapɔrte] *s.m.* ready-to-wear garments.

prêté [prɛte] *s.m.* thing lent; *c'est un* ~ *pour un rendu*, it is tit for tat, a Roland for an Oliver.

prétendant, -e [pretɑ̃dɑ̃] *s.m.f.* **1.** claimant, applicant; pretender (to the throne); **2.** suitor, wooer.

prétendre [pretɑ̃dr] *v.t.* to claim; to aspire (*à*, to); to intend, to mean, to affirm, to maintain, to assert, to mean to say; to make out; *que prétendez-vous* (*obtenir*) *de moi?*, what do you think you can expect from me?; *il prétend partir demain*, he intends to leave tomorrow; *on prétend que*, it is said that; it is rumoured that; **se** ~ *v.refl.* to make oneself out; ⚠ not 'to pretend' in senses 'to feign', or 'to dissimulate'.

prétendu, -e [pretɑ̃dy] *adj.* supposed, alleged, so-called, would-be; proposed, intended, future, to-be; ~*s.m.* suitor, wooer; **~ment** [pretɑ̃dymɑ̃] *adv.* falsely.

prête-nom [prɛtnɔ̃] *s.m.* (pl. *prête-noms*) person lending his or her name, man of straw, figure-head.

prétentaine, prétantaine [pretɑ̃tɛn] *s.f. courir la* ~, to gad about, to be on the loose.

prétentieu-x, -se [pretɑ̃sjø] *adj.* pretentious, affected; ostentatious; (of style) stilted; **~sement** [pretɑ̃sjøzmɑ̃] *adv.* pretentiously.

prétention [pretɑ̃sjɔ̃] *s.f.* **1.** pretension, claim (*à*, to); **2.** affectedness, pretentiousness.

prêter [prɛte] *v.t.* to lend; to attribute, to ascribe; to give rise, to be open, (*à*, to); ~ *à*, to lay oneself open to, to lend itself to; ~ *la main à*, to help, to further; ~ *l'oreille*, to listen; to lend an ear; ~ *serment*, to take the oath; *ce cuir prête bien*, this leather stretches easily; **se** ~ *v.refl.* to submit, to lend oneself (*à*, to), to be suitable (*à*, for); to countenance, to accept; to adapt oneself.

prétérit [preterit] *s.m.* (gram.) preterite.

préteur [pretœr] *s.m.* (Rom. hist.) praetor.
prêteu-r, -se [prɛtœr] *s.m.f.* lender, money-lender; *~r sur gages*, pawnbroker; *adj.* of a lending disposition, generous.
prétexte [pretɛkst] *s.m.* pretext, excuse, plea; reason, grounds; pretence; *sous ~ de*, on the pretext of, under the pretence of; *sous ~ que*, alleging, pretending; *ne sortez sous aucun ~*, do not go out under any circumstances.
prétexte [pretɛkst] *s.f.* (Rom. ant.) (toga) praetexta.
prétexter [pretɛkste] *v.t.* to use as a pretext, to advance as an excuse; to allege, to pretend.
prétoir [pretwar] *s.m.* **1.** (Rom. hist.) praetorium; **2.** (law) court, tribunal.
prétorien, -ne [pretɔrjɛ̃] *adj.* praetorian; *~ s.m.* (fig.) soldier.
prêtraille [prɛtrɑj] *s.f.* (pej.) the clergy.
prêtre [prɛtr] *s.m.* priest; (fam.) clergyman, vicar; *grand ~*, high priest.
prêtresse [prɛtrɛs] *s.f.* priestess.
prêtrise [prɛtriz] *s.f.* priesthood; *recevoir la ~*, to take (holy) orders.
préture [pretyr] *s.f.* praetorship.
preuve [prœv] *s.f.* proof, evidence, token; *faire ~ de*, to show, to display, to give proof of; *faire ses ~s*, to give proof of one's ability; to show one's mettle; *à ~*, witness, as evidenced by.
preux [prø] *adj.* gallant, valiant; *~ s.m.* gallant knight.
prévaloir [prevalwar] *v.i.* to prevail, to have the upper hand; **se ~** *v.refl. se ~ de*, to avail oneself of, to make use of, to turn to account; to presume on.
prévaricat-eur, -rice [prevarikatœr] *adj., s.m.f.* corrupt (official), unjust (judge).
prévarication [prevarikɑsjɔ̃] *s.f.* betrayal of trust or office, breach of trust, maladministration; ⚠ not 'prevarication'.
prévariquer [prevarike] *v.i.* to betray or abuse one's trust, to depart from justice; ⚠ not 'to prevaricate'.
prévenance [prevnɑ̃s] *s.f.* kind attention, obligingness, kindness; *avoir des ~s pour*, to be specially attentive or kind to.
prévenant, -e [prevnɑ̃] *adj.* obliging, nice, attentive, kind, engaging, prepossessing.
prévenir [prevnir] *v.t.* **1.** to forestall, to anticipate; to avert, to prevent, to ward off, to counter, to parry; *~ les désirs de qn.*, to anticipate someone's wishes; *~ la peste*, to ward off the plague; *mieux vaut ~ que guérir*, prevention is better than cure; **2.** to predispose, to prejudice; **3.** to warn, to forewarn; to inform, to give (prior) notice; *te voilà prévenu*, you have been warned, now you know; *tu aurais dû m'en ~*, you ought to have told me beforehand; *il faut ~ la police*, you must inform the police.
préventi-f, -ve [prevɑ̃tif] *adj.* preventive; (law) *détention ~ve*, detention awaiting trial.
prévention [prevɑ̃sjɔ̃] *s.f.* **1.** bias, prejudice, prepossession; *avoir des ~s contre*, to be prejudiced against; **2.** (law) detention awaiting trial; accusation, charge; *être en ~*, to be on remand, to be committed for trial; **3.** prevention, preventive measures.
préventivement [prevɑ̃tivmɑ̃] *adv.* preventively; (law) on suspicion, on remand, awaiting trial; *détenu ~*, committed for trial.
prévenu, -e [prevny] *adj.* preceded, forestalled, anticipated; informed, forewarned; prejudiced, biased; (law) accused, committed for trial; *s.m.f.* (the) accused.
prévisible [previzibl] *adj.* foreseeable.
prévision [previzjɔ̃] *s.f.* prevision, anticipation, conjecture; forecast; prophecy; what is foreseen or provided for; *~s météorologiques*, weather forecast; *en ~ de*, in anticipation of; in expectation of; *en ~ des mauvais jours*, against a rainy day.
prévisionnel, -le [previzjɔnɛl] *adj.* estimated, forecast(ed).
prévoir [prevwar] *v.t.* to foresee, to anticipate, to conjecture, to forecast, to look forward to; to provide for, to arrange for; to estimate; to destine.
prévôt [prevo] *s.m.* provost; *~ des marchands*, provost of the guilds; *~ d'armes*, fencing-master's assistant; (mil.) provost-marshal.
prévôté [prevote] *s.f.* provostship.
prévoyance [prevwajɑ̃s] *s.f.* foresight, forethought, caution; *société de ~*, provident society.
prévoyant, -e [prevwajɑ̃] *adj.* prudent, far-seeing, provident, cautious, careful.
prévu, -e [prevy] *adj.* foreseen; provided for; *tout est ~*, everything is provided for; everything is fixed; *~ s.m.* (the) foreseen.
priapée [priape] *s.f.* obscene poem, picture, etc.
prie-dieu [pridjø] *s.m.invar.* prie-dieu; prayer-stool; devotional chair.
prier [prie] **1.** *v.i.* to pray; *v.t.* to pray to; **2.** *v.t.* to pray, to beg, to ask, to invite; *je vous en prie*, please do; not at all, don't mention it; *je vous prie, montrez-le-moi*, please show it me; *croyez-vous je vous prie, que?*, do you think, I ask you, that?; *se faire ~*, to need pressing, to require much persuasion, to make a show of reluctance.
prière [priɛr] *s.f.* prayer, request, entreaty, petition, supplication; *~ de répondre*, kindly answer; *à la ~ de qn.*, by the request of s.o.
prieur, -e [priœr] *s.m.f.* prior, superior, prioress.
prieuré [priœre] *s.m.* priory.
primaire [primɛr] *adj.* primary; (fig.) immature, of limited outlook; (electr.) *enroulement ~*, primary winding.
primat [prima] *s.m.* **1.** (eccles.) primate, archbishop; **2.** primacy.
primate [primat] *s.m.* (zool.) primate, member of the Primates.
primatie [primasi] *s.f.* (eccles.) primacy.
primauté [primote] *s.f.* primacy, supremacy, pre-eminence, superior power.
prime [prim] *s.f.* premium; bonus, bounty, prize; free gift (esp. in exchange for coupons, stamps, etc.); subsidy; *faire ~*, to be highly appreciated, to be at a premium; (eccles., fencing) prime.
prime [prim] *adj.* first, early, initial; *la ~ jeunesse*, early youth; *de ~ abord*, at first sight; *de ~ saut*, at the first try; at once; (math.) prime.
primé, -e [prime] *adj.* prize, prize-winning.
primer [prime] *v.t.* **1.** to surpass, to excel, to beat; *sagesse prime richesse*, wisdom is better than riches; **2.** to award a medal or prize to.
primerose [primroz] *s.f.* (bot.) hollyhock; ⚠ not 'primrose'.
primesauti-er, -ère [primsotje] *adj.* impulsive, off-hand, spontaneous.
primeur [primœr] *s.f.* **1.** prime, early bloom or fruit; first (and best) part; novelty, new idea; **2.** (pl.) early fruit or vegetables.
primeuriste [primœrist] *s.m.f.* cultivator or purveyor of early vegetables (see PRIMEUR 2).
primevère [primvɛr] *s.f.* (bot.) primrose.
primidi [primidi] *s.m.* (hist.) first day of *décade* in calendar of 1st French Republic.
primiti-f, -ve [primitif] *adj.* primitive, original, first, primeval; pristine, simple, uncultivated, unrefined; primary (colour, rock); *s.m.f.* (anthrop., paint.) primitive; **~vement** [primitivmɑ̃] *adv.* originally, initially.
primo [primo] *adv.* firstly, in the first place, first.
primogéniture [primoʒenityr] *s.f.* primogeniture.
primordial, -e, (aux) [primɔrdjal] *adj.*

primordial, primeval, primary; prime; *c'est d'une importance ~e*, it is of prime importance.
primulacées [primylase] *s.f.pl.* (bot.) Primulaceae.
prince [prɛ̃s] *s.m.* prince, sovereign; (fig.) first in rank or merit; (pl.) the great; *être bon ~*, to be magnanimous, to show toleration; *le fait du ~*, arbitrary act of government; *le ~ des ténèbres*, the Prince of Darkness.
princeps [prɛ̃sɛps] *adj.* (of edition, etc.) earliest or original.
princesse [prɛ̃sɛs] *s.f.* princess; (fig., fam.) *aux frais de la ~*, at the expense of the State; free.
princi-er, -ère [prɛ̃sje] *adj.* princely, of a prince; **~èrement** [prɛ̃sjɛrmɑ̃] *adv.* in princely fashion, like a lord.
principal, -e, (**aux**) [prɛ̃sipal] *adj.* principal, chief, head, capital, essential, main; *~ s.m.* **1.** (money) capital, principal; **2.** (person) chief, head; headmaster, principal; **3.** main thing, principal thing; **~ement** [prɛ̃sipalmɑ̃] *adv.* principally, particularly.
principat [prɛ̃sipa] *s.m.* principate, sovereignty; reign (of Rom. emperor).
principauté [prɛ̃sipote] *s.f.* principality; princedom.
principe [prɛ̃sip] *s.m.* principle, source, beginning, origin; basis, reason, elements; essential matter; natural agent; principle, rule; *dès le ~*, from the beginning, from the outset; *les ~s de la géométrie*, the rudiments of geometry; *sans ~s*, unprincipled; *par ~*, on principle; *en ~*, in theory, in general, as a rule, on the whole.
printani-er, -ère [prɛ̃tanje] *adj.* spring-like, vernal, spring.
printemps [prɛ̃tɑ̃] *s.m.* spring, springtime; (fig.) bloom, prime.
priorat [prijɔra] *s.m.* priorship.
(**a**) **priori** [aprijɔri] *adv.loc., s.m.* a priori.
prioritaire [prijɔritɛr] *adj., s.m.f.* (person) having priority or right of way.
priorité [prijɔrite] *s.f.* priority, precedence; (of traffic) right of way; (fin.) *actions de ~*, preference shares.
pris, -e [pri] *adj.* taken, caught; attacked, overcome, smitten, afflicted, (*de*, by, with); occupied, engaged; set, congealed, frozen; *être ~ de fièvre*, to have a fever; *~ de peur*, overcome by fear; *avoir la gorge ~e*, to have an infected throat; *~ de vin*, the worse for drink; *avoir sa journée ~e*, to have a full day, to be fully booked-up; *les flaques d'eau étaient ~es*, the puddles had frozen over; *bien ~*, well-built, slim.
prise [priz] *s.f.* **1.** taking, capture, capturing; drawing of a supply (of), tapping; pinch (of snuff); *la ~ de la Bastille*, the storming of the Bastille; *~ de voile*, (of novice) taking the veil; *~ de vue(s)*, taking of photograph, photographing, snapping; *~ de son*, sound-mixing, synchronization (of sound-track); *~ de sang*, blood-sample; *~ d'eau*, tap, stand-pipe, water-point; (electr.) *~ de courant*, plug, socket, power-point; *~ d'air*, air-intake; (law) *~ de corps*, arrest; (fig.) *~ de bec*, altercation; *~ de conscience*, realization, awareness; **2.** something taken or caught, prize; (naut. law) *cour des ~s*, prize court; **3.** hold, grip, grasp; *lâcher ~*, to let go; *chercher une ~*, to seek a handhold or foothold; *être aux ~s avec*, to be at grips with, to be struggling with; *avoir une ~ sur*, to have a hold on; *donner ~ à qn.*, to give s.o. a hold (on one); *donner ~ à la malignité*, to lay oneself open to spiteful remarks; (of car) *en ~*, in gear; *~ directe*, direct drive.
prisée [prize] *s.f.* (law) appraisement.
priser[1] [prize] *v.t.* to appraise, to estimate, to value, to esteem (highly).
priser[2] [prize] *v.t.* to take (drugs); to take a pinch or small quantity of; *~ v.i.* to take snuff.
priseu-r, -se [prizœr] *s.m.f.* **1.** snuff-taker; **2.** appraiser; *commissaire ~r*, auctioneer, valuer.
prismatique [prismatik] *adj.* prismatic.
prisme [prism] *s.m.* prism; (fig.) *voir à travers un ~*, to see things distorted, to take a distorted view.
prison [prizɔ̃] *s.f.* prison, gaol, jail, imprisonment; *faire de la ~*, to do time, to be in prison.
prisonni-er, -ère [prizɔnje] *s.m.f.* prisoner, detainee, captive; *adj.* captive.
privati-f, -ve [privatif] *adj.* (of particle, prefix, etc.) privative; involving deprivation (of liberty, etc.).
privation [privɑsjɔ̃] *s.f.* privation, deprivation, loss; want, hardship; *~ des droits civils*, loss of civil rights; *vivre de ~s*, to lead a miserable life; to be hard up; to suffer many privations.
privauté [privote] *s.f.* excessive familiarity; *se permettre des ~s*, to take liberties.
privé, -e [prive] *adj.* private; unofficial; familiar; tame; privy; *de source ~e on apprend que*, it is learnt from an unofficial source that; *en ~*, in private, privately; *~ s.m.* private life; *dans le ~*, in private; in private life; (of job, etc.) in the private sector; in the home.
priver [prive] *v.t.* to deprive; **se** *~ v.refl.* to deprive oneself, to go without things, to stint oneself; *se ~ de*, to go without, to deprive oneself of; to refrain from.
privilège [privilɛʒ] *s.m.* privilege, prerogative; licence; (fin.) preference, prior charge.
privilégié, -e [privileʒje] *adj.* privileged, licensed; (of share, etc.) preference, preferential; entitled to preference; *s.m.f.* privileged person.
prix [pri] *s.m.* **1.** price, cost, value, worth; *au ~ de*, (i.) at the cost of; in exchange for; (ii.) in comparison with; *~ affiché*, marked price, posted price; *~ d'ami*, special or preferential price; *à bas ~*, at a low price, cheap; *à ~ coûtant, au ~ d'achat*, at cost price; *~ de revient*, selling-price, cost price; *~ de gros*, wholesale price; *~ fixe*, fixed price, net price; *~-fixe*, (i.) fixed-price store or restaurant; (ii.) table d'hôte menu; *~ courant*, (i.) market price; (ii.) catalogue, price--list; *~ unique*, one-price store; (*hors*) *de ~*, (extremely) expensive; *à tout ~*, at any price; at any cost; *à vil ~*, dirt-cheap; *une chose sans ~*, an invaluable thing; *mettre à ~*, to price (for sale); *mise à ~*, reserve price (at auction); *mettre à ~ la tête de qn.*, to put a price on someone's head; *donner du ~ à*, to put a high value or premium on; *j'attache beaucoup de ~ à*, I set great value upon, I value highly; (fam.) *au ~ où est le beurre*, as things are; **2.** prize, reward, stakes; prize-winning award; race for a prize.
probabilité [prɔbabilite] *s.f.* probability, likelihood.
probable [prɔbabl] *adj.* probable, likely; **~ment** [prɔbabləmɑ̃] *adv.* probably, very likely.
probant, -e [prɔbɑ̃] *adj.* convincing, conclusive.
probation [prɔbɑsjɔ̃] *s.f.* probation.
probatoire [prɔbatwar] *adj.* preliminary; probationary.
probe [prɔb] *adj.* honest, upright, loyal.
probité [prɔbite] *s.f.* probity, honesty, uprightness, integrity.
problématique [prɔblematik] *adj.* problematic(al), doubtful, questionable; *~ s.f.* science of devising problems; **~ment** [prɔblematikmɑ̃] *adv.* problematically, doubtfully.
problème [prɔblɛm] *s.m.* problem; puzzle.
proboscidiens [prɔbɔsidjɛ̃] *s.m.pl.* (zool.) Proboscidea, proboscidians.
procédé [prɔsede] *s.m.* proceeding, behaviour, dealing, trick; process, system, operation;

(billiards) cue-tip; *il a toujours eu de bons* ~*s à mon égard*, he has always behaved well to me.
procéder [prɔsede] *v.i.* to proceed, to behave, to operate, to do, to go on, to act, to deal; (law) to take proceedings; ~ *de bonne foi avec qn.*, to deal honestly with s.o.; ~ *à*, to proceed with, to institute, (inquiry, etc.), to proceed to (do sth.); ~ *de*, to proceed from, to arise from, to originate in.
procédure [prɔsedyr] *s.f.* procedure, practice, proceedings.
procéduri-er, -ère [prɔsedyrje] *adj.*, *s.m.f.* pettifogging, litigious (person).
procès [prɔsɛ] *s.m.* (law) proceedings, action; lawsuit; trial; cause, case; ~ *civil*, civil suit; ~ *criminel*, criminal trial; *engager un* ~, to engage in a lawsuit; *faire* or *intenter un* ~ *à qn.*, to take proceedings, or to bring an action, against s.o., to sue s.o., to go to law with s.o.; *être en* ~, to be at law, to be engaged in litigation; *plaider un* ~, to plead a case; (fig.) *faire le* ~ *de qn.*, to criticize s.o.; *sans autre forme de* ~, summarily, without more ado; ⚠ not 'process' exc. in sense 'the processes of the law'.
processi-f, -ve [prɔsɛsif] *adj.* litigious.
procession [prɔsɛsjɔ̃] *s.f.* procession.
processionnaire [prɔsɛsjɔnɛr] *s.f.* (ent.) processionary caterpillar.
processionnal (pl. **aux**) [prɔsɛsjɔnal] *s.m.* (eccles.) processional (prayer-book).
processionnel, -le [prɔsɛsjɔnɛl] *adj.* processional; ~**lement** [prɔsɛsjɔnɛlmɑ̃] *adv.* in procession.
processus [prɔsɛsys] *s.m.* process; progress, course.
procès-verbal (pl. **aux**) [prɔsɛvɛrbal] *s.m.* **1.** report (esp. with a view to legal proceedings); *dresser* ~, to report, to make a report, to take down particulars; *dresser* ~ *contre qn.*, to report s.o. (for minor offence), to take someone's particulars; **2.** report, minutes.
prochain [prɔʃɛ̃] *s.m.* neighbour, brother, fellow human being.
prochain, -e [prɔʃɛ̃] *adj.* near, nearest, next, coming, approaching, near at hand; (phil.) proximate; *l'année* ~*e*, next year; *sentant sa fin* ~*e*, feeling that his end was near; *le* ~ *village*, the next or neighbouring village; ~**ement** [prɔʃɛnmɑ̃] *adv.* shortly, soon, at an early date.
proche [prɔʃ] *adj.* neighbouring, near, (obs.) near to; approaching, close at hand; *de* ~ *en* ~, step by step; from place to place; nearer and nearer; ~**s** *s.m.pl.* near relatives, kindred.
proclamation [prɔklamɑsjɔ̃] *s.f.* proclamation.
proclamer [prɔklame] *v.t.* to proclaim.
proclitique [prɔklitik] *adj.*, *s.m.* (lang.) proclitic.
proconsul [prɔkɔ̃syl] *s.m.* (Rom. ant.) proconsul; ~**aire** [prɔkɔ̃sylɛr] *adj.* proconsular; ~**at** [prɔkɔ̃syla] *s.m.* proconsulate.
procréat-eur, -rice [prɔkreatœr] *adj.* procreative.
procréation [prɔkreɑsjɔ̃] *s.f.* procreation, generation.
procréer [prɔkree] *v.t.* to procreate, to beget, to engender.
procurateur [prɔkyratœr] *s.m.* procurator.
procuration [prɔkyrɑsjɔ̃] *s.f.* procuration, proxy, power of attorney; *donner* ~, to empower; *par* ~, by proxy.
procuratrice [prɔkyratris] *s.f.* woman holding power of attorney.
procurer [prɔkyre] *v.t.* to procure, to get, to acquire, to obtain (*à qn.*, for s.o.); *cela lui a procuré bien des désagréments*, this has caused him much unpleasantness.
procureur [prɔkyrœr] *s.m.* **1.** attorney, proxy, procurator; **2.** prosecutor; ~ *de la République*, Public Prosecutor; **3.** bursar (of religious establishment); ⚠ not 'procurer' in sense 'pimp'.
procureuse [prɔkyrøz] *s.f.* procuress.
prodigalité [prɔdigalite] *s.f.* prodigality, lavishness, extravagance; superabundance.
prodige [prɔdiʒ] *s.m.* prodigy, marvel, wonder, miracle; enigma; ~ *adj. enfant* ~, child prodigy.
prodigieu-x, -se [prɔdiʒjø] *adj.* prodigious, wonderful, stupendous, tremendous; ~**sement** [prɔdiʒjøzmɑ̃] *adv.* prodigiously, astoundingly.
prodigue [prɔdig] *adj.* prodigal, lavish, extravagant, wasteful; *l'enfant* ~, the prodigal son; ~ *s.m.* spendthrift, prodigal.
prodiguer [prɔdige] *v.t.* to lavish, to give freely of, to squander; **se** ~ *v.refl.* (i.) to spare no effort; (ii.) to advertise oneself, to push oneself forward.
prodrome [prɔdrom] *s.m.* (pathol.) premonitory symptom, prodrome; introduction, preamble.
product-eur, -rice [prɔdyktœr] *s.m.f.* producer; *adj.* producing, creative, productive.
productible [prɔdyktibl] *adj.* producible, that can be produced.
producti-f, -ve [prɔdyktif] *adj.* productive, yielding, bearing.
production [prɔdyksjɔ̃] *s.f.* **1.** production, producing, exhibition; (art, etc.) work; **2.** produce, product, output.
productivité [prɔdyktivite] *s.f.* productiveness, productivity.
produire [prɔdɥir] *v.t.* to produce, to bring forth, to bear, to make, to create; to exhibit, to show; to cause, to beget; to yield, to bring; ~ *intérêt*, to yield interest; *la guerre produit de grands maux*, war causes much misery; *cela n'a produit aucun effet*, it has had no effect; ~ *un titre*, to show one's title-deeds; **se** ~ *v.refl.* **1.** to occur, to happen; **2.** to make oneself known; to appear (on the stage); ⚠ not 'to produce' (a play, etc.).
produit [prɔdɥi] *s.m.* produce, production; product, result; profit, yield; proceeds; exhibit; (math.) product.
proéminence [prɔeminɑ̃s] *s.f.* **1.** prominence; **2.** protuberance.
proéminent, -e [prɔeminɑ̃] *adj.* prominent, protuberant.
prof [prɔf] *s.m.f.* abbrev. (fam.) *professeur*, prof.
profanat-eur, -rice [prɔfanatœr] *s.m.f.* profaner; *adj.* profanatory, profaning.
profanation [prɔfanɑsjɔ̃] *s.f.* profanation; desecration, violation; defacement.
profane [prɔfan] *adj.* **1.** profane, secular; **2.** uninitiated, lay; ~ *s.m.f.* uninitiated person, layman, not an expert.
profaner [prɔfane] *v.t.* to profane; to pollute, to violate, to desecrate; to deface; to misuse, to debase.
proférer [prɔfere] *v.t.* to utter; ⚠ not 'to proffer'.
prof-ès, -esse [prɔfɛ] *adj.*, *s.m.f.* professed (monk, nun).
professer [prɔfese] *v.t.* to profess, to declare; to teach, to be a professor of; ~ *l'histoire*, to teach history.
professeur [prɔfɛsœr] *s.m.* (man or woman) professor, (university) lecturer; teacher, master, mistress (at *lycée* or *collège*).
profession [prɔfɛsjɔ̃] *s.f.* **1.** profession, declaration; *faire* ~ *de*, to profess, to declare; ~ *de foi*, profession of faith, declaration of one's convictions; **2.** profession, occupation, business; *faire* ~ *de*, to make a profession of.
professionnel, -le [prɔfɛsjɔnɛl] *adj.* professional, vocational; by profession; *s.m.f.* professional.
professoral, -e, (**aux**) [prɔfɛsɔral] *adj.* professorial.
professorat [prɔfɛsɔra] *s.m.* professorship, lectureship; teaching (profession).

profil [prɔfil] *s.m.* profile, contour, outline; section; *de* ~, in profile, from the side.
profilé, -e [prɔfile] *adj.* (techn.) shaped, streamlined; ~ *s.m.* (rolled or extended) section, extrusion.
profiler [prɔfile] *v.t.* to profile, to draw the profile or outline of, to cut or machine to shape, to cut out, to cut to pattern; **se** ~ *v.refl.* to stand out, to be outlined or silhouetted.
profit [prɔfi] *s.m.* profit, advantage, gain; account; *faire* ~ *de*, to profit by, to make (good) use of; *tirer* ~ *de*, to gain an advantage from, to exploit; *mettre à* ~, to turn to account; *au* ~ *de*, to the advantage of, for the benefit of; on (someone's) account; on behalf of.
profitable [prɔfitabl] *adj.* profitable, advantageous; **~ment** [prɔfitabləmɑ̃] *adv.* profitably.
profitant, -e [prɔfitɑ̃] *adj.* (fam.) profitable, economical.
profiter [prɔfite] *v.t.i.* **1.** to profit, to be profitable, to gain; ~ *de*, to profit from, to take advantage of, to turn (sth.) to account, to make use of; ~ *dans*, or *en* or *à*, to profit by, to gain from (doing sth.); ~ *à qn.*, to be of profit or advantage to s.o.; to be useful to s.o.; **2.** to thrive, to prosper, to grow, to be a good proposition, to last, to wear well.
profiteu-r, -se [prɔfitœr] *s.m.f.* profiteer.
profond, -e [prɔfɔ̃] *adj.* deep, deep-seated, profound; dark; ~ *sommeil*, sound sleep; *~e révérence*, low bow or curtsy; *un esprit* ~, a profound mind; *une voix ~e*, a deep voice; *une nuit ~e*, a pitch-dark night; *une solitude ~e*, perfect solitude; *un* ~ *scélérat*, a consummate rascal; *peu* ~, shallow; **~e** *s.f.* (slang) pocket.
profondément [prɔfɔ̃demɑ̃] *adv.* deeply, profoundly, soundly, utterly.
profondeur [prɔfɔ̃dœr] *s.f.* depth; profundity, profoundness.
profus, -e [prɔfy] *adj.* profuse.
profusément [prɔfyzemɑ̃] *adv.* profusely.
profusion [prɔfyzjɔ̃] *s.f.* profusion, profuseness, abundance, lavishness; *à* ~, in profusion, lavishly.
progéniture [prɔʒenityr] *s.f.* progeny, offspring.
progestérone [prɔʒɛsterɔn] *s.f.* (physiol.) progesterone.
prognathe [prɔgnat] *adj.* prognathous, having projecting jaws.
prognathisme [prɔgnatism] *s.m.* prognathism.
programmat-eur, -rice [prɔgramatœr] *s.m.f.* compiler of programmes; **~eur** *s.m.* programmer (in e.g. automatic washing-machine).
programmation [prɔgramɑsjɔ̃] *s.f.* **1.** compilation of programmes; **2.** (computer) programming.
programme [prɔgram] *s.m.* **1.** programme; scheme, playbill; political statement; plan, planning; ~ *d'un examen*, examination syllabus; ~ *d'études*, syllabus, curriculum; **2.** (computer) program.
programmeu-r, -se [prɔgramœr] *s.m.f.* (computer) programmer.
progrès [prɔgrɛ] *s.m.* progress, improvement, headway; progression; *faire des* ~, to make progress; to improve; *en* ~, progressing, going forward, improving.
progresser [prɔgrese] *v.i.* to progress, to get on, to improve; to develop; to gain ground; *le mal progresse*, the disease is taking hold.
progressi-f, -ve [prɔgresif] *adj.* progressive; gradual; graduated; **~vement** [prɔgresivmɑ̃] *adv.* progressively, gradually.
progression [prɔgrɛsjɔ̃] *s.f.* progression, development, advancement; progress.
progressiste [prɔgresist] *s.m.f.*, *adj.* (Fr. pol.) progressive.
progressivité [prɔgresivite] *s.f.* progressiveness.
prohiber [prɔibe] *v.t.* to prohibit, to forbid; (shooting, etc.) *temps prohibé*, close season.
prohibiti-f, -ve [prɔibitif] *adj.* prohibitive, prohibitory.
prohibition [prɔibisjɔ̃] *s.f.* prohibition; **~nisme** [prɔibisjɔnism] *s.m.* prohibitionism; **~niste** [prɔibisjɔnist] *adj.*, *s.m.f.* prohibitionist.
proie [prwa] *s.f.* prey; booty, victim; *être en* ~ *à*, to be a prey to; *lâcher la* ~ *pour l'ombre*, to sacrifice the substance for the shadow.
projecteur [prɔʒɛktœr] *s.m.* projector, projection-apparatus; searchlight; spotlight.
projecti-f, -ve [prɔʒɛktif] *adj.* projective.
projectile [prɔʒɛktil] *s.m.* projectile, missile.
projection [prɔʒɛksjɔ̃] *s.f.* projection, plan; throwing; (geom.) projection; projected picture; (pl.) slides, film-show; ⚠ not 'projection' in sense of sth. sticking out.
projectionniste [prɔʒɛksjɔnist] *s.m.f.* (cin.) projectionist.
projecture [prɔʒɛktyr] *s.f.* (arch.) projection, ledge.
projet [prɔʒɛ] *s.m.* project, scheme, design, idea, plan, draft, sketch; *faire des ~s*, to form projects.
projeter [prɔʒte] *v.t.* **1.** to project, to throw, to hurl, to fling; **2.** to intend, to plan, to contemplate, to propose.
prolapsus [prɔlapsys] *s.m.* (med.) prolapsus, prolapse.
prolégomènes [prɔlegɔmɛn] *s.m.pl.* prolegomena, prefatory matter.
prolepse [prɔlɛps] *s.f.* (rhet.) prolepsis.
prolétaire [prɔletɛr] *s.m.* proletarian.
prolétariat [prɔletarja] *s.m.* proletariat.
prolétarien, -ne [prɔletarjɛ̃] *adj.* proletarian.
prolifération [prɔliferɑsjɔ̃] *s.f.* proliferation, multiplying.
prolifère [prɔlifɛr] *adj.* (bot.) proliferous.
proliférer [prɔlifere] *v.i.* to proliferate.
prolifique [prɔlifik] *adj.* prolific.
prolixe [prɔliks] *adj.* prolix, verbose, wordy; **~ment** [prɔliksəmɑ̃] *adv.* at great length.
prolixité [prɔliksite] *s.f.* prolixity.
prologue [prɔlɔg] *s.m.* prologue.
prolongation [prɔlɔ̃gɑsjɔ̃] *s.f.* prolongation; lengthening, extension of time, delay; postponement; protraction.
prolonge [prɔlɔ̃ʒ] *s.f.* ammunition-wagon; lashing-rope.
prolongement [prɔlɔ̃ʒmɑ̃] *s.m.* lengthening, extension, continuation.
prolonger [prɔlɔ̃ʒe] *v.t.* to prolong, to lengthen, to extend; (geom.) to extend, to produce; to protract, to spin out; to be an extension of.
promenade [prɔmenad] *s.f.* **1.** walk, walking, stroll; trip, excursion, ride; *faire une* ~ *(à pied)*, to go for a walk; *faire une* ~ *à cheval*, to go riding; ~ *en bateau*, boat-trip; **2.** promenade, walk.
promener [prɔmne] *v.t.* to take for a walk, drive, trip, etc.; to carry, to wheel, to propel; ~ *son chien*, to take one's dog for a walk; ~ *qn. par la ville*, to take s.o. round the town; ~ *son ennui avec soi*, to carry one's gloom around with one; ~ *ses mains sur*, to pass one's hands over; ~ *ses regards sur*, to let one's glance stray over; **se** ~ *v.refl.* to walk, to go for a walk, drive, trip, etc.; to move, to pass; *allez-vous ~!*, go away!, be off!; *envoyer* ~ *qn.*, to send s.o. about his business; *envoyer tout* ~, to abandon everything, to let everything go.
promeneu-r, -se [prɔmnœr] *s.m.f.* walker, promenader, stroller; one who takes (e.g. children) for a walk.
promenoir [prɔmnwar] *s.m.* covered walk; (theatr.) gallery; promenade.
promesse [prɔmɛs] *s.f.* promise, assurance,

undertaking; promissory note, note of hand, undertaking to pay.
prometteu-r, -se [prɔmɛtœr] *adj.* promising; *s.m.f.* one ready to make promises.
promettre [prɔmɛtr] *v.t.* to promise, to announce, to forebode; to give hopes of; ~ *et tenir font deux*, it is one thing to promise, another to perform; fair words butter no parsnips; ~ *monts et merveilles*, to promise wonders; *un enfant qui promet*, a promising child; *cela ne promet rien de bon*, this forebodes no good; **se** ~ *v.refl.* to promise (one's presence, support, etc.); to promise one another; *se ~ qch.*, to promise oneself sth., to count on having sth., to set one's heart on sth.; *se ~ de faire qch.*, to plan to do sth.
promis, -e [prɔmi] *adj.* promised; ~ *à*, destined for; *s.m.f.* fiancé(e), betrothed.
promiscuité [prɔmiskɥite] *s.f.* **1.** motley crew; squalid agglomeration; **2.** unpleasant proximity, rubbing shoulders with all sorts; ⚠ not usu. sexual 'promiscuity', or indiscriminateness.
promontoire [prɔmɔ̃twar] *s.m.* promontory, headland.
promot-eur, -rice [prɔmɔtœr] *s.m.f.* promoter, originator, instigator.
promotion [prɔmosjɔ̃] *s.f.* promotion, preferment; those promoted together, class, term; promotion (of sales, of a product).
promotionnel, -le [prɔmosjɔnɛl] *adj.* promotional, promoting sales (of merchandise).
promouvoir [prɔmuvwar] *v.t.* to promote, to advance; to encourage.
prompt, -e [prɔ̃] *adj.* prompt, quick, sudden, swift; *avoir l'esprit* ~, to have a quick understanding; *avoir la répartie ~e*, to be quick at repartee; *avoir l'humeur ~e*, to be quick-tempered; **~ement** [prɔ̃tmɑ̃] *adv.* promptly, quickly, swiftly, without delay.
promptitude [prɔ̃tityd] *s.f.* prompitude, swiftness, quickness, readiness.
promu, -e [prɔmy] *adj.* promoted.
promulgation [prɔmylgɑsjɔ̃] *s.f.* promulgation.
promulguer [prɔmylge] *v.t.* to promulgate.
pronation [prɔnɑsjɔ̃] *s.f.* pronation.
prône [pron] *s.m.* sermon, homily; prayers (for s.o.).
prôner [prone] *v.t.* to extol, to praise.
pronom [prɔnɔ̃] *s.m.* (gram.) pronoun.
pronominal, -e, (aux) [prɔnɔminal] *adj.*, ~ *s.m.* pronominal, reflexive, (verb).
prononçable [prɔnɔ̃sabl] *adj.* pronounceable.
prononcé, -e [prɔnɔ̃se] *adj.* pronounced; marked, decided, sharply defined; prominent; ~ *s.m.* delivering (of judgement).
prononcer [prɔnɔ̃se] *v.t.* to pronounce, to utter, to declare; to decide; to deliver (judgement); ~ *v.i.* to deliver judgement; **se** ~ *v.refl.* **1.** to declare oneself, to speak out, to make one's choice; **2.** to be pronounced.
prononciation [prɔnɔ̃sjɑsjɔ̃] *s.f.* **1.** pronunciation; **2.** (obs.) delivery of judgement.
pronostic [prɔnɔstik] *s.m.* prognostic, prognostication, prognosis; forecast.
pronostiquer [prɔnɔstike] *v.t.* to prognosticate; to foretell.
pronostiqueu-r, -se [prɔnɔstikœr] *s.m.f.* prognosticator, forecaster, tipster.
propagande [prɔpagɑ̃d] *s.f.* propaganda.
propagandiste [prɔpagɑ̃dist] *adj.*, *s.m.f.* propagandist.
propagat-eur, -rice [prɔpagatœr] *s.m.f.* propagator, spreader.
propagation [prɔpagɑsjɔ̃] *s.f.* propagation, spreading.
propager [prɔpaʒe] *v.t.* to propagate, to spread; **se** ~ *v.refl.* to spread, to be propagated; to reproduce, to multiply.
propane [prɔpan] *s.m.* (chem.) propane.
propédeute [prɔpedøt] *s.m.f.* student undertaking a *propédeutique* course.
propédeutique [prɔpedøtik] *s.f.* preliminary instruction; foundation course (prior to university entry), fam. abbrev. *propé.*
propension [prɔpɑ̃sjɔ̃] *s.f.* propensity, tendency, inclination.
propergol [prɔpɛrgɔl] *s.m.* (chem.) propellant.
prophète, prophétesse [prɔfɛt] *s.m.f.* prophet, prophetess, soothsayer; ~ *de malheur*, prophet of evil; bird of ill omen.
prophétie [prɔfesi] *s.f.* prophecy; prophetic utterance; prophesying.
prophétique [prɔfetik] *adj.* prophetic, prophetical; **~ment** [prɔfetikmɑ̃] *adv.* prophetically.
prophétiser [prɔfetize] *v.t.* to prophesy; to foretell.
prophylactique [prɔfilaktik] *adj.* prophylactic.
prophylaxie [prɔfilaksi] *s.f.* prophylaxis, preventive treatment.
propice [prɔpis] *adj.* propitious, favourable; suitable; *le ciel vous soit* ~, may fortune smile on you; *rendre* ~, to propitiate.
propitiation [prɔpisjɑsjɔ̃] *s.f.* propitiation.
propitiatoire [prɔpisjatwar] *adj.* propitiatory.
proportion [prɔpɔrsjɔ̃] *s.f.* proportion, (math.) ratio, proportion, percentage; extent; (pl.) proportions, dimensions; *en* (or *à*) ~ *de*, in proportion to; *en* ~, proportionally; *toutes ~s gardées*, with due proportion; everything considered; all allowances being made.
proportionnalité [prɔpɔrsjɔnalite] *s.f.* proportionality, proportional division or allocation.
proportionné, -e [prɔpɔrsjɔne] *adj.* proportioned, proportionate.
proportionnel, -le [prɔpɔrsjɔnɛl] *adj.* proportional; **~le** *s.f.* proportional representation; **~lement** [prɔpɔrsjɔnɛlmɑ̃] *adv.* proportionally, in proportion.
proportionner [prɔpɔrsjɔne] *v.t.* to proportion, to adjust, to adapt.
propos [prɔpo] *s.m.* **1.** purpose, resolution; **2.** talk, remark, discourse; *à* ~, opportune(ly), timely, in good time; at the right time; to the point, pertinent(ly), appropriate, fitting; by the way; *juger à ~ de*, to think fit to, to deem it advisable to; *à ~ de*, about; in reference to; with regard to; speaking of; *à ~ de bottes*, with reference to nothing in particular; *à quel ~?*, what about?, for what reason?; what are you referring to?; *à tout* ~, continually, at every turn, on every occasion; *mal à* ~, at the wrong time; unseasonably; inopportunely; *de ~ délibéré*, of set purpose, on purpose, purposely; deliberately; *hors de* ~, ill-timed, unseasonable, irrelevant.
proposer [prɔpoze] *v.t.* to propose, to offer; to propound, to move; to put forward; to suggest; **se** ~ *v.refl.* **1.** to offer oneself; **2.** to resolve, to intend, to mean; *je me propose de rester quelques jours ici*, I intend staying a few days here.
proposition [prɔpozisjɔ̃] *s.f.* offer, proposal; proposition; statement; (gram.) clause; (in parliament) motion.
propre [prɔpr] *adj.* own, characteristic, very, same, self-same, proper, peculiar; clean, neat; respectable, honest; suitable (*à*, for); *des qualités ~s*, characteristic qualities; *ses ~s paroles*, his very words; *remettre en main ~ à qn.*, to deliver to s.o. personally, to deliver into someone's own hands; *sa ~ fille*, his own daughter; *le mot* ~, the right word, a fitting description; *le sens ~ d'un mot*, (i.) the right meaning of a word; (ii.) the literal sense of a word; *au* ~, in the strict or literal sense, literally (opp. figuratively); *un nom* ~, a proper name; a proper noun; *bois ~ à la construction*, timber suitable for building; *biens ~s*, personal property;

un ~ à rien, a good-for-nothing; *~ à tout et bon à rien*, Jack-of-all-trades and master of none; *il ne possède rien en ~*, he has nothing of his own; *un hôtel modeste mais ~*, a modest but clean hotel; *c'est un homme ~*, he is a decent sort of man; (iron.) *c'est du ~!*, this is a fine state of affairs!, it's disgusting!; *vous voilà ~*, now you are in a pretty mess; *~ s.m.* characteristic, nature, peculiar quality; property; (law) separate property (of husband or wife); *le ~ de l'homme est de penser*, it is in the nature of man to think; **~ment** [prɔprəmɑ̃] *adv.* properly, exactly, correctly, rightly, well and truly; *à ~ment parler*, strictly speaking; *~ment dit*, in the strict sense of the word; *entrer dans le temple ~ment dit*, to enter the temple proper.

propret, -te [prɔprɛ] *adj.* neat, tidy, trim.

propreté [prɔprəte] *s.f.* cleanliness, neatness.

propriétaire [prɔprietɛr] *s.m.f.* owner, proprietor, proprietress, landlord, landlady, landowner; *~ foncier*, landowner.

propriété [prɔpriete] *s.f.* **1.** ownership, proprietorship, possession; *~ littéraire*, copyright; **2.** property, estate; **3.** property, characteristic, special quality; **4.** propriety, correctness, (of word, etc.).

proprio [prɔprio] *s.m.* (fam.) owner, landlord.

propulser [prɔpylse] *v.t.* to propel; **se ~**, *v.refl.* (pop.) *se ~ dans la nature*, to take a walk.

propulseur [prɔpylsœr] *s.m.* propeller; mechan, ism or means of propulsion, engine, motor, jet, thruster; *~ auxiliaire*, booster; *~ adj.* propelling, propulsive.

propulsi-f, -ve [prɔpylsif] *adj.* propulsive, propelling, driving.

propulsion [prɔpylsjɔ̃] *s.f.* propulsion, propelling, drive.

propylée [prɔpile] *s.m.* (Gr. hist.) propylaeum.

prorata [prɔrata] *s.m.invar.* proportion; *au ~ de*, in proportion to.

prorogation [prɔrɔgɑsjɔ̃] *s.f.* prorogation, adjournment.

proroger [prɔrɔʒe] *v.t.* to prorogue, to adjourn; to prolong, to extend (time-limit).

prosaïque [prozaik] *adj.* prosaic, commonplace, unimaginative; **~ment** [prozaikmɑ̃] *adv.* prosaically.

prosaïsme [prozaism] *s.m.* prosaic, unpoetical style; commonplaceness, banality, matter-of--factness.

prosateur [prozatœr] *s.m.* prose-writer.

proscription [prɔskripsjɔ̃] *s.f.* proscription, banishment, banishing; banning.

proscrire [prɔskrir] *v.t.* to proscribe, to banish, to exile, to outlaw; to forbid, to ban.

proscrit, -e [prɔskri] *adj.* proscribed, banished, abolished, forbidden, banned; *s.m.f.* exile, outcast, refugee, outlaw.

prose [proz] *s.f.* prose, prose writing, prose style.

prosélyt-e [prɔzelit] *s.m.f.* proselyte; **~isme** [prɔzelitism] *s.m.* proselytism.

proso-die [prɔzɔdi] *s.f.* prosody; **~dique** [prɔzɔdik] *adj.* prosodic; **~popée** [prɔzɔpɔpe] *s.f.* prosopopoeia.

prospecter [prɔspɛkte] *v.t.* to prospect, to make a survey of, to investigate (for marketing possibilities).

prospect-eur, -rice [prɔspɛktœr] *s.m.f.* prospector, researcher, investigator.

prospecti-f, -ve [prɔspɛktif] *adj.* prospective; **~ve** *s.f.* consideration of future developments.

prospection [prɔspɛksjɔ̃] *s.f.* prospecting, exploration; (market) research, canvassing (for custom).

prospectus [prɔspɛktys] *s.m.* prospectus, brochure.

prospère [prɔspɛr] *adj.* prosperous, thriving, flourishing, successful, favourable.

prospérer [prɔspere] *v.i.* to prosper, to thrive, to be successful.

prospérité [prɔsperite] *s.f.* prosperity, success, prosperousness.

prostat-e [prɔstat] *s.f.* (anat.) prostate (gland); **~ectomie** [prɔstatɛktɔmi] *s.f.* (surg.) prostatectomy; **~ique** [prɔstatik] *adj.* of the prostate.

prostern-ation [prɔstɛrnɑsjɔ̃] *s.f.* prostration; (fig.) self-abasement, grovelling; **~ement** [prɔstɛrnəmɑ̃] *s.m.* prostration, prostrate position; (fig.) abasement, humiliation; **~er** [prɔstɛrne] *v.t.* to prostrate; (Lit.) to bend down, to bow low; **se ~er** *v.refl.* to prostrate oneself, to bow low; *se ~er devant*, to grovel before, to bow down and worship.

prosthèse [prɔstɛz] *s.f.* (gram.) prosthesis, addition of prefix (also *prothèse*).

prosthétique, prothétique [prɔ(s)tetik] *adj.* (gram., biochem.) prosthetic.

prostitué, -e [prɔstitɥe] *s.m.f.* prostitute.

prostituer [prɔstitɥe] *v.t.* to prostitute; (fig.) to debase; **se ~** *v.refl.* to prostitute oneself; to become a prostitute.

prostitution [prɔstitysjɔ̃] *s.f.* prostitution; (fig.) degradation, debasement; *maison de ~*, brothel, disorderly house.

prostration [prɔstrɑsjɔ̃] *s.f.* **1.** (liturg.) prostration; **2.** (med.) exhaustion, prostration.

prostré, -e [prɔstre] *adj.* reduced to utter dejection; dispirited, prostrate, physically exhausted.

prostyle [prɔstil] *s.m.* (arch.) prostyle.

protactinium [prɔtaktinjɔm] *s.m.* (chem.) protactinium.

protagoniste [prɔtagɔnist] *s.m.* protagonist.

prote [prɔt] *s.m.* (print.) overseer.

protect-eur, -rice [prɔtɛktœr] *s.m.f.* protector, protectress, patron, patroness; *adj.* patronizing; protective, protecting; *droits ~eurs*, protective taxes.

protection [prɔtɛksjɔ̃] *s.f.* protection, support, shelter; patronage; protectionism.

protectionn-isme [prɔtɛksjɔnism] *s.m.* protectionism; **~iste** [prɔtɛksjɔnist] *adj., s.m.f.* protectionist.

protectorat [prɔtɛktɔra] *s.m.* protectorate.

protée [prɔte] *s.m.* (Gr. myth.) Proteus; (fig.) turncoat, chameleon; (zool.) proteus.

protégé, -e [prɔteʒe] *s.m.f.* protégé(e), dependant.

protéger [prɔteʒe] *v.t.* to protect, to give protection to, to shield, to shelter, to defend; to patronize, to be a patron of, to encourage.

protège-tibia [prɔtɛʒtibja] *s.m.* (pl. *~-tibias*) shin-guard.

protéiforme [prɔteifɔrm] *adj.* protean.

protéine [prɔtein] *s.f.* (chem.) protein.

protéique [prɔteik] *adj.* (chem.) proteinic.

protestant, -e [prɔtɛstɑ̃] *s.m.f., adj.* Protestant, protestant.

protestantisme [prɔtɛstɑ̃tism] *s.m.* Protestantism.

protestataire [prɔtɛstatɛr] *adj.* protesting.

protestation [prɔtɛstɑsjɔ̃] *s.f.* protestation, declaration; protest; *~s d'amitié*, profession of friendship, marks of affection, polite effusions.

protester [prɔtɛste] *v.t.* **1.** (law) to make a solemn declaration, to affirm; **2.** to protest (*contre*, against), to contest, to challenge; *~ de*, to protest, to affirm, (one's innocence, etc.) to make formal complaint of; *~ v.i.* to protest, to make a protest.

protêt [prɔtɛ] *s.m.* protest (for non-payment).

prothèse [prɔtɛz] *s.f.* prosthesis, fitting of artificial limbs, dentures, etc.; see also PROSTHÈSE.

protocolaire [prɔtɔkɔlɛr] *adj.* formal, in

accordance with protocol, in keeping with etiquette, in the approved way.
protocole [prɔtɔkɔl] *s.m.* **1.** protocol, formalities; official formula; etiquette; (print.) house-style; **2.** proceedings, official communiqué.
proton [prɔtɔ̃] *s.m.* (phys.) proton.
protoplasma [prɔtɔplasma], **protoplasme** [prɔtɔplasm] *s.m.* protoplasm.
prototype [prɔtɔtip] *s.m.* prototype.
protozoaire [prɔtɔzɔɛr] *s.m.* protozoon, protozoan; (pl.) protozoa; *adj.* protozoan.
protubérance [prɔtyberɑ̃s] *s.f.* protuberance; (astron.) ~ (*solaire*), solar prominence.
protubérant, -e [prɔtyberɑ̃] *adj.* protuberant, bulging.
prou [pru] *adv.* much; *peu ou* ~, little or much, more or less; to a certain extent; *ni peu ni* ~, not at all.
proue [pru] *s.f.* (naut.) prow, stem; (fig.) *s'avancer en* ~, to project.
prouesse [pruɛs] *s.f.* prowess, feat, exploit.
prouvable [pruvabl] *adj.* provable.
prouver [pruve] *v.t.* to prove, to give proof of, to show; *cela prouve sa bonne volonté*, this shows his good intention.
provenance [prɔvnɑ̃s] *s.f.* origin, source, provenance; place of production; (pl.) imported products; *en* ~ *d'Angleterre*, of English origin, imported from England.
provençal, -e, (aux) [prɔvɑ̃sal] *adj., s.m.f.* Provençal; ~ *s.m.* Provençal (language).
provende [prɔvɑ̃d] *s.f.* fodder, provender, (for animals).
provenir [prɔvnir] *v.i.* to come (*de*, from), to have its source, to issue, to spring, to arise, to proceed, to result.
proverbe [prɔvɛrb] *s.m.* proverb, saying; *passer en* ~, to become a proverb, or proverbial.
proverbial, -e, (aux) [prɔvɛrbjal] *adj.* proverbial; **~ement** [prɔvɛrbjalmɑ̃] *adv.* proverbially.
providence [prɔvidɑ̃s] *s.f.* providence; (fig.) protector, good angel, fairy godmother.
providentiel, -le [prɔvidɑ̃sjɛl] *adj.* providential; **~lement** [prɔvidɑ̃sjɛlmɑ̃] *adv.* providentially.
provignage [prɔviɲaʒ], **provignement** [prɔviɲmɑ̃] *s.m.* layering (of vines, rose-trees, etc.).
provigner [prɔviɲe] *v.t.* to layer (vines, rose--trees, etc.); ~ *v.i.* to layer, to increase by layering.
provin [prɔvɛ̃] *s.m.* (viticulture) layer.
province [prɔvɛ̃s] *s.f.* province; (the) provinces, (the) country; *de* ~, provincial, country.
provincial, -e, (aux) [prɔvɛ̃sjal] *adj.* provincial, of the provinces; country, countrified; *s.m.f.* provincial, one who lives in the provinces; ~ *s.m.* (eccles.) Provincial.
provincialisme [prɔvɛ̃sjalism] *s.m.* provincialism.
proviseur [prɔvizœr] *s.m.* headmaster, principal.
provision [prɔvizjɔ̃] *s.f.* provision, store, stock, supply; (pl.) provisions, supplies; (fin.) funds, provision, cover, reserve, margin; (law) advance of damages (before final assessment); payment on account (to lawyer); *jugement par* ~, provisional judgement; *avoir une* ~ *de*, (lit. & fig.) to have a good stock, a reserve, of; *faire* ~ *de qch.*, to lay in a stock of sth.
provisionnel, -le [prɔvizjɔnɛl] *adj.* provisional.
provisoire [prɔvizwar] *adj.* provisional, temporary; acting; *à titre* ~, provisionally, on a temporary basis; ~ *s.m.* the temporary; **~ment** [prɔvizwarmɑ̃] *adv.* provisionally, temporarily, for the time being.
provisorat [prɔvizɔra] *s.m.* headmastership.
provocant, -e [prɔvɔkɑ̃] *adj.* provocative, exciting, alluring; provoking.
provocat-eur, -rice [prɔvɔkatœr] *s.m.f.* provoker, instigator, aggressor; *adj.* provoking, provocative; *agent* ~*eur*, hired agitator, agent provocateur.
provocation [prɔvɔkɑsjɔ̃] *s.f.* provocation, instigation.
provoquer [prɔvɔke] *v.t.* to provoke, to rouse, to stir up; to challenge, to incite (*à*, to), to instigate, to inflame; to bring on, to cause; ~ *un adversaire*, to challenge an adversary; ~ *la sueur*, to cause to perspire.
proxénète [prɔksenɛt] *s.m.f.* go-between, procurer, procuress; ~ *s.m.* one who lives on immoral earnings, ponce.
proxénétisme [prɔksenetism] *s.m.* living on immoral earnings.
proximité [prɔksimite] *s.f.* proximity, propinquity, nearness, vicinity; near relationship; imminence; *à* ~ *de*, near; in the neighbourhood of.
proyer [prwaje] *s.m.* (ornith.) bunting.
prude [pryd] *adj.* prudish; ~ *s.f.* prude.
prudemment [prydamɑ̃] *adv.* prudently, cautiously, warily.
prudence [prydɑ̃s] *s.f.* prudence, caution, wariness, discretion, wisdom, advisability.
prudent, -e [prydɑ̃] *adj.* prudent, cautious, wary, discreet; advisable, wise, sensible.
pruderie [prydri] *s.f.* prudishness, prudery.
prud'homie [prydɔmi] *s.f.* jurisdiction of *conseil de prud'hommes* (see PRUD'HOMME 2).
prud'homme [prydɔm] *s.m.* **1.** wise, honest man; **2.** member of board of arbitration (*conseil de* ~*s*) between employers and workers; **3.** pompous ass.
prudhommesque [prydɔmɛsk] *adj.* pompous and sententious (see PRUD'HOMME 3).
pruine [prɥin] *s.f.* (bot.) pruina, dust or bloom of fruit, mushrooms, etc.
prune [pryn] *s.f.* plum; ~ *de Damas*, damson; ~ *de Monsieur*, Orleans plum; (fig.) *pour des* ~*s*, for nothing; (pop.) *des* ~*s!*, nothing doing!; ⚠ not 'prune'.
pruneau (pl. **-x**) [pryno] *s.m.* prune, dried plum; (fam.) shot, bullet.
prunelle [prynɛl] *s.f.* **1.** (bot.) prunella, sloe; **2.** (anat.) eyeball, pupil; (fig.) apple of one's eye; *jouer de la* ~, to ogle, to make eyes.
prunellier [prynɛlje] *s.m.* (bot.) sloe-tree, blackthorn.
prunier [prynje] *s.m.* (bot.) plum-tree.
prunus [prynys] *s.m.* (bot.) Prunus, ornamental plum(-tree).
prurigineu-x, -se [pryriʒinø] *adj.* (pathol.) pruriginous.
prurigo [pryrigo] *s.m.* (pathol.) prurigo.
prurit [pryrit] *s.m.* pruritus, itching.
Prusse [prys] *s.f.* (geog.) Prussia.
prussien, -ne [prysjɛ̃] *adj., s.m.f.* Prussian.
prussique [prysik] *adj.* (chem.) prussic.
prytanée [pritane] *s.m.* **1.** (Gr. hist.) prytaneum; **2.** school for sons of servicemen.
P.-S. [peɛs] abbrev. *post-scriptum*, P.S.
psallette [psalɛt] *s.f.* choir school; choir, choirboys.
psalliote [psaljɔt] *s.f.* (bot.) field mushroom.
psalmiste [psalmist] *s.m.* psalmist.
psalmodie [psalmɔdi] *s.f.* psalmody; (fig.) singsong.
psalmodier [psalmɔdje] *v.t.i.* to chant, to sing psalms; (fig.) to drone out, to recite monotonously or in a singsong voice.
psaltérion [psalterjɔ̃] *s.m.* (mus.) psaltery.
psaume [psom] *s.m.* psalm.
psautier [psotje] *s.m.* psalter.
pseudo- [psødo] *pref.* pseudo-.
pseudonyme [psødɔnim] *s.m.* pseudonym, assumed name, nom-de-plume; ~ *adj.* pseudonymous.

psitt [psit] *interj.* (attracting attention) hello!; look here!; hi!, hey!, I say!
psittacidés [psitaside] *s.m.pl.* (ornith.) Psittacidae, the parrot family.
psittacose [psitakoz] *s.f.* (pathol.) psittacosis.
psoas [psɔas] *s.m.* (anat.) psoas (muscle).
psoriasis [psɔrjazis] *s.m.* (pathol.) psoriasis.
P.S.V. [peɛsve] abbrev. *pilotage sans visibilité*, flying blind.
psychanaly-se [psikanaliz] *s.f.* psychoanalysis; **~ser** [psikanalize] *v.t.* to psychoanalyse; **~ste** [psikanalist] *s.m.f.* psychoanalyst; **~tique** [psikanalitik] *adj.* psychoanalytical.
psyché[1] [psiʃe] *s.f.* cheval-glass.
psyché[2] [psiʃe], **psychè** [psiʃɛ] *s.f.* (phil.) psyche.
psychiatr-e [psikjatr] *s.m.f.* psychiatrist; **~ie** [psikjatri] *s.f.* psychiatry; **~ique** [psikjatrik] *adj.* psychiatric.
psychique [psiʃik] *adj.* psychical, psychic.
psycholog-ie [psikɔlɔʒi] *s.f.* psychology; **~ique** [psikɔlɔʒik] *adj.* psychological; **~iquement** [psikɔlɔʒikmɑ̃] *adv.* psychologically, from the psychological point of view; **~ue** [psikɔlɔg] *s.m.f.* psychologist.
psychopath-e [psikɔpat] *s.m.f.* psychopath, one who is mentally ill; **~ie** [psikɔpati] *s.f.* psychopathy, mental illness.
psychose [psikoz] *s.f.* (psychol.) psychosis; (fig.) obsession.
psychosomatique [psikɔsɔmatik] *adj.* psychosomatic.
psychothérapie [psikoterapi] *s.f.* psychotherapy.
psychotique [psikɔtik] *adj.*, *s.m.f.* psychotic (person).
psychromètre [psikrɔmɛtr] *s.m.* (techn.) psychrometer, hygrometer.
psylle [psil] *s.m.* snake-charmer.
ptérodactyle [pterodaktil] *s.m.* (zool.) pterodactyl.
ptéropode [pteropɔd] *adj.* (zool.) pteropodial; **~s** *s.m.pl.* pteropods.
ptolémaïque [ptɔlemaik] *adj.* (hist.) Ptolemaic.
ptomaïne [ptomain] *s.f.* (biochem.) ptomaine.
ptose, ptôse [ptoz] *s.f.* (pathol.) ptosis.
P.T.T. [petete] abbrev. (hist.) *Postes, Télégraphes et Téléphones*; see P. ET T.
ptyaline [ptialin] *s.f.* (biochem.) ptyalin.
puant, -e [pɥɑ̃] *adj.* stinking; (of skunks, etc.) emitting a disagreable odour; (fig.) impudent.
puanteur [pɥɑ̃tœr] *s.f.* stink, stench.
pubère [pybɛr] *adj.* arrived at puberty, pubescent.
puberté [pybɛrte] *s.f.* puberty.
pubescence [pybesɑ̃s] *s.f.* (bot.) pubescence.
pubescent, -e [pybesɑ̃] *adj.* (bot.) pubescent, downy.
pubien, -ne [pybjɛ̃] *adj.* (anat.) pubic.
pubis [pybis] *s.m.* (anat.) pubis.
publiable [pybliabl] *adj.* publishable.
publi-c, -que [pyblik] *adj.* public, common; *la chose ~que*, the common weal, the State, public welfare or policy, public service; *l'intérêt ~c*, the public (or common) interest; *le bien ~c*, the public welfare; *le bruit ~c*, public opinion; public rumour; open secret; *fille* or *femme ~que*, prostitute; *maison ~que*, brothel (⚠ not 'public house'); **~c** *s.m.* public; audience; *en ~c*, publicly, in public; *le grand ~c*, the general public, people in general.
publicain [pyblikɛ̃] *s.m.* (bibl.) publican, tax-gatherer.
publication [pyblikɑsjɔ̃] *s.f.* **1.** publishing, publication, issuing, promulgation, proclamation; **2.** publication, published work; *~ périodique*, periodical.
publiciste [pyblisist] *s.m.f.* (obs.) political writer, journalist.
publicitaire [pyblisitɛr] *adj.* publicity, advertising; *~ s.m.f.* advertising or publicity agent.
publicité [pyblisite] *s.f.* **1.** publicity; **2.** advertising, advertising matter.
publier [pyblie] *v.t.* to publish, to make public.
publipostage [pyblipɔstaʒ] *s.m.* mailing (of advertising matter, samples, etc.).
publiquement [pyblikmɑ̃] *adv.* publicly, in public, openly.
puce [pys] *s.f.* flea; *marché aux ~s* (or *les ~s*), flea-market, second-hand market; *jeu de ~*, tiddly-winks; (fig.) *mettre la ~ à l'oreille de qn.*, to arouse someone's attention or suspicions; *secouer ses ~s*, to bestir oneself (and get out of bed); *secouer les ~s à qn.*, to reprimand s.o.; to catch s.o. out; *~ adj.* puce(-coloured).
puceau (pl. **-x**) [pyso] *adj.*, *s.m.* virgin (boy or man).
pucelage [pyslaʒ] *s.m.* maidenhood, virginity.
pucelle [pysɛl] *adj.* virgin; *~ s.f.* maiden, maid, virgin; *la ~ d'Orléans*, the Maid of Orleans, Joan of Arc.
puceron [pysrɔ̃] *s.m.* (ent.) puceron, aphis, blight (insect), greenfly, plant-louse.
puche [pyʃ] *s.f.* shrimping-net.
pucier [pysje] *s.m.* (pop.) bed, flea-bag.
pudding, pouding [pudiŋ] *s.m.* plum pudding.
puddl-age [pydlaʒ] *s.m.* (metall.) puddling; **~er** [pydle] *v.t.* (metall.) to puddle; **~eur** [pydlœr] *s.m.* (metall.) puddler.
pudeur [pydœr] *s.f.* modesty, bashfulness; decency; *sans ~*, shameless.
pudibond, -e [pydibɔ̃] *adj.* bashful, prudish.
pudibonderie [pydibɔ̃dri] *s.f.* excessive modesty, prudishness.
pudicité [pydisite] *s.f.* modesty, chastity, purity.
pudique [pydik] *adj.* modest, chaste, bashful; **~ment** [pydikmɑ̃] *adv.* modestly, chastely, bashfully.
puer [pɥe] *v.t.i.* to smell or stink (of); *il pue le vin*, he smells strongly of wine.
puériculture [pɥerikyltyr] *s.f.* rearing of children, infant management.
puéril, -e [pɥeril] *adj.* puerile, childish; trifling; **~ement** [pɥerilmɑ̃] *adv.* childishly, in a childish fashion.
puérilité [pɥerilite] *s.f.* puerility, childishness, puerile action, childish talk.
puerpéral, -e, (aux) [pɥɛrperal] *adj.* puerperal.
puffin [pyfɛ̃] *s.m.* (ornith.) shearwater; ⚠ not 'puffin'.
pugilat [pyʒila] *s.m.* pugilism, boxing; boxing-bout; fist-fight.
pugiliste [pyʒilist] *s.m.* pugilist, boxer.
puîné, -e [pɥine] *adj.*, *s.m.f.* younger, second, next, (child), younger (brother or sister).
puis [pɥi] *adv.* then, after that, afterwards, besides; *et ~*, and then; *et ~?*, what next?, so what?
puisage [pɥizaʒ] *s.m.* drawing up, pumping.
puisard [pɥizar] *s.m.* cesspool; drain-tank, sump.
puisatier [pɥizatje] *s.m.* well-digger.
puiser [pɥize] *v.t.* to draw, to pump up; (fig.) to fetch out (*dans*, of), to borrow, to extract, to derive.
puisque [pɥisk] *conj.* as, since, because, seeing that.
puissamment [pɥisamɑ̃] *adv.* powerfully, forcibly; extremely.
puissance [pɥisɑ̃s] *s.f.* power, might, force, energy; sway, authority, command; (math.) power; (obs.) powerful person; (pol.) power, powerful nation; *~ en chevaux*, horsepower; *~ au frein*, brake horsepower; (pol.) *grande ~*, major power; *en ~*, potential(ly), in reserve.

puissant, -e [pɥisɑ̃] *adj.* powerful, strong, potent, mighty; *les ~s*, the great, the mighty.
puits [pɥi] *s.m.* well; pit; shaft; *~ d'aération*, air-shaft; *~ de mine*, mine-shaft; *~ de science*, walking encyclopaedia; mine of information.
pulicaire [pylikɛr] *s.f.* (bot.) fleawort.
pull [pul] *s.m.* abbrev. of *pull-over*, pullover.
pullman [pulman] *s.m.* (rail.) Pullman car.
pull-over [pulɔvœr; pulɔvɛr] *s.m.* pullover.
pullulation [pylylɑsjɔ̃] *s.f.*, **pullulement** [pylylmɑ̃] *s.m.* pullulation, swarming.
pulluler [pylyle] *v.i.* to pullulate, to swarm, to multiply rapidly, to abound.
pulmonaire [pylmɔnɛr] *s.f.* (bot.) lungwort, Pulmonaria.
pulmonaire [pylmɔnɛr] *adj.* pulmonary.
pulpe [pylp] *s.f.* pulp.
pulpeu-x, -se [pylpø] *adj.* pulpous, pulpy.
pulsar [pylsar] *s.m.* (astron.) pulsar.
pulsatille [pylsatij] *s.f.* (bot.) pasque-flower, pulsatilla.
pulsation [pylsasjɔ̃] *s.f.* pulsation; throbbing, beating (of the pulse); vibration.
pulsative [pylsativ] *adj.f.* throbbing.
pulsion [pylsjɔ̃] *s.f.* (psychol.) urge, instinct.
pulsionnel, -le [pylsjɔnɛl] *adj.* (psychol.) instinctual.
pulsomètre [pyslsɔmɛtr] *s.m.* (techn.) pulsometer, (steam-condensing) vacuum pump.
pulsoréacteur [pylsɔreaktœr] *s.m.* (aeron.) pulso-jet.
pultacé, -e [pyltase] *adj.* (pathol.) pultaceous, pulpy.
pulvérisateur [pylverizatœr] *s.m.* pulverizer; atomizer, vaporizer, spray.
pulvérisation [pylverizɑsjɔ̃] *s.f.* pulverization, pulverizing; atomizing, spraying.
pulvériser [pylverize] *v.t.* to pulverize, to grind to powder; to atomize, to vaporize; (fig.) to annihilate, to crush completely, to cut to pieces.
pulvériseur [pylverizœr] *s.m.* (agric.) disc harrow.
pulvérulent, -e [pylverylɑ̃] *adj.* pulverulent, in dust, dust-covered, powdery.
puma [pyma] *s.m.* (zool.) puma, cougar.
punaise [pynɛz] *s.f.* **1.** (ent.) bug; **2.** drawing-pin.
punch[1] [pɔ̃ʃ] *s.m.* punch (drink).
punch[2] [pœnʃ] *s.m.* (boxing) ability to deliver punches; (fig.) drive, punch.
puncheur [pœnʃœr] *s.m.* boxer who delivers hard punches.
punching-ball [pœnʃiŋbol] *s.m.* punch-ball.
punique [pynik] *adj.* Punic; (fig.) treacherous; *foi ~*, Punic faith, treachery.
punir [pynir] *v.t.* to punish, to bring to punishment, to inflict punishment, or a penalty, on; to avenge; to penalize; *~ qn. de prison*, to punish s.o. with imprisonment; *~ qn. de* or *pour un crime*, to punish s.o. for a crime; *être puni par où l'on a péché*, to be justly punished for one's sins, to reap what one has sown; *un temps où la charité est punie*, a time when kindness is penalized; *un puni*, one undergoing punishment; (mil.) defaulter.
punissable [pynisabl] *adj.* punishable, liable to punishment or sanction.
punition [pynisjɔ̃] *s.f.* punishment; *en ~*, for a punishment, as a punishment.
punka see PANCA.
pupe [pyp] *s.f.* (ent.) pupa, chrysalis.
pupillaire [pypilɛr] *adj.* (law, anat.) pupillary, of the pupil.
pupillarité [pypilarite] *s.f.* (law) wardship, pupillage.
pupille [pypij] *s.m.f.* ward, pupil, minor; *~ s.f.* (anat.) pupil.
pupitre [pypitr] *s.m.* desk, reading-desk, lectern; music-stand.
pur, -e [pyr] *adj.* pure, unmingled, unalloyed, unadulterated, genuine, true, chaste, innocent, unsullied; clean, spotless; sheer, downright; *ciel ~*, clear sky; *~e bêtise*, downright foolishness; *par ~e malice*, out of sheer malice; *un ~ caprice*, a mere whim; *du vin ~*, wine without water; *conscience ~e*, clear conscience; *cheval ~-sang*, blood-horse, thoroughbred; *c'est la ~e vérité*, it's the plain unvarnished truth; *en ~e perte*, to no purpose, uselessly, with nothing to show for it; *en ~e nature*, in a state of nature, stark naked; **~ement** [pyrmɑ̃] *adv.* purely, simply, entirely, solely; *~ement et simplement*, unconditionally, without any reservations.
purée [pyre] *s.f.* (cook.) purée; *~ de pommes de terre*, or *pommes ~s*, mashed potatoes; (fam.) *être dans la ~*, to be hard up.
pureté [pyrte] *s.f.* purity, pureness, genuineness; innocence, chastity.
purgati-f, -ve [pyrgatif] *adj.* purgative; **~f** *s.m.* purgative.
purgation [pyrgɑsjɔ̃] *s.f.* purgation, purge.
purgatoire [pyrgatwar] *s.m.* purgatory.
purge [pyrʒ] *s.f.* purge, purging; clearing, draining-off; (law) paying off (mortgage, etc.); *robinet de ~*, drain-cock, blow-off cock.
purger [pyrʒe] *v.t.* to purge, to purify, to refine, to cleanse, to clear, to wipe off, to purge (sins, contempt, etc.); to drain off, to blow out; to administer a purgative to; **se ~** *v.refl.* to take a purgative.
purgeur [pyrʒœr] *s.m.* (techn.) blow-off cock, air-cock.
purifiant, -e [pyrifjɑ̃] *adj.* purifying.
purificat-eur, -rice [pyrifikatœr] *adj.* purifying.
purification [pyrifikɑsjɔ̃] *s.f.* purifying, purification; (liturg.) ceremony of purification; *la Purification*, the Purification of the Blessed Virgin Mary.
purificatoire [pyrifikatwar] *s.m.* (eccles.) purificator; *~ adj.* purifying.
purifier [pyrifje] *v.t.* to purify; to cleanse; to refine (gold, etc.).
purin [pyrɛ̃] *s.m.* liquid manure.
purisme [pyrism] *s.m.* purism.
puriste [pyrist] *s.m.f., adj.* purist.
puritain, -e [pyritɛ̃] *s.m.f.* puritan; *adj.* puritan(ical).
puritanisme [pyritanism] *s.m.* puritanism.
purotin [pyrɔtɛ̃] *s.m.* (pop.) one who is hard up, pauper.
purpurin, -e [pyrpyrɛ̃] *adj.* reddish, ruby-coloured, purplish.
purpurine [pyrpyrin] *s.f.* purpurin.
purulence [pyrylɑ̃s] *s.f.* purulence.
purulent, -e [pyrylɑ̃] *adj.* purulent.
pus [py] *s.m.* (pathol.) pus, matter.
push-pull [puʃpul] *s.m.* (electr.) push-pull (triode circuit).
pusillanime [pyzilanim] *adj.* pusillanimous, faint-hearted.
pusillanimité [pyzilanimite] *s.f.* pusillanimity.
pustule [pystyl] *s.f.* pustule, pimple.
pustuleu-x, -se [pystylø] *adj.* pustulous, pimply.
putain [pytɛ̃] *s.f.* prostitute, whore; (fig.) bitch; *quelle ~ de temps!*, what bloody awful weather!; *~ adj.invar.* accommodating, obliging.
putati-f, -ve [pytatif] *adj.* (law) putative, reputed, supposed.
pute [pyt] *s.f.* (vulg.) = PUTAIN.
putois [pytwa] *s.m.* (zool.) polecat, skunk.
putréfaction [pytrefaksjɔ̃] *s.f.* putrefaction, decomposition.
putréfier [pytrefje] *v.t.* to putrefy, to rot, to decompose; **se ~** *v.refl.* to putrefy, to rot.

putrescence [pytresɑ̃s] *s.f.* putrescence.
putrescent, -e [pytresɑ̃] *adj.* putrescent.
putride [pytrid] *adj.* putrid.
putridité [pytridite] *s.f.* putridity.
putsch [putʃ] *s.m.* (pol.) putsch, military coup d'état.
puy [pyi] *s.m.* mountain, conical peak, (in Auvergne).
p.-v. abbrev. *procès-verbal.*
pygargue [pigarg] *s.m.* (ornith.) sea-eagle.
pygmée [pigme] *s.m.* pygmy; (fig.) dwarf, midget, insignificant little man.
pyjama [piʒama] *s.m.* pyjamas, pyjama suit.
pylône [pilon] *s.m.* pylon.
pylore [pilɔr] *s.m.* (anat.) pylorus.
pyorrhée [pjɔre] *s.f.* (med.) pyorrhoea; discharge of pus.
pyracanthe [pirakɑ̃t] *s.f.* (bot.) pyracanth.
pyrale [piral] *s.f.* (ent.) Pyralis.
pyramidal, -e, (**aux**) [piramidal] *adj.* pyramidal; (fig.) astounding, tremendous.
pyramide [piramid] *s.f.* pyramid.
pyramider [piramide] *v.i.* to rise like a pyramid.
pyramidion [piramidjɔ̃] *s.m.* (arch.) pyramidian (at top of obelisk, etc.).
pyrénéen, -ne [pireneɛ̃] *adj., s.m.f.* Pyrenean; (native or inhabitant) of the Pyrenees.
pyrénéite [pireneit] *s.f.* (min.) pyreneite, a variety of garnet.
pyrèthre [pirɛtr] *s.m.* (bot.) pyrethrum; *poudre de* ~, pyrethrum (powder).
pyrexie [pirɛksi] *s.f.* (pathol.) pyrexia; feverish condition.
pyrite [pirit] *s.f.* (chem.) pyrites.
pyrogallique [pirɔgalik] *adj.* (chem.) pyrogallic.
pyrogallol [pirɔgal(l)ɔl] *s.m.* (chem., photo.) pyrogallol, pyro.
pyrogravure [pirɔgravyr] *s.f.* pyrography, poker-work.
pyroligneux [pirɔliɲø] *adj., s.m.* pyroligneous (acid).
pyroman-e [pirɔman] *s.m.f.* pyromaniac, incendiary, arsonist; ~**ie** [pirɔmani] *s.f.* pyromania, incendiarism.
pyromètre [pirɔmɛtr] *s.m.* pyrometer.
pyrosis [pirozis] *s.m.* (med.) pyrosis, heartburn.
pyrotechn-ie [pirɔtɛkni] *s.f.* pyrotechnics; ~**ique** [pirɔtɛknik] *adj.* pyrotechnic.
pyroxène [pirɔksɛn] *s.m.* (min.) pyroxene, a metal occurring in lavas.
pyroxylé, -e [pirɔksile] *adj.* (chem.) *poudre* ~*e*, gun-cotton.
pyroxyline [pirɔksilin] *s.f.* (chem.) pyroxylin; gun-cotton.
pyrrhique [pirik] *s.f.* pyrrhic dance.
pyrrhonien, -ne [pirɔnjɛ̃] *adj., s.m.f.* Pyrrhonian, Pyrrhonic.
pyrrhonisme [pirɔnism] *s.m.* Pyrrhonism.
Pythagore [pitagɔr] *s.m.* Pythagoras.
pythagoricien, -ne [pitagɔrisjɛ̃] *adj., s.m.f.* Pythagorean.
pythagor-ique [pitagɔrik] *adj.* Pythagorean; *silence* ~, prolonged silence; ~**isme** [pitagɔrism] *s.m.* Pythagorean philosophy, Pythagorism.
python [pitɔ̃] *s.m.* (zool.) python.
pythonisse [pitɔnis] *s.f.* (ant.) pythoness; (colloq.) fortune-teller, prophetess.
pyxide [piksid] *s.f.* (bot.) pyxidium; (eccles.) pyx.

Q

Q, q [ky] *s.m.* the letter Q, q.
Q.G. [kyʒe] abbrev. *Quartier général*, H.Q., G.H.Q.
Q.I. [kyi] abbrev. *quotient intellectuel*, I.Q.
qu' see QUE.
quadragénaire [kwadraʒenɛr] *adj., s.m.* quadragenarian.
quadragésimal, -e, (**aux**) [kwadraʒezimal] *adj.* quadragesimal, Lenten.
Quadragésime [kwadraʒezim] *s.f.* Quadragesima (Sunday).
quadrangulaire [kwadrɑ̃gylɛr] *adj.* quadrangular.
quadrant [k(w)adrɑ̃] *s.m.* quadrant.
quadratique [kwadratik] *adj.* (math.) quadratic; (crystallography) tetragonal.
quadrature [kwadratyr] *s.f.* (math., astron.) quadrature, squaring; *la* ~ *du cercle*, squaring the circle; (fig.) an insoluble problem, an unattainable objective; *les* ~*s de la Lune*, the (first and last) quarters of the moon; *marée de* ~, neap-tide.
quadriennal, -e, (**aux**) [kwadrijenal] *adj.* quadrennial, four-yearly.
quadrifide [kwadrifid] *adj.* (bot.) quadrifid, cleft into four divisions or lobes.
quadrifolié, -e [kwadrifɔlje] *adj.* (bot.) quadrifoliate.
quadrige [k(w)adriʒ] *s.m.* (Rom. ant.) quadriga.
quadri-jumeaux [kwadriʒymo] *adj.m.pl.* (anat.) quadrigeminal; ~**latère** [k(w)adrilatɛr] *s.m.* quadrilateral.
quadrillage [kadrijaʒ] *s.m.* **1.** cross-ruling, squaring (of paper); pattern of checks or squares or right-angled intersections, chequer-work; **2.** (mil., police) division of territory into sections for close supervision.
quadrille [kadrij] *s.f.* **1.** (obs.) group of riders in a tournament; **2.** (bullfighting) team of toreros working with a matador; ~ *s.m.* **1.** quadrille (dance); **2.** set of dancers in a country dance (Fr. *contredanse*).
quadrillé, -e [kadrije] *adj.* (of materials) chequered; (of paper) ruled in squares.
quadriller [kadrije] *v.t.* to divide into squares, to cross-rule; to divide into sections (see QUADRILLAGE 2).
quadrimoteur [k(w)adrimɔtœr] *adj.m., s.m.* four-engined (aircraft).
quadriparti, -e [kwadriparti], **quadripartite** [kwadripartit] *adj.* (bot., pol.) quadripartite.
quadrique [kwadrik] *adj., s.f.* (math.) quadric.
quadri-réacteur [k(w)adrireaktœr] *s.m.* four-engined jet aircraft; ~**syllabe** [kwadrisil(l)ab] *s.m.* quadrisyllable; ~**syllabique** [kwadrisil(l)abik] *adj.* quadrisyllabic.
quadrumane [k(w)adryman] *s.m.* quadrumane; ~ *adj.* quadrumanous.
quadrupède [k(w)adrypɛd] *s.m., adj.* quadruped.
quadruple [k(w)adrypl] *adj., s.m.* quadruple, fourfold, (number or amount).
quadrupler [k(w)adryple] *v.t.i.* to quadruple, to increase fourfold.
quadrupl-és, -ées [k(w)adryple] *s.m.f.pl.* quadruplets, quads.
quai [ke] *s.m.* quay, wharf; embankment (beside

river); (rail.) platform; *droit de* ~, wharfage; *le Quai* (*d'Orsay*), the French Foreign Office.
quaker [kwɛkœr] *s.m.*, **quakeresse** [kwɛkrɛs] *s.f.* Quaker.
qualifiable [kalifjabl] *adj.* **1.** that may be characterized or described (*de*, as); *pas* ~, indescribable, outrageous, that defies description; **2.** (sport) able to qualify.
qualificateur [kalifikatœr] *s.m.* (eccles. hist.) qualificator.
qualificati-f, -ve [kalifikatif] *adj.* (gram.) qualificative, qualifying; qualificatory; ~**f** *s.m.* epithet; significant appellation.
qualification [kalifikɑsjɔ̃] *s.f.* **1.** qualifying; description, designation, name, calling (s.o. sth.), giving a name to (s.o., sth.); epithet; title; **2.** (sport) qualifying; **3.** qualification (for job, etc.); ⚠ not 'qualification' in senses 'modification', 'restriction', 'reservation'.
qualifié, -e [kalifje] *adj.* **1.** (law, of crime, etc.) aggravated, with aggravating circumstances; **2.** qualified; qualifying.
qualifier [kalifje] *v.t.* **1.** to describe, to term, to call; ~ *qn. d'imbécile*, to call s.o. a fool; **2.** to qualify; to be suitable (*pour*, for); (sport) to (cause to) qualify; **se** ~ *v.refl.* to qualify.
qualitati-f, -ve [kalitatif] *adj.* qualitative; ~**vement** [kalitativmɑ̃] *adv.* qualitatively.
qualité [kalite] *s.f.* quality, characteristic, trait; attribute; excellence, skill, accomplishment; rank, nobility; title; *un vin de* ~, a choice wine; *en* ~ *de*, in the capacity of; as; under the name of; *nom, prénom et* ~, name, forename, and style; *avoir* ~ *de citoyen*, to rank as a citizen; *avoir* ~ *d'électeur*, to be qualified to vote; *avoir* ~ *d'agir*, to be empowered to act.
quand [kɑ̃] *adv., conj.* when, whenever; what time?; while, whilst; though, even though, although; *depuis* ~?, how long?, since when?; *jusqu'à* ~?, till when?; *à* ~ *le mariage?*, when is the wedding?; *c'est pour* ~ *la prochaine réunion?*, when, what is the date of, the next meeting?; ~ *bien même*, even though; ~ *même*, all the same, nevertheless; even though.
quanta see QUANTUM.
quant à [kɑ̃ta] *prep.* as for, with regard to, respecting; ~ *moi, je le ferai*, for my part, I have decided to do it.
quant-à-soi [kɑ̃taswa] *s.m.* reserve, dignity; *se tenir sur son* ~, to stand on one's dignity; to behave with reserve; to keep oneself to oneself.
quantième [kɑ̃tjɛm] *adj., s.m.* day (of the month).
quanti-fiable [kɑ̃tifjabl] *adj.* quantifiable; ~**fication** [kɑ̃tifikɑsjɔ̃] *s.f.* quantification; ~**fier** [kɑ̃tifje] *v.t.* to quantify, to determine the quantity of.
quantique [k(w)ɑ̃tik] *adj.* quantic.
quantitati-f, -ve [kɑ̃titatif] *adj.* quantitative; ~**vement** [kɑ̃titativmɑ̃] *adv.* quantitatively.
quantité [kɑ̃tite] *s.f.* quantity; great deal, amount, abundance, numbers; (math.) quantity; (pros.) quantity; ~ *de gens*, quite a number of people, a great many people; *en* ~, in quantity, in abundance, in bulk; *par grandes* ~*s*, in large quantities.
quantum [kwɑ̃tɔm] *s.m.* (pl. *quanta*) quantum; *théorie des quanta*, (phys.) quantum theory.
quarantaine [karɑ̃tɛn] *s.f.* **1.** forty, about forty; age of forty, fortieth year; **2.** quarantine; *mettre en* ~, to put in quarantine, to quarantine; (fig.) to boycott; **3.** (bot.) stock.
quarante [karɑ̃t] *adj., s.m.invar.* forty; *je m'en moque comme de l'an* ~, I don't care two hoots about it; *les années* ~, the (nineteen-)forties; (econ.) *les* ~ *heures*, the forty-hour week.
quarantenaire [karɑ̃tnɛr] *adj.* **1.** of forty years; **2.** (naut.) pertaining to quarantine; ~ *s.m.* quarantine-station.
quarantième [karɑ̃tjɛm] *adj., s.m.f.* fortieth.
quarderonner [kardərɔne] *v.t.* (arch.) to round off (an angle).
quart [kar] *s.m.* fourth part, quarter; quarter litre, quarter pound; quarter-litre receptacle (esp. mil. quarter-litre mug); (naut.) (i.) watch; (ii.) point of the compass; ~ *de cercle*, quadrant; ~ *d'heure*, quarter of an hour; *pour le* ~ *d'heure*, for the present, presently; *passer un mauvais* ~ *d'heure*, to have a bad time of it; *le* ~ *d'heure de Rabelais*, the moment of payment or reckoning, the critical moment, the moment of truth, the crunch; *le dernier* ~ *d'heure*, the final (and decisive) phase (of a battle, etc.); *les trois* ~*s du temps*, most of the time, mostly, usually; *aux trois* ~*s ivre*, three parts drunk; *manteau trois* ~*s*, three-quarter length coat; *portrait trois* ~*s*, three-quarter face portrait; (arch.) ~ *de rond*, quarter-round, ovolo; (mus.) ~ *de soupir*, semiquaver rest; *deux heures un* ~, a quarter past two; *deux heures trois* ~*s* or *trois heures moins le* ~, a quarter to three; *officier de* ~, officer of the watch; *maître de* ~, boatswain's mate; *être de* ~, *faire le* ~, to keep a watch.
quartanier, quartannier [kartanje] *s.m.* wild boar four years old.
quartation see INQUARTATION.
quartaut [karto] *s.m.* (obs.) octave-cask, quarter-cask.
quart-de-rond [kardərɔ̃] *s.m.* (pl. ~*s-de-rond*) (techn.) quarter-hollow moulding-plane.
quarte [kart] *adj.* quartan; *fièvre* ~, quartan fever or ague; ~ *s.f.* **1.** (mus.) fourth; **2.** (fenc.) quart; (piquet) quart, carte; **3.** (obs.) quarter gallon.
quartenier [kartənje] *s.m.* (obs.) police officer (in charge of a quarter).
quarteron[1] [kartərɔ̃] *s.m.* fourth part of 100; quarter-pound.
quarteron[2]**, -ne** [kartərɔ̃] *s.m.f.* quadroon.
quartette [kwartɛt] *s.m.* (jazz) quartet.
quartidi [kwartidi] *s.m.* (hist.) fourth day of *décade* in Fr. Republican calendar.
quartier [kartje] *s.m.* quarter; piece, portion, sector, slice, block, lump; gammon (of bacon); district, neighbourhood; *mettre en* ~*s*, to tear to pieces; *faire* ~ *à*, to spare; to give quarter to; *demander* ~, to cry for quarter; ~ *général*, headquarters; ~*-maître*, (naut., obs. mil.) quartermaster, (nav.) leading seaman; ~ *de selle*, saddle-flap; *prendre ses* ~*s d'hiver*, to take up one's winter quarters; *les bas* ~*s*, the lower, or the poorer, parts (of the town).
quarto [kwarto] *adv.* fourthly.
quartz [kwarts] *s.m.* quartz.
quartzite [kwartsit] *s.m.* quartzite.
quasar [kwazar] *s.m.* (astron.) quasar.
quasi [kazi] *s.m.* (butch.) thick end of loin of veal.
quasi [kazi] *adv.* almost, virtually, more or less; so to speak, as it were; ~**-contrat** [kazikɔ̃tra] *s.m.* (law) quasi-contract, implied contract; ~**-délit** [kazideli] *s.m.* (law) quasi-delict, technical offence; ~**ment** [kazimɑ̃] *adv.* (fam.) almost, more or less.
Quasimodo [kazimɔdo] *s.f.* Low Sunday.
quassia [kwasja], **quassier** [kwasje] *s.m.* (bot.) quassia.
quaternaire [kwatɛrnɛr] *adj.* quaternary.
quaterne [kwatɛrn] *s.m.* quarternion (at games).
quaternion [kwatɛrnjɔ̃] *s.m.* (math.) quaternion.
quatorze [katɔrz] *adj., s.m.* fourteen; fourteenth.
quatorzième [katɔrzjɛm] *adj., s.m.* fourteenth.
quatrain [katrɛ̃] *s.m.* quatrain; four-line stanza.
quatre [katr] *adj.* four; a few; *marcher à* ~ *pattes*, to go on all fours; *Henri* ~, Henry the Fourth;

marchand(e) des ~ saisons, costermonger, greengrocer; *entre ~ (z') yeux*, between ourselves, in strict confidence; *monter ~ à ~*, to run upstairs four at a time, to rush upstairs; *à ~ pas d'ici*, a few steps away, just round the corner; *travailler comme ~*, to work like a horse; *un restaurant de ~ sous*, a cheap, or very ordinary, restaurant; (fam.) *un de ces ~ jours*, one of these days, before very long; (fig.) (obs.) *mettre en ~*, to quarter, to dismember, to cut to pieces; (fig.) *se mettre en ~ pour faire*, to exert every muscle to do; *se mettre en ~ pour qn.*, to go through fire and water for s.o., to be prepared to do anything for s.o.; ~ *s.m.* (rowing, math., cards) four.

Quatre-Cantons [katrəkɑ̃tɔ̃] *s.m.pl.* (geog.) *le lac des ~*, the Lake of Lucerne.

quatre-épices [katrepis] *s.m.* or *f.invar.* (bot.) fennel-flower; **~-feuilles** [katrəfœj] *s.m.invar.* (arch.) quatrefoil; **~-huit** [katrəɥit] *s.m.invar.* (mus.) (*à*) *~-huit*, (in) common time; **~-mâts** [katrəmɑ] *s.m. invar.* (naut.) four-master; **~-saisons** [katrəsɛzɔ̃] *s.f.invar.* kind of strawberry; **~-temps** [katrətɑ̃] *s.m.pl.invar.* (eccles.) ember days.

quatre-vingtième [katrəvɛ̃tjɛm] *adj.*, *s.m.* eightieth.

quatre-vingt(s) [katrəvɛ̃] *adj.* eighty, fourscore.

quatrième [katrijɛm] *adj.* fourth; ~ *s.m.* fourth; fourth floor; fourth player; ~ *s.f.* (at school) fourth form, fourth class; (cards) *une ~ au roi*, four to the king; **~ment** [katrijɛmmɑ̃] *adv.* fourthly.

quatrillion [katriljɔ̃] *s.m.* quadrillion.

quatuor [kwatɥɔr] *s.m.* (mus.) quartet, quartette.

que [kə] (**qu'** before vowel or h-mute) *rel.* & *int. pron.* whom, which, that, (Eng. equivalents often omitted); as, when; what; *un homme ~ je connais*, a man (whom) I know; *le livre ~ vous cherchiez*, the book (that) you were looking for, the book for which you were looking; *fatigué ~ je suis*, tired as I am; *~ je sache*, as far as I know; *l'été qu'il a fait si chaud*, the summer when it was so hot; *~ dites-vous?*, what are you saying?; *qu'est-ce ~ tu cherches?*, what are you looking for?; *qu'est-ce ~ c'est?*, what is it?; *qu'est-ce qui se passe?*, what is going on?; *~ faire?*, what shall we do?, what's to be done?; *il ne sait ~ faire*, he doesn't know what to do; *ce ~ je ne supporterai jamais*, what I will never put up with.

que [kə] (**qu'** before vowel or h-mute) *adv.* **1.** (exclamatory) how much, how many; *vous êtes bon!*, how kind you are!; *~ de difficultés!*, what a lot of difficulties!; (fam.) *ce qu'il est bête!*, how stupid he is!; *~ si!*, yes, indeed!, of course!; *~ non!*, certainly n,t!; **2.** (int.) *~ ne le disiez-vous?*, why did you not say so?

que [kə] (**qu'** before vowel or h-mute) *conj.* that (Eng. equivalent often omitted), than, as, if, whether, in order that, as though, although, so that, etc.; *je crois qu'il est honnête*, I believe (that) he is an honest man; *vous dites ~ oui*, you say yes; you say (that) it is so; *il croit ~ non*, he thinks not; *est-il possible ~ vous partiez?*, is it possible that you are really going?; *plus vite ~ lui*, quicker than he; *aussi grand ~ moi*, as big as I; *qu'il accepte ou non*, whether he agrees or no; *~ son nom soit béni*, blessed be his name; *qu'il fasse comme il lui plaît*, let him do as he likes; *qu'il me soit permis de*, might I be allowed to?; *quand il pleuvait et qu'on ne pouvait pas sortir*, when it was raining and they couldn't go out; *parce que je suis malade et ~ je ne sors guère*, because I am unwell and (because I) don't often go out; *s'il vient et qu'il veuille me voir*, if he comes and (if he) wants to see me; *j'attendrai qu'il vienne*, I shall wait until he comes; *je ne te quitterai pas ~ l'orage soit terminé*, I won't leave you till the storm is over; *deux minutes s'étaient à peine écoulées qu'il entendit arriver le taxi*, scarcely two minutes had elapsed when he heard the taxi arrive; *c'est une drôle d'affaire ~ cela*, that is a queer business; *ne...~*, only, nothing but; *il n'en restait ~ les os*, there were only the bones left.

quel, -le [kɛl] *adj.* what; which; of what kind, what sort of; who; whatever; *~le heure est-il?*, what time is it?, what is the time?; *~le horreur!*, what a horrible thing!, how horrible!; *je ne sais ~le robe choisir*, I do not know which dress to choose; *~s sont ces types-là?*, who are those chaps?; *~le que soit la différence*, whatever the difference may be.

quelconque [kɛlkɔ̃k] *adj. ind.* whatever; any; some or other; ordinary; without characteristics; *en un point ~ du cercle*, at any point on the circle; *un livre ~*, any book, some book or other; *il faut donner une raison ~*, you must give a reason of some sort; *d'une manière ~*, anyhow; *un homme ~*, an ordinary man, an unremarkable man; *c'est très ~*, it is very ordinary, it is quite unexciting.

quelque [kɛlk(ə)] *ind. adj.* some, any; (pl.) a few; *~ indiscret aura dit cela*, some busybody has probably said that; *~ jour*, some day or other; *il a dû avoir ~ sujet de se plaindre*, very likely he had some ground for complaint; *~s amis*, a few friends; *ces ~s lignes*, these few lines; *~ chose*, something; *~ part*, somewhere; *~ peu*, somewhat; *il y a ~s années*, a few years ago; *quarante et ~s*, rather over forty, forty plus; ~ *adv.* about, some, nearly; *avoir ~ cinquante ans*, to be about fifty; *~...que*, however . . .; *~ grands qu'ils soient*, however great they may be.

quelquefois [kɛlkəfwa] *adv.* sometimes.

quelqu'un, -e [kɛlkœ̃] *ind. pron.* somebody, someone; anybody, anyone; (pl.) some, a few; *se croire ~*, to think oneself somebody; to be conceited; *quelques-uns de mes amis*, a few of my friends.

quémander [kemɑ̃de] *v.t.i.* to beg for, to solicit, to beg, to go begging.

qu'en-dira-t-on [kɑ̃diratɔ̃] *s.m.invar.* what people say, people's opinion; public talk; *se moquer du ~*, not to care a rap for what people say.

quenelle [kənɛl] *s.f.* (cook.) quenelle, fish- or meat-ball.

quenotte [kənɔt] *s.f.* (child. lang.) tooth.

quenouille [kənuj] *s.f.* **1.** distaff; (fig.) *tomber en ~*, to be ruled by women; **2.** pyramid-shaped fruit-tree; **3.** bed-post (of four-poster).

quérable [kerabl] *adj.* (law) demandable; that must be collected in person.

quercitron [kɛrsitrɔ̃] *s.m.* (bot.) quercitron, dyer's oak.

querelle [kərɛl] *s.f.* quarrel, quarrelling, row, brawl; dispute; *chercher ~ à*, to pick a quarrel with; *~ d'Allemand*, groundless quarrel; *vider une ~*, to fight it out; to settle a dispute.

quereller [kərɛle] *v.t.* **1.** (obs.) to abuse; to reproach; **2. se ~** *v.refl.* to quarrel, to fall out.

querelleu-r, -se [kərɛlœr] *adj.* quarrelsome, disputatious, aggressive.

quérir [kerir] *v.t.* to fetch; to look for.

questeur [kɥɛstœr] *s.m.* **1.** (Rom. hist.) quaestor; **2.** questor (treasurer of Fr. parliamentary assembly).

question [kɛstjɔ̃] *s.f.* **1.** question; query; point, matter, issue; *mettre en ~*, to call in question; *de quoi est-il ~?*, what is the matter?; *il n'est pas ~ de cela*, (i.) that is not the point; (ii.) that is out of the question; *vous sortez de la ~*, you are not sticking to the point; *là n'est pas la ~*, that's not the point, or the question; *la ~ préalable*, the previous question; (pol.) *~ de confiance*, motion of confidence; *ensuite, il fut ~ du mariage*, next, the question of the wedding came up; *qu'il n'en soit plus ~!*, (i.) let bygones be bygones; let us

say no more about it; (ii.) do not bother me any more; *c'est une ~ de vie ou de mort*, it's a matter of life and death; **2.** judicial torture, interrogation under torture; the rack.
questionnaire [kɛstjɔnɛr] *s.m.* questionnaire.
questionner [kɛstjɔne] *v.t.* to question, to interrogate; ⚠ not 'to question' in sense 'to cast doubts on'.
questionneu-r, -se [kɛstjɔnœr] *adj.* inquisitive.
questure [kɥɛstyr] *s.f.* **1.** quaestorship; **2.** office of *questeur*.
quête [kɛt] *s.f.* **1.** quest, search; (hunt.) beating; *en ~ de travail*, looking for work; *se mettre en ~ de*, to look for, to go in quest of; **2.** collection; begging; *faire la ~*, to make a collection.
quêter [kɛte] *v.t.* **1.** to seek, to solicit, to beg for, to fish for (compliments, etc.); (hunt.) to seek; **2.** to collect (alms, etc.), to make a collection.
quêteu-r, -se [kɛtœr] *s.m.f.* **1.** (Lit.) one who seeks (favours, etc.); **2.** one who takes the collection, collector.
quetsche [kwɛtʃ] *s.f.* quetsch plum.
queue [kø] *s.f.* tail; tail-piece, pigtail; any appendix shaped like a tail; end (of piece of material, etc.); latter end, fag end; rear; queue; string; handle; stalk, stem, (of plants, fruit, flowers, etc.); label (of documents); train (of a dress); (billiards) cue; *faire (la) ~*, to queue, to form a queue; *être à la ~ de*, to be at the bottom or end of; *en* or *de ~*, (of vehicles) at the tail end, at the back; *commencer par la ~*, to begin at the end; *produits de ~*, (distilling) tailings; (fig.) inferior products; *à la ~ leu leu*, one after another; in Indian file; *finir en ~ de poisson*, to fizzle out, to peter out, to end in a fiasco; *cela n'a ni ~ ni tête*, one cannot make head or tail of it; *tirer le diable par la ~*, to live from hand to mouth; to be hard up; *piano à ~*, grand piano; (fig.) *tenir la ~ de la poêle*, to be the boss; *~ de cheveux*, pigtail; *porte-~*, train-bearer; *à la ~ gît le venin*, the sting is in the tail; *~ de cheval*, horse-tail; pony-tail (hair style); *~(-)de(-)morue* or *~(-)de(-)pie*, swallow-tailed coat, morning coat, cutaway jacket.
queue(-)d'aronde [kødarɔ̃d] *s.f.* (techn.) dovetail.
queue-de-cochon [kødkɔʃɔ̃] *s.f.* (techn.) auger-bit, gimlet, borer; **~-de-rat** [kødra] *s.f.* (techn.) rat-tail file; **~-de-renard** [kødrənar] *s.f.* **1.** (bot.) love-lies-bleeding; **2.** (techn.) firmer chisel.
queuter [køte] *v.i.* (billiards) to make a push-stroke.
queux [kø] *s.f.* whetstone.
qui [ki] *rel.* & *int. pron.* who, whom, which, that, whoever, whomsoever, he who, she who; *à ~*, to whom; *à ~ est ce livre?*, whose book is this?; *à ~ mieux mieux*, in competition, one against the other, each louder, faster, etc., than the other; *c'est à ~ arrivera le premier*, the one who gets there first wins, they are competing to see who gets there first; *pour ~ s'y connaît*, to anyone who knows; *c'est à ~ le fera*, they all wish to do it; *je ne sais ~ vous voulez dire*, I do not know whom you mean; *je n'ai parlé à ~ que ce soit*, I spoke to nobody; *aimez ~ vous aime*, love those who love you; *à ~ le tour?*, whose turn is it?; *~ avez-vous vu?*, whom have you seen?; *~ est là?*, who is there?; *~ est-ce qu'il a rencontré?*, whom did he meet?; *ils s'échappèrent ~ par la porte, ~ par la fenêtre*, some escaped through the door, others through the window; *~ perd, gagne*, he who loses, wins.
(à) quia [akɥija] *adv. mettre* or *réduire qn. à ~*, to put s.o. in a quandary.
quiche [kiʃ] *s.f.* (cook.) quiche, flan with filling of eggs, cream, bacon, etc.
Quichotte [kiʃɔt] *s.m.* (Don) Quixote.
quichottisme [kiʃɔtism] *s.m.* quixotic behaviour.
quiconque [kikɔ̃k] *ind. pron.* whoever, whosoever, whomsoever, anyone who; anybody, anyone at all.
quidam [kɥidam] *s.m.* individual, (a) certain person, someone who shall be nameless.
quiddité [kɥid(d)ite] *s.f.* (phil.) quiddity.
quiet, quiète [kjɛ] *adj.* (obs.) quiet, tranquil, calm.
quiét-isme [kɥietism; kjetism] *s.m.* quietism; **~iste** [kɥijetist; kjetist] *adj., s.m.f.* quietist; **~ude** [kɥietyd; kjetyd] *s.f.* quietude; tranquillity, calm; *en toute ~ude*, in peace and quiet.
quignon [kiɲɔ̃] *s.m.* hunk, chunk, (of bread).
quille[1] [kij] *s.f.* **1.** skittle, ninepin; *un jeu de ~s*, a game of skittles, bowling; **2.** (fam.) leg; (mil. slang) demobilization; *être sur ses ~s*, to be on one's feet, to be restored to health; *jouer des ~s*, to take to one's heels; (mil.) *à nous la ~*, it's demob for us; **2.** tall, slim bottle (e.g. of hock).
quille[2] [kij] *s.f.* (naut.) keel.
quillier [kije] *s.m.* skittle-alley; set of ninepins.
quillon [kijɔ̃] **1.** crossbar (of sword); **2.** piling-swivel (on rifle).
quinaire [kinɛr] *adj.* quinary.
quinaud, -e [kino] *adj.* (obs.) abashed, ashamed.
quincaillerie [kɛ̃kɑjri] *s.f.* ironmongery, hardware, ironmongery shop or trade; imitation jewellery.
quincailli-er, -ère [kɛ̃kɑje] *s.m.f.* ironmonger.
quinconce [kɛ̃kɔ̃s] *s.m.* quincunx; trees planted in fives, or in alternate rows; *en ~*, quincuncial; planted in fives, or in quincunxes.
quine [kin] *s.m.* **1.** (obs.) series of five winning numbers; **2.** (fig.) big win, great victory; (backgammon) two fives.
quiné, -e [kine] *adj.* (bot.) quinate.
quinine [kinin] *s.f.* (pharm.) quinine, sulphate of quinine.
quinquagénaire [kɛ̃kaʒenɛr] *adj., s.m.f.* (person) fifty years old; quinquagenarian.
quinquagésime [kɥɛ̃kwaʒezim] *s.f.* Quinquagesima Sunday.
quinquennal, -e, (aux) [kɥɛ̃kɥenal] *adj.* quinquennial, every five years, of five years duration; *plan ~*, five-year plan.
quinquet [kɛ̃kɛ] *s.m.* **1.** Argand lamp, lamp; **2.** (pop.) eye.
quinquina [kɛ̃kina] *s.m.* Peruvian bark, quinquina, cinchona.
quint [kɛ̃] *adj.m.* (Fr. hist.) *Charles-~*, Charles the Fifth.
quintaine [kɛ̃tɛn] *s.f.* (hist.) quintain.
quintal, (aux) [kɛ̃tal] *s.m.* quintal (=(obs.) 50 kg; (mod.) 100 kg).
quinte [kɛ̃t] *s.f.* **1.** (mus.) fifth; (cards) quint; (fenc.) quint(e); **2.** fit of coughing (esp. in whooping-cough); (fig.) whim, fit of temper, tantrum.
quintefeuille [kɛ̃tfœj] *s.f.* (bot., herald.) cinquefoil; (arch.) cinquefoil window.
quintessence [kɛ̃tesɑ̃s] *s.f.* quintessence; pith.
quintessencié, -e [kɛ̃tesɑ̃sje] *adj.* hypercritical, quintessential, over-subtle.
quintessencier [kɛ̃tesɑ̃sje] *v.t.* to extract the quintessence of, to subtilize, to refine excessively.
quintette [k(ɥ)ɛ̃tɛt] *s.m.* (mus.) quintet, quintette.
quinteu-x, -se [kɛ̃tø] *adj.* peevish, fitful, capricious, (fam.) contrary; (of horse) restive.
quintidi [k(ɥ)ɛ̃tidi] *s.m.* (hist.) fifth day of *décade* in Fr. Republican calendar.
quintillion [k(ɥ)ɛ̃tiljɔ̃] *s.m.* quintillion.
quintuple [kɛ̃typl] *adj., s.m.* quintuple, fivefold.
quintupler [kɛ̃typle] *v.t.i.* to quintuple, to increase fivefold.

quintupl-és, -ées [kɛ̃typle] *s.m.f.pl.* quintuplets, quins.
quinzaine [kɛ̃zɛn] *s.f.* fifteen, about fifteen; period of fifteen days; fortnight; two weeks of paid work; two weeks' pay; the fourteenth day after; *remettre à ~*, to put off for a fortnight.
quinze [kɛ̃z] *adj.* fifteen; fifteenth; *d'aujourd'hui en ~*, today fortnight; *il y a eu ~ jours hier*, a fortnight yesterday; *tous les ~ jours*, every fortnight; once a fortnight; *Louis ~*, Louis the Fifteenth.
Quinze-Vingts [kɛ̃zvɛ̃] *s.m.pl.* hospital in Paris for the blind; *un quinze-vingts*, (i.) an inmate of the *Quinze-Vingts*; (ii.) a blind person.
quinzième [kɛ̃zjɛm] *adj., s.m.* fifteenth; fifteenth part; **~ment** [kɛ̃zjɛmmɑ̃] *adv.* fifteenthly, in fifteenth place.
quiproquo [kiprɔko] *s.m.* mistake, misunderstanding; mistaken identity.
quittance [kitɑ̃s] *s.f.* receipt, discharge (of debt, etc.); (obs.) *donner ~ de qch. à qn.*, to let s.o. off sth., to release s.o. from sth.
quittancer [kitɑ̃se] *v.t.* to give a receipt for; to receipt.
quitte [kit] *adj.* quit, free, discharged, clear, out of debt; *me voilà ~ envers vous*, I owe you nothing now; now we are quits; *il en est ~ à bon marché*, he gets off lightly; *elle en fut ~ pour la peur*, she escaped with nothing more than fright; *je le ferai, ~ à être puni*, I shall do it and chance the punishment; *jouer ~ ou double*, to play double or quits; *~ à ~*, quits; *tenir ~*, to release from payment or obligation.
quitter [kite] *v.t.* **1.** to leave, to quit, to abandon, to give up, to renounce, to forsake; *~ la place*, to leave, to make oneself scarce; to give up; *il ne la quitte pas des yeux*, he can't stop looking at her; (telephone) *ne quittez pas*, hold the line, hold on; *~ ses habits*, to take off one's clothes; *~ la partie*, to leave the game; (fig.) to give up, to throw in the sponge; *~ la vie*, to depart (this life); *~ prise*, to let go one's hold; *~ le deuil*, to go out of mourning; **2.** (obs.) to release (s.o. from a debt, etc.); to give up (sth. to s.o.); **se ~** *v.refl.* to separate, to part.
quitus [k(ɥ)itys] *s.m.* (law, comm.) discharge, receipt in full.
qui-vive [kiviv] *interj.* *~?*, who goes there?; *~ s.m.* alert; *être toujours sur le ~*, to be constantly on the look-out; to be always on the alert.
quoi [kwa] *rel.* & *int. pron.* what, which; *à ~ pensez-vous?*, what are you thinking of?; *à propos de ~?*, what is it about?; with respect to what?; *ce à ~ je fais allusion*, what I am referring to; *il n'y a pas de ~ rire*, it's no laughing matter; (fam.) *il n'y a pas de ~!*, don't mention it; no apology needed; *il y a de ~ vous faire enrager*, it's enough to drive you mad; *il n'a pas de ~ vivre*, he has not enough to live on; *de ~ vous mêlez-vous?*, what business is that of yours?; *c'est en ~ vous vous trompez*, that is just where you are mistaken; *en ~ puis-je vous servir?*, what can I do for you?; *~! vous partez?*, what! are you really going?; *~?*, what (did you say)?, eh?; *tu t'amuses bien, ~?*, having a good time, eh?; *~!*, well!; *enfin, ~, c'est la vie!*, well, well, that is life!; (pop.) *tu vas te coucher. De ~?*, you will go to bed. Oh, I will, will I?; *ce n'est rien. Quoi, rien?*, it's nothing. What do you mean, nothing?; *vous désirez ~?*, what is it you want?; *~ de neuf?*, anything new?; what's the news?; *à ~ bon?*, what's the point?; will it do any good?; *un je ne sais ~*, something, a certain quality, a touch (of sth.); *et je ne sais ~ encore*, and heaven knows what besides; *~ que ce soit*, anything whatever, whatever (it may be); *~ qu'il en soit*, be that as it may, whatever may be the case; at all events; *~ qu'il fasse*, whatever he may do; *~ qu'il en ait*, whether he wants it or not.
quoique [kwak(ə)] *conj.* although, though.
quolibet [kɔlibɛ] *s.m.* jeer, gibe.
quorum [k(w)ɔrɔm] *s.m.* quorum.
quota [k(w)ɔta] *s.m.* quota.
quote-part [kɔtpar] *s.f.* share, portion; quota; contribution pro rata.
quotidien, -ne [kɔtidjɛ̃] *adj.* daily, everyday, of daily occurrence; *~ s.m.* daily (newspaper); **~nement** [kɔtidjɛnmɑ̃] *adv.* daily, every day.
quotient [kɔsjɑ̃] *s.m.* quotient; *~ intellectuel*, intelligence quotient (abbrev. I.Q.); *~ électoral*, electoral quota.
quotité [kɔtite] *s.f.* quota, share, proportion.

R

R, r [ɛr] *s.m.* the letter R, r.
ra [ra] *s.m.* ruffle (of a drum).
rab [rab] abbrev. see RABIOT.
rabâchage [rabɑʃaʒ] *s.m.* tiresome repetition, drivel.
rabâcher [rabɑʃe] *v.t.i.* to repeat over and over again, to harp on; to talk drivel.
rabâcheu-r, -se [rabɑʃœr] *s.m.f.* one who is always repeating himself, who drivels on and on.
rabais [rabɛ] *s.m.* reduction in price, abatement, rebate, allowance, discount; *au ~*, at a reduced price, at a discount; on the cheap, badly paid; *vente au ~*, bargain sale.
rabaissement [rabɛsmɑ̃] *s.m.* lowering, depreciation.
rabaisser [rabɛse] *v.t.* to lower, to depreciate, to disparage, to belittle; to cut back, to trim; *~ l'orgueil de qn.*, to humble someone's pride; *~ les prétentions de qn.*, to cut s.o. down to size; **se ~** *v.refl.* to humble or belittle oneself.
raban [rabɑ̃] *s.m.* (naut.) lanyard, furling-line.
rabane [raban] *s.f.* raffia matting.
rabat [raba] *s.m.* **1.** (hunt.) = RABATTAGE; **2.** (obs.) turn-down collar; (mod.) (eccles., academic, etc.) bands; **3.** turn-down flap.
rabattage [rabataʒ] *s.m.* beating for game.
rabattement [rabatmɑ̃] *s.m.* **1.** (law) reduction, annulment; **2.** (geom.) projection.
rabatteu-r, -se [rabatœr] *s.m.f.* **1.** (hunt.) beater; (fig.) tout; **2.** (techn.) beater blades (of reaper).
rabattre [rabatr] *v.t.* to beat down, to bring down, to put down, to turn down, to fold down or back; to lower, to reduce, to cut back; to discount; (techn.) to flange, to flatten; (hunt.) to beat up (game); to humble, to disparage; to turn off (to left or right); to replace or close (lid, car bonnet, etc.); *~ de son prix*, to knock sth. off the price; *il vous faut en ~*, you must come down a peg or two; *~ une couture*, to turn down a seam; (fig.) *~ le caquet à qn.*, to silence s.o.; **se ~** *v.refl.* (of door, etc.) to close; (of vehicle) to turn off or to cut in sharply; *se ~ sur*, to compromise on (sth.), to accept (sth.) faute de mieux.

rabbi [rabi] *s.m.* = RABBIN.
rabbin [rabɛ̃] *s.m.* rabbi; *grand* ~, Chief Rabbi.
rabbinique [rabinik] *adj.* rabbinical.
rabbinisme [rabinism] *s.m.* rabbinism.
rabdomancie see RHABDOMANCIE.
rabelaisien, -ne [rablɛzjɛ̃] *adj.* Rabelaisian.
rabibochage [rabibɔʃaʒ] *s.m.* patching-up, temporary repair.
rabibocher [rabibɔʃe] *v.t.* to patch up; (fig.) to reconcile; **se** ~ *v.refl.* to be reconciled.
rabiot [rabjo] *s.m.* (mil. slang) remains of food or drink; supplementary period of service in the army; overtime; (fig., fam.) small bonus, windfall, something to the good, surplus; abbrev. *rab*; (fam.) *en rab*, extra, free, buckshee.
rabioter [rabjɔte] *v.i.* (fam.) to make a bit on the side; ~ *v.t.* to scrounge, to appropriate (the surplus).
rabique [rabik] *adj.* rabid.
râble[1] [rabl] *s.m.* back (of hare, etc.); (fam.) (of person) small of the back.
râble[2] [rɑbl] *s.m.* fire-rake; rabble, stirrer.
râblé, -e [rɑble] *adj.* (of hare, etc.) thick-backed; (of person) broad-backed, strong-backed; (fig.) sturdy.
râblure [rɑblyr] *s.f.* (naut.) rabbet (of keel).
rabot [rabo] *s.m.* plane, scraper.
rabotage [rabɔtaʒ], **rabotement** [rabɔtmɑ̃] *s.m.* planing.
raboter [rabɔte] *v.t.* to plane, to smooth, to machine.
raboteur [rabɔtœr] *s.m.* planer.
raboteuse [rabɔtøz] *s.f.* planing-machine.
raboteu-x, -se [rabɔtø] *adj.* knotty, rugged, rough, uneven; (fig.) harsh, unpolished.
rabougri, -e [rabugri] *adj.* stunted.
rabougrir [rabugrir] *v.t.* to stunt; **se** ~ *v.refl.* to become stunted.
rabougrissement [rabugrismɑ̃] *s.m.* stuntedness, sickliness, etiolation.
rabouillère [rabujɛr] *s.f.* rabbit's burrow.
rabouter [rabute] *v.t.* to join end to end, to butt together; to piece.
rabrouer [rabrue] *v.t.* to snub, to rebuke, to snap at.
racage [rakaʒ] *s.m.* (naut.) parrel.
racaille [rakɑj] *s.f.* rabble, riff-raff, scum.
raccommodable [rakɔmɔdabl] *adj.* mendable.
raccommodage [rakɔmɔdaʒ] *s.m.* mending, darning, repairing; mend, repair.
raccommodement [rakɔmɔdmɑ̃] *s.m.* reconciliation; making up (of quarrel).
raccommoder [rakɔmɔde] *v.t.* **1.** (obs.) to repair; (mod.) to mend, to patch, to darn; **2.** to reconcile; **se** ~ *v.refl.* to be reconciled, to make it up.
raccommodeu-r, -se [rakɔmɔdœr] *s.m.f.* mender.
raccompagner [rakɔ̃paɲe] *v.t.* to accompany back (home), to see home, to take back.
raccord [rakɔr] *s.m.* **1.** joining, junction, linking-up; joint; levelling; **2.** (mech., electr.) pipe-connection, union, coupling, socket; nipple; connector, adaptor; *bride de* ~, joint-flange; *bouchon de* ~, adaptor plug; **3.** (theatr., Lit., paint.) *faire un* ~, to connect up, to unify, to establish continuity, to provide a link; (fam.) to touch up one's make-up.
raccordement [rakɔrdəmɑ̃] *s.m.* junction, joining, levelling, squaring-off, connecting.
raccorder [rakɔrde] *v.t.* to join, to connect, to link; to make square or flush; **se** ~ (*à*) *v.refl.* (lit. & fig.) to fit in (with), to relate (to).
raccourci [rakursi] *s.m.* **1.** (obs.) abridgement, résumé, shortened account; (mod.) *en* ~, abridged, in shortened form, in miniature; **2.** ellipsis, epitome, simplification; (drawing) foreshortening; **3.** short cut.
raccourcir [rakursir] *v.t.* to shorten, to abridge, to curtail; (drawing) to foreshorten; (fam.) *tomber à bras raccourcis sur qn.*, to go for s.o. tooth and nail; ~ *v.i.* to get shorter, to shrink, to diminish.
raccourcissement [rakursismɑ̃] *s.m.* shortening, abridging, shrinking.
raccoutumer [rakutyme] *v.t.* = RÉACCOUTUMER.
raccroc [rakro] *s.m.* (obs.) fluke, lucky shot; (mod.) *par* ~, by a fluke.
raccrochage [rakrɔʃaʒ] *s.m.* **1.** catching hold of, buttonholing; **2.** = RACOLAGE 2.
raccrochement [rakrɔʃmɑ̃] *s.m.* clinging to.
raccrocher [rakrɔʃe] *v.t.i.* **1.** to hang up again, to replace on hook; (teleph.) ~ (*le récepteur*), to replace (the receiver), to ring off; (of boxer) ~ (*les gants*), to hang up (his gloves), to retire; **2.** to get hold of (sth.) again, to recover; **3.** to catch hold of, to buttonhole, to accost, to pick up (see RACOLER 2.); **se** ~ **à** *v.refl.* (i.) to catch hold of, (lit. & fig.) to cling to; (ii.) to be connected with, to be relevant to.
race [ras] *s.f.* race; stock, breed; line, lineage, ancestry, family; kind; *de* ~ (*pure*), thoroughbred; ~ *bovine*, cattle; ~ *chevaline*, horse species; (proverb) *bon chien chasse de* ~, breeding tells; like sire, like son; it runs in the blood.
racé, -e [rase] *adj.* thoroughbred; (fig.) distinguished, of breeding.
racème [rasɛm] *s.m.* (bot.) raceme.
racémique [rasemik] *adj.* (chem.) racemic.
racer [rɛsœr] *s.m.* racing yacht or motor boat; light racing-car.
rachat [raʃa] *s.m.* buying in, repurchase, redeeming; redemption; recovery; ransom; *vendre avec faculté de* ~, to sell with option of repurchase; *valeur de* ~, surrender value (of insurance policy).
rachetable [raʃtabl] *adj.* redeemable.
racheter [raʃte] *v.t.* to buy back, to buy again, to buy off, to buy in; to repurchase; (fig.) to redeem, to ransom, to atone for; ~ *des captifs*, to ransom prisoners; ~ *un défaut*, to atone for one's faults; ~ *son honneur*, to retrieve one's reputation; **se** ~ *v.refl.* to redeem oneself; to buy one's freedom; to be compensated; to be atoned for.
rachidien, -ne [raʃidjɛ̃] *adj.* (anat.) spinal.
rachis [raʃis] *s.m.* (anat., bot.) rachis, spine, axis.
rachitique [raʃitik] *adj., s.m.f.* rachitic, rickety, (person).
rachitisme [raʃitism] *s.m.* rachitis, rickets.
racial, -e, (aux) [rasjal] *adj.* racial.
racinage [rasinaʒ] *s.m.* (bookb.) marbling.
racinal (pl. **aux**) [rasinal] *s.m.* (carp.) beam, rafter, sleeper.
racine [rasin] *s.f.* root; (fig.) root, beginning, origin; (math.) ~ *carrée*, square root; ~ *quatrième*, fourth, or biquadratic root; *couper le mal dans sa* ~, to eradicate the evil; to get to the very root of the evil; *prendre* ~, to take root, to root; (fig.) to establish oneself; to cling like a limpet; to have come to stay; to stick.
raciner [rasine] *v.i.* (obs.) to root; ~ *v.t.* **1.** (obs.) to grain; **2.** (bookb.) to marble.
racinien, -ne [rasinjɛ̃] *adj.* after the style of Racine.
racisme [rasism] *s.m.* racialism.
raciste [rasist] *adj., s.m.f.* racialist.
racket [rakɛt] *s.m.* racket, swindle; **~teur** [rakɛtœr] *s.m.* racketeer.
raclage [rɑklaʒ] *s.m.* scraping.
racle [rɑkl] *s.f.* scraper.
raclée [rɑkle] *s.f.* (fam.) volley of blows; rout.
racler [rɑkle] *v.t.* to scrape, to scrape clean; to saw away (on a violin, etc.); to ransack, to make a clean sweep of; *se* ~ *la gorge*, to clear one's throat.

raclette [rɑklɛt] *s.f.* **1.** small scraper; **2.** cheese fondue.
racloir [rɑklwar] *s.m.* scraper; strike.
raclure [rɑklyr] *s.f.* scrapings.
racolage [rakɔlaʒ] *s.m.* **1.** recruiting; **2.** (of prostitute) soliciting.
racoler [rakɔle] *v.t.* **1.** to recruit forcibly, to impress; **2.** to tout for; (of prostitute) to solicit, to pick up.
racoleu-r, -se [rakɔlœr] *s.m.f.* **1.** crimp, recruiting-sergeant; **2.** tout; prostitute.
racontable [rakɔ̃tabl] *adj.* relatable, fit to be told.
racontar [rakɔ̃tar] *s.m.* gossip, rumour, report, hearsay, statement of doubtful accuracy.
raconter [rakɔ̃te] *v.t.* to tell, to relate, to narrate; *qu'est-ce que vous racontez là?*, what are you talking about?; *il en raconte de belles!*, he tells fine tales!; *il raconte bien*, he is a good story-teller; *allons donc! vous voulez m'en ~!*, now then! you are pulling my leg!, that's a tall story!
raconteu-r, -se [rakɔ̃tœr] *s.m.f.* story-teller.
racorni, -e [rakɔrni] *adj.* hard, hardened, tough, horny; shrunken.
racornir [rakɔrnir] *v.t.* **1.** to harden, to make hard or tough; **2.** to shrink, to shrivel; **se ~** *v.refl.* **1.** to harden, to become tough; to lose elasticity; (fig.) to become set in one's ideas; **2.** to shrink, to shrivel up.
racornissement [rakɔrnismɑ̃] *s.m.* hardening, shrivelling.
radar [radar] *s.m.* radar, radar station.
radariste [radarist] *s.m.f.* radar operator or technician.
rade [rad] *s.f.* (naut.) roads, roadstead; *en* or *sur ~*, in the roads.
radeau (pl. **-x**) [rado] *s.m.* raft, float.
rader [rade] *v.t.* **1.** to strike (a measure of grain); **2.** to score (a block of stone for cutting).
radiaire [radjɛr] *adj.* radiate.
radial, -e, (aux) [radjal] *adj.* radial.
radian [radjɑ̃] *s.m.* (math.) radian.
radiance [radjɑ̃s] *s.f.* radiance.
radiant, -e [radjɑ̃] *adj.* radiant; *~ s.m.* (astron.) radiant point, apparent focal point of meteoric shower.
radiateur [radjatœr] *s.m.* radiator; heater.
radiati-f, -ve [radjatif] *adj.* (phys.) radiation, radioactive.
radiation[1] [radjɑsjɔ̃] *s.f.* radiation, irradiation.
radiation[2] [radjɑsjɔ̃] *s.f.* striking-out, striking-off, erasure, obliteration, cancelling.
radical, -e, (aux) [radikal] *adj.* (lit. & fig.) radical; *~ s.m.* (gram., math., chem., pol.) radical; **~ement** [radikalmɑ̃] *adv.* radically, (fig.) absolutely.
radicalisme [radikalism] *s.m.* radicalism.
radicelle [radisɛl] *s.f.* (bot.) radicle, rootlet.
radiculaire [radikylɛr] *adj.* radicular.
radicule [radikyl] *s.f.* (bot.) radicle.
radié, -e [radje] *adj.* radiate, radiant, radiated.
radier [radje] *v.t.* to strike out, to obliterate, to cancel.
radier [radje] *s.m.* (build.) floor, apron, invert (of sewer, etc.); revetment.
radiesthésie [radjɛstezi] *s.f.* dowsing, water-divining.
radiesthésiste [radjɛstezist] *s.m.f.* dowser, water-diviner.
radieu-x, -se [radjø] *adj.* radiant, beaming, shining; dazzling, splendid; *ciel ~x*, cloudless sky, glorious weather; **~sement** [radjøzmɑ̃] *adv.* radiantly.
radin, -e [radɛ̃] *adj.* miserly; *s.m.f.* miser.
radiner [radine] *v.i.* (pop.) to turn up.
radio [radjo] **1.** *s.m.* radiogram, radio message; wireless navigator; radio-telegraphist; **2.** *s.f.* radio, wireless, broadcasting; radio-telephony, radio-telegraphy; radiography, X-ray (picture); radioscopy.
radioactif, -ve [radjɔaktif] *adj.* radioactive.
radio-activité [radjɔaktivite] *s.f.* radioactivity; **~alignement** [radjɔaliɲmɑ̃] *s.m.* (aeron.) radio navigation system; **~astronomie** [radjɔastrɔnɔmi] *s.f.* radio-astronomy; **~balisage** [radjɔbalizaʒ] *s.m.* radio beacon signalling; **~carbone** [radjɔkarbɔn] *s.m.* radio-carbon; **~communication** [radjɔkɔmynikɑsjɔ̃] *s.f.* radio-communication; **~compas** [radjɔkɔ̃pa] *s.m.* (aeron.) radio-compass, radio navigation system; **~diffusion** [radjɔdifyzjɔ̃] *s.f.* broadcasting, broadcast; radio; **~électricité** [radjɔelɛktrisite] *s.f.* radio-electricity; **~électrique** [radjɔelɛktrik] *adj.* radio-electric; **~élément** [radjɔelemɑ̃] *s.m.* radio-element; **~goniomètre** [radjɔgɔnjɔmɛtr] *s.m.* radio-goniometer, wireless direction-finding apparatus; **~goniométrie** [radjɔgɔnjɔmetri] *s.f.* radiogoniometry, wireless navigation; **~gramme** [radjɔgram] *s.m.* radiogram, radio message; **~graphie** [radjɔgrafi] *s.f.* radiography, X-ray; **~graphier** [radjɔgrafje] *v.t.* to X-ray; **~guidage** [radjɔgidaʒ] *s.m.* (naut., aeron.) radio control, wireless navigation; **~-isotope** [radjɔizɔtɔp] *s.m.* radio-isotope.
radiolaires [radjɔlɛr] *s.m.pl.* (zool.) Radiolaria.
radio-logie [radjɔlɔʒi] *s.f.* radiology; **~logue** [radjɔlɔg], **~logiste** [radjɔlɔʒist] *s.m.f.* radiologist; **~navigant** [radjɔnavigɑ̃] *s.m.* (aeron.) wireless navigator; **~navigation** [radjɔnavigɑsjɔ̃] *s.f.* wireless navigation; **~phare** [radjɔfar] *s.m.* radio beacon; **~phonie** [radjɔfɔni] *s.f.* wireless telephony, radio-telephony; broadcasting; **~phonique** [radjɔfɔnik] *adj.* radiophonic, wireless; **~photographie** [radjɔfɔtɔgrafi] *s.f.* photofluorography; **~scopie** [radjɔskɔpi] *s.f.* radioscopy, X-ray examination; **~sondage** [radjɔsɔ̃daʒ] *s.m.* radiosonde measurements; **~sonde** [radjɔsɔ̃d] *s.f.* radiosonde.
radiotélé-graphie [radjɔtelegrafi] *s.f.* radiotelegraphy; **~graphique** [radjɔtelegrafik] *adj.* radio-telegraphy; **~graphiste** [radjɔtelegrafist] *s.m.f.* (obs.) wireless telegraphist; **~phonie** [radjɔtelefɔni] *s.f.* = RADIOPHONIE.
radiotélescope [radjɔtelɛskɔp] *s.m.* radio telescope.
radiotélévisé, -e [radjɔtelevize] *adj.* broadcast on sound and vision.
radiothérapie [radjɔterapi] *s.f.* radiotherapy.
radis [radi] *s.m.* radish; (fig.) *il n'a plus un ~*, he has not a brass farthing left.
radium [radjɔm] *s.m.* radium.
radius [radjys] *s.m.* (anat.) radius.
radja(h) see RAJA(H).
radome, radôme [radom] *s.m.* radar dome.
radotage [radɔtaʒ] *s.m.* **1.** (obs.) dotage; **2.** silly nonsense.
radoter [radɔte] *v.i.* to talk nonsense.
radoteu-r, -se [radɔtœr] *s.m.f.* dotard; one who talks nonsense.
radoub [radu] *s.m.* (naut.) graving; *bassin de ~*, graving-dock; *en ~*, under repair.
radouber [radube] *v.t.* (naut.) to grave; **se ~** *v.refl.* to go into dock.
radoucir [radusir] *v.t.* to soften, to make milder, to mitigate; **se ~** *v.refl.* to grow milder, to calm down.
radoucissement [radusismɑ̃] *s.m.* softening; becoming milder; relenting, abatement.
rafale [rafal] *s.f.* squall, gust; burst (of small-arms fire).
raffermir [rafɛrmir] *v.t.* to strengthen, to make firmer, to fortify; **se ~** *v.refl.* to grow stronger; to harden, to become more confident.
raffermissement [rafɛrmismɑ̃] *s.m.* hardening,

strengthening; becoming firmer; (cook.) setting.

raffinage [rafinaʒ] *s.m.* refining.

raffiné, -e [rafine] *adj.* refined, delicate, exquisite; *s.m.f.* person of exquisite tastes.

raffinement [rafinmɑ̃] *s.m.* refinement; subtlety; sophistication.

raffiner [rafine] *v.t.* to refine; ~ *v.i.* to be over--subtle, to be punctilious.

raffinerie [rafinri] *s.f.* refinery.

raffineu-r, -se [rafinœr] *s.m.f.* refiner.

raffoler [rafɔle] *v.i.* to dote (*de*, on); to be passionately fond (*de*, of).

raffut [rafy] *s.m.* (fam.) row, din, uproar.

raffûter [rafyte] *v.t.* to resharpen.

rafiot [rafjo] *s.m.* skiff, small boat with lateen sail; (pej.) old tub.

rafistolage [rafistɔlaʒ] *s.m.* (fam.) patching-up.

rafistoler [rafistɔle] *v.t.* to patch up, to make a rough repair to.

rafle[1] [rafl] *s.f.* **1.** (obs.) looting, foray; **2.** (mod.) sweep by police.

rafle[2] [rɑfl] *s.f.* **1.** grape-stalk; **2.** corn-cob.

rafler [rɑfle] *v.t.* to sweep off; to carry away, to make a clean sweep of; ⚠ not 'to raffle'.

rafraîchir [rafreʃir] *v.t.* to refresh, to cool, to chill, to freshen; to renovate, to revive; to trim (the hair); ~ *une robe*, to do up a dress; ~ *v.i.* to cool; **se** ~ *v.refl.* **1.** to get cooler; **2.** to have a drink, to take refreshment.

rafraîchissant, -e [rafreʃisɑ̃] *adj.* refreshing, cooling, thirst-quenching.

rafraîchissement [rafreʃismɑ̃] *s.m.* refreshment; cooling, cooling effect; renovating; (pl.) refreshments, drinks.

rafraîchissoir [rafreʃiswar] *s.m.* wine-cooler.

ragaillardir [ragajardir] *v.t.* to cheer up, to enliven.

rage [raʒ] *s.f.* **1.** rage; violent desire, mania, passion; violent pain; *mettre en* ~, to enrage; *faire* ~, to rage, to be raging; (fig.) to be all the rage; *avoir la* ~ *du jeu*, to have a passion for gambling; ~ *de dents*, violent toothache; **2.** rabies, hydrophobia; madness, frenzy.

rager [raʒe] *v.i.* (fam.) to fume, to be in a passion, to be enraged.

rageu-r, -se [raʒœr] *adj.* ill-tempered, passionate, choleric; angry.

rageusement [raʒøzmɑ̃] *adv.* angrily, passionately.

raglan [raglɑ̃] *s.m.* raglan (coat); ~ *adj. invar. manches* ~, raglan sleeves.

ragot [rago] *s.m.* **1.** gossip, slander; **2.** two-year--old wild boar.

ragot, -e [rago] *adj.*, *s.m.f.* dumpy, thick-set, stumpy, (person).

ragoût [ragu] *s.m.* ragout, stew; (fig.) zest, piquancy, relish; ~ *de mouton*, Irish stew.

ragoûtant, -e [ragutɑ̃] *adj.* (usu. iron.) tempting, pleasing.

ragréer [ragree] *v.t.* (build.) to finish off; to re-face.

rag-time [ragtajm] *s.m.* (mus.) ragtime.

raguer [rage] (naut.) *v.t.i.* to chafe, to gall, to rub; to be chafed.

rai [rɛ] *s.m.* ray; spoke; point (of star, gem).

raid [rɛd] *s.m.* **1.** raid; **2.** long-distance flight or run, endurance test.

raide [rɛd] *adj.* stiff, rigid, tight, taut; (fig.) inflexible, stiff, steep; hard to accept or believe; exorbitant; broad, free, coarse; *c'est un peu* ~*!*, that's coming it rather strong; that's going a bit too far!; *une pente* ~, a steep slope; *corde* ~, (lit. & fig.) tightrope; *des propos* ~*s*, risqué remarks; *en avoir vu de* ~*s*, to have had some incredible experiences; ~ *adv.* steeply; hard, violently; stone (dead); *grimper* ~, to climb steeply; (fam.) *piocher* ~, to swot hard; (tennis) *renvoyer la balle* ~, to return the ball hard; *tomber* ~ *par terre*, to fall flat on the ground.

raideur [rɛdœr] *s.f.* stiffness, rigidity, inflexibility, tightness; steepness.

raidillon [rɛdijɔ̃] *s.m.* short, steep rise, steep path.

raidir [redir], **roidir** [rwadir] *v.t.* to stiffen, to make rigid, to tighten; (naut.) to haul taut; **se** ~ *v.refl.* to stiffen, to grow stiff or rigid; to harden oneself, to brace oneself, (*contre*, against).

raidissement [redismɑ̃] *s.m.* stiffening; tightening.

raidisseur [redisœr] *s.m.* (techn.) wire-strainer.

raie[1] [rɛ] *s.f.* line, stripe, stroke, streak; parting (of the hair); (agric.) ridge (between furrows); *à* ~*s*, striped; (opt.) ray (of spectrum).

raie[2] [rɛ] *s.f.* (ichth.) ray, skate; ~ *bouclée*, thorn--back; (pop.) *gueule de* ~, ugly- or nasty-looking person.

raifort [rɛfɔr] *s.m.* (bot.) horse-radish.

rail [rɑj] *s.m.* (rail., etc.) rail; ⚠ not fencing 'rail'.

railler [rɑje] *v.t.i.* to mock, to jeer at, to deride, to scoff at, to laugh at; *se* ~ *de*, to laugh at, to make fun of.

raillerie [rɑjri] *s.f.* raillery, mockery, mocking, banter, joke, chaffing, scoff; *entendre* ~, to know how to take a joke; *sans* ~ or ~ *à part*, seriously, joking apart.

railleu-r, -se [rɑjœr] *adj.* mocking, jesting, scoffing, satirical; *s.m.f.* joker, mocker, scoffer, banterer; ~**sement** [rɑjøzmɑ̃] *adv.* mockingly, jeeringly, scoffingly.

rainer [rene] *v.t.* to groove.

rainette [rɛnɛt] *s.f.* **1.** tree-frog, frog; **2.** = REINETTE.

rainure [renyr] *s.f.* groove, slot, channel, rabbet.

rainurer [renyre] *v.t.* = RAINER.

raiponce [rɛpɔ̃s] *s.f.* (bot.) rampion.

rais [rɛ] *s.m.* = RAI.

raisin [rɛzɛ̃] *s.m.* grape, grapes; ~*s secs*, raisins; *grain de* ~, grape; *grappe de* ~, bunch of grapes; ~*s de Corinthe*, currants, ~*s de Smyrne*, sultanas; ~*s de mer*, cuttle-fish eggs.

raisiné [rɛzine] *s.m.* a jam made of pears or quince, sugar, and grape-juice.

raison [rɛzɔ̃] *s.f.* reason; grounds, cause, motive; good sense, judgement; sanity; (math.) ratio; rate; ~ *sociale*, trading name of firm; *à* ~ *de*, at the rate of; *à plus forte* ~, a fortiori; all the more (so), with greater reason; ~ *de plus*, all the more reason; *comme de* ~, as is reasonable; *en* ~ *de*, (i.) in proportion to; (ii.) by reason of, on account of, owing to; in consideration of; *par la* ~ *que*, because; *avoir* ~, to be right; to be in the right; *avoir* ~ *de*, to get the better of; to receive satisfaction for; *avoir de bonnes* ~*s pour*, to have good ground to; *donner* ~ *à qn.*, to decide in someone's favour, to admit that s.o. is right, to side with s.o.; *entendre* ~, *se rendre à la* ~, to listen to reason, to be amenable, tractable; *se faire une* ~, to accept the inevitable, to reconcile oneself to one's fate; *faire* ~ *de*, to give satisfaction for; *demander* ~ *d'une insulte*, to demand satisfaction for an insult; *demander* ~ *de sa conduite à qn.*, to call s.o. to account for his behaviour; *mettre qn. à la* ~, to call s.o. to his senses; *parler* ~, to talk sense; *plus que de* ~, more than is reasonable; *la* ~ *du plus fort est toujours la meilleure*, God is on the side of the big battalions; might is right; *perdre la* ~, to lose one's reason, to become insane, to go mad; *point tant de* ~*s*, do not argue so much; ~ *d'être*, justification, reason for existence, object; *vous m'en rendrez* ~*!*, you will answer to me for that!; *cela n'a ni rime ni* ~, it is without rhyme or reason, there's no sense in it.

raisonnable [rɛzɔnabl] *adj.* **1.** reasoning, capable of reason; **2.** reasonable, rational,

sensible; moderate, within bounds; **~ment** [rεzɔnabləmɑ̃] *adv.* reasonably, sensibly; moderately, within reason.
raisonné, -e [rεzɔne] *adj.* reasoned, rational; calculated.
raisonnement [rεzɔnmɑ̃] *s.m.* reasoning, argument; reason.
raisonner [rεzɔne] *v.i.* to reason; to argue; ~ *v.t.* to reason about, to bring reason to bear on, to rationalize; ~ *qn.*, to get s.o. to see reason, to reason with s.o.; **se** ~ *v.refl.* to see reason; to be rational, to reason.
raisonneu-r, -se [rεzɔnœr] *adj.* reasoning; argumentative; *s.m.f.* reasoner, arguer, dialectician.
raja(h) [raʒa], **radja(h)** [radʒa] *s.m.* raja(h).
rajeunir [raʒœnir] *v.i.* to grow young again, to recover one's freshness; ~ *v.t.* to rejuvenate, to make young again, to make look younger; to renew, to modernize; **se** ~ *v.refl.* to make oneself look, or to make oneself out, younger than one is.
rajeunissant, -e [raʒœnisɑ̃] *adj.* rejuvenating.
rajeunissement [raʒœnismɑ̃] *s.m.* growing young again, rejuvenation; modernizing, revival renovation.
rajout [raʒu] *s.m.* addition, annexe, (to building, mechanism, text).
rajouter [raʒute] *v.t.* to add (sth.); (fam.) to add a further quantity of.
rajustement [raʒystəmɑ̃] *s.m.* readjustment; revision (of salary scales, etc.).
rajuster [raʒyste] *v.t.* to readjust; to adjust; to check, to correct; to put in right position, to put straight; to revise (salary scales, etc.); (obs.) to settle (difference), to reconcile; **se** ~ *v.refl.* to tidy oneself up.
râle[1] [rɑl] *s.m.* (ornith.) rail; ~ *d'eau*, water-rail; ~ *des genêts*, land-rail, corncrake.
râle[2] [rɑl], **râlement** [rɑlmɑ̃] *s.m.* (death-) rattle; (pathol.) râle.
ralenti, -e [ralɑ̃ti] *adj.* slow, slowed down, at reduced speed; ~ *s.m.* reduced speed or rate; (cin.) slow-motion picture; *au* ~, at reduced speed, throttled down, ticking over; *prendre le* ~, to slow down; (industry) *travail au* ~, go-slow (strike); *marcher au* ~, to go slow, to slow down production.
ralentir [ralɑ̃tir] *v.t.i.* to slow down, to slacken, to reduce speed; to ease; to lessen; to moderate, to abate; ~ *le pas*, to slacken one's pace; **se** ~ *v.refl.* to slow down, to slacken, to lose impetus, to relent.
ralentissement [ralɑ̃tismɑ̃] *s.m.* slackening; slowing-down; relaxation; easing; abatement, relenting; flagging; (fig.) cooling.
râler [rɑle] *v.i.* to rattle in one's throat; to be in one's death-throes, to be at one's last gasp; (of tiger) to growl; (of person) to rage, to fume, to growl; (obs., pop.) to haggle.
râleu-r, -se [rɑlœr] *adj., s.m.f.* bad-tempered, grumbling, (person).
ralingue [ralɛ̃g] *s.f.* (naut.) bolt-rope; pitch--rope (of tent); (naut.) *tenir les voiles en* ~, to keep the sails shivering.
ralinguer [ralɛ̃ge] (naut.) *v.t.* **1.** to luff, to sail close to the wind; **2.** to fix bolt-ropes (to sail); ~ *v.i.* (of sail) to shiver, to hang slack.
ralliement [ralimɑ̃] *s.m.* **1.** rallying, rally; joining (a cause, a party); *mot de* ~, rallying-cry; *point de* ~, rallying-point; rallying-place; **2.** (pol.) union, alliance; movement.
rallier [ralje] *v.t.* **1.** to rally, to bring together; to win over; **2.** to return to, to rejoin; ~ *son poste*, to return to one's post; (naut.) ~ *le bord*, to return on board, to rejoin one's ship; ~ *la terre*, to stand into the land; to haul in; ~ *le navire au vent*, to haul the ship into the wind; **se** ~ *v.refl.* to rally, to join; *se* ~ *à*, to adhere to; to come round to (an opinion, etc.); (naut.) *se* ~ *à terre*, to hug the shore.
rallonge [ralɔ̃ʒ] *s.f.* lengthening-piece, extension (-piece); leaf (of table); (fig., fam.) additional payment.
rallongement [ralɔ̃ʒmɑ̃] *s.m.* lengthening.
rallonger [ralɔ̃ʒe] *v.t.* to lengthen; ~ *v.i.* to get longer.
rallumer [ralyme] *v.t.* to relight; (fig.) to rekindle, to revive; **se** ~ *v.refl.* to burn up, to flare up again; (fig.) to break out again.
rallye [rali] *s.m.* **1.** (car) rally; **2.** young people's club.
ramadan [ramadɑ̃] *s.m.* Ramadan; (fig.) (also **ramdam** [ramdam]) din, row.
ramage [ramaʒ] *s.m.* **1.** (obs.) bough, branches; (pl.) branched or floral pattern; **2.** bird-song; (fig., jest) talk; **3.** (text.) stretching and drying.
ramager [ramaʒe] *v.i.* (of birds) to sing; ~ *v.t.* to make branched or floral patterns on (material).
ramas [ramɑ] *s.m.* heap, lot, collection, pile, set, mass; *un* ~ *de bandits*, a pack of robbers.
ramassage [ramɑsaʒ] *s.m.* gathering, picking up.
ramassé, -e [ramɑse] *adj.* crouching; squat, stocky; compact, close-knit; concise, pithy.
ramasse-miettes [ramɑsmjεt] *s.m.invar.* crumb--scoop; **~-monnaie** [ramɑsmɔnε] *s.m.invar.* coin-scoop; **~-poussière** [ramɑspusjεr] *s.m. invar.* dustpan.
ramasser [ramɑse] *v.t.* to gather up, to collect; to gather together, to amass, to acquire; to pick up; to take up; ~ *ses forces*, to muster all one's strength; ~ *une bûche* or *une pelle*, to come a cropper; ~ *une engueulade*, to come in for a volley of abuse; (fam.) *se faire* ~, to get caught or arrested; **se** ~ *v.refl.* to crouch, to gather oneself (for a spring); (pop.) to pick oneself up (after a fall); to fall down.
ramasseu-r, -se [ramɑsœr] *s.m.f.* picker, collector; **~r** *s.m.* (mech.) scoop, shovel.
ramassis [ramɑsi] *s.m.* heap, lot, mass; rabble, gang.
rambarde [rɑ̃bard] *s.f.* hand-rail, guard.
ramdam see RAMADAN.
rame[1] [ram] *s.f.* oar; *faire force de* ~*s*, to row hard.
rame[2] [ram] *s.f.* **1.** (obs.) branch, bough; **2.** (hort.) stake, prop, stick.
rame[3] [ram] *s.f.* **1.** ream (of paper); set of 20 rolls (of wallpaper); **2.** (rail.) set of carriages or trucks, train (esp. *métro*); string, convoy, train, (of barges, etc.).
rame[4] [ram] *s.f.* drying-frame.
ramé, -e [rame] *adj.* (obs.) with branches; ~ *adj.m.* (hunt., herald.) (of stag) ramé.
rameau (pl. **-x**) [ramo] *s.m.* bough, branch; sprig; (fig.) branch, subdivision; ramification; *Dimanche des* ~*x*, Palm Sunday.
ramée [rame] *s.f.* green boughs, branches, arbour; *danser sous la* ~, to dance under the greenwood tree.
ramender [ramɑ̃de] *v.t.* **1.** to mend (nets); to regild (with gold leaf); **2.** (agric.) to apply further dressing of manure.
ramener [ramne] *v.t.* to bring back, to bring home, to recall; to return, to bring again, to bring round; to relate; to restore; ~ *son châle sur ses épaules*, to pull one's shawl round one's shoulders; *son raisonnement se ramène à ceci*, his argument comes down to this.
ramequin [ramkɛ̃] *s.m.* (cook.) ramekin.
ramer[1] [rame] *v.i.* to row; *vol ramé*, slow-winged flight (of large birds).
ramer[2] [rame] *v.t.* (hort.) to stick, to stake, to train on sticks.
ramer[3] [rame] *v.t.* to stretch on a frame to dry.

ramereau (pl. **-x**), **ramerot** [ramro] *s.m.* (ornith.) young ring-dove.
ramette [ramɛt] *s.f.* **1.** ream (of note-paper); **2.** (print.) job-chase.
rameu-r, -se [ramœr] *s.m.f.* **1.** rower, oarsman, oarswoman; (also refers to insects, e.g. water-bugs, which walk on the water); **2.** birds with slow flight.
rameu-x, -se [ramø] *adj.* branchy, branched, ramose.
rami [rami] *s.m.* (cards) rummy.
ramie [rami] *s.f.* (bot.) ramee, grasscloth plant.
ramier [ramje] *s.m.* (ornith.) ring-dove, wood-pigeon.
ramification [ramifikɑsjɔ̃] *s.f.* ramification, branch, subdivision.
ramifié, -e [ramifje] *adj.* branched, with branches or ramifications.
(**se**) **ramifier** [ramifje] *v.refl.* to branch out, to divide, to have ramifications.
ramille [ramij] *s.f.* twig.
ramingue [ramɛ̃g] *adj.* (of horse) restive, stubborn.
ramolli, -e [ramɔli] *adj.* that has become soft; (fig.) weak in the head, (of brain) addled; passive, spineless.
ramollir [ramɔlir] *v.t.* (lit. & fig.) to soften; to weaken.
ramollissant, -e [ramɔlisɑ̃] *adj.* (med.) emollient.
ramollissement [ramɔlismɑ̃] *s.m.* softening; (pathol.) ~ *cérébral*, softening of the brain.
ramollo [ramɔlo] *s.m.f., adj.* (pop.) (one) weak in the head; *un vieux* ~, an old dodderer.
ramonage [ramɔnaʒ] *s.m.* chimney-sweeping.
ramoner [ramɔne] *v.t.* **1.** to sweep (a chimney); **2.** (mountaineering) to negotiate a chimney.
ramoneur [ramɔnœr] *s.m.* sweep, chimney-sweep.
rampant, -e [rɑ̃pɑ̃] *adj.* crawling, creeping; (herald.) rampant; (fig.) servile, grovelling, fawning, cringing; (arch.) sloping; ~ *s.m.* inclined portion, slope; (aeron. slang) *les* ~*s*, ground staff; ⚠ not 'rampant' in sense 'raging'.
rampe [rɑ̃p] *s.f.* **1.** banisters; stair handrail; (fig., fam.) *lâcher la* ~, to die; **2.** slope, incline, gradient; ramp; ~ *de lancement*, (rocket-) launcher, launching ramp or pad; **3.** (theatr.) footlights, bank (of projectors, spotlights, etc.); (aeron.) ~ *de balisage*, flare-path, line of beacons.
rampement [rɑ̃pmɑ̃] *s.m.* crawling, creeping.
ramper [rɑ̃pe] *v.i.* to crawl, to creep; to crouch; (fig.) to grovel, to crawl, to cringe; (arch.) to ramp, to slope, to incline.
ramponneau (pl. **-x**) [rɑ̃pɔno] *s.m.* (pop.) blow, knock, shock.
ramure [ramyr] *s.f.* **1.** branches, green boughs, foliage; **2.** antlers (of stag).
rancard, rencard [rɑ̃kar] *s.m.* **1.** (slang) confidential information, tip-off; **2.** (pop.) secret meeting-place, rendezvous.
rancarder, rencarder [rɑ̃karde] *v.t.* (pop.) to tip off (s.o.).
rancart [rɑ̃kar] *s.m.* *mettre au* ~, to throw aside, to get rid of.
rance [rɑ̃s] *adj.* rancid, rank; (lit. & fig.) stale, old; ~ *s.m.* rancidness; *sentir le* ~, to smell rancid.
ranch [rɑ̃tʃ] *s.m.* ranch.
rancir [rɑ̃sir] *v.i.* to grow rancid; (lit. & fig.) to become stale.
rancissement [rɑ̃sismɑ̃] *s.m.* growing rancid; rancidness, rancidity.
rancœur [rɑ̃kœr] *s.f.* rancour, bitterness.
rançon [rɑ̃sɔ̃] *s.f.* ransom; (fig.) price; *c'est la* ~ *de la célébrité*, it is the price of fame; *payer* ~ *pour qn.*, to ransom s.o.
rançonnement [rɑ̃sɔnmɑ̃] *s.m.* exaction of ransom, protection-money, etc.; extortion, fleecing.
rançonner [rɑ̃sɔne] *v.t.* **1.** (obs.) to hold to ransom; to set a ransom on; **2.** to exact ransom for, to extort payment for; (obs.) to overcharge, to exploit, to rob; ⚠ not 'to ransom'; see RANÇON.
rançonneu-r, -se [rɑ̃sɔnœr] *s.m.f.* extortioner, one who charges extortionate prices, robber, exploiter.
rancune [rɑ̃kyn] *s.f.* rancour, spite, malice, resentment, grudge; *sans* ~*!*, no ill feelings!, let bygones be bygones!, let's say no more about it!; *avoir de la* ~, or *garder* ~, *contre qn.*, to have or to harbour a grudge against s.o.
rancuni-er, -ère [rɑ̃kynje] *adj., s.m.f.* rancorous, spiteful, resentful, vindictive, (person); (person) having a grudge.
randonnée [rɑ̃dɔne] *s.f.* **1.** (hunt.) circuit (of game); **2.** (long) walk, ride, drive, trip, excursion, tour.
rang [rɑ̃] *s.m.* row, line, rank, range; place, station, order, class; (print.) frame; (theatr.) tier, row; *un* ~ *de perles*, a string of pearls; *à son* ~, in one's place; *en* ~ *de taille*, in order of size, according to size; *garder* or *tenir son* ~, to keep one's place, to keep up one's social position; *sortir du* ~, (mil.) to rise from the ranks; (fig.) to get out of the rut; *de premier* ~, first-class, first-rate; *se mettre sur les* ~*s*, to enter the lists; to compete, to come forward as a candidate; *mettre qn. au* ~ *de*, to rank s.o. among or with; *prendre* ~ *avant qn.*, to rank before, or above, s.o., to take precedence over s.o.; *par* ~ *d'âge, de taille*, according to age, to size; *une personne de haut* ~, a person of rank; *rompre les* ~*s*, to break rank; *rentrer dans le* ~, to return to the ranks; *en* ~ *d'oignons*, all in a line.
rangé, -e [rɑ̃ʒe] *adj.* in good order, tidy; (fig.) steady, leading a serious life; *bataille* ~*e*, pitched battle.
rangée [rɑ̃ʒe] *s.f.* row, line, array, file, tier, set, string.
rangement [rɑ̃ʒmɑ̃] *s.m.* putting in order, tidying, classifying, arranging.
ranger [rɑ̃ʒe] *v.t.* to put in order, to put in its place; to position; to put away; to arrange, to array; to range, to count, to rank, to classify, (*parmi*, among); to put aside, to keep back; to tidy (up); to bring under, to subdue; (naut.) to sail close to; ~ *sa voiture*, to position, to park, one's car; to move one's car aside; ~ *un pays sous sa loi*, to bring a country under one's law, to subdue a country; **se** ~ *v.refl.* **1.** to line up, to fall into ranks; (fig.) to rally; (mil.) *se* ~ *par trois*, to fall in in threes; (fig.) *se* ~ *à l'avis de*, to fall in with the ideas of; *se* ~ *sous l'autorité de*, to submit to the authority of; *se* ~ *sous le drapeau*, to rally to the flag; *se* ~ *du côté de*, to rally to (the side of), to join; **2.** to position oneself; to draw in, to move aside, to make room, to give way; (naut.) *se* ~ *à bord*, to come alongside; *se* ~ *contre le trottoir*, to draw in to the pavement; **3.** to settle down, to be sensible, to behave in an orderly way; **4.** to be put; *où cela se range-t-il?*, where does that go?
rani [rani] *s.f.* ranee.
ranimation [ranimɑsjɔ̃] *s.f.* = RÉANIMATION.
ranimer [ranime] *v.t.* to revive, to restore to life; (fig.) to stir up, to enliven, to put fresh heart into; **se** ~ *v.refl.* to revive, to come to life again; (fig.) to brighten up, to cheer up.
ranz [rɑ̃z, rɑ̃ts] *s.m.* Swiss pastoral song.
raout [raut] *s.m.* (obs.) party, social gathering.
rapace [rapas] *adj.* rapacious, greedy; ~ *s.m.* bird of prey, raptor.
rapacité [rapasite] *s.f.* rapacity.
râpage [rɑpaʒ] *s.m.* rasping, grating.

rapatrié, -e [rapatrije] *adj.* repatriated; *s.m.f.* repatriate.

rapatriement [rapatrimɑ̃] *s.m.* repatriation, sending back to one's native country.

rapatrier [rapatrie] *v.t.* **1.** to repatriate; **2.** (obs.) to reconcile; **se** ~ *v.refl.* (fam.) to be reconciled, to make it up.

râpe [rɑp] *s.f.* **1.** grater; rasp; **2.** corn-cob.

râpé, -e [rɑpe] *adj.* grated; threadbare, worn out.

râpé [rɑpe] *s.m.* **1.** rape (refuse of wine-making); **2.** grated cheese.

râper [rɑpe] *v.t.* to grate; to rasp; to wear threadbare; ⚠ not 'to rape'.

râperie [rɑpri] *s.f.* pulping-mill.

rapetasser [raptase] *v.t.* (fam.) to patch up, to mend roughly; (fig.) to touch up, to tinker at.

rapetissement [raptismɑ̃] *s.m.* shortening, reducing; dwarfing, belittling; shrinking.

rapetisser [raptise] *v.t.* to make smaller, to shorten, to reduce; (fig.) to diminish, to belittle; ~ *v.i.* to become smaller or shorter, to diminish.

râpeu-x, -se [rapø] *adj.* rough, grating.

raphia [rafja] *s.m.* (bot.) raffia.

rapide [rapid] *adj.* rapid, speedy, swift; fast; steep; ~ *s.m.* **1.** (geog.) rapid; **2.** (rail.) fast train, express; **~ment** [rapidmɑ̃] *adv.* rapidly, swiftly, fast; with great speed; by the fastest method.

rapidité [rapidite] *s.f.* rapidity, swiftness, speed; steepness.

rapiéçage [rapjesaʒ], **rapiècement** [rapjɛsmɑ̃] *s.m.* piecing, patching, mending.

rapiécer [rapjese] *v.t.* to piece, to patch, to mend.

rapière [rapjɛr] *s.f.* rapier.

rapin [rapɛ̃] *s.m.* art student, junior in studio; (usu. pej.) painter, dauber.

rapine [rapin] *s.f.* plundering, rapine, robbery; spoil, plunder.

rapiner [rapine] *v.t.i.* (obs.) to plunder, to pillage.

rapointir [rapwɛ̃tir] *v.t.* to resharpen.

rappariement [raparimɑ̃] *s.m.* matching; match.

rapparier [raparje] *v.t.* to match, to pair; to find a mate for.

rappel [rapɛl] *s.m.* recall, recalling; reminder; evocation, (fig.) echo; (theatr.) curtain-call; summoning up; rallying, gathering together; repeal; readjustment; (techn.) return; adjusting; ~ *à l'ordre*, call to order; *signal de* ~, (rail.) repeater signal; (road) reminder sign; (med.) *injection de* ~, booster injection; *vis de* ~, adjusting or resetting screw; *ressort de* ~, return spring; (typewriting) ~ *arrière*, carriage return; back-space key; (mountaineering) *descente en* ~, roping down, abseiling; *battre le* ~, to beat to arms; (fig.) to gather, to summon, to call up.

rappeler [raple] *v.t.* to recall, to call back; to call home; to evoke, to remind (one) of; to repeal; to bring back, to draw back; to return; to summon up; to muster; ~ *à la vie*, to restore to life; ~ *à l'ordre*, to call to order; *rappelez-moi à son souvenir*, remember me kindly to him; **se** ~ *v.refl.* (also *se* ~ *de*) to remember, to recall, to recollect; *se* ~ *à qn.*, or *au bon souvenir de qn.*, to send s.o. one's kind regards, to ask to be remembered to s.o.

rappliquer [raplike] *v.t.* to re-apply; ~ *v.i.* (pop.) to come back; to turn up.

rapport [rapɔr] *s.m.* **1.** product, return, yield, profit, revenue; *en plein* ~, fully profitable, producing a good yield; *maison de* ~, investment property; **2.** report, account, statement; **3.** relation, connection, respect; correspondence; ratio; *dans le* ~ *de*, in the ratio of; *avoir* ~ *à*, to relate to, to be connected with; *sous ce* ~, in this connection; *par* ~ *à*, in proportion to; in relation to, with regard to; compared with; (pop.) ~ *à*, as regards; because of; *en* ~ *avec*, in keeping or harmony with; **4.** (usu. pl.) relationship, connection; relations; communication; *avoir de bons* ~*s avec*, to have good relations with, to be on good terms with; *mettre qn. en* ~ *avec*, to put s.o. in touch with.

rapportable [rapɔrtabl] *adj.* returnable; replaceable; that can be fitted on; referable, attributable; reportable.

rapportage [rapɔrtaʒ] *s.m.* (school slang) reporting, sneaking.

rapporter [rapɔrte] *v.t.* **1.** to bring back, to bring home; to gain; (hunt.) to retrieve; to return, to refund; **2.** to produce, to yield, to bring in; to be profitable; **3.** to add, to supplement with; to insert, to join on, to fit; to bring (soil to a site); *terre rapportée*, made-up ground; *pièces rapportées*, inlay work, mosaic; **4.** to report, to state, to tell, to give an account of, to quote; to repeat or report (maliciously); **5.** to refer, to assign, to ascribe; **6.** to plot (measurements, angle, etc.); **7.** to repeal; **se** ~ **à** *v.refl.* **1.** (obs.) to compare to, to be like, to be in keeping with; **2.** to concern, to relate to, to be connected with; **3.** to rely on, to refer to (someone's judgement, etc.), (*de*, in, as regards); *je m'en rapporte à vous*, I rely on you, I refer to you, I leave that to you.

rapporteu-r, -se [rapɔrtœr] *s.m.f.* tell-tale, tale-bearer, informer; sneak; **~r** *s.m.* **1.** one who makes a report; rapporteur; chairman (of commission); *juge* ~*r*, judge in charge of legal inquiry; **2.** (geom.) protractor.

rapprendre [raprɑ̃dr] *v.t.* to learn again, to relearn.

rapprêter [raprɛte] *v.t.* (text., etc.) to give a second dressing to.

rapproché, -e [raprɔʃe] *adj.* near, close, nearby, neighbouring.

rapprochement [raprɔʃmɑ̃] *s.m.* bringing together; drawing closer; nearness, proximity; (fig.) reconciliation; comparison; parallel.

rapprocher [raprɔʃe] *v.t.* to bring nearer or closer, to make appear nearer; to bring together; to reconcile; to compare; **se** ~ *v.refl.* to be brought together, to become reconciled; *se* ~ *de*, to draw nearer or closer to; to approximate to, to approach.

rapsode see RHAPSODE.

rapsodie see RHAPSODIE.

rapt [rapt] *s.m.* **1.** (law) abduction; enticement; **2.** (nuclear phys.) pick-up.

râpure [rɑpyr] *s.f.* raspings, scrapings, filings.

raquer [rake] *v.t.* (pop.) to pay.

raquette [rakɛt] *s.f.* **1.** racket, racquet, battledore; tennis-player; (fig.) *coup de* ~, jolt, jar, back-kick (of starting-handle); **2.** snow-shoe; **3.** (bot.) opuntia, prickly pear; **4.** (hunt.) small trap.

rare [rar] *adj.* rare, exceptional, unusual, infrequent; sparse; of rare quality; rarefied; *vous vous faites bien* ~, we see very little of you; you are quite a stranger; **~ment** [rarmɑ̃] *adv.* rarely, seldom; occasionally.

raréfaction [rarefaksjɔ̃] *s.f.* rarefaction, rarefication; depletion; growing scarcity.

raréfiable [rarefjabl] *adj.* (phys.) rarefiable.

raréfier [rarefje] *v.t.* **1.** to rarefy; **2.** to deplete, to make scarce; **se** ~ *v.refl.* to become scarce; *l'argent s'est raréfié*, money is short.

rareté [rarte] *s.f.* rareness, rarity; scarcity; rare object, rarity.

rarissime [rarisim] *adj.* most rare.

ras, -e [rɑ] *adj.* close-cropped, close-shaven; short-napped, with short pile; bare, smooth, flat; level (with edge, etc.); *faire table* ~*e*, to clear the board; (fig.) to sweep away all pre-

conceptions; to begin anew; *en ~e campagne*, in open country; *à poil ~*, short-haired; *mesure ~e*, level measure; *à ~ bords*, up to the brim; *à* or *au ~ de*, level with; (naut.) *chargé à ~ d'eau*, laden to the water-line.
rasade [rɑzad] *s.f.* glass filled to the brim.
rasage [rɑzaʒ] *s.m.* shaving; (text.) shearing.
rasant, -e [rɑzɑ̃] *adj.* level with, or skimming, the ground; passing close, skirting; (fam.) boring; (mil.) *tir ~*, grazing fire.
rascasse [raskas] *s.f.* (ichth.) scorpion-fish.
rasé, -e [rɑze] *adj.* shaved, (clean-)shaven, close-cropped.
rase-mottes [rɑzmɔt] *s.m.* (aeron.) flying close to the ground, contour flying, hedge-hopping.
raser [rɑze] *v.t.* **1.** to shave; **2.** to graze, just to touch; to skim, to skirt; to keep close to, (fig.) to hug; **3.** to pull down, to demolish; to raze to the ground; **4.** (fam.) to bore, to pester, to weary; **se ~** *v.refl.* **1.** to shave; **2.** to crouch, to squat close to the ground; **3.** (fam.) to be bored.
raseu-r, -se [rɑzœr] *s.m.f.* **1.** (text.) shearer; **2.** (fam.) boring or tiresome person.
rash [raʃ] *s.m.* (med.) rash.
rasibus [rɑzibys] *adv.* quite close, grazing.
rasoir [rɑzwar] *s.m.* **1.** razor; *~ de sûreté*, safety razor; *cuir à ~*, razor-strop; **2.** = RASEUR 2.
rassasié, -e [rasazje] *adj.* replete, satisfied.
rassasiement [rasazimɑ̃] *s.m.* satiety, satiating.
rassasier [rasazje] *v.t.* to sate, to fill, to satiate, to gorge; to surfeit; to glut; *~ sa faim*, to satisfy one's hunger; *~ ses yeux de*, to feast one's eyes on; *être rassasié de*, to have one's fill of; to be sick of; to be fed up with; **se ~** *v.refl.* to satisfy or sate oneself, to eat, drink, etc., one's fill, to gorge oneself; to have enough (*de*, of).
rassemblé, -e [rasɑ̃ble] *adj.* assembled.
rassemblement [rasɑ̃bləmɑ̃] *s.m.* gathering, assembling, mustering, collecting; assemblage, gathering, crowd; collection; union.
rassembler [rasɑ̃ble] *v.t.* to gather, to assemble, to muster, to call up, to collect, to put together; *~ son courage*, to summon up courage; *~ un cheval*, to gather up a horse (for a jump); **se ~** *v.refl.* to assemble, to gather, to collect, to congregate, to muster.
rassembleur [rasɑ̃blœr] *s.m.* (fig.) collector, gatherer.
rasseoir [raswar] *v.t.* **1.** to re-seat, to re-position; (fig.) to re-establish; **2.** to calm, to compose; *~ v.i.* (of liquids) to settle; **se ~** *v.refl.* **1.** to sit down again; **2.** (fig., obs.) to calm down, to recover one's composure.
rasséréner [raserene] *v.t.* to clear up, to calm down, to restore serenity to; **se ~** *v.refl.* to clear up, to calm down.
rassis, -e [rasi] *adj.* **1.** (of bread) stale; **2.** staid, sober, reflective, sedate; *un homme de sens ~*, a man of calm judgement.
rassortiment [rasɔrtimɑ̃] *s.m.* = RÉASSORTIMENT.
rassortir [rasɔrtir] *v.t.* = RÉASSORTIR.
rassurant, -e [rasyrɑ̃] *adj.* reassuring; calming, soothing.
rassurer [rasyre] *v.t.* to reassure, to calm down, to restore confidence to; **se ~** *v.refl.* to feel or be reassured, to get over one's apprehensions; *rassurez-vous*, don't be afraid, set your mind at rest.
rastaquouère [rastakwɛr], **rasta** [rasta] *s.m.* (fam.) flashy-looking foreigner.
rat [ra] *s.m.* rat; (fig.) miser; *~ de cave*, (i.) (obs.) excise-man; (ii.) taper; *~ d'opéra*, pupil ballet-dancer; *~ d'église*, devout church-goer; *~ d'hôtel*, hotel-thief; *~ musqué*, musk-rat, musquash; *~ palmiste*, ground squirrel; *à bon chat bon ~*, set a thief to catch a thief.
rata [rata] *s.m.* (mil. slang) stew, grub, food.
ratafia [ratafja] *s.m.* ratafia (liqueur).
ratage [rataʒ] *s.m.* failure.
ratatiné, -e [ratatine] *adj.* dried up, shrivelled; wizened; crinkled.
ratatiner [ratatine] *v.t.* to shrivel, to shrink; **se ~** *v.refl.* to shrink, to shrivel up.
ratatouille [ratatuj] *s.f.* **1.** (cook.) ratatouille; **2.** (fam., pej.) inferior stew; bad cooking; **3.** (fig., fam.) hail of blows.
rate[1] [rat] *s.f.* (anat.) spleen; (fig., fam.) *ne pas se fouler la ~*, to take things easy; *dilater la ~ de qn.*, to make s.o. have a really good laugh; *se décharger la ~*, to vent one's spleen; ⚠ not 'rate'.
rate[2] [rat] *s.f.* female rat.
raté, -e [rate] *s.m.f.* unsuccessful person, failure; *~ s.m.* misfire; *~, -e adj.* missed, miscarried, defective, spoiled, lost, unsuccessful; mismanaged, bungled.
râteau (pl. **-x**) [rɑto] *s.m.* rake; (text.) warping-comb; (naut.) *~ de pont*, squeegee.
ratel [ratɛl] *s.m.* (zool.) ratel, honey-badger.
râteler [rɑtle] *v.t.* to rake.
râteleu-r, -se [rɑtlœr] *s.m.f.* raker; **~se** *s.f.* (agric.) mechanical rake.
râtelier [rɑtlje] *s.m.* **1.** rack, manger; (fig.) *manger au ~ de qn.*, to live at someone's expense; *manger à plusieurs ~s*, to have several irons in the fire, to have more than one string to one's bow, to have more than one source of income; **2.** (obs.) set of (natural) teeth; (mod.) set of false teeth, denture.
rater [rate] *v.i.* to misfire; to fail, to be a failure, not to come off; (fam.) *ça n'a pas raté!*, it was bound to happen!; *~ v.t.* to miss, to fail (to hit, to achieve, to obtain, etc.); to make a mess or failure of; *~ une balle, un train, une occasion*, to miss the ball, a train, an opportunity; *~ qn.*, to miss (i.e. to fail to meet) s.o.; *~ son coup*, to miss one's shot, to miss the mark, to fail to bring sth. off; *~ un examen*, to fail an examination; *~ une place*, to fail to secure a place or position; *il a raté son affaire*, he has bungled the job; *la mayonnaise est ratée*, the mayonnaise hasn't come off, is a failure; (fam.) *il n'en rate pas une*, he makes one faux pas after another.
ratiboiser [ratibwaze] *v.t.* **1.** (fam.) to clean out (s.o.), to make a clean sweep (at cards); to steal, to rob (s.o.) of; **2.** to ruin (s.o.).
ratichon [ratiʃɔ̃] *s.m.* (pop., pej.) priest.
ratier [ratje] *s.m.* rat-catcher (dog), ratter.
ratière [ratjɛr] *s.f.* rat-trap.
ratification [ratifikɑsjɔ̃] *s.f.* ratification, confirmation, approval.
ratifier [ratifje] *v.t.* to ratify, to confirm.
ratine [ratin] *s.f.* (text.) frieze-cloth.
ratiocination [rasjɔsinɑsjɔ̃] *s.f.* (Lit.) ratiocination.
ratiociner [rasjɔsine] *v.i.* (obs.) to reason; (mod.) to argue interminably.
ration [rɑsjɔ̃] *s.f.* ration, allowance; *mettre à la ~*, to ration, to put on short rations, to put on an allowance.
rational-isation [rasjɔnalizɑsjɔ̃] *s.f.* rationalization; **~iser** [rasjɔnalize] *v.t.* to rationalize, to organize on a rational basis, to reorganize; **~isme** [rasjɔnalism] *s.m.* rationalism; **~iste** [rasjɔnalist] *adj.*, *s.m.f.* rationalist.
rationalité [rasjɔnalite] *s.f.* rationality.
rationnaire [rasjɔnɛr] *adj.* one entitled to a ration or allowance.
rationnel, -le [rasjɔnɛl] *adj.* rational; theoretic(al); *mécanique ~le*, pure or theoretical mechanics; *organisation ~le*, rationalization; *~ s.m.* (log.) *le ~*, the rational; **~lement** [rasjɔnɛlmɑ̃] *adv.* rationally.
rationnement [rasjɔnmɑ̃] *s.m.* rationing; putting on rations or an allowance.

rationner [rasjɔne] *v.t.* to ration; to put on short rations; **se ~** *v.refl.* to ration, to restrict, oneself.
ratissage [ratisaʒ] *s.m.* raking, scraping; combing (of an area).
ratisser [ratise] *v.t.* **1.** to rake, to rake up or in; (mil., etc.) to comb (an area); **2.** to ruin, to clean out, (s.o. at cards).
ratissoire [ratiswar] *s.f.* hoe, light rake.
raton[1] [ratɔ̃] *s.m.* **1.** young rat; **2.** ~ *laveur,* raccoon.
raton[2] [ratɔ̃] *s.m.* a kind of cheesecake.
R.A.T.P. [ɛrɑtepe] abbrev. *Régie autonome des transports parisiens,* Paris transport authority.
rattachement [rataʃmɑ̃] *s.m.* tying up again, connection; connecting, linking; recovering.
rattacher [rataʃe] *v.t.* to tie up again, to refasten, to (re-)connect, to attach, to link; **se ~** *v.refl.* to be attached, to be connected or linked, (*à*, to); to belong (*à*, to).
rattrapage [ratrapaʒ] *s.m.* making up for, correcting; catching up.
rattraper [ratrape] *v.t.* to catch again, to recapture; to catch up, to overtake; to recover, to make up for; to rescue, to redeem; to get even with; *bien fin qui m'y rattrapera,* once bitten twice shy; they won't catch me doing that again; **se ~** *v.refl.* to catch hold (*à*, of), to recover, to make up (for lost time, etc.).
rature [ratyr] *s.f.* erasure, deletion, crossing out.
raturer [ratyre] *v.t.* to erase, to cross out, to delete; to annul; *tout raturé,* full of crossings-out, a mass of deletions.
R.A.U. [ɛray] abbrev. *République arabe unie,* U.A.R.
raucité [rosite] *s.f.* hoarseness; raucousness.
rauque [rok] *adj.* hoarse; harsh, raucous.
ravage [ravaʒ] *s.m.* ravages (pl.), devastation, destruction, havoc, ruin; *faire des ~s,* to cause havoc; (fam.) to break someone's heart.
ravager [ravaʒe] *v.t.* to ravage, to spoil, to devastate, to ruin, to lay waste; to leave its mark on.
ravageu-r, -se [ravaʒœr] *s.m.f.* destroyer, plunderer, pillager; *adj.* destroying, consuming.
ravalement [ravalmɑ̃] *s.m.* **1.** cleaning(-down), resurfacing, re-dressing; scraping; roughcasting, rendering, plastering; **2.** lopping (of trees); **3.** (obs.) cutting-down, reducing; **4.** (fig.) disparagement.
ravaler [ravale] *v.t.* **1.** to clean down, to scrape; to resurface; to render, to plaster, to roughcast; **2.** to lop (tree); **3.** (techn.) to reduce (in height or thickness), to plane down; (fig.) to reduce, to depreciate, to disparage; **4.** to swallow again, to gulp down; (lit. & fig.) to swallow, to choke back, to repress; ~ *sa salive,* to swallow; ~ *ses paroles,* (i.) to eat one's words; (ii.) to check oneself, to resist the temptation to speak; ~ *un sanglot,* to choke back a sob; **se ~** *v.refl.* to debase oneself, to reduce oneself (*au niveau de,* to the level of).
ravaleur [ravalœr] *s.m.* plasterer.
ravaudage [ravodaʒ] *s.m.* mending, patching up, darning; patch, rough repair.
ravauder [ravode] *v.t.* to mend, to darn, to patch up.
ravaudeu-r, -se [ravodœr] *s.m.f.* mender, darning-woman.
rave [rav] *s.f.* any of various root vegetables, esp. turnip; *bette* ~ (also *betterave*), beet, beetroot; *chou* ~, kohlrabi; ~ *céléri,* celeriac.
ravelin [ravlɛ̃] *s.m.* (fort.) ravelin.
ravenelle [ravnɛl] *s.f.* (bot.) **1.** wallflower; **2.** wild radish.
ravier [ravje] *s.m.* hors-d'œuvre dish.
ravière [ravjɛr] *s.f.* ground planted with root vegetables.
ravigote [ravigɔt] *s.f.* (cook.) ravigote sauce.
ravigoter [ravigɔte] *v.t.* to enliven, to invigorate.
ravin [ravɛ̃] *s.m.* ravine, gully.
ravine [ravin] *s.f.* small mountain stream; ravine, gully.
ravinement [ravinmɑ̃] *s.m.* wearing away, erosion.
raviner [ravine] *v.t.* to wear away, to erode, to score; (lit. & fig.) to furrow.
ravir [ravir] *v.t.* **1.** (obs.) to carry off, to take away, to abduct; to rob of; **2.** to enchant, to transport, to delight, to ravish; *à* ~, wonderfully well, admirably.
(**se**) **raviser** [ravize] *v.refl.* to change one's mind, to think better of it; to go back on a decision or promise.
ravissant, -e [ravisɑ̃] *adj.* ravishing, delightful, lovely, exquisite, enchanting, captivating.
ravissement [ravismɑ̃] *s.m.* **1.** (obs.) rape, carrying off, abduction; **2.** rapture, delight, ecstasy; *être dans le* ~, to be in raptures, in ecstasies.
ravisseu-r, -se [ravisœr] *s.m.f.* abductor.
ravitaillement [ravitɑjmɑ̃] *s.m.* supplying, provisioning, replenishment, revictualling; (mil.) supply.
ravitailler [ravitɑje] *v.t.* to supply, to provision, to provide, to revictual.
ravitailleur [ravitɑjœr] *adj., s.m.* supply (ship, convoy, plane, etc.); ~ *d'aviation,* aircraft refuelling tender.
ravivage [ravivaʒ] *s.m.* **1.** cleaning, filing up, (of metal surfaces); **2.** reviving (of colours).
raviver [ravive] *v.t.* **1.** to revive, to enliven, to brighten up; **2.** to clean or to file up (metal surfaces); **3.** (surg. & fig.) to reopen (a wound).
ravoir [ravwar] *v.t.* (used only in the infinitive) to get back, to have back; (fam.) to get (sth.) clean again.
rayage [rɛjaʒ] *s.m.* **1.** rifling (of guns); **2.** striking off, deletion, erasure.
rayé, -e [rɛje] *adj.* streaked, striped; (of firearms) rifled.
rayer [rɛje] *v.t.* **1.** to scratch, to score; to line; to rule (paper); **2.** to strike out or off; to cross out, to erase, to draw a line through.
rayère [rɛjɛr] *s.f.* loop-hole.
rayon [rɛjɔ̃] *s.m.* ray, beam; radius; range; sphere (of influence or activity); spoke (of wheel); furrow; shelf; department (of shop, etc.); *dix mètres de* ~, ten metres in radius; ~*s X,* X-rays; ~ *de miel,* honeycomb; *ce n'est pas de mon* ~, that's not within my province.
rayonnage [rɛjɔnaʒ] *s.m.* shelving; shelves; (agric.) drilling, furrowing.
rayonnant, -e [rɛjɔnɑ̃] *adj.* radiating; radiant, beaming; (arch.) rayonnant, Middle Gothic.
rayonne [rɛjɔn] *s.f.* (text.) rayon.
rayonné, -e [rɛjɔne] *adj.* **1.** radial, arranged radially; **2.** encircled by rays of light.
rayonnement [rɛjɔnmɑ̃] *s.m.* radiation; radiance; diffusion; (fig.) influence.
rayonner [rɛjɔne] *v.i.* to radiate, to spread in every direction, to depart from a central point; to shine, to shine forth, to beam.
rayure [rɛjyr] *s.f.* stripe, striping; rifling (of firearms); scratch, scratching; crossing out.
raz [rɑ] *s.m.* race, tide-race; ~ *de marée,* bore, tidal wave.
razzia [razja] *s.f.* razzia, raid, incursion.
razzier [razje] *v.t.* to raid (village, store, etc.), to make a raid on; to carry off.
R.D.A. [ɛrdeɑ] abbrev. *République démocratique allemande,* G.D.R.
ré [re] *s.m.* (mus.) D, ray, re.
réa [rea] *s.m.* sheave (of a pulley).

réabonnement [reabɔnmɑ̃] *s.m.* renewal of subscription.
réabonner [reabɔne] *v.t.* to renew (a person's) subscription; **se** ~ *v.refl.* to renew one's subscription.
réabsorber [reapsɔrbe] *v.t.* to reabsorb.
réabsorption [reapsɔrpsjɔ̃] *s.f.* reabsorption.
réac [reak] *adj., s.m.f.* abbrev. *réactionnaire.*
réaccoutumer [reakutyme] *v.t.* to reaccustom; **se** ~ *v.refl.* to reaccustom oneself; *se* ~ *au travail*, to get back into the routine of work.
réacteur [reaktœr] *s.m.* **1.** (obs.) reactionary; **2.** (phys., chem.) reactor; **3.** (aeron.) jet engine.
réacti-f, -ve [reaktif] *adj.* reactive; reagent; *s.m.f.* one who reacts, ~**f** *s.m.* (chem.) reagent.
réaction [reaksjɔ̃] *s.f.* (phys., chem., mech., pol.) reaction; (physiol.) reflex; (fig.) reaction, response; *avion, moteur, à* ~, jet aircraft, jet engine.
réactionnaire [reaksjɔnɛr] *adj., s.m.f.* reactionary.
réactionnel, -le [reaksjɔnɛl] *adj.* (med., psychol.) reactive, reflex.
réactiv-er [reaktive] *v.t.* to reactivate, to revive; ~**ité** [reaktivite] *s.f.* (nuclear chem., med.) reactivity; (psychol.) response, ability to react.
réadapt-ation [readaptɑsjɔ̃] *s.f.* readjustment; rehabilitation (treatment, therapy), retraining; ~**er** [readapte] *v.t.* to readjust, to rehabilitate, to retrain; **se** ~**er** *v.refl.* to adjust (to sth.).
réadmettre [readmɛtr] *v.t.* to readmit.
réadmission [readmisjɔ̃] *s.f.* readmission, readmittance.
réaffirmer [reafirme] *v.t.* to reaffirm.
réagir [reaʒir] *v.t.* to react (*sur*, on, *contre*, against, *à*, to).
réajustement [reaʒystmɑ̃] *s.m.* = RAJUSTEMENT.
réajuster [reaʒyste] *v.t.* = RAJUSTER.
réal (pl. **aux**) [real] *s.m.* (hist.) real (Spanish coin).
réaléser [realeze] *v.t.* to rebore (cylinders).
réalgar [realgar] *s.m.* (chem.) realgar.
réalisable [realizabl] *adj.* realizable, feasible.
réalisat-eur, -rice [realizatœr] *adj.* realizing, putting into effect, bringing to reality; *s.m.f.* realizer; (cin., etc.) producer.
réalisation [realizɑsjɔ̃] *s.f.* **1.** realization, putting into effect, execution; **2.** (cin., theatr.) production; screening, staging; **3.** (fin.) realizing, conversion into cash, selling out (of shares), capitalization (of debt).
réaliser [realize] *v.t.* **1.** to realize, to bring to reality, to put into effect, to execute, to fulfil, to carry out, to achieve; **2.** (fin.) to realize, to convert into cash, to sell out (shares), to capitalize (debt); **3.** (cin., theatr.) to produce; to stage, to screen; **4.** to realize, to grasp; **se** ~ *v.refl.* to be realized, to materialize, to come true; to realize or fulfil oneself.
réalisme [realism] *s.m.* realism.
réaliste [realist] *adj.* realistic; ~ *s.m.f.* realist.
réalité [realite] *s.f.* reality; *en* ~, in fact; in reality.
réanimation [reanimɑsjɔ̃] *s.f.* reviving, resuscitation, bringing to life again.
réanimer [reanime] *v.t.* to revive, to resuscitate.
réapparaître [reaparɛtr] *v.i.* to reappear.
réapparition [reaparisjɔ̃] *s.f.* reappearance.
réapprendre [reaprɑ̃dr] *v.t.* = RAPPRENDRE.
réapprovisionnement [reaprɔvizjɔnmɑ̃] *s.m.* replenishing, reprovisioning; reordering, restocking.
réapprovisionner [reaprɔvizjɔne] *v.t.* to supply again, to reprovision; to reorder, to restock.
réargenter [rearʒɑ̃te] *v.t.* to resilver, to replate.
réarmement [rearməmɑ̃] *s.m.* rearming, rearmament.
réarmer [rearme] *v.t.* **1.** to reload; **2.** (naut.) to refit; ~ *v.i.* to rearm.
réarrangement [rearɑ̃ʒmɑ̃] *s.m.* rearrangement.
réarranger [rearɑ̃ʒe] *v.t.* to rearrange.
réassignation [reasiɲɑsjɔ̃] *s.f.* **1.** (law) further summons, new summons; **2.** (fin.) reassignment, remortgaging.
réassigner [reasiɲe] *v.t.* **1.** (law) to resummon, to issue a further summons; **2.** (fin.) to reassign, to remortgage.
réassortiment [reasɔrtimɑ̃] *s.m.* matching, matching-up; making up (of tea-service, etc.).
réassortir [reasɔrtir] *v.t.* to match (material, etc.); to make up (set).
réassurance [reasyrɑ̃s] *s.f.* reinsurance.
réassurer [reasyre] *v.t.* to reinsure; ⚠ not 'to reassure'.
rebaisser [rəbese] *v.i.* to go down again.
rebaptiser [rəbatize] *v.t.* to rebaptize, to rename.
rébarbati-f, -ve [rebarbatif] *adj.* surly, stern, forbidding, rebarbative.
rebâtir [rəbɑtir] *v.t.* to rebuild, to reconstruct.
rebattre [rəbatr] *v.t.* to beat again; (cards) to reshuffle; to remake (mattress); ~ *les oreilles à qn. de qch.*, to be always on at s.o. about sth., to be dinning sth. into s.o.
rebattu, -e [rəbaty] *adj.* (fig.) hackneyed, trite, stale; oft-told; *sentier* ~, well-worn path.
rebec [rəbɛk] *s.m.* (mus.) rebec(k).
rebelle [rəbɛl] *adj.* rebellious, rebelling, refractory, intractable, disobedient; ~ *s.m.f.* rebel.
(**se**) **rebeller** [rəbɛlle] *v.refl.* to rebel, to protest.
rébellion [rebɛlljɔ̃] *s.f.* rebellion, revolt; the rebels.
(**se**) **rebiffer** [rəbife] *v.refl.* (fam.) to be refractory, to dig one's heels in, to be up in arms, to jib; *se* ~ *contre*, to strike back at, to rebel against.
rebiquer [rəbike] *v.i.* (fam.) to turn up, to curl, the wrong way.
reblochon [rəblɔʃɔ̃] *s.m.* reblochon (cheese).
reboisement [rəbwazmɑ̃] *s.m.* replanting, reafforestation, retimbering.
reboiser [rəbwaze] *v.t.* to replant, to reafforest.
rebond [rəbɔ̃] *s.m.* rebound, bounce.
rebondi, -e [rəbɔ̃di] *adj.* chubby, plump, buxom; (of purse, etc.) well-filled.
rebondir [rəbɔ̃dir] *v.i.* to rebound, to bounce. (of business activity, etc.) to revive, to pick up,
rebondissement [rəbɔ̃dismɑ̃ *s.m.* rebounding; rebound; (fig.) revival, new development.
rebord [rəbɔr] *s.m.* edge, brim, rim, flange, ledge, raised edge, brink; border; hem.
reborder [rəbɔrde] *v.t.* to put a new border on, to rehem, to re-edge; ~ *un enfant dans son lit*, to tuck a child up in bed again.
reboucher [rəbuʃe] *v.t.* **1.** to stop up again; to recork; to block again; **2.** to stop, to fill, (holes); **se** ~ *v.refl.* to get stopped up again.
rebours [rəbur] *adj.* cross-grained; ~ *s.m.* wrong way, wrong side; reverse, opposite; *à* ~, *au* ~, against the grain, against the nap; backwards, in the wrong direction; (of disposition, etc.) contrary; *au* ~ *de*, contrary to, against; *prendre qch. au* ~, to take sth. the wrong way, to misconstrue sth.
rebouter [rəbute] **1.** (obs.) to replace; **2.** to (re)set (bones).
rebouteur [rəbutœr], **rebouteu-x, -se** [rəbutø] *s.m.f.* (fam.) bone-setter.
reboutonner [rəbutɔne] *v.t.* to rebutton; **se** ~ *v.refl.* to button oneself up again.

rebras [rəbra] *s.m.* cuff; gauntlet (of glove).
rebroder [rəbrɔde] *v.t.* to add embroidery to.
rebroussement [rəbrusmɑ̃] *s.m.* turning back, stroking backwards; back-brushing; graining (of leather).
rebrousser [rəbruse] *v.t.* to turn back, to stroke backwards, to turn up (hair), to brush up (hair, nap); to grain (leather); ~ *chemin*, to retrace one's steps; *à rebrousse poil*, against the hair, against the nap; (fig.) against the grain, the wrong way; ~ *v.i.* (of edge of cutting tool) to turn back.
rebuffade [rəbyfad] *s.f.* rebuff, rebuke, snub, (fig.) slap in the face; *essuyer des ~s*, to meet with a rebuff, to be snubbed.
rébus [rebys] *s.m.* rebus; (fig.) riddle, enigma, puzzle.
rebut [rəby] *s.m.* reject; refuse, rubbish, waste; *mettre au* ~, to throw away; *de* ~, rubbishy; to be thrown away; reject; ~ *de la société*, social outcast or reject, drop-out, scum of the earth.
rebutant, -e [rəbytɑ̃] *adj.* repulsive, disgusting; tedious, disheartening, discouraging; *des démarches ~es*, moves aimed at discouraging (sth.).
rebuter [rəbyte] *v.t.* **1.** (obs.) to reject, to rebuff; **2.** (obs.) to throw away; **3.** to discourage, to deflect; **4.** to repel, to disgust, to be repellent or disgusting; ⚠ not 'to rebut' (an argument).
recacheter [rəkaʃte] *v.t.* to seal again.
recalage [rəkalaʒ] *s.m.* (fam.) failing (an examination), failure.
récalcitrant, -e [rekalsitrɑ̃] *adj.* refractory, recalcitrant, rebellious, obstinate, resisting.
recaler [rəkale] *v.t.* **1.** to wedge again; **2.** (fam.) to fail (an examination); *un recalé*, one who has failed, a failure.
récapitulati-f, -ve [rekapitylatif] *adj.* recapitulatory.
récapitulation [rekapitylɑsjɔ̃] *s.f.* recapitulation, summing up.
récapituler [rekapityle] *v.t.* to recapitulate, to sum up.
recarreler [rəkarle] *v.t.* to repave, to retile.
recaser [rəkɑze] *v.t.* (fam.) to find another job for; to re-house.
recauser [rəkoze] *v.i.* to talk again or later (*de*, about).
recéder [rəsede] *v.t.* **1.** to give in again; **2.** to let (s.o.) have (sth.) back again; to resell, to sell back; ⚠ not 'to recede'.
recel [rəsɛl] *s.m.* receiving stolen goods; harbouring (of malefactor); concealment (of child).
recélé [rəsele], **recelé** [rəsle] *s.m.* (law) concealment (of inheritance, of child).
receler [rəsle], **recéler** [rəsele] *v.t.* **1.** to conceal, to keep secret or hidden, to have concealed or tucked away; to harbour; **2.** to receive (stolen goods).
receleu-r, -se [rəs(ə)lœr] *s.m.f.* receiver (of stolen goods).
récemment [resamɑ̃] *adv.* lately, recently; freshly, newly.
recensement [rəsɑ̃smɑ̃] *s.m.* census, register of those liable for conscription; inventory; review.
recenser [rəsɑ̃se] *v.t.* to take the census of; to check off; to list, to inventory.
recenseur [rəsɑ̃sœr] *s.m.* **1.** (obs.) returning officer; **2.** census official.
recension [rəsɑ̃sjɔ̃] *s.f.* recension, collation (of texts, etc.); critical examination.
récent, -e [resɑ̃] *adj.* recent, fresh, late, new.
recepage [rəspaʒ], **recépage** [rəsepaʒ] *s.m.* cutting down (of vines, etc.) close to the ground.
receper [rəspe], **recéper** [rəsepe] *v.t.* **1.** to cut down close to the ground; **2.** (techn.) to saw down level, to raze.
récépissé [resepise] *s.m.* receipt, acknowledgement.
réceptacle [resɛptakl] *s.m.* receptacle; (bot.) thalamus.
récept-eur, -rice [resɛptœr] *adj.* receiving; *poste ~eur*, (radio) receiving station or set, receiver; (mech.) *arbre ~eur*, driven shaft; (electr.) *dynamo ~rice*, dynamo driven as motor; motor transmitter; **~eur** *s.m.* **1.** receiver, collector; **2.** (radio, telephone) receiver, receiving apparatus.
récepti-f, -ve [resɛptif] *adj.* receptive.
réception [resɛpsjɔ̃] *s.f.* reception; reception (-desk); receiving, taking over, admission; acceptance (by inspector, of building work done); welcoming; party, entertainment; *accuser ~ de*, to acknowledge receipt of.
réceptionnaire [resɛpsjɔnɛr] *s.m.f.* receiver, consignee; reception clerk.
réceptionner [resɛpsjɔne] *v.t.* (comm., etc.) to check and sign for, to take over, (goods).
réceptivité [resɛptivite] *s.f.* receptivity.
recerclage [rəsɛrklaʒ] *s.m.* rehooping (of casks).
recercler [rəsɛrkle] *v.t.* to rehoop (casks).
récessi-f, -ve [resesif] *adj.* (biol.) recessive.
récession [resesjɔ̃] *s.f.* receding, recession, contraction; (econ.) recession.
récessivité [resesivite] *s.f.* (biol.) recessive character, recessiveness.
recette [rəsɛt] *s.f.* **1.** receipts, takings, monies received, gate money; ~ (*nette*), profit; *faire* ~, to give a good return, to be a box-office success; **2.** tax collector's office, tax collection, receivership of taxes; **3.** receiving, receipt; recovery (of funds, etc.); (comm., etc.) taking delivery, checking and acceptance, (of goods); *faire la ~ des contributions*, to receive taxes; **4.** (mining) landing (for collection of material extracted); **5.** (cook.) recipe; (med.) prescription.
recevabilité [rəsvabilite] *s.f.* (law) admissibility, receivability.
recevable [rəsvabl] *adj.* receivable, acceptable, admissible.
receveu-r, -se [rəsvœr] *s.m.f.* receiver; collector; postmaster, postmistress; (bus, etc.) conductor, conductress; *~r*, *~se*, *des contributions*, tax-collector; *~r*, *~se*, *buraliste*, tobacconist (in kiosk).
recevoir [rəsvwar] *v.t.* to receive, to admit, to take, to take in, to accept; to welcome; to meet with; to entertain; *ils reçoivent beaucoup*, they entertain a good deal; *recevrez-vous demain?* will you be at home tomorrow?; ~ *un mauvais accueil*, to meet with a bad reception; ~ *les excuses de qn.*, to accept someone's apologies; *être reçu à un examen*, to pass an examination; *être reçu bachelier* = to pass A-Level; *être reçu médecin*, to qualify as a doctor; (comm.) *reçu votre lettre du 20 courant*, your letter of the 20th to hand.
réchampir [reʃɑ̃pir] *v.t.* (paint.) to pick out (with another colour); to set off.
rechange [rəʃɑ̃ʒ] *s.m.* change; (comm.) renewal (of bill of exchange); *pièces de* ~, spare parts; *roue de* ~, spare wheel; *vêtements de* ~, spare garments, change of clothes; ~ *de vêtements*, change of clothes.
rechanger [rəʃɑ̃ʒe] *v.t.* to change again.
rechanter [rəʃɑ̃te] *v.t.* to sing again; to repeat.
rechapage [rəʃapaʒ] *s.m.* retreading (of tyre); retread.
rechaper [rəʃape] *v.t.* to retread (tyre).
réchappé, -e [reʃape] *s.m.f.* one who has escaped, survivor.
réchapper [reʃape] *v.i.* ~ *de* or *à*, to escape from (great danger), to survive, to be a survivor of (a disaster); to recover from (serious illness); *en* ~, to recover; to escape with one's life, to get out alive.
recharge [rəʃarʒ] *s.f.* reloading; refill; (electr.) recharging; *mettre en* ~, to recharge.

rechargement [rəʃarʒəmɑ̃] *s.m.* reloading, reshipment; remetalling (of roads); (electr.) recharging.
recharger [rəʃarʒe] *v.t.* to reload, to reship; to remetal (roads); to refill, to fill up again; (electr.) to recharge.
réchaud [reʃo] *s.m.* dish-warmer, hotplate; methylated-spirit stove, spirit-lamp; small charcoal stove; (hort.) layer of fresh manure (on hotbed); *mettre un plat au* ~, to keep a dish hot.
réchauffage [reʃofaʒ] *s.m.* reheating, warming up again; (techn.) pre-heating.
réchauffé, -e [reʃofe] *adj.* warmed up again; (fig., pej.) needlessly revived; ~ *s.m.* old stuff; stale news; rehash.
réchauffement [reʃofmɑ̃] *s.m.* warming up; (hort.) lining a hotbed anew.
réchauffer [reʃofe] *v.t.* to warm up again; to stir up, to rekindle, to revive, (enthusiasm, courage, etc.); (hort.) to put fresh manure on (a hotbed); ~ *un serpent dans son sein*, to nurse a viper in one's bosom; **se** ~ *v.refl.* to get warm again; to warm oneself up.
rechauffeur [reʃofœr] *s.m.* (techn.) (re)heater, pre-heater, feed-water heater.
rechausser [rəʃose] *v.t.* to put shoes or stockings on (s.o.) again; to reshoe (a horse); (build.) to underpin; to line the foot of (a wall); (agric.) to bank up (the base of a tree); **se** ~ *v.refl.* to put one's shoes, etc., on again.
rêche [rɛʃ] *adj.* rough, harsh.
recherche [rəʃɛrʃ] *s.f* **1.** research, investigation; search, quest, pursuit, inquiry, examination; *faire de la* ~, to do research (work); *faire des* ~*s*, to research, to undertake research(es), to make inquiries (*sur*, into), to carry out investigations; *aller à la* ~ *de*, to go in quest of; to search for; **2.** refinement, affectation; *s'habiller avec* ~, to dress with studied elegance.
recherché, -e [rəʃɛrʃe] *adj.* refined, choice, fastidious, exquisite; much sought after, in great demand; *une expression trop* ~*e*, a far--fetched or affected expression.
rechercher [rəʃɛrʃe] *v.t.* to seek again, to look for again; to research into; to make the subject of research; to seek after, to search for; to (try to) find; to look up (a word); to inquire after; ~ *une femme en mariage*, to court a woman, to seek a woman's hand in marriage; ~ *l'amitié de qn.*, to seek someone's friendship; *tout le monde la recherche*, she is very much sought after, she is in great demand.
rechigné, -e [rəʃiɲe] *adj.* cross, surly, sullen, grim; bad-tempered.
rechigner [rəʃiɲe] *v.i.* **1.** (obs.) to look sullen, to sulk; *en rechignant*, with a bad grace; **2.** ~ *à*, to jib at.
rechute [rəʃyt] *s.f.* relapse, set-back; fresh fall.
rechuter [rəʃyte] *v.i.* to have a relapse.
récidive [residiv] *s.f.* repetition of an offence; recurrence (of an illness).
récidiver [residive] *v.i.* to repeat an offence; (of illness) to recur.
récidiviste [residivist] *s.m.f.* previous, old, or hardened offender, recidivist.
récidivité [residivite] *s.f.* (med.) tendency to recur.
récif [resif] *s.m.* reef (of rocks).
récipiendaire [resipjɑ̃dɛr] *s.m.f.* new member, member elect; recipient (of degree, etc.).
récipient [resipjɑ̃] *s.m.* **1.** (chem., etc.) recipient; **2.** receptacle, container, vessel; ⚠ not 'recipient' referring to a person.
réciprocité [resiprɔsite] *s.f.* reciprocity, reciprocation.
réciproque [resiprɔk] *adj.* reciprocal, mutual; (math.) reciprocal; inverse; *raison* ~, inverse ratio; ~ *s.f.* (log.) converse, reciprocal proposition; (fam.) the opposite, return; *rendre la* ~, to give tit for tat, to do the same (to s.o.), to get even (with s.o.); ~**ment** [resiprɔkmɑ̃] *adv.* reciprocally, mutually; vice-versa; (math.) conversely.
récit [resi] *s.m.* tale; recital, report, account, narration, relation; (mus.) recitative; *faire un* ~ *de*, to give an account of.
récital [resital] *s.m.* recital.
récitant, -e [resitɑ̃] *adj.* (mus.) solo; *s.m.f.* one who sings solo recitative; narrator.
récitatif [resitatif] *s.m.* (mus.) recitative.
récitation [resitɑsjɔ̃] *s.f.* recitation, reciting, recital, repeating (of lesson, etc.); recitation, piece learnt by heart.
réciter [resite] *v.t.* to recite, to repeat (prayers, lessons, etc.); (pej.) to reel off; (mus.) to sing (recitative).
réclamant, -e [reklamɑ̃] *s.m.f.* claimant; plaintiff, complainer.
réclamation [reklamɑsjɔ̃] *s.f.* claim, complaint, demand, protest, objection; *faire une* ~, to put in a claim, to lodge a complaint.
réclame [reklam] *s.f.* **1.** (print.) catchword; (theatr.) cue; **2.** advertisement, advertising, publicity; puff; advertisement sign; *faire de la* ~, to advertise, to mount an advertising or publicity campaign; *faire de la* ~ *pour*, to advertise, to publicize, to boost; *cela ne lui fait pas de* ~, that is not a good advertisement for him; *article qui est en* ~, article which is being sold cheap (to attract custom), loss-leader.
réclamer [reklame] *v.t.* to claim, to demand, to call for, to clamour for; to require; (obs.) to implore, to beg for; ~ *v.i.* to complain, to protest or appeal; **se** ~ **de** *v.refl.* to invoke, to refer to, to rely on (for support, etc.), to use (someone's) name.
reclassement [rəklɑsmɑ̃] *s.m.* reclassification, regrouping; redistribution; regrading (of salaried posts, etc.).
reclasser [rəklɑse] *v.t.* to reclassify, to regroup, to regrade (civil servants, etc.).
reclouer [rəklue] *v.t.* to nail again, to nail up, to nail down.
reclus, -e [rəkly] *adj.* shut up, sequestered, secluded; *s.m.f.* recluse.
réclusion [reklyzjɔ̃] *s.f.* seclusion, confinement; (law) solitary confinement.
réclusionnaire [reklyzjɔnɛr] *s.m.f.* (law) one in solitary confinement.
recogniti-f, -ve [rəkɔɲitif] *adj.* (law) recognitory.
recognition [rəkɔɲisjɔ̃] *s.f.* recognition, identification.
recoiffer [rəkwafe] *v.t.* to dress (the head or hair) again; **se** ~ *v.refl.* to do one's hair again; to put one's hat back on.
recoin [rəkwɛ̃] *s.m.* corner, nook; (fig.) innermost recess; *les coins et* ~*s d'une maison*, the nooks and crannies of a house.
récolement [rekɔlmɑ̃] *s.m.* (law) **1.** verification; inventory; **2.** reading over of their depositions to witnesses.
récoler [rekɔle] (law) **1.** to verify; to inventory; **2.** to read over their depositions to witnesses.
recollage [rəkɔlaʒ] *s.m.* re-pasting or re--gluing, sticking on again.
récollection [rekɔlɛksjɔ̃] *s.f.* (relig.) contemplation; self-communion, private meditation; ⚠ not 'recollection' in senses 'remembering', 'memory'.
recollement [rəkɔlmɑ̃] *s.m.* adhering again.
recoller [rəkɔle] *v.t.* to stick on or up, to paste, to glue, again; to mend (with adhesive), to stick together again; ~ *v.i.* (sport) to catch up with the main body of runners; **se** ~ *v.refl.* (pop.) to go and live with each other again.

récoltant, -e [rekɔltɑ̃] *s.m.f., adj.* (agric.) grower; (one) who harvests his own crop.
récolte [rekɔlt] *s.f.* harvest, crop, gathering; (fig.) harvest, collection; *~s sur pied,* standing crops; *faire rentrer la ~,* to get in the harvest.
récolter [rekɔlte] *v.t.* to get in, to reap; to harvest, to gather in; to receive, to get (sth. out of sth.); *je n'en ai récolté que des injures,* all I got out of it was a lot of abuse.
recommandable [rəkɔmɑ̃dabl] *adj.* commendable, worthy of commendation; respectable.
recommandation [rəkɔmɑ̃dɑsjɔ̃] *s.f.* recommendation, introduction; reference; injunction, advice, order; (post-office) registration.
recommander [rəkɔmɑ̃de] *v.t.* to recommend, to introduce, to commend; to enjoin, to order, to request, to exhort, to beg, to advise; to register (letter, etc.); **se ~** *v.refl. se ~ de,* to rely on the support or evidence, of; *se ~ à,* to commend oneself to (e.g. God's protection), to implore the help and protection of; *se ~ par,* to commend oneself by (a quality).
recommencement [rəkɔmɑ̃smɑ̃] *s.m.* recommencement, beginning again, fresh start.
recommencer [rəkɔmɑ̃se] *v.t.i.* to recommence, to begin or start again; *c'est toujours à ~,* there's no end to it; *le voilà qui recommence!,* he's at it again!; *~ sur nouveaux frais,* to begin all over again.
récompense [rekɔ̃pɑ̃s] *s.f.* reward; recompense, compensation; presentation (for long service, etc.); *en ~ de,* in return for; *recevoir une juste ~,* to be justly rewarded.
récompenser [rekɔ̃pɑ̃se] *v.t.* to reward, to repay, to recompense; to compensate.
recomposer [rəkɔ̃poze] *v.t.* to recompose, to put together again, to reconstitute; (print.) to re-set.
recomposition [rəkɔ̃pɔzisjɔ̃] *s.f.* recomposition, reconstitution; (print.) resetting.
recompter [rəkɔ̃te] *v.t.* to count again, to add up again, to re-count.
réconciliat-eur, -rice [rekɔ̃siljatœr] *s.m.f.* reconciler, conciliator.
réconciliation [rekɔ̃siljɑsjɔ̃] *s.f.* reconciliation; (eccles.) reconsecration.
réconcilier [rekɔ̃silje] *v.t.* to reconcile, to make (s.o.) reconciled, (*avec,* to, with); (eccles.) to reconsecrate; **se ~** *v.refl. se ~ (avec qn.),* to be reconciled (with s.o.), to make it up.
reconduction [rəkɔ̃dyksjɔ̃] *s.f.* renewal (of a lease, etc.); extension; prorogation.
reconduire [rəkɔ̃dɥir] *v.t.* **1.** to take back; to see home; to accompany to the door; to show out; to drive back; **2.** to renew (lease, etc.); to extend; to prorogue.
réconfort [rekɔ̃fɔr] *s.m.* comfort, relief, help, consolation.
réconfortant, -e [rekɔ̃fɔrtɑ̃] *adj.* comforting, relieving, consolatory, reviving; stimulating.
réconforter [rekɔ̃fɔrte] *v.t.* to comfort, to help, to relieve, to console, to revive, to fortify, to cheer up.
reconnaissable [rəkɔnɛsabl] *adj.* recognizable (*à,* by).
reconnaissance [rəkɔnɛsɑ̃s] *s.f.* recognition; gratitude, thankfulness; acknowledgement; (mil.) reconnoitring, reconnaissance; *manquer de ~,* to be ungrateful; *en ~ de vos services,* in recognition of your services; (mil.) *envoyer en ~,* to send on reconnaissance, to send out to reconnoitre; *~ du mont de piété,* pawn-ticket.
reconnaissant, -e [rəkɔnɛsɑ̃] *adj.* grateful, thankful.
reconnaître [rəkɔnɛtr] *v.t.* to recognize (*à,* by), to know, to identify; to find out; to acknowledge; to admit, to be grateful for, to make return for; (mil.) to reconnoitre; *reconnu coupable,* found guilty; *se faire ~,* to make oneself known (*de,* to); *je vous reconnais bien là,* that's just like you; **se ~** *v.refl.* to know oneself, to know each other; to be recognized, to recognize oneself; *s'y ~,* to get one's bearings; to take sth. in; *je ne m'y reconnais plus,* I am all at sea; *se ~ coupable,* to admit one's guilt; *donnez-moi le temps de me ~,* give me time to get my bearings.
reconnu, -e [r(ə)kɔny] *adj.* recognized, accepted, acknowledged.
reconquérir [rəkɔ̃kerir] *v.t.* to reconquer, to win back.
reconquête [rəkɔ̃kɛt] *s.f.* reconquest, regaining.
reconsidérer [rəkɔ̃sidere] *v.t.* to reconsider, to give further thought to.
reconstituant, -e [rəkɔ̃stitɥɑ̃] *adj.* tonic, bracing, invigorating; *~ s.m.* tonic.
reconstituer [rəkɔ̃stitɥe] *v.t.* to reconstitute, to re-create, to restore, to re-establish, to reconstruct.
reconstitution [rəkɔ̃stitysjɔ̃] *s.f.* reconstitution, reconstruction, restoration, reorganization; *~ de carrière,* (employee's) service record, curriculum vitae.
reconstruction [rəkɔ̃stryksjɔ̃] *s.f.* reconstruction, rebuilding.
reconstruire [rəkɔ̃strɥir] *v.t.* to reconstruct, to rebuild.
reconversion [r(ə)kɔ̃vɛrsjɔ̃] *s.f.* conversion; redeployment.
reconvertir [r(ə)kɔ̃vɛrtir] *v.t.* to convert (factory, etc. to new production); to redeploy (personnel); **se ~** *v.refl.* to be converted, to change over; *se ~ dans,* to change to (another type of production, a different job).
recopier [rəkɔpje] *v.t.* to copy over again, to copy out; to make a duplicate, or further copy, of; to write out, to make a fair copy of.
record [rəkɔr] *s.m.* record; *détenir un ~,* to hold a record; *battre le ~,* to break the record; *chiffre ~,* record figure; ⚠ not 'record' (of events) or gramophone 'record'.
recordage [rəkɔrdaʒ] *s.m.* restringing, restring.
recorder [rəkɔrde] *v.t.* to restring; ⚠ not to 'record'.
recordman [rəkɔrdman] *s.m.,* **recordwoman** [rəkɔrdwɔman] *s.f.* (pl. *recordmen, recordwomen*) (sport) record-holder, champion.
recors [rəkɔr] *s.m.* (hist.) bailiff's man.
recoucher [rəkuʃe] *v.t.* to put to bed again; to lay down again; **se ~** *v.refl.* to go to bed again, to lie down again.
recoudre [rəkudr] *v.t.* to sew up again; (surg.) to stitch (a wound, etc.).
recoupe [rəkup] *s.f.* **1.** (pl.) chippings, chips, cuttings, offcuts, scraps, odd ends; **2.** second cutting of hay; **3.** (milling) second flour, sharps, middlings.
recoupement [rəkupmɑ̃] *s.m.* **1.** (build.) set-off, stepping; **2.** intersecting, intersection; checking by intersection; (cross-)checking; cross-check.
recouper [rəkupe] *v.t.* **1.** to cut again, to recut; **2.** to blend (wines); **3.** to cut, to intersect; **4.** to check with, to corroborate; **se ~** *v.refl.* **1.** to intersect; **2.** to check, to agree.
recoupette [rəkupɛt] *s.f.* (milling) sharps (coarse flour), thirds.
recourbé, -e [rəkurbe] *adj.* curved, bent.
recourber [rəkurbe] *v.t.* to bend, to bend round, to bend back; **se ~** *v.refl.* to be curved, to bend, to curl.
recourir [rəkurir] *v.i.* **1.** to run again, to race again; **2.** to have recourse (*à,* to); to turn (to).
recours [rəkur] *s.m.* recourse, resort; resource, refuge; (law) appeal; recourse; lien; *avoir ~ à,* to have recourse to, to turn to; *~ en grâce,* recommendation to mercy.

recouvrable [rəkuvrabl] *adj.* recoverable.
recouvrage [rəkuvraʒ] *s.m.* covering again; re-covering; changing the cover of.
recouvrement[1] [rəkuvrəmɑ̃] *s.m.* recovery; collection (of debts, etc.).
recouvrement[2] [rəkuvrəmɑ̃] *s.m.* **1.** re-covering, covering again; **2.** lap, overlap; (mech.) lap (of slide-valve).
recouvrer [rəkuvre] *v.t.* to recover, to regain; to collect (debts, etc.).
recouvrir [rəkuvrir] *v.t.* to re-cover, to cover over, to hide, to conceal; to include, to involve; to overlap.
recracher [rəkraʃe] *v.t.i.* to spit out again.
récréance [rekreɑ̃s] *s.f.* provisional possession; *lettres de* ~, letters of recall (of an ambassador).
récréati-f, -ve [rekreatif] *adj.* recreative, amusing.
récréation [rəkreɑsjɔ̃] *s.f.* recreation, amusement; pastime; recreation time, (school) break (abbrev. *récré*); *cour de* ~, playground.
recréer [rəkree] *v.t.* to re-create, to reconstruct.
récréer [rekree] *v.t.* to amuse, to divert; **se** ~ *v.refl.* to amuse oneself.
récrément [rekremɑ̃] *s.m.* (physiol.) recrement.
recrépir [rəkrepir] to replaster, to reface.
recrépissage [rəkrepisaʒ] *s.m.* replastering, refacing.
recreuser [rəkrøze] *v.t.* to dig (hole, etc.) deeper.
(**se**) **récrier** [rekrije] *v.refl.* to cry out, to protest, to expostulate (*contre*, against; *sur*, upon), to exclaim.
récrimination [rekriminɑsjɔ̃] *s.f.* **1.** (obs.) counter-charge; **2.** (pl.) recriminations, reproaches.
récriminat-eur, -rice [rekriminatœr] *adj.* recriminative, given to recrimination.
récriminer [rekrimine] *v.i.* **1.** (obs.) to make countercharges; **2.** to make recriminations.
récrire [rekrir] *v.t.* to rewrite; to write again (*à*, to).
recristallisation [rəkristalizɑsjɔ̃] *s.f.* (min.) recrystallization.
recroquevillé, -e [rəkrɔkvije] *adj.* shrivelled up; bent, hunched.
(**se**) **recroqueviller** [rəkrɔkvije] *v.refl.* to shrivel up, to curl up; to hunch up, to double up.
recru, -e [rəkry] *adj.* tired out, worn out, dead tired.
recrû [rəkry] *s.m.* new growth (of copse-wood).
recrudescence [rəkrydesɑ̃s] *s.f.* recrudescence, fresh outbreak.
recrue [rəkry] *s.f.* recruit (*de*, to).
recrutement [rəkrytmɑ̃] *s.m.* recruiting, recruitment; recruits.
recruter [rəkryte] *v.t.* to recruit, to enlist; to enrol; **se** ~ *v.refl.* to be recruited, to be enlisted; to gain recruits (*dans*, *parmi*, from).
recruteur [rəkrytœr] *s.m.* recruiter, recruiting officer.
recta [rɛkta] *adv.* exactly, punctually.
rectal, -e, (aux) [rɛktal] *adj.* (anat.) rectal.
rectangle [rɛktɑ̃gl] *adj.* rectangular, right-angled; ~ *s.m.* rectangle.
rectangulaire [rɛktɑ̃gylɛr] *adj.* rectangular; at right angles, right-angled.
recteur [rɛktœr] *s.m.* rector (of university or Jesuit college); (in Brittany) parish priest.
rect-eur, -rice [rɛktœr] *adj.* directing; ~**rices** *s.f.pl.* (ornith.) tail feathers.
rectifiable [rɛktifjabl] *adj.* rectifiable.
rectificat-eur, -rice [rɛktifikatœr] *adj.* rectifying; *s.m.f.* rectifier; ~**eur** *s.m.* (chem.) rectifier.
rectificati-f, -ve [rɛktifikatif] *adj.* rectifying; ~**f** *s.m.* correction, amendment.
rectification [rɛktifikɑsjɔ̃] *s.f.* rectification; correction.
rectifier [rɛktifje] *v.t.* to rectify; to correct, to straighten; to refine, to purify.
rectifieu-r, -se [rɛktifjœr] *s.m.f.* (techn.) finisher; ~**se** *s.f.* finishing-machine.
rectiligne [rɛktiliɲ] *adj.* rectilinear, in a straight line, bounded by straight lines; perpendicular; ~ *s.m.* rectilinear angle; perpendicular.
rectilinéaire [rɛktilineɛr] *adj.* (photo., of lens) rectilinear.
rectitude [rɛktityd] *s.f.* rectitude, integrity, uprightness.
recto [rɛkto] *s.m.* recto, right-hand page of open book, front side (of page, card, etc.).
rectoral, -e, (aux) [rɛktɔral] *adj.* rectorial.
rectorat [rɛktɔra] *s.m.* rectorship, rectorate.
rectum [rɛktɔm] *s.m.* (anat.) rectum.
reçu [rəsy] *s.m.* receipt, written acknowledgement; *au* ~ *de votre lettre*, on receipt of your letter; ~, ~**e** *adj.* usual, customary, accepted; *idées* ~*es*, conventional opinions.
recueil [rəkœj] *s.m.* collection, compilation, selection, anthology; miscellany.
recueillement [rəkœjmɑ̃] *s.m.* silent reflection, devout meditation; composure, concentration of thought, calm meditation; awe.
recueilli, -e [rəkœji] *adj.* concentrated, devout, silent, calm and collected.
recueillir [rəkœjir] *v.t.* to gather, to collect; to reap, to receive; to shelter, to harbour; to inherit; **se** ~ *v.refl.* to concentrate one's thoughts, to commune with oneself, to meditate devoutly.
recuire [rəkɥir] *v.t.* to bake or cook again; to anneal, to reheat (glass, metals, etc.); ~ *v.i.* to be cooked again; (fig.) to stew; *faire* ~, to cook again.
recuit [rəkɥi] *s.m.* reheating, annealing.
recul [rəkyl] *s.m.* recoil; backing, backward movement; (of firearm) kick, recoil; drawing back; standing back (esp. to judge pictures, past events, etc.), remoteness, perspective; room to move back, run-back.
reculade [rəkylad] *s.f.* backing, falling back; (fig.) retreat, climb-down; *une honteuse* ~, a shameful retreat, or climb-down; *faire une* ~, to beat a retreat, to turn tail.
reculé, -e [rəkyle] *adj.* distant, remote.
reculement [rəkylmɑ̃] *s.m.* **1.** (obs.) backing, drawing back; **2.** (harness) breeching.
reculer [rəkyle] *v.t.i.* to draw back, to back, to move back, to go backwards; to put off, to delay, to postpone; to fall back, to back out, to retreat, to recoil, to shrink, to flinch; (of firearm) to recoil, to kick; ~ *les frontières*, to push back, to extend, the frontiers; *ne* ~ *devant rien*, to stick at nothing; *il n'est plus temps de* ~, there is no going back now; (see also SAUTER).
reculons [rəkylɔ̃] *adv.loc.* *à* ~, backwards; *entrer à* ~ *dans*, to back into; *marcher à* ~, to move backwards; (fig.) to retrogress.
récupérable [rekyperabl] *adj.* recoverable, retrievable, redeemable.
récupérateur [rekyperatœr] *s.m.* (techn.) recuperator, regenerator; (artill.) recuperator.
récupération [rekyperɑsjɔ̃] *s.f.* recuperation, recovery.
récupérer [rekypere] *v.t.* to recover, to retrieve, to salvage; to make up for; to find alternative employment for (s.o.).
récurage [rekyraʒ] *s.m.* scouring, scrubbing.
récurer [rekyre] *v.t.* to scour, to scrub.
récurrence [rekyrɑ̃s] *s.f.* recurrence.
récurrent, -e [rekyrɑ̃] *adj.* recurrent, recurring.
récursoire [rekyrswar] *adj.* (law) that can give rise to an appeal.
récusable [rekyzabl] *adj.* (law) exceptionable, challangeable, impugnable.
récusation [rekyzɑsjɔ̃] *s.f.* (law) challenge (of judges, jurors, etc.); exception, impugnment.

récuser [rekyze] *v.t.* (law) to challenge; to take exception to; not to admit; **se ~** *v.refl.* to excuse oneself, to decline (to judge, pronounce, etc.), to declare oneself incompetent (to judge).

recyclage [rəsiklaʒ] *s.m.* recycling, reprogramming; (school) reorientation (of study).

recycler [rəsikle] *v.t.* to retrain; to reorientate (a pupil); (techn.) to recycle; **se ~** *v.refl.* to retrain, to go on a refresher course.

rédact-eur, -rice [redaktœr] *s.m.f.* writer, author, editor; clerk; drafter.

rédaction [redaksjɔ̃] *s.f.* drawing up (of a deed, etc.); wording, writing; (school) composition; editing (of newspaper); the editors, editorial staff; offices (of newspaper).

rédactionnel, -le [redaksjɔnɛl] *adj.* editorial; esp. *publicité ~le*, advertisement feature in format of news item.

redan [rədɑ̃] *s.m.* **1.** (fort.) redan; (build.) step, lodge; **2.** (arch.) dog-tooth ornamentation.

reddition [rɛd(d)isjɔ̃] *s.f.* surrender; (law) *~ de comptes*, rendering of accounts.

redécouvrir [rədekuvrir] *v.t.* to rediscover.

redéfaire [rədefɛr] *v.t.* to undo again.

redemander [rədəmɑ̃de] *v.t.* to ask for (sth.) back; *~ de qch.*, to ask for more, or for a second helping of sth.

rédempt-eur, -rice [redɑ̃ptœr] *adj.* redeeming, redemptive; **~eur** *s.m.* redeemer, saviour.

rédemption [redɑ̃psjɔ̃] *s.f.* (theol., law) redemption.

redent [rədɑ̃] *s.m.* = REDAN 2.

redescendre [rədesɑ̃dr] *v.i.* to come or go down again; *~ v.t.* to take or bring down again.

redevable [rədəvabl *adj.* indebted; *être ~ de 100 francs*, to owe 100 francs; *être ~ de l'impôt*, to be liable for tax; *être ~ de la vie à qn.*, to owe one's life to s.o.

redevance [rədəvɑ̃s] *s.f.* rent, quit-rent, dues, royalty.

redevenir [rədəvənir] *v.i.* to become (sth.) again.

redevoir [rədəvwar] *v.t.* to owe a balance of (a sum on account); *il me redoit 20 francs*, he still owes me 20 francs; *la somme redue*, the balance outstanding.

rédhibition [redibisjɔ̃] *s.f.* (law) annulment (of sale of defective article).

rédhibitoire [redibitwar] *adj.* that annuls the transaction.

rédiger [rediʒe] *v.t.* to draw up, to write out, to word, to indite, to write; to edit (a newspaper).

rédimer [redime] *v.t.* to redeem; **se ~** *v.refl.* to redeem oneself.

redingote [rədɛ̃gɔt] *s.f.* **1.** (obs.) frock coat; **2.** woman's overcoat (fitted at the waist).

redire [rədir] *v.t.* to tell again, to say again, to repeat; to criticize; *trouver à ~ à tout*, to find fault with everything; *il n'y a rien à ~ à cela*, there is nothing wrong with that.

rediscuter [rədiskyte] *v.t.* to debate or discuss further.

redistribuer [rədistribɥe] *v.t.* to redistribute; to redeal (cards).

redistribution [rədistribysjɔ̃] *s.f.* redistribution.

redite [rədit] *s.f.* repetition, tautology.

redondance [rədɔ̃dɑ̃s] *s.f.* redundancy, redundance; bombast.

redondant, -e [rədɔ̃dɑ̃] *adj.* redundant, superfluous, otiose; bombastic.

redonner [rədɔne] *v.t.* to give back again, to restore; *~ v.i. ~ dans*, to fall into (e.g. old habits) again.

redorer [redɔre] *v.t.* to regild.

redormir [rədɔrmir] *v.t.* to sleep again, to go to sleep again.

redoublant, -e [rədublɑ̃] *s.m.f.* pupil sitting a class for a second year.

redoublé, -e [rəduble] *adj.* redoubled, double; repeated; accelerated, intensified; (mil.) *au pas ~*, at the double; *frapper à coups ~s*, to rain blows on, to make a (sudden and) violent attack on.

redoublement [rədubləmɑ̃] *s.m.* redoubling; increase; intensification, repetition; reduplication.

redoubler [rəduble] *v.t.i.* **1.** to double, to duplicate; **2.** to begin again, to start over again; to do (e.g. school class) over again; **3.** (dressm.) to reline; **4.** to redouble, to increase (considerably); *le vent redouble ses efforts*, the wind is getting up again; *je redoublai d'attention*, I was doubly attentive, I became even more attentive; *son angoisse redoubla*, his anxiety became acute.

redoutable [rədutabl] *adj.* formidable, terrible, redoubtable, dreadful, forbidding.

redoute [rədut] *s.f.* (obs.) **1.** (fort.) redoubt; **2.** party, dance; place where dance was given.

redouter [rədute] *v.t.* to dread, to fear, to be afraid of; *une plante qui redoute la chaleur*, a plant which cannot stand heat.

redresse [rədrɛs), *s.f.* (naut.) righting tackle.

redressement [rədrɛsmɑ̃] *s.m.* straightening; righting; re-erection; (electr.) rectifying; (fig.) renascence, re-establishment, re-forming; reform.

redresser [rədrɛse] *v.t.* to straighten, to make straight again; to re-erect, to set up again, to re-establish, to re-form; (electr.) to rectify; to right (a ship); (fig.) to redress, to reform, to put right; **se ~** *v.refl.* to become straight again, to stand erect, to stand up; to hold up one's head; (of a ship) to right herself.

redresseur [rədrɛsœr] *s.m.* **1.** redresser, righter; (often iron.) *un grand ~ de torts*, a great righter of wrongs; **2.** (techn.) straightener; **3.** (electr.) rectifier; *~ adj. m.* (electr.) rectifying; (opt.) erecting (prism); (anat.) *muscle ~*, erector (muscle).

réductase [redyktɑz] *s.f.* (chem.) reductase.

réduct-eur, -rice [redyktœr] *adj.* reducing, reduction (gear); *~ s.m.* (chem.) reducer; (mech.) reduction gear.

réductibilité [redyktibilite] *s.f.* reducibleness.

réductible [redyktibl] *adj.* reducible.

réduction [redyksjɔ̃] *s.f.* reduction, reducing; conversion; (arith., surg.) reduction; diminution; smaller edition, small-scale version, scale model; abatement; (price) concession; subjugation, conquest; *échelle de ~*, reducing scale, scale of reduction; (log.) *~ à l'absurde*, reductio ad absurdum.

réduire [redɥir] *v.t.* to reduce, to diminish, to abate, to curtail, to bring down; to transform, to condense, to abridge, to boil down; to subjugate, to drive, to compel; (math., surg.) to reduce; *~ en poudre, en cendres*, to reduce to dust, to ashes; *~ les rebelles*, to subdue the rebels; **se ~** *v.refl.* to be reduced, to reduce oneself; to reduce one's expenditure; to become of less importance; to diminish, to dwindle, to consume away, to boil down or away; to amount; *tout cela se réduit à peu de chose*, all this amounts to very little; *se ~ en poussière*, to crumble to dust.

réduit, -e [redɥi] *adj.* reduced, restricted, limited; small; scaled down.

réduit [redɥi] *s.m.* little nook, hole; hovel; retreat; poor lodging; (fort.) keep, redoubt.

réduplicati-f, -ve [redyplikatif] *adj.* reduplicative.

réduplication [redyplikɑsjɔ̃] *s.f.* reduplication, repetition.

réédification [reedifikɑsjɔ̃] *s.f.* rebuilding.

réédifier [reedifje] *v.t.* to rebuild.

rééditer [reedite] *v.t.* to republish, to reissue.

réédition [reedisjɔ̃] *s.f.* new edition; republishing, reissuing; (fig., fam.) repetition.

rééducation [reedykɑsjɔ̃] *s.f.* re-education, retraining; rehabilitation; remedial therapy.
rééduquer [reedyke] *v.t.* to re-educate, to retrain, to rehabilitate.
réel, -le [reɛl] *adj.* real, actual; (law) relating to things, not to persons; in esse; ~ *s.m.* reality, the real; **~lement** [reɛlmɑ̃] *adv.* really, actually, in reality, in fact; truly.
réélection [reelɛksjɔ̃] *s.f.* re-election.
rééligible [reeliʒibl] *adj.* re-eligible.
réélire [reelir] *v.t.* to re-elect.
réemploi, réemployer see REMPLOI, REMPLOYER.
réensemencement [reɑ̃smɑ̃smɑ̃] *s.m.* re-sowing.
réensemencer [reɑ̃smɑ̃se] *v.t.* to resow.
réescompte [reɛskɔ̃t] *s.m.* rediscount.
réescompter [reɛskɔ̃te] *v.t.* to rediscount.
réessayer see RESSAYER.
réévaluation [reevalɥɑsjɔ̃] *s.f.* revaluation, reappraisal, fresh valuation.
réévaluer [reevalɥe] *v.t.* to revalue, to make a new appraisal (of).
réexamen [reɛgzamɛ̃] *s.m.* re-examination, reconsideration.
réexaminer [reɛgzamine] *v.t.* to re-examine.
réexpédier [reɛkspedje] *v.t.* to send on, to forward; to send back.
réexpédition [reɛkspedisjɔ̃] *s.f.* sending on, forwarding; sending back.
réexportation [reɛkspɔrtɑsjɔ̃] *s.f.* re-exportation, re-export.
réexporter [reɛkspɔrte] *v.t.* to re-export.
refaçonner [rəfasɔne] *v.t.* to refashion, to remould.
réfaction [refaksjɔ̃] *s.f.* (comm.) allowance, rebate.
refaire [rəfɛr] *v.t.* to do again, to make again, to remake, to do over again; to restore, to renew; (fam.) to cheat, to take in, to deceive; **se** ~ *v.refl.* to recover one's strength; to pick up; to retrieve one's losses; (of person) to change.
réfection [refɛksjɔ̃] *s.f.* **1.** rebuilding, repairs; **2.** collation, repast.
réfectoire [refɛktwar] *s.m.* refectory, dining-room, dining-hall.
refend [rəfɑ̃] *s.m. bois de* ~, sawn timber; *mur de* ~, partition wall; *lignes de* ~, lines imitating joints between bricks, etc.
refendre [rəfɑ̃dr] *v.t.* to cleave, to split, to saw lengthwise.
référé [refere] *s.m.* (law) plea of urgency; provisional injunction; *en* ~, provisionally; sitting in chambers.
référence [referɑ̃s] *s.f.* reference; referring; (pl.) references (as to character).
referendum, référendum [referɛ̃dɔm] *s.m.* referendum.
référer [refere] *v.t. en* (or *s'en*) ~ *à*, to report or refer to (superior for decision); to submit the matter to; **se** ~ *v.refl. se* ~ *à*, to refer to; to rely on (evidence, opinion, etc.); *s'en* ~ *à*, see *en* ~ *à*.
refermer [rəfɛrme] *v.t.* to shut again, to close again, to reclose; **se** ~ *v.refl.* to close again, to close, to shut.
referrer [rəfɛre] *v.t.* to reshoe (horse, etc.).
refiler [rəfile] *v.t.* (pop.) to palm off, to foist.
réfléchi, -e [refleʃi] *adj.* reflected; (gram.) reflexive; (fig.) reflective, thoughtful, serious-minded; deliberate, considered, premeditated.
réfléchir [refleʃir] *v.t.* to reflect, to reflect back; ~ *v.i.* to think, to ponder, to reflect, to consider; *réfléchissez à cela*, think it over; **se** ~ *v.refl.* to be reflected.
réfléchissant, -e [refleʃisɑ̃] *adj.* reflecting.
réflecteur [reflɛktœr] *s.m.* reflector; ~, **réflectrice** *adj.* reflecting.
reflet [rəflɛ] *s.m.* reflection; flash; (paint.) reflex; reflected light; (fig.) reflection, reflex, replica, duplicate, reproduction, secondary manifestation.
refléter [rəflete] *v.t.* to reflect; **se** ~ *v.refl.* to be reflected.
refleurir [rəflœrir] *v.i.* to blossom again, to flower again; (fig.) to flourish again, *faire* ~, to revive; ~ *v.t.* to put fresh flowers on.
refleurissement [rəflœrismɑ̃] *s.m.* second flowering or blooming, reflorescence.
reflex [reflɛks] *adj.* reflex; ~ *s.m.* reflex camera.
réflexe [reflɛks] *s.m.* reflex, reaction.
réflexibilité [reflɛksibilite] *s.f.* reflexibility.
réflexible [reflɛksibl] *adj.* reflexible.
réflexion [reflɛksjɔ̃] *s.f.* **1.** reflection; *angle de* ~, angle of reflection; **2.** reflection, thought, consideration; ~ *faite*, on thinking it over; on second thoughts; *faire des* ~*s*, to make a comment; *cela mérite* ~, that's worth thinking about.
refluer [rəflɥe] to flow back; to ebb; (fig.) to flow back, to be driven back, to fall back; *faire* ~, to drive back.
reflux [rəfly] *s.m.* reflux, ebb; refluence, flowing back; surging back; *le flux et le* ~, the ebb and flow.
refondre [rəfɔ̃dr] *v.t.* to refound; (lit. & fig.) to recast; ~ *v.i.* to melt again.
refonte [rəfɔ̃t] *s.f.* refounding, recoining; (lit. & fig.) recasting.
réformable [refɔrmabl] *adj.* reformable; that needs reform.
réformat-eur, -rice [refɔrmatœr] *s.m.f.* reformer; *adj.* reforming.
réformation [refɔrmɑsjɔ̃] *s.f.* reform, reformation, amendment.
réforme [refɔrm] *s.f.* **1.** reform, reformation; (hist.) Reformation, amendment; **2.** *mettre à la* ~, to invalid out, to discharge, to cashier; to dispose of, to scrap.
réformé, -e [refɔrme] *adj.* **1.** (relig.) Reformed, Protestant; **2.** invalided out, discharged; scrapped; ~ *s.m.* discharged soldier.
reformer [rəfɔrme] *v.a.* to form again, to re-form; **se** ~ *v.refl.* to re-form.
réformer [refɔrme] *v.t.* **1.** to re-form; to reform, to recast, to remodel; **2.** to retire, to discharge, to scrap; **se** ~ *v.refl.* to reform, to mend one's ways.
reformeur [rəfɔrmœr] *s.m.* (petrochemical) reformer.
réformiste [refɔrmist] *adj.*, *s.m.f.* (pol.) reformist.
refouillement [rəfujmɑ̃] *s.m.* deepening; chiselling.
refoulé, -e [rəfule] *adj.*, *s.m.f.* repressed or inhibited (person).
refoulement [rəfulmɑ̃] *s.m.* driving back, forcing back; repression, inhibition.
refouler [rəfule] *v.t.* to drive back, to force back; to back (a train); to repel; to expel (immigrants, etc.); (naut.) to stem (current, etc.); to repress.
refouloir [rəfulwar] *s.m.* rammer (for guns), tamping-rod.
réfractaire [refraktɛr] *adj.* **1.** refractory, rebellious, insubordinate, recalcitrant; *être* ~ *aux ordres, aux lois*, to refuse to take orders, to obey the laws; **2.** (metall.) refractory, fireproof; (fam.) still hard after cooking; *argile* ~, fire-clay, ~ *s.m.* refractory person, insubordinate character; non-cooperator (esp. under German occupation 1940–1944); (mil.) defaulter; *les* ~*s*, the awkward squad.
réfracter [refrakte] *v.t.* to refract.
réfract-eur, -rice [refraktœr] *adj.* refracting.
réfraction [refraksjɔ̃] *s.f.* (phys.) refraction.
refrain [rəfrɛ̃] *s.m.* burden (of a song), refrain; chorus; *toujours le même* ~*!*, the same old story again!; *changez de* ~*!*, talk about sth. else!

réfrangibilité [refrɑ̃ʒibilite] *s.f.* refrangibility.
réfrangible [refrɑ̃ʒibl] *adj.* refrangible.
refréner [rəfrene] *v.t.* to curb, to restrain, to bridle, to master.
réfrigérant, -e [refriʒerɑ̃] *adj.* cooling, refrigerant, freezing; (fig.) freezing, chilling, distant; ~ *s.m.* **1.** refrigerant; **2.** refrigerator.
réfrigérateur [refriʒeratœr] *s.m.* refrigerator; *mettre au* ~, to put in the refrigerator; (fig.) to put into cold storage, to forget all about.
réfrigération [refriʒerɑsjɔ̃] *s.f.* refrigeration.
réfrigérer [refriʒere] *v.t.* to refrigerate, to cool, to freeze; (fig.) to give a cool reception to.
réfringence [refrɛ̃ʒɑ̃s] *s.f.* (phys.) refractive power, refringency, refractivity.
réfringent, -e [refrɛ̃ʒɑ̃] *adj.* refracting, refractive.
refroidir [rəfrwadir] *v.t.i.* to cool, to get cold, to chill; (fig.) to chill, to damp, to discourage; (pop.) to murder; **se** ~ *v.refl.* to get cold; (lit. & fig.) to cool.
refroidissement [rəfrwadismɑ̃] *s.m.* **1.** chilling, refrigeration; (lit. & fig.) cooling, coolness; *moteur à* ~ *par air*, air-cooled engine; **2.** cold, chill; *prendre un* ~, to catch a chill.
refuge [rəfyʒ] *s.m.* refuge, shelter, asylum; (street) refuge; (mountaineering) refuge (hut).
réfugié, -e [refyʒje] *adj.*, *s.m.f.* refugee.
(**se**) **réfugier** [refyʒje] *v.refl.* to take refuge; (fig.) to fall back (*dans*, on).
refus [rəfy] *s.m.* refusal, denial; rebuff; (fam.) *ce n'est pas de* ~, I won't say no to that; *essuyer un* ~, to meet with a rebuff; *jusqu'à* ~, to rejection point, as far as it will go, (of screw) tight; ~ *d'obéissance*, non-compliance (with order).
refuser [rəfyze] *v.t.* to refuse, to decline to accept, to reject, to turn down, to decline, (of horse) to refuse (obstacle); to deny; ~ *un candidat*, to reject a candidate; ~ *v.i.* **1.** (naut.) (of wind) to veer forward; (of stake, etc.) to refuse (to go in further); **se** ~ *v.refl.* **1.** to be refused, to be denied, to elude; *un apéritif ne se refuse pas*, I won't say no to an aperitif; **2.** *se* ~ *à*, to refuse, to decline, to shrink from, to resist; *se* ~ *à l'évidence*, to shut one's eyes to the evidence.
réfutable [refytabl] *adj.* refutable.
réfutation [refytasjɔ̃] *s.f.* refutation, rebuttal.
réfuter [refyte] *v.t.* to refute, to confute.
regagner [rəgɑɲe] *v.t.* **1.** to regain, to recover, to win back; to make up for; **2.** to get back to, to reach (again).
regain [rəgɛ̃] *s.m.* aftermath, second crop of grass; (fig.) renewal, revival.
régal [regal] *s.m.* feast, treat.
régalade [regalad] *s.f.* *boire à la* ~, to pour (wine, etc., from a bottle) down one's throat, without putting the bottle to one's lips.
régalage see RÉGALEMENT.
régalant [regalɑ̃] *adj.* entertaining, pleasant; *ce n'est pas très* ~, it's no great fun.
régale [regal] *s.m.* vox humana (organ stop); ~ *s.f.* (hist.) régale, right of Fr. kings to receive revenues of vacant bishoprics; ~ *adj.f.* (chem.) *eau* ~, aqua regia.
régalement [regalmɑ̃], **régalage** [regalaʒ] *s.m.* levelling (of ground).
régaler[1] [regale] *v.t.* to level (ground).
régaler[2] [regale] *v.t.* **1.** (obs.) to give a feast or entertainment to; **2.** to regale (*de*, with), to treat (*de*, to); to give (s.o.) a good dinner; to treat, to pay (for the drinks, etc.); **se** ~ *v.refl.* to treat oneself (to a good meal, etc.), to give oneself a treat, to feast (*de*, on); (fam.) to make a nice profit.
régalien, -ne [regaljɛ̃] *adj.* pertaining to the royal prerogative; *droits* ~*s*, regalia.
regard [rəgar] *s.m.* **1.** look, glance; notice, attention; *attirer tous les* ~*s*, to attract everybody's attention; *suivre du* ~, to follow with one's eyes; *chercher qn. du* ~, to look round for s.o.; *interroger qn. du* ~, to look inquiringly at s.o., to give s.o. a questioning look; *abaisser son* ~ *sur*, to look down at; *d'un seul* ~, at a glance; *en* ~, opposite, on the opposite page; *au* ~ *de*, in comparison with; with regard to; **2.** opening, manhole, inspection cover; ⚠ not 'regard' in senses 'esteem' or 'greeting'.
regardant, -e [rəgardɑ̃] *adj.* particular, nice; close-fisted, stingy, niggardly, near, (fam.) as mean as they make them.
regarder [rəgarde] *v.t.* to look at, to glance at, to look on, to gaze at, to see; to face; to mind, to consider; to concern; *cela ne me regarde pas*, that does not concern me; *cette maison regarde le sud*, this house faces south; ~ *qn. de travers*, to scowl or frown at s.o., to look at s.o. askance; ~ *fixement*, to stare at; ~ *d'un bon œil*, to look benevolently upon; *je le regarde comme mon principal ennemi*, I consider him my chief enemy; *vous allez vous faire* ~, you will attract attention, you will make yourself conspicuous; *il regarde à deux sous*, he looks at every penny he spends; *j'y regarderai à deux fois*, I shall think twice before doing it; *je ne m'y regarde pas de si près*, I am not so particular; *à bien y* ~, on thinking it over; **se** ~ *v.refl.* to look at oneself, to examine oneself; to look at each other; to front, to face, each other.
regarnir [rəgarnir] *v.t.* to regarnish, to refill, to restock, to retrim.
régate [regat] *s.f.* **1.** (pl.) regatta; **2.** a kind of necktie.
regazonner [rəgazone] *v.t.* to returf.
regel [rəʒɛl] *s.m.* renewed frost, freezing again; (phys.) regelation.
regeler [rəʒle] *v.t.* to freeze again.
régence [reʒɑ̃s] *s.f.*, *adj.* Regency (esp. of Philippe d'Orléans).
régénérat-eur, -rice [reʒeneratœr] *adj.* regenerating; *s.m.f.* regenerator.
régénération [reʒenerɑsjɔ̃] *s.f.* regeneration.
régéneré, -e [reʒenere] *adj.* regenerated, reconstituted.
régénérer [reʒenere] *v.t.* to regenerate; (fig.) to renew.
régent, -e [reʒɑ̃] *s.m.f.* **1.** Regent (esp. Philippe d'Orléans); **2.** governor; **3.** (school) form-master, tutor.
régenter [reʒɑ̃te] *v.t.* **1.** (obs.) to direct, to teach; **2.** to govern arbitrarily.
régicide [reʒisid] *s.m.* regicide (deed); ~ *s.m.f.* regicide (person); ~ *adj.* regicidal.
régie [reʒi] *s.f.* **1.** state management; public corporation; *en* ~, under State control, administered by the State; **2.** (theatr.) stage management, production.
regimbement [rəʒɛ̃bmɑ̃] *s.m.* resistance, kicking.
regimber [rəʒɛ̃be] *v.i.* to kick, to resist; to kick over the traces; ~ *contre*, to kick against, to baulk at.
régime [reʒim] *s.m.* **1.** regime, form of government or administration; system; organization; rules, regulations; conditions; ~ *climatérique*, climatic conditions; **2.** diet; *suivre un* ~, to be on a diet; **3.** (mech.) speed (of engine in revolutions); (hydraulics) regime, flow, (of watercourse); ~ *normal*, or *vitesse de* ~, normal running speed, working speed; (electr.) ~ *de chargement*, charging rate; *marcher à plein* ~, (lit. & fig.) to work at top speed, at full pressure; **4.** (gram.) object; ~ *direct*, direct object; **5.** hand, cluster, (of bananas, etc.).
régiment [reʒimɑ̃] *s.m.* regiment; (fam.) army; (pop.) military service; (fig.) mass.
régimentaire [reʒimɑ̃tɛr] *adj.* regimental.
région [reʒjɔ̃] *s.f.* region, area, sphere, (fig.) field.

régional, -e, (aux) [reʒjɔnal] *adj.* local, regional, of the district; ~ *s.m.* local telephone network.
régionalisme [reʒjɔnalism] *s.m.* **1.** regionalism; (admin.) regionalization, decentralization, devolution; **2.** (lang.) regionalism, local expression.
régionaliste [reʒjɔnalist] *adj., s.m.f.* (pol., Lit., etc.) regionalist.
régir [reʒir] *v.t.* to rule, to govern, to manage, to administer; (gram.) to govern.
régisseur [reʒisœr] *s.m.* manager, agent, steward, bailiff, factor; (theatr.) stage-manager; (cin.) assistant director.
registre [rəʒistr] *s.m.* **1.** register, account-book; (mus.) register; (print.) register; **2.** (mech.) flap, damper, register; inlet valve, throttle.
réglable [reglabl] *adj.* adjustable.
réglage [reglaʒ] *s.m.* ruling (of paper); regulating, setting, timing, adjusting, tuning; *vis de* ~, adjusting screw; *à* ~ *automatique*, self-regulating; (mil.) *tir de* ~, ranging; *coup de* ~, sighting shot.
règle [rɛgl] *s.f.* **1.** ruler, rule; ~ *à calcul*, slide-rule; **2.** rule, order, pattern; principle, law; (pl.) (physiol.) (monthly) period; *il est de* ~ *de*, it is customary to; *en* ~, in order, right, correct, regular; systematic; *se faire une* ~ *de*, to make a practice of; *dans toutes les* ~*s*, according to rule; *en* ~ *générale*, as a rule.
réglé, -e [regle] *adj.* regular, steady, well-ordered; regulated, adjusted, fixed, settled, decided, (of case, etc.) closed; (of paper) ruled; (physiol.) having periods.
règlement [rɛgləmɑ̃] *s.m.* ruling; rule, regulation; ordering; settlement; ~ *de comptes*, (lit. & fig.) settling of accounts.
réglementaire [regləmɑ̃tɛr] *adj.* regulation, according to regulations, statutory; prescribed; regular, correct, standard; ~**ment** [rɛglə-mɑ̃tɛrmɑ̃] *adv.* according to regulations, in the prescribed manner.
réglementation [regləmɑ̃tɑsjɔ̃] *s.f.* regulation, control; system of regulations.
réglementer [regləmɑ̃te] *v.t.* to regulate, to make regulations for.
régler [regle] *v.t.* **1.** to rule (paper, etc.); **2.** to regulate, to arrange, to order; to settle, to pay (account); to time, to set, to adjust; ~ *son compte avec*, to settle one's account with, to square up with; ~ *ses affaires*, to put one's affairs in order; ~ *sa montre*, to set one's watch; ~ *ses désirs*, to control one's aspirations; ~ *sa dépense*, to cut down one's expenses; ~ *les préséances*, to fix the order of precedence; (techn.) ~ *la carburation*, to regulate the mixture; ~ *l'allumage*, to time the ignition; (mil.) ~ (*le tir*), to range; **se** ~ *v.refl.* to model oneself, to be guided; (of account) to be settled; *je me réglerai sur vous*, I shall go by what you say.
réglet [reglɛ] *s.m.* (techn., print.) rule; (arch.) reglet; (carp.) fillet.
réglette [reglɛt] *s.f.* small ruler; (typ.) setting stick, reglet.
régleu-r, -se [reglœr] *s.m.f.* regulator, adjuster; ~**se**, *s.f.* (paper) ruling machine.
réglisse [reglis] *s.m.* or *f.* liquorice.
réglure [reglyr] *s.f.* ruling (of paper).
régnant, -e [reɲɑ̃] *adj.* reigning, prevailing, usual, predominant, current, prevalent; *le goût* ~, the prevailing fashion.
règne [rɛɲ] *s.m.* reign; sway; (fig.) vogue, predominance; ~ *animal*, animal kingdom; *sous le* ~ *de*, in the reign of.
régner [reɲe] *v.i.* to reign; to be prevalent, to prevail, to hold sway; (of disease, etc.) to rage, to be rife.
regonflage [rəgɔ̃flaʒ], **regonflement** [rəgɔ̃-fləmɑ̃] *s.m.* reinflation.
regonfler [rəgɔ̃fle] *v.i.* to swell again; (of river) to become swollen again; ~ *v.t.* to reinflate, to refill, (with air, etc.), to pump up; (fig., fam.) ~ (*le moral de*) *qn.*, to boost someone's morale.
regorger [rəgɔrʒe] *v.i.* to overflow, to be brim-full, (fig.) to be plentiful, to be replete; ~ *de*, to brim with, to abound with, to have an excess of; to wallow in.
regrat [rəgra] *s.m.* huckstering, second-hand dealing (in food).
regrattage [rəgrataʒ] *s.m.* scraping again, re-scraping.
regratter [rəgrate] *v.t.* to rescrape, to scrape down.
regratti-er, -ère [rəgratje] *s.m.f.* huckster, petty second-hand dealer; (fam.) petty embezzler.
regréer [rəgree] *v.t.* to re-rig (ship).
regreffer [rəgrefe] *v.t.* to regraft, to graft again.
régresser [regrese] *v.i.* to regress, to retrogress.
régressi-f, -ve [regresif] *adj.* regressive, retrogressive, on a descending scale.
régression [regresjɔ̃] *s.f.* regression, recession, retrogression, throw-back.
regret [rəgrɛ] *s.m.* regret; yearning, repining; repentance, sorrow; *à* ~, reluctantly, with regret; *avoir du* ~, to feel regret, to feel sorry; *tous mes* ~*s*, I am very sorry; *exprimez vos* ~*s*, make your apologies; *être au* ~, to feel sorry.
regrettable [rəgrɛtabl] *adj.* regrettable, deplorable, unfortunate, to be regretted.
regretter [rəgrete] *v.t.* to regret, to lament, to grieve for, to miss, to be sorry to have lost, to be sorry for; to repent; *je regrette*, (i.) I am sorry; (ii.) excuse me (you are wrong).
regrimper [rəgrɛ̃pe] *v.i.* to climb (up) again.
regros [rəgro] *s.m.* thick bark of oak tree.
regrossir [rəgrosir] *v.i.* to get big, or fat, again.
regroupement [rəgrupmɑ̃] *s.m.* regrouping.
regrouper [rəgrupe] *v.t.* to regroup, to reassemble
régularisation [regylarizɑsjɔ̃] *s.f.* putting in order, regulating, regularization.
régulariser [regylarize] *v.t.* to regularize, to regulate; to put in proper form.
régularité [regylarite] *s.f.* regularity.
régulat-eur, -rice [regylatœr] *adj.* regulating, standard; ~**eur** *s.m.* regulator; governor; throttle; (horol.) balance-wheel, escapement.
régulation [regylɑsjɔ̃] *s.f.* regulating, adjusting, regulation; control.
régule [regyl] *s.m.* (chem.) regulus; (mech.) Babbitt metal, white metal.
réguli-er, -ère [regylje] *adj.* regular; right, correct; punctual, reliable; even, uniform; ~**er** *s.m.* regular (monk, soldier); ~**èrement** [regyljɛrmɑ̃] *adv.* regularly; punctually; correctly; completely; every time; normally; evenly, uniformly.
régurgitation [regurʒitɑsjɔ̃] *s.f.* regurgitation.
régurgiter [regyrʒite] *v.t.* to regurgitate.
réhabilitation [reabilitɑsjɔ̃] *s.f.* rehabilitation; re-establishment.
réhabiliter [reabilite] *v.t.* to rehabilitate; to re-establish (one's reputation, etc.); **se** ~ *v.refl.* to rehabilitate oneself, to recover one's good name.
réhabituer [reabitɥe] *v.t.* to reaccustom; **se** ~ *v.refl.* to become reaccustomed.
rehaussement [rəosmɑ̃] *s.m.* raising up, raising; heightening, enhancing, increase (in value); (paint.) touching up.
rehausser [rəose] *v.t.* to raise up; to raise; to heighten, to enhance; to enrich; to touch up.
rehaut [rəo] *s.m.* (paint.) light, lights.
réimportation [reɛ̃pɔrtɑsjɔ̃] *s.f.* reimportation, reimport.
réimporter [reɛ̃pɔrte] *v.t.* to reimport.
réimposer [reɛ̃poze] *v.t.* to reassess (taxes); (print.) to reimpose.

réimposition [reɛ̃pozisjɔ̃] *s.f.* further assessment; (print.) reimposition.
réimpression [reɛ̃prɛsjɔ̃] *s.f.* reprinting, reprint, reimpression.
réimprimer [reɛ̃prime] *v.t.* to reprint.
Reims [rɛ̃s] *s.m.* (geog.) Rheims.
rein [rɛ̃] *s.m.* kidney; (pl.) loins; (arch.) extrados; *se casser les ~s*, to break one's back; (fig.) to ruin oneself, to kill oneself (esp. with work); *casser les ~s à qn.*, to ruin, to break, s.o.; *ceindre ses ~s*, to gird up one's loins; *la chute des ~s*, the small of the back; *avoir les ~s solides*, to have a strong back, to be strongly built; to be able to take it; *douleur, maux, de ~s*, backache, lumbago; *coup de ~s*, hard, back-breaking effort; *se donner un tour de ~s*, to strain one's back; *mettre à qn. l'epée dans les ~s*, (fig.) to prod s.o.; to harry s.o.; ⚠ not 'rein'.
réincarcération [reɛ̃karserasjɔ̃] *s.f.* reincarceration.
réincarcérer [reɛ̃karsere] *v.t.* to reincarcerate.
réincarnation [reɛ̃karnasjɔ̃] *s.f.* reincarnation.
(**se**) **réincarner** [reɛ̃karne] *v.refl.* to be reincarnated.
réincorporer [reɛ̃kɔrpɔre] *v.t.* to reincorporate; (mil.) to re-embody.
reine [rɛn] *s.f.* queen.
reine-claude [rɛnklod] *s.f.* (pl. *~(s)-claudes*) (bot.) greengage.
reine-des-prés [rɛndepre] *s.f.* (bot.) meadowsweet.
reine-marguerite [rɛnmargərit] *s.f.* (bot.) China aster.
reinette [rɛnɛt] *s.f.* rennet (apple).
réinfecter [reɛ̃fɛkte] *v.t.* to reinfect.
réinscription [reɛ̃skripsjɔ̃] *s.f.* reregistration, re-enrolment.
réinscrire [reɛ̃skrir] *v.t.* to reregister, to re-enrol.
réinstaller [reɛ̃stale] *v.t.* to reinstall, to re-establish; to resettle; **se** ~ *v.refl.* to reinstall or re-establish oneself.
réintégration [reɛ̃tegrasjɔ̃] *s.f.* reinstatement.
réintégrer [reɛ̃tegre] *v.t.* to reinstate, to take back, to bring back, to return to; ~ *le domicile conjugal*, to return to the conjugal residence, to go back to one's husband or wife; ⚠ not 'to reintegrate'.
réintroduction [reɛ̃trɔdyksjɔ̃] *s.f.* reintroduction.
réintroduire [reɛ̃trɔdɥir] *v.t.* to reintroduce, to reinsert.
réinventer [reɛ̃vɑ̃te] *v.t.* to rediscover, to give a new meaning to.
réinvention [reɛ̃vɑ̃sjɔ̃] *s.f.* rediscovery.
réinviter [reɛ̃vite] *v.t.* to invite again.
réitérati-f, -ve [reiteratif] *adj.* reiterative.
réitération [reiterasjɔ̃] *s.f.* reiteration.
réitérer [reitere] *v.t.* to reiterate, to repeat.
reître [rɛtr] *s.m.* (hist.) reiter; (fig.) rough soldier.
rejaillir [rəʒajir] *v.i.* to spurt up or out, to gush out, to fly; to rebound (*contre*, against), to be reflected.
rejaillissement [rəʒajismɑ̃] *s.m.* gushing up, spurting out, spouting; rebounding, rebound; reflection.
rejet [rəʒɛ] *s.m.* **1.** rejection, throwing back; throwing away, casting (away), throwing up; spoil (earth); (geol.) throw; **2.** carrying, transfer; **3.** new shoot (of plant, tree); **4.** (pros.) enjambment; running on into the next line.
rejetable [rəʒətabl] *adj.* that should be thrown away; *cela est difficilement ~*, that is difficult to get rid of.
rejeter [rəʒəte] *v.t.* to reject, to throw out, to throw or fling back; to set aside; to dismiss, to refuse; to throw up; to cast; ~ *la responsabilité sur qn.*, to shift the responsibility on to s.o.; ~ *le blâme sur qn.*, to lay the blame on s.o.; *se ~ en arrière*, to jump back, to fall back.
rejeton [rəʒətɔ̃] *s.m.* shoot, offshoot, runner; (fig.) offspring, scion.
rejoindre [rəʒwɛ̃dr] *v.t.* to join again, to rejoin; to join, to meet, to meet again; to connect; to reunite; to overtake, to catch up; **se** ~ *v.refl.* to meet, to join.
rejointoiement [rəʒwɛ̃twamɑ̃] *s.m.* rejointing.
rejointoyer [rəʒwɛ̃twaje] *v.t.* (mason.) to rejoint; to repoint (a wall).
rejouer [rəʒwe] *v.t.i.* to play again; to start playing again.
réjoui, -e [reʒwi] *adj.* cheerful, merry, jolly.
réjouir [reʒwir] *v.t.* to cheer, to rejoice, to enliven, to gladden, to please, to delight, to give pleasure to; **se** ~ *v.refl.* **1.** (obs.) to enjoy oneself, to make merry; **2.** to rejoice, to be glad, to be delighted, (*à*, at; *de*, in, at, with); *je me réjouis de voir cela*, I am delighted to see that.
réjouissance [reʒwisɑ̃s] *s.f.* rejoicing; rejoicings, merry-making, amusement, festivities; (butch.) makeweight (of bones thrown in with the meat).
réjouissant, -e [reʒwisɑ̃] *adj.* jolly, amusing, diverting, cheering, merry, jovial; (iron.) *eh bien, c'est ~!*, well, that's all very jolly!
relâche (rəlɑʃ] *s.m.* or *f.* respite, remission, interruption; relaxation, intermission; *travailler sans ~*, to work unremittingly; *donnez-vous un ~*, take some rest; take it easy for a bit; *son mal ne lui laisse pas de ~*, his pain gives him no respite; (theatr.) no performance, (house) closed; *faire ~*, to have no performance, to be closed.
relâche [rəlɑʃ] *s.f.* (naut.) putting into port, call, stay; port of call; *faire ~ à Durban*, to put into Durban.
relâché, -e [rəlɑʃe] *adj.* loose, lax, relaxed, slack.
relâchement [rəlɑʃmɑ̃] *s.m.* relaxation, slackness, slackening, loosening; falling-off; laxness, laxity; looseness (of the bowels); intermission, respite, abatement, easing (off).
relâcher [rəlɑʃe] *v.t.* to loosen, to slacken; to relax; to release, to set at liberty; to abate; ~ *v.i.* (naut.) to put into port; **se** ~ *v.refl.* to slacken, to get loose; to become lax; to get milder, to ease off, to become less acute; to relax, to unbend.
relais [rəlɛ] *s.m.* relay; stage; change of horses; posting-house; (hunt.) relay; (*course de*) ~, relay-race; (electr.) relay; (radio, etc.) relay station, booster; *travail par ~*, working in relays or shifts, shift work.
relance [rəlɑ̃s] *s.f.* **1.** (cards) raising the stakes, raise; **2.** (fig.) resurgence, new impetus.
relancer [rəlɑ̃se] *v.t.* to throw back, to throw again; (sport) to return (ball, service, etc.); to start again, to restart; to boost, to give new impetus to; (cards) to raise (the bid); (fig.) to importune, to hunt out, to badger.
relaps, -e [rəlaps] *adj., s.m.f.* (relig.) relapsed (person); ⚠ not 'relapse'.
relater [rəlate] *v.t.* to relate, to state (the facts), to report (fact, circumstances); ⚠ not 'to relate' in senses 'to refer', 'to connect'.
relati-f, -ve [rəlatif] *adj.* relative, relating (*à*, to), related; comparative; (gram.) relative; **~vement** [rəlativmɑ̃] *adv.* relatively; comparatively; *~vement à*, concerning.
relation [rəlasjɔ̃] *s.f.* **1.** relation, connection, correspondence; proportion; narration, narrative, statement; (pl.) relations, relationship, connection, contact; acquaintanceship; *avoir de nombreuses ~s*, to know a number of influential people, to have a number of good contacts; *être en ~(s) avec*, to be in touch or contact with, to be acquainted with; to be on (good, bad) terms with; to have dealings with; **2.** acquaintance, (business, etc.) connection.

relativisme [rəlativism] *s.m.* relativism.
relativité [rəlativite] *s.f.* relativity, relativeness.
relaver [rəlave] *v.t.* to wash again.
relaxation [rəlaksɑsjɔ̃] *s.f.* relaxation.
relaxe [rəlaks] *s.f.* (law) order of nolle prosequi.
relaxer [rəlakse] *v.t.* to release, to relax; **se ~** *v.refl.* to relax.
relayer [rəlɛje] *v.t.i.* to relay, to relieve, to take the place of; to change horses; **se ~** *v.refl.* to take it in turns, to work in shifts.
relayeu-r, -se [rəlɛjœr] *s.m.f.* relay runner.
relecture [rəlɛktyr] *s.f.* rereading; second reading.
relégation [rəlegɑsjɔ̃] *s.f.* relegation, banishment to a remote place, exile; transportation (to a penal colony).
reléguer [rəlege] *v.t.* to relegate, to exile, to banish, to shut up, to seclude, to consign (sth. to e.g. attic).
relent [rəlɑ̃] *s.m.* musty smell; nasty smell.
relevable [rəlvabl] *adj.* that can be raised, rising; hinged; retractable.
relevage [rəlvaʒ] *s.m.* raising, lifting; salving (of vessel); collection (from letter-box).
relevailles [rələvɑj] *s.f.pl.* churching (of a woman).
relève [rəlɛv] *s.f.* shift, relief, relieving.
relevé, -e [rələve] *adj.* raised, erect; turned-up; (cook.) highly seasoned; (fig.) exalted, lofty, refined; *virage ~*, banked corner.
relevé [rəlve] *s.m.* extract, abstract, summary; reading (of meter).
relevée [rəlve] *s.f.* (obs.) afternoon.
relèvement [rəlɛvmɑ̃] *s.m.* **1.** raising; (fig.) revival, re-establishment; rise, increase; **2.** collection, abstraction, or summarizing (of information); establishment of position, compass bearings.
relever [rəlve] *v.t.* **1.** to raise (again), to lift, to pick up; to increase; (fig.) to restore, to revive, to redeem; to collect, to take in, (pupils' work, etc.); **2.** to pick out, to take or pick up (a point, etc.); to point out; to note, to make a note of; to read (meter); to take (reading, fingerprints, bearings); to survey, to plot (ground); **3.** (cook.) to season; (fig.) to enliven (*de*, with), to underline, to enhance; **4.** to relieve (s.o. at work); **5. ~** *qn. de qch.*, to relieve s.o. of sth., to release s.o. from sth; **~** *v.i.* **~** *de*, **1.** to recover from; **2.** to be dependent on; to be derived from; to belong to; **se ~** *v.refl.* to stand up (again), to get up, to get to one's feet; to be raised, to turn up; to be raisable; to relieve each other, to work in shifts; (fig.) to recover; *un col qui se relève*, a collar that can be turned up.
releveu-r, -se [rəlvœr] *adj.* raising, lifting; (anat.) *muscle ~r*, levator (muscle); *chaîne ~se*, endless cable (for hauling trucks up incline); **~r** *s.m.* **1.** (nav.) minesweeper; **2.** raising or lifting mechanism; (anat.) levator; **3.** collector; one who notes figures, readings, etc., one who plots or surveys; (meter) reader.
reliage [rəljaʒ] *s.m.* hooping (of casks).
relief (rəljɛf] *s.m.* relief, embossment; set-off, setting off; (fig.) enhancement; (pl.) scraps; *avoir du ~*, to stand out; *donner du ~ à*, to set off, to give relief to; *manquer de ~*, to be flat, dull; *en ~*, in relief; raised, prominent; ⚠ not 'relief' in sense 'alleviation'.
relier [rəlje] *v.t.* to bind again, to refasten, to connect, to unite; to bind (books); to hoop (casks).
relieu-r, -se [rəljœr] *s.m.f.* bookbinder.
religieu-x, -se [rəliʒjø] *adj.* religious, devout, pious; scrupulous; **~x** *s.m.* monk; **~se** *s.f.* nun; **~sement** [rəliʒjøzmɑ̃] *adv.* religiously, scrupulously.
religion [rəliʒjɔ̃] *s.f.* religion; *entrer en ~*, to take one's vows; to become a monk or a nun; *se faire une ~ de*, to make it a point of honour to.
religionnaire [rəliʒjɔnɛr] (obs.) *s.m.f.* Huguenot.
religiosité [rəliʒjozite] *s.f.* religiosity.
reliquaire [rəlikɛr] *s.m.* reliquary, shrine.
reliquat [rəlika] *s.m.* balance, rest, remainder.
relique [rəlik] *s.f.* relic; (fig.) *garder comme des ~s*, to treasure up.
relire [rəlir] *v.t.* to read again, to read over again, to reread.
reliure [rəljyr] *s.f.* bookbinding; binding.
relogement [rəlɔʒmɑ̃] *s.m.* rehousing; obtaining new accommodation.
reloger [rəlɔʒe] *v.t.* to rehouse, to find new accommodation for.
relouer [rəlue] *v.t.* to relet, to let again; to sublet.
réluctance [relyktɑ̃s] *s.f.* (electr.) reluctance.
reluire [rəlɥir] *v.i.* to shine, to glisten, to be bright; *faire ~*, to polish; *brosse à ~*, polishing brush.
reluisant, -e [rəlɥizɑ̃] *adj.* shining, glittering, glossy; (fig.) brilliant.
reluquer [rəlyke] *v.t.* to eye; to have an eye on; to covet.
remâcher [rəmɑʃe] *v.t.* (fig.) to ruminate, to revolve in one's mind, to chew over, to brood over.
remaillage [rəmɑjaʒ] *s.m.* mending (of knitting or nets).
remailler [rəmɑje] *v.t.* to mend (knitting or nets).
remake [rimɛk] *s.m.* (cin.) remake (of film).
rémanence [remanɑ̃s] *s.f.* (magnetism) remanence; (psychol.) retention (of visual images).
rémanent, -e [remanɑ̃] *adj.* (magnetism) remanent; (psychol.) *image ~e*, after-image.
remanger [rəmɑ̃ʒe] *v.t.* to eat (the same thing) again.
remaniable [rəmanjabl] *adj.* alterable; capable of modification, of rearrangement.
remaniement [rəmanimɑ̃] *s.m.* altering, rearrangement, doing over again, modification; reshuffle (of cabinet, etc.).
remanier [rəmanje] *v.t.* to alter, to rearrange, to recast, to modify, to reshuffle (cabinet, etc.).
remaquiller [rəmakije] *v.t.* to make up (face) again; **se ~** *v.refl.* to do one's face again.
remariage [rəmarjaʒ] *s.m.* marrying again, remarriage.
remarier (rəmarje] *v.t.* to marry off (daughter, etc.) again; **se ~** *v.refl.* to get married again.
remarquable [rəmarkabl] *adj.* remarkable, noticeable, worthy of note; **~ment** [rəmarkabləmɑ̃] *adv.* remarkably.
remarque [rəmark] *s.f.* remark, observation, notice, note; mark; *faire la ~ que*, to remark, to observe, that; *faire une ~ sur*, to comment on.
remarquer [rəmarke] *v.t.* to remark, to notice, to observe, to distinguish; to mark again; *remarquez!*, mind you!; *faire ~*, to point out; to to call attention to; *se faire ~*, to distinguish oneself; (pej.) to attract attention, to make oneself conspicuous; to show off.
remballage [rɑ̃balaʒ] *s.m.* repacking, repackaging.
remballer [rɑ̃bale] *v.t.* to repack, to repackage, to pack up again; (fig., fam.) *il peut ~ ses compliments*, he can keep his compliments.
rembarquement [rɑ̃barkəmɑ̃] *s.m.* re-embarking; reshipment.
rembarquer [rɑ̃barke] *v.t.* to re-embark (passengers); to reship (goods); (**se**) **~** *v.refl.* & *v.i.* to re-embark.
rembarrer [rɑ̃bare] *v.t.* to rebuke, to repulse, to snub; to put (s.o.) in his place, to bite (someone's) head off.

remblai [rɑ̃blɛ] *s.m.* embanking, filling in, packing; filling material, fill; embankment.
remblayage [rɑ̃blɛjaʒ] *s.m.* filling up, embanking.
remblayer [rɑ̃blɛje] *v.t.* to fill up, to embank.
remblayeuse [rɑ̃blɛjøz] *s.f.* back-filler, trench-filler.
remboîtage [rɑ̃bwataʒ] *s.m.* (bookb.) recasing.
remboîtement [rɑ̃bwatmɑ̃] *s.m.* resetting (of bone).
remboîter [rɑ̃bwate] *v.t.* to reset (bone); (bookb.) to recase.
rembouger [rɑ̃buʒe] *v.t.* to fill up, to keep full, to top up (cask, etc.).
rembourrage [rɑ̃buraʒ] *s.m.* stuffing, padding.
rembourrer [rɑ̃bure] *v.t.* to stuff, to pad, to fill; (fam.) (of person) *être bien rembourré*, to be well upholstered.
remboursable [rɑ̃bursabl] *adj.* repayable, refundable; reimbursable, redeemable.
remboursement [rɑ̃bursəmɑ̃] *s.m.* repayment, reimbursement; *contre* ~, cash on delivery.
rembourser [rɑ̃burse] *v.t.* to repay, to reimburse, to refund; ~ *une rente*, to redeem an annuity; ~ *un créancier*, to pay a creditor.
rembrunir (rɑ̃brynir] *v.t.* to darken; **se** ~ *v.refl.* to darken, to cloud over, to become gloomy.
rembucher [rɑ̃byʃe] *v.t.* to pursue into covert; **se** ~ *v.refl.* to return to covert.
remède [rəmɛd] *s.m.* remedy; cure, medicine; *c'est sans* ~, it can't be helped, there is nothing to be done about it; *porter* ~ *à*, to remedy; ~ *de bonne femme*, old wives' remedy.
remédier [rəmedje] *v.t.* ~ *à*, to cure, to be a remedy for; to remedy, to put right, to help.
remembrer [rəmɑ̃bre] *v.t.* to consolidate, to combine, (smallholdings).
remémorer [rəmemɔre] *v.t.* to call to mind, to recall, to evoke; **se** ~ *v.refl.* to recollect, to remember.
remerciement [rəmɛrsimɑ̃] *s.m.* thanks; thank you, acknowledgement; *lettre de* ~, letter of thanks or acknowledgement, thank-you letter.
remercier [rəmɛrsje] *v.t.* **1.** to thank (*de, pour*, for); **2.** to dismiss, to discharge, to sack.
réméré [remere] *s.m.* (law) right of repurchase; *vente à* ~, sale with option to repurchase.
remettre [rəmɛtr] *v.t.* to put back, to put back again; to put on again; to set (bone, etc.); to bring, to deliver, to remit, to hand over; to entrust; to pardon; to remit (penalty, etc.); to postpone, to put off, to adjourn; to cure, to make right again, to reconcile; to recall; ~ *à neuf*, to make as good as new, to renovate, to recondition; ~ *en état*, to overhaul; ~ *en ordre*, to put in order; (footb.) ~ *en jeu*, to throw in; ~ *qch. en question*, to call sth. to question again, to reopen the question (of sth.); **se** ~ *v.refl.* to be all right again, to pull oneself together, to recover one's composure; *se* ~ *de*, to recover from, to get over; *se* ~ *avec qn.*, to become reconciled, to make it up, with s.o.; *je m'en remets à vous*, I leave it to you; *se* ~ *au travail*, to start work again, to resume one's work, to get to work again.
remeubler [rəmœble] *v.t.* to refurnish.
rémige [remiʒ] *s.f.* remex, quill-feather (of bird's wing).
remilitarisation [rəmilitarizasjɔ̃] *s.f.* remilitarization.
réminiscence [reminisɑ̃s] *s.f.* reminiscence; unconscious recollection; *théorie platonicienne de la* ~, Plato's theory of ideas.
remisage [rəmizaʒ] *s.m.* putting away, putting into garage, coach-house, shed, etc., (of vehicle, farm implements, etc.).
remise [rəmiz] *s.f.* **1.** putting back; ~ *en état*, overhauling; ~ *en marche*, restarting; ~ *en ordre*, rearranging, putting in order; (football) ~ *en jeu*, throw-in; **2.** delivery, handing over; **3.** remission (of debt, etc.); pardon; rebate, reduction; **4.** remission, deferment; **5.** coach-house, shed, outbuilding, garage; *voiture de* ~, hired carriage or car.
remiser[1] [rəmize] *v.t.* **1.** to put (vehicle, etc.) into coach-house, shed, garage, etc.; (fig.) to stow or store away, to shelve; **2.** (fig.) = REMBARRER; **se** ~ *v.refl.* (hunt.) to take cover, to go to covert.
remiser[2] [rəmize] *v.i.* (cards) to make a new stake.
remisier [rəmizje] *s.m.* (Stock Exchange) broker's agent; half-commission man.
rémissible [remisibl] *adj.* remissible, pardonable.
rémission [remisjɔ̃] *s.f.* remission, forgiveness; (med.) remission, abatement.
rémittent, -e [remitɑ̃] *adj.* (med.) remittent.
remmaillage [rɑ̃mɑjaʒ] *s.m.* = REMAILLAGE.
remmailler [rɑ̃mɑje] *v.t.* = REMAILLER.
remmailloter [rɑ̃mɑjɔte] *v.t.* to change (a baby('s nappies)).
remmancher [rɑ̃mɑ̃ʃe] *v.t.* to put a new handle to.
remmener [rɑ̃mne] *v.t.* to take or bring back.
rémois, -e [remwɑ] *adj., s.m.f.* (native or inhabitant) of Rheims.
remontage [rəmɔ̃taʒ] *s.m.* resetting; remounting, putting together again, reassembly, refitting (of parts); winding up (of clock, etc.).
remontant, -e [rəmɔ̃tɑ̃] *adj.* **1.** (hort.) flowering twice (or more), perpetual flowering; **2.** invigorating, bracing, tonic; ~ *s.m.* tonic.
remonte [rəmɔ̃t] *s.f.* **1.** going upstream; **2.** remounting, remount.
remontée [rəmɔ̃te] *s.f.* **1.** going up (again), ascent, climbing, raising, rise; (mining) bringing to the surface; (sport) recovery (in race); **2.** ski-lift.
remonte-pente [rəmɔ̃tpɑ̃t] (pl. *remonte-pentes*) *s.m.* ski-lift.
remonter [rəmɔ̃te] *v.i.* **1.** to go or come up again, to go or come back up, to rise or climb again; to go back northwards; to go upstream; to extend upwards; (hort.) to flower a second time; ~ *à cheval*, to remount; ~ *sur le trône*, to reascend the throne; **2.** to go back; ~ *dans le temps*, to go back in time; *cela remonte à 1400*, that goes back to, or dates from, 1400; ~ *v.t.* **1.** to go or come up (sth.) again, to reascend; (of shirt, etc.) to ride up; (fig.) ~ *la pente*, to turn the corner, to recover lost ground; **2.** to take or bring up (again); to put back up, to put higher, to raise the height of; **3.** to wind up (clock, etc.); **4.** to restore, to revive, to put new heart into; *se* ~ *le moral*, to restore one's morale; **5.** to reassemble (machine, etc.); to restock, to re-equip; to remount (horseman).
remonteur [rəmɔ̃tœr] *s.m.* mounter (of guns, clocks, etc.).
remontoir [rəmɔ̃twar] *s.m.* winder; winding-mechanism.
remontrance [rəmɔ̃trɑ̃s] *s.f.* remonstrance, reproof.
remontrer [rəmɔ̃tre] *v.t.* **1.** (obs.) to point out (error, etc., *à*, to); **2.** *en* ~ *à qn.*, to (try to) show oneself superior to s.o.; to teach s.o. a lesson; **3.** to show again; *il n'ose plus se* ~, he doesn't dare show his face again.
rémora [remɔra] *s.m.* (ichth.) remora; sucking fish; (fig.) hindrance, obstacle.
remordre [rəmɔrdr] *v.t.* to bite again, to have another bite (at); (fig.) to have another go at.
remords [rəmɔr] *s.m.* remorse.
remorquage [rəmɔrkaʒ] *s.m.* towing, hauling.
remorque [rəmɔrk] *s.f.* towing, tow, hauling;

tow-rope, towing-hawser; trailer; *se mettre à la ~ (de)*, to get into tow; (fig.) to let oneself be led (by), to follow in the wake (of), to be under the thumb (of).

remorquer [rəmɔrke] *v.t.* to tow, to haul, to take in tow; to drag, to tug.

remorqueur [rəmɔrkœr] *s.m.* (naut.) tug.

remoudre [rəmudr] *v.t.* to grind again.

remouiller [rəmuje] *v.t.* **1.** to wet again; **2.** *~ (l'ancre)*, to reanchor.

rémoulade [remulad] *s,f.* remoulade (sauce), mayonnaise flavoured with mustard and herbs.

remouler [rəmule] *v.t.* to remould.

rémouleur [remulœr] *s.m.* grinder, knife-grinder.

remous [rəmu] *s.m.* eddy, whirlpool; backwash, slipstream; surge; (fig.) upheaval.

rempaillage [rɑ̃pɑjaʒ] *s.m.* reseating, rebottoming, (of chairs).

rempailler [rɑ̃paje] *v.t.* to reseat, to rebottom, (chairs).

rempailleu-r, -se [rɑ̃pɑjœr] *s.m.f.* chair-mender, chair-bottomer.

rempaqueter [rɑ̃pakte] *v.t.* to repack, to pack up again.

rempart [rɑ̃par] *s.m.* rampart; (fig.) bulwark, safeguard, defence.

rempiéter [rɑ̃pjete] *v.t.* to refoot (wall, stocking).

rempiler [rɑ̃pile] *v.i.* (mil. slang) to re-enlist for military service; *~ v.t.* to restack.

remplaçable [rɑ̃plasabl] *adj.* replaceable, interchangeable.

remplaçant, -e [rɑ̃plasɑ̃] *s.m.f.* substitute, deputy, locum, stand-in.

remplacement [rɑ̃plasmɑ̃] *s.m.* replacing, substituting, replacement, substitution, change; *en ~ de*, in the place of.

remplacer [rɑ̃plase] *v.t.* to replace, to substitute, to act as substitute for, to stand in for, to take or fill the place of, to supersede, to do instead of, to be a substitute for; to reinvest; *se faire ~*, to find oneself a substitute.

remplage [rɑ̃plaʒ] *s.m.* (build.) rubble filling; (arch.) tracery, open-work ornamentation (in Gothic window).

rempli [rɑ̃pli] *s.m.* tuck, hem.

remplier [rɑ̃plie] *v.t.* to take in, to take a tuck in; to turn in.

remplir [rɑ̃plir] *v.t.* to fill, to fill up, to refill, to replenish; to cram, to crowd; to cover completely; to fulfil, to perform; to answer; to complete; *bien ~ son temps*, to employ one's time well; **se** *~ v.refl.* to fill or cram oneself, to fill, to be filled, to be thronged, to be crowded.

remplissage [rɑ̃plisaʒ] *s.m.* filling; filling up; filling in; (fig.) padding, verbiage.

remplisseu-r, -se [rɑ̃plisœr] *s.m.f.* filler-in (of patterns on china, etc., or in lace); **~se** *s.f.* bottle-filling machine

remploi [rɑ̃plwa], **réemploi** [reɑ̃plwa] *s.m.* **1.** re-use (esp. of building stone); **2.** (law) reinvestment.

remployer [rɑ̃plwaje], **réemployer** [reɑ̃plwaje] *v.t.* **1.** to re-use; **2.** (law) to reinvest.

(**se**) **remplumer** [rɑ̃plyme] *v.refl.* (of birds) to get new feathers; (fam.) to put on flesh, to pick up again (in health, spirits, money, etc.).

rempocher [rɑ̃pɔʃe] *v.t.* to put back in one's pocket.

rempoissonnement [rɑ̃pwasɔnmɑ̃] *s.m.* restocking with fish.

rempoissonner [rɑ̃pwasɔne] *v.t.* to restock with fish.

remporter [rɑ̃pɔrte] *v.t.* **1.** to take away (again), to take back; **2.** to gain, to carry off, (prize, etc.).

rempotage [rɑ̃pɔtaʒ] *s.m.* repotting.

rempoter [rɑ̃pɔte] *v.t.* to repot.

remuable [rəmɥabl] movable.

remuage [rəmɥaʒ] *s.m.* moving, stirring, turning.

remuant, -e [rəmɥɑ̃] *adj.* moving; restless, bustling.

remue-ménage [rəmymenaʒ] *s.m. invar.* bustle, stir, upset, fuss, to-do, confusion, excitement.

remuement [rəmymɑ̃] *s.m.* moving, stirring.

remuer [rəmɥe] *v.t.i.* to move, to keep moving; to be loose; to stir, to turn, to stir up, to shake; to affect, to touch; to wag (the tail); to shake (the head); *~ ciel et terre*, to move heaven and earth; to leave no stone unturned; *ne ~ ni pied ni patte*, to be quite motionless, not to move a muscle; (fig.) *~ l'argent à la pelle*, to be disgustingly rich; **se** *~ v.refl.* to bestir oneself, to be busy, to move, to get a move on; to make an effort.

remugle [rəmygl] *s.m.* musty or stuffy smell.

rémunérat-eur, -rice [remyneratœr] *adj.* remunerative, paying, profitable; **~eur** *s.m.* rewarder.

rémunération [remynerɑsjɔ̃] *s.f.* remuneration, reward, payment.

rémunératoire [remyneratwar] *adj.* (law) remuneratory.

rémunérer [remynere] *v.t.* to remunerate, to reward, to pay, to recompense.

renâcler [rənɑkle] *v.i.* to snuffle, to snort; (fig.) to show reluctance or repugnance, to snort (at having to do sth.).

renaissance [rənɛsɑ̃s] *s.f.* renascence, rebirth; revival, renewal, regeneration; Renaissance (16th c.); *~ adj.invar.* Renaissance.

renaissant, -e [rənɛsɑ̃] *adj.* renascent, revived, reviving, recurring, returning; Renaissance.

renaître [rənɛtr] *v.i.* to be born again, to revive, to spring up again, to rise again, to reappear, to to return, to be restored (*à*, to).

rénal, -e, (**aux**) [renal] *adj.* (anat.) renal.

renard [rənar] *s.m.* **1.** fox; fox-fur; (fig.) sly fox, cunning fellow, blackleg; **2.** crack, fissure.

renarde [rənard] *s.f.* she-fox, vixen.

renardeau (pl. **-x**) [rənardo] *s.m.* young fox, fox cub.

renarder [rənarde] *v.i.* to play the fox, to act cunningly; (pop. and obs.) to vomit.

renardière [rənardjɛr] *s.f.* fox's hole, earth.

rencaissage [rɑ̃kɛsaʒ] *s.m.* (hort.) putting into new tubs.

rencaissement [rɑ̃kɛsmɑ̃] *s.m.* paying (money) back in, receiving repayment.

rencaisser [rɑ̃kese] *v.t.* **1.** (hort.) to put into new tubs; **2.** to pay (money) back in.

rencard see RANCARD.

rencarder see RANCARDER.

renchaîner [rɑ̃ʃene] *v.t.* to chain up again.

renchéri, -e [rɑ̃ʃeri] *adj.* fastidious, difficult, finicky; contemptuous.

renchérir [rɑ̃ʃerir] *v.t.i.* to raise the price of, to make dearer; to become dearer, to rise in price; to add, to confirm (by speaking); *~ sur*, to outdo, to improve upon; to go one better than; to add to, to confirm, to stress (a previous remark).

renchérissement [rɑ̃ʃerismɑ̃] *s.m.* rise (in price).

rencogner [rɑ̃kɔɲe] *v.t.* to drive into a corner; **se** *~ v.refl.* to retreat into a corner; to ensconce oneself.

rencontre [rɑ̃kɔ̃tr] *s.f.* meeting, encounter, hit; collision, duel, fight; conjuncture, juncture, occasion; chance meeting or discovery; *aller à la ~ de qn.*, to go to meet s.o.; *faire une mauvaise ~*, to have an unpleasant encounter; to be held up (by bandits, etc.); *en toute ~*, on any occasion; *une connaissance de ~*, a casual acquaintance; *un monsieur de ~*, a gentleman I happened to meet; *un bibelot de ~*, a curio I picked up; (horol.) *roue de ~*, balance-wheel.

rencontrer [rɑ̃kɔ̃tre] *v.t.* to meet, to meet with, to

encounter, to come across, to fall in with; to hit upon; to run into, to collide with; to experience; *vous avez rencontré juste*, you have hit the nail on the head; you have been lucky; **se ~** *v.refl.* to meet, to meet each other; to collide, to come into collision; to be met with, to be found; to be of the same mind (*avec*, with); to arrive at the same result; *les grands esprits se rencontrent*, great minds think alike; *cela ne se rencontre pas tous les jours*, that is not something you come across every day.

rendement [rɑ̃dmɑ̃] *s.m.* **1.** yield, output, return(s); performance; efficiency; (mech.) work; productivity; *à plein ~*, at full output, at maximum load, at full blast; **2.** (sport) handicap,

rendez-vous [rɑ̃devu] *s.m. invar.* appointment, tryst, rendezvous; clandestine meeting; meeting--place; *donner, fixer, un ~ à qn.*, to make an appointment with s.o., to arrange to meet s.o.; *~ de chasse*, hunting-lodge; place of the meet.

rendormir [rɑ̃dɔrmir] *v.t.* to put to sleep again; **se ~** *v.refl.* to go to sleep again.

rendosser [rɑ̃dose] *v.t.* to put on (coat, etc.), to put on again.

rendre [rɑ̃dr] *v.t.* to give back, to return, to restore; to render; to deliver; to bring in, to yield; to bring up, to vomit; to exhale, to emit; to express, to convey, to translate; to give up; *~ l'âme*, to give up the ghost; *~ un arrêt*, to issue a decree; *~ un jugement*, to deliver a judgement; *~ compte*, to give an account (*de*, of); *~ gorge*, to disgorge; *~ grâce (à)*, to thank, to return thanks (to); *~ hommage à*, to pay homage to; *~ la justice*, to dispense justice; *~ justice à qn.*, to do s.o. justice; *rendre sa parole à qn.*, to release s.o. from his promise; *~ service à qn.*, to do s.o. a good turn; *~ témoignage*, to bear witness; *~ visite à qn.*, to pay s.o. a visit; to call on s.o.; *il m'en rendra raison*, he will have to apologise for that; *Dieu vous le rende!*, may God reward you!; **se ~** *v.refl.* to go, to make one's way, (*à*, to); to surrender, to yield; to make oneself; to be translated; *se ~ maître de*, to master; *se ~ agréable*, to make oneself pleasant; *je me rends à vos raisons*, I admit you are right; I yield to your arguments; *tous les fleuves se rendent à la mer*, all rivers flow into the sea; *cela ne peut se rendre en français*, that cannot be accurately translated into French.

rendu, -e [rɑ̃dy] *adj.* rendered, brought back, returned; tired out, exhausted, spent; arrived at one's destination; *prix ~*, delivery price, price delivered; *compte ~*, account, report; *~ s.m.* **1.** return; sth. returned; *un prêté pour un ~*, tit for tat; **2.** finish, execution, (of a work of art).

rêne [rɛn] *s.f.* (lit. & fig.) rein; *lâcher les ~s*, to give the horse his head, (fig.) to slacken the reins.

renégat, -e [rənega] *s.m.f.* renegade, turncoat.

rénette [renɛt] *s.f.* (techn.) paring-knife.

renfaîter [rɑ̃fɛte] *v.t.* to repair the ridge of, to new-ridge, (a roof).

renfermé [rɑ̃fɛrme] *s.m.* stuffiness.

renfermer [rɑ̃fɛrme] *v.t.* (obs.) to close or lock up again, to confine, to shut up; to contain, to comprise, to include; (mod.) to conceal, to restrict; **se ~** *v.refl.* to confine oneself, to limit oneself; *se ~ en soi-même*, to retire into oneself; to keep one's thoughts to oneself.

renfiler [rɑ̃file] *v.t.* to rethread, to restring.

renflammer [rɑ̃flame] *v.t.* to rekindle.

renflé, -e [rɑ̃fle] *adj.* swollen, swelling out; bulbous.

renflement [rɑ̃fləmɑ̃] *s.m.* swelling; bulging; bulge; (arch.) entasis.

renfler [rɑ̃fle] *v.t.i.* & *refl.* to swell, to enlarge, to bulge.

renflouement [rɑ̃flumɑ̃] *s.m.* (lit. & fig.) refloating.

renflouer [rɑ̃flue] *v.t.* (naut.) to refloat; (fin.) to refloat, to give a new injection of funds to.

renfoncement [rɑ̃fɔ̃smɑ̃] *s.m.* hollow, cavity, dent, indentation; hollowing out, denting; (art) depth, perspective; driving in (of nail, etc.); niche, nook, retreat.

renfoncer [rɑ̃fɔ̃se] *v.t.* to drive deeper, to sink; to pull down (a hat, etc.); (techn.) to indent.

renforçage [rɑ̃fɔrsaʒ] *s.m.* strengthening, reinforcement; (photo.) intensifying.

renforçateur [rɑ̃fɔrsatœr] *s.m.* (photo.) intensifier.

renforcement [rɑ̃fɔrsmɑ̃] *s.m.* reinforcement, strengthening, stiffening, bracing; (fig.) intensifying; (photo.) intensification.

renforcer [rɑ̃fɔrse] *v.t.* to strengthen, to reinforce, to intensify, to confirm, to concentrate.

renfort [rɑ̃fɔr] *s.m.* reinforcement, strengthening, stiffening; reinforce (of gun); fresh supply; fresh strength, help, relief; *de ~*, extra, additional; *à grand ~ de*, by dint of, with the aid of much, with plenty of; *pour ~ de potage*, to make matters worse, to crown everything.

renfrogné, -e [rɑ̃frɔɲe] *adj.* frowning; gloomy, sullen, glum.

renfrognement [rɑ̃frɔɲmɑ̃] *s.m.* scowl, frown, frowning.

(**se**) **renfrogner** [rɑ̃frɔɲe] *v.refl.* to frown, to scowl, to look sullen.

rengagé [rɑ̃gaʒe] *s.m.* (mil.) re-engaged, re--enlisted, man.

rengagement [rɑ̃gaʒmɑ̃] *s.m.* re-enlistment; re-engagement.

rengager [rɑ̃gaʒe] *v.t.* to re-enlist; to re-engage; (fig., fam.) to start again.

rengaine [rɑ̃gɛn] *s.f.* tiresome repetition, same old story; refrain of popular song.

rengainer [rɑ̃gene] *v.t.* **1.** (obs.) to sheathe one's sword; **2.** (fig., fam.) to suppress, to refrain from (saying sth.).

(**se**) **rengorger** [rɑ̃gɔrʒe] *v.refl.* (lit. & fig.) to puff oneself up; to put on airs, to swagger; *se ~ de*, to pride oneself on.

rengraisser [rɑ̃grese] *v.i.* to put on flesh again, to grow fat again.

rengréner [rɑ̃grene], **rengrener** [rɑ̃grəne] *v.t.* **1.** to fill (hopper) again with corn; **2.** (techn.) to put in gear again, to re-engage.

reniement [rənimɑ̃] *s.m.* denying, disowning, denial.

renier [rənje] *v.t.* to deny, to disown, to repudiate, to go back on (promise, etc.); to renounce.

reniflard [rəniflar] *s.m.* (techn.) air-valve, blow--valve, breather.

reniflement [rənifləmɑ̃] *s.m.* sniffling, sniff.

renifler [rənifle] *v.t.i.* to sniffle, to sniff; to nose; *~ du tabac*, to take snuff; (fig.) *~ une vilaine affaire*, to smell a rat.

renifleu-r, -se [rəniflœr] *adj., s.m.f.* sniffling, snivelling, (child, etc.).

réniforme [renifɔrm] *adj.* reniform, kidney--shaped.

rénitence [renitɑ̃s] *s.f.* (med.) renitency.

rénitent, -e [renitɑ̃] *adj.* (med.) renitent.

renne [rɛn] *s.m.* reindeer.

renom [rənɔ̃] *s.m.* reputation, repute, fame, renown; *en ~*, famous, fashionable.

renommé, -e [rənɔme] *adj.* renowned, famed, celebrated, noted, famous, well-known, reputed.

renommée [rənɔme] *s.f.* renown, fame, celebrity; reputation; report; *bonne ~ vaut mieux que ceinture dorée*, a good name is better than riches; (law) *preuve par ~*, hearsay evidence, common report.

renommer [rənɔme] *v.t.* **1.** to name again, to nominate again, to re-elect; **2.** (obs.) to extol.

renoncement [rənɔ̃smɑ̃] *s.m.* renouncement,

renunciation, self-denial; ~ *à soi-même*, self--denial, self-abnegation.
renoncer [rənɔ̃se] *v.t.* ~ (*à*), to renounce, to give up, to abandon, to relinquish, to disown, to repudiate; ~ *à soi-même*, to forget oneself, to abandon all selfish considerations.
renonciataire [rənɔ̃sjatɛr] *s.m.f.* (law) releasee.
renonciat-eur, -rice [rənɔ̃sjatœr] *s.m.f.* renouncer.
renonciation [renɔ̃sjasjɔ̃] *s.f.* renunciation, waiver, disclaimer, renouncement, self-denial.
renonculacées [rənɔ̃kylase] *s.f.pl.* (bot.) Ranunculaceae.
renoncule [rənɔ̃kyl] *s.f.* (bot.) ranunculus, buttercup, crowfoot, spearwort.
renouée [rənwe] *s.f.* (bot.) knot-grass; polygonum; spotted persicaria.
renouer [rənwe] *v.t.* to tie again, to bind again; to renew, to resume; to resume relations (*avec*, with); ~ *le fil de la conversation*, to pick up the thread of the conversation.
renouveau (pl. **-x**) [rənuvo] *s.m.* springtime; (fig.) renewal.
renouvelable [rənuvlabl] *adj.* renewable; extendible; that can be repeated.
renouveler [rənuvle] *v.t.* to renew, to renovate; to revive, to regenerate; to repeat, to do again; to replace; **se** ~ *v.refl.* to be revived, renewed, refreshed; to occur again; to change, to be replaced.
renouvellement [rənuvɛlmɑ̃] *s.m.* renewal, renewing; renovating; replacing, refurnishing, restocking; repetition.
rénovat-eur, -rice [renɔvatœr] *adj., s.m.f.* renovating, renewing; renovator, reviver; ~**eur** *s.m.* renovator (product).
rénovation [renɔvɑsjɔ̃] *s.f.* renovation, renewal, revival, refreshing; restoration.
rénover [renɔve] *v.t.* to renovate, to revive; to restore.
renseignement [rɑ̃sɛɲəmɑ̃] *s.m.* information, indication, account; particulars; inquiries; intelligence; *aller aux* ~*s*, to make inquiries, to seek information; *service des* ~*s*, intelligence service; *aviation de* ~, aerial reconnaissance.
renseigner [rɑ̃seɲe] *v.t.* to give information to, to direct; **se** ~ *v.refl.* to seek information, to make inquiries; to inquire, to ask (*sur*, about).
rentabilité [rɑ̃tabilite] *s.f.* profitability.
rentable [rɑ̃tabl] *adj.* profitable, paying.
rente [rɑ̃t] *s.f.* **1.** revenue; income, investment income, private means; fixed interest payment; regular payment or outgoing; allowance; pension; ~ *viagère*, annuity; *avoir des* ~*s*, to have private means; **2.** loan stock, government stock, funds; ⚠ not 'rent' as paid by tenant.
renté, -e [rɑ̃te] *adj.* with private means; endowed; *bien* ~, comfortably off.
renter [rɑ̃te] *v.t.* to endow; ⚠ not 'to rent' as a tenant.
renti-er, -ère [rɑ̃tje] *s.m.f.* stockholder; person who lives on *rentes*.
rentoilage [rɑ̃twalaʒ] *s.m.* putting canvas to, backing, (a picture).
rentoiler [rɑ̃twale] *v.t.* to put canvas to, to back, (a picture).
rentrage [rɑ̃traʒ] *s.m.* taking in, housing, carrying home.
rentraiture [rɑ̃trɛtyr] *s.f.* invisible mending or sewing.
rentrant, -e [rɑ̃trɑ̃] *adj.* re-entrant, pointing inwards; retractable; (geom.) *angle* ~, reflex angle; ~ *s.m.* (sport) new player; pupil returning after holidays.
rentré, -e [rɑ̃tre] *adj.* driven in; sunken, hollow; suppressed, restrained, checked.
rentrée [rɑ̃tre] *s.f.* **1.** re-entering; re-entry; coming home or back, return; reopening, beginning of new session or term; resumption (of work, etc.) after holidays; reappearance, come-back; **2.** bringing in, gathering in, storing; **3.** (pl.) monies paid in, receipts, takings; **4.** (cards) card drawn from the pile; **5.** (football) ~ *en touche*, throw-in.
rentrer [rɑ̃tre] *v.i.* to re-enter, to go in, to come or go home; to come or go back (into); to sink; to return; to make a reappearance; *faire* ~, to to bring in, to fetch or call in; ~ *dans*, (i.) to go or come back into; to fit into; to collide with; to penetrate; to hurl oneself on; (ii.) to recover (possession, etc., of); (lit. & fig.) ~ *dans sa coquille*, to withdraw into one's shell; *vouloir* ~ *sous terre*, to wish that the ground would swallow one up; ~ *dans son bien*, to recover one's property; ~ *dans l'ordre*, to be restored to order; ~ *en grâce*, to come into favour again; ~ *en possession de*, to recover, to regain possession of; ~ *en soi-même*, to reflect, or consider seriously; to commune with oneself; ~ *v.t.* to bring back, to bring in (again), to gather in, to bring home, to get in, to house; to draw in, to retract; to tuck in; to check, to suppress; ~ *les foins*, to get in the hay; *rentrez vos larmes*, check your tears; stop crying; *rentrez les avirons*, ship the oars; (slang) *il va lui* ~ *dedans*, or *lui* ~ *dans le chou*, he will pitch into him.
renversable [rɑ̃vɛrsabl] *adj.* easily upset; reversible.
renversant, -e [rɑ̃vɛrsɑ̃] *adj.* (fig.) startling, staggering, disconcerting.
renverse [rɑ̃vɛrs] *s.f.* reversal; *tomber à la* ~, to fall on one's back; (fig., fam.) to be struck all of a heap, to be staggered.
renversé, -e [rɑ̃vɛrse] *adj.* reversed, inverted; turned upside down; overthrown; lying on one's back; slanting; tipped back; staggered, utterly disconcerted; *c'est le monde* ~*!*, everything is upside down!, things have come to a pretty pass!
renversement [rɑ̃vɛrsmɑ̃] *s.m.* overturning, upsetting, turning upside down; inversion, reversing; subversion, destruction, ruin, overthrow; (mus.) inversion; *mécanisme de* ~, reversing gear.
renverser [rɑ̃vɛrse] *v.t.* to upset, to overturn, to overthrow, to turn upside down, to knock down; to spill (liquids); to reverse; (mus., arith.) to invert; (fig.) to stupefy, to astound, to amaze, to disarrange, to turn topsy-turvy, to turn (a person's head); (lit. & fig.) ~ *la vapeur*, to reverse the engine; **se** ~ *v.refl.* to be upset, overturned; to throw oneself back, to fall back; to capsize.
renvidage [rɑ̃vidaʒ] *s.m.* (techn.) winding (on bobbins).
renvider [rɑ̃vide] *v.t.* (techn.) to wind (on bobbins).
renvideur [rɑ̃vidœr] *s.m.* (techn.) **1.** winder (operative); **2.** mule (jenny).
renvoi [rɑ̃vwa] *s.m.* returning, return, sending back; dismissal, turning out, discharge; postponement, adjournment, reference; (print.) reference-mark; reverberation (of sound); (mech.) reversing; (med.) eructation.
renvoyer [rɑ̃vwaje] *v.t.* to return, to send back; to dismiss, to discharge; to dispatch; to turn out, (fam.) to throw out; to put off, to postpone, to adjourn, to refer; to reverberate, to reflect, to throw back; ~ *la balle*, (sport) to return the ball, to hit the ball back; (fig.) to give tit for tat, to put the ball back in opponent's court.
réoccupation [reɔkypɑsjɔ̃] *s.f.* reoccupation.
réoccuper [reɔkype] *v.t.* to reoccupy.
réorchestration [reɔrkɛstrɑsjɔ̃] *s.f.* reorchestration.
réorchestrer [reɔrkɛstre] *v.t.* to reorchestrate, to rescore.

réordonner [reɔrdɔne] *v.t.* **1.** to reordain; **2.** to put in order again.

réorganisat-eur, -rice [reɔrganizatœr] *s.m.f.* reorganizer.

réorganisation [reɔrganizɑsjɔ̃] *s.f.* reorganization.

réorganiser [reɔrganize] *v.t.* to reorganize; **se** ~ *v.refl.* to be reorganized.

réorientation [reɔriɑ̃tɑsjɔ̃] *s.f.* reorientation.

réorienter [reɔriɑ̃te] *v.t.* to reorientate.

réouverture [reuvɛrtyr] *s.f.* reopening.

repaire [rəpɛr] *s.m.* lair; den, haunt; ~ *de brigands*, den of thieves.

repaître [rəpɛtr] *v.t.* to feed, to nourish, to feast; **se** ~ *v.refl.* to eat one's fill; (of animals) to feed; (fig.) *se* ~ *de*, to feed on, to be sated with; *se* ~ *de chimères*, to feed on vain hopes, to indulge in idle fancies.

répandre [repɑ̃dr] *v.t.* to pour, to shed, to spill, to sprinkle; to spread, to scatter, to diffuse, to circulate, to propagate; to exhale; to lavish, to distribute; **se** ~ *v.refl.* to spread, to be scattered, to be propagated, diffused; to run out, to burst out; to be lavish (*en*, with); *se* ~ *en invectives*, to launch into abuse; *se* ~ *en excuses*, to be profuse in one's apologies; *se* ~ *dans le monde*, to go out a great deal, to be well known in society; *le bruit se répand que*, it is rumoured that.

répandu, -e [repɑ̃dy] *adj.* rumoured, propagated, spread, widespread, widely distributed; poured out, spilt; prevalent, current, in general use; *l'opinion la plus* ~*e*, the commonly held opinion; *un homme très* ~, a man well known in society circles.

réparable [reparabl] *adj.* reparable, repairable, that can be mended.

reparaître [rəparɛtr] *v.i.* to reappear, to make one's reappearance, to turn up again, to recur.

réparat-eur, -rice [reparatœr] *adj.* restorative, refreshing; *s.m.f.* repairer, restorer, mender.

réparation [reparɑsjɔ̃] *s.f.* repair, mending, repairing; reparation, atonement, amends, indemnification, compensation; ~*s courantes*, running repairs; *en* ~, under repair; *atelier de* ~*s*, repair shop; *demander* ~ *à qn.*, to demand satisfaction or reparation from s.o.; ~ *par les armes*, duel; (football) *coup de pied de* ~, penalty kick; *surface de* ~, penalty area.

réparer [repare] *v.t.* to repair, to mend; to make amends for; to make up for; to restore, to retrieve; to make reparation for; to redress (wrongs).

reparler [rəparle] *v.i.* to speak again, to talk again; *nous en reparlerons*, we shall see about that; let us think it over; we'll discuss that later; **se** ~ *v.refl.* to speak to each other again, to be on speaking terms again.

répartement [repartəmɑ̃] *s.m.* assessment (of taxes).

repartie [rəparti] *s.f.* repartee, rejoinder, retort, reply; *avoir la* ~ *prompte*, *être prompt à la* ~, to be quick at repartee, never to be at a loss for an answer.

repartir[1] [rəpartir] *v.t.* to answer, to retort, to rejoin.

repartir[2] [rəpartir] *v.i.* to leave again, to set out again; to start again; to set off back.

répartir [repartir] *v.t.* to distribute, to share out, to allocate, to divide.

répartiteur [repartitœr] *s.m.* **1.** distributor, apportioner; assessor (of taxes); **2.** dispatcher (of goods).

répartition [repartisjɔ̃] *s.f.* distribution, sharing out; allotment, apportionment.

repas [rəpɑ] *s.m.* meal, repast.

repassage [rəpɑsaʒ] *s.m.* **1.** ironing (of clothes etc.); **2.** sharpening, grinding, (of knives, etc.); **3.** passing again.

repasser [rəpɑse] *v i.* to pass again, to cross, to cross again, to come again, to look in again, to call again; ~ *v.t.* to iron (clothes, etc.), to sharpen, to grind, to set, (knives, etc.), to strop (razors); *fer à* ~, iron; *planche à* ~, ironing-board; ~ *une leçon*, to look over a lesson; ~ *un examen*, to sit or take an examination again; ~ *quelque chose dans son esprit*, to turn over something in one's mind; ~ *les Alpes*, to recross the Alps; ~ *dans son pays*, to visit one's country again.

repasseur [rəpɑsœr] *s.m.* grinder (of knives, scissors, etc.).

repasseuse [rəpɑsøz] *s.f.* ironer (person or machine), laundress.

repavage [rəpavaʒ], **repavement** [rəpavmɑ̃] *s.m.* repaving.

repaver [rəpave] *v.t.* to repave.

repayer [rəpeje] *v.t.* to pay over again.

repêchage [rəpɛʃaʒ] *s.m.* fishing up again, fishing out; (fig.) letting (doubtful candidate) through; supplementary examination for failures at main examination; (rowing) repêchage.

repêcher [rəpɛʃe] *v.t.* to fish up again, to fish out; (fig.) to help out of a difficulty; to let (a doubtful candidate) through; ~ *un candidat à deux points*, to let through a candidate who is two below pass-mark.

repeindre [rəpɛ̃dr] *v.t.* to repaint.

repeint [rəpɛ̃] *s.m.* retouched part (of a picture).

repenser [rəpɑ̃se] *v.t.i.* to think again (of something), to think over, to reconsider; *je n'y ai pas repensé*, I didn't give it another thought, I forgot all about it.

repentance [rəpɑ̃tɑ̃s] *s.f.* repentance, contrition, regret.

repentant, -e [rəpɑ̃tɑ̃] *adj.* repentant, penitent.

repenti, -e [rəpɑ̃ti] *adj.* penitent.

(**se**) **repentir** [rəpɑ̃tir] *v.refl.* to repent, to be sorry; *se* ~ *de ses fautes*, to repent one's sins; *se* ~ *d'avoir fait cela*, to be sorry to have done that; *je l'en ferai* ~, I will make him regret it.

repentir [rəpɑ̃tir] *s.m.* repentance, remorse, regret, contrition; alteration, correction, (in painting); (pl.) ringlets, curls.

repérable [rəperabl] *adj.* detectable, ascertainable, that can be located.

repérage [rəperaʒ] *s.m.* fitting to a mark, finding the bearings, taking up guiding marks, identifying the origin or the spot (*de*, of); locating, location; ranging; logging; making a guiding mark.

repercer [rəpɛrse] *v.t.* to pierce again, to bore again; to pierce (metal).

répercussion [repɛrkysjɔ̃] *s.f.* (lit. & fig.) repercussion, backlash; consequence, reaction.

répercuter [repɛrkyte] *v.t.* (lit. & fig.) to have repercussions, to reverberate, to echo; to reflect (back).

reperdre [rəpɛrdr] *v.t.* to lose again.

repère [rəpɛr] *s.m.* guiding mark; assembly mark, bench mark; landmark; *point de* ~, guide mark, setting mark, reference mark, landmark; *ligne de* ~, datum line.

repérer [rəpere] *v.t.* to mark; to adjust; to discover; to locate; to spot, to pin-point.

répertoire [repɛrtwar] *s.m.* repertory, repertoire, repository, catalogue, index; (theatr.) stock plays, repertory; *un vivant* ~, a walking encyclopaedia.

répertorier [repɛrtɔrje] *v.t.* to index.

répéter [repete] *v.t.* to repeat, to say again, to tell again; to rehearse (a play, part, etc.); to do again, to recommence; to reproduce, to repeat; to reflect; (law) to demand back; *il ne se l'est pas fait* ~ *deux fois*, he did not wait to be told twice; ~ *une expérience*, to repeat an experiment; **se** ~ *v.refl.* to repeat oneself, to say the same thing over and over again; to occur again; to be repeated.

répétit-eur, -rice [repetitœr] *s.m.f.* private teacher, coach, tutor, assistant teacher; ~**eur** *s.m.* (teleph.) repeater.

répétition [repetisjɔ̃] *s.f.* **1.** repetition, repeating, recurrence; reiteration; reproduction, duplicate; *montre à* ~, repeater; *fusil à* ~, magazine-rifle, repeater rifle; **2.** rehearsal; **3.** private lesson, tuition; **4.** (law) claim for recovery of money.

répétitorat [repetitɔra] *s.m.* tutorship.

repeuplement [rəpœpləmɑ̃] *s.m.* repeopling, repopulation; restocking.

repeupler [rəpœple] *v.t.* to repeople, to repopulate; to restock; **se** ~ *v.refl.* to become full of people again, to become repopulated.

repic [rəpik] *s.m.* (at piquet) repique.

repincer [rəpɛ̃se] *v.t.* to pinch again; (fig.) to catch again; *si je t'y repince*, if I catch you at it again.

repiquage [rəpikaʒ] *s.m.* **1.** (hort.) planting out, pricking out; **2.** repair (of roads); (photo.) retouching; retouched print.

repiquer [rəpike] *v.t.* **1.** to prick or pierce again, to stick (sth.) in again; **2.** (hort.) to plant out, to prick out; **3.** to repair (road), to have (the road) up; (photo.) to retouch; to rewrite (an article, etc.); to make a new recording of; **4.** (pop.) to catch again; **5.** (pop.) to come back (to sth.), to start again; ~ *au truc*, to start again, to have another go, to go back to the old job, or one's old ways.

répit [repi] *s.m.* respite, rest, break, intermission, breathing-space, delay; *sans* ~, without respite, unceasingly, unremittingly.

replacement [rəplasmɑ̃] *s.m.* replacing; reinvestment.

replacer [rəplase] *v.t.* to replace, to put back (again); to find a new position or job for; to reinvest (funds).

replantation [rəplɑ̃tɑsjɔ̃] *s.f.* replanting.

replanter [rəplɑ̃te] *v.t.* to replant.

replat [rəpla] *s.m.* (geog., mountaineering) shelf.

replâtrage [rəplɑtraʒ] *s.m.* replastering, plastering up; (fig.) patched-up arrangement.

replâtrer [rəplɑtre] *v.t.* to replaster, to plaster up; (fig.) to patch up.

repl-et, -ète [rəplɛ] *adj.* stout, chubby, podgy; ⚠ not 'replete'.

réplétì-f, -ve [repletif] *adj.* replenishing; (med.) *injection* ~*ve*, booster injection.

réplétion [replesjɔ̃] *s.f.* **1.** obesity, corpulence, stoutness; **2.** repletion, plethora; (astrophysics) mascon.

repleuvoir [rəplœvwar] *v.i. impers.* to rain again.

repli [rəpli] *s.m.* fold, crease, turn, winding, coil (of snake); (pl.) (fig.) secret places, innermost recesses.

repliement [rəplimɑ̃] *s.m.* folding back, folding up; withdrawal, falling back.

replier [rəplie] *v.t.* to fold up again, to turn in, to turn back; to withdraw, to pull or draw back; **se** ~ *v.refl.* to twist, to bend, to coil; (mil.) to fall back, to retreat; (fig.) to withdraw into oneself, to shut everything out.

réplique [replik] *s.f.* **1.** retort, rejoinder, repartee, reply, answer; objection, protest; question; (theatr.) cue; (theatr.) feed; *argument sans* ~, unanswerable argument; *obéissance sans* ~, unquestioning obedience; *pas de* ~*!*, no back answer!; (theatr.) *donner la* ~ *à un acteur*, to give an actor his cue; to feed an actor; to rehearse an actor in his part (by reading); *se donner la* ~, to answer each other, to argue; **2.** replica, counterpart; (mus.) replicate.

répliquer [replike] *v.t.* to reply, to retort, to answer (back), to rejoin, to protest, to object; ~ *à*, to answer (s.o., sth.).

replisser [rəplise] *v.t.* to repleat.

reploiement [rəplwamɑ̃] *s.m.* = REPLIEMENT.

replonger [rəplɔ̃ʒe] *v.t.i.* to plunge again, to dip again; to reimmerse; **se** ~ *v.refl.* to plunge or dive again; to be immersed; (fig.) to be involved or absorbed.

reployer [rəplwaje] *v.t.* = REPLIER.

repolir [rəpɔlir] *v.t.* to repolish; to retouch.

repolissage [rəpɔlisaʒ] *s.m.* repolishing.

répondant, -e [repɔ̃dɑ̃] *s.m.f.* respondent; surety, bail, guarantor, referee; ~ *s.m.* (eccles.) server.

répondeu-r, -se [repɔ̃dœr] *s.m.f., adj.* (one) who answers back; cheeky.

répondre [repɔ̃dr] *v.t.* to answer, to give an answer, to reply (*à*, to), to write back; ~ *à*, to respond to, to reciprocate, to comply with, to correspond to or with, to be in accordance with; to come up to (expectations, etc.); to be in proportion to; to be symmetrical with; to echo; ~ *de*, to be security or bail for, to be answerable for, to be responsible for, to guarantee; ~ *une impertinence*, to give an impertinent reply; *le succès n'a pas répondu à mes espérances*, the result fell short of my expectations; ~ *à la tendresse de qn.*, to return someone's affection; *je réponds de son honnêteté*, I will guarantee his honesty; *je vous en réponds*, take my word for it; I can tell you!; and no mistake!; **se** ~ *v.refl.* to answer each other; to correspond, to be symmetrical.

répons [repɔ̃] *s.m.* (eccles.) response.

réponse [repɔ̃s] *s.f.* answer, reply, retort, response, rejoinder; responsiveness; refutation; *en* ~, in reply, by way of answer, for (an) answer; *avoir* ~ *à tout*, never to be at a loss for an answer; *rendre* ~, to return an answer, to give a reply; ~ *de Normand*, equivocal or evasive answer.

repopulation [rəpɔpylɑsjɔ̃] *s.f.* repeopling, repopulation.

report [rəpɔr] *s.m.* carrying forward, bringing forward; amount brought forward; (Stock Exchange) continuation, contango; (accounting) posting; (lithography, etc.) transfer; ⚠ not 'report'.

reportage [rəpɔrtaʒ] *s.m.* (journalism) reporting; report, article.

reporter [rəpɔrtɛr] *s.m.* reporter.

reporter [rəpɔrte] *v.t.* to carry back, to take back, to bring back; to transfer (*sur*, to); (accounting) to carry or bring forward; to post; (lithography, etc.) to transfer; (Stock Exchange) to carry over; **se** ~ *v.refl.* to be carried back; to go back (in imagination, memory, etc.); to refer; ⚠ not 'to report'.

reporteur [rəpɔrtœr] *s.m.* **1.** (Stock Exchange) taker of stock, receiver of contango; **2.** (lithography, etc.) transfer operator.

repos [rəpo] *s.m.* rest, repose, quiet, respite; rest day or period, period off work; peace, sleep; (mus., pros.) pause, hold, caesura; (mil.) ~*!*, stand at ease!; *au* ~, at rest, when resting, (mil.) at ease; *champ de* ~, churchyard; *avoir l'esprit en* ~, to be easy in one's mind; *mettre sa conscience en* ~, to ease one's conscience; *laissez-moi en* ~, let me alone; *valeurs de tout* ~, gilt-edged securities; *mettre un moteur au* ~, to disengage an engine, to let an engine idle.

reposé, -e [rəpoze] *adj.* refreshed, rested, calm, quiet; *à tête* ~*e*, coolly, at leisure, deliberately; after thinking it over.

reposée [rəpoze] *s.f.* (hunt.) lair.

reposer[1] [rəpoze] *v.i.* to rest, to lie; (of liquids) to be left to settle; ~ *sur*, to rest on, to be based on, to be supported by; ~ *v.t.* to rest; to leave (liquids) to settle; **se** ~ *v.refl.* to rest, to refresh oneself; (of land) to lie fallow; (of liquids) to settle; (fig.) *se* ~ *sur*, to be based on; to rely on,

to trust in; *se ~ sur qn. de qch.*, to rely on s.o. as regards sth., to count on s.o. seeing to sth.
reposer[2] [rəpoze] *v.t.* to put down again, to put back; to re-lay, to reposition; to put (a question, etc.) again; (mil.) *reposez armes!*, order arms!; *le problème se repose*, the problem comes up again.
reposoir [rəpozwar] *s.m.* temporary altar.
repoussage [rəpusaʒ] *s.m.* embossing, chasing, repoussé work; (typ.) hand-stamping.
repoussant, -e [rəpusɑ̃] *adj.* repulsive, repellent, loathsome.
repousse [rəpus] *s.f.* regrowth, new growth.
repoussé [rəpuse] *adj., s.m.* repoussé, embossed, (work).
repoussement [rəpusmɑ̃] *s.m.* pushing back, repelling, repulsing; recoil (of firearm).
repousser[1] [rəpuse] *v.t.* to push back, to push away; to repulse, to repel; to throw away or out; to reject; to drive back; to thrust aside; to postpone.
repousser[2] [rəpuse] *v.t.* to put forth (new branches, etc.); *~ v.i.* to grow again.
repoussoir [rəpuswar] *s.m.* **1.** driving-bolt, punch, embossing-tool; spatula for pressing back cuticle; **2.** (fig.) set-off, contrast, foil.
répréhensible [repreɑ̃sibl] *adj.* reprehensible, culpable.
répréhension [repreɑ̃sjɔ̃] *s.f.* reprehension, censure, reprimand.
reprendre [rəprɑ̃dr] *v.t.* to take back, to take (staff) on again, to get back, to retake, to recover, to resume possession of, to catch again; to take up, to go on with; to go back over; to recapitulate; to find fault with, to reprove; to begin again; to resume; to answer, to rejoin; *~ haleine*, to recover one's breath; to take breath; (fig.) to get a respite; to pause; *~ la parole*, to resume, to go on speaking, to find one's tongue again; *~ courage*, to pluck up courage; to take heart again; *~ le dessus*, to get the upper hand again; to regain self-control; *~ des forces*, to recover one's strength; *la goutte l'a repris*, he is suffering from gout again; *~ ses habits d'été*, to go back to summer clothes; *reprenez de ce plat*, have some more; *on ne m'y reprendra pas de sitôt*, they won't catch me at it again; *~ en sous-œuvre*, to underpin; *on n'y trouve rien à ~*, there's nothing to find fault with; *~ sa parole*, to take back one's word; *~ v.i.* **1.** to recover, to get well again, (of business, etc.) to look up; **2.** to start again, to resume; to set or to go solid again; to take root again; *le froid a repris*, the cold weather has set in again; **se ~** *v.refl.* **1.** to regain self-control; to correct oneself; to check oneself; **2.** to begin again.
représaille [rəprezaj] *s.f.* (usu. pl.) reprisal; retaliation; *user* or *exercer des ~s*, to retaliate.
représentable [rəprezɑ̃tabl] *adj.* representable; (of candidate) suitable.
représentant, -e [rəprezɑ̃tɑ̃] *s.m.f.* representative, delegate, deputy; *~ de commerce*, commercial traveller, agent.
représentati-f, -ve [rəprezɑ̃tatif] *adj.* representative, typical.
représentation [rəprezɑ̃tasjɔ̃] *s.f.* representation; presentation, show, production; performance; likeness, image, picture; display, show, entertainment; (comm.) agency; remonstrance; *faire des ~s à qn.*, to remonstrate with s.o.; (comm.) *faire de la ~*, to be sales representative; *frais de ~*, entertainment allowance; *la ~ nationale*, the representatives of the people (i.e. parliament); *la ~ syndicale*, the trade(s) union representatives.
représenter [rəprezɑ̃te] *v.t.* to present (again), to reintroduce, to represent; to show, to display; to picture, to offer the likeness of, to portray, to describe, to typify, to symbolize; to act, to perform, to personate; to be the delegate of, to stand in the place of; to stand for; (comm.) to travel for, to be agent for, to represent; **se ~** *v.refl.* to imagine, to picture to oneself; to present oneself again; to occur again.
répressible [represibl] *adj.* repressible.
répressi-f, -ve [represif] *adj.* repressive.
répression [represjɔ̃] *s.f.* repression, suppression.
réprimande [reprimɑ̃d] *s.f.* reprimand, rebuke.
réprimander [reprimɑ̃de] *v.t.* to reprimand, to reprove, to rebuke.
réprimer [reprime] *v.t.* to repress, to restrain, to curb, to quell, to check, to hold in check, to suppress.
repris [rəpri] *s.m.* *~ de justice*, old offender.
reprisage [rəprizaʒ] *s.m.* darning, mending.
reprise [rəpriz] *s.f.* retaking, taking back, recapture, resumption, renewal, revival, improvement; darning, mending; (techn.) acceleration, pick-up (of engine); (theatr.) reperformance, revival; (mus.) repeat; (build.) underpinning; (law) reprisal; (boxing) round; (fenc.) bout; (rid.) reprise; *à plusieurs ~s*, several times, over and over again, repeatedly; at more than one go; *à diverses ~s*, at different times, on various occasions; *à deux ~s*, twice, twice over.
repriser [rəprize] *v.t.* to darn, to mend.
réprobat-eur, -rice [reprɔbatœr] *adj.* reproachful, reproving.
réprobation [reprɔbɑsjɔ̃] *s.f.* reprobation, censure, condemnation.
reprochable [rəprɔʃabl] *adj.* reproachable, calling for censure; (law) *témoin ~*, witness to whom exception could be taken.
reproche [rəprɔʃ] *s.m.* reproach, blame; (law) objection to (witnesses, evidence); *sans ~*, blameless; above reproach, irreproachable; unimpeachable.
reprocher [rəprɔʃe] *v.t.* to reproach, (law) to object to (witnesses, etc.); *~ qch à qn.*, to reproach s.o. with or for sth., *~ de*, to reproach with or for, to charge with, to blame, to criticize, to censure, for; **se ~** *v.refl.* to reproach oneself.
reproduct-eur, -rice [rəprɔdyktœr] *adj.* reproductive, reproductory; used for breeding; (fig.) productive, fertile; **~eur** *s.m.* animal used for breeding; **~rice** *s.f.* punched-card machine.
reproduction [rəprɔdyksjɔ̃] *s.f.* reproduction; imitation; republication; copy; manifolding; reproducing, reprinting; breeding (of stock), reproduction.
reproduire [rəprɔdɥir] *v.t.* to reproduce; to imitate, to copy; to republish, to reprint; **se ~** *v.refl.* to be reproduced; to reappear, to occur again, to recur; to breed, to reproduce, to generate offspring; to propagate; to multiply.
réprouvé, -e [repruve] *s.m.f.* reprobate, outcast.
réprouver [repruve] *v.t.* to reprobate, to reprove, to condemn, to disapprove of.
reps [rɛps] *s.m.* (text.) rep, repp.
reptation [rɛptɑsjɔ̃] *s.f.* creeping, crawling.
reptile [rɛptil] *s.m.* reptile; (fig.) slimy creature.
repu, -e [rəpy] *adj.* satiated.
républicain, -e [repyblikɛ̃] *adj., s.m.f.* republican; *~ s.m.* (ornith.) sociable weaver-bird.
(se) républicaniser [repyblikanize] *v.refl.* to become a republican.
républicanisme [repyblikanism] *s.m.* republicanism.
république [repyblik] *s.f.* republic, commonwealth; legitimate government (opp. dictatorship).
répudiation [repydjɑsjɔ̃] *s.f.* repudiation; (law) renunciation.
répudier [repydje] *v.t.* to repudiate; to renounce.
répugnance [repyɲɑ̃s] *s.f.* repulsion, repugnance, reluctance, aversion, unwillingness;

avec ~, unwillingly, reluctantly; *avoir de la* ~ *à faire cela*, to be loath to do that.
répugnant, -e [repyɲɑ̃] *adj.* repugnant, repulsive, disgusting, loathsome.
répugner [repyɲe] *v.t.* to disgust, to repel; ~ *à*, (i.) to be repugnant, repulsive, loathsome, to; (ii.) to feel repugnance, repulsion, loathing, for; to loathe, to abhor.
répulsi-f, -ve [repylsif] *adj.* repulsive, repellent.
répulsion [repylsjɔ̃] *s.f.* repulsion, disgust, aversion.
réputation [repytɑsjɔ̃] *s.f.* reputation, repute, character, name, fame; *perdu de* ~, disreputable; disgraced; of tarnished reputation; *avoir la* ~ *de*, to pass for; to be known for, to be famous or famed for.
réputé, -e [repyte] *adj.* reputed, considered, known (*pour*, for), famous, renowned, of repute.
réputer [repyte] *v.t.* to deem, to esteem, to repute, to hold, to account.
requérable [rəkerabl] *adj.* (law) to be demanded.
requérant, -e [rəkerɑ̃] *adj.* claiming, suing; *s.m.f.* applicant, petitioner, plaintiff.
requérir [rəkerir] *v.t.* to require, to ask, to summon, to call upon; to request, to solicit; (law) to put the case for the prosecution; to demand (penalty, etc.); to fetch, to summon, to call in; ~ *la force publique*, to call in the police.
requête [rəkɛt] *s.f.* request, demand, petition, application; *présenter sa* ~, to present a petition; to make a request; *Maître des requêtes*, master of petitions (in French *Conseil d'État*).
requêter [rəkete] *v.t.* (hunt.) to search again.
requiem [rekɥijɛm] *s.m.invar.* requiem.
requin [rəkɛ̃] *s.m.* (zool. & fig.) shark.
requinquer [rəkɛ̃ke] *v.t.* (fam.) to smarten up; **se** ~ *v.refl.* **1.** to smarten oneself up; **2.** to recover health, strength, spirits, etc., to pick up.
requis, -e [rəki] *adj.* required; requisite, necessary, due; conscripted (for forced labour); ~ *s.m.* labour conscript.
réquisition [rekizisjɔ̃] *s.f.* requisition, demand, application, summons; levy; conscription; commandeering; calling in (of army to assist civil power); *mettre en* ~, to requisition, to commandeer.
réquisitionner [rekizisjɔne] *v.t.* to requisition, to levy, to commandeer.
réquisitoire [rekizitwar] *s.m.* speech for the prosecution, list of charges; list of grievances, series of accusations, indictment.
rescapé, -e [rɛskape] *adj.* surviving; *s.m.f.* survivor.
rescinder [resɛ̃de] *v.t.* (law) to rescind, to annul.
rescision [resizjɔ̃] *s.f.* (law) rescission; annulment; avoiding of contract (owing to misrepresentation, etc.).
rescisoire [resizwar] *adj.* (law) rescissory.
rescousse [rɛskus] *s.f.* retaking, recapture; *à la* ~ *de*, to the rescue of, to the aid of, in support of.
rescription [rɛskripsjɔ̃] *s.f.* (obs.) money order.
rescrit [rɛskri] *s.m.* rescript.
réseau (pl. **-x**) [rezo] *s.m.* net, network, grid; (wire) entanglement; (fig.) web, tangle, system (esp. communications and supply services); (arch.) tracery; (anat) plexus, ganglion; (opt.) diffraction grating, screen; (phys.) structure (of crystals in atom); (zool.) paunch, rumen.
résection [resɛksjɔ̃] *s.f.* (surg.) resection.
réséda [rezeda] *s.m.* (bot.) mignonette; reseda (green).
réséquer [reseke] *v.t.* (surg.) to resect.
réservation [rezɛrvɑsjɔ̃] *s.f.* reservation, booking.
réserve [rezɛrv] *s.f.* reserve, reservation; guardedness; discretion, reticence, wariness; store, reserve; (hunt.) preserve; (mil.) reserves; (dyeing, etc.) resist; (mech.) *pièces de* ~, spare parts; *machine de* ~, stand-by engine; *à la* ~ *de*, except; with reservation of; *mettre en* ~, to lay by, to put by; *se tenir sur la* ~, to be on one's guard, to maintain an attitude of reserve; to be reticent; *sans* ~*s*, without any reservations, unreservedly; *sous toutes* ~*es*, without committing oneself.
réservé, -e [rezɛrve] *adj.* reserved, guarded, reticent, cautious; private; engaged.
réserver [rezɛrve] *v.t.* to reserve, to lay by, to keep back; to spare, to set apart; to keep in store; to destine; **se** ~ *v.refl.* to reserve for oneself; to bide one's time; to wait for an opportunity; *je me réserve de le lui dire*, I shall wait for a more suitable opportunity to tell him.
réserviste [rezɛrvist] *s.m.* (mil.) reservist.
réservoir [rezɛrvwar] *s.m.* tank, cistern, reservoir; *plume à* ~, fountain-pen; ~ *à huile*, oil-tank; ~ *à gaz*, gasholder, gasometer; ~ *à vapeur*, steam-chamber; *wagon-*~, tank-wagon, bulk liquid conveyor.
résidant, -e [rezidɑ̃] *adj.* resident.
résidence [rezidɑ̃s] *s.f.* residence, dwelling, home; residency; *établir sa* ~, to make one's home, to take up residence; ~ *surveillée*, house-arrest.
résident, -e [rezidɑ̃] *s.m.f.* Resident (diplomat, governor, etc.); resident (in foreign country).
résidentiel, -le [rezidɑ̃sjɛl] *adj.* residential.
résider [rezide] *v.i.* to reside, to have one's home or residence; to be based; to consist, to lie; *la difficulté réside en ceci*, the difficulty lies in this.
résidu [rezidy] *s.m.* residue; (chem.) residuum; (arith.) remainder.
résiduaire [rezidɥɛr] *adj.* waste; *eaux* ~*s*, waste water, process water.
résiduel, -le [rezidɥɛl] *adj.* residual.
résignataire [reziɲatɛr] *s.m.* (law) beneficiary.
résignation [reziɲɑsjɔ̃] *s.f.* resigning, resignation.
résigné, -e [reziɲe] *adj.* resigned, submissive, meek.
résigner [reziɲe] *v.t.* to resign; **se** ~ *v.refl.* to resign oneself, to submit, to be resigned.
résiliation [reziljɑsjɔ̃] *s.f.* cancelling, annulling.
résilience [reziljɑ̃s] *s.f.* (phys.) ductility.
résilient, -te [reziljɑ̃] *adj.* (phys.) ductile.
résilier [rezilje] *v.t.* to cancel, to annul.
résille [rezij] *s.f.* hair-net; network; lattice; leads (in stained-glass window).
résine [rezin] *s.f.* resin.
résiné [rezine] *adj.*, *s.m.* (*vin*) ~, retsina (wine).
résiner [rezine] *v.t.* **1.** to extract resin from (pines); **2.** to rosin; to treat with resin.
résineu-x, -se [rezinø] *adj.* resinous.
résini-er, -ère [rezinje] *s.m.* person who extracts resin from pines; *adj.* resin; *industrie* ~*ère*, resin industry.
résinifère [rezinifɛr] *adj.* resiniferous.
résipiscence [rezipisɑ̃s] *s.f.* resipiscence, repentance; *venir à* ~, to mend one's ways, to repent.
résistance [rezistɑ̃s] *s.f.* resistance, endurance, stamina, strength, resistant quality, opposition, resisting, impeding or stopping effect; (aeron.) drag; (electr.) resistance; *bobine de* ~, resistance-coil; *faire* ~, to offer resistance, to resist, to rebel; *éprouver une* ~, to meet with some resistance; *sans* ~, unresistingly; *pièce de* ~, main course (of meal), principal feature, pièce de résistance; (mech.) ~ *à l'écrasement*, compressive strength; *acier à haute* ~, high-tensile, high-resistance, steel; (hist.) *la Résistance*, the Resistance, the resistance movement.
résistant, -e [rezistɑ̃] *adj.* unyielding, resisting;

strong, lasting, firm, tough, resistant; *couleur ~e*, fast colour; ~ *s.m.* (hist.) resister, member of resistance movement.
résister [reziste] *v.i.* to resist, to hold out, not to yield; ~ *à*, to resist, to oppose, to withstand, to endure, to bear, to hold out against, to be resistant to, to be proof against; *vaisselle qui résiste au feu*, fireproof vessel.
résisteur [rezistœr] *s.m.* (phys.) resistor.
résistivité [rezistivite] *s.f.* (electr.) resistivity.
résolu, -e [rezɔly] *adj.* resolute, unwavering, determined, firm of purpose; (of problems, etc.) resolved, solved; **~ment** [rezɔlymɑ̃] *adv.* resolutely, firmly, stoutly.
résoluble [rezɔlybl] *adj.* **1.** resolvable, soluble, resoluble; **2.** (law) annullable, cancellable, terminable.
résoluti-f, -ve [rezɔlytif] *adj.* (med.) resolutive.
résolution [rezɔlysjɔ̃] *s.f.* resolution, solution, solving; (math.) resolution, reduction (of an equation); ~ *d'un contrat*, cancelling of an agreement; *prendre la ~ de*, to make up one's mind to; *changer de ~*, to change one's mind; *agir avec ~*, to act resolutely; *manquer de ~*, to be irresolute.
résolutoire [rezɔlytwar] *adj.* (law) cancelling, resolutive.
résolvant, -e [rezɔlvɑ̃] *adj.* = RÉSOLUTIF.
résolvante [rezɔlvɑ̃t] *s.f.* (math.) resolvent.
résonance [rezɔnɑ̃s] *s.f.* resonance, sympathetic vibration; (electr.) responsiveness; (fig.) echo, response.
résonateur [rezɔnatœr] *s.m.* resonator.
résonnant, -e [rezɔnɑ̃] *adj.* resonant, resounding, echoing; sonorous; (electr.) responsive.
résonnement [rezɔnmɑ̃] *s.m.* (obs.) = RÉSONANCE.
résonner [rezɔne] *v.i.* to resound, to sound, to ring, to echo (*de*, with); *faire ~*, to ring, to sound, (bell, etc.).
résorber [rezɔrbe] *v.t.* to reabsorb, to resorb; (fig.) to solve from within; **se** ~ *v.refl.* to be cured by resorption, to resorb; to be cured or solved internally.
résorcine [rezɔrsin] *s.f.* (chem.) resorcinol.
résorption [rezɔrpsjɔ̃] *s.f.* resorption, reabsorption; (fig.) cure or solution by internal means.
résoudre [rezudr] *v.t.* **1.** to resolve, to solve, to dissolve, to disintegrate, to melt, to dissipate, to break up into parts, to convert (into), to reduce by mental analysis; to cancel; ~ *une équation*, to solve, or reduce, an equation; *cela ne résout pas la question*, that does not settle the question; *nous avons résolu notre bail*, we have cancelled our lease; **2.** to resolve, to determine, to make up one's mind, (*à faire*, to do); *être résolu* (obs.) *de*, (mod.) *à*, *faire qch.*, to be resolved, determined, to have made up one's mind, to do sth.; **3.** to decide (on), to determine, to decree; **se** ~ *v.refl.* **1.** to be dissolved or converted; to be solved; **2.** to decide, to come to a decision, to make up one's mind, to resign oneself, (*à faire*, to do).
respect [rɛspɛ] *s.m.* respect, reverence, regard; (pl.) regards, respects, compliments; *porter ~ à*, to have respect for; ~ *humain*, regard for public opinion; *présenter ses ~s à* to pay one's respects to; *manquer de ~ à*, to be disrespectful towards, to show insufficient courtesy to, to slight; *tenir qn. en ~*, to intimidate s.o., to put s.o. in awe; *sauf votre ~*, begging your pardon, with all due respect, saving your presence, if I may be allowed to say so; *le ~ de soi*(*-même*), self-respect; ⚠ not 'respect' as in 'with respect to'.
respectabilité [rɛspɛktabilite] *s.f.* respectability.
respectable [rɛspɛktabl] *adj.* respectable, worthy of respect; considerable.
respecter [rɛspɛkte] *v.t.* to respect, to have respect for; to spare, to refrain from damaging, offending, interrupting, etc.; **se** ~ *v.refl.* to have respect for oneself, to be self-respecting, to be worthy of one's name; *tout soldat qui se respecte*, any self-respecting soldier, any soldier worthy of the name.
respecti-f, -ve [rɛspɛktif] *adj.* respective; reciprocal, mutual; **~vement** [rɛspɛktivmɑ̃] *adv.* respectively; mutually.
respectueu-x, -se [rɛspɛktɥø] *adj.* respectful, deferential; **~sement** [rɛspɛktɥøzmɑ̃] *adv.* respectfully, deferentially.
respirable [rɛspirabl] *adj.* fit to be breathed, breathable.
respirateur [rɛspiratœr] *s.m.* respirator; machine for ensuring artificial respiration.
respiration [rɛspirɑsjɔ̃] *s.f.* respiration, breathing; *difficulté de ~*, shortness of breath; *avoir la ~ coupée*, to be out of breath; *ce vent vous coupe la ~*, this wind takes one's breath away.
respiratoire [rɛspiratwar] *adj.* respiratory; *appareil ~*, respiratory system; breathing apparatus.
respirer [rɛspire] *v.t.i.* to breathe, to respire; to live; to exhale; to express, to manifest; to rest, to have a respite; *ah! je respire!*, ah, that's better!; *laissez-moi ~*, let me take breath; give me some respite; *elle respire la santé*, she is the living embodiment of health.
resplendir [rɛsplɑ̃dir] *v.i.* to be resplendent, to shine.
resplendissant, -e [rɛsplɑ̃disɑ̃] *adj.* resplendent, dazzling, bright, shining.
responsabilité [rɛspɔ̃sabilite] *s.f.* responsibility; liability.
responsable [rɛspɔ̃sabl] *adj.* responsible, answerable, accountable, liable, (*de*, for; *envers*, to).
resquille [rɛskij] *s.f.*, **resquillage** [rɛskijaʒ] *s.m.* entry or travelling without payment, gate-crashing; *en ~*, without payment.
resquiller [rɛskije] *v.i.* to go in or travel without payment, to have a free ride, to gate-crash; ~ *v.t.* ~ *une place*, not to pay for one's seat.
resquilleu-r, -se [rɛskijœr] *s.m.f.* one who gets a free place or ride (illicitly), gate-crasher.
ressac [rəsak] *s.m.* surf; undertow.
ressaisir [rəsezir] *v.t.* to seize again, to catch again, to recover, to regain; **se** ~ *v.refl.* to regain one's self-control; to regain control of the situation; *se ~ de qch.*, to recapture, to regain possession of, sth.
ressasser [rəsase] *v.t.* **1.** to resift; **2.** to keep on repeating, to say over and over again.
ressasseur [rəsasœr] *s.m.* one who is constantly saying the same thing.
ressaut [rəso] *s.m.* projection; abrupt fall or rise, dip, difference of level.
ressauter [rəsote] *v.t.i.* to jump again.
ressayer [reseje], **réessayer** [reeseje] *v.t.* to try again, to reattempt, to try on again.
ressemblance [rəsɑ̃blɑ̃s] *s.f.* resemblance, likeness.
ressemblant, -e [rəsɑ̃blɑ̃] *adj.* like, similar, very much alike; true to life.
ressembler [rəsɑ̃ble] *v.t.* ~ *à*, to be like, to resemble, to be similar to, to be akin to, to be a true picture of; (fig.) to match, to be worthy of; (fam.) *à quoi ressemble-t-il?*, what does he look like?; *ne ~ à rien*, (i.) to be like nothing else, to be quite out of the ordinary; (ii.) to be like nothing on earth, to be shapeless or awful; *le style ressemble à l'homme*, the style is worthy of the man; **se** ~ *v.refl.* to be alike, to resemble or be like each other; *les jours se suivent et ne se ressemblent pas*, no two days are alike; *qui se ressemble s'assemble*, birds of a feather flock together.
ressemelage [rəsəmlaʒ] *s.m.* resoling, resole.
ressemeler [rəsəmle] *v.t.* to resole.
ressemer [rəsme] *v.t.* to sow again, to resow; **se** ~ *v.refl.* to seed itself.

ressentiment [rəsɑ̃timɑ̃] *s.m.* resentment, grievance; (obs.) twinge (of old pain, etc.), sudden painful remembrance; (obs.) feeling of gratitude.

ressentir [rəsɑ̃tir] *v.t.* to feel, to feel the effects of, to be much affected or upset by, to suffer; to resent; **se** ~ *v.refl.* **1.** (obs.) to remember with resentment or with gratitude; **2.** to feel, to (continue to) feel the effects of; *se ~ d'une chute*, to be still suffering the effects of a fall; **3.** (pop.) *s'en ~ pour*, to be in good form for (doing sth.), to be all set to (do sth.).

resserre [rəsɛr] *s.f.* lock-up store, store-room.

resserré, -e [rəsere] *adj.* narrow, confined, cramped, shut in.

resserrement [rəsɛrmɑ̃] *s.m.* tightening, contraction, closeness, tightness; confinement.

resserrer [rəsere] *v.t.* to contract, to tighten, to draw together, to close (up), to abridge, to condense; to bind; to lock up again, to put back again in its place; *~ les liens de l'amitié*, to strengthen the bonds of friendship; **se** ~ *v.refl.* to contract, to shrink, to become narrower or tighter; (of fog, etc.) to get thicker; to draw together, to huddle; (fig.) to become closer.

resservir [rəsɛrvir] *v.t.* to serve (a dish) again; (fig.) to serve up again; ~ *v.i.* to be used again, to be still useful; **se ~ de** *v.refl.* to use again.

ressort [rəsɔr] *s.m.* **1.** spring, elasticity; (fig.) energy, means; *faire ~*, to spring, to bounce, to fly, back; *avoir du ~*, to be springy or elastic; *~ à boudin* or *hélicoïdal*, coil-spring; *~ à lames*, leaf-spring; *~ de choc*, buffer-spring; *main de ~*, shackle; *~ de rappel*, reaction-spring; *faire jouer tous les ~s*, to set every wheel in motion; to pull out all the stops; to leave no stone unturned; **2.** jurisdiction, department, province; *cela n'est pas de mon ~*, that does not come within my province; that is not in my line; *en dernier ~*, in the last resort; without appeal.

ressortir[1] [rəsɔrtir] *v.i.* to go or come out again; to stand out; to result; to appear, to emerge; *faire ~*, to show off, to make to stand out, to bring out, to emphasize.

ressortir[2] [rəsɔrtir] *v.i.* ~ *à*, to be under the jurisdiction of, to be within the province of, to pertain to; to concern; to be related to; *cette affaire ressortit au juge de paix*, this case falls under the jurisdiction of the magistrate.

ressortissant, -e [rəsɔrtisɑ̃] *adj., s.m.f.* (person) under the jurisdiction (*à*, of).

ressouder [rəsude] *v.t.* to resolder; (fig.) to unite again, to mend.

ressource [rəsurs] *s.f.* **1.** resource, device, shift, expedient; *en dernière ~*, as a last resort; **2.** (pl.) resources, money, means, fortune; *se trouver sans ~s*, to be without means; to be impoverished.

(**se**) **ressouvenir** [rəsuvnir] *v.refl.* to remember; *se ~ de*, to call to mind again; *faire ~*, to remind.

ressusciter [resysite] *v.t.* to resuscitate, to revive, to restore to life, consciousness, vigour, etc.; ~ *v.i.* to revive, to return to life, to resuscitate, to be resuscitated.

ressuyer [resɥije] *v.t.* to dry.

restant, -e [rɛstɑ̃] *adj.* left, remaining, surviving; *poste ~e*, poste restante; ~ *s.m.* rest, remainder.

restaurant [rɛstɔrɑ̃] *s.m.* restaurant, (hotel, etc.) dining-room.

restaurat-eur, -rice [rɛstɔratœr] *s.m.f.* **1.** restorer, repairer; **2.** restaurant proprietor, restaurateur.

restauration [rɛstɔrɑsjɔ̃] *s.f.* **1.** restoration, restoring, repair; (hist.) *la Restauration*, the Restoration (of the Bourbons, 1814–1830); **2.** restaurant-keeping; restaurant.

restaurer [rɛstɔre] *v.t.* to restore, to re-establish, to repair; **se** ~ *v.refl.* to refresh oneself, to have something to eat (esp. in order to regain strength); ⚠ not 'to restore' in sense 'to give back'.

reste [rɛst] *s.m.* rest, residue, remainder, remnant, remains; leavings; scraps; (math.) remainder; *paix à ses ~s*, peace to his ashes; *être en ~ avec*, to owe to, to be indebted to; *je ne veux pas être en ~ avec vous*, I do not want to be in your debt; *ne pas demander son ~*, to have had enough of it, not to wait for any more, to disappear abruptly; *jouir de son ~*, to make the most of what is left to one (of time, money, life, etc.); *jouer son ~*, to stake all that is left to one; *j'en ai de ~*, I have more than enough; *il a de la bonté de ~!*, it's a case of misplaced kindness!; *au ~*, *du ~*, besides, moreoever, also.

rester [rɛste] *v.i.* to remain, to stay, to stay behind, to stop; to live; to be left; to continue, to stand, to last, to keep, to endure; *~ en arrière* to remain behind, to fall or lag behind; *une œuvre qui restera*, a work which will last; *~ debout*, to remain standing, to stand; *~ court*, not to know what to say; to stop short; *il est resté interloqué*, he stood there nonplussed; *je suis resté deux heures à faire cela*, I spent two hours doing that; *~ chez soi*, to stay at home, to be at home; *~ sur la bonne bouche*, to keep something nice for the finish; (fig.) to remember only the nice parts; *~ sur sa faim*, to stop eating before one is full; *reste à savoir si*, it remains to be seen whether; *le seul ami qui me reste*, the only friend I have left; *il ne lui restait rien à faire que de*, all he could do was to; *il ne me reste que 20 francs*, I have only 20 francs left; *je reste votre fidèlement dévoué*, I remain yours truly; *restons-en là*, let us stop at that; that will do; let us say no more about it; *j'en étais resté à*, I had just been telling (or saying), I had got to the point where; *où en est-il resté dans sa lecture?*, where did he get to, or stop, in his reading?; *ils en sont restés aux lampes à pétrole*, they are still in the era of paraffin lamps; *elle n'en restera pas là*, she will not be content with that; *comme vous êtes resté lontemps!*, what a long time you have been!; (car) *~ en panne*, to break down; *~ en route*, to stop on the way, (fig.) to get stuck, to come to a full stop, to fall by the wayside; *il n'en reste pas moins que*, it is none the less true that; *reste qu'il faudra lui parler*, all the same, we shall have to speak to him.

restituable [rɛstitɥabl] *adj* repayable, refundable.

restituer [rɛstitɥe] *v.t.* to make restitution of; to restore, to return, to give back.

restitution [rɛstitysjɔ̃] *s.f.* restitution; restoring; reparation; *opérer la ~ de*, to make restitution of.

restoroute [rɛstɔrut] *s.m.* restaurant on main road or motorway.

restreindre [rɛstrɛ̃dr] *v.t.* to restrict, to limit, to shorten, to curtail, to cut down; to restrain; **se** ~ *v.refl.* to restrain oneself; to limit oneself; to cut down expenses, to retrench.

restricti-f, -ve [rɛstriktif] *adj.* restrictive.

restriction [rɛstriksjɔ̃] *s.f.* restraint, restriction, cutting down; reserve, reservation; *~ mentale*, mental reservation; *sans ~s*, without restriction, unrestricted, unreservedly.

restringent, -e [rɛstrɛ̃ʒɑ̃] *adj.* (med.) astringent.

restructuration [rəstryktyrɑsjɔ̃] *s.f.* restructuring.

restructurer [rəstryktyre] *v.t.* to restructure.

resucée [rəsyse] *s.f.* **1.** (fam.) another drink; **2.** repeat, rehash.

résultant, -e [rezyltɑ̃] *adj.* resulting; *~e s.f.* (math., phys.) resultant; (fig.) result, product.

résultat [rezylta] *s.m.* result, issue, consequence, outcome; (math.) result; *sans ~*, without result, in vain, fruitless, fruitlessly, ineffectual; (sport) *match sans ~*, draw.

résulter [rezylte] *v.i.* to result; ~ *de*, to result from, to be the outcome of, to arise from, to follow from; to emerge or appear from; *ce qui en résulte*, the result or outcome (of it); *il en résulte que*, consequently, the result is that, it follows that; *il résulte des aveux du prévenu que*, it appears from the admissions of the accused that.

résumé [rezyme] *s.m.* summary, résumé, epitome, abstract, synopsis, abridgement, compendium; *faire le* ~ *de*, to sum up; *en* ~, in short, to sum up, in brief.

résumer [rezyme] *v.t.* to sum up, to recapitulate, to abridge, to give a summary of, to summarize, to resume; **se** ~ *v.refl.* to be summed up, to be reduced (*à*, to); ⚠ not 'to resume' as in 'to resume work', 'to resume one's place'.

résurgence [rezyrʒɑ̃s] *s.f.* resurgence, reappearance (of underground stream).

resurgir [rəsyrʒir] *v.i.* to rise again; to arise suddenly, to re-emerge.

résurrection [rezyrɛksjɔ̃] *s.f.* resurrection, revival, resurrecting.

rétable [retabl] *s.m.* retable, reredos.

rétabli, -e [retabli] *adj.* re-established; cured.

rétablir [retablir] *v.t.* to re-establish, to restore, to repair, to retrieve, to readjust; to restore to health; ~ *ses affaires*, to retrieve one's losses; ~ *sa santé*, to recover one's health; ~ *la vérité*, to correct false statements; to state the real truth; to establish the truth; **se** ~ *v.refl.* to recover one's health; to be re-established or restored.

rétablissement [retablismɑ̃] *s.m.* re-establishment, restoration, recovery, recovery of balance, return to health; revival; (gymn.) pull-up.

retaille [rətɑj] *s.f.* parings, cuttings, shreds, waste bits.

retailler [rətɑje] *v.t.* to cut again, to prune again, to resharpen (pencil), to recut (file).

rétamage [retamaʒ] *s.m.* retinning, mending of saucepans, etc.; resilvering (of glass).

rétamer [retame] *v.t.* to retin; to resilver (glass); to tinker.

rétameur [retamœr] *s.m.* tinker.

retaper [rətape] *v.t.* to do up; to mend, to patch up; to fluff up; (fam.) to fix up, to put right.

retapisser [rətapise] *v.t.* to repaper (walls).

retard [rətar] *s.m.* delay, slowness; lateness; backwardness; (techn.) retardation, lag, retarding device; *en* ~, late, behind time, behindhand, overdue, in arrears; *avoir du* ~, to be late, overdue, etc., (of watch) to be slow; *être en* ~ *de dix minutes*, to be ten minutes late; *votre montre est en* ~ *de cinq minutes*, your watch is five minutes slow; ~ *à l'allumage*, retarded ignition; *fusée à* ~, delayed-action fuse.

retardataire [rətardatɛr] *adj.* late, behindhand, in arrears; ~ *s.m.f.* late comer, loiterer, laggard, one who is in arrears; out-of-date person; (mil.) one who overstays leave.

retardat-eur, -rice [rətardatœr] *adj.* (phys., techn.) retarding.

retardation [rətardɑsjɔ̃] *s.f.* (phys.) retardation.

retardé, -e [rətarde] *adj.* **1.** delayed; **2.** retarded, backward; *un* ~, a backward child.

retardement [rətardəmɑ̃] *s.m.* delay, putting off; retardment; *à* ~, with or by delayed action; *bombe à* ~, time-bomb; (photo.) *dispositif à* ~, delayed-action shutter.

retarder [rətarde] *v.t.* to retard, to delay, to make late, to hold up, to keep back, to hinder; ~ *sa montre*, to put one's watch back; ~ *v.i.* to be slow, to be late; tol ag, to fall behind; to be old-fashioned or behind the times; (fam.) not to be up to date (on the latest news); (of watch) to be slow; *vous retardez de cinq minutes*, you are five minutes late; your watch is five minutes slow.

retâter [rətɑte] *v.t.* to touch again; ~ *de*, to have another taste of, to try again.

reteindre [rətɛ̃dr] *v.t.* to dye again, to redye.

retendre [rətɑ̃dr] *v.t.* to stretch again; to hang up (line, etc.) again; to hold out (hand, etc.) again; to tighten; to reset (spring, etc.).

retenir [rətənir] *v.t.* to keep back, to return, to keep, to detain, to hold, to hold back, to withhold, to delay; to remember, to recollect; to hold in, to check, to restrain, to prevent, to hinder; to deduct; to reserve or book (seats); to engage (servants, etc.), to have (sth.) reserved; (arith.) to carry; ~ *sa langue*, to hold one's tongue, to put a curb on one's tongue; ~ *sa colère*, to restrain one's anger; *qu'est-ce qui vous retient?*, what is stopping you?; *retenez bien ceci*, be sure to remember this; ~ *par cœur*, to memorize; *donner et* ~ *ne vaut*, one cannot have one's cake and eat it; ~ *l'eau*, to hold water, to be watertight; ~ *les eaux d'une rivière*, to impound the water of a river; ~ *prisonnier*, to keep prisoner; ~ *en ôtage*, to hold as a hostage; **se** ~ *v.refl.* to restrain oneself, to keep back, to refrain, (*de*, from), to stop (oneself), to check oneself; to control oneself; *se* ~ *à*, to catch hold of, to cling to, to clutch at.

retenter [rətɑ̃te] *v.t.* to try again, to reattempt.

rétent-eur, -rice [retɑ̃tœr] *adj.* retentive, retaining; restraining.

rétention [retɑ̃sjɔ̃] *s.f.* retention, reservation; keeping back; (arith.) carrying over.

retentir [rətɑ̃tir] *v.i.* to resound, to ring, to re-echo; (fig.) to have repercussions.

retentissant, -e [rətɑ̃tisɑ̃] *adj.* resounding, ringing, sonorous, echoing; (fig.) sensational.

retentissement [rətɑ̃tismɑ̃] *s.m.* resounding, ringing; echo, fame, sensation; *avoir un grand* ~, to cause a great stir, to arouse widespread interest.

retenu, -e [rətny] *adj.* **1.** reserved, put aside; **2.** restrained, inhibited; (fig.) restrained, discreet.

retenue [rətny] *s.f.* reserve, moderation, modesty, discretion; caution, self-control, wariness; stoppage of pay; deduction; detention (of goods); damming back, dam; (naut.) stay; (at school) *être en* ~, to be kept in; (arith.) *et 3 de* ~, and 3 to carry; (techn.) *palan de* ~, staying-tackle; ~ *d'air*, airlock, air pocket (in pipe, etc.).

retercer, reterser [rətɛrse] *v.t.* to give the fourth dressing to (vines).

réticence [retisɑ̃s] *s.f.* reticence, reserve, hesitation; reservation; concealment, non-disclosure (of fact, etc.); leaving the rest of one's sentence to be understood.

réticent, -e [retisɑ̃] *adj.* **1.** not saying all one means; (of statement, etc.) unrevealing, incomplete, containing omissions; **2.** reticent, reserved, uncommunicative, not forthcoming.

réticulaire [retikylɛr] *adj.* reticular.

réticule [retikyl] *s.m.* vanity bag; (ant.) hair-net; (opt.) reticle, graticule.

réticulé, -e [retikyle] *adj.* reticulated.

réti-f, -ve [retif] *adj.* restive; unmanageable, mulish.

rétine [retin] *s.f.* (anat.) retina.

retirable [rətirabl] *adj.* removable, which can be drawn back.

retiration [rətirɑsjɔ̃] *s.f.* (print.) backing, printing of verso; *presse à* ~, perfecting-machine.

retiré, -e [rətire] *adj.* isolated, remote, secluded, retired; *vivre très* ~, to lead a secluded life; ~ *des affaires*, retired from business.

retirement [rətirmɑ̃] *s.m.* **1.** withdrawal; **2.** contraction, retraction.

retirer [rətire] *v.t.* to pull back again, to draw back; to extract, to draw out, to get, to obtain, to derive; to withdraw; to take back, to remove; to retract, to recall; ~ *grand profit de*, to profit greatly by; ~ *sa parole*, to go back on one's word;

~ *ses paroles*, to retract one's words; ~ *son vêtement*, to take off one's coat, etc.; **se** ~ *v.refl.* to retire, to withdraw, to retreat, to recede; to go home; to go to bed; to ebb; to go away; to contract, to shrink; *retirez-vous!*, leave the room! be off!; *vous pouvez vous* ~, you may go; *se* ~ *des affaires*, to retire from business; *cette étoffe se retire au lavage*, this material shrinks in the wash.

retombe [rətɔ̃b] *s.f.* **1.** (arch.) springing; **2.** *feuille de* ~, annexe (to document, plan, etc.).

retombée [rətɔ̃be] *s.f.* **1.** (arch.) springing; fall, drop, hang (of curtains, etc.); **2.** fall, falling; (radioactive) fall-out.

retomber [rətɔ̃be] *v.i.* to fall again, to fall back, to sink back, to subside, to relapse, to have a relapse; to hang down; *la conversation retombe sur les mêmes sujets*, the conversation comes back to the same theme; *la responsabilité retombe sur vous*, the responsibility falls on you; ~ *toujours sur ses pieds*, always to fall on one's feet.

retondre [rətɔ̃dr] *v.t.* to shear again; (arch.) to clean off.

retordage [rətɔrdaʒ], **retordement** [rətɔrdəmɑ̃] *s.m.* retwisting.

retordeu-r, -se [rətɔrdœr] *s.m.f.* (text.) twister; ~**se** *s.f.* twister (machine).

retordoir [rətɔrdwar], **retorsoir** [rətɔrswar] *s.m.* (text.) doubling and twisting machine.

retordre [rətɔrdr] *v.t.* to twist again; (text.) to twist; (fig.). *donner du fil à* ~ *à qn.*, to give s.o. a lot of bother, to cause s.o. headaches.

rétorquer [retɔrke] *v.t.* to retort, to make an argument tell against its user; *cet argument peut se* ~, that argument can be thrown back at you.

retors, -e [rətɔr] *adj.* twisted; crafty, cunning, shrewd; *un homme* ~, a wily bird, a slippery customer.

rétorsion [retɔrsjɔ̃] *s.f.* **1.** turning an argument against its user; **2.** retaliation, reprisals; *mesures de* ~, retaliatory measures.

retouche [rətuʃ] *s.f.* retouch, retouching; correction; touching up; alteration (of garment).

retoucher [rətuʃe] *v.t.* to touch again; to touch up, to retouch; to improve; to alter (garment).

retoucheu-r, -se [rətuʃœr] *s.m.f.* (photo.) retoucher, finisher.

retour [rətur] *s.m.* return, coming back, coming home; repetition, recurrence; backfire, backlash; (law) reversion; winding; decline, wane; reciprocity; recompense; (arch.) return; vicissitude; *billet d'aller et* ~, return ticket; *son amour n'est pas payé de* ~, his love is not returned, or reciprocated; *sans esprit de* ~, for good; irretrievably; *perdu sans* ~, past all hope; *il n'est pas encore de* ~, he is not yet back; *à votre* ~, on your return; *en* ~, in return (*de*, for); *faire* ~ *à*, to revert to; *faire un* ~ *sur soi-même*, to look into one's heart; to examine one's conscience; *les* ~*s de la fortune*, the vicissitudes of fortune; *les tours et* ~*s de la rivière*, the windings and turnings of the river; *chargement de* ~, return cargo; *par* ~ (*du courrier*), by return (of post); *être sur le* ~, to be on the wrong side of forty; to be on the wane; *beauté sur le* ~, beauty on the wane; (fig.) *un vieux cheval de* ~, an old offender; ~ *d'âge*, menopause, change of life; *en* ~ *d'équerre*, at right angles; (car) ~ *de manivelle*, kickback (of starting-handle); ~ *de flamme*, (lit. & fig.) backfire; ~ *de gaz*, blow-back; (electr.) ~ *par la terre*, earth return, earthing, earth circuit; (comm.) *avec facilité de* ~, on sale or return basis; (cin.) ~ *en arrière*, flashback; ⚠ not 'return' in sense 'yield'.

retournage [rəturnaʒ] *s.m.* turning (of garment).

retourne [rəturn] *s.f.* turn-up card; *la* ~ *est de pique*, spades are trumps.

retournement [rəturnəmɑ̃] *s.m.* turning, turning over, turning round or back, turning inside out; turning upside down, being upside down; (photo.) reversal (of negative); (fig.) complete transformation, reversal, volte-face, U-turn.

retourner [rəturne] *v.t.i.* to turn again, to turn back, to send back; to turn over, to turn upside down; (lit. & fig.) to turn inside out; to turn round; to return, to go back; to be brought back, to be returned; to turn up (card); ~ *sur ses pas*, to retrace one's steps; ~ *un projet*, to turn over, to examine, a proposal; ~ *un vêtement*, to turn a garment; ~ *sa casaque*, to turn one's coat, to change sides; **se** ~ *v.refl.* to turn round, to turn over or upside down; (fig.) *avoir le temps de se* ~, to have time to look round, to find one's feet; *il sait se* ~, he can speedily adapt himself (to change); *s'en* ~, to go back; *se* ~ *contre* to turn against (ally, etc.).

retracer [rətrase] *v.t.* to retrace; to relate, to picture, to evoke, to conjure up.

rétractable [retraktabl] *adj.* retractable.

rétractation [retraktɑsjɔ̃] *s.f.* retractation, retraction, recantation.

rétracter [retrakte] *v.t.* to retract; to unsay, to withdraw, to recall, to recant; **se** ~ *v.refl.* to contract; to retract, to eat one's words.

rétractile [retraktil] *adj.* retractile.

rétractilité [retraktilite] *s.f.* retractility.

rétraction [retraksjɔ̃] *s.f.* retraction, contraction, drawing-in.

retraduire [rətradɥir] *v.t.* to retranslate.

retrait, -e [rətrɛ] *adj.* shrunk, shrivelled, contracted, warped; retracted; (law) redeemed.

retrait [rətrɛ] *s.m.* shrinkage, contraction; withdrawal; (law) redemption; recess; ~ *d'emploi*, dismissal, discharge, compulsory retirement; *en* ~, receding, retreating, withdrawn, set back; (print.) indented.

retraite[1] [rətrɛt] *s.f.* retreat, retiring; shelter, seclusion; superannuation; retiring pension; retirement (from business, world, etc.); (eccles.) retreat; (mil.) retreat; drum-beat or bugle-call as the signal for retreat; *battre en* ~, to beat a retreat, to retreat; *battre la* ~, to beat the tattoo, to beat retreat; *sonner la* ~, to sound the retreat; *mettre à la* ~, to pension off, to superannuate; *prendre sa* ~, to retire on a pension; *en* ~, retired; *couper la* ~ *à qn.*, to cut off someone's retreat; *vivre dans la* ~, to live in retirement; *donner* ~ *à qn.*, to harbour or shelter s.o.; ~ *des vieux*, old-age pension; ~ *de voleurs*, den of thieves.

retraite[2] [rətrɛt] *s.f.* (comm.) redraft, renewed bill.

retraité, -e [rətrete] *adj.* pensioned off, on the retired list, retired, superannuated; *s.m.f.* one who is retired, pensioner.

retraitement [rətrɛtmɑ̃] *s.m.* (nuclear phys.) fuel reprocessing.

retranchement [rətrɑ̃ʃmɑ̃] *s.m.* retrenchment, suppression; excision; curtailment; (mil.) entrenchment, retrenchment.

retrancher [rətrɑ̃ʃe] *v.t.* to retrench, to cut off, to suppress, to curtail; to deduct, to subtract, to take away; (mil.) to entrench; ~ *qch. à qn.*, to deprive s.o. of sth.; **se** ~ *v.refl.* to entrench oneself, to dig in, to shelter, to take refuge, to shut oneself up; to cut oneself off.

retranscrire [rətrɑ̃skrir] *v.t.* to recopy, to retranscribe.

retransmetteur [rətrɑ̃smɛtœr] *s.m.* (radio, TV) retransmitter, booster.

retransmettre [rətrɑ̃smɛtr] *v.t.* to retransmit; to pass on (message, etc.).

retransmission [rətrɑ̃smisjɔ̃] *s.f.* (radio, TV) retransmission, rebroadcast; transmission of pre-recorded programme.

retravailler [rətravaje] *v.t.* (also ~ *à*) to do

further work on, to go over (sth.) again, (fig.) to polish; ~ *v.i.* to work again, to resume work.
retraverser [rətravɛrse] *v.t.* to cross again, to recross, to go over or through again.
rétréci, -e [retresi] *adj.* narrow, shrunk, contracted; limited.
rétrécir [retresir] *v.t.i.* to narrow, to make narrower, to make smaller; to diminish, to contract; **se** ~ *v.refl.* to become narrower, to diminish, to contract.
rétrécissement [retresismɑ̃] *s.m.* narrowing, narrowness, shrinking, contraction; narrow portion, neck; (med.) stricture, constriction.
retrempe [rətrɑ̃p] *s.f.* retempering (of steel).
retremper [rətrɑ̃pe] *v.t.* **1.** to retemper (steel); (fig.) ~ *qch.*, to give new vigour to sth. (*à*, through); **2.** to soak again; **se** ~ *v.refl. se* ~ *à*, to acquire new vigour from; *se* ~ *dans*, (i.) to plunge again into; (ii.) to gain fresh strength from, to steel oneself through.
rétribuer [retribɥe] *v.t.* to remunerate, to pay, to reward; to pay for (services, etc.).
rétribution [retribysjɔ̃] *s.f.* remuneration, fee, pay, salary, reward; (fig.) reward, recompense; ⚠ not 'retribution' in sense 'punishment'.
retriever [retrivœr] *s.m.* retriever (dog).
rétro [retro] *adj.invar.* old-fashioned (esp. of Twenties style).
rétro [retro] *s.m.* abbrev. *rétroviseur*; *d'effet rétrograde*.
rétroacti-f, -ve [retroaktif] *adj.* retroactive; retrospective.
rétro-action [retrɔaksjɔ̃] *s.f.* retroaction, reaction; ~**activement** [retrɔaktivmɑ̃] *adv.* retroactively, retrospectively; ~**activité** [retrɔaktivite] *s.f.* retroactivity, retrospective effect, back-dating; ~**céder** [retrɔsede] *v.t.* to give or cede back again; (law) to reconvey, to reassign; ~**cession** [retrɔsesjɔ̃] *s.f.* retrocession, ceding back; (law) reconveyance, reassignment; ~**chargeuse** [retrɔʃarʒøz] *s.f.* back-loader (machine); ~**diffusion** [retrɔdifyzjɔ̃] *s.f.* (nuclear phys.) back-scatter; ~**fusée** [retrɔfyze] *s.f.* retro-rocket, rocket exerting braking effect; ~**gradation** [retrɔgradɑsjɔ̃] *s.f.* retrogradation, retrogression; downgrading (of official, etc.), demotion; (mil.) reduction in rank; ~**grade** [retrɔgrad] *adj.* retrograde, backward, reversed; reactionary; *mouvement* ~*grade*, reverse motion, movement in reverse; (billiards) *effet* ~*grade*, screw-back; *faire l'effet de* ~*grade*, to put bottom on the ball; ~**grader** [retrɔgrade] *v.i.* to retrogress, to go backwards, to regress; (car) to change down; *v.t.* to downgrade, to demote; (mil.) to reduce to lower rank; ~**gression** [retrɔgresjɔ̃] *s.f.* retrogression, motion in reverse, backward movement; ~**pédalage** [retrɔpedalaʒ] *s.m.* back-pedalling.
rétrospecti-f, -ve [retrɔspɛktif] *adj.* retrospective; ~**vement** [retrɔspɛktivmɑ̃] *adv.* retrospectively, after the event.
rétrospective [retrospɛktiv] *s.f.* retrospective or historical exhibition of artist's work; series of films by well-known producer.
retroussé, -e [rətruse] *adj.* turned up, tucked up; *un nez* ~, a snub or up-tilted nose.
retroussement [rətrusmɑ̃] *s.m.* turning up, tucking up.
retrousser [rətruse] *v.t.* to turn up, to tuck up; **se** ~ *v.refl.* to tuck up one's dress; to be turned up.
retroussis [rətrusi] *s.m.* tucking-up; turn-up; (turned back) facings; *botte à* ~, top-boot.
retrouvailles [rətruvɑj] *s.f.pl.* (fam.) reunion.
retrouver [rətruve] *v.t.* to find again, to recover, to meet (again), to come back for (s.o.), to come and pick (s.o.) up; to recognize; **se** ~ *v.refl.* to find each other again, to meet again; to find one's way again, to get one's bearings; *je n'arrive pas à m'y* ~, I cannot make head or tail of it; I am all at sea; *comme on se retrouve!*, how small the world is!
rétroversion [retrovɛrsjɔ̃] *s.f.* (med.) retroversion.
rétroviseur [retrɔvizœr] *s.m.* (car) driving mirror.
rets [rɛ] *s.m.* net; (fig.) snare, trap, toils; *pris dans les* ~, ensnared.
réuni, -e [reyni] *adj.* reunited, united, together, put together.
réunification [reynifikɑsjɔ̃] *s.f.* reunification.
réunifier [reynifje] *v.t.* to reunite.
réunion [reynjɔ̃] *s.f.* reunion, collection, body, gathering, assembly, meeting, party, joining again, junction; reconciliation.
réunir [reynir] *v.t.* to reunite, to unite, to join together, to join again, to join; to gather, to assemble, to muster; to collect; to bring together; to combine; to reconcile; to connect; **se** ~ *v.refl.* to gather, to meet, to assemble, to be reunited; to combine; to amalgamate; to concur.
réussi, -e [reysi] *adj.* successful, well done, which is a success, which comes off; *mal* ~(*e*), unsuccessful, spoilt; (fam.) *une pièce mal* ~*e*, a play which is a flop.
réussir [reysir] *v.i.* to be successful, to be a success, to succeed; to turn out well; to prosper. to thrive; *mal* ~, to be a failure, to turn out badly; ~ *à passer*, to succeed in getting through; *tout lui a réussi*, everything went all right for him, he carried it off; ~ *v.t.* to do (sth.) well, to be successful at, to succeed in, to pass (examination etc.); ~ *le coup*, to bring it off, to do the trick; *elle réussit bien les omelettes*, she is a good hand at omelettes; *ce qu'il réussit le mieux, c'est*, what he is best at is.
réussite [reysit] *s.f.* **1.** success, upshot, happy issue or result; **2.** (card-game) patience,
revacciner [rəvaksine] *v.t.* to revaccinate.
revaloir [rəvalwar] *v.t.* to return, to repay; *je lui revaudrai ça*, I shall make him pay for it; I will get even with him; I will pay him out.
revalorisation [rəvalɔrizɑsjɔ̃] *s.f.* revaluation; enhanced value.
revaloriser [rəvalɔrize] *v.t.* to revalue; to enhance the value of.
revanchard, -e [rəvɑ̃ʃar] *adj., s.m.f.* revengeful (person); (pol.) revanchist.
revanche [rəvɑ̃ʃ) *s.f.* revenge, return, return match; *à charge de* ~, on condition of a like return; one good turn deserves another; *en* ~, in return; on the other hand; *prendre sa* ~, to take one's revenge; to play the return match; to have another try at it.
(**se**) **revancher** [rəvɑ̃ʃe] *v.refl.* to revenge oneself, to give as good as one gets; to take the upper hand.
rêvasser [rɛvase] *v.i.* to dream idly; to muse, to day-dream; to have one dream after another; to have confused dreams.
rêvasserie [rɛvasri] *s.f.* musing, day-dreaming, idle fancies.
rêvasseu-r, -se [rɛvasœr] *s.m.f.* idle dreamer, muser.
rêve [rɛv] *s.m.* dream; idle fancy, day-dream, illusion.
revêche [rəvɛʃ] *adj.* harsh, rough; cross, ill--tempered, cantankerous.
réveil [revɛj] *s.m.* waking, awakening; alarm (clock); (mil.) reveille; (fig.) awakening; disillusionment; *à mon* ~, *au* ~, on waking.
réveille-matin [revɛjmatɛ̃] *s.m.invar.* alarm clock; (bot.) variety of spurge.
réveiller [reveje] *v.t.* to wake, to wake up, to rouse; to revive, to quicken, to stir up; to recall;

to evoke; ~ *des souvenirs,* to reawaken memories; **se** ~ *v.refl.* to wake, to wake up, to be roused, to be revived.
réveillon [revɛjɔ̃] *s.m.* Christmas or New Year's Eve (midnight) supper; New Year's Eve party.
réveillonner [revɛjɔne] *v.i.* to have a midnight party.
révélat-eur, -rice [revelatœr] *adj.* revealing, tell-tale, disclosing; **~eur** *s.m.* informer; detector, indicator, warning (light, etc.); (photo.) developer.
révélation [revelɑsjɔ̃] *s.f.* revelation, disclosure, discovery.
révéler [revele] *v.t.* to reveal, to disclose, to betray, to give away (secret, etc.); to betoken, to indicate; (photo.) to develop; **se** ~ *v.refl.* to reveal itself, to show itself, to be disclosed, to come to light.
revenant, -e [rəvnɑ̃] *adj.* pleasing, prepossessing; *physionomie ~e,* prepossessing appearance; ~ *s.m.* ghost.
revenant-bon [rəvnɑ̃bɔ̃] *s.m.* profit, bonus.
revendeu-r, -se [rəvɑ̃dœr] *s.m.f.* dealer, retailer, *~se à la toilette,* second-hand clothes dealer.
revendicati-f, -ve [rəvɑ̃dikatif] *adj.* demanding, claiming, in support of claim, by way of protest; *programme ~f,* programme of demands; *mouvement ~f,* movement in support of claims, protest movement.
revendication [rəvɑ̃dikɑsjɔ̃] *s.f.* revendication, claiming, claim.
revendiquer [rəvɑ̃dike] *v.t.* to claim, to enter a claim to; (fig.) to lay claim to; ~ *une responsabilité,* to assume (full) responsibility.
revendre [rəvɑ̃dr] *v.t.* to resell, to sell again, to sell what one has bought; (fig.) *avoir qch. à ~,* to have enough and to spare of sth.
revenez-y [rəvənezi] *s.m.invar.* repetition, return, another go; *avoir un petit goût de ~,* to be appetizing, to make one want to have some more.
revenir [rəvənir] *v.i.* to come back, to return, to revert, to come again, to come on again, to recur, to come round again; to cost, ~ *à,* (of price) to come out at; to please; to be equivalent to; to be owing to; to be due (as a right) to; ~ *à soi,* to come to oneself, to come to; to revive; to recover consciousness; to come back to one's senses, to recover one's composure; *son nom ne me revient pas,* I cannot remember his name; *voilà des façons qui ne me reviennent pas,* these manners do not please me; *cela revient au même,* it comes to the same thing; *cela revient à dire que,* that amounts to saying that; *je n'en reviens pas!,* I cannot get over it; I am utterly amazed; that beats me; *n'y revenez plus,* do not do that again; *il n'y a pas à y ~,* that is definitely settled, you can't change it now, it is gone once and for all; ~ *sur un sujet,* to hark back to a subject, to bring a subject up again; *en ~ à,* to revert to, to hark back to, to keep harping on; *il revient de loin,* he had a narrow escape; that was a hairbreadth escape; he very nearly died; *je suis bien revenu sur son compte,* I have lost all the illusions I had about him; *la parole lui est revenue,* he can speak again, he has recovered his speech; ~ *de sa surprise, de sa frayeur,* to get over one's surprise, to recover from one's fright; ~ *d'une erreur,* to realize one's mistake, to renounce an error; *il me revient que,* I hear that, I am told that; *ce qui m'en revient est bien peu de chose,* the profit I get from it is pretty small; *sa maison lui revient à,* his house costs him; *s'en ~,* to come back; *faire ~ de la viande,* to brown meat; *il revient sur ce qu'il avait dit,* he retracts what he said; *cet aliment revient,* this food repeats (in the stomach); ~ *sur ses pas,* to retrace one's steps; *faire ~ qn.,* to bring s.o. round (from faint, etc.).
revente [rəvɑ̃t] *s.f.* resale; selling again.
revenu [rəveny] *s.m.* **1.** income; (~ *d'État*) revenue; interest, incomings; *impôt sur le ~,* income-tax; **2** (metall.) tempering.
revenue [rəvəny] *s.f.* young growth (of wood).
rêver [rɛve] *v.i.* to dream (*de,* of); to muse, to ponder, to think deeply; to rave, to be delirious; ~ *tout éveillé,* to day-dream, to indulge in idle fancies; *on croit ~,* it is incredible; ~ *v.t.* to imagine, to dream of, to long for; to dream (sth.); *il ne rêve que cela,* that is his only thought or desire, he hankers after that.
réverbération [revɛrberɑsjɔ̃] *s.f.* reverberation, re-echoing; reflection.
réverbère [revɛrbɛr] *s.m.* **1.** reveberator; reflector; *four à ~,* reverberatory furnace; **2.** street lamp.
réverbérer [revɛrbere] *v.t.* to reflect (light or heat); ⚠ not 'to reverberate' (of sound).
revercher [rəvɛrʃe] *v.t.* to solder (tin), to mend by soldering.
reverdir [rəvɛrdir] *v.i.* to grow green again; (fig.) to reblossom, to grow young again; ~ *v.t.* **1.** to paint green again; **2** (techn.) to soak, to soften, (hides).
reverdissage [rəvɛrdisaʒ] *s.m.* (techn.) soaking, softening, (of hides).
reverdissement [rəvɛrdismɑ̃] *s.m.* growing green again.
reverdoir [rəvɛrdwar] *s.m.* (brewing) steeping-vat.
révérence [reverɑ̃s] *s.f.* **1.** reverence; ~ *parler, sauf ~,* with all due respect, if I may be allowed to say so; **2.** curtsy, courtesy, bow, obeisance; *faire la ~,* to curtsy, to bow; *tirer sa ~ à qn.,* to bow to s.o. and leave him, to leave s.o., to bid s.o. a very good day.
révérenciel, -le [reverɑ̃sjɛl] *adj.* reverential; *crainte ~le,* awe, awed respect.
révérencieu-x, -se [reverɑ̃sjø] *adj.* reverential, deferential.
révérend, -e [reverɑ̃] *adj., s.m.f.* reverend.
révérendissime [reverɑ̃disim] *adj.* right reverend, most reverend.
révérer [revere] *v.t.* to revere, to honour, to venerate.
rêverie [rɛvri] *s.f.* reverie, day-dream, musing, fantasy.
revers [rəvɛr] *s.m.* back, reverse, other side, wrong side, counterpart; (tailoring) revers, lapel, facing, turn-up; top (of top-boot); (tennis) backhand stroke, backhander; misfortune, reverse, disaster, ruin, losses of money; *le ~ de la médaille,* the reverse of the medal, the dark side of the picture; *à ~,* on the other side; *prendre l'ennemi à ~,* to outflank the enemy; to attack the enemy in the rear; ⚠ not 'reverse' in senses 'contrary' or 'reverse (direction)', 'reverse (gear)'.
réversal, -e (aux) [revɛrsal] *adj.* (comm.) of mutual concession.
reversement [rəvɛrsmɑ̃] *s.m.* (accounting) transfer, transferring.
reverser [rəvɛrse] *v.t.* to pour out again, to pour into the same vessel, bottle, etc.; (accounting) to transfer, to carry over; to pay back; ⚠ not 'to reverse'.
reversi(s) [rəvɛrsi] *s.m.* reversi (card-game).
réversibilité [revɛrsibilite] *s.f.* reversibility; revertibility.
réversible [revɛrsibl] *adj.* reversible, revertible (*sur,* to).
réversion [revɛrsjɔ̃] *s.f.* reversion.
reversoir [rəvɛrswar] *s.m.* weir.
revêtement [rəvɛtmɑ̃] *s.m.* revetment, facing (of masonry), casing, cladding, lining; retaining wall.
revêtir [rəvɛtir] *v.t.* to put on; to clothe; to cover, to coat; to case, to line; ~ *un habit,* to put on a coat; *revêtu de son armure,* clad in armour;

mur revêtu de marbre, wall faced with marble; ~ *une apparence de,* to assume the appearance of; ~ *la forme humaine,* to take on human shape; *l'autorité dont il est revêtu,* the authority he is invested with; **se** ~ *v.refl. se* ~ *de,* to put on; to assume.

rêveu-r, -se [rɛvœr] *adj.* dreamy, musing; absent-minded; *s.m.f.* dreamer; ~**sement** [rɛvøzmɑ̃] *adv.* dreamily, pensively, absent-mindedly.

revient [rəvjɛ̃] *s.m.* cost; *prix de* ~, cost price, cost of manufacture, prime cost.

revif [rəvif] *s.m.* rising tide; (fig.) new lease of life, second blooming.

revirement [rəvirmɑ̃] *s.m.* (naut.) tacking about; sudden change, complete change, turn-about; about-turn; changing sides, turning round.

révisable [revizabl] *adj.* revisable.

réviser [revize] *v.t.* to revise, to examine afresh, to reconsider; to inspect (for repairs), to check.

réviseur [revizœr] *s.m.* reviser; proof-reader; auditor.

révision [revizjɔ̃] *s.f.* revision, revisal, reconsideration; (proof-)reading; inspection, checking; ~ *d'un procès,* rehearing of a case (in law-court); (mil.) *Conseil de* ~, medical examination board for recruits.

revisionnisme [revizjɔnism] *s.m.* (pol.) revisionism.

révisionniste [revizjɔnist] *adj., s.m.f.* (pol.) revisionist.

revisser [rəvise] *v.t.* to screw up (again), to tighten up.

revitaliser [rəvitalize] *v.t.* to revitalize.

revivification [rəvivifikɑsjɔ̃] *s.f.* revivification, regeneration.

revivifier [rəvivifje] *v.t.* to revivify, to vitalize, to revive, to regenerate.

reviviscence [rəvivisɑ̃s] *s.f.* reviviscence.

reviviscent, -e [rəvivisɑ̃] *adj.* reviviscent.

revivre [rəvivr] *v.i.* to live again, to come to life again, to have new life; *faire* ~, to revive, to bring to life again; ~ *v.t.* to relive, to live over again.

révocable [revɔkabl] *adj.* revocable, subject to repeal; subject to dismissal, removable; terminable.

révocation [revɔkɑsjɔ̃] *s.f.* revocation, dismissal, removal from office; repeal, annulment.

révocatoire [revɔkatwar] *adj.* revocatory.

revoici [rəvwasi] *prep.*, **revoilà** [rəvwala] *prep.* here, there, (s.o. or sth.) is again, *nous revoilà dans les mêmes difficultés,* there we are in the same difficulties again.

revoir [rəvwar] *v.t.* to see again, to examine again, to review, to revise; to meet again, to behold again; *à* ~, to be re-examined, for review, to be revised; *au* ~, goodbye (for the present), (fam.) see you later; *faire au* ~ *de la main,* to wave goodbye; **se** ~ *v.refl.* to meet again; to be again on good terms.

revoler [rəvɔle] *v.i.* to fly back, (fig.) to hurry back; to fly again.

revoler [rəvɔle] *v.t.* to steal again, to steal back.

révoltant, -e [revɔltɑ̃] *adj.* revolting, shocking.

révolte [revɔlt] *s.f.* revolt, rebellion, mutiny; indignation, outrage.

révolté, -e [revɔlte] *adj.* in revolt, rebellious, protesting; outraged; *s.m.f.* rebel, protester.

révolter [revɔlte] *v.t.* to revolt; to cause to revolt, to rouse, to shock, to arouse indignation in; to outrage; ~ *la conscience,* to be repugnant to the conscience; **se** ~ *v.refl.* to revolt, to rebel, to mutiny, to rise (*contre,* against); to be shocked, to be outraged.

révolu, -e [revɔly] *adj.* revolved, past, accomplished, full, completed; *il a trente ans* ~*s,* he has completed his 30th year; *époques* ~*es,* past ages.

révolution [revɔlysjɔ̃] *s.f.* revolution; revolving motion; complete change, upheaval.

révolutionnaire [revɔlysjɔnɛr] *adj., s.m.f.* revolutionary.

révolutionner [revɔlysjɔne] *v.t.* to revolutionize, to upset (violently), to overturn; to put in a state of revolution.

revolver [revɔlvɛr] *s.m.* **1.** revolver; **2.** (techn.) revolving head, turret, capstan (of lathe).

revolvériser [revɔlverize] *v.t.* (fam.) to shoot with a revolver; *se* ~, to shoot oneself.

révoquer [revɔke] *v.t.* to repeal, to annul, to revoke; to rescind, to withdraw; to dismiss, to remove from office, to recall; ~ *en doute,* to question, to call in question, to contest; ⚠ not 'to revoke' as in card-game.

revoter [rəvɔte] *v.t.* to vote (sth.) again; ~ *v.i.* to vote again.

revouloir [rəvulwar] *v.t.* (fam.) to want (sth.) again, to want some more (of sth.); *j'en reveux,* I want some more.

revoyure [rəvwajyr] *s.f.* (pop.) *à la* ~ = *au* REVOIR.

revue [rəvy] *s.f.* review, reviewing; magazine; survey, revising, inspection; (theatr.) revue; (mil.) *passer en* ~, to review; *passer une* ~ *de,* to review, to make a review of; (mil.) to hold a review of; *faire la* ~ *de,* to look over, to go through; (fam.) *nous sommes gens de* ~, *nous sommes de* ~, we shall see each other again before long; ~ *hebdomadaire,* weekly review; weekly.

revuiste [rəvɥist] *s.m.* writer of revues.

révulsé, -e [revylse] *adj.* much upset, much distressed; *yeux* ~*s,* eyes turned up (in horror, etc.).

(**se**) **révulser** [revylse] *v.refl.* (of face) to become contorted; (of eyes) to turn up.

révulsi-f, -ve [revylsif] *adj.* revulsive; ~**f** *s.m.* counter-irritant, revulsive.

révulsion [revylsjɔ̃] *s.f.* revulsion, counter-irritation.

rez-de-chaussée [redʃose] *s.m.invar.* ground floor, ground level; *au* ~, on the ground floor.

R.F. [ɛrɛf] abbrev. *République française.*

R.F.A. [ɛrɛfɑ] abbrev. *République fédérale allemande,* Federal Republic of Germany.

rhabdomancie, rabdomancie [rabdɔmɑ̃si] *s.f.* rhabdomancy, divining (by rod).

rhabillage [rabijaʒ], **rhabillement** [rabijmɑ̃] *s.m.* **1.** repairing, overhauling, repairs; **2.** dressing (s.o.) again, getting dressed again.

rhabiller [rabije] *v.t.* **1.** to repair, to overhaul; to restore (building); (fig.) to revive in a new form; **2.** to dress (s.o.) again; **se** ~ *v.refl.* to get dressed again; (fig., fam.) (of actor, athlete, etc.) *il peut se* ~, he can change back (because he is no good).

rhabilleu-r, -se [rabijœr] *s.m.f.* mender, repairer.

rhapsode, rapsode [rapsɔd] *s.m.* rhapsode; rhapsodist.

rhapsodie, rapsodie [rapsɔdi] *s.f.* rhapsody.

rhénan, -e [renɑ̃] *adj.* Rhenish.

rhéomètre [reɔmɛtr] *s.m.* rheometer, galvanometer.

rhéostat [reɔsta] *s.m.* (electr.) rheostat.

rhésus [rezys] *s.m.* (zool.) rhesus monkey; (physiol.) *facteur* ~, Rhesus factor.

rhéteur [retœr] *s.m.* rhetor, rhetorical orator; (iron.) tub-thumper, gas-bag.

rhétien, -ne [retjɛ̃] *adj.* (geol.) Rhaetic.

rhétique [retik] *adj.* (geog.) Rhaetian; ~ *s.m.* Rhaetian (language).

rhétoricien [retɔrisjɛ̃] *s.m.* **1.** rhetorician; **2.** (school) pupil in the (*classe de*) *rhétorique.*

rhétorique [retɔrik] *s.f.* rhetoric; (fig., pej.) fine words, bombast; *figure de* ~, rhetorical figure; figure of speech; fifth form on classical side in Fr. *lycée.*

Rhin [rɛ̃] *s.m.* (geog.) *le Rhin*, the Rhine.
rhinanthe [rinɑ̃t] *s.m.* (bot.) Rhinanthus, yellow rattle.
rhingrave [ringrav, rɛ̃grav] *s.m.* (hist.) Rhingrave, count of the Rhine; ~ *s.f.* type of ornate breeches popular in 17th cent.
rhinite [rinit] *s.f.* (med.) rhinitis, coryza, common cold.
rhinocéros [rinɔserɔs] *s.m.* (zool.) rhinoceros.
rhinoplastie [rinɔplasti] *s.f.* (surg.) rhinoplasty.
rhinoscopie [rinɔskɔpi] *s.f.* (med.) rhinoscopy.
rhizocarpé, -e [rizokarpe] *adj.* (bot.) rhizocarpous.
rhizome [rizom] *s.m.* (bot.) rhizome.
rhizo-phage [rizɔfaʒ] *adj.* rhizophagous, feeding on roots; **~phore** [rizɔfɔr] *s.m.* (bot.) rhizophore; **~podes** [rizɔpɔd] *s.m.pl.* (zool.) Rhizopoda; **~stome** [rizɔstɔm] *s.m.* (zool.) medusa; **~tome** [rizɔtɔm] *s.m.* (techn.) root-cutter.
rhodanien, -ne [rɔdanjɛ̃] *adj.* (geog.) Rhodanian, of the Rhone.
rhodium [rɔdjɔm] *s.m.* (chem.) rhodium.
rhododendron [rɔdɔdɛ̃drɔ̃] *s.m.* (bot.) rhododendron.
rhombe [rɔ̃b] *s.m.* rhomb, rhombus.
rhombique [rɔ̃bik] *adj.* rhombic, diamond-shaped.
rhomboèdre [rɔ̃bɔɛdr] *s.m.* (geom.) rhombohedron.
rhomboïdal, -e, (aux) [rɔ̃bɔidal] *adj.* rhomboid(al).
rhomboïde [rɔ̃bɔid] *s.m.* (geom.) rhomboid.
Rhône [ron] *s.m.* (geog.) Rhone (river).
rhubarbe [rybarb] *s.f.* rhubarb.
rhum [rɔm] *s.m.* rum.
rhumatisant, -e [rymatizɑ̃] *adj.*, *s.m.f.* (one) affected with rheumatism, rheumatic (sufferer).
rhumatismal, -e, (aux) [rymatismal] *adj.* rheumatic.
rhumatisme [rymatism] *s.m.* rheumatism.
rhumatologie [rymatɔlɔʒi] *s.f.* rheumatology.
rhumb see RUMB.
rhume [rym] *s.m.* cold; ~ *de cerveau*, cold in the head; ~ *des foins*, hay fever.
rhumerie [rɔmri] *s.f.* rum distillery.
riant, -e [rjɑ̃] *adj.* smiling, cheerful, pleasant, prepossessing.
ribambelle [ribɑ̃bɛl] *s.f.* swarm, long string, whole lot, hordes.
ribaud, -e [ribo] *s.m.f.*, *adj.* (obs.) debauched (person).
ribler [rible] *v.t.* (techn.) to dress (a millstone).
riblon [riblɔ̃] *s.m.* (usu. pl.) steel scrap, swarf.
ribonucléique [ribonykleik] *adj.* (biochem.) ribonucleic.
ribord [ribɔr] *s.m.* (naut.) garboard (strake), bottom planking.
ribote [ribɔt] *s.f.* orgy (of eating and drinking).
ribouis [ribwi] *s.m.* (pop.) old shoe, shoe.
ricain, -e [rikɛ̃] *adj.* (pop.) American.
ricanement [rikanmɑ̃] *s.m.* sneering, tittering, sneer, derisive laughter.
ricaner [rikane] *v.i.* to sneer, to titter, to giggle, to laugh derisively.
ricaneu-r, -se [rikanœr] *s.m.f.* sneerer; *adj.* sneering, giggling, mocking, derisive.
richard, -e [riʃar] *s.m.f.* (fam., pej.) wealthy person.
riche [riʃ] *adj.* rich, wealthy, well off, prosperous; copious, abundant, fertile, fruitful; costly, valuable; ~ *en*, rich in, fertile in; ~ *de*, rich in, full of, abounding in; *il est* ~ *à millions*, he is worth millions; ~ *s.m.* rich person; *les* ~*s*, the wealthy, the rich; **~ment** [riʃmɑ̃] *adv.* richly, copiously, abundantly, sumptuously, opulently.
richesse [riʃɛs] *s.f.* richness; riches (pl.); wealth, opulence; fertility, abundance; magnificence; valuable object; fortune; ~ *en matières premières*, wealth in raw materials; *contentement passe* ~, enough is as good as a feast; content is better than riches.
richissime [riʃisim] *adj.* rolling in money; extremely rich.
ricin [risɛ̃] *s.m.* (bot.) castor-oil plant; *huile de* ~, castor oil.
ricocher [rikɔʃe] *v.i.* to ricochet, to rebound.
ricochet [rikɔʃɛ] *s.m.* ricochet; ducks and drakes (stone skimming on water); (fig.) *par* ~, indirectly, in a roundabout way.
ric-rac [rikrak] *adv.loc.* strictly, exactly, sharp, on the nail.
rictus [riktys] *s.m.* grin; (anat., zool.) rictus.
ridage [ridaʒ] *s.m.* (naut.) tightening, hauling taut.
ride [rid] *s.f.* wrinkle; ripple (on water); ridge (on snow, or sand); (naut.) lanyard; *nœud de* ~, Matthew Walker knot, stopper knot; ⚠ not 'ride'.
ridé, -e [ride] *adj.* wrinkled, shrivelled; rippled, ripply, covered with ripples; corrugated.
rideau (pl. **-x**) [rido] *s.m.* curtain; rolling shutter; roll-top (of desk); register (in chimney); (fig.) screen, veil; ~ *de fer*, (theatr.) safety curtain; (pol. & fig.) iron curtain; *baisser le* ~, to drop the curtain; (theatr.) *un lever de* ~, a short opening play; a curtain-raiser; *tirer le* ~, to draw the curtain; (fig.) *tirer le* ~ *sur*, to draw a veil over, to dismiss from one's thoughts.
ridée [ride] *s.f.* net for catching larks.
ridelle [ridɛl] *s.f.* rack (forming side of a cart).
rider [ride] *v.t.* to wrinkle; to shrivel; to ripple or ruffle (water); to corrugate; (naut.) to tighten, to haul taut; **se** ~ *v.refl.* to become wrinkled or lined, to shrivel; to ripple.
ridicule [ridikyl] *adj.* ridiculous, laughable, ludicrous; *se rendre* ~, to make oneself ridiculous or a laughing-stock; ~ *s.m.* ridicule, ridiculousness, absurdity; *d'un* ~ *achevé*, perfectly ridiculous; *tomber dans le* ~, to become ridiculous; *tourner qn. en* ~, to ridicule s.o., to hold s.o. up to ridicule; **~ment** [ridikylmɑ̃] *adv.* ridiculously, ludicrously.
ridiculiser [ridikylize] *v.t.* to ridicule.
rien [rjɛ̃] *ind.pron.* anything, nothing, not anything; ~ *autre*, ~ *d'autre*, nothing else; ~ *de moins*, nothing less; ~ *moins que*, nothing less than; no less than; anything but; *en moins de* ~, in a trice; in less than no time; *moins que* ~, next to nothing; *pour* ~, (i.) for nothing; for no reason; (ii.) dirt cheap; for a song; given away; *cela ne fait* ~, it does not matter; *si cela ne vous fait* ~, if you have no objection; *il n'en est* ~, nothing of the kind; *ne faire semblant de* ~, to pretend not to notice; *comme si de* ~ *n'était*, as though nothing had happened; *cela ne vaut* ~, it's worth nothing; *il n'est* ~ *moins que sot*, he is anything but a fool; ~ *moins que cela*, anything but that; *n'en faites* ~, do nothing of the sort; *cela ne servira à* ~, that will be no use; *n'aboutir à* ~, to come to nothing; *un homme de* ~, a nobody; *une affaire de* ~, a matter of no importance; *un propre-à-*~, a good-for-nothing; *il ne faut jurer de* ~, you never can tell; never prophesy unless you know; *qui ne risque* ~ *n'a* ~, nothing venture, nothing win; *pour* ~ *au monde*, not for anything; not to save my life!; *il n'est pour* ~ *dans l'affaire*, he has nothing to do with the business; *il n'y a* ~ *à dire à cela*, there is nothing to be said to that; that is unanswerable; *si peu que* ~, next to nothing; *il ne reste plus* ~, there is nothing left; *est-il* ~ *de plus beau que cela?*, is there anything more beautiful than that?; ~ *que d'y penser, j'en ai le frisson*, I shudder at the mere thought of it; *il est parti de* ~, he rose from nothing; ~ *de tel que la santé*, there is nothing like health; (slang) *elle est* ~ *moche*, she is frightfully ugly; ~ *s.m.* mere nothing, trifle, trace, nothingness;

c'est un ~, it's a trifle; *en un* ~ *de temps*, in no time at all; *un* ~ *d'ail*, a touch of garlic.

rieu-r, -se [rjœr] *adj.* laughing, given to laughter, merry; ~**r** *s.m.* laugher; *avoir les* ~*rs de son côté*, to have the laugh on one's side.

rieuse [rjøz] *s.f.* (ornith.) kind of sea-gull.

riflard [riflar] *s.m.* **1.** (carp.) jack-plane; **2.** (mason.) paring-chisel; **3.** longest wool in a fleece; **4.** rough file (for metals); **5.** (fam.) umbrella.

rifler [rifle] *v.t.* to plane, to file.

rigaudon, rigodon [rigodɔ̃] *s.m.* rigadoon.

rigide [riʒid] *adj.* rigid, stiff, tense; (fig.) rigid, inflexible, hidebound; ~**ment** [riʒidmɑ̃] *adv.* rigidly, strictly.

rigidité [riʒidite] *s.f.* rigidity, stiffness, tenseness; (fig.) rigidity, strictness, severity.

rigodon see RIGAUDON.

rigolade [rigɔlad] *s.f.* (fam.) lark, fun, good time, good laugh, revelry, buffoonery; *à la* ~, light-heartedly, just for fun.

rigolage [rigɔlaʒ] *s.m.* (agric.) trenching, furrowing, making seed-drills.

rigolard, -e [rigɔlar] *adj.* full of fun, fond of a lark.

rigole [rigɔl] *s.f.* small trench, drill, furrow, gutter, rill, irrigating channel.

rigoler[1] [rigɔle] *v.t.* to have a good laugh, to have fun, to have a lark, to joke, to speak in jest; to revel.

rigoler[2] [rigɔle] *v.t.* (agric.) to trench, to drill, to furrow, to channel.

rigolo, -te [rigɔlo] *adj.* (fam.) funny, jolly, comic; *s.m.f.* humorous person, joker; ~ *s.m.* (pop.) revolver.

rigorisme [rigɔrism] *s.m.* rigorism, rigour, strictness, austerity.

rigoriste [rigɔrist] *adj.* rigorist.

rigoureu-x, -se [rigurø] *adj.* rigorous, strict, exact; (of winter, etc.) severe, harsh, inclement; *démonstration* ~*se*, exact, rigorous, or accurate demonstration; *un* ~*x examen*, a close or thorough examination; ~**sement** [rigurøzmɑ̃] *adv.* rigorously, strictly, exactly.

rigueur [rigœr] *s.f.* rigour, strictness, accuracy; harshness, inclemency; hardship; *à la* ~, (i.) strictly; strictly speaking; (ii.) in case of absolute necessity, if the worst comes to the worst, at a pinch; *de* ~, indispensable, obligatory; *l'habit est de* ~, evening dress must be worn; *tenir* ~ *à qn.*, to refuse to relent towards s.o., to remain at daggers drawn with s.o.

rillettes [rijɛt] *s.f.pl.* rillettes (minced pork cooked in fat, special dish of Touraine).

rillons [rijɔ̃] *s.m.pl.* rillons (pieces of pork or goose-meat cooked in fat).

rimailler [rimɑje] *v.i.* to write doggerel verse.

rimailleu-r, -se [rimɑjœr] *s.m.f.* bad poet.

rimaye [rimɑj] *s.f.* (mountaineering) berg-schrund.

rime [rim] *s.f.* rhyme; ~*s croisées*, alternate masculine and feminine rhymes; *cela n'a ni* ~ *ni raison*, there is neither rhyme nor reason in that; that is incoherent, or unacccountable, or self-contradictory.

rimer [rime] *v.i.* to rhyme; to write verse; *cela ne rime à rien*, there is no sense in that; *à quoi cela rime-t-il?*, what can you make of that?, what's the meaning of that?; ~ *v.t.* to put into verse.

rimeu-r, -se [rimœr] *s.m.f.* rhymer, rhymester, versifier.

rimmel [rimɛl] *s.m.* mascara.

rinçage [rɛ̃saʒ] *s.m.* rinsing.

rinceau (pl. **-x**) [rɛ̃so] *s.m.* scroll pattern, foliage ornament.

rince-bouteilles [rɛ̃sbutɛj] *s.m.invar.* bottle-brush; bottle-washing machine.

rince-doigts [rɛsdwɑ] *s.m.invar.* finger-bowl.

rincée [rɛ̃se] *s.f.* **1.** (pop.) hail of blows; (fig.) defeat; **2.** downpour.

rincer [rɛ̃se] *v.t.* to rinse, to wash out; **se** ~ *v.refl.* (pop.) *se* ~ *l'œil*, to take a good look, to be all eyes; *se* ~ *la dalle* or *le gosier*, to have a drink, to wet one's whistle; (pop.) *se faire* ~, to be robbed or cleaned out (at cards).

rincette [rɛ̃sɛt] *s.f.* **1.** (fam.) extra drop of wine (allegedly to wash out the glass); nip of spirits (in bottom of wineglass or coffee-cup); **2.** (pop.) spirits.

rinceu-r, -se [rɛ̃sœr] *s.m.f.* rinser, washer; ~**se** *s.f.* bottle-washing machine.

rinçure [rɛ̃syr] *s.f.* rinsings, slops.

ring [riŋ] *s.m.* (obs.) circus ring; (mod.) boxing or wrestling ring.

ringard [rɛ̃gar] *s.m.* fire-rake, clinker-bar.

ringarder [rɛ̃garde] *v.t.* to poke, to rake out (clinker).

ripaille [ripɑj] *s.f.* feast, feasting, carousal, revelry.

ripailler [ripɑje] *v.i.* to feast, to carouse.

ripailleu-r, -se [ripɑjœr] *s.m.f.* reveller, carouser.

ripaton [ripatɔ̃] *s.m.* (pop.) foot.

ripe [rip] *s.f.* (mason., sculpt.) scraper.

riper [ripe] *v.t.* **1.** (mason., sculpt.) to scrape; (naut.) to slip, to let slip (cable); **2.** to drag or shift sideways; ~ *v.i.* **1.** to scrape; **2.** to slip, to skid.

riposte [ripɔst] *s.f.* (fenc.) riposte, parry and thrust; (fig.) repartee, smart reply; counter-stroke, retort; *prompt à la* ~, quick at repartee.

riposter [ripɔste] *v.i.* to riposte, to parry and thrust; (fig.) to retort, to answer smartly.

ripuaire [ripɥɛr] *adj.* riparian.

riquiqui [rikiki] *adj.invar.* (fam.) undersized, tiny; mean, stingy.

rire [rir] *v.i.* to laugh (*de*, at), to smile, to look pleasant, auspicious; *aimer à* ~, to like fun; to like a joke; ~ *aux larmes*, to laugh till the tears come; ~ *aux éclats, à gorge déployée*, to roar with laughter; *éclater de* ~, to burst out laughing; ~ *sous cape*, to laugh up one's sleeve; *il a toujours le mot pour* ~, he is always ready with a joke; *il lui a ri au nez*, he laughed in his face; ~ *du bout des lèvres*, ~ *jaune*, to force a laugh; to give a sickly smile; *rira bien qui rira le dernier*, he laughs best who laughs last; *faire* ~, to make people laugh; to raise a laugh; *vous me faites rire*, you make me laugh, you are being ridiculous; *prêter à* ~, to cause amusement, to raise a smile, to be a laughing-stock; *se tordre de* ~, to split one's sides with laughing; *pour* ~, for fun; not seriously; in jest, comic, sham; *histoire de* ~, just for a joke, for fun; *vous voulez* ~*!*, you are not serious!, you must be joking!; *il n'y a pas de quoi* ~, it's nothing to laugh at; it's no laughing matter; **se** ~ *v.refl.* *se* ~ *de*, to laugh at; to mock at.

rire [rir] *s.m.* laugh, laughing, laughter; *éclat de* ~, burst of laughter; peal of laughter; *un gros* ~, a loud laugh, a guffaw; a horse-laugh; *le fou* ~, uncontrollable laughter, the giggles; *avoir le fou* ~, to be convulsed with laughter, to get the giggles.

ris[1] [ri] *s.m.* laugh, laughter.

ris[2] [ri] *s.m.* (naut.) reef; *prendre un* ~, to take in a reef; *prendre le bas* ~, to close-reef; *avec deux* ~ *aux huniers*, with double-reefed topsails.

ris[3] [ri] *s.m.* (butch.) sweetbread.

risberme [risbɛrm] *s.f.* (techn.) berm (of a dam).

risée[1] [rize] *s.f.* laugh, guffaw; derision; laughing-stock; *être un objet de* ~, to be a laughing-stock; *sous les huées et les* ~*s*, pursued by boos and catcalls.

risée[2] [rize] *s.f.* (naut.) squall, gust, flurry.

risette [rizɛt] *s.f.* nice little smile; forced smile.

risible [rizibl] *adj.* risible, laughable, ridiculous; **~ment** [rizibləmɑ̃] *adv.* laughably, ridiculously.
risque [risk] *s.m.* risk, hazard; *à tout ~*, at all hazards; *à ses ~s et périls*, at one's own risk; *j'en courrai le ~*, I will chance it.
risquer [riske] *v.t.* to risk, to run the risk of, to hazard, to chance; *~ la bataille*, to chance the fight; *qui ne risque rien n'a rien*, nothing venture nothing win; *~ le tout pour le tout*, to risk all to win all; *~ le coup*, to chance it; *~ le paquet*, to stake all; *~ gros*, to play for high stakes; *risqué*, (i.) hazardous; (ii.) improper, risqué, near the bone; *risque-tout*, daredevil; **se ~** *v.refl.* to take a risk, to venture.
rissole[1] [risɔl] *s.f.* (cook.) rissole; *~ de poisson*, fish-cake.
rissole[2] [risɔl] *s.f.* anchovy-net.
rissoler [risɔle] *v.t.i.* (cook.) to brown; *~ v.i.* (fig.) *se faire ~*, to get sunburnt.
ristourne [risturn] *s.f.* rebate, discount, reduction (of insurance contributions); bonus payment, dividend (from co-operative society).
rit, rite [rit] *s.m.* rite, ritual.
Rital [rital] *s.m.* (pop.) Italian.
ritournelle [riturnɛl] *s.f.* (mus.) ritornello; (fig.) tiresome repetition.
ritualisme [ritɥalism] *s.m.* ritualism.
ritualiste [ritɥalist] *adj., s.m.f.* ritualist.
rituel, -le [ritɥɛl] *adj.* ritual; *~ s.m.* prayer-book; ritual; **~lement** [ritɥɛlmɑ̃] *adv.* religiously; invariably, unfailingly.
rivage [rivaʒ] *s.m.* strand, beach, shore, bank, coast.
rival, -e, (**aux**) [rival] *adj.* rival; *s.m.f.* rival; competitor; *sans ~*, without rival, unrivalled.
rivaliser [rivalize] *v.i.* *~ avec*, to rival, to compete with; *~ d'adresse avec qn.*, to vie in skill with s.o.
rivalité [rivalite] *s.f.* rivalry, competition, emulation, opposition.
rive [riv] *s.f.* bank (of river, etc.), shore, beach, coast; border, edge, skirt; *la ~ du bois*, the edge of the wood.
rivelaine [rivlɛn] *s.f.* miner's pick.
river [rive] *v.t.* to rivet; to clench (nail); (fig.) to bind, to rivet; *~ son clou à qn.*, to reduce s.o. to silence, to shut someone's month.
riverain, -e [rivrɛ̃] *adj.* riparian, riverside, adjoining (road, etc.); *s.m.f.* owner of riverside property; owner of property bordering wood, road, street.
riveraineté [rivrɛnte] *s.f.* (law) riparian rights.
rivet [rivɛ] *s.m.* rivet.
rivetage [rivtaʒ] *s.m.* riveting.
riveter [rivte] *v.t.* to rivet.
riveur [rivœr] *s.m.* riveter.
riveuse [rivøz] *s.f.* riveter, riveting-machine.
rivière [rivjɛr] *s.f.* river, stream; water-jump; *~ de diamants*, diamond necklace; *les petits ruisseaux font les grandes ~s*, little strokes fell great oaks.
rivoir [rivwar] *s.m.* riveting-hammer, riveter.
rivure [rivyr] *s.f.* **1.** riveting, clenching (of nail); **2.** hinge-pin.
rixe [riks] *s.f.* brawl, row, scuffle, fight, quarrel, affray, squabble.
riz [ri] *s.m.* rice; *poudre de ~*, face-powder.
rizerie [rizri] *s.f.* rice-mill.
riziculture [rizikyltyr] *s.f.* rice-growing, cultivation of rice.
rizière [rizjɛr] *s.f.* rice plantation, ricefield.
riz-pain-sel [ripɛ̃sɛl] *s.m.invar.* (mil.) nickname for commissariat personnel.
R.N. [ɛrɛn] abbrev. *route nationale.*
rob[1] [rɔb] *s.m.* (pharm.) rob (a fruit syrup).
rob[2] [rɔb], **robre** [rɔbr] *s.m.* rubber (at whist and bridge).
robage [rɔbaʒ], **robelage** [rɔblaʒ] *s.m.* barking, decortication, (of trees, madder).
robe [rɔb] *s.f.* gown, dress, frock, robe; coat (of animal); *~ de chambre*, dressing-gown; *~ d'intérieur*, housecoat; *~ de plage*, sun-dress, beach--robe; *pommes de terre en ~ de chambre*, or *en ~ des champs*, potatoes cooked in their jackets; *les gens de ~*, the magistrature, the legal profession.
rober [rɔbe] *v.t.* **1.** to bark (madder); **2.** to wrap (cigars).
roberts [rɔbɛr] *s.m.pl.* (pop.) woman's breasts.
robeuse [rɔbøz] *s.f.* cigar-wrapper (operative).
robin [rɔbɛ̃] *s.m.* (obs., pej.) lawyer, one of the legal fraternity.
robinet [rɔbinɛ] *s.m.* tap, cock, faucet, spigot; *ouvrir, fermer, le ~*, to turn the tap on, off; *~ de vidange* or *de purge*, draw-off cock, drain-cock, waste-cock; (fig.) *un ~ d'eau tiède*, an old bore, a driveller.
robinetier [rɔbinɛtje] *s.m.* brass founder; tap or valve maker.
robinetterie [rɔbinɛtri] *s.f.* brass-founding, manufacture of taps and valves; factory for taps, etc.; array of taps or valves.
robinier [rɔbinje] *s.m.* (bot.) robinia, false acacia.
roborati-f, -ve [rɔbɔratif] *adj.* (med.) tonic, fortifying, invigorating.
robot [rɔbo] *s.m.* robot, automaton, automatic device; *avion-~*, remote-controlled (target) plane; *portrait-* or *photo-~*, identikit picture.
robre see ROB[2].
robuste [rɔbyst] *adj.* robust, sturdy, strong, hardy; **~ment** [rɔbystəmɑ̃] *adv.* robustly, stoutly, solidly, sturdily.
robustesse [rɔbystɛs] *s.f.* robustness, solidness.
roc [rɔk] *s.m.* rock; *avoir un cœur de ~*, to be hard--hearted, to have a heart of flint.
rocade [rɔkad] *s.f.* (mil.) *voie de ~*, road parallel to the front line; (civ.) by-pass.
rocaille [rɔkɑj] *s.f.* stones (on ground), stony ground; (arch.) rock-work, grotto work; *style ~*, rococo-style work in shells and stones; *jardin de ~*, rockery.
rocailleur [rɔkɑjœr] *s.m.* specialist in *rocaille* work.
rocailleu-x, -se [rɔkɑjø] *adj.* stony, pebbly; (fig.) harsh, rough, rugged.
rocambole [rɔkɑ̃bɔl] *s.f.* (bot.) Spanish garlic.
rocambolesque [rɔkɑ̃bɔlɛsk] *adj.* fantastic, melodramatic.
roccella [rɔksɛla], **rocelle** [rɔsɛl] *s.f.* (bot.) archil, orchil.
roche [rɔʃ] *s.f.* rock, boulder; (fig.) rock, flint, stone; *clair comme de l'eau de ~*, as clear as crystal; (geol.) *~-mère*, parent rock, gangue; *un homme de vieille ~*, a man of the old school; a man who belongs to the good old stock; *il a un cœur de ~*, he has a heart of flint.
rochelois, -e [rɔʃəlwa] *s.m.f., adj.* (native or inhabitant) of La Rochelle.
rocher [rɔʃe] *s.m.* rock, crag, boulder, cliff; *~ branlant*, logan-stone, rocking-stone; (zool.) murex; (anat.) hard part of temporal bone.
rocher [rɔʃe] *v.i.* **1.** (of fermenting beer) to froth; **2.** (of molten silver) to vegetate.
rochet[1] [rɔʃe] *s.m.* (eccles.) rochet.
rochet[2] [rɔʃɛ] *s.m.* **1.** bobbin (for silk); **2.** ratchet; *roue à ~*, ratchet-wheel.
rocheu-x, -se [rɔʃø] *adj.* rocky, abounding in rocks, rugged.
rock [rɔk] *s.m.* **1.** roc (fabulous bird); **2.** rock (music).
rococo [rɔkɔko, rɔkoko] *s.m.* rococo, rococo style; *~ adj.* rococo; (fig.) old-fashioned, antiquated.
rocou [rɔku] *s.m.* anatta; roucou (a dye).
rocouyer [rɔkuje] *s.m.* (bot.) anatta-tree, roucou(-tree).

rodage [rɔdaʒ] *s.m.* (techn.) grinding-in; smoothing by friction; *en ~*, (of car) being run in.
roder [rɔde] *v.t.* to grind in; to smooth by friction; to run in (car engine); (fig.) to try out.
rôder [rode] *v.i.* to prowl, to lurk, to roam, to hang about.
rôdeu-r, -se [rodœr] *s.m.f.* prowler, lounger, vagrant.
rodoir [rɔdwar] *s.m.* valve-grinder (tool).
rodomont [rɔdɔmɔ̃] *s.m.* swashbuckler, braggart; *faire le ~*, to bully, to hector; to swagger.
rodomontade [rɔdɔmɔ̃tad] *s.f.* rodomontade, bluster, braggadocio, swagger.
rogations [rɔgɑsjɔ̃] *s.f.pl.* (eccles.) rogation days.
rogatoire [rɔgatwar] *adj.* of inquiry; *commission ~*, judicial commission of inquiry.
rogaton [rɔgatɔ̃] *s.m.* scraps, rubbish, leavings.
rognage [rɔɲaʒ] *s.m.* paring, clipping.
rogne [rɔɲ] *s.f.* (fam.) bad temper.
rogne-pied [rɔɲpje] *s.m.invar.* farrier's knife.
rogner [rɔɲe] *v.t.* to clip, to pare, to cut, to curtail, to whittle down, to skimp (*sur*, on).
rogner [rɔɲe] *v.i.* (fam.) to be in a bad temper.
rogneu-r, -se [rɔɲœr] *s.m.f.* cutter, clipper; **~se** *s.f.* trimming-machine, trimmer.
rognoir [rɔɲwar] *s.m.* (bookb.) cutting-press.
rognon [rɔɲɔ̃] *s.m.* kidney; (geol.) nodule (of flint).
rognonner [rɔɲɔne] *v.i.* (fam.) to grumble, to mutter, to grouse.
rognures [rɔɲyr] *s.f.pl.* parings, clippings, scraps, leavings; shavings; refuse; *~s de verre*, cullet.
rogomme [rɔgɔm] *s.m.* (pop.) spirits; *une voix de ~*, husky, drunken voice.
rogue [rɔg] *adj.* arrogant, haughty, offensive.
rogue [rɔg] *s.f.* roe (of cod or herring).
rogué, -e [rɔge] *adj.* (of fish) roed.
rohart [rɔar] *s.m.* hippopotamus or walrus ivory.
roi [rwa] *s.m.* king; *~ d'armes*, king-at-arms; *~ de la nature*, lord of creation; *~ de cœur*, king of hearts; *de par le ~*, in the king's name; *les ~s, le jour des ~s*, Twelfth Night, Epiphany; *tirer* (or *fêter*) *les ~s*, to keep Twelfth Night; *travailler pour le ~ de Prusse*, to work for nothing, to have one's trouble for nothing; *morceau de ~*, dish fit for a king.
roide [rwad] *adj.* = RAIDE.
roideur [rwadœr] *s.f.* = RAIDEUR.
roidir see RAIDIR.
roitelet [rwatlɛ] *s.m.* **1.** petty king; **2.** (ornith.) wren.
rôle [rol] *s.m.* roll, list, catalogue; roster; (theatr.) part, role; *jouer un ~*, to play a part, to perform or fulfil a function, to occupy a position; *sortir de son ~*, to exceed one's functions; *ce n'est pas mon ~ de*, it is not my business to; (theatr.) *distribution des ~s*, casting, cast; *à tour de ~*, in turn, by turns; (naut.) *~ d'équipage*, muster-roll; register of the ship's company, ship's articles.
rollier [rɔlje] *s.m.* (ornith.) roller.
romain, -e [rɔmɛ̃] *adj.*, *s.m.f.* Roman; (print.) roman; **~e** *s.f.* **1.** steel-yard; **2.** cos lettuce.
romaïque [rɔmaik] *adj.*, *s.m.* Romaic, modern Greek.
roman, -e [rɔmɑ̃] *adj.* (lang.) Romance, Romanic; (arch.) Romanesque, Norman; (Lit.) neo-classical.
roman [rɔmɑ̃] *s.m.* novel, work of fiction, romance, adventure story; (arch.) romanesque; *~-feuilleton*, serial; *~-policier*, detective or crime story, thriller; *~-fleuve*, saga (novel); *cela tient du ~*, this is like a romantic or adventure story, it might be in a novel; ⚠ not 'Roman'.
romance [rɔmɑ̃s] *s.f.* song, ballad, romanza; ⚠ not 'romance'.
romancé, -e [rɔmɑ̃se] *adj.* in the form of a novel, fictionalized; *biographie ~e*, biographical novel; *histoire ~e*, historical romance.
romanche [rɔmɑ̃ʃ] *s.m.* Romansh, language spoken in the Grisons, East Switzerland.
romanci-er, -ère [rɔmɑ̃sje] *s.m.f.* novelist.
romand, -e [rɔmɑ̃] *adj.* *Suisse ~e*, French Switzerland.
romanesque [rɔmanɛsk] *adj.* romantic, imaginative, passionate; *~ s.m.* romanticism, romance; ⚠ not (arch.) 'romanesque'.
romani [rɔmani], **romano** [rɔmano] *s.m.* = ROMANICHEL.
romanichel, -le [rɔmaniʃɛl] *s.m.f.*, *adj.* gipsy, tzigane, romany; vagrant.
romaniser [rɔmanize] *v.t.* (eccles.) to romanize; *~ v.i.* to belong to the Roman Catholic church.
romaniste [rɔmanist] *s.m.f.* **1.** (eccles.) Romanist; **2.** (law) specialist in Roman law; **3.** (philol.) specialist in Romance languages.
romantique [rɔmɑ̃tik] *adj.*, *s.m.* **1.** (art) romantic; **2.** imaginative, emotional; (of disposition) romantic.
romantisme [rɔmɑ̃tism] *s.m.* romanticism.
romarin [rɔmarɛ̃] *s.m.* (bot.) rosemary.
rombière [rɔ̃bjɛr] *s.f.* (fam.) old frump.
rompre [rɔ̃pr] *v.t.i.* to break, to break in two, to burst, to snap; to disrupt, to break up; to interrupt, to break off, to divert, to break the force of; to break in (horse, etc.), to train, to accustom (to sth.); to upset (plans, balance, etc.); to deaden; (med.) to rupture; *être rompu aux affaires*, to have experience and skill in business, to be a good business man; *~ ses chaînes*, to break out of prison; (hunt.) *~ les chiens*, to call off the hounds; (fig.) to change the subject, to divert the conversation; (lit. & fig.) *~ la glace*, to break the ice; *~ une lance pour qn.*, to defend s.o.; to say a good word for s.o.; to take up the cudgels for s.o.; (fenc.) *~*, to draw back; (fenc.) *ne pas ~ d'une semelle*, not to draw back one step; *~ la tête à qn.*, to deafen s.o., to drive s.o. crazy (with questions, etc.); *~ avec qn.*, to break or fall out with s.o.; *~ à l'amiable*, to part friends; to part on good terms; *~ en visière à qn.*, to come to an open quarrel with s.o., to disagree fundamentally with s.o.; *rompez!*, off with you!, that will do!; *rompu de fatigue*, worn out; *~ des couleurs*, to soften, to tone down, colours; *applaudir à tout ~*, to applaud frantically; to bring the house down with applause; *à bâtons rompus*, by fits and starts; by snatches, desultory, rambling; **se** *~ v.refl.* to be broken, to be interrupted, to break; to part, to be refracted; *se ~ le cou*, to break one's neck; (fig.) to be ruined; *se ~ la tête*, to rack one's brains; *se ~ à la fatigue*, to train oneself to endure fatigue.
rompu, -e [rɔ̃py] *adj.* broken; tired out; trained, experienced, broken in.
romsteck, rumsteck [rɔmstɛk] *s.m.* rump steak.
ronce [rɔ̃s] *s.f.* (bot.) bramble, blackberry-bush; (fig.) thorn, obstacle; curl (in wood grain); *~s artificielles*, barbed wire.
ronceraie [rɔ̃srɛ] *s.f.* bramble thicket, ground covered with brambles.
ronceu-x, -se [rɔ̃sø] *adj.* brambly, thorny; (of wood) curl-grained.
ronchon [rɔ̃ʃɔ̃] *s.m.* grumbler.
ronchonnement [rɔ̃ʃɔnmɑ̃] *s.m.* grumbling, grousing, muttering; grumble, grouse.
ronchonner [rɔ̃ʃɔne] *v.i.* (fam.) to grumble, to grouse, to mutter.
ronchonneu-r, -se [rɔ̃ʃɔnœr] *s.m.f.* grumbler, grouser.

roncier [rɔ̃sje] *s.m.*, **roncière** [rɔ̃sjɛr] *s.f.* bramble-bush.

rond, -e [rɔ̃] *adj.* round, circular, rounded, rotund; plump; frank, open; even; (pop.) drunk; *un compte ~*, a round sum; *en nombres ~s*, in round numbers; *être ~ en affaires*, to be plain-dealing and brisk; to be businesslike and frank; *un homme tout ~*, a straightforward, plain-speaking man; *un petit homme tout ~*, a plump little man, a fat little chap; *tourner ~*, to run true, to run smoothly; (fam.) *une fortune ~e*, a tidy fortune.

rond [rɔ̃] *s.m.* round, ring, circle, orb, disc; washer; (fig., fam.) sou, money; *danser en ~*, to dance in a ring; *tourner en ~*, to turn round, to go round in circles; *s'asseoir en ~*, to sit in a circle; *~ de cuir*, round leather cushion (esp. on desk chair); (fig., pej.) bureaucrat, civil service clerk; *~ de serviette*, napkin-ring; (fam.) *il n'a plus un ~*, he hasn't a penny to his name.

rondache [rɔ̃daʃ] *s.f.* round shield, round buckler.

ronde [rɔ̃d] *s.f.* round; tour of inspection; patrol; (dance, mus.) round, roundelay; (mus.) semibreve; (writing) round hand; *à la ~*, round about; around; all round; in turn (round the circle); *passer à la ~*, to hand round; *faire la ~*, to go the rounds; *faire sa ~*, to make one's round, to inspect; *à 10 milles à la ~*, for 10 miles round.

rondeau (pl. **-x**) [rɔ̃do], **rondel** [rɔ̃dɛl] *s.m.* roundelay, rondeau; (mus.) rondo; (agric.) roller.

rondelet, -te [rɔ̃dlɛ] *adj.* plump, plumpish, podgy; rounded; *une bourse ~te*, a well-filled purse; *une somme ~te*, a tidy sum.

rondelle [rɔ̃dɛl] *s.f.* ring; round shield; roundel; small round or slice; disc; (techn.) collar, washer; *~ fusible*, fusible plug.

rondement [rɔ̃dmɑ̃] *adv.* roundly, promptly, briskly, frankly, bluntly, thoroughly; *mener (une affaire) ~*, to waste no time, to set about it smartly; *y aller ~*, to make a proper job of it.

rondeur [rɔ̃dœr] *s.f.* roundness, rotundity; (fig.) plain dealing, briskness, frankness, straightforwardness.

rondin [rɔ̃dɛ̃] *s.m.* round log; cudgel; (metall.) round bar, billet.

rond-point [rɔ̃pwɛ̃] *s.m.* circus (at intersection of roads); (traffic) roundabout; (arch.) apse.

ronéoter [rɔneɔte], **ronéotyper** [rɔneɔtipe] *v.t.* to roneo.

ronflant, -e [rɔ̃flɑ̃] *adj.* snoring, making a snoring or rattling noise; (fig.) sonorous, booming, bombastic, exaggerated; (of words, etc.) high-sounding (and empty).

ronflement [rɔ̃fləmɑ̃] *s.m.* snore, snoring; roar, rumbling, boom, roaring (of wind), humming (of top); (electr.) hum (in mains).

ronfler [rɔ̃fle] *v.i.* to snore; to roar, to boom, to rumble, to snort, to hum, to whir; (fam.) to sleep like a log; *ça ronfle, les affaires*, things are humming, we are doing a roaring trade; *il faut que ça ronfle*, we have got to make things hum.

ronfleu-r, -se [rɔ̃flœr] *s.m.f.* snorer; **~r** *s.m.* (electr.) buzzer.

rongeant, -e [rɔ̃ʒɑ̃] *adj.* gnawing, corroding; tormenting; (med., of ulcer) rodent; *soucis ~s*, tormenting cares; anxieties.

rongement [rɔ̃ʒmɑ̃] *s.m.* gnawing, corrosion, torment.

ronger [rɔ̃ʒe] *v.t.* to gnaw, to nibble, to eat; to corrode, to eat away, to erode; to etch; to wear away; *~ son mors*, or *son frein*, (of horse) to champ at the bit; *~ ses ongles*, to bite one's nails, *des soucis qui rongent le cœur*, anxieties which prey on the mind; **se** *~ v.refl.* to fret, to chafe; to be corroded; *se ~ les poings*, to fume, to fret (*de*, with).

rongeu-r, -se [rɔ̃ʒœr] *adj.* gnawing; corroding; heart-consuming; **~r** *s.m.* rodent.

ronron [rɔ̃rɔ̃], **ronronnement** [rɔ̃rɔnmɑ̃] *s.m.* purr, purring; hum, drone; *faire ~*, to purr.

ronronner [rɔ̃rɔne] *v.i.* to purr; to hum.

Röntgen [rœntgɛn] *s.m.* (phys.) *rayons ~*, X-rays.

roque [rɔk] *s.m.* (chess) castling.

roquefort [rɔkfɔr] *s.m.* Roquefort cheese.

roquelaure [rɔklɔr] *s.f.* (obs.) roquelaure (cloak worn by men in the 17th cent.).

roquer [rɔke] *v.i.* (chess) to castle.

roquet [rɔkɛ] *s.m.* **1.** pug(-dog); **2.** mongrel, cur.

roquette [rɔkɛt] *s.f.* **1.** (bot.) rocket; **2.** rocket (projectile).

rorqual [rɔrkwal] *s.m.* (zool.) rorqual.

rosace [rozas] *s.f.* rose, rose-window.

rosacé, -e [rozase] *adj.* (bot.) rosaceous; **~es** *s.f.pl.* (bot.) Rosaceae.

rosage [rozaʒ] *s.m.* rhododendron.

rosaire [rozɛr] *s.m.* rosary.

rosaniline [rozanilin] *s.f.* (chem.) rosaniline.

rosat [roza] *adj.invar.* (pharm.) of roses; *miel ~*, rose honey.

rosâtre [rozɑtr] *adj.* dusty pink, old rose (colour).

rosbif [rɔsbif] *s.m.* roast beef.

rose [roz] *s.f.* rose, rose-window, rose diamond; *~ des vents*, compass-card; *découvrir le pot aux ~s*, to find out the secret, to unmask the intrigue, to reveal the foul play; *pas de ~ sans épines*, there is no rose without a thorn; *bois de ~*, tulip-wood; *~ trémière*, hollyhock; *diamant taillé en ~*, rose-cut diamond; *~ s.m.* rose-colour, pink; *voir tout en ~*, to see only the bright side of things; to see everything through rose-coloured spectacles; *le ~ vous va bien*, pink suits you.

rose [roz] *adj.* rosy, pink, rose, rose-coloured, roseate; *tout n'est pas ~ en ce monde*, all is not sunshine in this world; life is not a bed of roses.

rosé, -e [roze] *adj.* rosy, roseate, pink, light pink; *vin ~*, rosé (wine).

roseau (pl. **-x**) [rozo] *s.m.* (bot.) reed.

rose-croix [rozkrwa] *s.f.invar.* Rosicrucian brotherhood; *~ s.m.invar.* Rosicrucian.

rosée [roze] *s.f.* dew; (bot.) *~ du soleil*, sundew.

roselet [rozlɛ] *s.m.* ermine.

roseli-er, -ère [rozəlje] *adj.* reed-producing, reedy; **~ère** *s.f.* reed-bed.

roséole [rozeɔl] *s.f.* roseola.

roser [roze] *v.t.* to make pink or rose-coloured; to give a roseate tint to.

roseraie [rozrɛ] *s.f.* rose-garden, rosery.

rosette [rozɛt] *s.f.* **1.** (arch., etc.) rose-shaped ornament, rosette; **2.** bow (of ribbon); (decoration) rosette (esp. of *Légion d'honneur*); **3.** (bot.) rosette.

rosier [rozje] *s.m.* (bot.) rose-tree, rose-bush.

rosière [rozjɛr] *s.f.* winner of the rose as the most virtuous girl of her village; (fam., jest) elderly spinster.

rosiériste [rozjerist] *s.m.f.* rose-grower.

rosir [rozir] *v.t.i.* to grow pink, to paint pink; to blush.

rossard, -e [rɔsar] *adj.*, *s.m.f.* spiteful, malicious, (person).

rosse [rɔs] *s.f.* miserable hack, worn-out old horse; (fig.) jade, shrew; regular brute; *~ adj.* malicious, malignant, spiteful, ironic; satirical, cruel.

rossée [rɔse] *s.f.* hail of blows, thrashing.

rosser [rɔse] *v.t.* to thrash, to beat up; (fam.) to beat, to defeat, to give a thrashing to.

rossignol [rɔsiɲɔl] *s.m.* **1.** nightingale; **2.** pick-lock, skeleton key; **3.** waste, scrap, unsaleable stock; **4.** (nav.) bosun's pipe.

rossinante [rɔsinɑ̃t] *s.f.* old nag, broken-winded horse.

rossolis [rɔsɔli] *s.m.* (bot.) sundew.

rostral, -e (aux) [rɔstral] *adj.* (Rom. ant.) rostral.
rostre [rɔstr] *s.m.* **1.** (zool., bot.) rostrum, beak; **2.** (Rom. ant.) *les ~s*, the rostra.
rot[1] [ro] *s.m.* belch, eructation.
rot[2] [rɔt] *s.m.* (agric.) rot (in vines).
rôt [ro] *s.m.* = RÔTI.
rotacé, -e [rɔtase] *adj.* (bot.) rotate.
rotang [rɔtɑ̃g] *s.m.* (bot.) rattan (tree); (see also ROTIN).
rotarien [rɔtarjɛ̃] *s.m., adj.m.* Rotarian.
rotary [rɔtari] *s.m.* **1.** (techn.) rotary sounding device; **2.** (teleph.) automatic system.
rotat-eur, -rice [rɔtatœr] *adj.* rotatory; **~eur** *s.m.* (anat.) rotator.
rotati-f, -ve [rɔtatif] *adj.* rotary, rotative, rotatory; **~ve** *s.f.* rotary press.
rotation [rɔtɑsjɔ̃] *s.f.* rotation; turnover (of stock); turn-round (of ship); (aeron., etc.) frequency of departures; (agric.) rotation (of crops); (mech.) *pièce à ~*, rotating part.
rotatoire [rɔtatwar] *adj.* rotatory.
rote [rɔt] *s.f.* **1.** (Cath.) Rota; **2.** (hist.) rote (mus. instrument); ⚠ not 'rote' exc. as in 2. above.
roter [rɔte] *v.i.* to belch; (pop., fig.) *en ~*, to sweat (at unpleasant task, etc.).
rôti [roti] *s.m.* roast meat, roast.
rotifères [rɔtifɛr] *s.m.pl.* (zool.) Rotifera.
rotin [rɔtɛ̃] *s.m.* **1.** rattan, rattan cane, rattan stick; **2.** penny, money.
rôtir [rotir] *v.t.i.* to roast, to bake, to toast; (lit. & fig.) to grill, to scorch.
rôtissage [rotisaʒ] *s.m.* roasting.
rôtisserie [rotisri] *s.f.* (obs.) cook-shop; (mod.) restaurant, grill.
rôtisseu-r, -se [rotisœr] *s.m.f.* (obs.) cook-shop keeper; (mod.) keeper of restaurant, of grill.
rôtissoire [rotiswar] *s.f.* (roasting) spit; rotisserie.
rotogravure [rɔtɔgravyr] *s.f.* rotogravure.
rotonde [rɔtɔ̃d] *s.f.* **1.** (arch.) rotunda; **2.** (rail.) round-house (engine-shed).
rotondité [rɔtɔ̃dite] *s.f.* rotundity, roundness; plumpness.
rotor [rɔtɔr] *s.m.* rotor.
rotule [rɔtyl] *s.f.* (anat.) kneecap, patella; (techn.) knuckle end, ball-shaped end; universal joint.
rotulien, -ne [rɔtyljɛ̃] *adj.* (anat.) pertaining to the kneecap, patellar.
roture [rɔtyr] *s.f.* plebeian rank, commoners' estate, humble folk; land held by commoners.
roturi-er, -ère [rɔtyrje] *s.m.f.* plebeian, commoner; *adj.* plebeian, common, of the common people.
rouage [ruaʒ] *s.m.* wheel, cog, gear-wheel, wheelwork, machinery; (horol.) movement; (fig.) machinery, wheels, workings; means.
rouan, -ne [ruɑ̃] *adj.* roan; *~ s.m.* roan horse.
rouanne [ruan] *s.f.* **1.** marking-tool (for casks); **2.** gouge.
roublard, -e [rublar] *adj., s.m.f.* deep, knowing, sharp, cute, cunning, double-dealing, artful, (person).
roublardise [rublardiz] *s.f.* cunning, trickery, double-dealing, craftiness.
rouble [rubl] *s.m.* rouble.
roucoulement [rukulmɑ̃] *s.m.* cooing; (fig.) billing and cooing, endearments.
roucouler [rukule] *v.t.i.* to coo; (fig.) to bill and coo, to whisper endearments.
roue [ru] *s.f.* wheel, pulley; (torture) wheel; *faire la ~*, to strut about; to show off; (fig.) *mettre des bâtons dans les ~s à qn.*, to put a spoke into someone's wheel; *pousser à la ~*, to put one's shoulder to the wheel; *la cinquième ~ du carrosse*, a thing of no use; *~ libre*, free wheel; *~ parasite*, idle(r) wheel; *~ dentée*, cog-wheel, toothed wheel; *~ motrice*, driving wheel; *moyeu de ~*, wheel boss or hub; *bloquer les ~s*, to lock wheels; *~ à aubes*, paddle-wheel, undershot wheel; (admin.) *deux ~s*, two-wheeled vehicles; (gymn.) *faire la ~*, to turn a cart-wheel.
roué, -e [rue] *adj.* **1.** broken (on the wheel); beaten; *~ de coups*, beaten unmercifully; **2.** (obs.) debauched, profligate; (mod.) cunning, calculating; *~ s.m.* (obs.) debauchee, rake; (mod.) calculating, unscrupulous person.
rouelle [ruɛl] *s.f.* round slice; *~ de veau*, fillet of veal.
rouennais, -e [rwanɛ] *adj., s.m.f.* (native or inhabitant) of Rouen.
rouennerie [rwanri] *s.f.* cotton print.
rouer [rue] *v.t.* (hist.) to break upon the wheel; (mod.) to beat; *~ de coups*, to beat unmercifully.
rouerie [ruri] *s.f.* **1.** (obs.) debauchery, profligacy; **2.** cunning, deceitfulness; calculating and cynical behaviour.
rouet [ruɛ] *s.m.* **1.** spinning-wheel; **2.** (obs.) flint-wheel, flintlock (on gun); **3.** (techn.) curb (surrounding well); ward (of lock); sheave (of pulley); (naut.) gin; (agric.) centrifugal well--pump.
rouette [ruɛt] *s.f.* osier-band, withe.
rouf [ruf] *s.m.* (naut.) deck-house, bridge-house, cuddy.
rouflaquettes [ruflakɛt] *s.f.pl.* (fam.) side--whiskers, sideburns.
rouge [ruʒ] *adj.* red; red-hot, ruddy, flushed; *du ~*, red wine; *boire un coup de ~*, to drink a glass of red wine; *perdrix ~*, red-legged partridge; *~ de honte*, blushing with shame; *~ de colère*, flushed with anger; *fer ~*, red-hot iron; *se fâcher tout ~*, to get downright angry; *voir ~*, to see red, to be mad with rage.
rouge [ruʒ] *s.m.* red colour, red, redness; rouge, paint; red republican, red; plate-powder, jewellers' rouge; *le ~ lui monte au visage*, he is turning red (with shame), he is blushing scarlet; *porter* or *chauffer au ~*, to make red-hot, to heat to red heat; *bâton de ~*, lipstick; *se mettre du ~*, to put on rouge.
rougeâtre [ruʒɑtr] *adj.* reddish.
rougeaud, -e [ruʒo] *adj., s.m.f.* ruddy, red--faced, (person).
rouge-gorge [ruʒgɔrʒ] *s.m.* (ornith.) robin.
rougeole [ruʒɔl] *s.f.* measles; (agric.) rust.
rougeoyer [ruʒwaje] *v.i.* to turn red, to burn red, to glow.
rouge-queue [ruʒkø] *s.m.* (ornith.) redstart.
rouget [ruʒɛ] *s.m.* **1.** (ichth.) red mullet, red gurnard; **2.** (vet.) swine-fever.
rouget, -te [ruʒɛ] *adj.* (fam.) slightly red.
rougeur [ruʒœr] *s.f.* redness, blush, flush, glow; (pl.) red blotches (on the skin).
rougir [ruʒir] *v.t.i.* to turn red, to redden, to tinge with red, to make red, to paint red; to make red-hot; to blush, to colour; (fig.) to be ashamed (*de*, of); *faire ~*, to make (s.o.) blush; *~ son eau*, to put a little red wine in one's water.
rougissant, -e [ruʒisɑ̃] *adj.* blushing, reddening.
rouille [ruj] *s.f.* rust, rustiness; (of plants) rust, mildew, blight; *~ adj.* red-brown, russet.
rouillé, -e [ruje] *adj.* rusted; (lit. & fig.) rusty; (agric.) affected by rust.
rouiller [ruje] *v.t.i.* to rust, to get rusty, to make rusty; to blight; to corrupt; to atrophy; **se ~** *v.refl.* (lit. & fig.) to become rusty; (agric.) to be affected by rust.
rouillure [rujyr] *s.f.* rustiness; (agric.) rust.
rouir [ruir] *v.t.i.* to ret (flax); to soak.
rouissage [ruisaʒ] *s.m.* retting (of flax).
roulade [rulad] *s.f.* **1.** (mus.) roulade; **2.** (cook.) roulade, rolled portion of meat, etc.; *~ de bœuf*, beef-olive.

roulage [rulaʒ] *s.m.* rolling; carting, cartage, carriage of goods; haulage; *entreprise de ~*, haulage contractor's business.
roulant, -e [rulɑ̃] *adj.* **1.** rolling, sliding, moving, mobile; *matériel ~*, rolling-stock; *bien ~*, smooth-running; (mil.) *cuisine ~e*, field-kitchen; *escalier ~*, moving staircase, escalator; *tapis ~*, conveyor belt, travelator; *affaire ~e*, going concern; *fonds ~*, working capital; *feu ~*, running fire; **2.** (fam.) screamingly funny; **~s** *s.m.pl.* (fam.) (rail.) train crews.
roulé, -e [rule] *adj.* rolled, curved; (cook.) rolled; (phon.) *R ~*, rolled R; *une femme bien ~e*, a woman with a good figure; *~ s.m.* (cook.) Swiss roll; (meat) roll; **~e** *s.f.* (pop.) hail of blows, thrashing.
rouleau (pl. **-x**) [rulo] *s.m.* roll, roller; reel; rolling-pin; scroll; piece (of wallpaper); twist, plug, (of tobacco); *~ essuie-mains*, roller-towel; (fig.) *être au bout de son ~*, to be at the end of one's tether; to be at one's wit's end.
roulement [rulmɑ̃] *s.m.* rolling, roll, circulation, rotation; running (of machinery, etc.); tread (of tyre); rumbling, rattle; *~ à billes*, ball-bearings; *voie* or *chemin de ~*, ball-race; *fonds de ~*, working capital.
rouler [rule] *v.t.* to roll, to roll up, to roll out (pastry, etc.); to push, to propel; to swing, to swivel; (fig.) to turn over (idea, etc.); (fam.) to swindle, to cheat; *~ sa bosse*, to travel around, to knock about the world; *se ~ les pouces*, or (fam.) *se les ~*, to twiddle one's thumbs, to do nothing; (fam.) *se faire ~*, to be swindled, to be robbed; *~ v.i.* to roll, to roll over, to move or run (esp. on wheels), to go; to go round, to revolve; to move around, to circulate, to keep moving; *~ à 100 km à l'heure*, to travel at, to do, 100 km per hour; *~ à droite*, to drive on the right; *~ sur*, (obs.) to be based on; (mod.) (of conversation, etc.) to turn on; **se~** *v.refl.* to roll, to twist, to writhe; to roll oneself up, to coil (up); *une tente qui se roule*, a tent which can be rolled up.
roulette [rulɛt] *s.f.* small wheel; roulette (game); roll; castor (of armchairs, etc.), trundle, roller, truckle; *comme sur des ~s*, smoothly, like clockwork; (dressm.) *~ à patrons*, pattern-marker, marking-wheel; *~ à pâte*, pastry-wheel; *patin à ~s*, roller-skate; *planche à ~s*, skateboard; *lit à ~s*, truckle-bed.
rouleu-r, -se [rulœr] *adj.* rolling; that rolls; **~r** *s.m.* **1.** ship that rolls heavily; **2.** workman who rolls casks, etc.; (in mine) haulage-man, roller, trammer; **3.** (obs.) tramp, rolling stone; **4.** (cycle-racing, etc.) runner; **~se** *s.f.* (ent.) leaf-roller (caterpillar).
roulier [rulje] *s.m.* (obs.) carter, wagoner, haulier.
roulis [ruli] *s.m.* rolling; rocking, swinging.
roulotte [rulɔt] *s.f.* (gipsy's) caravan; (obs.) caravan (for camping).
roulotter [rulɔte] *v.t.* to roll the edges of; (dressm.) to roll, to roll a hem on.
roulure [rulyr] *s.f.* **1.** rolling, curling; **2.** disease of trees causing splitting; **3.** prostitute.
roumain, -e [rumɛ̃] *adj., s.m.f.* Rumanian.
roumanie [rumani] *s.f.* (geog.) Rumania.
roupie[1] [rupi] *s.f.* rupee.
roupie[2] [rupi] *s.f.* (vulg.) nasal mucus; (fam.) *ce n'est pas de la ~ de sansonnet*, it's a bit of all right.
roupiller [rupije] *v.i.* (fam.) to doze, to snooze, to sleep.
roupillon [rupijɔ̃] *s.m.* (fam.) nap, forty winks, snooze, short sleep, doze; *faire* or *piquer un ~*, to snooze, to have forty winks.
rouquin, -e [rukɛ̃] *adj.* (fam.) red-haired, (of hair) red; *s.m.f.* (fam.) redhead; *~ s.m.* (pop.) red wine.
rouspétance [ruspetɑ̃s] *s.f.* violent protest, opposition, resistance, answering back, making a fuss.
rouspéter [ruspete] *v.i.* (fam.) to protest, to answer back, to make a fuss, to grouse.
roussâtre [rusɑtr] *adj.* russet, reddish.
rousse [rus] *s.f.* (pop.) police; *~ adj.f.* see ROUX.
rousselet [ruslɛ] *s.m.* (bot.) russet pear.
rousserolle [rusrɔl] *s.f.* (ornith.) great sedge warbler; reed warbler.
roussette [rusɛt] *s.f.* **1.** a kind of frog; **2.** dogfish; **3.** (zool.) large tropical bat; **4.** (cook.) fritter.
rousseur [rusœr] *s.f.* redness, russet colour; *taches de ~*, freckles.
roussi [rusi] *s.m.* burnt smell, scorching; *sentir le ~*, to smell of burning; (fig.) (i.) (obs.) to smack of heresy; (ii.) to be going wrong.
roussin [rusɛ̃] *s.m.* thickset horse; warhorse; (obs.) policeman.
roussir [rusir] *v.t.i.* to redden, to brown; to burn superficially, to scorch, to singe; *faire ~ de la viande*, to brown meat.
roussissement [rusismɑ̃] *s.m.* scorching, singeing.
routage [rutaʒ] *s.m.* sorting, dispatching, routing (of parcels, etc.).
route [rut] *s.f.* road; highway; way, course, orbit, direction, path, pathway, track; *grande ~*, main road, highway; *~ nationale*, trunk road; *~ départementale*, secondary road; *~ de ceinture*, orbital road, ring-road; *en ~*, on the way; on one's way; go ahead!, let us start!; *faire ~*, to go ahead; *faire ~ avec*, to travel along with; *faire ~ pour*, to make for; to steer for; *faire fausse ~*, to take the wrong road; (fig.) to take a wrong step; to bark up the wrong tree; to blunder; *code de la ~*, traffic regulations, highway code; *frais de ~*, travelling expenses; *se mettre en ~*, to set out, to start; *mettre en ~*, to start, to dispatch, to initiate; (mil.) *feuille de ~*, route(-order); *la ~ lui a été tracée*, his course has been marked out for him; *la ~ du soleil*, the course of the sun; *la ~ des Indes*, the way to India.
router [rute] *v.t.* to sort, to dispatch, to route.
routier [rutje] *s.m.* **1.** old hand, old stager, one with long experience; **2.** (naut.) track-chart; **3.** long-distance lorry-driver; **4.** (cycling) competitor in road-race; **5.** rover scout.
routi-er, -ère [rutje] *adj.* road, of roads; by road; *transports ~ers*, road transport, transport by road; *réseau ~er*, road system; *gare ~ère*, coach station; **~ère** *s.f. une* (*grande* or *bonne*) *~*, a good car for long-distance driving.
routine [rutin] *s.f.* routine, rote, practice, tradition, custom.
routini-er, -ère [rutinje] *adj.* routine, by routine, bound by routine; *s.m.f.* one who sticks to the routine, stick-in-the-mud, routinist.
rouverain, rouverin [ruvrɛ̃] *adj.m.* (of iron) brittle, hot-short.
rouvieu-x, -se [ruvjø] *adj.* mangy; **~x** *s.m.* mange.
rouvraie [ruvrɛ] *s.f.* plantation of English oaks.
rouvre [ruvr] *s.m.* (bot.) English oak.
rouvrir [ruvrir] *v.t.i.* to reopen.
rou-x, -sse [ru] *adj.* russet, red, red-haired, reddish, reddish-brown; *la lune ~sse*, April moon; **~x** *s.m.* **1.** russet colour; **2.** (cook.) roux; **3.** red-haired person, redhead.
royal, -e (**aux**) [rwajal] *adj.* royal, kingly, kinglike, regal; (fig.) splendid, fit for a king; *prince ~*, crown prince; (cook.) *lièvre à la ~e*, hare cooked with onions, garlic, etc. and red wine; *~e s.f.* tuft of beard below underlip; **~ement** [rwajalmɑ̃] *adv.* royally, regally; in a princely manner, splendidly; (fam.) completely.
royalisme [rwajalism] *s.m.* royalism.

royaliste [rwajalist] *adj., s.m.f.* royalist; (fig.) *être plus ~ que le roi*, to out-Herod Herod, to be excessively doctrinaire.
royalties [rwajalti] *s.f.pl.* (mining, etc.) royalties; ⚠ not author's 'royalties'.
royaume [rwajom] *s.m.* kingdom, realm; *le ~ des Cieux*, the Kingdom of Heaven; *le sombre ~*, Hades; *le Royaume-Uni*, the United Kingdom.
royauté [rwajote] *s.f.* royalty; kingship; monarchy.
ru [ry] *s.m.* tiny stream or channel, rivulet.
ruade [rɥad] *s.f.* kick (of horse).
ruban [rybɑ̃] *s.m.* ribbon; band, tape; narrow strip; (fig.) decoration; *scie à ~*, band-saw; *~ de cotton*, cotton tape; *~ gros grain*, petersham; *un long ~ de route*, a long road, a long strip of road; (bot.) *~ d'eau*, ribbon-grass.
rubané, -e [rybane] *adj.* **1.** covered with ribbons; **2.** striped, streaked; (of stem of glass) twisted; (of gun barrel) strip-wound.
rubaner [rybane] *v.t.* to trim with ribbons; (techn.) to roll into strips.
rubanerie [rybanri] *s.f.* ribbon-weaving; ribbon trade; ribbon manufacture.
rubani-er, -ère [rybanje] *adj.* ribbon; *s.m.f.* ribbon-maker, ribbon-dealer; **~er** *s.m.* = RUBAN *d'eau.*
rubéfaction [rybefaksjɔ̃] *s.f.* (med.) rubefaction.
rubéfiant, -e [rybefjɑ̃] *adj.*, *~ s.m.* rubefacient.
rubéfier [rybefje] *v.t.* (med.) to rubefy.
rubellite [rybelit] *s.f.* (min.) rubellite (a kind of tourmaline).
rubéole [rybeɔl] *s.f.* rubella, German measles.
rubescent, -e [rybɛssɑ̃] *adj.* reddish; growing red.
rubiacées [rybjase] *s.f.pl.* (bot.) Rubiaceae, the madder family.
rubican [rybikɑ̃] *adj.m.* (of horse) flecked with white and grey.
rubicelle [rybisɛl] *s.f.* **1.** spinel ruby; **2.** rose--quartz.
rubicond, -e [rybikɔ̃] *adj.* rubicund, ruddy, florid.
rubidium [rybidjɔm] *s.m.* (chem.) rubidium.
rubigineu-x, -se [rybiʒinø] *adj.* rubiginous, rusty, rust-coloured.
rubis [rybi] *s.m.* ruby; *faire ~ sur l'ongle*, to drink to the last drop; *payer ~ sur l'ongle*, to pay promptly and to the last farthing; *~ balais*, balas-ruby; (horol.) *monté sur ~*, jewelled.
rubrique [rybrik] *s.f.* **1.** rubric, head, chapter--heading, heading, caption; (journalism) regular article (on sport, social news, etc.); (publishing) imprint; **2.** (pl.) rubric (directions for conduct of divine service).
ruche [ryʃ] *s.f.* **1.** hive, beehive; *~ à cadres*, frame-hive; (fig.) swarm, hive of activity; **2.** ruche, ruching, frilling.
ruchée [ryʃe] *s.f.* hiveful of bees; honey obtained from one hive.
rucher [ryʃe] *s.m.* apiary, row of hives.
rucher [ryʃe] *v.t.* (dressm.) to ruche, to goffer.
rudbeckie [rydbeki] *s.f.* (bot.) rudbeckia.
rude [ryd] *adj.* rough, harsh, rugged; arduous, severe; violent, strong; formidable; shapeless; unpolished, uncouth; rude, primitive; *~ adversaire*, formidable opponent; *~ appétit*, hearty appetite; **~ment** [rydmɑ̃] *adv.* roughly, brutally, cruelly, harshly; very, a great deal; hard; *vous dansez ~ment bien*, you dance jolly well; *travailler ~ment*, to work hard; ⚠ not 'rude(ly)' in sense 'uncivil(ly)'.
rudenté, -e [rydɑ̃te] *adj.* (arch.) cabled.
rudenture [rydɑ̃tyr] *s.f.* (arch.) cabling.
rudéral, -e (aux) [ryderal] *adj.* (bot.) ruderal, growing in rubbish.
rudération [ryderɑsjɔ̃] *s.f.* paving with pebbles.
rudesse [rydɛs] *s.f.* roughness, harshness, unevenness, ruggedness; severity, fierceness; coarseness.
rudiment [rydimɑ̃] *s.m.* rudiment.
rudimentaire [rydimɑ̃tɛr] *adj.* rudimentary, primitive; imperfectly developed; elementary.
rudoiement [rydwamɑ̃] *s.m.* ill usage, bullying, brow-beating, rough handling.
rudoyer [rydwaje] *v.t.* to use roughly, to bully, to ill-treat, to treat harshly.
rue[1] [ry] *s.f.* street; *courir les ~s*, to roam the streets; (fig.) to be common talk, to be rife or current; *fille des ~s*, prostitute, street-walker; *être à la ~*, to be walking the streets, to have nowhere to live; *jeter qn. à la ~*, to throw s.o. out (into the street); *~ barrée*, no thoroughfare.
rue[2] [ry] *s.f.* (bot.) rue; ⚠ not 'rue' in sense 'repentance', 'regret'.
ruée [rɥe] *s.f.* rush, charge, onslaught, inrush; stampede; hurrying crowd.
ruelle [rɥɛl] *s.f.* **1.** narrow street, lane, alley; **2.** space between bed and wall; (Fr. Lit. hist.) alcove.
ruer [rɥe] *v.i.* to kick (as horse, etc.); (fig.) *~ dans les brancards*, to protest, to resist, to kick against the pricks; **se ~** *v.refl.* to rush, to hurl oneself (*sur*, on, at); to charge, to attack impetuously, to dash; to stampede.
rufian, ruffian [ryfjɑ̃] *s.m.* (obs.) procurer, pimp, whoremaster.
rugbyman [rygbiman] *s.m.* (pl. *rugbymen*) Rugby (football) player.
rugine [ryʒin] *s.f.* (surg.) raspatory, rasp.
rugir [ryʒir] *v.t.i.* to roar; to bellow.
rugissant, -e [ryʒisɑ̃] *adj.* roaring; (fig.) (of engine) noisy.
rugissement [ryʒismɑ̃] *s.m.* roar, roaring.
rugosité [rygozite] *s.f.* rugosity, roughness, rough spot.
rugueu-x, -se [rygø] *adj.* rugged, rugose, gnarled, wrinkled, corrugated, rough, uneven; (fig.) rough, harsh; **~x** *s.m.* (mil.) striker, percussion--pin.
ruine [rɥin] *s.f.* ruin, downfall, collapse, destruction, decay; *courir à sa ~*, to be on the road to ruin; *menacer ~*, to threaten to collapse, to be on the point of falling down; *cela causera sa ~*, that will be the ruination of him, that will bring ruin on him; *elle n'est plus qu'une ~*, she is a wreck, she is the shadow of her former self.
ruiner [rɥine] *v.t.* to ruin, to destroy, to spoil, to invalidate, to disprove; to overthrow; to bring to ruin; **se ~** *v.refl.* to ruin oneself; to go to ruin, to fall into ruins, to collapse.
ruineu-x, -se [rɥinø] *adj.* disastrous, bringing ruin or destruction, destructive; (fig.) (of expense, etc.) ruinous; in ruins, dilapidated, about to collapse, shaky; (fig.) unreliable; **~sement** [rɥinøzmɑ̃] *adv.* ruinously (expensive).
ruinure [rɥinyr] *s.f.* (carp.) notch; housing.
ruisseau (pl. **-x**) [rɥiso] *s.m.* stream, brook, creek, rivulet; (street & fig.) gutter; (fig.) stream, floods.
ruisselant, -e [rɥislɑ̃] *adj.* streaming, running, dripping, (*de*, with).
ruisseler [rɥisle] *v.i.* to stream, to run, to pour down, to run in streams; to be dripping wet; to trickle down.
ruisselet [rɥislɛ] *s.m.* rivulet, little brook.
ruissellement [rɥisɛlmɑ̃] *s.m.* streaming, running, pouring down, dripping; (geol.) *~ pluvial*, run-off; *terre de ~*, alluvium.
rumb, rhumb [rɔ̃b] *s.m.* (naut.) rhumb.
rumen [rymɛn] *s.m.* (zool.) rumen, paunch.
rumeur [rymœr] *s.f.* confused noise, rumbling; murmurings (of discontent); uproar, clamour; (fig.) rumour, report; *la ~ publique l'accuse*, it is rumoured that he is guilty.
rumex [rymɛks] *s.m.* (bot.) Rumex, dock.

ruminant, -e [rymінɑ̃] *adj.* ruminant, ruminating; ~ *s.m.* ruminant.
rumination [ryminɑsjɔ̃] *s.f.* rumination; chewing the cud.
ruminer [rymine] *v.t.* to ruminate, to chew the cud; (fig.) to meditate, to reflect on, to ponder, to revolve (sth.) slowly in one's mind.
rumsteck see ROMSTECK.
runabout [rœnabawt] *s.m.* small motor boat.
runes [ryn] *s.f.pl.* runes, runic letters.
runique [rynik] *adj.* runic.
ruolz [rɥɔls] *s.m.* plated metal, electroplate.
rupestre [rypɛstr] *adj.* (bot.) rupestral, rupestrine, rock; (art) on rock; *dessins ~s*, rock drawings; *figures ~s*, figures cut in the rock.
rupicole [rypikɔl] *s.f.* (ornith.) cock of the rock, grouse.
rupin, -e [rypɛ̃] (slang) *adj.* rich, luxurious; *s.m.f.* rich person, one living in luxury.
rupiner [rypine] (fam.) *v.i.* to do well, to succeed (*à*, in); ~ *v.t.* to succeed in.
rupteur [ryptœr] *s.m.* (electr.) contact-breaker, circuit-breaker, trip; interrupter.
rupture [ryptyr] *s.f.* rupture, breaking, parting, bursting, fracture, breach; (fig.) rupture, breaking-off; ~ *du contrat*, breach of contract; ~ *d'un mariage*, breaking-off of an engagement; *en ~ avec*, in defiance of, going against, contrary to; *en ~ de ban*, breaking bounds; in defiance of restrictions.
rural, -e, (aux) [ryral] *adj.* rural, country; ~ *s.m.* countryman; *les ruraux*, those living in the country, country people.
ruse [ryz] *s.f.* craft, cunning, guile, wile; ruse stratagem, feint, trick, dodge; *une ~ grossière*, a blatant piece of deception, a transparent ruse; ~ *de guerre*, stratagem of war; *~s innocentes*, harmless tricks.
rusé, -e [ryze] *adj.* wily, sly, artful, cunning.
ruser [ryze] *v.i.* to use cunning or deceit, to be wily, to resort to cunning or to a ruse, to finesse; (hunt.) to double.
rush [rœs] *s.m.* **1.** (sport) final dash or sprint; **2.** rush.
russe [rys] *adj.*, *s.m.f.* Russian.
russie [rysi] *s.f.* (geog.) Russia.
russifier [rysifje] *v.t.* to Russify, to Russianize.
russophile [rysɔfil] *adj.*, *s.m.f.* Russophile.
russule [rysyl] *s.f.* (bot.) a kind of reddish poisonous mushroom.
rustaud, -e [rysto] *adj.* boorish, rustic, clownish, coarse; *s.m.f.* boor, rustic, clod-hopper, clown.
rusticage [rystikaʒ] *s.m.* roughcasting, rough coat (for walls).
rusticité [rystisite] *s.f.* rusticity, simplicity; country manners; boorishness; (of plants) hardiness.
rustine [rystin] *s.f.* patch (for cycle tyre).
rustique [rystik] *adj.* rustic, rural, country; homely, simple, of simple workmanship, unrefined; boorish; (of plants) hardy; *maison ~*, country cottage; *des plaisirs ~s*, country pastimes; ~ *s.m.* mason's hammer.
rustiquer [rystike] *v.t.* to roughcast (wall, etc.); to give a rustic finish to; ⚠ not 'to rusticate' in senses 'to live a country life' or 'to send down temporarily' from the university.
rustre [rystr] *adj.* rustic, boorish, loutish; ~ *s.m.* boor, lout, clod-hopper.
rut [ryt] *s.m.* rut, rutting; *être en ~*, to rut, to be on heat.
rutabaga [rytabaga] *s.m.* (bot.) rutabaga, swede (turnip).
ruthénium [rytenjɔm] *s.m.* (chem.) ruthenium.
rutilant, -e [rytilɑ̃] *adj.* glowing, shining, bright red; ruddy.
rutile [rytil] *s.m.* (chem.) rutile (an ore of titanium).
rutiler [rytile] *v.i.* to glow, to shine, to glitter.
rythme [ritm] *s.m.* rhythm; (fam.) tempo.
rythmé, -e [ritme] *adj.* rhythmic.
rythmer [ritme] *v.t.* to give rhythm to; (fig.) to punctuate.
rythmique [ritmik] *adj.* rhythmic(al).

S

S, s [ɛs] *s.m.* the letter S, s; abbrev. *Sud*; *faire des s*, to zigzag; *en s*, winding, zigzag; *en S*, S-shaped; *S de suspension*, S-hook.
s' see SE; SI *conj.*
S.A. [ɛsɑ] abbrev. *Son Altesse*; *Societé anonyme*.
sa see SON *poss. adj.*
sabayon [sabajɔ̃] *s.m.* (cook.) zabaglione.
sabbat [saba] *s.m.* **1.** sabbath; **2.** (witches') sabbath; wild dance; tumult, uproar.
sabbatique [sabatik] *adj.* sabbatic(al).
sabin, -e [sabɛ̃] *adj.*, *s.m.f.* (ant.) Sabine.
sabine [sabin] *s.f.* (bot.) savin.
sabir [sabir] *s.m.* a lingua franca spoken in Levant and North Africa; jargon.
sable[1] [sɑbl] *s.m.* sand; (med.) gravel; *~s mouvants*, quicksands; (fig., fam.) *être sur le ~*, to be on the rocks; ~ *adj.* sand-coloured.
sable[2] [sɑbl] *s.m.* (herald.) sable.
sablé, -e [sɑble] *adj.* sanded, covered with sand; *allée ~e*, gravel walk; ~ *s.m.* (cook.) a kind of shortbread.
sabler [sɑble] *v.t.* **1.** to cover with sand, to sand, to gravel; **2.** to drink freely, to gulp down, to toss off; **3.** (techn.) to sand--blast.
sableu-x, -se [sɑblø] *adj.* sandy, gravelly, containing sand.
sablier [sɑblie] *s.m.* sand-glass, hourglass, egg--timer.
sablière [sɑbliɛr] *s.f.* **1.** sand-pit, gravel-pit; **2.** (carp.) wall-plate; purlin; **3.** sand-box (on locomotive).
sablon [sɑblɔ̃] *s.m.* fine white sand; scouring--sand.
sablonner [sɑblɔne] *v.t.* to scour with fine sand; (techn.) to sprinkle with welding sand.
sablonneu-x, -se [sɑblɔnø] *adj.* sandy.
sablonnière [sɑblɔnjɛr] *s.f.* sand-pit.
sabord [sabɔr] *s.m.* (naut.) porthole, port; port (side); ~ *de charge*, loading-port, cargo door; *faux ~*, deadlight; *contre-~*, port-lid.
sabordage [sabɔrdaʒ], **sabordement** [sabɔrdəmɑ̃] *s.m.* scuttling.
saborder [sabɔrde] *v.t.* (naut.) to scuttle (a ship); **se ~** *v.refl.* to scuttle (one's ship).
sabot [sabo] *s.m.* **1.** wooden shoe, clog, sabot; (techn.) brake-shoe, brake-block; skid, drag; shoe, glider (on foot of furniture); (electr.) collecting-shoe; overrider (on car bumper); *baignoire ~*, slipper bath; (fig.) *je le vois venir avec ses grands ~s*, it is easy to see what he is after; **2.** hoof; **3.** (whipping-)top; **4.** old, worn-out or inferior ship, vehicle, mus. instrument, etc.; *travailler comme un ~*, to do poor work.

sabotage [sabɔtaʒ] *s.m.* **1.** clog-making; **2.** sabotage; scamped or spoiled work.
saboter [sabɔte] *v.t.* **1.** (rail.) to chair (sleeper); **2.** to scamp (work), to perform badly; **3.** to sabotage.
saboterie [sabɔtri] *s.f.* clog factory; manufacture of clogs.
saboteu-r, -se [sabɔtœr] *s.m.f.* **1.** saboteur; **2.** bad worker.
saboti-er, -ère [sabɔtje] *s.m.f.* clog maker; clog seller.
sabouler [sabule] *v.t.* (fam.) to jostle, to rough-handle, to give a shaking to.
sabrage [sɑbraʒ] *s.m.* carding (of wool).
sabre [sɑbr] *s.m.* sabre, sword; (fam.) cut-throat razor; *~-baïonnette*, sword-bayonet; *~ au clair*, with sabres drawn; (fig.) *bruit de ~*, sabre-rattling, aggressive policy; *le ~ et le goupillon*, the Army and the Church.
sabrer [sɑbre] *v.t.* to strike with a sabre, to slash about, to cut, to sabre; (fig.) to strike out, to slash, to make drastic cuts in; to sack; to fail (candidates) wholesale; (text.) to card.
sabretache [sɑbrətaʃ] *s.f.* sabretache.
sabreur [sɑbrœr] *s.m.* swordsman; tough fighter.
saburral, -e (aux) [sabyral] *adj.* (med.) (of tongue) coated.
saburre [sabyr] *s.f.* (med.) saburra (foul granular matter in stomach).
sac[1] [sak] *s.m.* bag, sack, pouch; knapsack; *~ à main*, handbag; *~ de voyage*, soft bag, grip; *~ à ouvrage*, work-bag; *~ de sable*, sandbag, punch-ball; *~ de soldat*, knapsack, haversack; *~ de marin*, kitbag; *~ de couchage*, sleeping-bag; *~ de montagne* or *à dos*, rucksack; (fig.) *~ à vin*, habitual drunkard; *il en a plein le ~*, he has had a skinful (of drink); *prendre qn. la main dans le ~*, to catch s.o. red-handed, in the act; *donner le ~ à qn.*, to sack s.o.; *ils sont à mettre dans le même ~*, they are birds of a feather, one is as bad as the other; *l'affaire est dans le ~*, it is as good as done, it is all tied up, it is in the bag; *un homme de ~ et de corde*, a criminal type, one of the criminal fraternity; *vider son ~*, to speak one's mind, to get it off one's chest, to make a clean breast of it; *tirer d'un ~ deux moutures*, (fig.) to make double profits; *avoir le ~*, to be rich; *épouser un ~*, to marry money; to marry for money.
sac[2] [sak] *s.m.* sack, sacking, plunder, pillage; *mettre à ~*, to sack.
saccade [sakad] *s.f.* jerk, check, shock, bump; *par ~s*, by fits and starts.
saccadé, -e [sakade] *adj.* jerky, in jerks, irregular, interrupted, broken; (fig.) (of style) abrupt.
saccader [sakade] *v.t.* to jerk, to check.
saccage [sakaʒ] *s.m.* pillage, devastation, havoc.
saccager [sakaʒe] *v.t.* to devastate; to plunder; to throw into complete confusion, to ransack.
saccageu-r, -se [sakaʒœr] *s.m.f.* plunderer, pillager.
sacchar-ate [sakarat] *s.m.* (chem.) saccharate; **~ides** [sakarid] *s.m.pl.* (chem.) saccharides; **~ification** [sakarifikɑsjɔ̃] *s.f.* (chem.), conversion into sugar; **~ifier** [sakarifje] *v.t.* (chem.) to convert into sugar; **~imètre** [sakarimɛtr] *s.m.* saccharimeter; **~ine** [sakarin] *s.f.* saccharine; **~ique** [sakarik] *adj.* (chem.) saccharic; **~ose** [sakaroz] *s.m.* (chem.) saccarose, sucrose.
saccule [sakyl] *s.m.* (anat.) saccule.
sacculiforme [sakylifɔrm] *adj.* bag-shaped, sacciform.
sacerdoce [sasɛrdɔs] *s.m.* priesthood, the ministry; the ecclesiastical body.
sacerdotal, -e (aux) [sasɛrdɔtal] *adj.* sacerdotal.
sachée [saʃe] *s.f.* bagful, sackful.
sachem [saʃɛm] *s.m.* sachem (American Indian chief).
sachet [saʃɛ] *s.m.* sachet, scented bag; small paper bag; small packet.
sacoche [sakɔʃ] *s.f.* satchel; money-bag; courier's bag, saddle-bag, tool-bag.
sacolève [sakɔlɛv] *s.f.* sackalever, sacoleva (Levantine cargo-boat).
sacquer, saquer [sake] *v.t.* (fam.) to sack, to give the sack to, to dismiss, to kick out.
sacramentel, -le [sakramɑ̃tɛl] *adj.* sacramental.
sacre[1] [sakr] *s.m.* (rite of) consecration or coronation; (fig.) rite.
sacre[2] [sakr] *s.m.* (ornith.) saker (kind of falcon).
sacré[1], **-e** [sakre] *adj.* **1.** sacred, holy, consecrated, venerable, inviolable; *les livres ~s*, Holy Writ; **2.** (fam.) (in front of noun) damned, bloody (vulg. slang); *un ~ menteur*, a bloody liar; (also reinforces oaths, as in *~ bon Dieu!*); *~ s.m. le ~*, the sacred.
sacré[2], **-e** [sakre] *adj.* (anat.) sacral.
sacrebleu [sakrəblø] *interj.* mild expletive expressing surprise or indignation.
sacré-cœur [sakrekœr] *s.m.* (Cath.) Sacred Heart; *le Sacré-Cœur* (Catholic basilica at Montmartre, Paris).
sacrement [sakrəmɑ̃] *s.m.* sacrament; *les derniers ~s*, the last rites; *fréquenter les ~s*, to go to confession and communion regularly.
sacrer [sakre] *v.t.* to anoint; to consecrate; to crown; *~ v.i.* (fam.) to swear.
sacret [sakrɛ] *s.m.* (ornith.) sakeret, young tercel.
sacrificateur [sakrifikatœr] *s.m.* sacrificer; *Grand ~*, Jewish High Priest.
sacrificatoire [sakrifikatwar] *adj.* sacrificial.
sacrifice [sakrifis] *s.m.* sacrifice, offering; renunciation, self-denial.
sacrifier [sakrifje] *v.t.* to sacrifice, to immolate, to offer up, to give up, to devote, to throw away; *~ à*, to conform to, to give way to; **se ~** *v.refl.* to sacrifice oneself, to devote oneself.
sacrilège [sakrilɛʒ] *s.m.* sacrilege; *~ s.m.f.* sacrilegious person; *~ adj.* sacrilegious.
sacripant [sakripɑ̃] *s.m.* downright rascal, blackguard, good-for-nothing.
sacristain [sakristɛ̃] *s.m.* sexton, sacristan.
sacristi [sakristi] *interj.* mild expletive expressing surprise or indignation.
sacristie [sakristi] *s.f.* vestry, sacristy.
sacro-saint, -e [sakrɔsɛ̃] *adj.* (often iron.) sacrosanct.
sacrum [sakrɔm] *s.m.* (anat.) sacrum.
sadducéen, -ne [sadyseɛ̃] *adj.* Sadducean; *s.m.f.* Sadducee.
sadique [sadik] *adj.* sadistic; (fig.) cruel; *~ s.m.f.* sadist; **~ment** [sadikmɑ̃] *adv.* sadistically.
sadisme [sadism] *s.m.* sadism; (fig.) wanton cruelty.
safari [safari] *s.m.* safari.
safran[1] [safrɑ̃] *s.m.* (bot.) saffron; *~ adj. invar.* saffron(-coloured).
safran[2] [safrɑ̃] *s.m.* (naut.) after-piece, cheek, (of rudder).
safrané, -e [safrane] *adj.* flavoured or coloured with saffron; saffron(-coloured).
safraner [safrane] *v.t.* to flavour with saffron.
safre [safr] *s.m.* (chem.) zaffre.
saga [saga] *s.f.* saga, epic.
sagace [sagas] *adj.* sagacious, shrewd, clever.
sagacité [sagasite] *s.f.* sagacity.
sagaie [sagɛ] *s.f.* assegai.
sage [saʒ] *adj.* wise, sage, prudent, discreet, judicious, sensible; good, well-behaved; chaste, modest, restrained; (to children) *soyez ~s!*, be good!; *un enfant ~*, a well-behaved child; *~ s.m.* sage, wise man, sane or sensible person; ⚠ not 'sage' (bot.).
sage-femme [saʒfam] *s.f.* midwife.
sagement [saʒmɑ̃] *adv.* wisely, prudently,

judiciously; well, discreetly, soberly, virtuously, chastely.
sagesse [saʒɛs] *s.f.* wisdom, good sense, judiciousness, discretion; good behaviour, goodness; gentleness, restraint, modesty; chastity, virtue.
sagette [saʒɛt] *s.f.* **1.** (obs.) arrow; **2.** (bot.) arrowhead.
sagittaire [saʒitɛr] *s.m.* (astron.) Sagittarius; ~ *s.f.* = SAGETTE 2.
sagittal, -e, (aux) [saʒital] *adj.* arrow-shaped; (anat.) sagittal.
sagou [sagu] *s.m.* sago.
sagouin [sagwɛ̃] *s.m.* (zool.) sagoin, squirrel-monkey; (fig.) slovenly person.
sagoutier [sagutje] *s.m.* (bot.) sago-palm.
sagum [sagɔm] *s.m.* (ant.) sagum (Gaulish woollen cloak).
saharien, -ne [saarjɛ̃] *adj.* Saharan, Saharian, Saharic; *s.m.f.* Saharan, Saharian; **~ne** *s.f.* bush-shirt.
saï [sai] *s.m.* (zool.) sai, kind of (South American) monkey.
saie[1] [sɛ] *s.f.* = SAGUM.
saie[2] [sɛ] *s.f.* goldsmith's brush.
saïga [saiga] *s.m.* (zool.) saiga (kind of antelope).
saignant, -e [sɛɲɑ̃] *adj.* bleeding, bloody; (cook.) underdone, rare.
saignée [seɲe] *s.f.* blood-letting, bleeding, phlebotomy; bend of the arm; (fig.) heavy drawing (of funds, etc.), heavy sacrifice; extortion; (techn.) irrigation-trench, oil-groove.
saignement [sɛɲəmɑ̃] *s.m.* bleeding.
saigner [seɲe] *v.t.* to bleed, to kill (animal) by bleeding; (fig.) to drain, to exact heavy payment from, to extort from; ~ *à blanc*, to bleed to death; (fig.) to bleed white; ~ *v.i.* to bleed, to lose blood; (fig.) to cause pain; **se** ~ *v.refl.* (fig.) to make sacrifices; *se ~ aux quatre veines*, to make every sacrifice, to pinch and scrape.
saigneu-x, -se [sɛɲø] adj. bloody; *bout ~x*, scrag-end (of mutton, etc.).
saillant, -e [sajɑ̃] *adj.* projecting, jutting out; (herald.) salient; (fig.) striking, remarkable, noticeable, prominent, outstanding, salient; ~ *s.m.* salient.
saillie [saji] *s.f.* **1.** standing out, jutting out, projection, ledge, salient; *en* ~, sticking out; *faire* ~, to jut out; **2.** start, spurt, flash, impulse, outburst, witticism, sally; gush; **3.** (of animals) copulation, covering.
saillir [sajir] *v.i. irreg.* to stand out, to project, to jut out, to stick out, to protrude; to gush, to spurt; *faire* ~, to bring out; ~ *v.t.* (of animals) to cover, to serve.
sain, -e [sɛ̃] *adj.* sound, hale, healthy; normal; wholesome, salubrious, health-giving; clean; *~ d'esprit*, sane; *~ et sauf*, safe and sound; (naut.) *côte ~e*, clear coast.
saindoux [sɛ̃du] *s.m.* lard.
sainement [sɛnmɑ̃] *adv.* soundly; wholesomely, healthily, normally; (fig.) judiciously, sanely.
sainfoin [sɛ̃fwɛ̃] *s.m.* (bot.) sainfoin.
saint, -e [sɛ̃] *adj.* (abbrev. *S.*, *Ste*) holy, sacred, consecrated, saintly, sainted, sanctified; *S. André*, Saint Andrew; *Vendredi Saint*, Good Friday; *l'Écriture Sainte*, Holy Writ, the Scriptures; *le Saint-Esprit*, the Holy Ghost, the Holy Spirit; *toute la ~e journée*, the whole blessed day; *la Terre Sainte*, the Holy Land; *s.m.f.* saint; *ne savoir à quel ~ se vouer*, not to know which way to turn; *le ~ des ~s*, holy of holies; *chacun prêche pour son ~*, every one tries to further his own interests; *coiffer Ste Catherine*, to be 25 and unmarried; *la Saint-Jean, s.f.* midsummer; *la Saint-Médard, s.f.* St. Swithin's day; *la Saint-Michel, s.f.* Michaelmas; (colloq.) *la sainte-touche*, pay-day.
saint-bernard [sɛ̃bɛrnar] *s.m. invar.* St. Bernard (dog).
saint-crépin [sɛ̃krepɛ̃] *s.m.* (obs.) **1.** cobbler's tools, grindery; **2.** = SAINT-FRUSQUIN.
saint-cyrien [sɛ̃sirjɛ̃] *s.m.* (pl. *~-cyriens*) pupil of Saint-Cyr (mil. school).
Saint-Domingue [sɛ̃dɔmɛ̃g] *s.m.* (geog.) Santo Domingo.
Sainte-Hélène [sɛ̃telɛn] *s.f.* (geog.) St. Helena.
saintement [sɛ̃tmɑ̃] *adv.* holily, piously, righteously, in godly fashion.
sainte nitouche [sɛ̃tnituʃ] *s.f.* hypocrite, one who affects innocence, prude.
sainteté [sɛ̃təte] *s.f.* holiness, sacredness, sanctity, saintliness; *Sa Sainteté*, His Holiness (the Pope); *sujet de ~*, religious theme.
saint-frusquin [sɛ̃fryskɛ̃] *s.m. tout le* or *son ~*, one's belongings, one's worldly goods, all one possesses; the lot.
saint-germain [sɛ̃ʒɛrmɛ̃] *s.m.invar.* a kind of pear.
saint-glinglin [sɛ̃glɛ̃glɛ̃] *à la ~ adv.loc.* never, till the cows come home, till the year dot.
saint-honoré [sɛ̃tɔnɔre] *s.m.* (pl. *~-honoré(s)*) a kind of cake.
Saint-Laurent [sɛ̃lɔrɑ̃] *s.m.* (geog.) St. Lawrence (river).
saint-nectaire [sɛ̃nɛktɛr] *s.m.* a cheese from the Auvergne.
Saint-Office [sɛ̃tɔfis] *s.m.* the Holy Office.
saint-paulin [sɛ̃polɛ̃] *s.m.* a kind of cheese.
Saint-Père [sɛ̃pɛr] *s.m. le ~*, the Holy Father, the Pope.
saint-pierre [sɛ̃pjɛr] *s.m.invar.* (ichth.) John Dory.
Saint-Siège [sɛ̃sjɛʒ] *s.m.* the Holy See.
saisi, -e [sezi] *adj.* seized, gripped; struck, startled; (cook.) sealed; (law) distrained upon; ~ *s.m.* distrainee.
saisie [sezi] *s.f.* (law) seizure; execution, distraint, foreclosure, sequestration; *~-arrêt*, attachment; *~ immobilière*, attachment of real property; *~-brandon*, execution on crops; *~-exécution*, execution, distraint; *~-gagerie*, distraint; *~-revendication*, seizure under prior claim; *~ conservatoire*, seizure of goods under dispute.
saisine [sezin] *s.f.* **1.** (law) seisin; **2.** (naut.) gripe, slings, lashing.
saisir [sezir] *v.t.* **1.** to seize; to seize upon, to grasp, to lay hold of, to catch, to snatch; to avail oneself of; to understand, to perceive, to apprehend; *mal ~*, to be under a misapprehension about; *je n'ai pas bien saisi*, I did not quite catch it; **2.** to strike with amazement, to give a shock to, to startle, to strike dumb, to overwhelm, to overcome, to grip; *elle en est restée toute saisie*, she was awestruck; she was staggered; **3.** ~ *de*, to make (s.o.) cognizant of; to put (sth.) in the hands of; to refer (sth.) to, to bring (sth.) before, (a tribunal, etc.); to call on (s.o.) to consider (sth.); *le tribunal en est saisi*, it has been laid before the court; *on est saisi de deux questions*, we have two questions to consider; **4.** (law) to seize, to attach, to distrain, to sequestrate, to foreclose (mortgage, etc.), to vest (*de*, with); **5.** (naut.) to stow, to secure; to gripe; **6.** (cook.) to seal (by plunging in hot fat); **se** ~ *v.refl.* to seize, to snatch (*de*, at), to lay hold (of), to possess oneself (of).
saisissable [sezisabl] *adj.* **1.** (law) that can be seized, distrainable; **2.** perceptible, distinguishable, comprehensible.
saisissant, -e [sezisɑ̃] *adj.* striking, thrilling, startling; (of cold) piercing; ~ *s.m.* (law) distrainer.
saisissement [sezismɑ̃] *s.m.* shock, pang, shudder, thrill.

saison [sɛzɔ̃] *s.f.* season, time (of year), period, spell, (right or appropriate) time (*de*, for); *la ~ des vacances*, holiday time or season; *en cette ~*, at this time; *en toute(s) ~(s)*, all the year round; *de ~*, in season; (fig.) well-timed, seasonable; *en temps et ~*, in due season; *hors de ~*, out of season; (fig.) ill-timed, unseasonable; *arrière-~ s.f.* autumn; fall (U.S.); *la morte ~*, the dead season, the slack time; *la ~ nouvelle*, springtime; *marchand des quatre ~s*, costermonger; *faire une ~ à Vichy*, to take the cure at Vichy.
saisonni-er, -ère [sɛzɔnje] *adj.* seasonal, during the season; seasonable; *s.m.f.* seasonal worker.
sajou [saʒu] *s.m.* = SAPAJOU.
saké [sake], **saki** [saki] *s.m.* sake, fermented liquor made from rice.
saki [saki] *s.m.* (zool.) saki (monkey).
salace [salas] *adj.* salacious, lustful.
salacité [salasite] *s.f.* salacity, salaciousness, lustfulness.
salade[1] [salad] *s.f.* salad; lettuce, endive, etc.; (fig.) medley, jumble, mess, hotchpotch; (pl.) (fam.) stories, lies; (fam.) *mettre tout en ~*, to jumble everything up; *panier à ~*, salad-basket; (fam.) police van, Black Maria.
salade[2] [salad] *s.f.* (hist.) sallet, helmet.
saladier [saladje] *s.m.* salad bowl, salad dish, bowl of salad.
salage [salaʒ] *s.m.* salting.
salaire [salɛr] *s.m.* wages, wage, pay, fees; (fig.) reward, recompense, retribution; ⚠ not 'salary' (paid monthly).
salaison [salɛzɔ̃] *s.f.* salting, pickling; (pl.) salt provisions, goods preserved in brine.
salamalec [salamalɛk] *s.m.* salaam; (fam.) sweeping bow, excessively polite greeting, (fig.) prostration.
salamandre [salamɑ̃dr] *s.f.* **1.** (zool.) salamander; **2.** slow-combustion stove.
salangane [salɑ̃gan] *s.f.* salangane, swift that makes edible nest.
salant [salɑ̃] *adj.m.* salt, saline; *~ s.m.* salt-marsh, salt-pans.
salarial, -e, (aux) *adj.* relating to wages or pay; *politique ~e*, pay policy.
salariat [salarja] *s.m.* payment by weekly wage; wage-earning status; wage-earners, workers.
salarié, -e [salarje] *adj.* wage-earning; *s.m.f.* wage-earner, worker.
salarier [salarje] *v.t.* to pay wages to.
salaud [salo] *s.m.* (pop.) dirty, mean, low person, shit (vulg.).
sale [sal] *adj.* dirty, foul, unclean, filthy, soiled; (fig.) low(-down), dirty, coarse, obscene; mean; offensive, nasty, beastly.
salé, -e [sale] *adj.* salt, salted, briny; (fig.) broad, spicy, salty, near the bone; witty, biting; (of criticism) severe; (of price, sentence, etc.) stiff.
salé [sale] *s.m.* (*petit-*)~ salt pork; (pop.) small child, brat.
salement [salmɑ̃] *adv.* dirtily, filthily, nastily, disgustingly, in a low-down manner, in a mean way; (pop.) very much, awfully; *~ ennuyé*, worried stiff.
salep [salɛp] *s.m.* (cook.) salep.
saler [sale] *v.t.* to salt, to sprinkle with salt; to preserve with salt, to cure, to pickle; (fam.) to give a stiff punishment to; to overcharge, to fleece; *~ la note*, to inflate the bill.
saleron [salrɔ̃] *s.m.* salt-bowl, salt-cellar.
saleté [salte] *s.f.* dirt, filth, dirtiness, filthiness, dirty thing; coarse expression, dirty remark or story, obscenity, indecency; (fam.) dirty trick; bit of rubbish.
saleu-r, -se [salœr] *s.m.f.* salter.
sali-cacées [salikase], **~cinées** [salisine] *s.f.pl.* (bot.) Salicaceae; **~caire** [salikɛr] *s.f.* (bot.) spiked purple loosestrife; **~cine** [salisin] *s.m.* (chem.) salicin; **~cole** [salikɔl] *adj.* salt, salt-bearing; **~coque** [salikɔk] *s.f.* shrimp; (fam.) prawn; **~corne** [salikɔrn] *s.f.* (bot.) saltwort; **~coside** [salikozid] *s.m.* = *~cine*; **~cylate** [salisilat] *s.m.* (chem.) salicylate; **~cylique** [salisilik] *adj.* (chem.) salicylic.
salière [saljɛr] *s.f.* **1.** salt-cellar, salt-box; **2.** recess, hollow (i.) above eye of horse, (ii.) of eyes or temples, (iii.) (fam.) adjacent to collar-bone.
salifi-able [salifjabl] *adj.* (chem.) salifiable; **~fication** [salifikɑsjɔ̃] *s.f.* (chem.) salification; **~er** [salifje] *v.t.* (chem.) to salify.
saligaud [saligo] *s.m.* = SALAUD.
salignon [saliɲɔ̃] *s.m.* cake or bar of salt.
salin, -e [salɛ̃] *adj.* saline, salt; briny; *~ s.m.* salt-marsh.
salinage [salinaʒ] *s.m.* **1.** (techn.) evaporation or concentration of the brine; **2.** (commercial) salt-deposit.
saline [salin] *s.f.* salt-marsh; salt-mine; salt-extraction.
salini-er, -ère [salinje] *s.m.f.* extractor of sea-salt.
salinité [salinite] *s.f.* salinity.
salique [salik] *adj.* (hist.) Salic, Salian.
salir [salir] *v.t.* to dirty, to soil, to stain, to foul; (fig.) to defile, to defame, to sully, to tarnish, to degrade, to disgrace; **se** *~ v.refl.* to debase or degrade oneself.
salissant, -e [salisɑ̃] *adj.* easily soiled; (of work, etc.) that dirties, dirty.
salisson [salisɔ̃] *s.f.* (fam.) little slut.
salissure [salisyr] *s.f.* soil, stain, dirty mark, dirt.
salivaire [salivɛr] *adj.* salivary.
salivation [salivɑsjɔ̃] *s.f.* salivation.
salive [saliv] *s.f.* saliva, spit, spittle; *avaler sa ~*, to swallow; (fig.) to check oneself (from saying sth.).
saliver [salive] *v.i.* to salivate.
salle [sal] *s.f.* hall, entrance-hall, large room, assembly room; ward (in hospitals); (theatr.) house, auditorium, audience; *faire crouler la ~*, to bring down the house; *~ d'armes*, (i.) armoury; (ii.) fencing-school; *~ de bain*, bathroom; *~ d'eau*, wash-place, shower-room; *~ d'attente*, waiting-room; *~ d'audience*, audience-chamber; *~ d'études*, schoolroom; *~ de cours*, lecture-room; *~ à manger*, dining-room; *~ des pas perdus*, entrance-hall (to public building), (station) concourse; (mil.) *~ de police*, guardroom, military prison; *~ des ventes*, auction-room, sale-room.
salmigondis [salmigɔ̃di] *s.m.* (cook.) hotchpotch, salmagundi; (fig.) medley, farrago, hotchpotch.
salmis [salmi] *s.m.* (cook.) salmi, ragout of game.
salmon-ellose [salmɔneloz] *s.f.* (med.) salmonellosis; **~iculture** [salmɔnikyltyr] *s.f.* rearing of salmon and/or trout; **~idés** [salmɔnide] *s.m.pl.* (zool.) Salmonidae.
saloir [salwar] *s.m.* salting-tub; salt-box or -pot.
Salomon [salɔmɔ̃] *s.m.* Solomon; (geog.) *les îles ~*, the Solomon Islands.
salon [salɔ̃] *s.m.* drawing-room, living-room, sitting-room, lounge, parlour, fashionable (place of) reception; (annual) exhibition or show; saloon; lounge suite (of furniture); *fréquenter les ~s*, to move in fashionable circles; *~ d'attente*, waiting-room; *le Salon de l'Automobile*, the Motor Show; *~ de thé*, tea-room; *wagon-* or *voiture-~*, saloon carriage; ⚠ not 'saloon' as in saloon-bar, saloon car, billiard, dancing, etc., saloon.
saloon [salun] *s.m.* saloon (esp. Far West type).
salopard [salɔpar] *s.m.* **1.** (mil. slang) Moroccan rebel (during 1920–1933 campaigns); **2.** (pop.) = SALAUD.

salope [salɔp] *s.f.* slut, trollop; harlot, prostitute.
saloper [salɔpe] *v.t.* to bungle, to spoil (one's work).
saloperie [salɔpri] *s.f.* dirty trick; beastliness; filthiness, filth.
salopette [salɔpɛt] *s.f.* (workmen's) overalls, slops, dungarees.
salpêtre [salpɛtr] *s.m.* saltpetre, potassium nitrate; ~ *du Chili*, sodium nitrate.
salpêtrer [salpetre] *v.t.* **1.** to treat (ground) with saltpetre; **2. se** ~ *v.refl.* (of damp walls) to become covered with an efflorescence of saltpetre.
salpêtreu-x, -se [salpɛtrø] *adj.* affected with efflorescence of saltpetre (see SALPÊTRER 2).
salpêtrière [salpɛtrjɛr] *s.f.* saltpetre works; *la Salpêtrière*, hospital in Paris.
salpingite [salpɛ̃ʒit] *s.f.* (pathol.) salpingitis.
salse [sals] *s.f.* (geol.) salse, mud volcano.
salsepareille [salsəparɛj] *s.f.* (bot.) sarsaparilla.
salsifis [salsifi] *s.m.* salsify.
saltarelle [saltarɛl] *s.f.* saltarello (a dance).
saltimbanque [saltɛ̃bɑ̃k] *s.m.f.* juggler, acrobat; (lit. & fig.) clown, mountebank; buffoon; humbug, charlatan.
salubre [salybr] *adj.* salubrious, healthy, wholesome.
salubrité [salybrite] *s.f.* salubrity, healthiness, wholesomeness; ~ *publique*, public health.
saluer [salɥe] *v.t.* to bow to, to pay one's respects to, to take off one's hat to; to greet, to offer one's greetings or compliments to, to proclaim, to hail; (naut.) to salute (by dipping the flag); *saluez-le de ma part*, remember me to him.
salure [salyr] *s.f.* saltness, salinity.
salut [saly] *s.m.* **1.** preservation, salvation, well-being, welfare; escape, safety; *le ~ public*, the safety of the State; *il n'a dû son ~ qu'à sa fuite*, he found safety in flight; he only just escaped; *Armée du Salut*, Salvation Army; **2.** bow, greeting, salute, salutation; ~*!*, good day!; (fam.) ~ *à tous!*, hullo, everybody!, goodbye, all!; *faire un* ~, to bow, to nod; *à bon entendeur ~!*, a word to the wise; **3.** (Cath. liturg.) benediction.
salutaire [salytɛr] *adj.* salutary, wholesome, useful, beneficial, advantageous; ~**ment** [salytɛrmɑ̃] *adv.* usefully, advantageously.
salutation [salytɑsjɔ̃] *s.f.* salutation, greeting, salute; (pl.) (in letter) ~*s sincères* = yours sincerely; ~*s distinguées* = yours faithfully.
salutiste [salytist] *s.m.f.*, *adj.* (member) of Salvation Army, Salvationist.
salvat-eur, -rice [salvatœr] *adj.* saving.
salve [salv] *s.f.* volley, salvo, burst; salute; (fig.) ~ *d'applaudissements*, round of applause.
samaritain, -e [samaritɛ̃] *adj.*, *s.m.f.* Samaritan.
sambuque [sɑ̃byk] *s.f.* (anc. mus.) sambuca; (Rom. ant.) sambuca.
samedi [samdi] *s.m.* Saturday; ~ *Saint*, Easter Eve; (fam.) *être né un* ~, to be born idle.
samien, -ne [samjɛ̃] *adj.*, *s.m.f.* Samian, (native or inhabitant) of Samos.
samole [samɔl] *s.m.* (bot.) brookweed.
samovar [samɔvar] *s.m.* samovar.
sampan, sampang [sɑ̃pɑ̃] *s.m.* sampan.
sana [sana] *s.m.* abbrev. SANATORIUM.
sanatorium [sanatɔrjɔm] *s.m.* sanatorium.
san-benito [sɑ̃benito] *s.m.* (relig. hist.) sanbenito.
sanctifiant, -e [sɑ̃ktifjɑ̃] *adj.* sanctifying.
sanctificat-eur, -rice [sɑ̃ktifikatœr] *adj.* sanctifying; *s.m.f.* sanctifier.
sanctification [sɑ̃ktifikɑsjɔ̃] *s.f.* sanctification.
sanctifier [sɑ̃ktifje] *v.t.* to sanctify, to hallow, to keep holy.
sanction [sɑ̃ksjɔ̃] *s.f.* **1.** sanction, assent, ratification, approval; **2.** penalty, punishment, (pol.) sanction.
sanctionner [sɑ̃ksjɔne] *v.t.* **1.** to sanction; to approve of, to ratify; **2.** to punish; to be a punishment for.
sanctuaire [sɑ̃ktɥɛr] *s.m.* sanctuary, chancel (of church); (fig.) sanctuary, sanctum; secret recesses.
sandal [sɑ̃dal] *s.m.* = SANTAL.
sandale [sɑ̃dal] *s.f.* sandal.
sandalette [sɑ̃dalɛt] *s.f.* light sandal.
sandalier [sɑ̃dalje], **sandaliste** [sɑ̃dalist] *s.m.* sandal-maker.
sandaraque [sɑ̃darak] *s.f.* sandarac.
sandow [sɑ̃do] *s.m.* (proprietary name) **1.** elastic straps (for attaching luggage to roof-rack); **2.** (aeron.) catapult.
sandwich [sɑ̃dwitʃ] *s.m* (pl. *sandwich(e)s*) sandwich; *être en* ~, to be sandwiched or jammed (*entre*, between); *homme-*~, sandwich-man.
sang [sɑ̃] *s.m.* blood; (fig.) race, breed, pedigree, birth, parentage, kindred, lineage, consanguinity; *à ~ froid*, cold-blooded; *coup de* ~, stroke, congestion of the brain; *prise de* ~, blood-letting, taking of blood sample; *écoulement* or *flux de* ~, haemorrhage; *en* ~, *tout en* ~, covered with blood; *buveur de* ~, bloodthirsty man; (fig.) *avoir le ~ chaud*, to be ardent, to be hot-tempered; *il n'a pas de ~ dans les veines*, he is a spineless individual, he is lacking in guts; *cela glace le* ~, it makes one's blood run cold; *suer ~ et eau*, to strain every nerve; to sweat blood; to work oneself to the bone; *le ~ lui monte à la tête*, the blood rushes to his head; *se faire une pinte de bon* ~, to have a jolly time; *se faire du mauvais* ~, to fret, to worry; to get into a state; *mon ~ n'a fait qu'un tour*, I was quite overcome; *brûler* or *fouetter le ~ de*, to excite, to stimulate; *mettre à feu et à* ~, to put to fire and sword; *pur* ~, thoroughbred; *la voix du* ~, the call of the blood; *bon ~ ne peut mentir*, good breeding always tells; like father like son; *il a cela dans le* ~, it runs in his blood; *se battre au premier* ~, to fight till blood is drawn.
sang-dragon [sɑ̃dragɔ̃], **sang-de-dragon** [sɑ̃ddragɔ̃] *s.m. invar.* dragon's blood (a resin); (bot.) bloodwort.
sang-froid [sɑ̃frwa] *s.m.invar.* coolness, sang-froid, composure, self-control; *de* ~, coolly, deliberately, in cold blood; *garder son* ~, to keep cool; *perdre son* ~, to lose one's presence of mind, one's head, or one's self-control.
sanglant, -e [sɑ̃glɑ̃] *adj.* bloody; bleeding, blood-covered, blood-stained; caused or accompanied by bloodshed; (fig.) cruel, biting, bitter.
sangle (sɑ̃gl] *s.f.* girth, saddle-girth; strap, belt, thong; webbing; *lit de* ~, camp-bed.
sangler [sɑ̃gle] *v.t.* to gird, to bind with a girth, to strap up, to lace tightly; to lash.
sanglier [sɑ̃glje] *s.m.* wild boar.
sanglot [sɑ̃glo] *s.m.* sob; *éclater en ~s*, to burst into tears, to burst out sobbing.
sangloter [sɑ̃glɔte] *v.i.* to sob.
sang-mêlé [sɑ̃mele] *s.m.f.invar.* person of mixed blood, half-caste.
sangsue [sɑ̃sy] *s.f.* (zool.) leech; (fig.) bloodsucker, leech; (fam.) clinging type (of woman).
sanguin, -e [sɑ̃gɛ̃] *adj.* of blood, pertaining to blood; sanguine; choleric; blood-coloured, ruddy, red-faced; *groupe* ~, blood group; *vaisseaux ~s*, blood-vessels; *orange ~e*, blood orange.
sanguinaire [sɑ̃ginɛr] *adj.* sanguinary, bloodthirsty; ~ *s.f.* (bot.) bloodwort.
sanguine [sɑ̃gin] *s.f.* **1.** red haematite, bloodstone, red chalk; red chalk drawing; **2.** a kind of pear; **3.** blood orange.

sanguinelle [sãginɛl] *s.f.* (bot.) cornel, dogwood.
sanguinolent, -e [sãginɔlã] *adj.* tinged with blood, blood-red.
sanhedrin [sanedrɛ̃] *s.m.* sanhedrin, sanhedrim.
sanicle [sanikl] *s.f.* (bot.) sanicle.
sanie [sani] *s.f.* (pathol.) sanies.
sanieu-x, -se [sanjø] *adj.* sanious.
sanitaire [sanitɛr] *adj.* sanitary, pertaining to health, to hygiene, to sanitation, to health or medical services; *train* ~, ambulance train; *police* ~, health inspectors; *formation* ~, hospital or medical unit; ~ *s.m.* plumbing, sanitary installations.
sans [sã] *prep.* without, excluding, were it not for, but for; ~ *ailes*, wingless; ~ *amis*, friendless; ~ *le* or *un sou*, penniless; ~ *cesse*, incessantly, unceasingly, repeatedly; ~ *cela*, ~ *quoi*, otherwise; ~ *doute*, doubtless, no doubt; ~ *que*, without, unless; ~ *que je le sache*, without my knowing it; ~ *plus*, and that's all, and nothing else; *cela va* ~ *dire*, of course, that is understood; *ne le dites pas* ~ *qu'on vous le demande*, don't say it unless you are asked.
sans-abri [sãzabri] *s.m.f.invar.* homeless person.
sans-cœur [sãkœr] *s.m.f.invar.* heartless person.
sanscrit, sanskrit, -e [sãskri] *adj.*, *s.m.* Sanskrit.
sanscritiste, sanskritiste [sãskritist] *s.m.* Sanskrit scholar.
sans-culotte [sãkylɔt] *s.m* (Fr. hist.) sansculotte, sansculottist, violent republican; **~-façon** [sãfasɔ̃] *s.m.invar.* straightforwardness, bluntness, lack of ceremony, off-handedness, homeliness; **~-fil** [sãfil] **1.** *s.f.* wireless telegraphy, radio; **2.** *s.m.* radio-telegram, radiogram; **~-filiste** [sãfilist] *s.m.f.* **1.** radio operator; **2.** radio enthusiast, radio ham; **~-gêne** [sãʒɛn] *adj.*, *s.m.invar.* off-handed, over-familiar, blunt, (person); *s.m.* lack of ceremony, familiarity, casualness, off-handedness, unconcern, indifference; **~-le-sou** [sãlsu] *s.m.f.invar.* penniless person; **~-logis** [sãlɔʒi] *s.m.f.invar.* homeless person, one with no permanent address.
sansonnet [sãsɔnɛ] *s.m.* (ornith.) starling.
sans-souci [sãsusi] *s.m.f.*, *adj. invar.* carefree, easy-going, happy-go-lucky, (person); **~-travail** [sãtravaj] *s.m.f.invar.* unemployed (person).
santal (pl. **-s**) [sãtal] *s.m.* (bot.) sandalwood; sandalwood tree.
santé [sãte] *s.f.* health; health services; (mil.) army medical service or corps; (naut.) quarantine service; *patente de* ~, bill of health; *une* ~ *de fer*, an iron constitution; *être de* ~ *faible*, *avoir une faible*, or *une petite*, ~, to be delicate; *maison de* ~, nursing home, private clinic; *à ta* ~*!*, your health!; *boire à la* ~ *de qn.*, to drink someone's health, to toast s.o.; *porter une* ~, to drink a toast.
santoline [sãtɔlin] *s.f.* (bot.) lavender-cotton, santolina.
santon [sãtɔ̃] *s.m.* **1.** santon, Muslim monk or hermit, marabout; **2.** figure of a saint in a Christmas crib.
santonine [sãtɔnin] *s.f.* (bot.) santonica; (chem.) santonin.
sanve [sãv] *s.f.* (bot.) charlock, wild mustard.
saoul, -e see SOÛL.
saouler see SOÛLER.
saoulerie see SOÛLERIE.
sapajou (pl. **-s**) [sapaʒu] *s.m.* (zool.) sapajou (South American monkey); (fig.) baboon, ugly old man.
sape [sap] *s.f.* **1.** (obs.) hoe, mattock; scythe; (mod.) pick with spade-end, miner's pick; **2.** (mil.) sap, sapping, undermining; (fig.) undermining.
sapement [sapmã] *s.m.* sapping, undermining.
saper [sape] *v.t.* to sap, to mine; to undermine, to wear away the base of; (fig.) to undermine, to destroy the basis of; **se** ~ *v.refl.* (pop.) to dress; *être bien sapé*, to be well turned out.
sapeur [sapœr] *s.m.* (mil.) sapper, engineer; (fam.) *fumer comme un* ~, to smoke like a chimney.
sapeur-pompier [sapœrpɔ̃pje] *s.m.* fireman, member of fire brigade.
saphique [safik] *adj.* Sapphic.
saphir [safir] *s.m.* sapphire.
saphirine [safirin] *s.f.* blue chalcedony.
saphisme [safism] *s.m* Sapphism, lesbianism.
sapide [sapid] *adj.* sapid, palatable.
sapidité [sapidite] *s.f.* sapidity, tastiness.
sapience [sapjãs] *s.f.* sapience, wisdom.
sapientiaux [sapjãsjo] *adj.m.pl.*, *s.m.pl.* (bibl.) sapiential (books).
sapin [sapɛ̃] *s.m.* fir, fir-tree; *bois de* ~, deal; ~ *de Nord*, Scotch fir, Scotch pine; ~ *épicéa*, spruce; ~ *de Noël*, Christmas tree; *vert* ~, pine-green; (fam.) *sentir déjà le* ~, to have one foot in the grave.
sapine [sapin] *s.f.* deal plank, deal board; (build.) scaffold for crane, scaffold-pole.
sapinette [sapinɛt] *s.f.* **1.** (bot.) spruce; **2.** spruce-beer.
sapinière [sapinjɛr] *s.f.* fir-plantation, fir-grove.
saponacé, -e [sapɔnase] *adj.* saponaceous.
sapon-aire [sapɔnɛr] *s.f.* (bot.) Saponaria, soapwort; **~ifiable** [sapɔnifjabl] *adj.* saponifiable; **~ification** [sapɔnifikɑsjɔ̃] *s.f.* saponification; **~ifier** [sapɔnifje] *v.t.* to saponify; **~ine** [sapɔnin] *s.f.* (chem.) saponin.
sapote [sapɔt], **sapotille** [sapɔtij] *s.f.* (bot.) sapodilla.
sapotier [sapɔtje], **sapotillier** [sapɔtije] *s.m.* (bot.) sapodilla-tree.
sapristi [sapristi], **saprelotte** [saprəlɔt] *interj.* mild expletive expressing surprise or indignation.
saquer see SACQUER.
sarabande [sarabãd] *s.f.* saraband.
sarbacane [sarbakan] *s.f.* pea-shooter, blowpipe.
sarcasme [sarkasm] *s.m.* sarcasm, gibe, taunt.
sarcastique [sarkastik] *adj.* sarcastic; **~ment** [sarkastikmã] *adv.* sarcastically.
sarcelle [sarsɛl] *s.f.* (ornith.) teal.
sarclage [sarklaʒ] *s.m.* weeding.
sarcler [sarkle] *v.t.* to weed, to hoe, to clear of weeds.
sarcloir [sarklwar] *s.m.* spud, hoe, weeder.
sarclure [sarklyr] *s.f.* weedings, (uprooted) weeds.
sarcomateu-x, -se [sarkɔmatø] *adj.* sarcomatous.
sarcome [sarkom] *s.m.* (pathol.) sarcoma.
sarcophage [sarkɔfaʒ] *s.m.* **1.** sarcophagus; **2.** (ent.) flesh-fly.
sarcopte [sarkɔpt] *s.m.* (ent.) itch-mite.
Sardaigne [sardɛɲ] *s.f.* (geog.) Sardinia.
sarde [sard] *adj.*, *s.m.f.* Sardinian.
sardine [sardin] *s.f.* sardine; pilchard; (mil. slang) N.C.O.'s stripe.
sardini-er, -ère [sardinje] *adj.* sardine; *s.m.f.* sardine-packer; **~er** *s.m.* sardine-fisher; sardine-net.
sardoine [sardwan] *s.f.* sardonyx.
sardonique [sardɔnik] *adj.* sardonic; **~ment** [sardɔnikmã] *adv.* sardonically.
sargasse [sargas] *s.f.* sargasso, gulf-weed; *mer des Sargasses*, Sargasso Sea.
sari [sari] *s.m.* sari.
sarigue [sarig] *s.m.f.* (zool.) sarigue, South American opossum.
sarisse [saris] *s.f.* (Gr. ant.) sarissa.

S.A.R.L. [ɛsaɛrɛl] abbrev. *Société à responsabilité limitée.*

sarment [sarmɑ̃] *s.m.* vine-branch, vine-shoot; sarmentum, bine.

sarmenteu-x, -se [sarmɑ̃tø] *adj.* (bot.) sarmentose, sarmentous.

sarong [sarɔ̃] *s.m.* sarong.

saros [saros] *s.m.* (astron.) saros.

sarracénique [sarasenik] *adj.* Saracenic.

sarrasin [sarazɛ̃] *s.m.* (bot.) Saracen corn, buckwheat.

sarrasin, -e [sarazɛ̃] *s.m.f.* Saracen; *adj.* Saracenic.

sarrasine [sarazin] *s.f.* (arch.) portcullis.

sarrau (pl. **-x**) [saro] *s.m.* smock.

Sarre [sar] *s.f.* (geog.) Saar (river & region).

sarriette [sarjɛt] *s.f.* (bot.) savory.

sarrois, -e [sarwa] *adj., s.m.f.* (native or inhabitant) of the Saar.

sas [sɑ] *s.m.* sieve, screen, riddle, bolt(er); lock-chamber; coffer; airlock; immersion-chamber (of submarine).

sassafras [sasafrɑ] *s.m.* (bot.) sassafras.

sassage [sɑsaʒ] *s.m.* sieving, screening, bolting, sifting.

sassement [sɑsmɑ̃] *s.m.* **1.** = SASSAGE; **2.** passing through a lock (on canal, etc.); passing through an airlock; flooding (of submarine immersion-chambers).

sasser [sase] *v.t.* **1.** to sift, to sieve, to screen, to riddle; **2.** to pass (a boat) through a lock; to pass (s.o.) through an airlock.

sasseu-r, -se [sɑsœr] *s.m.f.* sifter, winnower; **~r** *s.m.* winnowing-machine.

satané, -e [satane] *adj.* infernal, confounded, damned.

satanique [satanik] *adj.* satanic, diabolical.

satellisation [satelizɑsjɔ̃] *s.f.* **1.** (astronaut.) production and launching of satellites; **2.** (pol.) making (a country) into a satellite.

satelliser [satelize] *v.t.* **1.** (astronaut.) to put into orbit; **2.** (pol.) to make (a country) a satellite.

satellite [satelit] *s.m.* satellite; (obs.) henchman; dependant; (techn.) planet wheel; *agglomération* **~**, satellite town.

satî [sati] *adj.f., s.m.* (hist.) suttee.

satiété [sasjete] *s.f.* satiety, repletion; *manger (jusqu') à* **~**, to eat one's fill, to eat till one can eat no more; *avoir d'une chose à* **~**, to have as much as one can take of a thing; *répéter qch. à* **~**, to repeat sth. until people are sick of the sound of it.

satin [satɛ̃] *s.m.* satin.

satinage [satinaʒ] *s.m.* satining, glazing, hot-pressing.

satiné, -e [satine] *adj.* satin-like, satiny, glazed, (of paper) hot-pressed, high-glazed; **~** *s.m.* satin-like gloss.

satiner [satine] *v.t.* to satin; to glaze (paper), to put a gloss on.

satinette [satinɛt] *s.f.* sateen.

satire [satir] *s.f.* satire; lampoon; satirizing; *faire la* **~** *de*, to satirize.

satirique [satirik] *adj.* satirical; **~ment** [satirikmɑ̃] *adv.* satirically.

satiriser [satirize] *v.t.* to satirize.

satisfaction [satisfaksjɔ̃] *s.f.* **1.** satisfaction, gratification, pleasure, contentment; **2** satisfying, indulging, indulgence; fulfilment (of obligation); (theol.) atonement.

satisfaire [satisfɛr] *v.t.* to satisfy, to please, to gratify, to suit; to fill (need, etc.); **~** *à*, to satisfy, to give satisfaction to; to fulfil (undertaking, etc.), to meet (requirement, objection), to answer, to comply with; **se ~** *v.refl.* to satisfy one's needs or desires; *se* **~** *de peu*, to be content with little.

satisfaisant, -e [satisfəzɑ̃] *adj.* satisfying, satisfactory, pleasing, gratifying.

satisfait, -e [satisfɛ] *adj.* satisfied, pleased, gratified, contented.

satisfecit [satisfesit] *s.m.* (school) good mark, good report; (Lit.) mark of approbation.

satrape [satrap] *s.m.* (hist.) satrap; (fig.) wealthy despot.

satrapie [satrapi] *s.f.* (hist.) satrapy.

saturable [satyrabl] *adj.* saturable.

saturant, -e [satyrɑ̃] *adj.* saturating.

saturateur [satyratœr] *s.m.* **1.** (chem.) saturator; **2.** humidifier.

saturation [satyrɑsjɔ̃] *s.f.* saturation.

saturé, -e [satyre] *adj.* saturated; (fig.) surfeited.

saturer [satyre] *v.t.* to saturate; (fig.) to satiate, to surfeit.

saturnales [satyrnal] *s.f.pl.* **1.** (Rom. ant.) Saturnalia; **2.** saturnalia.

saturne [satyrn] *s.m.* **1.** *Saturne*, Saturn (planet and god); **2.** (alchemy) lead; (pharm.) *extract* or *sel de* **~**, lead acetate, Goulard's extract.

saturnien, -ne [satyrnjɛ̃] *adj.* Saturnian.

saturnin, -e [satyrnɛ̃] *adj.* (med.) caused by lead or lead compounds; *colique* **~***e*, lead colic; ⚠ not 'saturnine' in sense 'gloomy'.

saturnisme [satyrnism] *s.m.* saturnism, lead-poisoning.

satyre [satir] *s.m.* **1.** satyr; (fig.) dirty old man, old goat; **2.** (ent.) satyrid butterfly.

satyrique [satirik] *adj.* satyric, of satyrs.

sauce [sos] *s.f.* **1.** sauce, gravy; (fig.) *on le met à toutes les* **~***s*, he is given every kind of job, he gets every sort of treatment; *accommoder avec une* **~** *blanche*, to serve, to do up, with white sauce; *accommoder avec toutes les* **~***s*, to dish up in every shape, to serve in a variety of guises; *(r)allonger la* **~**, to thin the sauce, (fig.) to water down, to pad out; (fig.) *la* **~** *fait manger le poisson*, the details are better than the thing itself; *trop de cuisiniers gâtent la* **~**, too many cooks spoil the broth; **2.** (fam.) rain, downpour; *recevoir la* **~**, to get a soaking; **3.** soft, black crayon.

saucé, -e [sose] *adj.* (of coins) thinly plated.

saucée [sose] *s.f.* downpour; soaking, drenching.

saucer [sose] *v.t.* **1.** (obs.) to dip in sauce, to put sauce on; **2.** **~** *son assiette*, to mop up the sauce from one's plate; **3.** (fam.) *se faire* **~**, *être saucé*, to get drenched.

saucier [sosje] *s.m.* sauce-cook, sauce-chef.

saucière [sosjɛr] *s.f.* sauce-boat; gravy-boat.

saucisse [sosis] *s.f.* sausage (served hot); captive balloon, barrage-balloon, sausage (-balloon); (pop.) fool; (fig.) *il n'attache pas ses chiens avec des* **~***s*, he watches every penny.

saucisson [sosisɔ̃] *s.m.* **1.** sausage (eaten cold and sliced); **2.** stick of explosive; **3.** long round loaf.

saucissonner [sosisɔne] *v.i.* (fam.) to picnic on sausage.

sauf [sof], fem. **sauve** [sov] *adj.* safe, unhurt, unscathed; *sain et* **~**, safe and sound; *avoir la vie sauve*, to escape with one's life; *laisser la vie sauve à qn.*, to spare someone's life; *obtenir la vie sauve*, to be spared, to obtain an assurance that one's life will be spared; *l'honneur est* **~**, honour is saved.

sauf [sof] *prep.* save, except, except for, except in case of, apart from, excluding, but, under, excepting, excepted; **~** *correction*, subject to correction; **~** *erreur*, errors excepted; **~** *à*, subject to (the right or possibility of); **~** *si*, even if, to the point of; **~** *à corriger plus tard*, subject to later correction or revision; **~** *votre respect*, with all due respect.

sauf-conduit [sofkɔ̃dɥi] *s.m.* (pl. *sauf-conduits*) safe conduct.

sauge [soʒ] *s.f.* (bot.) sage; salvia.

saugrenu, -e [sogrəny] *adj.* absurd, irrelevant, ridiculous, far-fetched.

saulaie [solɛ] *s.f.* willow-grove.
saule [sol] *s.m.* willow; ~ *pleureur*, weeping willow.
saulée [sole] *s.f.* row of willows.
saumâtre [somɑtr] *adj.* brackish, briny.
saumon [somɔ̃] *s.m.* **1.** salmon; **2.** (metall.) pig, ingot, block; ~ *de fonte*, pig-iron; ~ *adj. invar.* salmon-coloured.
saumoné, -e [somɔne] *adj.* salmon; *truite ~e*, salmon trout.
saumoneau (pl. **-x**) [somɔno] *s.m.* young salmon, samlet.
saumurage [somyraʒ] *s.m.* pickling (in brine).
saumure [somyr] *s.f.* brine, pickle, salt water.
saumuré, -e [somyre] *adj.* pickled, soused.
sauna [sona] *s.m.* or *f.* sauna (bath or establishment).
saunage [sonaʒ] *s.m.* extraction of salt from sea-water; (hist.) *faux ~*, illicit salt trade.
sauner [sone] *v.i.* to produce or deposit salt.
saunier [sonje] *s.m.* salt-maker, salt-trader; (hist.) *faux ~*, salt-smuggler.
saupiquet [sopikɛ] *s.m.* (cook.) sharp sauce.
saupoudrer [sopudre] *v.t.* to sprinkle (*de*, with), to powder, to dust, to dredge.
saupoudreuse [sopudrøz] *s.f.*, **saupoudroir** [sopudrwar] *s.m.* sprinkler, caster, sifter, dredger.
saur [sɔr] *adj.m.* smoked, dried; *hareng ~*, smoked herring, bloater.
saurer [sore] *v.t.* to smoke (herrings); to cure (ham).
saurien [sorjɛ̃] *s.m.* (zool.) saurian; *les ~s*, the Sauria.
saurin [sorɛ̃] *s.m.* freshly-smoked herring, bloater.
saurissage [sorisaʒ] *s.m.* smoking (of herrings, etc.).
saurisserie [sorisri] *s.f.* place where herrings are cured.
saussaie [sosɛ] *s.f.* = SAULAIE.
saut [so] *s.m.* jump, leap, vault, bound, hop, skip; fall, waterfall; plunge, dive; *faire un ~*, to take a leap; *au ~ du lit*, the minute one gets out of bed; on first getting up; *~ de lit*, dressing-gown, wrap, kimono, wrapper; *de plein ~*, at one go, straight away, abruptly; *faire le ~*, (i.) to take the plunge; (ii.) to give in; *faire un ~ de carpe*, to leap up, to somersault; *~ de loup*, ha-ha, sunk fence; *~ du Niagara*, Niagara Falls; *~ périlleux*, somersault; *~ en longueur, en largeur, à la perche*, long-jump, high-jump, pole-vault; *triple ~*, hop, skip, and jump; *~ de l'ange*, swallow-dive; *il ne fit qu'un ~ vers la porte*, he leapt for the door, he reached the door in a single bound.
saut-de-mouton [sodmutɔ̃] *s.m.* (pl. *sauts-de-mouton*) flyover, overpass.
saute [sot] *s.f.* sudden change (esp. of wind), shift, jump, freak, caprice.
sauté, -e [sote] *adj.* (cook.) fried, sauté; ~ *s.m.* sauté dish, sauté.
sautelle [sotɛl] *s.f.* vine-shoot.
saute-mouton [sotmutɔ̃] *s.m.* leap-frog.
sauter [sote] *v.t.i.* to leap, to jump, to hop, to skip, to spring; (fam.) to fling oneself, to fly; to jump over, to clear; to blow up; to explode, to burst, to go up, to fly off, (of fuse) to blow, (of cork) to pop; to miss out, to omit, to skip, to drop (a stitch); to veer, to shift; to get the sack; to go bust; *faire ~*, to make (s.o., sth.) jump, etc.; to toss; to explode; to break open, to spring (lock); to sack, to cause to lose job; (cook.) to sauté, to fry; *~ en parachute*, to make a parachute jump; *faire ~ la banque*, to break the bank; *~ au collet* or *à la gorge de qn.*, to fly at someone's throat; *se faire ~ la cervelle*, to blow one's brains out; *cela saute aux yeux*, it is obvious, it hits you in the eye; *reculer pour mieux ~*, to step back in order to take a better leap; (fig.) to bide one's time; (iron.) to slip back (into a worse position); (fig.) *~ le pas*, to take the plunge; (of condemned criminal) to die, to pay with one's neck.
sauterelle [sotrɛl] *s.f.* grasshopper; locust; (techn.) bevel; portable belt conveyor.
sauterie [sotri] *s.f.* informal dance, hop.
sauternes [sotɛrn] *s.m.* Sauterne(s) (wine).
saute-ruisseau [sotrɥiso] *s.m.invar.* errand-boy; (obs.) office-boy.
sauteu-r, -se [sotœr] *adj.* leaping, jumping; *s.m.f.* leaper, jumper, (fig.) turncoat, unreliable person; **~se** *s.f.* loose woman.
sauteuse [sotøz] *s.f.* shallow stew-pan.
sautillant, -e [sotijɑ̃] *adj.* hopping, skipping, jerky, lively, capricious.
sautillement [sotijmɑ̃] *s.m.* hopping, darting about, flitting.
sautiller [sotije] to hop, to skip (around).
sautoir [sotwar] *s.m.* **1.** (herald.) St. Andrew's Cross, saltire; **2.** (obs.) stirrup-leather; (mod.) long necklace or chain; ribbon (of order, worn round neck); *en ~*, crossed, crosswise, diagonally; round the neck; *épées en ~*, crossed swords; *porter un bijou en ~*, to wear a piece of jewellery on a chain.
sauvage [sovaʒ] *adj.* savage, wild, untamed, uncivilized; uninhabited, desert; (of plants) wild; unsociable, shy; ferocious, brutal, barbarous, savage; ~ *s.m.f.* savage; **~ment** [sovaʒmɑ̃] *adv.* savagely.
sauvageon, -ne [sovaʒɔ̃] *s.m.f.* wild child, little savage; ~ *s.m.* (hort.) wild stock (opp. graft).
sauvagerie [sovaʒri] *s.f.* wildness; unsociableness, shyness; ferocity, savagery, savageness.
sauvagesse [sovaʒɛs] *s.f.* (obs.) savage woman, female savage; (fig.) rough, uneducated woman.
sauvagin, -e [sovaʒɛ̃] *adj.* (of taste or smell of certain birds) strong, gamy, fishy; **~e** *s.f.* **1.** water-fowl (having strong flavour); **2.** (fur trade) common pelts.
sauvegarde [sovgard] *s.f.* safeguard, protection; safe conduct; safety rope, rail, etc., lifeline.
sauvegarder [sovgarde] *v.t.* to protect, to safeguard, to guard, to shield.
sauve-qui-peut [sovkipø] *s.m.invar.* panic, stampede, headlong flight, rout; *~!*, every man for himself!
sauver [sove] *v.t.* to save, to rescue, to preserve, to salve, to redeem; to conceal, to cover up, to palliate, (fault, etc.); to deliver, to spare; to bring back to life, to cure; **se ~** *v.refl.* to take to flight; to (make one's) escape; to take refuge; to run away, to hurry off; to work out one's salvation.
sauvetage [sovtaʒ] *s.m.* rescue, saving; salvage; *bateau de ~*, lifeboat; *bouée de ~*, lifebuoy; *ceinture de ~*, lifebelt; *médaille de ~*, life-saving medal; *échelle de ~*, fire-escape.
sauveteur [sovtœr] *adj.m.* saving, salvage; ~ *s.m.* rescuer, lifeboatman, salvager; *canot ~*, lifeboat.
sauveur [sovœr] *s.m.* saver, deliverer, rescuer; saviour, redeemer; *Notre Sauveur*, Our Saviour; ~ *adj.m.* saving, redeeming, restoring.
(**à la**) **sauvette** [alasovɛt] *adv.loc.* (pej.) hastily, in a hurry, on the sly.
sauve-vie [sovvi] *s.f.invar.* (bot.) wall-rue.
savamment [savamɑ̃] *adv.* learnedly; cleverly, knowingly, from knowledge, as an expert.
savane [savan] *s.f.* savanna(h); (in Canada) swamp.
savant, -e [savɑ̃] *adj.* learned, erudite, intellectual, clever, well-informed, expert; (of terms, etc.) technical, scientific; *un chien ~*, a performing dog; *une femme ~e*, (i.) a learned woman; (ii.)

(iron.) a bluestocking; *s.m.f.* learned person, scholar, scientist, expert; pedant.
savarin [savarɛ̃] *s.m.* (cook.) savarin (cake).
savate [savat] *s.f.* **1.** down-at-heel slipper or shoe; (fig.) clumsy oaf; *traîner ses ~s*, to shuffle around in slippers; (fig.) *traîner la ~*, to be down at heel, to live in abject poverty; **2.** (techn.) sole-piece, protective shoe; (naut.) shoe (of anchor); (shipbuilding) launching-block or -key.
savetier [savtje] *s.m.* (obs.) cobbler.
saveur [savœr] *s.f.* savour, flavour, savouriness, taste; (fig.) savour, smack; *plein de ~*, well--flavoured, tasty, savoury, pungent.
Savoie [savwa] *s.f.* (geog.) Savoy.
savoir [savwar] *v.t.* to know, to be informed of, to be aware of, to be practised in, to be trained in, to understand, to be acquainted with; to be able to, to manage to, to know how to; *~ l'anglais*, to know English; *~ son métier*, to know one's job; *savez-vous danser?*, can you dance?; *je n'en sais rien*, I don't know at all; I don't know anything about it; *à ~*, namely, to wit; *c'est à ~*, *reste à ~*, that remains to be seen; (*pour autant*) *que je sache*, to the best of my belief; as far as I know; *~ mieux qu'on ne dit*, to know more than one says; *je ne sais trop*, I am not quite sure; *~ c'est pouvoir*, knowledge is power; *un je ne sais quoi*, a slight touch (of sth.), a nuance, an indefinable something; *sachez que*, I would have you know that, please note that; *sachez bien que*, bear in mind that, you can be certain that, you can rest assured that; *on fait ~ que*, notice is hereby given that; *nous croyons ~*, we have reason to believe; it is rumoured; *je ne saurais me figurer*, I cannot imagine; *je ne saurais flatter*, I am incapable of flattery, do not expect flattery from me; (Lit.) *je ne sache pas* (*que*), I do not know, I am not aware, (that); *pas que je sache*, not that I know of; not to my knowledge; *il en sait trop long*, he knows too much; *sans le ~*, unwittingly, unconsciously; *Dieu sait comme*, goodness knows how; *je suis tout je ne sais comment*, I feel a bit off-colour; *faites-lui ~ que*, let him know that; *je vous sais incapable de mentir*, I know you are incapable of lying; *je lui savais une grande fortune*, I knew he was very wealthy; *tout se sait à la longue*, truth is sure to come out; everything gets found out in the end.
savoir [savwar] *s.m.* knowledge, erudition, learning; skill, competence, know-how.
savoir-faire [savwarfɛr] *s.m.invar.* experience, skill, competence.
savoir-vivre [savwarvivr] *s.m.invar.* (obs.) knowing how to live, how to conduct one's affairs; (mod.) good manners, good breeding, politeness, tact.
savon [savɔ̃] *s.m.* soap; cake of soap; *bulle de ~*, soap-bubble; *eau de ~*, soap-suds; *pain de ~*, cake of soap; *~ de Marseille*, household soap; *~ en paillettes*, soap-flakes; (fam.) *donner* or *passer un ~ à qn.*, to give s.o. a good talking-to, to give s.o. a piece of one's mind.
savonnage [savɔnaʒ] *s.m.* washing with soap; soaping.
savonner [savɔne] *v.t.* to wash with soap; to soap; (fig.) *~ la tête à qn.*, to haul s.o. over the coals, to give s.o. a good blowing-up; **se ~** *v.refl.* to wash oneself with soap, to soap oneself.
savonnerie [savɔnri] *s.f.* soap-works; soap-trade; *tapis de la Savonnerie*, 'Savonnerie' carpet.
savonnette [savɔnɛt] *s.f.* cake of toilet-soap; (obs.) *montre à ~*, hunter (watch).
savonneu-x, -se [savɔnø] *adj.* soapy, smelling of soap, soap-like; *terre ~se*, fuller's earth.
savonni-er, -ère [savɔnje] *adj.* pertaining to soap-manufacturing; **~ier** *s.m.* **1.** soap--manufacturer; **2.** soapberry-tree.
savourer [savure] *v.t.* to taste, to savour, to relish, to eat or drink with enjoyment; (fig.) to enjoy, to take delight in.
savoureu-x, -se [savurø] *adj.* savoury, tasty, well-flavoured, of full flavour; (fig.) spicy; **~sement** [savurøzmɑ̃] *adv.* in a savoury way; with relish, with gusto; (fig.) spicily.
savoyard, -e [savwajar] *adj., s.m.f.* (native or inhabitant) of Savoy.
saxatile [saksatil] *adj.* (biol.) saxatile, living or growing among rocks.
Saxe [saks] *s.f.* (geog.) Saxony.
saxe [saks] *s.m.* Dresden china.
saxhorn [sakshɔrn] *s.m.* (mus.) saxhorn.
saxicole [saksikɔl] *adj.* (biol.) = SAXATILE.
saxifrage [saksifraʒ] *s.f.* (bot.) saxifrage.
saxo [sakso] *s.m.* abbrev. *saxophone, saxophoniste.*
saxon, -ne [saksɔ̃] *adj., s.m.f.* Saxon; (native or inhabitant) of Saxony.
saxophone [saksɔfɔn] *s.m.* (mus.) saxophone.
saxophoniste [saksɔfɔnist] *s.m.f.* saxophone--player.
saynète [sɛnɛt] *s.f.* short comedy, sketch.
sayon [sɛjɔ̃] *s.m.* **1.** (ant.) sagum (Gaulish woollen cloak); **2.** shepherd's cloak.
sbire [sbir] *s.m.* (pej.) policeman (with implication of rough methods), myrmidon (of the law); hireling.
scabieuse [skabjøz] *s.f.* (bot.) scabious.
scabieu-x, -se [skabjø] *adj.* scabious, scabby.
scabreu-x, -se [skɑbrø] *adj.* scabrous; indecent; (of subject, etc.) risky, dangerous, delicate.
scaferlati [skafɛrlati] *s.m.* scaferlati (tobacco).
scalaire [skalɛr] *adj.* (math.) scalar.
scalde [skald] *s.m.* scald, skald (Scandinavian bard).
scalène [skalɛn] *adj.* (geom., anat.) scalene.
scalp [skalp] *s.m.* scalping; scalp (as a trophy).
scalpel [skalpɛl] *s.m.* scalpel.
scalper [skalpe] *v.t.* to scalp.
scandale [skɑ̃dal] *s.m.* scandal, public exposure, shame, offence to public opinion, (scandalous) scene; *au grand ~ des honnêtes gens*, to the indignation or disgust of decent people; *pierre de ~*, stumbling-block.
scandaleu-x, -se [skɑ̃dalø] *adj.* scandalous, shameful; notorious; **~sement** [skɑ̃daløzmɑ̃] *adv.* scandalously, to a scandalous degree, shockingly.
scandaliser [skɑ̃dalize] *v.t.* to scandalize, to shock, to cause offence to; **se ~** *v.refl.* to be scandalized, to take offence, to be shocked.
scander [skɑ̃de] *v.t.* (pros.) to scan; (mus.) to mark, to stress; (fig.) to accentuate, to punctuate (one's remarks, etc.), to stress.
scandinave [skɑ̃dinav] *adj., s.m.f.* Scandinavian.
Scandinavie [skɑ̃dinavi] *s.f.* (geog.) Scandinavia.
scansion [skɑ̃sjɔ̃] *s.f.* scansion, scanning.
scaphandre [skafɑ̃dr] *s.m.* diving-suit; *~* (*de cosmonaute*), space-suit; *~ autonome*, aqualung.
scaphandrier [skafɑ̃drije] *s.m.* diver (working under water).
scaphoïde [skafɔid] *adj.s.m.* (anat.) scaphoid.
scapulaire [skapylɛr] *s.m.* (eccles., anat.) scapular, scapulary; *~ adj.* (anat.) scapular.
scapulo-huméral, -e, (aux) [skapyloymeral] *adj.* (anat.) scapulo-humeral.
scarabée [skarabe] *s.m.* (ent.) scarabaeid, scarab (beetle); (ant.) scarab.
scarabéidés [skarabeide] *s.m.pl.* (ent.) Scarabaeidae.
scare [skar] *s.m.* (ichth.) scarus, parrot-fish.
scarieu-x, -se [skarjø] *adj.* (bot.) scarious.
scari-fiage [skarifjaʒ] *s.m.* scarifying; **~ficateur** [skarifikatœr] *s.m.* (agric.) scarifier; (surg.) scarificator; **~fication** [skarifikɑsjɔ̃] *s.f.* scarification; **~fier** [skarifje] *v.t.* to scarify.
scarlatine [skarlatin] *s.f.* scarlet fever, scarlatina.

scatologie [skatɔlɔʒi] *s.f.* scatology.
scatologique [skatɔlɔʒik] *adj.* scatological.
sceau (pl. **-x**) [so] *s.m.* seal; (fig.) mark; *mettre le ~ à*, to seal, to put the, or one's, seal to; (fig.) to set the seal on, to stamp, to crown; *porter le ~ du génie*, to bear the stamp or hallmark of genius; *sous le ~ du secret*, under the seal of secrecy; *le Garde des Sceaux* = the Lord Chancellor; (bot.) *~-de-Salomon*, Solomon's seal.
scélérat, -e [selera] *adj.* villainous, wicked, criminal; *s.m.f.* rascal, villain, scoundrel, criminal.
scélératesse [seleratɛs] *s.f.* villainy, wickedness; act of villainy, criminal act.
scellage [sɛlaʒ] *s.m.* sealing, fixing.
scellé [sele] *s.m.* seal; *apposer les ~s*, to affix the seals; *lever les ~s*, to take off the seals.
scellement [sɛlmɑ̃] *s.m.* fastening, fixing; seating (of joist, etc. in wall); sealing.
sceller [sele] *v.t.* **1.** to seal, to seal up; **2.** to fix, to fasten, to cement in, to plaster up; (fig.) to close, to ratify, to confirm.
scénario [senarjo] *s.m.* scenario, (film) script.
scénariste [senarist] *s.m.f.* (cin.) script-writer.
scène [sɛn] *s.f.* **1.** scene, stage, scenery; theatre; *être en ~*, to be on (the stage); *entrer en ~*, to enter, to come on; *sortir de ~*, to exit, to go off; *par ordre d'entrée en ~*, in order of appearance; *mettre en ~*, to stage, to produce (a play); *mise en ~*, (i.) staging, producing; (ii.) scenery; **2.** row, quarrel, scene; *faire une ~*, to make a scene, to have a row (*à qn.*, with or in front of s.o.); *avoir une ~ avec qn.*, to have a row with s.o.
scenic railway [senikrɛlwɛ] *s.m.* switchback.
scénique [senik] *adj.* scenic, theatrical, picturesque; *indications ~s*, stage directions; *art ~*, production (as an art); **~ment** [senikmɑ̃] *adv.* theatrically.
scénographie [senɔgrafi] *s.f.* scene-painting; (painting in) perspective.
scepticisme [sɛptisism] *s.m.* scepticism; (phil.) scepsis.
sceptique [sɛptik] *adj.* sceptical; *~ s.m.f.* sceptic.
sceptre [sɛptr] *s.m.* sceptre; (fig.) sovereignty, sway; *tenir le ~ de*, to be pre-eminent in, to hold the crown or to take the palm for.
schah, shah [ʃa] *s.m* shah.
schako [ʃako] *s.m.* = SHAKO.
schapska see CHAPSKA.
schelem see CHELEM.
schelling see SCHILLING.
schéma [ʃema] *s.m.* diagram, model, sketch, outline, draft; ⚠ not 'scheme' in senses '(detailed) plan', 'machination'.
schématique [ʃematik] *adj.* schematic, diagrammatic; (fig.) sketchy, over-simplified; **~ment** [ʃematikmɑ̃] *adv.* schematically, diagrammatically; (fig.) in outline, in simplified form, roughly sketched.
schématiser [ʃematize] *v.t.* to present in diagram, in diagrammatic form; to outline, to present the essentials of, to simplify.
schème [sɛm] *s.m.* scheme, diagram of positions; (art) style; ⚠ 'scheme' only in given sense of 'diagram of positions'.
scherzo [skɛrzo] *s.m.* scherzo.
schibboleth [ʃibɔlɛt] *s.m.* shibboleth.
schiedam [skidam] *s.m.* Schiedam, Hollands gin.
schilling [ʃiliŋ], **schelling** [ʃɛliŋ] *s.m.* (Austrian) schilling.
schismatique [ʃismatik] *adj., s.m.f.* schismatic.
schisme [ʃism] *s.m.* schism.
schiste [ʃist] *s.m.* (geol.) schist; *~ (argileux)*, shale.
schisteu-x, -se [ʃistø] *adj.* (geol.) schistose, schistous, foliated.
schistoïde [ʃistɔid] *adj.* schistlike, schistoid.
schizoïde [skizɔid] *adj., s.m.f.* schizoid (person).
schizophrène [skizɔfrɛn] *adj., s.m.f.* schizophrenic.
schizophrénie [skizɔfreni] *s.f.* schizophrenia.
schlague [ʃlag] *s.f.* flogging; (fig.) *conduire qn. à la ~*, to beat s.o. into submission, to rule s.o. with a rod of iron.
schlamm [ʃlam] *s.m.* (min.) sludge, tailings.
schlass [ʃlɑs, ʃlas] (pop.) *adj.invar.* drunk; *~ s.m.* knife.
schlich [ʃliʃ] *s.m.* (metall.) schlich, pulverized ore.
schlittage [ʃlitaʒ] *s.m.* transport of felled trees on a *schlitte*.
schlitte [ʃlit] *s.f.* timber-sledge.
schlitter [ʃlite] *v.t.* to transport (timber) on a *schlitte*.
schlitteur [ʃlitœr] *s.m.* lumber-man (using a *schlitte*).
schnaps [ʃnaps] *s.m.* schnapps, grain or potato liquor; inferior spirits.
schnauzer [ʃnawzɛr] *s.m.* schnauzer (dog).
schnorchel, schnorkel, [ʃnɔrkɛl] *s.m.* snorkel (-tube).
schnouff [ʃnuf] *s.f.* (slang) drug.
schooner [skunœr, ʃunœr] *s.m.* (naut.) schooner.
schupo [ʃupo] *s.m.* German policeman.
schuss [ʃus] *s.m.* (skiing) schuss, direct descent.
sciable [sjabl] *adj.* that can be sawn.
sciage [sjaʒ] *s.m.* sawing; cutting (of diamond); *bois de ~*, sawn timber.
sciant, -e [sjɑ̃] *adj.* (fam.) boring, tedious.
sciatique [sjatik] *adj.* sciatic; *~ s.f.* (pathol.) sciatica.
scie [si] *s.f.* **1.** saw, *~ à ruban*, band-saw; *~ de scieur de long*, pit-saw, rip-saw; *trait de ~*, saw-mark; *lame de ~*, saw-blade; *dent de ~*, saw-tooth, serration; *en dent de ~*, serrated, jagged; (ichth.) *(poisson)~*, sawfish; **2.** (fam.) (i.) boring person or thing, bore, tiresome person; (ii.) catchword, cliché, latest tune; *quelle ~!*, what a bore!
sciemment [sjamɑ̃] *adv.* knowingly, deliberately, wittingly, purposely.
science [sjɑ̃s] *s.f.* science, knowledge, learning, skill; *avoir la ~ infuse*, to know everything intuitively; *un homme de ~*, a scientist; a scientific man; *~s appliquées*, applied sciences; *savoir de ~ certaine*, to know for a certainty; (fig.) *un puits de ~*, a mine of information, a walking encyclopaedia.
sciène [sjɛn] *s.f.* (ichth.) Sciaena.
scientifique [sjɑ̃tifik] *adj.* scientific; *~ s.m.f.* scientist; **~ment** [sjɑ̃tifikmɑ̃] *adv.* scientifically.
scientisme [sjɑ̃tism] *s.m.* (phil.) scientism.
scientiste [sjɑ̃tist] *s.m.f.* (phil.) scientist, adept of scientism.
scier [sje] *v.t.* **1.** to saw, to saw off; *~ en long*, to rip; **2.** (naut.) to back (water); **3.** (fam.) to bore; (pop.) to astonish, to overwhelm.
scierie [siri] *s.f.* sawmill, saw-yard.
scieur [sjœr] *s.m.* sawyer; *~ de long*, (pit-) sawyer; *fosse de ~ de long*, saw-pit.
scieuse [sjøz] *s.f.* mechanical saw.
scille [sij] *s.f.* (bot.) squill, scilla.
scinder [sɛ̃de] *v.t.* to divide, to split up, to break up.
scinque [sɛ̃k] *s.m.* (zool.) skink.
scintillant, -e [sɛ̃tijɑ̃] *adj.* scintillant, scintillating, sparkling; twinkling, winking; *~ s.m.* bright ornament (on Christmas tree).
scintillation [sɛ̃tijɑsjɔ̃] *s.f.* twinkling (of star); (phys.) scintillation.
scintillement [sɛ̃tijmɑ̃] *s.m.* twinkling (of star); sparkling, flashing, flickering.
scintiller [sɛ̃tije] *v.i.* to scintillate, to sparkle, to flash, to flicker; (of star) to twinkle.

scion [sjɔ̃] *s.m.* **1.** scion, shoot; **2.** top part of fishing-rod; ⚠ not 'scion' in sense 'descendant'.
sciotte [sjɔt] *s.f.* stone-cutter's saw.
scirpe [sirp] *s.m.* (bot.) club-rush.
scissile [sisil] *adj.* (geol.) scissile.
scission [sisjɔ̃] *s.f.* scission, split, secession; (biol., phys.) fission, division; *faire* ~, to secede; to split off, to break away.
scissionniste [sisjɔnist] *adj.* seceding; ~ *s.m.f.* secessionist, seceder.
scissipare [sisipar] *adj.* (zool.) fissiparous.
scissiparité [sisiparite] *s.f.* (biol.) schizogenesis, fissiparity, scissiparity.
scissure [sisyr] *s.f.* fissure, cleft.
sciure [sjyr] *s.f.* sawdust.
scléreu-x, -se [sklerø] *adj.* (path.) sclerous.
sclérose [skleroz] *s.f.* (pathol.) sclerosis; (fig.) fossilization, ossification, antiquation; ~ *artérielle*, arteriosclerosis; ~ *en plaques*, disseminated, or multiple sclerosis.
(**se**) **scléroser** [skleroze] *v.refl.* (pathol.) to harden, to develop sclerosis; (fig.) to become ossified or fossilized.
sclérotique [sklerɔtik] *s.f.* (anat.) sclerotic.
scolaire [skɔlɛr] *adj.* school-; of schools, pertaining to schools; academic; scholastic; (pej.) as though repeating a lesson; *année* ~, school year; academic year; *obligation* ~, compulsory school attendance.
scolarisation [skɔlarizɑsjɔ̃] *s.f.* attendance at school; provision of schools.
scolariser [skɔlarize] *v.t.* to provide schools; to provide school education.
scolarité [skɔlarite] *s.f.* school attendance, attendance in full-time education; period of school attendance, (duration of) course of study; (numbers of) children receiving school education; *frais de* ~, school fees; *prolonger la* ~, to raise the school-leaving age.
scolasticat [skɔlastika] *s.m.* (relig.) seminary.
scolastique [skɔlastik] *adj.* scholastic, of schools, academic; ~ *s.f.* scholasticism; ~ *s.m.* scholastic, (medieval) schoolman; (relig.) seminarist.
scoliaste [skɔljast] *s.m.* scholiast.
scolie [skɔli] *s.f.* scholium, gloss, explanatory note.
scoliose [skɔljoz] *s.f.* (pathol.) scoliosis.
scolopendre [skɔlɔpɑ̃dr] *s.f.* **1.** (bot.) hart's-tongue; **2.** (ent.) Scolopendra, centipede.
scombridés [skɔ̃bride] *s.m.pl.* (ichth.) Scombridae, scombrids, (mackerel, etc.).
sconse [skɔ̃s] *s.m.* skunk (fur).
scooter [skutœr, skutɛr] *s.m.* (motor) scooter; ~**iste** [skuterist] *s.m.f.* scooter-rider.
scopie [skɔpi] *s.f.* (fam.) abbrev. RADIOSCOPIE.
scops [skɔps] *s.m.* (ornith.) scops owl.
scorbut [skɔrbyt] *s.m.* scurvy.
scorbutique [skɔrbytik] *adj.* scorbutic, scurvied; ~ *s.m.f.* person suffering from scurvy.
score [skɔr] *s.m.* (sport) score.
scorie [skɔri] *s.f.* scoria, dross, slag; ~*s*, clinkers.
scorpène [skɔrpɛn] *s.f.* (ichth.) scorpion-fish.
scorpion [skɔrpjɔ̃] *s.m.* (ent.) scorpion; (astron.) Scorpio.
scorsonère [skɔrsɔnɛr] *s.f.* (bot.) scorzonera, black salsify.
scotie [skɔsi] *s.f.* (arch.) scotia.
scotch [skɔtʃ] *s.m.* **1.** Scotch (whisky); **2.** Scotch tape (proprietary brand of adhesive tape).
scottish [skɔtiʃ] *s.f.* (mus.) schottische (dance).
scout, -e [skut] *adj. s.m.* Scout (formerly Boy Scout).
scoutisme [skutism] *s.m.* scouting, Scout movement.
scraper [skrɛpœr] *s.m.* (civil eng.) scraper.
scratch [skratʃ] *s.m., adj.* (sport) scratch(-line).
scratcher [skratʃe] *v.t.* to scratch (a competitor).
scribe [skrib] *s.m.* scribe; (iron.) pen-pusher, bureaucrat, quill-driver.
script[1] [skript] *s.m.* (fin.) scrip.
script[2] [skript] *s.m.* **1.** script (handwriting); **2.** (film-)script; **3.** *s.f.* = SCRIPT-GIRL.
script-girl [skriptgœrl] *s.f.* (cin.) continuity girl.
scriptural, -e, (**aux**) [skriptyral] *adj.* scriptural.
scrofulaire [skrɔfylɛr] *s.f.* (bot.) figwort.
scrofulariacées [skrɔfylarjase] *s.f.pl.* (bot.) Scrophulariaceae.
scrofule [skrɔfyl] *s.f.* (pathol.) scrofula.
scrofuleu-x, -se [skrɔfylø] *adj.* scrofulous.
scrotum [skrɔtɔm] *s.m.* (anat.) scrotum.
scrubber [skrœbœr, skrybœr] *s.m.* (chem. eng.) scrubber.
scrupule [skrypyl] *s.m.* scruple, doubt, qualm; *jusqu'au* ~, scrupulously, to a point of scruple; *ne vous faites pas tant de* ~*s à ce propos*, have no scruples about that; *il a trop de* ~*s*, he is over-scrupulous; *je m'en ferais* ~, I would have scruples about doing that.
scrupuleu-x, -se [skrypylø] *adj.* scrupulous, strict, exact, precise, punctilious, conscientious; ~**sement** [skrypyløzmɑ̃] *adv.* scrupulously, strictly.
scrutateur [skrytatœr] *s.m.* scrutineer, teller, searcher, investigator; ~ *adj.* searching.
scruter [skryte] *v.t.* to search, to scrutinize, to pry into, to delve into, to investigate, to make a detailed examination of.
scrutin [skrytɛ̃] *s.m.* ballot, poll, vote, voting; ~ *de liste*, simultaneous ballot for a number of names; *dépouiller le* ~, to count the votes.
sculpté, -e [skylte] *adj.* carved; engraved; chiselled.
sculpter [skylte] *v.t.* to sculpture, to carve, to engrave, to chisel; to sculpt; to fashion, to mould.
sculpteur [skyltœr] *s.m.* sculptor, carver; sculptress.
sculptural, -e, (**aux**) [skyltyral] *adj.* sculptural, sculpturesque.
sculpture [skyltyr] *s.f.* sculpture, carving; carved work.
scutellaire [skytɛlɛr] *s.f.* (bot.) Scutellaria, skullcap.
scythe [sit] *adj., s.m.f.,* **scythique** [sitik] *adj.* Scythian.
S.D.N. [ɛsdeɛn] abbrev. (hist.) *Société des Nations*, League of Nations.
se [sə] (**s'** before vowel or h-mute) *pron.* **1.** (direct object) himself, herself, itself, oneself, themselves; each other, one another; *elle s'est blessée*, she has hurt herself; *il* ~ *regarda dans la glace*, he looked at himself in the mirror; *ils* ~ *regardèrent étonnés*, they looked at each other in astonishment; **2.** (indirect object) (to) himself, etc.; *il s'est dit*, he said to himself; *ils ne* ~ *parlent plus*, they no longer speak to each other; *il* ~ *demanda*, he wondered, he asked himself; *elle s'est coupé le doigt*, she has cut her finger; (*se, s'* is often omitted, or rendered by passive, in Eng.; e.g. *il s'habilla vite*, he dressed quickly; *ils* ~ *sont mariés*, they got married; *cela peut* ~ *manger froid*, it can be eaten cold).
S.E. [ɛse] abbrev. *Son Excellence.*
S.É. [ɛse] abbrev. *Son Éminence.*
S.-E. [ɛse] abbrev. *Sud-Est, sud-est.*
séance [seɑ̃s] *s.f.* sitting, meeting; session, (cin., etc.) performance; attendance (for med., etc., treatment); *en* ~, sitting; *lever la* ~, to close the meeting; *suspendre la* ~, to adjourn the meeting; ~ *tenante*, on the spot; there and then; forthwith.
séant, -e [seɑ̃] *adj.* **1.** sitting; **2.** fitting, decent, seemly, proper.
séant [seɑ̃] *s.m.* (anat.) bottom, behind; *être sur son* ~, to be in a sitting posture; *se mettre* or *se dresser sur son* ~, to sit up (from a lying position).

seau (pl. **-x**) [so] *s.m.* pail, bucket; bucketful; *~ à charbon*, coal-scuttle; *~ de toilette*, slop-pail; *il pleut à ~x*, it is raining in torrents, it's coming down in buckets.

sébacé, -e [sebase] *adj.* sebaceous.

sébile [sebil] *s.f.* wooden bowl.

séborrhée [sebɔre] *s.f.* seborrhoea.

sec [sɛk], (fem.) **sèche** [sɛʃ] *adj.* dry, dried up, arid, hard; stiff, harsh; curt, sharp(ly); plain, without accompaniment; without rain; lean, thin, gaunt, spare; *avoir la gorge sèche*, to have a parched throat; *boire ~*, to take one's drink neat; to be a hard drinker; *un bruit ~*, a snap, a click; *un coup ~*, a tap; *couper ~*, to cut off, (cin.) to cut; *un orage ~*, a storm without rain; *avoir le cœur ~*, to be hard-hearted; to be unfeeling; *d'un œil ~*, unmoved, without emotion, unfeelingly; (cards) *roi ~*, king bare; *partie sèche*, one game only (no revenge); (art) *pointe sèche*, dry-point; (fig.) *fruit ~*, (of a person) failure; *mettre au pain ~*, to put on dry bread; *à pied ~*, dry-shod; *un merci tout ~*, a curt thank you; *un homme grand et ~*, a gaunt fellow; *~ et nerveux*, wiry; *à ~*, dried up; high and dry, on dry ground, aground; (fig., fam.) broke, on the rocks; *mettre un étang à ~*, to drain a pond; *perte sèche*, dead loss; (fam.) *rester ~*, to be unable to answer, to be nonplussed; *tout ~*, hard and fast; (naut.) *à ~ de toile*, under bare poles; *en cinq ~*, (at écarté) one game of five points only; (fig.) quickly, in next to no time; *~ s.m.* dryness, dry weather, drought; dry place; dry feed; *au ~*, in a dry place; *mettre au ~*, to put to dry, to put in a dry place, to put on dry feed.

sécant, -e [sekɑ̃] *adj.* (geom.) secant; *~e s.f.* (geom.) secant.

sécateur [sekatœr] *s.m.* pruning-scissors; pruning-shears, secateurs.

sécession [sesesjɔ̃] *s.f.* secession.

sécessionniste [sesesjɔnist] *adj., s.m.f.* secessionist.

séchage [seʃaʒ] *s.m.* drying; seasoning (of wood).

sèche [sɛʃ] *s.f.* (naut.) dry shelf; flat exposed at low tide; (fam.) cigarette.

sèche *adj* see SEC.

sèche-cheveux [sɛʃʃ(ə)vø] *s.m.invar.* hair-dryer.

sèche-linge [sɛʃlɛ̃ʒ] *s.m.invar.* drying cabinet.

sèchement [sɛʃmɑ̃] *adv.* dryly; curtly, baldly, harshly.

sécher [seʃe] *v.t.i.* to dry, to dry up; to season (wood); (fig.) to wither, to pine away; (fam.) to be stumped for an answer, to dry up; to fail (in an examination); (fig.) *~ les larmes de qn.*, to console s.o.; *~ sur pied*, to eat one's heart out; to pine away; *~ d'envie*, to be green with envy; *~ un cours*, to cut a lecture; **se ~** *v.refl.* to dry oneself; to dry (up), to be dried.

sécheresse [seʃrɛs] *s.f.* dryness, drought; barrenness; (fig.) dryness, curtness, harshness, coldness, insensibility; lack of charm; meagreness, baldness.

sécherie [seʃri] *s.f.* drying-house.

séchoir [seʃwar] *s.m.* drying-room; drier, towel-horse, clothes-airer, drying-apparatus.

second, -e [səgɔ̃] *adj.* second, other; assistant, secondary; *sans ~*, matchless, peerless, unique, unparalleled; *au ~ étage, au ~*, on the second floor; *voyager en ~e (classe)*, to travel second (class); *de ~e main*, (at) second hand; *en ~*, second in command; *en ~ lieu*, in the second place, secondly; then; on the other hand; *au ~ plan*, in the middle distance; *un ~ Alexandre*, another Alexander; *~ s.m.* second officer, principal assistant, second in command, right-hand man; (naut.) first officer, mate; second floor; second object; *ne venir qu'en ~*, to play second fiddle; *passer en ~*, to take second place, to be inferior (in rank); **~ement** [səgɔ̃dmɑ̃] *adv.* secondly, in the second place, secundo.

secondaire [səgɔ̃dɛr] *adj.* secondary, accessory, subordinate, minor; **~ment** [səgɔ̃dɛrmɑ̃] *adv.* secondarily, in a subordinate role.

seconde [səgɔ̃d] *s.f.* second; (mus.) second; (in schools) second (the class below the first); (fenc.) seconde; (print.) second proof, revise; (math., geom., astron., geog.) second.

seconder [səgɔ̃de] *v.t.* to second, to assist, to help, to support, to back, to further, to favour.

secouement [səkumɑ̃] *s.m.* (Lit.) shaking, tossing.

secouer [səkwe] *v.t.* to shake, to shake up, to shake off, to discard, to jolt, to toss; to rouse, to blow up; *secouez-le donc un peu!*, stir him up a bit!; **se ~** *v.refl.* to shake oneself; (fig.) to bestir or to exert oneself.

secourable [səkurabl] *adj.* helpful, willing to help or aid; *tendre une main ~*, to give a helping hand.

secourir [səkurir] *v.t.* to succour, to help, to assist, to relieve, to support, to protect.

secourisme [səkurism] *s.m.* first aid, life-saving.

secours [səkur] *s.m.* help, succour, assistance, relief, aid; (mil.) reinforcements; subsidy; *crier au ~*, to cry for help; *porter* or *prêter ~ à*, to give help, assistance, support to; to come to the aid of; *donner, accorder, un ~*, to give a subsidy; *société de ~ mutuel*, friendly society; sick-fund; *de ~*, emergency, spare, relief, rescue; *porte de ~*, emergency exit; *poste, boîte, de ~*, first-aid post, box; *roue de ~*, spare wheel; *train de ~*, relief train.

secousse [səkus] *s.f.* shake, jolt, shock, jog, jerk; tremor; *~ sismique* or *tellurique*, earth tremor; *par ~s*, in spasms or gasps, (fig.) spasmodically; (fam.) *il n'en fiche pas une ~*, he does not do a stroke of work.

secr-et, -ète [səkrɛ] *adj.* secret, hidden, private, inward; intimate, reserved, reticent, discreet; occult; esoteric; *fonds ~ets*, secret service funds; *en ~et*, secretly.

secret [səkrɛ] *s.m.* secret; secrecy, discreet silence, mystery; explanation, trick; secret recipe; secret mechanism; privacy; close confinement; *dans le ~*, in secret, on the sly; *cela se ferme à ~*, it has a secret lock; *faire jouer le ~*, to operate the hidden mechanism, to press the secret button; *je ne suis pas du ~*, I am not in the secret; *gardez-moi le ~*, keep it secret; *c'est le ~ de Polichinelle*, it's an open secret; *mettre dans le ~*, to let into the secret; *mettre au ~*, to keep in close custody; *avoir le ~ de plaire*, to have the gift of pleasing everybody.

secrétaire [səkretɛr] *s.m.f.* secretary, clerk; *~ de mairie*, town clerk; *~ de rédaction*, editor's assistant, sub-editor; *~ s.m.* **1.** writing-desk, secretaire; **2.** (ornith.) = SERPENTAIRE.

secrétariat [səkretarja] *s.m.* secretariat; secretaryship; secretary's office.

secrètement [səkrɛtmɑ̃] *adv.* secretly, in secret, privately, discreetly, inwardly, under cover, furtively, in a clandestine manner.

sécréter [sekrete] *v.t.* to secrete; to produce by secretion; to exude; (fig.) to generate; ⚠ not to 'secrete' in sense 'to hide'.

sécréteu-r, -se (also fem. **sécrétrice**) [sekretœr] *adj.* secretory.

sécrétion [sekresjɔ̃] *s.f.* secretion, exuding.

sécrétoire [sekretwar] *adj.* secretory.

sectaire [sɛktɛr] *s.m.f., adj.* sectarian.

sectat-eur, -rice [sɛktatœr] *s.m.f.* follower, disciple, votary.

secte [sɛkt] *s.f.* sect; *faire ~*, to form a sect; to form a little coterie.

secteur [sɛktœr] *s.m.* sector, section; area, zone;

quadrant; segment; ~ *denté*, toothed sector; ~ *à crans*, notched quadrant.
section [sɛksjɔ̃] *s.f.* section, cutting, sectioning; the part cut off; division, department, branch; (mil.) platoon (of infantry), section (of artillery, etc.); (nuclear phys.) ~ *efficace*, cross-section; ~ *de tramway*, *autobus*, fare stage; ~ *de vote*, polling-station.
sectionnement [sɛksjɔnmɑ̃] *s.m.* sectioning, dividing, severing, division into parts or stages.
sectionner [sɛksjɔne] *v.t.* to section, to divide into sections, to sever; (electr.) to isolate; **se** ~ *v.refl.* to snap, to break in several places.
sectionneur [sɛksjɔnœr] *s.m.* (electr.) isolating--switch, overload trip.
séculaire [sekylɛr] *adj.* secular; occurring once in a century; a hundred years old, centuries old; that has stood for centuries, time-honoured, ancient, venerable; *année* ~, the last year in a century; **~ment** [sekylɛrmɑ̃] *adv.* from time immemorial; ⚠ not 'secular' opp. 'ecclesiastical'; see SÉCULIER.
sécularisation [sekylarizɑsjɔ̃] *s.f.* secularization.
séculariser [sekylarize] *v.t.* to secularize.
sécularité [sekylarite] *s.f.* secularity.
séculi-er, -ère [sekylje] *adj.* secular, temporal; *le bras* ~, the temporal authority, the secular jurisdiction.
secundo [səgɔ̃do] *adv.* secondly, in the second place.
sécuriser [sekyrize] *v.t.* to give (a feeling of) security to.
sécurité [sekyrite] *s.f.* security, safety, confidence; ~ *sociale*, social security (services); social insurance; ⚠ not 'security', 'securities' in fin. senses.
sedan [sədɑ̃] *s.m.* (text.) Sedan cloth; ⚠ not 'sedan-chair' or 'sedan car'.
sédati-f, -ve [sedatif] *adj.* sedative; **~f** *s.m.* sedative.
sédation [sedɑsjɔ̃] *s.f.* (med.) sedation.
sédentaire [sedɑ̃tɛr] *adj.* sedentary, fixed, stay--at-home, tied to the house; (mil.) non-mobile, garrison; **~ment** [sedɑ̃tɛrmɑ̃] *adv.* sedentarily.
sédiment [sedimɑ̃] *s.m.* sediment; **~aire** [sedimɑ̃tɛr] *adj.* sedimentary; **~ation** [sedimɑ̃tɑsjɔ̃] *s.f.* sedimentation, formation of sediment.
séditieu-x, -se [sedisjø] *adj., s.m.f.* seditious, rebellious, mutinous, subversive, (person).
sédition [sedisjɔ̃] *s.f.* sedition, rebellion, mutiny, revolt.
séduct-eur, -rice [sedyktœr] *s.m.f.* seducer, deluder, enticer, corrupter; *adj.* seductive, deluding, enticing, tempting.
séduction [sedyksjɔ̃] *s.f.* seduction, enticement; charm, seductiveness, allurement; ensnaring; seducing; bribing, corruption, subornation.
séduire [sedɥir] *v.t.* to seduce; to entice, to charm, to beguile, to fascinate, to allure, to delude, to ensnare, to win over; to bribe, to corrupt, to suborn.
séduisant, -e [sedɥizɑ̃] *adj.* seductive, fascinating, charming, bewitching, prepossessing; tempting.
sedum [sedɔm] *s.m.* (bot.) sedum, stonecrop.
segment [sɛgmɑ̃] *s.m.* segment; ~ *de piston*, piston-ring; ~ *de frein*, brake-shoe.
segmentaire [sɛgmɑ̃tɛr] *adj.* segmental, segmented.
segmental, -e, (aux) [sɛgmɑ̃tal] *adj.* segmentary.
segmenter [sɛgmɑ̃te] *v.t.* to segment, to divide into segments; **se** ~ *v.refl.* to segment.
ségrégati-f, -ve [segregatif] *adj.* segregative.
ségrégation [segregɑsjɔ̃] *s.f.* segregation, separation; **~nisme** [segregɑsjɔnism] *s.m.* policy of segregation; **~niste** [segregɑsjɔnist] *adj., s.m.f.* segregationist.
seiche[1] [sɛʃ] *s.f.* (zool.) cuttle(-fish).
seiche[2] [sɛʃ] *s.f.* (geog.) tidal wave (on Swiss lakes).
séïde [seid] *s.m.* fanatical supporter.
seigle [sɛgl] *s.m.* rye, (pl.) rye-fields; ~ *ergoté*, spurred rye.
seigneur [sɛɲœr] *s.m.* lord, squire, noble, nobleman; *le Seigneur (Dieu)*, the Lord; *Notre Seigneur*, Our Lord; *trancher du grand* ~, *faire le grand* ~, (i.) to give oneself airs; (ii.) to throw one's money around; *vivre en grand* ~, to live in luxury; *à tout* ~, *tout honneur*, honour to whom honour is due.
seigneurial, -e, (aux) [sɛɲœrjal] *adj.* lordly, princely, baronial, manorial; *droits seigneuriaux* manorial rights.
seigneurie [sɛɲœri] *s.f.* seigniory, lordship, manor; domain; *Votre Seigneurie*, Your Lordship.
seille [sɛj] *s.f.* wooden bucket; large wooden or canvas container.
seime [sɛm] *s.f.* (vet.) sandcrack.
sein [sɛ̃] *s.m.* breast; bosom; (fig.) bosom, midst, heart, womb, depths, bowels; *donner le* ~ *à un enfant*, to give a child the breast; to suckle or nurse a child; *nourrir au* ~, to breast-feed; *vivre au* ~ *de l'opulence*, to live in the midst of plenty; *le* ~ *de l'Église*, the bosom of the Church; the faithful; *le* ~ *de Dieu*, paradise.
seine [sɛn] *s.f.* seine(-net).
seing [sɛ̃] *s.m.* (obs.) signature, sign manual; (law) *sous* ~ *privé*, by private deed.
séisme [seism] *s.m.* earthquake; (fig.) upheaval.
séismique [seismik] *adj.* = SISMIQUE.
séismographe see SISMOGRAPHE.
séismologie see SISMOLOGIE.
seize [sɛz] *adj.* sixteen; sixteenth; *Louis* ~, Louis the Sixteenth.
seizième [sɛzjɛm] *adj., s.m.* sixteenth.
séjour [seʒur] *s.m.* **1.** stay, sojourn, spell, visit; break of journey, stop-over; *taxe de* ~, visitor's tax; **2.** abode, residence, regions; (*salle de*) ~, living-room; *permis de* ~, residence permit; *un interdit de* ~, a person forbidden to reside (in a certain area); ~ *forcé*, enforced stay, compulsory residence; *un* ~ *délicieux*, an enchanting abode; *le céleste* ~, the celestial regions; the abode of the gods.
séjourner [seʒurne] *v.i.* to stay, to sojourn, to dwell temporarily, to remain, to stop, to lie.
sel [sɛl] *s.m.* salt; ~ *fin*, table salt; *gros* ~, coarse salt; (fig.) wit, piquancy, pungency, humour; (pl.) (chem.) salts; smelling salts, medicinal salts.
sélacien, -ne [selasjɛ̃] *adj.* (ichth.) selachian.
sélagine [selaʒin] *s.f.* (bot.) Selaginella.
select, sélect [selɛkt] *adj.invar.* select, choice, smart.
sélecteur [selɛktœr] *s.m.* (techn.) selector; (motor cycle) gear-change lever.
sélecti-f, -ve [selɛktif] *adj.* selective.
sélection [selɛksjɔ̃] *s.f.* selection, choice.
sélectionné, -e [selɛksjɔne] *adj.* selected, chosen, choice.
sélectionner [selɛksjɔne] *v.t.* to select.
sélectionneu-r, -se [selɛksjɔnœr] *s.m.f.* selector, grader; psychologist operating selection test.
sélectivité [selɛktivite] *s.f.* (radio) selectivity.
sélén-iate [selenjat] *s.m.* (chem.) selenate; **~ieux** [selenjø] *adj.m.* (chem.) (of acid) selenious; **~ique** [selenik] *adj.m.* (chem.) (of acid) selenic; **~ite** [selenit] *s.m.* (chem.) selenite; **~ium** [selenjɔm] (chem.) selenium; **~ographie** [selenɔgrafi] *s.f.* (astron.) selenography; **~ographique** [selenɔgrafik] *adj.* (astron.) selenographic(al).
self [sɛlf] *s.f.* **1.** = SELF-INDUCTION 2; **2.** abbrev. SELF-SERVICE; **~-control** [sɛlfkɔ̃trol] *s.m.* self--control; **~-inductance** [sɛlfɛ̃dyktɑ̃s] *s.f.*

(phys.) self-inductance; **~-induction** [sɛlfɛ̃dyksjɔ̃] *s.f.* (electr.) **1.** self-induction; **2.** (self-)induction coil, choke; **~-made-man** [sɛlfmɛdman] *s.m.* (pl. *~-made-men*) self-made man; **~-service** [sɛlfsɛrvis] *s.m.* (pl. *~-services*) self-service shop or restaurant.

selle [sɛl] *s.f.* **1.** saddle; *en ~*, in or into, the saddle; *monter en ~*, to mount; (fig.) *se remettre en ~*, to re-establish one's position; *remettre qn. en ~*, to give s.o. a helping hand, to set s.o. up (again); **2.** (med.) opening of the bowels, motion, evacuation, stool; *aller à la ~*, to have a motion.

seller [sɛle] *v.t.* to saddle.

sellerie [sɛlri] *s.f.* saddlery; harness room.

sellette [sɛlɛt] *s.f.* **1.** seat for suspects under interrogation; (fig.) *être sur la ~*, to be under interrogation or examination; *mettre* or *tenir qn. sur la ~*, to interrogate or cross-examine s.o.; **2.** saddle (of draught-horse); **3.** small stand for statue; **4.** (build.) painter's cradle.

sellier [sɛlje] *s.m.* saddle-maker, saddler.

selon [səlɔ̃] *prep.* according to; after; pursuant to; *~ moi*, to my mind; *~ lui*, according to him, from what he says; *~ toute apparence*, from all appearances; *~ toute vraisemblance*, in all probability; *c'est ~*, that depends; *~ que*, according as.

selve [sɛlv] *s.f.* (geog.) virgin forest.

semailles [səmɑj] *s.f.pl.* sowing; seed-time, sowing-time.

semaine [səmɛn] *s.f.* week; week's wages; *à la ~*, by the week, weekly; *gagner tant par ~*, to earn so much a week; *la ~ prochaine*, next week; *être de ~*, to be on duty for the week; *jours de ~*, working-days; weekdays; *la ~ anglaise*, five-day week; *prêter à la petite ~*, to lend money at a high rate of interest; *une politique à la petite ~*, a makeshift policy, a policy of shifts and expedients.

semainier [səmɛnje] *s.m.* **1.** person on duty for the week; **2.** desk-calendar (showing a week at a time); **3.** cabinet with seven drawers.

sémantique [semɑ̃tik] *adj.* semantic; *~ s.f.* semantics.

sémaphore [semafɔr] *s.m.* semaphore, signal-post.

sémaphorique [semafɔrik] *adj.* semaphoric.

semblable [sɑ̃blabl] *adj.* alike, like, such, similar; fellow; *a-t-on jamais vu rien de ~?*, did you ever see such a thing?; *rien de ~!*, nothing of the sort!; **~ment** [sɑ̃blabləmɑ̃] *adv.* similarly, likewise; *~ s.m.* fellow creature.

semblant [sɑ̃blɑ̃] *s.m.* semblance, outward appearance; show, pretence; *faux ~*, pretence, sham; *faire ~ de*, to pretend to; *ne faire ~ de rien*, to appear to be taking no notice; to pretend to know nothing about it.

sembler [sɑ̃ble] *v.i.* to appear, to seem, to look; *si bon vous semble*, if you think fit; if it is your wish; *comme bon vous semblera*, just as you please; *il semble que*, it appears that; it looks as if; *il me semble le voir*, I fancy I see him; *c'est ce qu'il me semble*, that's just what I think; *à ce qu'il me semble*, to my mind; in my opinion; *que vous en semble?*, what do you think of that?

semé, -e [səme] *adj.* sown; strewn (*de*, with), sprinkled, spangled, interspersed; (herald.) semée.

séméiologie see SÉMIOLOGIE.

semelle [səmɛl] *s.f.* sole (of shoe), foot (of stocking), sock (inside shoe); (techn.) sole-plate, bed-plate; chair, seat; (fenc.) step; (fig.) *ne pas reculer d'une ~*, not to budge an inch; *battre la ~*, to stamp one's feet (in order to warm them); (fenc.) *rompre la ~*, to retire in parrying.

semence [səmɑ̃s] *s.f.* seed; semen, sperm; (fig.) seed, germ; (tin-)tack; *~ de perles*, seed-pearls; *~ de diamants*, diamond sparks.

semen-contra [semɛnkɔ̃tra] *s.m.* (pharm.) worm-seed.

semer [səme] *v.t.* to sow; to strew, to sprinkle, to scatter, to spread, to broadcast, to disseminate; (obs.) to shed, to drop, to leave behind; (fig.) *qui sème le vent récolte la tempête*, he who sows the wind shall reap the whirlwind; *~ l'argent follement*, to squander one's money.

semestre [səmɛstr] *s.m.* half year; semester; half-yearly payment; six months' pay; six months' duty or leave.

semestriel, -le [səmɛstrjɛl] *adj.* half-yearly.

semeu-r, -se [səmœr] *s.m.f.* sower.

semi-automatique [səmiɔtɔmatik] *adj.* semi-automatic.

semi-chenillé, -e [səmiʃnije] *adj.*, *s.m.* half-track (vehicle).

semi-coke [səmikɔk] *s.m.* semi-coke.

semi-conduct-eur, -rice [səmikɔ̃dyktœr] *adj.* (electr.) semiconducting; **~eur** *s.m.* (electr.) semiconductor.

semi-fini, -e [səmifini] *adj.* (of goods) semi-finished.

sémillant, -e [semijɑ̃] *adj.* sprightly, lively, bright, of gay disposition.

séminaire [seminɛr] *s.m.* seminary.

séminal, -e, (aux) [seminal] *adj.* seminal.

séminariste [seminarist] *s.m.* seminarist.

sémiologie [semjɔlɔʒi], **séméiologie** [semejɔlɔʒi] *s.f.* semiology, semeiology.

semi-remorque [səmir(ə)mɔrk] *s.f.* half-trailer, half-trailer lorry.

semis [səmi] *s.m.* sowing; seed-bed; seedling.

sémite [semit] *s.m.f.* Semite.

sémitique [semitik] *adj.* Semitic.

semi-voyelle [səmivwajɛl] *s.f.* semivowel.

semnopithèque [sɛmnɔpitɛk] *s.m.* (zool.) Semnopithecus.

semoir [səmwar] *s.m.* (agric.) seed bag; sowing-machine; spreader.

semonce [səmɔ̃s] *s.f.* (obs.) summons; (naut.) call (to heave to, etc.); reprimand, admonition.

semoncer [səmɔ̃se] *v.t.* to reprimand, to rebuke; (naut.) to call to heave to.

semoule [səmul] *s.f.* semolina.

sempiternel, -le [sɛ̃pitɛrnɛl] *adj.* everlasting, never-ending; **~lement** [sɛ̃pitɛrnɛlmɑ̃] *adv.* eternally, everlastingly.

semple [sɑ̃pl] *s.m.* simple (of loom).

sénat [sena] *s.m.* senate.

sénateur [senatœr] *s.m.* senator; (fig.) one holding a secure position.

sénatorial, -e, (aux) [senatɔrjal] *adj.* senatorial.

senatus-consulte [senatyskɔ̃sylt] *s.m.* (Rom. & Fr. hist.) senatus-consultum, decree of the Senate.

senau [səno] *s.m.* (naut.) snow (a vessel); *voile de ~*, try-sail.

séné [sene] *s.m.* (bot.) senna; (fig.) *passe-moi la casse, je te passerai le ~*, scratch my back and I will scratch yours.

sénéchal (pl. **aux**) [seneʃal] *s.m.* seneschal.

sénéchaussée [seneʃose] *s.f.* court or jurisdiction of a seneschal.

séneçon [sensɔ̃] *s.m.* (bot.) groundsel.

Sénégal [senɛgal] *s.m.* (geog.) Senegal.

sénégalais, -e [senegalɛ] *adj.*, *s.m.f.* Senegalese.

sénescence [senesɑ̃s] *s.f.* senescence.

senestre [sənɛstr], **sénestre** [senɛstr] *adj.* left; (herald.) sinister.

sénevé [senve] *s.m.* (bot.) mustard; mustard-seed.

sénile [senil] *adj.* senile.

sénilité [senilite] *s.f.* senility.

senne [sɛn] *s.f.* = SEINE.

señorita [seɲɔrita] *s.m.* type of small cigar.

sens [sɑ̃s] *s.m.* **1.** sense, senses, instinct; *cela tombe sous les ~*, that's obvious; that's self-evident; **2.** judgement, interpretation, meaning, acceptance; opinion; (good) sense, reason; *à mon* ~, in my opinion; *j'abonde dans votre* ~, I entirely agree with you; *le bon* ~, good sense; *il n'est pas dans son bon* ~, he is not in his right mind; *n'avoir pas le* ~ *commun*, to be absurd; to have no common sense; *expression à double* ~, word with double meaning, pun, ambiguous expression; double-entendre; ~ *figuré*, figurative sense; ~ *propre*, proper meaning; *un homme de* ~ *rassis*, a staid, sober man; **3.** direction, way; *dans le (bon)* ~, in the right direction; *dans le* ~ *de*, in the same direction as, with (the current, etc.); *dans le* ~ *de la longueur*, lengthways; ~ *devant derrière*, back to front, wrong way round; ~ *dessus dessous*, upside down, topsy-turvy, in a muddle; *dans tous les* ~, in all directions; *(rue à)* ~ *unique*, one-way street; ~ *interdit*, no entry.

sensation [sɑ̃sɑsjɔ̃] *s.f.* sensation, feeling, excitement; *faire* ~, to make a sensation; *à* ~, sensational.

sensationnel, -e [sɑ̃sɑsjɔnɛl] *adj.* sensational, thrilling, exciting.

sensé, -e [sɑ̃se] *adj.* sensible, judicious, rational, reasonable; **~ment** [sɑ̃semɑ̃] *adv.* sensibly.

sensibilisat-eur, -rice [sɑ̃sibilizatœr] *adj.* sensitizing; **~eur** *s.m.* (photo.) sensitizer; **~rice** *s.f.* (biol.) sensitizing agent.

sensibilis-ation [sɑ̃sibilizɑsjɔ̃] *s.f.* sensitization; (fig.) *~ation à*, becoming sensitive to or aware of; **~er** [sɑ̃sibilize] *v.t.* **1.** (obs.) to instil sensitiveness into; **2.** to sensitize; **3.** (fig.) *être sensibilisé à*, to be sensitive to or aware of.

sensibilité [sɑ̃sibilite] *s.f.* sensibility, sensitiveness, feeling.

sensible [sɑ̃sibl] *adj.* sensible, perceptible, appreciable; sensitive, susceptible, receptive, (*à*, to); kind, compassionate; tender, sore; (mus.) *note* ~, leading note; **~ment** [sɑ̃sibləmɑ̃] *adv.* (obs.) perceptibly; (mod.) roughly, as far as one can judge; appreciably, considerably; ⚠ not 'sensible' in senses 'judicious', 'showing good sense', 'moderate'.

sensiblerie [sɑ̃sibləri] *s.f.* sentimentalism, (excessive) sentimentality.

sensiti-f, -ve [sɑ̃sitif] *adj.* sensitive; sensory.

sensitive [sɑ̃sitiv] *s.f.* (bot.) sensitive plant; ~ *s.m.f.* sensitive person.

sensitivité [sɑ̃sitivite] *s.f.* sensitivity.

sensoriel, -le [sɑ̃sɔrjɛl] *adj.* sensorial.

sensualisme [sɑ̃sɥalism] *s.m.* (phil.) sensualism.

sensualiste [sɑ̃sɥalist] *adj.* (phil.) sensualist, sensual; ~ *s.m.f.* sensualist.

sensualité [sɑ̃sɥalite] *s.f.* sensuality.

sensuel, -le [sɑ̃sɥɛl] *adj.* sensual, voluptuous.

sente [sɑ̃t] *s.f.* path.

sentence [sɑ̃tɑ̃s] *s.f.* sentence, judgement, verdict; aphorism, maxim; *rendre une* ~, to pass sentence; to bring in a verdict; ⚠ not 'sentence' as a grammatical structure.

sentencieu-x, -se [sɑ̃tɑ̃sjø] *adj.* sententious; **~sement** [sɑ̃tɑ̃sjøzmɑ̃] *adv.* sententiously.

senteur [sɑ̃tœr] *s.f.* scent, perfume, smell; (bot.) *pois de* ~, sweet pea.

senti, -e [sɑ̃ti] *adj.* heartfelt, deeply felt; strongly expressed, strongly worded; *quelques paroles bien ~es*, a few strong, or well-chosen, words.

sentier [sɑ̃tje] *s.m.* path, footpath; (fig.) track, path; road; *~s battus*, beaten tracks; well--trodden ways.

sentiment [sɑ̃timɑ̃] *s.m.* feeling, sense, instinct, sentiment, impression, sensation; opinion; *avoir le* ~ *de sa force*, to be conscious of one's strength; *juger par* ~, to judge by personal feeling or impression, to make a subjective judgement; *être animé de bons ~s*, to be well-meaning.

sentimental, -e, (aux) [sɑ̃timɑ̃tal] *adj.* sentimental, love; *sa vie ~e*, his love life; **~ement** [sɑ̃timɑ̃talmɑ̃] *adv.* sentimentally.

sentimentalité [sɑ̃timɑ̃talite] *s.f.* sentimentality.

sentine [sɑ̃tin] *s.f.* (naut.) well, bilge; (fig.) sink, sewer.

sentinelle [sɑ̃tinɛl] *s.f.* sentinel, sentry; *être en* ~, *faire* ~, to stand sentry; to mount guard; (fig.) to be on the watch.

sentir [sɑ̃tir] *v.t.* **1.** to feel, to perceive, to be conscious of, to be aware of, to have a sensation of, to have a feeling for; to be affected by; to experience; ~ *sa propre faiblesse*, to be conscious of one's weakness; ~ *ses jambes*, to feel (tiredness or pain in) one's legs; **2.** to smell, to smell bad; to scent; to smell of, to smack of, to savour of, to evoke (a feeling of); to perceive the smell of, to detect by smell; (fig.) to find out, to suspect, to detect; *cela sent bon*, this smells nice; *cela sent mauvais ici*, there is a bad smell here; (fig.) *cela ne sent pas bon*, I don't like the look of it, that does not look promising; ~ *l'ail*, to smell of garlic; (fig.) *je ne peux pas le* ~, I cannot bear, or stand, him; I hate the sight of him; ~ *le fagot*, to be tainted with heresy; **se** ~ *v.refl.* to feel, to be conscious of (being sth., being in a certain position); to make itself felt; to be affected (*de*, by); *je ne me sens pas bien*, I don't feel quite well; *il s'est senti mourir*, he was conscious that he was dying; *elle ne se sent pas de joie*, she is beside herself with joy; *les effets s'en font encore* ~, the consequences are still making themselves felt; *je ne me sens pas beaucoup de courage*, I don't feel very brave; *on se sent toujours de sa première éducation*, one is always conditioned by one's early upbringing.

seoir[1] [swar] *v.i.* to sit.

seoir[2] [swar] *v.i.* to suit, to be becoming or fitting; *ce chapeau vous sied*, this hat suits you well; *il vous sied mal de parler ainsi*, it ill becomes you to speak in that way; *comme il sied*, as is right and proper.

sep [sɛp] *s.m.* = CEP 2, 3.

sépale [sepal] *s.m.* (bot.) sepal.

séparable [separabl] *adj.* separable, detachable.

séparation [separɑsjɔ̃] *s.f.* separation, parting, severing, dispersion, dispersal; distinction, demarcation; *mur de* ~, partition-wall; (law) ~ *de biens*, separate maintenance; ~ *de corps et de biens*, judicial separation.

séparat-isme [separatism] *s.m.* separatism; **~iste** [separatist] *adj., s.m.f.* separatist.

séparé, -e [separe] *adj.* separate, distinct, apart; **~ment** [separemɑ̃] *adv.* separately.

séparer [separe] *v.t.* to separate, to part, to divide, to disunite, to disjoin, to break up, to set apart, to put on one side; to distinguish or differentiate between; to sever; **se** ~ *v.refl.* to part; to break up, to disperse, to part company; to be judicially separated.

sépia [sepja] *s.f.* sepia; sepia drawing.

seps [sɛps] *s.m.* (zool.) seps, serpent-lizard.

sept [sɛt] *adj.* seven; seventh.

septain [sɛtɛ̃] *s.m.* seven-line stanza.

septante [sɛptɑ̃t] *adj.* (dial.) seventy; *la Version des Septante*, the Septuagint.

septembre [sɛptɑ̃br] *s.m.* September.

septembriseur [sɛptɑ̃brizœr] *s.m.* Septembrist (agent of the massacres in France in September 1792).

septénaire [sɛptenɛr] *s.m., adj.* septenary, set of seven (days or years).

septennal, -e, (aux) [sɛptenal] *adj.* septennial.

septennat [sɛptena] *s.m.* seven years' office (esp. presidency).

septentrion [sɛptɑ̃trjɔ̃] *s.m.* (Lit.) north.

septentrional, -e, (aux) [sɛptɑ̃trjɔnal] *adj.* north, northern.

septicémie [sɛptisemi] *s.f.* (pathol.) septicaemia, blood-poisoning.

septicité [sɛptisite] *s.f.* septicity, septic condition, infection.
septidi [sɛptidi] *s.m.* (hist.) Septidi, 7th day of *décade* in Fr. Republican Calendar.
septième [sɛtjɛm] *adj.* seventh; (fig.) *être au ~ ciel*, to be in the seventh heaven; to walk on air; *~ s.m.* seventh floor; seventh part; *~ s.f.* (mus.) seventh; (at school) seventh form; **~ment** [sɛtjɛmmɑ̃] *adj.* seventhly.
septique [sɛptik] *adj.* septic.
septuagénaire [sɛptɥaʒenɛr] *adj., s.m.f.* septuagenarian.
septuagésime [sɛptɥaʒesim] *s.f.* Septuagesima.
septuor [sɛptɥɔr] *s.m.* (mus.) septet.
septuple [sɛptypl] *adj., s.m.* septuple, sevenfold (amount).
septupler [sɛptyple] *v.t.i.* to septuple, to increase sevenfold.
sépulcral, -e, (aux) [sepylkral] *adj.* sepulchral.
sépulcre [sepylkr] *s.m.* sepulchre.
sépulture [sepyltyr] *s.f.* sepulture, vault, tomb, burial-place; burial.
séquelle [sekɛl] *s.f.* **1.** (obs., pej.) gang; **2.** consequence, after-effect, (fig.) backlash.
séquence [sekɑ̃s] *s.f.* sequence; (at cards) sequence, run.
séquestration [sekɛstrɑsjɔ̃] *s.f.* sequestration, confinement.
séquestre [sekɛstr] *s.m.* (law) **1.** sequestration; **2.** sequestrator, assignee.
séquestrer [sekɛstre] *v.t.* to sequester, to confine, to isolate, to shut up illegally.
sequin [səkɛ̃] *s.m.* sequin.
sequoia [sekɔja] *s.m.* (bot.) sequoia.
sérac [serak] *s.m.* serac (in a glacier).
sérail (pl. **-s**) [seraj] *s.m.* seraglio.
sérancer [serɑ̃se] *v.t.* (text.) to hackle, to comb.
séraphin [serafɛ̃] *s.m.* seraph.
séraphique [serafik] *adj.* seraphic, angelic.
serbe [sɛrb] *adj., s.m.f.* Serb, Serbian.
Serbie [sɛrbi] *s.f.* (geog.) Serbia.
serein [sərɛ̃] *s.m.* (Lit.) dew-fall, evening damp; *prendre le ~*, to catch a chill (from the night air).
serein, -e [sərɛ̃] *adj.* serene, calm (and collected), unruffled, undisturbed, clear, tranquil, happy, cool, detached; *jours ~s*, halcyon days; **~ement** [sərɛnmɑ̃] *adv.* calmly, coolly, impartially.
sérénade [serenad] *s.f.* serenade; (fam.) uproar, shouting.
sérénissime [serenisim] *adj.* (as a title) Most Serene.
sérénite [serenite] *s.f.* serenity, calmness, placidity, equanimity, detachment.
séreu-x, -se [serø] *adj.* serous.
ser-f, -ve [sɛrf] *adj.* in bondage; *s.m.f.* serf.
serfouette [sɛrfwɛt] *s.f.* hoe.
serfouir [sɛrfwir] *v.t.* to hoe.
serfouissage [sɛrfwisaʒ] *s.m.* hoeing.
serge [sɛrʒ] *s.f.* serge.
sergé [sɛrʒe] *s.m.* twill (weave); serge-type material.
sergent [sɛrʒɑ̃] *s.m.* **1.** (obs.) bailiff; **2.** sergeant; (obs.) *~ de ville*, policeman; *~ fourrier*, quartermaster-sergeant; *~ instructeur*, drill-sergeant, sergeant-instructor; *~-chef*, staff-sergeant; *~-major*, quartermaster-sergeant; **3.** (join.) cramp, holdfast, clamp.
sérici-cole [serisikɔl] *adj.* sericultural; **~culteur** [serisikyltœr] *s.m.* sericulturist, breeder of silkworms; **~culture** [serisikyltyr] *s.f.* sericulture, breeding of silkworms.
série [seri] *s.f.* series, succession, spell, range, line; (sport) rating; *en* or *par ~*, in series, serially; *fabrication de ~*, mass-production, standardized production; *voiture de ~*, mass-produced car, standard model; *hors ~*, specially made, (made to) special order; out of the ordinary, outstanding; specialized; (comm.) *fins de ~*, discontinued lines, end-of-range bargains, (publisher's) remainders; (build.) *prix de ~*, contract price; *~ de prix*, cost schedule.
sérier [serje] *v.t.* to classify, to sort, to arrange in series, to file.
sérieu-x, -se [serjø] *adj.* serious, serious-minded, earnest, grave; momentous, important, considerable; severe; thorough; responsible; **~x** *s.m.* seriousness, gravity, responsibility; *garder son ~x*, to keep one's countenance; to refrain from laughing; *prendre au ~x*, to take seriously; (fam.) *alors c'était ~x?*, did you really mean it? you weren't joking?; **~sement** [serjøzmɑ̃] *adv.* seriously, in earnest; hard; gravely.
sérigraphie [serigrafi] *s.f.* (art) serigraphy, silk-screen printing.
serin [srɛ̃] *s.m.* canary; (fig., pej.) silly fool, silly goose; *~*, **~e** *adj.* silly.
seriner [serine] *v.t.* to teach (cage-bird) with serinette; (fig.) to din it into, to teach by repeating over and over again.
serinette [sərinɛt] *s.f.* serinette, bird-organ.
seringa, seringat [sərɛ̃ga] *s.m.* (bot.) syringa (= mock-orange, not lilac).
seringue [sərɛ̃g] *s.f.* syringe, squirt, spray.
seringuer [sərɛ̃ge] *v.t.* to syringe, to squirt, to spray; (slang) to spray with machine-gun fire.
sérique [serik] *adj.* (med.) serum, of or from injections.
serment [sɛrmɑ̃] *s.m.* oath, swearing; *prêter ~*, to take one's oath; to be sworn; *faire prêter ~ à qn.*, to put s.o. on his oath, to administer the oath to s.o.; *prestation de ~*, taking of oath; *faire ~*, to swear; *faux ~*, false oath, perjury; *sous ~*, on oath, under oath; *déclaration sous ~*, sworn statement; *violer ses ~s*, to break one's promises; *~ d'ivrogne*, drunkard's oath, empty promise.
sermon [sɛrmɔ̃] *s.m.* sermon, homily; (fig.) lecture; admonition, reprimand; *faire un ~*, to preach a sermon; to lecture.
sermonner [sɛrmɔne] *v.t.* to lecture, to sermonize; to reprimand, to take to task.
sermonneu-r, -se [sɛrmɔnœr] *s.m.f.* sermonizer, lecturer, fault-finder; *adj.* censorious, prone to find fault.
séro-logie [serɔlɔʒi] *s.f.* serology; **~sité** [serɔsite] *s.f.* serosity; **~thérapie** [serɔterapi] *s.f.* serotherapy, serum treatment.
serpe [sɛrp] *s.f.* billhook; *taillé à la ~*, rough(ly) hewn.
serpent [sɛrpɑ̃] *s.m.* snake, serpent; (mus.) serpent; (zool.) *~ à sonnettes*, rattlesnake; *~ à lunettes*, cobra; *avoir une langue de ~*, to have a venomous tongue.
serpentaire [sɛrpɑ̃tɛr] *s.m.* (ornith.) serpent-eater, secretary-bird; *~ s.f.* (bot.) snake-weed.
serpente [sɛrpɑ̃t] *s.f.* tissue-paper.
serpenteau (pl. **-x**) [sɛrpɑ̃to] *s.m.* young snake; (firework) squib.
serpenter [sɛrpɑ̃te] *v.i.* to wind in and out, to meander; *chemin qui monte en serpentant*, path that winds uphill.
serpentin [sɛrpɑ̃tɛ̃] *s.m.* **1.** worm (of a still); coiled tube; **2.** paper streamer; **~, -e** *adj.* snake-like, serpentine, sinuous, wavy, meandering; (of marble) serpentine, veined.
serpentine [sɛrpɑ̃tin] *s.f.* serpentine stone, serpentine marble.
serpette [sɛrpɛt] *s.f.* pruning-knife; small bill-hook.
serpillière [sɛrpijɛr] *s.f.* packing-cloth, sack-cloth; floor-cloth.
serpolet [sɛrpɔlɛ] *s.m.* (bot.) wild thyme.
serrage [sɛraʒ] *s.m.* tightening; fastening, securing; pressing; application (of brakes); *vis de ~*, clamping-screw.
serrate [sɛrat] *adj.* serrated; (of coins) milled.

serratule [sɛratyl] *s.f.* (bot.) saw-wort.
serre [sɛr] *s.f.* **1.** talon, claw; (fig.) clutch, grip; **2.** hot-house, greenhouse, conservatory; **3.** (techn.) pressing; **4.** (nav. arch.) stringer.
serré, -e [sere] *adj., adv.* tight, close, close together, enclosed, constricted, crowded, serried, concise, compact; (fig.) close-fisted; *vivre* ~, to live in straitened circumstances; *avoir le cœur* ~, to have a heavy heart, to be sad at heart; *critique* ~*e*, closely-reasoned criticism; *une partie* ~*e*, a hard-fought game; *jouer* ~, to play a cautious game, to hold one's cards close to one's chest; *mentir* ~, to lie persistently; (cin., TV) *montage* ~, drastic editing; *un tissu* ~, a closely woven material; *un nœud* ~, a tight knot.
serre-file [sɛrfil] *s.m.invar.* person bringing up the rear; (naut.) sternmost vessel.
serre-fils [sɛrfil] *s.m.invar.* (electr.) connector.
serre-frein(s) [sɛrfrɛ̃] *s.m.invar.* brake(s)man.
serre-joint(s) [sɛrʒwɛ̃] *s.m.invar.* (join.) cramp, clamp.
serre-livres [sɛrlivr] *s.m.invar.* book-end.
serrement [sɛrmɑ̃] *s.m.* pressing, squeezing, constriction; (mining) dam, watertight partition; ~ *de cœur*, pang, heaviness of heart, anguish; ~ *de main*, handshake.
serre-nez [sɛrne] *s.m.invar.* (for horses) twitch.
serre-papiers [sɛrpapje] *s.m.invar.* set of pigeon-holes.
serrer [sere] *v.t.* to press, to squeeze, to crush, to jam, to tighten, to tie tight(ly), to screw up, to pull in, to put close together, to crowd, to close; to pass or keep close to, to cling to, to hug, to condense, to shorten; to put away, to put by, to stow away, to lock up; ~ *la main à qn.*, to shake hands with s.o.; ~ *les dents*, to clench one's teeth; *cela serre le cœur*, that's heart-rending; ~ *les rangs*, to close the ranks; (naut.) ~ *le vent*, to haul close to the wind; ~ *la terre*, to hug the land; to keep close in to shore; ~ *de près*, to press hard; ~ *du linge*, to put away linen; ~ *son argent*, to lock up one's money; ~ *son style*, to condense one's style; ~ *son jeu*, to play a cautious game; ~ *un nœud*, to tighten a knot; **se** ~ *v.refl.* to crowd (together), to squeeze, to press, to cling (*contre*, to); *se* ~ *la ceinture*, (lit. & fig.) to tighten one's belt.
serre-tête [sɛrtɛt] *s.m.invar.* headband, headscarf; crash-helmet, safety helmet.
serrure [seryr] *s.f.* lock; *crocheter une* ~, to pick a lock.
serrurerie [seryrri] *s.f.* locksmith's trade, locksmith's work; blacksmith's work, forging; ~ *d'art*, wrought-iron work; *grosse* ~, heavy ironwork.
serrurier [seryrje] *s.m.* locksmith; ~ *en bâtiment*, supplier of builder's ironwork.
serte [sɛrt] *s.f.* = SERTISSAGE.
sertir [sɛrtir] *v.t.* to set, to mount; to crimp (cartridge).
sertissage [sɛrtisaʒ] *s.m.* setting, mounting.
sertisseu-r, -se [sɛrtisœr] *s.m.f.* setter, mounter; crimper (instrument).
sertissure [sɛrtisyr] *s.f.* setting.
sérum [serɔm] *s.m.* serum.
servage [sɛrvaʒ] *s.m.* serfdom, servitude, bondage.
serval [sɛrval] *s.m.* (zool.) serval.
servant [sɛrvɑ̃] *adj.m.* serving, in waiting, in attendance; (relig.) *frère* ~, lay brother; ~ *s.m.* (liturg.) server; (artill.) member of gun crew.
servante [sɛrvɑ̃t] *s.f.* **1.** (obs.) servant, maid-servant, serving-maid; (fig.) handmaid; **2.** side-table, serving-table, butler's tray, trolley; (techn.) adjustable support.
serve see SERF.
serveu-r, -se [sɛrvœr] *s.m.f.* server, waiter, waitress; (indust.) server (of a machine).
serviabilité [sɛrvjabilite] *s.f.* obligingness, willingness.
serviable [sɛrvjabl] *adj.* obliging, helpful.
service [sɛrvis] *s.m.* service, serving; service charge, tip; duty, attendance; help; function, office; department, staff; disposal; set; course; (air, bus, etc.) line, route; supply; *au* ~ *de*, in the service of; *être de* ~, to be on duty; *à votre* ~, at your disposal; at your service; *faire le* ~, to perform duty; to wait at table; (of buses, etc.) to run; *hors de* ~, worn out, out of use, out of action, not working; *escalier de* ~, back stairs; *en* ~, in service, in use, in commission; *entrer au* ~, to enlist, to join the (diplomatic, etc.) service; *faire son* ~, to do one's military service; *qu'y a-t-il pour votre* ~ ?, what can I do for you?; *rendre un* ~ *à qn.*, to do s.o. a favour; *rendre un mauvais* ~ *à qn.*, to do s.o. a bad turn; ~ *divin*, divine service; ~ *public*, civil service, public administration, public utility; *repas à 3* ~*s*, three-course meal; ~ *à thé*, tea-service; ~ *à liqueurs*, set of liqueur glasses; ~ *de table*, (set of) table-linen; *libre* ~, self-service.
serviette [sɛrvjɛt] *s.f.* **1.** towel; (table-)napkin, serviette; ~ *de toilette*, face-towel, hand-towel; ~ *de bain*, bath-towel; ~ *éponge*, Turkish towel(ling), bath-towel; ~ *d'enfant*, feeder, bib; ~ *hygiénique*, sanitary towel; **2.** brief-case, document-case, portfolio, dispatch-case.
servile [sɛrvil] *adj.* servile, menial; (fig.) slavish, cringing, mean-spirited, ~**ment** [sɛrvilmɑ̃] *adv.* in a servile manner, slavishly.
servilité [sɛrvilite] *s.f.* servility, slavishness, baseness, servileness.
servir [sɛrvir] *v.t.* to serve; to wait upon, to attend, to be in the service of; to be of assistance to, to further; to supply or serve with; to serve (dishes, etc.), to serve up; to wait at table; to be serviceable, to be of use; ~ *à*, to be used for, to be useful for; *à quoi cela servira-t-il?*, what is the use of that?; *cela ne sert à rien*, that serves no purpose, it is useless, or pointless; *il ne sert à rien de parler*, it is useless to talk; *elle m'a servi de mère*, she has been a mother to me; ~ *à table*, to wait at table; *servez à 8 heures*, serve the meal at 8 o'clock; *servez chaud*, serve hot; *madame est servie*, dinner is ready; dinner is served; ~ *une pompe*, to work a pump; ~ *une rente*, to pay an annuity; ~ *de jouet à qn.*, to serve as someone's plaything; ~ *de prétexte*, to serve as a pretext; *que ceci vous serve de leçon*, let this be a lesson to you; *que vous sert de pleurer?*, what's the use of crying?; ~ *à boire à qn.*, to fill someone's glass; **se** ~ *v.refl.* to help oneself; to do for oneself; to be served up; *se* ~ *de*, to use, to make use of; to avail oneself of; *se* ~ *chez* (*qn.*), to buy at, to get one's supplies from, (a shop).
serviteur [sɛrvitœr] *s.m.* servant, manservant; (obs.) *votre* ~, your humble servant (i.e. the speaker); (*je suis votre*) ~, I bid you good day; I am obliged to you; (iron.) thank you, no!
servitude [sɛrvityd] *s.f.* **1.** servitude, slavery; **2.** conditions, charge (upon an estate, etc.), easement, restrictive covenant; **3.** (naut.) *bateau de* ~, harbour craft.
servo-commande [sɛrvɔkɔmɑ̃d] *s.f.* servo-control; ~**frein** [sɛrvɔfrɛ̃] *s.m.* servo-brake; ~**mécanisme** [sɛrvɔmekanism] servo-mechanism; ~**moteur** [sɛrvɔmɔtœr] *s.m.* servo-motor, auxiliary motor, thruster.
ses see SON *poss. adj.*
sésame [sezam] *s.m.* (bot.) sesame; (fig.) ~ *ouvre-toi*, open sesame.
sésamoïde [sezamɔid] *adj.* (anat.) sesamoid.
séséli [sezeli] *s.m.* (bot.) meadow saxifrage.
sesquialtère [sɛskɥialtɛr] *adj.* (math.) sesquialter.
sesquioxyde [sɛskɥiɔksid] *s.m.* (chem.) sesquioxide.

sessile [sesil] *adj.* (bot.) sessile.
session [sesjɔ̃] *s.f.* session.
sesterce [sɛstɛrs] *s.m.* (Rom. ant.) sesterce, sestertius; *grand ~*, sestertium.
set [sɛt] *s.m.* (tennis, etc.) set; *balle de ~*, set-point.
sétacé, -e [setase] *adj.* setaceous, bristle-shaped.
setier [sətje] *s.m.* (obs.) measure of (i.) 150–300 litres of grain, (ii.) 8 *pintes* of liquid.
séton [setɔ̃] *s.m.* seton.
setter [setɛr] *s.m.* setter (dog).
seuil [sœj] *s.m.* sill, door-sill, threshold; (geol.) sill; (geog.) shelf; (fig.) threshold, dawn, beginning, entrance; (psychol.) limen.
seul, -e [sœl] *adj.* alone, single, lonely, on one's own, only, unaided, sole, mere, bare; *~ à ~*, face to face, by ourselves, by themselves; *il tremble au ~ nom de la mort*, the mere mention of death makes him tremble; *il est le ~ qui l'ait vu*, he alone saw him; *s.m.f.* (the) only person, (a) single person; *~ adv.* one only, only a; *~ un héros ferait cela*, only a hero, none but a hero, would do it; *tout ~*, by itself, unaided, without any trouble; **~ement** [sœlmɑ̃] *adv.* only, solely, merely; only just; but, yet; *sans ~ement le regarder*, without so much as looking at him; *il ne savait ~ement pas comment s'y prendre*, he didn't even know how to set about it.
seulet, -te [sœlɛ] *adj.* all alone, on one's own.
sève [sɛv] *s.f.* sap; (fig.) vigour, strength, vitality.
sévère [sevɛr] *adj.* severe, austere, rigid, harsh, stern, strict; (of losses, etc.) heavy; **~ment** [sevɛrmɑ̃] *adv.* severely, harshly, sternly, rigidly; gravely, seriously.
sévérité [severite] *s.f.* severity, austerity, rigour, rigidness, harshness; inclemency (of climate, season, etc.), severe measure, harsh decision.
sévices [sevis] *s.m.pl.* ill-treatment, cruelty.
sévir [sevir] *v.i.* **1.** *~ contre*, to punish severely, to to take severe measures against; **2.** to rage, to prevail, to be prevalent or rife, to be acute; (fig.) to be a plague.
sevrage [səvraʒ] *s.m.* **1.** weaning; **2.** (hort.) layering.
sevrer [səvre] *v.t.* **1.** to wean; (fig.) *~ de*, to wean from, to deprive of; **2.** (hort.) to layer.
sèvres [sɛvr] *s.m.* Sèvres (porcelain).
sexagénaire [sɛgzaʒenɛr] *adj.*, *s.m.f.* sexagenarian.
sexagésime [sɛgzaʒezim] *s.f.* Sexagesima.
sexe [sɛks] *s.m.* sex; sexual organs; sexuality, sex; *le ~ fort*, the sterner sex; *le ~ faible*, *le deuxième* or *le beau ~*, the weaker, second, or fair sex.
sexologie [sɛksɔlɔʒi] *s.f.* sexology, study of sexuality.
sextant [sɛkstɑ̃] *s.m.* (naut.) sextant.
sexte [sɛkst] *s.f.* (liturg.) sext.
sextidi [sɛkstidi] *s.m.* (hist.) Sextidi, sixth day of *décade* in Fr. Republican Calendar.
sextolet [sɛkstɔlɛ] *s.m.* (mus.) sextuplet.
sextuor [sɛkstɥɔr] *s.m.* (mus.) sextet.
sextuple [sɛkstypl] *adj.*, *s.m.* sextuple, sixfold.
sextupler [sɛkstyple] *v.t.i.* to sextuple, to increase sixfold, to multiply by six.
sexualité [sɛksɥalite] *s.f.* sexuality; sexual behaviour; (biol.) sexual characteristics.
sexué, -e [sɛksɥe] *adj.* sexual.
sexuel, -le [sɛksɥɛl] *adj.* sexual; **~lement** [sɛksɥɛlmɑ̃] *adv.* sexually.
seyant, -e [sɛjɑ̃] *adj.* becoming.
S.G.D.G. [ɛsʒedeʒe] abbrev. *Sans garantie du gouvernement.*
sgraffite [sgrafit] *s.m.* graffito, sgraffito.
shah see SCHAH.
shake-hand [ʃɛkɑ̃d] *s.m.invar.* handshake.
shaker [ʃɛkœr] *s.m.* cocktail-shaker.
shakespearien, -ne [ʃɛkspirjɛ̃] *adj.* Shakespearian.
shako [ʃako] *s.m.* shako.
shampooing [ʃɑ̃pwɛ̃] *s.m.* shampoo, shampooing.
shant(o)ung [ʃɑ̃tuŋ] *s.m.* (text.) shantung.
shérif [ʃerif] *s.m.* sheriff.
shetland [ʃɛtlɑ̃d] *s.m.* Shetland wool.
shimmy [ʃimi] *s.m.* **1.** (obs.) shimmy (American dance); **2.** (U.S.) shimmy, front-wheel wobble.
shirting [ʃirtɛ̃g] *s.m.* (text.) shirting.
shoot [ʃut] *s.m.* (footb.) powerful shot or kick.
shooter [ʃute] *v.i.* to shoot or kick hard; *~ v.t. ~ un penalty*, to take a penalty kick; **se** *~ v.refl.* (slang) to give oneself a fix (of a drug).
shopping [ʃɔpiŋ] *s.m.* looking round the shops, window-shopping.
short [ʃɔrt] *s.m.* shorts.
show [ʃo] *s.m.* variety show.
shrapnel [ʃrapnɛl] *s.m.* shrapnel (shell).
shunt [ʃœ̃t] *s.m.* (electr.) shunt (resistance).
shunter [ʃœ̃te] *v.t.* (electr.) to shunt.
si [si] *conj.* (**s'** before *il(s)*) if, whether, supposing that, what if; *~ ce n'est*, except for, but for, were it not for, unless; *~ ce n'est que*, except that, were it not that; *il viendra ~ cela est nécessaire*, he will come if necessary; *je ne sais s'il viendra*, I don't know whether he will come; *~ ce n'était la crainte de vous déplaire*, were it not for the fear of displeasing you; *~ s.m. invar. des ~ et des mais*, ifs and buts.
si [si] *adv.* so, so much, as, such, however, however much; yes, yes indeed; *que ~!*, yes, to be sure!; *une si belle femme!*, such a beautiful woman!; *je crois que ~*, I think it is so; *il n'est pas ~ prudent que moi*, he is not as careful as I; *~ grand qu'il soit*, however big it may be; *vous ne l'avez pas vu? Si*, you didn't see it? Yes, I did.
si [si] *s.m.* (mus.) B, te.
siamois, -e [sjamwa] *adj.*, *s.m.f.* Siamese; *frères ~, sœurs ~es*, Siamese twins.
Sibérie [siberi] *s.f.* (geog.) Siberia.
sibérien, -ne [siberjɛ̃] *adj.*, *s.m.f.* Siberian; *un froid ~*, biting cold.
sibilant, -e [sibilɑ̃] *adj.* (med.) sibilant, hissing.
sibylle [sibil] *s.f.* sibyl.
sibyllin, -e [sibilɛ̃] *adj.* sibylline.
sicaire [sikɛr] *s.m.* hired assassin.
siccati-f, -ve [sikatif] *adj.* siccative, desiccative; **~f** *s.m.* siccative, drier(s).
siccité [siksite] *s.f.* dryness.
Sicile [sisil] *s.f.* (geog.) Sicily.
sicilien, -ne [sisiljɛ̃] *adj.*, *s.m.f.* Sicilian; **~ne** *s.f.* Sicilienne (dance).
sicle [sikl] *s.m.* shekel.
side-car [sidkar, sajdkar] *s.m.* side-car; motor-cycle combination.
sidéral, -e, (aux) [sideral] *adj.* sidereal, pertaining to stars.
sidérer [sidere] *v.t.* (fam.) to flabbergast.
sidérite [siderit] *s.f.* **1.** (obs.) magnet; **2.** = SIDÉROSE 1.
sidérose [sideroz] *s.f.* **1.** (min.) siderite; **2.** (med.) siderosis.
sidérurgie [sideryrʒi] *s.f.* iron and steel metallurgy; steel-making, iron and steel production.
sidérurgique [sideryrʒik] *adj.* iron and steel; *industrie ~*, iron and steel industry.
sidi [sidi] *s.m.* (pej.) North African immigrant.
siècle [sjɛkl] *s.m.* century; age, period, times, world; *le ~ de Périclès*, the age of Pericles; *il y a un ~ que nous ne vous avons vu*, we have not seen you for ages; *dans les ~s des ~s*, for ever and ever; (fig.) *vivre dans le ~*, to live in the world (not in religious seclusion); *le ~ où nous vivons*, the age we live in; (fig.) *fin de ~*, *adj.* decadent.
siège [sjɛʒ] *s.m.* seat, chair; centre; box (of a coach); bench (of a tribunal); (eccles.) see; (mil.) siege; (anat.) seat, bottom; *prenez un ~*,

sit down; (car) ~ *d'arrière* or *spider*, dickey; *le Saint-Siège*, the Holy See; *bain de* ~, hip-bath; *mettre le* ~ *devant une ville*, to besiege a town; *lever le* ~, to raise the siege; *mettre en état de* ~, to lay under martial law; ~ *social d'une société*, registered offices of a company; head office; *le* ~ *du mal*, the seat of the malady.

siéger [sjeʒe] *v.i.* to sit; to be in session; (of a bishop) to hold a see; to lie, to be seated, to be located, to have its (head) office or headquarters.

sien, -ne [sjɛ̃] *poss.adj.* his, hers, its, one's; *pron. le* ~, *la* ~*ne*, his own, her own, his, hers; *il fait encore des siennes*, he is up to his old tricks again; *un* ~ *parent*, a relative of his; *les* ~*s*, one's own people; *y mettre du* ~, to work with a will; to do one's part, to contribute one's share.

sieste [sjɛst] *s.f.* siesta, afternoon nap.

sieur [sjœr] *s.m.* (obs.) Mr.; (iron.) *le* ~ *Lheureux*, the Lheureux gentleman, the said Mr. Lheureux.

sifflant, -e [siflɑ̃] *adj.* hissing, whistling, wheezing; ~**e** *s.f.* (phon.) sibilant.

sifflement [sifləmɑ̃] *s.m.* hiss, hissing, whistling, whizz; wheezing; singing (of kettle; in ears).

siffler [sifle] *v.t.i.* to whistle, to blow a whistle, to whistle to, to whistle up; (nav.) to pipe; to hiss, to boo; (fam.) ~ *un verre de vin*, to toss off a glass of wine; *l'arbitre a sifflé la mi-temps*, the referee blew for half-time; *l'agent a sifflé un contrevenant*, the policeman blew his whistle at an offender.

sifflet [siflɛ] *s.m.* whistle; hiss, catcall; *un coup de* ~, a whistle, a boatswain's call, (nav.) pipe; *couper le* ~ *à qn.*, to leave s.o. speechless.

siffleu-r, -se [siflœr] *adj.* whistling; *s.m.f.* whistler; hisser, booer.

sifflotement [siflɔtmɑ̃] *s.m.* whistling softly.

siffloter [siflɔte] *v.t.i.* to whistle softly, to whistle to oneself.

sigillaire [siʒilɛr] *adj.* of seals, sigillary; *anneau* ~, signet-ring; ~ *s.f.* (palaeont.) Sigillaria.

sigillé, -e [siʒile] *adj.* (bot., palaeont.) sigillate(d).

sigillographie [siʒillɔgrafi] *s.f.* sigillography.

sigisbée [siʒisbe] *s.m.* (obs. exc. iron.) cicisbeo, attendant swain.

sigle [sigl] *s.m.* group of initial letters, initial, initial letters; acronym.

signal (pl. **aux**) [siɲal] *s.m.* signal, sign; *donner le* ~ *de*, to give the signal for, to start, to launch, to provoke; *signaux de route*, road signs; (telephone) ~ *de numérotation*, dialling-tone.

signalé, -e [siɲale] *adj.* signal, notable, conspicuous, memorable.

signalement [siɲalmɑ̃] *s.m.* description (for identification).

signaler [siɲale] *v.t.* to signal; to point out, to call attention to, to mark out, to describe, to give a description of, to record, to report, to notify, to show; **se** ~ *v.refl.* to draw attention to oneself; to distinguish oneself.

signalétique [siɲaletik] *adj.* descriptive; *bulletin* ~, history sheet, record.

signaleur [siɲalœr] *s.m.* (mil., nav.) signaller, signalman.

signalisation [siɲalizɑsjɔ̃] *s.f.* marking with signposts, signals, buoys, etc., signposting, signalling; system of signs, signalling system; *appareil de* ~, signalling-apparatus, traffic lights, traffic signals.

signaliser [siɲalize] *v.t.* to mark with signals, signposts, signs, buoys, etc.; to mark, to signpost, to install signs, signals, indicators; to buoy.

signataire [siɲatɛr] *s.m.f.* signer; subscriber; signatory.

signature [siɲatyr] *s.f.* signature, signing; *honorer sa* ~, to honour one's undertaking.

signe [siɲ] *s.m.* sign, token, mark, indication; nod; wink; *faire* ~, to wink, to make signs, to give a sign or signal; *faire un* ~ *(de la main)*, to wave, to beckon, to sign; *faire un* ~ *(de tête)*, to nod; *c'est mauvais* ~, it looks bad, that's a bad sign.

signer [siɲe] *v.t.* to sign, to mark, to stamp; **se** ~ *v.refl.* to cross oneself, to make the sign of the cross.

signet [siɲɛ] *s.m.* bookmark; ⚠ not 'signet'.

significati-f, -ve [siɲifikatif] *adj.* significant, expressive, revealing.

signification [siɲifikɑsjɔ̃] *s.f.* signification, meaning, import, sense, significance; (law) legal notice, service (of writ).

signifier [siɲifje] *v.t.* to signify, to mean, to have the sense of, to denote, to imply; to notify, to give notice of; (law) to serve; ⚠ not 'to signify' in sense 'to be of significance'.

sil [sil] *s.m.* ochre.

silence [silɑ̃s] *s.m.* silence, stillness; secrecy; (mus.) rest; *faire* ~, to be silent, to stop speaking; *passer sous* ~, to make no mention of, to fail to mention, to pass over, to omit; *réduire qn. au* ~, or *imposer* ~ *à qn.*, to silence s.o.

silencieu-x, -se [silɑ̃sjø] *adj.* silent; noiseless, wordless, still; ~**x** *s.m.* (car) silencer; ~**sement** [silɑ̃sjøzmɑ̃] *adv.* silently.

silène [silɛn] *s.f.* (bot.) catchfly, Silene.

Silésie [silezi] *s.f.* (geog.) Silesia.

silésien, -ne [silezjɛ̃] *adj., s.m.f.* Silesian; ~**ne** *s.f.* silesia (a thin, twilled cloth used for linings).

silex [silɛks] *s.m.* silex, flint.

silhouette [silwɛt] *s.f.* silhouette, outline, profile, shape, figure, line.

silhouetter [silwete] *v.t.* to outline, to draw in outline, to silhouette; **se** ~ *v.refl.* to be silhouetted, to stand out, to show up.

silicate [silikat] *s.m.* (chem.) silicate.

silice [silis] *s.f.* (chem.) silica.

siliceu-x, -se [silisø] *adj.* silicious, siliceous.

silicique [silisik] *adj.* (chem.) silicic.

silicium [silisjɔm] *s.m.* (chem.) silicon.

silicone [silikon] *s.f.* (chem.) silicone.

silicose [silikoz] *s.f.* silicosis.

silicule [silikyl] *s.f.* (bot.) silicula, silicle.

silique [silik] *s.f.* (bot.) siliqua.

sillage [sijaʒ] *s.m.* (naut.) wake, track, course; headway; (fig.) wake; *dans le* ~ *de*, in the footsteps of.

sillet [sijɛ] *s.m.* nut (of violin-bow).

sillon [sijɔ̃] *s.m.* furrow, drill; track, trace; wrinkle; (poet.) fields; groove (in gramophone record); (anat.) groove.

sillonner [sijɔne] *v.t.* to plough; to furrow; to wrinkle; to score, to make lines or cracks in; to criss-cross; to streak, to hurtle, along or through.

silo [silo] *s.m.* silo.

silotage [silɔtaʒ] *s.m.* (agric.) ensilage, silage.

silure [silyr] *s.m.* (ichth.) Silurus, sheat-fish.

silurien, -ne [silyrjɛ̃] *adj., s.m.* (geol.) Silurian.

simagrée [simagre] *s.f.* (usu. pl.) grimace, affectation, pretence, fuss, affected ways.

simbleau (pl. **-x**) [sɛ̃blo] *s.m.* (carp.) radius line.

simien, -ne [simjɛ̃] *adj.* (zool.) simian.

simiesque [simjɛsk] *adj.* ape-like, monkey-like, apish.

similaire [similɛr] *adj.* similar, like.

simili [simili] *s.m.* **1.** (obs.) facsimile; **2.** half-tone print; ~ *s.f.* (fam.) abbrev. ~*gravure*; ~**gravure** [similigravyr] *s.f.* process-engraving; half-tone engraving or block; ~**sage** [similizaʒ] *s.m.* (text.) mercerizing; ~**ser** [similize] *v.t.* (text.) to mercerize; ~**ste** [similist] *s.m.* process-engraver, retoucher.

similitude [similityd] *s.f.* similitude, likeness, resemblance, analogy, similarity; simile, comparison; *parler par* ~*s*, to talk in similitudes.

similor [similɔr] *s.m.* imitation gold, pinchbeck.

simonie [simɔni] *s.f.* simony.

simoun [simun] *s.m.* simoom, simoon.

simple [sɛ̃pl] *adj.* simple, not compound, indivisible; elementary, unsophisticated, straightforward; single, only, alone, mere; plain, easy, unadorned; artless, sincere, simple-hearted; weak in intellect, silly, naïve, credulous, foolish; *billet* ~, single ticket; ~ *soldat*, private soldier; ~ *matelot*, ordinary seaman; ~ *s.m.* **1.** simple or simple-minded person, simpleton, half-wit; *les* ~*s*, the simple; **2.** (pharm.) simple, medicinal herb; **3.** (tennis, etc.) single(s); ~**ment** [sɛ̃pləmɑ̃] *adv.* simply, solely, merely, barely, plainly; only, just; with simplicity.

simplesse [sɛ̃plɛs] *s.f.* simpleness, artlessness.

simplet, -te [sɛ̃plɛ] *adj.* rather simple, naïve; with nothing much to it.

simplicité [sɛ̃plisite] *s.f.* **1.** simplicity; plainness, elementary nature; straightforwardness, openness, artlessness; **2.** silliness, simpleness.

simplifiable [sɛ̃plifjabl] *adj.* that can be simplified.

simplificat-eur, -rice [sɛ̃plifikatœr] *adj.* simplifying.

simplification [sɛ̃plifikɑsjɔ̃] *s.f.* simplification.

simplifier [sɛ̃plifje] *v.t.* to simplify.

simplisme [sɛ̃plism] *s.m.* simplism.

simpliste [sɛ̃plist] *adj.* simplist, simplistic, over--simplified.

simulacre [simylakr] *s.m.* simulacrum, image, phantom, semblance, mockery, illusion; *un* ~ *de combat*, a sham fight.

simulat-eur, -rice [simylatœr] *s.m.f.* simulator, malingerer; ~**eur** *s.m.* simulator (machine).

simulation [simylɑsjɔ̃] *s.f.* simulation, feigning, feint.

simulé, -e [simyle] *adj.* sham, feigned, counterfeit, fictitious.

simuler [simyle] *v.t.* to simulate, to give the effect or appearance of, to feign; to pretend to be, to have, or to feel; to sham.

simultané, -e [simyltane] *adj.* simultaneous.

simultanéité [simyltaneite] *s.f.* simultaneity, simultaneousness.

simultanément [simyltanemɑ̃] *adv.* simultaneously.

sinapisé, -e [sinapize] *adj.* infused with mustard.

sinapisme [sinapism] *s.m.* sinapism, mustard plaster.

sincère [sɛ̃sɛr] *adj.* sincere, true, truthful, ingenuous, honest, candid, frank, genuine, open--hearted; ~**ment** [sɛ̃sɛrmɑ̃] *adv.* sincerely, candidly, frankly.

sincérité [sɛ̃serite] *s.f.* sincerity, truthfulness, frankness, open-heartedness, ingenuousness, candour, genuineness.

sincipital, -e, (aux) [sɛ̃sipital] *adj.* (anat.) sincipital.

sinciput [sɛ̃sipyt] *s.m.* (anat.) sinciput (head from forehead to top, front part of skull).

sinécure [sinekyr] *s.f.* sinecure.

Singapour [sɛ̃gapur] *s.m.* (geog.) Singapore.

singe [sɛ̃ʒ] monkey, ape; (mech., naut.) windlass, hoist; (fig.) ape; imitator, copy-cat; ugly creature; malicious character; (pop.) boss, employer; (mil. slang) bully-beef; *payer qn. en monnaie de* ~, to pay s.o. with empty promises or fair words

singer [sɛ̃ʒe] *v.t.* to ape, to mimic; to imitate servilely.

singerie [sɛ̃ʒri] *s.f.* apish trick, antic, buffoonery, grimace, mimicry, monkey trick; troop of monkeys; monkey-house (at zoo).

single [siŋgəl] *s.m., adj.* **1.** (tennis) single; **2.** single (room, cabin, etc.).

singleton [sɛ̃glətɔ̃] *s.m.* singleton.

singulariser [sɛ̃gylarize] *v.t.* to singularize, to make appear peculiar, to make conspicuous; **se** ~ *v.refl.* to make oneself conspicuous, to draw attention to oneself.

singularité [sɛ̃gylarite] *s.f.* singularity, peculiarity, particular feature; queerness, oddness, eccentricity, unusual feature; single entity.

singuli-er, -ère [sɛ̃gylje] *adj.* singular, peculiar, queer, odd, remarkable, unusual, special; *combat* ~*er*, single combat; duel; ~**er** *s.m.* (gram.) singular; ~**èrement** [sɛ̃gyljɛrmɑ̃] *adv.* singularly, strangely, oddly; particularly.

sinistre [sinistr] *adj.* sinister, inauspicious; evil, wicked; gloomy; of ill omen, menacing, doom--laden; ~ *s.m.* disaster; damage or loss (under insurance policy).

sinistré, -e [sinistre] *adj.* that has suffered disaster; *région* ~*e*, disaster area; *s.m.f.* victim of a disaster; person suffering loss or damage (under insurance policy).

sinistrement [sinistrəmɑ̃] *adv.* in (a) sinister fashion, dismally, inauspiciously.

sinologie [sinɔlɔʒi] *s.f.* sinology.

sinologue [sinɔlɔg] *s.m.f.* sinologue, sinologist.

sinon [sinɔ̃] *conj.* else, or else, otherwise, if not; save, except; *je n'ai plus rien su* ~ *qu'il a été tué*, I did not hear anything more, except that he was killed.

sinople [sinɔpl] *s.m.* (herald.) vert.

sinueu-x, -se [sinɥø] *adj.* sinuous, winding, undulating, circuitous, meandering.

sinuosité [sinɥozite] *s.f.* sinuosity, winding, bend.

sinus [sinys] *s.m.* (anat.) sinus; (geom.) sine.

sinusite [sinyzit] *s.f.* (pathol.) sinusitis.

sinusoïdal, -e, (aux) [sinyzɔidal] *adj.* sinusoidal.

sinusoïde [sinyzɔid] *s.f.* (geom.) sinusoid.

sionisme [sjɔnism] *s.m.* Zionism.

sioniste [sjɔnist] *adj., s.m f.* Zionist.

siphon [sifɔ̃] *s.m* siphon; (in drain-pipe) trap, S-bend, interceptor.

siphonné, -e [sifɔne] *adj.* (fam.) mad.

siphonner [sifɔne] *v.t.* to siphon (off).

sire [sir] *s.m.* (obs.) sir, lord; sire; (mod.) *un pauvre* ~, a poor wretch; *un triste* ~, a sorry--looking individual; ⚠ not 'sire' as in horse--breeding, etc.

sirène [sirɛn] *s.f.* **1.** siren, mermaid; (fig.) siren, charmer, seductress; **2.** siren, fog-horn, hooter.

sirocco, siroco [sirɔko] *s.m.* sirocco.

sirop [siro] *s.m.* syrup.

siroter [sirɔte] *v.t.* to sip (esp. slowly and appreciatively).

sirupeu-x, -se [sirypø] *adj.* syrupy; (fig.) sickly, sentimental.

sirvente [sirvɑ̃t], **sirventès** [sirvɑ̃tɛs], **sirventois** [sirvɑ̃twa] *s.m.* sirvente (poem of Provençal troubadours).

sis, -e [si] *adj.* situated, situate.

sismal, -e, (aux) [sismal] *adj.* seismal.

sismique [sismik] *adj.* seismic.

sismographe [sismɔgraf], **séismographe** [seismɔgraf] *s.m* seismograph.

sismologie [sismɔlɔʒi], **séismologie** [seismɔlɔʒi] *s.f.* seismology.

sison [sizɔ̃] *s.m.* (bot.) stone parsley.

sistre [sistr] *s.m.* (mus.) sistrum.

sisymbre [sizɛ̃br] *s.m* (bot.) Sisymbrium, hedge mustard.

site [sit] *s.m* site, situation, lie of the ground, beauty spot; (archaeol.) site, siting, location; *angle de* ~, angle of sight (in relation to horizontal).

sitôt [sito] *adv.* as soon, so soon; ~ *dit*, ~ *fait*, no sooner said than done; ~ *pris* ~ *pendu*, caught and hanged forthwith; ~ *après*, immediately after; ~ *entré, il . . .*, as soon as he had come in he . . .; ~ *que*, as soon as; *il ne reviendra pas de* ~, it will be some time before he comes back.

sittelle, sittèle [sitɛl] *s.f.* (ornith.) nuthatch.

situation [sitɥɑsjɔ̃] *s.f.* situation, site, position,

environment; state, state of affairs, circumstances, predicament; (fin.) balance sheet, statement of assets and liabilities; (naut.) bearing.
situé, -e [sitɥe] *adj.* situated.
situer [sitɥe] *v.t.* to place, to locate, to site, to situate; to seat; to assign a place to; **se ~** *v.refl.* (fig.) to project oneself, to put oneself (in the picture, the atmosphere, etc.).
sium [sjɔm] *s.m.* (bot.) **1.** caraway; **2.** water--parsnip, skirret.
six [sis, si before consonant, siz before vowel or h-mute] *adj., s.m.* six, the sixth.
sixain see SIZAIN.
six-huit [sisɥit] *s.m.invar.* (mus.) six-eight time.
sixième [sizjɛm] *adj., s.m.f.* sixth; **~** *s.m.* sixth part; sixth floor; **~** *s.f.* sixth class (bottom but one); **~ment** [sizjɛmmɑ̃] *adv.* sixthly.
sixte [sikst] *s.f.* (mus.) sixth; (fenc.) sixte.
sizain, sixain [sizɛ̃] *s.m.* **1.** (pros.) sestina, sextain; **2.** packet of six packs (of cards).
skaï [skaj] *s.m.* (proprietary name) (text.) Skai cloth, leatherette.
skating [skɛtiŋ] *s.m.* roller-skating; roller--skating rink.
sketch [skɛtʃ] *s.m.* (pl. *sketches*) (theatr.) sketch.
ski [ski] *s.m.* ski, skiing; **~** *nautique*, water-skiing.
skier [skje] *v.i.* to ski.
skieu-r, -se [skjœr] *s.m.f.* skier.
skiff [skif] *s.m.* (naut.) skiff.
skunks, skungs [skɔ̃gs] *s.m.* = SCONSE.
slalom [slalɔm] *s.m.* (ski-ing) slalom; **~er** [slalɔme] *v.i.* to slalom; (fig.) to zigzag.
slalomeu-r, -se [slalɔmœr] *s.m.f.* slalom skier.
slave [slav] *adj., s.m.f.* Slav; Slavonic (language).
slavon [slavɔ̃] *s.m.* (lang.) Slavonic.
sleeping [slipiŋ] *s.m.* (obs.) (rail.) sleeping-car.
slip [slip] *s.m.* **1.** (naut.) slip(way); **2.** (under-) pants, pantie(s), briefs; ⚠ not 'slip', a full--length undergarment, nor 'slip' in senses 'slipping' or 'error'.
slogan [slɔgɑ̃] *s.m.* slogan, catch-phrase.
sloop [slup] *s.m.* sloop.
sloughi [slugi] *s.m.* (zool.) saluki, gazelle-hound.
slow [slo] *s.m.* slow foxtrot (dance).
slovaque [slɔvak] *adj., s.m.f.* Slovak.
Slovaquie [slɔvaki] *s.f.* (geog.) Slovakia.
slovène [slɔvɛn] *adj., s.m.f.* Slovene, Slovenian.
S.M. [ɛsɛm] abbrev. *Sa Majesté.*
smala [smala] *s.f.* (esp. Arab) tribe, family.
smalt [smalt] *s.m.* smalt (blue glass).
smaragdin, -e [smaragdɛ̃] *adj.* smaragdine, emerald green.
smash [smaʃ] *s.m.* (tennis) smash; **~er** [smaʃe] *v.t.i.* to smash, to deliver a smash.
smicard, -e [smikar] *s.m.f.* minimum wage earner.
smilax [smilaks] *s.m.* (bot.) smilax.
smille [smij] *s.f.* (techn.) scappling-hammer; pick.
smocks [smɔk] *s.m.pl.* (dressm.) smocking.
smoking [smɔkiŋ] *s.m.* dinner-jacket.
snack(-bar) [snak(bar)] *s.m.* snack-bar; ⚠ not 'snack' (meal).
S.N.C.F. [ɛsɛnseɛf] abbrev. *Société nationale des chemins de fer français.*
snob [snɔb] *s.m.f.* snob, social climber, devotee of fashion; **~** *adj.* smart, elegant, pretentious.
snober [snɔbe] *v.t.* to cold-shoulder, to snub.
snobisme [snɔbism] *s.m.* snobbishness, snobbery, devotion to fashion.
snow-boot [snobut] *s.m.* (obs.) galosh, overshoe.
sobre [sɔbr] *adj.* sober, temperate, abstemious; moderate, restrained; sparing, economical, frugal, plain; quiet, inconspicuous; **~ment** *adv.* soberly, temperately, moderately, frugally, plainly; ⚠ not 'sober' as opp. 'drunk'.
sobriété [sɔbriete] *s.f.* sobriety; temperance; moderation, restraint, discretion; economy, frugality.
sobriquet [sɔbrikɛ] *s.m.* nickname.
soc [sɔk] *s.m.* ploughshare.
sociabilité [sɔsjabilite] *s.f.* sociability, sociableness, sociable existence.
sociable [sɔsjabl] *adj.* sociable, companionable; **~ment** [sɔsjabləmɑ̃] *adv.* sociably.
social, -e, (aux) [sɔsjal] *adj.* social, of society; welfare; public; company, of a company or firm; *siège* **~**, company offices, registered office; *raison* **~***e*, name or style (of company); *capital* **~**, registered capital; **~ement** [sɔsjalmɑ̃] *adv.* socially.
social-isation [sɔsjalizɑsjɔ̃] *s.f.* socialization, collectivization; **~iser** [sɔsjalize] *v.t.* to socialize; to make socialist; **~isme** [sɔsjalism] *s.m.* socialism; **~iste** [sɔsjalist] *adj., s.m.f.* socialist.
sociétaire [sɔsjetɛr] *s.m.f.* member, society--member, associate, fellow, partner, shareholder; **~** *adj.* associate.
sociétariat [sɔsjetarja] *s.m.* membership, association.
société [sɔsjete] *s.f.* society; association; club; community; assembled company, gathering; (fashionable) society; companionship; company, firm, partnership; *jeux de* **~**, party games, round games; **~** *anonyme*, or *à responsabilité limitée*, company limited, limited (liability) company.
socinianisme [sɔsinjanism] *s.m.* Socinianism.
socio-logie [sɔsjɔlɔʒi] *s.f.* sociology; **~logique** [sɔsjɔlɔʒik] *adj.* sociological; **~logiquement** *adv.* sociologically; **~logue** [sɔsjɔlɔg] *s.m.f.* sociologist.
socle [sɔkl] *s.m.* socle, stand, pedestal, plinth, base; bed; (geog.) shelf; (fig.) basis, foundation.
socque [sɔk] *s.m.* clog, patten; (fig., as symbol of classical comedy) sock.
socquette [sɔkɛt] *s.f.* ankle-sock.
Socrate [sɔkrat] *s.m.* Socrates.
socratique [sɔkratik] *adj.* Socratic.
soda [sɔda] *s.m.* soda-water, fizzy lemonade, etc.
sodé, -e [sɔde] *adj.* containing soda.
sodique [sɔdik] *adj.* (chem.) sodic, sodium, soda.
sodium [sɔdjɔm] *s.m.* (chem.) sodium.
sodomie [sɔdɔmi] *s.f.* sodomy.
sodomite [sɔdɔmit] *s.m.* one given to sodomy, sodomite.
sœur [sœr] *s.f.* sister; sister (of religious order); *belle-***~**, sister-in-law; **~** *de lait*, foster-sister; *âme* **~**, kindred spirit; *les neuf* **~***s*, the Muses; *les trois* **~***s*, the Fates.
sœurette [sœrɛt] *s.f.* little sister.
sofa [sɔfa] *s.m.* sofa.
soffite [sɔfit] *s.m.* (arch.) soffit.
soi [swa] *pron.* oneself, himself, herself, itself; *en* **~**, in itself; *avoir son argent sur* **~**, to have money about, or on, one; *chacun pour* **~**, every man for himself; *chez* **~**, at home; *un chez-***~**, a home; *prendre sur* **~**, to make oneself responsible for; to take upon oneself; *rentrer en* **~***-même*; to withdraw into oneself; *revenir à* **~**, to come to, to come round; *cela va de* **~**, that goes without saying; of course; *hors de* **~**, beside oneself; (existential phil.) *le pour-***~**, self-awareness, conscious existence, self-determination; *l'en-***~**, basic or subconscious personality; **~** *s.m* self, personality, ego, essence.
soi-disant [swadizɑ̃] *adj.invar.* would-be; so--called; self-styled; *adv.* presumably, ostensibly.
soie[1] [swa] *s.f.* **1.** silk; *papier de* **~**, tissue paper; **2.** bristle (of hog, etc.).
soie[2] [swa] *s.f.* tang (of knife); tongue (of sword).
soierie [swari] *s.f.* silk stuff, silks; silk trade; *marchand de* **~**, silk-mercer.
soif [swaf] *s.f.* thirst; *avoir* **~**, to be thirsty, to

thirst (*de*, for); *boire à sa ~, étancher sa ~*, to drink one's fill, to quench one's thirst; *garder une poire pour la ~*, to put something by for a rainy day; (fig., fam.) *jusqu'à plus ~*, to satiety; *boire jusqu'à plus ~*, to drink immoderately.

soiffard, -e [swafar] *s.m.f.* (pop.) boozer; *adj.* given to drink.

soigné, -e [swaɲe] *adj.* carefully done, well finished, conscientious; well cared for, neat, trim, well-groomed; elaborate, well got up; (fam.) overdoing it, a bit steep.

soigner [swaɲe] *v.t.* to take care of, to look after; to take care with, to be careful about; to do (something) carefully; to attend to, to see to; to nurse, to treat (a patient); **se** ~ *v.refl.* to take care of oneself, to look after oneself; (of illness) to respond to treatment, to be curable with treatment.

soigneu-x, -se [swaɲø] *adj.* careful, conscientious, mindful, attentive, solicitous; **~sement** [swaɲøzmɑ̃] *adv.* carefully.

soin [swɛ̃] *s.m.* care, attention, concern, preoccupation, worry; attendance, nursing, treatment; *avoir* or *prendre ~ de qch.*, to take care of sth., to see to sth., to look after sth., to be careful about sth., to be mindful of sth., to worry about sth., to take the responsibility for sth.; *avoir* or *prendre ~ de faire qch.*, to see to or about doing sth., to be careful to do sth.; *ne pas prendre ~ de faire qch.*, to fail or neglect to do sth.; *avoir ~ que*, to take care that, to see to it that; *laisser à qn. le ~ de*, to leave it to s.o., to leave to s.o. the business of; *premiers ~s*, first-aid; *aux bons ~s de*, care of, c/o; *être aux petits ~s pour qn.*, to be very attentive to s.o., to wait on s.o. hand and foot.

soir [swar] *s.m.* evening, night; time p.m.; (fig.) evening, declining days; *du matin au ~*, from morning to night.

soirée [sware] *s.f.* evening; (evening) party, reception, at-home; evening performance; *donner une ~ dansante*, to give a dance; (iron.) *charmante ~!*, what a party!, a nasty experience!

soit [swa] *conj.* **1.** ~ ... ~, either ... or; ~ *l'un*, ~ *l'autre*, either the one or the other; ~ *indifférence*, ~ *crainte, elle ne parlait jamais*, whether through indifference or timidity, she never spoke; ~ *que* ... ~ *que*, either because ... or because; ~ *que ... ou*, whether ... or; ~ *qu'il se meuve ou non*, whether he moves or not; **2.** suppose, given, say; that is to say; for instance; ~ *un rectangle ABCD*, let ABCD be a rectangle; ~ *les hypothèses suivantes*, given the following hypotheses; *invitez quelques amis*, ~ *une douzaine*, invite some friends, say a dozen; ~ [swat] *adv.* all right, agreed, O.K.

soixantaine [swasɑ̃tɛn] *s.f.* sixty, about sixty; some sixty (years of age).

soixante [swasɑ̃t] *adj.* sixty; *~-dix*, seventy.

soixantième [swasɑ̃tjɛm] *adj.*, *s.m.* sixtieth, sixtieth part.

soja [sɔʒa], **soya** [sɔja] *s.m* soya (bean.).

sol¹ [sɔl] *s.m.* **1.** soil, ground; *cloué au ~*, rooted to the spot; **2.** (obs.) = SOU.

sol² [sɔl] *s.m.* (mus.) G, soh; *clef de ~*, treble clef, G clef.

solaire [sɔlɛr] *adj.* solar, of the sun; *lunettes ~s*, sun-glasses; *crème ~*, sun-tan lotion; *cadran ~*, sun-dial.

solanacées [sɔlanase] *s.f.pl.* (bot.) Solanaceae.

soldanelle [sɔldanɛl] *s.f.* (bot.) soldanella.

soldat [sɔlda] *s.m.* soldier, serviceman; (*simple*) ~, private soldier (or equivalent, e.g. gunner, aircraftman, etc.).

soldate [sɔldat] *s.f.* servicewoman.

soldatesque [sɔldatɛsk] *s.f.* (pej.) (undisciplined) soldiery; ~ *adj.* (pej.) barrack-room.

solde [sɔld] *s.f.* pay (esp. mil.); *être à la ~ de qn.*, to be in someone's pay, to have been bought by s.o.

solde [sɔld] *s.m.* (comm.) **1.** settlement, balance; *pour ~ (de compte)*, in settlement, in payment of balance, as final instalment; ~ *débiteur, créditeur*, debit, credit, balance; **2.** (bargain) sale; (pl.) bargains, sale goods, remainders, job-lots; *en ~*, in the sale, reduced, at a discount.

solder [sɔlde] *v.t.* **1.** to pay, to have in one's pay; **2.** to settle, to discharge, to pay (off), to balance (an account); **3.** to sell at a reduced price, to sell off, to clear; **se** ~ *v.refl.* to be balanced; (fig.) to turn out, to result (*par*, in); *se ~ par* or *en un déficit de*, to show a deficit of.

soldeu-r, -se [sɔldœr] *s.m.f.* dealer in surplus goods.

sole¹ [sɔl] *s.f.* (agric.) portion of ground to receive a succession of different crops.

sole² [sɔl] *s.f.* sole (of animal's foot); (ichth.) sole; (techn.) sole, sole-plate, bed(-plate), sill, floor (of furnace).

soléaire [sɔleɛr] *adj.* (anat.) *muscle ~*, soleus.

solécisme [sɔlesism] *s.m.* solecism.

soleil [sɔlɛj] *s.m.* sun, sunlight, sunshine; (bot.) sunflower; (fireworks) catherine-wheel; *au ~*, in the sun; *se chauffer au ~*, to sun oneself; to bask in the sun; *au ~ couchant*, at sunset; (fig.) *avoir du bien au ~*, to have landed property; *coup de ~*, sunstroke; *il fait du ~*, the sun is shining; (fam.) *piquer un ~*, to blush furiously.

solen [sɔlɛn] *s.m.* (ichth.) solen, razor-shell.

solennel, -le [sɔlanɛl] *adj.* solemn, formal; official; **~lement** [sɔlanɛlmɑ̃] *adv.* solemnly, in state; publicly, officially.

solenniser [sɔlanize] *v.t.* to solemnize, to celebrate, to mark (an event).

solennité [sɔlanite] *s.f.* solemnity, ceremony, celebration.

solénoïde [sɔlenɔid] *s.m.* (electr.) solenoid.

solfatare [sɔlfatar] *s.f.* solfatara.

solfège [sɔlfɛʒ] *s.m.* **1.** (mus.) solfeggio, sol-fa, solmization; **2.** (book on) rudiments of music.

solfier [sɔlfje] *v.t.* (mus.) to sol-fa.

solidaire [sɔlidɛr] *adj.* jointly responsible, jointly liable; binding on all parties; interdependent, closely-linked; ~ *de*, bound up with, linked to, integral with; (techn.) locked to, fixed to; **~ment** [sɔlidɛrmɑ̃] *adv.* jointly (and severally).

solidariser [sɔlidarize] *v.t.* to render jointly liable; **se** ~ *v.refl.* to join together in liability; (fig.) *se ~ avec qn.*, to make common cause with s.o.

solidarité [sɔlidarite] *s.f.* solidarity, fellowship, interdependence; joint or mutual responsibility.

solide [sɔlid] *adj.* solid, strong, substantial, firm, stout, tough, hefty, robust, trustworthy, dependable, weighty; *avoir la tête ~*, to have sound judgement, to be able to keep one's head; to have a good head (for drink); to be strong-minded; *être ~ au poste*, to stick to one's post, to keep going (through thick and thin); ~ *s.m.* (chem., geom.) solid; (fam.) reliability, reality, durable character; (fig.) solid ground; **~ment** [sɔlidmɑ̃] *adv.* solidly, firmly, strongly, soundly.

solidification [sɔlidifikɑsjɔ̃] *s.f.* solidification.

solidifier [sɔlidifje] *v.t.* to solidify; **se** ~ *v.refl.* to become solid, to solidify.

solidité [sɔlidite] *s.f.* solidity; solidness; firmness, strength, durability; stability, soundness.

soliloque [sɔlilɔk] *s.m.* soliloquy.

soliloquer [sɔlilɔke] *v.i.* to soliloquize.

solin [sɔlɛ̃] *s.m.* (build.) **1.** space between joists; **2.** plaster filling, plaster joint.

solipède [sɔlipɛd] *adj.*, *s.m.* (zool.) soliped.

soliste [sɔlist] *s.m.f.* soloist.

solitaire [sɔlitɛr] *adj.* solitary; isolated; alone, on one's own; lonely; preferring one's own company; *ver ~*, tapeworm, taenia; ~ *s.m.* **1.** hermit, recluse; **2.** solitaire (diamond); **3.** old boar;

4. solitaire (game); **~ment** [sɔlitɛrmɑ̃] *adv.* solitarily, in solitude.
solitude [sɔlityd] *s.f.* solitude, loneliness, isolation, being on one's own, being alone; (obs.) lonely spot.
solive [sɔliv] *s.f.* joist.
soliveau (pl. **-x**) [sɔlivo] *s.m.* small joist; (fig.) *un roi Soliveau*, a King Log, a (mere) figurehead.
sollicitation [sɔlisitɑsjɔ̃] *s.f.* entreaty, solicitation, request; attraction, stimulus.
solliciter [sɔlisite] *v.t.* to incite, to attract; to entreat, to solicit, to canvass, to request, to beg, to beseech, to ask earnestly.
solliciteu-r, -se [sɔlisitœr] *s.m.f.* petitioner, applicant, seeker (of favours, money, etc.).
sollicitude [sɔlisityd] *s.f.* solicitude, care, concern.
solo [sɔlo] *s.m.* solo; *jouer, chanter, en* ~; to play, to sing, solo; (*spectacle*) ~, one-man show.
solstice [sɔlstis] *s.m.* solstice.
solsticial, -e, (aux) [sɔlstisjal] *adj.* solstitial.
solubiliser [sɔlybilize] *v.t.* to render soluble.
solubilité [sɔlybilite] *s.f.* solubility.
soluble [sɔlybl] *adj.* soluble; solvable; *problème* ~, problem that can be (re)solved.
soluté [sɔlyte] *s.m.* (pharm.) solution.
solution [sɔlysjɔ̃] *s.f.* **1.** solution, dissolving; **2.** solution, mixture containing a substance in solution; **3.** resolution, solution; solving, answer (to problem, etc.); **4.** separation; ~ *de continuité*, break of continuity; (car) ~ *anti-gel*, anti-freeze (mixture).
solutionner [sɔlysjɔne] *v.t.* to solve.
solvabilité [sɔlvabilite] *s.f.* solvency.
solvable [sɔlvabl] *adj.* solvent; ⚠ not 'solvable'.
solvant [sɔlvɑ̃] *s.m.* (chem.) solvent.
somatique [sɔmatik] *adj.* somatic, bodily, corporeal.
sombre [sɔ̃br] *adj.* dark; sombre, dim, gloomy, menacing, forbidding, sinister, cloudy, overcast, melancholy, dismal, lamentable; *rouge* ~, dark red; *il fait nuit* ~, it is pitch-black.
sombrer [sɔ̃bre] *v.i.* (naut.) to founder, to go down, to sink; (fig.) to collapse, to fail, to fall in ruins, to relapse; *faire* ~, to be the ruin, or the end, of; *sa raison sombre*, his mind is going.
sombrero [sɔ̃brero] *s.m.* sombrero.
sommaire [sɔm(m)ɛr] *adj.* summary, abridged, concise, succinct, sketchy, hasty, improvised, scanty; ~ *s.m.* summary, synopsis, résumé, abstract, abridgement; **~ment** [sɔm(m)ɛrmɑ̃] *adv.* summarily, briefly, sketchily, cursorily, scantily.
sommation¹ [sɔm(m)ɑsjɔ̃] *s.f.* summons, demand, notice.
sommation² [sɔm(m)ɑsjɔ̃] *s.f.* (math.) summation; accumulation.
somme¹ [sɔm] *s.f.* sum, total, amount; summary, handbook, compendium; *en* ~, ~ *toute*, on the whole, finally, after all, in short.
somme² [sɔm] *s.f.* burden; *bête de* ~, beast of burden.
somme³ [sɔm] *s.m.* nap, sleep; *faire un petit* ~, to have forty winks.
sommeil [sɔmɛj] *s.m.* sleep, slumber; inactivity, lethargy; *avoir* ~, to be sleepy; *avoir le* ~ *léger* (*dur*), to be a light (heavy) sleeper; *tomber de* ~, to be overcome with sleep; *dormir d'un* ~ *de plomb*, to sleep like a log; *maladie du* ~, sleeping sickness.
sommeiller [sɔmɛje] *v.i.* to slumber, to doze; (fig.) to lie dormant, to be latent.
sommeilleu-x, -se [sɔmɛjø] *adj., s.m.f.* sleepy (person); (person) suffering from sleeping sickness.
sommelier [sɔmlje] *s.m.* butler, cellarman, wine-waiter.
sommer¹ [sɔme] *v.t.* to summon, to call upon.
sommer² [sɔme] *v.t.* (math.) to find the sum of.
sommet [sɔmɛ] *s.m.* top, summit; (fig.) acme, pinnacle, zenith; (bot.) apex; (geom.) vertex; *au* ~, at the summit, at the peak, at the top, among the top people; *conférence au* ~, summit conference.
sommier [sɔmje] *s.m.* box-spring mattress, mattress-base; (arch., build., eng.) breast-summer, springer, transom, lintel, bearer, stringer, stretcher, cross-beam, bed; (comm.) cash-book, register.
sommité [sɔmite] *s.f.* top, head; prominent person, leader, leading light, top personality.
somnambule [sɔmnɑ̃byl] *s.m.f.* somnambulist, sleep-walker; hypnotic subject; ~ *adj.* somnambulant.
somnambulisme [sɔmnɑ̃bylism] *s.m.* somnambulism, sleep-walking; ~ *provoqué*, hypnotic state.
somnifère [sɔmnifɛr] *adj.* somniferous, soporific; ~ *s.m.* sleeping-pill.
somnolence [sɔmnɔlɑ̃s] *s.f.* somnolence, drowsiness, lethargy.
somnolent, -e [sɔmnɔlɑ̃] *adj.* somnolent, drowsy, lethargic, dormant.
somnoler [sɔmnɔle] *v.i.* to doze; (fig.) to lie dormant.
somptuaire [sɔ̃ptɥɛr] *adj.* sumptuary.
somptueu-x, -se [sɔ̃ptɥø] *adj.* sumptuous, magnificent, gorgeous, lavish, luxurious; **~sement** [sɔ̃ptɥøzmɑ̃] *adv.* sumptuously, lavishly, luxuriously.
somptuosité [sɔ̃ptɥozite] *s.f.* sumptuousness, magnificence, richness.
son [sɔ̃] (also used instead of *sa* before vowel or h-mute), (fem.) **sa** [sa], (pl.) **ses** [se] *poss. adj.* his, her, its, one's, of it; *il faut chercher son explication*, we must look for an explanation of it.
son¹ [sɔ̃] *s.m.* sound, sounding; ringing; note, tone; *mur du* ~, sound-barrier.
son² [sɔ̃] *s.m.* bran; *taches de* ~, freckles.
sonar [sɔnar] *s.m.* (nav.) sonar (equipment).
sonate [sɔnat] *s.f.* sonata.
sondage [sɔ̃daʒ] *s.m.* (naut.) sounding; (mining) boring, drilling; (meteor.) sondage, use of aerial sonde, investigation of air-currents; (med.) probing, use of catheter; (fig.) sounding, testing, probing; sampling, survey, investigation, opinion poll; *faire un* ~, to sound; (fig.) to sound, to probe, to investigate, to (take a) sample.
sonde [sɔ̃d] *s.f.* (naut.) sounding-line, sounding--rod, lead; sounding; (nav., meteor.) sonde; (comm.) sampler, (cheese-)taster; (mining) bore, drilling, drill; (surg.) probe, catheter; ~ *spatiale*, space probe.
sonder [sɔ̃de] *v.t.* to sound, to take soundings; to probe, to try, to test, to sample, to see into, to fathom; ~ *le terrain*, to make trial borings; (fig.) to see how the land lies, to feel one's way.
sondeur [sɔ̃dœr] *s.m.* (naut.) leadsman; sounder, tester, sampler, investigator; sounding apparatus, sounder.
sondeuse [sɔ̃døz] *s.f.* test-drill.
songe [sɔ̃ʒ] *s.m.* dream; illusion.
songe-creux [sɔ̃ʒkrø] *s.m.invar.* dreamer, visionary.
songer [sɔ̃ʒe] *v.t.i.* to dream, to have dreams, to think idly (of), to reflect, to muse; ~ *à*, to think of, to give thought to, to reflect on; to intend, to propose, to consider; *songez à ce que vous allez faire*, mind what you are about; *maintenant que j'y songe*, now that I think of it; *vous n'y songez pas!*, you don't mean it!; you would not think of such a thing!; *il ne faut pas y* ~, it is out of the question; *songes-y bien*, think it over carefully, you had better think twice (before doing it); ~ *à faire*, to think of, to propose, to consider,

doing; *elle ne songe qu'à se marier*, her one idea is to get married.

songerie [sɔ̃ʒri] *s.f.* day-dream, musing, reverie.

songeu-r, -se [sɔ̃ʒœr] *adj.* dreamy, preoccupied, thoughtful, lost in thought; *s.m.f.* dreamer, thinker, thoughtful person.

sonique [sɔnik] *adj.* sonic; *mur* ~, sound-barrier; *détonation* ~, sonic boom.

sonnaille [sɔnɑj] *s.f.* cowbell; noise of cowbells.

sonnailler [sɔnɑje] *v.i.* (pej.) to keep ringing.

sonnailler [sɔnɑje] *s.m.* bell-wether, animal wearing a bell.

sonnant, -e [sɔnɑ̃] *adj.* sounding, ringing; *à 6 heures* ~*es*, at 6 o'clock sharp, on the stroke of 6; *espèces* ~*es*, hard cash.

sonné, -e [sɔne] *adj.* past; (fam.) (of boxer) knocked-out; (fig., fam.) round the bend; *il est 6 heures* ~*es*, it has struck 6, it is past 6; (fig., fam.) *c'est midi* ~, it is too late; *il a 50 ans* ~*s*, he has turned 50; he is over 50.

sonner [sɔne] *v.t.i.* **1.** to ring, to sound, to resound, to tinkle, to peel, to blow (bugle, etc.), to ring for; *on sonne*, there is a ring at the door; *midi sonne*, it is striking 12; *ce mot sonne mal*, this word has a nasty sound; *faire* ~ *ses mérites*, to sing one's own praises, to blow one's own trumpet; *cela sonne creux*, that sounds hollow; *il n'a plus sonné mot*, after that he did not utter a word; **2.** (fam.) to knock (s.o.) out (esp. by banging his head on the ground); (fig.) *se faire* ~, to be reprimanded, to be put in one's place.

sonnerie [sɔnri] *s.f.* ring, ringing, chime; sounding (of bugle-call); striking mechanism, bell(s), set of bells.

sonnet [sɔnɛ] *s.m.* sonnet.

sonnette [sɔnɛt] *s.f.* bell, hand-bell; bell-push; (mech.) pile-driver; *serpent à* ~*s*, rattlesnake.

sonneur [sɔnœr] *s.m.* bell-ringer; pile-driver operator.

sono [sɔno] *s.f.* abbrev. SONORISATION.

sonomètre [sɔnɔmɛtr] *s.m.* sonometer, audiometer.

sonore [sɔnɔr] *adj.* sonorous, resonant, loud-sounding; (of film, track, effect, wave, etc.) sound; (phon.) voiced, vocal, sounded; (fig.) emphatic, high-sounding.

sonorisation [sɔnɔrizɑsjɔ̃] *s.f.* addition of sound(-track) or sound effects; equipping (of hall, etc.) for sound (fam. abbrev. *sono*); (phon.) vocalization.

sonoriser [sɔnɔrize] *v.t.* to add sound(-track) or sound effects to; to equip (hall, etc.) for sound; (phon.) to vocalize.

sonorité [sɔnɔrite] *s.f.* sonorousness, sonority, quality of sound, timbre, tone, volume of sound (emitted), output, acoustic quality, resonance, conductivity of sound; (poetry, etc.) harmony; (phon.) vocality.

sonothèque [sɔnɔtɛk] *s.f.* sound (effects) library.

sophisme [sɔfism] *s.m.* sophism, fallacious or specious argument.

sophiste [sɔfist] *s.m.f.* sophist, one who uses specious arguments.

sophistication [sɔfistikɑsjɔ̃] *s.f.* sophistication; artificial or affected character; (obs.) adulteration.

sophistique [sɔfistik] *adj.* sophistical; ~ *s.f.* sophistry.

sophistiqué, -e [sɔfistike] *adj.* affected, artificial, contrived, elaborately got up; (obs.) adulterated.

sophistiquer [sɔfistike] *v.t.* (obs.) to adulterate.

soporifique [sɔpɔrifik] *adj.* soporific; (fig.) tedious; ~ *s.m.* soporific, sleeping-pill.

sopraniste [sɔpranist] *s.m.* male soprano.

soprano [sɔprano] *s.m.* soprano, treble; ~ *s.m.f.* soprano (singer).

sorbe [sɔrb] *s.f.* sorb-apple.

sorbet [sɔrbɛ] *s.m.* (obs.) sherbet; (mod.) sorbet.

sorbetière [sɔrbətjɛr] *s.f.* ice-mould, ice-pail, ice-maker.

sorbier [sɔrbje] *s.m.* (bot.) sorb-tree, service-tree; ~ *commun* or *des oiseleurs*, mountain-ash, rowan-tree.

sorbonnard, -e [sɔrbɔnar] *s.m.f.*, *adj.* (fam., pej.) (student or professor) of the Sorbonne.

sorcellerie [sɔrsɛlri] *s.f.* witchcraft, sorcery.

sorci-er, -ère [sɔrsje] *s.m.f.* sorcerer, sorceress, wizard, witch, magician, enchanter, enchantress; (fam.) *une (vieille)* ~*ère*, an old hag, an old witch; (fig.) *il ne faut pas être* ~*er pour faire cela*, you don't have to be very clever to do that; ~**er** *adj.m.* difficult; *ce n'est pas bien* ~*er ce que je vous demande*, it is nothing very difficult that I am asking you.

sordide [sɔrdid] *adj.* sordid, mean, squalid, filthy; ~**ment** [sɔrdidmɑ̃] *adv.* meanly, stingily, in squalor.

sordidité [sɔrdidite] *s.f.* sordidness, filth, squalor.

sore [sɔr] *s.m.* (bot.) sorus (reproductive organ in ferns).

sorgho [sɔrgo] *s.m.* (bot.) sorghum; Indian millet.

sorite [sɔrit] *s.m.* (log.) sorites.

sornette [sɔrnɛt] *s.f.* nonsense, idle talk, stupid talk; ~*s que tout cela!*, nonsense!

sort [sɔr] *s.m.* fate, lot, destiny, state, chance; spell, charm; hazard, chance; *jeter un* ~ *à qn.*, to cast a spell over s.o.; *le* ~ *en est jeté!*, the die is cast!; *tirer au* ~, to draw lots; *améliorer son* ~, to improve one's condition; *le* ~ *des armes*, the fortunes of war; *faire un* ~ *à qch.*, to emphasize sth.; (fam.) to finish with sth. completely, to finish sth. off; ⚠ not 'sort'.

sortable [sɔrtabl] *adj.* suitable, acceptable, eligible, presentable.

sortant, -e [sɔrtɑ̃] *adj.* outgoing, retiring, leaving office; (of number in lottery, etc.) drawn; *les entrants et les* ~*s*, those coming in and those going out.

sorte [sɔrt] *s.f.* sort, kind, species; manner, way; *toutes* ~*s de*, all kinds of; *de toute* ~, of every kind; of every description; *de la* ~, thus, in this way; *je n'ai rien fait de la* ~, I did nothing of the kind; *de telle* ~, in such a manner; *de la bonne* ~, properly, firmly; *d'aucune* ~, in no wise; *de* ~ *à*, so as to, in such a way as to; *de* ~ *que*, *en* ~ *que*, so that, in such a way that; *faites en* ~ *que le dîner soit bon*, make sure the dinner is a good one; *en quelque* ~, in a way, in some sort, in some degree.

sortie [sɔrti] *s.f.* going out, coming out, departure; (theatr.) exit; way out; egress; outlet; outing, excursion; export; money paid out, outgoings; result, answer (from calculations, etc.), response; sally, outburst, tirade; *faire une* ~ *à qn.*, to let fly at s.o., to pitch into s.o.; *se ménager une* ~, to keep a way out open, to manage so as to be able to back out; *droit de* ~, export duty; ~ *de bain*, bath-robe; ~ *de bal*, opera-cloak; *la* ~ *de l'école*, *des théâtres*, at the end of school, when the theatres come out; *à ma* ~ *d'école*, when I left school; *jour de* ~, day out, day off.

sortilège [sɔrtilɛʒ] *s.m.* witchcraft, charm, spell.

sortir [sɔrtir] *v.i.* to go out, to come out, to come forth, to leave, to leave the room, to make one's exit, to depart, to come away; to emerge, to come up, (of card, number, etc.) to turn up; to issue, to spring, to take rise, to have origin; (paint.) to stand out; to go out for social occasions; *il sort d'ici*, he has just gone out; *je ne sors guère*, I hardly ever go out; (fam.) *je sors de travailler*, I have just finished work; *je sors d'en prendre*, I have just had some; ~ *de l'enfance*, to be no longer a child; to be growing up; ~ *de* *maladie*, to recover from an illness; ~ *de son sujet, de la question*, to wander from one's subject, from the question; *le travail, l'argent, il ne sort jamais de là*, work, money, he can never get away from it; ~ *de Polytechnique*, to have been a pupil of the *École Polytechnique*; ~ *d'une bonne famille*, to come of a good family; *il le fait* ~ *de ses gonds*, he makes him fly into a passion; *les yeux lui sortent de la tête*, his eyes are starting out of their sockets; *vous vous en êtes bien sorti!*, you came out of it all right; *mais d'où sortez-vous?*, where have you come from?; don't you know that?; ~ *v.t.* to bring out, to take out, to pull out, to extricate; (fam.) to expel, to chuck out; (law) to have, to obtain; ~ *s.m.* coming out; *au* ~ *de l'enfance*, on ceasing to be a child; *au* ~ *du lit*, on getting out of bed.

sosie [sozi] *s.m.* very image, double, second self, exact counterpart.

sot, -te [so, sɔt] *adj.* foolish, silly, stupid, senseless, ridiculous; sheepish; *demeurer tout* ~, to look rather foolish; *à* ~*te question point de réponse*, a silly question deserves no answer; *s.m.f.* fool, ass, blockhead, dolt; *un* ~ *en trois lettres*, a downright fool; ⚠ not 'sot'.

sotie [sɔti] *s.f.* satirical farce.

sot-l'y-laisse [solilɛs] *s.m.invar.* parson's nose (on cooked fowl).

sottement [sɔtmɑ̃] *adv.* foolishly, stupidly.

sottise [sɔtiz] *s.f.* foolishness, silliness, stupidity; foolery, nonsense, childish behaviour, silly trick, stupid blunder; offensive remark, insult; *dire des* ~*s*, to make silly remarks; *dire des* ~*s à qn.*, to say rude things to s.o.; *commettre une* ~, to do something stupid, to make a stupid blunder.

sottisier [sɔtizje] *s.m.* collection of sayings 'that might have been better expressed'.

sou [su] *s.m.* sou (small coin = 5 centimes); (fig.) penny, cash; ~ *à* ~, a penny at a time, counting every penny; *n'avoir pas le* ~, *être sans le* ~, *n'avoir pas un* ~ *vaillant*, to be penniless; *il n'a pas le* ~, he is broke; *une petite robe de quatre* ~*s*, a cheap little frock; *cela vaut 100 francs comme un* ~, it's worth 100 francs if it's worth a sou; *il n'est pas ambitieux pour un* ~, he is not the least bit ambitious; *le* ~ *du franc*, 5 per cent commission; (fam.) *gros* ~, commission, rake-off.

Souabe [swab] *s.f.* (geog.) Swabia; ~ *s.m.f.* Swabian.

souabe [swab] *adj.* Swabian.

souahéli, -e [swaeli] *adj.*, *s.m.* Swahili.

soubassement [subɑsmɑ̃] *s.m.* base, substructure, pedestal, stylobate, lower portion (of wall or window); valance (of bedstead); (geol.) substratum; (fig.) basis.

soubresaut [subrəso] *s.m.* start, jolt, shock, jerk.

soubrette [subrɛt] *s.f.* lady's maid; (theatr.) soubrette.

souche [suʃ] *s.f.* **1.** stump, stock; **2.** counterfoil, stub; **3.** chimney-stack; **4.** (fig.) stock, root, origin, family; *faire* ~, to found a family, to be the first of a line; **5.** blockhead.

souchet [suʃɛ] *s.m.* **1.** (bot.) galingale, sedge; **2.** (ornith.) shoveller duck.

souci[1] [susi] *s.m.* care, anxiety, concern, trouble, worry, solicitude; *c'est là le moindre* (or *le cadet*) *de mes* ~*s*, that is the least of my worries; I am not letting that worry me; *se faire du* ~, to worry.

souci[2] [susi] *s.m.* (bot.) marigold; ~ *d'eau*, marsh marigold.

(**se**) **soucier** [susje] *v.refl.* to care; ~ *de*, to care about or for, to concern oneself with, to bother with or about, to be concerned with, to take account of, to mind; *il ne se soucie pas de cela*, that is no concern of his, he doesn't bother his head about that; *ne vous souciez pas du qu'en dira-t-on*, don't mind what people say; *il s'en soucie comme de l'an quarante* or *comme de sa première chemise*, he does not care a damn about it.

soucieu-x, -se [susjø] *adj.* worried, concerned, anxious, thoughtful, uneasy, weighed down with care; ~**sement** [susjøzmɑ̃] *adv.* anxiously; with great care.

soucoupe [sukup] *s.f.* saucer.

soudage [sudaʒ] *s.m.* soldering, welding, brazing; soldered joint, weld.

soudain, -e [sudɛ̃] *adj.* sudden; ~ *adv.* suddenly, all of a sudden.

soudainement [sudɛnmɑ̃] *adv.* suddenly, all of a sudden, unexpectedly.

soudaineté [sudɛnte] *s.f.* suddenness, unexpectedness.

Soudan [sudɑ̃] *s.m.* (geog.) Sudan.

soudanais, -e [sudanɛ] *adj.*, *s.m.f.* Sudanese.

soudard [sudar] *s.m.* (pej.) mercenary, ruffian, rough soldier.

soude [sud] *s.f.* (bot.) saltwort; (chem.) soda.

soudé, -e [sude] *adj.* welded; (fig.) fixed, rooted.

souder [sude] *v.t.* to solder; to braze, to weld; (fig.) to unite, to join; *fer à* ~, soldering-iron; *lampe à* ~, blowlamp; **se** ~ *v.refl.* to unite, to be soldered, joined, to fuse together.

soudeu-r, -se [sudœr] *s.m.f.* welder; ~**se** *s.f.* welding-machine.

soudoyer [sudwaje] *v.t.* to keep in one's pay; to hire, to subsidize; to bribe, to buy.

soudure [sudyr] *s.f.* **1.** solder; **2.** soldering; welding; soldered joint, weld; (fig.) joining; ~ *autogène*, autogenous welding (by oxy-acetylene); (fig.) *faire la* ~, to bridge the gap, to fill the need.

soue [su] *s.f.* pigsty.

soufflage [suflaʒ] *s.m.* **1.** glass-blowing; (metall.) blow, blast (of furnace); **2.** (naut.) sheathing, furring.

soufflant, -e [suflɑ̃] *adj.* **1.** blowing; *machine* ~*e*, blower; **2.** (fig., fam.) breathtaking; ~ *s.m.* (pop.) pistol, revolver; ~**e** *s.f.* (metall.) blower, blast-engine.

soufflard [suflar] *s.m* (geol.) air-volcano, mud--volcano.

souffle [sufl] *s.m.* breath, breathing, puff, blow, blast, wind; expiration; exhalation; gentle breeze; (med.) murmur; (fig.) inspiration; *il n'a plus que le* ~, he is at his last gasp; *jusqu'à mon dernier* ~, till my last breath; *être à bout de* ~, to be out of breath; (fig.) to be exhausted; (fig., fam.) *il a un certain* ~*!*, he has got a nerve!; *couper le* ~ *à qn.*, to wind s.o., to take someone's breath away.

soufflé [sufle] *s.m.* (cook.) soufflé dish, soufflé.

soufflé, -e [sufle] *adj.* puffed; aerated; (mining) containing pockets of gas; (fig., fam.) dumbfounded.

souffler [sufle] *v.t.i.* to breathe, to blow, to pant, to puff, to draw breath; (obs.) to speak, to breathe or utter (a word); *laissez-moi* ~ *un peu*, just let me get my breath; *les enfants ne soufflaient plus*, the children didn't utter another word; ~ *v.t.* **1.** to blow, to blow out; to blow down, to blast; to blow up, to inflate; to send a gust or stream of; ~ (or ~ *à*) *l'orgue*, to blow the organ; ~ *la bougie*, to blow out the candle; *l'explosion a soufflé deux maisons*, the explosion blew two houses down; ~ *un ballon*, to inflate a balloon; *la porte battait, soufflait un air chaud*, the door, as it opened and closed, sent in blasts of hot air; **2.** to steal; (at draughts) to huff; ~ *qch. à qn.*, to steal sth. from s.o., to do s.o. out of sth.; **3.** to whisper (sth.), to suggest; (theatr.) to prompt; *ne pas* ~ *mot*, not to breathe a word; ~ *un acteur*, ~ *une réplique à un acteur*, to prompt an actor; *je te soufflerai tes mots*, I will prompt you, I will tell you what to say.

soufflerie [sufləri] *s.f.* bellows (of organ, etc.); (techn.) blower; ~ (*aérodynamique*) wind-tunnel.

soufflet [suflɛ] *s.m.* **1.** bellows, blower; bellows (of camera); (rail.) concertina (connecting corridors of two carriages); *un sac à ~s*, a bag with gusseted sides; **2.** slap, box on the ears; (fig.) slap in the face, insult, affront.

souffleter [suflәte] *v.t.* to slap, to box the ears of, to give a slap in the face to; (fig.) to insult, to outrage.

souffleu-r, -se [suflœr] *s.m.f.* (theatr.) prompter; **~r** *s.m.* (glass-, etc.) blower; (zool.) blower (e.g. cachalot, dolphin); **2.** supplier of building stone; **~se** *s.f.* (agric.) seeder.

soufflure [suflyr] *s.f.* (techn.) blow-hole, air-hole; flaw, bubble, bulge.

souffrance [sufrɑ̃s] *s.f.* suffering, pain, ache; sufferance, delay, suspense; *en ~*, in suspense, at a standstill, in abeyance, outstanding, held over, to be called for.

souffrant, -e [sufrɑ̃] *adj.* unwell, ill, in pain, sickly; suffering, long-suffering, ailing; patient; (med.) *la partie ~e*, the part affected; *elle est toujours ~e*, she has always got something wrong with her.

souffre-douleur [sufrәdulœr] *s.m.invar.* butt, laughing-stock, victim.

souffreteu-x, -se [sufrәtø] *adj.* miserable, ailing, sickly, weakly.

souffrir [sufrir] *v.t.i.* to suffer, to be in pain, to feel pain; to bear, to endure, to sustain, to stand; *~ de*, to suffer from the effects of; to allow, to tolerate, to put up with, to admit of; *~ mort et passion*, *~ le martyre*, to endure excruciating pain; to be on the rack; to be racked with pain; *souffrez que je vous aide*, allow me to help you; *cette affaire ne souffre aucun retard*, this matter admits of no delay; *ma jambe me fait ~*, my leg is hurting; *pourquoi me faites-vous ~ ainsi?*, why are you causing me so much pain?; *ils ne peuvent se ~*, they cannot bear each other.

soufrage [sufraʒ] *s.m.* sulphuring.

soufre [sufr] *s.m.* sulphur; brimstone; *fleur de ~*, flowers of sulphur.

soufré, -e [sufre] *adj.* dipped in sulphur; sulphur-yellow.

soufrer [sufre] *v.t.* to sulphur, to sulphurate, to dip in sulphur; to fumigate or sprinkle with sulphur.

soufreu-r, -se [sufrœr] *s.m.f.* worker in sulphur-works; (agric.) one who dresses vines with sulphur; **~se** *s.f.* (agric.) sulphurator, sulphuring apparatus.

soufrière [sufriɛr] *s.f.* sulphur-mine.

soufroir [sufrwar] *s.m.* (text.) sulphuring-chamber or -stove.

souhait [swɛ] *s.m.* wish, desire, hope; *~s de bonne année*, New Year's greetings; *à ~*, to perfection, just right, as much as anyone could wish for; *jolie à ~*, as pretty as could be.

souhaitable [swɛtabl] *adj.* desirable.

souhaiter [swete] *v.t.* to wish, to wish for, to desire; to hope for, to hope (to or that); *~ bonne chance à qn.*, to wish s.o. luck; *~ de*, to have a wish to; (fam., iron.) *je vous en souhaite*, much good may it do you!; (pop.) *je vous la souhaite bonne et heureuse*, a happy and prosperous New Year!

souillard [sujar] *s.m.* drain-hole, gulley.

souillarde [sujard] *s.f.* scullery.

souille [suj] *s.f.* **1.** (hunt.) wallowing-place (of wild boar, etc.); **2.** (naut.) bed (of ship.); **3.** strike (made by projectile which ricochets).

souiller [suje] *v.t.* to soil, to dirty; to pollute, to sully, to defile, to contaminate, to tarnish.

souillon [sujɔ̃] *s.m.* (obs.) scullion; *~ s.f.* slut, slattern.

souillure [sujyr] *s.f.* stain, dirt; defilement, pollution, contamination; (fig.) blot, blemish, taint, defilement.

souk [suk] *s.m.* (North African) market, souk; (fig.) bedlam.

soûl, -e, saoul, -e [su] *adj.* full, drunk; (fig.) glutted, satiated; sick (of); surfeited (*de*, with); *tout son ~*, to one's heart's content, as much as one wants.

soulagement [sulaʒmɑ̃] *s.m.* alleviation, ease, relief, comfort, solace.

soulager [sulaʒe] *v.t.* to relieve, to alleviate, to comfort, to solace, to ease, to ease pressure on, to blow off (steam), to allay, to help, to succour; **se ~** *v.refl.* to relieve one's feelings; (fam.) to relieve oneself, to attend to nature.

soûlard, -e [sular] *s.m.f.* drunkard; *adj.* drunken.

soûler, saouler [sule] *v.t.* to make drunk; to surfeit, to glut; (fig.) to intoxicate; **se ~** *v.refl.* to get drunk.

soûlerie, saoulerie [sulri] *s.f.* drinking-bout, drunkenness.

soulèvement [sulɛvmɑ̃] *s.m.* rising, swelling, heaving, upheaval; uplift, upthrust; riot, revolt, insurrection.

soulever [sulve] *v.t.* to raise, to lift; to take up; to excite, to agitate, to stir up, to rouse, to provoke, to urge to insurrection; *cela me soulève le cœur, le cœur me soulève*, this turns my stomach; it makes me sick; *~ une question*, to raise a point; **se ~** *v.refl.* to revolt, to rise in rebellion.

soulier [sulje] *s.m.* shoe; *être dans ses petits ~s*, to be on pins and needles, to be in an uncomfortable situation.

soulignage [suliɲaʒ], **soulignement** [suliɲmɑ̃] *s.m.* underlining, stressing.

souligner [suliɲe] *v.t.* to underline; (fig.) to lay stress on, to emphasize, to accentuate, to show up.

soulte [sult] *s.f.* balance, adjustment, compensation.

soumettre [sumɛtr] *v.t.* to subdue, to overcome, to bring into subjection; to make to undergo; to subject; to submit (proposal, etc.); **se ~** *v.refl.* to submit, to yield, to surrender, to give way, to comply.

soumis, -e [sumi] *adj.* submissive, obedient, humble, dutiful; subject, liable; (obs.) *fille ~e*, registered prostitute.

soumission [sumisjɔ̃] *s.f.* **1.** submissiveness; surrender; **2.** (comm.) tender.

soumissionnaire [sumisjɔnɛr] *s.m.f.* tendering party, tenderer.

soumissionner [sumisjɔne] *v.t.* to tender.

soupape [supap] *s.f.* valve; *~ d'admission*, inlet-valve; intake; *~ d'alimentation*, supply-valve; *~ d'arrêt*, stop-valve, tide-flap; *~ d'échappement*, exhaust-valve, outlet-valve, escape-valve; *~ à gorge, à papillon, de réglage*, throttle, choke, regulator, regulating-valve; *~ de sûreté*, safety-valve; *~ à tiroir*, slide-valve; *~s commandées*, mechanically operated valves; (fig.) safety-valve; *~s latérales, en tête*, side-valves, overhead valves.

soupçon [supsɔ̃] *s.m.* suspicion; distrust; surmise, conjecture; trace, touch, very small quantity, the least drop; *pas un ~ de preuve*, not a shadow of proof, not a shred of evidence; *concevoir des ~s*, to have suspicions.

soupçonner [supsɔne] *v.t.* to suspect, to regard with suspicion, to have suspicions of, to surmise; *on ne peut le ~*, suspicion does not fall on him.

soupçonneu-x, -se [supsɔnø] *adj.* suspicious, distrustful; **~sement** [supsɔnøzmɑ̃] *adv.* suspiciously.

soupe [sup] *s.f.* (obs.) sop; soup; (in army) stew; *~ grasse*, meat soup, broth; *~ maigre*, vegetable soup; *tailler la ~*, to slice bread for the soup; *tremper la ~*, to pour the soup over slices of bread; (fig.) *monter comme une ~ au lait*, to flare up; to fly into a temper; *trempé comme une ~*, drenched to the skin.

soupente [supɑ̃t] *s.f.* cupboard, (U.S.) closet, (under the stairs); (techn.) brace (for a chimney--hood).
souper [supe] *s.m.* supper.
souper [supe] *v.i.* to have supper, to take supper; (fig., fam.) *j'en ai soupé!*, I have had more than enough of it.
soupeser [supəze] *v.t.* to try the weight of; to weigh, to weight; (fig.) to weigh up.
soupière [supjɛr] *s.f.* soup tureen.
soupir [supir] *s.m.* sigh, gasp; (mus.) crotchet rest; *demi-~*, quaver rest; *quart de ~*, semiquaver rest; *rendre le dernier ~*, to breathe one's last.
soupirail (pl. **aux**) [supiraj] *s.m.* air-hole, ventilator, vent.
soupirant [supirɑ̃] *s.m.* wooer, suitor, lover, admirer.
soupirer [supire] *v.i.* to sigh, to fetch sighs, to breathe; to whisper; *~ après, pour, vers*, to long for, to yearn for, to hanker after; *~ v.t.* to sigh, to say with a sigh.
souple [supl] *adj.* supple, soft, pliant, resilient, flexible, lissom; (bookb.) limp; (fig.) yielding, pliant, tractable, docile, adaptable, versatile; *avoir l'échine ~*, to cringe, to be servile; **~ment** [supləmɑ̃] *adv.* lithely, supplely, flexibly, adroitly, agilely.
souplesse [suplɛs] *s.f.* suppleness, flexibility, pliability, versatility, facility, litheness; ready compliance, pliancy.
souquenille [sukənij] *s.f.* smock.
souquer [suke] *v.t.i.* (naut.) to pull taut; to row hard, to pull away.
source [surs] *s.f.* source, spring, fountain; fount, rise; origin; *avoir, prendre, sa ~ à*, to rise in or at, (fig.) to arise from, to have its origins in; (fig.) *couler de ~*, to flow naturally; *je tiens cela de bonne ~*, I have it on good authority; *remonter à la ~ du mal*, to get to the root of the trouble.
sourci-er, -ère [sursje] *s.m.f.* water-diviner.
sourcil [sursi] *s.m.* eyebrow; *froncer les ~s*, to frown.
sourcili-er, -ère [sursilje] *adj.* (anat.) superciliary.
sourciller [sursije] *v.i.* to frown, to wince; *sans ~*, without moving a muscle, without turning a hair.
sourcilleu-x, -se [sursijø] *adj.* supercilious, haughty, lofty; punctilious, fussy.
sourd, -e [sur] *adj.* deaf; muffled; (fig.) deaf, insensible; underhand, clandestine, secret; vague; (phon.) voiceless; *un bruit ~*, a muffled sound; *douleur ~e*, dull pain; *faire la ~e oreille*, to turn a deaf ear; *de ~es menées*, underhand dealings; *lanterne ~e*, dark lantern; *crier comme un ~*, to speak too loud; *frapper comme un ~*, to beat or strike unmercifully; *~ comme un pot*, as deaf as a post; *être ~ à*, to turn a deaf ear to; **~ement** [surdəmɑ̃] *adv.* indistinctly, vaguely, dully; secretly.
sourdine [surdin] *s.f.* (mus.) mute; *jouer en ~*, to play pianissimo; *mettre une ~ à*, to mute; (fig.) to moderate, to put a check on; *en ~*, discreetly, secretly, on the quiet, on the sly.
sourd-muet [surmɥɛ], **sourde-muette** [surdmɥɛt] *s.m.f., adj.* deaf and dumb (person), deaf--mute.
sourdre [surdr] *v.i.* to spring up, to rise, to gush forth, to well up.
souriant, -e [surjɑ̃] *adj.* smiling; prepossessing, attractive.
souriceau (pl. **-x**) [suriso] *s.m.* little mouse.
souricier [surisje] *s.m., adj.* (*chat*) ~, mouser.
souricière [surisjɛr] *s.f.* mouse-trap; (fig.) police-trap.
sourire [surir] *v.i.* to smile (*de qch.*, at sth.; *à qn.* at s.o.); *cela me sourit assez*, I am rather taken with this; *cela ne me sourit pas*, the idea doesn't appeal to me; *la fortune lui sourit toujours*, fortune always smiles on him.
sourire [surir] *s.m.* smile; *~ moqueur*, sneer; (fam.) *avoir le ~*, to beam, to be wreathed in smiles; *garder le ~*, to keep smiling, to keep cheerful.
souris [suri] *s.m.* (obs.) = SOURIRE *s.m.*
souris [suri] *s.f.* mouse; knuckle (of leg of mutton); (fam.) female hotel-thief; (pop.) girl, girl-friend; *gris ~*, mouse-grey, mouse-colour; *on entendrait trotter une ~*, you could hear a pin drop; *~ qui n'a qu'un trou est bientôt prise*, it is well to have more than one string to one's bow.
sournois, -e [surnwa] *adj.* sly, deep, crafty, hypocritical; underhand; **~sement** [surnwazmɑ̃] *adv.* slyly, cunningly, artfully, in an underhand manner.
sournoiserie [surnwazri] *s.f.* slyness, dissembling, hypocrisy, trickery.
sous [su] *prep.* under; beneath, below; before; *~ les armes*, under arms; *~ le règne de*, in the reign of; *avoir qch. ~ la main*, to have sth. ready to hand; *ça vous regarde ~ le nez*, it is staring you in the face; *~ peu de jours, ~ peu*, in a few days, in a short time; shortly; soon; *~ prétexte de*, on the pretence of, under the pretext of; *~ les traits de*, in the guise of; *~ couleur de*, in the colour of, in the light of; *~ cet angle* or *cet aspect*, from this angle, from this point of view; *~ ce rapport*, in this connection, in this respect; *~ le sceau du secret*, under the seal of secrecy; *~ serment*, upon oath; *~ peine de mort*, upon pain of death; *~ peine d'amende*, under penalty of a fine; *travailler ~ la pluie*, to work in the rain; *mettre ~ enveloppe*, to put in an envelope or cover; *~ presse*, in the press; *~ un faux nom*, under a false name; *connu ~ le nom de*, known by the name of, known as; *cela s'est passé ~ mes yeux*, it happened before my very eyes; *mettre qch. ~ les yeux de qn.*, to put sth. before s.o., to bring sth. to someone's attention.
sous-alimentation [suzalimɑ̃tɑsjɔ̃] *s.f.* under-nourishment, malnutrition.
sous-alimenté, -e [suzalimɑ̃te] *adj.* under-nourished.
sous-amendement [suzamɑ̃dmɑ̃] *s.m.* amendment to an amendment.
sous-barbe [subarb] *s.f.invar.* **1.** under-jaw of a horse; **2.** backstay of bridle; **3.** (naut.) bobstay.
sous-bibliothécaire [subibliotekɛr] *s.m.f.* assistant librarian; **~-bois** [subwa] *s.m.invar.* undergrowth, underwood; (paint.) forest scene; **~-brigadier** [subrigadje] *s.m.* (excise & police) deputy sergeant; **~-chef** [suʃɛf] *s.m.* deputy head clerk; *~-chef de gare*, assistant station--master; **~-classe** [suklɑs] *s.f.* (biol.) sub-division, subclass.
sous-clavi-er, -ère [suklavje] *adj.* (anat.) subclavian.
sous-commission [sukɔmisjɔ̃] *s.f.* subcommittee; **~-comptoir** [sukɔ̃twar] *s.m.* (comm.) sub-branch; **~-consommation** [sukɔ̃sɔmɑsjɔ̃] *s.f.* (econ.) under-consumption.
souscript-eur, -rice [suskriptœr] *s.m.f.* **1.** signatory; drawer (of cheque); **2.** subscriber.
souscription [suskripsjɔ̃] *s.f.* **1.** subscription, signature; **2.** subscription; amount subscribed.
souscrire [suskrir] *v.t.* **1.** to sign, to put one's signature to; **2.** *~ à*, to subscribe to; to apply for (share issue, etc.); (fig.) to consent to, to acquiesce in.
sous-cutané, -e [sukytane] *adj.* subcutaneous, hypodermic.
sous-développé, -e [sudɛvlɔpe] *adj.* (econ.) underdeveloped; inadequately exploited.
sous-développement [sudɛvlɔpmɑ̃] *s.m.* under-developed economy, state of underdevelopment.
sous-direct-eur, -rice [sudirɛktœr] *s.m.f.* assistant-manager or manageress; vice-principal; deputy headmaster or headmistress.

sous-dominante [sudɔminɑ̃t] *s.f.* (mus.) subdominant; **~-économe** [suzekɔnɔm] *s.m.f.* deputy treasurer; assistant bursar; **~-embranchement** [suzɑ̃brɑ̃ʃmɑ̃] *s.m.* (biol.) subphylum; **~-emploi** [suzɑ̃plwa] *s.m.* underemployment; **~-entendre** [suzɑ̃tɑ̃dr] *v.t.* to imply; **~-entendu** [suzɑ̃tɑ̃dy] *s.m.* implying; implication, insinuation; mental reservation; **~-entrepreneur** [suzɑ̃trəprənœr] *s.m.* subcontractor.

sous-équipé, -e [suzekipe] *adj.* underequipped, with insufficient industrial resources.

sous-estimation [suzɛstimɑsjɔ̃] *s.f.* underestimating, underestimation; **~-estimer** [suzɛstime], **~-évaluer** [suzevalɥe] *v.t.* to underestimate, to underrate, to undervalue; **~-exposer** [suzɛkspoze] *v.t.* (photo.) to underexpose; **~-exposition** [suzɛkspozisjɔ̃] *s.f.* underexposing, underexposure; **~-faîte** [sufɛt] *s.m.* (build.) under-ridgeboard; **~-garde** [sugard] *s.f.* trigger-guard; **~-genre** [suʒɑ̃r] *s.m.* (biol.) subgenus; **~-gorge** [sugɔrʒ] *s.f.* throat-lash (of harness); **~-gouverneur** [suguvɛrnœr] *s.m.* deputy governor; **~-homme** [suzɔm] *s.m.* member of depressed class.

sous-inspect-eur, -rice [suzɛ̃spɛktœr] *s.m.f.* assistant inspector, assistant inspectress.

sous-jacent, -e [suʒasɑ̃] *adj.* subjacent, underlying.

sous-lieutenant [suljœtnɑ̃] *s.m.* second lieutenant; sub-lieutenant; ensign; **~-locataire** [sulɔkatɛr] *s.m.f.* subtenant, undertenant; **~-location** [sulɔkɑsjɔ̃] *s.f.* subletting; subtenancy; **~-louer** [sulwe] *v.t.* **1.** to sublet; **2.** to rent from the tenant; **~-main** [sumɛ̃] *s.m.invar.* **1.** blotting-pad; **2.** *en ~-main,* in secret.

sous-maître [sumɛtr] *s.m.* (obs.) assistant master; **~-maîtresse** [sumɛtrɛs] *s.f.* (obs.) assistant mistress; (mod.) madam (of a brothel).

sous-marinier [sumarinje] *s.m.* submariner, member of submarine crew; **~-maxillaire** [sumaksi(l)lɛr *adj.* (anat.) submaxillary; **~-multiple** [sumyltipl] *adj., s.m.* submultiple; **~-normale** [sunɔrmal] *s.f.* (geom.) subnormal; **~-œuvre** [suzœvr] *s.m.* (constr.) underpinning; *reprendre en ~-œuvre,* to underpin; (fig.) to make a basic reconstruction of; **~-officier** [suzɔfisje], (fam.) **~-off** [suzɔf] *s.m.* non-commissioned officer, N.C.O.; **~-ordre** [suzɔrdr] *s.m.invar.* subordinate; (fin.) *créancier en ~ordre,* creditor of a creditor (in bankruptcy); *s.m.* (biol.) suborder; **~-pied** [supje] *s.m.* trouser-strap, gaiter-strap; **~-préfecture** [suprefɛktyr] *s.f.* (admin.) sub-prefecture; **~-préfet** [suprefɛ] *s.m.* sub-prefect, sous-préfet; **~-préfète** [suprefɛt] *s.f.* wife of sous-préfet; **~-production** [suprɔdyksjɔ̃] *s.f.* (econ.) underproduction; **~-produit** [suprɔdɥi] *s.m.* by-product; (fig.) inferior imitation; **~-secrétaire** [sus(ə)kretɛr] *s.m.* (admin.) under-secretary; **~-secrétariat** [sus(ə)kretarja] *s.m.* under-secretaryship; **~-seing** [susɛ̃] *s.m.invar.* (law) private deed.

soussigné, -e [susiɲe] *adj., s.m.f.* undersigned; *je, ~,* I, the undersigned; *les ~s,* the undersigned.

sous-sol [susɔl] *s.m.* **1.** basement; **2.** subsoil, substratum; **~-station** [sustɑsjɔ̃] *s.f.* (electr.) substation; **~-tangente** [sutɑ̃ʒɑ̃t] *s.f.* (geom.) subtangent; **~-tendre** [sutɑ̃dr] *v.t.* (geom.) to subtend; **~-titre** [sutitr] *s.m.* subtitle, subheading; (cin.) subtitle; **~-titrer** [sutitre] *v.t.* (cin.) to subtitle.

soustracti-f, -ve [sustraktif] *adj.* (alg.) subtractive.

sous-traction [sustraksjɔ̃] *s.f.* abstraction; taking away; theft; (arith.) subtraction; **~traire** [sustrɛr] *v.t.* to remove, to take away, to abstract, to steal, to purloin; to withdraw, to protect, to screen, (*à,* from); to subtract, to deduct; *les pièces soustraites du dossier,* the documents removed, or abstracted, from the file; *se ~traire à,* to free oneself from, to avoid, to escape from (obligation, etc.); **~-traitant** [sutrɛtɑ̃] *s.m.* subcontractor; **~-traiter** [sutrete] *v.i.* to be a subcontractor, to subcontract; **~-ventrière** [suvɑ̃trijɛr] *s.f.* belly-band (of harness); **~-verge** [suvɛrʒ] *s.m.invar.* unridden off-horse (of a pair); (fig.) second in command, subordinate; **~-vêtement** [suvɛtmɑ̃] *s.m.* undergarment; (pl.) underwear.

soutache [sutaʃ] *s.f.* braid.

soutacher [sutaʃe] *v.t.* to braid.

soutane [sutan] *s.f.* cassock; (fig.) *la ~,* the cloth; *prendre la ~,* to become a priest, to take holy orders.

soute [sut] *s.f.* (naut.) bunker; coal-bunker, oil-bunker; (pl.) bunker oils; store(-room); (aeron.) cargo-hold; *~ aux poudres,* powder-magazine.

soutenable [sutnabl] *adj.* tenable; tolerable; sustainable.

soutenance [sutnɑ̃s] *s.f.* sustaining, defence, maintaining, (of a thesis); viva (on a thesis).

soutenant [sutnɑ̃] *s.m.* sustainer, defender, (of a thesis).

soutènement [sutɛnmɑ̃] *s.m.* prop, support; *mur de ~,* retaining-wall, breast-wall; (mining) *bois de ~,* pit-props.

souteneur [sutnœr] *s.m.* **1.** (obs.) defender; **2.** pimp, ponce.

soutenir [sutnir] *v.t.* to support, to maintain, to sustain, to endure, to keep up, to bear up; to prop, to prop up; to uphold, to affirm, to maintain, to back (up), to countenance, to stand by; *~ la conversation,* to keep up the conversation, *~ sa famille,* to support one's family; *~ une thèse,* to sustain, to defend, to undergo a viva on, a thesis; **se ~** *v.refl.* to last, to keep going, to hold out.

soutenu, -e [sutny] *adj.* sustained; lofty, grand, noble; steady, unfailing, constant, unremitting; accentuated, pronounced.

souterrain, -e [sutɛrɛ̃] *adj.* subterranean; underground; (fig.) concealed, underhand; *~ s.m.* underground passage, vault, dug-out; tunnel, subway.

soutien [sutjɛ̃] *s.m.* support, mainstay, prop; supporter, upholder; *~ de famille,* bread-winner.

soutien-gorge [sutjɛ̃gɔrʒ] *s.m.* (pl. *~s-gorge*) brassière, bra.

soutier [sutje] *s.m.* (naut.) stoker; trimmer.

soutirage [sutiraʒ] *s.m.* drawing-off (of wine, etc.), decanting.

soutirer [sutire] *v.t.* to draw off; to decant; *~ qch. à qn.,* to worm sth. out of s.o., to extract sth. from s.o.

souvenance [suvnɑ̃s] *s.f.* (obs.) remembrance; (mod.) *avoir ~ de,* to recollect.

souvenir [suvnir] *s.m.* remembrance, recollection, memory, reminder, memento, souvenir, keepsake, token of remembrance; memorial; *mon bon ~ à votre frère,* remember me to your brother; *garder un bon ~ de qch.,* to have pleasant memories of sth., to remember sth. with pleasure; *perdre le ~ de qch.,* to have no recollection of sth.

souvenir [suvnir] *v.i.impers.* (Lit.) to come to mind, to be recollected; *te souvient-il de cette occasion?,* do you recall that occasion?; **se ~** *v.refl. se ~ de,* to remember, to recollect, to recall, to call to mind; to bear in mind, not to forget; *je m'en souviendrai!,* I shall not forget it! (kindness or insult, etc.); *faire ~ qn. de qch.,* to remind s.o. of sth.

souvent [suvɑ̃] *adv.* often, frequently; *peu ~,* rarely; (pop.) *plus ~!,* not on your life!

souventes fois, souventefois [suvɑ̃tfwa] *adv.* (obs.) often, oft-times.
souverain, -e [suvrɛ̃] *adj.* sovereign, supreme, paramount; final, without appeal; *remède ~*, infallible remedy, sovereign remedy; *~ bien*, sovereign good, summum bonum; *cour ~e*, *tribunal ~*, supreme court; *avec un ~ mépris*, with supreme contempt; *s.m.f.* sovereign, monarch, ruler; *~ s.m.* sovereign (coin); **~ement** [suvrɛnmɑ̃] *adv.* supremely, extremely, without appeal.
souveraineté [suvrɛnte] *s.f.* sovereignty, supremacy, infallibility; dominions; *tenir en ~*, to hold sway over.
soviet [sɔvjɛt] *s.m.* soviet.
soviétique [sɔvjetik] *adj.* Soviet.
soya see SOJA.
soyeu-x, -se [swajø] *adj.* silky, silken.
spacieu-x, -se [spasjø] *adj.* spacious, vast, roomy; **~sement** [spasjøzmɑ̃] *adv.* spaciously.
spadassin [spadasɛ̃] *s.m.* (obs.) swashbuckler, swordsman; (mod.) hired assassin.
spadice [spadis] *s.f.* (bot.) spadix.
spahi [spai] *s.m.* spahi (Algerian trooper).
spalax [spalaks] *s.m.* (zool.) Spalax, mole rat.
spallation [spalɑsjɔ̃] *s.f.* (phys.) spallation.
spalter [spaltɛr] *s.m.* graining-brush.
sparadrap [sparadra] *s.m.* sticking-plaster.
spardeck [spardɛk] *s.m.* (naut.) spar-deck.
spart, sparte [spart] *s.m.* (bot.) esparto (grass).
Sparte [spart] *s.f.* (anc. geog.) Sparta.
sparterie [spartəri] *s.f.* esparto goods; manufacture of esparto.
spartiate [sparsjat] *adj., s.m.f.* Spartan.
spasme [spasm] *s.m.* spasm.
spasmodique [spasmɔdik] *adj.* spasmodic.
spath [spat] *s.m.* (min.) spar; *~ fluor*, fluorspar, fluorite.
spatial, -e, (aux) [spasjal] *adj.* spatial; *navire ~*, spacecraft.
spatialiser [spasjalize] *v.t.* to give a spatial character to; to adapt (astronauts) to space conditions.
spatio-naute [spasjɔnot] *s.m.f.* astronaut; **~nautique** [spasjɔnotik] *s.f.* astronautics, space-navigation.
spatule [spatyl] *s.f.* **1.** spatula, spreader; *en ~*, or *spatulé(e)*, spatulate; **2.** (ornith.) spoonbill.
speaker [spikœr] *s.m.* **1.** Speaker (of House of Commons); **2.** (radio) announcer (fem. *speakerine* [spikrin]).
spécial, -e, (aux) [spesjal] *adj.* special, especial, particular; peculiar; (fam.) queer (esp. homosexual); *~ à*, special, etc., to, characteristic of, specially made, designed, or intended, for; **~ement** [spesjalmɑ̃] *adv.* specially, especially, particularly; peculiarly.
spécialisation [spesjalizɑsjɔ̃] *s.f.* specialization, specializing.
spécialisé, -e [spesjalize] *adj.* specialized; *s.m.f.* specialist (*dans*, in).
spécialiser [spesjalize] *v.t.* to specialize; **se ~** *v.refl.* to specialize, to become a specialist.
spécialiste [spesjalist] *s.m.f., adj.* specialist; expert.
spécialité [spesjalite] *s.f.* specialty, peculiarity, speciality, special feature; specialized knowledge; line of business; particular function; patent medicine.
spécieu-x, -se [spesjø] *adj.* specious, plausible; **~sement** [spesjøzmɑ̃] *adv.* speciously, plausibly.
spécification [spesifikɑsjɔ̃] *s.f.* specification, specifying, detailed description or enumeration.
spécificité [spesifisite] *s.f.* specificity.
spécifier [spesifje] *v.t.* to specify, to mention specially, to state specifically.
spécifique [spesifik] *adj.* specific; **~ment** [spesifikmɑ̃] *adv.* specifically.
spécimen [spesimɛn] *s.m.* specimen.
spéciosité [spesjozite] *s.f.* speciousness.
spectacle [spɛktakl] *s.m.* spectacle, show, sight, scene, performance, parade, pageant, exhibition; (theatr.) play; *pièce à grand ~*, spectacular, lavishly produced show; *se donner en ~*, to make oneself conspicuous, to make an exhibition of oneself; *aller au ~*, to go to the theatre.
spectat-eur, -rice [spɛktatœr] *s.m.f.* spectator, looker-on, bystander, eye-witness; *les ~eurs*, the audience.
spectral, -e, (aux) [spɛktral] *adj.* **1.** spectral, ghostly; **2.** spectral, pertaining to the spectrum; *analyse ~e*, spectrum analysis.
spectre [spɛktr] *s.m.* **1.** spectre, ghost, phantom; **2.** (phys.) spectrum.
spectro-gramme [spɛktrɔgram] *s.m.* (phys.) spectrogram; **~graphe** [spɛktrɔgraf] *s.m.* (phys.) spectrograph; **~heliographe** [spɛktrɔeljɔgraf] *s.m.* (astron.) spectroheliograph; **~scope** [spɛktrɔskop] *s.m.* (phys.) spectroscope; **~scopie** [spɛktroskɔpi] *s.f.* spectroscopy; **~scopique** [spɛktrɔskɔpik] *adj.* spectroscopic.
spéculaire [spekylɛr] *adj.* specular; *écriture ~*, mirror-writing; (min.) *fer ~*, specular iron; *~ s.f.* (bot.) Venus's looking-glass.
speculat-eur, -rice [spekylatœr] *s.m.f.* speculator, gambler; (stock exchange) *~eur, ~rice, à la baisse*, bear; *~eur, ~rice, à la hausse*, bull.
spéculati-f, -ve [spekylatif] *adj.* speculative.
spéculation [spekylɑsjɔ̃] *s.f.* **1.** speculation, conjecture; meditation; **2.** speculation, speculative investment.
spéculer [spekyle] *v.i.* to speculate, to meditate; to speculate, to make investments that involve risk; to gamble; *~ sur qch.*, to speculate on, or about, sth.; to speculate in sth., to gamble on sth.
speculum, spéculum [spekylɔm] *s.m.* (surg.) speculum.
speiss [spɛs] *s.m.* (metall.) speiss.
spéléo-logie [speleɔlɔʒi] *s.f.* speleology; caving, pot-holing; **~logue** [speleɔlɔg] *s.m.f.* (fam. abbrev. *spéléo*) speleologist; caver, pot-holer.
spergule [spɛrgyl] *s.f.* (bot.) spurry, spurrey.
spermaceti [spɛrmaseti] *s.m.* spermaceti.
spermatie [spɛrmati] *s.f.* (bot.) spermatium.
spermatique [spɛrmatik] *adj.* (anat.) spermatic.
spermato-génèse [spɛrmatɔʒenɛz] *s.f.* (biol.) spermatogenesis; **~phytes** [spɛrmatɔfit] *s.f.pl.* (bot.) spermatophyta, spermaphyta, spermophyta; **~zoïde** [spɛrmatozɔid] *s.m.* (biol.) spermatozoon, spermatozoid.
sperme [spɛrm] *s.m.* sperm, semen.
spermophile [spɛrmɔfil] *s.m.* (zool.) gopher.
sphacèle [sfasɛl] *s.m.* (pathol.) necrosis, gangrene.
sphénoïdal, -e, (aux) [sfenɔidal] *adj.* sphenoidal.
sphénoïde [sfenɔid] *s.m.* (anat.) sphenoid.
sphère [sfɛr] *s.f.* sphere, globe, ball; (fig.) sphere, field of action or influence, circle, orbit.
sphéricité [sferisite] *s.f.* sphericity.
sphérique [sferik] *adj.* spherical.
sphéroïdal, -e, (aux) [sferɔidal] *adj.* spheroidal.
sphéroïde [sferɔid] *s.m.* spheroid.
sphéromètre [sferɔmɛtr] *s.m.* spherometer.
sphincter [sfɛ̃ktɛr] *s.m.* (anat.) sphincter.
sphinx [sfɛ̃ks] *s.m.* sphinx; (fig.) sphinx, enigmatic person; (ent.) hawk-moth.
spic [spik] *s.m.* (also *aspic*) (bot.) spike-lavender; *huile de ~*, spike-oil.
spica [spika] *s.m.* (surg.) spica (bandage).
spiciforme [spisifɔrm] *adj.* (bot.) spike-shaped.
spicule [spikyl] *s.m.* (zool.) spicule.
spider [spidɛr] *s.m.* (car) dickey (seat); ⚠ not 'spider'.
spiegel [spigɛl] *s.m.* (metall.) spiegeleisen.
spin [spin] *s.m.* (atomic phys.) spin.

spinal, -e, (aux) [spinal] *adj.* spinal.

spinelle [spinɛl] *s.m.* spinel (ruby).

spinozisme, spinosisme [spinozism] *s.m.* Spinozism.

spiral, -e, (aux) [spiral] *adj.* spiral.

spirale [spiral] *s.f.* spiral, helix; curl, ring; *des cheveux en* ~, hair in ringlets.

spirant, -e [spirɑ̃] *adj.*, **~e** *s.f.* (phon.) spirant.

spire [spir] *s.f.* spiral, coil, turn of a spiral; spiral formation; ⚠ not 'spire' as on a church.

spirée [spire] *s.f.* (bot.) spiraea, meadowsweet.

spirite [spirit] *s.m.f.* spiritualist; spiritist; ~ *adj.* spiritualistic.

spiritisme [spiritism] *s.m.* spiritualism; spiritism.

spiritualiser [spiritɥalize] *v.t.* to give a spiritual quality to.

spiritualisme [spiritɥalism] *s.m.* (phil.) spiritualism (opp. materialism); ⚠ not 'spiritualism' in sense 'spiritism'.

spiritualiste [spiritɥalist] *adj.* (phil.) spiritualistic; ~ *s.m.f.* spiritualist (opp. materialist).

spiritualité [spiritɥalite] *s.f.* spirituality; spiritual life.

spirituel, -le [spiritɥɛl] *adj.* **1.** spiritual; sacred; **2.** witty, sprightly, lively, humorous, sharp, incisive, clever; **~lement** [spiritɥɛlmɑ̃] *adv.* **1.** spiritually; **2.** wittily, cleverly.

spiritueu-x, -se [spiritɥø] *adj.* spirituous; **~x** *s.m.* (alcoholic) spirit, spirits.

spirochète [spirɔkɛt] *s.m.* (pathol.) spirochete.

spiroïdal, -e, (aux) [spirɔidal] *adj.* spiral, spiroid.

spiromètre [spirɔmɛtr] *s.m.* spirometer.

Spitzberg [spitsbɛrg] *s.m.* (geog.) Spitzbergen.

splanchnique [splɑ̃knik] *adj.* (anat.) splanchnic.

splanchnologie [splɑ̃knɔlɔʒi] *s.f.* (anat.) splanchnology.

spleen [splin] *s.m.* (fit of) depression, melancholy, gloom; *avoir le* ~, to be fed up (with life); ⚠ not 'spleen' the organ, nor in sense 'spite', 'venom'.

splendeur [splɑ̃dœr] *s.f.* splendour, magnificence, brilliance, brightness.

splendide [splɑ̃did] *adj.* splendid, magnificent, sumptuous, gorgeous, glorious, brilliant; **~ment** [splɑ̃didmɑ̃] *adv.* splendidly.

splénétique [splenetik] *adj.* gloomy; ~ *s.m.* gloom.

splénique [splenik] *adj.* (anat.) splenetic.

splénite [splenit] *s.f.* (pathol.) splenitis.

spoliat-eur, -rice [spɔljatœr] *s.m.f.* despoiler, spoliator; spoiler; *adj.* spoliatory.

spoliation [spɔljɑsjɔ̃] *s.f.* spoliation, despoiling, plundering.

spolier [spɔlje] *v.t.* to despoil, to deprive, to frustrate.

spondaïque [spɔ̃daik] *adj.* spondaic.

spondée [spɔ̃de] *s.m.* spondee.

spongiaires [spɔ̃ʒjɛr] *s.m.pl.* (zool.) sponges.

spongieu-x, -se [spɔ̃ʒjø] *adj.* spongy, absorbent.

spongiosité [spɔ̃ʒjozite] *s.f.* sponginess.

spontané, -e [spɔ̃tane] *adj.* spontaneous, natural.

spontanéité [spɔ̃taneite] *s.f.* spontaneity, spontaneousness.

spontanément [spɔ̃tanemɑ̃] *adv.* spontaneously.

sporadicité [spɔradisite] *s.f.* sporadic character or incidence.

sporadique [spɔradik] *adj.* sporadic; **~ment** [spɔradikmɑ̃] *adv.* sporadically.

sporange [spɔrɑ̃ʒ] *s.m.* (bot.) sporangium.

spore [spɔr] *s.f.* (bot.) spore.

sport [spɔr] *s.m.* sport, game(s), (sporting or recreational) activity; *les* ~*s*, sport; ~ *adj.invar.* sporting, sport(s), casual; *être* ~, to be sporting, to play fair; *vêtements* ~, games clothes, sportswear, casual clothes; ⚠ not 'sport' as in 'sport of nature', 'to make sport of', 'to have good sport'.

sporti-f, -ve [spɔrtif] *adj.* sporting, sports, sportsmanlike, relating to sport, fond of sport; **~vement** [spɔrtivmɑ̃] *adv.* in a sporting spirit.

sportivité [spɔrtivite] *s.f.* sportsmanship, sporting spirit.

sportsman [spɔrtsman] *s.m.* (pl. *sportsmen*) **1.** (obs.) sportsman; **2.** racegoer, patron of the turf.

spot [spɔt] *s.m.* **1.** (phys.) light-spot (on recording instrument); (radar) scanning-spot; (TV) spot (produced by electrons on screen); **2.** spotlight.

spoutnik [sputnik] *s.m.* sputnik, artificial satellite.

spray [sprɛ] *s.m.* spray, aerosol.

sprint [sprint] *s.m.* sprint, dash, rush; sprint race.

sprinter [sprintœr] *s.m.* sprinter.

sprinter [sprinte] *v.i.* to sprint.

spumescent, -e [spymesɑ̃] *adj.* spumescent.

spumeu-x, -se [spymø] *adj.* spumy, spumous, frothy.

squale [skwal] *s.m.* shark; dogfish.

squame [skwam] *s.f.* (bot., zool.) squama; scale.

squameu-x, -se [skwamø] *adj.* squamose, squamous, scaly.

square [skwar] *s.m.* enclosed public garden, square; ⚠ not a 'square' without a garden, nor geom. 'square'.

squatter [skwatœr, skwatɛr] *s.m.* squatter.

squelette [skəlɛt] *s.m.* skeleton, carapace, shell; (fig.) skeleton, outline; (of person) skeleton, nothing but skin and bones.

squelettique [skəlɛtik] *adj.* skeleton-like, as thin as a skeleton; skeletal; (fig.) skeleton (staff, etc.); sketchy, skimpy.

squille [skij] *s.f.* (zool.) squill.

squirr(h)e [skir] *s.m.* (pathol.) scirrhus, scirrhosity.

S.S. [ɛsɛs] *s.f.* abbrev. *Sécurité Sociale*; (hist.) (Nazi) S.S.

stabilisat-eur, -rice [stabilizatœr] *adj.* stabilizing; **~eur** *s.m.* stabilizer; balancer.

stabilisation [stabilizɑsjɔ̃] *s.f.* stabilization; steadying; consolidation; attitude control (of spaceship).

stabiliser [stabilize] *v.t.* to stabilize, to consolidate.

stabilité [stabilite] *s.f.* stability, stableness; durability, steadfastness, firmness, permanence.

stable [stabl] *adj.* stable, firm, durable; steadfast, permanent, lasting.

stabulation [stabylɑsjɔ̃] *s.f.* keeping cattle in sheds.

stade [stad] *s.m.* stadium; (fig.) period, stage.

staff [staf] *s.m.* (constr.) staff (build. material).

stage [staʒ] *s.m.* (period of) training, course of instruction; *faire son* ~, to do one's training; (law, etc.) to keep one's terms; ⚠ not theatr. 'stage', nor 'stage' in sense 'point in time'.

stagiaire [staʒjɛr] *s.m.f.* trainee; ~ *adj.* under instruction, undergoing training, keeping terms.

stagnant, -e [stagnɑ̃] *adj.* stagnant; *eau* ~*e*, stagnant or standing water; (fig.) *mare* ~*e*, backwater; *le commerce est* ~, business is very slack.

stagnation [stagnɑsjɔ̃] *s.f.* stagnation, stagnancy; (fig.) inactivity.

stagner [stagne] *v.i.* to stagnate; (fig.) to be inactive, to languish.

stalactite [stalaktit] *s.f.* stalactite.

stalagmite [stalagmit] *s.f.* stalagmite.

stalinien, -ne [stalinjɛ̃] *adj.*, *s.m.f.* Stalinist.

stalinisme [stalinism] *s.m.* Stalinism.

stalle [stal] *s.f.* stall, seat; stall, box (for horses), compartment in garage.

staminé, -e [stamine] *adj.* (bot.) staminate.

stance [stɑ̃s] *s.f.* stanza; (pl.) solemn (moral or elegiac) poem; ⚠ not 'stance'.

stand [stɑ̃d] *s.m.* stand, stall; shooting-stand; shooting-range.

standard[1] [stɑ̃dar] *s.m., adj.invar.* standard; *échange* ~, standard replacement (part); *pression* ~, working pressure.
standard[2] [stɑ̃dar] *s.m.* (telephone) exchange, switchboard.
standardisation [stɑ̃dardizɑsjɔ̃] *s.f.* standardization, mass-production, normalization.
standardiser [stɑ̃dardize] *v.t.* to standardize, to make uniform, to normalize.
standardiste [stɑ̃dardist] *s.m.f.* switchboard operator.
standing [stɑ̃diŋ] *s.m.* standing, status; *immeuble de grand* ~, high-class property.
stannate [stanat] *s.m.* (chem.) stannate.
stanneu-x, -se [stanø] *adj.* (chem.) stannous.
stannifère [stanifɛr] *adj.* (min.) stanniferous.
stannique [stanik] *adj.* (chem.) stannic.
staphisaigre [stafizɛgr] *s.f.* (bot.) stavesacre; larkspur.
staphylin [stafilɛ̃] *s.m.* (ent.) devil's coach-horse.
staphylin, -e [stafilɛ̃] *adj.* (anat.) staphyline.
staphylocoque [stafilɔkɔk] *s.m.* staphylococcus.
staphylôme [stafilom] *s.m.* (pathol.) staphyloma.
star [star] *s.f.* film star.
starter [startɛr] *s.m.* **1.** starter (of race); **2.** (car) choke; ⚠ not (car) 'starter'.
stase [stɑz] *s.f.* (pathol.) stasis.
statère [statɛr] *s.m.* (Gk. ant.) stater.
stathouder [statudɛr] *s.m.* (Dutch hist.) stadtholder.
statice [statis] *s.m.* (bot.) thrift.
station [stɑsjɔ̃] *s.f.* standing, pause, short stay, break of journey; halt, station, stopping-place; (taxi) rank, stand; ~ *d'hiver*, winter resort; ~ *thermale*, health resort, spa, watering-place; *faire une longue* ~, to make a long stay, to stand (waiting) a long time; ~ *verticale*, standing position; ~ *spatiale*, space station.
stationnaire [stasjɔnɛr] *adj.* at a standstill, stationary; unchanged, invariable; *rester* ~, to remain at a standstill; ~ *s.m.* (naut.) block-ship, guard-ship.
stationnement [stasjɔnmɑ̃] *s.m.* stationing, standing still, standing; (car) parking, waiting; parking-place; ~ *interdit*, no parking, no waiting; *droit de* ~, parking fee; right to erect stall, etc. on public ground.
stationner [stasjɔne] *v.i.* to stop, to stand about, to stand still, to take up a position; (of vehicle) to stand, to wait, to park, to be parked; ⚠ not 'to station'.
station-service [stasjɔ̃sɛrvis] *s.f.* (pl. *stations-service*) service-station; filling-station.
statique [statik] *adj.* static; ~ *s.f.* statics.
statisticien, -ne [statistisjɛ̃] *s.m.f.* statistician.
statistique [statistik] *s.f.* statistic; *la* ~, statistics; ~ *adj.* statistical; **~ment** [statistikmɑ̃] *adv.* statistically.
stator [statɔr] *s.m.* (electr.) stator.
statoréacteur [statɔreaktœr] *s.m.* (aeron.) ram-jet.
statuaire [statɥɛr] *s.m.f.* sculptor, sculptress; ~ *s.f.* statuary, sculpture; ~ *adj.* statuary, of or for statues.
statue [staty] *s.f.* statue; (fig.) figure (e.g. of grief).
statuer [statɥe] *v.t.i.* to rule, to decree, to enact; to come to a decision (*sur*, upon).
statuette [statɥɛt] *s.f.* statuette.
statufier [statyfje] *v.t.* **1.** (fam.) to make or put up a statue of; **2.** (fig.) to transform into statues, to freeze.
statu quo [statykwo] *s.m.* status quo.
stature [statyr] *s.f.* stature, height; (fig.) status, importance.
statut [staty] *s.m.* statute, by(e)-law, regulation, code; (legal, diplomatic, etc.) status; (pl.) statutes, articles (of association).
statutaire [statytɛr] *adj.* statutory; **~ment** [statytɛrmɑ̃] *adv.* statutorily, in accordance with the statutes or articles.
stayer [stɛjœr] *s.m.* **1.** (racing) stayer; horse good for long-distance racing; **2.** middle-distance racing cyclist.
Sté [ste] *s.f.* abbrev. *société*.
steamer [stimœr] *s.m.* steamer, steamship.
stéarine [stearin] *s.f.* stearin.
stéarique [stearik] *adj.* stearic.
stéatite [steatit] *s.f.* (min.) steatite.
stéatopyge [steatɔpiʒ] *adj.* steatopygous.
steeple-chase [stipəlʃɛz], **steeple** [stipl] *s.m.* **1.** (racing) steeple-chase; **2.** (athletics) long-distance obstacle-race, cross-country (race).
stèle [stɛl] *s.f.* stela, stele.
stellaire [stɛllɛr] *adj.* stellar, of stars; ~ *s.f.* (bot.) chickweed.
stemmate [stɛmmat] *s.m.* (zool.) stemma.
stencil [stɛnsil] *s.m.* (duplicating) stencil.
sténo [steno] *s.m.f.* abbrev. *sténographe*, *sténographie*; **~dactylo** [stenɔdaktilo] *s.m.f.* shorthand typist; **~dactylo(graphie)** [stenɔdaktilɔ(grafi)] *s.f.* shorthand and typing; **~graphe** [stenɔgraf] *s.m.f.* stenographer, shorthand writer; **~graphie** [stenɔgrafi] *s.f.* stenography, shorthand, shorthand record; **~graphier** [stenɔgrafje] *v.t.* to take down in shorthand; **~graphique** [stenɔgrafik] *adj.* stenographic, (in) shorthand; *compte rendu ~graphique*, verbatim report; **~graphiquement** [stenɔgrafikmɑ̃] *adv.* in shorthand; **~type** [stenɔtip] *s.f.* stenotype, shorthand typewriter; **~typie** [stenɔtipi] typing in shorthand; **~typiste** [stenɔtipist] *s.m.f.* stenotypist, stenotype operator.
stentor [stɑ̃tɔr] *s.m.* Stentor; *voix de* ~, stentorian voice.
steppe [stɛp] *s.f.* steppe.
stepper [stɛpœr] *s.m.* (equitation) high-stepper.
steppique [stepik] *adj.* of the steppes.
stercoraire [stɛrkɔrɛr] *adj.* stercoraceous.
stercoral, -e, (aux) [stɛrkɔral] *adj.* stercoral.
stère [stɛr] *s.m.* stere, cubic metre of firewood, cord.
stéréo [stereo] abbrev. *stéréophonie*, *stéréophonique*, stereo.
stéréo-bate [stereɔbat] *s.m.* (arch.) stereobate; **~chimie** [stereɔʃimi] *s.f.* stereochemistry; **~chromie** [stereɔkrɔmi] *s.f.* stereochromy; **~gramme** [stereɔgram] *s.m.* stereographic representation; **~graphie** [stereɔgrafi] *s.f.* stereography; **~graphique** [stereɔgrafik] *adj.* stereographic; **~métrie** [stereɔmetri] *s.f.* stereometry, measurement of solids; **~phonie** [stereɔfɔni] *s.f.* stereophony, stereophonic sound, stereo; **~phonique** [stereɔfɔnik] *adj.* stereophonic; **~scope** [stereɔskɔp] *s.m.* stereoscope; **~scopie** [stereɔskɔpi] *s.f.* stereoscopy; **~scopique** [stereɔskɔpik] *adj.* stereoscopic; **~tomie** [stereɔtɔmi] *s.f.* stereotomy; **~type** [stereɔtip] *adj.* (typ.) stereotype; *s.m.* (fig.) stereotyped opinion, conventional view, cliché.
stéréotypé, -e [stereɔtipe] *adj.* stereotyped.
stéréotypie [stereɔtipi] *s.f.* stereotyping; (psychol.) stereotype reaction.
stérer [stere] *v.t.* to measure in steres.
stérile [steril] *adj.* sterile, barren, unfruitful, unproductive, fruitless, vain, unprofitable; *discussion* ~, sterile or unprofitable discussion, pointless argument; *mariage* ~, childless marriage; **~ment** [sterilmɑ̃] *adv.* sterilely, unprofitably, vainly.
stérilisateur [sterilizatœr] *s.m.* sterilizer.
stérilisation [sterilizɑsjɔ̃] *s.f.* sterilization.
stériliser [sterilize] *v.t.* to sterilize.
stérilité [sterilite] *s.f.* sterility, barrenness,

unfruitfulness, unproductiveness; (fig.) paucity, dearth, poverty.
sterlet [stɛrlɛ] *s.m.* (ichth.) sterlet.
sternal, -e, (**aux**) [stɛrnal] *adj.* (anat.) sternal.
sterne [stɛrn] *s.f.* (ornith.) tern.
sternum [stɛrnɔm] *s.m.* (anat.) sternum, breastbone.
sternutation [stɛrnytɑsjɔ̃] *s.f.* (med.) sternutation, repeated sneezing.
sternutatoire [stɛrnytatwar] *adj.* sternutatory.
stérol [sterɔl] *s.m.* (chem., physiol.) sterol.
stéthoscope [stetɔskɔp] *s.m.* stethoscope.
steward [stiwart] *s.m.* (naut., aeron.) steward.
stibié, -e [stibje] *adj.* containing antimony, antimonious.
stick [stik] *s.m.* cane, walking-stick.
stigmate [stigmat] *s.m.* **1.** scar, mark, pock-mark; brand; (theol.) (pl.) stigmata; **2.** (bot.) stigma; **3.** (ent.) spiracle.
stigmatiser [stigmatize] *v.t.* (fig. & pej.) to stigmatize, to brand, to condemn.
stil-de-grain [stildəgrɛ̃] *s.m.* (paint.) yellow lake.
stillation [stilɑsjɔ̃] *s.f.* dripping, falling drop by drop.
stimulant, -e [stimylɑ̃] *adj.* stimulating; ~ *s.m.* stimulus, stimulant.
stimulation [stimylɑsjɔ̃] *s.f.* stimulation, excitation.
stimuler [stimyle] *v.t.* to stimulate, to urge, to spur on, to arouse, to excite, to prod.
stimulus [stimylys] *s.m.* (pl. *stimuli*) stimulus.
stipe [stip] *s.m.* (bot.) stipe, stem.
stipendié, -e [stipɑ̃dje] *s.m.f., adj.* (one who is) corrupt, bought, in someone's pay.
stipendier [stipɑ̃dje] *v.t.* to keep in one's pay, to hire; to buy, to bribe, to corrupt.
stipulation [stipylɑsjɔ̃] *s.f.* stipulation, condition.
stipule [stipyl] *s.f.* (bot.) stipule.
stipuler [stipyle] *v.t.* to stipulate, to lay down, to specify, to make clear.
stock [stɔk] *s.m.* stock(-in-trade), supply, reserve(s).
stockage [stɔkaʒ] *s.m* (comm.) stocking, keeping in stock, stockpiling.
stocker [stɔke] *v.t.* to stock, to put into stock, to stockpile, to store.
stockiste [stɔkist] *s.m.* wholesaler, stockist, stockholder, (car) distributor.
stoïcien, -ne [stɔisjɛ̃] *adj., s.m.f.* stoic.
stoïcisme [stɔisism] *s.m.* stoicism.
stoïque [stɔik] *adj.* stoical, stoic; **~ment** [stɔikmɑ̃] *adv.* stoically.
stoker [stɔkœr] *s.m.* (mech.) stoker.
stokes [stɔks] *s.m.* (phys.) stokes.
stolon [stɔlɔ̃] *s.m.* (bot.) stolon.
stomacal, -e, (**aux**) [stɔmakal] *adj.* stomachal, gastric.
stomachique [stɔmaʃik] *adj., s.m.* stomachic, digestive.
stomatite [stɔmatit] *s.f.* (pathol.) stomatitis.
stomato-logie [stɔmatɔlɔʒi] *s.f.* stomatology; **~logiste** [stɔmatɔlɔʒist], **stomatologue** [stɔmatɔlɔg] *s.m.f.* stomatologist.
stop [stɔp] *interj., s.m.* **1.** (as imperative and on road-signs) stop!, halt!; **2.** (in telegrams, etc.) stop; ~ *s.m.* stop, check, arrestation; (*signal de*) ~, stop-light (on car), red traffic-light; (fam.) (*auto-*)~, hitch-hiking; *faire du* ~, to hitch-hike, to thumb lifts.
stoppage [stɔpaʒ] *s.m.* invisible mending; ⚠ not 'stoppage'.
stopper[1] [stɔpe] *v.t.* to mend (invisibly), to fine-darn, to catch up (a run in a stocking).
stopper[2] [stɔpe] *v.t.i.* to stop, to come to a stop, to bring to a standstill, to arrest (movement or progress of).
stoppeu-r, -se [stɔpœr] *s.m.f.* **1.** darner; one who does invisible mending; **2.** = AUTO-STOPPEUR.
storax [stɔraks] *s.m.* (pharm.) storax.
store [stɔr] *s.m.* blind, Venetian blind, awning, folding partition; ⚠ not 'store'.
strabisme [strabism] *s.m.* strabismus, squinting, squint.
strabotomie [strabɔtɔmi] *s.f.* strabotomy.
stradivarius [stradivarjys] *s.m.* Stradivarius (violin, etc.).
stramoine [stramwan] *s.f.*, **stramonium** [stramɔnjɔm] *s.m.* (bot.) stramonium, thorn-apple.
strangulation [strɑ̃gylɑsjɔ̃] *s.f.* strangulation, strangling, throttling.
strapontin [strapɔ̃tɛ̃] *s.m.* bracket-seat, flap-seat, tip-up seat.
strass [stras] *s.m.* paste, strass.
strasse [stras] *s.f.* silk-waste (used for packing).
stratagème [strataʒɛm] *s.m.* stratagem, device, trick, artifice, dodge.
strate [strat] *s.f.* (geol.) stratum, layer.
stratège [stratɛʒ] *s.m.* **1.** (ant.) strategus; **2.** general, military leader, strategist.
stratégie [strateʒi] *s.f.* strategy, generalship.
stratégique [strateʒik] *adj.* strategic; **~ment** [strateʒikmɑ̃] *adv.* strategically.
stratégiste [strateʒist] *s.m.* (obs.) = STRATÈGE 2.
stratification [stratifikɑsjɔ̃] *s.f.* stratification.
stratifier [stratifje] *v.t.* to stratify.
stratigraphie [stratigrafi] *s.f.* stratigraphy.
strato-sphère [stratɔsfɛr] *s.f.* stratosphere; **~sphérique** [stratɔsferik] *adj.* stratospheric, operating in the stratosphere.
stratus [stratys] *s.m.* (meteor.) stratus.
strepto-coque [strɛptɔkɔk] *s.m.* (bacteriology) streptococcus; **~mycine** [strɛptɔmisin] *s.f.* (pharm.) streptomycin.
stress [strɛs] *s.m.* (physiol., psychol.) stress, shock.
strette [strɛt] *s.f.* (mus.) stretto (of a fugue).
striation [strijɑsjɔ̃] *s.f.* striation.
strict, -e [strikt] *adj.* strict, exact; *le* ~ *nécessaire*, no more than is necessary, only what is strictly necessary; *le* ~ *minimum*, the absolute minimum; **~ement** [striktəmɑ̃] *adv.* strictly, severely.
strident, -e [stridɑ̃] *adj.* shrill, strident, harsh, screeching.
stridulation [stridylɑsjɔ̃] *s.f.* stridulation, chirring, (of grasshoppers, etc.).
strie [stri] *s.f.* score, groove, channel; (pl.) fluting; (arch.) stria, listel, fillet; (conch., geol.) stria.
strié, -e [strie] *adj.* striate(d), fluted; striped, streaked.
strier [strie] *v.t.* to striate, to score, to stripe, to streak.
strige [striʒ] *s.f.* vampire.
strigile [striʒil] *s.m.* (ant.) strigil.
stripage [stripaʒ] *s.m.* (atomic phys.) stripping.
strip-tease [striptiz] *s.m.* strip-tease (performance).
strip-teaseuse [striptizøz], **strippeuse** [stripøz] *s.f.* strip-tease artist, stripper.
striure [striyr] *s.f.* striation, stria, fluting.
strix [striks] *s.m.* (ornith.) tawny owl.
strobile [strɔbil] *s.m.* strobile, pine-cone.
stroboscope [strɔbɔskɔp] *s.m.* stroboscope.
strontiane [strɔ̃sjan] *s.f.* (chem.) strontia.
strontium [strɔ̃sjɔm] *s.m.* (chem.) strontium.
strophe [strɔf] *s.f.* strophe, stanza.
structural, -e, (**aux**) [stryktyral] *adj.* structural.
structure [stryktyr] *s.f.* structure, make, arrangement, disposition, build.
structurel, -le [stryktyrɛl] *adj.* structural.
structurer [stryktyre] *v.t.* to give a structure to, to structure; **se** ~ *v.refl.* to acquire a structure.
strume [strym] *s.f.* (med.) struma, scrofula.

strychnine [striknin] *s.f.* strychnine.
stuc [styk] *s.m.* stucco.
stucateur [stykatœr] *s.m.* stucco-worker.
studieu-x, -se [stydjø] *adj.* studious, painstaking; **~sement** [stydjøzmɑ̃] *adv.* studiously.
studio [stydjo] *s.m.* **1.** (artist's) studio; **2.** one-room flat, bed-sitter; main room of one-room flat (i.e. not kitchen, W.C., etc.); suite of furniture for one-room flat.
stupéfaction [stypefaksjɔ̃] *s.f.* amazement, great astonishment, stupefaction.
stupéfaire [stypefɛr] *v.t.* to stupefy, to dumbfound, to amaze.
stupéfait, -e [stypefɛ] *adj.* amazed, dumbfounded, astounded; astonished; stupefied.
stupéfiant, -e [stypefjɑ̃] *adj.* stupefying, stupefacient; astounding, amazing; ~ *s.m.* narcotic, drug.
stupéfier [stypefje] *v.t.* **1.** to stupefy, to numb, to paralyse; **2.** to astound, to amaze.
stupeur [stypœr] *s.f.* stupor, daze, amazement; *être frappé de ~*, to be dumbfounded.
stupide [stypid] *adj.* in a state of stupor, dumbfounded; stupid, silly, obtuse, crass, slow-witted, unintelligent; **~ment** [stypidmɑ̃] *adv.* stupidly, foolishly.
stupidité [stypidite] *s.f.* stupidity, piece of stupidity, stupid behaviour or remark, stupid incident.
stupre [stypr] *s.m.* defilement, debauching; debauchery.
stuquer [styke] *v.t.* to stucco.
style [stil] **1.** style; ~ *sublime*, exalted style; *meubles de ~*, period furniture; *en* or *de grand ~*, large-scale, on a grand scale, in style; **2.** (bot.) style; **3.** style, pin, gnomon, of sun-dial; **4.** stylus, graver, etching-needle.
styler [stile] *v.t.* to train, to form; *domestique bien stylé*, well-trained servant.
stylet [stilɛ] *s.m.* stiletto; (ent.) stylet; (surg.) probe.
styl-isation [stilizɑsjɔ̃] *s.f.* stylization; **~iser** [stilize] *v.t.* to stylize, to conventionalize, to present stylistically; **~iste** [stilist] *s.m.f.* stylist, master of style; (indust.) styling specialist; **~istique** [stilistik] *s.f.* stylistics, study of style; *adj.* stylistic, of style.
stylite [stilit] *s.m.* stylite.
stylo [stilo], (obs.) **stylographe** [stilɔgraf] *s.m.* fountain-pen; *stylo à bille*, ball-point (pen).
stylobate [stilɔbat] *s.m.* (arch.) stylobate.
styloïde [stilɔid] *adj.* (anat.) styloid.
styptique [stiptik] *adj.* styptic, that checks bleeding; ~ *s.m.* styptic.
styrax [stiraks] *s.m.* **1.** (bot.) styrax; **2.** = STORAX.
styrène [stirɛn], **styrolène** [stirɔlɛn] *s.m.* (chem.) styrene.
Styrie [stiri] *s.f.* (geog.) Styria.
su [sy] *s.m.* knowledge; *au ~ de qn.*, to the knowledge of s.o.; *au vu et au ~ de tous*, openly, publicly.
suage[1] [sɥaʒ] *s.m.* humidity oozing from new timber, or damp wood burning.
suage[2] [sɥaʒ] *s.m.* rim (to dish or candle-stick).
suaire [sɥɛr] *s.m.* shroud, winding-sheet.
suant, -e [sɥɑ̃] *adj.* **1.** (fam.) sweating, dripping with sweat; **2.** (pop.) boring.
suave [sɥav] *adj.* suave, sweet, soft, delicate, pleasant, delicious, charming, bland; **~ment** [sɥavmɑ̃] *adv.* suavely, sweetly, gently.
suavité [sɥavite] *s.f.* suavity, sweetness, delicate charm, grace, blandness.
subaigu, -ë [sybegy] *adj.* (med.) subacute.
subalpin, -e [sybalpɛ̃] *adj.* subalpine.
subalterne [sybaltɛrn] *adj.* subordinate, secondary; ~ *s.m.f.* subordinate; (mil.) subaltern.
subconscient, -e [sypkɔ̃sjɑ̃] *adj.* **1.** half-aware; **2.** unconscious, subconscious; ~ *s.m.* subconscious.
subdéléguer [sybdelege] *v.t.* to subdelegate.
subdivis-er [sybdivize] *v.t.* to subdivide; **se ~er** *v.refl.* to be subdivided; **~ion** [sybdivizjɔ̃] *s.f.* subdivision.
suber [sybɛr] *s.m.* **1.** cork; **2.** (bot.) suber, cork-oak.
subir [sybir] *v.t.* to undergo, to go through, to submit to, to be subjected to, to suffer, to bear, to sustain; ~ *un examen*, to undergo an examination, to take an examination.
subit, -e [sybi] *adj.* sudden; **~ement** [sybitmɑ̃] *adv.* suddenly, all of a sudden.
subito [sybito] *adv.* (fam.) all of a sudden, at once.
subjacent, -e [sybʒasɑ̃] *adj.* = SOUS-JACENT.
subjecti-f, -ve [sybʒɛktif] *adj.* subjective; (gram.) (relating to) subject; *cas ~f*, nominative case; **~vement** [sybʒɛktivmɑ̃] *adv.* subjectively.
subjectivité [sybʒɛktivite] *s.f.* subjectivity.
subjoncti-f, -ve [sybʒɔ̃ktif] *adj.*, **~f** *s.m.* subjunctive; *au ~f*, in the subjunctive.
subjuguer [sybʒyge] *v.t.* to subjugate; to subdue, to overcome, to master, to get the upper hand of, to dominate, to enslave, to break in (horse), to win over, to vanquish.
sublimation [syblimɑsjɔ̃] *s.f.* sublimation; vaporization, gasification.
sublime [syblim] *adj.* sublime, grand, noble, perfect, lofty, of the most exalted kind; ~ *s.m.* the sublime; exalted diction.
sublimé, -e [syblime] *adj.* sublimated; ~ *s.m.* (chem.) sublimate.
sublimement [syblimǝmɑ̃] *adv.* sublimely.
sublimer [syblime] *v.t.* (chem., & fig.) to sublimate, to make sublime; (chem.) to gasify.
subliminal, -e, (aux) [sybliminal] *adj.* (psychol.) subliminal, subconscious.
sublimité [syblimite] *s.f.* sublimity, sublimeness.
sublingual, -e, (aux) [syblɛ̃gwal] *adj.* (anat.) sublingual.
sublunaire [syblynɛr] *adj.* sublunary.
submerger [sybmɛrʒe] *v.t.* to submerge, to swamp, to immerse, to flood with water; (fig.) to submerge, to overwhelm; *il est submergé de travail*, he is up to his ears in work.
submers-ible [sybmɛrsibl] *adj.* submersible; *s.m.* submarine; **~ion** [sybmɛrsjɔ̃] *s.f.* submersion, immersion, flooding, drowning; sinking.
subodorer [sybɔdɔre] *v.t.* to scent at a distance, (fig.) to guess, to suspect.
subordination [sybɔrdinɑsjɔ̃] *s.f.* subordination, being subject, submission.
subordonné, -e [sybɔrdɔne] *adj.* subordinate (*à*, to); (gram.) *proposition ~e*, subordinate clause; *s.m.f.* subordinate.
subordonner [sybɔrdɔne] *v.t.* to subordinate (*à*, to).
subornation [sybɔrnɑsjɔ̃] *s.f.* subornation, bribery.
suborner [sybɔrne] *v.t.* to suborn, to tamper with, to bribe, to corrupt, to seduce.
suborneu-r, -se [sybɔrnœr] *s.m.f.* suborner, corrupter; *adj.* suborning, seductive.
subrécargue [sybrekarg] *s.m.* supercargo.
subreptice [sybrɛptis] *adj.* surreptitious, stealthy, furtive, clandestine; **~ment** [sybrɛptismɑ̃] *adv.* surreptitiously, furtively.
subreption [sybrɛpsjɔ̃] *s.f.* subreption.
subrogation [sybrɔgɑsjɔ̃] *s.f.* (law) subrogation.
subrogé, -e [sybrɔʒe] *adj.* surrogate; ~ *tuteur*, trustee, surrogate guardian; ~ *s.m.* surrogate.
subroger [sybrɔʒe] *v.t.* to substitute.

subséquemment [sypsekamɑ̃] *adv.* subsequently.
subséquent, -e [sypsekɑ̃] *adj.* subsequent.
subside [sypsid] *s.m.* subsidy.
subsidence [sypsidɑ̃s] *s.f.* subsidence.
subsidiaire [sypsidjɛr] *adj.* subsidiary, additional, accessory; **~ment** [sypsidjɛrmɑ̃] *adv.* furthermore, subsidiarily, in addition.
subsistance [sybzistɑ̃s] *s.f.* subsistence, sustenance, maintenance, feeding, keep, neccessities of life; **~s** *s.f.pl.* provisions, supplies; (mil.) supply service.
subsistant, -e [sybzistɑ̃] *adj.* subsisting, existing; remaining, (still) extant; *s.m.f.* person in receipt of public assistance; ~*s.m.* (mil.) soldier on ration strength.
subsister [sybziste] *v.i.* to subsist, to continue to exist, to be extant, to keep oneself alive; to be kept alive; to hold good.
subsonique [sypsɔnik] *adj.* (aeron.) subsonic.
substance [sypstɑ̃s] *s.f.* substance, matter, material; *en* ~, in short, in the main, substantially.
substantiel, -le [sypstɑ̃sjɛl] *adj.* substantial, essential; **~lement** [sypstɑ̃sjɛlmɑ̃] *adv.* substantially.
substanti-f, -ve [sypstɑ̃tif] *adj.* substantive; **~f** *s.m.* substantive, noun; **~vement** [sypstɑ̃tivmɑ̃] *adv.* substantively, as a noun.
substituer [sypstitɥe] *v.t.* to substitute; (law) to entail; to appoint; ~ *une chose à une autre*, to substitute one thing for another, to replace one thing by another; **se** ~ (*à*) *v.refl.* to take the place of, to put oneself in (someone's) place or situation.
substitut [sypstity] *s.m.* substitute, deputy.
substitution [sypstitysjɔ̃] *s.f.* substitution, delegation; change; (law) entail.
substrat [sypstra], **substratum** [sypstratɔm] *s.m.* substratum, foundation.
subterfuge [syptɛrfyʒ] *s.m.* subterfuge, shift; *user de* ~, to resort to subterfuge, to evade the issue.
subtil, -e [syptil] *adj.* subtle, evasive, tenuous, fine; nice, refined, rarefied; acute, discerning, keen, crafty, smart; *avoir la vue ~e*, to have keen vision; *avoir l'ouïe ~e*, to have a quick ear; *un esprit* ~, a discerning mind; *une distinction ~e*, a subtle or nice distinction; **~ement** [syptilmɑ̃] *adv.* subtly, cunningly, indefinably.
subtilisation [syptilizɑsjɔ̃] *s.f.* stealing, filching.
subtiliser [syptilize] *v.t.* to steal, to filch; ~ *v.i.* (Lit.) to be over-subtle.
subtilité [syptilite] *s.f.* subtlety, refinement, discernment, delicacy.
subtropical, -e, (aux) [syptrɔpical] *adj.* subtropical.
subulé, -e [sybyle] *adj.* (bot., zool.) subulate, awl-shaped.
suburbain, -e [sybyrbɛ̃] *adj.* suburban.
subvenir [sybvənir] *v.i.* ~ *à*, to provide for, to meet, to defray (expenses).
subvention [sybvɑ̃sjɔ̃] *s.f.* subvention, subsidy, grant of money, financial aid.
subventionner [sybvɑ̃sjɔne] *v.t.* to subsidize, to endow, to grant aid to.
subversi-f, -ve [sybvɛrsif] *adj.* subversive.
subversion [sybvɛrsjɔ̃] *s.f.* subversion; overthrow.
subversivement [sybvɛrsivmɑ̃] *adv.* subversively.
subvertir [sybvɛrtir] *v.t.* to subvert, to overthrow, to upset.
suc [syk] *s.m.* juice, extract, secretion; (fig.) essence.
succédané, -e [syksedane] *adj.* substitute; ~ *s.m.* substitute, succedaneum; (pej.) poor substitute, second best, inferior imitation.
succéder [syksede] *v.t.* ~ *à*, to succeed (to), to follow, to come after, to come into (an inheritance); **se** ~ *v.refl.* to succeed each other, to follow one another, to come one after the other, to occur in succession, (of days, etc.) to pass; ⚠ not 'to succeed' in sense 'to be successful'.
succès [syksɛ] *s.m.* success, result, issue, successful outcome; *mauvais* ~, lack of success, failure; *avoir du* ~, to be a success, to go (down) well, to be well received; ~ *fou*, tremendous success; *il a eu un* ~ *d'estime*, it was well reviewed but did not catch on; *pièce à* ~, hit; *sans* ~, without success, unsuccessfully.
successeur [syksesœr] *s.m.* successor.
successibilité [syksesibilite] *s.f.* (law) right of succession.
successible [syksesibl] *adj.* (law) entitled to succeed or inherit; giving entitlement to (share in) succession.
successi-f, -ve [syksesif] *adj.* successive, running, following one another; alternate; **~vement** [syksesivmɑ̃] *adv.* successively, alternately.
succession [syksesjɔ̃] *s.f.* succession, series; following in order; sequence; sequel; succeeding (to the throne); inheritance, estate; *recueillir une* ~, to come into an inheritance; *renoncer à une* ~, to give up one's right to a succession; *prendre la* ~ *de qn.*, to take over someone's business; *droits de* ~, estate duties, death duties.
successivement [syksesivmɑ̃] *adv.* successively, in succession, alternately.
successoral, -e, (aux) [syksesɔral] *adj.* successional.
succin [syksɛ̃] *s.m.* amber.
succinct, -e [syksɛ̃] *adj.* succinct, terse, concise, short; (fig., fam.) meagre, scanty; **~ement** [syksɛ̃ktəmɑ̃] *adv.* succinctly, concisely, briefly.
succinique [syksinik] *adj.* (chem.) succinic.
succion [syksjɔ̃] *s.f.* suction, sucking.
succomber [sykɔ̃be] *v.i.* to succumb, to be overcome, to be defeated, to yield; to give way (*à*, to), to collapse, to die, to perish.
succube [sykyb] *s.m.* succuba, succubus.
succulence [sykylɑ̃s] *s.f.* succulence.
succulent, -e [sykylɑ̃] *adj.* succulent, rich, juicy,
succursale [sykyrsal] *s.f.* branch office, shop. etc., local branch, subsidiary; *magasin à ~s multiples*, multiple or chain store.
sucement [sysmɑ̃] *s.m.* sucking.
sucer [syse] *v.t.* to suck, to suck in or up, to exhaust, to drain; (fig.) to imbibe, to suck in.
sucette [sysɛt] *s.f.* **1.** lollipop, lolly; **2.** (baby's) dummy.
suceu-r, -se [sysœr] *s.m.f.* sucker; (fig.) *~r de sang*, bloodsucker, extortioner; (pl.) (zool.) suctorians; *adj.* (zool.) suctorial; **~se** *s.f.* suction pump.
suçoir [syswar] *s.m.* sucker.
suçon [sysɔ̃] *s.m.* mark left on skin by sucking, kiss-mark.
suçoter [sysɔte] *v.t.* to keep sucking.
sucrage [sykraʒ] *s.m.* sweetening, sugaring, adding of sugar to.
sucrant, -e [sykrɑ̃] *adj.* sweetening.
sucrase [sykrɑz] *s.f.* (chem.) invert sugar.
sucrate [sykrat] *s.m.* saccharate.
sucre [sykr] *s.m.* sugar, lump of sugar; ~ *candi*, sugar-candy; ~ *de canne*, cane sugar; ~ *cristallisé*, granulated sugar; ~ *en morceaux*, lump-sugar; *~-glace*, icing-sugar; ~ *de lait, de fruit*, lactose, fructose; ~ *d'orge*, barley sugar; ~ *de pomme*, barley sugar with apple flavouring; *pain de* ~, sugar-loaf; ~ *en poudre*, powdered sugar, castor sugar; *il est tout ~ et tout miel*, he is all honey; (fig.) *casser du* ~ *sur la tête de qn.*, to slander s.o., to run s.o. down.
sucré, -e [sykre] *adj.* sugared, sweetened; (fig.)

sugary, hypocritical; *faire le* ~, to be all sweetness, to put on a sweet manner.
sucrer [sykre] *v.t.* to sugar, to sweeten; (pop.) to cancel (leave, etc.), to suppress; **se** ~ *v.refl.* (fam.) to help oneself to sugar; (fig.) to feather one's nest.
sucrerie [sykrəri] *s.f.* sugar-refinery; (pl.) sweets, confectionery.
sucri-er, -ère [sykrie] *adj.* sugar; *industrie* ~*ère*, sugar industry, sugar manufacture; *betterave* ~*ère*, sugar-beet; ~**er** *s.m.* sugar-basin or -bowl.
sucrin [sykrɛ̃] *s.m.* (bot.) sweet melon.
sud [syd] *s.m.* south; *vent du* ~, south wind; *vers le* ~, southwards, towards the south; ~ *adj.invar.* south, southern; *Pôle Sud*, South Pole; *Hémisphère* ~, Southern Hemisphere; *côté* ~, south side.
Sud [syd] *s.m.* South, Southern Hemisphere, southern part; *l'Afrique du* ~, South Africa; *le Pacifique* ~, the South Pacific; *le* ~ *de l'Europe*, Southern Europe.
sud-africain, -e [sydafrikɛ̃] *adj.*, *s.m.f.* South African.
sud-américain, -e [sydamerikɛ̃] *adj.*, *s.m.f.* South American.
sudation [sydɑsjɔ̃] *s.f.* sweating.
sudatoire [sydatwar] *adj.* sudatory.
sud-coréen, -ne [sydkɔreɛ̃] *adj.*, *s.m.f.* South Korean.
sud-est [sydɛst] *s.m.* south-east.
sudiste [sydist] *adj.* (U.S. Civil War) of the South, Southern; *s.m.f.* Southerner.
sudorifique [sydɔrifik] *adj.* sudorific.
sudoripare [sydɔripar], **sudorifère** [sydɔrifɛr] *adj.* (anat.) sudoriferous.
sud-ouest [sydwɛst] *s.m.* south-west.
suède [sɥɛd] *s.m.* suede (leather).
Suède [sɥɛd] *s.f.* (geog.) Sweden.
suédois, -e [sɥedwɑ] *adj.* Swedish; *s.m.f.* Swede.
suée [sɥe] *s.f.* (fam.) sweating, sweat, (from effort or anxiety); *prendre une* ~, to get into a sweat; *en avoir la* ~, to sweat (at the thought of sth.).
suer [sɥe] *v.t.i.* to sweat, to perspire, to be in a sweat; to sweat away, to toil; to ooze, to exude; (fig.) to reek of; ~ *à grosses gouttes*, to sweat profusely; (fam.) *vous me faites* ~, you get on my nerves; you make me sick; I am fed up with you; (fig.) ~ *sang et eau*, to sweat blood, to strain every nerve; (pop.) *en* ~ *une*, to dance.
suette [sɥɛt] *s.f.* (hist.) sweating-sickness; ~ *miliaire*, miliary fever, sweating-fever.
sueur [sɥœr] *s.f.* sweat, perspiration; *à la* ~ *de son front*, by the sweat of one's brow.
suffire [syfir] *v.i.* to be sufficient or enough; *cela suffit*, that is enough, that will do; ~ *à*, to be sufficient or enough for, to suffice for, to be equal to, to be able to meet or to cope with; *cela suffit à mes besoins*, that suffices for my needs, that is all I require; *son lopin de terre lui suffit*, he is entirely happy with his little plot of ground; ~ *à ses devoirs*, to be equal to one's duties, to be up to one's task; ~ *à ses dépenses*, to be able to meet one's expenses; *je n'y suffis plus*, I can't cope; ~ *à* or *pour* with infin., *pour que* with subjunc., to be enough or sufficient to; *cela suffit à le tuer*, that is enough to kill him; *le moindre bruit suffit pour qu'ils se précipitent*, the slightest noise is enough to make them rush off; *il suffit de*, it only requires; *il suffit que*, it is enough that; *il suffit d'un seul coup pour* ..., it only takes one blow to ...; *il suffit d'une fois*, once is enough; *il vous suffit de lui dire*, you need only tell him; *il me suffit de peu*, my needs are small; **se** ~ *v.refl.* to be self-sufficient, to be self-supporting, to fend for oneself; to be sufficient unto itself.
suffisamment [syfizamɑ̃] *adv.* sufficiently, enough, adequately.
suffisance [syfizɑ̃s] *s.f.* **1.** sufficiency; **2.** conceit, self-satisfaction, conceitedness; *en* ~, sufficiently, enough.
suffisant, -e [syfizɑ̃] *adj.* **1.** sufficient, enough, adequate, satisfactory; competent; **2.** conceited, self-satisfied, pompous.
suffixe [syfiks] *s.m.* suffix.
suffocant, -e [syfɔkɑ̃] *adj.* suffocating, stifling.
suffocation [syfɔkɑsjɔ̃] *s.f.* suffocation, choking, stifling; choking fit.
suffoquer [syfɔke] *v.t.i.* to suffocate, to choke; (fig.) to overwhelm, to oppress, to take (someone's) breath away.
suffragant [syfragɑ̃] *adj.m.*, *s.m.* (eccles.) suffragan (bishop); (Protestant) assistant (minister); ~, ~**e** *s.m.f.* one with right to vote (in assembly, etc.).
suffrage [syfraʒ] *s.m.* suffrage, vote, voting, franchise; (fig.) approbation, approval, consent.
suffragette [syfraʒɛt] *s.f.* suffragette.
suffusion [syfyzjɔ̃] *s.f.* suffusion.
suggérer [sygʒere] *v.t.* to suggest, to hint, to insinuate; to inspire; ~ *une réponse à qn.*, to suggest or supply an answer to s.o., to prompt s.o. (with an answer).
suggestibilité [sygʒɛstibilite] *s.f.* suggestibility.
suggestible [sygʒɛstibl] *adj.* suggestible, liable to suggestion.
suggesti-f, -ve [sygʒɛstif] *adj.* suggestive; evocative, thought-provoking; sexy.
suggestion [sygʒɛstjɔ̃] *s.f.* suggestion, hint, suggesting, incitement, influence, instigation.
suggestionner [sygʒɛstjɔne] *v.t.* to influence by suggestion; to suggest (an idea to); **se** ~ *v.refl.* to suggest to oneself, to get an idea into one's head.
suggestivité [sygʒɛstivite] *s.f.* suggestiveness.
suicidaire [sɥisidɛr] *adj.* suicidal, conducive to suicide; ~ *s.m.f.* one with suicidal tendencies.
suicide [sɥisid] *s.m.* suicide.
suicidé, -e [sɥiside] *adj.* who has committed suicide; *s.m.f.* (of person) suicide.
(se) suicider [sɥiside] *v.refl.* to commit suicide, to kill oneself.
suie [sɥi] *s.f.* soot, carbon.
suif [sɥif] *s.m.* tallow, animal fat, suet; (pej.) fat (on human being).
suiffer [sɥife] *v.t.* to tallow, to grease, to smear with tallow.
suint [sɥɛ̃] *s.m.* grease (of sheep's wool); (glass-making) sandiver; *laine en* ~, natural, greasy wool.
suintement [sɥɛ̃tmɑ̃] *s.m.* oozing, running, leaking, trickling, condensation.
suinter [sɥɛ̃te] *v.i.* to ooze, to leak, to run, to trickle, (of wound) to weep.
suisse [sɥis] *adj.*, *s.m.* Swiss; ~ *s.m.* beadle, verger; Swiss guard (at Vatican); (*petit-*)~, petit-suisse (cheese); *boire, manger, en* ~, to drink, to eat, alone.
Suisse [sɥis] *s.f.* (geog.) Switzerland.
suissesse [sɥisɛs] *s.f.* Swiss woman or girl (nowadays iron.; *dame, femme, suisse* preferred).
suite [sɥit] *s.f.* **1.** retinue, train, attendants, following; **2.** pursuit, following; suite, sequel, sequence, series, set; continuation; what follows; course; coherence; consequence, result; *à la* ~ *de*, after, behind, coming after, following close upon; in consequence of, as a result of; in the retinue of; in pursuit of; *à sa* ~, in pursuit of, following, coming after, him (her, it); *et ainsi de* ~, and so on; *de* ~, in succession, uninterruptedly; *tout de* ~, at once, directly, immediately; *par* ~, consequently; *par* ~ *de*, in consequence of; *attendons la* ~, let us see what happens; *cela peut avoir des* ~*s* (*fâcheuses*), that may be attended with (unpleasant) consequences; *dans la* ~, afterwards; later on; *donner* ~ *à une commande, à une décision*, to carry

out an order, to implement a decision; *faire* ~ *à*, to be a continuation of, to follow; *la* ~ *au prochain numéro*, to be continued in our next; *esprit de* ~, sense of continuity, fixity of purpose; *il a de* ~ *dans ses idées*, he is a persevering type, (iron.) there's nothing you can do with him; *sans* ~, inconsequential, incoherent, disconnected, rambling.

suivant [sɥivɑ̃] *prep.* according to, in proportion to, in conformity with; ~ *la ligne*, *l'axe*, along the line, the axis.

suivant, -e [sɥivɑ̃] *adj.* following, next, subsequent; *au* ~*!*, next one!, who's next?; ~ *s.m.* follower, attendant, partisan, disciple; ~**e** *s.f.* (theatr.) maid, attendant.

suiveur [sɥivœr] *s.m.* man who follows women in the street; official follower of race (e.g. observer, journalist); (astronaut.) tracker; follower, imitator.

suivi, -e [sɥivi] *adj.* coherent, consistent, steady, sustained, persevering; popular, sought after, well attended; *travail* ~, regular work.

suivre [sɥivr] *v.t.* to follow, to come after, to come later, to succeed, to go after, to keep up with; to attend, to accompany; to observe, to understand, to pay attention to, to conform to; to practise (a profession); ~ *une affaire*, to follow up a matter; *à* ~, to be continued; *à faire* ~, to be forwarded; *prière de faire* ~, please forward; ~ *un cours*, to attend a class; *faire* ~ *qn.*, to have s.o. followed; ~ *de près*, to follow close on the heels of; to examine closely; ~ *son chemin*, to go one's way; *il suit de là que*, it follows from this that; it follows that; *voyez ce qui suit*, see what happens next; **se** ~ *v.refl.* to follow one another, to follow in order; to come in succession; to be coherent.

sujet, -te [syʒɛ] *adj.* subject, subjected, liable, (*à*, to); addicted (to); ~ *à caution*, unreliable, not to be relied on, that cannot be guaranteed, unconfirmed.

sujet, -te [syʒɛ] *s.m.f.* subject; ~ *s.m.* subject, topic, object, matter, theme; ground, cause; (gram.) subject; *bon* ~, good fellow; *mauvais* ~, bad lot; *avoir* ~ *de se plaindre*, to have cause to complain; *assez sur ce* ~, let us say no more on that matter; ~ *de discussion*, subject of discussion; *sortir de son* ~, to wander from one's subject; *au* ~ *de*, about, concerning.

sujétion [syʒesjɔ̃] *s.f.* subjection, liability, bondage, burden.

sulfamide [sylfamid] *s.m.* sulphonamide, sulpha drug.

sulfatage [sylfataʒ] *s.m.* sulphating, acid corrosion.

sulfate [sylfat] *s.m* (chem.) sulphate.

sulfaté, -e [sylfate] *adj.* sulphated.

sulfater [sylfate] *v.t.* to sulphate, to steep in copper sulphate, to spray or dress with sulphate.

sulfateu-r, -se [sylfatœr] *s.m.f.* (agric.) one who dresses vines with copper sulphate; ~**se** *s.f.* **1.** spray or pulverizer for applying copper sulphate; **2.** (mil. slang) sub-machine-gun.

sulfite [sylfit] *s.m.* (chem.) sulphite.

sulfitage [sulfitaʒ] *s.m.* treating (wine) with sulphite.

sulfocarbonate [sylfɔkarbɔnat] *s.m.* (chem.) thiocarbonate.

sulfone [sylfɔn] *s.m.* (chem.) sulphone.

sulfoné, -e [sylfɔne] *adj.* sulphonated.

sulfuration [sylfyrɑsjɔ̃] *s.f.* sulphuration.

sulfure [sylfyr] *s.m.* (chem.) sulphide.

sulfuré, -e [sylfyre] *adj.* **1.** (chem.) sulphuretted; **2.** treated with sulphur.

sulfurer [sylfyre] *v.t.* to sulphurize, to sulphurate; to dress (vines) with sulphide.

sulfureu-x, -se [sylfyrø] *adj.* sulphureous, sulphur-; sulphurous (acid).

sulfurique [sylfyrik] *adj.* (chem.) sulphuric.

sulfurisé, -e [sylfyrize] *adj.* treated with sulphuric acid; *papier* ~, greaseproof paper.

sultan [syltɑ̃] *s.m.* sultan.

sultanat [syltana] *s.m.* sultanate.

sultane [syltan] *s.f.* sultana; (ornith.) sultana; *poule* ~, sultana hen; ⚠ not 'sultana' (dried fruit).

sumac [symak] *s.m.* (bot.) sumac, sumach.

summum [sɔmmɔm] *s.m.* acme, summit, highest point or degree.

sunnite [synit] *adj.*, *s.m.* Sunnite, Sunni, (Muslim).

super [sype] *v.t.* to suck in (esp. food or drink); (naut.) (of pump) to suck; ~ *v.i.* (naut.) to become obstructed; *navire supé*, vessel stuck in the mud.

super [sypɛr] *s.m.* (fam.) abbrev. of *supercarburant*.

superbe [sypɛrb] *adj.* superb, grand-looking, stately, splendid, proud, excellent; *s.f.* vainglory, pride, haughtiness, arrogance; ~**ment** [sypɛrbəmɑ̃] *adv.* superbly, magnificently.

supercarburant [sypɛrkarbyrɑ̃] *s.m.* premium-grade petrol.

supercarré [sypɛrkare] *adj.* (of car cylinder) over-square.

supercherie [sypɛrʃəri] *s.f.* deceit, cheat, trickery, fraud, hoax.

supère [sypɛr] *adj.* (bot.) superior, placed above.

superfétation [sypɛrfetɑsjɔ̃] *s.f.* (physiol.) superfetation; (fig.) superfluity.

superfétatoire [sypɛrfetatwar] *adj.* superfluous.

superficialité [sypɛrfisjalite] *s.f.* superficialness, superficiality.

superficie [sypɛrfisi] *s.f.* superficies, area, surface; (fig.) exterior.

superficiel, -le [sypɛrfisjɛl] *adj.* superficial, of the surface; on the surface; (fig.) skin-deep, shallow; *couche* ~*le*, surface layer; *elle est un peu* ~*le*, there is not much in her; ~**lement** [sypɛrfisjɛlmɑ̃] *adv.* superficially.

superfin, -e [sypɛrfɛ̃] *adj.* superfine, A1, of superior quality, high-grade.

superflu, -e [sypɛrfly] *adj.* superfluous, needless; redundant; ~ *s.m.* superfluity, excess, unnecessary luxuries.

superfluité [sypɛrflɥite] *s.f.* superfluity, superfluousness.

supergrand [sypɛrgrɑ̃] *adj.m.* (pol.) *les* ~*s*, the superpowers.

supérieur, -e [syperjœr] *adj.* superior, upper, higher, above; of high quality; *l'étage* ~, the floor above; *les étages* ~*s*, the upper storeys; *les classes* ~*es*, the upper classes; *se montrer* ~ *aux événements*, to rise above events; *être* ~ *à sa tâche*, to be more than equal to one's task; ~ *s.m.* superior, chief; ~**ement** [syperjœrmɑ̃] *adv.* in a superior way, superlatively.

supériorité [syperjɔrite] *s.f.* superiority, excellence, pre-eminence.

superlati-f, -ve [sypɛrlatif] *adj.* superlative; ~**f** *s.m.* (gram.) superlative; *au* ~*f*, in the superlative; ~**vement** [sypɛrlativmɑ̃] *adv.* superlatively.

supermarché [sypɛrmarʃe] *s.m.* supermarket.

supernova [sypɛrnɔva] *s.f.* (astron.) supernova.

superphosphate [sypɛrfɔsfat] *s.m.* superphosphate.

superposable [sypɛrpozabl] *adj.* superposable, superimposable.

superposer [sypɛrpoze] *v.t.* to superpose, to superimpose, to pile (up), to lay upon something; **se** ~ *v.refl.* to pile up; (fig.) to be combined, to be added together.

superposition [sypɛrpozisjɔ̃] *s.f.* superposition, piling-up; (geom.) coincidence.

supersonique [sypɛrsɔnik] *adj.* (phys., aeron.) supersonic.

superstitieu-x, -se [sypɛrstisjø] *adj.* superstitious; **~sement** [sypɛrstisjøzmɑ̃] *adv.* superstitiously.
superstition [sypɛrstisjɔ̃] *s.f.* superstition.
superstructure [sypɛrstryktyr] *s.f.* superstructure; (naut.) upper works, deck fittings.
superviser [sypɛrvize] *v.t.* to supervise, to check.
superviseur [sypɛrvizœr] *s.m.* supervisor, inspector.
supervision [sypɛrvizjɔ̃] *s.f.* supervision, checking.
supin [sypɛ̃] *s.m.* (gram.) supine.
supinateur [sypinatœr] *adj.*, *s.m.* (anat.) supinator (muscle).
supination [sypinɑsjɔ̃] *s.f.* supination.
supplanter [syplɑ̃te] *v.t.* to supplant, to supersede.
suppléance [sypleɑ̃s] *s.f.* deputyship; filling vacancy as a substitute; temporary appointment; standing-in.
suppléant, -e [sypleɑ̃] *adj.*, *s.m.f.* deputy; assistant; substitute; supply; temporary.
suppléer [syplee] *v.t.* to do duty for, to take the place of; to make up for; to supplement, to complete; to fill (post, need); *~ une lacune*, to fill a gap, a hiatus; *~ (à) un manque, un défaut*, to make up for a lack, for a defect; *~ un collègue*, to take a colleague's place, to do the work of a colleague; *~ à une vacance*, to fill a vacancy; *l'enseignement ne saurait ~ à l'inspiration*, education cannot make up for lack of inspiration; *se faire ~*, to find a substitute (for oneself).
supplément [syplemɑ̃] *s.m.* supplement, additional quantity; extra charge, extra; (geom.) supplement; *en ~*, extra, as an extra, on additional payment.
supplémentaire [syplemɑ̃tɛr] *adj.* supplementary, additional, extra; *heures ~s*, overtime; **~ment** [syplemɑ̃tɛrmɑ̃] *adv.* as an extra, additionally; besides, in addition.
supplémenter [syplemɑ̃te] *v.t.* to charge extra, to make an additional charge, to demand excess fare; *faire ~ un billet*, to pay the excess on a ticket; ⚠ not 'to supplement'.
supplléti-f, -ve [sypletif] *adj.* suppletive.
suppliant, -e [sypliɑ̃] *adj.* supplicating, beseeching, entreating, appealing, pleading, suppliant; *s.m.f.* suppliant.
supplication [syplikɑsjɔ̃] *s.f.* supplication, entreaty.
supplice [syplis] *s.m.* punishment; (lit. & fig.) torture, torment; *le dernier ~*, the extreme penalty; death; *être au ~*, to be tortured, to be racked, to be in agonies; *mettre au ~*, to torture; *c'est le ~ de Tantale*, it is tantalizing.
supplicié, -e [syplisje] *s.m.f.* executed criminal.
supplicier [syplisje] *v.t.* to torture, to torment, to execute (a criminal), to put to death.
supplier [syplie] *v.t.* to beseech, to entreat, to implore, to beg, to pray, to supplicate.
supplique [syplik] *s.f.* petition, supplication; *présenter une ~*, to make humble petition; to petition.
support [sypɔr] *s.m.* prop, stand, stay, rest, pillar, base, mount; (fig.) support, pillar, prop, foundation; (herald.) supporter; *sans ~, sans amis, sans retraite*, without help, without friends, without a refuge.
supportable [sypɔrtabl] *adj.* bearable, tolerable, endurable.
supporter [sypɔrte] *v.t.* to bear, to support, to hold up, to prop, to sustain, to uphold; (fig.) to suffer, to stand, to endure, to bear (with), to put up with, to tolerate, to find acceptable; *cela ne supporte pas l'examen*, that does not stand close examination; that's easily seen through; *cela ne saurait se ~*, that cannot be tolerated; *ils ne peuvent se ~*, they cannot bear each other; ⚠ not 'to support' a suggestion, etc.
supposable [sypozabl] *adj.* supposable, imaginable.
supposé, -e [sypoze] *adj.* **1.** pretended, counterfeit, supposititious, false, assumed; **2.** supposed, admitted, presumed, alleged; *~ qu'il le fasse*, supposing that he does it; suppose he does so.
supposer [sypoze] *v.t.* to suppose, to conjecture, to assume, to take for granted, to presume, to imagine; to imply; to substitute for what is genuine, to forge; *je lui suppose une grande intelligence*, I credit him with great intelligence.
supposition [sypozisjɔ̃] *s.f.* **1.** supposition, conjecture, hypothesis, assumption; **2.** supposititiousness, forgery, substitution.
suppositoire [sypozitwar] *s.m.* (pharm.) suppository.
suppôt [sypo] *s.m.* instrument, tool, agent, henchman; *un ~ de Satan*, a fiend, a diabolical person, a limb of Satan.
suppression [sypresjɔ̃] *s.f.* suppressing, suppression, abolition, cancellation, discontinuance, deletion.
supprimable [syprimabl] *adj.* liable to cancellation.
supprimer [syprime] *v.t.* to suppress, to inhibit, to stop, to abolish, to cut off, to omit, to delete, to cancel, to do away with; *~ une phrase*, to take out a sentence; *~ les vivres à qn.*, to deprive s.o. of food, to cut off someone's supply of food.
suppurant, -e [sypyrɑ̃] *adj.* suppurating.
suppurati-f, -ve [sypyratif] *adj.*, *s.m.* suppurative.
suppuration [sypyrɑsjɔ̃] *s.f.* suppuration.
suppurer [sypyre] *v.i.* to suppurate.
supputation [sypytɑsjɔ̃] *s.f.* calculation, computation.
supputer [sypyte] *v.t.* to calculate, to compute, to reckon; to weigh.
supraconductivité [syprakɔ̃dyktivite], **supraconductibilité** [syprakɔ̃dyktibilite], **supraconduction** [syprakɔ̃dyksjɔ̃] *s.f.* (phys.) superconductivity.
supraconducteur [syprakɔ̃dyktœr] *s.m.* (phys.) superconductor.
suprasensible [syprasɑ̃sibl] *adj.* supersensible.
suprématie [sypremasi] *s.f.* supremacy, pre-eminence.
suprême [syprɛm] *adj.* supreme, highest, last, final, crowning; *au ~ degré*, in the highest degree, eminently; *les honneurs ~s*, the last honours, funeral ceremonies; *volontés ~s*, last will (of a dying person); **~ment** [syprɛmmɑ̃] *adv.* supremely, in the highest degree, extremely.
suprême [syprɛm] *s.m.* (cook.) supreme; chicken, game or fish served in *sauce suprême*.
sur [syr] *prep.* on, upon, above, over; on to, towards; out of, in; concerning, respecting; *avoir de l'argent ~ soi*, to have money about or on one; *la clef est ~ la porte*, the key is in the door; *prendre ~ le rayon*, to take off the shelf; *vérifier ~ la carte*, to check from the map; *payer ~ les fonds*, to pay from the funds; *une fenêtre qui donne ~ un jardin*, a window which looks out on a garden; *tirer ~*, to fire on or at; (fig.) to be somewhat like, to be getting on for; *l'emporter ~*, to beat, to defeat, to triumph over; *je compte ~ vous*, I rely on you; *un ~ cent*, one out of, or in, a hundred; *je prends cela ~ moi*, I take it upon myself; *~ le fait*, in the act; red-handed; *~ le moment*, at once, at first; *~ le tard*, rather late; late at night; *~ les 3 heures*, about three o'clock; *elle allait ~ ses vingt ans*, she was about twenty; *~ lest*, in ballast; *~ mer*, by sea; *juger ~*, to go by; to judge from; *~ ce sujet*, on this matter; concerning this; *trois mètres ~ quatre*, three metres by four; *revenir ~*

ses pas, to retrace one's steps; *tourner ~ la gauche*, to turn left; *~ toute chose*, above all; *~ la fin*, towards the end; *il est ~ son départ*, he is on the point of leaving; *~ ce*, *~ quoi*, thereupon, whereupon, on this, and now; *page ~ page*, page after page; *recevoir visite ~ visite*, to have one visit after another; *coup ~ coup*, in quick succession; *~ un ton*, in a tone; *~ un air*, to a tune.

sur, -e [syr] *adj.* sour, acid.

sûr, -e [syr] *adj.* certain, sure, positive, unerring, unfailing; secure, steady, safe, reliable; *un ami ~*, a trustworthy friend; *avoir le pied ~*, to be sure-footed; *le temps n'est pas ~*, the weather is uncertain; *mettre en lieu ~*, to put in a place of safety; *avoir le goût ~*, to have good taste; *le plus ~ est de*, the safest course is to; *pour le plus ~*, to be on the safe side, to make quite certain; *être ~ de son fait*, to be sure of one's facts; to know what one is talking about; *à coup ~*, (i.) surely, certainly, assuredly; (ii.) to a certainty; with certainty; *bien ~!*, certainly!; (fam.) *pour ~!*, to be sure!; sure enough; I should think so!; *j'en suis ~ et certain*, I am positive about that; I am perfectly sure of that; *soyez ~ que*, you may be perfectly sure that.

surabondamment [syrabɔ̃damɑ̃] *adv.* superabundantly.

surabondance [syrabɔ̃dɑ̃s] *s.f.* superabundance, excess, glut.

surabondant, -e [syrabɔ̃dɑ̃] *adj.* superabundant, overabundant.

surabonder [syrabɔ̃de] *v.i.* to superabound, to overflow; to be glutted.

surah [syra] *s.m.* surah, twilled silk.

suraigu, -ë [syregy] *adj.* over-shrill, over-sharp; intense.

surajouter [syraʒute] *v.t.* to superadd, to add over and above.

suralimentation [syralimɑ̃tɑsjɔ̃] *s.f.* intensive feeding, extra nourishment; (techn.) boosting, supercharging.

suralimenter [syralimɑ̃te] *v.t.* to feed up; to give extra nourishment to; (techn.) to boost, to supercharge.

suranné, -e [syrane] *adj.* out of date, antiquated; old-fashioned; obsolete; (law) expired, superannuated.

surbaissé, -e [syrbese] *adj.* (arch.) surbased; (of car frame) dropped, underslung.

surbaisser [syrbese] *v.t.* to lower; (arch.) to surbase.

surboum [syrbum] *s.f.* (fam.) = SURPRISE-PARTIE.

surcharge [syrʃarʒ] *s.f.* **1.** overload, overloading, overcharge (of battery), added burden, excess; **2.** word written over another; **3.** overcharge, surcharge, excess charge.

surcharger [syrʃarʒe] *v.t.* **1.** to overload, to overburden, to weigh down; **2.** to write (a word) over another, to overprint.

surchauffe [syrʃof] *s.f.* overheating; superheating; (fig.) overheating (of economy).

surchauffer [syrʃofe] *v.t.* to overheat, to superheat.

surchauffeur [surʃofœr] *s.m.* (techn.) superheater.

surchoix [syrʃwɑ] *s.m.* prime quality, first choice.

surclasser [syrklɑse] *v.t.* to outclass.

surcompensation [syrkɔ̃pɑ̃sɑsjɔ̃] *s.f.* (psychol.) overcompensation.

surcomposé, -e [syrkɔ̃poze] *adj.* (gram.) double compound.

surcompression [syrkɔ̃presjɔ̃] *s.f.* (techn.) supercharging.

surcomprimer [syrkɔ̃prime] *v.t.* (techn.) to supercharge.

surcot [syrko] *s.m.* surcoat.

surcouper [syrkupe] *v.t.* (at cards) to overtrump.

surcroît [syrkrwa] *s.m.* addition, increase, surplus, overmeasure; *par ~*, in addition; into the bargain; moreover; *pour ~ de malheur*, to make matters worse, as a crowning misfortune.

surdent [syrdɑ̃] *s.f.* wolf-tooth (in horses).

surdi-mutité [syrdimytite] *s.f.* deaf-mutism.

surdité [syrdite] *s.f.* deafness.

surdorer [syrdɔre] *v.t.* to double-gild.

surdos [syrdo] *s.m.* (harness) back-strap.

sureau (pl. **-x**) [syro] *s.m.* (bot.) elder, elder-tree.

surélévation [syrelevɑsjɔ̃] *s.f.* increase, raising, heightening.

surélever [syrelve] *v.t.* to raise, to heighten, to increase.

surelle [syrɛl] *s.f.* (dial.) = OSEILLE (bot.).

sûrement [syrmɑ̃] *adv.* **1.** surely, certainly; **2.** safely, securely, reliably, unerringly.

surémission [syremisjɔ̃] *s.f.* (fin.) over-issue.

surenchère [syrɑ̃ʃɛr] *s.f.* higher bid; outbidding; (fig.) stepping-up, escalation; *faire une ~ sur*, to outbid.

surenchérir [syrɑ̃ʃerir] *v.i.* **1.** to bid higher, to increase the offer; **2.** to become even more expensive.

surenchérissement [syrɑ̃ʃerismɑ̃] *s.m.* further increase in costs or prices; *~ de la vie*, increase in cost of living.

surenchérisseu-r, -se [syrɑ̃ʃerisœr] *s.m.f.* overbidder.

surentraîner [syrɑ̃trene] *v.t.* to overtrain.

suréquiper [syrekipe] *v.t.* to over-equip.

surérogation [syrerɔgɑsjɔ̃] *s.f.* supererogation.

surérogatoire [syrerɔgatwar] *adj.* supererogatory.

surestarie [syrɛstari] *s.f.* (naut.) demurrage.

surestimation [syrɛstimɑsjɔ̃] *s.f.* overvaluation, overestimate.

surestimer [syrɛstime] *v.t.* to overvalue, to overestimate.

suret, -te [syrɛ] *adj.* sourish, acid.

sûreté [syrte] *s.f.* safety, secureness; safety device; sure touch; security, surety, guarantee, warranty, warrant; certainty; *serrure de ~*, safety lock; *mettre en ~*, to put in safe keeping; to put out of harm's way; *~ de main*, steadiness of hand; *en ~ de conscience*, with an easy conscience; *prendre ses ~s*, to take every precaution; *la Sûreté*, = the Criminal Investigation Department, Scotland Yard.

surévaluer [syrevalɥe] *v.t.* to overvalue, to overestimate.

surexcitable [syrɛksitabl] *adj.* excitable, easily excited.

surexcitation [syrɛksitɑsjɔ̃] *s.f.* excitement.

surexciter [surɛksite] *v.t.* to excite, to excite greatly, to overstimulate.

surexposer [syrɛkspoze] *v.t.* (photo.) to overexpose.

surexposition [syrɛkspozisjɔ̃] *s.f.* (photo.) overexposure.

surface [syrfas] *s.f.* surface, superficies, area; (fig.) surface, outside, appearance, outward show; *~ portante*, (aeron.) aerofoil.

surfaire [syrfɛr] *v.t.* to overrate, to overpraise; (Lit.) to overcharge, to charge too much.

surfait, -e [syrfɛ] *adj.* overrated.

surfaix [syrfɛ] *s.m.* (harness) surcingle, girth.

surfilage [syrfilaʒ] *s.m.* (needlew.) overcasting, oversewing; (techn.) extra twist (to thread).

surfiler [syrfile] *v.t.* (needlew.) to oversew, to overcast; (techn.) to give extra twist to (thread).

surfin, -e [surfɛ̃] *adj.* superfine.

surgelé, -e [syrʒəle] *adj.* *aliments ~s*, frozen food.

surgeon [syrʒɔ̃] *s.m.* sucker, shoot (of tree); ⚠ not 'surgeon'.

surgeonner [syrʒɔne] *v.i.* to shoot, to put forth suckers.
surgir [syrʒir] *v.i.* to spring up, to arise, to crop up, to surge, to appear; *faire* ~, to bring about; to give rise to, to provoke, to evoke.
surgissement [syrʒismɑ̃] *s.m.* arising, appearing.
surhaussement [syrosmɑ̃] *s.m.* raising.
surhausser [syrose] *v.t.* to raise; to force up the price of.
surhomme [syrɔm] *s.m.* superman; giant.
surhumain, -e [syrymɛ̃] *adj.* superhuman.
suricate [syrikat] *s.m.* (zool.) suricate.
surimposer [syrɛ̃poze] *v.t.* to increase the tax on; to overtax; (obs.) to superimpose.
surimposition [syrɛ̃pozisjɔ̃] *s.f.* surtax; excessive tax.
surimpression [syrɛ̃presjɔ̃] *s.f.* superimposition (of images), overprinting.
surin [syrɛ̃] *s.m.* (slang) knife, dagger.
suriner [syrine] *v.t.* (pop.) to knife.
surintendance [syrɛ̃tɑ̃dɑ̃s] *s.f.* superintendence; superintendent's office or residence.
surintendant [syrɛ̃tɑ̃dɑ̃] *s.m.* superintendent, overseer; ~**e** *s.f.* (woman) superintendent; social worker.
surir [syrir] *v.i.* to turn sour.
surjaler [syrʒale] *v.i.* (naut.) to foul an anchor.
surjet [syrʒe] *s.m.* (needlew.) overcasting, whipping, oversewing.
surjeter [syrʒəte] *v.t.* (needlew.) to overcast, to whip, to oversew.
surjeu [syrʒø] *s.m.* (TV, etc.) play-back.
sur-le-champ see CHAMP.
surlendemain [syrlɑ̃dmɛ̃] *s.m* second day after, the next day but one (*de*, after).
surlonge [syrlɔ̃ʒ] *s.f.* (butch.) chuck, chuck--steak.
surmenage [syrmənaʒ] *s.m.* overwork, mental or physical strain.
surmenant, -e [syrmənɑ̃] *adj.* strenuous, overtiring, exhausting.
surmener [syrməne] *v.t.* to overwork, to drive too hard, to wear out; **se** ~ *v.refl* to drive oneself too hard, to overwork.
sur-moi [syrmwa] *s.m.* (psychol.) super-ego.
surmontable [syrmɔ̃tabl] *adj.* surmountable.
surmonter [syrmɔ̃te] *v.t.* to surmount, to overcome, to conquer, to master, to get over; to rise above, to top; **se** ~ *v.refl.* to overcome one's weaknesses; to be surmountable.
surmouler [syrmule] *v.t.* to cast in a duplicated mould; to remould.
surmulet [syrmylɛ] *s.m.* (ichth.) surmullet; ~ *rouget*, red mullet.
surmulot [syrmylo] *s.m.* (zool.) brown rat, Norway rat.
surmultiplication [syrmyltiplikɑsjɔ̃] *s.f.* (techn.) overdrive.
surmultiplié, -e [syrmyltiplije] *adj. vitesse* ~*e*, overdrive (gear).
surnager [syrnaʒe] *v.i.* to float, or to swim on the surface; (fig.) to survive, to remain.
surnaturel, -le [syrnatyrɛl] *adj.* supernatural; preternatural, miraculous; ~ *s.m.* supernatural.
surnom [syrnɔ̃] *s.m.* cognomen, nickname, pet name; ⚠ not 'surname'.
surnombre [synɔ̃br] *s.m.* excess, surplus.
surnommer [syrnɔme] *v.t.* to name, to call, to know (s.o.) as, to nickname.
surnuméraire [syrnymerɛr] *adj.*, *s.m.f.* supernumerary.
suroît [syrwa] *s.m.* (naut.) **1.** sou'wester (wind); **2.** sou'wester (waterproof hat or garment); (obs.) sailor's jersey.
suros [syro] *s.m.* (vet.) splint (of horses).
suroxyder [syrɔkside] *v.t.* (chem.) to peroxide.
surpasser [syrpɑse] *v.t.* to be higher than, to surpass, to exceed; to excel, to outdo; **se** ~ *v.refl.* to surpass oneself, to outdo oneself.
surpaye [syrpɛj] *s.f.* extra pay, bonus.
surpayer [syrpeje] *v.t.* to overpay, to pay (s.o.) too much, to pay too much for.
surpeuplé, -e [syrpœple] *adj.* over-populated, overcrowded.
surpeuplement [syrpœpləmɑ̃] *s.m.* overpopulation.
sur-place [syrplas] *s.m. faire du* ~, to mark time; (of traffic, etc.) to crawl along.
surplis [syrpli] *s.m.* surplice.
surplomb [syrplɔ̃] *s.m.* overhang; *en* ~, overhanging; jutting out.
surplombement [syrplɔ̃bmɑ̃] *s.m.* overhanging, overhang.
surplomber [syrplɔ̃be] *v.t.i.* to overhang, to hang or project over.
surplus [syrply] *s.m.* surplus, surplus stock, excess, overplus; remainder, rest; *au* ~, moreover; furthermore; besides.
surpopulation [syrpɔpylɑsjɔ̃] *s.f.* (geog.) excess population.
surprenant, -e [syrprənɑ̃] *adj.* surprising, amazing, astonishing, remarkable, strange.
surprendre [syrprɑ̃dr] *v.t.* to surprise, to take by surprise, to catch; to amaze, to astonish; to entrap, to deceive; to intercept, to detect, to find out, to perceive, ~ *qn. chez lui*, to pay s.o. a surprise visit; ~ *la bonne foi de qn.*, to abuse someone's good faith; **se** ~ *v.refl.* to catch oneself; to find oneself; to surprise each other.
surpression [syrpresjɔ̃] *s.f.* (techn.) excess pressure; (fig.) pressure, strain.
surprime [syrprim] *s.f.* (insurance) additional premium.
surprise [syrpriz] *s.f.* surprise, amazement; *revenir de sa* ~, to recover from one's surprise; *prendre par* ~, to come upon unawares; to take (s.o. or sth.) by surprise; to startle; *ménager une* ~ *à qn.*, to prepare a surprise for s.o.; *boîte à* ~, jack-in-the-box.
surprise-partie, surprise-party [syrprizparti] *s.f.* **1.** party (usu. at short notice) where guests contribute food; **2.** teenage party (at house of one of them).
surproduction [syrprɔdyksjɔ̃] *s.f.* over-production.
surproduire [syrprɔdɥir] *v.t.* to over-produce.
surréalisme [syrrealism] *s.m.* surrealism.
surréaliste [syrrealist] *adj.*, *s.m.f.* surrealist.
surrection [syrrɛksjɔ̃] *s.f.* (geol.) upheaval, uplift.
surrégénérateur [syrreʒeneratœr] *adj.* (atomic phys.) breeder (reactor).
surrénal, -e, (**aux**) [syrrenal] *adj.* (anat.) suprarenal, adrenal.
sursaturation [syrsatyrɑsjɔ̃] *s.f.* (chem.) supersaturation.
sursaturé, -e [syrsatyre] *adj.* supersaturated; (fig.) saturated, soaked (in), surfeited (with).
sursaut [syrso] *s.m.* start, jump; access, sudden outbreak; *se réveiller en* ~, to wake with a start; *se lever, se dresser, en* ~, to jump up, to start up.
sursauter [syrsote] *v.i.* to start (up), to start aside, to spring, to jump.
surséance [syrseɑ̃s] *s.f.* delay, suspension, stay of proceedings.
sursemer [syrsəme] *v.t.* to sow over again.
surseoir [syrswar] *v.t.* to suspend, to postpone, to delay, to put off; ~ *à des poursuites*, to stay proceedings; ~ *une délibération*, to postpone a deliberation.
sursis [syrsi] *s.m.* delay (of execution), respite; suspension; reprieve; postponement; (mil.) ~ *d'appel*, deferment of call-up.
sursitaire [syrsitɛr] *adj.*, *s.m.f.* (one) who has been granted a delay, or respite, or deferment.

surtaux [syrto] *s.m.* (law) overassessment, excessive rate.
surtaxe [syrtaks] *s.f.* surtax, extra tax; exorbitant tax.
surtaxer [syrtakse] *v.t.* to put an extra tax on, to impose surtax, to overtax.
surtension [syrtɑ̃sjɔ̃] *s.f.* (electr.) over-voltage, volt rise; (*onde de*) ~, surge; (fig.) tension, strain, pressure.
surtout [syrtu] *s.m.* **1.** overcoat, overall; **2.** ~ (*de table*), épergne, centre-piece.
surtout [syrtu] *adv.* above all, especially, particularly; (fam.) ~ *que*, especially as.
surveillance (syrvɛjɑ̃s] *s.f.* superintendence, supervision, watch, vigilance, inspection; ~ *de la police*, police supervision.
surveillant, -e [syrvɛjɑ̃] *s.m.f.* overseer, superintendent, supervisor, guardian, watcher, watchman, keeper, guard, sentry; (in schools) master or mistress on duty; ~*-général*, master in charge of discipline.
surveillé, -e [syrveje] *adj.* under supervision.
surveiller [syrveje] *v.t.* to supervise, to watch, to keep an eye on, to see to, to watch over, to look after; **se** ~ *v.refl.* to keep a watch or check on oneself, to mind one's step.
survenance [syrvənɑ̃s] *s.f.* unforeseen arrival, supervening; (law) unexpected birth.
survenir [syrvənir] *v.i.* to arrive unexpectedly, to happen unexpectedly, to occur, to arise; to turn up.
survente [syrvɑ̃t] *s.f.* sale at excessive price.
survêtement [syrvɛtmɑ̃] *s.m.* track suit.
survie [syrvi] *s.f.* survival, outliving, survivorship.
survivance [syrvivɑ̃s] *s.f.* survival; reversion (of office or estate).
survivant, -e [syrvivɑ̃] *adj.* surviving; *s.m.f.* survivor.
survivre [syrvivr] *v.i.* to survive, to escape death; ~ *v.t.* (obs.) to survive (s.o.); (mod.) ~ *à*, to survive, to outlive; **se** ~ *v.refl.* to survive, to live on; to have outlived one's day; *se* ~ *à soi-même*, to have outlived one's faculties.
survoler [syrvɔle] *v.t.* to fly over; (fig.) to skim through.
survoltage [syrvɔltaʒ] *s.m.* (electr.) boost, raising of voltage.
survolté, -e [syrvɔlte] *adj.* (electr.) boosted, with increased voltage; (of lamp) overrun; (fig.) excited, highly-charged.
survolter [syrvɔlte] *v.t.* (electr.) to boost (current), to increase voltage (in a circuit).
survolteur [syrvɔltœr] *s.m.* (electr.) booster, step-up transformer.
sus [sy(s)] *prep.* upon; *courir* ~ *à l'ennemi*, to fall upon the enemy; ~*!* ~*!*, come on!, at 'em!, let 'em have it!, get cracking!; *en* ~, above; in addition; extra; to boot.
susceptibilité [sysɛptibilite] *s.f.* susceptibility, capability, liability; sensitiveness, touchiness, sore spot; *blesser la* ~ *de qn.*, to hurt someone's feelings.
susceptible [sysɛptibl] *adj.* susceptible, touchy, sensitive, easily offended, irritable; ~ *de*, capable of, liable to.
susciter [sysite] *v.t.* to raise up, to create, to provoke, to cause, to occasion, to stir up.
suscription [syskripsjɔ̃] *s.f.* superscription, address.
susdit, -e [sysdi] *adj.*, *s.m.f.* aforesaid.
susmentionné, -e [sysmɑ̃sjɔne] *adj.* above-mentioned.
susnommé, -e [sysnɔme] *adj.*, *s.m.f.* above-named.
suspect, -e [syspɛ(kt)] *adj.* suspicious, suspected, suspect; *s.m.f.* suspect, suspected person.
suspecter [syspɛkte] *v.t.* to consider suspect, to suspect, to call in question.
suspendre [syspɑ̃dr] *v.t.* to hang (up); to suspend, to interrupt, to postpone, to delay.
suspendu, -e [syspɑ̃dy] *adj.* suspended; hung (up), hanging, delayed, postponed, halted; *pont* ~, suspension bridge; *voiture non* ~*e*, carriage without springs.
suspens [syspɑ̃] *adj.invar.* suspended; ~ *s.m.* suspense; *en* ~, in suspense, suspended, held over, deferred, undecided, in a state of uncertainty.
suspense [syspɑ̃s] *s.f.* **1.** (obs.) suspension (of an ecclesiastic); **2.** suspense.
suspenseur [syspɑ̃sœr] *adj.m.* (anat.) suspensory, suspending; ~ *s.m.* (bot.) suspensor.
suspensi-f, ve [syspɑ̃sif] *adj.* suspensive, suspending; (gram.) *points* ~*fs* = *points de* SUSPENSION.
suspension [syspɑ̃sjɔ̃] *s.f.* suspension, interruption; hanging lamp; suspension, springs, springing, (of vehicle); ~ *à roues indépendantes*, independent suspension; *points de* ~, marks of omission, ellipsis.
suspensoir [syspɑ̃swar] *s.m.* suspensory bandage, sling; (naut.) sling, tricing-line.
suspente [syspɑ̃t] *s.f.* (naut.) sling (of a yard); (aeron.) suspending-cords (of balloon-gondola or parachute harness).
suspicieu-x, -se [syspisjø] *adj.* suspicious.
suspicion [syspisjɔ̃] *s.f.* suspicion; *tenir en* ~, to distrust.
sustentat-eur, -rice [systɑ̃tatœr] *adj.* lifting.
sustentation [systɑ̃tɑsjɔ̃] *s.f.* (obs.) sustaining, nourishing; (mod.) support, maintenance, equilibrium; (aeron.) lift.
sustenter [systɑ̃te] *v.t.* (obs.) to sustain, to feed; **se** ~ *v.refl.* (fam.) to feed oneself, to take nourishment.
susurrement [sysyrmɑ̃] *s.m.* susurration, whispering, whisper.
susurrer [sysyre] *v.t.i.* to murmur, to whisper.
susvisé, -e [syvize] *adj.* (admin.) above-mentioned.
sutural, -e, (aux) [sytyral] *adj.* (anat., bot., zool.) sutural.
suture [sytyr] *s.f.* (anat., bot., zool., surg.) suture.
suturer [sytyre] *v.t.* (surg.) to suture, to stitch, (wound).
suzerain, -e [syzrɛ̃] *s.m.f.* suzerain; *adj.* paramount, sovereign.
suzeraineté [syzrɛnte] *s.f.* suzerainty, lordship, sovereignty.
svastika [svastika], **swastika** [swastika] *s.m.* swastika.
svelte [svɛlt] *adj.* svelte, slender, with delicate lines, lissom, slim, lithe.
sveltesse [svɛltɛs] *s.f.* slenderness, litheness, lissomness.
S.V.P. [ɛsvepe] abbrev. *s'il vous plaît.*
swahéli [swaeli] *adj.*, *s.m.* = SOUAHÉLI.
sweater [switœr] *s.m.* sweater.
swing [swiŋ] *s.m.* (boxing, golf, mus., danc.) swing; ~ *adj.* swinging, swing.
swinguer [swiŋge] *v.i.* (mus.) to swing, to swing it, to hot it up.
sybar-ite [sibarit] *adj.*, *s.m.f.* sybarite; sybaritic (person); ~**itique** [sibaritik] *adj.* sybaritic; ~**itisme** [sibaritism] *s.m.* sybaritism, sensuality.
sycomore [sikɔmɔr] *s.m.* (bot.) sycamore; sycomore (fig).
sycophante [sikɔfɑ̃t] *s.m.* sycophant, rogue: (obs.) informer.
syénite [sjenit] *s.f.* (min.) syenite.
syllabaire [sil(l)abɛr] *s.m.* spelling-book.
syllabe [sil(l)ab] *s.f.* syllable.

syllabique [sil(l)abik] *adj.* syllabic.
syllabisme [sil(l)abism] *s.m.* syllabic writing.
syllabus [sil(l)abys] *s.m.* (Cath.) syllabus; ⚠ not school, etc. 'syllabus'.
syllepse [sil(l)ɛps] *s.f.* (rhet.) syllepsis.
sylleptique [sil(l)ɛptik] *adj.* sylleptic.
syllogisme [sil(l)ɔʒism] *s.m.* syllogism.
syllogistique [sil(l)ɔʒistik] *adj.* syllogistic.
sylphe [silf] *s.m.* sylph.
sylphide [silfid] *s.f.* sylph, sylphid.
sylvestre [silvɛstr] *adj.* sylvan, silvan, pertaining to forests, growing in forests.
sylvi-cole [silvikɔl] *adj.* of forestry; **~culteur** [silvikyltœr] *s.m.* forest owner; **~culture** [silvikyltyr] *s.f.* forestry, silviculture.
sylvinite [silvinit] *s.f.* (chem., agric.) native potassium chloride.
sym-biose [sɛ̃bjoz] *s.f.* (biol.) symbiosis; **~biote** [sɛ̃bjɔt] *s.m.* symbiont; *adj.* symbiotic; **~biotique** [sɛ̃bjɔtik] *adj.* symbiotic.
symbole [sɛ̃bɔl] *s.m.* symbol; *Symbole des apôtres*, Apostles' Creed.
symbol-ique [sɛ̃bɔlik] *adj.* symbolic, symbolical, in symbols, token; *s.f.* symbology, system of symbols; **~iquement** [sɛ̃bɔlikmɑ̃] *adv.* symbolically; **~isation** [sɛ̃bɔlizɑsjɔ̃] *s.f.* symbolization, symbolizing; (psychoanalysis) development of dream symbols; **~iser** [sɛ̃bɔlize] *v.t.* to symbolize; to present by a symbol; **~isme** [sɛ̃bɔlism] *s.m.* symbolism; **~iste** [sɛ̃bɔlist] *adj.*, *s.m f.* symbolist.
symétrie [simetri] *s.f.* symmetry.
symétrique [simetrik] *adj.* symmetrical; ~ *s.m.* symmetry (of muscular and nervous system); ~ *s.f.* (geom.) symmetrical figure; **~ment** [simetrikmɑ̃] *adv.* symmetrically.
sympath-ie [sɛ̃pati] *s.f.* sympathy, fellow-feeling, congeniality, (mutual or instinctive) attraction, affection; **~ique** [sɛ̃patik] *adj.* **1.** sympathetic; **2.** likeable, congenial, attractive, sympathetic; *s.m.* (anat.) *le (grand) ~ique*, the sympathetic nerve system; **~iquement** [sɛ̃patikmɑ̃] *adv.* sympathetically, congenially, in a friendly way.
sympathisant, -e [sɛ̃patizɑ̃] *adj.* sympathetic (*avec*, to, towards); *s.m.f.* sympathizer.
sympathiser [sɛ̃patize] *v.i.* **1.** to sympathize; to get on well (together), to have similar tastes; **2.** to identify (oneself) (*avec*, with), to have a sympathetic understanding (*avec*, of).
symphon-ie [sɛ̃fɔni] *s.f.* symphony; **~ique** [sɛ̃fɔnik] *adj.* symphonic, symphony; **~iste** [sɛ̃fɔnist] *s.m.f.* symphonist; composer of symphonies; player in symphony orchestra.
symphyse [sɛ̃fiz] *s.f.* (anat.) symphysis.
symposium [sɛ̃pozjɔm] *s.m.* symposium.
symptom-atique [sɛ̃ptɔmatik] *adj.* symptomatic; **~atiquement** [sɛ̃ptɔmatikmɑ̃] *adv.* symptomatically; **~atologie** [sɛ̃ptɔmatɔlɔʒi] *s.f.* symptomatology.
symptôme [sɛ̃ptom] *s.m.* symptom; (fig.) sign, indication.
synagogue [sinagɔg] *s.f.* synagogue.
synalèphe [sinalɛf] *s.f.* synaloepha, coalescence of two syllables in pronunciation.
synallagmatique [sinalagmatik] *adj.* (law) synallagmatic, reciprocal.
synanthéré, -e [sinɑ̃tere] *adj.* (bot.) synantherous.
synarthrose [sinartroz] *s.f.* (anat.) synarthrosis.
synchrone [sɛ̃kron] *adj.* synchronous, simultaneous, coeval.
synchronique [sɛ̃krɔnik] *adj.* synchronic.
synchronisation [sɛ̃krɔnizɑsjɔ̃] *s.f.* synchronization, synchronizing.
synchroniser [sɛ̃krɔnize] *v.t.* to synchronize.
synchroniseur [sɛ̃krɔnizœr] *s.m.* (electr.) synchronizer; (mech.) synchromesh gearbox; **~se** *s.f.* (sound-film) synchronizer.
synchronisme [sɛ̃krɔnism] *s.m.* synchronism.
synchrotron [sɛ̃krɔtrɔ̃] *s.m.* (phys.) synchrotron.
synclinal, -e, (**aux**) [sɛ̃klinal] *adj.* (geog.) synclinal; ~ *s.m.* syncline.
syncopal, -e, (**aux**) [sɛ̃kɔpal] *adj.* syncopal.
syncope [sɛ̃kɔp] *s.f.* syncope, fainting-fit; *tomber en ~*, to faint; (gram.) syncope; (mus.) syncopation.
syncopé, -e [sɛ̃kɔpe] *adj.* syncopated; (fam.) astounded.
syncoper [sɛ̃kɔpe] *v.t.* to syncopate.
syncrétisme [sɛ̃kretism] *s.m.* syncretism, ecumenism.
syndactile [sɛ̃daktil] *adj.* (zool.) syndactyl.
syndic [sɛ̃dik] *s.m.* syndic; receiver (in bankruptcy); official trustee.
syndical, -e, (**aux**) [sɛ̃dikal] *adj.* pertaining to syndicates, trade union; *chambre ~e*, trade or professional association, trade union committee.
syndicalisme [sɛ̃dikalism] *s.m.* syndicalism, trade unionism.
syndicaliste (sɛ̃dikalist] *adj.*, *s.m.f.* syndicalist, trade unionist.
syndicat [sɛ̃dikat] *s.m.* syndicate, trade union.
syndicataire [sɛ̃dikatɛr] *adj.*, *s.m.f.* (member) of a syndicate.
syndiqué, -e [sɛ̃dike] *adj.*, *s.m.f.* (trade) union (member).
syndiquer [sɛ̃dike] *v.t.* to form into a syndicate or association; **se** ~ *v.refl.* to form or join a syndicate or association.
syndrome [sɛ̃drom] *s.m.* syndrome, set of concurrent symptoms in a disease.
synecdoque [sinɛkdɔk] *s.f.* (rhet.) synecdoche.
synérèse [sinerɛz] *s.f.* **1.** (phon.) synaeresis; contraction of two syllables into one; **2.** (chem.) syneresis.
synergie [sinɛrʒi] *s.f.* (physiol.) synergy, synergism.
synesthésie [sinɛstezi] *s.f.* synaesthesia.
syngnathe [sɛ̃gnat] *s.m.* (ichth.) Syngnathus, pipe-fish.
synodal, -e, (**aux**) [sinɔdal] *adj.* synodal, of the Synod.
synode [sinɔd] *s.m.* synod.
synodique [sinɔdik] *adj.* synodic(al), synodal.
synonyme [sinɔnim] *s.m.* synonym; ~ *adj.* synonymous.
synonymie [sinɔnimi] *s.f.* synonymy, synonymity.
synonymique [sinɔnimik] *adj.* synonymic.
synopsis [sinɔpsis] *s.f.* synopsis.
synoptique [sinɔptik] *adj.* synoptic; **~s** *s.m.pl.* *Les ~s*, the Synoptic Gospels.
synovial, -e, (**aux**) [sinɔvjal] *adj.* (anat.) synovial.
synovie [sinɔvi] *s.f.* (physiol.) synovia.
synovite [sinɔvite] *s.f.* (med.) synovitis.
syntaxe [sɛ̃taks] *s.f.* syntax.
syntaxique [sɛ̃taksik], **syntactique** [sɛ̃taktik] *adj.* syntactic, syntactical.
synthèse [sɛ̃tɛz] *s.f.* synthesis.
synthétique [sɛ̃tetik] *adj.* synthetic(al); **~ment** [sɛ̃tetikmɑ̃] *adv.* synthetically, by synthesis.
synthétiser [sɛ̃tetize] *v.t.* to synthesize, to synthetize.
syphilis [sifilis] *s.f.* (pathol.) syphilis.
syphilitique [sifilitik] *adj.*, *s.m.f.* syphilitic.
syriaque [sirjak] *adj.*, *s.m.* Syriac (language).
Syrie [siri] *s.f.* (geog.) Syria.
syrien, -ne [sirjɛ̃] *adj.*, *s.m.f.* Syrian.
syringa [sirɛ̃ga] *s.m.* (bot.) Syringa (=lilac).
syringe [sirɛ̃ʒ] *s.f.* syrinx.
syrte [sirt] *s.f.* (ant.) Syrtis; (anc. geog.) *les Syrtes*, the Syrtes; (obs.) *des syrtes*, quicksands.

systématique [sistematik] *adj.* systematic, methodical, deliberate, persistent; (pej.) hide-bound, doctrinaire; ~ *s.f.* systematic classification, taxonomy; **~ment** [sistematikmɑ̃] *adv.* systematically.

systématiser [sistematize] *v.t.* to systematize.

système [sistɛm] *s.m.* system, method, device, contraption; *par* ~, systematically, in a stereotyped way, in accordance with preconceived ideas; *esprit de* ~, tendency to classify or organize, tidy mind; (pej.) pig-headedness; (pop.) *le* ~ *D* (=*débrouille-toi*), resourcefulness, wangling, looking after No. 1, 'I'm all right, Jack'; *courir, porter, taper, sur le* ~ *à qn.*, to get on someone's nerves, to be getting s.o. down.

systole [sistɔl] *s.f.* (physiol.) systole.

systolique [sistɔlik], **systaltique** [sistaltik] *adj.* (physiol.) systolic, systaltic.

systyle [sistil] *adj.*, *s.m.* (arch.) systyle.

syzygie [siziʒi] *s.f.* (astron.) syzygy.

T

T, t [te] *s.m.* the letter T, t; often used for euphony as in: *a-t-il, aime-t-elle, ne voilà-t-il pas*; abbrev. *tonne*; *T*, T-shaped; *bandage en T*, T--bandage.

t' see TE.

ta see TON *poss. adj.*

tabac [taba] *s.m.* **1.** tobacco, snuff; tobacconist's (shop); ~ *à chiquer*, chewing-tobacco; ~ *en carotte*, twist; ~ *en poudre, à priser*, snuff; *bureau* or *débit de* ~, tobacconist's shop; *marchand de* ~, tobacconist; *blague à* ~, tobacco-pouch; (fam.) *c'est toujours le même* ~, it's always the same, it goes on and on; **2.** (obs.) fight, hail of blows, beating; (obs., fam.) *donner du* ~ *à qn.*, to beat s.o.; (mod., fam.) *passage à* ~, beating-up; *passer qn. à* ~, to beat s.o. up; *coup de* ~, storm, bad weather; (theatr. slang) *avoir le gros* ~, to be a big hit, to hit the jackpot.

tabagie [tabaʒi] *s.f.* **1.** smoking-room, smoking--den; **2.** (fam.) place reeking of tobacco-smoke.

tabard [tabar] *s.m.* tabard.

tabarin [tabarɛ̃] *s.m.* buffoon, clown.

tabasser [tabase] *v.t.* (pop.) to beat, to beat up.

tabatière [tabatjɛr] *s.f.* snuff-box; skylight; *fenêtre, châssis, à* ~, hinged skylight.

tabellaire [tabelɛr] *adj.* tabular.

tabellion [tabeljɔ̃] *s.m.* (obs.) scrivener; (fam., pej.) lawyer.

tabernacle [tabɛrnakl] *s.m* tabernacle.

tabès [tabɛs] *s.m.* (pathol.) tabes.

tabis [tabi] *s.m.* (text.) tabby, watered silk.

tablature [tablatyr] *s.f.* (mus.) tablature, fingering chart; tabulation; *donner de la* ~ *à qn.*, to put s.o. in a difficult position.

table [tabl] *s.f.* table, board, slab, level or plane surface, bed, face; (telephone) switch-board; ~ *alphabétique*, alphabetical list, index; ~ *d'hôte*, table d'hôte, set menu; ~ *à ouvrage*, work-table; ~ *à rallonges*, extending table; ~ *de dix couverts*, table laid for ten; ~ *ronde*, round table, round-table conference; ~ *d'harmonie*, sound-board; ~ *de jeu*, card-table, gaming--table; ~ *des matières*, table of contents; ~ *de nuit*, bedside table; *la sainte* ~, communion--table, Holy Communion; ~*s tournantes*, table-turning; ~ *volante*, occasional table; ~ *roulante*, (tea-)trolley; ~*s-gigogne*, nest of tables; *aimer la* ~, to be fond of good living, of one's food; *avoir une* ~ *frugale*, to live frugally; *la* ~ *et le logement*, board and lodging; *bénir la* ~, to say grace before meat; *mettre* or *dresser la* ~, to lay the table; *faire* ~ *rase*, to make a clean sweep; *jouer cartes sur* ~, to put one's cards on the table, to be frank; *se lever* or *sortir de* ~, *quitter la* ~, to get up from dinner, etc., to rise from table; *se mettre à* ~, to sit down to table; (pop.) *se mettre à* ~, to give the game away, to inform (on one's accomplices); *tenir* ~ *ouverte*, to keep open house; *propos de* ~, table-talk; *haut bout de la* ~, head of the table; ~ *d'écoute*, telephone-tapping apparatus; *diamant taillé en* ~, table-cut diamond; ~ *de lancement*, launching-pad.

tableau (pl. **-x**) [tablo] *s.m.* picture, painting, scene, scenery, view; list, catalogue, table, roll, schedule, board; (law) rolls, panel; (rail.) ~ *indicateur*, indicator; ~ *de chasse*, bag, list of victories or conquests; score; (electr.) ~ *de distribution*, switchboard, fuse-board; ~ *noir*, black-board; (law) *rayé du* ~, struck off the rolls; (fam.) *vous voyez d'ici le* ~, you can just imagine what it was like; *pour achever le* ~, to complete the picture, as the last straw; ~ *de bord*, dash-board, instrument panel; ~ *d'honneur*, roll of honour; ~ *vivant*, tableau; *une ombre au* ~, a dark side to the picture.

tableautin [tablotɛ̃] *s.m.* small picture, miniature, vignette.

tablée [table] *s.f.* table, company at table.

tabler [table] *v.i.* **1.** (obs.) (at backgammon) to set the board; **2.** ~ *sur*, to count on, to rely on, to base (estimate, etc.) on.

tableti-er, -ère [tablətje] *s.m.f.* maker of inlaid chess-boards, etc., worker in marquetry, ivory, bone, etc.

tablette [tablɛt] *s.f.* shelf, flap (of writing-desk); sill, coping-stone; tablet, cake, bar, block, (of soap, chocolate, etc.); lozenge; (soup-, etc.) cube; (ant.) tablet(s); notebook; ~ *de cheminée*, mantelpiece; *rayez cela de vos* ~*s*, get that out of your head.

tabletterie [tablɛtri] *s.f.* marquetry, inlaid work, work in ivory, mother-of-pearl, etc.

tablier [tablie] *s.m.* **1.** apron (garment); *rendre son* ~, to give notice; **2.** flooring, decking, roadway, (of a bridge); **3.** chess- or draught--board; **4.** shutter; top of roll-top desk; register (in fireplace); (car) ~ *de bord*, dashboard.

tabou [tabu] *s.m.*, *adj. invar.* taboo.

tabouret [taburɛ] *s.m.* stool, footstool; (bot.) shepherd's purse; ~ *de piano*, music-stool.

tabulaire [tabylɛr] *adj.* tabular, tabulated, in tabular form.

tabulateur [tabylatœr] *s.m.* tabulator (on typewriter).

tabulatrice [tabylatris] *s.f.* tabulator (for punched cards).

tac [tak] *s.m.* (onom.) tick, tap, tapping, click (esp. of foils in fenc.); (fenc.) *riposter du* ~ *au* ~, to parry with the riposte; (fig.) *répondre* or *riposter du* ~ *au* ~, to give as good as one gets.

tachant, -e [taʃɑ̃] *adj.* (of materials) easily marked or dirtied.

tache [taʃ] *s.f.* spot, stain, flaw, (fig.) blot, blemish, stigma; *sans* ~, blameless, pure, spot-less, undefiled, unblemished; ~ *solaire*, sunspot; ~ *de naissance*, birthmark, mole; ~ *de rousseur* or *de son*, freckle; ~ *de vin*, (i.) winestain; (ii.) birth-

mark; strawberry mark; *faire* ~, to strike a discordant note, to be a misfit.
tâche [tɑʃ] *s.f.* task, job, duty; *à la* ~, by the job, by the piece; on piece-work, on piece-rates; *ouvrage à la* ~, jobbing, piece-work; *ouvrier à la* ~, jobbing workman, worker on piece-rates; (fig.) *prendre à* ~ *de faire une chose*, to make it one's business to do a thing, to make a point of doing a thing.
tachéo-graphe [takeɔgraf] *s.m.* (surv.) tacheometer; ~**mètre** [takeɔmɛtr] *s.m.* (surv.) tacheometer, tachymeter; ~**métrie** [takeɔmetri] *s.f.* tacheometry, tachymetry.
tacher [taʃe] *v.t.* to stain, to spot, to dirty, to slur, to sully, to tarnish, to blemish; **se** ~, *v.refl.* to make a mess on one's clothes, to mess oneself up; to become dirty, stained, spotted; to stain, to spot.
tâcher [tɑʃe] *v.i.* to try, to endeavour, to strive; to seek, to do one's best, to make an effort, (*de*, to).
tâcheron [tɑʃrɔ̃] *s.m.* jobbing workman, piece--worker; subcontractor; (fig., pej.) drudge.
tacheter [taʃte] *v.t.* to mark with spots, to fleck, to speckle.
tachygraphe [takigraf] *s.m.* tachograph.
tachymètre [takimɛtr] *s.m.* tachometer, revolution-counter, speedometer; ⚠ not 'tacheometer', 'tachymeter'.
tacite [tasit] *adj.* tacit, implied, implicit, understood; ~**ment** [tasitmɑ̃] *adv.* tacitly, implicitly.
taciturne [tasityrn] *adj.* taciturn; silent, uncommunicative; *Guillaume le* ~, William the Silent.
taciturnité [tasityrnite] *s.f.* taciturnity.
tacot [tako] *s.m.* (fam.) (of car) old crock, banger.
tact [takt] *s.m.* **1.** (obs.) touch, contact; (mod.) sense of touch; **2.** (obs.) perception; (mod.) tact, intuition.
tacticien [taktisjɛ̃] *s.m.* tactician.
tactile [taktil] *adj.* tactile; tactual.
tactique [taktik] *s.f.* tactics (pl.); (fig.) plan of action; ~ *adj.* tactical.
tadorne [tadɔrn] *s.m.* (ornith.) sheldrake, shelduck.
taenia [tenja] *s.m.* = TÉNIA.
taffetas [tafta] *s.m.* taffeta; (pharm.) ~ *anglais* or *gommé*, court plaster, sticking-plaster.
tafia [tafja] *s.m.* tafia (rum).
Tage [taʒ] *s.m.* (geog.) Tagus (river).
tagète, tagette [taʒɛt] *s.m.* (bot.) tagetes.
taïaut, tayaut [tajo] *s.m.* (hunt.) tally-ho.
taie [tɛ] *s.f.* **1.** ~ *d'oreiller*, pillow-case; **2.** (med.) leucoma, speck (on the eye); (fig.) *avoir une* ~ *sur l'œil*, to be prejudiced, to wear blinkers.
taïga [tajga] *s.f.* taiga (forest-land).
taillable [tɑjabl] *adj.* (feud. law) taxable; subject to tallage, talliable; *être* ~ *et corvéable*, (of serfs) to be obliged to work at their lord's pleasure; (fig.) to come in for all the hard work, to be the one who has to pay.
taillade [tɑjad] *s.f.* cut, gash, slash, incision; (dressm.) slit.
taillader [tɑjade] *v.t.* to slash, to cut, to gash; *jupe tailladée*, slit or slashed skirt.
taillage [tɑjaʒ] *s.m.* dressing, trimming, slicing; milling (of gear-wheels).
taillanderie [tɑjɑ̃dri] *s.f.* edge-tool trade, edge tools.
taillandier [tɑjɑ̃dje] *s.m.* edge-tool maker.
taillant [tɑjɑ̃] *s.m.* edge (of a knife, etc.).
taille [tɑj] *s.f.* cutting, cut, clipping, trimming, pointing, sharpening; incision; engraving; fashion; edge (of a sword); height, stature, size, shape, figure; waist; tally(-stick); copsewood; coppice; (hort.) pruning, dressing of vines; (surg.) cystotomy; (mus.) tenor part; (feud. law) tallage; deal (at cards); *quelle est sa* ~*?*, how tall is he, what size does he take?; *par rang de* ~, in order of height or size; (*tour de*) ~, waist measurement; *avoir la* ~ *fine*, to have a small waist; *prendre bien la* ~, to fit very well; *n'avoir point de* ~, to be shapeless, to have no figure; *avoir la* ~ *bien prise*, to be well-proportioned, to have a good figure; *être de* ~ *à*, to be big enough to; to be fully able to, to be up to; *être de* ~ *à lutter contre*, to be a match for; *à* or *de la* ~ *de*, equal to, corresponding to; *une tâche à sa* ~, a task worthy of him; *une erreur de* ~, an error of sizeable proportions; *frapper d'estoc et de* ~, to cut and thrust, to hit right and left, to lay about one; *se tenant par la* ~, with their arms round each other's waists; *sortir en* ~, to go out without a coat; *faire des coches sur une* ~, to make notches in a tally; *pierre de* ~, freestone; *outils de* ~, stone-cutter's tools.
taillé, -e [tɑje] *adj.* cut, trimmed, pruned; built, proportioned, shaped; *être* ~ *pour*, to be cut out for, to be fit for; *cote mal* ~*e*, rough compromise.
taille-buissons [tɑjbɥisɔ̃] *s.m.invar.* hedge--shears; ~**-crayon,** ~**-crayons** [tɑjkrɛjɔ̃] *s.m.invar.* pencil-sharpener; ~**-douce** [tɑjdus] *s.f.* copper-plate engraving; ~**-légumes** [tɑjlegym] *s.m.invar.* (cook.) vegetable cutter; ~**-mer** [tɑjmɛr] *s.m.* (naut.) cutwater.
tailler [tɑje] *v.t.* to hew, to trim, to prune, (hort.) to dress; to cut, to make an incision in, to cut out, (surg.) to operate on for stone; to carve, to sharpen; to frame, to shape; to deal (cards); ~ *une robe*, to cut out a dress; ~ *sur un patron*, to cut on or from a pattern; ~ *des torchons dans un drap usagé*, to cut up an old sheet for cleaning rags; (fam.) ~ *une bavette*, to chat, to gossip; to have a chat; ~ *de la besogne à qn.*, to cause s.o. a great deal of trouble; ~ *en plein drap*, to have ample means, to have enough and to spare, to spare no expense; *se* ~ *qch.*, to carve sth. out for oneself, to acquire sth.; **se** ~ *v.refl.* (pop.) to go away, to vanish.
taille-racines [tɑjrasin] *s.m.invar.* = TAILLE--LÉGUMES.
taillerie [tɑjri] *s.f.* gem-cutting; gem-cutter's workshop.
tailleur [tɑjœr] *s.m.* tailor, cutter; dealer (at cards); *en* ~, cross-legged; ~ *à façon*, jobbing tailor; ~ *de pierres*, stone-cutter; (jest) sculptor; ~ *de vignes*, vine-dresser; (*costume*) ~, coat and skirt, two-piece.
tailleuse [tɑjøz] *s.f.* tailoress, dressmaker.
taillis [taji] *s.m.* copse, coppice, copsewood, undergrowth, brushwood.
tailloir [tɑjwar] *s.m.* trencher, platter; (arch.) abacus.
tain [tɛ̃] *s.m.* **1.** silvering (of mirror); **2.** tinning--bath.
taire [tɛr] *v.t.* to say nothing about, to be silent about, not to mention, to keep to oneself, to suppress, to conceal, to pass over in silence, to overlook, to leave unsaid; *faire* ~, to silence, to hush, to reduce to silence; **se** ~ *v.refl.* to be silent, to hold one's tongue; to fall silent, to be hushed; *taisez-vous*, hold your tongue!, be quiet; (fam.) shut up; *qui plus sait, plus se tait*, a still tongue shows a wise head; *mieux vaut se* ~ *que mal parler*, least said, soonest mended; *qui se tait consent*, silence gives consent.
talc [talk] *s.m.* talc, talcum.
talé, -e [tale] *adj.* (of fruit) bruised.
talent [talɑ̃] *s.m.* **1.** talent, skill, ability, faculty, gift, attainments, parts; ~*s de société*, polite accomplishments; **2.** (ant.) talent (weight, money).
talentueu-x, -se [talɑ̃tɥø] *adj.* talented; ~**sement** [talɑ̃tɥøzmɑ̃] *adv.* in a talented fashion.

taler [tale] *v.t.* to trample, to bruise (esp. fruit); (fig.) to bother, to harass.
talion [taljɔ̃] *s.m.* talion, retaliation; *loi du ~*, law of retaliation, lex talionis, an eye for an eye, a tooth for a tooth.
talisman [talismɑ̃] *s.m.* talisman, charm, amulet.
talismanique [talismanik] *adj.* talismanic.
talle [tal] *s.f.* (bot., hort.) sucker.
taller [tale] *v.i.* (hort.) to throw out suckers.
tallipot [talipo] *s.m.* (bot.) talipot, fan palm.
talmouse [talmuz] *s.f.* **1.** (cook.) cheese-cake; **2.** (fam.) slap, punch on the nose.
talmud [talmyd] *s.m.* Talmud.
taloche[1] [talɔʃ] *s.f.* cuff, thump, punch, clout on the head.
taloche[2] [talɔʃ] *s.f.* mason's mortar-board or hawk.
talocher [talɔʃe] *v.t.* to cuff, to thump.
talon [talɔ̃] *s.m.* heel; heel-piece; butt-end, fag-end, remnant, left-over; bead; flange (of tyre); (at cards) talon (cards left after deal); (fin., comm.) counterfoil; *marcher sur les ~s de qn.*, to follow close behind s.o.; *être toujours sur les ~s de qn.*, to dog someone's footsteps, to be always close on someone's heels; *jouer des ~s, montrer les ~s*, to show a clean pair of heels, to take to one's heels; *tourner les ~s*, to make off, to run away; *se sentir* or *avoir l'estomac dans les ~s*, to be famished; *un ~-rouge*, an aristocrat, a courtier, a dandy; *~ de chèque*, counterfoil, stub; ⚠ not 'talon'.
talonnage [talɔnaʒ] *s.m.* **1.** (naut.) grounding, touching bottom; **2.** (Rugby football) heeling.
talonner [talɔne] *v.t.* to be close on the heels of, to press hard, to urge, to dun; to bother, to pursue, to harry; to spur; (Rugby football) to heel, to pass back; *~ v.i.* (naut.) to touch bottom.
talonnette [talɔnɛt] *s.f.* heel-piece (of a stocking or shoe); insole; binding (inside trouser bottom).
talonneur [talɔnœr] *s.m.* (Rugby football) hooker.
talonnière [talɔnjɛr] *s.f.* (myth.) talaria (pl.); (art) heel-support (for live model).
talpack [talpak] *s.m.* (mil., obs.) busby.
talquer [talke] *v.t.* to powder with talc.
talqueu-x, -se [talkœ] *adj.* talcose.
talure [talyr] *s.f.* bruising (of fruit).
talus [taly] *s.m.* slope, bank, declivity, embankment; (fort.) talus; (geol.) talus, scree; *en ~*, shelving; ⚠ not anat. 'talus'.
tamandua [tamandɥa] *s.m.* (zool.) tamandua, ant-eater.
tamanoir [tamanwar] *s.m.* (zool.) tamanoir, ant-bear.
tamarin[1] [tamarɛ̃] *s.m.* (bot.) tamarind(-tree).
tamarin[2] [tamarɛ̃] *s.m.* (zool.) tamarin, marmoset.
tamarinier [tamarinje] *s.m.* (bot.) tamarind (-tree).
tamaris [tamari] *s.m.* (bot.) tamarisk.
tambouille [tɑ̃buj] *s.f.* (fam.) badly-prepared food, cheap stew; (pop.) cooking.
tambour [tɑ̃bur] *s.m.* drum, drummer; (anat.) tympanum; (mech.) cylinder, barrel, paddle--box; (arch.) tambour, drum, lobby; (embroidery) tambour, frame; *baguette de ~*, drumstick; *peau de ~*, drumhead; *~ de basque*, tambourine; *~-major*, drum major; *~ voilé*, muffled drum; *~ de ville*, town crier; *~ battant*, with drums beating, (fig.) ostentatiously, in a loud and vulgar fashion; *sans ~ ni trompette*, quietly; (fam.) on the q.t.; *partir sans ~ ni trompette*, to slip away, to flit; *ce qui vient de la flûte s'en va par le ~*, easy come, easy go.
tambourin [tɑ̃burɛ̃] *s.m.* tambourine.
tambourinage [tɑ̃burinaʒ], **tambourinement** [tɑ̃burinmɑ̃] *s.m.* drumming, tattooing; (mech.) hammering, knocking; (fig.) advertising, puffing.
tambourinaire [tɑ̃burinɛr] *s.m.* **1.** tambourine--player; (in Africa) drummer; **2.** town crier.
tambouriner [tɑ̃burine] *v.i.* to drum, to beat, to tattoo; *~ v.t.* to drum, to proclaim by beat of drum, to cry, to advertise.
tamier [tamje] *s.m.* (bot.) black bryony.
tamil see TAMOUL.
tamis [tami] *s.m.* sieve, sifter, strainer, filter, screen, riddle; *~ de crin*, hair sieve; *passer au ~*, to sift, to sieve, to sort (out); (fig.) to sift, to examine thoroughly.
tamisage [tamisaʒ] *s.m.* sifting, straining, sieving, filtering, screening.
Tamise [tamiz] *s.f.* (geog.) Thames (river).
tamiser [tamize] *v.t.* to sift, to sieve, to strain; to filter; to soften (light).
tamiserie [tamizri] *s.f.* sieve-making, sieve factory.
tamiseu-r, -se [tamizœr] *s.m.f.* sifter; **~r** *s.m.* cinder-riddle; **~se** *s.f.* sifting-machine.
tamisi-er, -ère [tamizje] *s.m.f.* sieve-maker; dealer in sieves.
tamoul [tamul], **tamil** [tamil] *adj., s.m.* Tamil.
tampon [tɑ̃pɔ̃] *s.m.* stopper, plug, bung, man-hole-cover, tampion (of gun); (surg.) tampon, plug; (rail., naut.) buffer; pad, rubber stamp; (mil. slang) officer's servant, batman.
tamponnement [tɑ̃pɔnmɑ̃] *s.m.* **1.** collision, clash (of buffers); **2.** tamponade, tamponage (of wound, etc.).
tamponner [tɑ̃pɔne] *v.t.* **1.** to plug, to stop up, to tampon; to stamp; **2.** to dab; **3.** to collide, to run into; **se ~** *v.refl.* to collide.
tamponneu-r, -se [tɑ̃pɔnœr] *adj.* in collision, colliding; (fam.) *autos ~ses*, bumper-cars, dodgems.
tamponnier [tɑ̃pɔnje], **tamponnoir** [tɑ̃pɔnwar] *s.m.* plugging-tool, wall-bit.
tam-tam [tam-tam] *s.m.* tom-tom; gong; *faire du ~*, to advertise, to puff, to make a fuss, to create a sensation.
tan [tɑ̃] *s.m.* tan, tan-bark; *fosse à ~*, tan-pit.
tanaisie [tanɛzi] *s.f.* (bot.) tansy.
tancer [tɑ̃se] *v.t.* to scold, to reprimand.
tanche [tɑ̃ʃ] *s.f.* (ichth.) tench.
tandem [tɑ̃dɛm] *s.m.* tandem, tandem bicycle; (fig., fam.) inseparable pair (of people).
tandis que [tɑ̃dikə] *conj.loc.* whilst, whereas, while.
tangage [tɑ̃gaʒ] *s.m.* (naut.) pitching.
tangence [tɑ̃ʒɑ̃s] *s.f.* (geom.) tangency; *point de ~*, tangential point.
tangent, -e [tɑ̃ʒɑ̃] *adj.* (geom.) tangent, tangential.
tangente [tɑ̃ʒɑ̃t] *s.f.* (geom.) tangent; (fig.) *s'échapper par la ~*, to go off at a tangent.
tangentiel, -le [tɑ̃ʒɑ̃sjɛl] *adj.* (geom.) tangential; **~lement** [tɑ̃ʒɑ̃sjɛlmɑ̃] *adv.* tangentially.
Tanger [tɑ̃ʒe] *s.m.* (geog.) Tangier.
tangibilité [tɑ̃ʒibilite] *s.f.* tangibility, tangibleness.
tangible [tɑ̃ʒibl] *adj.* tangible; palpable; corporeal; **~ment** [tɑ̃ʒibləmɑ̃] *adv.* tangibly.
tango [tɑ̃go] *s.m.* tango (dance, mus.); bright orange (colour).
tangon [tɑ̃gɔ̃] *s.m.* (naut.) (swinging) boom.
tangue [tɑ̃g] *s.f.* sea-sand, calcareous sand, (from Channel beaches, used as manure).
tanguer [tɑ̃ge] *v.i.* to pitch, to roll, to sway.
tanière [tanjɛr] *s.f.* den, lair, hole.
tanin, tannin [tanɛ̃] *s.m.* tannin.
taniser, tanniser [tanize] *v.t.* to add tan-bark or tannin to.
tank [tɑ̃k] *s.m.* **1.** tank; water-container, jerrican; **2.** (obs., mil.) tank.

tanker [tɑ̃kɛr] *s.m.* (naut.) tanker.
tankiste [tɑ̃kist] *s.m.* (mil.) member of tank crew.
tannage [tanaʒ] *s.m.* tanning.
tannant, -e [tanɑ̃] *adj.* tanning; (fig., fam.) wearisome, tiresome, provoking, boring.
tanne [tan] *s.f.* pimple, blackhead; spot (on tanned leather).
tanné, -e [tane] *adj.* tanned, tawny, tan (-coloured); sunburnt.
tannée [tane] *s.f.* spent bark, waste tan; (pop.) thrashing.
tanner [tane] *v.t.* to tan; (fig.) to annoy, to pester; ~ *le cuir à qn.*, to give s.o. a hiding.
tannerie [tanri] *s.f.* tanyard, tannery; tanning.
tanneur [tanœr] *s.m.* tanner.
tannin see TANIN.
tannique [tanik] *adj.* (chem.) tannic.
tanniser see TANISER.
tan-sad [tɑ̃sad] *s.m.* pillion (on motor cycle).
tant [tɑ̃] *adv.* so much, so many, such, so, as much; ~ *et* ~, so very much; ~ *et plus*, more than enough, any amount of, over and over again; *faire* ~ *que*, to ensure that, to bring it about that; *faire* ~ (*et si bien*) *que*, to work to such good purpose that; *faire* ~ *que de*, to go as far as to, to decide to; ~ *pour cent*, percentage; ~ *bons que mauvais*, good as well as bad; ~ *mieux*, all the better; that's right; I'm glad of it; ~ *pis*, it's a pity; I'm sorry about it; it can't be helped; never mind; (obs.) ~ *plus*, the more, so much the more; ~ *soit peu*, very little, just a bit, however little; ~ *s'en faut*, far from it; ~ *bien que mal*, as well as one can; middling, so-so, anyhow; after a fashion; ~ *il est stupide*, such is his stupidity, so stupid is he; ~ *il est vrai que*, so true it is that, so much so that, to such an extent is this so, that; *vous tous*, ~ *que vous êtes*, every one of you, the whole lot of you; ~ *que*, as far as, as long as; so far as, so long as; ~ *qu'à*, as for, as far as . . . is concerned; *pour* ~ *faire*, if it comes to that; *à* ~ *faire qu'acheter une maison*, if it comes to buying a house; *en* ~ *que*, in so far as; as; considered as; *si* ~ *est que*, if, supposing it to be that; ~ *s'en faut que*, so far from, far from; ~ *il y a que*, however, at all events; (fam.) *vous m'en direz* ~, you don't have to tell me, you can say that again, you're telling me!
tantale[1] [tɑ̃tal] *s.m.* (chem.) tantalum.
tantale[2] [tɑ̃tal] *s.m.* (ornith.) tantalus, wood ibis.
Tantale [tɑ̃tal] *s.m.* (myth.) Tantalus.
tante [tɑ̃t] *s.f.* **1.** aunt; ~ *à la mode de Bretagne*, father's or mother's first cousin; (fam.) *chez ma* ~, at the pawnshop; **2.** (pop.) pederast.
tantième [tɑ̃tjɛm] *adj.* such and such a, given, required, (fraction, part, etc.); *le* ~ *jour, le* ~ *courant*, the day of the month; ~ *s.m.* percentage, share, quota.
tantinet [tɑ̃tinɛ] *s.m. un* ~, a little, a little bit, a scrap or drop (of); **un** ~ *adv.loc.* somewhat, rather, just a little.
tantôt [tɑ̃to] *adv.* presently, by and by, shortly, soon; a little while ago, just now, nearly (two days, etc., ago), this afternoon; today; sometimes; ~ *plus* ~ *moins*, sometimes more, sometimes less; ~ *l'un*, ~ *l'autre*, first one, then the other; alternately; ~ *ceci* ~ *cela*, now this, now that; *à* ~, see you later (in the same day); *sur le* ~, late in the day, towards evening.
Tanzanie [tɑ̃zani] *s.f.* (geog.) Tanzania.
taoïsme [taɔism], **taôisme** [taoism] *s.m.* Taoism.
taon [tɑ̃] *s.m.* (ent.) gadfly, horse-fly.
tapage [tapaʒ] *s.m.* noise, fuss, racket, row; controversy; clash (of colours); *faire du* ~, to make an uproar, (fam.) to kick up a row; *voilà bien du* ~ *pour rien!*, what a fuss about nothing!; (fig.) *faire du* ~, to create a stir.
tapageu-r, -se [tapaʒœr] *s.m.f.* noisy person, rowdy, brawler; *adj.* noisy, riotous, loud; glaring, gaudy, showy, flashy; **~sement** [tapaʒøzmɑ̃] *adv.* noisily, rowdily.
tapant, -e [tapɑ̃] *adj.* on the stroke of; *neuf heures* ~(*es*), on the stroke of nine; *à l'heure* ~*e*, at the stroke of the hour, (fam.) on the dot, on the tick.
tape [tap] *s.f.* tap, pat, rap, slap; plug, stopper, bung; (nav.) tompion, tampion; (naut.) ~ *d'écubier*, buckler; (fig.) failure; (obs., fam.) *ramasser une* ~, to fail, to come a cropper, (theatr.) to be hissed and booed.
tapé, -e [tape] *adj.* (of fruit) dried, over-ripe; worn, lined (with age); (fam.) *bien* ~, well done, well executed, well served; *une réponse bien* ~*e*, a smart reply, a pat answer, a crushing rejoinder.
tapecul, tape-cul [tapky] *s.m.* **1.** counterpoise--weight (for closing gate); **2.** see-saw; **3.** (naut.) jigger (sail); **4.** (vehicle) bone-shaker, rattle--trap; **5.** bumping (in the saddle); bumping (form of schoolboy bullying).
tapée [tape] *s.f.* (fam.) large quantity, host, masses, (of).
taper[1] [tape] *v.t.* **1.** to tap, to strike, to beat, to smack, to slap; (fam.) *c'est à se* ~ *la tête contre les murs*, it's enough to drive you up the wall; (pop.) *se* ~ *la cloche*, to have a good feed; **2.** to tap, to knock, to tap out (tune, etc.), to type; ~ *trois coups à la porte*, to give three knocks on the door; **3.** (fam.) to touch s.o. (for money); ~ *v.i.* **1.** to tap, to beat, to strike; ~ *sur l'épaule à qn.*, to tap s.o. on the shoulder; ~ *des mains*, to strike with the hand; ~ *des poings, des pieds*, to punch, to kick; ~ *sur qn.*, to strike s.o.; (fig.) to say rude things about s.o. behind his back; ~ *sur le ventre à qn.*, to be over-familiar with s.o.; ~ *sur les nerfs à qn.*, to get on someone's nerves; ~ *dans les mains*, to clap, to clap in time; ~ *dans l'œil de qn.*, to be a hit with s.o.; ~ *dans le mille*, to be successful, to hit the jackpot; to guess right; **2.** to type; **3.** (fig.) (of wine) to go to the head; (pop.) to stink; (of sun) to be burning hot; **4.** (fam.) ~ *dans*, to help oneself to (sth.); **se** ~ *v.refl.* **1.** to come to blows; **2.** (pop.) to put away (quantities of food, drink, etc.); **3.** (fam.) to come in for, to have to do, (sth. unpleasant); (pop.) to do without (sth.).
taper[2] [tape] *v.t.* (techn., naut., mil.) to plug, to stop up, to tamp; to insert tampon in.
tapette [tapɛt] *s.f.* little tap, pat, carpet-beater, fly-swat, engraver's pad; cooper's bat or mallet; (fam.) glib tongue; *avoir une fière* ~, to be a terrible chatterbox.
tapeu-r, -se [tapœr] *s.m.f.* constant borrower, cadger, sponger.
tapi, -e [tapi] *adj.* crouched, crouching; (fig.) lurking.
tapin [tapɛ̃] *s.m.* (fam.) drummer; (pop.) (of prostitute) *faire le* ~, to solicit.
tapinois [tapinwɑ] *s.m. en* ~ *adv.loc.* slyly, on the sly, clandestinely, stealthily.
tapioca [tapjɔka] *s.m.* tapioca.
tapir [tapir] *s.m.* (zool.) tapir; (fig., *École Normale* slang) one taking private tuition.
(**se**) **tapir** [tapir] *v.refl.* to squat, to crouch, to cower, to nestle; to lurk, to hide.
tapis [tapi] *s.m.* carpet, matting, rug, cloth, cover, tapestry; ~ *de billard*, billiard-cloth; ~*-brosse*, doormat; ~ *de foyer*, hearth-rug; ~ *de sol*, groundsheet; ~ *roulant*, conveyor-belt, travelling band; (hort.) ~ *de gazon*, greensward, grass-plot; (fig.) *amuser le* ~, to keep the company entertained; (fig.) *faire* ~ *net*, to sweep the board; *sur le* ~, talked of, under

discussion; *mettre sur le* ~, to bring up, to bring forward, to broach (a subject, etc.).

tapisser [tapise] *v.t.* to upholster (furniture), to paper or line (a wall), to hang (with tapestry), to cover, to adorn; (fig.) to carpet, to cover thickly.

tapisserie [tapisri] *s.f.* tapestry, arras, hangings, upholstery, tapestry-weaving, tapestry-work, embroidery; *faire de la* ~, to do tapestry-work or embroidery; (fig.) *faire* ~, to be a wallflower.

tapissie-r, -ère [tapisje] *s.m.f.* upholsterer, tapestry-worker.

tapon [tapɔ̃] *s.m.* bundle of rags or screwed-up paper.

tapotement [tapɔtmɑ̃] *s.m.* tapping, strumming.

tapoter [tapɔte] *v.t.* to pat, to tap; to strum (piano).

taquer [take] *v.t.* (print.) to plane down.

taquet [takɛ] *s.m.* wedge, peg, picket, angle-block, bracket, catch, stop; (naut.) cleat, belaying-pin; ~ *de soupape*, tappet.

taquin, -e [takɛ̃] *adj.* teasing; *s.m.f.* tease, teaser, pest.

taquiner [takine] *v.t.* to tease; to plague, to torment, to worry, to trouble.

taquinerie [takinri] *s.f.* teasing, worrying.

taquoir [takwar] *s.m.* (print.) plane.

tarabiscot [tarabisko] *s.m.* (join.) groove, hollow; grooving-plane, moulding-plane.

tarabiscotage [tarabiskɔtaʒ] *s.m.* over-elaboration.

tarabiscoté, -e [tarabiskɔte] *adj.* with elaborate mouldings; (fig.) affected, over-elaborate.

tarabiscoter [tarabiskɔte] *v.t.* to adorn with elaborate mouldings; (fig.) to over-refine, to over-elaborate.

tarabuster [tarabyste] *v.t.* to worry, to bother, to vex, to plague, to pester.

tarage [taraʒ] *s.m.* (comm.) taring, establishing weight of container or wrapping.

tarare [tarar] *s.m.* winnowing-machine.

taraud [taro] *s.m.* (techn.) (screw-)tap, screw-cutter.

taraudage [tarodaʒ] *s.m.* (techn.) screw-cutting, tapping, threading.

tarauder [tarode] *v.t.* (techn.) to tap, to screw-cut, to worm, to cut a thread in; to bore through, to pierce.

taraudeu-r, -se [tarodœr] *adj.* tapping, piercing, boring; (fig.) agonizing; *s.m.f.* tapper, borer; **~se** *s.f.* tapper, tap, screw-cutter, thread-cutter.

tarbouche [tarbuʃ] *s.m.* tarboosh.

tard [tar] *adv.* late; *se coucher* ~, to go to bed late; *arriver trop* ~, to arrive late; *tôt ou* ~, sooner or later; *plus* ~, later on; in after years, afterwards; *pas plus* ~ *que*, at the latest, as recently as; *pas plus* ~ *qu'hier*, only yesterday; *il se fait* ~, it's getting late; *mieux vaut* ~ *que jamais*, better late than never; *il n'est jamais trop* ~ *pour bien faire*, it's never too late to mend; ~ *s.m.* (lit. & fig.) *sur le* ~, late in the day.

tarder [tarde] *v.i.* to delay, to put off, to linger, to loiter, to wait, to dally, to be long, to be slow; *il me tarde de*, I long to; *il me tarde que cet ouvrage soit fini*, I am most anxious for this work to be finished; *il ne tardera pas à venir*, he will soon be here; *qu'il tarde à venir!*, what a long time he is!

tardi-f, -ve [tardif] *adj.* tardy, late, belated; slow, sluggish, backward.

tardigrade [tardigrad] *adj., s.m.* (zool.) tardigrade.

tardivement [tardivmɑ̃] *adv.* tardily, belatedly; slowly.

tare [tar] *s.f.* **1.** waste, loss, deficiency, (fig.) defect, blemish, fault, vice; **2.** tare (weight of container or wrapping); *faire la* ~, to allow for the tare weight.

taré, -e [tare] *adj.* damaged, defective; (fig.) tainted, disreputable; (of vessel, box, etc.) tared.

tarentelle [tarɑ̃tɛl] *s.f.* tarantella, tarantelle.

tarentule [tarɑ̃tyl] *s.f.* (ent.) tarantula; (fig.) *être piqué* or *mordu de la* ~, to be highly excited, to be bitten (with sth.).

tarer [tare] *v.t.* (comm.) to tare, to specify weight of container or wrapping.

taret [tarɛ] *s.m* (zool.) teredo; ship-worm, borer.

targe [tarʒ] *s.f.* (hist.) targe, buckler.

targette [tarʒɛt] *s.f.* small bolt, sash bolt.

(se) targuer [targe] *v.refl. se* ~ *de*, to pride oneself on, to boast or brag of.

tari, -e [tari] *adj.* dry, dried up, exhausted.

tarière [tarjɛr] *s.f.* **1.** auger, bore, drill; **2.** (ent.) terebra.

tarif [tarif] *s.m.* tariff, rate, price-list, list of charges, scale or schedule of fares; *plein* ~, full rate, full fare; *c'est le* ~, it is the fixed price, the agreed figure, it is what you have to pay, it is the usual (price or punishment).

tarifaire [tarifɛr] *adj.* (comm.) tariff, price.

tarifé, -e [tarife] *adj.* at a fixed or tariff price.

tarifer [tarife] *v.t.* to price, to fix a price for.

tarification [tarifikɑsjɔ̃] *s.f.* price-fixing, pricing; price.

tarin [tarɛ̃] *s.m.* **1.** (ornith.) siskin; **2.** (pop.) nose.

tarir [tarir] *v.t.i.* to dry (up), to run dry, to be exhausted, to exhaust, to drain, to cease, to stop; (fig.) to atrophy; *ne pas* ~ *sur qch.*, never to stop talking about sth.

tarissable [tarisabl] *adj.* exhaustible, not inexhaustible.

tarissement [tarismɑ̃] *s.m.* exhausting, drying up, draining; exhaustion.

tarlatane [tarlatan] *s.f.* tarlatan.

tarmacadam [tarmakadam] *s.m.* tar macadam, tarmac.

taroté, -e [tarɔte] *adj.* (of playing-cards) spotted, chequered (on the back, like tarot cards).

tarots [taro] *s.m.pl.* (also *tarot* sing.) (cards) tarots, (game of) tarot.

tarpan [tarpɑ̃] *s.m.* tarpan, wild horse.

tarpon [tarpɔ̃] *s.m.* (ichth.) tarpon.

tarse [tars] *s.m.* (anat.) tarsus.

tarsien, -ne [tarsjɛ̃] *adj.* (anat.) tarsal.

tarsier [tarsje] *s.m.* (zool.) tarsier.

tartan [tartɑ̃] *s.m.* tartan, plaid.

tartane [tartan] *s.f.* (naut.) tartan, tartane, tartana.

tartare [tartar] *adj., s.m.f.* Tartar; (cook.) tartare (sauce, steak).

tarte [tart] *s.f.* tart; (fig.) *c'est sa* ~ *à la crème*, that's one of his favourite remarks; ~ *adj.* (fam.) ugly; silly; sluggish; gauche.

tartelette [tartəlɛt] *s.f.* small tart, tartlet.

tartine [tartin] *s.f.* slice of bread and butter; (fig.) interminable discourse; ~ *de confiture*, slice of bread, butter, and jam.

tartiner [tartine] *v.t.* to spread with butter; *fromage à* ~, cheese-spread.

tartrate [tartrat] *s.m.* (chem.) tartrate.

tartre [tartr] *s.m.* (chem.) tartar; (in boilers, pipes, etc.) fur, scale.

tartrique [tartrik] *adj.* (chem.) tartaric.

tartufe, tartuffe [tartyf] *s.m.* hypocrite.

tartuferie, tartufferie [tartyfri] *s.f.* hypocrisy, cant, piece of hypocrisy.

tas [tɑ] *s.m.* heap, pile, mass; cluster, bundle; crowd, set, lot, pack, gang; building-site, place of work; (techn.) hand-anvil; ~ *à river*, dolly; ~*-étampe*, swage-block; (arch.) ~ *de charge*, springing-stones (for piers of arch); *un* ~ *de foin*, a haycock; *un* ~ *de gerbes*, a shock of sheaves; *un* ~ *de blé*, a heap of corn; (fam.) *il y en* *a des* ~ *et des* ~, there are bags and bags of them; (fam.) ~ *de salauds!*, you're a lot of bastards!; *un* ~ *de mensonges*, a pack of lies; *prendre* or *piquer au* ~, to help oneself; *dans le* ~, in the mass; *tirer dans le* ~, to fire into the crowd, to shoot at random; *sur le* ~, on the site, at work; *apprentissage sur le* ~, learning the trade on the job; *crier famine sur un* ~ *de blé*, to cry famine in the midst of plenty.

Tasmanie [tasmani] *s.f.* (geog.) Tasmania.

tasmanien, -ne [tasmanjɛ̃] *adj.*, *s.m.f.* Tasmanian.

tassage [tɑsaʒ] *s.m.* (sport) crowding, bumping, (an opponent).

tasse [tɑs] *s.f.* cup, cupful; *une demi-*~, half a cup; ~ *à thé*, tea-cup; *boire dans une* ~, to drink from a cup; (fig.) *boire une* or *la* ~, to swallow water (while bathing); *boire à la grande* ~, to be drowned in the sea, to go to Davy Jones's locker.

tasseau (pl. **-x**) [tɑso] *s.m.* (techn.) bracket, ledge; stop; guard, lug, cleat.

tassé, -e [tɑse] *adj.* collapsed, subsided; hunched, thickset, crowded, jam-packed; *bien* ~, full to the brim; (of drinks) stiff.

tassement [tɑsmɑ̃] *s.m.* **1.** cramming, squeezing, compressing, packing down; **2.** settling (down), consolidation; sinking, subsidence.

tasser [tɑse] *v.t.* to compress, to press down, to ram down; to heap up, to pile up; to squeeze, to cram; (sport) to crowd, to bump, (an opponent); ~ *v.i.* (hort.) to grow thick, to bunch; **se** ~ *v.refl.* to subside, to sink, to settle; (fig., fam.) to settle down, to return to normal; (pop.) to stuff oneself (with food).

tassette [tɑsɛt] *s.f.* tasset, armour for thighs.

taste-vin [tastəvɛ̃], **tâte-vin** [tɑtvɛ̃] *s.m.invar.* wine-taster (instrument).

tâter [tɑte] *v.t.* to feel, to taste, to handle, to touch, to finger; (fig.) to try, to sound, to put to the test, to prove; ~ *de*, to taste, to sample, to experience; ~ *le mur*, to feel one's way along the wall, to grope along the wall; ~ *le terrain*, to reconnoitre the ground, to see how the land lies, to put out a feeler; **se** ~ *v.refl.* to examine oneself, to take stock of one's position, to think things over.

tâteur [tɑtœr] *s.m* (techn.) feeler, sensor.

tatillon, -ne [tatijɔ̃] *adj.* fussy, finical, finicky.

tâtonnant, -e [tɑtɔnɑ̃] *adj.* groping, tentative.

tâtonnement [tɑtɔnmɑ̃] *s.m.* groping, feeling one's way, tentative move or effort; *expérience de* ~, tentative experiment; *par* ~*s*, by trial and error.

tâtonner [tɑtɔne] *v.i.* to fumble, to grope, to feel one's way, to hesitate, to waver, to probe away, to proceed cautiously.

(à) tâtons [atɑtɔ̃] *adv.loc.* groping about, feeling one's way, tentatively, blindly, at random.

tatou [tatu] *s.m.* (zool.) armadillo.

tatouage [tatwaʒ] *s.m.* tattooing, tattoo.

tatouer [tatwe] *v.t.* to tattoo.

tatoueur [tatwœr] *s.m.* tattooer.

tau [to] *s.m.* **1.** (Gr. letter, herald.) tau; **2.** T-shaped (shepherd's) stick.

taud [to] *s.m.*, **taude** [tod] *s.f.* (naut.) tarpaulin, awning.

taudis [todi] *s.m.* hovel, filthy lodgings, slum.

taule, tôle [tol] *s.f.* **1.** (pop.) bedroom, hotel room; **2.** (mil. slang) prison; *aller en* ~, *faire de la* ~, to do a stretch in prison.

taupe [top] *s.f.* (zool.) Mole; moleskin; (civ. eng.) mole; *vivre comme une* ~, to be a recluse, never to go out; *vieille* ~, old hag; *myope comme une* ~, blind as a bat; (student slang) *être en* ~, to be swotting for admission to the *École Polytechnique*.

taupe-grillon [topgrijɔ̃] *s.m.* (ent.) mole-cricket.

taupier [topje] *s.m.* mole-catcher.

taupière [topjɛr] *s.f.* mole-trap.

taupin [topɛ̃] *s.m.* (ent.) skipjack, click beetle; (obs. mil.) sapper; student reading for the *École Polytechnique*.

taupinière [topinjɛr], **taupinée** [topine] *s.f.* mole-hill, mole-tunnel; (fig.) subterranean maze.

taure [tɔr] *s.f.* heifer, young cow.

taureau (pl. **-x**) [tɔro] *s.m.* bull; (astron.) Taurus, the Bull; *jeune* ~, steer; *combat de* ~*x*, bullfight.

taurillon [tɔrijɔ̃] *s.m.* young bull, yearling bull.

taurin, e [tɔrɛ̃] *adj.* of bullfighting.

tauromachie [tɔromaʃi] *s.f.* bullfighting, bullfight.

tauromachique [tɔromaʃik] *adj.* of bullfighting.

tautologie [totɔlɔʒi] *s.f.* tautology.

tautologique [totɔlɔʒik *adj.* tautological.

taux [to] *s.m.* price, rate (of exchange, interest, tax); assessment; percentage, proportion, figure.

tavaïolle [tavajɔl] *s.f.* (eccles.) chrisom(-cloth).

tavelé, -e [tavle] *adj.* spotted.

taveler [tavle] *v.t.* to spot, to speckle; **se** ~ *v.refl.* to become spotted.

tavelure [tavlyr] *s.f.* spots, speckles; (hort.) spot.

taverne [tavɛrn] *s.f.* tavern, public house; café-restaurant (of 'ye olde' type).

taverni-er, -ère [tavɛrnje] *s.m.f.* (obs., jest) publican, innkeeper.

taxable [taksabl] *adj.* taxable, liable to tax.

taxateur [taksatœr] *s.m.* taxer, assessor; (law) taxing-master; ~ *adj.* (law) taxing.

taxati-f, -ve [taksatif] *adj.* taxable.

taxation [taksɑsjɔ̃] *s.f.* taxation, taxing, assessment, fixing of prices.

taxe [taks] *s.f.* tax, taxation, fixed price, controlled price, rate, charge, fee, dues; postage due; ~ *de séjour*, visitors' tax.

taxer [takse] *v.t.* to fix the price of, to tax, to rate, to assess, to charge; (fig.) ~ *qn. de*, to accuse s.o. of, to tax s.o. with

taxi [taksi] *s.m.* taxi, taxi-cab; (fam.) *faire le* ~, *être* ~, to be a taxi-driver.

taxidermie [taksidɛrmi] *s.f.* taxidermy.

taxidermiste [taksidɛrmist] *s.m.* taxidermist.

taxi-girl [taksigœrl] *s.f.* taxi-girl, (club) dance--hostess.

taximètre [taksimɛtr] *s.m.* taximeter; taxi with taximeter

taxiphone [taksifɔn] *s.m.* public call-box, coin--box (telephone).

taxonomie [taksɔnɔmi], **taxinomie** [taksinɔmi] *s.f.* taxonomy.

taxonomique [taksɔnɔmik] *adj.* taxonomic(al).

tchécoslovaque [tʃekɔslɔvak] *adj.* Czechoslovak.

Tchécoslovaquie [tʃekɔslɔvaki] *s.f.* (geog.) Czechoslovakia.

tchèque (tʃɛk] *adj.*, *s.m.f.* Czech.

te [tə] (**t'** before vowel or h-mute) *pers.pron.* thee, you, thyself, yourself.

té [te] *s.m.* T; ~ *à dessin*, or *équerre à* ~, T-square; *en* ~, T-shaped, T-section; *fer en* ~, T-iron, T-girder.

technicien, -ne [tɛknisjɛ̃] *s.m.f.* technician, (technical) expert, technologist.

technicité [tɛknisite] *s.f.* technicality, technical character.

technique [tɛknik] *adj.* technical, of technique; ~ *s.f.* technique, technic, technology; ~**ment** [tɛknikmɑ̃] *adv.* technically.

technocrate [tɛknɔkrat] *s.m.* technocrat.

technocratie [tɛknɔkrasi] *s.f.* technocracy.

technologie [tɛknɔlɔʒi] *s.f.* technology.
technologique [tɛknɔlɔʒik] *adj.* technological.
teck, tek [tɛk] *s.m.* (bot.) teak.
tectonique [tɛktɔnik] *adj.* (geol.) tectonic; ~ *s.f.* tectonics.
tectrice [tɛktris] *s.f., adj.* (ornith.) tectrix, covert, covering feather of wing or tail.
tee [ti] *s.m.* (golf) tee.
T.E.E. [teee] abbrev. *Trans-Europ-Express.*
tégument [tegymɑ̃] *s.m.* (anat.) tegument; (bot.) integument.
tégumentaire [tegymɑ̃tɛr] *adj.* tegumentary, tegumental; integumentary.
teigne [tɛɲ] *s.f.* (ent.) moth, clothes-moth; (med.) ringworm, tinea; (vet.) thrush; (fig.) pest.
teigneu-x, -se [tɛɲø] *adj.* suffering from ringworm.
teillage [tɛjaʒ], **tillage** [tijaʒ] *s.m.* stripping (of hemp, flax, etc.), scutching.
teille [tɛj], **tille** [tij] *s.f.* lime-bark, bast, bass, harl.
teiller [tɛje], **tiller** [tije] *v.t.* to strip, to scutch.
teilleu-r, -se [tɛjœr] *s.m.f.* worker who scutches; (flax, etc.); ~**se** *s.f.* scutcher, scutch-blade.
teindre [tɛ̃dr] *v.t.* to dye, to stain, to tinge (*en, de*, with), to colour, to tincture, (fig.) to tinge, to imbue; ~ *en rouge*, to dye red; to tinge with red; *se* ~ *de violet*, to become tinged with violet, to take on a violet hue.
teint [tɛ̃] *s.m.* **1.** complexion; **2.** dye, colour; *bon* or *grand* ~, fast colour; (fig.) staunch, dyed in the wool.
teint, -e [tɛ̃] *adj.* dyed, tinted; tinged.
teinte [tɛ̃t] *s.f.* tint, shade, tone, hue; (fig.) touch, tinge; *demi-*~, half-tint, chiaroscuro; *une* ~ *d'ironie*, a hint of irony, an ironical touch; *gravure en demi-*~, mezzotint.
teinter [tɛ̃te] *v.t.* to tint, to tinge, to colour.
teinture [tɛ̃tyr] *s.f.* dye, dyeing, tinting; tinge; (pharm.) tincture; colouring, hue; (fig.) smattering.
teinturerie [tɛ̃tyrri] *s.f.* dye-works, dyer's trade, dyeing, (dyers and) cleaners.
teinturi-er, -ère [tɛ̃tyrje] *s.m.f.* dyer, (dyer and) cleaner.
tek see TECK.
tel, -le [tɛl] *adj., pron.* such, like, similar, such a one, as such, in this form, of such a kind, so great; *rien de* ~, nothing of the kind, nothing like (it), nothing so good; ~ *fait ceci*, ~ *autre fait cela*, one person does this, another that; ~ *ou* ~, such and such; *comme* ~, as such; ~ *que*, such as, like; ~ *père*, ~ *fils*, like father, like son; *à* ~*le heure*, at such (a) time; ~ *quel*, such as it is, just as it is; *Monsieur un* ~, Mr. So-and-So; *de* ~*le sorte que*, in such a way that, so that.
télamon [telamɔ̃] *s.m.* (arch.) telamon.
télé [tele] *s.f.* (fam.) abbrev. of *télévision, poste de télévision.*
télébenne [telebɛn], **télécabine** [telekabin] *s.f.* ski-lift; cabin of ski-lift.
télécinéma [telesinema] *s.m* telecine, TV films.
télécom-mande [telekɔmɑ̃d] *s.f.* remote control, operation by remote control; ~**mander** [telekɔmɑ̃de] *v.t.* to operate by remote control.
télécommunication [telekɔmynikɑsjɔ̃] *s.f.* telecommunication.
télécran [telekrɑ̃] *s.m.* TV projection screen.
téléférique, téléphérique [teleferik] *s.m.* cable-way, telpher, cable-lift; *adj.* cable-.
télégénique [teleʒenik] *adj.* who comes over well on television.
télé-gramme [telegram] *s.m.* telegram, cable, cablegram; ~**graphe** [telegraf] *s.m.* telegraph; ~**graphie** [telegrafi] *s.f.* telegraphy; (obs.) ~*graphie sans fil*, wireless, wireless telegraphy; ~**graphier** [telegrafje] *v.t.* to telegraph, to send a telegram; ~**graphique** [telegrafik] *adj.* telegraphic, by telegraph, by telegram, etc.; *poteau* ~*graphique*, telegraph-pole; ~**graphiquement** [telegrafikmɑ̃] *adv.* telegraphically, by telegram, etc. ~**graphiste** [telegrafist] *s.m.f.* telegraphist; *s.m.* telegraph-boy.
téléguidage [telegidaʒ] *s.m.* radio-control.
téléguidé, -e [telegide] *adj.* radio-controlled; (of missile) guided.
téléguider [telegide] *v.t.* to radio-control, to direct by radio.
téléimprimeur [teleɛ̃primœr] *s.m* teleprinter.
télé-mètre [telemɛtr] *s.m.* telemeter, range--finder; ~**métreur** [telemetrœr] *s.m.* telemetrist, range-taker; ~**métrie** [telemetri] *s.f.* telemetry, range-finding.
téléobjectif [teleɔbʒɛktif] *s.m* telephoto lens.
téléolo-gie [teleɔlɔʒi] *s.f.* teleology; ~**gique** [teleɔlɔʒik] *adj.* teleologic(al).
téléosaure [teleɔsor] *s.m.* (palaeont.) teleosaur, fossil crocodile.
télépathie [telepati] *s.f.* telepathy.
télépathique [telepatik] *adj.* telepathic.
téléphérage [teleferaʒ] *s.m.* transport by cable--way, by telpher.
téléphérique see TÉLÉFÉRIQUE.
télé-phone [telefɔn] *s.m.* telephone; (fam.) *coup de* ~*phone*, phone-call, ring; (fig.) ~*phone arabe* or *de brousse*, bush-telegraph; ~**phoner** [telefɔne] *v.t.i.* to telephone, to phone (message, etc.); ~*phoner à, chez*, to telephone, to phone (s.o.), to ring (s.o.) up; ~**phonie** [telefɔni] *s.f.* telephony; ~*phonie sans fil*, radio-telephony; ~**phonique** [telefɔnik] *adj.* telephonic, telephone, phone; by telephone; *appareil* ~*phonique*, receiver, instrument; *cabine* ~*phonique*, public call-box; ~**phoniquement** [telefɔnikmɑ̃] *adv.* telephonically, by telephone; ~**phoniste** [telefɔnist] *s.m.f.* telephonist, telephone operator.
téléphotographie [telefotografi] *s.f.* telephotography, photography with telephoto lens; telephoto.
télépointage [telepwɛ̃taʒ] *s.m.* (nav.) (equipment for) remote control of fire.
téle-scopage [telɛskɔpaʒ] *s.m.* telescoping; ~**scope** [telɛskɔp] *s.m.* telescope; ~**scoper** [telɛskɔpe] *v.t.* to telescope, to crumple up (a vehicle); **se** ~**scoper** *v.refl.* (of vehicles) to telescope, to concertina; (fig.) to be telescoped, to merge; ~**scopique** [telɛskɔpik] *adj.* telescopic; (fig.) telescopic, telescoping, retracting.
téléscripteur [teleskriptœr] *s.m.* = TÉLÉIMPRIMEUR.
télésiège [telesjɛʒ] *s.m.* chair-lift.
téléski [teleski] *s.m.* ski-lift.
téléspectat-eur, -rice [telespɛktatœr] *s.m.f.* (television) viewer.
télétype [teletip] *s.m.* = TÉLÉIMPRIMEUR.
téléviser [televize] *v.t.* to televise.
téléviseur [televizœr] *s.m.* television set.
télévision [televizjɔ̃] *s.f.* television.
télex [telɛks] *s.m.* telex.
tellement [tɛlmɑ̃] *adv.* so, so much, so far, to such a degree, to such an extent, in such a way; (fam.) ~ *de*, so much, so many, such a lot of; *pas* ~, not particularly, not all that much; (obs.) ~ *quellement*, after a fashion, indifferently.
tellure [tel(l)yr] *s.m.* (chem.) tellurium.
tellureu-x, -se [tel(l)yrø] *adj.* (chem.) tellurous.
tellurien, -ne [tel(l)yrjɛ̃] *adj.* tellurian, of or from the earth.
tellurique [tel(l)yrik] *adj.* telluric, of or from the earth; (chem.) telluric; *secousse* ~, earth tremor; (electr.) *courant* ~, earth current; (geog.) *eaux* ~*s*, underground streams.
téméraire [temerɛr] *adj.* daring, rash, bold, headstrong, reckless, foolhardy; *Charles le* ~,

Charles the Bold; **~ment** [temerɛrmɑ̃] *adv.* daringly, rashly, boldly, recklessly.

témérité [temerite] *s.f.* temerity, rashness, boldness.

témoignage [temwaɲaz] *s.m.* evidence, witness, testimony; testimonial, character; mark, token; *faux ~*, false witness, perjury; *en ~ de*, in witness of; *appeler en ~*, to call to witness, to call upon to give evidence; *porter, rendre ~*, to bear witness, to give an eye-witness account (*sur*, of); to give evidence; *rendre ~ à la vérité de*, to testify to the truth of; *~ d'estime*, testimonial; *~ d'affection*, token of affection, love, etc.

témoigner [temwaɲe] *v.t.* to testify, to bear witness, to give evidence, to attest, to evince, to show, to express, to prove; *tout témoignait pour lui*, everything told in his favour; *~ de*, to bear witness to, to give evidence of, to manifest, to give proof of, to confirm; to vouch for.

témoin [temwɛ̃] *s.m.* witness; testimony, evidence, sign, token, proof; sample; check; pilot, control, (in experiment); marker, boundary-mark; second (in duel); baton (in relay race); *~ à charge*, witness for the prosecution; *~ à décharge*, witness for the defence; *lampe ~*, warning light, pilot light; (geol.) *butte ~*, outlier; *~ oculaire*, eye-witness; *parler sans ~s*, to speak privately (with s.o.); *parler devant ~s*, to speak before witnesses, in the presence of a third party; *il faut en être ~ pour le croire*, it must be seen to be believed; *mes yeux en sont ~s*, I saw it with my own eyes; *prendre qn. à ~*, to call s.o. to witness.

tempe [tɑ̃p] *s.f.* (anat.) temple.

tempérament [tɑ̃peramɑ̃] *s.m.* **1.** constitution, temperament, temper, character, disposition, nature, humour; *de ~*, by nature, temperamentally; *avoir du ~*, to be of an amorous disposition, to be highly-sexed; **2.** moderation, reasonableness, compromise; (comm.) easy terms; *vente à ~*, hire-purchase, sale on easy terms, credit sale.

tempérance [tɑ̃perɑ̃s] *s.f.* temperance, moderation, sobriety, soberness; teetotalism.

tempérant, -e [tɑ̃perɑ̃] *adj.* temperate, moderate, sober, teetotal; (med.) sedative.

température [tɑ̃peratyr] *s.f.* temperature.

tempéré, -e [tɑ̃pere] *adj.* temperate, moderate, sober, tempered; *monarchie ~e*, constitutional monarchy.

tempérer [tɑ̃pere] *v.t.* to temper, to moderate; to cool, to allay; to check, to mitigate, to have a sobering or restraining effect on.

tempête [tɑ̃pɛt] *s.f.* tempest, storm; agitation, tumult, commotion, disturbance; *une ~ dans un verre d'eau*, a storm in a teacup.

tempêter [tɑ̃pete] *v.i.* to storm, to rage, to bluster, to fume.

tempétueu-x, -se [tɑ̃petɥø] *adj.* tempestuous, stormy, boisterous.

temple [tɑ̃pl] *s.m.* temple; (Protestant) church.

templier [tɑ̃plije] *s.m.* Knight Templar, Templar.

tempo [tɛmpo, tɛ̃po] *s.m.* (mus.) tempo, time; (fig.) tempo, pace.

temporaire [tɑ̃pɔrɛr] *adj.* temporary, provisional; **~ment** [tɑ̃pɔrɛrmɑ̃] temporarily, on a temporary basis, for the time being.

temporal, -e, (aux) [tɑ̃pɔral] *adj.* (anat.) temporal.

temporalité [tɑ̃pɔralite] *s.f.* temporality.

temporel, -le [tɑ̃pɔrɛl] *adj.* temporal, transient, wordly.

temporisat-eur, -rice [tɑ̃pɔrizatœr] *adj.* temporizing; *s.m.f.* temporizer, procrastinator.

temporisation [tɑ̃pɔrizɑsjɔ̃] *s.f.* temporizing, procrastination, delaying tactics.

temporiser [tɑ̃pɔrize] *v.i.* to temporize, to delay, to procrastinate.

temps[1] [tɑ̃] *s.m.* time, term, space of time, duration, period, age, epoch, era; occasion, opportunity; days, season, times; (mil.) movement; (gram.) tense; (mus.) measure, time, beat; *le bon ~, le vieux ~, le bon vieux ~*, the good old days (times); *ces derniers ~*, lately, of late; *du ~ de*, in the time of; *du ~ que*, when; *dans les derniers ~ de*, in the last days of; *de mon ~*, in my day, when I was young; *être de son ~*, to keep up with the times; (mus.) *mesure à deux ~*, common time or measure (two or four beats in a bar); *marquer* or *prendre un ~*, to pause; *un ~ d'arrêt*, a pause, a halt; *travailler à plein-~*, to work full-time; *la plupart du ~*, mostly, generally; *à ~*, in time; for a time, for a term; just in time; in the nick of time; *avec le ~*, with time, in course of time; *dans le ~*, formerly, in days gone by; *dans son ~*, in due course; *en son ~*, when it suits him, in his own good time; *en ~ utile*, in due course, at the appropriate time; *de tout ~*, at all times, at any time; ever, always; *de ~ en ~, de ~ à autre*, from time to time, now and then; *entre ~*, meanwhile, meantime; *en même ~*, at the same time, at once; *en ~ et lieu*, in due time and place; *il est (grand) ~ de*, it is (high) time to; *le ~ de mettre mon manteau et j'arrive*, just let me put my coat on and I'm coming; *cela a fait son ~*, it's had its day, it has seen better days; *cela n'aura qu'un ~*, that won't last for ever, or long; *avoir tout le ~*, to have plenty of time; *il y a peu de ~*, a little while ago, recently; *en peu de ~*, shortly, soon, quickly; *il y a beau ~ de tout cela*, that's a long time ago; *le ~ lui dure*, time hangs heavy on his hands; *se donner du bon ~*, to take things easy, to have a good time; *prendre son ~*, to take one's time; to choose one's time; *prendre du ~*, to take time; *prendre bien* (or *mal*) *son ~*, choose one's time well (or badly); *par le ~ qui court*, as things are, nowadays; *pour quelque ~*, for a short time, for a little while; *selon le ~*, according to circumstances; *usé par le ~*, timeworn, weather-beaten; *autres ~ autres mœurs*, customs change with the times; *le ~ est un grand maître*, time is a great teacher; *en deux ~ trois mouvements*, in double quick time; *moteur à 4 ~*, 4-stroke engine.

temps[2] [tɑ̃] *s.m.* weather; *quel ~ fait-il?*, what is the weather like?; *il fait beau (~)*, it is fine; *le ~ est couvert*, the weather is cloudy or overcast; *~ gris (sombre)*, dull weather; *gros ~, ~ orageux*, stormy, thundery weather, dirty weather; *le ~ s'éclaircit*, it is clearing up; *le ~ se met au beau*, it is becoming settled; *le ~ se gâte*, the weather is breaking up; *le ~ est au beau fixe*, it's fine, settled weather; the weather is set fair; *par tous les ~*, in all weathers; *prévision(s) du ~*, weather forecast; *le ~ se brouille*, the sky is getting overcast; *~ clair* or *serein*, clear sky; *couleur du ~*, sky-blue; (fig.) *faire la pluie et le beau ~*, to be all-powerful, (fam.) to be God Almighty; *parler de la pluie et du beau ~*, to talk of insignificant things; *prendre le ~ comme il vient*, to take things as they come; *le ~ ne tiendra pas*, this weather won't last; (fam.) *il fera beau ~ quand je ferai cela*, it will be a long time before I do that.

tenable [tənabl] *adj.* tenable, habitable; bearable; *la position n'est plus ~*, the position is no longer tenable; ⚠ not usu. 'tenable' of an argument, etc.

tenace [tənas] *adj.* tenacious, obstinate, stubborn, persistent, difficult to eradicate; sticky, adhesive; **~ment** [tənasmɑ̃] *adv.* tenaciously, obstinately.

ténacité [tenasite] *s.f.* tenacity; retentiveness; adhesive quality.

tenaillement [tənɑjmɑ̃] *s.m.* (fig.) torment.

tenailler [tənɑje] *v.t.* (hist.) to torture with red-hot pincers; (fig.) to torment, torture, to rack.

tenailles [tənɑj] *s.f.pl.* pincers, nippers, pliers, tongs.
tenanci-er, -ère [tənɑ̃sje] *s.m.f.* (feud.) holder of fief; (mod.) tenant (esp. farmer); lessee, licensee, keeper (of gaming-house or brothel).
tenant, -e [tənɑ̃] *adj.* contiguous to, adjoining, attached; following, sitting; *séance tenante*, there and then, on the spot, at once; *chemise à col ~*, shirt with collar attached; *s.m.f.* champion, title-holder; upholder, supporter, partisan; ~ *s.m.* (herald.) supporter; (of property) *tout d'un ~, d'un seul ~*, in a block, continuous; *les ~s*, adjacent property, lands marching with (an estate); *les ~s et les aboutissants*, (i.) adjacent property; (ii.) the details, the ins and outs.
tendance [tɑ̃dɑ̃s] *s.f.* tendency, inclination, leaning, bent, propensity, trend; *avoir ~ à*, to tend to, to be apt to.
tendanciel, -le [tɑ̃dɑ̃sjɛl] *adj.* with a purpose.
tendancieu-x, -se [tɑ̃dɑ̃sjø] *adj.* intentionally misleading, insinuating, suggestive, tendentious; not impartial; (law) *question ~se*, leading question; **~sement** [tɑ̃dɑ̃sjøzmɑ̃] *adv.* tendentiously.
tender [tɑ̃dɛr] *s.m.* (rail.) tender.
tendeur [tɑ̃dœr] *s.m.* spreader, layer, setter (of snares); (trouser-)press, stretcher, hanger; (rail.) tightener; tightening-bolt, wire-strainer.
tendineu-x, -se [tɑ̃dinø] *adj.* tendinous, sinewy.
tendoir [tɑ̃dwar] *s.m.* clothes-line, drying-line, stretcher; (weaving) tenter.
tendon [tɑ̃dɔ̃] *s.m.* (anat.) tendon, sinew, hamstring.
tendre [tɑ̃dr] *adj.* tender; soft, delicate, touching, new; sensitive, affectionate, loving; kind, compassionate; early, young, fresh; ~ *s.m.* (obs.) affection; **~ment** [tɑ̃drəmɑ̃] *adv.* tenderly, affectionately, kindly, lovingly.
tendre [tɑ̃dr] *v.t.* to stretch, to strain, to tighten; to bend (a bow), to spread (a net), to lay (a snare), to set (a trap), to pitch (a tent), to hang (curtains, etc.), to put up, to hold out, to offer, to present, to put forth, to throw out; *~ la main*, to hold or put out one's hand, (fig.) to beg; *~ la main à*, to hold out one's hand to, to give a helping hand to, to put out one's hand for; *~ à*, to tend to, to be conducive to, to lead to; *à quoi tend ce discours?*, what is all this talk leading to?, what are you aiming at?
tendresse [tɑ̃drɛs] *s.f.* tenderness, fondness, love, sensibility, kindness, affection, delicacy; (pl.) caresses, endearments.
tendreté [tɑ̃drəte] *s.f.* (of eatables, plants) tenderness.
tendron [tɑ̃drɔ̃] *s.m.* tender shoot; (fam.) young girl.
tendu, -e [tɑ̃dy] *adj.* tense, tight, taut, stretched, outstretched, (of spring) wound up; distended; hung, (wall-)papered; bent, intent, strained, stiff; difficult, delicate; *la main ~e*, the hand stretched out, the outstretched hand, the hand of friendship; *bras ~s*, arms outstretched, at arm's length; *poings ~s*, fists raised; *l'esprit ~*, the mind concentrated or focused (on); *style ~*, stilted style.
ténèbres [tenɛbr] *s.f.pl.* darkness, gloom, night, mystery, obscurity; (eccles.) Tenebrae.
ténébreu-x, -se [tenebrø] *adj.* dark, gloomy; secret, sad, obscure, mysterious; sinister, evil; (jest) *un beau ~x*, a Byronic lover; **~sement** [tenebrøzmɑ̃] *adv.* darkly, mysteriously, perfidiously.
ténébrion [tenebrijɔ̃] *s.m.* (ent.) Tenebrio, meal-beetle.
tènement [tɛnmɑ̃] *s.m.* (feud. law) tenement, holding.
ténesme [tenɛm] *s.m.* (med.) tenesmus.
teneur [tənœr] *s.f.* tenor, terms, text, import, content; (chem.) amount, percentage, degree; grade (of ore); (nuclear phys.) *~ isotopique*, isotopic abundance.
teneu-r, -se [tənœr] *s.m.f.* keeper; *~r de livres*, bookkeeper, accountant.
ténia [tenja] *s.m.* taenia, tapeworm.
tenir [tənir] *v.t.* **1.** to hold, to lay hands on, to keep hold of, to grip; to restrain; to keep to; to possess, to have in one's grasp, to get; *~ un verre*, to hold a glass; *~ sa langue*, to hold one's tongue; *~ la droite*, to keep to the right; *nous tenons les voleurs*, we have got the thieves; *~ un territoire*, to hold or possess territory; (fam.) *~ un rhume*, to have got a cold; *faire ~ qch. à qn.*, to transmit sth. to s.o.; *tiens!, tenez!*, look!, here!, wait!, I say!; *~ qn. en estime*, to hold s.o. in esteem; *~ qch. de qn.*, to get, to have received, sth. from s.o.; **2.** to keep, to maintain, to keep or hold in place, to retain; *~ sa promesse*, to keep one's promise; *~ un plat chaud*, to keep a dish hot; *tenu par des courroies*, held in place by straps; *~ table ouverte*, to keep open house; **3.** to resist, to stand up (to sth.); *~ bon* or *ferme*, to hold fast, to stick it out, to hold out; *~ tête à qn.*, to resist s.o., to stand up to s.o., to keep up with s.o.; *~ le coup*, to hold out (against fatigue, attacks, etc.); **4.** to hold, to contain; to take up (space), to occupy, to keep to; *la bouteille tient un litre*, the bottle holds a litre; *~ une si grande place*, to take up so much room, to occupy so large a place; *~ son rang*, to keep one's position; (naut.) *~ le large*, to keep out to sea; **5.** to hold, to occupy (position, etc.); to keep (hotel, record, etc.), to take (notes); to deliver (speech, etc.); *~ la charge de*, to hold the office of; *~ la comptabilité*, to be in charge of the accounts; *~ un hôtel*, to keep a hotel; *~ un registre*, to keep a register; *~ un discours*, to make a speech; *~ des propos désobligeants*, to make offensive remarks; *quel langage tenez-vous là!*, that's a nice way to talk!; **6.** to consider, to hold, to deem; *~ pour probable*, to consider likely; *tenez-vous-le pour dit*, take it as said, that's settled once and for all, I won't tell you again; *~ qn. comme un frère*, to look on s.o. as a brother; *~ qn. quitte de qch.*, to acquit s.o. of sth.; **7.** *~ à*, to be attached to, to be intent on, to be determined on or to, to insist on; to prize, to value; to cling to; to depend on, to be due to, to hang by, to be derived from; *je tiens à les inviter*, I am determined to invite them; *si vous y tenez*, if you insist; *~ à la liberté*, to value liberty; *~ à la vie* to cling to life; *cela ne tient qu'à vous*, that is up to you; *je n'y tiens plus*, I am no longer interested in, or worried about, it; *qu'à cela ne tienne!*, don't let that stop you!; *à quoi tient cette idée?*, where does this idea come from?, how did you get that into your head?; **8.** *~ de qn.*, to take after s.o., to be like s.o.; *~ de qch.*, to partake (of the quality) of sth.; *cela tient du miracle*, it is something of a miracle; ~ *v.i.* **1.** to hold, to hold fast, to stay put or fixed, to be held or fixed; to last, to persist; to stand; *je ne tiens plus debout*, I can no longer keep on my feet; *la corde tient*, the rope is holding; *leur mariage ne tint pas*, their marriage didn't last; *je n'y puis plus ~*, I can't hold out any longer; (fig.) *l'histoire ne tient pas debout*, the story doesn't hold water; *il n'y a pas de raison qui tienne*, there is no valid reason, or objection; there is nothing to stop one (doing sth.); **2.** *~ pour*, to hold with (an opinion, etc.); *~ dans*, to be contained in, to go into (a box, etc.); *nous ne tiendrons pas tous dans la voiture*, we shan't all get into the car; **se** ~ *v.refl.* **1.** to hold one another; (fig.) to go together, to be linked; to be held; *se ~ par la main*, to hold hands; *tout cela se tient*, it all hangs together; *la foire se tient ici*, the fair is held here; **2.** to stand,

to be, to remain, to stay, to keep; *se ~ auprès du mur*, to stand, to remain, by the wall; *se ~ droit*, to stand up straight; *se ~ immobile*, to stand or remain still; *se ~ tranquille*, to keep quiet, not to move; **3.** to hold good; *son raisonnement se tient*, his argument is valid; **4.** to behave; *se ~ (bien)*, to behave oneself, to behave properly; **5.** to restrain oneself, to refrain (*de*, from); **6.** *se ~ à*, to cling to, to keep close to; to keep to (an instruction, etc.); *s'en ~ à*, to keep to, not to go beyond, to stop at, (a point); *ils s'en tinrent là*, they stopped (there); *tenez-vous-en là*, stop there; *savoir à quoi s'en ~*, to know what to make of it.

tennis [tenis] *s.m.* **1.** (lawn) tennis; tennis court; tennis-shoes, gym-shoes; *~ s.f.pl.* tennis shoes, gym shoes; **2.** (text.) flannel serge.

tennisman [tenisman] *s.m.* (pl. *tennismen*) (obs.) tennis-player.

tenon [tənɔ̃] *s.m.* tenon, lug, shoulder; bolt (of firearms); nut (of an anchor).

ténor [tenɔr] *s.m.* (mus.) tenor; (fig.) leading light, star performer.

ténorino [tenɔrino] *s.m.* falsetto tenor.

ténorisant, -e [tenɔrizɑ̃] *adj.* resembling a tenor voice.

ténoriser [tenɔrize] *v.i.* to sing like a tenor, in the tenor register.

ténotomie [tenɔtɔmi] *s.f.* (surg.) tenotomy.

tenseur [tɑ̃sœr] *s.m.* (anat., math.) tensor; (techn.) stretcher, tightener.

tension [tɑ̃sjɔ̃] *s.f.* tension; tensing; tenseness, application, strain, straining, intensity; (techn.) tensile stress, strain, pressure; (electr.) tension, voltage; (fam.) high blood-pressure; (electr.) *en ~*, in series; (phys.) *~ superficielle*, surface tension; *une ~ vers*, a striving towards.

tenson [tɑ̃sɔ̃] *s.f.* tenson.

tentaculaire [tɑ̃takylɛr] *adj.* tentacular; (fig.) sprawling.

tentacule [tɑ̃takyl] *s.m.* tentacle, feeler.

tentant, -e [tɑ̃tɑ̃] *adj.* tempting, enticing; attractive, alluring, inviting.

tentat-eur, -rice [tɑ̃tatœr] *s.m.f.* tempter, temptress; *adj.* tempting.

tentation [tɑ̃tɑsjɔ̃] *s.f.* temptation.

tentative [tɑ̃tativ] *s.f.* attempt, try, trial, endeavour; *~ de meurtre*, attempted murder.

tente [tɑ̃t] *s.f.* tent, pavilion, awning; *dresser une ~*, to pitch a tent; (fig.) *se retirer sous sa ~*, to withdraw in a huff, to go away and sulk.

tente-abri [tɑ̃tabri] *s.f.* individual shelter-tent.

tenter[1] [tɑ̃te] *v.t.* **1.** to attempt, to try, to venture; *~ la chance*, *~ le coup*, to make the attempt; to risk it, to venture; **2.** to tempt, to entice, to attract; *être tenté*, to be tempted, to be attracted, to be inclined.

tenter[2] [tɑ̃te] *v.t.* to erect an awning over.

tenture [tɑ̃tyr] *s.f.* hangings, tapestry, draperies; wallpaper.

tenu, -e [təny] *adj.* **1.** maintained, kept, held; steady, firm, sustained; *une maison bien ~e*, a well-maintained house, a house kept in good order; (fin.) *valeurs bien ~es*, shares maintaining a firm price; (mus.) *note ~e*, sustained note; **2.** bound, obliged; *être ~ à*, to be bound or obliged to; *être ~ au secret professionnel*, to be bound to official secrecy; *à l'impossible nul n'est ~*, no one is expected to achieve the impossible; *être ~ de ne pas quitter son poste*, to be under an obligation not to leave one's post; *être ~ de*, to be obliged to, to be responsible for; *être ~ des dégradations*, to be responsible for damage, for repairs.

ténu, -e [teny] *adj.* thin, tenuous, attenuated, slight, slender, frail, faint; (fig.) subtle, over-refined, minimal.

tenue [təny] *s.f.* holding, sitting, session; attitude; (of a person) behaviour, deportment, carriage, bearing, dress, appearance, seat (on horseback); (of race-horse) staying power; firmness (of share prices); bookkeeping; (mus.) holding (of a note); (naut.) anchor-hold; (mil.) *en ~*, in uniform; *grande ~*, *petite ~*, full-dress, undress, uniform; *~de campagne*, service dress, full marching kit; *se mettre en ~*, to change, to dress (for the occasion); *~ de livres en partie double*, *en partie simple*, bookkeeping by double entry, by single entry; *avoir de la ~*, to have manners, to know how to behave; *avoir une bonne ~*, to have good manners, to behave well; *tout d'une ~*, *d'une seule ~*, all of a piece; *en ~ de soirée*, in evening dress; (car) *~ de route*, road-holding, steering.

ténuirostre [tenɥirɔstr] *adj.* (ornith.) slender-billed.

ténuité [tenɥite] *s.f.* tenuity, tenuousness, thinness, slenderness, smallness.

tenure [tənyr] *s.f.* (feud.) tenure.

teocalli [teɔkali] *s.m.* teocalli, temple of Mexican aborigines, usually on truncated pyramid.

téorbe see THÉORBE.

ter [tɛr] *adv.* three times, thrice-repeated, occurring a third time; (house number) *5 ~*, 5b.

térato-logie [teratɔlɔʒi] *s.f.* teratology; **~logique** [teratɔlɔʒik] *adj.* teratological; **~logiste** [teratɔlɔʒist]; **~logue** [teratɔlɔg] *s.m.* teratologist.

terbium [tɛrbiɔm] *s.m.* (chem.) terbium.

tercet [tɛrsɛ] *s.m.* (pros.) tercet, tiercet, triplet.

térébenthène [terebɑ̃tɛn] *s.m.* (chem.) terebenthene.

térébenthine [terebɑ̃tin] *s.f.* turpentine; *essence de ~*, (oil of) turpentine.

térébinthe [terebɛ̃t] *s.m.* (bot.) terebinth; turpentine-tree.

térébrant, -e [terebrɑ̃] *adj.* (zool.) terebrant, boring; (fig.) piercing.

tergal [tɛrgal] *s.m.* (text.) (proprietary name) = TÉRYLÈNE.

tergiversation [tɛrʒivɛrsɑsjɔ̃] *s.f.* tergiversation; evasion, shuffling.

tergiverser [terʒivɛrse] *v.i.* to tergiversate; to beat about the bush, to be evasive.

terme [tɛrm] *s.m.* term, expression, word; limit, boundary, goal, end, outcome, aim; time, due date, date of completion; rent, quarter, quarter-day; (arch.) terminus; (comm., fin.) *à ~*, on account, by instalments; *à deux ~s*, in two instalments; (Stock Exchange) *opérations à ~*, forward dealings; (med.) *à ~*, (at) full-term; *avant ~*, prematurely, untimely, before one's time; *à court ~*, short-dated; *dans toute la force du ~*, in the full meaning of the word; *moyen ~*, middle course; *approcher de son ~*, to draw to a close; *être planté comme un ~*, to stand like a statue, like a block of stone; *mesurer, ménager, peser, ses ~s*, to weigh one's words; *parler de qn. en bons ~s*, to speak favourably of s.o.; *payer son ~*, to pay one's rent; *toucher à son ~*, to be near one's end; *mener à ~*, to bring to a conclusion, to carry through; *mon ~ était échu*, my time was up, my lease had run out; *il y a ~ à tout*, all things come to an end; *qui a ~ ne doit rien*, no one need pay till a debt is due; *le ~ vaut l'argent*, time is money.

terminaison [tɛrminɛzɔ̃] *s.f.* termination, ending; end, conclusion.

terminal, -e, (aux) [tɛrminal] *adj.* terminal; concluding; (bot., hort.) terminal, leader; (at school) (*classe*) *~e* = upper sixth; *~ s.m.* terminal.

terminer [tɛrmine] *v.t.* to terminate, to end, to form the end of, to round off, to bound, to limit, to finish, to complete, to conclude, to close; *~ un différend*, to settle a quarrel; **se ~** *v.refl.* to end, to terminate, to come to an end.

terminologie [tɛrminɔlɔʒi] *s.f.* terminology.

terminus [tɛrminys] *s.m* terminus.
termite [tɛrmit] *s.m.* (ent.) termite, white ant; (fig.) *travail de ~*, destructive or subversive underground activity.
termitière [tɛrmitjɛr] *s.f.* termitarium, termitary, nest of termites, termite mound, ant-hill; (fig.) ant-heap.
ternaire [tɛrnɛr] *adj.* ternary; (bot.) ternate; (mus.) *mesure ~*, triple time.
terne [tɛrn] *s.m.* tern, three winning numbers, (at dice) two threes; (electr.) triple-phase conductor.
terne [tɛrn] *adj.* dull, leaden, wan, dim, colourless, dingy; flat, lifeless, drab, dreary.
ternir [tɛrnir] *v.t.* to tarnish, to dull, to diminish the lustre of; to dirty, to stain; to dim, to deaden, to fade; to sully, to cast a slur on; **se ~** *v.refl.* to grow dull, or dim, to lose lustre, to fade.
ternissure [tɛrnisyr] *s.f.* **ternissement** [tɛrnismɑ̃] *s.m.* tarnish, tarnishing, dullness, dimming, fading, blemish, stain, dull spot or patch.
terpène [tɛrpɛn] *s.m.* (chem.) terpene.
terrain [tɛrɛ̃] *s.m.* soil, earth, land, site, plot, ground, piece of ground, (geog.) formation, terrain; field; pitch; tennis-court; *aller sur le ~*, to fight a duel; *céder le ~*, to yield ground, to give way; *connaître le ~*, to know one's ground, to be on familiar ground; *reconnaître le ~*, to reconnoitre the ground; *disputer le ~*, to dispute every inch of ground; *être sur son ~*, to be on one's own ground, to be at home; (fig.) *ménager le ~*, to make the most of one's resources; *perdre du ~*, to lose ground; *tâter, sonder, le ~*, to feel one's way; to see how the land lies; *~s à vendre*, plots of land for sale.
terramare [tɛramar] *s.f.* terramare, terramara.
terraqué, -e [tɛrake] *adj.* terraqueous.
terrasse [tɛras] *s.f.* terrace, raised bank; earthwork; flat roof, wide balcony; pavement (in front of a café); *assis à la ~*, sitting outside; ⚠ not 'terrace' of houses.
terrassement [tɛrasmɑ̃] *s.m.* earthwork(s), embankment, excavation, spoil.
terrasser [tɛrase] *v.t.* **1.** to bank up, to dig, to embank; **2.** to throw to the ground, to fell, to knock down; (fig.) to overwhelm, to floor, to lay low; *être terrassé*, to be crushed or prostrated.
terrassier [tɛrasje] *s.m.* navvy, labourer.
terre [tɛr] *s.f.* earth, land, shore, ground, soil, loam, clay, mould; country, dominions, territory, grounds, estate, property; the world; *bien avant dans les ~s*, far inland; *à ~*, on land, ashore; *~ cuite*, terracotta; *~ ferme*, terra firma, dry land; *~ à foulon*, fuller's earth; *~ forte*, heavy soil; *~ glaise*, clay; *~-noix*, pignut, earth-nut; *~ d'ambre*, umber; *~ de pipe*, pipe-clay; *pipe en ~*, clay pipe; *~ à porcelaine*, china clay; *~ à potier*, potter's clay; *~ pourrie*, rotten-stone; *charbon de ~*, coal (opp. charcoal); (electr.) (*prise de*) *~*, earth, earth-wire, earth connection; *mettre à la ~*, to earth; (of plants) *en pleine ~*, (growing) in the open, in the wild, on unfenced ground; *~ sainte*, consecrated ground; *la Terre Sainte*, the Holy Land; *~ à ~*, dull, matter-of-fact, commonplace, vulgar, down-to-earth, earthy; *tremblement de ~*, earthquake; *ventre à ~*, at full gallop; *tomber à* or *par ~*, to fall to the ground; *coucher par ~*, to sleep on the ground; *aller par ~*, to go by land, overland; *chasser sur les ~s d'autrui*, to trespass, to encroach on other people's rights; *cultiver la ~*, to till the ground; (naut.) *être à ~*, to be on shore; *mettre à ~*, to land; *mettre un ennemi à ~*, to vanquish an enemy; *mettre pied à ~*, to alight; *être sous ~*, to be dead and buried, to be in one's grave; *être encore sur ~*, to be still alive; *sur la ~*, on earth, in the world; *mettre un genou en ~*, to go down on one knee; *mettre en ~*, or *porter en ~*, to bury; *perdre ~*, to lose sight of land; *aller à ~*, to go ashore, to land; *remuer ciel et ~*, to move heaven and earth, to leave no stone unturned; *tenir aux choses de la ~*, to care for creature comforts; *vivre sur ses ~s*, to live on one's estate; *politique de la ~ brûlée*, scorched-earth policy.
terreau (pl. **-x**) [tɛro] *s.m.* leaf-mould, humus, compost.
terreauter [tɛrote] *v.t.* to compost.
Terre-Neuve [tɛrnœv] *s.f.* (geog.) Newfoundland; **terre-neuve** *s.m.invar.*, Newfoundland (dog).
terre-neuvien, -neuvier, or **-neuvas** [tɛrnœvjɛ̃, -nœvje, -nœva] *s.m., adj.* (fisherman or vessel) fishing off Newfoundland.
terre-plein [tɛrplɛ̃] *s.m.* (pl. *terre-pleins*) open space, platform, raised walk, terrace; (fort.) terreplein.
terrer [tɛre] *v.t.* (hort.) to earth up, to earth over, to fill with soil; to compost, to spread mould on, to renew the soil of, to full (cloth); **se ~** *v.refl.* to burrow; to entrench oneself; (fig.) to dig oneself in, to go to ground, to bury oneself.
terrestre [tɛrɛstr] *adj.* terrestrial, earthly, land; (fig.) worldly.
terreur [tɛrœr] *s.f.* terror; fear, dread, fright; object of dread, one who inspires terror; *la ~*, the reign of terror, the Terror; *pris de ~*, terror-stricken; (slang) *jouer les ~s*, to terrorize, to work a protection racket.
terreu-x, -se [tɛrø] *adj.* earthy, dull, dirty, muddy, sickly.
terri [tɛri] *s.m.* = TERRIL.
terrible [tɛribl] *adj.* terrible, dreadful, awful, frightful; *enfant ~*, enfant terrible, little devil, holy terror; **~ment** [tɛribləmɑ̃] *adv.* terribly; (lit. & fig.) dreadfully, awfully, frightfully.
terrien, -ne [tɛrjɛ̃] *s.m.f.* land-owner, landed proprietor; inhabitant of the Earth; (naut.) landlubber; *adj.* land-owning, of the soil, country.
terrier [tɛrje] *s.m.* burrow, hole, earth; (dog) terrier; *sortir de son ~*, to break cover.
terrifiant, -e [tɛrifjɑ̃] *adj.* terrifying, awe-inspiring; (fig.) terrific, astonishing, remarkable.
terrifier [tɛrifje] *v.t.* to terrify, to frighten, to fill with terror.
terril [tɛri(l)] *s.m.* (coal mining) slag heap.
terrine [tɛrin] *s.f.* earthenware pan, basin, pot, terrine, dish, pie-dish; potted meat, pâté; ⚠ not 'tureen'.
terrir [tɛrir] *v.i.* (naut.) to make land; (of fish) to come close inshore.
territoire [tɛritwar] *s.m.* territory, zone, area; jurisdiction; *~ maritime*, territorial waters.
territorial, -e, (**aux**) [tɛritɔrjal] *adj.* territorial; *~ s.m.* territorial, soldier of the territorial army; **~e** *s.f.* territorial army.
territorialité [tɛritɔrjalite] *s.f.* territoriality, territorial condition or quality.
terroir [tɛrwar] *s.m.* soil, ground; locality, part of the country; *goût de ~*, special local flavour; *il sent son ~*, he is a real local type, you can tell where he comes from; *accent de ~*, local accent.
terroriser [tɛrɔrize] *v.t.* to terrorize, to intimidate, to terrify.
terrorisme [tɛrɔrism] *s.m.* terrorism, terrorization.
terroriste [tɛrɔrist] *s.m.f., adj.* terrorist.
tertiaire [tɛrsjɛr] *adj.* tertiary; *~ s.m.* (geol.) Tertiary period or system.
tertio [tɛrsjo] *adv.* thirdly.
tertre [tɛrtr] *s.m.* hillock, mound, knoll.
térylène [terilɛn] *s.m.* (text.) terylene (proprietary name).
tes see TON *poss. adj.*

tessère [tesɛr] *s.f.* (Rom. ant.) tessera.
Tessin [tesɛ̃] *s.m.* (geog.) Ticino (river and canton).
tessiture [tessityr] *s.f.* (mus.) tessitura.
tesson [tesɔ̃] *s.m.* (pot)sherd, shard; piece of broken glass; *~s de bouteilles*, broken bottles.
test[1] [tɛst] *s.m.* (zool.) test, shell.
test[2] [tɛst] *s.m.* test, trial.
test[3] [tɛst] *s.m.* = TÊT.
testacé, -é [tɛstase] *adj.* testaceous.
testament [tɛstamɑ̃] *s.m.* will, testament; *le Nouveau Testament*, the New Testament; *léguer par ~*, to leave in a will; *mourir sans ~*, to die intestate.
testamentaire [tɛstamɑ̃tɛr] *adj.* testamentary, under a will.
testat-eur [tɛstatœr] *s.m.* testator; **~rice** [tɛstatris] *s.f.* testatrix.
tester[1] [tɛste] *v.i.* to make a will.
tester[2] [tɛste] *v.t.* to test.
testicule [tɛstikyl] *s.m.* testicle, testis.
testimonial, -e, (**aux**) [tɛstimɔnjal] *adj.* witnessing, testifying, supported by evidence.
teston [tɛstɔ̃] *s.m.* (hist.) tester (coin).
testostérone [tɛstɔsterɔn] *s.f.* (biol.) testosterone.
têt [tɛ] *s.m.* **1.** (pot)sherd, shard; earthenware pot; **2.** (chem.) test, cupel; **3.** (bot., zool.) test, testa, shell.
tétanie [tetani] *s.f.* (med.) tetany.
tétanique [tetanik) *adj.* (med.) tetanic; (fig.) convulsive.
tétaniser [tetanize] *v.t.* to tetanize.
tétanos [tetanos] *s.m.* (pathol.) tetanus, lockjaw.
têtard [tetar] *s.m.* **1.** tadpole; **2.** pollard tree; **3.** (slang) child.
tête [tɛt] *s.f.* head; top; (fig.) brain(s); sense, mind, intellect, wit, judgement, presence of mind; face, expression, appearance; life; *donner ~ baissée dans*, to rush headlong, full tilt, into; *~ carrée*, stubborn, obstinate person; *coup de ~*, rash act; (mil.) *~ droite!*, eyes right!; *de la ~ aux pieds*, from head to foot, from top to toe; *en ~*, in front, ahead, foremost; (techn.) *soupapes en ~*, overhead valves; *un en-~* a heading; (journalism) *article de ~*, leading article, leader; *yeux à fleur de ~*, prominent, staring eyes; *~ de ligne*, starting-point, terminus; *de linotte*, empty-headed person; *mal de ~*, headache; *mauvaise ~*, obstinate, stubborn person; *par ~*, per head, a head; *en avoir par-dessus la ~*, to have had more than enough; *~ à perruque*, barber's block, (fig.) blockhead; *à ~ reposée*, at leisure; (*en*) *~ à ~*, tête-à-tête, close together, privately; *un ~ à ~*, a private interview, a private occasion; *il y va de votre ~*, your life is at stake; *avoir sa ~*, or *toute sa ~*, to be in one's senses, to be completely rational, to know what one is doing; (fam.) *avoir la ~ fêlée*, to be cracked; *avoir de la ~*, to have one's head screwed on the right way; *avoir la ~ dure*, to be obstinate; *avoir la ~ solide*, to be steady, to have a good head; *ce sont deux ~s dans le même bonnet*, they are hand in glove; *avoir une chose en ~*, to be bent on a thing; *se mettre en ~ de faire*, to take it into one's head to do; *se mettre dans la ~ que*, to get it into one's head that; *avoir la ~ chaude, la ~ pres du bonnet*, to be hot-headed; *avoir la ~ qui tourne*, to be giddy; *avoir martel en ~*, to be much bothered; *avoir mal à la ~*, to have a headache; *avoir la ~ à ce qu'on fait*, to have one's mind on what one is doing; *calculer de ~*, to work out in one's head; *donner de la ~ contre un mur*, to run one's head against a wall; (fig.) *se casser* or *se creuser la ~*, to rack one's brains; *crier à tue-~*, to yell or shout at the top of one's voice; *donner sa ~ à couper*, to stake one's life (on sth.); *en avoir par-dessus la ~*, to be heartily sick of it, to have had more than enough of it; *ne savoir où donner de la ~*, not to know what to do, to be at one's wits end; *faire ~ à*, to face, to stand up to; *faire à sa ~*, to have one's own way, to do as one likes; *faire une ~*, or *une sale ~*, to pull a long face; *faire un signe de ~*, to nod; (footb.) *faire une ~*, *jouer de la ~*, to head the ball; *faire un-~-à queue*, to make a quick turn-round, to dash in and out again, to make a U-turn; *virer ~ à queue*, to turn in its own length; *hocher la ~*, to toss one's head, to shake one's head; *jeter qch. à la ~ de qn.*, (i.) to flaunt sth. before s.o.; (ii.) to cast sth. in someone's teeth; (fig.) *se jeter à la ~ de qn.*, to throw oneself at s.o.; (of wine, excitement, etc.) *monter à la ~*, to go to one's head; *piquer une ~*, to dive, to plunge headlong; *prendre la ~*, to take the lead, to assume leadership; *tenir ~ à qn.*, to stand up to s.o., to turn and face s.o.; (fam.) *se payer la ~ de qn.*, to take a rise out of s.o., to have s.o. on, to pull someone's leg; *faire la ~*, to sulk; *~ d'un missile*, missile warhead; *~ d'ail*, bulb of garlic; *~ de bielle*, crank-head; (mil.) *~ de pont*, bridgehead, beach-head; *avoir une ~ sympathique*, to have a nice face; *faire une drôle de ~*, to put on a silly or peculiar expression; *faire une ~ de six pieds de long*, to pull a very long face; *il a une bonne ~*, he looks a decent sort; *je connais cette ~*, I know that chap.
têteau (pl. **-x**) [tɛto] *s.m.* end of a main branch.
tête-bêche [tɛtbɛʃ] *adv.* (lying) head to foot, head to tail; (joined) bottom to top.
tête-de-mort [tɛtdəmɔr] *s.f.* (pl. *têtes-de-mort*) **1.** death's-head, skull and crossbones; **2.** (also *tête de Maure*) a kind of Dutch cheese.
tête-de-moineau [tɛtdəmwano] *s.m.* (pl. *têtes-de-moineau*) (anthracite, etc.) nut.
tête-de-nègre [tɛtdənɛgr] *adj.*, *s.m.invar.* very dark brown (colour).
tétée [tete] *s.f.* suck, feed (from breast or feeding-bottle).
téter [tete] *v.t.* to suck; *donner à ~ à*, to suckle, to feed.
têtière [tɛtjɛr] *s.f.* **1.** (naut.) head (of sail); **2.** headstall; **3.** antimacassar.
tétin [tetɛ̃] *s.m.* nipple, teat, dug.
tétine [tetin] *s.f.* **1.** teat, dummy; **2.** udder, dug; (pop., pej.) breast.
téton [tetɔ̃] *s.m.* (fam.) breast; (techn.) nipple.
tétonnière [tetɔnjɛr] *s.f.* (fam.) woman with big bosom.
tétra-chlorure [tetraklɔryr] *s.m.* (chem.) tetrachloride; **~corde** [tetrakɔrd] *s.m.* (mus.) tetrachord; **~èdre** [tetraɛdr] *s.m.* tetrahedron; *adj.* tetrahedral; **~gone** [tetragɔn] *s.f.* (bot.) New Zealand spinach; **~logie** [tetralɔʒi] *s.f.* tetralogy; **~mère** [tetramɛr] *adj.* (ent.) tetramerous; **~mètre** [tetramɛtr] *s.m.* (pros.) tetrameter; **~pode** [tetrapɔd] *s.m.* (zool.) tetrapod; *adj.* tetrapod(ous); **~ptère** [tetraptɛr] *adj.*, *s.m.f.* (ent.) tetrapterous (insect).
tétrarchat [tetrarka] *s.m.* tetrarchate.
tétrarchie [tetrarʃi] *s.f.* tetrarchy.
tétrarque [tetrark] *s.m.* tetrarch.
tétras [tetrɑ] *s.m.* (ornith.) grouse; *grand ~*, capercaillie.
tétrastyle [tetrastil] *s.m.* tetrastyle.
tétrasyllabe [tetrasilab] *s.m* tetrasyllable; *~ adj.* tetrasyllabic.
tétrasyllabique [tetrasilabik] *adj.* tetrasyllabic.
tétrodon [tetrɔdɔ̃] *s.m.* (ichth.) tetrodon, globe-fish.
tette [tɛt] *s.f.* teat, dug, (of animals).
têtu, -e [tɛty] *adj.* headstrong, stubborn, obstinate, pig-headed, mulish.
teuf-teuf [tœftœf] *s.m.* vintage car, old crock.
teuton, -ne [tøtɔ̃] *adj.* Teutonic; *s.m.f.* Teuton.
teutonique [tøtɔnik] *adj.* Teutonic.
Texas [tɛksas] *s.m.* (geog.) Texas.
texan, -e [tɛksɑ̃] *adj.*, *s.m.f.* Texan.

texte [tɛkst] *s.m.* **1.** text, original; *lire dans le* ~, to read in the original; *tiré du* ~, (of quotation) textual; **2.** text; words (of song, etc.), libretto; script; theme, matter, subject; **3.** print, type; *gravure hors-*~, plate, full-page engraving; *revenir à son* ~, to return to the point; *restituer un* ~, to restore a text.

textile [tɛkstil] *adj.*, *s.m.* textile.

textuel, -le [tɛkstɥɛl] *adj.* textual, verbatim, word for word; **~lement** [tɛkstɥɛlmɑ̃] *adv.* textually, in the exact words (of the text, etc.), word for word.

texture [tɛkstyr] *s.f.* texture; (fig.) construction, arrangement.

thaï [tai] *adj.invar.* Thai.

thaïlandais, -e [tailɑ̃dɛ] *adj.* Thai; *s.m.f.* Thai, Thailander.

Thaïlande [tailɑ̃d] *s.f.* (geog.) Thailand.

thalamus [talamys] *s.m.* (anat.) thalamus.

thaler [talɛr] *s.m.* (hist.) thaler (German coin).

thalle [tal] *s.m.* (bot.) thallus.

thallium [talliɔm] *s.m.* (chem.) thallium.

thallophytes [tallɔfit] *s.f.pl.* (bot.) thallophytes.

thalweg [talvɛg] *s.m.* (geog.) thalweg, lowest line of a valley.

thaumaturge [tomatyrʒ] *s.m.f.* thaumaturge, worker of miracles; ~ *adj.* thaumaturgic(al).

thaumaturgie [tomatyrʒi] *s.f.* thaumaturgy.

thé [te] *s.m.* tea; tea-party; tea-plant; *boîte à* ~, tea-caddy, tea-canister; *salon de* ~, tea-room.

théatin [teatɛ̃] *s.m.* Theatine (monk).

théâtral, -e, (**aux**) [teɑtral] *adj.* theatrical, dramatic; **~ement** [teɑtrikalmɑ̃] *adv.* theatrically, dramatically; (fig.) in a theatrical manner.

théâtralisme [teɑtralism] *s.m.* theatricality (of behaviour); (psychol.) exhibitionism.

théâtre [teɑtr] *s.m.* theatre, playhouse, stage, drama, plays, dramatic works; dramatic art, acting; scene, show; setting, background; field of action; *coup de* ~, unexpected event; striking stage-effect; striking change; *pièce de* ~, play, stage piece; ~ *de la guerre*, theatre of war; *faire du* ~, to be or go on the stage, to act, to be an actor; *le* ~ *de Molière*, Molière's plays; ⚠ not (operating) 'theatre'.

thébaïde [tebaid] *s.f.* (Lit.) deep solitude.

thébain, -e [tebɛ̃] *adj.*, *s.m.f.* Theban.

théier [teje] *s.m.* (bot.) tea-plant, tea-shrub.

théière [tejɛr] *s.f.* teapot.

théisme[1] [teism] *s.m.* (med.) poisoning through excessive tea-drinking.

théisme[2] [teism] *s.m.* theism.

théiste [teist] *s.m.f.* theist; ~ *adj.* theistic.

thématique [tematik] *adj.* (gram., mus.) thematic; ~ *s.f.* set of themes.

thème [tɛm] *s.m.* theme, topic, subject; exercise, composition (translation from one's own language into another); (fam.) *un fort en* ~, a brilliant pupil; (pej.) a swot, a bookish type.

thénar [tenar] *s.m.* (anat.) thenar.

théobrome [teɔbrɔm] *s.m.* (bot.) Theobroma.

théobromine [teɔbrɔmin] *s.m.* (pharm.) theobromine.

théocratie [teɔkrasi] *s.f.* theocracy.

théocratique [teɔkratik] *adj.* theocratic.

théodicée [teɔdise] *s.f.* theodicy.

théodolite [teɔdɔlit] *s.m.* theodolite.

théogonie [teɔgɔni] *s.f.* theogony.

théogonique [teɔgɔnik] *adj.* theogonic.

théologal, -e, (**aux**) [teɔlɔgal] *adj.* theological; *les trois vertus* ~*es*, the three theological virtues (faith, hope, charity); ~ *s.m.* lecturer in divinity.

théolog-ie [teɔlɔʒi] *s.f.* theology, divinity; **~ien** [teɔlɔʒjɛ̃] *s.m.* theologian; **~ique** [teɔlɔʒik] *adj.* theological; **~iquement** [teɔlɔʒikmɑ̃] *adv.* theologically.

théorbe, téorbe [teɔrb] *s.m.* (mus.) theorbo.

théorème [teɔrɛm] *s.m.* (math.) theorem.

théoricien, -ne [teɔrisjɛ̃] *s.m.f.* theorist, theoretician.

théorie [teɔri] *s.f.* theory, speculation, theoretical instruction; (mil.) training-manual; principles of manœuvre; procession; *en* ~, theoretically, in theory, (fig.) on paper; *faire des* ~*s*, to speculate; *une longue* ~ *de moines*, a procession of monks.

théorique [teɔrik] *adj.* theoretic, theoretical, speculative; **~ment** [teɔrikmɑ̃] *adv.* theoretically, in theory.

théosophe [teɔzɔf] *s.m.f.* theosophist.

théosophie [teɔzɔfi] *s.f.* theosophy.

thèque [tɛk] *s.f.* (bot.) theca.

thérapeute [terapøt] *s.m.* therapeutist, therapist.

thérapeutique [terapøtik] *adj.* therapeutic; ~ *s.f.* therapeutics, therapy.

thérapie [terapi] *s.f.* therapy.

thermal, -e, (**aux**) [tɛrmal] *adj.* thermal; *eaux* ~*es*, hot springs; *station* ~*e*, health resort, spa, watering-place; *établissement* ~, thermal establishment, hydro.

thermalité [tɛrmalite] *s.f.* quality of thermal waters.

thermes [tɛrm] *s.m.pl.* (ant.) thermae, hot springs; (mod.) hot baths, thermal establishment.

thermidor [tɛrmidɔr] *s.m.* (hist.) Thermidor (eleventh month in Fr. Republican Calendar, July–August).

thermidorien, -ne [tɛrmidɔrjɛ̃] (hist.) *adj.*, *s.m.f.* Thermidorian.

thermie [tɛrmi] *s.f.* thermal unit of heat (1000 great calories); ⚠ does not = either (British) 'therm' or 'British Thermal Unit'.

thermique [tɛrmik] *adj.* thermic, thermal.

thermistor [tɛrmistɔr], **thermisteur** [tɛrmistœr] *s.m.* (phys.) thermistor.

thermo-chimie [tɛrmɔʃimi] *s.f.* thermochemistry; **~durcissable** [tɛrmɔdyrsisabl] *adj.* (of resins, etc.) heat-setting; **~dynamique** [tɛrmɔdinamik] *s.f.* thermodynamics; *adj.* thermodynamic; **~électricité** [tɛrmɔelɛktrisite] *s.f.* thermoelectricity; **~électrique** [tɛrmɔelɛktrik] *adj.* thermoelectric; **~graphe** [tɛrmɔgraf] *s.m.* thermograph; **~mètre** [tɛrmɔmɛtr] *s.m.* thermometer; **~métrique** [tɛrmɔmetrik] *adj.* thermometric(al); **~nucléaire** [tɛrmɔnykleɛr] *adj.* thermonuclear; **~plastique** [tɛrmɔplastik] *adj.* (chem.) thermoplastic, heat-resistant; **~pompe** [tɛrmɔpɔ̃p] *s.f.* heat-pump; **~propulsion** [tɛrmɔprɔpylsjɔ̃] *s.f.* thermo-propulsion.

thermorésistant, -e [tɛrmɔrezistɑ̃] *adj.* heat-resisting.

thermos [tɛrmos] *s.f.* thermos, proprietary brand of vacuum flask or jar.

thermoscope [tɛrmɔskɔp] *s.m.* (phys.) thermoscope.

thermosiphon [tɛrmosifɔ̃] *s.m.* (techn.) thermo-siphon.

thermostat [tɛrmɔsta] *s.m.* thermostat.

thésauriser [tezorize] *v.t.i.* to hoard, to treasure up money, to amass money, to salt away.

thésauriseu-r, -se [tezɔrizœr] *s.m.f.* hoarder.

thèse [tɛz] *s.f.* **1.** thesis, argument, proposition, (fam.) line, discussion; subject; *cela change la* ~, that alters the case; *en* ~ *générale*, as a general rule; **2.** (obs.) graduation or doctoral thesis; (mod.) *soutenance de* ~, oral examination on thesis submitted.

théurgie [teyrʒi] *s.f.* theurgy.

thibaude [tibod] *s.f.* felt, underlay, (for carpets).

thionique [tiɔnik] *adj.* (chem.) *acide* ~, thio-acid.

thiosulfate [tjɔsylfat] *s.m.* (chem.) thiosulphate.

thixotropie [tiksɔtrɔpi] *s.f.* thixotropy.

thlaspi [tlaspi] *s.m.* (bot.) Thlaspi, penny-cress.

thomisme [tɔmism] *s.m.* Thomism.
thomiste [tɔmist] *s.m.f., adj.* Thomist.
thon [tɔ̃] *s.m.* (ichth.) tunny(-fish); **~aire** [tɔnɛr] *s.m.* net for tunny-fishing; **~ier** [tɔnje] *s.m.* tunny-boat; **~ine** [tɔnin] *s.f.* (ichth.) Mediterranean tunny.
thoracique [tɔrasik] *adj.* (anat.) thoracic.
thorax [tɔraks] *s.m.* (anat.) thorax, chest.
thorite [tɔrit] *s.f.* (min.) thorite.
thorium [tɔriɔm] *s.m.* (chem.) thorium.
thrips [trips] *s.m.* (ent.) thrips.
thrombose [trɔ̃boz] (pathol.) thrombosis.
thrombus [trɔmbys] *s.m.* (pathol.) thrombus, blood-clot.
thuriféraire [tyriferɛr] *s.m.* thurifer, censer--bearer, (fig.) flatterer.
thurne [tyrn] *s.f.* = TURNE 2.
thuya [tyja] *s.m.* (bot.) thuja, thuya, arbor vitae.
thyade [tjad] *s.f.* Bacchante.
thym [tɛ̃] *s.m.* (bot.) thyme.
thymique [timik] *adj.* (anat.) thymic.
thymol [timɔl] *s.m.* thymol.
thymus [timys] *s.m.* (anat.) thymus (gland).
thyroïde [tirɔid] *adj.* (anat.) thyroid.
thyroïdien, -ne [tirɔidjɛ̃] *adj.* (anat.) thyroid.
thyroxine [tirɔksin] *s.f.* (chem.) thyroxin(e).
thyrse [tirs] *s.m.* (anat., bot.) thyrsus.
tiare [tjar] *s.f.* tiara; (fig.) papal office; *coiffer la ~*, to become pope.
Tibet [tibɛ] *s.m.* (geog.) Tibet.
tibétain, -e [tibetɛ̃] *adj., s.m.f.* Tibetan.
tibia [tibja] *s.m.* (anat.) tibia.
tibial, -e, (aux) [tibjal] *adj.* (anat.) tibial.
Tibre [tibr] *s.m.* (geog.) Tiber (river).
tic [tik] *s.m.* tic, twitching; nervous habit or mannerism; (fig.) obsession, mania.
ticket [tikɛ] *s.m.* ticket, check, slip, coupon; (pop.) 1000-franc note (pre-1958 francs); (pop.) *avoir le ~*, to be getting on very well (with s.o.).
tic-tac [tik-tak] *s.m.* tick-tock, ticking.
tictaquer [tiktake] *v.i.* to tick.
tiédasse [tjedas] *adj.* (pej.) lukewarm.
tiède [tjɛd] *adj.* lukewarm, tepid, mild, soft; (fig.) indifferent, half-hearted; *~ s.m.f.* (pej.) lukewarm or fainthearted person; **~ment** [tjɛdmɑ̃] *adv.* coolly, without enthusiasm, half--heartedly.
tiédeur [tjedœr] *s.f.* **1.** tepidity, lukewarmness, mildness, pleasant warmth (after cold); (fig.) indifference, half-heartedness; **2.** warmth, cosiness.
tiédir [tjedir] *v.i.* to become warm, to become lukewarm or tepid; (fig.) to cool off; *faire ~ des assiettes*, to warm plates; *~ v.t.* to warm.
tiédissement [tjedismɑ̃] *s.m.* becoming tepid or lukewarm; (fig.) cooling(-off).
tien, -ne [tjɛ̃] *poss. adj.* & *pron.* yours, your own; (fam.) *à la ~ ne!*, your health!; *~ s.m.* your property, yours; *le ~ et le mien*, what is yours and what is mine, mine and thine; *les ~s*, your relations, family, friends, supporters; *il faut y mettre du ~*, you must make an effort, you must you put your back into it; you must contribute something.
tierce [tjɛrs] *s.f.* (mus., astron.) third; (fenc.) tierce (thrust or parry); (print.) last revise, final (proof); (cards, herald.) tierce; (eccles.) terce, tierce.
tiercé, -e [tjɛrse] *adj.* (herald.) divided into three parts; (agric.) ploughed or dressed three times; (betting) *pari ~*, triple forecast.
tiercelet [tjɛrsəlɛ] *s.m.* (ornith.) tercel, male hawk.
tiercer [tjɛrse] *v.t.* (agric.) to plough or dress three times; (techn.) to space at 120°.
tierceron [tjɛrsərɔ̃] *s.m.* (arch.) tierceron.
tier-s, -ce [tjɛr] *adj.* third, (med.) tertian; *fièvre ~ce*, tertian fever; *~s état*, tiers état, third estate, the commonalty, the commons, the people; (pol.) *Tiers Monde*, Third World; (law) *~s-arbitre*, referee.
tiers [tjɛr] *s.m.* third, third party, third person; *les deux ~*, two-thirds; *être en ~*, to make a third, to be odd man out; *le ~ et le quart*, any-body and everybody.
tiers-point [tjɛrpwɛ̃] *s.m.* **1.** (arch.) tierce-point; **2.** (techn.) triangular file.
tif, tiffe [tif] *s.m.* (usu. pl.) (pop.) hair.
tige [tiʒ] *s.f.* stem, stalk, trunk (of tree), straw (of corn); shank (of key); shaft (of column); (fig.) leg of a boot; stock (of a family); (techn.) rod; *~ de piston*, piston-rod; *haute ~*, standard (tree); *~ de communication*, connecting-rod; *~ de soupape*, valve-stem; valve-tappet, valve-spindle.
tigelle [tiʒɛl] *s.f.* (bot.) tigellum.
tigette [tiʒɛt] *s.f.* (arch.) honeysuckle ornament.
tignasse [tiɲas] *s.f.* (fam.) hair; untidy head of hair, shock or mop of hair.
tigre, -sse [tigr] *s.m.f.* (zool.) tiger, tigress.
Tigre [tigr] *s.m.* (geog.) Tigris (river).
tigré, -e [tigre] *adj.* spotted, speckled; striped; (bot.) *lis ~*, tiger-lily.
tigron [tigrɔ̃], **tiglon** [tiglɔ̃] *s.m.* (zool.) tigon.
tilbury [tilbyri] *s.m.* (hist.) tilbury, two-wheeled carriage.
tilde [tild, tilde] *s.m.* tilde.
tillac [tijak] *s.m.* deck; *franc ~*, main deck, flush-deck; *faux ~*, half-deck.
tillage, tille, tiller see TEILLAGE, etc.
tilleul [tijœl] *s.m.* lime-tree, linden-tree, lime--tree flowers; infusion of lime-tree flowers.
timbale [tɛ̃bal] *s.f.* **1.** kettledrum; (pl.) timpani; **2.** metal cup or mug; (cook.) round pie-dish; pie.
timbalier [tɛ̃balje] *s.m.* timpanist.
timbrage [tɛ̃braʒ] *s.m.* stamping, cancelling, cancellation, post-marking; (techn.) test-stamp.
timbre [tɛ̃br] *s.m.* **1.** bell, sound, tone, quality, timbre; (fam.) *avoir le ~ fêlé*, to be cracked; to have a screw loose; **2.** postage-stamp, stamp; *~ d'affranchissement*, postage-stamp; *~ acquit*, receipt-stamp; *~ dateur* or *du jour*, date-stamp; *droit de ~*, stamp-duty; *~ de la poste*, post-office stamp, postmark; *~-poste*, stamp, postage--stamp; *~ quittance*, receipt stamp; *~ sec*, plain relief stamp; embossing-press; **3.** (herald.) crest, helmet.
timbré, -e [tɛ̃bre] *adj.* stamped; sonorous, having a rich timbre; (herald.) crested; (fam.) cracked, dotty.
timbrer [tɛ̃bre] *v.t.* to stamp, (law) to docket, (herald.) to crest.
timide [timid] *adj.* timid, shy, apprehensive, bashful, diffident, cautious; *~ s.m.* timid be-haviour, shy manner; **~ment** [timidmɑ̃] *adv.* timidly, shyly, bashfully.
timidité [timidite] *s.f.* timidity, timorousness, bashfulness, shyness, diffidence.
timon [timɔ̃] *s.m.* pole (of carriage), beam (of plough), (naut.) tiller, helm; (fig.) helm, direction, government.
timonerie [timɔnri] *s.f.* (naut.) steerage; *poste de ~*, signal-station; *kiosque de ~*, wheelhouse; *chef de ~*, chief quartermaster; (car) steering--gear; brake system.
timonier [timɔnje] *s.m.* **1.** steersman, signalman; helmsman; *~ de quart*, quartermaster; **2.** shaft--horse.
timoré, -e [timɔre] *adj.* timorous, fearful.
tin [tɛ̃] *s.m.* (naut.) keel-block.
tinamou [tinamu] *s.m.* (ornith.) tinamou.
tincal [tɛ̃kal] *s.m.* (chem.) tincal, tinkal, crude borax.
tinctorial, -e, (aux) [tɛ̃ktɔrjal] *adj.* tinctorial.
tinette [tinɛt] *s.f.* tub, firkin; soil-tub (for night-soil).

tintamarre [tɛ̃tamar] *s.m.* noise, din, racket; chatter; (fig.) fuss.
tintement [tɛ̃tmɑ̃] *s.m.* ringing, tinkling, jingling; tolling, chiming; singing, ringing, (in the ears).
tinter [tɛ̃te] *v.i.* to ring, to toll, to jingle, to clink, to tingle, to tinkle; *les oreilles me tintent*, there is a ringing in my ears; (fig.) my ears are burning.
tintinnabuler [tɛ̃tinabyle] *v.i.* to tinkle, to tintinnabulate.
tintouin [tɛ̃twɛ̃] *s.m.* (fam.) din, trying noise; (fig.) disquiet, trouble, bother, nuisance.
tipule [tipyl] *s.f.* (ent.) crane-fly, daddy-long--legs.
tique [tik] *s.f.* (ent.) tick.
tiquer [tike] *v.i.* to have a nervous twitch, to twitch; (of horse) to bite the crib, to be vicious; (fam.) to wince; to crib (*sur*, at), to make a wry face.
tiqueté, -e [tikte] *adj.* variegated, spotted, speckled
tiqueture [tiktyr] *s.f.* variegation, speckles.
tiqueu-r, -se [tikœr] *adj.* having a nervous twitch or habit; (of horse) crib-biting, vicious.
tir [tir] *s.m.* firing, shooting; (footb., etc.) shot; fire; line of fire, trajectory; archery, target- or shooting-practice; shooting-gallery, -range, or -ground, rifle-range, rifle match or competition; ~ *à la cible*, target-firing; *canon à ~ rapide*, quick-firing gun; *armes à ~ automatique*, automatic weapons; *concours de ~*, shooting--match; *société de ~*, rifle club; ~ *à longue portée*, long-range fire.
T.I.R. [teiɛr] abbrev. *Transports internationaux routiers.*
tirade [tirad] *s.f.* tirade, lengthy speech, torrent of words; (fam.) lecture; (fam.) *d'une ~*, *tout d'une ~*, at a stretch, without pausing for breath.
tirage [tiraʒ] *s.m.* draught, drawing, pulling, dragging, tug; pull, tugging, pulling; tow, towing-path; winding off (of silk); extraction (of ores, etc.); (print.) working off, impression, edition; (newspapers) circulation, issue; (photo.) printing; (fig.) difficulty, obstacle; ~ *élevé*, large circulation (of newspapers); ~ *au sort*, drawing lots; *mauvais ~*, bad draught (of a chimney); (fam.) *il y a du ~*, things are not going smoothly.
tiraillement [tirɑjmɑ̃] *s.m.* pulling, hauling about; constriction, spasm, cramp, gnawing pain, twinge; (fig.) discord, wrangling, tug-of--war.
tirailler [tirɑje] *v.t.* to pull about, to pull in contrary directions, to tug (at); (fig.) to tease, to plague, to pester; ~ *v.i.* to fire wildly, to shoot at random; **se** ~ *v.refl.* to squabble.
tiraillerie [tirɑjri] *s.f.* desultory firing, skirmishing; constant tugging.
tirailleur [tirajœr] *s.m.* sharpshooter, skirmisher.
tirant [tirɑ̃] *s.m.* strap, purse-string, tie (of shoes); (arch.) brace, (techn.) stay, rod; (naut.) draught.
tirasse [tiras] *s.f.* draw-net (for quails, etc.); (organ) pedal-coupler.
tire [tir] *s.f.* **1.** (pop.) tug, pull, snatch; *voleur à la ~*, pick-pocket; **2.** (slang) car.
tiré, -e [tire] *adj.* drawn, fatigued, worn out; printed, issued; saved (from danger); (fig.) ~ *par les cheveux*, far-fetched; ~ *à quatre épingles*, spick and span; *à couteaux ~s*, at daggers drawn; ~ *s.m.* **1.** (usu. pl.) coverts; shooting-ground; **2.** (comm.) drawee (of a bill).
tire-au-cul [tiroky], **tire-au-flanc** [tiroflɑ̃] *s.m.invar.* (pop.) scrimshanker.
tire-balle(s) [tirbal] *s.m.* (surg.) bullet-extractor; **~-botte** [tirbɔt] *s.m.* (pl. *~-bottes*) boot--hook; boot-jack; **~-bouchon** [tirbuʃɔ̃] *s.m.* (pl. *~-bouchons*) corkscrew; (of hair) corkscrew curls, ringlets; *en ~-bouchon*, winding, spiral; **~-bouton** [tirbutɔ̃] *s.m.* (pl. *~-boutons*) button--hook; **~-braise** [tirbrɛz] *s.m.invar.* (baker's) oven-rake; **~-clou** [tirklu] *s.m.* (pl. *~-clous*) (techn.) nail-puller.
(**à**) **tire-d'aile** [atirdɛl] *adv.loc.* in swift flight, swiftly away.
tirée [tire] *s.f.* (fam.) long and difficult journey, hard slog.
tire-fesses [tirfɛs] *s.m.invar.* (pop.) ski-lift; **~-feu** [tirfø] *s.m.invar.* (artill.) lanyard; **~-filet** [tirfilɛ] *s.m.* (pl. *~-filets*) (techn.) scribe, scriber; **~-fond** [tirfɔ̃] *s.m.invar.* **1.** long bolt, screw--spike, coach-bolt; (rail.) sleeper-bolt; **2.** ring (screwed into ceiling), eye-bolt; **~-jus** [tirʒy] *s.m.invar.* (pop.) handkerchief; **~-laine** [tirlɛn] *s.m.invar.* (obs.) thief, prowler; **~-lait** [tirlɛ] *s.m.invar.* breast-reliever
(**à**) **tire-larigot** [atirlarigo] *adv.loc.* (fam.) in great quantities.
tire-ligne [tirliɲ] *s.m.* (pl. *~-lignes*) drawing-pen; **~lire** [tirlir] *s.f.* money-box (with slot); (pop.) stomach; head; **~-pied** [tirpje] *s.m.* (pl. *~-pieds*) (shoemaker's) stirrup.
tirer [tire] *v.t.i.* to draw, to pull, to tow, to drag, to pull in, out, on, up, etc.; to extract, to save, to get, to obtain, to derive, to extort, to snatch, to take away, out, off; to let (blood), to tap (liquors); (at cards) to cut; to stretch, to strain, to tighten, to wire-draw; (naut.) to draw; (print. and photo.) to print, to work off, to take (photo, etc.); to fire, to shoot, to discharge, to let off; to fence; to deduce, to infer, to conclude, to elicit; to trace, to delineate; ~ *avantage de tout*, to turn everything to account; ~ *les cartes*, to tell fortunes (with cards); ~ *gloire* (or *vanité*) *de*, to take pride in; to glory in; to boast of; ~ *la langue*, to put out one's tongue, to have one's tongue hanging out, (fig.) to be in a bad way; ~ *le diable par la queue*, to be hard up; ~ *qn. d'erreur*, to disabuse s.o.; ~ *son épingle du jeu*, to save one's stake; to be well out of sth.; ~ *les marrons du feu*, to be the cat's-paw; *tiré à quatre chevaux*, drawn and quartered; ~ *une ligne*, to draw a line; *il se fera ~ l'oreille*, he will require pressing; he is very reluctant; (fig.) ~ *sa poudre aux moineaux*, to waste time and money on trifles; ~ *parti de qch.*, to turn sth. to advantage, to make the best of sth.; ~ *au sort*, or *à la courte paille*, to draw lots; ~ *sa source de*, to spring from; ~ *les vers du nez à qn.*, to pump s.o. (for information); ~ *à blanc*, to fire with blank cartridges; *bien ~*, to be a good shot, a good fencer; *bon à ~*, ready for the press; ~ *une épreuve*, *un plâtre*, to make a print, a cast; ~ *à sa fin*, to be drawing to an end; to be on one's last legs; to be nearly over; ~ *au clair*, to elucidate, to throw light on, to clear up; ~ *en longueur*, to drag out, to be long or slow; *ce vert tire sur le jaune*, this green has a yellowish tinge; ~ *sur* or *vers*, to make for, to turn towards; (naut.) ~ *au large*, to stand out to sea; ~ *à soi*, to adapt, to make use of, to manipulate; *cela ne tire pas à conséquence*, that is of no importance; (pop.) ~ *six mois de prison*, to get six months (in prison); **se** ~ *v.refl.* to drag or haul oneself; to be drawn; to extract oneself; *se ~ d'affaire* or *s'en ~*, to escape; to recover; to come off, to manage to get through or over it; *s'en ~ à bon compte*, to come off well, to do well (out of it); (fam.) *ça se tire*, it's nearly finished; (pop.) *se ~ des pieds*, or *des pattes*, or *des flûtes*, to be off, to make tracks, to show a clean pair of heels.
tire-sou [tirsu] *s.m.* (pl. *~-sous*) money--grubber.
tiret [tirɛ] *s.m.* dash, hyphen.

tiretaine [tirtɛn] *s.f.* (obs.) linsey-woolsey, wincey.
tirette [tirɛt] *s.f.* **1.** (obs.) cord, pull (for bell, etc.); **2.** pull-out surface or flap (on desk, etc.), slide; **3.** flue-damper.
tireu-r, -se [tirœr] *s.m.f.* shooter, firer, fencer, wire-drawer, marksman, rifleman, shot; (comm.) drawer (of a bill); printer; *~r d'armes*, fencing-master; *~r d'élite*, crack shot, marksman; *~se de cartes*, fortune-teller.
tireuse [tirøz] *s.f.* **1.** (photo.) printer, printing--box; **2.** bottle-filler.
tire-veille(**s**) [tirvɛj] *s.m.* (naut.) ladder-rope, man-rope, side-rope; yoke-lines (of rudder).
tiroir [tirwar] *s.m.* drawer; (mech.) slide, slide--valve; *pièce, roman, à ~s*, play, novel, composed of unconnected episodes; *fond de ~s*, forgotten objects, junk; *racler ses fonds de ~*, to turn out one's junk, to scrape the bottom of the barrel.
tiroir-caisse [tirwarkɛs] *s.m.* cash-register, till.
tisane [tizan] *s.f.* **1.** infusion, herb-tea, decoction; *~ de champagne*, light, cheap champagne; *~ d'orge*, barley-water; *~ de menthe*, mint-tea; **2.** (pop.) blow, beating, reprimand, ticking--off.
tison [tizɔ̃] *s.m.* firebrand, ember(s), half-burnt log; *allumette ~*, fusee; (fig.) *~ de discorde*, mischief-maker, firebrand.
tisonné, -e [tizɔne] *adj.* (of horse) marked with black spots.
tisonner [tizɔne] *v.t.* to stir or poke (the fire).
tisonnier [tizɔnje] *s.m.* poker.
tissage [tisaʒ] *s.m* weaving; cloth-mill, weaving--mill.
tisser [tise] *v.t.* to weave; (fig.) to contrive, to compose, to elaborate; *métier à ~*, loom; (of spider) *~ une toile*, to spin a web.
tisserand, -e [tisrɑ̃] *s.m.f.* weaver.
tisserin [tisrɛ̃] *s.m.* (ornith.) weaver(-bird).
tisseu-r, -se [tisœr] *s.m.f.* weaver.
tissu [tisy] *s.m.* texture, textile, fabric, tissue, web, cloth, material, stuff; (biol.) tissue; (fig.) tissue, concoction, succession; *~*, **~e** *adj.* woven; (fig.) composed, elaborated.
tissulaire [tisylɛr] *adj.* (biol.) of tissue.
tissure [tisyr] *s.f.* texture, weave.
titan [titɑ̃] *s.m.* Titan.
titane [titan] *s.m.* (chem.) titanium.
titanesque [titanɛsk], **titanique** [titanik] *adj.* (obs.) titanic, gigantic, colossal.
Tite-Live [titliv] *s.m.* Livy.
titi [titi] *s.m.* (pop.) street-urchin.
Titien [tisjɛ̃] *s.m.* Titian.
titillation [titil(l)ɑsjɔ̃] *s.f.* titillation, tickling.
titiller [titil(l)e] *v.t.* to titillate, to tickle.
titrage [titraʒ] *s.m.* testing, assaying, sizing, standardizing, titration; (cin.) titling.
titre [titr] *s.m.* title; title-page; head, heading; inscription, caption; chapter, division, section (of regulations, etc.); style, name, form of address, title; status, rank, position; title (to office, etc.); proof, evidence; title(-deed); (share) certificate, security, bond, voucher, scrip; diploma, certificate; entitlement; claim; reason, grounds; qualification; grade, size, gauge; (chem.) strength (of solution), titre, standard; *à bon ~, à juste ~*, rightly, justly, justifiably; *à ~ de*, by right of, by virtue of, on the score of, on the basis of, by way of; *à ~ de grâce*, as a favour; *à ~ gracieux*, complimentary, free; *à ~ gratuit*, free, gratis, gratuitous(ly); *envoi à ~ d'essai*, trial lot, sample lot; *à quel ~?*, by what right?, on what ground?; *à plus d'un ~*, for several reasons, on more counts than one; *à ~ d'ami*, as a friend; *à ~ d'office*, ex officio; *avoir des ~s à*, to be entitled to; *donner des ~s à*, to entitle to; *en ~*, titular, regular, official, by appointment; *~s de noblesse*, patents of nobility.
titré, -e *adj.* titled; conferring a title; (chem.) of standard strength, titrated.
titrer [titre] *v.t.* to give a title to; (cin.) to title; (chem.) to determine the strength of (a solution), to titrate; to size, to number, to assay, to determine.
titubant, -e [titybɑ̃] *adj.* staggering, reeling, tottering, lurching.
tituber [titybe] *v.i.* to stagger, to reel, to stumble.
titulaire [titylɛr] *adj.* titulary, pertaining to a title; titular, regular; head; *~ s.m.f.* titular incumbent, head, or chief; holder, bearer, occupant.
titularisation [titylarizɑsjɔ̃] *s.f.* appointment to permanent post, establishment.
titulariser [titylarize] *v.t.* to appoint to a permanent post, to put on the establishment, to confirm (an appointment); *fonctionnaire titularisé*, established civil servant.
tmèse [tmɛz] *s.f.* (gram.) tmesis.
toarcien, -ne [toarsjɛ̃] *adj., s.m.* (geol.) Toarcian.
toast [tost] *s.m.* **1.** toast; health; *porter un ~*, to drink a toast; to propose a toast; **2.** toast, piece of toast.
toboggan [tobɔgɑ̃] *s.m.* toboggan, sledge, sleigh; toboggan-run; chute.
toc [tɔk] *s.m.* (onom.) *~, ~!*, knock, knock!; fake, trash; *~ adj.* sham, imitation; (fam.) *être ~*, or *~-~*, or *toctoc*, to be mad.
tocante, toquante [tɔkɑ̃t] *s.f.* (fam.) watch, ticker.
tocard, -e [tɔkar] *adj.* (fam.) stupid, ugly; *~ s.m.* (of race-horse) bad runner; (pop.) (of person) nobody, dud; *il n'est pas ~*, he is no fool, there are no flies on him.
tocsin [tɔksɛ̃] *s.m.* tocsin, alarm-bell; *sonner le ~*, to sound the alarm; (fig.) to stir up anger; *sonner le ~ contre*, to raise a hue and cry after; to raise an outcry against.
toge [tɔʒ] *s.f.* (Rom. ant.) toga; (mod.) gown, robe.
tohu-bohu [tɔybɔy] *s.m.* primeval chaos; chaos; confusion, clutter, disorder; uproar, hubbub; to-do; din.
toi [twa] (**t'** before *y* or *en*) *pers. pron.* you, yourself, to yourself; *qui, ~?*, who, you?; *aide-~*, help yourself; *dis-~*, say to yourself; *sans ~*, without you; *garde t'en bien*, beware of it.
toile [twal] *s.f.* cloth; linen; canvas, sail-cloth; textile fabric; (naut.) sail; (spider's) web; (theatr.) curtain; *~ cirée*, oilcloth; American cloth; *~ fine*, fine linen; *~ à bâche*, tarpaulin; *~ vernie*, oilskin, oiled cloth; *~ émeri*, emery--paper; *~ métallique*, wire gauze; *~ ouvrée, ~ damassée*, damask linen; *~ peinte*, print; *~ à calquer*, tracing-paper; *~ à matelas*, tick, ticking; *~ à peindre*, artists' canvas; *~ de maître*, valuable picture; *~ à sac*, sackcloth; *~ à voiles*, sail--cloth; *~ de chanvre*, canvas; *~ de coton*, calico; shirting; *~ d'emballage*, packing-sheet; *~ écrue*, holland; *~ d'Irlande*, Irish linen; *~ de lin*, linen; *~ à draps*, sheeting; *commerce des ~s*, linen trade; *marchand de ~s*, linen-draper; (naut.) *faire de la ~*, to make sail; *réduire la ~*, to shorten sail; *à sec de ~*, with bare poles; *~ de panneau*, hatchway screen; *~ d'araignée*, spider's web, cobweb; *~ (de pneu)* canvas (of a tyre); (theatr.) *~ de fond*, backcloth, drop-scene.
toilerie [twalri] *s.f.* cloth (linen, cotton, hemp) trade or manufacture; linen goods.
toilette [twalɛt] *s.f.* **1.** (*table de*) *~*, (obs.) wash-stand; (mod.) dressing-table; **2.** the act of washing, dressing, etc.; *faire sa ~*, to wash (oneself), to dress; *faire un bout* or *brin de ~*, to tidy oneself up, to have a quick wash; *produits de ~*, toilet goods, toiletries; *trousse de ~*, washing-

-things, sponge-bag; *faire de la* ~, to dress up; **3.** clothes, dress, way of dressing, style of dress, dresses, turn-out; *grande* ~, full dress, full evening dress; *parler* ~, to talk clothes; *revendeuse, marchande, à la* ~, wardrobe dealer, old-clothes woman; *cabinet de* ~, (obs.) dressing-room; (mod.) toilet; **4.** (often pl.) lavatory, W.C., toilet; wash-room, wash-place; **5.** (cook.) caul, membrane used as a wrapper for sausages, etc.; **6.** packing-cloth used by dressmakers for carrying garments, material, etc.

toili-er, -ère [twalje] *s.m.f.* linen manufacturer; linen draper; *adj.* linen.

toise [twaz] *s.f.* (obs.) fathom; toise, lineal measure of six French feet (roughly = 6½ feet); (mod.) apparatus for measuring a person's height; (fig.) standard; *passer à la* ~, to be measured for height; (fig.) *mesurer les autres à sa* ~, to judge others by one's own standards.

toisé [twaze] *s.m.* measuring; mensuration; quantity surveying, evaluation.

toiser [twaze] *v.t.* to measure, to estimate, to survey (for quantities); (fig.) to scan, to scrutinize, to sum up; ~ *qn. de la tête aux pieds*, to look s.o. up and down.

toison [twazɔ̃] *s.f.* fleece; (fig.) shock of hair, mane.

toit [twa] *s.m.* roof; (fig.) house, home; ~ *ouvrant*, sunshine-roof; ~ *à cochons*, pigsty; *habiter sous les* ~*s*, to live in a garret; *crier, dire*, or *prêcher qch. sur les* ~*s*, to proclaim sth. from the house-tops.

toiture [twatyr] *s.f.* roofing, roof.

tokai, tokay [tɔkɛ], **tokaï** [tɔkaj] *s.m.* Tokay (wine).

tôle[1] [tol] *s.f.* sheet metal, metal plate; ~ *ondulée*, corrugated iron; ~ *d'acier*, steel plate; ~ *émaillée*, vitreous enamel.

tôle[2] see TAULE.

tôlé, -e [tole] *adj.* made of sheet metal, (of car) with pressed-steel body; (of snow) hard-packed.

Tolède [tɔlɛd] *s.m.* (geog.) Toledo.

tolérable [tɔlerabl] *adj.* bearable, tolerable; excusable, permissible, acceptable, passable; (mech.) *jeu* ~, permissible clearance or play, tolerance.

tolérance [tɔlerɑ̃s] *s.f.* tolerance, indulgence; toleration, sufferance, permission, permitted variation (from rule, etc.), latitude; religious toleration, freedom of worship; *par* ~, on sufferance; (coinage, mech.) tolerance, allowance, margin, limit(s); (med.) tolerance (of drug, etc.); *maison de* ~, licensed brothel.

tolérant, -e [tɔlerɑ̃] *adj.* tolerant, indulgent.

tolérantisme [tɔlerɑ̃tism] *s.m.* religious toleration, latitudinarianism.

tolérer [tɔlere] *v.t.* to tolerate, to allow, to suffer, to put up with, to endure.

tôlerie [tolri] *s.f.* sheet-iron trade or manufacture; (pl.) rolling-mills, boiler-plate works.

tolet [tɔlɛ] *s.m.* (naut.) thole, tholepin, swivel.

toletière [tɔltiɛr] *s.f.* (naut.) rowlock.

tôlier [tolje] *s.m.* manufacturer of sheet metal; sheet-metal worker; (pressed-steel car) body-builder, body-worker.

tollé [tɔlle] *s.m.* outcry; *crier* ~ *contre, sur*, to raise an outcry against.

toluène [tɔlɥɛn] *s.m.* (chem.) toluene.

T.O.M. [teoɛm] abbrev. *Territoire d'Outre-Mer.*

tomahawk [tɔmaok, tɔmawak] *s.m.* tomahawk.

tomaison [tomɛzɔ̃] *s.f.* (print.) volume number (with each signature).

tomate [tɔmat] *s.f.* tomato.

tombac [tɔ̃bak] *s.m.* (metall.) tombac.

tombal, -e [tɔ̃bal] *adj.* of the tomb, sepulchral; *pierre* ~*e*, tombstone.

tombant, -e [tɔ̃bɑ̃] *adj.* falling, drooping, flowing; dying away; fading away; *des cheveux* ~*s*, flowing locks; *épaules* ~*es*, sloping shoulders; *à la nuit* ~*e*, at nightfall.

tombe [tɔ̃b] *s.f.* tomb, grave, sepulchre; tombstone, gravestone, headstone.

tombeau (pl. **-x**) [tɔ̃bo] *s.m.* tomb, grave; tombstone, monument; (fig.) tomb, death, end; *descendre au* ~, to die; *conduire à* ~ *ouvert*, to drive at breakneck speed; *l'intérêt est le* ~ *de l'amitié*, self-interest is stronger than friendship.

tombé, -e [tɔ̃be] *adj.* (lit. & fig.) fallen; *fruits* ~*s*, windfalls; (Rugby football) *coup de pied* ~, drop-kick.

tombée [tɔ̃be] *s.f.* fall; *la* ~ *du jour* or *de la nuit*, nightfall.

tombelle [tɔ̃bɛl] *s.f.* (archaeol.) barrow; mound, tomb.

tomber [tɔ̃be] *v.i.* to fall, to fall down, to drop (down); to tumble, (of aircraft) to crash; to droop, to hang down; to throw oneself; to decay, to degenerate, to flag, to subside, to die down, to die out, to collapse, to be a failure; to become, to turn out; to fall due; to lead, to flow, (*dans*, into); ~ *sur*, to meet, to run into, to come across; to occur; ~ *en panne*, to break down, to have a breakdown; ~ *de fatigue, de sommeil*, to be ready to drop with fatigue, with sleep; (fig.) ~ *de son haut*, to be amazed; to be humbled; ~ *des nues*, to be astounded; *faire* ~, to knock over, to push down; *laisser* ~, to let fall, to drop, to abandon, to give up, to let down, to allow to lapse; *les bras m'en tombèrent*, you could have knocked me down with a feather!; (impers.) *il tombe de l'eau*, it is raining; *le jour tombe*, the day is closing in; *la fièvre tombe*, the fever is abating; *la mer tombe*, the sea is growing calmer; *la malade est tombée bien bas*, the patient is in a very bad way; *c'est un homme qui est bien tombé*, he is not the man he was; he has seen better days; *cela tombe dans le maniéré*, that degenerates into mere affectation; *cette pièce est tombée*, that play was a failure; ~ *amoureux de*, to fall in love with; ~ *d'accord*, to agree; *faire* ~ *qn. en confusion*, to put s.o. to confusion, to make s.o. look silly; ~ *de la poêle dans la braise*, to jump out of the frying-pan into the fire; *le sort tomba sur lui*, it fell to his lot; *cela tombe sous le sens*, that is evident; *cela lui est tombé entre les mains*, it came into his hands; ~ *bien*, to be fortunate, to be opportune, to come at a good time; ~ *mal*, to be unfortunate, to be inopportune, to come at the wrong moment; ~ *juste*, to happen at the right time, to come just in time, to come at the right moment; ~ *v.t.* to knock down, to floor; (pop.) to seduce, to lay (a woman); (fam.) to take off (jacket, etc.).

tombereau (pl. **-x**) [tɔ̃bro] *s.m.* **1.** cart; dumper, tip-cart; (hist.) tumbril; **2.** cartload.

tombeur [tɔ̃bœr] *s.m.* (professional) wrestler; (pop.) seducer.

tombola [tɔ̃bɔla] *s.f.* tombola.

tome [tɔm] *s.m.* tome, volume; (fig.) part, section; *le premier* ~ *de sa vie*, the early chapters of his life; ~ *s.f.* = TOMME.

tomenteu-x, -se [tɔmɑ̃tø] *adj.* (bot.) tomentose, downy, hairy.

tomme [tɔm] *s.f.* tomme (cheese).

tommette [tɔmɛt] *s.f.* (red hexagonal) floor-tile.

ton [tɔ̃] (used also instead of *ta* before vowel or h-mute), (fem.) **ta** [ta], (pl.) **tes** [te] *poss. adj.* your; (relig.) thy.

ton [tɔ̃] *s.m.* tone (of voice), intonation; pitch; colour, tone, tint, shade; inflexion; trend, tone, air; style, manner; fashion; (mus.) key; tone (interval); *hausser le* ~, *baisser le* ~, to raise, to lower, the voice; *le bon* ~, good form, polite behaviour; *de bon* ~, well-bred, well-mannered, in good taste; *parler d'un* ~ *de maître*, to speak dictatorially; *mettre au* ~ *de*, to attune to; *changer*

de ~, (fam.) *chanter sur un autre* ~, to change one's tone, or one's tune; *le prendre sur un* ~ (*bien haut*), to be superior, to be uppish, about it, to sit on one's high horse; *mauvais* ~, bad taste; ill breeding; *donner le* ~, to pitch the key, to give the note; (fig.) to set the fashion.
tonal, -e [tɔnal] *adj.* tonal.
tonalité [tɔnalite] *s.f.* (mus.) tonality; (fig.) tone, character, atmosphere, impression.
tonca see TONKA.
tondage [tɔ̃daʒ] *s.m.* shearing (of cloth).
tondailles [tɔ̃dɑj] *s.f.pl.* (obs.) sheep-shearing (time).
tondaison [tɔ̃dɛzɔ̃] *s.f.* (obs.) = TONTE.
tondeu-r, -se [tɔ̃dœr] *s.m.f.* shearer.
tondeuse [tɔ̃døz] *s.f.* shears, shearing-machine, clippers; ~ *à gazon*, lawn-mower; ~ *de toilette*, hair-clippers.
tondre [tɔ̃dr] *v.t.* to shear, to clip, to mow, to cut, to crop, to pare; to graze; (fig.) to fleece; (fig.) *se laisser* ~ *la laine sur le dos*, to put up with anything; ~ *la brebis de trop près*, to cut it too fine, *il tondrait un œuf*, he's a regular skinflint; (fam.) *se faire* ~, to have one's hair cropped short.
tondu, -e [tɔ̃dy] *adj.* shorn, (of head) shaven; *à brebis* ~*e Dieu mesure le vent*, God tempers the wind to the shorn lamb. ~ *s.m. le petit* ~, Napoleon; *il n'y avait que trois pelés et un tondu*, there was only a handful (of nonentities) there; there were just two men and a boy.
tonicité [tɔnisite] *s.f.* tonicity, tonic quality.
tonifiant, -e [tɔnifjɑ̃] *adj.* bracing, tonic.
tonifier [tɔnifje] *v.t.* to brace, to fortify, to tone up, to give tone to.
tonique [tɔnik] *adj.* tonic, bracing, stimulating; ~ *s.m.* (med.) tonic; ~ *s.f.* (mus.) tonic, key-note.
tonitruant, -e [tɔnitryɑ̃] *adj.* thundering, thunderous; *voix* ~*e*, stentorian voice.
tonitruer [tɔnitrye] *v.i.* to shout, to thunder, to speak in a stentorian voice.
tonka, tonca [tɔ̃ka] *s.f.* (bot.) tonka bean.
tonnage [tɔnaʒ] *s.m.* (naut.) tonnage; *droit de* ~, tonnage-dues; ~ *brut*, gross tonnage; ~ *net*, net tonnage, register; ~ *réel*, dead weight.
tonnant, -e [tɔnɑ̃] *adj.* thundering; thunderous, loud, sonorous.
tonne [tɔn] *s.f.* **1.** tun, cask, barrel (larger than *un tonneau*); **2.** (metric) ton (= 1000 kg), tonne; ~ *kilométrique*, ton-kilometre (unit of transport pricing); **3.** (naut.) buoy.
tonneau (pl. **-x**) [tɔno] *s.m.* tun, cask (smaller than *une tonne*); (naut.) ton; tonneau (of car); (aeron.) horizontal spin; (of car) *faire un* ~, to roll over; *être d'un bon* ~, to be of the best quality; *fond de* ~, (bad) wine from bottom of barrel, lees; (fig.) residue; *mettre un* ~ *en perce*, to broach a cask; ~ *d'arrosage*, water-cart; ~ *percé*, leaky cask; (fig.) spendthrift; *ce sont gens du même* ~, they are birds of a feather.
tonnelage [tɔnlaʒ] *s.m.* cooperage; *marchandises de* ~, goods in barrel.
tonnelet [tɔnlɛ] *s.m.* small cask, keg.
tonnelier [tɔnəlje] *s.m.* cooper.
tonnelle [tɔnɛl] *s.f.* arbour, bower; barrel-vault.
tonnellerie [tɔnɛlri] *s.f.* **1.** cooperage; **2.** cooper's shop.
tonner [tɔne] *v.i.* to thunder, to boom; (fig.) to inveigh, to fulminate.
tonnerre [tɔnɛr] *s.m.* thunder; (fig.) thunderbolt, thunderclap, bolt from the blue; loud noise, *un éclat de* ~, *un coup de* ~, a clap, a peal, of thunder; a thunderbolt; *le* ~ *est tombé sur le théâtre*, the theatre has been struck by lightning; *un* ~ *d'applaudissements*, thunderous applause; *une voix de* ~, a stentorian voice; (fam.) *du* ~, splendid, first-rate; *une fille du* ~, a smashing girl; *la voiture a marché le* ~, the car went like a bomb; *mille* ~*s!*, in heaven's name!, for God's sake!
tonométrie [tɔnɔmetri] *s.f.* (med.) measurement of blood, etc., pressure.
tonsure [tɔ̃syr] *s.f.* tonsure; (fam.) bald patch on top of head; *recevoir la* ~, to take the first step towards holy orders.
tonsuré [tɔ̃syre] *adj.* tonsured; ~ *s.m.* priest.
tonsurer [tɔ̃syre] *v.t.* to tonsure, to shave (head).
tonte [tɔ̃t] *s.f.* sheep-shearing; shearing-time; shearing(s).
tontine [tɔ̃tin] *s.f.* **1.** tontine; **2.** (hort.) basket of moss, etc. for protecting shrubs in transit.
tontiner [tɔ̃tine] *v.t.* (hort.) to pack in a *tontine*.
tontisse [tɔ̃tis] *s.f.* shearings (of cloth); hangings coated with shearings; flocks; *bourre* ~, shoddy; *papier* ~, flock-paper.
tonton [tɔ̃tɔ̃] *s.m.* (child. lang.) uncle.
tonture [tɔ̃tyr] *s.f.* shearings, flocks; clippings; (naut.) sheer.
tonus [tɔnys] *s.m.* (physiol.) tone; (fig.) energy, dynamism.
top [tɔp] *s.m.* electronic time, etc., signal, pip, ping, bleep.
topaze [tɔpaz] *s.f.* topaz.
tope [tɔp] *interj.* Done!, agreed!, all right!, shake!
toper [tɔpe] *v.i.* to agree, to shake hands on a bargain, to accept a challenge.
topette [tɔpɛt] *s.f.* very narrow phial or glass tube.
tophacé, -e [tɔfase] *adj.* (med.) gritty.
tophus [tɔfys] *s.m.* (med.) tophus.
topinambour [tɔpinɑ̃bur] *s.m.* (bot.) Jerusalem artichoke.
topique [tɔpik] *adj.* topical; local; relevant, to the point; ~ *s.m.* topic, subject; (pl.) (rhet.) topics.
topo [tɔpo] *s.m.* (fam. abbrev. of *topographie*) **1.** plan, sketch; **2.** short speech or lecture, disquisition; *c'est toujours le même* ~, it is always the same story.
topo-graphe [tɔpɔgraf] *s.m.* topographer; ~**graphie** [tɔpɔgrafi] *s.f.* topography; topographical presentation; ~**graphique** [tɔpɔgrafik] *adj.* topographical; ~**graphiquement** [tɔpɔgrafikmɑ̃] *adv.* topographically; ~**logie** [tɔpɔlɔʒi] *s.f.* (math.) topology; ~**nymie** [tɔpɔnimi] *s.f.* toponymy, study of place-names.
toquade [tɔkad] *s.f.* whim, fancy, craze, fad; *avoir une* ~ *pour qn.*, to be crazy about s.o., to be infatuated with s.o.
toquante see TOCANTE.
toquard, -e [tɔkar] *adj.*, *s.m.* = TOCARD.
toque [tɔk] *s.f.* toque, flat cap, small hat, bonnet; ~ *de magistrat*, judge's cap.
toqué, -e [tɔke] *adj.* (fam.) crazy, a bit touched, cracked; infatuated, madly in love, (*de*, with); *il est* ~, he is not quite all there.
toquer [tɔke] *v.t.* to touch, to hit, to tap, to strike lightly; **se** ~ *v.refl.* to be or to become infatuated (*de*, with).
toquet [tɔkɛ] *s.m.* small toque, cap.
torche [tɔrʃ] *s.f.* **1.** torch, (fig.) torch; **2.** straw plaiting, straw packing; **3.** reel (of wire).
torche-cul [tɔrʃəky] *s.m.* (pl. ~*-culs*) (vulg.) toilet paper, bumf (vulg.); (fig.) worthless writing, crap (vulg.).
torche-pot [tɔrʃəpo] *s.m.* (pl. ~*-pots*) (ornith.) nuthatch.
torcher [tɔrʃe] *v.t.* **1.** to wipe, to rub; to daub (wall); **2.** (fig.) to scamp, to botch, to leave half-done; to give a lick and a promise to; **3.** (pop.) to hit, to beat; **se** ~ *v.refl.* to wipe oneself; (pop.) to have a fight; (vulg.) *je m'en*

torche, I couldn't care less, you can stuff it (vulg.).
torchère [tɔrʃɛr] *s.f.* cresset; candelabrum, floor-lamp, standard lamp.
torchette [tɔrʃɛt] *s.f.* small cleaning rag.
torchis [tɔrʃi] *s.m.* loam, clay, mud, daub; *mur de ~,* mud wall.
torchon [tɔrʃɔ̃] *s.m.* **1.** duster; dish-cloth, clout; *un coup de ~,* cleaning-up; (fig.) dust-up, fight; *le ~ brûle,* there is trouble (between them); **2.** straw packing; **3.** (fig., vulg.) shit; (fam.) worthless writing.
torchonner [tɔrʃɔne] *v.t.* **1.** (obs.) to wipe, to clean, to dust; **2.** (fam.) to scamp (work).
torcol [tɔrkɔl] *s.m.* (ornith.) wryneck.
tordage [tɔrdaʒ] *s.m.* twist, twisting (of silk, etc.).
tordant, -e [tɔrdɑ̃] *adj.* (fam.) very funny, killing, screamingly funny.
tord-boyaux [tɔrbwajo] *s.m.* (fam.) strong brandy, rot-gut, hooch.
tordeu-r, -se [tɔrdœr] *s.m.f.* twister, throwster; **~se** *s.f.* (ent.) tortrix, leaf-roller moth.
tordeuse [tɔrdøs] *s.f.* machine for twisting silk.
tord-nez [tɔrne] *s.m.* (vet.) horse-twitch.
tordoir [tɔrdwar] *s.m.* wire-tightener, stick for tightening cords, packing-stick; cable-twister, twisting-machine; wringer.
tordre [tɔrdr] *v.t.* to twist, to wring; to wring out; to wrench, to wrest; to distort, to pull out of shape; *se ~ de douleur,* to be racked with pain; *rire à se ~,* to split one's sides (with laughter); *c'était à se ~,* it was screamingly funny; *~ la bouche,* to make a wry face; *~ le nez,* to turn up one's nose.
tordu, -e [tɔrdy] *adj.* twisted, wrung, bent, buckled, deformed, distorted; (fig.) queer, twisted, devious; (fam.) mad; (pop.) *avoir la gueule ~e,* to have an ugly face; *un ~,* a deformed person, a cripple.
tore [tɔr] *s.m.* (arch.) tore, torus; (bot.) torus.
toréador [tɔreadɔr] *s.m.* toreador, bullfighter.
toréer [tɔree] *v.i.* to fight (as a toreador).
toréro [tɔrero] *s.m.* bullfighter, torero.
toreutique [tɔrøtik] *s.f.* toreutics.
torgnole [tɔrɲɔl] *s.f.* blow, cuff, slap; clout.
toril [tɔril] *s.m.* bull-pen.
tormentille [tɔrmɑ̃til] *s.f.* (bot.) tormentil.
tornade [tɔrnad] *s.f.* tornado.
toron [tɔrɔ̃] *s.m.* (naut.) strand of rope.
torpédo [tɔrpedo] *s.m.* open touring car, roadster; ⚠ not 'torpedo'.
torpeur [tɔrpœr] *s.f.* torpor.
torpide [tɔrpid] *adj.* torpid; (med.) dormant.
torpillage [tɔrpijaʒ] *s.m.* torpedoing.
torpille [tɔrpij] *s.f.* torpedo; (ichth.) torpedo, electric ray.
torpiller [tɔrpije] *v.t.* to torpedo; (fig.) to undermine, to torpedo.
torpillerie [tɔrpijri] *s.f.* torpedo-chamber, torpedo-compartment.
torpilleur [tɔrpijœr] *s.m.* torpedo-boat; (obs.) torpedo-officer.
torque [tɔrk] *s.m.* (archaeol.) torque; *~ s.f.* coil of wire.
torré-facteur [tɔr(r)efaktœr] *s.m.* roaster (esp. for coffee), drier; **~faction** [tɔr(r)efaksjɔ̃] *s.f.* torrefaction, roasting, drying; **~fier** [tɔr(r)efje] *v.t.* to roast, to dry, to torrefy; (obs.) to grill, to toast.
torrent [tɔrɑ̃] *s.m.* torrent, stream, flood; flow; rush; *un ~ de larmes,* a flood of tears; *un ~ d'injures,* a stream of invective; *le ~ des affaires,* the rush of business; *céder au ~, suivre le ~,* to drift with the stream, (fig.) to swim with the tide.
torrentiel, -le [tɔrɑ̃sjɛl] *adj.* torrential.
torrentueu-x, se [tɔrɑ̃tɥø] *adj.* torrent-like, rushing; (fig.) impetuous, headlong, rushed.
torride [tɔrid] *adj.* torrid, scorching.
tors, -e [tɔr] *adj.* twisted, twined, wreathed, contorted, deformed, crooked; tortuous; *cou ~,* wry neck; (fig.) hypocrite.
tors [tɔr] *s.m.* torsion, twist, (of thread).
torsade [tɔrsad] *s.f.* twisted fringe or cord; bullion (cord); (arch.) rope-moulding.
torse [tɔrs] *s.m.* torso, trunk, bust; *le ~ nu,* stripped to the waist; *bomber le ~,* to stick out one's chest.
torsion [tɔrsjɔ̃] *s.f.* torsion, torque, twisting, twist.
tort [tɔr] *s.m.* wrong, injustice, mischief, harm, injury, hurt; error, fault; *avoir ~,* to be wrong; *avoir grand ~,* to be very wrong; *avoir tous les ~s,* to be absolutely wrong; *avoir le ~ de,* to make the mistake of; *à ~,* wrongfully; *à ~ et à travers,* at random; without rhyme or reason; thoughtlessly; *à ~ ou à raison,* rightly or wrongly; *dans son ~,* in the wrong; *donner ~ à qn.,* to decide against s.o., to prove s.o. to be in the wrong; *mettre qn. dans son ~,* to put s.o. in the wrong; *le ~ est de votre côté,* you are in the wrong; *reconnaître ses ~s,* (i.) to acknowledge oneself to be wrong; (ii.) to admit having wronged somebody; *faire ~ à,* to wrong, to do an injustice to, to harm the interests of; *se faire du ~,* to do oneself no good; *avoir des ~s envers qn.,* to behave badly towards s.o.; *réparer ses ~s,* to redeem one's faults; to make amends.
torte [tɔrt] *adj.* rare fem. of TORS *adj.*
torticolis [tɔrtikɔli] *s.m.* stiff neck, crick in the neck; torticollis.
tortil [tɔrtil] *s.m.* (herald.) torse; string of pearls circling a baron's coronet.
tortillage [tɔrtijaʒ] *s.m.* twisting, contortion; entwining; twisted appearance.
tortillard [tɔrtijar] *adj.m.* (bot.) *orme ~,* small--leaved elm; *~ s.m.* (obs.) (rail.) branch line; (mod., fam.) local train.
tortille [tɔrtij] *s.f.* winding path, serpentine walk.
tortillement [tɔrtijmɑ̃] *s.m.* twisting, waggling, wriggling.
tortiller [tɔrtije] *v.t.* **1.** to twist; **2.** (fig., pop.) to eat up quickly, to scoff up; to defeat; *~ v.i.* (fig.) to be evasive, to wriggle; *~ des hanches,* to waggle one's hips; (fig.) *il n'y a pas à ~,* there's no getting out of, or away from, it, it's no use beating about the bush; **se ~** *v.refl.* to waddle; to wriggle, to twist; to be twisted or convoluted; (fig.) to make frenzied efforts.
tortillon [tɔrtijɔ̃] *s.m.* **1.** head-pad; **2.** sweet--paper twisted at ends, screw of paper; (drawing) paper-stump.
tortionnaire [tɔrsjɔnɛr] *adj.* of torture, cruel, oppressive, extortionate; *~ s.m.* torturer.
tortis [tɔrti] *s.m.* twisted threads, twist.
tortorer [tɔrtɔre] *v.t.* (pop.) to eat.
tortu, -e [tɔrty] *adj.* crooked; tortuous; *jambes ~es,* bandy legs.
tortue [tɔrty] *s.f.* (zool.) tortoise, turtle; (ant.) testudo; *à pas de ~,* at a snail's pace.
tortueu-x, -se [tɔrtɥø] *adj.* crooked, winding, tortuous; (fig.) underhand, deceitful, devious, tortuous, circuitous; **~sement** [tɔrtɥøzmɑ̃] *adv.* tortuously.
tortuosité [tɔrtɥozite] *s.f.* tortuousness.
torturant, -e [tɔrtyrɑ̃] *adj.* torturing, tormenting.
torture [tɔrtyr] *s.f.* torture, torment, agony; *être à la ~,* to be in (mental) torment; *se mettre l'esprit à la ~,* to rack one's brains.
torturer [tɔrtyre] *v.t.* to torture, to torment; to strain, to distort, to pervert, to do violence to (text, etc.), to ravage (features, etc.).

torve [tɔrv] *adj.* glowering, menacing; *un regard ~*, a nasty sly look, a sideways look.
tory [tɔri] *s.m., adj.* Tory.
torysme [tɔrism] *s.m.* Toryism.
toscan, -e [tɔskɑ̃] *adj., s.m.f.* Tuscan.
Toscane [tɔskan] *s.f.* (geog.) Tuscany.
tôt [to] *adv.* **1.** Soon, quickly, promptly, speedily; *plus ~*, sooner, earlier, before; *au plus ~*, as soon as possible; at the latest; at the earliest; *~ ou tard*, sooner or later; *le plus ~ possible*, as soon as possible; *~ après*, soon after; **2.** early; *réveillez-moi très ~*, wake me very early.
total, -e, (**aux**) [tɔtal] *adj.* total, complete, entire, whole, utter, absolute; *~ s.m.* total, whole, sum total; *au ~*, on the whole, after all; (pop., fig.) *~, tu as perdu ton emploi*, net result, you have lost your job; **~ement** [tɔtalmɑ̃] *adv.* totally, entirely, absolutely, utterly, completely, wholly.
totalisat-eur, -rice [tɔtalizatœr] *adj.* calculating, reckoning, adding, totalizing; **~eur** *s.m.* totalizator; adding-machine.
totalisation [tɔtalizɑsjɔ̃] *s.f.* totalization, adding-up.
totaliser [tɔtalize] *v.t.* to reckon up, to total, to add up.
totalitaire [tɔtalitɛr] *adj.* totalitarian.
totalitarisme [tɔtalitarism] *s.m.* totalitarianism.
totalité [tɔtalite] *s.f.* entirety, whole, entire amount, totality; *en ~*, entirely, completely, in its entirety, taken as a whole.
totem [tɔtɛm] *s.m.* totem.
totémisme [tɔtemism] *s.m.* totemism.
toton [tɔtɔ̃] *s.m.* teetotum.
touage [twaʒ] *s.m.* towage, chain-towing, warping, kedging.
touaille [twaj] *s.f.* roller-towel.
toubib [tubib] *s.m.* (fam.) doctor.
toucan [tukɑ̃] *s.m.* (ornith.) toucan.
touchant, -e [tuʃɑ̃] *adj.* touching, moving, appealing, pathetic; (iron.) *il est ~ de maladresse*, he is so awkward, it makes you weep; *~ prep.* concerning, respecting, touching, in the matter of, about, with regard to, with respect to, relating to.
touche [tuʃ] *s.f.* **1.** touch, contact; (fish.) nibble; trial, assay; (fam.) *faire une ~*, to make contact, to pick (a woman) up; *pierre de ~*, touchstone; **2.** (mus.) fingerboard (of violin, etc.), key (of piano, etc.); (typewriter) key; **3.** (art) manner; **4.** (fenc.) hit; **5.** (pop.) appearance; **6.** (football) touch, touch-line; throw-in; *il y a ~*, in touch; *jouer la ~*, to throw in; (fig.) *rester sur la ~*, to remain on the side-lines.
touche-à-tout [tuʃatu] *s.m.invar.* busybody; child who can't keep his fingers off things.
toucher [tuʃe] *v.t.* to touch; to feel; to strike, to hit, to tap; to finger, to play (an instrument); to adjoin; to offend; to concern, to interest; to touch on, to mention; to express, to depict, to draw, to collect, to receive; to move, to affect; *~ juste*, to hit the nail on the head; *cela ne me touche pas*, it is no concern of mine, it does not affect me; *~ un mot de*, to say a word about, to drop a hint about; (naut.) *~ (le fond)*, to strike bottom, to ground; *~ un port*, to touch at, to call at, a port; *~ ses appointements, un chèque, des rations*, to draw one's salary, a cheque, rations; *ne faire que ~ barre à*, to be only paying a flying visit to; *il a été touché de* (or *par*) *votre repentir*, your repentance moved him; *ne touchez pas cette corde*, keep quiet about that; *cela vous touche de près*, this closely affects you; *touché, bien touché!*, a hit!; (fig.) that got home, that was a nasty crack; *il me toucha l'épaule*, he touched me on the shoulder; *son jardin touche le mien*, his garden is next to mine; *vos paroles l'ont touché au vif*, your words have touched him on the raw, have gone home; *~ son chapeau*, to touch one's hat (as salutation); *touchez-moi la main*, let's shake hands; *touchez là!*, your hand on it!; *~ la main à qn.*, to shake hands with s.o. (on a bargain); *le cocher toucha ses chevaux*, the driver gave his horses a touch of the whip; *~ à*, to touch, to handle; to reach; to meddle or tamper with, to involve oneself in, to have a finger in; to be related to (a person); to affect, to change, to alter, to concern, to allude to, to adjoin, to draw near; *ne touchez pas aux fils*, don't touch, or don't tamper with, the wires; *ne touchez pas à la religion*, do not meddle with religious matters, keep off religion; *on n'ose ~ à cette coutume*, one dare not lay a finger on this observance; *il a touché à cette affaire*, he had a hand in this business; *elle a un petit air de n'y pas ~*, she looks as if butter would not melt in her mouth, she looks all innocence; *nous touchons à la révolution*, we are heading for a revolution; *~ à sa fin*, to draw to a close; to be at the point of death; *~ au but*, *~ au port*, to be on the verge of success, to be in sight of one's goal, to be nearly there; *cela touche à la folie*, that borders on lunacy; *je touche à la quarantaine*, I am getting on for forty; **se ~** *v.refl.* to touch, to be in or come into contact, to come next; to meet, to join; to be akin; *les extrêmes se touchent*, extremes meet; *ces maisons se touchent*, these houses adjoin.
toucher [tuʃe] *s.m.* touch, feel; feeling, sensation; contact; touching; (mus.) touch.
toucheur [tuʃœr] *s.m.* **1.** cattle-drover; **2.** (print.) inking-roller.
toue [tu] *s.f.* **1.** towing, warping; **2.** barge, ferry-boat.
touée [twe] *s.f.* (naut.) towing, towage, warping; tow-line; scope (length of cable used in towing or anchoring); (fig.) stretch (of journey to be done); *ancre de ~*, kedge.
touer [twe] *v.t.* (naut.) to tow, to warp, to kedge.
toueu-r, -se [twœr] *adj.* towing (esp. by chain); **~r** *s.m.* tow-boat, tug.
touffe [tuf] *s.f.* tuft, bunch, wisp, clump, cluster.
touffeur [tufœr] *s.f.* stifling heat.
touffu, -e [tufy] *adj.* **1.** bushy, thick, full, luxuriant; tufted; *cheveux ~s*, bushy hair; **2.** (fig.) too detailed, overloaded, meaty.
toujours [tuʒur] *adv.* always, ever, still, constantly, perpetually, frequently, usually; anyhow, at any rate, all the same; *pour ~*, for ever; evermore; *de ~*, lifelong, unchanging, everlasting; *depuis ~*, from time immemorial; *comme ~*, as usual; *il vit ~*, he is still alive, or living; *allez ~*, go on, never mind!; *racontez ~*, go on, tell us!, tell us all the same!; *payez ~, on verra après*, pay up now, we'll see about it later; *~ est-il que*, still the fact remains that; however; *~ plus*, more and more; *c'est ~ ça!*, that's something, that's better than nothing; *êtes-vous ~ content de lui?*, are you still pleased with him?
touloupe [tulup] *s.f.* lambskin greatcoat.
toundra [tundra] *s.f.* tundra.
toupet [tupɛ] *s.m.* tuft, lock of hair; forelock, toupet, toupee, transformation; (fig.) impertinence, cheek, impudence, effrontery; *avoir du ~*, to be impudent, cheeky; *il a eu le ~ de*, he has had the effrontery to; *il en a un ~!*, he's got a nerve!
toupie [tupi] *s.f.* top, peg-top, spinning-top; (techn.) milling-cutter (of moulding-machine); splayed foot (of furniture); (fig.) old frump; *~ d'Allemagne*, humming-top.
toupiller [tupije] *v.i.* to spin, to gyrate; *~ v.t.* to shape (wood on moulding-machine).
tour [tur] *s.f.* tower, turret; (at chess) castle;

(build.) tower block; (fam.) (of person) great lump; (obs.) ~ *à feu*, lighthouse.

tour [tur] *s.m.* **1.** turn, turning; tour, circuit; trip; circumference, girth, measurement round; revolution, rotation; turn (of duty); (fig.) direction; complexion; *fermer à double* ~, to double-lock; ~ *de reins*, strained back; *mon sang n'a fait qu'un* ~, my heart missed a beat; *les* ~*s et retours d'un chemin*, the twists and turns of a road; *à chacun son* ~, every dog has his day; ~ *à* ~, in turn, turn and turn about; *à* ~ *de rôle*, in turn, by roster, on a rota; *à son* ~, in turn; *à qui le* ~?, whose turn is it?; *c'était au* ~ *du monsieur de*, it was the gentleman's turn to; *avoir un* ~ *de faveur*, to go out of one's turn; ~ *de scrutin*, ballot; ~ *de phrase*, expression, turn of phrase; ~ *d'esprit*, turn of mind; ~ *d'horizon*, survey; *donner un bon* ~ *à*, to give a favourable turn to, to put a favourable complexion on; ~ (*de piste*), lap, stage; *faire un* ~, to take a short walk, to take a trip; *faire le* ~ *de*, to go round, to take a trip round; *faire un* ~ *de jardin, de ville*, to take a turn in the garden, a trip round the town; *faire le* ~ *du monde*, to take a world tour, to go round the world; (fig.) *faire ses quinze* ~*s*, to dawdle; *faire le grand* ~, to take the longest way round; *avoir deux mètres de* ~, to be two metres round; ~ *de taille*, girth, waist measurement; ~ *de poitrine*, chest or bust measurement; ~ *de tête*, hat size; ~ *de cou*, neck-band; ~ *de lit*, (bed) valance; *faire le* ~ *du cadran*, to sleep the clock round; *à* ~ *de bras*, with all one's might; *en un* ~ *de main*, in the twinkling of an eye; **2.** trick, feat, stunt; *il savait plus d'un tour*, he was up to a good many tricks; ~ *de cartes*, card-trick; *jouer un bon* ~ *à*, to play a trick on; *un mauvais* ~, a dirty trick; ~ *d'adresse*, feat of skill, acrobatic feat, sleight-of-hand; ~ *de force*, feat of strength, tour de force, remarkable performance; ~ *de main*, trick(s) of the trade; manual skill, dexterity, knack; **3.** lathe, turning-lathe; ~ *de potier*, potter's wheel; *fait au* ~, engine-turned; (fig.) well-turned, shapely, nicely rounded.

touraille [turɑj] *s.f.* malt-kiln.

tourange-au (pl. **-x**) [turɑ̃ʒo], (fem.) ~**lle** [turɑ̃ʒɛl] *adj., s.m.f.* (native or inhabitant) of Touraine or of Tours.

touranien, -ne [turanjɛ̃] *adj.*, ~ *s.m.* Turanian (language).

tourbe[1] [turb] *s.f.* peat, turf.

tourbe[2] [turb] *s.f.* rabble, mob.

tourber [turbe] *v.i.* to cut peat or turf.

tourbeu-x, -se [turbø] *adj.* peaty, turfy.

tourbi-er, -ère [turbje] *s.m.f.* peat-cutter; owner of peat bog; *adj.* peaty, containing peat.

tourbière [turbjɛr] *s.f.* peat-bog, peat-moss.

tourbillon [turbijɔ̃] *s.m.* whirlwind, eddy; vortex; whirlpool; whirling cloud; (fig.) whirl, bustle, seething mass.

tourbillonnant, -e [turbijɔnɑ̃] *adj.* whirling, eddying.

tourbillonnement [turbijɔnmɑ̃] *s.m.* whirling, eddying.

tourbillonner [turbijɔne] *v.i.* to whirl round, to eddy; (fig.) to whirl or spin round.

tourd [tur] *s.m.* **1.** (ornith.) thrush; **2.** (ichth.) Labrus, wrasse.

tourdille [turdij] *adj. gris* ~, dirty grey.

tourelle [turɛl] *s.f.* turret; (conning-)tower; revolving head (of camera, containing different lenses).

touret [turɛ] *s.m.* (techn.) small wheel; polishing-wheel; reel, drum.

tourie [turi] *s.f.* carboy, demijohn, wicker-covered jar.

tourillon [turijɔ̃] *s.m.* **1.** axle, axle-shaft, spindle, pivot; **2.** (artill.) trunnion; **3.** crank-pin, gudgeon.

tourisme [turism] *s.m.* touring, travel, tourism; tourist industry.

touriste [turist] *s.m.f.* tourist.

touristique [turistik] *adj.* tourist, travel.

tourmaline [turmalin] *s.f.* tourmaline.

tourment [turmɑ̃] *s.m.* torment, torture, pain, anguish, agony; (fig.) anxiety, care, trouble, worry.

tourmentant, -e [turmɑ̃tɑ̃] *adj.* tormenting, torturing, troublesome.

tourmente [turmɑ̃t] *s.f.* **1.** tempest, storm; ~ *de neige*, blizzard; **2.** (fig.) disturbance, turmoil, upheaval.

tourmenté, -e [turmɑ̃te] *adj.* **1.** stormy, tempestuous, tempest-tossed; **2.** agitated, anxious, worried, disturbed, harassed, plagued, tormented; restless; **3.** twisted, distorted; laboured, exaggerated.

tourmenter [turmɑ̃te] *v.t.* to torture, to torment; to pain, to distress, to harass, to pester, to plague, to molest, to annoy, to dun, to bully; to toss, to shake, to agitate; to lash; to jolt; to twist, to warp; **se** ~ *v.refl.* to worry, to fret, to torment oneself; to toss about, to be agitated, to be restless, to fidget; to warp; (of ship) to strain.

tourmenteu-r, -se [turmɑ̃tœr] *s.m.f.* torturer, (fig.) tormentor; ~**r** *s.m.* (obs.) executioner.

tourmentin [turmɑ̃tɛ̃] *s.m.* (naut.) forestay sail, storm-jib; (ornith.) stormy petrel.

tournage [turnaʒ] *s.m.* **1.** turning; **2.** (naut.) belaying; *taquet de* ~, belaying-cleat; **3.** (cin.) filming, making (a film).

tournailler [turnɑje] *v.i.* to keep wandering round and round, to hover.

tournant, -e [turnɑ̃] *adj.* turning, revolving, winding; *escalier* ~, spiral staircase; *plaque* ~*e*, turntable; *mouvement* ~, (mil.) turning movement; (fig.) move to circumvent; *grève* ~*e*, staggered strike (first in one department then in another); *pont* ~, swing-bridge; *les tables* ~*es*, table-turning; ~ *s.m.* turn, turning; bend, corner (of street); turn, turning-point; eddy, whirlpool; water-wheel; *attendre qn. au* ~, to be waiting for an opportunity to catch s.o.; *avoir* or *rattraper qn. au* ~, to pay off old scores with s.o.

tourne [turn] *s.f.* continuation (of an article on a later page).

tourné, -e [turne] *adj.* **1.** turned; made, shaped, formed, directed; disposed, inclined; *bien* ~, shapely, handsome, neatly turned; *mal* ~, awkward; uncouth; badly turned; ill made; misshapen; *avoir l'esprit mal* ~, to be quick to take offence, to have a nasty disposition; **2.** (of milk) turned, sour.

tourne-à-gauche [turnagoʃ] *s.m.invar.* (techn.) wrench; ~**bouler** [turnəbule] *v.t.* (fig., fam.) to bowl over, to knock all of a heap; ~**-bride** [turnəbrid] *s.m.* (obs.) wayside inn; ~**-broche** [turnəbrɔʃ] *s.m.* roasting-jack; turnspit; ~**-disque** [turnədisk] *s.m.* (pl. ~*-disques*) (gramophone) turntable; record-player, playing-deck; ~**dos** [turnədo] *s.m.* fillet steak.

tournée [turne] *s.f.* **1.** tour, walk, round, visit, journey, excursion, turn; circuit, beat; **2.** round of drinks; *c'est ma* ~, it's my round!; *la* ~ *du patron*, drinks on the house; **3.** (pop.) hail of blows, thrashing.

tourne-feuille [turnəfœj] *s.m.* (pl. ~*-feuilles*) (mus.) page-turner.

(**en un**) **tournemain** [ɑ̃nœ̃turnəmɛ̃] *adv.loc.* in a trice, in the twinkling of an eye.

tourne-pierre [turnpjɛr] *s.m.* (pl. ~*-pierres*) (ornith.) turnstone.

tourner [turne] *v.t.* to turn, to revolve, to rotate, to twist, to twirl, to wind; to bend; to turn over, to turn round; to go round, to round; to outflank; to direct, to apply, to manage, to interpret, to construe; to change, to transform, to convert, to turn, to shape; to infatuate; ~ *casaque*, to turn one's coat, to change sides, to desert to the enemy; ~ *ses pas d'un certain côté*, to bend one's steps in a certain direction; ~ *tout en mal*, to put a bad construction on everything; ~ *une carte*, to turn up a card; ~ *une difficulté*, to get over a difficulty, hindrance, etc.; (lit. & fig.) ~ *le dos à*, to turn one's back on, to cold-shoulder, to be facing the other way from; (fig.) ~ *les talons*, to make off, to take to one's heels; ~ *des olives*, to stone olives; ~ *le coin*, to turn the corner (of a street); ~ *la page*, or *le feuillet*, to turn (over) the page; *le succès, le vin, lui a tourné la tête*, success, the wine, has gone to his head; *cette fille lui a tourné la tête*, he is infatuated with that girl; (fam.) ~ *le sang* or *les sangs*, to upset (emotionally); ~ *le cœur*, to upset (the stomach); *il tourne carreau*, diamonds are trumps; ~ *la loi*, to evade the law, to get round the law; to defeat the intention of the law; ~ *un pot*, to throw a pot (on the wheel); *on le tourne à toutes sauces*, they put every kind of job on to him; ~ *v.i.* to turn, to revolve, to twist round, to move, to veer, to change, to alter; to become, to turn out; to turn sour; ~ (*un film*), to make a film, to act or star in a film; ~ *autour de*, to turn on, to be concerned with, to revolve about; ~ *autour d'une femme*, to be running after, to be making advances to, a woman; ~ *autour du pot*, to beat about the bush; ~ *bien*, to turn out well, to be going well; ~ *mal*, to turn out badly, to go wrong, to be going badly; *ce jeune homme tournera mal*, this young man will come to a bad end; ~ *de l'œil*, (i.) to faint; (ii.) to die; *la tête me tourne*, I feel giddy; *le pied m'a tourné*, I have wrenched my foot; *nous verrons comment les choses tourneront*, we shall see how things turn out; ~ *court*, (i.) to turn sharply; (ii.) to stop abruptly, to end suddenly, to be cut short; ~ *rond*, to turn round; (of engine) to run smoothly; ~ *à vide*, to run in neutral; *la chance a tourné*, the tables are turned; the luck has changed; *le temps tourne au froid*, it is turning cold; *le vent tourne à l'ouest*, the wind is getting round to the west; *elle tourne à la bigoterie*, she is becoming something of a bigot; *faire* ~ *le moteur*, to start or to run the engine; *faire* ~ *un disque*, to play or to put on a record; **se** ~ *v.refl.* to turn round, about; *se* ~ *en*, to be changed into; *se* ~ *contre qn.*, to turn against s.o., to round on s.o.

tournesol [turnəsɔl] *s.m.* (bot.) sunflower; purple dye; (chem.) litmus.

tournette [turnɛt] *s.f.* **1.** squirrel's cage; **2.** wool--winder, skein-holder; **3.** glass-cutter's wheel.

tourneur [turnœr] *s.m.* turner; ~ *adj. ouvrier* ~, turner; *derviche* ~, whirling dervish.

tournevis [turnəvis] *s.m.* screw-driver.

tourniole [turnjɔl] *s.f.* (pathol.) whitlow.

tourniquet [turnikɛ] *s.m.* **1.** turnstile, revolving door, turnpike; **2.** (med.) tourniquet; **3.** sash--pulley; windlass; pulley-sheave; swivel; (fish.) winch, reel; (naut.) roller; **3.** whirligig (beetle); **4.** whirligig (toy); garden sprinkler.

tournis [turni] *s.m.* (vet.) staggers (in horses and cattle); sturdy (in sheep); turnside (in dogs); (fig., fam.) *vous me donnez le* ~, you are making me giddy.

tournisse [turnis] *s.f.* (carp.) stud, stud-piece.

tournoi [turnwa] *s.m.* tournament; tourney.

turnoiement [turnwamɑ̃] *s.m.* turning, whirling round, wheeling round.

tournois [turnwa] *adj. invar.* (hist.) (of coins) minted at Tours.

tournoyant, -e [turnwajɑ̃] *adj.* eddying, turning about, whirling round.

tournoyer [turnwaje] *v.i.* to whirl round, to spin, to pivot, to wheel about; to eddy.

tournure [turnyr] *s.f.* **1.** shape, figure; *elle a une jolie* ~, she has a good figure; **2.** turn; cast; appearance; tendency, direction, course; ~ *d'esprit*, turn of mind, attitude, disposition; ~ *d'une phrase*, turn, construction, of a sentence; *il en cherchait la* ~, he was thinking of how to put it; **3.** (dressm.) bustle; **4.** metal turnings.

tourte [turt] *s.f.* **1.** pie; **2.** round loaf of bread; ~ *adj.* (pop.) stupid, not blessed with brains.

tourteau[1] (pl. **-x**) [turto] *s.m.* (agric.) oil-cake; (herald.) roundel, torteau.

tourteau[2] (pl. **-x**) [turto] *s.m.* edible crab.

tourtereau (pl. **-x**) [turtəro] *s.m.* (ornith.) young turtle-dove; (pl.) (fig.) young lovers.

tourterelle [turtərɛl] *s.f.* (ornith.) turtle-dove.

tourtière [turtjɛr] *s.f.* pie-dish, baking-tin.

tous [tu, tus] see TOUT.

touselle [tuzɛl] *s.f.* (bot.) beardless wheat.

Toussaint [tusɛ̃] *s.f.* All Saints' Day.

tousser [tuse] *v.i.* to cough; to clear one's throat; (of engine) to splutter.

tousserie [tusri] *s.f.* coughing; persistent coughing.

tousseu-r, -se [tusœr] *s.m.f.* one who coughs, cougher.

toussoter [tusɔte] *v.i.* to cough slightly, to give a small cough, to hem.

tout, -e [tu], (pl.) **tous, toutes** *adj.* all, the whole, the whole of, every, any; full, complete, whole, entire; only, sole; ~ *le jour*, all day, the whole day long; *tous les jours*, every day; *tous les deux jours*, every other day; ~*es les fois que*, whenever; *tous* (*les*) *deux, trois*, both, all three; ~ *le monde*, everybody; ~ *le monde et son père*, all the world and his wife; ~*e autre chose*, anything else, anything but that; ~ *son possible*, one's very utmost; *par tous pays*, in all countries; *à* ~*e force*, at any cost; *à* ~ *hasard*, come what may, on the off-chance, to be on the safe side; *de* ~ *temps*, from time immemorial, right from the beginning; *à* ~ *propos*, at every turn; ~ *autre que lui*, any one but him; *courir à* ~*es jambes*, to run at full speed; *donner tous pouvoirs à*, to give full powers to; *somme* ~*e*, on the whole; *pour* ~*e réponse il*, his only reply was to; *pour* ~ *mobilier il y avait*, the sole furniture was; *dans sa* ~*e jeunesse*, in his early youth; *elle a été* ~*e bienveillance*, she has shown nothing but kindness; ~ *adv.* wholly, entirely, quite, just, thoroughly, fully, absolutely, altogether, all, pure; although, however, for all, for all that; *le* ~ *premier*, the foremost, the very first, the first of all; *c'est* ~ *un*, it's all the same; *c'est* ~ *comme vous voudrez*, just as you like; *il était* ~ *à son travail*, he was engrossed in his work; ~ *à coup*, suddenly; ~ *à fait*, absolutely, entirely; ~ *à l'heure*, just now; in a minute, shortly; ~ *d'abord*, first of all, straight away; ~ *au moins*, at least; ~ *au plus*, at most; ~ *à vous*, yours sincerely; ~ *allumé*, ready lighted; ~ *autant*, quite as much, as many; ~ *autre chose*, (something) quite different; ~ *au long*, at full length; ~ *beau*, ~ *doux*, gently!, softly!, not so fast!, wait a minute!; ~ *chaud*, piping hot; ~ *contre*, hard by; close; ~ *court*, and nothing more, full stop, period (U.S.); *c'est imbécile*, ~ *court*, it's lunatic, full stop; ~ *de bon*, in earnest; ~ *de go*, straight off, point--blank; ~ *de même*, all the same; ~ *de suite*, at once, immediately; ~ *doucement*, gently; ~ *du long*, from beginning to end; ~ *d'un coup*, all at once, suddenly; *tout en regardant*, whilst watching; ~ *ensemble*, together, all together, at the same time; ~ *éveillé*, wide awake; ~ *fait*, ready made; (fig.) cut and dried; ~ *grand*, wide (open); ~ *grand ouvert*, wide open; ~ *haut*, aloud, boldly, openly; ~ *le long de*, all along; ~ *nu*, stark naked; ~ *près*, quite near, close at hand; ~ *prêt*, quite ready; ~ *soie, laine*, pure silk, pure wool; *dans nos ~ commencements*, in our early beginnings; *~es bonnes qu'elles sont*, however good they are, for all their goodness, although they are very good, good as they are; *~ nouveau, ~ beau*, new brooms sweep clean; *~ pron.indef.* everything, anything, all, everybody; *après ~*, after all; *à ~ prendre*, all things considered, on the whole; *pour ~ dire*, to sum up, in a word; *c'est ~ dire*, that sums it up, there's no more to be said; *comme ~*, extremely, out and out, and no mistake; *~ est là*, it is all there, that is the sum of it, that is the whole problem; *ce n'est pas ~ de*, it is not just a matter of, it is not enough to; (fam.) *ce n'est pas ~, ça*, there is more to it than that, there are other things to do than that; (fam.) *et ~* (*et ~*), and so on, and all that; *~ dormait dans la voiture*, everyone in the car was asleep; *en ~*, in all, wholly; *en ~ et pour ~*, wholly, entirely; *du ~*, at all; *pas* (or *point*) *du ~*, not at all, not in the least; *rien du ~*, nothing at all; *plus du ~*, never again, no more, now no longer; *se faire à ~*, to adapt oneself to any circumstances; *pardessus ~*, above all; *~ bien considéré*, all things considered; *propre à ~*, fit for anything, equal to anything; *voilà ~*, that's all; *il y a ~ à parier que*, the odds are that; *nous tous*, all of us, *je les vois tous*, I see them all, all of them; *~ s.m.* the whole, all, everything, the main thing, the chief point; *le ~ pour le ~*, neck or nothing; *risquer le ~ pour le ~*, to risk all to win all; to stake everything; *le ~ est de*, the main, the essential, thing is to; *il en fait son ~, c'est son ~*, it means everything to him; it is vital to him; *du ~ au ~*, completely, fundamentally; *~ ce qu'il y a de plus aimable*, most, extremely, kind; *des gens ~ ce qu'il y a de plus honorable(s)*, highly respectable people.

tout-à-l'égout [tutalegu] *s.m.invar.* main drainage; flush system.

toute [tut] see TOUT.

toute-bonne [tutbɔn] *s.f.* **1.** (bot.) clary; **2.** (hort.) toute-bonne (pear).

toute-épice [tutepis] *s.f.* allspice, pimento.

toutefois [tutfwa] *adv.* yet, nevertheless, still, however, all the same; *si ~ la chose est possible*, if the thing is at all possible; *excepté ~ que*, always excepting that.

toute-puissance [tutpɥisɑ̃s] *s.f.* omnipotence, almighty power, absolute authority.

toutou [tutu] *s.m.* (child. lang.) dog, doggie; *suivre qn. comme un ~*, to follow s.o. like a little dog.

tout-puissant [tupɥisɑ̃], (fem.) **toute-puissante** [tutpɥisɑ̃t] *adj.* almighty, all-powerful, omnipotent; autocratic.

tout-venant [tuvənɑ̃] *s.m.invar.* ungraded product (esp. coal); (fig.) assortment, oddments, what-have-you.

toux [tu] *s.f.* cough; *une quinte de ~*, a violent fit of coughing, a paroxysm of coughing; *une ~ qui sent le sapin*, a graveyard cough.

toxémie [tɔksemi] *s.f.* toxaemia, blood-poisoning.

toxicité [tɔksisite] *s.f.* poisonousness, toxicity.

toxico-logie [tɔksikɔlɔʒi] *s.f.* toxicology; **~logique** [tɔksikɔlɔʒik] *adj.* toxicological; **~logue** [tɔksikɔlɔg] *s.m.f.* toxicologist; **~mane** [tɔksikɔman] *s.m.f.* drug-addict; *adj.* addicted to drugs; **~manie** [tɔksikɔmani] *s.f.* toxicomania, drug-addiction.

toxine [tɔksin] *s.f.* toxin.

toxique [tɔksik] *adj.* toxic; *gaz ~*, poison gas; *~ s.m.* toxin, poison.

traban [trabɑ̃] *s.m.* (hist.) halberdier or pikeman in Swiss or Scandinavian troops.

trabée [trabe] *s.f.* (ant.) trabea, ceremonial toga.

trac[1] [trak] *s.m. tout à ~*, blindly, without reflection.

trac[2] [trak] *s.m.* fear (esp. before public appearance, examination, etc.); *avoir le ~*, to have cold feet, to be in a cold sweat, to have butterflies in the stomach; *~ de théâtre*, stage-fright.

traçage [trasaʒ] *s.m.* tracing, drawing, marking-out.

traçant, -e [trasɑ̃] *adj.* (bot.) (of plants) running, creeping; (mil.) tracer (bullet or shot).

tracas [traka] *s.m.* bustle, stir, disturbance, turmoil; hurry, flurry; worry, annoyance, bother, trouble.

tracasser [trakase] *v.t.* to worry, to pester, to plague, to bother, to tease, to torment; to interfere with; **se ~** *v.refl.* to worry, to fuss, to get into a state.

tracasserie [trakasri] *s.f.* bustle, bother, worry; bickering, cavil; mischief-making; annoyance, vexation, pestering, harassment, persecution, plaguing, teasing, chicanery.

tracassi-er, -ère [trakasje] *adj.* teasing, bothering, fidgety, cantankerous, interfering; *s.m.f.* meddler, busybody, mischief-maker.

tracassin [trakasɛ̃] *s.m.* (fam.) worry, depression, restlessness; *il lui faut un ~*, he has to have something to worry about.

trace [tras] *s.f.* **1.** trace, track, trail, footprint, (pl.) spoor; *suivre les ~s de qn.*, to follow in someone's steps, to follow someone's example; **2.** trace, mark, evidence, (visible) outlines; (chem.) trace.

tracé [trase] *s.m.* outline, sketch, trace, tracing, draught, plan, lay-out; line, direction; *faire le ~ de*, (i.) to sketch; (ii.) to lay out.

tracement [trasmɑ̃] *s.m.* tracing, drawing, marking-out.

tracer [trase] *v.t.* **1.** to trace, to draw, to mark out, to delineate, to portray; **2.** to lay out; (fig.) to lay down (policy, etc.); *~ v.i.* (of plant) to send out runners; (pop.) to hurry, to get a move on.

traceret [trasrɛ] *s.m.* tracer, tracing-point, scribe.

traceu-r, -se [trasœr] *s.m.f.* tracer.

trachéal, -e, (**aux**) [trakeal] *adj.* (anat.) tracheal.

trachée [traʃe] *s.f.* **1.** (anat.) trachea, windpipe; **2.** (bot.) trachea, spiral vessel, wood-vessel; **3.** (ent.) trachea, air-tube (of insects).

trachée-artère [traʃeartɛr] *s.f.* (anat.) trachea, windpipe.

trachéen, -ne [trakeɛ̃] *adj.* tracheal.

trachéite [trakeit] *s.f.* (pathol.) tracheitis.

trachéotomie [trakeɔtɔmi] *s.f.* tracheotomy.

trachome [trakom] *s.m.* trachoma.

trachyte [trakit] *s.m.* (min.) trachyte.

traçoir [traswar] *s.m.* =TRACERET.

tract [trakt] *s.m.* tract, pamphlet.

tractations [traktɑsjɔ̃] *s.f.pl.* (pej.) bargaining, dealing, horse-trading.

tracteur [traktœr] *s.m.* tractor.

traction [traksjɔ̃] *s.f.* traction; draught; tension; *effort de ~*, pull, tractive effort; *résistance à la ~*, tensile strength; *~ avant*, front-wheel drive.

traditeur [traditœr] *s.m.* (eccles. hist.) traditor.

tradition [tradisjɔ̃] *s.f.* tradition; (law) delivery, handing-over; *de ~*, traditional.

traditionalisme [tradisjɔnalism] *s.m.* traditionalism.

traditionaliste [tradisjɔnalist] *adj., s.m.f.* traditionalist.

traditionnel, -le [tradisjɔnɛl] *adj.* traditional; orthodox; **~lement** [tradisjɔnɛlmɑ̃] *adv.* traditionally, in conformity with tradition.

traduct-eur, -rice [tradyktœr] *s.m.f.* translator; **~eur** *s.m.* (electr.) transformer.

traduction [tradyksjɔ̃] *s.f.* translation; (automation) *~ automatique*, automatic transfer; *~ des informations*, data reduction.

traduire [tradɥir] *v.t.* **1.** to translate, to construe; to explain, to interpret, to render; to turn (*en*, into); to show, to voice, to express; **2.** (law) to deliver; to indict, to arraign; ~ *en justice*, to indict; **se** ~ *v.refl.* to be translated; to be expressed, to be shown.

traduisible [tradɥizibl] *adj.* translatable.

trafic [trafik] *s.m.* (often pej.) traffic, trade, dealings, traffickings, commerce; (rail, air, etc.) traffic; (pej.) *faire le ~ de*, to make money out of, to put up for sale; ~ *d'influence*, corrupt practice (over offices, contracts, etc.).

trafiquant, -e [trafikɑ̃] *s.m.f.* trader, merchant; (pej.) trafficker.

trafiquer [trafike] *v.t.* **1.** (also ~ *de*) (often pej.) to deal (in), to trade, to make money out of, to buy and sell, to barter away; **2.** (pop.) to fiddle, to fix, to adulterate, to doctor, to rig; (slang) to ring (a car engine).

trafiqueu-r, -se [trafikœr] *s.m.f.* = TRAFIQUANT.

tragédie [traʒedi] *s.f.* tragedy.

tragédien, -ne [traʒedjɛ̃] *s.m.f.* tragedian.

tragi-comédie [traʒikɔmedi] *s.f.* tragi-comedy.

tragi-comique [traʒikɔmik] *adj.* tragi-comic, tragi-comical.

tragique [traʒik] *adj.* tragic, tragical; ~ *s.m.* tragic style; tragicalness, tragedy; tragic writer or poet; *prendre les choses au ~*, to look on the dark side, to take things too seriously; **~ment** [traʒikmɑ̃] *adv.* tragically.

trahir [trair] *v.t.* to betray, to be false to; to deceive, to mislead; to give away, to disclose; to abandon, to fail, to let down; to misrepresent, to traduce; **se** ~ *v.refl.* to betray oneself, to give oneself away; to reveal involuntarily one's presence, plans, real nature, etc.

trahison [traizɔ̃] *s.f.* treason, treachery, perfidy, betrayal, gross deception, foul play, treacherousness; *haute* ~, high treason.

traille [trɑj] *s.f.* ferry cable, ferry.

train [trɛ̃] *s.m.* **1.** pace, rate, speed; course, way; movement, motion, process, progress; mood, spirits, humour, inclination; train (of events), series, succession; *à* (or *de*) *ce* ~, at this rate; *au ~ dont il va, du ~ où il va*, the way he is going; *aller à fond de ~, aller un ~ d'enfer*, to go at breakneck speed, to go hell for leather; *aller son ~*, to go on, to go one's way, to take its course, to keep on just the same; *bon ~*, at a good speed; with a high hand; *grand ~*, very fast; *dans le ~*, in the swim; *en ~*, in good form, in the mood, slightly tipsy; *être en ~ de faire*, to be on the way to do; to be engaged in or busy doing, to be in the act or the process of doing; *mener un bon ~*, to go at a good pace; *mener un grand ~*, to live in style; (sport) *mener le ~*, to set the pace, to lead the field; *mener un ~ d'enfer*, to go the pace, to lead a killing life; *en bon ~*, off to a good start, making good progress; *mettre en bon ~*, to help to the success of; *mettre en ~*, to start off; to make ready, to get ready; *mise en ~*, making ready, preparatory work; *pas en ~, mal en ~*, not going well, started badly, out of sorts; ~ *de maison*, style of living, domestic staff; **2.** noise, row; *faire du ~*, to make a lot of noise, to cause a commotion; **3.** (rail., artill., mule, etc.) train; string, line, procession, retinue; ~ *de marchandises*, goods train; ~ *de voyageurs*, passenger train; ~ *direct*, through train; *~-poste*, mail train; *~-omnibus*, stopping train; (~)*rapide*, express; (mil.) *le Train des équipages*, service corps, supply services; **4.** undercarriage, frame; quarters (of horse); (pop.) bottom, backside; ~ *de devant*, forecarriage, forequarters; (vehicle) ~ *avant*, front wheels, front suspension; ~ *arrière*, rear wheels, rear suspension; ~ *de pneus*, set of tyres; (aeron.) ~ *d'atterrissage*, landing-wheels, landing-gear; (fam.) *c'est le diable et son ~*, it's the hell of a business; **5.** (horol.) train; (mech.) train of gears.

traînage [trɛnaʒ] *s.m.* dragging; sledging, sleighing; (cable-) haulage.

traînant, -e [trɛnɑ̃] *adj.* trailing, dragging, shuffling; drawling; slow, languid, flagging; prolix, dull.

traînard [trɛnar] *s.m* laggard, straggler, loiterer, slow worker.

traînasser [trɛnase] *v.t.* (pej.) to spin out, to drag out, to protract, to delay; ~ *v.i.* to linger, to dawdle, to be dilatory, to lag behind, to loiter.

traîne [trɛn] *s.f.* **1.** train (of a dress); **2.** drag-net, drift-net, seine(-net); **3.** (naut.) rope's end; **4.** rope-maker's sledge; **5.** hedgerow (along lane or watercourse); **6.** being towed; *à la ~*, in tow, at the rear, lagging behind; left lying around.

traîneau (pl. **-x**) [trɛno] *s.m.* sledge, sleigh, sled; dray, drag; (agric.) bush-harrow; (hunt., fish.) drag-net.

traînée [trene] *s.f.* **1.** trail, train (of gunpowder); **2.** track, trail, streak; **3.** (aeron.) *effort, force, de ~*, drag; **4.** (pop.) prostitute.

traîne-malheur [trɛnmalœr], **traîne-misère** [trɛnmizɛr] *s.m.invar.* unfortunate wretch.

traîner [trene] *v.t.* **1.** to drag, to draw, to pull along, to tow; to lead to, to entail; ~ *la jambe*, to limp, to be lame; ~ *le pas*, to shuffle along, to dawdle; ~ *qn. dans la boue*, to defame s.o.; ~ *qn. partout*, to have s.o. constantly at one's heels; **2.** to drag out, to lead, to protract, to spin out, to delay, to put off; to drawl; *faire ~*, to delay, to drag out; ~ *en longueur*, to spin out; ~ *v.i.* **1.** to drag, to trail; to hang down; **2.** to lie around, to kick about, to knock about; *ne laissez rien ~*, do not leave anything about; **3.** to be found; *cela traîne dans tous les livres*, that is in all the books; *ça traîne partout*, it is hackneyed, trite, old hat; **4.** to droop, to flag, to languish, to linger; to become dull; to progress very slowly, to drag on; to cling, to survive; to lag, to loiter, to drop behind, to dawdle; *je ne vis pas, je traîne*, I do not live, I exist; *cette affaire traîne*, this affair doesn't make much progress; (theatr.) *cet acte traîne*, this act drags; ~ *par les rues*, (fam.) ~ *les rues*, to wander round the streets, to loaf; **5.** (billiards) to follow one's ball; **se** ~ *v.refl.* **1.** to creep along, to crawl, to drag oneself along; to trudge, to wade; **2.** to drag on, to stretch out; to be long-drawn-out, to be lengthy; to be heavy, dull.

traîne-savates [trɛnsavat] *s.m.invar.* tramp.

traîneu-r, -se [trɛnœr] *s.m.f.* straggler, laggard, loafer, one who hangs around; **~r** *s.m.* sledge-driver; drayman; (mining) hauler; *~r d'épée, ~r de sabre*, swashbuckler.

trainglot see TRINGLOT.

train-train, traintrain [trɛ̃trɛ̃] *s.m.* routine, regular habits, jog-trot.

traire [trɛr] *v.t.* **1.** (obs.) to draw; (mod.) *or trait*, wire-drawn or spun gold, gold wire; **2.** to milk.

trait [trɛ] *s.m.* **1.** dart, arrow, bolt; flash, gleam, beam, shaft, glint, ray, burst; pull, pulling, draught, gulp; *comme un ~*, like a flash, like a shot, like an arrow from the bow; *lancer un ~ à qn.*, to have a dig at s.o.; *d'un ~, d'un seul ~, tout d'un ~*, at a draught, at one go, straight off; without stopping; ~ *d'esprit*, witticism, clever hit; ~ *de scie*, kerf, saw-cut; *cheval de ~*, draught horse; **2.** stroke, move, act, deed, touch; turn (of the scale); ~ *d'éclat*, brilliant stroke; **3.** line; outline; link; trace, leash; ~ *d'union*, hyphen; (fig.) connecting-link; *au ~*, in outline; *décrire à grands ~s*, to sketch; *avoir ~ à*, to relate to; **4.** trait, characteristic, feature, lineament; ~ *pour ~*, to a T.

trait, -e [trɛ] p.p. of TRAIRE

traitable [trɛtabl] *adj.* tractable, manageable, docile; ductile, malleable, amenable.

traitant [trɛtɑ̃] *s.m.* **1.** (hist.) tax-farmer; **2.** (obs.) slave-trader; ~ *adj.m. médecin* ~, general practitioner (opp. consultant).

traite [trɛt] *s.f.* **1.** journey, stage, stretch, distance; *trente milles d'une* ~, thirty miles at a stretch; **2.** trade, traffic; ~ *des noirs, des nègres*, slave trade; ~ *des blanches*, white slave traffic; *faire la* ~, to carry on the slave trade; **3.** draft, bill, drawing (of cheque, etc.); *faire* ~ *sur*, to draw a bill on; **4.** milking.

traité [trete] *s.m.* **1.** treatise; **2.** treaty, agreement, contract.

traitement [trɛtmɑ̃] *s.m.* **1.** treatment, usage; manipulation; (techn.) processing; *mauvais* ~*s*, ill-treatment; **2.** salary, stipend, pay; *toucher, recevoir son* ~, to recive one's salary.

traiter [trete] *v.t.* **1.** to treat, to use, to deal with, to behave towards; ~ *en ami*, to treat as a friend; ~ *en enfant*, to treat (s.o.) as though he were a child; ~ *qn. de haut en bas*, to treat s.o. with scorn; *se faire* ~ (*de qch.*), to undergo treatment (for sth.); **2.** to treat of, to deal with; to render, to depict, to represent, to manage, to handle, to discuss, to negotiate; to execute, to transact; **3.** ~ *de*, to call, to style, to regard as; ~ *qn. d'imbécile*, to call s.o. a fool; *il l'a traité de tous les noms*, he called him every name under the sun; **4.** to treat, to entertain; ~ *v.i.* to deal, to negotiate, to come to terms; **se** ~ *v.refl.* to treat oneself; to live (well, etc.); to treat one another; *se* ~ *de*, to call one another (names, etc.).

traiteur [trɛtœr] *s.m.* (obs.) restaurant-keeper; (mod.) caterer.

traître, -sse [trɛtr] *s.m.f.* traitor, traitress; (fig., theatr.) villain; *en* ~, treacherously, perfidiously; *adj.* treacherous, false, perfidious, faithless; *jouer un tour bien* ~, to play a very dirty trick; (fam.) *pas un* ~ *mot*, not a single word, not a syllable.

traîtreusement [trɛtrøzmɑ̃] *adv.* treacherously, perfidiously.

traîtrise [tretriz] *s.f.* treachery, treacherousness; hidden danger; (fig.) pitfall.

trajectographie [traʒɛktɔgrafi] *s.f.* tracking (of space vehicle).

trajectoire [traʒɛktwar] *s.f.* trajectory.

trajet [trajɛ] *s.m.* passage, journey, course, way, path, voyage, distance; (anat.) course (of artery, etc.); *c'est un* ~ *de deux heures*, it is a two-hours' journey, run, etc., it takes two hours; *le* ~ *n'est pas long*, it is quite a short distance.

tralala [tralala] *s.m.* (fam.) fuss, ado, show; *faire du* ~, to make an ostentatious display; *en grand* ~, dressed up to the nines.

tram [tram] *s.m.* abbrev. of TRAMWAY.

tramail [tramaj] *s.m.* (fish.) trammel, drag-net.

trame [tram] *s.f.* weft, woof; (TV) frame; (photo.) screen; (fig.) course, thread; (fig.) plot.

tramer [trame] *v.t.* to weave; (fig.) to plot; to lay, to hatch, to work out (cunning scheme, etc.); **se** ~ *v.refl.* to be plotted; *il se trame qch.*, a plot is being hatched, there is sth. afoot, there is sth. fishy going on.

trameu-r, -se [tramœr] *s.m.f.* weaver; ~**se** *s.f.* weft-winding machine.

tramontane [tramɔ̃taɲ] *s.f.* north; pole star; tramontane, north wind; (fig.) *perdre la* ~, to lose one's head, or one's presence of mind.

tramp [trɑ̃p] *s.m.* tramp (steamer).

tramway [tramwɛ] *s.m.* **1.** tram; **2.** tramway.

tranchage [trɑ̃ʃaʒ] *s.m.* cutting, slicing.

tranchant, -e [trɑ̃ʃɑ̃] *adj.* sharp, cutting, keen; (fig.) trenchant, peremptory, decisive; glaring; ~ *s.m.* edge, cutting edge; (fig.) bite, effect; *à deux* ~*s*, double-edged, that cuts both ways.

tranche [trɑ̃ʃ] *s.f.* **1.** slice, round, slab, rasher, chop, steak; earth turned by the plough; *cela prend de larges* ~*s de temps*, that takes up a good slice of one's time; *s'en payer une* ~, to give oneself a good time; ~ *grasse*, thick flank (of beef); ~ *de filet*, fillet steak (of beef); **2.** edge; *doré sur* ~*s*, gilt-edged, (fam.) rolling in money; **3.** series, set, group, (of figures); block or issue (of shares), draw (of lottery); instalment; section, cross--section; **4.** face, surface; (artill.) face (of guns); **5.** chisel.

tranché, -e [trɑ̃ʃe] *adj.* cut, sliced; clear-cut, distinct, well-defined.

tranchée [trɑ̃ʃe] *s.f.* **1.** trench; cut, groove, slot; cutting, excavation, ditch; entrenchment; *sortir de la* ~, to go over the top; **2.** (med.) pl. colic, gripes.

tranchefile [trɑ̃ʃfil] *s.f.* (bookbind.) headband.

tranchefiler [trɑ̃ʃfile] *v.t.* (bookbind.) to put on the headband of.

tranchelard [trɑ̃ʃlar] *s.m.* cook's knife.

tranche-montagne [trɑ̃ʃmɔ̃taɲ] *s.m.* (pl. *tranche--montagnes*) swaggerer, bully.

trancher [trɑ̃ʃe] *v.t.* **1.** to cut off, to cut short; to divide, to sever; to put an end to; to cut, to carve, to slice; ~ *la tête à qn.*, to cut off someone's head; ~ *son discours*, to cut short one's speech; *le* ~ *en un mot*, to cut matters short, not to mince matters; ~ *net*, to speak plainly; *tranchons là*, let's say no more about it; **2.** to decide, to determine, to solve, to come to a (quick) decision about; ~ *une difficulté*, to solve a difficulty; ~ *v.i.* **1.** to cut; ~ *dans le vif*, (surg.) to operate, to use the knife; (fig.) to take drastic measures; **2.** to decide; *il faut* ~, you must make a decision; **3.** ~ *du* or *de la*, to behave like; ~ *du seigneur*, to lord it; **4.** ~ *sur*, to stand out against, to contrast with; ~ *avec*, to contrast with, to be in contrast to.

tranchet [trɑ̃ʃɛ] *s.m.* paring-knife, hacking-knife.

trancheu-r, -se [trɑ̃ʃœr] *s.m.f.* (tailor's) cutter; ~**r** *s.m.* (coal-)cutter; (fishery) gutter; ~**se** *s.f.* stone-cutting machine; ditcher, trench--digger.

tranchoir [trɑ̃ʃwar] *s.m.* **1.** trencher, platter, plate; **2.** chopper; **3.** (ichth.) Zanclus, Moorish idol.

tranquille [trɑ̃kil] *adj.* quiet, tranquil, calm, peaceful, still, steady, stable, at peace, at rest, at ease, serene, undisturbed; *laissez-moi* ~, leave me alone; don't bother me; *laissez cela* ~, leave it alone, don't bother your head about it; *restez* ~, *tenez-vous* ~, be quiet; keep still; *soyez* ~, don't worry; set your mind at rest; never fear; *vous pouvez être* ~ *qu'il n'est pas là*, you may be certain he is not there; ~**ment** [trɑ̃kilmɑ̃] *adv.* quietly, calmly, tranquilly, peacefully, placidly.

tranquillisant, -e [trɑ̃kilizɑ̃] *adj.* soothing, tranquillizing, reassuring; ~ *s.m.* tranquillizer.

tranquilliser [trɑ̃kilize] *v.t.* to soothe, to calm, to quiet, to still, to tranquillize, to set at rest; **se** ~ *v.refl.* to feel calmer, to be easier in one's mind.

tranquillité [trɑ̃kilite] *s.f.* quiet, calm, stillness, peace, tranquillity, peace of mind, stability, order.

transaction [trɑ̃zaksjɔ̃] *s.f.* **1.** compromise, agreement, arrangement; (law) adjustment; **2.** transaction.

transactionnel, -le [trɑ̃zaksjɔnɛl] *adj.* of the nature of a compromise; *règlement* ~, compromise arrangement

transalpin, -e [trɑ̃salpɛ̃] *adj.* transalpine.

transat [trɑ̃zat] *s.f.* abbrev. of *Compagnie générale transatlantique*; ~ *s.m.* abbrev. of TRANSATLANTIQUE 2.
transatlantique [trɑ̃zatlɑ̃tik] *adj.* transatlantic; ~ *s.m.* **1.** transatlantic liner; **2.** deck-chair.
transbahuter [trɑ̃sbayte] *v.t.* to shift, to lug along; **se** ~ *v.refl.* to move (oneself), to drag along.
transbord-ement [trɑ̃sbɔrdəmɑ̃] *s.m.* transhipment; **~er** [trɑ̃sbɔrde] *v.t.* to tranship, to transfer; **~eur** [trɑ̃sbɔrdœr] *s.m.* (obs.) ferry-boat; (mod.) (*pont*) *~eur*, transporter-bridge.
transcendance [trɑ̃sɑ̃dɑ̃s] *s.f.* transcendency, transcendence.
transcendant, -e [trɑ̃sɑ̃dɑ̃] *adj.* transcendent; transcendental; (fam.) outstanding.
transcendantal, -e, (aux) [trɑ̃sɑ̃dɑ̃tal] *adj.* transcendental.
transcendantalisme [trɑ̃sɑ̃dɑ̃talism] *s.m.* transcendentalism.
transcender [trɑ̃sɑ̃de] *v.t.* to transcend; (fam.) to excel; **se** ~ *v.refl.* to excel oneself.
transcodage [trɑ̃skɔdaʒ] *s.m.* conversion (of code).
transcoder [trɑ̃skɔde] *v.t.* to convert (computer program).
transcontinental, -e, (aux) [trɑ̃scɔ̃tinɑ̃tal] *adj.* transcontinental.
transcripteur [trɑ̃skriptœr] *s.m.* transcriber, copyist.
transcription [trɑ̃skripsjɔ̃] *s.f.* **1.** transcription; (law) registration; **2.** copy, transcript.
transcrire [trɑ̃skrir] *v.t.* to copy out, to transscribe; (law) to register.
transe [trɑ̃s] *s.f.* **1.** apprehension, anxiety, fright, dread, fear; (fam.) scare; *être dans des ~s mortelles*, to be in mortal terror; **2.** trance.
transept [trɑ̃sɛpt] *s.m.* (arch.) transept.
transfèrement [trɑ̃sfɛrmɑ̃] *s.m.* = TRANSFERT.
transférer [trɑ̃sfere] *v.t.* to transfer, to transport, to convey; to make over; to translate (a bishop).
transfert [trɑ̃sfer] *s.m.* transfer, transference; (law) conveyance, transfer, assignment, alienation; *machine à* ~, automatic transfer machine.
transfigur-ation [trɑ̃sfigyrɑsjɔ̃] *s.f.* transfiguration, transformation; **~er** [trɑ̃sfigyre] *v.t.* to transfigure, to transform, to make a new man of.
transfiler [trɑ̃sfile] *v.t.* (naut.) to lace; to lash.
transformable [trɑ̃sfɔrmabl] *adj.* transformable, convertible.
transformat-eur, -rice [trɑ̃sfɔmatœr] *adj.* transforming, transformative; **~eur** *s.m.* (electr.) transformer, converter.
transform-ation [trɑ̃sfɔrmɑsjɔ̃] *s.f.* transformation, metamorphosis, transmutation, conversion; (Rugby football) converting (of try); *~ation chimique*, chemical change; *industrie de ~ation*, processing industry; **~er** [trɑ̃sfɔrme] *v.t.* to transform, to change, to turn, to convert; **se ~er** *v.refl.* to be transformed; **~isme** [trɑ̃sfɔrmism] *s.m.* transformism; **~iste** [trɑ̃sfɔrmist] *adj.*, *s.m.f.* transformist.
transfuge [trɑ̃sfyʒ], *s.m.* deserter; turn-coat, dissident.
transfus-er [trɑ̃sfyze], *v.t.* to transfuse; (fig.) to instil, to inject; **~ion** [trɑ̃sfyzjɔ̃], *s.f.* transfusion.
transgress-er [trɑ̃sgrese] *v.t.* to transgress, to violate, to infringe, to contravene; **~eur** [trɑ̃sgrɛsœr] *s.m.* transgressor, offender; **~ion** [trɑ̃sgrɛsjɔ̃] *s.f.* transgression, violation; (geog.) encroachment, transgression.
transhumance [trɑ̃zymɑ̃s] *s.f.* change of pasture, moving to new pastures.
transhumant, -e [trɑ̃zymɑ̃] *adj.* (of flocks and herds) changing pasture.
transhumer [trɑ̃zyme] *v.t.i.* to move to new pastures.
transi, -e [trɑ̃zi] *adj.* chilled, numbed; paralysed; *un amoureux* ~, a faint-hearted lover; ~ *de froid*, frozen; ~ *de peur*, petrified (with fear).
transiger [trɑ̃ziʒe] *v.i.* to compromise, to come to terms, to compound (*avec*, with), to make concessions, to give way; ~ *sur l'honneur*, to barter away one's honour.
transir [trɑ̃zir] *v.t.* to numb; (fig.) to freeze, to penetrate; *~v.i.* to be numbed or frozen.
transistor [trɑ̃zistɔr] *s.m.* transistor; transistor radio.
transistorisé, -e [trɑ̃zistɔrize] *adj.* transistorized.
transit [trɑ̃zit] *s.m.* transit; transit free of customs duty; through traffic; **~aire** [trɑ̃zitɛr] *adj.* transit; *s.m.* forwarding agent; **~er** [trɑ̃zite] *v.t.* to convey (goods) in transit; **~er** *v.i.* to be in transit.
transiti-f, -ve [trɑ̃zitif] *adj.* transitive.
transition [trɑ̃zisjɔ̃] *s.f.* transition; gradual passage, change; *de* ~, transitional; *sans* ~, abruptly.
transitivement [trɑ̃zitivmɑ̃] *adv.* transitively.
transitoire [trɑ̃zitwar] *adj.* transitory, transient, transitional, temporary, provisional; **~ment** [trɑ̃zitwarmɑ̃] *adv.* transiently, provisionally.
translati-f, -ve [trɑ̃slatif] *adj.* (law) transferring; *acte ~f de propriété*, conveyance.
translation [trɑ̃slɑsjɔ̃] *s.f.* translation, removal, transfer; ⚠ not 'translation' of languages.
translit(t)ération [trɑ̃sliterɑsjɔ̃] *s.f.* transliteration.
translucide [trɑ̃slysid] *adj.* translucent; diaphanous.
translucidité [trɑ̃slysidite] *s.f.* translucence, translucency.
transmetteur [trɑ̃smɛtœr] *s.m.* transmitter; (naut.) engine-room telegraph.
transmettre [trɑ̃smɛtr] *v.t.* to transmit, to send on, to convey, to forward; to hand on, to make over, to transfer; (Rugby football) to pass (the ball); to broadcast; to pass on; (fig.) to hand down; ~ *son nom à la postérité*, to hand down one's name to posterity.
transmigration [trɑ̃smigrɑsjɔ̃] *s.f.* transmigration; ~ *des âmes*, metempsychosis, transmigration of souls.
transmiss-ibilité [trɑ̃smisibilite] *s.f.* transmissibility; **~ible** [trɑ̃smisibl] *adj.* transmissible; (law) heritable; **~ion** [trɑ̃smisjɔ̃] *s.f.* transmission, passing on, handing down, handing over, transfer, forwarding; (pl.) communications; (mil.) signals; (mech.) transmission (gear), drive.
transmuable [trɑ̃smɥabl], **transmutable** [trɑ̃smytabl] *adj.* transmutable.
transmuer [trɑ̃smɥe], **transmuter** [trɑ̃smyte] *v.t.* to transmute.
transmutation [trɑ̃smytɑsjɔ̃] *s.f.* transmutation.
transparaître [trɑ̃sparɛtr] *v.i.* to be visible (through something); to appear, to become apparent or clear, to show through.
transparence [trɑ̃sparɑ̃s] *s.f.* transparence, transparency, transparentness.
transparent, -e [trɑ̃sparɑ̃] *adj.* transparent; (fig.) easily seen through, unsubtle, uncomplicated; ~ *s.m.* **1.** paper with black guiding lines (placed under unruled writing-paper); **2.** transparency.
transpercer [trɑ̃sperse] *v.t.* to run through, to pierce, to transfix, to transpierce; (fig.) to penetrate, to pierce to the heart, to cut to the quick; (of rain, etc.) to drench.
transpir-ation [trɑ̃spirɑsjɔ̃] *s.f.* sweat, perspiration; (bot.) transpiration; **~er** [trɑ̃spire] *v.i.* to perspire, to sweat; (bot.) to transpire; (fig.)

to transpire, to become known; (fam.) *~er sur,* to sweat away at.

transplant [trɑ̃splɑ̃] *s.m.* (biol., surg.) transplant; **~ation** [trɑ̃splɑ̃tɑsjɔ̃] *s.f.* transplantation, transplanting, transplant; **~er** [trɑ̃splɑ̃te] *v.t.* to transplant; (fig.) to uproot; **se ~er** *v.refl.* to be transplanted, to emigrate.

transport [trɑ̃spɔr] *s.m.* **1.** (often pl.) transport, conveyance, carrying; removal; traffic; *compagnie de ~,* carrying company, forwarding company; *~s en commun,* public transport; *frais de ~,* carriage; *ce malade n'est pas en état de souffrir le ~,* this patient is too ill to be moved; **2.** transport ship; (hist.) *~ de condamnés,* convict ship; *~ de ravitaillement,* store ship; transport; **3.** fit, violent emotion, transport, rapture, rage; *avec ~,* enthusiastically; *~ au cerveau,* congestion of the brain; **4.** (law) *~ de justice, ~ sur les lieux,* visit by court to scene of crime; **5.** (comm.) carrying forward; **~able** [trɑ̃spɔrtabl] *adj.* transportable, movable; **~ation** [trɑ̃spɔrtasjɔ̃] *s.f.* (hist.) transportation.

transporté, -e [trɑ̃spɔrte] *adj.* carried away, overcome (*de,* with); *s.m.f.* (hist.) transported convict.

transporter [trɑ̃spɔrte] *v.t.* **1.** to transport, to convey, to remove; to transfer, to make over; (comm.) to carry over; (law) to deport, to transport; **2.** (fig.) to carry away, to overcome; **se ~** *v.refl.* to be transported; to go, to move.

transporteur [trɑ̃spɔrtœr] *s.m.* haulier, carrier; (techn.) conveyor.

transposable [trɑ̃spozabl] *adj.* transposable, transferable.

transposer [trɑ̃spoze] *v.t.* to transpose.

transpositeur [trɑ̃spozitœr] *adj., s.m.* (mus.) transposing (instrument).

transposition [trɑ̃spozisjɔ̃] *s.f.* transposition.

transsaharien, -ne [trɑ̃ssaarjɛ̃] *adj.* (geog.) Trans-Saharan.

transsibérien, -ne [trɑ̃ssiberjɛ̃] *adj.* (geog.) Trans-Siberian.

transsonique [trɑ̃ssɔnik] *adj.* transonic, trans-sonic.

transsubstantiation [trɑ̃ssypstɑ̃sjɑsjɔ̃] *s.f.* transubstantiation.

transsudation [trɑ̃ssydɑsjɔ̃] *s.f.* transudation.

transsuder [trɑ̃ssyde] *v.t.i.* to transude, to ooze through.

transvasement [trɑ̃svɑzmɑ̃] *s.m.* decanting.

transvaser [trɑ̃svɑze] *v.t.* to decant.

transversal, -e, (aux) [trɑ̃svɛrsal] *adj.* transverse, transversal, cross; horizontal; *rue ~e,* side-street; **~ement** [trɑ̃svɛrsalmɑ̃] *adv.* transversely, across, crosswise; horizontally.

transverse [trɑ̃svɛrs] *adj.* transverse; *~ s.m.* (anat.) transverse muscle.

transvestisme [trɑ̃svɛstism] *s.m.* = TRAVESTISME.

transvider [trɑ̃svide] *v.t.* to pour off.

transylvain, -e [trɑ̃silvɛ̃] *adj., s.m.f.* Transylvanian.

trantran [trɑ̃trɑ̃] *s.m.* = TRAIN-TRAIN.

trapèze [trapɛz] *s.m.* (geom.) trapezium; (U.S.) trapezoid; (anat.) trapezium (bone); trapezius (muscle); (gymn.) trapeze.

trapéziste [trapezist] *s.m.f.* trapeze-artist.

trapézoèdre [trapezɔɛdr] *s.m.* trapezohedron.

trapézoïdal, -e, (aux) [trapezɔidal] *adj.* trapezoidal.

trappe[1] [trap] *s.f.* trapdoor; trap, pitfall; *tendre, dresser, une ~,* to set a trap.

trappe[2] [trap] *s.f.* Trappist order; Trappist monastery.

trappeur [trapœr] *s.m.* trapper.

trappiste [trapist] *s.m.* Trappist.

trappistine [trapistin] *s.f.* Trappistine, Trappist nun; trappistine (liqueur).

trapu, -e [trapy] *adj.* thickset, dumpy, squat, stocky, solid; (slang) *candidat ~,* strong candidate; *problème ~,* thorny problem.

traque [trak] *s.f.* (hunt.) driving, beating.

traquenard [traknar] *s.m.* trap, snare; (fig.) pitfall; *se laisser prendre au ~,* to walk into a trap.

traquer [trake] *v.t.* (hunt.) to drive, to beat; to hunt, to hunt down, to track down, to run to earth, to surround.

traquet [trakɛ] *s.m.* **1.** trap; **2.** (ornith.) stonechat, wheatear.

traqueur [trakœr] *s.m.* (hunt.) beater.

trauma [troma] *s.m.* (med., psychol.) trauma; **~tique** [tromatik] *adj.* traumatic; **~tiser** [tromatize] *v.t.* (med.) to cause a state of shock; (fig.) to give a shock to; **~tisme** [tromatism] *s.m.* (med.) traumatism, shock; (psychol.) traumatic state; **~-tologie** [tromatɔlɔʒi] *s.f.* traumatology.

travail[1] (pl. **aux**) [travaj] *s.m.* **1.** work, job, employment; task, labour, toil; effort, fatigue, trouble; piece of work; workmanship, execution; industry; working, operation; fermenting; practice, drill; (pl.) works, public works; earthworks; (mine) workings; feats, deeds; *à force de ~,* by (sheer) hard work; *c'est un beau ~,* it is a fine piece of work; *d'un ~ exquis,* of exquisite workmanship; *cabinet de ~,* study; *les sans-~,* the unemployed; *se mettre au ~,* to set to work; *~ servile,* menial work; *travaux forcés,* hard labour, penal servitude; *~ à la pièce,* or *aux pièces,* piece-work; *travaux ménagers,* household duties, housework; *vivre de son ~,* to live by one's work, to work for a living; *travaux d'art,* public works, major construction projects; **2.** labour, childbirth; **3.** (pl.) proceedings, transactions, deliberations.

travail[2] (pl. **-s**) [travaj] *s.m.* (vet.) trave.

travaillé, -e [travaje] *adj.* **1.** worked, wrought; laboured; elaborate; finished; **2.** tormented, obsessed (*par,* by, with); *~ par la peur,* distracted with fear; *~ par l'ambition,* obsessed with ambition.

travailler [travaje] *v.t.i.* **1.** to work, to labour, to take pains, to take trouble over, to make an effort (*à,* to), to exert oneself; to be active; to study; to practise; *~ pour vivre,* to work for one's living; *il a travaillé pour le roi de Prusse,* he has done it all for nothing, he has got nothing for his trouble; *faire ~ une machine,* to operate, to run, a machine; *faire ~ sa matière grise,* to put one's mind to work; *faire ~ son argent,* to get interest on one's money; **2.** to undergo a change; (of wine) to ferment; (of wood) to warp; (of walls) to crack; (of paint) to fade; **3.** to be agitated; *son esprit travaille,* his mind is in a ferment, he is thinking hard; **4.** *~ pour,* to be on the side of, to use one's influence on behalf of; *~ contre,* to operate against, to intrigue against; **5.** to torment, to worry, to distress, to disturb, to agitate; to stir up, to subvert; to work upon, to influence, to excite; *l'ambition ne me travaille point,* I am not a prey to ambition; (tennis, etc.) *~ une balle,* to cut a ball; *~ les esprits,* to excite public opinion; **6.** to work at, to be engaged on, to be occupied with, to elaborate; *~ son style,* to elaborate one's style; to work, to fashion; to knead (dough); to train, to exercise (horses); **se ~** *v.refl.* **1.** to be worked, to be wrought; **2.** to endeavour; to worry; to strain; *se ~ l'esprit,* to fret; to rack one's brains.

travailleu-r, -se [travajœr] *adj.* industrious, hardworking, painstaking; labouring, toiling; *s.m.f.* **1.** hard worker; conscientious student; **2.** working man, workman, labourer, operative, worker.

travailleuse [travajøz] *s.f.* work-table.

travaillisme [travajism] *s.m.* socialism, socialist policy.

travailliste [travajist] *adj.* (in United Kingdom) Labour; *s.m.f.* Labour politician, member of Labour Party.

travée [trave] *s.f.* (constr.) span, bay, truss.

travelling [travliŋ] *s.m.* (cin., TV) travelling platform (for camera), dolly; use of travelling platform; travel.

travers [travɛr] *s.m.* **1.** breadth, width; broadside (of a ship); *à ~*, across; through; *à ~ champs*, across country; *à ~ les âges*, down the ages; (adv.) *au ~*, through (it or them); *au ~ de*, through, by means of; *à tort et à ~*, like a bull in a china shop; recklessly; at random; indiscreetly; indiscriminately; heedlessly; rashly; *de ~*, askew, awry, crooked, wrong; *faire qch. de ~*, to do sth. wrong, in the wrong way; *il s'y est pris tout de ~*, he went about it the wrong way; *regarder qn. de ~*, to look askance at s.o., to give s.o. an odd look; (fig.) *il a mis son bonnet de ~ aujourd'hui*, he has got out of bed on the wrong side; he is in a bad temper; *il prend de ~ tout ce qu'on dit*, he takes everything the wrong way; (naut.) *feu de ~*, broadside; *vent de ~*, wind abeam; *par le ~*, abeam, athwart; *prendre la lame par le ~*, to keep broadside on to the sea, to broach to; *se mettre en ~ de*, to block, to obstruct, to oppose; (naut.) *venir en ~*, to broach to; *mettre un navire en ~*, to bring a ship to; *en ~ du courant*, athwart the tide; *en ~*, across, crosswise, transversely; athwart, sideways, obliquely; **2.** fault, defect, bad habit, oddity, eccentricity; *donner dans le ~*, to have taken to bad habits.

traversable [travɛrsabl] *adj.* traversable, fordable.

traverse [travɛrs] *s.f.* **1.** traverse, crossbar, cross-piece, transom, ground-sill, stretcher; buffer-beam; (harbour) bar; sleeper (of a railway); girder; stay; cross-member; cross--bearer; cross-head; *se jeter à la ~ de*, to obstruct, to counter, to thwart; *venir à la ~ de*, to upset, to run counter to; **2.** hindrance, obstacle, set--back, hitch, disappointment; **3.** crossing; cross-road; short cut; *prendre la ~*, to take a short cut; *chemin de ~*, cross-road, short cut; **4.** (fort.) traverse; (geom.) traverse, transversal line.

traversée [travɛrse] *s.f.* passage, voyage, crossing; (rail.) cross-over; *mauvaise ~*, rough passage.

traverser [travɛrse] *v.t.* **1.** to traverse; to cross, to travel across, to travel through, to go through, to make a way through; (rid.) to traverse; to span, to lie across, to run through; **2.** to run through (with a sword); to penetrate; **3.** to cross, to thwart, to foil, to frustrate, to hinder, to obstruct; *~ la rue*, to cross the street; *~ l'esprit*, to cross the mind, to occur (to); *~ un projet*, to thwart a project.

traversi-er, -ère [travɛrsje] *adj.* cross, crossing traversing, going across; *flûte ~ère*, transverse flute; *navire ~er*, ship passing across one's course; *barque ~ère*, ferry; (naut.) *barres ~ères*, cross-trees; **~er** *s.m.* (naut.) thwart; **~ère** *s.f.* (naut.) fish; *bossoir de ~ère*, fish-head, fish--davit.

traversin [travɛrsɛ̃] *s.m.* **1.** bolster; **2.** cross--piece, stretcher, thwart, (of boat); **3.** beam (of balance).

traversine [travɛrsin] *s.f.* cross-beam, cross--board; sleeper; transom; girder; (naut.) gang-plank.

travertin [travɛrtɛ̃] *s.m.* (min.) travertine.

travesti, -e [travɛsti] *adj.* **1.** disguised, dressed up (in a part), in fancy dress; *acteur ~*, actor taking woman's part; **2.** (obs.) burlesqued, parodied; *~ s.m.* fancy dress; (psychol.) transvestite.

travest-ir [travɛstir] *v.t.* **1.** to disguise, to dress up; **2.** to parody, to burlesque, to make a travesty of; to misrepresent, to falsify; **se ~ir** *v.refl.* to disguise oneself, to dress up as the other sex, to put on fancy dress; **~isme** [travɛstism] *s.m.* (psychol.) transvestism; **~issement** [travɛstismɑ̃] *s.m.* **1.** disguise, fancy dress; **2.** = TRAVESTISME; **3.** travesty, parody.

trayeu-r, -se [trɛjœr] *s.m.f.* milker, milkmaid; **~se** *s.f.* milking-machine.

trayon [trɛjɔ̃] *s.m.* dug, teat, (of cows, etc.).

trébuchant, -e [trebyʃɑ̃] *adj.* **1.** (of coins) of full weight; **2.** stumbling, faltering.

trébuchement [trebyʃmɑ̃] *s.m.* stumbling, falling; hesitation.

trébucher [trebuʃe] *v.i.* to stumble; to trip, to fall; (fig.) to err, to fail; *~ v.t.* to weigh (coins).

trébuchet [trebyʃɛ] *s.m.* **1.** bird-trap, snare, gin; *prendre au ~*, to ensnare; **2.** assay-balance, trebuchet.

tréfilage [trefilaʒ] *s.m.* wire-drawing, extrusion.

tréfiler [trefile] *v.t.* to wire-draw, to extrude.

tréfilerie [trefilri] *s.f.* wire-mill.

tréfileur [trefilœr] *s.m.* wire-drawer, wire-maker.

tréfileuse [trefiløz] *s.f.* wire-drawing bench.

trèfle [trɛfl] *s.m.* (bot.) trefoil; clover; shamrock; (at cards) clubs; (arch.) trefoil; *croisement en ~*, clover-leaf intersection (road-junction).

tréflé, -e [trefle] *adj.* (herald.) treflé, treflee.

tréflière [treflijɛr] *s.f.* clover-field.

tréfonci-er, -ère [trefɔ̃sje] *adj.* of the soil and subsoil; *redevance ~ère*, mining royalty.

tréfonds [trefɔ̃] *s.m.* subsoil; (fig.) bottom, deepest parts, heart (of a matter); *savoir le fond et le ~ d'une affaire*; to know the ins and outs of an affair.

treillage [trɛjaʒ] *s.m.* trellis(-work), lattice-work, wire netting or fencing.

treillager [trɛjaʒe] *v.t.* to trellis, to lattice, to cover with a criss-cross pattern.

treillageur [trɛjaʒœr], **treillagiste** [trɛjaʒist] *s.m.* trellis-maker, lattice-maker.

treille [trɛj] *s.f.* **1.** vine arbour; vine growing on trellis; (fam.) *le jus de la ~*, wine; **2.** (text.) tulle net.

treillis[1] [treji] *s.m.* trellis, trellis-work, lattice--work; metal grille; *pont en ~*, lattice girder bridge.

treillis[2] [treji] *s.m.* coarse canvas, denim.

treillisser [trejise] *v.t.* to trellis.

treize [trɛz] *adj.*, *s.m.* thirteen; thirteenth (of the month).

treizième [trɛzjɛm] *adj.* thirteenth.

trélingage [trelɛ̃gaʒ] *s.m.* (naut.) cat-harpings.

tréma [trema] *s.m.* diaeresis.

trémail [tremaj] *s.m.* = TRAMAIL.

trématode [trematɔd] *s.m.* (zool.) trematode (worm), fluke.

tremblaie [trɑ̃ble] *s.f.* aspen-grove.

tremblant, -e [trɑ̃blɑ̃] *adj.* trembling, tremulous, quivering, flickering, faltering, quavering, shaky, tottering, shivering, wavering.

tremble [trɑ̃bl] *s.m.* (bot.) aspen.

tremblé, -e [trɑ̃ble] *adj.* wavy, waved, shaky; *écriture ~e*, shaky writing; (mus.) tremolo; *~ s.m.* (print.) waved rule.

tremblement [trɑ̃bləmɑ̃] *s.m.* trembling, shaking, shivering, quivering, quaking, tremor, trepidation, quavering, agitation, flickering, fluttering; (mus.) shake; trill; (fam.) *et tout le ~*, and so on and so on, the whole bag of tricks, and all that stuff; *~ de terre*, earthquake.

trembler [trɑ̃ble] *v.i.* to tremble, to shake, to shiver, to quake, to quiver, to shudder, to totter, to waver, to flutter, to flicker, to twinkle;

je tremble de le voir, I tremble at the thought of seeing him; *il tremblait qu'on ne le découvrît;* he was in mortal fear of discovery; *à faire ~,* terrifying, frightful, awful.

trembleu-r, -se [trɑ̃blœr] *s.m.f.* apprehensive person; **~r** *s.m.* (electr.) trembler, vibrator; *bobine à ~r,* buzzer; **~se** *s.f.* (fishing) *pêche à la ~se,* dapping.

tremblotant, -e [trɑ̃blɔtɑ̃] *adj.* tremulous; quivering, flickering.

tremblote [trɑ̃blɔt] *s.f.* (fam.) fear, shivers; *avoir la ~,* to be all of a tremble.

tremblotement [trɑ̃blɔtmɑ̃] *s.m.* tremulousness, trembling, shakiness.

trembloter [trɑ̃blɔte] *v.i.* to tremble, to shake, to shiver, to quiver.

trémie [tremi] *s.f.* hopper, mill-hopper; funnel; (build.) space for hearth.

trémière [tremjɛr] *adj.f.* (bot.) *rose ~,* hollyhock, rose-mallow.

tremolo, trémolo [tremɔlo] *s.m.* (mus.) tremolo.

trémoussement [tremusmɑ̃] *s.m.* fluttering, fidgeting, twitching, frisking about.

(**se**) **trémousser** [tremuse] *v.refl.* to fidget, to dance about, to flutter.

trempage [trɑ̃paʒ] *s.m.* steeping, soaking; (print.) wetting.

trempe [trɑ̃p] *s.f.* steeping, soaking; (print.) wetting down; (metall.) tempering, hardening, quench; (pop.) thrashing; (brewing) malting--water; temper (of a metal); (fig.) temper, stamp, cast, character, calibre; grit, guts; *un corps d'une bonne ~,* a sound constitution; *un homme de cette ~,* a man of that calibre, a man with that sort of guts; *ils ne sont pas de la même ~,* they are not in the same class.

tremper [trɑ̃pe] *v.t.* to soak, to wet, to drench, to moisten, to steep, to dip (into a liquid), to dunk; (print.) to wet; to dilute; (metall., & fig.) to temper (steel); *il est tout trempé,* he is wet to the skin; (pop.) *~ la soupe,* to pour the soup on to the bread; *l'expérience l'a trempé,* experience has made a man of him; *~ v.i.* to soak, to be steeped; to be stained; to be implicated; to be concerned (in), to have a hand (in); *il a trempé là-dedans,* he has had a hand in that; **se** *~ v.refl.* to get wet, to immerse oneself, to take a dip.

trempette [trɑ̃pɛt] *s.f. faire ~,* **1.** to dip (piece of bread, sugar, etc.) in wine, coffee, etc., to dunk; **2.** to take a little dip, to wet one's feet.

trempeur [trɑ̃pœr] *s.m.* temperer; (print.) wetter.

tremplin [trɑ̃plɛ̃] *s.m.* spring-board; (fig.) stepping-stone, jumping-off place.

trémulation [tremylɑsjɔ̃] *s.f.* tremor, trembling.

trémuler [tremyle] *v.i.* to shake, to tremble.

trenail [trənaj] *s.m.* (techn.) treenail, trenail.

trench-coat [trɛnʃkot] *s.m.* (pl. *trench-coats*) trench coat, raincoat.

trentaine [trɑ̃tɛn] *s.f.* some thirty, about thirty, thirty or so; the age of thirty; *avoir passé la ~,* to be on the wrong side of thirty.

trente [trɑ̃t] *adj., s.m.* thirty; thirtieth (of the month); *~-et-quarante,* (game of) rouge et noir; *se mettre, être, sur son ~-et-un,* to put on, to be wearing, one's best clothes; *il n'y en a pas ~-six,* there isn't more than one of them; (fig.) *en voir ~-six chandelles,* to see stars; *tous les ~-six du mois,* once in a blue moon; (tennis) *~ à ~,* thirty all.

Trente [trɑ̃t] *s.m.* (geog.) Trento, Trent, (in Italy).

trentenaire [trɑ̃tənɛr] *adj.* for thirty years, lasting thirty years.

trentième [tratjɛm] *adj.* thirtieth; *~ s.m.* thirtieth part.

trépan [trepɑ̃] *s.m.* **1.** (surg.) trepan; **2.** rock--drill; **~ation** [trepanɑsjɔ̃] *s.f.* (surg.) trepanning; **~er** [trepane] *v.t.* (surg.) to trepan.

trépang [trepɑ̃] *s.m.* = TRIPANG.

trépas [trepɑ] *s.m.* death; *passer de vie à ~,* to die; ⚠ not 'trespass'.

trépassé, -e [trepɑse] *s.m.f.* dead, deceased; *les ~s,* the dead; *le jour, la fête, des Trépassés,* All Souls' Day.

trépasser [trepɑse] *v.i.* to die, to pass away, to depart this life; ⚠ not 'to trespass'.

trépidant, -e [trepidɑ̃] *adj.* shaking, quivering, vibrating; (fig.) agitated, in a flurry, excited.

trépidation [trepidɑsjɔ̃] *s.f.* shaking, trembling, quivering, vibration; (med.) trepidation; (astron.) trepidation; (fig.) agitation, flurry; excitement.

trépied [trepje] *s.m.* trivet; tripod, three-legged stool, stand, etc.

trépider [trepide] *v.i.* to vibrate.

trépignement [trepiɲmɑ̃] *s.m.* stamping (of the feet); pawing the ground.

trépigner [trepiɲe] *v.i.* to stamp (one's feet); *~ v.t.* to trample upon.

trépointe [trepwɛ̃t] *s.f.* welt (of shoe).

très [trɛ] *adv.* very, most, very much; *~ bien,* very well; all right; *voilà qui est ~ bien,* that's just the thing; *le Très-Haut,* the Most High; (fam.) *avoir ~ faim, ~ soif,* to be very hungry, very thirsty; *faire ~ attention,* to be very careful, to listen very carefully.

trésaille [trezɑj] *s.f.* cross-piece, upper rail, (on cart, etc.).

trésor [trezɔr] *s.m.* treasure, riches, wealth, fortune; treasury; (law) treasure trove; *Trésor,* Treasury, funds, (public or privy) purse.

trésorerie [trezɔrri] *s.f.* treasury, treasury department, exchequer, funds, resources; treasurership, office of treasurer.

trésori-er, -ère [trezɔrje] *s.m.f.* treasurer, cashier, paymaster; (eccles.) custodian (of the treasury).

tressage [trɛsaʒ] *s.m.* plaiting, braiding; weaving.

tressaillement [tresajmɑ̃] *s.m.* start; tremor, thrill; shudder.

tressaillir [tresajir] *v.i.* to start, to give a start, to thrill; to wince, to shudder; to tremble, to quake; *~ de joie,* to tremble with joy.

tressautement [tresotmɑ̃] *s.m.* starting, jumping, agitation.

tressauter [tresote] *v.i.* to jump; to start, to tremble, to jump about; to be bumped or jolted about.

tresse [trɛs] *s.f.* plait, tress, braid, pigtail; (arch.) strap-work; (naut.) sinnet; (techn.) packing, gasket.

tresser [trese] *v.t.* to plait, to tress, to braid, to weave.

tresseu-r, -se [trɛsœr] *s.m.f.* plaiter, braider.

tréteau (pl. **-x**) [treto] *s.m.* trestle, support; (pl.) boards, stage; (fig.) *monter sur les ~x,* to go on the stage; to tread the boards.

treuil [trœj] *s.m.* windlass, winch, hoist, winding-gear; crab (hoisting gear).

trêve [trɛv] *s.f.* truce, cessation, rest, relief; *sans ~,* relentless(ly); *faire ~,* to stop, to cease, to give a respite; *demander une ~,* to ask for a truce; *~ de questions,* no more of your questions; *son mal ne lui laisse pas de ~,* the pain gives him no rest.

Trèves [trɛv] *s.m.* (geog.) Treves, Trier.

trévire [trevir] *s.f.* (naut.) parbuckle.

trévirer [trevire] *v.t.* (naut.) to parbuckle; to slew.

tri [tri] *s.m.* sorting, picking; *faire le ~* or *un ~,* to sort; to select.

triade [trijad] *s.f.* triad, group of three, trinity.

triage [trijaʒ] *s.m.* sorting; selection, choice;

(rail.) shunting, marshalling; *voie de ~*, siding; (indust.) sorting-shed.
tri-alcool [trialkɔl], **triol** [trijɔl] *s.m.* (chem.) tri-alcohol.
triandre [triɑ̃dr] *adj.* (bot.) triandrous.
triangle [trijɑ̃gl] *s.m.* triangle, triangular space or shape; (naut.) triangular flag; (mus.) triangle.
triangul-aire [trijɑ̃gylɛr] *adj.* triangular; (fig.) three-cornered; **~ation** [trijɑ̃gylɑsjɔ̃] *s.f.* (survey.) triangulation; **~er** [trijɑ̃gyle] *v.t.* to triangulate.
trias [trijɑs] *s.m.* (geol.) Trias.
triasique [trijɑzik] *adj.* (geol.) Triassic.
triatomique [triatɔmik] *adj.* (chem.) triatomic.
tribal, -e, (aux) [tribal] *adj.* tribal.
tribalisme [tribalism] *s.m.* tribalism.
tribart [tribar] *s.m.* triangular yoke (to prevent animals getting through holes in hedges).
tribasique [tribɑzik] *adj.* (chem.) tribasic.
tribo-électricité [tribɔelɛktrisite] *s.f.* static electricity (produced by friction); **~mètre** [tribɔmɛtr] *s.m.* tribometer; **~métrie** [tribɔmetri] *s.f.* tribometry, measurement of friction.
tribord [tribɔr] *s.m.* (naut.) starboard; *quart de ~*, starboard watch; (rowing) bow side.
tribordais [tribɔrdɛ] *s.m.* (naut.) member of starboard watch.
triboulet [tribulɛ] *s.m.* (techn.) triblet, mandrel; ring-gauge.
tribraque [tribrak] *s.m.* (pros.) tribrach.
tribu [triby] *s.f.* tribe, family, clan; (fam.) horde, whole tribe (of).
tribulation [tribylɑsjɔ̃] *s.f.* tribulation, affliction, trial.
tribun [tribœ̃] *s.m.* (Rom. hist.) tribune; (mod.) democratic leader, champion (of the people), upholder (of rights, etc.).
tribunal, (aux) [tribynal] *s.m.* tribunal, court, lawcourt, court of justice; judge's or magistrates' bench; the judges, the magistrature; commission; (fig.) arbiter; *devant le ~ de l'opinion publique*, before the bar of public opinion.
tribunat [tribyna] *s.m.* (hist.) tribunate.
tribune [tribyn] *s.f.* tribune, rostrum, platform, hustings; gallery, grandstand; parliamentary or forensic oratory, public speaking; (fig.) forum, platform, voice; *~ sacrée*, pulpit; *~ aux enchères*, auctioneer's rostrum; *~ d'orgue*, organ--loft; *~ publique*, strangers' gallery; *~ des journalistes*, press gallery; *monter à la ~*, to mount the rostrum.
tribunitien, -ne [tribynisjɛ̃] *adj.* (hist.) tribunicial, tribunitian; demagogic.
tribut [triby] *s.m.* tribute, grant; contribution; tax; *payer ~ à la nature*, to die; *payer ~ à la mer*, to be seasick.
tributaire [tribytɛr] *adj.* tributary, subject, dependent; (of river) tributary; *~ s.m.f.* (fig.) one who pays tribute (*de*, to), devotee (*de*, of).
tricéphale [trisefal] *adj.* three-headed.
triceps [trisɛps] *s.m.* (anat.) triceps.
tricher [triʃe] *v.i.* to deceive, to be dishonest, to cheat; *~ sur le poids*, to give short weight.
tricherie [triʃri] *s.f.* cheating, deception, trickery, trick, dishonesty.
tricheu-r, -se [triʃœr] *s.m.f.* cheat, trickster; (obs.) deceiver.
trichiasis [trikjazis] *s.f.* (med.) trichiasis.
trichine [trikin] *s.f.* (med.) threadworm, trichina.
trichiné, -e [trikine] *adj.* (med.) trichinous.
trichinose [trikinoz] *s.f.* (med.) trichinosis.
trichloréthylène [triklɔretilɛn] *s.m.* (chem.) trichlorethylene.
trichrome [trikrom] *adj.* trichromatic, (printed) in three colours.
trichromie [trikrɔmi] *s.f.* (photo., typ.) three--colour process.
trick [trik] *s.m.* (at whist, bridge) odd trick.
tricoises [trikwas] *s.f.pl.* farrier's pincers.
tricolore [trikɔlɔr] *adj.* tricolour; *drapeau ~*, tricolour, French flag.
tricorne [trikɔrn] *adj.*, *s.m.* three-cornered (hat).
tricot [triko] *s.m.* knitting; knitted jersey, cardigan, or vest; knitwear.
tricotage [trikɔtaʒ] *s.m.* knitting.
tricoter [trikɔte] *v.t.* to knit; *aiguilles à ~*, knitting-needles; (pop.) *~ les côtes à qn.*, to give s.o. a thrashing; *~ v.i.* (obs.) to dance, to jig about; (mod.) *~ (des jambes)*, to skip off; to pedal.
tricoteu-r, -se [trikɔtœr] *s.m.f.* knitter; (hist.) *les ~ses*, in the time of the Fr. Revolution, women who sat and knitted during the trials of the Revolutionary Tribunal; **~se** *s.f.* knitting--machine.
tric-trac [triktrak] *s.m.* backgammon, backgammon-board.
tricuspide [trikyspid] *adj.* tricuspid, three--pointed.
tricycle [trisikl] *s.m.* tricycle.
tridactyle [tridaktil *adj.* (zool.) tridactyl, tridactylous, three-toed.
trident [tridɑ̃] *s.m.* trident; harpoon.
tridenté, -e [tridɑ̃te] *adj.* tridentate, three--pronged, three-toothed.
tridi [tridi] *s.m.* (hist.) Tridi, third day of *décade* in Fr. Republican calendar.
tridimensionnel, -le [tridimɑ̃sjɔnɛl] *adj.* three--dimensional.
triduum [tridyɔm] *s.m.* (eccles.) three days of prayer, triduum.
trièdre [triɛdr] *adj.*, *s.m* trihedral.
triennal, -e, (aux) [triɛnal] *adj.* **1.** triennial; **2.** lasting for three years, elected for three years; *plan ~*, three-year plan.
trier [trije] *v.t.* to sort, to sort out; to pick, to pick out, to choose, to select; (rail.) to marshal, to shunt; *des hommes triés*, picked men; *triés sur le volet*, carefully selected, hand-picked; (fig.) élite.
triérarque [trierark] *s.m.* (Gr. ant.) trierarch.
trière [triɛr] *s.f.* (ant.) trireme.
trieu-r, -se [trijœr] *s.m.f.* sorter, picker, grader; **~r** *s.m.* separator, screening-machine; **~se** *s.f.* wool-picker (machine), grader, machine for selecting punched cards.
trifide [trifid] *adj.* (bot., zool.) trifid, three-cleft.
trifoliolé, -e [trifɔljɔle] *adj.* (bot.) trifoliate.
triforium [trifɔrjɔm] *s.m.* (arch.) triforium.
trifouiller [trifuje] *v.t.i.* (fam.) to rummage, to fumble; to fiddle with, to disarrange.
trigémellaire [triʒemelɛr] *adj.* (med.) carrying triplets; *accouchement ~*, birth of triplets.
trigéminé, -e [triʒemine] *adj.* arranged or occurring in three groups of two.
trigle [trigl] *s.m.* (ichth.) gurnard, gurnet.
triglyphe [triglif] *s.m.* (arch.) triglyph.
trigone [trigɔn] *adj.* trigonal, having three angles; *~ s.m.* (astrol.) trigon; (anat.) trigon.
trigonomé-trie [trigɔnɔmetri] *s.f.* trigonometry; *~trie rectiligne*, plane trigonometry; **~trique** [trigɔnɔmetrik], *adj.* trigonometrical; **~triquement** [trigɔnɔmetrikmɑ̃] *adv.* trigonometrically.
trijumeau (pl. **-x**) [triʒymo] *adj.*, *s.m.* (anat.) trigeminal.
trilatéral, -e (aux) (trilateral] *adj.* trilateral, three-sided.
trilingue [trilɛ̃g] *adj.* trilingual.
trilittère [trilitɛr] *adj.* triliteral.
trille [trij] *s.m.* (mus.) trill, shake.
triller [trije] *v.t.i.* (mus.) to trill, to shake.
trillion [triljɔ̃] *s.m.* trillion (a million million millions); (obs.) billion (a million millions).
trilobé, -e [trilɔbe] *adj.* trilobate.

trilobites [trilɔbit] *s.m.pl.* (palaeont.) trilobites.
triloculaire [trilɔkylɛr] *adj.* (bot.) trilocular, three-celled.
trilogie [trilɔʒi] *s.f.* trilogy.
trimard [trimar] *s.m.* (slang) *être sur le* ~, to be a tramp, to be on the road; **~er** [trimarde] *v.i.* to trudge, to tramp the roads; *~v.t.* to transport, to carry, to hump; **~eur** [trimardœr] *s.m.* (pop.) gipsy, tramp. vagabond.
trimbalage, trimballage [trɛ̃balaʒ], **trimbalement, trimballement** [trɛ̃balmɑ̃] *s.m.* (fam.) lugging around.
trimbal(l)er [trɛ̃bale] *v.t.* (fam.) to lug around; (pop.) *qu'est-ce qu'il trimballe!*, isn't he a fool!; **se** ~ *v.refl.* to trail around, to wander about.
trimer [trime] *v.i.* to slave, to work very hard, to drudge; to wear oneself out; ~ *toute une journée*, to slave away all day.
trimestre [trimɛstr] *s.m.* three months, quarter (of a year), term, trimester; quarter's rent; quarter's pay.
trimestriel, -le [trimɛstrijɛl] *adj.* quarterly, term's; of three months (duration); *bulletin* ~, quarterly report, term's report; **~lement** [trimɛstrijɛlmɑ̃] *adv.* quarterly.
trimètre [trimɛtr] *s.m.* (pros.) trimeter.
trimmer [trimɛr, trimœr] *s.m.* (fish.) trimmer.
trimoteur [trimɔtœr] *s.m.* three-engined plane.
trin [trɛ̃], **trine** [trin] *adj.* (relig.) threefold, triune; (astrol.) trine.
trinervé, -e [trinɛrve] *adj.* (bot.) trinervate.
tringle [trɛ̃gl] *s.f.* rod, curtain-rod; (carp.) measuring-rod; mark; (arch.) tringle.
tringlot, trainglot [trɛ̃glo] *s.m.* (mil. slang) soldier of the Fr. service corps.
trinitaire [trinitɛr] *adj.*, *s.m.f.* Trinitarian; (member) of order of Holy Trinity.
trinité [trinite] *s.f.* trinity; *la (Sainte) Trinité*, the (Holy) Trinity; *la Trinité*, (i.) Trinity Sunday; (ii.) (geog.) Trinidad.
trinôme [trinom] *s.m.* (alg.) trinomial.
trinquart [trɛ̃kar] *s.m.* (naut.) herring-boat.
trinquer [trɛ̃ke] *v.i.* to clink glasses, to have a drink (with s.o. as token of friendship); (pop.) to drink a lot, to booze; to clink, to clash; ~ *à*, to drink to; ~ *de*, to experience, to suffer (loss, etc.); *si nous trinquons de quinze jours de prison*, if we get fourteen days' prison.
trinquet [trɛ̃kɛ] *s.m.* (naut.) foremast in a lateen vessel.
trinquette [trɛ̃kɛt] *s.f.* (naut.) fore stay-sail.
trinqueur [trɛ̃kœr] *s.m.* drinker.
trio [trio] *s.m.* trio.
triode [triɔd] *s.f.* (phys.) triode; valve having three electrodes.
triolet [trijɔlɛ] *s.m.* (pros.) triolet; (mus.) triplet.
triomphal, -e, (aux) [trijɔ̃fal] *adj.* triumphal, triumphant; (fig.) resounding; **~ement** [trijɔ̃falmɑ̃] *adv.* triumphantly, in triumph.
triomphant, -e [trijɔ̃fɑ̃] *adj.* triumphant, victorious; full of self-confidence.
triomphat-eur, -rice [trijɔ̃fatœr] *adj.* triumphant, having triumphed, victorious, conquering; *s.m.f.* conqueror, victor; **~eur** *s.m.* (Rom. ant.) general accorded a triumph.
triomphe [trijɔ̃f] *s.m.* **1.** triumph, victory, success, greatest success; (fig.) height, acme; **2.** (obs.) trump, kind of card-game.
triompher [trijɔ̃fe] *v.t.* ~ *de*, to overcome, to vanquish, to surmount, to master, to triumph over, to gloat over; ~ *v.i.* to triumph, to be victorious or triumphant, to be jubilant; to win, to conquer, to prevail; to excel; (Rom. ant.) to be accorded a triumph.
tripaille [tripɑj] *s.f.* (fam.) garbage, offal; tripe.
tripang [tripɑ̃] *s.m.* (zool.) trepang, sea-cucumber, bêche-de-mer.
tripale [tripal] *adj.* (of propeller) three-bladed.
triparti, -e or **-te** [triparti] *adj.* tripartite; three-power, three-party; divided into three parts.
tripartisme [tripartism] *s.m.* three-party government.
tripartition [tripartisjɔ̃] *s.f.* tripartition.
tripatouiller [tripatuje] *v.t.* (pop.) to falsify (text, accounts, etc.) to fiddle, to cook, to garble.
tripe [trip] *s.f.* (usually pl.) **1.** tripe, guts, belly, innards; (fig.) heart, core; *avoir la* ~ *républicaine*, to be a republican to the core; *cela me saisit aux* ~*s*, it went to my heart; *rendres* ~*s et boyaux*, to bring up one's inside, to be violently sick; **2.** ~ *de velours*, velveteen.
triperie [tripri] *s.f.* tripe-shop; tripe-selling.
tripette [tripɛt] *s.f.* small piece of tripe; *ça ne vaut pas* ~, it is absolutely worthless or useless.
triphasé, -e [trifaze] *adj.* (electr.) three-phase.
triphtongue [triftɔ̃g] *s.f.* triphthong.
tripi-er, -ère [tripje] *s.m.f.* tripe-seller, seller of offal.
triplace [triplas] *adj.* three-seater (plane).
triplan [triplɑ̃] *s.m.* (aeron.) triplane.
triple [tripl] *s.m.* triple, treble, triplicate; *plier en* ~, to fold in three; ~ *adj.* triple, treble, threefold; (fam.) out and out, complete, utter, thorough, arrant, double-dyed, very great; *un* ~ *sot*, a complete idiot; *un* ~ *coquin*, a thorough scoundrel; *au* ~ *galop*, at full gallop; (mus.) ~ *croche*, demi-semiquaver; **~ment** [tripləmɑ̃] *adv.* triply, trebly, in three ways; three times.
triplement [tripləmɑ̃] *s.m.* tripling, trebling, triplicating.
tripler [triple] *v.t.i.* to triple, to treble, to triplicate; to increase threefold.
tripl-és, -ées [triple] *s.m.f.pl.* triplets.
triplet [triplɛ] *s.m.* **1.** (pl.) = TRIPLÉS, TRIPLÉES; **2.** (opt.) triplet lens; ⚠ not (mus.) 'triplet'.
triplicata [triplikata] *s.m.invar.* triplicate, third copy.
triplure [triplyr] *s.f.* (dressm.) interlining.
tripode [tripɔd] *adj.* tripod (mast.)
tripoli [tripoli] *s.m.* tripoli, rotten-stone.
triporteur [tripɔrtœr] *s.m.* delivery tricycle (for goods).
tripot [tripo] *s.m.* gaming-house, gambling-den.
tripotage [tripɔtaʒ] *s.m.* (pej.) intrigue, underhand dealings, shady business, jobbery, fiddle, fiddling, rigging, cooking (of accounts, etc.), manipulation.
tripotée [tripɔte] *s.f.* (fam.) **1.** thrashing, beating, drubbing; **2.** large number; ~ *d'enfants*, swarm of children.
tripoter [tripɔte] *v.t.* to paw, to handle, to finger, to play with; (fig.) to meddle with, to tamper with; to speculate with; ~ *l'argent des autres*, to speculate with other people's money; ~ *v.i.*, to mess about; to have dealings, to engage in shady deals, to speculate or gamble (*sur*, in).
tripoteu-r, -se [tripɔtœr] *s.m.f.* intriguer, schemer, (shady) speculator, one operating a swindle; *adj. des mains* ~*ses*, hands that paw.
triptyque [triptik] *s.m.* (paint.) triptych.
trique [trik] *s.f.* cudgel, stick, bludgeon; (fig.) *à coups de* ~, *à la* ~, with the big stick, by brute force; *maigre comme un coup de* ~, as thin as a rake.
triqueballe [trikbal] *s.m.* lumber-waggon.
trique-madame [trikmadam] *s.f. invar.* (bot.) white stonecrop.
triquer [trike] *v.t.* (pop.) to beat, to cudgel.
triquet [trikɛ] *s.m* trestle; pair of steps.
trirectangle [trirɛkɑ̃gl] *adj.* (geom.) trirectangular, having three right angles.
trirème [trirɛm] *s.f.* (ant.) trireme.

trisaïeul, -e [trizajœl] *s.m.f.* great-great--grandfather, -grandmother.
trisannuel, -le [trizanɥɛl] *adj.* triennial.
trisect-eur, -rice [trisɛktœr] *adj.* trisecting.
trisection [trisɛksjɔ̃] *s.f.* (geom.) trisection.
trismus [trismys], **trisme** [trism] *s.m.* (pathol.) trismus, lockjaw.
trisoc [trisɔk] *s.m.* plough with three shares.
trisser[1] [trise] *v.i.* (of swallows) to twitter.
trisser[2] [trise] *v.t.* to encore a second time; to give a second encore.
trisser[3] [trise] *v.i.* (pop.) to go away, to set off; **se** ~ *v.refl.* (pop.) to skip off, to do a bunk.
triste [trist] *adj.* sad, sorrowful, deplorable, unhappy, calamitous, tragic, heart-breaking; gloomy, depressing, mournful, dejected, melancholy, dismal; dull, dreary, bleak, miserable; sorry, wretched, (pej.) pathetic; *mon ~ devoir*, my painful duty; *c'est une ~ affaire*, it is a bad, or sorry, business; *faire ~ figure*, to pull a long face; to cut a sorry figure; *faire ~ mine à*, to look glumly at, to receive without enthusiasm; **~ment** [tristəmɑ̃] *adv.* sadly, gloomily, mournfully, wretchedly, miserably, tragically.
tristesse [tristɛs] *s.f.* sadness, melancholy, sorrow, unhappiness; dreariness, gloom, cheerlessness; sad event; sad side.
trisyllabe, trissyllabe [trisilab] *s.m.* trisyllable; ~ *adj.* trisyllabic.
trisyllabique, trissyllabique [trisilabik] *adj.* trisyllablic.
tritium [tritjɔm] *s.m.* (chem.) tritium.
triton[1] [tritɔ̃] *s.m.* (Gr. myth.) Triton; (zool.) triton, trumpet-shell.
triton[2] [tritɔ̃] *s.m.* (mus.) tritone, interval of three whole tones.
tritur-able [trityrabl] *adj.* triturable; **~ateur** [trityratœr] *s.m.* triturator; **~ation** [trityrɑsjɔ̃] *s.f.* trituration, mastication; **~er** [trityre] *v.t.* to triturate, to grind to a fine powder, to masticate; to handle roughly, to browbeat; *se ~er les méninges* or *la cervelle*, to rack one's brains.
triumvir [triɔmvir] *s.m.* (Rom. hist.) triumvir.
triumviral, -e, (aux) [triɔmviral] *adj.* (Rom. hist.) triumviral.
triumvirat [triɔmvira] *s.m.* (Rom. hist.) triumvirate.
trivial, -e, (aux) [trivjal] *adj.* trivial, trifling; vulgar; trite, hackneyed; ~ *s.m.* the trivial, triviality; vulgarity, coarseness; **~ement** [trivjalmɑ̃] *adv.* (obs.) in a trivial way; (mod.) vulgarly, coarsely.
trivialité [trivjalite] *s.f.* triviality; coarseness, vulgarity; truism, commonplace; coarse expression.
troc [trɔk] *s.m.* truck, exchange, barter, swap; *faire ~ de*, to swap; *~ pour ~*, a fair exchange.
trocart [trɔkar] *s.m.* (surg.) trocar.
trochaïque [trɔkaik] *adj.* (pros.) trochaic.
trochanter [trɔkɑ̃tɛr] *s.m.* (anat., ent.) trochanter.
trochée [trɔʃe] *s.m.* (pros.) trochee.
trochée [trɔʃe] *s.f.* bunch of leaves sprouting from a tree-stump.
trochet [trɔʃɛ] *s.m.* cluster (of fruit or flowers).
trochile [trɔkil] *s.m.* (ornith.) trochilus (humming-bird).
trochisque [trɔʃisk] *s.m.* (pharm.) troche, lozenge.
trochlée [trɔkle] *s.f.* (anat.) trochlea.
trochure [trɔʃyr] *s.f.* fourth antler of deer.
troène [trɔɛn] *s.m.* (bot.) privet.
troglodyte [trɔglɔdit] *s.m.* troglodyte, cave--dweller; (ornith.) wren.
troglodytique [trɔglɔditik] *adj.* troglodytic.
trogne [trɔɲ] *s.f.* (fam.) face, bloated or beery face, rubicund countenance.
trognon [trɔɲɔ̃] *s.m.* core (of fruit); stump or stalk (of vegetable); (fig., pop.) *jusqu'au ~*, utterly, completely, to the core; (pop.) *petit ~*, term of endearment.
Troie [trwa] *s.f.* (anc., geog.) Troy.
trois [trwɑ] *adj., s.m.* three; third (of the month); *je demeure au ~*, I live at number three.
trois-deux [trwadø] *s.m.* (mus.) three-two time.
trois étoiles [trwɑzetwal] *s.loc.* X; *Monsieur ~* (usu. written *M.* ***), Mr. X.
trois-huit [trwaɥit] *s.m.* (mus.) three-eight time.
troisième [trwɑzjɛm] *adj.* third; ~ *s.m.f.* third; (rail., school) third class; third floor; **~ment** [trwɑzjɛmmɑ̃] *adv.* thirdly.
trois-mâts [trwɑmɑ] *s.m.* (naut.) three--master (ship.); **~-points** [trwɑpwɛ̃] *adj.loc. invar. les frères ~-points*, the Freemasons; **~-quarts** [trwɑkar] *s.m.invar.* three-quarter violin; three-quarter length coat; (Rugby football) three-quarter; **~-quatre** [trwɑkatr] *s.m.* (mus.) three-four time; **~-six** [trwɑsis] *s.m.invar.* (obs. or dial.) proof spirit.
troll [trɔl] *s.m.* troll, gnome.
trolle [trɔl] *s.f.* (hunt.) unleashing hounds to allow them to quest for game.
trolley [trɔlɛ] *s.m.* trolley (of tram or trolley-bus); (fam.) trolleybus.
trolleybus [trɔlɛbys] *s.m.* trolleybus.
trombe [trɔ̃b] *s.f.* waterspout; downpour, deluge; *~ de vent*, whirlwind; (fig.) *entrer en ~*, to rush in like a whirlwind.
trombidion [trɔ̃bidjɔ̃] *s.m.* (ent.) harvest-bug.
trombine [trɔ̃bin] *s.f.* (pop.) head, face.
tromblon [trɔ̃blɔ̃] *s.m.* **1.** blunderbuss; grenade--discharger cup; **2.** (pop.) hat.
trombone [trɔ̃bɔn] *s.m.* **1.** (mus.) trombone; trombone-player; **2.** paper-clip.
trompe [trɔ̃p] *s.f.* **1.** trumpet, horn, hunting--horn; *à son de ~*, to the sound of the trumpet, (fig.) with the full blare of publicity; *proclamer à son de ~*, to publish abroad; *~ de Béarn* or *à laquais*, Jew's harp; **2.** (techn.) aspirator, pump, trompe; **3.** proboscis, (elephant's) trunk; (pop.) big nose, proboscis; (anat.) tube; *~ de Fallope*, Fallopian tube; **4.** (arch.) pendentive.
trompe-la-mort [trɔ̃plamɔr] *s.m.f.invar.* one who has escaped certain death or survived a critical illness, one who seems indestructible.
trompe-l'œil [trɔ̃plœj] *s.m.invar.* trompe-l'œil (painting); (fig.) deceptive appearance, eye-wash, window-dressing, bluff; *en ~*, in trompe--l'œil, dummy.
tromper [trɔ̃pe] *v.t.* to deceive, to mislead, to delude, to cheat, to take in, to impose on, to abuse; to disappoint, to falsify (hopes, etc.), to betray; to elude; to baffle; to divert, to beguile; to be unfaithful to (husband, wife); to divert, to stave off; *mari trompé*, husband whose wife is unfaithful; *~ le temps*, to while away the time; **se** ~ *v.refl.* to mistake, to be mistaken, to make a mistake; to err; to deceive each other, to deceive oneself; *je puis me ~*, I may be wrong, or mistaken; *on peut se ~ sans pécher*, a mistake is not a crime; *ils se ressemblent à s'y ~*, you cannot tell them apart; *il n'y a pas à s'y ~*, there is no mistake about it, there is no mistaking it; *se ~ de*, to mistake (sth.), to make a mistake about, to make an error of (a certain amount); *je me suis trompé de chambre*, I mistook the room; *se ~ de chemin*, to take the wrong road; *se ~ d'adresse*, to go to the wrong address, to apply to the wrong person or place; *se ~ de 100 francs*, to make an error of 100 francs.
tromperie [trɔ̃pri] *s.f.* deceit, cheat, fraud, imposture; delusion, illusion, mirage.
trompeter [trɔ̃pəte] *v.i.* to sound the trumpet; (of eagle) to scream; ~ *v.t.* to summon, to

proclaim by trumpet; to proclaim, to publish, to spread abroad; to divulge.

trompette [trɔ̃pɛt] *s.f.* trumpet, bugle; (zool.) trumpet-shell; *déloger sans tambour ni* ~, to slip away quietly; to do a moonlight flit; *un nez en* ~, a turned-up nose; ~ *s.m.* trumpeter, trumpet--player.

trompettiste [trɔ̃petist] *s.m.f.* trumpet-player.

trompeu-r, -se [trɔ̃pœr] *adj.* deceptive; deceitful; delusive, false, misleading; **~r** *s.m.* deceiver, cheat; impostor; betrayer; *le ~r trompé*, the biter bit; *à ~r ~r et demi*, diamond cut diamond; set a thief to catch a thief; **~sement** [trɔ̃pøzmɑ̃] *adv.* deceptively, deceitfully.

trompillon [trɔ̃pijɔ̃] *s.m.* (arch.) small pendentive.

tronc [trɔ̃] *s.m.* trunk; stock, parent stock; poor-box, alms-box; collecting-box; (arch.) drum; broken shaft (of column); (geom.) frustrum (of cone or pyramid); ~ *commun*, common origin, (school) common curriculum; ~ *de cône*, truncated cone.

troncature [trɔ̃katyr] *s.f.* truncation.

tronche [trɔ̃ʃ] *s.f.* stump (of a tree); (pop.) head.

tronchet [trɔ̃ʃɛ] *s.m.* block, cooper's block.

tronçon [trɔ̃sɔ̃] *s.m.* fragment, stump, broken piece, length; (rail.) section, portion, (signalling) block; base (of horse's tail).

tronçonnage [trɔ̃sɔnaʒ], **tronçonnement** [trɔ̃sɔnmɑ̃] *s.m.* cutting up.

tronçonner [trɔ̃sɔne] *v.t.* to cut up, to cut into pieces or lengths.

tronçonneuse [trɔ̃sɔnøz] *s.f.* (techn.) chain saw.

trône [tron] *s.m.* throne; (fig.) sovereign power; the sovereign; (pl.) (theol.) Thrones.

trôner [trone] *v.i.* to sit on a throne or as on a throne; to reign, to hold sway, to be supreme; (fig.) to lord it (over), to domineer; to sit in state, to preside; to be prominent or conspicuous.

tronqué, -e [trɔ̃ke] *adj.* truncated, cut off, cut short; mutilated, maimed; (of phrases, etc.) garbled; (bot.) truncate.

tronquer [trɔ̃ke] *v.t.* to truncate, to cut off, to lop off; to mutilate, to maim; to garble, to mangle.

trop [tro] *adv.* too; too much (*de*, of, of a); too many; too far; too high; too long; too often; to excess; too well; over; very; much, very much, very well; ~ *peu*, too little; too few; not enough; ~ *peu nombreuse*, too small; *de* ~, too much, too many; superfluous; unwanted; *être de* ~, to be in the way, to intrude; *par* ~, rather too, rather too much, far too, all too; *c'est par ~ exiger*, that is being over-exacting; *pas* ~, not too much, not too many; not over, not very; (fam.) *rien de* ~, nothing very much; *c'en est* ~, that's enough, that's more than one can bear; *c'est ~ que* (*de*), it's overdoing it to; *il n'a pas ~ d'une heure de*, it takes him a good hour to; *je ne m'y fierais pas* ~, I would not trust to it; *il ne va pas ~ bien*, he is not very well; ~ *est* ~, enough is as good as a feast; *je ne sais* ~, I hardly know; ~ *s.m.* excess, superfluity.

trope [trɔp] *s.m.* (rhet.) trope.

trophée [trɔfe] *s.m.* trophy; decorative motif formed of weapons, instruments, etc.; (fig.) *faire ~ de*, to glory in.

trophique [trɔfik] *adj.* trophic; nourishing, nutritious; nutritional; *troubles* ~*s*, dystrophy, digestive ailments.

tropical, -e, (**aux**) [trɔpikal] *adj.* tropical.

tropique [trɔpik] *s.m.* (geog., astron.) tropic; (pl.) the tropics; ~ *adj.* (astron.) tropical.

tropisme [trɔpism] *s.m.* tropism.

troposphère [trɔpɔsfɛr] *s.f.* troposphere.

trop-perçu [trɔpɛrsy] *s.m.* (pl. *trop-perçus*) over--assessment (of taxes).

trop-plein [trɔplɛ̃] *s.m.* (pl. *trop-pleins*) overflow, overspill, waste; surplus, overplus, excess; *tuyau de* ~, waste-pipe, overflow (pipe).

troquer [trɔke] *v.t.* to truck, to barter, to exchange, to swap; ~ *son cheval borgne contre un aveugle*, to change for the worse.

troquet [trɔkɛ] *s.m.* (pop.) small café.

trot [tro] *s.m.* trot, trotting; *au grand* ~, at full trot; *au petit* ~, at a jogtrot; (fig., fam.) *au* ~, briskly, at the double; *et au* ~*!*, and get a move on!

trotskyste [trɔtskist] *adj.*, *s.m.f.* Trotskyite.

trotte [trɔt] *s.f.* (fam.) distance, stretch, run, walk; *faire de grandes* ~*s*, to take long trips; *jusqu'à chez vous, ça fait une* ~, it is a fair distance to your place.

trotte-menu [trɔtməny] *adj.invar.* (jest) *la gent* ~, the tribe of tiny trotters (i.e. mice).

trotter [trɔte] *v.i.* to trot; to run about, to be on the go; *on entendrait une souris* ~, one could hear a pin drop; *il a trotté toute la journée*, he has been running about all day; *cet air me trotte par* (*dans*) *la tête*, that tune keeps running in my head; **se** ~ *v.refl.* (pop.) to make off, to be on one's way.

trotteu-r, -se [trɔtœr] *s.m.f.* trotter; **~se** *s.f.* second-hand (of a watch, etc.).

trottin [trɔtɛ̃] *s.m.* errand-girl.

trottinement [trɔtinmɑ̃] *s.m.* pitter-patter.

trottiner [trɔtine] *v.i.* to jog along, to trot along, to patter along.

trottinette [trɔtinɛt] *s.f.* scooter (toy).

trottoir [trɔtwar] *s.m.* pavement, footway, footpath; *bordure du* ~, kerb; ~ *roulant*, moving footway; *faire le* ~, to walk the streets (as a prostitute).

trou [tru] *s.m.* hole; gap; cave; opening, orifice, mouth (of bottle); eye (of needle); pot--hole; hiding-place; pit (in the skin); empty place, vacuum; *le ~ de la serrure, de la porte*, keyhole; ~ *d'homme*, manhole; (naut.) ~ *du chat*, lubber's hole; ~ *d'air*, air-pocket; ~ *d'aération*, air-vent; ~ *de mémoire*, a blank in one's mind; ~ *du souffleur*, prompter's box; (pop.) *être au* ~, to be in prison; *boucher un* ~, to stop up a hole; (fig.) to pay a debt; *faire son* ~, to get on in the world; *faire un ~ pour en boucher un autre*, to rob Peter to pay Paul; *un petit* ~, a nice quiet little place in the country; *mettre la pièce à côté du* ~, to use the wrong means, to set about it the wrong way; *faire un ~ à la lune*, to shoot the moon, to fly from one's creditors; *boire comme un* ~, to drink like a fish; *il est logé dans un* ~, he lives in a hovel; *à chaque ~ une cheville*, there is an answer to, or a cure for, everything.

troubadour [trubadur] *s.m.* troubadour.

troublant, -e [trublɑ̃] *adj.* disquieting, disturbing; disconcerting, provocative.

trouble [trubl] *s.m.* disorder, disturbance, confusion; misunderstanding, dissension, disagreement, dispute, quarrel; perplexity, uneasiness; (pl.) commotions, troubles; *cause de* ~, disturbing factor; (law) ~ *de la possession* or *de jouissance*, disturbance of possession, prevention of enjoyment of possession; *susciter des* ~*s*, to provoke disturbances or disorder; ~ *s.f.* see TRUBLE.

trouble [trubl] *adj.* troubled; turbid; muddy, thick; dim; dull; murky; obscure; confused; blurred; uneasy; of a dubious character or quality, ambiguous; overcast, hazy, foggy; *avoir la vue* ~, to be dim-sighted, near-sighted; (fig.) to have a blurred vision, to have an imperfect understanding; *pêcher en eau* ~, to fish in troubled waters; to be engaged in shady business.

troublé, -e [truble] *adj.* **1.** troubled, muddy, murky; **2.** troubled, confused, perplexed.

trouble-fête [trubləfɛt] *s.m.invar.* kill-joy, spoil--sport, damper, wet blanket; skeleton at the feast.

troubler [truble] *v.t.* to stir (up), to disturb; to make thick, to make muddy; to muddle; to turn; to disturb, to disarrange; to confuse, to upset, to disorder, to agitate, to make uneasy; to perplex, to disconcert, to worry, to unsettle; to unhinge; to trouble; to excite, to provoke; to interrupt, to break in upon; to destroy the harmony of, to bring discord into; to ruffle, to annoy; to discompose; to dim, to dull; ~ *le royaume*, to bring discord into the kingdom; ~ *la fête*, to interrupt the festivities; ~ *la retraite d'une armée*, to harass a retreating army; ~ *quelqu'un dans la possession d'un bien*, to contest a person's right to a thing; **se** ~ *v.refl.* to be confused, to be disconcerted; to become agitated, to get flustered; to be foggy, to become overcast, cloudy; to grow dim; to grow muddy, thick; *sans se* ~, unconcerned, unruffled, without turning a hair; *sa mémoire se trouble*, his memory fails him; *ma vue se trouble*, my sight is growing dim; *le temps commence à se* ~, it is getting cloudy, or overcast.

troué, -e [true] *adj.* tattered, in holes, perforated, pitted.

trouée [true] *s.f.* opening, gap, breach; pass; *faire sa* ~, to cut one's way; (fig.) to make one's mark.

trouer [true] *v.t.* to make a hole or opening in, to bore, to pierce; to perforate.

troufignon [trufiɲɔ̃] *s.m.* (vulg.) back, backside, arse (vulg.).

trouille [truj] *s.f.* (pop.) funk, fear, panic; *avoir la* ~, to be in a funk, to have an attack of cold feet; *ficher* or *flanquer la* ~ *à qn.*, to put the wind up s.o.

trou-madame [trumadam] *s.m.* (pl. *trous-madame*) nine-holes (game).

troupe [trup] *s.f.* troop, band, company; set, gang, crew; (theatr.) company, troupe; crowd, number; force, soldiers, military, body of troops; other ranks; squad; herd, drove (of animals); flock, flight (of birds); shoal (of fish); ~*s de mer*, sea-forces; ~*s de terre*, land-forces; *le gros de la* ~, the main body; *aller en* ~, to herd together.

troupeau (pl. **-x**) [trupo] *s.m.* herd, flock, drove; (fig.) set, pack, crowd.

troupiale [trupjal] *s.m.* (ornith.) troupial, troopial.

troupier [trupje] *s.m.* (obs.) soldier, trooper.

troussage [trusaʒ] *s.m.* (cook.) trussing.

trousse [trus] *s.f.* truss, bundle; case (for razors, toilet articles, needles, surgical instruments, pencils, etc.); *je suis à ses* ~*s*, I am at his heels; *avoir la police à ses* ~*s*, to have the police on one's track, after one; ⚠ not constr. or surg. 'truss'.

trousseau (pl. **-x**) [truso] *s.m.* bunch (of keys); outfit, uniform, kit; trousseau, wedding outfit; (anat.) fasciculus.

trousse-galant [trusgalɑ̃] *s.m.* (obs.) cholera.

trousse-queue [truskø] *s.m.invar.* (harness) tail-leather.

troussequin [truskɛ̃] *s.m.* **1.** cantle (of saddle); **2.** = TRUSQUIN.

trousser [truse] *v.t.* to tuck up, to pin up, to turn up; to tie up, to pack up; (cook.) to truss; (fig.) to dispatch, to expedite, to polish off, to dash off (sth.); **se** ~ *v.refl.* to tuck up one's skirt, etc.

trouvable [truvabl] *adj.* findable, that can be found, to be found, to be met.

trouvaille [truvɑj] *s.f.* lucky find, windfall, godsend; find, discovery; invention, new idea, happy thought.

trouvé, -e [truve] *adj.* found; *enfant* ~, foundling; *objets* ~*s*, lost property; *bien* ~*(e)*, happy, felicitous.

trouver [truve] *v.t.* to find, to discover, to meet with, to hit upon; to think up; to find out, to detect, to get; to think, to consider, to deem, to judge, to contrive, to manage; *j'ai trouvé à propos de*, I thought fit to, I took the occasion to; ~ *à qui parler*, ~ *son maître*, to meet one's match; ~ *la mort*, to meet one's death; ~ *grâce aux yeux de qn.*, to find favour in somebody's eyes; *aller* ~, to go and see, to go and fetch, to meet; *venir* ~, to come and see, to come and fetch, to come to meet; *comment trouvez-vous ça?*, how do you like it?; *je lui trouve bon visage*, I think he looks well; *où avez-vous trouvé cela?*, what made you think of that?, what put that into your head?; ~ *à dire*, ~ *à redire*, to find fault (*à* with); *il trouve toujours à placer son mot*, he always manages to have his say; *nous trouverons bien à vous aider*, we shall certainly find a way to help you; ~ *beau*, to admire; ~ *bon*, to think (it) right, to approve, to think fit; ~ *mauvais*, to think it wrong, to disapprove, to censure; (fam.) *la* ~ *mauvaise*, to take a poor view of it; *vous trouvez?*, do you think so?; **se** ~ *v.refl.* to meet, to meet with; to be present; to be situated or located; to be; to happen to be, to chance to be; to be found, to be found to be, to prove, to turn out; to feel, to feel oneself, to consider oneself, to find oneself; *il s'est trouvé là quand je suis arrivé*, he chanced to be there when I arrived; *la nouvelle s'est trouvée fausse*, the news turned out to be false; *se* ~ *bien*, to feel well; *se* ~ *mal*, to feel ill, to faint; *se* ~ *pris*, to be caught; *je me trouve dans l'impossibilité de*, I find I am quite unable to; *comment vous trouvez-vous aujourd'hui?*, how are you to-day?; *cela se trouve bien*, that is lucky; *je me trouve bien de la campagne*, I am all the better for being in the country; *il ne se trouva personne d'assez courageux*, there was nobody brave enough; *il se trouve que*, it so happens that, it turns out that; *il se trouve qu'il y a*, there happens to be; *se* ~ *malheureux*, to consider oneself unfortunate.

trouvère [truvɛr] *s.m.* trouvère, minstrel.

trouveu-r, -se [truvœr] *s.m.f.* discoverer, finder; inventor.

troyen, -ne [trwajɛ̃] *adj., s.m.f.* Trojan.

truand, -e [tryɑ̃] *s.m.f.* (obs.) vagrant, beggar; ~ *s.m.* (mod.) criminal type (esp. pimp, ponce, thief).

truander [tryɑ̃de] *v.i.* (obs.) to beg; ~ *v.t.* (mod.) to rob, to cheat.

truanderie [tryɑ̃dri] *s.f.* vagrancy; vagabonds.

truble [trybl], **trouble** [trubl] *s.f.* (fish.) hoop--net.

trublion [tryblijɔ̃] *s.m.* trouble-maker, agitator; tiresome and stupid person.

truc[1] [tryk] *s.m.* knack, dodge, deception; trick; secret; craft, ingenuity, cunning; (theatr.) stage effect, machinery, trap; (fam.) thing, gadget, contraption; what-d'you-call-it; *connaître le* ~, to be in the know, to be knowing, to know all the tricks, to know the tricks of the trade.

truc[2] **truck** [tryk] *s.m.* truck, trolley.

trucage [trykaʒ] *s.m.* = TRUQUAGE.

truchement [tryʃmɑ̃] *s.m.* interpreter; spokesman, representative; go-between.

trucider [tryside] *v.t.* (fam.) to kill.

truculence [trykylɑ̃s] *s.f.* truculence, truculency.

truculent, -e [trykylɑ̃] *adj.* truculent; (fig.) highly-coloured, flamboyant, picturesque.

truelle [tryɛl] *s.f.* (build.) trowel; (artist's) palette-knife; ~ *à poisson*, fish-slice; ⚠ not gardener's 'trowel'.

truellée [tryele] *s.f.* trowelful.
truffe [truf] *s.f.* **1.** truffle; **2.** dog's nose; **3.** (fam.) idiot.
truffer [tryfe] *v.t.* to stuff (full), to fill; to pad out (a speech).
trufficulture [tryfikyltyr] *s.f.* culture, growing, of truffles.
truffi-er, -ère [tryfje] *adj.* *terrain ~er*, truffle-bearing ground; *chien ~er*, truffle-hound; *chêne ~er*, oak-tree near which truffles are found; **~ère** *s.f.* truffle-bed.
truie [trɥi] *s.f.* (zool.) sow; (ichth.) ~ (*de mer*), hog-fish.
truisme [tryism] *s.m.* truism.
truite [trɥit] *s.f.* (ichth.) trout; ~ *saumonée*, salmon trout.
truité, -e [trɥite] *adj.* red-spotted, red-speckled; spotted, speckled, mottled; *porcelaine, poterie, ~e*, crackle-ware; *fonte ~e*, white and grey pig-iron.
trumeau (pl. **-x**) [trymo] *s.m.* **1.** (arch.) wall between two windows, pier, panel; pier-glass; **2.** leg or shin of beef.
truquage [trykaʒ] *s.m.* faking, trickery, rigging; fake; *~électoral*, gerrymandering.
truqué, -e [truke] *adj.* fake(d), rigged, fixed; (of dice) loaded.
truquer [tryke] *v.i.* to use deception; ~ *v.t.* to fake, to fix, to rig, to cook (accounts), to load (dice).
truqueu-r, -se [trykœr] *s.m.f.* cheat, fake, swindler.
trusquin [tryskɛ̃] *s.m.* (techn.) mortise-gauge, beam-compass.
trusquiner [tryskine] *v.t.* (techn.) to trace with a mortise-gauge or beam-compass.
trust [trœst] *s.m.* (comm.) trust.
truster [trœste] *v.t.* to form into a trust; to take over; to monopolize, to have the monopoly of.
trusteur [trœstœr] *s.m.* one who forms a trust; (fig., fam.) one who takes over or monopolizes (sth.).
trypanosome [tripanozɔm] *s.m.* trypanosome.
trypanosomiase [tripanozɔmjaz] *s.f.* (med.) trypanosomiasis, sleeping-sickness.
trypsine [tripsin] *s.f.* (biol.) trypsin.
tsar [tsar] *s.m.* tsar, czar; **~évitch** [tsarevitʃ] *s.m.* tsarevich, czarevich; **~ine** [tsarin] *s.f.* tsarine, czarina; **~isme** [tsarism] tsarism; **~iste** [tsarist] *adj.* tsarist.
tsé-tsé [tsetse] *s.f.* (ent.) tsetse(-fly).
T.S.F. [teɛsɛf] abbrev. *télégraphie sans fil*; ~ *s.f.* wireless set.
tsigane [tsigan], **tzigane** [dzigan] *adj., s.m.f.* tzigane.
T.S.V.P. [teɛsvepe] abbrev. *tournez s'il vous plaît*, P.T.O.
tu [ty] *pers. pron. m.f.* thou; you.
tuable [tyabl] *adj.* that may be killed; fit for slaughter; (fig.) expendable.
tuant, -e [tyɑ̃] *adj.* killing, fatiguing, harassing, toilsome, laborious; wearisome, tiresome, tedious.
tub [tœb] *s.m.* tub, bath.
tuba [tyba] *s.m.* (mus.) tuba.
tubage [tybaʒ] *s.m.* tubing; tubes; placing of tubes.
tubard, -e [tybar] *adj., s.m.f.* (pop.) = TUBERCULEUX.
tube [tyb] *s.m.* tube; pipe, canal, conduit; (anat.) duct; (paint.) tube; (obs.) top-hat, chimney-pot hat; ~ *acoustique*, speaking-tube; ~ *à essai*, test-tube; ~ *digestif*, alimentary canal; (pop.) *coup de ~*, phone-call; ⚠ not 'tube' = underground railway.
tuber [tybe] *v.t.* to tube, to fit with tubes; to case (shaft, etc.).
tubéracé, -e [tyberase] *adj.* (bot.) tuberaceous; **~es** *s.f.pl.* Tuberaceae.
tubercule [tybɛrkyl] *s.m.* (bot.) tuber, tubercle; (med.) tubercle.
tuberculeu-x, -se [tybɛrkylø] *adj.* (bot.) tuberculate, tuberculous; (med.) tubercular; *s.m.f.* tubercular, tuberculosis patient.
tubercul-ination [tybɛrkylinɑsjɔ̃]; **~inisation** [tybɛrkylinizɑsjɔ̃] *s.f.* tuberculization; **~ine** [tybɛrkylin] *s.f.* tuberculin; **~iner** [tyberkyline]; **~iniser** [tybɛrkylinize] *v.t.* to tuberculize; **~isation** [tybɛrkylizɑsjɔ̃] *s.f.* (med.) tuberculization; **se ~iser** [tybɛrkylize] *v.refl.* (med.) to tuberculize; **~ose** [tybɛrkyloz] *s.f.* (pulmonary) tuberculosis.
tubéreuse [tyberøz] *s.f.* (bot.) tuberose.
tubéreu-x, -se [tyberø] *adj.* (bot.) tuberous, tuberose.
tubériforme [tyberifɔrm] *adj.* (bot.) (of mushroom) tuberiform; tuberoid.
tubérosité [tyberozite] *s.f.* tuberosity.
tubicole [tybikɔl] *adj.* (zool.) tubicolous.
tubitèles [tybitɛl] *s.m.pl.* (zool.) Tubitelae (spiders).
tubulaire [tybylɛr] *adj.* tubular; fitted with or made from tubes.
tubulé, -e [tybyle] *adj.* tubulated.
tubuleu-x, -se [tybylø] *adj.* tubulous, tubular.
tubulure [tybylyr] *s.f.* (techn.) tubulature, neck, nozzle; ~ *d'admission des gaz*, inlet manifold.
tudesque [tydɛsk] *adj.* Old German; (pej.) Teutonic, Hunnish.
tudieu [tydjø] *interj.* archaic oath.
tue-chien [tyʃjɛ̃] *s.m.invar.* (bot.) autumn crocus, colchicum; **~-loup** [tylu] *s.m.invar.* (bot.) aconite; **~-mouche** [tymuʃ] *s.m.invar.* (bot.) fly agaric; *adj. papier ~-mouche(s)*, fly-paper.
tuer [tɥe] *v.t.* to kill; to slay, to slaughter, to butcher; to murder, to destroy; to make or do away with, to be the death or end of; (fig.) to sign the death-warrant of, to finish off; to cause the death of; to bore, to tire to death; to ruin; to while away; ~ *dans l'œuf*, to nip in the bud; (in war) *les tués*, the dead, the fallen; *tué à l'ennemi* or *au combat*, killed in action; *un coup à bien ~ un bœuf*, a blow that would have felled an ox; *se faire ~*, to get killed, to risk one's life; *le chagrin la tue*, she is dying of grief; *le grand bruit me tue*, I cannot bear a loud noise; *il me tue avec ses compliments*, he bores me to death with his compliments; *les acteurs ont tué la pièce*, the actors murdered the play; (pop.) ~ *le ver*, to take a nip of spirits first thing in the morning; **se ~** *v.refl.* to kill oneself, to commit suicide; to be killed; to destroy one's health, to wear oneself out; to rack one's brains, to tie oneself in knots; to kill each other; *il s'est tué à la chasse*, he was killed while hunting; *vous vous tuez à mener une pareille vie*, you are wearing yourself out leading such a life.
tuerie [tyri] *s.f.* slaughter, massacre, butchery, carnage; slaughter-house.
(**à**) **tue-tête** [atytɛt] *adv.loc.* at the top of one's voice.
tueu-r, -se [tɥœr] *s.m.f.* killer, slayer; butcher, slaughterer; *~r à gages*, hired assassin.
tuf [tyf] *s.m.* (geol.) tufa, tuff; (fig.) bedrock, bottom, heart; *trouver le ~*, to get to the bottom, to get down to fundamentals.
tuffeau, tufeau (pl. **-x**) [tyfo] *s.m.* (geol.) tufa-stone; micaceous chalk (from Touraine).
tufi-er, -ère [tyfje] *adj.* (geol.) tufaceous; chalky.
tuile [tɥil] *s.f.* **1.** tile; ~ *creuse*, gutter-tile; ~ *faîtière*, ridge-tile; ~ *flamande*, pantile; *couvreur en ~*, tiler; *loger sous les ~s*, to live in an attic; **2.** (techn.) sleeking-board; **3.** (fig., fam.) sudden misfortune, piece of bad luck.

tuileau (pl. **-x**) [tɥilo] *s.m.* broken tile.
tuilerie [tɥilri] *s.f.* tile-making, tile-factory, tile-kiln; *les Tuileries,* the Tuileries (gardens and former palace in Paris).
tuilette [tɥilɛt] *s.f.* small tile.
tuilier [tɥilje] *s.m.* tile-maker.
tulipe [tylip] *s.f.* **1.** (bot.) tulip; **2.** (tulip--shaped) glass, globe, etc.
tulipier [tylipje] *s.m.* (bot.) tulip-tree.
tulle [tyl] *s.m.* (text.) tulle, net.
tullerie [tylri] *s.f.* tulle-manufacture, tulle factory.
tulli-er, -ère [tylje] *adj.* tulle.
tulliste [tylist] *s.m.f.* net- or tulle-maker.
tuméfaction [tymefaksjɔ̃] *s.f.* (med.) tumefaction.
tuméfié, -e [tymefje] *adj.* swollen, puffy, puffed-up; (fig.) inflated.
tuméfier [tymefje] *v.t.* (med.) to tumefy, to cause to swell; **se ~** *v.refl.* to swell up.
tumescence [tymesɑ̃s] *s.f.* (med.) tumescence.
tumescent, -e [tymesɑ̃] *adj.* (med.) tumescent, swelling.
tumeur [tymœr] *s.f.* (med.) tumour, growth.
tumulaire [tymylɛr] *adj.* tumulary; *pierre ~,* tombstone; *inscription ~,* inscription on tombstone.
tumulte [tymylt] *s.m.* tumult, uproar, clamour, riot, hubbub, agitation, commotion, turmoil; clash; bustle, hurry; *apaiser le ~,* to calm the tumult; *le ~ du monde,* the hurry and bustle of life; *en ~,* in a tumult, in confusion; in an uproar.
tumultuaire [tymyltɥɛr] *adj.* tumultuary; disorderly, riotous.
tumultueu-x, -se [tymyltɥø] *adj.* tumultuous, noisy, riotous, seething, disorderly, chaotic; **~sement** [tymyltɥøzmɑ̃] *adv.* tumultuously, noisily, in disorder.
tumulus [tymylys] (pl. ~ or *tumuli*) *s.m.* (archaeol.) tumulus, barrow.
tune [tyn] *s.f.* = THUNE.
tungstate [tœ̃kstat] *s.m.* (chem.) tungstate.
tungstène [tœ̃kstɛn] *s.m.* (chem.) tungsten.
tungstique [tœ̃kstik] *adj.* tungstic.
tuniciers [tynisje] *s.m.pl.* (zool.) Tunicata.
tunique [tynik] *s.f.* tunic, coat; (bot.) coat, integument; (anat.) wall, membrane.
tuniqué, -e [tynike] *adj.* (bot.) tunicate.
Tunisie [tynizi] *s.f.* (geog.) Tunisia.
tunisien, -ne [tynizjɛ̃] *adj., s.m.f.* Tunisian.
tunnel [tynɛl] *s.m.* tunnel.
tupinambis [typinɑ̃bi] *s.m.* tupinambis (lizard).
turban [tyrbɑ̃] *s.m.* turban; turban-shaped hat, etc.; (bot.) *lis ~,* martagon.
turbé [tyrbe], **turbeh** [tyrbɛ] *s.m.* (Muslim arch.) turbeh.
turbellariés [tyrbelarje] *s.m.pl.* (zool.) Turbellaria, a class of flatworms.
turbidité [tyrbidite] *s.f.* turbidity.
turbin [tyrbɛ̃] *s.m.* (pop.) work, paid work.
turbinage [tyrbinaʒ] *s.m.* separation by centrifuge.
turbine [tyrbin] *s.f.* turbine.
turbiné, -e [tyrbine] *adj.* (nat. hist.) turbinate, top-shaped.
turbinelle [tybinɛl] *s.f.* (zool.) turbinella.
turbiner [tyrbine] (pop.) to work hard, to slave away.
turbith [tyrbit] *s.m.* (pharm.) turpeth.
turbo-alternateur [tyrbɔaltɛrnatœr] *s.m.* (techn.) turbo-alternator; **~compresseur** [tyrbɔkɔ̃presœr] *s.m.* (techn.) turbo-compressor; **~moteur** [tyrbɔmɔtœr] *s.m.* (techn.) turbo--motor, turbine; **~pompe** [tyrbɔpɔ̃p] *s.f.* (mech.) turbo-pump; **~propulseur** [tyrbɔprɔpylsœr] *s.m.* (techn.) propeller-turbine, propeller jet, turbo-propeller, turbo-prop; **~réacteur** [tyrbɔreaktœr] *s.m.* (aeron.) turbo--jet.
turbot [tyrbo] *s.m.* (ichth.) turbot.
turbotière [tyrbɔtjɛr] *s.f.* (cook.) fish-kettle.
turbotin [tyrbɔtɛ̃] *s.m.* young turbot.
turbulence [tyrbylɑ̃s] *s.f.* turbulence; wildness, boisterousness.
turbulent, -e [tyrbylɑ̃] *adj.* turbulent; wild.
turc, turque [tyrk] *adj.* Turkish; *s.m.f.* Turk; ~ *s.m.* (lang.) Turkish; (obs.) Muhammadan; (obs., pej.) cruel man; *à la turque,* in Turkish fashion; cross-legged, squatting; (mus.) alla turca; *latrines à la turque,* latrines on which one squats; (hist.) *le Grand Turc,* the Sultan of Turkey; (pol.) *jeunes ~s,* young Turks, ginger group; *fort comme un ~,* strong as a horse; *tête de Turc,* try-your-strength-machine; (fig.) butt, scapegoat.
turc [tyrk] *s.m.* (ent.) larva of may-bug, grub.
turco [tyrko] *s.m.* (obs.) Algerian soldier.
turdidés [tyrdide] *s.m.pl.* (ornith.) Turdidae.
turf [tyrf] *s.m.* turf, racecourse, racing.
turfiste [tyrfist] *s.m.* devotee of the turf; racing man.
turgescence [tyrʒesɑ̃s] *s.f.* (med.) turgescence, turgidity.
turgescent, -e [tyrʒesɑ̃] *adj.* turgescent, turgid.
turgide [tyrʒid] *adj.* turgid, swollen, congested.
turion [tyrjɔ̃] *s.m.* (bot.) turion.
turlupin [tyrlypɛ̃] *s.m.* (obs.) buffoon, clown; practical joker.
turlupinade [tyrlypinad] *s.f.* (obs.) pun; practical joke.
turlupiner [tyrlypine] *v.i.* (obs.) to play practical jokes; *v.t.* (mod., fam.) to tease, to torment.
turlurette [tyrlyrɛt] *s.f.* (obs.) **1.** kind of guitar, hurdy-gurdy, bagpipes, flageolet; **2.** refrain, burden of a song.
turlutaine [tyrlytɛn] *s.f.* mania, bee in one's bonnet; hobby; everlasting theme.
turlutte [tyrlyt] *s.f.* lump of lead covered with hooks used for sea-fishing.
turlututu [tyrlytyty] imitation of sound of flute (esp. to mock pomposity).
turne [tyrn] *s.f.* **1.** (pop.) squalid house or room; work-place; **2.** (university slang) digs.
turnep(s) [tyrnɛp(s)] *s.m.* (bot.) kohlrabi.
turonien, -ne [tyronjɛ̃] *adj.* (geol.) Turonian.
turpitude [tyrpityd] *s.f.* turpitude, baseness, ignominy, vileness, shameful action.
turquerie [tyrkri] *s.f.* **1.** harshness, cruelty; **2.** (Lit.) work of Turkish inspiration or background.
turquette [tyrkɛt] *s.f.* (bot.) rupturewort.
Turquie [tyrki] *s.f.* (geog.) Turkey.
turquin [tyrkɛ̃] *adj.* dark blue, slate-blue (esp. of marble).
turquoise [tyrkwaz] *s.f.* turquoise; ~ *s.m.* turquoise (colour); ~ *adj.invar.* turquoise(-coloured).
turriculé, -e [tyrikyle] *adj.* (conch.) turriculated.
turritelle [tyritɛl] *s.f.* (conch.) Turritella.
tussah [tysa] *s.m.* = TUSSOR.
tussilage [tysilaʒ] *s.m.* (bot.) coltsfoot.
tussor, tussore [tysɔr] *s.m.* tussore silk.
tutélaire [tytelɛr] *adj.* tutelar, tutelary; guardian, protecting; (pol.) *puissance ~,* protecting power, trustee.
tutelle [tytɛl] *s.f.* (law) tutelage, guardianship; trusteeship; protection; oversight, supervisory powers; *en ~,* in a state of dependence, under supervision; *enfant en ~,* minor, ward; *être sous la ~ des lois,* to be under the protection of the law.
tut-eur, -rice [tytœr] *s.m.f.* (law) guardian, trustee; protector, protectress; *il n'a pas besoin de ~eur,* he can manage for himself; **~eur** *s.m.*

(hort.) prop, stake; *corset ~eur*, tree-guard, tree-fence; ⚠ not 'tutor' in sense 'private teacher'.
tuteurer [tytœre] *v.t.* (hort.) to prop up, to stake.
tuthie, tutie [tyti] *s.f.* (obs. chem.) zinc oxide, tutty.
tutoiement [tytwamɑ̃] *s.m.* use of *tu, ton*, etc.; addressing (s.o.) familiarly.
tutoyer [tytwaje] *v.t.* to use *tu, ton*, etc.; to speak familiarly to, to speak contemptuously or rudely to; to be on familiar terms with; **se ~** *v.refl.* to be on familiar terms.
tutti quanti [tu(t)tikwɑ̃ti] *s.loc.* (and) the whole lot.
tutu [tyty] *s.m.* tutu, ballet-dancer's short skirt.
tuyau (pl. **-x**) [tɥijo] *s.m.* pipe, tube; hose; chimney flue; shaft, funnel; stalk (of corn); stem (of feather, pipe); nozzle; flute, goffer, (of frills); (fam.) stomach, throat; *~ d'alimentation*, feed-pipe; *~ d'aspiration*, suction-pipe; *~ de conduite*, delivery-pipe, spout; *~ de descente*, rainwater-pipe, downspout; (fam.) *parler dans le ~ de l'oreille*, to whisper something in someone's ear; *~ de poêle*, stove-pipe; stove-pipe (hat); (fam.) private information; source of information, contact; *un ~ increvable*, a hot tip.
tuyautage [tɥijotaʒ] *s.m.* frilling, goffering; (fam.) giving confidential information or tips, putting in the know.
tuyauter [tɥijote] *v.t.* to frill, to flute, to goffer; (fam.) to give confidential information or tips to; to put in the picture; *se faire ~*, to pick up tips, to get oneself in the picture; *~ v.i.* (agric.) to show a stem.
tuyauterie [tɥijotri] *s.f.* pipes, piping, pipework, tubing; manufacture of pipes; tube works.
tuyauteu-r, -se [tɥijotœr] *s.m.f.* tipster, one who gives tips.
tuyère [tɥijɛr] *s.f.* tuyere, twyer.
T.V.A. [teveɑ] abbrev. *taxe à la valeur ajoutée*, V.A.T.
tweed [twid] *s.m.* (text.) tweed.
twist [twist] *s.m.* twist (dance).
tympan [tɛ̃pɑ̃] *s.m.* (anat.) tympanum, ear-drum; (arch.) tympanum, tympan; (print.) tympan; (mech.) tread-wheel, scoop-wheel; tympanum; pinion; *un bruit à briser le ~*, a deafening noise.
tympanal, -e, (aux) [tɛ̃panal] *adj.* (anat.) tympanic.
tympanique [tɛ̃panik] *adj.* (anat.) tympanic; (med.) *son ~*, tympanitic sound.
tympaniser [tɛ̃panize] *v.t.* (obs.) to criticize, to ridicule, to run down.
tympanon [tɛ̃panɔ̃] *s.m.* (mus.) dulcimer.
type [tip] *s.m.* type; model, form; symbol, emblem, personification; standard, pattern, prototype; plan, drawing; (fam.) fellow, character; personality, chap; (pop.) boy-friend.
typé, -e [tipe] *adj.* conforming to a type, stereotyped, true to type, true bred.
typer [tipe] *v.t.* to stamp, to mark, to brand; to type (a character, film-star, etc.).
typesse [tipɛs] *s.f.* (pop., pej.) woman, girl.
typha [tifa] *s.m.* (bot.) cat's-tail, reed-mace.
typhacées [tifase] *s.f.pl.* (bot.) Typhaceae.
typhique [tifik] *adj.* (med.) typhous; typhoid(al).
typhlite [tiflit] *s.f.* (med.) typhlitis.
typhoïde [tifɔid] *adj., s.f.* typhoid.
typhoïdique [tifɔidik] *adj.* (med.) typhoidal.
typhon [tifɔ̃] *s.m.* typhoon.
typhus [tifys] *s.m.* (med.) typhus.
typique [tipik] *adj.* typical, characteristic; symbolical, emblematic; original, true to type.
typo [tipɔ] *s.m.* abbrev. *typographe*.
typo-chromie [tipɔkrɔmi] *s.f.* (print.) typochromy; **~graphe** [tipɔgraf] *s.m.f.* typographer, printer, compositor; **~graphie** [tipɔgrafi] *s.f.* typography, printing, print, letter-press; printing-works; **~graphique** [tipɔgrafik] *adj.* typographic(al); **~graphiquement** [tipɔgrafikmɑ̃] *adv.* typographically; **~lithographie** [tipɔlitɔgrafi] *s.f.* typolithography; **~logie** [tipɔlɔʒi] *s.f.* typology; **~logique** [tipɔlɔʒik] *adj.* typological; **~mètre** [tipɔmɛtr] *s.m.* (print.) typometer.
typtologie [tiptɔlɔʒi] *s.f.* spirit-rapping.
tyran [tirɑ̃] *s.m.* **1.** tyrant, despot; **2.** (ornith.) tyrant fly-catcher, king-bird; **~neau** (pl. **-x**) [tirano] *s.m.* petty tyrant; **~nicide** [tiranisid] *s.m.f.* tyrannicide (person); *s.m.* tyrannicide (deed); **~nie** [tirani] *s.f.* tyranny, oppression; **~nique** [tiranik] *adj.* tyrannical, despotic; **~niquement** [tiranikmɑ̃] *adv.* tyrannically, despotically; **~niser** [tiranize] *v.t.* to tyrannize, to tyrannize over, to oppress, to dominate.
tyrolien, -ne [tirɔljɛ̃] *adj., s.m.f.* Tyrolean, Tyrolese; **~ne** *s.f.* (mus.) Tyrolienne (song); Tyrolean dance.
tyrosinase [tirɔzinɑz] *s.f.* (chem.) tyrosinase.
tyrosine [tirɔzin] *s.f.* (chem.) tyrosine.
tyrrhénien, -ne [tirenjɛ̃] *adj., s.m.f.* Tyrrhenian, Etruscan.
tzigane see TSIGANE.

U

U, u [y] *s.m.* the letter U, u; *en U*, U-shaped.
ubiquiste [ybikɥist] *s.m., adj.* ubiquitous (person).
ubiquité [ybikɥite] *s.f.* ubiquity, omnipresence.
uhlan [ylɑ̃] *s.m.* uhlan.
ukase [ykɑz], **oukase** [ukɑz] *s.m.* ukase; fiat; (fig.) arbitrary decision, strict order.
Ukraine [ykrɛn] *s.f.* (geog.) Ukraine.
ukrainien, -ne [ykrɛnjɛ̃] *s.m.f., adj.* Ukrainian.
ulcérati-f, -ve [ylseratif] *adj.* ulcerative.
ulcération [ylserɑsjɔ̃] *s.f.* ulceration.
ulcère [ylsɛr] *s.m.* ulcer, open sore, running sore.
ulcéré, -e [ylsere] *adj.* ulcerated, ulcerous; (fig.) embittered, resentful, rankling.
ulcérer [ylsere] *v.t.* to ulcerate; (fig.) to wound, to gall, to envenom.
ulcéreu-x, -se [ylserø] *adj.* ulcerous, ulcerated.
uliginaire [yliʒinɛr], **uligineu-x, -se** [yliʒinø] *adj.* (of ground) marshy; (bot.) uliginose, uliginous, growing in marshes.
ulmacées [ylmase] *s.f.pl.* (bot.) Ulmaceae, the elm family.
ulmaire [ylmɛr] *s.f.* (bot.) meadow-sweet.
ulnaire [ylnɛr] *adj.* (anat.) ulnar.
ulster [ylstɛr] *s.m.* ulster (coat).
ultérieur, -e [ylterjœr] *adj.* ulterior; further, of the remoter parts of; later, subsequent, future, to come; **~ement** [ylterjœrmɑ̃] *adv.* further,

later, at a later or future date, subsequently, afterwards.
ultimatum [yltimatɔm] *s.m.* ultimatum.
ultime [yltim] *adj.* ultimate, last, final.
ultra [yltra] *s.m.f.*, *adj.* extremist, ultra, ultra--reactionary (person.).
ultra-court, -e [yltrakur] *adj.* (phys.) (of waves) ultra-short.
ultramoderne [yltramɔdɛrn] *adj.* ultra-modern.
ultramontain, -e [yltramɔ̃tɛ̃] *s.m.f.* ultramontanist, Vaticanist; *adj.* ultramontane, beyond the Alps.
ultramontanisme [yltramɔ̃tanism] *s.m.* ultramontanism, Vaticanism.
ultra-sensible [yltrasɑ̃sibl] *adj.* extremely sensitive, hypersensitive, (of) high sensitivity.
ultra-son [yltrasɔ̃] *s.m.* ultrasound, ultrasonic or supersonic echo; *sondage par* ~, ultrasonic sounding.
ultra-sonique [yltrasɔnik] *adj.* ultrasonic.
ultra-violet, -te [yltravjɔlɛ] *adj.* ultraviolet.
ululement [ylylmɑ̃] *s.m.* = HULULEMENT.
ululer [ylyle] *v.i.* = HULULER.
ulve [ylv] *s.f.* (bot.) Ulva, sea-lettuce.
Ulysse [ylis] *s.m.* Ulysses.
un [œ̃], (fem.) **une** [yn] *ind.art.*, *adj.*, *pron.*, a, an, any, some; one; single; unique, unified, whole; an entity; ~*jour*, a day, one day, some day, some time; *il n'y en a qu'*~, there is only one, it is unique; *ne faire qu'*~ *avec*, to be indistinguishable from; *ils ne font qu'*~, they are indistinguishable, or inseparable; *de deux jours l'*~, every other day; *sur les* ~*e heure*, about one o'clock; *deux francs l'*~*(e)*, two francs apiece; (pop.) *sans* ~ *sou*, broke; *de deux choses l'*~*e*, it's one thing or the other; *c'est d'*~ *ennuyeux!*, it is just too boring!; *il fait* ~ *chaud*, it's frightfully hot; *il y a* ~ *monde!*, there are so many people!, there's such a crowd!; *c'est tout* ~, it's the same thing; it's all the same, it doesn't really matter; ~ *Figaro l'eût vite fait*, a (man like) Figaro would have quickly done it; (pop.) ~*e gentille de bonne*, a nice (type of) maid; *il a rencontré un Dubois*, he met a certain Dubois; *en voilà* ~ *qui a du toupet*, he's got some nerve, there's a cheeky fellow for you; ~ *que je plains, c'est*, a person I'm sorry for is; *tout produit doit être* ~, everything produced must be a single whole; *l'action doit être* ~*e*, there must be unity of action; *l'*~ *et l'autre*, both; *les* ~*s et les autres*, both, everybody, all, all together; *l'*~ *ou l'autre*, either (the one or the other); *ni l'*~ *ni l'autre*, neither; *les* ~*s . . . les autres*, some . . . others; *l'*~ *l'autre*, *les* ~*s les autres*, each other, one another; *l'*~ *dans l'autre*, on an average, taken as a whole; *ne faire ni* ~*e ni deux*, not to hesitate, not to think twice; ~ *à* ~, one by one; *comme pas* ~, like nobody else; *et d'*~, that's that done, that settles that one.
unanime [ynanim] *adj.* unanimous; ~**ment** [ynanimmɑ̃] *adv.* unanimously, by common consent.
unanimité [ynanimite] *s.f.* unanimity, agreement, conformity (of opinion); *à l'*~, unanimously, without dissentient, without a dissenting voice.
unau [yno] *s.m.* (zool.) sloth.
unciforme [ɔ̃sifɔrm] *adj.* unciform, hook--shaped.
unciné, -e [ɔ̃sine] *adj.* (bot.) uncinate.
une [yn] *s.f.* front page (of newspaper); *à la* ~, on the front page.
unguéal, -e (**aux**) [ɔ̃gɥeal] *adj.* ungual, unguiculate.
unguis [ɔ̃gɥis] *s.m.* (anat.) unguis.
uni, -e [yni] *adj.* **1.** smooth, even, level, uniform; equable, quiet, calm, uneventful; plain, self--coloured, without pattern or decoration; *du linge* ~, plain linen; **2.** joined, linked, united, harmonious, affectionate; *ils sont très* ~*s*, they are very fond of each other; they are a very happy couple, they make a perfect pair.
uniate [ynjat] *s.m.*, *adj.* Uniate.
unicaule [ynikol] *adj.* (bot.) having one stalk, uniaxial.
unicellulaire [yniselylɛr] *adj.* unicellular.
unicolore [ynikɔlɔr] *adj.* unicolour(ed).
unicorne [ynikɔrn] *s.m.* unicorn; (obs.) narwhal.
unidirectionnel, -le [ynidirɛksjɔnɛl] *adj.* (of transmitter, etc.) unidirectional.
unième [ynjɛm] *adj.* first (as in twenty-first, thirty-first, etc.); ~**ment** [ynjɛmmɑ̃] *adv.* firstly (as in twenty-firstly, etc.).
unificat-eur, -rice [ynifikatœr] *adj.* unifying.
unification [ynifikɑsjɔ̃] *s.f.* unification, amalgamation; consolidation (of debt, etc.); standardization.
unifier [ynifje] *v.t.* to unify, to amalgamate; to unite; to make level, to make uniform; to standize; to consolidate; **se** ~ *v.refl.* to become united; to merge, to coalesce.
uniforme [ynifɔrm] *adj.* uniform; even, equal; standard, of the same type, unvarying; ~ *s.m.* uniform, regimentals; *d'*~, regimental; regulation; standard; (fig.) *quitter l'*~, to leave the service; *en grand* ~, in full uniform.
uniformément [ynifɔrmemɑ̃] *adv.* uniformly, evenly, equally, throughout, unvaryingly; *vêtus* ~, all dressed alike; *corps* ~ *compact*, body of uniform density.
uniform-isation [ynifɔrmizɑsjɔ̃] *s.f.* making uniform, standardization; ~**iser** [ynifɔrmize] *v.t.* to make uniform, to standardize; ~**ité** [ynifɔrmite] *s.f.* uniformity, sameness, monotony, consistency.
unijambiste [yniʒɑ̃bist] *s.m.f.*, *adj.* (one) who has lost a leg.
unilatéral, -e, (**aux**) [ynilateral] *adj.* unilateral, one-sided; *stationnement* ~, parking on one side only; ~**ement** [ynilateralmɑ̃] *adv.* unilaterally.
uniloculaire [ynilɔkylɛr] *adj.* (bot.) unilocular.
uniment [ynimɑ̃] *adv.* evenly, plainly, smoothly, simply; regularly; uniformly.
uninominal, -e, (**aux**) [yninɔminal] *adj.* containing or bearing one name only; *scrutin* ~, voting for one candidate.
union [ynjɔ̃] *s.f.* union, uniting, unification, link, conjunction, combination, blending; agreement, harmony, attachment, fellowship; match, marriage; alliance, society, association; (techn.) union, coupling, joint; *trait d'*~, hyphen; (obs.) ~*s ouvrières*, trade unions; *l'*~ *fait la force*, union is strength; united we stand, divided we fall; ~**isme** [ynjɔnism] *s.m.* (pol.) unionism; (obs.) trade unionism; ~**iste** [ynjɔnist] *s.m.f.*, *adj.* **1.** (U.S. hist., U.K. pol.) unionist; **2.** (obs.) trade unionist.
unipare [ynipar] *adj.* uniparous.
unipersonnel, -le [ynipɛrsɔnɛl] *adj.*, *s.m.* (gram.) impersonal (verb).
uniphasé [ynifɑze] *adj.* (electr.) single-phase, monophase.
unipolaire [ynipɔlɛr] *adj.* (electr.) unipolar, single-pole.
unique [ynik] *adj.* unique, sole, single; only; unequalled; uncommon, singular, odd, unrivalled, unprecedented, matchless, unparalleled; *fils* ~, only son; (*rue à*) *sens* ~, one-way street; ~**ment** [ynikmɑ̃] *adv.* uniquely, solely, only.
unir [ynir] *v.t.* to unite, to join, to link, to ally, to combine, to match; to smooth, to level; **s'**~ *v.refl.* to unite, to join, to combine; *s'*~ *à*, to join forces with, to marry.
unisexe [ynisɛks] *adj.invar.* unisex
unisexualité [ynisɛksɥalite] *s.f.* unisexuality.
unisexué, -e [ynisɛksɥe] *adj.* unisexual.

unisson [ynisɔ̃] *s.m.* unison; (fig.) harmony; *à l'~*, in unison; (fig.) in harmony.
unitaire [ynitɛr] **1.** *adj.* forming a single unit, unit, unitary, united, combined, single, uniform; **2.** *s.m.f.*, *adj.* (relig.) Unitarian.
unitarisme [ynitarism] *s.m.* Unitarianism.
unité [ynite] *s.f.* unity; unit; digit; (fig.) uniformity, community, harmony, agreement; unique quality; *prix d'~*, unit price, price of a single item.
uniti-f, -ve [ynitif] *adj.* unitive, uniting.
univalve [ynivalv] *adj.* (zool.) univalve.
univers [ynivɛr] *s.m.* universe, earth, world, mankind; (fig.) realm, sphere; (print.) large sheet of paper (1 m × 1·30 m).
universal-isation [ynivɛrsalizɑsjɔ̃] *s.f.* universalization, dissemination; **~iser** [ynivɛrsalize] *v.t.* to universalize, to make universal or general; **~isme** [ynivɛrsalism] *s.m.* universalism; **~iste** [ynivɛrsalist] *adj.*, *s.m.f.* universalist; **~ité** [ynivɛrsalite] *s.f.* universality; sum total, whole, totality.
universaux [ynivɛrso] *s.m.pl.* (phil.) universals.
universel, -le [ynivɛrsɛl] *adj.* universal, of the universe, general, (of legatees) sole or residuary; world-wide, widely known or accepted; (techn.) (of joint, spanner, etc.) universal; all-purpose; *homme ~*, a man who knows everything, polymath; **~lement** [ynivɛrsɛlmɑ̃] *adv.* universally, generally, without exception.
universitaire [ynivɛrsitɛr] *adj.* university; academic; *le corps ~*, the teaching body of the university; *~ s.m.f.* university man or woman; member of the university, university professor.
université [ynivɛrsite] *s.f.* university.
univoque [ynivɔk] *adj.* univocal.
upas [ypɑs] *s.m.* upas, upas-tree.
uppercut [ypɛrkyt] *s.m.* (boxing) upper-cut.
urane [yran] *s.m.* (chem.) oxide of uranium.
uranique [yranik] *adj.* (chem.) uranic.
uranium [yranjɔm] *s.m.* (chem.) uranium.
uranographie [yranɔgrafi] *s.f.* (obs.) uranography.
uranoscope [yranɔskɔp] *s.m.* (ichth.) Uranoscopus, star-gazer.
urate [yrat] *s.m.* (chem.) urate.
urbain, -e [yrbɛ̃] *adj.* urban, town, city, city-dwelling; (fig.) urbane, townified.
urban-isation [yrbanizɑsjɔ̃] *s.f.* urbanization; **~iser** [yrbanize] *v.t.* to urbanize; **~isme** [yrbanism] *s.m.* town planning; **~iste** [yrbanist] *s.m.f.* town planner; *adj.* (town) planning; **~istique** [yrbanistik] *adj.* relating to town planning.
urbanité [yrbanite] *s.f.* urbanity, courtesy.
urcéolé, -e [yrseɔle] *adj.* (bot.) urceolate.
ure [yr] *s.m.* = URUS.
urée [yre] *s.f.* (chem.) urea.
urémie [yremi] *s.f.* (pathol.) uraemia.
urémique [yremik] *adj.* uraemic.
uréomètre [yreɔmɛtr] *s.m.* = UROMÈTRE.
uretère [yrtɛr] *s.m.* (anat.) ureter.
uretérite [yrterit] *s.f.* (pathol.) ureteritis.
urétral, -e, (aux) [yretral] *adj.* (anat.) urethral.
urètre, urèthre [yrɛtr] *s.m.* (anat.) urethra.
urétrite [yretrit] *s.f.* urethritis.
urgence [yrʒɑ̃s] *s.f.* urgency; emergency; (med.) emergency case; *d'~*, urgent, immediately, without delay; *il y a ~*, it is urgent, it is a pressing matter; *il y a ~ qu'il vienne*, it is essential that he comes; *en cas d'~*, in case of emergency, in an emergency.
urgent, -e [yrʒɑ̃] *adj.* urgent, pressing, insistent.
urger [yrʒe] *v.i.* (fam.) to be urgent.
urinaire [yrinɛr] *adj.* (anat.) urinary.
urinal [yrinal] *s.m.* urinal (bottle).
urine [yrin] *s.f.* urine.
uriner [yrine] *v.i.* to urinate, to pass water.
urinoir [yrinwar] *s.m.* (public) urinal.
urique [yrik] *adj.* (chem.) uric.
urne [yrn] *s.f.* urn; *~ funéraire*, sepulchral urn; *~ du scrutin*, *~ électorale*, ballot-box; *aller aux ~s*, to go to the polls, to vote in an election.
urobiline [yrɔbilin] *s.f.* (chem., pharm.) urobilin.
urogénital, -e, (aux) [yrɔʒenital] *adj.* urogenital.
uro-graphie [yrɔgrafi] *s.f.* urography; **~logie** [yrɔlɔʒi] *s.f.* urology; **~logue** [yrɔlɔg] *s.m.f.* urologist; **~mètre** [yrɔmɛtr] *s.m.* ureometer; **~scopie** [yrɔskɔpi] *s.f.* uroscopy.
U.R.S.S. [yɛrɛsɛs, yrs] *s.f.* abbrev. *Union des Républiques Socialistes Soviétiques*, U.S.S.R.
ursuline [yrsylin] *s.f.* Ursuline.
urticacées [yrtikase] *s.f.pl.* (bot.) Urticaceae.
urticaire [yrtikɛr] *s.f.* (pathol.) nettle-rash, urticaria.
urticant, -e [yrtikɑ̃] *adj.* urticating, stinging.
urtication [yrtikɑsjɔ̃] *s.f.* urtication.
urubu [yryby] *s.m.* (ornith.) urubu, American black vulture.
Uruguay [yrygwɛ, yrygɛ] *s.m.* (geog.) Uruguay.
uruguayen, -ne [yrygwɛɛ̃, yrygɛɛ̃] *adj.*, *s.m.f.* Uruguayan.
urus [yrys] *s.m.* (zool.) urus, aurochs.
us [ys] *s.m.pl.* usages, ways; esp. in *les ~ et coutumes*, the (traditional) manners and customs.
usage [yzaʒ] *s.m.* use, custom; usage; formality; usefulness, purpose; practice, habit, way, employment, enjoyment, wear; *à ~ externe*, for external application; *bâtiment à ~ de collège*, building intended for use as a school; *à l'~*, in use, in practice; *à l'~ de*, for the use of, for use in, for use by, intended for; *d'~*, usual, habitual; for everyday use; customary, conventional; *en ~*, in use, used, usual, common; *avoir l'~ de*, to be practised or experienced in; *coefficient d'~*, frequency count or index (of a word); (fam.) *faire de l'~*, to wear well; *garanti à l'~*, guaranteed to wear; *le bon ~*, proper use, good practice, correct usage; *de bon ~*, (i.) very serviceable; (ii.) in the approved way; in good taste; *hors d'~*, worn out, no longer usable, useless, threadbare; obsolete; *sans ~*, (i.) (of) no use; (ii.) ill-mannered; *peu en ~*, little used, uncommon; *avoir de l'~*, to be well-bred; *manquer d'~*, to lack breeding; to have no manners; *faire ~ de*, to make use of, to avail oneself of; to use; *mettre en ~*, to bring into use; *mettre tout en ~*, to spare no pains; *~ fait droit*, custom becomes law; *~ rend maître*, practice makes perfect; *il est d'~ de*, it is customary to; *il n'est pas d'~ de . . .*, it's not done, it's not customary to . . .; *conforme à l'~*, customary, usual, in accordance with general practice; *aller à l'encontre de l'~*, to defy convention, to act unconventionally.
usagé, -e [yzaʒe] *adj.* that has been used, not new, second-hand; (fig.) threadbare.
usager [yzaʒe] *s.m.* user; *les ~s de la route*, road-users; *les ~s du français*, French-speakers.
usant, -e [yzɑ̃] *adj.* exhausting, tiring, wearing; (law) using, enjoying.
usé, -e [yze] *adj.* worn-out, threadbare, frayed; stale, trite, hackneyed, the worse for wear, broken, broken down, outworn, lifeless; (fig.) dead, blunted; decrepit; (of soil, etc.) exhausted.
user [yze] *v.t.* **1.** to use, to use up, to consume, to wear, to wear out; to weaken, to diminish, to blunt; to destroy, to exhaust; **2.** *~ de*, to use, to make use of, to utilize, to employ, to have recourse to, to resort to, to avail oneself of, to exercise; to put into operation; to treat; *~ d'un droit*, to exercise a right; *~ de qn.*, or *en ~ avec qn.*, to treat s.o. (well, badly, etc.);

vous en usez mal avec lui, you are behaving badly towards him, you are treating him badly; **s'~** *v.refl.* to wear out, to wear away, to diminish, to grow old or weak, to deteriorate, to become worn out or exhausted; to wear oneself out.

usinage [yzinaʒ] *s.m.* machining; manufacture.

usine [yzin] *s.f.* factory, plant, works, mill; ~ *à gaz*, gasworks.

usiner [yzine] *v.t.* to machine, to manufacture; (pop.) to be hard at work; *ça usine ici!*, what a hive of industry!, everyone sweating away!

usini-er, -ère [yzinje] *adj.* manufacturing, factory.

usité, -e [yzite] *adj.* customary, used, in use, current, normal, common; *peu* ~, rare, seldom used, not in current use.

ustensile [ystɑ̃sil] *s.m.* utensil, implement, tool; *~s de toilette*, toilet requisites.

usucapion [yzykapjɔ̃] *s.f.* (law) usucaption, usucapion.

usuel, -le [yzɥɛl] *adj.* usual, customary, ordinary, common, current, everyday; **~lement** [yzɥɛlmɑ̃] *adv.* usually, commonly, ordinarily, customarily.

usufructuaire [yzyfryktɥɛr] *adj.* (law) usufructuary, giving only the usufruct.

usufruit [yzyfrɥi] *s.m.* (law) usufruct, use, enjoyment, life-interest.

usufruiti-er, -ère [yzyfrɥitje] *s.m.f.*, *adj.* usufructuary.

usuraire [yzyrɛr] *adj.* usurious; **~ment** [yzyrɛrmɑ̃] *adv.* usuriously, with usury.

usure[1] [yzyr] *s.f.* usury, (lending at) exorbitant interest; *prêter à* ~, to practise usury; (fig.) *rendre avec* ~, to repay with interest or in full measure.

usure[2] [yzyr] *s.f.* wear, wear and tear, erosion, exhaustion, dissipation (of energy); *guerre d'~*, war of attrition.

usuri-er, -ère [yzyrje] *s.m.f.* usurer, money-lender.

usurpat-eur, -rice [yzyrpatœr] *s.m.f.* usurper; *adj.* usurping, encroaching.

usurpation [yzyrpɑsjɔ̃] *s.f.* usurpation, usurping, encroachment.

usurpatoire [yzyrpatwar] *adj.* usurping, encroaching, usurpatory, illegal.

usurper [yzyrpe] *v.t.* to usurp; ~ *v.i.* ~ *sur*, to encroach upon.

ut [yt] *s.m.* (mus.) C, doh.

utérin, -e [yterɛ̃] *adj.* uterine; *sœur ~e*, half-sister on the mother's side.

utérus [yterys] *s.m.* (anat.) uterus, womb.

utile [ytil] *adj.* useful, serviceable, of use, of utility, profitable, valuable, advantageous, due, expedient, beneficial; necessary, indispensable; *en temps* ~, in due or in good time, at a suitable moment; *il serait* ~ *de*, it would be well to; *puis-je vous être ~?*, can I be of assistance to you?; (techn.) *travail* ~, effective or useful work; *charge* ~, useful load; (law) *jours ~s*, days reckoned in judicial proceedings; **~ment** [ytilmɑ̃] *adv.* usefully, advantageously, profitably, to good purpose.

utile [ytil] *s.m.* utility, usefulness; expediency, the expedient; *joindre l'~ à l'agréable*, to combine business with pleasure.

utilisable [ytilizabl] *adj.* utilizable, that can be used, practical, that can be turned to account.

utilisat-eur, -rice [ytilizatœr] *s.m.f.* user.

utilisation [ytilizɑsjɔ̃] *s.f.* utilization, use, employment, method of use, turning to account.

utiliser [ytilize] *v.t.* to utilize, to turn to account, to make use of, to employ.

utilitaire [ytilitɛr] *adj.*, *s.m.f.* utilitarian; materialistic (person); utility (vehicle, etc.).

utilitarisme [ytilitarism] *s.m.* utilitarianism.

utilité [ytilite] *s.f.* utility, usefulness, profitableness, profit, advantage, purpose, service; (theatr.) minor part; *d'aucune ~*, useless.

utopie [ytɔpi] *s.f.* Utopia; Utopian scheme; (fig.) dream; *créer des ~s*, to build castles in the air.

utopique [ytɔpik] *adj.* Utopian.

utopiste [ytɔpist] *s.m.f.* Utopian; dreamer.

utriculaire [ytrikylɛr] *adj.* utricular; ~ *s.m.* (bot.) Utricularia, bladderwort.

utricule [ytrikyl] *s.m.* (anat., bot.) utricle.

utriculeu-x, -se [ytrikylø] *adj.* utricular.

uval, -e, (aux) [yval] *adj.* relating to the grape.

uva-ursi [yvayrsi] *s.m.* (bot.) uva-ursi, bearberry.

uvée [yve] *s.f.* (anat.) uvea.

uvéite [yveit] *s.f.* inflammation of the uvea.

uvulaire [yvylɛr] *adj.* (anat., phon.) uvular.

uvule [yvyl] *s.f.* (anat.) uvula.

V

V, v [ve] *s.m.* the letter V, v; V-shaped object; V-sign; abbrev. (i.) *votre* (e.g. before *Excellence*, *Altesse*); (ii.) *volt*; *en V*, V-shaped; *décolleté en V*, V-neck.

va [va] 3rd pers. sing. pres. indic. & 2nd pers. sing. imperat. of ALLER.

vacance [vakɑ̃s] *s.f.* **1.** vacancy, vacant post; availability; (university) *déclarer la ~ d'une chaire*, to declare a chair vacant; **2.** (pl.) holidays; vacation, recess; *en ~(s)*, on holiday; *entrer en ~s*, (school) to break up, (parliament) to rise, to go into recess; *les grandes ~s*, the summer holidays, the long vacation; *vous avez besoin de ~s*, you need a holiday.

vacanci-er, -ère [vakɑ̃sje] *s.m.f.* holiday-maker, visitor.

vacant, -e [vakɑ̃] *adj.* vacant, unoccupied, unfilled, empty.

vacarme [vakarm] *s.m.* noise, uproar, din, hubbub; *faire du ~*, to create a disturbance.

vacation [vakɑsjɔ̃] *s.f.* **1.** sitting; attendance (of public officers, etc.); **2.** (professional) fee; **3.** (pl.) vacation, recess (of law courts).

vaccin [vaksɛ̃] *s.m.* vaccine, serum, lymph; (lit. & fig.) inoculation.

vaccinal, -e, (aux) [vaksinal] *adj.* vaccinal.

vaccinat-eur, -rice [vaksinatœr] *s.m.f.* vaccinator; *adj.* vaccinating.

vaccination [vaksinɑsjɔ̃] *s.f.* vaccination.

vaccine [vaksin] *s.f.* **1.** (obs.) vaccination; **2.** vaccinia, cowpox; ⚠ not 'vaccine'.

vacciner [vaksine] *v.t.* to vaccinate, to inoculate; *être vacciné contre*, to have been inoculated against; to be immune to.

vachard, -e [vaʃar] *adj.* (pop.) nasty, spiteful, swinish.

vache [vaʃ] *s.f.* cow; ~ *laitière*, or *à lait*, dairy cow, milch cow; (obs., fig.) fat woman, lethargic or flabby person; (slang) policeman; (fig., fam.) nasty, spiteful individual, swine, bastard; (fig.) *ils ont fait de vous une belle ~ à lait*, they are exploiting you, they are making a good thing out of you; *les ~s grasses*, years of plenty; *les ~s maigres*, lean years, famine; *~ marine*, sea--cow, dugong, manatee; *le plancher des ~s*, dry land, terra firma; *manger de la ~ enragée*, to go through hard times; *donner des coups (de pied) en ~*, to give a side-kick; (fig.) to lash out unexpectedly, to deal a treacherous blow; *parler français comme une ~ espagnole*, to speak appalling French; *chacun son métier et les ~s seront bien gardées*, if everyone minds his own business, all will be well; *c'est une ~ de belle maison*, it's a really super house; (*peau* or *cuir de*) *~*, cowhide; *queue de ~*, red-haired; *~ adj.* (fam.) nasty, mean; super; *c'est ~*, (i.) it's a dirty trick, it's a brute, it's a wretched piece of luck; (ii.) it's super, smashing.

vachement [vaʃmɑ̃] *adv.* (fam.) **1.** (obs.) nastily, brutally; **2.** tremendously.

vach-er, -ère [vaʃe] *s.m.f.* cowherd, cowman, cowgirl; (fig.) *des manières de ~er*, bucolic behaviour, rustic ways.

vacherie [vaʃri] *s.f.* cow-house, byre; (obs.) flabbiness, lethargy, inertia; (fam.) dirty trick, nasty remark.

vacherin [vaʃrɛ̃] *s.m.* **1.** kind of meringue; **2.** (in Franche-Comté) gruyère cheese.

vachette [vaʃɛt] *s.f.* calf; calfskin.

vacillant, -e [vasijɑ̃] *adj.* vacillating, flickering, wavering; unsteady, shaky, wobbly; (fig.) vacillating, irresolute.

vacillation [vasijɑsjɔ̃] *s.f.* vacillation, unsteadiness, wobbling, flickering, indecisiveness.

vacillement [vasijmɑ̃] *s.m.* vacillation, vacillating.

vaciller [vasije] *v.i.* to vacillate, to flicker; to be unsteady, to stagger, to reel; (fig.) to hesitate, to waver, to hover, to vacillate.

vacuité [vakɥite] *s.f.* vacuity, emptiness.

vacuum [vakɥɔm] *s.m.* vacuum.

vade-mecum [vademekɔm] *s.m.invar.* vade--mecum.

vadrouille [vadruj] *s.f.* **1.** (naut.) swab; **2.** (fam.) stroll, loafing about; (pop.) loose woman.

vadrouiller [vadruje] *v.i.* (fam.) to loaf about, to stroll around.

va-et-vient [vaevjɛ̃] *s.m.invar.* **1.** oscillation, swing, see-saw motion, reciprocal motion, two--way movement; coming and going; **2.** ferry; *faire le ~ entre*, to ply between; **3.** (naut.) hauling-rope; **4.** (electr.) two-way wiring, two--way switch.

vagabond, -e [vagabɔ̃] *s.m.f.* vagabond, vagrant, tramp; *adj.* wandering, roving, flighty.

vagabondage [vagabɔ̃daʒ] *s.m.* vagabondage, vagabondism; vagrancy; roaming.

vagabonder [vagabɔ̃de] *v.i.* to be a vagabond, to wander, to roam, to rove.

vagin [vaʒɛ̃] *s.m.* (anat.) vagina.

vaginal, -e, (aux) [vaʒinal] *adj.* vaginal.

vaginite [vaʒinit] *s.f.* (pathol.) vaginitis.

vagir [vaʒir] *v.i.* to wail, to cry.

vagissement [vaʒismɑ̃] *s.m.* wail (of an infant); bark (of a crocodile); squeal (of a hare).

vague[1] [vag] *s.f.* wave, billow, surge; (fig.) *la nouvelle ~*, the new generation (of writers, etc.).

vague[2] [vag] *adj.* empty, vacant; *terrains ~s*, waste ground; *~ s.m.* empty space; *regarder dans le ~*, to gaze into space.

vague[3] [vag] *adj.* vague, indefinite, hazy, undefined, shadowy, sketchy; *~ s.m.* vagueness, uncertainty, indefiniteness; **~ment** [vagmɑ̃] *adv.* vaguely, dimly, faintly, sketchily.

vaguemestre [vagmɛstr] *s.m.* (mil.) post orderly, post corporal.

vaguer [vage] *v.i.* to ramble, to wander, to stray, to rove.

vahiné [vaine] *s.f.* Tahitian girl or woman.

vaigrage [vɛgraʒ] *s.m.* inner planking or casing (of a ship).

vaigre [vɛgr] *s.f.* (naut.) plank or plate (for inner lining of a ship).

vaillamment [vajamɑ̃] *adv.* valiantly, courageously, gallantly, stoutly.

vaillance [vajɑ̃s] *s.f.* courage, bravery, valour.

vaillant, -e [vajɑ̃] *adj.* valiant, gallant, courageous, valorous; spirited, fit, in good health, up to the mark; *n'avoir pas un sou ~*, not to have a penny to one's name.

vaille que vaille [vajkəvaj] *adv.loc.* see VALOIR.

vain, -e [vɛ̃] *adj.* vain, fruitless, ineffectual; to no purpose, futile, idle; frivolous, trifling; vainglorious, conceited; empty, hollow, shadowy; *en ~*, vainly, in vain.

vaincre [vɛ̃kr] *v.t.* to vanquish, to conquer, to overcome, to defeat, to get the better of, to master, to subdue; to surpass, to outdo; to win, to be the victor; *se laisser ~*, to give way, to yield; **se ~** *v.refl.* to control oneself, to conquer one's passions.

vaincu, -e [vɛ̃ky] *adj.* vanquished, conquered, defeated; *s'avouer ~*, to admit defeat; *il était ~ d'avance*, he hadn't a hope of success; *les ~s*, the vanquished; *une attitude de ~*, a defeatist attitude.

vainement [vɛnmɑ̃] *adv.* vainly, in vain, to no purpose.

vainqueur [vɛ̃kœr] *s.m.* conqueror, victor, vanquisher; prize-winner, winner; *~ adj.m.* conquering, victorious, triumphant.

vair [vɛr] *s.m.* squirrel's fur; (herald.) vair.

vairé, -e [vɛre] *adj.* (herald.) vairy, charged with vair.

vairon [vɛrɔ̃] *adj.m.* (of eyes) of different colour.

vairon [vɛrɔ̃] *s.m.* (ichth.) minnow.

vaisseau (pl. **-x**) [vɛso] *s.m.* **1.** vessel, receptacle; **2.** vessel, ship; *~ spatial*, space-ship, spacecraft; (fig.) *conduire le ~*, to be at the helm; *brûler ses ~x*, to burn one's boats; **3.** interior (of large building), nave; **4.** (anat.) vessel, duct.

vaisselier [vɛsəlje] *s.m.* dresser, sideboard.

vaisselle [vɛsɛl] *s.f.* **1.** plates and dishes, crockery; *laver* or *faire la ~*, to wash up; *~ d'or, d'argent*, gold, silver, plate; *~ plate*, gold or silver dishes.

val (pl. *vaux* or *vals*) [val] *s.m.* dale, vale, valley; *par monts et par vaux*, up hill and down dale.

valable [valabl] *adj.* valid, good, cogent; available, sound; (law) good and sufficient; **~ment** [valabləmɑ̃] *adv.* validly, on solid grounds, with good reason.

Valence [valɑ̃s] *s.f.* (geog.) **1.** Valence (France); **2.** Valencia (Spain).

valence[1] [valɑ̃s] *s.f.* Valencia orange.

valence[2] [valɑ̃s] *s.f.* (chem.) valency.

valence-gramme [valɑ̃sgram] *s.f.* (phys.) gramme-equivalent.

valenciennes [valɑ̃sjɛn] *s.f.* Valenciennes (lace).

valériane [valerjan] *s.f.* (bot.) valerian.

valet [valɛ] *s.m.* **1.** valet, footman, manservant; *~ de chambre*, valet; *~ de pied*, footman; *~ de ferme*, farm-hand; (agric.) *maître ~*, head man; (hunt.) *~ de chiens*, whipper-in, whip; (fig.) *âme de ~*, servile nature; *faire le plat ~*, to cringe; (proverb) *tel maître, tel ~*, like master, like man; (proverb) *il n'y a pas de grand homme pour son ~ de chambre*, no man is a hero to his valet; *~ de comédie*, stage valet (i.e. highly resourceful); *je suis votre ~*, I am yours to command; **2.** (cards) knave, jack; **3.** door counterweight; **4.** (techn.) clamp, stand, support, holder; (surg.) *~ à Patin*, ligature, forceps.

valetaille [valtɑj] *s.f.* (pej.) menials, flunkeys.

valétudinaire [valetydinɛr] *adj., s.m.f.* valetudinarian; invalid, (person) in poor health.

valeur [valœr] *s.f.* **1.** value, worth, price; equivalent; merit, (high) quality; useful person, asset; consideration, weight, importance; import, meaning; *de* ~, valuable, (of) quality, gifted; *avoir de la* ~, to be of value; (fig.) to carry weight; *sans* ~, valueless, worthless; *objets de* ~, valuables; (fig.) *attacher de la* ~ *à*, to set store by, to attach importance to; *être en* ~, to be thriving; *mettre en* ~, to make the most of, to put to good use, to develop, to exploit, to make profitable, to bring into production; to emphasize, to bring to notice; *remettre en* ~, to bring back into production, to restore, (land); to improve (land); **2.** valour, courage, gallantry; **3.** (pl.) bills, paper stocks, shares, securities, scrip; ~ *en espèces*, cash, bullion; ~*s mobilières*, transferable securities.

valeureu-x, se [valœrø] *adj.* brave, valiant; ~**sement** [valœrøzmɑ̃] *adv.* bravely, valiantly.

validation [validɑsjɔ̃] *s.f.* validation, rendering valid.

valide [valid] *adj.* **1.** valid, good; **2.** able-bodied, healthy, fit for duty; ~**ment** [validmɑ̃] *adv.* validly.

valider [valide] *v.t.* to make valid, to declare valid, to validate, to ratify.

validité [validite] *s.f.* validity; period of validity, availability.

valise [valiz] *s.f.* valise, suitcase, travelling-bag; *faire sa* ~, to pack, to pack one's bags (and depart); *la* ~ *diplomatique*, the diplomatic bag.

vallée [vale] *s.f.* valley.

valleuse [valøz] *s.f.* small dry valley, forming cleft in sea-cliff.

vallon [valɔ̃] *s.m.* little valley; vale; *le sacré* ~, the sacred vale (of the Muses), (fig.) poetry.

vallonnement [valɔnmɑ̃] *s.m.* undulation; (landscape gardening) creating an undulating landscape.

valoir [valwar] *v.i.* to be worth, to be as good as, to be equal or equivalent to; (fig.) to deserve, to merit; *cela ne vaut rien*, that is worthless; *il ne vaut pas grand'chose*, he, or it, is nothing much; *l'un vaut l'autre*, there is nothing to choose between them, one is as good, or as bad, as the other; *se* ~, to be as good as each other; *tous les métiers se valent*, one trade is as good as another; *faire* ~, to make the most of, to put to good use, to make profitable, to exploit, to develop, to set off (to advantage), to bring out, to emphasize; *faire* ~ *ses droits*, to assert one's claim; *se faire* ~, to make the most of oneself, to push oneself forward; *personne qui vaut qu'on s'occupe d'elle*, person who deserves attention; *cela ne vaut pas la peine*, it is not worth while; (fam.) *cela vaut le coup*, it's worth a go; *à* ~ (*sur une somme*), on account (of a sum); *à* ~ *sur Dubois*, on Dubois' account, to the account of Dubois; *le climat ne vous vaut rien*, this climate is not good for you; ~ *v.t.* to procure, to assure; to gain, to earn; to yield; *ses exploits lui ont valu une gloire immortelle*, his exploits have earned him immortal fame; *sa condamnation lui a valu cinq ans de prison*, his conviction meant five years in prison; ~ *v.impers. il vaut* (*vaudrait*) *mieux*, it is (would be) better (to do sth.); *autant vaudrait*, one might as well; (proverb) *mieux vaut tard que jamais*, better late than never; *vaille que vaille, adv.loc.* for better or for worse, come what may, at all costs, as best one can; *ne faire rien qui vaille*, to be doing nothing worth while; *un rien qui vaille*, a good-for-nothing.

valorisation [valɔrizɑsjɔ̃] *s.f.* valorization, valuing; fixing (of price); development (of economy).

valoriser [valɔrize] *v.t.* to valorize, to value; to fix the price of; to increase the price of, to re-value; to develop the economy of.

valse [vals] *s.f.* waltz, valse; (fig.) change-round (of ministries, posts, etc.).

valser [valse] *v.i.* to waltz; (fig.) *faire* ~ *des employés*, to shift personnel around; *envoyer* ~, to sack.

valseu-r, -se [valsœr] *s.m.f.* waltzer.

valvaire [valvɛr] *adj.* (bot., anat.) valvate.

valve [valv] *s.f.* (techn., anat., zool., bot.) valve; clack (of pump); (electr.) rectifier valve.

valvulaire [valvylɛr] *adj.* valvular.

valvule [valvyl] *s.f.* (anat.) valvula.

vamper [vɑ̃pe] *v.t.* (fam.) to vamp, to seduce.

vampire [vɑ̃pir] *s.m.* vampire.

vampirisme [vɑ̃pirism] *s.m.* vampirism.

van[1] [vɑ̃] *s.m.* winnowing-basket.

van[2] [vɑ̃] *s.m.* horse-box.

vanadique [vanadik] *adj.* (chem.) vanadic.

vanadium [vanadjɔm] *s.m.* (chem.) vanadium.

vandale [vɑ̃dal] *s.m.f.* (hist.) Vandal; (mod.) vandal.

vandalisme [vɑ̃dalism] *s.m.* vandalism.

vandoise [vɑ̃dwaz] *s.f.* (ichth.) dace.

vanesse [vanɛs] *s.f.* (ent.) vanessa.

vanille [vanij] *s.f.* (bot., cook.) vanilla, vanilla--bean.

vanillé, -e [vanije] *adj.* vanilla, flavoured with vanilla.

vanillier [vanije] *s.m.* (bot.) vanilla plant.

vanité [vanite] *s.f.* **1.** vanity, conceit; *faire* or *tirer* ~ *de*, to pride oneself on, to take (vain or excessive) pride in, to preen oneself on; *sans* ~, in all due modesty, without wishing to boast; **2.** nothingness, futility; emptiness, unreality, uselessness; worthlessness; *la* ~ *des œuvres humaines*, the vanity of human achievements.

vaniteu-x, -se [vanitø] *adj.* vain, vainglorious, conceited; ~**sement** [vanitøzmɑ̃] *adv.* vainly, presumptuously, vaingloriously.

vannage[1] [vanaʒ] *s.m.* system of water-gates; damming; gating (of turbine).

vannage[2] [vanaʒ] *s.m.* winnowing; winnowings, chaff.

vanne[1] [van] *s.f.* water-gate, sluice-gate, sluice; gate (of turbine); (techn.) butterfly-valve, regulator.

vanne[2] [van] *s.m.* or *f.* (pop.) rude remark.

vanné, -e [vane] *adj.* (fam.) see VANNER[3].

vanneau (pl. **-x**) [vano] *s.m.* **1.** (ornith.) lapwing, peewit; **2.** flight feathers of bird of prey.

vanner[1] [vane] *v.t.* to winnow.

vanner[2] [vane] *v.t.* to fit or dam with sluices; to gate (a turbine).

vanner[3] [vane] *v.t.* (fam.) to wear out, to exhaust.

vannerie [vanri] *s.f.* basket-making; basket trade; basketwork; *chaise en* ~, basket chair, wicker chair.

vannette [vanɛt] *s.f.* winnowing-basket.

vanneu-r, -se [vanœr] *s.m.f.* winnower.

vannier [vanje] *s.m.* basket-maker.

vannure [vanyr] *s.f.* winnowings, chaff.

vantail [vɑ̃taj] *s.m.* (pl. *vantaux*) leaf, hinged flap of a door or window.

vantard, -e [vɑ̃tar] *s.m.f.* boaster, braggart; *adj.* boasting, bragging.

vantardise [vɑ̃tardiz] *s.f.* boasting, boastfulness, boast, bragging; pretension, bluff.

vanter [vɑ̃te] *v.t.* to extol, to commend, to eulogize, to vaunt, to praise; **se** ~ *v.refl.* to boast; to brag; to exaggerate, to make a good story; *sans me* ~, without wishing to boast; (fam.) *il ne s'en est pas vanté*, he kept quiet about it, he was none too pleased with himself; *il n'y a pas de quoi se* ~, that is nothing to be proud of.

vanterie [vɑ̃tri] *s.f.* boasting, bragging; boast.

va-nu-pieds [vanypje] *s.m.f.invar.* vagabond, ragamuffin.
vapes [vap] *s.f.pl.* (pop.) *être dans les* ~, to be knocked out, to be in a daze, a stupor, (including from drugs).
vapeur [vapœr] *s.f.* **1.** steam; water vapour; *à la* ~, by steam; (fig.) hurriedly, hastily; *à toute* ~, at full speed; *bateau à* ~, steamer; **2.** vapour, haze, mist; (pl.) fumes, exhalations; (obs. med.) vapours.
vapeur [vapœr] *s.m.* steamer.
vapocraquage [vapɔkrakaʒ] *s.m.* (techn.) steam-cracking.
vaporeu-x, -se [vapɔrø] *adj.* vaporous, steamy, misty, nebulous; (fig.) ethereal.
vaporisage [vapɔrizaʒ] *s.m.* (techn.) steam treatment (of textiles).
vaporisateur [vapɔrizatœr] *s.m.* vaporizer, atomizer, scent-spray.
vaporisation [vapɔrizɑsjɔ̃] *s.f.* vaporization, evaporation.
vaporiser [vapɔrize] *v.t.* to spray, to sprinkle (with); to vaporize, to cause to evaporate; **se** ~ *v.refl.* to turn to vapour, to vaporize, to evaporate.
vaquer [vake] *v.i.* **1.** to be vacant; **2.** to be on vacation; ~ *à*, to apply oneself to, to devote one's attention to, to be occupied with, to busy oneself with.
varaigne [varɛɲ] *s.f.* tide-sluice (in a salt--marsh).
varan [varɑ̃] *s.m.* (zool.) varan (lizard).
varangue [varɑ̃g] *s.f.* (naut.) floor frame.
varappeu-r, -se [varapœr] *s.m.f.* (rock-)-climber.
varech, varec [varɛk] *s.m.* (bot.) seaweed, sea--wrack, dulse, varec, Irish moss.
vareuse [varøz] *s.f.* (sailor's) jersey; reefer(-jacket); pilot-jacket, pea-jacket; tunic.
varia [varja] *s.m.pl.* (journalism) features.
variabilité [varjabilite] *s.f.* variability, changeableness.
variable [varjabl] *adj.* variable, changeable; unsteady; ~ *s.f.* variable.
variance [varjɑ̃s] *s.f.* (sci., math.) variance.
variante [varjɑ̃t] *s.f.* variant; variant reading.
variateur [varjatœr] *s.m.* ~ *de vitesse*, infinitely variable speed change.
variation [varjɑsjɔ̃] *s.f.* variation, varying, fluctuation, deviation, divergence, (compass) error.
varice [varis] *s.f.* (pathol.) varix, varicose vein.
varicelle [varisɛl] *s.f.* (pathol.) varicella, chicken-pox.
varicocèle [varikɔsɛl] *s.f.* (pathol.) varicocele.
varié, -e [varje] *adj.* varied, varying, diverse, diversified, miscellaneous; varicoloured; (bot.) variegated; *terrain* ~, broken country; (mus.) *air* ~, air with variations; (mech.) *mouvement* ~, variable movement.
varier [varje] *v.t.* to vary, to change, to variegate, to diversify; ~ *v.i.* to vary, to change, to fluctuate, to be inconsistent; (of wind) to veer; *sur ce point les opinions varient*, opinions differ on this point.
variété [varjete] *s.f.* **1.** variety, diversity, many--sidedness; **2.** variety, specimen, kind, (pl.) miscellanea, varieties; *spectacle de* ~*s*, variety show.
variole [varjɔl] *s.f.* (pathol.) variola, smallpox.
variolé, -e [varjɔle] *adj.* pock-marked.
varioleu-x, -se [varjɔlø] *adj.* suffering from smallpox, variolous; *s.m.f.* smallpox case.
variolique [varjɔlik] *adj.* variolous; *éruption* ~, smallpox pustule or spot.
varioloïde [varjɔlɔid] *s.f.* varioloid.
variomètre [varjɔmɛtr] *s.m.* (electr., aeron.) variometer.
variqueu-x, -se [varikø] *adj.* (pathol.) varicose.
varlet [varlɛ] *s.m.* (feud.) varlet.
varlope [varlɔp] *s.f.* jointing-plane, try-plane.
varloper [varlɔpe] *v.t.* to plane (with the jointing-plane).
Varsovie [varsɔvi] *s.f.* (geog.) Warsaw.
vasard, -e [vɑzar] *adj.* muddy; ~ *s.m.* muddy bottom.
vasculaire [vaskylɛr] *adj.* (anat., bot.) vascular.
vase [vɑz] *s.f.* mud, mire, slime, ooze.
vase [vɑz] *s.m.* vase; vessel; ~ *d'élection*, chosen vessel; (phys.) ~*s communicants*, communicating vessels (linked by U-tube); ~ *de nuit*, chamber--pot.
vaseline [vazlin] *s.f.* vaseline.
vaseu-x, -se [vɑzø] *adj.* muddy, slimy; (fig., obs.) vile; (fig.) out-of-sorts, weak, weary; woolly, murky.
vasière [vɑzjɛr] *s.f.* **1.** bog, marshy ground; **2.** basin in salt-marsh; **3.** mussel-bed.
vasistas [vazistɑs] *s.m.* small hinged panel in door or window.
vaso-mot-eur, -rice [vɑzɔmɔtœr] *adj.* (physiol.) vaso-motor.
vasouiller [vazuje] *v.t.* (fam.) to hesitate, to fumble; to go badly, to go wrong.
vasque [vask] *s.f.* basin (of a fountain); shallow bowl.
vassal, -e, (**aux**) [vasal] *s.m.f.* (feud. & fig.) vassal.
vassalité [vasalite] *s.f.*, **vasselage** [vaslaʒ] *s.m.* vassalage, bondage, subjection.
vaste [vast] *adj.* vast, wide, spacious; capacious; comprehensive; (anat.) *muscle* ~, vastus muscle.
vaticane [vatikan] *adj.f.* Vatican.
vaticination [vatisinɑsjɔ̃] *s.f.* vaticination, prophecy.
vaticiner [vatisine] *v.i.* to vaticinate, to prophesy.
va-tout [vatu] *s.m.invar.* (cards) *faire* ~, to stake everything; (fig.) *jouer son* ~, to stake or risk all.
vaudeville [vodvil] *s.m.* vaudeville.
vaudevilliste [vodvilist] *s.m.* writer of vaudeville.
vaudois, -e [vodwɑ] *adj.*, *s.m.f.* Vaudois, (native or inhabitant) of the Canton de Vaud (Switzerland); *adj.* (eccles. hist.) Waldensian; ~ *s.m.pl.* Waldenses, Vaudois.
(**à**) **vau-l'eau** [avolo] *adv.loc.* with the current, downstream; adrift; (fig.) into thin air; *aller à* ~, to drift, to have lost one's bearings.
vaurien, -ne [vorjɛ̃] *s.m.f.* good-for-nothing; rogue, vagabond, scamp.
vautour [votur] *s.m.* (ornith. & fig.) vulture.
vautrait [votrɛ] *s.m.* pack of boar-hounds.
(**se**) **vautrer** [votre] *v.refl.* to wallow, to sprawl; (fig.) to revel (in).
(**à**) **vau-vent** [avovɑ̃] *adv.loc.* (hunt.) downwind.
vavasseur [vavasœr] *s.m.* (feud.) vavasour.
V.D.Q.S. [vedekyɛs] abbrev. *Vin Délimité de Qualité Supérieure.*
veau (pl. **-x**) [vo] *s.m.* **1.** calf; *tuer le* ~ *gras*, to kill the fatted calf; *le* ~ *d'or*, the golden calf, worldly wealth; **2.** (meat) veal; **3.** (leather) calf, calfskin; **4.** (fig.) dolt; **5.** ~ *marin*, seal; sealskin; **6.** *pleurer comme un* ~, to cry like a baby; *faire le* ~, *s'étendre comme un* ~, to sprawl, to lounge, to loll.
vecteur [vɛktœr] *s.m.*, *adj.m.* (geom.) vector; *rayon* ~, radius vector.
vectoriel, -le [vɛktɔrjɛl] *adj.* vectorial.
vécu, -e [veky] *adj.* true to life, real, sincere; *histoire* ~*e*, true(-life) story; ~ *s.m.* actual experience.
vedette [vədɛt] *s.f.* **1.** vedette, scout, mounted sentinel; motor boat, launch; **2.** (film, etc.)

star; *avoir la* ~, to star, to have one's name in big letters; (fig.) *tenir la* ~, to be the main attraction or interest; **3.** (print.) *mettre en* ~, to print on a line by itself; to print in large type; (fig.) to give prominence to, to highlight.

védique [vedik] *adj.* Vedic.

végétal, -e, (**aux**) [veʒetal] *adj.* vegetal, plant, vegetable (as distinct from *animal* and *mineral*); ~ *s.m.* plant, vegetable.

végétalisme [veʒetalism] *s.m.* veganism.

végétarien, -ne [veʒetarjɛ̃] *adj., s.m.f.* vegetarian.

végétarisme [veʒetarism] *s.m.* vegetarianism.

végétati-f, -ve [veʒetatif] *adj.* vegetative; *mener une vie* ~*ve*, to vegetate; to lead a monotonous life.

végétation [veʒetɑsjɔ̃] *s.f.* **1.** vegetation; **2.** (pathol.) ~*s* (*adénoïdes*), adenoids, adenoidal growth.

végéter [veʒete] *v.i.* to vegetate, to grow; (fig.) to vegetate.

véhémence [veemɑ̃s] *s.f.* vehemence, impetuosity.

véhément, -e [veemɑ̃] *adj.* vehement, ardent, impetuous, fiery; ~**ement** [veemɑ̃tmɑ̃] *adv.* vehemently.

véhicule [veikyl] *s.m.* vehicle, conveyance; (fig.) carrier, vehicle, medium; ~ *spatial*, space vehicle.

véhiculer [veikyle] *v.t.* to transport; (fig.) to convey, to act as a carrier of.

veille [vɛj] *s.f.* **1.** watching, waking, sleeplessness; (pl.) working at night; staying up, sitting up; late hours; **2.** waking, being awake, wakefulness; watchman; (naut.) *homme de* ~, watch; *entre le sommeil et la* ~, between sleeping and waking; **3.** vigil, eve, day before; *à la* ~ *de*, on the day before, on the eve of; (fig.) on the point or verge or brink of, just before; (naut.) *ancre de* ~, sheet-anchor.

veillée [veje] *s.f.* **1.** evening (in company); time between the last meal and bedtime; *les* ~*s d'hiver*, the winter evenings; *passer la* ~ *chez son voisin*, to pass the evening with one's neighbour; ~ (also *veille*) *d'armes*, vigil (of knight before receiving arms); (fig.) period of moral or spiritual preparation; **2.** sitting up (with the sick); vigil (by a dead body), wake.

veiller [veje] *v.t.i.* **1.** to sit up, to keep watch; to be awake, to be watchful or alert; *faire* ~ *qn.*, to keep s.o. up; **2.** to be on the watch (*à*, for), to have an eye (*à*, to), to keep an eye (*sur*, on), to watch (*sur*, *à*, over); ~ *à faire*, to be careful to do; ~ *à ce que*, to see to it that; ~ *au grain*, (i.) (naut.) to look out for squalls; (ii.) to spare expense, to live sparingly; **3.** to watch by (the dead); to sit up with, to nurse at night.

veilleu-r, -se [vɛjœr] *s.m.f.* one who sits up or keeps watch or vigil; ~**r** *s.m.* guard, watchman; ~*r de nuit*, night-watchman, night-porter; ~**se** *s.f.* night-light, night-lamp; pilot-light; *mettre en* ~*se*, to turn down, to dim.

veinard, -e [vɛnar] *adj., s.m.f.* (fam.) lucky (person).

veine [vɛn] *s.f.* **1.** (anat., bot.) vein; ~ *cave*, vena cava; ~ *porte*, vena portae, portal vein; *être en* ~, to be inspired, to be in good form; (fig.) *se saigner aux quatre* ~*s*, to bleed oneself white; **2.** (geol.) seam, vein; **3.** (poetic, etc.) inspiration; **4.** (fig.) luck; ~ *de cocu* or *de pendu*, the devil's own luck.

veiné, -e [vene] *adj.* veined, veiny.

veiner [vene] *v.t.* to vein, to grain; to streak.

veinette [vɛnɛt] *s.f.* graining-brush.

veineu-x, -se [vɛnø] *adj.* venous, venose; veined, strongly-grained.

veinule [venyl] *s.f.* small vein.

veinure [venyr] *s.f.* grain (of wood); veining.

vêlage [vɛlaʒ], **vêlement** [vɛlmɑ̃] *s.m.* calving.

vélaire [velɛr] *adj., s.f.* (phon.) velar.

velche, welche [vɛlʃ] *s.m.* foreigner (esp. used by Germans of French and Italians).

veld, veldt [vɛlt] *s.m.* veld(t).

vêler [vele] *v.i.* to calve.

vélin [velɛ̃] *s.m.* parchment, vellum.

vélite [velit] *s.m.* **1.** (Rom. ant.) veles; **2.** (pl.) corps of volunteers organized by Napoleon.

velléitaire [veleitɛr] *adj., s.m.f.* indecisive (person).

velléité [veleite] *s.f.* whim, vague inclination; faint attempt; trace; *une* ~ *de sourire*, a ghost of a smile.

vélo [velo] *s.m.* bicycle, bike; cycling.

véloce [velɔs] *adj.* swift, agile; ~**ment** [velɔsmɑ̃] *adv.* swiftly, rapidly.

vélocipède [velɔsipɛd] *s.m.* bicycle, velocipede.

vélocité [velɔsite] *s.f.* velocity, speed.

vélodrome [velɔdrɔm] *s.m.* cycling-stadium, cycle-track.

vélomoteur [velɔmɔtœr] *s.m.* motor cycle (50–125 c.c.).

vélo-pousse [velɔpus] *s.m.* (pl. *vélos-pousse*) bicycle-rickshaw, trishaw.

velot [vəlo] *s.m.* skin of stillborn calf.

velours [vəlur] *s.m.* velvet (also fig.); ~ *côtelé* or *à côtes*, ribbed velvet, corduroy; ~ *de coton*, velveteen; *faire patte de* ~, to draw in one's claws, (fig.) to show the velvet glove; *jouer sur le* ~, to play on velvet, to run no risk of failure.

velouté, -e [vəlute] *adj.* velvety, velvet, soft as velvet; mellow, bland, smooth, creamy; ~ *s.m.* velvet texture, velvety feel; bloom (of peach); blandness, creaminess; cream soup; velouté (sauce); ~ *d'asperges*, cream of asparagus soup.

velouter [vəlute] *v.t.* to give (a material) the appearance of velvet; to make soft as velvet; (fig.) to soften; (cook.) to cream; **se** ~ *v.refl.* to show a velvety texture or bloom, to take on a mellow tone.

velouteu-x, -se [vəlutø] *adj.* velvety, soft as velvet.

veloutier [vəlutje] *s.m.* velvet-weaver.

veloutine [vəlutin] *s.f.* flannelette.

velu, -e [vəly] *adj.* hairy; shaggy; (bot.) pubescent.

velum, vélum [velɔm] *s.m.* awning, canopy.

velvet [vɛlvɛt] *s.m. s.f.* velveteen.

velvote [vɛlvɔt] *s.f.* (bot.) toadflax.

venaison [vənɛzɔ̃] *s.f.* venison.

vénal, -e, (**aux**) [venal] *adj.* venal, that can be bought, corrupt, mercenary; (comm.) *valeur* ~*e*, market value; ~**ement** [venalmɑ̃] *adv.* venally, corruptly.

vénalité [venalite] *s.f.* venality, corruption.

venant, -e [vənɑ̃] *adj.* coming; ~ *s.m.* comer; *les allants et les* ~*s*, those coming and going, passers-by; *à tout* ~, to the first comer, to all and sundry.

vendable [vɑ̃dabl] *adj.* saleable, vendible.

vendange [vɑ̃dɑ̃ʒ] *s.f.* grape-harvest; grape-gathering; the grapes harvested, wine-harvest, vintage; (pl.) *les* ~*s*, the vintage, the season of grape-harvest; (proverb) *adieu paniers,* ~*s sont faites*, all good things come to an end.

vendanger [vɑ̃dɑ̃ʒe] *v.t.i.* to harvest the grapes; to gather the grapes from the vineyard.

vendangette [vɑ̃dɑ̃ʒɛt] *s.f.* (dial.) thrush (bird).

vendangeu-r, -se [vɑ̃dɑ̃ʒœr] *s.m.f.* vintager, grape-gatherer, grape-harvester.

vendéen, -ne [vɑ̃deɛ̃] *adj., s.m.f.* Vendean, (native or inhabitant) of la Vendée.

vendémiaire [vɑ̃demjɛr] *s.m.* (hist.) Vendémiaire (first month in Fr. Republican Calendar, September–October).

vendetta [vãdeta] *s.f.* vendetta.
vendeu-r, -se [vãdœr] *s.m.f.* salesman, saleswoman; shop assistant, shop-girl; vendor.
vendre [vãdr] *v.t.* to sell, to vend; (fig.) to sell; to betray; (law) to sell up (a person); ~ *cher*, to sell at a high price, to exact a high price for; (fig.) ~ *cher* or *chèrement sa vie*, to sell one's life dearly; ~ *la mèche*, to betray the plot; to let the cat out of the bag; **se** ~ *v.refl.* to sell oneself; to sell, to be sold, to be on, or for, sale.
vendredi [vãdrədi] *s.m.* Friday; ~ *saint*, Good Friday.
vendu, -e [vãdy] *adj.* sold; (fig., pej.) corrupt, venal; ~ *s.m.* traitor.
venelle [vənɛl] *s.f.* alley; *enfiler la* ~, to take to one's heels.
vénéneu-x, -se [venenø] *adj.* poisonous, venomous.
vénérable [venerabl] *adj.* venerable.
vénération [venerɑsjɔ̃] *s.f.* veneration, reverence, worship.
vénérer [venere] *v.t.* to venerate, to reverence, to worship.
vénerie [venri] *s.f.* hunting; administration of hunts.
vénérien, -ne [venerjɛ̃] *adj.* venereal; *s.m.f.* one suffering from venereal disease.
vénéréologie [venereɔlɔʒi], **vénérologie** [venerɔlɔʒi] *s.f.* venereology.
venette [vənɛt] *s.f.* (fam.) fear; *avoir la* ~, to get the wind up.
veneur [vənœr] *s.m.* huntsman; *Grand* ~, King's huntsman.
vénézuélien, -ne [venezɥeljɛ̃] *adj., s.m.f.* Venezuelan.
vengeance [vãʒɑ̃s] *s.f.* vengeance, revenge, retribution; *crier* ~, to cry aloud for vengeance; *tirer* ~ *de*, to be avenged for; *exercer* or *tirer sa* ~ *sur*, to avenge oneself on, to be revenged on; *ne respirer que la* ~, to breathe vengeance.
venger [vãʒe] *v.t.* to avenge, to revenge; **se** ~ *v.refl.* to avenge oneself (*de*, upon), to be revenged, to take vengeance.
vengeur [vãʒœr], **vengeresse** [vãʒrɛs] *s.m.f.* avenger, revenger; *adj.* avenging, revengeful.
véniel, -le [venjɛl] *adj.* venial; **~lement** [venjɛlmã] *adv.* venially.
venimeu-x, -se [vənimø] *adj.* venomous; (fig.) spiteful, malignant.
venimosité [vənimozite] *s.f.* venomousness.
venin [vənɛ̃] *s.m.* poison, venom; (fig.) venom, rancour, malice, spite; *il a jeté tout son* ~, he has vented all his spite.
venir [vənir] *v.i.* to come, to be coming, to arrive, to approach, to appear, to occur; ~ *à*, *jusqu'à*, to reach, to come to, to arrive at, to approach; ~ *à faire*, to happen to, to chance to do; ~ *de*, to come from, to issue, to emanate, to be derived from; ~ *de faire*, to have just done; ~ *trouver*, to come and see; ~ *prendre*, to come and fetch; (naut.) ~ *sur bâbord*, *tribord*, to turn to port, to starboard; *voici mon ami qui vient*, *voici* ~ *mon ami*, here comes my friend, here is my friend coming; *les jours qui viennent*, the days to come; *le train venu de Paris*, the train from Paris; *le premier venu*, the first comer, the first thing to hand; *un nouveau-venu*, a newcomer; *être bien*, *mal*, *venu*, to be welcome, unwelcome; *il serait mal venu d'insister*, it would be improper, or ungracious, to insist; *d'où vient cela?*, what is the cause of that?; *d'où vient que?*, how is it that?; *il prend le temps comme il vient*, he takes things as they come; (fig.) ~ *à bout de*, to master, to overcome, to cope with; to see the end of; to accomplish, to achieve, to bring to a conclusion; ~ *à rien*, to come to nothing, to fail; *laisser* ~ *les choses*, to let things take their course; *voir* ~ *les événements*, to await developments, to see how things turn out; *je vous vois* ~*!*, I see what you're after, what you are getting at!; *il me vint une pensée*, a thought struck me; it occurred to me, *il me vient à l'esprit* or *dans l'idée*, it occurs to me, the idea enters my head; *il vient de sortir*, he has just gone out; *je viens le voir*, I have come to see him; (in writing) *je viens vous remercier*, I am writing to thank you; *se faire bien* ~ *(de)*, to ingratiate oneself (with); *faire* ~, to send for, to call, to summon, to have fetched or sent; *en* ~ *à*, to come to, to come to the point of, to be reduced to; *en* ~ *aux mains*, to come to blows; *les choses en sont-elles venues là?*, have things come to such a pass?; *où voulez-vous en* ~*?*, what are you driving at?; *il s'en est allé comme il est venu*, he made his journey, his effort, for nothing; ~ *au monde*, to be born; (proverb) *tout vient à point à qui sait attendre*, everything comes to him who waits; *je ne ferai qu'aller et* ~, I'll be back in a minute; ~ *bien*, to thrive, to do well, to come out well; *on vint à parler de la guerre*, the conversation turned upon the war; *si ma lettre venait à se perdre*, if my letter should get lost; *vienne une maladie*, should illness occur.
Venise [v(ə)niz] *s.f.* (geog.) Venice.
vénitien, -ne [venisjɛ̃] *adj., s.m.f.* Venetian; *lanterne* ~*ne*, Chinese lantern.
vent [vã] *s.m.* **1.** wind, breeze; (fig.) wind, vanity, emptiness; *être logé aux quatre* ~*s*, to be exposed to every wind of heaven; ~ *fort*, gale; ~ *frais*, stiff breeze; *coup de* ~, gust of wind; ~*s alizés*, trade-winds; *faire* or *aller* ~ *arrière*, to run before the wind; ~ *debout*, head wind; wind in the teeth; *aller contre* ~*s et marées*, to have wind and tide against one; (fig.) to be up against it; *avoir le* ~ *en poupe*, to sail before the wind; (fig.) to be on the high road to success; *pincer*, *serrer*, *tenir*, *le* ~, to hug the wind; *au plus près du* ~, close-hauled; *passer au* ~ *de*, to keep to windward of; *bord du* ~, weather side; windward; *bord sous le* ~, lee side; leeward; *au gré du* ~, at the mercy of the wind, floating in the breeze; (fig.) *regarder de quel côté vient le* ~, to see how the land lies; (proverb) *autant en emporte le* ~, words, words, words!, it is all idle talk; *tout cela n'est que du* ~, that's all moonshine; *en coup de* ~, precipitately; *arbre de* (or *en*) *plein* ~, standard tree; *quel bon* ~ *vous amène?*, what lucky chance brings you here?; *en plein* ~, in the open air; *venir des quatre* ~*s*, to come from the four corners of the earth; (fig.) *avoir du* ~ *dans les voiles*, to be tipsy, to be three sheets in the wind; (proverb) *qui sème le* ~ *récolte la tempête*, he that sows the wind shall reap the whirlwind; (proverb) *selon le* ~ *la voile*, one must cut one's coat according to one's cloth; (techn.) *machine à* ~, blower; *il fait du* ~, it is windy, there is a wind; *avec le* ~ *qu'il fait*, in a wind like this; (fig.) *tourner à tout* ~, to be a weathercock; (fig.) *le nez au* ~, with one's head in the clouds; *avoir des* ~*s*, to be troubled with wind; to break wind; **2.** (hunt.) scent, wind; *avoir le* ~ *de*, to get the scent of; (fig.) *avoir* ~ *de*, to get wind of, to suspect; *n'avoir ni* ~ *ni nouvelle de qn.*, not to hear a word from s.o.
ventage [vãtaʒ] winnowing.
vente [vãt] *s.f.* sale; selling, auction; *en* ~, for sale; (of book) now published; *hors de* ~, unsaleable, no longer on sale, withdrawn; *marchandises de bonne* ~, goods that sell well; *mettre en* ~, to put up for sale, to publish (book); *en* ~ *chez*, sold by, on sale at; ~ *de charité*, charity bazaar; *salle des* ~*s*, auction-rooms, sale-rooms, auction-mart.
venteau (pl. **-x**) [vãto] *s.m.* (techn.) air-hole (in bellows).
venter [vãte] *v.impers.* (of wind) to blow; to be

windy; *qu'il pleuve ou qu'il vente*, whatever the weather, come rain or shine.
venteu-x, -se [vɑ̃tø] *adj.* windy.
ventilateur [vɑ̃tilatœr] *s.m.* ventilator, fan, blower, ventilation duct or aperture.
ventilation [vɑ̃tilɑsjɔ̃] *s.f.* **1.** ventilation; **2.** (law) see VENTILER 2.
ventiler [vɑ̃tile] *v.t.* **1.** to ventilate, to air; **2.** (law) to value separately (objects sold together); (fin.) to apportion (a total under different heads of account).
ventis [vɑ̃ti] *s.m.pl.* (forest.) fallen trees, wind-fallen timber.
ventôse [vɑ̃toz] *s.m.* (hist.) Ventose (6th month in Fr. Republican Calendar, February–March).
ventouse [vɑ̃tuz] *s.f.* **1.** cupping-glass; cupping; **2.** (zool.) sucker; (techn.) suction-cup; *faire* ~, to adhere by suction; **3.** vent, vent-hole, air-hole.
ventral, -e, (aux) [vɑ̃tral] *adj.* abdominal; (anat., zool.) ventral.
ventre [vɑ̃tr] *s.m.* abdomen, belly; stomach, tummy (fam.); paunch; guts; womb; bowels; bulge; hollow portion or space; *à plat* ~, flat on the face; *se mettre à plat* ~ *devant*, to abase oneself before, to crawl to; *courir* ~ *à terre*, to go at full gallop, to run like a hare; to ride hell for leather; *avoir mal au* ~, to have internal pains; to have a stomach-ache; *bas-*~, abdomen, genital organs (esp. female); *avoir du* ~, to be getting fat, to be getting a paunch or a tummy; to be pot-bellied; *prendre du* ~, to get stout, to develop a paunch; (fig.) *il a quelque chose dans le* ~, he has something about him, he has got guts; *il n'a rien dans le* ~, he is starving; he is a useless sort of person; *je sais ce qu'il a dans le* ~, I know what he has got in him; I know what he is up to; (proverb) ~ *affamé n'a point d'oreilles*, it is no use preaching to a hungry man; (fig.) *se serrer le* ~, to tighten one's belt; *au large* ~, squat, fat; *faire* ~, to bulge out; *il n'a pas trois mois dans le* ~, he hasn't three months to live; (fig.) *à* ~ *déboutonné*, to excess; in an unrestrained way; *dès le* ~ *de sa mère*, from his mother's womb.
ventrebleu [vɑ̃trəblø], **ventre-saint-gris** [vɑ̃trəsɛ̃gri] *interj.* archaic expletives.
ventrée [vɑ̃tre] *s.f.* bellyful.
ventriculaire [vɑ̃trikylɛr] *adj.* ventricular.
ventricule [vɑ̃trikyl] *s.m.* (anat.) ventricle.
ventrière [vɑ̃trijɛr] *s.f.* girth (of horse); (techn.) purlin, cross-tree; (naut.) bilge-block.
ventriloque [vɑ̃trilɔk] *adj.* ventriloquous; ~ *s.m.f.* ventriloquist.
ventriloquie [vɑ̃trilɔki] *s.f.* ventriloquy.
ventripotent, -e [vɑ̃tripɔtɑ̃] *adj.* corpulent, big-bellied.
ventru, -e [vɑ̃try] *adj.* corpulent, obese, pot-bellied; bulging, (well-)rounded, protruding, projecting; (techn.) dished.
venturi [vɑ̃tyri] *s.m.* (techn.) venturi(-tube), choke (of carburettor).
venu, -e [vəny] *adj.* see VENIR.
venue [vəny] *s.f.* **1.** coming, arrival, advent; (pl.) *allées et* ~*s*, comings and goings; **2.** growth; *arbre d'une belle* ~, well-grown tree; *tout d'une* ~, in a single piece, (lit. & fig.) straight up and down; ⚠ not 'venue' in sense 'meeting-place'.
vénusté [venyste] *s.f.* charm, beauty, sex-appeal.
vêpres [vɛpr] *s.f.pl.* vespers.
ver [vɛr] *s.m.* worm; maggot, grub, larva; moth; *mangé* or *rongé des* ~*s*, moth-eaten; ~ *solitaire*, tapeworm; ~ *luisant*, glow-worm; (fig.) ~ *rongeur*, canker, thorn in the flesh, remorse; (fam.) *tirer les* ~*s du nez à qn.*, to worm secrets out of s.o.; *nu comme un* ~, stark naked; *tuer le* ~, to keep the damp out (by drinking an early glass of spirits).
véracité [verasite] *s.f.* veracity, truthfulness; truth.
véraison [verɛzɔ̃] *s.f.* turning, ripening (especially of grapes).
véranda [verɑ̃da] *s.f.* veranda(h).
vératre [veratr] *s.m.* (bot.) Veratrum.
verbal, -e, (aux) [vɛrbal] *adj.* verbal; oral, by word of mouth; ~**ement** [vɛrbalmɑ̃] *adv.* verbally, orally, by word of mouth, in words.
verbalisation [vɛrbalizɑsjɔ̃] *s.f.* verbalization; (police) making of a report, taking of particulars.
verbaliser [vɛrbalize] *v.i.* to make a report (with a view to prosecution), to take down particulars (of an accident, etc.).
verbe [vɛrb] *s.m.* **1.** verb; **2.** tone of voice, speech; *avoir le* ~ *haut*, to have a domineering way of talking; **3.** (theol.) *le Verbe*, the Word.
verbénacées [vɛrbenase] *s.f.pl.* (bot.) Verbenaceae.
verbeu-x, -se [vɛrbø] *adj.* verbose, long-winded, prolix.
verbiage [vɛrbjaʒ] *s.m.* verbiage, prattle, nonsense.
verbosité [vɛrbozite] *s.f.* verbosity.
ver-coquin [vɛrkɔkɛ̃] *s.m.* **1.** (vet.) staggers; worm causing staggers; **2.** vine-grub.
verdâtre [vɛrdɑtr] *adj.* greenish.
verdelet, -te [vɛrdəlɛ] *adj.* (of wine) tart, acid.
verdet [vɛrdɛ] *s.m.* verdigris.
verdeur [vɛrdœr] *s.f.* **1.** greenness; viridity; sap (of wood); **2.** acidity, tartness, (of wine); **3.** (fig.) vigour, vitality, (of the not-so-young); **4.** (in speech) spicinesss, freedom, frankness.
verdict [vɛrdikt] *s.m.* verdict.
verdier[1] [vɛrdje] *s.m.* (ornith.) greenfinch.
verdier[2] [vɛrdje] *s.m.* verderer, ranger.
verdir [vɛrdir] *v.t.* to make or paint green; ~ *v.i.* to grow green, to turn green.
verdissant, -e [vɛrdisɑ̃] *adj.* turning green, verdant.
verdoyant, -e [vɛrdwajɑ̃] *adj.* verdant, green.
verdoyer [vɛrdwaje] *v.i.* to be verdant, to show green.
verdure [vɛrdyr] *s.f.* **1.** verdure, greenness; **2.** greenery, greenstuff, salad; **3.** tapestry representing mainly foliage.
véreu-x, -se [verø] *adj.* **1.** worm-eaten, maggoty; rotten; **2.** (fig.) dubious, suspect, shady; shaky.
verge [verʒ] *s.f.* rod, staff, verge; switch, wand, whisk; (mech.) spindle, pin; shank (of an anchor); (anat.) penis; (fig.) *donner des* ~*s pour se faire fouetter*, to lay up a rod for one's own back; *huissier à* ~, verger; (bot.) ~ *d'or*, golden-rod; ⚠ not 'verge' in sense 'edge'.
vergé, -e [verʒe] *adj.* **1.** (of paper) laid; **2.** (of textile fabrics) streaky.
verger [vɛrʒe] *s.m.* orchard.
vergetier [vɛrʒətje] *s.m.* **1.** broom-maker, brush-maker; **2.** (metall.) drawer of iron rods.
vergette [vɛrʒɛt] *s.f.* **1.** small cane or switch; **2.** (obs.) clothes-brush.
vergeture [vɛrʒətyr] *s.f.* (usu. pl.) streak, stria.
verglacé, -e [vɛrglase] *adj.* covered with thin, slippery ice; *routes* ~*es*, icy roads.
verglas [vɛrgla] *s.m.* ice, black ice, icy surface, icy conditions, glazed frost, frozen rain.
vergne [vɛrɲ] *s.m.* alder.
vergogne [vɛrgɔɲ] *s.f.* (obs.) shame, modesty; *sans* ~, shamelessly.
vergue [vɛrg] *s.f.* (naut.) yard; *bout de* ~, yard-arm.
véridicité [veridisite] *s.f.* veracity, truthfulness, truth; accuracy.
véridique [veridik] *adj.* veracious, veridical, truthful, honest, credible, true, accurate; ~**ment** [veridikmɑ̃] *adv.* truthfully, honestly, accurately.

vérifiable [verifjabl] *adj.* verifiable, ascertainable.

vérificat-eur, -rice [verifikatœr] *s.m.f.* verifier, inspector, examiner, checker, tester, auditor (of accounts); gauge; (*appareil*) *~eur*, testing-machine, tester.

vérification [verifikasjɔ̃] *s.f.* verification; examining, auditing.

vérifier [verifje] *v.t.* to verify, to inspect, to examine, to check, to test; to audit (accounts); to prove, to confirm, to justify.

vérin [verɛ̃] *s.m.* (car, etc.) jack.

vérine [verin], **verrine** [vɛrin] *s.f.* (naut.) tripping-line.

véritable [veritabl] *adj.* true, genuine, real, lifelike; staunch; (fig.) thorough, regular, complete, downright; **~ment** [veritabləmɑ̃] *adv.* truthfully, in truth, really, truly, veritably.

vérité [verite] *s.f.* truth, verity, truthfulness, sincerity; fact; certainty; *sa réponse avait l'accent de la ~*, his answer rang true; *dire à qn. ses ~s*, to tell s.o. a few home truths; *à la ~*, I confess; to tell the truth; as a matter of fact; *en ~*, indeed, truly; in point of fact; (proverb) *toutes ~s ne sont pas bonnes à dire*, it is not always wise to speak the truth; *~ banale*, truism; *il n'y a que la ~ qui offense*, nothing hurts like the truth.

verjus [vɛrʒy] *s.m.* verjuice; juice of unripe grapes.

vermeil, -le [vɛrmɛj] *adj.* vermilion, bright red; rosy, ruddy; *lèvres ~les*, ruby lips; *~ s.m.* silver gilt, vermeil.

vermicelle [vɛrmisɛl] *s.m.* vermicelli.

vermiculaire [vɛrmikylɛr] *adj.* vermicular, vermiform.

vermiculé, -e [vɛrmikyle] *adj.* vermiculated.

vermiculure [vɛrmikylyr] *s.f.* (arch.) vermiculation.

vermiforme [vɛrmifɔrm] *adj.* vermiform.

vermifuge [vɛrmifyʒ] *s.m.* (pharm.) vermifuge; *~ adj.* vermifugal.

vermiller [vɛrmije] *v.i.* (of boars, pigs, etc.) to root.

vermillon [vɛrmijɔ̃] *s.m.* vermilion.

vermine [vɛrmin] *s.f.* vermin; (fig.) rabble, pest.

vermineu-x, -se [vɛrminø] *adj.* verminous.

vermisseau (pl. **-x**) [vɛrmiso] *s.m.* small worm, grub; (fig.) (mere) worm.

vermivore [vɛrmivɔr] *adj.* vermivorous.

(se) vermouler [vɛrmule] *v.refl.* to become worm-eaten.

vermoulu, -e [vɛrmuly] *adj.* worm-eaten; dilapidated; (fig.) decrepit, mouldering.

vermoulure [vɛrmulyr] *s.f.* worm-hole; dust from worm-holes, worm-eaten state.

vermout, vermouth [vɛrmut] *s.m.* vermouth.

vernaculaire [vɛrnakylɛr] *adj.* vernacular.

vernal, -e, (aux) [vɛrnal] *adj.* vernal, spring, springlike.

vernalisation [vɛrnalizasjɔ̃] *s.f.* (agric.) vernalization.

verni, -e [vɛrni] *adj.* varnished, japanned, glazed; shiny, shining; *souliers ~s*, patent-leather shoes; (fig., fam.) *être ~(e)*, to be very lucky, to bear a charmed life.

vernier [vɛrnje] *s.m.* vernier (instrument).

vernir [vɛrnir] *v.t.* to varnish; to glaze, to polish; to lacquer, to japan; (fig.) to gloss over.

vernis [vɛrni] *s.m.* varnish, polish, glaze, gloss, glazings; (fig., pej.) veneer; *donner un ~ à*, to give a gloss to, to set off; (pej.) to varnish over.

vernissage [vɛrnisaʒ] *s.m.* **1.** varnishing, glazing; **2.** private view of a picture-exhibition.

vernissé, -e [vɛrnise] *adj.* glazed, glossy.

vernisser [vɛrnise] *v.t.* to glaze (pottery).

vernisseu-r, -se [vɛrnisœr] *s.m.f.* varnisher.

vérole [verɔl] *s.f.* (pathol.) (*petite*) ~ = VARIOLE; (pop.) pox, syphilis.

vérolé, -e [verɔle] *adj.* (pop.) syphilitic.

Vérone [verɔn] *s.f.* (geog.) Verona.

véronique [verɔnik] *s.f.* **1.** (relig. relic) veronica; **2.** (bot.) veronica; **3.** pass (in bullfighting).

verrat [vɛra] *s.m.* breeding boar.

verre [vɛr] *s.m.* glass; lens; (pl.) glasses, spectacles; *~ à boire*, glass, drinking-glass, tumbler; *~ à pied*, rummer, wineglass, stemmed glass; *~ à vitre*, window glass, sheet glass; *~ dépoli*, frosted glass; *papier de ~*, glass-paper, sandpaper; *une tempête dans un ~ d'eau*, a storm in a teacup; *boire un petit ~*, to have a brandy, to drink a liqueur, to take a nip; *~ grossissant*, magnifying-glass; *laine* or *coton de ~*, glass-fibre.

verré, -e [vɛre] *adj.* coated with powdered glass; *papier ~*, glass-paper, sandpaper.

verrerie [vɛrri] *s.f.* glassware; glass-works; glass-making.

verrier [vɛrje] *s.m.* **1.** glass-maker, glass-blower; *peintre ~*, artist in stained glass; **2.** dealer in glassware.

verrière [vɛrjɛr] *s.f.* **1.** (obs.) large stained-glass window; (mod.) large glass window, glass wall, glass roof, glass casing; **2.** (aeron.) cockpit-cover, perspex dome.

verrine[1] [vɛrin] *s.f.* **1.** (naut.) binnacle-lamp; **2.** (techn.) bulkhead fitting (protecting lamp).

verrine[2] [vɛrin] *s.f.* see VERINE.

verroterie [vɛrɔtri] *s.f.* glass beads, glass trinkets; small glassware.

verrou [vɛru] *s.m.* bolt, bar; breech-bolt (of shot-gun); (rail.) point-lock; (mil.) plugging (a gap); *s'enfermer au ~*, to bolt oneself in; *fermer une porte au ~*, to bolt a door; *pousser* or *fermer le ~*, to slip the bolt; (fig.) *sous les ~s*, locked up, in prison, behind bars.

verrouillage [vɛrujaʒ] *s.m.* bolting, locking; (mil.) plugging (of a gap).

verrouiller [vɛruje] *v.t.* to bolt, to lock; to block, to stop, to plug (a gap); to lock in or up, to shut up, to put behind bars.

verrucaire [vɛrykɛr] *s.f.* (bot.) wartwort.

verrue [vɛry] *s.f.* wart, verruca; (fig.) blemish, scar.

verruqueu-x, -se [vɛrykø] *adj.* verrucous, verrucose.

vers [vɛr] *s.m.* **1.** line (of poetry); **2.** (pl. in Fr.) verse, poetry; *faire des ~*, to write poetry; *écrire en ~*, to write in verse; *~ blancs*, blank verse; *mauvais* or *méchants ~*, doggerel; *~ libres*, vers libre, free verse; ⚠ not 'verse' in sense of a group of lines, nor 'verse' of the Bible.

vers [vɛr] *prep.* **1.** towards, to, in the direction of; **2.** (of time, age) about, around.

versant [vɛrsɑ̃] *s.m.* watershed, slope, declivity, side; *le ~ sud des Alpes*, the southern slopes of the Alps.

versatile [vɛrsatil] *adj.* fickle, inconstant; changeable; ⚠ not 'versatile'.

versatilité [vɛrsatilite] *s.f.* fickleness, changeableness; ⚠ not 'versatility'.

verse [vɛrs] *s.f.* **1.** *à ~*, in torrents; *il pleut à ~*, it is pouring, it's raining cats and dogs; **2.** beating down (of crops by rain, etc.).

versé, -e [vɛrse] *adj.* **1.** poured; spilt; (of crops) laid, beaten down, flattened; **2.** versed, experienced, conversant, (*dans*, in, with).

versement [vɛrsəmɑ̃] *s.m.* **1.** payment; instalment; *en plusieurs ~s*, by instalments; **2.** deposit.

verser *v.t.* [vɛrse] *v.t.* **1.** to pour, to pour out; to pour forth, to discharge, to empty; to shed; (mil.) to post, to draft, (to a unit, etc.); *~ à pleines mains*, to lavish; *~ une pièce au dossier*, to attach a document to the file; *versez-lui à boire*, fill his glass, or see that he has something to drink; *~ le sang de qn.*, to shed someone's blood;

~ *son sang*, to be wounded or die (for a cause); **2.** to spill, to upset, to overturn; to beat down, to lay, (crops); **3.** to pay in, to deposit (money); ~ *v.i.* to overturn; (of crops) to be beaten down.
verset [vɛrsɛ] *s.m.* verse (of Bible, psalm, etc.); (liturg.) versicle.
verseur [vɛrsœr] *s.m.* pourer, filler, dispenser, tipper.
verseuse [vɛrsøz] *s.f.* coffee-pot (with straight handle).
versicolore [vɛrsikɔlɔr] *adj.* versicoloured, variegated, of changing hue.
versiculet [vɛrsikylɛ] *s.m.* versicle, little verse.
versificateur [vɛrsifikatœr] *s.m.* versifier (esp. pej., opp. 'poet').
versification [vɛrsifikɑsjɔ̃] *s.f.* versification, poetic technique.
versifier [vɛrsifje] *v.i.* to write verse; ~ *v.t.* to put into verse.
version [vɛrsjɔ̃] *s.f.* translation (from foreign language); version, account.
verso [vɛrso] *s.m.* verso, back, reverse.
versoir [vɛrswar] *s.m.* mould-board (of a plough).
verste [vɛrst] *s.f.* verst, Russian measure of length = 3,500 feet.
vert, -e [vɛr] *adj.* **1.** green; verdant, grassy; (fig.) sharp, harsh; unripe, raw; sour, tart; *ils sont trop ~s*, sour grapes!, the grapes are sour; *bois ~*, green, unseasoned wood; *cuir ~*, rawhide, untanned leather; *le feu ~*, the green (traffic-) light; (fig.) *donner le feu ~ à*, to give the go--ahead to; ~ *de froid*, blue with cold; ~ *de peur*, white with fear; *une ~e réponse*, a sharp retort; *une ~e réprimande*, a severe reprimand, a stiff talking-to; **2.** (fig.) vigorous, hearty; spicy; *un vieillard encore ~*, a vigorous old man; *la ~e jeunesse*, the bloom of youth; (fam.) *en dire de ~es*, to tell dirty or risqué stories; *en dire de(s) ~es et de(s) pas mûres*, to tell scandalous stories; *une volée de bois ~*, a hail of blows; ~ *s.m.* green; *mettre un cheval au ~*, to put a horse out to grass; (fig.) *se mettre au ~*, to recuperate in the country; to lead, or to settle down to, a quiet life; *prendre qn. sans ~*, to catch s.o. napping, to catch s.o. out.
vert-de-gris [vɛrdəgri] *s.m.invar.* verdigris, copper acetate; ~ *adj.invar.* grey-green.
vert-de-grisé, -e [vɛrdegrize] *adj.* (pl. *vert-de--grisé(e)s*) covered with verdigris, or with a patina.
vertébral, -e, (**aux**) [vɛrtebral] *adj.* vertebral.
vertèbre [vɛrtɛbr] *s.f.* (anat.) vertebra.
vertébré, -e [vɛrtebre] *adj., s.m.* vertebrate; *les ~s*, the Vertebrata.
vertement [vɛrtəmɑ̃] *adv.* vigorously, briskly; sharply, soundly; harshly, severely; *je l'ai tancé ~*, I gave him a good dressing-down.
vertical, -e, (**aux**) [vɛrtikal] *adj.* vertical, plumb, upright; *plan ~*, vertical plane; ~ *s.m.* (astron.) vertical (circle); **~e** *s.f.* vertical, vertical line, plumb-line; **~ement** [vɛrtikalmɑ̃] *adv.* vertically.
verticalité [vɛrtikalite] *s.f.* verticality, vertical or upright position.
verticille [vɛrtisil] *s.m.* (bot.) verticil, whorl.
verticillé, -e [vɛrtisile] *adj.* (bot.) verticillate.
vertige [vɛrtiʒ] *s.m.* dizziness, vertigo, giddiness; (fig.) madness, intoxication; *à donner le ~*, (of heights, etc.) dizzy, impressive, stupendous.
vertigineu-x, -se [vɛrtiʒinø] *adj.* giddy, dizzy, vertiginous; (of speed) mad; *une hausse ~se*, an astronomic rise (of prices, etc.).
vertigo [vɛrtigo] *s.m.* **1.** (vet.) staggers; **2.** (fig.) whim; ⚠ not 'vertigo'.
vertu [vɛrty] *s.f.* **1.** virtue; (obs.) valour, moral courage; *faire de nécessité ~*, to make a virtue of necessity; **2.** chastity, virtue; **3.** quality, property, faculty, force; *en ~ de*, by virtue of; in pursuance of; on the strength of; on the ground of, on grounds of; in the name of; under (the terms of).
vertueu-x, -se [vɛrtɥø] *adj.* virtuous, chaste; **~sement** [vɛrtɥøzmɑ̃] *adv.* virtuously.
vertugadin [vɛrtygadɛ̃] *s.m.* farthingale.
verve [vɛrv] *s.f.* verve, spirit, animation, warmth, mettle, dash, go, gusto, zest; *être en ~*, to be animated; (fam.) to be in good form; *jouer avec ~*, to give a spirited performance.
verveine [vɛrvɛn] *s.f.* (bot.) vervain, verbena.
vervelle [vɛrvɛl] *s.f.* (falc.) varvel.
verveu-x, -se [vɛrvø] *adj.* animated, full of go, dashing, witty, lively, in high spirits.
verveux [vɛrvø] *s.m.* (fish.) hoop-net.
vésanie [vezani] *s.f.* (pathol.) insanity.
vesce [vɛs] *s.f.* (bot.) vetch, tare.
vésical, -e, (**aux**) [vezikal] *adj.* vesical, of the bladder, in the bladder.
vésicant, -e [vezikɑ̃] *adj., s.m.* (med.) vesicant.
vésication [vezikɑsjɔ̃] *s.f.* vesication.
vésicatoire [vezikatwar] *s.m.* vesicant; ~ *adj.* vesicatory.
vésiculaire [vezikylɛr] *adj.* vesicular.
vésicule [vezikyl] *s.f.* vesicle; bladder; blister (on the skin); ~ *biliaire*, gall-bladder.
vesou [vəzu] *s.m.* sugar-cane juice.
vespasienne [vɛspazjɛn] *s.f.* public urinal.
vespéral, -e, (**aux**) [vɛsperal] *adj.* vespertine.
vespertilion [vɛspɛrtiljɔ̃] *s.m.* (zool.) Vespertilio (bat).
vesse [vɛs] *s.f.* (vulg.) silent fart.
vesse-de-loup [vɛsdəlu] *s.m.* (pl. *vesses-de-loup*) (bot.) puff-ball, devil's snuff-box.
vesser [vese] *v.i.* (vulg.) to let out a silent fart.
vessie [vɛsi] *s.f.* bladder; blister; (ichth.) ~ *natatoire*, air-bladder, swimming-bladder; *il veut nous faire prendre des ~s pour des lanternes*, he is trying to persuade us that black is white.
vessigon [vɛsigɔ̃] *s.m.* (vet.) wind-gall.
vestale [vɛstal] *s.f.* vestal (virgin); (fig.) chaste woman.
veste [vɛst] *s.f.* coat (of suit), jacket; (fam.) *changer de ~*, to change one's views, to change sides; (fig.) *remporter, ramasser*, or *prendre, une ~*, to fail, to meet with a rebuff; *retourner sa ~*, to change sides; ⚠ not 'vest' (undergarment).
vestiaire [vɛstjɛr] *s.m.* cloakroom, clothes--lobby; coat-rack, one's hat and coat (left in cloakroom); wardrobe (i.e. one's collection of clothes); ⚠ not (station, etc.) 'cloakroom'.
vestibule [vɛstibyl] *s.m.* hall, lobby, vestibule.
vestige [vɛstiʒ] *s.m.* vestige, trace, mark, remains; footprint, sign.
veston [vɛstɔ̃] *s.m.* jacket, coat (of suit); *complet ~*, lounge suit.
Vésuve [vezyv] *s.m.* (geog.) Vesuvius.
vêtement [vɛtmɑ̃] *s.m.* **1.** garment, dress, (pl.) clothes, garb; (woman's) outdoor coat; (poet.) vesture, apparel; (fig.) cloak, disguise; *je vais chercher un ~*, I'll just go and get my coat, I'll just put something on.
vétéran [veterɑ̃] *s.m.* veteran; (fam.) old hand.
vétérinaire [veterinɛr] *adj.* veterinary; ~ *s.m.f.* veterinary surgeon, vet.
vétillard, -e [vetijar] *adj.* who quibbles, who stands on trifles; *s.m.f.* quibbler.
vétille [vetij] *s.f.* trifle, quibble.
vétiller [vetije] *v.i.* to trifle; to stand on trifles, to quibble, to niggle.
vétilleu-r, -se [vetijœr] *adj., s.m.f.* (obs.) = VÉTILLARD.
vétilleu-x, -se [vetijø] *adj.* captious, fastidious, finicky, niggling; over-nice, over-punctilious.
vêtir [vetir] *v.t.* to clothe, to dress, to array; to array oneself in, to put on; *légèrement vêtu*, lightly clad; **se ~** *v.refl.* to dress (oneself), to put on

one's clothes; *se ~ d'une robe noire*, to put on a black dress.
vétiver [vetivɛr] *s.m.* (bot.) vetiver, cuscus (grass).
véto [veto] *s.m.* veto; *mettre son ~ à*, to interpose or to put one's veto on, to veto.
vêture [vɛtyr] *s.f.* vesture; (of a nun) taking of the veil.
vétuste [vetyst] *adj.* antiquated, decayed, falling to pieces.
vétusté [vetyste] *s.f.* age, old age, decrepitude.
veu-f, -ve [vœf] *adj.* widowed, bereft, bereaved, deprived; **~f** *s.m.* widower; **~ve** *s.f.* widow; (ornith.) widow-bird, whidah; (slang) *la Veuve*, the guillotine, *épouser la Veuve*, to be guillotined.
veuillez [vœje] see VOULOIR *v.t.*
veule [vœl] *adj.* **1.** soft, without energy, slack, weak, spineless, flabby, sluggish; **2.** (of soil) too light, sandy.
veulerie [vœlri] *s.f.* slackness, sluggishness, flabbiness, apathy.
veuvage [vœvaʒ] *s.m.* widowhood; being a grass-widow.
veuve [vœv] *adj.*, *s.f.* see VEUF.
vexant, -e [vɛksɑ̃] *adj.* vexing, provoking.
vexat-eur, -rice [vɛksatœr] *adj.* vexatious.
vexation [vɛksɑsjɔ̃] *s.f.* vexation; irritation; harassment; vexatious or oppressive measure; humiliation.
vexatoire [vɛksatwar] *adj.* vexatious.
vexer [vɛkse] *v.t.* to vex, to annoy; to provoke, to offend; to humiliate; to harass; **se ~** *v.refl.* to be offended, to take offence.
vexillaire [vɛksil(l)ɛr] *s.m.* (Rom. ant.) vexillary, standard-bearer.
vexille [vɛksil] *s.m.* vexillum.
viabilisé, -e [vjabilize] *adj.* (of building plot, etc.) with services laid on.
viabilité[1] [vjabilite] *s.f.* condition or practicability (of road, etc.); provision of services (access roads, sewers, etc.).
viabilité[2] [vjabilite] *s.f.* viability (of foetus); (fig.) viability.
viable [vjabl] *adj.* (of foetus) viable; (fig.) having prospects of survival or development.
viaduc [vjadyk] *s.m.* viaduct.
viag-er, -ère [vjaʒe] *adj.* for life; *rente ~ère*, life annuity; **~er** *s.m.* life interest; *placer en ~er*, to invest in a life annuity.
viande [vjɑ̃d] *s.f.* meat, flesh; (pop.) human body; *~ noire*, game; (pop.) *amène ta ~!*, come on! shift your carcass!; *montrer sa ~*, to strip; *sac à ~*, bed, sleeping-bag; ⚠ not 'viand'.
viander [vjɑ̃de] *v.i.* (of deer, etc.) to graze.
viatique [vjatik] *s.m.* **1.** viaticum, provisions, money for journey; (fig.) support, solace; essential equipment; **2.** (liturg.) viaticum, last sacrament.
vibord [vibɔr] *s.m.* (naut.) waist-board.
vibrage [vibraʒ] *s.m.* (techn.) vibration; *~ du béton*, vibration treatment of concrete.
vibrant, -e [vibrɑ̃] *adj.* vibrating, vibrant, shaking, resonant, ringing; (fig.) thrilling, moving, quivering; *une nature ~e*, a sensitive or emotional disposition; **~e** *s.f.* (phon.) liquid.
vibrateur [vibratœr] *s.m.* vibrator; buzzer.
vibratile [vibratil] *adj.* vibratile.
vibration [vibrɑsjɔ̃] *s.f.* vibration, oscillation; shimmering.
vibratoire [vibratwar] *adj.* vibratory, oscillatory.
vibrer [vibre] *v.i.* to vibrate; (fig.) to thrill, to quiver, to be thrilled, moved, etc.
vibreur [vibrœr] *s.m.* (electr.) vibrator, trembler, buzzer.
vibrion [vibrijɔ̃] *s.m.* (bacteriology] vibrio.
vibrionner [vibrijɔne] *v.i.* (fig., fam.) to be in a ferment.
vibromasseur [vibrɔmasœr] *s.m.* vibro-massage apparatus.
vicaire [vikɛr] *s.m.* curate, assistant priest; deputy, delegate; ⚠ not 'vicar' except in *vicaire apostolique*, vicar apostolic; and *Vicaire du Christ*, Vicar of Christ (the Pope).
vicarial, -e, (aux) [vikarjal] *adj.* vicarial; curate's.
vicariat [vikarja] *s.m.* (eccles.) curacy.
vice [vis] *s.m.* vice, fault, defect, flaw, blemish; evil, depravity; (sexual) perversion; viciousness; *~ de construction*, flaw in construction; *~ de conformation*, malformation, physical defect; *~ de style*, defect of style; *~ de prononciation*, impediment (in speech); *pauvreté n'est pas ~*, poverty is no crime; ⚠ not carpenter's, etc., 'vice'.
vice-amiral [visamiral] *s.m.* (pl. *vice-amiraux*) vice-admiral.
vice-chancelier [visʃɑ̃səlje] *s.m.* (pl. *vice--chanceliers*) vice-chancellor; **~-consul** [viskɔ̃syl] *s.m.* (pl. *vice-consuls*) vice-consul; **~-consulat** [viskɔ̃syla] *s.m.* (pl. *vice-consulats*) vice--consulate; **~-légat** [vislega] *s.m.* (pl. *vice-légats*) vice-legate.
vicennal, -e, (aux) [visenal] *adj.* vicennial.
vice-présidence [visprezidɑ̃s] *s.f.* (pl. *vice--présidences*) vice-presidency.
vice-président, -e [visprezidɑ̃] *s.m.f.* (pl. *vice-président(e)s*) vice-president.
vice-reine [visrɛn] *s.f.* (pl. *vice-reines*) vicereine; **~-roi** [visrwa] *s.m.* (pl. *vice-rois*) viceroy; **~-royauté** [visrwajote] *s.f.* (pl. *vice-royautés*) viceroyalty.
vice versa [viseversa] *adv.loc.* vice versa.
vichy [viʃi] *s.m.* cheap cotton material; *eau de ~*, Vichy water, Vichy.
viciat-eur, -rice [visjatœr] *adj.* vitiating, polluting.
viciation [visjɑsjɔ̃] *s.f.* vitiation, contamination, pollution, poverty (of blood).
vicier [visje] *v.t.* to vitiate, to taint, to contaminate, to pollute, to corrupt, to make depraved; *~ un accord*, to vitiate a contract; **se ~** *v.refl.* to become vitiated, tainted, polluted, contaminated; to become depraved.
vicieu-x, -se [visjø] *adj.* **1.** vicious, depraved; **2.** faulty, defective, imperfect; **~sement** [visjøzmɑ̃] *adv.* viciously; defectively; depravedly; ⚠ not 'vicious' in senses 'spiteful', savage'.
vicinal, -e, (aux) [visinal] *adj. chemin ~*, local road, by-road.
vicissitude [visisityd] *s.f.* vicissitude, change, ever-changing succession; (pl.) vicissitudes, ups and downs.
vicomte [vikɔ̃t] *s.m.* viscount.
vicomté [vikɔ̃te] *s.f.* viscountcy, viscounty, viscountship.
vicomtesse [vikɔ̃tɛs] *s.f.* viscountess.
victime [viktim] *s.f.* victim, sufferer; *être ~ de*, to be the, or a, victim of, to suffer from, to be victimized by.
victoire [viktwar] *s.f.* victory; *remporter la ~*, to gain the victory (*sur*, over), to win the day; *chanter ~*, to triumph, to exult.
victoria [viktɔrja] *s.f.* **1.** victoria (carriage); **2.** (bot.) victoria (water-lily).
victorien, -ne [viktɔrjɛ̃] *adj.* Victorian.
victorieu-x, -se [viktɔrjø] *adj.* victorious; *preuve ~se*, decisive proof; **~sement** [viktɔrjøzmɑ̃] *adv.* victoriously; *réfuter ~sement*, to refute conclusively.
victuaille [viktɥɑj] *s.f.* (usu. pl.) victuals, provisions.
vidage [vidaʒ] *s.m.* emptying, cleaning-out; waste (pipe or tap).
vidange [vidɑ̃ʒ] *s.f.* emptying, removing, evacuation, drawing-off, draining; blowing-off (steam, etc.); clearance, clearing-out; (pl.)

night-soil; sediment, sludge; ullage (of wine); *tonneau en ~*, half-filled or half-empty cask.

vidanger [vidɑ̃ʒe] *v.t.* to empty, to evacuate, to clear out, to drain off, to blow off or release (steam, etc.).

vidangeur [vidɑ̃ʒœr] *s.m.* man employed to empty cesspools.

vide [vid] *adj.* empty; void, vacant, unoccupied; devoid, destitute, (*de*, of); hollow; *à ~*, empty, to no purpose; (mech.) *tourner à ~*, to run in neutral, to run with no load; *frapper à ~*, to hit out and miss; *travailler l'estomac ~*, to work on an empty stomach; (fig.) *cœur ~*, stony-hearted; *~ s.m.* empty space, blank, void; vacuum; gap, hole; (fig.) emptiness, vanity, nothingness; *regarder dans le ~*, to stare into space; *le ~ de son esprit*, the blankness of his mind; *~ de l'âme*, loneliness; *nettoyage par le ~*, vacuum-cleaning; *pompe à ~*, vaccuum pump; *faire le ~ autour de*, to isolate.

vide-bouteille [vidbutɛj] (pl. *vide-bouteilles*) syphon-top (to a bottle).

vide-gousset [vidgusɛ] *s.m.* (pl. *vide-goussets*) pickpocket.

vidéo [video] *s.f.* (TV) video, recording on video; **~-cassette** [videokaset] *s.f.* video-cassette; **~-gramme** [videogram] *s.m.* video-recording.

vide-poches [vidpɔʃ] *s.m.invar.* tidy, receptacle for odds and ends; glove-compartment (in car).

vide-pomme [vidpɔm] *s.m.* (pl. *vide-pommes*) apple-corer.

vider [vide] *v.t.* to empty; to draw off, to drain (of liquids), to bail out, to evacuate, to clear out; to bore, to hollow out (solid objects); to draw (game, poultry); to gut (fish); (fig.) to settle, to decide, to end; to vacate, to clear out of; (fam.) to exhaust; *~ les lieux*, to vacate the premises; (fig.) to clear off, to quit, to decamp; *~ les arçons*, (of horseback rider) to be thrown; *~ une question*, to settle a question.

videu-r, -se [vidœr] *s.m.f.* emptier; (at night club, etc.) bouncer, chucker-out.

vidimer [vidime] *v.t.* (law) to certify (as a true copy).

vidimus [vidimys] *s.m.* vidimus, certification, attestation.

vidrecome [vidrəkɔm] *s.m.* (hist.) hanap, large drinking-glass.

viduité [vidɥite] *s.f.* (law) viduity, widowhood.

vidure [vidyr] *s.f.* offal, giblets; rubbish (tipped from dustbin, etc.).

vie [vi] *s.f.* life; existence, days, lifetime; vitality, liveliness, spirit, animation; livelihood, living, food, sustenance; life, biography, memoir; *sa ~ durant*, throughout his life; *de (toute) ma ~*, in all my life, in all my born days, till my dying day; *jamais de la ~!*, never!, there's no question of it!, not on your life!; *style plein de ~*, lively style; *gagner sa ~*, to earn one's living, to get one's livelihood; *devoir sa ~ à*, to owe one's life or existence to; *faire la ~*, to live fast; (fam.) *il nous a fait la ~*, he leads us a life, he is for ever on at us; *ce n'est pas une ~*, it's no sort of life, you can't live under those conditions; *femme de mauvaise ~*, loose woman, prostitute; *prix de la ~*, cost of living; *prime* or *indemnité de ~ chère*, cost-of-living bonus; *en ~*, alive, living; *faire la ~ dure à qn.*, to make someone's life a misery; *avoir la ~ dure*, to be tenacious of life; to be hard to kill; (fam., pej.) to be a long time dying; *train de ~*, way of living, establishment; *la ~ des champs*, country life; *~ probable*, expectation of life; *à ~*, for life; *la ~ future*, the life to come; *arbre de ~*, arbor vitae; *il y va de la ~*, it's a matter of life and death; *donner la ~ à*, to give birth to.

vieil see VIEUX.

vieillard [vjɛjar] *s.m.* old man, aged man; (pl.) the aged, elderly people.

vieille see VIEUX.

vieillerie [vjɛjri] *s.f.* lumber, rubbish, old clothes; work (of art, etc.) no longer in fashion; (pl.) (fig.) outworn ideas, old-fashioned notions; (fam.) = VIEILLESSE.

vieillesse [vjɛjɛs] *s.f.* old age; age, antiquity (of buildings, etc.); the aged, old people.

vieilli, -e [vjeji] *adj.* old-fashioned, obsolescent, no longer in common use, out-of-date; aged; *~ dans*, grown old (and wise and experienced) in.

vieillir [vjejir] *v.i.* to grow old, to age, to look old; (of wine) to mellow; to become obsolete or old-fashioned; to fall into disuse; *il a vieilli*, he has aged, he looks much older; *~ v.t.* to age, to make older, to make look older; *cette robe vous vieillit*, that dress makes you look older (than you are); *vous me vieillissez de deux ans*, you are making me out two years older than I am; **se ~** *v.refl.* to make oneself out older than one is, to make oneself look older.

vieillissant, -e [vjejisɑ̃] *adj.* ageing, growing old.

vieillissement [vjejismɑ̃] *s.m.* ageing, growing old; becoming out-of-date.

vieillot, -te [vjɛjo] *adj.* quaint, old-fashioned; (obs.) elderly, old-looking.

vielle [vjɛl] *s.f.* (mus.) hurdy-gurdy; ⚠ not 'hurdy-gurdy' = 'barrel-organ'.

vielleu-r, -se [vjɛlœr] *s.m.f.* hurdy-gurdy player.

vielleux [vjɛlø] *s.m.* = VIELLEUR.

Vienne [vjɛn] *s.f.* **1.** Vienne (in France); **2.** Vienna (Austria).

viennois, -e [vjɛnwa] *adj.*, *s.m.f.* **1.** (native or inhabitant) of Vienne; **2.** Viennese.

vierge [vjɛrʒ] *s.f.* virgin, maid; (astron.) Virgo; *~ adj.* virgin; maiden; infertile; spotless, untarnished; *page ~*, virgin or blank page; *casier (judiciaire) ~*, clear record (no convictions), clean sheet; *film ~*, unexposed film; *cassette ~*, blank cassette; *fil de la ~*, gossamer; *vigne ~*, Virginia creeper.

Viet-nam, Viet-nâm [vjɛtnam] *s.f.* (geog.) Vietnam.

vietnamien, -ne [vjɛtnamjɛ̃] *adj.*, *s.m.f.* Vietnamese.

vieux [vjø], **vieil** [vjɛj] (before vowel or h-mute), *fem.* **vieille** [vjɛj] *adj.* old, aged, ancient, venerable, advanced in years; old-fashioned, antiquated, out of date, obsolete, stale; veteran; *~ jeu*, old-fashioned, antiquated, old hat; *~ soldat*, veteran, old soldier; *~ comme le temps, le monde*, as old as the hills, as Adam; *~ garçon*, (old) bachelor; *vieille fille*, old maid; spinster; *vieil homme*, old man; *c'est toujours la vieille question*, it is always the same old question; *il faut être ~ dans le métier*, one has got to be experienced in the business; **~, vieille** *s.m.f.* old man, old woman, old age; (pop.) *elle a reçu un sacré coup de ~, cet été*, she has suddenly aged during this summer; (fam.) *mon ~*, old chap, my dear fellow; *un ~ de la vieille*, a veteran of the Old Guard; *coudre du ~ avec du neuf*, to put a new patch on an old garment, to put new wine into old bottles; *mes vieux*, my parents, the old people.

vi-f, -ve [vif] *adj.* live, living, alive; quick; animated, lively, spirited, sprightly; fiery, (of horses) mettlesome; eager, passionate, ardent, hasty; bright, vivid, intense; bracing, piercing, keen; acute; (of pain) shooting; *de vive voix*, by word of mouth; *des yeux ~fs*, sparkling eyes; *eau vive*, spring-water; *vives eaux*, spring tides; *chaux vive*, quicklime; *haie vive*, quickset hedge; *plaie vive*, open sore or wound; *ils ont échangé des propos fort ~fs*, angry words passed between them; *foi vive*, burning faith; *vive arête*, sharp angle or edge; *pierres vives*, drystone (walling); *joints ~fs*, dry joints (no mortar); *vive allure* or *allure vive*, smart pace; rapid gait; *geler ~f*, to freeze hard; *de vive force*, by main force; *avoir l'esprit ~f*, to be quick-witted; **~f** *s.m.* quick (live flesh); living person; life, lifelike quality; (fig.) *blessé au ~f*, stung to the quick; *trancher dans le ~f*, to cut to the quick; (fig.) to set to work in earnest; *avoir les nerfs à ~f*, to have one's nerves on edge, to be on edge; (law) *acte entre ~fs*, agreement between living persons; (fig.) *entrer dans le ~f de la question*, to get to the heart of the matter or to the bottom of the question; *peindre sur le ~f*, to paint or draw from life; *le ~f de l'eau*, high water, the top of the tide; (fam.) *prendre sur le ~f*, to catch a likeness; *il l'a pris sur le ~f*, he has got him to the life; *c'est pris sur le ~f*, that's lifelike; (fam.) *cela l'a piqué au ~f*, that thrust went home.

vif-argent [vifarʒɑ̃] *s.m.* mercury, quicksilver; (fig.) *être du ~*, to be like quicksilver, to be never still.

vigie [viʒi] *s.f.* **1.** look-out (man); **2.** look-out post; observation-box (on guard's van); *être en ~*, to be on the look-out; **3.** danger-buoy.

vigilamment [viʒilamɑ̃] *adv.* vigilantly.

vigilance [viʒilɑ̃s] *s.f.* vigilance, wakefulness, lying awake; *endormir* or *tromper la ~ de qn.*, to put s.o. off his guard.

vigilant, -e [viʒilɑ̃] *adj.* vigilant, watchful, on one's guard; ~ *s.m.* one who cannot sleep, watcher (in the night).

vigile [viʒil] *s.m.* **1.** (Rom. hist.) night-watchman; **2.** = VIGILANT *s.m.*

vigile [viʒil] *s.f.* vigil; ~ *adj.* of the day before.

vigne [viɲ] *s.f.* vine; vineyard; *raisin de ~*, wine-grape; ~ *vierge*, Virginia creeper; ~ *blanche* or *de Salomon*, wild clematis, traveller's joy, old man's beard; ~ *de Judas*, woody nightshade, bittersweet.

vigneau, vignot [viɲo] *s.m.* (moll.) winkle.

vigneron, -ne [viɲərɔ̃] *s.m.f.* vine-dresser, vine-grower, wine-grower.

vignette [viɲɛt] *s.f.* **1.** vignette; illustration in text, head-and-tail piece; ornamented border; engraving embellished with a scroll; emblem or badge (of firm); official stamp; (on car) ~ *de l'impôt*, licence; **2.** (bot.) meadow-sweet.

vignoble [viɲɔbl] *s.m.* vineyard; ~ *adj.* wine-growing.

vignot see VIGNEAU.

vigogne [vigɔɲ] *s.f.* (zool.) vicuña; vicuña-wool.

vigoureu-x, -se [vigurø] *adj.* vigorous, strong, lusty, sturdy, stout, stalwart, robust; forceful, energetic; forcible; *opposition ~se*, strong opposition; *haine ~se*, violent or intense hatred; (art) *touche ~se*, firm touch, strong line; **~sement** [vigurøzmɑ̃] *adv.* vigorously, energetically.

vigueur [vigœr] *s.f.* vigour, strength; force, energy, power; forcibleness; ~ *d'esprit*, strength of mind; *la ~ de la réaction*, the violence of the reaction; *entrer en ~*, to take effect; (of law) to come into force; *mettre en ~*, to enforce, to put in force.

vil, -e [vil] *adj.* vile, mean, base; abject, low; paltry, worthless, contemptible; *à ~ prix*, (dirt-)cheap, at a low price; *âme ~e*, base mind.

vilain, -e [vilɛ̃] *adj.* nasty, bad, unpleasant; naughty; mean, scurvy, dirty; rude, shameful, ugly; (fam.) *il fait ~*, it's nasty weather; ~ *s.m.* (feud.) villein, serf; (hist.) peasant; **~ement** [vilɛnmɑ̃] *adv.* in an ugly fashion; villainously, basely, shamefully.

vilebrequin [vilbrəkɛ̃] *s.m.* (techn.) centre-bit, brace (and bit), breast-drill, wimble; (mech.) crank, crankshaft.

vilement [vilmɑ̃] *adv.* (Lit.) vilely, in a servile manner.

vilenie [vilni] *s.f.* vile action, base deed; meanness, baseness.

vilipender [vilipɑ̃de] *v.t.* to vilify, to run down, to abuse.

villa [vila] *s.f.* villa; street, etc., of villas.

village [vilaʒ] *s.m.* village; tented town, camp (with services laid on).

villageois, -e [vilaʒwa] *s.m.f.* villager; *adj.* rustic, country, village.

villanelle [vilanɛl] *s.f.* (pros., mus.) villanelle.

ville [vil] *s.f.* town, city; *être à la* or *en ~*, to be in town; *dîner en ~*, to dine out; *costume de ~*, plain clothes, mufti; *hôtel de ~*, town hall; *toilette de ~*, town dress; (on letters) *en ~*, local; ~ *d'eau(x)*, watering-place, spa; (obs.) *sergent de ~*, policeman; *la haute, la basse, ~*, the upper, the lower, (part of the) town.

villégiateur [vileʒjatœr] *s.m.* (obs.) (holiday) visitor.

villégiature [vileʒjatyr] *s.f.* holiday (in country or at a resort); holiday resort.

villégiaturer [vileʒjatyre] *v.i.* (obs.) to be on holiday, to holiday, to have a quiet holiday.

villeu-x, -se [vilø] *adj.* (bot., anat.) hairy, villous, villose.

villosité [vilozite] *s.f.* (bot., anat.) villosity.

vin [vɛ̃] *s.m.* wine; ~ *mousseux*, sparkling wine; ~ *de Bordeaux*, (if red) claret; ~ *du Rhin*, hock; ~ *rosé* or *gris*, rosé (wine); *être pris de ~*, to be in liquor, to be the worse for drink; (fam.) *sac à ~*, drunken sot; *être entre deux ~s*, to be tipsy; *cuver son ~*, to sleep it off; *mettre de l'eau dans son ~*, to come down a peg or two, to cut down expenses, to go easy for a bit; *quand le ~ est tiré, il faut le boire*, he has put his hand to the plough, it's too late to turn back; *à bon ~ point d'enseigne*, good wine needs no bush; *chaque ~ a sa lie*, there's no rose without a thorn; *un doigt de ~*, a thimbleful of wine; *avoir le ~ gai, triste, mauvais*, to be merry, dull, quarrelsome, in one's cups; *porter bien le ~*, to have a good head (for drinking); *marchand de ~*, (i.) wine-merchant; (ii.) keeper of public house or wine bar; *négociant en ~s*, wholesale wine-merchant.

vinage [vinaʒ] *s.m.* fortifying of wine.

vinaigre [vinɛgr] *s.m.* vinegar; *sel de ~*, smelling-salts.

vinaigré, -e [vinɛgre] *adj.* with vinegar added, vinegary.

vinaigrer [vinɛgre] *v.t.* to add vinegar to.

vinaigrerie [vinɛgrəri] *s.f.* vinegar-works; vinegar-making.

vinaigrette [vinɛgrɛt] *s.f.* **1.** vinegar sauce, oil and vinegar dressing, French dressing; (*à la*) ~, in oil and vinegar; **2.** (obs.) kind of bath-chair; ⚠ not 'vinaigrette' (bottle).

vinaigrier [vinɛgrije] *s.m.* **1.** vinegar-merchant; **2.** cruet.

vinaire [vinɛr] *adj. industrie ~*, wine trade, wine-growing.

vinasse [vinas] *s.f.* residuary liquor; cheap or poor wine, hog-wash.

vindas [vɛ̃das] *s.m.* windlass, winch; (gymn.) giant-stride.

vindicati-f, -ve [vɛ̃dikatif] *adj.* vindictive, revengeful; **~vement** [vɛ̃dikativmɑ̃] *adv.* vindictively.

vindicte [vɛ̃dikt] *s.f.* prosecution (of crime); *désigner qn. à la ~*, to expose s.o. to public condemnation.

vinée [vine] *s.f.* grape-harvest, vintage; fruit-bearing branch (of vine).

viner [vine] *v.t.* to fortify (wine).

vineu-x, -se [vinø] *adj.* vinous, winy, wine-coloured, smelling of wine, wine-flavoured; rich in wines.

vingt [vɛ̃] *adj., s.m.* twenty, a score; twentieth (of the month); *faire ~ pas*, to take a stroll or a turn; (pop.) *~-deux!*, watch out!
vingtaine [vɛ̃tɛn] *s.f. une ~*, a score, about twenty.
vingtième [vɛ̃tjɛm] *adj., s.m.* twentieth.
vinicole [vinikɔl] *adj.* wine-growing, wine--producing.
vinifère [vinifɛr] *adj.* (esp. of soil) viniferous, vine-bearing, wine-producing.
vinification [vinifikɑsjɔ̃] *s.f.* wine-making, fermenting.
vinyle [vinil] *s.m.* (chem.) vinyl.
viol [vjɔl] *s.m.* rape, violation; (fig.) violation; ⚠ not (mus.) 'viol'.
violacé, -e [vjɔlase] *adj.* **1.** purplish; blue (with cold), reddened (by alcohol); **2.** (bot.) violaceous.
violacer [vjɔlase] *v.i.*, **se** *~ v.refl.* (of complexion or flowers) to turn purple.
violat [vjɔla] *adj.m.* of violets, violet; *sirop ~*, syrup of violets.
violat-eur, -rice [vjɔlatœr] *s.m.f.* violator; transgressor; ravisher.
violation [vjɔlɑsjɔ̃] *s.f.* violation, infringement, desecration.
violâtre [vjɔlɑtr] *adj.* purplish.
viole [vjɔl] *s.f.* viol; *~ d'amour*, viola d'amore; *~ de gambe*, viola da gamba.
violemment [vjɔlamɑ̃] *adv.* violently, with violence; ardently.
violence [vjɔlɑ̃s] *s.f.* violence; act of violence; (law) force, duress; (fig.) stress, violence, height, fury, vehemence, virulence; *faire ~ à*, to do violence to, to outrage, to abuse, to rape; *faire ~ à la loi*, to stretch, (fam.) to bend, the law; *se faire ~*, to act contrary to one's feelings.
violent, -e [vjɔlɑ̃] *adj.* violent, strong, excessive, intense, impetuous, passionate; *faire des efforts ~s*, to make strenuous efforts; *des remèdes ~s*, harsh remedies; *c'est un peu ~!*, that's too much!, that is going too far!
violenter [vjɔlɑ̃te] *v.t.* to force, to constrain, to outrage, to do violence to; to violate, to assault, to commit rape upon.
violer [vjɔle] *v.t.* to violate, to desecrate, to ravish; to rape; to outrage, to break, to transgress (treaties, laws, etc.); *~ le domicile de qn.*, to make forcible entry into someone's house.
violet, -te [vjɔlɛ] *adj.* violet(-coloured), purple; *~ s.m.* violet, purple, (colour); *~te s.f.* (bot.) violet; *bois de ~te*, violet-wood, rosewood.
violier [vjɔlje] *s.m.* (bot.) wallflower, gillyflower.
violine [vjɔlin] *s.f.* (chem.) violet colouring; *~ adj.* violet.
violiste [vjɔlist] *s.m.f.* violist.
violon [vjɔlɔ̃] *s.m.* **1.** violin, (fam.) fiddle; (pl.) (naut.) fiddles; *~ d'Ingres*, hobby (esp. artistic), spare-time activity; *payer les ~s*, to pay the piper; **2.** (fam.) lock-up (in police-station).
violoncelle [vjɔlɔ̃sɛl] *s.m* violoncello, cello.
violoncelliste [vjɔlɔ̃selist] *s.m.f.* violoncellist, cellist.
violoneux [vjɔlɔnø] *s.m.* (pej.) fiddler.
violoniste [vjɔlɔnist] *s.m.f.* violinist.
viorne [vjɔrn] *s.f.* (bot.) viburnum, wayfaring--tree; wild clematis.
vipère [vipɛr] *s.f.* adder, viper.
vipereau (pl. **-x**) [vipro] *s.m.* young viper.
vipérin, -e [viperɛ̃] *adj.* viperine; (fig.) viperish, venomous; *~e s.f.* **1** viperine snake; **2.** (bot.) viper's bugloss.
virage [viraʒ] *s.m.* **1.** turning, cornering; curve, bend; *déraper dans un ~*, to skid on a bend; *prendre le ~*, to take the curve or corner, to corner; (naut.) tacking; **2.** (photo.) toning; **3.** change (of colour).
virago [virago] *s.f.* virago, termagant.
viral, -e (**aux**) [viral] *adj.* viral.
virée [vire] *s.f.* (fam.) trip, run (around).
virelai [virlɛ] *s.m.* virelay.
virement [virmɑ̃] *s.m.* **1.** turning; (naut.) tacking; **2.** (book-keep.) transfer, clearing; *comptoir général de ~*, bankers' clearing-house.
virer [vire] *v.i.* **1.** to turn, to take a bend, to corner; (aeron.) to bank; to twist and turn, to turn about, to gyrate; to turn colour; to change sides; *~ au noir, à l'aigre*, to turn black, sour; **2.** (naut.) to tack about, to veer about; *~ de bord*, to tack, to go about; *~ vent arrière*, to wear ship; *~ vent devant*, to tack ship; *~ au cabestan*, to heave, to haul; *~ v.t.* **1.** to transfer, to clear (a sum of money); **2.** (photo.) to tone; **3.** (naut.) to turn (capstan), to haul in (cable); *~ l'ancre*, to weigh anchor; **4.** (fam.) *~ qn.*, to send, to chase, s.o. away.
vireur [virœr] *s.m.* (mech.) turning-gear.
vireu-x, -se [virø] *adj.* poisonous, noxious.
virevolte [virvɔlt] *s.f.* quick turning or wheeling (of a horse); (fig.) sudden change (of fortune); about-face.
Virgile [virʒil] *s.m.* Virgil, Vergil.
virginal, -e, (**aux**) [virʒinal] *adj.* virginal, maidenly.
virginal (**aux**) [virʒinal] *s.m.* (mus.) virginal, (pair of) virginals.
virginie [virʒini] *s.m.* Virginia tobacco or snuff.
virginité [virʒinite] *s.f.* virginity, maidenhood, (fig.) purity, innocence.
virgule [virgyl] *s.f.* comma; (decimal) point; (fig.) *moustaches en ~*, drooping moustache.
virguler [virgyle] *v.t.* to punctuate or decorate with commas.
viril, -e [viril] *adj.* virile, male, masculine, manly; *âge ~*, manhood, man's estate; **~ement** [virilmɑ̃] *adv.* like a man, in a virile fashion.
virilité [virilite] *s.f.* virility; manhood; vigour, energy.
virole [virɔl] *s.f.* **1.** (techn.) ferrule, collar, sleeve, sleeve-joint; **2.** die (for stamping).
viroler [virɔle] *v.t.* **1.** (techn.) to ferrule, to fit with a sleeve, to hoop; **2.** (die-stamping) to put into the stamping-machine.
virtualité [virtɥalite] *s.f.* virtuality.
virtuel, -le [virtɥɛl] *adj.* virtual, potential, probable; **~lement** [virtɥɛlmɑ̃] *adv.* virtually.
virtuose [virtɥoz] *s.m.f.* virtuoso.
virtuosite [virtɥozite] *s.f.* virtuosity.
virulence [virylɑ̃s] *s.f.* virulence.
virulent, -e [virylɑ̃] *adj.* virulent.
virure [viryr] *s.f.* (naut.) strake.
virus [virys] *s.m.* virus; (fig.) virus, poison.
vis [vis] *s.f.* screw; (*escalier à*) *~*, spiral staircase; *pas de ~*, pitch of screw; thread; *serrer une ~*, to screw up, to tighten, a screw; *~ sans fin*, worm--screw; *~ platinée*, platinum-head screw; *fermer à ~*, to screw down (lid, etc.); *~ de réglage*, adjusting-screw; *commande par ~ sans fin*, worm-drive; *~ de serrage*, locking-screw; *tige à ~*, screwed rod, threaded rod; (fam.) *serrer la ~ à qn.*, to apply pressure to s.o., to put the screw(s) on s.o.
visa [viza] *s.m.* stamp, endorsement; visa (on passport, etc.).
visage [vizaʒ] *s.m.* face, countenance; visage; expression; image; aspect; *changer de ~*, to change countenance, to turn pale; *trouver ~ de bois*, to find the door shut, or nobody there; *à deux ~s*, two-faced, double-sided, double--faced; *sans ~*, faceless, anonymous; *toute vérité a deux ~s*, there are two aspects of every truth; *à ~ découvert*, barefacedly; *avoir bon ~*, to look well; *faire son ~*, to make up one's face; *faire bon, mauvais, ~ à*, to smile at, to frown on, to behave in a friendly, an unfriendly, way to; *visages pâles*, pale-faces.

visagiste [vizaʒist] *s.m.f.* beautician.
vis-à-vis [vizavi] *adv., prep.loc.* (obs.) face to face; (mod.) opposite, over against; facing; (fig.) towards, as regards; in face of, before, in the presence of; compared to; ~ *s.m.* **1.** the person or thing facing another; **2.** S-shaped settee.
viscéral, -e, (aux) [viseral] *adj.* visceral, intestinal; (fig.) inner, inward.
viscère [visɛr] *s.m.* any of the viscera or vital organs; (pl.) viscera.
viscose [viskoz] *s.f.* viscose.
viscosimètre [viskozimɛtr] *s.m.* viscometer, viscosimeter.
viscosité [viskozite] *s.f.* viscosity, viscidity.
visée [vize] *s.f.* **1.** aiming; **2.** (usu. pl.) aims, intentions, designs, plans.
viser[1] [vize] *v.t.* to aim at; to aspire to, to be directed at, to relate to, to refer to; *des négociations visant une alliance,* negotiations with a view to merger; *être visé,* to be the person referred to; *je ne vise personne,* I am not referring to anyone in particular; (slang) *vise-moi ça!,* just look at that!; ~ *v.i.* to take aim; *il visait à ce but,* that was his object; ~ *juste,* to aim straight; ~ *à l'effet,* to aim at effect.
viser[2] [vize] *v.t.* to visa, to stamp, to countersign, to endorse; *faire ~ un passeport,* to get a passport visa'd, to have a visa stamped on one's passport.
viseur [vizœr] *s.m.* (photo.) viewfinder; (mil.) sight (of a gun, etc.).
visibilité [vizibilite] *s.f.* visibility; conspicuousness; *virage sans ~,* blind corner; *pilotage sans ~,* flying blind.
visible [vizibl] *adj.* **1.** visible, perceptible, observable; (fig.) manifest, obvious, evident; **2.** visible, ready to receive visitors; at home; (fam.) dressed; on view; **~ment** [viziblәmɑ̃] *adv.* visibly, obviously, conspicuously.
visière [vizjɛr] *s.f.* **1.** (medieval) visor, vizor; **2.** peak (of cap, etc.); (fig.) *rompre en ~ à,* to fly at, to fly in the face of, to contradict flatly.
vision [vizjɔ̃] *s.f.* **1.** sight, vision, eyesight, view; **2.** vision, dream, phantom, fancy; fantasy.
visionnaire [vizjɔnɛr] *s.m.f.* visionary, seer; dreamer; ~ *adj.* visionary, fanciful.
visionner [vizjɔne] *v.t.* to view (a film).
visionneuse [vizjɔnøz] *s.f.* viewer (for viewing films or transparencies).
visitation [vizitɑsjɔ̃] *s.f.* visitation.
visite [vizit] *s.f.* **1.** visit, call; visitor, caller; *être en ~ chez,* to be staying with, to be on a visit to; *faire des ~s,* to pay calls; *recevoir des ~s,* to have callers; **2.** inspection, visit of inspection, examination, search; visitation (of a bishop, etc.); *la ~ des bagages,* the examination of luggage; *droit de ~,* right of search; (law) *droit de ~ aux enfants,* right of access to the children; *trou de ~,* manhole cover, inspection cover.
visiter [vizite] *v.t.* **1.** to visit, to pay a visit to; to call on; **2.** to search, to examine, to inspect.
visiteu-r, -se [vizitœr] *s.m.f.* **1.** caller, visitor; **2.** inspector, searcher.
vison [vizɔ̃] *s.m.* (zool.) mink; mink (fur).
visqueu-x, -se [viskø] *adj.* viscous, sticky.
vissage [visaʒ] *s.m.* screwing.
visser [vise] *v.t.* to screw, to screw up or down; (fig., fam.) to apply pressure to, to put the screw(s) on; ~ *à bloc,* to screw tight; **se** ~ *v.refl. ce bouchon se visse,* this is a screw stopper.
visserie [visri] *s.f.* **1.** nuts and bolts, screws, etc; **2.** screw factory.
Vistule [vistyl] *s.f.* (geog.) Vistula.
visualisation [vizɥalizɑsjɔ̃] *s.f.* visualizing, making visual.
visualiser [vizɥalize] *v.t.* **1.** to make visible; **2.** to put in visual form.
visuel, -le [vizɥɛl] *adj.* visual; **~lement** [vizɥɛlmɑ̃] *adv.* visually.
vital, -e, (aux) [vital] *adj.* vital; (fig.) vital, essential.
vitalité [vitalite] *s.f.* vitality, vigour.
vitamine [vitamin] *s.f.* vitamin.
vitaminé, -e [vitamine] *adj.* vitaminized, with added vitamins.
vite [vit] *adj.* swift, quick, speedy, rapid, fast; ~ *adv.* quickly, fast, rapidly, speedily; soon; *au plus ~,* as fast as possible; *il a eu, il aura, ~ fait de,* it didn't, won't, take him long to; *~!,* quick!, hurry up!, get a move on!, look sharp (about it)!
vitellin, -e [vitelɛ̃] *adj.* (biol.) of the vitellus, vitelline.
vitellus [vitelys] *s.m.* (biol.) vitellus, yolk of egg.
vitelotte [vitlɔt] *s.f.* kidney-potato.
vitesse [vitɛs] *s.f.* quickness, rapidity, swiftness, speed, celerity; *à toute* or *grande* or *pleine ~,* at top speed, at high speed; (fam.) *en ~!,* and be quick about it!; (*train de*) *grande ~,* express train; *expédier en petite ~,* to send by goods train; *gagner de ~,* to outstrip; (car) *boîte des ~s,* gear-box; *changer de ~,* to change gear; *~ en prise directe,* direct drive; *compteur de ~,* speedometer, speed indicator; *~ à l'heure,* speed per hour; (aeron.) *en perte de ~,* stalling, at stalling speeds, (fig.) running down, moribund.
viticole [vitikɔl] *adj.* wine-growing.
viticult-eur [vitikyltœr] *s.m.* viticulturist, wine-grower; **~ure** [vitikyltyr] *s.f.* viticulture, wine-growing.
vitrage [vitraʒ] *s.m.* glazing; glass windows; glazed portion (of partition, etc.).
vitrail, (aux) [vitraj] *s.m.* stained-glass window, large leaded window.
vitre [vitr] *s.f.* pane, window; (fig., fam.) *casser les ~s,* to fly into a rage, to make a scene; *ça ne casse pas les ~s,* that's nothing to write home about.
vitré, -e [vitre] *adj.* **1.** glazed; *porte ~e,* glass door; **2.** (anat.) vitreous.
vitrer [vitre] *v.t.* to glaze, to put glass in(to).
vitrerie [vitrәri] *s.f.* glazing, glaziery.
vitreu-x, -se [vitrø] *adj.* (of eyes, etc.) glassy, glazed, vitreous.
vitrier [vitrije] *s.m.* glazier.
vitrière [vitrijɛr] *s.f.* metal framing (for windows).
vitrifiable [vitrifjabl] *adj.* vitrifiable.
vitrification [vitrifikɑsjɔ̃] *s.f.* vitrification, vitrifaction.
vitrifier [vitrifje] *v.t.* to vitrify.
vitrine [vitrin] *s.f.* shop window; glass case, show-case; glass cabinet; *regarder* or *lécher les ~s,* to go window-shopping.
vitriol [vitrijɔl] *s.m.* (chem.) vitriol, concentrated sulphuric acid; (obs.) gut-rot (spirit); **~er** [vitrijɔle] *v.t.* **1.** (techn.) to vitriolize; **2.** to throw acid at (s.o.).
vitrioleu-r, -se [vitriɔlœr] *s.m.f.* acid-thrower.
vitupération [vityperɑsjɔ̃] *s.f.* vituperation.
vitupérer [vitypere] *v.t.* to vituperate, to abuse; ~ *contre,* to criticize violently, to inveigh against.
vivable [vivabl] *adj.* liveable with; fit to live in.
vivace[1] [vivas] *adj.* long-lived, tenacious of life; (bot.) perennial; (fig.) inveterate, deep-rooted, undying, enduring; ⚠ not 'vivacious'.
vivace[2] [vivatʃe] *adv., adj.* (mus.) vivace.
vivacité [vivasite] *s.f.* vivacity, liveliness, sprightliness; spirit, ardour, brightness, vividness; acuteness; keenness (of air); heat, heatedness (of argument, etc.); *j'ai eu des ~s,* I spoke rather hastily.
vivant, -e [vivɑ̃] *adj.* alive, living; (fig.) lively, animated, lifelike; *s.m.f.* living person; *les ~s,*

the living; *bon* ~, one who likes to do himself well, jolly fellow; ~ *s.m.* life, lifetime; *de son* ~, in his lifetime; *du* ~ *de son frère*, while his brother was alive.

vivat [viva] *interj.* hurrah!, bravo!; ~ *s.m.* cheer; *pousser des* ~*s*, to cheer.

vive[1] [viv] see VIVRE.

vive[2] [viv] *s.f.* (ichth.) weever.

vivement [vivmɑ̃] *adv.* quickly, briskly, sharply, vigorously; keenly, acutely, deeply, poignantly; warmly; ~ *que ça finisse!*, stop doing that immediately!

viveur [vivœr] *s.m.* (of person) fast liver.

vivier [vivje] *s.m.* fish-pond; fish-well (in boat),

vivifiant, -e [vivifjɑ̃] *adj.* vivifying, quickening. bracing, life-giving, refreshing, invigorating.

vivification [vivifikɑsjɔ̃] *s.f.* vivification, vivifying, revival.

vivifier [vivifje] *v.t.* to vivify, to quicken, to give life to; to animate, to revive, to brace.

vivi-pare [vivipar] *adj.* viviparous; **~-parité** [viviparite] *s.f.* viviparity, viviparousness.

vivisection [viviseksjɔ̃] *s.f.* vivisection.

vivoter [vivɔte] *v.i.* to live in a small way; (fam.) to rub along.

vivre [vivr] *v.i.* to live, to be alive, to exist, to subsist; to board; to behave; to last, to endure; *vive le roi!*, long live the king!; *vive la liberté!*, up with liberty!; *vive la mariée!*, three cheers for the bride!; *je vous apprendrai à* ~*!*, I'll teach you some manners!; ~ *de*, to live on, from, off, (fig.) to be nourished on, to be fed on; ~ *d'expédients*, to live by one's wits; *se laisser* ~, to take life easy; *le savoir-*~, good manners; *qui vive?*, who goes there; *faire* ~, to support; *il fait bon* ~, it is good to be alive; *bien* ~, (i.) to lead an upright life, (ii.) to live well; *il n'a pas de quoi* ~, he has not enough to live on; *on vivait bien juste*, we just about managed to live; *chercher à* ~, to look for food; *il fait cher* ~ *ici*, living is expensive here; *être sur le qui-vive*, to be on the look-out or qui vive; *le bien* ~, fat living; *être facile à* ~, to be easy to get on with; ~ *en prince*, to live like a prince; *qui vivra, verra*, time will show; *ne trouver âme qui vive*, not to find a living soul; ~ *v.t.* to live, to experience; *une histoire vécue*, a true-life story; ~ *s.m.* living, board, food; *les* ~*s*, provisions, victuals; *couper les* ~*s à qn.*, to cut off someone's supplies or money.

vivri-er, -ère [vivrije] *adj.* food-producing; *cultures* ~*ères*, food crops.

vizir [vizir] *s.m.* vizier.

vlan, v'lan [vlɑ̃] *interj.* bang!

vocable [vɔkabl] *s.m.* **1.** vocable, word; **2.** patronage; *église sous le* ~ *de Saint-Jean*, church dedicated to Saint John.

vocabulaire [vɔkabylɛr] *s.m.* vocabulary, terminology; word-list, word-book.

vocal, -e, (aux) [vɔkal] *adj.* vocal; **~ment** [vɔkalmɑ̃] *adv.* vocally.

vocalique [vɔkalik] *adj.* vocalic, vowel.

vocalisation [vɔkalizɑsjɔ̃] *s.f.* vocalization.

vocalise [vɔkaliz] *s.f.* vocalization exercise.

vocaliser [vɔkalize] *v.t.i.* to vocalize; (mus.) to practise vocalization.

vocatif [vɔkatif] *s.m.* (gram.) vocative (case).

vocation [vɔkɑsjɔ̃] *s.f.* vocation, calling; call; dedicating; sense of vocation; ⚠ not 'vocation' in sense 'occupation'.

vocifération [vɔsiferɑsjɔ̃] *s.f.* (usu. pl.) loud and angry words, shouts of anger, outcry.

vociférer [vɔsifere] *v.i.* to shout angrily; ~ *v.t.* to shout, to scream, (abuse, etc.).

vodka [vɔdka] *s.m.* vodka.

vœu (pl. **-x**) [vø] *s.m.* **1.** wish, will, prayer; *être au comble de ses* ~*x*, to have reached the summit of one's hopes; *faire des* ~*x pour*, to pray for, to wish for; *je fais des* ~*x pour ton bonheur*, I wish you happiness; ~*x de Nouvel An*, New Year wishes; *tous mes* ~*x*, my best wishes; *émettre un* ~, (i.) to express a desire; (ii.) (of an assembly) to pass a resolution; *nos* ~*x sont exaucés*, our wishes are fulfilled, our prayers are granted; **2.** vow; votive offering; suffrage; *faire* ~ *de*, to make a vow to, to swear to; *prononcer ses* ~*x*, to take the vows.

vogue [vɔg] *s.f.* vogue, fashion; repute, reputation; *en* ~, in or into fashion; *avoir la* or *de la* ~, to be in fashion, to be popular.

voguer [vɔge] *v.i.* to sail, (of boats) to move, to float; to be rowed; to glide; (fig.) *et vogue la galère!*, come what will!, let's chance it!

voici [vwasi] *prep.* here is, here are, this is, these are; ~*!*, look!, see here!, here it is!; *me* ~, here I am; *monsieur, notre ami, que* ~, this gentleman, our friend, here; ~ *venir*, here comes; *nous y* ~, here we are, now we have come to the point; *en* ~ *bien d'une autre!*, this is something new, this puts a new complexion on it; ~ *que l'aube arrive*, now comes the dawn; ~ *trois mois que j'habite ici*, I have now been living here for three months; ~ *cinq ans*, five years ago; *me* ~ *à trembler*, I'm starting to tremble.

voie [vwa] *s.f.* **1.** way, road, highway; line, route, path, track, trail; (rail.) track, permanent way, line, gauge; (of vehicle) track, axle width; set (of saw); (electr.) circuit; *mettre sur la* ~, to put on the right way, to give directions; *la bonne, la mauvaise,* ~, the right, the wrong, road, (fig.) the right, the wrong, course; *par* ~ *de terre, de mer*, by land, by sea route; *par* ~ *aérienne*, by air, *par* ~ *de* or ~ *Londres*, via London, routed through London; *la* ~ *lactée*, the Milky Way; ~ *à sens unique*, one-way street, (rail.) single-line track; *route à trois* ~*s*, three--lane highway; (rail.) ~ *de garage*, siding; (aeron.) ~ *de départ*, runway; (naut.) ~ *d'eau*, leak; **2.** (fig.) way, means, process, method, course, medium, channel; *en bonne* ~, going well, making good progress; *en* ~ *de*, in process of; *en* ~ *de réparation*, under repair; *être en* (*bonne*) ~ *de*, to be (well) on the way to; *par* ~ *diplomatique*, through (the normal) diplomatic channels; *savoir par les* ~*s les plus sûres*, to have it on the best authority; *par la* ~ *de la persuasion*, by means of persuasion; (law) ~*s de droit*, recourse to legal proceedings; ~(*s*) *de fait*, act of violence, assault, taking the law into one's own hands; ~*s de recours*, grounds for appeal; ~*s d'accommodement*; measures of conciliation; **3.** (anat.) duct, canal; **4.** portable load (of wood, coal, water).

voilà [vwala] *prep.* there is, there are; that is, those are; ~*!*, there!; ~ *comme elle est*, that is what she is like; *en* ~ *assez!*, that will do!, no more of that!, stop it!; ~ *trois ans*, three years ago; ~ *une heure qu'il parle*, he has been talking for an hour; ~ *ce que c'est de vivre seul*, that is what it means to live on one's own; ~ *qui est bien!*, good!, that's a good thing!; ~ *bien les hommes*, that's what men are like, there's the human race for you!; *comme te* ~ *grande!*, how tall you are!; *me* ~ *bien!*, I am in a fine mess; *te* ~ *content*, now you're happy; ~ *tout*, that's all; *en* ~ *une blague*, that is a piece of nonsense; (pop.) *en* ~ *une de femme!*, what a woman!, some woman!; *nous y* ~, there we are, now we have got to the problem; (in café) ~, *monsieur!*, coming, sir!; *en veux-tu en* ~, more than enough, as much as you want; *en* ~ *pour un an*, that will last or take a year; (fam.) (*ne*) ~*-t-il pas qu'il pleut!*, well, if it isn't raining!

voilage [vwalaʒ] *s.m.* veiling; net curtain.

voile[1] [vwal] *s.m.* **1.** veil; (text.) voile, veiling; (fig.) cover, disguise, mask; show, pretence;

mist (before the eyes); obscuring of vision, black-out; (photo.) fogging; (pathol.) shadow (on lung); (of novice) *prendre le ~*, to take the veil; (fig.) *sous le ~ de*, under cloak of, under a mask of; *les ~s de la nuit*, the shades of night; **2.** (anat.) *~ du palais*, soft palate, velum.

voile[2] [vwal] *s.f.* sail, canvas; (naut.) course; *à la ~*, sailing, by sail; *faire la ~*, to sail, to do sailing; *mettre à la ~*, to set or make sail; *faire force de ~s* or *mettre toutes ~s dehors*, to crowd on all sail, (fig.) to make every effort; *amener les ~s*, to strike sail; *diminuer les ~s*, to shorten sail; *naviguer à la ~*, to sail; *navire à ~s*, sailing-ship; (fig.) *avoir le vent dans les ~s*, to be doing well, to be on the high road to success; (aeron.) *vol à ~*, gliding.

voilé, -e [vwale] *adj.* veiled; clouded, blurred, dull, dim; soft; muffled; (photo.) fogged; *temps ~*, hazy weather; *ton ~*, subdued or muffled voice; *roue ~e*, buckled wheel, wheel out of true.

voilement [vwalmɑ̃] *s.m.* buckle (in wheel); warp (in wood).

voiler [vwale] *v.t.* **1.** to veil, to cover, to cloak; to disguise, to conceal; to muffle, to cloud; *~ une roue*, to buckle a wheel; **2.** (naut.) to rig; **se ~** *v.refl.* to be veiled, to wear a veil; to be concealed, covered, or disguised; (of sky) to become overcast; to buckle, to warp.

voilerie [vwalri] *s.f.* **1.** sail-loft; **2.** sail-making.

voilette [vwalɛt] *s.f.* hat-veil, fine veil; veiling.

voilier [vwalje] *s.m.* **1.** sail-maker; **2.** sailing-ship, sailor; *fin ~*, good sailor; *grand ~*, large sea-bird (esp. albatross).

voilure [vwalyr] *s.f.* **1.** set of sails, canvas, the sails; (aeron.) wings, wing surface, aerofoils; *carguer la ~*, to take in sail, to slew up sail; **2.** warping (of boards, etc.), buckling (of wheel).

voir [vwar] *v.t.* to see; to look at, to watch, to behold; to view, to inspect, to examine, to study; to find out; to perceive, to realise; to be on visiting terms with, to visit, to meet; to attend to, to deal with; to go into; *à ~*, to be seen, worth seeing; *c'est à ~!*, we shall see about that!; *on verra*, we shall see, we shall decide later; *~ le jour*, to be born, (fig.) to appear, to emerge; *aller ~*, to go and see; to call on; *allez-y ~*, (i.) go and see about it; (ii.) believe it if you can!; *voyez à ce que cela soit fait*, see to it that it is done; (pop.) *il faudrait ~ à faire ce que j'ordonne*, see that you do what I tell you; *n'avoir rien à ~ avec*, to be irrelevant to; to have nothing to do with, to have no connection with, not to affect; *voyons!*, come!; *faire ~*, to show; *faites ~*, let me see, show it me; *~ du pays*, to travel, to see something of the world; *faire ~ du pays à qn.*, to lead s.o. a pretty dance; *elle lui en a fait ~ de toutes les couleurs*, she plagued him, she made life a burden to him; *je vous vois venir*, I can see what you are driving at, I can guess what you are after; *se faire bien ~*, to make oneself agreeable, to ingratiate oneself; *se faire mal ~*, to make oneself conspicuous (in a bad way), to incur censure; *être bien vu*, to be well thought of, to be highly esteemed; *il ne voit personne.*, he sees nobody, he lives in complete retirement; *nous ne voyons plus ces gens-là*, we are no longer on visiting terms with those people; *vous n'avez rien à y ~*, it's no business of yours; *tu vois bien!*, now you see!, didn't I tell you?; *les enfants, voyez-vous, ça ne dit pas toujours la vérité*, children, you know, don't always speak the truth; *se faire ~*, to show oneself, to make an appearance; *j'en ai vu bien d'autres*, I have seen or experienced a lot worse; *essaie un peu, pour ~!*, just try it and see!; *on lui voit beaucoup d'argent*, he seems to have a lot of money; *voyez si elle est partie*, find out if she has gone; *je ne vois plus rien à dire*, I can find nothing more to say; (of printer's proof) *vu et corrigé*, read and corrected; (pop.) *écoute ~!*, just listen!; *dites ~!*, come on, tell us!; **se ~** *v.refl.* to see oneself; to find oneself; to see each other; to be apparent or conspicuous; to occur, to happen; *cela se voit tous les jours*, that happens or can occur any day, that is an everyday occurence; *cela se voit*, that is plain, evident, obvious, noticeable; *cela se voit comme le nez au milieu du visage*, it is as plain as a pikestaff, it is very obvious or noticeable; *ils ne se voient pas*, they are not on visiting terms; *je me vois forcé de*, I find myself compelled to; *je ne me vois pas habiter là*, I can't see myself living there.

voire [vwar] *adv.* even, indeed, truly; nay, not to say; (obs.) *~?*, really?.

voirie [vwari] *s.f.* **1.** highways, public roads, road system; **2.** administration of roads and streets; *le service de ~*, the highways or streets department, sanitary services, refuse collection; **3.** rubbish-dump, refuse-tip.

voisé, -e [vwaze] *adj.* (phon.) voiced.

voisement [vwazmɑ̃] *s.m.* (phon.) voicing.

voisin, -e [vwazɛ̃] *adj.* neighbouring, bordering (*de*, on), next, next door, adjacent, adjoining; *~ de*, akin to, similar to, closely related to, in the area of, around; *s.m.f.* neighbour; *en ~*, as a neighbour, in a neighbourly manner.

voisinage [vwazinaʒ] *s.m.* neighbourhood; neighbourliness; proximity, vicinity, nearness; *détesté de tout le ~*, an object of hatred to all the neighbours; *avoir des relations de bon ~*, to be on good terms with one's neighbours.

voisiner [vwazine] *v.i.* to visit one's neighbours; *~ avec*, to be next door to, to be sitting beside, to be adjacent to.

voiturage [vwatyraʒ] *s.m.* cartage; conveying, transporting.

voiture [vwatyr] *s.f.* **1.** conveyance, method of transport; cartage; *lettre de ~*, consignment note, way-bill; *prix de ~*, fare, transport charge, carriage; **2.** car, carriage, vehicle, conveyance, coach; cart, van, wagon, truck, taxi(-cab), hackney cab; *~ à deux chevaux*, carriage and pair; *~ deux chevaux* (abbrev. *2 c.v.*) two horse-power car; *~ de remise*, hired car or carriage; *~ d'enfant*, perambulator, pram; *~ de malade*, invalid car or carriage, Bath chair; *~ de livraison*, delivery-van; *~ cellulaire*, prison van; *à bras*, handcart; *~-restaurant*, dining car; *en ~*, by car, by cart; *aller en ~*, to go by car, to drive; *emporter en ~*, to cart away; *transport par ~*, cartage; (rail.) *en ~!*, take your seats!

voiturer [vwatyre] *v.t.* to cart, to convey, to transport, to carry, to carry by car, to take in the car, to drive (s.o.) in the car.

voiturette [vwatyrɛt] *s.f.* small car or van.

voiturier [vwatyrje] *s.m.* carrier, carter, wagoner, driver.

voiturin [vwatyrɛ̃] *s.m.* (obs.) driver, cab-man.

voix [vwa] *s.f.* **1.** voice; tone, utterance, speech, words, sound, cry (of animals, hounds); *à ~ basse*, in an undertone, in a low voice, under one's breath, in a whisper; *à haute ~* or *à ~ haute*, in a loud voice, aloud; *élever sa ~*, to raise one's voice, to speak out, to voice one's opinion; *être sans ~*, to be silent, to be unable to speak, (fig.) to be speechless; *à portée de ~*, within shouting distance; *de vive ~*, by word of mouth, orally, verbally; *faire la grosse ~*, to speak gruffly, to put on an angry tone; (hunt.) *donner de la ~*, to give tongue; *~ de fausset*, falsetto; **2.** vote, voting, voice, say, opinion; *aller aux ~*, to put to the vote; *aux ~!*, divide!, put it to the vote!; *je n'ai pas ~ au chapitre*, I have no say, or voice, in the matter; *donner sa ~ à*, to give one's vote to, to vote for; **3.** (gram.) voice.

vol[1] [vɔl] *s.m.* flying, flight; soaring; flock (of birds), swarm (of flying insects); ~ *plané*, volplane, glide, gliding descent (with engines off); (of birds) soaring; ~ *à voile*, gliding (in glider); *à ~ d'oiseau*, as the crow flies; bird's-eye, from a bird's-eye view; *au ~*, on the wing; flying; (fig.) fleetingly, as it passes; *cueillir une impression au ~*, to gain a fleeting impression.

vol[2] [vɔl] *s.m.* theft, stealing, robbery, larceny, defrauding; (law) ~ *avec effraction*, burglary, housebreaking, theft with breaking and entering; ~ *de grand chemin*, highway robbery; ~ *à l'étalage*, shoplifting.

volable [vɔlabl] *adj.* liable to be stolen; (of person) easy to rob.

volage [vɔlaʒ] *adj.* fickle, inconstant, flighty.

volaille [vɔlɑj] *s.f.* poultry, fowl, fowls; (pop., pej.) a lot of women or girls; *marchand de ~*, poulterer.

volailler [vɔlɑje] *s.m.* poulterer.

volant, -e [vɔlɑ̃] *adj.* flying; loose, detachable, movable, shifting, temporary, travelling; floating, fluttering; (aeron.) *personnel ~*, flight personnel; *feuille ~e*, loose sheet, detachable slip, detached portion; *tapis ~*, magic carpet; *en camp ~*, temporarily; on a flying visit; *pont ~*, flying bridge; (naut.) spar-deck.

volant [vɔlɑ̃] *s.m.* **1.** shuttlecock; ~ (*au filet*), badminton; sail (of windmill); detachable portion (of book of tickets, etc.); *jouer au ~*, to play at battledore and shuttlecock, to play badminton; **2.** (dressm.) flounce, shaped panel; **3.** (mech.) fly-wheel; (hand-operated) control wheel; (car) steering-wheel; (fig.) reserve of stocks or power; ~ *de sécurité*, governor, regulator.

volatil, -e [vɔlatil] *adj.* volatile, evaporating rapidly, (fig.) evanescent; ⚠ not 'volatile' in fig. sense 'lively'.

volatile [vɔlatil] *s.m.* fowl, bird, winged creature; ~ *adj.* winged, flying.

volatilis-able [vɔlatilizabl] *adj.* volatilizable; **~ation** [vɔlatilizɑsjɔ̃] *s.f.* volatilization; **~er** [vɔlatilizc] *v.t.* to volatilize; **se ~er** *v.refl.* to become volatilized, to evaporate; (fig.) to vanish into thin air.

volatilité [vɔlatilite] *s.f.* volatileness, volatility.

vol-au-vent [vɔlovɑ̃] *s.m.invar.* (cook.) vol-au--vent, puff pastry case filled with quenelles, mushrooms, sauce, etc.

volcan [vɔlkɑ̃] *s.m.* volcano; (fig.) seething cauldron; (of person) ball of fire.

volcanique [vɔlkanik] *adj.* volcanic; (fig.) fiery.

volcan-isme [vɔlkanism] *s.m.* volcanism; **~ologie** [vɔlkanɔlɔʒi] *s.f.* vulcanology; **~ologue** [vɔlkanɔlɔg] *s.m.f.* vulcanologist.

volée [vɔle] *s.f.* flight, flock; volley; volley of blows, (fam.) thrashing; pealing (of bells); rank, class, standing; (fam.) band, bevy; *prendre sa ~*, to take wing or flight, to leave the nest; *à la ~*, on the volley, full-pitch; (fig.) instantly, promptly; *à pleine ~*, full-pitch, at full tilt, as hard as one can go; *semer à la ~*, to scatter, to sow broadcast; *de haute ~*, of the first order, in the top class; *cheval de ~*, leader-horse.

voler[1] [vɔle] *v.i.* to fly, to soar, to take wing; to make a flight; to float; (fig.) to run at top speed or like mad, to move fast, to tear away; to dart; (of news, rumours, etc.) to spread rapidly; *faire ~*, to send flying, to blow around or along; ~ *en éclats*, to fly into pieces; *on entendrait ~ une mouche*, you could hear a pin drop; ~ *de ses propres ailes*, to shift for oneself, to stand on one's own feet.

voler[2] [vɔle] *v.t.* to steal, to rob, to thieve, to take away; to kidnap; to usurp; to plagiarize; to swindle, to cheat; (fam.) to pinch, to scrounge; (fig.) *il ne l'a pas volé*, it serves him right, he has got what he deserves; *je suis volé!*, I have been done!; *il se croit volé de ses vacances*, he thinks he has been done out of his holiday.

volerie[1] [vɔlri] *s.f.* flying (of falcons, etc.).

volerie[2] [vɔlri] *s.f.* (obs. exc. dial.) larceny, theft, robbery, stealing; swindle; fleecing.

volet [vɔlɛ] *s.m.* shutter, window-shutter; sorting-tray; (mech.) butterfly-valve; (aeron.) flap; (fig.) *triés sur le ~*, hand-picked, specially selected, choice.

voleter [vɔlte] *v.i.* to flutter about; to flicker.

voleu-r, -se [vɔlœr] *s.m.f.* thief, robber, buglar; plunderer, stealer; *au ~r!*, stop thief!; *~r à la tire*, pickpocket; *~r de grand chemin*, highwayman, footpad; *~r* (*commettant effraction*), burglar; *à ~r, ~r et demi*, set a thief to catch a thief; (jest) *il est fait comme un ~r*, he is dressed like a scarecrow; *adj.* thieving, dishonest.

volière [vɔljɛr] *s.f.* aviary, large bird-cage.

volige [vɔliʒ] *s.f.* (carp.) batten, scantling, slate-lath.

voligeage [vɔliʒaʒ] *s.m.* battening, fitting battens.

voliger [vɔliʒe] *v.t.* to batten, to fit battens to.

voliti-f, -ve [vɔlitif] *adj.* volitive, volitional.

volition [vɔlisjɔ̃] *s.f.* volition.

volley-ball [vɔlɛbol] *s.m.* volley-ball (abbrev. *volley*).

volleyeu-r, -se [vɔlɛjœr] *s.m.f.* volley-ball player; (tennis) volleyer.

volontaire [vɔlɔ̃tɛr] *adj.* **1.** voluntary, of one's free will; intentional, deliberate; spontaneous; **2.** self-willed, wilful, headstrong; ~ *s.m.f.* volunteer; **~ment** [vɔlɔ̃tɛrmɑ̃] *adv.* voluntarily, willingly; deliberately, intentionally; wilfully.

volontariat [vɔlɔ̃tarja] *s.m.* voluntary (military) service.

volonté [vɔlɔ̃te] *s.f.* will, will-power, determination, stubbornness; mind, pleasure, wish, desire; (pl.) whims, caprices; *à ~*, at will, at pleasure, as much as you wish; just as you like; to order; *avoir de la bonne ~*, or *être plein de bonne ~*, to be quite willing, to be full of good will; *y mettre de la mauvaise ~*, to do (sth.) with a bad grace or reluctantly; *dernières ~s*, last will and testament; *faire ses quatre ~s* or *toutes ses ~s*, to act according to one's own sweet will; to have one's own way in everything; *on demande un homme de bonne ~*, a volunteer is required.

volontiers [vɔlɔ̃tje] *adv.* willingly, gladly, with pleasure; readily; frequently; *on croit ~ que*, one is apt, anxious, to think that; *il est ~ taciturne*, he is inclined to be silent; (fam.) *je boirais ~ un coup*, I could do with a glass of something.

volt [vɔlt] *s.m.* (electr.) volt.

voltage [vɔltaʒ] *s.m.* voltage.

voltaïque [vɔltaik] *adj.* voltaic.

voltaire [vɔltɛr] *s.m.* ~, or *fauteuil Voltaire*, a type of armchair.

voltairien, -ne [vɔltɛrjɛ̃] *adj., s.m.f.* Voltairian, Voltairean.

voltamètre [vɔltamɛtr] *s.m.* (electr.) voltameter.

volte [vɔlt] *s.f.* (rid., fenc.) volte; (naut.) turn (to change course).

volte-face [vɔltəfas] *s.f.invar.* (mil.) turning about; *~!*, about turn!; (fig.) *faire ~*, to change sides; to wheel around; to make a complete change of front.

volter [vɔlte] *v.i.* (rid., fenc.) to volt.

voltige [vɔltiʒ] *s.f.* acrobatics on slack-rope or flying trapeze; trick riding.

voltigement [vɔltiʒmɑ̃] *s.m.* flutter, fluttering, hovering, flying about, flitting.

voltiger [vɔltiʒe] *v.i.* to flutter about, to fly

about, to flit, to hover; to perform acrobatics (see VOLTIGE).

voltigeur [vɔltiʒœr] *s.m.* **1.** performer on slack-rope or flying trapeze; **2.** light infantryman, sharp-shooter; **3.** a kind of cigar.

voltmètre [vɔltmɛtr] *s.m.* (electr.) voltmeter.

volubile [vɔlybil] *adj.* **1.** (bot.) voluble; **2.** voluble, glib.

volubilis [vɔlybilis] *s.m.* (bot.) convolvulus.

volubilité [vɔlybilite] *s.f.* volubility, volubleness; *parler avec* ~, to talk volubly, to have a glib tongue.

volucompteur [vɔlykɔ̃tœr] *s.m.* counter, register, (on petrol-pump).

volume [vɔlym] *s.m.* **1.** volume, book, part of a book, tome; **2.** volume, bulk, size, capacity, mass; (geom.) solid; *cela fera beaucoup de* ~, that will take up a lot of room; (fig., fam.) *faire du* ~, to throw one's weight about.

volumétrique [vɔlymetrik] *adj.* volumetric; **~ment** [vɔlymetrikmɑ̃] *adv.* volumetrically.

volumineu-x, -se [vɔlyminø] *adj.* voluminous, bulky.

volupté [vɔlypte] *s.f.* voluptuousness, pleasure, sensuality, sensual pleasure.

voluptuaire [vɔlyptɥɛr] *adj.* voluptuary, of luxury, for embellishment.

voluptueu-x, -se [vɔlyptɥø] *adj.* voluptuous, sensual, luxurious, epicurean; *s.m.f.* epicurean, sensualist, voluptuary; **~sement** [vɔlyptɥøzmɑ̃] *adv.* voluptuously, luxuriously.

volute [vɔlyt] *s.f.* volute, scroll; spiral, curl; (zool.) volute.

volve [vɔlv] *s.f.* (bot.) volva.

vomer [vɔmɛr] *s.m.* (anat.) vomer (bone in nose).

vomique [vɔmik] *adj.f. noix* ~, nux vomica.

vomi [vɔmi] *s.m.* vomit.

vomir [vɔmir] *v.t.i.* to vomit (up); to spew, to cast up, to belch out, to bring up, to throw up; *avoir envie de* ~, to feel sick, to have nausea; (fig.) *cela donne envie de* ~, or *c'est à* ~, it makes you sick, it is utterly repulsive; ~ *des injures*, to let out a stream of invective.

vomissement [vɔmismɑ̃] *s.m.* vomiting, vomit; (fig.) belching out.

vomissure [vɔmisyr] *s.f.* vomit.

vomiti-f, -ve [vɔmitif] *adj.* vomitory; **~f** *s.m.* vomitory, emetic.

vomitoire [vɔmitwar] *s.m.* (Rom. ant.) vomitory.

vomito negro [vɔmitonegro] *s.m.* (pathol.) black vomit, yellow fever.

vorace [vɔras] *adj.* voracious, greedy, ravenous; (fig.) destructive; **~ment** [vɔrasmɑ̃] *adv.* voraciously, greedily, ravenously.

voracité [vɔrasite] *s.f.* voraciousness, voracity, greediness, greed.

vortex [vɔrtɛks] *s.m.* vortex; ⚠ not 'eddy' or 'whirlpool'.

vos see VOTRE.

votant, -e [vɔtɑ̃] *s.m.f.* voter, elector.

vote [vɔt] *s.m.* vote, suffrage, voting; poll; *droit de* ~, franchise; ~ *à main levée*, vote by show of hands; *bulletin de* ~, voting-paper, ballot-paper; ~ *au scrutin secret*, (secret) ballot.

voter [vɔte] *v.t.i.* to vote, to give one's vote, to poll; (pop.) ~ *qn.*, to vote for s.o.; ~ *des remerciements à qn.*, to pass a vote of thanks to s.o.; ~ *une loi*, to enact a law.

voti-f, -ve [vɔtif] *adj.* votive.

votre [vɔtr], (pl.) **vos** [vo] *poss.adj.* your, your own.

vôtre [votr] *poss.pron.* yours, your own; *le* ~, *la* ~, *les* ~*s*, yours; your property; your part; *il a emporté son chapeau et le* ~ *aussi*, he has gone off with his hat and yours too; *je suis tout* ~, I am entirely at your service; *je suis des* ~*s*, I am with you, I am on your side; *vous en avez encore fait des* ~*s*, you have been up to your tricks again; *je serai des* ~*s jeudi*, I shall be one of your party on Thursday; (pop.) *à la* ~*!*, your health!; *allons, mettez-y du* ~, now, show your good will; *aimez les* ~*s*, love your family.

vouer [vwe] *v.t.* to vow, to promise solemnly; to devote, to dedicate, to consecrate; to doom, to condemn, to consign; ~ *à l'exécration publique*, to consign to public hatred; ~ *au bleu*, to dedicate to the Virgin; **se** ~ *v.refl.* to devote oneself; (fam.) *ne savoir à quel sant se* ~, not to know which way to turn.

vouge [vuʒ] *s.m.* **1.** billhook; **2.** (obs.) halberd.

vouloir [vulwar] *v.t.* to will, to be determined on, to want, to require, to wish, to be willing, to have a will; to choose; to demand; to ask; to expect; to mean, to intend; to decree; to maintain; to admit; *je veux du silence*, I must have silence; *je ne le veux pas*, I won't have it; *qu'il le veuille ou non*, whether he likes it or not; ~ *qn. pour roi*, to want s.o. as king; *veux-tu te taire!*, will you shut up!; *faites comme vous voudrez*, do as you like; *je lui voudrais plus de courage*, I wish he had more courage; *vous ne voulez pas de ma compagnie?*, you don't want my company?; *je n'en veux pas*, I don't want it, I don't want anything to do with it; *un cruel sort a voulu que*, a cruel fate decreed that; *Descartes a voulu que les animaux fussent des machines*, Descartes maintained that animals were machines; *que voulez-vous?*, (i.) what do you want?, what can I do for you?; (ii.) what do you expect? that's how it is; it can't be helped; ~ *bien*, to be willing, to be prepared, to be so kind as to; *je (le) veux bien*, I am willing, willingly, I don't mind, I have no objection, all right, then!; *vous l'avez (bien) voulu*, you would have it, it serves you right, you have brought it on yourself; ~ *du bien à qn.*, to bear good will to s.o., to wish s.o. well; *que voulez-vous dire?*, what do you mean?; *que veut dire cela?*, what does it mean?; *je veux dire que*, I mean (to say) that; *il m'en veut*, he has, he bears, a grudge against me; *je m'en veux de n'avoir pas*, I reproach myself for not having; *que me voulez-vous?*, what do you want of me?; *il faut savoir ce qu'on veut*, one must make up one's mind; *ce bois ne veut pas brûler*, this wood won't burn; *Dieu veuille que*, God grant that; *il veut absolument qu'elle parte*, he insists on her leaving; *veuillez me faire savoir*, kindly let me know; *veuillez faire ceci*, please, have the goodness to, do this; *il veut 100 francs de son chien*, he wants 100 francs for his dog; *je veux que vous parliez*, I want you to speak; *comment voulez-vous qu'il y arrive?*, how do you expect him to manage it?; *demandez-lui s'il voudrait dire*, ask him if he wouldn't mind saying; ~ *c'est pouvoir*, where there's a will there's a way; *c'est triste, je veux bien, mais*, it is sad, I admit, but; *je veux bien que vous ayez raison*, I grant you may be right.

vouloir [vulwar] *s.m.* will, will-power; *bon* ~, goodwill; willingness; *mauvais* ~, ill will, reluctance, bad grace, unwillingness.

voulu, -e [vuly] *adj.* deliberate, intended, intentional, done on purpose; required, requisite, necessary.

vous [vu] *pers.pron.* you; to you; one; *je* ~ *l'ai dit*, I told you so; *je* ~ *le porterai*, I will bring it (to) you; *bien à* ~, yours sincerely; *à* ~, to you, yours, belonging to you; it's your turn, you begin; *à* ~ *de savoir si*, it is up to you to know whether; *il ne tient qu'à* ~, it is up to you, it all depends on you; *ça* ~ *fait peur*, it frightens one; *de* ~ *à moi*, between ourselves; from you to me; ~*-même*, yourself; ~*-mêmes*, yourselves.

vousseau (pl. **-x**) [vuso], **voussoir** [vuswar]

s.m. (arch.) voussoir, wedge-shaped stone (forming arch).
voussure [vusyr] *s.f.* (arch.) coving; (anat.) arching.
voûte [vut] *s.f.* vault, arch; (fig.) canopy, vault; ~ *d'arête*, groined vault; *clef de* ~, keystone; (anat.) ~ *du palais*, roof of the mouth.
voûté, -e [vute] *adj.* vaulted, arched; (of person) bent, stooping, round-shouldered.
voûter [vute] *v.t.* to vault, to arch over; to make round-shouldered; **se** ~ *v.refl.* to become bent or round-shouldered, to stoop.
vouvray [vuvrɛ] *s.m.* Vouvray (wine).
vouvoyer [vuvwaje], **vousoyer** [vuzwaje] *v.t.* to use *vous* (and not *tu*) in speaking to (s.o.).
voyage [vwajaʒ] *s.m.* journey, travel, voyage, trip, tour, excursion; *bon* ~*!*, a pleasant journey (to you)!; *partir en* ~, to go on a (long) journey, to set off on one's travels, to leave home; *aimer les* ~*s*, to be fond of travelling; *faire un* ~, to travel, to be travelling, to make a journey or trip; ~ *de noces*, honeymoon; ~ *d'agrément*, pleasure trip; ~ *d'essai*, trial trip; *le grand* ~, the last journey, death; *en* ~, on a journey, travelling, away; *compagnon de* ~, travelling-companion, fellow-traveller.
voyager [vwajaze] *v.i.* to travel, to journey, to make a trip; to be travelling; to be a traveller or representative (for a firm); (of goods) to be transported; ~ *par mer*, to travel by sea, to voyage; *marchandises qui s'abîment en voyageant*, goods which are liable to damage in transit.
voyageu-r, -se [vwajaʒœr] *s.m.f.* traveller; passenger; ~*r de commerce* or *commis-*~*r*, commercial traveller, bagman; *adj.* travelling, migratory, nomadic; *oiseaux* ~*rs*, migratory birds, migrants.
voyant, -e [vwajɑ̃] *adj.* **1.** seeing; sighted; **2.** showy, glaring, gaudy, loud; conspicuous; *s.m.f.* seer, clairvoyant(e), prophet, prophetess; ~ *s.m.* signal-light, warning-light; mark; signal; (surv.) sighting-board.
voyelle [vwajɛl] *s.f.* vowel.
voyer [vwaje] *s.m. agent* ~, road-surveyor, inspector of roads.
voyou [vwaju] *s.m.* hooligan, rough, rowdy; street urchin.
voyoucratie [vwajukrasi] *s.f.* (iron.) mobocracy, mob-rule.
(**en**) **vrac** [ɑ̃vrak] *adv.loc.* pell-mell, in disorder; in bulk, unpacked, loose; *charger en* ~, to load in bulk.
vrai, -e [vrɛ] *adj.* true, real, exact, right, genuine, correct, accurate, veritable, true to life; veracious, truthful, sincere; thorough, arrant, regular; *c'est la vérité* ~*e*, that is gospel, not a word of a lie!; ~ *de* ~, genuine, hundred-per-cent; (pop.) *c'est pas* ~*!*, impossible!, no kidding?; ~ *s.m.* truth, reality; *être dans le* ~, to be (in the) right; ~ *adv.* truly, true, really; *à* ~ *dire*, or *au* ~, to tell the truth, in truth; *pour de* ~, really, truly, in earnest; *vous me dites cela pour de* ~*?*, do you really mean it?; *pas* ~*?*, is it not so?, isn't that a fact?, eh?; *vous m'écrirez, pas* ~*?*, you will write to me, won't you? (fam.) *eh, ben* ~, *c'est du propre!*, well, really! that's a pretty state of affairs!; ~**ment** [vrɛmɑ̃] *adv.* truly, veritably, really; indeed, in truth; ~*ment?*, really?, is that so?
vraisemblable [vrɛsɑ̃blabl] *adj.* likely, credible, probable, expected, believable, plausible; *le vrai peut quelquefois n'être pas* ~, truth is stranger than fiction; *peu* ~, unlikely, unconvincing; ~**ment** [vrɛsɑ̃blabləmɑ̃] *adv.* very likely, probably; in all probability; to all appearances, apparently.
vraisemblance [vrɛsɑ̃blɑ̃s] *s.f.* likelihood, probability, plausibility; verisimilitude, credibility; *selon toute* ~, to all appearances, in all probability; according to every reasonable expectation.
vrillage [vrijaʒ] *s.m.* (weaving) snarling, kinking; twist, torsion.
vrille [vrij] *s.f.* **1.** (bot.) tendril; **2.** (mech.) borer, piercer, gimlet; **3.** spiral; (aeron.) spin, tail-spin; *escalier en* ~, spiral staircase; (aeron.) *tomber en* ~, to spin, to get into a spin.
vrillé, -e [vrije] *adj.* bored, pierced, twisted, kinked; spiral; (bot.) having tendrils, twisted.
vrillée [vrije] *s.f.* (bot.) bindweed.
vriller [vrije] *v.t.* to pierce, to bore; to twist, to kink, to snarl; ~ *v.i.* to ascend spirally, to cork--screw.
vrillette [vrijɛt] *s.f.* (ent.) boring-beetle, death-watch beetle, anobium.
vrombir [vrɔ̃bir] *v.i.* to buzz, to hum, to throb.
vrombissement [vrɔ̃bismɑ̃] *s.m.* buzzing, humming, throbbing; purring (of engine).
vu, -e [vy] *adj.* seen, considered, regarded, deemed; *ni* ~ *ni connu*, you won't discover anything, nobody is any the wiser; (fam.) *c'est bien* ~*?*, understood?, got it?; *bien* ~, well liked, appreciated, regarded with favour; *mal* ~, held in very poor, or no, esteem, meets with disapproval; ~ *d'avion*, aerial view, bird's-eye view; ~ *prep.* ~ *la difficulté*, considering, or in view of, the difficulty; ~ *qu'il ne le connaît pas*, in view of the fact that he doesn't know him, seeing that he is not acquainted with him.
vu [vy] *s.m. au* ~ *et au su de tout le monde*, openly, with everyone's knowledge; as everybody knows.
vue [vy] *s.f.* sight, eyesight, vision, eyes, eye; view, aspect, look; prospect; survey; design, aim, schemes; (fig.) insight, penetration, reckoning; (photo.) slide; *à* ~, at sight; (of drawing) freehand; (comm.) *payable à* ~, payable on sight, on presentation; *jeter la* ~ *sur*, to cast one's eye over; (cin.) *prise de* ~*s*, filming, take; *à* ~ *de pays*, according to the lie of the land; (fig.) cursorily, at a cursory glance; *à* ~ *de nez*, at a rough guess, by rule of thumb; at first glance; *à* ~ *d'œil*, visibly, very rapidly, in no time; *garder à* ~, not to let out of one's sight, to watch closely; to keep in custody; *changement à* ~, (theatr.) change of scenery without lowering curtain; (fig.) sudden and complete change; *à perte de* ~, as far as the eye can see; (fig.) endlessly, going on and on; *je le connais de* ~, I know him by sight; *avoir la* ~ *basse* or *courte*, to be short-sighted; *sa* ~ *baisse*, his sight is failing; *avoir la* ~ *faible*, to have poor eyesight; *perdre la* ~, to lose one's sight; *perdre de* ~, to lose sight of; (law) *droit de* ~*s*, ancient lights; *en* ~, visible, in sight, in prospect, conspicuous, prominent; *en* ~ *de*, (i.) with a view to, in order to; (ii.) within sight of; *avoir en* ~, to have in view or in mind, to propose (*de*, to); *avoir des* ~*s sur*, to have views, or designs, on; to aim at; *avoir* ~ *sur*, (of window, etc.) to have a view of, to look over; ~ *d'en face*, *de côté*, front, side, view; ~ *en coupe*, cross--section; *prendre des* ~*s*, to take photos, snapshots, etc; *point de* ~, point of view, view-point; *au point de* ~ *de*, as to, in respect of, regarding, from the standpoint or angle of; *avoir le don de seconde* ~, to be clairvoyant, to have second sight; (mus.) *jouer à première* ~, to play at sight; (slang) *en mettre plein la* ~ *de qn.*, to dazzle s.o.
vulcain [vylkɛ̃] *s.m.* red admiral (butterfly).
vulcanisation [vylkanizɑsjɔ̃] *s.f.* vulcanization, vulcanizing.
vulcaniser [vylkanize] *v.t.* to vulcanize, to cure (rubber).
vulcanite [vylkanit] *s.f.* vulcanite, ebonite.
vulcanologie [vylkanɔlɔʒi] *s.f.* = VOLCANOLOGIE.

vulcanologue [vylkanɔlɔg] *s.m.f.* = VOLCANOLOGUE.

vulgaire [vylgɛr] *adj.* **1.** vulgar, common; in common use, everyday, ordinary; *langue* ~, vulgar tongue, vernacular; **2.** vulgar, coarse, low, plebeian; in bad taste; ~ *s.m.* the common people, the common herd; populace; the common run; **~ment** [vylgɛrmɑ̃] *adv.* vulgarly, coarsely, in a vulgar way; commonly.

vulgarisat-eur, -rice [vylgarizatœr] *s.m.f.* popularizer.

vulgarisation [vylgarizɑsjɔ̃] *s.f.* popularization; dissemination.

vulgariser [vylgarize] *v.t.* to popularize, to disseminate; to coarsen, to vulgarize.

vulgarité [vylgarite] *s.f.* commonness, ordinariness; vulgarity, coarseness.

vulgate [vylgat] *s.f.* Vulgate.

vulnérabilité [vylnerabilite] *s.f.* vulnerability, vulnerableness.

vulnérable [vylnerabl] *adj.* vulnerable.

vulnéraire [vylnerɛr] *adj.* vulnerary, useful for healing wounds; ~ *s.m.* vulnerary; ~ *s.f.* (bot.) kidney-vetch, ladies' fingers.

vulpin [vylpɛ̃] *s.m.* (bot.) foxtail (grass).

vultueu-x, -se [vyltɥø] *adj.* (of the face) red and swollen, congested, bloated.

vulvaire [vylvɛr] *adj.* (anat.) vulvar.

vulve [vylv] *s.f.* (anat.) vulva.

vulvite [vylvit] *s.f.* (med.) vulvitis.

W

W, w [dubləve] *s.m.* the letter W, w.

wagnérien, -ne [vagnerjɛ̃] *adj.*, *s.m.f.* Wagnerian.

wagon [vagɔ̃] *s.m.* railway coach or carriage, truck; ~*-poste*, mail-van; ~*-restaurant*, restaurant-car, dining-car; ~*-salon*, pullman car; ~*-lit*, sleeping-car, sleeper; ~*-citerne* or ~*-réservoir* or ~*-foudre*, tank-car, tank-wagon; ~*-trémie*, hopper-truck; ⚠ not 'wagon' in sense 'heavy cart'.

wagonnet [vagɔnɛ] *s.m.* (mining) tub, tip-truck.

walk-over [walkɔvœr] *s.m.* (sport) walk-over.

walkyrie [valkiri] *s.f.* (myth.) Valkyrie; *la Walkyrie*, the Valkyrie (opera).

wallace [valas] *s.f.* drinking-fountain (of kind erected in Paris by Richard Wallace).

wallon, -ne [valɔ̃] *adj.*, *s.m.f.* Walloon.

wapiti [wapiti] *s.m.* (zool.) wapiti.

warrant [warɑ̃t, varɑ̃(t)] *s.m.* (comm.) warrant, voucher; **~age** [varɑ̃taʒ] *s.m.* issuing of warrant; **~er** [varɑ̃te] *v.t.* to issue (goods) with a warrant.

water-closet [watɛrklozɛt] *s.m.* (pl. *water-closets*) = WATERS.

watergang [watɛrgɑ̃] *s.m.* canal beside dyke or road.

wateringue [watrɛ̃g] *s.f.* reclaiming and draining system.

waterproof [watɛrpruf] *s.m.*, *adj.invar.* waterproof.

waters [watɛr, vater] *s.m.pl.* water-closet, W.C.

watt [wat] *s.m.* (electr.) watt; **~-heure** [watœr] *s.m.* watt-hour; **~man** [watman] *s.m.* (obs.) tram-driver; **~mètre** [watmɛtr] *s.m.* watt-hour meter, wattmeter.

week-end [wikɛnd] *s.m.* week-end.

welche see VELCHE.

western [wɛstɛrn] *s.m.* western (film).

wharf [warf] *s.m.* wharf.

whig [wig] *s.m.*, *adj.* (Eng. hist.) Whig.

whisky [wiski] *s.m.* (pl. *whiskies*) whisky, whiskey.

whist [wist] *s.m.* whist.

wigwam [wigwam] *s.m.* wigwam.

wisigoth, -e [visigo] *adj.*, *s.m.f.* Visigoth(ic).

wisigothique [vizigɔtik] *adj.* Visigothic.

wolfram [vɔlfram] *s.m.* wolfram, tungsten ore.

wombat [wɔ̃ba] *s.m.* (zool.) wombat.

wyandotte [vjɑ̃dɔt] *s.m.f.*, *adj.* Wyandotte (fowl).

X

X, x [iks] *s.m.* the letter X, x; *avoir les jambes en X*, to be knock-kneed; *rayons-X*, X-rays; (students' slang) *l'X* = the *École Polytechnique*; *un X*, a student of the *École Polytechnique*, a Polytechnician; *les X*, mathematics.

xanth-ine [gsɑ̃tin] *s.f.* (chem.) xanthine; **~ophylle** [gsɑ̃tɔfil] *s.f.* xanthophyll.

xénon [ksenɔ̃] *s.m.* (chem.) xenon.

xéno-phobe [ksenɔfɔb] *s.m.f.*, *adj.* xenophobe; **~phobie** [ksenɔfɔbi] *s.f.* xenophobia.

xéranthème [kserɑ̃tɛm] *s.m.* (bot.) xeranthemum, immortelle.

xérès [gzerɛs] *s.m.* sherry (wine); *Xérès*, (geog.) Jerez.

xérodermie [kserɔdermi] *s.f.* (pathol.) xeroderm(i)a.

xiphoïde [ksifɔid] *adj.* (anat.) xiphoid, sword-shaped.

xylène [ksilɛn] *s.m.* (chem.) xylene.

xylocope [ksilɔkɔp] *s.m.* (ent.) carpenter-bee.

xylo-graphe [ksilɔgraf] *s.m.* wood-engraver, xylographer; **~graphie** [ksilɔgrafi] *s.f.* wood-engraving, xylography; **~graphique** [ksilɔgrafik] *adj.* xylographic.

xylol [ksilɔl] *s.m.* = XYLÈNE.

xylophage [ksilɔfaʒ] *adj.* (ent.) xylophagous.

xylophone [ksilɔfɔn] *s.m.* xylophone.

Y

Y, y [igrɛk] *s.m.* the letter Y, y.

y [i] *pron.*, *adv.* **1.** here, there, thither; to, in, at, on, it or them; at home; *allez-~*, go there, (fam.) go on! get moving!; *vas-~!*, go on! go it!; *je l'~ ai vu*, I saw him there; *j'~ cours*, I'll be there, I'll go, right away; *j'~ suis, j'~ reste*, possession is nine points of the law; *il ~ a*, there is, there are, there exists; *il n'~ voit pas*, his sight is bad; *j'~ vois clair*, I see it, I understand it; *j'~ suis*, I get it, I see what you mean, I understand; *ça ~ est*, it's done, that's it, all right! done! now it's happened!; *le compte ~ est*, the account, the total, is right, it is correct; *je n'~ suis pour rien*, I have nothing to do with it, it is nothing to do with me; *il ~ va de sa tête*, his life is at stake; (pop.) *je l'~ ai flanqué une gifle*, I gave him a slap; **2.** pron. object in construction using *à*; *~ penser*, to think of it or them; *sans ~ penser*, without thinking; *s'~ fier*, to rely on it; *s'~ décider*, to make up one's mind (to do it); *~ compris*, including; *je n'~ comprends rien*, I don't understand it, I can't make head or tail of it; *~ regarder de près*, to be very particular; *~ ajouter foi*, to give it credence; *s'~ engager*, to undertake (it), to commit oneself to it, to pledge one's word; *s'~ refuser*, to refuse to undertake it.

yacht [jɔt] *s.m.* yacht.

yachtman [jɔtman], **yachtsman** [jɔtsman] *s.m.* (pl. *yachtmen, yachtsmen*) (obs.) yachtsman.

yack, yak [jak] *s.m.* (zool.) yak.

yaourt [jaur] *s.m.* = YOGHOURT.

yatagan [jatagɑ̃] *s.m.* yataghan.

yèble [jɛbl] *s.f.* = HIÈBLE.

Yémen [jemen] *s.m.* (geog.) Yemen.

yéménite [jemenit] *adj.*, *s.m.f.* (native or inhabitant) of the Yemen, Yemeni.

yeuse [jøz] *s.f.* (bot.) ilex, holm-oak, evergreen oak.

yeux [jø] *s.m.pl.* see ŒIL.

yé-yé [jeje] (pl. *yé-yés*) *s.m.f.* (obs., used about 1960) = teenager; *~ adj.* teen-age.

yoghourt, yogourt [jɔgur] *s.m.* yoghurt, yogurt, yaourt.

yole [jɔl] *s.f.* (naut.) yawl, gig, skiff.

yougoslave [jugɔslav] *adj.*, *s.m.f.* Yugoslavian, Yugoslav.

Yougoslavie [jugɔslavi] *s.f.* (geog.) Yugoslavia.

youpin [jupɛ̃] *s.m.* (slang, pej.) Jew.

youyou [juju] *s.m.* (naut.) dinghy.

ypérite [iperit] *s.f.* mustard-gas.

ypréau (pl. **-x**) [ipreo] *s.m.* (bot.) broad-leaved elm.

yucca [juka] *s.m.* (bot.) yucca.

Z

Z, z [zɛd] *s.m.* the letter Z, z; (fig., fam.) *être fait comme un ~*, to be as crooked as they're made.

zagaie [zagɛ] *s.f.* = SAGAIE.

zain [zɛ̃] *adj.m.* (of horses and dogs) whole-coloured, with no speck of white.

Zambèze [zɑ̃bɛz] *s.m.* (geog.) Zambezi.

Zambie [zɑ̃bi] *s.f.* (geog.) Zambia.

zani, zanni [zani] *s.m.* zany.

zanzibar [zɑ̃zibar] *s.m.* a kind of dice game (abbrev. *zanzi*).

Zanzibar [zɑ̃zibar] *s.m.* (geog.) Zanzibar.

zazou, -e [zazu] *s.m.f.* nickname for off-beat youth in years following 2nd World War.

zèbre [zɛbr] *s.m.* zebra; (pop.) individual.

zébrer [zebre] *v.t.* to mark with stripes, to stripe, to streak.

zébrure [zebryr] *s.f.* **1.** stripe, striped marking (on fur); **2.** weal, stripe.

zébu [zeby] *s.m.* (zool.) zebu, humped ox.

Zélande [zelɑ̃d] *s.f.* (geog.) Zeeland, Zealand; *la Nouvelle ~*, New Zealand.

zélat-eur, -rice [zelatœr] *s.m.f.* **1.** Zealot; **2.** zealous supporter or defender.

zèle [zɛl] *s.m.* zeal, devotion, enthusiasm, fervour; *faire du ~*, to be over-zealous; (indust.) *grève de ~*, go-slow.

zélé, -e [zele] *adj.* zealous, full of zeal.

zélote [zelɔt] *s.m.* = ZÉLATEUR 1.

zend, -e [zɛ̃d] *adj.*, *~ s.m.* (lang.) Zend.

zénith [zenit] *s.m.* zenith.

zéolite, zéolithe [zeɔlit] *s.f.* zeolite.

zéphyr [zefir] *s.m.* **1.** zephyr, west wind, gentle breeze; **2.** soft wool or brushed cotton material.

zéro [zero] *s.m.*, *adj.* zero, nought, nothing, nil; no; (fig.) nonentity; *~ heure*, 12 midnight (abbrev. *0.h.*); *mettre au point ~*, to zero or calibrate (an instrument); *il a fait ~ faute*, he made no mistakes; *~ de recette aujourd'hui*, nil receipts today; **~tage** [zerɔtaʒ] *s.m.* calibration or zeroing (of instrument).

zest [zɛst] *interj.* (obs.) phew!; *~ s.m. entre le zist et le ~*, (i.) neither one thing nor the other, so-so; (ii.) dithering, unable to make up one's mind.

zeste [zɛst] *s.m.* (of orange, lemon, etc.) peel, rind, zest; slice of lemon, etc., added to drink; dividing membrane (in walnut); (fig.) *cela ne vaut pas un ~*, it's not worth a straw; *cela n'y fera pas un ~*, that won't make an iota of difference; ⚠ not 'zest' in sense 'keen enjoyment'.

zester [zɛste] *v.t.* to remove the rind of (an orange, etc.).

zeugma [zœgma], **zeugme** [zœgm] *s.m.* zeugma.

zézaiement [zezɛmɑ̃] *s.m* lisping, lisp.

zézayer [zezeje] *v.i.* to lisp.

zibeline [ziblin] *s.f.* sable.

zieuter, zyeuter [zjøte] *v.t.* (pop.) to watch, to keep an eye on.

zig, zigue [zig], **zigoto** [zigɔto] *s.m.* (pop.) individual.

zigouiller [ziguje] *v.t.* (slang) to stick a knife into, to kill.

zigzag [zigzag] *s.m.* zigzag; *faire des ~s*, to zigzag, to stagger along; *ligne en ~*, zigzag line;

éclairs en ~, forked lightning; **~ué** [zigzage] *adj.* zigzag, in zigzags; **~uer** [zigzage] *v.i.* to zigzag, to drive erratically, to weave from side to side.

zinc [zɛ̃g] *s.m.* **1.** zinc; **2.** (slang) bar-counter; **3.** (pop.) aeroplane, (fam.) crate; **~ographie** [zɛ̃kɔgrafi], **~ogravure** [zɛ̃kɔgravyr] *s.f.* zincography.

zingage [zɛ̃gaʒ] *s.m.* zincing, zinc-plating.

zingaro [dzingaro] *s.m.* Zingaro, gipsy.

zinguer [zɛ̃ge] *v.t.* to cover or plate with zinc, to zinc; to galvanize.

zingueur [zɛ̃gœr] *s.m.* zinc-worker, zinc-roofer.

zinnia [zinja] *s.m.* (bot.) zinnia.

zinzin [zɛ̃zɛ̃] *adj.* (pop.) mad, cracked; ~ *s.m.* (pop.) gadget, thingummy.

zinzinuler [zɛ̃zinyle] *v.i.* (of small birds) to trill.

zinzolin [zɛ̃zɔlɛ̃] *s.m.*, *adj.invar.* reddish violet.

zircon [zirkɔ̃] *s.m.* zircon; **~ium** [zirkɔnjɔm] *s.m.* (chem.) zirconium.

zist [zist] *s.m.* see ZEST *s.m.*

zizanie [zizani] *s.f.* (bot.) tare, darnel-grass; zizania, wild rice; (fig.) dissension, discord, strife; (fig.) *semer la* ~, to sow dissension.

zodiacal, -e, (**aux**) [zɔdjakal] *adj.* zodiacal.

zodiaque [zɔdjak] *s.m.* zodiac.

zoé [zɔe] *s.f.* zoea, larva of certain crustaceans.

zoïle [zɔil] *s.m.* carping critic.

zona [zona] *s.m.* (pathol.) shingles.

zonage [zonaʒ] *s.m.* (town-planning) zoning.

zone [zon] *s.f.* zone, belt, sector, area; ~ *franche*, duty-free zone; ~ *bleue*, restricted parking zone; ~ *verte*, green belt; ~ *de salaire*, pay-scale; *de seconde* ~, inferior, second-class; *la Zone*, haphazard development (in former military zone of Paris fortifications); *une* ~, a run-down district.

zoné, -e [zone] *adj.* zoned, zonate.

zoni-er, -ère [zonje] *s.m.f.* frontier-dweller.

zoo [zoo] *s.m.* zoo.

zoolite, zoolithe [zɔɔlit] *s.m.* zoolite.

zoolog-ie [zɔɔlɔʒi] *s.f.* zoology; **~ique** [zɔɔlɔʒik] *adj.* zoological; **~iquement** [zɔɔlɔʒikmɑ̃] *adv.* zoologically; **~iste** [zɔɔlɔʒist] *s.m.* zoologist.

zoophyte [zɔɔfit] *s.m.* (sci.) zoophyte.

zoospore [zɔɔspɔr] *s.f.* (bot.) zoospore.

zootrope [zɔɔtrɔp] *s.m.* zoetrope, wheel of life.

zorille [zɔril] *s.f.* (zool.) zoril.

zoroastrie-n, -ne [zɔrɔastrijɛ̃] *s.m.f.*, *adj.* Zoroastrian.

zoroastrisme [zɔrɔastrism] *s.m.* Zoroastrianism.

zostère [zɔstɛr] *s.f.* (bot.) sea-grass.

zouave [zwav] *s.m.* zouave (soldier); (fig., fam.) *faire le* ~, to lark about, to play the buffoon.

zou [zu] *interj.* gee up!, let's go!

zozo [zozo] *s.m.* (pop.) fool.

zut [zyt] *interj.* (pop.) expressing anger or contempt; ~ *pour les scrupules!*, to hell with scruples!

zyeuter see ZIEUTER.

zygène [ziʒen] *s.f.* **1.** (ent.) burnet moth; **2.** (zool.) hammer-head shark.

zygoma [zigɔma] *s.m.* (anat.) zygoma.

zygomatique [zigɔmatik] *adj.* (anat.) zygomatic.

zygo-morphe [zigɔmɔrf] *adj.* (bot.) zygomorphic, zygomorphous; **~spore** [zigɔspɔr] *s.m.* (bot.) zygospore.

zygote [zigɔt] *s.m.* (biol.) zygote.

zymase [zimaz] *s.f.* (chem.) zymase.

zymotique [zimɔtik] *adj.* zymotic, of fermentation.

THE CONCISE OXFORD ENGLISH–FRENCH DICTIONARY

First edited by
G. W. F. R. Goodridge

SECOND EDITION
edited by
Joyce A. Hutchinson, Ph.D. (Cantab.)
and
Jean-Dominique Biard, Ph.D. (London)

PREFACE

THE most difficult task facing the compiler of a concise English–French dictionary must be to decide which English words to include and which to omit, and then to find ways of presenting the material clearly and at the same time succinctly. This was the challenge ably met by G. W. F. R. Goodridge, who edited the first edition of the *Concise Oxford English–French Dictionary* in 1940. The same task, nearly forty years later, is immeasurably greater, when one considers the increase in everyday vocabulary brought about by technological progress and the vast extension of mass communications.

This edition of the *Concise Oxford English–French Dictionary* therefore represents a complete revision of the 1940 edition. It is based on a detailed scrutiny of the original edition, which has inevitably led to the elimination of a mass of material, either because it is now obsolete or because the words were too uncommon or too technical to justify inclusion. The opportunity has been taken to bring the vocabulary completely up-to-date, with the addition of many new words, phrases and meanings, including additional derivatives. These include the more common technical terms and also some contemporary colloquialisms. Also included in the main body of the text are certain common Proper Names, including those of countries, as well as the more common acronyms (e.g. NATO).

Like the first edition, this dictionary is designed primarily for the English-speaking user who wishes to write or speak French; but, unlike the original edition, which mentions particularly 'the general requirements of schools, commercial phraseology and modern war terms', no special attention has been paid to the requirements of any group of users.

The methods used in the selection of vocabulary and its presentation are explained more fully in the Introduction, which the reader is urged to consult in order to make the best use of the dictionary. We should like to reiterate the principle stated by Goodridge in his Preface: 'In many old-fashioned glossaries, synonyms, or what passed for such, were arranged in groups divided by semicolons. The investigator was left to his own beclouded choice as to which term in which group was precisely the one he was seeking. I have endeavoured to lessen this difficulty in the first place by dispensing with all synonyms; secondly by explaining in brackets the exact meaning of words . . .'

We also agree with Goodridge that a dictionary can have no pretensions to fulfil the uses of a grammar and grammatical information has been kept to a minimum. Considerations of space also prevent the inclusion of numerous examples but these are given where they seem essential to illustrate the difference between French and English usage, or to show the difference between two possible constructions.

Lengthy paraphrases to explain English concepts which do not exist in French (e.g. cricketing terms) have also been avoided.

In conclusion, we should like to express our gratitude to all our friends and colleagues, both English- and French-speaking, who have shown a continued interest in this work, have encouraged us and helped us to track down stubborn translations, either by their own research, or in discussion. They are too numerous to mention by name and so must remain anonymous. We should however particularly like to thank Monsieur Bernard LeGros, assistant at the *Institut d'Études Anglaises et Nord-Américaines* of the University of Caen, who, with the help of his colleagues, has seldom failed to find an answer to the most thorny problem. Finally, we should like to put on record our gratitude to the late Professor S. Ullmann, who introduced us both to this project and without whose unfailing advice and encouragement it would never have got off the ground.

J.A.H.
J.-D.B.

INTRODUCTION

1. VOCABULARY

The criterion for the selection of the vocabulary has been to include only words which can be considered to form part of the everyday, non-specialized working vocabulary of the average English user. This selection is based on the vocabulary offered in the *Concise Oxford Dictionary* (6th edition). While some common technical, commercial, legal, scientific and other specialized terms are included, it is assumed that the reader seeking more specialized terms in these fields will consult a specialist dictionary. Such words, when included, are preceded by the appropriate subject label. Since the dictionary is intended for the user wishing to speak as well as to write French, a reasonable number of current colloquial expressions is included and every effort has been made to offer a French equivalent on the same level. Words used in the spoken language by educated speakers are labelled (*fam.*), those generally used only by uneducated speakers are marked (*pop.*). Although the French equivalent of an English word can often be used both literally and figuratively, it is sometimes necessary to use two different French words where the same English word covers both uses. This is indicated by the labels (*lit.*) or (*fig.*) before the French words. Names of countries, as well as the corresponding adjectives, are now included in the text (and not in a separate appendix), as are most common acronyms. These are given in their alphabetical place in the dictionary. For some acronyms or abbreviations which refer to English institutions (e.g. TUC), it has been necessary to given an approximate French equivalent and this is marked (*approx.*).

Many English words have several different senses and in most cases these, even if very close in meaning, are translated by different French words. A concise gloss, indicating the sense of the English word, is given before each French word. The French word given is the most usual French equivalent, except in a few cases where two French words are equally current. In a few entries, where no glosses are given for an English word with several senses, it may be assumed that the one French word given covers all the senses of the English word.

2. ARRANGEMENT OF ENTRIES

For conciseness, entries have been condensed so that all derivatives and compounds are included in the entry of which the headword is their first element, even if this places them out of alphabetical sequence. Cross references are given where the placing of a word may not be obvious, and also for phrases, such as '**let sleeping dogs lie**', which are translated under only one of their constituent words. In all cross references the word to be referred to is printed in SMALL CAPITALS, e.g. '**let sleeping** DOGS **lie**'.

3. STRUCTURE OF ENTRIES

a. *Parts of speech.*

When the English headword can be used as several different parts of speech, the *s.* form is usually given first, and the other forms later in the same entry. Only very occasionally, in the case of very long entries, are *s.* and *v.* the subject of separate entries.

b. *Numbering.*

Most French words are preceded either by a gloss or an abbreviated subject label (see section 1). The several distinct senses of the English headword, indicated in this way, may be numbered **1.**, **2.**, **3.**, etc. The same numbers repeated, (1), (2), (3), etc. before the French words for other parts of speech or derivatives, indicate a corresponding field of meaning.

c. *Phrases and compounds.*

All phrases and compounds in which the headword is the main element follow in the same entry. In these cases, the headword is represented by the swung dash ~, e.g. under SPOT, **on the ~**; **in a ~**; **~-on**; **~light**, etc.

d. *Derivatives.*

All derivatives formed from the headword with suffixes, e.g. *-able*, *-ance*, *-ly*, *-ness*, are also given in the same entry. The headword, or the part of the headword preceding the oblique dash, /, is represented by the swung dash, e.g. under ACCEPT, **~able**; **~ance**; under AMIAB/LE, **~ility**, **~ly**. In the case of adverbs formed with *-ly*, an asterisk, *, indicates that the French adverb is regularly formed by adding -ment to the feminine form of the French adjective. The French adverb is given in full only if its formation is irregular or if it is necessary to translate the English adverb by a phrase.

e. *Transitive and intransitive verbs.*

When a French verb, like the corresponding English verb, can be used both transitively and intransitively, this is indicated by the abbreviation *v.t.* & *i.* after the verb, e.g. **blow** *v.t.* & *i.* souffler. Where the transitive and intransitive forms vary slightly in French, this is indicated as follows: **abate** *v.t.* & *i.* (*make or become less*) (s')affaiblir. The (s') shows that the reflexive form of the French verb corresponds to the English intransitive. Similarly, **abort** *v.t.* & *i.* (faire) avorter; in this case (faire) provides the transitive form (*to cause an abortion*). When two different French verbs are required to translate the transitive and intransitive forms of the English verb, these are given separately, e.g. **believe** *v.t.* croire; *v.i.* avoir la foi; **bolt** *v.t.* (*lock*) verrouiller; *v.i.* (*flee*) décamper. It also happens that a French verb is used transitively while its English equivalent is not, and vice versa, e.g. **approve of**, approuver; **ask for**, demander; **obey**, obéir (à qn.); **please**, plaire (à qn.). These cases are usually marked with the danger signal (see below, section 4).

f. *Verbs with prepositions or adverbs.*
Particular attention has been paid to the English construction, verb + preposition or, verb + adverb, since this construction is much less common in French and can present a major translation problem. Verbs used in this way are translated under the entry for the verb itself, e.g. under TAKE, ~ **after**, ~ **against**, ~ **away**, ~ **back**, ~ **down**, ~ **from**, ~ **in**, ~ **off**, ~ **on**, ~ **out**, ~ **to**, ~ **up**.

4. THE DANGER SIGNAL

The danger signal, ⚠, used by Goodridge to indicate a 'faux ami', has been retained and its use extended to give warning of possible syntactical error.

5. INFLEXION AND SYNTAX

For conciseness, the plural of a *s.* or *adj.* and the feminine form of an *adj.* are given only if they are irregular. When a *s.* may refer to both sexes, it is presented as *s.m.f.* and the feminine ending given in brackets, e.g. assistant(e). A few essential reminders of syntactical constructions are included, e.g. verbs or constructions followed by the subjunctive, the use of the partitive article. These are usually illustrated by examples.

6. CROSS-CHECKING

A basic rule for the use of a bilingual dictionary is to cross-check the translation of a word by looking it up in a dictionary in the opposite direction. While every effort has been made to present the material in this dictionary in a clear, concise and practical way, avoiding possible ambiguities, the user is recommended, if in doubt, to cross-check in the *French–English dictionary*, where he may also find more information on feminine and plural forms, as well as a phonetic transcript of the French word as a guide to pronunciation.

ABBREVIATIONS USED IN THE DICTIONARY

ABBREVIATIONS in general use (including acronyms, e.g. NATO) appear in the dictionary itself. The addition of 'etc.' to the full form in this list means that the abbreviation may also stand for a related word, e.g. sometimes *fin.* = financial, *parl.* = parliamentary.

abbrev./iation
acad./emic
adj./ective
admin./istrative
adv./erb
agric./ulture
anat./omy
antiq./uity
approx./imate(ly)
arch./itecture
archeol./ogy
art./icle
astron./omy
auto./mobile, motoring
aux./iliary
aviat./ion

biol./ogy
bot./any

chem./istry
comm./erce
comp./arative
cond./itional tense
conj./unction
constr./uction
cook./ery
crit./icism

def./inite
dem./onstrative
dept. department
dialect./al
dressm./aking

eccles./iastical
econ./omics
electr./ical, electricity
e.g. for example
Eng./lish
ent./omology
esp./ecially
etc. etcetera
exc./ept
exclam./atory

f./eminine
fam./iliar
fig./urative(ly)

fin./ance, etc.
fort./ification
Fr./ench
freq./uently
fut./ure tense

gen./erally
geog./raphy, etc.
geol./ogy, etc.
geom./etry
govt. government
gym./nastics

herald./ry
hist./ory, etc.
hort./iculture
hunt./ing

i./ntransitive
impers./onal
indef./inite
indic./ative
ind./irect
inf./initive
interrog./ative
interj./ection
invar./iable
iron./ically
irreg./ular(ly)

joc./ular

kg. kilogram
km. kilometre

lang./uage (a language)
ling./uistics, etc.
lit./erally
liter./ature

m./asculine
math./ematics
mech./anical(ly)
med./icine
metall./urgy
meteor./ology
micro./phone
mil./itary
mineral./ogy

mod./ern
ms. manuscript
mus./ic, etc.
myth./ology

naut./ical
n.b. note
neg./ative
no. number

obj./ect
obs./olete
opt./ical
orat./ory
ornith./ology

paint./ing
parl./iament, etc.
part./iciple
pej./orative(ly)
pers./onal
pharm./acy, etc.
photo./graphy
phys./ics, physical
pl./ural
poet./ical
polit./ics, etc.
pop./ular
poss./essive
p.p. past participle
pref./ix
prep./osition
pres./ent
print./ing
pron./oun
psych./ology
P. proprietary name. see note below.

qch. quelque chose
qn. quelqu'un

rail./ways
refl./exive
rel./ative
relig./ious
rhet./oric
Rom./an

s./ubstantive, noun
sc./ience, etc.
sew./ing
sing./ular
s.o. someone
sth. something
subj./unctive
surg./ery

t./ransitive
techn./ical(ly)
temp./erature
text./iles
theat./re
theol./ogical
TV television

univ./ersity
usu./ally

v./erb
veg./etable
vet./erinary
vulg./ar

zool./ogy, etc.

Symbols
The following symbols are used in the dictionary:

~ (swung dash)—represents headword or part of headword (see Introduction 3)

* indicates regularly formed *adv.* (see Introduction 3)

≠ indicates opposite meaning e.g. **right** (≠ *left*)

⚠ danger signal (see Introduction 4)

¹. ². ³. etc. used to differentiate unrelated homonyms

1. 2. 3. etc. & (1), (2), (3) etc. see Introduction 3.

NOTE ON PROPRIETARY TERMS

THIS dictionary includes some words which are or are asserted to be proprietary names or trade marks. Their inclusion does not imply that they have acquired for legal purposes a non-proprietary or general significance, nor is any other judgement implied concerning their legal status. In cases where the editor has some evidence that a word is used as a proprietary name or trade mark this is indicated by the letter **P**, but no judgement concerning the legal status of such words is made or implied thereby.

A

a (**an**) *indef. art.* un(e) *m.f.*; *s.* (*mus.*) la *m.*; (*in house number*) **6a** = 6 bis; **A1** (*first class*) de première qualité; (*mil. med.*) bon pour le service.
aback *adv.* en arrière; **to be taken ~,** être décontenancé, interloqué.
abandon *s.* laisser-aller *m.*, désinvolture *f.*; *v.t.* abandonner, quitter; (*give up, fig.*) renoncer à; **~ oneself to,** se laisser aller à; **~ed** *adj.* (*deserted*) abandonné; (*wicked*) dépravé; **~ment** *s.* abandon *m.*
abase *v.t.* (*degrade*) abaisser; (*humiliate*) humilier; **~ment** *s.* humiliation *f.*
abash *v.t.* (*strike with shame*) confondre; (*astound*) déconcerter, dérouter; **~ed** *adj.* confondu, déconcerté.
abate *v.t.* & *i.* (*diminish*) diminuer; (*make or become less*) (s')affaiblir, (s')amoindrir; (*storm, pain etc.*) se calmer; (*law*) annuler; **~ment** *s.* diminution *f.*
abattoir *s.* abattoir *m.*
abb/ey *s.* abbaye *f.*; **~ot** *s.* abbé *m.*; **~ess** *s.* abbesse *f.*
abbreviat/e *v.t.* abréger; **~ion** *s.* abréviation *f.*
ABC *s.* (*alphabet*) a b c *m.*; (*first rudiments of music etc.*) l'a b c. de la musique etc.; (*railway time-table*) indicateur *m.* (des chemins de fer).
abdicat/e *v.t.* **1.** (*authority*) abdiquer; **2.** (*function*) se démettre de; **3.** (*rights*) renoncer à; **4.** (*throne*) déposer (la couronne); *v.i.* abdiquer; **~ion** *s.* (1) & (4) abdication *f.*; (2) démission *f.*; (3) renonciation *f.*
abdom/en *s.* abdomen *m.*; **~inal** *adj.* abdominal.
abduct *v.t.* enlever; **~ion** *s.* enlèvement *m.*
aberration *s.* (*deviation from normal*) aberration *f.*; (*mental lapse*) égarement *m.*
abet *v.t.* encourager, pousser (qn. à faire qch.); être complice de; **~ter, ~tor** *s.* complice *m.f.*
abeyance *s.* suspension (temporaire) *f.*; **in ~** (*custom*) en désuétude, (*question*) en suspens.
abhor *v.t.* exécrer, avoir en horreur; **~rence** *s.* horreur *f.*; **~rent** *adj.* odieux, exécrable, détestable.
abide *v.t.* & *i.* (*dwell, remain*) demeurer, habiter, séjourner; (*endure*) *v.t.* supporter; *v.i.* durer; (*submit to*) **~ by,** se soumettre à (*the rules*—aux règles), rester fidèle à (*a promise*—sa promesse), s'en tenir à; **I will ~ by what you say,** je m'en tiendrai à ce que vous dites; **abiding** *adj.* durable, persistant.
ability *s.* (*power or capacity*) capacité *f.*; (*talent*) talent *m.*, habileté *f.*; **to do sth. to the best of one's ~,** faire de son mieux.
abject *adj.* **1.** (*despicable*) abject; **2.** (*wretched*) misérable; **3.** (*degraded*) bas, vil; **~ly** *adv.* (1) abominablement; (2)*; (3)*; **~ness** *s.* (1) abjection *f.*; (2) misère *f.*; (3) bassesse *f.*
abjure *v.t.* (*eccles.*) abjurer; (*rights, etc.*) renoncer à.
ablaze *adj.* en feu; (*fig.*) enflammé (*with*—de); **to be ~,** flamber.
able *adj.* (*competent*) capable (*to*—de); (*talented*) habile; **to be ~,** pouvoir; (*in a position to*) être en mesure de; **~-bodied** *adj.* fort, vigoureux, (*fam.*) costaud; **ably** *adv.**;*.
ablution *s.* ablution *f.*; (*fam. usu. pl.*) ablutions; (*place, in camp, etc.*) sanitaires *m.pl.*
abnegation *s.* (*of doctrine etc.*) abjuration *f.*; (*self-*) abnégation *f.*
abnormal *adj.* anormal; **~ity** *s.* anomalie *f.*; (*med.*) difformité *f.*; **~ly** *adv.**.
aboard *adv.* (*ship, plane*) à bord, (*vehicles*) en voiture; *prep.* à bord de; **to go ~,** s'embarquer; **all ~!,** en voiture!
abode *s.* demeure *f.*, domicile *m.*
aboli/sh *v.t.* **1.** abolir; **2.** (*suppress*) supprimer; **~tion** *s.* (1) abolition *f.*; (2) suppression *f.*; **~tionist** *s.* abolitionniste *m.f.*
A-bomb *s.* bombe atomique *f.*
abomin/ate *v.t.* avoir en horreur; **~able** *adj.* abominable; **~ably** *adv.**; **~ation** *s.* horreur *f.*, abomination *f.*
aborigin/al *adj.* & *s.m.f.* aborigène; **~es** *s.pl.* aborigènes *m.f.pl.*
abort *v.t.* & *i.* (faire) avorter; **~ion** *s.* (*act*) avortement *m.*; (*person, plant, etc.*) avorton *m.*; (*thing*) œuvre manquée *f.*; **~ionist** *s.* avorteu/r, -se *m.f.*, (*fam.*) faiseuse d'anges *f.*; **~ive** *adj.* (*med.*) abortif; (*fig.*) avorté, manqué, raté.
abound *v.i.* abonder (*in*—en); foisonner, grouiller (de), **it ~s in worms,** cela grouille (foisonne) de vers.
about *adv.* & *prep.* (*all round*) (tout) autour (de); (*here and there*) çà et là; (*somewhere around*) quelque part; **dotted ~ the fields,** parsemé par les champs; **there is a rumour ~ that,** le bruit court que; **to be up and ~** (*of person*), être sur pied; (*approximately*) environ, à peu près; (*face in opposite direction*) **~ turn!,** demi-tour!; **~-face** *v.i.* faire volte-face; *s.* volte-face *f.*; (*in rotation*) à tour de rôle; (*occupied with*) **what are you ~?** (*fam.*) qu'est-ce que vous fabriquez?; **to be ~ to do sth.,** être sur le point de faire qch.; (*concerning*) au sujet de; **what is it all ~?,** de quoi s'agit-il?; **he told me ~ it,** il m'a mis au courant; **what** *or* **how ~ my lunch?,** et mon dèjeuner?; **what ~ a walk?,** si on faisait une promenade?; *see also certain verbs, e.g.* BEAT, GO, HANG, PUT, SEE.
above *prep.* au dessus de; *adv.* (*higher up*) au dessus, plus haut; (*overhead*) en haut; (*in addition*) de plus, davantage; **~ all,** surtout; **~-board** *adv.* cartes sur table.
abracadabra *s.* abracadabra *m.*; (*gibberish*) jargon *m.*
abras/ion *s.* abrasion *f.*; **~ive** *adj.* abrasif.
abreast *adv.* de front, côte à côte; **~ of,** en ligne avec; **four etc. ~,** par rangs de quatre etc.; **to keep ~ of the times,** se tenir au courant.
abridge *v.t.* **1.** (*summarize*) abréger; **2.** (*reduce*) diminuer; **~ment** *s.* (1) abrégé *m.*; (2) diminution *f.*
abroad *adv.* (*in foreign country*) à l'étranger; (*widely*) au loin; **to** PUBLISH **~; the report is ~ that . . .,** le bruit court que . . .
abrogat/e *v.t.* abroger; **~ion** *s.* abrogation *f.*
abrupt *adj.* **1.** (*sudden, hasty*) brusque, précipité; **2.** (*disconnected*) décousu, saccadé; **3.** (*steep*) escarpé; **4.** (*rude in manner*) brusque, bourru; **~ly** *adv.* (1)*; (2) d'une manière décousue; (3) à pic; (4) d'un ton cassant.
abscess *s.* abcès *m.*
abscond *v.i.* s'enfuir, (*fam.*) décamper.
absen/ce *s.* **1.** (*being away*) absence *f.*, éloignement *m.*; **2.** (*non-existence, want of*) manque *m.*; **3.** (*abstracted state*) distraction *f.*; **leave of ~ce,** permission *f.*; **sentenced in his ~ce,** con-

damné par contumace; **in the ~ce of** (*facts*) à défaut de; **~t** *adj.* (1) absent; (2) manquant; (3) distrait; *v.refl.* s'absenter; **~t-minded** *adj.* distrait; **~t-mindedly** *adv.**; **~t-mindedness** *s.* distraction *f.*; **~tee** *s.* absent *m.*, manquant *m.*

absinth *s.* absinthe *f.*

absolute *adj.* (*complete, pure; unrestricted; unqualified*) absolu, parfait, véritable; (*despotic*) autoritaire, despotique; **~ly** *adv.**,*,*; de façon autoritaire, despotiquement; (= *oh, yes!*) bien entendu, parfaitement; (*quite*) entièrement; **~ly forbidden,** formellement interdit.

absol/ve *v.t.* (*from sins*) absoudre; (*from promise etc.*) relever (de); **~ution** *s.* absolution *f.*

absor/b *v.t.* absorber; (*deaden shock or sound*) amortir; **~bed in,** absorbé dans; **~bent** *adj.* & *s.m.* absorbant; **~ber** *s.* amortisseur *m.*; **~bing** *adj.* absorbant; **~ption** *s.* absorption *f.*

abstain *v.i.* s'abstenir (*from*—de); (*voting*) **ten abstained,** dix se sont abstenus; **~er** *s.* abstinent *m.*

abstemious *adj.* sobre, frugal; **~ly** *adv.**,*.

abstention *s.* abstention *f.*

abstinen/ce *s.* (*eccles.*) abstinence *f.*; **total ~,** rejet (*m.*) de toute boisson alcoolique; **~t** *adj.* abstinent.

abstract *adj.* (≠ *concrete*) abstrait; (*theoretical*) théorique; *s.* (*summary*) abrégé *m.*; *v.t.* **1.** (*take away*) soustraire; **2.** (*steal*) dérober; **3.** (*summarize*) résumer; **~ion** *s.* (1) soustraction *f.*; (2) vol *m.*; **4.** (*absent-mindedness*) distraction *f.*; **~ed** *adj.* distrait.

abstruse *adj.* abstrus.

absurd *adj.* absurde, ridicule; **~ity** *s.* absurdité *f.*; **~ly** *adv.**,*.

abundan/ce *s.* (*plenty*) abondance *f.*; (*riches*) richesse *f.*, affluence *f.*; **~t** *adj.* abondant, copieux; **to be ~t,** abonder; **~tly** *adv.* abondamment,*.

abus/e *s.* **1.** (*insult*) injures *f.pl.*; **2.** (*misuse*) abus *m.*; *v.t.* (1) injurier, médire de; (2) abuser de; **~ive** *adj.* (*language*) injurieux; (*person*) grossier; ⚠ abusif = *excessive*.

abut *v.t.* **~ on,** être contigu à, toucher à.

abys/s *s.* abîme *m.*; **~mal** *adj.* insondable; (*fig.*) profond.

academ/y *s.* (*place of study*) académie *f.*; (*school*) collège *m.*; (*for special training*) école militaire *or* navale *f.*; (*arts*) académie *f.*; (*mus.*) conservatoire *m.*; **~ic** *adj.* académique; (*unpractical*) théorique; *s.* universitaire *m.*; **~ical** *adj.* universitaire; **~ician** *s.* académicien *m.*

accede *v.i.* (*to office*) arriver à; (*to throne*) monter sur (le trône); (*assent to*) consentir à; (*to treaty*) adhérer à.

accelerat/e *v.t.* & *i.* accélérer; (*fig.*) précipiter; **~ion** *s.* accélération *f.*; **~or** *s.* accélérateur *m.*; **~or pedal,** champignon *m.* (*fam.*).

accent *s.* (*stress, sign, dialect*) accent *m.*; *v.t.* accentuer, appuyer sur; **~uate** *v.t.* souligner; (*detail*) faire ressortir; (*effect*) rehausser; **~uation** *s.* accentuation *f.*

accept *v.t.* **1.** (*consent to receive*): (*present etc.*) accepter; (*compliments, greetings*) agréer; **2.** (*invitation*) accepter; **3.** (*admit as true*) admettre; **~able** *adj.* acceptable, possible, (*suitable*) convenable; **~ance** *s.* (1) & (2) acceptation *f.*, agrément *m.*; (3) créance *f.*, admission *f.*; **~ation** *s.* (*of word*) signification *f.*

access *s.* (*admission, approach*) accès *m.*; (*of illness*) attaque *f.*; **~ible** *adj.* accessible, (*person*) abordable; **~ible to all,** à la portée de tout le monde; **~ion** *s.* admission *f.*; (*to power*) accession *f.*; (*to throne*) avènement *m.*; (*to library*) addition *f.*; **~ory** *adj.* accessoire; *s.* (*optional extra*) accessoire *m.*; (*law*) complice *m.*, (*before the fact*) par instigation; (*after the fact*) après coup.

accident *s.* (*mishap, event without apparent cause*) accident *m.*; (*unexpected event*) événement *m.*; (*unintentional act*) hasard *m.*; **by ~,** par hasard, accidentellement; **a** CHAPTER **of ~s; ~al** *adj.* accidentel, fortuit; (*not essential*) secondaire; **~al** *s.* (*mus.*) accident *m.*; **~ally** *adv.**;*.

acclaim *s.* acclamation *f.* (*also* = **acclamation**); *v.t.* acclamer.

acclimatiz/e *v.t.* acclimater; **~ation** *s.* acclimatation *f.*

accommodat/e *v.t.* **1.** (*adapt, arrange*) accommoder, adapter (à); **2.** (*reconcile* (*oneself*)) (s')adapter, (s')accommoder; **3.** (*lodge*) loger, abriter; **4.** (*oblige*) obliger, rendre service à; **~ion** *s.* (1) & (2) adaptation *f.*; (3) logement *m.*; (4) commodités *f.pl.*, facilités *f.pl.*; **~ing** *adj.* obligeant, complaisant.

accompan/y *v.t.* accompagner; (*mus.*) accompagner (*on*—à); **~iment** *s.* accompagnement *m.*; **~ist** *s.* accompagnat/eur, -rice *m.f.*

accomplice *s.* complice *m.*

accomplish *v.t.* accomplir; (*an end*) atteindre (un but), arriver à (ses fins); (*a desire*) réaliser (un désir); (*successfully*) mener à bonne fin; **~ed** *adj.* accompli, achevé; **~ment** *s.* accomplissement *m.*, réalisation *f.*; **~ments** *s.pl.* (= *talents*) talents *m.pl.*

accord *s.* **1.** (*consent*) accord *m.*; **2.** (*agreement*) entente *f.*; **of one's own ~,** de son plein gré; **with one ~,** d'un commun accord; *v.t.* (1) (*grant*) concéder, octroyer; *v.i.* (2) s'accorder, être d'accord (sur, avec); **~ance** *s.* accord *m.*, conformité *f.*; **in ~ance with,** conformément à; **~ing as,** selon que, dans la mesure où, **you will be rewarded ~ing as to whether you work well or badly,** vous serez récompensé selon que vous travaillerez bien ou mal; **~ing to,** selon, d'après, **~ing to the rules,** selon les règles; **~ing to him, I was wrong,** d'après lui, j'ai eu tort; **it's all ~ing,** c'est selon; **~ingly** *adv.* (*therefore*) en conséquence; (*correspondingly*) conformément.

accordion *s.* accordéon *m.*; **~ist** *s.* accordéoniste *m.f.*; **~** PLEATS.

accost *v.t.* aborder; (*solicit*) racoler.

account *s.* (*reckoning*) calcul *m.*; (*fin.*) compte *m.*; (*explanation*) exposé *m.*, rapport *m.*; (*narration*) récit *m.*; **to pay** (**sth.**) **on ~,** donner un acompte; **on no ~,** dans aucun cas; **on ~ of,** à cause de (qn., qch.), par égard pour (qn.), en consideration de (qch.); **to take into ~,** tenir compte de; **to** CALL **to ~**; *v.t.* **~ for,** justifier, expliquer; **~able** *adj.* responsable (de); **~ant** *s.* comptable *m.*; CHARTER**ed ~ant; ~ancy** *s.* comptabilité *f.*

accredit *v.t.* accréditer (*to*—auprès de); attribuer (qch. à qn.).

accretion *s.* accroissement *m.*

accrue *v.i.* (*fall to*) revenir à; (*arise from*) provenir de.

accumulat/e *v.t.* & *i.* (s')amonceler, (s')entasser; **~ion** *s.* amoncellement *m.*, entassement *m.*, (*heap*) amas *m.*, tas *m.*; **~or** *s.* (*electr.*) accumulateur *m.*

accura/te *adj.* **1.** (*exact*) exact, précis; **2.** (*eye, aim*) juste; **3.** (*memory, translation*) fidèle; **~cy** *s.* (1) exactitude *f.*, précision *f.*; (2) justesse *f.*; (3) fidélité *f.*; **~tely** *adv.* avec précision.

accursed *adj.* maudit, (*fam.*) détestable.

accus/e *v.t.* **1.** accuser (qn. de qch. *or* de faire, d'avoir fait, qch.); **2.** (*law*) inculper, incriminer; **~ation** *s.* (1) accusation *f.*; (2) inculpation *f.*; **~er** *s.* accusat/eur, -rice *m.f.*; **~ed** *s.* (*during inquiry*) inculpé *m.*; (*in lower courts*) prévenu *m.*; (*at assizes*) accusé *m.*

accustom *v.t.* accoutumer (à); *v.refl.* s'accoutumer (à); **to be ~ed to sth.,** avoir l'habitude de qch.; **to be ~ed to doing sth.,** avoir l'habitude de faire qch.

ace *s.* (*cards, dice etc.*; *service at tennis*; *champion*) as *m.*; **within an ~ of,** à deux doigts de.
acerbity *s.* (*speech, temper*) âpreté *f.*; (*taste*) aigreur *f.*
acet/ic *adj.* acétique; **~ate** *s.* acétate *m.*; **~ylene** *s.* acétylène *m.*
ache *s.* douleur *f.*, mal *m.*, (*fig.*) peine *f.*; *v.i.* faire mal; **my head ~s,** j'ai mal à la tête; **my heart ~s,** je suis navré; **to be aching to do sth.,** brûler d'envie de faire qch.
achieve *v.t.* (*accomplish*) accomplir; (*attain*) atteindre; **~ment** *s.* accomplissement *m.*, réussite *f.*, exploit *m.*; ⚠ achever = **to finish.**
acid *adj.* & *s.m.* acide; (*fig.*) aigre; **the ~ test,** (*lit.* & *fig.*) la pierre de touche; **~ity** *s.* acidité *f.*; **~ly** *adv.* avec aigreur.
acknowledge *v.t.* **1.** (*admit truth of, own*) reconnaître, admettre; **2.** (*announce receipt of*) accuser réception de; **3.** (*thank*) remercier; **~ment** *s.* (1) (*of fact*) reconnaissance *f.*, (*of misdeed*) aveu *m.*; (2) accusé de réception *m.*; (3) remerciement *m.*
acme *s.* comble *m.*
acne *s.* acné *f.*
acorn *s.* gland *m.*
acoustic *adj.* acoustique; **~s** *s.* acoustique *f.* ⚠ *sing. in French.*
acquaint *v.t.* (*make aware of or familiar with*) informer de; (*inform*) renseigner (sur), faire part à qn. de qch., mettre qn. au courant de qch.; **to be ~ed with,** connaître, être au courant de; **to become ~ed with,** faire la connaissance de; **~ance** *s.* connaissance *f.*, (*persons*) relations *f.pl.*
acquiesce *v.i.* **1.** (*agree, esp. tacitly*) acquiescer (à); **2.** (*accept*) accepter, se soumettre à; **~nce** *s.* (1) consentement *m.*; (2) soumission *f.*
acqui/re *v.t.* gagner, acquérir, (ap)prendre; **he has ~red a taste for whisky,** il a pris goût au whisky; **~red** *adj.* acquis; **~sition** *s.* acquisition *f.*; **~sitive** *adj.* âpre au gain.
acquit *v.t.* acquitter; **~ oneself (of),** s'acquitter (de); **~tal** *s.* acquittement *m.*
acre *s.* (*approx.*) arpent *m.*; **~s** (*pl.* = *lands, fields*) terres *f.pl.*; **~age** *s.* superficie *f.*
acrid *adj.* âcre.
acrimon/y *s.* acrimonie *f.*; **~ious** *adj.* hargneux.
acrobat *s.* acrobate *m.*; **~ics** *s.* acrobatie *f.* ⚠ *sing. in French*; **~ic** *adj.* acrobatique.
across *prep.* à travers; **~ the fields,** à travers les champs; en travers de; **he put a chair ~ the door,** il mit une chaise en travers de la porte; (*on the other side of, position only*), **his house is ~ the street,** sa maison est de l'autre côté de la rue; **a bridge ~ a river,** un pont sur une rivière; **to get ~ s.o.,** se mettre en travers de qn.; **to run or come ~,** rencontrer par hasard; **to put sth. ~,** faire adopter qch.; ⚠ *for,* **to walk, run, etc. ~,** *use* traverser *with a phrase, e.g.* à pied, en courant, etc.; **he ran ~ the street,** il traversa la rue en courant; *adv.* en travers.
acrostic *s.* acrostiche *m.*
act *s.* **1.** (*thing done*) fait *m.*; (*objectively*) acte *m.*; **an ~ of courage,** un acte de courage; (*subjectively*) action *f.*; **a kind ~,** une bonne action; **2.** (*decree*) loi *f.*; **3.** (*theat.*) acte *m.*; **4.** (*item in programme*) numéro *m.*; **to put on an ~,** jouer la comédie (à qn.); **in the ~ of,** sur le point de; **caught in the ~,** pris sur le fait; *v.t.* & *i.* (1) agir; (3) jouer; **5.** (*behave*) se comporter; **6.** (*serve as*): (*thing*) servir de; (*person*) remplir les fonctions de; **~ on,** agir sur; **~ upon advice,** agir d'après un conseil; **~or** *s.* acteur *m.*, **~ress** actrice *f.*; **~ing** *adj.* intérimaire; **~ing** *s.* action *f.*; (*theat.*) jeu *m.*; (*fig.*) comédie *f.*
action *s.* acte *m.*, action *f.* (*see* ACT); (*style*) allure *f.*; (*mechanism*) marche *f.*, mouvement *m.*; (*law*) action *f.*, litige *m.*; (*battle*) action *f.*, combat *m.*; **to take ~,** prendre des mesures; (*law*) poursuivre en justice; **~able** *adj.* actionnable.
activ/e *adj.* actif; (*energetic*) alerte, dynamique; **~ate** *v.t.* activer; **~ely** *adv.**; **~ity** *s.* activité *f.*; (*sphere of action*) fonctions *f.pl.*
actual *adj.* **1.** (*real*) effectif, réel; **2.** (*current*) actuel (⚠ *this meaning only*); **~ity** *s.* réalité *f.*; **~ly** *adv.* (1)*,*; (2)*.
actuary *s.* actuaire *m.*
acumen *s.* perspicacité *f.*
acute *adj.* **1.** (*sharp, keen, penetrating*; *angle*; *accent*) aigu; **2.** (*clever*) avisé, perspicace; **3.** (*disease*) aigu; **4.** (*emotions*) intense, poignant; **~ly** *adv.* (1) vivement; (2) avec perspicacité; (3) & (4) intensément; **~ness** *s.* (1) acuité *f.*; (2) perspicacité *f.*; (3) & (4) intensité *f.*
A.D. (=**anno domini**) **1. A.D. 1972**—1972 après J.C.; **2.** (*Eng. fam.*) vieillesse *f.*
adamant *adj.* (*substance*) infrangible; (*person*) inflexible.
adapt *v.t.* & *i.* (*suit, fit*), (s')adapter (à) (pour); (*alter*) (se) modifier; **~able** *adj.* adaptable, (*person*) souple; **~ation** *s.* adaptation *f.*, modification *f.*; **~er, ~or** *s.*, adaptat/eur, -rice *m.f.*; (*electr.*) raccord *m.*
A.D.C. (*abbrev. aide-de-camp*) *s.* aide de camp *m.*
add *v.t.* ajouter; **~ to** *v.t.* augmenter; **~ up** *v.t.* & *i.* additionner; **~ up to,** se monter à; (*fam.*) signifier; **~endum** *s.* addendum *m.* (*pl.* addenda); **~ition** *s.* (*adding*) addition *f.*; (*thing added*) surcroît *m.*, supplément *m.*; **~itional** *adj.* additionnel, supplémentaire.
adder *s.* vipère *f.*
addict *s.* **1.** (*tobacco, drink*) intoxiqué *m.*; (*drugs*) toxicomane *m.*; **2.** (*sports, etc.*) fanatique *m.*; **~ed to,** adonné à; **~ion** *s.* (1) goût *m.*; (2) manie *f.*
addle *v.t.* pourrir; **~d** *adj.* (*eggs*) pourri; (*fig.* = *crazy*) brouillé, confus; **~-pated, -headed,** écervelé.
address *s.* (*speech*) discours *m.*; (*manner*) abord *m.*, air *m.*; (*residence*) adresse *f.*; *v.t.* (*speak to*) s'adresser à, haranguer, apostropher; (*write to*) adresser une lettre à qn.; (*an envelope*) mettre l'adresse sur; (*a meeting*) prendre la parole à; **~ oneself to,** se mettre à; **~ee** *s.* destinataire *m.*; **~ograph** *s.* adressographe *m.*; PUBLIC **~ system.**
adduce *v.t.* (*excuse, authority*) alléguer; (*proof*) fournir.
adenoids *s.* végétations (adénoïdes) *f.pl.*
adept *s.* expert *m.*; *adj.* **~ at,** expert en.
adequate *adj.* suffisant; **~ to,** proportionné à, (*person*) à la hauteur de; **~ly** *adv.* suffisamment.
adhe/re *v.i.* (*stick fast*) coller (à); (*fig.*) maintenir, persister dans; (*support*) adhérer; **~rence** *s.* adhérence *f.*; **~rent** *s.* adhérent *m.*; **~sion** *s.* adhésion *f.*; **~sive** *adj.* & *s.m.* adhésif.
adjacent *adj.* adjacent, voisin (de); (*of country*) limitrophe.
adjectiv/e *s.* adjectif *m.*; **~al** *adj.* adjectif; (*facetiously*) sacré (*before noun*).
adjoin *v.i.* être contigu à, toucher à; **~ing** *adj.* voisin.
adjourn *v.t.* & *i.* suspendre, ajourner; (*move to another place*) changer, passer à; **~ment** *s.* suspension *f.*, ajournement *m.*
adjudge *v.t.* (*award*) décerner; (*condemn*) condamner; (*judge*) juger.
adjudicat/e *v.t.* & *i.* (*give judgement*) juger; (*act as judge*) se prononcer sur; **~or** *s.* juge *m.*
adjunct *s.* accessoire *m.*
adjust *v.t.* (*arrange*) arranger; (*adapt*) ajuster (à); **~able** *adj.* réglable; **~ment** *s.* réglage *m.*, arrangement *m.*, adaptation *f.*
adjutant *s.* capitaine adjudant-major *m.*; ⚠ adjudant = **R.Q.M.S.** adjudant-chef = **R.S.M.**
ad lib *adv.* à volonté; *v.i.* improviser.

administ/er *v.t.* (*manage*) administrer, gérer; (*dispense*) rendre; (*apply, give*) administrer; **~ration** *s.* (*management*) administration *f.*, gestion *f.*; (*part of govt.*) administration *f.*, service public *m.*; **~rative** *adj.* administratif; **~rator** *s.* administrateur *m.*, gérant *m.*

admiral *s.* amiral *m.*; **~ty** *s.* amirauté *f.*; ministère de la marine *m.*

admir/e *v.t.* **1.** (*approve*) estimer; **2.** (*look with wonder at, compliment on*) admirer; **~able** *adj.* admirable; **~ably** *adv.**; **~ation** *s.* (1) estime *f.*; (2) admiration *f.*; **~er** *s.* admirateur *m.*, amoureux *m.*

admi/t *v.t.* **1.** (*let in*) laisser entrer; **2.** (*accept as true*) reconnaître; **3.** (*acknowledge*) admettre; **4.** (*~ of, lie open to*) permettre; **~ssible** *adj.* admissible; **~ssion** *s.* (1) accès *m.*; entrée *f.*; (3) aveu *m.*; **~ttance** *s.* (1) entrée *f.*, droit d'entrée *m.*; **no ~ttance!**, entrée interdite!; **~ttedly** *adv.* il est vrai, de l'aveu général.

admixture *s.* mélange *m.*

admoni/sh *v.t.* **1.** (*reprimand*) réprimander; **2.** (*warn*) avèrtir, prévenir; **~tion** *s.* (1) remontrance *f.*; (2) avertissement *m.*

ad nauseam *adv.* à satiété.

ado *s.* (*fuss*) agitation *f.*; (*difficulty*) difficulté *f.*; **without further ~**, sans plus de façons; **much ~ about nothing,** beaucoup de bruit pour rien.

adolescen/t *adj.* & *s.m.f.* adolescent(e); **~ce** *s.* adolescence *f.*

adopt *v.t.* (*child*) adopter; (*take over, e.g. idea*) adopter, embrasser; (*take up, e.g. resolution*) adopter, (*candidate*) choisir; **~ed child,** enfant adoptif; **~ed country,** pays d'adoption; **~ion** *s.* adoption *f.*; **~ive** *adj.* adoptif.

ador/e *v.t.* adorer; **~able** *adj.* adorable; **~ation** *s.* adoration *f.*; **~er** *s.* adorateur *m.*; (*iron.*) soupirant *m.*

adorn *v.t.* orner (de), parer (de); **~ment** *s.* parure *f.*

adrift *adj.* à la dérive; **to be ~** (*fig.*) divaguer, dérailler; **to cast ~**, laisser à l'abandon; **to come ~**, se détacher.

adroit *adj.* adroit; **~ly** *adv.**

adulation *s.* adulation *f.*

adult *adj.* & *s.m.f.* adulte.

adulterate *v.t.* frelater.

adulter/y *s.* adultère *m.*; **~er, -ess** *s.* adultère *m.f.*; **~ous** *adj.* adultère.

advance *s.* **1.** (*going forward*) avance *f.*; **2.** (*progress*) progrès *m.*; **3.** (*rise in price*) hausse *f.*; **4.** (*loan*) avances *f.pl.*; **in ~**, à l'avance; **two days in ~**, deux jours à l'avance; (*after a verb*) d'avance, **to pay in ~**, payer d'avance; (*as an attribute*) en avance, **he is in ~**, il est en avance; **~** NOTICE; **~ warning sign** (*auto.*) triangle de présignalisation *m.*; *v.t.* & *i.* (1) (s')avancer; (2) progresser; (3) augmenter, faire monter; (4) avancer, prêter; **5.** (*help on*) pousser; **6.** (*argue*) avancer, prétendre; **~ment** *s.* avancement *m.*, promotion *f.*

advantage *s.* avantage *m.*; (*superiority*) supériorité *f.*; (*tennis*) **~ in, out,** avantage dedans, dehors; **to turn sth. to ~**; tirer profit de qch.; **to have the ~ of s.o.,** l'emporter sur qn.; **to take ~ of,** profiter de (qch.), abuser de (qn.); **~ous** *adj.* avantageux, profitable.

advent *s.* (*coming*) venue *f.*; (*eccles.*) Avent *m.*

adventur/e *s.* aventure *f.*; **~er** *s.* explorateur *m.*; **~er, ~eress,** (*pej.*) aventur/ier, -ière *m.f.*; **~ous** *adj.* aventureux.

adverb *s.* adverbe *m.*

adversary *s.* adversaire *m.*

advers/e *adj.* (*opposite*) contraire, opposé; (*criticism*) hostile; (*opinion etc.*) défavorable; **~ity** *s.* adversité *f.*, malheur *m.*

advertise *v.t.* (*make known*) publier; (*by poster*) afficher; (*in press*) annoncer; (*comm.*) faire de la réclame pour; **~ for,** demander par voie d'annonce; *v.i.* faire de la publicité; (*in press*) mettre une annonce dans la presse; **~ment** *s.* (*advertising*) publicité *f.*, réclame *f.*; (*poster*) affiche *f.*; (*in press*) annonce *f.*; **classified ~ments,** petites annonces *f.pl.*; **~r** *s.* annonceur *m.*

advice *s.* (*opinion*) avis *m.*, conseil *m.*; (*information*) nouvelle *f.*; **to ask ~ from s.o.,** demander conseil à qn.; consulter qn.

advis/e *v.t.* (*give advice to*) conseiller (à qn. de faire qch.); (*recommend*) recommander; (*notify*) aviser, faire part à qn. de qch.; **~e against,** déconseiller (qch. à qn.); **~able** *adj.* prudent, opportun; **~ability** *s.* opportunité *f.*, convenance *f.*; **~ed** *adj.* délibéré; **well-~ed,** (*person*) bien avisé, (*action*) judicieux; **ill-~ed,** (*person* & *action*) malavisé; **~edly** *adv.* en (pleine) connaissance de cause; **to keep s.o. ~ed of sth.,** tenir qn. au courant de qch.; **~ory** *adj.* consultatif.

advocate *s.* (*law*) avocat *m.*; (*gen.*) défenseur, champion *m.*; *v.t.* conseiller, recommander.

adze *s.* herminette *f.*

aerate *v.t.* aérer; **~d water,** eau gazeuse *f.*

aerial *adj.* aérien; *s.* (*radio* & *TV*) antenne *f.*

aero- (*in combination*) **~batics,** acrobatie aérienne *f.* (*usu. pl.*); **~drome,** aérodrome *m.*; **~dynamics,** aérodynamique *f.* ⚠ *sing. in French*; **~nautics,** aéronautique *f.* ⚠ *sing. in French*; **~plane,** avion *m.*; **~sol,** aérosol *m.*

aesthet/e *s.* esthète *m.f.*; **~ic** *adj.* esthétique; **~ics** *s.* esthétique *f.* ⚠ *sing. in French.*

afar *adv.* au loin; **from ~**, de loin.

affab/le *adj.* affable; **~ility** *s.* affabilité *f.*

affair *s.* (*comm.*) affaire *f.*; (=*love* ~) liaison *f.*, affaire de cœur *f.*; (*fam.* = *thing, happening*) affaire *f.*; **that's his ~**, c'est son affaire.

affect *v.t.* **1.** (*pretend, assume*) affecter, feindre (de); **2.** (*attack*) atteindre; **3.** (*move, touch*) affecter, émouvoir; **4.** (*influence*) affecter, modifier; **5.** (*concern*) toucher, intéresser; **~ation** *s.* (1) affectation *f.*; **~ed** *adj.* (1) affecté; (2) atteint (de); (3) ému, touché; **~edly** *adv.* (1) avec affectation; **~ing** *adj.* (3) émouvant, touchant; **~ion** *s.* (*love*) affection *f.*; (*med.*) maladie *f.*; **~ionate** *adj.* affectueux; **~ionately** *adv.**; **~ive** *adj.* (4) affectif.

affidavit *s.* déclaration sous serment f.

affiliat/e *v.t.* & *i.* (s')affilier (*with, to*—à); **~ion** *s.* affiliation *f.*

affinity *s.* (*relationship*) parenté *f.*; (*resemblance*) ressemblance *f.*; (*attraction*) affinité *f.*

affirm *v.t.* affirmer; **~ation** *s.* affirmation *f.*; **~ative** *adj.* affirmatif; *s.* affirmative *f.*; **to reply in the ~ative,** répondre par l'affirmative.

affix *v.t.* (*a seal*) apposer (sur); (*to a document*) annexer à.

afflict *v.t.* (*distress, trouble*) troubler, peiner; (*cause mental or physical suffering*) affliger; **~ion** *s.* peine *f.*, détresse *f.*; (*med.*) maladie *f.*

affluen/ce *s.* (*crowd*) affluence *f.*; (*riches*) opulence *f.*; **~t** *adj.* opulent; *s.* (*of a river*) affluent *m.*

afford *v.t.* (*supply*) fournir, offrir; (*spare money for*) se permettre, être à même de, avoir les moyens de, **he cannot ~ to,** ses moyens ne lui permettent pas de; (*fig.* = *he dare not*) il n'ose pas.

afforest *v.t.* (re)boiser; **~ation** *s.* boisement *m.*

affray *s.* rixe *f.*, bagarre *f.*

affright *v.t.* effrayer.

affront *s.* affront *m.*; *v.t.* insulter; ⚠ affronter = **to confront.**

afield *adv.* aux champs; **far ~**, au loin.

aflame *adv.* en flammes; (*fig.*) embrasé.

afloat *adv.* (*floating*) à flot, flottant; (*at sea*) en mer; (*fig.*) (*out of debt*) (être) à flot; **to keep ~**, se maintenir à flot.

afoot *adv.* (*on foot*) à pied; (*in progress*) en train.
afore- (*in combination*), **~named,** susnommé; **~said,** susdit; **~thought,** prémédité.
afraid *adj.* effrayé; **to be ~ of, that,** avoir peur de, que; **I am ~ that it will bore you,** j'ai peur que cela ne vous ennuie; **I am ~ of the dark,** j'ai peur du noir; **to be ~** (=*to be sorry*) regretter, **I am ~ that I shall have to remind you that,** je regrette d'avoir à vous rappeler que.
afresh *adv.* de nouveau.
Africa *s.* Afrique *f.*; **~n** *adj.* & *s.m.f.* africain(e).
after *adv.* (*also* = **afterwards**) ensuite; *prep.* (*behind*) après; (*in pursuit of*) en quête de; (*concerning*) au sujet de; (*according to*) d'après, suivant; (*in imitation of*) à la manière de; **~ a** FASHION; *conj.* après que (+*indicative*) **~ he had eaten,** après qu'il eut mangé; après (+*past inf.*) **~ eating,** après avoir mangé.
after (*in combination*) **~-care** *s.* surveillance *f.*; **~-effect** *s.* séquelles *f.pl.*; **~life** *s.* vie future *f.*; **~math** *s.* suites *f.pl.*; **~shave** *s.* après-rasage *m.*; **~-taste** *s.* arrière-goût *m.*; **~thought** *s.* réflexion (*f.*) après coup.
afternoon *s.* après-midi *m.*; **~ tea,** thé *m.*, (*for children*) goûter *m.*
again *adv.* (*another time*) encore (une fois), de nouveau; (*in addition*) de plus; *N.B. the prefix* re *can be added to many verbs & is sufficient to translate* **~**, e.g. revenir = **to come ~**; **~ and ~,** maintes fois; **over and over ~,** maintes et maintes fois; NOW **and ~; as much ~,** deux fois autant; **half as much ~,** la moitié en plus.
against *prep.* contre.
agape *adv.* bouche bée.
age *s.* (*years of life*) âge *m.*; (*latter part of life*) vieillesse *f.*; (*long period*) âge *m.*; (*fam.* = *long time*) siècle *m.*, éternité *f.*; **what ~ are you?,** quel âge avez-vous?; **he is twenty years of ~,** il a vingt ans; **to be of ~,** être majeur; **to be under ~,** être mineur; **~-group** *s.* classe *f.*; **~-limit** *s.* limite d'âge *m.*; **~d** *adj.* âgé; **~d twenty,** âgé de vingt ans; **~less** *adj.* sans âge; *v.t.* & *i.* vieillir.
agen/cy *s.* (*action*) action *f.*, entremise *f.*; (*office*) agence *f.* **~t** *s.* agent *m.*; ESTATE **~**.
agenda *s.* ordre du jour *m.*; ⚠ agenda = **note-book.**
agglomerat/e *v.t.* agglomérer; **~ion** *s.* agglomération *f.*
agglutinat/e *v.t.* & *i.* (s')agglutiner; **~ion** *s.* agglutination *f.*
aggrandize *v.t.* aggrandir; **~ment** *s.* agrandissement *m.*
aggravat/e *v.t.* **1.** (*make worse*) aggraver; **2.** (*fam.* = *annoy*) agacer; **~ing** *adj.* (1) aggravant; (2) agaçant; **~ion** *s.* (1) aggravation *f.*; (2) agacement *m.*
aggregat/e *s.* total *m.*, masse *f.*; *v.t.* agréger; **~ion** *s.* assemblage *m.* ⚠ agrégation = **university degree.**
aggress/ion *s.* agression *f.*; **~ive** *adj.* agressif; **~or** *s.* agresseur *m.*
aggrieve *v.t.* peiner.
aghast *adj.* abasourdi, (*fam.*) sidéré.
agil/e *adj.* agile; **~ity** *s.* agilité *f.*
agitat/e *v.t.* & *i.* (*shake up*) agiter; (*disturb, excite*) agiter, exciter; (*create public disorder*) agiter, ameuter; **~ion** *s.* agitation *f.*; **~or** *s.* agitateur *m.*
agnostic *adj.* & *s.m.f.* agnostique; **~ism** *s.* agnosticisme *m.*
ago *adv.* il y a; **a week ~,** il y a une semaine; **long ~,** il y a longtemps; **a short time ~,** il y a peu de temps.
agog *adj.* impatient; **to be all ~ to,** brûler d'envie de.
agon/y *s.* angoisse *f.*; **~y column,** annonces personnelles *f.pl.*; **~ize** *v.i.* souffrir horriblement, être à la torture; ⚠ agonie = **moment of death;** agoniser = **to be dying.**
agree *v.t.* & *i.* (*consent to*) consentir à; (*concur with*) s'entendre sur, convenir de; (*be in harmony with*) être d'accord avec; (*of food,* **~** *with*) convenir à; **~d!,** d'accord! convenu!; **~able** *adj.* (*pleasant*) plaisant, agréable; (*well-disposed*) aimable; (*conformable*) conforme à; **~ably** *adv.* agréablement, conformément; **~ment** *s.* (*mutual understanding*) harmonie *f.*, accord *m.*; (*treaty*) convention *f.*; (*legal contract*) contrat *m.* ⚠ agrément = **approval; pleasure, charm.**
agricultur/e *s.* agriculture *f.*; **~al** *adj.* agricole; **~al** SHOW; **~alist** *s.* agriculteur *m.*, cultivateur *m.*
aground *adj.* échoué; **to go ~,** s'échouer.
ah! *interj.* ah!, oh!; **aha!** *interj.* haha!
ahead *adv.* (*in advance*) en avance; (*forward*) en avant; **to go ~,** aller de l'avant; **go ~!,** en avant!; **~ of,** en tête de, devant; **to be two hours ~ of s.o.,** avoir deux heures d'avance sur qn.; **to get ~ of,** dépasser, laisser loin derrière.
ahoy! *interj.* ohé!
aid *s.* (*help*) aide *f.*, secours *m.*; (*helper*) aide *m.*; (*useful things, usu. pl.*) aides *f.pl.*; **first ~,** premiers secours *m.pl.*; **in ~ of,** au profit de, en faveur de; **to come to the ~ of,** venir en aide à; **with the ~ of,** à l'aide de; *v.t.* aider, contribuer à.
ail *v.t.* **what ~s you?,** qu'avez-vous?; *v.i.* être souffrant; **~ing** *adj.* souffrant; **~ment** *s.* indisposition *f.*
aileron *s.* aileron *m.*
aim *s.* (*aiming*) visée *f.*, (*fig.*) visées *f.pl.*; (*object ~ed at*) but *m.*, objectif *m.*; (*purpose*) but *m.*, dessein *m.*; **~less** & **~lessly** *adj.* & *adv.* sans but; *v.t.* (*direct or point at*) braquer sur; (*take aim*) viser; **~ a blow,** allonger un coup; *v.i.* (*be ambitious*) viser, **~ high,** viser haut.
air *s.* air *m.*; (*appearance*) mine *f.*, aspect *m.*; (*tune*) air *m.*; **to give oneself ~s,** se donner des airs; **to be on the ~,** (*radio* & *TV*) (*material*) être radiodiffusé, (*person*) passer sur les ondes; **to** CLEAR **the ~; by ~,** par avion; **in the open ~,** en plein air; CASTLES **in the ~; ~borne** *adj.* aéroporté; **~ brake** *s.* frein à air comprimé *m.*; **~-conditioned** *adj.* climatisé; **~-conditioner** *s.* climatiseur *m.*; **~conditioning** *s.* climatisation *f.*; **~craft** *s.* avion *m.*; **~craft-carrier** *s.* porte-avions *m.*; **~field** *s.* champ d'aviation *m.*; **~ force** *s.* armée de l'air *f.*; **~ hostess** *s.* hôtesse de l'air *f.*; **~ letter** *s.* aérogramme *m.*; **~lift** *s.* pont aérien *m.*; **~line** *s.* service de transports aériens *m.*; **~ liner** *s.* avion de ligne *m.*; **~lock** *s.* poche d'air *f.*; **~ mail** *s.* poste aérienne *f.*; **~man** *s.* aviateur *m.*; **~ pocket** *s.* trou d'air *m.*; **~port** *s.* aéroport *m.*; **~ raid** *s.* attaque aérienne *f.*; **~–sea rescue** *s.* sauvetage aéro-maritime *m.*; **~ship** *s.* dirigeable *m.*; **~sickness** *s.* mal de l'air *m.*; **~strip** *s.* terrain d'atterrissage *m.*; **~tight** *adj.* hermétique; **~less** *adj.* privé d'air, (*of weather*) calme; **~y** *adj.* aéré, léger; **~ily** *adv.* légèrement; **~y-fairy** *adj.* (*ideas*) illusoire, chimérique, (*person*) fantaisiste, rêveur; *v.t.* (*ventilate*) aérer, ventiler; (*show feelings*) donner libre cours à; (*show off knowledge*) étaler, afficher; **~ing** *s.* aération *f.*, (*walk*) promenade *f.*
aisle *s.* (*church*) bas-côté *m.*; (*any gangway*) passage *m.*
ajar *adj.* entr'ouvert, entre-baillé.
akimbo (*of the arms*) *adv.* les poings sur les hanches.
akin *adj.* (*related by blood*) apparenté (à); (*of similar nature*) voisin (de).
alabaster *s.* albâtre *m.*

alacrity *s.* alacrité *f.*
alarm *s.* (*sound*) alerte *f.*; (*sound & emotion*) alarme *f.*; **to sound the ~,** sonner le tocsin *or* donner l'alarme; **~ clock** *s.* réveille(-matin) *m.*; **~ bell, ~ signal,** sonnette (*f.*) signal (*m.*) d'alarme, tocsin *m.*; *v.t.* alarmer, alerter; (*frighten*) effrayer; *v.refl.* (*be ~ed*) s'alarmer; **~ing** *adj.* alarmant; **~ist** *s.* alarmiste *m.f.*
alas *interj.* hélas!
albatross *s.* albatros *m.*
albeit *conj.* bien que, quoique.
albino *s.* albinos *m.f.*
album *s.* album *m.*
alcohol *s.* alcool *m.*; **~ic** *adj.* & *s.m.f.* alcoolique; **~ism** *s.* alcoolisme *m.*; **~ level** (*in blood*) alcoolémie *f.*
alcove *s.* (*in a room*) alcôve *m.*; (*in a wall*) enfoncement *m.*, niche *f.*; **dining ~** *s.* coin repas *m.*
alder *s.* aune *m.*
alderman *s.* échevin *m.*
ale *s.* bière *f.*; **pale ~,** bière blonde *f.*; GINGER **~**; **~house,** cabaret *m.*
alert *s.* alerte *f.*; **on the ~,** sur le qui vive; *adj.* (*watchful*) vigilant; (*nimble*) alerte; *v.t.* alerter.
alfresco *adv.* en plein air.
algebra *s.* algèbre *f.*; **~ic** *adj.* algébrique.
alias *adj.* alias; *s.* nom d'emprunt *m.*
alibi *s.* alibi *m.*
alien *adj.* & *s.m.f.* étrang/er, -ère; **~ate** *v.t.* s'aliéner (qn.); **~ation** *s.* désaffection *f.*
alight[1] *adj.* (*on fire*) allumé; (*illuminated*) éclairé; **to be ~,** brûler.
alight[2] *v.i.* (*dismount, descend*) descendre; (*as bird*) se poser; **~ on,** trouver par hasard.
align *v.t.* aligner; *v.refl.* s'aligner (sur); **~ment** *s.* alignement *m.*
alike *adj.* semblable; *adv.* également; **to be ~,** se ressembler.
aliment *s.* aliment *m.*; **~ary** *adj.* alimentaire.
alimony *s.* pension alimentaire *f.*
alive *adj.* (*living*) vivant; (*active*) vif, animé; (*aware of*) sensible (*to*—à); DEAD **or ~; to be ~ with,** grouiller de; **look ~!,** dépêchez-vous!
alkali *s.* alcali *m.*; **~ne** *adj.* alcalin.
all *adj.* (*whole, complete*) tout(e); **~ day,** tout le jour; **~ night,** toute la nuit; (*usu. no art. in phrases*) **in ~ simplicity,** en toute simplicité; (*with pl.*) tous, toutes; **~ the boys,** tous les garçons; **~ the girls,** toutes les filles; **on ~** FOURS; **on ~** HANDS; **A~ Saints', A~ Hallows' Day,** la Toussaint *f.*; **A~ Souls' Day,** le jour des morts *m.*; *s.pl.* tous *m.pl.*, toutes *f.pl.*; (*everybody*) tout le monde; **~ of you** (etc.), vous (etc.) tous; (*everything*) tout *m.*; **to take, to risk ~,** prendre, risquer le tout; **~'s well that ends well,** tout est bien qui finit bien; (*with rel. pron.*) tout ce qui/que; tous ceux, toutes celles qui/que; **~ that glitters is not gold,** tout ce qui brille n'est pas or; **take ~ that you find,** prenez tout ce que vous trouvez; **~ who came,** tous ceux (toutes celles) qui sont venu(e)s; **~ but,** *use* faillir + *inf.*, **she ~ but fell,** elle a failli tomber; **above ~,** surtout; **after ~,** après tout; **not at ~,** pas du tout; **~ told,** tout compte fait; **it's ~ up with him,** c'en est fait de lui; **~ included,** tout compris; **~ at** ONCE; ONCE **for ~; for ~ that,** malgré cela; **it's ~ over with,** c'en est fini; **~ the more,** d'autant plus; **~ the better,** tant mieux; *adv.* tout (*invar. before adj. exc. f. adj. beginning with a consonant or an aspirated 'h'*) **they are ~ upset,** ils sont tout confus; **she is ~ upset,** elle est toute confuse; **she was dressed ~ in black,** elle était habillée tout en noir; **~ in** (*exhausted*) éreinté; **~ out** *adj.* maximum; *adv.* à outrance; **~ right** *adj.* bon; *adv.* bien; *interj.* bon!; **~ there,** avisé; **~ the same,** tout de même; **it's ~ the same to me,** ça m'est égal; **~-clear** *s.* fin d'alerte *f.*; **-~-electric,** où tout marche à l'électricité; **~-important,** de la première importance; **~-in,** inclusif; **~-purpose,** à tout faire; **~-powerful,** tout-puissant; **~-round,** complet; **~-rounder** *s.* homme universel *m.*
allay *v.t.* (*storm, anger, thirst, hunger*) apaiser; (*pain, grief, fear*) alléger, soulager.
alleg/e *v.t.* alléguer; **~ation** *s.* allégation *f.*
allegiance *s.* fidélité *f.*
allegor/y *s.* allégorie *f.*; **~ical** *adj.* allégorique.
alleluia *interj.* & *s.m.* alléluia.
allerg/y *s.* allergie *f.*; **~ic** *adj.* allergique (*to*—à).
alleviat/e *v.t.* alléger; **~ion** *s.* allégement *m.*
alley *s.* ruelle *f.*; **blind ~,** cul-de-sac *m.*, impasse *f.*; ⚠ allée = **path in wood or park.**
alliance *s.* alliance *f.*
alligator *s.* alligator *m.*
alliteration *s.* allitération *f.*
allocat/e *v.t.* attribuer; **~ion** *s.* allocation *f.*
allocution *s.* allocution *f.*
allot *v.t.* assigner (qch. à qn.); (*seats, shares, etc.*) répartir (entre plusieurs personnes); **~ment** *s.* (*share*) répartition *f.*, part *f.*; (*plot of land*) terrain *m.*; **~ments,** jardins ouvriers *m.pl.*
allow *v.t.* permettre (à qn. de faire qch.), autoriser (qn. à faire qch.); (*admit of*) admettre; (*give periodically*) allouer; **~able** *adj.* permis, admissible; **~ance** *s.* ration *f.*, allocation *f.*, (*tax*) déduction *f.*; **to make ~ance for,** tenir compte de; **~ing for,** eu égard à.
alloy *s.* alliage *m.*
allu/de *v.i.* faire allusion (*to*—à); **~sion** *s.* allusion *f.*; **~sive** *adj.* allusif.
allur/e *v.t.* (*entice*) séduire; (*charm*) charmer; **~ement** *s.* séduction *f.*; **~ing** *adj.* séduisant, charmant; ⚠ allure = **gait, speed.**
alluvial *adj.* alluvial.
ally *s.* allié *m.*; *v.t.* allier; *v.refl.* (*~ oneself to or with*) s'allier à.
almanac *s.* almanach *m.*
almighty *adj.* (*all-powerful*) tout-puissant; (*Eng. fam. = very great*) formidable; *s.* **the A~,** le Tout-Puissant *m.*
almond *s.* amande *f.*; **~-tree,** amandier *m.*; **~-shaped** *adj.* en amande.
almoner *s.* assistante sociale *f.*
almost *adv.* presque.
alms *s.* aumône *f.*; **~house,** hospice *m.*
aloft *adv.* en haut.
alone *adj.* seul; **he ~ knows,** lui seul le sait; **to leave ~,** laisser tranquille; **let ~,** sans compter; **to let well ~,** le mieux est l'ennemi du bien; *adv.* (*= exclusively*) seulement.
along *prep.* le long de; *adv.* (*space*) d'un bout à l'autre; (*time*) **all ~,** tout le temps; **come ~!,** allons!; **to come or go ~ with,** accompagner; **~side** *adv.* & *prep.* bord à bord.
aloof *adj.* & *adv.* (*apart, in space*) à l'écart, éloigné; (*fig.*) distant, désintéressé; **~ness** *s.* distance *f.*
aloud *adv.* à haute voix.
alpaca *s.* alpaga *m.*
alphabet *s.* alphabet *m.*; **~ic(al)** *adj.* alphabétique; **~ically** *adv.**.
Alp/s *s.* Alpes *f.pl.*; **~ine** *adj.* alpin; **~inist** *s.* alpiniste *m.*
already *adv.* déjà.
Alsatian *s.* (*dog*) berger allemand *m.*
also *adv.* aussi, de plus; **~-ran** *adj.* & *s.m.* non-classé.
altar *s.* autel *m.*
alter *v.t.* & *i.* **1.** (*change in character, position, etc.*) changer; **2.** (*modify*) modifier; **~ation** *s.* (1) changement *m.*; (2) modification *f.*
altercation *s.* altercation *f.*
alternat/e *adj.* alternatif; *v.t.* & *i.* (faire) alterner; **~ely** *adv.**, tour à tour, successive-

ment; **~ive** *adj.* alternatif; *s.* alternative *f.*; **~ive route,** itinéraire de délestage *m.* **~ively** *adv.**.
although *conj.* bien que, quoique.
altimeter *s.* altimètre *m.*
altitude *s.* altitude *f.*
alto *s.* contralto *m.*
altogether *adv.* tout à fait, entièrement.
altruis/m *s.* altruisme *m.*; **~t** *s.* altruiste *m.*; **~tic** *adj.* altruiste.
aluminium *s.* aluminium *m.*
always *adv.* toujours.
a.m. *adv.* du matin; **7 a.m.** 7 heures du matin.
amalgam *s.* amalgame *m.*; **~ate** *v.t.* & *i.* (s')amalgamer; **~ation** *s.* fusion *f.*
amass *v.t.* & *i.* (s')amasser.
amateur *s.* amateur *m.*; **~ish** *adj.* d'amateur; **~ishly** *adv.* en amateur.
amatory *adj.* amoureux.
amaz/e *v.t.* stupéfier; **~ed** *adj.* stupéfait; **~ement** *s.* stupéfaction *f.*; **~ing** *adj.* stupéfiant.
amazon *s.* amazone *f.*
ambassad/or, -ress *s.* ambassad/eur, -rice *m.f.*
amber *s.* ambre *m.*
ambidextrous *adj.* ambidextre.
ambien/t *adj.* ambiant; **~ce** *s.* ambiance *f.*
ambigu/ous *adj.* (*with double meaning*) ambigu; (*uncertain*) équivoque; **~ity** *s.* ambiguité *f.*; **~ously** *adv.**.
ambit *s.* limites *f.pl.*; (*scope*) compétence *f.*
ambiti/on *s.* ambition *f.*; **~ous** *adj.* ambitieux.
amble *s.* déambulation *f.*; *v.i.* déambuler; (*horse*) aller à l'amble.
ambrosia *s.* ambroisie *f.*
ambulance *s.* ambulance *f.*
ambush *s.* (*mil.*) embuscade *f.*; (*fig.*) guet-apens *m.*; *v.t.* (*mil.*) embusquer; **to lie in ~,** se tenir en embuscade.
ameliorat/e *v.t.* améliorer; **~ion** *s.* amélioration *f.*
amen *interj.* & *s.m.* amen.
amenable *adj.* (*tractable*) soumis, docile; (*responsive to*) sensible à; (*responsible to*) responsable envers.
amend *v.t.* **1.** (*correct*) corriger; **2.** (*improve*) améliorer; **3.** (*alter*) modifier; *v.i.* se corriger; **~ment** *s.* (1) correction *f.*; (2) amélioration *f.*; (3) modification *f.*
amends *s.* compensation *f.*, dédommagement *m.*; **to make ~ for,** réparer qch., dédommager qn. de.
amenit/y *s.* (*person*) aménité *f.*; (*thing, place*) agrément *m.*; **~ies** *s.pl.* attraits *m.pl.*, agréments *m.pl.*
America *s.* Amérique *f.*; **North/South ~,** Amérique du Nord, du Sud; **United States of ~,** Etats-Unis (d'Amérique) *m.pl.*; **~n** *adj.* & *s.m.f.* américain(e); **~nism** *s.* américanisme *m.*; **~nize** *v.t.* américaniser.
amethyst *s.* améthyste *f.*
amiab/le *adj.* aimable, affable; **~ility** *s.* amabilité *f.*; **~ly** *adv.**,*.
amicab/le *adj.* amical; **~ly** *adv.**
amid, amidst *prep.* au milieu de; entre, parmi (*see* AMONG).
amiss *adv.* (*wrongly*) mal; (*out of order*) mal à propos; **there's sth. ~,** il y a qch. qui ne va pas, (*fam.*) il y a qch. qui cloche; **to take sth. ~,** prendre qch. en mauvaise part; **not to come ~,** venir à propos.
ammonia *s.* ammoniaque *f.*
ammunition *s.* munitions *f.pl.*
amnesia *s.* amnésie *f.*
amnesty *s.* amnistie *f.*
amœba *s.* amibe *f.*
amok, amuck *adv.* **to run ~,** devenir fou furieux; (*fam.*) voir rouge.
among, amongst *prep.* entre (*with two or more people or things of the same kind*); parmi (*in the middle of, never with a numeral*), **~ the spectators,** entre les spectateurs; **~ the crowd,** parmi la foule; (*with races & classes*) chez; **~ the Indians,** chez les Indiens.
amoral *adj.* amoral.
amorous *adj.* amoureux.
amorphous *adj.* amorphe.
amount *s.* (*money* & *fig.*) somme *f.*; (*total*) montant *m.*; (*quantity*) quantité *f.*; *v.i.* **~ to,** (*add up to*) se monter à; (*be equivalent to*) se réduire à.
amphibi/an *s.* amphibie *m.*; **~ous** *adj.* amphibie.
amphitheatre *s.* amphithéâtre *m.*
ampl/e *adj.* **1.** (*spacious, abundant*) ample; **2.** (*quite enough*) suffisant; **we have ~e time,** nous avons largement le temps; **~itude** *s.* ampleur *f.*; **~y** *adv.* (1)*; (2) suffisamment.
amplif/y *v.t.* & *i.* (*enlarge, electr.*) (s')amplifier; (*increase strength of*) renforcer; (*add details to*) amplifier; développer; **~ication** *s.* amplification *f.*; **~ier** *s.* amplificateur *m.*
amputat/e *v.t.* amputer; **~ion** *s.* amputation *f.*
amulet *s.* amulette *f.*
amuse *v.t.* **1.** (*interest pleasingly*) amuser; **2.** (*entertain*) divertir; **3.** (*cause to laugh*) faire rire; *v.refl.* s'amuser, se divertir; **~ment** *s.* (1) amusement *m.*; (2) divertissement *m.*
an *see* **A.**
anachron/ism *s.* anachronisme *m.*; **~istic** *adj.* anachronique.
anaem/ia *s.* anémie *f.*; **~ic** *adj.* (*also fig.*) anémique.
anæsthe/sia *s.* anesthésie *f.*; **~tic** *adj.* & *s.m.* anesthésique; **~tist** *s.* anesthésiste *m.f.*; **~tize** *v.t.* anesthésier.
anagram *s.* anagramme *f.*
analgesic *adj.* & *s.m.* analgésique.
analog/y *s.* analogie *f.*; **~ous** *adj.* analogue.
analy/se *v.t.* analyser; **~sis** *s.* analyse *f.*; **~st** *s.* analyste *m.f.*
anarch/y *s.* anarchie *f.*; (*gen. disorder, confusion*) désordre *m.*; **~ic(al)** *adj.* anarchique; **~ism** *s.* anarchisme *m.*; **~ist** *s.* anarchiste *m.f.*
anathema *s.* anathème *m.*; (*object of abhorrence*) bête noire *f.*
anatom/y *s.* anatomie *f.*; **~ical** *adj.* anatomique; **~ist** *s.* anatomiste *m.f.*
ancest/or *s.* ancêtre *m.f.*; **~ral** *adj.* ancestral; **~ry** *s.* lignée *f.*
anchor *s.* ancre *f.*; *v.t.* & *i.* mouiller; **to cast/raise ~,** jeter/lever l'ancre; **~age** *s.* (*action*) ancrage *m.*; (*place*) havre *m.*, mouillage *m.*
anchovy *s.* anchois *m.*
ancient *adj.* & *s.m.* ancien; ⚠ *adj. always follows noun in this sense*; **~ history,** l'histoire ancienne.
ancillary *adj.* subordonné (à), subsidiaire; ⚠ ancillaire (*lit.*) *refers to liaisons with servants.*
and *conj.* et; **better ~ better,** de mieux en mieux; **~ how!** *interj.* (*fam.*) et comment!; BOTH . . . ~; ⚠ *in the Eng. idiom come and see* (= *come to see*) **and** *is not translated into French*; **he came ~ saw me,** il est venu me voir; **try ~ rest,** essayez de vous reposer.
anecdot/e *s.* anecdote *f.*; **~al** *adj.* anecdotique.
anemone *s.* anémone *f.*
aneroid *adj.* & *s.m.* anéroïde.
anew *adv.* de nouveau.
angel *s.* (*lit.* & *fig.*) ange *m.* (*no f.*) **his wife is an ~,** sa femme est un ange; **~ic** *adj.* angélique.
angelica *s.* angélique *f.*
angelus *s.* angélus *m.*
ang/er *s.* colère *f.*; *v.t.* mettre (qn.) en colère; **~ry** *adj.* **1.** (*person*) en colère, fâché; (*look, tone*) courroucé; (*words*) aigre; **2.** (*wound*) enflammé; **3.** (*sea, wind*) en furie, furieux; **to be ~ry with s.o.,** être fâché contre qn.; **to get ~ry,** se fâcher, se mettre en colère; **~rily** *adv.* (1) en

colère; (3) furieusement; **~ry young man** *s.* révolté *m.*
angina *s.* angine *f.*; **~ pectoris** *s.* angine de poitrine *f.*
angle[1] *s.* (*lit.* & *fig.*) angle *m.*; **from a certain ~** (*fig.*) sous un certain angle; **~-iron** *s.* cornière *f.*; *v.t.* former un angle; (*fig.*) présenter sous un certain angle; **angular** *adj.* angulaire.
angl/e[2] *v.i.* pêcher à la ligne; **~er** *s.* pêcheur *m.* (à la ligne); **~ing** *s.* pêche *f.* (à la ligne).
Anglican *adj.* & *s.m.* anglican.
Anglic/ism *s.* anglicisme *m.*; **~ize** *v.t.* angliciser.
Anglo- (*in combination*): **~-Catholic** *adj.* & *s.* anglo-catholique; **~phile** *adj.* & *s.* anglophile; **~phobe** *adj.* & *s.* anglophobe; **~-Saxon** *adj.* & *s.* anglo-saxon.
angora *s.* angora *m.*
angry *see* ANGER.
anguish *s.* angoisse *f.*
aniline *s.* (*dye*) aniline *f.*
animal *s.* (*living* & *moving being*) animal *m.*; (*other than man*) bête *f.*; (*pop. slightly pej.*) animal *m.*; (*coarse person*) brute *f.*; *adj.* (*of animals*) animal; (*carnal, sensual*) bestial.
animat/e *v.t.* animer; *adj.* animé; **~ed** *adj.* animé; **~ion** *s.* animation *f.*
animosity, animus *s.* animosité *f.*
aniseed *s.* anis *m.*
ankle *s.* cheville *f.*; **~t** *s.* bracelet (de cheville) *m.*; socquette *f.*; **~-DEEP.**
annal/s *s.pl.* annales *f.pl.*; **~ist** *s.* annaliste *m.f.*
anneal *v.t.* (*glass, metal*) recuire.
annex *s.* annexe *f.*; *v.t.* annexer; (*fam.*) chiper; **~ation** *s.* annexion *f.*
annihilat/e *v.t.* (*lit.* & *fig.*) annihiler; **~ion** *s.* annihilation *f.*
anniversary *s.* anniversaire *m.*
annotat/e *v.t.* annoter; **~ion** *s.* annotation *f.*
announc/e *v.t.* annoncer; **~ement** *s.* annonce *f.*, communication *f.*; **~er** *s.* (*esp. radio* & *TV*) annonceur *m.*, présentateur *m.*, speaker *m.*, speakerine *f.*
annoy *v.t.* **1.** (*irritate*) agacer, énerver; **2.** (*molest*) importuner; **3.** (*vex*) ennuyer; **~ance** *s.* (1) agacement *m.*, énervement *m.*; (2) importunité *f.*; (3) ennui *m.*; **~ing** *adj.* (1) agaçant, énervant; (2) importun; (3) ennuyeux.
annual *s.* (*book*) annuaire *m.*; (*plant*) plante annuelle *f.*; *adj.* annuel.
annuity *s.* (*grant*) rente *f.*, pension *f.*; (*investment*) annuité *f.*
annul *v.t.* annuler.
annular *adj.* annulaire.
anodyne *s.* (*med.*) calmant *m.*; *adj.* anodin.
anoint *v.t.* (*with*) oindre (de).
anomal/y *s.* anomalie *f.*; **~ous** *adj.* anormal.
anon[1] *adv.* tout à l'heure.
anon[2] (*abbrev. for anonymous*) anonyme.
anonym/ous *adj.* anonyme; **~ity** *s.* anonymat *m.*
anorak *s.* anorak *m.*
another *pron.* & *adj.* (*a different one*) un(e) autre; (*an additional one*) un(e) de plus, encore un(e); **have ~ cup of tea,** prenez encore une tasse de thé; **one ~,** l'un(e) l'autre, les un(e)s les autres; *refl.pron.* se; **they hate one ~,** ils se détestent l'un l'autre.
answer *s.* **1.** (*reply*) réponse *f.*; **2.** (*solution*) solution *f.*; **know all the ~s,** avoir réponse à tout; **in ~ to,** en réponse à; *v.t.* (1) répondre à; (2) résoudre; *v.i.* répondre; (*succeed*) réussir, faire l'affaire; **that won't ~,** cela ne fera pas l'affaire; (*fam.*) ça ne rendra pas; **~ back,** répliquer; **~ the door,** aller ouvrir; **~ for,** répondre de; **~able** *adj.* responsable.
ant *s.* fourmi *f.*; **white ~,** termite *m.*; **~-eater** *s.* fourmilier *m.*; **~hill** *s.* fourmilière *f.*
antacid *adj.* & *s.m.* alcalin.
antagon/ism *s.* antagonisme *m.*; **~ist** *s.* antagoniste *m.*; **~istic** *adj.* antagonique; **~ize** *v.t.* provoquer l'hostilité de.
antarctic *adj.* & *s.m.* antarctique.
ante- (*in combination*): **~chamber, -room,** antichambre *f.*; **~date,** *v.t.* antidater; **~diluvian** *adj.* antédiluvien; **~natal** *adj.* prénatal; **~-penultimate** *adj.* antépénultième.
antecedent *adj.* antérieur (à); *s.* précédent *m.*; **~s** (*of person*) antécédents *m.pl.*
antelope *s.* antilope *f.*
antenna *s.* (*insects* & *radio*) antenne *f.*
anterior *adj.* antérieur (à).
anthem *s.* hymne *m.*
anthology *s.* anthologie *f.*
anthracite *s.* anthracite *m.*
anthrax *s.* (*of cattle*) charbon *m.*
anthropolog/y *s.* anthropologie *f.*; **~ist** *s.* anthropologiste *m.f.*
anti- (*in combination*): **~-aircraft** *adj.* anti-aérien, contre-avions, **~-aircraft guns** *s.* DCA (défense contre avions); **~biotic** *adj.* & *s.m.* antibiotique; **~body** *s.* anticorps *m.*; **~climax** *s.* (*liter. crit.*) retombée (*f.*) de la tension; (*orat.* & *style*) gradation descendante *f.*; (*gen.*) lendemain de la fête *m.*; **~clerical** *adj.* anticlérical; **~cyclone** *s.* anticyclone *m.*; **~freeze** *s.* antigel *m.*; **~-Semitism** *s.* antisémitisme *m.*; **~septic** *adj.* & *s.m.* antiseptique; **~social** *adj.* antisocial; **~toxin** *s.* antitoxine *f.*
antic *s.* gambade *f.*; *adj.* grotesque.
anticipat/e *v.t.* (*look forward to*) (*good things*), s'attendre (avec impatience) à; (*difficulties etc.*) prévoir; (*forestall, use in advance*) anticiper (sur); **~ion** *s.* anticipation *f.*; **in ~ion of,** en attendant.
antidote *s.* antidote *m.*
antipath/y *s.* antipathie *f.*; **~etic** *adj.* antipathique.
antipodes *s.pl.* antipodes *m.pl.*
antiquar/y *s.* antiquaire *m.*; **~ian** *adj.* d'antiquaire.
antiqu/e *adj.* antique; *s.* objet d'art, meuble ancien *m.*, antiquités *f.pl.*; **~e-dealer** *s.* antiquaire *m.*; **~ated** *adj.* (*out of date*) démodé; (+ *ridiculous*) vieillot; (*of ideas, person*) vieux jeu; (*old-fashioned, manners, etc.*) suranné; **~ity** *s.* antiquité *f.*
antirrhinum *s.* gueule de loup *f.*
antithe/sis *s.* antithèse *f.*; **~tic(al)** *adj.* antithétique.
antlers *s.pl.* bois (de cerf) *m.pl.*
antonym *s.* antonyme *m.*
anus *s.* anus *m.*
anvil *s.* enclume *f.*
anxi/ety *s.* anxiété *f.*, inquiétude *f.*; **~ous** *adj.* anxieux, inquiet; (*desirous*) anxieux, impatient (de); **~ously** *adv.**, avec inquiétude.
any *pron.* en (*with verb*), **have you ~?** en avez-vous?; **is there ~ left?** en reste-t-il?; *adj.* du, de la, des, *but* de *after a negative*: **have you ~ milk?** avez-vous du lait?; **I haven't ~ milk,** je n'ai pas de lait; tout; **~ man,** tout homme; n'importe quel, **take ~ book,** prenez n'importe quel livre; *adv.* un peu; aucunement; **~one, ~body,** qualqu'un, personne (*with neg.*), **I didn't see ~body,** je n'ai vu personne; n'importe qui, **~body will tell you,** n'importe qui vous dira; **~thing,** quelque chose, tout, n'importe quoi, rien; **have you ~thing to say?**, avez-vous quelque chose à dire?; **~thing you wish,** tout ce que vous voudrez; **say ~thing, but speak,** dites d'importe quoi, mais parlez; **is there ~thing better than,** y a-t-il rien de meilleur que; **~how,** en tout cas, de toute façon, **~how, you are right,** en tout cas, vous avez raison; n'importe comment, **do it**

~how, but do it, faites-le n'importe comment, mais faites-le; **~way,** de toute façon; n'importe comment; **~where,** n'importe où; **~ more,** plus; **~ time,** n'importe quand; **~ day,** n'importe quel jour; **~ old how** (*fam.*) (*action*) au petit bonheur; (*things*) en pagaïe; **to feel ~ old how** (*fam.*) se sentir tout chose.

apace *adv.* vite.

apanage *s.* apanage *m.*

apart *adv.* à part; **~ from,** en dehors de; **to set ~,** mettre de côté.

apartheid *s.* ségrégation (des races) *f.*, apartheid *m.* (*used only about South Africa*).

apartment *s.* (*room*) pièce *f.*; (*flat*) appartement *m.*

apath/y *s.* apathie *f.*; **~etic** *adj.* apathique.

ape *s.* singe *m.*; *v.t.* singer.

aperient *adj.* & *s.m.* laxatif.

aperture *s.* ouverture *f.*

apex *s.* sommet *m.*; (*fig.*) apogée *m.*

aphis *s.* puceron *m.*

aphorism *s.* aphorisme *m.*

aphrodisiac *s.* aphrodisiaque *m.*

api/ary *s.* rucher *m.*; **~arist** *s.* apiculteur *m.*; **~culture** *s.* apiculture *f.*

apiece *adv.* (*person*) par personne; (*things*) (par) pièce; chacun.

apocalypse *s.* apocalypse *f.*

Apocrypha *s.* livres apocryphes *m.pl.*; **~l** *adj.* apocryphe.

apogee *s.* apogée *m.*

apolog/y *s.* (*acknowledgement of offence*) excuses *f.pl.*; (*explanation*) excuse *f.*; (*defence*) apologie *f.*; (*poor specimen*) semblant de, **an ~y for a hat,** un semblant de chapeau; **~etic** *adj.* d'excuse; **~ist** *s.* apologiste *m.*; **~ize** *v.i.* s'excuser, (*for*) de, (*to*) auprès de; faire ses excuses (à qn.).

apople/xy *s.* apoplexie *f.*; **~ctic** *adj.* apoplectique.

aposta/sy *s.* apostasie *f.*; **~te** *s.* apostat *m.*

apost/le *s.* apôtre *m.*; **~olic** *adj.* apostolique.

apostroph/e *s.* apostrophe *f.*; **~ize** *v.t.* apostropher.

apotheosis *s.* apothéose *f.*

appal *v.t.* épouvanter; **~ling** *adj.* épouvantable.

apparatus *s.* appareil *m.*

apparel *s.* vêtements *m.pl.*; *v.t.* vêtir.

apparent *adj.* **1.** (*clear*) manifeste; **2.** (*seeming*) apparent; **~ly** *adv.* (1)*; (2) en apparence.

apparition *s.* apparition *f.*

appeal *s.* **1.** appel *m.*; **Court of A~,** Cour d'appel *f.*; **2.** (*attraction*) attrait *m.*; *v.i.* (1) faire appel (*to*—à); (2) (*~ to*) intéresser, séduire; **if it ~s to you,** si cela vous chante; **~ing** *adj.* séduisant.

appear *v.i.* **1.** (*become visible*) paraître; **2.** (*present oneself*) apparaître; **3.** (*be published*) paraître; **4.** (*seem*) sembler; **it ~s that,** il paraît que; **so it ~s,** paraît-il; **~ance** *s.* (1) & (2) apparition *f.*; (3) parution *f.*; (4) apparence *f.*; **5.** (*look, air*) air *m.*, aspect *m.*; **to keep up ~ances,** garder, sauver les apparences; **to judge by ~ances,** juger sur la mine.

appease *v.t.* **1.** (*pacify*) apaiser; **2.** (*satisfy*) satisfaire à; **~ment** *s.* (1) apaisement *m.*; (2) satisfaction *f.*

appellation *s.* appellation *f.*

append *v.t.* annexer, joindre; (*signature*) apposer; **~age** *s.* addition *f.*

appendicitis *s.* appendicite *f.*

appendix *s.* (*of book; anat.*) appendice *m.*

appertain to *v.i.* appartenir à.

appet/ite *s.* appétit *m.*; **~izer** *s.* apéritif *m.*; **~izing** *adj.* appétissant.

applau/d *v.t.* (*clap hands*) applaudir; (*commend*) applaudir à; **~se** *s.* applaudissements *m.pl.*

apple *s.* pomme *f.*; **~-tree** *s.* pommier *m.*; CRAB-**~**; **to upset s.o.'s ~-cart,** bouleverser (*pop.*) chambarder les plans de qn.; **~ jack** *s.* calvados *m.*; **~ of the eye,** prunelle *f.*; **~-pie bed,** lit en portefeuille *m.*; **in ~-pie order,** dans un ordre parfait.

appl/y *v.t.* & *i.* **1.** (*put in contact*) appliquer; **2.** (*administer*) mettre en pratique; **3.** (*devote to*) appliquer; **4.** (*be relevant to*) avoir rapport à; **5.** (*refl.*) s'appliquer à; **6. ~y for,** faire une demande de, solliciter; **~iance** *s.* appareil *m.*; **~icable** *adj.* applicable; **~icant** *s.* candidat *m.*, postulant *m.*; **~ication** *s.* (1) application *f.*; (2) mise en pratique *f.*; (3) application *f.*; (4) rapport *m.*; (6) demande *f.*; **letter of ~ication,** lettre de candidature *f.*

appoint *v.t.* (*to post*) nommer; (*fix, time etc.*) désigner; (*equip*) installer; *v.i.* (*ordain*) disposer; **at the ~ed time,** à l'heure convenue; **~ment** *s.* nomination *f.*; (*post*) poste *m.*; (*engagement*) rendez-vous *m.*; **to make an ~ment with,** donner un rendez-vous à, prendre un rendez-vous avec.

apportion *v.t.* répartir; **~ment** *s.* répartition *f.*

apposite *adj.* juste, à propos, approprié.

apprais/e *v.t.* **1.** (*fix price*) évaluer; **2.** (*estimate*) estimer; **~al** *s.* (1) évaluation *f.*; (2) estimation *f.*

apprecia/te *v.t.* **1.** (*set high value on*) apprécier, priser; **2.** (*estimate rightly*) évaluer, estimer; **3.** (*be aware of*) apprécier; **4.** *v.i.* (*rise in value*) s'améliorer, monter; **~ble** *adj.* appréciable; **~tion** *s.* (1) & (3) appréciation *f.*; (2) évaluation *f.*; (4) hausse *f.*; **~tive** *adj.* reconnaissant.

apprehen/d *v.t.* **1.** (*seize*) appréhender; **2.** (*understand*) comprendre; **3.** (*fear*) appréhender; **~sible** *adj.* (2) compréhensible; **~sion** *s.* (1) arrestation *f.*; (2) compréhension *f.*; (3) appréhension *f.*; **~sive** *adj.* (3) anxieux, craintif.

apprentice *s.* apprenti *m.*; (*before another noun in apposition*) **an ~ builder,** *or,* **a builder's ~,** un apprenti maçon; **~ship** *s.* apprentissage *m.*; *v.t.* mettre en apprentissage (*to*—chez).

apprise *v.t.* informer (de).

approach *s.* (*manner*) approche *f.*; (*access*) accès *m.*; **~es** *s.pl.* approches *f.pl.*; **to make ~es to,** faire des avances à; *v.t.* & *i.* (*come nearer*) (s')approcher (de); (*make overtures to*) aborder; (*resemble*) ressembler à; **~able** *adj.* (*person*) abordable; (*place*) accessible; **~ing** *adj.* prochain.

approbation *s.* approbation *f.*; **on ~,** à l'essai.

appropriate[1] *adj.* (*suitable*) propre, approprié (à); (*proper*) convenable; **~ly** *adv.**; **~ness** *s.* propriété *f.*

appropriate[2] *v.t.* (*take possession of*) s'approprier; (*devote to special use*) affecter à.

approv/e *v.t.* approuver; ⚠ **to ~e of,** approuver qn. ou qch., (*v.t. in French*); **~al** *s.* approbation *f.*; **on ~al** (*comm. of product*) à condition; (*of person, car etc.*) à l'essai; **~ing** *adj.* approbat/eur, -rice; **~ed school,** maison de rééducation (des jeunes délinquants) *f.*

approximat/e *adj.* approximatif; *v.t.* s'approcher (*to*—de); **~ely** *adv.**; **~ion** *s.* approximation *f.*

appurtenance *s.* (*building*) dépendance *f.*; (*thing*) accessoire *m.*; (*fam.*) attirail *m.*

apricot *s.* abricot *m.*; **~-tree** abricotier *m.*

April *s.* avril *m.*; **~ fool,** poisson d'avril *m.*; **~ shower,** giboulée de mars *f.*

apron *s.* (*garment*) tablier *m.*; (*theat.*) avant-scène *f.*; (*aviat. landing area*) aire d'atterrissage *f.*; **to be tied to s.o.'s, one's mother's, ~-strings,** être toujours pendu aux basques de qn., être toujours dans les jupes de sa mère.

apse *s.* abside *f.*

apt *adj.* **1.** (*appropriate*) approprié, à propos; **2.** (*quick*) doué; **3.** (*inclined, ~ to*) disposé à, susceptible de; **~itude** *s.* aptitude *f.*; **~ly** *adv.*

(1) avec à propos; (2) habilement; **~ness** *s.* (1) à propos *m.*; (2) aptitude *f.*; (3) disposition *f.*
aqualung *s.* scaphandre autonome *m.*
aquamarine *s.* aigue-marine *f.*
aquaplaning *s.* hydroplanage *m.*
aquarium *s.* aquarium *m.*
aquatic *adj.* aquatique.
aqueduct *s.* aqueduc *m.*
aquiline *adj.* aquilin.
Arab/ia *s.* Arabie *f.*; **~** *adj.* & *s.m.f.* arabe; **~ic** *adj.* & *s.m.* arabe; **~ian** *adj.* arabe; **street ~** (*fam.*) gavroche *m.*, titi *m.*
arabesque *s.* arabesque *m.*
arable *adj.* arable.
arbit/er *s.* arbitre *m.*; **~rate** *v.t.* & *i.* (*determine*) juger; (*settle dispute*) arbitrer (un différend); **~rator** *s.* arbitre *m.*; **~ration** *s.* arbitrage *m.*
arbitrary *adj.* arbitraire.
arboriculture *s.* arboriculture *f.*
arbour *s.* tonnelle *f.*
arc *s.* (*geom.* & *electr.*) arc *m.*; **~ lamp**; lampe à arc *f.*
arcade *s.* (*arch.*) arcade *f.*; (*shops*) passage *m.*, galerie(s) *f.*(*pl.*).
arch[1] *s.* (*bridge*) arche *f.*; (*vault*) voûte *f.*; **~way,** voûte *f.*; *v.t.* (*furnish with arch*) cintrer, voûter; (*form into arch*) arquer; **~ed** *adj.* arqué, voûté.
arch[2] *adj.* (*coy*) malin, espiègle; (*outstanding*) insigne, éminent; (*fam.*) fieffé (*before noun*); **~ enemy,** ennemi numéro un.
arch- (*in combination*) **~angel,** archange *m.*; **~bishop,** archevêque *m.*; **~duke,** archiduc *m.*; **~priest,** archiprêtre *m.*
archaeolog/y *s.* archéologie *f.*; **~ist** *s.* archéologue *m.f.*
archa/ic *adj.* archaïque; **~ism** *s.* archaïsme *m.*
archer *s.* archer *m.*; **~y** *s.* tir à l'arc *m.*
archipelago *s.* archipel *m.*
architect *s.* architecte *m.*; **~ure** *s.* architecture *f.*
archiv/es *s.pl.* archives *f.pl.*; **~ist** *s.* archiviste *m.f.*
arctic *adj.* & *s.m.* arctique.
ard/ent *adj.* (*lit.* & *fig.*) ardent; **~our** *s.* ardeur *f.*
arduous *adj.* ardu.
area *s.* (*extent of surface*) superficie *f.*; (*scope, range*) étendue *f.*; (*region*) territoire *m.*, région *f.*; (*court of house*) cour basse *f.*; ⚠ basse-cour = **farmyard.**
arena *s.* arène *f.*; (*Roman amphitheatre*) arènes *f.pl.*
Argentin/a (**the Argentine**) *s.* (*geog.*) Argentine *f.*; **~ian** *adj.* & *s.m.f.* argentin(e).
argu/e *v.t.* & *i.* **1.** (*maintain*) soutenir; **2.** (*prove*) prouver; **3.** (*reason*) plaider (*against, for*—contre, en faveur de); discuter; **4.** (*contend*) argumenter; **5.** (*infer*) conclure; **to ~e the toss** (*fam.*) discutailler; **~able** *adj.* (1) (*which can be maintained*) soutenable; (3) (*which is open to discussion*) discutable; **~ment** *s.* (1) & (2) argument *m.*; (3) raisonnement *m.*; (4) discussion *f.*, débat *m.*, altercation *f.*; (5) conclusion *f.*; **~mentation** *s.* discussion *f.*; **~mentative** *adj.* raisonneur.
aria *s.* aria *m.*
arid *adj.* aride; **~ity** *s.* aridité *f.*
aright *adv.* bien, correctement.
arise *v.i.* (*person*) se lever; (*building*) s'élever; (*occur*) surgir, survenir; (*come from*) provenir de.
aristocra/t *s.* aristocrate *m.f.*; **~cy** *s.* aristocratie *f.*; **~tic** *adj.* aristocratique.
arithmetic *s.* arithmétique *f.*; **~al** *adj.* arithmétique.
ark *s.* (*Noah's*) arche *f.* (de Noé).
arm[1] *s.* (*limb*) bras *m.*; (*sleeve*) manche *f.*; (*of tree*) branche *f.*; (*any ~-like thing*) bras *m.*; **with open ~s,** à bras ouverts; **to keep s.o. at ~'s length,** tenir qn. à distance; **~ in ~,** bras dessus bras dessous; **~chair,** fauteuil *m.*; **~ful** *s.* brassée *f.*; **~hole,** emmanchure *f.*; **~pit,** aisselle, *f.*
arm[2] *s.* (*weapon*) arme *f.*; **coat of ~s,** blason *m.*, armoiries *f.pl.*; **to be up in ~s,** se rebeller (contre); (*fam.*) être dans tous ses états; *v.t.* & *i.* (s')armer.
armada *s.* armada *f.*
armament *s.* armement *m.*
armature *s.* armure *f.*; (*electr.*) armature *f.*
armistice *s.* armistice *m.*
armour *s.* armure *f.*; (*on ships, tanks, cars etc.*) blindage *m.*; **~ed** *adj.* blindé; **~er** *s.* armurier *m.*; **~y** *s.* armurerie *f.*; (*on large scale*) arsenal *m.*
army *s.* armée *f.*
aroma *s.* arôme *m.*; **~tic** *adj.* aromatique.
around *prep.* autour de; *adv.* à l'entour; **to get ~ to sth., to doing sth.,** arriver à (faire) qch.
arouse *v.t.* (*awake*) réveiller; (*stir up passions*) éveiller; (*stir up person*) provoquer.
arpeggio *s.* arpège *m.*
arraign *v.t.* traduire (qn.) en justice; **~ment** *s.* accusation *f.*
arrange *v.t.* **1.** (*put in order*) arranger; **2.** (*settle*) arranger; **3.** (*form plans*) arranger, combiner; **4.** (*mus.*) adapter; **~ment** *s.* (1), (2), (4) arrangement *m.*; (3) mesures *f.pl.*
arrant *adj.* fieffé (*before noun*).
array *s.* **1.** (*dress*) atours *m.pl.*; parure *f.*; **2.** (*display*) étalage *m.*; **3.** (*mil.*) rang *m.*; *v.t.* (1) parer (*in*—de); (2) étaler; (3) ranger, déployer.
arrears *s.pl.* arriéré *m.sing.*; **to be in ~ with,** avoir du retard dans.
arrest *s.* **1.** (*stop*) arrêt *m.*; **2.** (*by authority*) arrestation *f.*; **to place under ~,** mettre en état d'arrestation; HOUSE **~**; *v.t.* (1) & (2) arrêter; **3.** (*catch attention*) retenir.
arriv/e *v.i.* (*lit.* & *fig.*) arriver, parvenir; **~al** *s.* arrivée *f.*; (*person*) nouveau-venu *m.*
arrogan/t *adj.* arrogant; **~ce** *s.* arrogance *f.*
arrow *s.* flèche *f.*
arrowroot *s.* arrow-root *m.*
arsenal *s.* arsenal *m.*
arsenic *s.* arsenic *m.*
arson *s.* incendie criminel *m.*
art *s.* **1.** art *m.*; **2.** (*skill*) art *m.*, adresse *f.*; **3.** (*cunning*) artifice *m.*; **~s** (*acad.*) lettres *f.pl.*; *see* B.A., M.A.; **fine ~s,** beaux arts *m.pl.*; **~ful** *adj.* (2) adroit; (3) malin; **~fully** *adv.* (2) habilement; (3) avec astuce; **~less** *adj.* ingénu; **~y** *adj.* (*usu. pej.*) artiste; **~y-crafty** *adj.* bohème.
artefact *s.* artefact *m.*
arter/y *s.* artère *f.*; **~ial** *adj.* artériel; **~ial road,** (route) nationale *f.*
artesian *adj.* (*well*) (puits) artésien.
arthrit/is *s.* arthrite *f.*; **~ic** *adj.* arthritique.
artichoke *s.* artichaut *m.*; **Jerusalem ~,** topinambour *m.*
article *s.* (*clause of bill etc.*; *short liter. work*; *thing*; *ling.*) article *m.*; **~s** *s.pl.* (*apprenticeship*) contrat d'apprentissage *m.*; *v.t.* mettre en apprentissage.
articulate *adj.* (*having joints*) articulé; (*distinct, of speech*) articulé; (*capable of effective speech*) capable de s'exprimer; *v.t.* & *i.* articuler; **~d** LORRY.
artific/e *s.* (*device*) expédient *m.*; (*cunning*) artifice *m.*; (*skill*) adresse *f.*; **~ial** *adj.* artificiel; **~ially** *adv.**; **~iality** *s.* manque de naturel *m.*; **~er** *s.* artisan *m.* ⚠ artificier *is used only of a technician concerned with fireworks or explosives.*
artillery *s.* artillerie *f.*
artisan *s.* artisan *m.*
artist *s.* artiste *m.f.*; **~ic** *adj.* artistique; **~ically** *adv.**
as *adv.* & *conj.* **1.** (*in same degree*) aussi, autant que; **he is ~ tall ~ you,** il est aussi grand que vous; **he works ~ much ~ he can,** il travaille autant qu'il peut; ⚠ *the first ~ is not translated in*

idiomatic phrases, see ~ **white** ~ **a** SHEET, etc.; **2.** (*similarly*) comme, ainsi que; **do** ~ **I do,** faites comme moi; ~ **has been said above,** ainsi qu'il a été dit plus haut; ~ **a friend,** en ami; **3.** (*while, when*) comme, tandis que; **we arrived** ~ **he was leaving,** nous sommes arrivés comme il partait; nous sommes arrivés tandis qu'il sortait; **4.** (*since, seeing that*) puisque, étant donné que; ~ **you insist, I accept,** puisque vous insistez, j'accepte; ~ **he isn't coming, we can go,** étant donné qu'il ne vient pas, nous pouvons partir; **5.** (*such* ~) comme; ~ **for,** ~ **to,** quant à; ~ **for him,** quant à lui; ~ **for that,** quant à cela; ~ **many,** ~ **much,** autant (de); ~ **soon** ~, aussitôt que; **such** ~, tel que; **a woman such** ~ **his mother,** une femme telle que sa mère; **such** ~ **it is,** tel quel; ~ **such,** comme tel; ~ WELL; ~ **from,** à partir de; ~ **of now,** dès maintenant; ~ **yet,** jusqu'ici; ~ **you like,** comme vous voudrez; **so stupid** ~ **to,** assez stupide pour; ~ **far** ~ **I know,** autant que je sache; ~ **it were,** pour ainsi dire, comme qui dirait; ~ **you were!** (*mil., sport*) revenez!; (*fig. fam.*) pardon!, recommençons!

asbestos *s.* amiante *m.*

ascen/d *v.t.* & *i.* monter; ~**dant** *s.* & ~**dancy** *s.* (*astron.* & *influence*) ascendant *m.*; **in the** ~**dant,** à l'ascendant; ~**sion** *s.* ascension *f.*; ~**t** *s.* ascension *f.*; (*slope*) côte *f.*, montée *f.*

ascertain *v.t.* (*find out*) constater, s'informer de; (*make sure*) s'assurer de, que; **I will** ~ **the truth of the report,** je vais m'assurer de l'exactitude de la nouvelle; ~ **that nothing is missing,** assurez-vous que rien ne manque.

ascetic *s.* ascète *m.f.*; *adj.* ascétique; ~**ism** *s.* ascétisme *m.*

ascribe *v.t.* (*to*) attribuer (à).

asdic *s.* asdic *m.*

asep/sis *s.* asepsie *f.*; ~**tic** *adj.* aseptique.

ash[1] *s.* (*tree*) frêne *m.*

ash[2] *s.* (*remains of fire, cigarette, etc.*) cendre *f.*; (*pl.* = *remains of body*) cendres *f.pl.*; ~ **blonde** *adj.* d'un blond cendré; ~**en** *adj.* cendré, blême; ~**tray** *s.* cendrier *m.*; **A**~ **Wednesday,** Mercredi des Cendres *m.*; ~**y** *adj.* cendreux.

ashamed *adj.* honteux; **to be** ~, avoir honte.

ashore *adv.* à terre.

Asia *s.* Asie *f.*; ~ **Minor,** Asie mineure *f.*; ~**n** *adj.* & *s.m.f.* asiatique; ~**tic** *adj.* asiatique.

aside *adv.* à part, à l'écart; *s.* aparté *m.*; **to stand** ~, se tenir à l'écart; **to take s.o.** ~, prendre qn. à part; **to set sth.** ~, mettre qch. de côté.

asinine *adj.* sot.

ask *v.t.* & *i.* **1.** (*inquire*) demander (qch. à qn.); **2.** (*a question*) poser (une question); **3.** (*request*) prier (qn. de faire qch.); **4.** (*invite*) inviter; **5.** (*interrogate*) interroger; ~ **after s.o.,** demander des nouvelles de qn.; ~ **for sth.,** demander qch.; ⚠ *v.t. in French*; **you're** ~**ing for it!,** vous chercher des embêtements!; **I** ~ **you!,** je vous le demande!

askance *adv.* **to look** ~ **at s.o.,** regarder qn. de travers.

askew *adv.* de travers.

aslant *prep.* en travers de; *adv.* de biais.

asleep *adj.* (*sleeping*) endormi; (*numb, of limbs etc.*) engourdi; **to** FALL ~; **sound** ~, profondément endormi.

aslope *adv.* en pente.

asparagus *s.* asperges *f.pl.*

aspect *s.* (*way of looking, point of view*) aspect *m.*; (*direction in which sth. fronts*) orientation *f.*

aspen *s.* tremble *m.*

asperity *s.* (*roughness*) aspérité *f.*; (*fig.*) âpreté *f.*

aspersion *s.* calomnie *f.*; ⚠ aspersion = **sprinkling with liquid.**

asphalt *s.* asphalte *m.*

asphyxia *s.* asphyxie *f.*; ~**te** *v.t.* & *i.* (s')asphyxier; ~**tion** *s.* suffocation *f.*

aspic *s.* (*cook.*) aspic *m.*

aspirate *s.* aspirée *f.*; ~ **h,** h aspiré; *v.t.* aspirer.

aspir/e *v.t.* (*ambition*) aspirer (à); (*reach high*) s'élever (à); ~**ant** *s.* aspirant *m.*; ~**ation** *s.* aspiration *f.*

aspirin *s.* aspirine *f.*; **an** ~, un comprimé d'aspirine *m.*

ass *s.* (*animal*) âne *m.*, ânesse *f.*; (*stupid person*) âne *m.*; **to be an** ~, **to make an** ~ **of oneself,** faire l'idiot.

assail *v.t.* assaillir; ~**ant** *s.* assaillant *m.*

assassin *s.* assassin *m.*; ~**ate** *v.t.* assassiner; ~**ation** *s.* assassinat *m.*

assault *s.* (*mil.*) assaut *m.*; (*personal attack*) attaque *f.*; *v.t.* attaquer.

assay *s.* essai *m.*; *v.t.* essayer.

assegai *s.* sagaie *f.*

assembl/e *v.t.* & *i.* **1.** (*bring or come together*) (s')assembler; **2.** (*collect*) rassembler; **3.** (*fit together parts, of machine etc.*) monter; ~**y** *s.* (1) (*usu. formal body*) assemblée *f.*; (2) réunion *f.*; (3) montage *m.*; ~**y line** *s.* chaîne de montage *f.*

assent *s.* assentiment *m.*; *v.i.* (*to*) consentir (à); (*approve*) approuver.

assert *v.t.* **1.** (*declare*) affirmer; **2.** (*claim rights*) revendiquer; ~ **oneself,** s'imposer; ~**ion** *s.* (1) assertion *f.*; (2) revendication *f.*

assess *v.t.* **1.** (*fix amount of fine, tax etc.*) établir le montant de; **2.** (*value, esp. for taxation*) évaluer; ~**ment** *s.* (1) imposition *f.*; (2) évaluation *f.*; ~**or** *s.* (1) (*valuer*) contrôleur *m.*; (2) (*adviser to judge*) assesseur *m.*

asset *s.* avantage *m.*; (*thing giving advantage*) atout *m.*; ~**s** *s.pl.* biens *m.pl.*

assidu/ity *s.* assiduité *f.*; ~**ous** *adj.* assidu; ~**ously** *adv.**

assign *v.t.* **1.** (*allot*) assigner; **2.** (*appoint*) désigner; **3.** (*make over formally*) céder; ~**ation** *s.* (1) attribution *f.*; (*meeting*) rendez-vous *m.*; ~**ment** *s.* (3) cession *f.*; (*task*) tâche *f.*

assimilat/e *v.t.* & *i.* (s')assimiler; ~**ion** *s.* assimilation *f.*

assist *v.t.* aider (qn. à faire qch.); ⚠ assister = **to be present;** ~**ance** *s.* aide *f.*; ⚠ assistance = **audience;** ~**ant** *s.* assistant(e), aide *m.f.*; adjoint *m.*; **shop** ~**ant** *s.* commis *m.*, vendeu/r, -se *m.f.*; ~**ant** *adj. often* sous + *noun.* sous-directeur, *etc.*; ~**ant-master** *s.* professeur *m.*; ⚠ professeur-adjoint = **unqualified teacher.**

assizes *s.pl.* assises *f.pl.*

associat/e *s.* (*partner*) partenaire *m.*; (*subordinate member of organization*) membre associé *m.*; *adj.* (*allied*) associé; *v.t.* & *i.* **1.** (*join, unite together*) associer, s'associer à qn.; **2.** (~ *with*) fréquenter; **3.** (*connect ideas*) associer; ~**ion** *s.* (1) & (3) association *f.*; (2) fréquentation *f.*; ~**ion football,** football *m.*, (*fam.*) foot *m.*

assort *v.t.* (*arrange in sorts*) classifier; *v.i.* (*harmonize,* ~ *with*) s'assortir à; ~**ed** *adj.* (*matching*) assorti; (*varied*) assortis *pl.*; ~**ment** *s.* assortiment *m.*

assuage *v.t.* (*fig. anger etc.*) apaiser; (*hunger, desires*) satisfaire; (*thirst*) étancher; (*pain*) soulager; **to be** ~**d,** se calmer.

assum/e *v.t.* **1.** (*take on, role, responsibility etc.*) assumer; (*take upon oneself unduly*) s'arroger; **2.** (*simulate*) affecter, feindre; (*name*) emprunter; **3.** (*take for granted*) supposer; ~**ed,** *adj.* feint, simulé, supposé; ~**ed name,** nom d'emprunt; ~**ing,** *adj.* présompteux; ~**ing it to be true,** en supposant que ce soit vrai; ~**ption** *s.* (1) appropriation *f.* (*arrogance*) prétention *f.*; (3) supposition *f.*; (*eccles.*) Assomption *f.*

assur/e *v.t.* assurer; ~**ance** *s.* assurance *f.*;

(*self-assurance*) assurance *f.*; (*impudence*) audace *f.*; (*insurance*) assurance *f.*; **~edly** *adv.* assurément.
aster *s.* (*bot.*) aster *m.*; **China ~**, reine-marguerite *f.*
asterisk *s.* astérisque *m.*
astern *adv.* à l'arrière.
asteroid *s.* astéroïde *m.*
asthma *s.* asthme *m.*; **~tic** *adj.* & *s.m.f.* asthmatique.
astir *adv.* (*out of bed*) debout; (*moving*) en mouvement.
astonish *v.t.* étonner; **~ing** *adj.* étonnant; **~ment** *s.* étonnement *m.*
astound *v.t.* stupéfier; (*fam.*) sidérer; **~ing** *adj.* stupéfiant.
astrakhan *s.* astrakan *m.*
astral *adj.* astral.
astray, to go ~ *v.i.* s'égarer.
astride *adv.* à califourchon (sur).
astringent *adj.* & *s.m.* astringent.
astrolog/y *s.* astrologie *f.*; **~er** *s.* astrologue *m.*; **~ical** *adj.* astrologique.
astronaut *s.* astronaute *m.*
astronom/y *s.* astronomie *f.*; **~er** *s.* astronome *m.*; **~ic(al)** *adj.* (*lit.* & *fig.*) astronomique.
astute *adj.* astucieux; **~ly** *adv.**
asunder *adv.* (*in two*) en deux; (*in pieces*) en morceaux.
asylum *s.* (*institution, refuge, sanctuary*) asile *m.*; **to ask for ~**, demander asile (à).
at *prep.* (*place* & *time*) à; (*house, shop*) chez; **~ home,** chez moi (toi, lui, elle, nous, vous, eux, elles); **~-home** *s.* réception *f.*; **~ all,** du tout; **~ that,** tel quel; *other possible translations*: **angry ~**, fâché contre; **~ a distance,** de loin; **to stop ~ nothing,** n'hésiter devant rien; **~ peace,** en paix; **~ sea,** sur mer; **to go in ~ the door,** entrer par la porte.
atheis/m *s.* athéisme *m.*; **~t** *s.* athée *m. f.*
athirst *adj.* (*thirsty*) assoiffé; (*eager for, knowledge, money, pleasure, power, etc.*) assoiffé (de connaissances, d'argent, de plaisirs, de pouvoir, etc.).
athlet/e *s.* athlète *m.f.*; **~ic** *adj.* athlétique; **~ic sports,** concours athlétique *m.*; **~icism** *s.* athlétisme *m.*, culte du sport *m.*
athwart *adv.* en travers; *prep.* en travers de.
Atlantic *adj.* & *s.m.* atlantique.
atlas *s.* atlas *m.*; **road ~**, guide routier *m.*
atmospher/e *s.* atmosphère *f.*; **~ic** *adj.* atmosphérique; **~ics** *s.pl.* (*electr., radio*) perturbations atmosphériques *f.pl.*, parasites *m.pl.*
atoll *s.* atoll *m.*
atom *s.* atome *m.*; *adj.* atomique; **~ic** *adj.* atomique; **~ize** *v.t.* atomiser; **~izer** *s.* atomiseur *m.*
atone *v.t.* & *i.* (*make amends*) compenser; (*redeem*) racheter; **~ for**, expier; **~ment** *s.* réparation *f.*, expiation *f.*
atroci/ous *adj.* atroce; **~ously** *adv.**; **~ty** *s.* (*action*) atrocité *f.*; (*object*) horreur *f.*
atrophy *s.* atrophie *f.*; *v.t.* & *i.* (s')atrophier.
attach *v.t.* & *i.* **1.** (*fasten, join*) (s')attacher, (se) fixer; **2.** (*attribute to*) (s')attacher, attribuer (à); **3.** (*bind in friendship*) (s')attacher, (se) lier; **~ment** *s.* (1) attache *f.*; (2) attribution *f.*; (3) attachement *m.*, attaches *f.pl.*; **~é case** *s.* serviette *f.*
attack *s.* (*assault, lit.* & *fig.*) attaque *f.*; (*onset of illness*) accès *m.*; *v.t.* attaquer.
attain *v.t.* & *i.* (*reach, gain, accomplish*) atteindre (à); **~ment** *s.* (*of hopes etc.*) réalisation *f.*; **~ments** *s.pl.* connaissances *f.pl.*
attar *s.* (*of roses*) essence de roses *f.*
attempt *s.* tentative *f.*; (*on life*) attentat *m.*; *v.t.* (*try*) tenter, essayer; (*try to accomplish*) entreprendre.
atten/d *v.t.* & *i.* **1.** (*be present at*) assister à; (*lectures*) suivre; **2.** (*apply mind to*) faire attention à; **3.** (*accompany*) accompagner; **4.** (*look after, ~ to*) s'occuper de; (*in shop*) servir; (*med.*) soigner; **~dance** *s.* (1) assistance *f.*; (3) service *m.*; **to be in ~dance on s.o.,** être de service auprès de qn.; (4) soins *m.pl.*; **to** DANCE **~dance on; ~dant** *s.* (1) assistant *m.*; (3) serviteur *m.*; (4) employé *m.*; **~dant** *adj.* concomitant; **~tion** *s.* (2) attention *f.*; **pay ~tion!**, faites attention!; (4) soins *m.pl.*; (*mil.*) garde-à-vous *m.*; (*order*) garde-à-vous!; **to** CALL **~tion to; ~tive** *adj.* (*listening*) attentif; (*careful*) soucieux.
attenuat/e *v.t.* **1.** (*make slender or thin*) affiner; **2.** (*reduce in force or value*) atténuer; **~ed** *adj.* (1) affiné; (2) atténué; **~ion** *s.* atténuation *f.*
attest *v.t.* attester; **~ation** *s.* attestation *f.*
attic *s.* grenier *m.*; (*with sloping roof*) mansarde *f.*
attire *s.* vêtements *m.pl.*; (*female*) toilette *f.*; *v.t.* & *i.* (se) vêtir, (se) parer; ⚠ attirer = **to attract.**
attitud/e *s.* (*posture* & *fig.*) attitude *f.*; **~ of mind,** état d'esprit *m.*; **~inize** *v.i.* poser.
attorney *s.* (*legal representative*) mandataire *m.*; (*solicitor*) avoué *m.*; **A~ General,** procureur-général *m.*; **power of ~**, délégation de pouvoir *f.*
attract *v.t.* **1.** (*draw to oneself*) attirer; **2.** (*allure, charm*) séduire; **~ion** *s.* (1) attraction *f.*; (2) séduction *f.*; **3.** (*object*) attraction *f.*; **4.** (*charm*) attrait *m.* charme *m.*; **~ive** *adj.* attirant, séduisant; ⚠ attractif *is used only of magnets, etc.*
attribut/e *s.* (*quality*) attribut *m.*; (*object appropriate to person or office, usu. pl.*) attributions *f.pl.*; *v.t.* attribuer (à); **~ion** *s.* attribution *f.*
attrition *s.* (*friction*) frottement *m.*; (*abrasion, techn.*) abrasion *f.*; (*wearing out*) usure *f.*; **war of ~**, guerre d'usure *f.*
attune *v.t.* (*mus.*) accorder; (*adapt*) harmoniser; **~d to,** en accord avec.
auburn *adj.* châtain.
auction *s.* (*sale*) vente aux enchères *f.*; (*bidding*) enchères *f.pl.*; *v.t.* vendre aux enchères; **~eer** *s.* commissaire-priseur *m.*; **~-room,** salle des ventes *f.*
audaci/ous *adj.* audacieux; **~ously** *adv.**; **~ty** *s.* audace *f.*
audib/le *adj.* (*sound*) audible; (*voice*) intelligible; **~ility** *s.* audibilité *f.*; **~ly** *adv.**,*.
audience *s.* **1.** (*formal interview*) & **2.** (*hearing*) audience *f.*; **3.** (*assembly*): (*concert, lecture*) auditoire *m.*; (*eccles. ceremony*) assistance *f.*; (*theatre*) public *m.* ⚠ audience *is never used in sense* (3).
audit *s.* vérification (des comptes) *f.*; *v.t.* vérifier (les comptes); **~or** *s.* commissaire aux comptes *m.*
audition *s.* audition *f.*; *v.t.* auditionner.
auditorium *s.* auditorium *m.*
auditory *adj.* auditif.
auger *s.* (*tool*) foret *m.*
aught *s.* quelque chose; **for ~ I know,** autant que je sache.
augment *v.t.* augmenter; **~ation** *s.* augmentation *f.*; **~ative** *adj.* augmentatif.
augur *s.* augure *m.*; *v.t.* & *i.* augurer; **to ~ well /ill for,** être de bon/de mauvais augure pour; **~y** *s.* augure *m.*
August[1] *s.* (*month*) août *m.*
august[2] *adj.* auguste.
aunt *s.* tante *f.*; **great-~**, grand-tante *f.*; **A~ Sally,** jeu de massacre *m.*
aura *s.* aura *f.*
aural *adj.* auriculaire.
aureole *s.* auréole *f.*
auspic/e(s) *s. usu. pl.* auspices *m.pl.*; **under the ~es of s.o.,** sous les auspices de qn.; **~ious** *adj.* propice, favorable, de bon augure.

auster/e *adj.* austère; **~ely** *adv.**; **~ity** *s.* austérité *f.*
austral *adj.* austral.
Austral/ia *s.* Australie *f.*; **A~ian** *adj.* & *s.m.f.* australien(ne); **A~asia** *s.* Australasie *f.*
Austria *s.* Autriche *f.*; **A~n** *adj.* & *s.m.f.* autrichien(ne).
authentic *adj.* authentique; **~ally** *adv.**; **~ate** *v.t.* authentiquer; **~ity** *s.* authenticité *f.*
author *s.* auteur *m.* (*no f.*); **~ess** *s.* femme auteur *f.*; **~ship** *s.* profession d'écrivain *f.*; (*of a deed*) paternité *f.*
author/ity *s.* (*power, influence, person, book, expert*) autorité *f.*; (*permission*) autorisation *f.*; **~itarian** *adj.* & *s.* autoritaire; **~itative** *adj.* **1.** (*commanding*) autoritaire; **2.** (*having ~ity*) autorisé; **~itatively** *adv.* (1) de façon autoritaire; (2) de bonne source; **~ization** *s.* autorisation *f.*; **~ize** *v.t.* autoriser.
autobiograph/y *s.* autobiographie *f.*; **~ical** *adj.* autobiographique.
autocra/cy *s.* autocratie *f.*; **~t** *s.* autocrate *m.*; **~tic** *adj.* autocratique.
autograph *s.* autographe *m.*; *v.t.* écrire de sa main; (*a book etc.*) signer.
automat/ic *adj.* automatique; *s.* (*pistol*) (pistolet) automatique *m.*; **~ion** *s.* automatisation *f.*; **~ism** *s.* automatisme *m.*; **~on** *s.* automate *m.*
autonom/y *s.* autonomie *f.*; **~ous** *adj.* autonome.
autopsy *s.* autopsie *f.*
autumn *s.* automne *m.*; **~al** *adj.* automnal.
auxiliary *adj.* & *s.m.f.* auxiliaire.
avail *s.* (*use*) utilité *f.*; (*profit*) profit *m.*; **it is of no ~ to,** ça ne sert à rien de; *v.t.* (*to be of use or assistance to*) servir à, être utile à; (*to help, to benefit*) profiter à; **to ~ oneself of,** profiter de; **~able** *adj.* disponible; **~ability** *s.* disponibilité *f.*
avalanche *s.* avalanche *f.*
avaric/e *s.* avarice *f.*; **~ious** *adj.* avare.
avenge *v.t.* venger, se venger de; **to ~ an insult,** venger un affront, se venger d'un affront; **to ~ oneself upon s.o.,** se venger de qn.; **to be ~d,** prendre sa revanche (*on*—sur); **~r** *s.* veng/eur, -eresse *m.f.*
avenue *s.* (*road*) avenue *f.*; (*way of approach*) voie d'accès *f.*; **to explore all ~s,** envisager toutes les possibilités.
aver *v.t.* affirmer.
average *s.* moyenne *f.*; **on the ~,** en moyenne; *adj.* moyen; *v.t.* prendre la moyenne de; (*amount on ~ to*) s'élever en moyenne à; **he ~s 8 hours work a day,** il travaille en moyenne 8 heures par jour.
avers/e *adj.* (*opposed*) opposé; (*disinclined*) peu disposé (*to*—à); **to be ~e to,** répugner à; **~ion** *s.* (*dislike*) aversion *f.*; (*object of dislike*) objet d'aversion *m.*; **pet ~ion,** bête noire *f.*
avert *v.t.* détourner.
aviary *s.* volière *f.*
aviat/ion *s.* aviation *f.*; **~or** *s.* aviat/eur, -rice *m.f.*
avid *adj.* avide (*for*—de); **~ity** *s.* avidité *f.*
avocado (pear) avocat *m.*
avoid *v.t.* éviter (de); **~able** *adj.* évitable; **~ance** *s.* dérobade *f.* (devant).
avow *v.t.* avouer; **~al** *s.* aveu *m.*; **~edly** *adv.* de son propre aveu, franchement.
await *v.t.* attendre.
awake *v.t.* réveiller; *v.i.* (*cease to sleep*) se réveiller; **~ to,** s'éveiller à; *adj.* (*not asleep*) éveillé; (*vigilant*) vigilant; **~ to** (*aware of*) conscient de; **~n** *v.t.* & *i.* (se) réveiller; **~ning** *s.* réveil *m.*
award *s.* (*judgement*) décision *f.*; (*prize*) récompense *f.*; *v.t.* (*adjudge*) adjuger; (*grant*) accorder; (*confer*) décerner.
aware *adj.* averti; **to be ~ of,** avoir conscience de; **to become ~ of,** se rendre compte de; **not to be ~ of,** ignorer; **not that I am ~,** pas que je sache; **~ness** *s.* conscience *f.*
awash *adv.* (*flush with water*) à fleur d'eau; *adj.* (*washed by water*) inondé.
away *adv.* (*at a distance*) au loin; (*continuously*) sans arrêt; **~ from home,** absent; **10 miles ~,** à une distance de 10 milles; **~ with!,** à bas!; **~ with you!,** allez-vous-en; **~ match,** match aller; *see also under verbs* GIVE, GO, THROW, *etc.*
awe *s.* crainte *f.*; **to be in ~ of,** être intimidé par; **~-inspiring, ~some** *adj.* terrifiant; **~-struck** *adj.* frappé de terreur; *v.t.* terrifier.
awful *adj.* (*inspiring awe*) terrifiant, imposant; (*fam. = very bad*) terrible, affreux; (*fam. = very great*) formidable; **an ~ accident,** un accident terrible; **an ~ lot (of),** un nombre formidable (de); **~ly** *adv.* terriblement; (*fam. = very*) bigrement, rudement; **~ly good,** rudement bon.
awhile *adv.* un moment, pendant quelque temps.
awkward *adj.* **1.** (*ill-adapted for use*) peu commode; **2.** (*hard to deal with*): (*question*) embarrassant, (*silence*) embarrassé, (*situation*) gênant; **3.** (*clumsy*) gauche, maladroit; **~ly** *adv.* (2) avec gêne; (3) gauchement; **~ness** *s.* (1) incommodité *f.*; (2) difficulté *f.*, embarras *m.*; (3) gaucherie *f.*, maladresse *f.*
awl *s.* alène *f.*
awning *s.* tente *f.*; (*on cart or van*) bâche *f.*
awry *adv.* de travers.
axe *s.* hache *f.*; **to have an ~ to grind,** prêcher pour son saint; **battle~,** (*mil.*) hache d'armes *f.*; (*fig.*) dragon *m.*; *v.t.* (*comm.*) faire une coupe sombre (dans le personnel).
axiom *s.* axiome *m.*; **~atic** *adj.* axiomatique.
axis *s.* axe *m.*
axle *s.* essieu *m.*
ay, aye *adv.* (=*yes*) oui, bien; **ayes** (*pl.*) les voix pour; **the ~es have it,** les oui l'emportent.
aye *adv.* (*always*) toujours, à jamais.
azalea *s.* azalée *f.*
azure *s.* azur *m.*; *adj.* azuré.

B

B *s.* (*mus. note*) si *m.*
B.A. (*approx.*) (*degree*) licence ès lettres *f.*; (*title*) licencié(e) ès lettres *m.f.*; (*abbrev.*) l. ès l.
baa *s.* bêlement *m.*; *v.i.* bêler.
babble *s.* **1.** (*idle talk*) babillage *m.*, bavardage *m.*; **2.** (*stream*) murmure *m.*, (*birds*) gazouillis *m.*; *v.i.* (1) babiller, bavarder; (*tell secrets*) jaser; (2) murmurer; gazouiller.
babe *s.* bébé *m.*; (*fam.*) bambin *m.*
babel *s.* (*fig.*) vacarme *m.*
baboon *s.* babouin *m.*
baby *s.* (*child*) bébé *m.*; (*childish person*) enfant *m.*; **don't be a ~,** ne faites pas l'enfant; (*pet project*) dada *m.*; **to be left holding the ~,** avoir l'affaire sur les bras; (*pop.*) rester en carafe avec; **~'s** BOTTLE; **~ grand piano,** piano demi-queue *m.*; **~hood** *s.* enfance *f.*; **~-linen** *s.* layette *f.*; **~-sitter** *s.* baby-sitter *m.f.*; **~-talk** *s.* babil *m.*
bachelor *s.* (*unmarried man*) célibataire *m.*; (*acad.*)

licencié(e) *m.f.*; ~ **of arts, of science,** *see* B.A., B.SC.; **~'s quarters,** garçonnière *f.*; ~ **girl** *s.* jeune fille émancipée *f.*; ⚠ bachelier = **person who has passed the** baccalauréat (**exam taken on leaving school**).

bacill/us *s.* bacille *m.*; **~ary** *adj.* bacillaire.

back[1] *s.* (*anat., of book*) dos *m.*; (*rear part*) derrière *m.*; (*of chair*) dossier *m.*; (*of hand*) revers *m.*; (*of stage*) fond *m.*; (*of page*) verso *m.*; (*sport*) arrière *m.*; **with one's ~ to the wall,** acculé; **to go behind s.o.'s ~,** agir dans le dos de qn.; **to get one's ~ up,** se hérisser; **to get s.o.'s ~ up,** agacer qn.; **to turn one's ~ on,** tourner le dos à; **to put one's ~ into,** faire un grand effort; **~-breaking** *adj.* éreintant; **~stroke** (*swimming*) brasse (*f.*) sur le dos; *adj.* de derrière, arrière; (*remote*) lointain; **~chat** *s.* réplique impertinente *f.*; **~cloth** *s.* toile de fond *f.*; **~ door** *s.* porte de derrière *f.*; **~-door** *adj.* clandestin; **~log** *s.* accumulation *f.*; **~ number** *s.* ancien numéro *m.*, (*fig. of person*) vieille baderne *f.*; **~ seat** *s.* siège arrière *m.*; **to take a ~ seat,** s'effacer; **~-stairs** *s.* escalier de service *m.*; **~ street** *s.* rue écartée, pauvre *f.*; **~yard** *s.* arrière-cour *f.*; *adv.* en arrière; **to be ~,** être de retour; **some years ~,** il y a quelques années; **there and ~,** aller et retour; *N.B. with many verbs the prefix* re- *is used to translate* **~, to come, to go, to take ~,** revenir, retourner, reprendre; **to** GIVE **~**; **~fire** *s.* (*of engine*) pétarade *f.*, *v.i.* pétarader; (*fig. of plan, etc.*) rater; **~lash** *s.* contrecoup *m.*; **~-pedal** *v.i.* rétropédaler, (*fig.*) faire volte-face; **~stitch** *s.* point arrière *m.*; **~wash** *s.* ressac *m.*

back[2] *v.t.* (*make horse, car, go ~wards*) faire reculer, faire faire marche arrière à; (*support*) soutenir; (*bet on*) parier sur; (*endorse bill*) avaliser; *v.i.* reculer, faire marche arrière; (*of wind*) ravaler; **~ down,** abandonner, lâcher la partie; **~ into sth.,** reculer contre; *v.i.* entrer à reculons; **~ out of,** se retirer de; **~ up,** *v.t.* seconder, appuyer; **~er** *s.* (*supporter*) partisan *m.*, soutien *m.*; **~ing** *s.* (*movement*) recul *m.*; (*support*) appui *m.*

backbit/e *v.t.* médire de; (*fam.*) débiner; **~er** *s.* médisant *m.*; **~ing** *s.* médisance *f.*; (*fam.*) ragot *m.*

backbone *s.* (*anat.*) épine dorsale *f.*; (*fig.*) (*main support*) pivot *m.*; (*firmness of character*) cran. *m.*; **without ~,** mollasse; **person without ~,** chiffe *f.*

backgammon *s.* jacquet *m.*

background *s.* fond *m.*; (*paint., theat. & fig.*) arrière-plan *m.*; **in the ~,** à l'arrière-plan; (*of a person*) milieu (*m.*) et formation (*f.*); (*relevant information*) documentation *f.*; **~ music,** musique de fond *f.*

backhand *s.* (*tennis*) revers (de main) *m.*; **~ed** *adj.* de revers; **~ed compliment,** compliment équivoque *m.*

backslid/e *v.i.* rechuter; **~ing** *s.* rechute *f.*

backward *adj.* **1.** (*undeveloped, child, etc.*) arriéré; **2.** (*towards rear*): (*movement*) en arrière; (*from back to front*) à rebours; (*not progressive*) rétrograde; **3.** (*season, plants, etc.*) retardé, tardif; **4.** (*shy*) peu disposé à; **~ness** *s.* (1) arriération *f.*; (3) retard *m.*; (4) répugnance *f.*; **~s** *adv.* (*walk*) à reculons; (*fall*) à la renverse; (*back to front*) à rebours; (*wrong end first*) à l'envers; **~s and forwards,** de long en large; **to lean** *or* **bend over ~s to do sth.** (*fam.*) se décarcasser pour faire qch.; **to go ~s,** rétrograder.

backwater *s.* (*river*) bras de décharge *m.*; (*gen. & fig.*) mare, eau, stagnante *f.*

backwoods *s.* forêt vierge *f.*; (*fig.*) brousse *f.*

bacon *s.* lard *m.*; **to save one's ~** (*fam.*) sauver sa peau.

bacteri/um *s.* bactérie *f.*; **~ology,** bactériologie *f.*; **~ological** *adj.* bactériologique.

bad *s.* mauvais *m.*; (*evil*) mal *m.*; **to go to the ~,** tourner mal; **from ~ to worse,** de mal en pis; *adj.* (≠*good*) mauvais; (*ill*) malade; (*evil*) méchant; (*decayed*) gâté, avarié; (*painful*) fort, grave; **to go ~,** se gâter, s'avarier; **a ~ hat, lot,** canaille *f.*; **a ~ egg** (*fig.*) vaurien *m.*; **a ~ time,** un mauvais moment, un mauvais quart d'heure; **I have a ~ finger,** j'ai mal au doigt; **it's too ~,** (*too much*) c'est trop fort; (*regrettable*) c'est dommage; **~-tempered,** de mauvaise humeur; **to be on ~ terms with s.o.,** être mal avec qn.; **to be in a ~ way,** être mal en point; (*fam.*) être mal fichu; **to come to a ~ end,** finir mal; **to give a** DOG **a ~ name; ~ly** *adv.* mal; (=*seriously*) gravement; **~ness** *s.* (*people*) méchanceté *f.*; (*things*) mauvaise qualité *f.*; mauvais état *m.*

badge *s.* (*of office, rank, etc.*) insigne *m.*; (*of identity, etc.*) plaque *f.*

badger *s.* (*animal*) blaireau *m.*; *v.t.* harceler.

badminton *s.* (*sport*) badminton *m.*

baffle *s.* déflecteur *m.*, cloison *f.*; *v.t.* (*fool*) déjouer; (*frustrate*) frustrer; (*perplex*) confondre.

bag *s.* (*small*) sac *m.*; (*large*) valise *f.*; HAND**~**; KIT**~**; SPONGE-**~**; TEA-**~**; VANITY **~**; (*hunt.*) tableau de chasse *m.*; **~s** *s.pl.* (*pop. trousers*) falzar *m.*; **~s of,** des tas de; **to depart ~ and baggage,** prendre ses cliques et ses claques; **to let the** CAT **out of the ~**; *v.t.* (*hunt.*) tuer; (*take possession of*) empocher; *v.i.* (*bulge*) bouffer; **to be ~gy** (*trousers*) faire des poches aux genoux.

bagatelle *s.* (*game*) petit billard *m.*; (*trifle*) bagatelle *f.*

baggage *s.* (*luggage*) bagages *m.pl.*; (*hussy*) friponne *f.*; BAG **and ~.**

bagpipe(s) *s.* cornemuse, *f.*; **~r,** joueur de cornemuse *m.*

bail[1] *s.* (*law*) caution *f.*; **on ~,** sous caution; **to go ~ for,** se porter garant de; ⚠ bail = **lease.**

bail[2], **bale** *v.t.* écoper; **to ~ out** (*aviat.*) sauter en parachute.

bailiff *s.* (*law*) huissier *m.*; (*farm, estate*) régisseur *m.*

bait *s.* amorce *f.*; (*prepared & fig.*) appât *m.*; *v.t.* (*tease*) harceler; (*put ~ on hook*) amorcer, appâter.

baize *s.* feutrine *f.*; **green ~,** tapis vert. *m.*

bak/e *v.t. & i.* (faire) cuire au four; (*fig.*) se dessécher; **~ehouse** *s.* fournil *m.*; **~er** *s.* boulanger *m.*; **~ery** *s.*, **~er's shop** *s.* boulangerie *f.*; **~ing powder** *s.* levure *f.*; **~ed** POTATO; HALF-**~ed.**

bakelite *s.* bakélite *f.* (**P.**)

baksheesh *s.* bakchich *m.*

balalaika *s.* balalaïka *f.*

balance *s.* **1.** (*fin.*) solde *m.* (*credit, debit ~*), solde créditeur, débiteur; **2.** (*comm. machine*) balance *f.*; **3.** (*equilibrium*) équilibre *m.*; **~ sheet,** bilan *m.*; **~ carried forward,** report *m.*; **~ of payments,** balance du commerce *f.*; **~ of power,** équilibre des forces, *m.*; *v.t.* (1) (*accounts*) balancer; (*budget*) équilibrer; (2) peser; (3) équilibrer; *v.i.* balancer.

balcony *s.* balcon *m.*

bald *adj.* **1.** (*hairless*) chauve; (*without feathers*) déplumé; **~ as a** COOT; **~** PATE; **2.** (*bare*) dénudé; **3.** (*meagre*) maigre; (*of style*) sec; **~ly** *adv.* (3)*.; **~ness** *s.* (1) calvitie *f.*; (2) nudité *f.*; (3) sécheresse *f.*

balderdash *s.* fariboles *f.pl.*

bale[1] *s.* (*evil*) mal *m.*; **~ful** *adj.* funeste.

bale[2] *s.* (*large, of wool, etc.*) balle *f.*; (*small*) ballot *m.*; (*of hay, straw*) botte *f.*; *v.t.* emballer; see BAIL.

balk *s.* (*timber*) billot *m.*; (*fig.*) obstacle *m.*; *v.t.* (*thwart*) frustrer; (*hinder*) entraver; *v.i.* (*horse*) se dérober; (*fig.* & *fam.*) caler (devant une difficulté).

ball[1] (*golf, tennis, rifle*) balle *f.*; (*football*) ballon *m.*; (*bowls, hockey, croquet, snow*) boule *f.*; (*billiards*) bille *f.*; (*cannon*) boulet *m.*; (*wool, silk, string*) pelote *f.*; (*thread*) peloton *m.*; (*of eye*) globe *m.*; **~-bearings,** roulement à billes *m.*; **~cock** *s.* valve à flotteur *f.*; **~-point pen** *s.* stylo à bille *m.*; **to keep the ~ rolling,** renvoyer la balle.

ball[2] *s.* (*dance*) bal *m.*; (*fam.*) **to have a ~,** rigoler.

ballad *s.* (*poem*) ballade *f.*; (*song*) romance *f.*

ballast *s.* lest *m.*; (*rail. slag*) ballast *m.*; *v.t.* lester.

ball/et *s.* ballet *m.*; **~et-dancer,** danseu/r, -se *m.f.*; **~erina,** ballerine *f.*

balloon *s.* (*large* & *toy*) ballon *m.*; (*in cartoon*) bulle *f.*; **~ist,** aéronaute *m.*

ballot *s.* scrutin *m.*; *v.i.* voter au scrutin secret; **~-box,** urne *f.*; ⚠ ballot = **bale.**

bally *adj.* (*fam.*) sacré, satané (*before the noun*); *adv.* sacrément; **~hoo** *s.* (*fam.*) battage *m.*

balm *s.* (*lit.* & *fig.*) baume *m.*; **~y** *adj.* (*fragrant*) embaumé; (*soothing*) calmant; (*fam.* = *silly*) toqué.

balsa *s.* (*wood*) balsa *m.*

balsam *s.* baume *m.*

Baltic *s.* (*sea*) Baltique *f.*; *adj.* balte.

balust/er *s.* (*pillar*) balustre *m.*; (*pl. handrail*) rampe *f.*; **~rade,** balustrade *f.*

bamboo *s.* bambou *m.*

bamboozle *v.t.* (*fam.*) embobiner.

ban *s.* interdiction *f.*; **to put a ~ on sth.,** frapper qch. d'interdiction; *v.t.* interdire.

banal *adj.* banal (*pl.* banals); **~ity** *s.* banalité *f.*

banana *s.* banane *f.*; **~-tree,** bananier *m.*

band *s.* (*strip of material, metal, rubber; stripe of colour; troop of persons*) bande *f.*; (*mus.*) orchestre *m.*; (*brass*) fanfare *f.*; (*radio*) bande (de fréquence) *f.*; **~box,** carton *m.*; **~master** *s.* chef de musique *m.*; **~sman** *s.* musicien *m.*; **~stand** *s.* kiosque à musique *m.*; **~ wagon** *s.* voiture de parade *f.*; (*fig. fam.*) **to jump on the ~ wagon,** se mettre du côté du manche; *v.t.* (*put ~s on*) bander; (*form into ~*) (se) liguer.

bandage *s.* pansement *m.*; *v.t.* panser.

bandanna *s.* madras *m.*

bandit *s.* (*outlaw*) bandit *m.*; (*robber*) brigand *m.*; (*gangster*) gangster *m.*; ONE-**armed ~**; **~ry** *s.* brigandage *m.*

bandoleer *s.* cartouchière *f.*

bandy *adj.* (*~-legged*) bancal; *v.t.* (*to pass to and fro*) se renvoyer; (*to spread about*) faire circuler.

bane *s.* **1.** (*ruin*) ruine *f.*; **2.** (*poison*) poison *m.*; **~ful** *adj.* (1) pernicieux; (2) empoisonné; **to be the ~ of s.o.'s life,** empoisonner la vie de qn.; **she is the ~ of his life,** elle lui empoisonne la vie.

bang[1] *s.* **1.** (*blow*) coup *m.* **2.** (*noise of door etc.*) claquement *m.*; **3.** (*loud noise*) détonation *f.*; *v.t.* & *i.* (1) rosser; (2) claquer; (3) détoner; **~ on** (=*quite right*), (*pop.*) dans le mille!

bang[2] *s.* (*hair*) frange *f.*

bangle *s.* bracelet *m.*

banish *v.t.* bannir; (*fig.*) chasser; **~ment** *s.* bannissement *m.*

banister(s) *s.* rampe *f.*

banjo *s.* banjo *m.*

bank[1] *s.* (*river*) rive *f.*; (*earth*) talus *m.*; (*sand, coral*) banc *m.*; (*clouds*) amoncellement *m.*; *v.t.* (*to heap up*) amonceler; (*to earth up*) endiguer; *v.i.* (*aviat.*) virer sur l'aile; **~ing** *s.* (*aviat.*) virage sur l'aile *m.*

bank[2] *s.* (*fin., comm.*) banque *f.*; (*store*) **blood ~, eye ~,** banque du sang, banque des yeux; **data ~,** centre (*m.*) de traitement de l'information; (*row of similar objects*) batterie *f.*; **to break the ~,** faire sauter la banque; **~ account** *s.* compte en banque *m.*; **~-book** *s.* carnet de banque *m.*; **~ card** *s.* carte de garantie *f.*; **~ holiday** *s.* jour férié *m.*; **~note** *s.* billet de banque *m.*; **B~ Rate** *s.* taux d'escompte *m.*; **~er** *s.* banquier *m.*; *v.t.* déposer en banque; **~ on,** compter sur; **don't ~ on it,** n'y comptez pas.

bankrupt *s.* failli *m.*; (*fraudulent*) banqueroutier *m.*; *adj.* failli, en faillite; **to go ~,** faire faillite; *v.t.* réduire à la faillite; **~cy** *s.* (*fin.* & *fig.*) faillite *f.*; (*fraudulent*) banqueroute *f.*

banner *s.* bannière *f.*; *adj.* **~** HEADLINES.

banns *s.* bans *m.pl.* (de mariage).

banquet *s.* banquet *m.*; *v.i.* banqueter; *v.t.* offrir un festin à qn.; **~ing-hall,** salle de festin *f.*

banshee *s.* la Dame blanche *f.*

bant *v.i.* se mettre au régime.

bantam *s.* coq nain *m.*; **~weight,** poids coq *m.*

banter *s.* raillerie *f.*; *v.t.* & *i.* railler, plaisanter avec; **~ing** *adj.* de raillerie.

Bantu *adj.* & *s.* bantou.

bapt/ism *s.* baptême *m.*; **~ismal** *adj.* baptismal; **~ist** *s.* baptiste *m.*; **~istery** *s.* baptistère *m.*; **~ize** *v.t.* baptiser.

bar *s.* (*iron, etc.; tribunal; harbour; mus.*) barre *f.*; (*of soap*) pain *m.*; (*of chocolate*) plaque *f.*; (*on window*) barreau *m.*; (*law*) barreau *m.*; **to be at the ~,** être inscrit au barreau; **to** CALL **to the ~**; (*obstacle*) barrière *f.*; (*drinking place*) buvette *f.*, bar *m.*; (*to medal*) palmes *f.pl.*; COLOUR **~**; **~man, ~maid, ~tender,** barman, garçon *m.*; barmaid, serveuse *f.*; *v.t.* (*door*) barricader; (*window*) grillager; (*the way*) barrer; (*exclude*) exclure; **~ring** *prep.* sauf, excepté.

barb *s.* barbillon *m.*; (*fig.*) traits *m.pl.*; **~ed wire,** fil de fer barbelé; (*usu.*) barbelés *m.pl.*

barbar/ian *adj.* & *s.m.* barbare; **~ic, ~ous** *adj.* barbare; **~ity** *s.* barbarie *f.*; **~ism** *s.* barbarisme *m.* (⚠ *used only of ling. faults*).

barbecue *s.* barbecue *m.*; *v.t.* rôtir en barbecue.

barber *s.* coiffeur *m.*; ⚠ barbier *is obs.* = **barber who also shaved.**

barbiturate *adj.* & *s.m.* barbiturique.

bard *s.* barde *m.*

bare *adj.* (*naked*) nu; (*mere*) simple; (*empty*) vide; (*unadorned*) dégarni; **~back,** à cru; **~ faced** (*fig.*) effronté; **~foot,** pieds nus; **~headed,** nu-tête; **~ly** *adv.* à peine, tout juste; **we have ~ly the time** (=*scarcely*), nous avons à peine le temps; **we have ~ly the time** (=*just*), nous avons toute juste le temps; **~ness** *s.* (*poverty*) misère *f.*; (*barrenness*) nudité *f.*; *v.t.* dénuder; (*strip*) dépouiller; (*fig.*) révéler.

bargain *s.* (*agreement*) marché *m.*; (*thing got cheaply*) occasion *f.*; **a great ~,** une bonne affaire *f.*; **that's a ~!,** conclu!; **into the ~,** par-dessus le marché; **~ counter,** rayon des soldes *m.*; *v.i.* marchander; (*fig. to be prepared for*) **~ for, with,** s'attendre à; **collective ~ing,** convention collective *f.*

barge[1] *s.* chaland *m.*; (*ceremonial*) chaloupe *f.*; **admiral's ~,** canot (*m.*) major; **~e** *s.* marinier *m.*

barge[2] *v.t.* **~ against,** se cogner à; **~ in** (*fig.*) mettre les pieds dans le plat.

baritone *adj.* & *s.m.* baryton.

bark *s.* **1.** (*of tree*) écorce *f.*; **2.** (*of dog, etc.*) aboiement *m.*; **his ~ is worse than his bite,** chien qui aboie ne mord pas; **3.** (*ship*) barque *f.*; *v.t.* (1) (*one's shin*) (s')écorcher *v.i.* (2) aboyer; (*cough*) tousser.

barley *s.* orge *f.*; **pearl ~,** orge perlé *m.*; **~corn,** grain d'orge *m.*; **~ sugar,** sucre d'orge *m.*; **~-water,** orgeat *m.*

barm *s.* levure *f.*

barn *s.* grange *f.*; **~ floor,** aire *f.*; **~** OWL; **~yard** basse-cour *f.*

barnacle *s.* anatife *m.*; (*pop.*) bernacle *f.*
baromet/er *s.* baromètre *m.*; **~ric** *adj.* barométrique.
baron, -ess *s.* baron *m.*, baronne *f.*; **~ of beef,** (double) aloyau *m.*; **~y,** baronnie *f.*; **~et,** baronnet *m.*
baroque *adj.* & *s.m.* baroque.
barrack *v.t.* (*pop.*) chahuter.
barracks *s.* (*mil.*) caserne *f.*; (*plain building*) (*fam.*) caserne *f.*; ⚠ baraque = **shack, wooden hut.**
barrage *s.* (*mil.*) tir de barrage *m.*; (*fig. of questions etc.*) flot *m.*
barrel *s.* (*small*) baril *m.*; (*wooden*) tonneau *m.*; (*for tar*) tonne *f.*; (*of rifle*) canon *m.*; **~-organ,** orgue de barbarie *m.*; DOUBLE-**~ed.**
barren *adj.* (*lit.* & *fig.*) stérile; **~ness** *s.* stérilité *f.*
barricade *s.* barricade *f.*; *v.t.* barricader.
barrier *s.* barrière *f.*; **crash ~,** glissière de sécurité *f.*; (*obstacle*) obstacle *m.*; **~ cream,** crème protectrice *f.*; **B~ Reef,** La Grande Barrière.
barrister *s.* avocat *m.*
barrow *s.* (*tumulus*) tumulus *m.*; (*wheel~*) brouette *f.*; **~ boy,** marchand des quatre saisons *m.*
barter *s.* troc *m.*; *v.t.* troquer.
basalt *s.* basalte *m.*
bas/e[1] *s.* (*foundation*) fondement *m.*; (*for operations*) base *f.*; **~eball,** baseball *m.*; **~ement** *s.* sous-sol *m.*; **~ic, ~al** *adj.* de base, fondamental; **~eless** *adj.* sans fondement; *v.t.* (*found on*) fonder, baser, sur; (*establish*) établir.
base[2] *adj.* **1.** (*low*) bas; **2.** (*mean*) vil; **3.** (*metal*) sans valeur; **4.** (*coin*) faux; **~ly** *adv.* (1)*; (2)*; **~ness** *s.* bassesse *f.*
bash *s.* coup violent *m.*; (*fam.*) gnon *m.*; *v.t.* cogner; **~ in,** enfoncer; **to have a ~,** tenter le coup.
bashful *adj.* timide; **~ly,** *adv.**; **~ness** *s.* timidité *f.*
basilica *s.* basilique *f.*
basilisk *s.* basilic *m.*
basin *s.* (*hand*) cuvette *f.*; (*bowl*) bol *m.*; (*river* & *dock*) bassin *m.*
basis *s.* (*foundation*) fondement *m.*; (*basic ingredient*) base *f.*
bask *v.i.* (*fam.*) faire le lézard.
basket *s.* (*with handle*) panier *m.*; (*usu. without handle*) corbeille *f.*; (*for back*) hotte *f.*; (*for game, fish, etc.*) bourriche *f.*; **~ball,** basket-ball, *m.*; **~-maker,** vannier *m.*
basque *adj.* & *s.m.f.* basque.
bass[1] *s.* (*fish*) (*freshwater*) perche *f.*; (*sea*) bar *m.*
bass[2] *s.* (*mus.*) basse *f.*; *adj.* de basse; DOUBLE-**~**.
bassinet *s.* berceau d'osier *m.*; (*Moses basket*) moïse *m.*
bassoon *s.* (*instrument* & *player*) basson *m.*
bastard *adj.* & *s.m.* bâtard; (*fig.* & *pop.*) salaud *m.*; **~ize** *v.t.* déclarer bâtard.
baste *v.t.* (*cook.*) arroser; (*sew.*) bâtir; (*thrash*) bâtonner.
bastinado *s.* bastonnade *f.*
bastion *s.* (*mil.* & *fig.*) bastion *m.*
bat[1] *s.* (*animal*) chauve-souris *f.*; **as** BLIND **as a ~; to have ~s in the belfry,** avoir une araignée dans le plafond; **~ty** *adj.* (*pop.*) cinglé.
bat[2] *s.* (*cricket, etc.*) batte *f.*; **~sman** *s.* batteur *m.*; **to do sth. off one's own ~,** prendre qch. sous son bonnet; *v.t.* (*wink*) cligner; **to ~ an eyelid,** sourciller.
batch *s.* (*bread* & *fig. of persons*) fournée *f.*; (*papers*) liasse *f.*
bate *v.t.* & *i.* (*restrain*) baisser; (*comm. deduct*) rabattre; **with ~d breath,** dans un souffle.
bath *s.* (*wash*) bain *m.*; (*container*) baignoire *f.*; **~s** (*public*) établissement de bains *m.*; SWIMMING-**~**; *v.t.* & *i.* donner, prendre, un bain; **B~ chair,** fauteuil roulant *m.*; **~room,** salle de bains *f.*; **~ towel,** serviette de toilette *f.*
bath/e *s.* bain *m.*, baignade *f.*; *v.t.* & *i.* (se) baigner; **~er** *s.* baigneu/r, -se *m.f.*; **~ing** *s.* bains de mer *m.pl.*; **~ing-costume,** maillot *m.*; **to be ~ed in** PERSPIRATION.
bathos *s.* pathos *m.*
batman *s.* (*mil.*) ordonnance *f.*
baton *s.* bâton *m.*
battalion *s.* bataillon *m.*
batten *s.* latte, *f.*; *v.t.* **~ on,** s'engraisser, s'enrichir, aux dépens de.
batter[1] *s.* (*cook.*) pâte *f.*
batter[2] *v.t.* (*beat*) battre, rouer de coups; (*ill--treat*) maltraiter; **~ down,** abattre; **~ in,** enfoncer; **~ed** *adj.* (*hat*) cabossé; (*furniture etc.*) abîmé; **~ing-ram,** bélier *m.*
battery *s.* (*mil.*) batterie *f.*; (*small, electr.*) pile *f.*; (*auto, etc.*) batterie *f.*
battle *s.* bataille *f.*; **~**AXE; **~dress,** tenue de campagne *f.*; **~field** *s.* champ de bataille *m.*; **~ment** *s.* créneaux *m.pl.*; **~ship** *s.* cuirassé *m.*; **that's half the ~** (*fig.*) c'est à moitié gagné; *v.t.* & *i.* lutter (*against, with*—contre, avec).
battledore *s.* (*and shuttlecock*) jeu de volant *m.*
bauble *s.* babiole *f.*
bauxite *s.* bauxite *f.*
Bavaria *s.* Bavière *f.*; **~n,** *adj.* & *s.m.f.* bavarois(e).
bawdy *adj.* obscène.
bawl *v.t.* & *i.* brailler; **to ~ s.o. out,** (*pop.*) engueuler qn.
bay *s.* **1.** (*tree*) laurier *m.*; **2.** (*geog.*) baie *f.*; **3.** (*arch.*) travée *f.*; **4.** (*bark*) aboiement *m.*; **5.** (*horse*) bai *m.*; **~ window,** baie *f.*; *v.i.* (4) aboyer; **at ~,** aux abois; **to keep at ~,** tenir en échec.
bayonet *s.* baïonnette *f.*; **fixed ~s,** baïonnette au canon.
bazaar *s.* (*oriental market*) bazar *m.*; (*charity sale*) vente de charité *f.*; (*big shop*) bazar *m.*
bazooka *s.* bazooka *m.*
B.B.C. *s.* la B B C.
B.C. avant Jésus-Christ; (*abbrev.*) av. J-C.
be *v.i.* être; (*exist*) exister; (*occur*) avoir lieu; (*time, it is 6 o'clock, etc.*), être, il est six heures, etc.; (*age*) avoir, **he is 6 years old,** il a six ans; (*to be hot, cold, hungry, thirsty etc.*) avoir chaud, froid, faim, soif, etc.; (*weather, to be fine, hot, cold etc.*) faire beau, chaud, froid, etc.; (*health, to be well, ill etc.*) aller bien, mal, etc.; (*to be situated*) se trouver; (*to be destined to*) devoir, **he is to go,** il doit s'en aller; **to ~ off,** s'en aller; **to ~ out,** être sorti; **~ that as it may,** quoi qu'il en soit; **that may ~,** cela se peut; **here I am, he is, etc.,** me, le, voici, etc.; **there it is, they are, etc.,** le, la, les voilà; *v.aux.* (*Eng. passive.*) **to be killed, heard, etc.,** être tué, entendu; **I am told that,** on me dit que; **the house is being repaired,** on est en train de réparer la maison; (*continuous present* & *past*) *the part of the verb* BE *is not translated in French,* **I am** (**you are etc.**) **singing,** je chante, tu chantes, etc.; **I was,** (**you were etc.**) **singing,** je chantais, tu chantais, etc.; **~ing** *s.* (*existence*) existence *f.*; (*person*) être *m.*
beach *s.* plage *f.*; **~comber** *s.* (*wave*) vague déferlante *f.*; (*fig. person*) propre à rien *m.*; **~-head** *s.* tête de pont *f.*; *v.t.* tirer à sec; (*wreck*) échouer.
beacon *s.* fanal *m.*; (*naut.*) balise *f.*; (*aviat.*) phare *m.*; (*fig.*) flambeau *m.*
bead *s.* (*jewellery*) grain *m.*; (*sweat, etc.*) goutte *f.*; (*arch.*) moulure *f.*; **~ing** *s.* (*arch.*) moulure *f.*; **~y** *adj.* (*eyes*) (des yeux) en vrille.
beagle *s.* briquet *m.*
beak *s.* bec *m.*; (*pop.* =*judge*) cigogne *f.*, curieux *m.*

beaker *s.* (*for drinking*) coupe *f.*; (*plastic*) gobelet *m.*; (*sc.*) vase *m.*

beam *s.* **1.** (*timber*) poutre *f.*; **2.** (*naut.*) bau *m.*; **3.** (*light*) rayon *m.*; **4.** (*smile*) sourire *m.*; *v.i.* (3) & (4) briller, rayonner; *v.t.* (*radio*) diriger (vers); **~ing** *adj.* rayonnant; **to be on one's ~-ends,** être à la côte.

bean *s.* (*broad*) fève *f.*; (*kidney*) haricot *m.*; (*French*) haricot vert *m.*; RUNNER **~**; (*coffee, etc.*) grain *m.*; (*pop.* = *coin*) **he hasn't a ~,** il n'a plus un radis; **to be full of ~s,** bouillonner d'énergie; **to** SPILL **the ~s**; **~feast, ~o** *s.* (*pop.*) gueuleton *m.*

bear[1] *s.* (*animal* & *fig.*) ours *m.*, ourse *f.*; TEDDY **~**; **~-cub** *s.* ourson *m.*; **~garden** *s.* pétaudière *f.*; **~skin** *s.* (*mil.*) bonnet à poil *m.*; **to be like a ~ with a sore head,** être d'une humeur massacrante.

bear[2] *v.t.* (*carry, hold*) porter; (*support*) soutenir; (*endure*) supporter; (*give birth to*) enfanter; (*produce*) porter; (*witness*) rendre (témoignage); *v.i.* (*turn right, left*) se diriger vers la droite, la gauche; **to** GRIN **and ~ it**; **~ down on,** foncer sur; **~ on,** se rapporter à; **~ out,** appuyer; **~ oneself,** se comporter; **~ in mind,** garder en mémoire; **bring to ~,** mettre en action; **~able** *adj.* supportable; **~er** *s.* porteur *m.*

beard *s.* barbe *f.*; **grey~** *s.* barbon *m.*; **~ed** *adj.* barbu; *v.t.* braver.

bearing *s.* (*connection*) rapport *m.*; (*carriage*) allure *f.*; (*behaviour*) comportement *m.*; (*herald.*) armoiries *f.pl.*; (*mech.*) coussinet *m.*; BALL-**~s**; **~s,** position *f.*; **to take one's ~s,** s'orienter; (*fig. fam.*) se repérer; **to lose one's ~s,** se désorienter.

beast *s.* **1.** (*animal*) bête *f.*; **~s** *s.pl.* bétail *m.sing.*; **2.** (*fig. person*) brute *f.*; **~ of burden,** bête de somme *f.*; **~liness** *s.* (1) bestialité *f.*; (2) obscénité *f.*; **~ly** *adj.* (1) bestial; (2) brutal; (*fam. of things*) infect; **~ly** *adv.* (*pop.*) rudement.

beat *s.* (*heart, pulse, drum, etc.*) battement *m.*; (*time, verse, mus.*) temps *m.*; (*police, etc.*) ronde *f.*; **it's off his ~** (*fig.*) ce n'est pas de son rayon; *v.t.* (*hit; strike metal; defeat; ~ time*) battre; (*thrash*) rosser; *v.i.* battre, taper, frapper; **that ~s me** (*pop.*) ça me dépasse; **~ it!** (*pop.*) fiche-moi le camp!; **~ about the bush,** tourner autour du pot; **~ black and blue,** battre comme plâtre; **~ hollow,** battre à plate couture; **~ at, on** (*door, etc.*) cogner à; **~ back,** repousser; **~ down** *v.t.* (*corn, etc.*) coucher; (*comm.*) rabattre, faire baisser (le prix); *v.i.* battre; **~ in,** enfoncer; **~ on,** frapper sur, contre; **~ up** (*cook.*) fouetter; (*pop. s.o.*) tabasser (qn.); **~ing** *s.* raclée *f.*; (*defeat*) défaite *f.*

beatif/y *v.t.* béatifier; **~ic** *adj.* béatifique; **~ication** *s.* béatification *f.*

beatitude *s.* béatitude *f.*

beatnik *s.* beatnik *m.*

beaut/y *s.* beauté *f.*; **~y parlour,** institut de beauté *m.*; **~y queen,** reine de beauté *f.*; **~y sleep,** sommeil d'avant minuit *m.*; **~y spot** *s.* (*natural*) grain de beauté *m.*, (*artificial*) mouche *f.*; (*locality*) site à voir *m.*; **the ~y of it all** (*fig.*) le plus beau de l'histoire; **~ify** *v.t.* embellir; **~iful** *adj.*, **~eous** *adj.* beau, belle; **~ician** *s.* esthéticienne *f.*

beaver *s.* (*animal* & *fur*) castor *m.*; (*armour*) visière (de casque) *m.*

becalmed *adj.* encalminé.

because *conj.* parce que; **he came home ~ it was raining,** il est rentré parce qu'il pleuvait; **~ of** *prep.* à cause de; **he came home ~ of the rain,** il est rentré à cause de la pluie.

beck[1] *s.* (*stream*) ruisseau *m.*

beck[2] *s.* (*nod*) signe de tête *m.*; **to be at s.o.'s ~ and call,** obéir à qn. au doigt et à l'œil.

beckon *v.t.* & *i.* faire signe (à).

becom/e *v.i.* (*come to be*) devenir; (*from choice*) se faire; *v.t.* (*suit*) aller à; (*fig.*) convenir à; **what will ~e of me?,** que vais-je devenir?; **~ing** *adj.* (*suitable*) convenable; (*attractive*) seyant.

bed *s.* (*furniture; of river, sea, etc.*) lit *m.*; (*geol.*) couche *f.*; (*constr.; fig.*) assise *f.*; **~ of roses** (*fig.*) lit de roses *m.*; FLOWER-**~**; APPLE-**pie ~**; **to go to ~,** se coucher; **to take to one's ~,** s'aliter; **to get out of ~ on the wrong side,** se lever du pied gauche; **~clothes,** literie *f.*; **~fellow,** camarade *m.*; **~pan,** bassin (hygiénique) *m.*; **~post,** colonne de lit *f.*; **~ridden** *adj.* alité; **~rock** *s.* (*geol.*) soubassement *m.*, (*fig.*) base *f.*, (*of price*) le plus bas; **~room,** chambre à coucher *f.*; **~side** *s.* chevet *m.*; **~side** RUG; **~-sitter** *s.* studio *m.*; **~spread,** dessus de lit *m.*; **~stead,** châlit *m.*; **~time,** heure de se coucher *f.*; **~ding** *s.* literie *f.*; *v.t.* coucher.

bedeck *v.t.* orner (de).

bedevil *v.t.* (*annoy*) harceler; (*torment*) tourmenter; (*bewitch*) posséder; **~led with** (*situation*), aggravé de.

bedizen *v.t.* attifer.

bedlam *s.* chahut *m.*

bedraggle *v.t.* tacher de boue; **~d** *adj.* dépenaillé.

bee *s.* abeille *f.*; (*meeting*) réunion *f.*; (*competition*) concours *m.*; **humble ~,** bourdon *m.*; **queen ~,** reine (des abeilles) *f.*; (*fig.*) présidente active *f.*; **~hive,** ruche *f.*; **~swax,** cire d'abeille *f.*; **~-line,** ligne droite à vol d'oiseau *f.*; **to make a ~-line for,** se diriger tout droit vers/sur; **to have a ~ in one's bonnet,** avoir une marotte.

beech *s.* hêtre *m.*; **~mast, ~-nut,** faine *f.*

beef *s.* bœuf *m.*; **~** OLIVE; **~steak** *s.* bifteck *m.*; **~ tea** *s.* consommé *m.*; **~y** *adj.* costaud; *v.i.* (*pop.*) râler.

beer *s.* bière *f.*; **~house,** brasserie *f.*; GINGER **~**.

beet *s.* bette *f.* *or* blette *f.*; **~root,** betterave *f.*; **sugar-~,** betterave sucrière *f.*

beetl/e *s.* (*instrument*) maillet *m.*; (*insect*) scarabée *m.*; **black-~e,** cafard *m.*; STAG-**~e**; **~ing** *adj.* surplombant; (*brows*) pro-éminent.

befall *v.t.* & *i.* arriver (à).

befit *v.t.* convenir à; **~ting** *adj.* convenable.

befogged *adj.* enveloppé de brouillard; (*fig.*) embrumé.

before *prep.* (*time, order*) avant, **~ noon,** avant midi; **~ you,** avant vous; (*place*) devant; **I have your letter ~ me,** j'ai votre letter sous les yeux; (*with verb*) avant de; **~ speaking,** avant de parler; (*in the presence of*) en présence de; *adv.* (*time, order, place*) avant; (*in front*) en avant; (*previously*) auparavant; *conj.* avant que; **~ he arrives,** avant qu'il n'arrive; **~hand,** d'avance, au préalable.

befriend *v.t.* traiter en ami; (*help*) aider.

beg *v.t.* & *i.* (*for charity*) mendier; (*ask*) demander, (*urgently*) solliciter; (*ending of letter*) prier, **I ~ to remain etc.,** je vous prie d'agréer . . .; **to ~ the question,** faire une pétition de principe; **~gar** *s.* mendiant *m.*; (*fam.*) coquin *m.*; *v.t.* ruiner; **~garly** *adj.* misérable, (*fig.*) piètre; **~ging** *s.* mendicité *f.*

beget *v.t.* (*lit.* & *fig.*) engendrer.

begin *v.t.* & *i.* commencer; (*set about*) se mettre à; **~ to,** commencer à, **he ~s to read,** il commence à lire; **~ with, by,** commencer par, **he ~s by reading,** il commence par lire; **~ again,** recommencer; **~ner** *s.* débutant(e) *m.f.*; **~ning** *s.* début *m.*, commencement *m.*

begone! *interj.* Va-t'en!, allez-vous-en!

begonia *s.* bégonia *m.*

begrudge *v.t.* (*envy*) envier; **I ~ him his success,** je lui envie son succès; (*be mean*)

lésiner sur; **he doesn't ~ what it costs to educate his children,** il ne lésine pas sur l'éducation de ses enfants.
beguile *v.t.* (*deceive*) tromper; (*pass time*) faire passer; (*amuse*) divertir; **~r** *s.* trompeur *m.*
behalf, on ~ of (*in the name of*) de la part de; **on my** (*etc.*) **~,** de ma (etc.) part; (*in favour of*) en faveur de.
behav/e *v.i.* se conduire, (*well*—comme il faut); **~iour** *s.* conduite *f.*, (*bearing*) comportement *m.*
behead *v.t.* décapiter.
behest *s.* ordre *m.*; **at his, your, etc. ~,** par son, votre, etc. ordre.
behind *s.* derrière *m.*; *prep.* derrière; *adv.* (*place*) en arrière; (*in arrears*) en retard; **from ~,** par derrière; **~ the times,** (*person* & *things*) en retard sur son temps; **~hand,** en retard.
behold *v.t.* voir; *interj.* voyez!, voici!, voilà!; **~er** *s.* spectat/eur, -rice *m.f.*
beholden, to be ~ to s.o. for sth., être redevable à qn. de qch.
behoves *v.impers.* (*necessity*) il vous incombe de; (*convenience*) il convient de.
beige *s.* (*material*) laine écrue *f.*; *adj.* (*colour*) beige.
belabour *v.t.* rosser.
belated *adj.* attardé.
belch *s.* éructation *f.*; (*pop.*) rot *m.*; *v.i.* éructer; (*pop.*) roter; **~ out,** (*fig.*) vomir.
beldam *s.* vieille sorcière *f.*
beleaguer *v.t.* assiéger.
belfry *s.* (*church*) clocher *m.*; (*any building, e.g. town hall*) beffroi *m.*; **to have** BATS **in the ~.**
Belg/ium *s.* Belgique *f.*; **~ian** *adj.* & *s.m.f.* belge.
belie *v.t.* (*fail to correspond, to hopes, etc.*) démentir; (*deceive*) tromper.
belief *s.* croyance *f.*; (*creed*) foi *f.*; (*confidence*) confiance *f.*; (*conviction*) conviction *f.*; **to the best of my ~,** pour autant que je sache.
believe *v.t.* croire, **I don't ~ you,** je ne vous crois pas; *v.i.* avoir la foi; **~ in,** croire à, **I don't ~ in ghosts,** je ne crois pas aux revenants; (*in God*) croire en Dieu; **I ~ he will come,** je crois qu'il viendra; **I don't ~ he will come,** je ne crois pas qu'il vienne; **to make ~** (**to**), faire semblant (de); s'imaginer que; **believable** *adj.* croyable; **~r** *s.* (*eccles.*) croyant *m.*; (*gen.*) partisan (de).
belittle *v.t.*.(*lit.* & *fig.*) rapetisser.
bell *s.* (*church*) cloche *f.*; **to** RING **a ~,** (*fig.*); (*cow*) grelot *m.*; (*door, small, hand*) sonnette *f.*; **~-bottomed** (*trousers*), (pantalon) à pattes d'éléphant; **~-pull** cordon de sonnette *m.*; **~-ringer** sonneur *m.*; **~-tower,** beffroi *m.*; **~-tent,** tente-marabout *f.*; *v.i.* (*stag*) bramer; **to ~ the cat,** attacher le grelot.
belladonna *s.* belladone *f.*
bellicose *adj.* belliqueux.
belligeren/t *adj.* & *s.m.* belligérant; **~cy** *s.* belligérance *f.*
bellow *v.i.* **1.** (*bull* & *pop. of person*) beugler; **2.** (*sea, wind*) mugir; **~ing** *s.* (1) beuglement *m.*; (2) mugissement *m.*
bellows *s.* soufflet *m.sing.*
belly *s.* ventre *m.*; **~ache** *s.* mal au ventre *m.*; **~ache** *v.i.* (*fam.*) rouspéter; **to have a ~ful** (*fig. fam.*) en avoir plein le dos; *v.i.* (*of sail*) se gonfler.
belong *v.i.* (*to*) (*be property of*) appartenir à; (*be connected with*) faire partie de; (*have origin from*) être (originaire) de; **~ings** *s.* affaires *f.pl.*
beloved *adj.* & *s.* bien-aimé(e) *m.f.*
below *adv.* (*stairs, etc.*) en bas; (*under*) en dessous; (*downstream*) en aval; (*on page*) ci-dessous, plus bas; *prep.* au-dessous de; (*fig.*) indigne (de).
belt *s.* **1.** (*round waist*) ceinture *f.*; **2.** (*district*) zone *f.*; **green ~,** zone verte; **hit below the ~,** coup bas; **to tighten one's ~,** se serrer la ceinture; **seat, safety ~,** ceinture de sécurité; **fan ~,** courroie de ventilateur *f.*; *v.t.* (1) ceindre; (*fam.* = *to thrash*) donner une râclée à; *v.i.* (*pop.* = *to hurry*) aller à toute vitesse; **~ up!** (*pop.*) ta gueule!
belvedere *s.* belvédère *m.*
bemoan *v.t.* (*person*) pleurer (qn.); (*thing*) déplorer (qch.).
bemused *adj.* hébété.
bench *s.* (*seat*) banc *m.*; (*law*) siège *m.*; (*carpenter's*) établi *m.*; (*theatre*) banquette *f.*
bend *s.* **1.** (*knot*) nœud *m.*; **2.** (*curve*) courbure *f.*; **3.** (*in road*) coude *m.*, virage *m.*; **4.** (*med.*) **the ~s,** maladie des caissons *f.*; **round the ~** (*fam.*) cinglé; *v.i.* (2) se courber; (3) faire un coude; **4.** (*under weight*) fléchir (sous); *v.t.* (2) courber; (*head*) pencher; (*knee*) fléchir; (*eyes*) diriger; (*archery*) tendre; (*twist*) tordre; **~ down,** se pencher; **~ over** BACKWARDS; **on ~ed knee,** à genoux.
beneath *adv.* au-dessous; *prep.* sous; (*fig.*) indigne (de).
Benedictine *adj.* & *s.m.* bénédictin; (*liqueur*) bénédictine *f.*
benediction *s.* (*eccles.* & *gen.*) bénédiction *f.*
benefact/or, -ress *s.* bienfait/eur, -rice *m.f.*; **~ion** *s.* bienfait *m.*
benefice *s.* (*eccles.*) bénéfice *m.*
benefic/ence *s.* bienfaisance *f.*; **~ent** *adj.* bienfaisant; **~ently** *adv.* avec bienfaisance; **~ial** *adj.* salutaire (à); **~iary** *s.* bénéficiaire *m.*
benefit *s.* (*gain*) bénéfice *m.*; (*advantage*) avantage *m.*; (*aid*) secours *m.*; (*privilege*) privilège *m.*; *v.t.* faire du bien à; (*be of use to*) profiter à; *v.i.* profiter (*by*—de).
benevolen/ce *s.* bienveillance *f.*; **~t** *adj.* bienveillant.
Bengal *s.* (*geog.*) Bengale *m.*; **~i** *s.* bengali.
benighted *adj.* surpris par la nuit; (*fig.*) ignorant.
benign *adj.* **1.** (*kindly*) affable; **2.** (*med.*) bénin (*f.* bénigne); **~ant** *adj.* bienveillant; **~ity** *s.* (1) affabilité *f.*; (2) bénignité *f.*
bent *s.* penchant *m.*; *adj.* courbé; **~ on doing sth.,** déterminé à faire qch.; **~ double,** plié en deux.
benzine *s.* benzine *f.*
bequeath *v.t.* léguer.
bequest *s.* legs *m.sing.*
bereave *v.t.* priver de; **~ment** *s.* deuil *m.*; **~d** *adj.* en deuil.
beret *s.* béret *m.*
berry *s.* baie *f.*; (*coffee*) grain *m.*
berserk, to go ~, devenir fou furieux.
berth *s.* (*ship*) cabine *f.*; (*train*) couchette *f.*; (*job*) emploi *m.*; (*dock*) mouillage *m.*; **to give s.o. a wide ~,** tenir qn. à distance respectueuse; *v.t.* amarrer; *v.i.* mouiller.
beryl *s.* béryl *m.*
beseech *v.t.* supplier; **I ~ you,** je vous en supplie; **~ing** *adj.* suppliant; **~ingly** *adv.* d'un ton suppliant.
beset *v.t.* (*surround*) entourer (de); (*fig. attack*) assaillir; (*scatter with*) parsemer de; **~ting** *adj.* habituel; **~ting sin,** péché mignon *m.*
beside *prep.* à côté de; (*near*) près de; (*in comparison with*) auprès de; (*except*) hors de; (*moreover*) de plus; **to be ~ oneself,** être hors de soi; (*fam.*) sortir de ses gonds; **~s** *adv.* en outre; (*also*) aussi; *prep.* **have you not any books ~s these?,** n'avez-vous pas d'autres livres que ceux-ci?
besiege *v.t.* (*mil.* & *fig.*) assiéger; **~d** *adj.* & *s.* assiégé; **~r** *s.* assiégeant *m.*
besmirch *v.t.* (*lit.* & *fig.*) salir.
besom *s.* balai *m.*
besotted *adj.* abruti.
bespatter *v.t.* éclabousser.

bespeak *v.t.* (*order*) commander; (*reserve*) retenir; (*be evidence of*) témoigner de.
best *adj.* le (la, les) meilleur((e)s); ~ **man,** garçon d'honneur *m.*; **the ~ part of,** la plupart de + *pl.* (*exc.* la plupart du temps); la majeure partie de + *sing.*; ~ **seller,** succès de librairie *m.*; *adv.* le mieux; **it is ~ to,** le mieux est de; *s.* le meilleur; **to have the ~ of it,** l'emporter (sur); **to make the ~ of it,** (*use to advantage*) tirer parti de; (*make do with*) prendre son parti de qch.; **at ~,** au mieux; **to do one's ~,** faire de son mieux; **in one's Sunday ~,** endimanché; *v.t.* (*fam.*) rouler.
bestial *adj.* bestial; **~ity** *s.* bestialité *f.*
bestir (*oneself*) *v.refl.* se remuer.
bestow *v.t.* (*grant*) accorder; (*confer on*) conférer à; (*devote*) consacrer; **~al** *s.* don *m.*
bestride *v.t.* enjamber; (*horse, bicycle*) enfourcher.
bet *s.* pari *m.*; *v.t.* parier (sur); **~ter, -tor** *s.* parieu/r, -se *m.f.*; **~ting** *s.* paris *m.pl.*; **~ting-shop,** P.M.U. (*abbrev. for* Pari Mutuel Urbain); **I ~ (you don't),** chiche!; **you ~!,** pour sûr!
betake (*oneself to*) *v.refl.* (*place*) se rendre à; (*have recourse to*) se livrer à.
bethink (*oneself of*) *v.refl.* s'aviser de.
betide, WOE ~.
betimes *adv.* (*early*) de bonne heure; (*in good time*) à temps.
betoken *v.t.* indiquer; (*foreshadow*) présager.
betray *v.t.* (*be false to*) trahir; (*hand over*) livrer; (*show*) révéler; (*plans, secrets, etc.*) dévoiler; **~al** *s.* trahison *f.*; **~er** *s.* traître, -sse *m.f.*
betroth *v.t.* fiancer; **~al** *s.* fiançailles *f.pl.*; **~ed** *adj.* & *s.* fiancé(e) *m.f.*
better *adj.* meilleur; *adv.* mieux; ~ **and ~,** de mieux en mieux; **for ~ or worse,** vaille que vaille; **so much the ~,** tant mieux; **it is ~ to,** il vaut mieux; **to be ~,** aller mieux; **to get ~,** se remettre; **to go one ~ than s.o.,** damer le pion à qn.; **to go one ~,** (*action, bid, etc.*) renchérir ur; **to get the ~ of,** l'emporter sur; **~s** *s.pl.* supérieurs *m.pl.*; *v.t.* (*make ~*) améliorer; (*do ~*) surpasser; **~ment** *s.* amélioration *f.*
between, betwixt *prep.* entre.
bevel *s.* biseau *m.*; **~led** *adj.* biseauté.
beverage *s.* (*gen.*) boisson *f.*; (*special*) breuvage *m.*
bevy *s.* (*birds*) volée *f.*; (*people*) essaim *m.*
bewail *v.t.* se lamenter sur; (*fig.*) déplorer.
beware *v.i.* faire attention; (*take heed of*) prendre garde à; (*guard against*) se méfier de; *interj.* attention!; prenez garde!; méfiez-vous!
bewilder *v.t.* **1.** (*lead astray*) égarer; **2.** (*frighten*) effarer; **3.** (*surprise*) déconcerter; **~ing** *adj.* (1) affolant; (2) effrayant; (3) déconcertant; **~ment** *s.* (1) égarement *m.*; (2) effarement *m.*; (3) surprise *f.*
bewitch *v.t.* (*magic*) ensorceler; (*charm*) enchanter; **~ing** *adj.* charmant.
beyond *s.* au-delà *m.*; **the back of ~,** le bout du monde; (*pop.*) en plein bled; *prep.* au delà de; ~ **all imagination,** au-delà de toute imagination; hors de; ~ **reach,** hors de portée; ~ **question,** hors de doute; plus que; ~ **what was needed,** plus qu'il ne faudrait; au dessus de; **he is ~ that,** il est au-dessus de ça; ~ **endurance,** intolérable; ~ **the sea,** outre-mer; ~ **measure,** outre mesure; **that's ~ me,** cela me dépasse; *adv.* plus loin, au-delà.
bezique *s.* bésigue *m.*
bias *s.* (*slant, diagonal*) biais *m.*; (*prejudice*) préjugé *m.*; (*fig.*) penchant *m.*; *v.t.* influencer; ⚠ biaiser = **to dodge.**
bib *s.* bavette *f.*; (*for baby*) bavoir *m.*; **in one's best ~ and tucker,** sur son trente-et-un.
bibber *s.* (*wine*) soiffard *m.*
Bibl/e *s.* bible *f.*; **~ical** *adj.* biblique.
bibliograph/y *s.* bibliographie *f.*; **~er** *s.* bibliographe *m.f.*
bibulous *adj.* (*person*) buveur *m.*
bicarbonate *s.* bicarbonate *m.*, (*pop.* = ~ *of soda*) bicarbonate (de soude).
biceps *s.* biceps *m.*
bicker *v.i.* se chamailler; (*water*) murmurer; **~ing** *s.* chamaillerie *f.*
bicycle *s.* bicyclette *f.*; (*more usu.*) vélo *m.*; *v.i.* aller à bicyclette, faire du vélo.
bid *s.* offre *m.*; (*at auction*) enchère *f.*; (*at bridge*) annonce *f.*; *v.t.* **1.** (*order*) ordonner (à qn. de faire qch.); **2.** (*invite*) inviter (à); **3.** (*money*) offrir; **4.** (*wish*) souhaiter, dire; **to ~ s.o. welcome,** souhaiter la bienvenue à qn.; **to ~ goodday, farewell,** dire bonjour, adieu; *v.i.* (*make a ~*) faire une offre, enchérir (sur qn.); ~ **fair to,** promettre de; **~ding** *s.* (1) ordre *m.*; (3) offre *f.*; **~der** *s.* (3) enchérisseur *m.*; **~dable** *adj.* docile.
bide *v.i. see* ABIDE; ~ **one's time,** attendre son heure.
biennial *adj.* (*two years long*) biennal; (*two yearly*) biennal, bisannuel; *s.* (*plant*) plante bisannuelle *f.*
bier *s.* bière *f.*
bifocal *adj.* bifocal; *s.* **~s,** lunettes à double--foyer *f.pl.*
big *adj.* (*large, adult*) grand; (*bulky*) gros; (*important*) important; ~ **end** (*auto.*) tête de bielle *f.*; ~ **game,** grands fauves *m.pl.*; ~ **noise, ~wig,** gros bonnet *m.*; (*fam.*) grand manitou *m.*; ~ **toe,** gros orteil *m.*; **to grow ~ger,** grossir; **~ness** *s.* grosseur *f.*
bigam/y *s.* bigamie *f.*; **~ist** *s.* & **~ous** *adj.* bigame.
bigot *s.* **1.** (*eccles.*) bigot(e) *m.f.*; **2.** (*gen.*) fanatique *m.f.*; **~ed** *adj.* (1) bigot; (2) fanatique; **~ry** *s.* (1) bigoterie *f.*; (2) fanatisme *m.*
bike *s.* vélo *m.*
bikini *s.* bikini *m.*
bilateral *adj.* bilatéral.
bilberry *s.* myrtille *f.*
bil/e *s.* (*med.* & *fig.*) bile *f.*; **~ious** *adj.* bilieux; **~iousness** *s.* accès de bile *m.*
bilge *s.* (*ship's bottom*) fond de cale *m.*; (*foulness*) eau stagnante *f.*; (*pop.* = *rot*) idioties *f.pl.*; **~-water,** eau de cale *f.*
bilharzia *s.* bilharziose *f.*
bilingual *adj.* bilingue.
bill[1] *s.* (*of bird*) bec *m.*; *v.i.* (*of doves*) becqueter; **to ~ and coo,** se bécoter.
bill[2] *s.* (*comm., professional, hotel, etc.*) note *f.*; (*restaurant*) addition *f.*; (*invoice*) facture *f.*; (*poster*) affiche *f.*; (*folder*) dépliant *m.*; (*parl.*) projet de loi *m.*; ~ **of exchange,** lettre de change *f.*; ~ **of lading,** connaissement *m.*; ~ **of fare,** menu *m.*; **hand~,** prospectus *m.*; **~head** *s.* en-tête de facture *f.*; **~sticker** *s.* colleur d'affiches *m.*; *v.t.* (*comm.*) facturer; (*publicity*) afficher.
billet *s.* (*mil.*) (*order*) billet de logement *m.*; (*lodging*) logement *m.*; (*job*) poste *m.*; (*of wood*) bûche *f.*; *v.t.* (*mil.*) cantonner; *v.i.* loger chez l'habitant; (*fig.*) loger.
billiard/s *s.* (*game*) billard *m.sing.*; **~-**BALL; **~-cue,** queue de billard *f.*; **~-table,** billard *m.*
billion *s.* billion *m.*
billow *s.* (*wave*) lame *f.*; (*of smoke etc.*) tourbillon *m.*; *v.i.* onduler; **~y** *adj.* houleux.
billy, billycan *s.* gamelle *f.*
billy-goat *s.* bouc *m.*
bin *s.* huche *f.*; **bread-~,** huche à pain *f.*; **dust~,** poubelle *f.*
binary *adj.* binaire.
bind *v.t.* (*tie*) lier; (*compel*) obliger (à); (*book*) relier; ~ **up** (*wound*) bander; ~ **oneself to,** s'engager à; **it's a ~,** (*pop.*) quelle barbe!; **~er,** (*person*) relieur *m.*; **~ing** *s.* (*braid*) liséré *m.*; (*books*) reliure *f.*; *adj.* obligatoire (*on*—pour).

binge, to go on the ~ (*pop.*) faire (la) noce.
binoculars *s.* jumelle *f.* (*sing. or pl.*).
binomial *adj.* binôme.
biochemistry *s.* biochimie *f.*
biograph/y *s.* biographie *f.*; **~er** *s.* biographe *m.f.*; **~ical** *adj.* biographique.
biolog/y *s.* biologie *f.*; **~ist** *s.* biologiste *m.f.*; **~ical** *adj.* biologique; (*warfare*) microbien.
biped *adj.* & *s.m.* bipède.
biplane *s.* biplan *m.*
birch *s.* (*tree*) bouleau *m.*; (*flogging*) verge *f.*; *v.t.* fouetter.
bird *s.* oiseau *m.*; (*fam.* = *woman*) poule *f.*; GALLOWS-~; GAME-~; GAOL~; NIGHT-~; ~ of PARADISE; ~ of PREY; **~'s eye view,** vue aérienne *f.*; **~s of a feather flock together,** qui se ressemble s'assemble; **a ~ in the hand is worth two in the bush,** un tiens vaut mieux que deux tu l'auras; **to kill two ~s with one stone,** faire d'une pierre deux coups; **the** EARLY **~ catches the worm.**
biretta *s.* barrette *f.*
birth *s.* naissance *f.*; (*origin*) extraction *f.*; CHILD~; **by ~,** de naissance; **~ control,** contrôle *m. or* limitation *f. or* régulation *f.*, des naissances; **~day** *s.* anniversaire *m.*; **~place** *s.* lieu de naissance *m.*; **~ rate** *s.* natalité *f.*; **~-right** *s.* patrimoine *m.*
biscuit *s.* biscuit *m.*
bisect *v.t.* diviser en deux.
bishop *s.* évêque *m.*; (*at chess*) fou *m.*; **~ric** *s.* évêché *m.*
bismuth *s.* bismuth *m.*
bison *s.* bison *m.*
bissextile *adj.* bissextile.
bit *s.* (*small amount*) morceau *m.*; (*of paper, wood*) bout *m.*; **a ~ of a letter,** un bout de lettre; **a ~ of the way,** un bout du chemin; **a ~ of a poet,** un peu poète; (*bridle*) mors *m.*; **to take the ~ between one's teeth,** prendre le mors aux dents; **to** CHAMP **at the ~**; (*coin*) pièce *f.*; (*mech.*) mèche *f.*; **~ by ~,** petit à petit; **not a ~ of it,** pas le moins du monde; **to do one's ~,** faire sa part; **~ty** *adj.* (*in ~s*) en morceaux; (*style*) sans suite.
bitch *s.* chienne *f.*; (*fig.fam.*) garce *f.*; *v.t.* **to ~ up** (*Eng.pop.*) gâter.
bit/e *s.* **1.** (*with teeth*) morsure *f.*; **2.** (*insect*) piqûre *f.*; **3.** (*mouthful*) bouchée *f.*; **4.** (*fishing*) touche *f.*; **his** BARK **is worse than his ~e**; *v.t.* (1) mordre; (*gnaw, nails, etc.*) ronger; (2) piquer; *v.i.* (4) mordre; **once bitten, twice shy,** chat échaudé craint l'eau froide; **what's ~ing you?,** quelle mouche vous pique?; **~ing** *adj.* (*fig.*) mordant; (*wind*) glacial; **~ingly** *adv.* d'un ton mordant.
bitter *adj.* **1.** (*taste*) amer; **2.** (*cold*) glacial; **3.** (*relentless*) acharné; **4.** (*style*) caustique; (*quarrel*) violent; (*enemy etc.*) cruel; **to the ~ end,** jusqu'au bout; **to be ~ cold,** faire un froid de loup; **~-sweet** *adj.* aigre-doux; **~ly** *adv.* (1)*; (2)*; (3) âprement; (4) avec acrimonie; **~ness** *s.* (1) & (3) amertume *f.*; (2) rigueur *f.*; (4) acrimonie *f.*
bittern *s.* butor *m.*
bitum/en *s.* bitume *m.*; **~inous** *adj.* bitumineux; (*covered with ~en*) bitumé.
bivalve *adj.* & *s.m.* bivalve.
bivouac *s.* bivouac *m.*; *v.t.* bivouaquer.
blab *v.t.* révéler; *v.i.* jaser.
black *s.* (*colour*) noir *m.*; (*person*) noir(e) *m.f.*; *adj.* noir; **~amoor** *s.* (*pej.*) moricaud(e) *m.f.*; **to** BEAT **~ and blue**; **~ball** *v.t.* blackbouler; **~berry** *s.* mûre *f.*; **~bird** *s.* merle *m.*; **~board** *s.* tableau noir *m.*; **~ currant** *s.* cassis *m.*; **~ eye,** œil poché *m.*; **~guard** *s.* fripouille *f.*; **~guardly trick,** canaillerie *f.*; **~leg** *s.* jaune *m.*; **~list** *v.t.* mettre à l'index; **~mail** *s.* chantage *m.*; *v.t.* faire chanter; **~mailer** *s.* maître chanteur *m.*; **B~ Maria** *s.* (*fam.*) panier à salade *m.*; **~ market** *s.* marché noir *m.*; ~ SHEEP; **~smith** *s.* forgeron *m.*; **~thorn** *s.* prunellier *m.*; **~en** *v.t.* noircir; **~ing** *s.* cirage noir *m.*; **~ness** *s.* noirceur *f.*; **~** *v.t.* noircir; **~ out** *v.t.* **1.** camoufler les lumières; **2.** (*electr.*) couper l'électricité; *v.i.* **3.** (*med.*) avoir un étourdissement; **~-out** *s.* (1) camouflage des lumières *m.*; (2) panne d'électricité *f.*; (3) étourdissement *m.*
bladder *s.* (*med.* & *techn.*) vessie *f.*; GALL-~.
blade *s.* (*of grass*) brin *m.*; (*of knife*) lame *f.*; (*oar*) pale *f.*; (*aviat. propeller*) pale *f.*; (*person*) joyeux drille *m.*; RAZOR-~.
blame *s.* blâme *m.*; *v.t.* blâmer (qn. de qch.); **I am to ~,** c'est ma faute; **~able** *adj.* blâmable; **~less** *adj.* **1.** irréprochable; **2.** (*not guilty*) innocent; **~lessness** *s.* (1) caractère irréprochable *m.*; (2) innocence *f.*
blanch *v.t.* (*agric., cook., techn.*) blanchir; *v.i.* pâlir.
blancmange *s.* blanc-manger *m.*
bland *adj.* (*person*) doux; (*manner*) suave; (*air, food, etc.*) doux; **~ishment** *s.* cajolerie *f.*; **~ness** *s.* douceur *f.*, suavité *f.*
blank *s.* (*space*) blanc *m.*; (*dash*) tiret *m.*; (*in memory*) trou *m.*; (*void*) vide *m.*; (*cartridge*) (cartouche *f.*) à blanc; *adj.* blanc; (*fig.*) absolu; **~ cheque,** chèque en blanc *m.*; **~ verse,** vers blancs *m.pl.*; **~ly** *adv.* sans expression; **to draw a ~,** tirer un numéro blanc; (*fig.*) faire chou blanc; POINT-~.
blanket *s.* couverture *f.*; **electric ~,** couverture électrique *f.*; **wet ~,** rabat-joie *m.*; *v.t.* (*fig.*) étouffer.
blare *s.* bruit sonore *m.*; *v.i.* claironner.
blasphem/e *v.t.* & *i.* blasphémer; **~er** *s.* blasphémateur *m.*; **~ous** *adj.* blasphématoire; **~y** *s.* blasphème *m.*
blast *s.* (*wind*) rafale *f.*; (*on instrument*) sonnerie *f.*; (*explosion*) explosion *f.*; *v.t.* (*wind*) flétrir; (*mine*) faire sauter; (*destroy*) détruire; (*fam.* = *curse*) maudire; *interj.* zut!; **~ you!,** que le diable vous emporte!; ~-FURNACE; **~-off** *s.* mise à feu *f.*; **at full ~,** à toute allure.
blatant *adj.* (*noisy*) braillard; (*showy*) voyant; (*fig.*) flagrant.
blaz/e[1] *s.* **1.** (*fire*) flamme *f.*; **2.** (*passion*) éclat *m.*; *v.i.* (1) flamber; (2) s'emporter; **~e abroad,** proclamer; **~er** *s.* blazer *m.*; **~ing** *adj.* flamboyant.
blaze[2] *s.* (*mark on horse*) étoile *f.*; (*on tree*) encoche *f.*; *v.t.* (*trail*) marquer, frayer (la piste).
blazon *s.* blason *m.*; *v.t.* blasonner.
bleach *s.* (*process*) blanchiment *m.*; (*substance*) décolorant *m.*; (*hydrogen peroxide*) eau oxygénée *f.*; *v.t.* blanchir; (*hair*) oxygéner; **~ing** *s.* blanchiment *m.*
bleak *adj.* (*dreary*) lugubre; (*bare*) dénudé; (*chilly*) glacial.
bleary(-eyed) (*med.*) aux yeux chassieux; (*pop.*) **to be ~-eyed,** n'avoir pas les yeux en face des trous.
bleat(ing) *s.* bêlement *m.*; *v.t.* bêler.
bleed *v.t.* & *i.* (*lit.* & *fig.*) saigner; **~ing** *adj.* saignant; (*fig.*) navré.
blemish *s.* tare *f.*; *v.t.* entacher.
blench *v.i.* (*draw back*) reculer; (*flinch*) broncher.
blend *s.* mélange *m.*; *v.t.* & *i.* (se) mélanger (à); (*colours*) (se) fondre; (*fig.*) fusionner; **~er** *s.* (*cook.*) mixeur *m.*
bless *v.t.* (*consecrate*) bénir; (*praise*) exalter; (*make happy*) rendre heureux; (*thank*) remercier; **God ~ you!** Dieu vous bénisse!; **~ed** *adj.* béni, heureux; (*eccles.*) bénit; (= *cursed*) fichu (*before noun*); **to be ~ed with,** jouir de; **~edness** *s.* bonheur *m.*; **~ing** *s.* bénédiction *f.*; (*at meals*) bénédicité *m.*; (*thing*) bonheur *m.*

blight *s.* **1.** (*plant disease*) rouille *f.*; **2.** (*fig.*) fléau *m.*; *v.t.* (1) (*wind*) flétrir; (*disease*) rouiller; (2) ruiner; **~er** *s.* (*pop. person*) poison *m.f.*; **lucky ~er,** veinard *m.*
blimey *interj.* (*pop.*) zut alors!
blind[1] *s.* store *m.*; **Venetian ~,** jalousie *f.*; (*pretext*) prétexte *m.*; (*pop.*) **to go on a ~,** faire la noce.
blind[2] *adj.* (*lit.* & *fig.*) aveugle (à); COLOUR-~; **~ as a bat,** myope comme une taupe; **~ in one eye,** borgne; **to turn a ~ eye to sth.,** fermer les yeux sur qch.; **~ alley** *s.* cul-de-sac *m.*; **~ corner** *s.* virage masqué *m.*; **~ man, ~ woman** *s.* aveugle *m.f.*; **~-man's buff,** colin-maillard *m.*; **~ spot** *s.* point faible *m.*; **~fold** *v.t.* bander les yeux à qn.; **~fold** *adj.* aux yeux bandés; **~ing** *adj.* aveuglant; **~ness** *s.* (*med.*) cécité *f.*; (*fig.*) aveuglement *m.*; *v.t.* aveugler.
blink *s.* clignotement *m.*; (*momentary gleam*) lueur *f.*; (*fig.*) aperçu *m.*; **on the ~,** (*electr.*) détraqué; **~er** *s.* (*horse*) œillère *f.*; (*auto.*) clignotant *m.*; *v.i.* clignoter; **~ing** *adj.* (*pop.* = *bloody*) sacré (*before the noun*).
bliss *s.* bonheur *m.*; (*eccles.*) béatitude *f.*; **~ful** *adj.* heureux.
blister *s.* ampoule *f.*; *v.t.* & *i.* faire venir des ampoules; (se) couvrir d'ampoules; **~ing** *adj.* (*heat*) brûlant; (*criticism*) acerbe.
blithe *adj.* gai.
blitz *s.* bombardement (aérien) *m.*; *v.t.* bombarder; **~krieg** *s.* guerre éclair *f.*
blizzard *s.* tourmente de neige *f.*
bloated *adj.* bouffi (*with*—de).
bloater *s.* hareng saur *m.*
blob *s.* tache *f.*
block *s.* **1.** (*of stone*) bloc *m.*; (*of wood*) bille *f.*; **2.** (*of flats*) immeuble *m.*; (*buildings*) pâté de maisons *m.*; **3.** (*traffic jam*) embouteillage *m.*; **4.** (*mould for hats*) forme *f.*; **5.** (*print.*) cliché *m.*; **a** CHIP **off the old ~**; STUMBLING-~; **~head** *s.* tête de bois *f.*; **~house** *s.* blockhaus *m.*; **~ letters, capitals,** majuscules (d'imprimerie) *m.pl.*; *v.t.* (3) embouteiller; (4) mettre à la forme; **~ up,** boucher; **~ out,** esquisser; **~ade** *s.* blocus *m.*; *v.t.* bloquer; **~age** *s.* obstruction *f.*
bloke *s.* (*pop.*) type *m.*
blonde *adj.* blond; *s.* blonde *f.*
blood *s.* sang *m.*; (*person*) dandy *m.*; **in** COLD **~**; FLESH **and ~**; **~ bank,** banque du sang *f.*; **~ count,** numération globulaire *f.*; **~-curdling** *adj.* à tourner le sang; **~-donor** *s.* donneur de sang *m.*; **~hound** *s.* limier *m.*; **~pressure** *s.* pression artérielle *f.*; **~-red** *adj.* rouge sang; **~shed** *s.* carnage *m.*; **~shot** *adj.* injecté de sang; **~-stained** *adj.* taché de sang; **~sucker** *s.* (*lit.* & *fig.*) sangsue *f.*; **~thirsty** *adj.* sanguinaire; **~-vessel** *s.* vaisseau sanguin *m.*; **it makes my ~ boil,** cela me fait bouillir; **~less** *adj.* exsangue; (*without ~shed*) sans effusion de sang; **~y** *adj.* sanglant; (*pop. before noun*) sacré; **~y** *adv.* (*intensive*) vachement.
bloom *s.* (*lit.* & *fig.*) fleur *f.*; *v.i.* fleurir; **~ing** *adj.* florissant; (*pop.* = *bloody*) fichu (*before the noun*).
bloomer *s.* (*pop.*) gaffe *f.*; **~s,** culotte *f.sing.*
blossom *s.* fleur *f.*; *v.i.* fleurir.
blot *s.* **1.** (*spot of ink*) pâté *m.*; **2.** (*blemish* & *fig.*) tache *f.*; *v.t.* (1) faire un pâté; (2) tacher; **3.** (*dry with ~ting-paper*) sécher; **~ one's copy-book,** ternir sa réputation; **~ out** *v.t.* effacer; **~ter** *s.* sous-main *m.*; **~ting-paper** *s.* buvard *m.*; **~to** *adj.* (*fam.*) rétamé.
blotch *s.* tache *f.*
blouse *s.* (*full, worn over skirt, etc.*) blouse *f.*; (*worn inside*) corsage *m.*; (*shirt ~*) chemisier *m.*
blow[1] *s.* souffle *m.*; (*fresh air*) coup de vent *m.*; *v.t.* & *i.* souffler; **the wind ~s,** le vent souffle; **it is ~ing,** il fait du vent; (*an instrument*) jouer de; (*a fuse*) faire sauter; (*pop.* = *squander*) gaspiller; (*pop.* = *curse*) se moquer de; (*auto. horn*) klaxonner; **to ~ one's** NOSE; **~ out** *v.t.* éteindre; **~ over** *v.i.* passer; **~ up** *v.t.* & *i.* (*detonate*) (faire) sauter; (*inflate*) gonfler; (*fam.*) passer un savon (à qn.); **~ hot and cold** (*fig.*) virer à tout vent; **to see which way the** WIND **~s; ~ one's own trumpet,** chanter ses propres louanges; (*fam.*) se faire mousser; **~fly** *s.* mouche à viande *f.*; **~-hole** *s.* évent *m.*; **~-lamp** *s.* lampe à souder *f.*; **~pipe** *s.* chalumeau *m.*
blow[2] *s.* (*lit.* & *fig.*) coup *m.*; **to come to ~s,** en venir aux coups; **without striking a ~,** sans coup férir.
blowzy *adj.* mal peigné.
blubber *s.* (*weeping*) pleurnicherie *f.*; (*whale fat*) graisse de baleine *f.*; *v.i.* pleurnicher; (*fam.*) chialer.
bludgeon *s.* matraque *f.*; *v.t.* (*lit.* & *fig.*) matraquer.
blue *adj.* & *s.m.* bleu; **the ~s,** le cafard; **~bell** *s.* jacinthe (des bois) *f.*; **~bottle** *s.* mouche à viande *f.*; **~ collar worker** *s.* salarié *m.*; **~** FUNK; **~jacket** *s.* (*fam.*) col-bleu *m.*; **~-jeans** *s.* blue-jean *m.*; **~ print** *s.* projet *m.*; **~stocking** *s.* bas-bleu *m.*; **bluish** *adj.* bleuâtre; *v.t.* bleuir; (*pop.*) **to ~ one's money,** gaspiller son argent.
bluff[1] *s.* (*steep bank*) escarpement *m.*; *adj.* à pic; (*fig.*) brusque.
bluff[2] *s.* bluff *m.*; *v.t.* & *i.* bluffer; **to call s.o.'s ~,** relever le défi de qn.
blunder *s.* bévue *f.*; (*fam.*) gaffe *f.*; *v.i.* faire un faux pas; (*fam.*) gaffer; **~er** *s.* gaffeur *m.*; **~ing** *adj.* maladroit.
blunderbuss *s.* espingole *f.*
blunt *adj.* **1.** (*knife*) émoussé; **2.** (*person*) brusque; **3.** (*insensitive*) obtus; **4.** (*thing or fact*) brutal; *v.t.* (1) émousser; (3) engourdir; **~ness** *s.* (1) état émoussé *m.*; (2) brusquerie *f.*
blur *s.* **1.** (*smear*) tache *f.*; **2.** (*dimness*) brouillard *m.*; *v.t.* (1) barbouiller; (2) brouiller.
blurb *s.* annonce sur le couvre-livre *f.*; (*fam.*) jus *m.*
blurt (**out**) *v.t.* lâcher; (*a secret*) laisser échapper.
blush *s.* rougeur *f.*; *v.i.* rougir; **~ing** *adj.* rougissant.
bluster *s.* fanfaronnade *f.*; *v.i.* faire le fanfaron; (*wind*) faire rage; **~ing** *adj.* fanfaron.
boa *s.* boa *m.*
boar *s.* (*pig*) verrat *m.*; (*wild*) sanglier *m.*; **~'s head,** hure *f.*
board *s.* **1.** (*piece of wood*) planche *f.*; FLOOR-~; BLACK~; CHESS~; **notice-~,** panneau d'affichage *m.*; SPRING~; (*thick paper*) carton *m.*; HARD~; **2.** (*food, etc.*) pension *f.*; **~ and lodging,** pension complète *f.*; ABOVE-~; **3.** (*polit.*) ministère *m.*; (*comm.*) conseil d'administration *m.*; **~ meeting,** réunion du conseil d'administration *f.*; **~ of inquiry,** commission d'enquête *f.*; **4.** (*ship's side*) bord *m.*; **on ~,** à bord (de); **to go by the ~,** (*naut.*) tomber à l'eau, (*fig.*) être négligé; *v.t.* (1) planchéier; **~ up,** boucher, (*door, window*) condamner; (2) prendre en pension; (4) monter à bord de; *v.i.* (2) être en pension (*with*—chez); **~er** *s.* (2) pensionnaire *m.f.*; **~ing** *s.* (1) planchéiage *m.*; (2) pension *f.*; **~ing-house** *s.* pension de famille *f.*; **~ing--school** *s.* pensionnat *m.*
boast *s.* vantardise *f.*; *v.i.* se vanter (*of*—de); **~er** *s.* vantard *m.*; **~ing** *s.* vantardise *f.*; **~ful** *adj.* vantard.
boat *s.* (*gen.*) bateau *m.*; (*small, open*) canot *m.*; LIFE~; MOTOR ~; STEAM~; (*receptacle*) saucière *f.*; GRAVY-~; SAUCE-~; **to be in the same ~,** être logé à la même enseigne; **to miss the ~** (*fig.*) manquer le coche; **~-hook** *s.* gaffe *f.*; **~-house** *s.* hangar (à bateau) *m.*; **~load** *s.*

batelée *f.*; **~man** *s.* batelier *m.*; **~-neck** *s.* encolure bateau *f.*; **~swain** *s.* maître d'équipage *m.*, bosco *m.*; **~-train** *s.* train-paquebot *m.*; *v.i.* faire du canotage; **~er** *s.* (*hat*) canotier *m.*; **~ing** *s.* canotage *m.*
bob *s.* (*hair*) coiffure à la Jeanne d'Arc; (*horse's tail*) queue écourtée *f.*; **~tailed** *adj.* à queue écourtée; (*curtsy*) révérence *f.*; *v.t.* (*hair*) coiffer à la Jeanne d'Arc; *v.i.* sautiller; **~-sleigh** *s.* bobsleigh (*abbrev.* bob) *m.*
bobbin *s.* (*reel*) bobine *f.*; (*spindle*) fuseau *m.*
bobby *s.* (*fam.*) flic *m.*
bode *v.t.* présager; **~ ill, well,** être de mauvais, de bon, augure.
bodice *s.* corsage *m.*
bodkin *s.* poinçon *m.*
bod/y *s.* (*of person or animal*; *group*; *substance*; *main part*) corps *m.*; (*dead*) cadavre *m.*; (*organization*) organisme *m.*, organe *m.*; (*of dress*) corsage *m.*; (*auto.*) carosserie *f.*; (*aviat.*) fuselage *m.*; **over my dead ~,** à mon corps défendant; **~-guard** *s.* garde du corps *m.*; ⚠ corps de garde = **guard-room**; **~ily** *adj.* corporel; *adv.* en personne.
bog *s.* marécage *m.*; *v.t.* embourber; **~ged down,** embourbé; **~gy** *adj.* marécageux.
bogey *s.* croque-mitaine *m.*
boggle *v.i.* hésiter; (*fumble*) patauger; **~ at,** reculer devant.
bogus *adj.* factice; **~ concern,** affaire véreuse *f.*
boil[1] *s.* furoncle *m.*
boil[2] *v.t.* faire bouillir; ⚠ *not* bouillir *alone*; *v.i.* (*come to the ~*) bouillir; (*fig.*) bouillir (*with*—de); **it makes my** BLOOD **~**; **~ away** *v.i.* s'évaporer; **~ down to** (*fig.*) se réduire à; **~ over** *v.i.* (*water*) déborder; (*milk*) se sauver; **~ed** EGG; **~ed** POTATO; **~er** *s.* (*cook.*) marmite *f.*; (*techn.*) chaudière *f.*; **~er-room** *s.* chaufferie *f.*; **~ing** *adj.* bouillant; *s.* ébullition *f.*; **~ing-**POINT.
boisterous *adj.* **1.** (*weather*) tumultueux; **2.** (*person*) tapageur; **3.** (*spirits*) exubérant; **~ly** *adv.* (1) violemment; (2) bruyamment; **~ness** *s.* (1) violence *f.*; (2) turbulence *f.*; (3) exubérance *f.*
bold *adj.* **1.** (*brave*) intrépide; **2.** (*daring*) audacieux; **3.** (*impudent*) impudent; **4.** (*type*) gros; **5.** (*fig.*) vigoureux; **to make ~ to,** (*dare*) oser; (*presume to*) se permettre de; **~ness** *s.* (2) audacité *f.*; (3) impudence *f.*; (5) vigueur *f.*; **~ly** *adv.* (1)*; (2)*; (3) impudemment; (5)*.
bole *s.* tronc *m.*
bollard *s.* poteau d'amarrage *m.*
bolster *s.* traversin *m.*; *v.t.* **~ up,** soutenir.
bolt *s.* **1.** (*lock*) verrou *m.*; **2.** (*mech.*) boulon *m.*; **3.** (*arrow*) trait *m.*; **4.** (*thunder~*) coup (de foudre) *m.*; **5.** (*flight*) fuite *f.*; **to do a ~,** décamper; **6.** (*fabric*) pièce *f.*; *v.t.* (1) verrouiller; (2) boulonner; **7.** (*gulp down*) avaler; *v.i.* (5) décamper; (*horse*) s'emballer.
bomb *s.* bombe *f.*; *v.t.* bombarder; **to go like a ~,** (*pop.*) chauffer; **~er** *s.* (*aviat.*) bombardier *m.*; **~shell** (*mil.*) obus *m.*; (*fig.*) coup de foudre *m.*
bombard *v.t.* bombarder (*with*—de); **~ment** *s.* bombardement *m.*
bombast *s.* emphase *f.*; (*style*) grandiloquence *f.*; **~ic** *adj.* emphatique; grandiloquent; **~ically** *adv.* avec emphase, avec grandiloquence.
bonanza *s.* (*techn.*) riche veine (de minérai) *f.*; (*fam.*) filon *m.*
bond *s.* (*tie*) lien *m.*; (*comm. law*) obligation *f.*; (*fin.*) bon *m.*, titre *m.*; **~s** *s.pl.* fers *m.pl.*; *v.t.* (*comm.*) entreposer; **~ed warehouse,** entrepôt *m.*; **~age** *s.* esclavage *m.*; **~man, maid,** esclave *m.f.*
bone *s.* os *m.*; (*fish*) arête *f.*; **~s** *s.pl.* ossements *m.pl.*; **~ of contention,** pomme de discorde *f.*; FUNNY-**~**; WISH**~**; **to have a ~ to pick with s.o.,** avoir maille à partir avec qn.; **to make no ~s about sth.,** ne pas y aller par quatre chemins; **to be nothing but skin and ~s,** n'avoir que la peau sur les os; **to make old ~s,** faire de vieux os; RAG-**and-~ man**; **~-dry** *adj.* archisec; **~head** *s.* (*pop.*) tête de bois *f.*; **~ idle** *adj.* paresseux comme une couleuvre; **~-setter** *s.* (*fam.*) rebouteux *m.*; **~-shaker** *s.* (*fam.*) vieille guimbarde *f.*; **~less** *adj.* sans os; **bony** *adj.* osseux; *v.t.* désosser, enlever les arêtes de.
bonfire *s.* feu de joie *m.*
bonnet *s.* (*child's hat*) bonnet *m.*; (*peasant's hat*) bavolet *m.*; (*auto.*) capot *m.*; **to have a** BEE **in one's ~.**
bonny *adj.* (*healthy*) éclatant de santé; (*well-made, of women*) plantureux.
bonus *s.* (*fin.*) boni *m.*; (*comm.*) (*extra pay for expenses etc.*) prime *f.*; (*free extra pay, at New Year etc.*) gratification *f.*
boo *interj.* hou!; *v.t.* huer; **she wouldn't say ~ to a goose,** elle a peur de son ombre.
booby *s.* nigaud *m.*; **~ trap** *s.* attrape-nigaud *m.*; (*mil.*) mine piégée *f.*; **~ prize** *s.* dernier *m.*
book *s.* (*printed*) livre *m.*; (*comm. usu. pl.*) livres *m.pl.*; (*of blank sheets*) carnet *m.*; CHEQUE-**~**; EXERCISE-**~**; NOTE**~**; TEXT**~**; **it's a closed ~ to me,** je n'y comprends rien; **to bring s.o. to ~,** demander des comptes à qn.; **to be in s.o.'s good ~s,** être dans les petits papiers de qn.; **to be in s.o.'s bad ~s,** être mal vu de qn.; **~**BINDER; **~**BINDING; **~case** *s.* bibliothèque *f.*; **~keeper** *s.* comptable *m.*; **~keeping** *s.* comptabilité *f.*; **~maker** *s.* (*betting*) bookmaker *m.*; (*fam.*) **~ie,** book *m.*; **~mark(er)** *s.* signet *m.*; **~-post,** imprimé *m.*; **~seller** *s.* libraire *m.*; **~shelf** *s.* rayon *m.*; **~shop** *s.* librairie *f.*; **~stall** *s.* étalage de livres *m.*; **~** TOKEN; **~worm** *s.* rat de bibliothèque *m.*; **~ish** *adj.* (*person*) studieux, (*thing, style*) livresque; **~let** *s.* opuscule *m.*, brochure *f.*; *v.t.* (*enter in ~*) inscrire; (*rail.*) prendre un billet; (*a seat*) retenir (une place); **~ing-office** *s.* guichet *m.*
boom *s.* **1.** (*naut.*) tangon *m.*; **2.** (*comm.*) boom *m.*; **3.** (*sound*) grondement *m.*; **sonic ~,** bang supersonique *m.*; *v.i.* (2) prospérer; (3) gronder.
boomerang *s.* boomerang *m.*
boon *s.* (*favour*) faveur *f.*; (*request*) requête *f.*; **~ companion,** joyeux compagnon *m.*
boor *s.* rustre *m.*; **~ish** *adj.* rustaud; **~ishness** *s.* grossièreté *f.*
boost *s.* relance *f.*; *v.t.* (*help*) renforcer; (*advertise*) faire de la réclame pour; (*increase, volume, pressure etc.*) amplifier; (*electr.*) survolter; **~er** *s.* (*radio*) amplificateur *m.*; (*electr.*) survolteur *m.*; (*on rocket*) moteurs latéraux *m.pl.*
boot *s.* (*shoe*) botte *f.*; (*auto.*) coffre *m.*; *v.t.* (*out*) *also* **to give s.o. the ~,** flanquer qn. à la porte; **~black** *s.* cireur (de chaussures) *m.*; **~lace,** lacet *m.*; **~leg** *v.i.* faire de la contrebande (d'alcool); **~legger,** contrebandier *m.*; **~less** *adj.* sans bottes; (*fig.*) sans profit; **~ee** *s.* chausson (d'enfant) *m.*; **~maker** *s.* bottier *m.*
booth *s.* (*at fair*) baraque *f.*; POLLING-**~**; TELEPHONE **~**.
booty *s.* butin *m.*
booze *s.* boisson alcoolique *f.*; *v.i.* se soûler; (*fam.*) s'imbiber (d'alcool); **~r** *s.* soûlaud *m.*
borage *s.* bourrache *f.*
bor/ax *s.* borax *m.*; **~ic** *adj.* borique.
border *s.* **1.** (*edge*) bord *m.*; **2.** (*edging*) bordure *f.*; **3.** (*frontier*) frontière *f.*; (*limit*) limite *f.*; **4.** (*hort.*) parterre *m.*; *adj.* (3) limitrophe; *v.t.* (1) border; *v.i.* (3) **~ on,** être limitrophe de; (*fig.*) avoisiner; **~line** *s.* ligne de démarcation *f.*; **~line case,** cas limite *m.*

bore[1] *s.* (*mine*) trou de sondage *m.*; (*river*) mascaret *m.*; *v.t.* sonder.
bor/e[2] *s.* (*person*) raseur *m.*; **what a ~e!** (*fam.*) la barbe!; *v.t.* ennuyer; (*fam.*) assommer; **to be ~ed to** DEATH; **~ing** *adj.* ennuyeux, assommant; **~edom** *s.* ennui *m.*
born, to be *v.i.* naître; ⚠ je suis né = **I was born;** *adj.* **a ~ poet, etc,** poète, etc., né.
borough *s.* bourg *m.*; (*approx.*) municipalité *f.*
borrow *v.t.* emprunter (qch. à qn.); **~er** *s.* emprunteur *m.*; **~ing** *s.* emprunt *m.*
boscage *s.* bocage *m.*
bosh *s.* (*pop.*) blague *m.*
bosom *s.* sein *m.*; **~ friend,** ami intime.
boss[1] *s.* (*protuberance*) bosse *f.*
boss[2] *s.* (*person*) patron *m.*, patronne *f.*; *v.t.* faire marcher; **~ s.o. about,** régenter qn.; **~y** *adj.* autoritaire.
botan/y *s.* botanique *f.*; **~ical** *adj.* botanique; **~ist** *s.* botaniste *m.f.*; **~ize** *v.i.* botaniser.
botch *s.* **1.** (*bad work*) bousillage *m.* **2.** (*bad repair*) rafistolage *m.*; *v.t.* (1) bousiller; (2) rafistoler; **~er** *s.* bousilleur *m.*
both *pron.* & *adj.* l'un et l'autre, tous les deux; **~ of us,** nous deux; **on ~ sides,** des deux côtés; *adv.* **~ . . . and . . .,** à la fois . . . et . . .; **he is ~ a writer and an artist,** il est à la fois écrivain et artiste.
bother *s.* **1.** (*trouble*) ennui *m.*; **2.** (*care*) souci *m.*; **3.** (*annoyance*) embêtement *m.*; *v.t.* & *i.* (1) ennuyer; (2) se soucier de; (*fuss*) se tracasser; (3) embêter; *interj.* zut!; **what a ~!,** quelle barbe!; **a spot of ~,** embarras *m.*; **don't ~,** ne vous tracassez pas; **~ation** *s.* embêtement *m.*; **~some** *adj.* gênant, agaçant.
bottle *s.* (*wine, etc.*) bouteille *f.*; (*water*) carafe *f.*; (*small*) flacon *m.*; (*baby's*) biberon *m.*; **hot--water ~,** bouillote *f.*; **~-green** *adj.* vert bouteille; **~-neck** *s.* goulot *m.*; (*traffic*) bouchon *m.*; **~-washer** *s.* plongeur *m.*; HEAD **cook and ~-washer**; *v.t.* mettre en bouteille; **~ up** *v.t.* (*fig.*) contenir.
bottom *s.* (*lower part*) bas *m.*; (*of sea, lake, etc.*) fond *m.*; (*foundation*) base *f.*; (*of ship*) carène *f.*; (*of table*) bas bout *m.*; (*of class*) queue *f.*; (*of body*) derrière *m.*; ROCK-**~**; **to be at the ~ of sth.,** être la cause de qch.; **to get to the ~ of sth.,** découvrir la cause de qch.; **from top to ~,** de fond en comble; **~less** *adj.* sans fond.
bough *s.* rameau *m.*
boulder *s.* roc *m.*
bounc/e *s.* **1.** (*leap*) saut *m.*; (*of ball*) bond *m.*; **2.** (*energy*) allant *m.*; (*boastfulness*) vantardise *f.*; *v.i.* (1) bondir; *v.t.* (1) faire rebondir; *v.i.* (2) être plein d'allant; se vanter; (*cheque*) être retourné pour non-provision; **~ing** *adj.* vigoureux.
bound[1] *s.* (*boundary*) borne *f.*; *v.t.* borner; **~less** *adj.* sans bornes, illimité; **out of ~s,** hors limites.
bound[2] *s.* **1.** (*leap*) saut *m.*; **2.** (*of ball*) rebondissement *m.*; *v.i.* (1) sauter; (2) rebondir; **by** LEAPS **and ~s.**
bound[3] *adj.* (*book*) relié; **to be ~ to,** être obligé de, devoir; **it's ~ to happen,** cela doit arriver; **to be ~ for** (*ship, plane, etc.*) être à destination de; **~en** *adj.* obligatoire; **~en duty,** devoir sacré *m.*
boundary *s.* limite *f.*
bounder *s.* (*fam.*) un m'as-tu vu *m.*
bount/eous, bountiful *adj.* généreux; **~eousness** *s.* générosité *f.*; **~y** *s.* (*liberality*) générosité *f.*; (*gift*) don *m.*; (*subsidy*) gratification *f.*, prime *f.*
bouquet *s.* bouquet *m.*
bourn *s.* (*boundary*) borne *f.*; (*goal*) but *m.*
bout *s.* (*spell of work*) tour *m.*; (*illness*) accès *m.*; (*sport*) assaut *m.*
bovine *adj.* (*lit.* & *fig.*) bovin.
bow[1] *s.* (*greeting*) salut *m.*; *v.t.* (*head*) incliner; (*back*) courber; (*knees*) plier; (*show in or out*) faire entrer, congédier en saluant; *v.i.* saluer, s'incliner, se courber; **~ to,** saluer; **~ down** *v.t.* courber; (*fig.*) accabler (sous); *v.i.* se prosterner; **~ and** SCRAPE.
bow[2] *s.* (*weapon*) arc *m.*; (*violin*) archet *m.*; (*knot*) nœud *m.*; (*saddle*) arçon *m.*; **to have two** STRINGS **to one's ~**; **~-legged** *adj.* les jambes en cerceau; **~man** *s.* archer *m.*; **~-window** *s.* oriel m.
bow[3] *s.* (*naut.*) proue *f.*; (*oarsman*) rameur d'avant *m.*
bowdlerize *v.t.* expurger.
bowels *s.* (*med.*) intestin *m.*; (*gen.* & *fig.*) entrailles *f.pl.*
bower *s.* tonnelle *f.*
bowl[1] *s.* bol *m.*; (*usu. glass*) coupe *f.*; (*for milk*) jatte *f.*; (*large*) cuvette *f.*, bassin *m.*; (*of pipe*) fourneau *m.*; SALAD-**~**; SUGAR-**~**.
bowl[2] *s.* (*wooden ball*) boule *f.*; **~s** (*game*) boules *f.pl.*; *v.i.* jouer aux boules; (*cricket*) lancer; *v.t.* lancer, rouler; **~ along,** rouler; **~ over,** renverser; **~er** *s.* (*hat*) chapeau melon *m.*; **~ing** & **~ing-alley,** bowling *m.*; **~ing-green,** boulingrin *m.*
bowline *s.* bouline *f.*
box[1] *s.* (*tree*) buis *m.*
box[2] *s.* boîte *f.*; (*cardboard*) carton *m.*; (*chest*) coffre *m.*; (*casket*) coffret *m.*; (*large, wooden*) caisse *f.*; (*horse*) box *m.* (*pl.* boxes); (*theat.*) loge *f.*; (*jury*) banc *m.*; (= *TV*) le petit écran *m.*; BALLOT-**~**; MONEY-**~**; POOR-**~**; SENTRY-**~**; SIGNAL-**~**; SNUFF-**~**; TELEPHONE-**~**; WINDOW-**~**; WITNESS-**~**; **~ girder** *s.* fer carré *m.*; **~-office** *s.* bureau de location *m.*; **~-**PLEAT; **~-room** *s.* débarras *m.*; **B~ing-Day** *s.* jour des étrennes *m.*; *v.t.* mettre en boite, en caisse.
box[3] *s.* (*slap on ear*) gifle *f.*; *v.t.* gifler; *v.i.* (*sport*) boxer; **to ~ s.o.'s** EARS; **~er** *s.* boxeur *m.*; **~ing** *s.* boxe *f.*; **~ing-gloves** *s.* gants de boxe *m.pl.*
boy *s.* garçon *m.*; **~ scout,** (boy)scout *m.*; **old ~,** (*of school, etc.*) ancien élève *m.*; (*fam.*) mon vieux; **~s will be ~s,** il, faut que jeunesse se passe; **tom~,** garçon manqué; **~ish** *adj.* garçonnier; **~hood** *s.* (*early*) enfance *f.*; (*late*) adolescence *f.*
boycott *s.* boycottage *m.*; *v.t.* boycotter.
brac/e *s.* (*pair*) paire *f.*; (*clasp*) agrafe *f.*; (*mus.*) accolade *f.*; (*naut.*) cordage de vergue *m.*; (*arch., auto., aviat.*) entretoise *f.*; (*dental*) appareil *m.*; **~es,** bretelles *f. pl.*; *v.t.* (*strengthen*) étayer; (*support*) soutenir; (*tighten*) attacher; (*invigorate*) fortifier; **~ing** *adj.* fortifiant.
bracelet *s.* bracelet *m.*; **~s** (*Eng. pop.* = *handcuffs*) menottes *f.pl.*
bracken *s.* fougère *f.*
bracket *s.* (*arch.*) console *f.*; (*electr., gas.*) applique *f.*; (*print*) crochet *m.*; **in ~s,** entre parenthèses; *v.t.* (*support*) soutenir; (*enclose in ~s*) mettre entre crochets; (*couple together*) coupler; (*fam.*) mettre dans le même sac.
brackish *adj.* saumâtre.
brad *s.* semence *f.*; **~awl** *s.* poinçon *m.*
brag *s.* vantardise *f.*; *v.i.* se vanter (de); **~ging** *s.* vantardise *f.*; **~gart** *s.* vantard *m.*
brahmin *s.* brahmane *m.*
braid *s.* **1.** (*hair*) tresse *f.*; (*plait*) natte *f.*; **2.** (*trimming*) passement *m.*; (*ribbon*) galon *m.*; *v.t.* (1) tresser; (2) galonner.
Braille *s.* braille *m.*
brain *s.* (*tissue, cook.*) cervelle *f.*; (*intellect*) *also* **~s,** cerveau *m.*; **to** CUDGEL **one's ~s; to** PICK **s.o.'s ~s; to have an idea on the ~,** avoir une idée dans la cervelle; **~ drain** (*fam.*) exode des cerveaux *m.*; **~ fever** *s.* fièvre cérébrale *f.*; **~-**PAN; **~storm** *s.* transport au cerveau *m.*;

~s trust *s.* brain-trust *m.*; **~wash** *v.t.* endoctriner, bourrer le crâne (à qn.); **~washing** *s.* lavage de cerveau *m.*, bourrage de crâne *m.*; **~wave** *s.* trouvaille *f.*; **~less** *adj.* sans cervelle; **~y** *adj.* intelligent; *v.t.* assommer.
braise *v.t.* (*cook.*) braiser.
brake[1] *s.* (*thicket*) fourré *m.*
brake[2] (*auto. etc.*) frein *m.*; **~-lever** *s.* levier de frein *m.*; **~ lights,** signaux de freinage *m.pl.*; **~ lining** *s.* garniture de frein *f.*; **~-van** *s.* wagon-frein *m.*; *v.t.* & *i.* (*lit.* & *fig.*) freiner.
bramble *s.* ronce *f.*
bran *s.* son *m.*
branch *s.* (*of tree* & *fig.*) branche *f.*; (*of bank, etc.*) succursale *f.*; OLIVE-~; VINE-~; **~ line, ~ road,** embranchement *m.*; *v.i.* **~ off,** (*road, etc.*) bifurquer; (*fig.*) diverger.
brand *s.* (*burning wood*) tison *m.*; (*iron stamp*) fer *m.*; (*mark, comm.*) marque *f.*; *v.t.* marquer; **~ed** *adj.* marqué; ~-NEW.
brandish *v.t.* brandir.
brandy *s.* cognac *m.*
brass *s.* (*metal*) cuivre jaune *m.*, laiton *m.*; (*mus.*) cuivres *m.pl.*; (*fam.* = *cheek*) culot *m.*; (*pop.* = *money*) pognon *m.*; (*pop. fig.*) **top ~,** les grosses légumes *f.pl.*; *adj.* de bronze, en laiton; **not to be worth a ~** FARTHING; **~ band** *s.* fanfare *f.*; **~ hat** *s.* (*mil.*) képi à étoiles *m.*; ~ TACKS.
brassière *s.* soutien-gorge *m.*; ⚠ brassière = **child's vest.**
brat *s.* (*fam.*) gosse *m.*, gamin, *m.*; **~s** *pl.* marmaille *f.*
bravado *s.* bravade *f.*
brave *s.* (*Red Indian*) guerrier *m.*; *adj.* **1.** (*courageous*) brave; ⚠ (*always follows the noun in this sense*); **2.** (*showy*) élégant; (*excellent*) fameux; **~ly** *adv.*; (1)*; (2) élégamment; remarquablement; **~ry** *s.* (1) bravoure *f.*; (2) élégance *f.*; *v.t.* braver, affronter.
bravo *interj.* bravo!
brawl *s.* bagarre *f.*; *v.i.* se bagarrer.
brawn *s.* muscle *m.*; (*cook.*) fromage de tête *m.*; **~y** *adj.* musclé; (*fam.*) costaud.
bray *s.* braiment *m.*; *v.i.* braire.
brazen *adj.* **1.** (*like brass*) de laiton; **2.** (*sound*) cuivré; **3.** (*shameless*) effronté; **~ly** *adv.* avec effronterie; **~ness** *s.* (3) effronterie *f.*; *v.t.* **~ it out,** crâner.
brazier *s.* brasero *m.*
Brazil *s.* Brésil *m.*; **~ian** *adj.* & *s.m.f.* brésilien(ne).
breach *s.* **1.** (*of law*) violation *f.*; (*of rules, minor offence*) infraction *f.*; **2.** (*in relations*) rupture *f.*; (*quarrel*) brouille *f.*; **3.** (*gap*) brèche *f.*; (*empty space*) vide *m.*; **~ of the peace,** attentat contre l'ordre public *m.*; **~ of promise,** rupture de promesse de mariage *f.*; *v.t.* (3) ouvrir une brèche dans.
bread *s.* pain *m.*; (*Eng. style*) pain de mie *m.*; ⚠ un pain = **a loaf of bread**; GINGER~; **~ and butter,** (*slice*) tartine *f.*; (*living*) pain *m.*; **to earn one's ~ and butter** (*fam.*) gagner sa croûte; **~-basket** *s.* panier à pain *m.*; ~-BIN; **~-fruit** *s.* fruit de l'arbre à pain *m.*; **~-winner** *s.* gagne-pain *m.*
breadth *s.* (*measurement*) largeur *f.*; (*fig.*) ampleur *f.*
break[1] *s.* (*action*) cassure *f.*; (*fig.*) rupture *f.*; (*broken place*) brèche *f.*; (*gap*) trou *m.*; (*fig.*) lacune *f.*; (*pause in work*) interruption *f.*, pause *f.*; TEA-~; (*quarrel*) brouille *f.*; **to get a ~** (*fam.*) avoir de la veine; **without a ~,** sans discontinuer.
break[2] *v.t.* & *i.* (*make or become discontinuous, divide into two or more parts*) (se) briser; (*of weather*) se gâter; (*of clouds*) se disperser; (*crack, shatter*) (se) casser; **~ one's leg, etc.,** se casser la jambe, etc.; (*surpass a record*) battre (un record); (*interrupt*) interrompre, suspendre; (*of voice*) muer; (*of day*) se lever; (*of news*) *v.t.* annoncer, *v.i.* devenir notoire; (*tame, subdue*) dresser, dompter; (*destroy*) briser; (*~ a bank*) faire sauter (une banque); (*of ground*) défoncer; (*become bankrupt*) faire faillite; (*of heart*) (se) briser; **~ s.o. of a habit,** corriger qn. d'une habitude; (*of law*) violer, enfreindre; (*of promise, etc.*) manquer à; **~ away,** (se) détacher (*from*—de); **~away** *adj.* détaché; **~ down** *v.t.* (*by force*) abattre, (*analyse*) détailler; *v.i.* (*cease to function*) s'interrompre, (*collapse*) s'effondrer, (*mech.*) rester en panne; **~down** *s.* (*med.*) dépression nerveuse *f.*, (*mech.*) panne *f.*; **~down lorry** *s.* dépanneuse *f.*; **~ in,** enfoncer, (*of burglar*) s'introduire par effraction, (*tame, discipline*) dresser, assouplir; **~-in** *s.* vol avec effraction *m.*; **~ off** *v.t.* rompre; *v.i.* se détacher; **~ out** *v.i.* (*war, etc.*) éclater; **~ through** *v.t.* percer; **~-through** *s.* percée *f.*, (*fig.*) progrès *m.*; **~ up** *v.t.* démolir; *v.i.* se disperser, se séparer, (*school*) entrer en vacances; **to drive at ~neck speed,** rouler à tombeau ouvert; **~water** *s.* brise-lames *m.*, digue *f.*; **~able** *adj.* cassable, fragile; **~age** *s.* casse *f.*; **~er** *s.* (*wave*) brisant *m.*; **~ing** *s.* rupture *f.*; **~ing-point** *s.* (*mech.*) limite de rupture *f.*; (*fig.*) **to be at ~ing-point,** être à bout de patience.
breakfast *s.* petit déjeuner *m.*; *v.i.* prendre son petit déjeuner.
bream *s.* brème *f.*
breast *s.* poitrine *f.*; (*woman's*) sein *m.*; (*of animal*) poitrail *m.*; (*fig.*) cœur *m.*; (*cook. poultry*) blanc *m.*; **to make a clean ~ of,** tout avouer; **~bone,** sternum *m.*; **~plate,** plastron *m.*; **~-pocket,** poche de poitrine *f.*; **~-stroke** (*swimming*) brasse *f.*; *v.t.* (*waves etc.*) fendre; (*fig.*) faire face à.
breath *s.* (*air*) haleine *f.*; (*single respiration*) souffle *m.*; **out of ~,** hors d'haleine, à bout de souffle; **~alyser** *s.* alcootest *m.*; **~less** *adj.* essoufflé; **~lessly** *adv.* sans haleine; **~-taking** *adj.* à en couper le souffle; (*fam.*) époustouflant.
breath/e *v.t.* (*air*) respirer; (*word*) murmurer; *v.i.* respirer; **don't ~e a word,** n'en soufflez pas mot; **~ing** *s.* respiration *f.*; *adj.* (*living*) vivant; (*exercises, apparatus, etc.*) respiratoire; **~ing space,** moment de répit *m.*
breech *s.* (*gun*) culasse *f.*; **~es** *s.* culotte *f. sing.*; **~es-**BUOY.
breed *s.* race *f.*; (*species*) espèce *f.*; *v.t.* (*propagate*) engendrer; (*raise cattle*) élever; *v.i.* se reproduire; **~er** *s.* éleveur *m.*; **~ing** *s.* élevage *m.*; **good ~ing,** savoir-vivre *m.*
breez/e *s.* brise *f.*; **~e-block** *s.* (*constr.*) parpaing *m.*; **~y** *adj.* exposé au vent.
Bren (**gun**) *s.* fusil-mitrailleur *m.*
Breton *adj.* & *s.m.f.* breton(ne).
breviary *s.* bréviaire *m.*
brevity *s.* brièveté *f.*; (*conciseness*) concision *f.*
brew *s.* infusion *f.*; *v.t.* (*tea*) infuser; (*beer*) brasser; *v.i.* (*storm*) se préparer; (*mischief*) se tramer; **~er** *s.* brasseur *m.*; **~ery** *s.* brasserie *f.*
briar, see BRIER.
bribe *s.* pot-de-vin *m.*; *v.t.* corrompre, suborner; **~ry** *s.* corruption *f.*; ⚠ bribe = **tiny piece.**
brick *s.* brique *f.*; (*pop.* = *person*) brave type *m.*; **to drop a ~,** faire une gaffe; **you can't make ~s without straw,** on ne fait pas d'omelette sans casser des œufs; **~bat** *s.* (*fig.*) pavé *m.*; **~-kiln** *s.* four à briques *m.*; **~layer** *s.* maçon *m.*; *v.t.* **~ up,** murer de briques.
brid/e *s.* mariée *f.*; **~egroom,** marié *m.*; **~esmaid,** demoiselle d'honneur *f.*; **~al** *s.* noce *f.*; *adj.* nuptial; ⚠ bride = **bridle.**
bridge *s.* (*over water, etc.*) pont *m.*; SUSPENSION ~; SWING ~; WEIGH~; (*naut.*) passerelle *f.*; (*of nose*) dos *m.*; (*game*) bridge *m.*; (*of violin*) chevalet *m.*;

~-head *s.* tête de pont *f.*; *v.t.* construire un pont sur; **to play ~,** bridger; **to ~ the gap,** faire la soudure.

bridle *s.* **1.** (*harness*) bride *f.*; **2.** (*restraint*) frein *m.*; **~-path,** piste cavalière *f.*; *v.t.* (1) brider; (2) freiner; *v.i.* (*fig.*) se raidir.

brief[1] *s.* (*law*) dossier *m.*; *v.t.* confier une cause à; **~-case,** serviette *f.*

brief[2] *adj.* bref; **~s** *s.* slip *m.*; **~ly** *adv.* brièvement.

brier, briar *s.* (*bush*) ronce *f.*; (*sweet*) églantier *m.*; (*pipe*) pipe de bruyère *f.*

brig *s.* (*naut.*) brick *m.*

brigad/e *s.* (*mil.* & *gen.*) brigade *f.*; *v.t.* embrigader; *v.refl.* s'embrigader; **~ier** *s.* général de brigade *m.*; ⚠ brigadier = **corporal.**

brigand *s.* brigand *m.*; **~age** *s.* brigandage *m.*

brigantine *s.* (*naut.*) brigantin *m.*; ⚠ brigantine = **spanker** (**sail**).

bright *adj.* **1.** (*giving light, shining*) brillant, éclatant; **2.** (*lit up, with joy, etc.*) étincelant, vif (de joie, etc.) **3.** (*vivid*) vif; **4.** (*illustrious*) glorieux; **5.** (*lively, intelligent*) gai, doué; **a ~ idea,** une idée lumineuse *f.*; **a ~ period** (*meteor.*) une éclaircie *f.*; **~en** *v.t.* (1) faire briller; (5) (*fig.*) égayer; *v.i.* (1) s'éclairer; (*weather*) s'éclaircir; (5) s'animer; **~ly** *adv.* (*also* ~) (1) brillamment; (2) vivement; (3) avec éclat; (5) gaiement, avec intelligence; **~ness** *s.* (1) éclat *m.*; (2) vivacité *f.*; (3) éclat *m.*; (4) splendeur *f.*; (5) gaieté *f.*, intelligence *f.*

Bright's disease *s.* (*med.*) brightisme *m.*; (*fam.*) mal de Bright *m.*

brill *s.* barbue *f.*

brillian/ce *s.* **1.** (*brightness*) éclat *m.*; **2.** (*vividness*) éclat *m.*; **3.** (*intelligence*) intelligence *f.*; **~t** *adj.* (1) brillant; (2) éclatant; (3) intelligent; *s.* brillant *m.*; **~tly** *adv.* (1) & (2) avec éclat; (3) brillamment; **~tine** *s.* brillantine *f.*

brim *s.* (*edge of cup, etc.*; *of hat*) bord *m.*; **~-full** *adj.* rempli jusqu'au bord; (*fig.*) débordant de; **to be ~-full of** (*fig.*) déborder de; *v.t.* remplir jusqu'au bord; *v.i.* être plein de; **~ over,** déborder.

brimstone *s.* soufre *m.*

brindled *adj.* moucheté.

brin/e *s.* (*salt water*) saumure *f.*; (*sea*) mer *f.*; *v.t.* mettre dans la saumure; **~y** *adj.* saumâtre; *s.* (*Eng. fam.*) mer *f.*

bring *v.t.* (*person*) amener; (*thing*) apporter; (*cause, result in*) faire venir, provoquer; (*law*) (~ *a charge*) porter une accusation, (~ *a case*) intenter un procès, (~ *to court*) traduire en justice; (*advance* (*an argument*)) avancer; **~ oneself to,** se résoudre à; **~ about** *v.t.* (*cause*) occasionner, (*achieve*) réaliser; **~ back** *v.t.* ramener, rapporter; **~ down** *v.t.* (*fell*) abattre, (*thing*) descendre, (*person*) faire descendre, (*price*) faire baisser; **~ down the house,** faire crouler la salle; **~ forth** *v.t.* (*give birth*) mettre au monde, (*agric.*) produire; **~ forward** *v.t.* (*idea*) avancer, (*fin.*) reporter; **~ in** *v.t.* (*person*) faire entrer; (*thing*) entrer, (*fin.*) rapporter, (*parl.*) déposer, (*fashion*) lancer; **~ off** *v.t.* réussir (un coup); **~ on,** causer, (*agric.*) faire pousser; **~ out** (*person*) faire sortir, (*thing*) sortir, (*book*) publier, (*words*) proférer, (*fig.*) faire ressortir; **~ round** (*med.*) ranimer, (*fig.*) convaincre; **~ to** (*med.*) ranimer, (*naut., aviat.*) mettre en panne; **~ together** *v.t.* (*collect*) rassembler, (*re-unite*) réunir, (*put in touch*) mettre en contact; **~ under** *v.t.* asujettir; **~ up** *v.t.* (*children, etc.*) élever, (*person*) faire monter, (*thing*) monter, (*med.*) vomir; (*fig.*) soulever; **~ing-up** *s.* éducation *f.*; *see also* BEAR, BOOK, DATE, HOME, LIGHT, MIND, PASS, PLAY.

brink *s.* (*lit.* & *fig.*) bord *m.*; **on the ~ of tears, etc.,** au bord des larmes, etc.; **on the ~ of doing sth.,** à deux doigts de faire qch.; **~manship** *s.* politique d'équilibre instable *f.*

briquet(te) *s.* briquette *f.*

brisk *adj.* (*lively movement, keen air, etc.*) vif; (*person*) animé; (*comm.*) **business is ~,** le marché est animé; **~ly** *adv.* vivement; **~ness** *s.* vivacité *f.*

brisket *s.* (*cook.*) poitrine (de bœuf) *f.*

bristl/e *s.* (*of hog or boar*) soie *f.*; (*of other animals*) poil *m.*; (*human*) poil (raide) *m.*; *v.t.* & *i.* (*lit.* & *fig.*) (se) hérisser; **to ~e with difficulties, etc.,** être hérissé de difficultés, etc.; **~y** *adj.* poilu, hérissé.

Brit/ain (**Great**) *s.* Grande-Bretagne *f.*; **B~annic** *adj.* britannique; **B~ish** *adj.* britannique; **the B~ish** *s.pl.* les Britanniques *m.pl.*; **the B~ish Isles,** les îles britanniques *f.pl.*; **B~on** *s.* Anglais(e) *m.f.*

Brittany *s.* Bretagne *f.*

brittle *adj.* (*apt to break*) cassant; (*fragile*) fragile; **~ness** *s.* fragilité *f.*

broach *s.* **1.** (*roasting-spit*) broche *f.*; **2.** (*church spire*) flèche *f.*; **3.** (*boring-bit*) foret *m.*; *v.t.* (1) embrocher; (3) forer; **4.** (*open* & *start using*; *begin discussion of*) entamer; **5.** (*cask*) mettre en perce.

broad *adj.* **1.** (*large across*) large; **2.** (*extensive*) vaste; **3.** (*daylight*) grand, plein; (*hint*) clair; **4.** (*accent*) fort; **5.** (*style*) ample; **6.** (*vulgar*) grossier; **it's as ~ as it's long,** c'est bonnet blanc et blanc bonnet; ~ BEAN; **~-brimmed** *adj.* à larges bords; **~cloth** *s.* drap fin *m.*; **~-loom** *s.* moquette en grande largeur *f.*; **~minded** *adj.* à l'esprit large; **~sheet** *s.* (*print. format*) in plano *m.*; (*newssheet*) canard *m.*; **~side** *s.* (*naut. guns*) bordée *f.*; (*of ship*) travers *m.*; **~sword** *s.* sabre *m.*; (*pop.* = *prostitute*) poule *f.*; **~s** (*East Anglia*) région lacustre *f.*; **~en** *v.t.* & *i.* (s')élargir; **~ly** *adv.* largement, d'une façon générale; **~ness** *s.* (1) largeur *f.*; (2) étendue *f.*; (5) ampleur *f.*; (6) grossièreté *f.*

broadcast *s.* (*radio* & *TV*) émission *f.*; *v.t.* **1.** (*sow seed*) semer à la volée; **2.** (*radio* & *TV*) radiodiffuser; **3.** (*fig.*) répandre; *adj.* & *adv.* (1) semé à la volée; (2) diffusé; (3) répandu; **~er** *s.* (2) (*apparatus*) émetteur *m.*; (2) (*person*) présentateur (de radio) *m.*; **~ing** *s.* (1) semaille à la volée *f.*; (2) radiodiffusion *f.*

brocade *s.* brocart *m.*

broccoli *s.* brocoli *m.*

brochure *s.* brochure *f.*; (*folder*) dépliant *m.*

brock *s.* (= *badger*) blaireau *m.*

brogue *s.* (*shoe*) soulier (de sport, de chasse) *m.*; (*accent*) accent (irlandais) *m.*

broil[1] *s.* (*quarrel*) brouille *f.*

broil[2] *v.t.* (*cook.*) griller; (*fam.*) griller; **~er** (*chicken*), poulet d'élevage forcé; (*fam.*) poulet aux hormones *m.*

broke *adj.* (*fam.*) *also* **stony ~,** fauché.

broken *adj.* (*in pieces*) brisé; (*infirm*) délabré; (*fig. humbled*) abattu; (*trained, e.g. horse*) rompu; **~ down** *adj.* (*techn.*) détraqué; (*auto. etc.*) en panne; **~ English, etc.,** mauvais anglais *m.* etc.; **~ ground,** terrain accidenté *m.*; **~-hearted** *adj.* au cœur brisé; **~ home,** foyer désuni *m.*; ~ REED; **~ sleep,** sommeil interrompu *m.*; **~ly** *adv.* sans suite, irrégulièrement.

broker *s.* (*dealer in secondhand goods*) brocanteur *m.*; (*fin.*) courtier *m.*; **~age** *s.* courtage *m.*

brolly *s.* (*abbrev. for umbrella*) (*fam.*) pépin *m.*

bromide *s.* (*sedative*) bromure *m.*; (*fig.*) platitude *f.*

bronch/itis *s.* bronchite *f.*; **~ial** *adj.* bronchique.

bronze *s.* bronze *m.*; *adj.* en bronze; *v.t.* bronzer; *v.t.* & *i.* (*tan*) (se) bronzer.

brooch *s.* broche *f.*

brood *s.* (*young birds*) couvée *f.*; (*pej. human family*) nichée *f.*; **~-mare** *s.* poulinière *f.*; *v.i.*

1. (*bird*) couver; 2. (*fig.* ~ *on, over*) ruminer (sombrement); 3. (*be near*) menacer; **~er** *s.* (1) couveuse *f.*, (*apparatus*) couveuse artificielle *f.*; **~y** *adj.* (1) qui va couver; (2) rêveur.
brook[1] *s.* (*small stream*) ruisseau *m.*; **~let** *s.* ruisselet *m.*
brook[2] *v.t.* (*tolerate, usu. in neg.*) (ne pas) souffrir.
broom *s.* (*brush*) balai *m.*; (*bush*) genêt *m.*; **~stick** *s.* manche à balai *m.*
broth *s.* bouillon *m.*
brothel *s.* bordel *m.*
brother *s.* **1.** (*family* & *eccles.*) frère *m.*; **2.** (*extended use*) compagnon *m.*, ami *m.*, collègue *m.*, confrère *m.*; **~-in-law,** beau-frère *m.*; **~hood** *s.* (1) fraternité *f.*; (2) confraternité *f.*; **3.** (*association*) confrérie *f.*; **~ly** *adj.* fraternel; **~liness** *s.* amour fraternel *m.*
brougham *s.* coupé *m.*
brow *s.* (*eye~*) sourcil *m.*; (*forehead*) front *m.*; (*top of hill*) sommet *m.*; **~beat** *v.t.* rudoyer.
brown *s.* brun *m.*; *adj.* brun; (*tanned*) hâlé; NIGGER-**~**; **to be in a ~ study,** rêver; **~ bread** *s.* pain bis *m.*; **~ paper** *s.* papier gris *m.*; **~ sugar** *s.* cassonnade *f.*; *v.t.* & *i.* brunir; (*cook.*) dorer; **to be ~ed off** (*fam.*) avoir le cafard; **~ed off** *adj.* cafardeux.
browse *v.t.* & *i.* brouter; (*fig.*) feuilleter des livres.
brucellosis *s.* brucellose *f.*
bruise *s.* **1.** (*on person*) contusion *f.*; **2.** (*on fruit, etc.*) talure *f.*; *v.t.* (1) contusionner; (2) taler; **3.** (*cook.*) écraser; **~r** *s.* boxeur *m.*
brunt *s.* choc *m.*; **to bear the ~ of,** (*attack*) soutenir le premier choc de; (*work*) payer de sa personne; (*expense*) payer la plupart des frais.
brush *s.* (*~wood*) brousse *f.*; (*instrument for*): (*scrubbing*) brosse *f.*, (*sweeping*) balai *m.*, (*painting*) pinceau *m.*, (*clothes, hair, nail, teeth, etc.*) brosse *f.*; (*tail of fox*) queue *f.*; (*electr.*; *opt.*) faisceau *m.*; (*skirmish*) escarmouche *f.*; TARR**ed with the same ~; a touch of the** TAR **~**; **~wood** *s.* broussailles *f.pl.*; *v.t.* (*sweep, scrub*) balayer, brosser; **~ against** *v.t.* frôler; **~ aside** *v.t.* écarter; **~ off** *v.t.* & *i.* (s')enlever à la brosse; (*fam.*) snober; **~ up** *v.t.* donner un coup de brosse à; (*fig. fam.*) rafraîchir; **~-up** *s.* coup de brosse *m.*
brusque *adj.* brusque; **~ly** *adv.**; **~ness** *s.* brusquerie *f.*
Brussels *s.* Bruxelles *f.*; **~** (*lace, sprouts*) (dentelle, choux) de Bruxelles.
brutal *adj.* brutal; **~ity** *s.* brutalité *f.*; **~ize** *v.t.* abrutir; **~ly** *adv.**.
brut/e *s.* (*lit.* & *fig.*) brute *f.*; *adj.* (*matter*) brute; (*rude, stupid*) grossier, brute; **by ~e force,** de vive force; **~ish** *adj.* bestial; **~ishly** *adv.**; **~ishness** *s.* bestialité *f.*
B.Sc. (*approx.*) (*degree*) licence ès sciences *f.*; (*title*) licencié(e) ès sciences *m.f.* (*abbrev.*) L. ès sc.
B.S.T. (*abbrev. British Summer Time*) heure d'été anglaise *f.*
B.t.u. (*abbrev. British Thermal Unit*) unité thermale anglaise *f.*
bubble *s.* bulle *f.*; (*fig.*) chimère *f.*; **to** PRICK **the ~**; *v.i.* faire des bulles; (*cook.*) bouillonner; **to ~ over** (*fig.*) déborder (de).
bubonic *adj.* bubonique.
buccaneer *s.* boucanier *m.*
buck *s.* daim *m.*; (*roe~*) chevreuil *m.*; (*male of antelope, chamois, hare, rabbit*) mâle *m.*; (*dandy*) élégant *m.*; **to pass the ~,** renvoyer la balle à qn.; **~skin** *s.* peau de daim *f.*; **~shot** *s.* chevrotine *f.*; *v.i.* (*horse*) faire un saut de mouton; **~ up** (*Eng. pop.*) *v.t.* ragaillardir; *v.i.* se ressaisir; **~ up!** (*pop.*) grouillez-vous!
bucket *s.* seau *m.*; (*pump piston*) piston *m.*; (*mech.*) auget *m.*; **to kick the ~** (*pop.*) casser sa pipe; **~ seat** (*auto. aviat.*) siège-baquet *m.*; **~-shop,** bureau de courtier marron *m.*
buckle *s.* boucle *f.*; *v.t.* boucler; (*~ on*) revêtir; *v.i.* (*wheel*) se voiler; **~ to** (*fam.*) se mettre au boulot; **~r** *s.* bouclier *m.*
buckram *s.* bougran *m.*
buckshee *adj.* & *adv.* (*fam.*) aux frais de la princesse.
buckwheat *s.* sarrasin *m.*
bucolic *adj.* bucolique.
bud *s.* **1.** (*plant*) bourgeon *m.*; **2.** (*flower*) bouton *m.*; **3.** (*agric.*) écusson *m.*; TASTE **~s**; *v.i.* (1) bourgeonner; *v.t.* (3) écussonner; **to be in ~,** bourgeonner; **to** NIP **in the ~**; **~ding** *adj.* (1) bourgeonnant; (*fig.*) en herbe; *s.* (1) bourgeonnement *m.*; (3) écussonnage *m.*
Buddh/a *s.* bouddha *m.*; **~ism** *s.* bouddhisme *m.*; **~ist** *s.* bouddhiste *m.*
buddy *s.* (*fam.*) copain *m.*
budge *v.i.* bouger.
budgerigar *s.* perruche *f.*
budget *s.* budget *m.*; *v.i.* (*fin.*) budgétiser; **~ for,** prévoir; **~ary** *adj.* budgétaire.
buff *s.* (*leather*) buffle *m.*; (*colour*) chamois *m.*; *adj.* chamois; *v.t.* polir.
buffalo *s.* buffle *m.*
buffer *s.* (*rail.*) tampon *m.*; (*fam.*) vieux bonze *m.*; **~ state,** état-tampon *m.*
buffet[1] *s.* **1.** (*blow*) soufflet *m.*; **2.** (*fig.*) coup *m.*; *v.t.* (1) souffleter; (2) frapper; **3.** (*contend with*) se débattre avec; **~ing** *s.* succession de coups *f.*
buffet[2] *s.* (*sideboard*) buffet *m.*; (*refreshments*) buffet *m.*; **~ car** *s.* wagon-restaurant *m.*
buffoon *s.* bouffon *m.*; **~ery** *s.* bouffonneries *f.pl.*
bug *s.* punaise *f.*; (*loosely*) insecte *m.*; (*germ*) microbe *m.*; (*fig.* = *craze*) marotte *f.*; (*hidden micro.*) microphone clandestin *m.*; (*lunar module*) module *m.*; **big ~** (*fam.*) gros bonnet *m.*; *v.t.* faire des écoutes téléphoniques chez; **~bear** *s.* épouvantail *m.*; **~gy** *s.* boghei *or* buggy *m.*
bugger *s.* (*law*) pédéraste *m.*; (*pop.*) bougre *m.*
bugle[1] *s.* (*instrument*) clairon *m.*; *v.i.* sonner du clairon; **~r** *s.* clairon *m.*
bugle[2] *s.* (*plant*) bugle *f.*
build *s.* taille *f.*; *v.t.* bâtir; **~ on,** fonder sur; **~ up** *v.t.* édifier, créer; (*health, strength, etc.*) affermir; **~up** *s.* organisation *f.*; (*publicity*) publicité *f.*; **~er** *s.* entrepreneur *m.*; **~ing** *s.* (*work*) construction *f.*; (*edifice*) bâtiment *m.*, édifice *m.*; **~ing society** *s.* société immobilière *f.*; **built-in** *adj.* encastré; (*fig.*) inhérent; **built-up area,** agglomération urbaine *f.*
bulb *s.* (*bot.*) bulbe *m.*; (*electr.*) ampoule *f.*; **~ous** *adj.* bulbeux.
Bulgar/ia *s.* Bulgarie *f.*; **~ian** *adj.* & *s.m.f.* bulgare.
bulge *s.* bosse *f.*; (*temporary increase in nos. or volume*) vague (de naissances, de scolarisation) *f.*; *v.t.* bourrer; *v.i.* faire une bosse; (*building*) faire ventre.
bulk *s.* (*cargo*) chargement *m.*; (*large shape*) volume *m.*; (*great size*) grandeur *f.*, grosseur *f.*; (*mass*) masse *f.*; **the ~ of,** le gros de; **in ~** (*comm.*) en vrac, en gros; **~ buying** *s.* achat massif *m.*; **~-carrier** *s.* vraquier *m.*; **~head** *s.* cloison *f.*; *v.i.* **~ large,** occuper une place importante; **~y** *adj.* **1.** (*thing*) gros; **2.** (*person*) corpulent; **~iness** *s.* (1) volume *m.*; (2) grosseur *f.*
bull *s.* (*male of cow*) taureau *m.*; (*of other animals*) mâle *m.*; (*Stock Exchange*) haussier *m.*; (*papal edict*) bulle *f.*; (*inconsistent talk*) fariboles *f.pl.*; **to take the ~ by the horns,** prendre le taureau par les cornes; **a ~ in a china shop,** un éléphant dans un magasin de porcelaine; **like a ~ at a gate,** tête baissée; **a** COCK **and ~ story; a** RED **rag to a ~**; **~-baiting** *s.* com-

bat de chiens et de taureaux *m.*; **~dog** *s.* bouledogue *m.*; **~doze** *v.t.* passer au bouldozeur; **~dozer** *s.* bouteur *m.*, bouledozeur *m.*; **~'s-eye** *s.* (*window*) œil de bœuf *m.*; (*sweet*) bonbon *m.*; **to hit the ~'s-eye,** faire mouche; **~fight** *s.* course de taureaux *f.*; **~finch** *s.* bouvreuil *m.*; **~frog** *s.* grenouille d'Amérique *f.*; **~ring** *s.* arène *f.*; **~ock** *s.* bœuf *m.*

bullet *s.* balle *f.*; **~-proof** *adj.* à l'épreuve des balles; **~-proof car,** voiture blindée *f.*; **~-proof jacket,** gilet pare-balles *m.*

bulletin *s.* bulletin *m.*

bullion *s.* lingot *m.*

bully *s.* tyran *m.*; *v.t.* tyranniser; (*school*) brimer; *v.i.* (*hockey*) **~ off,** engager le jeu; *adj.* (*fam.*) épatant; **~ beef** *s.* bœuf en conserve *m.*; (*fam.*) singe *m.*

bulrush *s.* jonc *m.*

bulwark *s.* (*rampart* & *fig.*) rempart *m.*; (*breakwater*) brise-lames *m.*; (*ship's side*) pavois *m.pl.*

bum *s.* (*pop.* = *buttocks*) cul *m.*; (*sheriff's officer*) recors *m.*; (*pop.* = *loafer*) clochard *m.*; **~-boat,** canot d'approvisionnement *m.*; *v.i.* **~ around,** fainéanter.

bumble-bee *s.* bourdon *m.*

bumf *s.* (*pej.* & *fam.*) paperasserie *f.*

bump *s.* **1.** (*blow*) coup *m.*; **2.** (*swelling*) bosse *f.*; **3.** (*aviat.*, *auto.*) cahot *m.*; *v.t.* (1) cogner; (3) cahoter; *v.i.* **~ against,** buter contre; **~ into** (*fig.*) rencontrer par hasard; **~ off** (*fam.*) démolir; **~er** *s.* (*drink*) rasade *f.*; (*auto.*) pare-choc *m.*; *adj.* exceptionnel; **~y** *adj.* (2) couvert de bosses; (3) cahoteux.

bumpkin *s.* péquenot *m.*

bumptious *adj.* suffisant.

bun *s.* (*cook.*) brioche *f.*; (*hair*) chignon *m.*

bunch *s.* (*flowers*) bouquet *m.*; (*veg.*) botte *f.*; (*grapes*) grappe *f.*; (*keys*) trousseau *m.*; (*bananas*) régime *m.*; (*people*) groupe *m.*; **the best of the ~,** le dessus du panier; *v.t.* lier en bouquet, en botte, etc.; *v.i.* se grouper; (*huddle*) se serrer.

bundle *s.* (*veg.*, *hay*, *straw*, *etc.*) botte *f.*; (*package*) paquet *m.*; (*papers*) liasse *f.*; (*wood*) fagot *m.*; *v.t.* empaqueter, emballer; (*in disorder*) entasser; **~ away, off,** renvoyer promener; **~ up,** mettre en liasse.

bung *s.* bondon *m.*; *v.t.* boucher; **~ed up** *adj.* (*sink*, *etc.*) bouché; (*eyes*) poché; **~-hole** *s.* bonde *f.*

bungalow *s.* bungalow *m.*

bungl/e *s.* gâchis *m.*; *v.t.* gâcher; (*fail to accomplish*) rater; **~er** *s.* bousilleur *m.*; **~ing** *adj.* maladroit.

bunion *s.* oignon *m.*

bunk *s.* couchette *f.*; **~-beds,** lits superposés *m.pl.*; (*pop.* = *rubbish*) sornettes *f.pl.*; *v.i.* **to do a ~,** filer.

bunker *s.* (*naut.*) soute *f.*; (*household*) charbonnier *m.*; (*golf*) banquette *f.*; (*mil.*) casemate (blindée) *f.*; *v.t.* mettre en soute; *v.i.* se trouver dans une impasse.

bunkum *s.* sornettes *f.pl.*

bunny *s.* (*fam.*) Jeannot lapin *m.*

Bunsen burner *s.* brûleur Bunsen *m.*

bunting *s.* (*bird*) bruant *m.*; (*flags*) drapeaux *m.pl.*

buoy *s.* bouée *f.*; **life~,** bouée de sauvetage *f.*; **breeches-~,** bouée-culotte *f.*; *v.t.* (*mark with* **~s**) baliser; **~ up,** faire flotter; (*fig.*) soutenir; **~ancy** *s.* légèreté *f.*, insubmersibilité *f.*; (*fig.*) gaieté *f.*, entrain *m.*; (*comm.*) fermeté *f.*; **~ant** *adj.* flottable; (*fig.*) gai, plein d'entrain; (*comm.*) soutenu; **~antly** *adv.* avec entrain.

bur(r) *s.* (*plant*) glouteron *m.*

burble *s.* **1.** (*murmur*) murmure *m.*; **2.** (*incoherent chatter*) bafouillage *m.*; *v.i.* (1) murmurer; (2) bafouiller.

burden *s.* (*load*) fardeau *m.*; (*song*) refrain *m.*; (*theme*) thème *m.*; (*naut.*) port *m.*; (*law*) charge (pécuniaire) *f.*; *v.t.* charger (*with*—de); **~some** *adj.* pesant; (*fig.*) onéreux.

burdock *s.* bardane *f.*

bureau *s.* (*desk*, *office*) bureau *m.*; (*dept.*) service *m.*; (*agency*) agence *f.*; **~cracy** *s.* bureaucratie *f.*; **~crat** *s.* bureaucrate *m.*; **~cratic** *adj.* bureaucratique.

burgee *s.* guidon *m.*

burgeon *v.i.* bourgeonner.

burgess *s.* (*citizen*) citoyen *m.*; (*M.P.*) député *m.*

burgher *s.* bourgeois *m.*; (*South Africa* = *European*) blanc *m.*

burgl/ar *s.* cambrioleur *m.*; **~ar-alarm,** dispositif anti-vol *m.*; **~ary** *s.* cambriolage *m.*; **~e** *v.t.* & *i.* cambrioler.

burgomaster *s.* bourgmestre *m.*

Burgundy *s.* (*geog.*) Bourgogne *f.*; (*wine*) bourgogne *m.*; **B~ian** *adj.* & *s.m.f.* bourguignon(ne).

burial *s.* enterrement *m.*; **~-ground,** cimetière *m.*; **~-service,** office des morts *m.*

burke *v.t.* (*avoid question*) escamoter (la question); (*hush up scandal*) étouffer (un scandale).

burlesque *adj.* & *s.m.* burlesque; *v.t.* parodier.

burly *adj.* de forte carrure.

Burm/a *s.* Birmanie *f.*; **B~ese** *adj.* & *s.m.f.* birman(e).

burn[1] *s.* (*stream*) ruisseau *m.*

burn[2] *s.* brûlure *f.*; *v.t.* brûler; (*tan*) bronzer; *v.i.* brûler, flamber; (*fig.*) brûler (de); **~ away** *v.t.* consumer; **~ alive** *v.t.* brûler vif; **~ down** *v.t.* incendier; *v.i.* baisser; **~ into** (*acid*) *v.t.* ronger; **~ out** *v.t.* brûler jusqu'au bout; *v.i.* s'éteindre; (*fig.*) se consumer; **~ up** *v.t.* consumer; *v.i.* flamber; **~ to ashes** *v.t.* réduire en cendres; **~ one's hand, etc.,** se brûler la main, etc.; **he ~t his fingers** (*fig.*) il lui en a cuit; **~ the candle at both ends,** brûler la chandelle par les deux bouts; **my ears ~,** les oreilles me tintent; **~er** *s.* brûleur *m.*; (*gas*) bec *m.*

burning *s.* brûlage *m.*; (*fire*) incendie *m.*; (*techn.*) cuite *f.*; (*cook.*) brûlé *m.*, **there's a smell of ~,** ça sent le brûlé; *adj.* brûlant, enflammé; (*desire*, *faith*) ardent; (*indignation*) violent; (*pain*) cuisant.

burnish *v.t.* brunir.

burr *s.* (*disc round star*) halo *m.*; (*ridge on metal or paper*) barbe *f.*; (*accent*) grasseyement. *m.*

burrow *s.* terrier *m.*; *v.t.* creuser; *v.i.* (*fig.*) **~ into,** fouiller.

bursar *s.* (*admin.*) économe *m.*; (*student*) boursier *m.*; **~'s office, ~ship,** économat *m.*; **~y** *s.* (*scholarship*) bourse *f.*

burst *s.* (*split*) éclatement *m.*; (*explosion*) explosion *f.*; (*sound*) éclat *m.*; (*of weeping*, *anger*, *etc.*) crise *f.*; (*of joy*, *etc.*) transport *m.*; *v.t.* éclater, crever; (*river*) rompre; (*express feelings*) s'exclamer; (*buttons*) faire sauter; *v.i.* (*boiler*) sauter; (*clouds*, *tyre*) crever; (*door*) s'ouvrir; (*overflow with*) déborder de; **~ in** *v.t.* enfoncer; **~ into,** se précipiter dans; (*laughter*) éclater (de rire); (*tears*) fondre (en larmes); **~ a blood vessel,** en prendre un coup de sang; **~ing** *s.* éclatement *m.*; (*tyre*) crevaison *f.*; (*river*) débordement *m.*

bury *v.t.* (*body*) enterrer; (*thing*) enfouir; (*hide*) cacher; (*fig.*) *v.refl.* se plonger dans; **~ the hatchet,** faire la paix.

bus *s.* autobus *m.*; (*fam.*) **old ~,** vieille bagnole *f.*; **to miss the ~** (*fig. fam.*) manquer le coche; **~-**CONDUCTOR; **~** LANE; **~-**STOP.

busby *s.* colback *m.*, bonnet à poils *m.*

bush[1] *s.* (*shrub*) buisson *m.*; (*woodland*, *etc.*) brousse *f.*; **to** BEAT **about the ~; a** BIRD **in the hand is worth two in the ~; good** WINE

needs no ~; to be ~ed (*fam.*) être claqué; **~-baby** *s.* galago *m.*; **B~man** (*native*) bushman *m.*; **~ telegraph,** téléphone arabe *m.*; **~y** *adj.* buissonneux; (*hair*) touffu; (*eyebrows*) en broussailles.

bush² *s.* (*techn.*) bague *f.*

bushel *s.* boisseau *m.*

business *s.* (*task*) besogne *f.*; (*duty*) devoir *m.*; (*occupation*) métier *m.*; (*profession*) profession *f.*; (*agenda*) ordre du jour *m.*; (*concern, problem*) affaire *f.*; (*comm.*) affaires *f.pl.*; (*firm*) affaire *f.*, maison de commerce *f.*; **on ~,** pour affaires; **to be in ~,** être dans les affaires; **to have ~ with,** avoir affaire à; **to** MEAN **~; to make it one's ~ to,** se faire un devoir de; **to send s.o. about his ~,** envoyer promener qn.; **it's no ~ of yours,** cela ne vous regarde pas; **mind your own ~,** mêlez-vous de ce qui vous regarde; **that's my ~,** c'est mon affaire; **~ hours,** heures d'ouverture *f.pl.*; **~ house,** maison de commerce *f.*; **~like** *adj.* (*person*) pratique; (*thing*) sérieux; **~man,** homme d'affaires *m.*; **~ premises,** locaux commerciaux *m.pl.*

bust *s.* (*sculpture*) buste *m.*; (*part of body*) poitrine *f.*

bustard *s.* outarde *f.*

bustl/e *s.* remue-ménage *m.*; *v.t.* bousculer; *v.i.* se remuer; **~ing** *adj.* (*active*) remuant; (*busy*) affairé.

bus/y *adj.* (*occupied, engaged, in, with, at*) occupé à; **she is ~y preparing the dinner,** elle est occupée à préparer le dîner; **she is ~y with the the preparation of the dinner,** elle est occupée à la préparation du dîner; (*day*) chargé; (*street*) passant; *s.* (*pop.* = *detective*) flic *m.*; *v.refl.* **~y oneself,** s'affairer; (*with, at*) s'occuper à; **~ily** *adv.* activement; (*hurriedly*) avec empressement; **~ybody** *s.* officieux *m.*; **to be a ~ybody,** faire la mouche du coche.

but *s.* mais *m.*; **~ me no ~s,** je ne veux pas de vos mais; *prep.* sauf, **all ~ he,** tous sauf lui; *adv.* ne . . . que, **she is ~ a child,** elle n'est qu'une enfant; *conj.* mais, **not one, ~ two,** pas un, mais deux; sans, **guilty ~ not guilty,** coupable sans être coupable; sans que, **he never goes out ~ that I see him,** il ne sort jamais sans que je m'en aperçoive; **it never rains ~ it pours,** un malheur ne vient jamais seul; **~ for,** sans, **~ for him, we should not be here,** sans lui, nous ne serions pas là; **all ~,** (*adj.*) presque, **all ~ dead,** presque mort; (+ *verb*) peu s'en faut que, **he all ~ lost his job,** peu s'en fallut qu'il ne perdît sa place; **not ~ that,** ce n'est pas à dire que, **he has gone, not ~ that he would have liked to stay,** il est parti, ce n'est pas à dire qu'il n'eût voulu rester.

butane *s.* butane *m.*

butcher *s.* (*lit.* & *fig.*) boucher *m.*; PORK-**~; ~'s shop,** boucherie *f.*; *v.t.* **1.** (*slaughter meat*) abattre; **2.** (*slaughter wantonly*) égorger; **3.** (*fig. ruin book or ms.*) massacrer; **~y** *s.* (1) abattage *m.*; (2) boucherie *f.*; (3) massacre *m.*

butler *s.* maître d'hôtel *m.*

butt *s.* (*wine cask*) tonneau *m.*; (*thicker end, of tool, of weapon*) bout *m.*; crosse *f.*; (*target*) cible *m.*; **~s** *pl.* (*shooting-range*) champ de tir *m.*; (*object of ridicule*) tête de turc *f.*; (*of cigarette*) mégot *m.*; **~-end,** gros bout *m.*; *v.t.* (*goat*) donner un coup de corne à; *v.i.* **~ against,** buter contre; **~ in,** intervenir sans façon.

butter *s.* beurre *m.*; BREAD **and ~; to look as if ~ wouldn't melt in one's mouth,** faire la sainte nitouche; **~-dish,** beurrier *m.*; **~--fingers** *s.* maladroit(e) *m.f.*; **~-fingered** *adj.* maladroit; **~milk** *s.* babeurre *m.*; **~scotch** *s.* caramel au beurre *m.*; **~y** *s.* dépense *f.*; *v.t.* (*cook.*) beurrer; **~ s.o. up** (*fam.*) passer de la pommade à qn.

buttercup *s.* bouton-d'or *m.*

butterfl/y s. papillon *m.*; CABBAGE-**~; to have ~ies in one's stomach,** (*pop.*) avoir la trouille.

buttock *s.* fesse *f.*; (*pl. of horse or cow*) croupe *f.*; (*cook.*) culotte *f.*

button *s.* bouton *m.*; **~hole** *s.* boutonnière *f.*; *v.t.* (*fam.*) cramponner; **~hook** *s.* tire-bouton *m.*; **~s** *s.* chasseur *m.*; *v.t.* & *i.* (**~ up**) (se) boutonner.

buttress *s.* contrefort *m.*; FLYING **~**; (*fig.*) soutien *m.*; *v.t.* arc-bouter; (*fig.*) soutenir.

buxom *adj.* (*plump*) grassouillet; (*comely*) avenant.

buy *s.* achat *m.*; *v.t.* (*lit.* & *fig.*) acheter; **I'll ~ it** (*fig.*) je l'avalerai!; **~ back** *v.t.* racheter; **~ in** *v.t.* acheter; **~ off** *v.t.* se débarasser (de qn.) à prix d'argent; **~ out** (*comm.*) désintéresser; **~ up** *v.t.* accaparer; **~er** *s.* acheteur *m.*; **~ing** *s.* achat *m.*

buzz *s.* bourdonnement *m.*; *v.i.* bourdonner; *v.t.* (*signal*) appeler, téléphoner à; (*spread rumour*) répandre; (*aviat.*) harceler; **~ off,** *v.i.* (*pop.*) filer; **~er** *s.* vibreur *m.*; **~ing** *s.* bourdonnement *m.*

buzzard *s.* busard *m.*, buse *f.*

by *prep.* **1.** (*agency*) par, de; **knocked down ~ a car,** renversé par une auto; **a book ~,** un livre de . . .; **loved ~ all,** aimé de tous; **2.** (*means*) par, à; **~ chance,** par hasard; **~ means of,** à l'aide de; **3.** (*nearness*) près, près de; **sit down ~ me,** asseyez-vous près de moi; **4.** (*measure*) de; **~ far,** de beaucoup; **taller ~ a head,** plus grand d'une tête; **5.** (*time*) **~ day,** pendant le jour; **~ next Monday,** avant lundi prochain; **~ the hour,** à l'heure; **6.** (*manner*) **~ mistake,** par erreur; **~ the rules,** selon les règles; **~ my watch,** d'après ma montre; **7.** (+ *doing, etc.*) en faisant, etc.; **you will find the number ~ looking in the directory,** vous trouverez le numéro en regardant dans l'annuaire; *adv.* de côté; **to put some money ~,** mettre de l'argent de côté; **near ~,** tout près; **~ and ~,** plus tard; **~ the ~,** & **~ the way,** à propos; **~ and large,** généralement; **~ oneself,** tout(e) seul(e).

by *adj.* (*in combination*); **~-election,** élection partielle *f.*; **~gone** *adj.* passé; **to let ~gones be ~gones,** oublier le passé; **~-law,** arrêté municipal *m.*; **~pass** *s.* périphérique *m.*; *v.t.* contourner; **~path,** chemin détourné *m.*; **~--product** *s.* sous-produit *m.*; **~-road, ~way,** ruelle *f.*; **~stander,** spectateur *m.*; **~-street,** rue écartée *f.*; **~word,** dicton *m.*; (*person*) risée *f.*; **to become a ~word,** passer en proverbe.

bye-bye *interj.* au revoir!; **~s** *s.pl.* (*fam.*) dodo *m.*; **go to ~s,** faire dodo.

byre *s.* étable *f.*

Byzantine *adj.* byzantin.

C

C *s.* (*mus.*): (*first note of scale*) do *m.*; (*key*) ut *m.*
cab *s.* **1.** (*taxi*): (*archaic*) fiacre *m.*; (*auto.*) taxi *m.*; HACKNEY **~**; **2.** (*driver's shelter*) cabine *f.*; **~man** *s.* (1) cocher *m.*, chauffeur de taxi *m.*; **~-rank** *s.* station de taxis *f.*
cabal *s.* cabale *f.*; **~istic** *adj.* cabalistique; *v.i.* cabaler.
cabaret *s.* spectacle de variétés *m.*; (*in a night-club*) attractions *f.pl.*
cabbage *s.* chou *m.*; SAVOY **~**; **~ butterfly** *s.* papillon blanc *m.*; **~ lettuce** *s.* laitue pommée *f.*
cabin *s.* (*hut*) cabane *f.*; (*native hut*) case *f.*; (*on ship*) cabine *f.*; (*aviat.*) cabine de pilotage *f.*; (*passenger*) carlingue *f.*; **~-boy** *s.* mousse *m.*; **~-crew** *s.* (*aviat.*) équipage de bord *m.*; **~ cruiser** *s.* petit yacht *m.*, cabin-cruiser *m.*
cabinet *s.* (*private room*; *parl.*; *furniture*) cabinet *m.*; **Shadow C~**, cabinet fantôme *m.*; **~-maker** *s.* ébéniste *m.*; **~-making** *s.* ébénisterie *f.*; **C~ Minister,** ministre *m.*
cable *s.* **1.** (*rope or chain*; *electr.*) câble *m.*; **2.** (*measure*) encablure *f.*; **3.** (*telegram*) câble *m.*; **~-car** *s.* téléférique *or* téléphérique *m.*; **~gram** *s.* câblogramme *m.*; *v.t.* & *i.* (3) câbler.
caboodle *s.* **the whole ~**, tout le tremblement *m.*
caboose *s.* (*ship's kitchen*) coquerie *f.*; (*rail.*) fourgon *m.*
cabotage *s.* cabotage *m.*
cabriole *s.* (*leg of furniture*) pied-de-biche *m.*
cacao *s.* (*seed*) cacao *m.*; (*tree*) cacaoyer *m.*
cachalot *s.* cachalot *m.*
cache *s.* (*hiding-place*) cachette *f.*; (*stores, etc. hidden*) provisions (cachées) *f.pl.*; *v.t.* mettre dans une cachette.
cachet *s.* (*lit.* & *fig.*; *med.*) cachet *m.*
cackle *s.* (*hens*) caquet *m.*; (*geese*) cacardement *m.*; (*fig.*) caquet *m.*; **to cut s.o.'s ~** (*fam.*) clouer le bec à qn.; *v.t.* & *i.* caqueter, cacarder; (*laugh*) glousser.
cacophon/y *s.* cacophonie *f.*; **~ous** *adj.* cacophonique.
cactus *s.* cactus *m.*
cad *s.* mufle *m.*; **~dish** *adj.* mufle.
cadastral *adj.* cadastral.
cadaverous *adj.* cadavéreux.
caddie *s.* (*golf*) caddie *m.*
caddy *s.* boîte à thé *f.*
cadence *s.* (*rhet.*) chute *f.*; (*mus.*) cadence *f.*
cadenza *s.* (*mus.*) cadence *f.*
cadet *s.* (*younger son*) cadet *m.*; (*mil.*) élève-officier *m.*; **~ corps,** préparation militaire supérieure *f.*; **to be in the ~ corps,** faire de la P.M.S.
cadge *v.t.* & *i.* **1.** (*peddle*) colporter; **2.** (*beg*) quémander; (*fam.*) écornifler; **~r** *s.* (1) colporteur *m.*; (2) quémandeur *m.*; (*fam.*) écornifleur *m.*
cadi *s.* cadi *m.*
cadmium *s.* cadmium *m.*
cadre *s.* (*framework*; *mil.*) cadre *m.*
caduc/ity *s.* caducité *f.*; **~ous** *adj.* cad/uc, -uque.
Caesarean, -ian *adj.* **1.** (*relating to Caesar*) césarien; **2. ~ birth,** césarienne *s.f.*
caesura *s.* césure *f.*
caf/é *s.* café-restaurant *m.*; **~eteria,** cafétéria *f.*
caffeine *s.* caféine *f.*
caftan *s.* cafetan *or* caftan *m.*
cage *s.* cage *f.*; *v.t.* encager.
cag/ey *adj.* (*shrewd*) madré; (*unapproachable*) renfermé; (*secretive*) retors; **~ily** *adv.* sans franchise; **~iness** *s.* manque de franchise *m.*
cahoots *s.* **to be in ~ with s.o.** (*fam.*) être de mèche avec qn.
Cain *s.* (*name* & *fig.*) Caïn *m.*; **to** RAISE **~**.
caique *s.* caïque *m.*
cairn *s.* (*heap of stones*) cairn *m.*; (*dog*) terrier cairn *m.*
Cairo *s.* le Caire *m.*
cajol/e *v.t.* (*kindly*) cajoler; (*with flattery*) amadouer; **to ~e s.o. into or out of doing sth.,** amener qn. à faire qch., empêcher qn. de faire qch., par la douceur; **to ~e sth.** (*usu. information*) **out of s.o.** (*fam.*) tirer les vers du nez de qn.; **~ery** *s.* cajolerie *f.*
cake *s.* (*cook.*) gâteau *m.*, (*bread*) galette *f.*; (*fish, etc.*) croquette *f.*; (*soap*) pain *m.*; (*tobacco*) pavé *m.*; **you can't have your ~ and eat it,** on ne peut pas tout avoir; **it's a piece of ~** (*fam.*) c'est du gâteau; **to sell like hot ~s,** se vendre comme des petits pains; **~shop** *s.* pâtisserie *f.*; **~walk** *s.* cake-walk *m.*; *v.t.* couvrir d'une croûte; *v.i.* former une croûte; (*blood, etc.*) se coaguler.
calabash *s.* calebasse *f.*
calamine *s.* calamine *f.*
calamit/y *s.* (*disaster*) calamité *f.*; (*state*) malheur *m.*; **~ous** *adj.* calamiteux.
calcareous *adj.* calcaire.
calc/ium *s.* calcium *m.*; **~ify** *v.t.* & *i.* (se) calcifier; **~ine** *v.t.* & *i.* (se) calciner.
calcul/ate *v.t.* & *i.* (*with figures*) calculer, faire des calculs; (*estimate*) estimer; (*be confident*) compter (sur); (*fam. = suppose, believe*) prévoir; **~able** *adj.* calculable; **~ated** *adj.* (*intentional*) prémédité; (*suited for purpose*) de nature à, fait pour; **~ating** *adj.* (*pej. scheming*) combinard, (*selfish*) intéressé; **~ation** *s.* calcul *m.*; **~ator** *s.* (*pers.* & *machine*) calculateur *m.*; **~ating-machine,** calculatrice *f.*
calculus *s.* (*math.*; *med.*) calcul *m.*
calendar *s.* calendrier *m.*; *v.t.* classer.
calends *s.pl.* (*Roman calendar*) calendes *f.pl.*; **to put sth. off till the Greek C~,** renvoyer qch. aux calendes grecques.
calf *s.* **1.** (*animal*): (*of cow*) veau *m.*, (*other animals*) petit *m.*; **2.** (*part of leg*) mollet *m.*; **cow in ~,** vache qui va vêler; **to kill the fatted ~,** tuer le veau gras; **~-leather,** veau *m.*; **~-love,** amours enfantines *f.pl.*; **to calve** *v.i.* vêler.
calibr/e *s.* (*lit.* & *fig.*) calibre *m.*; **~ate** *v.t.* calibrer, étalonner; **~ation** *s.* étalonnage *m.*
calico *s.* calicot *m.*
California *s.* Californie *f.*
caliph *s.* calife *m.*
calix *s.* calice *m.*
call[1] *s.* **1.** (*shout*; *of bird*) cri *m.*; **2.** (*signal*) appel *m.*; **3.** (*telephone*) coup de téléphone *m.*; **4.** (*vocation*) vocation *f.*; **5.** (*need*) besoin *m.*, raison *f.*; **you have no ~ to,** vous n'avez aucune raison de; **6.** (*short visit*) (courte) visite *f.*; **7.** (*demand*): (*for payment*) appel *m.*; (*for goods*) demande *f.*; **8.** (*at cards*) annonce *f.*; **9.** (*naut., aviat.*) escale *f.*; PORT **of ~**; BECK **and ~**; **on ~**

(*fin.*) à court terme; (*available*) disponible; **within ~**; à portée de voix; **~-box** *see* TELEPHONE; **~-boy** *s.* avertisseur *m.*; **~-girl** *s.* call--girl *f.*; **~-sign** (*radio, aviat.*) indicatif (d'appel) *m.*

call[2] *v.t.* & *i.* (1), (2), (3) appeler; (6) rendre visite, passer; (7) lancer un appel; (8) annoncer; (9) faire escale (à); **10.** (*awaken*) réveiller; **11.** (*~ a meeting*) convoquer; **12.** (*name, describe as; summon*) appeler; **~ again** *v.i.* repasser; **~ away** *v.t.* appeler; (*attention*) distraire; **~ back** *v.t.* rappeler; **~ for** *v.t.* appeler (qn.), aller/venir, chercher (qn.); commander (qch.); (*necessitate*) réclamer; **~ forth** *v.t.* (*emotions*) exciter; (*memories, spirits*) évoquer; (*protests, doubts*) soulever; **~ in** *v.t.* (*fin.*) faire rentrer; (*doctor, etc.*) faire venir; **~ in question** *v.t.* mettre en doute; **~ off** *v.t.* (*cancel*) décommander; (*dog*) rappeler; **~ on** *v.t.* (*visit*) rendre visite à; (*appeal to*) faire appel à; **~ out** *v.t.* faire sortir; (*in duel*) provoquer; (*troops, etc.*) faire intervenir; *v.i.* crier, s'écrier; **~ over** *v.t.* faire l'appel; **~ up** *v.t.* appeler au téléphone; (*mobilise*) mobiliser; **~-up** *s.* appel sous les drapeaux *m.*; **~ upon** *v.t.* (*God*) invoquer; (*s.o. for sth.*) demander (qch. à qn.); (*s.o. to do sth.*) inviter (qn. à faire qch.); **~ to account,** demander des comptes à; **~ attention to,** attirer l'attention de qn. sur qch.; **~ to the bar,** inscrire au barreau; **~ a halt,** crier halte; **~ to mind,** se rappeler; **~ s.o. names,** traiter qn. de tous les noms, traiter qn. d'imbécile etc.; **~ to order,** rappeler à l'ordre; **~ a spade a spade,** appeler les choses par leur nom; **~ to** WITNESS; **to be ~ed,** s'appeler; **so-~ed** *adj.* soi-disant; **~er** *s.* visiteur *m.*; (*telephone*) correspondant *m.*, personne en ligne *f.*; **~ing** *s.* appel *m.*; (*trade, profession*) métier *m.*, profession *f.*; **London ~ing,** ici Londres.

calligraphy *s.* calligraphie *f.*

cal(l)iper *s.* **1.** (*compasses*) compas d'épaisseur *m.*; **2.** (*support for injured leg*) attelle *f.*; *v.t.* (1) calibrer.

call/ous *adj.* **1.** (*of skin*) calleux; **2.** (*fig.*) dur; **~osity** *s.* (1) callosité *f.*; **~ousness** *s.* (2) dureté *f.*

callow *adj.* (*lit.*) sans plumes; (*fig.*) novice; **~ youth** *s.* blanc-bec *m.*

calm *s.* (*also* = CALMNESS) (*lit.* & *fig.*) calme *m.*; **dead ~,** calme plat *m.*; *adj.* calme; (*Eng. fam.* = *impudent*) effronté; **~ly** *adv.**; *v.t.* & *i.* (se) calmer; (*naut.*) *v.i.* calmir; **to ~ down** *v.t.* & *i.* (s') apaiser.

calomel *s.* calomel *m.*

calor/ie *s.* calorie *f.*; **~ific** *adj.* calorifique.

calumn/y *s.* calomnie *f.*; **~iate** *v.t.* calomnier; **~ious** *adj.* calomnieux.

Calvary *s.* Calvaire *m.*

calve *see* CALF.

calypso *s.* calypso *m.*

calyx *s.* calice *m.*

cam *s.* (*mech.*) came *f.*; **~shaft** *s.* arbre à cames *m.*

camber *s.* **1.** (*naut.*) tonture *f.*; **2.** (*road*) bombement *m.*; **3.** (*arch.*) cambrure *f.*; *v.t.* (2) bomber; (3) cambrer.

Cambodia *s.* (*geog.*) Cambodge *m.*; **~n** *adj.* & *s.m.f.* cambodgien(ne).

cambric *s.* batiste *f.*; **~-muslin,** percale *f.*

camel *s.* chameau, chamelle *m.f.*; **~eer** *s.* chamelier *m.*; **~-hair,** poil de chameau *m.*

camellia *s.* camélia *m.*

cameo *s.* camée *m.*

camera *s.* **1.** (*law* = *room*) chambre *f.*; **in ~,** à huis clos; **2.** (*photo.*) appareil photographique *m.*; (*cinema* & *TV*) caméra *f.*; **~man** (*press, cinema, TV*) cadreur *m.*; **~ obscura,** chambre noire *f.*

Cameroon *s.* (République fédérale du) Cameroun; **~ian** *adj.* & *s.m.f.* camerounais(e).

camisole *s.* (*obs.*) cache-corset *m.*; ⚠ camisole (*also obs.*) = **loose jacket.**

camomile *s.* camomille *f.*

camouflage *s.* (*mil.* & *fig.*) camouflage *m.*; *v.t.* camoufler.

camp *s.* (*mil.* & *gen.*) camp *m.*; **holiday ~** (*for children*) colonie de vacances *f.*; (*adult*) club de vacances *m.*; **~-bed** *s.* lit de camp *m.*; **~-chair** *s.* chaise pliante *f.*; **~-follower** *s.* (*hist.*) ribaud(e) *m.f.*; (*fig.*) suiveur *m.*; **~-stool** *s.* pliant *m.*; *v.i.* camper, faire du camping; **~ing** *s.* camping *m.*; **to go ~ing,** faire du camping; *adj.* (*fam.* = *affected*) précieux; (*pop.* = *homosexual*) pédé.

campaign *s.* (*mil.* & *gen., polit.*) campagne *f.*; *v.i.* (*mil.*) faire campagne; (*fig.*) faire campagne (*for, against*—pour, contre); **old ~er** *s.* vétéran *m.*

campan/ile *s.* campanile *m.*; **~ology** *s.* art du carillon *m.*

camphor *s.* camphre *m.*

campion *s.* lychnis *m.*

campus *s.* campus *m.*

can[1] *v.i.* (*be able to*) pouvoir; **~ you see?,** pouvez-vous voir?; (*know how to*) savoir, **~ you swim?,** savez-vous nager?; (*have the right to*) **~ you come out?,** pouvez-vous sortir?; (*be in a position to*) (*person*) être à même de; (*thing*) être possible de; **this ~ be said,** il est possible de dire cela; **this ~ happen,** il est possible que cela arrive.

can[2] *s.* **1.** (*metal container, for milk, etc.*) bidon *m.*; WATER**ing-~**; **2.** (*tin, of food, beer, etc.*) boîte *f.*; **to carry the ~** (*pop.*) payer les pots cassés; **~-**OPENER; *v.t.* (2) mettre en conserve; **~ it!,** (*pop.*) ta gueule!; **~ned music** (*fam.*) musique de conserve *f.*

Canad/a *s.* Canada *m.*; **~ian** *adj.* & *s.m.f.* canadien(ne); **French ~ian,** canadien français *m.*

canal *s.* canal *m.*; **~ize** *v.t.* (*lit.* & *fig.*) canaliser.

canary *s.* (*bird*) serin *m.*, canari *m.*; (*wine*) vin des Canaries *m.*; **C~ Islands** (*or* **Canaries**), îles Canaries *f.pl.*

canasta *s.* canasta *m.*

cancel *v.t.* **1.** (*cross out*) biffer; **2.** (*annul*) annuler; **3.** (*countermand*): (*order, invitation*) décommander; (*plan*) supprimer; **4. ~ each other out,** s'annuler; **5.** (*stamp*) oblitérer; **~lation** *s.* (1) biffure *f.*; (2), (3), (4) annulation *f.*; (5) oblitération *f.*

cancer *s.* cancer *m.*; **~ous** *adj.* cancéreux.

candelabrum *s.* candélabre *m.*

candid *adj.* **1.** (*unprejudiced*) impartial; **2.** (*unreserved*) sincère; **3.** (*outspoken*) franc; **~ly** *adv.* (1)*; (2)*; (3)*; ⚠ candide = **innocent, pure.**

candida/te *s.* candidat(e) *m.f.* (*for, in*—à); **~cy, ~ture** *s.* candidature *f.*

candle *s.* (*tallow*) chandelle *f.*; (*wax*) bougie *f.*; (*church*) cierge *m.*; (*electr.*) bougie *f.*; **not to be** FIT **to hold a ~ to; to** BURN **the ~ at both ends; by ~-light,** à la chandelle; **~ grease** *s.* suif *m.*; **C~mas** *s.* Chandeleur *f.*; **~-power** *s.* bougie *f.*; **~stick** *s.* chandelier *m.*; (*flat*) bougeoir *m.*

candour *s.* (*freedom from prejudice*) impartialité *f.*; (*sincerity*) franchise *f.*; ⚠ candeur = **purity.**

cand/y *s.* sucre candi *m.*; (*U.S.*) bonbon *m.*; **~y-**FLOSS; *v.t.* (*fruit*) glacer; (*sugar*) faire cristalliser; **~ied** *adj.* (*fruit*) glacé, confit; (*fig.*) mielleux.

cane *s.* **1.** (*bamboo, sugar, walking stick*) canne *f.*; **2.** (*used for punishment*) verge *m.*; **sugar-~,** canne à sucre *f.*; **~-sugar,** sucre de canne *m.*; *v.t.* (1) (*weave ~; for chair, etc.*) canner; (2) fouetter.

canine *adj.* canin; ~ **tooth,** canine *s.f.*
canister *s.* (*tea*) boîte (à thé) *f.*; (*shot*) boîte à mitraille *f.*
canker *s.* **1.** (*disease, human & animal*) ulcère *f.*; **2.** (*bot.* & *fig.*) chancre *m.*; **3.** (*caterpillar*) ver rongeur *m.*; *v.t.* (1) ulcérer; (2) corrompre; (3) ronger; ~**ed** *adj.* ulcéré.
cannabis *s.* chanvre indien *m.*
cannibal *adj.* & *s.m.f.* anthropophage, cannibale; ~**ism** *s.* anthropophagie *f.*, cannibalisme *m.*; ~**ize** *v.t.* (*mech.*) démonter pour fournir des pièces de rechange.
cannon *s.* **1.** (*gun, mech.*) canon *m.*; **2.** (*billiards*) carambolage *m.*; ~**ade** *s.* canonnade *f.*; ~**-ball,** boulet de canon *m.*; ~**-fodder** (*fam.*) chair à canon *f.*; *v.i.* (2) caramboler; ~ **into** *v.i.* se heurter contre.
cannot *see* CAN.
canoe *s.* canoë *m.*; (*native*) pirogue *f.*; **to** PADDLE **one's own** ~; *v.i.* faire du canoë; ~**ist** *s.* canoéiste *m.f.*
canon *s.* **1.** (*principle*) canon *m.*; **2.** (*churchman*) chanoine *m.*; **3.** (*mus.*) canon *m.*; *adj.* (*church law*) droit canon *m.*; ~**ical** *adj.* (1) canonial; (*eccles.*) canonique; ~**icals** *s.pl.* vêtements sacerdotaux *m.pl.*; ~**ize** *v.t.* canoniser.
canopy *s.* (*over bed, throne*) baldaquin *m.*; (*over doorway*) marquise *f.*; (*arch.*) baldaquin *m.*; (*aviat.*) verrière *f.*; (*fig.* = *sky*) voûte *f.*
cant[1] *s.* (*slanting surface, position*) inclinaison *f.*; (*oblique push*) poussée déviatrice *f.*; *v.t.* & *i.* pencher, s'incliner.
cant[2] *s.* (*special lang.*) jargon *m.*; (*hypocrisy*) tartuferie *f.*
cantaloup *s.* cantaloup *m.*
cantankerous *adj.* hargneux.
cantata *s.* cantate *f.*
canteen *s.* (*mil.*; *bar*) cantine *f.*; (*box of cutlery*) ménagère *f.*
canter *s.* petit galop *m.*; *v.t.* & *i.* mener, aller au petit galop.
canticle *s.* cantique *m.*
cantilever *adj.* & *s.m.* (*techn.*) cantilever; ~ **bridge,** pont cantilever *m.*
canto *s.* chant *m.*
canton *s.* (*Swiss state*) canton *m.*; *v.t.* (*mil.*) cantonner; ~**ment** *s.* (*mil.*) cantonnement *m.*
cantor *s.* chantre *m.*
canvas *s.* (*cloth for sails, tents, painting*) toile *f.*; (*for embroidery*) canevas *m.*; (= *a picture*) toile *f.*; **under** ~, (*camping*) sous la tente; (*naut.*) à la voile.
canvass *v.t.* & *i.* (*discuss*) discuter; (*ask for votes*) solliciter la voix de qn.; (*ask for custom*) visiter la clientèle, faire du porte à porte.
canyon *s.* gorge *f.*; (*in foreign countries*) cañon *m.*
cap *s.* **1.** (*headgear*) bonnet *m.*, (*indoor, of female servants*) coiffe *f.*, (*outdoor*) casquette *f.*, (*law, acad.*) toque *f.*, (*mil.*) képi *m.*, casquette *f.*, (*naut.*) bonnet *m.*, béret *m.*, (*skull-*~) calotte *f.*; FORAGE-~; **if the** ~ FITS **wear it; to set one's** ~ **at,** jeter son dévolu sur; ~ **in hand,** chapeau bas; **2.** (*lid*) couvercle *m.*; (*of bottle*) capsule *f.*, (*of pipe, fountain-pen*) capuchon *m.*; *v.t.* (1) (*fig., crown*) couronner; (2) couvrir; (*bottle*) capsuler; **3.** (*fig. outdo*) surpasser.
capab/le *adj.* **1.** (*susceptible of*) susceptible de; **2.** (*having power for*) capable de; **3.** (*competent*) compétent; ~**ility** *s.* (1) possibilité *f.*; (2) capacité *f.*; (3) compétence *f.*
capac/ity *s.* (*power to contain, to produce, cubic content, mental power*) capacité *f.*; (*function or character*) qualité *f.* ~**ious** *adj.* spacieux; ~**itate** *v.t.* rendre capable de; (*law*) habiliter à.
caparison *s.* caparaçon *m.*; *v.t.* caparaçonner.
cape[1] *s.* (*short cloak*) cape *f.*; (*eccles.*) chape *f.*
cape[2] *s.* (*headland*) cap *m.*; **C~ Town,** le Cap; **C~ of Good Hope,** cap de Bonne Espérance *m.*; **C~ Coloured** *s.* métis(se) du Cap *m.f.*; **C~ gooseberry** *s.* (*fam.*) amour-en-cage *m.*
caper[1] *s.* (*cook.*) câpre *f.*
caper[2] *s.* (*jump*) cabriole *f.*; **to cut a** ~, faire des cabrioles; *v.i.* cabrioler.
capillary *adj.* capillaire.
capital *s.* (*city*) capitale *f.*; (*letter*) majuscule *f.*; (*comm.*) capital *m.*; (*arch.*) chapiteau *m.*; **to make** ~ **out of sth.,** tirer parti de qch.; *adj.* **1.** (*principal*) principal; **2.** (*fam.* = *excellent*) formidable; **3.** (*law*; *fig.*) capital; ~ **punishment,** peine de mort *f.*; *interj.* parfait!; ~**ism** *s.* capitalisme *m.*; ~**ist** *s.* capitaliste *m.f.*; ~**ize** *v.t.* (*fin.*) capitaliser; (*fig.*) tourner à son profit; ~**ly** *adv.* (1)*, (2)*.
capitation *s.* capitation *f.*
capitul/ate *v.i.* (*mil.* & *fig.*) capituler; ~**ation** *s.* capitulation *f.*; (*summary*) résumé *m.*
capon *s.* chapon *m.*
capric/e *s.* (*whim*) caprice *m.*; (*art*) capriccio *m.*; ~**ious** *adj.* capricieux; ~**iously** *adv.**.
capsicum *s.* (*red*) piment *m.*; (*green*) poivron *m.*
capsize *v.t.* & *i.* (faire) chavirer.
capstan *s.* cabestan *m.*
capsule *s.* (*bot., pharm., med.*) capsule *f.*; (*space*) module *m.*
captain *s.* (*mil., sport, of industry*) capitaine *m.*; (*navy*) capitaine de vaisseau *m.*; (*merchant navy*) commandant *m.*; (*aviat.*) commandant de bord *m.*; *v.t.* (*mil., naut., aviat.*) commander; (*sport*) mener; (*comm.*) diriger.
caption *s.* **1.** (*law*) arrestation *f.*; **2.** (*legend under picture*) légende *f.*; (*cinema*) sous-titre *m.*
captious *adj.* (*fallacious*) captieux; (*ready to find fault*) pointilleux.
captiv/e *s.* capti/f, -ve *m.f.*; (*in confinement*) prisonni/er, -ère *m.f.*; *adj.* (*lit.* & *fig.*) captif; **to take, to lead, to hold** ~**e,** faire, tenir, prisonnier; ~**ate** *v.t.* captiver; ~**ating** *adj.* captivant; ~**ity** *s.* captivité *f.*
capt/or *s.* (*f. -ress*) celui (celle) qui a capturé; ravisseur *m.*; ~**ture** *s.* (*action & thing*) capture *f.*; *v.t.* capturer.
Capuchin *s.* (*friar*) capucin *m.*; (c~ *monkey*) sapajou *m.*
car *s.* voiture *f.*; (*motor*) auto(mobile) *f.*; DINING-~; SALOON ~; SLEEPING-~; TRAM~; ~-PARK; ~**port** *s.* auvent *m.*
caracole *s.* caracole *f.*; *v.i.* caracoler.
carafe *s.* carafe *f.*
caramel *s.* caramel *m.*; *adj. invar.* caramel; ~**ize** *v.t.* (*cook.*) caraméliser.
carapace *s.* carapace *f.*
carat *s.* carat *m.*
caravan *s.* (*company* & *vehicle*) caravane *f.*; ~**serai** *s.* caravansérail *m.*
caraway *s.* (*cook.*) carvi *m.*; ~ **seed,** graine de carvi *f.*
carbine *s.* carabine *f.*
carbo- (*in combination*); ~**hydrate,** hydrate de carbone *m.*; ~**lic** (*acid*), phénol *m.*; ~**rundum,** carborundum *m.*
carbon *s.* carbone *m.*; ~ **copy** *s.* carbone *m.*; ~ **dating,** datation à l'aide du carbone 14 *f.*; ~ **paper** *s.* papier carbone *m.*; ~**ize** *v.t.* carboniser.
carboy *s.* bonbonne *f.*
carbuncle *s.* (*precious stone*) escarboucle *f.*; (*tumour*) anthrax *m.*
carburettor *s.* (*auto.*) carburateur *m.*
carcass *s.* (*of animal*; *pej. of person*; *fig.*) carcasse *f.*
card[1] *s.* carte *f.*; **admission** ~, carte d'entrée *f.*; **Christmas** ~, carte de Noël *f.*; **credit** ~, carte de garantie *f.*; **dance** ~, carnet de bal *m.*; **identity** ~, carte d'identité *f.*; **playing-**~,

carte à jouer *f.*; **post~,** carte postale *f.*; **punched ~,** carte perforée *f.*; **race-~,** programme (des courses) *m.*; **ration ~,** carte d'alimentation *f.*; **record ~,** fiche *f.*; **visiting-~,** carte de visite *f.*; **wedding-, funeral- etc. ~,** faire-part *m.*; (*fig.* = *eccentric*) original *m.*; **~s** (*game*) jeu de cartes *m.*; **to** PLAY **~s; it's on the ~s,** il est probable; **to have a ~ up one's sleeve,** avoir plus d'une carte dans son jeu; **to get one's ~s,** être congédié; **~board** *s.* carton *m.*; **~ index** *s.* fichier *m.*; **~-index** *v.t.* classer; **~-sharper** *s.* tricheur *m.*; **~-table** *s.* table de jeu *f.*; **~-trick** *s.* tour de cartes *m.*

card[2] *s.* (*text.*) carde *f.*; *v.t.* carder.

card/iac *adj.* & *s.m.f.* cardiaque; **~iograph** *s.* cardiographe *m.*; **~iogram** *s.* cardiogramme *m.*

cardigan *s.* cardigan *m.*

cardinal *s.* cardinal *m.*; *adj.* cardinal.

care *s.* **1.** (*sorrow*) souci *m.*; **2.** (*anxiety*) sollicitude *f.*, (*worry*) inquiétude *f.*; **3.** (*task*) charge *f.*, (*act*) soin *m.*; **4.** (*attention*) attention *f.*; **~ of** (*abbrev. c/o*) aux bons soins de (*abbrev.* a.b.s.); **take ~!,** attention!; **take ~ of,** prendre soin de; *v.t.* & *i.* (1), (2) se soucier (de), s'inquiéter (de); (3) (**~** *for*) s'occuper de; (*child, invalid*) soigner; **5.** (*be inclined to*) trouver plaisir (à); **I don't ~,** ça m'est égal; **I couldn't ~ less,** je m'en fiche; **not to ~ a** FIG; **~ for** (= *like*) trouver (qch., qn.) sympathique; **~taker** *s.* gardien *m.*; (*of block of flats*) concierge *m.f.*; **~free** *adj.* insouciant; **~ful** *adj.* (*person*) soigneux, prudent; (*work, appearance, etc.*) soigné; **to be ~ful,** faire attention, prendre garde (à); **~fully** *adv.* avec soin, avec prudence; **~fulness** *s.* soin *m.*, attention *f.*; **~less** *adj.* **1.** (*without ~*) insouciant; **2.** (*negligent*) négligent; **3.** (*inattentive*) inattentif; **4.** (*not artificial*) spontané; **5.** (*without thought*) irréfléchi; **~lessly** *adv.* (1) avec insouciance; (2) avec négligence; (3) sans faire attention; (4)*; (5) sans réfléchir; **~lessness** *s.* (1) insouciance *f.*; (2) négligence *f.*; (3) inattention *f.*; (4) spontanéité *f.*; (5) imprévoyance *f.*; **~-worn** *adj.* rongé par le souci.

careen *v.t.* & *i.* caréner.

career *s.* **1.** (*rapid progression*) course *f.*; **2.** (*profession, etc.*) carrière *f.*; *v.i.* (1) aller à toute vitesse; *adj.* (**~** *diplomat, etc.*) de carrière; **~ist** *s.* arriviste *m.f.*

caress *s.* caresse *f.*; *v.t.* caresser.

caret *s.* (*techn.*) signe d'omission *m.*

cargo *s.* cargaison *f.*; **~ ship** *s.* cargo *m.*

Carib *adj.* & *s.m.f.* caraïbe; **~bean** *adj.* caraïbe; *s.* (*geog.*) les Antilles *f.pl.*

caribou *s.* caribou *m.*

caricatur/e *s.* caricature *f.*; *v.t.* caricaturer; **~ist** *s.* caricaturiste *m.f.*

carmine *adj.* & *s.m.* carmin.

carmelite *s.* carmélite *f.*

carn/age *s.* carnage *m.*; **~al** *adj.* charnel; (*law*) sexuel; **~ivore** *s.* carnivore *m.*; **~ivorous** *adj.* carnivore.

carnation *s.* œillet *m.*

carnival *s.* (*eccles.*) carnaval *m.*; (*gen.*) fête *f.*

carol *s.* chant *m.*; (*Christmas ~*) noël *m.*; (*of birds*) ramage *m.*; *v.i.* chanter.

carotid *s.* carotide *f.*; *adj.* carotidien.

carouse *s.* (& **carousal**) beuverie *f.*; *v.i.* faire la noce.

carp[1] *s.* (*fish*) carpe *f.*

carp[2] *v.i.* (*find fault*) trouver à redire (à).

carpent/er *s.* charpentier *m.*; (*joiner*) menuisier *m.*; *v.t.* & *i.* charpenter, menuiser; **~ry** *s.* charpenterie *f.*, menuiserie *f.*

carpet *s.* (*floor covering* & *fig.*) tapis *m.*; (*of flowers etc.*) parterre *m.*; **to be on the ~,** être sur la sellette; **to put out the** RED **~; to sweep sth. under the ~** (*fig.*) enterrer qch., étouffer (un scandale), jeter le manteau de Noé sur qch.; **~-bagger** *s.* aventurier politique *m.*; **~-sweeper** *s.* balai mécanique *m.*; *v.t.* recouvrir d'un tapis.

carriage *s.* (*of goods*) transport *m.*; (*cost of*) port *m.*; (*bearing*) maintien *m.*; (*vehicle*) voiture *f.*; **gun-~,** affût *m.*; HACKNEY **~; railway ~,** wagon *m.*; (*mech. of typewriter, etc.*) chariot *m.*; **~ forward,** port-dû; **~ free,** franco de port; **~ paid,** port payé; **~** CLOCK; **~way** *s.* chemin carrossable *m.*; (*traffic lane*) voie *f.*

carrier *s.* (*person*) transporteur *m.*; (*on bicycle, etc.*) porte-bagages *m.*; (*conveyor of disease*) vecteur *m.*; **~-bag** *s.* sac (en papier) *m.*; **~** PIGEON; AIRCRAFT-**~**.

carrion *s.* (*lit.* & *fig.*) charogne *f.*

carrot *s.* carotte *f.*; **~y** *adj.* (*colour of hair*) roux.

carry *v.t.* (*convey*) porter; (*water*) amener; (*sound*) conduire; (*transport*) transporter; (*support*) supporter; (*have on person*) porter sur soi; (*take by force*) emporter; (*parl. admin.* = *vote*) voter; (*fin.*) reporter; (*math.*) retenir; *v.i.* porter; **~ all before one,** triompher; **~ one's audience with one,** entraîner ses auditeurs; **~ the** CAN; **~** COALS **to Newcastle; ~ conviction,** emporter la conviction; **~ the day,** l'emporter; **~ oneself,** se comporter; **~ a point,** faire adopter un avis; **~ the war into the enemy's camp,** porter la guerre chez l'ennemi; **~ weight,** avoir du poids; CASH **and ~**; FETCH **and ~**; **~-**COT; **~ away** *v.t.* emporter; **be carried away** (*fig.*) être transporté; **~ back** *v.t.* (*person*) ramener; (*thing*) rapporter; **~ forward** *v.t.* (*fin.*) reporter; (*math.*) retenir; **~ off** *v.t.* (*prize*) remporter, (*person*) enlever, (*fig.*) faire accepter; **~ it off** (*fig.*) s'imposer; **~ on** *v.t.* (*business*) diriger, (*profession, trade*) exercer, (*conversation*) soutenir, (*correspondence*) entretenir; **~ on** *v.i.* (*continue*) continuer, poursuivre; (*fig. fam.*) se comporter mal, flirter; **~ out** *v.t.* emporter, (*order*) exécuter, (*experiment*) effectuer, (*obligation*) satisfaire à, (*theory*) mettre en pratique, (*idea*) réaliser; **~ over** *v.t.* reporter; **~ through** *v.t.* mener à terme.

cart *s.* charrette *f.*; PUSH-**~**; **to put the ~ before the horse,** mettre la charrue devant les bœufs; **in the ~** (*fam.*) dans le pétrin; **~-horse** *s.* cheval de trait *m.*; **~-**WHEEL; **~age** *s.* transport *m.*; **~er** *s.* camionneur *m.*; *v.t.* & *i.* transporter.

cartilag/e *s.* cartilage *m.*; **~inous** *adj.* cartilagineux.

cartograph/y *s.* cartographie *f.*; **~er** *s.* cartographe *m.f.*

carton *s.* carton *m.*

cartoon *s.* (*painting*) carton *m.*; (*humorous drawing*) dessin satirique *m.*; (*cinema*) dessin animé *m.*; **strip ~,** bande dessinée *f.*

cartridge *s.* cartouche *f.*; **~ paper,** bristol *m.*

carv/e *v.t.* & *i.* **1.** (*meat*) découper; **2.** (*wood* & *stone*) sculpter, tailler; **~e out** *v.t.* tailler; **~e up** *v.t.* (*animal*) dépecer; (*fig.*) diviser; **~er** *s.* (1) couteau à découper *m.*; (2) sculpteur *m.*; **~ing** *s.* (1) découpage *m.* (2) sculpture *f.*; *adj.* **~ing knife** *s.* couteau à découper *m.*

caryatid *s.* cariatide *f.*

cascade *s.* (*lit.* & *fig.*) cascade *f.*; *v.i.* tomber en cascade.

case[1] *s.* (*instance*) cas *m.*; (*situation*) situation *f.*; (*condition*) état *m.*; (*law*) cause *f.*; (*ling.*) cas *m.*; **in any ~,** en tout cas; **in that ~,** dans ce cas-là, en ce cas; **that is not the ~,** il n'en est pas ainsi; **in ~ he comes,** en cas qu'il vienne, au cas où il viendrait; **in ~ of need, etc.,** en cas de besoin, etc.; **~-book** *s.* recueil de jurisprudence *m.*; **~ history** *s.* dossier (médical) *m.*; **~-law** *s.* précédents *m.pl.*; **~work** *s.* étude sur dossier *f.* ; TEST **~**.

case[2] *s.* (*box*) boîte *f.*; (*packing*) caisse *f.*; (*suit*~) valise *f.*; (*for cigarettes, glasses, etc.*) étui *m.*; (*for watch, torch, etc.*) boîtier *m.*; (*auto.*) carter *m.*; (*display*) vitrine *f.*; (*med.*) trousse *f.*; (*covering*) enveloppe *f.*; PILLOW~; VANITY ~; (*print.*) casse *f.*; **upper ~, lower ~,** haut de casse, bas de casse; **~-harden** *v.t.* aciérer; (*fig.*) endurcir; *v.t.* mettre en caisse, envelopper; **casing** *s.* enveloppe *f.*; (*techn.*) revêtement *m.*
casemate *s.* casemate *f.*
casement *s.* croisée *f.*
cash *s.* argent *m.*; (*ready money*) espèces *f.pl.*; **~ on delivery,** livraison contre remboursement *f.*; **~ and carry (store),** libre service de gros *m.*; **~-book** *s.* livre de caisse *m.*; **~-box** *s.* caisse *f.*; **~ desk** *s.* caisse *f.*; **~ price** *s.* prix au comptant *m.*; **~ register** *s.* caisse enregistreuse *f.*; **~ier** *s.* caissier *m.*; *v.t.* **~ a cheque,** (*of bank*) encaisser, changer; (*of customer*) toucher (un chèque); **~ in on,** tirer profit de.
cashew (nut) *s.* anacarde *m.*
cashier *v.t.* (*mil.*) casser.
cashmere *s.* cachemire *m.*
casino *s.* casino *m.*
cask *s.* tonneau *m.*; **~et** *s.* coffret *m.*
cassava *s.* manioc *m.*
casserole *s.* braisière *f.*, (*fam.*) cocotte, terrine *f.*; (*cook.*) daube *f.* ⚠ casserole = **saucepan.**
cassette *s.* cassette *f.*
cassock *s.* soutane *f.*
cast *s.* **1.** (*throw*) (*of missile*) jet *m.*; (*of dice, line*) coup *m.*; **2.** (*mould*): (*container*) moule *m.*; (*result*) moulage *m.*; (*plaster*) plâtre *m.*; **3.** (*theat.*) distribution *f.*; **4.** (*type*) caractère *m.*, disposition *f.*; **5.** (*squint*) **to have a ~,** loucher; *adj.* (2) fondu; **~-** IRON; *v.t.* & *i.* (1) (*dice, spell, anchor, glance*) jeter; (*line*) lancer; (*vote*) donner; (*light, shadow*) projeter; (*lots*) tirer au sort; (*shed skin, horns*) se dépouiller de, (*bird*) muer; (*add up*) additionner; **ne'er ~ a** CLOUT; **the** DIE **is ~**; (2) couler; (3) distribuer (les rôles); **~ about for,** chercher le moyen de; **~ ashore** *v.t.* échouer; **be ~ ashore,** faire naufrage; **~ aside** *v.t.* rejeter; **~ away** *v.t.* repousser; **~-away** *s.* naufragé *m.*; **~ down** *v.t.* (*eyes, etc.*) baisser; (*fig.*) abattre; **~ off** *v.t.* rejeter, se dépouiller de, (*knitting*) arrêter les mailles; (*naut.*) larguer; **~ -off clothing,** *s.* défroque *f.*; **~ on** *v.t.* (*knitting*) monter les mailles; **~ out** *v.t.* expulser, chasser; **~ing vote** *s.* voix prépondérante *f.*
castanet *s.* (*usu. pl.*) castagnette *f.*
caste *s.* caste *f.*; **to lose ~,** déroger.
castigat/e *v.t.* (*chastise*) châtier; (*criticise*) critiquer (sévèrement); **~ion** *s.* châtiment *m.*
cast/le *s.* (*building*) château *m.*; (*chess*) tour *f.*; **~s in the air, in Spain,** châteaux en Espagne; **~ellated** *adj.* crénelé; *v.t.* & *i.* (*chess*) roquer.
castor *s.* (*for sugar, etc.*) saupoudroir *m.*; (*on furniture*) roulette *f.*; **~** SUGAR; **~ oil,** huile de ricin *f.*
castrat/e *v.t.* (*lit.* & *fig.*) châtrer; **~ion** *s.* castration *f.*
casual *adj.* **1.** (*by chance*) fortuit; **2.** (*irregular, impermanent*) temporaire; **3.** (*easy-going, unmethodical*) désinvolte; **4.** (*clothes*) (vêtements) de repos; *s.* (*workman*) travailleur temporaire *m.*; **~ly** *adv.* (1)*, par hasard; (2)*; (3) avec désinvolture; **~ty** *s.* (*mishap*) accident *m.*; (*injured person*) accidenté(e) *m.f.*; **~ties** *s.pl.* (*in war*) pertes, *f.pl.*, morts et blessés *m.pl.*; **~ty department, ward** *s.* salle des accidentés *f.*
casuist *s.* casuiste *m.*; **~ry** *s.* casuistique *f.*
cat *s.* chat(te) *m.f.*; (*tom*) matou *m.*; (*wild*) félin *m.*; (*fig. usu. of woman*) chipie *f.*; WILD ~; **~-o'-nine-tails** *s.* chat à neuf queues *m.*; **to put the ~ among the pigeons,** mettre le loup dans la bergerie; **a ~ may look at a king,** un chien regarde bien un évêque; **to wait and see which way the ~ jumps,** attendre pour voir où souffle le vent; **to let the ~ out of the bag,** vendre la mèche; **room to swing a ~,** de la place pour se retourner; **to lead a ~-and-dog life,** vivre comme chien et chat; **to play ~ and mouse with s.o.,** jouer au chat et à la souris avec qn.; **to** BELL **the ~**; **~ burglar** *s.* monte-en-l'air *m.*; **~call** *s.* sifflet *m.*; **~gut** *s.* corde be boyau *f.*; **~kin** *s.* (*bot.*) chaton *m.*; **~mint** *s.* (*bot.*) cataire *f.*; **~nap** *s.* sommeil léger *m.*; **~nap** *v.i.* ne dormir que d'un œil; **~walk** *s.* (*naut., aviat.*) passavant *m.*, coursive *f.*; **~'s-cradle** *s.* jeu du berceau *m.*; **~'s-eye** (*in road*) cataphote *m.*; **~'s-paw** *s.* dupe *f.*; **~ty** *adj.* sournois.
cataclysm *s.* cataclysme *m.*
catacomb *s.* catacombe *f.*
catafalque *s.* catafalque *m.*
catalepsy *s.* catalepsie *f.*
catalogue *s.* catalogue *m.*; *v.t.* cataloguer.
catalyst *s.* (*lit.* & *fig.*) catalyseur *m.*
catamaran *s.* catamaran *m.*
catapult *s.* (*hist., mil., aviat.*) catapulte *f.*; (*weapon, child's toy*) fronde *f.*, lance-pierres *m.*; *v.t.* & *i.* catapulter.
cataract *s.* (*waterfall*; *eye disease*) cataracte *f.*; (*downpour*) déluge *m.*
catarrh *s.* catarrhe *m.*
catastroph/e *s.* catastrophe *f.*; **~ic** *adj.* (*lit.* & *fig. fam.*) catastrophique.
catch *s.* **1.** (*act of ~ing*) prise *f.*, (*cricket*) prise de la balle *f.*, (*fish caught*) pêche *f.*; **2.** (*trick*) attrape *f.*; **3.** (*mech.*): (*buckle*) ardillon *m.*, (*door*) loquet *m.*, (*lock*) mentonnet *m.*; SAFETY ~; **4.** (*mus.*) canon *m.*; **5.** (*fam. person*) parti *m.*; **6.** (*fragment of conversation*) bribe *f.*; **with a ~ in one's voice,** d'une voix entrecoupée; *v.t.* & *i.* (1) (*lit.* & *fig.*) saisir; (*attention*) attirer; (*ball*) prendre; (*overtake*, **~** *up with*) rattraper; (*train, etc.*; *fish*; *cold, disease*) attraper; (*grip* & *tear*) accrocher; (*become entangled in*) s'enchevêtrer dans; (*of fire, etc., begin to burn*) prendre (feu); (2) attraper; (*detect, surprise*) surprendre (*at, in*— à); **~ it** *v.i.* (*fam.*) écoper; **~ at,** s'accrocher à; **~ on** *v.i.* (*fam.*) prendre; **~ out** *v.t.* (*fam.*) pincer; **~-phrase** *s.* rengaine *f.*; **~word** *s.* slogan *m.*; **~ing** *adj.* contagieux; **~ment** *s.* captage *m.*
catech/ize *v.t.* (*eccles.*) catéchiser; (*gen.*) interroger; **~ism,** catéchisme *m.*
categor/y *s.* catégorie *f.*; **~ical** *adj.* catégorique; **~ically** *adv.**; **~ize** *v.t.* classer par catégories.
cater *v.i.* approvisionner; **~ for,** pourvoir à; **~er** *s.* fournisseur *m.*; **~ing** *s.* approvisionnement *m.*; (*food*) alimentation *f.*
caterpillar *s.* (*bot., mech.*) chenille *f.*; **~ tractor,** tracteur à chenilles *m.*
caterwaul *v.i.* miauler; (*fig.*) faire du chahut; **~ing** *s.* miaulement *m.*; (*fig.*) sabbat *m.*
cathedral *s.* cathédrale *f.*
cathode *s.* (*electr.*) cathode *f.*; *adj.* cathodique.
catholic *adj.* (*eccles.*) catholique; (*universal*) universel; *s.m.f.* catholique; **~ism** *s.* catholicisme *m.*
cattle *s.* bétail *m.*; **~-breeder,** éleveur (de bétail) *m.*; **~-breeding** *s.* élevage (de bétail) *m.*; **~-shed,** étable *f.*; **~-truck** *s.* bétaillère *f.*
caucus *s.* comité électoral *m.*
cauldron *s.* chaudron *m.*
cauliflòwer *s.* chou-fleur *m.*
caulk *v.t.* (*naut.*) calfater.
caus/e *s.* (*person or thing that produces effect*) cause *f.*; (*reason for action*) motif *m.*; (*justification*) raison *f.*, **there is no ~e to,** il n'y a pas de raison de; (*law*) cause *f.*; (*object of efforts*) but *m.*; **to make common ~e with,** faire cause commune avec; *v.t.* (*have as result*) causer; (*cause to be done*)

faire faire; **he ~ed him to fall,** il l'a fait tomber; **he ~ed him to do it,** il le lui a fait faire; **~al** *adj.* causal; **~ation** *s.* causalité *f.*; **~eless** *adj.* sans cause.
causeway *s.* chaussée *f.*
caustic *adj.* (*lit.* & *fig.*) caustique.
cauteriz/e *v.t.* cautériser; **~ation** *s.* cautérisation *f.*
caut/ion *s.* (*prudence*) prudence *f.*; (*warning*) avertissement *m.*; (*pop.* = *person*) numéro *m.*; **~ money,** cautionnement *m.*; **~ionary** *adj.* avertisseur; **~ious** *adj.* prudent; **~iously** *adv.* prudemment; *v.t.* (*warn against*) mettre en garde (contre); (*admonish*) avertir; ⚠ cautionner = (*law*) **to go bail for.**
cavalcade *s.* cavalcade *f.*
cavalier *s.* cavalier *m.*; *adj.* (*offhand*) cavalier; **in a ~ fashion,** cavalièrement.
cavalry *s.* cavalerie *f.*
cave *s.* caverne *f.*; ⚠ cave = **cellar; ~-dweller,** habitant des cavernes *m.*; **~-man,** homme des cavernes *m.*; *v.t.* & *i.* creuser; **to ~ in,** s'affaisser; (*fig.*) céder; (*fig. fam.*) caner.
cavern *s.* caverne *f.*; **~ous** *adj.* (*voice*) caverneux; (*eye*) cave.
caviar(e) *s.* caviar *m.*; **~ to the general,** de la confiture aux cochons.
cavil *s.* chicane *f.*; *v.i.* ergoter; **~ at,** chicaner sur.
cavity *s.* cavité *f.*; **~ wall,** mur alvéolé *m.*
cavort *v.i.* (*pop.*) cabrioler.
caw *s.* (& **cawing**) croassement *m.*; *v.i.* croasser.
cayenne *s.* (*cook.*) poivre de Cayenne *m.*
cayman, caiman *s.* caïman *m.*
cease *v.t.* & *i.* (*stop doing*) cesser; (*come to an end*) (s')arrêter (*from*—de); **~-fire** *s.* cessez-le-feu *m.*; **without ~**, sans cesse; **~less** *adj.* incessant.
cedar *s.* cèdre *m.*
cede *v.t.* céder.
cedilla *s.* cédille *f.*
ceil *v.t.* plafonner; **~ing** *s.* (*arch.*, *aviat.*, *comm.*) plafond *m.*
celandine *s.* chélidoine *f.*
celanese *s.* soie artificielle *f.*
celebr/ate *v.t.* & *i.* **1.** (*perform rite*) célébrer; **2.** (*keep festival*) commémorer; **3.** (*extol*) célébrer; **~ated** *adj.* (*famous*) célèbre; **~ation** *s.* (1) célébration *f.*; (2) commémoration *f.*; (3) louange *m.*; **~ity** *s.* célébrité *f.*
celerity *s.* célérité *f.*
celer/y *s.* céleri *m.*; **~iac** *s.* céléri-rave *m.*
celestial *adj.* céleste.
celib/acy *s.* célibat *m.*; **~ate** *adj.* & *s.m.f.* célibataire.
cell *s.* (*hermit's*, *monk's*, *prison*; *cavity in brain*; *biol.*) cellule *f.*; (*in honeycomb*) alvéole *f.*; (*nucleus of people*) noyau *m.*; (*electr.*) élément *m.*, cellule (*f.*) (photo-électrique).
cellar *s.* (*underground room*; *store of wine*) cave *f.*; SALT-~; **~age** *s.* caves *f.pl.*; ⚠ cellier = **store--room.**
cell/o *s.* violoncelle *m.*; **~ist** *s.* violoncelliste *m.f.*
cellophane *s.* cellophane *f.* (**P.**)
cellul/ar *adj.* cellulaire; **~oid** *s.* celluloïd *m.*; **~ose** *s.* cellulose *f.*
Celsius *adj.* celsius.
Celt, Kelt *s.* celte *m.f.*; **~ic,** *adj.* celte *or* celtique.
cement *s.* **1.** (*constr.* & *fig.*) ciment *m.*; **2.** (*metall.*, *med.*) cément *m.*; *v.t.* (1) cimenter; (2) cémenter.
cemetery *s.* cimetière *m.*
cenotaph *s.* cénotaphe *m.*
cense *v.t.* encenser; **~r** *s.* encensoir *m.*
censor *s.* censeur *m.*; **~ial** *adj.* censorial; **~ious** *adj.* pointilleux; **~ship** *s.* censure *f.*; *v.t.* censurer.
censure *s.* (*disapproval*) censure *f.*; (*reprimand*) blâme *m.*; *v.t.* réprimander, blâmer.
census *s.* recensement *m.*
cent *s.* (*coin*) cent *m.*; **per ~**, pour cent.
centaur *s.* centaure *m.*
centen/ary *adj.* & *s.m.* centenaire; **~arian** *s.* centenaire *m.f.*; **~nial** *adj.* centenaire; (*occurring every 100 years*) centennal; *s.* centenaire *m.*
centi- (*in combination*) **~gram,** centigramme *m.*; **~litre,** centilitre *m.*; **~metre,** centimètre *m.*
centigrade *adj.* centigrade (*now replaced by* Celsius).
centipede *s.* mille-pattes *m.invar.*
centr/e *s.* centre *m.*; **~e of attraction** *s.* (*lit.*) clou du spectacle *m.*; (*fig.*) centre d'attraction *m.*; **~e of gravity** *s.* centre de gravité *m.*; **~e-board** *s.* (*naut.*) dérive *f.*; **~e-forward** *s.* (*sport*) avant-centre *m.*; **~e-half** *s.* (*sport*) demi--centre *m.*; **~al** *adj.* central; **~alization** *s.* centralisation *f.*; **~alize** *v.t.* centraliser; **~ifugal** *adj.* centrifuge; **~ifuge** *s.* centrifugeur *m.*, centrifugeuse *f.*; *v.t.* centrer; (*fig.*) concentrer.
centur/y *s.* siècle *m.*; (*sport*) cent points; (*Roman army*) centurie *f.*; **~ion** *s.* centurion *m.*
ceramic *adj.* céramique; **~s** *s.* céramique *f.* ⚠ *sing. in French.*
cereal *s.* (*grain*) céréale *f.*; (*breakfast food*) flocons d'avoine *m.pl.*; *adj.* céréalier.
cerebral *adj.* cérébral.
ceremon/y *s.* (*rite*) rite *m.*; (*formal procedure*) cérémonie *f.*; (*formalities*) cérémonies *f.pl.*; **without ~y,** sans cérémonies; **to stand on ~y,** faire des cérémonies; **Master of C~ies** (*M.C.*) maître de cérémonie *m.*; **~ial** *adj.* de cérémonie; *s.* rituel *m*, étiquette *f.*; **~ious** *adj.* cérémonieux.
certain *adj.* certain; (*before the noun* = *unspecified*) **of a ~ age,** d'un certain âge; **a ~ lady,** une certaine dame; **~ly** *adv.**; **~ty** *s.* certitude *f.*
certificate *s.* (*med.*, *law*) certificat *m.*; (*acad.*) certificat *m.*, diplôme *m.*; (*birth, death, etc.*) acte *m.*
certif/y *v.t.* **1.** (*attest formally*) certifier; **2.** (*med. declare insane*) déclarer (qn.) atteint d'aliénation mentale; **~iable** *adj.* digne d'être déclaré atteint d'aliénation mentale.
certitude *s.* certitude *f.*
cerulean *adj.* céruléen.
cervical *adj.* cervical.
cessation *s.* (*ceasing*) cessation *f.*; (*pause*) interruption *f.*
cession *s.* cession *f.*
cesspool (cesspit) *s.* fosse d'aisances *f.*; (*fig.*) cloaque *m.*
Ceylon *s.* Ceylan *m.*; **C~ese** *adj.* & *s.m.f.* cingalais(e).
chaf/e *v.t.* & *i.* (*rub to make warm*) frictionner; (*rub and make sore*) frotter; (*fig. irritate, become irritated*) (s')irriter; (*of animal—against bars*) se frotter contre; (*naut.*) raguer; **~ing-dish** *s.* chauffe-plat *m.*
chaff *s.* **1.** (*grain husks*) balle *or* bale *f.*; **2.** (*chopped hay or straw*) paille hachée *f.*; **3.** (*banter*) taquinerie *f.*; *v.t.* (3) taquiner.
chaffinch *s.* pinson *m.*
chagrin *s.* chagrin *m.*; *v.t.* chagriner.
chain *s.* chaîne *f.*; (*series*) enchaînement *m.*; (*pl. fetters*) chaînes *f.pl.*; **~-armour** *s.* cotte de mailles *f.*; **~ reaction** *s.* réaction en chaîne *f.*; **~-smoke** *v.i.* fumer des cigarettes à la file; **~-smoker** *s.* fumeur de cigarettes à la file *m.*; **~-stitch** *s.* point de chaînette *m.*; **~ store** *s.* magasin à succursales multiples *m.*; *v.t.* enchaîner.
chair *s.* chaise *f.*; **arm~, easy ~** *s.* fauteuil *m.*; DECK-~; PUSH-~; WHEEL~; (*univ.*) chaire *f.*; (*authority*) siège *m.*; (*mech.*, *rail.*) coussinet *m.*; **to take the ~**, présider; **~man** *s.* président *m.*; *v.t.* présider à.
chalet *s.* chalet *m.*
chalice *s.* calice *m.*
chalk *s.* craie *f.*; **by a long ~,** de beaucoup;

they're as different as ~ and cheese, c'est le jour et la nuit; ~y *adj.* (*soil* & *fig.*) crayeux; (*water*) calcaire; *v.t.* marquer à la craie; ~ **out** *v.t.* tracer; ~ **up** *v.t.* (*fig. fam.*) porter sur l'ardoise.

challeng/e *s.* **1.** (*of sentry*) sommation *f.*; **2.** (*to duel*) défi *m.*; **3.** (*difficulty*) gageure *f.*; *v.t.* (1) faire une sommation; (2) défier; (*dispute statement, etc.*) contester; **~er,** provocateur *m.*

chamber *s.* chambre *f.*, salle *f.*; (*admin., parl., comm., mech.*) chambre *f.*; **~s** (*set of rooms*) (*of* avocat) cabinet *m.*; (*of* avoué) étude *f.*; **~lain** *s.* chambellan *m.*; **~-maid** *s.* femme de chambre *f.*; ~ **music** *s.* musique de chambre *f.*; **~-pot** *s.* pot de chambre *m.*

chameleon *s.* caméléon *m.*

chamfer *s.* chanfrein *m.*; *v.t.* chanfreiner.

chamois *s.* (*animal*) chamois *m.*; (*leather*) peau de chamois *f.*

champ[1] *v.t.* & *i.* (*munch noisily*) mâcher; ~ **at the bit** (*fig.*) ronger son frein.

champ[2] *s.* (*pop. abbrev. of champion*) as *m.*

champion *s.* **1.** (*supporter*) défenseur *m.*; **2.** (*winner*) champion *m.*; *adj.* de première classe; **~ship** *s.* (1) défense *f.*; (2) championnat *m.*; *v.t.* (1) défendre.

chance *s.* (*fortune*) hasard *m.*; (*opportunity*) occasion *f.*; (*possibility*) possibilité *f.*; ⚠ chance = (*usu. good*) **luck; by ~,** par hasard; **on the ~ of finding,** dans l'espoir de trouver; **to stand a good ~,** avoir des chances de; **to have an eye to the main ~,** savoir saisir la balle au bond; **to give s.o. a ~,** donner, laisser, une chance à qn., (*comm.*) prendre à l'essai; **to give s.o. a ~ to do sth.,** donner à qn. l'occasion de faire qch.; *adj.* fortuit; *v.t.* & *i.* (*risk*) risquer; (*happen to do*) arriver (*impers.*) **I ~d to see him,** il m'est arrivé de le voir; **if you ~ to do sth.,** s'il vous arrive de faire qch.; **~ one's arm,** risquer le coup; **chancy** *adj.* hasardeux.

chancel *s.* chœur *m.*, sanctuaire *m.*

chancell/or *s.* (*law, univ.*) Chancelier *m.*; **Lord C~or,** Grand Chancelier *m.*; **C~or of the Exchequer,** Chancelier de l'Echiquier *m.*; **~ery** *s.* chancellerie *f.*

chandelier *s.* lustre *m.*

chandler *s.* (*dealer in candles, oil, soap, paint, etc.*) droguiste *m.*, marchand de couleurs *m.*; **corn-~,** marchand de blé *m.*; **ship('s)-~,** fournisseur *m.*

change *s.* **1.** (*becoming or making different, difference*) changement *m.*; **2.** (*substitution*) échange *m.*; (*variety*) variété *f.*; **3.** (*money*) monnaie *f.*; **a ~ of air,** un changement d'air; **a ~ for the better,** une amélioration; **a ~ of clothes,** linge de rechange *m.*; **to get no ~ out of** (*fig. fam.*) perdre sa peine avec; **to** RING **the ~s;** *v.t.* & *i.* (1) *v.i.* changer; *v.t.* transformer (*into*—en); (2) échanger (*for*—contre); (3) changer, rendre la monnaie; ~ **over,** passer de; (*mil.*) relever; CHOP **and ~; all ~!,** toute le monde descend!; ~ **clothes, course, hands, one's mind, trains,** changer de vêtements, de cap, de mains, d'avis, de train; ~ **one's tune** (*fig.*) chanter sur un autre ton; **~able** *adj.* changeant; **~less** *adj.* constant; **~ling** *s.* enfant substitué *m.*

channel *s.* (*watercourse*) canal *m.*; (*strait*) détroit *m.*; **the** ENGLISH **C~; the C~ Islands,** les îles anglo-normandes *f.pl.*; (*radio, T.V.*) chaîne *f.*; (*direction*) voie *f.*; **~s** *pl.* (*medium or agency*) voie *f.*; **through the usual ~s,** par la voie hiérarchique; *v.t.* (*make* ~) creuser un canal; (*convey through*) faire passer par; (*direct*) diriger.

chant *s.* **1.** (*mus.*) mélodie *f.*; **2.** (*eccles.*) psalmodie *f.*; *v.t.* & *i.* (1) chanter; (2) psalmodier; **~ry** *s.* chapelle *f.*

chanticleer *s.* chantecler *m.*

chao/s *s.* (*lit.* & *fig.*) chaos *m.*; **~tic** *adj.* chaotique.

chap *s.* **1.** (*pop. = fellow*) type *m.*; OLD **~; 2.** (*cook.*) joue *f.*; **3.** (*crack in skin*) gerçure *f.*; **4. ~s** *pl.* (*of animal*) babines *f.pl.*; (*of person*) mâchoires *f.pl.*; **to lick one's ~s** (*fam.*) s'en lécher les babines; *v.t.* & *i.* (3) (se) gercer.

chapel *s.* (*subordinate to church*) chapelle *f.*; (*private*) oratoire *m.*; (*non-conformist*) temple *m.*; (*printers' union*) atelier *m.*; **Lady C~,** chapelle de la Sainte Vierge *f.*

chaperon(e) *s.* chaperon *m.*; *v.t.* chaperonner.

chaplain *s.* **1.** (*of an institution*) aumônier *m.*; **2.** (*priest*) chapelain *m.*; **~cy** *s.* (1) aumônerie *f.*; (2) chapellenie *f.*

chaplet *s.* (*of flowers, etc.*) guirlande *f.*; (*eccles.*) chapelet *m.*

chapter *s.* (*eccles., division of book*) chapitre *m.*; **to give ~ and verse,** citer ses références; **a ~ of accidents,** une kyrielle d'accidents.

char[1] *v.t.* & *i.* (*to burn*) carboniser.

char[2] *v.i.* (*fam.*) faire le ménage de qn.; *s.* femme de ménage *f.*

charabanc *s.* autocar *m.*

character *s.* (*distinctive mark; written symbol*) caractère *m.*; (*reputation*) réputation *f.*; (*status*) rôle *m.*, genre *m.*; (*in book or play*) personnage *m.*; (*fam. eccentric*) original *m.*; **in ~,** dans son rôle; **out of ~,** en désaccord avec; **~istic** *adj.* & *s.f.* caractéristique; *adj.* typique; **~istically** *adv.* typiquement; **~ize** *v.t.* caractériser; **~ization** s. caractérisation *f.*

charade *s.* charade *f.*

charcoal *s.* charbon de bois *m.*

charge *s.* **1.** (*load; explosive; mil.; electr.*) charge *f.*; **2.** (*expense*) frais *m.pl.*; **3.** (*price asked*) prix *m.*; **4.** (*task, duty; care, custody; object of care*) charge *f.*; **5.** (*accusation*) plainte *f.*; **6.** (*instructions*) recommandations *f.pl.*; **to be in ~ of** (*oversee*) être chargé de; (*be in care of*) être confié à; **to take ~ of,** se charger de; **to give in ~,** faire arrêter; **~-sheet** *s.* cahier des délits et écrous *m.* ⚠ cahier des charges = **clauses of a contract;** REVERSE **~s;** *v.t.* & *i.* (1) charger; (2) payer; (3) demander; (4) charger de; (5) porter une plainte contre; ~ **with,** accuser de; (6) enjoindre à; **~able** *adj.* à la charge, aux frais (*to*—de); (*fin.*) imputable (à); **~r** *s.* (*mil.*) cheval de guerre *m.*; (*techn.*) chargeur *m.*

chariot *s.* chariot *m.*

charit/y *s.* (*kindness*) bienveillance *f.*; (*leniency*) indulgence *f.*; (*almsgiving*) charité *f.*; (*institution*) société *f.*, institution *f.* (philanthropique, de bienfaisance); **~y begins at home,** charité bien ordonnée commence par soi-même; **~able** *adj.* (*person*) charitable; (*thing*) de bienfaisance.

charlatan *s.* (*med.* & *gen.*) charlatan *m.*

charlock *s.* sénevé *m.*

charm *s.* **1.** (*spell; attractiveness*) charme *m.*; **2.** (*amulet*) amulette *f.*; **3.** (*trinket*) breloque *f.*; *v.t.* (1) enchanter; **~ed** *adj.* (1) enchanté; **to lead a ~ed life** (*fam.*) être verni; **~er** *s.* charmeu/r, -se *m.f.*; **~ing** *adj.* charmant.

chart *s.* **1.** (*naut.*) carte marine *f.*; **2.** (*tabulated information*) tableau *m.*, graphique *m.*, (*med.*) courbe (de température) *f.*; **~room** *s.* cabine des cartes *f.*; *v.t.* (1) porter sur la carte; (2) inscrire sur un graphique.

charter *s.* **1.** (*of rights, etc.*) charte *f.*; (*law*) statuts *m.pl.*; *v.t.* (1) accorder une charte à; **2.** (*let or hire*) affréter; **~ed accountant** *s.* expert comptable *m.*; ~ **flight** *s.* vol à la demande *m.*; ~ **plane** *s.* avion de transport à la demande *m.*

charwoman *see* CHAR.

char/y *adj.* **1.** (*cautious*) circonspect; **2.** (*mean*) chiche (*with*—de); **~ily** *adv.* (1) avec circonspection; (2)*.

chase[1] *s.* (*pursuit, hunting*) chasse *f.*; (*game hunted*) gibier chassé *m.*; **to go on a wild-goose ~,** courir après le vent; *v.t.* chasser; *v.i.* (*fam.*) s'affairer; **go and ~ yourself** (*pop.*) va te faire pendre ailleurs.

chase[2] *v.t.* (*engrave*) ciseler; (*stone*) enchâsser (dans).

chasm *s.* (*lit.* & *fig.*) abîme *m.*

chassis *s.* (*auto.*) châssis *m.*; (*aviat.*) train d'atterrissage *m.*

chast/e *adj.* **1.** (*sexually*) chaste; **2.** (*refined in taste, etc.*) pur; **~en** *v.t.* (*punish, purify*) châtier; (*moderate*) modérer; **~ity** *s.* (1) chasteté *f.*; (2) pureté *f.*

chastise *v.t.* **1.** (*punish*) châtier; **2.** (*discipline*) corriger; **~ment** *s.* (1) châtiment *m.*; (2) correction *f.*

chasuble *s.* chasuble *f.*

chat *s.* bavardage *m.*; **to have a ~,** faire un brin de causette; *v.i.* bavarder; **to ~ s.o. up** (*pop.*) faire du baratin à qn.; **~ty** *adj.* (*person*) bavard; (*style*) familier.

chattel *s.* (*usu. pl.*) biens meubles *m.pl.*; **goods and ~s,** biens et effets *m.pl.*

chatter *s.* **1.** (*talk*) bavardage *m.*; **2.** (*teeth; mech.*) claquement *m.*; *v.i.* (1) bavarder; (2) claquer; **~er** *s.* bavard(e) *m.f.*; **~box,** moulin à paroles *m.*

chauffeur *s.* chauffeur *m.*

chauvin/ism *s.* chauvinisme *m.*; **~ist** *adj.* & *s.m.f.* chauvin(e).

cheap *adj.* (*low in price*) bon marché; (*easily got*) facile; (*of small value*) sans grande valeur; *adv.* à bon marché; **dirt ~,** d'un prix dérisoire; **on the ~,** au rabais; **~er** (*comp.*) meilleur marché; **~en** *v.t.* (*lit.*) baisser le prix; (*fig.*) (se) déprécier; **~ly** *adv.* à bon marché.

cheat *s.* (*person*) **1.** (*deceiver*) trompeu/r, -se *m.f.*; **2.** (*swindler*) escroc *m.*; **3.** (*at cards*) tricheu/r, -se *m.f.*; (*thing*) tromperie *f.*, escroquerie *f.*; *v.t.* (1) tromper; (2) escroquer; *v.i.* (3) tricher; **~ing** *s.* (1) tromperie *f.*; (2) escroquerie *f.*; (3) tricherie *f.*

check *s.* **1.** (*gen.*) échec *m.*, (*chess*) échec au roi *m.*; **2.** (*curb*) frein *m.*; **3.** (*control*) vérification *f.*; **4.** (*ticket, counterfoil*) bulletin (de consigne) *m.*; **5.** (*text.*) tissu à carreaux *m.*; *adj.* (*also* **~ed**) à carreaux; **to hold in ~,** tenir en échec; *v.t.* (1) (*chess*) faire échec à; (2) freiner; (3) vérifier, contrôler; **~ in** *v.i.* s'inscrire; **~ off** *v.t.* (*on list*) cocher; **~ out** *v.i.* (*at hotel*) régler sa note; **~ up** *v.t.* vérifier, contrôler; **~-up** *s.* examen *m.*; **~mate** *s.* (*chess*) échec et mat *m.*, (*fig.*) échec *m.*; **~mate** *v.t.* mater; (*fig.*) damer le pion à qn.

cheek *s.* **1.** (*anat.*) joue *f.*; **2.** (*fam. impudence*) toupet *m.*; **damned ~,** sacré culot *m.*; **with** TONGUE **in ~; to be ~ by jowl with s.o.** (*pop.*) être amis comme cochons; **~-bone** *s.* pommette *f.*; *v.t.* (2) parler à, agir envers, qn. avec effronterie; **~y** *adj.* effronté.

cheep (*of young birds*) *s.* piaulement *m.*; *v.i.* piauler.

cheer *s.* **1.** (*food*) chère *f.*; **2.** (*pl. applause*) acclamations *f.pl.*; **3.** (*comfort*) consolation *f.*; **~s!,** à la vôtre!; **be of good ~!,** soyez heureux!; **~ful** *adj.* (*person*) joyeux; (*thing*) gai; **~fully** *adv.* avec bonne grâce, gaiement; **~fulness** *s.* bonne humeur *f.*; **~ily** *adv.* gaiement; **~ing** *adj.* réconfortant, encourageant; *s.* acclamations *f.pl.*; **~less** *adj.* triste; **~y** *adj.* gai; **~io!,** au revoir!; *v.t.* (2) acclamer; (3) réconforter; *v.i.* (2) pousser des vivats; **~ up** *v.t.* égayer; *v.i.* prendre courage.

cheese *s.* fromage *m.*; CREAM **~**; CHALK **and ~**; **~cake** *s.* tartelette *f.*; **~-paring** *s.* économies de bouts de chandelles *f.pl.*; *adj.* qui fait des économies etc.; **to be ~d off** (*fam.*) en avoir marre.

cheetah *s.* guépard *m.*

chef *s.* chef (de cuisine) *m.*

chemical *s.* produit chimique *m.*; *adj.* chimique; **~ warfare,** guerre chimique *f.*; **~ly** *adv.**

chemist *s.* **1.** (*sc.*) chimiste *m.f.*; **2.** (*pharm.*) pharmacien(ne) *m.f.*; **~ry** *s.* (1) chimie *f.*; **~'s shop,** pharmacie *f.*

cheque *s.* chèque *m.*; BLANK **~**; **crossed ~,** chèque barré *m.*; **~-book** *s.* carnet de chèques *m.*

chequered *adj.* (= *checked*) à carreaux; (*variegated*) bariolé; (*eventful*) mouvementé.

cherish *v.t.* (*care for*) choyer; (*love tenderly* & *fig.*) chérir; (*consider, an idea, etc.*) entretenir.

cheroot *s.* cigare de Manille *m.*, manille *m.*

cherry *s.* cerise *f.*; **wild ~,** merise *f.*; **~-tree,** cerisier *m.* **~-coloured,** cerise *invar.*

cherub *s.* (*angel* & *child*) chérubin *m.*; **~ic** *adj.* de chérubin.

chess *s.* (*game*) échecs *m.pl.*; **~-board** *s.* échiquier *m.*; **~-man,** pièce *f.*; (*pawn*) pion *m.*

chest *s.* **1.** (*box*) coffre *m.*; **2.** (*anat.*) poitrine *f.*; **~ of drawers,** commode *f.*; **to get sth. off one's ~** (*fam.*) déballer (ses secrets, etc.), vider son sac.

chestnut *s.* (*bot.*) châtaigne *f.*; **~-tree,** châtaignier *m.*; **horse-~** (*tree*) marronnier *m.*; (*fruit*) marron d'Inde *m.*; **edible ~,** marron *m.*; *adj.* châtain; (*horse*) *s.* alezan *m.*; **to pull s.o's ~s out of the fire,** tirer les marrons du feu pour qn.

cheval-glass *s.* psyché *f.*

chevron *s.* (*herald; mil.*) chevron *m.*

chew *v.t.* (*with teeth*) mâcher; (*tobacco*) chiquer; (*fig.*) **~ over,** ruminer; **~ the** CUD; **~ing-gum,** chewing-gum *m.*

chiaroscuro *s.* clair-obscur *m.*

chicanery *s.* chicane *f.*

chichi *adj.* (*person*) chichiteux; (*thing*) à falbalas; *s.* (*person*) personne chichiteuse *f.*; (*thing*) falbala *m.*

chick *s.* (*young fowl*) poussin *m.*; (*term of endearment*) poulet *m.*; **~-pea,** pois chiche *m.*; **~-weed,** mouron *m.*

chicken *s.* poulet *m.*; (*cook.*) volaille *f.*; **to count one's ~s before they are hatched,** vendre la peau de l'ours; **to be ~** (*fam.*) être poule mouillée; **to ~ out of sth.** (*fam.*) caner devant qch.; **~-feed** (*fig. fam.*) des poussières *f.pl.*; **~-pox,** varicelle *f.*

chicory *s.* (*in salad*) endive *f.*; (*in coffee*) chicorée *f.*

chid/e *v.t.* gronder; **~ing** *s.* gronderie *f.*

chief *s.* chef *m.*; (*fam.* = *boss*) patron *m.*; *adj.* principal; **~ly** *adv.* (*in the first place*) avant tout; (*for the most part*) principalement; **~tain** *s.* chef *m.*

chilblain *s.* engelure *f.*

child *s.* enfant *m.f.*; **with ~,** enceinte; **~birth** *s.* couches *f.pl.*; **~hood** *s.* enfance *f.*; **to be in one's second ~hood,** retomber en enfance; **~'s play** (*fig.*) jeu d'enfant *m.*; **~ish** *adj.* puéril; **~ishly** *adv.**; **~ishness** *s.* puérilité *f.*; **~less** *adj.* sans enfant; **~like** *adj.* enfantin; (*fig.*) innocent.

Chile *s.* Chili *m.*; **~an** *adj.* & *s.m.f.* chilien(ne).

chil(l)i *s.* piment *m.*

chill *s.* (*cold sensation*) froid *m.*, frisson *m.*; (*feverish cold*) refroidissement *m.*; (*cold air*) fraîcheur *f.*; **to catch a ~,** prendre froid; **to take the ~ off,** (*water*) faire tiédir, (*wine*) chambrer; *adj.* froid; *v.t.* (*lit.* & *fig.*) refroidir; (*cook.*) frigorifier; **~y** *adj.* **1.** (*temperature*) froid, frais; **2.** (*sensitive to cold, of person*) frileux; **3.** (*fig. of manner*) froid; **~iness** *s.* (1) fraîcheur *f.*; (3) froideur *f.*

chime *s.* **1.** (*bells*) carrillon *m.*; **2.** (*harmony*) harmonie *f.*; *v.t.* (1) sonner; *v.i.* (1) carillonner; (2) s'harmoniser (avec).

chimera *s.* chimère *f.*; **~ical** *adj.* chimérique.
chimney *s.* cheminée *f.*; (*of lamp*) verre *m.*; **~-piece, ~-pot,** cheminée *f.*; **~-**SWEEP.
chimpanzee *s.* chimpanzé *m.*
chin *s.* menton *m.*; **~-wag** *s.* bavardage *m.*; *v.i.* bavarder.
china[1] *s.* porcelaine *f.*; *adj.* de porcelaine; **~ clay,** kaolin *m.*; **a** BULL **in a ~ shop.**
Chin/a[2] *s.* (*geog.*) Chine *f.*; **~ese** *adj.* & *s.m.f.* chinois(e); **~ese lantern,** (lanterne) vénitienne *f.*
chine *s.* **1.** (*ravine*) ravin *m.*; **2.** (*backbone*) échine *f.*; **3.** (*cook.*) échine *f.*; *v.t.* (3) échiner.
chink *s.* **1.** (*crevice*) crevasse *f.*; (*opening*) fente *f.*; (*in curtains, door, etc.*) entrebâillement *m.*; **2.** (*sound*) tintement *m.*; *v.t.* & *i.* (2) (faire) tinter; (*glasses*) trinquer.
chintz *s.* perse *f.*
chip *s.* (*of wood or metal*) copeau *m.*; (*of glass or stone*) éclat *m.*; (*on edge of plate, etc.*) ébréchure *f.*; (*cook.*) frite *f.*; (*at poker*) jeton *m.*; **he's a ~ off the old block,** il est bien le fils de son père; **to have a ~ on one's shoulder** (*fam.*) avoir un complexe; *v.t.* & *i.* (*cut or break at edge*) (s')ébrécher; (*shape*) tailler; **~ped** *adj.* ébréché.
chipolata *s.* (*sausage*) chipolata *f.*
chiropod/ist *s.* pédicure *m.f.*; **~y** *s.* soins du pédicure *m.pl.*
chirp *s.* **1.** (*of birds*) gazouillement *m.*, (*collective*) gazouillis *m.*; **2.** (*of insects*) chant *m.*, cri *m.*; *v.i.* (1) gazouiller; (2) chanter, crier; (*fig.*) gazouiller; **~y** (*fig.*) gai.
chisel *s.* ciseau *m.*; *v.t.* ciseler; (*fig.fam.*) extorquer (qch. à qn.).
chit *s.* **1.** (*child*) gosse *m.f.*, **a ~ of a girl,** une gamine; **2.** (*note*) note *f.*; **~-chat** *s.* bavardage *m.*
chitterlings *s.* (*cook.*) andouille *f.*
chivalr/y *s.* **1.** (*medieval knightly system*) chevalerie *f.*; **2.** (*gallantry*) courtoisie *f.*; **~ous** *adj.* (1) chevaleresque; (2) courtois; **~ously** *adv.* (1)*; (2)*.
chive *s.* (*bot.*) ciboulette *f.*
chivy *v.t.* (*fam.*) harceler.
chlor/al *s.* chloral *m.*; **~ate** *s.* chlorate *m.*; **~ide** *s.* chlorure *m.*, (*commonly*) eau de Javel *f.*; **~ine** *s.* chlore *m.*; **~inate** *v.t.* javelliser; **~ination** *s.* javellisation *f.*; **~oform** *s.* chloroforme *m.*; *v.t.* chloroformer; **~ophyll** *s.* chlorophylle *f.*
chock *s.* cale *f.*; *v.t.* caler; **~-a-block** *adj.* bondé; **~-full** *adj.* archiplein.
chocolate *s.* chocolat *m.*; *adj.* au chocolat; (*colour*) chocolat *invar.*
choice *s.* (*act of choosing, thing chosen*) choix *m.*; (*assortment*) assortiment *m.*; *adj.* de choix, d'élite; **for ~,** de préférence; **from ~,** de son propre gré; **Hobson's ~,** carte forcée *f.*
choir *s.* (*singers; arch.*) chœur *m.*; (*musical society*) chorale *f.*; **~boy** *s.* enfant de chœur *m.*; **~ school** *s.* maîtrise *f.*; **~ stalls,** stalles *f.pl.*
chok/e *s.* (*auto.*) starter *m.*; *v.t.* & *i.* (*suffocate*) (s')étouffer; **~e up** boucher; **~er** *s.* (*collar*) col dur *m.*, (*cravat*) foulard *m.*, (*necklace*) collier *m.*; **~ing** *s.* étouffement *m.*
choler *s.* (*med.*) bile *f.*; (*fig.*) colère *f.*; **~ic** *adj.* coléreux.
cholera *s.* choléra *m.*
cholesterol *s.* cholestérol *m.*
choos/e *v.t.* choisir (*between*—entre); (*theol.*) élire; **the chosen people,** le peuple élu; *v.i.* (*wish to*) vouloir; (*think fit to*) décider de; **~y** *adj.* difficile.
chop *s.* (*cook.*) côtelette *f.* (de porc, d'agneau, etc.); *see* CHAP (2); *v.t.* couper; (*wood*) fendre; (*cook.*) hacher; **~ and change,** changer d'avis comme une girouette; **~ up** *v.t.* couper en morceaux, hacher; **~per** *s.* hache *f.*; **~ping-board** *s.* hachoir *m.*; **~ping-knife** *s.* hachoir *m.*, hache-légumes *m.*, hache-viande *m.*; **~py** *adj.* (*sea*) agité.
chopstick *s.* baguette *f.*
choral *adj.* choral; **~e** *s.* choral *m.* (*pl.* chorals); ⚠ chorale *s.f.* = **music society.**
chord *s.* (*mus.*) accord *m.*; (*string of harp*) corde *f.*; (*fig.*) **to strike a ~,** faire vibrer la corde sensible.
chore *s.* travail de ménage *m.*; (*fam.*) corvée *f.*
choreograph/y *s.* choréographie *f.*; **~er** *s.* choréographe *m.f.*
chorister *s.* choriste *m.*
chortle *v.i.* glousser.
chorus *s.* (*of singers or dancers*) chœur *m.*; (*song, refrain of song*) refrain *m.*; (*of protest, etc.*) concert *m.*; **~-girl,** girl *f.*
chosen *see* CHOOSE.
Christ *s.* le Christ *m.*, Jésus-Christ *m.*
christen *v.t.* baptiser; **~ing** *s.* baptême *m.*
Christendom *s.* chrétienté *f.*
Christian *adj.* & *s.m.f.* chrétien(ne); **to be a ~,** être chrétien; **~ name,** nom de baptême *m.*; **~ity** *s.* christianisme *m.*; **~ize** *v.t.* christianiser.
Christmas *s.* Noël *m.*; **Father ~,** le père Noël; **~-box,** étrennes *f.pl.*; **~** CARD; **~** CAROL; **~ Day,** jour de Noël *m.*; **~ Eve,** veille de Noël *f.*, (*evening party*) réveillon *m.*; **~ tree,** arbre de Noël *m.*
chromatic *adj.* chromatique; **~s** *s.* chromatique *f.* ⚠ *singular in French.*
chrome, chromium *s.* chrome *m.*; **~ plate** *s.* acier chromé *m.*; **~-plated** *adj.* chromé.
chronic *adj.* chronique; (*Eng.pop.* = *very bad, intense*) insupportable, affreux; **~ally** *adv.**;*,*; **~ity** *s.* chronicité *f.*
chronicle *s.* chronique *f.*; *v.t.* faire la chronique de; **~r** *s.* chroniqueur *m.*
chronolog/y *s.* chronologie *f.*; **~ical** *adj.* chronologique; **~ically** *adv.**.
chronometer *s.* chronomètre *m.*
chrysalis *s.* chrysalide *f.*
chrysanthemum *s.* chrysanthème *m.*
chubby *adj.* joufflu.
chuck *s.* (*mech.*) mandrin *m.*; (*cook.*) paleron de bœuf *m.*; *v.i.* (*sound*) glousser; *v.t.* balancer; **~ away** *v.t.* jeter; **~ out** *v.t.* (faire) sortir; **~ up** *v.t.* lâcher; **~ under the chin,** donner une petite tape sous le menton; **~ it!** (*pop.* = *stop*) assez!
chuckle *s.* gloussement *m.*; *v.i.* glousser.
chug *v.i.* (*auto.*) cogner; **~ along** *v.i.* tourner en cognant; (*fig.*) avancer en haletant.
chum *s.* (*fam.*) copain *m.*
chump *s.* (*wood*) bloc de bois *m.*; (*meat*) côte (de mouton) *f.*; (*pop.* = *head*) boule *f.*; **to go off one's ~** (*fam.*) perdre la boule.
chunk *s.* gros morceau *m.*; (*of bread*) quignon *m.*; **~y** *adj.* (*of build*) trapu; en gros morceaux.
church *s.* (*building & society*) église *f.*; (*protestant, in France*) temple *m.*; (*profession*) ordres *m.pl.*; **~-goer** *s.* pratiquant(e) *m.f.*; **~man** (*cleric*) ecclésiastique *m.*; (*in Eng. sense, not chapel*) anglican *m.*; **~ service,** office *m.*; **~warden,** marguillier *m.*; **~yard,** cimetière *m.*
churl *s.* (*hist.*) manant *m.*; (*ill-bred*) rustre *m.*; **~ish** *adj.* grincheux; **~ishly** *adv.* d'une manière grincheuse.
churn *s.* (*for milk*) bidon *m.*; (*for butter*) baratte *f.*; *v.t.* (*butter*) baratter; *v.i.* (*seethe*) bouillonner; **~ out** *v.t.* (*fig.*) produire en série.
chute *s.* (*waterfall*) chute d'eau *f.*; (*techn.*) tuyau de descente *m.*; (*for children*) toboggan *m.*
cicada *s.* cigale *f.*
cicerone *s.* cicerone *m.*
C.I.D (*abbrev. for Criminal Investigation Department*), Police Judiciaire *f.*, (*abbrev.*) P.J.
cider *s.* cidre *m.*; **~-**PRESS.

cigar *s.* cigare *m.*; ~**ette** *s.* cigarette *f.*; ~**ette--case,** étui à cigarettes *m.*; ~**ette-end,** mégot *m.*; ~**ette-holder,** fume-cigarette *m.*; ~**ette--LIGHTER.**
cinch *s.* **it's a** ~ (*pop.*) c'est du tout cuit.
cincture *s.* ceinture *f.*
cinder(s) *s.* escarbilles *f.pl.*; (*of volcano, of furnace*) scories *f.pl.*; (*ashes*) cendres *f.pl.*; ~**-track,** piste cendrée *f.*
Cinderella *s.* Cendrillon *f.*
cine/ma *s.* cinéma *m.*; ~ **camera,** caméra *f.*; ~**matics** *s.* cinématique *f.* ⚠ *sing. in French*; ~**matograph** *s.* cinématographe *m.*; ~**matography** *s.* cinématographie *f.*
cinnamon *s.* cannelle *f.*
cinq(ue) foil *s.* (*arch., bot.*) quinte-feuille *f.*
cipher *s.* **1.** (*numeral*) chiffre arabe *m.*; (*math. symbol*) zéro *m.*; **2.** (*worthless person or thing*) zéro *m.*; **3.** (*disguised writing*) chiffre *m.*; **in** ~, en chiffre; *v.t.* & *i.* (1) & (3) chiffrer.
circle *s.* (*figure; ring*) cercle *m.*; (*theat.*) balcon *m.*; (*set, class*) cercle *m.*, club *m.*, milieu *m.*; (*period*) cycle *m.*; (*under eyes*) cerne *m.*; (*underground rail.*) **inner/outer** ~, petite, grande, ceinture *f.*; **vicious** ~, cercle vicieux *m.*; **to run round in** ~**s,** ne pas savoir où donner de la tête; **to come full** ~, revenir à zéro; ~**t** *s.* bandeau *m.*; *v.t.* entourer (*with*—de); *v.i.* circuler.
circuit *s.* (*course*) circuit *m.*; (*deviation*) détour *m.*; (*law*) tournée *f.*; (*electr.*) circuit *m.*; **short** ~, court-circuit *m.*; ~**-breaker** (*electr.*) disjoncteur *m.*; ~**ous** *adj.* qui fait un détour; (*fig.*) détourné.
circular *adj.* & *s.f.* circulaire; ~ **letter,** circulaire *f.*; ~**ize** *v.t.* adresser une circulaire à.
circulat/e *v.t.* & *i.* (faire) circuler; (*spread*) répandre; ~**ing** *adj.* circulant; (*math.*) périodique; ~**ion** *s.* (*of blood*) circulation *f.*; (*spreading*) diffusion *f.*; (*sales of paper*) tirage *m.*
circum- (*in combination*): ~**cise** *v.t.* circoncire; ~**cision** *s.* circoncision *f.*; ~**ference** *s.* circonférence *f.*; ~**flex** *adj.* circonflexe; ~**locution** *s.* circonlocution *f.*; ~**navigate** *v.t.* faire le tour de; ~**navigation** *s.* circumnavigation *f.*; ~**scribe** *v.t.* circonscrire; ~**scription** *s.* circonscription *f.*; ~**spect** *adj.* circonspect; ~**spection** *s.* circonspection *f.*; ~**vent** *v.t.* circonvenir.
circumstanc/e *s.* circonstance *f.*; (*ceremony*) pompe *f.*; (*pl. = means*) moyens *m.pl.*; **in easy** ~**es,** à l'aise; **in reduced** ~**es,** gêné; ~**es permitting,** sauf imprévu; **force of** ~**es,** ~**es beyond our control,** force majeure *f.*; **in the** ~**es,** dans les circonstances actuelles; ~**ed** *adj.* dans une situation donnée; ~**tial** *adj.* (*detailed*) circonstancié; (*incidental*) accessoire; (*evidence*) indirect; ⚠ circonstanciel *is used in ling. only*; ~**tiate** *v.t.* donner des détails circonstanciés sur.
circus *s.* cirque *m.*; (*square, e.g. Piccadilly*) rond--point *m.*
cirrus *s.* (*clouds*) cirrus *m.*
cistern *s.* (*on roof*) réservoir *m.*; (*underground*) citerne *f.*
citadel *s.* citadelle *f.*
cit/e *v.t.* (*quote* & *law*) citer; ~**ation** *s.* citation *f.*
cithern, cittern *s.* cithare *f.*
citizen *s.* (*national*) citoyen *m.*; (*of a city*) habitant *m.*; (*law*) ressortissant *m.*; ~**ship** *s.* (*of city*) droit de cité *m.*; (*of country*) nationalité *f.*
citric *adj.* citrique.
citron *s.* cédrat *m.*; ~ **tree** cédratier *m.*; ⚠ citron = **lemon.**
citrus *s.* (*fruit*) agrumes *m.pl.*
city *s.* ville *f.*; **the C**~, la cité *f.* (de Londres).
civet (*cat*) *s.* civette *f.*
civic *adj.* civique; ~**s,** instruction civique *f.*; ~ **authorities,** autorités municipales *f.pl.*
civil *adj.* **1.** (≠ *mil. or eccles.*) civil; ~ **engineer** *s.* ingénieur civil *m.*; ~ **list** *s.* liste civile *f.*; ~ **marriage,** mariage civil *m.*; **C**~ **servant** *s.* fonctionnaire *m.f.*; **C**~ **Service** *s.* fonction publique *f.*; ~ **war** *s.* guerre civile *f.*; **the American C**~ **War,** la Guerre de Sécession *f.*; ~**ian** *s.* civil *m.*; *adj.* de civil; **in** ~**ian dress,** en civil; **2.** (*polite*) poli; ~**ity** *s.* civilité *f.*; ~**ization** *s.* civilisation *f.*; ~**ize** *v.t.* civiliser; ~**ly** *adv.**.
clack *s.* claquement *m.*; *v.t.* claquer.
clad *adj.* (*in*) vêtu (de).
claim *s.* **1.** (*demand as due*) réclamation *f.*; **2.** (*right*) droit *m.*; **3.** (*title*) titre *m.*; **4.** (*mining*) concession *f.*; **to lay** ~ **to sth.,** prétendre à qch.; *v.t.* (1) réclamer; (2) revendiquer; (3) prétendre (à qch.); ~ **to,** prétendre + *inf.*, **he** ~**s to be very clever,** il prétend être fort habile; ~ **that,** prétendre que, **he** ~**s that he hasn't seen it,** il prétend qu'il ne l'a pas vu; **I don't** ~ **that he said it,** je ne prétends pas qu'il l'ait dit (*subj. after neg. or interrog.*); ~**ant** *s.* prétendant(e) *m.f.*
clairvoyan/ce *s.* **1.** (*fig.*) clairvoyance *f.*; **2.** (*fortune-telling*) voyance *f.*; ~**t** *s.* (1) clairvoyant *m.*; (2) voyant(e) *m.f.*
clam *s.* (*zool.*) palourde *f.*; **to be like, to shut up like, a** ~ (*fig.*) être muet comme la tombe.
clamber *v.i.* grimper; ~ **over** *v.t.* escalader.
clammy *adj.* humide et froid.
clam/our *s.* (*shout*) clameur *f.*; (*of protest, etc.*) réclamation *f.*; ~**orous** *adj.* bruyant, (*person*) criard; ~**orously** *adv.* bruyamment, à grands cris.
clamp *s.* **1.** (*wood*) serre-joint *m.*; **2.** (*metal*) crampon *m.*; *v.t.* (1) serrer; (2) cramponner; ~ **down on** *v.t.* (*fig.*) visser.
clan *s.* clan *m.*; (*fig.*) clique *f.*; ~**sman** *s.* membre d'un clan; ~**nish** *adj.* dévoué au clan, à la clique.
clandestine *adj.* clandestin.
clang *s.* bruit métallique *m.*; *v.i.* retentir; ~**er** (*fig. fam.*) gaffe *f.*; ~**our** *s.* bruit métallique *m.*; ~**orous** *adj.* retentissant.
clank *s.* cliquetis *m.*; *v.i.* cliqueter.
clap *s.* **1.** (*applause*) applaudissement *m.*, battement de mains *m.*; **2.** (*of thunder*) coup (de tonnerre) *m.*; *v.t.* & *i.* applaudir; ~ **hands,** battre des mains; (*fam.*) (~ *into prison, etc.*) *v.t.* flanquer; ~**board** *s.* bardeau *m.*; ~**trap** *s.* (*fam.*) bobards *m.pl.* ~**per** *s.* (*of bell*) battant *m.*; ~**ping** *s.* applaudissements *m.pl.*, battement de mains *m.*
claret *s.* (*wine*) bordeaux *m.*
clarif/y *v.t.* clarifier; (*fig.*) éclaircir; ~**ication** *s.* clarification *f.*; éclaircissement *m.*
clarinet *s.* clarinette *f.*
clarion *s.* clairon *m.*
clarity *s.* clarté *f.*
clash *s.* **1.** (*sound*) heurt sonore *m.*; **2.** (*collision*) choc *m.*; **3.** (*discord, colours, etc.*) désaccord *m.*; (*of opinions*) conflit *m.*; *v.t.* (2) (se) heurter; *v.i.* (1) résonner; (3) (*colours*) jurer; (*fig.*) être en contradiction avec.
clasp *s.* **1.** (*hook*) agrafe *f.*; **2.** (*closing device*) fermoir *m.*; **3.** (*embrace*) étreinte *f.*; ~**-knife,** couteau pliant *m.*; *v.t.* (1) agrafer; (2) fermer; (3) étreindre; ~ **hands,** joindre les mains (*one's own*), serrer la main à qn. (*s.o. else*).
class *s.* (*school, species, mil., rail.*) classe *f.*; (*rank*) rang *m.*; (*in exams*) classement *m.*; (*comm.*) qualité *f.*; (*lesson*) cours *m.*; **lower** ~ *s.* classe ouvrière *f.*; **working** ~ *s.* classe laborieuse *f.*; **middle** ~ *s.* bourgeoisie *f.*; **upper** ~ *s.* classe dirigeante *f.*; ~**-conscious** *adj.* qui a l'esprit de caste; ~**-room** *s.* salle de classe *f.*; ~**y** *adj.* (*pop.*) chic; *v.t.* classer.
classic *adj.* classique; *s.pl.* **1.** (*authors*) classiques *m.pl.* **2.** (*studies*) humanités *f.pl.*; ~**al** *adj.*

classique; **~ism** *s.* (1) classicisme *m.*; (2) humanisme *m.*; **~ist** *s.* (2) humaniste *m.f.*
classif/y *v.t.* (*arrange*) classer; (*in species*) classifier; **~ication** *s.* classement *m.*; classification *f.*; **~ied information,** document secret *m.*
clatter *s.* fracas *m.*; (*of dishes*) cliquetis de vaisselle *m.*; (*of voices*) brouhaha *m.*; *v.t.* entre-choquer; *v.i.* résonner.
clause *s.* (*law*) disposition *f.*; (*of treaty*) clause *f.*; (*ling.*) proposition *f.*
claustr/al *adj.* claustral; **~ophobia** *s.* claustrophobie *f.*
clavichord *s.* clavecin *m.*
clavicle *s.* clavicule *f.*
claw *s.* (*of cats, etc.*) griffe *f.*; (*of birds of prey*) serre *f.*; (*of small birds*) ongle *m.*; (*of crabs, etc.*) pince *f.*; (*mech. of machine, hammer, etc.*) pied-de--biche *m.*; *v.t.* griffer, déchirer.
clay *s.* argile *f.*, glaise *f.*; **with feet of ~** (*fig.*) aux pieds d'argile; **~** PIGEON; **~** PIPE; **~-pit** *s.* glaisière *f.*
clean *adj.* (≠ *dirty*) propre; (*pure*) pur; (*clear-cut, decisive*) net; **~ bill of health** (*naut.*) patente nette *f.*; **~ slate,** casier vierge *m.*; **make a ~** SWEEP; *adv.* (*completely*) nettement; **to come ~** (*fam.*) tout déballer; **~-shaven** *adj.* glabre; *v.t.* nettoyer; **~ out, up,** nettoyer à fond; **~ed out** *adj.* (*pop.*) mis à sec; **~-up** *s.* nettoyage *m.*; (*fam.*) rafle *f.*; **~er** *s.* (*person*) femme de ménage *f.*; (*of clothes*) dégraisseur *m.*; **vacuum ~er,** aspirateur *m.*; **~ing** *s.* nettoyage *m.*; DRY **~ing**; **~ly** *adj.* propre; *adv.* proprement; **~liness** *s.* propreté *f.*; **~ness** *s.* propreté *f.*
cleans/e *v.t.* nettoyer; (*fig.*) purifier; **~ing** *s.* nettoyage *m.*, purification *f.*; *adj.* détersif; **~ing cream,** crème de démaquillage *f.*; **~ing department,** service de voirie *m.*
clear[1] *adj.* (*sound, water, weather*) clair; (*evident, bright*) clair; (*transparent*) transparent; (*unobstructed*) dégagé; (*sure*) convaincu; (*complete*) entier; (*free from*) libre de; (*distinct*) net; (*profit, conscience*) net; **all-~** *s.* fin d'alerte *f.*; **the coast is ~,** le champ est libre; **to make it ~ to s.o. that,** faire comprendre à qn. que; **to make oneself ~,** se faire comprendre; **to keep ~ of s.o.,** éviter qn.; **~-cut** *adj.* net; **road ~!** (*sign*) fin des travaux! **~way** (*road sign*) arrêt interdit!; **~ly** *adv.* clairement; (*evidently*) évidemment; **~ness** *s.* (*brightness*) clarté *f.*; (*transparence*) transparence *f.*; (*distinctness*) netteté *f.*
clear[2] *v.t.* **1.** (*rubbish, etc.*) déblayer; **2.** (*ground*) défricher; **3.** (*debt*) acquitter; **4.** (*account*) liquider; **5.** (*letters*) lever; **6.** (*cheque*) virer; **7.** (*comm.*) gagner net; **8.** (*comm. goods*) solder; **9.** (*goods at customs*) dédouaner; **10.** (*decode*) déchiffrer; **11.** (*of guilt*) disculper; **12.** (*leap over*) franchir; **13.** (*fig.*) décharger; **~ the table,** débarrasser la table; **~ the ground** (*fig.*) déblayer le terrain; **~ the air** (*fig.*) mettre les choses au point; *v.i.* (*of sky*) se dégager; (*of weather*) s'éclaircir; (*fig.*) s'éclairer; **~ away** *v.t.* enlever; *v.i.* se dissiper; **~ off** *v.i.* (*fam.*) filer; **~ out** *v.t.* nettoyer; **~ up** *v.t.* ranger; *v.i.* s'éclaircir; **~ance,** (1) débarras *m.*; (5) levée *f.*; (9) dédouanement *m.*; **~ance sale,** (8) soldes *m.pl.*; **~ing** *s.* (3) acquittement *m.*; (4) liquidation *f.*; (6) virement *m.*; (11) disculpation *f.*; (*in forest*) clairière *f.*; **~ing-house,** banque de virement *f.*
cleat *s.* (*techn.*) taquet *m.*
cleav/e *v.t.* & *i.* **1.** (*split*) (se) fendre; **2.** (*stick*) coller (*to*—à); **~age** *s.* (1) division *f.*, (*fam.*) décolleté *m.*
clef *s.* (*mus.*) clef *f.*
cleft *s.* fente *f.*; *adj.* fourchu; (*palate*) fendu; **in a ~ stick,** dans une impasse.
clematis *s.* clématite *f.*
clemen/t *adj.* **1.** (*mild*) doux; **2.** (*merciful*) clément; **~cy** *s.* (1) douceur *f.*; (2) clémence *f.*
clench, clinch *v.t.* (*nail*) rabattre; (*teeth, fist*) serrer; (*bargain*) conclure.
clerestory *s.* claire-voie *f.*
clergy *s.* clergé *m.*; **~man,** prêtre *m.*; (*protestant*) pasteur *m.*
clerical *adj.* **1.** (*of clergy*) clérical; **2.** (*comm.*) de commis; **3.** (*admin., bank*) de bureau, d'employé; **~ error** *s.* (*in ms.*) faute de copiste *f.*; (*in typing*) faute de frappe *f.*; ⚠ clérical = (1) *only*.
clerk *s.* (*eccles., law*) clerc *m.*; (*admin., bank*) employé *m.*; (*comm.*) commis *m.*; **~ of the court,** greffier *m.*; **Town C~,** secrétaire de mairie *m.*; **C~ of the Council,** secrétaire général de la Préfecture *m.*
clever *adj.* **1.** (*skilful*) adroit; **2.** (*talented*) capable; **3.** (*intelligent*) intelligent; **4.** (*ingenious*) ingénieux; **~ at** (*school subject*) fort en (*math. etc.*); **~ly** *adv.* (1)*; (2)*; (3) intelligemment; (4)*; **~ness** *s.* (1) adresse *f.*; (2) capacité *f.*; (3) intelligence *f.*; (4) ingéniosité *f.*
click *s.* bruit de déclic *m.*; (*ling.*) clappement de langue *m.*; *v.i.* faire un bruit sec.
client *s.* client(e) *m.f.*; **~èle** *s.* clientèle *f.*
cliff *s.* falaise *f.*; **~-hanger** *s.* coup de poker *m.*
climacteric *s.* climatérique *f.*
climat/e *s.* (*lit.* & *fig.*) climat *m.*; **~ic** *adj.* climatique.
climax *s.* (*rhet.*) gradation *f.*; (*theat.*) crise *f.*; (*apex*) point culminant *m.*; (*extreme case of*) comble *m.*
climb *s.* (*ascent*) ascension *f.*; (*place to be climbed*) montée *f.*; *v.t.* (*hill, stairs*) monter; (*tree, ladder, etc.*) grimper sur; (*mountain*) faire l'ascension de; (*wall*) escalader; *v.i.* (*road, etc.*) monter; (*plants*) grimper; (*fig.*) s'élever; **~ down,** *v.i.* descendre; (*fig.*) se dégonfler; **~-down** *s.* descente *f.*; (*fig.*) reculade *f.*; **~ over** *v.t.* escalader; **~ up** *v.t.* gravir; **~er** *s.* (*bot.*) plante grimpante *f.*; (*sport*) alpiniste *m.f.*; (*zool.*) grimpeur *m.*; (*fig.*) arriviste *m.f.*; **~ing** *adj.* (*ascending*) montant; (*plant*) grimpant.
clime *s.* région *f.*
clinch *see* CLENCH.
cling *v.i.* (*to*) se cramponner (à); (*fig.*) rester fidèle à (*principles, beliefs*); ne pas démordre de (*ideas, theory*); **~ing** *adj.* (*clothes*) collant; (*smell*) tenace; **~stone** PEACH.
clinic *s.* (*med. school*) clinique *f.*; (*for outpatients*) dispensaire *m.*; ⚠ clinique = **private nursing--home**; **~al** *adj.* clinique.
clink *s.* tintement *m.*; (*pop.* = *prison*) violon *m.*; *v.t.* & *i.* (faire) tinter.
clinker *s.* mâchefer *m.*
clip *s.* **1.** (*act of clipping*) coupe *f.*; **2.** (*yield of wool*) tonte *f.*; **3.** (*cinema*) extrait (d'un film) *m.*; **4.** (*holder*) agrafe *f.*; **paper-~,** trombone *m.*; **5.** (*jewellery*) clip *m.*; *v.t.* (1) (*hair, etc.*) couper; (2) tondre; (4) agrafer; (*tickets*) poinçonner; (*speech*) manger (ses mots); **to ~ the wings of s.o.,** rogner les ailes à qn.; **~per** *s.* (*naut., aviat.*) clipper *m.*; (*person*) tondeur *m.*; **~pers** *s.* (*tool*) tondeuse *f.*; **~pie** *s.* (*pop.*) receveuse *f.*; **~ping** *s.* (1) coupe *f.*; (2) tonte *f.*; (*press*) coupure de presse *f.*; (*pl. pieces cut*) rognures *f.pl.*
cloak *s.* capote *f.*; (*fig.*) masque *m.*, couvert *m.*; **~room** *s.* (*rail. etc.*) consigne *f.*; (*theat. etc.*) vestiaire *m.*; **~ and dagger,** de cape et d'épée; *v.t.* (*fig.*) masquer.
cloche *s.* (*hort.* & *hat*) cloche *f.*
clock *s.* (*church, etc.*) horloge *f.*; (*small*) pendule *f.*; ALARM **~**; **carriage ~,** pendulette *f.*; **o'~,** heure *f.*; **four o'~,** quatre heures; **against the ~,** contre la montre; **round the ~,** vingt--quatre heures sur vingt-quatre; **to put the ~ back** (*fig.*) remonter dans le temps; **to watch the ~** (*pop.*) ne pas faire de rabiot; **~maker** *s.*

horloger *m.*; **~wise,** dans le sens des aiguilles d'une montre; COUNTER **~wise**; **~work** *s.* mécanisme *m.*, *adj.* mécanique; **regular as ~work** (*fig.*) réglé comme un chronomètre; *v.t.* & *i.* chronométrer; **~ in/out, on/off** *v.t.* & *i.* (se faire) pointer à l'arrivée, au départ.

clod *s.* (*of earth*) motte *f.*; (*fig. person*) lourdaud *m.*; **~hopper** *s.* rustre *m.*

clog *s.* **1.** (*shoe*) *m.*; **2.** (*hobble* & *fig.*) entrave *f.*; *v.t.* (2) entraver; (*a pipe*) boucher; *v.i.* s'agglomérer; **become ~ged,** s'obstruer.

cloister *s.* cloître *m.*; *v.t.* cloîtrer.

close[1] *s.* enclos *m.*; (*cathedral ~*) parvis *m.*, place *f.*; *adj.* **1.** (*shut up*) fermé; **2.** (*confined*) renfermé; **3.** (*weather*) étouffant; **4.** (*narrow, tight*) étroit; **5.** (*fam. stingy*) serré; **6.** (*near in time or place*) proche; **7.** (*intimate*) intime; **8.** (*compact*) dense; **9.** (*crowded*) serré; **10.** (*private*) discret; (*secret*) exclusif; **11.** (*attentive*) attentif; **12.** (*sport*) presque égal; **13.** (*ling.*) fermé; **at ~** QUARTERS; **a ~** SHAVE; **sail ~ to the** WIND; **~-fisted** *adj.* grippe-sou; **~-fitting** *adj.* collant; **~-up** *s.* (*cinema*) plan rapproché *m.*; (*TV*) plan serré *m.*; *adv.* (4) étroitement; (6) tout près; (10) au secret; **~ly** *adv.* (4)*; (7)*; (10)*,*; (11)*; **~ness** *s.* (1), (2) manque d'air *m.*, odeur de renfermé *f.*; (3) lourdeur *f.*; (4) étroitesse *f.*; (5) avarice *f.*; (6) proximité *f.*; (7) intimité *f.*; (8), (9) densité *f.*, épaisseur *f.*; (10) caractère privé *m.*; (11) rigueur *f.*

close[2] *s.* (*end*) fin *f.*; *v.t.* & *i.* (*draw together*) serrer; (*end, come to an end*) terminer; **~ a session,** lever une séance; (*shut*) fermer; (*mil. ranks*) serrer; (*bargain*) conclure; **~ down** *v.t.* & *i.* fermer boutique; (*radio, TV*) terminer l'émission; **~ in** *v.i.* (*night*) tomber; **~ up** *v.t.* boucher; *v.i.* (*wound*) se fermer; **~d** *adj.* (*shut*) fermé; (*blocked*) barré; (*exclusive*) fermé; **with ~ed** DOORS; **~d shop,** qui n'admet que les travailleurs syndiqués; **~d circuit TV,** télévision en circuit fermé; **closing** *s.* fermeture *f.*, fin *f.*; *adj.* terminal, dernier; **closure** *s.* (*law, admin.*) clôture *f.*

closet *s.* (*small room*) cabinet *m.*; (*cupboard*) penderie *f.*; **~ed** *adj.* (*with*) enfermé (avec).

clot *s.* (*of earth*) motte *f.*; (*in milk, blood*) caillot *m.*; (*in flour, sauce, etc.*) grumeau *m.*; (*pop.* = *fool*) idiot *m.*; *v.i.* (*med.*) se coaguler; (*cook.*) se cailler, **~ted cream,** crème caillée *f.*

cloth *s.* drap *m.*; **table-~** (*linen*) nappe *f.*; (*heavy*) tapis *m.*; (*duster*) torchon *m.*

cloth/e *v.t.* habiller (*in, with*—de); (*fig.*) couvrir (de); **~ier** *s.* (*maker* & *dealer*) drapier *m.*; **~ing** *s.* vêtements *m.pl.*

clothes *s.pl.* habits *m.pl.*; vêtements *m.pl.*; **old ~,** défroque *f.*; **in plain ~,** en civil; **to** CHANGE **one's ~**; **~-**BRUSH; **~-horse** *s.* séchoir *m.*; **~-line** *s.* corde *f.*; **~-**PEG.

cloud *s.* (*in sky, of dust, etc.*) nuage *m.*; (*large number*) nuée *f.*; (*fig.*) ombre *m.*; **to be under a ~,** être en butte aux soupçons; **~burst** *s.* averse *f.*; **~less** *adj.* sans nuages; **~y** *adj.* (*weather*) nuageux; (*sky*) couvert; (*liquid*) trouble; (*fig.*) sombre; **it is ~y,** il y a des nuages; *v.t.* couvrir de nuages; (*a liquid*) troubler; (*fig.*) assombrir, obscurcir; *v.i.* se couvrir de nuages; **~ over** *v.i.* (*sky*) s'obscurcir; (*fig.*) s'assombrir.

clout *s.* **1.** (*cloth*) bout d'étoffe *m.*; **2.** (*blow*) gifle *f.*; **ne'er cast a ~ till May is out,** en avril ne te découvre pas d'un fil; *v.t.* (2) gifler.

clove *s.* clou de girofle *m.*; (*of garlic*) gousse (d'ail) *f.*

cloven *adj.* fourchu; **~-hoofed** (*fig.*) au pied fourchu.

clover *s.* trèfle *m.*; **to be in ~** (*fig.*) être comme un coq en pâte.

clown *s.* (*lout*) rustre *m.*; (*circus*) clown *m.*; *v.i.* faire le pitre.

cloy *v.t.* & *i.* rassasier.

club *s.* (*stick*) massue *f.*; (*golf*) club *m.*; (*society*) club *m.*, cercle *m.*, société *f.*; NIGHT-~; (*at cards*) trèfle *m.*; **~-footed** *adj.* qui a un pied-bot; **~house** *s.* club *m.*, cercle *m.*; *v.t.* (*hit*) matraquer; **~ together,** mettre en commun, agir en commun.

cluck *s.* gloussement *m.*; *v.i.* glousser.

clue *s.* indice *m.*, piste *f.*; (*crossword*) définition *f.*

clump *s.* (*of trees*) bouquet *m.*; (*of flowers, shrubs*) massif *m.*; *v.i.* **~ about,** marcher lourdement.

clums/y *adj.* **1.** (*person, physically*) maladroit; **2.** (*person, fig.*) gauche; **3.** (*thing*) incommode; **~ily** *adv.* (1)*, (2)*; **~iness** *s.* (1) maladresse *f.*; (2) gaucherie *f.*; (3) incommodité *f.*

cluster *s.* (*of fruit*) grappe *f.*; (*of flowers, trees*) bouquet *m.*; (*of houses*) pâté *m.*; (*of people*) groupe *m.*; (*of bananas*) régime *m.*; (*of bees*) essaim *m.*; *v.i.* se grouper.

clutch *s.* **1.** (*grasp*) étreinte *f.*, prise *f.*; **2.** (*of eggs*) couvée *f.*; **3.** (*auto.*) embrayage *m.*; **in the ~es of s.o.,** sous la griffe de qn.; **to let the ~ in** (*auto.*) embrayer; **to disengage the ~,** débrayer; *v.t.* (1) saisir, (*grasp*) empoigner.

clutter *s.* désordre *m.*; (*fam.*) pagaïe *f.*; *v.t.* jeter en désordre.

co- *pref.* co-, con-.

c/o (*abbrev. care of*) aux bons soins de.

coach *s.* **1.** (*gen.*) voiture *f.*; (*hist.*) carosse *f.*; (*rail.*) wagon *m.*; (*large bus*) autocar *m.*, car *m.*; STAGE-~; **2.** (*tutor*) répétiteur *m.*; **3.** (*sport*) entraîneur *m.*; SLOW **~**; **~-house** *s.* remise *f.*; **~man** *s.* cocher *m.*; **~work** *s.* (*auto.*) carosserie *f.*; *v.t.* (2) préparer à un examen; (3) entraîner.

coadjutor *s.* coadjuteur *m.*

coagulat/e *v.t.* & *i.* (se) coaguler; **~ion** *s.* coagulation *f.*

coal *s.* charbon *m.*, houille *f.*; **live ~s,** charbons ardents *m.pl.*; **to carry ~s to Newcastle,** porter de l'eau à la mer; **to haul s.o. over the ~s,** passer un savon à qn.; **~-black** *adj.* charbonneux; **~-cellar** *s.* cave à charbon *f.*; **~field** *s.* bassin houiller *m.*; **~-house** *s.* réduit à charbon *m.*; **~-mine, ~-pit** *s.* mine *f.*, houillère *f.*; **~-scuttle** *s.* seau à charbon *m.*; **~tar** *s.* goudron *m.*; *v.t.* & *i.* (*naut.*) (s')approvisionner en charbon.

coalesce *v.i.* se combiner; (*fin.*) fusionner; (*fig.*) s'unir.

coalition *s.* coalition *f.*

coarse *adj.* (*common, inferior*) commun; (*rough*) grossier; (*unrefined*) gros, rude; (*vulgar*) vulgaire; **~ly** *adv.* grossièrement; **~n** *v.t.* rendre grossier; **~ness** *s.* grossièreté *f.*

coast *s.* côte *f.*; **the ~ is** CLEAR; **~guard** *s.* garde-côte *m.*; **~line** *s.* littoral *m.*; **~al** *adj.* côtier; **~er** *s.* (*naut.*) caboteur *m.*; (*small mat*) dessous de bouteille, de carafe, de verre *m.*; *v.i.* (*bicycle, auto.*) descendre en roue libre.

coat *s.* (*clothing*) manteau *m.*; FROCK-~; **great-~,** manteau *m.*; **over~, top~,** pardessus *m.*; (*of animal*) pelage *m.*; (*of horse*) robe *f.*; (*of paint*) couche *f.*; **~ of** ARMS; **~ of mail** *s.* cotte de maille *f.*; **~-hanger** *s.* cintre *m.*; **~-tails,** basques *f.pl.*; *v.t.* **~ with,** enduire de; (*med., cook.*) enrober de; **~ing** *s.* (*paint*) couche *f.*; (*covering*) revêtement *m.*

coax *v.t.* cajoler; **~ing** *s.* câlinerie *f.*

cob *s.* (*horse*) bidet *m.*; (*nut*) grosse noisette *f.*; (*male swan*) cygne mâle *m.*; (*corn*) épi de maïs *m.*; (*building material*) torchis *m.*, bousillage *m.*

cobalt *s.* cobalt *m.*

cobble *s.* (*paving stone*) pavé *m.*; *v.t.* (*mend roughly*) rapetasser; **~r** *s.* cordonnier *m.*

cobra *s.* cobra *m.*

cobweb *s.* toile d'araignée *f.*

cocaine *s.* cocaïne *f.*

cochineal *s.* cochenille *f.*

cock *s.* **1.** (*male of hen*) coq *m.*; **2.** (*other male bird*) mâle *m.*; **3.** (*tap*) robinet *m.*; **4.** (*of gun*) chien *m.*; **5.** (*of hay*) meulon *m.*; **~-and-bull story,** histoire à dormir debout *f.*; **~-crow** *s.* chant du coq *m.*; **~-eyed** *adj.* (*pop.*) tout de traviole; **~-fight** *s.* combat de coqs *m.*; **~-a-doodle-do,** cocorico; **~-a-hoop** *adj.* jubilant; **~sure** *adj.* outrecuidant; **~y** *adj.* arrogant; *v.t.* (*erect*) dresser; (4) (*gun*) armer; (5) (*hay*) mettre en meule; **~ a** SNOOK; **~ed hat** *s.* chapeau à cornes *m.*, bicorne *m.*, tricorne *m.*; **to knock s.o. into a ~ed hat** (*fig.*) abasourdir qn.
cockade *s.* cocarde *f.*
cockatoo *s.* cacatoès *m.*
cockatrice *s.* basilic *m.*
cockchafer *s.* hanneton *m.*
cockerel *s.* petit coq *m.*
cockle *s.* (*shell*) clovisse *f.*; **the ~s of the heart,** le tréfonds du cœur *m.sing.*; *v.t.* & *i.* (se) recoquiller.
cockney *adj.* & *s.* cockney.
cockpit *s.* arène *f.*; (*fig.*) arènes *f.pl.*; (*aviat.*) cabine de pilotage *f.*; (*naut.*) poste des blessés *m.*; (*yacht*) cockpit *m.*
cockroach *s.* cafard *m.*
cockscomb, coxcomb *s.* crête *f.*; (*fam. person*) fat *m.*
cocktail *s.* cocktail *m.*; **~ party,** cocktail *m.*
coconut *s.* noix de coco *f.*; **~-tree,** cocotier *m.*; **~ matting,** tapis en fibres de coco *m.*
cocoa *s.* cacao *m.*
cocoon *s.* cocon *m.*
C.O.D. (*abbrev. for 'cash on delivery'*), livraison contre remboursement
cod *s.* (*fish*) morue *f.*; **~-liver oil,** huile de foie de morue *f.*
coddle *v.t.* choyer; (*cook.*) faire bouillir doucement.
code *s.* **1.** (*laws, set of rules; signals*) code *m.*; **2.** (*secret writing*) chiffre *m.*; **Highway C~,** code de la route *m.*; **~-word** *s.* mot convenu *m.*; *v.t.* (2) chiffrer; **codify** *v.t.* codifier.
codeine *s.* codéine *f.*
codicil *s.* codicille *m.*
coeducation *s.* enseignement mixte *m.*
coefficient *s.* (*math.*) coefficient *m.*
coequal *adj.* & *s.m.f.* égal(e).
coerc/e *v.t.* contraindre (à); **~ion** *s.* contrainte *f.*; **~ive** *adj.* coercitif.
coeval *adj.* contemporain (*with*—de).
coexist *v.i.* coexister; **~ence** *s.* coexistence *f.*
C. of E. (*abbrev. for Church of England*) église anglicane *f.*
coffee *s.* café *m.*; **white ~,** café au lait *m.*; **black ~,** café noir *m.*; **~-**BEAN; **~-coloured** *adj.* café au lait; **~-**GROUNDS; **~-house** *s.* café *m.*; **~-**MILL; **~-pot** *s.* cafetière *f.*
coffer *s.* coffre *m.*; (*for money*) caisse *f.*; **~s** *s.pl.* (= *funds*) Trésor public *m.*; **~-dam** *s.* cloison de sûreté *m.*
coffin *s.* cercueil *m.*
cog *s.* (*techn.*) dent *f.*; **~-wheel,** roue dentée *f.*; *v.t.* denter.
cogen/cy *s.* force *f.*; (*law*) bien-fondé *m.*; **~t** *adj.* puissant.
cogitat/e *v.i.* méditer; **~ion** *s.* méditation *f.*
cognate *adj.* (*law*) parent; (*ling.*) apparenté.
cognizan/ce *s.* **1.** connaissance *f.*; **2.** (*law*) compétence *f.*; **to take ~ of,** prendre connaissance de; **~t** *adj.* (1) instruit (*of*—de); (2) compétent (pour).
cohabit *v.i.* cohabiter.
coheir(ess) *s.* cohérit/ier, -ière *m.f.*
coher/e *v.i.* **1.** (*stick to*) adhérer à; **2.** (*fig. be lucid*) être cohérent; **~ence** *s.* (1) adhérence *f.*; (2) cohérence *f.*; **~ent** *adj.* (1) adhérent; (2) cohérent; **~ently** *adv.* (2) avec cohérence.
cohes/ion *s.* cohésion *f.*; **~ive** *adj.* cohésif.
cohort *s.* cohorte *f.*
coil *s.* **1.** (*rope, etc.*) rouleau *m.*, (*naut.*) glène *f.*; **2.** (*snake*) anneau *m.*; **3.** (*electr.*) bobine *f.*; *v.t.* (1) enrouler; (*naut.*) lover; (3) bobiner; *v.i.* (2) se lover.
coin *s.* monnaie *f.*, pièce de monnaie *f.*; *v.t.* frapper; (*fig.*) inventer; **~ money** (*fig.*) faire des affaires d'or; **~age** *s.* (*act*) frappe *f.*; (*coins*) monnaie *f.*; (*system*) système monétaire *m.*; **~er** *s.* monnayeur *m.*; (*counterfeit*) faux-monnayeur *m.*; (*fig.*) inventeur *m.*
coincid/e *v.i.* coïncider; **~e with,** s'accorder avec; **~ence** *s.* coïncidence *f.*; **~ental** *adj.* par coïncidence.
coke *s.* (*fuel*) coke *m.*; (*pop. abbrev. for cocaine*) coco *m.*; (*pop. abbrev. for coca-cola*) coca-cola *f.*
colander *s.* passoire *f.*
cold *s.* (*temperature*) froid *m.*; (*med.*) rhume *m.*; **~ in the head,** rhume de cerveau *m.*; **to catch a ~,** s'enrhumer; *adj.* (*lit.* & *fig.*) froid; **in ~ blood,** de sang-froid; **~-blooded** *adj.* (*fig.*) insensible; **to be ~** (*person*) avoir froid; (*weather*) **it is ~,** il fait froid; **to get ~,** se refroidir; **my feet are ~,** j'ai froid aux pieds; **to have ~ feet** (*fig. fam.*) avoir la frousse; **that leaves me ~,** cela ne me dit rien; **~ cream** *s.* crème de beauté *f.*; **~-shoulder** *v.t.* (*fig.*) faire grise mine à qn.; **~ storage** *s.* entrepôt frigorifique *m.*; **~ war** *s.* guerre froide *f.*; **~ly** *adv.* froidement; (*calmly*) calmement; **~ness** *s.* (*fig.*) froideur *f.*
colic *s.* colique *f.*
collaborat/e *v.i.* collaborer (*in sth.*—à qch.), (*with s.o.*—avec qn.); **~ion** *s.* collaboration *f.*; **~or** *s.* collaborat/eur, -rice *m.f.*
collaps/e *s.* (*lit.* & *fig.*) effondrement *m.*; *v.i.* s'effondrer; **~ible** *adj.* pliant.
collar *s.* (*shirt, etc.*) col *m.*; (*coat*) collet *m.*; (*detachable*) faux-col *m.*; (*lace, etc.*) collerette *f.*; (*for dog, etc.*) collier *m.*; **~-bone** *s.* clavicule *f.*; **~-**STUD; *v.t.* (*pop.*) cramponner (qn.); rafler (qch.).
collat/e *v.t.* **1.** (*compare*) comparer (à); **2.** (*place in order*) collationner (avec); **~ion** *s.* (1) comparaison *f.*; (2) collation *f.*; **3.** (*light meal*) collation *f.*
collateral *s.* (*relation*) collatéral *m.*; (*fin.*) nantissement *m.*; *adj.* collatéral.
colleague *s.* collègue *m.f.*
collect[1] *s.* (*prayer*) collecte *f.*
collect[2] *v.t.* **1.** (*gather*) rassembler; (*eggs, etc.*) ramasser; (*wealth*) amasser; **2.** (*stamps, etc.*) collectionner; **3.** (*letters*) faire la levée de; **4.** (*taxes*) percevoir; **5.** (*debts*) recouvrer; **6.** (*tickets*) contrôler; **7.** (*thoughts*) rassembler; **8.** (*news, etc.*) recueillir; *v.i.* (*people*) se rassembler; (*things*) s'amasser; **~ed** *adj.* calme; **~ion** *s.* (1) rassemblement *m.*, ramassage *m.*, amas *m.*; (2) collection *f.*; (3) levée *f.*; (4) perception *f.*; (5) recouvrement *m.*; (6) contrôle *m.*; (8) recueil *m.*; **9.** (*in church*) quête *f.*; **to take the ~ion,** faire la quête; **~ive** *adj.* collectif; **~ive** BARGAIN**ing**; **~ivity** *s.* collectivité *f.*; **~or** *s.* (1) ramasseur *m.*; (2) collectionneur *m.*; (4) percepteur *m.*; (5) encaisseur *m.*; (6) contrôleur *m.*; RENT **~or.**
colleg/e *s.* (*univ.*) collège universitaire *m.*, faculté *f.*; (*mus.*) conservatoire *f.*; (*learned society*) institut *m.*, académie *f.*; (*school*) collège *m.*; TECHNICAL **~e**; TRAINING **~e**; **~iate** *adj.* de collège.
collide *v.i.* se heurter; **~ with,** entrer en collision avec.
collier *s.* (*person*) mineur *m.*; (*ship*) charbonnier *m.*; **~y** *s.* houillère *f.*
collision *s.* collision *f.*; (*rail.*) tamponnement *m.*; (*naut.*) abordage *m.*; (*fig.*) conflit *m.*; **~ course** (*fig.*) trajectoire de collision *f.*

collocate *v.t.* arranger.
colloqu/y *s.* (*discussion*) colloque *m.*; (conversation) entretien *m.*; **~ial** *adj.* familier, (*ling.*) parlé; **~ialism** *s.* expression familière *f.*; **~ially** *adv.* familièrement, dans la langue parlée.
collu/de *v.i.* s'entendre secrètement; **~sion** *s.* collusion *f.*; **~sive** *adj.* collusoire.
collywobbles *s.* (*fam.*) colique *f.*
colon *s.* **1.** (*ling.*) deux points *m.pl.*; **2.** (*med.*) colon *m.*
colonel *s.* colonel *m.*
colonnade *s.* colonnade *f.*
colon/y *s.* colonie *f.*; **~ial** *adj.* & *s.m.* colonial; **~ialism** *s.* colonialisme *m.*; **~ist** *s.* (*settler*) colon *m.*; **~ize** *v.t.* coloniser; **~ization** *s.* colonisation *f.*
colo(u)ration *s.* coloration *f.*
coloss/al *adj.* colossal; **~us** *s.* colosse *m.*
colour *s.* couleur *f.*; (*complexion*) teint *m.*; **~s** *s.pl.* (*flag*) couleurs *f.pl.*, drapeau *m.*, (*naut.*) pavillon *m.*; (*paints*) couleurs *f.pl.*; **under ~ of** (*fig.*) sous prétexte de; **to be off ~** (*fam.*) ne pas être bien dans son assiette; TROOPING **the ~; with flying ~s** (*fig.*) brillamment; **~ bar** *s.* ségrégation *f.*; **~-blind** *adj.* daltonien; **~-blindness** *s.* daltonisme *m.*; **~-bearer** *s.* porte-drapeau *m.*; **~ful** *adj.* vif; (*character*) original; (*story*) intéressant; **~less** *adj.* incolore; *v.t.* (*paint* & *fig.*) colorer; (*crayon*) colorier; (*dye*) teindre; *v.i.* se colorer; (*blush*) rougir; **~ed** *adj.* coloré; (*person*) de couleur; **~ing** *s.* coloration *f.*, coloris *m.*; **~ist** *s.* coloriste *m.*
colt *s.* (*young horse*) poulain *m.*; (*at sport, novice*) débutant *m.*
columbine *s.* (*bot.*) ancolie *f.*
column *s.* (*arch., mil., newspaper*) colonne *f.*; **~ist** *s.* journaliste *m.f.*
coma *s.* coma *m.*; **~tose** *adj.* comateux.
comb *s.* peigne *m.*; (*techn. for wool*) carde *f.*; (*cock's*) crête *f.*; HONEY~; *v.t.* peigner; **~ one's hair,** se peigner; (*techn.*) carder; (*mil., police*) battre, fouiller; **~ out** *v.t.* démêler.
combat *s.* combat *m.*; *v.t.* & *i.* combattre; **~ant** *s.* combattant *m.*; **~ive** *adj.* combatif.
combin/e *s.* (*law*) corporation *f.*; (*comm.*) cartel *m.*; *v.t.* combiner; *v.i.* s'unir; (*comm.*) fusionner; (*chem.*) se combiner; (*fig.*) se liguer (contre); **~e harvester** *s.* moissonneuse-batteuse(-lieuse) *f.*; **~ation** *s.* combinaison *f.*
combust/ible *adj.* & *s.m.* combustible; **~ibility** *s.* combustibilité *f.*; **~ion** *s.* combustion *f.*
come *v.i.* (*draw near*) venir; (*arrive, occur*) arriver; (*become*) devenir; **~ and go,** aller et venir; **~ about** *v.i.* arriver; **~ across** *v.t.* rencontrer; **~ along** *v.i.* avancer; **~ at** *v.i.* arriver à; **~ away** *v.i.* partir; (*thing*) se détacher; **~ back** *v.i.* revenir; **~-back** *s.* retour *m.*; **~ by** *v.t.* se procurer; **~ down** *v.i.* descendre; **~-down** *s.* chute *f.*; **~ down in the world,** se déclasser; **~ down to** *v.i.* se ramener à; **~ for** *v.t.* venir chercher; **~ from** *v.i.* venir de; (*nationality*) être originaire de; **~ hither look** *s.* geste d'appel *m.*; **~ home** *v.i.* rentrer (à la maison); **~ in** *v.i.* entrer; (*tide*) monter; **~ in handy,** se révéler utile; **~ into** *v.i.* entrer dans; *v.t.* (*inherit*) entrer en possession de; **~ near** *v.t.* & *i.* approcher (de); **~ near to doing sth.,** faillir faire qch.; **~ of** *v.i.* descendre de; **~ off** *v.i.* se détacher; (*happen*) avoir lieu; (*succeed*) réussir; **~ off it!** (*pop.*) la barbe!; **~ on** *v.t.* tomber sur; *v.i.* avancer, arriver; (*fig.*) progresser; **it came on to rain,** il se mit à pleuvoir; **~ out** *v.i.* sortir; (*book*) paraître; (*flower*) fleurir; (*show oneself*) se révéler; (*on strike*) se mettre en grève; **~ over** *v.i.* passer de l'autre côté; *v.t.* traverser; **~ round** *v.i.* (*periodically*) revenir; (*med.*) revenir à soi; (*fig.*) retrouver son calme; **~ through** *v.t.* passer par; (*successfully*) venir à bout de; **~ to** *v.i.* arriver à; (*finally*) aboutir à; (*decision*) prendre; (*fin.*) revenir à; (*med.*) reprendre connaissance; **~ to nothing,** n'aboutir à rien; **~ to the same thing,** revenir au même; **~ to pass,** arriver; **~ up** *v.i.* monter; (*fig.*) apparaître; (*plant*) pousser; (*law*) comparaître; (*arise*) se soulever; **~ up to** *v.t.* (*goal*) atteindre; (*hopes, etc.*) réaliser, répondre à; (*be capable of*) être à la hauteur de; **~ up with** *v.t.* (*reach*) atteindre; (*propose*) proposer; **~r** *s.* (*first, last, new*) premier, dernier, nouveau venu *m.*
comed/y *s.* comédie *f.*; **~ian** *s.* (*theat.* & *fig.*) comédien(ne) *m.f.*; (*music-hall*) comique *m.f.*
comel/y *adj.* avenant; (*fitting*) bienséant; **~iness** *s.* grâce *f.*
comestible *adj.* & *s.m.* (*usu. pl.*) comestible.
comet *s.* comète *f.*
comfit *s.* dragée *f*
comfort *s.* **1.** (*consolation*) consolation *f.*; **2.** (*relief*) soulagement *m.*; **3.** (*ease*) confort *m.*, aises *f.pl.*; **4.** (*satisfaction*) satisfaction *f.*; *v.t.* (1) consoler; (2) soulager; (3) réconforter; (4) satisfaire à; **~able** *adj.* (3) (⚠ *only of sth. which provides* ~) confortable; (*person*) à l'aise, confortablement installé, assis, etc.; **to make oneself ~able,** se mettre à l'aise; (4) rassuré; (*fin.*) aisé; **~ably** *adv.* (3) confortablement, à l'aise; (*fin.*) dans l'aisance; **~er** *s.* (1) consolat/eur, -rice *m.f.*; (*muffler*) cache-nez *m.*; (*child's*) sucette *f.*; **~less** *adj.* (*thing or place*) sans confort, incommode; (*person*) délaissé.
comic *s.* (*quality*) comique *m.*; (*actor*) *see* COMEDIAN; (*fam.*) comédien *m.*; (*paper*) journal humoristique *m.*, (*child's*) journal pour enfant *m.*; *adj.* comique; **~ally** *adv.**.
coming *s.* venue *f.*; **~(s) and going(s)**, va-et-vient *m.*, allées et venues *f.pl.*; (*eccles.*) avènement *m.*; **~-back** *s.* retour *m.*; **~-in** *s.* entrée *f.*; **~-out** *s.* sortie *f.*; *adj.* (*to come*) à venir; (*future*) futur; (*next*) prochain; UP **and ~**; *interj.* j'arrive!
comity *s.* courtoisie *f.*; ⚠ comité = **committee.**
comma *s.* virgule *f.*; **inverted ~s,** guillemets *m.pl.*
command *s.* **1.** (*order*) ordre *m.*; **2.** (*authority*) commandement *m.*; **3.** (*district*) région *f.*, zone *f.*; **4.** (*fig. of language etc.*) maîtrise *f.*; **self-~,** maîtrise de soi *f.*; **to have at one's ~**, avoir à sa disposition; **second in ~**, adjoint *m.*; (*mil.*) en second; **~ performance** *s.* spectacle donné sur l'ordre de qn. *m.*; *v.t.* (1) ordonner (à qn. de faire qch.); (2) contrôler; (*dominate*) dominer; (*overlook*) donner sur; (*~ respect*) inspirer; (*have available*) disposer de; *v.i.* commander; **~ant** *s.* commandant *m.*; **~eer** *v.t.* réquisitionner; **~er** *s.* commandant *m.*; (*of an order*) commandeur *m.*; (*naut.*) capitaine de frégate *m.*; (*mil., aviat.*) lieutenant-colonel *m.*; (*civil aviat.*) chef de bord *m.*; **~ing** *adj.* (*air, etc.*) imposant; (*position*) dominant; **~ment** *s.* commandement *m.*; **~o** *s.* commando *m.*
commemorat/e *v.t.* commémorer; **~ion** *s.* commémoration *f.*; **~ive** *adj.* commémoratif.
commence *v.t.* & *i.* commencer (à, de); **~ment** *s.* commencement *m.*; (*law*) date d'entrée en vigueur *f.*
commend *v.t.* **1.** (*praise*) louer; **2. ~ sth. to s.o.**, confier qch. aux soins de qn.; **~able** *adj.* louable; **~ably** *adv.* d'une manière louable; **~ation** *s.* (1) louange *f.*; (2) recommandation *f.*; **~atory** *adj.* élogieux.
commensurab/le *adj.* commensurable (avec); **~ility** *s.* commensurabilité *f.*
commensurate *adj.* (*with*) proportionné (à), de même mesure (que).
comment *s.* remarque *f.*; (*extended*) commen-

taire *m.*; *v.t.* & *i.* (~ *on*) commenter; **~ary** *s.* commentaire *m.*; (*radio, TV*) **live ~ary,** reportage en direct *m.*; **~ator** *s.* commentat/eur, -rice, *m.f.*

commerc/e *s.* commerce *m.*; **~ial** *adj.* (*relating to ~e*) commercial, de commerce; (*nation, street, etc.*) commerçant; *s.* (*TV, radio, cinema*) message publicitaire *m.*; **~ial traveller** *s.* commis-voyageur *m.*; **~ially** *adv.* commercialement.

commiserat/e *v.i.* (*with*) compatir (à); **~ion** *s.* commisération *f.*

commissar *s.* (*U.S.S.R.*) commissaire du peuple *m.*

commissariat *s.* (*mil.*) intendance *f.*

commissary *s.* (*mil.*) officier d'intendance *m.*; (*gen.*) commissaire *m.*

commission *s.* **1.** (*order, task; order for piece of work*) commande *f.*; **2.** (*of crime, etc.*) perpétration *f.*; **3.** (*mil., etc.*) brevet *m.*; **4.** (*comm.*) commission *f.*; **5.** (*body of people*) commission *f.*; **6.** (*naut.*) armement *m.*; *v.t.* (1) charger de; donner une commande pour; (3) nommer au commandement; (6) armer; **take out of ~,** désarmer; **~aire** *s.* porteur *m.*; (*hotel*) chasseur *m.*; **~er** *s.* commissaire *m.*

commit *v.t.* (*crime, act*) commettre; (*hand over*) livrer; (*entrust*) confier (*to*—à); **~ to memory,** apprendre par cœur; **~ to prison,** condamner à la prison; **~ to writing,** coucher par écrit; **~ oneself,** s'engager (*to*—à); **~ment** *s.* engagement *m.*; **~tal** *s.* (*order*) mandat *m.*; (*act*) perpétration *f.*; **~tee** *s.* comité *m.*; (*parl.*) commission *f.*; (*of a society*) bureau *m.*

commode *s.* (*chest*) commode *f.*; (*night*) chaise percée *f.*

commodious *adj.* spacieux; **~ly** *adv.**.

commodity *s.* (*manufactured*) produit *m.*; (*raw*) denrée *f.*; ⚠ commodité = **convenience, utility.**

commodore *s.* (*naut.*) (*approx.*) capitaine de vaisseau *m.*; (*air ~*) général de brigade aérienne *m.*; (*of yacht-club*) président *m.*

common *s.* (*land*) terrain communal *m.*; **out of the ~,** hors du commun, extraordinaire; **in ~,** en commun; (*pl.*) **the (House of) C~s,** la Chambre des Communes *f.*; *adj.* **1.** (*shared by all*) commun; **2.** (*ordinary*) ordinaire; **3.** (*frequent*) habituel; **4.** (*inferior*) commun; **5.** (*vulgar*) vulgaire; **~ or garden,** le plus ordinaire; **~ law** *s.* droit coutumier *m.*; **~place** *s.* lieu commun *m.*, *adj.* banal; **~ sense** *s.* sens commun *m.*; **~weal** *s.* intérêt public *m.*; **~wealth** *s.* (*British*) Commonwealth *m.*, (*gen.*) république *f.*; **~er** *s.* rotur/ier, -ière *m.f.*; **~ly** *adv.* (1) communément; (2)*; (3)*; (4) de façon inférieure; (5)*; **~ness** *s.* (1) caractère commun *m.*; (2) caractère ordinaire *m.*; (3) fréquence *f.*; (4) infériorité *f.*; (5) vulgarité *f.*

commotion *s.* (*phys.* & *emotional, of person*) commotion *f.*; (*noise*) brouhaha *m.*; (*revolt*) insurrection *f.*

communal *adj.* communal (*only = relating to a* 'commune'); commun, collectif.

commune *v.i.* (*with*) parler intimement (avec).

communicant *s.* (*eccles.*) communiant(e) *m.f.*; (*churchgoer*) fidèle *m.f.*

communic/ate *v.t.* communiquer, transmettre; *v.i.* communiquer (*with*—avec); (*eccles.*) communier; **~able** *adj.* communicable; **~ating** *adj.* communicant; **~ation** *s.* communication *f.*; **~ation cord** (*rail.*) signal d'alarme *m.*; **~ative** *adj.* communicatif.

communion *s.* (*eccles. service* & *church*) communion *f.*; (*comm.*) relations *f.pl.*

commun/ism *s.* communisme *m.*; **~ist** *s.* communiste *m.f.*

community *s.* (*society, relig. order,* & *fig.*) communauté *f.*; (*gen.*) collectivité *f.*; ville *f.*, nation *f.*; *adj.* communautaire.

commut/e *v.t.* **1.** (*exchange*) échanger; (*law*) commuer (*into*—en); **2.** (*travel*) voyager avec une carte d'abonnement; **~able** *adj.* (1) échangeable; (*law*) commuable; **~ation** *s.* (1) échange *f.*; (*law*) commutation *f.*; **~ator** *s.* (*electr.*) commutateur *m.*; **~er** *s.* (2) banlieusard(e) *m.f.*

compact *s.* (*treaty*) pacte *m.*; (*for powder*) poudrier *m.*; *adj.* compact; (*fig.*) concis; **~ly** *adv.* d'une façon compacte; **~ness** *s.* compacité *f.*; *v.t.* rendre compact.

companion *s.* compagnon *m.*, compagne *f.*; (*employee*) dame de compagnie *f.*; (*one of pair*) pendant *m.*; **~able** *adj.* sociable; **~ship** *s.* camaraderie *f.*; (*company*) compagnie *f.*; **~-way** *s.* (*naut.*) échelle *f.*

company *s.* (*society, theat., mil.*) compagnie *f.*; REPERTORY **~**; (*naut. ship's ~*) équipage *m.*; (*guests*) du monde, **our neighbours have ~,** il y a du monde chez les voisins; **to part ~ with s.o.,** quitter qn.; (*comm.*) société *f.*; **limited ~,** société à responsabilité limitée *f.*; (*abbrev.*) S.A.R.L.; **& Co.,** et Cie.

compar/e *v.t.* comparer (*to, with*—à, avec); *v.i.* être comparable à; **~ed with,** en comparaison de; **~able** *adj.* comparable (à); **~ative** *adj.* comparatif; *s.* (*ling.*) comparatif *m.*; **~atively** *adv.* relativement; **~ison** *s.* comparaison *f.*

compartment *s.* compartiment *m.*

compass *s.* (*range*) étendue *f.*; (*scope*) portée *f.*; **within the ~ of,** à la portée de; (*limits*) limites *f.pl.*; (*instrument*) boussole *f.*; (*math.*) compas *m.*; **~ points,** points cardinaux *m.pl.*; *v.t.* (*go round*) faire le tour de; (*surround*) entourer de.

compassion *s.* compassion *f.*; **to have ~ on,** avoir pitié de; **~ate** *adj.* compatissant; **~ate leave,** congé (*m.*) pour convenance personnelle.

compatib/le *adj.* compatible (avec); **~ility** *s.* compatibilité *f.*

compatriot *s.* compatriote *m.f.*

compel *v.t.* (*force*) forcer (à, de); (*bring about inevitably*) imposer; (*command attention, etc.*) commander.

compend/ium *s.* abrégé *m.*; **~ious** *adj.* abrégé.

compensat/e *v.t.* **1.** (*counterbalance*) compenser; **2.** (*recompense*) indemniser; **3. ~ for,** dédommager de; **~ion** *s.* (1) compensation *f.*; (2) indemnité *f.*; (3) dédommagement *m.*

compère *s.* présentateur *m.*, meneur de jeu *m.*; ⚠ compère = **comrade; conjuror's assistant**; *v.t.* présenter.

compet/e *v.i.* concourir (*for*—pour); **~e with,** faire concurrence à; **~ition** *s.* (*competing, sport*) compétition *f.*; (*rivalry*) concurrence *f.*; (*exam., etc.*) concours *m.*; **~itive** *adj.* de concours; **~itor** *s.* concurrent(e) *m.f.*

compet/ence *s.* **1.** (*means*) aisance *f.*; **2.** (*ability*) capacité *f.*; **3.** (*law*) compétence *f.*; **~ent** *adj.* (2) capable; (3) compétent; **~ently** *adv.* avec compétence; ⚠ compétence, compétent, *properly = 3 only but are also currently used for 2.*

compil/e *v.t.* compiler; **~ation** *s.* (*act* & *thing ~ed*) compilation *f.*; **~er** *s.* compilat/eur, -rice *m.f.*

complacen/t *adj.* **1.** (*self-satisfied*) content de soi; **2.** (*good-humoured*) complaisant; **~cy** *s.* (1) contentement de soi *m.*; (2) complaisance *f.*

complain *v.i.* (*whimper*) gémir; (*make ~t*) se plaindre (de); **~t** *s.* (*objection*) plainte *f.*; (*subject of ~*) grief *m.*; (*illness*) maladie *f.*

complaisan/ce *s.* **1.** (*civility*) courtoisie *f.*; **2.** (*desire to please*) complaisance *f.*; **~t** *adj.* (1) courtois; (2) complaisant.

complement *s.* (*math., ling.*) complément *m.*;

(*naut.*) effectif *m.*; *v.t.* compléter; **~ary** *adj.* complémentaire.

complet/e *adj.* **1.** (*having all its parts*) complet; **2.** (*finished*) achevé; **3.** (*thorough*) parfait; *v.t.* (1) compléter; (2) achever; (3) parfaire; **~ely** *adv.* complètement, parfaitement; **~eness** *s.* (1) plénitude *f.*; **~ion** *s.* (2) (*act*) achèvement *m.*; (*result*) accomplissement *m.*

complex *s.* (*group of parts*; *psych.*) complexe *m.*; *adj.* **1.** (*consisting of parts*) complexe; **2.** (*complicated*) compliqué; **~ity** *s.* (1) complexité *f.*; (2) complication *f.*

complexion *s.* (*colour of skin*) teint *m.*; (*character*) caractère *m.*; ⚠ complexion = (*physical*) **constitution.**

complian/ce *s.* (*agreement*) acquiescement *m.*; (*agreeing*) conformité *f.*; **in ~ce with,** conformément à; **~t** *adj.* accommodant.

complicat/e *v.t.* compliquer; **~ed** *adj.* compliqué; **~ion** *s.* complication *f.*

complicity *s.* complicité *f.*

compliment *s.* compliment *m.*; **~s** (*pl.* = *greetings*) hommages *m.pl.*; **~ary** *adj.* (*expressing praise*) flatteur; (*free*) à titre gracieux; **~ary-ticket** *s.* billet de faveur *m.*; *v.t.* complimenter (*on*—pour).

compline *s.* (*eccles.*) complies *f.pl.*

comply *v.i.* se plier; **~ with,** se conformer à.

component *s.* (*chem.*) composant *m.*; (*techn.*) composante *f.*; *adj.* composant.

comport (*oneself*) *v.refl.* se comporter; **~ment** *s.* comportement *m.*

compos/e *v.t.* (*form, constitute*; *liter., mus.*; *print.*) composer; (*settle, adjust*) arranger; (*make calm*) calmer; (*reconcile*) apaiser; **be ~ed of,** se composer de; **~ed** *adj.* (*quiet*) tranquille, (*calm*) calme; **~er** *s.* (*mus.*) compositeur *m.*

composite *adj.* & *s.m.* composé; (*arch.*) composite.

composition *s.* (*act of composing*; *thing composed*; *nature of a thing*) composition *f.*; (*agreement*) arrangement *m.*; (*artificial substance*) composé *m.*

compositor *s.* (*print.*) compositeur *m.*

compost *s.* humus *m.*

composure *s.* sang-froid *m.*

compote *s.* (*cook.*) compote *f.*

compound *s.* (*mixture*; *chem.*) composé *m.*; (*ling.*) mot composé *m.*; (*overseas* = *enclosure*) enclos *m.*; *adj.* (*composite*) composé; (≠ *simple*) compliqué; (*math.*) composé; (*med.*) compliqué; (*techn.*) compound; *v.t.* (*mix*) composer; (*settle*) arranger; *v.i.* (*come to terms*) s'arranger; **~ a felony,** pactiser avec un crime.

comprehen/d *v.t.* **1.** (*understand*) & **2.** (*comprise*) comprendre; **~sible** *adj.* (1) compréhensible; **~sion** *s.* (1) compréhension *f.*; (2) portée *f.*; **~sive** *adj.* (2) étendu; **~sive school** *s.* collège *m.* *or* lycée *m.* polyvalent.

compress *s.* (*med.*) compresse *f.*; *v.t.* **1.** (*squeeze together*) comprimer; **2.** (*make smaller*) condenser; **~ed** *adj.* (1) comprimé; (2) concis; **~ible** *adj.* compressible; **~ion** *s.* (1) compression *f.*; (2) concentration *f.*; **~or** *s.* compresseur *m.*

comprise *v.t.* comprendre.

compromise *s.* compromis *m.*; *v.t.* régler par un compromis; (*bring under suspicion*) compromettre; *v.i.* transiger.

comptroller *s.* (*fin.*) économe *m.*; (*admin.*) auditeur à la cour des comptes *m.*

compuls/ion *s.* **1.** (*force*) contrainte *f.*; **under ~ion,** de force; **2.** (*impulse*) impulsion *f.*; **~ive** *adj.* (1) coercitif; (2) impulsif; **~ory** *adj.* obligatoire; **~orily** adv.*.

compunction *s.* remords *m.*

comput/e *v.t.* **1.** (*calculate*) calculer; **2.** (*estimate*) évaluer; **~ation** *s.* (1) calcul *m.*; (2) évaluation *f.*; **~er** *s.* (*electr.*) ordinateur *m.*

comrade *s.* camarade *m.*; **~ship** *s.* camaraderie *f.*

con[1] *s.* contre *m.*; **the pros and ~s,** le pour et le contre.

con[2] *v.t.* (*study*) étudier; (*naut.*) gouverner; (*pop.* = *dupe*) escroquer.

concatenation *s.* enchaînement *m.*

concav/e *adj.* concave; **~ity** *s.* concavité *f.*

conceal *v.t.* **1.** (*hide*) cacher; **2.** (*dissimulate*) dissimuler; **3.** (*not reveal*) garder secret; **~ment** *s.* (1) (*act of hiding*) action de cacher *f.*; (2) (*secrecy*) dissimulation *f.*; (*hiding-place*) cachette *f.*

concede *v.t.* (*grant*) concéder; (*admit as true*) admettre; (*allow*) accorder.

conceit *s.* (*vanity*) vanité *f.*; (*liter. far-fetched ideas*) concetti *m.pl.*; **~ed** *adj.* vaniteux; **~edly** *adv.**.

conceiv/e *v.t.* & *i.* (*lit.* & *fig.*) concevoir; **~able** *adj.* concevable.

concentrat/e *s.* concentré *m.*; *v.t.* & *i.* (se) concentrer; **~ion** *s.* concentration *f.*; **~ion camp,** camp de concentration *m.*

concentric *adj.* concentrique.

concept *s.* concept *m.*

conception *s.* conception *f.*

concern *s.* (*matter, question*) affaire *f.*; (*importance*) importance *f.*; (*anxiety*) souci *m.*; (*comm.*) entreprise *f.*; *v.t.* (*affect*) intéresser; (*trouble*) inquiéter; (*interest, involve*) être l'affaire de; (*be relevant to*) regarder; (*relate to*) concerner; ⚠ concerner *is not used with a person subject*; **as far as I am ~ed,** en ce qui me concerne; **to whom it may ~,** à qui de droit; **~ oneself about,** s'inquiéter de; **~ oneself with,** s'intéresser à; **~ed** *adj.* (*involved*) intéressé; (*troubled*) soucieux; **to be ~ed,** être soucieux (*about*—de); **those ~ed,** les intéressés *m.pl.*; **~ing** *prep.* en ce qui concerne.

concert *s.* (*mus.*) concert *m.*; (*agreement*) concorde *f.*; **in ~ with,** d'accord avec; **~ hall,** salle de concert *f.*; ~ PITCH; *v.t.* concerter.

concertina *s.* concertina *m.*

concerto *s.* concerto *m.*

concession *s.* concession *f.*; **~aire** *s.* concessionnaire *m.*; **~ary** *adj.* concédé.

conch *s.* conque *f.*; **~ology** *s.* conchyliologie *f.*; **~ologist** *s.* conchyliologiste *m.f.*

conciliat/e *v.t.* **1.** (*propitiate*) réconcilier; **2.** (*win over*) gagner (à); **3.** (*reconcile*) concilier; **~ion** *s.* (1) réconciliation *f.*; (3) conciliation *f.*; **~ory** *adj.* conciliant, de conciliation.

concise *adj.* concis; **~ly** *adv.* avec concision; **~ness** *s.* concision *f.*

conclave *s.* (*papal*) conclave *m.*; (*private meeting*) conférence *f.*; (*secret meeting*) conciliabule *m.*

conclude *v.t.* & *i.* (*bring or come to an end*) conclure; (*finish*) achever; (*infer*) conclure.

conclus/ion *s.* (*ending, inference*) conclusion *f.*; (*final opinion*) décision *f.*; **in ~ion,** pour conclure; **it is, was, a** FOREGONE **~ion**; **~ive** *adj.* concluant; **~ively** *adv.* d'une manière concluante.

concoct *v.t.* **1.** (*cook.*) confectionner; **2.** (*fig.*) fabriquer; **~ion** *s.* (1) confection *f.*; (2) combinaison *f.*

concomitant *adj.* & *s.m.* concomitant.

concord *s.* (*agreement*) concorde *f.*; (*ling., mus.*) accord *m.*; **~ance** *s.* (*ling., Bible*) concordance *f.*; **~at** *s.* concordat *m.*

concourse *s.* (*flocking together*) concours *m.*; (*crowd*) foule *f.*; (*open space at, e.g., railway station*) cours *m.*

concrete *s.* béton *m.*; PRECAST ~; REINFORCED ~; **~-mixer** *s.* bétonnière *f.*; *adj.* en béton; (≠ *abstract*) concret; *v.t.* bétonner.

concubine *s.* concubine *f.*

concupiscen/ce *s.* concupiscence *f.*; **~t** *adj.* concupiscent.

concur *v.i.* **1.** (*coincide*) coïncider; **2.** (*agree*) être d'accord; **~rence** *s.* (1) coïncidence *f.*; (2) accord *m.*; (*of circumstances*) concours *m.*; **~rent**

adj. (1) simultané; (2) d'accord; (*math.*) concourant; **~rently** *adv.* (1) simultanément; (2) conjointement; ⚠ concurrence, concurrent = **competition, competitor.**

concuss *v.t.* secouer; (*med.*) commotionner; **to be ~ed,** être étourdi; **~ion** *s.* secousse *f.*; (*med.*) commotion (cérébrale) *f.*

condemn *v.t.* (*blame* & *law*) condamner (à); (*pronounce unfit—housing, etc.*) déclarer inutilisable; **~able** *adj.* condamnable; **~ation** *s.* condamnation *f.*; **~atory** *adj.* condamnatoire.

condens/e *v.t.* & *i.* (*lit.* & *fig.*) (se) condenser; **~ation** *s.* condensation *f.*; **~ed milk,** lait condensé *m.*; **~er** *s.* (*electr.*, *techn.*) condensateur *m.*; (*phys.*, *gas*) condenseur *m.*

condescen/d *v.i.* condescendre; **~d to do sth.,** daigner faire qch.; **~d to s.o.,** se montrer condescendant envers qn.; **~ding** *adj.* condescendant; **~dingly** *adv.* avec condescendance; **~sion** *s.* condescendance *f.*

condiment *s.* condiment *m.*

condition *s.* **1.** (*stipulation*) condition *f.*; **2.** (*state*) état *m.*; (*sport*) forme *f.*; **3.** (*rank*) rang *m.*; **4.** (*pl. = circumstances*) conditions *f.pl.*; **in a ~ to,** en état de; **in good ~,** (*things*) en bon état; (*persons*) en pleine forme; **out of ~,** en mauvais état; **on ~ that,** à condition de (+*inf.*) à condition que (+*fut.indic. or subj.*); **you may have a bicycle on ~ that you pass your exam,** vous aurez un vélo à condition de réussir à votre examen; **I agree on ~ that you tell your father,** j'y consens à condition que vous en parlerez à votre père; **I will see her on ~ that she comes at 9 a.m.,** je la verrai à condition qu'elle vienne à 9 heures du matin; *v.t.* (1) conditionner; (2) conditionner, mettre en forme; **~al** *s.* (*ling.*) conditionnel *m.*; *adj.* dépendant (*on*—de); **~ally** *adv.* sous condition.

condole *v.i.* (*with*) offrir ses condoléances à; **~nce** *s.* condoléance *f.*

condominium *s.* condominium *m.*

condon/e *v.t.* **1.** (*forgive*) pardonner; **2.** (*atone for*) réparer; **~ation** *s.* (1) pardon *m.*; (2) réparation *f.*

conduc/e *v.t.* conduire à; **be ~ive to,** être favorable à.

conduct *s.* **1.** (*behaviour*) conduite *f.*; **2.** (*management*) direction *f.*; **3.** (*guidance*) conduite *f.*; *v.t.* (1) **~ oneself,** se conduire; (2) diriger; (3) conduire; (*mus.*, *electr.*) conduire; **~ing** *s.* conduite *f.*; *adj.* (*electr.*) conducteur; **~ion** *s.* (*electr.*) conduction *f.*; **~or** *s.* (*leader*) guide *m.*, directeur *m.*; (*mus.*) chef d'orchestre *m.*; (*bus, etc.*) receveur *m.*; (*electr.*) conducteur *m.*; LIGHTNING-**~or.**

conduit *s.* conduit *m.*

cone *s.* (*shape* & *object*) cône *m.*; (*pine-~*) cône *m.*, pomme (*f.*) de pin; (*cook.*) cornet *m.*

confabulation *s.* conciliabule *m.*; (*fam.*) **confab** *s.* causette *f.*

confection *s.* **1.** (*process* & *dress*) confection *f.*; **2.** (*dish*) mélange *m.*; **3.** (*sweet*) friandise *f.*; **~er** *s.* (3) confiseur *m.*; **~ery** *s.* (3) confiserie *f.*

confeder/acy *s.* fédération *f.*; **~ation** *s.* confédération *f.*; **~ate** *s.* & *adj.* confédéré; (*pej.*) complice *m.*; *v.t.* & *i.* (se) confédérer.

confer *v.t.* **1.** (*bestow*) accorder; **2.** *v.i.* (*discuss*) conférer (*with*—avec); **~ence** *s.* (2) conférence *f.*; **~ment** *s.* (1) collation *f.*

confess *v.t.* avouer; (*of priest*) confesser qn.; (*of penitent*) confesser qch.; *v.i.* (*eccles.*) se confesser; **~ed** *adj.* (*avowed*) de son propre aveu; **~edly** *adv.* de l'aveu général; **~ion** *s.* (*admission of guilt*) aveu *m.*, confession *f.*; (*statement of belief*) confession *f.*; ⚠ confesse *f. is used only in the expression* aller à confesse (*to go to confession*); **~ional** *adj.* confessionnel; *s.* confessional *m.*; **~or** *s.* confesseur *m.*

confetti *s.pl.* confettis *m.pl.*

confid/e *v.t.* **1.** (*tell secrets to, entrust sth. to*) confier (qch. à qn.); *v.i.* **1.** se confier (*in*—à); **2.** (*trust*) se fier (*in*—à); **~ant** *s.* confident(e) *m.f.*; **~ence** *s.* (1) confidence *f.*; (2) confiance *f.*; (*impudence*) prétention *f.*; **self-~,** confiance en soi *f.*; **~ence trick,** escroquerie *f.*; **~ence (con) man, trickster** *s.* escroc *m.*; **~ent** *adj.* (*trusting*) confiant; (*impudent*) prétentieux; (*convinced*) persuadé; **~ential** *adj.* (*talk, letter, etc.*) confidentiel; (*person*) de confiance; **~ently** *adv.* avec assurance; **~ing** *adj.* confiant.

configuration *s.* configuration *f.*

confine *s.* (*usu. pl.*) confins *m.pl.*; *v.t.* confiner (*to*—à, dans); (*imprison*) enfermer; *v.i.* confiner (*on*—à); **~ oneself to,** se borner à; **~d to bed,** alité; **~ment** *s.* détention *f.*; (*childbirth*) accouchement *m.*; (*to bed*) alitement *m.*

confirm *v.t.* **1.** (*make stronger*) renforcer; **2.** (*ratify*) confirmer; **3.** (*corroborate*) corroborer; **4.** (*eccles.*) confirmer; **~ed** *adj.* invétéré; **~ation** *s.* (1) renforcement *m.*; (2), (3), (4) confirmation *f.*; **~ative** *adj.* de confirmation.

confiscat/e *v.t.* confisquer; **~ion** *s.* confiscation *f.*

conflagration *s.* (*fire*) incendie *m.*; (*fig.*) conflagration *f.*

conflict *s.* **1.** (*fight*) conflit *m.*; **2.** (*clash*) lutte *f.*; **in ~,** en désaccord; *v.i.* (1) entrer en conflit avec; (2) se heurter, lutter; **~ing** *adj.* opposé; en conflit avec, en contradiction avec.

confluence *s.* confluent *m.*

conform *v.t.* (*adapt*) conformer; *v.i.* **~ to,** se conformer à; **~able** *adj.* conforme à; (*person*) accommodant; **~ation** *s.* conformation *f.*; **~ity** *s.* (*likeness*) conformité *f.*; (*compliance*) soumission *f.*; **in ~ity with,** conformément à.

confound *v.t.* confondre; **~ him!,** le diable l'emporte!; **~ed** *adj.* (*fam.* = *damned*) sacré (*before noun*); **~edly** *adv.* diablement.

confraternity *s.* confrérie *f.*

confront *v.t.* (*bring face to face* (*with*)) confronter (avec); (*face defiantly*) affronter; **~ation** *s.* confrontation *f.*

confus/e *v.t.* **1.** (*muddle*) brouiller; **2.** (*perplex*) troubler; **3.** (*mix up*) confondre; **~ed** *adj.* (1) brouillé; (2) troublé, confus; (3) confus; **to get ~ed,** s'embrouiller; **~ion** *s.* (1) désordre *m.*; (2) & (3) confusion *f.*

confut/e *v.t.* réfuter; **~ation** *s.* réfutation *f.*

congeal *v.t.* & *i.* (*freeze*) (se) congeler; (*blood, etc.*) (se) coaguler.

congenial *adj.* (*person*) sympathique; (*thing*) approprié.

congenital *adj.* congénital.

conger (eel) *s.* congre *m.*

congest *v.t.* **1.** (*med.*) congestionner; **2.** (*streets, etc.*) embouteiller, (*fam.*) congestionner; **~ed** *adj.* (1) congestionné; (2) surpeuplé, embouteillé; **~ion** *s.* (1) congestion *f.*; (2) encombrement *m.*

conglomerat/e *adj.* congloméré; *s.* (*geol.*) conglomérat *m.*; *v.t.* & *i.* (se) conglomérer; **~ion** *s.* conglomérat *m.*

Congo *s.* (*geog.*) Congo *m.*; **~lese** *adj.* & *s.m.f.* congolais(e).

congratulat/e *v.t.* féliciter (*on*—de); **~ions** *s.pl.* félicitations *f.pl.*; **~ory** *adj.* de félicitation.

congregat/e *v.t.* & *i.* (se) rassembler; **~ion** *s.* (*assembly, univ., church*) assemblée *f.*; (*of priests, etc.*) congrégation *f.*; **~ional church,** congrégationalisme *m.*

congress *s.* congrès *m.*; (*U.S. parl.*) Congrès *m.*; (*Trades Union*) confédération (*f.*) des syndicats britanniques.

congru/ity *s.* (*accordance*) conformité *f.*; (*harmony*) harmonie *f.*; (*correspondence*) correspondance *f.*; **~ous** *adj.* convenable; **~ously** *adv.**

conic(al) *adj.* conique.

conifer *s.* conifère *m.*; **~ous** *adj.* conifère.
conjectur/e *s.* conjecture *f.*; *v.t.* conjecturer; **~al** *adj.* conjectural; **~ally** *adv.* par conjecture.
conjoint *adj.* conjoint; **~ly** *adv.**.
conjugal *adj.* conjugal; **~ly** *adv.**.
conjugat/e *v.t.* conjuguer; **~ion** *s.* conjugaison *f.*
conjunct/ion *s.* (*action of joining* & *ling.*) conjonction *f.*; (*simultaneous event*) coïncidence *f.*; **in ~ion with,** conjointement avec; **~ive** *adj.* conjonctif.
conjunctivitis *s.* conjonctivite *f.*
conjuncture *s.* conjoncture *f.*
conjur/e[1] *v.t.* (*appeal solemnly to*) conjurer; **~ation** *s.* supplication *f.*
conjur/e[2] *v.i.* **~e up,** évoquer; **~e away,** escamoter; **~er** *s.* prestidigitateur *m.*; **~ing** *s.* prestidigitation *f.*; **~ing trick** *s.* tour de prestidigitation *m.*
connect *v.t.* **1.** (*join*) joindre; *v.i.* se joindre à; **2.** (*techn.*) (*pipes*) accorder; (*shaft*) embrayer; **3.** (*rail.*) assurer la correspondance avec; *v.i.* correspondre; **4.** (*people*) mettre en relations avec; (*by marriage*) apparenter; **5.** (*telephone*) mettre en communication avec; **6.** (*electr.*) mettre en contact; brancher (sur); **7.** (*fig.*) (*ideas*) associer; (*arguments*) enchaîner; **~ed** *adj.* (1) en rapport avec; (4) apparenté; (7) cohérent; **~ion** (**connexion**) *s.* (1) union *f.*, liaison *f.*; (2) raccord *m.*, embrayage *m.*; (3) correspondance *f.*; (4) relations *f.pl.*; parenté *f.*; (*a relative*) parent(e) *m.f.*; (5) communication (téléphonique) *f.*; (6) connexion *f.*, prise *f.*; (7) association *f.*, enchaînement *m.*; (*relevance*) rapport *m.*
conning-tower *s.* kiosque *m.*
conniv/e (*at*) *v.i.* (*take part in*) être de connivence avec qn. (dans); (*ignore*) fermer les yeux (sur); **~ance** *s.* connivence *f.*
connoisseur *s.m.f.* connaiss/eur, -euse (*of*—en).
connot/e *v.t.* **1.** (*imply*) impliquer; **2.** (*mean*) signifier; **~ation** *s.* (1) implication *f.*; (2) signification *f.*
connubial *adj.* conjugal.
conquer *v.t.* (*overcome, lit.* & *fig.*) vaincre; (*acquire by conquest*) conquérir; **~or** *s.* vainqueur *m.*; **William the C~or,** Guillaume le Conquérant.
conquest *s.* (*act, thing conquered, person*) conquête *f.*
consanguinity *s.* consanguinité *f.*
conscien/ce *s.* conscience *f.*; **~ce money,** somme restituée par remords de conscience *f.*; **~ce-stricken** *adj.* pris de remords; **~tious** *adj.* consciencieux; **~tious objector** *s.* objecteur de conscience *m.*; **~tiousness** *s.* droiture *f.*; **~tiously** *adv.**.
conscious *adj.* **1.** (*med.*) qui a sa connaissance; **2.** (*aware*) conscient; **3.** (*done ~ly*) voulu; **~ of,** conscient de; **to be ~ of,** avoir conscience de; **self-~,** gêné; **~ly** *adv.* sciemment; **~ness** *s.* (1) connaissance *f.*; (2) conscience *f.*
conscript *adj.* & *s.m.* conscrit; *v.t.* enrôler par conscription; **~ion** *s.* conscription *f.*
consecrat/e *v.t.* **1.** (*make sacred to, devote to*) consacrer (à); **2.** (*sanctify*) sacrer; **~ed** *adj.* (*water*) bénit; **~ion** *s.* (1) consécration *f.*; (2) sacre *m.*
consecutive *adj.* consécutif; **~ly** *adv.**.
consensus *s.* consentement *m.*
consent *s.* **1.** (*agreement*) accord *m.*; **2.** (*permission*) consentement *m.*; **by common ~,** d'un commun accord; **age of ~,** âge légal *m.*; *v.i.* (1) & (2) consentir (à).
consequen/ce *s.* (*result, importance, influence*) conséquence *f.*; **of no ~ce,** sans importance; **in ~ce of,** par suite de; **~t** *adj.* conséquent; **~tial** *adj.* (*resulting*) consécutif; (*important*) prétentieux; **~tly** *adv.* (*as a result*) en conséquence de; (*therefore*) par conséquent.
conservative *s.* (*pol.*) conservat/eur, -rice *m.f.*; *adj.* (*polit.* & *gen.*) conservat/eur, -rice *m.f.*; **~ estimate,** appréciation modérée.
conserv/e *s.* confiture *f.*; *v.t.* (*preserve*) conserver; (*keep safe*) préserver; **~ancy board** (*rivers*) commission fluviale *f.*; **~ation** *s.* conservation *f.*; **~atoire** *s.* conservatoire *m.*; **~ator** *s.* conservateur *m.*; **~atory** *s.* (*attached to house*) jardin d'hiver *m.*; (*greenhouse*) serre *f.*; (*mus., art, etc.*) conservatoire *m.*
consider *v.t.* **1.** (*contemplate*) considérer; **2.** (*deliberate on*) considérer; **3.** (*take into account*) tenir compte de; **4.** (*show ~ation for*) avoir des égards pour; **5.** (*regard as*) considérer; **~able** *adj.* considérable; **~ably** *adv.**; **~ate** *adj.* (4) prévenant; **~ateness** *s.* (4) prévenance *f.*; **~ation** *s.* (1) considération *f.*; (2) examen *m.*; (4) égards *m.pl.*; (*inducement*) compensation *f.*; **under ~ation,** à l'étude; **in ~ation of,** (3) eu égard à; (4) par égard pour; **in ~ation of which** (= *in exchange for*) moyennant quoi; **~ing** *prep.* eu égard à; **he is unusually well preserved ~ing his age,** il est remarquablement bien conservé, eu égard à son âge.
consign *v.t.* **1.** (*hand over*) livrer; **2.** (*transmit, by road, rail, etc.*) expédier; **~ee** *s.* (2) destinataire *m.*; **~or** *s.* (2) expéditeur *m.*; **~ment** *s.* (*act*) expédition *f.*; (*goods*) arrivage *m.*
consist *v.i.* se composer (*of*—de); consister (*of*—en), **the house ~s of five rooms,** la maison consiste en cinq pièces; consister (*in*—à + *inf.*), **the difficulty ~s in getting the piano into the house,** la difficulté consiste à faire entrer le piano dans la maison.
consisten/ce, ~cy *s.* consistance *f.*; **~t** *adj.* (*solid*) consistant; (*not contradictory*) conséquent; **~t with,** compatible avec; **~tly** *adv.* avec consistance; avec conséquence.
consistory *s.* (*eccles.*) consistoire *m.*
consol/e *s.* console *f.*; *v.t.* consoler; **~ation** *s.* consolation *f.*; **~ation prize,** prix de consolation *m.*; **~atory** *adj.* consolant.
consolidat/e *v.t.* & *i.* **1.** (*solidify, strengthen*) (se) consolider; **2.** (*comm. combine*) fusionner; **~ion** *s.* (1) consolidation *f.*; (2) fusion *f.*
consols *s.pl.* (*fin.*) consolidés *m.pl.*
consonance *s.* (*mus.*) consonance *f.*; (*fig.*) accord *m.*
consonant *s.* (*ling.*) consonne *f.*
consort *s.* époux *m.*, épouse *f.*; **prince ~,** prince-consort *m.*; *v.t.* (*~ with*) fréquenter; *v.i.* (*~ with*) s'accorder avec; **~ium** *s.* consortium *m.*
conspicuous *adj.* **1.** (*readily seen*) évident; **2.** (*outstanding*) éminent; **3.** (*striking*) remarquable; **to make oneself ~,** se faire remarquer; **~ly** *adv.* (1) visiblement; (2) éminemment; (3)*.
conspir/e *v.t.* comploter; *v.i.* conspirer; **~acy** *s.* conspiration *f.*; **~ator** *s.* conspirat/eur, -rice *m.f.*
constab/le *s.* (*hist.*) connétable *m.*; (*police*) agent *m.*; **Chief C~le,** commissaire de police *m.*; **special ~le,** auxiliaire de la police *m.*; **~ulary** *s.* police *f.*
constan/cy *s.* **1.** (*faithfulness*) constance *f.*; **2.** (*steadiness*) stabilité *f.*; **~t** *adj.* (1) & (2) constant; *s.* (*math.*) constante *f.*; **~tly** *adv.* (*always*) constamment; (*often*) à maintes reprises.
constellation *s.* constellation *f.*
consternation *s.* consternation *f.*
constipat/e *v.t.* (*lit.* & *fig.*) constiper; **~ed** *adj.* constipé; **~ion** *s.* constipation *f.*
constituen/cy *s.* circonscription électorale *f.*; (*people*) électeurs *m.pl.*; **~t** *s.* (*voter*) élect/eur, -rice *m.f.*; (*part*) élément *m.*; *adj.* constituant.
constitut/e *v.t.* (*appoint*) nommer; (*establish*)

constituer; (*be part of*) composer; **~ion** *s.* (*nature, health, govt.*) constitution *f.*; (*of a society, etc.*) statuts *m.pl.*; **~ional** *adj.* constitutionnel; *s.* promenade hygiénique *f.*; **~ionally** *adv.**; **~ionalist** *s.* constitutionnel *m.*; **~ive** *adj.* constitutif.

constrain *v.t.* **1.** (*compel—to*) contraindre (à); **2.** (*confine*) emprisonner; **~ed** *adj.* (1) contraint; **~t** *s.* (1) & (2) contrainte *f.*; (*repression of feeling*) retenue *f.*; (*uneasiness*) gêne *f.*

constrict *v.t.* serrer; **~ion** *s.* constriction *f.*; **~or** *adj.* & *s.* constricteur *m.*; BOA **~**.

construct *v.t.* construire; **~ion** *s.* construction *f.*; (*interpretation*) interprétation *f.*; **~ional** *adj.* de construction; **~ive** *adj.* de la construction; (*positive*) constructif; **~or** *s.* constructeur *m.*

construe *v.t.* (*ling.*) construire; (*explain*) expliquer.

consubstant/ial *adj.* consubstantiel; **~iation** *s.* consubstantiation *f.*

consul *s.* consul *m.*; **~ar** *adj.* consulaire; **~ate** *s.* consulat *m.*

consult *v.t.* consulter; *v.i.* **~ with,** conférer avec; **~ant** *s.* consultant *m.*; *adj.* consultant; (*doctor*) médecin consultant *m.*, (*engineer*) ingénieur-conseil *m.*; **~ation** *s.* consultation *f.*; **~ative** *adj.* consultatif; **~ing** *adj.* consultant, -conseil; **~ing room** *s.* cabinet *m.*

consum/e *v.t.* (*destroy*) consumer; (*eat or drink, use up*) consommer; (*waste*) gaspiller; **to be ~ed,** se consumer, se consommer; (*fig.*) brûler (*with*—de); **~er** *s.* consommat/eur, -rice *m.f.*; **~er goods,** denrées de consommation (courante) *f.pl.*

consummat/e *v.t.* consommer; *adj.* parfait; **~ely** *adv.**; **~ion** *s.* consommation *f.*; (*end*) fin *f.*; (*final success*) couronnement *m.*

consumpt/ion *s.* **1.** (*consuming*) consommation *f.*; **2.** (*med.*) tuberculose *f.*; **~ive** *adj.* (2) tuberculeux.

contact *s.* (*touch, connection, med.*) contact *m.*; **~s** *pl.* relations *f.pl.*; *v.t.* prendre contact avec (qn.); **~ lens** verre(s) de contact *m.*; lentille cornéenne *f.*

contag/ion *s.* (*med.* & *fig.*) contagion *f.*; **~ious** *adj.* contagieux.

contain *v.t.* (*have within*) contenir; (*comprise*) comporter; (*restrain*) maîtriser; (*mil.*) contenir; **not to be able to ~ oneself for joy, etc.,** ne pas pouvoir se tenir de joie, etc.; **~er** *s.* récipient *m.*; (*comm. transport*) conteneur *m.*; **~erization** *s.* conteneurisation *f.*; **~erize** *v.t.* conteneuriser.

contaminat/e *v.t.* contaminer; **~ion** *s.* contamination *f.*

contango *s.* (*fin.*) report *m.*

contemplat/e *v.t.* **1.** (*look at*) contempler; **2.** (*think about*) méditer; **3.** (*intend*) projeter, envisager de + *inf.*; *v.i.* réfléchir; **~ion** *s.* (1) contemplation *f.*; (2) méditation *f.*; (3) prévision *f.*; **~ive** *adj.* pensif; (*eccles.*) contemplatif.

contempor/aneous *adj.* contemporain (*with*—de); **~aneously** *adv.* à la même époque (que); **~ary** *adj.* & *s.m.* contemporain.

contempt *s.* (*scorn*) mépris *m.*; (*disrespect*) dédain *m.*; (*law*) **~ of court,** outrage à magistrat *m.*, offense à la cour *f.*; (*non-appearance*) non-comparution *f.*; **~ible** *adj.* méprisable; **~ibility** *s.* caractère méprisable *m.*; **~ibly** *adv.* de manière méprisable; **~uous** *adj.* méprisant (*of*—de); **~uously** *adv.* avec mépris.

contend *v.t.* **1.** (*compete for*) disputer (qch. à qn.); **2.** (*argue*) discuter; **3.** (*maintain*) soutenir; *v.i.* **4.** (*struggle*) lutter (pour qch., contre qn.); **~er** *s.* rival *m.*; **~ing** *adj.* (1) rival; (4) opposé.

content[1] *s.* (*satisfaction*) contentement *m.*; *adj.* (*satisfied* (*with*)) content (de); (*willing* (*to*)) disposé (à); *v.t.* contenter; **~ oneself with,** se contenter de; **~ed** *adj.* content (*with*—de); **~edly** *adv.* avec satisfaction; **~ment** *s.* contentement *m.*

content[2] *s.* (*capacity*) contenance *f.*; **~s** *s.pl.* contenu *m.sing.*

content/ion *s.* (*controversy*) controverse *m.*; BONE **of ~ion**; (*claim*) prétention *f.*; **my ~ion is that,** je prétends que; **~ious** *adj.* contentieux; (*person*) querelleur.

contest *s.* (*discussion*) débat *m.*; (*struggle*) lutte *f.*; (*sport*) épreuve *f.*, (*boxing*) match *m.*; *v.t.* (*dispute*) contester; (*compete for*) disputer; **~able** *adj.* contestable; **~ant** *s.* adversaire *m.*; (*sport*) concurrent *m.*

context *s.* contexte *m.*

contigu/ity *s.* contiguïté *f.*; **~ous** *adj.* conti/gu, -guë.

continen/ce *s.* **1.** (*temperance*) modération *f.*; **2.** (*chastity*) continence *f.*; **~t** *adj.* (1) modéré; (2) continent.

continent *s.* (*geog.*) continent *m.*; **the C~** (*freq.* = *Europe*), le Continent; **~al** *adj.* continental; *s.* habitant de l'Europe.

contingen/cy *s.* **1.** (*being ~t*) contingence *f.*; **2.** (*~t event*) éventualité *f.*; **3.** (*chance occurrence*) événement imprévu *m.*, aléa *m.*; **~t** *adj.* (1) dépendant (*on*—de), **to be ~t upon,** dépendre de; (2) éventuel; (3) aléatoire; *s.* (*mil.*) contingent *m.*; **~tly** *adv.* (1) à la condition que; (3) fortuitement.

continu/e *v.t.* **1.** (*go on with*) continuer; **2.** (*take up again*) reprendre; **3.** (*keep*) maintenir; *v.i.* continuer à; demeurer + *adj.*; **to be ~ed,** à suivre; **~al** *adj.* continuel; **~ally** *adv.**; **~ance** *s.* (3) (*duration*) durée *f.*, (*stay*) séjour *m.*; **~ation** *s.* (1) & (2) continuation *f.*; (*thing, that ~es*) suite *f.*; **~ity** *s.* continuité *f.*; **~uous** *adj.* continu; (*cinema performance*) permanent; **~ously** *adv.* sans arrêt.

contort *v.t.* (*features, etc.*) tordre; *v.refl.* (*do ~ions*) se contorsionner; **~ion** *s.* contorsion *f.*; **~ionist** *s.* contorsionniste *m.f.*

contour *s.* (*outline*) contour *m.*; (*line on map*) courbe de niveau *f.*

contraband *s.* contrebande *f.*; *adj.* de contrebande.

contracept/ion *s.* contraception *f.*; **~ive** *adj.* & *s.m.* contraceptif.

contract *s.* (*agreement, law, cards*) contrat *m.*; (*comm.*) forfait *m.*; **on ~** (*comm.*) à forfait; *v.t.* & *i.* (se) contracter; **~ out of,** se dégager de; **~ed** *adj.* contracté; **~ion** *s.* contraction *f.*; **~or** *s.* entrepreneur *m.*

contradict *v.t.* **1.** (*deny*) contredire; **2.** (*be at variance with*) démentir; **~ion** *s.* **1.** contradiction *f.*; (2) démenti *m.*; **~ory** *adj.* (1) & (2) contradictoire.

contradistinction *s.* contraste *m.*

contralto *s.* contralto *m.*

contraption *s.* (*pop.*) truc *m.*; (*fam.*) machin *m.*

contrar/y *s.* contraire *m.*; **on the ~y,** au contraire; *adj.* **1.** (*opposed*) contraire (à); **2.** (*perverse*) contrariant; **~iety** *s.* (2) opposition *f.*; **~iness** *s.* (2) esprit de contradiction *m.*; **~iwise** *adv.* (*on the other hand*) de l'autre côté; (*in the opposite way*) en sens opposé.

contrast *s.* contraste *m.*; **in ~ with,** par contraste avec; *v.t.* mettre en contraste; *v.i.* contraster; **~ing** *adj.* (*colours*) couleurs qui contrastent entre elles.

contraven/e *v.t.* (*law*) contrevenir; (*oppose*) s'opposer à; **~tion** *s.* contravention *f.*

contribut/e *v.t.* & *i.* contribuer (*to*—à); **~ion** *s.* contribution *f.*; (*in newspaper*) article *m.*; **~or** *s.* collaborat/eur, -rice *m.f.*, souscript/eur, -rice *m.f.*; **~ory** *adj.* accessoire.

contrit/e *adj.* contrit; **~ely** *adv.* avec contrition; **~ion** *s.* contrition *f.*

contriv/e *v.t.* **1.** (*devise*) inventer; (*plan*) organiser; *v.i.* **2.** (*manage*) s'ingénier (à), s'arranger (pour); **~ance** *s.* (1) invention *f.*, appareil *m.*; (2) ingéniosité *f.*

control *s.* **1.** (*check*) contrôle *m.*, restriction *f.*; BIRTH **~**; **2.** (*supervision*) autorité *f.*; **3.** (*mastery*) maîtrise *f.*; **self-~**, maîtrise de soi *f.*; **4.** (*techn.*) direction *f.*, commande *f.*; REMOTE **~**; **~s** *s.pl.* (*mech.*) commandes *f.pl.*; **~ room** *s.* poste des commandes *f.*; **~ tower** (*aviat.*) tour de contrôle *f.*; *v.t.* (1) contrôler; (2) (*have ~ of*) commander; (3) maîtriser; **~ler** *s.* contrôleur *m.*

controvers/y *s.* controverse *m.*; **~ial** *adj.* discutable.

contumac/y *s.* entêtement *m.*; (*law*) contumace *f.*; **~ious** *adj.* entêté; **~iously** *adv.* obstinément.

contumely *s.* mépris *m.*

contusion *s.* contusion *f.*

conundrum *s.* devinette *f.*

conurbation *s.* agglomération urbaine *f.*

convalesc/e *v.i.* être en convalescence; **~ence** *s.* convalescence *f.*; **~ent** *adj.* & *s.m.f.* convalescent(e).

convect/ion *s.* convection *f.*; **~or** *s.* (*heating apparatus*) appareil de chauffage par convection *m.*

convene *v.t.* convoquer; *v.i.* se rassembler.

conveni/ence *s.* (*what is suitable*) convenance *f.*; (*useful appliance*) commodité *f.*; (= *W.C.*) toilettes *f.pl.*; (*comforts*) aises *m.pl.*; **at your ~ence,** quand vous le pourrez; **at your earliest ~ence,** dans le plus bref délai possible; **~ent** *adj.* (*suitable*) commode; (*easy*) pratique; (*near*) commode; **~ently** *adv.* sans inconvénient.

convent *s.* couvent *m.*; **~ual** *adj.* conventuel.

convention *s.* **1.** (*meeting*) assemblée *f.*; **2.** (*accepted usage*) usage *m.*; **3.** (*agreement*) convention *f.*; **~al** *adj.* (2) conventionnel; **~ality** *s.* caractère conventionnel *m.*

converg/e *v.i.* converger (*on*—vers, sur); **~ence** *s.* convergence *f.*; **~ent** *adj.* convergent.

conversant *adj.* (*with*) (*person*) familier avec; (*thing*) versé dans; (*facts, news*) au courant de.

convers/e[1] *v.i.* s'entretenir, (*with s.o. about sth.*) avec qn. de qch.; **~ation** *s.* conversation *f.*; **~ational** *adj.* (*person*) causeur; (*thing*) de conversation; **~ationalist** *s.* causeur *m.*; **~azione** *s.* réunion artistique ou littéraire *f.*

converse[2] *adj.* & *s.m.* contraire; (*math.*) *adj.* & *s.f.* réciproque.

conver/t *s.* converti(e) *m.f.*; *v.t.* **1.** (*change into*) transformer (en); **2.** (*cause to change faith or opinion*) convertir; **3.** (*rugby*) **~t a try,** transformer un essai; **~sion** *s.* (1), (3) transformation *f.*; (2) conversion *f.*; **~tible** *adj.* convertible; *s.* (*auto.*) voiture décapotable *f.*

convex *adj.* convexe.

convey *v.t.* **1.** (*carry*) transporter; **2.** (*transmit*) transmettre; **3.** (*seem to mean*) exprimer; **4.** (*law*) céder; **5.** (*~ compliments, etc.*) présenter; **~ance** *s.* (1) (*act*) transport *m.*, (*vehicle*) voiture *f.*; (2) transmission *f.*; (4) acte de cession *f.*, transfert *m.*; **~ancing** *s.* (4) cession *f.*

convict *s.* forçat *m.*; *v.t.* déclarer coupable, condamner; **~ion** *s.* (*verdict of guilty*) condamnation *f.*; (*firm belief*) conviction *f.*

convinc/e *v.t.* convaincre (*of*—de); **~ing** *adj.* convaincant; **~ingly** *adv.* de manière convaincante.

convivial *adj.* **1.** (*atmosphere, etc.*) de festin; **2.** (*person*) jovial; **~ity** *s.* (1) festins *m.pl.*; (2) jovialité *f.*

convo/ke *v.t.* convoquer; **~cation** *s.* (*act*) convocation *f.*; (*assembly*) assemblée *f.*; (*univ.*) assemblée universitaire *f.*

convolution *s.* (*coiled state*) enroulement *m.*; (*one turn of spiral*) spire *f.*; (*med.*) circonvolution *f.*

convolvulus *s.* volubilis *m.*

convoy *s.* convoi *m.*; *v.t.* convoyer.

convuls/e *v.t.* convulser; (*fig.*) bouleverser; **to be ~ed with** (*laughter, etc.*), se tordre de (rire); **~ion** *s.* convulsion *f.*; **~ive** *adj.* convulsif; **~ively** *adv.**.

cony, coney *s.* lapin *m.*

coo *v.t.* roucouler; **~ing** *s.* roucoulement *m.*; BILL **and ~.**

cook *s.* cuisin/ier, -ière *m.f.*; HEAD **~ and bottle washer**; *v.t.* faire cuire; (*fam.* = *falsify*) cuisiner; *v.i.* (*be ~ed*) cuire; (*do the ~ing*) cuisiner, faire la cuisine; **~ s.o.'s** GOOSE; **~er** *s.* (*stove*) cuisinière *f.* (électrique, à gaz, etc.); (*fruit suitable for ~ing*) fruit à cuire *m.*; PRESSURE--~er; **~ery** *s.* cuisine *f.*; **~ery book,** livre de cuisine *m.*; **~ing** *s.* (*process*) cuisson *m.*; (*art*) cuisine *f.*

cool *s.* frais *m.*; **to keep one's ~,** garder son sang-froid; *adj.* **1.** (*slightly cold*) frais; **2.** (*calm*) calme; **3.** (*lacking cordiality*) froid; **4.** (*impudent*) sans gêne; **~ly** *adv.* (1) fraîchement; (3) froidement; (4) sans gêne; **~ness** *s.* (1) frais *m*, (3) froideur *f.*; **~ant** *adj.* & *s.* refroidisseur, refrigérateur *m.*; *v.t.* (1) rafraîchir; (2) calmer; *v.i.* (1) se rafraîchir; (2) se calmer; **to (be left to) ~ one's heels** (*fig. fam.*) faire le poireau.

coolie *s.* coolie *m.*

coomb, combe *s.* combe *f.*

coon *s.* (*animal*) raton laveur *m.*; (*negro*) (*fam. pej.*) moricaud(e) *m.f.*

coop *s.* (*agric.*) mue *f.*; *v.t.* mettre en cage; **~ up,** claquemurer.

co-operat/e *v.i.* coopérer (*with, in*—avec, à); **~ion** *s.* coopération *f.*; **~ive** *adj.* coopératif; (*helpful*) accommodant; *s.* (*~ive society*) coopérative *f.*; (*abbrev. co-op*) coopé *f.*; **~or** *s.* coopérateur *m.*

co-opt *v.t.* coopter; **~ation, ~ing** cooptation *f.*

co-ordinat/e *v.t.* coordonner; *adj.* coordonné; *s.* (*math.*) coordonnée *f.*; **~ion** *s.* coordination *f.*

coot *s.* foulque *f.*; **bald as a ~,** chauve comme un œuf.

cop *s.* (*pop.* = *policeman*) flic *m.*; **to play ~s and robbers,** jouer aux gendarmes et aux voleurs; *v.t.* (*pop.*) choper.

copal *s.* copal *m.*

cope[1] *s.* (*eccles.*) chape *f.*; (*fig.*) voûte *f.*

cope[2] *v.i.* se débrouiller; **~ with,** venir à bout de.

coping *s.* (*arch. of wall*) chaperon *m.*; **~-stone** *s.* couronnement *m.*

copious *adj.* **1.** (*plentiful*) copieux; **2.** (*fig.*) riche; **~ly** *adv.* (1)*; (2)*; **~ness** *s.* (1) abondance *f.*; (2) richesse *f.*

copper *s.* (*mineral*) cuivre *m.*; (*coin*) sou *m.*; (*boiler*) chaudron *m.*; (*pop.* = *policeman*) flic *m.*; *adj.* de cuivre; (*coloured*) cuivré; **~ beech,** hêtre rouge *m.*; **~plate** *s.* (*art*) gravure en taille--douce; (*handwriting*) écriture calligraphiée *f.*

coppice, copse *s.* taillis *m.*

copra *s.* copra *m.*

copulat/e *v.i.* s'accoupler; **~ion** *s.* copulation *f.*

copy *s.* (*reproduction; for printing*) copie *f.*; CARBON **~**; FAIR **~**; ROUGH **~**; (*of book*) exemplaire *m.*; (*of newspaper*) numéro *m.*; **~-book** *s.* cahier *m.*; **~-cat** *s.* (*fam.*) singe *m.*; **~right** *s.* copyright *m.*, droits de reproduction *m.pl.*; **~--writer** *s.* rédacteur publicitaire *m.*; *v.t.* copier.

coquet/te *s.* coquette *f.*; **~ry** *s.* coquetterie *f.*

coral *s.* corail *m.* (*pl.* coraux); **~ island,** île coralienne *f.*; **~ reef,** récif de corail *m.*

corbel *s.* (*arch.*) corbeau *m.*

cord *s.* **1.** (*rope*) corde *f.*; **2.** (*measure of cut wood*) corde *f.*; **3.** (*pl.* = *corduroy trousers*) pantalon en velours côtelé *m.*; *v.t.* (1) & (2) corder; **~age** *s.* (*naut.*) cordages *m.pl.*

cordial *s.* cordial *m.*; *adj.* (*stimulating, sincere*) cordial; **~ity** *s.* cordialité *f.*; **~ly** *adv.**.

cordite *s.* cordite *f.*

cordon *s.* (*line of police, troops, etc.*; *braid*) cordon *m.*; *v.t.* ~ **off,** établir un cordon autour de.
corduroy *s.* velours côtelé *m.*; **~s,** *pl.* pantalon en velours côtelé *m.*
core *s.* cœur *m.*; HARD ~; **rotten to the ~,** pourri jusqu'à la moëlle; *v.t.* enlever le cœur de.
co-respondent *s.* (*law*) complice *m.f.*
coriander *s.* coriandre *f.*
cork *s.* (*bark of ~-oak*) liège *m.*; (*bottle stopper*) bouchon *m.*; ~-OAK; **~screw** *s.* tire-bouchon *m.*; *v.t.* boucher; **~age** *s.* droit (*m.*) de débouchage (d'un vin apporté de l'extérieur).
corm *s.* (*bot.*) bulbe *m.*
cormorant *s.* cormoran *m.*
corn[1] *s.* (*grain*) grain *m.*; (*cereals*) céréales *f.pl.*; (*wheat*) blé *m.*; (*maize*) maïs *m.*; PEPPER~; SEED-~; **~-chandler** *s.* grainetier *m.*; ~-COB; **~ exchange** *s.* halle au blé *f.*; **~field** *s.* champ de blé *m.*; **~flakes,** flocons d'avoine *m.pl.*; **~flour** *s.* farine de blé *f.*; **~flower** *s.* bleuet *or* bluet *m.*; *v.t.* (*preserve meat*) saler; **~ed beef,** bœuf en conserve *m.*
corn[2] *s.* (*on foot*) cor *m.*; **to tread on s.o's ~s,** marcher sur les pieds de qn.
cornea *s.* cornée *f.*
cornelian *s.* cornaline *f.*
corner *s.* **1.** (*angle*) & **2.** (*remote place*) coin *m.*; **3.** (*comm. monopoly*) accaparement *m.*; **to drive s.o. into a ~,** mettre qn. au pied du mur; TIGHT ~; HOLE-**and**-~; **~-stone** *s.* (*lit.* & *fig.*) pierre angulaire *f.*; *v.t.* (3) accaparer; *v.i.* (*auto.*) prendre un virage.
cornet *s.* (*mus.*) cornet à pistons *m.*; (*cook.*) cornet *m.*
cornice *s.* (*arch.*) corniche *f.*
cornucopia *s.* corne d'abondance *f.*
Corn/wall *s.* (*geog.*) Cornouailles *f.pl.*; ⚠ Cornouaille *f.sing. is a part of Brittany*; **~ish** *adj.* cornique; *s.m.* (*language*) cornique.
corolla *s.* corolle *f.*
corollary *s.* corollaire *m.*
coronary *adj.* coronaire; *s.* (= ~ *thrombosis*) thrombose coronaire *f.*, (*usu.*) infarctus *m.*
coronation *s.* couronnement *m.*; (*of king*) sacre *m.*
coroner *s.* coroner *m.*
coronet *s.* couronne *f.*
corporal *s.* (*cavalry, artillery*) brigadier *m.*; (*infantry, aviat.*) caporal *m.*; *adj.* corporel; ~ PUNISHMENT.
corporate *adj.* (*law*) constitué.
corporation *s.* (*civic authority*) conseil municipal *m.*; ⚠ corporation = (*hist.*) **trade guild;** (*pop.* = *large belly*) bedaine *f.*
corps *s.* corps *m.*
corpse *s.* cadavre *m.*
corpulen/ce *s.* corpulence *f.*; **~t** *adj.* corpulent.
corpuscle *s.* (*med.*) globule *f.*
correct *adj.* (*in accordance with facts*) correct; (*true, accurate*) exact; (*proper, in good taste*) correct; **~ion** *s.* correction *f.*; **~ive** *adj.* & *s.m.* correctif; **~ly** *adv.* correctement, exactement; **~ness** *s.* correction *f.*, exactitude *f.*; *v.t.* corriger.
correlat/e *v.t.* mettre en corrélation (*with*—avec); **~ion** *s.* corrélation *f.*; **~ive** *adj.* corrélatif.
correspond *v.i.* (*be similar to*; *exchange letters*) correspondre (avec); (*agree with*) s'accorder avec; **~ence** *s.* correspondance *f.*; **~ence course** *s.* cours par correspondance *m.*; **~ent** *s.* correspondant *m.*; **~ing** *adj.* correspondant.
corridor *s.* (*passage in building, territory, air*) corridor *m.*, couloir *m.*; (*in train*) couloir *m.*; **~s** (*fig. of power, etc.*) coulisses *f.pl.*
corroborat/e *v.t.* corroborer; **~ion** *s.* corroboration *f.*
corro/de *v.t.* & *i.* (se) corroder; **~sion** *s.* corrosion *f.*; **~sive** *adj.* & *s.m.* corrosif.
corrugat/e *v.t.* plisser; (*cardboard, iron*) onduler; *v.i.* se plisser, onduler; **~ed** *adj.* plissé, ondulé; **~ed iron,** tôle ondulée *f.*; **~ion** *s.* plissement *m.*, ondulation *f.*
corrupt *adj.* **1.** (*rotten*) pourri; **2.** (*depraved*) corrompu; **3.** (*venal*) vénal; *v.t.* (1) pourrir; (2) corrompre; (3) suborner; **~ible** *adj.* corruptible; **~ion** *s.* (1) putréfaction *f.*; (2) & (3) corruption *f.*
corsair *s.* corsaire *m.*
cors/et *s.* (*boned*) corset *m.*; (*elastic*) gaine *f.*; **~elet** *s.* (*garment* & *armour*) corselet *m.*
Corsica *s.* (*geog.*) Corse *f.*; **~n** *adj.* & *s.m.f.* corse.
corvette *s.* corvette *f.*
cos *s.* (*lettuce*) romaine *f.*
cosh *s.* (*Eng. fam.*) matraque *f.*; *v.t.* matraquer.
cosine *s.* (*math.*) cosinus *m.*
cosmetic *s.* fard *m.*; *adj.* cosmétique; ⚠ cosmétique *s.m.* = *only* **hair cream; ~s** *pl.* produits de beauté *m.pl.*
cosm/os *s.* cosmos *m.*; **~ic** *adj.* cosmique; **~ography** *s.* cosmographie *f.*; **~onaut** *s.* cosmonaute *m.f.*
cosmopolitan *adj.* & *s.m.f.* cosmopolite.
cosset *v.t.* chouchouter.
cost *s.* (*price*) prix *m.*; (*comm.*) coût *m.*; **~s** *s.pl.* (*expenses*) frais *m.pl.*; (*law*) frais et dépenses *m.pl.*; **at all ~s,** à tout prix; **to one's ~,** à ses dépens; **at the ~ of,** au prix de; **~ of living,** coût de la vie *m.*; ~ PRICE; **~ly** *adj.* coûteux; **~liness** *s.* prix élevé *m.*; (= *luxury*) somptuosité *f.*; *v.t.* évaluer le prix de; *v.i.* coûter.
coster(**monger**) *s.* marchand des quatre-saisons *m.*
costume *s.* costume *m.*; ~ JEWELLERY; *v.t.* costumer.
cos/y *adj.* (*place*) confortable; (*person*) à son aise; **tea-~y,** couvre-théière *m.*; **~ily** *adv.* confortablement, à l'aise; **~iness** *s.* confort *m.*
cot *s.* lit d'enfant *m.*; (*naut.*) cadre *m.*; **carry-~,** porte-bébé (berceau) *m.*
cottage *s.* chaumière *f.*; ⚠ cottage = **small country house; ~ hospital,** hôpital rural *m.*; **~ industry** *s.* artisanat *m.*; **~r** *s.* paysan *m.*
cotton *s.* (*raw material, thread*) coton *m.*; (*cloth*) cotonnade *f.*; **~ wool** *s.* ouate *f.*, (*pharm.*) coton hydrophile *m.*; *v.t.* & *i.* **~ on to** (*understand*) (*fam.*) piger.
couch *s.* (*bed*) lit *m.*; (*sofa*) divan *m.*; *v.t.* (*express*) rédiger; *v.refl.* (*lie in wait*) s'embusquer; **~-grass** *s.* chiendent *m.*
cough *s.* toux *f.*; WHOOPING ~; *v.i.* tousser; **~ out, ~ up,** cracher; (*fam.*) cracher.
council *s.* conseil *m.*; **~ estate,** cité ouvrière *f.*; **~-house** (*approx.*) H.L.M. *m.* (habitation à loyer modéré); **~lor** *s.* conseiller *m.*
counsel *s.* **1.** (*debate*) consultation *f.*; **2.** (*advice*) conseil *m.*; **3.** (*barrister*) avocat *m.*; **to take ~ of,** consulter; **to keep one's own ~,** garder ses idées pour soi; *v.t.* (2) conseiller (*to*—de); **~lor** *s.* (2) conseiller *m.*
count[1] *s.* (*rank*) comte *m.*; **~ess** *s.* comtesse *f.*
count[2] *s.* (*counting*) calcul *m.*; (*total*) montant *m.*; (*charge in indictment*) chef d'accusation *m.*; (*boxing*) compte *m.*; **to be out for the ~,** rester sur le tapis pour le compte; *v.t.* & *i.* (*reckon*) calculer; (*repeat nos. in order*) compter; (*include or be included*) compter; (*consider*) estimer; **~-down** *s.* compte à rebours *m.*; **~ in** *v.t.* comprendre; **~ on** *v.t.* compter sur; **~ out** *v.t.* compter un à un; (*boxing*) **to be ~ed out,** rester sur le tapis pour le compte; **~ing** *s.* compte *m.*; (*act*) dénombrement *m.*; **~ing-house** *s.* bureau (de la comptabilité) *m.*; **~less** *adj.* innombrable.

countenance *s.* (*face*) visage *m.*; (*gen. bearing*) contenance *f.*; **to keep one's ~,** se donner une contenance; *v.t.* (*sanction*) approuver (qch.); (*encourage*) appuyer (qn.).
counter *s.* (*token in games*) jeton *m.*; (*in shop*) comptoir *m.*; (*in bank, etc.*) guichet *m.*; *adj.* opposé (à); *adv.* à l'encontre (de); **~-clockwise,** en sens inverse des aiguilles d'une montre; *v.t.* aller à l'encontre de; (*fig.*) déjouer.
counter- (*in combination*): **~act** *v.t.* neutraliser; **~-attack** *s.* contre-attaque *f.*; *v.i.* contre--attaquer; **~-attraction** *s.* attraction concurrente *f.*; **~balance** *s.* contrepoids *m.*; *v.t.* contrebalancer; **~charge** *s.* (*law*) contre--dénonciation *f.*; **~-claim** *s.* (*law*) demande reconventionnelle *f.*; **~-current** *s.* contre--courant *m.*; **~feit** *adj.* faux, contrefait; *v.t.* contrefaire; **~-espionage** *s.* contre-espionnage *m.*; **~foil** *s.* talon *m.*; **~-irritant** *s.* (*med.*) révulsif *m.*; **~mand** *v.t.* contremander; **~march** *s.* contremarche *f.*; **~mine** *s.* contre--mine *f.*; *v.t.* contreminer; **~-offensive** *s.* contre-offensive *f.*; **~part** *s.* contre-partie *f.*, (*person*) homologue *m.*; **~point** *s.* (*mus.*) contrepoint *m.*; **~poise** *s.* contrepoids *m.*; **~sign** *v.t.* contresigner; **~sink** *v.t.* (*mech.*) fraiser; **~-tenor** *s.* (mus.) haut-contre *f.*
counterpane *s.* couvre-lit *m.*
countr/y *s.* **1.** (*nation*) pays *m.*; **2.** (*region*) pays *m.*; (≠ *capital*) province *f.*; **3.** (*fatherland*) patrie *f.*; **4.** (≠ *town*) campagne *f.*; **~y dance** *s.* contredanse *f.*; **~y house,** maison de campagne *f.*; **~yman, ~ywoman** *s.* (3) compatriote *m.f.*; (4) campagnard(e) *m.f.*; **~y seat** *s.* château *m.*; **~yside** *s.* paysage *m.*; **~ified** *adj.* (2) provincial; (4) campagnard.
county *s.* comté *m.*; **~ town,** chef-lieu de comté *m.*
coupl/e *s.* couple *m.* (*used only of a man & a woman*); (*of things*) paire *f.* (*or use* deux); *v.t.* coupler; (*mate*) accoupler; (*fig.*) associer (*with*—à), **~et** *s.* distique *m.*; **~ing** *s.* accouplement *m.*; (*rail.*) bielle *f.*
coupon *s.* ticket *m.*; (*token, to be cut out, in newspapers etc.*) bon *m.*; (*fin.*) coupon *m.*
courage *s.* courage *m.*; **~ous** *adj.* courageux; **~ously** *adv.**.
courier *s.* (*messenger*) courrier *m.*; (*guide*) guide *m.*
cours/e *s.* (*space or time*) cours *m.*, courant *m.*; (*line of conduct*) ligne de conduite *f.*; (*series*) série *f.*; (*sport*): (*racing*) champ de courses *m.*, (*golf*) terrain (de golf) *m.*; (*part of meal*) plat *m.*; (*acad.*) cours *m.*; (*med.*) cure *f.*; (*ship's*) route *f.*; (*fig.*) voie *f.*; **~e of events,** cours des événements *m.*; **to** CHANGE **~e; of ~e,** bien entendu; *v.t.* (*hunting*) courir; *v.i.* (*liquids*) couler; **~er** *s.* coursier *m.*; **~ing** *s.* (*hunt.*) chasse au lièvre *f.*
court *s.* **1.** (*arch.*; *of king*) cour *f.*; **2.** (*sport*) terrain *m.*, (*tennis*) court *m.*; **3.** (*law*) cour *f.*, tribunal *m.*; (*of enquiry, etc.*) commission *f.*; **4.** (*attentions*) cour *f.*; **at ~** (1) à la cour; **in ~** (3) au palais; CONTEMPT **of ~**; **~-house** *s.* palais de justice *m.*; **~ martial** *s.* conseil de guerre *m.*; **~--martial** *v.t.* traduire en conseil de guerre; **~yard** *s.* cour *f.*; **~esan** *s.* courtisane *f.*; **~ier** *s.* courtisan *m.*; **~liness** *s.* courtoisie *f.*; **~ly** *adj.* courtois; **~ship** *s.* (4) cour *f.*; *v.t.* (4) (*also pay ~ to*) faire la cour à; (*solicit*) rechercher; (*invite*) aller au-devant de.
courte/ous *adj.* courtois; **~ously** *adv.**; **~sy** *s.* courtoisie *f.*
cousin *s.* cousin(e) *m.f.*; **first ~,** cousin(e) germain(e) *m.f.*; SECOND **~.**
cove *s.* (*bay*) anse *f.*; (*pop.* =*fellow*) type *m.*
covenant *s.* (*polit.*) pacte *m.*; (*law*) contrat *m.*; (*eccles.*) Alliance *f.*; *v.t.* promettre par contrat; s'engager par contrat (à faire qch.).
Coventry, to send s.o. to ~, mettre qn. en quarantaine.
cover *s.* **1.** (*~ing*) couverture *f.*, (*lid*) couvercle *m.*, (*for chair*) housse *f.*; **2.** (*shelter*) abri *m.*; **to take ~,** se mettre à l'abri; **3.** (*pretence*) couvert *m.*; **4.** (*funds to meet liability*) couverture *f.*; **under ~** (2) à l'abri (*of*—de); **under ~ of** (3) sous couvert de; **under separate ~,** sous pli séparé; **~let** *s.* couvre-lit *m.*; *v.t.* (1) couvrir; (2) abriter; (3) dissimuler; (4) couvrir; (*with gun*) mettre (qn.) en joue; (*~ distance*) parcourir; **~ up** *v.t.* (*fam.*) maquiller; **~age** *s.* (*insurance*) risques couverts *m.pl.*, (*advertising, radio, TV*) couverture *f.*; **~ing** *s.* couverture *f.*; **~ing letter,** lettre avec pièce jointe *f.*; **~-up** *s.* (*fam.*) maquillage *m.*
covert *s.* fourré *m.*; (*of animal*) gîte *m.*; *adj.* voilé; **~ly** *adv.* en secret.
covet *v.t.* convoiter; **~ous** *adj.* avide (de); **~ousness** *s.* convoitise *f.*
covey *s.* (*of partridges & fig. of family*) couvée *f.*
coving *s.* (*arch.*) voussure *f.*
cow *s.* (*female ox*) vache *f.*; (*of other animals*) femelle *f.*; **to wait until the ~s come home,** attendre jusqu'à la semaine des quatre jeudis; **~herd, ~man** *s.* vacher *m.*; **~shed** *s.* étable *f.*; *v.t.* intimider.
coward *s.* lâche *m.*; **~ice, ~liness** *s.* lâcheté *f.*; **~ly** *adj.* & *adv.* lâche, lâchement.
cowboy *s.* cow-boy *m.*
cower *v.i.* s'accroupir; (*fig.*) plier l'échine (devant qn.).
cowl *s.* (*hood*) capuchon *m.*; (*monk's habit*) coule *f.*; (*on chimney*) mitre *f.*
cowrie *s.* (*shell*) porcelaine *f.*
cowslip *s.* coucou *m.*
cox *s.* *see* COXSWAIN; *v.t.* barrer.
coxcomb *s.* fat *m.*
coxswain *s.* barreur *m.*
coy *adj.* timide; **to be ~** (*pej. of girl*) faire la Sainte Nitouche; **~ly** *adv.**; **~ness** *s.* timidité *f.*
cozen *v.t.* extorquer (qch. à qn.); (*fam.*) empiler qn.
crab *s.* crabe *m.*; HERMIT-**~**; **to catch a ~** (*rowing*) engager un aviron; **~-apple** *s.* pomme sauvage *f.*; **~-apple tree** *s.* pommier sauvage *m.*; **~bed** *adj.* (*person*) acariâtre; (*writing*) illisible; **to write a ~bed hand,** écrire comme un chat.
crack *s.* **1.** (*sound*) craquement *m.*, (*of whip*) claquement *m.*; **2.** (*blow*) coup *m.*; **3.** (*fissure*) fente *f.*; **4.** (*partial break*) fêlure *f.*; **5.** (*fam. witty remark*) bon mot *m.*; **6.** (*sport, good player*) crack *m.*; *adj.* (*pop.*) de première classe, d'élite; *v.t.* (1) faire craquer, faire claquer; (3) fendre; (4) fêler; (5) (*~ a joke*) lancer; (*voice, nut*) casser; *v.i.* (1) craquer, claquer; (3) (*earth*) se fendiller, (*wall*) se lézarder; (4) se fêler; (*voice*) muer; (*break down*) s'effondrer; **~ up** *v.t.* vanter; *v.i.* (*fam.*) flancher; **to get ~ing** (*fam.*) s'activer; **get ~ing!** activons!; **to be a ~pot** (*fig. fam.*) avoir le cerveau fêlé; **~ed** *adj.* (*china*) fêlé; (*fig. fam.*) cinglé; **~er** *s.* (*firework*) pétard *m.*; (*paper toy*) diablotin *m.*; (*biscuit*) biscuit sec *m.*
crackl/e *s.* crépitement *m.*; (*on telephone*) friture *f.*; (*on radio*) parasites *m.pl.*; *v.i.* crépiter; **~ing** *s.* crépitement *m.*; (*of pork*) couenne *f.*
cradle *s.* (*child's bed & fig.*) berceau *m.*; (*med.*) arceau *m.*; *v.t.* bercer.
craft *s.* (*skill*) adresse *f.*; (*cunning*) ruse *f.*; (*trade*) métier *m.*; (*boat*) embarcation *f.*; (*aviat.*) appareil *m.*; **~y** *adj.* astucieux, rusé; **~ily** *adv.* astucieusement; **~sman** *s.* artisan *m.*; **~smanship** *s.* habileté *f.*
crag *s.* rocher escarpé; **~gy** *adj.* escarpé.
cram *v.t.* **1.** (*fill to repletion*) bourrer, (*with food*) gaver (*with*—de); **2.** *v.i.* (*for exam*) bachoter, (*fam.*) potasser; **3.** (*pack tightly*) bourrer; **4.**

(*thrust in*) fourrer (qch. dans); **5.** (*eat greedily*) se bourrer (de); **~med full** (3) (archi)bondé (de); **~mer** *s.* (2) répétiteur *m.*, **~mer's** (*fam.*) boîte à bachot *f.*; **~ming** *s.* (2) bachotage *m.*

cramp *s.* **1.** (*med.*) crampe *f.*; **2.** (*techn.*) crampon *m.*; *v.t.* (1) donner des crampes à; (2) cramponner; **~ed** *adj.* à l'étroit; **to ~ s.o's style,** couper les ailes à qn.

cranberry *s.* canneberge *f.*

crane *s.* (*bird* & *mech.*) grue *f.*; *v.t.* (*the neck*) tendre (le cou).

cranium *s.* crâne *m.*

crank *s.* **1.** (*mech.*) manivelle *f.*; **2.** (*person*) excentrique *m.*; **~shaft,** vilebrequin *m.*; **~y** *adj.* excentrique; *v.t.* (*auto.*) faire démarrer à la manivelle.

cranny *s.* fissure *f.*

crape *s.* crêpe *m.*

crash *s.* **1.** (*noise*) fracas *m.*; **2.** (*violent breakage*) heurt *m.*; **3.** (*violent fall or collision*) chute *f.*, collision *f.*; accident *m.*; **4.** (*fig.*) débâcle *m.*; (*fin.*) krach *m.*; **5.** (*coarse linen*) toile *f.*; ~ BARRIER; ~-HELMET; **~-land** *v.i.* (*aviat.*) atterir sur le ventre; **~-landing** *s.* atterissage forcé *m.*; *v.t.* (1) fracasser; (2) heurter; (3) (*auto.*) endommager; *v.i.* (1) retentir avec fracas; (2) se fracasser, se heurter; (3) (*auto.*) se tamponner; (*aviat.*) s'écraser sur le sol; (4) s'effondrer, faire un krach; **~ into,** se heurter contre, percuter contre; GATE~.

crass *adj.* épais; (*fig.* ~ *ignorance*) crasse.

crate *s.* cageot *m.*; (*for glass, china*) caisse *f.*; (*fam. auto.*) vieille bagnole *f.*; *v.t.* mettre en cageot, emballer.

crater *s.* cratère *m.*

cravat *s.* foulard *m.*

crav/e *v.t.* **1.** (*beg for*) implorer; **2.** (*long for*) désirer ardemment; **~ing** *s.* (2) désir ardent *m.*; soif *f.* (*for*—de).

craven *adj.* poltron.

crawl *s.* (*movement*) marche lente *f.*; (*of snake*) reptation *f.*; (*swimming stroke*) crawl *m.*; *v.i.* (*on hands and knees*) se traîner à quatre pattes; (*move slowly*) se traîner; (*snake*) ramper; (*fig.*) ramper; (*swim.*) crawler; **to be ~ing with,** grouiller de.

crayfish, crawfish *s.* écrevisse *f.*, langouste *f.*

crayon *s.* crayon de couleur *m.*; (*art*) fusain *m.*; *v.t.* crayonner.

craz/e *s.* (*mania*) manie *f.*; (*temporary fashion*) marotte *f.*; **to have a ~ for,** avoir la marotte de; **~y** *adj.* (*mad*) toqué; (*eager about*) passionné de; (*idea, etc.*) fou; **~iness** *s.* folie *f.*

creak *s.* grincement *m.*; *v.i.* grincer.

cream *s.* (*of milk*) crème *f.*; CLOT**ted ~**; (*cook.*) crème *f.*, purée *f.*; (*cosmetics*) crème de beauté *f.*; (*fig.*) crème *f.*, le dessus du panier; **the ~ of the joke,** le sel de l'histoire; (*colour*) crème (*invar.*); **~ cheese,** fromage blanc *m.*; **~ puff,** chou à la crème *m.*; **~ery** *s.* crémerie *f.*; **~y** *adj.* crémeux; *v.t.* (*lit.* & *fig.*) écrémer; (*cook.*) battre en crème.

crease *s.* **1.** (*fold*) pli *m.*; **2.** (*wrinkle*) faux pli *m.*; *v.t.* & *i.* (1) (se) plisser; (2) (se) froisser; **~-resistant** *adj.* infroissable.

creat/e *v.t.* créer; *v.i.* (*fam.*) rouspéter, faire une scène à qn.; **~ion** *s.* création *f.*; **~ive** *adj.* créat/eur, -rice; **~or** *s.* créat/eur, -rice *m.f.*

creature *s.* créature *f.*; (*fig.*) créature *f.*, âme damnée *f.*

credence *s.* (*belief*) créance *f.*; (*credit*) crédit *m.*; **to give ~ to,** ajouter foi à; **letters of ~,** lettres de créance *f.pl.*

credentials *s.pl.* (*diplomatic*) lettres de créance *f.pl.*; (*of servant*) certificat *m.*; (*proof of identity*) pièces d'identité *f.pl.*

credib/le *adj.* croyable; **~ility** *s.* crédibilité *f.*

credit *s.* **1.** (*belief, trust*) créance *f.*, foi *f.*; **2.** (*reputation*) crédit *m.*; **3.** (*deferred payment; fin.*) crédit *m.*; **4.** (*in exam.*) mention *f.*; **5.** (*cinema*) générique *m.*; **6.** (*source of honour*) honneur *m.*; **on ~,** à crédit; **to give s.o. ~ for sth.,** attribuer qch. à qn.; **to be a ~ to,** faire honneur à; ~ CARD; **~ side** *s.* crédit *m.*; *v.t.* (1) ajouter foi à; (3) créditer (*with*—de); **~ with** (*fig.*) imputer à; **~able** *adj.* honorable; **~ably** *adv.**; **~or** *s.* créancier *m.*

credul/ity *s.* crédulité *f.*; **~ous** *adj.* crédule.

creed *s.* (*eccles.*) credo *m.*; (*belief*) croyance *f.*

creek *s.* crique *f.*; **to be up the ~** (*pop.*) (*crazy*) être complètement dingue; (*in trouble*) faire fausse route.

creel *s.* panier de pêche *m.*

creep *v.i.* (*crawl*) ramper; (*move stealthily*) se glisser; (*plant*) grimper; (*skin*) se hérisser; **to make one's flesh ~, to give one the ~s,** donner la chair de poule à; **~er** *s.* (*plant*) plante grimpante *f.*; VIRGINIA **~er; ~ing** *adj.* rampant; **~y** *adj.* horrifiant.

cremat/e *v.t.* incinérer; **~ion** *s.* crémation *f.*; **~orium** *s.* (four) crématoire *m.*

crenellated *adj.* crénelé.

Creole *adj.* & *s.m.f.* créole.

creosote *s.* créosote *f.*; *v.t.* créosoter.

crêpe *s.* crêpe *m.*; **~ de chine,** crêpe de Chine *m.*; **~ paper,** papier gaufré *m.*; **~ rubber,** crêpe *m.*

crepitat/e *v.i.* crépiter; **~ion** *s.* crépitation *f.*

crescent *s.* (*moon* & *Islam*) croissant *m.*; (*street*) rue en demi-lune *f.*; *adj.* (*moon*) croissant; (*shape*) en croissant.

cress *s.* cresson *m.*

crest *s.* (*of animal*) crête *f.*; (*of bird*) huppe *f.*; (*of helmet*) cimier *m.*; (*of mountain, of wave*) crête *f.*; (*herald.*) armoiries *f.pl.*; **~ed** *adj.* (*birds*) huppé; **~fallen** *adj.* confus; **to look ~fallen,** avoir l'oreille basse.

Cret/e *s.* (*geog.*) Crète *f.*; **~an** *adj.* & *s.m.f.* crétois(e).

cretin *s.* crétin *m.*; **~ous** *adj.* idiot.

cretonne *s.* (*text.*) cretonne *f.*

crevasse *s.* crevasse *f.*

crevice *s.* (*in rock*) fente *f.*; (*in wall*) lézarde *f.*

crew *s.* (*naut., aviat.*) équipage *m.*; (*fig.*) bande *f.*; *v.i.* être membre de l'équipage; **~ cut** (*hair*) *s.* coiffure en brosse *f.*; *adj.* coiffé en brosse.

crib *s.* (*rack for animal fodder*) râtelier *m.*; (*child's bed*) berceau *m.*, (*eccles.*) crèche *f.*; (*school*) (*pop.*) traduc *f.*, pompe *f.*; *v.t.* (*confine*) claquemurer; *v.i.* (*cheat*) copier.

crick *s.* (*in neck*) torticolis *m.*

cricket[1] *s.* (*insect*) grillon *m.*

cricket[2] *s.* (*game*) cricket *m.*; **~ ball,** balle de cricket *f.*; **~ ground,** terrain de cricket *m.*

crier *see* CRY.

crim/e *s.* crime *m.*; (*law*) délit *m.*; **~inal** *s.* coupable *m.*; *adj.* criminel; **~inally** *adv.**; **~inology** *s.* criminologie *f.*

crimp *v.t.* (*cloth*) gaufrer; (*hair*) friser.

crimson *adj.* & *s.m.* cramoisi.

cring/e *v.i.* (*fig.*) s'aplatir (devant qn.); **~ing** *s.* attitude servile *f.*

crinkle *v.t.* & *i.* onduler; (*crease*) (se) froisser.

crinoline *s.* crinoline *f.*

cripple *s.* boit/eux, -euse *m.f.*; *v.t.* estropier; (*fig.*) paralyser; (*naut.*) désemparer; **~d** *adj.* (*with rheumatism, pain, etc.*) perclus (de rhumatismes, de douleurs, etc.); (*fig.*) (*~d with fear, grief, etc.*) terrassé (par la peur, le chagrin, etc.).

crisis *s.* (*turning point*) moment crucial *m.*; (*time of acute danger*) crise *f.*

crisp *s.* (*cook.*) (pomme de terre) frite *f.*; *adj.* (*brittle*) fragile; (*bracing*) vif; (*brisk*) net (*of style*), alerte (*of manner*); (*cook.*) croustillant, croquant; (*snow*) craquant; **~ly** *adv.* vivement; **~ness** *s.* (*air*) froid piquant *m.*; (*snow*) dureté

craquante *f.*; (*cook.*) qualité croustillante *f.*; (*fig.*) vivacité *f.*; *v.t.* (*hair*) crêper; (*cook.*) rendre croustillant; *v.i.* se crêper; devenir croustillant.
criterion *s.* critère *m.*
critic *s.* critique *m.*; **~al** *adj.* critique; **~ally** *adv.**; (*med.*) gravement; **~ism** *s.* critique *f.*; **~ize** *v.t.* critiquer.
croak *s.* **1.** (*frogs*) coassement *m.* **2.** (*birds*) croassement *m.*; *v.i.* (1) coasser; (2) croasser.
Croat/ia *s.* (*geog.*) Croatie *f.*; **~** *adj.* & *s.m.f.* croate.
crochet *s.* crochet *m.*; **~-needle,** crochet *m.*; *v.t.* faire qch. au crochet; *v.i.* faire du crochet.
crock *s.* (*pot or jar*) pot de terre *m.*; (*broken piece*) tesson *m.*; (*fig.*) (*auto.*) guimbarde *f.*; **~ery** *s.* faïence *f.*
crocodile *s.* crocodile *m.*; **~ tears,** larmes de crocodile *f.pl.*
crocus *s.* crocus *m.*
croft *s.* petite ferme *f.*
cromlech *s.* cromlech *m.*
crone *s.* (*fam.*) vieille taupe *f.*
crony *s.* copain *m.*
crook *s.* **1.** (*staff*) (*of bishop*) crosse *f.*; (*of shepherd*) houlette *f.*; **2.** (*bend, curve*) courbe *f.*; **3.** (*pop.* = *criminal*) escroc *m.*; **by** HOOK **or by ~**; **~-backed** *adj.* bossu; *v.t.* (2) recourber.
crooked *adj.* **1.** (*not straight*) tordu; **2.** (*winding*) tortueux; **3.** (*fig. dishonest*) malhonnête; **~ly** *adv.* (1) de travers; (2)*; (3)*; **~ness** *s.* (1) (*of body*) difformité *f.*; (2) détour *m.*; (3) malhonnêteté *f.*
croon *v.t.* & *i.* fredonner.
crop *s.* **1.** (*of bird*) jabot *m.*; **2.** (*whip-handle*) manche *m.*; **3.** (*produce*) récolte *f.*; **4.** (*hair*) coupe *f.*; **5.** (*hunting*) stick de chasse *m.*; *v.t.* (3) récolter; (4) couper court; (*graze*) brouter; *v.i.* **~ up** (*fig.*) surgir; **to come a ~per** (*lit.*) ramasser une pelle; (*fig.*) tomber sur un bec.
croquet *s.* croquet *m.*
crosier *s.* crosse *f.*
cross[1] *s.* (*relig. symbol*; *figure*; *fig.*) croix *f.*; (*hybrid*) croisement *m.*; **on the ~,** de biais; *adj.* (*transverse*) transversal; (*breed*) croisé; (*annoyed*) fâché; **to be/get ~,** se fâcher (*with s.o.*—contre qn.); **~ly** *adv.* avec mauvaise humeur; **~ness** *s.* mauvaise humeur *f.*; **at ~ purposes** *adv.* en désaccord.
cross[2]**-** (*in combination*) **~-bones,** tibias en croix *m.pl.*; SKULL **and ~-bones; ~bow** *s.* arbalète *f.*; **~-breed** *v.t.* croiser; **~-bred** *adj.* croisé; **~-country** *s.* (*sport*) cross *m.*; **~-examine** *v.t.* interroger; **~-examination** *s.* interrogatoire contradictoire *m.*; **~-eyed** *adj.* louche; **~-fire** *s.* feux croisés *m.pl.*; **~-grained** (*fig.*) *adj.* hargneux; **~-legged** *adj.* les jambes croisées; **~-patch** *s.* grincheux *m.*; chipie *f.*; **~-question** *v.t.* (*fam.*) mettre sur la sellette; **~-reference** *s.* renvoi *m.*; **~road** *s.* carrefour *m.* **~-section** *s.* section transversale *f.*; **~-stitch** *s.* point de croix *m.*; **~word** *s.* (problème de) mots croisés *m.*
cross[3] *v.t.* (*legs, arms, etc.*) croiser; (*draw line across, a cheque*) barrer; (*road, etc.*) traverser; (*thwart*) contrecarrer; (*interbreed*) croiser; **~ oneself,** se signer; **~ one's fingers, keep one's fingers ~ed** (*fig.*) toucher du bois; **~** SWORDS; *v.i.* (*meet* & **~**) se croiser; (*go across*) traverser; **~ off** *v.t.* biffer; **~ out** *v.t.* rayer; **~ over** *v.t.* & *i.* traverser; **~ing** *s.* croisement *m.*; (*of sea*) traversée *f.*; LEVEL **~ing**; PEDESTRIAN **~ing.**
crotch *s.* fourche *f.*
crotchet *s.* (*mus.*) noire *f.*; ⚠ croche = **quaver; ~y** *adj.* capricieux.
crouch *v.i.* s'accroupir; **~ing** *adj.* accroupi.
croup (*med.*) croup *m.*; (*of horse*) croupe *f.*
crow *s.* (*bird*) corneille *f.*; (*of cock*) chant *m.*; **as the ~ flies,** à vol d'oiseau; **~bar** *s.* levier *m.*, anspect *m.*; **~'s-foot** (*wrinkle*) patte d'oie *f.*; **~'s-nest** (*naut.*) nid de pie *m.*; *v.i.* (*cock*) chanter; (*fig.*) jubiler; **~ over s.o.,** triompher de qn.
crowd *s.* foule *f.*; (*heap of things*) tas *m.*; (*fam.*) bande *f.*; *v.t.* bourrer (dans, de); *v.i.* s'assembler, s'attrouper; **~ out** *v.t.* repousser; **~ round** *v.t.* se presser autour de; **~ with** *v.t.* encombrer de; **~ed** *adj.* encombré (de); bondé.
crown *s.* **1.** (*lit.* & *fig.*; *of sovereign*) couronne *f.*; (*top*) sommet *m.*; (*of hat*) calotte *f.*; **C~ prince(ss),** prince héritier *m.*, princesse héritière *f.*; *v.t.* couronner (de); (*fig.*) combler.
crucial *adj.* crucial.
crucible *s.* creuset *m.*
cruci/fix *s.* crucifix *m.*; **~fixion** *s.* crucifixion *f.*; **~form** *adj.* cruciforme; **~fy** *v.t.* crucifier.
crud/e *adj.* **1.** (*in raw state*) brut; **2.** (*fig.*) grossier; **~ely** *adv.* (1) crûment; (2) grossièrement; **~ity** *s.* (1) état naturel *m.*; **~eness** *s.* (2) crudité *f.*
cruel *adj.* cruel; **~ly** *adv.**; **~ty** *s.* cruauté *f.*
cruet *s.* huilier *m.*
cruis/e *s.* croisière *f.*; *v.i.* (*naut.*) croiser; (*taxi*) marauder; **~er** *s.* (*naut.*) croiseur *m.*; CABIN **~er; ~ing speed,** vitesse économique *f.*
crumb *s.* (*fragment of bread* & *fig.*) miette *f.*; (≠ *crust*) mie *f.*
crumbl/e *v.t.* & *i.* (s')émietter; (*stone*) (s')effriter; **~y** *adj.* friable.
crumple *v.t.* & *i.* (se) chiffonner.
crunch *s.* (*sound, of eating*) bruit sec *m.*; (*of footsteps*) piétinement *m.*; (*fig.* = *test*) pierre de touche *f.*; *v.t.* (*food*) croquer; (*with feet*) écraser.
crupper *s.* (*of horse*) croupe *f.*
crusade *s.* (*lit.* & *fig.*) croisade *f.*; **~r** *s.* croisé *m.*
crush *s.* (*crowd*) presse *f.*; (*drink*) jus de fruits *m.*; (*pop. infatuation*) béguin *m.*; **to have a ~ on s.o.,** en pincer pour qn; *v.t.* (*compress, subdue*) écraser; (*crumple*) froisser.
crust *s.* (*of bread* ≠ *crumb*; *pastry*) croûte *f.*; (*piece of bread*) croûton *m.*; (*of earth*) écorce *f.*; **the upper ~,** (*fig. fam.*) le gratin *m.*; **~y** *adj.* (*cook.*) croquant; (*person*) bourru.
crustacean *adj.* & *s.* crustacé *m.*
crutch *s.* béquille *f.*
crux *s.* point crucial *m.*; (*of problem*) nœud *m.*
cry *s.* **1.** (*loud utterance*) cri *m.*; **2.** (*of birds*) cri *m.*; **3.** (*fit of weeping*) crise de larmes *f.*; **4.** (*appeal*) appel *m.*; HUE **and ~; it's a far ~ to,** il y a loin d'ici à; **in full ~** (*fig.*) acharné (contre); *v.t.* (1) & (2) crier, pousser un cri; *v.i.* (1) s'écrier; (3) pleurer; **~ down** *v.t.* décrier; **~ for** *v.t.* implorer; **~ off** *v.i.* se retirer; **~ out** *v.i.* s'écrier; **~ up** *v.t.* vanter; **crier** *s.* (*street*) crieur *m.*, (*town*) tambour de ville *m.*; **~ing** *adj.* (*fig.*) criant; **~ing** *s.* larmes *f.pl.*; **it's no use ~ing over** SPILT **milk.**
crypt *s.* crypte *f.*
cryptic *adj.* occulte.
crystal *s.* cristal *m.*; *adj.* de cristal; **~ clear,** clair comme de l'eau de roche; **~lize** *v.t.* & *i.* (se) cristalliser.
cub *s.* (*bear*) ourson *m.*; (*lion*) lionceau *m.*; (*fox*) renardeau *m.*; (*wolf* & *C~ Scout*) louveteau *m.*; (*other animals*) petit *m.*; (*fig.*) novice *m.*; *v.t.* mettre bas.
Cuba *s.* (*geog.*) Cuba *m.*; **~n** *adj.* & *s.m.f.* cubain(e).
cub/e *s.* cube *m.*; **~e root,** racine cubique *f.*; **~ic** *adj.* cubique; **~ism** *s.* cubisme *m.*; *v.t.* cuber.
cubicle *s.* box *m.* (*pl.* boxes).
cuckold *s.* cocu *m.*; *v.t.* cocufier.
cuckoo *s.* coucou *m.*
cucumber *s.* concombre *m.*
cud, to chew the ~, ruminer.
cuddle *s.* étreinte *f.*; *v.t.* câliner; (*fam.* & *pej.*) peloter.

cudgel *s.* gourdin *m.*; **to take up the ~s for s.o.,** (*fig.*) prendre fait et cause pour qn.; *v.t.* bâtonner; **~ one's brains,** (*fam.*) se creuser la cervelle.
cue *s.* (*theat.*) réplique *f.*; (*billiards*) queue *f.*; **to take one's ~ from s.o.,** se mettre à la remorque de qn.
cuff *s.* **1.** (*blow*) taloche *f.*; **2.** (*dress*) (*ornamental*) parement *m.*; (*part of garment*) poignet *m.*; (*of shirt*) manchette *f.*; ~-LINK; **off the ~** *adj.* impromptu, improvisé; *adv.* sans préparation, de but en blanc; *v.t.* (1) talocher.
cuirass *s.* cuirasse *f.*
culinary *adj.* culinaire.
cull *v.t.* **1.** (*pick flower, etc.*) cueillir; **2.** (*select*) choisir; **3.** (*select & kill*) abattre sélectivement; *s.* (3) abattage sélectif *m.*
culminat/e *v.i.* (*astron. & fig.*) atteindre son point culminant; **~e in** (*fig.*) se terminer en *or* par (+*s.*); **~ion** *s.* zénith *m.*, point culminant *m.*
culpab/le *adj.* coupable; **~ility** *s.* culpabilité *f.*; **~ly** *adv.* d'une façon coupable.
culprit *s.* coupable *m.*
cult *s.* (*eccles. & homage*) culte *m.*; (*fad*) marotte *f.*; (*of*—de).
cultivat/e *v.t.* (*agric. & fig.*) cultiver; **~ed** *adj.* cultivé; **~ion** *s.* culture *f.*; **~or** *s.* (*person*) cultivat/eur, -rice *m.f.*; (*machine*) cultivateur *m.*
cultur/e *s.* culture *f.*; **~al** *adj.* culturel.
culvert *s.* conduit *m.*
cumb/er *v.t.* encombrer (*with*—de); **~ersome, ~rous** *adj.* encombrant.
cumulative *adj.* cumulatif.
cumulus *s.* (*cloud*) cumulus *m.*
cuneiform *adj.* cunéiforme.
cunning *s.* **1.** (*skill*) adresse *f.*; **2.** (*slyness*) ruse *f.*; *adj.* (1) adroit; (2) rusé; **~ly** *adv.* (1) avec adresse; (2) avec ruse.
cup *s.* (*for drinking*) tasse *f.*; (*ornamental, prize*) coupe *f.*; (*hollow*) cuvette *f.*; (*eccles.*) calice *f.*; **a ~ of tea, coffee, etc.,** une tasse de thé, de café, etc.; **a tea~, coffee-~, etc.,** une tasse à thé, à café, etc.; **another ~ of** TEA; **one's ~ of tea** (*fig.*) son rayon; **it's not my ~ of tea,** ce n'est pas de mon rayon; **that's just my ~ of tea** (*fam.*) ça me va; **to be in one's ~s,** être dans les vignes du Seigneur; **there's many a slip twixt ~ and lip,** il y a loin de la coupe aux lèvres; *v.t.* mettre en forme de coupe.
cupboard *s.* (*gen.*) armoire *f.*; (*in wall*) placard *m.*; **~ love,** amour intéressé *m.*; SKELETON **in ~.**
Cupid *s.* Cupidon *m.*; (*art*) amour *m.*
cupidity *s.* cupidité *f.*
cupola *s.* coupole *f.*
cur *s.* chien mâtiné; (*fig.*) chien *m.*
cur/ate *s.* vicaire *m.*; **~acy** *s.* vicariat *m.*; ⚠ curé = **priest.**
curator *s.* conservateur *m.*
curb *s.* **1.** (*on horse*) gourmette *f.*; **2.** (*fig.*) frein *m.*; *see* KERB; *v.t.* (1) gourmer; (2) freiner.
curd(s) *s.* lait caillé *m.*; **~le** *v.t. & i.* (se) cailler.
cur/e *s.* **1.** (*remedy*) remède *m.*, (*course of treatment*) cure *f.*, (*recovery*) guérison *f.*; **2.** (*spiritual charge*) charge *f.*; *v.t.* (1) guérir; (*fig.*) remédier à; (*preserve meat*): (*salt*) saler, (*smoke*) fumer; ⚠ curer = **to clean out, to pick teeth; ~able** *adj.* curable; **~ative** *adj.* curatif.
curfew *s.* couvre-feu *m.*
curio *s.* curiosité *f.*
curio/sity *s.* curiosité *f.*; **~us** *adj.* curieux; **~usly** *adv.**.
curl *s.* (*hair*) boucle *f.*; (*spiral form*) spirale *f.*; *v.t. & i.* boucler; **~ up** *v.i.* (*paper, etc.*) s'enrouler; se mettre en boule; (*person*) se coucher en chien de fusil; **~er** *s.* bigoudi *m.*; **~y** *adj.* (*hair*) bouclé.
curlew *s.* courlis *m.*
curmudgeon *s.* (*fam.*) mauvais coucheur *m.*
currant *s.* groseille *f.*; (*dried*) raisin de Corinthe *m.*; **black ~,** cassis *m.*; **red ~,** groseille rouge *f.*; **white ~,** groseille blanche *f.*; **~ bush** *s.* groseillier *m.*
curren/cy *s.* (*period of time*) cours *m.*; (*circulation*) circulation *f.*; (*prevalance*) cours *m.*; (*money*) monnaie *f.*; (*foreign ~cy*) devises *f.pl.*; **~t** *s.* (*water, air, electr.*) courant *m.*; (*fig.*) cours *m.*; **~t** *adj.* (*in general use*) courant; (*present*) actuel; **~t affairs,** actualités *f.pl.*; **~tly** *adv.* couramment, actuellement.
curricul/um *s.* programme scolaire *m.*; **~ar** *adj.* au programme.
curry *s.* (*cook.*) curry *m.*; *v.t.* (*cook.*) préparer qch. au curry; (*horse*) étriller; **~-comb** *s.* étrille *f.*; **to ~ favour,** chercher à se mettre bien avec qn.
curse *s.* malédiction *f.*; (*oath*) juron *m.*; (*fig. scourge*) fléau *m.*; *v.t.* maudire; *v.i.* jurer; **to be ~d with** (*fig.*) être affligé de; **~d** *adj.* maudit, (*fam.*) sacré (*both always before the noun*).
cursive *adj.* cursif.
cursor/y *adj.* rapide et superficiel; **~ily** *adv.* rapidement et superficiellement.
curt *adj.* brusque, sec; **~ly,** *adv.**,*.
curtail *v.t.* **1.** (*shorten*) raccourcir; **2.** (*expenses*) réduire; **3.** (*fig.*) rogner (qch. à qn.); **~ment** *s.* (1) raccourcissement *m.*; (2) diminution *f.*
curtain *s.* rideau *m.*; **iron ~,** rideau de fer *m.*; **~-call** *s.* (*theat.*) rappel *m.*; **~ hook** *s.* agrafe *f.*; **~-raiser** *s.* (*theat.*) lever de rideau *m.*; **~ ring** *s.* anneau *m.*; **~ rod** *s.* tringle *m.*
curts(e)y *s.* révérence *f.*; *v.i.* faire la révérence.
curv/e *s.* courbe *f.*; *v.t. & i.* (se) courber; **~aceous** *adj.* bien arrondi.
curvet *s.* courbette *f.*
cushion *s.* (*furnishing & techn.*) coussin *m.*; (*billiards*) bande *f.*; PIN~; *v.t.* matelasser; (*fig.*) amortir.
cusp *s.* pointe *f.*; (*arch.*) lobe *m.*
custard *s.* (*cook.*) crème anglaise *f.*, crème renversée *f.*; **~ tart,** flan *m.*
custod/y *s.* (*care*) garde *f.*; (*prison*) emprisonnement *m.*; **in ~y,** en état d'arrestation; **to take into ~y,** arrêter; **~ian** *s.* (*museums, etc.*) conservateur *m.*; (*building*) concierge *m.*
custom *s.* **1.** (*established usage*) coutume *f.*; **2.** (*comm.*) clientèle *f.*; **~-built,** hors série; **~-made,** sur mesure; **~ary** *adj.* (1) coutumier; **~er** *s.* (2) client(e) *m.f.*
customs *s.pl.* douane *f.sing.*; **~-house/post,** douane *f.*; **~-officer,** douanier *m.*
cut[1] *s.* **1.** (*act of ~ting*) coupe *f.*; (*blow with sword or whip*) coup *m.*; **2.** (*fig. insult*) affront *m.*; **3.** (*way sth. is ~*) coupe *f.*; **to be a ~ above,** être supérieur à; **4.** (*wound; ~ in book or play*) coupure *f.*; **5.** (*of meat*) morceau *m.*; **6.** (*fin., comm. reduction*) réduction *f.*; **power ~,** coupure de courant *f.*; (*pop. share of profit*) pourcentage *m.*; **short ~,** raccourci *m.*
cut[2] *v.t. & i.* (1) & (4) (se) couper; (*slice*) trancher; (*carve*) tailler; **~ one's finger, etc.,** se couper le doigt, etc.; **~ both ways,** être à deux tranchants; **~ no** ICE; (2) & **~ dead,** tourner le dos à qn.; (*cards*) couper; (*hair, etc.*) couper; **to have one's hair ~,** se faire couper les cheveux; (5) découper; (6) réduire, couper; (**~** *a lesson, etc.*) sécher; **~ one's losses,** faire la part du feu; **~ short,** couper court (à qch.), couper la parole (à qn.); (3) couper; **~ a** DASH; **~** GLASS; (*of tooth*) percer, **to ~ a tooth,** avoir une dent qui perce; **~ back** *v.t.* réduire; **~ down** *v.t.* abattre, (*fig.*) réduire; **~ in** *v.i.* intervenir; **~ off** *v.t.* détacher, (*telephone*) couper la communication, (*disinherit*) déshériter, (*exclude*) exclure; **~ off one's** NOSE **to spite one's face; ~ out** *v.t.* couper, tailler, (*s.o.*) éliminer (qn.); **~ it out!,** ça suffit!; **be ~ out**

for, être de taille à; **~-out** *s.* (*electr.*) coupe-circuit *m.*; **~ up** *v.t.* couper, découper, tailler en pièces; **~ up** *adj.* (*fig.*) désolé; **~ and dried,** tout fait; **~throat** *adj.* (*fig.*) acharné; **~ter** *s.* (*person*) coupeur *m.*, tailleur *m.*, (*tool*) coupoir *m.*, (*boat*) cotre *m.*; **~ting** *s.* (*press*) coupure *f.*, (*agric.*) bouture *f.*, (*rail.*) voie encaissée *f.*; **~ting** *adj.* tranchant, (*wind*) glacial, (*fig.*) mordant.

cutaneous *adj.* cutané.

cute *adj.* (*clever*) malin; (*sweet*) gentil.

cuticles *s.* envies *f.pl.*

cutlass *s.* coutelas *m.*

cutler *s.* coutelier *m.*; **~y** *s.* (*manufacture*) coutellerie *f.*; (*household*) couverts *m.pl.*

cutlet *s.* côtelette *f.*; (*minced fish or meat*) croquette *f.*

cwt *s.* (*hundredweight*) quintal *m.*

cyanide *s.* cyanure *m.*

cybernetics *s.* cybernétique *f.* ⚠ *singular in French.*

cycl/e *s.* (*recurrent period, vibration, electr.*) cycle *m.*; (*bicycle*) vélo *m.*; **~ing** *s.* cyclisme *m.*; **~ist** *s.* cycliste *m.f.*; *v.i.* aller à bicyclette, faire du vélo.

cyclone *s.* cyclone *m.*

Cyclops *s.* cyclope *m.*

cyclostyle *s.* appareil à polycopier; *v.t.* polycopier.

cygnet *s.* jeune cygne *m.*

cylind/er *s.* cylindre *m.*; **~rical** *adj.* cylindrique.

cymbal *s.* cymbale *f.*

cynic *s.* cynique *m.*; **~al** *adj.* sceptique, caustique; ⚠ cynique *adj.* = **immoral, shameless;** **~ally** *adv.* avec scepticisme; **~ism** *s.* scepticisme *m.*

cynosure *s.* point de mire *m.*

cypher *see* CIPHER.

cypress *s.* (*tree*) cyprès *m.*

Cypr/us *s.* (*geog.*) Chypre *f.*; **~iot** *adj.* & *s.m.f* cypriote.

cyst *s.* kyste *m.*

czar, tsar *s.* tsar *m.*; **~ina** *s.* tsarine *f.*

Czech/oslovakia *s.* Tchécoslovaquie *f.*; **~** *adj.* & *s.m.f.* tchèque; **~oslovak** *adj.* & *s.m.f.* tchécoslovaque.

D

D, d *s.* (*mus.*) ré *m.*

dab[1] *s.* **1.** (*small amount*) petit morceau *m.*; (*of paint*) tache *f.*; **2.** (*gentle tap*) tape *f.*; **3.** (*brief application with cloth*) coup d'éponge *m.*; *v.t.* (2) tapoter; (3) tamponner, éponger, donner un coup d'éponge à; **to be a ~ hand at sth., at doing sth.,** s'entendre à qch., à faire qch.; (*fam.*) avoir du chic pour faire qch.

dab[2] *s.* (*fish*) limande *f.*

dabbl/e *v.t.* (*wet*) mouiller, humecter; (*soil*) souiller; *v.i.* (*paddle*) barboter, patauger; (*on Stock Exchange*) boursicoter; (*do in a dilettante way*) faire (de la poésie, de la politique, etc.) en amateur; **~e in,** se mêler de; **~er** *s.* amateur *m.* (*f. rare*).

dachshund *s.* basset allemand *m.*

dacron *s.* (*text.*) dacron *m.* (**P.**)

dactyl *s.* dactyle *m.*

dad, daddy *s.* papa *m.*; **~-long-legs,** faucheux *m.*, tipule *f.*

dado *s.* (*arch.*) lambris *m.*

daffodil *s.* (*wild*) narcisse *m.*; (*garden*) jonquille *f.*

daft *adj.* (*pop.*) cinglé; (*fam.*) écervelé; **to go ~ about,** s'enticher de.

dagger *s.* poignard *m.*; **at ~s drawn,** à couteaux tirés; **to look ~s at s.o.,** lancer un regard furibond à qn.; CLOAK **and ~.**

dago *s.* Sud-américain (de race latine) *m.*, métèque *m.*

dahlia *s.* dahlia *m.*

daily *s.* (*newspaper*) quotidien *m.*; (*domestic*) femme de ménage *f.*; *adj.* (*happening every day*) quotidien; (*done every day*) journalier; **~ bread,** pain quotidien *m.*; **~** DOZEN; **~** ROUND; **~ worker,** ouvrier à la journée *m.*; *adv.* quotidiennement, tous les jours.

daint/y *s.* (*delicacy*) friandise *f.*; (*titbit*) morceau de choix *m.*; *adj.* (*taste, shape*) délicat; (*person*) mignon, coquet; (*hard to please*) difficile; **~ily** *adv.* délicatement; **~iness** *s.* délicatesse *f.*

dairy *s.* laiterie *f.*, crémerie *f.*; *adj.* laitier; **~ herd,** troupeau de vaches laitières *m.*; **~maid,** laitière *f.*; **~man,** laitier *m.*

dais *s.* estrade *f.*; ⚠ dais = **canopy.**

dais/y *s.* (*small*) pâquerette *f.*; (*ox-eyed*) marguerite *f.*; MICHAELMAS **~**; (*fam.*) (*person*) perle *f.*; (*thing*) merveille *f.*; **to push up the ~ies,** (*fam.*) manger les pissenlits par la racine; **~-chain** *s.* guirlande de pâquerettes *f.*; **~-cutter** *s.* vol en rase-motte *m.*

dale *s.* vallon *m.*, vallée *f.*; **up hill and down ~,** par monts et par vaux.

dall/y *v.i.* (*trifle*) s'amuser; (*play*) folâtrer, badiner, flirter; **~y away** (*time*), gaspiller (son temps); **~y with** (*fig.*) jouer avec, caresser (une idée); **~iance** *s.* badinage *m.*, flirt *m.*

daltonism *s.* (*med.*) daltonisme *m.*

dam[1] *s.* (*animals*) mère *f.*

dam[2] *s.* (*water barrier*) digue *f.*; (*river*) barrage *m.*; (*mill*) écluse *f.*; *v.t.* barrer, endiguer; **~ up,** établir un barrage sur, contenir.

damag/e *s.* **1.** (*harm*) dommage *m.*, dégâts *m.pl.*; **rain/frost ~e,** dégâts dûs à la pluie/au gel; **2.** (*fig. to person*) préjudice *m.*; **cause ~e to s.o.,** porter préjudice à qn.; **3.** (*naut. mishap or loss*) avaries *f.pl.*; **~e in transit** avaries de route *f.pl.* **4. ~es** (*law*) dommages-intérêts *m.pl.*; **5.** (*pop.* = *cost*) **what's the ~e?** c'est combien?; *v.t.* (1) endommager, abîmer; (2) nuire à, faire tort à; (3) avarier; **~eable** *adj.* avariable; **~ed** *adj.* avarié, endommagé; **~ing** *adj.* (1) dévastateur; (2) nuisible, préjudiciable.

damask *s.* (*linen, silk, steel*) damas *m.*; (*colour*) incarnat *m.*; *adj.* damassé; **~ rose** *s.* rose de Damas *f.*

dame *s.* dame *f.*

damn *s.* juron *m.*; **it's not worth a ~**, cela ne vaut pas un clou; **I don't care a ~**, je m'en fiche; *interj.* zut!, sapristi!; *v.t.* **1.** (*eccles.*) damner; **2.** (*fig.*) condamner, perdre; **3.** (*condemn to*) condamner à; **4.** (*curse*) maudire envoyer au diable; **~able** *adj.* (1) damnable; (4) maudit; **~ation** *s.* damnation *f.*; **~ed** *adj.* (1) damné; (2) perdu; (4) (*fam.*) sacré (*before the noun*); **the ~ed** *s.* les damnés *m.pl.*; **~ed** *adv.* (*also* **~ably**) (*pop.*) vachement; (*fam.*) diablement; **it's ~ed difficult,** c'est vachement difficile; **~ing** *adj.* **~ing evidence,** preuve accablante *f.*

damp *s.* (*also* **~ness**) humidité *f.*; *adj.* humide; (*skin*) moite; **~ course** *s.* couche isolante, couche hydrofuge *f.*; **~-proof** *adj.* hydrofuge, imperméable; **~en** *v.t.* humecter; *v.i.* devenir humide; *v.t.* (*make* ~) mouiller, humecter; (*fig. discourage*) décourager; ~ **s.o.'s ardour,** tempérer l'ardeur de qn.; (*mus.*) assourdir; ~ **down** (*a furnace*) boucher; ~ **off** *v.i.* (*hort.*) périr par excès d'humidité.

damper *s.* (*chimneys*) registre *m.*; (*person*) rabat--joie *m.*; (*piano*) étouffoir *m.*; **to put a ~ on the proceedings,** jeter un froid sur la compagnie.

damsel *s.* demoiselle *f.*

damson *s.* prune de damas *f.*; **~-coloured,** prune.

danc/e *s.* danse *f.*; (*ball*) bal *m.*; FOLK-**~e**; **she'll lead you a ~e,** elle vous en fera voir de toutes les couleurs; **~e-hall** *s.* dancing *m.*; **~e music** *s.* musique de danse *f.*; *v.t.* & *i.* danser; **~e with s.o.,** faire danser qn.; **~e attendance on s.o.,** faire l'empressé auprès de qn.; **~e to s.o.'s tune,** se faire mener par qn.; **make s.o. ~e to another tune,** faire chanter qn. sur un autre ton; **~er** *s.* dans/eur, -euse *m.f.*; **~ing** *s.* danse *f.*; **~ing--girl** *s.* danseuse de cabaret *f.*; **~ing-master** *s.* maître de danse *m.*; **~ing partner** *s.* partenaire *m.f.*, cavali/er, -ère *m.f.*

dandelion *s.* dent-de-lion *f.*, (*fam.*) pissenlit *m.*

dander *s.* (*fam.*) **to get s.o.'s ~ up,** mettre qn. en colère; **he got his ~ up,** la moutarde lui a monté au nez.

dandle *v.t.* bercer, dorloter.

dandruff *s.* pellicules *f.pl.*

dandy *s.* élégant *m.*, dandy *m.*; *adj.* (*U.S.A.*) élégant, chic, (*pop.*) chouette.

Dan/e *s.m.f.* Danois(e); **Great ~e,** danois *m.*; **~ish** *adj.* danois; *s.m.* (*lang.*) danois; **~ish blue** (*cheese*) fromage bleu *m.*

danger *s.* (*liability to harm*) péril *m.*, risque *m.*; (*thing liable to cause harm*) danger *m.*; **in ~ of,** en danger de; **to be in ~ of,** risquer de; ~ **money** *s.* prime de danger *f.*; ~ **signal** *s.* signal d'arrêt *m.*; **~ous** *adj.* dangereux; **~-ously** *adv.**.

dangle *v.t.* & *i.* pendiller, se balancer, faire balancer; ~ **sth. alluringly before s.o.,** faire miroiter qch. aux yeux de qn.

dank *adj.* humide (et froid).

dapper *adj.* fringant, soigné; (*fam.*) tiré à quatre épingles.

dapple *v.t.* tacheter; **~-grey** *adj.* gris pommelé *invar*; **~d** *adj.* pommelé.

dar/e *s.* défi *m.*; *v.t.* (*venture*) oser; (*challenge*) braver, défier (*to*—de); **I ~ say,** sans doute, j'ose dire; **~edevil** *s.* risque-tout *m.invar.*; **~ing** *s.* audace *f.*; *adj.* audacieux; **~ingly** *adv.**.

dark *s.* noir *m.*, obscurité *f.*; **to be in the ~ about sth.,** ignorer tout de qch.; **a leap in the ~,** un saut dans l'inconnu *m.*; *adj.* **1.** (*obscure*) obscur, sombre; **2.** (*colours*) foncé *invar.*; **3.** (*skin*) brun; **4.** (*fig.*) triste; **to be ~,** faire sombre; **to get ~,** s'assombrir; **to keep sth. ~,** tenir qch. secret; **keep it ~!,** gardez le secret!; **the D~ ages,** les temps obscurs du Moyen Age *m.pl.*; **the D~ Continent,** le continent noir *m.*; ~ **horse** (*fam.*) concurrent inconnu mais dangereux *m.*; **~-room,** chambre noire *f.*; **~en** *v.t.* & *i.* (1) (s')obscurcir; (2) foncer; (3) brunir; (4) (s')attrister; **never ~en my door again,** ne mettez plus les pieds chez moi; **~ly** *adv.* obscurément; **~ness** *s.* obscurité *f.*, ténèbres *m.pl.*; **~y** *s.* (*fam.*) nègre *m.*, négresse *f.*

darling *adj.* & *s.m.f.* chéri(e).

darn[1] *s.* (*repair*) reprise *f.*; *v.t.* repriser; **~ing--needle** *s.* aiguille à repriser *f.*

darn[2] *s.* (*pop.* = *damn*) juron *m.*; *interj.* (*fam.*) ~ **it!** (*emphasis*) bon Dieu!; (*frustration*) zut!

dart *s.* **1.** (*missile*) dard *m.*, flèche *f.*; **2.** (*motion*) brusque élan *m.*; **3.** (*fold in garment*) pince *f.*; **4.** (*game, pl.*) fléchettes *f.pl.*; **~board,** cible *f.*; *v.t.* (1) darder, lancer; (3) faire une pince (à une robe); *v.i.* (2) se précipiter, foncer; ~ **away** *v.i.* partir comme une flèche.

dash *s.* (*stroke of pen*) trait *m.*, tiret *m.*; (*rush*) précipitation *f.*; (*vigour*) fougue *f.*, brio *m.*, allant *m.*; (*splash of water*) goutte *f.*; (*slight infusion*) goutte *f.*, (*of brandy*) doigt *m.*, (*of garlic*) pointe *f.*; (= *~board*) tableau de bord *m.*; **to cut a ~** (*fam.*) faire de l'épate; *interj.* (= *damn*) zut!, sapristi!; *v.t.* (*to pieces*) briser (en morceaux); (*discourage*) décourager; *v.i.* se précipiter, se sauver; ~ **against** *v.t.* & *i.* (se) heurter contre; ~ **away** *v.t.* écarter vivement; *v.i.* filer; ~ **down** *v.t.* jeter à terre; ~ **in**(**to**), se précipiter dans; ~ **off** *v.t.* dessiner en un tour de main; (*rush work*) bâcler; **~ing** *adj.* fougueux; **~ingly** *adv.* avec brio.

dastard *s.* lâche *m.*; **~ly** *adj.* lâche; **~liness** *s.* lâcheté *f.*

data *s.* données *f.pl.*; ~ **processing,** traitement de l'information *m.*

date[1] *s.* (*fruit*) datte *f.*; **~-palm** (*tree*) dattier *m.*

date[2] *s.* (*time*) date *f.*; (*fam.* = *appointment*) rendez-vous *m.*; (*fam. person*) flirt *m.f.*; **out of ~,** démodé; **up to ~,** (*thing*) contemporain, (*person, on facts*) au courant; **to be up to ~,** être **à la page; to bring up to ~,** (*accounts*) mettre à jour, (*on facts*) mettre au courant; **~-line** *s.* ligne de changement de date *f.*; **~less** *adj.* (*letter*) sans date, (*fame, etc.*) immémorial; *v.t.* (*mark with ~*) dater; (*refer to ~*) assigner une date à; (*make appear old-fashioned*) dater; (*fam.*) donner rendez-vous à; ~ **from,** dater de, remonter à; *v.i.* (*become recognizable as past*) dater (de loin), être démodé; **dated** *adj.* (*letter*) en date de; (=*out of ~*) démodé; CARBON **dating.**

dative *adj.* & *s.* datif *m.*

daub *s.* (*painting*) croûte *f.*, barbouillage *m.*; *v.t.* enduire (*with*—de); *v.i.* barbouiller; **~er** *s.* barbouilleur *m.*

daughter *s.* fille *f.*; **~-in-law,** belle-fille *f.*; **~ly** *adj.* filial.

daunt *v.t.* (*discourage*) décourager; (*frighten*) intimider; **nothing ~ed,** nullement intimidé; **~less** *adj.* intrépide; **~lessly** *adv.**; **~lessness** *s.* intrépidité *f.*

dauphin *s.* dauphin *m.*; **~ess** *s.* dauphine *f.*

davit *s.* porte-manteau *m.*

dawdle *v.i.* traîner, flâner; ~ **away** *v.t.* (*time, life, etc.*) gaspiller; **~r** *s.* traînard *m.*, flâneur *m.*

dawn *s.* (*daybreak*) point du jour *m.*; (*fig.*) aurore *f.*, aube *f.*; **at the ~ of his life,** à l'aube de sa vie; *v.i.* (*grow light*) poindre; (*appear faintly*) naître; **it ~ed on me that,** j'eus soudain l'idée que; **~ing** *adj.* naissant.

day *s.* (*hours of ~light*) jour *m.*; (*whole ~*) journée *f.*; (*period, era*) temps *m.*; ~ **before,** veille *f.*; ~ **after,** lendemain *m.*; ~ **before yesterday,** avant-hier; ~ **after tomorrow,** après-demain; **one ~, one of these ~s,** un de ces jours; **every ~,** tous les jours; **every other ~,** tous les deux jours; **from ~ to ~,** de jour en jour; **in these ~s,** de nos jours; **in ~s gone by,** au temps jadis; **by ~,** de jour; ~ **in,** ~ **out,** du matin au soir; **the ~ when,** le jour où; ~ **off,** jour de congé; **twice a ~,** deux fois par jour; QUARTER ~; RAINY ~; RED **letter ~**; WORKING ~; **to call it a ~,** débrayer pour le reste de la journée; **to** CARRY **the ~**; **~-boarder** *s.* demi--pensionnaire *m.*; **~-book** *s.* journal *m.*; **~-boy** *s.* externe *m.*; **~break** *s.* point du jour *m.*; **~--dream** *s.* rêverie *f.*; **~light** *s.* jour *m.*, lumière *f.*; **~light saving** *s.* heure d'été *f.*; ~ **nursery** *s.* crèche *f.*; **~-school** *s.* externat *m.*; **~time** *s.* jour *m.*, journée *f.*

daze *s.* **1.** (*from blow*) étourdissement *m.*; **2.** (*from light*) éblouissement *m.*; **in a ~,** stupéfait; *v.t.* (1) étourdir; (2) éblouir.
dazzl/e *s.* éblouissement *m.*; *v.t.* éblouir, aveugler; (*fig.*) éblouir; (*fam.*) épater; **~ing** *adj.* éblouissant, (*fam.*) épatant.
D-Day *s.* Jour J *m.*
D.D.T. *s.* D.D.T. *m.*
deacon *s.* diacre *m.*; **~ess** *s.* diaconesse *f.*
dead *s.pl.* **the ~,** les morts *m.pl.*; *s.* (*inactive time*) **at ~ of night, winter, etc.,** en pleine nuit, en plein hiver; *adj.* (*no longer alive*) mort; **~ as a doornail,** mort et bien mort; **~ or alive,** mort ou vif; (*insensible*) sourd, insensible (*to*—à); (*numb, lit.* & *fig.*) engourdi; (*obsolete*) mort; (*dull, inactive, inanimate*): (*colours*) mat; (*sounds*) lourd, sourd; (*ball*) mort; (*fire, etc.*) éteint; (*motor, etc.*) mort; (*trade, etc.*) stagnant; (*complete*) net, sec; **~ loss,** perte sèche *f.*; **~-and-alive** *adj.* mort, triste; **~ centre,** point mort *m.*; **~ end** *s.* impasse *f.*; **~-end** (*fig. of job, etc.*) sans avenir; **~head** *s.* (*theatr.*) détenteur d'un billet de faveur *m.*; **~ heat,** manche nulle *f.*; **~ language,** langue morte *f.*; **~ letter** (*law*) lettre morte *f.*, (*unclaimed letter*) lettre tombée au rebut *f.*; **~line** *s.* (*space*) dernière limite *f.*, (*time*) date limite *f.*; **~lock** *s.* impasse *f.*; **~locked** *adj.* dans l'impasse; **~ march,** marche funèbre *f.*; **~ men** (*fam.*) cadavre de bouteilles *m.pl.*; **~ nettle,** ortie blanche *f.*; **~ pan** (*pop.*) (à la) face hébétée; **~ reckoning** *s.* (*naut.*) estime *f.*; **D~ Sea,** la Mer Morte *f.*; **~ season,** morte-saison *f.*; **~ shot** *s.* tireur d'élite *m.*; **~ weight** *s.* (*naut.*) chargement en lourd *m.*; (*fig.*) boulet aux pieds *m.*; **~ wood,** bois mort *m.*; **to cut out the ~ wood** (*fig.*) réduire le personnel; *adv.* (*exactly*) droit, en plein, juste; **~ on time,** juste à l'heure; (*completely*) complètement; **~ against,** complètement opposé à; **~-beat** *adj.* rompu, éreinté; **~ drunk,** ivre mort; **~ tired** (*fam.*) claqué, crevé; **~en** *v.t.* (*blow, shock*) amortir, (*sound*) assourdir, étouffer, (*fig.*) émousser; **~ly** *adj.* mortel, (*sin*) capital; **~ly** *adv.* mortellement; **~ly nightshade** *s.* belladone *f.*
deaf *adj.* sourd; (*fig.*) insensible (*to*—à); **~ as a post,** sourd comme un pot; **to turn a ~ ear to,** faire la sourde oreille à; **~-and-dumb** *adj.* & *s.m.f.*, & **~ mute** *s.m.f.* sourd(e)-muet(te); **~-aid** *s.* sonotone *m.*; **~en** *v.t.* assourdir; **~ening** *adj.* assourdissant; **~ness** *s.* surdité *f.*
deal[1] *s.* (*wood*) bois de sapin *m.*
deal[2] *s.* (*comm.*) opération *f.*, affaire *f.*; **it's a ~!,** affaire conclue!; (*quantity*) quantité *f.*; **a good ~ of,** beaucoup de; (*cards*) donne *f.*; **to have a raw ~,** ne pas avoir la vie facile; **to give s.o. a raw ~,** en faire voir de dures à qn.; *v.t.* (**~ out**) distribuer; (*cards*) donner; *v.i.* (*comm.*) traiter; **~ in,** faire le commerce de; **~ with** (*thing*) traiter (une affaire, une question), (*person*) avoir affaire à, (*person or problem*) s'occuper de; **~er** *s.* marchand *m.*; (*wholesale*) négociant *m.*; **~ings** *s.pl.* relations *f.pl.*, négociations *f.pl.*; **double ~ings,** duplicité *f.*
dean *s.* doyen *m.*
dear *s.* cher, chère *m.f.*, chéri(e) *m.f.*; *adj.* **1.** (*beloved*) cher (*before noun*), **a ~ friend,** un cher ami; **2.** (*expensive*) cher (*after noun*), **a ~ meal,** un repas cher; **Oh ~!,** Mon Dieu!; **~ me!,** vraiment!; *adv.* cher; **it will cost you ~,** cela vous coûtera cher; **~ly** *adv.* (*affection*) tendrement; (*at a high price*) chèrement; **~ness** *s.* cherté *f.*
dearth *s.* (*scarcity, of food* & *essentials*) disette *f.*; (*lack*) manque (de) *m.*
death *s.* mort *f.*; **Black D~,** peste noire *f.*; **to be bored, frightened, starved, etc. to ~,** mourir, (*fam.*) crever, d'ennui, de peur, de faim, etc.; **to** RIDE **to ~; to be the ~ of s.o.,** faire mourir qn.; **to be at ~'s door,** être à l'agonie; **to be in at the ~,** être présent au bon moment; **~-blow** *s.* coup de grâce *m.*; **~ duties** *s.* droits de succession *m.pl.*; **~'s head** *s.* tête de mort *f.*; **~-mask** *s.* masque mortuaire *m.*; **~ penalty** *s.* peine de mort *f.*; **~ rate** *s.* taux de mortalité *m.*; **~-rattle** *s.* râle *m.*; **~-roll** *s.* liste de morts *f.*, nécrologe *m.*; **~ struggles** *s.* agonie *f.*; **~-trap** *s.* souricière *f.*; **~-warrant** *s.* arrêt de mort *m.*; **~-watch (beetle)** *s.* psoque *m.*, (*fam.*) horloge de la mort *f.*; **~less** *adj.* immortel; **~ly** *adj.* mortel; *adv.**.
debar *v.t.* exclure, empêcher, interdire (*from*—de).
debase *v.t.* (*degrade*) avilir; (*comm.*) altérer; **~ment** *s.* avilissement *m.*
debat/e *s.* discussion *f.*; (*parl. etc.*) débats *m.pl.*; *v.t.* discuter, débattre; *v.i.* délibérer (sur); **~able** *adj.* discutable; **~er** *s.* argumentat/eur, -rice *m.f.*
debauch, debauchery *s.* débauche *f.*; *v.t.* (*pervert*) débaucher; (*taste, etc.*) corrompre; **~ee** *s.* débauché(e) *m.f.*
debenture *s.* obligation *f.*; **~ holder** *s.* obligataire *m.f.*; **~ stock** *s.* obligations sans garantie *f.pl.*
debilit/y *s.* débilité *f.*, faiblesse *f.*; **~ate** *v.t.* débiliter.
debit *s.* débit *m.*; **~ account** *s.* compte débiteur *m.*; **~ side** *s.* débit *m.*; *v.t.* **~ with, against,** porter au débit de; **~ to,** débiter à.
debouch *v.i.* déboucher.
debris *s.* débris *m.pl.*
debt *s.* dette *f.*; **to get or run into ~,** s'endetter; **to be up to the eyes in ~,** être criblé de dettes; **National D~,** dette publique *f.*; **~ of honour,** dette d'honneur *f.*; **I am in your ~,** je vous suis obligé; **~-collector** *s.* (*private*) agent de recouvrement *m.*, (*official*) huissier *m.*; **~or** *s.* débit/eur, -rice *m.f.*
debunk *v.t.* (*person*) démystifier; (*pop. reputation, etc.*) dégonfler; **~ing** *s.* démystification *f.*
decade *s.* (*10 days, pop. = 10 years*) décade *f.*; (*10 years*) décennie *f.*
decaden/ce *s.* décadence *f.*; **~t** *adj.* décadent.
decaffeinated *adj.* décaféiné.
decagon *s.* décagone *m.*
Decalogue *s.* décalogue *m.*
decamp *v.t.* (*raise camp*) lever le camp; *v.i.* (*leave suddenly*) déguerpir, décamper, filer.
decant *v.t.* transvaser; **~er** *s.* carafe *f.*
decapitat/e *v.t.* décapiter; **~ion** *s.* décapitation *f.*
decarbonize *v.t.* (*an engine*) décalaminer; (*a metal*) décarburer.
decay *s.* **1.** (*decline*) décadence *f.*, déclin *m.*; **2.** (*ruinous state*) ruine *f.*, délabrement *m.*; **3.** (*veg. matter*) décomposition *f.*; **4.** (*teeth, bones, etc.*) carie *f.*; *v.i.* (1) (*arch.* & *fig.*) tomber en ruines, (*comm.*) péricliter; (2) se délabrer; (3) pourrir, se décomposer; (4) se gâter; **5.** (*fig.*) dépérir.
decease *s.* décès *m.*; *v.i.* décéder; **~d** *adj.* & *s.m.f.* défunt(e).
deceit *s.* (*action*) supercherie *f.*, duperie *f.*; (*~fulness*) tromperie *f.*, duplicité *f.*, fraude *f.*; **~ful** *adj.* (*person*) trompeur; (*character*) faux; (*action*) perfide; **~fully** *adv.* d'une manière trompeuse; **~fulness** *s.* tromperie *f.*, perfidie *f.*
deceive *v.t.* **1.** (*persuade* (*oneself*) *of what is false*) (se) tromper, (s')abuser; **2.** (*mislead*) induire en erreur; **3.** (*disappoint*) décevoir; ⚠ décevoir = *only* (3); **~r** *s.* trompeu/r, -se *m.f.*
decelerat/e *v.t.* & *i.* ralentir; **~ion** *s.* décélération *f.*; **~ion** LANE.
December *s.* décembre *m.*
decen/t *adj.* **1.** (*not immodest*) décent, pudique ⚠ décent = *this meaning only*; **2.** (*respectable*) bien-

séant; **3.** (*good enough*) convenable, passable; **4.** (*fam.* = *kindly*) honnête, gentil; **5.** (*pop.* = *clothed*) habillé; **~cy** *s.* (1) décence *f.*, pudeur *f.*; (2) bienséance *f.*, convenance *f.*; (4) gentillesse *f.*; **~cies** *s.pl.* convenances *f.pl.*; **in common ~cy,** par simple politesse; **~tly** *adv.* (1) décemment; (2) convenablement; (3) passablement; (4) gentiment.

decentraliz/e *v.t.* décentraliser; **~ation** *s.* décentralisation *f.*

decept/ion *s.* (*being deceived*) erreur *f.*, mécompte *m.*; (*which deceives*) tromperie *f.*, duperie *f.*; ⚠ déception = **disappointment**; **~ive** *adj.* trompeur; **~ively** *adv.* d'une manière trompeuse.

deci- (*in combination*) **~bel** *s.* décibel *m.*; **~gram** *s.* décigramme *m.*; **~litre** *s.* décilitre *m.*; **~metre** *s.* décimètre *m.*

decid/e *v.t.* & *i.* (*settle an issue*) régler, trancher (une question); (*between conflicting opinions*) départager (les opinions); (*give judgement*) décider, statuer; (*come to a decision*) se décider à, se résoudre à; **~e to, on,** décider de; **~e against s.o., sth.** se prononcer contre qn., qch.; **~e in favour of s.o.,** donner gain de cause à qn.; **~ed** *adj.* (*conspicuous*) marqué, net; (*resolute*) résolu, décidé; **~edly** *adv.* décidément, catégoriquement; **~ing** *adj.* **~ing game,** la belle.

deciduous *adj.* caduc, caduque *m.f.*; **~ tree,** arbre à feuillage caduc *m.*

decimal *s.* décimale *f.*; *adj.* décimal; **~ coinage, currency,** système monétaire décimal *m.*; **~ point,** virgule *f.* ⚠ (*Eng.* 10·37 = *French* 10,37); **~ize** *v.t.* décimaliser; **~ization** *s.* décimalisation *f.*

decimate *v.t.* décimer.

decipher *v.t.* déchiffrer; **~able** *adj.* déchiffrable; **~ing** *s.* déchiffrement *m.*

decis/ion *s.* (*act of deciding*) décision *f.*; (*firmness*) décision *f.*, fermeté *f.*; (*formal judgement*) arrêt *m.*; **~ive** *adj.* **1.** (*conclusive*) décisif; **2.** (*resolute*) résolu; **3.** (*unequivocal*) catégorique, incontestable **~ively** *adv.* (1) définitivement; (2)*; (3)*,*.

deck *s.* (*of ship*) pont *m.*; QUARTER**~**; (*of bus*) impériale *f.* (*fam.* = *ground*) sol *m.*; (*of cards*) jeu *m.*; **to clear the ~s,** faire le branle-bas; **~ cargo** *s.* pontée *f.*; **~-chair** *s.* chaise-longue (de bord) *f.*, (*fam.*) transat *m.*; **~-hand** *s.* homme de pont *m.*; **~-house** *s.* (*naut.*) rouf *m.*; **~ tennis** *s.* tennis de bord *m.*; **~er** *s.* (*bus*) **single-~er,** autobus sans impériale *m.*, **double-~er,** autobus à impériale *m.*; (*ship*) vaisseau à 2 ou 3 ponts *m.*; *v.t.* parer, orner; (*cover*) couvrir.

deckle-edge *s.* barbes *f.pl.*; **~d paper,** papier à bords non ébarbés *m.*

decla/im *v.t.* & *i.* déclamer; **~mation** *s.* déclamation *f.* **~matory** *adj.* déclamatoire.

declar/e *v.t.* & *i.* **1.** (*proclaim*; *to customs*; *war, etc.*) déclarer, annoncer; **2.** (*cricket*) fermer son jeu; **3.** (*cards*) annoncer son jeu; **~ation** *s.* (1) déclaration *f.*; (3) annonce *f.*; **~ed** *adj.* avoué déclaré; **~er** *s.* déclarat/eur, -rice *m.f.*; (*at bridge*) déclarant *m.*

declension *s.* (*ling.*) déclinaison *f.*; (*deviation*) déviation *f.*; (*decay*) décadence *f.*

declin/e *s.* (*decrease or deterioration*) déclin *m.*; (*of temperature, price, etc.*) baisse *f.*; (*decay*) décadence *f.*; (*med.*) maladie de langueur *f.*, phtisie *f.*; *v.t.* & *i.* (*incline, slope*) descendre (en pente), baisser, s'incliner; (*refuse*) refuser (*to do sth.*—de faire qch.); (*ling.*) décliner; (*decrease, lower*) baisser; (*med.*) décliner; (*fig.*) tomber en décadence; **~ation** *s.* (*slope*) pente *f.*; (*non-acceptance*) refus *m.*; (*astron.*) déclinaison *f.*; **~ing** *adj.* sur son déclin.

declivity *s.* pente *f.*

declutch *v.i.* débrayer.

decode *v.t.* déchiffrer; **~d** *adj.* en clair.

decoke *v.t.* *see* DECARBONIZE.

decompos/e *v.t.* (*separate, analyse*) décomposer, analyser; *v.i.* (*rot*) se décomposer, pourrir; **~ition** *s.* décomposition *f.*, putréfaction *f.*

decompress *v.t.* décomprimer; **~ion** *s.* décompression *f.*

decontaminat/e *v.t.* désinfecter, décontaminer; **~ion** *s.* désinfection *f.*, décontamination *f.*

decontrol *v.t.* décontrôler; (*trade, prices*) libérer.

decorat/e *v.t.* **1.** (*adorn*) décorer, parer, orner; (*with flags*) pavoiser; **2.** (*paint, paper*) peindre, tapisser; **3.** (*with medal*) décorer; **~ed** *adj.* (*arch. style*) flamboyant; (*with medal*) médaillé; **~ion** *s.* (1) décoration *f.*; (3) médaille *f.*; **~ive** *adj.* décoratif; **~or** *s.* décorateur *m.*; (*house*) peintre *m.*, tapissier *m.*

decor/um *s.* bienséance *f.*, étiquette *f.*, décorum *m.*; **~ous** *adj.* bienséant, comme il faut; **~ously** *adv.* convenablement.

decoy *s.* (*trap*) leurre *m.*, piège *m.*; (*person*) agent provocateur *m.*; *v.t.* leurrer, attirer (qn.) dans un piège.

decrease *s.* diminution *f.*; *v.t.* & *i.* diminuer, décroître.

decree *s.* (*law*) arrêt *m.*; (*gen.*) décret *m.*; **~ in bankruptcy,** jugement de faillite *m.*; **~ nisi,** divorce sous conditions *m.*; *v.t.* décréter.

decrepit *adj.* **1.** (*person*) décrépit; **2.** (*thing*) caduc, délabré; **~ude** *s.* (1) décrépitude *f.*; (2) caducité *f.*

decry *v.t.* décrier, dénigrer, huer.

dedicat/e *v.t.* **1.** (*devote* (*oneself*) *to*) (se) consacrer à; **2.** (*church, book, etc.*) dédier; **~ion** *s.* (1) dévouement *m.*; (2) (*church*) consécration *f.*, (*book*) dédicace *f.*; **~ory** *adj.* dédicatoire.

deduce *v.t.* (*trace descent from*) déduire de; (*infer from*) conclure de.

deduct *v.t.* déduire, retrancher, soustraire; **~ion** *s.* (*in price*) rabais *m.*; (*inference*) déduction *f.*; **~ive** *adj.* déductif.

deed *s.* (*action*) acte *m.*; (*legal document*) contrat *m.*; (*exploit*) exploit *m.*; **~ poll,** acte unilatéral *m.*

deem *v.t.* juger, estimer; **~ed** (= *considered*) censé (+ *inf.* + *s.* *or adj.*), **she is ~ed to be intelligent,** elle est censée être intelligente.

deep *s.* (*poet.* = *sea*) mer *f.*; (*pit*) abîme *m.*, gouffre *m.*; *adj.* (*extending far down*, (*lit.* & *fig.*) *profound, intense*) profond; **to go off the ~ end** (*fig.*) s'emballer; **to be in ~ water(s)** (*fam. fig.*) faire de mauvaises affaires; **~-freeze** *s.* congélateur *m.*; **~-freeze** *v.t.* surgeler; (*of colours*) foncé (*invar.*); (*of voice*) de basse; (*immersed in*) enfoncé dans; **to be 10 feet ~,** avoir 10 pieds de profondeur; **ankle-~, knee-~,** *etc.* enfoncé jusqu'à la cheville, au genou, etc.; (*fig. absorbed in*) absorbé, plongé, perdu, dans; *adv.* & **~ly** *adv.* profondément; STILL **waters run ~**; **~-fry** *v.t.* cuire en friteuse; **~-laid,** ténébreux; **~-rooted, ~-seated,** profondément enraciné; **~ly read,** versé (dans); **~en** *v.t.* approfondir; (*colours*) foncer; *v.i.* devenir plus profond; (*grow darker*) s'assombrir; **~ness** *s.* profondeur *f.*

deer *s.* (*gen.*) bête fauve *f.*; (*red*) cerf *m.*; (*fallow* **~**) daim *m.*; MUSK **~**; **~skin** *s.* peau de daim *f.*; **~stalker** *s.* casquette de chasseur *f.*; **~-stalking** *s.* chasse au chevreuil *f.*

deface *v.t.* **1.** (*disfigure*) défigurer; **2.** (*make illegible*) effacer, oblitérer; **~ment** *s.* (1) défiguration *f.*; (2) oblitération *f.*

defalcat/e *v.i.* détourner (des fonds); **~ion** *s.* détournement (de fonds) *m.*, déficit *m.*; **~or** *s.* détourneur *m.*; ⚠ défalquer = **to deduct**; défalcation = **deduction.**

defam/e *v.t.* diffamer; **~ation** *s.* diffamation *f.*; **~atory** *adj.* diffamatoire.

default *s.* défaut *m.*; **in ~ of,** à défaut de; **by ~,** (*law*) par contumace; (*sport*) **to win by ~,**

gagner par forfait; *v.i.* faire défaut; **~er** *s.* défaillant *m.*, délinquant *m.*, retardaire *m.*

defeat *s.* **1.** (*in battle*) défaite *f.*; **2.** (*failure, frustration*) insuccès *m.*, échec *m.*; **3.** (*of government*) mise en minorité *f.*; **4.** (*law*) annulation *f.*; *v.t.* (1) vaincre; (2) frustrer, déjouer; (3) mettre en minorité; (4) annuler; **~ism** *s.* défaitisme *m.*; **~ist** *s.* défaitiste *m.*

defecat/e *v.t.* & *i.* (faire) déféquer; **~ion** *s.* défécation *f.*

defect *s.* (*material* & *moral*) défaut *m.*, manque *m.*; *v.i.* déserter; **~ion** *s.* défection *f.*; **~ive** *adj.* défectueux; MENTAL **~ive**; **~ively** *adv.**.

defence *s.* défense *f.*; **~less** *adj.* sans défense, désarmé.

defen/d *v.t.* (*ward off attack*; *law*) défendre; (*keep safe*) protéger; **~dable** *adj.* défendable; **~dant** *s.* (*law*) défend/eur, -eresse *m.f.*; **~der** *s.* défenseur *m.*; **~sible** *adj.* défendable, (*fig.*) soutenable; **~sive** *s.* défensive *f.*; *adj.* défensif.

defer *v.t.* **1.** (*put off*) différer, ajourner; *v.i.* **2.** (*submit to*) déférer à; ⚠ déférer = (2) *only*; **~ence** *s.* (2) déférence *f.*; **in ~ence to,** par déférence pour; **~ential** *adj.* (2) respectueux; **~entially** *adv.* (2)*; **~ment** *s.* (1) ajournement *m.*

defian/ce *s.* (*challenge*) défi *m.*; (*open disobedience*) révolte *f.*; **in ~ce of,** au mépris de; **~t** *adj.* rebelle; **~tly** *adv.* d'un air de défi; ⚠ défiance, défiant = **distrust, distrustful.**

deficien/cy *s.* (*lack*) manque *m.*; (*deficit*) insuffisance *f.*; **~cy disease,** maladie de carence *f.*; **~t** *adj.* (*lacking*) insuffisant; (*mentally*) faible d'esprit; **to be ~t in,** manquer de.

deficit *s.* déficit *m.*; **to have a ~,** être en déficit.

defile[1] *s.* défilé *m.*; *v.i.* (*march in file*) défiler.

defile[2] *v.t.* **1.** (*make dirty*) souiller; **2.** (*profane*) profaner; **~ment** *s.* (1) souillure *f.*; (2) profanation *f.*

defin/e *v.t.* **1.** (*mark out limits*) déterminer, délimiter; **2.** (*show clearly*) préciser, dessiner; **3.** (*explain meaning of*) définir; **~able** *adj.* définissable; **ill-~ed,** mal défini, flou; **well-~ed,** clair, précis; **~ition** *s.* (2) netteté *f.*, précision *f.*; (3) définition *f.*

definit/e *adj.* (*with exact limits*) déterminé; (*distinct, precise*) net, défini; (*certain*) définitif; **~e article** (*ling.*) article défini *m.*; **~ely** *adv.* (*clearly*) précisément; (*certainly*) définitivement; (*fam.* = *yes, indeed!*) bien entendu!; **~eness** *s.* netteté *f.*, précision *f.*; **~ive** *adj.* définitif; **~ively** *adv.**.

deflat/e *v.t.* **1.** (*let air out of tyre*) dégonfler (un pneu); **2.** (*reduce value of currency*) amener la déflation de la monnaie; **~ion** *s.* (1) dégonflement *m.*; (2) déflation *f.*

deflect *v.t.* détourner; *v.i.* **~** (*from*) dévier (de); **~ion** *s.* déviation *f.*; **wind ~or** *s.* volet déflecteur d'air *m.*

defloration *s.* défloration *f.*

deflower *v.t.* (*deprive of virginity*) (*fam.*) dépuceler; (*ravage*) déflorer, gâter.

defoliat/e *v.t.* défeuiller; **~ion** *s.* défeuillaison *f.*, défoliation *f.*

deforest *v.t.* déboiser, défricher; **~ation** *s.* déboisement *m.*, défrichement *m.*

deform *v.t.* (*spoil look of*) déformer; (*disfigure*) défigurer; **~ation** *s.* déformation *f.*; **~ed** *adj.* contrefait, difforme; **~ity** *s.* difformité *f.*

defraud *v.t.* (*law*) frauder (*of*—de); (*fig.*) voler; **~er** *s.* fraudeu/r, -se *m.f.*

defray *v.t.* payer, défrayer, rembourser.

defrock *v.t.* défroquer.

defrost *v.t.* (*auto, aviat., tech.*) dégivrer; (*cook.*) décongeler.

deft *adj.* adroit; **~ly** *adv.**; **~ness** *s.* adresse *f.*

defunct *adj.* (*person*) défunt; (*thing*) tombé en désuétude.

defuse *v.t.* désamorcer.

defy *v.t.* (*challenge*) défier (*to*—de); (*resist openly*) braver; **~ solution, etc.,** présenter de sérieuses difficultés.

degenera/te *adj.* & *s.m.f.* dégénéré(e); *v.i.* dégénérer; **~cy** *s.* & **~tion** *s.* dégénération *f.*

degrad/e *v.t.* **1.** (*reduce to lower rank*) dégrader, casser; **2.** (*debase*) avilir; **~ation** *s.* (1) dégradation *f.*; (2) avilissement *m.*; **~ed** *adj.* dégradé; **~ing** *adj.* (2) avilissant.

degree *s.* (*stage in scale*; *class, rank*; *unit of measurement*) degré *m.*; (*acad.*) grade universitaire *m.*; *see* B.A., B.SC., *etc.*; **to** GRANT **a ~**; **by ~s,** petit à petit; **in some ~,** dans une certaine mesure; **in a high ~,** dans une large mesure.

dehydrate *v.t.* & *i.* (se) déshydrater; **~d** *adj.* (*cook.*): (*veg.*) déshydraté; (*eggs, milk*) en poudre.

de-ice *v.t.* dégivrer; **~r** *s.* dégivreur *m.*

deif/y *v.t.* diviniser, déifier; **~ication** *s.* déification *f.*

deign *v.t.* daigner.

dei/ty *s.* (*fig.* & *eccles.*) divinité *f.*; (*myth.*) déité *f.*; **~sm** *s.* déisme *m.*; **~st** *s.* déiste *m.*

deject *v.t.* abattre; **~ed** *adj.* abattu; **~edly** *adv.* d'un air abattu; **~ion** *s.* abattement *m.*; ⚠ déjection = (*med.*) **evacuation.**

delay *s.* (*lack of haste, time overdue*) retard *m.*; (*period of time, time forecast*) délai *m.*; **without ~,** sans tarder; **without further ~,** sans plus tarder; **with the least possible ~,** dans le plus bref délai; *v.t.* (*person*) retenir, retarder; (*thing*) différer, remettre; *v.i.* tarder; **~ed-action,** à retardement; **~ing tactics,** tactique de retardement *f.*

delect/able *adj.* délectable; **~ation** *s.* délectation *f.*

delegat/e *s.* délégué(e) *m.f.*; *v.t.* déléguer; **~ion** *s.* délégation *f.*

delet/e *v.t.* biffer, rayer, supprimer; **~ion** *s.* rature *f.*, suppression *f.*

deleterious *adj.* délétère, nuisible.

delft *s.* faïence de Delft *f.*

deliberat/e *v.t.* & *i.* discuter, délibérer; *adj.* **1.** (*intentional*) délibéré; **2.** (*after consideration*) réfléchi; **~ely** *adv.* (1) exprès, à dessein; (2) sans hâte, posément; **~ion** *s.* (1) délibération *f.*; (2) circonspection *f.*

delica/te *adj.* (*dainty, fragile*) délicat; (*fastidious*) raffiné; (*slender*) fin; (*sensitive*) épineux; **~cy** *s.* (*feeling*) délicatesse *f.*, finesse *f.*; (*choice food*) friandise *f.*; **~tely** *adv.* délicatement, (*fig.*) avec délicatesse.

delicatessen *s.* (*shop* & *food*) charcuterie *f.*

delicious *adj.* délicieux; **~ly** *adv.**.

delight *s.* (*thing giving pleasure*) délices *f.pl.*; (*emotion*) joie *f.*; **to the ~ of,** à la grande joie de; **to take ~ in,** se délecter à, se complaire à faire qch.; TURK**ish ~**; *v.t.* (*please greatly*) enchanter, ravir; **be ~ed to,** être enchanté de, ravi de; *v.i.* (*take pleasure in*) se plaire à; **~ful** *adj.* délicieux, ravissant; **~fully** *adv.* délicieusement.

delimit *v.t.* délimiter; **~ation** *s.* délimitation *f.*

delineat/e *v.t.* tracer, esquisser, dessiner; **~ion** *s.* délinéation *f.*, dessin *m.*

delinquen/cy *s.* (*being ~t*) culpabilité *f.*, délinquence *f.*; (*neglect of duty*) faute *f.*, négligence *f.*; (*guilt*) délit *m.*; **~t** *adj.* & *s.m.f.* délinquant(e), coupable.

deliquesc/e *v.i.* tomber en déliquescence; **~ence** *s.* déliquescence *f.*; **~ent** *adj.* déliquescent.

deliri/um *s.* (*med.* & *fig.*) délire *m.*; **~um tremens** *s.* delirium tremens *m.*; **~ous** *adj.* délirant; **to be ~ous,** délirer; (*madly excited with joy, etc.*) être fou de joie, etc.

deliver *v.t.* **1.** (*liberate*) (dé)livrer, libérer (*from*—de); **2.** (*message*) remettre; **3.** (*letters*) distribuer;

4. (*goods*) livrer; **5.** (*ball*) lancer; **6.** (*blow*) asséner; **7.** (*speech*) prononcer; **8.** (*woman of child*) faire accoucher; **~ the goods** (*fig.*) remplir ses engagements; **be ~ed of,** accoucher de; **~ance** *s.* (1) délivrance *f.*, libération *f.*; **~er** *s.* (1) libérat/eur, -rice *m.f.*; **~y** *s.* (2) remise *f.*; (3) distribution *f.*; (4) livraison *f.*; (7) débit *m.*, élocution *f.*; (8) accouchement *m.*; **for immediate ~y,** à livrer tout de suite; CASH **on ~y; ~y van** *s.* camion de livraison *m.*

dell *s.* vallon *m.*

delphinium *s.* pied d'alouette *m.*; (*pl.* pieds d'alouette).

delta *s.* delta *m.*; **~ wing aircraft,** avion aux ailes en delta *m.*

delu/de *v.t.* (*deceive*) tromper; (*impose upon*) abuser; (*trick*) duper; **~de oneself,** se tromper; **~sion** *s.* illusion *f.*, hallucination *f.*; ⚠ délusion *is not a French word*; **to be under a ~sion,** se faire illusion, s'abuser; **~sive** *adj.* illusoire.

deluge *s.* déluge *m.*; *v.t.* (*lit.* & *fig.*) inonder (*with*—de).

delve *v.i.* (*dig, archeol.*) creuser, fouiller le sol; (*fig. research*) fouiller.

demagnetize *v.t.* démagnétiser, désaimanter.

demagog/ue *s.* démagogue *m.*; **~ic** *adj.* démagogique; **~ism** *s.* démagogisme *m.*; **~y** *s.* démagogie *f.*

demand *s.* (*request*) demande *f.*; (*peremptory, one's rights, etc.*) revendication *f.*; (*excessive*) exigence *f.*; (*comm. call for commodity*) demande *f.*; **in ~,** recherché; **on ~,** sur simple demande; **to make ~s on s.o.,** se montrer exigeant avec qn.; **work which makes ~s on one's time,** travail qui exige beaucoup de temps; ⚠ demande *usu.* = **request** & *is weaker than Eng. demand*; *v.t.* (*request*) demander; **~ sth. from** *or* **of s.o.,** demander qch. à qn.; **~ that s.o. does sth.,** demander à qn. de faire qch.; (*as of right*) exiger, réclamer; ⚠ demander *usu.* = **to ask (for)**.

demarcat/e *v.t.* délimiter; **~ion** *s.* délimitation *f.*, démarcation *f.*; **~ion dispute,** querelle de compétence *f.*

demean *v.t.* (*lower dignity of*) abaisser; **~ oneself,** se comporter; (*lower oneself to*) s'abaisser jusqu'à; **~our** *s.* conduite *f.*

dement/ed *adj.* fou *m.*, folle *f.*; **~ia** *s.* démence *f.*

demerara *see* SUGAR.

demigod *s.* demi-dieu *m.*

demijohn *s.* dame-jeanne *f.* (*pl.* dames-jeannes); (*fam.*) bonbonne *or* bombonne *f.*

demilitarize *v.t.* démilitariser.

demise *s.* **1.** (*death*) décès *m.*; **2.** (*fin.*) transfert *m.*; *v.t.* (2) transférer.

demist *v.t.* (*auto., aviat.*) enlever la buée (du pare-brise etc.); **~er** *s.* dispositif antibuée *m.*

demobiliz/e *v.t.* démobiliser; **~ation** *s.* démobilisation *f.*

democra/t *s.* démocrate *m.f.*; **~cy** *s.* démocratie *f.*; **~tic** *adj.* démocratique; **~tically** *adv.**.

demograph/y *s.* démographie *f.*; **~er** *s.* démographe *m.f.*; **~ic** *adj.* démographique.

demoli/sh *v.t.* (*destroy*) démolir; (*fam.* = *eat up*) dévorer; **~tion** *s.* démolition *f.*

demon *s.* démon *m.*; **~ic** *adj.* diabolique; **~iac** *adj.* démoniaque; **~ology** *s.* démonologie *f.*

demonstra/te *v.t.* & *i.* **1.** (*give or be proof of; establish truth of*) démontrer; **2.** (*take part in public ~tion*) manifester; **3.** (*comm. show off goods*) faire la démonstration de; **4.** (*show feelings, qualities*) témoigner, faire preuve de; **~ble** *adj.* démontrable; **~tion** *s.* (1) & (3) démonstration *f.*; (2) manifestation *f.*; (4) témoignage *m.*; **~tive** *adj.* (1) démonstratif; (4) expansif; (*ling.*) *adj.* & *s.m.* démonstratif; **~tor** *s.* (1) (*in laboratory*) démonstrateur *m.*, préparateur *m.*; (2) manifestant(e) *m.f.*

demorali/ze *v.t.* (*morals*) corrompre; (*morale*) démoraliser; **~zation** *s.* démoralisation *f.*

demot/e *v.t.* rétrograder; **~ion** *s.* rétrogradation *f.*

demur *v.i.* hésiter; **~ at,** faire des objections à; **without ~,** sans hésitation.

demure *adj.* grave, composé; (*iron.*) faussement modeste; **~ly** *adv.* modestement; **~ness** *s.* modestie *f.*

demurrage *s.* (*naut.*) indemnité de surestarie *f.*; (*rail.*) droits de magasinage *m.pl.*

den *s.* (*of wild beasts*) antre *m.*; (*of robbers*) repaire *m.*; (*private room*) cabinet de travail *m.*

denationalize *v.t.* dénationaliser.

denial *see* DENY.

denigrat/e *v.t.* dénigrer; **~ion** *s.* dénigrement *m.*

denim *s.* (*cloth*) treillis *m.*; (*clothing*) pantalon de treillis *m.*

Denmark *s.* Danemark *m.*

denominat/e *v.t.* (*name*) appeler; (*designate*) dénommer; **~ion** *s.* (*title*) dénomination *f.*; (*religion*) secte *f.*; (*money*) coupure *f.*; **~or** *s.* dénominateur *m.*

denote *v.t.* (*indicate*) dénoter; (*signify*) signifier.

denounce *v.t.* (*inveigh against*) dénoncer, attaquer; (*end treaty*) dénoncer.

dens/e *adj.* **1.** (*compact*) dense, épais; **2.** (*crowded together*) serré; **3.** (*stupid*) bête; ⚠ dense ≠ (3); **~ity** *s.* (1) densité *f.*; (2) épaisseur *f.*; (3) bêtise *f.*; **~ely** *adv.* **~ely packed,** très serré; **~ely populated,** très peuplé.

dent *s.* enfoncement *m.*; *v.t.* cabosser.

dental *s.* (*ling.*) dentale *f.*; *adj.* (*of a tooth*) dentaire; (*of sound*) dental.

dentist *s.* dentiste *m.*; **~ry** *s.* art dentaire *m.*

dentition *s.* dentition *f.*

denture *s.* dentier *m.*; (*fam.*) râtelier *m.*

denude *v.t.* (*make bare*) dénuder; (*deprive* (*of*)) dépouiller (de).

denunciat/ion *s.* dénonciation *f.*; (*invective*) attaque *m.*; **~or** *s.* dénonciat/eur, -rice *m.f.*

den/y *v.t.* **1.** (*declare untrue*) nier; **2.** (*refute*) démentir; **3.** (*disavow*) désavouer; **4.** (*refuse*) refuser; **~y oneself,** se priver (de); **~iable** *adj.* niable; **~ial** *s.* (1) dénégation *f.*; (2) démenti *m.*; (3) désaveu *m.*; (4) refus *m.*; **self ~ial,** abnégation *f.*

deodor/ant *s.* déodorant *m.*; *adj.* désodorisant; **~ize** *v.t.* désodoriser.

depart *v.i.* partir; (*diverge from*) se départir de; **~ed** *adj.* & *s.m.f.*; mort(e); **~ure** *s.* départ *m.*

department *s.* (*admin. division*) département *m.*; (*in shop*) rayon *m.*; (*in office*) bureau *m.*, service *m.*; **~ store** *s.* bazar *m.*, grand magasin *m.*; **~al** *adj.* départemental.

depend *v.i.* **1.** (*be contingent on*) dépendre de; **2.** (*rely on*) compter sur, se fier à; **3.** (*be dependent on*) être à la charge de; **it (all) ~s,** ça dépend; **~able** *adj.* (2) sûr; **~ant** *s.* (3) dépendant *m.*; **~ence** *s.* (1) dépendance *f.*; (2) confiance *f.*; **~ency** *s.* dépendance *f.*; **~ent** *adj.* (1) dépendant (de); (*contingent*) connexe; (*subordinate*) subordonné; (3) à la charge de.

depict *v.t.* peindre; (*fig.*) dépeindre.

depilat/e *v.t.* dépiler; **~ory** *adj.* & *s.m.* dépilatoire.

deplet/e *v.t.* (*exhaust*) épuiser; (*empty*) vider; (*diminish*) dégarnir; **~ion** *s.* épuisement *m.*

deplor/e *v.t.* **1.** (*grieve over*) pleurer sur; **2.** (*regret*) déplorer; **3.** (*deprecate*) désapprouver; **~able** *adj.* (1) pitoyable; (2) lamentable; (3) regrettable; **~ably** *adv.**;*;*.

deploy *v.t.* & *i.* (*mil., naut.*) (se) déployer; **~ment** *s.* déploiement *m.*

depopulat/e *v.t.* dépeupler; **~ion** *s.* dépopulation *f.*

deport *v.t.* **1.** (*expel from country*): (*convict*) déporter; (*alien*) expulser; **2.** *v.refl.* (*behave*) se comporter; **~ation** *s.* (1) déportation *f.*, expulsion *f.*; **~ee** *s. m.f.* (1) déporté(e), expulsé(e); **~ment** *s.* (2) maintien *m.*; (*fig.*) comportement *m.*

depos/e *v.t.* **1.** (*dethrone*) détrôner; **2.** *v.i.* (*testify*) déposer; **~ition** *s.* (1), (2) déposition.

deposit *s.* **1.** (*in bank*) dépôt *m.*; **2.** (*earnest money*) arrhes *f.pl.*; **3.** (*accumulated matter*) dépôt *m.*; **~ account,** compte de dépôts *m.*; *v.t.* (1) mettre en dépôt; (2) laisser comme arrhes; (3) déposer; **~ary** *s.* dépositaire *m.*, consignataire *m.*; **~or** *s.* déposant *m.*; **~ory** *s.* dépôt *m.*, entrepôt *m.*

depot *s.* dépôt *m.*

deprav/e *v.t.* dépraver; **~ed** *adj.* & *s.m.f.* (*habits, person*) dépravé(e); **~ity** *s.* dépravation *f.*

deprecat/e *v.t.* désapprouver; **~ory** *adj.* désapprobateur.

depreciat/e *v.t.* **1.** (*disparage*) dénigrer; **2.** (*lower in value*) dévaloriser; *v.i.* se déprécier; **~ion** *s.* (1) dénigrement *m.*; (2) dépréciation *f.*, dévalorisation *f.*

depredation *s.* déprédation *f.*

depress *v.t.* **1.** (*lower or reduce*) abaisser; (*pedal, button, etc.*) appuyer sur; **2.** (*comm.*) faire baisser (les prix); **3.** (*dispirit*) abattre, décourager, déprimer; **~ed** *adj.* (1) & (2) en baisse; (3) abattu, découragé, déprimé. **~ion** *s.* (1) (*hollow* & *barometric pressure*) dépression *f.*; (2) (*comm.*) baisse *f.*, crise économique *f.*; (3) découragement *m.*, dépression *f.*

depriv/e *v.t.* priver (*of*—de); **~ation** *s.* privation *f.*

depth *s.* profondeur *f.*; (*intensity*) intensité *f.*, gravité *f.*; (*middle of*) cœur *m.*; **in the ~ of winter, etc.,** au plus profond de l'hiver etc.; **to get out of one's ~,** perdre pied; **in ~** *adv.* profondément; **~s** *s.pl.* (= *sea*) profondeurs *f.pl.*; **in the ~s of despair, etc.,** au comble du désespoir, etc.; **~-charge** *s.* grenade sous-marine *f.*

deput/e *v.t.* déléguer; **~ation** *s.* délégation *f.*; **~ize (for)** *v.i.* assurer l'intérim (à la place de); **~y** *s.* (*polit.* = *M.P.*) député *m.*; (*delegate*) délégué *m.*; **~y** *adj.* (= *vice* (*chairman*)) vice-président *m.*; (*governor, manager, etc.*) directeur-adjoint *m.*

derail *v.t.* & *i.* (faire) dérailler; **~ment** *s.* déraillement *m.*

derange *v.t.* **1.** (*disorganise*) déranger; **2.** (*make insane*) détraquer; **~d** *adj.* (1) dérangé; (2) détraqué; **~d person** *s.m.f.* aliéné(e); **~ment** *s.* (1) dérangement *m.*; (2) aliénation (mentale) *f.*

derelict *adj.* **1.** (*ownerless, esp. ship*) abandonné; **2.** (*abandoned by society*) délaissé; *s.* (1) épave *f.*; (2) épave humaine *f.*; **~ion** *s.* abandon *m.*; (*of duty*) negligence *f.*

deri/de *v.t.* tourner en dérision; ⚠ dérider = *to* **smooth; ~sion** *s.* dérision *f.*; **~sive** *adj.* moqueur; **~sively** *adv.* d'un ton moqueur; **~sory** *adj.* dérisoire.

deriv/e *v.t.* (*obtain from*) retirer de; *v.i.* (*have origin from*) provenir, découler de; (*ling.*) dériver de; **~ation** *s.* dérivation *f.*; **~ative** *adj.* & *s.m.* dérivé.

dermat/itis *s.* dermatite *f.*, dermite *f.*; **~ology** *s.* dermatologie *f.*

derogat/e *v.i.* **1.** (*detract from*) porter atteinte à; **2.** (*do sth. unworthy*) déroger (à); **~ion** *s.* dérogation *f.*; **~ory** *adj.* (1) de dénigrement; (2) indigne.

derrick *s.* (*on ship*) mât de charge *m.*; (*of oil-well*) tour de forage *f.*

derv *s.* (*Diesel-engined road vehicle*) carburant diesel *m.*

dervish *s.* derviche *m.*

descant *s.* déchant *m.*; *v.i.* accompagner en déchant; (*talk at large*) disserter.

descend *v.t.* & *i.* descendre; (*be derived from*) descendre de, être issu de; (*fig. stoop to*) s'abaisser à; **~ upon,** tomber sur; **~ance** *s.* descendance *f.*; **~ant** *s.* descendant *m.*

descent *s.* (*going down, way down, slope*) descente *f.*; (*lineage*) descendance *f.*; (*attack*) descente *f.*

descri/be *v.t.* décrire; (*mark out, as in geom.*) tracer; **~ption** *s.* description *f.*; (*police*) signalement *m.*; (*sort, kind*) sorte *f.*; **~ptive** *adj.* descriptif; **~ptively** *adv.**.

descry *v.t.* discerner.

desecrat/e *v.t.* profaner; **~ion** *s.* profanation *f.*

desert[1] *s.* (*usu. pl.* = *merits*) mérite *m.*; **one's ~s,** ce qu'on mérite.

desert[2] *s.* (*uninhabited region*) désert *m.*; *adj.* (*uninhabited*) désert; (*belonging to ~*) désertique; *v.t.* (*abandon*) abandonner; *v.i.* (*run away*) déserter; **~er** *s.* déserteur *m.*; **~ion** *s.* abandon *m.*, désertion *f.*

deserv/e *v.t.* mériter; **~edly** *adv.* à juste titre; **~ing** *adj.* (*person*) méritant; (*action*) méritoire.

desiccate *v.t.* & *i.* (se) dessécher.

design *s.* **1.** (*plan*) projet *m.*, dessein *m.*; **2.** (*sketch*) dessin *m.*, esquisse *f.*; **3.** (*construction*) plan *m.*; **4.** (*pattern*) motif *m.*; **5.** (*comm.*) modèle *m.*; **to have ~s on s.o., sth.** jeter son dévolu sur qn., qch.; **by ~,** exprès; *v.t.* & *i.* (1) projeter, avoir l'intention de; (2) dessiner, esquisser; **~ed for,** destiné à; **~edly** *adv.* à dessein; **~er** *s.* dessinateur *m.*; **~ing** *adj* intrigant, comploteur.

designat/e *adj.* désigné (*after the noun*); *v.t.* **1.** (*describe as, specify*) désigner; **2.** (*appoint to office*) nommer; **~ion** *s.* (1) désignation *f.*; (2) (*appointment*) nomination *f.*

desir/e *s.* désir *m.*; (*expressed wish*) souhait *m.*; *v.t.* désirer, souhaiter; (*request*) demander; **~able** *adj.* désirable, souhaitable; **~ability** *s.* caractère désirable *m.*; (*comm.*) désidérabilité *f.*; **~ous** *adj.* désireux (*of*—de).

desist *v.i.* cesser (*from*—de); ⚠ se désister de = **to renounce.**

desk *s.* (*furniture*) pupitre *m.*, bureau *m.*; (*subdivision of office*) bureau *m.*, service *m.*

desolat/e *adj.* **1.** (*abandoned*) solitaire, abandonné; **2.** (*uninhabited*) désert; **3.** (*sad*) désolé; **4.** (*laid waste*) ravagé; *v.t.* (2) (*depopulate*) dépeupler; (3) désoler; (4) ravager; **~ion** *s.* (1) abandon *m.*; (3) désolation *f.*; (4) dévastation *f.*

despair *s.* désespoir *m.*; **drive to ~,** pousser au désespoir; *v.i.* désespérer (*of*—de); **~ing(ly)** *adj.* & *adv.* sans espoir.

despatch *see* DISPATCH.

desperado *s.* risque-tout *m.*, aventurier *m.*

desperat/e *adj.* (*hopelessly bad*) désespéré; (*dangerous*) dangereux; (*reckless*) capable de tout; **~ion** *s.* désespérance *f.*

despicab/le *adj.* méprisable; **~ly** *adv.* d'une façon méprisable.

despise *v.t.* (*regard with contempt*) dédaigner; (*look down on*) mépriser.

despite *s.* dépit *m.*; **in ~ of,** en dépit de, malgré.

despoil *v.t.* dépouiller; **~er** *s.* spoliateur *m.*

despond *v.i.* (*lose hope*) désespérer; (*be dejected*) se décourager; **~ency** *s.* désespoir *m.*; découragement *m.*; **~ent** *adj.* découragé; **~ently** *adv.* avec découragement.

despot *s.* despote *m.*; **~ic** *adj.* despotique; **~ically** *adv.**; **~ism** *s.* despotisme *m.*

dessert *s.* dessert *m.*; ⚠ desserte = **serving-table; ~**-SPOON.

destin/e *v.t.* destiner (*to, for*—à); **~ed for** (*ship, plane, etc.*) à destination de; **~ation** *s.* destination *f.*; **~y** *s.* (*future*) destin *m.*; (*power that fore-ordains*) destin *m.*, (*liter.*) destinée *f.*

destitut/e *adj.* **1.** (*in want*) indigent; **2.** (*resource-less*) dénué, dépourvu (de); **~ion** *s.* (1) indigence *f.*; (2) dénuement *m.*; ⚠ destitution = **dismissal.**
destroy *v.t.* détruire; (*an animal*) abattre; (*refl. oneself*) se suicider; **~er** *s.* (*person*) destructeur *m.*; (*ship*) contre-torpilleur *m.*
destruct/ion *s.* destruction *f.*; (*damage*) ravages *f.pl.*; (*ruin*) perte *f.*, ruine *f.*; **~ible** *adj.* destructible; **~ive** *adj.* destructif.
desultor/y *adj.* décousu, sans méthode; **~ily** *adv.* sans suite, à bâtons rompus; **~iness** *s.* manque de suite *m.*, manque de méthode *m.*
detach *v.t.* détacher (*from*—de); **~able** *adj.* détachable; **~ed house,** maison individuelle *f.*; **semi-~ed house,** maison individuelle jumelée *f.*; **~ment** *s.* détachement *m.*
detail *s.* **1.** (*item*) détail *m.*; **2.** (*small party*) détachment *m.*; **in ~,** en détail; **go into ~s,** donner des précisions; *v.t.* (1) (*give ~s of*) détailler; (2) (*tell off for special duty*) détacher; **~ed** *adj.* (1) détaillé; (2) détaché.
detain *v.t.* (*keep person in custody*) détenir; (*withhold*) retenir, garder; (*keep waiting*) retenir; **~ee** *s.m.f.* détenu(e).
detect *v.t.* découvrir, dépister; **~ion** *s.* découverte *f.*, dépistage *m.*, détection *f.*; **~ive** *s.* (*private*) détective *m.*; (*police*) agent de la Sûreté *m.*; *adj.* détecteur; **~ive novel,** roman policier *m.*; **~or** *s.* détecteur *m.*
detention *s.* détention *f.*; (*school*) consigne *f.*, (*fam.*) colle *f.*
deter *v.t.* détourner, empêcher (*from*—de); **~rent** *s.* force de dissuasion *f.*; (*weapon*) arme de dissuasion *f.*
detergent *adj.* & *s.m.* détersif, détergent.
deteriorat/e *v.i.* **1.** (*health etc.*) dégénérer; **2.** (*things*) se détériorer; **3.** (*situation*) empirer; **~ion** *s.* (1) dégénérescence *f.*; (2) détérioration *f.*; (3) aggravation *f.*
determin/e *v.t.* (*end*) régler, résoudre; (*fix precisely*) déterminer; *v.i.* (*decide*) décider (*to*—de); **~ant** *adj.* & *s.m.* déterminant; **~ation** *s.* (*decision*) détermination *f.*; (*resolution*) résolution *f.*; **~ed** *adj.* déterminé, résolu.
detest *v.t.* détester; **~able** *adj.* détestable; **~ably** *adv.**; **~ation** *s.* détestation *f.*
detonat/e *v.t.* & *i.* (faire) détoner, éclater; **~ion** *s.* détonation *f.*; **~or** *s.* détonateur *m.*
detour *s.* détour *m.*
detract (*from*) *v.t.* (*value*) amoindrir; (*merit*) dénigrer; **~ion** *s.* amoindrissement *m.*; dénigrement *m.*; **~or** *s.* détracteur *m.*
detriment *s.* détriment *m.*; **to the ~ of,** au détriment de, au préjudice de; **without ~,** sans préjudice (*to s.o.*—pour qn., *to sth.*—de qch.); **~al** *adj.* préjudiciable; **~ally** *adv.* d'une manière préjudiciable.
deuce *s.* (*devil*) diable *m.*; (*at dice/cards*) deux; (*at tennis*) quarante A; *interj.* diantre!; **~d** *adj.* sacré (*before noun*); *adv.* diablement.
devalu/e, devalu/ate *v.t.* dévaluer; **~ation** *s.* dévaluation *f.*
devastat/e *v.t.* dévaster; **~ing** *adj.* dévastateur; **~ingly** *adv.* d'une manière dévastatrice; **~ion** *s.* dévastation *f.*
develop *v.t.* & *i.* **1.** (*unfold; photo.*) développer; **2.** (*become or make bigger*) (s')amplifier; **3.** (*come or bring to maturity*) (se) développer; **4.** (*make usable or profitable*) exploiter; **~er** *s.* (*photo.*) révélateur *m.*; **~ing** *adj.* **~ing countries,** pays en voie de développement *m.pl.*; **~ment** *s.* (1), (3) développement *m.*; (2) amplification *f.*; (4) exploitation *f.*; RIBBON **~ment.**
deviant *s.* espèce aberrante *f.*
deviat/e *v.i.* (*turn aside*) dévier; (*digress*) s'écarter; (*from*—de); **~ion** *s.* déviation *f.*; écart *m.*
device *s.* (*plan, trick*) expédient *m.*, (*fam.*) truc *m.*, (*pop.*) combine *f.*; (*design, invention*) invention *f.*, appareil *m.*, dispositif *m.*; (*motto*) devise *f.*; (*method*) procédé *m.*; **to leave s.o. to his own ~s,** laisser qn. agir à sa guise.
devil *s.* diable *m.*, diablesse *f.*; (*wretched person*) pauvre diable *m.*; (*lawyer's, author's*) nègre *m.*; **between the ~ and the deep blue sea,** entre l'enclume et le marteau; **talk of the ~,** quand on parle du loup, on en voit la queue; **the ~ of a noise,** un bruit de tous les diables; **there'll be the ~ to pay,** il faudra payer la casse; **what the ~ are you doing?,** que diable faites-vous?; **how the ~ did you do it?,** comment diable l'avez-vous fait? **~-may-care** *adj.* je m'en-fichiste; **~ish** *adj.* diabolique; **~ishly** *adv.* diablement; **~ment** *s.* diablerie *f.*; **to be full of ~ment,** avoir le diable au corps; **~ry** *s.* magie noire *f.*, diablerie *f.*; *v.t.* (*cook.*) griller au poivre.
devious *adj.* tortueux, détourné; **~ly** *adv.* d'une manière tortueuse.
devise *v.t.* (*think out*) concevoir, projeter; (*contrive*) combiner; (*law*) léguer par testament.
devoid *adj.* dépourvu (*of*—de).
devolution *s.* dévolution *f.*
devolve (*on*) *v.t.* & *i.* incomber à; **it ~s on you to,** c'est à vous qu'il incombe de.
devot/e *v.t.* **1.** (*dedicate*) vouer; **2.** (*give up, time etc., exclusively to*) consacrer (à); **~e oneself to,** se consacrer à; **~ed** *adj.* (1) voué; (2) (*time*) consacré; (*person*) dévoué, fidèle; **~edly** *adv.* avec dévouement; **~ee** *s.* (*relig. fanatic*) dévot(e) *m.f.*; (*enthusiast*) fervent *m.*; **~ion** *s.* (*relig.*) dévotion *f.*; (*self-surrender*) dévouement *m.*; **~s** *pl.* (*relig. exercises*) dévotions *f.pl.*
devour *v.t.* (*eat up, eat greedily, consume, destroy,* & *fig.*) dévorer; **~ing** *adj.* dévorant, avide.
devout *adj.* **1.** (*pious*) dévot; **2.** (*sincere, hearty*) fervent; **~ly** *adv.* (1) avec dévotion; (2) avec ferveur.
dew *s.* rosée *f.*; **~-drop,** goutte de rosée *f.*; **~y** *adj.* humide de rosée.
dewlap *s.* (*cow*) fanon *m.*; (*fam. of person*) double menton *m.*
dext/erity *s.* dextérité *f.*; **~(e)rous** *adj.* (*neat-handed*) adroit; (*clever*) habile; **~(e)rously** *adv.**;*.
diabet/es *s.* diabète *m.*; **~ic** *adj.* & *s.m.f.* diabétique.
diabolic(al) *adj.* (*lit.* & *fig.*) diabolique; **~ally** *adv.**.
diadem *s.* diadème *m.*
diaeresis *s.* tréma *m.*
diagnos/e *v.t.* diagnostiquer; **~is** *s.* diagnostic *m.*; **~tic** *adj.* diagnostique; **~tician** *s.* diagnostiqueur *m.*
diagonal *s.* diagonale *f.*; *adj.* diagonal; **~ly** *adv.* en diagonale.
diagram *s.* schéma *m.*; **~atic** *adj.* schématique.
dial *s.* (*sundial, clock face, of telephone etc.*) cadran *m.*; (*fam.* = *face*) gueule *f.*; *v.t.* (*telephone*) composer un numéro au téléphone.
dialect *s.* dialecte *m.*; **~ic(s)** dialectique *f.*; ⚠ *singular in French.*
dialogue *s.* dialogue *m.*
diamet/er *s.* diamètre *m.*; **~rical** *adj.* diamétral; **~rically** *adv.**; **~rically opposed to,** diamétralement opposé à.
diamond *s.* (*precious stone*) diamant *m.*; (*cards*) carreau *m.*; (*shape*) losange *m.*; (*for cutting*) diamant de vitrier *m.*; **rough ~** (*fig.*) cœur d'or sous des dehors frustes *m.*; **~-cutter** *or* **-seller** *s.* diamantaire *m.*; **~ panes,** carreaux en losange *m.pl.*
diaphanous *adj.* diaphane.
diaphragm *s.* diaphragme *m.*
diarrhoea *s.* diarrhée *f.*

diary *s.* (*record of events*) journal *m.*; (*book for same*) agenda *m.*
diatonic *adj.* (*mus.*) diatonique.
diatribe *s.* diatribe *f.*
dibber (dibble) *s.* plantoir *m.*; *v.t.* planter au plantoir.
dice *s. see* DIE; *v.i.* (*game*) jouer aux dés; *v.t.* (*cook.*) couper en petits cubes.
dichotomy *s.* dichotomie *f.*
dicky *s.* (*bird*) oisillon *m.*; (*false shirt front*) plastron *m.*; *adj.* (*fam.* = *shaky*) faible; (*person*) patraque; (*thing*) branlant.
dictaphone *s.* dictaphone *m.*
dictat/e *s.* (*usu. pl.*) précepte *m.*, ordre *m.*; *v.t.* & *i.* **1.** (*say aloud matter to be written*) dicter; **2.** (*give orders*) donner des ordres; **3.** (*lay down authoritatively*) dicter, stipuler; **~ion** *s.* (1) dictée *f.*; (2) ordre *m.*; (3) stipulation *f.*; **~or** *s.* dictateur *m.*; **~orial** *adj.* dictatorial; **~orially** *adv.**; **~orship** *s.* dictature *f.*
diction *s.* diction *f.*
dictionary *s.* dictionnaire *m.*
dictum *s.* dicton *m.*
didactic *adj.* didactique; **~ally** *adv.**.
diddle *v.t.* (*fam.*) carotter; **to be ~d,** être chocolat; **I have been ~d,** on m'a eu.
die[1] *s.* (*pl.* DICE) dé *m.*; (*pl.* DIES) (*engraved stamp*) coin *m.*; **the ~ is cast,** les dés sont jetés.
die[2] *v.i.* (*cease to exist*) mourir; (*fade*) s'éteindre, dépérir; (*fig.*) mourir, s'éteindre; **~ away, ~ out,** s'éteindre; **~ down,** tomber, s'apaiser; **~ with** *or* **of,** mourir de; **be dying to,** mourir d'envie de; **~-hard** *s.* jusqu'au boutiste *m.*
diesel *s.* diesel *m.*; **~ engine,** moteur diesel *m.*
diet *s.* **1.** (*foreign parl.*) diète *f.*; **2.** (*way of feeding*) alimentation *f.*; **3.** (*prescribed course of food*) régime *m.*; ⚠ diète = **poor ~**; *v.t.* & *i.* (3) (se) mettre au régime, être au régime; **~ary** *adj.* (2) alimentaire; **~etics** *s.* diététique *f.* ⚠ *sing. in French*; **~ician** *s.* diététicien *m.*
differ *v.i.* **1.** (*be unlike*) différer (*from*—de); **2.** (*diverge in opinion*) être en désaccord; ne pas s'entendre; **they ~ as to which road to take,** ils ne s'entendent pas sur la route à suivre; **~ence** *s.* (1) différence *f.*; (2) différend *m.*; **to** SPLIT **the ~ence; ~ent** *adj.* (1) différent; (*various*) plusieurs, **there are ~ent ways of doing it,** il y a plusieurs façons de le faire; **~ential** *adj.* & *s.m.* (*maths.*, *med.*, *techn.*, *fin.*) différentiel; **~entiate** *v.t.* & *i.* (se) différencier.
difficult *adj.* (*hard to understand or deal with*) difficile; (*troublesome*) difficile, peu commode; **~y** *s.* difficulté *f.*; **to be in ~ies,** être dans l'embarras; **to make ~ies,** faire le difficile; **with ~y,** difficilement.
diffiden/ce *s.* manque de confiance (en soi) *m.*; **~t** *adj.* qui manque de confiance, timide, hésitant.
diffus/e *v.t.* & *i.* (se) diffuser; *adj.* diffus; **~ion** *s.* diffusion *f.*
dig *s.* **1.** (*turning up soil*) bêchage *m.*; **2.** (*fam. archeol.*) fouilles *f.pl.*; **3.** (*poke*) bourrade *f.*; **4.** (*gibe*) coup de patte *m.*; **5.** (*pl.* = *lodgings*) meublé *m.*; **to have a ~ at s.o.,** lancer une pierre dans le jardin de qn.; *v.t.* & *i.* (1) bêcher, piocher; (2) creuser; (3) (*s.o. in ribs*) bourrer les côtes à qn.; **6.** (*fam.* = *like*) piger, **I don't ~ that music,** je ne pige rien à cette musique; **~ down,** approfondir; **~ for,** faire des fouilles (pour trouver); **~ into,** enfoncer dans; **~ oneself in** (*fig.*) s'accrocher; **~ out,** déterrer; **~up,** exhumer; **~ger** *s.* (1) bêcheur *m.*, (*tool*) plantoir *m.*; (2) chercheur *m.*; (*navvy*) terrassier *m.*; GOLD-**~ger;** GRAVE-**~ger; ~ging** *s.* (2) fouilles *f.pl.*; **~gings** *s.* (*fam.* = *lodgings*) meublé *m.*

digest *s.* résumé *m.*, condensé *m.*; *v.t.* (*summarize*) résumer; (*arrange*) classer; (*food, etc.*) digérer; (*assimilate*) assimiler; **~ible** *adj.* digestible; **~ion** *s.* digestion *f.*; **~ive** *adj.* digestif.
digit *s.* (*numeral*) chiffre *m.*; (*finger or toe*) doigt *m.*; **~al** *adj.* digital; (*clock, computer, etc.*) (à affichage) numérique.
digitalis *s.* digitale *f.*
dignif/y *v.t.* donner de la dignité à; (*iron.*) décorer de; **~ied** *adj.* digne.
dignit/y *s.* dignité *f.*; **beneath one's ~y,** indigne de soi; **to stand on one's ~y,** rester sur son quant-à-soi; **~ary** *s.* dignitaire *m.*
digress *v.i.* dévier, s'écarter (*from*—de), faire une digression; **~ion** *s.* digression *f.*
dike, dyke *s.* (*ditch*) fossé *m.*; (*dam*) digue *f.*; (*causeway*) chaussée *f.*; *v.t.* endiguer.
dilapidat/e *v.t.* & *i.* (se) délabrer; (*squander*) dilapider; **~ed** *adj.* délabré; **~ion** *s.* (*~ed state*) délabrement *m.*; **~ions** *s.pl.* dégâts *m.pl.*
dilat/e *v.t.* & *i.* (*widen or expand*) (se) dilater; (*enlarge upon*) s'étendre sur; **~ation** *s.* dilatation *f.*
dilator/y *adj.* lent; **~iness** *s.* lenteur *f.*
dilemma *s.* dilemme *m.*
dilettante *s.* dilettante *m.*, amateur *m.*
diligen/ce *s.* diligence *f.*; **~t** *adj.* diligent; **~tly** *adv.* diligemment.
dilly-dally *v.i.* (*fam.*) (*walk*) baguenauder; (*act*) lambiner, lanterner.
dilut/e *v.t.* (*reduce in strength*) diluer; (*thin down*) délayer; *adj.* (*acid, etc.*) dilué; (*colour*) délavé; (*fig.*) atténué; **~ion** *s.* dilution *f.*
diluvial *adj.* diluvien.
dim *adj.* **1.** (*lacking brightness or clearness*) terne, faible; **2.** (*obscure*) obscur; **3.** (*indistinct*) indistinct, confus; **4.** (*fam.* = *stupid*, *~-witted*) bête; **~-wit** *s.* bêta, bêtasse *m.f.*; **to take a ~ view of sth.,** envisager qch. sans enthousiasme; *v.t.* & *i.* (1) (se) ternir; (2) (s')obscurcir; **~ly** *adv.* (1) faiblement; (2) obscurément; (3) indistinctement, confusément; (4)*; **~ness** *s.* (1) faiblesse *f.*; (2) obscurité *f.*; (3) imprécision *f.*; (4) bêtise *f.*
dime *s.* (*U.S.A. coin*) dime *f.*; (*fig.*) sou *m.*
dimension *s.* dimension *f.*
dimin/ish *v.t.* & *i.* (*make or become less*) diminuer; (*impair*) réduire; **~ution** *s.* diminution *f.*; **~utive** *adj.* (*ling.*) diminutif; (*tiny*) minuscule.
dimple *s.* fossette *f.*; *v.t.* creuser des fossettes dans; *v.i.* se creuser de fossettes.
din *s.* fracas *m.*, vacarme *m.*, tapage *m.*; *v.t.* **~ sth. into s.o.'s ears,** corner qch. aux oreilles de qn.
dine *v.i.* dîner; **~ off** *or* **on,** faire son repas de; **~ out,** dîner en ville; **dining-car,** wagon-restaurant *m.*; **dining-room, dining-hall,** salle à manger *f.*; **~r** *s.* dîneur *m.*
ding-dong *s.* (*sound of bells*) tintement *m.*; *adj.* (*desperate, neck and neck*) acharné; **~ battle,** partie durement disputée.
dinghy *s.* you-you *m.*
ding/y *adj.* **1.** (*dull-coloured*) fade; **2.** (*dirty*) sale, mal tenu; **~iness** *s.* (1) fadeur *f.*; (2) saleté *f.*
dinky *adj.* (*fam.*) coquet.
dinner *s.* dîner *m.*; **~-jacket,** smoking *m.*; **~-party** *s.* dîner *m.*
dinosaur *s.* dinosaure *m.*
dint *s.* marque (*m.*) d'un coup *or* d'un choc; *v.t.* cabosser; **by ~ of,** à force de.
dioces/e *s.* diocèse *m.*; **~an** *adj.* diocésain.
dip *s.* (*act*) plongée *f.*; (*downward slope*) pente *f.*, inclinaison *f.*; (*short bathe*) baignade *f.*; (*tallow candle*) chandelle *f.*; (*sheep-~*) bain parasiticide *m.*; *v.t.* & *i.* (*put into liquid*) tremper; (*go under water*) plonger; (*headlights*) (se) mettre en code, (se) mettre en feux de croisement; (*magnetic*

needle) incliner; ~ **into** (*hand*) puiser dans; (*fig.*) ~ **into a book,** feuilleter un livre; ~**-stick** *s.* jauge *f.*
diphtheria *s.* diphtérie *f.*
diphthong *s.* diphtongue *f.*
diploma *s.* diplôme *m.*
diploma/cy *s.* diplomatie *f.*; ~**t** *s.* diplomate *m.*; ~**tic** *adj.* diplomatique.
dipsomania *s.* dipsomanie *f.*; ~**c** *adj.* & *s.m.f.* dipsomane.
diptych *s.* diptyque *m.*
dire *adj.* affreux.
direct[1] *adj.* **1.** (*straight*) direct, droit; **2.** (*frank*) droit, net; ~ **current,** courant continu *m.*; *adv.* (1) directement; ~**ly** *adv.* (1) (*manner*) directement, (*straight away*) tout de suite; (2) nettement; ~**ness** *s.* (1) mouvement direct *m.*; (2) droiture *f.*, netteté *f.*
direct[2] *v.t.* (*control*) diriger; (*order s.o. to do sth.*) commander à qn. de faire qch.; (*address letter*) adresser; (*give instructions for route*) diriger; (*focus on*) braquer sur.
direct/ion *s.* (*course, way*) direction *f.*, sens *m.*; (*control*) conduite *f.*; (*address*) adresse *f.*; (*pl. instructions*) directions *f.pl.*; ~**ion-finder** *s.* radiogoniomètre *m.*; ~**ion-**INDICATOR; ~**ive** *s.* directive *f.*; *adj.* direct/eur, -rice; ~**or** *s.* directeur *m.*, administrateur *m.*, (*of film*) réalisateur *m.*; **managing** ~**or,** directeur-général *m.*; **chairman & managing** ~**or,** président-directeur-général *m.* (*abbrev.* P.D.G.); ~**orate** *s.* (*board of* ~*ors*) conseil d'administration *m.*; ~**ory** *s.* (*polit.*) directoire *m.*; annuaire *m.*, (*telephone*) bottin *m.*
dirge *s.* chant funèbre *m.*
dirigible *adj.* & *s.m.* dirigeable.
dirk *s.* dague *m.*
dirt *s.* (*mud*) boue *f.*; (*mire, soil, etc.*) crotte *f.*, (*on clothes, skin, etc.*) crasse *f.*; (*fig.*) ordure *f.*; **to treat s.o. like** ~, traiter qn. comme la dernière des créatures; ~ CHEAP; ~ **road,** chemin de terre battue *m.*; ~**y** *adj.* (*unclean*) sale, crasseux; (*foul*) malpropre, dégoûtant; (*obscene*) ordurier, grossier; (*mean*) vilain; (*weather*) sale; **a** ~**y trick,** un sale tour *m.*; **don't wash your** ~**y linen in public,** il faut laver son linge sale en famille; ~**ily** *adv.* salement; ~**iness** *s.* saleté *f.*; ~**y** *v.t.* & *i.* crotter, (se) souiller.
disab/le *v.t.* rendre incapable (*from*—de); (*injure*) estropier; (*ship*) désemparer; ~**led,** *adj.* & *s.m.f.* invalide; ~**ility** *s.* incapacité *f.*, invalidité *f.* ~**ility pension,** pension d'invalidité *f.*
disabuse *v.t.* désabuser.
disaccord *s.* désaccord *m.*
disadvantage *s.* désavantage *m.*; **at a** ~, dans un mauvais moment; (*compared with another*) dans une position désavantageuse; ~**ous** *adj.* désavantageux.
disaffect *v.t.* (se) détacher de, aliéner; ~**ed** *adj.* mal disposé; ~**ion** *s.* désaffection *f.*
disagree *v.i.* (*differ*) différer (*with*—de); (*quarrel*) se brouiller; ~ **with s.o.,** ne pas être d'accord avec qn.; ~ **with** (*of food, climate, etc.*) ne pas convenir à; ~**able** *adj.* désagréable; ~**ably** *adv.**; ~**ment** *s.* désaccord *m.*; ⚠ désagrément = **an unpleasing thing.**
disallow *v.t.* (*reject*) rejeter; (*prohibit*) défendre.
disappear *v.i.* disparaître; ~**ance** *s.* disparition *f.*
disappoint *v.t.* (*fail to fulfil desire or hope*) tromper, décevoir, désappointer; (*frustrate*) faire échouer; ~**ed** *adj.* déçu; ~**ing** *adj.* décevant; ~**ment** *s.* déception *f.*
disappro/ve, of *v.t.* désapprouver; ~**val** *s.* & ~**bation** *s.* désapprobation *f.*
disarm *v.t.* désarmer; ~**ament** *s.* désarmement *m.*; ~**ing** *adj.* désarmant; ~**ingly** *adv.* d'une manière désarmante.
disarrange *v.t.* déranger; ~**ment** *s.* dérangement *m.*
disarray *s.* **1.** désordre *m.*; **2.** (*fig.*) désarroi *m.*; *v.t.* (1) mettre en désordre; (2) jeter dans le désarroi.
disast/er *s.* désastre *m.*; ~**er area,** zone sinistrée *f.*; ~**rous** *adj.* désastreux; ~**rously** *adv.**.
disavow *v.t.* **1.** (*disown; repudiate*) désavouer; **2.** (*deny knowledge of*) renier; ~**al** *s.* (1) désaveu *m.*; (2) reniement *m.*
disband *v.t.* & *i.* (*mil.*) licencier; (se) séparer; ⚠ débander = **to unbind.**
disbelie/f *s.* incrédulité *f.*; ~**ve** *v.t.* ne pas croire; (*words*) ne pas ajouter foi à; ~**ver** *s.* incrédule *m.f.*
disbud *v.t.* débourgeonner.
disburden *v.t.* décharger; ~ **oneself of,** se décharger de.
disburse *v.t.* débourser; ~**ment** *s.* (*act*) déboursement *m.*; (*money*) débours *m.* (*usu. pl.*)
disc, disk *s.* disque *m.*; **slipped** ~, hernie discale *f.*; ~ **brakes,** freins à disques *m.pl.*; ~ **jockey** *s.* animateur *m.*
discard *s.* (*cards*) écart *m.*; *v.t.* (*throw out*) mettre au rebut; (*cards*) écarter; (*give up*) abandonner; (*dismiss*) renvoyer.
discern *v.t.* discerner; ~**ible** *adj.* visible, perceptible; ~**ing** *adj.* judicieux; ~**ment** *s.* discernement *m.*
discharge *s.* **1.** (*unloading; firing of gun*) déchargement *m.*; **2.** (*from employment*) congé *m.*, renvoi *m.*; **3.** (*from prison*) libération *f.*; **4.** (*from wound*) suppuration *f.*; **5.** (*of duty*) accomplissement *m.*; *v.t.* & *i.* (1) (se) décharger; (2) congédier; (3) libérer; (4) suppurer; (5) s'acquitter de; **6.** (*disembark*) débarquer.
disciple *s.* disciple *m.*
disciplin/e *s.* (*order; branch of learning*) discipline *f.*; (*punishment*) châtiment *m.*; *v.t.* (*train to obey*) discipliner; (*punish*) punir; ~**ary** *adj.* disciplinaire.
disclaim *v.t.* (*disavow*) désavouer; (*renounce*) renier; ~**er** *s.* désaveu *m.*
disclos/e *v.t.* (*uncover*) découvrir; (*divulge*) révéler; ~**ure** *s.* (*act*) découverte *f.*; (*thing* ~*ed*) révélation *f.*
discolour *v.t.* & *i.* (se) décolorer; ~**ation** *s.* décoloration *f.*
discomfit *v.t.* **1.** (*defeat*) battre; **2.** (*thwart*) frustrer; **3.** (*disconcert*) déconcerter; ~**ure** *s.* (1) défaite *f.*; (2) échec *m.*; (3) déconvenue *f.*
discomfort *s.* malaise *m.*
discompos/e *v.t.* défaire; (*fig.*) troubler; ~**ure** *s.* trouble *m.*
disconcert *v.t.* **1.** (*upset*) déconcerter; **2.** (*embarrass*) gêner; ~**ing** *adj.* (1) déconcertant; (2) gênant.
disconnect *v.t.* (*gen.*) détacher (*from*—de); (*mech.*) débrayer; (*electr.*) débrancher; (*telephone*) couper; ~**ed** *adj.* (*electr.*) débranché; (*style*) décousu; ~**ion** (*disconnexion*) *s.* débrayage *m.*
disconsolate *adj.* (*inconsolable*) désolé; (*unhappy*) triste; ~**ly** *adv.* d'une manière désolée.
discontent *s.* mécontentement *m.*; *v.t.* mécontenter; ~**ed** *adj.* mécontent (de).
discontinu/e *v.t.* & *i.* mettre fin à, suspendre; ~**ance** *s.* interruption *f.*; ~**ity** *s.* discontinuité *f.*; ~**ous** *adj.* discontinu.
discord *s.* (*disagreement*) discorde *f.*; (*harsh noise*) bruit discordant *m.*; (*mus. lack of harmony*) dissonance *f.*; ~**ance** *s.* discordance *f.*; ~**ant** *adj.* discordant.
discothèque *s.* discothèque *f.*
discount *s.* **1.** (*comm.*) rabais *m.*; **2.** (*fin.*) escompte *m.*; (*reduction*) remise *f.*; **at a** ~, au rabais; ~ **for cash,** escompte au comptant; *v.t.* (1) rabattre; (2) escompter; **3.** (*ignore*) ne pas

tenir compte de; **4.** (*allow for exaggeration*) faire la part de l'exagération dans; **5.** (*take account of*) tenir compte de, **to arrive at this figure, I have ~ed my probable losses,** pour arriver à cette somme, j'ai tenu compte de mes pertes probables; **6.** (*use up effect, of news, etc., beforehand*) **this possibility has already been ~ed,** on avait déjà envisagé cette possibilité.

discountenance *v.t.* (*refuse approval*) désapprouver; (*discourage*) décourager.

discourag/e *v.t.* (*reduce confidence*) décourager; (*deter from*) dissuader de; **~ement** *s.* découragement *m.*; **~ing** *adj.* décourageant.

discourse *s.* (*lecture or sermon*) discours *m.*; (*talk*) allocution *f.*; *v.i.* discourir (sur); s'entretenir.

discourte/ous *adj.* impoli; **~ously** *adv.**; **~sy** *s.* impolitesse *f.*

discover *v.t.* (*find out*) découvrir; (*reveal*) révéler; **~er** *s.* découvreur *m.*; **~y** *s.* découverte *f.*

discredit *s.* discrédit *m.*; *v.t.* (*refuse belief*) ne pas croire, mettre en doute; (*bring ~ on*) discréditer; **~able** *adj.* peu honorable.

discre/et *adj.* **1.** (*prudent*) avisé, circonspect; **2.** (*cautious in speech or action*) discret; **~etly** *adv.* (1) avec circonspection; (2)*; **~tion** *s.* (1) circonspection *f.*; (*liberty*) discrétion *f.*; **it is at your ~ion,** il dépend de vous de; **~tionary** *adj.* discrétionnaire.

discrepan/cy *s.* **1.** (*difference*) contradiction *f.*; **2.** (*failure to agree*) désaccord *m.*; **~t** *adj.* (1) différent; (2) en contradiction avec.

discrete *adj.* distinct.

discriminat/e *v.t.* & *i.* discriminer, distinguer (*between*—entre; *among*—parmi; *against*—contre); **~ing** *adj.* (*distinctive*) distinctif; (*against s.o.*) discriminatoire; (*thoughtful*) avisé; **~ion** *s.* discrimination *f.*, distinction *f.*; (*thoughtfulness*) perception *f.*

discursive *adj.* discursif, décousu.

discus *s.* disque *m.*

discuss *v.t.* discuter; **~ible** *adj.* discutable; **~ion** *s.* discussion *f.*

disdain *s.* **1.** (*treating with scorn*) dédain *m.*; **2.** (*treating as below notice*) mépris *m.*; *v.t.* (1) dédaigner; (2) mépriser; **~ful** *adj.* dédaigneux; **~fully** *adv.**.

disease *s.* maladie *f.*; **~d** *adj.* malade.

disembark *v.t.* & *i.* débarquer; **~ation** *s.* débarquement *m.*

disembarrass *v.t.* (*free from embarrassment, rid of*) débarrasser (de); (*disentangle*) démêler.

disembody *v.t.* désincorporer.

disembowel *v.t.* vider, éventrer; **~led** *adj.* éventré.

disembroil *v.t.* débrouiller.

disenchant *v.t.* désenchanter; **~ed** *adj.* désenchanté; **~ment** *s.* désenchantement *m.*

disencumber *v.t.* désencombrer.

disengage *v.t.* **1.** (*detach, loosen*) dégager; (*gear*) débrayer; *v.i.* **2.** (*withdraw from action*) décrocher; **~d** *adj.* libre; **~ment** *s.* (1) dégagement *m.*; (2) décrochage *m.*

disentangle *v.t.* (*unravel threads*) démêler; (*extricate oneself*) (se) dépêtrer; (*fig.*) débrouiller.

disestablish *v.t.* séparer de l'état; **~ment** *s.* séparation (*f.*) de l'église et de l'état.

disfavour *s.* (*dislike*) défaveur *f.*; (*disapproval*) désapprobation *f.*

disfigure *v.t.* (*deform*) défigurer; (*mar beauty of*) gâter, enlaidir; **~ment** *s.* enlaidissement *m.*

disfranchise *v.t.* priver du droit de vote; **~ment** *s.* privation du droit de vote *f.*

disfrock *v.t.* défroquer.

disgorge *v.t.* (*eject, food, water*) dégorger, vomir; (*give up, booty*) rendre; (*discharge, river*) déverser.

disgrace *s.* **1.** (*loss of favour*) disgrâce *f.*; **2.** (*shame*) honte *f.*; **3.** (*cause of reproach*) déshonneur *m.*; **in ~,** en disgrâce; *v.t.* (1) (*dismiss from favour*) disgrâcier; (2) (*bring shame on*) déshonorer; **~ful** *adj.* honteux; **~fully** *adv.**.

disgruntled *adj.* fâché, contrarié.

disguise *s.* (*state*) déguisement *m.*; (*garments used*) travesti *m.*; **in ~,** déguisé; *v.t.* déguiser; (*hide*) dissimuler; **~d as,** déguisé en.

disgust *s.* **1.** (*profound dislike*) dégoût *m.*; **2.** (*profound discontent*) écœurement *m.*; *v.t.* (1) dégoûter; (2) écœurer; **~ing** *adj.* (1) dégoûtant; (2) écœurant.

dish *s.* (*plate*) plat *m.*, PIE ~; (*food*) mets *m.*; (*concave vessel*) cuvette *f.*; (*fam. attractive person*) beau morceau (de fille) *m.*, (*pop.*) pépée *f.*; **~es,** vaisselle *f.*, **to wash up the ~es,** faire la vaisselle; **~cloth** *s.* (*for washing*) lavette *f.*, (*for drying*) torchon *m.*; **~-warmer** *s.* réchaud *m.*; **~washer** *s.* lave-vaisselle *m.*; **~-water** *s.* eau de vaisselle *f.*, (*fam.*) lavasse *f.*; *v.t.* (*make concave*) creuser; (*fam. = defeat*) enfoncer; **~ up,** servir.

disharmony *s.* (*sound*) dissonance *f.*; (*fig.*) désaccord *m.*

dishearten *v.t.* décourager; **~ing** *adj.* décourageant; **~ment** *s.* découragement *m.*

dishevelled *adj.* (*of person*) échevelé; (*of hair*) ébouriffé.

dishonest *adj.* malhonnête; **~ly** *adv.**; **~y** *s.* malhonnêteté *f.*

dishonour *s.* déshonneur *m.*; *v.t.* (*treat with scorn*) traiter irrespectueusement; (*bring ~ on*) déshonorer; (*refuse cheque*) refuser de payer; **~able** *adj.* (*act*) déshonorant; (*person*) sans honneur; **~ably** *adv.* d'une manière déshonorante.

disillusion *v.t.* désabuser; **~ment** *s.* déception *f.*

disincentive *adj.* & *s.m.* préventif.

disinclin/e *v.t.* inspirer peu d'empressement (pour); **~ation** *s.* manque d'empressement *m.*; **~ed to** *adj.* peu disposé à.

disinfect *v.t.* désinfecter; **~ant** *adj.* & *s.m.* désinfectant; **~ion** *s.* désinfection *f.*

disingenuous *adj.* qui manque de franchise; **~ly** *adv.* sans franchise; **~ness** *s.* manque de franchise *m.*

disinherit *v.t.* déshériter; **~ance** *s.* déshéritement *m.*

disintegrat/e *v.t.* & *i.* (se) désagréger; **~ion** *s.* désagrégation *f.*

disinter *v.t.* exhumer; **~ment** *s.* exhumation *f.*

disinterested *adj.* **1.** (*impartial*) désintéressé; **2.** (*fam. not interested*) indifférent; **~ly** *adv.* (1) avec désintéressement; (2) avec indifférence; **~ness** *s.* (1) désintéressement *m.*; (2) indifférence *f.*

disjoin *v.t.* disjoindre.

disjoint *v.t.* disloquer; **~ed** *adj.* (*style*) décousu; **~edly** *adv.* d'une manière décousue.

disjuncti/on *s.* séparation *f.*; **~ve** *adj.* disjonctif.

disk *see* DISC.

dislike *s.* aversion *f.*, antipathie *f.*; **to have a ~ for,** avoir de l'aversion pour; **to take a ~ to,** prendre en aversion; *v.t.* ne pas aimer.

dislocat/e *v.t.* disloquer; **~ion** *s.* dislocation *f.*

dislodge *v.t.* déloger.

disloyal *adj.* **1.** (*person*) infidèle; **2.** (*act*) déloyal; **3.** (*disaffected*) mal disposé (envers); **~ly** *adv.* (1)*; (2) traîtreusement, de façon déloyale; **~ty** *s.* (1) infidélité *f.*; (2) trahison *f.*

dismal *adj.* **1.** (*dark*) sombre; **2.** (*sad*) triste; **~ly** *adv.* (1)*; (2)*.

dismantl/e *v.t.* **1.** (*also fig.*) démanteler; **2.** (*machine*) démonter; **~ing** *s.* (1) démantèlement *m.*; (2) démontage *m.*

dismast *v.t.* démâter.

dismay *s.* **1.** (*loss of courage*) effroi *m.*; **2.** (*horrified amazement*) consternation *f.*; *v.t.* (1) effrayer; (2) consterner.

dismember *v.t.* démembrer; **~ment** *s.* démembrement *m.*
dismiss *v.t.* **1.** (*send away*) renvoyer; **2.** (*discharge*): (*employee*) congédier, (*official*) destituer; **3.** (*put out of mind*) écarter; *v.i.* (*break ranks*) rompre; **~!,** rompez!; **~al** *s.* (1) renvoi *m.*; (2) congédiement *m.*, destitution *f.*
dismount *v.t.* démonter; *v.i.* descendre de.
disobe/y *v.t.* désobéir à; **~dience** *s.* désobéissance *f.*; **civil ~dience,** désobéissance civile *f.*; **~dient** *adj.* désobéissant.
disoblig/e *v.t.* désobliger; **~ing** *adj.* désobligeant.
disorder *s.* **1.** (*confusion*) désordre *m.*; **2.** (*bodily or mental ailment*) trouble *m.*; *v.t.* déranger; **~ed** *adj.* (1) en désordre; (2) dérangé; **~ly** *adj.* en désordre, déréglé.
disorganiz/e *v.t.* désorganiser; **~ation** *s.* désorganisation *f.*
disorientate *v.t.* désorienter.
disown *v.t.* désavouer.
disparag/e *v.t.* **1.** (*speak slightingly of*) dénigrer; **2.** (*depreciate*) déprécier; **~ement** *s.* (1) dénigrement *m.*; (2) dépréciation *f.*; **~ing** *adj.* peu flatteur; **~ingly** *adv.* avec mépris.
dispar/ate *adj.* disparate; **~ity** *s.* disparité *f.*
dispassionate *adj.* **1.** (*free from emotion*) calme; **2.** (*impartial*) impartial; **~ly** *adv.* (1)*; (2)*.
dispatch, despatch *s.* **1.** (*comm.*) expédition *f.*, envoi *m.*; **2.** (*speed*) promptitude *f.*; **3.** (*official communication*) bulletin *m.*, (*diplomatic*) dépêche *f.*; **~-box/case** *s.* serviette *f.*; **~-rider** *s.* estafette *f.*; *v.t.* (1) expédier, envoyer; (2) expédier; **4.** (*kill*) achever.
dispel *v.t.* dissiper.
dispensary *s.* (*clinic*) dispensaire *m.*; (*chemist*) pharmacie *f.*
dispensation *s.* (*distribution*) distribution *f.*; (*exemption*) dispense *f.*; (*of Providence*) décret *m.*
dispense *v.t.* **1.** (*distribute*) dispenser; **2.** (*administer* (*justice*)) administrer; **3.** (*med.*) préparer; ⚠ dispenser ≠ (*3*); **~ from,** exempter de; **~ with** se passer de; **~r** *s.* pharmacien(ne) *m.f.*
dispers/e *v.t.* & *i.* **1.** (*scatter*) (se) disperser; **2.** (*dispel*) (se) dissiper; **~al** *s.* dispersion *f.*
dispirit *v.t.* décourager; **~ed** *adj.* découragé; **~edness** *s.* découragement *m.*; **~ing** *adj.* décourageant.
displace *v.t.* **1.** (*move from position*) déplacer; **2.** (*remove from office*) destituer, (*replace*) remplacer; **~d person,** personne déplacée *f.*; **~ment** *s.* (1) déplacement *m.*; (2) destitution *f.*
display *s.* **1.** (*exhibition*) exposition *f.*; **2.** (*ostentation*) étalage *m.*, parade *f.*, (*in shop*) vitrine *f.*; **3.** (*show of affection etc.*) preuve *f.*; *v.t.* (1) exposer; (2) étaler; (3) manifester, faire preuve de.
displeas/e *v.t.* (*offend, vex*) vexer; (*not please*) déplaire à; **be ~ed,** être mécontent (*at, with*—de); **~ing** *adj.* déplaisant; **~ure** *s.* déplaisir *m.*
disport *v.refl.* (*archaic*) s'ébattre.
dispos/e *v.t.* **1.** (*place in order*) placer; **2.** (*incline to*) (se) disposer à; **~e of,** se débarrasser de; **~able** *adj.* (*available*) disponible; (*that can be ~ed of*) à jeter après usage; **~al** *s.* disposition *f.*; (*sale*) vente *f.*; **to have at one's ~al,** avoir à sa disposition; **to be at s.o.'s ~al,** être à la disposition de qn.; **~ed to,** disposé à; **kindly ~ed,** bien disposé; **~ition** *s.* (1) organisation *f.*; (2) caractère *m.*
dispossess *v.t.* déposséder (*of*—de); **~ion** *s.* dépossession *f.*
dispro/of *s.* réfutation *f.*; **~ve** *v.t.* réfuter.
disproportion *s.* disproportion *f.*; **~ate** *adj.* disproportionné; **~ately** *adv.* d'une manière disproportionnée.
disput/e *s.* **1.** (*debate*) discussion *f.*; **2.** (*quarrel*) querelle *f.*; **3.** (*difference of opinion*) dispute *f.*; **beyond ~e** *adj.* & *adv.* incontestable(ment); *v.t.* & *i.* (1) discuter; (2) se quereller; (3) contester; **4.** (*contend for*) disputer; **~able** *adj.* discutable; **~ation** *s.* débat *m.*
disqualif/y *v.t.* **1.** frapper d'incapacité; **2.** (*sports*) disqualifier; **~ication** *s.* (1) incapacité *f.*; (2) disqualification *f.*
disquiet *s.* inquiétude *f.* (*also* = **~ude**); *v.t.* inquiéter.
disquisition *s.* dissertation *f.*
disregard *s.* **1.** (*indifference*) indifférence *f.*; **2.** (*neglect*) négligence *f.*; *v.t.* (1) ne pas tenir compte de; (2) négliger.
disrepair *s.* délabrement *m.*; **in a state of ~,** délabré.
disreput/e *s.* discrédit *m.*; **fall into ~e,** tomber dans le discrédit; **~able** *adj.* (*person*) perdu de réputation; (*thing*) déshonorant.
disrespect *s.* manque de respect *m.*; **~ful** *adj.* irrespectueux; **~fully** *adv.**.
disrobe *v.t.* & *i.* (se) déshabiller.
disrupt *v.t.* **1.** (*shatter*) faire éclater; **2.** (*separate forcibly*) disloquer; **3.** (*interrupt*) interrompre; **~ion** *s.* (1) éclatement *m.*; (2) dislocation *f.*; (3) interruption *f.*; **~ive** *adj.* disruptif.
dissatis/fy *v.t.* mécontenter; **~fied with,** mécontent de; **~faction** *s.* mécontentement *m.*
dissect *v.t.* (*lit.* & *fig.*) disséquer; **~ion** *s.* dissection *f.*
dissemble *v.t.* dissimuler; *v.i.* feindre; **~r** *s.* dissimulateur *m.*
disseminat/e *v.t.* (*lit.* & *fig.*) disséminer; **~ion** *s.* dissémination *f.*
dissen/t *s.* **1.** (*difference of opinion*) dissentiment *m.*; **2.** (*nonconformity*) dissidence *f.*; *v.i.* (1) ne pas être du même avis que (*about*—sur); (2) être dissident; **~sion** *s.* dissension *f.*; **~ter** *s.* dissident *m.*; **~tient** *adj.* opposé; *s.* opposant *m.*
dissertation *s.* dissertation *f.*
disservice *s.* mauvais service *m.*
dissiden/t *adj.* & *s.m.f.* dissident(e); **~ce** *s.* dissidence *f.*
dissimilar *adj.* dissemblable (*to*—à); **~ity** *s.* dissemblance *f.*
dissimulat/e *v.t.* & *i.* dissimuler; **~ion** *s.* dissimulation *f.*
dissipat/e *v.t.* & *i.* (*squander*) (se) dissiper, gaspiller; (*waste* (*energy*)) disperser (ses efforts); **~ed** *adj.* débauché; ⚠ dissipé (*more usually* = **inattentive**); **~ion** *s.* dissipation *f.*
dissociat/e *v.t.* séparer; *v.refl.* se désolidariser (*from*—de/d'avec qch. *or* qn.); **~ion** *s.* séparation *f.*
dissolub/le *adj.* dissoluble; **~ility** *s.* dissolubilité *f.*
dissolute *adj.* dissolu; **~ness** *s.* débauche *f.*
dissolution *s.* dissolution *f.*
dissolve *v.t.* & *i.* (*mix into*) (se) dissoudre; (*fade away*) (se) dissiper, (se) disperser; (*into tears*) fondre (en larmes); (*parl.*) dissoudre; **~nt** *adj.* & *s.m.* dissolvant.
dissonan/t *adj.* dissonant; **~ce** *s.* dissonance *f.*
dissua/de *v.t.* dissuader (*from*—de); **~sion** *s.* dissuasion *f.*
distaff *s.* quenouille *f.*; **on the ~ side,** du côté maternel.
distan/ce *s.* (*length from A—B*) distance *f.*; (*remoteness*) éloignement *m.*; (*~t point*) lointain *m.*; (*fig. coldness*) distance *f.*; **in the ~ce,** au loin; **from a ~ce,** de loin; **at a ~ce of 2 km.,** à 2 km. de distance; **to keep at a ~ce,** garder ses distances; **to keep s.o. at a ~ce,** tenir qn. à une distance respectueuse; *v.t.* distancer; **~t** *adj.* (*remote, place* & *time*) distant; (*fig.*) distant; (*relatives*) éloigné; **3 miles ~t,** distant de 3 milles; **~tly** *adv.* de loin; (*fig.*) froidement.
distaste *s.* dégoût *m.*; **~ful** *adj.* dégoûtant.
distemper[1] *s.* (*illness*) maladie *f.*, malaise *m.*

distemper[2] *s.* (*paint*) détrempe *f.*; *v.t.* peindre à la détrempe.
disten/d *v.t.* & *i.* (se) distendre; (*med.*) dilater; **~sion** *s.* distension *f.*; dilatation *f.*
distil *v.t.* & *i.* (se) distiller; **~lation** *s.* distillation *f.*; **~ler** *s.* distillateur *m.*; **~lery** *s.* distillerie *f.*
distinct *adj.* **1.** (*clearly perceptible*) distinct, net; **2.** (*different*) différent (*from*—de); **3.** (*decided*) marqué; **~ion** *s.* (2) distinction *f.*, différence *f.*; (*mark of honour*) récompense honorifique *f*,; (*excellence*) valeur *f.*; **to pass (an exam) with ~ion,** être reçu avec mention; **~ive** *adj.* distinctif; **~ly** *adv.* (1)*,*; (2) séparément; **~ness** *s.* (1) netteté *f.*
distinguish *v.t.* & *i.* (*make distinctions between*) distinguer (entre); (*characterize*) classer; (*recognize*) apercevoir; (*become eminent*) se distinguer; **~able** *adj.* (*clear*) distinct, net; (*recognizable*) reconnaissable; **~ed** *adj.* distingué; **~ing mark** *s.* signe distinctif *m.*
distort *v.t.* (*deform*) déformer; (*misrepresent*) défigurer; (*of features*) décomposer; **~ed** *adj.* tordu; **~ion** *s.* déformation *f.*
distract *v.t.* **1.** (*divert*) & **2.** (*draw away*) distraire; **3.** (*bewilder*) bouleverser; **4.** (*drive mad*) rendre fou; **~ed** *adj.* fou; ⚠ distrait = **absent-minded**; **~ion** *s.* (1) divertissement *m.*; (3) trouble *m.*; (4) agitation *f.*; **to drive to ~ion,** rendre fou; ⚠ distraction = **absent-mindedness.**
distraught *adj.* égaré.
distress *s.* (*emotional*) détresse *f.*; (*poverty*) misère *f.*; *v.t.* désoler, affliger; **~ed** *adj.* (*impoverished*) indigent; (*area*) misérable; **~ing** *adj.* désolant.
distribut/e *v.t.* (*deal out*) distribuer, répartir; (*classify*) classer; **~ion** *s.* distribution *f.*, répartition *f.*; **~ive** *adj.* distributif; **~or** *s.* distribut/eur, -rice *m.f.*; (*comm.*) concessionnaire *m.*; (*auto.*) delco *m.*
district *s.* (*region of town*) quartier *m.*; (*admin. division*) canton *m.*; (*province*) région *f.*; *adj.* du quartier, régional; **~ attorney** (*U.S.*) *s.* Procureur de la République *m.*; **~ nurse, ~ visitor** *s.* infirmière visiteuse *f.*
distrust *s.* **1.** (*want of trust*) défiance *f.*; **2.** (*suspicion*) méfiance *f.*; *v.t.* (1) se défier de; (2) se méfier de; **~ful** *adj.* (1) défiant; (2) méfiant; **~fully** *adv.* (1) avec défiance; (2) avec méfiance.
disturb *v.t.* **1.** (*incommode*) déranger; **2.** (*agitate*) troubler, agiter; **3.** (*worry*) inquiéter; **~ance** *s.* (1) dérangement *m.*; (2) agitation *f.*, (*polit.*) troubles *m.pl.*, (*meteor.*) perturbation *f.*; (3) inquiétude *f.*; **~ing** *adj.* (2) troublant; (3) inquiétant.
disun/ite *v.t.* désunir; **~ion** *s.* désunion *f.*
disuse *s.* désuétude *f.*; **to fall into ~,** tomber en désétude; **~d** *adj.* abandonné.
ditch *s.* fossé *m.*; **to the last ~,** (*fig.*) jusqu'au bout; DULL **as ~-water**; *v.t.* & *i.* (*make ~es*) creuser; (*auto.*) faire verser dans le fossé; (*aviat.*) faire un amerrissage forcé; (*fam.* = *abandon*) laisser tomber; **~er** *s.* (*mech.*) trancheuse *f.*, (*person*) terrassier *m.*
dither *v.i.* (*tremble*) trembler; (*hesitate*) hésiter; **to be all of a ~,** être dans tous ses états.
ditto *adv.* idem; (*comm.*) dito.
ditty *s.* chansonnette *f.*
ditty-bag *s.* trousse *f.*
diurnal *adj.* diurne.
divan *s.* (*oriental council* & *sofa*) divan *m.*; **~-bed** *s.* lit-divan *m.*
div/e *s.* **1.** (*~ing*) plongeon *m.*; **2.** (*of submarine*) plongée *f.*; **3.** (*rush*) élan *m.*; **4.** (*fam. disreputable place*) boîte *f.*; **5.** (*aviat.*) chute en piqué *f.*, abattée *f.*; *v.i.* (1) & (2) plonger; (3) se plonger dans, s'élancer; (5) tomber en piqué; **~e-bomb** *v.t.* bombarder en piqué; **~er** *s.* (*person*) plongeur *m.*, scaphandrier *m.*, (*bird*) plongeon *m.*; **~ing-bell** *s.* cloche à plonger *f.*; **~ing-board** *s.* plongeoir *m.*; **~ing-suit** *s.* scaphandre *m.*
diverge *v.t.* & *i.* (*proceed or cause to proceed in different directions*) diverger; (*become further apart*) s'écarter (*from*—de); **~nce** *s.* divergence *f.*; **~nt** *adj.* divergent.
divers *adj.* divers.
divers/e *adj.* (*of different kinds*) varié; (*unlike*) différent, divers (*usu. pl.*); **~ify** *v.t.* diversifier; **~ity** *s.* diversité *f.*
diver/t *v.t.* (*turn in another direction*) détourner; **2.** (*ward off*) écarter; **3.** (*distract attention*) distraire; **4.** (*entertain*) divertir; **~sion** *s.* (1) détournement *m.*, déviation *f.*; (4) distraction *f.*, divertissement *m.*; **5.** (*misappropriation, of funds*) détournement *m.*; **~ting** *adj.* (4) divertissant.
divest *v.t.* dépouiller, déposséder (*of*—de); *v.refl.* se dépouiller de; **~ment, ~iture** *s.* (*state*) dépouillement *m.*, (*law*) dépossession *f.*
divi/de *v.t.* & *i.* **1.** (*into parts*) (se) diviser (en); **2.** (*share*) partager; **3.** (*cut off, separate*) séparer; **4.** (*parl.*) voter; **~ders** *s.* compas à pointes sèches *m.*; **~sible** *adj.* divisible; **~sibility** *s.* divisibilité *f.*; **~sion** *s.* (1) division *f.*; (2) partage *m.*; (3) séparation *f.*; (4) vote *m.*; **5.** (*quarrel*) désaccord *m.*; **6.** (*admin. part of country*) circonscription *f.*; **7.** (*mil.*) division *f.*; **~sor** *s.* diviseur *m.*
dividend *s.* dividende *f.*; **~-warrant,** chèque-dividende *m.*
divine[1] *s.* écclésiastique *m.*; *adj.* (*holy* & *fam.*) divin; **~ service** *s.* office *m.*
divin/e[2] *v.t.* & *i.* deviner; **~ation** *s.* divination *f.*; **~er** *s.* devin *m.*; **~ing-rod** *s.* baguette divinatoire *f.*
divinity *s.* (*state*) divinité *f.*; (*god*) dieu *m.*, déesse *f.*; (*theology*) théologie *f.* ⚠ *not* divinité; **doctor of ~,** docteur en théologie *m.*
division *s. see* DIVIDE.
divorce *s.* **1.** (*end of marriage*) & **2.** (*separation of parts*) divorce *m.*; *v.i.* (1) divorcer; **~ s.o.,** divorcer (d')avec qn.; *v.t.* & *i.* (2) (se) séparer; **~e** *s.* divorcé(e) *m.f.*
divulge *v.t.* (*let out secret*) dévoiler; (*make public*) divulguer.
dixie, dixy *s.* bouteillon *m.*
dizz/y *adj.* (*speed, height, etc.*) vertigineux; (*person*) frappé de vertige; **I feel ~y,** j'ai le vertige; **~iness** *s.* vertige *m.*
do[1] *v.t.* **1.** (*perform*) (*a good deed, work, duty, task, military service etc.*) faire, accomplir, effectuer, s'acquitter de, (une bonne action, le travail, son devoir, une tâche, son service militaire etc.), (*fam.*) **~ 10 years,** faire dix ans de prison; **~ German,** faire de l'allemand; **~ Hamlet,** (*actor*) jouer H., (*producer*) donner H., (*at school*) étudier H.; **~ a sum,** faire un calcul, résoudre un problème; **what ~ you ~ for a living?,** quel est votre métier?; (*pop.*) **what are you ~ing?,** qu'est-ce que tu fabriques?; **2.** (*complete*) terminer, finir; **has she ~ne crying?,** a-t-elle fini de pleurer?; **3.** (*cause*) faire, occasionner, causer; **~ harm to s.o.,** faire du tort (du mal) à qn.; **who did that to you?,** qui vous a fait cela?; **it will ~ you no harm,** cela ne vous fera pas de mal; **4.** (*arrange, put in order*) faire, arranger, (*a room*) nettoyer (une chambre); (*hair*) coiffer qn., se coiffer; (*nails*) se faire les ongles; **5.** (*travel, cover distance*) faire, parcourir, couvrir; **~ 10 miles on foot,** faire 10 milles à pied; (*auto.*) **~ 100 km.p.h.**; faire du cent à l'heure; **6.** (*visit*) faire, visiter; **we did the châteaux de la Loire, etc.,** nous avons fait les châteaux . . . etc.; **7.** (*suit*) convenir; **will that ~ for you?,** est-ce que cela vous convient?;

8. (*render, give*) (*service, justice, the honours*), rendre (un service, justice, les honneurs); **9.** (*cooking*) cuire, **well done,** bien cuit; **done to a turn,** cuit à point; **10.** (*of hotel*) traiter; **they ~ you well here,** on vous traite bien ici; **he does himself well,** il ne se prive de rien; **11.** (*fam. cheat*) rouler; **you've been done,** on vous a eu; (*fam.*) refaire; **he's done me out of 10 francs,** il m'a refait de dix francs; *v.i.* **1.** (*behave*) faire, agir, se comporter; **he did well to refuse,** il a bien fait de refuser; **you would ~ better to keep quiet,** vous feriez mieux de vous taire; **2.** (*finish*) finir, en finir; **it's done,** c'en est fini; **3.** (*be suitable*) convenir, aller; **that will ~,** ça ira; **4.** (*be adequate*) suffire, faire l'affaire; **that will ~,** cela suffit; **5.** (*fare*) aller, se porter; **how ~ you ~?,** comment allez-vous?; (*fam.*) **how are you doing?,** comment ça va?; **do** (*with some prepositions and adverbs*): **~ again,** refaire; **I won't ~ it again,** je ne le referai pas, je ne recommencerai pas; **~ away with,** (*a custom*) abolir (un usage); (*a building*) détruire; (*a person*) tuer, assassiner, supprimer, qn.; **~ by,** traiter, user de; **~ well/ill by s.o.,** en user bien/mal avec qn.; **he has been hard done by,** il en a vu de dures; **~ down,** rouler, refaire; **~ for,** tuer, ruiner, détruire; **I'm done for,** je suis perdu; **~ for** (*domestic*) faire le ménage de qn.; **~ in** (*kill*) tuer, (*pop.*) buter, refroidir, zigouiller; (*exhaust*) épuiser, éreinter; **done in,** épuisé, éreinté; **~ out** (*room*) nettoyer (une chambre); **~ out of** (*deprive*) priver qn. de qch.; (*steal*) soutirer qch. à qn.; (*in a job*) supplanter; **~ over** (*again*) refaire, recommencer; (*cover with*) couvrir de, enduire de; **~ up** (*goods*) emballer; (*parcel*) envelopper, ficeler; (*repair*) réparer, mettre à neuf; **~ oneself up,** faire toilette; **~ up one's face,** se maquiller; **done up to kill,** sur son trente-et-un; (*exhaust*) *see* **~ in; to be done up,** être éreinté, n'en pouvoir plus; **make ~ with,** se contenter, s'arranger (de); **you must make ~ with what you have,** il faut vous contenter de ce que vous avez; **I'll make ~,** je m'arrangerai; **~ with, I could ~ with a cup of tea,** une tasse de thé ne serait pas de refus; **~ with,** (*control, usu. neg.*) **he can ~ nothing with this boy,** il ne peut rien faire de ce garçon; (*endure*) **I can't ~ with this noise,** je ne peux pas supporter ce bruit; **have to ~ with** (*person*) avoir affaire à qn.; (*affair*) être mêlé à qch.; **I have nothing to ~ with it,** je n'y suis pour rien; (*concern*) (*person*) regarder, **that has nothing to ~ with you,** cela ne vous regarde pas; (*thing*) avoir rapport à; **that has nothing to ~ with the case,** cela n'a pas de rapport avec la question; **~ without,** se passer de; **~ well,** prospérer, aller bien; **his business is doing well,** son affaire prospère; **he did well in his exam,** il a bien réussi à son examen; **do** (*elliptic*) (*various methods of translation*): **1.** *repeat verb,* (*they promise to pay*) **but they never ~,** mais ils ne payent jamais; **2.** *use adverbs such as* comme, aussi (*positive*) (*he reads a lot*) **and so ~ I,** et moi aussi, (*you haven't studied*) **as he did,** comme lui; pas, non plus (*negative*), (*you believe it?*) **I don't,** pas moi; (*you don't believe it*) **nor ~ I,** moi non plus; **3.** *use* faire, (*he said he would write*) **but he didn't,** mais il ne l'a pas fait; **4.** *in answer to questions, use* oui *and* non, (*did you sell it?*) **I did,** oui; (*did he say he would come?*) **he didn't,** non; **5.** *use* et vous (lui, etc.), **I like coffee, ~ you?,** j'aime bien le café, et vous?; **6.** *use* n'est-ce pas, **you like him, don't you?,** vous l'aimez, n'est-ce-pas?; **do** (*emphatic*): **1.** *affirmative imperative, use* je vous en prie, *or* donc, **~ tell me,** dites-le-moi, je vous en prie; **~ be quiet,** restez donc tranquille; **2.** *negative imperative, use* n'en faites rien, (*I shall tell him*), **Don't!,** N'en faites rien!; **3.** *in the present or past tenses, use a strengthening adverb or clause,* **he did see me, but he did not speak,** il m'a vu en effet, mais il n'a pas parlé; **you did say that,** vous l'avez dit, j'en suis sûr; **do** (*auxiliary*) *in sentences such as,* **what did they find?: ~ not say that,** *the form of DO is not translated, use only the appropriate tense of the verb*; **do** (*miscellaneous expressions*), **done!,** tope-là! c'est fait! conclu! entendu!; **well done!,** bravo!; **have done!, be done!,** finissez donc!; **what is to be done?, what am I to ~?,** que faire?; **that's done it,** ça, c'est la fin (de tout); **that's not done,** cela ne se fait pas; **no sooner said than done,** aussitôt dit, aussitôt fait; **to ~ one's best,** faire de son mieux; **to ~ nothing but,** ne rien faire que, **she did nothing but cry,** elle ne faisait que pleurer; **nothing doing** (*gen.*) rien à faire; (*comm.*) le marché est mort; **I've done with him,** j'en ai fini avec lui; **never ~ things by halves,** ne faites jamais rien à moitié; **up and doing,** plein d'allant; **well-to-~,** aisé, cossu; **the well-to-~,** les gens riches; **~-nothing,** fainéant; **it's all over and done with,** c'est fini, tout cela; **what can I ~ for you?,** en quoi puis-je vous aider, servir, être utile?, (*comm.*) qu'y a-t-il pour votre service?; **do** *s.* (*fam.*) (*hoax*) escroquerie *f.*, duperie *f.*; (*fam.*) (*entertainment*) affaire *f.*, fête *f.*; (*pl.*) **the ~'s and don'ts,** ce qui se fait et ce qui ne se fait pas, les prescriptions et les proscriptions; **to have a hair-~,** se faire coiffer; **a to-~,** remue-ménage *m.*; **what a to-~,** que de manières!; **~able** *adj.* faisable; **~er** *s.* personne active, agissante *f.*; (*author of an action*) faiseur, auteur *m.*; **evil/wrong ~er,** malfaiteur *m.*; **~-gooder** *s.* (*pej.*) dame patronnesse *f.*, belle âme *f.*; **~ing** *s.* fait *m.*, œuvre *f.*, action *f.*; **it's none of my ~ing,** je n'y suis pour rien; **it's all your ~ing,** c'est vous qui êtes la cause de tout cela; **that takes some ~ing,** ce n'est pas facile à faire; **~ings** *s.* (*pl. actions*) faits et gestes *m.pl.*; (*fam.*) gala *m.*, fête *f.*; (*pop. anything*) truc *m.*, machin *m.*; **~ing-up** *s.* remise à neuf *f.*, réparation *f.*; **~ing-away** *s.* abolition *f.*

do²(h) *s.* (*mus.*) do *m.invar.*

dobbin *s.* percheron *m.*

docil/e *adj.* docile; **~ely** *adv.**; **~ity** *s.* docilité *f.*

dock¹ *s.* (*weed*) oseille *f.*

dock² *s.* (*naut.*) bassin *m.*, dock *m.*; (*comm. bay for unloading*) dock *m.*, quai de déchargement *m.*; (*in police court*) banc des prévenus *m.*; **dry ~,** cale sèche *f.*; **wet ~,** bassin à flot *m.*; **in ~,** (*ship*) à quai, (*in court*) au banc des prévenus; (*fam. auto., etc.*) en réparation; *v.t.* & *i.* (faire) entrer en bassin; *v.i.* amarrer; **~yard** *s.* chantier naval *m.*; **~er** *s.* docker *m.*; **~ing** *s.* (*naut., space*) amarrage *m.*

dock³ *v.t.* (*tail*) couper la queue à; (*money*) retrancher.

docket *s.* **1.** (*label*) étiquette *f.*; **2.** (*voucher*) fiche *f.*; *v.t.* (1) étiqueter; (2) faire une fiche pour.

doctor *s.* (*acad.*) docteur *m.*, doctoresse *f.*; (*med.*) médecin *m.*; (*as a title*) **Dr. Dubois,** le docteur Dubois; **~ of law, letters, medicine, science, etc.,** docteur en droit, ès lettres, en médecine, ès sciences; **~al** *adj.* doctoral; **~ate** *s.* doctorat *m.*; *v.t.* (*care for*) soigner; (*fam. = patch up*) rafistoler; (*garble*) tripatouiller; (*castrate, a cat*) châtrer, couper; (*dilute*) frelater; (*modify with view to cheating customer*) trafiquer; **~ a drink,** droguer une boisson.

doctrin/e *s.* doctrine *f.*; **~aire** *adj.* & *s.m.f.* doctrinaire; **~al** *adj.* doctrinal.

document *s.* document *m.*; *v.t.* documenter;

~ary *adj.* documentaire; *s.* (= *film*) documentaire *m.*; **~ation** *s.* documentation *f.*
dodder *v.t.* avancer en tremblotant, (*fam.*) traîner la patte; (*old*) **~er** *s.* (*fam.*) croulant *m.*; **~ing** *adj.* tremblotant.
dodg/e *s.* (*trick*) ruse *f.*, truc *m.*; (*ingenious method*) invention *f.*, combine *f.*; (*movement*) saut *m.*; *v.t.* & *i.* (*elude*) éluder, échapper; (*blow*) esquiver; (*treat evasively*) user de détours, chercher des faux-fuyants; **~e about,** faire des tours et des détours; **~er** *s.* (*fam.*) roublard *m.*; **~y** *adj.* (*situation*) délicat.
doe *s.* (*female*): (*deer*) daine *f.*, (*rabbit*) lapine *f.*, (*hare*) hase *f.*; **~skin** *s.* peau de daim *f.*
doff *v.t.* ôter.
dog *s.* chien *m.*; (*male of other species, fox, etc.*) mâle *m.*; (*gay or rascally fellow*) type *m.*; **dirty ~,** sale type *m.*; **fire ~s,** chenet *m.*; **hang ~ look,** mine patibulaire *f.*; SHAGGY **~ story; ~ in the manger,** chien du jardinier qui ne mange pas de choux et n'en laisse pas manger aux autres; **to go to the ~s,** se ruiner; **give a ~ a bad name,** qui veut noyer son chien, l'accuse de la rage; **let sleeping ~s lie,** n'éveillez pas le chat qui dort; **to lead a ~'s life,** mener une vie de chien; **to lead a** CAT **and ~ life; ~'s-body** *s.* sous-fifre *m.*; **~-collar** *s.* collier *m.*; (*Eng. fam. eccles.*) col romain *m.*; **~ days** *s.* canicule *f.*; **~-eared** *adj.* corné; **~ fight** *s.* (*aviat.*) combat aérien *m.*; **~fish** *s.* chien de mer *m.*; **~ Latin** *s.* latin de cuisine *m.*; **~-lead** *s.* laisse *f.*; **~rose** *s.* églantine *f.*; **~-star** *s.* sirius *m.*; **~-tired** *adj.* fourbu; **~-watch** *s.* petit quart *m.*; *v.t.* emboîter le pas à qn., se cramponner à qn.
dogged *adj.* opiniâtre; **~ness** *s.* opiniâtreté *f.*
doggerel *s.* vers de mirliton *m.pl.*
doggo *adv.* **to lie ~** (*pop.*) se tenir peinard.
doggy *s.* (*fam.*) toutou *m.*; *adj.* canin.
dogma *s.* dogme *m.*; **~tic** *adj.* dogmatique; **~tism** *s.* dogmatisme *m.*; **~tize** *v.i.* dogmatiser.
doh *see* DO[2].
doily, doyley *s.* napperon *m.*
doing *see* DO[1].
doldrums *s.* calme plat *m.*; **in the ~** (*comm.*) dans le marasme; (*pers. fam.*) (avoir) le cafard.
dole *s.* (*charity*) aumône *f.*; (*unemployment benefit*) allocation de chômage *f.*; **on the ~,** en chômage; *v.t.* **~ out,** distribuer.
doleful *adj.* lugubre, triste; **~ly** *adv.**,*; **~ness** *s.* tristesse *f.*
doll *s.* (*toy*) poupée *f.*; (*pop.* = *pretty woman*) pépée *f.*; *v.t.* **~** (*oneself*) **up** (se) bichonner.
dollar *s.* dollar *m.*
dollop *s.* masse *f.* (informe); (*of jam, etc.*) cuillerée *f.*
dolly *s.* (= *doll*) poupée *f.*; (*for clothes-washing*) agitateur *m.*; (*TV* & *cinema platform*) travelling *m.*; (*mech. for pile-driving*) mouton *m.*
dolmen *s.* dolmen *m.*
dolo/ur *s.* douleur *f.*; **~rous** *adj.* douloureux.
dolphin *s.* (*mammal*) dauphin *m.*; (*fish*) daurade *f.*; (*buoy*) balise *f.*; (*mooring post*) poteau d'amarrage *m.*
dolt *s.* lourdaud *m.*, (*fam.*) gourde *f.*; **~ish** *adj.* lourdaud.
domain *s.* (*lit.* & *fig.*) domaine *m.*
dome *s.* (*arch.*) dôme *m.*; (*natural vault*) voûte *f.*; **~d** *adj.* couvert d'un dôme; (*person*) voûté.
Domesday Book *s.* cadastre national anglais (1086) *m.*
domestic *s.* domestique *m.f.*; *adj.* domestique; **~ science,** arts ménagers *m.pl.*; **~ate** *v.t.* **1.** (*people*) accoutumer à la vie d'intérieur; **2.** (*animals*) domestiquer; **3.** (*plants*) acclimater; ⚠ domestiquer = *only* (2); **~ated** *adj.* (1) (*pej.*) casanier, **~ated woman,** femme d'intérieur *f.*; (2) domestiqué; (3) acclimaté; **~ity** *s.* vie de famille *f.*; ⚠ domesticité = **staff of servants.**
domicil/e *s.* domicile *m.*; *v.t.* domicilier; **~iary** *adj.* domiciliaire.
domina/nt *s.* (*mus., biol.*) dominante *f.*; *adj.* dominant; **~nce** *s.* prédominance *f.*; **~te** *v.t.* & *i.* (*influence* & *overlook*) dominer; **~tion** *s.* domination *f.*
domineer *v.i.* **~ over s.o.,** tyranniser qn.; **~ing** *adj.* autoritaire.
Dominican *s.* dominicain *m.*
dominion *s.* (*sovereignty*) empire *f.*; (*domination*) domination *f.*; (*territory*) dominion *m.* ⚠ *used only of British* **~s,** *otherwise* colonie *f.*
domino *s.* (*costume* & *person*; *piece used in game*) domino *m.*; (*game, pl.*) dominos *m.pl.*
don[1] *s.* (*acad.*) universitaire *m.*; (*Spanish title*) don *m.*; **~nish** *adj.* professoral; (*iron.*) pédant.
don[2] *v.t.* revêtir.
don/ate *v.t.* faire don de; **~ation** *s.* don *m.*; **~or** *s.* donateur *m.*; BLOOD **~or.**
done *see* DO[1].
donkey *s.* (*animal* & *fam. idiot*) âne *m.*; **~-work** *s.* travail de routine *m.*; **to talk the hind leg off a ~,** bavarder comme une pie.
don't *s.* interdiction *f.*; **~-care** *adj.* & *s.m.f.* (*fam.*) je m'en fichiste; **~-care attitude,** je m'en fichisme *m.*
doodle *s.* gribouillage *m.*; *v.i.* gribouiller.
doom *s.* (*fate*) destin *m.*; (*sentence*) sentence *f.*; (*death*) mort *f.*; **~sday** *s.* (jour du) Jugement dernier *m.*; *v.t.* condamner (*to*—à); **~ed to,** destiné à.
door *s.* (*of building*) porte *f.*; (*of vehicle*) portière *f.*; **next ~** *adv.* à côté; **at** DEATH**'s ~;** TRAP **~; to lay at the ~ of** (*fig.*) mettre sur le dos de; **out of ~s,** dehors; **within ~s,** dedans; **with closed ~s,** à huis clos; **never** DARKEN **my ~ again; to keep the** WOLF **from the ~; ~bell** *s.* sonnette *f.*; **~-handle** *s.* poignée *f.*; **~-keeper** *s.* portier *m.*; **~knob** *s.* bouton *m.*; **~**MAT; DEAD **as a ~nail; ~post** *s.* montant *m.*; **~step** *s.* seuil *m.*; **~way** *s.* entrée *f.*
dope *s.* **1.** (*varnish*) enduit *m.*; **2.** (*drug*) stupéfiant *m.*; **3.** (*fam. inside information*) tuyau *m.*; **4.** (*fam. stupid person*) crétin *m.*; *v.t.* & *i.* (2) (se) droguer; **~-pedlar** *s.* trafiquant de stupéfiants *m.*; **~y** *adj.* abruti.
dorman/t *adj.* (*inactive*) en désuétude; (*sleeping*) endormi; (*heraldry*) dormant; **~cy** *s.* sommeil *m.*
dormer *s.* (*window*) lucarne *f.*
dormitory *s.* dortoir *m.*; **~-suburb,** commune-dortoir *f.*
dormouse *s.* loir *m.*
dorsal *adj.* dorsal.
dory *s.* (*fish*) daurade *or* dorade *f.*; (*boat*) doris *m.*
dos/e *s.* (*lit.* & *fig.*) dose *f.*; *v.t.* & *i.* (faire) prendre des médicaments (à); ⚠ doser = **to measure out; ~age** *s.* (*action*) administration des médicaments *f.*; (*amount*) dosage *m.*; (*med., pharm.*) posologie *f.*
doss *v.i.* (*pop.*) pioncer; **~ down** (*pop.*) aller au plumard; **~-house,** asile de nuit *m.*
dossier *s.* dossier *m.*
dot *s.* point *m.*; **polka ~** *s.* pois *m.*, *adj.* à pois; **on the ~** *adv.* (*fam.*) pile, **to arrive on the ~,** arriver pile, **that's right on the ~,** ça tombe pile; *v.t.* (*mark with a ~*) pointer; (*mark with ~s*) pointiller; (*place ~ over i*) mettre un point sur; (*scatter like ~s*) parsemer (*with*—de); (*pop.* = *hit s.o.*) flanquer un gnon à qn.; **~ted line** *s.* pointillé *m.*; **~ty** *adj.* (*fam.*) cinglé.
dot/e *v.i.* radoter; **~e on,** raffoler de; **~age** *s.* radotage *m.*; **~ard** *s.* radoteur *m.*; **~ing** *adj.* qui raffole.
dottle *s.* culot *m.*
double *s.* (*person like another*; *game*; *twice the amount*) double *m.*; (*thing like another*) réplique *f.*; (*darts*) doublé *m.*; (*racing*) pari jumelé *m.*; **at the ~,** au pas de course; *adj.* (*twofold, of two*

kinds, etc.) double; (*deceitful*) faux; *adv.* **to see ~,** voir double; **~ or quits,** quitte ou double; **~-barrelled,** à deux coups; **~-bass** *s.* contrebasse *m.*; **~ bed** *s.* grand lit *m.*; **~-bottomed,** à double fond; **~-breasted,** croisé; **~ chin** *s.* menton double *m.*; **~-cross** *v.t.* rouler; **~-dealer** *s.* fourbe *m.*; **~-dealing** *s.* duplicité *f.*; **~-declutch** *v.i.* faire un double débrayage; **~-edged,** à deux tranchants; **~ figures,** nombre de deux chiffres; **~** GLAZ**ing; ~-jointed,** désarticulé; **~-lock** *v.t.* fermer à double tour; **~-quick** *adv.* au pas gymnastique; **~-talk** *s.* paroles creuses *f.pl.*; **to talk ~ Dutch,** baragouiner; **doubly** *adv.* doublement; **~ton** *s.* (*cards*) doubleton *m.*; *v.t.* & *i.* (*make or become ~; play two parts*) doubler; (*fold letter*) plier; (*clench fist*) serrer; (*at bridge*) contrer; **~ back** *v.i.* revenir sur ses pas; **~ over, ~ up,** (se) plier en deux; **~ up with laughter, pain, etc.,** se tordre de rire, de douleur, etc.

doublet *s.* (*garment*) pourpoint *m.*; (*one of pair of words*) doublet *m.*

doubloon *s.* doublon *m.*

doubt *s.* (*uncertainty*) doute *m.*; (*uncertain state*) incertitude *f.*; **no ~,** sans doute; **without ~,** sans aucun doute; **~ful** *adj.* douteux, incertain; **~fully** *adv.* avec doute, d'une manière indécise; **~fulness** *s.* incertitude *f.*; **~less** *adj.* indubitable; **~less** *adv.* indubitablement; *v.t.* & *i.* (*mistrust*) (*s.o.*) se méfier de (qn.), (*sth.*) douter de (qch.); **I ~ whether he will come,** je doute qu'il vienne; **I don't ~ that he will win,** je ne doute pas qu'il gagnera; (*call in question*) mettre en doute; (*be uncertain*) se demander.

douche *s.* douche *f.*; *v.t.* & *i.* (se) doucher.

dough *s.* pâte *f.*; (*pop.* = *money*) fric *m.*; **~nut** *s.* beignet *m.*, pet-de-nonne *m.*; **~y** *adj.* pâteux.

doughty *adj.* vaillant.

dour *adj.* austère.

douse, dowse *v.t.* (*extinguish light*) éteindre; (*drench*) tremper.

dove *s.* (*bird* & *fig.*) colombe *f.*; RING-**~**; **~-coloured** *adj.* gorge de pigeon; **~cot**(**e**) *s.* colombier *m.*; **to flutter the ~cots,** jeter une pierre dans la mare aux grenouilles; **~tail** *s.* queue d'aronde *f.*; *v.t.* assembler à queue d'aronde; (*fig.*) *v.t.* & *i.* (se) raccorder.

Dover *s.* (*geog.*) Douvres *m.*

dowager *adj.* & *s.f.* douairière.

dowdy *adj.* mal fagoté.

dower, dowry *s.* **1.** (*widow's share*) douaire *m.*; **2.** (*marriage portion*) dot *f.*; **3.** (*natural talent*) don *m.*; *v.t.* (1) assigner un douaire à; (2) doter; (3) douer.

down[1] *s.* (*open high land*) colline *f.*, dune *f.*

down[2] *s.* (*fine, soft hair*) duvet *m.*; **~y** *adj.* duveteux.

down[3] *s.* **ups and ~s,** les hauts et les bas *m.pl.*; **to have a ~ on s.o.,** avoir une dent contre qn.; **~** *prep.* (*along*) le long de; **~ stage** *adv.* sur le devant; **~stream,** en aval de; **~ the street,** en bas de la rue; **~ town** *s.* quartier des affaires *m.*; **~ to,** jusqu'à; **~** *adv.* (*towards lower place*) en bas; (*in lower place*) en bas; (*fig. of shares, prices, etc.*) en baisse; (*sun*) couché; (*wind*) baissé; **up and ~,** de long en large, de haut en bas; (*command, to dog*) couchez!; **~ with the government!,** à bas le gouvernement!; COME, GO, LOOK, WRITE, *etc. see relevant verb*; **to be ~ on s.o.,** être monté contre qn.; **to be ~ with sth.** (*illness*) être alité avec; **~ in the** DUMPS; **~ at heel** (*shoes*) éculé, (*gen.*) à l'air miteux; **to be ~ on one's luck,** avoir la déveine; **~ and out** *adj.* pouilleux; **~ under** *adv.* aux antipodes; **to win** HANDS **~**; **~-hearted** *adj.* découragé; **~trodden** *adj.* foulé aux pieds; **~** *adj.* descendant; **~ draught** *s.* courant d'air descendant *m.*; **~ grade** *s.* déclin *m.*; **~grade** *v.t.* rétrograder; **~ payment** *s.* paiement en espèces *m.*; **~ train** *s.* train descendant *m.*; **~** *v.t.* (*fam.*) descendre; **~ tools,** se mettre en grève.

downcast *adj.* (*eyes*) baissé; (*dejected*) abattu.

downfall *s.* (*from position*; *storm etc.*) chute *f.*

downhill *adj.* en pente; *adv.* **the road goes ~,** la route descend; **his work is going ~,** son travail est sur le déclin.

downpour *s.* pluie battante *f.*

downright *adj.* (*sincere*) franc, droit, net; (*arrant*) véritable; *adv.* nettement; **~ness** *s.* droiture *f.*

downstairs *adv.*, *adj.* & *s.m.* en bas.

downward(**s**) *adj.* descendant; *adv.* en descendant.

dowry *s. see* DOWER.

dows/er *s.* radiesthésiste *m.*; **~ing** *s.* radiesthésie *f.*; **~ing-rod** *s.* baguette de sourcier *m.*

doze *s.* somme *f.*; *v.i.* sommeiller; **~ off,** s'assoupir.

dozen *s.* douzaine *f.*; **daily ~,** réveil musculaire *m.*

drab *s.* (*colour*) terne *m.*; (*person*) souillon *m.*; *adj.* gris, terne.

drachm *s.* drachme *f.*

drachma *s.* drachme *f.*

draft *s.* **1.** (*mil.*) détachement *m.*, contingent *m.*; **2.** (*U.S.* = *conscription*) conscription *f.*; **3.** (*order for money*) traite *f.*; **4.** (*sketch of work*) esquisse *f.*; **5.** (*rough copy of letter, etc.*) brouillon *m.*; (*of document*) **~ resolution, etc.,** projet de résolution, etc.; *v.t.* (1) détacher; (2) enrôler; (4) esquisser; (5) rédiger, (*parl.*) dresser un projet; **~sman** *s.* (4) dessinateur *m.*; (5) rédacteur *m.*

drag *s.* (*check on motion*) entrave *f.*; (*net*) drague *f.*; *v.t.* (*pull along*) traîner; (*search bottom of water*) draguer; (*anchor*) chasser sur; **the ship ~s its anchor,** le navire chasse sur son ancre; *v.i.* se traîner; **~ one's feet, ~ along,** traîner les pieds; **~ down,** entraîner; **~ in,** introduire de force; **~ on,** traîner; **~ out,** faire sortir de force; **~ up,** extraire, déterrer; (*child*) **~ged up,** mal élevé.

dragon *s.* (*animal* & *person*) dragon *m.*; **~-fly,** libellule *f.*

dragoon *s.* dragon *m.*; *v.t.* contraindre (à), mener à coups de trique.

drain *s.* (*ditch*) fossé d'écoulement *m.*; (*sewer*) égoût *m.*; (*loss of energy, etc.*) perte *f.*, (*fam.*) saignée *f.*; BRAIN **~**; **to throw one's money down the ~,** jeter son argent par les fenêtres; **~-pipe** *s.* tuyau d'écoulement *m.*; *v.t.* (*liquid*) drainer, assécher; (*auto., tank, etc.*) vidanger; (*drink to dregs*) vider; (*exhaust*) épuiser; *v.i.* s'écouler, s'égoutter; **~age** *s.* drainage *m.*; **~ing-board** *s.* égouttoir *m.*

drake *s.* canard *m.*; **to play** DUCKS **and ~s.**

dram *s.* drachme *f.*, (*fam.*) goutte *f.*, petit verre *m.*

drama *s.* (*the ~*) théâtre *m.*; (*a play, ~tic events*) drame *m.*; **~tic** *adj.* dramatique; **~tist** *s.* dramaturge *m.*; **~tization** *s.* dramatisation *f.*; **~tize** *v.t.* dramatiser.

drape *s.pl.* rideaux *m.pl.*; *v.t.* & *i.* (se) draper; **~r** *s.* marchand de nouveautés *m.*; **~ry** *s.* (*material*) draperie *f.*; (*shop*) marchand de nouveautés *m.*

drastic *adj.* énergique, rigoureux; **~ally** *adv.**,*; ⚠ drastique *is used only in medicine.*

drat *interj.* diable!; **~ted** *adj.* maudit (*before noun*).

draught *s.* **1.** (*act of drawing*) traction *f.*, tirage *m.*; **2.** (*of fish*) coup de filet *m.*; **3.** (*drink*) trait *m.*, gorgée *f.*; **4.** (*of ship*) tirant d'eau *m.*; **5.** (*of air*) courant d'air *m.*; **6.** (*of chimney*) tirage *m.*; **7.** (*plan*) projet *m.*; **8.** (*med.*) potion *f.*; **9.** (*game, pl.*) dames *f.pl.*; **~ beer,** bière à la pression *f.*;

~-board *s.* damier *m.*; **~horse** *s.* cheval de trait *m.*; **~sman** *s.* dessinat/eur, -rice *m.f.*; **~y** *adj.* (5) exposé aux courants d'air.

draw *s.* **1.** (*action*) tirage *m.*, traction *f.*; **2.** (*attraction*) attraction *f.*; **3.** (*lots*) tirage *m.*; **4.** (*~n game*) match nul *m.*; QUICK **on the ~**; *v.t.* & *i.* (1) tirer, (*drag*) traîner; (2) attirer; (3) tirer au sort; (4) faire match nul; **5.** (*deduce*) retirer; **6.** (*extract teeth*) arracher; **7.** (*take from or out of*) puiser (dans); **8.** (*sketch*) dessiner; **9.** (*ship*) jauger; **10.** (*search undergrowth*) battre; **11.** (*cheque*) tirer; **~ a** BLANK; **~ aside** *v.t.* tirer à l'écart, *v.i.* s'écarter; **~ back** *v.t.* & *i.* reculer; **~ in** *v.t.* & *i.* rentrer, (*days*) raccourcir; **~ near** *v.t.* & *i.* s'approcher (de); **~ off** *v.t.* retirer; **~ on** *v.t.* mettre, (*encourage*) entraîner; **~ out** *v.t.* & *i.* (s')allonger; **~ up** *v.t.* remonter, (*draft*) rédiger; **~ oneself up,** se redresser.

drawback *s.* (*inconvenience*) inconvénient *m.*; (*of customs duty*) remise *f.* (des droits de douane).

drawbridge *s.* pont-levis *m.*

drawer *s.* (*person*) tireur *m.*; (*in furniture*) tiroir *m.*; **~s** *s.* caleçon *m.* ⚠ caleçon *is usu. singular.*

drawing *s.* (*action*) & (*lots*) tirage *m.*; (*sketch*) dessin *m.*; **~-board** *s.* planche à dessin *f.*; ~-PIN; ~-PAPER.

drawing-room *s.* salon *m.*

drawl *s.* voix traînante *f.*; *v.t.* & *i.* parler d'une voix traînante.

dray *s.* haquet *m.*

dread *s.* crainte *f.*; *v.t.* & *i.* craindre, redouter; *adj.* craint, redoutable; **~ful** (*frightening* & *intensive*) effroyable; **~fully** *adv.**.

dreadnought *s.* cuirassé *m.*

dream *s.* (*lit.* & *fig.*) rêve *m.*; (*sth. delightful*) merveille *f.*; DAY-~; PIPE-~; *v.t.* & *i.* (*during sleep*) rêver; (*think*) songer (*of*—à); (*waste time*) rêvasser; **~er** *s.* rêveur *m.*, visionnaire *m.*; **~y** *adj.* rêveur.

drear/y *adj.* lugubre; (*dull*) morne; **~ily** *adv.* lugubrement.

dredge[1] *s.* drague *f.*; *v.t.* draguer; **~r** *s.* dragueur *m.*

dredge[2] *v.t.* (*sprinkle*) saupoudrer (*with*—de); **~r** *s.* saupoudreuse *f.*

dregs *s.* (*lit.* & *fig.*) lie *f.*, rebut *m.*; **to drink to the ~,** boire jusqu'à la lie.

drench *s.* (*vet.*) breuvage *m.*; *v.t.* (*vet.*) purger; (*wet all over*) tremper.

dress *s.* (*clothing*) habits *m.pl.*; (*gown*) robe *f.*; (*costume, style*) toilette *f.*, tenue *f.*; FANCY **~**; **~ circle** *s.* corbeille *f.*; **~ coat** *s.* habit *m.*; **~-designer** *s.* modéliste *m.f.*; **~maker** *s.* coutur/ier, -ière *m.f.*; **~ rehearsal** *s.* répétition générale *f.*; *v.t.* & *i.* (*mil.*) (s')aligner; (*clothe*) (s')habiller; (*wound*) panser; (*food*) apprêter, assaisonner; (*ship with flags*) pavoiser; (*shop window*) faire la vitrine; (*hair*) (se) coiffer; **~ down** *v.t.* chapitrer; **~ up** *v.i.* faire toilette, se bichonner; **well-~ed** *adj.* bien mis; **~y** *adj.* chic.

dressage *s.* dressage *m.*

dresser *s.* (*kitchen cupboard*) vaisselier *m.*; (*person*) (*theatre*) habilleuse *f.*; (*med.*) assistant en chirurgie *m.*

dressing *s.* (*action*) toilette *f.*; (*of wound*) pansement *m.*; (*manure*) engrais *m.*; (*cook.*) assaisonnement *m.*; (*mil.*) alignement *m.*; SALAD **~**; WINDOW **~**; **to give s.o. a ~ down** (*fam.*) passer un savon à qn.; **~-case** *s.* nécessaire de toilette *m.*; **~-gown** *s.* robe de chambre *f.*; **~-room** *s.* vestiaire *m.*; **~table** *s.* coiffeuse *f.*

dribble *s.* **1.** (*drops*) dégouttement *m.*; **2.** (*at the mouth*) bave *f.*; *v.i.* (1) s'écouler; (2) baver; *v.t.* (*football*) dribbler.

drift *s.* **1.** (*deviation due to current, wind, etc.*) dérive *f.*; **2.** (*inaction*) laisser-aller *m.*; **3.** (*meaning*) sens *m.*; **4.** (*deposit of snow, sand, etc.*) amoncellement *m.*; *v.i.* (1) aller à la dérive; (2) aller à vau l'eau; (4) s'amonceler; **~-net** *s.* seine *f.*; **~-wood,** bois flotté *m.*

drill *s.* **1.** (*tool*) perceuse *f.*, (*techn.*) foret *m.*; **2.** (*exercise*) exercice *m.*; **3.** (*seed-sowing machine*) semoir *m.*; **4.** (*small furrow*) sillon *m.*; **5.** (*text.*) coutil *m.*; **pneumatic ~,** marteau pneumatique *m.*; *v.t.* (1) percer, forer; (2) exercer; (3) semer; **~ing** *s.* (1) forage *m.*

drink *s.* (*liquid*) boisson *f.*; (*glass or portion*) verre *m.*; (*intemperance*) alcoolisme *m.*; **strong ~,** spiritueux *m.*; **to have a ~,** prendre un verre; **to** STAND **s.o. a ~**; *v.t.* & *i.* boire; (*to excess*) se livrer à la boisson; **~ like a** FISH; **~ down, ~ off,** avaler, boire d'un trait; **~ in** (*fig.*) boire; **~ to,** boire à; **~ up,** vider; **~able** *adj.* (*good to ~*) buvable; (*without risk to health*) potable; **~ing** *s.* (*act*) boire *m.*; (*drunkenness*) ivrognerie *f.*; **~ing-water** *s.* eau potable *f.*; **~ing-fountain** *s.* fontaine *f.*

drip *s.* **1.** (*process*) chute goutte à goutte *f.*; **2.** (*small amount*) goutte *f.*; **3.** (*pop. boring person*) raseu/r, -se *m.f.*; *v.t.* & *i.* dégoutter, (faire) écouler goutte à goutte; **~-dry** *adj.* sèche sur cintre; **~ping** *s.* as (1); (*fat from meat*) graisse *f.*; *adj.* trempé.

driv/e *s.* (*excursion in vehicle*) promenade en voiture *f.*; (*private road*) avenue *f.*, allée *f.*; (*cricket, golf*) drive *m.*; (*energy*) dynamisme *m.*, allant *m.*; (*card party*) tournoi *m.*; **front-wheel ~e** (*auto.*) traction avant *f.*; **left-, right-hand ~e,** conduite à gauche, à droite *f.*; POWER **~**; *v.t.* (*impel*) pousser; (*hunt game*) chasser; (*vehicle, animals*) conduire; (*machine*) faire marcher; (*a bargain*) conclure; **~e mad, etc.,** rendre fou, etc.; *v.i.* (*of person*) conduire, **can you ~e?,** savez-vous conduire?; (*of vehicle*) rouler; **~e away, ~e off,** chasser; **~e back,** repousser; **~e in** *v.t.* enfoncer; **~e-in cinema, restaurant,** cinéma (*m.*), restaurant (*m.*) pour automobilistes; **~ing** *s.* conduite *f.*; *adj.* **~ing rain,** pluie battante *f.*; **~ing force,** force motrice *f.*; **~ing** LICENCE; **~ing school,** auto-école *f.*; **~ing test,** examen de permis de conduire *m.*; **what is he ~ing at?** (*fig.*) où veut-il en venir?

drivel *s.* **1.** (*from mouth*) bave *f.*; **2.** (*aimless talk*) radotage *m.*; *v.i.* (1) baver; (2) radoter.

driver *s.* (*horse*) cocher *m.*; (*cattle*) bouvier *m.*; (*engine*) mécanicien *m.*; (*car*) conducteur *m.*, chauffeur *m.*; (*bus*) conducteur *m.*; LORRY-~.

drizzle *s.* bruine *f.*; *v.i.* bruiner.

drogue *s.* (*naut.*) ancre flottante *f.*; (*aviat.*) parachute de queue *m.*

droll *adj.* drôle; **~ery** *s.* drôlerie *f.*

dromedary *s.* dromadaire *m.*

drone *s.* **1.** (*male bee*) bourdon *m.*; **2.** (*fig. person*) parasite *m.f.*; **3.** (*sound*) bourdonnement *m.*; *v.t.* & *i.* (3) bourdonner.

drool *s.* **1.** (*from mouth*) bave *f.*; **2.** (*foolish talk*) radotage *m.*; *v.i.* (1) baver; (2) radoter.

droop *s.* **1.** (*hanging down*) inclinaison *f.*, abaissement *m.*; **2.** (*weariness*) langueur *f.*; *v.t.* (1) (*head, eyes*) pencher, baisser; *v.i.* (1) se pencher, se voûter; (2) languir; **~ing** *adj.* (1) baissé; (2) languissant; (*shoulders*) voûté.

drop *s.* (*liquid; med., fig.*) goutte *f.*; (*ear-ring*) pendant *m.*; (*sweet*) pastille *f.*; (*fall in price, temp. etc.*) baisse *f.*; chute *f.*; (*descent*) descente *f.*; **~ by ~,** goutte à goutte; *v.t.* (*liquid, tears, etc.*) verser; (*let fall*) laisser tomber; (*give up*) renoncer à; (*lower*) baisser; (*deposit, a person, packet, etc.*) déposer; **~ it!,** laisse tomber!; **~ s.o. a hint,** toucher un mot à qn.; **~ a** BRICK; *v.i.* (*drip*) goutter, s'égoutter; (*fall*) tomber; (*lose value*) baisser; **~ behind** *v.i.* rester en arrière; **~ in** *v.i.* entrer en passant; **~ off** *v.i.* tomber, (*fall asleep*) sommeiller; **~ out** *v.i.* sortir des rangs; **~-out** *s.* hippie *m.f.*; **~ goal** *s.* (*rugby*)

drop-goal *m.*; **~let** *s.* gouttelette *f.*; **~pings** *s.* crottes *f.pl.*; (*of horse*) crottin *m.*
drops/y *s.* hydropsie *f.*; **~ical** *adj.* hydropique.
dross *s.* (*scum of molten metal*) scories *f.pl.*; (*impurities*) impuretés *f.pl.*; (*refuse* & *fig.*) lie *f.*, rebut *m.*
drought *s.* (*lack of rain*) sécheresse *f.*; (*thirst*) soif *f.*
drove *s.* (*cattle*) troupeau *m.*; (*crowd*) foule *f.*; **~r** *s.* toucheur de bœufs *m.*
drown *v.t.* & *i.* (*by submersion*) (se) noyer; (*flood*) inonder; (*overpower sound*) étouffer; **~ one's sorrows in drink,** noyer son chagrin dans l'alcool.
drows/e *v.i.* somnoler; **~y** *adj.* somnolent; **~iness** *s.* somnolence *f.*
drub *v.t.* rosser; **~bing** *s.* rossée *f.*
drudge *s.* homme *m.* or femme *f.* de peine; *v.i.* (*pop.*) trimer; **~ry** *s.* corvée *f.*
drug *s.* (*med.*) produit pharmaceutique *m.*; (*narcotic*) drogue *f.*, stupéfiant *m.*; **a ~ on the market,** article invendable *m.*, (*pop.*) rossignol *m.*; **~ addict** *s.* drogué(e) *m.f.*; **~store** *s.* droguerie *f.*, pharmacie *f.*; **~ traffic,** trafic des stupéfiants *m.*; **~gist** *s.* droguiste *m.*; *v.t.* & *i.* (se) droguer.
drugget *s.* droguet *m.*
Druid, Druidess *s.* druide *m.*, druidesse *f.*; **~ic** *adj.* druidique.
drum *s.* (*mus.*) tambour *m.*; **big ~,** grosse caisse *f.*; **African ~,** tam-tam *m.*; KETTLE-**~**; (*of ear*) tympan *m.*; (*cylindrical container*) bidon *m.*; OIL **~**; **~ major** *s.* tambour-major *m.*; **~stick** *s.* baguette de tambour *f.*, (*of poultry*) pilon *m.*; *v.i.* (*mus.*) battre du tambour; (*tap continuously*) tambouriner; **~ out** *v.t.* dégrader; **~ up** (*custom, support*) racoler (les clients, les partisans); **~mer** *s.* tambour *m.*, (*U.S. comm.*) commis voyageur *m.*; **~ming** *s.* tambourinage *m.*
drunk *s.* (*pop.*) soûlaud *m.*; *adj.* (*lit.* & *fig.*) ivre (*with*—de); **~ard** *s.* ivrogne *m.*; **~en** *adj.* ivrogne; **~enness** *s.* ivrognerie *f.*, (*pop.*) soûlerie *f.*
dry *adj.* **1.** (*lacking moisture, rain*) sec, sèche; **to be ~** (*of weather*) faire sec; **2.** (*arid*; *fig.*) aride, froide; **3.** (*thirsty*) altéré; **to be ~** (*of person*) avoir soif; **4.** (*sarcastic*) caustique; **5.** (*teetotal*) sec; **~-clean** *v.t.* nettoyer à sec; **~-cleaning** *s.* nettoyage à sec *m.*; **~ goods,** nouveautés *m.pl.*; **~** ICE; **~ land,** terre ferme *f.*; **~ rot** *s.* (*fungi*) salpêtre *m.*, (*formation*) salpêtrisation *f.*; **~-shod** *adv.* à pied sec; **drily** *adv.* (4) ironiquement; **~ness** *s.* (1) sécheresse *f.*; (2) aridité *f.*; (3) soif *f.*; (4) ironie *f.*; **~** *v.t.* & *i.* sécher, (s')assécher; **~ up** (*dishes*) essuyer (la vaisselle); **~ up** *v.t.* & *i.* (se) dessécher, tarir, (*fam. stop talking*) sécher; **dried up,** à sec; CUT **and dried; ~er, drier** *s.* (*hair*) séchoir *m.*, (*spin*) essoreuse *f.*
dryad *s.* dryade *m.*
dual *adj.* double; **~ carriageway,** route à quatre voies *f.*; **~ control,** à double commande; **~-purpose,** à deux fins.
dub *v.t.* (*a knight*) armer; (*give nickname*) baptiser; (*film*) doubler.
dubi/ous *adj.* (*doubtful*) douteux; (*equivocal*) ambigu; (*shady*) suspect; **~ety** *s.* doute *m.*, caractère douteux *m.*; **~ously** *adv.* avec doute; **~tative** *adj.* dubitatif.
ducal *adj.* ducal.
ducat *s.* ducat *m.*
duchess *s.* duchesse *f.*
duchy *s.* duché *f.*
duck *s.* (*bird*) cane *f.*; (*generic*) canard *m.*; **lame ~,** canard boîteux *m.*; (*darling*) chou *m.*; (*score*) zéro *m.*; (*text.*) coutil *m.*; **~s** *pl.* (*clothing*) pantalon de coutil *m.*; **to play ~s and drakes,** faire des ricochets; **to make ~s and drakes of,** jeter par les fenêtres; **that runs off me like water off a ~'s back,** cela glisse sur moi comme la pluie sur un imperméable de caoutchouc; **~-boards** *s.* caillebottis *m.*; **~ling** *s.* caneton *m.*; **ugly ~ling** *s.* laideron *m.*; **~ing** *s.* bain forcé *m.*; *v.t.* & *i.* (*dip under water*) plonger; (*to avoid blow*) esquiver.
duct *s.* (*small*) conduit *m.*, (*large*) conduite *f.*
ductile *adj.* (*metals*) ductile; (*supple*) souple.
dud *s.* (*pl. clothes*) frusques *f.pl.*; (*shell that fails to go off*) obus non éclaté *m.*; (*stupid person*) raté *m.*, (*fam.*) cancre *m.* (*at maths.*) en math.; *adj.* (*counterfeit*) faux; (*useless*): (*person*) incapable; (*pop. idea*) moche; (*cheque*) sans provision.
dudgeon *s.* ressentiment *m.*; **in high ~,** dans une colère bleue.
due *s.* dû *m.*; (*pl.*) droits *m.pl.*; **to give s.o. his ~,** rendre justice à qn.; *adj.* (*owing*) dû; (*proper*) juste, convenable; (*under contract to be ready*) prévu; (*attributed to*) dû à; **train ~ at 7 o'clock,** train qui doit arriver à 7 heures; **in ~ form,** en bonne et due forme; **in ~ course,** en temps voulu; **to fall ~,** arriver à échéance; *adv.* (*of compass point*), **~ north,** en plein nord; **~ to,** à cause de; **duly** *adv.* dûment, directement.
duel *s.* duel *m.*; *v.i.* se battre en duel; **~list** *s.* duelliste *m.*
duenna *s.* duègne *f.*
duet *s.* duo *m.*
duff *adj.* sans valeur.
duffer *s.* (*pop.*) gourde *m.*; (*schoolboy*) cancre *m.*
duffle, duffel *s.* molleton *m.*; **~-coat,** duffel-coat *m.*
dug *s.* tétine *f.*
dug-out *s.* (*shelter*) abri *m.*; (*canoe*) pirogue *f.*
duke *s.* duc *m.*; **~dom** *s.* duché *f.*
dulcet *adj.* mélodieux.
dull *adj.* **1.** (*stupid*) borné; **2.** (*boring*) ennuyeux; **3.** (*colour*) terne, mat; **4.** (*weather*) gris, triste; **5.** (*light*) faible; **6.** (*sound*) sourd; **~ as ditch water,** ennuyeux comme la pluie; **~-eyed** *adj.* à l'œil éteint; **~-witted,** à l'esprit lourd; **~ard** *s.* balourd *m.*; **~ness** *s.* (1) lourdeur d'esprit *f.*; (2) monotonie *f.*; (3) & (5) faiblesse *f.*; (4) tristesse *f.*; **7.** (*comm.*) inactivité *f.*; **~y** *adv.* (2)*; (5)*; (6)*; *v.t.* & *i.* (*blunt*) (s')émousser; (*tarnish*) (se) ternir; (*stupefy*) hébéter; (*ease pain*) endormir.
dumb *adj.* muet; DEAF **and ~**; (*pop.* = *stupid*) gourde (*also s.*) **a ~ person,** une gourde *f.*; **~-bell** *s.* haltère *m.*, barre à disques *f.*; **~ show** *s.* pantomime *f.*; **~ waiter** *s.* table roulante *f.*; **~ly** *adv.* sans parler; **~ness** *s.* mutisme *m.*
dumbfound *v.t.* confondre.
dummy *s.* (*sham article*) simulacre *m.*; (*mere tool*) homme de paille *m.*; (*lay figure*) mannequin *m.*; (*at cards*) mort *m.*; (*child's comforter*) sucette *f.*; **to sell a ~** (*rugby*) faire une feinte de passe; **~ run,** galop d'essai *m.*
dump *s.* (*heap of refuse*) amas *m.*, dépotoir *m.*; RUBBISH **~**; (*munitions*) dépôt *m.*; (*depressing place*) trou *m.*; **~s** (= *depression*) cafard *m.*, **to be down in the ~s,** avoir le cafard; *v.t.* (*deposit*) décharger; (*throw down*) déverser; (*comm.*) faire du dumping.
dumpy *adj.* (*persons* & *things*) trapu.
dun[1] *adj.* (*colour*) gris-brun.
dun[2] *s.* (*creditor*) créancier impatient *m.*; *v.t.* relancer.
dunce *s.* (*schoolboy*) cancre *m.*; (*pop.*) âne *m.*
dunderhead *s.* crétin *m.*
dune *s.* dune *f.*
dung *s.* (*animal excrement*) bouse *f.*; (*manure*) fumier *m.*; **~hill,** fumier *m.*; *v.t.* fumer.
dungaree *s.* (*cloth*) treillis *m.*; **~s** (*pl.* = *overalls*) bleu *m.*; salopette *f.*
dungeon *s.* cachot *m.*
dunk *v.t.* tremper.
Dunkirk *s.* (*geog.*) Dunkerque *m.*
duo- (*in combination*): **~decimal** *adj.* duodécimal;

~**denal** *adj.* duodénal; ~**denum** *s.* duodénum *m.*; ~**logue** *s.* dialogue *m.*
dupe *s.* dupe *f.*; *v.t.* duper.
duplex *s.* (appartement) duplex *m.*; *adj.* double.
duplicat/e *s.* duplicata *m.*; *adj.* (*double*) double; (*exactly like*) identique; (*spare, key, etc.*) de rechange; **in** ~**e,** en deux exemplaires; *v.t.* (*make exact copy of*) copier; (*double*) doubler; (*make many copies of*) polycopier; ~**ion** *s.* duplication *f.*; ~**or** *s.* duplicateur *m.*
duplicity *s.* duplicité *f.*
durab/le *adj.* durable; ~**ility** *s.* durabilité *f.*
duration *s.* durée *f.*
duress *s.* contrainte *f.*; **to act under** ~, agir sous la contrainte.
during *prep.* pendant.
dusk *s.* crépuscule *m.*; ~**y** *adj.* (*dim*) sombre; (*skin, person*): (*by air & sun*) hâlé, (*by pigmentation*) bistré.
dust *s.* (*fine powder*) poussière *f.*; (*of metal*) poudre *f.*; (*household refuse*) balayures *f.pl.*; (*corpse*) cendres *f.pl.*; SAW~; **to throw** ~ **in s.o.'s eyes,** jeter de la poudre aux yeux de qn.; ~BIN; ~ **bowl** *s.* région dénudée *f.*; ~**-cart** *s.* voiture des boueux *f.*; ~**-cover,** ~**-jacket** *s.* couvre-livre *m.*; ~**man** *s.* boueux *m.*; ~**pan** *s.* pelle à ordures *f.*; ~**-sheet** *s.* housse *f.*; ~**-up** *s.* prise de bec *f.*; ~**y** *adj.* poussiéreux; **not so** ~**y** (*fam. fig.*) pas si moche que ça; *v.t.* & *i.* (*clear away* ~) épousseter; (*sprinkle with powder*) saupoudrer de; ~**er** *s.* torchon *m.*
Dutch *adj.* hollandais; ~**man,** ~**woman** *s.* Hollandais(e); DOUBLE ~; **to go** ~, payer chacun son écot; ~ **auction** *s.* vente à la baisse *f.*; **full of** ~ **courage,** avec un aplomb d'ivrogne; ~ **hoe** *s.* serfouette *f.*; ~ **oven** *s.* rôtissoire *f.*
dut/y *s.* (*obligation*) devoir *m.*; (*customs*) droits (de douane) *m.pl.*; (*office or function, usu. pl.*) fonctions *f.pl.*; **to be on** ~**y,** être de service; **to be off** ~**y,** être libre; **to do** ~**y for,** servir de; ~**y-free,** en franchise; ~**y-free shop** *s.* boutique franche *f.*; ~**iable** *adj.* soumis aux droits de douane; ~**iful** *adj.* (*obedient*) obéissant; (*respectful*) déférent; ~**ifully** *adv.* avec soumission, avec déférence; ~**ifulness** *s.* obéissance *f.*, déférence *f.*
dwarf *s.* nain *m.*; *adj.* (*small*) nain; (*stunted*) rabougri; *v.t.* (*stunt*) rabougrir; (*make look small*) rapetisser.
dwell *v.i.* (*reside*) habiter; (*stay*) rester; ~ **on,** s'appesantir sur; ~**er** *s.* habitant *m.*; ~**ing** *s.*, ~**-house,** maison d'habitation *f.*; ~**-place,** demeure *f.*
dwindle *v.i.* (*grow less*) diminuer; (*fade away*) dépérir.
dye *s.* (*colour*) teinte *f.*; (*colouring matter*) teinture *f.*; **of the deepest** ~, de la pire noirceur; *v.t.* & *i.* (se) teindre; ~ **black, green, etc.,** teindre en noir, en vert, etc.; ~**-works** *s.* teinturerie *f.*; ~**r** *s.* teinturier *m.*
dyke *see* DIKE
dynam/ic *adj.* dynamique; ~**ics** *s.* dynamique *f.* ⚠ *singular in French*; ~**ism** *s.* dynamisme *m.*
dynamite *s.* dynamite *m.*; *v.t.* dynamiter.
dynamo *s.* dynamo *m.*
dynast *s.* dynaste *m.*; ~**ic** *adj.* dynastique; ~**y** *s.* dynastie *f.*
dysentery *s.* dysenterie *f.*
dyslex/ia *s.* dyslexie *f.*; ~**ic** *adj.* & *s.m.f.* dyslexique.
dyspep/sia *s.* dyspepsie *f.*; ~**tic** *adj.* dyspeptique.
dystrophy *s.* dystrophie *f.*

E

E, e *s.* (*mus.*) mi *m.*
each *pron.* (*of two or more*) chacun(e); (*comm.*) **two francs** ~, deux fr. pièce, deux fr. chacun; *adj.* chaque; ~ **other,** l'un(e) l'autre, les un(e)s les autres; **they love** ~ **other,** ils s'aiment l'un l'autre; **they struggle against** ~ **other,** ils luttent les uns contre les autres; **they make fun of** ~ **other,** ils se moquent l'un de l'autre; ~ **way** (*betting*) gagnant et placé.
eager *adj.* **1.** (*keenly desirous, excessively so*) avide (*for*—de); **2.** (*keen to do*) empressé de faire; **3.** (*impatient for, about*) impatient de + *inf.*; **4.** (*desire, look, etc.*) ardent; **to be** ~ **to do sth.** brûler de faire qch.; ~**ly** *adv.* (1) avec avidité; (2) avec empressement; (3) avec impatience; (4) ardemment; ~**ness** *s.* (1) avidité *f.*; (2) empressement *m.*; (3) impatience *f.*; (4) ardeur *f.*
eag/le *s.* (*bird*) aigle *m.*; (*Roman ensign*) aigle *f.*; (*eccles.*) lutrin *m.*; ~**let** *s.* aiglon *m.*
E. & O. E. (*abbrev. of errors and omissions excepted*) sauf erreur ou omission.
ear *s.* (*organ of hearing; mus.; ling.*) oreille *f.*; (*sense of hearing*) ouïe *f.*; (*handle*) anse *f.*; (*of corn*) épi *m.*; **to give** ~ **to,** prêter l'oreille à; **to be all** ~**s,** être tout oreilles; **to box s.o.'s** ~**s,** souffleter qn.; **to turn a** DEAF ~ **to; to get a** FLEA **in one's** ~; **to bring a** HORNET**'s nest about one's** ~**s; to be up to the** ~**s in work etc.,** être débordé de travail, etc.; ~**ache** *s.* mal à l'oreille *m.*; ~**-drum** *s.* tympan *m.*; ~**mark** *v.t.* (*agric.*) marquer à l'oreille, (*fin.*) affecter (*for*—à), (*fig.*) (se) réserver; ~**phone** *s.* écouteur *m.*; ~**-ring** *s.* boucle d'oreille *f.*; **out of** ~**shot,** hors de portée de voix; **within** ~**-shot,** à portée de voix; ~**-trumpet** *s.* cornet acoustique *m.*- ~**wig** *s.* perce-oreille *m.*
earl *s.* comte *m.*; ~**dom** comté *m.*
early *adv.* **1.** (*near the beginning of*) au commencement de; **2.** (*in advance*) avant l'heure, en avance, tôt; **3.** (*in good time*) de bonne heure; **you are** ~, vous êtes en avance; **to get up** ~, se lever tôt; *adj.* (1) premier, matinal; (2) précoce, prématuré; (3) prompt; **the** ~ **bird catches the worm,** le monde appartient à ceux qui se lèvent tôt; ~ **closing day** *s.* demi-journée de fermeture *f.*; **at an** ~ **date,** à une date prochaine; **to be an** ~ **riser,** être matinal; ~ **fruit, vegetables,** primeurs *m.pl.*; ~ **warning** (*radar*), radar de veille lointaine *m.*; **earliness** *s.* (1) heure peu avancée *f.*; (2) arrivée prématurée *f.*; (3) ponctualité *f.*
earn *v.t.* (*gain money from work*) gagner; (*deserve*) mériter; ~**ed income,** revenus salariaux *m.pl.*; ~**ings** *s.* salaire *m.*
earnest *s.* (*money*) arrhes *f.pl.*; (*foretaste*) avant-goût *m.*; **in** ~; sérieusement; pour de bon; *adj.* **1.** (*serious*) sérieux; **2.** (*eager*) empressé; ~**ly** *adv.* (1)*; (2) avec empressement; ~**ness** *s.* (1) sérieux *m.*; (2) empressement *m.*
earth *s.* (*planet*; ≠ *sea or air*; *soil*) terre *f.*; (*ground*) sol *m.*; (*fox-hole*) terrier *m.*; (*electr.*) mise à la masse *f.*; **down-to-**~, (*thing*) terre à terre, (*person*) qui a les pieds sur terre, réaliste; **how on** ~**?,** comment diable?; **why on** ~**?,** pourquoi diable?; **to go to** ~ *v.i.* (*lit.* & *fig.*)

se terrer; **to run to ~** *v.t.* (*lit.*) acculer au terrier, (*fig.*) déterrer; **to move** HEAVEN **and ~**; **~quake** *s.* tremblement de terre *m.*; **~work** *s.* (*techn.*) terrassement *m.*; **~worm** *s.* ver de terre *m.*; **~en** *adj.* de terre, en terre; **~enware** *s.* poterie *f.*, faïence *f.*; **~ly** *adj.* terrestre; **not to stand an ~ly** (*pop.*) ne pas avoir la moindre chance (de réussir); **it's no ~ly use** (*fam.*) ça ne sert à rien du tout; **~y** *adj.* terreux; (*vulgar*) grossier; *v.t.* (*electr.*) mettre à la masse; **~ up** *v.t.* (*agric.*) butter.

ease *s.* **1.** (*freedom from pain or trouble*) aise *f.*; **2.** (*quiet*) repos *m.*; **3.** (*facility*) facilité *f.*; **4.** (*comfort*) aises *f.pl.*; **at ~**, à l'aise; **stand at ~!**, repos!; **ill at ~**, mal à l'aise; **with ~**, avec facilité; *v.t.* (1) soulager; (2) tranquilliser; (3) faciliter; (*move gently*) relâcher doucement; *v.i.* se détendre; **~ off** *v.i.* (*person*) se reposer; (*situation*) se détendre.

easel *s.* chevalet *m.*

east *s.* (*compass point*) est *m.*; **the E~** (*part of world*) Orient *m.*; **Middle E~, Near E~, Far E~**, (*geog.*) Moyen-, Proche-, Extrême-Orient *m.*; *adj.* (*geog.*) oriental; **E~ Africa,** Afrique Orientale *f.*; (*polit.*) est, de l'est; **E~ Berlin,** Berlin-Est *m.*, **E~ Germany,** Allemagne de l'Est *f.*; **~erly** *adj.* d'est; **~ern** *adj.* de l'Est, oriental; **~wards** *adv.* vers l'est.

Easter *s.* Pâques *m.sing. or f.pl.*; *adj.* de Pâques; **~ egg,** œuf de Pâques *m.*

eas/y *adj.* **1.** (*peaceful, quiet*) tranquille; **2.** (≠ *difficult*) facile; **3.** (*comfortable*) aisé; **4.** (*compliant*) docile, tolérant, doux; **5.** (*informal*) sans gêne; **6.** (*~ily obtained*) disponible; **~y** CHAIR; **~y-going** *adj.* accommodant; **to take it ~y** *v.i.* en prendre à son aise; (*fam.*) se la couler douce; **take it ~y!**, calmez-vous!; **~ily** *adv.* (1)*; (2)*; (3) confortablement; (4) docilement, avec tolérance, doucement; (5) sans gêne; **~iness** *s.* (1) tranquillité *f.*; (2) facilité *f.*; (3) aisance *f.*; (4) tolérance *f.*, douceur *f.*; (5) aisance *f.*; (6) disponibilité *f.*

eat *v.t.* (*lit.* & *fig.*) manger; *v.i.* se manger; **~ away** *v.t.* corroder; **~ into** *v.t.* ronger; **~ up** *v.t.* (*lit.* & *fig.*) dévorer; **~ your** CAKE **and have it; ~ one's** WORDS; **~s** *s.* manger *m.sing.*, (*fam.*) mangeaille *f.*; **~able** *adj.* mangeable; **~ables** *s.pl.* comestibles *m.pl.*; **~er** *s.* (*person*) mangeur *m.*, (*fruit*) fruit de table *m.*; **~ing** *s.* chère *f.*; **~ing-house** *s.* restaurant *m.*

eave(s) *s.* larmier *m.sing.*; **to ~sdrop** *v.i.* écouter aux portes; **~sdropper** *s.* personne qui écoute aux portes.

ebb *s.* **1.** (*tide*) reflux *m.*; **2.** (*fig. decline*) déclin *m.*; *v.i.* (1) refluer; (2) décliner.

ebony *s.* ébène *m.*; *adj.* d'ébène.

ebulli/ence *s.* **1.** (*boiling*) ébullition *f.*; **2.** (*exuberance*) exubérance *f.*; **~ent** *adj.* (1) bouillonnant; (2) exubérant; **~tion** *s.* (1) (*boiling*) ébullition *f.*; (2) (*outburst*) explosion *f.*

eccentric *adj.* (*math., techn., fig.*) excentrique; *s.* (*person*) excentrique *m.f.*; **~ity** *s.* excentricité *f.*

ecclesiastic *s.* ecclésiastique *m.*; *adj.* (& **~al**) ecclésiastique.

echo *s.* **1.** (*sound*) écho *m.*; **2.** (*imitation*) écho *m.*; *v.t.* (1) faire écho à; (2) répéter; *v.i.* (1) faire écho, résonner; (2) se faire l'écho de; **~-sounding device,** sondeur *m.*

eclectic *adj.* éclectique; **~ism** *s.* éclectisme *m.*

eclip/se *s.* (*lit.* & *fig.*) éclipse *f.*; *v.t.* (*lit.* & *fig.*) éclipser; **~tic** *adj.* & *s.f.* écliptique.

eclogue *s.* églogue *f.*

ecolog/y *s.* écologie *f.*; **~ical** *adj.* écologique.

econom/ic *adj.* économique; **~s** *s.* économique *f.*; (*science*) économie politique *f.*; ⚠ *sing. in French*; **~ical** *adj.* (*thrifty*) économe; (*things*) économique; **~ically** *adv.**; **~ist** *s.* personne économe; (*specialist*) économiste *m.f.*; **~ize** *v.t.* & *i.* (*use sparingly, avoid expense*) économiser; (*practise ~y*) faire des économies; **~y** *s.* économie *f.*

E.C.S.C. (*European Coal* & *Steel Community*) C.E.C.A. (Communauté européenne Charbon--Acier) *f.*

ecsta/sy *s.* (*relig., med., fig.*) extase *f.*; **to go into ~sies** (*over, about*) s'extasier (sur, devant); **~tic** *adj.* extatique.

Ecuador *s.* (*geog.*) Équateur *m.*; **~ian** *adj.* & *s.m.f.* équatorien(ne).

ecumenic(al) *adj.* œcuménique.

eczema *s.* eczéma *m.*

eddy *s.* (*whirlpool*) remous *m.*; (*smoke, etc.*) tourbillon *m.*; *v.i.* tourbillonner.

Eden *s.* (*lit.* & *fig.*) Eden *m.*, paradis terrestre *m.*

edentate *adj.* édenté.

edg/e *s.* **1.** (*cutting ~e of knife, etc.*) tranchant *m.*, (*of sword*) fil *m.*, (*of razor*) tête de coupe *f.*; **2.** (*sharpness, lit.* & *fig.*) mordant m.; **3.** (*crest*) arête *f.*; **4.** (*rim, border*) marge *f.*, bord *m.*; **5.** (*boundary*) lisière *f.*; **6.** (*of page of book, etc.*) tranche *f.*; **to be on ~e,** (*fig.*) avoir les nerfs à vif; **to give an ~e to sth.,** aiguiser qch.; **to have the ~e on s.o.** (*fig.*) avoir l'avantage sur qn.; **to take the ~e off sth.,** émousser qch.; *v.t.* (2) aiguiser; (4) border (*with*—de); **7.** (*move imperceptibly*) *v.t.* & *i.* (se) glisser, (s')insinuer; **~ed** *adj.* (1) tranchant; (4) bordé; GILT-**~ed**; **~eways** *adv.* de côté; **to be unable to get a word in ~eways,** trouver impossible de placer un mot; **~ing** *s.* bordure *f.*; **~y** *adj.* nerveux, à cran.

edib/le *adj.* comestible; (*fats, etc.*) alimentaire; **~ility** *s.* nature comestible *f.*

edict *s.* (*hist.*) édit *m.*; décret *m.*

edifice *s.* (*usu. large*) édifice *m.*

edif/y *v.t.* édifier; **~ication** *s.* édification *f.*

edit *v.t.* (*prepare for publication*) préparer pour la publication; (*act as ~or of*) diriger, être le rédacteur en chef de; (*modify*) adapter; (*cinema, TV*) monter; ⚠ éditer = **to publish; ~ing** *s.* (*film, TV*) montage *m.*; **~ion** *s.* (*form of work*) édition *f.*, (*no. of copies*) tirage *m.*; **~or** *s.* (*of newspaper*) rédacteur en chef *m.*, (*of book*) éditeur *m.*, (*of film, TV*) monteur *m.*; ⚠ éditeur = **publisher; ~orial** *s.* éditorial *m.*

educa/te *v.t.* **1.** (*bring up child*) élever; **2.** (*train*) former; **3.** (*instruct*) instruire; **well-~ted,** bien instruit; **~ble** *adj.* éducable; **~tion** *s.* (1) éducation *f.*; (2) formation *f.*; (3) enseignement *m.*, instruction *f.*; **~tional** *adj.* éducatif; **~tive** *adj.* éducatif; **~tor** *s.* éducat/eur, -rice *m.f.*

E.E.C. (*European Economic Community*) C.E.E. (Communauté européenne économique) *f.*

eel *s.* anguille *f.*

eerie *adj.* mystérieux.

efface *v.t.* effacer; **~ oneself,** s'effacer; **~ment** *s.* effacement *m.*; **self ~ment,** effacement de soi *m.*

effect *s.* effet *m.*; **~s** *s.pl.* (*property*; *theat.*) effets *m.pl.*; **in ~**, en effet; **to that ~**, à cet effet; **to bring** *or* **carry into ~**, mettre à effet; **to take ~**, prendre effet; **with ~ from,** à dater de; **to do sth. for ~**, faire des effets; **~ive** *adj.* (*having ~*) efficace; (*striking*) frappant; (*existing*) effectif; (*serviceable*): (*person*) valide, (*thing*) en service; **~ual** *adj.* efficace; *v.t.* (*bring about*) effectuer; (*accomplish*) exécuter.

effemin/acy *s.* caractère efféminé *m.*; **~ate** *adj.* efféminé.

effervesce *v.i.* (*lit.* & *fig.*) être en effervescence; **~nce** *s.* effervescence *f.*; **~nt** *adj.* (*lit.* & *fig.*) effervescent.

effete *adj.* (*worn out*) épuisé; (*feeble*) stérile.

efficac/ious *adj.* efficace; **~y, ~iousness** *s.* efficacité *f.*

efficien/cy *s.* **1.** (*competence, of person*) compétence *f.*; **2.** (*of thing*) efficacité *f.*; **~t** *adj.* (1) compétent, capable; (2) efficace; **~tly** *adv.* (1) avec compétence; (2) efficacement.

effigy *s.* effigie *f.*

effloresce *v.i.* (*chem. mineral*) effleurir; **~nce** *s.* (*lit.* & *fig.*) efflorescence *f.*; **~nt** *adj.* efflorescent.

effluen/ce *s.* émanation *f.*; **~t** *adj.* & *s.m.* effluent.

effluvium *s.* effluve *m.*

efflux *s.* écoulement *m.*

effort *s.* (*exertion*; *endeavour*) effort *m.*; (*Eng. fam. piece of work*) essai *m.*; **~less,** sans effort.

effrontery *s.* effronterie *f.*

effulgen/ce *s.* éclat *m.*; **~t** *adj.* resplendissant.

effus/ion *s.* (*lit.* & *fig.*) effusion *f.*; **~ive** *adj.* (*fig.*) exubérant.

eft *s.* triton *m.*

E.F.T.A. (*European Free Trade Association*) A.E.L.E. (Association euoropéenne de libre échange) *f.*

e.g. (*for example*) par ex. (par exemple).

egalitarian *adj.* égalitaire; *s.* égalitariste *m.f.*

egg *s.* œuf *m.*; **boiled ~,** œuf à la coque; **hard-boiled ~,** œuf dur; **fried ~,** œuf sur le plat; **poached ~,** œuf poché; **scrambled ~s,** œufs brouillés; BAD **~**; **good ~!** *interj.* (*fam.*) chic alors!; **to have all one's ~s in the same basket,** mettre tous ses œufs dans le même panier; **to teach one's grandmother to suck ~s,** apprendre à un vieux singe à faire la grimace; GOOSE **with the golden ~s**; **~-beater** *s.* batteur à œufs *m.*; **~-cup** *s.* coquetier *m.*; **~head** *s.* (*fam.*) grosse tête *f.*; **~-plant** *s.* aubergine *f.*; **~shell** *s.* coquille *f.*; **~-whisk** *s.* fouet *m.*; *v.t.* **~ s.o. on,** pousser qn. (*to do sth.*— à faire qch.).

eglantine *s.* églantine *f.*

ego *s.* ego *m.*, moi *m.*; **~centric** *adj.* & *s.m.f.* égocentrique.

ego/ism *s.* égoïsme *m.*; **~ist** *s.* égoïste *m.f.*; **~istic** *adj.* égoïste; **~tism** *s.* égotisme *m.*; **~tist** *s.* égotiste *m.f.*; **~tistical** *adj.* égotiste.

egregious *adj.* (*pej.*) (*outrageous*) insigne; (*notorious*) notoire.

egress *s.* (*going out, way out*) sortie *f.*

egret *s.* (*bird*) aigrette *f.*

Egypt *s.* Egypte *f.*; **~ian** *adj.* & *s.m.f.* égyptien (ne); **~ologist** *s.* égyptologue *m.f.*

eh *interj.* (*inquiry*) hein?; (*surprise*) hé!, eh!

eider *s.* (*bird*) eider *m.*; **~down** *s.* édredon *m.*

eight *s.* & *adj.* huit; **to have one over the ~** (*pop.*) prendre une biture; **~fold,** huit fois autant; **~h** *adj.* & *s.m.f.* huitième.

eighteen *s.* & *adj.* dix-huit; **~th** *adj.* & *s.m.f.* dix-huitième.

eight/y *s.* & *adj.* quatre-vingts; *N.B. no 's' if another number follows,* **~y five,** quatre-vingt-cinq; **~ieth** *adj.* & *s.m.f.* quatre-vingtième.

either *pron.* (*each of two*) l'un et l'autre; *adj.* (*one or other of two*) l'un ou l'autre; **~ . . . or,** ou (bien) . . . ou (bien), soit . . . soit; **it's ~ right or wrong, you must decide,** ou bien c'est vrai, ou bien c'est faux, il faut décider; **we shall have dinner ~ before or after the meeting,** on dînera soit avant, soit après, la réunion; *adv.* non plus; **I haven't seen him ~,** je ne l'ai pas vu, non plus.

ejaculat/e *v.i.* **1.** (*cry out*) s'écrier; **2.** *v.t.* (*eject fluids from body*) éjaculer; **~ion** *s.* (1) exclamation *f.*; (2) éjaculation *f.*; **~ory** *adj.* (*eccles.*) (oraison) jaculatoire.

eject *v.t.* (*throw out*) chasser; (*person*) expulser; (*thing*) rejeter; (*emit*) émettre; *v.i.* (*aviat.*) se faire éjecter; **~ion** *s.* expulsion *f.*; éjection *f.*; **~or** *s.* (*mil.*) éjecteur *m.*; (*aviat.*) siège éjectable *m.*

eke, ~out *v.t.* économiser.

elaborat/e *v.t.* élaborer; *adj.* **1.** (*detailed*) détaillé, minutieux; **2.** (*highly finished*) soigné, travaillé; **~eness** *s.* (1) minutie *f.*; (2) travail *m.*; **~ion** *s.* élaboration *f.*

elapse *v.i.* s'écouler.

elastic *adj.* & *s.m.* (*lit.* & *fig.*) élastique; **~ band** *s.* élastique *m.*; **~ity** *s.* élasticité *f.*

elat/e *v.t.* **1.** (*delight*) ravir; **2.** (*make proud*) enorgueillir; **be ~ed about,** s'enorgueillir de; **~ion** *s.* (1) transport *m.*; (2) orgueil *m.*

elbow *s.* (*part of body, ~-shaped thing*) coude *m.*; **to lean one's ~s on,** s'accouder sur; **~-grease** *s.* (*fam.*) huile de coude *f.*; **~-rest** *s.* accoudoir *m.*; **to have ~-room,** avoir ses coudées franches; *v.t.* coudoyer; *v.i.* jouer des coudes.

eld/er[1] *adj.* plus âgé; *adj.* & *s.m.f.* aîné(e); **~ers** (*of a tribe or society*) anciens *m.pl.*; (*older people*) personnes plus âgées *f.pl.*; **~erly** *adj.* d'un certain âge; **~est** *adj.* le plus âgé; *adj.* & *s.m.f.* l'aîné(e).

elder[2] *s.* (*tree*) sureau *m.*; **~-berry** *s.* baie de sureau *f.*

E.L.D.O. (*abbrev. European Launcher Development Organisation*) CECLES *m.* (Conseil Européen pour la construction des lanceurs d'engins spatiaux).

Eldorado *s.* Eldorado *m.*

elect *v.t.* **1.** (*choose*) choisir; **2.** (*by vote*) élire; **3.** (*eccles.*) élire; *adj.* futur (*before the noun*); *s. pl.* les élus *m.pl.*; **~ed** *adj.* élu; **~ion** *s.* (2) élection *f.*; **by -~ion,** élection partielle *f.*; **~ioneer** *v.i.* (2) faire de la propagande électorale; **~ioneering** *s.* propagande électorale *f.*; **~or** *s.* élect/eur, -rice *m.f.*; **~oral** *adj.* électoral; **~orate** *s.* (hist.) électorat *m.*; (2) électeurs *m.pl.*; **~ive** *adj.* électif.

electr/ic *adj.* (*lit.* & *fig.*) électrique; **~ic** BLANKET; **~ic chair** *s.* chaise électrique *f.*; **~ic current** *s.* courant électrique *m.*; **~ic fire/heater** *s.* radiateur électrique *m.*; **~ic lamp** *s.* lampe électrique *f.*; **~ic shock** *s.* secousse électrique *m.*; **~ic torch** *s.* lampe électrique *f.*; **~ical** *adj.* électrique; **~ical engineer** *s.* ingénieur électricien *m.*; **~ician** *s.* électricien *m.*; **~icity** *s.* électricité *f.*; **~ify** *v.t.* électrifier, (*fig.*) électriser; **~ification** *s.* électrification *f.*, (*fig.*) galvanisation *f.*

electro- (*in combination*) **~cardiogram** *s.* électrocardiogramme *m.*; **~cardiograph** *s.* électrocardiographe *m.*; **~cute** *v.t.* électrocuter; **~cution** *s.* électrocution *f.*; **~dynamics** *s.* électrodynamique *f.* ⚠ *sing. in French*; **~lysis** *s.* électrolyse *f.*; **~magnet** *s.* électro-aimant *m.*; **~magnetic** *adj.* électromagnétique; **~meter** *s.* électromètre *m.*; **~plate(d)** *adj.* & *s.m.* plaqué à l'électricité.

electr/ode *s.* électrode *f.*; **~on** *s.* électron *m.*; **~onic** *adj.* électronique; **~onics** *s.* électronique *f.* ⚠ *sing. in French*; **~um** *s.* électrum *m.*

elegan/ce *s.* élégance *f.*; **~t** *adj.* élégant.

eleg/y *s.* élégie *f.*; **~iac** *adj.* élégiaque.

element *s.* **1.** (*chem.*; *component part*; *fig.*) élément *m.*; **to be in one's ~,** être dans son élement; **~s** *pl.* **2.** (*weather*) éléments *m.pl.*; **3.** (*rudiments*) éléments *m.pl.*; **~al** *adj.* (1) élémentaire; (2) des éléments; (3) primordial; **~ary** *adj.* (3) (*rudimentary*) élémentaire; (*unanalysable*) simple.

elephant *s.* éléphant *m.*; **a white ~** (*fig.*) un objet inutile et encombrant *m.*; **~iasis** *s.* éléphantiasis *f.*; **~ine** *adj.* éléphantesque.

elevat/e *v.t.* (*lit.* & *fig.*) élever; **~ion** *s.* (*raising*; *exaltation*; *height*) élévation *f.*; (*arch.*) coupe transversale *f.*; **~or** *s.* (*hoisting machine*) monte-charge *m.*, élévateur *m.*; (*grain-store*) silo *m.*; (*aviat.*) gouvernail d'altitude (*or* de profondeur) *m.*; (*U.S. lift*) ascenseur *m.*

eleven *adj.* & *s.* onze *m.*; (*sport* = *team*) équipe *f.*; **~ses** *s.* (*pop.*) casse-croûte *f.*; **~th** *adj.* & *s.*

onzième; ⚠ le onze, le onzième (*no elision*); **at the ~th hour,** au dernier moment.
elf *s.* elfe *m.*; **~in** *adj.* féerique.
elicit *v.t.* (*obtain, answer, etc.*) obtenir; (*discover, truth, facts*) dévoiler; (*cause*) provoquer.
elide *v.t.* élider.
eligib/le *adj.* (*fit to be chosen, etc.*) éligible (à); (*desirable*) désirable; **~ility** *s.* éligibilité *f.*
eliminat/e *v.t.* éliminer; **~ion** *s.* élimination *f.*
elision *s.* élision *f.*
élite *s.* élite *f.*
elixir *s.* élixir *m.*
elk *s.* élan *m.*
ell *s.* (*obs.*) aune *f.*; **give him an** INCH **and he'll take an ~.**
ellip/se *s.* ellipse *f.*; **~tic(al)** *adj.* elliptique.
ellip/sis *s.* ellipse *f.*; **~tical** *adj.* elliptique.
elm *s.* (*tree*) orme *m.*
elocution *s.* élocution *f.*; (*manner of speaking, art*) diction *f.*; **~ist** *s.* professeur de diction *m.f.*
elongat/e *v.t.* allonger; **~ion** *s.* allongement *m.*
elope *v.i.* s'enfuir (de la maison paternelle avec un amant), se laisser enlever; **~ment** *s.* enlèvement *m.*
eloquen/ce *s.* éloquence *f.*; **~t** *adj.* éloquent; **~tly** *adv.* avec éloquence.
else *adj.* autre; **anything, something ~,** qch. d'autre; **anybody, somebody ~,** qn. d'autre; **nobody ~,** personne d'autre; **nothing ~,** rien d'autre; **what ~?** quoi de plus?; *adv.* (*of place*) ailleurs; **nowhere ~,** nulle part ailleurs; **somewhere, anywhere ~,** n'importe où ailleurs; (*of manner*) autrement; **or ~,** ou bien, autrement; **~where** *adv.* ailleurs.
elucidat/e *v.t.* élucider; **~ion** *s.* élucidation *f.*
elu/de *v.t.* (*escape from*) éluder; (*avoid*) éviter; (*fig. baffle*) dépasser; **~sive** *adj.* évasif, difficile à saisir; **~siveness** *s.* caractère évasif *m.*, nature insaisissable *f.*; **~sory** *adj.* fuyant.
Elysi/um *s.* Élysée *m.*; **~an** *adj.* élyséen; **~an Fields,** Champs Élysées.
emaciat/e *v.t.* (*of face*) émacier; amaigrir; **~ed** *adj.* émacié; **~ion** *s.* émaciation *f.*, amaigrissement *m.*
emanat/e *v.i.* émaner (*from*—de); **~ion** *s.* émanation *f.*
emancipat/e *v.t.* (*law, fig.*) émanciper; **~ion** *s.* émancipation *f.*; **~or** *s.* émancipateur *m.*
emasculat/e *v.t.* (*lit. & fig.*) émasculer; *adj.* émasculé; **~ion** *s.* émasculation *f.*
embalm *v.t.* (*preserve, lit. & fig.*; *make fragrant*) embaumer; **~ing** *s.* embaumement *m.*
embank *v.t.* **1.** (*river*) endiguer; **2.** (*road*) remblayer; **~ment** *s.* (1) digue *f.*; (2) remblai *m.*
embargo *s.* embargo *m.*; **to lay an ~ on,** mettre l'embargo sur.
embark *v.t.* & *i.* **1.** (*on ship*) (s')embarquer; **2.** (*on course*) s'embarquer (dans); **~ation** *s.* embarquement *m.*; ⚠ embarcation = **small boat.**
embarrass *v.t.* **1.** (*encumber, esp. with debt*) embarrasser; **2.** (*confuse*) gêner; **~ment** *s.* (1) embarras *m.*; (2) gêne *f.*
embassy *s.* ambassade *f.*
embattle *v.t.* (*mil.*) ranger en bataille; **~d** *adj.* (*herald.*) bastillé; (*arch.*) crénelé.
embed *v.t.* (*techn.*) encastrer; (*fig.*) fixer.
embellish *v.t.* (*adorn*) embellir; (*enrich*) enrichir; **~ment** *s.* embellissement *m.*
ember *s.* (*live coal or wood*) tison *m.*; **~s** *pl.* (*hot ashes*) braises *f.pl.*; **~ days,** Quatre-Temps *m.pl.*
embezzle *v.t.* détourner; **~ment** *s.* détournement (de fonds) *m.*
embitter *v.t.* (*quarrel, etc.*) envenimer; (*person*) aigrir.
emblazon *v.t.* (*herald.*) blasonner; (*fig.*) exalter.
emblem *s.* emblème *m.*
embod/y *v.t.* (*clothe with body, & fig.*) incarner; (*give concrete form to*) concrétiser; (*incorporate in*) incorporer (à, dans); **~iment** *s.* incarnation *f.*
embolden *v.t.* enhardir.
embolism *s.* embolie *f.*
emboss *v.t.* (*paper*) gaufrer; (*art*) travailler en relief; ⚠ embosser *is a naut. term.*
embrace *s.* étreinte *f.*; *v.t.* (*lit. & fig.*) embrasser.
embrasure *s.* embrasure *f.*
embrocation *s.* embrocation *f.*
embroider *v.t.* **1.** (*needlework*) broder; **2.** (*embellish, with fictitious detail*) enjoliver; **~y** *s.* (1) broderie *f.*; (2) enjolivement *m.*
embroil *v.t.* **1.** (*bring into confusion*) embrouiller; **2.** (*involve in hostility*) brouiller; **~ment** *s.* (1) embrouillement *m.*; (2) brouille *f.*
embryo *s.* (*lit.* & *fig.*) embryon *m.*; **~nic** *adj.* embryonnaire.
emend *v.t.* émender; **~ation** *s.* émendation *f.*
emerald *s.* émeraude *f.*
emerge *v.i.* apparaître; **~ from** (*lit.* & *fig.*) émerger de; **~nce** *s.* émergence *f.*; **~ncy** *s.* crise *f.*; (*unexpected event*) éventualité *f.*; **case of ~ncy,** cas d'urgence, *m.*; **state of ~ncy,** état d'urgence *m.*; **~ncy** *adj.* provisoire, de fortune; **~ncy exit,** sortie de secours *f.*; **~nt** *adj.* qui émerge; (*nation*) en voie de développement.
emeritus *adj.* honoraire.
emery *s.* émeri *m.*; **~-cloth, -paper,** toile *f.*, papier *m.* (d')émeri.
emetic *adj.* & *s.m.* émétique.
emigr/ant *s.* émigrant(e) *m.f.*; (*polit. hist.*) émigré(e) *m.f.*; **~ate** *v.i.* émigrer; **~ation** *s.* émigration *f.*
eminen/ce *s.* (*high ground*; *superiority*; *cardinal's title*), éminence *f.*; **~t** *adj.* éminent; **~tly** *adv.* éminemment.
emir *s.* émir *m.*; **~ate** *s.* émirat *m.*
emissary *s.* émissaire *m.*
emi/t *v.t.* émettre; **~ssion** *s.* émission *f.*
emollient *adj.* & *s.m.* émollient.
emoluments *s.pl.* émoluments *m.pl.*
emot/ion *s.* (*feeling*) émotion *f.*; (*excited state*) émoi *m.*; **~ional** *adj.* (*concerning the ~s*) émotionnel; (*given to ~*) émotionnable; (*causing ~*) émotif; **~ive** *adj.* émotif.
empanel *v.t.* inscrire sur la liste du jury.
empathy *s.* compréhension *f.*
emperor *s.* empereur *m.*; *see* EMPRESS.
empha/sis *s.* **1.** (*stress on words*) accent *m.*; **2.** (*vigour of expression*) force *f.*; **3.** (*importance*) importance *f.*, poids *m.*; ⚠ emphase = **pomposity; ~size** *v.t.* (1) accentuer; (2) donner de la force à; (3) appuyer sur, souligner; **~tic** *adj.* (1) accentué; (2) énergique.
empire *s.* (*lit.* & *fig.*) empire *m.*
empiric/al *adj.* empirique; **~ism** *s.* empirisme *m.*
emplacement *s.* emplacement *m.*
employ *s.* service *m.*; *v.t.* employer (*as, for*—comme, à); **~ee** *s.* employé(e) *m.f.*; **~ment** *s.* emploi *m.*; **~or** *s.* employ/eur, -euse *m.f.*, patron(ne) *m.f.*
emporium *s.* grand magasin *m.*
empower *v.t.* (*authorize*) autoriser (à); (*law*) habiliter (à); (*enable*) rendre capable de.
empress *s.* impératrice *f.*
empt/y *adj.* (*containing nothing*) vide; (*void of*) vide de; (*vacant*) libre; (*fam. hungry*) qui a un creux dans l'estomac; (*fam. frivolous*) vain, creux; (*of ships, etc.*) à vide; *s.* (*bottle*) cadavre de bouteille *m.*; *v.t.* & *i.* (se) vider; (*river*) se jeter; **~iness** *s.* vide *m.*
empyrean *adj.* & *s.m.* empyrée.
emu *s.* émeu *m.*
emulat/e *v.t.* rivaliser avec; (*imitate*) imiter; **~ion** *s.* émulation *f.*; **~or** *s.* émule *m.f.*

emuls/ion *s.* émulsion *f.*; **~ion paint,** peinture vinylique *f.*; **~ify** *v.t.* émulsionner.
enable *v.t.* (*empower*) mettre à même de, rendre capable de; (*supply with means*) donner (à qn.) les moyens de.
enact *v.t.* **1.** (*make law*) promulguer; **2.** (*ordain*) décréter; **3.** (*play part*) représenter; **~ment** *s.* (1) promulgation *f.*; (2) décret *m.*
enamel *s.* émail *m.* (*pl.* émaux); *v.t.* émailler.
enamour *v.t.* séduire; **to become ~ed of,** s'éprendre de; **to be ~ed of,** être épris de.
encage *v.t.* mettre en cage.
encamp *v.t.* & *i.* (faire) camper; **~ment** *s.* campement *m.*
encase *v.t.* (*put in case*) emballer (*in*—dans); (*surround*) revêtir (*in*—de).
encash *v.t.* encaisser; **~ment** *s.* encaissement *m.*
encephal/ic *adj.* encéphalique; **~ogram** *s.* & **~ograph** *s.* encéphalogramme *m.*; **~ography** *s.* encéphalographie *f.*
enchant *v.t.* (*lit.* & *fig.*) enchanter; **~er, ~ress** *s.* enchant/eur, -eresse *m.f.*; **~ing** *adj.* ravissant; **~ment** *s.* enchantement *m.*
encircle *v.t.* encercler.
enclave *s.* enclave *f.*
enclitic *adj.* & *s.m.* (*ling.*) enclitique.
enclos/e *v.t.* **1.** (*surround*) entourer; **2.** (*shut up*) enfermer; **3.** (*hem in*) renfermer; **4.** (*frame*) encadrer; **5.** (*put in letter*) joindre (à); **~ed** *adj.* (5) ci-joint; **the ~ed copy,** la copie ci-jointe; **please find ~ed a copy,** vous trouverez ci--joint une copie; **~ed order** (*eccles.*) ordre cloîtré *m.*; **~ure** *s.* (1) clôture *f.*, enclos *m.*; (5) pièce jointe *f.*
enconium *s.* panégyrique *m.*
encompass *v.t.* (*surround*) entourer; (*contain*) renfermer; (*bring about*) occasionner.
encore *interj.* bis!; *v.t.* bisser; *s.* rappel *m.*
encounter *s.* **1.** (*hostile*) combat *m.*; **2.** (*casual*) rencontre *f.*; *v.t.* (1) affronter; (2) rencontrer (par hasard).
encourag/e *v.t.* encourager; (*promote*) appuyer; **~ement** *s.* encouragement *m.*; **~ing** *adj.* encourageant.
encroach *v.t.* (*on*) **1.** (*on property, rights*) empiéter sur; **2.** (*on s.o.'s time, etc.*) abuser de; **~ment** *s.* (1) empiétement *m.*; (2) abus *m.*
encumb/er *v.t.* **1.** (*hamper, impede*) encombrer, entraver; **2.** (*burden with debt*) accabler; (*law* & *fin.*) grever; **~rance** *s.* (1) encombrement *m.*, entrave *f.*; (2) (*mortgage, etc.*) charge *f.*
encyclical *s.* encyclique *f.*
encycloped/ia *s.* encyclopédie *f.*; **~ic** *adj.* encyclopédique; **~ist** *s.* encyclopédiste *m.f.*
end *s.* (*limit*) limite *f.*; (*extreme point; remnant*) bout *m.*; (*conclusion*) fin *f.*; (*destruction*) fin *f.*; (*death*) mort *f.*; (*result*) résultat *m.*; (*object*) but *m.*; **in the ~,** enfin, après tout; DEAD **~**; **thin ~ of** WEDGE; **wrong ~ of the** STICK; **odds and ~s,** bouts *m.pl.*; **to make both ~s meet,** joindre les deux bouts; **to be at one's wits' ~,** ne pas savoir où donner de la tête; **to be at a loose ~,** être désœuvré; **to come to a** BAD **~**; **to go off the** DEEP **~**; **to put an ~ to,** mettre fin à; **to be on one's** BEAM **~s**; **to** BURN **the candle at both ~s**; **on ~** (*upright*) debout; (*continuously*) de suite, **for months on ~,** des mois de suite; **to stand on ~** (*hair*) se dresser; **~-game** *s.* (*chess*) fin de partie *f.*; **~-paper** *s.* feuille de garde *f.*; **~-product** *s.* produit fini *m.*; **~ing** *s.* fin *f.*, (*ling.*) terminaison *f.*; **never-~ing** *adj.* interminable; **~less** *adj.* sans fin, incessant; **~ways,** bout à bout; *v.t.* finir, achever; *v.i.* finir, prendre fin; **~ by, ~ in,** finir par, en; **he will ~ by killing himself in an accident,** il finira par se faire tuer dans un accident; **he will ~ in having nothing left,** il finira par ne plus rien avoir; **he ~ed by winning the game,** il finit le jeu en gagnant la partie; ALL**'s well that ~s well.**
endanger *v.t.* mettre en danger.
endear *v.t.* rendre cher; **~ oneself to s.o.,** se faire aimer de qn.; **~ing** *adj.* attachant; **~ment** *s.* tendresse *f.*; *pl.* (*words*) mots tendres *m.pl.*
endeavour *s.* effort *m.*; (*attempt*) tentative *f.*; *v.i.* **~ to,** s'efforcer de.
endemic *adj.* endémique.
endive *s.* escarole *or* scarole *f.*; ⚠ endive = **chicory.**
endorse *v.t.* **1.** (*cheque or document*) endosser; **2.** (*make payable to s.o.*) transmettre à qn. par voie d'endossement; **3.** (*law, driving licence*) porter une contravention sur le permis de conduire; **4.** (*confirm*) confirmer; **5.** (*approve*) approuver; **~ment** *s.* (1) & (2) endos *m.*; (3) inscription d'une contravention sur le permis de conduire *f.*; (4) confirmation *f.*; (5) approbation *f.*
endow *v.t.* **1.** (*give permanent income to*) doter; **2.** (*invest with powers*) revêtir de, (*with qualities*) douer de; **~ment** *s.* (1) dotation *f.*; (2) don *m.*
endue *v.t.* (*with*) habiller (de); (*fig.*) douer de.
endur/e *v.t.* (*undergo*) souffrir; (*bear*) supporter; *v.i.* (*last*) durer; **~able** *adj.* supportable; **~ance** *s.* (*resistance to pain, fatigue, etc.*) endurance *f.*; (*hardship*) épreuves *f.pl.*; **~ing** *adj.* (*resistant*) endurant; (*lasting*) durable.
enema *s.* lavement *m.*
enemy *adj.* & *s.m.f.* ennemi(e); **to** CARRY **the war into the ~'s camp.**
energ/y *s.* énergie *f.*; **~etic** *adj.* énergique; **~etically** *adv.**; ⚠ énergétique = **relating to energy (power)**; **~ize** *v.t.* activer.
enervat/e *v.t.* affaiblir; ⚠ énerver = **to exasperate**; **~ion** *s.* affaiblissement *m.*
enfeeble *v.t.* affaiblir; **~ment** *s.* affaiblissement *m.*
enfold *v.t.* (*wrap*) envelopper (*in*—dans); (*embrace*) étreindre.
enforce *v.t.* **1.** (*press, urge*) forcer; **2.** (*compel observance of*) imposer qch. à qn.; (*law*) faire exécuter, faire respecter; **3.** (*strengthen*) renforcer, appuyer; **~ment** *s.* (1) contrainte *f.*; (2) application *f.*; (3) renforcement *m.*
enfranchise *v.t.* **1.** (*set free*) affranchir; **2.** (*give vote to*) donner le droit de vote à; **~ment** *s.* (1) affranchissement *m.*; (2) octroi du droit de vote *m.*
engag/e *v.t.* & *i.* **1.** (*bind by promise*) (s')engager, (*of marriage*) (se) fiancer; **2.** (*pledge oneself to*) s'engager à; **3.** (*hire*) louer, (*reserve*) retenir, réserver; **4.** (*fit, interlock, with*) (s')engager; **5.** (*gear*) (s')embrayer; **6.** (*mil.*) **~e the enemy,** engager le combat; **7.** (*employ*) engager, (*keep busy*) occuper; **8. ~ in,** se mêler de, s'occuper de; **~ed** (*notice on door*) occupé; **~ement** *s.* (1) engagement *m.*, fiançailles *f.pl.*; (6), (7). engagement *m.*; (*appointment*) rendez-vous *m.*; **~ing** *adj.* engageant.
engender *v.t.* engendrer.
engine *s.* (*mech.*) machine *f.*; (*auto.*) moteur *m.*; (*rail.*) locomotive *f.*; (*means*) engin *m.*; FIRE-**~**; STEAM-**~**; **~-driver** *s.* mécanicien *m.*; **~-room** *s.* chambre des machines *f.*; **~** SPEED; **~er** *s.* ingénieur *m.*; (*mil.*) soldat, officier, etc. du génie *m.*; (*civil*) ingénieur civil *m.*; (*mech.*) mécanicien *m.*; (*electr.*) électricien *m.*; **~er** *v.t.* (construct) construire; (*contrive*) manigancer; **~ering** *s.* génie civil *m.*
Engl/and *s.* Angleterre *f.*; **~ish** *adj.* & *s.m.* (*language*) anglais; **~man, ~woman,** Anglais(e) *m.f.*; **~ish Channel,** la Manche.
engrain *v.t.* teindre, imprégner; (*fig.*) enraciner.
engrav/e *v.t.* (*lit.* & *fig.*) graver; **~er** *s.* graveur *m.*; **~ing** *s.* gravure *f.*
engross *v.t.* (*law: document*) grossoyer; (*monopolize*) monopoliser; (*absorb*) absorber.

engulf *v.t.* engloutir.
enhance *v.t.* **1.** (*heighten*) rehausser; **2.** (*exaggerate*) exagérer; **~ment** *s.* (1) rehaussement *m.*; (2) embellissement *m.*
enigma *s.* énigme *f.*; **~tic** *adj.* énigmatique.
enjoin *v.t.* (*prescribe*) prescrire (qch. à qn.); (*command s.o. to do sth.*) enjoindre à qn. de faire qch.
enjoy *v.t.* (*find pleasure in*) prendre plaisir à; **2.** (*have benefit of*) jouir de; **~ oneself,** s'amuser; **~able** *adj.* agréable; **~ment** *s.* (1) plaisir *m.*; (2) jouissance *f.*
enlace *v.t.* enlacer.
enlarge *v.t.* & *i.* (s')agrandir; (*expatiate on*) discourir longuement sur; **~ment** *s.* agrandissement *m.*
enlighten *v.t.* **1.** (*instruct*) éclairer, (*eccles.*) édifier; **2.** (*inform*) mettre au courant; **3.** (*shed light on*) éclairer; **~ment** *s.* (1) lumières *f.pl.*; (2) renseignements *m.pl.*; (3) éclaircissement *m.*
enlist *v.t.* & *i.* (*mil.*) (s')enrôler; (*get support of*) gagner qn. à sa cause; **~ment** *s.* enrôlement *m.*
enliven *v.t.* animer; (*cheer*) égayer; (*stimulate*) stimuler.
enmesh *v.t.* (*lit.*) prendre dans les rets; (*mech.*) engrener; (*fig.*) empêtrer.
enmity *s.* inimitié *f.*
ennoble *v.t.* **1.** (*lit.*) anoblir; **2.** (*fig.*) ennoblir; **~ment** *s.* (1) anoblissement *m.*; (2) ennoblissement *m.*
enorm/ity *s.* **1.** (*great wickedness*) monstruosité *f.*; **2.** (*crime*) atrocité *f.*; **3.** (*hugeness*) énormité *f.*; **~ous** *adj.* (3) énorme; (*fig.*) monstrueux; **~ously** *adv.* énormément.
enough *adj.* assez de; *adv.* assez, suffisamment; **to be ~,** suffire; *s.* suffisance *f.*; **~ apples,** assez de pommes; **I have had ~,** j'en ai assez; **that's ~,** cela suffit; **five men are ~,** cinq hommes suffisent; **he is rich ~ to pay,** il est suffisamment riche pour payer.
enquire *see* INQUIRE.
enrage *v.t.* rendre furieux; faire enrager; ⚠ enrager *v.i.* = **to be very angry**; **~d** *adj.* enragé.
enrapture *v.t.* ravir.
enrich *v.t.* enrichir (*with*—de); (*agric.*) fertiliser; **~ment** *s.* enrichissement *m.*
enrol *v.t.* & *i.* **1.** (*mil.*) (s')enrôler; **2.** (*as member*) (s')inscrire; **3.** (*register, deed, etc.*) enregistrer; **~ment** *s.* (1) enrôlement *m.*; (2) inscription *f.*; (3) enregistrement *m.*
ensconce, oneself *v.refl.* se blottir.
ensemble *s.* ensemble *m.*
enshrine *v.t.* enchâsser; (*fig.*) conserver; (*fam.*) mettre sous globe.
enshroud *v.t.* envelopper.
ensign *s.* (*badge, emblem*) insigne *m.*; (*flag, naut.*) pavillon *m.*; (*hist. mil. rank*) porte-drapeau *m.*; (*U.S. navy*) enseigne de vaisseau *m.*
enslave *v.t.* asservir; **~ment** *s.* asservissement *m.*
ensnare *v.t.* prendre au piège.
ensu/e *v.i.* **1.** (*happen later*) suivre; **2.** (*result from*) s'ensuivre de; **~ing** *adj.* (1) suivant; (2) qui s'ensuit.
ensure *v.t.* assurer (*against*—contre); **~ that,** s'assurer que.
entail *v.t.* **1.** (*law—property*) substituer; **2.** (*necessitate*) entraîner; **~ment** *s.* (1) substitution *f.*; (2) suite *f.*
entangle *v.t.* **1.** (*lit.* & *fig. snare*) empêtrer; **2.** (*make tangled*) emmêler; **3.** (*complicate*) embrouiller; **~ment** *s.* (1) enchevêtrement *m.*; (2) emmêlement *m.*; (3) embrouillement *m.*
enter *v.t.* (*admit, procure admission for*) faire entrer; (*insert record of*) inscrire; ⚠ entrer *is not transitive in French*; **~ a room** = entrer dans une pièce; *v.i.* (*go or come in*(*to*)) entrer; (*penetrate*) pénétrer (dans); (*theat.*) entrer; (*become member of club, etc.*) adhérer à; (*put name on list, etc.*) se faire inscrire; **~** (*for*) **a competition,** se porter concurrent; **~ into,** (*bargain*) faire, conclure (un marché); (*feelings*) partager (les sentiments de qn.); **~ (up)on,** (*begin*) commencer, (*undertake*) entreprendre, (*inherit*) entrer en jouissance de.
enter/itis *s.* entérite *f.*; **~ic** *adj.* entérique.
enterpris/e *s.* (*bold undertaking*) entreprise *f.*; (*initiative*) esprit d'entreprise *m.*; **~ing** *adj.* entreprenant, aventureux.
entertain *v.t.* **1.** (*as guest*) recevoir; **2.** (*amuse*) amuser; **3.** (*harbour, doubts, etc.*) nourrir; **4.** (*consider*) entretenir; **~er** *s.* (2) amuseur *m.*; **~ing** *adj.* (2) divertissant; **~ment** *s.* (1) hospitalité *f.*; (2) divertissement *m.*
enthral *v.t.* (*enslave*) asservir; (*captivate*) captiver.
enthrone *v.t.* introniser; **~ment** *s.* intronisation *f.*
enthus/e *v.i.* s'enthousiasmer (*about*—pour); **~iasm** *s.* enthousiasme *m.*; **~iast** *s.* enthousiaste *m.f.*; **~iastic** *adj.* enthousiaste; **~iastically** *adv.* avec enthousiasme.
entic/e *v.t.* **1.** (*attract*) attirer; **2.** (*seduce*) séduire; **~ement** *s.* (1) attrait *m.*; (2) séduction *f.*; **~ing** *adj.* séduisant; **~ingly** *adv.* d'une manière séduisante.
entire *adj.* (*complete, of one piece, not castrated* (*animal*)) entier; (*not broken*) complet; **~ly** *adv.* entièrement; **~ty** *s.* totalité *f.*; **in its ~ty,** dans son entier.
entitle *v.t.* **1.** (*give title to book, etc.*) intituler; **2.** (*give right or claim to*) donner droit à qn. de; **to be ~d to,** avoir le droit de; **~ment** *s.* (2) droit *m.*
entity *s.* entité *f.*
entomb *v.t.* (*place in tomb*) enterrer; (*serve as tomb for*) ensevelir.
entomolog/y *s.* entomologie *f.*; **~ical** *adj.* entomologique; **~ist** *s.* entomologiste *m.f.*
entrails *s.pl.* (*lit.* & *fig.*) entrailles *f.pl.*
entrain *v.t.* & *i.* (s')embarquer en chemin de fer; (*fig.*) entraîner.
entran/ce[1] *s.* (*coming in, right of admission, door*) entrée *f.*; **no ~ce,** entrée interdite; *adj.* d'entrée; **~ce fee,** droits d'entrée *m.pl.*; **~ce-hall,** vestibule *m.*; **~t** *s.* arrivant *m.*; (*sport*) participant *m.*
entranc/e[2] *v.t.* transporter (de); **~ing** *adj.* ravissant.
entreat *v.t.* (*ask earnestly*) supplier; (*beg*) implorer (*to do*—de faire); **~ingly** *adv.* d'un ton suppliant, avec instance; **~y** *s.* supplication *f.*
entrench *v.t.* (*surround with trench*) retrancher; (*encroach upon*) empiéter sur; *v.refl.* se retrancher.
entrust *v.t.* (*charge s.o. with sth.*) charger qn. de qch.; (*confide sth. to s.o.*) confier qch. à qn.
entry *s.* (*coming or going in, entrance, item entered*) entrée *f.*; (*alley*) ruelle *f.*; (*for exam.*) inscription *f.*; **~ fee,** droits d'inscription *m.pl.*; **no ~,** entrée interdite; (*road sign*) sens interdit.
entwine *v.t.* entrelacer.
enumerat/e *v.t.* énumérer; **~ion** *s.* énumération *f.*
enunciat/e *v.t.* **1.** (*state definitely*) énoncer; **2.** (*proclaim*) proclamer; **3.** (*pronounce distinctly*) articuler; **~ion** *s.* (1) énonciation *f.*; (2) proclamation *f.*; (3) articulation *f.*
envelop *v.t.* envelopper (*in*—de); **~ment** *s.* enveloppement *m.*
envelope *s.* enveloppe *f.*
enviable, envious *see* ENVY.
environ *v.t.* environner (de); **~s** *s.pl.* environs *m.pl.*; **~ment** *s.* environnement *m.*, (*fig.*) milieu *m.*; **~mental** *adj.* de l'environnement; dû au milieu.
envisage *v.t.* (*face*) faire face à; (*visualize, contemplate*) envisager.
envoy *s.* émissaire *m.*, plénipotentiaire *m.*

env/y *s.* (*emotion*) envie *f.*; (*thing* **~***ied*) objet d'envie *m.*; **to be** GREEN **with ~y**; *v.t.* envier qn.; envier qch. à qn.; **~iable** *adj.* enviable; **~ious** *adj.* envieux (de).
enzyme *s.* (*chem.*) enzyme *f.*
epaulet(**te**) *s.* épaulette *f.*
ephemera *s.* éphémère *m.*; **~l** *adj.* éphémère.
epic *s.* épopée *f.*; *adj.* épique.
epicur/e *s.* gourmet *m.*; **~ean** *adj.* & *s.m.f.* épicurien(ne).
epidemic *s.* épidémie *f.*; *adj.* épidémique.
epiderm/is *s.* épiderme *m.*; **~ic** *adj.* épidermique.
epidiascope *s.* lanterne magique *f.*
epigram *s.* épigramme *m.*; **~matic** *adj.* épigrammatique.
epigraph *s.* épigraphe *f.*
epilep/sy *s.* épilepsie *f.*; **~tic** *adj.* & *s.m.f.* épileptique.
epilogue *s.* épilogue *m.*
epiphany *s.* Épiphanie *f.*
episcop/acy *s.* **1.** (*govt. by bishops*) gouvernement par les évêques *m.*; **2.** (*bishops*) épiscopat *m.*; **~al** *adj.* (1) & (2) épiscopal; **~alian** *adj.* épiscopal; **~ate** *s.* épiscopat *m.*
episod/e *s.* épisode *m.*; **~ic** *adj.* épisodique.
epist/le *s.* (*lit.* & *fam.*) épître *f.*; **~olary** *adj.* épistolaire.
epitaph *s.* épitaphe *f.*
epithet *s.* épithète *f.*
epitom/e *s.* abrégé *m.*; **~ize** *v.t.* abréger.
E.P.N.S. (*electroplated nickel silver*) *adj.* argenté; *s.* plaqué *m.*
epoch *s.* époque *f.*; **~-making** *adj.* qui fait époque.
eponymous *adj.* éponyme.
equable *adj.* (*uniform*) égal, uniforme; (*not easily disturbed*) d'humeur égale.
equal *s.* égal(e) *m.f.*; *adj.* (*same, evenly matched*) égal; (*adequate for*) de force à (+*inf.*), à la hauteur de (+*noun*), **to be, to feel ~ to doing sth.,** être, se sentir, de force à faire qch.; **to be ~ to the task,** être à la hauteur de la tâche; **other things being ~,** toutes choses égales; **on ~ terms,** sur un pied d'égalité; *v.t.* égaler, équivaloir à; **~ity** *s.* égalité *f.*; **~ization** *s.* égalisation *f.*; **~ize** *v.t.* égaliser; *v.i.* (*sport*) égaliser; **~ly** *adv.* également.
equanimity *s.* égalité d'humeur *f.*; (*calmness*) sérénité *f.*
equat/e *v.t.* (*state equality of*) déclarer équivalent (*to or with*—à); (*treat as equivalent*) rendre équivalent (à); **~ion,** *s.* (*making equal*) égalisation *f.*; (*math.*) équation *f.*
equator *s.* équateur *m.*; **~ial** *adj.* équatorial.
equerry *s.* écuyer *m.*
equestrian *adj.* équestre.
equi- (*in combination*): **~distant** *adj.* équidistant; **~lateral** *adj.* équilatéral; **~librium** *s.* équilibre *m.*; **~nox** *s.* équinoxe *m.*; **~poise** *s.* équilibre *m.*, contrepoids *m.*
equine *adj.* équin.
equip *v.t.* équiper; (*mech.*) outiller; *v.refl.* s'équiper; **~ with,** munir de; **~age** *s.* (*carriage, horses, etc.*) équipage *m.*; (*outfit*) équipement *m.*; **~ment** *s.* équipement *m.*; (*mech.*) outillage *m.*; KITCHEN **~ment.**
equitabl/e *adj.* équitable; **~y** *adv.**.
equitation *s.* équitation *f.*
equit/y *s.* (*fairness, principles of justice*) équité *f.*; (*law*) esprit d'une loi *m.*; (*property*) part résiduaire *f.*; **~ies** *s.pl.* (*stocks*) actions ordinaires *f.pl.*
equivalen/ce *s.* équivalence *f.*; **~t** *adj.* & *s.m.* équivalent; **to be ~t to,** équivaloir à.
equivoc/al *adj.* (*of doubtful meaning*) équivoque; (*dubious*) douteux; **~ate** *v.i.* user d'équivoques; **~ation** *s.* équivoque *f.*
era *s.* ère *f.*
eradicat/e *v.t.* (*lit.* & *fig.*) déraciner; **~ion** *s.* déracinement *m.*
eras/e *v.t.* (*lit.* & *fig.*) effacer; **~er** *s.* (*knife*) grattoir *m.*, (*rubber*) gomme *f.*; **~ure** *s.* rature *f.*
ere *prep.* (*archaic*) avant; *conj.* avant que.
erect *adj.* droit; *adv.* debout; *v.t.* **1.** (*set upright*) dresser; **2.** (*build*) ériger; (*fig.*) élever; **3.** (*techn.*) assembler; **~ion** *s.* (2) construction *f.*; (3) assemblage *m.*
eremite *s.* ermite *m.*
erg *s.* erg *m.*
ergot *s.* ergot *m.*; **~ism** *s.* ergotisme *m.*
ermine *s.* (*animal* & *fur*) hermine *f.*
ero/de *v.t.* (*of water*) éroder; (*of acid*) corroder; **~sion** *s.* érosion *f.*
erotic *adj.* érotique; **~a** *s.pl.* œuvres érotiques *f.pl.*
err *v.i.* (*make mistake*) se tromper; (*be incorrect*) être, tomber, dans l'erreur; (*go astray*) s'égarer; **~ on the side of,** pécher par; ⚠ errer = **to wander; ~ant** *adj.* (*itinerant*) errant, (**~***ing*) tombé dans l'erreur; **~atic** *adj.* (*irregular*) irrégulier; (*uncertain*) douteux; (*med., geol.*) erratique; **~atically** *adv.* irrégulièrement; **~atum** *s.* erratum *m.* (*pl.* errata); **~ing** *adj.* dans l'erreur, égaré; **~oneous** *adj.* erroné; **~oneously** *adv.**.
errand *s.* (*short journey*) course *f.*; (*message*) message *m.*; **to run ~s,** faire des courses; **to go on a fool's ~,** y aller, se déplacer, pour des prunes; **~-boy,** garçon de courses *m.*
error *s.* (*mistake, mistaken opinion*) erreur *f.*; (*transgression*) faute *f.*; (*deviation*) égarement *m.*
Erse *adj.* & *s.m.* erse.
erstwhile *adj.* d'autrefois; *adv.* autrefois.
eructation *s.* éructation *f.*
erudit/e *adj.* érudit; **~ion** *s.* érudition *f.*
erupt *v.i.* (*volcano*) faire éruption; (*lava, water*) jaillir; (*fig.*) exploser; **~ion** *s.* (*volcano* & *med.*) éruption *f.*; **~ive** *adj.* éruptif.
erysipelas *s.* érysipèle *m.*
escalade *s.* escalade *f.*
escalat/e *v.t.* & *i.* (s')accroître, escalader; **~ion** *s.* accroissement *m.*, escalade *f.*; **~or** *s.* escalier roulant *or* mécanique *m.*
escap/e *s.* **1.** (**~***ing*) fuite *f.*; **2.** (*leakage*) fuite *f.*; **3.** (*outlet*) échappement *m.*; **fire-~e,** escalier de secours *m.*; **to have a narrow ~e,** l'échapper belle; **~e clause,** clause échappatoire *f.*; *v.i.* (1) s'échapper (*from*—de); (2) fuir, s'échapper; *v.t.* éviter, échapper à; **~ade** *s.* escapade *f.*; **~ee** *s.* évadé *m.*; **~ement** *s.* (*mech.*) échappement *m.*; **~ism** *s.* évasion *f.*; **~ist** *adj.* qui aime l'évasion.
escarpment *s.* escarpement *m.*
eschatology *s.* eschatologie *f.*
eschew *v.t.* éviter.
escort *s.* **1.** (*bodyguard*); & **2.** (*naut.*) escorte *f.*; **3.** (*of woman*) cavalier *m.*; **4.** (*people accompanying*) cortège *m.*; *v.t.* (1) & (2) escorter; (3) & (4) accompagner.
escritoire *s.* secrétaire *m.*
escudo *s.* escudo *m.*
escutcheon *s.* écu *m.*; **a blot on the ~,** une tache sur son nom.
Eskimo *adj.* & *s.m.f.* esquimau (de).
esoteric *adj.* ésotérique.
espalier *s.* espalier *m.*
esparto *s.* (*grass*) spart *m.*
especial *adj.* spécial; **~ly** *adv.**.
Esperanto *s.* espéranto *m.*
espionage *s.* espionnage *m.*
esplanade *s.* esplanade *f.*
espous/e *v.t.* **1.** (*marry*) épouser; **2.** (*fig. adopt*) épouser; **~al** *s.* (1) épousailles *f.pl.*; (2) adoption *f.*
espresso *s.* café express *m.*
espy *v.t.* apercevoir.

esquire (*form of address*) Monsieur . . .
E.S.R.O. (*abbrev. European Space Research Organisation*) *m.* CERS (Conseil Européen pour la Recherche Spatiale).
essay *s.* **1.** (*thesis*) dissertation *f.*; (*exercise*) composition *f.*; (*liter. work*) essai *m.*; **2.** (*attempt*) essai *m.*; *v.t.* & *i.* (2) essayer (de); **~ist,** essayiste *m.*
essen/ce *s.* essence *f.*; **~tial** *adj.* & *s.m.* essentiel; **~tially** *adv.**.
establish *v.t.* **1.** (*set up*; *place beyond dispute*) établir; **2.** (*settle* (*oneself*)) (s')installer; **3.** (*church*) reconnaître comme institution d'état; **~ment** *s.* (1) établissement *m.*; (3) église établie *f.*; (*staff, household etc.*) train de vie *m.*; (*fig.*) **the E~ment,** le pouvoir, les classes dirigeantes *f.pl.*
estate *s.* (*status*) rang *m.*; (*condition*) état *m.*; (*class*) état *m.*; (*land*) propriété *f.*; (*law*) biens *m.pl.*; **housing ~,** cité *f.*; **~ agent** *s.* agent immobilier *m.*; **~ car** *s.* break *m.*
esteem *s.* estime *f.*; *v.t.* (*think highly of*; *consider*) estimer.
estimable *adj.* estimable.
estimat/e *s.* **1.** (*judgement of value*) estimation *f.*, évaluation *f.*; **2.** (*price quoted for work*) devis *m.*; **the E~es** *s.pl.* (*parl. fin.*) crédits budgétaires *m.pl.*; *v.t.* & *i.* (1) évaluer; (2) établir un devis; **~ion** *s.* (*judgement*) jugement *m.*; (*opinion*) avis *m.*; (*esteem*) estime *f.*; **~ive** *adj.* estimatif.
estrange *v.t.* (*alienate*) aliéner l'affection, l'estime, de qn.; (*make enemy of*) rendre hostile; **become ~d,** se détacher de; **~ment** *s.* désaffection *f.*; détachement *m.*
estuary *s.* estuaire *m.*
E.T.A. (*abbrev. estimated time of arrival*) heure d'arrivée prévue *f.*
etc. (*abbrev.*) etc.; **etceteras** *s.pl.* tout le tralala *m.*
etch *v.t.* (*art*) graver à l'eau-forte; (*fig.*) graver; **~er** *s.* aquafortiste *m.f.*; **~ing** *s.* gravure à l'eau-forte *f.*
etern/al *adj.* éternel; (*incessant*) incessant; (*pej.*) sempiternel; **~ally** *adv.* éternellement, sans cesse; ⚠ incessamment = **without delay;** **~ity** *s.* éternité *f.*
ether *s.* (*upper air*; *chem.*) éther *m.*; **~eal** *adj.* éthéré.
ethic/al *adj.* (*relating to ~s*) éthique; (*moral*) moral; **~s** *s.* (*science of morals*) éthique *f.* ⚠ *sing. in French*; (*moral principles*) moralité *f.*
Ethiopia *s.* Éthiopie *f.*; **~n** *adj.* & *s.m.f.* éthiopien(ne).
ethnic(al) *adj.* ethnique.
ethno/graphy *s.* ethnographie *f.*; **~grapher** *s.* ethnographe *m.f.*; **~graphic** *adj.* ethnographique; **~logical** *adj.* ethnologique; **~logist** *s.* ethnologue *m.f.*; **~logy** *s.* ethnologie *f.*
ethology *s.* éthologie *f.*
ethos *s.* (*morals*) morale *f.*; (*customs*) mœurs *f.pl.*
etiolat/e *v.t.* & *i.* (s')étioler; **~ion** *s.* étiolement *m.*
etiquette *s.* étiquette *f.*, protocole *m.*
Etruscan *adj.* & *s.m.f.* étrusque.
etymolog/y *s.* étymologie *f.*; **~ical** *adj.* étymologique.
eucalyptus *s.* eucalyptus *m.*
Eucharist *s.* eucharistie *f.*
eugenics *s.* eugénisme *m.*
eulog/y *s.* panégyrique *m.*; **~ist** *s.* panégyriste *m.*; **~istic** *adj.* élogieux; **~ize** *v.t.* composer le panégyrique de, célébrer.
eunuch *s.* eunuque *m.*
euphem/ism *s.* euphémisme *m.*; **~istic** *adj.* euphémique.
euphon/y *s.* euphonie *f.*; **~ic** *adj.* euphonique.
euphor/ia *s.* euphorie *f.*; **~ic** *adj.* euphorique.
Eurasian *adj.* & *s.m.f.* eurasien(ne).
Euratom (*abbrev. European Atomic Energy Community*) Euratom *f.*
eureka! *interj.* eurêka!
Europe *s.* Europe *f.*; **~an** *adj.* & *s.m.f.* européen(ne).
euthanasia *s.* euthanasie *f.*
evacu/ate *v.t.* évacuer; **~ation** *s.* évacuation *f.*; **~ee** *s.* évacué(e) *m.f.*
evade *v.t.* (*escape from*) échapper à, esquiver; (*elude*) éluder.
evaluat/e *v.t.* évaluer; **~ion** *s.* évaluation *f.*
evanescen/ce *s.* évanescence *f.*; **~t** *adj.* évanescent.
evangel/ical *adj.* évangélique; **~ism** *s.* évangélisme *m.*; **~ist** *s.*; évangéliste *m.*; **~ize** *v.t.* évangéliser.
evaporat/e *v.t.* & *i.* (s')évaporer; **~ion** *s.* évaporation *f.*
evas/ion *s.* évasion *f.*; (*excuse*) échappatoire *m.*; **~ive** *adj.* évasif; **~ively** *adv.**.
eve *s.* veille *f.*; **New Year's E~,** la Saint Sylvestre.
even[1] *adj.* (*level, smooth*) uni; (*uniform*) uniforme, régulier; (*equal*) égal; (*calm*) calme; (*number*) pair; **~ money,** compte rond *m.*; **to get ~ with s.o.,** être quitte avec qn.; *adv.* même; **~ if, ~ though,** même si; **~ly** *adv.* uniformément, régulièrement; **~ness** *s.* égalité *f.*; *v.t.* unifier.
even[2] *s.* & **evening** *s.* soir *m.*, (*whole ~ing*) soirée *f.*; **~song,** vêpres *f.pl.*; **~tide,** soir *m.*; **~ing dress,** tenue de soirée *f.*; **good ~ing,** bonsoir!
event *s.* (*happening*) événement *m.*; (*result*) conséquence *f.*; (*sport*) épreuve *f.*; **in the ~ of,** en cas de; **at all ~s,** en tout cas; **in any ~,** de toute façon; **~ful** *adj.* (*occasion*) mémorable; (*life*) mouvementé; **~ual** *adj.* (*likely to happen*) éventuel; (*ultimately resulting*) définitif; **~uality** *s.* (*possible ~*) éventualité *f.*; **~ually** *adv.* éventuellement; finalement; **~uate** *v.i.* (*turn out*) aboutir à; (*end*) finir; (*happen*) arriver.
ever *adv.* (*always*) toujours; (*at any time*) jamais; **if ~,** si jamais; **for ~,** à jamais; WHAT~; WHEN~; WHERE~; WHO~; **~ so** (*fam.* = *very*) énormément; **~green** *adj.* toujours vert; *s.* arbre vert *m.*; **~lasting** *adj.* éternel; (*pej.*) sempiternel; **~lasting flower** *s.* immortelle *f.*; **~more** *adv.* toujours.
every *adj.* chaque, tout; **~** DAY; **~body, ~one,** tout le monde; **~thing,** tout; **~ way,** de toutes les façons; **~where** *adv.* partout.
evict *v.t.* expulser; (*law*) évincer; **~ion** *s.* éviction *f.*
eviden/ce *s.* **1.** (*sign*) indication *f.*; **2.** (*information*) preuve *f.*, témoignage *m.*; **3.** (*law*) déposition *f.*; **4.** (*conspicuousness*) évidence *f.*; **to be in ~ce** (4) être en évidence; **to give ~ce** (3) déposer; *v.t.* (1) indiquer; **~t** *adj.* évident; **~tly** *adv.* évidemment.
evil *s.* (*~ thing, sin*) mal *m.*; (*harm*) malheur *m.*; *adj.* mauvais, méchant; *adv.* (& *~ly*) mal; **~-doer** *s.* méchant *m.*; **~ eye** *s.* mauvais œil *m.*
evince *v.t.* manifester; ⚠ évincer = **to evict** (*law*).
eviscerate *v.t.* éventrer; (*fig.*) affaiblir.
evo/ke *v.t.* évoquer; **~cation** *s.* évocation *f.*; **~cative** *adj.* évocat/eur, -rice.
evolution *s.* évolution *f.*
evolve *v.t.* & *i.* (*open out*) (faire) évoluer; (*develop*) (se) développer; *v.t.* (*produce heat, etc.*) émettre; (*gas*) dégager.
ewe *s.* brebis *f.*; **~ lamb,** agnelle *f.*; (*fig.*) trésor *m.*
ewer *s.* aiguière *f.*
ex *s.* (*pop. former husband or wife*) ex *m.f.*; *prep.* (*comm.*) **~ works** (prix) départ-usine; (*in combination* = *former*) *adj.* ancien (*before the noun*);

the ~Prime Minister, l'ancien Premier Ministre.

exacerbat/e *v.t.* **1.** (*aggravate*) exacerber; **2.** (*irritate s.o.*) exaspérer (qn.); **~ion** *s.* (1) exacerbation *f.*; (2) exaspération *f.*

exact[1] *adj.* exact; (*time*) précis; **~ly** *adv.* exactement, précisément; **~ness, ~itude** *s.* exactitude *f.*, précision *f.*

exact[2] *v.t.* (*demand*) exiger; (*obtain*) extorquer; **~ing** *adj.* (*person*) exigeant, (*work*) ardu; **~ion** *s.* exaction *f.*

exaggerat/e *v.t.* & *i.* exagérer; **~ion** *s.* exagération *f.*

exalt *v.t.* **1.** (*raise in rank, etc.*) élever; **2.** (*extol*) exalter; **~ation** *s.* (1) promotion *f.*; (2) (*elation*) exaltation *f.*; **~ed** *adj.* (1) élevé; (2) exalté.

exam *s.* (*abbrev. for examination*) examen *m.*

examin/e *v.t.* **1.** (*inspect; med., acad.*) examiner; **2.** (*law*) (*defendant*) interroger, (*witness*) faire déposer; **3.** (*customs*) visiter; **~ation** *s.* (1) examen *m.*; (2) interrogatoire *m.*, audition *f.*; (3) visite *f.*; **to sit for, to take, an ~ation,** passer un examen; **to** PASS **an ~ation; ~ation-paper** *s.* épreuve *f.* (d'examen); **~ee** *s.* candidat *m.*; **~er** *s.* examinat/eur, -rice *m.f.*

example *s.* (*illustration, model*) exemple *m.*; (*specimen*) spécimen *m.*; (*precedent*) précédent *m.*; **for ~,** par exemple.

exasperat/e *v.t.* exaspérer; **~ing** *adj.* exaspérant; **~ion** *s.* exaspération *f.*

excavat/e *v.t.* (*dig*) creuser; (*dig up*) déterrer; *v.i.* (*archeol.*) faire des fouilles; **~ion** *s.* (*hole*) excavation *f.*; (*act*) fouille *f.*; (*archeol.*) fouilles *f.pl.*; **~or** *s.* excavateur *m.*

exceed *v.t.* (*go beyond*) dépasser; (*be greater than*) excéder; (*surpass*) surpasser; *v.i.* (*be immoderate*) dépasser les bornes; **~ingly** *adv.* excessivement.

excel *v.t.* surpasser; *v.i.* exceller (*at, in*—à, dans); **~lence** *s.* excellence *f.*; **~lency** *s.* (*title*) excellence *f.*; **~lent** *adj.* excellent; **~lently** *adv.* parfaitement.

except *v.t.* (*exclude from*) excepter; (*object to*) soulever des objections contre; **~ed** *adj.* excepté; *prep.* (*also* **~ing**) à l'exception de; *conj.* sauf que; **~ for,** exception faite de; **~ that,** sauf que.

exception *s.* exception *f.*; (*objection*) objection *f.*; **to be an ~,** faire exception; **to take ~ to,** trouver à redire à; se formaliser (de, que); **with the ~ of,** exception faite de; **the ~ proves the rule,** l'exception confirme la règle; **~able** *adj.* qui prête à l'objection; **~al** *adj.* exceptionnel; **~ally** *adv.**.

excerpt *s.* extrait *m.*; *v.t.* extraire.

excess *s.* (*fact of exceeding*) excès *m.*; (*amount in* ~) excédent *m.*; (*over-indulgence, usu. pl.*) excès *m.pl.*; **in ~,** en excédent; **to ~,** à l'excès; *adj.* excédentaire; **~ fare,** supplément *m.*; **~ luggage,** excédent de bagages *m.*; **~ profits,** surplus de bénéfices *m.*; **~ive** *adj.* excessif; **~ively** *adv.**.

exchange *s.* (*substitution*) échange *m.* (*for*—contre, de); (*thing ~d*) objet d'échange *m.*; (*fin.*) change *m.*; (*building*) bourse *f.*; (*telephone*) central *m.*; LABOUR **~; in ~ for,** en échange de; **~ control** (*fin.*) contrôle des changes *m.*; **~ rate** (*fin.*) taux du change *m.*; *v.t.* échanger (*for*—contre).

exchequer *s.* (*law*) échiquier *m.*; (*fin.*) trésor public *m.*; CHANCELLOR **of the E~.**

excise[1] *s.* (service des) contributions indirectes *f.pl.*; **~ duty,** impôt indirect *m.*

excis/e[2] *v.t.* (*med.*) exciser; (*fig.*) découper; **~ion** *s.* excision *f.*

excit/e *v.t.* (*set in motion*) agiter; (*stir up*) exciter; (*stimulate*) activer; **~able** *adj.* excitable; **~ability** *s.* excitabilité *f.*; **~ant** *s.* (*stimulant*) excitant *m.*; **~ation** *s.* excitation *f.*; **~ed** *adj.* excité, agité; **~edly** *adv.* avec agitation; **~ement** *s.* excitation *f.*, agitation *f.*, animation *f.*; **~ing** *adj.* excitant, passionnant.

excla/im *v.t.* & *i.* s'exclamer; **~mation** *s.* exclamation *f.*; **~mation mark,** point d'exclamation *f.*; **~matory** *adj.* exclamatif.

exclu/de *v.t.* (*shut out from*) exclure de; (*leave out*) exclure; (*make impossible*) empêcher (de); **~sion** *s.* exclusion *f.*; **~sive** *adj.* (**~ding**) exclusif; (*closed* (*society*)) fermé; (*not to be had* elsewhere) exclusif; **~sive of,** non compris; **~siveness** *s.* exclusivité *f.*; **~sively** *adv.* exclusivement.

excommunicat/e *v.t.* excommunier; **~ion** *s.* excommunication *f.*

excoriate *v.t.* excorier.

excrement *s.* excrément *m.*

excrescence *s.* excroissance *f.*

excret/e *v.t.* excréter; **~a** *s.pl.* excréments *m.pl.*; **~ion** *s.* excrétion *f.*; **~ive, ~ory** *adjs.* excréteur, -trice.

excruciating *adj.* atroce.

exculpat/e *v.t.* disculper; **~ion** *s.* disculpation *f.*; **~ory** *adj.* justificatif.

excursion *s.* (*short journey, pleasure trip*) excursion *f.*; (*mil.*) sortie *f.*; (*fig.*) digression *f.*; **~ ticket,** billet d'excursion *m.*; **~ train** *s.* train d'excursion *m.*

excursive *adj.* digressif.

excus/e *s.* excuse *f.*; **to make ~es,** s'excuser; *v.t.* excuser; (*forgive*) pardonner (qch. à qn.); (*grant exemption*) dispenser (*from*—de); *v.refl.* s'excuser; **~e me!,** excusez-moi!, pardon!; **~able** *adj.* excusable; **~atory** *adj.* justificatif.

exeat *s.* permission de sortie *f.*

execra/te *v.t.* exécrer; (*curse*) maudire; **~ble** *adj.* exécrable; **~tion** *s.* exécration *f.*

execut/e *v.t.* **1.** (*perform*) exécuter; (*duties*) exercer; **2.** (*put to death*) exécuter; **3.** (*fin.*) effectuer; **~ant** *s.* (*mus.*) exécutant *m.*; **~ion** *s.* (1) & (2) exécution *f.*; (*duties*) exercice *m.*; **~ioner** *s.* (2) bourreau *m.*; **~ive** *adj.* & *s.m.* exécutif; (*person*) administrateur *m.*; **~or** *s.* exécut/eur, -rice (testamentaire) *m.f.*

exege/sis *s.* exégèse *f.*; **~tic** *adj.* exégétique.

exemplar *s.* (*to be copied*) modèle *m.*; (*specimen*) spécimen *m.*; **~y** *adj.* exemplaire.

exemplif/y *v.t.* (*give example*) démontrer par son exemple; (*be example*) servir d'exemple (à); **~ication** *s.* démonstration *f.*

exempt *adj.* exempt (*from*—de); *v.t.* exempter (*from*—de); **~ion** *s.* exemption *f.*

exercise *s.* exercice *m.*; **~-book** *s.* cahier *m.*; *v.t.* (*use*) exercer; (*give ~ to*) faire prendre de l'exercice à; *v.i.* (*take ~*) s'exercer; (*perplex, worry*) embarrasser.

exert *v.t.* (*exercise*) exercer; (*bring to bear*) mettre en œuvre; (*put forth*) déployer; *v.refl.* se donner du mal, se dépenser; **~ion** *s.* effort *m.*

exeunt (*theat.*) sortent.

exhal/e *v.t.* & *i.* (s')exhaler; **~ation** *s.* (*skin*) exhalation *f.*; (*smell, etc.*) exhalaison *f.*

exhaust *s.* (*mech.*) échappement *m.*; **~-pipe** *s.* tuyau d'échappement *m.*; *v.t.* (*draw off*) soutirer (*from*—de); (*consume*) consommer; (*empty of contents*) vider; (*deal with ~ively*) épuiser; (*drain of energy*) épuiser; **~ible** *adj.* (*rare*) épuisable; **~ing** *adj.* épuisant; **~ion** *s.* (*lit.* & *fig.*) épuisement *m.*; **~ive** *adj.* exhaustif.

exhibit *s.* objet exposé *m.*; (*law*) document *m.*, pièce à conviction *f.*; *v.t.* (*art*) exposer; (*law*) exhiber; (*show off*) exhiber; (*manifest*) faire preuve de; **~ion** *s.* exposition *f.*; exhibition *f.*; (*scholarship*) bourse *f.*; **~ionism** *s.* exhibitionnisme *m.*; **~ionist** *s.* exhibitionniste *m.f.*; **~or** *s.* exposant *m.*

exhilarat/e *v.t.* (*enliven*) animer; (*strengthen*) fortifier; **~ing** *adj.* fortifiant; ⚠ exhilarant

(*obs.*) = **arousing laughter; ~ion** *s.* animation *f.*
exhort *v.t.* exhorter; **~ation** *s.* exhortation *f.*
exhum/e *v.t.* exhumer; **~ation** *s.* exhumation *f.*
exigen/ce, exigency *s.* (*urgent need*) exigence *f.*; (*emergency*) état d'urgence *m.*; **~t** *adj.* (*urgent*) urgent; (*exacting*) exigeant.
exigu/ous *adj.* exigu; **~ity** *s.* exiguïté *f.*
exile *s.* (*banishment, long absence from country*) exil *m.*; (*person*) exilé(e) *m.f.*; *v.t.* exiler.
exist *v.i.* exister; **~ence** *s.* (*mode of life*) vie *f.*; (*all that ~s*) existence *f.*; **~ent** *adj.* existant; **~ential** *adj.* existentiel; **~entialism** *s.* existentialisme *m.*
exit *s.* (*going out, way out*) sortie *f.*; (*departure*) départ *m.*; (*death*) fin *f.*; (*theat.*) (*stage direction*) sort; *v.i.* s'en aller.
exodus *s.* (*lit.* & *fig.*) exode *m.*
ex officio *adj.* à titre d'office; *adv.* (*to act*—agir) de par ses fonctions.
exonerat/e *v.t.* **1.** (*free from blame*) disculper; **2.** (*release from*) dispenser de; **~ion** *s.* (1) disculpation *f.*; (2) dispense *f.*
exorbitan/ce *s.* énormité *f.*; **~t** *adj.* exorbitant.
exorci/ze *v.t.* exorciser; **~sm** *s.* exorcisme *m.*; **~st** *s.* exorciste *m.*
exotic *adj.* exotique.
expan/d *v.t.* & *i.* **1.** (*spread out*) (s')étendre; (*med.*) dilater; **2.** (*develop*) (se) développer; **3.** (*increase*) (s')élargir; **4.** *v.i.* (*become genial*) devenir expansif; **~se** *s.* étendue *f.*; **~sion** *s.* (1) expansion *f.*; dilatation *f.*; (2) développement *m.*; (3) élargissement *m.*; **~sive** *adj.* (1) étendu; expansif; (4) expansif; **~siveness** *s.* (1) expansibilité *f.*; (4) expansivité *f.*
expatiat/e *v.i.* disserter (*on*—sur); **~ion** *s.* discours *m.*
expatriat/e *adj.* & *s.m.f.* expatrié(e); *v.t.* exiler; **~ion** *s.* expatriation *f.*
expect *v.t.* **1.** (*reckon on*) compter sur; **2.** (*anticipate*) s'attendre à; **3.** (*look for*) espérer; **4.** (*suppose*) supposer; **~ancy** *s.* (2) attente *f.*; (3) espérance *f.*; **~ant** *adj.* qui attend; **~ant mother,** femme enceinte *f.*; **~ation** *s.* (2) attente *f.*; (3) prévision *f.*; (4) probabilité *f.*
expectora/te *v.i.* expectorer; **~nt** *adj.* & *s.m.* expectorant; **~tion** *s.* expectoration *f.*
expedien/cy *s.* convenance *f.*; (*pej.*) opportunisme *m.*; **~t** *adj.* (*suitable*) convenable, utile; (*advisable*) opportun; (*politic*) politique; *s.* expédient *m.*
expedit/e *v.t.* **1.** (*help on progress of*) hâter; **2.** (*dispatch*) expédier; ⚠ expédier ≠ (1); **~ion** *s.* (*promptness*) promptitude *f.*; (*group of men, ships, etc.*) expédition *f.*; **~ionary** *adj.* expéditionnaire; **~ious** *adj.* expéditif.
expel *v.t.* expulser; (*drive out*) chasser.
expend *v.t.* (*spend, money, efforts*) dépenser; (*use up*) épuiser; **~able** *adj.* dont on peut se dispenser; **~iture** *s.* dépense *f.*
expens/e *s.* dépense *f.*; **~es** *pl.* frais *m.pl.*; **at my ~e,** à mes frais; **at the ~e of** (*fig.*) aux dépens de; **~e account,** indemnité pour frais professionnels *f.*; **~ive** *adj.* (*dear*) coûteux; (*tastes, etc.*) dispendieux; **~ively** *adv.* coûteusement; dispendieusement; **~iveness** *s.* cherté *f.*
experience *s.* expérience *f.*; **by ~,** par expérience; **from ~,** en connaissance de cause; *v.t.* faire l'expérience de; (*feelings*) éprouver; **~d** *adj.* expérimenté; qui a de l'expérience.
experiment *s.* expérience *f.*; **~al** *adj.* expérimental; **~ally** *adv.**; *v.i.* faire des expériences.
expert *s.* expert *m.*; *adj.* expert (dans *or* en qch.; à faire qch.); **~ise** *s.* compétence *f.*; ⚠ expertise = **test by experts, assessment of value of work of art; ~ness** *s.* habileté *f.*
expia/te *v.t.* expier; **~ble** *adj.* expiable; **~tion** *s.* expiation *f.*; **~tory** *adj.* expiatoire.
expir/e *v.i.* (*breathe out, die, come to an end*) expirer; **~ation** *s.* expiration *f.*; **~y** *s.* expiration *f.*
expla/in *v.t.* & *i.* (*make known, account for*) expliquer; (*make intelligible*) éclaircir; **~in away,** justifier (par ses explications); **~nation** *s.* explication *f.*; **~natory** *adj.* explicatif.
expletive *adj.* & *s.m.* explétif.
explic/ate *v.t.* élucider; **~able** *adj.* explicable; **~ation** *s.* explication *f.*; **~atory** *adj.* explicatif.
explicit *adj.* (*expressly stated, outspoken*) explicite; (*definite*) défini; **~ly** *adv.* explicitement; **~ness** *s.* précision *f.*
explode *v.t.* (*detonate*) faire sauter; (*discredit*) discréditer; *v.i.* (*lit.* & *fig.*) exploser.
exploit *s.* exploit *m.*; *v.t.* exploiter; **~ation** *s.* exploitation *f.*
explor/e *v.t.* **1.** (*unknown country*) explorer; **2.** (*examine, med.*) sonder; **3.** (*inquire into*) scruter; **~ation** *s.* (1) exploration *f.*; (2) sondage *m.*; (3) recherche *f.*; **~atory** *adj.* exploratif; **~er** *s.* explorat/eur, -rice *m.f.*
explos/ion *s.* explosion *f.*; **~ive** *adj.* & *s.m.* explosif; **high ~ive** *s.* explosif brisant *m.*
exponent *s.* (*who or which interprets*) interprète *m.*; (*type*) représentant *m.*
export *s.* (*act*) exportation *f.*; (*goods*) article d'exportation *m.*; *v.t.* exporter; **~able** *adj.* exportable; **~ation** *s.* exportation *f.*; **~er** *s.* exportat/eur, -rice *m.f.*
expos/e *v.t.* **1.** (*put in unsheltered position*) exposer; **2.** (*subject to*) exposer à; **3.** (*exhibit*) mettre en montre; **4.** (*disclose*) dévoiler; **5.** (*unmask*) démasquer; **6.** (*photo.*) exposer; **~d** *adj.* (1) exposé; **~é** *s.* exposé *m.*; **~ition** *s.* exposition *f.*; **~ure** *s.* (1), (2), (3), (6) exposition *f.*; (4), (5) révélation *f.*; **to die of ~ure,** mourir de froid.
expostulat/e *v.i.* (*with s.o.*) faire des remontrances à qn., raisonner qn.; **~ion** *s.* remontrance *f.*; **~ory** *adj.* de remontrance.
expound *v.t.* (*set out in detail*) exposer; (*explain*) expliquer.
express *s.* (*train*) express *m.*, rapide *m.*; *adj.* (*definitely stated*) explicite; (*done for purpose*) exprès; (*travelling at speed*) rapide; (*letters, etc.*) exprès (*invar.*); *v.t.* (*represent in symbols, words, reveal*) exprimer; (*send by ~*) expédier par exprès; **~ible** *adj.* exprimable; **~ion** *s.* expression *f.*; **~ive** *adj.* expressif; **~ly** *adv.* expressément.
expropriat/e *v.t.* exproprier; **~ion** *s.* expropriation *f.*
expuls/ion *s.* expulsion *f.*; (*from school*) renvoi *m.*; **~ive** *adj.* expulsif.
expunge *v.t.* effacer.
expurgat/e *v.t.* expurger; **~ion** *s.* expurgation *f.*; **~ory** *adj.* expurgatoire.
exquisite *adj.* exquis; (*of pain, etc.*) atroce; (*refined*) raffiné; (*perfect*) parfait; **~ly** *adv.* délicatement, parfaitement; **~ness** *s.* délicatesse *f.*, perfection *f.*
extant *adj.* existant encore.
extempor/e *adj.* & *adv.* impromptu; **~arily** *adv.* impromptu; **~ize** *v.i.* improviser; **~ization** *s.* improvisation *f.*
extend *v.t.* (*stretch out*): (*arm*) allonger, (*hand*) tendre; (*space and time*) prolonger; (*enlarge*) étendre; (*accord to*) offrir, accorder, à; *v.i.* se prolonger; s'étendre.
extens/ion *s.* (*extending*) extension *f.*; (*enlargement*): (*space*) prolongement *m.*; (*time*) prolongation *f.*; (*additional part*) (*techn.*) rallonge *f.*; (*fig.*) extension *f.*; (*telephone*) poste *m.*; **~ion ladder,** échelle à coulisse *f.*; **~ible** *adj.* extensible; **~ive** *adj.* vaste, étendu, large; **~ively** *adv.* largement, d'une manière étendue.
extent *s.* étendue *f.*; (*fig.*) portée *f.*; **to some ~,** dans une certaine mesure; **to a great ~,** dans

une large mesure; **to such an ~ that,** jusqu'au point où.
extenuat/e *v.t.* atténuer; ⚠ exténuer = **to tire out; ~ing** *adj.* atténuant; **~ion** *s.* atténuation *f.*
exterior *adj.* & *s.m.* extérieur.
exterminat/e *v.t.* exterminer; **~ing** *adj.* exterminateur; **~ion** *s.* extermination *f.*; **~or** *s.* exterminat/eur, -rice *m.f.*
external *adj.* extérieur; (*med. of remedy, etc.* ≠ *internal*) externe; **~ly** *adv.* extérieurement.
extinct *adj.* (*volcano, etc.*) éteint; (*race, species*) disparu; **~ion** *s.* extinction *f.*
extinguish *v.t.* (*put out* (*fire*), *wipe out* (*debt*) éteindre; (*eclipse*) anéantir; **~er** *s.* (*fire*) extincteur *m.*; (*candle snuffer* & *fig.*) éteignoir *m.*
extirpat/e *v.t.* extirper; **~ion** *s.* extirpation *f.*
extol *v.t.* (*liter.*) exalter; célébrer.
extort *v.t.* extorquer (qch. à qn.); (*fig.*) arracher (qch. à qn.); **~ion** *s.* extorsion *f.*; **~ionate** *adj.* exorbitant.
extra *s.* (*additional thing, charge*) supplément *m.*; (*theat.*) figurant *m.*; (*newspaper*) édition spéciale *f.*; *adj.* (*additional*) supplémentaire; (*larger, better*) extra; *adv.* en plus; **~curricular** *adj.* extra-scolaire; **~marital** *adj.* extra-conjugal; **~mural** *adj.* hors-faculté; **~-sensory** *adj.* extra-sensoriel; **~-special** *adj.* tout(e) particulier(ière); **~territorial** *adj.* exterritorial; **~ time** *s.* (*sport*) prolongations *f.pl.*
extract *s.* extrait *m.*; *v.t.* (*take out*) extraire; (*by force, tooth, etc.*) arracher; (*deduce, derive from*) tirer de; (*quote*) citer; **~ion** *s.* extraction *f.*
extradit/e *v.t.* extrader; **~able** *adj.* susceptible d'extradition; **~ion** *s.* extradition *f.*
extraneous *adj.* étranger (à).
extraordinar/y *adj.* extraordinaire; **~ily** *adv.**; **~iness** *s.* extraordinaire *m.*
extravagan/ce *s.* **1.** (*of behaviour, speech, etc.*) extravagance *f.*; **2.** (*wastefulness*) prodigalité *f.*; **~t** *adj.* (1) extravagant; (2) prodigue; **3.** (*exorbitant*) exorbitant; **~tly** *adv.* (1) d'une manière extravagante; (2) prodigalement; **~za** *s.* (*art*) fantaisie *f.*
extrem/e *s.* extrême *m.*; **to go to ~es,** pousser à l'extrême; **in ~is,** à l'agonie; *adj.* extrême; **~ unction** *s.* extrême-onction *f.*; **~ely** *adv.**; **~ist** *s.* extrémiste *m.f.*; **~ity** *s.* extrémité *f.*
extricate *v.t.* dégager; (*from*—de); *v.refl.* se libérer (de).
extrinsic *adj.* extrinsèque.
extrover/t *adj.* & *s.m.f.* extraverti(e); **~sion** *s.* extroversion *f.*
extru/de *v.t.* expulser; (*techn.*) projeter; **~sion** *s.* expulsion *f.*; (*techn.*) extrusion *f.*
exuberan/ce *s.* exubérance *f.*; **~t** *adj.* (*luxurious, prolific*) luxuriant; (*copious, lavish, demonstrative*) exubérant; **~tly** *adv.* avec exubérance.
exude *v.t.* & *i.* exsuder.
exult *v.i.* exulter (*over*—de); **~ation** *s.* exultation *f.*; **~ing, ~ant** *adjs.* triomphant.
eye *s.* (*organ of sight*) œil *m.* (*pl.* yeux); **to be all ~s,** être tout yeux; **to turn a** BLIND **~; ~s right!,** tête à droite!; EVIL **~**; GLAD **~**; (*fig. of thing*) **to hit** (*s.o.*) **in the ~,** sauter aux yeux (de qn.); **in the ~s of,** aux yeux de; **to keep an ~ on s.o.,** tenir qn. à l'œil; **to keep one's ~s skinned,** n'avoir pas les yeux dans la poche; **to look s.o. in the ~,** regarder qn. dans le blanc des yeux; **my ~!** (*pop.*) mon œil!; **to run one's ~ over,** jeter un coup d'œil sur; **to see ~ to ~ with s.o.,** voir du même œil que qn.; **to shut or close one's ~s to,** fermer les yeux sur; **to be up to the ~s in** (*work, debt, etc.*), avoir (du travail, des dettes, etc.) par dessus la tête; **with an ~ to,** en vue de; **to pull the** WOOL **over s.o.'s ~s**; (*faculty of sight*) vue *f.*; (*look, gaze*) coup d'œil *m.*; **to have an ~ for,** avoir le coup d'œil pour; (*thing like an* ~): (*of needle*) chas *m.*, (*of shoe*) œillet *m.*, (*of hook*) porte *f.*, (*of potato*) œil *m.*; BULL**'s-~**; APPLE **of the ~**; **~ball** *s.* globe de l'œil *m.*; **~brow** *s.* sourcil *m.*; **~glass** *s.* monocle *m.*; **~hole** *s.* judas *m.*; ~LASH; **~let** *s.* œillet *m.*; **~lid** *s.* paupière *f.*; **~-opener** *s.* (*fig.*) révélation *f.*; **~-shadow** *s.* fard *m.*; **~sight** *s.* vue *f.*; **~sore** *s.* objet déplaisant *m.*; **~-tooth** *s.* canine *f.*; **~wash** *s.* (*fam. fig.*) du tape-l'œil; **~witness** *s.* témoin oculaire *m.*; **to get an ~ful** (*pop.*) se rincer l'œil; *v.t.* observer; (*inspect*) mesurer du regard, toiser.
eyot *s.* îlot *m.*
eyrie *s.* nid d'aigle *m.*

F

F, f *s.* (*mus.*) fa *m.*
fa(h) *s.* (*mus.*) fa *m.*
fab/le *s.* **1.** (*myth, legend*) mythe *m.*, légende *f.*; **2.** (*moral story*) fable *f.*; **3.** (*falsehood*) invention *f.*; **~led** *adj.* (1) fabuleux; **~ulist** *s.* (2) fabuliste *m.*; **~ulous** *adj.* (2) fabuleux; (3) incroyable; (*pop.*) fabuleux; **~ulously** *adv.* (2)*; (3)*.
fabric *s.* (*thing put together*) construction *f.*; (*building* & *fig.*) édifice *m.*; (*structure*) structure *f.*; (*construction*) ouvrage *m.*; (*text.*) tissu *m.*; (*eccles.*) fabrique *f.*; ⚠ fabrique = **factory, manufacture; ~ate** *v.t.* **1.** (*construct*) construire; **2.** (*invent* (*fact*), *forge* (*document*)) inventer, forger; **~ation** *s.* (1) construction *f.*; (2) invention *f.*, fabrication *f.*; **~ator** *s.* (1) constructeur *m.*; (2) inventeur *m.*, faussaire *m.*
façade *s.* (*lit.* & *fig.*) façade *f.*
face[1] *s.* (*of person*) figure *f.*, visage *m.*; **~ to ~,** face à face; **in the ~ of,** devant (qch.), au nez de (qn.); **in ~ of,** en dépit de; **full in the ~,** en pleine figure; **to set one's ~ against sth.,** se buter au sujet de qch.; **he said it to my ~,** il me l'a dit en face; **to cut off one's** NOSE **to spite one's ~**; (*expression*) mine *f.*; (*grimace*) grimace *f.*; (*fam. effrontery*) culot *m.*; **to have the ~ to,** avoir le culot de; **to lose/save ~,** perdre, sauver, la face; (*aspect*) apparence *f.*; **on the ~ of it**; au premier coup d'œil; **to put a good ~ on sth.,** payer d'audace; (*surface*) surface *f.*; (*front, right side*) face *f.*; (*of clock*) cadran *m.*; (*of bat, club, etc.*) plat *m.*; **~ card,** figure *f.*; ~-FLANNEL; **~-lift(ing)** *s.* lifting *m.*; **~ powder** *s.* poudre (de riz) *f.*; **~ value,** valeur nominale *f.*, (*philately*) valeur faciale *f.*; **~less** *adj.* anonyme; **~r** *s.* (*Eng. pop.*) (*blow*) gifle *f.*, (*insult*) affront *m.*
face[2] *v.t.* & *i.* **1.** (*meet firmly*) faire face à, braver; **~ the music,** tenir tête à l'orage; (*present itself*) se poser; **the problem which ~s us,** le problème qui se pose pour nous; **2.** (*be opposite to*) se présenter à; (*look towards*) être orienté, exposé, vers; **3.** (*dressm.*) mettre un revers, un parement à; **4.** (*techn.*) revêtir (*with*—de), (*stone*) aplanir; **5.** (*turn left, right, etc.*) faire

demi-tour (à gauche, à droite, etc.); ABOUT ~; **facing** *s.* (3) revers *m.*; (4) revêtement *m.*; **facing** *prep.* en face de, face à.

facet *s.* (*small surface, of crystal etc.*) facette *f.*; (*fig. aspect*) face *f.*

facetious *adj.* facétieux; **~ly** *adv.* d'une manière facétieuse; **~ness** *s.* (*action, words*) facétie *f.*; (*humour*) humeur facétieuse *f.*

fa(s)cia *s.* (*arch.*) cordon *m.*, bandeau *m.*; (*shop*) enseigne *m.*; (*auto.*) tableau de bord *m.*

facial *adj.* facial; *s.* (*Eng. fam.*) traitement esthétique pour le visage *m.*

facile *adj.* (*easy*) facile; (*working easily*) commode; (*fluent, usu. pej.*) facile; (*flexible, of person*) accommodant.

facilit/ate *v.t.* faciliter (qch. à qn.); **~y** *s.* (*absence of difficulty*) facilité *f.*; (*dexterity*) habileté *f.*; (*pl. opportunities*) facilités *f.pl.*

facsimile *s.* fac-similé *m.*

fact *s.* (*thing done; thing known to be true*) fait *m.*; (*reality*) réalité *f.*; **in ~,** en effet; **the ~ is that,** le fait est que; **~-finding mission,** enquête *f.*

facti/on *s.* (*break-away group within party*) faction *f.*; (*prevalence of party spirit*) esprit de faction *m.*; **~ous** *adj.* factieux; **~ously** *adv.* en factieux; **~ousness** *s.* esprit de faction *m.*

factitious *adj.* factice.

factor *s.* **1.** (*agent*) agent *m.*, (*comm.*) commissionaire *m.*; (*Scottish land agent*) régisseur *m.*; **2.** (*math., med., techn., fig.*) facteur *m.*; **~age** *s.* (1) (*commission*) commission *f.*; **~ize** *v.t.* (*math.*) mettre en facteurs.

factory *s.* (*small*) fabrique *f.*; (*large*) usine *f.*; (*specialized, e.g. china*) manufacture *f.*

factotum *s.* factotum *m.*

factual *adj.* réel, positif.

facult/y *s.* faculté *f.*; **~ative** *adj.* conditionnel; (*optional*) facultatif.

fad *s.* caprice *m.*

fade *v.t.* & *i.* (*droop, wither*) (se) faner, (se) flétrir; ((*cause to*) *lose colour, sun, etc.*) déteindre; (*disappear gradually, colour, etc.*) passer; (*grow faint, sound*) s'éteindre; (*fig. lose power*) s'évanouir; **~ away,** s'évanouir, s'éteindre; **~-in, ~-out** *s.* ouverture (*f.*), fermeture (*f.*) en fondu; **~-up** *s.* (*cinema*) fondu *m.*; **fading** *s.* (*radio*) évanouissement (du son) *m.*

faeces *s.pl.* matières fécales *f.pl.*

fag *s.* **1.** (*drudgery*) corvée *f.*; **2.** (*at school*) bizuth *m.*; **3.** (*pop. cigarette*) sèche *f.*; **~-end** *s.* bout *m.* (*of cigarette*) mégot *m.*; *v.t.* & *i* (1) (*grow or make weary*) (s')éreinter; (2) servir comme bizuth; **~ged (out)** (*fam.*) éreinté.

fag(g)ot *s.* (*bundle of sticks*) fagot *m.*; (*mech.*) faisceau *m.*; (*cook.*) crépinette *f.*; *v.t.* (*needlework*) orner d'un point de chausson.

Fahrenheit *adj.* & *s. invar.* fahrenheit.

fail *s.* **without ~,** sans faute; *v.t.* (*disappoint*) décevoir; (*neglect*) négliger; (*candidate in exam*) faire échouer; *v.i.* (*be missing*) manquer; (*be deficient*) faire défaut; (*break down*) tomber en panne; (*not succeed*) échouer; (*go bankrupt*) faire faillite; (*fig.*) baisser, diminuer; (*come to nothing*) faire fiasco; **~ to do,** omettre, manquer, de faire; **~ in,** échouer (à un examen, en maths, etc.), rater qch.; **~-safe** *adj.* à sûreté intégrée; **~-safe mechanism,** disjoncteur automatique *m.*; **~ing** *s.* (*deficiency*) manque *m.*; (*fault*) défaut *m.*; (*weakness*) faiblesse *f.*; (*foible*) faible *m.*; **~ing** *adj.* défaillant; **~ing** *prep.* faute de, à défaut de; **~ure** *s.* (*non-performance*) défaut *m.*; (*≠ success*) échec *m.*, insuccès *m.*; (*bankruptcy*) faillite *f.*; (*unsuccessful person*) raté *m.*; (*unsuccessful thing*) échec *m.*; (*techn.*) panne *f.*

fain *adj.* (*archaic*) **to be ~ to,** être disposé à.

faint *s.* évanouissement *m.*; *v.i.* s'évanouir, se trouver mal; *adj.* **1.** (*feeble*) faible; **2.** (*timid*) timide; **3.** (*dim, pale*) faible, vague; **4.** (*liable to* ~) prêt à s'évanouir; **~-hearted** *adj.* timoré; **~-heartedness** *s.* faiblesse *f.*; **~ly** *adv.* (1)*; (2)*; (3)*,*; **~ness** *s.* (1), (2), (3), (4) faiblesse *f.*

fair[1] *s.* (*annual, trade*) foire *f.*; (*bazaar*) vente de charité *f.*; FUN-~; **~ground** *s.* champ de foire *m.*

fair[2] *adj.* **1.** (*beautiful*) beau; **2.** (*blond*) blond; **3.** (*just*) juste; **4.** (*of moderate quality or amount*) moyen, passable; **5.** (*weather*) clair; **~ copy,** copie au net *f.*; **to be ~ game** (*fig.*) mériter qu'on se moque; **~ play** *s.* franc-jeu *m.*; **~ share,** bonne part *f.*; **~way** *s.* (channel) chenal navigable *m.*, (*golf*) chemin normal *m.*; **~-weather** *adj.* (*fig.*) des beaux jours; *adv.* **to bid ~ to,** (*of person*) être en passe de, (*of thing*) s'annoncer bien; **to play ~,** jouer franc-jeu; **~ly** *adv.* (3) équitablement; (4) passablement; (*rather*) assez; (*completely*) complètement; **~ness** *s.* (1) beauté *f.*; (2) blondeur *f.*; (3) justice *f.*; (5) clarté *f.*

fairy *s.* fée *f.*; *adj.* féerique; **F~land** *s.* pays de fées *m.*; **~ lights** *s.* guirlande électrique *f.*; **~ ring** *s.* cercle magique *m.*; **~-tale** *s.* conte de fées *m.*, (*fam. tall story*) blague *f.*, (*falsehood*) mensonge *m.*

faith *s.* **1.** (*trust*) foi *f.*; **2.** (*relig. belief*) croyance *f.*; **3.** (*religion*) foi *f.*; **4.** (*loyalty*) fidélité *f.*, bonne foi *f.*; **to have ~ in s.o.,** avoir foi en qn.; **to have ~ in sth.,** avoir confiance en qch.; **in good ~,** en toute bonne foi; **~-healer,** guérisseur mystique *m.*; **~ful** *adj.* (1) & (4) fidèle; (*true*) fidèle; (*accurate*) exact; **~fully** *adv.* fidèlement; **yours ~fully** (*at end of letter*), veuillez agréer, Monsieur/Madame, l'expression de mes sentiments distingués; **~fulness** *s.* fidélité *f.*; **~less** *adj.* infidèle, perfide; **~lessly** *adv.**,*; **~lessness** *s.* infidélité *f.*

fake *s.* (*act*) contrefaçon *f.*; (*thing*) objet (meuble, document) truqué *m.*, faux *m.*; *v.t.* truquer.

fakir *s.* fakir *m.*

Falang/e *s.* (*Spanish polit.*) phalange *f.*; **~ist** *s.* phalangiste *m.f.*

falcon *s.* faucon *m.*; **~er** *s.* fauconnier *m.*; **~ry** *s.* fauconnerie *f.*

faldstool *s.* (*bishop's chair*) faldistoire *m.*; (*kneeling desk*) prie-dieu *m.*

fall *s.* **1.** (*~ing; amount of snow, etc.; fig. down~*) chute *f.*; **2.** (*drop in price, temperature, etc.*) baisse *f.*; **3.** (*descent*) pente *f.*; **4.** (*autumn*) automne *m.*; **5.** (*cataract, Eng. often pl.*) cascade *f.*; **6.** (*approach, of night, etc.*) tombée *f.*; **to** RIDE **for a ~**; *v.i.* (1) & (6) tomber; (2) baisser; (3) descendre; **7.** (*droop*) s'incliner; **8.** (*of face*) s'allonger; **9.** (*collapse*) s'écrouler, s'effondrer; **10.** (*sin*) pécher; **11.** (*happen*) arriver; **12.** (*become*) devenir; **~ asleep,** s'endormir; **~ in love with,** tomber amoureux de; **~** FOUL **of**; **~ away** *v.i.* (*ground*) descendre, (*med.*) maigrir; **~ back** *v.i.* (*mil.*) se replier, (*fig.*) reculer; **~ back on,** se rabattre sur; **~ behind,** rester en arrière; **~ down** *v.i.* tomber, s'écrouler, (*fig.*) échouer; **~ down on sth.** (*fig.*) rater qch.; **~ for s.o.,** s'amouracher de qn.; **~ for sth.,** se laisser prendre à qch.; **~ in** (*mil.*) former les rangs, (*collapse*) s'effondrer; **~ into conversation with,** entrer en conversation avec; **~ in with,** (*meet*) rencontrer, (*agree to*) se conformer à; **~ off,** décliner, baisser, (*fin.*) diminuer; **~ out** (*mil.*) rompre les rangs, (*happen*) se passer; **~ out with s.o.,** se brouiller avec qn.; (*radio-active*) **~-out** *s.* retombées (radioactives) *f.pl.*; **~ to,** se mettre à; **~ through** (*fail*) échouer; **~ under,** tomber sous; **~ upon,** tomber sur; **~ short,** ne pas (se) réaliser; **~en** *adj.* tombé, (*fig.*) déchu; **~ing** *s.* chute *f.*; **~ing-away** *s.* amaigrissement *m.*, (*fig.*) défection *f.*; **~ing-back** *s.* repli *m.*; **~ing-in** *s.* écroulement *m.*, (*fig.*) accord *m.*;

~ing-off *s.* fléchissement *m.*; **~ing-out** *s.* (*hair, etc.*) chute *f.*, (*fig.*) brouille *f.*; **~ing sickness** *s.* épilepsie *f.*; **~ing star,** étoile filante *f.*

fallac/y *s.* **1.** (*misleading argument*) raisonnement fallacieux *m.*; **2.** (*delusiveness*) caractère trompeur *m.*; **3.** (*error*) erreur *f.*; **~ious** *adj.* (1) fallacieux; (2) trompeur; (3) erroné; **~iously** *adv.* (1) d'une manière fallacieuse; (2) d'une manière trompeuse; (3)*.

fallib/le *adj.* faillible; **~ility** *s.* faillibilité *f.*

fallow *adj.* en jachère; **to leave ~,** laisser (une terre) en jachère.

fallow deer *see* DEER.

false *adj.* **1.** (*erroneous*) faux; **2.** (*deceitful, spurious*) trompeur; **3.** (*artificial*) artificiel; **4.** (*mus.*) faux; *adv.* (1), (2), (3) faussement; (4) (chanter, jouer, sonner) faux; **to play s.o. ~,** tromper qn.; **~ alarm,** fausse alerte *f.*; **~ bottom,** double fond *m.*; **~ hair,** postiche *m.*; **~ pretences,** moyens frauduleux *m.pl.*; **~hood** *s.* mensonge *m.*; **~ly** *adv.* faussement; **~ness** *s.* fausseté *f.*; **falsity** *s.* fausseté. *f.*

falsetto *s.* (*mus.*) fausset *m.*; *adj.* de fausset.

falsif/y *v.t.* (*alter fraudulently, misrepresent*) falsifier; (*disappoint*) tromper; **~ication** *s.* falsification *f.*

falter *v.i.* **1.** (*motion*) chanceler; **2.** (*speech*) balbutier; **3.** (*waver*) hésiter; **~ing** *adj.* (1) chancelant; (2) balbutiant; (3) hésitant.

fam/e *s.* (*rumour*) bruit *m.*; (*reputation*) réputation *f.*; (*renown*) renommée *f.*; **~ed** *adj.* célèbre; **~ous** *adj.* célèbre; (*fam.* = *excellent*) fameux; **~ously** *adv.* (*fam.*) fameusement.

familiar *s.* (*friend*) ami intime *m.*; (*in witchcraft*) esprit familier *m.*; *adj.* (*intimate*) intime; (*well known*) familier (*to*—à), bien connu (*to*—de); **to be ~ with sth.,** bien connaître qch.; (*common*) ordinaire; (*informal; amorously intimate*) familier; **~ity** *s.* familiarité *f.*; **~ize** *v.t.* familiariser (*with*—avec); **~ly** *adv.* familièrement.

family *s.* famille *f.*; *adj.* de famille, familial; **~ allowance,** allocation familiale *f.*; **~ man,** père de famille *m.*; **~ planning,** contrôle des naissances *m.*; **~ tree,** arbre généalogique *m.*

famine *s.* (*scarcity*) disette *f.*; (*starvation*) famine *f.*

famish *v.t.* affamer; **to be ~ed** (*Eng. fam.*) mourir de faim.

famous *see* FAME.

fan[1] *s.* **1.** (*winnowing machine*) van *m.*; **2.** (*to cool face*) éventail *m.*; **3.** (*mech.*) ventilateur *m.*; **~-shaped,** en éventail; ~BELT; **~light** *s.* fenêtre en éventail *f.*, (*above door*) imposte *f.*; **~tail** (*pigeon*) pigeon-paon *m.*; **~ vaulting** *s.* (*arch.*) voûte en éventail *f.*; *v.t.* (1) vanner; (2) (s')éventer; **4.** (*increase flames, etc.*) attiser, (*fig.*) exciter; *v.i.* **~ out,** se déployer en éventail.

fan[2] *s.* (*pop.* = *enthusiast*) fervent, fanatique *m.f.*; **~ mail,** courrier des admirateurs *m.*

fanatic *adj.* & *s.m.f.* fanatique; **~al** *adj.* fanatique; **~ally** *adv.**; **~ism** *s.* fanatisme *m.*

fanc/y *s.* **1.** (*imagination*) imagination *f.*; **2.** (*delusion; supposition; caprice, whim*) fantaisie *f.*; **3.** (*taste, liking*) goût *m.*; **to take a ~y to s.o., sth.,** se sentir attiré par qn., se sentir du goût pour qch.; **to take s.o.'s ~y,** captiver qn.; FLIGHT **of ~y**; *adj.* (≠ *plain*) extravagant; (*whimsical*) fantaisiste; **~y dress** *s.* travesti *m.*; **~ydress ball,** bal costumé *m.*; **~y-free** *adj.* libre; **~y goods,** articles de Paris *m.pl.*; **~y price,** prix exorbitant *m.*; *v.t.* & *i.* (1) (s') imaginer; (2) supposer, se figurer; (3) trouver plaisant, avoir envie de; **~y oneself** (*pop.*) se prendre pour qn.; **just ~y!, ~y that!,** figurez-vous!; **~ier** *s.* amateur *m.*; **~iful** *adj.* (*person*) rêveur, capricieux; (*thing*) fantaisiste.

fane *s.* (*poet.*) temple *m.*

fanfare *s.* fanfare *f.*

fang *s.* (*canine*) croc *m.*; (*of serpent*) crochet *m.*; (*prong of tooth*) racine *f.*

fantasia *s.* (*mus.*) fantaisie *f.*

fantastic *adj.* **1.** (*extravagantly fanciful*) fantastique; **2.** (*grotesque, quaint*) fantasque, bizarre; **3.** (*pop.* = *excellent*) fantastique; **~ally** *adv.* (1) & (3)*; (2) bizarrement.

fantasy *s.* (*imagination*) imagination *f.*; (*fancy*) fantaisie *f.*; (*illusion*) fantasme *m.*; (*fantastic design, etc.*) fantaisie *f.*

F.A.O. (*Food & Agriculture Organization*) F.A.O. *f.*

far *adj.* (*distant*) lointain; (*remote*) éloigné; ~ EAST; *adv.* (*at, to, by, a great distance, in space or time*) loin; (*fig. by a great deal*) de loin; **~ away, ~ off,** au loin; **~ into the night,** bien avant dans la nuit; **~ the best,** de loin le meilleur; **as ~ as,** aussi loin que; **as ~ as I know,** autant que je sache; **as ~ as he is concerned,** en ce qui le concerne, quant à lui; **~ and away,** de loin; **~ and near,** partout; **~ and wide,** de tous côtés; **by ~,** de loin; **~ from,** loin de; **~ from it,** loin de là; **~ from being,** loin d'être; **to go ~** (*lit.* & *fig.*) aller loin; **to go too ~** (*fig.*) dépasser les bornes; **how ~?** (*to what extent*) jusqu'à quel point?; **how ~ is it?** (*from A to B*) quelle est la distance? (entre A et B); **in so ~ as,** dans la mesure où; **so ~,** jusqu'ici; **so ~ as to,** jusqu'à; **~-away** *adj.* (*remote*) éloigné, (*dreamy*) rêveur; **few and ~ between,** rare(s); **~-fetched** *adj.* recherché; **~-flung** *adj.* étendu; **~-off** *adj.* lointain; **not to be ~ out,** ne pas se tromper de beaucoup; **~-reaching** *adj.* de grande portée; **~-seeing, ~-sighted** *adj.* prévoyant.

farc/e *s.* **1.** (*theat.*) farce *f.*; **2.** (*pretence*) comédie *f.*; **~ical** *adj.* (1) burlesque; (2) ridicule.

fare *s.* (*cost of conveyance*): (*bus, train*) prix de la place *m.*, (*taxi*) prix de la course *m.*; (*passenger*) (*on bus, train*) voyageur *m.*, (*in taxi*) client *m.*; (*food*) chère *f.*; *v.i.* (*poet. to go, travel*) voyager; (*get on*) aller; (*be fed*) manger, faire bonne/maigre chère; **~well** *s.* & *interj.* adieu *m.*; *adj.* d'adieu.

farinaceous *adj.* farinacé.

farm *s.* (*land* & *house*) ferme *f.*; **oyster-~,** *etc.* élevage *m.*; **sewage-~,** champ d'épandage *m.*; **~-labourer** *s.* travailleur agricole *m.*; **~yard** *s.* cour de ferme *f.*; *v.t.* cultiver; *v.i.* être fermier, cultivateur; **~er** *s.* cultivateur *m.*, fermier *m.*; **~er's wife,** fermière *f.*; **~ing** *s.* (*cultivation*) culture *f.*, (*agriculture*) agriculture *f.*

farrago *s.* salmigondis *m.*

farrier *s.* maréchal-ferrant *m.*

farrow *s.* portée (de petits cochons) *f.*; *v.i.* mettre bas.

farth/er *adj.* plus éloigné; *adv.* plus loin; **~est** *adj.* le plus éloigné; *adv.* le plus loin.

farthing *s.* sou *m.*; **not to be worth a brass ~,** (*person*) n'avoir pas un liard; (*thing*) (*fam.*) ne pas valoir tripette.

fascia *see* FACIA.

fascicle, fascicule *s.* (*bot.*) bouquet *m.*; (*instalment of book*) fascicule *m.*

fascinat/e *v.t.* fasciner; **~ing** *adj.* fascinant; **~ion** *s.* fascination *f.*

Fasc/ism *s.* fascisme *m.*; **~ist** *adj.* & *s.m.f.* fasciste.

fashion *s.* **1.** (*make, shape, style*) forme *f.*, coupe *f.*; **2.** (*way, manner*) façon *f.*, manière *f.*; **3.** (*in dress or habit*) mode *f.*; **in ~,** à la mode; **out of ~,** démodé; **the height of ~,** le dernier cri; **after a ~,** en quelque sorte, tant bien que mal; **in the French ~,** à la française; **~ house,** maison de haute couture *f.*; **~-plate** *s.* gravure de mode *f.*; **~able** *adj.* & **~ably** *adv.* à la mode; *v.t.* (1) former, façonner; FULLY **~ed; new-~ed** *adj.* à la mode; **old-~ed** *adj.* démodé.

fast[1] *s.* (~*ing*) jeûne *m.*; *v.i.* jeûner; **~-day,** jour de jeûne *m.*

fast[2] *adj.* **1.** (*firm, fixed*) ferme, stable; **2.** (*rapid*) rapide; **3.** (*pleasure-seeking*) libre; **4.** (*sleep*) profond; **5.** (*colour*) solide; **hard and ~,** absolu, immuable; **to pull a ~ one on s.o.** (*fam.*) avoir qn. au culot; *adv.* (1) fermement; (2) vite; **~ asleep,** profondément endormi; **to be ~** (*clock*) avancer; **to make ~,** (*naut.*) amarrer, (*fix*) attacher solidement; **to stand ~,** tenir ferme; **to stick ~,** coller; **to play ~ and loose,** jouer double jeu; **~ness** *s.* (*mil.*) forteresse *f.*

fasten *v.t.* & *i.* (*fix*) (s')attacher; (*bind*) (se) lier; (*door, etc.*) (se) fermer; (*hook*) agrafer; (*button*) boutonner; (*fig. gaze, etc.*) (se) fixer; **~ off,** arrêter; **~ on to,** se cramponner à; **~er** *s.*, **~ing** *s.* attache *f.*, agrafe *f.*, fermeture *f.*, ZIP **~er.**

fastidious *adj.* délicat, difficile (à plaire); **~ly** *adv.**,*; **~ness** *s.* délicatesse *f.*; ⚠ fastidieux = **tedious.**

fat *s.* graisse *f.*; (*of meat, etc.*) gras *m.*; (~ *content of food*) matières grasses *f.pl.*; **to live on the ~ of the land,** vivre comme coq en pâte; **the ~ is in the fire,** le feu est aux poudres; *adj.* **1.** (*plump*) gros; **2.** (*greasy*) gras; **3.** (*fertile, rich*) gras, riche; **to grow ~,** (s')engraisser; **a ~ lot of good that's done you!,** vous voilà bien avancé!; **a ~ lot I care,** je ne m'en fiche pas mal; **~-head** *s.* niais *m.*; **~stock** *s.* bétail de boucherie *m.*; **~ness** *s.* (1) embonpoint *m.*; (2) graisse *f.*; (3) fertilité *f.*; **~ten** *v.t.* & *i.* (s')engraisser; **~ted** CALF; **~ty** *adj.* graisseux.

fatal *adj.* (*destructive, ruinous*) fatal, funeste; (*deadly*) mortel; **~ism** *s.* fatalisme *m.*; **~ist** *s.* fataliste *m.f.*; **~ity** *s.* (*accident*) désastre *m.*; (*death*) mort (accidentelle) *f.*; **~ly** *adv.* fatalement; mortellement.

fate *s.* (*myth. power*) destin *m.*, sort *m.*; (*destiny*) destinée *f.*; (*death*) mort *f.*; **~d** *adj.* destiné (à); **ill-~d** *adj.* infortuné; **~ful** *adj.* fatal; (*decisive*) décisif.

father *s.* (*parent, originator, eccles.*) père *m.*; GRAND~; GREAT-**grand~**; **F~** CHRISTMAS; **~-in--law, step~,** beau-père *m.*; **~s** *s.pl.* (*ancestors*) aïeux *m.pl.*; **~hood** *s.* paternité *f.*; **~land** *s.* patrie *f.*; **~less** *adj.* sans père; **~liness** *s.* attitude paternelle *f.*; **~ly** *adj.* paternel; *v.t.* (*beget*) engendrer; (*originate*) inventer.

fathom *s.* toise *f.*; (*naut.*) brasse *f.*; *v.t.* (*sound*) sonder; (*comprehend*) pénétrer; **~less** *adj.* insondable.

fatigue *s.* (*weariness*) fatigue *f.*; (*wearying task or duty*) corvée *f.*; *v.t.* fatiguer.

fatu/ous *adj.* **1.** (*silly*) sot; **2.** (*purposeless*) inepte; **~ity** *s.*, **~ousness** *s.* (1) sottise *f.*; (2) ineptie *f.*

faucet *s.* fausset *m.*

fault *s.* **1.** (*defect*) défaut *m.*; **2.** (*culpability, offence*) faute *f.*; **3.** (*tennis*) faute *f.*; **4.** (*geol.*) faille *f.*; **to a ~,** à l'excès; **to be at ~,** être en défaut; **to find ~ with,** trouver à redire à; **whose ~ is it?,** à qui la faute?; *v.t.* & *i.* (*find ~ with*) critiquer; (4) provoquer, présenter, une faille; **~finder** *s.* censeur *m.*; **~iness** *s.* imperfection *f.*; **~less** *adj.* sans faute, sans défaut; **~lessly** *adv.* sans faute, sans défaut; **~lessness** *s.* perfection *f.*; **~y** *adj.* défectueux.

faun *s.* (*myth.*) faune(sse) *m.f.*

fauna *s.* faune *f.*

favour *s.* **1.** (*liking, approval; mark of* ~) faveur *f.*; **2.** (*partiality; aid*) faveur *f.*; **by ~ of,** à la faveur de; **in ~ of,** en faveur de; **to do s.o. a ~,** accorder une faveur à qn.; **to** CURRY **~**; *v.t.* (1) considérer avec faveur; (2) favoriser; **3.** (*resemble*) ressembler à; **~ s.o. with,** gratifier qn. de; **~able** *adj.* (*well-disposed*) bien disposé; (*approving*) favorable; (*promising*) favorable; **~ably** *adv.* favorablement; **~ite** *adj.* & *s.m.f.* favori, -te, (*sport*) favori *m.*; **~itism** *s.* favoritisme *m.*

fawn *s.* faon *m.*; *adj.* fauve; *v.t.* (*of dogs*) ramper; **~ upon s.o.,** courber l'échine, (*fam.*) s'aplatir, devant qn.; **~ing** *s.* servilité *f.*; *adj.* servile.

fay *s.* (*poet.*) fée *f.*

fealty *s.* fidélité *f.*

fear *s.* (*emotion*) peur *f.*, crainte *f.*; (*object or cause of alarm*) danger *m.*; **for ~ of,** de peur de; **for ~ that,** de peur que; **no ~ (of),** pas de danger (de + *s.*, que + *v.*); *v.t.* & *i.* craindre, redouter, avoir peur, **~ sth.,** avoir peur de qch.; **~ that sth. will happen,** avoir peur que qch. arrive (*subjunctive*); **~ful** *adj.* (*state*) peureux, craintif; (*cause*) effrayant; (*pop.* = *annoying*) effroyable; **~fully** *adv.* craintivement; terriblement; (*pop.*) terriblement; **~fulness** *s.* (*state*) nature timorée *f.*, (*cause*) horreur *f.*; **~less** *adj.* & **~lessly** *adv.* sans peur; **~lessness** *s.* intrépidité *f.*; **~some** *adj.* effrayant.

feasib/le *adj.* (*practicable*) faisable, possible; (*plausible*) admissible; **~ility** *s.* possibilité *f.*

feast *s.* **1.** (*eccles.* & *annual festival*) fête *f.*; **2.** (*meal*) festin *m.*; **3.** (*fig. treat*) régal *m.*; *v.t.* (2) fêter; (3) régaler (*fig.*) enchanter; *v.i.* (2) festoyer; (3) se régaler (de).

feat *s.* (*notable act*) haut fait *m.*, exploit *m.*; (*surprising performance*) tour de force *m.*

feather *s.* plume *f.*; **wing-~,** penne *f.*; **to show the white ~,** être poltron, (*fam.*) avoir la frousse; BIRDS **of a ~**; **~ bed** *s.* duvet *m.*; **~-bed** *v.t.* (*fig.*) favoriser; **~-brained** *adj.* écervelé; **~weight** *s.* poids plume *m.*; **~y** *adj.* couvert de plumes, (*like* ~*s*) plumeux, (*soft, light*) duveteux; *v.t.* emplumer; (*rowing*) plumer; **~ one's nest,** faire sa pelote; TAR **and ~.**

feature *s.* **1.** (*usu. pl. of face*) trait *m.*, caractéristique *f.*; **2.** (*prominent part*) trait saillant *m.*; **3.** (*cinema*) grand film *m.*; **4.** (*newspaper*) gros titre *m.*; *v.t.* (*portray*) dépeindre; (2) dominer; (3) mettre en vedette; *v.i.* (*take part in*) figurer au programme.

febrifuge *s.* fébrifuge *m.*

febrile *adj.* fébrile.

February *s.* février *m.*

feckless *adj.* (*ineffective*) incapable; (*careless*) insouciant; (*thoughtless*) irréfléchi.

fecund *adj.* fécond; **~ity** *s.* fécondité *f.*

fed, to be ~ up (with) (*pop.*) en avoir marre (de).

feder/al *adj.* fédéral; **~ate** *v.t.* & *i.* (se) fédérer; **~ation** *s.* fédération *f.*

fee *s.* (*for professional services*) honoraires *m.pl.*; (*school*) frais de scolarité *m.pl.*; (*boarding*) pension *f.*; *v.t.* (*pay ~ to*) rétribuer; (*engage for* ~) acheter.

feebl/e *adj.* (*physically* & *mentally*) faible; (*fam. fig.*) pas fort; **~e-minded** *adj.* faible d'esprit; **~eness** *s.* faiblesse *f.*; **~y** *adv.**.

feed *s.* **1.** (~*ing*) action de nourrir *f.*; **2.** (*pasturage*) pâturage *m.*; **3.** (*fodder*) fourrage *m.*; **4.** (*pop.* = *feast*) gueuleton *m.*; **5.** (*techn.*) alimentation *f.*; *v.t.* & *i.* (1) (se) nourrir (*on*—de); (2) (faire) paître; (3) donner à manger à; (5) alimenter; **~back** *s.* (*electr.*) rétroaction *f.*; **~-pipe** *s.* tuyau d'alimentation *m.*; **~er** *s.* (*child's bib*) bavoir *m.*, (*tributary*) affluent *m.*, (*mech.*) conduite d'alimentation *f.*, (*gas*) gazoduc *m.*; **~ing bottle** (*for baby*) biberon *m.*; **~ing cup** (*for invalids*) canard *m.*

feel *s.* (*sense of touch*) toucher *m.*; (*sensation*) sensation *f.*; *v.t.* **1.** (*explore or perceive by touch*) tâter; **2.** (*be conscious of*) sentir; **3.** (*experience, be affected by*) ressentir; *v.i.* (1) tâtonner; (2) se sentir; (3) avoir le sentiment, l'impression (de); **~ hot, cold,** (*person*) avoir chaud, froid; (*thing*) être chaud, froid, au toucher; **~ like** (= *wish* *for*) avoir envie de; ~ **for s.o.,** éprouver de la pitié pour qn.; **~er** *s.* (*organ of touch*) antenne *f.*; (*fig.*) ballon d'essai *m.*; **~ing** *s.* (*touch*) toucher *m.*; (*sensation*) sensation *f.*; (*emotion*) sentiment *m.*; (*expression*) expression *f.*; (*impression*) impression *f.*; **~ings** *s.pl.* sensibilité *f.*; **~ing** *adj.* sensible; **~ingly** *adv.* avec sentiment.

feign *v.t.* (*pretend*) feindre; (*simulate*) simuler.

feint *s.* (*sham attack*) feinte *f.*; (*pretence*) faux semblant *m.*; *v.i.* faire semblant (de).

fel(d)spar *s.* feldspath *m.*

felicit/ate *v.t.* féliciter (de); **~ation** *s.* félicitation *f.*; **~ous** *adj.* heureux; **~ously** *adv.**; **~y** *s.* bonheur *m.*; (*in style*) bonheur d'expression *m.*

feline *adj.* & *s.m.* félin.

fell *s.* (*animal's coat*) peau *f.*; (*thick wool*) laine *f.*; (*hill country*) lande *f.*; *v.t.* (*cut down*) abattre; (*dressm.*) rabattre; *adj.* (*fierce*) féroce; (*destructive*) meurtrier.

fellow *s.* **1.** (*comrade*) camarade *m.*, compagnon *m.*, compagne *f.*; **2.** (*counterpart*): (*person*) égal *m.*, (*thing*) pendant *m.*; **3.** (*acad.*) professeur *m.*, membre *m.* (*of a college*); **4.** (*of a learned society*) membre *m.*; **5.** (*fam.*) type *m.*; **my dear, my good, ~,** mon cher (ami); OLD ~; **poor ~,** pauvre diable; **to be hail-~-well-met with,** être à tu et à toi avec; *adj.* pareil; **~ citizen,** concitoyen(ne) *m.f.*; **~-countryman,** compatriote *m.*; **~ creature,** semblable *m.*; **~-feeling** *s.* sympathie *f.*, compréhension *f.*; **~-student,** condisciple *m.*; **~-traveller,** compagnon de voyage *m.*, (*polit.*) communisant *m.*; **~ship** *s.* (1) camaraderie *f.*; (3) poste de professeur *m.*, bourse de recherches *f.*; (4) titre de membre *m.*; (*group*) compagnie *f.*, société *f.*, association *f.*

felo de se *s.* suicide *m.*

felon *s.* criminel *m.*; **~ious** *adj.* criminel; **~y** *s.* crime *m.*, délit majeur *m.*; **to** COMPOUND **a ~y.**

felspar *see* FELDSPAR.

felt *s.* feutre *m.*; *v.t.* & *i.* (se) feutrer; *adj.* de feutre.

felucca *s.* felouque *f.*

female *s.* (*person*) femme *f.*; (*animal* & *pej. of person*) femelle *f.*; *adj.* femelle; des femmes.

femin/ine *adj.* & *s.m.* féminin; **~inity** *s.* féminité *f.*; **~ism** *s.* féminisme *m.*; **~ist** *s.* féministe *m.f.*

femoral *adj.* fémoral.

femur *s.* fémur *m.*

fen *s.* marais *m.*; **~ny** *adj.* marécageux.

fence[1] *s.* **1.** (*hedge, etc.*) clôture *f.*, palissade *f.*; **2.** (*mech.*) garde *m.*; **3.** (*Eng. fam. receiver of stolen goods*) receleur *m.*; **to sit on the ~,** ménager la chèvre et le chou; *v.t.* (1) clôturer, palissader; (3) receler.

fenc/e[2] *v.i.* (*sword play*) faire de l'escrime; **~ with,** lutter, (*fig.*) esquiver; **~er** *s.* escrimeur *m.*; **~ing** *s.* escrime *f.*; **~ing glove,** gant d'escrime *m.*; **~ing master,** maître d'armes *m.*; **~ing school,** salle d'armes *f.*

fend *v.t.* **~ off,** parer; *v.i.* **~ for oneself,** se débrouiller (tout seul).

fender *s.* (*for fire*) foyer *m.*; (*naut.*) boudin *m.*; (*auto.*) pare-chocs *m.*

fennel *s.* fenouil *m.*

feral *adj.* féroce; (*wild*) sauvage.

ferment *s.* (*leaven, etc.*) ferment *m.*; (*state, lit.* & *fig.*) fermentation *f.*; *v.t.* & *i.* (faire) fermenter; (*fig.*) mettre en effervescence; **~ation** *s.* fermentation *f.*

fern *s.* fougère *f.*; **~ery** *s.* fougeraie *f.*

feroc/ious *adj.* féroce; **~iously** *adv.**; **~ity** *s.* férocité *f.*

ferret *s.* furet; *m.*; (*pej. police*) sbire *m.*; *v.t.* prendre au furet; (*fig.*) **~ out,** dénicher, dépister; **~y** *adj.* de furet.

ferr/ic *adj.* ferrique; **~ous.** *adj.* & **~iferous** *adj.* ferreux; **~uginous** *adj.* ferrugineux.

ferrule *s.* (*ring*) virole *f.*; (*cap*) bout ferré *m.*

ferry *s.* (*place*) passage en bac *m.*; (*boat*) bac *m.*; **air ~,** bac aérien *m.*; **car ~,** navire transbordeur *m.*; **train ~,** ferry-boat *m.*; *v.t.* & *i.* (faire) traverser en bac; **~-boat** *s.* bac *m.*; **~man** *s.* passeur *m.*

fertil/e *adj.* fertile (*in*—en); (*egg, etc.*) fécondé; **~ity** *s.* fertilité *f.*; **~ize** *v.t.* **1.** (*agric.*) fertiliser; **2.** (*med., bot.*) féconder; **~ization** *s.* (1) fertilisation *f.*, (2) fécondation *f.*; **~izer** *s.* (*agric.*) engrais *m.*

ferule *s.* (*cane for punishment*) férule *f.*

ferv/ent *adj.* **1.** (*hot, glowing*) ardent; **2.** (*fig. ardent*) fervent; **~ency** *s.* (1) ardeur *f.*; (2) ferveur *f.*; **~ently** *adv.* (1) ardemment; (2) avec ferveur; **~id** *adj.* fervent; **~our** *s.* (1) ardeur *f.*; (2) ferveur *f.*

festal *adj.* (*of feast*) de fête; (*gay*) gai.

fester *v.t.* & *i.* (s')envenimer; (*fig.*) envenimer, (s')aigrir.

festiv/al *s.* (*day, celebration*) fête *f.*; (*mus. etc.*) festival *m.* ⚠ *this meaning only*; **~e** *adj.* de fête, gai; **~ity** *s.* gaieté *f.*; **~ities** *s.pl.* festivités *f.pl.*

festoon *s.* feston *m.*; *v.t.* festonner.

fetch *v.t.* (*go and bring*) aller chercher (qch., qn.); (*blood, water*) tirer; (*sigh*) pousser; (*tears*) arracher; (*a price*) atteindre (un prix); (*deal blow*) asséner (un coup); **~ and carry,** faire des commissions; **~ing** *adj.* (*fam.*) chic, séduisant.

fête *s.* fête *f.*; *v.t.* fêter.

fetid *adj.* fétide; **~ity** *s.* & **~ness** *s.* fétidité *f.*

fetish *s.* fétiche *m.*; **~ism** *s.* fétichisme *m.*

fetlock *s.* (*of horse*) boulet *m.*

fetter *s.* (*lit.* & *fig.*) entrave *f.*; **~s** *s.pl.* fers *m.pl.*; *v.t.* (*lit.* & *fig.*) entraver.

fettle *s.* forme *f.*; **in fine ~,** en pleine forme.

feud *s.* querelle *f.*; (*enmity*) inimitié *f.*; *v.i.* se quereller.

feudal *adj.* féodal; **~ism** *s.* féodalisme *m.*; **~ system** *s.* féodalité *f.*

fever *s.* (*lit.* & *fig.*) fièvre *f.*; SCARLET **~**; **~ed** *adj.* (*lit.*) fiévreux; (*fig.*) enfiévré; **~ish** *adj.* (*lit.*) fiévreux; (*fig.*) fébrile; **~ishly** *adv.* fiévreusement; **~ishness** *s.* (*med.*) fièvre légère *f.*; (*fig.*) fébrilité *f.*

few *pron.* peu; *adj.* peu de, rare, peu nombreux, quelques; **~ people know that,** il y a peu de gens qui savent cela; **give me a ~ nails,** donnez-moi quelques clous; **the happy ~,** les rares initiés; **a good ~,** un assez grand nombre; **quite a ~,** pas mal de; **~ and** FAR **between**; **~er,** moins de.

fez *s.* fez *m.*

fiasco *s.* (*failure*) échec *m.*; (*ignominious result*) fiasco *m.*

fiat *s.* (*authorization*) autorisation *f.*; (*decree*) décret *m.*

fib *s.* petit mensonge *m.*; (*pop.*) craque *f.*; *v.i.* & **to tell ~s,** dire des craques; **~ber** *s.* blagueur *m.*

fibr/e *s.* fibre *f.*; **~eglass** *s.* (*for insulation*) laine de verre *f.*; (*solid substance*) fibre de verre *f.*; **~oid** *s.* fibrome *m.*; *adj.* fibreux; **~ositis** *s.* cellulite *f.*; **~ous** *adj.* fibreux.

fibula *s.* péroné *m.*

fickle *adj.* inconstant; **~ness** *s.* inconstance *f.*

fiction *s.* (*invention*) fiction *f.*; (*type of liter.*) roman *m.*; **~al** *adj.* d'imagination.

fictitious *adj.* (*not genuine*) fictif; (*imaginary*) imaginaire; **~ly** *adv.* fictivement.

fiddle *s.* **1.** (*violin*) violon *m.*; **2.** (*naut.*) violon *m.*; **3.** (*fam.*) combine *f.*; **to play second ~,** (*fig.*) jouer un rôle secondaire; **as fit as a ~,** en pleine forme; **~-de-dee!,** chansons!; **~-faddle, ~sticks,** balivernes *f.pl.*; *v.t.* & *i.* (1) jouer du violon; (3) falsifier, (*fam.*) maquiller; **~ about,**

bricoler; ~ **with,** tripoter; ~**r** *s.* joueur de violon *m.*; **fiddling** *adj.* (*petty*) insignificant.
fidelity *s.* fidélité *f.*
fidget *s.* (*state*) agitation *f.*; (*person*) agité *m.*; **to have the ~s** (*fam.*) avoir la bougeotte; *v.t.* agacer; *v.i.* s'impatienter, ne pas tenir en place; ~**y** *adj.* agité, nerveux.
Fido (*Fog Investigation Dispersal Operation*) dénébulateur *m.*
fiduciary *adj.* fiduciaire.
fie! *interj.* fi donc!, pouah!
fief *s.* fief *m.*
field *s.* (*agric., of battle, electr.*) champ *m.*; (*sport*) terrain *m.*; (*coal~, etc.*) bassin *m.*; OIL~; (*expanse of sea, snow, etc.*) étendue *f.*; (*area of action*) terrain *m.*, (*fig.*) champ *m.*, plan *m.*; (*racing*) concurrents *m.pl.*; ~**-day** *s.* (mil.) jour de grandes manœuvres *m.*, (*fig.*) grand jour *m.*; ~ **events,** épreuves de sauts et de lancers *f.pl.*; ~**-glasses,** jumelles *f.pl.*; **F~ Marshal** *s.* maréchal *m.*; ~**-mouse** *s.* mulot *m.*; ~**-study** *s.* enquête sur les lieux *f.*; ~**-work** *s.* travaux pratiques *m.pl.*; *v.i.* (*cricket*) tenir le champ.
fiend *s.* (*devil, wicked person*) démon *m.*; (*pop. addict*) fanatique *m.*; ~**ish** *adj.* diabolique; ~**ishly** *adv.**.
fierce *adj.* **1.** (*violent, storm, passion, etc.*) violent, (*person*) cruel, féroce; **2.** (*vehement*) acharné, furieux; **3.** (≠ *smooth*) brutal; **4.** (*intense*) (*desire*) ardent, (*look*) farouche; ~**ly** *adv.* (1) violemment, férocement; (2) furieusement; (3)*; (4) ardemment,*; ~**ness** *s.* (1) violence *f.*, férocité *f.*; (2) fureur *f.*; (3) brutalité *f.*; (4) ardeur *f.*
fier/y *adj.* **1.** (*flaming*) enflammé; **2.** (*flashing*) ardent; **3.** (*irritable*) fougueux; ~**iness** *s.* (1) flamme *f.*; (2) ardeur *f.*; (3) fougue *f.*
fife *s.* (*instrument* & *player*) fifre *m.*
fifteen *adj.* & *s.m.* quinze; (*rugby*) équipe *f.*, quinze *m.*; ~**th** *adj.* & *s.m.* quinzième; (*with date* & *name*) quinze.
fifth *adj.* & *s.m.* cinquième; (*with date* & *name*) cinq; ~**ly** *adv.* cinquièmement, en cinquième lie.
fift/y *adj.* & *s.m.* cinquante; ~**y-~y,** moitié moitié; **to be in one's ~ies,** avoir la cinquantaine; ~**ieth** *adj.* & *s.m.* cinquantième.
fig *s.* figue *f.*; ~**-tree,** figuier *m.*; **not to care a ~** (*for*) (*pop.*) se ficher (de).
fight *s.* (~*ing, boxing*) combat *m.*; (*battle*) bataille *f.*; (*fig. conflict*) lutte *f.*; RUN**ning ~; ~ to a finish** *s.* combat à outrance *m.*; **to show ~,** montrer les dents; *v.t.* & *i.* (*in battle*) combattre, livrer bataille (à), se battre; (*struggle for*) lutter (pour); (*Eng. fam.*) se quereller; ~ **to a finish,** lutter jusqu'au bout; ~ **shy of,** éviter; ~**er** *s.* (*mil.*) combattant *m.*, (*aviat.*) chasseur *m.*, (*fig. person*) batailleur *m.*; ~**ing** *s.* combats *m.pl.*, lutte *f.*; *adj.* combattant, de combat; ~**ing cock** *s.* coq de combat *m.*; ~**ing fit** *adj.* en pleine forme; **to have a ~ing chance,** avoir encore une chance.
figment *s.* (*invented statement*) invention *f.*; (*imaginary thing*) fiction *f.*
figur/e *s.* (*external form*) figure *f.*; (*bodily shape*) ligne *f.*; (*image*) image *m.*; (*emblem*) symbole *m.*; (*diagram*) illustration *f.*; (*number*) chiffre *m.*; (*person*) figure *f.*; ~**e-head** (*lit.* & *fig.*) figure de proue *f.*; ~**ation** *s.* (*act*) figuration *f.*; (*shape*) configuration *f.*; ~**ative** *adj.* figuratif; *s.* figuré *m.*; ~**atively** *adv.* au figuré; ~**ine** *s.* figurine *f.*; ~**e of speech,** figure de rhétorique *f.*; *v.t.* (*represent in diagram*) représenter; (*imagine*) se figurer; (*calculate, estimate*) calculer, estimer; *v.i.* figurer.
Fiji (Islands) *s.pl.* (*geog.*) îles Fidji *f.pl.*; ~**an** *adj.* & *s.m.* (*lang.*) fidjien; *s.m.f.* Fidjien(ne).
filament *s.* filament *m.*
filbert *s.* aveline *f.*; ~**-tree,** avelinier *m.*
filch *v.t.* (*fam.*) chiper.
fil/e 1. (*instrument*) lime *f.*; **2.** (*for papers*) (*stiff cover*) chemise *f.*, (*box*) classeur *m.*, (*contents*) dossier *m.*; **3.** (*mil.*) file *f.*, (*gen. row*) queue *f.*; **rank and ~e,** hommes de troupe *m.pl.*, (*fig.*) la masse; *v.t.* (1) limer; (2) classer; (3) *v.i.* marcher à la file; ~**e off,** défiler; ~**er** *s.* (1) limeur *m.*; ~**ing** *s.* (1) limage *m.*; (2) classement *m.*; ~**ings** *s.* (1) limaille (de fer) *f.*
filial *adj.* filial.
filiation *s.* filiation *f.*
filibuster *s.* **1.** (*pirate*) flibustier *m.*; **2.** (*polit.*) obstruction *f.*; obstructionniste *m.f.*; *v.i.* (1) flibuster; (2) faire de l'obstruction.
filigree *s.* filigrane *m.*; *adj.* en filigrane; ~**d** *adj.* filigrané.
fill *s.* (*full supply*) saoul (soûl) *m.*; **to eat one's ~,** manger son saoul; (*enough to ~ sth.*) quantité pour remplir *f.*; *v.t.* & *i.* (*make or become full, pervade*) (se) remplir; (*block up*) boucher; (*tooth*) plomber; (*satisfy*) combler; (*occupy, time, post*) occuper; ~ **in** *v.t.* (*form, etc.*) remplir, (*time, etc.*) occuper, (*hole, etc.*) combler; ~ **out** *v.t.* & *i.* (se) gonfler, (*fam. of person*) (se) remplumer; ~ **up** *v.t.* & *i.* (se) remplir, (*with petrol*) faire le plein (d'essence); ~**er** *s.* (*for drops*) compte-gouttes *m.*, (*funnel*) entonnoir *m.*, (*techn.*) mastic *m.*; ~**ing** *s.* remplissage *m.*, (*techn.*) remblayage *m.*, (*tooth*) obturation *f.*, (*fam.*) plombage *m.*; ~**ing** *adj.* (*fam. of food*) bourratif; ~**ing station** *s.* poste d'essence *m.*, station-service *f.*
fillet *s.* **1.** (*round head*) bandeau *m.*; **2.** (*of beef*) filet *m.*, (*of veal*) rouelle *f.*, (*of fish*) filet *m.*; **3.** (*arch.*) filet *m.*, moulure *f.*; *v.t.* (2) découper en filets.
fillip *s.* (*flip*) chiquenaude *f.*; (*fig.*) stimulant *m.*
filly *s.* (*foal*) pouliche *f.*; (*pop. girl*) jouvencelle *f.*
film *s.* **1.** (*thin layer*) membrane *f.*; **2.** (*photo.*) pellicule *f.*; **3.** (*cinema*) film *m.*; **to make, shoot, a ~,** tourner un film; *adj.* cinématographique (*industry, studio, etc.*); ~ **director, producer,** cinéaste *m.*; ~ **star** *s.* vedette *f.*; **4.** (*over eyes*) taie *f.*; **5.** (*haze*) voile *f.*; ~**y** *adj.* transparent; embrumé, voilé; *v.t.* (1) couvrir d'une pellicule; (2) photographier; (3) filmer.
filter *s.* **1.** (*for liquids, porous substance, electr.*) filtre *m.*; **2.** (*road sign*) flèche de dégagement à droite *f.*; ~**-tip** (*cigarette*) filtre *m.*; *v.t.* & *i.* (1) filtrer; (*fig.*) filtrer; (2) suivre la flèche verte; ~**ing** *s.* (*lit.* & *fig.*) filtrage *m.*, (*techn.*) filtration *f.*
filth *s.* **1.** (*dirt, garbage*) ordure *f.*; **2.** (*obscenity*) obscénité *f.*; ~**y** *adj.* (1) sale; (2) obscène; ~**ily** *adv.* salement; ~**iness** *s.* (1) saleté *f.*; (2) obscénité *f.*
filtrat/e *s.* filtrat *m.*; *v.t.* filtrer; ~**ion** *s.* filtration *f.*
fin *s.* (*of fish*) nageoire *f.*; (*of shark, aviat.*) aileron *m.*
final *s.* (*sport*) finale *f.*; (*pl. exam.*) examens de fin d'études *m.pl.*; (*newspaper*) dernière édition *f.*; *adj.* (*last*) final, dernier; (*conclusive*) définitif; (*ling.*) final; ~**ist** *s.* (*sport*) finaliste *m.f.*; ~**ity** *s.* (*last act, state*) caractère décisif *m.*, (*being ~*) irrévocabilité *f.*; ~**ize** *v.t.* (*put in ~ form*) mettre la dernière main à; (*approve*) décider, trancher; ~**ly** *adv.* enfin, finalement; définitivement.
finale *s.* (*mus.*) finale *m.*; (*gen.*) conclusion *f.*
financ/e *s.* finance *f.*; ~**es** *pl.* (*public*) finances *f.pl.*; (*private*) ressources *f.pl.*; *v.t.* financer; (*comm.*) commanditer; ~**ial** *adj.* financier; ~**ial year,** exercice *m.*; ~**ially** *adv.**; ~**ier** *s.* financier *m.*; ~**ing** *s.* financement *m.*
finch *s.* (*bird*) pinson *m.*
find *s.* trouvaille *f.*; *v.t.* (*come across, acknowledge, recognize*) trouver; (*obtain*) se procurer; (*discover*) découvrir; (*ascertain*) constater; (*supply*) fournir;

(~ *guilty, etc.*) déclarer; (*think*) estimer; ~ **it impossible to,** se trouver dans l'impossibilité de; ~ **out (about)**, apprendre; ~ **out about sth.** (*inquire*) se renseigner sur qch.; **~er** *s.* trouveur *m.*; (*photo.*) viseur *m.*; (*telescope*) chercheur *m.*; **~ing** *s.* (*verdict*) décision *f.*

fin/e[1] *s.* (*penalty*) amende *f.*; *v.t.* condamner (qn.) à une amende; **~able** *adj.* passible d'amende.

fine[2] *adj.* (*of high quality*) beau; (*pure, refined*) pur, fin; (*thin, in small pieces*) mince, fin; (*excellent*) excellent; (*handsome*) beau; (*weather*) beau, **to be** ~ (*weather*) faire beau; (*smart*) élégant; (*fastidious*) délicat; (*fig.*) fin; ~ **arts,** beaux--arts *m.pl.*; *adv.* bien; **to chop** ~, hacher menu; **~-drawn** *adj.* ténu, (*fig.*) subtil; **~ly** *adv.* finement, magnifiquement; **~ness** *s.* finesse *f.*, beauté *f.*, élégance *f.*; **~ry** *s.* atours *m.pl.*; *v.t.* & *i.* ~ **down,** (se) clarifier; ~ **away, down, off,** (s')amincir, (s')effiler.

finesse *s.* **1.** (*subtle management*) finesse *f.*; **2.** (*artfulness*) finesse *f.*; **3.** (*cards*) impasse *f.*; *v.t.* & *i.* (1) user de finesse; (2) finasser; (3) faire l'impasse de.

finger *s.* (*on hand, of glove, measure, ~-like object*) doigt *m.*; **fore-~**, index *m.*; **little ~**, petit doigt *m.*; **middle ~**, médius *m.*; **ring ~**, annulaire *m.*; **to burn one's ~s,** se faire échauder; **to have a ~ in the pie,** avoir part au gâteau, y être pour qch.; **to put one's ~ on sth.,** mettre le doigt sur qch.; **to** CROSS **one's ~s; to have** GREEN **~s; ~-bowl** *s.* rince-doigts *m.invar.*; **~-mark** *s.* empreinte *f.*; **~print** *s.* empreinte digitale *f.*; **to the ~tips,** jusqu'au bout des doigts; **to have sth. at one's ~tips,** savoir qch. sur le bout du doigt; *v.t.* manier; (*mus.*) (*instrument*) toucher de, (*indicate ~ing*) indiquer le doigté de; **light-~ed** *adj.* voleur.

finial *s.* (*arch.*) fleuron *m.*

finic/al *adj.* (*fastidious*) difficile; (*too detailed*) précieux; **~ky** *adj.* (*person*) pointilleux; (*thing*) soigné.

finish *s.* (*last stage*) fin *f.*; (*completed state*) fini *m.*; PHOTO ~; FIGHT **to a** ~; *v.t.* & *i.* finir, (se) terminer; (*perfect*) parfaire; ~ **doing sth.,** finir de faire qch.; ~ **by doing sth.,** finir par faire qch.; ~ **off,** mener à bonne fin, (*fam.* = *kill*) achever; **~ed** *adj.* fini, achevé, accompli; **~er** *s.* (*techn.*) finisseur *m.*; **~ing** *s.* achèvement *m.*; (*techn.*) finissage *m.*; **~ing** *adj.* qui touche à sa fin; **~ing-post** *s.* (*sport*) ligne d'arrivée *f.*; **~ing touch** (*pop.*) coup de fion *m.*, **to put the ~ing touch to sth.,** mettre la dernière main à qch.

finite *adj.* fini; (*ling.*) ~ **verb,** verbe à un mode personnel.

Fin/land *s.* (*geog.*) Finlande *f.*; **~n** *s.m.f.* Finlandais(e); **~nish** *adj.* & *s.m.* (*lang.*) finnois.

fiord, fjord *s.* fjord, fiord *m.*

fir *s.* (*tree*) sapin *m.*; ~-CONE, ~-NEEDLE.

fire *s.* **1.** (*combustion, burning fuel, heat*) feu *m.*; **electric ~, gas ~,** radiateur électrique, à gaz *m.*; (*flame*) flamme *f.*; **to set ~ to,** mettre le feu à; **on ~**, en feu; **to be on ~**, (*lit.* & *fig.*) brûler; **to catch ~**, prendre feu; **the** FAT **is in the ~; to pull** CHESTNUTS **out of the ~; out of the** FRY**ing pan into the ~; to have too many** IRONS **in the ~**; WILD ~; **2.** (*conflagration, destructive burning*) incendie *f.*; **to set on ~**, incendier; **3.** (*fig.*) flamme *f.*, ardeur *f.*; **4.** (*discharge of gun*) feu *m.*; CEASE ~; **to hang ~**, faire long feu; **to miss ~**, rater; **to open ~**, ouvrir le feu; **to be under ~**, essuyer le feu (de l'ennemi); **~-alarm** *s.* avertisseur d'incendie *m.*; **~arm** *s.* arme à feu *f.*; **~-bomb** *s.* bombe incendiaire *f.*; **~brand** *s.* tison *m.*, (*fig.*) brandon de discorde *m.*; ~ **brigade,** sapeurs--pompiers *m.pl.*; **~damp** *s.* grisou *m.*; **~--engine** *s.* autopompe *f.* **~-escape** *s.* escalier de secours *m.*; ~ **extinguisher** *s.* extincteur *m.*; **~fly** *s.* luciole *f.*; **~-guard** *s.* garde-feu *m.*; ~ **insurance** *s.* assurance contre l'incendie *f.*; **~-irons,** garniture de foyer *f.*; **~-lighter** *s.* allume-feu *m.*; **~man** *s.* pompier *m.*; **~place** *s.* cheminée *f.*; **~proof** *adj.* incombustible, (*techn.*) ignifuge, *v.t.* ignifuger; **~-screen** *s.* garde-feu *m.*; **~side** *s.* foyer *m.*; ~ **station** *s.* poste de sapeurs-pompiers *m.*; **~work** *s.* (*fam.*) pétard *m.*, **~works,** feu d'artifice *m.*; *v.t.* (1) mettre le feu à; (2) incendier; (3) enflammer; (4) tirer; **5.** (*pottery*) mettre au four; **6.** (*cure*) sécher au feu; **7.** (*supply with fuel*) chauffer; **8.** (*dismiss*) renvoyer; *v.i.* (1) prendre feu; (4) tirer, (*of weapon*) partir; (*of motor*) se mettre à tourner; **firing** *s.* (*fuel*) combustible *m.*; (4) tir *m.*; (*auto.*) allumage *m.*; **firing-line** *s.* ligne de feu *f.*; **firing-squad** *s.* peloton d'exécution *m.*

firm[1] *s.* (*comm.*) maison de commerce *f.*

firm[2] *adj.* (*solid, steadfast*) ferme; (*steady*) stable; **to hold ~**, tenir bon; **~ly** *adv.* fermement; **~ness** *s.* fermeté *f.*

firmament *s.* firmament *m.*

first *s.* (*of month*) premier *m.*; (*edition*) édition originale *f.*; (*beginning*) début *m.*; (*in exam.*) mention *f.*; (*in race etc.*) premi/er, -ère *m.f.*; (*comm. best quality*) marchandises de choix *f.pl.*; *adj.* (*time, order, position, rank*) premier; *in dates* & *titles use* premier *without article*, **Charles the ~**, Charles premier; **twenty-~**, vingt-et--unième; ~ AID; **~-born** *adj.* & *s.m.* premier--né; **~-fruits** (*hist.*) prémices *f.pl.*, (*veg. etc.*) primeurs *m.pl.*; **~-rate** *adj.* de premier ordre; *adv.* (*before all else*) avant tout, d'abord; (*for the ~ time*) pour la première fois; **~ly** *adv.* premièrement.

firth *s.* embouchure *f.*

fiscal *adj.* fiscal.

fish *s.* (*animal* & *flesh*) poisson *m.*; (*pop. person*) type *m.*; **to drink like a ~**, boire comme un trou; **to have other ~ to fry,** avoir d'autres chats à fouetter; **a pretty kettle of ~**, un beau gâchis; **another kettle of ~**, une autre paire de manches; ~-BONE; ~ **finger** *s.* croquette de poisson *f.*; **~-hook** *s.* hameçon, *m.*; **~-kettle** *s.* poissonnière *f.*; **~monger** *s.* poissonnier *m.*; **~-pond** *s.* vivier *m.*; **~wife** *s.* poissarde *f.*; *v.t.* & *i.* pêcher; ~ **for** (*lit.* & *fig.*) pêcher; ~ **out,** repêcher; ~ **in troubled waters,** pêcher en eau trouble; **~erman** *s.* pêcheur *m.*; **~ery** *s.* pêcherie *f.*; **~ing** *s.* pêche *f.*; **~ingboat** *s.* bateau de pêche *m.*; **~ing-line** *s.* ligne *f.*; **~ing-rod** *s.* canne à pêche *f.*; **~ing tackle** *s.* engins de pêche *m.pl.*; **~y** *adj.* (*smell, taste*) de poisson; (*full of fish*) poissonneux; (*eye, look*) vitreux; (*fig. fam.*) louche.

fiss/ile *adj.* fissile; **~ion** *s.* fission *f.*

fissure *s.* fissure *f.*

fist *s.* poing *m.*; (*fam. handwriting*) écriture *f.*; **to** CLENCH **one's ~s; ~icuffs** *s.* coups de poing *m.pl.*

fistula *s.* fistule *f.*

fit[1] *s.* (*med.* & *fig. of anger, etc.*) accès *m.*, attaque *f.*; (*of coughing*) quinte *f.*; **by ~s and starts,** par à-coups; **~ful** *adj.* capricieux; **~fully** *adv.* par à-coups.

fit[2] *adj.* **1.** (*worthy*) digne; **2.** (*proper*) convenable; **3.** (*in good health*) en forme; **as ~ as a** FIDDLE; ~ **for,** propre à, capable de; ~ **to,** en état de; **not to be ~ to hold a candle to s.o.,** ne pas arriver à la cheville de qn.; **to think ~**, juger bon (*to*—de); **~ly** *adv.* convenablement, à propos; **~ness** *s.* (1) à-propos *m.*; (2) convenance *f.*; (3) forme *f.*; **~ting** *adj.* convenable, à propos.

fit[3] *s.* **to be a good, a bad ~,** aller bien, mal; *v.t.* (*adjust to shape* & *size*) ajuster; (*join together*) emboîter; (*adapt*) adapter; (*make competent*) préparer; (*supply with*) équiper; *v.i.* s'accorder; **if the cap ~s wear it,** à bon entendeur, salut!; **~ for** *v.t.* préparer à; **~ in** *v.t.* & *i.* (s')emboîter; **~ in with** (*fig.*) s'accorder avec; **~ on** *v.t.* essayer; **~ out** *v.t.* équiper; **~ up** *v.t.* (*house*) aménager, (*techn.*) monter; **~ with** *v.t.* munir de; **~ter** *s.* (*tailoring*) essayeur *m.*; (*techn.*) monteur *m.*; **~ting** *s.* ajustage *m.*; **~tings** *s.pl.* aménagements *m.pl.*; **~ting-out** *s.* équipement *m.*; **~ment** *s.* meuble *m.*

five *adj.* & *s.m.* cinq; **~fold,** quintuple; **~-year plan,** plan quinquennal *m.*

fix *s.* (*fam. dilemma*) mauvaise passe *f.*; **to be in a ~,** être dans le pétrin; (*naut.*, *aviat.*) point *m.*, **to take a ~,** faire le point; (*pop. drug*) dose *f.*, **to give oneself a ~,** se piquer; *v.t.* & *i.* (*make firm*) fixer; (*fasten*) fermer; (*focus on*) fixer sur; (*locate*) (s')orienter; (*settle*) déterminer; (*arrange*) arranger; (*repair*) réparer; (*fam. get even with s.o.*) avoir qn.; (*tamper with*) truquer; (*bribe*) graisser la patte à qn.; **~ on,** se décider pour; **~ up,** arranger; **~ation** *s.* idée fixe *f.*; **~ative** *s.* fixatif *m.*; **~ed** *adj.* fixe, (*fin.*) à terme; **~edly** *adv.* fixement; **~ing** *s.* fixation *f.*, (*photo.*) fixage *m.*; **~ity** *s.* invariabilité *f.*; **~ture** *s.* objet fixe *m.*, (*sport*) match *m.*; **~tures** *s.pl.* (*law*) biens immeubles par destination *m.pl.*

fizz *s.* **1.** (*sound*) pétillement *m.*; **2.** (*effervescence*) mousse *f.*; *v.i.* (1) pétiller; (2) mousser; **~y** *adj.* gazeux.

fizzle *s.* (*sound*) pétillement *m.*; (*fig. fam.*) fiasco *m.*; *v.i.* fuser; **~ out** (*fig.*) faire fiasco.

flabbergast *v.t.* (*pop.*) époustoufler; **~ing** *adj.* époustouflant.

flabb/y *adj.* **1.** (*limp*) flasque; **2.** (*feeble, worn out*) avachi; **~iness** *s.* (1) mollesse *f.*; (2) avachissement *m.*

flaccid *adj.* flasque; **~ity** *s.* flaccidité *f.*

flag *s.* **1.** (*bot.*) iris *m.*; **2.** (*stone*) dalle *f.*; **3.** (*standard*) drapeau *m.*, (*naut.*) pavillon *m.*; **~-day** *s.* journée de bienfaisance *f.* (*in aid of*—au profit de); **~-pole** *s.* mât *m.*; **~ship** *s.* vaisseau amiral *m.*; **~staff** *s.* hampe *f.*; **~stone** *s.* dalle *f.*; *v.t.* (2) daller; (3) pavoiser, (*signal with ~s*) transmettre par signaux; *v.i.* (*hang down*) pendre; (*droop*) languir; (*lose vigour*) défaillir; (*fall off in interest*) faiblir; **~ down** *v.t.* arrêter au drapeau; **~ging** *s.* dallage *m.*; **~ging** *adj.* languissant, défaillant.

flagella/te *v.t.* flageller; **~nt** *s.* flagellant *m.*; **~tion** *s.* flagellation *f.*

flageolet *s.* flageolet *m.*

flagon *s.* grosse bouteille *f.*

flagrant *adj.* flagrant; **flagrante delicto,** flagrant délit.

flail *s.* fléau *m.*; *v.t.* & *i.* battre au fléau.

flair *s.* flair *m.*

flak/e *s.* **1.** (*snow, etc.*) flocon *m.*; **2.** (*thin, broad piece, layer*) écaille *f.*; CORN**~es**; *v.i.* (1) tomber en flocons; (2) s'écailler; **~y** *adj.* (1) floconneux; (2) écailleux; (*pastry*) feuilleté.

flamboyant *adj.* flamboyant.

flam/e *s.* (*lit.* & *fig.*) flamme *f.*; (*bright light*) éclat *m.*; (*sweetheart*) petite amie *f.*; *v.i.* flamber; (*shine*) briller; (*lit.* & *fig. blaze*) s'enflammer; **~ing** *adj.* flambant, en flammes; (*pop.* = *damned*) sacré (*before noun*).

flamingo *s.* flamant *m.*

flan *s.* (*cook.*) flan *m.*

Flanders *s.* (*geog.*) Flandre *f.*, Flandres *f.pl.*

flange *s.* rebord *m.*; (*mech.*) collet *m.*; (*of wheel*) boudin *m.*; *v.t.* border.

flank *s.* (*of body, building, mountain, army, etc.*) flanc *m.*; *adj.* de flanc; *v.t.* flanquer.

flannel *s.* (*text.*) flanelle *f.*; *adj.* en flanelle; (*face-*)**~**, gant de toilette *m.*; **~s** *s.pl.* (*trousers*) pantalon de flanelle *m.*; **~ette** *s.* pilou *m.*

flap *s.* **1.** (*light stroke*) tape *f.*; **2.** (*of wing*) coup *m.*; **3.** (*hanging piece*): (*of coat*) pan *m.*, (*of hat*) bord *m.*, (*of pocket*) patte *f.*, (*of table*) battant *m.*, (*of envelope*) rabat *m.*, (*mud-~, auto.*) bavette (de protection) *f.*; **4.** (*aviat. wing ~*) aileron *m.*; **5.** (*pop.* = *fuss*) affolement *m.*; *v.t.* & *i.* (1) taper; (2) battre (des ailes); (3) (*hang loose*) claquer, battre; (5) s'affoler; **~jack** *s.* (*cook.*) crêpe *f.*, (*powder compact*) poudrier *m.*; **~per** *s.* (*fam.*) gamine *f.*

flare *s.* **1.** (*bright, unsteady flame*) flamme vacillante *f.*; **2.** (*signal*) fusée *f.*; **3.** (*outburst of flame*) flambée *f.*; **4.** (*shape*) évasement *m.*; *v.i.* (1) briller irrégulièrement; (3) flamboyer; (4) s'évaser; **~ up** (*fig.*) s'emporter; **~-up** *s.* flambée *f.*; **~-path** *s.* (*aviat.*) piste balisée *f.*; **flaring** *adj.* (1) brillant; (3) éclatant; (4) évasé.

flash *s.* **1.** (*sudden short blaze*) éclair *m.*; **2.** (*sudden attack*): (*of hope*) rayon *m.*, (*of genius*) trait *m.*, (*of wit*) saillie *f.*; **3.** (*on uniform*) écusson *m.*; **4.** (*news*) dernière nouvelle *f.*, flash *m.*; **5.** (*photo.*) (lampe) éclair *f.*, flash *m.*; **6.** (*ostentation*) tape-à-l'œil *m.*; **a ~ in the pan,** feu de paille *m.*; **in a ~,** dans un éclair; *v.t.* (1) faire briller; (2) lancer; *v.i.* (1) étinceler, jeter des éclairs; (*move swiftly*) aller comme un éclair; **~back** *s.* (*cinema, liter.*) retour en arrière *m.*; **~ bulb** *s.* (*photo.*) flash *m.*; **~light** *s.* (*torch*) lampe de poche *f.*; **~-point** *s.* (*chem.*) point de combustion *m.*; **~y** *adj.* voyant.

flask *s.* (*small, for perfume, etc.*) flacon *m.*; (*for drinking*) gourde *f.*; **vacuum ~,** bouteille thermos *f.*, thermos *m.*

flat *s.* (*rooms*) appartement *m.*; (*~ surface*) plat *m.*; (*level ground*) plaine *f.*; (*tyre*) crevaison *f.*; (*mus.*) bémol *m.*; **~s** *s.pl.* (*shallows*) marais *m.pl.*, bas-fonds *m.pl.*; **~let** *s.* studio *m.*; *adj.* **1.** (*lying at full length*) étendu à plat; **2.** (*horizontal, level; smooth, even*) plat; **3.** (*unqualified*) catégorique; **4.** (*dull*) fade; **5.** (*stale, ≠ effervescent*) plat, éventé; **6.** (*mus.*) bémol; **7.** (*unvarying*) uniforme, monotone; **~-bottomed** *adj.* à fond plat; **~-fish** *s.* poissons plats *m.pl.*; **~-footed** *adj.* aux pieds plats; **~-iron** *s.* fer à repasser *m.*; **~ race** *s.* plat *m.*; **~ rate** *s.* tarif uniforme *m.*; *adv.* (1) à plat; (3) catégoriquement; (6) faux; **~ out** *adv.* à toute vitesse; **to fall ~,** tomber à plat, (*fig.*) rater son effet; **~ly** *adv.* (1) à plat; (3)*; **~ness** *s.* (2) aplatissement *m.*; (4) platitude *f.*; (7) monotonie *f.*; **~ten** *v.t.* & *i.* (2) (s')aplatir; (4) affadir.

flatter *v.t.* flatter; **~er** *s.* flatteur *m.*; **~ing** *adj.* flatteur; **~y** *s.* flatterie *f.*

flatulen/ce *s.* flatulence *f.*; **~t** *adj.* flatulent.

flaunt *v.t.* (*wave proudly*) brandir, faire flotter; (*show off*) étaler; **~ing** *adj.* (*fig.*) prétentieux.

flautist *s.* flûtiste *m.f.*

flavour *s.* (*sensation*) goût *m.*; (*distinctive taste, quality*) saveur *f.*, arôme *m.*, bouquet *m.*; *v.t.* assaisonner (de); **~ing** *s.* assaisonnement *m.*; **~less** *adj.* sans saveur.

flaw *s.* **1.** (*crack*): (*in china, glass*) fêlure *f.*; (*in metal*) paille *f.*; **2.** (*defect*) défaut *m.*; *v.t.* & *i.* (1) (se) fêler; (2) (s')abîmer; **~less** *adj.* sans défaut.

flax *s.* lin *m.*; **~en** *adj.* de lin; (*hair*) filasse.

flay *v.t.* écorcher; (*fig.*) s'acharner sur.

flea *s.* puce *f.*; **to get a ~ in one's ear** (*fam.*) essuyer une rebuffade; ⚠ mettre la puce à l'oreille = **to arouse suspicion or curiosity; ~-bite** *s.* piqûre de puce *f.*, (*fig.*) bagatelle *f.*; **~-bitten** *adj.* & *s.m.* (*horse*) aubère; **~ market** *s.* marché aux puces *m.*

fleck *s.* (*spot*) petite tache *f.*; (*of dust, etc.*) particule *f.*; *v.t.* tacheter (de).

fledge *v.t.* pourvoir de plumes; **fully-~d,**

emplumé; (*fig.*) à part entière; **~ling** *s.* oisillon *m.*; (*fig.*) blanc-bec *m.*

flee *v.t.* (*shun*) éviter; (*run away from*) fuir; *v.i.* fuir, s'enfuir.

fleec/e *s.* (*of animal*) toison *f.*; (*text.*) ouatine *f.*; *v.t.* tondre; (*fig.*) dépouiller de, plumer; **~y** *adj.* laineux; (*sky*) moutonneux.

fleet[1] *s.* (*naut.*) flotte *f.*; (*aviat.*) flotte aérienne *f.*; (*of cars*) parc automobile *m.*

fleet[2] *adj.* (*poet.*) rapide; **~ of foot,** au pied léger; **~ing** *adj.* éphémère, fugitif; **~ness** *s.* rapidité *f.*

Flem/ing *s.m.f.* Flamand(e); **~ish** *adj.* & *s.m.* (*lang.*) flamand.

flesh *s.* (*of body, of fruit; fig. the body*) chair *f.*; (*meat*) viande *f.*; (*fat*) embonpoint *m.*; **~ and blood** *s.* nature humaine *f.*, *adj.* humain; **in the ~,** en chair et en os; **to make one's ~** CREEP; **~-coloured,** couleur chair; **~-pots,** bonne chère *f.*; **~iness** *s.* embonpoint *m.*; **~less** *adj.* décharné; **~ly** *adj.* charnel; **~y** *adj.* charnu.

flex[1] *v.t.* fléchir.

flex[2] *s.* (*electr.*) fil *m.*

flexib/le *adj.* (*lit.* & *fig.*) flexible; **~ility** *s.* flexibilité *f.*

flick *s.* **1.** (*light blow*) petit coup *m.*; **2.** (*with finger*) chiquenaude *f.*; **3.** (*turn of wrist*) tour *m.*; **~-knife** *s.* couteau à cran d'arrêt *m.*, (*pop.*) eustache *m.*; *v.t.* (1) & (2) donner un petit coup, une chiquenaude, à; (3) donner un coup de poignet; **~ away** *v.t.* chasser; **~ off** *v.t.* faire envoler.

flicker *s.* (*light*) lueur vacillante *f.*; (*oscillation*) vacillement *m.*; (*fig. of fear, etc.*) frisson *m.*; *v.i.* (*flame*) vaciller; (*needle*) osciller; **~ing** *adj.* vacillant.

flight *s.* (*movement, way of flying, journey by air*) vol *m.*; (*of birds, insects*) vol *m.*, volée *f.*; (*of time*) fuite *f.*; (*of stairs, arrows*) volée *f.*; (*running away*) fuite *f.*, **to take ~,** prendre la fuite, **to put to ~,** mettre en fuite; **~ of fancy,** essor de l'imagination *m.*; **~-deck** *s.* (*naut.*) pont d'envol *m.*; **~ lieutenant** *s.* (*aviat.*) capitaine *m.*; **~iness** *s.* légèreté *f.*; **~y** *adj.* léger, frivole.

flims/y *s.* (*paper*) papier pelure *m.*; *adj.* (*frail*) fragile; (*paltry*) maigre, pauvre; **~iness** *s.* fragilité *f.*

flinch *v.i.* (*draw back*) reculer; (*wince*) broncher.

fling *s.* **1.** (*throw*) jet *m.*; **2.** (*dance*) pas écossais *m.*; **3.** (*spell of indulgence*) fête *f.*, **to have one's ~,** faire la noce, (*youth*) jeter sa gourme; *v.t.* (1) jeter; **~ away, ~ down,** jeter; **~ off,** rejeter; **~ open,** ouvrir brusquement; **~ out,** jeter dehors.

flint *s.* **1.** (*stone*) silex *m.*; **2.** (*to produce fire*) pierre *f.*; (*in petrol lighter*) pierre à briquet *f.*; **~y** *adj.* (1) siliceux; (*fig.*) de pierre.

flip *s.* chiquenaude *f.*; *v.t.* donner une chiquenaude à.

flippan/cy *s.* **1.** (*disrespect*) désinvolture *f.*; **2.** (*lack of seriousness*) légèreté *f.*; **~t** *adj.* (1) désinvolte; (2) sans-gêne; **~tly** *adv.* (1) d'un air dégagé; (2) cavalièrement.

flirt *s.* flirteu/r, -se *m.f.*; *v.i.* flirter; **~ with s.o.,** avoir un flirt avec qn.; **~ation** *s.* flirt *m.*

flit *s.* déménagement *m.*; *v.i.* (*move house*) déménager; (*fam.*) filer; (*move about*) aller et venir; (*fly about*) voltiger.

flitch *s.* (*bacon*) flèche *f.*

float *s.* (*thing that ~s*) flotte *f.*; (*raft*) radeau *m.*; (*cart*) char (de cortège) *m.*; **milk-~,** voiture de laitier *f.*; (*pl. footlights*) rampe *f.*; (*money for change*) fonds de roulement *m.pl.*; *v.t.* (*of water, to carry*) porter, faire flotter; (*launch, scheme, etc.*) lancer, créer; *v.i.* flotter; **~able** *adj.* flottable; **~ation** *s.* (*comm.*) lancement *m.*, (*fin.*) émission *f.*; **~ing** *s.* flottement *m.*, (*timber*) flottage *m.*; **~ing** *adj.* flottant; **~ing dock** *s.* bassin à flot *m.*; **~ing vote** *s.* vote flottant *m.*, voix flottantes *f.pl.*

flock *s.* **1.** (*crowd*) foule *f.*; **2.** (*birds, etc.*) volée *f.*; **3.** (*animals*) troupeau *m.*; **4.** (*eccles.*) ouailles *f.pl.*; **5.** (*wool*) flocon *m.*; **6.** (*stuffing*) bourre *f.*; *v.i.* (1) s'attrouper; (2) former un vol; (3) s'assembler en troupeau.

floe *s.* glace flottante *f.*, banquise *f.*

flog *v.t.* fouetter; (*pop. = sell*) bazarder, brader; **~ging** *s.* fouet *m.*

flood *s.* **1.** (*tide*) flux *m.*; **2.** (*inundation*) inondation *f.*; **3.** (*downpour*) torrent *m.*; **4.** (*eccles. the F~*) le Déluge *m.*; **5.** (*fig.*) flot *m.*; **to be in ~,** déborder; **~gate** *s.* écluse *f.*; **~light** *v.t.* illuminer par projecteurs; **~lighting** *s.* illumination (par projecteurs) *f.*; **~-tide** *s.* flux *m.*; *v.t.* (2) inonder; *v.i.* (2) déborder.

floor *s.* **1.** (*of room*) plancher *m.*, parquet *m.*; **2.** (*storey*) étage *m.*, GROUND **~**; **3.** (*right to speak*) parole *f.*; **to take the ~,** prendre la parole; **on the ~,** par terre; *v.t.* (1) planchéier; **4.** (*knock down*) terrasser, (*fig.*) désarçonner; **~board** *s.* lame *f.*; **~ show** *s.* attractions *f.pl.*; **~ing** *s.* plancher *m.*, parquet *m.*, carrelage *m.*

flop *s.* (*motion*) chute lourde *f.*; (*sound*) bruit mat *m.*; (*pop. = failure*) four *m.*; *v.i.* (*sway about*) vaciller; (*move, sit down, awkwardly*) s'affaler; (*pop.*) faire un four.

flora *s.* flore *f.*

floral *adj.* floral.

Floren/ce *s.* (*geog.*) Florence *f.*; **~tine** *adj.* & *s.m.f.* florentin(e).

florescence *s.* floraison *f.*

floret *s.* fleuron *m.*

florid *adj.* fleuri; **~ity** *s.*, **~ness** *s.* teint fleuri *m.*; **~ly** *adv.* d'une manière fleurie.

florin *s.* florin *m.*

florist *s.* fleuriste *m.f.*; **~ry** *s.* art du fleuriste *m.*

floss *s.* bourre de soie *f.*; **candy-~,** barbe à papa *f.*

flotation *s.* *see* FLOAT.

flotilla *s.* flotille *f.*

flotsam *s.* épave flottante *f.*

flounce *s.* (*movement*) mouvement brusque *m.*; (*dress*) volant *m.*; *v.i.* sursauter; **~ about,** se démener.

flounder[1] *s.* (*fish*) flet *m.*

flounder[2] *v.i.* patauger; (*fig.*) s'embarrasser.

flour *s.* farine *f.*; CORN**~**; *v.t.* (*cook.*) fariner; **~y** *adj.* farineux.

flourish *s.* (*curve, in writing*) parafe *f.*; (*gesture*) geste large *m.*; (*florid passage*) fioriture *f.*; *v.t.* brandir; *v.i.* fleurir; (*prosper*) prospérer; **~ing** *adj.* florissant, prospère.

flout *v.t.* (*defy*) défier; (*not care about*) se moquer de.

flow *s.* **1.** (*~ing*) flot *m.*, courant *m.*, (*of river*) cours *m.*; **2.** (*tide*) flux *m.*, **ebb and ~,** le flux et le reflux; **3.** (*copious supply*) abondance *f.*; *v.i.* (1) couler; (2) monter; **4.** (*circulate*) circuler; **5.** (*style*) couler avec aisance; **6.** (*dress*) se draper; **7.** (*gush out*) s'écouler; **~ from,** découler de; **~ing** *adj.* (1) coulant; (2) montant; (6) flottant.

flower *s.* (*bot.* & *fig.*) fleur *f.*; (*state of ~ing*) floraison *f.*; **in ~,** en fleur(s); **~-bed** *s.* massif *m.*; **~** GARDEN; **~pot** *s.* pot de fleurs *m.*; **~-show** *s.* exposition de fleurs *f.*, floralies *f.pl.*; **~-stand** *s.* jardinière *f.*; *v.i.* fleurir; **~ed** *adj.* fleuri; **~et** *s.* fleurette *f.*; **~ing** *s.* floraison *f.*; **~ing** *adj.* fleuri, à fleurs; **~y** *adj.* fleuri.

fluctuat/e *v.i.* flotter, être fluctuant; **~ion** *s.* fluctuation *f.*

flu *s.* (*short for influenza*) grippe *f.*

flue *s.* (*of chimney*) tuyau *m.*

fluen/cy *s.* facilité *f.*; **~t** *adj.* facile; (*flowing*) coulant; **to be ~t in a language,** parler une

langue couramment; **~tly** *adv.* facilement; (*of a lang.*) couramment.
fluff *s.* (*cloth*) peluche *f.*; (*dust, fur*) duvet *m.*; *v.t.* rendre pelucheux; *v.i.* pelucher; **~y** *adj.* pelucheux; duveteux; (*blurred*) flou.
fluid *adj.* & *s.m.* fluide; **~ity** *s.* fluidité *f.*
fluke *s.* (*worm in sheep*) douve *f.*; (*fish*) flet *m.*; (*on anchor*) patte d'ancre *f.*; (*head of lance*) fer *m.*; (*lucky accident*) coup de chance *m.*
flume *s.* canalisation *f.*
flummery *s.* (*cook.*) crème aux œufs *f.*; (*empty compliments*) flagornerie *f.*; (*trifles*) vétilles *f.pl.*
flummox *v.t.* (*pop.*) désarçonner.
flunkey *s.* (*servant*) laquais *m.*; (*snob*) flagorneur *m.*
fluorescen/ce *s.* fluorescence *f.*; **~t** *adj.* fluorescent.
fluorid/e *s.* fluorure *m.*; **~ate** *v.t.* fluorer; **~ation** *s.* fluorisation *f.*
flurry *s.* **1.** (*nervous agitation*) émoi *m.*; **2.** (*of snow, etc.*) rafale *f.*; *v.t.* (1) agiter.
flush *s.* **1.** (*rush of water*) cascade *f.*; **2.** (*sudden abundance*) avalanche *f.*; **3.** (*of emotion*) transport *m.*; **4.** (*of W.C.*) chasse d'eau *f.*; **5.** (*blush*) rougeur *f.*; **6.** (*freshness, vigour*) fraîcheur *f.*, éclat *m.*; **7.** (*cards*) flush *m.*; *v.i.* (1) jaillir; (4) tirer la chasse d'eau; (5) rougir; *v.t.* (*game*) faire se lever; *adj.* (*full*) plein à déborder; (*abundant*) abondant; **~ with,** bien pourvu de; (*level with*) au même niveau que.
fluster *s.* agitation *f.*; (*mentally*) trouble *m.*; *v.t.* agiter; troubler.
flut/e *s.* **1.** (*mus.*) flûte *f.*; **2.** (*arch.*) cannelure *f.*; *v.i.* (1) jouer de la flûte; *v.t.* (2) canneler; **~ed** *adj.* (2) cannelé; **~ing** *s.* (2) cannelure *f.*; **~y** *adj.* flûté.
flutter *s.* **1.** (*of wings*) battement (des ailes) *m.*; **2.** (*fig.*) agitation *f.*; **3.** (*pop. gamble*) spéculation *f.*, (*bet*) pari *m.*; *v.t.* & *i.* (1) battre (des ailes); (2) (s')agiter; **4.** (*descend*) descendre; **5.** (*hover*) voltiger; **6.** (*heart, etc.*) palpiter; **~ the** DOVE**cots; ~ in the wind,** flotter (au vent); **~ing** *s. as* **~** (1), (6) palpitation *f.*; **~ing** *adj.* flottant.
fluvial *adj.* fluvial.
flux *s.* (*med., tide*) flux *m.*; (*continuous change*) instabilité *f.*
fluxion *s.* (*math.*) fluxion *f.*
fly[1] *s.* (*insect*) mouche *f.*; (*on garment*) braguette *f.*; (*on tent*) auvent *m.*; **~ in the ointment,** ombre au tableau *f.*; **~-blown** *adj.* couvert de chiures de mouches; **~catcher** *s.* (*bird*) attrape-mouches *m.*; **~-trap** *s.* (*plant*) attrape-mouches *m.*; **~weight** *s.* (*boxing*) poids-mouche *m.*
fly[2] *v.t.* (*jump over*) escalader; (*wave flag*) arborer, (*naut.*) battre pavillon; (*kite*) faire voler; (*aviat.*) (*pilot plane*) piloter, (*cross in plane*) survoler; (*avoid*) fuir; *v.i.* (*bird, plane, etc.*) voler; **as the** CROW **flies;** (*travel by air*) voyager en avion; (*travel fast*) filer; (*hurry*) se dépêcher; (*flee*) s'enfuir; (*flag, etc.*) flotter; **let ~** *v.t.* décocher; **~ away** *v.i.* s'envoler; **~ off** *v.i.* s'envoler, (*button*) sauter; **~ off the handle,** sortir de ses gonds; **~ open** *v.i.* s'ouvrir brusquement; **~ over** *v.t.* survoler; **~-half** *s.* (*rugby*) demi d'ouverture *m.*; **~leaf** *s.* (*of book*) feuille de garde *f.*; **~over** *s.* (*aviat.*) survol *m.*; **~over** *s.* (*road*) voie surélevée *f.*, autopont *m.*; **~-past** *s.* (*aviat.*) défilé aérien *m.*; **~wheel** *s.* volant *m.*; **~ing** *s.* vol *m.*, aviation *f.*; **~ing** *adj.* volant, d'aviation; **~ing boat** *s.* hydravion *m.*; **~ing buttress** *s.* arc-boutant *m.*; **with ~ing** COLOURS**; ~ing fish** *s.* poisson volant *m.*; **~ing fox** *s.* roussette *f.*; **F~ing Officer** *s.* lieutenant *m.*; **~ing saucer** *s.* soucoupe volante *f.*; **~ing squad** (*police*) brigade mobile *f.*; **~ing start** *s.* bon départ *m.*; **~ing visit** *s.* visite éclair *f.*
foal *s.* poulain *m.*. pouliche *f.*; *v.i.* pouliner.
foam *s.* **1.** écume *f.*; **2.** (*on beer, etc.*) mousse *f.*; **~ rubber,** caoutchouc mousse *m.*; **~ing, ~y** *adj.* écumeux; *v.i.* (1) écumer; (2) mousser; **~ at the mouth,** écumer de rage.
fob *s.* (*watch*) gousset *m.*; *v.t.* **to ~ s.o. off with sth.,** refiler qch. à qn.
f.o.b. (*free on board*) franco à bord.
focal *adj.* focal; **~ize** *v.t.* mettre au point.
fo'c's'le *see* FORECASTLE.
focus *s.* foyer *m.*; **in ~,** au point, net; **out of ~,** pas au point, flou; *v.t.* & *i.* mettre au point, (faire) converger; (*fig.*) (se) concentrer; **~sing** *s.* mise au point *f.*
fodder *s.* fourrage *m.*; CANNON-**~.**
foe *s.* ennemi *m.*
foet/us, fetus *s.* fœtus *m.*; **~al** *adj.* fœtal.
fog *s.* brouillard *m.*; **freezing ~,** brouillard givrant *m.*; **~ dispersal** *s.* dénébulation *f.*; **~-horn** *s.* signal de brume *m.*; **~-lights** (*auto.*) feux de brouillard *m.pl.*; *v.t.* (*fig.*) embrumer; **~gy** *adj.* brumeux; (*fig.*) vague; **to be ~gy** (*weather*) faire du brouillard; **not to have the ~giest idea about sth.** (*fam.*) ne rien piger à qch.
fogy, fogey *s.* (*usu. old* **~**), vieille baderne *f.*
foible *s.* (*weakness, failing*) faiblesse *f.*; (*penchant*) faible *m.*
foil *s.* (*metal*) feuille *f.*; **tin ~** *s.* feuille d'aluminium *f.*; (*of mirror*) tain *m.*; (*contrast*) repoussoir *m.*; (*sword*) fleuret *m.*; *v.t.* (*baffle*) déjouer; (*frustrate*) faire échouer.
foist *v.t.* (*introduce secretly*) insérer (dans); (*palm sth. off on s.o.*) refiler qch. à qn.
fold[1] *s.* (*sheep*) bergerie *f.*; (*eccles.*) bercail *m.*
fold[2] *s.* pli *m.*; (*hollow*) repli *m.*; *v.t.* & *i.* (se) (re)plier; (*arms*) croiser; (*clasp*) serrer; (*wrap up*) envelopper; **~ up** (*fig.*) *v.i.* plier boutique, s'effondrer; **~er** *s.* (*circular*) dépliant *m.*, (*file*) chemise *f.*; **~ing doors,** porte pliante *f.*
-fold *suffix* **ten~,** *etc.* dix, etc. fois.
foliage *s.* feuillage *m.*
foliate *v.t.* (*mirror*) étamer; (*metal*) battre en feuilles; *adj.* folié.
folio *s.* folio *m.*; *adj.* in-folio.
folk *s.* (*nation*) nation *f.*; (*race*) peuple *m.*; (*relatives*) famille *f.*; (*people*) gens *m.pl.*, **old ~,** vieilles gens *f. pl.*, **young ~,** jeunes gens; ⚠ *preceding adj. is f.*; (*people of one class or profession*) gens, **church ~,** gens d'Eglise, **legal ~,** gens de loi; *adj.* populaire; **~-dance** *s.* contredanse *f.*; **~lore** *s.* folklore *m.*; **~-song** *s.* chanson populaire *f.*; **~-tale** *s.* conte *m.*
follow *v.t.* & *i.* **1.** (*go or come after*) suivre; **2.** (*pursue*) poursuivre; **3.** (*take as model*) prendre pour modèle; **4.** (*result from*) s'ensuivre, découler (de); **5.** (*understand*) comprendre; **as ~s,** comme suit; **it ~s that** (4) il s'ensuit que; **~ through,** poursuivre jusqu'à la fin, (*sport*) suivre le coup; **~ up** *v.t.* donner suite à, exploiter; **~-up** *s.* suite *f.*; **~ suit** (*cards*) jouer dans la couleur, (*fig.*) faire de même; **~ in s.o.'s** FOOT**steps; ~er** *s.* (1) suivant *m.*; (2) poursuivant *m.*; (3) disciple *m.*, partisan *m.*; **6.** (*fam.*) galant *m.*; **~ing** *s.* suite *f.*; *adj.* suivant.
folly *s.* (*foolishness*) sottise *f.*; (*foolish act, idea; costly structure*) folie *f.*
foment *v.t.* & *i.* (*lit.* & *fig.*) fomenter; **~ation** *s.* (*lit.* & *fig.*) fomentation *f.*
fond *adj.* **1.** (*tender*) tendre; **2.** (*doting*) faible, indulgent; **to be ~ of,** (*food*) être gourmand de; (*mus. etc.*) être amateur de; (*s.o.*) être attaché à (qn.); **~ly** *adv.* (1)*; **~ness** *s.* (1) tendresse *f.*; (*liking*) goût *m.*
fondle *v.t.* caresser.
font *s.* (*eccles.*) fonts baptismaux *m.pl.*; (*fig.*) source *f.*
food *s.* (*lit.* & *fig.*) nourriture *f.*; (=**~***stuffs*) aliments *m.pl.*; (*agric.*) pâture *f.*; SEA**~**; **~ for**

thought, matière à réflexion *f.*; **~stuff** *s.* denrée alimentaire *f.*

fool *s.* (*simpleton*) idiot *m.*; (*unwise person*) imbécile *m.*; (*hist. jester*) bouffon *m.*; (*dupe*) dupe *f.*; (*cook.*) mousse *f.*; APRIL **~; to act, play, the ~,** faire l'idiot; **to make a ~ of oneself,** se conduire comme un imbécile, se rendre ridicule; **to make a ~ of s.o.,** duper qn.; **to go on a ~'s** ERRAND; **~'s paradise,** bonheur illusoire *m.*; **~hardy** *adj.* (*action*) téméraire, (*person*) risque-tout; **~hardiness** *s.* témérité *f.*; **~proof** *adj.* (*mech.*) indéréglable, (*fig.*) à toute épreuve; **~ery** *s.* sottise *f.*, idiotie *f.*; **~ish** *adj.* bête, sot, stupide; **~ishly** *adv.* sottement; **~ishness** *s.* sottise *f.*; **to be** PENNY **wise and pound ~ish;** *v.t.* duper; *v.i.* faire l'idiot; **~ about,** faire l'idiot, (*waste time*) baguenauder; **~ away** *v.t.* gaspiller.

foolscap *s.* papier ministre *m.*; **~'s-cap** *s.* bonnet d'âne *m.*

foot *s.* (*of human body*; *metre*; *measure*) pied *m.*; (*of animal*) patte *f.*; (*step*) pas *m.*; (*infantry*) infanterie *f.*; (*base*) bas *m.*, pied *m.*; **on ~,** à pied; **from head to ~,** de la tête aux pieds; **to have one ~ in the grave,** avoir un pied dans la tombe; **to put one's ~ in it,** mettre les pieds dans le plat; **to put one's ~ down,** prendre une attitude énergique; **to put one's best ~ forward,** partir du bon pied; **to set on ~,** mettre sur pied; **to fall on one's feet** (*fig.*) retomber sur ses pieds; **to be swept off one's feet,** être transporté (*by sth.*—de qch., *by s.o.*—par qn.); **to** DRAG **one's feet; to** STAND **on one's own feet; to let the** GRASS **grow under one's feet; to have** COLD **feet; ~-and-mouth disease** *s.* fièvre aphteuse *f.*; **~ball** *s.* (*sport*) football *m.*, (*ball*) ballon *m.*; **~board** *s.* marchepied *m.*; **~-brake** *s.* frein à pédale *m.*; **~-bridge** *s.* passerelle *f.*; **~fall** *s.* bruit de pas *m.*; **~-gear, ~wear** *s.* chaussures *f.pl.*; **~hills** *s.* avant-mont *m.*; **~hold** *s.* point d'appui *m.*; **to lose one's ~hold,** perdre pied; **~lights** *s.* rampe *f.*; **~loose** *adj.* (*fig.*) libre comme l'air; **~man** *s.* valet de pied *m.*; **~note** *s.* note au bas de la page *f.*; **~pad** *s.* voleur *m.*; **~-passenger** *s.* piéton *m.*; **~path** *s.* sentier *m.*; **~plate** *s.* (*rail.*) plateforme *f.*; **~print** *s.* empreinte (de pas) *f.*; **~-rule** *s.* règle d'un pied *f.*; **~-soldier** *s.* fantassin *m.*; **~sore** *adj.* aux pieds meurtris; **~step** *s.* pas *m.*; **to follow in s.o.'s ~steps,** emboîter le pas à qn.; **~stool** *s.* tabouret *m.*; **four-~ed** *adj.* quadrupède, à quatre pattes; **light-~ed** *adj.* au pied léger; **sure-~ed** *adj.* au pied sûr; **~ing** *s.* (*~hold*) point d'appui *m.*, (*secure position*) position *f.*; (*status*) pied *m.*, **on an equal ~ing,** sur pied d'égalité; *v.t.* (*add up*) additionner; **~ the bill,** régler la note; **~ it,** aller à pied.

footling *adj.* (*Eng. fam.*) insignifiant.

fop *s.* fat *m.*; **~pery** *s.* fatuité *f.*; **~pish** *adj.* fat.

for *prep.* (*in place of*) pour, à la place de; (*in defence of*) pour; (*in favour of*) pour, au profit de; (*with a view to*) pour, en vue de; (*as regards*) pour, en ce qui concerne; (*because of*) à cause de; (*in exchange ~*) pour, en échange de; (*distance*) **the road climbed ~ 3 km.,** la route montait pendant 3 km.; **the view stretches ~ 3 km.,** la vue s'étend sur 3 km.; (*time*) **it rained ~ 3 days,** il a plu pendant 3 jours; **he came to stay ~ 3 days,** il est venu pour 3 jours; **he has been here ~ 3 weeks,** il est ici depuis 3 semaines (*n.b. use present tense*); **but ~ me, etc.,** sans moi, etc.; **it is not ~ me, etc. to,** ce n'est pas à moi, etc. de; *see also under appropriate verb, adj. etc. e.g.* CRY **~,** FAMOUS **~;** *conj.* (*seeing that*) vu que; (*since*) car.

forage *s.* fourrage *m.*; **~-cap** *s.* calot *m.*; *v.t.* & *i.* fouragger; **~ for,** chercher en fouillant dans tous les coins.

foray *s.* incursion *f.*

forbear *v.i.* **1.** (*abstain, refrain, from*) s'abstenir de; **2.** (*be patient*) se montrer patient; montrer de l'indulgence (*with*—pour); **~ance** *s.* (1) abstention *f.*; (2) patience *f.*; **~ing** *adj.* (2) patient, indulgent, tolérant.

forbears *s.pl.* ancêtres *m.pl.*

forbid *v.t.* (*command s.o. not to do*) défendre à qn. de faire qch.; (*prohibit sth.*) interdire qch.; (*prevent*) empêcher; **God ~ !,** à Dieu ne plaise!; **~den** *adj.* défendu, interdit; **~ding** *adj.* (*uninviting*) rébarbatif.

force *s.* force *f.*; **to bring into ~,** mettre en vigueur; **to come into ~,** entrer en vigueur; **by ~ of,** à force de; **in ~,** (*in large numbers*) en force, (*valid*) en vigueur; *v.t.* (*compel, strain, drive*; *agric.*) forcer; (*break open*): (*door, etc.*) enfoncer, (*lock*) forcer; **~ sth. upon s.o.,** imposer qch. à qn.; **~ s.o.'s hand,** forcer la main à qn.; **~ in** *v.t.* enfoncer; **~ open** *v.t.* forcer; **~d** *adj.* forcé; **~ful** *adj.* vigoureux; **forcible** *adj.* forcé.

forcemeat *s.* (*cook.*) farce *f.*

forceps *s.* pince *f.*; (*obstetrics*) forceps *m.*; (*dentistry*) davier *m.*

ford *s.* gué *m.*; *v.t.* passer à gué; **~able** *adj.* guéable.

fore *s.* (*~ part*; *bow of ship*) avant *m.*; **to come to the ~** (*fig.*) se faire connaître; *adj.* de devant; (*naut.*) d'avant; *adv.* à l'avant; **~ and aft,** de l'avant à l'arrière.

fore- (*in combination*) **~arm** *s.* avant-bras *m.*; **~arm** *v.t.* prémunir; **~bode** *v.t.* présager; **~boding** *s.* mauvais présage *m.*; **~cast** *s.* prévision *f.*, WEATHER **~cast; ~cast** *v.t.* prévoir, prédire; **~castle** *s.* gaillard d'avant *m.*; **~close** *v.t.* (*fin.*) forclore; **~closure** *s.* forclusion *f.*; **~court** *s.* avant-cour *f.*; **~doom** *v.t.* prédestiner; **~father** *s.* ancêtre *m.*; **~finger** *s.* index *m.*; **~foot** *s.* patte de devant *f.*; **~front** *s.* premier plan *m.*, premier rang *m.*; **~go** *v.t.* précéder; **~going** *s.* ce qui précède; **~going** *adj.* précédent; **~gone** *adj.* prévu, **it was a ~gone conclusion,** c'était à prévoir; **~ground** *s.* premier plan *m.*; **~hand** *s.* (*horse*) avant-main *f.*, (*tennis*) coup droit *m.*; **~head** *s.* front *m.*; **~judge** *v.t.* préjuger; **~knowledge** *s.* prescience *f.*; **~land** *s.* promontoire *m.*; **~leg** *s.* patte, jambe, de devant *f.*; **~lock** *s.* toupet *m.*; **~man** *s.* contremaître *m.*; **~mast** *s.* mât de misaine *m.*; **~most** *adj.* premier; *adv.* au premier rang; **~name** *s.* prénom *m.*; **~noon** *s.* matinée *f.*; **~ordain** *v.t.* prédestiner; **~runner** *s.* (*person*) précurseur *m.*; (*thing*) *adj.* avant-coureur; **~see** *v.t.* prévoir; **~seeing** *adj.* prévoyant; **~shadow** *v.t.* présager; **~shore** *s.* plage *f.*; **~shorten** *v.t.* raccourcir; **~sight** *s.* prévoyance *f.*; **~skin** *s.* prépuce *m.*; **~stall** *v.t.* prévenir; **~taste** *s.* avant-goût *m.*; **~tell** *v.t.* prédire; **~thought** *s.* prévoyance *f.*; **~top** *s.* hune de misaine *f.*; **~warn** *v.t.* prévenir; **~woman** *s.* première *f.*; **~word** *s.* avant-propos *m.*

foreign *adj.* (*of different country, alien, irrelevant*) étranger; (*comm. affairs*) extérieur; **F~ Office** *s.* ministère des affaires étrangères *m.*; **F~ Legion** *s.* légion étrangère *f.*; **~er** *s.* étrang/er, -ère *m.f.*

forensic *adj.* médico-légal.

forest *s.* forêt *f.*; *adj.* forestier; **~-tree,** arbre de haute futaie *m.*; **~er** *s.* (garde-)forestier *m.*; **~ry** *s.* (*science*) sylviculture *f.*; (*admin.*) (eaux et) forêts.

forfeit *s.* (*thing ~ed*) objet confisqué *m.*; (*law*) dédit *m.*; (*fine*) amende *f.*; (*in game*) gage *m.*; *v.t.* perdre; (*law*) être déchu de ses droits; **~ure** *s.* (*property*) confiscation *f.*; (*rights*) déchéance *f.*; (*licence*) retrait *m.*; (*title*) forfaiture *f.*

forgather *v.i.* s'assembler.

forge *s.* forge *f.*; *v.t.* **1.** (*beat into shape*) forger; **2.** (*invent*) inventer; **3.** (*counterfeit*) contrefaire; *v.i.* avancer; **~ ahead,** foncer, dépasser (qn.); **~r** *s.* (1) forgeur *m.*; (2) inventeur *m.*; (3) faussaire *m.*; **~ry** *s.* (*act*) falsification *f.*, (*document*) faux *m.*, (*money*) contrefaçon *f.*

forget *v.t.* oublier; (*neglect*) négliger; **~ about** *v.t.* oublier **~ oneself** *v.refl.* s'oublier; **~ful** *adj.* oublieux, négligent; **~fulness** *s.* oubli *m.*, négligence *f.*; **~table** *adj.* oubliable; **~-me-not** *s.* myosotis *m.*

forgiv/e *v.t.* **~e s.o. sth.,** pardonner qch. à qn.; **~e s.o. for doing sth.,** pardonner à qn. d'avoir fait qch.; (*debt*) remettre; **~able** *adj.* pardonnable; **~eness** *s.* pardon *m.*; (*debt*) remise *f.*; **~ing** *adj.* clément, indulgent.

forgo *v.t.* (*give up*) renoncer à; (*go without*) s'abstenir de.

fork *s.* **1.** (*for digging*) fourche *f.*; **2.** (*for eating*) fourchette *f.*; **3.** (*mus. tuning-~*) diapason *m.*; **4.** (*bifurcation*): (*of road*) bifurcation *f.*, (*rail.*) embranchement *m.*; **5.** (*~ed part, of tree, etc.*) fourche *f.*; **~-lift** *s.* chariot élévateur *m.*; *v.t.* & *i.* (1) fourcher; (4) bifurquer; (5) être en forme de fourche; **~ out** (*pop.*) *v.t.* allonger, *v.i.* casquer; **~ed** *adj.* fourchu (*road*) bifurqué; (*with teeth*) à dents; **~ed** LIGHTNING.

forlorn *adj.* (*forsaken*) abandonné; (*in pitiful state*) désespéré, misérable; **~ hope** (*fig.*) tentative désespérée *f.*

form *s.* (*shape, sort, aspect, good condition*) forme *f.*; (*school*) classe *f.*; **~-master** *s.* professeur *m.*; (*set order of words*) formule *f.*; (*document*) formulaire *m.*; (*formality*) formalité *f.*; **a matter of ~,** une simple formalité; (*bench*) banc *m.*; (*of hare*) gîte *m.*; **good ~,** bon ton *m.*; *v.t.* former; (*fig.*) concevoir; *v.i.* prendre forme, se former; **~ fours!,** en colonne par quatre!; **~ation** *s.* formation *f.*; **~ative** *adj.* formateur; **~less** *adj.* informe.

formal *adj.* **1.** (*explicit*) formel; **2.** (*according to rules*) en bonne forme; **3.** (*ceremonial, conventional*) cérémonieux, traditionnel; **4.** (*prim, stiff*) formaliste, raide; **5.** (*done as a matter of form*) de pure forme; **~ism** *s.* formalisme *m.*; **~ist** *s.* formaliste *m.*; **~ity** *s.* (2) formalité *f.*; (3) cérémonie *f.*; (4) raideur *f.*; **~ly** *adv.* (2) en bonne et due forme; (3) cérémonieusement.

formaldehyde *s.* formaldéhyde *m.*

format *s.* format *m.*

former *pron.* (*the first of two*) le (la) premi/er, -ère; celui (celle)-là; *adj.* (*the earlier of two*) premier; (*of the past*) d'autrefois; (*earlier*) antérieur, précédent; ancien (*before the noun*); **~ly** *adv.* autrefois.

formic *adj.* formique.

formidabl/e *adj.* (*dreadful*) terrifiant; (*difficult to overcome*) redoutable; (*fam. = very big, very good*) formidable; **~eness** *s.* caractère redoutable *m.* **~y** *adv.* redoutablement; (*fam.*) formidablement.

formula *s.* formule *f.*; **~ry** *s.* formulaire *m.*; **~te** *v.t.* formuler.

fornicat/e *v.i.* forniquer; **~ion** *s.* fornication *f.*; **~or** *s.* fornicateur *m.*

forsake *v.t.* (*give up*) renoncer à, abandonner; (*desert*) abandonner, délaisser; **God-~n,** *adj.* misérable, du diable.

forswear *v.t.* (*renounce*) abjurer; (*perjure oneself*) se parjurer.

forsworn *adj.* parjure.

forsythia *s.* forsythia *m.*

fort *s.* fort *m.*; **to hold the ~,** (*fig.*) assurer l'intérim; **~ify** *v.t.* (*lit.* & *fig.*) fortifier; (*with spirits*) alcooliser; **~ification** *s.* fortification *f.*; **~itude** *s.* courage *m.*; **~ress** *s.* forteresse *f.*

forte *s.* fort *m.*

forth *adv.* (*forwards*) en avant; (*out of doors*) en dehors; **from this time ~,** désormais; **and so ~,** et ainsi de suite; **~coming** *adj.* (*about to happen*) prochain, à venir; (*of person, approachable*) abordable; **~right** *adj.* franc, net; **~with** *adv.* sur-le-champ.

fortnight *s.* quinzaine *f.*; **~ly** *adj.* bimensuel; *adv.* tous les quinze jours.

fortuitous *adj.* fortuit; **~ly,** *adv.**; **~ness** *s.* hasard *m.*

fortunate *adj.* heureux; **~ly** *adv.**.

fortune *s.* (*chance, luck*) chance *f.*; (*prosperity, wealth*) fortune *f.*; (*future*) destin *m.*; **to make a ~,** faire fortune; **to tell s.o.'s ~,** dire la bonne aventure à qn.; **~-hunter** *s.* coureur de dot *m.*; **~-teller** *s.* diseuse de bonne aventure *f.*

fort/y *s.* & *adj.* quarante *m.*; **the ~ies,** les années quarante; **to be in one's ~ies,** avoir la quarantaine; **the roaring ~ies** (*geog.*) les grand frais d'Ouest *m.pl.*; **to have ~y winks,** faire dodo; **~ieth** *s.* & *adj.* quarantième.

forum *s.* (*hist.* & *fig.*) forum *m.*

forward *s.* (*sport*) avant *m.*; *adj.* **1.** (*in front*) en avant; **2.** (*well-advanced*) avancé, précoce; **3.** (*ready*) prêt; **4.** (*pert*) audacieux, effronté; **~ness** *s.* (1) avancement *m.*; (2) précocité *f.*; (3) empressement *m.*; (4) hardiesse *f.*; *adv.* en avant; *see under verbs,* COME **~,** *etc.*; *v.t.* (*promote*) soutenir; (*send on*) faire suivre; (*comm.*) expédier; **~ing** *s.* expédition *f.*

fossil *s.* fossile *m.*; (*fig. fam.*) (vieux) fossile *m.*; **~ize** *v.t.* & *i.* (se) fossiliser.

foster *v.t.* **1.** (*bring up child*) nourrir; **2.** (*put child into care*) mettre (un enfant) en nourrice; **3.** (*encourage, harbour*) encourager, protéger; **4.** (*cherish, lit.* & *fig.*) nourrir; **~-brother,** frère adoptif *m.*; **~-child,** nourrisson *m.*; **~-father,** père adoptif *m.*; **~-mother,** mère adoptive *f.*; **~-sister,** sœur adoptive *f.*

foul *s.* (*collision*) collision *f.*; (*~ stroke*) faute *f.*, coup interdit *m.*; *adj.* **1.** (*offensive, stinking*) infect, puant, dégoûtant; **2.** (*dirty*) sale, (*water*) trouble; **3.** (*choked*) bouché; **4.** (*morally*) impur, honteux, infâme; **5.** (*obscene*) obscène, grossier; **6.** (*unfair*) déloyal; **7.** (*weather*) sale; **~ play,** tricherie *f.*; **to fall ~ of s.o.,** se brouiller avec qn.; *v.t.* & *i.* (*make or become ~*) (se) salir, (se) souiller; (*entangle*) (s')engager; (*collide with*) (se) heurter (contre); **~ly** *adv.* (2) salement; (4) honteusement; (5) grossièrement; (6) déloyalement; **~ness** *s.* (1) puanteur *f.*; (2) saleté *f.*; (4) infamie *f.*; (5) obscénité *f.*

found *v.t.* **1.** (*lay base of, establish*) fonder; **2.** (*metal*) fondre; **ill-~ed** *adj.* sans fondement, mal appuyé; **~ation** *s.* (1) fondation *f.*; (*reason*) fondement *m.*; **~ation garment** *s.* gaîne *f.*; **~ation-stone,** première pierre *f.*; **~er** *s.* (1) fondat/eur, -rice *m.f.*; (2) fondeur *m.*; **~ry** *s.* (2) fonderie *f.*

founder *v.i.* (*sink*) sombrer; (*collapse*) s'effondrer; (*horse*) être atteint de fourbure; **~ed** *adj.* (*horse*) fourbu.

foundling *s.* enfant trouvé *m.*

fount *s.* source *f.*; (*print.*) fonte *f.*

fountain *s.* (*spring*) source *f.*; (*artificial jet of water*) fontaine *f.*; **~-head** *s.* source *f.*; **~-pen** *s.* stylo *m.*

four *adj.* & *s.* quatre; (*rowing*) quatre *m.*; **on all ~s,** à quatre pattes; **~-**CORNER**ed; ~-**FOOT**ed; ~fold,** quadruple; **~-poster** *s.* lit à colonnes *m.*; **~score,** quatre-vingts; **~-square** *adv.* carrément; **~th** *adj.* & *s.* quatrième, (*dates* & *names*) quatre; **~thly** *adv.**.

fourteen *adj.* & *s.* quatorze; **~th** *s.* & *adj.* quatorzième; (*dates* & *names*) quatorze; **Louis 14th.,** Louis quatorze.

fowl *s.* volaille *f.*; GUINEA-**~**; **~ pest** *s.* peste aviaire *f.*; **~er** *s.* (*with net*) oiseleur *m.*, (*with*

gun) chasseur *m.*; **~ing piece** *s.* fusil de chasse *m.*
fox *s.* (*animal* & *fig.*) renard *m.*; **~glove** *s.* digitale *f.*; **~hole** *s.* terrier *m.*; **~hound** *s.* foxhound *m.*; **~-hunt(ing)**, chasse au renard *f.*; **~trot** *s.* fox-trot *m.*; **~y** *adj.* rusé; (*colour*) roux; *v.t.* mystifier, tromper; *v.i.* ruser.
fraction *s.* fraction *f.*; **~al** *adj.* fractionnaire.
fractious *adj.* (*difficult*) rétif; (*peevish*) revêche.
fracture *s.* fracture *f.*; *v.t.* fracturer.
fragil/e *adj.* fragile; **~ity** *s.* fragilité *f.*
fragment *s.* fragment *m.*; **~ary** *adj.* fragmentaire; *v.t.* fragmenter.
fragran/ce *s.* parfum *m.*; **~t** *adj.* parfumé.
frail *adj.* **1.** (*brittle*) fragile; **2.** (*health*) faible, frêle; **~ty** *s.* (1) fragilité *f.*; (2) faiblesse *f.*
frame *s.* (*construction*) charpente *f.*; (*build*) taille *f.*; (*skeleton of sth. e.g. umbrella*) carcasse *f.*; (*for tapestry*) métier *m.*; (*of spectacles*) monture *f.*; (*of car, of window; hort.*) châssis *m.*; (*of door*) chambranle *m.*; (*of picture*) cadre *m.*; (*TV*) trame *f.*; (*cinema*) photogramme *m.*; (*fig.*) **~ of mind,** disposition *f.*; **~work** *s.* charpente *f.*, (*fig.*) cadre *m.*; *v.t.* (*shape*) former, (*fig.*) formuler; (*adapt*) ajuster; (*construct*) construire; (*articulate*) articuler; (*put in ~, serve as ~ for*) encadrer; (*fam.*) manigancer qch., monter un coup contre qn.; **~-up** *s.* coup monté *m.*; **~r** *s.* encadreur *m.*, (*fig.*) auteur *m.*; **framing** *s.* construction *f.*, encadrement *m.*, (*fig.*) conception *f.*, élaboration *f.*
franc *s.* franc *m.*
France *s.* (*geog.*) France *f.*
franchise *s.* droit de vote *m.*; (*comm.*) droit de vente *m.*; ⚠ franchise = **frankness.**
Franciscan *adj.* & *s.m.* franciscain.
frangipane, frangipani *s.* frangipane *f.*
frank[1] *adj.* (*candid*) franc; (*undisguised*) sincère; **~ly** *adv.* franchement; **~ness** *s.* franchise *f.*
frank[2] *v.t.* (*letter*) affranchir; **~ing** *s.* affranchissement *m.*
frankfurter *s.* (*cook.*) saucisse de Francfort *f.*
frankincense *s.* encens *m.*
frantic *adj.* frénétique; **~ with,** fou de; **~ally** *adv.**.
fratern/al *adj.* fraternel; **~ally** *adv.**; **~ity** *s.* (*spirit* & *eccles.*) fraternité *f.*; (*group*) confrérie *f.*; **~ize** *v.i.* fraterniser.
fratricid/e *s.* fratricide *m.*; **~al** *adj.* fratricide.
fraud *s.* (*criminal deception*) fraude *f.*; (*dishonest trick*) tromperie *f.*; (*disappointing person*) imposteur *m.*, (*thing*) attrape-nigaud *m.*; (*fam.*) fumiste *m.*; **~ulent** *adj.* frauduleux.
fraught *adj.* **~ with** (*containing*) lourd de; (*liable to produce*) fertile en.
fray *s.* bagarre *f.*; *v.t.*& *i.* (*rub*) (s')effranger; (*make or become ragged at edge*) (s')érailler.
freak *s.* **1.** (*caprice*) caprice *m.*; **2.** (*monstrosity*) monstre *m.*; **3.** (*eccentric*) excentrique *m.*; *adj.* (1) phénoménal; (2) anormal; **~ish** *adj.* (1) capricieux; (2) monstrueux.
freckle *s.* tache de rousseur *f.*; *v.t.* & *i.* (se) couvrir de taches de rousseur; **~d** *adj.* couvert de taches de rousseur.
free *adj.* (*at liberty, disengaged, not literal* (*of translation*), *lavish*) libre; (*~ from obstruction*) dégagé; (*spontaneous*) spontané; (*not charged for*) gratuit; **~ from,** exempt de; **~ with,** prodigue de; **tax-~**, exempt d'impôt; POST-~; DUTY-~; **to give ~** REIN **to; to set ~**, (*slaves, etc.*) affranchir, (*prisoner, etc.*) libérer; **~board** *s.* franc-bord *m.* **~booter** *s.* pirate *m.*; **~-hand** *adj.* à main levée; **~hold** *s.* propriété foncière *f.* (à perpétuité); **~ kick** *s.* coup franc *m.*; **~lance** *s.* franc-tireur *m.*, *adj.* indépendant, **~lance journalist,** pigiste *m.*, **~-lance** *v.i.* travailler à la pige; **~man** *s.* (*of city*) citoyen d'honneur *m.*; **F~**MASON; **~ pass** *s.* billet de faveur *m.*; **~ port** *s.* port franc *m.*; **~ thinker** *s.* libre penseur *m.*; **~ trade** *s.* libre-échange *m.*; **~-wheel** *v.i.* rouler en roue libre; **~ will** *s.* libre arbitre *m.*; **~dom** *s.* liberté *f.*, (*excessive*) sans-gêne *m.*; *adv.* & **~ly** *adv.* (*without charge*) gratuitement; (*without hindrance*) librement, sans contrainte; (*openly*) franchement; (*generously*) largement, abondamment; (*willingly*) volontiers; *v.t.* libérer; (*disentangle*) débarrasser (*from*—de); (*exempt from*) exempter de.
freez/e *s.* gel *m.*, gelée *f.*; (*comm.*) blocage *m.*; *v.t.* & *i.* geler, (se) glacer; (*preserve by ~ing, deep ~e*) congeler, surgeler; (*comm.*) bloquer; **~e out** *v.t.* boycotter; **~e up** *v.t.* geler; DEEP-**-~er; ~ing** *s.* congélation *f.*; **~ing** *adj.* glacial; **~ing** FOG; **~ing-**POINT.
freight *s.* (*transport of goods, load, cost*) fret *m.*; *v.t.* affréter; **~er** *s.* (*naut.*) cargo *m.*, (*aviat.*) avion de fret *m.*; **~ing** *s.* affrètement *m.*
French *adj.* & *s.m.* (*lang.*) français *m.*; **~** BEAN; **to take ~ leave,** filer à l'anglaise; **~ chalk** *s.* craie de tailleur *f.*; **~ horn** *s.* cor d'harmonie *m.*; **~man, ~woman,** Français(e) *m.f.*; **~ polish** *s.* vernis *m.*; **~ window** *s.* porte-fenêtre *f.*; **~ify** *v.t.* franciser.
frenetic *adj.* frénétique.
frenz/y *s.* (*med.*) délire *m.*; (*violent emotion*) frénésie *f.*; (*of despair*) fureur *f.*; (*of delight*) transport *m.*; **~ied** *adj.* frénétique.
frequen/cy *s.* (*occurrence; phys.; electr.*) fréquence *f.*; **~t** *adj.* (*occurring often*) fréquent; (*numerous*) nombreux; (*habitual*) habituel; **~tly** *adv.* fréquemment, souvent.
frequent *v.t.* fréquenter.
fresco *s.* fresque *f.*
fresh *adj.* **1.** (*new, novel*) nouveau; **2.** (*≠ stale or preserved*) frais; **3.** (*vigorous*) vigoureux; **4.** (*inexperienced*) novice; **5.** (*refreshing*) rafraîchissant; **6.** (*impertinent*) effronté; **~man** *s.* étudiant de première année *m.*; **~ water,** eau douce *f.*; **~-water** *adj.* d'eau douce; *adv.* & **~ly** *adv.* fraîchement; (*recently*) récemment; **~en** *v.t.* rafraîchir; **~en up** *v.i.* se rafraîchir; **~et** *s.* courant d'eau douce *m.*; **~ness** *s.* (1) nouveauté *f.*; (2) fraîcheur *f.*; (3) vigueur *f.*; (6) effronterie *f.*
fret *s.* **1.** (*worried state*) inquiétude *f.*; **2.** (*arch.*) frette *f.*; **3.** (*mus.*) touchette *f.*; *v.t.* (1) inquiéter, agacer; *v.i.* (1) se tracasser, se ronger (*with*—de); (*chafe*) se ronger; (*of child*) pleurnicher; **~saw** *s.* scie à chantourner *f.*; **~work** *s.* découpage *m.*; **~ful** *adj.* maussade, agacé, (*child*) pleurnicheur; **~fulness** *s.* irritabilité *f.*, mauvaise humeur *f.*
friab/le *adj.* friable; **~ility** *s.* friabilité *f.*
friar *s.* moine *m.*; **~y** *s.* monastère *m.*
fricassee *s.* (*cook.*) fricassée *f.*; *v.t.* fricasser.
friction *s.* (*med., mech., fig.*) friction *f.*
Friday *s.* vendredi *m.*; **Good ~**, vendredi saint; **man ~**, Vendredi *m.*
fridge, frig *s.* (*fam.*) frigo *m.*
friend *s.* ami(e) *m.f.*; (*F~*) quaker(esse) *m.f.*; **to be ~s with s.o.,** être lié d'amitié avec qn.; **to make ~s with s.o.,** se lier d'amitié avec qn.; **Society of F~s,** secte des Quakers *f.*; **a ~ in need is a ~ indeed,** c'est dans le besoin qu'on connaît ses amis; **~less** *adj.* sans ami; **~ly** *adj.* (*thing*) amical, ami; (*person*) aimable, sympathique; **F~ly Society** *s.* amicale *f.*; **~liness** *s.* disposition amicale *f.*; (*kindness*) bienveillance *f.*; **~ship** *s.* amitié *f.*
Friesian *adj.* (*geog.*) frison(ne); (*cattle*) de race frisonne.
frieze *s.* (*text.*) ratine *f.*; (*arch.*) frise *f.*
frigate *s.* frégate *f.*
fright *s.* (*fear*) frayeur *f.*; (*person*) horreur *f.*; STAGE **~; to take ~**, s'effrayer; **~en** *v.t.* effrayer; **~en away** *v.t.* effaroucher; **~ened**

adj. effrayé, **to be ~ened of,** avoir peur de; **~ful** *adj.* effroyable, (*ugly*) affreux, (*pop.*) effroyable; **~fully** *adv.* affreusement; **~fulness** *s.* horreur *f.*
frigid *adj.* **1.** (*intensely cold*) glacial; **2.** (*lacking ardour, med.*) frigide; **3.** (*repellent*) glacial; **~ly** *adv.* froidement; **~ity** *s.* **~ness** *s.* (1), (3) froideur *f.*; (2) frigidité *f.*
frill *s.* (*dress*) jabot *m.*, ruche *f.*; **~s** *pl.* (*fam.*) fioritures *f.pl.*; **~y** *adj.* ruché.
fringe *s.* **1.** (*ornamental border, hair*) frange *f.*; **2.** (*border, outskirts*) lisière *f.*; **3.** (*fig.*) marge *f.*; *adj.* marginal, supplémentaire; *v.t.* & *i.* (1) franger; (2) border.
frippery *s.* (*cheap goods*) camelote *f.*; (*cheap finery*) falbalas *m.pl.*
frisk *v.i.* gambader; *v.t.* (*pop.* = *search person*) fouiller; **~y** *adj.* (*person*) folâtre; (*horse*) fringant; (*dog*) frétillant; **~iness** *s.* gaieté *f.*
fritillary *s.* (*bot.*) fritillaire *f.*; (*butterfly*) argynne *m.*
fritter *s.* (*cook.*) beignet *m.*; *v.t.* effriter; **~ away** *v.t.* gaspiller; (*fig.*) s'effriter.
frivol/ous *adj.* (*trifling*) frivole; (*futile*) futile; (*silly*) stupide; **~ity** *s.* frivolité *f.*
frizzle *v.t.* (*cook.*) faire frire, faire griller; (*hair*) friser; *v.i.* grésiller.
fro *adv.* **to and ~,** de long en large; **to go to and ~,** aller et venir.
frock *s.* (*eccles.*) froc *m.*; (*woman's dress*) robe *f.*; **~-coat,** redingote *f.*
frog *s.* grenouille *f.*; (*on mil. dress*) brandebourg *m.*; **to have a ~ in one's throat** (*fam.*) avoir un chat dans la gorge; LEAP-~; **~man** *s.* homme-grenouille *m.*; **~-march** *v.t.* évacuer de force.
frolic *s.* gambade *f.*; (*prank*) fredaine *f.*; *v.i.* gambader; **~some** *adj.* folâtre.
from *prep.* (*out of*) de; (*goods, ships, planes, etc.*) en provenance de; (*because of*) à cause de; (*at a distance of*) à . . . km de; (*since*) depuis; (*according to*) d'après; **~ above, etc.** (de *or* d') d'en haut etc.; **~ time to time,** de temps en temps; *see also certain verbs.*
frond *s.* (*bot.*) fronde *f.*
front *s.* (*face*) face *f.*; (*fore part*) devant *m.*; (*forward position*) premier rang *m.*; (*mil., polit., meteor.*) front *m.*; (*at seaside*) promenade *f.*; (*theat.*) côté de la salle *m.*; (*disguise*) contenance *f.*; (*arch.*) façade *f.*; (*shop*) devanture *f.*; **in ~ of,** devant, en face de; *adj.* de face, de devant; (*auto. wheel, etc.*) avant; **~ bench** *s.* (*parl.*) banc des ministres *m.*; **~ door** *s.* porte de devant *f.*; **~ page** *s.* (*of newspaper*) la une; **~ page news,** nouvelle à la une, nouvelle sensationnelle *f.*; **~-wheel** DRIVE; *v.t.* (*face*) faire face à, donner sur; (*confront*) affronter, faire front à; **~age** *s.* terrain en bordure *m.*; (*arch.*) façade *f.*; **~al** *s.* (*eccles.*) devant d'autel *m.*; **~al** *adj.* (*med.*) frontal, (*mil.*) de front.
frontier *s.* frontière *f.*; *adj.* frontière (*invar.*)
frontispiece *s.* frontispice *m.*
frost *s.* (*freezing*) gelée *f.*; **hoar-~,** givre *m.*; (*pop.* = *failure*) four *m.*; **~-bite** *s.* gelure *f.*; *v.t.* (*damage with* ~) geler; (*cover with* ~) givrer; (*cook.*) glacer; **~ed glass** *s.* verre dépoli *m.*; **~ily** *adv.* froidement; **~iness** *s.* froid glacial *m.*, (*fig.*) froideur *f.*; **~y** *adj.* givré; glacé.
froth *s.* **1.** (*med., naut., cook.*) écume *f.*; **2.** (*on drinks*) mousse *f.*; *v.i.* (1) écumer; (2) mousser; **~y** *adj.* (1) écumeux; (2) mousseux.
frown *s.* **1.** (*contraction of brows*) froncement des sourcils *m.*; **2.** (*severe look*) regard sévère *m.*; (*fig.*) hostilité *f.*; *v.i.* (1) froncer les sourcils; (2) se renfrogner; **~ upon** regarder d'un œil sévère; **~ing** *adj.* (1) sourcilleux; (2) renfrogné.
frowzy *adj.* (*fusty*) qui sent le renfermé; (*dingy*) mal tenu.
frozen *adj.* gelé; (*food*) congelé, surgelé.
fructif/erous *adj.* fructifère; **~y** *v.t.* & *i.* (faire) fructifier.
frugal *adj.* frugal; **~ity** *s.* frugalité *f.*; **~ly** *adv.**.
fruit *s.* (*lit.* & *fig.*) fruit *m.* ⚠ *usu. pl. sense in Eng.*, **some ~** = des fruits; un fruit = **a piece of ~**; **first ~s,** prémices *f.pl.*; **~ machine** *s.* machine à sous *f.*; **~ shop** *s.* fruiterie *f.*; **~-tree** *s.* arbre fruitier *m.*; **~erer** *s.* fruitier *m.*; **~ful** *adj.* fertile, fécond, (*fig.*) fructueux; **~fulness** *d.* fertilité *f.*, fécondité *f.*; **~less** *adj.* stérile, (*fig.*) infructueux, vain; **~y** *adj.* de fruit, fruité; *v.i.* porter des fruits, fructifier.
fruition *s.* (*fig.*) réalisation *f.*; **to come to ~,** se réaliser.
frump *s.* (*pop.*) vieille toupie *f.*; **~ish** *adj.* (*fam.*) mal fagoté.
frustrat/e *v.t.* décevoir (qn.); contrecarrer (qn., *s.o.'s efforts*); (*plans*) faire échouer; (*plot*) déjouer; (*hopes*) frustrer; **~ion** *s.* (*act*) déception *f.*; (*feeling*) frustration *f.*
fr/y *s.* (*young fish*) alevin *m.*; (*cook.*) friture *f.*; (*offal*) fressure *f.*; (*people*) **small ~y,** menu fretin *m.*; *v.t.* & *i.* (faire) frire; **to have other** FISH **to ~y**; **~yer** *s.* (*cook.*) friteuse *f.*; **~ied** *adj.* frit; **~ied** EGG; **~ying** *s.* friture *f.*; **~ying-pan** *s.* poêle à frire *f.*; **to fall out of the ~ying--pan into the fire,** tomber de Charybde en Scylla.
fuchsia *s.* fuchsia *m.*
fuddle *v.t.* & *i.* **1.** (*intoxicate*) (se) griser; **2.** (*fig. confuse*) (s')embrouiller; **~d** *adj.* (1) grisé; (2) embrouillé.
fuddy-duddy *s.* (*fam.*) vieille baderne *f.*
fudge *s.* (*nonsense*) blague *f.*; (*toffee*) fondant *m.*; *v.t.* (*fam.*) rafistoler.
fuel *s.* (*lit.*) combustible *m.*; (*fig.*) aliment *m.*; **high-**OCTANE **~**; **~-oil** *s.* mazout *m.*, (*techn.*) gasoil, gazole *m.*; *v.t.* & *i.* (se) pourvoir en combustible.
fug *s.* renfermé *m.*
fugitive *adj.* & *s.m.f.* fugit/if, -ive.
fugue *s.* (*mus., psych.*) fugue *f.*
fulcrum *s.* point d'appui *m.*
fulfil *v.t.* **1.** (*bring to pass*) réaliser; **2.** (*carry out*) accomplir, remplir, exécuter; **3.** (*satisfy*) combler, répondre à; **4.** (*bring to an end*) achever; **~ment** *s.* (1) réalisation *f.*; (2) accomplissement *m.*, exécution *f.*
full[1] *s.* plein *m.*; **to the ~,** complètement; **in ~,** en entier, **write in ~,** écrivez en toutes lettres; *adj.* (*filled to capacity*) plein, rempli; (*bus, cinema, etc.*) complet; (*replete*) rempli; (*crowded*) bondé; (*copious*) abondant; (*complete*) complet, entier; (*plump; of garment*) ample; **~ of,** plein de, comblé de; *adv.* (*also* **~ly**) (*quite*) pleinement; (*exactly*) juste; **~ back** *s.* (*sport*) arrière *m.*; **~-blooded** *adj.* (*fig.*) vigoureux; **~-blown** *adj.* (*flower*) épanoui, (*fig.*) qualifié; **~ daylight** *s.* plein jour *m.*; **~-grown** *adj.* adulte; **~-length** *adv.* en pied; **~ name,** nom et prénoms; **~ play** (*fig.*) libre carrière *f.*; **~ share,** bonne part *f.*; **at ~ speed,** à toute vitesse; **~ stop** *s.* point *m.*; **~-time** *adj.* à temps entier; **~y fashioned** (*dressm.*) proportionné; **~y-**FLEDGED; **~ness** *s.* plénitude *f.*; (*dress, details*) ampleur *f.*
full[2] *v.t.* (*text.*) fouler; **~er** *s.* foulon *m.*; **~er's earth,** terre à foulon *f.*
fulminate *v.t.* & *i.* (*detonate*) exploser; (*fig.*) fulminer.
fulsome *adj.* servile; **~ness** *s.* servilité *f.*
fumble *v.t.* manipuler maladroitement; *v.i.* tâtonner; **~r** *s.* maladroit *m.*
fume *s.* fumée *f.*; *v.t.* exposer à la fumée; *v.i.* (*lit.*) fumer; (*fig.*) écumer, baver (*with*—de).
fumigat/e *v.t.* désinfecter; **~ion** *s.* fumigation *f.*

fun *s.* (*amusement*) amusement *m.*; (*jocularity*) plaisanterie *f.*; **in ~, for ~, for the ~ of it,** pour rire; **to make ~ of,** se moquer de; **to** POKE **~ at s.o.; ~-fair,** vogue *f.*; **~ny** *adj.* (*amusing*) drôle; (*queer*) bizarre; **~ny-bone** *s.* petit juif *m.*

funambulist *s.* funambule *m.*

function *s.* **1.** (*work sth. is designed to do*) fonction *f.*; **2.** (*official duty*) fonction *f.*; **3.** (*math.*) fonction *f.*; **4.** (*meeting*) cérémonie *f.*, réception *f.*; *v.i.* (1) fonctionner; **~al** *adj.* fonctionnel; **~ary** *s.* (2) fonctionnaire *m.*

fund *s.* fonds *m.*; **~s,** *s.pl.* fonds *m.pl.*; *v.t.* (*fin.*) consolider.

fundamental *s.* principe fondamental *m.*; (*mus.*) fondamentale *f.*; *adj.* (*serving as base*) fondamental; (*essential, primary*) essentiel, foncier; **~ly** *adv.* fondamentalement; foncièrement.

funeral *s.* funérailles *f.pl.*; (*official*) obsèques *m.pl.*; (*burial*) enterrement *m.*; **~ service,** office des morts *m.*; *adj.* (*ceremony, march, oration*) funèbre; (*column, stone, urn*) funéraire; (*wreath*) mortuaire; **it's your/my, etc. ~,** tant pis pour vous/moi, etc.

funereal *adj.* (*fig.*) funèbre, lugubre.

fung/us *s.* (*bot.*) champignon vénéneux *m.*; (*med.*) fongus *m.*; **~icide** *s.* substance fongicide *f.*

funicular *adj.* & *s.m.* funiculaire.

funk *s.* (*fam.*) frousse *f.*; (*coward*) froussard *m.*; **to be in a (blue) ~,** (*fam.*) avoir la frousse; *v.t.* (*shirk*) (*pop.*) se dégonfler devant; (*be afraid of*) avoir la frousse de; *v.i.* avoir la frousse.

funnel *s.* (*of ship*) cheminée *f.*; (*tube*) entonnoir *m.*

funny *see* FUN.

fur *s.* **1.** (*animal's coat*) pelage *m.*; **2.** (*clothing*) fourrure *f.*; **3.** (*crust*): (*med.*) empâtement *m.*; (*techn.*) tartre *m.*; *v.t.* & *i.* (2) couvrir, doubler, de fourrure; (3) (s')empâter, (s')entartrer; **~red** *adj.* (2) fourré; (3) empâté; entartré; **~below** *s.* falbala *m.*; **~rier** *s.* fourreur *m.*

furbish *v.t.* (*polish*) fourbir; (*fam. renovate*) retaper.

furious *adj.* (*angry, violent, uproarious*) furieux (*with*—contre); **~ly** *adv.**.

furl *v.t.* (*sail*) ferler; (*fold up*) replier.

furlong *s.* furlong *m.*

furlough *s.* congé *m.*; (*mil.*) permission *f.*

furnace *s.* (*techn.*) fourneau *m.*; (*fig.*) fournaise *f.*; (*domestic*) calorifère *m.*; **blast-~,** haut fourneau *m.*

furnish *v.t.* **1.** (*supply*) fournir (*with*—de); **2.** (*supply with furniture, & fig.*) meubler (*with*—de); **~ed,** *adj.* meublé; **~ing** *s.* (1) fourniture *f.*; (2) *pl.* ameublement *m.*

furniture *s.* (*complete*) ameublement *m.*; (*piece of*) meuble *m.*; (*set of*) mobilier *m.*

furore *s.* fureur *f.*

furrow *s.* **1.** (*agric.*) sillon *m.*; **2.** (*wrinkle*) ride *f.*; **3.** (*naut.*) sillage *m.*; *v.t.* (1) labourer; (2) rider; (3) sillonner.

further *adj.* **1.** (*more remote*) plus éloigné; **2.** (*additional*) additionnel, supplémentaire, encore un(e) autre; **until ~ notice,** jusqu'à nouvel avis; **~ information,** de plus amples renseignements; *adv.* (1) plus loin; (2) davantage, de plus; **~ up, down, etc.,** plus haut, plus bas, etc.; **furthest** *adj.* & *adv. see* FARTHER; **~more** *adv.* de plus; encore (*followed by inversion*); *v.t.* (*promote*) seconder; (*favour*) favoriser; **~ance** *s.* avancement *m.*, aide *f.*

furtive *adj.* furtif; **~ly** *adv.**.

fury *s.* (*anger*) fureur *f.*; (*violence*) furie *f.*; (*angry woman*) furie *f.*; **like ~,** furieusement; (*swiftly*) à toute vitesse.

furze *s.* ajonc *m.*

fuse *s.* (*electr.*) coupe-circuit *m.*, plomb *m.*; (*wire*) fusible *m.*; (*for explosive*) fusée *f.*; *v.t.* & *i.* (*electr.*) (faire) sauter, **you will blow a ~,** vous ferez sauter les plombs; **there has been a ~,** les plombs ont sauté; (*melt with heat*) fondre; (*blend*) fusionner.

fusee *s.* (*mil., techn.*) fusée *f.*; (*match*) tison *m.*

fuselage *s.* fuselage *m.*

fusilier *s.* fusilier *m.*

fusillade *s.* fusillade *f.*

fusion *s.* (*lit.* & *fig.*) fusion *f.*; (*fused mass*) fonte *f.*

fuss *s.* (*bustle*) agitation *f.*; (*excessive concern*) (*fam.*) histoires *f.pl.*; (*ostentatious activity*) importance *f.*; **what a ~!,** que d'histoires!; **to make a ~,** faire des histoires; **to make a ~ of s.o.,** faire grand cas de qn.; **~-pot** *s.* (*pop.*) faiseu/r, -se d'histoires *m.f.*; *v.i.* faire des histoires; (*move ~ily*) s'affairer; (*worry*) se tracasser; **~ over s.o.,** être aux petits soins pour qn.; **~y** *adj.* (*busy*) affairé; (*worrying*) tracassier; (*showy*) voyant; (*fastidious*) tâtillon.

fustian *s.* **1.** (*text.*) futaine *f.*; **2.** (*bombast*) grandiloquence *f.*; *adj.* (1) de futaine; (2) grandiloquent.

fust/y *adj.* **1.** (*stale smelling*) qui sent le renfermé; **2.** (*antiquated*) vieux jeu; **~iness** *s.* (1) renfermé *m.*

futil/e *adj.* futile; **~ity** *s.* futilité *f.*

futur/e *s.* avenir *m.*; (*ling.*) futur *m.*; **in the ~,** à l'avenir; *adj.* futur, à venir; **~ity** *s.* avenir *m.*

fuzz *s.* (*fluff*) duvet *m.*, bourre *m.*; (*pop. = police*) flics *m.pl.*; **~y** *adj.* duveteux; (*blurred*) flou.

G

G, g *s.* (*mus.*) sol *m.*

gab *s.* (*fam.*) bagou(t) *m.*; **to have the gift of the ~,** avoir du bagou(t).

gabble *s.* bredouillement *m.*; *v.t.* & *i.* bredouiller.

gaberdine, gabardine *s.* (*text.*) gabardine *f.*; (*coat*) imperméable *m.*, gabardine *f.*

gable *s.* (*arch.*) pignon *m.*

gad *v.i.* (*usu. ~ about*) galoper (de côté et d'autre); **~about** *s.* (*pop.*) vadrouilleur, -se *m.f.*

gadfly *s.* taon *m.*

gadget *s.* (*fam.*) truc *m.*

Gael *s.* Gaël *m.*; **~ic** *adj.* & *s.m.* (*language*) gaélique.

gaff *s.* **1.** (*fishing spear*) harpon *m.*; **2.** (*hook for landing fish*) gaffe *f.*; **3.** (*pop.*) **to blow the ~,** vendre la mèche; *v.t.* (2) gaffer.

gaffer *s.* (*old man*) vieux *m.*; (*foreman, boss*) patron *m.*

gag *s.* **1.** (*in mouth*) bâillon *m.*; **2.** (*joke*) gag *m.*, blague *f.*; *v.t.* & *i.* (1) (*lit.* & *fig.*) bâillonner; (2) blaguer; **3.** (*retch*) avoir des haut-le-cœur.

gaga *adj.* (*pop.*) gaga, gâteux.

gage[1] *s.* (*pledge*) gage *m.*; (*challenge*) défi *m.*

gage[2] *s.* (=*greengage*) reine-claude *f.*

gaggle *s.* (*of geese* & *people*) troupeau *m.*

gaiety *s. see* GAY.

gain *s.* (*profit*) bénéfice *m.*, avantage *m.*; (*money-making*) gain *m.*; *v.t.* (*obtain, secure*) obtenir,

acquérir; (*win*) gagner; (*reach*) atteindre; (*persuade s.o. to sth.*) gagner qn. à qch.; *v.i.* (*profit*) gagner; (*of clock*) avancer; ~ **on s.o.,** gagner sur qn.; ~**er** *s.* gagnant *m.*; ~**ful** *adj.* rémunérateur, lucratif; ~**fully** *adv.* de façon rémunératrice.
gainsay *v.t.* (*deny*) nier; (*contradict*) contredire.
gait *s.* démarche *f.*; (*of horse*) allure *f.*
gaiter *s.* guêtre *f.*
gala *s.* gala *m.*
galantine *s.* (*cook.*) galantine *f.*
galaxy *s.* (*astron.*) galaxie *f.*; (*the Milky Way*) la Voie lactée *f.*; (*of islands*) groupe *m.*; (*fig.*) constellation *f.*
gale *s.* vent fort *m.*; **to blow a** ~, souffler violemment.
gall *s.* **1.** (*bile*) bile *f.*; **2.** (*asperity, rancour, bitterness*) fiel *m.*, amertume *f.*; **3.** (*pop. impudence*) culot *m.*; **4.** (*blister*) écorchure *f.*; **5.** (*on trees, etc.*) galle *f.*; ~**-bladder,** vésicule biliaire *f.*; ~**stone,** calcul biliaire *m.*; *v.t.* (2) (*fig.*) agacer, irriter, blesser; (4) écorcher; ~**ing** *adj.* (*fig.*) irritant.
gallant *s.* **1.** (*smart young man*) élégant *m.*; **2.** (*attentive man*) galant *m.*; *adj.* (1) élégant; (2) galant; **3.** (*brave*) vaillant; ~**ly** *adv.* (2) galamment; (3) vaillamment; ~**ry** *s.* (2) galanterie *f.*; (3) vaillance *f.*
galleon *s.* galion *m.*
gallery *s.* (*covered walk, raised balcony; underground passage; art, etc.*) galerie *f.*; (*corridor*) couloir *m.*; (*theat. pop.*) poulailler *m.*; **to play to the** ~, parler, poser, pour la galerie.
galley *s.* (*naut.*) galère *f.*; (*ship's kitchen*) coquerie *f.*; (*print.*) galée *f.*; ~ **proofs,** épreuves en placard *f.pl.*, placards *m.pl.*
Gallic *adj.* gaulois; ~**ism** *s.* gallicisme *m.*; ~**ize** *v.t.* franciser.
gallivant *v.i.* courir la prétentaine (prétantaine).
gallon *s.* gallon *m.*
galloon *s.* galon *m.*
gallop *s.* (*pace*) galop *m.*; (*track*) piste *f.*; *v.t.* & *i.* (faire) galoper; ~**ing** *s.* galop *m.*; *adj.* galopant.
gallows *s.pl.* potence *f.* ⚠ *sing. in French*; ~**-bird,** gibier de potence *m.*
galore *adv.* (*fam.*) à la pelle, à gogo.
galoshes, goloshes *s.pl.* caoutchoucs *m.pl.*
galumph *v.i.* caracoler.
galvan/ic *adj.* (*lit.* & *fig.*) galvanique; ~**ism** *s.* galvanisme *m.*; ~**ization** *s.* galvanisation *f.*; ~**ize** *v.t.* (*lit.* & *fig.*) galvaniser; ~**ized** *adj.* galvanisé.
gambit *s.* (*chess*) gambit *m.*; (*fig.*) risque calculé *m.*
gambl/e *s.* **1.** (*game*) jeu *m.*; **2.** (*risk, risky undertaking*) risque *m.*, entreprise risquée *f.*; *v.i.* (1) jouer; (2) prendre des risques; ~**er** *s.* joueur *m.*; ~**ing** *s.* jeu *m.*
gamboge *s.* gomme-gutte *f.*
gambol *s.* gambade *f.*; *v.i.* gambader.
game *s.* (*sport, pastime*) jeu *m.*; (*jest*) plaisanterie *f.*; (*trick*) manège *m.*; (*subdivision at tennis, bridge, etc.*) partie *f.*; (*animals*) gibier *m.*; BIG ~; FAIR ~; **to play the** ~ (*fig.*) jouer franc jeu; **to give the** ~ **away,** vendre la mèche; **to make** ~ **of s.o.,** se moquer de qn.; **the** ~ **is up (with)**, c'en est fini, fait, (de); ~**-bag** *s.* gibecière *f.*; ~**-bird** *s.* gibier à plumes *m.*; ~**-cock** *s.* coq de combat *m.*; ~KEEPER; ~ LICENCE; ~ PARK; *adj.* (*spirited*) courageux; (*ready to or for*) de force à; (*crippled*) estropié; **to be** ~, avoir du cran; ~**ly** *adv.* crânement; **gamy** *adj.* faisandé; *v.t.* & *i.* jouer; **gaming-house** *s.* maison de jeu *f.*; **gaming-table** *s.* table de jeu *f.*; ~**ster** *s.* joueur *m.*
gamma *s.* gamma *m.*; ~ **rays,** rayons gamma *m.pl.*
gammon *s.* **1.** (*ham*) jambon fumé *m.*; **2.** (*humbug*) baliverne *f.*; *v.t.* (2) (*fam.*) mettre en boîte.
gammy *adj.* (*pop.*) amoché.
gamp *s.* (*fam.*) riflard *m.*
gamut *s.* (*mus., range, scope*) gamme *f.*
gander *s.* jars *m.*
gang *s.* (*of workmen*) équipe *f.*; (*of prisoners*) convoi *m.*; (*usu. criminal*) bande *f.*; ~**plank** *s.* planche de débarquement *f.*; ~**ster** *s.* gangster *m.*; *v.i.* (~ *up*) s'associer; ~ **up on s.o.,** se liguer contre qn.
gangling *adj.* dégingandé.
ganglion *s.* ganglion *m.*
gangren/e *s.* gangrène *f.*; *v.i.* se gangrener; ~**ous** *adj.* gangreneux.
gangway *s.* (*naut., aviat.*) passerelle *f.*; (*passage*) passage *m.*; (*in bus*) couloir *m.*; (*in theat.*) allée *f.*
gannet *s.* fou *m.*
gantry *s.* (*stand for barrels*) chantier *m.*; (*platform for crane, etc.*) portique *m.*
gaol, jail *s.* prison *f.*; *v.t.* emprisonner; ~**bird,** gibier de potence *m.*; ~**er** *s.* geôlier *m.*
gap *s.* (*breach*) brèche *f.*; (*empty space*) vide *m.*, blanc *m.*, (*fig.*) lacune *f.*; (*hole*) trou *m.*; (*fig. wide divergence*) abîme *m.*; **to** BRIDGE **the** ~.
gap/e *s.* **1.** (*yawn*) bâillement *m.*; **2.** (*stare*) badauderie *f.*; *v.i.* (1) bâiller; (2) rester bouche bée (devant); **3.** (*open wide, of thing*) bâiller, s'ouvrir; ~**ing** *adj.* (*person*) bouche bée; (*thing*) béant.
garage *s.* garage *m.*; *v.t.* garer; ~ **proprietor,** garagiste *m.*
garb *s.* costume *m.*; *v.t.* vêtir (de).
garbage *s.* (*offal, fam.*) tripaille *f.*; (*refuse*) détritus *m.*, déchets *m.pl.*; (*filth*) ordures *f.pl.*
garble *v.t.* (*facts*) dénaturer; (*text, quotation*) tronquer; ~**d version,** version fantaisiste *f.*
garden *s.* jardin *m.*; **flower** ~, jardin d'agrément; **kitchen** ~, jardin potager; **market** ~, jardin maraîcher; *adj.* de jardin; COMMON **or** ~; ~ **city,** cité-jardin *f.*; ~ **party,** garden-party *m.*; ~ **path,** allée *f.*; **to lead s.o. up the** ~ **path** (*fig.*) leurrer qn.; *v.i.* jardiner; ~**er** *s.* jardinier *m.*; **market** ~**er** *s.* maraîcher *m.*; ~**ing** *s.* jardinage *m.*
gardenia *s.* (*bot.*) gardénia *m.*
gargantuan *adj.* gargantuesque.
gargle *s.* gargarisme *m.*; *v.i.* se gargariser.
gargoyle *s.* gargouille *f.*
garish *adj.* (*dazzling*) éblouissant; (*showy*) voyant.
garland *s.* guirlande *f.*; *v.t.* enguirlander.
garlic *s.* ail *m.* (*pl.* ails); CLOVE **of** ~.
garment *s.* vêtement *m.*
garner *s.* grenier *m.*; *v.t.* (*usu. fig.*) accumuler; (*rarely lit.*) engranger.
garnet *s.* grenat *m.*
garnish *s.* (*cook.*) garniture *f.*; *v.t.* (*cook.*) garnir.
garret *s.* grenier *m.*; (*hovel*) galetas *m.*
garrison *s.* garnison *f.*; *v.t.* mettre une garnison dans (une ville).
garrotte *s.* (*torture*) garrotte *f.*; (*instrument*) garrot *m.*; *v.t.* étrangler.
garrul/ity *s.* loquacité *f.*; ~**ous** *adj.* loquace.
garter *s.* jarretière *f.*; **Order of the G**~, Ordre de la Jarretière *m.*
gas *s.* **1.** (*chem., for light, heat, etc.*) gaz *m.*; **2.** (*anaesthetic*) anesthésique *m.*; **3.** (*poison* ~) gaz asphyxiant *m.*; **tear** ~, gaz lacrymogène *m.*; MUSTARD ~; **4.** (*fig. fam. empty talk*) baratin *m.*; **5.** (*fam. = petrol*) essence *f.*; **to step on the** ~ (*fam.*) gazer, aller à pleins gaz; ~**bag** *s.* (*fig. fam.*) baratineur *m.*; ~ **chamber** *s.* chambre à gaz *f.*; ~ COOKER; ~ FIRE; ~**-mantle** *s.* manchon *m.*; ~ **mask** *s.* masque à gaz *m.*; ~ METER; ~**ometer** *s.* gazomètre *m.*; ~ **pipe** *s.* tuyau à gaz *m.*; ~ **ring** *s.* réchaud à gaz *m.*; ~**works** *s.* usine à gaz *f.*; ~**eous,** ~**sy** *adj.* gazeux; *v.t.* & *i.* (3) gazer; (4) baratiner.

gash *s.* (*scar*) balafre *f.*; (*wound*) estafilade *f.*; *v.t.* balafrer.
gasket *s.* (*naut.*) raban *m.*; (*auto.*) joint de culasse *m.*
gasp *s.* halètement *m.*; **at one's last ~,** (*lit.*) à son dernier soupir; (*fig.*) à la dernière extrémité; *v.i.* haleter; *v.t.* dire en haletant; **~er** *s.* (*pop. cigarette*) sèche *f.*
gast/ric *adj.* gastrique; **~ritis** *s.* gastrite *f.*; **~ronomy** *s.* gastronomie *f.*; **~ronomic** *adj.* gastronomique.
gate *s.* (*opening*) porte *f.*; (*barrier*) barrière *f.*, (*of metal*) grille *f.*; (*of lock, etc.*) vanne *f.*; (*electr.*) grille *f.*; (*sport*) (*numbers*) entrée *f.*, (*receipts*) recette *f.*; FLOOD~; **like a** BULL **at a ~**; **~-crash** *v.i.* resquiller; **~crasher** *s.* resquilleur *m.*; **~house** *s.* loge *f.*; **~legged table,** table à abattants *f.*; **~post** *s.* montant *m.*; **~way** *s.* portail *m.*; *v.t.* (*confine*) consigner.
gather *v.t.* & *i.* **1.** (*bring or come together*) (s')assembler; **2.** (*collect*) recueillir; **3.** (*pluck*) cueillir; **4.** (*draw together in folds*) froncer; **5.** (*fig. pick up, infer*) conclure, déduire (*from*—de) **6.** (*med.*) former un abcès; **~ in** *v.t.* recueillir; **~ together** *v.t.* & *i.* (s')assembler; **~ up** *v.t.* ramasser; **~ing** *s.* (1) rassemblement *m.*, assemblage *m.*; (4) fronces *f.pl.*; (6) abcès *m.*; **~s** *s.pl.* (4) fronces *f.pl.*
G.A.T.T. *s.* (*General Agreement on Tarriffs & Trade*) Accord (*m.*) général sur les tarifs et le commerce.
gaud/y *adj.* voyant; **~iness** *s.* clinquant *m.*; (*ostentation*) tape-à-l'œil *m.*
gauge *s.* **1.** (*standard measure, capacity, instrument*) jauge *f.*; **2.** (*fig. criterion, test*) capacité *f.*; **3.** (*rail.*) écartement *m.*; *v.t.* (1) jauger.
Gaul *s.* (*hist.*) Gaule *f.*; (*person*) Gaulois(e) *m.f.*
Gaull/ist *s.* gaulliste *m.f.*; **~ism** *s.* gaullisme *m.*
gaunt *adj.* décharné; (*cheek*) creux; **~ness** *s.* extrême maigreur *f.*
gauntlet *s.* (*hist.*) gantelet *m.*; (*glove*) (gant à) crispin *m.*; **to throw down, to pick up, the ~,** jeter, relever, le gant; **to run the ~ of** (*fig.*) subir l'assaut de.
gauze *s.* gaze *f.*; (*wire*) toile métallique *f.*
gavel *s.* marteau *m.*
gawk *s.* empoté *m.*; **~y** *adj.* gauche.
ga/y *adj.* (*light-hearted*; *showy*) gai; (*dissolute*) débauché; **~iety** *s.* gaieté *f.*; **~ily** *adv.* gaiement.
gaze *s.* regard fixe *m.*; *v.i.* contempler; **~ at** *v.t.* regarder fixement.
gazebo *s.* belvédère *m.*
gazelle *s.* gazelle *f.*
gazett/e *s.* revue *f.*; (*govt.*) Journal Officiel *m.*; **~eer** *s.* dictionnaire géographique *m.*
G.B. (*Great Britain*) Grande-Bretagne *f.*
G.C.E. (*General Certificate of Education*) baccalauréat *m.* (*approx.*).
G.C.F., G.C.M. (*math.*) le plus grand commun diviseur.
gear *s.* (*apparatus, tackle*) équipement *m.*, (*fam.*) attirail *m.*; (*harness*) harnachement *m.*; (*household effects*) appareils *m.pl.*; (*mech.*) engrenage *m.*; (*auto.*) embrayage *m.*, **low ~,** première vitesse *f.*, **top ~,** quatrième vitesse *f.*; **to engage ~,** embrayer; **to disengage ~,** débrayer; **to change ~,** changer de vitesse; **out of ~,** (*auto.*) au point mort, (*mech.*) désengrené, (*fig.*) détraqué; **~box** *s.* boîte de vitesses *f.*; **~-lever** *s.* levier des vitesses *m.*; *v.t.* **~ to** (*fig.*) adapter à.
gee! *interj.* mince alors!
geezer *s.* (*pop. usu. old ~*) vieille baderne *f.*
Geiger-counter *s.* compteur geiger *m.*
geisha *s.* geisha, ghesha *f.*
gelatin(e) *s.* gélatine *f.*; **~ous** *adj.* gélatineux.
gelding *adj.* & *s.m.* hongre.
gelid *adj.* glacé.
gelignite *s.* nitroglycérine *f.*
gem *s.* (*precious stone*) pierre précieuse *f.*; (*jewel, thing of beauty*) bijou *m.*
gen *s.* (*pop.*) tuyau *m.*; *v.t.* & *i.* **~ up,** tuyauter, se faire tuyauter.
gender *s.* (*ling.*) genre *m.*
gene *s.* (*biol.*) gène *m.*
genealog/y *s.* généalogie *f.*; **~ical** *adj.* généalogique; **~ist** *s.* généalogiste *m.f.*
general *s.* (*mil.*) général *m.*; (*servant*) bonne à tout faire *f.*; CAVIAR **to the ~**; *adj.* général; **in ~,** en général; **~issimo** *s.* généralissime *m.*; **~ity** *s.* généralité *f.*, (*the majority of*) la plupart de (des + *pl.*); **~ization** *s.* généralisation *f.*; **~ize** *v.i.* généraliser; **~ly** *adv.**; **~ship** *s.* (*office, rare*) généralat *m.*, (*fig.*) stratégie *f.*
generat/e *v.t.* engendrer; **~ion** *s.* génération *f.*; **~ive** *adj.* générateur; **~or** *s.* générateur *m.*
generic *adj.* générique.
gener/ous *adj.* **1.** (*noble-minded,* ≠ *mean*) généreux; **2.** (*abundant*) abondant; **~osity** *s.* générosité *f.*; **~ously** *adv.* (1) généreusement; (2) abondamment.
genesis *s.* (*lit.* & *fig.*) genèse *f.*
genetic *adj.* génétique; **~s** *s.pl.* génétique *f.* ⚠ *sing. in French.*
Geneva *s.* **1.** (*geog.*) Genève *f.*; **2.** (*gin*) genièvre *m.*; **~n** *adj.* & *s.m.f.* genevois(e).
genial *adj.* **1.** (*mild, warm*) doux; **2.** (*cheering*) réconfortant; **3.** (*sociable*) affable; **~ity** *s.* (1) douceur *f.*; (2) confort *m.*; (3) cordialité *f.*; **~ly** *adv.* (1) doucement; (3) cordialement; ⚠ génial, génialement = **of genius, ingenious(ly).**
genie *s.* génie *m.*
genital *adj.* génital; **~s** *s.pl.* parties génitales *f.pl.*
genitive *s.* (*ling.*) génitif *m.*
genius *s.* génie *m.*
Genoa *s.* (*geog.*) Gênes *f.*
genocide *s.* génocide *m.*
gent *s.* homme *m.*
genteel *adj.* (*archaic, pop.*) comme il faut; (*usu. pej.*) bien élevé, (petit) bourgeois; **~ly** *adv.* comme il faut.
gentian *s.* gentiane *f.*
gentile *s.* (≠ *Jew*) gentil *m.*; (*heathen*) infidèle *m.f.*
gentility *s.* (*birth*) bonne famille *f.*; (*social superiority* & *habits*) distinction *f.*
gentle *adj.* **1.** (*well-born*) de bonne famille; **2.** (*mild, quiet*) doux, aimable; **3.** (≠ *rough or severe*) léger, gentil; **~folk** *s.pl.* personnes de bonne famille *f.pl.*; **~man** *s.* (*status*) gentilhomme *m.*, homme distingué *m.*, (*gen.*) monsieur *m.*; **~manly** *adj.* distingué, courtois; **~woman** *s.* dame *f.*, femme distinguée *f.*; **~ness** *s.*; (2) douceur *f.*; (3) légèreté *f.*, gentillesse *f.*; **gently** *adv.* (2) doucement; (3) légèrement.
gentry *s.* (*class*) petite noblesse *f.*; (*pej.*) **those ~,** ces gens-là *f.pl.*
genufle/ct *v.i.* faire des génuflexions; **~xion** *s.* génuflexion *f.*
genuine *adj.* **1.** (*pure bred*) de race pure; **2.** (*not counterfeit*) vrai, de bon aloi, véritable; **3.** (*authentic*) authentique; **4.** (*of person, sincere*) sincère; **~ly** *adv.*; (2) véritablement; (3)*; (4)*; **~ness** *s.* (3) authenticité *f.*; (4) sincérité *f.*
genus *s.* genre *m.*
geocentric *adj.* géocentrique.
geograph/y *s.* géographie *f.*; **~er** *s.* géographe *m.f.*; **~ical** *adj.* géographique.
geolog/y *s.* géologie *f.*; **~ical** *adj.* géologique; **~ist** *s.* géologue *m.f.*
geometr/y *s.* géométrie *f.*; **~ical** *adj.* géométrique; **~ician** *s.* géomètre *m.f.*
geophysics *s.* géophysique *f.* ⚠ *sing. in French.*

georgette *s.* (*text.*) crêpe georgette *m.*
geranium *s.* géranium *m.*
gerfalcon *s.* gerfaut *m.*
geriatric *adj.* de gériatrie; **~s** *s.pl.* gériatrie *f.*, gérontologie *f.* ⚠ *sing. in French.*
germ *s.* (*growing organism*, (*fig.*) *rudiment*) germe *m.*; (*microbe*) bacille *m.*, microbe *m.*; **~ warfare,** guerre bactériologique; **~icide** *s.* bactéricide *m.*, microbicide *m.*; **~inal** *adj.* (*of germs*) germinal, (*embryonic*) embryonnaire; **~inate** *v.t.* & *i.* (faire) germer; **~ination** *s.* germination *f.*
german *adj.* (*of relationship*) germain; **~e** *adj.* se rapportant à.
German/y *s.* (*geog.*) Allemagne *f.*; **~** *adj.* & *s.m.f.* allemand(e); *s.m.* (*language*) allemand; **~ic** *adj.* germanique; **~** MEASLES.
gerrymander *v.t.* (*of elections*) truquer; **~ing** *s.* manipulations électorales *f.pl.*
gerund *s.* (*ling.*) gérondif *m.*; **~ive** *s.* (*ling.*) adjectif verbal *m.*
gestation *s.* gestation *f.*
gesticulat/e *v.i.* gesticuler; **~ion** *s.* gesticulation *f.*
gesture *s.* geste *m.*
get *v.t.* **1.** (*obtain*) obtenir; **2.** (*earn, gain, win*) gagner; **3.** (*procure*) (se)procurer; **4.** (*receive*) recevoir; **5.** (*fetch*) aller chercher; **6.** (*learn*) apprendre; **7.** (*induce*) persuader (à qn. de faire qch.); **8.** (*beget*) engendrer; **9.** (*suffer, experience*) subir; **10.** (*catch, contract*) attraper; **11.** (*have inflicted*) recevoir; **12.** (*pop. trick*) avoir; **13.** (*fam. understand*) piger; *v.i.* (*arrive*) arriver; (*become*) devenir; **~ about** *v.i.* (*news, etc.*) circuler; (*person*) se déplacer; **~ across** *v.t.* (*pop.* = *annoy*) agacer; (*fam. make acceptable*) faire accepter; **~ along** *v.i.* avancer; **~ along with s.o.,** s'accorder avec qn.; **~ along without sth.,** se passer de qch.; **~ at** *v.t.* (*reach*) atteindre, (*fig.*) découvrir, (*pop.*) **~ at s.o.,** avoir qn.; **what is he ~ting at?,** où veut-il en venir?; **~-at-able** *adj.* accessible; **~ away** *v.t.* arracher (qch. à qn.); *v.i.* se sauver; **~-away** *s.* départ *m.*, fuite *f.*; **~ away with sth.,** (*fig.*) faire accepter qch.; **~ away with it,** s'en tirer; **~ back** *v.t.* recouvrer; *v.i.* revenir; **~ one's own back,** prendre sa revanche; **~ by** *v.i.* (*fig.*) s'en tirer, se débrouiller; **~ down** *v.t.* descendre, (*note*) noter, (*swallow*) avaler, (*fig.*) agacer; **don't let it ~ you down,** ne vous en faites pas; **~ down** *v.i.* descendre; **~ down to sth.,** s'attaquer à qch.; **~ in** *v.t.* rentrer; *v.i.* entrer, (*elections*) être élu; **~ into** *v.t.* introduire; *v.i.* pénétrer dans; (*car, etc.*) monter dans; (*habit*) prendre l'habitude de; **~ off** *v.t.* enlever, (*law*) faire acquitter, (*fam.*) tirer d'affaire; *v.i.* (*bus, etc.*) descendre de, (*aviat.*) décoller, (*fig.*) se dégager de, (*fam.*) s'en tirer; **~ on** *v.i.* (s')avancer, (*bus, etc.*) monter dans, (*fig.*) **~ on with s.o.,** s'entendre avec qn., (*grow old*) vieillir; **how are you ~ting on?,** comment ça va?; **~ on s.o.'s nerves,** porter sur les nerfs de qn.; **~ out** *v.t.* sortir, (*cork*) tirer, (*nail*) arracher, (*fig. plans, etc.*) dresser; **~ sth. out of s.o.,** soutirer qch. à qn.; **~ out** *v.i.* sortir, (*news*) s'ébruiter; **~ out of** *v.i.* descendre de, (*fig. of mess*) se tirer de, (*of duty*) se soustraire à, (*of habit*) se défaire de; **~ out!,** (*pop.*) fiche-moi le camp!; **~ over** *v.t.* franchir, (*illness*) se remettre de, (*fig.*) se faire à; **~ round** *v.t.* tourner, (*law*) contourner, (*fam. s.o.*) embobiner qn.; **~ round to** *v.i.* arriver à; **~ through** *v.t.* (*fig.*) faire adopter; *v.i.* passer par, se frayer un chemin à travers, (*exam.*) être reçu, (*phone*) obtenir la communication; **~ to** *v.i.* arriver à; **~ together** *v.i.* se réunir; **~-together** *s.* réunion *f.*; **~ under** *v.t.* passer par dessous; **~ up** *v.t.* monter; **~ one's** BACK **up;** *v.i.* se lever, (*wind*) s'élever, (*sea*) grossir; **~-up** *s.* accoutrement *m.*
gew-gaw *s.* babiole *f.*
geyser *s.* (*spring*) geyser *m.*; (*mech.*) chauffe-bain *m.*, chauffe-eau *m.*
Ghana *s.* (*geog.*) Ghana *m.*; **~ian** *adj.* & *s.m.f.* ghanéen(ne).
ghastl/y *adj.* **1.** (*horrible, frightful*) horrible, effrayant; **2.** (*deathly*) blême; **3.** (*fam. deplorable*) effroyable; **~iness** *s.* (1) aspect effrayant *m.*; (2) pâleur *f.*
gherkin *s.* cornichon *m.*
ghetto *s.* ghetto *m.*
ghost *s.* (*spectre*) spectre *m.*, revenant *m.*; (*pale person*) fantôme *m.*; (*fig. semblance*) ombre *f.*; (*spirit*) souffle *m.*, esprit *m.*; **Holy G~,** Saint-Esprit *m.*; **to give up the ~,** rendre l'âme; **~ story** *s.* histoire de revenants *f.*; **~ town** *s.* ville morte *f.*; **~ writer** *s.* nègre *m.*; **~ly** *adj.* spectral, (*eccles.*) spirituel.
G.H.Q. (*abbrev. General Headquarters*) G.Q.G. *m.* (Grand Quartier Général).
ghoul *s.* goule *f.*; (*fig.*) vampire *m.*
giant(ess) *s.m.f.* (*lit.* & *fig.*) géant(e); *adj.* géant; **~ism** *s.* gigantisme *m.*
gibber *v.t.* & *i.* baragouiner; **~ish** *s.* baragouinage *m.*
gibbet *s.* gibet *m.*
gibbon *s.* gibbon *m.*
gibbous *adj.* gibbeux; **~ moon,** lune entre le plein et le quartier.
gib/e, jibe *s.* **1.** (*jeer*) raillerie *f.*; **2.** (*taunt*) sarcasme *m.*; *v.i.* (1) railler; (2) se moquer (de); **~er** *s.* railleur *m.*; **~ing** *adj.* (1) railleur; (2) moqueur.
giblets *s.pl.* abbatis *m.pl.*
Gibraltar *s.* (*geog.*) Gibraltar *m.*; **straits of ~,** détroit de Gibraltar *m.*; **~ian** *adj.* de Gibraltar; *s.m.f.* habitant(e) de Gibraltar.
gidd/y *adj.* **1.** (*person, dizzy*) pris de vertige, (*thing*) vertigineux; **2.** (*staggering*) étourdi; **3.** (*excitable*) écervelé; **~ily** *adv.* étourdiment; **~iness** *s.* (1) vertige *m.*; (2) étourdissement *m.*; (3) étourderie *f.*
gift *s.* (*present*) cadeau *m.*; (*natural endowment*) don *m.*; **~ of the** GAB; **you don't look a ~-horse in the mouth,** à cheval donné on ne regarde pas la bouche; **~ed** *adj.* doué.
gig *s.* (*carriage*) cabriolet *m.*; (*boat*) yole *f.*
gigant/ic *adj.* gigantesque; **~ism** *s.* gigantisme *m.*
giggle *s.* rire bête *m.*, (*scornful*) ricanement *m.*; *v.i.* rire bêtement, ricaner.
gigolo *s.* gigolo *m.*
gild *v.t.* (*lit.* & *fig.*) dorer; **~er** *s.* doreur *m.*; **~ing** *s.* dorure *f.*
gills *s.pl.* (*of fish*) ouïes *f.pl.*, branchies *f.pl.*; (*fam. of person*) bajoue *f.*
gillyflower *s.* giroflée *f.*
gilt *s.* dorure *f.*; **to take the ~ off the gingerbread,** enlever l'attrait de qch.; **~-edged** *adj.* (*book*) doré sur tranches, (*shares*) de tout repos; *adj.* doré.
gimcrack *s.* babiole *f.*; *adj.* de bazar.
gimlet *s.* vrille *f.*
gimmick *s.* (*pop.*) (*thing*) machin, truc *m.*; (*trick*) tour *m.*
gin[1] *s.* **1.** (*snare, trap*) trébuchet *m.*; **2.** (*kind of crane*) treuil *m.*; **3.** (*cotton*) égreneuse *f.*; *v.t.* (1) prendre au piège; (3) égrener.
gin[2] *s.* (*spirit*) gin *m.*
ginger *s.* **1.** (*bot.*) gingembre *m.*; **2.** (*fig.*) entrain *m.*; **3.** (*person with ~ hair*) rouquin *m.*; *adj.* roux, (*hair*) rouquin; **~-ale, ~-beer,** boisson gazeuse *f.*; **~bread** *s.* pain d'épice *m.*; **to take the** GILT **off the ~bread; ~ly** *adv.* doucement; *v.t.* (2) dégourdir.
gingham *s.* (*text.*) vichy *m.*
gipsy, gypsy *adj.* & *s.m.f.* bohémien(ne); *adj.* (*of mus. ling.*) tsigane.

giraffe *s.* girafe *f.*
girandole *s.* girandole *f.*
gird *v.t.* ceindre; ~ **up one's loins** (*Bible*) ceindre ses reins, (*fig. fam.*) retrousser ses manches; ~**er** *s.* poutre *f.*; BOX ~**er.**
girdle *s.* (*lit.* & *fig.*) ceinture *f.*; (*corset*) gaine *f.*; *v.t.* ceinturer.
girl *s.* (jeune) fille *f.*; fillette *f.*; ~ **guide,** guide *f.*; ~**hood** *s.* jeunesse *f.*; ~**ish** *adj.* de petite fille; ~**ishness** *s.* manières de petite fille *f.pl.*
giro *s.* (*fin.*) (chèque de) virement postal *m.*
girth *s.* (*of horse*) sangle *f.*; (*measurement*) circonférence *f.* (*of person*) tour de taille *m.*
gist *s.* fond *m.*
give[1] *v.t.* (*bestow, make present of*) donner, offrir, faire cadeau de; (*grant, confer*) accorder, conférer; (*deliver*) remettre, (*speech, etc.*) prononcer, (*judgment, thanks, etc.*) rendre; (*administer*) administrer, (*punishment, etc.*) infliger; **give s.o. his** DUE; ~ **as good as one gets,** rendre la pareille, payer de retour; (*consign, put*) remettre; (*make pledge*) formuler; (*devote*) consacrer; (*present, offer, hand, arm, etc.*) offrir; (*impart*) transmettre, présenter; (*assume*) supposer; (*cause*) occasionner; (*pleasure*) faire; ~ **oneself** AIRS; ~ GROUND; ~ PLACE; ~ RISE; ~ WAY; *v.i.* (*collapse*) s'écrouler; (*yield*) céder; ~ **and take,** *v.i.* & *s.* (faire des) concessions mutuelles *f.pl.*; ~ **away** *v.t.* distribuer, faire cadeau de, (*betray*) dénoncer, trahir; ~ **oneself away,** se trahir; ~ **bride away,** accompagner la mariée à l'autel; ~**-away** *s.* (*fam.*) trahison *f.*, dénonciation *f.*; ~**-away price,** prix dérisoire *m.*; ~ **back** *v.t.* rendre; ~ **forth** *v.t.* publier, émettre; ~ **in** *v.t.* remettre, *v.i.* céder; ~ **off** *v.t.* émettre, dégager, exhaler; ~ **out** *v.t.* distribuer, émettre, annoncer, *v.i.* manquer, s'épuiser; ~ **over** *v.t.* remettre, *v.i.* finir; ~ **up** *v.t.* abandonner, renoncer à, (*seat*) céder; ~ **up the** GHOST; (*withdraw from*) se retirer de, (*fig. fam.*) abandonner la partie; ~ **oneself up,** se rendre; **given** *adj.* (*disposed to*) adonné à, enclin à, (*fixed*) déterminé; **given name,** prénom *m.*; **given (that)** *conj.* étant donné (que); **giver** *s.* donat/eur, -rice *m.f.*; **giving** *s.* don *m.*
give[2] *s.* élasticité *f.*
gizzard *s.* gésier *m.*
glac/ial *adj.* glacial (*m.pl. rare* **-als** *or* **-aux**); (*geol.*) glaciaire; ~**iated** *adj.* glaciaire; ~**ier** *s.* glacier, *m.*; ~**is** *s.* glacis *m.*
glad *adj.* (*pleased*) content (*of*—de); (*joyful*) joyeux; **to give s.o. the** ~ **eye,** faire les yeux doux à qn.; ~**den** *v.t.* réjouir; ~**ly** *adv.* avec plaisir, avec joie, (*willingly*) volontiers; ~**ness** *s.* joie *f.*; ~**some** *adj.* joyeux; (*thing*) réjouissant.
glade *s.* clairière *f.*
gladiator *s.* gladiateur *m.*
gladiolus *s.* glaïeul *m.*
glam/our *s.* enchantement *m.*, charme *m.*; ~**our boy,** ~**our girl** *s.* (*pop.*) ensorcel/eur, -euse *m.f.*; ~**orize** *v.t.* embellir; ~**orous** *adj.* enchant/eur, -eresse, ensorcelant.
glanc/e *s.* **1.** (*movement*) ricochet *m.*; **2.** (*flash*) éclair *m.*; **3.** (*brief look*) coup d'œil *m.*; *v.t.* & *i.* (1) effleurer; (3) jeter un coup d'œil à; ~**e at** *v.t.* parcourir; ~**ing** *adj.* oblique.
gland *s.* glande *f.*; ~**ular** *adj.* glandulaire.
glar/e *s.* **1.** (*light*) éclat éblouissant *m.*; (*fig.*) lumière crue *f.*; **2.** (*tawdry brilliance*) clinquant *m.*; **3.** (*fierce look*) regard enflammé *m.*; **4.** (*of headlights*) éblouissement *m.*; *v.i.* (1) étinceler; (3) jeter un regard furieux (à); ~**ing** *adj.* (*light*) éblouissant, aveuglant; (*colour*) éclatant; (*fig,*) qui crève les yeux.
glass *s.* (*substance, container, quantity*) verre *m.*; (*mirror*) glace *f.*, miroir *m.*; (*barometer*) baromètre *m.*; (*pane of* ~) vitre *f.*; **cut** ~, cristal taillé *m.*; FIBRE~; FIELD-~**es;** OPERA-~**es;** PLATE~; STAINED ~; ~**es** *s.pl.* lunettes *f.pl.*; *adj.* de verre, en verre; (*door, etc.*) vitré; ~**-blower** *s.* verrier-souffleur *m.*; ~ **case** *s.* vitrine *f.*; ~**-cutter** *s.* (*tool*) diamant *m.*; ~**-door** *s.* porte vitrée *f.*; ~**house** *s.* (*hort.*) serre *f.*, (*pop.* = *prison*) taule *f.*; ~**ware** *s.* verrerie *f.*; ~**works** *s.*, verrerie *f.*; ~**y** *adj.* (*eye*) vitreux, (*smooth*) lisse, uni; *v.t.* (*reflect*) mirer; (*door, etc.*) vitrer.
glaucoma *s.* glaucome *m.*
glaucous *adj.* glauque.
glaz/e *s.* **1.** (*substance*) vernis *m.*; (*surface*) lustre *m.*; **2.** (*cook.*) glace *f.*; *v.t.* (1) (*pottery*) vernisser; (*text.*) satiner; (2) glacer; **3.** (*fit with glass*) vitrer; *v.i.* (*eye*) devenir vitreux; ~**ier** *s.* vitrier *m.*; ~**ing** *s.* (1) vernissage *m.*, (*product*) vernis *m.*; (3) vitrerie; *f.*; **double** ~**ing** *s.* vitre (thermopan) à double paroi *m.*
G.L.C. (*Greater London Council*) Conseil municipal de Londres *m.*
gleam *s.* (*lit.* & *fig.*) lueur *m.*; *v.i.* luire; ~**ing,** *adj.* luisant.
glean *v.t.* **1.** (*corn*) glaner; **2.** (*fig. facts*) grapiller; ~**er** *s.* (1) glaneu/r, -se *m.f.*; ~**ing** *s.* glanage *m.*; ~**ings** *s.pl.* glanure *f.*
glebe *s.* glèbe *f.*
glee *s.* **1.** (*mus.*) chant (*m.*) à plusieurs parties (sans accompagnement); **2.** (*mirth*) allégresse *f.*; ~**ful,** ~**some** *adj.* (2) joyeux.
glen *s.* vallée (profondément encaissée) *f.*
glib *adj.* (*speech*) coulant; (*tongue*) délié; (*person*) beau parleur, (*fam.*) qui a du bagou(t); ~**ly** *adv.* facilement, (*fam.*) avec du bagou(t); ~**ness** *s.* faconde *f.*
glid/e *s.* (*aviat.*) vol plané *m.*; *v.i.* (*pass smoothly*) (se) glisser, couler; (*go stealthily*) avancer à pas de loup; (*bird*) planer; (*aviat.*) faire du vol plané; ~**er** *s.* (*aviat.*) planeur *m.*; ~**ing** *s.* vol plané *m.*
glimmer *s.* (*lit.* & *fig.*) lueur *f.*; *v.i.* jeter une lueur faible; ~**ing** *s.* (*usu. fig.*) lueur *f.*
glimpse *s.* aperçu *m.*; *v.t.* & **to catch a** ~ **of,** entrevoir.
glint *s.* reflet *m.*; *v.i.* étinceler.
glisten *v.i.* scintiller; (*water*) miroiter.
glitter *s.* scintillement *m.*; (*fig.*) éclat *m.*; *v.i.* scintiller; **all that** ~**s is not gold,** tout ce qui brille n'est pas or; ~**ing** *adj.* scintillant.
gloaming *s.* crépuscule *m.*
gloat *v.i.* dévorer des yeux; jeter des regards avides sur; ~ **over,** jubiler (de + *inf.*), faire des gorges chaudes (de qch.).
glob/e *s.* (*sphere; earth*) globe *m.*; (*chart of earth*) globe terrestre *m.*; (*lamp glass*) ampoule *f.*; ~**e-trotter** *s.* bourlingueu/r, -se *m.f.*; **to go** ~**e-trotting** (*fam.*) bourlinguer; ~**al** *adj.* sphérique; (*world-wide*) global; ~**ular** *adj.* globulaire; ~**ule** *s.* globule *f.*
gloom *s.* (*darkness*) obscurité *f.*, ténèbres *f.pl.*; (*melancholy*) mélancolie *f.*; ~**y** *adj.* (*lit.* & *fig.*) sombre.
glor/y *s.* (*fame*) gloire *f.*; (*majesty, beauty*) splendeur *f.*; ~**y-hole** *s.* (*fam.*) capharnaüm *m.*; ~**ification** *s.* glorification *f.*; ~**ify** *v.t.* glorifier, (*fam.*) embellir; ~**iole** *s.* auréole *f.*; ⚠ gloriole = **vanity, pride;** ~**ious** *adj.* glorieux, (*fig.*) splendide, (*weather*) radieux, (*fam.*) fameux; ~**iously** *adv.* glorieusement, magnifiquement; *v.i.* ~**y in sth.,** se faire gloire de qch.
gloss *s.* **1.** (*superficial lustre*) lustre *m.*; **2.** (*specious appearance*) vernis *m.*; **3.** (*marginal explanation*) commentaire, *m.*; **4.** (*comment, interpretation*) glose *f.*; *v.t.* (1) lustrer; (2) édulcorer; (3) commenter; (4) gloser; ~ **over** (*fig. fam.*) maquiller; ~**ary** *s.* glossaire *m.*; ~**y** *adj.* lustré, luisant; *s.* (*fam.* = *magazine*) illustré *m.*
glove *s.* gant *m.*; **to be hand in** ~ (*fig.*) être

comme les deux doigts de la main; **to handle with** KID **~s;** *v.t.* ganter.

glow *s.* **1.** (*heat or light*) incandescence *f.*; **2.** (*fig.*) ardeur *f.*, chaleur *f.*; **3.** (*of face*) rougeur *f.*; *v.i.* (1) être incandescent; (2) s'embraser; (3) rayonner, briller; **~ing** *adj.* (1) incandescent; (2) chaleureux; (3) vermeil; **~-worm** *s.* ver luisant *m.*

glower *v.i.* se renfrogner.

glucose *s.* glucose *m.*

glue *s.* colle (forte) *f.*; *v.t.* coller.

glum *adj.* renfrogné; **~ly** *adv.* d'un air renfrogné.

glut *s.* **1.** (*surfeit*) rassasiement *m.*; **2.** (*excessive supply*) surabondance *f.*, (*comm.*) engorgement *m.*; *v.t.* (1) gorger; (2) engorger; **~ton** *s.* glouton *m.*; **to be a ~ton for work,** être un bourreau de travail; **~tonous** *adj.* glouton; **~tony** *s.* gloutonnerie *f.*

glutinous *adj.* glutineux.

glycerin(**e**) *s.* glycérine *f.*

G.M.T. (*Greenwich Mean Time*) Heure (*f.*) (du méridien) de Greenwich.

gnarled *adj.* noueux.

gnash *v.t.* & *i.* grincer (*teeth*—des dents); **~ing** *s.* grincement *m.*

gnat *s.* cousin *m.*

gnaw *v.t.* (*lit.* & *fig.*) ronger; **~ing** *s.* rongement *m.*; (*fig.*) torture *f.*; *adj.* rongeu/r, -se.

gneiss *s.* gneiss *m.*

gnom/e *s.* **1.** (*fairy*) gnome *m.*; **2.** (*pithy saying*) sentence *f.*; **~ic** *adj.* (2) gnomique.

gnomon *s.* gnomon *m.*

gnostic *s.* gnostique *m.f.*; **~ism** *s.* gnosticisme *m.*

G.N.P. (*gross national product*) produit national brut *m.*

gnu *s.* gnou *m.*

go[1] *s.* (*animation*) allant *m.*; (*success*) succès *m.*; **to make a ~ of sth.,** réussir qch.; (*turn*) coup *m.*, tentative *f.*; **to have a ~,** tenter le coup; (*pop. state of affairs*) affaire *f.*; **to be all the ~,** faire fureur; **here's a ~,** voilà un joli gâchis; **it's no ~,** rien à faire, ça ne marche pas; **to be always on the ~,** être toujours sur la brèche; TOUCH **and ~.**

go[2] *v.t.* & *i.* (*walk, move, travel*) aller; (*depart*) s'en aller; **~** FAR; **~** EASY; **~ for a** WALK; **~ slow** *v.i.* (*esp. at work*) faire la grève perlée; **~-slow** *s.* grève perlée *f.*; (*lead to, ~ in a certain direction*) conduire à; (*extend to, reach*) atteindre; (*be guided by*) suivre; (*techn. work*) marcher, fonctionner; (*make sound*) faire; (*of time*) passer; (*cover distance*) faire; (*of events, turn out*) aller; **how goes it?, how is it going?,** comment ça va?; **it goes without saying,** cela va sans dire; (*begin motion*) partir; **~!** (*at start of race*) partez!; **from the word ~,** dès le départ; **to let ~,** lâcher prise; (*of money*) passer; (*be sold*) se vendre; (*at auction*) **going!, going!, gone!,** une fois, deux fois, adjugé!; (*fail, give way, collapse*) céder, se briser; **to let oneself ~,** se laisser aller; (*proceed to do*) aller; **he went to find him,** il alla le chercher; ⚠ **~ and do** = aller faire; **to be ~ing to do,** aller faire, être sur le point de faire; (*become*) devenir; **~** MAD; **~** RED; **~ to** SLEEP; **as far as that goes,** quant à cela; **~ it** (*pop.*) y aller (fort), exagérer; (*with preps.* & *advs.*) **~ about** *v.i.* (*naut.*) virer de bord; **~ about sth.,** se mettre, se prendre, à qch.; **~ after,** poursuivre; **~ against s.o.,** se tourner contre qn.; **~ against advice, etc.,** agir contre l'avis de qn., etc.; **~ ahead** *v.i.* avancer; **~ along,** continuer; **~ along with s.o.,** accompagner qn., (*fig.*) être d'accord avec (qn., qch.); **~ around with,** fréquenter; **~ at,** s'attaquer à; **~ away,** s'en aller; **~ back,** retourner, (*in memory*) remonter; **~ back on** (*word, etc.*) manquer à; **~ beyond,** dépasser; **~ by** *v.i.* (*person, time*) passer; **~ by the name of,** être connu sous le nom de; **~ by s.o.'s advice,** agir d'après l'avis de qn.; **~ down** *v.i.* descendre, (*tide, price, temperature*) baisser, (*wind*) tomber, (*naut.*) sombrer, (*tyre*) se dégonfler, (*fig.*) déchoir; **~ down with** (*sickness*) tomber malade de; **~ for,** aller chercher (qn. or qch.); (*be sold for*) être vendu pour; (*fam. attack*) tomber sur (qn.); **~ forward** *v.i.* avancer; **~ in,** entrer, (*of sun*) se cacher; **~ in for,** poser sa candidature à, se présenter à, (*take part in*) se mêler de, (*specialize in*) s'adonner à; **~ into,** entrer dans, (*fig. examine*) approfondir; **~ off** *v.i.* s'en aller, (*happen*) se passer, (= **~** *bad*) se gâter, (*of gun*) partir; **~ on,** continuer, (*take place*) se passer; **~ on!** (*encouragement*) vas-y!, allez-y!, (*doubt*) allons donc!; **~ out** *v.i.* sortir, (*flame, etc.*) s'éteindre; **~ over** *v.t.* traverser, (*change sides*) passer dans l'autre camp, (*check*) vérifier, (*revise*) revoir, repasser; **~ round** *v.t.* faire le tour de, *v.i.* tourner, (*be sufficient*) suffire; **~ through** *v.t.* traverser, (*rehearse*) réciter, (*look at*) parcourir, (*endure*) subir; **~ through with sth.,** mener qch. à bien; **~ together,** s'assortir, se compléter; **~ under,** couler, sombrer; **~ up** (*person, price, temperature*) monter, (*explosive*) sauter; **~ with** *v.t.* accompagner, (*mix well with*) s'assortir avec; **~ without,** se passer de; **~-ahead** *adj.* entreprenant; **~-ahead** *s.* signal de départ *m.*; **~-between** *s.* intermédiaire *m.f.*; **~-cart** *s.* charrette *f.*; **~-getter** *s.* (*pop.*) arriviste *m.f.*; **~-kart** *s.* kart *m.*; **~er** *s.* bon marcheur *m.*

Goa *s.* (*geog.*) Goa *m.*; **~nese** *adj.* & *s.m.f.* de Goa; habitant de Goa.

goad *s.* (*lit.* & *fig.*) aiguillon *m.*; *v.t.* (*lit.* & *fig.*) aiguillonner.

goal *s.* (*object, destination, sport*) but *m.*; **~**KEEPER; **~-post** *s.* montant de but *m.*

goat *s.* (*animal*) bouc *m.*, chèvre *f.*; (*person*) idiot *m.*; **to get s.o.'s ~,** agacer qn.; **~herd** *s.* chevri/er, -ère *m.f.*; **~skin** *s.* peau de bouc *f.*; **~ee** *s.* barbiche *f.*, bouc *m.*

gobbet *s.* morceau *m.*

gobbl/e *v.t.* & *i.* **1.** (*turkey*) glouglouter; **2.** (*fam.*) bâfrer; **~er** (1) dindon *m.*; **~ing** *s.* (1) glouglou *m.*

goblet *s.* gobelet *m.*; (*silver, gold*) timbale *f.*

goblin *s.* lutin *m.*

god *s.* (*creator, supreme being, superhuman being*) dieu *m.*; (*idol*) idole *f.*; (*pl. theat.*) poulailler *m.*; **the** LAP **of the ~s; thank G~!,** Dieu merci!; **my G~!,** mon Dieu!; **for G~'s sake!,** pour l'amour de Dieu; **G~** FORBID; **G~ willing,** s'il plaît à Dieu; **~child, ~son** *s.* filleul *m.*, **~-daughter** *s.* filleule *f.*; **~father** *s.* parrain *m.*; **~mother** *s.* marraine *f.*; **G~-fearing** *adj.* religieux; **G~-forsaken** *adj.* misérable; **~head** *s.* divinité *f.*; **~less** *adj.* impie; **~like** *adj.* divin; **~liness** *s.* piété *f.*; **~ly** *adj.* pieux; **~send** *s.* aubaine *f.*; **~wit** *s.* (*bird*) barge *f.*

goddess *s.* déesse *f.*

goffer, gopher *v.t.* gauffrer.

goggle *v.i.* rouler de gros yeux; (*of eyes*) sortir de la tête; **~s** *s.pl.* (*fam.*) bésicles *m.pl.*; (*mech., auto.*) lunettes de protection *f.pl.*

going *s.* (*departure*) départ *m.*; COMING **and ~;** (*condition of ground*) état du terrain *m.*; **while the ~ is good** (*fam.*) tant que ça marche; *adj.* (*in action*) en marche; (*existing*) existant; **to set ~,** mettre en marche; **~ away** *s.* départ *m.*; **~ back** *s.* retour *m.*; **~ down** *s.* descente *f.*, (*of sun, moon*) coucher *m.*, (*in temperature, price*) baisse *f.*; **~ in** *s.* entrée *f.*; **~ off** *s.* (*person, gun*) départ *m.*; **~s-on** *s.* conduite *f.*; **~ out** *s.* sortie *f.*; **~-over** *s.* (*fam.*) inspection *f.*, (*pop.* thrashing) rossée *f.*; **~ up** *s.* montée *f.*, (*price, temperature*) hausse *f.*

goitr/e *s.* goitre *m.*; **~ous** *adj.* goitreux.

gold *s.* (*metal, wealth, colour*) or *m.*; **as good as ~,** sage comme une image; **all that** GLITTERS **is not ~; ~-digger** *s.* chercheur d'or *m.*, (*fig.*) sangsue *f.*; **~-dust** *s.* poussière d'or *f.*; **~-field** *s.* terrain aurifère *m.*; **~finch** *s.* chardonneret *m.*; **~fish** *s.* poisson rouge *m.*; **~ lace** *s.* galon d'or *m.*; **~ leaf** *s.* feuille d'or *f.*; **~ plate** *s.* vaisselle d'or *f.*; **~smith** *s.* orfèvre *m.*; **~ standard** *s.* étalon-or *m.*; *adj.* & **~en** *adj.* d'or, en or, (*colour*) doré; **~en handshake** (*fig.*) prime de retraite anticipée *m.*; **~en mean,** juste milieu *m.*; **~en opportunity,** occasion exceptionnelle *f.*; **~en syrup** *s.* mélasse *f.*; GOOSE **with ~en eggs.**

golf *s.* golf *m.*; **~-club,** crosse de golf *f.*; **~-course,** terrain de golf *m.*; **~er** *s.* joueur de golf *m.*

gondol/a *s.* gondole *f.*; **~ier** *s.* gondolier *m.*

gone *adj.* (*lost*) perdu; (*dead*) parti; **it is just ~ 6 p.m.,** il est six heures passées; **to be ~ on** (*fam.*) être épris de; **be ~!,** va-t-en!, allez-vous-en!; **~ with the wind,** autant en emporte le vent; **goner** *s.* (*pop.*) **he's a goner,** il est fichu.

gonfalon *s.* gonfalon *m.*

gong *s.* gong *m.*; (*pop.* = *medal*) banane *f.*, (*pl.*) batterie de cuisine *f.*

gonorrhoea *s.* blennorrhagie *f.*

good *s.* (*profit*) avantage *m.*; (*well-being*) bien *m.*; **what's the ~?,** à quoi bon?; **a lot of ~ that will do you (has done you),** vous voilà bien avancé; **for ~,** pour de bon; **~s** *s.pl.* marchandises *f.pl.*; CONSUMER **~s;** PIECE **~s;** SOFT **~s;** (*law*) biens meubles *m.pl.*, **~s and** CHATTELS; *adj.* (*satisfactory, pleasing*) bon; (*adequate*) convenable, suffisant; **in ~ time,** avant l'heure; **all in ~ time,** en son temps; (*worthy*) brave (*before s.*); (*right, proper*) convenable; (*virtuous*) bon; (*benevolent*) bienveillant, aimable; **be so ~ as to, ~ enough to,** avoir l'amabilité de; (*well-behaved*) sage; **as ~ as** GOLD; (*agreeable, gratifying*) agréable, bon; **~ day, ~ morning,** bonjour; **~ evening,** bonsoir; **to take sth. in ~ part,** ne pas s'offenser de qch.; **to have a ~ time,** s'amuser (bien); (*suitable*) bon, favorable; **to be ~ at sth.,** savoir bien faire qch., (*at a school subject*) être bon en; (*considerable*) bon; **a ~** DEAL; **as ~ as,** (*practically*) pour ainsi dire; **to make ~,** indemniser; **to hold ~,** être valable; **~-for-nothing** *adj.* & *s.m.* bon-à-rien; **~-looking** *adj.* beau; **~-natured** *adj.* aimable; **~-tempered,** de bonne humeur; **~ly** *adj.* (*handsome*) beau, (*considerable*) grand, important; **~ness** *s.* (*of person*) bonté *f.*, (*of thing*) qualité *f.*; **my ~ness!,** bonté divine!; **for ~ness' sake!,** pour l'amour de Dieu!; **to have the ~ness to,** avoir l'obligeance de.

goodbye *interj.* & *s.m.* adieu.

goodwill *s.* (*kindliness*) bonne volonté *f.*; (*heartiness*) bon cœur *m.*; (*comm.*) clientèle *f.*; (*law*) achalandage *m.*

goody *s.* bonbon *m.*; *interj.* chouette!; **~-~** *s.* Sainte Nitouche *f.* (*of man or woman*); *adj.* de sainte-Nitouche.

goose *s.* (*lit.* & *fig.*) oie *f.*; **the ~ with the golden eggs,** la poule aux œufs d'or; **to cook s.o.'s ~** (*fig.*) régler son compte à qn.; **to say** BOO **to a ~; wild-~** CHASE; **~-flesh** *s.* chair de poule *f.*; **~ step** *s.* pas de l'oie *m.*

gooseberry *s.* groseille *f.*; CAPE **~; ~ bush** *s.* groseiller épineux *m.*; **to play ~,** se trouver en tiers (avec un couple), gêner.

Gordian *adj.* **~ knot,** nœud gordien *m.*

gor/e *s.* **1.** (*blood*) sang *m.*; **2.** (*dressm.*) godet *m.*; *v.t.* (1) (*of bull*) blesser d'un coup de cornes; (2) tailler à godet; **~y** *adj.* (*covered with blood*) ensanglanté; (*bloody*) sanglant.

gorge *s.* **1.** (*throat*) gorge *f.*; **2.** (*contents of stomach*) cœur *m.*; **3.** (*surfeit, fam.*) gavage *m.*; **4.** (*opening in hills, ravine*) gorge *f.*; *v.t.* & *i.* (3) (se) gorger (*with*—de).

gorgeous *adj.* **1.** (*luxurious*) somptueux; **2.** (*beautiful*) ravissant; **~ly** *adv.* (1) somptueusement; (2) splendidement; **~ness** *s.* (1) somptuosité *f.*; (2) splendeur *f.*

gorget *s.* (*armour*) hausse-col *m.*; (*dress*) gorgerette *f.*

gorgon *s.* gorgone *f.*

gorilla *s.* gorille *m.*

gorse *s.* genêt *m.*

gosh *interj.* (*fam.*) nom d'un chien!

goshawk *s.* autour *m.*

gosling *s.* oison *m.*

gospel *s.* (*eccles.*) évangile *m.*; (*thing to be believed*) *also* **~ truth,** parole d'évangile *f.*

gossamer *s.* (*cobweb*) fils (*m.pl.*) de la Vierge; (*text.*) gaze *f.*

gossip *s.* (*person*) compère *m.*, commère *f.*; bavard(e) *m.f.*; (*talk*) commérage *m.*, bavardage *m.*; (*malicious*) cancans *m.pl.*; *v.i.* bavarder; cancaner.

Goth *s.* Goth *m.*; **~ic** *s.* (*ling.*) gotique *m.*; *adj.* (*arch.*) gothique; (*type, script*) *adj.* & *s.f.* gothique.

gouge *s.* gouge *f.*; *v.t.* inciser; **~ out** (*eyes*) arracher (les yeux).

goulash *s.* (*cook.*) goulasch, goulache *m. or f.*

gourd *s.* (*fruit*) courge *f.*; (*bottle*) gourde *f.*

gout *s.* (*med.* & *drop of blood*) goutte *f.*; **~y** *adj.* goutteux.

govern *v.t.* (*rule, direct, administer*) gouverner, diriger, administrer; (*control*) diriger, maîtriser; (*sway, influence*) déterminer; (*ling.*) gouverner; **~ance** *s.* (*manner of ~ing*) direction *f.*, (*control*) empire *m.*; **~ess** *s.* gouvernante *f.*; **~ing** *adj.* gouvernant, (*fig.*) dominant; **~ing body,** conseil d'administration *m.*; **~ment** *s.* (*of state*) gouvernement *m.*, (*administration*) régime *m.*, ministère *m.*, (*fig.*) empire *m.*; **~mental** *adj.* gouvernemental; **~or** *s.* (*ruler, administrator*) gouverneur *m.*, directeur *m.*, administrateur *m.* (*member of ~ing body*) membre du conseil *m.*, (*pop. father, employer*) patron *m.*, (*mech.*) régulateur *m.*

gown *s.* (*woman's dress*) robe *f.*; (*robe, civic, acad. etc.*) robe *f.*, toge *f.*

grab *s.* **1.** (*attempt to seize*) mouvement pour saisir *m.*; **2.** (*rapacious conduct*) rapacité *f.*; **3.** (*mech.*) pelle mécanique *f.*, pelleteuse *f.*; *v.t.* (1) agripper; (2) accaparer; SMASH-**and-~; ~ber** *s.* (2) accapareur *m.*, homme rapace *m.*

grace *s.* (*attractiveness, charm; divine influence*) grâce *f.*; (*favour*) faveur *f.*; (*goodwill*) bonne volonté *f.*; (*delay granted*) grâce *f.*, répit *m.*; (*mercy*) grâce *f.*, clémence *f.*; (*at meals*): (*before*) bénédicité *f.*, (*after*) grâces *f. pl.*; (*form of address*) sa, votre, grâce; (*mus.*) **~-note** *s.* agrément *m.*; *v.t.* (*adorn*) orner (*with*—de); (*honour*) honorer (*with*—de); **~ful** *adj.* gracieux; **~fully** *adv.**; **~fulness** *s.* grâce *f.*; **~less** *adj.* sans grâce, (*fig.*) effronté.

gracious *adj.* **1.** (*condescending, haughty*) condescendant, hautain; **2.** (*kindly*) bienveillant; **3.** (*merciful*) miséricordieux; ⚠ gracieux = **graceful; good ~!,** juste ciel!; **~ly** *adv.* (1) avec condescendance; (2) avec bienveillance; (3) avec miséricorde; **~ness** *s.* (1) condescendance *f.*; (2) bienveillance *f.*; (3) miséricorde *f.*

gradat/e *v.t.* (*of colours*) arranger (des couleurs) en dégradé; **~ion** *s.* dégradé *m.*, effet de dégradé *m.*

grade *s.* (*degree*) degré *m.*; (*of persons*) rang *m.*, grade *m.*; (*of things*) classe *f.*; (*comm.*) qualité *f.*; (*slope*) pente *f.*; **to make the ~,** être à la hauteur de la situation; *v.t.* (*arrange in ~s*) trier, classer; (*road*) régulariser la pente (d'une route).

gradient *s.* pente *f.*, profil *m.*

gradual *s.* (*mus. eccles.*) graduel *m.*; *adj.* graduel; **~ly** *adv.**.
graduat/e *s.* (*acad.*) diplômé(e) *m.f.*; *v.t.* **1.** (*arrange in grades*) graduer; (*colours*) arranger en dégradé; *v.i.* **2.** (*acad.*) prendre ses diplômes; **3.** (*change gradually*) passer graduellement à; **~ion** *s.* (1) gradation *f.*, (*of instrument*) graduation *f.*; (2) remise de diplômes *f.*
graffiti *s.pl.* graffiti *m.pl.*
graft *s.* **1.** (*hort., med.*) greffe *f.*; **2.** (*illicit practices*) pots-de-vin *m.pl.*; *v.t.* (1) greffer; **~er** *s.* (1) greffeur *m.*; **~ing** *s.* greffage *m.*; **~ing-knife** *s.* greffoir *m.*
Grail *s.* Graal *m.*
grain *s.* (*corn*) grain *m.*; (*wheat*) blé *m.*; (*particle, unit of weight*) grain *m.*; **to take sth. with a ~ of** SALT; (*texture*) (*of skin*) grain *m.*, (*of wood*) fibres *m.pl.*, (*of stone*) fil *m.*; **against the ~,** (*lit.* & *fig. fam.*) à rebrousse-poil; *v.t.* (*wood*) marbrer.
gram(me) *s.* gramme *m.*
gramm/ar *s.* grammaire *f.*; **~ar** SCHOOL; **~-arian** *s.* grammairien *m.*; **~atical** *adj.* grammatical; **~atically** *adv.**.
gramophone *s.* phonographe *m.*; **~ record,** disque *m.*
grampus *s.* (*zool.*) épaulard *m.*; (*fam.*) gros poussif *m.*
granary *s.* grenier *m.*
grand *adj.* grand; (*imposing*) grandiose; (*fam. = excellent*) formidable; **~ aunt,** grand-tante *f.*; **~father,** grand-père *m.*; **~mother,** grand-mère *f.*, **to teach one's ~mother to suck** EGGS; **~uncle,** grand-oncle *m.*; **~parents,** grands parents *m.pl.*; **~children,** petits-enfants *m.pl.*; **~daughter,** petite-fille *f.*; **~nephew,** petit-neveu *m.*; **~niece,** petite-nièce *f.*; **~son,** petit-fils *m.*; **~** PIANO; **~stand** *s.* tribune *f.*; **~ee** *s.* (*Spanish*) grand (d'Espagne) *m.*, (*fig. fam.*) grand manitou *m.*; **~eur** *s.* grandeur *f.*, magnificence *f.*; **~ly** *adv.* avec grandeur.
grandiloquen/ce *s.* grandiloquence *f.*; **~t** *adj.* grandiloquent.
grandiose *adj.* grandiose.
grange *s.* (*barn*) grange *f.*; (*house*) manoir *m.*
granite *s.* granit *m.*
granivorous *adj.* granivore.
granny *s.* (*relation*) grand-maman *f.*, (*fam.*) mémé *f.*; (*old woman*) mémère *f.*
grant *s.* (*~ing*) octroi *m.*, concession *f.*; (*thing ~ed*) don *m.*; (*aid*) subvention *f.*; *v.t.* (*consent to give*) accorder; (*a favour*) octroyer; (*degree*) conférer; (*concede*) concéder; (*a request*) accéder à; (*law, transfer*) céder; (*allow*) admettre; **to take sth. for ~ed,** considérer qch. comme allant de soi; **~ee** *s.* donataire *m.*; **~or** *s.* donateur *m.*
granul/e *s.* granule *m.*; **~ar** *adj.* granulaire; **~ate** *v.t.* granuler; **~ated** *adj.* granulé; **~ated** SUGAR; **~ation** *s.* granulation *f.*; **~ous** *adj.* granuleux.
grape *s.* grain de raisin *m.*, **~s** *pl.* raisin *m.*; ⚠ grappe = **a bunch of ~s; to cry sour ~s** (*fig.*) faire la petite bouche, trouver les raisins trop verts; **~fruit** *s.* pamplemousse *m.*; **~-harvest** *s.* vendage *f.*; **~-picker** *s.* vendangeu/r, -se *m.f.*; **~-shot** *s.* mitraille *f.*; **~-vine** (*fig.*) téléphone arabe *m.*
graph *s.* graphique *m.*; **~ic** *adj.* **1.** (*of drawing, of graphs*) graphique; **2.** (*vividly descriptive*) pittoresque; **~ically** *adv.* (1)*; (2)*; **~ology** *s.* graphologie *f.*
graphite *s.* graphite *m.*
grapnel *s.* grappin *m.*
grappl/e *v.t.* (*seize with hook*) saisir au grappin; (*with hands*) agripper; (*come to close quarters with*) empoigner à bras le corps; (*contend with*) lutter corps à corps avec; (*fig.*) affronter corps à corps; **~ing** *s.* corps à corps *m.*; **~ing-iron,** grappin *m.*
grasp *s.* **1.** (*grip*) étreinte *f.*; **2.** (*clutch*) prise *f.*; (*fig.*) compréhension *f.*; **within one's ~,** en son pouvoir; *v.t.* (1) étreindre; (2) saisir; (3) comprendre; **~ing** *adj.* avare, avide.
grass *s.* herbe *f.*; (*lawn*) pelouse *f.*; (*turf*) gazon *m.*; (*grazing*) pâturage *m.*; **to let the ~ grow under one's feet,** rester les deux pieds dans le même sabot; SNAKE **in the ~**; **~-green** *adj.* vert pré; **~hopper** *s.* sauterelle *f.*; **~land** *s.* prairie *f.*; **~roots** *adj.* local; **~ verge** *s.* accotement *m.*; **~ widow** (*pop.*) veuve temporaire *f.*; **~y** *adj.* herbeux; *v.t.* gazonner.
grat/e[1] *s.* (*for fire*) foyer *m.*; (*bars*) grille *f.*; **~ing** *s.* grillage *m.*
grat/e[2] *v.t.* & *i.* **1.** (*rub small*) râper; **2.** (*grind, creak*) grincer; **3.** (*fig. irritate*) agacer; **~er** *s.* (1) râpe *f.*; **~ing** *adj.* (2) grinçant; (3) agaçant.
grateful *adj.* reconnaissant (*to*—envers); (*pleasant*) agréable; **~ly** *adv.* avec reconnaissance; **~ness** *s.* reconnaissance *f.*
gratif/y *v.t.* (*please*) faire plaisir à; (*indulge*) satisfaire à; se laisser aller à; **~ication** *s.* satisfaction *f.*; **~ying** *adj.* agréable.
gratis *adv.* gratis.
gratitude *s.* gratitude *f.*
gratuit/ous *adj.* (*done or got gratis; uncalled for*) gratuit; **~ously** *adv.**; **~y** *s.* (*tip*) gratification *f.*, pourboire *m.*; (*bounty, to soldier etc.*) prime *f.* (de démobilisation).
gravamen *s.* grief *m.*
grave[1] *s.* (*pit*) fosse *f.*; (*mound*) tombe *f.*; (*fig.*) tombeau *m.*; **have one** FOOT **in the ~**; **~-digger** *s.* fossoyeur *m.*; **~stone** *s.* dalle *f.*, pierre tombale *f.*; **~yard** *s.* cimetière *m.*
grav/e[2] *adj.* (*serious*) grave, inquiétant; (*solemn*) grave, sévère; (*low-pitched*) grave; (*accent*) grave; **~ely** *adv.* gravement; **~ity** *s.* (*solemnity, importance*) gravité *f.*; **force of ~ity,** gravité, *f.*
grav/e[3] *v.t.* (*engrave, carve, fig.*) graver; (*naut.*) radouber; **~en** *adj.* gravé; **~er** *s.* (*tool*) burin *m.*
gravel *s.* (*coarse sand*) gravier *m.*; (*med.*) gravelle *f.*; **~-pit** *s.* sablière *f.*; **~ly** *adj.* sablé, (*stony*) caillouteux; *v.t.* sabler; (*fam. = puzzle*) coller.
gravitat/e *v.i.* graviter; (*be drawn down*) être attiré vers le bas; (*fig.*) être attiré vers, graviter (autour de qn., de qch.); **~ion** *s.* gravitation *f.*
gravy *s.* jus *m.*, sauce *f.*; **~-boat,** saucière *f.*
gray *see* GREY.
graz/e *s.* (*scratch*) égratignure *f.*; *v.t.* **1.** (*touch in passing*) frôler; **2.** (*abrade skin*) égratigner; *v.i.* **3.** (*agric.*) paître; **~ier** *s.* (3) éleveur *m.*; **~ing** *s.* (3) élevage *m.*; (*grass*) pâturage *m.*
greas/e *s.* graisse *f.*; **~e-gun** *s.* graisseur *m.*; **~e-**PAINT; **~e-proof paper,** papier parcheminé; **~iness** *s.* graisse *f.*; **~y** *adj.* graisseux; *v.t.* graisser; **~e s.o.'s palm** (*fam.*) graisser la patte à qn.
great *s.* **the ~,** *s.pl.* les grands *m.pl.*; *adj.* (*large in size or number, important, of great ability, habitual, serious*) grand; (*hard, grievous*) grave; (*pregnant*) enceinte (*with*—de); (*relations*) arrière-, **~-grandfather,** arrière-grand-père *m.*; **~coat** *s.* pardessus *m.*, (*mil.*) capote *f.*; **~ly** *adv.* grandement, beaucoup; **~ness** *s.* grandeur *f.*
greave *s.* (*armour*) jambière *f.*
grebe *s.* (*bird*) grèbe *m.*
Greece *s.* (*geog.*) Grèce *f.*; **Grecian** *adj.* grec, grecque.
greed *s.* **1.** (*avarice*) avidité *f.*; **2.** (*for food*) gloutonnerie *f.*; **~ily** *adv.* avidement; **~iness** *s.* (1) avidité *f.*; (2) gloutonnerie *f.*; **~y** *adj.* (1) avide (*for*—de); (2) glouton.
Greek *adj.* & *s.m.f.* grec, grecque; *s.m.* (*lang.*) grec; **it's all ~ to me,** c'est de l'hébreu, du chinois, pour moi.
green *s.* vert *m.*; (*village ~*) place du village *f.*; **~s** *pl.* légumes verts *m.pl.*; *adj.* (*colour, unripe*)

vert; (*inexperienced*) naïf, inexpérimenté; (*fresh, not dried*) frais; **to be ~ with envy,** en faire une jaunisse; **to have ~ fingers,** être un virtuose du jardinage; **to give the ~ light to,** donner le feu vert à; **~finch** *s.* verdier *m.*; **~fly** *s.* puceron *m.*; **~gage** *s.* reine-claude *f.*; **~-grocer** *s.* fruitier *m.*; **~horn** *s.* (*fig.*) blanc-bec *m.*; **~house** *s.* serre *f.*; **~** PEAS; **~-room** *s.* foyer des artistes *m.*; **~sward** *s.* gazon *m.*; **~wood** *s.* forêt verte *f.*; **~ery** *s.* verdure *f.*; **~ish** *adj.* verdâtre; **~ness** *s.* verdeur *f.*, (*fig.*) naïveté *f.*

Greenland *s.* (*geog.*) Groenland *m.*; **~er** *s.m.f.* Groenlandais(e).

greet *v.t.* **1.** (*salute*) saluer; **2.** (*receive*) accueillir; **3.** (*meet, eyes, ears, etc.*) s'offrir (aux yeux, aux oreilles); **~ing** *s.* (1) salut *m.*; (2) accueil *m.*; **~ings** *s.pl.* salutations *f.pl.*; souhaits *m.pl.*

gregarious *adj.* (*living in communities*) grégaire; (*fond of company*) sociable; **~ness** *s.* grégarisme *m.*

Gregorian *adj.* grégorien.

gremlin *s.* mauvais génie *m.*

grenad/e *s.* grenade *f.*; **~ier** *s.* grenadier *m.*

grenadine *s.* (*text.* & *syrup*) grenadine *f.*

grey *s.* gris *m.*; (*horse*) cheval gris *m.*; *adj.* gris; (*aged*) aux cheveux gris; **to turn ~,** grisonner; **~beard** *s.* barbon *m.*, (*pop.*) vieux birbe *m.*; **~hound,** lévrier *m.*, levrette *f.*; **~lag,** bernacle *f.*; **~ matter** (*fig.*) matière grise *f.*; **~ish** *adj.* grisâtre; **~ness** *s.* teinte grise *f.*

grid *s.* (*framework*) grille *f.*; (*mapping*) quadrillage *m.*; (*network of lines*) réseau *m.*; (*electr.*) grille *f.*; **national ~** (*electr.*) réseau électrique national *m.*; **~iron** *s.* gril *m.*

grief *s.* chagrin *m.*; **to come to ~,** tourner mal; ⚠ grief = **grievance.**

griev/e *v.t.* & *i.* (s')affliger, (se) désoler; **~ance** *s.* grief *m.*; **~ous** *adj.* (*painful*) douloureux, pénible; (*flagrant, heinous*) atroce, odieux; **~ous bodily harm** (*law*) coups et blessures *m.pl.*; **~ously** *adv.* douloureusement; atrocement.

griffin, griffon, gryphon *s.* griffon *m.*

griffon *s.* (*dog*) griffon *m.*

grig *s.* (*small eel*) (petite) anguille *f.*; (*cricket*) grillon *m.*

grill *s.* **1.** (*gridiron*) gril *m.*; (*food*) grillade *f.*; **2.** (*screen*) grille *f.*; *v.t.* (1) griller; (*fig. fam. question*) cuisiner.

grim *adj.* **1.** (*stern, merciless*) sévère, impitoyable; **2.** (*of harsh aspect*) macabre, menaçant; **3.** (*joyless*) lugubre; **~ly** *adv.* (1) inflexiblement; (2) d'un air menaçant; (3)*; **~ness** *s.* (1) sévérité *f.*, implacabilité *f.*; (2) air menaçant *m.*; (3) aspect lugubre *m.*

grimace *s.* grimace *f.*; *v.i.* grimacer.

grimalkin *s.* (*cat*) mistigri *m.*; (*person*) vieille toupie *f.*

grim/e *s.* crasse *f.*; **~iness** *s.* saleté *f.*; **~y** *adj.* crasseux.

grin *s.* **1.** (*of pleasure*) large sourire *m.*; **2.** (*of pain, etc.*) grimace *f.*; **3.** (*sneer*) ricanement *m.*; *v.i.* (1) sourire; (2) grimacer; (3) ricaner; **~ and bear it,** faire contre mauvaise fortune bon cœur.

grind *s.* (*~ing*) broyage *m.*; (*fam. dull work*) boulot *m.*; *v.t.* & *i.* **1.** (*crush small*) broyer, (*coffee, etc.*) moudre; **2.** (*harass*) pressurer; **3.** (*sharpen*) aiguiser, affûter; **4.** (*grate*) grincer; **5.** (*fam.*) potasser; **~stone** *s.* meule *f.*; **~er** *s.* (1) (*for coffee, etc.*) moulin *m.*; (3) (*person*) rémouleur *m.*, (*mech.*) affûteuse *f.*; **~ing** *s.* (1) broyage *m.*; (3) affûtage *m.*; (4) grincement *m.*

grip *s.* **1.** (*firm hold*) étreinte *f.*; **2.** (*way of holding*) prise *f.*; **3.** (*fig. mastery, understanding*) emprise *f.*, compréhension *f.*; **4.** (*small bag*) trousse *f.*; **to come to ~s with,** en venir aux prises avec; *v.t.* (1) étreindre; (3) saisir.

gripe *s.* **1.** (*pl. pains*) coliques *f.pl.*; **2.** (*pop. complaint*) grief *m.*; *v.t.* & *i.* (1) donner, avoir des coliques; (2) *v.i.* rouspéter.

grisly *adj.* horrible, macabre.

grist *s.* blé à moudre *m.*; **all is ~ to his mill,** il fait flèche de tout bois.

gristl/e *s.* cartilage *m.*; **~y** *adj.* cartilagineux.

grit *s.* (*sand*) sable *m.*; (*~stone*) grès *m.*; (*fam.*) cran *m.*; **~ty** *adj.* sablonneux, graveleux; *v.t.* (*teeth*) serrer (les dents).

grizzle *v.i.* (*fam.*) pleurnicher.

grizzl/ed *adj.* grisonnant; **~y** *adj.* (*hair*) grisonnant; (*bear*) gris; *s.m.* (*bear*) grizzli *m.*

groan *s.* **1.** (*of pain, etc.*) gémissement *m.*; **2.** (*grunt*) grognement *m.*; *v.i.* (1) gémir; (2) grogner; **~ing** *s.* gémissement *m.*

groats *s.* gruau d'avoine *m.*

grocer *s.* épicier *m.*; **~y** *s.* épicerie *f.*; **~'s shop,** épicerie *f.*, alimentation *f.*

grog *s.* grog *m.*; **~gy** *adj.* (*drunk*) gris; (*unsteady, shaky*) chancelant, titubant.

groin *s.* (*anat.*) aine *f.*; (*arch.*) arête *f.*; ⚠ groin = **pig's snout.**

groom *s.* (*servant*) valet d'écurie *m.*; (*bridegroom*) marié *m.*; *v.t.* (*horse*) panser; (*make neat*) (*fam.*) (se) bichonner, (*fig. prepare for special job or occasion*) préparer à; **well-~ed** *adj.* bien astiqué.

groov/e *s.* rainure *f.*; (*arch.*) cannelure *f.*; (*techn.*) gorge *f.*; (*of gram. record*) sillon *m.*; *v.t.* (*arch.*) canneler; (*techn.*) rainer; **~y** *adj.* (*pop.*) bath (*invar.*).

grope *v.i.* tâtonner; **~ for sth.,** chercher qch. à tâtons.

gross *s.* (*12 dozen*) grosse *f.*; (*bulk*) gros *m.*; *adj.* **1.** (*luxuriant, rank*) dense, épais; **2.** (*flagrant*) flagrant; **3.** ($\neq$ *net*) brut **4.** (*coarse, indecent*) grossier; **5.** (*fat*) gros; **~ly** *adv.* (4) grossièrement; **~ness** *s.* (2) énormité *f.*; (4) grossièreté *f.*

grotesque *adj.* grotesque; **~ly** *adv.**.

grotto *s.* grotte *f.*

grotty *adj.* (*pop.*) mal foutu.

ground *s.* (*bottom of sea or river*) fond *m.*; (*base, foundation*) fondement *m.*; (*motive, justification*) raison *f.*; **on the ~ of, that,** sous prétexte de, que; **to have no ~(s) to do, for doing sth.,** n'avoir pas de raison de faire qch.; (*underlying part, background*) fond *m.*; (*surface of earth,* $\neq$ *air*) sol *m.*, terre *f.*; **to cut the ~ from under s.o.'s feet,** couper l'herbe sous les pieds de qn.; **to get off the ~** (*fig.*) démarrer; (*pl.*) (*of house*) jardins *m.pl.*, parc *m.*, (*dregs, esp. of coffee*) marc *m.*; (*land*) territoire *m.*, terrain *m.*; **to give or lose ~,** perdre du terrain; **to gain ~,** gagner du terrain; **on one's own ~** (*fig.*) sur son terrain; **common ~** (*fig.*) terrain d'entente *m.*; **to** CLEAR **the ~; to break new ~,** (*lit.*) défricher une terre vierge, (*fig.*) innover; **to stand one's ~,** tenir bon; (*field or area for special use*) terrain *m.*; **~-bait** *s.* amorce de fond *f.*; **~ bass** *s.* basse contrainte *f.*; **~ floor** *s.* rez-de-chaussée *m.*; **~ ivy** *s.* lierre terrestre *m.*; **~ nut** *s.* arachide *f.*; **~-plan** *s.* plan (horizontal) *m.*; **~-rent** *s.* redevance foncière *f.*; **~sheet** *s.* tapis de sol *m.*; **~sman** *s.* jardinier *m.*; **~ staff** *s.* personnel rampant *m.*; **~ swell** *s.* lame de fond *f.*; **~work** *s.* fondement *m.*; *v.t.* (*place on ~*) mettre par terre; (*aviat.*) empêcher de voler; (*base on principle*) fonder; (*instruct*) donner des connaissances solides (en); *v.i.* (*run ashore*) s'échouer; **~ing** *s.* connaissance fondamentale *f.*; **~less** *adj.* sans fondement.

groundsel *s.* séneçon *m.*

group *s.* groupe *m.*; **~ captain** *s.* colonel *m.*; *v.t.* & *i.* (se) grouper; **~ing** *s.* groupement *m.*

grouse *s.* **1.** (*bird*) tétras *m.*; **2.** (*pop. grumble*) rogne *f.*; *v.i.* (2) rouspéter.

grout *s.* coulis *m.*; *v.t.* jointoyer; **~ing** *s.* jointoiement *m.*

grove *s.* bocage *m.*; (*clump*) bosquet *m.*

grovel *v.i.* (*lie prone*) se vautrer; (*fig. abase oneself*) ramper, s'aplatir (devant qn.); **~ling** *adj.* rampant.
grow *v.t.* cultiver; *v.i.* (*bot.*) pousser; (*person*) grandir; (*increase in size, etc.*) augmenter; (*come by degrees*) se développer; (*become*) devenir, *see* DARK, OLD, *etc.*; **~ less,** diminuer; **~ on** (*fig.*) s'imposer à, plaire de plus en plus à; **~ up,** grandir, devenir adulte; **~n-up** *s.* grande personne *f.*, *adj.* & *s.m.f.* adulte; **to let the** GRASS **~ under one's feet; ~er** *s.* cultivateur *m.*; **~ing** *s.* (*agric.*) culture *f.*, croissance *f.*; *adj.* croissant, grandissant; **~ing pains** (*fig.*) maladie de croissance *f.*; **~th** *s.* croissance *f.*, (*crop*) récolte *f.*, (*med.*) excroissance *f.*, (*comm.*) développement *m.*, (*fig.*) accroissement *m.*
growl *s.* **1.** (*anger*) grondement *m.*; **2.** (*complaint*) grognement *m.*; *v.i.* (1) gronder; (2) grogner; **~er** *s.* (*fam.*) (2) grognon *m.*; (*fam. cab*) fiacre *m.*
groyne *s.* épi *m.*
grub *s.* (*of insect*) larve *f.*; (*pop. food*) mangeaille *f.*; *v.t.* fouir; **~ up** *v.t.* défricher, déraciner; **money-~ber,** grippe-sou *m.*; **~by** *adj.* sale.
grudg/e *s.* (*resentment*) ressentiment *m.*; (*ill will*) rancune *f.*; **to have a ~e against s.o.,** en vouloir à qn.; *v.t.* donner à contre-cœur, lésiner sur qch.; **~ing** *adj.* donné à contre-cœur, (*person*) lésineur; **~ingly** *adv.* à contre-cœur.
gruel *s.* gruau *m.*; **~ling** *adj.* (*exhausting*) éreintant.
gruesome *adj.* macabre.
gruff *adj.* (*surly*) bourru; (*rough-voiced*) (à la voix) rauque; **~ly** *adv.* d'un ton bourru.
grumbl/e *s.* **1.** (*faint growl*) grondement *m.*; **2.** (*murmur*) murmure *m.*; **3.** (*complaint*) grognement *m.*; *v.i.* (1) gronder; (2) murmurer; (3) grogner, ronchonner; **~er** *s.* (3) ronchon *m.*, grognon *m.*; **~ing** *s.* grognement *m.*
grumpy *adj.* grincheux.
grunt *s.* grognement *m.*; *v.i.* grogner; **~er** *s.* (*pig*) cochon *m.*; (*fig.*) grognon *m.*
G-string *s.* cache-sexe *m.*
guano *s.* guano *m.*
guarant/ee *s.* (*person providing ~ee*) garant(e) *m.f.*; (*person receiving ~ee*) bénéficiaire *m.f.*; (*guaranty*) garantie *f.*; *v.t.* (*be ~ee for*) se porter garant de; (*answer for*) répondre de; (*engage, secure*) garantir; **~or** *s.* garant(e) *m.f.*
guard *s.* (*posture, state*) garde *f.*; (*protector, sentry*) garde *m.*; (*rail.*) chef de train *m.*; (*mil. body of men*) garde *f.*; **~s** *pl.* (*mil.*) gardes *f.pl.*; (*security device*) dispositif de sécurité *m.*; **on ~,** sur ses gardes; **on ~!** (*command*) en garde!; **off ~,** au dépourvu; **to mount ~,** monter la garde; **~room** *s.* (*mil.*) corps de garde *m.*; **~sman** *s.* soldat de la garde *m.*; **~'s van** *s.* fourgon *m.*; *v.t.* garder; (*techn.*) protéger; (*fig.*) surveiller; **~ against** *v.t.* mettre en garde contre, *v.i.* se tenir sur ses gardes contre; **~ed** *adj.* circonspect.
guardian *s.* **1.** (*protector, caretaker*) gardien(ne) *m.f.*; **2.** (*law*) tut/eur, -rice *m.f.*; **3.** (*of museum, etc.*) conservat/eur, -rice *m.f.*; **~ angel** *s.* ange gardien *m.*; **~ianship** *s.* (1) garde *f.*; (2) tutelle *f.*; (3) conservation *f.*
guava *s.* goyave *f.*; **~-tree,** goyavier *m.*
gudgeon *s.* (*fish*) goujon *m.*; (*fam. credulous person*) jobard(e) *m.f.*; (*mech.*) goujon *m.*; **~-pin,** tourillon *m.*
guerdon *s.* (*poet.*) récompense *f.*
Guernsey *s.* (*geog.*) Guernesey *m.*; (*jersey*) vareuse *f.*; (*cattle*) vache de guernesey *f.*
guerrilla *s.* franc-tireur *m.*, partisan *m.*; **~ warfare,** guerre de guérilla *f.*, guérilla *f.*
guess *s.* (*rough estimate*) hypothèse *f.*; (*conjecture*) conjecture *f.*; *v.t.* & *i.* deviner, conjecturer; (*think likely*) estimer; **~ work** *s.* simple conjecture *f.*; **by ~ work,** au jugé.
guest *s.* invité *m.*; (*at meal*) convive *m.*; (*in hotel*) hôte *m.*; **paying ~,** pensionnaire *m.*; **~-house,** pension *f.*; **~-room,** chambre des invités *f.*
guffaw *s.* gros rire *m.*; *v.i.* s'esclaffer.
guide *s.* guide *m.*; (*adviser*) conseiller *m.*; (*principle*) principe *m.*; (*techn.*) glissière *f.*; **~-book** *s.* guide *m.*; **~-dog** *s.* chien pour aveugle *m.*; **~-line** (*fig. usu. pl.*) directive *f.*; *v.t.* guider; (*advise*) diriger; **~d missile,** engin téléguidé *m.*; **guidance** *s.* conduite *f.*, direction *f.*
guild *s.* (*hist., of craftsmen*) corporation *f.*; (*hist., of merchants*) guilde *f.*; **~hall,** hôtel de ville *m.*
guile *s.* (*cunning*) ruse *f.*; (*deceit*) tromperie *f.*; **~ful** *adj.* rusé, trompeur; **~fully** *adv.* avec ruse; **~less** *adj.* naïf.
guillemot *s.* guillemot *m.*
guillotine *s.* guillotine *f.*; (*for paper*) massicot *m.*; (*parl.*) clôture imposée des débats *f.*; *v.t.* guillotiner; (*paper*) rogner; (*parl.*) imposer la clôture des débats.
guilt *s.* culpabilité *f.*; **~iness** *s.* culpabilité *f.*; **~less** *adj.* innocent; **~lessness** *s.* innocence *f.*; **~y** *adj.* coupable.
Guinea[1] *s.* (*geog.*) Guinée *f.*; **~n** *adj.* & *s.m.f.* guinéen(ne); **g~-fowl** *s.* pintade *f.*; **g~-pig** *s.* (*lit.* & *fig.*) cobaye *m.*
guinea[2] *s.* (*coin*) guinée *f.*
guise *s.* (*external appearance*) costume *m.*, aspect *m.*; (*pretence*) semblant *m.*; **in the ~ of,** sous l'apparence de; ⚠ en guise de = **instead of.**
guitar *s.* guitare *f.*; **~-player, ~ist** *s.* guitariste *m.f.*
gules *s.* (*herald.*) gueules *m.pl.*
gulf *s.* golfe *m.*; (*fig.*) gouffre *m.*; **the G~ Stream,** le Gulf-Stream *m.*
gull *s.* **1.** (*bird*) (*large*) goéland *m.*, (*small*) mouette *f.*; **2.** (*fool*) jobard *m.*; *v.t.* (*dupe*) (2) duper, rouler; **~ible** *adj.* crédule; **~ibility** *s.* crédulité *f.*
gullet *s.* gosier *m.*
gully *s.* (*geol.*) couloir *m.*, ravin *m.*; (*gutter*) rigole *f.*; *v.t.* raviner.
gulp *s.* (*effort to swallow*) serrement de gorge *m.*; (*mouthful of food*) bouchée *f.*; (*of drink*) lampée *f.*; **at a ~,** d'un trait; *v.i.* s'étouffer; *v.t.* **~ down,** avaler, (*tears, etc.*) ravaler.
gum *s.* **1.** (*in mouth*) gencive *f.*; **2.** (*glue*) gomme *f.*; **3.** (*tree*) gommier *m.*; **to be up a ~-tree** (*fig.*) être dans le pétrin; CHEWING-**~**; **~boil** *s.* abcès (aux gencives) *m.*; **~boot** *s.* botte (en caoutchouc) *f.*; **~my** *adj.* (2) gommeux; *v.t.* (2) gommer, coller.
gumption *s.* (*fam.*) jugeotte *f.*; **to show ~,** se montrer débrouillard.
gun *s.* (*firearm*) fusil *m.*, canon *m.*; TOMMY-**~**; (*member of shoot*) fusil *m.*; (*for spraying*) pistolet *m.*; (*fig. fam.*) **big ~,** gros bonnet *m.*; **it's blowing great ~s** (*fam.*) il fait un vent à décorner les bœufs; **to stick to one's ~s** (*fig.*) ne pas démordre de sa position; **to** JUMP **the ~; to** SPIKE **s.o.'s ~s; ~boat** *s.* canonnière *f.*; **~-carriage** *s.* affût *m.*; **~-cotton** *s.* fulmicoton *m.*; **~ dog** *s.* chien de chasse *m.*; **~-fire** *s.* (*artillery*) canonnade *f.*, (*rifle*) tir *m.*; **~man** *s.* bandit *m.*, gangster *m.*; **~-metal** *s.* bronze à canon *m.*; **~powder** *s.* poudre *f.*; **~room** *s.* (*naut.*) poste des aspirants *m.*, (*sport*) armurerie *f.*; **~-running** *s.* contrebande d'armes *f.*; **~shot** *s.* coup de feu *m.*; **~smith** *s.* armurier *m.*; **~ner** *s.* (*mil.*) canonnier *m.*, (*sport*) chasseur *m.*; **~nery** *s.* (*mil.*) artillerie *f.*, (*manufacture*) fabrication de canons *f.*; *v.t.* tuer d'un coup de revolver; **~ for** *v.t.* chasser, (*fig.*) pourchasser.
gunny *s.* toile de jute *f.*
gunwale *s.* (*naut.*) plat-bord *m.*
gurgl/e *s.* **1.** (*liquid*) glouglou *m.*; **2.** (*person*) gloussement *m.*; **3.** (*stream, etc.*) murmure *m.*; *v.i.* (1) glouglouter; (2) glousser; (3) murmurer; **~ing** *s.* *as* GURGLE.

guru *s.* gourou *m.*
gush *s.* (**gushing** *s.*) **1.** (*sudden stream*) jaillissement *m.*; **2.** (*effusiveness*) exubérance *f.*; *v.i.* (1) jaillir; (2) être exubérant; **~ing** *adj.* (1) jaillissant; (2) exubérant; **~ingly** *adv.* (1) en jaillissant; (2) avec exubérance.
gusset *s.* soufflet *m.*
gust *s.* (*of wind*) rafale *f.*; (*of rain*) ondée *f.*; (*of smoke*) bouffée *f.*; (*of anger, etc.*) accès *m.*; **~y** *adj.* venteux, orageux.
gusto *s.* (*vigour*) entrain *m.*; (*enjoyment*) plaisir *m.*
gut *s.* (*mus.*) corde *f.*; CAT~; (*fishing*) crin de Florence *m.*; (*narrow water passage*) goulet *m.*; **~s** *s.pl.* boyaux *m.pl.* (*pop.*) cran *m.sing.*; **to hate s.o.'s ~s** (*pop.*) ne pas pouvoir blairer qn.; *adj.* (*fundamental, instinctive*) viscéral; *v.t.* (*remove ~s*) vider; (*by fire*) ne laisser que les quatre murs; **~ted** *adj.* vidé; entièrement brûlé sauf les murs.
gutta-percha *s.* gutta-percha *f.*
gutter *s.* (*on roof*) gouttière *f.*; (*in street*) caniveau *m.*, rigole *f.*; (*water in ~*) ruisseau *m.*; **to end in the ~** (*fig.*) tomber dans le ruisseau; **~ press,** presse à scandales *f.*; **~snipe** *s.* gamin des rues *m.*; *v.t.* creuser; *v.i.* (*candle*) couler.
guttural *s.* (*ling.*) gutturale *f.*; *adj.* guttural.
guy *s.* **1.** (*rope, chain*) (*naut.*) hauban *m.*; (*tent, etc.*) corde, chaîne, de retenue *f.*; **2.** (*person*) épouvantail *m.*, (*G~ Fawkes*) effigie *f.*; **3.** (*fam.*) type *m.*; **to look a ~** (2) être mal fagoté; *v.t.* (1) retenir; (*naut.*) haubanner; (2) tourner en ridicule.
guzzl/e *v.t.* & *i.* (*food*) bâfrer; (*drink*) lamper; **~er** *s.* (*fam.*) bâfreur *m.*, soiffard *m.*
gybe *v.i.* (*naut.*) empanner.
gym *s.* (*gymnasium*) gymnase *m.*; (*gymnastics*) gymnastique *f.*; **~-shoe,** chaussure de tennis *f.*
gymkhana *s.* concours hippique *m.*
gymnas/ium *s.* (*sport*) gymnase *m.*; (*acad.*) lycée *m.*; **~t** *s.* gymnaste *m.f.*; **~tic** *adj.* gymnastique; **~tics** *s.* gymnastique *f.* ⚠ *sing. in French.*
gynaecolog/y *s.* gynécologie *f.*; **~ical** *adj.* gynécologique; **~ist** *s.* gynécologue *m.f.*
gyps/um *s.* gypse *m.*; **~eous** *adj.* gypseux.
gypsy *see* GIPSY.
gyrat/e *v.i.* tournoyer; **~ion** *s.* giration *f.*; **~ory** *adj.* giratoire.
gyro- (*in combination*) **~-compass,** gyrocompas *m.*; **~meter,** gyromètre *m.*; **~-pilot,** gyropilote *m.*; **~scope,** gyroscope *m.*
gyves *s.pl.* fers *m.pl.*

H

ha *interj.* ha!; **~! ~!,** ha! ha!
habeas corpus *s.* habeas corpus *m.*
haberdasher *s.* mercier *m.*; **~y** *s.* mercerie *f.*
habiliment *s.* accoutrement *m.*; **~s** *s.pl.* (*dress*) vêtements *m.pl.*
habit *s.* (*practice*) habitude *f.*; (*constitution*): (*of body*) tempérament *m.*, (*of mind*) tournure d'esprit *f.*; (*dress*) costume *m.*, (*lady's riding-~*) amazone *f.*; (*eccles.*) habit *m.*; **to be in the ~ of,** avoir l'habitude de; **to make a ~ of,** prendre l'habitude de; **from (force of) ~,** par habitude; **~-forming** *adj.* qui crée un effet de besoin; **~ual** *adj.* (*customary*) habituel; (*given to special ~*) d'habitude, (*pej.*) invétéré; **~ually** *adv.**; **~uate** *v.t.* & *i.* (s')habituer (à); **~ude** *s.* (*custom*) habitude *f.*, (*tendency*) tendance *f.*; **~ué** *s.* habitué *m.*
habit/able *adj.* habitable; **~ation** *s.* habitation *f.*
habitat *s.* habitat *m.*
hack *s.* (*wound*) blessure *f.*; (*gash*) entaille *f.*; (*kick*) coup de pied *m.*; (*hired horse*) cheval de louage *m.*; (*liter. drudge*) nègre *m.*; (*scribbler*) écrivain à gages *m.*; (*tool*) pioche *f.*; *v.t.* (*cut*) entailler; (*kick*) donner un coup de pied à; **~-saw** *s.* scie à métaux *f.*; **~ writer,** nègre *m.*; **~ work,** travail de nègre *m.*; **~ing** *adj.* **~ing cough,** toux sèche *f.*
hackle *s.* (*on cock*) camail *m.*; (*of dog*) **with its ~s up,** (chien) hérissé de colère; **to make s.o.'s ~s rise,** faire se hérisser qn. de colère.
hackney *s.* (*horse*) cheval de louage *m.*; **~ cab, carriage, coach,** voiture de louage *f.*; *v.t.* banaliser; **~ed** *adj.* banal (*pl.* -als); **to become ~ed,** se banaliser.
haddock *s.* (*usu.*) églefin *m.*; (*also*) aiglefin, aigrefin *m.*; **smoked ~,** églefin fumé *m.*, haddock *m.*
Hades *s.* enfers *m.pl.*
haemo/globin *s.* hémoglobine *f.*; **~philia** *s.* hémophilie *f.*; **~rrhage** *s.* hémorragie *f.*; **~rrhoids** *s.pl.* hémorroïdes *f.pl.*
haft *s.* (*of knife*) manche *m.*; (*of sword*) poignée *f.*
hag *s.* (*lit.* & *fig.*) sorcière *f.*; **~ridden** *adj.* hanté de cauchemars.
haggard *adj.* hagard.
haggl/e *v.i.* marchander; **~e over** *v.t.* marchander; **~er** *s.* marchandeur *m.*; **~ing** *s.* marchandage *m.*
hagiograph/y *s.* hagiographie *f.*; **~er** *s.* hagiographe *m.f.*
Hague (*the*) *s.* (*geog.*) la Haye *f.*
ha-ha *s.* saut de loup *m.*; *interj. see* HA.
hail[1] *s.* (*frozen rain*) grêle *f.*; (*fig. of questions, etc.*) pluie *f.*; *v.i.* grêler; **~stone** *s.* grêlon *m.*
hail[2] *v.t.* (*greet*) saluer; (*call to*) héler; **~ from** *v.i.* venir de; **within ~,** à portée de voix; *interj.* salut!; **to be ~-**FELLOW**-well-met with.**
hair *s.* (*one ~ on head*; *~like thing*) cheveu *m.*; (*head of ~*) cheveux *m.pl.*; (*of animal*; *on human body*) poil *m.*; (*of horse*) crin *m.*; FALSE **~**; **to do one's ~,** se coiffer; **to have one's ~ done,** se faire coiffer; **to get in s.o.'s ~,** porter sur les nerfs de qn.; **to** KEEP **one's ~ on; to let one's ~ down,** en prendre à son aise; **to make one's ~ stand on end,** faire dresser les cheveux sur la tête; **to split ~s,** couper les cheveux en quatre; **to tear one's ~,** s'arracher les cheveux; **~'s breadth,** épaisseur d'un cheveu *f.*, **by a ~'s breadth,** à un cheveu près; **~**BRUSH; **~cloth** *s.* étoffe de crin *f.*; **~-do** *s.* coiffure *f.*; **~dresser** *s.* coiffeur *m.*; **~** DRIER; **~-line** *s.* (*lit.*) naissance des cheveux *f.*, (*fig. very thin line*) fil *m.*, **~-line** *adj.* subtil; **~-net** *s.* résille *f.*; **~pin** *s.* épingle à cheveux *f.*, **~pin bend,** lacet *m.*; **~-raising** *adj.* à faire dresser les cheveux sur la tête; **~ shirt** *s.* cilice *m.*; **~-splitting** *s.* ergotage *m.*; **~ spring** *s.* (*of watch*) spiral *m.*; **~y** *adj.* (*of head*) chevelu, (*of body*) poilu.
hake *s.* merluche *f.*
halberd *s.* hallebarde *f.*
halcyon *s.* (*kingfisher*) alcyon *m.*; *adj.* serein; **~ days,** jours de bonheur *m.pl.*
hale *adj.* vigoureux; **to be ~ and hearty,** se porter comme un charme.
half *s.* moitié *f.*; **~ of his time,** la moitié de son temps; **~ the class,** la moitié de la classe; **the first ~ of the nineteenth century,** la première moitié du dix-neuvième siècle; **~ and ~,**

moitié moitié; **too long by ~,** trop long de moitié; **to do things by halves,** faire les choses à moitié; (~ *of one, with numbers*) demi(e), **three and a ~,** trois et demi; **three and a ~ hours,** trois heures et demie; **a dozen and a ~,** une douzaine et demie; **~ past four** (*etc.*), quatre (*etc.*) heures et demie; (*pop. school term*) semestre *m.*; (*sport*) demi *m.*, **scrum-~,** demi de mêlée *m.*, **stand-off ~,** demi d'ouverture *m.*; *adj.* demi(e); **~ a cup,** une demi-tasse *f.*; **~ a dozen,** une demi-douzaine *f.*; **~ an hour,** une demi-heure *f.*; *adv.* demi, à demi; **not ~** (*pop.*) tout à fait; **~-baked** *adj.* (*fig.*) incomplet, immature; idiot; **~-blood, ~-breed, ~-caste** *adj.* & *s.m.f.* métis(se); **~-brother, ~-sister** *s.* demi-frère *m.*, demi-sœur *f.*; **~-hearted** *adj.* peu empressé; **~-heartedly** *adv.* avec peu d'empressement; **~ hitch,** demi-clef *f.*; **~ holiday** *s.* congé de l'après-midi *m.*; **at ~-mast** (*flag*) en berne; **~ moon** *s.* demi-lune *f.*; **~-open** *adj.* entr'ouvert; **~ pay** *s.* demi-solde *f.*; **~penny** *s.* sou *m.*; **at ~** PRICE; **~-time** *s.* (*sport*) mi-temps *f.*; **~-tone,** (*art*) demi-teinte *f.*; (*mus.*) demi-ton *m.*; **~-truth,** demi-vérité *f.*; **~-way** *s.* mi-chemin *f.*, *adv.* à mi-chemin; **~-yearly** *adj.* semestriel, *adv.**.

halibut *s.* flétan *m.*

halitosis *s.* mauvaise haleine *f.*

hall *s.* (*large public room*) salle *f.*; (*dining-room*) réfectoire *m.*; (*students' residence*) pavillon *m.*; (*country house*) château *m.*; (*passage*) vestibule *m.*; TOWN ~; ⚠ halle = **market hall; ~mark** *s.* poinçon (de garantie) *m.*, (*fig.*) sceau *m.*; **~mark** *v.t.* poinçonner.

hallelujah *see* ALLELUIA.

halliard *see* HALYARD.

hallo *interj.* holà!; (*telephone*) allô!; **~o** *interj.* (*hunting*) taïaut; *v.i.* huer.

hallow *s.* (*obs.*) saint *m.*; **All H~s** *s.* Toussaint *f.*; **H~e'en** *s.* veille de la Toussaint *f.*; *v.t.* sanctifier; **~ed** *adj.* sanctifié.

hallucinat/e *v.t.* halluciner; **~ion** *s.* hallucination *f.*; **~ory** *adj.* hallucinatoire.

halo *s.* (*round sun, moon, etc.*) halo *m.*; (*eccles., fig.*) auréole *f.*

halt[1] *s.* (*temporary stop; small railway station*) halte *f.*; **to** CALL **a ~;** (*command*) halte!; *v.t.* & *i.* (s')arrêter.

halt[2] *adj.* (*lame*) boiteux; *s.pl.* les estropiés *m.pl.*; **~ing** *adj.* boiteux; (*hesitating*) hésitant.

halter *s.* (*for horse*) licou *m.*; (*for hanging*) (*obs.*) hart *f.*, corde *f.*

halve *v.t.* (*divide into two*) partager, diviser en deux; (*reduce*) diminuer de moitié.

halyard *s.* (*naut.*) drisse *f.*

ham *s.* **1.** (*anat.*) jarret *m.*; **2.** (*cook.*) jambon *m.*; **3.** (*radio*) radio-amateur *m.*; **4.** (*fam. theat.*) cabotin *m.*; *v.i.* (4) (*fam.*) cabotiner; **~-fisted** *adj.* maladroit; **~string** *s.* tendon du jarret *m.*; **~strung** *adj.* (*fig.*) pieds et poings liés.

hamadryad *s.* hamadryade *f.*

hamburger *s.* (*cook.*) hamburger *m.*, biftek hâché *m.*

hamlet *s.* hameau *m.*

hammer *s.* **1.** (*tool; auctioneer's; sport; in clock, piano, etc.*) marteau *m.*; **2.** (*in gun*) percuteur *m.*; **~ and sickle,** la faucille et le marteau; **to come under the ~,** être vendu aux enchères; **to go at it ~ and tongs,** y aller à bras raccourcis; *v.t.* (1) marteler; **~ in,** enfoncer; **~ into,** faire entrer dans; **~ out** *v.t.* (*techn.*) étendre au marteau, (*fig.*) élaborer, (*problem*) résoudre; **~ing** *s.* (*act*) martelage *m.*, (*noise*) martèlement *m.*

hammock *s.* hamac *m.*

hamper[1] *s.* manne *f.*; (*fish, etc.*) bourriche *f.*

hamper[2] *v.t.* (*hinder*) gêner; (*obstruct*) entraver; (*fig.*) empêtrer.

hamster *s.* hamster *m.*

hand *s.* (*anat.*) main *f.*; **a** BIRD **in the ~;** (*fig.*) **right ~,** bras droit *m.*; (*authority, custody*) main *f.*; **to be in good ~s,** être en bonnes mains; **by the ~(s) of** (*in the care of*) aux bons soins de; (*share in action*) partie *f.*, participation *f.*; **to bear, have, a ~ in sth.,** participer à qch., y être pour qch.; **to lend, give, s.o. a ~,** donner un coup de main à qn.; (*in marriage*) main *f.*; (*manual worker*) ouvrier *m.*, (*naut.*) marin *m.*; **all ~s,** main-d'œuvre *f.*, (*naut.*) équipage *m.*; **an** OLD **~; at first ~,** de première main; **second ~,** *adj.* & *adv.* d'occasion; (*writing*) écriture *f.*; (*~like thing*): (*of clock, etc.*) aiguille *f.*, (*of bananas*) régime *m.*; (*side or direction*) côté *m.*, **right ~,** droite *f.*, **left ~,** gauche *f.*; (*measure*) main *f.*; (*at cards*) jeu *m.*; **to show one's ~,** jouer cartes sur table; **to play a** LONE **~;** (*fam. applause*) ovation *f.*; **to** CLAP **~s; at ~,** (*within reach*) à portée de main, (*about to happen*) imminent, proche; **by ~,** de la main de (qn.), (*done by ~*) à la main; **from ~ to mouth,** au jour le jour; **in ~,** (*comm.*) en magasin, (*cash*) en caisse, (*fig.*) en chantier, en train; **to take in ~,** prendre en main, entreprendre; **to have in ~,** avoir en main; **to fall into the ~s of,** tomber aux/dans les, mains de; **off~,** (*rude*) brusque, (*extempore*) impromptu, incontinent; **on ~,** sous la main, (*available*) disponible; **on all ~s,** de tous côtés; **on the one ~, on the other ~,** d'une part, d'autre part; **out of ~,** indiscipliné; **to ~,** sous le main; **not to do a ~'s turn,** ne pas remuer le petit doigt; **bound ~ and foot,** pieds et poings liés; **~ in** GLOVE **with; ~ in ~,** la main dans la main; **~ to ~ fighting,** combat corps à corps; **to get one's ~ in,** se faire la main (à); **to win ~s down,** arriver dans un fauteuil; **~s off!,** ne touchez pas!; **~s up!,** haut les mains!; **to lay ~s on,** mettre la main sur, (*illegally*) faire main basse sur; **to get the upper ~ of s.o.,** prendre l'avantage sur qn.; **to wash one's ~s of,** se laver les mains de; **~bag** *s.* sac à main *m.*; **~bell** *s.* sonnette *f.* **~bill** *s.* prospectus *m.*; **~book** *s.* guide *m.*, manuel *m.*; **~-brake** *s.* frein à main *m.*; **~cart** *s.* charrette à bras *f.*; **~clap** *s.* battement de mains *m.*; **~cuffs** *s.* menottes *f.pl.*, **~cuff** *v.t.* mettre les menottes à; **~-grenade** *s.* grenade à main *f.*; **~-luggage,** bagages à main *m.pl.*; **~made** *adj.* fait à la main; **~maid** *s.* servante *f.*; **~-picked** *adj.* (*fam.*) trié sur le volet; **~rail** *s.* garde-fou *m.*; **~shake** *s.* poignée de main *f.*; GOLDen **~shake; to do a ~stand,** faire le poirier; **~writing** *s.* écriture *f.*; **heavy-~ed,** oppressif; **high-~ed,** autoritaire; **left-~ed,** gaucher; **open-~ed,** généreux; **red-~ed,** en flagrant délit; **right--~ed,** droitier; **to be short-~ed,** manquer de personnel; **~ful** *s.* (*amount*) poignée *f.*, (*naughty child*) enfant terrible *m.*; *v.t.* (~ *s.o. into or out of bus, etc.*) donner la main à qn. (pour monter, descendre, etc.); (*deliver by ~*) remettre; **~ down, ~ on,** transmettre; **~ in,** déposer, donner; **~ out,** distribuer; **~-out** *s.* (*charity*) aumône *f.*, (*news*) communiqué *m.*; **~ over,** remettre; **~ round,** passer, faire circuler; **~ it to s.o.** (*fam.*) reconnaître l'habileté de qn., **you have to ~ it to him, he can play,** il faut le reconnaître, il sait jouer.

h. & c. (*abbrev. for hot & cold running water*) eau courante chaude et froide.

handicap *s.* handicap *m.*; *v.t.* handicaper; **~ped** *adj.* handicapé.

handicraft *s.* travail manuel *m.*

handiwork *s.* (*lit.* & *fig.*) ouvrage *m.*

handkerchief *s.* mouchoir *m.*; (*scarf*) foulard *m.*

handl/e *s.* (*of basket*) anse *f.*; (*of implement*) manche *m.*; (*of door, etc.*) poignée *f.*; (*of pan, etc.*)

queue *f.*; (*of barrow*) bras *m.*; (*auto.*) manivelle *f.*; (*fig.*) avantage *m.*; **to** FLY **off the ~e; ~e-bars** *s.* (*bicycle*) guidon *m.*; *v.t.* **1.** (*touch with hands*) manier, manipuler; **2.** (*manage, deal with*) contrôler, (*techn.*) manœuvrer; **3.** (*treat in talk*) traiter; **4.** (*comm.*) faire le commerce de, vendre; **~er** *s.* (*dog*) dresseur *m.*; **~ing** *s.* (1) maniement *m.*, manipulation *f.*; (2) contrôle *m.*; (3) traitement *m.*; (4) commerce *m.*

handsome *adj.* **1.** (*in appearance*) beau, belle *m.f.*; **2.** (*generous*) généreux; **3.** (*considerable*) considérable; **~ly** *adv.* (1) avec beauté; (2)*; (3) largement; **~ness** *s.* (1) beauté *f.*; (2) générosité *f.*

hand/y *adj.* **1.** (*ready to hand*) accessible; **2.** (*convenient to use*) commode, pratique; **3.** (*person clever with hands*) adroit; **~ily** *adv.* (2) commodément; (3)*; **~iness** *s.* (1) accessibilité *f.*; (2) commodité *f.*; (3) adresse *f.*; **~yman** *s.* bricoleur *m.*

hang *s.* (*way thing ~s*) ligne *f.*; **to get the ~ of sth.,** avoir le chic pour faire qch.; *v.t.* & *i.* (*on hooks*) suspendre (à); (*wallpaper*) tapisser; (*door*) poser; (*by the neck*) pendre; (*be ~ed*) être pendu; (*droop*) pencher; (*hover*) planer; (*of dress, curtains, etc.*) tomber; **~ about** *v.i.* traînasser; **~ back** *v.i.* hésiter; **~ down** *v.i.* pendre; **~ fire** *v.i.* faire long feu; **~ on** *v.i.* tenir bon; (*wait*) attendre; **~ on to,** se cramponner à; **~ out** *v.t.* (*washing*) étendre; **to have a ~over** (*pop.*) avoir la G.D.B. (gueule de bois); **~ together** *v.i.* (se) tenir; **~ up** *v.t.* accrocher, suspendre; (*telephone*) raccrocher; **~**DOG; **~-glider** *s.* deltaplane *m.*; **~man** *s.* bourreau *m.*; **~er** *s.* (*hook*) crochet *m.*; (*clothes*) cintre *m.*; **~er-on** *s.* parasite *m.*; **~ing** *s.* (*of person*) pendaison *f.*; (*of things*) suspension *f.*; **~ings** *s.pl.* tentures *f.pl.*; **~ing** *adj.* suspendu.

hangar *s.* (*aviat.*) hangar *m.*

hank *s.* écheveau *m.*

hanker *v.i.* languir (*after, for*—après); **~ing** *s.* (*desire*) envie violente *f.*; (*nostalgia*) nostalgie *f.*

hanky-panky *s.* méchant coup *m.*; **there is some ~ here,** il y a anguille sous roche.

Hanseatic *adj.* hanséatique.

hansom *s.* cab *m.*

haphazard *adj.* & **~ly** *adv.* au hasard.

hapless *adj.* infortuné.

happen *v.i.* (*occur*) arriver; *n.b. with a person as subject the verb is impersonal,* **if I ~ to see him,** s'il m'arrive de le voir; **if you ~ to come to Paris,** s'il vous arrive de venir à Paris; (*chance to be*) se trouver par hasard, **I ~ed to be in London,** je me trouvais par hasard à Londres; **~ing** *s.* événement *m.*

happy *adj.* **1.** (*lucky, fortunate*) heureux; **2.** (*content, glad*) content; **3.** (*felicitous*) heureux; **power,** *etc.* **-~,** ivre de pouvoir, etc.; **trigger--~,** à la gâchette facile; **~-go-lucky** *adj.* (*person*) insouciant; (*manner*) à la va comme je te pousse; **happily** *adv.* heureusement; **happiness** *s.* (1), (2) bonheur *m.*; (3) félicité *f.*

hara-kiri *s.* harakiri *m.*

harangue *s.* harangue *f.*; *v.t.* & *i.* haranguer.

harass *v.t.* **1.** (*worry, trouble*) tourmenter; **2.** (*attack repeatedly*) harceler; **~ment** *s.* (1) tourment *m.*; (2) harcèlement *m.*; ⚠ harasser = **to exhaust.**

harbinger *s.* avant-coureur *m.*

harbour *s.* (*naut.*) port *m.*; (*shelter*) asile *m.*; **inner ~,** arrière-port *m.*; **outer ~,** avant-port *m.*; **~ dues** *s.pl.* droits de mouillage *m.pl.*; **~-master** *s.* capitaine de port *m.*; *v.t.* (*shelter*) héberger; (*fig.*) nourrir; *v.i.* (*naut.*) se mettre à l'abri.

hard *s.* (*sloping roadway across foreshore*) cale *f.*; *adj.* **1.** (*firm, solid*) dur; **2.** (*stern, cruel*) sévère; **~ as nails,** impitoyable; **3.** (*difficult to do or bear*) difficile; **4.** (*water*) calcaire; **5.** (*drug*) toxique; **6.** (*weather*) rigoureux; **7.** (*frost*) fort; **~ and** FAST; **~board** *s.* isorel *m.*; **~ cash** *s.* espèces sonnantes *f.pl.*; **~ core** *s.* noyau *m.*, (*fig. fam.*) les durs *m.pl.*; **~ court** *s.* court en terre battue *m.*; **~-hearted** *adj.* au cœur dur; **~ labour** *s.* travaux forcés *m.pl.*; **~ lines,** pas de chance; **~ luck** *s.* malchance *f.*; **~ up** *adj.* gêné; **~ware** *s.* quincaillerie *f.*; **~wood** *s.* bois dur *m.*; *adv.* (2) fort, dur; (3) difficilement; **to freeze ~,** geler ferme; **to rain ~,** pleuvoir dru; **to be ~ put to it to do sth.,** avoir beaucoup de mal à faire qch.; **~ by** *adv.* tout près; **~-boiled** *adj.* (*cook.*) dur, (*fig.*) expérimenté; **~-working** *adj.* laborieux; **~en** *v.t.* & *i.* (*make or become ~*) durcir; (*techn.*) tremper; (*fig.*) endurcir; **~ening** *s.* durcissement *m.*, endurcissement *m.*; **~ly** *adv.* (*with difficulty*) durement, difficilement; (*scarcely*) à peine; **~ness** *s.* (1) dureté *f.*; (2) sévérité *f.*; (3) difficulté *f.*; (4) dureté *f.*; (6) rigueur *f.*

hardship *s.* (*circumstances*) rigueur *f.*; (*severe suffering*) épreuve *f.*, privation *f.*

hard/y *adj.* **1.** (*bold*) hardi; **2.** (*robust*) robuste; **3.** (*able to resist cold, etc.*) résistant; ⚠ hardi = (1) *only*; **~ihood** *s.* (1) hardiesse *f.*; **~ily** *adv.* (1) hardiment; (2) vigoureusement; **~iness** *s.* (2) vigueur *f.*; (3) robustesse *f.*

hare *s.* lièvre *m.*; JUGged **~**; **~bell** *s.* campanule *f.*; **~lip** *s.* bec de lièvre *m.*

harem *s.* harem *m.*

hark *v.i.* (*usu.* **~** *to*) écouter; **~ back to,** revenir toujours sur.

harlequin *s.* arlequin *m.*; **~ade** *s.* arlequinade *f.*

harlot *s.* prostituée *f.*

harm *s.* **1.** (*injury*) mal *m.*; **2.** (*moral wrong*) tort *m.*, préjudice *f.*; *v.t.* (1) faire du mal à; (2) faire du tort à, porter préjudice à; **~ful** *adj.* nuisible; **~fully** *adv.* d'une manière nuisible; **~fulness** *s.* (*of person*) caractère malfaisant *m.*, (*of thing*) nocivité *f.*; **~less** *adj.* inoffensif; **~lessly** *adv.* sans mal; **~lessness** *s.* caractère inoffensif *m.*

harmattan *s.* harmattan *m.*

harmonic *adj.* & *s.* (*mus.*) harmonique *m. or f.*; **~s** *s.* harmonie *f.*; **~ally** *adv.**.

harmonica *s.* harmonica *m.*

harmonium *s.* harmonium *m.*

harmon/y *s.* (*mus.*; *pleasant sound*; *fig.*) harmonie *f.*; **in ~ with,** en harmonie avec; **~ious** *adj.* harmonieux; **~iously** *adv.**; **~ist** *s.* harmoniste *m.f.*; **~ize** *v.t.* & *i.* (s')harmoniser (*with*—avec).

harness *s.* (*for horse, for baby*) harnais *m.*; (*parachute*) ceinture *f.*; **in ~** (*fig.*) attelé à la besogne; **~-maker** *s.* bourrelier *m.*; **~-room** *s.* sellerie *f.*; *v.t.* (*horse*) harnacher; (*use power, etc.*) aménager.

harp *s.* harpe *f.*; *v.i.* (*play the ~*) jouer de la harpe; (*fig.* **~** *on*) chanter toujours la même antienne, rabâcher; **~ist** *s.* harpiste *m.f.*

harpoon *s.* harpon *m.*; *v.t.* harponner.

harpsichord *s.* clavecin *m.*

harpy *s.* (*monster* & *woman*) harpie *f.*

harquebus *s.* arquebuse *f.*

harridan *s.* vieille sorcière *f.*

harrier *s.* (*dog*) lévrier *m.*; (*sport*) coureur de cross *m.*

harrow *s.* (*agric.*) herse *f.*; *v.t.* (*agric.*) herser; (*distress, heart, etc.*) déchirer; (*person*) affliger, navrer; **~ing** *adj.* déchirant, navrant.

harry *v.t.* (*ravage*) ravager; (*harass*) harceler.

harsh *adj.* **1.** (*unfeeling, severe, strict*) rude, sévère, dur; **2.** (*rough*): (*to ear*) discordant, (*to taste*) âpre, (*to eye*) déplaisant, (*to touch*) rêche; **~ly** *adv.* (1), (2) durement; **~ness** *s.* (1) dureté *f.*; (2) discordance *f.*; âpreté *f.*; aspect déplaisant *m.*; rudesse *f.*

hart *s.* cerf *m.*; **~shorn** *s.* ammoniaque *m.*

harum-scarum *s.* tête de linotte *f.*; *adj.* écervelé.

harvest *s.* **1.** (*season* & *fig.*) moisson *f.*; **2.** (*yield, crops*) récolte *f.*; GRAPE **~**; **~-bug** *s.* aoûtat *m.*; **~ home** *s.* fête de la moisson *f.*; *v.t.* (1) moissonner; (2) récolter; *v.i.* faire la moisson; **~er** *s.* (*person*) moissonneur *m.*, (*machine*) moissonneuse *f.*; COMBINE **~er.**

has-been *s.* (*fam.*) croulant(e) *m.f.*; *adj.* (*fam.*) décati(e).

hash *s.* **1.** (*cook.*) hachis *m.*; **2.** (*mess*) gâchis *m.*; **to make a ~ of sth.,** faire un joli gâchis de qch.; **to settle s.o.'s ~,** régler son compte à qn.; *v.t.* (1) hacher.

hashish *s.* haschisch *or* haschich *m.*

hasp *s.* moraillon *m.*; (*of door*) loquet *m.*

hassle *s.* (*pop.*) (*quarrel*) chamaillerie *f.*, (*bustle*) pagaille *f.*; *v.i.* discutailler.

hassock *s.* (*church*) agenouilloir *m.*; pouf *m.*

hast/e *s.* (*quick movement*) précipitation *f.*; (*hurry*) hâte *f.*; **in ~e,** en hâte, à la hâte; **to make ~e,** se dépêcher; **post ~e,** en toute hâte; **more ~e less speed,** hâte-toi lentement; **~en** *v.t.* & *i.* (se) hâter; **~y** *adj.* **1.** (*hurried*) précipité; **2.** (*rash*) irréfléchi; **3.** (*quick-tempered*) emporté; **~ily** *adv.* (1) à la hâte; (2) à la légère; (3) vivement; **~iness** *s.* (1) précipitation *f.*; (2) impatience *f.*; (3) vivacité *f.*

hat *s.* chapeau *m.*; **bowler ~,** chapeau melon *m.*; OPERA **~**; **top ~,** chapeau haut-de-forme *m.*; BAD **~**; BRASS **~**; COCK**ed ~**; TIN **~**; **to take off one's ~ to s.o.,** tirer son chapeau à qn.; **~band** *s.* ruban *m.*; **~-box** *s.* carton à chapeaux *m.*; **~**-PIN; **~ shop** *s.* modiste *f.*; **~-stand** *s.* porte-chapeau *m.*; **~ter** *s.* chapelier *m.*; **mad as a ~ter,** fou à lier.

hatch *s.* (*lower half of door*) demi-battant *m.*; (*hole in floor, trap-door*) trappe *f.*; (*for food*) passe-plat *m.*; (*in office, etc.*) guichet *m.*; (*floodgate*) vanne *f.*; (*naut.*) panneau (de cale) *m.*; **~way** *s.* (*naut.*) écoutille *f.*; *v.t.* (*eggs*) faire couver; (*incubate*) faire éclore; (*fig.*) couver, tramer; *v.i.* éclore; **to count one's chickens before they are ~ed,** vendre la peau de l'ours avant de l'avoir mis à terre; **~ery** *s.* (*fish*) alevinier *m. or* alevinière *f.*

hatchet *s.* hachette *f.*; **to** BURY **the ~**; **~-faced** *adj.* à la figure en lame de couteau.

hatchment *s.* (*herald.*) écusson funéraire *m.*

hat/e *s.* haine *f.*; *v.t.* (*dislike strongly, detest*) haïr, avoir en horreur; (*bear malice*) en vouloir à qn. (à cause de qch.); **~eful** *adj.* haïssable; **~efully** *adv.* odieusement; **~efulness** *s.* caractère odieux *m.*; **~red** *s.* haine *f.*; **man-~er** *s.* misanthrope *m.*; **woman-~er** *s.* misogyne *m.*

haught/y *adj.* hautain; (*lofty*) altier; **~ily** *adv.* avec hauteur; d'un air altier; **~iness** *s.* hauteur *f.*

haul *s.* (*~ing*) traction *f.*; (*distance*) trajet *m.*; (*catch of fish*) coup de filet *m.*; (*booty*) prise *f.*; *v.t.* (*pull or drag*) traîner; (*tow*) remorquer; (*transport by cart, etc.*) camionner; (*naut. ~ in*) haler; **~ down** *v.t.* amener; **~ s.o. over the** COALS; **~age** *s.* camionnage *m.*; **~ier** *s.* routier *m.*

ha(u)lm *s.* fane *f.*

haunch *s.* (*anat.*) hanche *f.*; **~es** (*fam.*) derrière *m.*; **~ of venison,** cuissot *m.*

haunt *s.* lieu fréquenté *m.* (par); (*of criminals, etc.*) repaire *m.*; *v.t.* (*ghosts*) hanter; (*be frequently in a place or with s.o.*) fréquenter; (*obsess*) obséder; **to be ~ed by,** être hanté par.

hautboy *s.* hautbois *m.*

have *s.* (*pop. = swindle*) blague *f.*; **the ~s and the ~-nots,** les riches et les pauvres; *v.t.* (*possess*) avoir, posséder; (*meals*) prendre; (*enjoy*) jouir de; (*endure*) supporter, tolérer; (*know*) savoir; (*maintain, state*) soutenir, prétendre; (*fam. cheat*) rouler; **~ a good time,** s'amuser; **I won't ~ this nonsense,** je ne veux pas de cette idiotie; **~ sth. done,** faire faire qch., **we are having our car repaired,** nous faisons réparer notre auto; **you had better go,** vous feriez mieux de partir; **~ just,** venir de, **he has just arrived,** il vient d'arriver; **he's had it** (*fam.*) il est fichu; **~ it in for s.o.,** avoir une dent contre qn.; **~ it out with s.o.,** vider une affaire avec qn.; **~ on** (*wear*) porter, (*fam. trick*) rouler; **~ up,** arrêter; **~ to** (*obligation*) devoir, il faut, **I ~ to leave,** je dois partir, il faut que je parte; *aux. verb. compound tenses as in Eng.*, **I ~ done, I had done, I shall ~ done, I should ~ done,** j'ai fait, j'avais fait, j'aurai fait, j'aurais fait; *similar tenses of* être *with refl.* & *certain other verbs*, **I ~ rested, I had rested, I shall ~ rested, I should ~ rested,** je me suis reposé, je m'étais reposé, je me serai reposé, je me serais reposé; **I ~ come, I had come, I shall ~ come, I should ~ come,** je suis venu, j'étais venu, je serai venu, je serais venu; ⚠ **I ~ been here for two days,** *see* FOR.

haven *s.* (*harbour*) havre *m.*; (*refuge*) asile *m.*

haversack *s.* havresac *m.*

havoc *s.* ravages *m.pl.*; **to play ~ with,** causer des dégâts à.

haw[1] *s.* (*bot.*) cenelle *f.*; **~thorn** *s.* aubépine *f.*

haw[2] *v.i.* **to** HEM **and ~.**

Hawaii *s.* (*geog.*) îles Hawaii *f.pl.*; **~an** *adj.* & *s.m.f.* hawaien(ne).

hawk[1] *s.* (*bird*) faucon *m.*; (*fig. person*) vautour *m.*; **~ing** *s.* chasse au faucon *f.*

hawk[2] *v.t.* & *i.* **1.** (*clear throat*) graillonner; **2.** (*carry about for sale*) colporter; **~er** *s.* (2) colporteur *m.*; (*door to door*) camelot *m.*; **~ing** *s.* (1) graillonnement *m.*; (2) colportage *m.*

hawser *s.* haussière *f.*

hawthorn see HAW.

hay *s.* foin *m.*; **to make ~,** faire les foins; **to make ~ while the sun shines** (*fig.*) battre le fer pendant qu'il est chaud; **~cock** *s.* meulon *m.*; **~ fever** *s.* rhume des foins *m.*; **~-fork** *s.* fourche à foin *f.*; **~loft** *s.* fenil *m.*; **~maker** *s.* faneur *m.*; **~making** *s.* fenaison *f.*; **~rick, ~stack** *s.* meule de foin *f.*; **to look for a** NEEDLE **in a ~stack; ~wire** *adj.* (*fam.*) (*in disorder*) chambardé, (*crazy*) écervelé.

hazard *s.* (*game, chance*) hasard *m.*; (*risk*) risque *m.*; **at all ~s,** à tout hasard; *v.t.* (*expose to ~*) hasarder; (*run risk of*) risquer (de); (*venture, guess*) hasarder; **~ous** *adj.* hasardeux.

haz/e *s.* **1.** (*mist*) brume *f.*; **2.** (*fig. mental daze*) brouillard *m.*; **~iness** *s.* (1) état brumeux *m.*; (2) vague *m.*; **~y** *adj.* (1) brumeux; (2) vague.

hazel *s.* (*tree*) noisetier *m.*; (*colour*) couleur noisette; **~-nut** *s.* noisette *f.*

H.C.F. (*highest common factor*) P.G.C.D. (plus grand comun diviseur) *m.*

he *pron.* (*subject*) il; **~** *did it*, il l'a fait; (*emphatic*) lui; **it was ~ who did it,** c'est lui qui l'a fait; **~ and I,** lui et moi; (*with* être) ce; **~ is my father,** c'est mon père; **~ is a writer, etc.,** c'est un écrivain, etc.; *s.* mâle *m.*, homme *m.*; **~-man,** homme à poigne *m.*; **~-goat, etc.** bouc *m.*; *usu. special word, e.g.* **~-bear,** ours *m.*

H.E. (*His Excellency*) S.E. (son Excellence) *f.*

head *s.* (*anat.*) tête *f.*; (*as measure*) tête *f.*; BEAR **with sore ~; to make neither ~ nor tail of sth.,** n'y comprendre rien; (*intellect*) tête *f.*; **to have a good ~ on one's shoulders,** avoir de la tête; **to have a good ~ for business, etc.,** s'entendre aux affaires, etc.; (*of coin or medal*) face *f.*; **~s or tails,** pile ou face; **crowned ~,** tête couronnée *f.*; **twenty ~ of cattle,** vingt têtes de bétail; (*thing like ~*): (*of nail, pin*) tête *f.*, **hit the** NAIL **on the ~,** (*of arrow*) pointe *f.*, (*of hammer*) fer *m.*, (*of stick*) pommeau *m.*, (*foam* *on beer, etc.*) mousse *f.*, faux-col *m.*, (*of record--player, etc.*) tête *f.*; (*top, of list, page, etc.*) haut *m.*, tête *f.*; (*of table*) bout *m.*; PIT-~; (*promontory*) cap *m.*; (*ruler, chief*) chef *m.*; *adj.* principal; **at the ~ of,** à la tête de; (*~ing, category*) chef *m.*, rubrique *f.*; (*title*) en-tête *m.*; (*culmination*) aboutissement *m.*, (*crisis*) crise *f.*; **to come to a ~,** aboutir; **to bring to a ~,** faire aboutir, amener une crise; **to get or take it into one's ~ that,** se mettre dans la tête que/de; **to let s.o. have his ~,** donner libre carrière à qn.; **to go to a person's ~** (*of liquor, success, etc.*) monter à la tête de qn.; **~ first,** la tête la première; (*fig.*) précipitamment; **to keep one's ~,** garder son sang-froid; **to keep one's ~ above water** (*fig.*) être à flot; **to put ~s together,** se consulter; **to lose one's ~** (*lit.* & *fig.*) perdre sa tête; **to go off one's ~,** perdre la boule; **~ache** *s.* mal de tête *m.*; **~board** *s.* tête de lit *f.*; **~ clerk** *s.* chef de bureau *m.*; **~ cook and bottle washer,** factotum *m.*; **~-dress** *s.* coiffure *f.*; **~gear** *s.* couvre-chef *m.*; **~land** *s.* promontoire *m.*; **~light, ~lamp** *s.* (*auto.*) phare *m.*; **~line** *s.* manchette *f.*, titre *m.*, BANNER **~lines; ~long** *adv.* la tête la première; **~man** *s.* chef *m.*; **~sman** *s.* bourreau *m.*; **~master, ~mistress,** directeur *m.*, directrice *f.*; ~ OFFICE; **~-on,** de front; **~quarters** *s.* quartier--général *m.*; **~-rest** *s.* appui-tête *m.*; **~room** *s.* hauteur libre *f.*; **~stone** *s.* pierre tombale *f.*; **~strong** *adj.* entêté; **~way** *s.* progrès *m.*; **~ wind** *s.* vent debout *m.*; *v.t.* (*lead, direct*) diriger, tourner (*towards*—vers); (*be at ~ of*) être à la tête de; (*football*) jouer de la tête; **~ for,** se diriger vers; (*naut.*) mettre le cap sur; **~ off** (*fig.*) détourner; **~er** *s.* (*dive*) plongeon *m.*, (*football*) tête *f.*; **~ing** *s.* en-tête *m.*; **~y** *adj.* (*impetuous*) impétueux, (*wine*) capiteux, (*scent*) entêtant.

heal *v.t.* & *i.* (se) guérir; (*fig.*) (s')apaiser; **~er** *s.* (*unqualified*) guérisseur *m.*; **~ing** *s.* guérison *f.*

health *s.* santé *f.*; (*toast*) toast *m.*; **to drink s.o.'s ~,** boire à la santé de qn.; **National H~,** (service de) Sécurité Sociale; **public ~,** santé publique *f.*; ~ RESORT; **~ful** *adj.* (*air*) salubre, (*effect*) salutaire; **~y** *adj.* sain; **~ily** *adv.**; **~iness** *s.* santé *f.*, (*of climate, etc.*) salubrité *f.*

heap *s.* (*pile*) amas *m.*; (*pop. large no. or amount*) tas *m.*; *v.t.* (*load*) charger (de); (*accumulate*) **~ up,** entasser.

hear *v.t.* (*perceive with ear* & *be willing to ~*) entendre; (*listen to*) écouter; *v.i.* apprendre; **~ of,** entendre dire qch. (à, par, qn.); entendre parler de qch.; **~ from,** recevoir des nouvelles de; **~! ~!,** bravo!; **~er** *s.* audit/eur, -rice *m.f.*; **~ers** *s.pl.* auditoire *m.*; **~ing** *s.* (*sense*) ouïe *f.*; (*law, etc.*) audition *f.*; **hard of ~ing,** dur d'oreille; **in my ~ing,** en ma présence; **~ing aid** *s. see* DEAF-**aid; ~say** *s.* ouï-dire *m.*

hearken *v.i.* prêter l'oreille (*to*—à).

hearse *s.* corbillard *m.*

heart *s.* (*anat.*; *emotion, affection*; *soul, mind*; *courage*; *central part*; *~-shaped thing*; *cards*) cœur *m.*; **~ to ~** *adj.* & *s.m.* tête à tête; **after one's own ~,** selon son cœur; **at ~,** au fond; **by ~,** par cœur; **to lose ~,** perdre courage; **to take ~,** prendre courage; **to take to ~,** prendre à cœur; **with all one's ~,** de tout son cœur; **not to have the ~ to,** ne pas avoir le courage de; COCKLES **of the ~; ~ache** *s.* chagrin *m.*; **~-break** *s.* chagrin *m.*; **~-breaking** *adj.* déchirant; **~-broken** *adj.* navré; **~burn** *s.* brûlures d'estomac *f.pl.*; **~felt** *adj.* du fond du cœur; **~-rending** *adj.* navrant; **~-searching** *s.* scrupule *m.*, *adj.* pénétrant; **~en** *v.t.* encourager; **~less** *adj.* impitoyable; **~lessly** *adv.**; **~less-ness** *s.* dureté *f.*, insensibilité *f.*

hearth *s.* foyer *m.*; **~ rug,** carpette *f.*

heart/y *adj.* **1.** (*vigorous*) vigoureux; HALE **and ~y; 2.** (*genial*) cordial, chaleureux; **3.** (*sincere*) sincère; **4.** (*copious*) copieux, (*eater*) gros; **~ily** *adv.* (1)*; (2)*,*; (3)*; (4)*; **~iness** *s.* (1) vigueur *f.*; (2) cordialité *f.*; (3) sincérité *f.*

heat *s.* (*lit.* & *fig.*) chaleur *f.*; (*in competition*) manche *f.*; (*fam. fig. pressure*) pression *f.*; **~--stroke** *s.* coup de chaleur *m.*; **~ wave** *s.* vague de chaleur *f.*; *v.t.* chauffer; (*fig.*) échauffer; *v.i.* s'échauffer; **~ed** *adj.* chauffé, (*fig.*) chaud, (*person*) échauffé; **~er** *s.* appareil de chauffage *m.*, radiateur *m.*; **immersion ~er,** chauffe-eau électrique *m.invar.*; STORAGE **~er; ~ing** *s.* chauffage *m.*; **central ~ing** *s.* chauffage central *m.*

heath *s.* (*tract of land*) lande *f.*; (*heather*) bruyère *f.*; **~er** *s.* bruyère *f.*

heathen *adj.* & *s.m.f.* païen(ne).

heave *s.* soulèvement *m.*; *v.t.* (*lift, raise*) lever, soulever; (*throw*) lancer; (*sigh*) pousser; (*naut.*) haler; *v.i.* (*swell, rise*) se soulever; (*pant*) haleter; **~ to** (*naut.*) se mettre en panne; **~ in sight,** apparaître.

heaven *s.* (*sky*) ciel *m.* (*pl.* ciels); (*eccles.*) ciel *m.* (*pl. collective* cieux), paradis *m.*; (*fig.*) béatitude *f.*; **good ~s!** *interj.* bonté divine!; **~ forbid!,** plût à Dieu que non!; **to move ~ and earth,** remuer ciel et terre; **~ly** *adj.* céleste, (*fam.*) divin.

heav/y *adj.* (*of great weight*) lourd, pesant; (*compact, dense*) gros; (*laden*) chargé (*with*—de); (*abundant*) lourd; (*food*) lourd; (*ground*) gras; (*fig. dull, tedious*) lourd, triste; **~y** WEATHER; **~y-handed** *adj.* (*clumsy*) maladroit, (*severe*) oppressif; **~yweight** *s.* poids lourd *m.*; **~ily** *adv.* lourdement, pesamment; **~iness** *s.* lourdeur *f.*, (*weight*) poids *m.*, (*fig.*) abattement *m.*

hebdomadal *adj.* hebdomadaire.

Hebr/ew *s.* (*lang.*) hébreu *m.*; *adj.* & *s.m.* hébreu, ♀ israélite, juive *f.* **~aic** *adj.* hébraïque; **~aism** *s.* hébraïsme *m.*; **~aist** *s.* hébraïsant *m.*

hecatomb *s.* hécatombe *f.*

heckle *v.t.* (*harass*) harceler; (*interrupt*) interrompre; **~r** *s.* contradicteur *m.*

hectic *adj.* (*med.*) hectique; (*fam.*) (*person*) agité, (*time*) mouvementé, (*thing*) enivrant.

hecto/gram *s.* hectogramme *m.*; **~litre** *s.* hectolitre *m.*; **~metre** *s.* hectomètre *m.*

hector *s.* matamore *m.*; *v.t.* malmener; *v.i.* faire le matamore.

hedge *s.* haie *f.*; (*fence*) barrière *f.*; **~hog** *s.* hérisson *m.*; **~row** *s.* bordure de haies *f.*; **~--sparrow** *s.* troglodyte *m.*; *v.t.* (*surround with ~*) entourer d'une haie; (*cut ~*) tailler les haies; (*secure against loss*) compenser; *v.i.* (*avoid committing oneself*) chercher des échappatoires; **~r** *s.* tailleur de haies *m.*

hedon/ism *s.* hédonisme *m.*; **~ist** *s.* hédoniste *m.*

heed *s.* attention *f.*; **to pay ~ to,** faire attention à; **to take ~ of,** prendre garde à; *v.t.* (*take notice of*) prendre garde à; (*attend to*) faire attention à; **~ful** *adj.* attentif; (*careful*) prudent; **~fully** *adv.**,*; **~fulness** *s.* attention *f.*; prudence *f.*; **~less** *adj.* inattentif, insouciant; **~lessly** *adv.* sans faire attention; avec insouciance; **~lessness** *s.* inattention *f.*; insouciance *f.*

hee-haw *s.* hi-han *m.*; *v.i.* braire.

heel *s.* (*anat.* & *of sock, shoe, etc.*) talon *m.*; (*fam. person*) canaille *f.*; DOWN **at ~; to** COOL **or** KICK **one's ~s; to take to one's ~s,** tourner les talons; *v.t.* & *i.* (*shoes*) remettre des talons à; (*rugby*) talonner; (*naut.*) donner de la bande; **well-~ed** *adj.* bien pourvu.

hefty *adj.* robuste; (*fam. sturdy*) costaud.

hegemony *s.* hégémonie *f.*

heifer *s.* génisse *f.*

heigh-ho *interj.* (*boredom, disappointment*) oh!; (*surprise*) eh!; (*ironic*) ça y est!
height *s.* (*from base to top*) hauteur *f.*; (*elevation*) élévation *f.*; (*high point*) éminence *f.*; (*top*) sommet *m.*; (*fig.*) comble *m.*; **to be at its ~,** battre son plein; **~ of fashion,** (à la) toute dernière mode; **at the ~ of the season,** en pleine saison; **~en** *v.t.* (*raise higher*) relever; (*intensify*) rehausser; (*exaggerate*) augmenter.
heinous *adj.* odieux; **~ly** *adv.**; **~ness** *s.* atrocité *f.*
heir(ess) *s.m.f.* héritier *m.*, héritière *f.*; **~ apparent,** héritier naturel *m.*; **~ presumptive,** héritier présomptif *m.*; **~dom** *s.* héritage *m.*; **~less** *adj.* sans héritier; **~loom** *s.* bijou, *m.* meuble, *m.* etc. de famille.
helicopter *s.* hélicoptère *m.*
helio/graph *s.* héliographe *m.*; **~scope** *s.* hélioscope *m.*
heliotrope *s.* héliotrope *m.*
heliport *s.* héliport *m.*
helium *s.* hélium *m.*
helix *s.* (*med.*) hélix *m.*; (*math.*) hélice *f.*
hell *s.* (*eccles.* & *fig.*) enfer *m.*; *interj.* zut!; **a ~ of a noise, etc.,** un bruit (etc.) infernal; **to go ~ for leather,** brûler les étapes; **to** RAISE **~**; **~ish** *adj.* infernal; **~ishly** *adv.**.
Hellen/e *adj.* & *s.m.f.* hellène; **~ic** *adj.* hellénique; **~ism** *s.* hellénisme *m.*; **~ist** *s.* helléniste *m.f.*
hello! *see* HALLO.
helm *s.* barre *f.*, gouvernail *m.*; **to be at, to take, the ~,** (*lit.* & *fig.*) être à la barre, tenir la barre; **~sman** *s.* homme de barre *m.*
helmet *s.* casque *m.*; **crash ~,** casque de motocycliste.
helot *s.* ilote *m.f.*; **~ism** *s.* ilotisme *m.*
help *s.* **1.** (*assistance*) aide *f.*; **2.** (*domestic servant*) aide ménagère *f.*; **3.** (*remedy*) remède *m.*; **4.** (*~er*) aide *m.*; *interj.* au secours!; *v.t.* (1) aider, secourir; (3) remédier (à); (*prevent*) empêcher; (*avoid*) éviter; **not to be able to ~ oneself,** ne pas pouvoir s'empêcher de; (*make easier*) faciliter, arranger; *v.refl.*; **~ oneself to food,** se servir; **it can't be ~ed,** il n'y a rien à faire; **~er** *s.* aide *m.*, assistant *m.*, collaborateur *m.*; **~ful** *adj.* (*person*) serviable, (*thing*) utile; **~fully** *adv.* utilement; **~fulness** *s.* aide *f.*; **~ing** *s.* (*of food*) portion *f.*, **to take a second ~ing of sth.,** en reprendre; **~ing** *adj.* secourable; **~less** *adj.* sans recours, (*incapable, powerless*) incapable, impuissant, (*abandoned*) désemparé, délaissé; **~lessly** *adv.* sans secours, sans espoir; **~lessness** *s.* impuissance *f.*, incapacité *f.*; **~mate** *s.* compagnon *m.*, compagne *f.*, (*wife*) épouse *f.*
helter-skelter *s.* tohu-bohu *m.*; *adv.* pêle-mêle.
Helvetian *s.m.f.* helvète; *adj.* helvétique.
hem[1] *s.* ourlet *m.*; (*edge*) bord *m.*; *v.t.* ourler; border; **~ about, in, round,** entourer (de); **~-stitch** *s.* ourlet à jour *m.*; *v.t.* ourler à jour.
hem[2] *interj.* hem!; **to ~ and haw,** ânonner.
hemi- (*in combination*), **~cycle** *s.* hémicycle *m.*; **~sphere** *s.* hémisphère *m.*; **~stitch** *s.* hémistiche *m.*
hemlock *s.* ciguë *f.*
hemorrhage *see* HAEM-.
hemp *s.* chanvre *m.*; (*drug*) chanvre indien *m.*, kif *m.*; **~en** *adj.* de chanvre.
hen *s.* poule *f.*; (*birds, etc.*) femelle *f.*; adj. femelle; **~-house,** poulailler *m.*; **~ pecked** *adj.* mené par le bout du nez.
hence *adv.* (*place*) d'ici; (*time*) d'ici, à partir d'aujourd'hui; (*result*) d'où; **~forth, ~-forward,** désormais.
henchman *s.* (*hist.*) écuyer *m.*, page *m.*; (*polit.*) partisan *m.*
henna *s.* henné *m.*
hept/agon *s.* heptagone *m.*; **~agonal** *adj.* heptagonal; **~archy** *s.* heptarchie *f.*
her (*pron.* (*direct object*) la; **I know ~,** je la connais; (*ind. object*) lui; **I speak to ~,** je lui parle; (*emphatic*) elle, **with ~,** avec elle; *adj.* son, sa, ses.
herald *s.* **1.** (*official*) héraut *m.*; **2.** (*messenger*) messager *m.*; **3.** (*forerunner*) avant-coureur *m.*; *v.t.* (2) annoncer; (3) proclamer; (*usher in*) introduire; **~ic** *adj.* héraldique; **~ry** *s.* blason *m.*
herb *s.* (*bot.*) herbe *f.*; (*cook.*) herbe potagère *f.*; (*med.*) herbe médicinale *f.*; **~aceous** *adj.* herbacé; **~age** *s.* herbage *m.*; **~al** *adj.* des herbes; *s.* herbier *m.*; **~alist** *s.* herboriste *m.f.*; **~arium** *s.* herbier *m.*; **~icide** *s.* herbicide *m.*; **~ivorous** *adj.* herbivore.
Hercul/es *s.* Hercule; **~ean** *adj.* herculéen.
herd *s.* (*of cattle*; & *pop. pej. of people*) troupeau *m.*; *v.t.* rassembler en troupeau; *v.i.* s'attrouper; **~sman** *s.* berger *m.*, bouvier *m.*
here *adv.* (*place, time*) ici; *interj.* (*answer to call*) présent!; (*wait*) tenez!; **look ~,** dites donc!; **~ and there,** çà et là; **~ is, are,** voici; **~ is my son,** voici mon fils; **~ are your gloves,** voici vos gants; **~ he, she, it, is,** le voici, la voici, le/la voici; **~ I am,** me voici; **~ they are,** les voici; **~ we are,** nous voici; **that is neither ~ nor there,** cela n'a rien à voir avec la chose; **~abouts** *adv.* aux environs; **~after** *s.* l'autre monde *m.*; *adv.* plus tard; **~by** *adv.* par ceci; par là; (*law*) par le présent acte; **~in** *adv.* en ceci; ci-inclus; **~inafter** *adv.* ci-après; **~of,** de ceci; à ce sujet; **~to** *adv.* en outre; ci-joint; **~tofore** *adv.* jusqu'ici; ci-devant; **~upon** *adv.* là-dessus; **~with** *adv.* ci-joint.
heredit/y *s.* hérédité *f.*; **~ament** *s.* (*law*) bien transmissible par héritage *m.*; **~ary** *adj.* héréditaire.
here/sy *s.* hérésie *f.*; **~tic** *adj.* & *s.m.f.* hérétique.
heritage *s.* héritage *m.*
hermaphrodite *adj.* & *s.m.* hermaphrodite.
hermetic *adj.* hermétique; **~ally** *adv.**.
hermit *s.* ermite *m.*; **~-crab,** bernard-l'ermite *m.*; **~age** *s.* ermitage *m.*
hernia *s.* hernie *f.*
hero *s.* héros *m.* (⚠ le *not* l'); **~-worship** *s.* culte du héros *m.*; *v.t.* avoir un véritable culte pour; **~ic** *adj.* héroïque; **~ically** *adv.**; **~ine** *s.* héroïne *f.* (l'); **~ism** *s.* héroïsme *m.*
heroin *s.* héroïne *f.*
heron *s.* héron *m.*; **~ry** *s.* héronnière *f.*
herpes *s.* herpès *m.*
herring *s.* hareng *m.*; RED **~**; **~-bone** *s.* (*stitch*) point de chausson *m.*; **~-bone** *adj.* (*pattern*) à chevrons.
hers *pron.* à elle; le sien, la sienne, les siens, les siennes; **this book is ~,** ce livre est à elle; **it is ~,** c'est le sien.
herself *pron.* elle-même; *refl. pron.* se.
hesit/ate *v.i.* hésiter (*to*—à); **~ancy** *s.* incertitude *f.*; **~ant** *adj.* hésitant; **~atingly** *adv.* avec hésitation; **~ation** *s.* hésitation *f.*
hetero- (*in combination*) **~clite** *adj.* hétéroclite; **~dox** *adj.* hétérodoxe; **~doxy** *s.* hétérodoxie *f.*; **~geneous** *adj.* hétérogène; **~geneity** *s.* hétérogénéité *f.*; **~sexual** *adj.* hétérosexuel.
hew *v.t.* (*cut with axe, etc.*) couper; (*cut into shape*) tailler; (*cut coal from seam*) attaquer au pic; **~er** *s.* tailleur *m.*
hexagon *s.* hexagone *m.*; **~al** *adj.* hexagonal.
hexameter *s.* hexamètre *m.*
hey *interj.* hé!; (*queston*) hein?
heyday *s.* (*of youth*) fleur *f.*; (*of life*) printemps *m.*; (*of achievements, etc.*) comble *m.*; **to be in its ~,** battre son plein.
hi! *interj.* ohé!
hiatus *s.* (*ling.*) hiatus *m.*; (*gap*) lacune *f.*

hibernat/e *v.i.* (*zool.*) hiberner; (*fig.*) somnoler; **~ion** *s.* hibernation *f.*
hiccup, hiccough *s.* hoquet *m.*; *v.i.* avoir le hoquet.
hid/e[1] *s.* (*animal's skin*) peau *f.*; (*dressed*) cuir *m.*; **~ebound** *adj.* (*fig.*) bigot; **~ing** *s.* (*fam. thrashing*) râclée *f.*
hid/e[2] *v.t.* & *i.* (*conceal*) (se) cacher; (*keep secret*) dissimuler; (*obstruct view*) dérober à la vue; **~e-and-seek** *s.* cache-cache *m.*; **~ing-place** *s.* cachette *f.*; **~e-out** *s.* (*pop.*) planque *f.*
hideous *adj.* **1.** (*ugly*) hideux; **2.** (*repulsive*) affreux; **3.** (*of crime, etc.*) atroce; **~ly** *adv.* (1)*; (2)*; (3)*; **~ness** *s.* (1) hideur *f.*; (3) atrocité *f.*
hie *v.i.* (*poet.*) se hâter (vers).
hierarch/y *s.* hiérarchie *f.*; **~ical** *adj.* hiérarchique.
hieroglyph *s.* hiéroglyphe *m.*; **~ic** *adj.* hiéroglyphique; **~ics** *s.pl.* hiéroglyphes *m.pl.*
hi-fi (*Eng. fam. for high-fidelity*) *s.* haute fidélité *f.*; *adj.* de haute fidélité.
higgledy-piggledy *adj.* & *adv.* pêle-mêle.
high *s.* (*degree, place*) haut *m.*; (*auto.* = *top gear*) quatrième vitesse *f.*; (*meteor.*) haute pression *f.*; *adj.* (*of great upward extent*) haut; **~ heels,** des talons hauts; **~ mountains,** de hautes montagnes; **a ~ collar,** un col haut; **2 metres ~,** haut de deux mètres; (*of exalted rank*) haut, élevé; **the Most H~,** le Très-Haut; **~ card,** haute carte; (*of ~ quality*) haut (*before the s.*); **~ society,** la haute société; **~er** (*in rank or quality*) supérieur; **~est** (*in rank or quality*) suprême; (*on drugs, etc.*) complètement parti; (*of meat, etc.*) avancé, faisandé; (*great, intense, extreme, powerful*) grand (*before the s.*), fort (*before the s.*), extrême, puissant; **~ temperature,** forte température; **~ esteem,** haute estime; (*of price*) élevé; (*of sound*) haut, aigu; *adv.* haut, en haut; (=*on ~*) en haut; (*in a ~ degree*) fortement; **~ altar** *s.* maître-autel *m.*; **~ball,** whisky-soda *m.*; **~-born** *adj.* de haute naissance; **~brow** *adj.* & *s.m.* intellectuel; **~-class** *adj.* de première qualité, supérieur; **~er education,** enseignement supérieur *m.*; **~ explosive,** *adj.* de haute puissance; **~ frequency** *adj.* à haute fréquence; **~-handed** *adj.* autoritaire; **~** JUMP (*sport* & *fig.*); **~land** *s.* pays montagneux *m.*; **~lands** *s.pl.* Hautes-Terres *f.pl.*; **~lander** *s.* montagnard *m.*; **~-level** *adj.* à un niveau supérieur; **~light** *v.t.* faire ressortir; **~lights** *s.* (*art*) rehaut *m.*, (*fig.*) trait marquant *m.*; **~-minded** *adj.* magnanime; **~-pitched** *adj.* aïgu; **~-powered** *adj.* à grande puissance; **~ priest,** grand-prêtre *m.*; **~-rise block,** tour (d'habitation) *f.*; **~road,** grand-route *f.*; **~school,** lycée *m.*; **~ seas,** le (grand) large; **~-spirited,** plein d'entrain; **~ spirits,** entrain *m.*; **H~ Street,** grand'rue, *f.*; **~ tea,** collation du soir *f.*; **it was ~ time,** il était temps; **~ water,** marée haute *f.*; **~way** *s.* grand-route *f.*; **H~way** CODE; **~wayman** *s.* voleur de grand chemin *m.*; **~ly** *adv.* (*degree*) hautement, extrêmement, (*favourably*) favorablement; **H~ness** *s.* (*title*) Altesse *f.*
hijack *s.* détournement (illicite) *m.*; *v.t.* détourner; **~er** *s.* pirate de l'air *m.*
hike *s.* excursion à pied *f.*; *v.i.* faire une excursion à pied; HITCH-~.
hilar/ity *s.* hilarité *f.*; **~ious** *adj.* hilare.
hill *s.* (*rising ground*) colline *f.*; (*slope*) montée *f.*, descente *f.*; (*heap, mound*) butte *f.*; **up ~ and down** DALE; **as old as the ~s,** vieux comme le monde; **~ock** *s.* monticule *m.*; **~side** *s.* flanc de colline *m.*; **~y** *adj.* vallonné, accidenté.
hilt *s.* poignée *f.*; **up to the ~,** (*fig.*) jusqu'à la garde.
him *pron.* (*direct obj.*) le, l'; **she loves ~, she sees ~,** elle l'aime, elle le voit; (*ind. obj.*) lui; **she speaks to ~,** elle lui parle; (*emphatic*) lui; **I think of ~,** je pense à lui; **for ~,** pour lui; **~self,** lui-même; ⚠ *refl. pron.* se.
Himalaya *s.* (*geog.*) Himalaya *m.*; **~n** *adj.* himalayen.
hind[1] *s.* biche *f.*
hind[2] *adj.* de derrière, postérieur; **~ leg** *s.* patte de derrière *f.*; **to talk the ~ leg off a** DONKEY; **~most** *adj.* dernier; **~quarters** *s.* arrière--train *m.*; **~sight** *s.* (*fig.*) rétrospective *f.*
hind/er *v.t.* **1.** (*impede*) gêner; **2.** (*prevent*) empêcher; **3.** (*delay*) retarder; **~rance** *s.* (1) gêne *f.*; (2) empêchement *m.*; (3) retard *m.*; (*obstruction*) obstacle *m.*
Hind/u *adj.* & *s.m.f.* hindou(e); **~uism** *s.* hindouisme *m.*; **~i** *s.* (*lang.*) hindî *m.*; **~ustani** *s.* (*lang.*) hindou *m.*
hinge *s.* (*of door, etc.*) gond *m.*; (*for stamps*) charnière *f.*; (*fig.*) pivot *m.*; *v.t.* munir de gonds (de charnières); *v.i.* (*fig.* ~ *on*) pivoter sur, être axé sur.
hint *s.* (*indirect suggestion*) allusion *f.*; (*slight indication*) avis *m.*; (*fig.*) nuance *f.*; **to drop a ~,** donner à entendre que; **to take a ~,** comprendre à demi-mot; *v.t.* insinuer; **~ at,** faire allusion à.
hinterland *s.* arrière-pays *m.*
hip *s.* (*anat.*) hanche *f.*; (*bot.*) gratte-cul *m.*; (*interj.*) hip!; **~-bath,** bain de siège *m.*
Hippocratic *adj.* hippocratique.
hippodrome *s.* hippodrome *m.*
hippopotamus *s.* hippopotame *m.*
hire *s.* (*payment*) loyer *m.*; (*hiring*) location *f.*; **on ~,** en location; **for ~,** à louer; **~-purchase,** achat *m.* *or* vente *f.*, à tempérament; *v.t.* & *i.* (*employ*) engager; (*grant or obtain use for payment*) louer; **~ling** *s.* mercenaire *m.*
hirsute *adj.* hirsute.
his *adj.* son, sa, ses; *pron.* à lui; le sien, la sienne, les siens, les siennes; **this car is ~,** cette auto est à lui; **it is ~,** c'est la sienne.
hiss *s.* (& *hissing*) sifflement *m.*; *v.t.* & *i.* siffler.
histamine *s.* histamine *f.*
histor/y *s.* histoire *f.*; (*background to situation, etc.*) historique *m.*; **~ian** *s.* historien *m.*; **~ic(al)** *adj.* historique; (*occasion*) mémorable; **~ically** *adv.**; **~iographer** *s.* historiographe *m.*
histrionic *adj.* théâtral; **~s** *s.* art du théâtre *m.*; (*fig.*) comédie *f.*
hit *s.* (*blow*) coup *m.*; (*fig. stroke*) trait *m.*; (*success*) succès m.; *v.t.* (*strike*) frapper; (*aim blow*) envoyer; (*reach target*) atteindre; (*fig.*) toucher, blesser; **~ upon,** trouver; **~ (it) off** (*likeness*) saisir; **~ below the** BELT; **~ the** NAIL **on the head**; **~ it off with s.o.,** s'entendre bien avec qn.; **~-or-miss** (*fam.*) vaille que vaille; **~ and run** *adj.* (*raid, etc.*) éclair; **~ and run driver** *s.* chauffard *m.*; **~ parade** *s.* palmarès *m.*
hitch *s.* **1.** (*jerk*) secousse *f.*; **2.** (*knot*) clef *f.*; **3.** (*temporary stoppage*) incident technique *m.*, anicroche *f.*; **4.** (*lift in vehicle*) trajet en auto--stop *m.*; *v.t.* (1) tirer brusquement; (2) accrocher, nouer; (*naut.*) amarrer; (4) faire de l'auto-stop; *v.i.* (1) clocher; (2) s'accrocher; **~-hike** *v.i.* faire de l'auto-stop; **~-hiker** *s.* auto-stoppeur *m.*
hither *adj.* de ce côté-ci; *adv.* ici; **~ and thither,** çà et là; **~to** *adv.* jusqu'ici.
hive *s.* (*bees* & *fig.*) ruche *f.*; *v.t.* mettre dans une ruche; *v.i.* entrer dans une ruche; vivre en communauté; **~ off,** *v.t.* & *i.* (*bees* & *fig.*) essaimer.
ho! *interj.* ho!
hoar *adj.* (*hair*) blanchi; **~**-FROST; **~y** *adj.* blanc; (*fig.*) vénérable.
hoard *s.* **1.** (*store*) provision *f.*; **2.** (*hidden stock*) amas *m.*; (*of money*) magot *m.*; **3.** (*treasure*)

trésor *m.*; *v.t.* (1) faire une provision de; (2) amasser; (3) garder comme un trésor; **~er** *s.* avare *m.*

hoarding *s.* (*temporary fence*) clôture (de chantier) *f.*, palissade *f.*; (*for posting bills*) panneau d'affichage *m.*

hoarse *adj.* (*voice*) rauque; (*person*) enroué; **~ly** *adv.* d'une voix rauque; **~ness** *s.* enrouement *m.*

hoax *s.* (*trick*) attrape *f.*; (*swindle*) farce *f.*; (*fam.*) canular *m.*; *v.t.* attraper.

hob *s.* plaque chauffante *f.*; **~nailed boots,** souliers à clous.

hobble *s.* **1.** (*limp*) claudication *f.*; **2.** (*for horse*) entrave *f.*; *v.t.* (2) entraver; *v.i.* (1) boiter, clopiner; **~dehoy** *s.* (grand) dadais *m.*

hobby *s.* (*serious*) passe-temps *m.*, violon d'Ingres *m.*; (*fad*) dada *m.*, marotte *f.*; **~-horse** *s.* (*lit.*) cheval de bois *m.*; (*fig.*) dada *m.*; **to get on one's ~-horse,** enfourcher son dada.

hobgoblin *s.* lutin *m.*

hob-nob *v.i.* **~ with,** être à tu et à toi avec.

hobo *s.* clochard *m.*

hock *s.* **1.** (*of animal*) jarret *m.*; **2.** (*wine*) vin du Rhin *m.*

hockey *s.* hockey *m.*

hocus-pocus *s.* tromperie *f.*

hod *s.* (*techn.*) oiseau *m.*

hoe *s.* (*agric.*) houe *f.*; **Dutch ~,** sarcloir *m.*; *v.t.* houer, sarcler.

hog *s.* (*animal*) porc *m.*; (*pej. of person*) cochon *m.*; **road-~,** chauffard *m.*; **to go the whole ~** (*fam.*) y mettre le paquet; **~shead** *s.* barrique *f.*; **~-wash** (*fam.*) lavasse *f.*; *v.t.* (*fam. take unfaire share of*) accaparer.

hogget *s.* agneau antenais *m.*

hogmanay *s.* la Saint-Sylvestre *f.*

hoick *v.t.* (*Eng. pop.* ~ *out*) arracher.

hoist *s.* (*act*) action de hisser; (*goods lift*) monte-charge *m.*; (*crane*) grue *f.*; (*of flag*) drisse *f.*; *v.t.* hisser; (*flag*) envoyer (les couleurs); **to be ~ with one's own petard,** se prendre à son propre piège.

hoity-toity *adj.* arrogant.

hold *s.* (*naut.*) cale *f.*; (*grasp, means of ~ing*) prise *f.*; (*fig.*) emprise *f.*; **to lay ~ of,** se saisir de; *v.t.* (*grasp*) tenir, saisir; (*possess*) avoir; (*contain*) contenir; (*celebrate*) célébrer; (*restrain*) retenir; (*think, believe*) tenir, maintenir; *v.i.* (*not give way*) tenir (bon); (*be valid*) demeurer valable, demeurer vrai; **~ the line!** (*telephone*) ne quittez pas!; **~ it against s.o.,** en vouloir à qn.; **~ water** (*fig.*) tenir debout; **to be left ~ing the** BABY; **~ back** *v.t.* & *i.* (se) retenir; **~ down** *v.t.* maintenir; **~ forth** *v.i.* pérorer; **~ in** *v.t.* retenir; **~ out** *v.t.* tendre, offrir; *v.i.* tenir; **~ over** *v.t.* différer; **~ up** *v.t.* (*raise*) lever; (*support*) porter; (*stop*) arrêter, bloquer; (*delay*) retarder; **~ with** *v.t.* approuver; **~all** *s.* fourre-tout *m.*; **~-up** *s.* (*attack*) attaque à main armée *f.* (*obstacle*) entrave *f.*; (*delay*) retard *m.*, (*traffic*) embouteillage *m.*; **~er** *s.* (*of post*) titulaire *m.*, (*fin.*) porteur *m.*, (*tenant*) locataire *m.*, (*owner*) détenteur *m.*; CIGARETTE-**~er**; PEN-**~er**; **small-~er** *s.* petit fermier *m.*; **~ing** *s.* tenue *f.*, possession *f.*, (*fin.*) portefeuille *f.*, fonds *m.pl.*; **small~ing** *s.* petite propriété *f.*

hole *s.* (*hollow place*; *perforation*; *golf*) trou *m.*; (*gap*) ouverture *f.*; (*burrow*) trou *m.*, terrier *m.*; (*pop.* = *wretched place*) trou *m.*, boîte *f.*; (*fig. dilemma, fix*) embarras *m.*, pétrin *m.*; **a square** PEG **in a round ~**; **~-and-corner** *adj.* fait en sous-main; *v.t.* trouer; (*techn.*) percer; (*golf*) mettre la balle au trou.

holiday *s.* congé *m.*; (*eccles.*) jour de fête *m.*; (*bank* & *public* ~) jour férié *m.*; **~s,** vacances *f.pl.*; **~s with pay,** congés payés *m.pl.*; *adj.* de congé, de vacances; **~-maker** *s.* estivant *m.*; ~ RESORT; ~ *v.i.* être en vacances, passer des vacances.

Holland *s.* (*geog.*) Hollande *f.*; (*text.*) toile de Hollande *f.*; **~er** *s.m.f.* Hollandais(e); **~s** *s.* (*gin*) schiedam *m.*; **~aise** *adj.* (*cook.*) hollandaise.

hollow *s.* (*depression*) creux *m.*; (*hole*) cavité *f.*; (*valley*) cuvette *f.*; *adj.* creux; (*empty*) vide; (*false*) faux; (*sound*) sourd; (*voice*) caverneux; *adv.* **to beat ~,** barrre à plate couture; *v.t.* creuser; **~ness** *s.* vide *m.*; (*fig.*) fausseté *f.*

holly *s.* houx *m.*; **~hock** *s.* rose trémière *f.*

holocaust *s.* holocauste *m.*

holster *s.* étui *m.*, gaine *f.*, (de revolver).

holy *adj.* (*eccles.*) saint, divin, bénit, sacré; (*of high moral excellence*) sacré; ⚠ sacré *after the noun in these senses*; **~ of holies** *s.* le Saint des Saints *m.*; **H~ Ghost** *s.* Saint-Esprit *m.*; **H~ Land** *s.* Terre Sainte *f.*; ~ ORDERS; **H~ See** *s.* Saint-Siège *m.*; **~ water** eau bénite *f.*; **H~ Week,** semaine sainte *f.*; **holiness** *s.* (*state* & *title*) sainteté *f.*

homage *s.* hommage *m.*

Homburg *s.* chapeau Morès *m.*

home *s.* (*residence*) demeure *f.*; (*abstract*) foyer *m.*; (*native land*) patrie *f.*; (*institution*): (*for the old*) asile *m.*, (*for the sick*) hospice *m.*, (*for students, etc.*) foyer *m.*; *adj.* de famille, familial, domestique; (≠ *foreign*) du pays, intérieur, indigène; **at ~,** chez soi, à la maison; **at-~** *s.* réception *f.*; **to be at ~ with,** être à son aise avec; **to make oneself at ~,** faire comme chez soi; CHARITY **begins at ~**; *adv.* chez soi, à la maison; **to go ~,** rentrer (à la maison, dans son pays); **to bring sth. ~ to s.o.,** faire comprendre qch. à qn. *or* faire comprendre à qn. que; **to wait till the** COWS **come ~**; **~ care** *s.* soins à domicile *m.pl.*; **~-coming** *s.* retour *m.*; **~-made** *adj.* fait à la maison; **H~ Office** *s.* ministère de l'intérieur *m.*; **~ port** *s.* port d'attache *m.*; **H~ Rule** *s.* autonomie *f.*; **~sick** *adj.* nostalgique; **~sickness** *s.* nostalgie *f.*; **~spun** *adj.* rustique; **~stead** *s.* ferme *f.*; **~ team** *s.* équipe locale *f.*; **to tell s.o. ~** TRUTHS; **~ward** *adv.* vers la maison, *adj.* de retour; **~work** *s.* devoir *m.*; **~less** *adj.* sans asile; **~ly** *adj.* simple, sans façons, (*cook.*) bourgeois, (*pej.*) inélégant; **~r** *s.* (*pigeon*) pigeon voyageur *m.*; *v.i.* (*pigeons*) revenir au colombier.

homicid/e *s.* homicide *m.*; **~al** *adj.* homicide.

homily *s.* homélie *f.*

homo- (*in combination*) **~geneous** *adj.* homogène; **~geneity** *s.* homogénéité *f.*; **~logous** *adj.* homologue; **~nym** *s.* homonyme *m.*; **~phone** *s.* homophone *m.*; **~sexual** *adj.* & *s.m.f.* homosexuel(le).

homoeopath *s.* homéopathe *m.*; **~ic** *adj.* homéopathique; **~y** *s.* homéopathie *f.*

hone *s.* pierre à aiguiser *f.*; *v.t.* affûter.

honest *adj.* franc, sincère; (*loyal*) fidèle; honnête (*after noun*); (*worthy*) brave (*before noun*); **~ly** *adv.* franchement; honnêtement; **~y** *s.* franchise *f.*; sincérité *f.*; honnêtetê *f.*; fidélité *f.*; intégrité *f.*

honey *s.* miel *m.*; (*fam.*) chéri(e) *m.f.*; **~ed** *adj.* mielleux; **~-bee** *s.* abeille *f.*; **~comb** *s.* rayon de miel *m.*, (*text.*) nid d'abeille *m.*, (*metal*) alvéole *f.*; **~comb** *v.t.* cribler de trous; **~-combed** *adj.* criblé de trous, (*text.*) disposé en nid d'abeille, (*metal*) alvéolé; **~moon** *s.* lune de miel *f.*, voyage de noces *m.*; **~suckle** *s.* chèvrefeuille *m.*

honk *s.* **1.** (*goose*) cri de l'oie *m.*; **2.** (*auto.*) coup de klaxon *m.*; *v.i.* (1) crier; (2) klaxonner.

honor/arium *s.* honoraires *m.pl.*; **~ary** *adj.* (*conferred as honour*) d'honneur; (*position or title*) honorifique; (*unpaid*) honoraire; **~ific** *adj.* honorifique.

honour *s.* honneur *m.*; **in ~ of,** en l'honneur de; **to have the ~ to,** avoir l'honneur de; **~s** *s.pl.* (*cards*) honneurs *m.pl.*; **to do the ~s,** faire les honneurs (de la maison); (*acad.*) **~s list,** palmarès *m.*; **~s course,** cours de licence *m.*; **~s degree,** licence *f.*; *v.t.* honorer; (*confer ~ on*) faire honneur à; **time ~ed** *adj.* consacré par l'usage; **~able** *adj.* honorable; **~ably** *adv.**.

hood *s.* (*dress*) capuchon *m.*; (*acad.*) épitoge *f.*; (*auto.*) capote *f.*; **Little Red Riding H~,** le petit chaperon rouge *m.*; *v.t.* encapuchonner; **~wink** *v.t.* bander les yeux à qn.; (*fig. fam.*) empaumer.

hoof *s.* sabot *m.*; **on the ~,** (*cattle*) sur pied; *v.i.* (*pop.*) **~ it,** aller à pied.

hook *s.* (*for hanging*) croc *m.*, crochet *m.*; (*agric. tool*) faucille *f.*; (*stroke*) coup tiré *m.*; (*boxing*) crochet *m.*; (*on dress*) agrafe *f.*; (*for fishing*) hameçon *m.*; **by ~ or by crook,** de bric et de broc; **~worm** *s.* ankylostome *m.*; *v.t.* (*fasten*) accrocher, agrafer; (*sport*) donner un crochet à; (*rugby*) talonner; (*fishing*) prendre; **~ it** *v.i.* (*pop.*) décamper; **~-up** *s.* (*radio*) relais radiophonique *m.*; **~ed** *adj.* (*~-shaped*) crochu; (*on drugs, etc.*) adonné à; **~er** *s.* (*rugby*) talonneur *m.*

hookah *s.* narguilé *m.*

hooligan *s.* voyou *m.*; **~ism** *s.* vandalisme *m.*

hoop *s.* (*for cask*) cercle *m.*; (*toy*) cerceau *m.*; (*croquet*) arceau *m.*

hoot *s.* **1.** (*derision*) huée *f.*; **2.** (*whistle, horn, etc.*) coup de sifflet, de klaxon *m.*; **3.** (*owl*) ululement *m.*; *v.t.* & *i.* (1) huer; (2) klaxonner; (3) ululer; **~er** *s.* (*auto.*) klaxon *m.*; (*ship*) sirène *f.*; (*train*) sifflet *m.*

Hoover *s.* aspirateur *m.*; *v.t.* passer l'aspirateur (sur les tapis, etc.).

hop[1] *s.* (*bot.*) houblon *m.*; **~-picker** *s.* cueilleur de houblon *m.*; **~-pole** *s.* échalas *m.*

hop[2] (*~ping movement*) saut *m.*, sautillement *m.*; (*fam. dance*) sauterie *f.*; (*aviat. distance travelled*) trajet *m.*; *v.i.* sauter à cloche-pied; (*birds*) sautiller; **~ it!** (*pop.*) fiche-moi le camp!; **~scotch** *s.* (*game*) marelle *f.*

hope *s.* (*expectation*) espérance *f.*; (*trust*) confiance *f.*; (*ground for ~, cause for ~*) espoir *m.*; *v.i.* espérer, **~ for** *v.t.* espérer; **~ to,** espérer + *inf.*; **~ against ~,** ne jamais désespérer; **~ful** *adj.* plein d'espoir; (*offering ~*) encourageant; (*promising*) qui promet bien; **~fully** *adv.* avec espoir; d'une façon encourageante; (*=it is hoped that*) on l'espère; **~fulness** *s.* espoir *m.*; **~less** *adj.* sans espoir, désespéré; (*offering no ~*) désespérant; (*incorrigible*) incorrigible; **~lessly** *adv.* sans espoir; (*without remedy*) irrémédiablement; **~lessness** *s.* désespoir *m.*; (*futility*) vanité *f.*

hopper *s.* (*techn.*) trémie *f.*

horde *s.* horde *f.*

horizon *s.* (*lit.* & *fig.*) horizon *m.*

horizontal *adj.* horizontal; **~ly** *adv.**.

hormone *s.* hormone *f.*

horn *s.* (*substance*; *of cattle*) corne *f.*; (*of deer*) bois *m.*; (*mus.*) cor *m.*; (*auto.*) corne *f.*, klaxon *m.*; FOG-~; FRENCH ~; SHOE~; **~ of plenty,** corne d'abondance *f.*; **to take the** BULL **by the ~s**; **~beam** *s.* charme *m.*; **~bill** *s.* calao *m.*; **~pipe** *s.* matelote *f.*; **~-rimmed** *adj.* à monture de corne; **~ed** *adj.* cornu; **~ed** OWL; **~y** *adj.* en corne, (*skin*) calleux.

hornet *s.* frelon *m.*; **to bring a ~'s nest about one's ears,** tomber dans un guêpier.

horology *s.* horlogerie *f.*

horoscope *s.* horoscope *m.*

horr/ible (*also* **horrid**) *adj.* (*ugly*) horrible; (*frightening*) affreux; **~ibly** *adv.* & **~idly** *adv.**;*; **~ific** *adj.* terrifiant; **~ified** *adj.* (*scandalised*) horrifié; **~ify** *v.t.* frapper d'horreur.

horror *s.* (*emotion* & *thing*) horreur *f.*

horse *s.* cheval *m.*; (*fam. = cavalry*) cavalerie *f.*; (*gym.*) cheval d'arçons *m.*; **white ~s** (*sea*) moutons *m.pl.*; HOBBY-~; SAW-~; SHIRE-~; **to get on one's high ~,** monter sur ses grands chevaux; **to put the** CART **before the ~**; **to look a** GIFT-**~ in the mouth**; **to have sth. from the ~'s mouth,** tenir un renseignement de bonne source; **on ~back,** à cheval; **~-box** *s.* van *m.*; ~-CHESTNUT; **~-fly** *s.* taon *m.*; **~hair** *s.* crin *m,*; **~man** *s.* cavalier *m.*; **~manship** *s.* équitation *f.*; **~play** *s.* jeu de mains *m.*; **~ power,** cheval vapeur; TAX**able ~ power**; **~-race** *a.* course de chevaux *f.*; **~-radish** *s.* raifort *m.*; **~shoe** *s.* fer à cheval *m.*; **~-tail** *s.* prèle *f.*; **~-trading** *s.* maquignonnage *m.*; **~whip** *s.* cravache *f.*; **~woman** *s.* amazone *f.*, écuyère *f.*; **horsy** *adj.* chevalin; (*affectedly interested in ~s*) hippomane.

hortat/ory *adj.* & **~ive** *adj.* d'exhortation.

horticultur/e *s.* horticulture *f.*; **~al** *adj.* horticole; **~ist** *s.* horticulteur *m.*

hosanna *s.* hosanna *m.*

hos/e *s.* **1.** *pl.* (*stockings*) bas *m.pl.*; **2.** (*~e-pipe*) tuyau *m.*; *v.t.* (2) arroser au tuyau; **~ier** *s.* (1) bonnetier *m.*; **~iery** *s.* bonneterie *f.*

hospice *s.* hospice *m.*

hospitabl/e *adj.* hospitalier; **~y** *adv.**.

hospital *s.* hôpital *m.*; **~ize** *v.t.* hospitaliser.

hospitality *s.* hospitalité *f.*

host[1] *s.* (*entertainer*) hôte *m.*; (*landlord of inn*) aubergiste *m.*; (*of parasite*) hôte *m.*; **~ess** *s.* hôtesse *f.*; **air ~ess** *s.* hôtesse de l'air *f.*

host[2] *s.* (*large number*) foule *f.*; (*army*) armée *f.*

host[3] *s.* (*eccles.*) hostie *f.*

hostage *s.* otage *m.*; (*fig.*) gage *m.*

hostel *s.* hôtellerie *f.*; (*acad.*) maison universitaire *f.*; **youth ~,** auberge de la jeunesse *f.*; **~ry** *s.* (*archaic*) hôtellerie *f.*

hostil/e *adj.* hostile; **~ely** *adv.**; **~ity** *s.* hostilité *f.*

hot *adj.* (*giving or feeling heat*) chaud, brûlant; (*cook.*) piquant; (*fig.*) ardent; (*fresh*) frais, récent; (*pop. = stolen*) compromettant; **red-~,** chauffé au rouge; **to be ~,** (*person*) avoir chaud, (*weather*) faire chaud; **to strike while the iron is ~,** battre le fer pendant qu'il est chaud; **~ air** (*fig. pop.*) bla-bla-bla *m.*; **~bed** *s.* couche *f.*, (*fig.*) foyer *m.*; **to sell like ~** CAKES; **~ dog** *s.* (*cook.*) saucisse chaude *f.*; **~foot** *adv.* à toute vitesse; **~head** *s.* (*fig.*) excité *m.*; **~house** *s.* serre *f.*; **~ line** *s.* téléphone rouge *m.*; ~PLATE; **~-pot** *s.* (*cook.*) ragoût *m.*; **~ seat** s. (*fig.*) sellette *f.*; **~ water** *s.* (*fig. fam.*) pétrin *m.*; **~-water** BOTTLE; **~ly** *adv.* chaudement; **~ness** *s.* chaleur *f.*

hotchpotch *s.* (*fig.*) salmigondis *m.*

hotel *s.* hôtel *m.*; **~ier** *s.* hôtelier *m.*

Hottentot *adj.* & *s.m.f.* hottentot(e).

hough *s.* (*of horse*) jarret *m.*

hound *s.* chien de meute *m.*; (*pej. pers.*) chien *m.*, **~s** *pl.* (*pack of ~s*) meute *f.*, *v.t.* chasser, (*fig.*) s'acharner sur qn.

hour *s.* heure *f.*; ELEVEN**th ~**; **half an ~** *s.* demi-heure *f.*; **quarter of an ~** *s.* quart d'heure *m.*; **~s** (*fixed time for work, etc.*) heures *f.pl.*; **in the small ~s,** bien avant dans la nuit; **~glass** *s.* sablier *m.*; **~ly** *adj.* à chaque heure, *adv.* d'heure en heure.

houri *s.* houri *f.*

house *s.* (*residence*) maison *f.*; (*parl.*) chambre *f.*; (*theat.*) salle *f.*; (*comm.*) maison *f.*; (*dynasty*) famille *f.*; (*~hold*) ménage *m.*; COUNCIL ~; HEN-~; LIGHT-~; PUBLIC ~; WARE~; **at, in, to, the ~ of,** chez; **at my ~,** chez moi; **to the Dubois' ~,** chez les Dubois; **to keep ~,** faire le ménage; **to place s.o. under ~ arrest,** consigner qn.; **~-to-~,** de porte en porte; **~-agent** *s.* agent de location *m.*; **~boat** *s.*

bateau-maison *m.*; **~breaker** *s.* cambrioleur *m.*; **H~ of Commons,** chambre des Communes *f.*; **~-dog** *s.* chien de garde *m.*; **~hold** *s.* ménage *m.*; **~holder** *s.* chef de famille *m.*; **~hold word,** mot, nom, dans toutes les bouches; **~keeper** *s.* ménagère *f.*, (*employee*): (*private*) gouvernante *f.*, (*public*) intendante *f.*; **~keeping** *s.* ménage *m.*; **~maid** *s.* femme de chambre *f.*; **~-proud woman,** femme d'intérieur *f.*; **~ surgeon** *s.* interne *m.*; **~-warm** *v.i.* pendre la crémaillère; **~wife** *s.* maîtresse de maison *f.*; **~work** *s.* travail ménager *m.*; *v.t.* (*receive*) recevoir; (*store*) héberger; (*shelter*) abriter; (*provide ~s for*) loger; (*naut.*) caler; (*agric.*) engranger; **housing** *s.* logement *m.*, (*techn.*) enchassure *f.*; **housing estate** *s.* cité ouvrière *f.*

hovel (*shed, outhouse*) appentis *m.*; (*mean dwelling*) taudis *m.*

hover *v.i.* (*bird*) voltiger, planer; (*loiter*) rôder; **~ about** *v.t.* & *i.* tourner autour (de); **~craft** *s.* aéroglisseur *m.*

how *adv.* comment; **and ~!** et comment! **~ on earth?, ~ the devil?,** comment donc?, comment diable?; **~ long?,** combien de temps?; **~ much?, ~ many?,** combien (de)?; **~ often?,** combien de fois?; **~ are you?,** comment allez-vous?; **~ old are you?,** quel âge avez-vous?; **~ is it that?,** comment se fait-il que?; **~ kind of you!,** que vous êtes aimable!; **~ hot it is!,** (ce) qu'il fait chaud!; **to know ~ to do sth.,** savoir faire qch.; **~ever** & **~soever** *adv.* de quelque manière que; **~ever clever he may be,** quelque ingénieux qu'il soit; **~ever that may be,** quoi qu'il en soit; **~ever** *conj.* cependant.

howitzer *s.* obusier *m.*

howl *s.* hurlement *m.*; *v.t.* & *i.* hurler; **~er** *s.* (*fig.*) bourde *f.*; **~ing** *s.* hurlement *m.*; **~ing** *adj.* (*fam.*) criant.

hoy *s.* (*naut.*) petit vaisseau côtier *m.*; *interj.* ohé!

hoyden *s.* garçon manqué *m.*; **~ish** *adj.* garçonnier.

h.p. 1. (*abbrev. for hire purchase*) vente *f.* *or* achat *m.*, à tempérament; **2.** (*abbrev. for horse power*) c.v. (cheval vapeur).

H.Q. (*abbrev. for headquarters*) Q.G. (quartier général) *m.*

H.R.H. (*abbrev. for His/Her Royal Highness*) S.A.R. (son Altesse Royale) *f.*

hub *s.* moyeu *m.*; (*fig.*) pivot *m.*; **~cap** *s.* (*auto.*) enjoliveur *m.*

hubbub *s.* vacarme *m.*

huckaback *s.* grosse toile *f.*

huckster *s.* colporteur *m.*

huddle *s.* **1.** (*confused heap*) fouillis *m.*; **2.** (*confusion, lit.* & *fig.*) méli-mélo *m.*; *v.t.* (1) entasser; (2) jeter pêle-mêle; *v.i.* s'entasser, se presser.

hue *s.* (*colour*) teinte *f.*; (*clamour*) huée *f.*; **~ and cry,** clameur *f.*

huff *s.* accès de colère *m.*; **to be in a ~,** prendre la mouche; *v.t.* & *i.* (*bully*) malmener; (*offend*) offenser; (*take offence*) se froisser; **~y** *adj.* susceptible.

hug *s.* étreinte *f.*; *v.t.* (*embrace*) étreindre, serrer dans ses bras; (*keep close to, shore, etc.*) serrer; (*cling to, fig.*) chérir.

huge *adj.* énorme; **~ly** *adv.* énormément; **~ness** *s.* énormité *f.*

hugger-mugger *adj.* secret; désordonné; *adv.* en secret; en désordre.

Huguenot *adj.* & *s.m.f.* huguenot(e).

hulk *s.* (*body of dismantled ship*) ponton *m.*; (*unwieldy vessel, fam.*) vieux rafiot *m.*; (*big person or mass*) mastodonte *m.* **~ing** *adj.* énorme, balourd.

hull[1] *s.* (*of peas, beans, etc.*) cosse *f.*; *v.t.* écosser.

hull[2] *s.* (*naut.*) coque *f.*

hullabaloo *s.* brouhaha *m.*

hullo *s.* & *interj.* (*call*) holà; (*greeting*) salut; (*telephone*) allô.

hum *s.* **1.** (*of animals, insects, voices*) bourdonnement *m.*; **2.** (*singing with closed lips*) fredonnement *m.*; **3.** (*of motors, etc.*) vrombissement *m.*; *v.i.* (1) bourdonner; (2) fredonner; (3) vrombir; (*top*) ronfler; *interj.* hem!; **~ming** *adj.* (1) bourdonnant; (2) fredonnant; (3) vrombissant; (*fig.*) en plein essor; **~ming-bird** *s.* colibri *m.*

human *s.* (& **~** *being*) être humain *m.*; *adj.* humain; **~ism** *s.* humanisme *m.*; **~ist** *s.* humaniste *m.*; **~itarian** *adj.* humanitaire; **~ities** *s.pl.* humanités *f.pl.*; **~ity** *s.* humanité *f.*; **~ize** *v.t.* humaniser; **~ly** *adv.**.

humane *adj.* humain; **~ly** *adv.**; **~ness** *s.* humanité *f.*

humbl/e *adj.* (*lowly*) humble; (*unpretentious*) modeste; **~e-bee** *s.* bourdon, *m.*; **to eat ~e pie,** faire amende honorable; **~eness** *s.* humilité *f.*; **~y** *adv.**; *; *v.t.* humilier.

humbug *s.* (*deception, sham*) supercherie *f.*, charlatanisme *m.*; (*impostor*) charlatan *m.*; (*sweet*) berlingot *m.*; *v.t.* embobeliner; *v.i.* blaguer.

humdrum *adj.* monotone.

humerus *s.* humérus *m.*

humid *adj.* humide; **~ifier** *s.* humidificateur *m.*; **~ity** *s.* humidité *f.*

humiliat/e *v.t.* humilier; **~ing** *adj.* humiliant; **~ion** *s.* humiliation *f.*

humility *s.* humilité *f.*

hummock *s.* mamelon *m.*

hum/our *s.* (*state of mind*) humeur *f.*; (*sense of ~*) humour *m.*; (*comic imagination*) drôlerie *f.*; **sense of ~our,** sens de l'humour *m.*; *v.t.* (*indulge s.o.'s fancy*) se prêter à; (*satisfy tastes, demands*) satisfaire à; (*be tolerant with s.o.*) ménager qn.; **~orist** *s.* humoriste *m.*; **~oristic** *adj.* humoristique; **~orous** *adj.* humoristique; (*witty*) spirituel; (*comic*) drôle; **~orously** *adv.* avec humour.

hump *s.* bosse *f.*; (*pop.* = *depression*) cafard *m.*; **~backed** *adj.* bossu; *v.t.* porter sur le dos.

humph *interj.* hum!

humus *s.* humus *m.*

Hun *s.* (*hist.*) Hun *m.*; (*fam. pej.*) boche *m.*

hunch *s.* (*hunk*) gros morceau *m.*; (*pop. intuition*) pressentiment *m.*; *v.t.* voûter; **~back** *s.* bossu(e) *m.f.*

hundred *s.* cent *m.*, centaine *f.*; **one ~,** cent *m.*; **~s,** des centaines *f.pl.*; *adj.* cent; **200,** deux cents; **220,** deux cent vingt; **~fold,** centuple; **~th** *adj.* & *s.m.* centième; **~weight** *s.* quintal *m.*

Hungar/y *s.* (*geog.*) Hongrie *f.*; **~ian** *adj.* & *s.m.f.* hongrois(e).

hung/er *s.* faim *f.*; (*fig.*) soif *f.* (de); *v.i.* avoir faim; (*fig.*) avoir soif (de); **~er-strike,** grève de la faim *f.*; **~ry** *adj.* affamé; (*fig.*) avide (de); **to be ~ry,** avoir faim; **~rily** *adv.* voracement; (*fig.*) avidement.

hunk *s.* gros morceau *m.*; (*of bread*) quignon *m.*

hunt *s.* chasse *f.*; *v.t.* & *i.* (*sport; drive out*) chasser; **~ down,** pourchasser; **~ for,** chercher; **~ out,** dénicher; **~er** *s.* chasseur *m.*; (*horse*) cheval de chasse *m.*; (*watch*) savonnette *f.*; **~ing** *s.* chasse (à courre) *f.*; **~ing-box** *s.* pavillon de chasse *m.*; **~ress** *s.* chasseresse *f.*; **~sman** *s.* chasseur *m.*; (*official*) piqueur *m.*

hurdle *s.* (*agric.*) claie *f.*; (*sport*) haie *f.*; (*fig.*) obstacle *m.*; *v.i.* (*sport*) faire la course de haies; **~r** *s.* coureur de haies *m.*

hurdy-gurdy *s.* orgue de barbarie *f.*

hurl *v.t.* lancer; **~ from, out of,** précipiter de.

hurly-burly *s.* tintamarre *m.*

hurrah, hurray, hooray *s.* & *interj.* hourra *m.*

hurricane *s.* ouragan *m.*; **~-lamp,** lampe-tempête *f.*

hurry *s.* (*undue haste*) hâte *f.*, précipitation *f.*; (*eagerness*) empressement *m.*; (*need for haste*) urgence *f.*; **to be in a ~,** être pressé; **there's no ~,** rien ne presse; *v.t.* presser, hâter; *v.i.* se presser, se dépêcher; **~ up!,** dépêchez-vous!; **hurried** *adj.* (*person*) pressé; (*thing*) fait à la va-vite; (*careless*) précipité.

hurt *s.* **1.** (*wound*) blessure *f.*; **2.** (*harm*) mal *m.*, (*fig.*) tort *m.*; *adj.* blessé; *v.t.* (1) blesser; (2) faire du mal à; (*fig.*) offenser; *v.i.* faire mal; **it ~s,** cela fait mal; **where it ~s most,** au point sensible; **~ful** *adj.* blessant, nocif; **~fully** *adv.* d'une manière blessante, nocive.

hurtle *v.t.* heurter; *v.i.* tomber avec fracas.

husband *s.* mari *m.*; *v.t.* (*conserve*) ménager; **~man** *s.* agriculteur *m.*; **~ry** *s.* culture *f.*

hush *s.* silence *m.*; (*peace*) calme *m.*; **~-money** *s.* prix du silence *m.*; *v.t.* faire taire, calmer; **~ up** *v.t.* étouffer; *interj.* chut!; **~-~** *adj.* (*fam.*) secret.

husk *s.* **1.** (*of peas*) cosse *f.*; **2.** (*of nuts*) coque *f.*; **3.** (*of cereal*) balle *f.*; *v.t.* (1) écosser; (2) écaler; (3) décortiquer; **~y** *s.* chien esquimau *m.*; *adj.* enroué.

hussar *s.* hussard *m.*

hussy, huzzy *s.* garce *f.*

hustings *s.pl.* élections *f.pl.*

hustle (& **hustling**) *s.* bousculade *f.*; *v.t.* (*jostle*) bousculer; (*push*) pousser; *v.i.* se bousculer; (*hurry*) se dépêcher.

hut *s.* cabane *f.*; **~ment** *s.* baraquement *m.*

hutch *s.* clapier *m.*

hyacinth *s.* (*bot.*) jacinthe *f.*

hybrid *adj.* & *s.m.* hybride.

hydra *s.* hydre *f.*

hydrangea *s.* hortensia *m.*

hydrant *s.* prise d'eau *f.*; **fire-~,** bouche d'incendie *f.*

hydraulic *adj.* hydraulique; **~s** *s.* hydraulique *f.* ⚠ *sing. in French.*

hydro *s.* (*fam.* = *hotel*) établissement thermal *m.*

hydro- (*in combination*) **~cephalous** *adj.* hydrocéphale; **~dynamics** *s.* hydrodynamique *f.* ⚠ *sing. in French*; **~electric** *adj.* hydro-électrique; **~foil** *s.* hydroptère *m.*; **~graphy** *s.* hydrographie *f.*; **~jet** *s.* hydroréacteur *m.*; **~logy** *s.* hydrologie *f.*; **~meter** *s.* hydromètre *m.*; **~pathy** *s.* hydrothérapie *f.*; **~phobia** *s.* hydrophobie *f.*; **~ponics** *s.* aquiculture *f.*; **~statics** *s.* hydrostatique *f.* ⚠ *sing. in French.*

hydrogen *s.* hydrogène *m.*; *adj.* à l'hydrogène.

hyena, hyaena *s.* hyène *f.*

hygien/e *s.* hygiène *f.*; **~ic** *adj.* hygiénique; **~ically** *adv.**.

hymn *s.* hymne *f.*, cantique *m.*; *v.t.* célébrer; **~al** *s.* recueil de cantiques *m.*; **~al** *adj.* de cantique, d'hymne.

hyperbole *s.* hyperbole *f.*

hyper- (*in combination*) **~critical** *adj.* hypercritique; **~market** *s.* hypermarché *m.*; **~sensitive** *adj.* hypersensible.

hyphen *s.* trait d'union *m.*; **~ate** *v.t.* mettre un trait d'union entre . . . et . . .

hypnosis *s.* hypnose *f.*

hypnot/ic *adj.* hypnotique; **~ism** *s.* hypnotisme *m.*; **~ist** *s.* hypnotiseur *m.*; **~ize** *v.t.* hypnotiser.

hypo- (*in combination*) **~chondria** *s.* hypocondrie *f.*; **~chondriac** *adj.* & *s.m.* (*med.*) hypocondriaque, *s.* (*fam.*) malade imaginaire *m.*; **~crisy** *s.* hypocrisie *f.*; **~crite** *s.* hypocrite *m.*; **~critical** *adj.* hypocrite; **~dermic** *adj.* hypodermique; **~phosphate** *s.* hypophosphate *m.*; **~sulfate** *s.* hyposulfite *m.*; **~tenuse** *s.* hypoténuse *f.*; **~thermia** *s.* hypothermie *f.*; **~thesis** *s.* hypothèse *f.*; **~thetical** *adj.* hypothétique.

hysterectomy *s.* hystérectomie *f.*

hyster/ia *s.* (*med.*) hystérie *f.*; (*fam.*) crise de nerfs *f.*; **~ical** *adj.* (*med.*) hystérique; (*fam.*) excité; **~ics** *s.* crise de nerfs (de rires, de larmes, etc.) *f.*

I

I NOTE. *This section contains many words* (*adjectives, adverbs, substantives*) *formed with negative prefixes* (il-, im-, in-, ir-). *These are frequently the same in the corresponding French words, e.g.* illégitime, immobile, inconstant, irréparable. *It should also be noted that the prefixes are often replaced by* 'peu' *or, more rarely,* 'non' *before the adjective, e.g.* peu sincère (**insincere**), non-décisif (**indecisive**). *The adverb is then* d'une manière peu sincère (**insincerely**), *or,* peu convenablement (**indecorously**), *or,* sans suite (**inconsistently**), *or,* sans causer d'offense (**inoffensively**). *The substantive becomes* manque de sincérité (**insincerity**).

I *pron.* je; moi (*used*): **1.** (*alone*) **who is there? I,** qui est là? moi; **2.** (*after* c'est) **it was I who did it,** c'est moi qui l'ai fait; **3.** (*for emphasis*) **I don't like,** moi, je n'aime pas; **4.** (*in comparisons*) **taller than I,** plus grand que moi; **5.** (*with another pronoun as subject*) **he and I are going out,** lui et moi, nous sortons.

I.A.E.A. (*International Atomic Energy Agency*) AIEA *f.* (Agence Internationale de l'Energie Atomique).

iambic *adj.* iambique.

I.A.T.A. (*International Air Transport Association*) AITA *f.* (Association Internationale des Transports Aériens).

Iberian *adj.* ibérique.

ibex *s.* bouquetin *m.*

ibis *s.* ibis *m.*

ice *s.* glace *f.*; (*cook.*) glace *f.*; **dry ~,** neige carbonique *f.*; **to break the ~,** (*fig.*) rompre la glace; **to cut no ~ with s.o.,** laisser qn. froid; **to put sth. on ~** (*fig.*) différer qch., (*fam.*) mettre qch. au frigidaire; **to be/skate, on thin ~** (*fig.*) toucher à un sujet délicat; **~-age** *s.* époque glaciaire *f.*; **~berg** *s.* iceberg *m.*; **~box** *s.* glacière *f.*; **~-breaker** *s.* brise-glace(s) *m.invar.*; **~-cap** *s.* calotte glaciaire *f.*; **~ cream** *s.* glace *f.*; **~ hockey,** hockey sur glace *m.*; **iciness** *s.* état glacé *m.*; **icing** *s.* (*cook.*) glaçage *m.*, glacé *m.*; **icy** *adj.* glacé, (*fig.*) glacial (*m.pl. rare* -als *or* -aux); *v.t.* (*cover with ~, cool in ~, cook.*) glacer; (*freeze*) congeler; (*wine*) frapper; *v.i.* (*~ up*) se givrer.

Iceland *s.* (*geog.*) Islande *f.*; **~ic** *adj.* & *s.m.* (*lang.*) islandais; **~er** *s.m.f.* Islandais(e).

ichthyology *s.* ichtyologie *f.*

icicle *s.* glaçon *m.*

icon, ikon *s.* icône *f.*; **~oclasm** *s.* iconoclasme *m.*; **~oclast** *s.* iconoclaste *m.f.*

icy *see* ICE.

idea *s.* idée *f.*; **not to have the** FOG**giest ~.**

ideal *s.* idéal *m.* (*pl.* -als *or* -aux); **~s** *s.pl.* valeurs *f.pl.*; *adj.* idéal; **~ism** *s.* idéalisme *m.*; **~ist** *s.* idéaliste *m.f.* **~ize** *v.t.* idéaliser; **~ly** *adv.* idéalement.

ident/ical *adj.* identique (*with, to*—à); **~ically**

*adv.**; **~ify** *v.t.* identifier (*with*—à); **~ification** *s.* identification *f.*; **~ikit** *s*, portrait-robot *m.*; **~ity** *s.* identité *f.*; **~ity** CARD.

ideogram & **ideograph** *s.* idéogramme *m.*

ideolog/y idéologie *f.*; **~ical** *adj.* idéologique; **~ist** *s.* idéologue *m.f.*

ides *s.pl.* ides *f.pl.*

idiom *s.* (*language*) idiome *m.*; (*phrase*) idiotisme *m.*; **~atic** *adj.* idiomatique; **~atically** *adv.* couramment.

idio/t *s.* idiot(e) *m.f.*; **~cy** *s.* idiotie *f.*; **~-syncrasy** *s.* (*med.*) idiosyncrasie *f.*; (*gen.*) particularité *f.*; **~tic** *adj.* idiot; **~tically** *adv.**.

idl/e *adj.* **1.** (*lazy*) paresseux; BONE **~**; **2.** (*unoccupied*) désœuvré; **3.** (*useless*) inutile, (*purposeless*) vain, (*trifling*) futile, (*baseless*) sans fondement; *v.t.* & *i.* (*be ~e*) être oisif; (*pass time ~y*) fainéanter; (*~e away time*) passer son temps à ne rien faire; (*auto.*) fonctionner, marcher, à vide; **~eness** *s.* (1) paresse *f.*; (2) désœuvrement *m.*; (3) inutilité *f.*, vanité *f.*, futilité f.; **~ er** *s.* fainéant *m.*; **~ly** *adv.* (1) paresseusement; (2) dans l'oisiveté; (3) inutilement, vainement, futilement.

idol *s.* idole *f.*; **~ater** *s.* idolâtre *m.f.*; **~atrous** *adj.* idolâtre; **~atry** *s.* idolâtrie *f.*; **~ize** *v.t.* idolâtrer.

idyll *s.* idylle *f.*; **~ic** *adj.* idyllique.

i.e. (*id est*) c'est-à-dire.

if *s.* si *m.invar.*; *conj.* (*on the condition or supposition that*; *whenever*; *whether*) si; (*provided that*) pourvu que; (*in exclamation*) **~ I had only known!,** si seulement j'avais su!; **as ~,** comme si; **~ any** (= *~ there are any*), s'il y en a; **~ not,** si non; **~ so,** si oui.

igloo *s.* igloo *m.*

igneous *adj.* igné.

ignis fatuus *s.* feu follet *m.*

ignit/e *v.t.* mettre le feu à; *v.i.* prendre feu, s'enflammer; **~ion** *s.* ignition *f.*; (*auto.*) allumage *m.*; **~ion key** (*auto.*) clef de contact *f.*

ignobl/e *adj.* **1.** (*of low birth*) roturier; **2.** (*mean, base*) ignoble; **~y** *adv.* (1) de basse naissance; (2)*.

ignomin/ious *adj.* **1.** (*mean, shameful*) méprisable; **2.** (*humiliating*) ignominieux; **~iously** *adv.* (1) de façon méprisable; (2)*; **~y** *s.* ignominie *f.*

ignoramus *s.* ignorant *m.*

ignoran/t *adj.* ignorant (de); **to be ~t of,** ignorer; **~ce** *s.* ignorance *f.*; **~tly** *adv.* par ignorance.

ignore *v.t.* refuser de voir, ne pas prêter attention à; ⚠ ignorer = **not to know.**

iguana *s.* iguane *m.*

ikon *see* ICON.

ilex *s.* yeuse *f.*

ilk *s.* *in phrase*, **of that ~,** de cette sorte.

ill *s.* (*evil*) mal *m.*; (*harm*) tort *m.*; **to speak ~ of s.o.,** médire de qn.; **~s** *pl.* (*misfortunes*) malheurs *m.pl.*; *adj.* (*evil, faulty, harmful*) mauvais; (*sick*) malade; **to be taken ~, to fall ~,** tomber malade; **to look ~,** avoir mauvaise mine; **~ feeling** *s.* malice *f.*; **~ humour, ~ temper** *s.* mauvaise humeur *f.*; **~ luck** *s.* malheur *m.*; **~ will** *s.* rancune *f.*; *adv.* (*badly*) mal; (*scarcely*) ne . . . guère; **to go ~ with,** mal tourner pour; **to take sth. ~,** mal prendre qch.; **~-advised** *adj.* peu judicieux; **~-bred** *adj.* mal élevé; **~-equipped** *adj.* mal préparé; **~-favoured** *adj.* laid; **~-gotten** *adj.* mal acquis; **~-judged** *adj.* peu judicieux; **~-natured** *adj.* méchant; **~omened** *adj.* de mauvaise augure; **~-tempered** *adj.* de mauvaise humeur; **~-timed** *adj.* inopportun; **~-treat** *v.t.* maltraiter; **~ness** *s.* maladie *f.*

illegal *adj.* illégal; **~ity** *s.* illégalité *f.*; **~ly** *adv.**.

illegib/le *adj.* illisible; **~ility** *s.* illisibilité *f.*; **~ly** *adv.**.

illegitima/te *adj.* illégitime; **~cy** *s.* illégitimité *f.*; **~tely** *adv.**.

illiberal *adj.* **1.** (*narrow-minded*) d'esprit étroit; **2.** (*stingy*) mesquin; (*sordid*) sordide; **~ly** *adv.* (1) sans libéralisme; (2) sans libéralité.

illicit *adj.* illicite; **~ly** *adv.**.

illimitable *adj.* illimité.

illitera/te *adj.* **1.** (*unable to read & write*) analphabète; **2.** (*uneducated*) illettré; *s.* (1) analphabète *m.f.*; (2) illettré *m.*; **~cy** *s.* (1) analphabétisme *m.*

illogical *adj.* illogique; **~ity** *s.* illogisme *m.*; **~ly** *adv.**.

illuminat/e, illumine *v.t.* **1.** (*light up, throw light on*) éclairer; **2.** (*decorate with lights*) illuminer; **3.** (*decorate ms.*) enluminer; **~ion** *s.* (1) éclairage *m.*, (*fig.*) lumière *f.*; (2) illumination *f.*; (3) enluminure *f.*; **~ive** *adj.* (1) éclairant; (2) illuminant; (3) d'enluminure; **~or** (3) enlumineur *m.*

illus/ion *s.* illusion *f.*; **~ionist** *s.* illusionniste *m.*; **~ive** *adj.* (*deceptive*) trompeur; (*unreal*) illusoire; **~ory** *adj.* illusoire.

illustrat/e *v.t.* (*with examples, pictures, etc.*) illustrer; **~ion** *s.* (*clarification*) éclaircissement *m.*; (*example*) exemple *m.*; (*drawing*) illustration *f.*; **~ive** *adj.* explicatif; qui illustre; **~or** *s.* illustrateur *m.*

illustrious *adj.* illustre.

I.L.O. (*International Labour Organisation*) O.I.T. *f.* (Organisation internationale du Travail).

image *s.* **1.** (*idol*) image *f.*; **2.** (*opt.*) image *f.*; **3.** (*idea*) image *f.*; **the living ~ of s.o.,** tout le portrait de qn,; *v.t.* (1) représenter; (2) refléter; (3) se figurer; **~ry** *s.* (1), (2), (3), images *f.pl.*

imagin/e *v.t.* & *i.* (*form mental image of*) imaginer; (*suppose, think*) supposer, croire; (*fancy*) se figurer; **~able** *adj.* imaginable; **~ary** *adj.* imaginaire; **~ation** *s.* imagination *f.*; **~ative** *adj.* (*person*) imaginatif; (*thing*) d'imagination.

imam *s.* imam *or* iman *m.*

imbalance *s.* déséquilibre *m.*

imbecil/e *adj.* & *s.m.f.* imbécile; **~ity** *s.* imbécillité *f.*

imbibe *v.t.* (*drink in*) absorber; (*inhale*) aspirer; (*absorb*) s'imbiber de; (*fig.*) assimiler.

imbroglio *s.* imbroglio *m.*

imbrue *v.t.* (*wet, moisten, soak*) tremper; (*stain, dye*) teindre.

imbue *v.t.* (*saturate*) imprégner (*with*—de); (*fig.*) pénétrer de.

I.M.F. (*International Monetary Fund*) F.M.I. *m.* (Fonds monétaire international).

imita/te *v.t.* (*mimic, follow example of*) imiter; (*be like*) ressembler à; **~ble** *adj.* imitable; **~tion** *s.* (*act, copy*) imitation *f.*; (*law*) contrefaçon *f.*; **~tive** *adj.* imitatif; **~tor** *s.* imitat/eur, -rice *m.f.*

immaculate *adj.* immaculé; (*fam.*) impeccable; **the I~ Conception,** l'Immaculée Conception *f.*; **~ly** *adv.* impeccablement.

immanen/t *adj.* (*inherent*) immanent; (*eccles.*) omniprésent; **~ce** *s.* immanence *f.*

immaterial *adj.* (*incorporeal*) immatériel; (*unimportant*) peu important.

immatur/e *adj.* prématuré; (*plan*) pas mûr; (*person*) encore enfant; **~ely** *adv.* prématurément; **~ity** *s.* immaturité *f.*

immeasurab/le *adj.* incommensurable; **~ility** *s.* incommensurabilité *f.*; **~ly** *adv.**.

immediate *adj.* (*direct*) immédiat; (*nearest, next*) proche; (*occurring at once*) immédiat, urgent; **~ly** *adv.**, urgemment.

immemorial *adj.* immémorial.

immens/e *adj.* immense; **~ely** *adv.* immensément; (*fam.* = *very much*) formidablement; **~ity** *s.* immensité *f.*

immers/e *v.t.* (*put under water*) immerger; (*plunge*; *fig. involve deeply*) plonger; **~ed in,** plongé dans; **~ion** *s.* immersion *f.*; **~ion** HEATER.
immigr/ant *adj.* immigré; *s.* immigrant *m.*; **~ate** *v.i.* immigrer; **~ation** *s.* immigration *f.*
imminen/t *adj.* imminent; **~ce** *s.* imminence *f.*
immitigable *adj.* implacable.
immobil/e *adj.* **1.** (*immovable*) fixe; **2.** (*motionless*) immobile; **~ity** *s.* (1) fixité *f.*; (2) immobilité *f.*; **~ize** *v.t.* immobiliser.
immoderate *adj.* immodéré; (*appetite*) démesuré; (*desire*) déréglé; **~ly** *adv.**.
immodest *adj.* **1.** (*indecent*) impudique; **2.** (*impudent*) impudent; **~ly** *adv.* (1)*; (2) impudemment; **~y** *s.* (1) impudeur *f.*; (2) impudence *f.*
immolat/e *v.t.* immoler; **~ion** *s.* immolation *f.*
immoral *adj.* (*morally wrong, evil*) immoral; (*dissolute*) débauché; **~ity** *s.* immoralité *f.*; **~ly** *adv.**.
immortal *adj.* immortel; *s.* (*antiq.*) immortel *m.*; **the I~s** (*members of l'Académie française*) les Immortels *m.pl.*; **~ity** *s.* immortalité *f.*; **~ize** *v.t.* immortaliser; **~ly** *adv.**.
immovab/le *adj.* **1.** (*not movable*) immuable; **2.** (*fig. unyielding*) inflexible; **~ility** *s.* (1) immuabilité *f.*; (2) inflexibilité *f.*; **~ly** *adv.* (1)*; (2) impitoyablement.
immun/e *adj.* exempt (*from, against, to*—de); (*from infection, etc.*) immunisé (contre); **~ity** *s.* exemption *f.*; (*med.*) immunité *f.*; **~ize** *v.t.* immuniser (contre); **~ization** *s.* immunisation *f.*
immure *v.t.* emmurer.
immutab/le *adj.* immuable; **~ility** *s.* immutabilité *f.*; **~ly** *adv.**.
imp *s.* (*little devil*) lutin *m.*; (*mischievous child*) polisson *m.*; **~ish** *adj.* espiègle.
impact *s.* (*collision*) heurt *m.*; (*effect, influence*) impact *m.*; *v.t.* enfoncer (dans); **~ed** *adj.* (*tooth*) (dent) barrée; (*fracture*) avec impaction.
impair *v.t.* (*damage*) endommager; (*weaken*) affaiblir; (*fig.*) diminuer, altérer; **~ment** *s.* détéroriation *f.*; (*fig.*) altération *f.*
impale *v.t.* empaler.
impalpab/le *adj.* impalpable; (*fig.*) imperceptible; **~ility** *s.* immatérialité *f.*
impart *v.t.* (*give share of*) attribuer; (*communicate*) faire part de.
impartial *adj.* impartial; **~ity** *s.* impartialité *f.*; **~ly** *adv.**.
impassable *adj.* infranchissable; (*water*) impassable; (*road*) impraticable.
impasse *s.* (*lit.* & *fig.*) impasse *f.*
impassib/le *adj.* impassible; **~ility** *s.* impassibilité *f.*
impassioned *adj.* passionné.
impassiv/e *adj.* insensible; **~ely** *adv.* sans émoi; **~ity** *s.* insensibilité *f.*
impasto *s.* empâtement *m.*
impatien/t *adj.* **1.** (≠ *patient*) impatient (de); **2.** (*intolerant*) intolérant (de); **~ce** *s.* (1) impatience *f.*; (2) intolérance *f.*; **~tly** *adv.* (1) impatiemment; (2) avec intolérance.
impeach *v.t.* (*law*) mettre en accusation; (*call in question*) mettre en doute; (*disparage*) dénigrer; **~ment** *s.* mise en accusation *f.*
impeccab/le *adj.* impeccable; **~ility** *s.* impeccabilité *f.*; **~ly** *adv.**.
impecuni/ous *adj.* besogneux; **~osity** *s.* besoin *m.*
imped/e *v.t.* (*retard*) retarder; (*hinder*) gêner, entraver; **~ance** *s.* (*electr.*) impédance *f.*; **~iment** *s.* (*hindrance*) gêne *f.*, entrave *f.*; obstacle *m.*, (*in speech*) bégayement *m.*; **~imenta** *s.pl.* impedimenta *m.pl.*
impel *v.t.* (*propel*) pousser; (*fig.*) forcer, obliger à.
impend *v.i.* (*hang over*) être suspendu sur; (*be imminent*) menacer; (*fig.*) planer; **~ing** *adj.* imminent, prochain.
impenetrab/le *adj.* impénétrable; **~ility** *s.* impénétrabilité *f.*; **~ly** *adv.**.
impeniten/t *adj.* impénitent; **~ce** *s.* impénitence *f.*
imperative *adj.* (*peremptory*) impératif; (*urgent*) impérieux; (*obligatory*) obligatoire; *s.* (*ling.*) impératif *m.*; **~ly** *adv.**;*;*.
imperceptib/le *adj.* imperceptible; **~ility** *s.* imperceptibilité *f.*; **~ly** *adv.**.
imperfect *s.* (*ling.*) imparfait *m.*; *adj.* (≠ *perfect*) imparfait; (*incomplete*) inachevé; (*faulty*) défectueux; **~ion** *s.* imperfection *f.*; **~ly** *adv.* imparfaitement.
imperial *s.* (*beard*) impériale *f.*; *adj.* impérial; **~ism** *s.* impérialisme *m.*; **~ist** *s.* impérialiste *m.f.*; **~istic** *adj.* impérialiste; **~ly** *adv.**.
imperil *v.t.* mettre en péril.
imperious *adj.* impérieux; **~ly** *adv.**; **~ness** *s.* (*commanding nature*) nature impérieuse *f.*; (*urgency*) urgence *f.*
imperishable *adj.* impérissable.
impermanent *adj.* transitoire.
impermeab/le *adj.* imperméable; **~ility** *s.* imperméabilité *f.*
impersonal *adj.* impersonnel; **~ly** *adv.**.
impersonat/e *v.t.* **1.** personnifier; **2.** (*theat.*) jouer le rôle de **3.** (*assume identity of*) se faire passer pour; **~ion** *s.* (1) personnification *f.*; (2) interprétation *f.*; (3) usurpation d'identité *f.*; **~or** *s.* (1) (*fig.*) incarnation *f.*; (2) interprète *m.f.*; (3) imposteur *m.*
impertinen/t *adj.* **1.** (*insolent*) impertinent; **2.** (*irrelevant*) hors de propos; **~ce** *s.* (1) impertinence *f.*; (2) manque de rapport *m.*; **~tly** *adv.* (1) avec impertinence; (2) hors de propos.
imperturbab/le *adj.* imperturbable; **~ility** *s.* imperturbabilité *f.*; **~ly** *adv.**.
impervious *adj.* imperméable (à); (*fig.*) insensible (à); **~ness** *s.* imperméabilité *f.*; (*fig.*) impénétrabilité *f.*
impetigo *s.* impétigo *m.*
impetu/ous *adj.* impétueux; **~osity** *s.* impétuosité *f.*; **~ously** *adv.**.
impetus *s.* (*moving force*) force impulsive *f.*; (*momentum*) vitesse acquise *f.*; (*impulse*) élan *m.*, impulsion *f.*
impinge *v.i.* se heurter (*on*—à).
impi/ous *adj.* impie; **~ety** *s.* impiété *f.*; **~ously** *adv.* avec impiété.
implacab/le *adj.* implacable; **~ility** *s.* implacabilité *f.*; **~ly** *adv.**.
implant *v.t.* implanter.
implausible *adj.* peu plausible.
implement *s.* (*piece of equipment*) équipement *m.*; (*tool*) outil *m.*; *v.t.* (*give effect to*) exécuter; (*fulfil*) accomplir; **~ation** *s.* exécution *f.*
implicat/e *v.t.* (*entwine*) entrelacer; (*involve, imply*) impliquer; **~ion** *s.* implication *f.*
implicit *adj.* (*not expressed*) implicite; (*unquestioning*) absolu; **~ly** *adv.**;*.
implore *v.t.* & *i.* implorer.
imply *v.t.* (*involve truth of*) impliquer; (*mean*) signifier; (*insinuate, hint*) sous-entendre.
impolite *adj.* impoli; **~ly** *adv.**; **~ness** *s.* impolitesse *f.*, manque de politesse *m.*
impolitic *adj.* peu politique.
imponderable *adj.* & *s.m.* impondérable.
import *s.* **1.** (*meaning*) signification *f.*; **2.** (*importance*) importance *f.*; **3.** (*comm.*) article d'importation *m.*; *v.t.* (1) signifier; (3) importer; *v.i.* (2) importer, avoir de l'importance; **~ation** *s.* importation *f.*; **~er** *s.* importateur *m.*
importan/t *adj.* important; **~ce** *s.* importance *f.*; **~tly** *adv.* avec importance.
importun/e *v.t.* importuner; (*harrass*) harceler;

~ate *adj.* importun; **~ately** *adv.* importunément; **~ity** *s.* importunité *f.*
impos/e *v.t.* imposer; *v.i.* en imposer à; **~ing** *adj.* imposant; **~ition** *s.* (*act*) imposition *f.*; (*thing*) abus *m.*
impossib/le *adj.* impossible; (*pop.* = *outrageous*) impayable; **~ility** *s.* impossibilité *f.*; **~ly** *adv.* de façon impossible.
impost/or *s.* imposteur *m.*; **~ure** *s.* imposture *f.*
impoten/t *adj.* **1.** (*powerless*) impuissant; **2.** (*decrepit*) impotent; **3.** (*males, without sexual power*) impuissant; **~ce** *s.* (1), (3) impuissance *f.*; (2) impotence *f.*; **~tly** *adv.* sans force.
impound *v.t.* (*shut up in pound*) enfermer; (*confiscate*) confisquer; (*animals*) mettre en fourrière; (*auto.*) emmener à la fourrière.
impoverish *v.t.* appauvrir.
impracticab/le *adj.* irréalisable; (*road* = *impassable*) impraticable; **~ility** *s.* nature irréalisable *f.*; (*of road*) état non carrossable *m.*
imprecation *s.* imprécation *f.*
imprecis/e *adj.* imprécis; **~ion** *s.* imprécision *f.*
impregnable *adj.* imprenable.
impregnat/e *v.t.* (*make pregnant*) féconder; (*saturate*) imprégner (*with*—de); **~ion** *s.* imprégnation *f.*
impresario *s.* imprésario *m.*
impress *s.* (*mark ~ed*) empreinte *f.*; (*characteristic mark*) marque *f.*; *v.t.* (*imprint, stamp*) imprimer, marquer; (*fig. fix*) inculquer (*on*—à); (*affect deeply*) impressionner; (*mil.* & *force into service*) enrôler de force; **~ion** *s.* (*mark*) empreinte *f.*; (*of book*) édition *f.*; (*effect on mind, belief*) impression *f.*; **~ionable** *adj.* impressionnable; **~ionism** *s.* impressionnisme *m.*; **~ive** *adj.* impressionnant; **~ively** *adv.* de façon impressionnante.
imprest *s.* avance de fonds *f.*
imprint *s.* empreinte *f.*; (*publisher's*) indication de l'éditeur *f.*; *v.t.* imprimer.
imprison *v.t.* emprisonner; **~ment** *s.* emprisonnement *m.*
improbab/le *adj.* **1.** (*not likely*) improbable; **2.** (*incredible*) invraisemblable; **~ility** *s.* (1) improbabilité *f.*; (2) invraisemblance *f.*; **~ly** *adv.* (1)*; (2)*.
impromptu *adj.* & *adv.* impromptu.
improp/er *adj.* **1.** (*inaccurate*) inexact; **2.** (*indecent*) inconvenant; **~erly** *adv.* (1) inexactement; (2) d'une manière inconvenante; **~riety** *s.* (1) inexactitude *f.*; (2) inconvenance *f.*
improv/e *v.t.* & *i.* (*make better*) (s')améliorer; (*make good use of*) profiter de; **~able** *adj.* améliorable; **~ement** *s.* amélioration *f.*; (*fig.*) embellissements *m.pl.*; **~ing** *adj.* améliorant; (*edifying*) édifiant; (*instructive*) instructif.
improviden/t *adj.* imprévoyant; **~ce** *s.* imprévoyance *f.*; **~tly** *adv.* sans prévoyance.
improvis/e *v.t.* improviser; **~ation** *s.* improvisation *f.*
impruden/t *adj.* imprudent; **~ce** *s.* imprudence *f.*; **~tly** *adv.* imprudemment.
impuden/t *adj.* impudent; **~ce** *s.* impudence *f.*; **~tly** *adv.* impudemment.
impugn *v.t.* (*s.o.*) attaquer (qn.); (*sth.*) mettre en doute (qch.).
impuls/e *s.* (*impelling*) impulsion *f.*; (*impetus*) élan *m.*; (*tendency to act rashly*) coup de tête *m.*; **~ion** *s.* impulsion *f.*; **~ive** *adj.* impulsif; **~ively** *adv.**.
impunity *s.* impunité *f.*
impur/e *adj.* (*dirty*) sale; (*unchaste*) impur; (*adulterated*) mélangé; **~ely** *adv.* d'une manière impure; **~ity** *s.* impureté *f.*
imput/e *v.t.* imputer (à); **~able** *adj.* imputable; **~ation** *s.* imputation *f.*
in *prep.* **1.** dans, **~ the house,** dans la maison; **~ my garden,** dans mon jardin; **~ a month,** dans un mois; **2.** en (*usu. without article*) **~ good health,** en bonne santé; **~ itself,** en soi; (*with f. countries*) **~ France,** en France; **3.** à, **~ his way,** à sa manière; **~ time,** à temps; (*with names of towns*) **~ Paris,** à Paris; (*with m. countries*) **~ Canada,** au Canada; **4.** chez, **~ animals,** chez les animaux; (~ *the works of*) **~ Balzac,** chez Balzac; **5.** de (*measurement*) **ten feet ~ height,** dix pieds de haut; (*time*) **ten o'clock ~ the evening,** dix heures du soir; (*after a superlative*) **the best ~ the class,** le meilleur de la classe; **~ a certain way,** d'une manière + *adj.*; **6.** entre (=*among*) **one day ~ a thousand,** un jour entre mille; **7.** par, (*weather*) **~ this weather,** par ce temps; **8.** pendant (=*during*) **~ the day,** pendant la journée; **9.** sous, **~ the rain,** sous la pluie; **10.** sur (=*out of*) **one man ~ ten,** un homme sur dix; **11.** **~ the morning, ~ the evening, etc.,** le matin, le soir, etc. (⚠ *no prep. in French*); *see also certain verbs,* BELIEVE ~, ENGAGE ~, etc.; *adv.* (*at home*) chez soi, à la maison; (*~side*) dedans; (*train, etc.*) arrivé; (*polit.*) au pouvoir; (*fam. fashion*) à la mode; **~ for,** engagé, inscrit, pour; **to be ~ for sth,.** être sur le point d'avoir qch.; **to have it ~ for s.o.,** avoir une dent contre qn.; ~-PATIENT; **~s and outs** *s.pl.* tenants et aboutissants *m.pl.*
inability *s.* incapacité *f.*
inaccessib/le *adj.* inaccessible; (*unapproachable*) inabordable; **~ility** *s.* inaccessibilité *f.*; **~ly** *adv.**.
inaccura/te *adj.* inexact; **~cy** *s.* inexactitude *f.*; **~tely** *adv.**.
inact/ion *s.* **1.** (*absence of action*) inaction *f.*; **2.** (*sluggishness*) oisiveté *f.*; **~ive** *adj.* (1) inactif; (2) oisif; **~ivity** *s.* inactivité *f.*
inadequa/te *adj.* insuffisant; **~cy** *s.* insuffisance *f.*; **~tely** *adv.* insuffisamment.
inadmissib/le *adj.* inadmissible; **~ility** *s.* inadmissibilité *f.*
inadverten/t *adj.* (*inattentive*) inattentif; (*unintentional*) commis par inadvertance; **~ce** *s.* inadvertance *f.*; **~tly** *adv.* par inadvertance.
inadvisable *adj.* à déconseiller.
inalienab/le *adj.* inaliénable; **~ility** *s.* inaliénabilité *f.*
inalterable *adj.* inaltérable.
inan/e *adj.* (*empty*) vide; (*silly, senseless*) sot, stupide; **~ely** *adv.* stupidement; **~ity** *s.* inanité *f.*
inanimate *adj.* inanimé.
inapplicable *adj.* inapplicable.
inapposite *adj.* inapproprié.
inappreciable *adj.* inappréciable.
inappropriate *adj.* impropre (à).
inapt *adj.* inapte; **~itude** *s.* inaptitude *f.*
inarticulate *adj.* (*not jointed*) désarticulé; (*not distinct*) inarticulé; (*dumb, unexpressed*) muet, inexprimé; (*unable to express thoughts*) incapable de s'exprimer.
inartistic *adj.* (*person*) peu artiste; (*thing*) peu artistique; **~ally** *adv.* sans art.
inasmuch as *conj.* (*seeing that*) vu que; (*the more so*) d'autant plus que.
inattent/ion *s.* **1.** (*lack of attention*) inattention *f.*; **2.** (*negligence*) négligence *f.*; **~ive** *adj.* (1) inattentif; (2) négligent; **~ively** *adv.* (1)*; (2) négligemment.
inaudib/le *adj.* inaudible; **~ility** *s.* manque d'audibilité *m.*; **~ly** *adv.* de manière inaudible.
inaugur/ate *v.t.* inaugurer; **~al** *adj.* inaugural; **~ation** *s.* inauguration *f.*
inauspicious *adj.* peu propice.
inborn *adj.* inné.
inbred *adj.* consanguin.
Inca *s.* & *adj.* *invar.* Inca.

incalculabl/e *adj.* incalculable; (*uncertain*) imprévisible; **~y** *adv.**;*.

in camera *see* CAMERA.

incandescen/t *adj.* incandescent; **~ce** *s.* incandescence *f.*

incantation *s.* incantation *f.*

incapab/le *adj.* incapable (de); (*disqualified*) peu susceptible (de); (*law*) incompétent; **~ility** *s.* incapacité *f.*

incapacit/ate *v.t.* rendre incapable (de); (*law*) frapper d'incapacité; **~y** *s.* incapacité *f.*

incarcerat/e *v.t.* incarcérer; **~ion** *s.* incarcération *f.*

incarnadine *adj.* incarnadin.

incarnat/e *adj.* incarné; *v.t.* (*lit.* & *fig.*) incarner; **~ion** *s.* (*lit.* & *fig.*) incarnation *f.*

incautious *adj.* imprudent; **~ly** *adv.* imprudemment.

incendiary *adj.* incendiaire; *s.* (*person*) incendiaire *m.f.*; (*bomb*) bombe incendiaire *f.*

incense *s.* encens *m.*; *v.t.* (*perfume with* ~) encenser, parfumer; (*inflame with anger*) pousser à bout; (*incite*) pousser.

incentive *s.* aiguillon *m.* (*stimulus*) stimulant *m.*; (*comm.*) prime d'entreprise *f.*

inception *s.* début *m.*

incertitude *s.* incertitude *f.*

incessant *adj.* incessant; **~ly** *adv.* sans cesse.

incest *s.* inceste *m.*; **~uous** *adj.* incestueux.

inch *s.* pouce *m.*; **~ by ~,** peu à peu; **give him an ~ and he'll take an ell,** donnez-lui en comme la main, il en prendra comme le bras; **within an ~ of,** à un doigt de, à deux doigts de; *v.i.* **~ forward,** avancer peu à peu.

inchoate *adj.* (*just begun*) naissant; (*undeveloped*) rudimentaire.

incidence *s.* (*contact with thing*) incidence *f.*; (*range, scope, extent*) portée *f.*

incident *s.* incident *m.*, épisode *m.*; **~al** *adj.* (*casual*) fortuit; (*not essential*) accidentel; (*mus.*) d'accompagnement; **~ally** *adv.* (*casually*) fortuitement; (*in addition*) soit dit en passant.

incinerat/e *v.t.* incinérer; **~ion** *s.* incinération *f.*; **~or** *s.* incinérateur *m.*

incipient *adj.* naissant.

incis/e *v.t.* (*make cut in*) inciser; (*engrave*) graver; **~ion** *s.* incision *f.*; **~ive** *adj.* incisif; **~or** *s.* (*tooth*) incisive *f.*

incite *v.t.* inciter (à); **~ment** *s.* incitation *f.*; (*stimulus*) stimulant *m.*

incivility *s.* incivilité *f.*

inclemen/t *adj.* (*weather*) inclément; **~cy** *s.* inclémence *f.*

inclin/e *s.* pente *f.*; *v.t.* **1.** (*cause to lean*) incliner; **2.** (*dispose to*) disposer à; *v.i.* (1) (*lean*) s'incliner; (*bend*) se pencher; (2) (*be disposed to*) être enclin à; (*tend to*) incliner à; **~ation** *s.* (1) (*slope*) inclinaison *f.*; (2) (*propensity*) inclination *f.*; (*liking*) penchant *m.* (pour).

inclu/de *v.t.* renfermer, comprendre; **~ded, ~ding** *adj.* (y) compris; **~sion** *s.* inclusion *f.*; **~sive** *adj.* (*~ding, comprehensive*) inclusif; (*~ding extra payments*) (tout) compris; **from the 1st. to the 4th. ~sive,** du premier au quatre (quatrième) inclusivement.

incognito *s.m.* & *adj.* & *adv.* incognito.

incoheren/t *adj.* incohérent; **~ce** *s.* incohérence *f.*; **~tly** *adv.* sans cohérence.

incohesive *adj.* sans cohésion.

incombustib/le *adj.* incombustible; **~ility** *s.* incombustibilité *f.*

income *s.* revenu *m.* (*often pl.*); EARN**ed ~**; **~ tax,** impôt sur le revenu *m.*

incoming *adj.* arrivant; (*beginning*) commençant; (*tide*) montant.

incommensurab/le *adj.* incommensurable; (*not comparable in size, value, etc.*) incomparable; **~ility** *s.* incommensurabilité *f.*

incommensurate *adj.* (*out of proportion*) disproportionné (*with, to*—à, avec); (*inadequate*) insuffisant.

incommod/e *v.t.* (*inconvenience*) incommoder; (*trouble, annoy*) gêner; **~ious** *adj.* incommode.

incommunic/able *adj.* incommunicable; **~ado** *adv.* au secret; **~ative** *adj.* réservé.

incommutable *adj.* immuable; (*law*) incommutable.

incomparab/le *adj.* incomparable; **~ly** *adv.**.

incompatib/le *adj.* (*opposed*) opposé; (*discordant*) discordant; (*inconsistent*) incompatible (avec); **~ility** *s.* incompatibilité *f.*

incompeten/t *adj.* (≠ *competent* & *law*) incompétent; **~ce** *s.* incompétence *f.*; **~tly** *adv.* de façon incompétente.

incomplete *adj.* incomplet; **~ly** *adv.**.

incomprehensib/le *adj.* incompréhensible; **~ility** *s.* incompréhensibilité *f.*; **~ly** *adv.**.

incomprehension *s.* incompréhension *f.*

inconceivab/le *adj.* inconcevable; **~ly** *adv.**.

inconclusive *adj.* peu concluant, non décisif.

incongru/ous *adj.* (*out of keeping with*) sans rapport avec; (*absurd*) absurde; **~ity** *s.* manque de rapport *m.*, absurdité *f.*; ⚠ incongru = **rude, ill-mannered.**

inconsequen/t *adj.* inconséquent; **~ce** *s.* inconséquence *f.*; **~tial** *adj.* inconséquent; (*unimportant*) sans importance.

inconsiderable *adj.* (*not worth considering*] peu considérable; (*of small size, value, etc.*) insignifiant.

inconsiderate *adj.* (*thoughtless, rash*) inconsidéré; (*not considerate of others*) sans égards (pour autrui).

inconsisten/t *adj.* **1.** (≠ *consistent*) inconséquent; **2.** (*incompatible*) sans rapport avec; **~cy** *s.* (1) inconséquence *f.*; (2) contradiction *f.*; **~tly** *adv.* sans conséquence, sans suite.

inconsolable *adj.* inconsolable.

inconspicuous *adj.* peu apparent; **~ly** *adv.* discrètement.

inconstan/t *adj.* **1.** (*fickle*) inconstant; **2.** (*variable, irregular*) instable, irrégulier; **~cy** *s.* (1) inconstance *f.*; (2) instabilité *f.*

incontestab/le *adj.* incontestable; **~ly** *adv.**.

incontinen/t *adj.* (*lacking self-restraint; med.*) incontinent; **~ce** *s.* incontinence *f.*; **~tly** *adv.* incontinent.

incontrovertib/le *adj.* incontestable; **~ly** *adv.**.

inconvenien/t *adj.* (*impracticable*) incommode; (*unsuitable*) inopportun; ⚠ inconvénient *is a s.* = **inconvenience**; **~ce** *s.* inconvénient *m.*; (*trouble*) dérangement *m.*; **~ce** *v.t.* déranger; **~tly** *adv.* inopportunément.

inconvertible *adj.* inconvertible.

incorporat/e *adj.* constitué en société; *v.t.* & *i.* (s') incorporer (*with, in*—à); **~ion** *s.* incorporation *f.*

incorporeal *adj.* incorporel.

incorrect *adj.* **1.** (*improper*) incorrect; **2.** (*inaccurate*) inexact; **~ly** *adv.* (1)*; (2)*; **~ness** *s.* (1) incorrection *f.*; (2) inexactitude *f.*

incorrigib/le *adj.* incorrigible; **~ly** *adv.**.

incorruptib/le *adj.* incorruptible; **~ility** *s.* incorruptibilité *f.*

increas/e *s.* (*growth*) augmentation *f.*; (*in price, tax, etc.*) majoration *f.*; (*~ed amount*) plus-value *m.*; (*fig.*) redoublement *m.*; **on the ~e,** en hausse; *v.t.* & *i.* (*become, make, greater*) augmenter; (*intensify*) (se) développer; **~e price by 10%,** majorer le prix de 10%; **~ing** *adj.* croissant.

incredib/le *adj.* incroyable; **~ility** *s.* incrédibilité *f.*; **~ly** *adv.**.

incredul/ous *adj.* incrédule; **~ity** *s.* incrédulité *f.*

increment *s.* (*increase*) augmentation *f.*; (*profit*) plus-value *m.*

incriminat/e *v.t.* (*charge with crime*) inculper;

(*involve in accusation*) incriminer; **~ion** *s.* accusation *f.*
incrust *v.t.* encroûter; (*with gems*) incruster; **~ation** *s.* incrustation *f.*
incubat/e *v.t.* & *i.* couver; **~ion** *s.* (*med.*) incubation *f.*; **~or** *s.* couveuse *f.*
incubus *s.* (*demon*) incube *m.*; (*nightmare*) cauchemar *m.*; (*burden*) fardeau *m.*
inculcate *v.t.* inculquer (qch. à qn.).
inculpat/e *v.t.* inculper; **~ion** *s.* inculpation *f.*
incumben/t *s.* (*eccles.*) titulaire *m.*; *adj.* **to be ~t on,** incomber à; **it is ~t on you to,** il vous incombe de; **~cy** *s.* (*eccles.*) bénéfice *m.*
incunabula *s.pl.* incunables *m.pl.*
incur *v.t.* (*become liable to*) contracter; (*bring upon self*) s'attirer; (*suffer*) subir; (*run risk, danger*) courir.
incurab/le *adj.* & *s.m.f.* incurable; **~ly** *adv.**.
incurious *adj.* (*not curious*) peu curieux; (*inattentive, careless*) inattentif; (*indifferent*) indifférent.
incursion *s.* incursion *f.*
indebted *adj.* (*fin.*) endetté (envers); (*fig.*) redevable (à).
indecen/t *adj.* **1.** (*unbecoming*) malséant; **2.** (*immodest*) indécent; **~cy** *s.* (1) inconvenance *f.*; (2) indécence *f.*; **~tly** *adv.* (1) avec inconvenance; (2) indécemment.
indecipherable *adj.* indéchiffrable.
indecis/ion *s.* indécision *f.*; **~ive** *adj.* (*person, battle*) indécis; (*inconclusive*) peu concluant; **~ively** *adv.* d'une manière indécise.
indecor/ous *adj.* peu convenable; **~um** *s.* inconvenance *f.*
indeed *adv.* (*in truth*) en vérité; (*intensifying*) vraiment, **yes, ~!,** oui, vraiment!; (*concessive*) en effet; (*interrog.*) vraiment?
indefatigab/le *adj.* infatigable; **~ly** *adv.**.
indefensible *adj.* indéfendable; (*fig.*) insoutenable.
indefinable *adj.* indéfinissable.
indefinite *adj.* (*ling.*; *vague*) indéfini; (*blurred*) indistinct; (*unlimited*) illimité; **~ly** *adv.* indéfiniment; vaguement.
indelib/le *adj.* indélébilc; **~ly** *adv.* d'une manière indélébile.
indelica/te *adj.* **1.** (*unrefined*) indélicat; **2.** (*coarse*) grossier; **3.** (*tactless*) sans tact; **~cy** *s.* (1) indélicatesse *f.*; (2) grossièreté *f.*; (3) manque de tact *m.*; **~tely** *adv.* (1) d'une manière indélicate; (2) grossièrement; (3) sans tact.
indemnif/y *v.t.* **1.** (*secure against loss*) garantir (contre); **2.** (*compensate for*) indemniser (de); **~ication** *s.* (1) garantie *f.*; **3** (*act*) indemnisation *f.*; (*sum*) indemnité *f.*
indemnity *s.* (*security against loss*) garantie *f.*; (*exemption from penalties*) immunité *f.*; (*compensation*) indemnité *f.*
indent *s.* **1.** (*~ation*) dentelure *f.*; **2.** (*official order*) contrat *m.*, commande *f.*; *v.t.* (1) denteler; (2) passer une commande; **3.** (*print*) rentrer; **~ation** *s.* dentelure *f.*; **~ure** *s.* (*law*) acte, contrat *m.* (en double expédition); **~ures** *s.pl.* contrat d'apprentissage *m.*
independen/t *adj.* indépendant (de); (*unwilling to take help*) suffisant; **person of ~ means,** rentier *m.*; **~ce** *s.* indépendance *f.*; **~tly** *adv.* avec indépendance; indépendamment (de); chacun de son côté.
indescribable *adj.* indescriptible; (*vague*) vague.
indestructib/le *adj.* indestructible; **~ility** *s.* indestructibilité *f.*
indetermin/able *adj.* indéterminable; **~ate** *adj.* indéterminé; **~ately** *adv.* de façon indéterminée; **~ation** *s.* indétermination *f.*
index *s.* **1.** (*forefinger*) index *m.*; **2.** (*pointer on instrument*) aiguille *f.*; **3.** (*math.*) exposant *m.*; **4.** (*list*) index *m.*; **5.** (*fig.*) indice *m.*; *v.t.* (4) faire un index.
India *s.* (*geog.*) Inde *f.*; **~ paper** *s.* papier bible *m.*; ~ RUBBER; **~n** *adj.* & *s.m.f.* indien(ne), hindou(e); *adj.* des Indes; RED **~n**; WEST **~n**; **~n corn** *s.* maïs *m.*; **~n file** *s.* file indienne *f.*; **~n summer** *s.* été de la Saint-Martin *m.*
indicat/e *v.t.* (*point out, show*) indiquer, signaler; (*be sign of*) indiquer, signifier; (*express*) exprimer; **~ion** *s.* indication *f.*; **~ive** *adj.* indicatif; **~or** *s.* (*person* & *techn.*) indicateur *m.*; **direction ~or** (*auto.*) flèche *f.*, clignotant *m.*; **~or light,** lampe-témoin *f.*
indict *v.t.* accuser; **~able** *adj.* tombant sous le coup de la loi; **~ment** *s.* (mise en) accusation *f.*
indifferen/t *adj.* **1.** (*impartial*) impartial; **2.** (*unconcerned*) indifférent (à); **3.** (*neither good nor bad*) médiocre, passable; **4.** (*rather bad*) pas fameux; **~ce** *s.* (1) neutralité *f.*; (2) indifférence *f.*; (3) (*unimportance*) peu d'importance *m.*; **~tly,** *adv.* (2) avec indifférence; (3) passablement.
indigenous *adj.* indigène.
indigen/t *adj.* indigent; **~ce** *s.* indigence *f.*
indigest/ible *adj.* indigeste; **~ion** *s.* indigestion *f.*
indign/ant *adj.* indigné (*at, with*—contre); **~antly** *adv.* avec indignation; **~ation** *s.* indignation *f.*; **~ity** *s.* affront *m.*
indigo *s.* indigo *m.*
indirect *adj.* indirect; **~ speech,** discours indirect *m.*; **~ly** *adv.**.
indiscernible *adj.* indiscernable.
indiscipline *s.* indiscipline *f.*
indiscr/eet *adj.* indiscret; (*imprudent*) imprudent; **~eetly** *adv.* indiscrètement; imprudemment; **~etion** *s.* (*imprudence*) imprudence *f.*; (*rashness*) manque de retenue *m.*; (*social offence*) indiscrétion *f.*
indiscriminate *adj.* (*confused*) confus; (*undiscriminating*) sans discrimination; **~ly** *adv.* sans discrimination; (*wildly*) aveuglément.
indispensab/le *adj.* indispensable; (*necessary*) obligatoire; (*that cannot be set aside*) inéluctable; **~ly** *adv.**;*;*.
indispos/e *v.t.* (*make unfit*) rendre incapable (*for sth.*—de qch., *to do sth.*—de faire qch.); (*make averse to*) indisposer contre; (*med.*) indisposer; **~ed** *adj.* souffrant; **~ition** *s.* (*illness*) indisposition *f.*, (*aversion*) aversion *f.* (*to*—pour).
indisputab/le *adj.* incontestable; **~ly** *adv.**.
indissolub/le *adj.* indissoluble; (*chem.*) insoluble; **~ility** *s.* indissolubilité *f.*; (*chem.*) insolubilité *f.*; **~ly** *adv.**;*.
indistinct *adj.* indistinct; **~ly** *adv.**; **~ness** *s.* imprécision *f.*
indistinguishable *adj.* indiscernable.
indite *v.t.* rédiger.
individual *s.* (*single member of class*) individu *m.*; (*single person*) particulier *m.*; (*pop. person*) type *m.*; *adj.* (*single*) individuel; (*particular*) particulier; **~ism** *s.* individualisme *m.*; **~ist** *s.* individualiste *m.f.*; **~ity** *s.* individualité *f.*; **~ly** *adv.* individuellement, personnellement.
indivisib/le *adj.* indivisible; **~ility** *s.* indivisibilité *f.*; **~ly** *adv.**.
Indo-China *s.* (*geog.*) Indo-Chine *f.*; **~-Chinese** *adj.* & *s.m.f.* indo-chinois(e).
indocil/e *adj.* indocile; **~ity** *s.* indocilité *f.*
indoctrinat/e *v.t.* endoctriner; **~ion** *s.* endoctrinement *m.*
indolen/t *adj.* indolent; **~ce** *s.* indolence *f.*; **~tly** *adv.* indolemment.
indomitable *adj.* indomptable.
Indonesia *s.* (*geog.*) Indonésie *f.*; **~n** *adj.* & *s.m.f.* indonésien(ne).
indoor *adj.* d'intérieur; (*plant*) d'appartement; **~s** *adv.* à la maison.

indubitab/le *adj.* indubitable; **~ly** *adv.**.
induce *v.t.* (*prevail on, persuade*) persuader (à qn. de faire qch.); (*bring about*) provoquer, occasionner; (*infer*) déduire; **~ment** *s.* incitation *f.* (à); attraits *m.pl.*
induct *v.t.* (*install*) installer; (*introduce to*) initier à; **~ion** *s.* installation *f.*; (*inference*) induction *f.*; (*med.*; *electr.*) induction *f.*; **~ive** *adj.* inductif; (*electr.*) inducteur; **~ively** *adv.* par induction.
indulg/e *v.t.* & *i.* (*gratify*) se prêter à; se montrer complaisant envers; (*give free course to*) donner libre cours à; (*take pleasure in*) s'abandonner à; (*fam. drink too much*) boire à l'excès; **~e in,** se permettre de, se payer le luxe de; **~ence** *s.* complaisance *f.*, indulgence *f.*; **~ent** *adj.* indulgent, complaisant; (≠ *strict*) faible; **~ently** *adv.* avec indulgence.
industr/y *s.* (*diligence*) assiduité *f.*; (*comm.*) industrie *f.*; COTTAGE **~y**; **~ial** *adj.* industriel; **~ialism** *s.* industrialisme *m.*; **~ialist** *s.* industriel *m.*; **~ialize** *v.t.* industrialiser; **~ious** *adj.* travailleur; **~iously** *adv.* laborieusement.
inebriat/e *s.* ivrogne *m.*; *v.t.* enivrer; **~ion** *s.* ivresse *f.*
inedible *adj.* (*not eatable*) non comestible; (*unfit to eat*) immangeable.
inedited *adj.* inédit.
ineducable *adj.* inéducable.
ineffab/le *adj.* ineffable; **~ly** *adv.**.
ineffaceable *adj.* ineffaçable.
ineffective *adj.* (*thing*) inefficace; (*person*) incapable; **~ly** *adv.* sans effet.
ineffectual *adj.* (*thing*) inefficace; (*person*) incapable; **~ly** *adv.**;*.
inefficacious *adj.* inefficace.
inefficien/t *adj.* incapable; **~cy** *s.* incapacité *f.*; **~tly** *adv.**.
inelastic *adj.* non élastique; (*rigid*) rigide.
inelegan/t *adj.* **1.** (*ungraceful*) inélégant; **2.** (*unpolished*) grossier; **~ce** *s.* (1) inélégance *f.*; (2) grossièreté *f.*; **~tly** *adv.* (1) sans élégance; (2) grossièrement.
ineligib/le *adj.* inéligible; **~ility** *s.* inéligibilité *f.*; **~ly** *adv.* de façon inéligible.
ineluctable *adj.* inéluctable.
inept *adj.* **1.** (*out of place*) peu à propos; **2.** (*absurd*) inepte; **~itude** *s.* (1) manque d'à propos *m.*; (2) ineptie *f.*; **~ly** *adv.* (1) peu à propos; (2) sottement.
inequality *s.* (*lack of equality*; *unevenness*) inégalité *f.*; (*variableness*) instabilité *f.*
inequitable *adj.* peu équitable.
ineradicable *adj.* indéracinable.
inert *adj.* inerte; **~ia** *s.*, **~ness** *s.* inertie *f.*
inescapable *adj.* inévitable.
inessential *adj.* peu essentiel.
inestimable *adj.* inestimable.
inevitab/le *adj.* inévitable; **~ly** *adv.**.
inexact *adj.* inexact; **~itude** *s.* inexactitude *f.*; **~ly** *adv.**.
inexcusable *adj.* inexcusable.
inexhaustib/le *adj.* inépuisable; **~ly** *adv.**.
inexorab/le *adj.* inexorable; **~ly** *adv.**.
inexpedien/t *adj.* inopportun; **~cy** *s.* inopportunité *f.*
inexpensive *adj.* peu coûteux.
inexperience *s.* inexpérience *f.*; **~d** *adj.* inexpérimenté.
inexpert *adj.* inexpert; **~ly** *adv.* de façon inexperte.
inexpiable *adj.* inexpiable.
inexplicab/le *adj.* inexplicable; **~ly** *adv.**.
inexplicit *adj.* indéfini, vague.
inexpressib/le *adj.* inexprimable; **~ly** *adv.**.
inexpressive *adj.* inexpressif.
inexpugnable *adj.* inexpugnable.
inextinguishable *adj.* inextinguible.
inextricab/le *adj.* inextricable; **~ly** *adv.**.
infallib/le *adj.* infaillible; **~ility** *s.* infaillibilité *f.*; **~ly** *adv.**.
infam/y *s.* infamie *f.*; **~ous** *adj.* infâme; **~ously** *adv.* de façon infâme.
infant *s.* enfant *m.*; *adj.* infantile; **~ school,** (école) maternelle *f.*; **infancy** *s.* enfance *f.*; **~icide** *s.* infanticide *m.*; **~ile** *adj.* infantile, enfantin; **~a** *s.* infante *f.*
infantry *s.* infanterie *f.*; **~man,** fantassin *m.*
infatuat/e *v.t.* rendre fou, affoler; **to be ~ed with,** s'enticher de; **~ion** *s.* engouement *m.*
infect *v.t.* **1.** (*contaminate*) contaminer; **2.** (*med.*) infecter; **3.** (*fig.*) pénétrer (*with*—de), communiquer (qch. à qn.); **~ion** *s.* (1) contamination *f.*; (2) infection *f.*; **~ious** *adj.* infectieux.
infelicit/ous *adj.* malheureux; **~ously** *adv.**; **~y** *s.* malheur *m.*
infer *v.t.* (*deduce*) déduire; (*imply*) inférer; **~ence** *s.* déduction *f.*
inferior *adj.* & *s.m.* inférieur; **~ity** *s.* infériorité *f.*; **~ity complex,** complexe d'infériorité *m.*
infernal *adj.* infernal; **~ly** *adv.**.
inferno *s.* enfer *m.*
infertil/e *adj.* **1.** infertile; **2.** (*fig.*) stérile; **~ity** *s.* (1) infertilité *f.*; (2) stérilité *f.*
infest *v.t.* infester (de); **~ation** *s.* infestation *f.*
infidel *s.* infidèle *m.*; **~ity** *s.* (*law*) infidélité *f.*; (*fig.*) déloyauté *f.*
infighting *s.* (*boxing*) corps à corps *m.*; (*fig.*) luttes secrètes (au sein d'une société) *f.pl.*
infiltrat/e *v.t.* & *i.* (s')infiltrer (dans); **~ion** *s.* infiltration *f.*
infin/ite *s.* infini *m.*; *adj.* infini; **~itely** *adv.**; **~itesimal** *adj.* infinitésimal; **~itive** *s.* infinitif *m.*; **~itude** *s.* infinité *f.*; **~ity** *s.* infinité *f.*
infirm *adj.* (*weak*) faible; (*irresolute*) irrésolu; **~ary** *s.* infirmerie *f.*; **~ity** *s.* (*med.*) infirmité *f.*; (*weakness*) faiblesse *f.*
in flagrante delicto *adv.* en flagrant délit.
inflam/e *v.t.* (*add heat or fuel to*) mettre le feu à; (*cause inflammation in*; *fig. with passion, etc.*) enflammer; **~mable** *adj.* inflammable; **~mation** *s.* inflammation *f.*; **~ matory** *adj.* inflammatoire; (*fig.*) incendiaire.
inflat/e *v.t.* **1.** (*with air or gas*) gonfler; **2.** (*puff up with*) gonfler de; **3.** (*raise price artificially*) enfler; **4.** (*fin.*) avoir recours à l'inflation; **~ion** *s.* (1) gonflement *m.*; (2) bouffissure *f.*; (3) & (4) inflation *f.*; **~ionary** *adj.* d'inflation.
inflect *v.t.* (*ling.*) (*noun*) décliner; (*verb*) conjuguer.
inflexib/le *adj.* inflexible; **~ility** *s.* inflexibilité *f.*; **~ly** *adv.**.
inflexion *s.* inflexion *f.*
inflict *v.t.* infliger (*on*—à); **~ oneself on s.o.,** imposer sa présence à qn.; **~ion** *s.* (*punishment*) châtiment *m.*; (*disaster*) calamité *f.*
inflow *s.* afflux *m.*
influen/ce *s.* influence *f.* (sur); *v.t.* (*exert ~ce on*) influencer; (*affect*) influer sur; **~tial** *adj.* influent.
influenza *s.* grippe *f.*
influx *s.* (*crowd*) affluence *f.*; (*water*) afflux *m.*
inform *v.t.* (*tell*) renseigner (*about*—sur); (*inspire*) animer (*with*—de); (*bring charge against*) dénoncer; **well-~ed** *adj.* au courant; **to keep s.o. ~ed,** tenir qn. au courant; **~ant** *s.* informat/eur, -rice *m.f.*; **~ation** *s.* information *f.*; (*knowledge*) connaissances *f.pl.*; (*piece of news*) renseignement *m.*; (*accusation*) dénonciation *f.*; **~ative** *adj.* instructif; **~er** *s.* dénonciat/eur, -rice *m.f.*; (*police*) indicateur (de police) *m.*
informal *adj.* (*not observing forms*) irrégulier; (*without formality*) sans cérémonie; (*unofficial*) officieux; **~ity** *s.* absence de cérémonie *f.*;

~ly *adv.* sans cérémonie; (*unofficially*) officieusement.
infraction *s.* infraction *f.*
infra dig *adj.* indigne de soi.
infra-red *adj.* infrarouge.
infrastructure *s.* infrastructure *f.*
infrequen/t *adj.* peu fréquent; **~cy** *s.* rareté *f.*; **~tly** *adv.* rarement.
infringe *v.t.* enfreindre; **~ment** *s.* infraction *f.*
infuriate *v.t.* rendre furieux.
infus/e *v.t.* & *i.* (s')infuser (dans); (*tea*) faire infuser; **~ion** *s.* infusion *f.*
ingenious *adj.* ingénieux; **~ly** *adv.**.
ingenuity *s.* ingéniosité *f.*; ⚠ ingénuité = **ingenuousness.**
ingenuous *adj.* (*frank*) franc; (*artless*) ingénu; **~ly** *adv.* franchement; ingénument; **~ness** *s.* ingénuité *f.*
ingest *v.t.* ingérer; **~ion** *s.* ingestion *f.*
ingle *s.* **~-nook,** coin du feu *m.*
inglorious *adj.* (*ignominious*) déshonorant; (*obscure*) obscur; **~ly** *adv.* sans gloire.
ingot *s.* lingot *m.*
ingrained *adj.* invétéré.
ingrate *s.* ingrat *m.*
ingratiat/e *v.t.* (*oneself with s.o.*) se faire bien voir de qn.; **~ing** *adj.* insinuant.
ingratitude *s.* ingratitude *f.*
ingredient *s.* ingrédient *m.*
ingress *s.* entrée *f.*
ingrowing *adj.* (*nail*) incarné.
ingurgitate *v.t.* ingurgiter.
inhabit *v.t.* habiter; **~able** *adj.* habitable; **~ant** *s.* habitant *m.*
inhal/e *v.t.* (*med.*) inhaler; (*fam.*) aspirer; (*tobacco*) avaler (la fumée); **~ant** *s.* (*med.*) inhalateur *m.*; **~ation** *s.* inhalation *f.*; **~er** *s.* inhalateur *m.*
inharmonious *adj.* inharmonieux; **~ly** *adv.* sans harmonie.
inherent *adj.* inhérent; **~ly** *adv.* par inhérence.
inherit *v.t.* & *i.* hériter (*from*—de); **~ance** *s.* héritage *m.*; **~or** *s.* héritier *m.*; **~ress, ~rix** *s.* héritière *f.*
inhibit *v.t.* (*prohibit*) interdire; (*hinder, restrain*) empêcher, retenir; **~ion** *s.* interdiction *f.*; (*med.*) inhibition *f.*
inhospitable *adj.* inhospitalier.
inhuman *adj.* inhumain; **~ity** *s.* inhumanité *f.*; **~ly** *adv.**.
inhum/e *v.t.* inhumer; **~ation** *s.* inhumation *f.*
inimical *adj.* hostile.
inimitable *adj.* inimitable.
iniquit/ous *adj.* (*unjust*) inéquitable; (*wicked*) inique; **~y** *s.* iniquité *f.*
initial *s.* initiale *f.*; *adj.* initial; (*fig.*) d'origine; *v.t.* parafer; **~ly** *adv.**.
initiat/e *s.* initié *m.*; *v.t.* **1.** (*originate*) inaugurer; **2.** (*admit to*) initier à; **~ion** *s.* (1) inauguration *f.*; (2) initiation *f.*; **~ive** *s.* initiative *f.*; **~or** *s.* initiat/eur, -rice *m.f.*
inject *v.t.* injecter; (*med.*) faire une piqûre à qn.; **~ion** *s.* injection *f.*; (*med.*) piqûre *f.*
injudicious *adj.* peu judicieux; **~ly** *adv.* peu judicieusement.
injunction *s.* (*order*) injonction *f.*; (*law*) mise en demeure *f.*
injur/e *v.t.* **1.** (*hurt, harm*) blesser, endommager; **2.** (*do wrong to*) faire du tort à; ⚠ injurier = **to insult**; **~ed** *adj.* blessé, **with multiple ~ies,** polytraumatisé; (*fig.*) offensé; **~ious** *adj.* (*wrongful*) nuisible, (*calumnious*) injurieux; **~y** *s.* (1) blessure *f.*, lésion *f.*, dommage *m.*; (2) tort *m.*; ⚠ injure = **insult**; **~y time** *s.* (*sport*) arrêts de jeu *m.pl.*
injustice *s.* injustice *f.*
ink *s.* encre *f.*: **~-pot, ~stand, ~-well** *s.* encrier *m.*; **~y** *adj.* couvert d'encre; (*colour*) noir d'encre.
inkling *s.* soupçon *m.*; **to have an ~ of,** avoir vent de.
inland *s.* intérieur *m.*; *adj.* d'intérieur; (*waterway*) fluvial; **~ revenue,** fisc *m.*; *adj.* fiscal.
in-laws *s.pl.* belle-famille *f.*, beaux-parents *m.pl.*
inlay *s.* incrustation *f.*; (*wood*) marqueterie *f.*; *v.t.* incruster; marqueter.
inlet *s.* bras de mer *m.*
inmate *s.* habitant *m.*; (*of asylum, home, etc.*) pensionnaire *m.*; (*of prison*) détenu *m.*
in(ner)most *adj.* (*deepest*) le plus profond; (*most secret*) le plus secret.
inn *s.* auberge *f.*; **I~s of Court,** ordre des avocats de Londres *m.*; **~keeper** *s.* aubergiste *m.*
innate *adj.* inné.
innavigable *adj.* non navigable.
inner *adj.* intérieur, interne; **~ tube** (*of tyre*) chambre à air *f.*; *s.* (*darts*) cercle près du centre de la cible *m.*
innings *s.* (*fig.*) tour *m.*
innocen/t *adj.* innocent; (*harmless*) inoffensif; *s.* innocent *m.*; **~ce** *s.* innocence *f.*; **~tly** *adv.* innocemment.
innocuous *adj.* inoffensif.
innovat/e *v.i.* innover; **~ion** *s.* innovation *f.*; **~or** *s.* innovat/eur, -rice *m.f.*
innuendo *s.* insinuation *f.*
innumerable *ad.* innombrable.
inobservan/t *adj.* inattentif; **~ce** *s.* inattention *f.*
inoculat/e *v.t.* inoculer; **~ion** *s.* inoculation *f.*
inodorous *adj.* inodore.
inoffensive *adj.* (*unoffending*) ne causant pas d'offense; (*not objectionable*) inoffensif; **~ly** *adv.* sans causer d'offense.
inoperable *adj.* inopérable.
inoperative *adj.* inopérant.
inopportune *adj.* inopportun; **~ly** *adv.* inopportunément; **~ness** *s.* inopportunité *f.*
inordinate *adj.* immodéré, irrégulier; **~ly** *adv.* immodérément, sans mesure.
inorganic *adj.* inorganique.
input *s.* entrée *f.*; **~-output table,** tableau entrées-sorties *m.*
inquest *s.* enquête (judiciaire) *f.*
inquir/e *v.t.* (*make search into*) faire une enquête sur; (*seek information about*) se renseigner sur; *v.i.* demander, s'informer de; **~ingly** *adv.* d'un air interrogateur; **~y** *s.* (*question*) demande *f.*; (*investigation*) enquête *f.*
inquisit/ion *s.* (*hist.*) Inquisition *f.*; (*official inquiry*) enquête *f.*; **~or** *s.* inquisiteur *m.*
inquisitive *adj.* curieux; **~ly** *adv.* indiscrètement; **~ness** *s.* curiosité *f.*
inroad *s.* (*incursion*) incursion *f.*; (*encroachment*) empiétement *m.*
inrush *s.* irruption *f.*
insalubri/ous *adj.* insalubre; **~ty** *s.* insalubrité *f.*
insan/e *adj.* fou; **~ely** *adv.* follement; **~ity** *s.* démence *f.*
insanitary *adj.* (*unhealthy*) malsain; (*unhygienic*) antihygiénique.
insatiab/le *adj.* insatiable; **~ility** *s.* insatiabilité *f.* **~ly** *adv.**.
inscri/be *v.t.* **1.** (*write in/on, enter on list*) inscrire (sur); **2.** (*book*) dédier; **~ption** *s.* (1) inscription *f.*; (2) dédicace *f.*
inscrutable *adj.* énigmatique.
insect *s.* insecte *m.*; **~icide** *s.* insecticide *m.*; **~ivore** *s.* insectivore *m.*; **~ivorous** *adj.* insectivore.
insecur/e *adj.* (*not secure*) peu sûr; (*not feeling safe*) inquiet; **~ely** *adv.* sans sécurité; **~ity** *s.* insécurité *f.*

inseminat/e *v.t.* inséminer; **~ion** *s.* insémination *f.*
insensate *adj.* (*unfeeling*) insensible; (*stupid, mad*) insensé.
insensib/le *adj.* **1.** (*imperceptible; unaware of*) insensible (à); **2.** (*unconscious*) inconscient; **~ility** *s.* (1) insensibilité *f.*; (2) inconscience *f.*; **~ly** *adv.* (1)*; (2)*.
insensitiv/e *adj.* peu sensible; **~ity** *s.* insensibilité *f.*
inseparab/le *adj.* inséparable; **~ility** *s.* inséparabilité *f.*; **~ly** *adv.**.
insert *s.* (*print.*) encart *m.*; pièce insérée *f.*; *v.t.* (*fit into*) insérer dans; (*introduce*) introduire; **~ion** *s.* insertion *f.*
inset *s.* encart *m.*; *v.t.* insérer; (*place between*) intercaler.
inshore *adj.* côtier; *adv.* près de la côte.
inside *s.* intérieur *m.*; **~s** *pl.* (*entrails*) estomac *m.*; *adj.* intérieur; (*fam.*) secret; *adv.* à l'intérieur; *prep.* à l'intérieur de; **~ out,** à l'envers; **~r** *s.* initié *m.*
insidious *adj.* **1.** (*treacherous*) perfide; **2.** (*proceeding subtly*) insidieux; **~ly** *adv.* (1)*; (2)*.; **~ness** *s.* (1) perfidie *f.*; (2) nature insidieuse *f.*
insight *s.* pénétration *f.*; (*awareness*) perspicacité *f.*; (*glimpse*) aperçu *m.*
insignia *s.pl.* insignes *m.pl.*
insignifican/t *adj.* insignifiant; **~ce** *s.* insignifiance *f.*
insincer/e *adj.* peu sincère; **~ely** *adv.* d'une manière peu sincère; **~ity** *s.* manque de sincérité *m.*
insinuat/e *v.t.* (*introduce gradually*) (s')insinuer; (*convey indirectly*) laisser entendre; **~ing** *adj.* insinuant; **~ion** *s.* insinuation *f.*
insipid *adj.* insipide; **~ity** *s.* insipidité *f.*
insist *v.i.* (*dwell on*) insister sur; (*maintain positively*) affirmer; (*demand urgently*) exiger; **~ence** *s.* insistance *f.*; **~ent** *adj.* insistant, pressant; **~ently** *adv.* avec insistance.
insobriety *s.* intempérance *f.*
in so far as, étant donné que.
insolen/t *adj.* insolent; **~ce** *s.* insolence *f.*; **~tly** *adv.* insolemment.
insolub/le *adj.* (*not to be solved, or dissolved*) insoluble; **~ility** *s.* insolubilité *f.*; **~ly** *adv.**.
insolven/t *adj.* insolvable; (*bankrupt*) en faillite; **~cy** *s.* insolvabilité *f.*; faillite *f.*
insomnia *s.* insomnie *f.*; **~c** *s.* insomniaque, insomnieu/x, -se *m.f.*
insomuch (*that*) à tel point (que).
inspect *v.t.* examiner avec attention; (*officially*) inspecter; **~ion** *s.* inspection *f.*; **~or** *s.* inspecteur *m.*; **~orate** *s.* inspectorat *m.*
inspir/e *v.t.* (*breathe in*) inspirer; (*s.o. with sth.*) inspirer qch. à qn.; (*animate*) animer (de); (*suggest*) suggérer; **~ation** *s.* inspiration *f.*; **~ing** *adj.* inspirant.
inspirit *v.t.* **1.** (*animate*) animer; **2.** (*encourage*) encourager; **~ing** *adj.* (1) vivifiant; (2) encourageant.
instability *s.* instabilité *f.*
install *v.t.* (*place in position, in office, etc.*) installer; **~ation** *s.* (*ceremony, apparatus*) installation *f.*
instalment *s.* (*comm.*) versement *m.*, **to pay by ~s,** régler à tempérament; (*of serial*) épisode *m.*
instance *s.* (*example*) exemple *m.*; (*particular case*) cas *m.*; (*request*) demande *f.*; **for ~,** par exemple; **in this ~,** dans ce cas; ⚠ instance = **entreaty**; *v.t.* donner en exemple.
instant *s.* instant *m.*; *adj.* (*urgent*) urgent, instant; (*immediate*) immédiat; **the 6th. ~,** le six courant; **~aneous** *adj.* instantané; **~ly** *adv.* instantanément.
instead *adv.* à la place; **~ of,** au lieu de.
instep *s.* cou-de-pied *m.*; ⚠ coup-de-pied = **kick.**
instigat/e *v.t.* provoquer, fomenter; (*incite*) inciter (à); **~ion** *s.* instigation *f.*; **~or** *s.* instigat/eur, -rice *m.f.*
instil *v.t.* inculquer (*into*—à).
instinct *s.* instinct *m.*; **~ive** *adj.* instinctif; **~ively** *adv.**.
institut/e *s.* (*society, building*) institut *m.*; *v.t* (*establish*) instituer; (*set on foot*) commencer, entamer; (*appoint*) investir; **~ion** *s.* (*act; established law or custom; building; fam. = familiar object*) institution *f.*; **~ional** *adj.* d'institution.
instruct *v.t.* **1.** (*teach*) instruire; **2.** (*inform*) avertir; **3.** (*give orders to*) donner des ordres à; **~ion** *s.* (1), (2), (3) instruction *f.*; **~ions** *s.pl.* (3) directives *f.pl.*; **~ions** (*for use of sth.*) mode d'emploi *m.*; **~ive** *adj.* instructif; **~or** *s.* maître *m.*, instructeur *m.*, professeur *m.*
instrument *s.* (*tool, implement, mus.*) instrument *m.*; (*law*) document officiel *m.*; **~al** *adj.* (*mus.*) instrumental; (*serving as ~ or means to*) contributif (à); **to be ~al in,** contribuer à; **~alist** *s.* (*mus.*) instrumentaliste *m.f.*; **~ality** s. intermédiaire *m.*; **~ation** *s.* (*mus.*) orchestration *f.*
insubordinat/e *adj.* insubordonné; **~ion** *s.* insubordination *f.*
insubstantial *adj.* peu substantiel; (*not real*) imaginaire.
insufferab/le *adj.* insupportable; **~ly** *adv.**.
insufficien/t *adj.* insuffisant; **~cy** *s.* insuffisance *f.*; **~tly** *adv.* insuffisamment.
insular *adj.* (*geog.*) insulaire; (*fig.*) borné; **~ity** *s.* insularité *f.*; (*fig.*) étroitesse d'esprit *f.*
insulat/e *v.t.* (*electr.*) isoler; **~ion** *s.* isolation *f.*; **~or** *s.* (*techn.*) isolateur *m.*; (*substance*) isolant *m.*
insulin *s.* insuline *f.*
insult *s.* (*abuse*) injure *f.*; (*indignity*) outrage *m.*; (*affront*) affront *m.*; *v.t.* injurier, insulter; **~ing** *adj.* injurieux, insultant; **~ingly** *adv.* d'une manière insultante.
insuperable *adj.* insurmontable.
insupportable *adj.* insupportable.
insur/e *v.t.* (*make sure, guarantee, fin.*) assurer; **~able** *adj.* assurable; **~ance** *s.* assurance *f.*; **car, life, fire, all risks ~ance,** assurance automobile, vie, incendie, tous risques; **~ance company,** compagnie d'assurances *f.*; **~ance policy,** police d'assurances *f.*
insurgen/t *adj.* & *s.m.* insurgé; **~ce** *s.* insurrection *f.*
insurmountable *adj.* insurmontable.
insurrection *s.* insurrection *f.*
insusceptible *adj.* non susceptible (*of, to*—de).
intact *adj.* intact.
intake *s.* (*techn.*): (*air*) appel *m.*, (*water*) prise *f.*; (*of people*) recrues *f.pl.*
intangib/le *adj.* intangible; (*fig.*) insaisissable; **~ility** *s.* intangibilité *f.*; **~ly** *adv.**.
integ/er *s.* nombre entier *m.*; **~ral** *s.* intégrale *f.*; *adj.* (*complete*) intégral; (*of or essential to whole*) intégrant; **to be an ~ral part of,** faire partie intégrante de; **~rally** *adv.* intégralement; **~rate** *v.t.* (*complete*) compléter; (*form into whole*) unifier; (*assimilate*) intégrer; **~ration** *s.* intégration *f.*; **~rity** *s.* (*lit.* & *fig.*) intégrité *f.*
integument *s.* tégument *m.*
intellect *s.* (*philos.*) intellect *m.*; (*ability*) intelligence *f.*; **~ual** *adj.* & *s.m.* intellectuel; **~ually** *adv.**.
intelligen/t *adj.* intelligent; **~ce** *s.* (*intellect*) intellect *m.*; (*ability*) intelligence *f.*; (*news*) renseignements *m.pl.*; (*mil.*) service des renseignements *m.*, service secret *m.*; **~ce quotient** (*I.Q.*) coefficient d'âge mental *m.*; **~tly** *adv.* avec intelligence; **~tsia** *s.* élite intellectuelle *f.*
intelligib/le *adj.* intelligible; **~ly** *adv.**.
intemper/ate *adj.* intempérant; (*excessive*) immodéré; **~ance** *s.* intempérance *f.*

intend *v.t.* (*purpose*) ~ **to,** avoir l'intention de; (*design*) ~ **for,** destiner à; *v.i.* (*mean*) vouloir dire.

intens/e *adj.* (*in high degree*; *strenuous*) intense; (*vehement*) fervent; (*strained*) tendu; ~**ely** *adv.* intensément; (*fam.*) extrêmement; ~**ify** *v.t.* & *i.* (s')intensifier; ~**ity** *s.* intensité *f.*; (*fig.*) ardeur *f.*; ~**ive** *adj.* intensif; **labour** (*etc.*) -~**ive,** à forte proportion de travail, (etc.).

intent *s.* intention *f.*; **to loiter with** ~, (*law*) rôder avec intention délictueuse; **to all** ~**s and purposes,** à toutes fins utiles; *adj.* (*resolved on*) résolu à; (*absorbed in*) absorbé par; (*eager*) ardent; ~**ly** *adv.* attentivement; ~**ness** *s.* attention soutenue *f.*

intention *s.* intention *f.*; ~**al** *adj.* intentionnel; ~**ally** *adv.**.

inter *v.t.* enterrer; ~**ment** *s.* enterrement *m.*

inter- *prefix* entre, inter; *in combination*: ~**-allied** *adj.* interallié; ~**-city** *adj.* interurbain; ~**-continental** *adj.* intercontinental; ~**-departmental** *adj.* interdépartemental; ~**planetary** *adj.* interplanétaire; *and see below in text.*

interact *v.t.* exercer une action réciproque; ~**ion** *s.* action réciproque *f.*

inter alia, entre autres.

interbreed *v.t.* & *i.* (se) croiser.

intercede *v.t.* intercéder, (*with s.o.*—auprès de qn., *for s.o.*—en faveur de qn.).

intercept *v.t.* intercepter; (*cut off*) couper; ~**ion** *s.* interception *f.*

intercess/ion *s.* intercession *f.*; ~**or** *s.* intercesseur *m.*

interchange *s.* **1.** (*exchange*) échange *m.*; **2.** (*alternation*) alternance *f.*; **3.** (*road junction*) échangeur *m.*; *v.t.* (1) échanger; (2) faire alterner; ~**able** *adj.* interchangeable.

intercom *s.* interphone *m.*

intercourse *s.* (*social*) relations *f.pl.*; (*sexual*) rapports (sexuels) *m.pl.*

interdependent *adj.* interdépendant.

interdict *s.* interdit *m.*; *v.t.* interdire (à qn de faire qch.); ~**ion** *s.* interdiction *f.*

interest *s.* (*title, right*) titre *m.*, droit *m.*; (*advantage, influence*) intérêt *m.*; (*fin.*) intérêts *m.pl.*; (*quality exciting attention*) intérêt *m.*; **in the** ~ **of,** dans l'intérêt de; **to take an** ~ **in,** s'intéresser à; **to have an** ~ **in,** avoir des intérêts dans; *v.t.* intéresser; ~**ing** *adj.* intéressant.

interfer/e *v.t.* & *i.* (*oppose*) contrecarrer, gêner; (*meddle with*) se mêler de; (*intervene*) intervenir (dans), s'ingérer (dans); ~**ence** *s.* intervention *f.*; (*radio etc.*) parasites *m.pl.*

interim *s.* intérim *m.*; *adj.* (*thing*) provisoire; (*person*) par intérim.

interior *s.* intérieur *m.*; *adj.* intérieur.

interjection *s.* interjection *f.*

interlace *v.t.* entrelacer; (*mingle with*) entremêler de.

interlard *v.t.* (*cook.*; *fig.*) entrelarder (*with*—de).

interlea/f *s.* page interfoliée *f.*; ~**ve** *v.t.* interfolier.

interline *v.t.* interligner.

interlock *v.t.* & *i.* (s')enclencher.

interlocutor *s.* interlocut/eur, -rice *m.f.*

interloper *s.* intrus *m.*; ⚠ interlope *adj.* = **suspect.**

interlude *s.* intervalle *m.*; (*theat.*) intermède *m.*; (*mus.*) interlude *m.*

intermarr/iage *s.* **1.** (*within family*) mariage consanguin *m.*; **2.** (*between races*) mariage entre races différentes *m.*; ~**y** *v.i.* (1) se marier entre proches parents; (2) se marier entre races différentes.

intermediary *adj.* & *s.m.* intermédiaire.

intermediate *adj.* intermédiaire.

intermezzo *s.* intermezzo *m.*

interminab/le *adj.* interminable; ~**ly** *adv.**.

intermingle *v.t.* entremêler (*with*—de); *v.i.* s'entremêler (*with*—à).

intermission *s.* pause *f.*; (*theat.*) entracte *m.*

intermit *v.t.* interrompre; ~**tence** *s.* intermittence *f.*; ~**tent** *adj.* intermittent; ~**tently** *adv.* par intermittence.

intermix *v.t.* & *i.* (s')entremêler.

intern *v.t.* interner; ~**ee,** *s.* interné(e) *m.f.*; ~**ment** *s.* internement *m.*

internal *adj.* (*techn., math.*) interne; (*domestic affairs, of State, etc.*) intérieur, de l'intérieur; (*med.*) interne, intestinal; ~**ly** *adv.* intérieurement.

international *s.* (*sport*) international *m.*; *adj.* international; ~**ly** *adv.* sur le plan international.

internecine *adj.* d'extermination réciproque.

interpellate *v.t.* interpeller.

interplay *s.* effets combinés *m.pl.*; réaction *f.*

Interpol *s.* Interpol *m.*

interpolat/e *v.t.* interpoler; ~**ion** *s.* interpolation *f.*

interpos/e *v.t.* (*thing*) interposer; (*argument*) faire état de; *v.i.* s'interposer; ~**ition** *s.* interposition *f.*

interpret *v.t.* interpréter; ~**ation** *s.* interprétation *f.*; ~**er** *s.* interprète *m.f.*

interracial *adj.* (*society, etc.*) composé de races différentes; (*relations, strife, etc.*) entre des races différentes.

interregnum *s.* interrègne *m.*

interrogat/e *v.t.* interroger; ~**ion** *s.* interrogation *f.*; ~**ive** *s.* (*ling.*) interrogatif *m.*; *adj.* interrogat/eur, -rice; ~**ory** *s.* interrogatoire *m.*; *adj.* interrogat/eur, -rice.

interrupt *v.t.* interrompre; (*break continuity of*) rompre; (*obstruct, view, etc.*) obstruer; ~**ion** *s.* interruption *f.*

intersect *v.t.* entrecouper; (*math.*) intersecter; ~**ion** *s.* intersection *f.*; (*road junction*) carrefour *m.*

intersperse *v.t.* (*scatter here & there*) parsemer (de); (*diversify*) émailler (de).

interstice *s.* interstice *m.*

intertwine *v.t.* & *i.* (s')entrelacer.

interval *s.* (*time, space*; *mus.*) intervalle *m.*; (*pause, break*) pause *f.*; (*theat.*) entracte *m.*; (*sport*) mi-temps *f.*; **at** ~**s,** par intervalles.

interven/e *v.i.* (*occur in meantime*) survenir; (*interfere, mediate*) intervenir; ~**tion** *s.* intervention *f.*

interview *s.* entrevue *f.*; (*press, etc.*) interview *m.*; *v.t.* interviewer, avoir un entretien avec.

interweave *v.t.* tisser ensemble; (*fig.*) entremêler.

intesta/te *adj.* & *s. invar.* intestat; ~**cy** *s.* absence de testament *f.*

intestin/e *s.* intestin *m.*; ~**al** *adj.* intestinal.

intima/te *s.* intime *m.f.*; *adj.* intime; (*familiar*) familier; *v.t.* (*make known*) annoncer; (*imply*) suggérer; ~**cy** *s.* intimité *f.*; ~**tely** *adv.**;*; ~**tion** *s.* annonce *f.*; suggestion *f.*

intimidat/e *v.t.* intimider; ~**ion** *s.* intimidation *f.*

into *prep.* dans; en (*usu. without art.*); **break** ~, **run** ~, *etc. see under relevant verb.*

intolerab/le *adj.* intolérable; ~**ly** *adv.**.

intoleran/t *adj.* intolérant; ~**ce** *s.* intolérance *f.*

inton/e *v.t.* & *i.* **1.** (*eccles.*) psalmodier; **2.** (*recite*) entonner; ~**ation** *s.* (1) psalmodie *f.*; (2) (*mus.*; *of speech*) intonation *f.*

intoxic/ant *s.* spiritueux *m.*; ~**ate** *v.t.* **1.** (*make drunk*) enivrer; **2.** (*excite*) enivrer; ~**ation** *s.* (1) ivresse *f.*; (2) enivrement *m.*; ~**ating** *adj.* enivrant.

intractable *adj.* (*not docile*) intraitable; (*not easily dealt with*) difficile à manier.

intransigent *adj.* intransigeant.

intransitive *adj.* intransitif.
intravenous *adj.* intraveineux.
intrepid *adj.* intrépide; **~ity** *s.* intrépidité *f.*; **~ly** *adv.**.
intric/ate *adj.* (*entangled*) embrouillé; (*involved*) compliqué; (*complicated, fig.*) complexe; **~acy** *s.* complication *f.*; complexité *f.*; **~ately** *adv.* d'une manière compliquée.
intrigu/e *s.* intrigue *f.*; *v.t.* & *i.* intriguer; **~er** *s.* intrigant(e) *m.f.*; **~ing** *adj.* intrigant.
intrinsic *adj.* intrinsèque; **~ally** *adv.**.
introduc/e *v.t.* **1.** (*usher in*) introduire; **2.** (*make known to s.o.*) (se) présenter; **3.** (*bring into use*) introduire; **4.** (*parl.*) déposer; **~tion** *s.* (1) & (3) introduction *f.*; (2) présentation *f.*; (*in book*) introduction *f.*; **~tory** *adj.* d'introduction, préliminaire.
introspect/ion *s.* introspection *f.*; **~ive** *adj.* introspectif.
introvert *adj.* & *s.m.f.* introverti(e).
intru/de *v.t.* introduire de force (dans); *v.i.* (*come uninvited*) imposer sa présence (à); (*be unwelcome*) être inopportun; (*inconvenience*) déranger; **~der** *s.* intrus *m.*; **~sion** *s.* intrusion *f.*; (*inconvenience*) dérangement *m.*; **~sive** *adj.* (*person*) importun, gênant; (*geol.*) intrusif.
intuit/ion *s.* intuition *f.*; **~ive** *adj.* intuitif; **~ively** *adv.**.
inundat/e *v.t.* (*lit.* & *fig.*) inonder (*with*—de); **~ion** *s.* inondation *f.*
inure *v.t.* aguerrir; (*harden*) endurcir (*to*—à).
inva/de *v.t.* envahir; (*encroach on*) empiéter sur; **~der** *s.* envahisseur *m.*; **~sion** *s.* invasion *f.*
invalid[1] *adj.* & *s.m.f.* (*ill*) malade; (*incapacitated*) infirme; (*incapacitated by injury*) invalide; *adj.* (*suitable for* ~*s*) de malade, d'infirme.
invalid[2] *adj.* (≠ *valid*) invalide; **~ate** *v.t.* invalider; **~ity** *s.* invalidité *f.*
invaluable *adj.* inappréciable.
invariab/le *adj.* invariable; **~ly** *adv.**.
invasion *see* INVADE.
invective *s.* invective *f.*
inveigh (*against*) *v.i.* invectiver (contre), *or* invectiver qn.
inveigle *v.t.* enjôler; **~ment** *s.* enjôlement *m.*
invent *v.t.* inventer; **~ion** *s.* (*act, product, ability*) invention *f.*; **~ive** *adj.* inventif; **~or** *s.* inventeur *m.*; **~ory** *s.* inventaire *m.*, *v.t.* inventorier.
inverse *adj.* & *s.m.* inverse; **~ly** *adv.**.
inver/t *v.t.* (*turn upside down*) renverser; (*order, etc.*) intervertir; **~ted** COMMAS; **~sion** *s.* interversion *f.*; (*ling.*) inversion *f.*
invertebrate *adj.* & *s.m.* invertébré.
invest *v.t.* **1.** (*clothe, dress*) vêtir (*in, with*—de); **2.** (*endue with*) investir de; **3.** (*lay siege to*) investir; **4.** (*fin.*) investir, placer; **~iture** *s.* (1), (2) investiture *f.*; **~ment** *s.* placement *m.*; **~or** *s.* actionnaire *m.*
investigat/e *v.t.* examiner en détail, étudier; **~ion** *s.* examen *m.*, enquête *f.*
invetera/te *adj.* invétéré; **~cy** *s.* obstination *f.*
invidious *adj.* (*conduct*) odieux; (*comparison, etc.*) blessant.
invigilat/e *v.t.* surveiller; **~ion** *s.* surveillance *f.*; **~or** *s.* surveillant(e) *m.f.*
invigorat/e *v.t.* fortifier; (*animate*) animer; **~ing** *adj.* fortifiant; (*air*) tonifiant.
invincib/le *adj.* invincible; **~ility** *s.* invincibilité *f.*; **~ly** *adv.**.
inviolab/le *adj.* inviolable; **~ility** *s.* inviolabilité *f.*; **~ly** *adv.**.
inviolate *adj.* (*not violated*) inviolé; (*unbroken*) intact.
invisib/le *adj.* invisible; **~ility** *s.* invisibilité *f.*; **~ly** *adv.**.
invit/e *v.t.* (*request s.o. to come, to do sth.*) inviter (qn. à faire qch.); (*solicit courteously*) solliciter; (*attract*) provoquer, susciter; **~ation** *s.* invitation *f.*; **~ ing** *adj.* (*food*) alléchant; encourageant; **~ingly** *adv.* d'une manière engageante.
invocation *s.* invocation *f.*
invoice *s.* facture *f.*; *v.t.* facturer.
invoke *v.t.* (*in prayer*) invoquer; (*appeal to, ask earnestly for*) implorer; (*summon by magic*) évoquer.
involuntar/y *adj.* involontaire; **~ily** *adv.**.
involve *v.t.* (*entangle, implicate in*) embrouiller, impliquer dans; (*entail*) entraîner; **~d** *adj.* embrouillé, compliqué; **~ment** *s.* complication *f.*; (*being* ~*d*) implication *f.*
invulnerab/le *adj.* invulnérable; **~ility** *s.* invulnérabilité *f.*; **~ly** *adv.**.
inward *adj.* intérieur, interne; (*fig.*) intime, profond; **~ly** *adv.* intérieurement; **~ness** *s.* essence *f.*; **~s** *adv.* intérieurement, en dedans.
inwrought *adj.* incrusté (de).
iodine *s.* iode *m.*
Ion/ian *adj.* ionien; **~ic** *adj.* (*arch.*) ionique.
iota *s.* iota *m.*
I O U. *s.* reconnaissance de dette *f.*
ipecacuanha *s.* ipéca *m.*
ipso facto *adv.* par le fait même.
I.Q. (*intelligence quotient*) *s.* coefficient d'âge mental *m.*
Iran *s.* (*geog.*) Iran *m.*; **~ian** *adj.* & *s.m.f.* iranien(ne).
Iraq *s.* (*geog.*) Irak *m.*; **~i** *adj.* & *s.m.f.* irakien(ne).
irascib/le *adj.* irascible; **~ility** *s.* irascibilité *f.*
ir/e *s.* ire *f.*; **~ate** *adj.* courroucé.
Ir/eland *s.* (*geog.*) Irlande *f.*; **~ish** *adj.*& *s.m.* (*lang.*) irlandais; **~ishman, ~ishwoman,** Irlandais(e) *m.f.*
iridescen/t *adj.* iridescent; **~ce** *s.* iridescence *f.*
iris *s.* (*bot.*; *of eye*) iris *m.*
irksome *adj.* ennuyeux.
iron *s.* (*metal*) fer *m.*, **cast ~**, fonte *f.*, CORRUGATED **~**; **scrap ~**, ferraille *f.*, **wrought ~**, fer forgé *m.*; (*tool*) fer *m.*; (*for clothes*) fer (à repasser) *m.*; **~s** *s.pl.* (*fetters*) fers *m.pl.*; **to strike while the ~ is** HOT; **to have too many ~s in the fire,** éparpiller ses efforts; **to rule s.o. with a rod of ~**, mener qn. avec une poigne de fer; *adj.* de fer, en fer; **I~ Age** *s.* âge du fer *m.*; **~clad** *s.* (*naut.*) cuirassé *m.*; **I~ Curtain** *s.* rideau de fer *m.*; **~-grey** *adj.* gris-fer (*invar.*); **~ lung** *s.* poumon d'acier *m.*; **~monger** *s.* quincaillier *m.*; **~mongery** *s.* quincaillerie *f.*; **~-mould** *s.* tache de rouille *f.*; **~works** *s.* industrie sidérurgique *f.*; *v.t.* repasser; **~ out** (*fig.*) aplanir; **~ing** *s.* repassage *m.*; **~ing-board** *s.* planche à repasser *f.*
iron/y *s.* ironie *f.*; **~ic(al)** *adj.* ironique.
irradiat/e *v.t.* illuminer; **~ion** *s.* illumination *f.*
irrational *adj.* (*illogical*) irrationnel; (*unreasonable*) déraisonnable; (*not endowed with reason*) dépourvu de raison; **~ly** *adv.* d'une manière irrationnelle; d'une manière déraisonnable.
irreclaimable *adj.* (*fig.*) incorrigible.
irreconcilable *adj.* (*implacably hostile*) irréconciliable; (*incompatible with*) inconciliable avec.
irrecoverable *adj.* (*law*; *fin.*) irrécouvrable; (*fig.*) irréparable.
irredeemable *adj.* (*fin.*) non amortissable; (*fig.*) irrémédiable.
irreducible *adj.* irréductible.
irrefutab/le *adj.* irréfutable; **~ly** *adv.**.
irregular *adj.* irrégulier; **~s** *s.pl.* (*mil.*) irréguliers *m.pl.*; **~ity** *s.* irrégularité *f.*; **~ly** *adv.**.
irrelevan/t *adj.* sans pertinence; (*out of context*) hors de propos; (*unconnected*) sans rapport (*to*—avec); **~ce** *s.* manque de pertinence *m.*; manque de rapport *m.*
irreligious *adj.* irréligieux.

irremediab/le *adj.* irrémédiable; **~ly** *adv.**.
irremovable *adj.* immuable; (*law*) inamovible.
irreparab/le *adj.* irréparable; **~ly** *adv.**.
irreplaceable *adj.* irremplaçable.
irrepressible *adj.* irrépressible; (*irresistible*) irrésistible.
irreproachab/le *adj.* irréprochable; **~ly** *adv.**.
irresistib/le *adj.* irrésistible; **~ly** *adv.**.
irresolut/e *adj.* irrésolu; **~ely** *adv.**.; **~ion** *s.* irrésolution *f.*
irrespective of, sans égard à.
irresponsib/le *adj.* irresponsable; (*act*) irréfléchi; **~ility** *s.* irresponsabilité *f.*; **~ly** *adv.**.
irresponsive *adj.* (*uncaring*) indifférent; (*unfeeling*) insensible (à).
irretrievab/le *adj.* irréparable; **~ly** *adv.**.
irreveren/t *adj.* irrévérencieux; **~ce** *s.* irrévérence *f.*; **~tly** *adv.**.
irreversible *adj.* irréversible; (*law*) irrévocable.
irrevocab/le *adj.* irrévocable; **~ly** *adv.**.
irrigat/e *v.t.* irriguer; (*med.*) arroser; **~ion** *s.* irrigation *f.*
irrit/ate *v.t.* (*lit.* & *fig.*) irriter; **~ability** *s.* irritabilité *f.*; **~able** *adj.* irritable; **~ant** *s.* irritant *m.*; **~ating** *adj.* irritant; **~ation** *s.* irritation *f.*
irruption *s.* irruption *f.*
-ish *suffix* (*with colours*) -âtre; *e.g.* **bluish,** bleuâtre.
isinglass *s.* colle de poisson *f.*
Islam *s.* Islam *m.*; **~ic** *adj.* islamique.
island *s.* (*geog.* & *fig.*) île *f.*; (*traffic*) refuge *m.*; *adj.* insulaire; **~er** *s.* insulaire *m.f.*
isle *s.* île *f.*; **I~ of Man,** île de Man *f.*; **I~ of Wight,** île de Wight *f.*; **~t** *s.* îlot *m.*
isobar *s.* isobare *f.*
isolat/e *v.t.* isoler; **~ion** *s.* isolement *m.*; (*phys. techn.*) isolation *f.*
isosceles *adj.* (*triangle*) isocèle.
isotherm *s.* isotherme *f.*
isotope *s.* isotope *m.*
Israel *s.* (*geog.*) Israël *m.*; **~i** *adj.* & *s.m.f.* israélien(ne); **~ite** *s.* israélite *m.f.*
issue *s.* **1.** (*going out*) sortie *f.*; **2.** (*outcome*) résultat *m.*; **3.** (*children*) postérité *f.*; **4.** (*question*) question *f.*; **5.** (*giving out*) distribution *f.*, émission *f.*; **6.** (*of newspaper*) numéro *m.*; **at ~,** en question; **to take ~ with s.o.,** prendre qn. à partie; *v.t.* (5) distribuer, émettre; (6) publier; (*an order*) donner; *v.i.* (1) sortir, jaillir; (*be derived from*) provenir de.
isthmus *s.* isthme *m.*
it *pron.* **1.** (*referring to sth. previously mentioned or implied*) (*subject*) il, elle; (*object*) le, la, l'; (*of ~*) en, **take some of ~,** prenez-en; (*to or in ~*) y, **the money is in ~,** l'argent y est, **he goes to ~,** il y va; **2.** (*as subject of impersonal v.*) il, **~ is raining,** il pleut; **~ is cold,** il fait froid; **~ is 6 o'clock,** il est 6 heures; **3.** (*as subject anticipating deferred subject*) (*with an adj.*) il, **~ is absurd to do that,** il est absurde de faire cela; **~ is incredible that he should refuse,** il est incroyable qu'il ait refusé; **~ is difficult to learn Greek,** il est difficile d'apprendre le grec; (*with a s.*) ce, **~'s an expensive business, these holidays,** c'est une affaire coûteuse, ces vacances; **4.** (*as subject representing deferred subject introduced by that* & *adv.*) ce, **~ is in vain that you argue,** c'est en vain que vous discutez, **~ is to him that you must apply,** c'est à lui qu' il faut vous adresser; **5.** (*as antecedent to a relative of any no. or gender*) ce, **~ was you who started,** c'est vous qui avez commencé; **~ was his glasses that he lost,** ce sont ses lunettes qu'il a perdues; **6.** (*as indefinite object with various v.* & *prep.*) *see these words*; **7.** *that's ~,* c'est cela (ça); **~self,** lui-même, elle-même, soi-même; (*with v.refl.*) se; (*emphatic*) même, **he is kindness ~self,** il est la bonté même; **by ~self,** de soi; **in ~self,** en soi.
italic/s *s.pl.* italique *m.* ⚠ *sing. in French*; **~ize** *v.t.* mettre en italique.
Ital/y *s.* (*geog.*) Italie *f.*; **~ian** *adj.* & *s.m.f.* italien(ne); *s.m.* (*lang.*) italien.
itch *s.* (*lit.* & *fig.*) démangeaison *f.*; *v.i.* démanger; (*fig.*) avoir grande envie (de).
item *s.* (*in list*) article *m.*; (*news*) fait divers *m.*; (*theat. etc.*) numéro *m.*; **~ize** *v.t.* détailler.
iterat/e *v.t.* répéter; **~ion** *s.* répétition *f.*
itineran/t *adj.* itinérant, ambulant; **~cy** *s.* (*law, eccles.*) fonctions itinérantes *f.pl.*
itinerary *s.* itinéraire *m.*
its *poss. pron.* son, sa, ses.
ivory *s.* ivoire *m.*; *adj.* d'ivoire, en ivoire.
Ivory Coast *s.* (*geog.*) Côte d'Ivoire *f.*; *adj.* ivoirien.
ivy *s.* lierre *m.*
izard *s.* isard *m.*

J

jab *s.* coup *m.*; (*med. fam.*) piqûre *f.*; *v.t.* piquer; (*thrust into*) enfoncer dans.
jabber *s.* **1.** (*chatter*) jacasserie *f.*; **2.** (*indistinct talk*) bredouillement *m.*; *v.i.* (1) jacasser; (2) bredouiller.
jabot *s.* jabot *m.*
jacaranda *s.* jacaranda *m.*
jacinth *s.* (*gem*) hyacinthe *f.*
jack *s.* (*mech.*) cric *m.*; (*small pike*) brocheton *m.*; (*ship's flag*) pavillon *m.*; UNION **J~**; (*cards*) valet *m.*; (*bowls*) cochonnet *m.*; **~ass** *s.* âne *m.*, (*fam. stupid person*) bourrique *f.*; **~boot** *s.* botte à l'écuyère *f.*; **~daw** *s.* choucas *m.*; **J~ Frost,** bonhomme Hiver *m.*; **~-in-office** *s.* bureaucrate *m.*; **~-knife** *s.* couteau pliant *m.*, (*dive*) saut de carpe *m.*, (*of articulated vehicle*) tête-à-queue *m.invar.*, *v.i.* faire un tête-à-queue; **~ of all trades** *s.* bricoleur *m.*; **~-o'-lantern** *s.* feu follet *m.*; **~pot** (*in lottery*) gros lot *m.*; *v.t.* **~ up** (*mech.*) soulever au cric.
jackal *s.* chacal *m.* (*pl.* -als.).
jackanapes *s.* freluquet *m.*
jacket *s.* (*garment*) veste *f.*, veston *m.*; LIFE-~; **strait ~,** camisole de force *f.*; (*of book*) jaquette *f.*; ⚠ jaquette = **man's morning coat, ladies' tailored jacket; ~** POTATOES.
Jacobin *s.* jacobin *m.*
Jacobite *s.* jacobite *m.*
jade *s.* (*worn-out horse*) rosse *f.*; (*gem, colour*) jade *m.*; **~d** *adj.* (*worn out*) éreinté; (*sated*) blasé.
jag *s.* **1.** (*sharp projection*) dent *f.*; **2.** (*fam. spree*) bamboche *f.*; *v.t.* (1) (*to cut, tear*) denteler; **~ged** *adj.* dentelé.
jaguar *s.* jaguar *m.*
jail *see* GAOL.
jalopy *s.* (vieille) bagnole *f.*
jalousie *s.* jalousie *f.*
jam *s.* **1.** (*cook.*) confiture *f.*; **2.** (*squeeze*) presse *f.*; **3.** (*traffic*) embouteillage *m.*; **in a ~** (*fig. fam.*) dans le pétrin; *v.t.* (1) confire; (2) serrer; (3)

embouteiller; **4.** (*radio*) brouiller; **5.** *v.t.* & *i.* (*mech.*) (se) coincer, (se) bloquer; **~ming** *s.* (*radio*) brouillage *m.*
Jamaica *s.* (*geog.*) Jamaïque *f.*; **~n** *adj.* & *s.m.f.* jamaïquain(e).
jamb *s.* montant *m.*
jamboree *s.* jamboree *m.*
jangle *s.* bruit discordant *m.*; *v.i.* faire un bruit de ferraille.
janissary *s.* janissaire *m.*
janitor *s.* (*of block of flats*) concierge *m.f.*; (*of other building*) portier *m.*
January *s.* janvier *m.*
japan[1] *s.* (*varnish*) laque *f.*; *v.t.* laquer.
Japan[2] *s.* (*geog.*) Japon *m.*; **~ese** *adj.* & *s.m.f.* japonais(e); *s.m.* (*lang.*) japonais.
jape *s.* (*joke*) plaisanterie *f.*; (*trick*) tour *m.*
japonica *s.* cognassier *m.*
jar[1] *s.* **1.** (*sound*) son discordant *m.*; **2.** (*shock*) choc *m.*; **3.** (*quarrel*) friction *f.*; *v.i.* (1) grincer; (2) (*fig.*) taper sur les nerfs de qn,; (3) (*colour*) jurer avec; **~ring** *adj.* discordant; (*colours*) disparate.
jar[2] *s.* (*vessel*) jarre *f.*; (*earthenware*) pot *m.*; (*glass*) bocal *m.*
jargon *s.* jargon *m.*
jasmin(e) *s.* jasmin *m.*
jasper *s.* jaspe *m.*
jaundice *s.* (*med.*) jaunisse *f.*; (*fig.*) envie *f.*; **~d** *adj.* (*fig.*) envieux.
jaunt *s.* excursion *f.*; (*fam.*) balade *f.*; *v.i.* faire une excursion.
jaunt/y *adj.* **1.** (*self-satisfied*) prétentieux; **2.** (*sprightly*) vif; **~iness** *s.* (1) prétention *f.*; (2) vivacité *f.*
Java *s.* (*geog.*) Java *m.*, île de Java *f.*; **~nese** *adj.* & *s.m.f.* javanais(e)
javelin *s.* javeline *f.*; (*sport*) javelot *m.*
jaw *s.* mâchoire *f.*; (*fam. = lecture*) laïus *m.*; **~s** *s.pl.* (*fam.*) gueule *f.*, (*of machine*) mâchoire *f.*; **~-bone** *s.* maxillaire *m.*; *v.i.* (*fam.*) gueuler.
jay *s.* geai *m.*; **~-walk** *v.i.* traverser en dehors des clous; **~-walker** *s.* piéton qui traverse en dehors du passage clouté *m.*
jazz *s.* jazz *m.*; *adj.* de jazz; *v.t.* jouer en jazz; (*brighten up*) animer.
jealous *adj.* jaloux (de); **~ly** *adv.**; **~y** *s.* jalousie *f.*
jean *s.* (*text.*) coutil *m.*; **~s** *s.pl.* bleu *m.*; blue--jean *m.*
jeep *s.* jeep *m.*
jeer *s.* (*~ing*) raillerie *f.*; (*booing*) huée *f.*; (*sarcasm*) sarcasme *m.*; *v.i.* railler; **~ing** *s.* raillerie *f.*; **~ing** *adj.* railleur.
Jehovah *s.* Jéhovah *m.*
jejune *adj.* (*agric.*) aride; (*fig.*) plat.
jell *v.i.* (*set as jelly*) se solidifier, prendre; (*take shape*) se cristalliser.
jell/y *s.* (*cook.*) gelée *f.*; (*pop. gelignite*) plastic *m.*; **~yfish** *s.* méduse *f.*; *v.t.* cuire en gelée; *v.i.* se solidifier; **~ied** *adj.* en gelée.
jemmy *s.* rossignol *m.*
jeopard/y *s.* danger *m.*; **~ize** *v.t.* mettre en danger.
jeremiad *s.* jérémiade *f.*
jerk *s.* **1.** (*sudden pull*) secousse *f.*, saccade *f.*; **2.** (*twitch of muscle*) tic *m.*; *v.t.* (1) donner une secousse à; (2) *v.i.* se crisper; **~y** *adj.* saccadé.
jerkin *s.* justaucorps *m.*
jerrican *s.* jerrican *m.*, nourrice *f.*, bidon *m.*
jerry-build/er *s.* constructeur de pacotille *m.*; **~ing** *s.* construction de pacotille *f.*
Jersey *s.* (*geog.*) île de Jersey *f.*; **j~** (*text.*) jersey *m.*; (*garment*) chandail *m.*
Jerusalem *s.* Jérusalem *f.*; **~ artichoke** *s.* topinambour *m.*
jest *s.* plaisanterie *f.*; (*object of derision*) risée *f.*; **in ~** pour rire; *v.i.* plaisanter; **~er** *s.* (*hist.*) bouffon *m.*; (*gen.*) farceur *m.*
Jesuit *s.* jésuite *m.*; **~ical** *adj.* jésuitique.
Jesus *s.* Jésus *m.*
jet *s.* **1.** (*stone*) jais *m.*; **~-black** *adj.* de jais; **2.** (*stream of water, etc.*) jet *m.*; **3.** (*aviat.*) avion à réaction *m.*; **~-propelled** *adj.* à réaction; **~ lag** *s.* fatigue (*f.*) due au décalage horaire; **~ set** *s.* jeunesse dorée *f.*; *v.i.* (2) gicler.
jetsam *s.* épaves *f.pl.*
jettison *v.t.* jeter par dessus bord; (*fig.*) se délester de.
jetty *s.* jetée *f.*
Jew *s.* juif *m.*; **~ess** *s.* juive *f.*; **~ish** *adj.* juif; **~ry** *s.* juiverie *f.*
jewel *s.* (*lit.* & *fig.*) bijou *m.*; **~-case** *s.* coffret à bijoux *m.*; **~led** *adj.* (*of watch*) à rubis; **~(l)er** *s.* bijoutier *m.*; **~(l)ery** *s.* bijouterie *f.*; **costume ~(l)ery** *s.* affiquets *m.pl.*
jib *s.* (*sail*) foc *m.*; (*techn.*) flèche *f.*; **the cut of his ~** (*fam.*) son allure *f.*; *v.i.* (*of horse* & *fig.*) se dérober (*at*—devant).
jiffy *s.* instant *m.*; **in a ~,** en un clin d'œil.
jig *s.* (*dance, mus.*) gigue *f.*; (*techn.*) gabarit de réglage *m.*; **~saw puzzle** *s.* jeu de patience *m.*; *v.i.* sautiller.
jigger *s.* (*flea*) chique *f.*; (*small glass*) goutte *f.*
jiggery-pokery *s.* manigance *f.* (*often pl.*).
jilt *s.* coquette *f.*; *v.t.* délaisser; (*fam.*) planter là.
jingle *s.* (*sound*) tintement *m.*; (*words*) verbiage *m.*; *v.i.* & *t.* (faire) tinter.
jingo *s.* chauvin *m.*; **~ism** *s.* chauvinisme *m.*
jinks (*high*) *s.pl.* ébats bruyants *m.pl.*
jinx *s.* (*fam.*) guigne *f.*
jitter *v.i.* avoir la frousse; **~s** *s.pl.* (*fam.*) frousse *f.*; **to have the ~s,** avoir la frousse; **~bug** *s.* alarmiste *m.*; **~y** *adj.* froussard.
jive *s.* swing *m.*; *v.i.* danser le swing.
Job *s.* (*person*) Job *m.*
job *s.* (*piece of work*) travail *m.*; (*task*) tâche *f.*; (*business*) affaire *f.*; (*post*) emploi *m.*, place *f.*; **a bad ~,** une mauvaise histoire *f.*; **it's a good ~ that,** heureusement que; **to make a good ~ of sth.,** mener qch. à bien, se tirer bien de qch.; ODD **~ (man)**; **~ lot** *s.* solde *m.*, occasion *f.*; *v.t.* & *i.* (*do ~s*) bricoler; (*hire out*) louer; (*stock exchange*) agioter; **~ber** *s.* (*stock exchange*) agioteur *m.*; **~bing** *adj.* (*of gardener, etc.*) à la tâche.
jockey *s.* jockey *m.*; DISC **~**; *v.i.* **~ for,** man-œuvrer.
jocose *adj.* jovial.
jocular *adj.* plaisant; **~ity** *s.* gaieté *f.*; **~ly** *adv.* en plaisantant.
jocund *adj.* enjoué; **~ity** *s.* enjouement *m.*
jodhpurs *s.* culotte de cheval *f.*
jog *s.* (*push, nudge*) secousse *f.*; (*slow walk*) petit trot *m.*; **~trot** *s.* petit-trot *m.*, (*fam.*) train-train *m.*; *v.t.* (*shake*) secouer; (*nudge*) pousser (du coude); (*~ memory*) rafraîchir; *v.i.* (*walk*) aller son petit train-train; (*for exercise*) faire du footing.
join *s.* réunion *f.*, jonction *f.*; *v.t.* (*put together*) unir, joindre; (*connect*) relier; (*become member of*) adhérer à; (*meet s.o.*) rejoindre qn.; **~ battle,** entrer en lutte; **~ hands,** se donner la main; *v.i.* se joindre, s'unir; **~ with others,** se joindre à d'autres; **~ in** *v.i.* participer à; **~ up** *v.i.* s'engager; s'enrôler (dans); **~er** *s.* menuisier *m.*; **~ery** *s.* menuiserie *f.*; **~ing** *s.* jonction *f.*
joint *s.* (*point of joining*) joint *m.*, jointure *f.*; (*anat.*) articulation *f.*; (*cook.*) rôti *m.*; (*pop. meeting place*) boui-boui *m.*; (*pop. marijuana cigarette*) dose *f.*; **out of ~,** disloqué, (*fig.*) désaxé; **to put s.o.'s nose out of ~,** jouer un sale tour à qn.; *adj.* réuni; (*fin.*) indivis; (*stock*) par actions; (*of persons*) co-, **~ author,** co--auteur *m.*, **~ heir,** co-héritier *m.*, **~ manager,**

co-directeur *m.*, ~ **owner,** co-propriétaire *m.*; (*of actions*) conjoint, ~ **venture,** opération conjointe *f.*; ~**ly** *adv.* conjointement; *v.t.* jointer, assembler; (*cook.*) découper.

jointure *s.* douaire *m.*

joist *s.* solive *f.*

joke *s.* plaisanterie *f.*, blague *f.*; **practical** ~, mauvais tour *m.*; **it's no** ~ **to,** ce n'est pas drôle de; **he cannot take a** ~, il ne comprend pas la plaisanterie; *v.i.* plaisanter; ~**r** *s.* blagueur *m.*; (*card*) joker *m.*

joll/y *adj.* (*joyful*) joyeux; (*festive*) gai; (*fam. delightful*) fameux; ~**y** ROGER; *adv.* (*fam.* = *very*) fameusement, drôlement; *v.t.* flatter; ~**ification** *s.* noce *f.*; ~**ity** *s.* gaieté *f.*

jolt *s.* cahot *m.*; *v.t.* & *i.* cahoter; ~**ing** *s.* cahotement *m.*; *adj.* cahotant.

Jones *s.* KEEP **up with the** ~**es.**

jonquil *s.* jonquille *f.*

Jordan *s.* (*geog.*) (*country*) Jordanie *f.*; (*river*) Jourdain *m.*; ~**ian** *adj.* & *s.m.f.* jordanien(ne).

jostl/e *v.t.* bousculer; *v.i.* se cogner (à); ~**ing** *s.* bousculade *f.*

jot *s.* brin *m.*; *v.t.* ~ **down,** noter; ~**tings** *s.pl.* notes *f.pl.*

journal *s.* (*diary, newspaper*) journal *m.*; ~**ese** *s.* langage journalistique *m.*; ~**ism** *s.* journalisme *m.*; ~**ist** *s.* journaliste *m.f.*

journey *s.* voyage *m.*; (*distance*) trajet *m.*; ⚠ journée = **day;** *v.i.* voyager.

joust *s.* joute *f.*; *v.i.* jouter.

jovial *adj.* jovial; ~**ity** *s.* jovialité *f.*; ~**ly** *adv.**.

jowl *s.* (*jaw*) mâchoire *f.*; (*heavy* ~) bajoue *f.*; CHEEK *by* ~.

joy *s.* joie *f.*; **to wish s.o.** ~ **of sth.,** féliciter qn. de qch.; ~**-ride** *s.* tour en voiture *m.*; ~**stick** *s.* (*pop. aviat.*) manche à balai *m.*; ~**ful** *adj.* & ~**ous** *adj.* joyeux; ~**fully** *adv.**; ~**fulness** *s.* joie *f.*; ~**less** *adj.* sans joie; ~**lessness** *s.* tristesse *f.*

J.P. (*abbrev. Justice of the Peace*) *s.* juge de paix *m.*

jubila/nt *adj.* radieux; ~**tion** *s.* jubilation *f.*

jubilee *s.* jubilé *m.*

Judai/sm *s.* judaïsme *m.*; ~**c** *adj.* judaïque.

Judas *s.* (*person,* (j~) *hole in door*) judas *m.*

judge *s.* juge *m.*, magistrat *m.*; (*sport*) juge *m.*; **to be a good** ~ **of,** se connaître en; *v.t.* juger; ~**ment** *s.* (*sentence, opinion*) jugement *m.*; (*good sense*) jugement *m.*; (*critical faculty*) discernement *m.*; **Last J~ment,** (jour du) jugement dernier m.

judic/ature *s.* (*administration of justice*) judicature *f.*; (*body of judges*) magistrature *f.*; ~**ial** *adj.* judiciaire; (*impartial*) impartial; ~**ially** *adv.**;*; ~**iary** *s.* judiciaire *m.*; ~**ious** *adj.* judicieux.

judo *s.* judo *m.*

jug *s.* pot *m.*; (*earthenware*) cruche *f.*; (*metal*) broc *m.*; (*pop.* = *prison*) taule *f.*; *v.t.* (*cook. hare*) étuver; ~**ged hare** *s.* civet de lièvre *m.*

juggernaut *s.* (*lorry*) poids lourd *m.*

juggl/e *v.t.* & *i.* (*lit.* & *fig.*) jongler (avec); ~**er** *s.* jongleur *m.*; ~**ing** *s.* jonglerie *f.*

jugular *adj.* & *s.f.* jugulaire.

juic/e *s.* (*cook.*) jus *m.*; (*fig.*) suc *m.*; (*pop. petrol, electr.*) jus *m.*; **to step on the** ~**e,** gazer; ~**y** *adj.* juteux, succulent; (*fig.*) savoureux.

ju-jitsu *s.* jiu-jitsu *m.*

ju-ju *s.* gris-gris *m.*

jujube *s.* jujube *m.*

juke-box *s.* phonographe à sous *m.*

julep *s.* (*med. obs.*) julep *m.*; (*mod.*) whisky glacé à la menthe.

July *s.* juillet *m.*

jumble *s.* fouillis *m.*; ~ **sale** *s.* vente de charité *f.*; *v.t.* brouiller.

jumbo *s.* éléphant *m.*; ~ **jet** *s.* (*aviat.*) gros-porteur *m.*, avion géant à réaction *m.*

jump *s.* (*leap*) saut *m.*; (*with shock*) sursaut *m.*; (*in price*) bond *m.*; (*obstacle to be ~ed*) obstacle *m.*; (*sport*) **high** ~, saut en hauteur *m.*, **long** ~, saut en longueur *m.*; **he's for the high** ~ (*fig.*) il va en prendre pour son grade; ~**-jet** *s.* (*aviat.*) avion à décollage vertical *m.*; *v.t.* & *i.* sauter, sursauter; (*price*) faire un bond; ~ **at sth.,** sauter sur qch.; ~ **the gun,** démarrer avant le signal; ~ **the queue,** passer avant son tour; ~ **to conclusions,** conclure sans réflexion; ~ **to it,** faire vite; **wait and see which way the** CAT ~**s;** ~**ed-up** *adj.* parvenu; SHOW ~**ing;** ~**ing-off place** *s.* base avancée *f.*; ~**y** *adj.* nerveux, (*fin.*) instable.

jumper *s.* (*garment*) chandail *m.*; (*sport*) sauteur *m.*

junction *s.* jonction *f.*; (*roads*) bifurcation *f.*; (*rail.*) embranchement *m.*; **spaghetti** ~, (*motorway*) échangeur *m.*

juncture *s.* (*techn.*) jointure *f.*; (*fig.*) conjoncture *f.*

June *s.* juin *m.*

jungle *s.* jungle *f.*

junior *s.* cadet *m.*; *adj.* plus jeune, cadet; (*in rank*) subalterne; (*comm.*) ~ **clerk, assistant,** petit commis; **W. R. Smith, jun.,** W. R. Smith, le jeune, W. R. Smith, fils.

juniper *s.* genièvre *m.*; (*tree*) genévrier *m.*

junk *s.* (*salt meat*) singe *m.*; (*oakum*) étoupe *f.*; (*scrap*) ferraille *f.*; (*fig. rubbish*) bêtises *f.pl.*; (*drug*) narcotiques *f.pl.*; (*Chinese boat*) jonque *f.*; ~**-shop** *s.* boutique de bric-à-brac *f.*; ~**ie** *s.* (*drug addict*) drogué *m.*

junket *s.* **1.** (*cook.*) lait caillé *m.*; **2.** (*feast*) gueuleton *m.*; *v.i.* (2) gueuletonner.

junta *s.* (*polit.*) junte *f.*

Jupiter *s.* jupiter *m.*

jur/idical *adj.* juridique; ~**isdiction** *s.* juridiction *f.*; ~**isprudence** *s.* jurisprudence *f.*; ~**ist** *s.* juriste *m.*; ~**or** *s.* juré *m.*; ~**y** *s.* jury *m.*; ~**y-man,** ~**ywoman,** juré *m.*, femme juré *f.*

just *adj.* (*fair, correct*) juste; (*of person*) équitable; (*deserved*) légitime; ~**ly** *adv.* justement, équitablement; (*with reason*) à juste titre; ~**ness** *s.* justice *f.*; (*accuracy*) justesse *f.*; *adv.* (*exactly*) exactement; (*barely*) à peine, tout juste; (*not long before*) il n'y a qu'un instant; (*fam.* = *quite*) franchement; **to have** ~, venir de + inf.; ~ **now,** récemment; ~ **one thing,** juste une chose; ~ **you,** vous seul; **we shall** ~ (= *only*) **say hello,** nous ne ferons que dire bonjour; ~ **the same,** (*however*) quand même.

justic/e *s.* justice *f.*; (*judge*) magistrat *m.*; (*magistrate*) juge *m.*; MISCARRIAGE **of** ~; ~**iary** *s.* justicier *m.*

justif/y *v.t.* justifier; ~**iable** *adj.* justifiable; ~**iably** *adv.* à juste titre; ~**ication** *s.* justification *f.*

jut *v.i.* (*out*) faire saillie.

jute *s.* jute *m.*

juvenile *s.* adolescent *m.*; *adj.* juvénile, pour enfants.

juxtapos/e *v.t.* juxtaposer; ~**ition** *s.* juxtaposition *f.*

K

Kaffir *s.* cafre *m.*
kale *s.* chou frisé *m.*
kaleidoscop/e *s.* kaléidoscope *m.*; **~ic** *adj.* kaléidoscopique.
kamikaze *s.* (*aircraft* & *pilot*) kamikaze *m.*
kangaroo *s.* kangourou *m.*; **~ court,** tribunal irrégulier *m.*
kaolin *s.* kaolin *m.*
kapok *s.* kapok *m.*
karate *s.* karaté *m.*
Kashmir *s.* (*geog.*) Cachemire *m.*
kayak *s.* kayak *m.*
kebab *s.* brochette *f.*
kedge (*anchor*) *s.* ancre à jet *f.*
keel *s.* quille *f.*; (*fig.*) **on an even ~,** en équilibre; **to ~ over** *v.i.* chavirer.
keen *adj.* **1.** (*sharp*): (*pointed*) aigu, (*cutting*) tranchant; **2.** (*air*) piquant; **3.** (*cold*) mordant; **4.** (*sound*) aigu; **5.** (*hearing*) fin; **6.** (*look*) perçant; **7.** (*emotion*) vif; **8.** (*mind*) pénétrant; **9.** (*eager*) ardent; **to be ~ on,** être passionné de; **to be ~ to,** être avide de; **~ly** *adv.* vivement; (*fig.*) avidement, ardemment; **~ness** *s.* (1) & (4) acuité *f.*; (2) & (3) sévérité *f.*; (5) finesse *f.*; (6) & (8) pénétration *f.*; (7) vivacité *f.*, profondeur *f.*; (9) ardeur *f.*; (*enthusiasm*) zèle *m.*
keep *s.* (*hist. tower*) donjon *m.*; (*maintenance, food*) subsistance *f.*, nourriture *f.*; **for ~s,** pour toujours; *v.t.* (*retain possession of, protect*) garder; (*have charge of, shop, house, accounts, diary, etc.*) tenir; (*maintain*) entretenir, maintenir; (*delay*) retarder, **~ s.o. waiting,** faire attendre qn.; (*reserve for future use*) retenir; conserver; (*observe, celebrate*) observer, célébrer, fêter; (*not reveal*) garder, **~ promise, word,** tenir (sa) parole; (*comm.* **~** *in stock*) tenir; *v.i.* (*continue doing sth.*) continuer à faire qch.; (*wait*) attendre; (*remain in good condition*) se conserver; (*remain*) rester; *v.refl* se tenir; **~** SILENT; **~ at,** s'acharner à; **~ away** *v.t.* & *i.* (se) tenir à l'écart; **~ back** *v.t.* retenir, (*enemy*) contenir, (*secrets*) taire; *v.i.* rester en arrière; **~ down** *v.t.* réprimer, maîtriser, (*price*) maintenir; *v.i.* se tapir; **~ from** *v.t.* & *i.* (s')empêcher; (*from doing sth.*—de faire qch.), (*information*) taire; **~ in** *v.t.* (*fire*) entretenir, (*at school*) mettre en retenue, (*feelings*) cacher; **~ in with s.o.,** rester en bons termes avec qn.; **~ in touch with,** rester en contact avec; **~ off** *v.t.* éloigner, écarter; *v.i.* rester à distance; **~ on** *v.t.* (*hat, etc.*) garder, **~ one's hair on,** ne pas perdre la tête; *v.i.* **~ on doing sth.,** continuer à faire qch.; **~ on at s.o.,** harceler qn.; **~ out** *v.t.* empêcher d'entrer; **~ time** (*clock*) donner l'heure exacte; **~ to** *v.t.* garder (*the right, etc.*—la droite, etc.); **~ to oneself,** garder pour soi; **~ oneself to oneself,** faire preuve de réserve; **~ together** *v.t.* & *i.* garder, rester, ensemble; **~ under** *v.t.* maîtriser, dominer; **~ up** *v.t.* soutenir, maintenir, entretenir; *v.i.* tenir bon; **~ up with s.o.,** ne pas se laisser distancer par qn.; **~ up with the Joneses,** chercher à épater les voisins; **~ up with sth.,** continuer à faire qch.; **~er** *s.* gardien *m.*, conservateur *m.*, **game~er,** garde-chasse *m.*, **goal~er,** gardien de but *m.*; **~ing** *s.* garde *f.*; **in safe ~ing,** sous bonne garde; **in ~ing with,** en harmonie avec; **~ing** *adj.* (*fruit*) de bonne conserve; **~sake** *s.* (*book*) keepsake *m.*, (*other things*) souvenir *m.*
keg *s.* baril *m.*
kelp *s.* varech *m.*
ken *s.* connaissance *f.*
kennel *s.* (*dog*) chenil *m.*; (*in street*) ruisseau *m.*
Kenya *s.* (*geog.*) Kenya *m.*; **~n** *adj.* & *s.m.f.* kenyan(e).
kerb *s.* bord du trottoir *m.*
kerchief *s.* fichu *m.*
kernel *s.* amande *f.*; (*fig.*) noyau *m.*
kerosene *s.* pétrole *m.*; (*chem.*) kérosène *m.*
kestrel *s.* émouchet *m.*
ketch *s.* ketch *m.*
kettle *s.* bouilloire *f.*; FISH-~; **a pretty ~ of** FISH; **another ~ of** FISH; **~drum** *s.* timbale *f.*
key *s.* (*for lock, for clock; solution*) clef *f.*; MASTER ~; PASS ~; SKELETON ~; (*code, crib*) corrigé *m.*; (*mus.*) clef *f.*, ton *m.*; (*of piano, typewriter, etc.*) touche *f.*; *adj.* clef, **~ industry,** industrie clef; **~ position,** position clef; **~board** *s.* clavier *m.*; **~hole** *s.* trou (de serrure) *m.*; **~note** *s.* (*mus.*) tonique *f.*, (*fig.*) dominante *f.*; **~stone** *s.* clef de voûte *f.*; **~ signature** *s.* armature *f.*; *v.t.* (*constr.*) claveter; **~ up** (*fig.*) surexciter.
khaki *s.* kaki *m.*; *adj.* kaki (*invar.*).
khan *s.* khan *m.*
Khedive *s.* khédive *m.*
kibbutz *s.* kibboutz *m.*
kick *s.* (*with foot*) coup de pied *m.*; (*of gun*) recul *m.*; (*fam. resilience*) allant *m.*; (*pop. thrill*) plaisir *m.*; **for ~s,** histoire de rire; *v.t.* donner des coups de pied à; (*football*) botter; *v.i.* donner un (des) coup(s) de pied; **~ over the** TRACES; **~ one's heels,** see COOL; (*gun*) reculer; **~ against** (*fig.*) rouspéter contre; **~ off,** donner le coup d'envoi; **~-off** *s.* (*sport*) coup d'envoi *m.*; **~ up** (*dust*) soulever; **~ up a row** (*fam.*) faire de boucan.
kickshaw *s.* colifichet *m.*
kid *s.* (*young goat*) chevreau *m.*, chevrette *f.*; (*child*) gosse *m.f.*; *adj.* (*leather*) de chevreau; **to handle s.o. with ~-gloves,** ménager qn.; *v.i.* mettre bas; *v.t.* (*pop.*) blaguer; *v.refl.* s'imaginer; **~dy** *s.* (*fam.*) mioche *m.f.*
kidnap *v.t.* kidnapper; **~per** *s.* kidnappeur *m.*
kidney *s.* (*anat.*) rein *m.*; (*cook.*) rognon *m.*; (*fig. sort, kind*) acabit *m.*; **~** BEAN; **~ machine** *s.* rein artificiel *m.*
kill *s.* (*act*) mise à mort *f.*; (*hunt. animals ~ed*) tableau de chasse *m.*; *v.t.* (*lit.* & *fig.*) tuer; **~ two** BIRDS **with one stone**; (*animals*) abattre; (*destroy*) détruire; (*auto.* ~ *engine*) bloquer; **dressed to ~,** habillé de façon mirobolante; **~joy** *s.* rabat-joie *m.*; **~er** *s.* (*person*) tueur *m.*; (*instrument, chem.*) insecticide *m.*, microbicide *m.*; **pain-~er** *s.* analgésique *m.*; **~ing** *adj.* (*exhausting*) éreintant, (*fam.* = *funny*) tordant.
kiln *s.* four *m.*
kilo- **~gramme** kilogramme *m.* (*abbrev.* kilo *m.*); **~metre** kilomètre *m.*; **~watt** *s.* kilowatt *m.*
kilt *s.* kilt *m.*
kimono *s.* kimono *m.*
kin *s.* parenté *f.*; parents *m.pl.*; KITH **and ~**; *adj.* apparenté; **next of ~,** le plus proche parent; **~dred** *s.* parenté *f.*, famille *f.*; **~ship** *s.* parenté *f.*; **~sfolk** *s.* parents *m.pl.*; **~sman, ~swoman,** parent(e) *m.f.*
kind[1] *s.* (*race*) espèce *f.*; (*class, sort*) classe *f.*, sorte *f.*; genre *m.*; **of a ~,** du même genre; **in ~,** en nature; (*fam.*) **~ of,** pour ainsi dire.

kind[2] *adj.* bon, aimable; **~liness** *s.* bienveillance *f.*; **~ly** *adj.* bienveillant; **~ly** *adv.* avec bienveillance, aimablement; **~ly do sth.,** avoir l'amabilité de faire qch.; **to take ~ly to,** prendre bien, (*be attracted by*) être attiré par; **~ness** *s.* bonté *f.*, amabilité *f.*, (*act*) bienfait *m.*
kindergarten *s.* jardin d'enfants *m.*
kindl/e *v.t.* & *i.* (s')allumer; (*fig.*) (s')enflammer, (s')exciter; **~ing** *s.* allumage *m.*
kine *s.* bétail *m.*
kinetic *adj.* cinétique; **~s** *s.* cinétique *f.* ⚠ *sing. in French.*
king *s.* (*ruler, chess, cards*) roi *m.*; (*draughts*) dame *f.*; ⚠ **K~ George,** le Roi Georges; **a** CAT **may look at a ~**; **~cup** *s.* bouton d'or *m.*; **~fisher** *s.* martin-pêcheur *m.*; **~pin** *s.* cheville ouvrière *f.*; **~-sized** *adj.* géant; **~dom** *s.* royaume *m.*, (*bot.*) règne *m.*; **~ly** *adj.* royal; **~ship** *s.* royauté *f.*
kink *s.* (*in wire, etc.*) nœud *m.*; (*in rope*) coque *f.*; (*fig.*) lubie *f.*
kiosk *s.* kiosque *m.*
kipper *s.* hareng saur *m.*; *v.t.* saurer.
kirk *s.* église *f.*
kirtle *s.* jupon *m.*
kismet *s.* destin *m.*
kiss *s.* baiser *m.*; **~ of life,** bouche à bouche *m.*; *v.t.* embrasser, donner un baiser à; ⚠ baiser qn. = **to make love to s.o.**; **~ing** *s.* embrassade *f.*; (*of feet*) baisement *m.*; (*of lady's hand*) baise-main *f.*
kit *s.* (*mil.*) paquetage *m.*; (*equipment*) équipement *m.*; (*outfit*) trousse *f.*; **first-aid ~,** trousse de premier secours *f.*; (*set of parts to be assembled*) prêt à monter, *e.g.* **aircraft ~,** avion prêt à monter, **model ~,** maquette prête à monter; **~bag** *s.* sac *m.*; *v.t.* équiper.
kitchen *s.* cuisine *f.*; **~ equipment** *s.* batterie de cuisine *f.*; **~** GARDEN; **~-maid** *s.* fille de cuisine *f.*; **~ sink** *s.* évier *m.*, (*fig.*) bourbier *m.*; **~ette** *s.* cuisinette *f.*
kite *s.* (*bird*) milan *m.*; (*toy*) cerf-volant *m.*; (*pop. aviat.*) zinc *m.*
kith *s.* connaissances *f.pl.*; **~ and kin,** amis et parents *m.pl.*
kitten *s.* chaton *m.*; *v.i.* mettre bas; **~ish** *adj.* enjoué.
kittiwake *s.* goéland tridactyle *m.*
kitty *s.* (*pet name for cat*) minou *m.*; (*fund*) cagnotte *f.*
kiwi *s.* kiwi *m.*
kleptomania *s.* kleptomanie *f.*; **~c** *s.* kleptomane *m.f.*
knack *s.* chic *m.*; **to have the ~ of doing sth.,** (*manually*) avoir le coup de main pour faire qch., (*mentally*) avoir le chic pour faire qch.
knacker *s.* (*horse*) équarisseur *m.*
knapsack *s.* havresac *m.*; sac tyrolien *m.*
knapweed *s.* centaurée *f.*
knav/e *s.* (*rogue*) fripon *m.*; (*cards*) valet *m.*; **~ery** *s.* friponnerie *f.*; **~ish** *adj.* malicieux.
knead *v.t.* pétrir.
knee *s.* genou *m.* (*pl.*—oux); **on one's ~s,** à genoux; **~cap** *s.* (*anat.*) rotule *f.*, (*protective padding*) genouillère *f.*; **~**-DEEP.
kneel *v.i.* (& *~ down*) s'agenouiller; **~ing** *adj.* agenouillé.
knell *s.* glas *m.*
knickers *s.* culotte *f.*
knick-knack *s.* colifichet *m.*
knife *s.* couteau *m.*; PEN**~**; **to get one's ~ into s.o.,** avoir une dent contre qn.; **~-edge** *s.* (*geog.*) arête *f.*; **~-rest** *s.* porte-couteau *m.*; *v.t.* poignarder.
knight *s.* chevalier *m.*; (*chess*) cavalier *m.*; **~hood** *s.* chevalerie *f.*, (*title*) qualité de chevalier *f.*; **~ly** *adj.* chevaleresque, (*order*) de chevalerie; *v.t.* armer chevalier.
knit *v.t.* tricoter; (*wrinkle brow*) froncer; *v.t.* & *i.* (*make or become compact*) (s')unir; (*med.*) souder; **~wear** *s.* lainages *m.pl.*; **~ter** *s.* tricoteuse *f.*; **~ting** *s.* (*act*) tricotage *m.*, (*work*) tricot *m.*, (*fig.*) union *f.*, (*med.*) soudure *f.*; **~ting**-NEEDLE.
knob *s.* (*swelling*) bosse *f.*; (*of door, etc.*) bouton *m.*; (*of stick*) pomme *f.*; (*of coal, sugar*) morceau *m.*
knock *s.* (*blow*) coup *m.*; (*on door*) coup à la porte *m.*; *v.t.* & *i.* (*strike*) frapper; (*make noise*) cogner; (*fam. disparage*) éreinter; **~ s.o. into a** COCK**ed hat**; **~ about** *v.t.* malmener, **~-about** *adj.* (*clothes, etc.*) de travail; **~ back** *v.t.* (*pop.*) avaler; **~ down** *v.t.* renverser, (*at auction*) adjuger; **~-down price,** prix de réclame *m.*; **~ off** *v.t.* & *i.* faire tomber, (*comm.*) rabattre, (*work*) cesser (son travail); **~ out** *v.t.* (*pipe*) débourrer, (*in competition*) éliminer, (*boxing*) mettre knock-out; **~-out** *s.* knock-out *m.*; **~ up** *v.t.* réveiller, (*fam.*) éreinter; **have a ~-up** (*tennis*) faire quelques balles; **~er** *s.* marteau *m.*; **~-kneed** *adj.* cagneux.
knoll *s.* monticule *m.*
knot *s.* nœud *m.*; REEF **~**; **~-grass** *s.* renouée *f.*; **~ty** *adj.* noueux, (*fig.*) épineux; *v.t.* nouer.
knout *s.* knout *m.*
know *v.t.* & *i.* (*be aware of*) savoir; (*be acquainted with*) connaître; (*recognize*) reconnaître; (*distinguish*) distinguer; **~ of,** connaître; **let s.o. ~ sth.,** faire savoir qch. à qn.; **~-all** *s.* (*fam.*) je-sais-tout *m.*; **~ better than to,** être trop avisé pour; **~ how to do sth.,** savoir faire qch.; **~-how** *s.* savoir-faire *m.*; **~ing** *adj.* malin, rusé; **~ingly** *adv.* habilement, (*on purpose*) en connaissance de cause; **in the ~,** au courant, à la page.
knowledge *s.* connaissance *f.*; (*learning*) savoir *m.*; **it's common ~ that,** tout le monde sait que; **not to my ~,** pas que je sache; **without my ~,** à mon insu; **~able** *adj.* bien instruit.
knuckle *s.* (*bone*) articulation *f.*; (*meat*) jarret *m.*; **~-bone** *s.* osselet *m.*; **~duster** *s.* coup-de-poing américain *m.*; *v.i.* **~ under,** flancher.
kodak *s.* kodak *m.* [P]
kohl *s.* khôl, kohol, koheul *m.*
kohlrabi *s.* chou-rave *m.*
kola *s.* (*tree*) kolatier *m.*; (*nut*) noix de kola *f.*; (*drink*) cola *m.*
Koran *s.* Coran *m.*
Korea *s.* (*geog.*) Corée *f.*; **~n** *adj.* & *s.m.f.* coréen(ne).
kosher *adj.* kascher.
kotow, kowtow *v.i.* se prosterner (*to*—devant).
kriegspiel *s.* exercice simulé *m.*
kudos *s.* (*pop.*) gloriole *f.*

L

la *see* LAH.
lab (*fam. abbrev. for laboratory*) labo *m.*
label *s.* (*lit.* & *fig.*) étiquette *f.*; *v.t.* (*lit.* & *fig.*) étiqueter.
labial *s.* (*ling.*) labiale *f.*; *adj.* labial.
labile *adj.* labile.
laboratory *s.* laboratoire *m.*
laborious *adj.* (*hard-working*; *style*) laborieux; (*difficult*) pénible; **~ly** *adv.**;*.
labour *s.* (*physical or mental exertion*) travail *m.*, peine *f.*; HARD **~**; (*task, duty*) tâche *f.*; **~s of Hercules,** les douze travaux d'Hercule; (*childbirth*) travail *m.*; (*workers*) main d'œuvre *f.*; **skilled ~,** main d'œuvre spécialisée *f.*; (*polit. L~*) parti travailliste *m.*; **L~ Exchange** *s.* bureau de placement *m.*; **L~ Party** *s.* parti travailliste *m.*; **~-saving** *adj.* qui simplifie le travail; *adj.* ouvrier; (*polit.*) travailliste; *v.t.* & *i.* travailler: (*fig.*) insister sur; (*work hard to*) s'efforcer de; (*be troubled*) peiner; **~ under,** être la victime de; ♤ labourer = **to plough; ~ed** *adj.* travaillé; **~er** *s.* travailleur *m.*, (*manual*) ouvrier *m.*, (*unskilled*) manœuvre *m.*; ♤ laboureur = **ploughman; ~ing** *adj.* ouvrier, (*fig.*) anxieux.
Labrador *s.* (*geog.*) Labrador *m.*; (*dog*) terre-neuve *m.invar.*
laburnum *s.* cytise *m.*
labyrinth *s.* (*lit.* & *fig.*) labyrinthe *m.*; **~ine** *adj.* de labyrinthe.
lace *s.* **1.** (*for boots, stays, etc.*) lacet *m.*; **2.** (*trimming*) galon *m.*; **3.** (*text.*) dentelle *f.*; *v.t.* (1) lacer; (2) galonner; **4.** (*flavour drink with spirit*) arroser; *v.i.* se lacer.
lacerat/e *v.t.* (*lit.* & *fig.*) lacérer; **~ion** *s.* lacération *f.*
lachrym/al *adj.* lachrymal; **~ose** *adj.* pleurnicheur.
lack *s.* (*deficiency*) manque *m.*; (*thing in short supply*) pénurie (de) *f.*; **for ~ of,** faute de; *v.t.* & *i.* manquer (de); être à court (de); **be ~ing,** manquer (*in*—de); **~ing** *adj.* qui manque; **~-lustre** *adj.* terne.
lackadaisical *adj.* mollasse.
lackey *s.* (*servant, obsequious person*) laquais *m.*
laconic *adj.* laconique; **~ally** *adv.**.
lacquer *s.* laque *f.*; **hair ~,** laque *f.*; *v.t.* laquer.
lacrosse *s.* crosse *f.*
lact/ation *s.* lactation *f.*; **~eal** *adj.* lacté; **~ic** *adj.* lactique; **~ose** *s.* lactose *m.*
lacuna *s.* lacune *f.*
lacustrine *adj.* lacustre.
lad *s.* garçon *m.*
ladder *s.* (*lit.* & *fig.*) échelle *f.*; SNAKES **and ~s**; STEP-**~; she has a ~ in her stocking,** son bas a filé; *v.t.* & *i.* (*of stocking*) (faire) filer.
lad/e *v.t.* charger; **~en** *adj.* chargé; (*fig.*) accablé (de); **~ing** *s,* chargement *m.*; **bill of ~ing** *s.* connaissement *m.*
la-di-da *adj.* prétentieux.
ladle *s.* louche *f.*; *v.t.* (**~** *out*) servir à la louche.
lady *s.* dame *f.*; (*title*) lady *f.*; **~-in-waiting,** dame d'honneur; **~ of the manor,** châtelaine *f.*; **my ~,** madame; **young ~,** jeune fille *f.*; **~bird** *s.* bête à bon Dieu *f.*; **L~ chapel** *s.* Chapelle de la Sainte Vierge *f.*; **L~ Day** *s.* Annonciation *f.*; **~-killer** *s.* bourreau de cœurs *m.*; **~like** *adj.* raffiné; **~ship** *s.* madame *f.*
lag *s.* (*pop. convict, usu. old ~*) forçat *m.*; JET-**~**; time-**~** *s.* retard *m.*; *v.i.* **1.** (*hang back*) traîner; **~ behind,** rester en arrière; **2.** (*insulate*) revêtir; **~gard** *s.* (1) traînard *m.*; **~ging** *s.* (2) enveloppe isolante *f.*
lager *s.* bière blonde *f.*
lagoon *s.* lagune *f.*
lah, la *s.* (*mus.*) la *m.*
laic *adj.* & *s.m.f.* laïc, laïque (*pl.* laïcs); **~ization** *s.* laïcisation *f.*; **~ize** *v.t.* laïciser.
laid *adj.* **new-~,** (*eggs*) frais.
lair *s.* tanière *f.*; (*fig.*) repaire *m.*
laity *s.* laïcs *m.pl.*
lake *s.* (*water*) lac *m.*; (*pigment*) laque *f.*; *adj.* lacustre; des lacs.
lakh *s.* lac *m.*
lama *s.* lama *m.*; **~sery** *s.* lamaserie *f.*
lamb *s.* (*animal*) agneau *m.*, agnelle *f.*; (*meat, person*) agneau *m.*; *v.i.* agneler; **~kin** *s.* agnelet *m.*; **~skin** *s.* peau d'agneau *f.*; **~'s-wool** *s.* laine d'agneau *f.*
lambast *v.t.* (*fam.*) rosser.
lambent *adj.* (*flame*) vacillant; (*style*) brillant.
lame *adj.* (*crippled*) estropié; (*limping*) boiteux; (*of metre*) boiteux; (*unsatisfactory*) insuffisant; (*of excuse*) piètre; **~ duck,** canard boiteux *m.*; *v.t.* estropier; **~ly** *adv.* en boitant; (*fig.*) piètrement; **~ness** *s.* claudication *f.*; (*fig.*) faiblesse *f.*
lament *s.* (*cry*) lamentation *f.*; (*elegy*) complainte *f.*; *v.t.* & *i.* (*wail*) pleurer; (*mourn*) se lamenter (*for, over*—sur); (*thing*) déplorer; **~able** *adj.* lamentable, (*fam.*) déplorable; **~ably** *adv.* lamentablement, (*fam.*) déplorablement; **~ation** *s.* lamentation *f.*; **~ed** *adj.* (= *late*) feu (*before noun*).
laminat/e *v.t.* laminer; **~ion** *s.* laminage *m.*
Lammas *s.* premier août *m.*
lamp *s.* lampe *f.*; STANDARD **~**; **by ~light,** à la lumière d'une lampe; **~post** *s.* réverbère *m.*; **~shade** *s.* abat-jour *m.*
lampoon *s.* libelle *f.*; *v.t.* chansonner.
lamprey *s.* lamproie *f.*
lance *s.* **1.** (*weapon*) lance *f.*; FREE **~**; **2.** (*surg.*) lancette *f.*; **~-corporal** *s.* soldat de première classe *m.*; **~r** *s.* lancier *m.*; **~rs** *s.* (*dance*) quadrille des lanciers *m.*; **~t** *s.* (*surg.*) lancette *f.*; **~t window,** fenêtre ogivale *f.*; *v.t.* (2) ouvrir; ♤ lancer = **to throw.**
land *s.* (*earth, ≠ sea*; *ground, soil*) terre *f.*; **to see how the ~ lies,** (*fig.*) sonder, tâter, le terrain; (*state, country*) pays *m.*; (*property*) propriété *f.*; **to live on the** FAT **of the ~**; **~-agent** *s.* (*steward*) régisseur *m.*, (*dealer*) agent foncier *m.*; **~fall** *s.* abordage *m.*; **~lady** *s.* logeuse *f.*; **~-locked** *adj.* entouré de terres; **~lord** *s.* logeur *m.*, hôtelier *m.*, (*owner*) propriétaire *m.*; **~lubber** *s.* marin d'eau douce *m.*; **~mark** *s.* (*stone*) borne *f.*, (*conspicuous object*) point de repère *m.*, (*fig.*) événement décisif *m.*; **~-mine** *s.* mine *f.*; **~-owner** *s.* propriétaire terrien *m.*; **~rover** *s.* (*auto.*) voiture tout terrain *f.*; **~scape** *s.* paysage *m.*, *v.t.* (*hort.*) dessiner un jardin d'agrément; **~scape gardener** *s.* jardinier paysagiste *m.*; **~scape gardening** *s.* art des jardins *m.*; **~scape painter** *s.* paysagiste *m.f.*; **~slide** *s.* glissement de terrain *m.*, *adj.* (*fig.*) **~slide victory,** victoire écrasante *f.*; *v.t.* & *i.* (*naut. aviat.*) débarquer, (faire) atterrir; CRASH **~**; *v.t.* (*a blow*) allonger; (*a fish*) prendre; (*fam.*

win prize, etc.) décrocher; *v.i.* (*alight*) se recevoir; **~ed** *adj.* (*property*) foncier, (*person*) terrien; **~ing** *s.* (*on stairs*) palier *m.*, (*aviat.*) atterrissage *m.*; **~ing-craft** *s.* péniche de débarquement *f.*; **~ing-stage** *s.* débarcadère *m.*; **~ing-strip** *s.* piste d'atterrissage *f.*

landau *s.* landau *m.*

lane *s.* (*in country*) sentier *m.*; (*in town*) ruelle *f.*; (*naut.*, *aviat.*) route *f.*; (*sport*) piste *f.*; (*traffic*) voie *f.*; **acceleration, deceleration ~,** bande d'accélération, de décélération *f.*; **bus ~,** couloir réservé (aux autobus), couloir de circulation des transports en commun *m.*

language *s.* (*speech, style*) langage *m.*; (*national*) langue *f.*; **~ laboratory,** laboratoire de langues *m.*

langu/id *adj.* languissant; (*weak*) faible; **~idly** *adv.* langoureusement; **~idness** *s.* langueur *f.*; **~ish** *v.i.* languir (*for*—de); **~or** *s.* langueur *f.*; **~orous** *adj.* langoureux.

lank(y) *adj.* (*hair*) raide; (*tall & lean*) dégingandé.

lanolin *s.* lanoline *f.*

lantern *s.* (*for light, for projecting pictures, arch.*) lanterne *f.*; **~ jawed** *adj.* aux joues décharnées; **~-slide** *s.* plaque *f.* (d'appareil à projection).

lanyard *s.* (*naut.*) amarrage *m.*; (*gun*) cordon tire-feu *m.*

lap¹ *s.* (*tail of skirt or coat*) pan *m.*; (*of sitting person*) genoux *m.pl.*; (*fig.*) sein *m.*; (*in race*) tour *m.*; **~ of honour** *s.* (*sport*) tour d'honneur *m.*; (*of rope*) tour *m.*; (*overlapping part*) battant *m.*, chevauchement *m.*; **to live in the ~ of luxury,** nager dans le luxe; **it is in the ~ of the gods,** Dieu seul le sait; **~-dog** *s.* bichon *m.*; *v.t.* (*enfold, wrap*) enrouler (dans), envelopper (dans); (*make overlap*) enchevaucher; (*sport, travel one ~*) faire un tour du circuit; (*racing, pass*) boucler; *v.i.* s'enrouler; se chevaucher.

lap² *s.* (*act or sound of drinking*) lapement *m.*; (*of waves*) clapotis *m.*; (*quantity*) lampée *f.*; *v.t.* & *i.* laper; (*waves*) clapoter; **~ up** *v.t.* (*lit.* & *fig.*) avaler.

lapel *s.* revers *m.*

lapidary *adj.* & *s.m.* lapidaire.

lapis lazuli *s.* lapis-lazuli *m.*

Lapland *s.* (*geog.*) Laponie *f.*; **~er** *s.m.f.* Lapon(ne); **Lapp** *adj.* & *s.m.* (*lang.*) lapon.

lapse *s.* (*of memory*) défaillance *f.*; (*slight mistake*) lapsus *m.*; (*backsliding*) chute *f.*; (*expiry*) expiration *f.*, déchéance *f.*; (*of time*) laps *m.*; *v.i.* (*fall back or away*) tomber (dans); (*become void*) n'être plus valable; (*elapse*) s'écouler; **~d** *adj.* (*of religion*) non-pratiquant, (*right, ticket, etc.*) périmé.

lapwing *s.* vanneau *m.*

larboard *s.* (*naut.*) bâbord *m.*

larceny *s.* vol *m.*; **petty ~,** larcin *m.*

larch *s.* mélèze *m.*

lard *s.* saindoux *m.*; *v.t.* (*cook.*) larder; (*fig.*) entrelarder (de); **~er** *s.* garde-manger *m.*

large *adj.* (*in size*) grand, gros; (*in range*) large; (*copious*) copieux; (*generous*) généreux; (*numerous*) nombreux; (*important*) important; (*fig.*) large; **at ~,** (*at liberty*) en liberté; (*in full*) en toutes lettres; **~ly** *adv.* (*copiously, generously*) largement, amplement; (*for the most part*) en grande partie; (*to a ~ extent*) considérablement; **~ness** *s.* (*in space*) grandeur *f.*; (*of mass*) grosseur *f.*; (*fig.*) largeur *f.*

larges(se) *s.* largesse *f.*

lark *s.* **1.** (*bird*) alouette *f.*; **2.** (*fam. spree*) rigolade *f.*; *v.i.* (2) rigoler; **~spur** *s.* pied-d'alouette *m.*

larva *s.* larve *f.*

laryn/x *s.* larynx *m.*; **~gitis** *s.* laryngite *f.*

lascivious *adj.* lascif; **~ly** *adv.**.; **~ness** *s.* lascivité *f.*

laser *s.* (*phys.*) laser *m.*

lash *s.* (*stroke*) coup de fouet *m.*; (*of whip*) mèche *f.*; **eye~,** cil *m.*; *v.t.* & *i.* (*beat*) fouetter; (*fig. with tongue*) cingler; (*tail, etc.*) battre (de la queue); (*tie tightly*) lier; (*naut.*) amarrer; (*pour, rush*) jaillir; **~ out,** (*horse*) ruer; (*fig.*) se livrer à; **~ing** *s.* (*naut.*) amarrage *m.*; **~ings** (*pop.* **~***ings of sth.*) à gogo.

lass *s.* jeune fille *f.*

lassitude *s.* lassitude *f.*

lasso *s.* lasso *m.*; *v.t.* prendre au lasso.

last¹ *s.* (*shoemaker's*) forme *f.* (à chaussure).

last² *s.* (*person or thing*) derni/er, -ère *m.f.*; (*end*) extrémité *f.*; **at ~** *adv.* enfin; **at long ~,** à la fin (des fins); **to the ~,** jusqu'au bout; **to see the ~ of,** voir pour la dernière fois, (*with intent*) ne plus revoir; *adj.* (*after all others, most recent, utmost*) dernier; (*coming at the end*) ultime; **~ but one,** avant-dernier; **~ night,** hier soir; **the ~ night,** la dernière nuit; **~ week,** la semaine dernière; **the ~ week of the holidays,** la dernière semaine des vacances; **the ~ two, three, etc.,** les deux, trois (etc.) derniers; **the ~** STRAW; **the L~ Supper,** la Cène; *adv.* la dernière fois; **~ly** *adv.* en dernier lieu.

last³ *v.i.* durer; **~ing** *adj.* permanent, durable.

latch *s.* loquet *m.*; **~key** *s.* clef de la porte *f.*; *v.t.* fermer; *v.i.* (*pop.*) **~ on to s.o.,** s'accrocher à qn.; **~et** *s.* cordon *m.*

late *adj.* (*after expected time*) tardif; (*far on in day or night*) avancé; (*backward*) retardé; (*dead*) feu (*before noun*); (*former*) ancien (*before noun*); (*recent*) récent, dernier; **of ~,** dernièrement; **at the ~st,** au plus tard; **the ~st** (*news*) la dernière nouvelle; **~ly** *adv.* dernièrement, récemment; **~ness** *s.* **1.** (*time of day*) heure avancée *f.*; **2.** (*with delay, being overdue*) retard *m.*, arrivée tardive *f.*; *adv.* (1) tard, **the train will arrive ~** (*in the day*), le train arrivera tard; (2) en retard, **the train will be ~,** le train arrivera en retard; **to be ~,** être en retard; **sooner or ~r,** tôt ou tard; **~comer** *s.* retardataire *m.*

lateen (*sail*) (voile) latine *f.*

latent *adj.* latent.

lateral *s.* (*hort.*) bourgeon latéral *m.*; *adj.* latéral; **~ly** *adv.**.

laterite *s.* latérite *f.*

latex *s.* latex *m.*

lath *s.* latte *f.*

lathe *s.* (*mech.*) tour *m.*

lather *s.* (*froth of soap, etc.*) mousse *f.*; (*on horse*) écume *f.*; *v.t.* savonner; *v.i.* mousser; **~ shaving cream,** crème à raser moussante *f.*

Latin *adj.* & *s.m.* (*lang.*) latin; **~ America** *s.* Amérique latine *f.*; **~ism** *s.* latinisme *m.*; **~ist** *s.* latiniste *m.f.*

latitud/e *s.* (*geog.*; *freedom, full extent*) latitude *f.*; **~es** *pl.* latitudes *f.pl.* (*in*—sous); **~inal** *adj.* latitudinal; **~inarian** *adj.* & *s.m.f.* latitudinaire.

latrine *s.* latrines *f.pl.*

latter *pron.* celui-ci, celle-ci, ceux-ci, celles-ci; *adj.* dernier **~ day** *adj.* moderne; **~ end,** fin *f.*; **~ly** *adv.* dernièrement.

lattice *s.* treillis *m.*; **~ window,** fenêtre à carreaux en losanges *f.*

Latvia *s.* (*geog.*) Lettonie *f.*; **~n** *adj.* & *s.m.f.* letton(ne).

laud *v.t.* louer; **~able** *adj.* louable; **~ably** *adv.**.; **~ation** *s.* louange *f.*; **~atory** *adj.* laudatif; **~s** *s.* (*eccles.*) laudes *f.pl.*

laudanum *s.* laudanum *m.*

laugh *s.* (*act, sound*) rire *m.*; *v.i.* rire; **~ at s.o.,** se moquer de qn.; **~ off sth.,** tourner qch. en plaisanterie; **~able** *adj.* risible; **~ing** *adj.* (*person*) rieur; (*thing*) riant; **it's no ~ing matter,** il n'y a pas de quoi rire; **~ing-gas,**

gaz hilarant *m.*; **~ing jackass,** martin-pêcheur géant *m.*; **~ing-stock** *s.* risée *f.*; **~ter** *s.* rire *m.*

launch *s.* (*~ing of ship*) lancement *m.*; (*large boat*) chaloupe *f.*; (*mech. propelled boat*) vedette *f.*; *v.t.* (*discharge, set afloat*) lancer; (*start*) déclencher; *v.i.* **~ out** (*into*) se lancer (dans des dépenses, des commentaires, etc.); **~ing pad** *s.* aire de lancement *f.*

laund/er *v.t.* blanchir; **~(e)rette** *s.* laverie automatique *f.*; **~ress** *s.* blanchisseuse *f.*; **~ry** *s.* (*place*) blanchisserie *f.*; (*clothes*) lessive *f.*; **to do the ~ry,** faire la lessive.

laureate *adj.* & *s.m.* lauréat; **Poet ~,** poète officiel *m.*

laurel *s.* laurier *m.*; **to rest on one's ~s,** se reposer sur ses lauriers.

lava *s.* lave *f.*

lavatory *s.* cabinet *m.* (de toilette); toilettes *f.pl.*; (*cloakroom*) lavabo *m.*

lavender *s.* lavande *f.*

lavish *adj.* (*person*) prodigue; (*expense, etc.*) extravagant; **~ly** *adv.* avec prodigalité; **~ness** *s.* prodigalité *f.*; *v.t.* prodiguer.

law *s.* (*established rule, science, etc.*) loi *f.*; (*of a state*) législation *f.*; (*rule of procedure*) règlement *m.*; (*legal profession, branch of study*) droit *m.*; (*courts, etc.*) jurisprudence *f.*; **~ and** ORDER; IN-**~**; **to lay down the ~,** faire la loi; **to take the ~ into one's own hands,** se faire justice (à soi-même); **to go to ~,** intenter une action (contre qn.); **possession is nine-tenths of the ~,** possession vaut titre; **~-abiding** *adj.* ami de l'ordre; **the L~ Courts,** le palais de justice *m.*; **~maker** *s.* législateur *m.*; **~suit** *s.* procès *m.*; **~ful** *adj.* (*concerning ~*) légal, (*permitted by ~*) légitime, (*not forbidden*) licite, (*authorised*) autorisé; **~fully** *adv.* légalement, légitimement; **~less** *adj.* sans loi, anarchique.

lawn *s.* (*text.*) linon *m.*; (*hort.*) pelouse *f.*; **~**-MOWER; **~**-ROLLER; **~ tennis** *s.* tennis *m.*

lawyer *s.* juriste *m.f.*; (*solicitor*) avoué *m.*; (*barrister*) avocat *m.*

lax *adj.* **1.** (*negligent*) négligent; (*morals*) relâché; **2.** (*not strict*) peu sévère; **3.** (*vague*) vague; **4.** (*not tight*) lâche; **~ity** *s.* (1) négligence *f.*; relâchement *m.*; (2) manque de sévérité *m.*; (3) vague *m.*; (4) laxité *f.*

laxative *adj.* & *s.m.* laxatif.

lay[1] *s.* (*song*) lai *m.*

lay[2] *adj.* (≠ *clerical*) laïque; (≠ *professional*) profane; **~ brother, ~ sister,** frère convers *m.*, sœur converse *f.*; **~ figure** *s.* mannequin *m.*, (*fig.*) fantoche *f.*; **~man** *s.* laïque *m.*, profane *m.*

lay[3] *v.t.* (*prostrate, ~ flat*) étendre, coucher; (*cause to subside*) faire tomber, (*of dust, etc.*) abattre; (*deposit, place*) poser, placer; **~ to rest** (=*bury*) enterrer; (*of eggs*) *v.t.* & *i.* pondre; **~ hold of,** saisir; (*locate*) situer; (*impose*) poser; **~ bare, ~ open,** révéler; **~** WASTE; (*dispose, arrange, ~ table, etc.*) mettre; (*~ a trap*) tendre; **~about** *s.* propre à rien *m.*; **~ aside, ~ by,** mettre de côté; **~-by** *s.* (*on road*) aire de stationnement *f.*; **~ down,** déposer, (*conditions*) imposer, (*rule, etc.*) établir; **~ down the** LAW; **~ in,** faire provision de; **~ off,** (*workmen*) congédier; **~ on,** appliquer, (*gas, water, etc.*) installer, (*organize*) organiser; **~ out,** disposer, (*goods*) étaler, (*money*) débourser; **~out** *s.* disposition *f.*; **~ up,** (*naut.*) mettre en rade, (*med.*) rendre malade; **to be laid up,** être alité; **~ing** *s.* (*eggs*) ponte *f.*, (*techn.*) pose *f.*

layer *s.* **1.** (*person*) poseur *m.*; (*hen*) pondeuse *f.*; **2.** (*of matter*) couche *f.*; **3.** (*hort.*) marcotte *f.*; *v.t.* (3) marcotter.

layette *s.* layette *f.*

lazaret(to) *s.* (*naut.*) lazaret *m.*

laz/y *adj.* paresseux; (*slow-moving*) indolent; **~y-bones** *s.* fainéant *m.*; **~e** *v.i.* fainéanter; **~ily** *adv.* paresseusement; **~iness** *s.* paresse *f.*, indolence *f.*

lead[1] *s.* (*metal*) plomb *m.*; (*for pencil*) mine *f.*; (*bullet*) balle *f.*; (*naut.*) sonde *f.*; **to swing the ~** (*pop.*) tirer au flanc; **black ~,** mine noire *f.*; **red ~,** minium *m.*; **white ~,** céruse *f.*; **~ pencil,** crayon *m.*; **~-poisoning** *s.* saturnisme *m.*; **~en** *adj.* de plomb, (*heavy*) lourd, (*slow*) de plomb, (*~-coloured*) couleur de plomb.

lead[2] *s.* (*example*) exemple *m.*; (*leadership*) direction *f.*; (*theat.*) premier rôle *m.*; (*cards*) main *f.*; (*electr.*) avance *f.*; (*for dog*) laisse *f.*; **in the ~,** à la tête; **to take the ~,** se mettre à la tête; *v.t.* (*conduct*) conduire; (*guide*) guider; (*persuade*) pousser (à); (*induce*) amener (à); (*spend* (*life*)) mener; (*be first*) être en tête de; (*be leader of*) être à la tête de; (*direct orchestra, etc.*) diriger; *v.i.* (*go to, e.g. road*) mener; (*cards*) avoir la main; **~ s.o. a** DANCE; **~ up the** GARDEN **path**; **~ astray** *v.t.* détourner, égarer; **~ away** *v.t.* emmener; **~ on** *v.t.* conduire, (*fam.*) inciter; **~ up to** (*fig.*) aboutir à; **~er** *s.* (*newspaper*) article de fond *m.*, (*law*) avocat principal *m.*, (*mus.*) chef d'orchestre *m.*, (*racing*) cheval de tête *m.*, (*hort.*) bourgeon terminal *m.*, (*of party*) dirigeant *m.*, chef *m.*; **~ership** *s.* direction *f.*; **~ing** *s.* direction *f.*, exemple *m.*; **~ing** *adj.* (*chief*) de tête, de fond, (*most important*) principal, (*guiding*) dominant; **~ing article,** article de fond *m.*; **~ing lady, ~ing man,** premi/er, -ère *m.f.*; **~ing question,** question qui suggère la réponse *f.*; **~ing strings** (*lit.* & *fig.*) laisse *f.*

leaf *s.* (*of plant, metal*) feuille *f.*; (*of paper*) feuillet *m.*; (*of door, etc.*) battant *m.*; (*of table*) rallonge *f.*; **to turn over a new ~,** faire peau neuve; **~-mould,** terreau *m.*; **~age** *s.* feuillage *m.*; **~less** *adj.* sans feuille; **~let** *s.* (*bot.*) foliole *f.*, (*publicity, etc.*) prospectus *m.*, dépliant *m.*; **~y** *adj.* feuillu.

league *s.* (*measure*) lieue *f.*; (*compact*) ligue *f.*; (*sport*) division *f.*; **in ~,** ligué; **L~ of Nations,** Société des Nations *f.*; *v.i.* (se) liguer.

leak *s.* (*of liquid, electr., fig.*) fuite *f.*; (*naut.*) voie d'eau *f.*; **to spring a ~** (*naut.*) faire eau; *v.t.* (*fig.*) faire savoir; *v.i.* (*liquid*) fuir; (*fig.*) & **~ out,** transpirer; **~age** *s.* fuite *f.*; **~y** *adj.* qui fuit, (*naut.*) qui fait eau, (*shoe*) qui prend l'eau.

lean[1] *s.* (*meat*) maigre *m.*; *adj.* (≠ *plump*, ≠ *fat, of meat*) maigre; (*meagre, poor*) frugal; **~ years** (*fig.*) période de vaches maigres *f.*; **~ness** *s.* maigreur *f.*

lean[2] *v.t.* & *i.* appuyer, pencher; (*be inclined to*) pencher vers; **~ on,** s'appuyer sur; **~ out of the window,** se pencher à la fenêtre; **~ing** *s.* inclinaison *f.*, (*fig.*) penchant *m.*; **~-to** *s.* appentis *m.*

leap *s.* saut *m.*; **~ in the** DARK; **by ~s and bounds,** par bonds et par sauts; **~ year** *s.* année bissextile *f.*; *v.t.* franchir; (*horse*) faire sauter; *v.i.* sauter; (*fig.*) bondir (*with*—de); **~ over** *v.t.* sauter; **~ up** *v.i.* jaillir, (*person*) bondir; **~-frog** *s.* saute-mouton *m.*

learn *v.t.* & *i.* apprendre; (*get knowledge*) s'instruire; **~ how to do sth.,** apprendre à faire qch.; **~ed** *adj.* érudit, savant; **~er** *s.* élève *m.f.*, (*beginner*) débutant(e) *m.f.*; **~ing** *s.* savoir *m.*

leas/e *s.* bail *m.* (*pl.* baux); **on ~,** à bail; **~hold** *s.* location (*f.*) à bail; *v.t.* donner, prendre, à bail; **~ing** *s.* crédit-bail *m.*

leash *s.* laisse *f.*; *v.t.* freiner.

least *s.* moins *m.*; **at ~,** au moins; **at the very ~,** tout au moins; **to say the ~,** pour le moins; **not in the ~,** pas le moins du monde; **~ said, soonest mended,** le moins on en dit, le mieux ça vaut; *adj.* (*size*) le (la, les) plus petit(e)(s); (*in importance*) le (la) moindre; *adv.* le moins.

leather *s.* (*material*) cuir *m.*; **patent ~,** cuir vernis *m.*; **wash ~,** peau de chamois *f.*; (*article*) objet de cuir *m.*; **to go** HELL **for ~;** *adj.* & **~n** *adj.* de cuir, en cuir; **~y** *adj.* semblable à du cuir.

leave *s.* (*permission*) autorisation *f.*; **by your ~,** avec votre permission; (*of absence*) permission *f.*, congé *m.*; **on ~,** en permission; (*farewell*) au revoir *m.*; **to take one's ~,** dire au revoir (*of*—à), faire ses adieux (*of*—à); FRENCH **~;** *v.t.* (*let remain*) laisser; (*bequeath*) léguer; (*go away from*) quitter; (*commit to another*) confier; (*abandon*) abandonner; **~ it to me,** je m'en charge; **~ it at that,** cela suffit; **it ~s me cold,** cela ne me dit pas grand'chose; *v.i.* (*depart*) partir; (*cease*) cesser; **be left,** rester; **be left with,** garder; **~ about,** laisser traîner; **~ alone,** laisser tranquille; **~ behind,** laisser, (*forget*) oublier; **~ off,** cesser de faire, renoncer à qch.; **~ out,** omettre (qch.), exclure (qn.); **~ no** STONE **unturned; ~ much to be desired,** laisser à désirer; **take it or ~ it,** c'est à prendre ou à laisser; **left-overs, leavings** *s.* restes *m.pl.*; **left** LUGGAGE.

leaven *s.* (*lit.* & *fig.*) levain *m.*; *v.t.* faire lever.

Leban/on *s.* (*geog.*) Liban *m.*; **~ese** *adj.* & *s.m.f.* libanais(e).

lecher/ous *adj.* débauché; **~y** *s.* débauche *f.*

lectern *s.* lutrin *m.*

lecture *s.* **1.** (*lesson*) cours *m.*, conférence *f.*; **~** THEATRE; **2.** (*admonition*) remontrance *f.*; ⚠ lecture = **reading;** *v.i.* (1) faire un cours, une conférence; *v.t.* (2) sermonner; **~r** *s.* (*acad.*) maître de conférences *m.*, (*gen.*) conférencier *m.*

ledge *s.* (*of window, etc.*) rebord *m.*; (*of rock*) saillie *f.*

ledger *s.* grand livre *m.*

lee *s.* abri *m.*; *adj.* sous le vent; **~ shore,** côté sous le vent *m.*; **~ward** *adv.* sous le vent; **~way** *s.* (*naut.*) dérive *f.*, (*fig.*) marge *f.*

leech *s.* (*archaic, physician*) médecin *m.*; (*worm*) sangsue *f.*; (*fam. person*) crampon *m.*; **to stick like a ~,** se cramponner.

leek *s.* poireau *m.*

leer *s.* regard sournois *m.*, (*often amatory*) œillade *f.*; *v.i.* jeter des regards sournois; jeter des œillades.

lees *s.* (*lit.* & *fig.*) lie *f.*

left[1] *s.* (*side, polit.*) gauche *f.*; **on the ~,** à gauche; **to keep to the ~,** garder sa gauche; *adj.* (≠ *right*) gauche, (*polit.*) de gauche; *adv.* à gauche; **~-handed** *adj.* gaucher; **~-winger** *s.* (*polit.*) gauchiste *m.*

left[2] *see* LEAVE.

leg *s.* (*limb*) jambe *f.*; (*of dog, fly*) patte *f.*; (*cook.*) (*of chicken*) cuisse *f.*, (*of mutton*) gigot *m.*, (*of veal*) cuisseau *m.*, (*of venison*) cuissot *m.*, (*of pork*) jambon *m.*; (*of chair, table, etc.*) pied *m.*; (*division of flight, game, etc.*) étape *f.*; **on one's last ~s,** à bout de course; **with** TAIL **between ~s; to pull s.o.'s ~,** faire une plaisanterie à qn.; **to stretch one's ~s,** se dégourdir les jambes; **not to have a ~ to stand on,** être à bout d'arguments; **~ging** *s.* guêtre *m.*, (*sport*) jambière *f.*; **~gy** *adj.* dégingandé.

legacy *s.* legs *m.*

legal *adj.* (*according to law*) légal; **~ tender,** monnaie légale *f.*; (*proceedings, aid, etc.*) judiciaire; (*department, adviser*) juridique; **~ity** *s.* légalité *f.*; **~ize** *v.t.* légaliser; **~ly** *adv.* légalement; juridiquement.

legat/e *s.* légat *m.*; **~ion** *s.* légation *f.*

legatee *s.* légataire *m.f.*

legend *s.* (*myth.* & *on coin, etc.*) légende *f.*; **~ary** *adj.* légendaire.

legerdemain *s.* prestidigitation *f.*

leghorn *s.* (*hat*) paille d'Italie *f.*; (*fowl*) leghorn *m.*

legib/le *adj.* lisible; **~ility** *s.* lisibilité *f.*; **~ly** *adv.**.

legion *s.* (*hist.*; *great number*) légion *f.*; **British L~,** Anciens Combattants *m.pl.*; **Foreign L~,** légion étrangère *f.*; **L~ of Honour,** Légion d'Honneur *f.*; **~ary** *s.* légionnaire *m.*

legislat/e *v.i.* légiférer; **~ion** *s.* législation *f.*; **~ive** *adj.* législatif; **~or** *s.* législateur *m.*; **~ure** *s.* législature *f.*

legitim/ate *adj.* légitime; **~acy** *s.* légitimité *f.*; (*fig.*) bien fondé *m.*; **~ately** *adv.**; **~ize** *v.t.* légitimer.

leguminous *adj.* légumineux.

lei *s.* guirlande *f.*

leisure *s.* loisir *m.*; **at ~,** à loisir; **at one's ~,** à ses moments de liberté; **~d** *adj.* (*people, classes*) aisé, (*life*) facile; **~ly** *adj.* lent, *adv.* à loisir.

lemming *s.* lemming *m.*

lemon *s.* (*fruit*) citron *m.*; (*tree*) citronnier *m.*; (*colour*) jaune citron *m.*; ⚠ limon = **lime; ~ade** *s.* limonade *f.*; **~** SOLE; **~ squash** *s.* citron pressé *m.*; **~-squeezer** *s.* presse-citron *m.*

lemur *s.* maki *m.*

lend *v.t.* (*grant use of*) prêter; (*hire*) louer; (*contribute*) donner; **~ oneself to,** se prêter à; **~ a** HAND **to s.o.; ~er** *s.* prêteu/r, -se *m.f.*

length *s.* (*in space*) longueur *f.*; (*in time*) durée *f.* (*ling. of vowel*) quantité *f.*; (*long stretch*) étendue *f.*; (*of cloth*) métrage *m.*, morceau *m.*; **at ~,** (*time*) enfin, (*in full*) en entier; **at full ~,** de tout son long; **full, short, ~** (*film*) long, court, métrage *m.*; **~en** *v.t.* & *i.* (s')allonger; **~wise** *adv.* en longueur; **~y** *adj.* long; **~ily** *adv.* longuement.

lenien/cy *s.* indulgence *f.*; **~t** *adj.* indulgent; **~tly** *adv.* avec indulgence.

lens *s.* (*glass*) lentille *f.*; (*of spectacles*) verre *m.*; CONTACT **~;** (*of eye*) cristallin *m.*; (*of camera*) objectif *m.*

Lent *s.* (*eccles.*) Carême *m.*

lentil *s.* lentille *f.*

leonine *adj.* léonin.

leopard *s.* léopard *m.*; **~ess** *s.* léopard femelle *f.*

leotard *s.* léotard *m.*

lep/er *s.* lépreu/x, -se *m.f.*; **~rosarium** *s.* léproserie *f.*; **~rosy** *s.* lèpre *f.*; **~rous** *adj.* lépreux.

lepidopterous *adj.* lépidoptère.

Lesbian *adj.* & *s.f.* lesbien(ne); **~ism** *s.* saphisme *m.*

lesion *s.* lésion *f.*

less *adj.* (*smaller*) moindre; (*of lower rank*) moins important; (*of smaller quantity*) moins de; *adv.* moins; *prep.* moins, (*excluding*) à part; **~ and ~,** de moins en moins; **to be none the ~** + *adj.*, n'en être pas moins + *adj.*, **I am none the ~ pleased to see you,** je n'en suis pas moins heureux de vous voir; **~ en** *v.t.* diminuer; **~er** *adj.* moindre.

-less *suffix* (*usu.*) sans + *s.*, **care~,** sans soin; **doubt~,** sans doute; **home~,** sans foyer; **penni~,** sans le sou; **tree~,** sans arbres; *see also under appropriate head word.*

less/ee *s.* locataire *m.f.*; **~or,** *s.* bailleur *m.*

lesson *s.* (*eccles., school, warning, example*) leçon *f.*; **to teach s.o. a ~,** (*fig.*) donner une leçon à qn.

lest *conj.* de peur de + *inf.*; de peur que + *subj.*

let *s.* (*tennis*) balle au ras du filet *f.*; (*act of letting*) location *f.*; *v.t.* (*allow*) laisser (+ *inf.*); (*permit*) permettre (à qn. de faire qch.); (*cause to*) faire; (*rent*) louer; (*imperative*) **~ him come!,** qu'il vienne!; **~ alone, ~ be,** *v.t.* (*person*) laisser tranquille, (*thing*) laisser de côté; **~ down** *v.t.* (*lengthen*) allonger, (*by rope, etc.*) descendre, (*deflate*) dégonfler, (*lower*) baisser, (*fam. fail*) décevoir; **~-down** *s.* déception *f.*; **~ go** *v.i.* lâcher prise; **~ in** *v.t.*

faire entrer; ~ **into** *v.t.* laisser entrer dans, (*secret*) mettre dans; ~ **in for** *v.t.* entraîner (qn. à); ~ **oneself in for,** s'engager à; ~ **loose** *v.t.* lâcher; ~ **off** *v.t.* (*missile*) décocher, (*gun*) faire partir, (*steam*) lâcher, (*excuse from*) dispenser qn. de qch., (*forgive*) faire grâce à qn. de qch.; **~-off** *s.* chance de s'en tirer sans mal *f.*; ~ **on** *v.i.* (*fam.*) moucharder; ~ **out** *v.t.* laisser sortir, (*water*) laisser fuir, (*garment*) élargir, (*hire*) louer, (*set free*) relâcher, (*cry, secret*) laisser échapper; ~ **slip** *v.t.* (*lit.* & *fig.*) laisser tomber; ~ **through** *v.t.* laisser passer; ~ **up** *v.i.* (*fig.*) ralentir; **~-up** *s.* ralentissement *m.*; ~ **well** ALONE.

lethal *adj.* mortel.

letharg/ic *adj.* léthargique; **~y** *s.* léthargie *f.*

letter *s.* (*print.*) caractère *m.*; (*symbol, message, literal meaning*) lettre *f.*; ~ **of credit,** lettre de crédit *f.*; **~s patent,** lettres patentes *f.pl.*; RED ~ **day; ~s** (*literature*) belles-lettres *f.pl.*; **man of ~s,** homme de lettres *m.*; **~-box** *s.* boîte aux lettres *f.*; **~-card** *s.* carte-lettre *f.*; **~press** *s.* texte imprimé *m.*; **~-writer** *s.* épistolier *m.*

lettuce *s.* laitue *f.*; CABBAGE ~; COS ~.

leukaemia *s.* leucémie *f.*

Levant *s.* (*geog.*) Levant *m.*; **~ine** *adj.* & *s.m.f.* levantin(e).

levée *s.* (*hist.*) lever *m.*; (*reception*) réception *f.*; (*embankment*) levée *f.*

level *s.* (*instrument*) niveau *m.*, **spirit ~,** niveau à bulle d'air *m.*; (*standard*) niveau *m.*; ~ **of alcohol** (*in blood*), alcoolémie *f.*; (*flat surface*) plaine *f.*; **on a ~ with,** de niveau avec, (*fig.*) au niveau de; **on the ~** (*fam.*) honnête; *adj.* (*horizontal*) horizontal; (*equal with*) de niveau avec; (*even*) plat, uni; (*in same plane with*) au niveau de; **to do one's ~ best,** faire de son mieux; ~ **crossing** *s.* (*rail.*) passage à niveau *m.*; **~-headed** *adj.* (bien) équilibré; *v.t.* (*make* ~) niveler; (*place on same* ~) égaliser; (*lay low, abolish*) raser, détruire; (*aim at*) diriger sur; (*gun*) braquer sur; **~ler** *s.* niveleur *m.*; **~ling** *s.* nivellement *m.*

lever *s.* levier *m.*; *v.t.* exercer des pesées sur; ~ **up,** soulever au levier; **~age** *s.* puissance de levier *f.*; (*fig.*) prise *f.*

leveret *s.* levraut *m.*

leviathan *s.* léviathan *m.*

levitat/e *v.t.* & *i.* (se) soulever par lévitation; **~ion** *s.* lévitation *f.*

Levite *s.* lévite *m.*

levity *s.* (*lit.* & *fig.*) légèreté *f.*

levy *s.* (*compulsory payment, enlistment, amount levied*) levée *f.*; *v.t.* lever.

lewd *adj.* impudique; **~ness** *s.* impudeur *f.*

lexicograph/y *s.* lexicographie *f.*; **~er** *s.* lexicographe *m.f.*; **~ical** *adj.* lexicographique.

lexicon *s.* lexique *m.*

liab/le *adj.* **1.** (*legally bound*) responsable (*for*—de), (*subject to*) passible de; **2.** (*exposed or apt to*) sujet à, enclin à; **~ility** *s.* (1) responsabilité *f.*; (2) disposition *f.*; **limited ~ility** COMPANY; **~ilities** *s.pl.* engagements *m.pl.*

liais/on *s.* liaison *f.*; **~e** *v.i.* (*Eng. fam.*) faire la liaison (*with s.o.*—avec qn.).

liana *s.* liane *f.*

liar *s.* menteu/r, -se *m.f.*

libation *s.* libation *f.*

libel *s.* diffamation *f.*; ~ **action,** procès en diffamation *m.*; *v.t.* diffamer; **~lous** *adj.* diffamatoire.

liberal *s.* libéral *m.*; *adj.* (*generous, abundant*) généreux; (*unprejudiced*) large; (*polit.*) libéral; **~ism** *s.* libéralisme *m.*; **~ity** *s.* libéralité *f.*; **~ize** *v.t.* rendre libéral; **~ly** *adv.* libéralement, généreusement.

liberat/e *v.t.* libérer; **~ion** *s.* libération *f.*; **~or** *s.* libérat/eur, -rice *m.f.*

libertine *s.* libertin *m.*

libert/y *s.* liberté *f.*; **at ~ to,** libre de; **~ies** *s.pl.* privilèges *m.pl.*; **to take ~ies with,** prendre des libertés avec.

libidinous *adj.* libidineux.

librar/y *s.* (*books, building, room*) bibliothèque *f.*; **lending ~,** bibliothèque de prêt *f.*; **travelling ~,** bibliobus *m.*; (*collection of records, etc.*) collection *f.*; ⚠ librairie = **bookshop; ~ian** *s.* bibliothécaire *m.f.*; ⚠ libraire = **bookseller.**

librett/o *s.* livret *m.*; **~ist** *s.* librettiste *m.f.*

Libya *s.* (*geog.*) Libye *f.*; **~n** *adj.* & *s.m.f.* libyen(ne).

licence *s.* (*formal authority*) autorisation *f.*; (*document*) permis *m.*; **driving ~, game ~,** permis de conduire, de chasse *m.*; **marriage ~,** dispense des bans *f.*; **pilot's ~,** brevet de pilote *m.*; (*excessive liberty*) licence *f.*

licens/e *v.t.* (*authorize*) autoriser; (*grant licence to or for*) donner un permis (à qn. de faire qch.); (*authorize use of, e.g. public house*) patenter; **~ed** *adj.* patenté; **~ed** VICTUALLER; **~ee** *s.* titulaire d'un permis *m.f.*, patenté *m.*

licentiate *s.* licencié(e) *m.f.*

licentious *adj.* licencieux; **~ly** *adv.**; **~ness** *s.* licence *f.*

lichen *s.* lichen *m.*

lick *s.* (*act*) coup de langue *m.*; (*blow*) coup *m.*; (*small quantity*) brin *m.*; **a ~ and a promise,** un bout de toilette *m.*; *v.t.* (*pass tongue over, play lightly over*) lécher; ~ **one's** CHAPS; (*pop.* = *defeat*) enfoncer; **~spittle** *s.* (*pop.*) lèche-cul *m.*; **~ing** *s.* (*pop.*) raclée *f.*

lid *s.* couvercle *m.*; **eye~,** paupière *f.*; **that puts the (tin) ~ on it** (*fam.*) ça, c'est le comble.

lido *s.* piscine *f.*

lie[1] *s.* (*false statement, belief, imposture*) mensonge *m.*; **to tell a ~,** mentir; **to give the ~ to,** démentir; *v.i.* mentir.

lie[2] *s.* (*of the land*) configuration *f.*; *v.i.* (*be in horizontal position*) être couché; **let sleeping** DOGS ~; (*rest on sth.*) reposer (sur qch.); (*be situated*) se trouver; **see how the** LAND **~s**; (*remain*) rester; (*be comprised in*) résider dans; (*be responsibility of*) appartenir à; ~ **about,** traîner; ~ **down,** se coucher; ~ **in** (*late, in bed*) faire la grasse matinée; ~ **in state,** être exposé sur un lit de parade; ~ **low,** dissimuler ses desseins.

lief *adv.* **I had as ~,** j'aimerais autant.

liege *s.* (*subject*) lige *m.*; (*lord*) suzerain *m.*

lien *s.* (*law*) droit de rétention *m.*; ⚠ lien = **bond.**

lieutenant *s.* lieutenant *m.*; **sub-, second-~,** (*army*) sous-lieutenant *m.*; (*navy*) enseigne *m.*; **~-colonel,** lieutenant-colonel *m.*; **~-commander,** capitaine de corvette *m.*; **~-general,** (*hist.*) lieutenant-général *m.*; (*mod.*) général de division *m.*; **lieutenancy** *s.* grade de lieutenant *m.*

life *s.* (*principle, state, living things, energy, story of, worldly pleasures*) vie *f.*; **still ~,** (*art*) nature morte *f.*; **a matter of ~ and death,** question de vie ou de mort *f.*; **the ~ and** SOUL **of; for ~,** à vie; **for the ~ of me,** parole d'honneur; **not on your ~,** (*fam.*) jamais de la vie; **to bring to ~,** animer; **to come to ~,** revenir à la vie, (*fig.*) s'animer; **to take one's ~,** se suicider; **~belt** *s.* ceinture de sauvetage *f.*; **~-blood** *s.* essence *f.*; **~boat** *s.* canot de sauvetage *m.*; **~buoy** *s.* bouée de sauvetage *f.*; **~-guard** *s.* (*army*) garde du corps *m.*, (*on beach*) sauveteur *m.*; ~ **insurance** *s.* assurance (sur la) vie *f.*; ~ **interest** *s.* usufruit *m.*; **~-jacket** *s.* gilet de sauvetage *m.*; **~-sized** *adj.* grandeur nature; **~less** *adj.* inanimé, (*fig.*) sans vie; **~lessness** *s.* manque de vie *m.*; **~like** *adj.* vivant; **~long** *adj.* de toute la vie; **~time** *s.* vie *f.*; **in my ~time,** de mon vivant.

lift *s.* (*act of ~ing*) levée *f.*, levage *m.*; (*for people*) ascenseur *m.*; (*for goods*) monte-charge *m.*;

(~*ing power*) force ascensionnelle *f.*, poussée *f.*; **to give s.o. a ~** (*in car*) prendre qn. en stop; **face-~**, déridage *m.*, (*fig.*) remise à neuf *f.*; FORK-~; *v.t.* (*raise*) lever; (*fig.*) élever; (*hoist*) soulever; (*elevate*) élever; (*fam. = steal*) faucher; (*agric.*) arracher; *v.i.* se lever, se soulever; (*fog, etc.*) se dissiper; **~-off** *s.* décollage *m.*

ligament *s.* ligament *m.*

ligature *s.* (*tie*) lien *m.*; (*bandage*) ligature *f.*; (*mus.*) liaison *f.*; (*print.*) ligature *f.*

light[1] *s.* (*natural*) jour *m.*; **it is ~**, il fait jour; (*source of*) éclairage *m.*; (*artificial*) lumière *f.*; (*for fire*) feu *m.*; (*brightness*) éclat *m.*; (*mental brightness*) lumière *f.*; (*aspect*) jour *m.*; **in an unfavourable ~**, sous un jour défavorable; (*fig. enlightenment*) éclaircissement *m.*; (*auto., naut.*) feu *m.*; **traffic ~s,** feux tricolores *m.pl.*; (*comm.*) enseignes lumineuses *f.pl.*; (*window*) fenêtre *f.*; FLOOD~; LIME~; NIGHT-~; PILOT-~; SEARCH~; SKY~; SPOT~; **to bring to ~**, dévoiler; **to come to ~**, se révéler; **~house** *s.* phare *m.*; **~house** KEEPER; **~ship** *s.* bateau-feu *m.*; **~-year** *s.* année lumière *f.*

light[2] *v.t.* **1.** (*cause to burn*) allumer; **2.** (*illuminate, lit. & fig.*) éclairer; *v.i.* (1) s'allumer; **~ up** *v.t.* & *i.* (s')allumer; **~ upon** *v.t.* tomber sur; **~er** *s.* (*cigarette, etc.*) briquet *m.*; FIRE **~er; ~ing** *s.* (1) allumage *m.*; (2) éclairage *m.*; **~ing-up time** *s.* heure d'éclairage obligatoire *f.*

light[3] *adj.* **1.** (*illuminated*) éclairé; **2.** (*colours*) pâle, clair; **3.** (≠ *heavy*, ≠ *ponderous*, ≠ *grave*, ≠ *tight*, ≠ *dense*) léger; **to make ~ of sth.,** faire peu de cas de qch.; **~-fingered** *adj.* (*fam.*) aux doigts longs; **~-headed** *adj.* (*med.*) délirant, (*fam.*) étourdi; **~-hearted** *adj.* insouciant; **~-weight** *s.* poids léger *m.*, *adj.* peu sérieux; **~en** *v.t.* & *i.* (1) (s')éclairer, (*flash*) lancer des éclairs; (3) (s')alléger; **~ly** *adv.* (3) légèrement; **~ness** *s.* (1) jour *m.*; (2) pâleur *f.*, clarté *f.*; (3) légèreté *f.*

lighter *s.* (*boat*) allège *f.*; **~age** *s.* transport par allège *m.*

lightning *s.* éclair *m.*; **forked ~**, éclair en zig-zag *m.*, éclair ramifié *m.*; **sheet ~**, éclair de chaleur *m.*; **~-conductor** *s.* paratonnerre *m.*; *adj.* éclair (*invar.*), **~ strike,** grève éclair.

lights *s.* (*of animal*) mou *m.*

ligneous *adj.* ligneux.

like[1] *s.* (*counterpart*) semblable *m.*; (*equal*) pareil *m.*; **the ~s of me, you, etc.,** les gens comme moi, vous, etc.; **and the ~**, et autres choses du même genre; *adj.* semblable (à); (*of picture, etc.*) ressemblant; **to be or look ~**, ressembler à; **~ father ~ son,** tel père, tel fils; **what is he ~?**, (*physically*) à quoi ressemble-t-il?, (*morally*) quel est son genre?; **what is it ~?**, comment est-ce?; **it's just ~ him,** c'est bien de lui (*to*—de); **you never saw anything ~ it,** vous n'avez jamais rien vu de pareil; **there will never be a party ~ it,** il n'y aura jamais de fête pareille; **that's something ~ a house,** ça, c'est une maison; (*in the mood for*) disposé à; **to feel ~ doing sth.,** être disposé à faire qch.; **to feel ~ a cup of tea,** avoir envie d'une tasse de thé; *prep.* comme; **drink ~ a** FISH; **swear ~ a** TROOPER; *conj.* (*Eng. fam.*) comme; **~ly** *adj.* probable, (*credible*) vraisemblable, (*suitable*) propre à, (*promising*) prometteur; **to be ~ly to,** avoir des chances de; **~ly** *adv.* probablement, vraisemblablement; **not ~ly!** (*fam.*) pas de danger!; **~lihood** *s.* probabilité *f.*, vraisemblance *f.*; **~en** *v.t.* comparer (*to*—à); **~ness** *s.* ressemblance *f.* (à), portrait *m.*; **~wise** *adv.* pareillement; **to do ~wise,** en faire autant.

like[2] *v.t.* aimer; (*enjoy*) se plaire à; **I should ~**, je voudrais; **when you ~**, quand vous voudrez; **~able** *adj.* (*person*) sympathique, (*thing*) attirant; **liking** *s.* goût *m.*

lilac *s.* lilas *m.*; *adj.* lilas *invar.*

lilliputian *adj.* lilliputien.

lilt *s.* cadence *f.*

lily *s.* lis *m.*; **~ of the valley** *s.* muguet *m.*; TIGER-~; WATER-~.

limb *s.* (*leg, arm, wing*) membre *m.*; (*of tree*) branche *f.*; **out on a ~** (*fig.*) sur la corde raide; **loose-~ed** *adj.* dégingandé; **~less** *adj.* mutilé.

limber *s.* prolonge *f.* (d'artillerie); *adj.* (*flexible*) souple; (*agile*) agile; *v.t.* assouplir; **~ up** *v.i.* faire des exercices d'assouplissement.

limbo *s.* (*eccles.*) limbes *m.pl.*; (*fam.*) oubli *m.*

lime *s.* **1.** (*substance*) chaux *f.*, (*bird*~) glu *f.*; **2.** (*fruit*) limon *m.*; **3.** (*tree*) tilleul *m.*; **~-juice** *s.* jus de limon *m.*; **~kiln** *s.* four à chaux *m.*; **~-lights** *s.* (*theat.*) (les feux de la) rampe *f.*, **to be in the ~light** (*fig.*) être en vedette; **~stone** *s.* calcaire *m.*; *v.t.* (1) (*agric.*) chauler, (*birds*) prendre à la glu.

limit *s.* limite *f.*; TIME **~; he's the ~** (*fam.*) il est impossible; **that's the ~**, il ne manquait plus que cela; **~s** (*faults*) points faibles *m.pl.*, désavantages *m.pl.*; **~less** *adj.* illimité; *v.t.* limiter; **~ed** *adj.* limité, restreint, (*fig.*) borné; **~ed** COMPANY; **~ation** *s.* limitation *f.*

limn *v.t.* peindre.

limousine *s.* limousine *f.*

limp[1] *s.* claudication *f.*; *v.i.* claudiquer, clopiner; **~ing** *adj.* clopinant.

limp[2] *adj.* (≠ *stiff*) mou, flasque; (*without energy*) abattu; **~ly** *adv.* mollement.

limpet *s.* patelle *f.*

limpid *adj.* limpide; **~ity** *s.* limpidité *f.*

linchpin *s.* esse *f.*

linctus *s.* sirop pharmaceutique *m.*

linden *s.* (LIME (3)) tilleul *m.*

line *s.* (*cord, fishing; telegraph, TV, etc.; row; course, direction; boundary; equator*) ligne *f.*; (*clothes-~*) corde *f.* (d'étendage); (*dash*) trait *m.*; (*of poetry*) vers *m.*; (*lineage*) lignée *f.*; (*out~*) contour *m.*; (*comm.*) article *m.*; (*transport co.*) compagnie *f.* (de navigation, aérienne); (*wrinkle*) ride *f.*; (*rail. track*) voie *f.*; (*short letter*) mot *m.*; (*area of activity, business*) **what's your ~?** (*fam.*) qu'cst-ce que vous faites?, **it's not my ~** (*fam.*) ce n'est pas mon rayon; HARD **~s; to** HOLD **the ~; to read between the ~s,** lire entre les lignes; **to shoot a ~** (*fam.*) baratiner; **to toe the ~**, se mettre en ligne, (*fig.*) rentrer dans le rang; **~sman** *s.* (*sport*) juge de touche *m.*; *v.t.* (*mark with ~s*) rayer; (*route*) aligner le long de la route; (*garment*) doubler; **~-out** *s.* (*rugby*) rentrée en touche *f.*; **~ up** *v.i.* s'aligner; **~-up** *s.* alignement *m.*; **lining** *s.* (*of garment*) doublure *f.*, (*of brake*) garniture *f.*

lineage *s.* lignée *f.*

lineal *adj.* & **~ly** *adv.* en ligne directe.

lineament *s.* linéament *m.*

linear *adj.* linéaire.

linen *s.* (*text.*) toile *f.*; (*household, table, personal*) linge *m.*; *adj.* de lin, de toile; **do not wash your** DIRTY **~ in public.**

liner *s.* (*naut.*) paquebot *m.*

ling *s.* (*fish*) lotte *f.*; (*heather*) bruyère *f.*

linger *v.i.* (*be slow to leave*) s'attarder; (*dally*) flâner, traîner; **~er** *s.* retardataire *m.*; **~ing** *adj.* (*look*) prolongé; (*death*) lent; (*hope, etc.*) persistant.

lingo *s.* (*fam.*) baragouin *m.*

lingu/al *adj.* lingual; **~ist** *s.* linguiste *m.f.*; **~istic** *adj.* linguistique; **~istics** *s.* linguistique *f.* ⚠ *sing. in French.*

liniment *s.* liniment *m.*

lining *s. see* LINE.

link *s.* (*loop or ring of chain*) anneau *m.*, chaînon *m.*; (*person or thing that unites*) lien *m.*; **cuff-~**, bouton de manchette *m.*; **missing ~**, lacune

f.; ~**s** *s.pl.* terrain de golf *m.*; *v.t.* (*connect*) lier, réunir; (*intertwine arms*) se donner le bras.
linnet *s.* linotte *f.*
linoleum *s.* linoléum *m.*; (*fam. lino*) lino *m.*
linotype *s.* linotype *f.*
linseed *s.* graine de lin *f.*; ~ **oil** *s.* huile de lin *f.*
lint *s.* (*med.*) charpie *f.*; (*fluff*) peluche *f.*
lintel *s.* linteau *m.*
lion *s.* (*animal* & *person*) lion *m.*; ~**ess** *s.* lionne *f.*; SEA-~; ~ CUB; ~**-hearted** *adj.* au cœur de lion; ~**ize** *v.t.* traiter en vedette.
lip *s.* (*human*) lèvre *f.*; HARE~; (*animal*) babine *f.*; (*of jug, etc.*) bec *m.*, bord *m.*; (*pop.* = *cheek*) culot *m.*; **to keep a stiff upper** ~, tenir le coup; **there's many a slip twixt** CUP **and** ~; **to** ~**-read** *v.t.* lire sur les lèvres; **to pay** ~**-service to,** dire qch. du bout des lèvres; ~**stick** *s.* rouge à lèvres *m.*; **thick-**~**ped** *adj.* lippu.
liquef/y *v.t.* & *i.* (se) liquéfier; ~**action** *s.* liquéfaction *f.*; ~**iable** *adj.* liquéfiable.
liqueur *s.* liqueur *f.*
liquid *s.* liquide *m.*; *adj.* (*lit.*, *fin.*) liquide; (*sounds*) clair; (*fig.*) limpide; ~**ate** *v.t.* (*fin.*, *kill*) liquider; ~**ation** *s.* liquidation *f.*; **to go into** ~**ation,** soumettre à une liquidation; ~**ator** *s.* liquidateur *m.*; ~**ity** *s.* liquidité *f.*
liquor *s.* (*gen.*) liquide *m.*; (*alcohol*) alcool *m.*
liquorice *s.* réglisse *f.*
lira *s.* (*Italian monetary unit*) lire *f.*
lisle *s.* fil *m.*
lisp *s.* zézaiement *m.*; *v.i.* zézayer.
lissom *adj.* souple.
list *s.* **1.** (*catalogue*) liste *f.*; **sick-**~, rôle des malades *m.*; **2.** (*naut.*) bande *f.*; **to have a** ~, donner de la bande; ~**s** (*arena*) lice *f.*; *v.t.* (1) porter sur une liste, cataloguer; *v.i.* (2) donner de la bande.
listen *v.i.* écouter; ~ **in,** ~ **to,** écouter; ~**er** *s.* (*radio, etc.*) audit/eur, -rice *m.f.*; (*pej.*) écouteur *m.*
listless *adj.* apathique; ~**ly** *adv.* avec apathie; ~**ness** *s.* apathie *f.*
litany *s.* litanie *f.*
liter/acy *s.* aptitude à lire et à écrire *f.*; (*process*) alphabétisation *f.*; ~**ate** *adj.* sachant lire et écrire.
literal *adj.* littéral; (*fig.*) prosaïque; ~**ly** *adv.**.
liter/ary *adj.* littéraire; ~**ature** *s.* littérature *f.*
lithe *adj.* souple; ~**ness** *s.* souplesse *f.*
lithograph *s.* lithographie *f.*; *v.t.* lithographier; ~**er** *s.* lithographe *m.f.*; ~**y** *s.* lithographie *f.*
Lithuania *s.* (*geog.*) Lituanie *f.*; ~**n** *adj.* & *s.m.f.* lituanien(ne).
litig/ant *s.* plaid/eur, -euse *m.f.*; ~**ation** *s.* litige *m.*
litmus *s.* tournesol *m.*; ~**-paper,** papier (de) tournesol *m.*
litotes *s.* litote *f.*
litre *s.* litre *m.*
litter *s.* **1.** (*stretcher*) litière *f.*, (*med.*) civière *f.*; **2.** (*bedding for animals*) litière *f.*; **3.** (*rubbish*) désordre *m.*, ordures *f.pl.*; ~**-basket** *s.* panier à ordures *m.*; ~**-bin** *s.* boîte à ordures *f.*; **4.** (*young animals*) portée *f.*; *v.t.* (2) faire la litière de; (3) jeter le désordre dans, encombrer (*with*—de); (4) mettre bas.
little *s.* (*amount*) (un) peu *m.*; (*time*) quelques instants *m.pl.*; (*duration*) courte durée *f.*; (*distance*) court trajet *m.*; ~ **by** ~, peu à peu, petit à petit; **to make or think** ~ **of sth.,** faire peu de cas de qch.; *adj.* (≠ *big, in size, distance, time, fig.*) petit; ~ FINGER; (*not much*) peu de; **there is very** ~ **butter left,** il reste très peu de beurre; **give me a** ~ **butter,** donnez-moi un peu de beurre; ~**ness** *s.* petitesse *f.*; *adv.* peu; (*not at all*) ne . . . guère.
littoral *s.* littoral *m.*; *adj.* du littoral.
liturg/y *s.* liturgie *f.*; ~**ical** *adj.* liturgique.
live[1] *v.i.* vivre; (*behave in certain way*) mener une vie + *adj.*, ~ **poorly,** mener une vie pauvre; (*dwell*) habiter; *v.t.* passer, mener; ~ **down** *v.t.* faire oublier; ~ **in** *v.t.* habiter; ~ **on** *v.t.* vivre de, *v.i.* persister; ~ **through** *v.t.* survivre à; ~ **together** *v.i.* cohabiter; ~ **it up** (*fam.*) mener une vie de patachon; ~ **with sth.,** supporter qch.; **long** ~ **the Queen!,** vive la Reine!; ~**able** *adj.* (*fam.*) vivable; ~**able with** *adj.* supportable; **short-**~**d** *adj.* passager; **all the** ~**long day,** toute la sainte journée; ~**lihood** *s.* gagne-pain *m.*
live[2] *adj.* (*alive, real, active*) vivant, en vie, actif; (*radio etc. not recorded*) en direct; (*explosive*) chargé; (*electr.*) électrisé; (*colour, air*) vif; ~**stock** *s.* bétail *m.*; ~ **wire** *s.* (*fig.*) type dynamique *m.*; ~**liness** *s.* vivacité *f.*; ~**ly** *adj.* vivant, animé, vif; ~**n up** *v.t.* animer.
liver *s.* (*anat.*, *cook.*) foie *m.*; COD-~ **oil;** ~**ish** *adj.* (*med.*) hépatique, (*fam.*) mal en train.
livery *s.* livrée *f.*; ~ **stable** *s.* pension (pour chevaux) *f.*; écuries de louage *f.pl.*
livid *adj.* livide; ~**ness** *s.* lividité *f.*
living *s.* (*livelihood*) vie *f.*; (*eccles.*) bénéfice *m.*; **the** ~, *s.pl.* les vivants *m.pl.*; COST **of** ~; **to earn one's** ~, gagner sa vie; *adj.* vivant; ~ IMAGE; **within** ~ **memory,** de mémoire d'homme; ~**-room** *s.* salle de séjour *f.*; ~ **wage** *s.* (salaire) minimum vital *m.*, S.M.I.C.
lizard *s.* lézard *m.*
llama *s.* lama *m.*
load *s.* **1.** (*burden*) fardeau *m.*, (*of ship, etc.*) charge *f.*; **2.** (*electr.*) charge *f.*; **3.** (*weight* & *fig.*) poids *m.*; ~**s** (*pop.* = *plenty*) des tas de; ~**stone** *s.* aimant *m.*; *v.t.* (1) charger; (3) accabler; (*gun*) charger; (*dice*) piper; ~ **with,** charger, (*fig.*) combler de; ~**ing** *s.* chargement *m.*
loaf[1] *s.* pain *m.*; (*pop. brains*) ciboulot *m.*
loaf[2] *v.i.* flâner; ~**er** *s.* fainéant *m.*
loam *s.* (*agric.*) terreau *m.*; (*constr.*) torchis *m.*
loan *s.* prêt *m.*; (*fin.*) emprunt *m.*; **on** ~, à titre de prêt; ~**-word,** mot d'emprunt *m.*; *v.t.* prêter.
lo(a)th *adj.* **I am** ~ **to do that,** il me répugne de faire cela.
loath/e *v.t.* détester; ~**ing** *s.* dégoût *m.*; ~**some** *adj.* repoussant, dégoûtant.
lob *s.* (*tennis*) lob *m.*; *v.t.* lober.
lobby *s.* (*entrance hall*) vestibule *m.*; (*corridor*) couloir *m.*; (*parl. hall open to public*) salle des pas perdus *f.*; (*parl. voting chamber*) vestibule *m.*; (*group of people*) groupe de pression *m.*; *v.t.* (*parl.* ~ *an M.P.*) relancer un député dans les couloirs.
lobe *s.* lobe *m.*
lobelia *s.* lobélie *f.*
lobster *s.* homard *m.*; ~**-pot** *s.* casier *m.*
local *s.* (*person*) homme du pays *m.*; (*pub.*) bistro du coin *m.*; *adj.* local; (*confined to one place*) localisé; ~**ity** *s.* lieu *m.*, région *f.*; ~**ize** *v.t.* localiser; ~**ly** *adv.**.
locat/e *v.t.* (*state locality of*) situer; (*find*) repérer; (*establish*) établir; **to be** ~**ed,** se trouver, être situé; ~**ion** *s.* emplacement *m.*; (*cinema*) extérieur *m.*; ⚠ location = **letting or hiring;** ~**ive** *s.* locatif *m.*
loch *s.* lac *m.*; **sea** ~, bras de mer *m.*
lock *s.* **1.** (*of hair*) mèche *f.*; **2.** (*on door*) serrure *f.*; **3.** (*rail. brakes*) verrou *m.*; **4.** (*of gun*) platine *f.*; **5.** (*on waterway*) écluse *f.*; **6.** (*auto.*) rayon de braquage *m.*; **7.** (*wrestling*) clef *f.*; ~**s** (*hair*) chevelure *f.*; ~, **stock and barrel** (*pop.*) et tout le fourbi; ~**-gate** *s.* porte d'écluse *f.*; ~**jaw** *s.* tetanos *m.*; ~**-keeper** *s.* éclusier *m.*; ~**smith** *s.* serrurier *m.*; *v.t.* & *i.* (2) fermer à clef; (3) (se) bloquer; ~ **in** *v.t.* enfermer; ~ **out** *v.t.* fermer la porte à; ~**-out** *s.* lock-out *m. invar.*; ~ **up** *v.t.* enfermer, (*fin.*) immobiliser; ~**-up** *s.*

(*fam.*) violon *m.*; **~er** *s.* armoire *f.*, case *f.*, (*naut.*) caisson *m.*
locket *s.* médaillon *m.*
locomot/ion *s.* locomotion *f.*; **~ive** *s.* locomotive *f.*; *adj.* locomot/eur, -rice.
locum (tenens) *s.* suppléant *m.*
locust *s.* sauterelle *f.*
locution *s.* locution *f.*
lodg/e *s.* (*of gatekeeper, porter; masonic*) loge *f.*; (*house*) pavillon *m.*; *v.t.* (*house*) loger; (*deposit*) déposer; (*fix in*) enfoncer; (*place*) poser; (*make complaint*) porter (plainte); *v.i.* (*live as ~er*) être logé; (*settle*) se loger; **~er** *s.* pensionnaire *m.f.*, (*tenant*) locataire *m.f.*; **~ement** *s.* (*mil.*) logement *m.*, (*comm.*) dépôt *m.*; **~ing** *s.* logement *m.*; **~ings** *s.* appartement meublé *m.*
loft *s.* grenier *m.*
loft/y *adj.* **1.** (*lit.* & *fig.*) élevé; **2.** (*haughty*) hautain; **~ily** *adv.* (1) en hauteur; (2) avec hauteur; **~iness** *s.* (1) élévation *f.*; (2) hauteur *f.*
log *s.* **1.** (*of wood*) bûche *f.*; **to sleep like a ~,** dormir comme un loir; **2.** (*apparatus*) loch *m.*; **3.** (*record*) journal *m.*; **~(-book)** (*naut., aviat.*) journal de bord *m.*; **~-book** (*auto.*) carte grise *f.*; **~ hut** *s.* cabane de bois *f.*; *v.t.* (3) enregistrer.
loganberry *s.* ronce-framboise *f.*
logarithm *s.* logarithme *m.*
loggerheads *adv.* **to be at ~ with s.o.,** être en bisbille avec qn.
logic *s.* logique *f.*; **~al** *adj.* logique; **~ally** *adv.**; **~ian** *s.* logicien *m.*
logistics *s.pl.* logistique *f.* ⚠ *sing. in French.*
loin *s.* (*of beef*) aloyau *m.*; (*of pork*) échine *f.*; (*of veal*) longe *f.*; **~s** *s.pl.* reins *m.pl.*; **to** GIRD **up one's ~s; ~cloth** *s.* pagne *m.*
loiter *v.i.* flâner; (*delay*) s'attarder; (*with intent*) rôder; **~er** *s.* flâneur *m.*; traînard *m.*; rôdeur *m.*
loll *v.i.* (*recline*) se prélasser; (*hang out—tongue*) pendre.
London *s.* Londres *m.*; **~er** *s.* londonien(ne) *m.f.*; *adj.* londonien, de Londres.
lone *adj.* **1.** (*solitary*) solitaire; **2.** (*single*) seul; **to play a ~ hand,** agir tout seul; **~liness** *s.* & **~ness** *s.* (1) solitude *f.*; (2) isolement *m.*; **~ly** *adj.* solitaire, isolé, seul; **~some** *adj.* (1) solitaire; (2) isolé.
long[1] *adj.* long; **thirty metres ~,** long de trente mètres; **a ~ time,** longtemps; **in the ~ run,** à la longue; **as** BROAD **as it's ~; ~ in the** TOOTH; **~-boat** *s.* chaloupe *f.*; **~-distance** *adj.* (*forecast*) à long terme, (*telephone, etc.*) à longue distance; **~-distance runner** *s.* coureur de (grand) fond *m.*; **~hand** *s.* écriture ordinaire *f.*; **~ jump** *s.* saut en longueur *m.*; **~-lived** *adj.* à longue vie; **~ sight** *s.* presbytie *f.*; **~-sighted** *adj.* presbyte, (*fig.*) prévoyant; **~-standing** *adj.* de longue date; **~-term** *adj.* (*fin.*) à longue date, (*fig.*) à longue échéance; **~-winded** *adj.* verbeux.
long[2] *adv.* longtemps; **~** LIVE; **to be ~ (in) doing sth.,** être long à faire qch.; **~-drawn--out** *adj.* prolongé; **~-playing** *adj.* de longue durée; **~-playing record** *s.* microsillon *m.*; **~-suffering** *adj.* patient; **before ~,** avant peu; **so ~!,** à bientôt!; **so** *or* **as ~ as,** (*time*) aussi longtemps que, (*provided that*) pourvu que; **how ~?,** combien de temps?; **how ~ have you been waiting?,** depuis combien de temps attendez-vous?; **~er** *adv.* plus longtemps; **no ~er,** ne . . . plus.
long[3] *v.i.* brûler (*to do sth.*—de faire qch.); **~ for sth.,** avoir grande envie de qch.; **I ~ to see you,** il me tarde de vous voir; **~ing** *s.* grande envie *f.*; (*home-sickness*) nostalgie *f.*; *adj.* impatient; **~ingly** *adv.* impatiemment.
longevity *s.* longévité *f.*
longitud/e *s.* longitude *f.*; **~inal** *adj.* longitudinal.
loo *s.* (*card game*) mouche *f.*; (*pop. lavatory*) toilettes *f.pl.*
loofah *s.* luffa *m.*
look *s.* **1.** (*act, gaze*) regard *m.*; **2.** (*expression*) air *m.*; **3.** (*appearance*) aspect *m.*; **~s** *s.pl.* beauté *f.*; *v.i.* (1) regarder; (2), (3) avoir l'air; **he ~s happy,** il a l'air heureux; **it ~s like rain,** on dirait qu'il va pleuvoir; **~ about,** regarder autour de soi; **~ after** *v.t.* (*care for*) soigner, (*take charge of*) s'occuper de; **~ at** *v.t.* regarder; **~ away,** détourner les yeux; **~ back,** regarder en arrière; **~ big** *v.i.* avoir l'air important; **~ blank** *v.i.* avoir l'air déconcerté; **~ down,** baisser les yeux; **~ down on** *v.t.* mépriser; **~ for** *v.t.* chercher, (*expect*) attendre; **~ed-for** *adj.* attendu; **~ forward to** *v.t.* attendre avec impatience; **~ here!,** dites donc!; **~-in** *s.* (*fig.*) chance *f.*; **~ into** *v.t.* examiner; **~ out** *v.i.* faire attention; **~ out!,** attention!; **~-out** *s.* guet *m.*, poste d'observation *f.*, (*fam.*) perspective *f.*; **that's my ~-out,** c'est mon affaire; **be on the ~-out for** *v.t.* guetter (qn.), s'attendre à (qch.); **~ over, ~ through** *v.t.* parcourir; **~ up** *v.i.* lever les yeux, (*seek*) *v.t.* chercher; *v.i.* (*improve*) reprendre; **~ up to** *v.t.* admirer; **~er-on** *s.* spectat/eur, -rice *m.f.*; **~ing-**GLASS.
loom *s.* métier *m.*; *v.i.* (*appear dimly*) se dessiner; (*threaten*) menacer.
loon *s.* (*bird*) plongeon *m.*; (*person*) idiot *m.*; **~y** *adj.* & *s.m.f.* (*pop.*) dingue.
loop *s.* boucle *f.*; *v.t.* boucler; **~ the ~,** boucler la boucle; **~hole** *s.* (*arch.*) meurtrière *f.*; (*fig.*) échappatoire *m.*
loose *adj.* **1.** (*unbound*) détaché, délié, libre, (*hair*) dénoué; **2.** (≠ *tight*, ≠ *compact*) lâche; **3.** (*not close-fitting*) large; **4.** (≠ *literal*) vague, approximatif; **5.** (*careless*) vague; **6.** (*wanton*) dissolu; **7.** (*techn.*) desserré; **8. ~ cash,** menue monnaie; **on the ~,** évadé; **to come, get, ~,** se détacher; **to work ~,** se desserrer; **to let ~,** donner libre cours à; **at a ~** END; **to play** FAST **and ~; ~ box** *s.* box *m.*; **~ cover** *s.* housse *f.*; **~-leaf** *s.* feuille volante *f.*; **~strife** *s.* lysimaque *f.*; **~ly** *adv.* (1) librement; (2)*; (4)*,*; (5)*; **~n** *v.t.* & *i.* (se) relâcher, (se) desserrer; **~n up** *v.t.* & *i.* (s')assouplir; **~ness** *s.* (1), (2) relâchement *m.*; (3) ampleur *f.*; (4), (5) vague *m.*, imprécision *f.*; (6) relâchement *m.*; (7) desserrage *m.*; *v.t.* (*let ~*) délier, détacher; (*free*) libérer, lâcher.
loot *s.* butin *m.*; *v.t.* piller.
lop *v.t.* (*branch*) élaguer; (*tree*) émonder; **~--eared** *adj.* aux oreilles pendantes; **~sided** *adj.* de guingois.
lope *v.i.* avancer en faisant de longues enjambées.
loquacious *adj.* loquace; **~ness** *s.* loquacité *f.*
lord *s.* (*God, ruler*) Seigneur *m.*; (*superior, chief*) chef *m.*; (*owner*) propriétaire *m.*; (*husband*) maître *m.*; (*nobleman*) milord *m.*; (*title*) lord *m.*; **my ~,** monseigneur; **oh L~-,** mon Dieu!; **L~'s Prayer,** Notre Père *m.*, oraison dominicale *f.*; **L~'s day** *s.* jour du Seigneur *m.*; *v.t.* **to ~ it over s.o.,** dominer qn.; **~liness** *s.* hauteur *f.*; **~ly** *adj.* hautain; **~ship** *s.* (*estate, title*) seigneurie *f.*; (*fig.*) autorité *f.*
lore *s.* doctrine *f.*; (*traditions*) traditions *f.pl.*
lorgnette *s.* face-à-main *m.*; ⚠ lorgnette = **opera-glasses.**
lorry *s.* camion *m.*; **articulated ~,** camion semi-remorque *m.*; **~-driver** *s.* camionneur *m.*
lose *v.t.* & *i.* perdre; (*get rid of*) se débarasser de; (*forfeit*) manquer; (*of watch*) retarder (de . . . minutes); **~ sight of,** perdre de vue; **~ one's temper,** perdre patience; **~ the way,** se perdre; **he has not lost by it,** il n'y a rien

perdu; **~r** *s.* perdant *m.*; **losing** *adj.* (*team*) perdant, (*comm.*) à perte.
loss *s.* (*act, thing lost*) perte *f.*; (*detriment*) dommage *m.*; **~ of voice,** extinction de voix *f.*; **to be at a ~,** être embarrassé; **to sell at a ~,** vendre à perte; **to** CUT **one's ~es; a** DEAD **~.**
lot *s.* (*chance selection*) tirage au sort *m.*; **to cast ~s,** tirer au sort; (*fortune, destiny*) sort *m.*; (*appointed task*) destin *m.*; (*piece of land*) parcelle *f.*; (*at auction*) lot *m.*; (*fam. large amount*) tas *m.*; **a ~ of, ~s of,** beaucoup de; BAD **~;** JOB **~.**
lotion *s.* lotion *f.*
lottery *s.* loterie *f.*
lotto *s.* loto *m.*
lotus *s.* lotus *m.*; **~-eater** *s.* (*fig.*) songe-creux *m.*
loud *adj.* **1.** (*strongly audible*) fort, haut; **2.** (*noisy*) bruyant; **3.** (*flashy*) criard, voyant; **~speaker** *s.* haut-parleur *m.*; **~ly** *adv.* (1) fort, haut, à haute voix; (2) bruyamment; **~ness** *s.* (1) force *f.*; (2) caractère bruyant *m.*; (3) caractère voyant *m.*; *adv.* haut, fort, à haute voix.
lounge *s.* (*idling*) flânerie *f.*; (*sofa*) divan *m.*; (*room*) salon *m.*; *v.i.* (*idle*) flâner; (*recline*) se prélasser; **~ suit** *s.* complet veston *m.*
lour, lower *v.i.* (*frown*) se renfrogner; (*of sky*) s'assombrir; **~ing** *adj.* menaçant.
lous/e *s.* (*insect*) pou *m.*; WOOD-**~e;** (*person*) salaud *m.*; **~y** *adj.* (*infested with lice*) pouilleux; (*pop. very bad*) moche; **~y with** (*pop.*) grouillant de.
lout *s.* lourdaud *m.*; **~ish** *adj.* lourdaud.
louver, louvre *s.* abat-vent *m.*
love *s.* (*affection*) amitié *f.*; **to send one's ~ to,** envoyer ses amitiés à; **for ~ nor money,** à aucun prix, pour rien au monde; (*passion, thing ~d*) amour *m.*; (*tennis score*) zéro *m.*; **to fall in ~ with,** tomber amoureux de; **to make ~ to,** faire la cour à; **~ affair** *s.* liaison *f.*; **~-birds** *s.* inséparables *m.pl.*; **~-in-a-mist** *s.* cheveux de Vénus *m.pl.*; **~-letter** *s.* billet-doux *m.*; **~lock** *s.* accroche-cœur *m.*; **~lorn** *adj.* délaissé; **~sick** *adj.* éperdu d'amour; **lovable** *adj.* aimable; **~liness** *s.* beauté *f.*; **~ly** *adj.* beau, agréable; *v.t.* avoir de l'amitié pour, aimer; (*admire*) adorer; **~r** *s.* amoureux *m.*, amant *m.*; (*devotee of*) amateur *m.* (de); **loving** *adj.* (*person*) aimant, (*act*) amical.
low[1] *adj.* (≠ *high,* ≠ *loud*) bas; (*humble*) humble; (*no longer full*) bas, à sec; (*lacking vigour*) bas, faible; (*vulgar*) bas, vil; (*deep*) profond; (*fig. poor*) défavorable; **the L~ Countries,** les Pays-Bas *m.pl.*; **~brow** *adj.* peu intellectuel; **~-down** *adj.* (*fig.*) bas, vil; **to give the ~-down on sth.** (*fig. fam.*) tuyauter sur qch.; **~land** *s.* plaine *f.*; **~-lying** *adj.* bas; **~ pressure** *s.* basse pression *f.*; **~-spirited** *adj.* découragé; **~ly** *adj.* humble; **~liness** *s.* humilité *f.*; **~ness** *s.* faible altitude *f.*, (*smallness*) petitesse *f.*, (*fig.*) abattement *m.*, (*meanness*) bassesse *f.*; *adv.* bas; **to bring ~,** abattre; **to lay ~,** terrasser; **to lie ~,** se tenir coi; **to run ~,** baisser.
low[2] *v.i.* (*of cow*) beugler; **~ing** *s.* beuglement *m.*
lower *adj.* plus bas, inférieur; **~ case** (*print.*) bas de casse *m.*; **~-class** *adj.* laborieux; *v.t.* (*let down*) descendre; (*flag, sail*) amener; (*make ~*) abaisser, diminuer; *v.i.* baisser, (*be degrading*) avilir.
loyal *adj.* **1.** (*faithful*) fidèle; **2.** (*patriotic*) loyal; **~ist** *s.* loyaliste *m.*; **~ty** *s.* (1) & (2) fidélité *f.*; (2) loyalisme *m.*
lozenge *s.* (*figure*) losange *m.*; (*small tablet*) pastille *f.*
L.S.D. *s.* LSD *m.*; (*fam.*) acide *m.*
lubber *s.* lourdaud *m.*
lubric/ant *adj.* & *s.m.* lubrifiant; **~ate** *v.t.* lubrifier.
lubricity *s.* (*techn.*) onctuosité *f.*; (*fig.*) lubricité *f.*
lucerne *s.* luzerne *f.*
lucid *adj.* **1.** (*free from obscurity*) transparent; **2.** (*clearly expressed*) lucide; **3.** (*bright*) lumineux; **~ity** *s.* (1) transparence *f.*; (2) lucidité *f.*, clarté *f.*; (3) luminosité *f.*; **~ly** *adv.* (2)*; (3)*.
Lucifer *s.* Lucifer *m.*
luck *s.* (*good*) chance *f.*; (*ill*) malchance *f.*; **to wish s.o. good ~,** souhaiter bonne chance à qn.; HARD **~;** TOUGH **~;** DOWN **on one's ~; to take** POT **~; as ~ would have it,** par bonheur, par malheur; **no ~,** pas de chance; **~ily** *adv.* heureusement, par bonheur; **~less** *adj.* (*event*) malencontreux, (*person*) malheureux; **~y** *adj.* (*event*) heureux, (*person*) fortuné, veinard; **~y charm,** porte-bonheur *m.*
lucr/e *s.* lucre *m.*; **~ative** *adj.* lucratif.
ludicrous *adj.* grotesque; **~ly** *adv.**
luff *s.* (*naut.*) lof *m.*; *v.i.* lofer.
lug *v.t.* traîner.
luge *s.* luge *f.*; *v.i.* luger.
luggage *s.* bagages *m.pl.*; **left-~ office** *s.* consigne *f.*; **~-rack** *s.* filet *m.*; **~-van** *s.* fourgon à bagages *m.*
lugger *s.* (*naut.*) lougre *m.*
lugubrious *adj.* lugubre; **~ly** *adv.**
lukewarm *adj.* (*lit.* & *fig.*) tiède; **~ness** *s.* tiédeur *f.*
lull *s.* (*in storm*) accalmie *f.*; *v.t.* (*send to sleep*) bercer, endormir; (*soothe*) calmer; (*hoodwink*) endormir; (*allay*) calmer; **~aby** *s.* berceuse *f.*
lumbago *s.* lumbago *m.*
lumbar *adj.* lombaire.
lumber *s.* **1.** (*disused articles*) bric-à-brac *m.*; **2.** (*rough timber*) bois de charpente *m.*; **~jack, ~man** *s.* (2) bûcheron *m.*; **~-room** *s.* (1) débarras *m.*; **~ing** *adj.* (1) encombrant, (*heavy*) lourd.
luminary *s.* (*sun, moon*) luminaire *m.*; (*person*) lumière *f.*
lumin/ous *adj.* lumineux; (*signs, etc.*) réflectorisé; **~osity** *s.* luminosité *f.*
lump *s.* (*mass*) masse *f.*; (*whole*) bloc *m.*, ensemble *m.*; (*swelling*) bosse *f.*; (*of earth*) motte *f.*; (*of stone*) bloc *m.*; (*of sugar*) morceau *m.*; (*in liquid, sauce, etc.*) grumeau *m.*; **~ sum,** somme globale *f.*; **~y** *adj.* (*earth*) plein de mottes; (*med.*) plein de bosses; (*sauce, etc.*) grumeleux; *v.t.* entasser; **~ together,** englober; **~ it** (*fig. fam.*) l'avaler.
lun/acy *s.* **1.** (*med.*) aliénation mentale *f.*; **2.** (*fig.*) folie *f.*; **~atic** *s.* (1) aliéné *m.*; (2) fou *m.*; *adj.* (1) d'aliéné; (2) de fou; (*fam.*) extravagant.
lunar *adj.* lunaire.
lunch(eon) *s.* déjeuner *m.*; *v.i.* déjeuner.
lung *s.* poumon *m.*
lunge *s.* **1.** (*thrust with sword*) botte *f.*; **2.** (*plunge*) mouvement brusque *m.*; *v.i.* (1) se fendre; (2) s'élancer brusquement.
lupin *s.* lupin *m.*
lurch[1] *s.* panne *f.*; **to leave s.o. in the ~,** planter qn. là.
lurch[2] *s.* (*naut., auto.*) embardée *f.*; *v.i.* faire une embardée; (*fam.*) tituber.
lure *s.* leurre *m.*; *v.t.* leurrer, berner.
lurid *adj.* (*ghastly*) blafard; (*glaring*) flamboyant; (*sensational*) sensationnel.
lurk *v.i.* se cacher; **~ing** *adj.* caché, secret; **~ing-place** *s.* cachette *f.*
luscious *adj.* succulent; (*fig.*) savoureux.
lush *adj.* (*bot.*) plein de sève.
lust *s.* luxure *f.*; (*fig.*) convoitise *f.*; *v.i.* désirer, convoiter; **~ful** *adj.* luxurieux.
lustr/e *s.* (*5 year period; polish, glaze; chandelier*) lustre *n.*; (*brilliance*) éclat *m.*; **~ous** *adj.* lustré; (*fig.*) éclatant.
lust/y *adj.* (*vigorous*) vigoureux; (*fam.*) costaud; **~ily** *adv.* vigoureusement; **~iness** *s.* vigueur *f.*

lut/e *s.* luth *m.*; **~anist** *s.* joueur de luth *m.*
Lutheran *adj.* & *s.m.f.* luthérien(ne).
Luxembourg[1] *s.* (*geog. province of Belgium*) Luxembourg *m.*
Luxemburg[2] *s.* (*geog.*) Grand-Duché de Luxembourg *m.*; **from** *or* **of ~** *adj.* luxembourgeois.
luxuri/ance *s.* luxuriance *f.*; **~ant** *adj.* luxuriant; **~antly** *adv.* avec exubérance; **~ate** *v.i.* (*bot.*) pousser avec exubérance; (*fig.*) se complaire (dans).
luxur/y *s.* (*self-indulgence*) luxe *m.*; (*desirable but not essential object*) objet de luxe *m.*; **~ies** *s.pl.* luxe *m.*; ⚠ luxure = **lust**; LAP **of ~y**; **~ious** *adj.* (*fond of ~*) qui aime le luxe, (*self-indulgent*) voluptueux, (*thing*) luxueux; ⚠ luxurieux = **lustful.**
lye *s.* lessive *f.*
lying *s.* mensonge *m.*; *adj.* (*person, appearance*) menteur; (*thing*) mensonger.
lymph *s.* lymphe *f.*; **~atic** *adj.* lymphatique.
lynch *v.t.* lyncher; **~ing** *s.* lynchage *m.*
lynx *s.* lynx *m.*
Lyons *s.* (*geog.*) Lyon *m.*; **of** *or* **from ~** *adj.* lyonnais.
lyre *s.* lyre *f.*; **~-bird** *s.* oiseau-lyre *m.*
lyric *s.* (*poem*) poème lyrique *m.*; (*words of song*) paroles *f.pl.*; *adj.* & **~al** *adj.* lyrique; **~ism** *s.* lyrisme *m.*

M

ma *s.* (*pop.*) maman *f.*
M.A. *s.* (*degree*) maîtrise *f.*
mac *see* MACK.
macabre *adj.* macabre.
macadam *s.* macadam *m.*; **~ize** *v.t.* macadamiser.
macaroni *s.* macaroni *m.*
macaroon *s.* macaron *m.*
macaw *s.* ara *m.*
mace *s.* **1.** (*hist.* & *staff of office*) masse *f.*; **~-bearer** *s.* massier *m.*; **2.** (*spice*) macis *m.*
macerat/e *v.t.* & *i.* macérer; **~ion** *s.* macération *f.*
Mach *s.* nombre de Mach *m.*; **to fly at ~ 1, 2, etc.,** voler à Mach 1, 2, etc.
machete *s.* machette *f.*
machiavellian *adj.* machiavélique.
machination *s.* (*usu. pl.*) machination *f.*
machine *s.* **1.** (*mech. apparatus*) machine *f.*, **sewing-~,** machine à coudre *f.*, (*bicycle, car, etc.*) machine *f.*, (*aircraft*) appareil *m.*; **2.** (*controlling system, polit. etc.*) noyau directeur *m.*; **~-gun** *s.* mitrailleuse *f.*; **~-gunner** *s.* mitrailleur *m.*; **~-made** *adj.* fait à la machine; **~ tool** *s.* machine-outil *f.*; *v.t.* (1) coudre à la machine; (*techn.*) usiner; **~ery** *s.* (1) machinerie *f.*; (2) organes *f.pl.*, mécanisme *m.*; **~ist** *s.* machiniste *m.f.*
mack, mac *s.* (*fam. abbrev. for mackintosh*) imper *m.*
mackerel *s.* maquereau *m.*; **~ sky,** ciel pommelé.
mackintosh *s.* (*text.*) tissu imperméable *m.*; (*garment*) imperméable *m.*
macro- (*in combination*) **~cephalic** *adj.* macrocéphale; **~cosm** *s.* macrocosme *m.*
mad *adj.* (*insane*) fou, folle; (*rabid*) enragé; (*foolish*): (*act*) insensé, (*person*) fou; (*fam.* = *annoyed*) furieux (*at s.o.*—contre qn., *at having done sth.*—d'avoir fait qch.); (*excited, infatuated*) fou (*about, for, on*—de); **~ with joy, etc.,** fou de joie, etc.; **~ as a** HATTER; **to go ~,** devenir fou; **~cap** *s.* écervelé(e) *m.f.*; **~house** *s.* (*fam.*) maison de fous *f.*; **~man, ~woman** *s.* aliéné(e) *m.f.*; **~den** *v.t.* rendre fou, (*annoy*) exaspérer; **~dening** *adj.* à rendre fou, exaspérant; **~ly** *adv.* follement; **~ness** *s.* folie *f.*, (*anger*) fureur *f.*
Madagascar *s.* (*geog.*) Madagascar *m.*; **of or from ~** *adj.* malgache; *see* MALAGASY.
madam (ma'am) *s.* madame *f.*
madder *s.* garance *f.*
made *p.p.adj.* fait; **~ (out) of,** fait de; **~ to measure,** fait sur mesure; **~ to order,** fait sur commande; **~-up** (*finished*) composé, (*invented*) inventé, (*with cosmetics*) maquillé; **~ up of,** composé de; **ready-~,** de confection; **ready-~ clothes** *s.* prêt-à-porter *m.*
Madeira *s.* (*geog.*) Madère *f.*; (*wine*) madère *m.*
madonna *s.* madone *f.*; **~ lily** *s.* lis blanc *m.*
Madrid *s.* (*geog.*) Madrid *f.*; **native of ~** *s.m.f.* Madrilène; **of ~** *adj.* madrilène.
madrigal *s.* madrigal *m.*
maelstrom *s.* (*lit.* & *fig.*) maelstrom *m.*
maenad *s.* (*myth.*) ménade *f.*; (*fury*) furie *f.*
maestro *s.* maestro *m.*
Mae West *s.* (*aviat.*) gilet de sauvetage *m.*
mafia *s.* maffia *f.*
magazine *s.* (*arms store*) magasin *m.*; POWDER-~; (*in rifle*) chargeur *m.*; (*periodical*) magazine *f.*, revue *f.*
magenta *adj.* & *s.m.* magenta.
maggot *s.* asticot *m.*; ⚠ magot = **savings**; **~y** *adj.* véreux.
Magi *s.pl.* les Rois Mages *m.pl.*
magic *s.* magie *f.*; **black ~, white ~,** magie noire, magie blanche; *adj.* & **~al** *adj.* magique; **~ian** *s.* magicien *m.*
magist/rate *s.* juge *m.*; **~erial** *adj.* (*of magistrate*) de magistrat, (*authoritative*) autoritaire, (*dictatorial*) impérieux; **~racy** *s.* magistrature *f.*
magma *s.* magma *m.*
Magna Carta, charta *s.* Grande Charte *f.*
magnanim/ous *adj.* magnanime; **~ity** *s.* magnanimité *f.*; **~ously** *adv.**.
magnate *s.* magnat *m.*
magnesi/a *s.* magnésie *f.*; **~um** *s.* magnésium *m.*
magnet *s.* (*lit.* & *fig.*) aimant *m.*; **~ic** *adj.* magnétique; **~ic needle,** aiguille aimantée *f.*; **~ism** *s.* magnétisme *m.*; **~ize** *v.t.* aimanter, (*fig.*) magnétiser, attirer.
magneto *s.* (*auto.*) magnéto *f.*
magnificat *s.* magnificat *m.invar.*
magnificen/t *adj.* (*splendid*) magnifique; (*imposing*) imposant; (*fam.*) fameux; **~ce** *s.* magnificence *f.*; **~tly** *adv.**.
magnif/y *v.t.* **1.** (*increase in size*) grossir; **2.** (*sound*) amplifier; **3.** (*exaggerate*) exagérer; **~ication** *s.* (1) grossissement *m.*; (2) amplification *f.*; **~ying glass** *s.* loupe *f.*
magnitude *s.* (*size*) grandeur *f.*; (*importance*) ampleur *f.*; (*astron.*) magnitude *f.*
magnolia *s.* magnolia *m.*
magnum *s.* magnum *m.*
magpie *s.* pie *f.*
Magyar *adj.* & *s.m.f.* magyar(e); (*lang.*) langue magyare *f.*
maharaja(h) *s.* maharajah *or* maharadjah *m.*
mah-jong(g) *s.* mah-jong *m.*
mahogany *s.* (*wood, colour*) acajou *m.*; *adj.* en acajou.

maid *s.* (*virgin*) vierge *f.*; (*young, unmarried, girl*) jeune fille *f.*; **old ~,** vieille fille *f.*; (*~servant*) bonne *f.*, domestique *f.*; **the M~ of Orleans,** la pucelle d'Orléans *f.*

maiden *s. as* MAID; *adj.* (*unmarried*) non mariée, (*untried, first*) vierge, premier; **~ speech,** premier discours *m.*; **~ name,** nom de jeune fille *m.*; **~hair** *s.* (*fern*) capillaire *m.*; **~hood** *s.* virginité *f.*; **~ly** *adj.* virginal.

mail *s.* (*armour*) cotte de maille *f.*; (*letters*) courrier *m.*; (*post*) poste *f.*; (*vehicle carrying ~*) train, avion, etc. postal; **~-bag** *s.* sac postal *m.*; **~-boat** *s.* bateau-poste *m.*; **~-coach** *s.* malle-poste *f.*; **~ order** *s.* commande par poste; *f.*; **~ed fist** (*fig.*) force armée *f.*; *v.t.* envoyer par la poste.

maim *v.t.* mutiler.

main *s.* (*high seas*) large *m.*; (*pipe for water, gas, etc.*) conduite principale *f.*; **in the ~,** en général, **the summer, in the ~, was fine,** l'été, en général, a été beau, (*after pl.s.*) pour la plupart, **men, in the ~, like the sun,** les hommes, pour la plupart, aiment le soleil; **with** MIGHT **and ~;** *adj.* grand, principal, essentiel; ~BRACE; **~land** *s.* continent *m.*; **~mast** *s.* grand mât *m.*; **~ point** *s.* essentiel *m.*; **~sail** *s.* grand-voile *f.*; **~spring** *s.* (*mech.*) grand ressort *m.*, (*fig.*) mobile principal *m.*; **~stay** *s.* (*naut.*) étai de grand mât *m.*, (*fig.*) fondement *m.*; **~top** *s.* grande-hune *f.*; **~ly** *adv.* principalement.

maintain *v.t.* (*keep up*) soutenir; (*keep going*) maintenir; (*keep in repair*) entretenir; (*support*) soutenir; (*assert*) soutenir; **~able** *adj.* (*position*) tenable; (*fig.*) soutenable.

maintenance *s.* (*maintaining*) entretien *m.*, maintien *m.*; (*subsistence*) pension alimentaire *f.*; ⚠ *avoid use of* maintenance *which is obs. or anglicism.*

maison(n)ette *s.* (*small house*) maisonnette *f.*; (*flat*) appartement *m.*

maize *s.* maïs *m.*

majest/y *s.* (*state, sovereign, title*) majesté *f.*; **~ic** *adj.* majestueux; **~ically** *adv.**.

majolica *s.* majolique *f.*

major *s.* (*mil.*) commandant *m.*; **~-general** *s.* général de division *m.*; (*person of full age*) majeur *m.*; (*mus.*) majeur *m.*; (*acad. subject*) matière principale *f.*; *adj.* majeur, principal; (*mil.*) **drum ~,** tambour major; SERGEANT-**~**; **~-domo** *s.* majordome *m.*; **~ road** *s.* route de priorité *f.*; **~ suit** (*at cards*) couleur majeure *f.*; *v.i.* **~ in** (*acad.*) se spécialiser dans.

Majorca *s.* (*geog.*) Majorque *f.*

majority *s.* (*greater number*; *full age*) majorité *f.*; (*mil. rank*) grade de commandant *m.*; *adj.* (*government, shareholder, etc.*) majoritaire.

make *s.* (*way sth. is made*) fabrication *f.*; (*shape*) forme *f.*; (*brand*) marque *f.*; **to be on the ~,** se pousser; *v.t.* (*create*) faire, construire; (*manufacture*) fabriquer; (*cause to exist*) créer; (*bring about*) provoquer; (*constitute*) constituer; (*amount to*) faire; (*represent as being or doing*) représenter; (*earn, win*) gagner; (*cook.*) faire, préparer; (*perform*) effectuer; (*utter*) faire; (*force s.o. to do sth.*) obliger qn. à faire qch.; **~ s.o. do,** faire + *inf.*, **you made her cry,** vous l'avez fait pleurer; **~ s.o. do sth.,** faire faire qch. à qn., **I made him write a letter,** je lui ai fait écrire une lettre; (*cause to be*) rendre, **he will ~ her happy,** il la rendra heureuse; **~** FRIENDS; **~** FUN **of; ~** HAY; **~ a** HABIT **of; ~ do,** se débrouiller, **~ do with,** se contenter de; **~ of,** (*understand*) comprendre; **~ away** *v.i.* s'éloigner; **~ away/off, with,** *v.t.* (*steal*) soustraire, (*destroy*) détruire; **~ for** *v.t.* (*proceed towards*) se diriger vers, (*be conducive to*) favoriser; **~ off** *v.i.* décamper; **~ out** *v.t.* (*list, etc.*) établir, (*decipher*) déchiffrer, (*understand*) comprendre, (*perceive*) distinguer, (*pretend*) prétendre (que); **~ over** *v.t.* céder; **~ up** *v.t.* (*list, etc.*) dresser, (*lost ground*) regagner, (*compose*) composer, (*med., cook.*) préparer, (*complete*) compléter, (*settle*) arranger, (*invent*) inventer, (*face*) (se) maquiller; **~-up** *s.* maquillage *m.*; **~ it up,** se réconcilier; **~ up for,** (*loss*) compenser, (*time*) rattraper; **~-believe** *s.* faux-semblant *m.*; **~shift** *s.* expédient *m.*, pis-aller *m.*, *adj.* provisoire, de fortune; **~weight** *s.* supplément *m.*, (*fam.*) bouche-trou *m.*; **~r** *s.* créateur *m.*, (*manufacturer*) fabricant *m.*; **making** *s.* fabrication *f.*, construction *f.*; **to be the making of s.o.,** être un élément de la réussite de qn.; **to have the makings of,** avoir l'étoffe de.

malachite *s.* malachite *f.*

maladjust/ed *adj.* **1.** (*techn.*) mal ajusté; **2.** (*fig.*) inadapté; **~ment** *s.* (1) mauvais ajustement *m.*; (2) inadaptation *f.*

maladministration *s.* mauvaise administration *f.*

maladroit *adj.* maladroit.

malady *s.* maladie *f.*

Malagasy *adj.* & *s.m.f.* malgache; *s.m.* (*lang.*) malgache.

malapropism *s.* impropriété (d'expression) *f.*

malapropos *adj.* inopportun; *adv.* mal à propos.

malaria *s.* paludisme *m.*; **~l** *adj.* paludéen.

Malay/a *s.* (*geog.*) Malaisie *f.*; **~** *adj.* & *s.m.f.* malais(e); *s.m.* (*lang.*) malais.

malcontent *adj.* & *s.m.* mécontent.

male *adj.* & *s.m.* mâle.

male- (*in combination*) **~diction** *s.* malédiction *f.*; **~factor** *s.* malfait/eur, -rice *m.f.*; **~volent** *adj.* malveillant; **~volence** *s.* malveillance *f.*; **~volently** *adv.* avec malveillance.

malform/ation *s.* malformation *f.*; **~ed** *adj.* difforme.

malic/e *s.* méchanceté *f.*; (*grudge*) rancune *f.*; (*law*) intention délictueuse *f.*; ⚠ malice *is less strong than Eng.*; **~ious** *adj.* méchant; rancunier; **~iously** *adv.* méchamment.

malign *v.t.* calomnier; *adj.* pernicieux; ⚠ malin = **shrewd**; **~ant** *adj.* malveillant; (*med.*) malin, maligne; **~ity** *s.* & **~ancy** *s.* malignité *f.*; **~antly** *adv.* malignement.

malinger *v.i.* tirer au flanc; **~er** *s.* (*fam.*) tireur au flanc *m.*

mallard *s.* canard sauvage *m.*

malleab/le *adj.* (*lit.* & *fig.*) malléable; **~ility** *s.* malléabilité *f.*

mallet *s.* maillet *m.*

mallow *s.* mauve *f.*

malmsey *s.* malvoisie *f.*

malnutrition *s.* sous-alimentation *f.*

malodorous *adj.* malodorant.

malpractice *s.* malversation *f.*; (*by doctor*) faute professionnelle *f.*

malt *s.* malt *m.*; *adj.* de malt.

Malt/a *s.* (*geog.*) Malte *f.*; **~ese** *adj.* & *s.m.f.* maltais(e) **~ese cross,** croix de Malte *f.*

maltreat *v.t.* maltraiter; **~ment** *s.* mauvais traitement *m.*

malversation *s.* malversation *f.*

mamba *s.* mamba *m.*

mam(m)a *s.* maman *f.*

mammal *s.* mammifère *m.*; **~ian** *adj.* mammifère.

Mammon *s.* Mammon *m.*

mammoth *s.* mammouth *m.*; *adj.* monstre, géant.

man *s.* (*human being, human race, ~kind*) homme *m.*; (*male adult*) homme *m.*; (*husbamd*) mari *m.*; (*servant*) domestique *m.*; (*workman*) ouvrier *m.*; (*chess, draughts*) pièce *f.*, pion *m.*; (*common soldier, sailor*) homme *m*; **~!,** mon vieux; **my good ~,** mon brave; **old ~,** vieillard *m.*; **young ~,** jeune homme *m.*; **~ in the street,**

homme moyen *m.*; ODD ~ **out**; ~ FRIDAY; ISLE **of M~**; ~ **to** ~, d'homme à homme; **~-eater** *s.* (*animal*) mangeur d'hommes *m.*, (*person*) anthropophage *m.*; **~handle** *v.t.* (*techn.*) manutentionner, (*fam.*) malmener; **~hole** *s.* regard *m.*; **~-hour** *s.* heure de main-d'œuvre ouvrière *f.*; **~kind** *s.* genre humain *m.*; **~-made** *adj.* artificiel; **~power** *s.* main-d'œuvre *f.*; **~servant** *s.* domestique *m.*; **~slaughter** *s.* homicide *m.*; **~-of-war** *s.* cuirassé *m.*; **~ful** *adj.* courageux; **~fully** *adv.**; **~hood** *s.* humanité *f.*, (*adult status*) maturité *f.*, (*virility*) virilité *f.*; **~like** *adj.* d'homme; **~liness** *s.* virilité *f.*; **~ly** *adj.* viril; **~nish** *adj.* homasse; *v.t.* (*with men*) équiper, (*guard*) armer.

manacle *s.* (*usu. pl.*) menottes *f.pl.*; *v.t.* passer les menottes à.

manag/e *v.t.* (*conduct working of*) diriger; (*have control of*) conduire; (*subdue*): (*animal*) maîtriser, (*person*) mater; (*cajole*) ménager; (*contrive*) arranger; (*techn.*) manier; *v.i.* venir à bout de qch., se débrouiller; **~e to do sth.,** parvenir à faire qch.; **~eable** *adj.* (*tool*) maniable, (*job*) faisable, (*person*) docile; **~ement** *s.* (*act*) gestion *f.*, (*staff*) direction *f.*; **~er** *s.* directeur *m.*, gérant *m.*; **~eress** *s.* directrice *f.*; **~erial** *adj.* directorial; **~ing** *adj.* directeur, (*fig.*) actif; **~ing** DIRECTOR.

mandarin *s.* **1.** (*Chinese official*; *influential person*) mandarin *m.*; **2.** (*orange*) mandarine *f.*

mandat/e *s.* mandat *m.*; *v.t.* (*international polit.*) mettre sous le mandat de; **~ary** *s.* mandataire *m.*; **~ory** *adj.* impératif.

mandible *s.* mandibule *f.*

mandolin(**e**) *s.* mandoline *f.*

mandrake *s.* mandragore *f.*

mane *s.* (*of horse, lion, fam. human hair*) crinière *f.*

manege *s.* manège *m.*

manganese *s.* manganèse *m.*

mang/e *s.* gale *f.*; **~y** *adj.* galeux; (*fam.*) moche.

mangel-wurzel *s.* betterave fourragère *f.*

manger *s.* mangeoire *f.*; (*eccles.*) crèche *f.*; DOG **in the ~.**

mangle *s.* (*for clothes*) calandre *f.*; *v.t.* (*clothes*) calandrer; (*mutilate*) mutiler; (*spoil*) abîmer.

mango *s.* mangue *f.*; **~-tree,** manguier *m.*

mangrove *s.* palétuvier *m.*

man/ia *s.* **1.** (*med.*) démence *f.*; **2.** (*craze*) manie *f.*; **~iac** *adj.* & *s.m.f.* (1) fou (folle) furieux (furieuse); (2) maniaque (de); **~iacal** *adj.* fou; **~ic** *adj.* maniaque; **~ic-depressive** *adj.* & *s.m.f.* cyclothymique.

manicur/e *s.* manucure *m.*; *v.t.* faire les mains (de qn.); **~ist** *s.* manucure *m.f.*

manifest *s.* (*naut.*) manifeste *m.*; *adj.* manifeste; (*indubitable*) incontestable; *v.t.* & *i.* (se) manifester; **~ation** *s.* manifestation *f.*; **~ly** *adv.**; **~o** *s.* manifeste *m.*

manifold *s.* (*techn.*) tubulure *f.*; *adj.* (*of various forms*) multiple; (*many & diverse*) nombreux.

manikin *s.* mannequin *m.*; (*dwarf*) nabot *m.*

Manila *s.* (*geog.*) Manille *f.*

manila *s.* (*fibre*) chanvre de Manille *m.*; ~ **paper,** papier bulle *m.*

manipulat/e *v.t.* (*handle*) manier; (*deal skilfully with*) manipuler; (*manage craftily*) manœuvrer; **~ion** *s.* manipulation *f.*; **~or** *s.* manipulateur *m.*

manna *s.* manne *f.*

mannequin *s.* mannequin *m.*

manner *s.* (*way sth. is done*) manière *f.*; (*sort, kind*) sorte *f.*; (*style*) allure *f.*; **~s** *s.pl.* (*social*) manières *f.pl.*; (*moral*) mœurs *f.pl.*; **after the ~ of,** à la manière de; **in a ~,** en quelque sorte; **no ~ of,** aucune espèce de; **~ed** *adj.* maniéré; **~ism** *s.* maniérisme *m.*; **~ly** *adj.* bien élevé.

manœuvr/e *s.* manœuvre *f.*; *v.t.* & *i.* (faire) manœuvrer; (*force into, out of*) amener à, dissuader de; **~able** *adj.* maniable.

manor *s.* (*feudal*) seigneurie *f.*; (*house*) manoir *m.*; **~ial** *adj.* seigneurial.

manse *s.* presbytère *m.*

mansion *s.* (*country*) château *m.*; (*town*) hôtel *m.*; △ mansion = **mansion** (*in medieval drama*).

mantel (**piece**) *s.* cheminée *f.*

mantilla *s.* mantille *f.*

mantis *s.* mante *f.*; **praying ~,** mante religieuse *f.*

mantle *s.* (*cloak*) cape *f.*; (*gas*) manchon *m.*; (*geol.*) manteau *m.*; *v.t.* couvrir.

manual *s.* (*handbook*) manuel *m.*; (*organ*) clavier *m.*; *adj.* manuel.

manufactur/e *s.* fabrication *f.*; *v.t.* (*lit.* & *fig.*) fabriquer; **~er** *s.* fabricant *m.*; **~ing** *adj.* industriel.

manure *s.* fumier *m.*; *v.t.* fumer.

manuscript *s.* manuscrit *m.*; *adj.* manuscrit.

Manx *s.m.* (*lang.*) manx *m.*; *adj.* de l'île de Man; ~ **cat,** chat sans queue *m.*

many *s.* **the ~,** la foule; *pron.* beaucoup; *adj.* beaucoup de, nombreux; **as ~,** autant (de); **so ~,** tant (de); **too ~,** trop (de); **~ a,** maint; **~ a time,** maintes fois; **~-coloured** *adj.* multicolore; **~-sided** *adj.* (*fig.*) complexe.

Mao/ist *s.m.f.* maoïste; **~ism** *s.* maoïsme *m.*

Maori *adj.* & *s.m.f.* maori(e); *s.m.* (*lang.*) maori.

map *s.* carte *f.*; (*of the world*) mappemonde *f.*; **off the ~,** (*fig.*) à l'autre bout du monde; *v.t.* faire la carte de; **~ out** *v.t.* organiser.

maple *s.* érable *m.*; **~-leaf, ~ sugar,** feuille (*f.*), sucre (*m.*), d'érable.

maquette *s.* maquette *f.*

Maquis *s.* maquis *m.*; (*person*) maquisard *m.*

mar *v.t.* gâcher.

marabou *s.* marabout *m.*

maraschino *s.* marasquin *m.*

marathon *s.* (*race, test of endurance*) marathon *m.*

maraud *v.t.* piller; *v.i.* marauder; **~er** *s.* maraudeur *m.*; **~ing** *s.* maraude *f.*; *adj.* maraudeur.

marble *s.* (*stone*) marbre *m.*; (*toy*) bille *f.*; **to play ~s,** jouer aux billes; *adj.* de marbre, en marbre; *v.t.* marbrer.

March[1] *s.* (*month*) mars *m.*

march[2] *s.* (*action, mus.*) marche *f.*; **forced ~,** marche forcée *f.*; **quick ~,** pas accéléré *m.*; **~ past** *s.* défilé *m.*; (*distance*) étape *f.*; (*progress*) progrès *m.*; STEAL **a ~ on**; *v.t.* faire marcher; *v.i.* faire une marche; (*progress*) avancer; FROG-~; **~ in,** entrer; **~ on,** avancer sur; **~ out,** sortir; **~ past,** défiler.

march[3] *s.* (*boundary, usu. pl.*) marche *f.*; *v.i.* **~ with,** être limitrophe de.

marchioness *s.* marquise *f.*

mare *s.* jument *f.*; **~'s nest** (*fig.*) découverte illusoire *f.*

margarine *s.* margarine *f.*

margin *s.* (*border*) bord *m.*; (*strip at edge of page*; *excess*) marge *f.*; (*comm., fin.*) couverture *f.*; **~ release** *s.* (*on typewriter*) touche passe-marge *f.*; **~al** *adj.* marginal; **~ally** *adv.**.

margrave *s.* margrave *m.*

marguerite *s.* marguerite *f.*

marigold *s.* souci *m.*

marijuana *s.* marihuana, marijuana *f.*

marinade *s.* marinade *f.*; *v.t.* (*also* MARINATE) faire mariner.

marine *s.* marine *f.*; (*mil.*) fusilier marin *m.*; *adj.* (*of, from, near, for use at, sea*) marin; (*of shipping*) maritime.

mariner *s.* marin *m.*; **~'s compass,** boussole *f.*

marionette *s.* marionnette *f.*

marital *adj.* marital.

maritime *adj.* maritime.

marjoram *s.* marjolaine *f.*

mark[1] *s.* (*German currency*) mark *m.*
mark[2] *s.* **1.** (*target*) but *m.*; **beside the ~, wide of the ~,** (*fig.* = *irrelevant*) hors de propos; **you are wide of the ~,** vous êtes loin de la vérité; **2.** (*sign, indication, of quality, feeling, etc.*) signe *m.*, marque *f.*, preuve *f.*; **3.** (*affixed sign, seal*) marque *f.*; TRADE ~; (*cross made by illiterate person*) marque *f.*, croix *f.*; **4.** (*for work, conduct, etc.*) note *f.*; (*numerical unit*) point *m.*; **to get a good ~,** avoir une bonne note; **to get 18 ~s,** gagner 18 points; EXCLAMATION ~; QUESTION ~; **5.** (*line indicating position*) marque *f.*; (*sport*) **on your ~s!,** à vos marques!; **to get off the ~,** partir, démarrer; **on the ~,** prêt; **up to the ~,** (*of health*) en forme; **6.** (*visible sign left by s.o. or sth.*; *trace, stain, spot, etc.*) marque *f.*; trace *f.*, tache *f.*; TIDE-~; **to make one's ~,** (*fig.*) se distinguer; **of ~,** de marque; *v.t.* (2) & (3) marquer; (4) coter; (6) marquer, tacher; **7.** (*see, notice*) remarquer; (*heed*) faire attention à; **8.** (*sport*) marquer; **~ down,** (*price*) baisser; **~ off,** (*distance*) mesurer, (*set limits to*) limiter; **~ out,** tracer; **~ out for,** désigner pour; **~ time,** (*lit.* & *fig.*) marquer le pas; **~ up,** augmenter; **~ed** *adj.* marqué; **~edly** *adv.* d'une manière marquante; **~er** *s.* (*book~*) signet *m.*, (*naut., aviat.*) balise *f.*; **~ing** *s.* (*of horse, bird, etc.*) particularité *f.*; **~ing-ink** *s.* encre indélébile *f.*
market *s.* (*sale, place, building*) marché *m.*; (*comm. outlet*) débouché *m.*; MONEY-~; **on the ~,** en vente; **to be in the ~ for,** être acheteur de; ~ GARDEN; ~ GARDENer; **~-hall** *s.* halle *f.*; **~-place** *s.* place du marché *f.*; **~ price** *s.* prix de vente *m.*; **~ town** *s.* bourg *m.*; *v.t.* (*sell*) vendre; (*buy*) acheter; (*fig. pej.*) trafiquer; **~able** *adj.* vendable; **~eer** *s.* trafiquant *m.*; **~ing** *s.* vente *f.*, achat *m.* (au marché); (*of a product*) commercialisation *f.*
marksman *s.* tireur d'élite *m.*
marl *s.* marne *f.*
marline-spike, marlinspike *s.* épissoir *m.*
marmalade *s.* confiture d'oranges *f.*; *adj.* orange; ⚠ marmelade = (*any*) **stewed fruit.**
marmoset *s.* ouistiti *m.*
marmot *s.* marmotte *f.*
maroon *s.* **1.** (*colour*) marron *m.*; **2.** (*firework*) pétard *m.*; *adj.* (1) marron; *v.t.* abandonner (sur une île déserte).
marquee *s.* grande tente *f.*
marquetry *s.* marqueterie *f.*
marquis *s.* marquis *m.*
marriage *s.* mariage *m.*; **~ bonds** *s.pl.* liens conjugaux *m.pl.*; ~ LICENCE; **~ portion** *s.* dot *f.*; **~able** *adj.* mariable.
marrow *s.* (*in bones*) moelle *f.*; (*veg.*) courge *f.*; **~bone,** os à moelle *m.*; **~fat pea,** pois cassé *m.*
marr/y *v.t.* (*of priest, unite*; *of parent or guardian, give in marriage*) marier; (*take s.o. in wedlock*) épouser; *v.i.* & **get ~ied,** se marier.
Mars *s.* mars *m.*
Marseillaise *s.* marseillaise *f.*
marsh *s.* marais *m.*; **salt-~,** marais salant *m.*; **~land** *s.* marécage *m.*; **~ mallow** *s.* (*bot.*) guimauve *f.*, (*sweet*) pâte de guimauve *f.*; **~y** *adj.* marécageux.
marshal *s.* maréchal *m.*; **Field M~, Air M~,** Maréchal (de France) *m.*; *v.t.* (*arrange in order*) disposer, ranger; (*conduct with ceremony*) conduire; **~ling yard** *s.* (*rail.*) gare de triage *f.*
marsupial *adj.* & *s.m.* marsupial.
mart *s.* marché *m.*; (*auction*) salle des ventes *f.*
marten *s.* martre *f.*
martial *adj.* martial; **~ law,** loi martiale *f.*
martin *s.* martinet *m.*
martinet *s.* chef autoritaire *m.*; (*fam.*) gendarme *m.*
Martinmas *s.* la St. Martin *f.*
martlet *s.* (*herald*) merlette *f.*
martyr *s.* martyr(e) *m.f.*; **he is a ~ to rheumatism,** ses rhumatismes le martyrisent; **to make a ~ of oneself,** jouer les martyrs; **~dom** *s.* martyre *m.*; **~ology** *s.* martyrologe *m.*; *v.t.* martyriser.
marvel *s.* merveille *f.*; *v.i.* s'émerveiller, s'étonner (*at*—de); **~lous** *adj.* merveilleux, étonnant; **~lously** *adv.**, étonnamment.
Marxist *adj.* & *s.m.f.* marxiste.
marzipan *s.* pâte d'amandes *f.*; (*small cake*) massepain *m.*
mascara *s.* mascara *m.*
mascot *s.* mascotte *f.*
masculin/e *s.* masculin *m.*; *adj.* (*gender*) masculin; (*male, manly*) mâle; (*vigorous*) viril; (*mannish*) hommasse; **~ity** *s.* masculinité *f.*
mash *s.* (*cook.*) purée *f.*; (*agric.*) pâtée *f.*; *v.t.* (*cook.*) faire une purée de, réduire en purée; **~ed** POTATO.
mask *s.* masque *m.*; (*of fox*) face *f.*; **gas ~,** masque à gaz *m.*; *v.t.* masquer.
masoch/ism *s.* masochisme *m.*; **~ist** *s.* masochiste *m.f.*
mason *s.* maçon *m.*; **Free~,** franc-maçon *m.*; **~ic** *adj.* maçonnique; **~ry** *s.* maçonnerie *f.*; **Free~ry** *s.* franc-maçonnerie *f.*
masque *s.* masque *m.*
masquerade *s.* **1.** (*masked ball*) bal masqué *m.*; **2.** (*pretence*) mascarade *f.*; *v.i.* **~ as** (2) se déguiser en, se faire passer pour; **~r** *s.* masque *m.*
mass[1] *s.* (*eccles.*) messe *f.*
mass[2] *s.* (*large body of matter*) masse *f.*; (*large number*) foule *f.*; **a ~ of,** un tas de; (*main part of*) majorité *f.*; **the ~es** *s.pl.* les masses *f.pl.*; **in the ~,** en masse; **~ communication,** moyens de communication collective *m.pl.*; **~ meeting,** rassemblement *m.*; **~ media,** moyens de diffusion collective *m.pl.*; **to ~ produce,** produire en série; **~ production** *s.* production en série *f.*; *v.t.* & *i.* (se) masser.
massacre *s.* massacre *m.*; *v.t.* massacrer.
mass/age *s.* massage *m.*; *v.t.* masser; **~eur, ~euse** *s.* masseu/r, -se *m.f.*
massif *s.* massif *m.*
massive *adj.* massif; **~ly** *adv.**.
mast[1] *s.* (*beech*) faines *f.pl.*; (*oak*) glands *m.pl.*
mast[2] *s.* (*of ship, for flag*) mât *m.*; HALF-~; (*for aerial, etc.*) pylône *m.*; **to serve before the ~,** être simple matelot.
master *s.* (*controller, head of household, owner, of dog, etc., skilled workman, great artist*) maître *m.*; (*of ship*) capitaine *m.*; (*teacher*) professeur *m.*; (*employer*) patron *m.*; **past ~ at,** passé maître en; **~ of arts** *s.* titulaire de la maîtrise *m.f.*; **~ of** CEREMONIES; TOAST-~; **to be one's own ~,** être son propre maître; **~-copy** *s.* original *m.*; **~-key** *s.* passe-partout *m.*; **~-mind** *s.* esprit supérieur *m.*, *v.t.* diriger; **~piece** *s.* chef d'œuvre *m.*; **~-stroke** *s.* coup de maître *m.*; **~-switch** *s.* interrupteur principal *m.*; *v.t.* **1.** (*acquire knowledge of*) acquérir la maîtrise de; **2.** (*subdue*) maîtriser; **~ful** *adj.* impérieux; **~ly** *adj.* de maître, magistral; **~y** *s.* (1) maîtrise *f.*; (2) empire *m.*
mastic *s.* mastic *m.*
masticat/e *v.t.* mastiquer; **~ion** *s.* mastication *f.*
mastiff *s.* dogue *m.*
mastodon *s.* mastodonte *m.*
mastoid *adj.* mastoïde; **~itis** *s.* mastoïdite *f.*
masturbat/e *v.i.* & *t.* (se) masturber; **~ion** *s.* masturbation *f.*
mat *s.* **1.** (*on floor*) tapis *m.*, (*door* & *fig.*) paillasson *m.*; (*table*) dessous de plat *m.*; **2.** (*tangle*) emmêlement *m.*; *v.t.* & *i.* (2) (s')emmêler; **~ting** *s.* nattes *f.pl.*
matador *s.* matador *m.*
match[1] *s.* (*for lighting*) allumette *f.*; SAFETY ~;

~box *s.* boîte à allumettes *f.*; **box of ~es,** boîte d'allumettes *f.*; **~wood** *s.* bois d'allumettes *m.*; éclats de bois *m.pl.*

match[2] *s.* **1.** (*like, equal*) égal *m.*; **2.** (*marriage*) mariage *m.*; **3.** (*person eligible for marriage*) parti *m.*; **4.** (*game, contest*) match *m.* (*pl.* matchs *or* matches); AWAY ~; **to be a ~ for,** être de taille à lutter contre; **~maker** *s.* (2) marieu/r, -se *m.f.*; **~ point** *s.* (*tennis*) balle de match *f.*; **~less** *adj.* incomparable; **~lessly** *adv.**; *v.t.* (1) égaler, correspondre à; (*make correspond*) assortir; (4) rivaliser avec; *v.i.* (1) s'assortir, s'harmoniser avec.

mate[1] *s.* (*chess*) mat *m.*; *v.t.* faire échec et mat.

mate[2] *s.* (*one of pair*) mâle *m.*, femelle *f.*; (*fellow workman*) camarade *m.*; (*fam. friend*) copain *m.*; (*naut.*) officier en second *m.*; *v.t.* & *i.* (*animals*) (s')accoupler, (*people*) (se) marier.

material *s.* (*from which sth. is made*) matière *f.*; (*text.*) tissu *m.*; (*elements*) matériaux *m.pl.*; **raw ~s** *s.pl.* matières premières *f.pl.*; *adj.* (*of matter*) matériel; (≠ *spiritual*) corporel; (*important*) important; (*essential*) essentiel; **~ism** *s.* matérialisme *m.*; **~ist** *s.* matérialiste *m.f.*; **~ize** *v.i.* prendre forme, se réaliser; *v.t.* matérialiser; **~ly** *adv.* matériellement, sensiblement.

matern/al *adj.* maternel; **~ally** *adv.**; **~ity** *s.* maternité *f.*; *adj.* (*dress*) de future maman; (*care, etc.*) pré-natal; **~ity hospital** *s.* maternité *f.*

mathemat/ics *s.pl.* mathématiques *f.pl.*; **~ical** *adj.* mathématique; **~ically** *adv.**.

matinée *s.* (*theat.*) matinée *f.*

matins *s.* matines *f.pl.*

matri- (*in combination*) **~arch** *s.* femme à poigne *f.*; **~archal** *adj.* matriarcal; **~archy** *s.* matriarcat *m.*; **~cide** *s.* matricide *m.*; **~lineal** *adj.* en ligne maternelle.

matriculat/e *v.i.* **1.** (*complete secondary school*) passer le baccalauréat; **2.** (*enter university*) se faire inscrire à l'université; **~ion** *s.* (1) baccalauréat *m.*; (2) inscription à l'université *f.*; matriculer = **to register.**

matrimon/y *s.* mariage *m.*; **~ial** *adj.* conjugal, matrimonial; **~ially** *adv.* conjugalement.

matrix *s.* matrice *f.*

matron *s.* (*older woman*) dame âgée *f.*; (*mother*) mère de famille *f.*; (*in hospital*) infirmière en chef *f.*; (*in school, etc.*) intendante *f.*; **~ly** *adj.* d'âge mûr.

matt *adj.* mat.

matter *s.* **1.** (*physical substance*) matière *f.*; **2.** (*content ≠ form*) fond *m.*; **3.** (*affair, concern*) affaire *f.*, sujet *m.*; **4.** (*discharge*) pus *m.*; PRINTED ~; **as a ~ of fact,** à vrai dire; **~-of-fact** *adj.* terre-à-terre; **as a ~ of course,** qui va de soi; **what's the ~?,** qu'est-ce qu'il y a?; **what's the ~ with you?,** qu'avez-vous?; *v.i.* (4) suppurer; *v.i.* (*impers.*) (*to be important*) importer; **it doesn't ~,** n'importe, cela ne fait rien.

mattock *s.* pioche *f.*

mattress *s.* matelas *m.*; **spring ~,** matelas à ressorts *m.*

matur/e *adj.* **1.** (*fully developed*) mûr; **2.** (*adult*) adulte, responsable; **3.** (*fin.*) échu; **~ely** *adv.* (1)*; (2) d'une manière responsable; **~ity** *s.* (1), (2) maturité *f.*; (3) échéance *f.*; *v.t.* & *i.* (1) (faire) mûrir; (3) échoir.

maudlin *adj.* larmoyant.

maul *v.t.* malmener; *s.* (*Rugby*) mêlée spontanée *f.*

maunder *v.i.* divaguer.

Maundy Thursday, jeudi saint *m.*

Mauriti/us *s.* (*geog.*) île Maurice *f.*; **~ian** *adj.* & *s.m.f.* mauricien(ne).

mausoleum *s.* mausolée *m.*

mauve *adj.* & *s.m.* mauve.

maverick *s.* indépendant *m.*

maw *s.* (*of birds, etc.*) jabot *m.*

mawkish *adj.* (*sickly*) écœurant; (*sentimental*) (*fam.*) gnangan.

maxillary *adj.* & *s.m.* maxillaire.

maxim *s.* maxime *f.*

maxim/um *s.* maximum *m.*; *adj.* & **~al** *adj.* maximum; (*temperature*) maximal; (*price*) (prix)-plafond.

May[1] *s.* (*month*) mai *m.*; (*hawthorn* (*blossom*)) aubépine *f.*; **~-bug** *s.* hanneton *m.*; **~ Day** *s.* fête du travail *f.*; **~day** *s.* (*distress signal*) signal international de détresse *m.*; **~fly** *s.* éphémère *m.*; **~pole** *s.* mai *m.*; **~-tree** *s.* aubépine *f.*

may[2] *v.aux.* **1.** (*possibility*) pouvoir; **that ~ be,** cela se peut; **he ~ not come,** il se peut qu'il ne vienne pas; **he ~ have made a mistake,** il a pu se tromper; **2.** (*permission*) pouvoir; **I ~ not tell you,** je ne puis vous le dire; **3.** (*request*) pouvoir; **~ I speak?,** puis-je parler?; **you might call at the baker's,** vous pourriez passer chez le boulanger; **4.** (*wish*) pouvoir; **~ he be happy!,** puisse-t-il être heureux!; **5.** *examples using the subjunctive*; **so that you ~ know,** pour que vous sachiez; **I fear he ~ not come,** j'ai peur qu'il ne vienne pas; **whatever you ~ say/do,** quoi que vous disiez/fassiez; **however rich he ~ be,** quelque riche qu'il soit; **whatever effort he ~ make,** quelque effort qu'il fasse; **whoever it ~ be,** qui que ce soit; **be that as it ~,** quoi qu'il en soit.

maybe *adv.* peut-être.

mayonnaise *s.* mayonnaise *f.*

mayor *s.* maire *m.*; **~ess** *s.* mairesse *f.*; **~alty** *s.* mairie *f.*

maze *s.* labyrinthe *m.*; (*fig.*) imbroglio *m.*

mazurka *s.* mazurka *f.*

M.C. (*master of ceremonies*) maître de cérémonie *m.*

me[1] *pron.* (*direct* & *indirect obj.*) me; (*alone*; *after a prep.*; *with another pronoun*) moi.

me[2], **mi** *s.* (*mus.*) mi *m.*

mead *s.* hydromel *m.*

meadow *s.* prairie *f.*; (*small*) pré *m.*; **~sweet** *s.* reine des prés *f.*

meagre *adj.* maigre; **~ly** *adv.**; **~ness** *s.* maigreur *f.*

meal *s.* (*grain*) farine *f.*; (*food*) repas *m.*; **~ies** *s.pl.* maïs *m.*; **~y** *adj.* farineux; **~y-mouthed** *adj.* doucereux.

mean[1] *s.* milieu *m.*, moyen *m.*; GOLDEN ~; (*maths.*) moyenne *f.*; **~s** *s.pl.* (*steps towards end*) moyen *m.*; **by ~s of,** au moyen de; **by all ~s,** certainement; **by no ~s,** en aucune façon; **~s** *s.pl.* (*resources*) moyens *m.pl.*, (*money*) ressources *f.pl.*; **~s test** *s.* prise en considération des revenus *f.*; *adj.* moyen; **~time, ~while** *adv.*, **in the ~time,** en attendant.

mean[2] *adj.* **1.** (*of poor quality*) pauvre; **2.** (*of low degree*) humble; **3.** (*ignoble, ungenerous*) mesquin; **4.** (*miserly*) avare; **~ly** *adv.* (1)*; (2)*; (3) chichement; (4)*; **~ness** *s.* (1) pauvreté *f.*; (2) bassesse *f.*; (3) mesquinerie *f.*; (4) avarice *f.*

mean[3] *v.t.* & *i.* (*intend to, wish to*) avoir l'intention de, compter + *inf.*, vouloir + *inf.*; (*be resolved on*) se proposer de; (*intend for*) destiner à; (*signify*) vouloir dire, signifier; (*entail, involve*) entraîner; **~ business** (*fig.*) avoir des intentions sérieuses; **~ well,** avoir de bonnes intentions; **~ well by s.o.,** vouloir du bien à qn.; **well-meant** *adj.* fait dans une bonne intention; **~ing** *s.* (*what is meant*) signification *f.*; (*what is intended*) intention *f.*; **~ing** *adj.* & **~ingful** *adj.* significatif; **well-~ing** *adj.* plein de bonnes intentions, bien intentionné; **~ingless** *adj.* sans signification.

meander *s.* (*usu. pl.*) méandres *m.pl.*; *v.i.* (*stream*) serpenter; (*person*) errer; **~ing** *s.* méandres *m.pl.*

measl/es *s.* rougeole *f.*; **German ~es,** rubéole *f.*; **~y** *adj.* (*pop.*) piètre.

measur/e *s.* (*size, quantity, extent, amount, vessel; rhythm; action; law*) mesure *f.*; (*tape-~*) mètre *m.*; *v.t.* mesurer; (*person for clothes*) prendre les mesures de qn.; *v.i.* (*be of certain length*) avoir . . . pieds de long; **~e out,** mesurer; **~e up to** (*fig.*) être à la hauteur de; **~e with s.o.,** se mesurer avec qn.; **~able** *adj.* mesurable; **~ed** *adj.* mesuré, rythmé; **~eless** *adj.* illimité, (*beyond ~*) démesuré; **~ement** *s.* (*act*) mesurage *m.*, (*size*) mensuration *f.*; **~ements** *s.pl.* mesures *f.pl.*; **~ing** *s.* mesurage *m.*, mensuration *f.*

meat *s.* viande *f.*; SAUSAGE-~; (*archaic = food*) nourriture *f.*; **~less day** (*eccles.*) jour maigre *m.*; **~y** *adj.* de viande, (*fig.*) plein de substance.

Mecca *s.* (*geog.*) la Mecque *f.*

mechan/ic *s.* artisan *m.*; (*techn.*) mécanicien *m.*; **~ics** *s.* mécanique *f.* ⚠ *sing. in French,* (*fig.*) mécanisme *m.*; **~ical** *adj.* (*working by machine*) mécanique, (*automatic*) machinal; **~ically** *adv.**; *; **~ician** s. mécanicien *m.*; **~ism** *s.* (*lit.* & *fig.*) mécanisme *m.*; **~ize** *v.t.* mécaniser.

medal *s.* médaille *f.*; **~lion** *s.* médaillon *m.*; **~list** *s.* médaillé(e) *m.f.*

meddl/e *v.i.* se mêler (*with, in*—de); **~e with** *v.t.* (*lit.*) toucher à, (*fig.*) s'ingérer dans; **~er** *s.* touche-à-tout *m.*; **~esome** *adj.* curieux; **~ing** *s.* ingérence *f.* (dans).

medi(a)eval *adj.* médiéval; (*suggesting Middle Ages, out of date*) moyenâgeux.

medial *adj.* médial.

median *s.* médiane *f.*

mediat/e *v.i.* intervenir (entre); servir d'intermédiaire; **~ion** *s.* médiation *f.*; **~or** *s.* médiateur *m.*

medi/cal *adj.* (*care, profession*) médical; (*school, book*) de médecine; (*student*) en médecine; **~cally** *adv.* médicalement; **~cament** *s.* médicament *m.*; **~cate** *v.t.* médicamenter; **~cinal** *adj.* médicinal; **~cine** *s.* (*science*) médecine *f.*, (*drugs, etc.*) médicament *m.*; PATENT **~cine; ~cine-man,** sorcier *m.*; **~co** *s.* (*fam.*) toubib *m.*

mediocr/e *adj.* médiocre; **~ity** *s.* médiocrité *f.*

meditat/e *v.i.* méditer (*on*—sur); *v.t.* projeter; **~ed** *adj.* projeté; **~ion** *s.* méditation *f.*; **~ive** *adj.* méditatif.

Mediterranean *s.* (*geog.*) Méditerranée *f.*; *adj.* (*sea*) méditerrané; (*climate, etc.*) méditerranéen.

medium *s.* (*middle quality, degree*) moyen *m.*; (*means, agency*) moyen *m.*, intermédiaire *m.*; (*spiritual*) médium *m.*; (*sea, air, etc.*) milieu *m.*; (*pl. means of communication*) moyens d'information *m.pl.*, média *m.*; *adj.* moyen.

medlar *s.* nèfle *f.*; **~-tree** *s.* néflier *m.*

medley *s.* mélange *m.*; (*mus.*) pot-pourri *m.*; *adj.* mélangé.

meed *s.* (*poet.*) récompense *f.*

meek *adj.* (*submissive*) résigné; (*gentle*) doux; **~ly** *adv.* avec douceur; **~ness** *s.* douceur *f.*

meerschaum *s.* (*clay*) écume de mer *f.*; (*pipe*) pipe en écume de mer *f.*

meet[1] *s.* (*hunt.*) rendez-vous de chasse *m.*; *v.t.* (*come into contact with*) rencontrer; (*get to know*) faire la connaissance de; (*confront*) affronter, faire face à; (*become visible to eye, audible to ear, etc.*) s'offrir (aux yeux, aux oreilles, etc.); (*satisfy need*) satisfaire à un besoin; (*experience*) trouver, subir; (*await arrival of*) aller chercher; **go to ~ s.o.,** aller au devant de qn.; (*comm.*) faire honneur à; *v.i.* se rencontrer; **make both** ENDS **~**; **~ with,** subir, (*sth. bad*) essuyer, (*sth. good*) recevoir; **~ing** *s.* (*contact*) rencontre *f.*; (*by appointment*) rendez-vous *m.*; (*assembly*) assemblée *f.*, réunion *f.*; (*session*) séance *f.*; (*duel*) duel *m.*; (*race*) courses *f.pl.*; **~ing-place** *s.* rendez-vous *m.*

meet[2] *adj.* (*archaic = fit, proper*) séant, convenable.

mega- (*in combination*) **~cycle** *s.* mégacycle *m.*; **~lith** *s.* mégalithe *m.*; **~phone** *s.* mégaphone *m.*; **~ton** *s.* mégatonne *f.*

megalomania *s.* mégalomanie *f.*; **~c** *s.* mégalomane *m.f.*

melamine *s.* mélamine *f.*

melanchol/y *s.* mélancolie *f.*; *adj.* mélancolique; **~ia** *s.* (*med.*) mélancolie *f.*; **~ic** *adj.* mélancolique.

Melanesia *s.* (*geog.*) Mélanésie *f.*; **~n** *adj.* & *s.m.f.* mélanésien(ne).

melliflu/ent *adj.* & **~ous** *adj.* mielleux.

mellow *adj.* **1.** (*soft & rich, flavour, sound*) moelleux; **2.** (*softened by age, etc.*) mûri; **3.** (*genial*) doux; **4.** (*drunk*) gris; *v.t.* & *i.* (1) rendre, devenir, moelleux; (2) (se) mûrir; (3) (s')adoucir; (4) griser; **~ness** *s.* (1) moelleux *m.*; (2) maturité *f.*; (3) douceur *f.*

melodrama *s.* mélodrame *m.*; **~tic** *adj.* mélodramatique.

melod/y *s.* mélodie *f.*; **~ic** *adj.* mélodique; **~ious** *adj.* mélodieux; **~iously** *adv.**; **~iousness** *s.* caractère mélodieux *m.*

melon *s.* melon *m.*; WATER-~.

melt *v.t.* fondre; (*fig.*) attendrir; **~ down,** faire fondre; *v.i.* fondre; (*dissolve*) se dissoudre; (*fig.*) s'adoucir; **~ away,** se dissiper; BUTTER **wouldn't ~ in his mouth; ~ing** *s.* fonte *f.*, fusion *f.*, (*fig.*) attendrissement *m.*; **~ing** *adj.* fondant, (*fig. causing to ~*) attendrissant, (*fig. effect*) attendri; **~ing-**POINT; **~ing-pot** *s.* (*fig.*) creuset *m.*

member *s.* membre *m.*; (*of society etc.*) adhérent *m.*; **M~ of Parliament** *s.* député *m.*; **~ship** *s.* qualité de membre *f.*

membrane *s.* membrane *f.*

memento *s.* souvenir *m.*

memo *s.* note *f.*

memoir *s.* (*record*) mémoire *m.*; (*autobiography*) mémoires *m.pl.*; (*essay*) étude *f.*

memor/y *s.* (*faculty, repute, computer*) mémoire *f.*; (*thing remembered*) souvenir *m.*; **in ~y of,** en mémoire de; **~able** *adj.* mémorable; **~ably** *adv.**; **~andum** *s.* mémorandum *m.*; **~ial** *s.* monument *m.* (commémoratif), *adj.* commémoratif; **~ialize** *v.t.* commémorer; **~ize** *v.t.* apprendre par cœur.

menac/e *s.* menace *f.*; *v.t.* menacer; **~ing** *adj.* menaçant.

menagerie *s.* ménagerie *f.*

mend *s.* raccommodage *m.*, (*in stockings, etc.*) reprise *f.*; **on the ~,** (*fig.*) en voie d'amélioration; *v.t.* raccommoder, réparer, repriser; (*put right*) réparer, arranger; *v.i.* s'améliorer; **~ing** *s.* raccommodage *m.*, (*stockings, etc.*) remaillage *m.*

mendaci/ous *adj.* mensonger; **~ty** *s.* mensonge *m.*

mendicant *adj.* & *s.m.f.* mendiant(e).

menhir *s.* menhir *m.*

menial *s.* domestique *m.f.*; *adj.* servile, de domestique.

meningitis *s.* méningite *f.*

menopause *s.* ménopause *f.*

menstru/al *adj.* menstruel; **~ate** *v.i.* avoir ses règles; **~ation** *s.* menstruation *f.*

mensur/able *adj.* mesurable; **~ation** *s.* mensuration *f.*

mental *adj.* mental; (*pop. = unbalanced*) toqué; **~ age,** âge mental *m.*; **~ defective** *s.* aliéné(e) *m.f.*; **~ home,** asile d'aliénés *m.*; **~ly** *adv.* mentalement; **~ity** *s.* mentalité *f.*

menthol *s.* menthol *m.*

mention *s.* mention *f.*; *v.t.* mentionner, citer; **not to ~,** sans parler dc; **don't ~ it,** je vous en prie, il n'y a pas de quoi.

mentor *s.* mentor *m.*

menu *s.* menu *m.*
Mephistophel/es *s.* Méphistophélès *m.*; **~ean** *adj.* méphistophélique.
mercantile *adj.* (*affairs*) commercial; (*nation*) commerçant; **~ marine,** marine marchande *f.*; ⚠ mercantile = **mercenary** (*pej.*).
mercenary *adj.* & *s.m.* mercenaire.
mercer *s.* marchand de tissus et de soieries *m.*; **~ized** *adj.* mercerisé.
merchandise *s.* marchandises *f.pl.*
merchant *s.* négociant *m.*; *adj.* marchand; **~-man** *s.* (*naut.*) navire marchand *m.*; **speed-~** (*pop.*) chauffard *m.*
mercur/y *s.* (*god, planet, liquid metal*) mercure *m.*; **~ial** *adj.* (*lit.*) mercuriel; (*fig.*) vif, changeant, inconstant.
merc/y *s.* **1.** (*abstention from punishment*) grâce *f.*, clémence *f.*; **2.** (*disposition to forgive*) miséricorde *f.*; **3.** (*act of ~*) bienfait *m.*; **to be at the ~y of s.o. or sth.,** être à la merci de qn. *or* de qch.; **to have ~y on,** avoir pitié de; **~iful** *adj.* (1) miséricordieux; (2) compatissant; **~ifully** *adv.* (1)*; (2) avec compassion; **~ifulness** *s.* (1) miséricorde *f.*; (2) compassion *f.*; **~iless** *adj.* impitoyable; **~ilessly** *adv.**.
mere[1] *s.* (*poet. lake*) lac *m.*
mere[2] *adj.* seul, simple; **~ly** *adv.* purement et simplement, ne . . . que, **I came ~ly to say,** je ne suis venu que pour dire.
meretricious *adj.* (*of style*) boursouflé, clinquant; **~ness** *s.*; boursouflure *f.*, clinquant *m.*
merge *v.i.* se fondre (dans), s'incorporer (à); (*comm.*) fusionner; *v.t.* incorporer (*in*—à); **~r** *s.* (*comm.*) fusion *f.*
meridian *s.* méridien *m.*; (*fig.*) apogée *m.*; *adj.* méridien.
meridional *adj.* méridional.
meringue *s.* meringue *f.*
merino *s.* (*sheep, yarn*) mérinos *m.*
merit *s.* mérite *m.*; **~s** *s.pl.* (*of person*) juste valeur *f.*, (*of case*) bien-fondé *m.*; *v.t.* mériter; **~ocracy** *s.* mandarinat *m.*; **~orious** *adj.* (*act*) méritoire, (*person*) méritant; **~oriously** *adv.* de façon méritoire.
merlin *s.* émerillon *m.*
mer/maid *s.* sirène *f.*; **~man** *s.* triton *m.*
merr/y *adj.* gai; (*slightly drunk*) gris; **to make ~y,** se réjouir; **~y-go-round** *s.* manège *m.* (de chevaux de bois); **~y-making** *s.* réjouissance *f.*; **~ily** *adv.**; **~iment** *s.* gaieté *f.*
mescalin(e) *s.* mescaline *f.*
mesh *s.* maille *f.*; (*net, network*) filet *m.*; *v.t.* prendre au filet; (*mech.*) engrener.
mesmer/ism *s.* hypnotisme *m.*; **~ize** *v.t.* hypnotiser.
mess *s.* **1.** (*spilt liquid, etc.*) saleté *f.*; **2.** (*untidiness*) fouillis *m.*, (*fig.*) gâchis *m.*; **to make a ~ of sth.,** gâcher qch.; **3.** (*fam. trouble*) pétrin *m.*; **to be in a ~** (*fig.*) être dans le pétrin; **4.** (*mil.*) mess *m.*, (*naut.*) table *f.*; **5.** (*dish of food*) plat *m.*, (*for animals*) pâtée *f.*; **~mate** *s.* camarade *m.*; **~ tin** *s.* gamelle *f.*; **~y** *adj.* (1) sale; (2) désordonné; *v.i.* (4) faire popote ensemble; **~ about** *v.t.* (*fam.*) tripoter, *v.i.* lambiner; **~ up** *v.t.* gâcher.
message *s.* message *m.*; (*errand*) commission *f.*; **to get the ~** (*pop.*) piger.
messenger *s.* messager *m.*, coursier *m.*
Messia/h *s.* Messie *m.*; **~nic** *adj.* messianique.
Messrs. (*abbrev.*) MM.
met *adj.* (*abbrev. for meteorological*) météo (*invar.*).
metabol/ism *s.* métabolisme *m.*; **~ic** *adj.* métabolique.
metacarpus *s.* métacarpe *m.*
metal *s.* métal *m.*; (*for road*) empierrement **m.**; (*for rail.*) ballast *m.*; SCRAP **~**; **~s** *s.pl.* (*rails*) rails *m.pl.*; *v.t.* (*road*) empierrer; **~lic** *adj.* métallique; **~lurgy** *s.* métallurgie *f.*; **~lurgist** *s.* métallurgiste *m.f.*
metamorph/ic *adj.* métamorphique; **~ism** *s.* métamorphisme *m.*; **~ose** *v.t.* & *i.* (se) métamorphoser; **~osis** *s.* métamorphose *f.*
metaphor *s.* métaphore *f.*; **~ical** *adj.* métaphorique; **~ically** *adv.**.
metaphysic/al *adj.* métaphysique; **~s** *s.* métaphysique *f.* ⚠ *sing. in French*; **~ian** *s.* métaphysicien *m.*
metatarsus *s.* métatarse *m.*
mete, ~ out *v.t.* distribuer.
metempsychosis *s.* métempsycose *f.*
meteor *s.* météore *m.*; **~ic** *adj.* météorique, (*fig.*) fulgurant; **~ite** *s.* météorite *m.*; **~ology** *s.* météorologie *f.*; **~ological** *adj.* météorologique, (*fam.*) météo; **~ologist** *s.* météorologue *m.f.*
meter *s.* compteur *m.*; *v.t.* mesurer au compteur.
methane *s.* méthane *m.*
methinks, il me semble.
method *s.* méthode *f.*; (*arrangements, for payment, etc.*) modalités *f.pl.*; **~ical** *adj.* méthodique; **~ically** *adv.**.
Method/ist *adj.* & *s.m.f.* méthodiste; **~ism** *s.* méthodisme *m.*
methylated *adj.* **~ spirit,** alcool à brûler *m.*
meticulous *adj.* méticuleux; **~ly** *adv.**.
metonymy *s.* métonymie *f.*
metr/e *s.* (*verse* & *measure*) mètre *m.*; **~ic** *adj.* métrique; **~ical** *adj.* métrique; **~icate** *v.t.* adapter au système métrique; **~onome** *s.* métronome *m.*
metropol/is *s.* (*capital city*) capitale *f.*; (*principal trade centre*) métropole *f.*; **~itan** *s.* (*bishop*) métropolitain *m.*; *adj.* métropolitain.
mettle *s.* tempérament *m.*; (*spirit, esp. of horse*) fougue *f.*; **to be on one's ~,** se piquer au jeu; **~some** *adj.* fougueux.
mew[1] *s.* (*bird*) mouette *f.*
mew[2] *s.* (*of cat*) miaulement *m.*; *v.i.* miauler.
mews *s.pl.* écuries *f.pl.* (en ville).
Mexic/o *s.* (*geog.*) (*country*) Mexique *m.*; (*city*) Mexico *f.*; **~an** *adj.* & *s.m.f.* mexicain(e).
mezzanine *s.* entre-sol *m.*
mezzotint *s.* mezzo-tinto *m.*
miaow *s.* miaou *m.*; *v.i.* miauler.
miasma *s.* miasme *m.* (*usu. pl.*).
mica *s.* mica *m.*
Michaelmas *s.* la St. Michel *f.*; **~ daisy** *s.* aster *m.*
mickey (*pop.*) **to take the ~ out of s.o.,** faire marcher qn.
micro- (*in combination*) **~biology** *s.* microbiologie *f.*; **~cosm** *s.* microcosme *m.*; **~dot** *s.* micropoint *m.*; **~film** *s.* microfilm *m.*; **~phone** *s.* microphone *m.*; **~scope** *s.* microscope *m.*; **~scopic** *adj.* microscopique; **~wave** *s.* hyperfréquence *f.*
microbe *s.* microbe *m.*
mid *adj.* au milieu de; *in combination,* **~-August,** mi-août *f.*; **~-Lent,** mi-Carême *f.*; **~day** *s.* midi *m.*; **~land** *s.* intérieur du pays *m.*; **~night** *s.* minuit *m.*; **~summer** *s.* milieu de l'été *m.*, **M~summer('s) Day,** la St. Jean, **M~summer Night's Dream,** Songe d'une nuit d'été *m.*; **~way** *s.* mi-chemin *m.*, *adv.* à mi-chemin; **~winter** *s.* cœur de l'hiver *m.*
midden *s.* fumier *m.*
middle *s.* milieu *m.*; (*of body*) taille *f.*; *adj.* du milieu, moyen; **M~ Ages** *s.* Moyen-âge *m.*; **~-aged** *adj.* entre deux âges; **~ class** *s.* bourgeoisie *f.*, *adj.* bourgeois; **M~ East** *s.* Moyen-Orient *m.*; **~** FINGER; **~ man** *s.* intermédiaire *m.*; **~-of-the-road** *adj.* (*fig.*) modéré; **~-sized** *adj.* de taille moyenne; **middling** *adj.* passable, *adv.**.
midge *s.* moucheron *m.*
midget *adj.* & *s.m.f.* nain(e).
midriff *s.* diaphragme *m.*

midship *s.* milieu du navire *m.*; **~man** *s.* aspirant *m.*
midst *s.* milieu *m.*; **in the ~ of,** au milieu de.
midwif/e *s.* sage-femme *f.*; **~ery** *s.* obstétrique *f.*
mien *s.* mine *f.*
might[1] *s.* **1.** (*strength*) force *f.*; **2.** (*power*) puissance *f.*; **with all one's ~,** de toutes ses forces; **with ~ and main,** de vive force; **~y** *adj.* (1) fort; (2) puissant; **~ily** *adv.* (1) avec force; (2) puissamment; (*fam.*) formidablement.
might[2] *for past tenses of verb see* MAY.
mignonette *s.* réséda *m.*
migraine *s.* migraine *f.*
migr/ate *v.i.* **1.** (*people*) & **2.** (*birds*) émigrer; **~ant** *adj.* & *s.* (1) émigrant; (2) migrateur; **~ation** *s.* (1) émigration *f.*; (2) migration *f.*; **~atory** *adj.* (1) émigrant; (2) migrateur.
mike *s.* (*pop.* = *microphone*) micro *m.*
milch *adj.* **~ cow,** vache laitière *f.*
mild *adj.* **1.** (*gentle, ≠ severe, ≠ harsh, ≠ bitter*) doux; **2.** (*med.*) bénin, bénigne; **~ly** *adv.* doucement; **~ness** *s.* (1) douceur, *f.*; (2) bénignité *f.*
mildew *s.* **1.** (*agric.*) rouille *f.*; **2.** (*on leather, paper, etc.*) moisissure *f.*; *v.t.* (1) nieller; *v.i.* (2) se piquer.
mile *s.* mille *m.*; **to** STAND **out a ~;** (*distance*) parcours *m.*; (*measured*) kilométrage *m.*; **~stone** *s.* borne *f.*; **~age** *s.* kilométrage *m.*
milfoil *s.* millefeuille *m.*
militan/t *adj.* & *s.m.* militant; **~cy** *s.* caractère militant *m.*
milit/ary *s.* troupes *f.pl.*; *adj.* militaire; **~arism** *s.* militarisme *m.*; **~arize** *v.t.* militariser; **~ate** *v.t.* militer (*against*—contre; *for*—pour, en faveur de); **~ia** *s.* milice *f.*; **~iaman** *s.* milicien *m.*
milk *s.* lait *m.*; **no use crying over** SPILT **~;** **~ bar** *s.* milk-bar *m.*; **~-can** *s.* boîte à lait *f.*; **~-**FLOAT; **~maid** *s.* laitière *f.*; **~man** *s.* laitier *m.*; **~ shake** *s.* milkshake *m.*; **~sop** *s.* poule mouillée *f.*; **~-tooth** *s.* dent de lait *f.*; **~y** *adj.* (*of ~*) lacté; (*colour*) laiteux; **M~y Way** *s.* voie lactée *f.*; **~iness** *s.* aspect laiteux *m.*; *v.t.* traire; (*fig.*) soutirer (qch. à qn.).
mill *s.* (*building or apparatus for grinding*) moulin *m.*; (*factory*) fabrique *f.*; ROLLING-**~;** SAW-**~;** **all is** GRIST **to his ~;** RUN **of the ~;** **~board** *s.* carton-pâte *m.*; **~-dam** *s.* écluse *f.*; **~-hand** *s.* ouvrier *m.*; **~-owner** *s.* fabricant *m.*; **~-pond** *s.* réservoir *m.*; **~-race** *s.* bief *m.*; **~stone** *s.* meule *f.*, (*fig.*) boulet *m.*; **~-wheel** *s.* roue de moulin *f.*; *v.t.* (*grind*) moudre; (*coin*) créneler; *v.i.* **~ around,** tournoyer; **~er** *s.* meunier *m.*
millennium *s.* millénium *m.*
millepede, millipede *s.* mille-pattes *m.*
millet *s.* millet *m.*
milli- (*in combination*) **~bar** *s.* millibar *m.*; **~gram** *s.* milligramme *m.*; **~metre** *s.* millimètre *m.*
milliard *s.* milliard *m.*
milliner *s.* modiste *f.*; **~y** *s.* (magasin de) modes *m.*
million *s.* million *m.*; *adj.* **ten ~ dollars,** dix millions de dollars; **~aire** *s.* millionnaire *m.f.*; **~th** *adj.* & *s.m.* millionième.
mime *s.* (*play, actor*) mime *m.*; *v.t.* mimer.
mimic *s.* mime *m.*, imitat/eur, -rice *m.f.*; *adj.* imitateur; (*mock*) simulé; *v.t.* imiter; **~ry** *s.* mimique *f.*
mimosa *s.* mimosa *m.*
minaret *s.* minaret *m.*
minatory *adj.* menaçant.
mince *s.* (*cook.*) hachis *m.*, viande hachée *f.*; **~meat** *s.* mélange de fruits *m.* (pour fourrer); **to make ~meat of** (*fig.*) réduire en marmelade; **~ pie** *s.* tourte aux fruits *f.*; *v.t.* hacher; *v.i.* (*walk*) minauder; **not to ~ matters,** ne pas y aller par quatre chemins; **~r** *s.* hachoir *m.*; **mincing** *adj.* minaudier.
mind[1] *s.* (*consciousness*) esprit *m.*; (*intellect*) intelligence *f.*; (*memory*) souvenir *m.*; (*opinion*) avis *m.*; (*intention*) envie *f.*; **presence of ~,** présence d'esprit *f.*; **to** BEAR **in ~;** **to** CALL **to ~;** **to** CHANGE **one's ~;** **to give one's ~ to,** faire attention à; **to have a good ~ to,** avoir envie de; **to make up one's ~,** se décider (*to*—à); **to put in ~ of,** rappeler; **to speak one's ~,** dire ce qu'on pense; **to take s.o.'s ~ off sth.,** changer les idées à qn.; MASTER-**~;** **~ed** *adj.* (*disposed to*) disposé à; ABSENT-**~ed;** NARROW-**-~ed;** **~ful** *adj.* (*heeding*) attentif (*of*—à); (*caring*) soucieux (*of*—de); (*aware*) conscient (*of*—de).
mind[2] *v.t.* & *i.* (*remember*) se rappeler; (*heed, attend*) faire attention (à); écouter; (*look out*) prendre garde (à); (*have charge of*) garder, surveiller; (*object to*) se plaindre de, trouver à redire à; (*care, trouble*) se soucier (*about*—de); (*be troubled by*) s'inquiéter de; **do you ~ if,** est-ce que cela vous dérange si; **never ~,** n'importe; **I don't ~,** cela m'est égal.
mine[1] *pron.* à moi; le mien, la mienne, les miens, les miennes; **a friend of ~,** un de mes amis.
mine[2] *s.* (*for minerals; explosive device*) mine *f.*; **~field** *s.* champ de mines *m.*; **~layer** *s.* mouilleur de mines *m.*; **~sweeper** *s.* dragueur de mines *m.*; *v.t.* (*dig.*) creuser; (*quarry*) extraire; (*lay ~s*) miner; **~r** *s.* mineur *m.*
mineral *adj.* & *s.m.* minéral; **~ water,** eau minérale *f.*; **~ogist** *s.* minéralogiste *m.f.*; **~ogy** *s.* minéralogie *f.*
mingl/e *v.t.* & *i.* (se) mêler (*with*—à); **~ing** *s.* mélange *m.*
mingy *adj.* (*pop.*) pingre.
mini *s.* (*car*) mini *f.*; (*skirt*) minijupe *f.*; *in combination*: **~bus** *s.* microbus *m.*; **~car** *s.* mini *f.*; **~skirt** *s.* minijupe *f.*
miniature *s.* miniature *f.*; *adj.* en miniature.
minim *s.* (*mus.*) blanche *f.*
minim/um *adj.* & *s.m.* minimum; **~um wage,** salaire minimum inter-professionnel de croissance *m.* (SMIC); **~al** *adj.* minimum, (*temperature*) minimal; **~ize** *v.t.* réduire au minimum, (*fig.*) minimiser.
minion *s.* favori *m.*
minist/er *s.* (*agent, admin., polit.*) ministre *m.*; (*clergyman*) ministre du culte *m.*; *v.i.* (*to*) subvenir aux besoins de; rendre service à; **~erial** *adj.* (*law*) ministériel; (*polit.*) gouvernemental; (*eccles.*) de ministre du culte; **~ration** *s.* service *m.*; (*med.*) administration *f.*; **~ry** *s.* ministère *m.*
mink *s.* (*animal, fur*) vison *m.*
minnow *s.* vairon *m.*
minor *s.* (*law; mus.*) mineur *m.*; *adj.* (*lesser of two*) inférieur; (*of lesser importance*) secondaire; (*mus.*) mineur; **~ity** *s.* minorité *f.*; *adj.* (*government*) minoritaire.
Minorca *s.* (*geog.*) Minorque *f.*
minster *s.* cathédrale *f.*
minstrel *s.* ménestrel *m.*; **~s' gallery** (*arch.*) tribune *f.*; **~sy** *s.* art des ménestrels *m.*
mint[1] *s.* hôtel de la monnaie *m.*; *adj.* **in ~ condition,** à l'état neuf; *v.t.* frapper, (*invent*) forger.
mint[2] *s.* (*herb*) menthe *f.*
minuet *s.* menuet *m.*
minus *s.* moins *m.*; *prep.* moins; *adj.* & *adv.* en moins.
minuscule *adj.* minuscule.
minute[1] *s.* minute *f.*; (*memo*) note *f.*; **~s** *s.pl.* procès-verbal *m.*; **up to the ~,** à la page; **just (wait) a ~!,** minute!; **~-hand** *s.* aiguille des minutes *f*;. *v.t.* prendre note de, dresser le procès-verbal de.
minute[2] *adj.* **1.** (*very small*) menu; **2.** (*precise*)

minutieux; **~ly** *adv.* (2) minutieusement; **~ness** *s.* (1) exiguïté *f.*; (2) minutie *f.*
minutiae *s.pl.* infimes détails *m.pl.*
minx *s.* coquine *f.*
mirac/le *s.* (*lit.* & *fig.*) miracle *m.*; **~le play,** miracle *m.*; **~ulous** *adj.* miraculeux; **~ulously** *adv.**.
mirage *s.* mirage *m.*
mir/e *s.* bourbe *f.*; **~y** *adj.* bourbeux.
mirror *s.* (*lit.* & *fig.*) miroir *m.*; *v.t.* refléter.
mirth *s.* gaieté *f.*; **~ful** *adj.* gai; **~less** *adj.* morne.
MIRV *s.* (*multiple independently targeted re-entry vehicle*) MIRV *m.*; fusée intercontinentale à ogives multiples *f.*
misadventure *s.* mésaventure *f.*; **by ~,** par accident.
misalliance *s.* mésalliance *f.*
misanthrop/e *s.* & **~ist** *s.* misanthrope *m.*; **~ic(al)** *adj.* misanthropique; **~y** *s.* misanthropie *f.*
misappl/y *v.t.* mal appliquer; **~ication** *s.* mauvaise application *f.*; (*misuse*) emploi erroné *m.*
misapprehen/d *v.t.* mal comprendre; **~sion** *s.* fausse idée *f.*
misappropriat/e *v.t.* détourner; **~ion** *s.* détournement *m.*
misbegotten *adj.* (*law*) illégitime; (*ill-formed*) rabougri.
misbehav/e *v.i.* se conduire mal; **~iour** *s.* mauvaise conduite *f.*
miscalculat/e *v.t.* mal calculer; **~ion** *s.* erreur de calcul *f.*, (*fig.*) mécompte *m.*
miscalled *adj.* appelé à tort.
miscarr/y *v.i.* **1.** (*letter*) s'égarer; **2.** (*med.*) faire une fausse couche; **3.** (*fig.*) avorter, échouer; **~iage** *s.* (1) perte *f.*; (2) fausse couche *f.*; (3) avortement *m.*, échec *m.*; **~iage of justice,** erreur judiciaire *f.*, mal-jugé *m.*
miscegenation *s.* métissage *m.*
miscellan/eous *adj.* divers; **~y** *s.* mélange *m.*
mischance *s.* mésaventure *f.*, malheur *m.*
mischief *s.* (*harm, injury*) mal *m.*, tort *m.*; (*discord*) discorde *f.*; **to make ~,** semer la discorde; (*childish scrape*) bêtises *f.pl.*; (*malice*) méchanceté *f.*; **~-maker** *s.* semeur de zizanie *m.*
mischievous *adj.* **1.** (*person*) méchant; **2.** (*thing*) nuisible; **3.** (*child*) espiègle; **~ly** *adv.* (1) méchamment; (2)*; **~ness** *s.* (1) méchanceté *f.*; (2) nature nuisible *f.*; (3) espièglerie *f.*
misconceive *v.t.* mal comprendre, avoir une fausse idée de.
misconception *s.* fausse idée *f.*, malentendu *m.*
misconduct *s.* mauvaise conduite *f.*; *v.t.* mal administrer; *v.refl.* se conduire mal.
misconstru/e *v.t.* mal interpréter; **~ction** *s.* fausse interprétation *f.*
miscount *s.* erreur de calcul *f.*; *v.t.* mal compter.
miscreant *s.* vaurien *m.*
misdated *adj.* mal daté.
misdeal *s.* maldonne *f.*; *v.t.* faire (une) maldonne.
misdeed *s.* méfait *m.*
misdemeanour *s.* méfait *m.*; (*law*) délit *m.*
misdirect *v.t.* **1.** (*letter, etc.*) mal adresser; **2.** (*person*) mal renseigner; **~ion** *s.* (1) erreur d'adresse *f.*; (2) mauvais renseignement *m.*
misdoing *s.* méfait *m.*
miser *s.* avare *m.*; **~ly** *adj.* avare; **~liness** *s.* avarice *f.*
miserabl/e *adj.* **1.** (*unhappy*) malheureux; **2.** (*poor*) misérable; **3.** (*uncomfortable*) misérable; **4.** (*pitiable*) lamentable; **5.** (*mean*) mesquin; **~y** *adv.* (1)*, (2)*, (3)*, (4)*, (5) chichement.
misery *s.* (*unhappiness*) malheur *m.*; (*poverty*) misère *f.*
misfeasance *s.* abus de pouvoir *m.*
misfire *v.t.* & *i.* (*auto.*) avoir des ratés; (*gun*) faire long feu; (*pop.*) foirer.
misfit *s.* (*garment*) vêtement qui ne va pas bien *m.*; (*person*) inadapté *m.*
misfortune *s.* (*calamity*) infortune *f.*; (*bad luck*) malheur *m.*
misgiv/e *v.t.* provoquer de l'appréhension chez; **~ing** *s.* appréhension *f.*; (*foreboding*) pressentiment *m.*
misgovern *v.t.* mal gouverner; **~ment** *s.* mauvais gouvernement *m.*
misguided *adj.* (*act*) malencontreux; (*person*) fourvoyé.
mishandle *v.t.* malmener.
mishap *s.* mésaventure *f.*; (*slight*) contretemps *m.*
misinform *v.t.* mal renseigner; **~ation** *s.* faux renseignement *m.*
misinterpret *v.t.* mal interpréter; **~ation** *s.* erreur d'interprétation *f.*
misjudge *v.t.* mal juger; (*be mistaken*) se tromper.
mislay *v.t.* égarer.
mislead *v.t.* (*deceive*) tromper; (*misguide*) fourvoyer; (*corrupt*) dévoyer; **~ing** *adj.* trompeur.
mismanage *v.t.* mal administrer; **~ment** *s.* mauvaise administration *f.*
misname *v.t.* mal nommer.
misnomer *s.* erreur de nom *f.*
misogyn/ist *s.* misogyne *m.*; **~y** *s.* misogynie *f.*
misplace *v.t.* (*lose*) égarer; (*place wrongly*) mal placer; **~d** *adj.* égaré; déplacé.
misprint *s.* faute d'impression *f.*; *v.t.* imprimer incorrectement.
mispro/nounce *v.t.* mal prononcer; **~nunciation** *s.* mauvaise prononciation *f.*
misquot/e *v.t.* citer inexactement.
misread *v.t.* mal lire.
misrepresent *v.t.* mal représenter; (*facts*) dénaturer; **~ation** *s.* distortion *f.* (des faits).
misrule *s.* mauvaise administration *f.*; *v.t.* mal administrer.
miss[1] *s.* (*failure*) échec *m.*; **to give sth. a ~,** laisser passer qch.; *v.t.* (*fail to hit, reach, meet, catch, find*) manquer, (*fam.*) rater; (*pass over*) ne pas voir, ne pas entendre, ne pas trouver; laisser passer; (*regret absence of*) regretter, éprouver le manque de; ♤ **I ~ you,** vous me manquez; **he ~es his father,** son père lui manque; **~ out** *v.t.* omettre; HIT **or ~**; **~ing** *adj.* (*thing*) manquant, (*lost*) égaré, (*person*) disparu; **to be ~ing** *v.i.* manquer.
miss[2] *s.* (*title*) mademoiselle *f.* (*pl.*) mesdemoiselles *f.pl.*
missal *s.* missel *m.*
misshapen *adj.* (*thing*) déformé; (*person*) difforme.
missile *s.* projectile *m.*; (*space*) fusée *f.*
mission *s.* (*errand, vocation, group of people, post*) mission *f.*; **~ary** *s.* missionnaire *m.f.*
missis, missus *s.* (*pop.*) (*by inferiors*) patronne *f.*; (*by husband*) moitié *f.*
missive *s.* missive *f.*
misspell *v.t.* mal orthographier; **~ing** *s.* faute d'orthographe *f.*
misspent *adj.* perdu.
misstate *v.t.* exposer d'une manière inexacte; **~ment** *s.* rapport inexact *m.*
mist *s.* (*lit.* & *fig.*) brume *f.*; **~ily** *adv.* vaguement; **~iness** *s.* brume *f.*; **~y** *adj.* brumeux; (*fig.*) vague; *v.t.* & *i.* (s')embrumer.
mistake *s.* erreur *f.*, faute *f.*; (*mistaken opinion*) méprise *f.*; **there's no ~,** il n'y a pas à dire; **to make a ~,** se tromper; **to make the ~ of doing sth.,** avoir le tort de faire qch.; **by ~,** par erreur; *v.t.* (*misinterpret*) mal comprendre; (*take for s.o. or sth. else*) se tromper sur qn., à propos de qch.; **~ s.o. for,** prendre qn. pour;

~n *adj.* erroné, faux; (*person*) dans l'erreur; **~nly** *adv.* par erreur.
mister *s.* monsieur *m.*
mistime *v.t.* faire mal à propos, mal calculer le moment de; **~d** *adj.* inopportun.
mistletoe *s.* gui *m.*
mistral *s.* mistral *m.*
mistranslat/e *v.t.* mal traduire; **~ion** *s.* traduction inexacte *f.*
mistress *s.* (*woman in charge*; *lover*) maîtresse *f.*; (*teacher*) institutrice *f.*, professeur *m.*
mistrust *s.* méfiance *f.*; *v.t.* se méfier de; **~ful** *adj.* méfiant.
misunderstand *v.t.* mal comprendre; **~ing** *s.* malentendu *m.*
misuse *s.* abus *m.*; *v.t.* faire mauvais usage de; (*ill-treat*) maltraiter.
mite *s.* (*insect*) mite *f.*; (*eccles.*) denier *m.*; (*fam.*) gosse *m.*
mitigat/e *v.t.* **1.** (*appease*) apaiser; **2.** (*reduce severity of*) adoucir; **3.** (*moderate*) atténuer; **~ion** *s.* (1) apaisement *m.*; (2) adoucissement *m.*; (3) atténuation *f.*
mitre *s.* **1.** (*of bishop*) mitre *f.*; **2.** (*joint*) onglet *m.*; *v.t.* (2) assembler à l'onglet.
mitten *s.* mitaine *f.*
mix *s.* mélange *m.*; *v.t.* & *i.* (se) mêler, mélanger (*with*—à); **~ up** *v.t.* (*fig.*) embrouiller; **be ~ed up in,** être mêlé à; **~ with** (*people*) fréquenter; **~ed** *adj.* mêlé, (*school, marriage, etc.*) mixte; **~ed-up** *adj.* (*fig.*) perplexe; **~er** *s.* (*cook.*) mixeur *m.*; **to be a good ~er,** être liant; **to be a bad ~er,** ne pas être sociable; **~ture** *s.* mélange *m.*, (*med.*) mixtion *f.*
miz(z)en *s.* artimon *m.*; ⚠ misaine = **foremast.**
mnemonic *adj.* & *s.f.* mnémonique.
moan *s.* **1.** (*sound*) gémissement *m.*; **2.** (*complaint*) plainte *f.*; *v.i.* (1) gémir; (2) se plaindre.
moat *s.* fossé *m.*
mob *s.* (*populace, rabble*) populace *f.*; (*crowd*) cohue *f.*; (*gang*) bande *f.*; *v.t.* (*attack*) molester; (*crowd round*) entourer; **~ster** *s.* (*pop.*) gangster *m.*
mob-cap *s.* charlotte *f.*
mobil/e *adj.* mobile; **~ity** *s.* mobilité *f.*; **~ize** *v.t.* mobiliser; **~ization** *s.* mobilisation *f.*
moccasin *s.* mocassin *m.*
mocha *s.* moka *m.*
mock[1] *s.* (*object of ~ery*) risée *f.*; *v.t.* (*ridicule*) tourner en dérision; (*imitate*) singer; *v.i.* se moquer (de); **~er** *s.* moqueu/r, -se *m.f.*; **~ery** *s.* moquerie *f.*, parodie *f.*; **~ing** *adj.* moqueur; **~ing-bird** *s.* oiseau-moqueur *m.*; **~-up** *s.* maquette *f.*
mock[2] *adj.* (*sham, counterfeit*) faux; **~ examination** *s.* examen blanc *m.*, (*fam.*) galop d'essai *m.*; **~-heroic** *adj.* & *s.m.* héroï-comique; **~ turtle soup** *s.* potage à la tête de veau *m.*
mod/e *s.* (*manner*) manière *f.*; (*fashion*) mode *f.*; (*mus.*) mode *m.*; **~al** *adj.* modal; **~ality** *s.* modalité *f.*; **~ish** *adj.* à la mode.
model *s.* (*representation of object*) modèle *m.*, maquette *f.*; (*pattern*) patron *m.*; (*design*) marque *f.*; (*object to be imitated*) modèle *m.*; (*person*) modèle *m.*, mannequin *m.*; *adj.* modèle, en miniature; *v.t.* modeler (sur); *v.refl.* se mouler sur; *v.i.* être mannequin; **~ler** *s.* (*techn.*) modeleur *m.*, (*fashion designer, maker of ~ trains, etc.*) modéliste *m.*; **~ling** *s.* (*techn.*) modelage *m.*, (*fashion*) profession de mannequin *f.*
moderat/e *s.* modéré *m.*; *adj.* (*temperate*) modéré; (*not excessive*) modeste; (*price*) modique; (*of middle quality*) moyen, médiocre; **~ely** *adv.* modérément; **~eness** *s.* & **~ion** *s.* modération *f.*, (*price*) modicité *f.*; **~or** *s.* modérateur *m.*, médiateur *m.*; *v.t.* & *i.* (se) modérer; (*mediate*) servir de médiateur.
modern *adj.* moderne; **~ languages,** langues vivantes *f.pl.*; **~ity** *s.* modernité *f.*; **~ize** *v.t.* moderniser.
modest *adj.* modeste; **~ly** *adv.**; **~y** *s.* modestie *f.*
modicum *s.* un peu *m.*
modif/y *v.t.* **1.** (*tone down*) atténuer; **2.** (*make less severe*) & **3.** (*make changes in*) modifier; **~ication** *s.* (1) atténuation *f.*; (2), (3) modification *f.*
modulat/e *v.t.* moduler; **~ion** *s.* modulation *f.*
module *s.* (*space*) engin spatial *m.*
Mogul *s.* mogol *m.*
M.O.H. (*Medical Officer of Health*) médecin de la santé publique *m.*
mohair *s.* mohair *m.*
Mohammedan *adj.* & *s.m.f.* musulman(e); **~ism** *s.* islamisme *m.*
moiety *s.* moitié *f.*
moiré *s.* moire *f.*
moist *adj.* (*damp*) moite; (*rainy*) humide; **~en** *v.t.* humecter; **~ness** *s*, moiteur *f.*; **~ure** *s.* humidité *f.*; **~urize** *v.t.* hydrater; **~urizer** *s.* (*cosmetic*) crème hydratante *f.*
molar *adj.* & *s.f.* molaire.
molasses *s.pl.* mélasse *f.* ⚠ *sing. in French.*
mole *s.* **1.** (*on skin*) grain de beauté *m.*; **2.** (*animal*) taupe *f.*; **3.** (*breakwater*) môle *m.*; **~hill** *s.* (2) taupinière *f.*; **to make a mountain out of a ~hill,** faire d'une mouche un éléphant; **~skin** *s.* (2) taupe *f.*
molecul/e *s.* molécule *f.*; **~ar** *adj.* moléculaire.
molest *v.t.* molester; **~ation** *s.* molestation *f.*
mollif/y *v.t.* adoucir; **~ication** *s.* adoucissement *m.*
mollusc *s.* mollusque *m.*
molly-coddle *v.t.* dorloter.
molten *adj.* en fusion, fondu.
moment *s.* **1.** (*time*) moment *m.*; **the very ~,** le moment même; **2.** (*importance*) importance *f.*; **of no ~,** sans importance; **~ary** *adj.* momentané; **~arily** *adv.**; **~ous** *adj.* important; **~um** *s.* force d'impulsion *f.*, (*fam.*) élan *m.*
Monaco *s.* (*geog.*) Monaco *f.*; **of ~** *adj.*, **inhabitant of ~** *s. m.f.* monégasque.
monarch *s.* monarque *m.*; **~ical** *adj.* monarchique; **~ism** *s.* monarchisme *m.*; **~ist** *s.* monarchiste *m.f.*; **~y** *s.* monarchie *f.*
monast/ery *s.* monastère *m.*; **~ic** *adj.* monastique; **~icism** *s.* monachisme *m.*
Monday *s.* lundi *m.*
monetary *adj.* monétaire.
money *s.* (*gen., fin.*) argent *m.*; (*coin*) pièce *f.* (de monnaie); (*note*) billet *m.*; (*wealth*) richesses *f.pl.*; **to have a good run for one's ~,** s'en payer pour son argent; **to get one's ~'s** WORTH; **~-box** *s.* tirelire *f.*; **~-changer** *s.* changeur *m.*; **~-**GRUBBER; **~-lender** *s.* bailleur de fonds *m.*; **~-market** *s.* bourse *f.*; **~ order** *s.* mandat *m.*; **~ed** *adj.* possédant, fortuné.
Mongol/ia *s.* (*geog.*) Mongolie *f.*; **~** *adj.* & *s.m.f.* mongol(e); (*med.*) mongolien(ne).
mongoose *s.* mangouste *f.*
mongrel *s.* métis *m.*; (*dog*) corniaud *m.*; *adj.* métis, bâtard.
monitor *s.* **1.** (*school*) chef de classe *m.*; **2.** (*radio, etc.*) contrôleur *m.*; **3.** (*lizard*) varan *m.*; *v.t.* (2) contrôler; **~ing** *s.* (2) contrôle *m.*
monk *s.* moine *m.*; **~ish** *adj.* (*pej.*) de moine.
monkey *s.* singe *m.*, guenon *f.*; (*person*) gamin *m.*; **~ business** *s.* sale tour *m.*; **~-nut** *s.* cacahuète *f.*; **~-puzzle (tree)** *s.* araucaria *m.*; **~-tricks** *s.* singeries *f.pl.*; *v.t.* **~ with,** tripoter.
mono- (*in combination*) **~chrome** *adj.* monochrome; **~gamy** *s.* monogamie *f.*; **~gamous** *adj.* monogame; **~gram** *s.* monogramme *m.*; **~graph** *s.* monographie *f.*; **~lith** *s.* monolithe *m.*; **~lithic** *adj.* monolithe; **~logue** *s.* monologue *m.*; **~mania** *s.* monomanie *f.*; **~-plane** *s.* monoplan *m.*; **~syllable** *s.* monosyllabe *m.*;

~**syllabic** *adj.* monosyllabique; ~**tone** *s.* ton monotone *m.*; ~**tonous** *adj.* monotone; ~**tony** *s.* monotonie *f.*
monocle *s.* monocle *m.*
monopol/y *s.* monopole *m.*; ~**ist** monopolisateur *m.*; ~**ize** *v.t.* monopoliser; ~**ization** *s.* monopolisation *f.*
monsoon *s.* mousson *f.*
monst/er *s.* monstre *m.*; ~**rosity** *s.* & ~**rousness** *s.* monstruosité *f.*; ~**rous** *adj.* monstrueux.
monstrance *s.* (*eccles.*) ostensoir *m.*
month *s.* mois *m.*; ~ **of** SUNDAYS; ~**ly** *adj.* mensuel; *adv.**; ~**ly** *s.* (*magazine*) revue mensuelle *f.*
monument *s.* monument *m.*; ~**al** *adj.* monumental.
moo *s.* meuglement *m.*; *v.i.* meugler.
mood *s.* (*ling.*) mode *m.*; (*state of mind*) humeur *f.*; ~**iness** *s.* mauvaise humeur *f.*; ~**y** *adj.* maussade.
moon *s.* lune *f.*; *adj.* lunaire; **the man in the** ~, l'homme de la lune; ~**beam** *s.* rayon de lune *m.*; ~**light** *s.* clair de lune *m.*; **by** ~**light,** au clair de la lune; ~**shine** *s.* clair de lune *m.*, (*fig.*) balivernes *f.pl.*; ~**struck** *adj.* lunatique; *v.i.* ~ **about,** musarder.
moor[1] *s.* (*heath*) lande *f.*
moor[2] *v.t.* & *i.* (*naut.*) (s')amarrer; ~**ing** *s.* amarrage *m.*
Moor[3] *s.* (*person*) Maure *m.*; ~**ish** *adj.* mauresque.
moose *s.* élan *m.*
moot *v.t.* débattre; *adj.* ~ **point,** point discutable *m.*
mop *s.* (*for cleaning*) balai *m.*; (*of hair*) tignasse *f.*; *v.t.* (*clean* (*as*) *with* ~) essuyer; ~ **up,** balayer.
mope *v.i.* avoir le cafard, broyer du noir.
moped *s.* vélomoteur *m.*
moquette *s.* moquette *f.*
moraine *s.* moraine *f.*
moral *s.* morale *f.*; ~**s** *s.pl.* mœurs *f.pl.*; *adj.* moral, de morale; ~**ist** *s.* moraliste *m.*; ~**ity** *s.* moralité *f.*, (*sc.*) morale *f.*; ~**ize** *v.i.* moraliser; ~**ly** *adv.* (*practically*) moralement, (*virtuously*) de façon morale, (*point of view*) du point de vue moral.
morale *s.* moral *m.*; ⚠ morale = **moral.**
morass *s.* marais *m.*; (*fig.*) abîme *m.*
moratorium *s.* moratoire *m.*
morbid *adj.* (≠ *natural*, ≠ *healthy*) malsain; (*med.*) morbide; ~**ness** *s.* morbidité *f.*
mordant *adj.* mordant.
more *adj.* plus de; *adv.* plus, davantage; ~ **than,** plus que, plus de; ~ **than I,** plus que moi; ~ **than ten,** plus de dix; **no** ~, pas plus; ~ **or less,** plus ou moins; ~ **and** ~, de plus en plus; **will you have some** ~?, en voulez-vous encore?; **will you have some** ~ **tea?,** voulez-vous encore du thé?; **I don't want any** ~, je n'en veux plus; ~**over** *adv.* de plus, qui plus est.
morganatic *adj.* morganatique.
morgue *s.* morgue *f.*
moribund *adj.* moribond.
morn(**ing**) *s.* matin *m.*; (*whole* ~) matinée *f.*; (*fig.*) aube *f.*; *adj.* du matin; **in the** ~**ing,** le matin; **good** ~**ing,** bonjour; ~**ing coat,** ~**ing dress,** jaquette *f.*
Morocc/o *s.* (*geog.*) Maroc *m.*; (*leather*) maroquin *m.*; ~**an** *adj.* & *s.m.f.* marocain(e).
moron *s.* (*med.*) arriéré *m.*; (*fam.*) crétin *m.*; ~**ic** *adj.* crétin.
morose *adj.* morose; ~**ness** *s.* morosité *f.*
morpheme *s.* morphème *m.*
morphia, morphine *s.* morphine *f.*
morphology *s.* morphologie *f.*
morrow *s.* lendemain *m.*
Morse *s.* (*code*) morse *m.*
morsel *s.* morceau *m.*
mortal *s.* mortel *m.*; *adj.* mortel; ~**ity** *s.* mortalité *f.*; ~**ly** *adv.**.
mortar *s.* (*vessel, gun, substance*) mortier *m.*; ~-**board** *s.* (*acad.*) toque *f.*, mortier *m.*
mortgage *s.* (*loan to buy house*) crédit personnalisé à long terme *m.*; (*loan raised on property*) hypothèque *f.*; *v.t.* hypothéquer.
mortif/y *v.t.* (*lit.* & *fig.*) mortifier; ~**ication** *s.* mortification *f.*; ~**ying** *adj.* mortifiant.
mortise *s.* mortaise *f.*; *v.t.* mortaiser; ~ **lock** *s.* serrure à mortaises *f.*
mortuary *s.* morgue *f.*; *adj.* mortuaire.
mosaic *s.* mosaïque *f.*; *adj.* en mosaïque; ⚠ mosaïque (*adj.*) = **of Moses.**
Mosc/ow *s.* (*geog.*) Moscou *m.*
Moses *s.* Moïse *m.*
mosque *s.* mosquée *f.*
mosquito *s.* moustique *m.*; ~-**net** *s.* moustiquaire *m.*
moss *s.* mousse *f.*; **a** ROLLING **stone gathers no** ~; ~-**rose** *s.* rose moussue *f.*; ~**y** *adj.* moussu.
most *adj.* le plus de; *s.* **to make the** ~ **of sth.,** tirer le meilleur parti de qch.; *adj.* & *s.* (*the majority* (*of*)) (*with pl.*) la plupart des, (*with sing.*) la plus grande partie de, la majorité de; ⚠ *except* ~ **of the time,** la plupart du temps; **for the** ~ **part** (*referring to pl.*) pour la plupart, (*referring to sing.*) dans sa majeure partie; *adv.* le plus, **what** ~ **annoys me,** ce qui m'ennuie le plus; (= *very*) très; (*forming superlative of adj.* & *adv.*) le plus; **at the** ~, tout au plus; ~**ly** *adv.* (*especially*) surtout, (*time*) la plupart du temps, (*for the* ~ *part*) en majeure partie.
mote *s.* grain de poussière *m.*; (*fig. in eye*) paille *f.*
motel *s.* motel *m.*
motet *s.* motet *m.*
moth *s.* (*ent.*) phalène *f.*; (*gen.*) papillon de nuit *m.*; (*clothes*) mite *f.*; ~-**ball** *s.* boule antimite *f.*; ~-**eaten** *adj.* mité.
mother *s.* (*parent, nun*) mère *f.*; ~ **country** *s.* patrie *f.*; ~-**in-law** *s.* belle-mère *f.*; ~-**of-pearl** *s.* nacre *f.*; ~ **tongue** *s.* langue maternelle *f.*; ~**hood** *s.* maternité *f.*; ~**less** *adj.* orphelin de mère; ~**ly** *adj.* maternel; *v.t.* servir de mère à, (*care for*) chérir.
motif *s.* motif *m.*
motion *s.* **1.** (*movement*) mouvement *m.*; **2.** (*gesture*) geste *m.*; **3.** (*proposition*) motion *f.*; **4.** (*med.*) selle *f.*; **to set in** ~, mettre en marche; ~**less** *adj.* immobile; *v.t.* & *i.* (2) faire signe (à).
motiv/e *s.* (*aim*) motif *m.*; (*of action*) mobile *m.*; *adj.* mot/eur, -rice; ~**ate** *v.t.* motiver; ~**ation** *s.* motivation *f.*
motley *s.* habit d'arlequin *m.*; *adj.* bigarré.
motor *s.* (*motive force, engine*) moteur *m.*; (*vehicle*) auto *f.*; *adj.* mot/eur, -rice; ~ **boat** *s.* canot automobile *m.*; ~ **cycle** *s.* motocyclette *f.*; ~-**cyclist** *s.* motocycliste *m.f.*, (*fam. esp. police*) motard *m.*; ~**cade** *s.* défilé de voitures *m.*; ~**rail** *s.* autorail *m.*; ~**way** *s.* autoroute *f.*; ~**ing** *s.* automobilisme *m.*; ~**ist** *s.* automobiliste *m.*; ~**ize** *v.t.* motoriser; *v.i.* aller en auto, faire de l'auto.
mottled *adj.* tacheté; (*text.*) chiné.
motto *s.* devise *f.*
moujik *s.* moujik *m.*
mould[1] *s.* (*earth, compost*) humus *m.*; ~**er** *v.i.* tomber en poussière.
mould[2] *s.* (*fungus*) moisissure *f.*; ~**iness** *s.* moisissure *f.*; ~**y** *adj.* moisi, (*fam.*) assommant.
mould[3] *s.* (*vessel*) moule *m.*; (*fig. character*) trempe *f.*; *v.t.* mouler; ~**er** *s.* mouleur *m.*; ~**ing** *s.* moulure *f.*
moult *v.i.* muer; ~**ing** *s.* mue *f.*
mound *s.* monticule *m.*; (*over grave*) tumulus *m.*
mount *s.* (*hill*) mont *m.*; (*of picture*) carton de montage *m.*; (*horse*) monture *f.*; *v.t.* (*climb on to, put person on animal, put in setting, organise*) monter;

v.i. monter, (*horse*) à cheval; (*throne*) sur le trône; **~ed** *adj.* (*police, etc.*) monté; **~ing-block** *s.* montoir *m.*

mountain *s.* (*lit.* & *fig.*) montagne *f.*; **to make a ~ out of a** MOLE-**hill**; *adj.* de montagne, montagnard; **~** RESORT; **~ ash** *s.* sorbier *m.*; **~eer** *s.* (*climber*) alpiniste *m.f.*, (*dweller in ~s*) montagnard *m.*; **~eering** *s.* alpinisme *m.*; **~ous** *adj.* montagneux.

mountebank *s.* (*acrobat*) saltimbanque *m.*; (*fig. pej.*) charlatan *m.*

mourn *v.t.* pleurer qn.; **~ over sth.,** déplorer qch.; *v.i.* se lamenter; (*wear ~ing*) porter le deuil; **~er** *s.* personne qui suit le cortège funèbre *f.*; **~ful** *adj.* (*person*) désolé, (*thing*) funèbre; **~fully** *adv.* tristement, lugubrement; **~fulness** *s.* tristesse *f.*, air funèbre *m.*; **~ing** *s.* (*emotion*) affliction *f.*, (*clothes*) deuil *m.*; **to be in ~ing,** porter le deuil.

mouse *s.* souris *f.*; (*person*) personne falote *f.*; **to play** CAT **and ~ with**; **~-coloured** *adj.* gris-souris; **~hole** *s.* trou de souris *m.*; **~trap** *s.* souricière *f.*; **mousy** *adj.* de souris, (*person*) effacé; *v.i.* faire la chasse aux souris; **~r** *s.* bon ratier *m.*

mousse *s.* (*cook.*) mousse *f.*

moustache *s.* moustache *f.*

mouth *s.* (*human, of horse, of cattle*) bouche *f.*; (*of other animals*) gueule *f.*; (*opening*) ouverture *f.*, entrée *f.*; (*of river*) embouchure *f.*; **to be down in the ~** (*fig.*) avoir l'oreille basse; **to** FOAM **at the ~**; **to make one's ~ water,** faire venir l'eau à la bouche; BUTTER **wouldn't melt in his ~**; FOOT-**and-~ disease**; **to look a** GIFT **horse in the ~**; **from** HAND **to ~**; **from the** HORSE**'s ~**; **to be born with a** SILVER **spoon in one's ~**; **~-organ** *s.* harmonica *m.*; **~piece** *s.* (*mus.*) embouchure *f.*, (*telephone*) microphone *m.*, (*person*) porte-parole *m.*; **~ful** *s.* bouchée *f.*; *v.t.* déclamer; *v.i.* grimacer.

move *s.* mouvement *m.*; (*step, proceeding*) mesure *f.*; (*at chess, etc.*) tour *m.*; (*change of residence*) déménagement *m.*; *v.t.* (*change position of*) déplacer; (*stir, rouse*) remuer, provoquer; (*affect*) émouvoir; (*propose*) proposer; **~** HEAVEN **and earth**; *v.i.* (*stir*) remuer, bouger; (*change place*) se déplacer; (*~ house*) déménager; (*at chess, etc.*) jouer; (*take action*) agir; **~ about** *v.t.* déplacer, *v.i.* aller et venir; **~ away** *v.t.* & *i.* (s')éloigner; **~ back** *v.t.* & *i.* (faire) reculer; **~ forward** *v.t.* & *i.* avancer; **~ in** *v.t.* rentrer *v.i.* (*house*) emménager; **~ off** *v.i.* s'éloigner; **~ on** *v.t.* & *i.* (faire) circuler; **~ out** *v.t.* sortir, *v.i.* déménager; **~ round** *v.t.* tourner; **~ up** *v.t.* & *i.* monter; **movable** *adj.* mobile, (*law*) meuble; **movability** *s.* mobilité *f.*; **~ment** *s.* mouvement *m.*; **~r** *s.* mobile *m.*, (*fig. person*) auteur *m.*; **movies** *s.* cinéma *m.*; **moving** *adj.* mobile, (*force*) moteur, (*affecting*) émouvant, touchant.

mow *s.* (*of hay, etc.*) meule *f.*; *v.t.* faucher; (*lawn*) tondre; **~er** *s.* (*person*) faucheur *m.*; (*machine*) faucheuse *f.*; (*lawn-~er*) tondeuse *f.* (à gazon).

M.P. (*Member of Parliament*) député *m.*

m.p.g. (*abbrev. miles per gallon*) (*approx. equivalent*) litres aux 100 (km.).

m.p.h. (*abbrev. miles per hour*) (*approx. equivalent*) km/h.

Mr. Monsieur *m.* (*abbrev.*) M.

Mrs. Madame *f.*; (*abbrev.*) Mme.

much *adj.* beaucoup de; **too ~,** trop de; **how ~?,** combien de?; **so ~,** tant de; **as ~ as,** autant de . . . que, **he has as ~ money as you,** il a autant d'argent que vous; *s.* beaucoup; **to make ~ of s.o.,** être aux petits soins pour qn.; **to think ~ of,** estimer; **not to be up to ~,** être très quelconque; *adv.* beaucoup; (*with p.p. = very*) très, **~ annoyed,** très fâché; **as ~ as,** autant que, **he works as ~ as he can,** il travaille autant qu'il peut; **so ~,** tellement; ⚠ **very ~** = beaucoup (*never* très beaucoup); **~ of a ~ness,** bonnet blanc et blanc bonnet.

mucilag/e *s.* mucilage *m.*; **~inous** *adj.* mucilagineux.

muck *s.* (*manure*) fumier *m.*; (*dirt, filth*) boue *f.*, ordure *f.*; **to make a ~ of sth.** (*pop.*) gâcher qch.; *v.t.* fumer; **~ about** *v.i.* traînailler; **~ out** *v.t.* nettoyer; **~ up** *v.t.* salir, (*fig.*) gâcher; **~y** *adj.* sale.

mucous *adj.* muqueux; **~ membrane** *s.* muqueuse *f.*

mucus *s.* mucus *m.*

mud *s.* boue *f.*; (*in river*) vase *f.*; **to stick in the ~,** s'embourber; **stick-in-the-~** *s.* (*fig.*) vieux croûton *m.*; **~guard** *s.* garde-boue *m.*; **~dy** *adj.* (*road*) boueux, (*river*) vaseux, (*clothes*) plein de boue, (*liquid*) trouble; **~diness** *s.* état boueux *m.*

muddle *s.* désordre *m.*; *v.t.* (*bungle*) brouiller; (*confuse, mix up*) embrouiller.

muezzin *s.* muezzin *m.*

muff *s.* manchon *m.*

muffle *v.t.* (*for warmth*) (s')emmitouffler; (*deaden sound*) assourdir; **~r** *s.* (*scarf*) cache-nez *m.*; (*auto.*) pot d'échappement *m.*

mufti *s.* costume civil *m.*; **in ~,** (*mil., eccles.*) en civil; (*pop. mil.*) en pékin.

mug[1] *s.* timbale *f.*; (*pop. = face*) bille *f.*; (*pop. = fool*) cornichon *m.*; *v.t.* **~ up,** bûcher.

mug[2] *v.t.* (*attack*) agresser; **~ging** *s.* agression *f.*

muggy *adj.* lourd.

mulatto *s.* mulâtre(sse) *m.f.*

mulberry *s.* mûre *f.*; **~-tree** *s.* mûrier *m.*; **~ harbour** *s.* port flottant *m.*

mulch *s.* paillis *m.*; *v.t.* pailler.

mulct *v.t.* (*law*) frapper d'une amende; (*fig.*) dépouiller (de).

mul/e *s.* (*animal*) mulet *m.*, mule *f.*; (*person*) mule *f.*; (*slipper*) mule *f.*; **~eteer** *s.* muletier *m.*; **~ish** *adj.* têtu comme un mulet.

mull *v.t.* (*drink*) chauffer et épicer; **~ed** *adj.* chaud et épicé; **~ over** (*fam.*) ruminer.

mullet *s.* muge *m.*; **red ~,** rouget *m.*

mullion *s.* meneau *m.*

multi- (*in combination*) **~coloured** *adj.* multicolore; **~farious** *adj.* multiple; **~fariously** *adv.* de diverses manières; **~form** *adj.* multiforme; **~lateral** *adj.* multilatéral; **~millionaire** *s.* multimillionnaire *m.*; **~-storey car park** *s.* parking-silo *m.*

multipl/e *adj.* & *s.m.* multiple; **~e-choice** (question) à choix multiple; **~e crash** *s.* (*auto.*) collisions en série *f.pl.*; **with ~e injuries** *adj.* polytraumatisé; **~ication** *s.* multiplication *f.*, (*techn.*) amplification *f.*; **~icity** *s.* multiplicité *f.*; **~y** *v.t.* & *i.* (se) multiplier.

multitud/e *s.* multitude *f.*; **~inous** *adj.* multiple, très nombreux.

mum[1] *s.* (*fam. = mother*) maman *f.*

mum[2]**, to keep ~,** se taire; **~'s the word!,** motus!

mumbl/e *v.i.* marmonner; **~ing** *s.* marmonnement *m.*

mumbo-jumbo *s.* (*object*) objet de vénération ridicule *m.*; (*ceremony*) rituel incompréhensible *m.*, momerie *f.*

mummer *s.* mime *m.*; **~y** *s.* pantomime *f.*

mumm/y *s.* **1.** (*fam. = mother*) maman *f.*; **2.** (*dead body*) momie *f.*; **~ify** *v.t.* (2) momifier.

mumps *s.* oreillons *m.pl.*

munch *v.t.* mâcher.

mundane *adj.* du monde; terre-à-terre; ⚠ mondain = **worldly.**

municipal *adj.* municipal; **~ity** *s.* municipalité *f.*

munificen/t *adj.* munificent; **~ce** *s.* munificence *f.*; **~tly** *adv.* avec munificence.
muniments *s.pl.* archives *f.pl.*
munitions *s.pl.* munitions *f.pl.*
mural *s.* peinture murale *f.*; *adj.* mural.
murder *s.* meurtre *m.*; *v.t.* assassiner; (*fam.*) massacrer; ⚠ meurtrir = **to bruise**; **~er, ~ess** *s.* meurtri/er, -ère *m.f.*; **~ous** *adj.* meurtrier.
murk *s.* ténèbres *f.pl.*; **~iness** *s.* obscurité *f.*; **~y** *adj.* ténébreux.
murmur *s.* murmure *m.*; *v.t.* & *i.* murmurer; **~ing** *adj.* & **~ous** *adj.* murmurant.
murrain *s.* (*med.*) épizootie *f.*; (*fam.*) peste *f.*
muscat(**el**) *s.* muscat *m.*
musc/le *s.* muscle *m.*; **~ular** *adj.* (*concerning ~s*) musculaire; (*body*) musclé, musculeux.
Muscovite *adj.* & *s.m.f.* moscovite.
mus/e *s.* (*myth.*) muse *f.*; *v.i.* méditer (sur), rêver (à); **~ing** *s.* rêverie *f.*
museum *s.* musée *m.*; **~ piece** *s.* pièce de collection *f.*
mushroom *s.* champignon *m.*; *adj.* aux champignons; (*fig.*) champignon; *v.i.* (*expand rapidly*) pousser comme un champignon; (*take ~ shape*) monter, s'élever (etc.) en forme de champignon.
music *s.* musique *f.*; **to** FACE **the ~**; **~-hall** *s.* music-hall *m.*; **~-master** *s.* professeur de musique *m.*; **~-stand** *s.* pupitre *m.*; **~-stool** *s.* tabouret *m.*; **~al** *s.* (& *~al comedy*) opérette *f.*; **~al** *adj.* musical, (*of person*) musicien; **~al box** *s.* boîte à musique *f.*; **~ally** *adv.* musicalement; **~ian** *s.* musicien(ne) *m.f.*
musk *s.* musc *m.*; **~-deer** *s.* musc *m.*; **~-ox** *s.* bœuf musqué *m.*; **~-rose** *s.* rose musquée *f.*
musket *s.* mousquet *m.*; **~eer** *s.* mousquetaire *m.*; **~ry** *s.* mousqueterie *f.*
Muslim, Moslem *adj.* & *s.m.f.* musulman(e).
muslin *s.* mousseline *f.*; *adj.* de mousseline.
musquash *s.* castor du Canada *m.*
mussel *s.* moule *f.*
Mussulman *see* MUSLIM.
must[1] *s.* (*new wine*) moût *m.*; **~y** *adj.* moisi.
must[2] *s.* (*essential*) impératif *m.*; *aux. v.* (*be obliged to*) devoir *or* il faut que + *subj.*, **I ~ see her,** je dois la voir *or* il faut que je la voie; **~ be** (*clearly is*) devoir, **he ~ be a stranger,** il doit être étranger; **~ have** (*clearly did or has done*), **it ~ have rained,** il a dû pleuvoir.
mustang *s.* mustang *m.*
mustard *s.* moutarde *f.*; **~ gas,** ypérite *f.*; **~-pot,** moutardier *m.*
muster *s.* assemblée *f.*; (*for inspection*) revue *f.*; **to pass ~,** passer; *v.t.* & *i.* (se) rassembler; **~ up** *v.t.* rassembler.
mutab/le *adj.* mutable; **~ility** *s.* mutabilité *f.*
muta/tion *s.* changement *m.*; (*med.*) mutation *f.*; **~nt** *s.* mutant(e) *m.f.*
mute *s.* **1.** (*person*) muet(te) *m.f.*; **2.** (*mus.*) sourdine *f.*; *v.t.* (2) mettre la sourdine à; *adj.* (*dumb*) muet; (*silent*) silencieux; **~ly** *adv.* en silence; **~ness** *s.* (*gen.* & *med.*) mutisme *m.*
mutilat/e *v.t.* mutiler; **~ion** *s.* mutilation *f.*
mutin/y *s.* mutinerie *f.*; *v.i.* se mutiner; **~eer** *s.* mutin *m.*; **~ous** *adj.* mutiné; (*fig.*) révolté.
mutter *s.* **1.** (*low tone*) marmonnement *m.*; **2.** (*grumble*) grommellement *m.*; *v.t.* & *i.* (1) marmonner; (2) grommeler.
mutton *s.* mouton *m.*; LEG **of ~**; NECK **of ~**.
mutual *adj.* (*consent, effort, service*) mutuel; (*aid, hate, love*) réciproque; **~ity** *s.* mutualité *f.*; **~ly** *adv.**; *.
muzzle *s.* (*of animal*) museau *m.*; (*put on animal*) muselière *f.*; (*of gun*) gueule *f.*; *v.t.* (*lit.* & *fig.*) museler.
my *adj.* mon, ma, mes; ⚠ **I have broken ~ arm, etc.,** je me suis cassé le bras, etc.
myop/ia *s.* myopie *f.*; **~ic** *adj.* myope.
myriad *s.* myriade *f.*
myrmidon *s.* myrmidon *m.*
myrrh *s.* myrrhe *f.*
myrtle *s.* myrte *m.*
myself *pron.* moi-même; *reflexive,* me; **by ~,** tout seul; **I am not ~,** je ne suis pas bien dans mon assiette.
myster/y *s.* mystère *m.*; **~ious** *adj.* mystérieux; **~iously** *adv.**; **~iousness** *s.* mystère *m.*, nature mystérieuse *f.*
mystic *s.* mystique *m.*; *adj.* mystique, magique, occulte; **~ism** *s.* mysticisme *m.*
mystif/y *v.t.* mystifier; (*confuse*) embrouiller; (*lead astray*) désorienter; **~ication** *s.* mystification *f.*
myth *s.* mythe *m.*; **~ical** *adj.* mythique; **~ology** *s.* mythologie *f.*; **~ological** *adj.* mythologique.
myxomatosis *s.* myxomatose *f.*

N

nab *v.t.* (*pop.*) pincer.
nabob *s.* nabab *m.*
nadir *s.* (astron.) nadir *m.*; (*gen.*) stade le plus bas *m.*
nag[1] *s.* (*horse*) bidet *m.*
nag[2] *v.t.* harceler; *v.i.* criailler; **~ging** *adj.* (*pain, etc.*) harcelant.
naiad *s.* naïade *f.*
nail *s.* **1.** (*human, bird, animal*) ongle *m.*; **2.** (*metal spike*) clou *m.*; TOOTH **and ~**; THUMB-**~ sketch;** HARD **as ~s; ~-brush,** *etc.* brosse *f.* (*etc.*) à ongles; **to hit the ~ on the head** (*fig.*) frapper juste; **to pay on the ~,** payer recta; *v.t.* (2) clouer; **~ down** *v.t.* (*fig. fam.*) coincer.
naïve *adj.* naïf; **~ly** *adv.**; **~ty** *s.* naïveté *f.*
naked *adj.* (*nude, defenceless, unadorned*) nu; (*of trees, etc.*) dénudé; (*of light, etc.*) non protégé; **to the ~ eye,** à l'œil nu; **~ly** *adv.* à nu, (*fig.*) crûment; **~ness** *s.* (*lit.* & *fig.*) nudité *f.*
namby-pamby *adj.* (*affected*) doucereux; sentimental.
name *s.* (*title, reputation*) nom *m.*; **Christian** *or* **given ~,** prénom *m.*; FULL **~**; (*comm.*) raison sociale *f.*; **by ~,** de nom; **in the ~ of,** au nom de; **to** CALL **s.o. ~s; give a** DOG **a bad ~; what is your ~?,** comment vous appelez-vous?; **his ~ is John,** il s'appelle Jean; **to make a ~ for oneself,** se faire un nom; **~-day** *s.* fête *f.*; **~sake** *s.* homologue *m.f.*; **~less** *adj.* (*unknown*) inconnu, (*anonymous*) anonyme, (*not to be ~d*) innommable, (*unspeakable*) indicible; **~ly** *adv.* à savoir; *v.t.* nommer; (*nominate*) désigner.
nankeen *s.* nankin *m.*
nanny *s.* nounou *f.*; **~-goat** *s.* chèvre *f.*
nap *s.* **1.** (*of cloth*) poil *m.*; **2.** (*short sleep*) somme *f.*; **3.** (*tip—racing*) tuyau increvable *m.*; *v.t.* (3) tuyauter; *v.i.* (2) somnoler; **to catch s.o. ~ping** (*fig.*) prendre le lièvre au gîte.

napalm *s.* napalm *m.*
nape *s.* nuque *f.*
napery *s.* linge (de table) *m.*
naphtha *s.* naphte *m.*; **~lene** *s.* naphtaline *f.*
napkin *s.* (*for baby*) couche *f.*; (*at table*) serviette *f.*; **~-ring** *s.* rond de serviette *m.*
Napoleon *s.* Napoléon *m.*; **~ic** *adj.* napoléonien.
nappy *s.* (*fam.*) couche *f.*
narciss/us *s.* narcisse *m.*; **~ism** *s.* narcissisme *m.*
narcosis *s.* narcose *f.*
narcotic *adj.* & *s.m.* narcotique.
narghile *s.* narguilé *m.*
nark *s.* (*pop.*) mouchard *m.*; *v.t.* embêter.
narrat/e *v.t.* raconter; **~ion** *s.* narration *f.*; **~ive** *adj.* narratif, *s.* récit *m.*; **~or** *s.* narrateur *m.*
narrow *s.* (*usu. pl.*) goulet *m.*; *adj.* (*small in width*) étroit; (*restricted*) borné; (*prejudiced*) étroit; (*searching*) minutieux; (*majority, etc.*) petit; **to have a ~** ESCAPE; **~-minded** *adj.* à l'esprit étroit; **~ly** *adv.* (*closely*) étroitement, minutieusement; (*only just*) tout juste; **~ness** *s.* (*size*) étroitesse *f.*, (*carefulness*) minutie *f.*; *v.t.* & *i.* (se) rétrécir, (se) reserrer.
nasal *s.* (*ling.*) nasale *f.*; *adj.* nasal; **~ly** *adv.* d'un ton nasal.
nascent *adj.* naissant.
nasturtium *s.* capucine *f.*
nast/y *adj.* **1.** (*dirty; trick, weather*) sale; **2.** (*obscene*) obscène; **3.** (*spiteful*) méchant; **4.** (*unpleasant*) désagréable, (*smell*) nauséabond, (*taste*) infect; **~ily** *adv.* (1)*; (2) de façon obscène; (3) méchamment; (4)*; de façon dégoûtante; **~iness** *s.* (1) saleté *f.*; (2) obscénité *f.*; (3) méchanceté *f.*; (4) goût (*m.*), odeur (*f.*), désagréable.
natal *adj.* (*concerning birth*) de naissance; (*country, lang.*) natal; **~ity** *s.* natalité *f.*
natation *s.* natation *f.*
nation *s.* nation *f.*; **~al** *s.* national *m.*, ressortissant *m.*; *adj.* national; **~al service**, service militaire *m.*; **N~al Socialist** *adj.* & *s.m.f.* national-socialiste; **~alism** *s.* nationalisme *m.*; **~alist** *s.* nationaliste *m.f.*; **~ally** *adv.* sur le plan national; **~ality** *s.* nationalité *f.*; **~alize** *v.t.* nationaliser; **~alization** *s.* nationalisation *f.*
nativ/e *s.* (*of place*) enfant *m.*; (*esp. non-European*) indigène *m.*; *adj.* (*inborn*) natif; (*by birth*) de naissance; (*country*) natal; (*lang.*) maternel; (*indigenous*) indigène, originaire (de); **~ity** *s.* nativité *f.*
N.A.T.O. (*North Atlantic Treaty Organization*) OTAN (Organisation du Traité de l'Atlantique Nord) *f.*
natter *s.* (*fam.*) bavardage *m.*; *v.i.* bavarder.
natty *adj.* (*smart*) coquet; (*skilful*), (*person*) adroit, (*thing*) commode.
natural *s.* (*half-wit*) innocent *m.*; (*person ~ly endowed for sth.*) personne douée pour qch. *f.*; (*mus.*) bécarre *m.*; *adj.* (*of nature, ≠ artificial, illegitimate*) naturel; (*mus.*) bécarre; **~ death** *s.* mort naturelle *f.*; **~ism** *s.* naturalisme *m.*; **~ist** *s.* naturaliste *m.f.*; **~ize** *v.t.* naturaliser; **~ization** *s.* naturalisation *f.*; **~ly** *adv.**; **~ness** *s.* naturel *m.*
nature *s.* (*external world, essential quality, kind, sort*) nature *f.*; (*character*) tempérament *m.*; **good-~d** *adj.* bienveillant; **ill-~d** *adj.* malveillant.
naught (*archaic*) *s.* rien *m.*; (*math.*) zéro *m.*; **to set at ~**, tenir pour rien, mépriser; **to come to ~**, échouer.
naught/y *adj.* (*child*) méchant; (*disobedient*) désobéissant; (*wicked*) vilain; (*fam. story*) salé; **~ily** *adv.* mal; **~iness** *s.* mauvaise conduite *f.*
nause/a *s.* nausée *f.*; **~ate** *v.t.* écœurer; **~ating** *adj.* & **~ous** *adj.* nauséabond, écœurant.
nautical *adj.* (*chart, mile*) marin; (*art, science*) nautique; (*of navy*) de marine.
naval *adj.* (*arch., battle*) naval (*pl.* -als); (*person*) de marine; (*state*) maritime.
nave *s.* (*eccles.*) nef *f.*; (*of wheel*) moyeu *m.*
navel *s.* (*anat.*) nombril *m.*; (*central point*) centre *m.*
navig/ate *v.t.* (*direct ship*) gouverner; (*direct plane*) piloter; (*sail on sea*) naviguer sur; (*fly in air*) voyager dans; *v.i.* naviguer; **~able** *adj.* (*river*) navigable, (*plane*) manœuvrable; **~ability** *s.* navigabilité *f.*, manœuvrabilité *f.*; **~ation** *s.* navigation *f.*; **~ator** *s.* (*naut., aviat.*) navigateur *m.*
navvy *s.* terrassier *m.*
navy *s.* marine *f.*; **merchant ~**, marine marchande *f.*; **~ blue,** bleu marine.
nay *s.* non *m.*, refus *m.*; *adv.* non; (*yet more*) bien plus, et même.
Nazarene *adj.* & *s.m.f.* Nazaréen(ne).
Nazi *adj.* & *s.m.f.* nazi(e); **~ism** *s.* nazisme *m.*
N.B. n.b.
N.C.O. (*non-commissioned officer*) sous-officier *m.*
Neanderthal *adj.* du néanderthal.
neap *adj.* de morte-eau; **~-tide** *s.* morte-eau *f.*
Neapolitan *adj.* & *s.m.f.* napolitain(e).
near *adj.* (*closely related*) proche; (*close to*) prochain; (*short*) direct; (*mean*) mesquin; **~by** *adj.* proche; **~ side** *s.* (*U.K.*) gauche *m.*, (*France, etc.*) droite *f.*; **~-sighted** *adj.* myope; **it was a ~ thing,** il s'en est fallu de peu (que), (*for me*) je l'ai échappé belle, (*for him*) il l'a échappé belle; **~ly** *adv.* presque, (*close to*) de près, **he ~ly died,** il a failli mourir; **~ness** *s.* (*in time, space*) proximité *f.*, (*relations*) intimité *f.*, (*meanness*) mesquinerie *f.*; *adv.* (*space, time*) près; (*=~ly*) presque; **to come ~ to doing sth., to being,** être à deux doigts de faire qch., d'être; FAR **and ~**; **~by** *adv.* tout près; *prep.* (*~ to*) près de; *v.t.* & *i.* s'approcher (de).
neat[1] *s.* bœuf *m.*; **~'s-foot,** pied de bœuf *m.*; **~'s-tongue,** langue de bœuf *f.*
neat[2] *adj.* **1.** (*undiluted*) pur, nature; **2.** (*nicely made*) bien fait; **3.** (*tidy*): (*person*) propre, soigné, (*house, book, etc.*) bien tenu; **4.** (*cleverly phrased*) élégant; **5.** (*deft*) adroit; **~ly** *adv.* (3) avec soin; (4) élégamment; (5)*; **~ness** *s.* (3) soin *m.*, ordre *m.*; (4) élégance *f.*; (5) adresse *f.*
nebul/ous *adj.* nébuleux; **~osity** *s.* nébulosité *f.*
necessar/y *s.* indispensable *m.*; (*≠ luxury*) le strict nécessaire *m.*; **~ies** *m.pl.* nécessaire *m.*; *adj.* nécessaire (*to, for*—à); (*indispensable*) indispensable; (*inevitable*) inévitable; **if ~y,** le cas échéant, en cas de nécessité; **it is ~y (for you) to do,** il (vous) faut faire; **it is ~y that you do,** il faut que vous fassiez; **~ily** *adv.**;*;*.
necessit/ate *v.t.* nécessiter; (*involve as condition or result*) imposer, entraîner; **~ous** *adj.* nécessiteux; **~y** *s.* nécessité *f.*; (*need*) besoin (de) *m.*; (*poverty*) indigence *f.*; **of ~y,** nécessairement.
neck *s.* (*anat.*) cou *m.*; (*of garment*) encolure *f.*; (*of bottle*) goulot *m.*; (*of land*) langue *f.*; (*of mutton*) collet *m.*; (*pop. impudence*) toupet *m.*; **~ and ~,** à égalité; **up to the ~ in debt,** endetté jusqu'au cou; **to stick one's ~ out** (*fam.*) se risquer (à); **to win by a ~** (*racing*) gagner par une encolure; STIFF **~**; STIFF-**~ed; ~cloth** *s.* cache-col *m.*; **~erchief** *s.* foulard *m.*; **~lace** *s.* & **~let** *s.* collier *m.*; ~TIE; *v.t.* & *i.* (*fam.*) se bécoter.
necro/logy *s.* nécrologie *f.*; **~mancer** *s.* nécromancien *m.*; **~mancy** *s.* nécromancie *f.*; **~polis** *s.* nécropole *f.*
nectar *s.* nectar *m.*
nectarine *s.* brugnon *m.*
need *s.* (*want, necessity of*) besoin *m.* (de); (*time of ~*) difficulté *f.*; (*poverty*) indigence *f.*; **a**

FRIEND **in ~**; **if ~ be,** au besoin; **in case of ~,** en cas de besoin; **to be in ~ of,** avoir besoin de; **~ful** *adj.* & *s.m.* nécessaire; **~iness** *s.* besoin *m.*; **~less** *adj.* inutile; **~lessly** *adv.**; **~y** *adj.* nécessiteux; *v.t.* (*want*) avoir besoin de; (*require*) demander, exiger; (*have to do*) devoir.

needle *s.* (*sewing, gramophone, indicator, peak, pine*) aiguille *f.*, **knitting ~,** aiguille à tricoter *f.*; (*obelisk*) obélisque *f.*; PINS **and ~s; to look for a ~ in a haystack,** chercher une aiguille dans une botte de foin; **~woman** *s.* couturière *f.*; **~work** *s.* couture *f.*; *v.t.* (*fam.*) (*goad*) harceler; (*irritate*) agacer.

nefarious *adj.* infâme; **~ly** *adv.* de façon infâme.

negat/e *v.t.* nier; **~ion** *s.* négation *f.*; **~ive** *s.* négative *f.*, (*photo.*) cliché *m.*; **in the ~ive,** négativement; *adj.* négatif; *v.t.* (*veto*) rejeter; (*contradict*) réfuter; (*neutralize*) neutraliser.

neglect *s.* (*act*) négligence *f.*, oubli *m.*; (*state*) abandon *m.*; (*careless treatment*) manque de soins *m.*; *v.t.* (*disregard*) négliger; (*leave uncared for*) laisser à l'abandon; (*leave undone*) négliger (*to*— de); **~ful** *adj.* négligent, oublieux; **~fully** *adv.* négligemment.

neglig/ence *s.* **1.** (*want of care*) négligence *f.*; **2.** (*carelessness*) insouciance *f.*; **~ent** *adj.* (1) négligent; (2) insouciant; **~ently** *adv.* (1) avec négligence; (2) avec insouciance; **~ible** *adj.* négligeable.

negoti/ate *v.t.* (*gen.* & *fin.*) négocier; (*auto*) **~ate a corner,** prendre un virage, **~ate a hill,** monter une colline; **~able** *adj.* négociable; **~ation** *s.* négociation *f.*; **~ator** *s.* négociateur *m.*

Negr/o *adj.* & *s.m.* nègre; **~ess** *s.* négresse *f.*; **~oid** *adj.* négroïde.

negus *s.* **1.** (*wine*) vin chaud et épicé *m.*; **2.** (*N~, emperor of Ethiopia*) négus *m.*

neigh *s.* hennissement *m.*; *v.i.* hennir.

neighbour *s.* voisin(e) *m.f.*; (*fig.*) prochain *m.*; *v.t.* & *i.* avoisiner, être voisin de; **~hood** *s.* voisinage *m.*; **in the ~hood of** (*fig.*) environ; **~ing** *adj.* avoisinant; **~ly** *adj.* (*person*) serviable, bon voisin, (*act*) de bon voisinage; **~liness** *s.* bon voisinage *m.*

neither *pron., adj.* ni l'un ni l'autre, aucun (de), **~ of them knows,** ni l'un ni l'autre ne sait; **~ answer is correct,** aucune de ces réponses n'est juste; *conj.* non plus; **he did not go, ~ did I,** il n'y est pas allé, (ni) moi non plus; *adv.* **~ . . . nor,** ni . . . ni, **he can ~ read nor write,** il ne sait ni lire ni écrire.

nem. con. *adv.* à l'unanimité.

nemesis *s.* châtiment *m.*

neo- (*in combination*) néo-; **~lithic** *adj.* néolithique; **~logism** *s.* néologisme *m.*; **~phyte** *s.* néophyte *m.f.*; **~plasm** *s.* néoplasme *m.*

neon *s.* néon *m.*; **~ lighting,** éclairage au néon *m.*

Nepal *s.* (*geog.*) Népal *m.*; **~ese, ~i** *adj.* & *s.m.f.* népalais(e).

nephew *s.* neveu *m.*

nephrit/ic *adj.* néphrétique; **~is** *s.* néphrite *f.*

nepotism *s.* népotisme *m.*

Neptune *s.* Neptune *m.*

nereid *s.* néréide *f.*

nerv/e *s.* (*anat., presence of mind, assurance*) nerf *m.*; (*bot.*) nervure *f.*; (*fam.*) toupet *m.*; **to get on s.o.'s ~es,** porter, taper, sur les nerfs de qn.; **~eless** *adj.* sans force; **~ous** *adj.* (*med.*) nerveux, (*fig.*) intimidé, craintif; **to feel ~ous,** avoir les nerfs tendus, (*fam.*) avoir le trac; **~ous** BREAKDOWN; **~ously** *adv.* timidement; **~ousness** *s.* (*med.*) nervosité *f.*, (*fig.*) timidité *f.*; **~y** *adj.* (*fam.*) énervé; *v.t.* donner du nerf à, encourager.

nest *s.* (*of bird*) nid *m.*; (*lair*) repaire *m.*; (*brood, swarm*) nichée *f.*; **to** FEATHER **one's ~; to bring a** HORNET**'s ~ about one's ears;** MARE**'s ~**; WASP**'s ~**; **~ of tables,** table gigogne *f.*; **~-egg** *s.* (*fam.*) magot *m.*; *v.i.* faire son nid, (se) nicher; **~ling** *s.* oisillon *m.*

nestle *v.t.* & *i.* (se) blottir.

net *s.* (*text.*) tulle *m.*; (*fishing, tennis*) filet *m.*; **~ball** *s.* net-ball *m.*; **~-cord** *s.* (*tennis*) au ras du filet; **~work** *s.* réseau *m.*, (*radio*) chaîne *f.*; **~ting** *s.* filet *m.*; WIRE **~ting**; *v.t.* prendre au filet.

net(t) *adj.* (≠ *gross, weight*) net; *v.t.* rapporter net.

nether *adj.* inférieur; **~most** *adj.* le plus bas.

Netherland/s *s.* (*geog.*) les Pays-Bas *m.pl.*; **~er** *s.m.f.* Néerlandais(e).

nettle *s.* ortie *f.*; **~-rash** *s.* urticaire *f.*; *v.t.* piquer; (*fig.*) piquer au vif.

neur- (*in combination*) **~algia** *s.* névralgie *f.*; **~asthenia** *s.* neurasthénie *f.*; **~itis** *s.* névrite *f.*; **~ology** *s.* neurologie *f.*; **~ologist** *s.* neurologue *m.f.*; **~osis** *s.* névrose *f.*; **~otic** *adj.* névrosé.

neut/er *adj.* & *s.m.* neutre; *v.t.* châtrer; **~ral** *s.* (*person*) neutre *m.*; (*gear*) point mort *m.*; *adj.* neutre; **~rality** *s.* neutralité *f.*; **~ralize** *v.t.* neutraliser.

neutron *s.* neutron *m.*

never *adv.* (ne) . . . jamais; (*not at all*) pas du tout; (*pop.* = *surely not*) pas possible!; **on the ~-~,** à tempérament; **~ mind,** n'importe; **~-ending** *adj.* incessant; interminable; **~more** *adv.* jamais plus; **~theless,** néanmoins.

new *adj.* (*fresh, additional, different, recent*) nouveau; (*unworn, unused*) neuf; **brand ~,** flambant neuf; (*cook.*) frais; **~-born** *adj.* nouveau-né; **~comer** *s.* nouveau-venu *m.*; **~fangled** *adj.* d'un nouveau genre; **~-**LAID; **turn over a ~** LEAF; **N~ Year** *s.* Nouvel An *m.*; **N~ Year's** EVE; **N~ Caledonia** *s.* (*geog.*) Nouvelle Calédonie *f.*; **N~ Guinea** *s.* (*geog.*) Nouvelle-Guinée *f.*; **N~ Hebrides** *s.* (*geog.*) Nouvelles Hébrides *f.pl.*; **N~ Orleans** *s.* la Nouvelle-Orléans *f.*; **~ly** *adv.* nouvellement; **~ness** *s.* nouveauté *f.*

newel *s.* noyau *m.*

Newfoundland *s.* (*geog.*) Terre-Neuve *f.*

news *s.* (*piece of*) nouvelle *f.*; (*in press*) nouvelles *f.pl.*; (*on radio*) informations *f.pl.*; (*in cinema, TV*) actualités *f.pl.*; **~agent** *s.* marchand de journaux *m.*; **~monger** *s.* colporteur de nouvelles *m.*; **~paper** *s.* journal *m.*, (*daily*) quotidien *m.*, (*weekly*) hebdomadaire *m.*; **~print** *s.* papier journal *m.*; **~-reader** *s.* (*radio, TV*) speaker-(ine) *m.f.*; **~-reel** (*cinema*) bande d'actualités *f.*; **~y** *adj.* (*fam.*) plein de nouvelles.

newt *s.* triton *m.*

New Zealand *s.* (*geog.*) Nouvelle-Zélande *f.*; **~er** *s.m.f.* néo-zélandais(e); *adj.* de Nouvelle-Zélande.

next *adj.* (*nearest*) le plus proche; (*time, place, reckoned from moment of speaking*) prochain; (*reckoned from point in past*) suivant; **~ Sunday I shall go to church,** dimanche prochain, j'irai à l'église; **the ~ Sunday he went to church,** le dimanche suivant il alla à l'église; **I shall get off at the ~ station,** je descendrai à la prochaine gare; **he got off at the ~ station,** il descendit à la gare suivante; **~ time I shall win,** la prochaine fois, je gagnerai; **the ~ time I won,** la fois suivante, j'ai gagné; *adv.* ensuite, la prochaine fois; *prep.* **~ to,** à côté de; **~ day** *s.* le lendemain; **~ door** *s.* la maison d'à côté, *adj.* voisin; **~ of kin,** les plus proches parents *m.pl.*

N.F.U. (*National Farmers' Union*) FNSA (Fédération nationale des Syndicats agricoles) *f.*

nib *s.* (*of pen*) bec *m.*; (*techn.*) pointe *f.*

nibble *s.* **1.** (*eating*) grignotage *m.*; **2.** (*fishing*) touche *f.*; *v.t.* (1) grignoter; (2) mordre.

nice *adj.* **1.** (*fastidious*) difficile, scrupuleux; **2.** (*subtle, fine*) subtil, délicat; **3.** (*agreable*) agréable;

4. (*kind, friendly*) aimable, gentil; **5.** (*cook. taste, smell*) bon; **~ and** + *adj. e.g.* **~ and warm,** agréablement chaud; **~-looking** *adj.* beau; **~ly** *adv.* (1) soigneusement; (2) justement; (3) agréablement; (4) aimablement, gentiment; **~ness** *s.* (1) difficulté *f.*, méticulosité *f.*; (2) subtilité *f.*, délicatesse *f.*; (3) agrément *m.*; (4) amabilité *f.*, gentillesse *f.*; **~ty** *s.* précision *f.*, subtilité *f.*

niche *s.* (*lit.* & *fig.*) niche *f.*

nick *s.* encoche *f.*; **in the ~ of time,** au bon moment; *v.t.* cocher; (*pop.* = *steal*) faucher.

nickel *s.* nickel *m.*; (*U.S. coin*) pièce de cinq cents *f.*; **~-plated** *adj.* nickelé; *v.t.* nickeler.

nickname *s.* sobriquet *m.*; *v.t.* surnommer.

nicotine *s.* nicotine *f.*

niece *s.* nièce *f.*

nifty *adj.* (*pop.*) adroit.

niggard/ly *adj.* mesquin; **~liness** *s.* mesquinerie *f.*

nigger *s.* nègre *m.*, négresse *f.*; **~-brown** *adj.* tête-de-nègre *invar.*

niggl/e *v.i.* couper les cheveux en quatre; **~ing** *adj.* (*detail*) insignifiant; (*person*) tatillon; (*doubt, fear*) persistant.

nigh *adj.* proche; *adv.* près; *prep.* près de.

night *s.* (*lit.* & *fig.*) nuit *f.*; **first ~** (*theat.*) première *f.*; *adj.* de nuit; **to work ~s,** travailler de nuit; **at ~,** la nuit; **by ~,** de nuit; **good-~,** bon soir; **to have a good ~,** bien dormir; **to be ~,** faire nuit; **~-bird** *s.* (*person*) noctambule *m.*; **~-blindness** *s.* nyctalopie *f.*; **~cap** *s.* (*garment*) bonnet de nuit *m.*, (*drink*) grog *m.*; **~-club** *s.* boîte de nuit *f.*; **~-dress, ~-gown** *s.* chemise de nuit *f.*; **at ~fall,** à la nuit tombante; **~jar** *s.* engoulevent *m.*; **~-light** *s.* veilleuse *f.*; **~mare** *s.* cauchemar *m.*; **~shade** *s.* morelle *f.*; **deadly ~shade** *s.* belladone *f.*; **~-watchman** *s.* gardien de nuit *m.*; **~ly** *adj.* (*at ~*) de nuit, (*every ~*) de toutes les nuits; **~ly** *adv.* toutes les nuits.

nightingale *s.* rossignol *m.*

nihil/ism *s.* nihilisme *m.*; **~ist** *s.* nihiliste *m.f.*

nil *s.* rien *m.*; (*sport*) zéro *m.*; (*on form*) néant *m.*; *adj.* nul.

Nil/e *s.* (*geog.*) Nil *m.*; **~otic** *adj.* nilotique.

nimbl/e *adj.* agile; (*of mind*) prompt, vif; **~eness** *s.* agilité *f.*; promptitude *f.*, vivacité *f.*; **~y** *adv.**;*,*.

nimbus *s.* (*halo*) nimbe *m.*; (*rain-cloud*) nimbus *m.*

nincompoop *s.* crétin *m.*

nine *adj.* & *s.m.* neuf; **to be dressed up to the ~s,** être sur son trente et un; **~fold** *adj.* & *adv.* neuf fois; **ninth** *adj.* & *s.m.* neuvième; **ninthly** *adv.**; **~pin** *s.* quille *f.*; **~pins** *s.* jeu de quilles *m.*; **~teen** *adj.* & *s.m.* dix-neuf **~teenth** *adj.* dix-neuvième; **~ty** *adj.* & *s.m.* quatre-vingt-dix; **~ty-one, -two,** *etc.* quatre-vingt-onze, quatre-vingt-douze, etc.

nip *s.* **1.** (*pinch*) pincement *m.*; **2.** (*bite*) morsure *f.*; **3.** (*cold*) piquant *m.*; **4.** (*of spirits*) goutte *f.*; *v.t.* (1) pincer; (2) mordre; (3) piquer; (*agric.*) brûler; **~ in the bud,** tuer dans l'œuf; **~per** *s.* (*pop.*) posse *m.*; (*claw of crustacean*) pince *f.*; **~pers** *s.* (*tool*) pince *f.*; **~ping** *adj.* (*cold, tool*) pinçant, piquant; (*wind, fig.*) mordant; **~py** *adj.* (*cold*) mordant; (*pop.*) preste; **to be ~py** (*fam.*) se grouiller.

nipple *s.* (*anat.*) mamelon *m.*; (*on baby's bottle*) tétine *f.*; (*mech.*) raccord *m.*

nirvana *s.* nirvâna *m.*

nit *s.* (*insect*) pou *m.*; (*fam.*) propre à rien *m.*

nitr/e *s.* nitre *m.*; **~ate** *s.* nitrate *m.*; **~ic** *adj.* nitrique; **~ogen** *s.* azote *m.*; **~ogenous** *adj.* azoté; **~ous** *adj.* azoteux.

no *particle* non; *adj.* aucun, **~ man,** aucun homme; pas de, **there is ~ bread,** il n'y a pas de pain; **in ~ way, in ~ wise,** aucunement; **in ~ circumstances,** en aucun cas; **it's ~ deal,** rien à faire; **it's ~ use,** cela ne sert à rien (de); **~ admittance,** entrée interdite; **~-claim bonus** *s.* bonus-malus *m.*; **~ man's land** *s.* no man's land *m.*, (*fig.*) terrain neutre *m.*; **~ smoking,** défense de fumer; **~ thoroughfare, ~ through road,** voie sans issue; *adv.* non; **~ less,** pas moins; **~ more,** pas plus.

Noah *s.* Noé *m.*; **~'s ark** *s.* arche de Noé *f.*

nob/le *s.* noble *m.*, aristocrate *m.*; *adj.* noble; (*building, etc.*) imposant; **~leman** *s.* gentilhomme *m.*; **~ility** *s.* noblesse *f.*; **~ly** *adv.* noblement, superbement.

nobody *pron.* personne . . . (ne); nul(le); *s.* (*fam.*) inconnu(e) *m.f.*

nocturn/al *adj.* nocturne; **~e** *s.* nocturne *m.*

nod *s.* (*of head, in assent*) signe de tête *m.*; (*in greeting*) inclination de tête *f.*; *v.t.* & *i.* (*in assent*) faire signe que oui; (*incline head*) incliner la tête; (*let head droop*) dodeliner (de la tête); (*be drowsy*) sommeiller.

nod/e *s.* nœud *m.*; **~al** *adj.* nodal.

nodul/e *s.* nodule *m.*; **~ar** *adj.* nodulaire; **~ose, ~ous** *adj.* noduleux.

noggin *s.* quart *m.*

noise *s.* bruit *m.*; BIG **~**; **~s off** (*theat.*) bruitage *m.*; **to make a ~,** faire de bruit; **noisy** *adj.* bruyant, trapageur; **noisily** *adv.* bruyamment; **noisiness** *s.* (*din*) vacarme *m.*, (*nature*) nature bruyante *f.*; **~less** *adj.* silencieux; **~lessly** *adv.* sans bruit; *v.t.* **~ abroad,** ébruiter.

noisome *adj.* puant; **~ness** *s.* puanteur *f.*

nomad *s.* nomade *m.f.*; **~ic** *adj.* nomade.

nomenclature *s.* nomenclature *f.*

nominal *adj.* (*in name only*) nominal; (*not real*) fictif; **~ly** *adv.**;*.

nomin/ate *v.t.* **1.** (*appoint*) nommer; **2.** (*propose*) désigner; **~ation** *s.* (1) nomination *f.*; (2) désignation *f.*; **~ative** *s.* nominatif *m.*; **~ee** *s.* candidat agréé *m.*

non- (*in combination*) **~-acceptance** *s.* refus *m.*; **~-aggression** *s.* non-agression *f.*; **~-aligned** *adj.* non-engagé; **~-appearance** *s.* absence *f.*, (*law*) non-comparution *f.*; **~-attendance** *s.* absence *f.*; **~-belligerent, ~-combatant** *adj.* & *s.m.* non-combattant; **~-compliance** *s.* refus d'obéissance *m.*; **~-commissioned** *see* N.C.O.; **~-committal** *adj.* qui n'engage à rien; **~-conducting** *adj.* non-conducteur; **~-cooperation** *s.* refus de coopération *m.*; **~-delivery** *s.* non-livraison *f.*; **~-existent** *adj.* non-existant; **~-fiction** *s.* littérature non-romanesque *f.*; **~-intervention** *s.* non-intervention *f.*; **~-negotiable** *adj.* non-négociable; **~-payment** *s.* non-paiement *m.*; **~-performance** *s.* non-exécution *f.*; **~-playing** *adj.* qui ne joue pas; **~-resident** *adj.* non-résident; **~-resistance** *s.* non-résistance *f.*; **~-returnable** *adj.* (*containers, etc.*) perdu; **~-skid** *adj.* antidérapant; **~-slip** *adj.* antidérapant; **~-smoker** *s.* non-fumeur *m.*; **~-stick** *adj.* antiadhérant; **~-stop** *adj.* permanent, (*rail.*) direct, (*aviat.*) sans escale; **~-violence** *s.* non-violence *f.*

nonage *s.* minorité *f.*

nonce, for the ~, pour la circonstance.

nonchalan/t *adj.* nonchalant; **~ce** *s.* nonchalance *f.*

nonconformist *adj.* & *s.m.f.* non-conformiste.

nondescript *adj.* quelconque.

none *pron.* aucun, personne; **~ of my friends,** aucun de mes amis; **I have ~,** je n'en ai pas; *adv.* **I like him ~ the better for it,** je ne l'en aime pas mieux; **I am ~ the wiser,** je n'en sais pas plus long.

nonentity *s.* nullité *f.*

nones *s.pl.* nones *f.pl.*

nonplus *v.t.* déconcerter; **~sed** *adj.* perplexe.

nonsens/e *s.* (*lacking sense or meaning*) non-sens

m.; (*absurdity*) absurdité *f.*; (*stupid act or words*) bêtise *f.*; **~ical** *adj.* absurde; **~ically** *adv.**.
non sequitur *s.* inconséquence *f.*
noodle *s.* (*cook.* & *fam.*) nouille *f.*
nook *s.* coin *m.*; INGLE **~**.
noon *s.* (& **~day, ~tide**) midi *m.*; *adj.* de midi.
noose *s.* nœud coulant *m.*; *v.t.* prendre au nœud coulant.
nor ni; **neither John ~ Peter,** ni Jean ni Pierre; **he neither eats ~ drinks,** il ne mange ni ne boit; non plus; **she doesn't like it, ~ do I,** elle ne l'aime pas (ni) moi non plus.
Nordic *adj.* nordique.
norm *s.* norme *f.*
normal *adj.* normal; *s.* normale *f.*; **~ity** *s.* normalité *f.*; **~ly** *adv.**.
Norman/dy *s.* Normandie *f.*; **~** *adj.* & *s.m.f.* normand(e); (*arch.*) roman; **~ Conquest,** conquête de l'Angleterre *f.* (par les Normands).
Norse *s.* (*lang.*) nor(r)ois *m.*
north *s.* nord *m.*; *adj.* du nord, septentrional; *adv.* au nord; **~-east** *s.* nord-est *m.*; **~-west** *s.* nord--ouest *m.*; **N~ Pole** *s.* pôle nord *m.*; **~erly** *adj.* du nord; **~ern** *adj.* du nord, septentrional; **~ern lights** *s.pl.* aurore boréale *f.*; **~ward** *adj.* au nord.
Norw/ay *s.* (*geog.*) Norvège *f.*; **~egian** *adj.* & *s.m.f.* norvégien(ne) *m.f.*; (*lang.*) norvégien *m.*
nor'-wester *s.* norois *m.*
nose *s.* (*anat., sense of smell, prow, front end of car, etc.*) nez *m.*; (*of some animals*) museau *m.*; (*of pipe*) bec *m.*; (*projecting part*) bout *m.*; **to blow one's ~,** se moucher; **to cut off one's ~ to spite one's face,** bouder contre son ventre; **to lead s.o. by the ~,** mener qn. par le bout du nez; **to put s.o.'s ~ out of** JOINT; **to turn up one's ~ at,** faire la nique à; **to** PAY **through the ~**; **~bag** *s.* musette-mangeoire *f.*; **~dive** *s.* piqué *m.*, *v.i.* descendre en piqué; **~gay** *s.* bouquet *m.*; **~(e)y** *adj.* (*fam.*) fureteur; *v.t.* **~ out,** flairer; *v.i.* **~ into** (*of ship, etc.*) manœuvrer.
nostalg/ia *s.* nostalgie *f.*; **~ic** *adj.* nostalgique.
nostril *s.* narine *f.*; (*of animal*) naseau *m.*
nostrum *s.* panacée *f.*
not *adv.* (*negative verbs*) ne . . . pas, ne . . . point; **I do ~ know,** je ne sais pas, je ne sais point; (*with infinitive*) **I asked him ~ to come,** je l'ai prié de ne pas venir; (*with participle*) **~ knowing, I can't say,** ne sachant pas, je ne peux le dire; (*elliptically*) pas; **~ at all,** pas du tout; **~ so,** pas vrai; **why ~?,** pourquoi pas?; **~ I,** pas moi; **you will do it, whether you like it or ~,** vous le ferez, que vous le vouliez ou pas, *or,* ou non; non pas, **he is your son and ~ mine,** il est votre fils, et non pas le mien; **~ only,** non seulement; **~ half!** (*pop.*) et comment; **~withstanding,** néanmoins.
notab/le *adj.* & *s.m.* notable; **~ility** *s.* notabilité *f.*; **~ly** *adv.**.
notary *s.* notaire *m.*
notation *s.* notation *f.*
notch *s.* **1.** (*made with knife, etc.*) entaille *f.*; **2.** (*made by accident*) brèche *f.*; *v.t.* (1) entailler; (2) ébrécher; **~ up** *v.t.* cocher.
note *s.* (*mus., brief record, comment*) note *f.*; GRACE **~**; (*sign*) signe *m.*; (*short letter, money*) billet *m.*; (*eminence*) marque *f.*; **~book** *s.* carnet *m.*; **~case** *s.* portefeuille *f.*; **~**PAPER; **~worthy** *adj.* remarquable; *v.t.* (*observe*) remarquer; (*notice, write down*) noter; **~d** *adj.* distingué.
nothing *s.* rien *m.*; **~ new, etc.,** rien de nouveau, etc.; **~ happened,** rien n'est arrivé; **I saw ~,** je n'ai rien vu; **to come to ~,** aboutir à rien; **to think ~ of doing sth.,** considérer comme naturel de faire qch.; **~ness** *s.* néant *m.*, (*unimportance*) insignifiance *f.*
notice *s.* (*warning*) avis *m.*; **advance ~,** préavis *m.*; (*announcement*) avertissement *m.*; (*attention*) attention *f.*; (*review*) notice *f.*; (*dismissal*) congé *m.*; **at short ~,** à bref delai; **to give ~ of,** avertir de; **to give ~ to** (*employee*) donner son congé à, (*employer*) donner sa démission à; **to take no ~ of,** ne pas faire attention à; **~**-BOARD; *v.t.* (*perceive, take ~ of*) remarquer; (*remark upon*) faire remarquer; **~able** *adj.* (*noteworthy*) remarquable, (*able to be ~d*) perceptible; **~ably** *adv.**,*.
notif/y *v.t.* avertir (qn. de qch.); annoncer (qch. à qn.); faire part (à qn. de qch.); (*law*) notifier; **~iable** *adj.* (*disease*) à déclarer obligatoirement; **~ication** *s.* notification *f.*
notion *s.* (*concept*) notion *f.*; (*idea*) idée *f.*; (*view, opinion*) sentiment *m.*, opinion *f.*; (*intention*) intention *f.*; **~al** *adj.* imaginaire; (*philos.*) spéculatif.
notori/ety *s.* notoriété *f.*; **~ous** *adj.* notoire; **~ously** *adv.**.
nougat *s.* nougat *m.*
nought *s.* zéro *m.*
noun *s.* nom *m.*
nourish *v.t.* (*lit.* & *fig.*) nourrir; **~ing** *adj.* nourrissant; **~ment** *s.* nourriture *f.*
nous *s.* esprit *m.*
novel[1] *s.* roman *m.*; **~ette** *s.* nouvelle *f.*; **~ist** *s.* romancier *m.*; ⚠ nouvelle = **short story.**
novel[2] *adj.* nouveau; **~ty** *s.* nouveauté *f.*
November *s.* novembre *m.*
novic/e *s.* novice *m.f.* **~iate** *s.* (*eccles. period* & *house*) noviciat *m.*; (*gen.*) apprentissage *m.*
now *adv.* maintenant; (*without temporal force*) donc; **~ hot, ~ cold,** tantôt chaud, tantôt froid; **~ and then (again),** de temps en temps; **~ then!,** allons!; **as of ~,** pour l'instant; **for ~,** jusqu'à nouvel ordre; **~adays** *adv.* de nos jours.
nowhere *adv.* nulle part.
noxious *adj.* nuisible.
nozzle *s.* bec *m.*; (*for water*) lance *f.*
N.S.P.C.C. (*National Society for the Prevention of Cruelty to Children*) Société pour la protection de l'enfance *f.* (*approx.*)
nuance *s.* nuance *f.*
nub *s.* noyau *m.*
nubile *adj.* nubile.
nuclear *adj.* nucléaire.
nucleus *s.* noyau *m.*
nud/e *s.* (*art*) nu *m.*; *adj.* nu; **~ist** *adj.* & *s.m.f.* nudiste; **~ity** *s.* nudité *f.*
nudge *s.* coup de coude *m.*; *v.t.* pousser du coude.
nugatory *adj.* (*futile*) futile; (*inoperative*) inefficace.
nugget *s.* pépite *f.*
nuisance *s.* (*thing*) ennui *m.*; (*law*) dommage *m.*; (*person*) peste *f.*; **what a ~!,** quel ennui!
N.U.J. (*National Union of Journalists*) (*approx.*) FNPF (Fédération nationale de la Presse française) *f. or* Fédération française des Travailleurs du livre *f.*
null *adj.* nul; **~ and void,** nul et non avenu; **~ify** *v.t.* annuler; **~ity** *s.* nullité *f.*
N.U.M. (*National Union of Miners*) Fédération nationale des Syndicats des Mineurs *f.* (*approx.*)
numb *adj.* engourdi; **to grow ~,** s'engourdir; **~ness** *s.* engourdissement *m.*; *v.t.* engourdir.
number *s.* (*quantity, math., ling.*) nombre *m.*; (*of house, ticket, telephone, auto. etc.*) numéro *m.*; (*of periodical, etc.*) numéro *m.*; (*item*) article *m.*; **~ one** (*pop.*) (= *me*) bibi, **he looks after ~ one,** il soigne sa petite personne; **~-plate** *s.* (*auto.*) plaque d'immatriculation *f.*; **~less** *adj.* innombrable; *v.t.* (*count*) compter; (*mark with ~*) numéroter; (*include with*) comprendre; **~ed** *adj.* compté, numéroté.
numer/al *s.* chiffre *m.*; *adj.* numéral; **~ation** *s.*

numération *f.*; **~ical** *adj.* numérique; **~ically** *adv.**; **~ous** *adj.* nombreux.
numismat/ic *adj.* numismatique; **~ics** *s.* numismatique *f.* ⚠ *sing. in French*; **~ist** *s.* numismate *m.f.*
num(b)skull *s.* benêt *m.*
nun *s.* religieuse *f.*; **~nery** *s.* couvent *m.*
nuncio *s.* nonce *m.*
N.U.P.E. (*National Union of Public Employees*) Fédération nationale des Syndicats des employés de la fonction publique *f.* (*approx.*).
nuptial *adj.* nuptial; **~s** *s.pl.* noces *f.pl.*
N.U.R. (*National Union of Railwaymen*) Fédération nationale des Syndicats des Cheminots *f.* (*approx.*).
nurse *s.* (*wet-~*) nourrice *f.*; (*for child* & *~maid*) bonne d'enfants *f.*; (*for sick*) infirmière *f.*, **male ~**, infirmier *m.*; *v.t.* & *i.* (*suckle*) allaiter; (*care for*) soigner; (*cherish*) nourrir; (*be sick-~*) être infirmière; **nursing** *s.* soins *m.pl.*; (*profession*) métier d'infirmière *m.*; **Nursing home** *s.* clinique *f.*; **~ling** *s.* nourrisson *m.*
nursery *s.* (*room*) chambre d'enfants *f.*; **day ~**, crèche *f.*; (*hort.*) pépinière *f.*; **~man** *s.* pépiniériste *m.*; **~ rhyme** *s.* chanson enfantine *f.*; **~ school** *s.* école maternelle *f.*; **~ slopes** (*for skiers*) pente (*f.*) pour débutants.
nurture *s.* nourriture *f.*; *v.t.* (*lit.* & *fig.*) nourrir.
N.U.S. (*National Union of Students*) Union nationale des étudiants d'Angleterre *f.*; (*approx. French equivalent*) FNEF (Fédération nationale des Etudiants de France) *f.*
nut *s.* **1.** (*edible*) noix *f.*, (*hazel-~*) noisette *f.*, MONKEY~, PEA~; **2.** (*mech.*) écrou *m.*; **3.** (*pop.* = *head*) ciboulot *m.*; **4.** (*pop.* = *idiot*) toqué *m.*; **~s** (*coal*) têtes-de-moineau *m.pl.*; **~crackers** *s.* casse-noisettes *m.*; **~meg** *s.* noix de muscade *f.*; **~shell** *s.* coquille de noix *f.*, **in a ~shell** (*fig.*) en un mot; **~ty** *adj.* abondant en noix; ayant un goût de noix; (*pop.*) entiché (*about*—de); *v.i.* (1) cueillir des noix.
N.U.T. (*National Union of Teachers*) FEN (Fédération de l'Education nationale) *f.*, *or* USNEF (Union Syndicale Nationale des Enseignants de France) *f.* (*approx.*)
nutri/ment *s.* aliments *m.pl.*; **~ent** *adj.* nutritif; *s.* aliment *m.*; **~tion** *s.* nutrition *f.*; **~tious** *adj.* & **~tive** *adj.* nutritif.
nuzzle *v.i.* (*pig*) fouiner; (*dog*) flairer; (*fam. person*) se blottir (contre).
nylon *s.* (*text.*) nylon *m.*; **~s** *s.pl.* bas de nylon *m.pl.*
nymph *s.* nymphe *f.*; **~omania** *s.* nymphomanie *f.*; **~omaniac** *adj.* & *s.f.* nymphomane.

O

O *interj.* (*invocation*) ô.
oaf *s.* lourdaud *m.*; **~ish** *adj.* rustre.
oak *s.* chêne *m.*; CORK-~; *adj.* & **~en,** de chêne, en chêne; **~-apple** *s.* galle de chêne *f.*
oakum *s.* étoupe *f.*
O.A.P. (*old-age pensioner*) *s.* personne du troisième âge *f.*
oar *s.* rame *f.*; (*naut. sport*) aviron *m.*; **to put one's ~ in** (*fig.*) intervenir; **~sman** *s.* rameur *m.*; *v.i.* ramer.
oasis *s.* (*lit.* & *fig.*) oasis *f.*
oast *s.* séchoir (à houblon) *m.*; **~-house** *s.* sécherie (pour le houblon) *f.*
oat(s) *s.* avoine *f.*; **wild ~s,** folle avoine *f.*; **to sow one's wild ~s** (*fig.*) jeter sa gourme; **~cake** *s.* galette d'avoine *f.*; **~meal** *s.* farine d'avoine *f.*
oath *s.* (*sworn promise*) serment *m.*; **to take the ~,** prêter serment; **on ~** (*evidence*) sous serment, (*witness*) assermenté; (*curse*) juron *m.*
O.A.U. (*Organization of African Unity*) O.U.A. *f.* (Organisation de l'Unité Africaine).
obbligato *s.* (*mus.*) accompagnement à volonté *m.*
obdura/cy *s.* **1.** (*stubbornness*) entêtement *m.*; **2.** (*hardness*) endurcissement *m.*; **~te** *adj.* (1) entêté; (2) endurci; **~tely** *adv.* obstinément.
obedien/ce *s.* (*obeying*) obéissance *f.* (*to*—à); (*sphere of authority*) autorité *f.*; **~t** *adj.* obéissant (*to*—à); **your ~t servant** (*archaic*) votre obéissant serviteur, (*mod.*) toujours à vos ordres; **~tly** *adv.* avec obéissance.
obeisance *s.* (*gesture*) salut *m.*; (*homage*) hommage *m.*; ⚠ obéissance = **obedience.**
obelisk *s.* (*stone shaft*) obélisque *m.*; (*sign*) obèle *m.*
obes/e *adj.* obèse; **~ity** *s.* obésité *f.*
obey *v.t.* & *i.* obéir (à qn., à qch.).
obi *s.* obi *f.*
obituary *s.* (*record of deaths*) nécrologe *m.*; (*brief biography*) nécrologie *f.*; *adj.* (*concerning death*) mortuaire; (*notice*) nécrologique; **~ column, ~ notice,** nécrologie *f.*
object[1] *s.* (*material thing*; *ling.*) objet *m.*; (*purpose*) but *m.*, fin *f.*; (*of attention, etc.*) objet *m.*, sujet *m.*; **expense no ~,** les frais importent peu, on ne regarde pas à la dépense; **~-lesson** *s.* démonstration *f.*; **~ive** *s.* (*ling.*) régime *m.*; (*aim*) objectif *m.*; **~ive** *adj.* objectif; **~ively** *adv.**; **~ivity** *s.* objectivité *f.*
object[2] *v.t.* (*state reason against*) formuler une objection à; (*state opposition to*) s'opposer **à;** **~ion** *s.* objection *f.*; (*disapproval, dislike*) opposition *f.*; **to have no ~ion to,** ne pas s'opposer à, ne pas voir d'inconvénient à; **~ionable** *adj.* désagréable; **~or** *s.* objecteur *m.*
oblation *s.* (*eccles.* & *gen.*) oblation *f.*
oblig/e *v.t.* & *i.* **1.** (*compel, constrain*) obliger, contraindre (à); **2.** (*confer favour on*) rendre service à; **3.** (*do sth. as favour*) avoir l'obligeance de faire qch.; **~ate** *v.t.* soumettre à une obligation; **~ation** *s.* (1) obligation *f.*; (*indebtedness*) obligations *f.pl.*; **to be under an ~ation to s.o.,** rester l'obligé de qn.; **~atory** *adj.* obligatoire; **~ing** *adj.* obligeant, serviable; **~ingly** *adv.* avec obligeance; **~ingness** *s.* obligeance *f.*
oblique *adj.* (*slanting, angle*) oblique; (*indirect*) indirect; **~ly** *adv.**;*.
obliterat/e *v.t.* effacer; ⚠ *of stamps only*, oblitérer; **~ion** *s.* rature *f.*; (*stamps*) oblitération *f.*
oblivi/on *s.* oubli *m.*; **~ous** *adj.* (*forgetful*) oublieux (*to or of*—de); (*unaware*) ignorant (*of*—de).
oblong *s.* rectangle *m.*; *adj.* oblong(ue).
obloquy *s.* critique malveillante *f.*
obnoxious *adj.* odieux; **~ to,** détesté par; **~ness** nature odieuse *f.*
oboe *s.* hautbois *m.*; **tenor ~,** cor anglais *m.*; **~-player, oboist** *s.* hautboïste *m.f.*
obscen/e *adj.* (*indecent*) obscène; (*repulsive*) répugnant; **~ely** *adv.* de façon obscène; **~ity** *s.* obscénité *f.*
obscur/e *adj.* obscur; (*not clear*) peu clair; **~antism** *s.* obscurantisme *m.*; **~ely** *adv.* obscurément; **~ity** *s.* obscurité *f.*; *v.t.* obscurcir.

obsequies *s.pl.* obsèques *f.pl.*
obsequious *adj.* obséquieux; **~ly** *adv.**; **~ness** *s.* obséquiosité *f.*
observ/e *v.t.* (*adhere to, comply with, notice, watch*) observer; *v.t.* & *i.* (*comment*) dire; **~able** *adj.* (*visible*) visible; (*noticeable*) remarquable; **~ably** *adv.**;*; **~ance** *s.* (*keeping of law, etc.*) observance *f.*; (*ceremonial act*) rite *m.*; **~ant** *adj.* observat/eur, -rice; **~ation** *s.* observation *f.*; **~atory** *s.* observatoire *m.*; **~er** *s.* observateur *m.*
obsess *v.t.* obséder (*with*—par); **be ~ed by,** vivre dans l'obsession de; **~ion** *s.* obsession *f.*; **~ional** *adj.* obsessional; **~ive** *adj.* d'obsession.
obsidian *s.* obsidienne *f.*
obsole/te *adj.* vieux; (*ticket, etc.*) périmé; (*techn.*) hors d'usage; **to become ~te,** tomber en désuétude; **~scent** *adj.* vieilli; **~scence** *s.* vieillissement *m.*
obstacle *s.* obstacle *m.*
obstetr/ics *s.* obstétrique *f.* ⚠ *sing. in French*; **~ic(al)** *adj.* obstétrical; **~ician** *s.* chirurgien obstétrique *m.*
obstina/cy *s.* obstination *f.*; entêtement *m.*; **~te** *adj.* obstiné, têtu; **~tely** *adv.* obstinément.
obstreperous *adj.* tapageur; (*noisy*) bruyant; **~ly** *adv.* tapageusement; bruyamment; **~ness** *s.* tapage *m.*, turbulence *f.*
obstruct *v.t.* (*block up*) obstruer; (*make impassable*) boucher; (*prevent progress of*) entraver, gêner; **~ion** *s.* (*act*) obstruction *f.*; (*obstacle*) obstacle *m.*, entrave *f.*; **~ionist** *s.* obstructionniste *m.f.*; **~ive** *adj.* qui cause une obstruction.
obtain *v.t.* (*acquire*) obtenir; (*get*) se procurer; (*receive*) recevoir; *v.i.* (*be established*) régner; (*hold good*) être en vigueur; **~able** *adj.* trouvable.
obtru/de *v.t.* mettre en avant; *v.i.* s'imposer (*on*—à); importuner; **~sion** *s.* importunité *f.*; **~sive** *adj.* importun; **~sively** *adv.* avec importunité.
obtuse *adj.* (*blunt*) émoussé; (*angle*) obtus; (*of mind*) à l'esprit obtus; **~ly** *adv.* stupidement.
obverse *s.* (*of coin*) avers *m.*; (*of statement*) envers *m.*
obviate *v.t.* obvier à; (*prevent*) prévenir.
obvious *adj.* évident; **~ly** *adv.* évidemment; **~ness** *s.* évidence *f.*
occasion *s.* (*opportunity*) occasion *f.*; (*reason*) raison *f.*, motif *m.*; (*special event*) circonstance *f.*; **you have no ~ to complain,** vous n'avez pas lieu de vous plaindre; *v.t.* occasionner; **~al** *adj.* (≠ *regular*) occasionnel, (*incidental*) fortuit, (*intended for special ~*) de circonstance; **~al table** *s.* petite table (basse) *f.*; **~ally** *adv.* de temps en temps.
Occident *s.* occident *m.*; **~al** *adj.* occidental.
occlu/de *v.t.* (*close, obstruct*) fermer, obstruer; (*chem.*) occlure; **~ded front** (*meteor.*) occlusion *f.*, front occlus *m.*; **~sion** *s.* (*of teeth*) emboîtement *m.*
occult *adj.* occulte; **~ism** *s.* occultisme *m.*
occup/y *v.t.* (*mil.*; *take up space or time*; *keep busy*) occuper; (*hold office*) tenir; (*reside in*) habiter; **~ oneself with,** s'occuper (de qch., à faire qch.); **~ancy** *s.* occupation *f.*; **~ant** *s.* (*of office*) titulaire *m.*, (*resident*) occupant *m.*; **~ation** *s.* occupation *f.*, (*trade, calling*) métier *m.*, profession *f.*; **~ational** *adj.* de métier, professionnel; **~ational therapy** (*for the disabled*) thérapie ré-éducative *f.*, (*psychiatric*) traitement par l'occupation *m.*; **~ier** *s.* locataire *m.*
occur *v.i.* (*happen*) arriver, avoir lieu; (*be found*) se trouver; (*come to mind*) venir à l'esprit; **it ~red to me that/to,** l'idée me vint que/de; **~rence** *s.* événement *m.*, incident *m.*; ⚠ occurrence = **circumstance;** *exc.* **in the ~rence,** en l'occurrence.
ocean *s.* (*lit.* & *fig.*) océan *m.*; **~-going** *adj.* (*naut.*) long-courrier; **O~ia** *s.* (*geog.*) Océanie *f.*; **~ic** *adj.* océanique; **~ographer** *s.* océanographe *m.f.*; **~ography** *s.* océanographie *f.*
ochre *s.* ocre *f.*
o'clock *s.* heure *f.*; **five ~,** cinq heures *f.pl.*
octagon *s.* octogone *m.*; **~al** *adj.* octogonal.
octane *s.* octane *m.*; **high ~ fuel** *s.* supercarburant *m.*; **~ number,** indice d'octane *m.*
octave *s.* (*eccles., mus.*) octave *f.*
octavo *s.* in-octavo *m.*
octet *s.* (*mus.*) octuor *m.*
October *s.* octobre *m.*
octogenarian *adj.* & *s.m.f.* octogénaire.
octopus *s.* pieuvre *f.*
ocul/ar *adj.* oculaire; **~ist** *s.* oculiste *m.*
odalisque *s.* odalisque *f.*
odd *adj.* (≠ *even*) impair; (*additional*) de surplus; (*casual*) singulier; (*strange*) bizarre; (*unmatched*) dépareillé; (*unmatched, of pair*) déparié; **£60 ~,** soixante et quelques livres; **~ jobs,** bricolage *m.*; **~ job man,** bricoleur *m.*; **to be the ~ man out,** faire cavalier seul; **~ity** *s.* (*strangeness*) bizarrerie *f.*; (*peculiar trait*) trait singulier *m.*, (*person*) original(e) *m.f.*; **~ly** *adv.* bizarrement; **~ments** *s.* bribes *f.pl.*, (*comm.*) fins de série *f.pl.*; **~ness** *s.* bizarrerie *f.*, singularité *f.*
odds *s.* (*inequalities*) inégalité *f.*; (*difference*) différence *f.*; (*betting*) pari *m.*; (*of horse*) cote *f.* (d'un cheval); **the ~ are that,** on peut parier que; **to be at ~ with s.o.,** (*fam.*) être en bisbille avec qn.; **to make no ~,** importer peu; (*chances in favour of*) chances *f.pl.*; **~ and** ENDS.
ode *s.* ode *f.*
odi/ous *adj.* odieux; **~ously** *adv.**; **~um** *s.* odieux *m.*
odor/iferous *adj.* odoriférant; **~ous** *adj.* (*good or bad*) odorant; (*sweet-smelling*) parfumé.
odour *s.* (*pleasant*) parfum *m.*; (*unpleasant*) odeur *f.*; **~less** *adj.* inodore.
Odyssey *s.* odyssée *f.*
O.E.C.D. (*Organization for Economic Co-operation and Development*) O.C.D.E. *f.* (Organisation de Coopération et Développement économique).
oecumenic(al) *adj.* œcuménique.
Oedipus *s.* Œdipe *m.*; **~ complex,** complexe d'Œdipe *m.*
O.E.E.C. (*Organization for European Economic Co-operation*) O.E.C.E. *f.* (Organisation européene de Coopération économique).
oesophagus *s.* œsophage *m.*
of *prep.* **1.** (*possession*) de; **the door ~ the house,** la porte de la maison; **2.** (*cause, origin*) de; **to die ~ hunger,** mourir de faim; **~ necessity,** nécessairement; **3.** (*quality*) de; **hard ~ hearing,** dur d'oreille; **4.** (*quantity*) de; **enough ~,** assez de; **too much ~,** trop de; **a cup ~,** une tasse de; **a kilo ~,** un kilo de; **5.** (*time*) de; **a meeting ~ eight hours,** une séance de huit heures; **~ an evening,** un soir; **~ late,** récemment; **6.** (*material*) en; **~ gold,** en or; **~ wood,** en bois; **7.** (*acad.*) en; **a student ~ medicine,** un étudiant en médecine; **bachelor ~ arts,** licencié ès lettres; **8.** (*distance*) de; **within a mile ~ the town,** à environ un mille de la ville; **9.** (*about, concerning*) de, au sujet de; **to hear ~,** entendre parler de; **10.** (*out of*) parmi, entre; **11.** (*agency*) de; **loved ~ all,** aimé de tous; **12.** *see also certain adjs.*; CAPABLE **~, etc.; 13.** *see also certain verbs*, **to** DREAM **~,** *etc.*
off *adv.* (*at a distance*) au loin; **3 km. ~,** à trois kilomètres de distance; (*out of position*) déplacé; (*loose*) détaché; (*discontinued, stopped*) rompu, annulé; **on and ~,** de temps à autre; **straight ~,** tout de suite, incontinent, (*fam.*) illico; **well ~,** à l'aise; *see also certain verbs*, SHOW **~,** TAKE **~, etc.;** *prep.* de; *adj.* (≠ *near* (*side*)), (côté) extérieur; (*subordinate*) secondaire; **~-beat** (*mus.*) hors de cadence, (*pop.*) cocasse; **on the ~ chance** *adv.* à tout hasard; **~ colour** *adj.*

malade, souffrant; **~-day,** jour où l'on n'est pas en forme; **~hand** (*extempore*) impromptu, (*casual*) cavalier; **~handed,** sans façon; **~-key** (*mus.*) faux; **~-licence** *s.* vente pour consommation à domicile *f.*; **~-load** *v.t.* déposer; **~-peak period,** heures creuses *f.pl.*; **~print** *s.* tirage à part *m.*; **~-putting** (*fam.*) déconcertant; **~-season** *s.* morte-saison *f.*; **~set** *s.* compensation *f.*, (*print.*) offset *m.*; **~set** *v.t.* compenser; **~shoot** *s.* rejeton *m.*; **~shore** *adj.* marin, *adv.* en mer; **~side** (*sport*) hors-jeu; **~spring** *s.* progéniture *f.*; **~-time** *s.* temps libre *m.*; **~ white** *adj.* blanchâtre.

offal *s.* (*edible*) abats *m.pl.*; (*refuse*) déchets *m.pl.*

offen/ce *s.* **1.** (*misdemeanour*) tort *m.*; **2.** (*illegal act*) délit *m.*, contravention *f.*; **second ~ce,** récidive *f.*; **3.** (*aggressive action*) agression *f.*; **4.** (*resentment*) offense *f.*; **to take ~ce,** s'offenser; **5.** (*hurt to feelings*) blessure *f.*; **to give ~ce to,** froisser; **~d** *v.t.* & *i.* (2) commettre un délit; (*against a law*) enfreindre (un règlement); (5) blesser, offenser; **~der** *s.* (2) délinquant *m.*; (5) offenseur *m.*; **~sive** *s.* offensive *f.*; **~sive** *adj.* (3) agressif, brusque; (5) injurieux; **6.** (*disgusting*) désagréable; **~sively** *adv.* (3) brusquement; (5) de façon blessante; (6) désagréablement; **~siveness** *s.* (5) caractère blessant *m.*, caractère injurieux *m.*; (6) caractère déplaisant *m.*

offer *s.* offre *f.*; (*of marriage*) demande *f.* (en mariage); (*attempt*) tentative *f.*; *v.t.* offrir; **~ to do sth.,** offrir de faire qch.; (*tender*) présenter; (*excuses*) faire (des excuses); **~ing** *s.* offre *f.*; (*eccles.* & *gift*) offrande *f.*; **~tory** *s.* (*collection*) quête *f.*; (*part of mass*) offertoire *m.*

offic/e *s.* (*duty*) devoir *m.*; (*task*) charge *f.*; (*function, official position*) fonction *f.*; (*eccles.*) office *m.*; (*place of bisiness*) bureau *m.*, **head ~e,** siège social *m.*; TICKET-**~e;** (*department*) bureau *m.*, service *m.*; (*government*) ministère *m.*; **~er** *s.* (*mil., naut.*) officier *m.*; (*eccles.*) dignitaire *m.*; (*public servant*) fonctionnaire *m.*; (*police*) agent *m.*; **~ial** *s.* fonctionnaire *m.*; **~ial** *adj.* officiel; **~ialdom** *s.* bureaucratie *f.*; **~ialese** *s.* jargon administratif *m.*; **~ially** *adv.**; **~iate** *v.i.* (*eccles.*) officier, (*admin.*) remplir les fonctions de, présider à; **~ious** *adj.* trop empressé, trop zélé; ⚠ officieux = **unofficial; ~iously** *adv.* avec trop de zèle; **~iousness** *s.* excès de zèle *m.*

offing *s.* **in the ~,** en perspective.

oft(en) *adv.* souvent; **every so ~en,** de temps en temps.

ogee *s.* cimaise *f.*

ogive *s.* ogive *f.*

ogle *v.t.* lorgner; *v.i.* lancer des œillades.

ogre(ss) *s.* ogre *m.*; ogresse *f.*

oh! *interj.* (*expressing surprise, admiration, entreaty, etc.*) oh!

ohm *s.* ohm *m.*

O.H.M.S. (*abbrev. for On Her/His Majesty's Service*) Service de la Reine/du Roi.

oil *s.* (*gen., cook., eccles., med.*) huile *f.*; CASTOR **~**; COD-**liver ~**; (*crude*) pétrole *m.*; **fuel ~,** fuel-oil *m.*; (*heating*) mazout *m.*; **~s** (*art*) peinture à l'huile *f.*; **to** STRIKE **~**; **~cake** *s.* (*agric.*) tourteau *m.*; **~can** *s.* burette *f.*; **~cloth** *s.* (*for table*) toile cirée *f.*, (*for floor*) linoléum *m.*; **~ drum** *s.* bidon *m.*; **~field** *s.* gisement pétrolifère *m.*; **~-fired** *adj.* chauffé au mazout; **~skin(s)** *s.* ciré *m.*; **~-slick** *s.* marée noire *f.*; **~stove** *s.* réchaud à pétrole *m.*; **~ sump** *s.* (*auto.*) carter d'huile *m.*; **~-tanker** *s.* pétrolier *m.*; **~-well** *s.* puits à pétrole *m.*; **~iness** *s.* aspect huileux *m.*, (*fam. fig.*) onctuosité *f.*; **~y** *adj.* huileux, (*fam. fig.*) onctueux; *v.t.* huiler.

ointment *s.* onguent *m.*, pommade *f.*

O.K. *s.* accord *m.*; *interj.* d'accord; *adj.* parfait; *adv.* très bien; *v.t.* approuver.

old *adj.* ($\neq$ *young*) vieux, âgé; (*worn out*) usé; (*dating from long ago, long established*) ancien (*after noun*); (*former*) ancien (*before noun*); **~ boy,** ancien élève; (*fam. affectionate*) brave (*before noun*); **~ Jim,** le (ce) brave Jim; (*fam. contemptuous*) vieux; **~ chap, ~ fellow, ~ thing, etc.,** mon vieux; **how ~ are you?,** quel âge avez-vous?; **I am ten years ~,** j'ai dix ans; **to grow ~,** vieillir; **to be an ~ hand at sth.,** se connaître à qch.; **~ age** *s.* vieillesse *f.*; **~-age pension,** pension de retraite *or* de vieillesse *f.*; **~** CLOTHES; **~-fashioned** *adj.* démodé; **~ hat** *adj.* (*fam.*) vieillot; **~ man** vieillard *m.*, (*fam.* = *boss*) patron *m.*; **~-time, ~-world** *adj.* d'autrefois; **~ woman** *s.* vieille *f.*; **of ~,** autrefois; **~en** *adj.* vieux, d'autrefois.

oleaginous *adj.* oléagineux.

oleander *s.* laurier-rose *m.*

olfactory *adj.* olfactif.

oligarch/y *s.* oligarchie *f.*; **~ic(al)** *adj.* oligarchique.

olive *s.* (*fruit*) olive *f.*; (*tree*) olivier *m.*; (*colour*) olive *m.invar.*; *adj.* olivâtre; **beef ~** (*cook.*) paupiette *f.*; **~-branch** *s.* (*eccles.*) rameau d'olivier *m.*, (*fig.*) branche d'olivier *f.*; **~-green,** vert olive (*invar.*); **~ oil** *s.* huile d'olive *f.*

Olymp/ia *s.* Olympie *f.*; **~us** (*mount*) Olympe *m.*; **~iad** *s.* olympiade *f.*; **~ian** *adj.* & *s.m.f.* olympien(ne); **~ic** *adj.* olympique; **~ic games,** jeux olympiques *m.pl.*

ombudsman *s.* médiateur *m.*

omega *s.* oméga *m.*

omelet(te) *s.* omelette *f.*

om/en *s.* présage *m.*; **~inous** *adj.* de mauvaise augure; **~inously** *adv.* de manière inquiétante.

omission *s.* omission *f.*

omit *v.t.* omettre; **~ to do sth.,** omettre, oublier, de faire qch.

omnibus *s.* autobus *m.*; (*book*) édition intégrale *f.*; *adj.* (*serving several purposes*) polyvalent; (*comprising several items*) global.

omni- (*in combination*) **~potence** *s.* omnipotence *f.*, toute-puissance *f.*; **~potent** *adj.* omnipotent, tout-puissant; **~present** *adj.* omniprésent; **~science** *s.* omniscience *f.*; **~scient** *adj.* omniscient; **~vorous** *adj.* omnivore.

on[1] *prep.* **1.** (*gen.*) sur; **~ to** (*movement*) sur; **2.** (=*off, out of*) de; **to live ~ bread,** vivre de pain; **3.** (*movement*) en; **~ the way,** en route; **~ one's travels,** en voyage; **4.** (*mus. instrument*) de; **to play ~ the piano,** jouer du piano; **to play sth. ~ the piano,** jouer qch. au piano; **5.** (*time*) *no prep. with days,* **~ Monday,** lundi; **~ Mondays,** le lundi; **~ the next day,** le lendemain; **~ a fine summer's day,** par un beau jour d'été; **~ his arrival, his departure, his death,** *etc.*, à son arrivée, à son départ, à sa mort, etc.; **6.** (*place*) **~ the right, ~ the left,** à droite, à gauche; **7.** *see certain verbs,* DEPEND **~, have** PITY **~,** *etc.*; **~ approval,** à l'essai, à condition; **~ business,** pour affaires; **~ foot,** à pied; **~ horseback,** à cheval; **~ holiday,** en vacances; **~ pain of,** sous peine de; **~ sale,** en vente; **~ strike,** en grève; **~ trust,** sur parole.

on[2] *adv.* en avant; **later ~,** plus tard; **~ and ~,** sans cesse; **and so ~,** et ainsi de suite; *see also certain verbs,* **to** GO **~, etc.; ~coming** *adj.* approchant, (*fig.*) imminent, (*traffic*) en sens inverse; **~looker** *s.* spectat/eur, -rice *m.f.*; **~set** *s.* (*med., mil.*) attaque *f.*, (*fig.*) abord *m.*; **at the ~set,** de prime abord; **~shore** *adj.* (*wind*) du large; **~slaught** *s.* (*med., mil., fig.*) attaque *f.*; **~ward** *adj.* progressif; **~wards** *adv.* en avant.

once *adv.* (*on one occasion*) une fois; (*formerly*) autrefois; **at ~,** (*immediately*) tout de suite, (*simultaneously*) à la fois; **all at ~,** tout à coup;

~ and for all, une fois pour toutes; **for this ~,** pour cette fois; **~ in a while,** de temps en temps; **~ a year, a month, etc.,** une fois par an, par mois, etc.; **~ upon a time,** (il y avait) une fois; **to give sth. the ~-over,** jeter un coup d'œil sur qch.

one *s., pron.* un; **1.** (*people*) (*subject*) on; (*object*) vous; (*possessive* ~'*s*) son, sa, ses; **~ must obey ~'s parents,** on doit obéir à ses parents; **2.** (*things*) un(e); **the big ~,** le (la) grand(e); **the red ~s,** les rouges; **I have ~,** j'en ai un; **he has some good ~s,** il en a de bons; **3.** (*dem. pron. people* & *things*) celui, celle, ceux, celles; **the ~ you saw,** celui que vous avez vu; **the ~s you found,** ceux que vous avez trouvés; **this ~, that ~,** celui-ci, celle-ci; celui-là, celle-là; **it's all ~ to me,** ça m'est égal; **~self,** soi-même; (*refl.*) se; **by ~self,** tout seul; **beside ~self,** hors de soi; NUMBER ~; *adj.* (*number*) un(e); (*single*) un(e) seul(e), unique; (*identical*) identique; **~-armed** *adj.* manchot; **~-armed bandit,** machine à sous *f.*; **~-eyed** *adj.* borgne; **~-horse** (*fam. fig.*) minable; **~-man job,** travail pour un seul homme; **~-man band,** homme-orchestre; **~-sided,** *adj.* unilatéral; **~-track** (*mind*), (esprit) à idée fixe; **~-way** (*street*) (rue) à sens unique; **~ness** *s.* unité *f.*

onerous *adj.* (*fig.*) lourd; ⚠ onéreux = **expensive, costly.**

onion *s.* oignon *m.*

only *adj.* seul, unique; **~ son, daughter,** fils, fille, unique; *adv.* seulement, ne . . . que; **not ~ but also,** non seulement . . . mais aussi, mais encore; **you know ~ too well,** vous ne savez que trop bien; *conj.* mais.

onomatopoeia *s.* onomatopée *f.*

onus *s.* charge *f.*; **the ~ is on you** (*etc.*) *to*, c'est à vous (*etc.*) de.

onyx *s.* onyx *m.*

ooz/e *s.* vase *f.*; *v.i.* suinter; **~ing** *s.* suintement *m.*; **~y** *adj.* vaseux, suintant.

opacity *s.* opacité *f.*

opal *s.* opale *f.*; *adj.* opalin; **~escence** *s.* opalescence *f.*; **~escent** *adj.* opalescent.

opaque *adj.* opaque.

O.P.E.C. (*Organization of Petroleum Exporting Countries*) O.P.E.P. *f.* (Organisation des Pays exportateurs de pétrole).

open[1] *s.* **in the ~** (*air*) en plein air; *adj.* (≠ *closed, unlocked*) ouvert; (*unconfined*) libre; (*exposed*) exposé, découvert; (≠ *exclusive*) accessible (à tous); (*clear*) manifeste; (*spread out*) étendu; (*unfolded*) ouvert, déplié; (*frank*) franc; (*cheque*) non barré; **wide ~,** grand ouvert; **~ boat** *s.* bateau non-ponté *m.*; **~cast** (*mining*) à découvert; **~ day** *s.* journée 'porte ouverte' *f.*; **~-handed** *adj.* généreux; **~ letter** *s.* lettre ouverte *f.*; **~-minded** *adj.* à l'esprit ouvert; **~-mouthed** *adj.* bouche bée; **on the ~ sea,** au grand large; **~-and-shut** *adj.* (*fam.*) peu complexe; **O~ University** *s.* université des ondes *f.*; **~ verdict** *s.* jugement sans conclusion *m.*; **~-work** *s.* broderie à jour *f.*; **~ly** *adv.* ouvertement, manifestement; **~ness** *s.* aspect découvert *m.*, franchise *f.*, libéralité *f.*

open[2] *v.t.* ouvrir; (*bottle*) déboucher; (*declare* ~) inaugurer; (*begin*) commencer, entamer; (*session*) ouvrir; *v.i.* s'ouvrir; (*shop*) ouvrir; **~ on to,** donner sur; **~ out** *v.t.* & *i.* (s')étendre; **~ up** *v.t.* & *i.* (s')ouvrir; **~er** *s.* (*tin, can*) ouvre-boîte *m.*, (*bottle*) décapsuleur *m.*; **~ing** *s.* (*gap*) ouverture *f.*, (*beginning*) commencement *m.*, (*opportunity*) chance *f.*, occasion *f.*; **~ing** *adj.* de début, d'inauguration.

opera *s.* opéra *m.*; **~-glass(es)** *s.* jumelles *f.pl.*; **~-hat** *s.* gibus *m.*; **~-house** *s.* opéra *m.*; **~tic** *adj.* d'opéra; **operetta** *s.* opérette *f.*

oper/ate *v.t.* opérer; (*mech.*) faire fonctionner; **~ate on s.o.,** opérer qn.; *v.i.* (*be in action*) marcher, agir; (*work*) fonctionner; **~able** *adj.* (*med.*) opérable; **~ating-theatre** *s.* salle d'opération *f.*; **~ation** *s.* (*action, fin., med., mil.*) opération *f.*; **to come into ~ation,** entrer en vigueur; **~ational** *adj.* en état de marche; **~ative** *s.* ouvrier *m.*; **~ative** *adj.* opérant, (*med.*) opératoire, (*fig.*) en vigueur, (*practical*) pratique; **~ator** *s.* (*techn.*) opérat/eur, -rice *m.f.*, (*telephone*) standardiste *m.f.*

ophidian *s.* ophidien *m.*

ophthalm/ia *s.* ophtalmie *f.*; **~ic** *adj.* (*concerning eyes, cure, etc.*) ophtalmique; (*concerning ~ology, hospital, etc.*) ophtalmologique; **~ology** *s.* ophtalmologie *f.*

opiate *s.* médicament opiacé *m.*

opine *v.i.* être d'avis (que).

opinion *s.* (*belief, professional advice*) opinion *f.*; (*view*) avis *m.*; **in my ~,** à mon avis; **to be of the ~ that,** estimer que; **to form an ~,** se faire une opinion; ~ POLL; **~ated** *adj.* opiniâtre.

opium *s.* opium *m.*

opossum *s.* opossum *m.*

opponent *s.* adversaire *m.*

opportun/e *adj.* (*suitable, of time*) opportun; (*done at suitable time*) à propos; **~ely** *adv.* opportunément, à propos; **~ism** *s.* opportunisme *m.*; **~ist** *s.* opportuniste *m.f.*

opportunity *s.* occasion *f.* (*for*—de); **to take the ~ of,** saisir l'occasion de; ⚠ opportunité = **expediency.**

oppos/e *v.t.* (*place in opposition to*) opposer (à); (*set oneself against*) s'opposer à; **be ~ed to,** être opposé à; **~ed** *adj.* (*contrasted*) opposé (à), (*hostile*) hostile (à); **~ite** *s.* contraire *m.*, (*~ite thing or term*) contre-pied *m.*; **~ite** *adj.* (*contrary*) opposé, (*facing*) en face, vis-à-vis; **~ite number** *s.* homologue *m.*; **~ite (to)** *prep.* en face de; **~ite** *adv.* en face; **~ition** *s.* opposition *f.*

oppress *v.t.* (*treat harshly, unjustly*) opprimer; (*weigh down*) oppresser, accabler; **~ion** *s.* oppression *f.*; **~ive** *adj.* oppressif; (*heat, etc.*) accablant; **~or** *s.* oppresseur *m.*

opprobr/ium *s.* opprobre *m.*; **~ious** *adj.* (*abusive*) injurieux; (*disgraceful*) infamant.

opt *v.i.* opter (*for*—pour); **~ out of,** se retirer de.

optative *s.* (*ling.*) optatif *m.*; *adj.* optatif.

optic *adj.* optique; **~s** *s.* optique *f.* ⚠ *sing. in French*; **~al** *adj.* d'optique; **~ian** *s.* opticien *m.*

optim/ism *s.* optimisme *m.*; **~ist** *s.* optimiste *m.f.*; **~istic** *adj.* optimiste.

optimum *s.* optimum *m.*; *adj.* optimum (optima).

option *s.* (*choice*) option *f.*; (*right to choose*) latitude *f.*, liberté de choix *f.*; (*right to buy or sell*) option *f.*, faculté *f.*; (*alternative to fine*) substitution *f.*; **~al** *adj.* facultatif.

opulen/ce *s.* opulence *f.*; **~t** *adj.* (*rich*) opulent; (*abundant*) abondant.

opus *s.* (*mus.*) opus *m.*

or *conj.* ou; (*with negative*) ni; **he cannot read ~ write,** il ne sait ni lire ni écrire; **whether . . . ~,** ou . . . ou; soit que . . . soit que.

orac/le *s.* oracle *m.*; **~ular** *adj.* d'oracle.

oral *s.* (*exam*) épreuve orale *f.*; (≠ *written exam*) oral *m.*; *adj.* oral; **~ly** *adv.* oralement; (*med.*) par voie buccale.

orange *s.* orange *f.*; (*tree*) oranger *m.*; (*colour*) orange *m.*; *adj.* orange (*invar.*), orangé; **~-blossom** fleur d'oranger *f.*; **~ade** *s.* orangeade *f.*; **~ry** *s.* orangerie *f.*

orang-utan, outang *s.* orang-outan *m.*

orat/e *v.i.* faire une allocution; (*fam.*) laïusser; **~ion** *s.* allocution *f.*; **funeral ~ion,** oraison funèbre *f.*; **~or** *s.* orat/eur, -rice *m.f.*; **~orical** *adj.* oratoire; **~orically** *adv.* d'une façon oratoire; **~orio** *s.* oratorio *m.*; **~ory** *s.* (*chapel*) oratoire *m.*; (*rhetoric*) art oratoire *m.*

orb *s.* orbe *m.*; (*regalia*) globe *m.*

orbit *s.* orbite *f.*; **in ~,** en orbite, sur son orbite; *v.t.* & *i.* décrire une orbite (autour de).
orchard *s.* verger *m.*
orchestra *s.* orchestre *m.*; **~l** *adj.* orchestral; **~te** *v.t.* orchestrer.
orchid, orchis *s.* orchidée *f.*
ordain *v.t.* (*eccles.* & *destine*) ordonner; (*decree*) décréter.
ordeal *s.* épreuve *f.*
order *s.* **1.** (*group*; *eccles.*, *of chivalry*, *biol.*, *zool.*) ordre *m.*; (*social class*) rang *m.*; **2.** (*sequence*) ordre *m.*; **3.** (*method, tidiness, efficient state*) ordre *m.*; **law and ~,** ordre public *m.*; (*rules of procedure*) règlement *m.*; (*techn.*) **working ~,** état de marche *m.*; APPLE-**pie ~**; CALL **to ~**; **4.** (*command*) ordre *m.*; (*authoritative*) consigne *f.*; (*admin.*, *polit.*) arrêté *m.*; **~ in Council,** décret-loi *m.*; MONEY **~**; TALL **~**; **5.** (*comm.*) commande *f.*; **6.** (*divine service*) office *m.*; **7. holy ~s,** ordres *m.pl.*; **in ~,** (2), (3) en ordre; (*law*) en règle; **out of ~,** (2), (3) en désordre, (*techn.*) en panne, détraqué; **to keep, put, in ~,** tenir, mettre, en ordre; **~ of the day,** ordre du jour *m.*; **to ~** (5) sur commande; **to place an ~** (5) faire passer une commande; **~-book** *s.* livre de commandes *m.*; **~-form** *s.* bulletin de commande *m.*; **in ~ to** *conj.* pour + *inf.*; **in ~ that** *conj.* pour que + *subj.*; **~ly** *s.* (*mil.*) ordonnance *f.*, (*hospital*) infirmier *m.*; **~ly** *adj.* (2) en ordre; (3) méthodique, ordonné, rangé, (*person*) ordonné, (≠ *unruly*) discipliné; **~liness** *s.* (2) ordre *m.*; (3) esprit de méthode *m.*, (≠ *unruliness*) discipline *f.*; *v.t.* (2), (3) mettre en ordre, ranger; (4) ordonner (à qn. de faire qch:) **~ arms**! (*mil.*) reposez armes!; (5) commander.
ordinal *adj.* & *s.m.* ordinal.
ordinance *s.* (*command*) ordonnance *f.*; (*relig. rite*) rite *m.*
ordinar/y *s.* ordinaire *m.*; *adj.* (*normal*) ordinaire; (≠ *exceptional*) habituel; (*commonplace*) quelconque; **out of the ~y,** peu commun; **in ~y** (*by permanent appointment*) ordinaire, attitré; **~ily** *adv.**;*.
ordination *s.* (*of priests*) ordination *f.*
ordnance *s.* (*guns*) artillerie *f.*; (*department for stores, etc.*) service du matériel *m.*; **~ survey,** service cartographique *m.*
ore *s.* minerai *m.*
organ *s.* **1.** (*mus.*) orgue *m.*, orgues *f.pl.*; BARREL-**~**; **2.** (*anat.*) organe *m.*; **3.** (*fig. medium*) organe *m.*; **~-blower** *s.* souffleur d'orgue *m.*; **~-builder** *s.* facteur d'orgues *m.*; **~-grinder** *s.* joueur d'orgue de Barbarie *m.*; **~-loft** *s.* tribune *f.*; **~ic** *adj.* (2) organique; **~ically** *adv.**; **~ism** *s.* organisme *m.*; **~ist** *s.* (1) organiste *m.f.*; **~ize** *v.t.* organiser; **~ization** *s.* (*act* & *result*) organisation *f.*; (*body*) organisme *m.*, organisation *f.*; **~izer** *s.* organisat/eur, -rice *m.f.*
organdie *s.* (*text.*) organdi *m.*
orgasm *s.* (*med.*) orgasme *m.*; (*fig.*) point culminant *m.*
orgy *s.* orgie *f.*
oriel window *s.* fenêtre en encorbellement *f.*
orient *s.* (*the O~*) l'Orient *m.*; **~al** *adj.* & *s.m.f.* oriental(e); **~alist** *s.* orientaliste *m.f.*; *v.t.* & **~ate,** orienter; *v.refl.* s'orienter; **~ation** *s.* orientation *f.*
orifice *s.* orifice *m.*
oriflamme *s.* oriflamme *f.*
origin *s.* origine *f.*; **~al** *s.* (*archetype, person*) original *m.*; **~al** *adj.* (*innate, initial*) originel; (*first-hand, not derived*) original; (*creative*) créateur; **~ality** *s.* originalité *f.*; **~ally** *adv.* à l'origine; **~ate** *v.t.* créer; *v.i.* provenir (*from*—de); **~ation** *s.* création *f.*, naissance *f.*; **~ator** *s.* créat/eur, -rice *m.f.*
oriole *s.* loriot *m.*
orison *s.* oraison *f.*
Orkneys *s.* (*geog.*) Orcades *f.pl.*
ormolu *s.* or moulu *m.*, dorure *f.*
ornament *s.* ornement *m.*; **~al** *adj.* ornemental; *v.t.* orner (*with*—de); **~ation** *s.* ornementation *f.*
ornate *adj.* orné; (*style*) fleuri; **~ly** *adv.* richement; **~ness** *s.* enjolivement *m.*
ornitholog/y *s.* ornithologie *f.*; **~ical** *adj.* ornithologique; **~ist** *s.* ornithologue *m.f.*
orphan *s.* orphelin(e) *m.f.*; *v.t.* rendre orphelin; **~age** *s.* orphelinat *m.*
orthodox *adj.* orthodoxe; **~y** *s.* orthodoxie *f.*
orthography *s.* orthographe *f.*; ⚠ orthographie (*rare*) = **elevation of building.**
orthopaedic *adj.* orthopédique; **~s** *s.* orthopédie *f.* ⚠ *sing. in French.*
ortolan *s.* ortolan *m.*
Oscar *s.* (*cinema*) oscar *m.*
oscillat/e *v.i.* osciller; **~ion** *s.* oscillation *f.*
osier *s.* osier *m.*; **~-bed** *s.* oseraie *f.*
osprey *s.* orfraie *f.*; (*feathers*) aigrette *f.*
ossify *v.t.* & *i.* (s')ossifier.
ostensibl/e *adj.* soi-disant, prétendu (*before noun*); **~y** *adv.* en apparence.
ostentat/ion *s.* ostentation *f.*; **~ious** *adj.* plein d'ostentation; **~iously** *adv.* avec ostentation.
osteopath *s.* chiropracteur *m.*; **~ic** *adj.* de chiropraxie; **~y** *s.* chiropraxie *f.*
ostler *s.* valet d'écurie *m.*
ostrac/ism *s.* ostracisme *m.*; **~ize** *v.t.* frapper d'ostracisme.
ostrich *s.* autruche *f.*
other *adj.* autre; (*additional*) encore un(e); **the ~ day,** l'autre jour; **every ~ day,** tous les deux jours; *s.* & *pron.* autre, d'autres, les autres, (*after prep. persons only*) autrui; **I have ~s,** j'en ai d'autres; *adv.* & **~wise** *adv.* autrement; **~-worldly** *adj.* détaché du siècle.
otiose *adj.* oiseux.
otter *s.* loutre *f.*
Ottoman[1] *adj.* & *s.m.f.* ottoman(e).
ottoman[2] *s.* (*sofa*) ottomane *f.*
ouch! *interj.* aïe!
ought *v.aux.* devoir; **you ~ to do it,** vous devriez le faire; **you ~ to have done it,** vous auriez dû le faire.
ounce *s.* (*measure*) once *f.*; (*animal*) once *f.*
our *adj.* notre, nos.
ours *pron.* le, la, les, nôtre(s); **a friend of ~,** un de nos amis; **that is ~,** c'est à nous.
ourselves *pron.* (*emphatic*) nous-mêmes; (*reflexive*) nous.
oust *v.t.* (*law*; *dispossess*) évincer; (*eject*) expulser.
out *adv.* (≠ *at home*) sorti; (*outside*) dehors; (*of secret*) dévoilé; (*not burning*) éteint; (*finished*) terminé; (*on strike*) en grève; (*in bloom*) épanoui; **to hear s.o. ~,** entendre qn. jusqu'au bout; **~ with it!,** dites-le-donc!; **~ and ~,** achevé; DOWN **and ~**; ODD **man ~**; **all ~,** à toute vitesse; **to be ~ for,** être en quête de; *see also certain verbs*, BE **~**, FIND **~**, SPEAK **~**, TURN **~**, *etc.*; *prep.* **~ of,** (*place*) hors de; (= *without*) sans; (*cause*) par (curiosité, etc.); (*sight*) loin de; **take ~ of** (*drawer, etc.*) prendre dans; (*numbers*) sur, **nine times ~ of ten,** neuf fois sur dix; (*at the end of, patience, etc.*) à bout de (patience, etc.); **~ of** BREATH, DATE, DOORS, FASHION, JOINT, ORDER, PLACE, PRINT, **the** QUESTION, SORTS, STEP, TEMPER, **the** WAY; *s.* INS **and ~s.**
outback *s.* (*Australia*) intérieur du pays *m.*
outbid *v.t.* enchérir (sur qn.); *v.i.* surenchérir.
outboard *s.* (*motor*) hors-bord *m.*
outbreak *s.* (*of volcano*) éruption *f.*; (*of epidemic*) manifestation *f.*; (*of fire*) incendie, *m.*; (*of war*) déchaînement *m.*; (*of emotions*) accès *m.*; (*revolt*) révolte *f.*
outbuildings *s.pl.* dépendances *f.pl.*
outburst *s.* (*temper, etc.*) accès *m.*; (*laughter*) éclat *m.*

outcast *s.* banni *m.*
outclassed *adj.* surclassé.
outcome *s.* conséquence *f.*, résultat *m.*
outcrop *s.* (*geol.*) affleurement *m.*
outcry *s.* clameur *f.*
outdated *adj.* démodé.
outdistance *v.t.* distancer.
outdo *v.t.* surpasser (*in*—en).
outdoor *adj.* extérieur; (*games*) de plein air; (*clothes*) de ville; **~s** *adv.* au-dehors, en plein air.
outer *adj.* extérieur; **~most** *adj.* le plus extérieur, maximum.
outfall *s.* (*of river*) embouchure *f.*; (*of sewer*) déversoir *m.*
outfit *s.* (*mil.*) équipement *m.*; (*clothes*) trousseau *m.*; (*techn.*) nécessaire *m.*; **~ter** *s.* marchand de confection *m*.
outflank *v.t.* (*mil.*) déborder.
outgoing *adj.* sortant; (*polit.*) démissionnaire; **~s** *s.pl.* frais *m.pl.*
outgrow *v.t.* (*grow faster than*) dépasser en hauteur; (*get rid of with age*) perdre en grandissant; (*grow too big for, clothes, etc.*) devenir trop grand pour.
outhouse *s.* remise *f.*
outing *s.* sortie *f.*; (*trip*) excursion *f.*; (*walk, ride*) promenade *f.*
outlandish *adj.* bizarre.
outlast *v.t.* durer plus longtemps que; (*person*) survivre à.
outlaw *s.* proscrit *m.*; *v.t.* proscrire; **~ry** *s.* proscription *f.*
outlay *s.* dépense *f.*
outlet *s.* (*exit*) sortie *f.*; (*comm.*) débouché *m.*; (*for energy, etc.*) exutoire *m.*
outline *s.* **1.** (*contour*) contour *m.*; (*of person*) silhouette *f.*; **2.** (*rough draft*) esquisse *f.*; **3.** (*rough idea*) aperçu *m.*; *v.t.* (1) (se) profiler; (2) esquisser; (3) donner un aperçu de.
outlive *v.t.* survivre à.
outlook *s.* (*view, prospect*) perspective *f.*; (*view of life*) vue *f.*
outlying *adj.* écarté.
outmanœuvre *v.t.* déjouer.
outmoded *adj.* démodé.
outnumber *v.t.* surpasser en nombre.
out-patient *s.* *see* PATIENT.
outpost *s.* avant-poste *m.*
outpouring *s.* (*of emotion*) épanchement *m.*; (*of abuse*) flot *m.*
output *s.* (*techn.*) rendement *m.*, production *f.*; (*fin.*) rendement *m.*; INPUT **~**.
outrage *s.* outrage *m.*; *v.t.* outrager; **~ous** *adj.* (*offensive*) outrageant; (*immoderate*) abusif; (*violent*) révoltant; (*price*) exorbitant; **~ously** *adv.* abusivement, abominablement; **~ousness** *s.* énormité *f.*; (*of price*) exorbitance *f.*
outrider *s.* (*on horse*) cavalier *or* (*motorized*) motard, d'escorte *m.*
outrigger *s.* outrigger *m.*
outright *adj.* total, net; *adv.* (*entirely*) tout à fait; (*once for all*) une fois pour toutes; (*without reservation*) carrément, nettement.
outrun *v.t.* (*outstrip*) courir plus vite que, distancer; (*overrun time*) dépasser.
outset *s.* début *m.*; **at the ~**, dès le début.
outshine *v.t.* éclipser.
outside *s.* extérieur *m.*; (*fig.*) maximum *m.*; **at the ~**, tout au plus; *adj.* du dehors, extérieur, (*price*) maximum; *adv.* au dehors, à l'extérieur; *prep.* en dehors de, à l'extérieur de; **~r** *s.* (*horse*) outsider *m.*; (*fam.* ≠ *professional*) profane *m.*; (*pej.*) voyou *m.*
outsize *s.* pointure hors série *f.*, taille exceptionnelle *f.*; *adj.* de taille exceptionnelle.
outskirts *s.* (*of town*) banlieue *f.*, périphérie *f.*; (*of wood*) lisière *f.*
outspoken *adj.* (*person*) franc; (*statement*) carré; **~ly** *adv.* carrément.
outstanding *adj.* (*conspicuous*) saillant; (*fig.*) éminent; (*still unsettled*) en suspens; (*fin.*) à payer.
outstay *v.t.* rester plus longtemps que.
outstretched *adj.* (*arms*) tendu; (*hands*) ouvert.
outstrip *v.t.* distancer; (*fig.*) dépasser.
outvote *v.t.* obtenir la majorité des voix contre.
outward *adj.* extérieur; (*application*) externe; (*train*) en partance; **~ly** *adv.* à l'extérieur.
outweigh *v.t.* peser plus que; (*fig.*) avoir plus de poids que, l'emporter sur.
outwit *v.t.* duper.
ouzel, ousel *s.* merle *m.*
oval *adj.* & *s.m.* ovale.
ovar/y *s.* ovaire *m.*; **~ian** *adj.* ovarien.
ovation *s.* ovation *f.*
oven *s.* (*cook.*) four *m.*; (*kiln*) étuve *f.*; **~ware,** plats allant au four *m.pl.*
over *adv.* (*above*) dessus; (*in excess*) davantage; (*covering surface*) partout; (= *P.T.O.*) voir au verso; *see also certain verbs*, CROSS **~**, FALL **~**, TURN **~**, *etc.*; **all ~**, (*covering whole surface*) partout, (*completely finished*) fini, passé; **~ again,** de nouveau; **~ and ~**, à plusieurs reprises; *prep.* (*position, above*) sur, au-dessus-de; (*motion, across*) par dessus, par; (*concerning*) sur, de; (*on other side*) de l'autre côté de; (*more than*) plus de.
overact *v.t.* & *i.* exagérer.
over-age, to be ~, avoir passé la limite d'âge.
overall *s.* blouse *f.*; **~s** *s.pl.* salopette *f.*, bleus *m.pl.*; *adj.* d'ensemble, global.
overawe *v.t.* intimider.
overbalance *v.i.* perdre l'équilibre; *v.t.* renverser.
overbearing *adj.* impérieux.
overboard *adv.* par-dessus bord; **to fall ~**, tomber à la mer; **to throw ~**, jeter par-dessus bord; **man ~!**, un homme à la mer!
overburden *v.t.* surcharger (de); (*fig.*) accabler (de).
overcall *v.t.* & *i.* (*cards*) monter sur l'annonce (de).
overcast *adj.* (*sky*) couvert.
overcharge *v.t.* faire payer trop cher.
overcoat *s.* pardessus *m.*
overcome *v.t.* vaincre, l'emporter sur; (*emotion, difficulty*) surmonter; *adj. p.p.* **~ by,** accablé de.
over(-)confiden/ce *s.* **1.** (*in self*) présomption *f.*; **2.** (*in s.o.*) confiance excessive *f.*; **~t** *adj.* (1) présompteux; (2) trop confiant.
overcrowd *v.t.* (*bus, room*) bonder; (*town, region*) surpeupler; **~ed** *adj.* bondé, surpeuplé; **~ing** *s.* encombrement *m.*; surpeuplement *m.*
overdo *v.t.* **1.** (*carry to excess*) exagérer; **2.** (*cook.*) faire trop cuire; **3.** (*overtax strength*) **~ it, things,** se surmener; **~ne** *adj.* (1) exagéré; (2) trop cuit; (3) surmené.
overdose *s.* dose excessive *f.*; surdosage *m.*
overdraft *s.* découvert *m.*
overdraw *v.t.* (*fin.*) tirer à découvert; **~n** *adj.* (*fin.*) à découvert; (*fig.*) exagéré.
overdress *v.i.* s'habiller d'une manière voyante.
overdrive *s.* (*auto.*) vitesse surmultipliée *f.*
overdue *adj.* (*train, ship, etc.*) en retard; (*fin.*) arriéré.
overeat *v.i.* trop manger.
overestimate *s.* surestimation *f.*; *v.t.* surestimer.
over-expose *v.t.* (*photo.*) surexposer.
overfill *v.t.* trop remplir.
overflow *s.* (*act*) débordement *m.*; (*excess, pipe*) trop-plein *m.*; *v.t.* inonder; *v.i.* déborder (*with*—de); **~ing** *adj.* débordant.
overfly *v.t.* survoler.
overgrown *adj.* (*with weeds, etc.*) envahi par; (*walls, house*) recouvert de.
overhang *s.* saillie *f.*; *v.t.* surplomber; **~ing** *adj.* surplombant.

overhaul *s.* (*inspection*) examen minutieux *m.*; *v.t.* examiner minutieusement; (*overtake*) dépasser.
overhead *adj.* (*cable, railway*) aérien; (*fin.*) général; *adv.* en haut; (*above*) au-dessus (de la tête); **~s** *s.pl.* frais généraux *m.pl.*
overhear *v.t.* entendre par hasard; (*conversation*) surprendre.
overheat *v.t.* surchauffer.
overjoyed *adj.* transporté de joie.
over-laden *adj.* surchargé (de).
overland *adj. adv.* de terre, par voie de terre.
overlap *s.* chevauchement *m.*; *v.t.* & *i.* (se) chevaucher.
overlay *v.t.* recouvrir (*with*—de).
overleaf *adv.* au verso.
overload *v.t.* surcharger; **~ing** *s.* surcharge *f.*
overlook *v.t.* (*have view of*) donner sur; (*take no notice of*) perdre de vue; (*ignore*) passer sous silence; (*superintend*) surveiller.
overlord *s.* suzerain *m.*
over-much *adj.* excessif; *adv.* excessivement.
overnight *adv.* (*during night*) la nuit; (*suddenly*) du jour au lendemain; *adj.* (*luggage*) (bagage) à main; (*journey*) voyage de nuit.
overpass *s.* (*road*) voie surélevée *f.*
overpay *v.t.* trop payer; **~ment** *s.* paiement excessif *m.*
over-populated *adj.* surpeuplé.
overpower *v.t.* **1.** (*subdue*) subjuguer; **2.** (*fig.*) accabler; **~ing** *adj.* (1) dominant; (2) accablant.
over-production *s.* surproduction *f.*
overrate *v.t.* surestimer.
overreach, oneself *v.refl.* surestimer ses forces.
override *v.t.* passer outre à.
overripe *adj.* trop mûr.
overrule *v.t.* (*set aside*) rejeter; (*annul*) annuler.
overrun *v.t.* (*spoil*) ravager; (*spread over*) envahir; (*exceed time allowed*) dépasser; (*print.*) chasser; (*infest*) infester (*with*—de).
oversea *adj.* d'outre-mer; **~s** *adv.* outre-mer.
oversee *v.t.* surveiller; **~r** *s.* surveillant *m.*; (*techn.*) contremaître *m.*
overshadow *v.t.* (*darken*) obscurcir; (*outshine*) éclipser.
overshoe *s.* caoutchouc *m.*
overshoot *v.t.* dépasser; (*aviat.*) **~ the runway,** atterrir trop long.
oversight *s.* (*failure to notice*) inadvertance *f.*; (*mistake*) faute d'attention *f.*; (*supervision*) surveillance *f.*; **through/by, an ~,** par mégarde.
oversleep *v.i.* dormir au delà de l'heure du réveil.
overspill *s.* (*of population*) trop-plein (des villes) *m.*
overstate *v.t.* exagérer; **~ment** *s.* exagération *f.*
overstep *v.t.* dépasser.
overstocked *adj.* encombré de marchandises.
overstrain *s.* surmenage *m.*; *v.t.* & *refl.* (se) surmener.
overstrung *adj.* (*piano*) à cordes croisées; (*person*) surexcité.
overt *adj.* manifeste, public; **~ly** *adv.* ouvertement.
overtake *v.t.* (*catch up*) rattraper; (*surprise*) surprendre; (*auto.*) doubler.
overtax *v.t.* surmener.
overthrow *s.* chute *f.*; *v.t.* (*lit.* & *fig.*) renverser; (*put an end to*) défaire.
overtime *s.* heures supplémentaires *f.pl.*; *adv.* en heures supplémentaires; **to work ~,** faire des heures supplémentaires.
overtired *adj.* excessivement fatigué.
overtone *s.* (*mus.*) harmonique *m.*; (*secondary quality*) arrière-goût *m.*; (*implication*) nuance *f.*
overture *s.* (*mus.* & *gen.*) ouverture *f.*
overturn *v.t.* & *i.* verser, (se) renverser; (*naut.*) (faire) chavirer; (*auto.*) (faire) capoter.
over-valu/e *v.t.* surestimer; **~ation** *s.* surestimation *f.*
overweening *adj.* outrecuidant.
overweight *s.* (*of luggage*) excédent *m.*; *adj.* (*thing*) qui excède le poids réglementaire; (*person*) qui excède le poids normal.
overwhelm *v.t.* (*submerge*) ensevelir; (*crush*) écraser; (*fig.*) accabler; (*deluge with*) combler de; **~ing** *adj.* accablant.
overwind *v.t.* (*watch*) trop remonter (une montre).
overwork *s.* surmenage *m.*; *v.t.* & *i.* (se) surmener.
overwrought *adj.* excédé.
ovum *s.* ovule *m.*
ow/e *v.t.* & *i.* (*lit.* & *fig.*) devoir; **~e sth. to s.o.,** être redevable à qn. de qch.; **~ing** *adj.* dû; **~ing to** *prep.* (*caused by*) à cause de; (*because of*) en raison de.
owl *s.* (*gen.*) hibou *m.*; **barn ~, screech ~,** effraie *m.*; **sparrow ~,** chat-huant *m.*; **tawny ~,** chouette *m.*; **horned ~,** duc *m.*; **~et** *s.* jeune hibou *m.*; **~ish** *adj.* de hibou.
own *adj.* propre (*before noun*), à soi; **of my, etc. ~,** à moi, etc.; **one's ~ people,** les siens *m.pl.*; **on one's ~,** de son propre chef; **to hold one's ~,** tenir bon; **to get one's ~ back,** se venger; *v.t.* (*possess*) posséder; (*acknowledge*) reconnaître; (*admit as true*) avouer; **~ up** (**to**) avouer; **~er** *s.* propriétaire *m.f.*; **~er-driver,** chauffeur-propriétaire *m.*; **~er-occupier,** propriétaire résident *m.*; **~ership** *s.* possession *f.*, propriété *f.*
ox *s.* bœuf *m.*; **~-bow** *s.* (*in river*) bras-mort *m.*; **~herd** *s.* bouvier *m.*; **~tail** *s.* (*cook.*) queue de bœuf *f.*
oxid/e *s.* oxyde *m.*; **~ize** *v.t.* & *i.* (s')oxyder.
oxy-acetylene *adj.* oxyacétylénique.
oxygen *s.* oxygène *m.*; **~ate, ~ize** *v.t.* oxygéner.
oxymoron *s.* alliance de mots *f.*
oyster *s.* huître *f.*; **~-bed** *s.* banc d'huîtres *m.*
ozone *s.* ozone *m.*

P

P.A. (*Public Address system*) système de diffusion publique *m.*
pace *s.* (*step*) pas *m.*; (*gait*) allure *f.*; (*speed*) pas *m.*; **at a slow ~,** à pas lents; **at a quick ~,** d'un pas rapide; **to put s.o. through his ~s,** mettre qn. à l'épreuve; **to keep ~ with,** aller de pair avec, (*fig.*) se tenir au courant de; **to set the ~,** régler l'allure; **~-maker** *s.* (*for heart*) stimulateur *m.*, (*sport*) lièvre *m.*, **to act as ~-maker for s.o.,** servir de lièvre à qn.; *v.i.* aller au pas; *v.t.* arpenter; (*measure distance*) mesurer au pas; (*test speed of*) régler l'allure de.
pachyderm *s.* pachyderme *m.*; **~atous** *adj.* pachyderme.
Pacific *s.* (*geog.*) (Océan) Pacifique *m.*
pacif/ic *adj.* pacifique; **~ication** *s.* pacification *f.*; **~ism** *s.* pacifisme *m.*; **~ist** *s.* pacifiste *m.f.*; **~y** *v.t.* pacifier; (*appease*) apaiser.

pack *s.* (*bundle*): (*pedlar's*) ballot *m.*, (*soldier's*) sac *m.*; (*packet*) paquet *m.*; (*lot*) tas *m.*, foule *f.*; (*of hounds*) meute *f.*; (*of wolves, thieves*) bande *f.*; (*rugby*) pack *m.*; (*of cards*) jeu *m.*; (*of ice*) (glace de) banquise *f.*; (*med., cosmetic*) masque *m.*; **~-horse** *s.* cheval de bât *m.*; *v.t.* (*goods*) emballer; (*cram, crowd*) bourrer, entasser, serrer; (*wrap tightly*) envelopper; (*fill meeting with partisans*) s'assurer une majorité de partisans; **~ one's bags,** faire ses valises; **~ together** *v.t.* & *i.* (se) serrer; **send ~ing** *v.t.* envoyer promener; **~ up** *v.t.* emballer, empaqueter, *v.i.* (*pop.*) se retirer, (*of machine*) être en panne; **~ it in!, ~ it up!,** ça suffit!; **~age** *s.* (*parcel*) colis *m.*; **~age deal** *s.* contrat global *m.*; **~age tour** *s.* voyage organisé *m.*; **~age** *v.t.* empaqueter; **~er** *s.* emballeu/r, -se *m.f.*; **~et** *s.* paquet *m.*, (*mail-boat*) paquebot *m.*; **to make a ~et** (*fam.*) gagner un argent fou; **~ing** *s.* emballage *m.*, (*filling*) bourrage *m.*, (*material*) matières pour emballage *f.pl.*; **~ing-case** *s.* caisse *f.* (d'emballage).

pact *s.* pacte *m.*

pad[1] *s.* (*piece of soft material*) tampon *m.*; (*leg-guard*) jambière *f.*; (*of paper*) bloc-correspondance *m.*; (*paw of animal*) patte *f.*; (*pop.* = *lodging*) piaule *f.*; *v.t.* (*stuff*) bourrer; (*upholstery*) capitonner; (*clothes*) ouater; (*make soft, protect*) matelasser; **~ded cell,** cellule capitonnée *f.*; **~ded envelope,** pochette matelassée *f.*; **~ding** *s.* rembourrage *m.*, capitonnage *m.*, ouate *f.*, (*fig.*) remplissage *m.*

pad[2] *v.i.* (*walk softly*) aller doucement.

paddle *s.* **1.** (*short oar*) pagaie *f.*; **2.** (*in water*) barbotage *m.*; **3.** (*of wheel*) palette *f.*; **4.** (*zool. fin, flipper*) nageoire *f.*; *v.t.* (1) pagayer; *v.i.* (1) ramer doucement; *v.i.* (2) barboter; **~ one's own canoe** (*fig.*) mener sa barque.

paddock *s.* (*small field*) enclos *m.*; (*enclosure for race-horses*) pesage *m.*

paddy[1] *s.* (*fam.* = *temper*) rogne *f.*; **in a ~,** en rogne.

paddy[2] *s.* (*growing rice*) paddy *m.*; **~-field** *s.* rizière *f.*

padlock *s.* cadenas *m.*; *v.t.* cadenasser.

padre *s.* (*fam. chaplain*) aumônier *m.*; (*fam. clergyman*) ministre du culte *m.*

paean *s.* péan *m.*

p(a)ediatric *adj.* de pédiatrie; **~s** *s.* pédiatrie *f.* ⚠ *sing. in French*; **~ian** *s.* pédiatre *m.f.*

pagan *adj.* & *s.m.f.* païen(ne); **~ism** *s.* paganisme *m.*

page *s.* **1.** (*boy attendant*) page *m.*; (*in hotel, etc.*) chasseur *m.*; **2.** (*of book*) page *f.*; *v.t.* (1) (*hotel*) faire appeler (qn. par un chasseur); (2) (*number*) paginer.

pageant *s.* spectacle *m.*; **~ry** *s.* pompe *f.*

paginat/e *v.t.* paginer; **~ion** *s.* pagination *f.*

pagoda *s.* pagode *f.*

paid *adj.* (*remunerated with money*) à gages; **~ holidays,** congés payés *m.pl.*; (*debt*) libéré, réglé, (*on bill*) payé; CARRIAGE **~**; **to put ~ to,** faire échouer.

pail *s.* seau *m.*

pain *s.* (*physical* & *mental*) douleur *f.*; **to have a ~ in one's stomach, etc.,** avoir mal à l'estomac, etc.; **~s** *pl.* (*trouble*) peine *f.*; **to take ~s,** se donner du mal; (*punishment*) peine *f.*; **on** *or* **under ~ of,** sous peine de; **~-**KILL**er**; **~staking** *adj.* assidu; **~ful** *adj.* douloureux, (*fig.*) pénible; **~fully** *adv.**,*; **~fulness** *s.* douleur *f.*; **~less** *adj.* indolore; **~lessly** *adv.* sans peine; *v.t.* (*physical*) faire du mal à; (*mental*) faire de la peine à; *v.i.* faire mal; **~ed** *adj.* (*look, etc.*) peiné.

paint *s.* peinture *f.*; **grease-~,** fard *m.*; **~box** *s.* boîte de couleurs *f.*; **~brush** *s.* pinceau *m.*; *v.t.* (*art* & *constr.*) peindre; (*one's face*) (se) farder; (*in words*) dépeindre; **~er** *s.* peintre *m.*, (*of boat*) amarre *f.*; **~ing** *s.* (*act*) peinture *f.*, (*picture*) tableau *m.*

pair *s.* **1.** (*set of two*) paire *f.*; **2.** (*couple, male & female*) couple *m.*; **3.** (*parl.*) adversaire avec qui on s'est entendu pour s'absenter *m.*; **4.** (*other member of ~*) pendant *m.*; ⚠ **a ~ of, compasses, pyjamas, trousers,** *sing. in French*—un compas, un pyjama, un pantalon; **au ~,** au pair; *v.t.* & *i.* (1) (s')assortir; (2) (s')accoupler; (3) s'entendre pour s'absenter; **~ off** *v.t.* & *i.* (s')arranger deux par deux; **~ing** *s.* accouplement *m.*

Pakistan *s.* (*geog.*) Pakistan *m.*; **~i** *adj.* & *s.m.f.* pakistanais(e).

pal *s.* (*fam.*) copain *m.*; *v.i.* **~ up (with),** se lier (avec).

palace *s.* palais *m.*; ⚠ palace = **luxury hotel.**

paladin *s.* paladin *m.*

pal(a)eo- (*in combination*) **~graphy** *s.* paléographie *f.*; **~lithic** *adj.* paléolithique; **~ntology** *s.* paléontologie *f.*

palat/e *s.* (*anat.* & *sense of taste*) palais *m.*; **hard, soft, ~e,** palais dur, palais mou; **~able** *adj.* agréable (au palais); **~al** *s.* (*ling.*) palatale *f.*; *adj.* palatal.

palatial *adj.* magnifique.

palatin/e *adj.* palatin; **~ate** *s.* palatinat *m.*

palaver *s.* **1.** (*conference*) palabre *m.*; **2.** (*empty* words) bavardage *m.*; *v.i.* (2) bavarder.

pal/e[1] *s.* (*stake*) pieu *m.*; (*boundary*) borne *f.*; **beyond the ~e,** (*fig.*) qui dépasse les bornes, insupportable; **~ing** *s.* palissade *f.*

pale[2] *adj.* (*whitish, wan*) blême; (*faintly coloured*) pâle; (*dim—of light*) blafard; **to grow or turn ~,** pâlir; **~-face** *s.* visage-pâle *m.*; **~ness** *s.* pâleur *f.*

paleo- *see* PALAEO-.

Palestin/e *s.* (*geog.*) Palestine *f.*; **~ian** *adj.* & *s.m.f.* palestinien(ne).

palette *s.* palette *f.*; **~-knife** *s.* (*art*) couteau de peintre *m.*; (*cook.*) spatule *f.*

palfrey *s.* palefroi *m.*

palimpsest *s.* palimpseste *m.*

palindrom/e *s.* palindrome *m.*; **~ic** *adj.* palindrome.

paling *see* PALE[1].

palisade *s.* palissade *f.*; *v.t.* palissader.

pall[1] *s.* (*over coffin*) drap mortuaire *m.*; (*eccles. vestement*) pallium *m.*; (*fig. of smoke, etc.*) voile *m.*, manteau *m.*; **~bearer** *s.* porteur d'un cordon du poêle *m.*

pall[2] *v.i.* devenir insipide; **it ~s on me,** je m'en lasse.

pallet[1] *s.* (*straw bed*) paillasse *f.*

pallet[2] *s.* (*flat wooden blade, artist's, mech., portable platform*) palette *f.*

palliasse *s.* paillasse *f.*

palliat/e *v.t.* **1.** (*alleviate*) pallier; **2.** (*excuse*) atténuer; **~ion** *s.* (1) soulagement *m.*; (2) atténuation *f.*; **~ive** *adj.* & *s.m.* palliatif.

pallid *adj.* (*face*) blême; (*light*) blafard.

pallor *s.* pâleur *f.*

palm *s.* (*of hand, of glove*) paume *f.*; (*tree*) palmier *m.*; (*branch*) palme *f.*; (*prize*) palme *f.*; **to** GREASE **s.o.'s ~**; **~-oil** *s.* huile de palme *f.*; **P~ Sunday,** dimanche des Rameaux *m.*; **~ wine** *s.* vin de palme *m.*; **~ate** *adj.* palmé; **~y** *adj.* (*fig.*) heureux; *v.t.* (*conceal in hand*) escamoter; **~ off (on),** faire passer (à).

palmist *s.* chiromancien(ne) *m.f.*; **~ry** *s.* chiromancie *f.*

palpabl/e *adj.* **1.** (*perceptible, to touch*) palpable; **2.** (*easily found out*) évident; **~y** *adv.* (1) de façon palpable; (2) évidemment.

palpitat/e *v.i.* (*throb*) palpiter; (*tremble*) frémir; **~ion** *s.* palpitation *f.*

pals/y *s.* paralysie *f.*; **~ied** *adj.* atteint de paralysie.
paltr/y *adj.* mesquin; **~iness** *s.* mesquinerie *f.*
pampas *s.pl.* pampas *f.pl.*; **~-grass** *s.* herbe des pampas *f.*
pamper *v.t.* choyer.
pamphlet *s.* brochure *f.*; ♤ pamphlet = **satirical, libellous work**; **~eer** *s.* auteur de brochures *m.*; pamphlétaire *m.* (*satirical*).
pan[1] *s.* (*saucepan*) casserole *f.*; (*frying*) poêle *f.*; (*shallow dish*) plat *m.*; (*~-shaped vessel, of W.C., hollow in ground*) cuvette *f.*; BRAIN-~; FLASH **in the ~**; *v.t.* (*for gold*) laver à la batée; **~ out** (*fig.*) réussir.
pan[2] (*T.V.* & *cinema*) *s.* panoramique *m.*; *v.t.* & *i.* (faire) faire un panoramique; *v.i.* panoramiquer.
pan- (*in combination*) pan; *e.g.* **~-African,** panafricain; **~-American,** panaméricain; **~-Hellenism,** panhellénisme *m.*
panacea *s.* panacée *f.*
Panama *s.* (*geog.*) Panama *m.*; **~nian** *adj.* & *s.m.f.* panaméen(ne); **p~ (hat)** panama *m.*
pancake *s.* crêpe *f.*; **~ landing** *s.* (*aviat.*) descente à plat *f.*; *v.i.* (*aviat.*) descendre à plat.
panchromatic *adj.* (*photo.*) panchromatique.
pancrea/s *s.* pancréas *m.*; **~tic** *adj.* pancréatique.
panda *s.* panda *m.*; **~ car,** voiture pie *f.*
pandemic *adj.* de pandémie.
pandemonium *s.* vacarme *m.*
pander *s.* (*pop.*) maquereau *m.*; *v.i.* **~ to,** (*person*) encourager; (*ideas, wishes*) se prêter à.
pane *s.* vitre *f.*
panegyr/ic *s.* panégyrique *m.*; **~ist** *s.* panégyriste *m.*
panel *s.* (*board, part of door, of dress, etc.*) panneau *m.*; (*for instruments*) planche de bord *f.*; (*of jurors, etc.*) liste *f.*; (*group*) groupe *m.*; **~ling** *s.* lambrissage *m.*; *v.t.* garnir de boiseries, lambrisser; **~led bath,** baignoire encastrée *f.*
pang *s.* (*short pain*) élancement *m.*; (*of emotion*) accès (de) *m.*; **~s of death,** affres de la mort *f.pl.*
panic *s.* (*fright*) affolement *m.*; (*alarm*) panique *f.*; **~-stricken** *adj.* pris de panique; *adj.* panique; *v.i.* être pris de panique; **~ky** *adj.* (*thing, news*) alarmiste; (*person*) affolé.
pannier *s.* panier *m.*
panoply *s.* (*armour*) panoplie *f.*; (*fig. brilliant array*) spectacle *m.*
panoram/a *s.* panorama *m.*; **~ic** *adj.* panoramique.
pansy *s.* (*bot.*) pensée *f.*; (*pop. homosexual*) tante *f.*
pant *v.i.* (*gasp for breath*) haleter; (*throb*) palpiter; (*fig. yearn for*) soupirer après.
pantaloon *s.* (*pantomime figure*; *tight trousers*) pantalon *m.*
pantechnicon *s.* fourgon de déménagement *m.*
panthei/sm *s.* panthéisme *m.*; **~st** *s.* panthéiste *m.f.*
pantheon *s.* panthéon *m.*
panther *s.* panthère *f.*
pantie/s *s.pl.* slip *m.* ♤ *singular in French*; **~-girdle** *s.* gaine-culotte *f.*
pantile *s.* tuile flamande *f.*
pantomime *s.* pantomime *f.*
pantry *s.* garde-manger *m.*
pants *s.* (*under*) caleçon *m.*; (*trousers*) pantalon *m.* ♤ *both sing. in French.*
pap *s.* (*soft food*) bouillie *f.*; (*mash*) pulpe *f.*
papa *s.* papa *m.*
pap/acy *s.* papauté *f.*; **~al** *adi.* papal; **~ist** *s.* papiste *m.f.*; **~istry** *s.* papisme *m.*
papaw, pawpaw *s.* papaye *f.*; (*tree*) papayer *m.*
paper *s.* papier *m.*; **drawing, printing, wrapping, writing ~,** papier à dessin, d'impression, d'emballage, à lettres; **brown ~,** papier gris *m.*; CARBON ~; CREPE ~; GREASE-**proof ~**; INDIA ~; MANILLA ~; SAND~; TISSUE-~; TOILET-~; TRACING-~; WALL~; WASTE-~; (*bank notes*) billets *m.pl.*; (*document*) pièce *f.*; (*pl. ~s, identity, etc.*) papiers *m.pl.*; (*exam*) épreuve *f.*; (*newspaper*) journal *m.*; (*essay*) étude *f.*; **on ~** (*fig.*) en théorie; *adj.* de papier; **~back** *s.* livre broché *m.*; **~-chase** *s.* rallye-papier *m.*; **~-**CLIP; **~-hanger** *s.* tapissier *m.*; **~-knife** *s.* coupe-papier *m.*; **~-mill** *s.* papeterie *f.*; **~ money** *s.* papier-monnaie *m.*; **~weight** *s.* presse-papier *m.*; **~work** *s.* paperasserie *f.*; *v.t.* (*wall~*) tapisser.
papier mâché *s.* papier mâché *m.*; *adj.* en papier mâché.
paprika *s.* paprika *m.*
Papua *s.* (*geog.*) Papua *m.*; (*hist.*) Papouasie *f.*; **~n** *adj.* & *s.m.f.* papou(e).
papyrus *s.* papyrus *m.*
par *s.* (*equality*) égalité *f.*; (*average or normal value*) moyen *m.*; (*fin. face value*) pair *m.*; (*golf*) normale *f.*; **at ~,** au pair; **above, below ~,** au-dessus, au-dessous, du pair; **to be below ~,** (*health*) ne pas être dans son assiette.
para *s.* (*pop. abbrev. ~chutist*) para *m.*
para- (*in combination*) para; **~military,** paramilitaire; **~typhoid,** paratyphoïde *f.*
parable *s.* parabole *f.*
parabola *s.* parabole *f.*
parachut/e *s.* parachute *m.*; *v.t.* parachuter; *v.i.* descendre en parachute; **~ist** *s.* parachutiste *m.*
paraclete *s.* paraclet *m.*
parade *s.* **1.** (*display, ostentation*) étalage *m.*, parade *f.*; **2.** (*mil.*) revue *f.*: (*procession*) défilé *m.*; **3.** (*public walk*) promenade publique *f.*; *v.t.* (1) faire parade de; (2) assembler; *v.i.* (1) parader; (2) défiler.
paradigm *s.* paradigme *m.*
paradis/e *s.* paradis *m.*; **bird of ~e,** paradisier *m.*; FOOL**'s ~e; ~al** *adj.* paradisiaque.
paradox *s.* paradoxe *m.*; **~ical** *adj.* paradoxal.
paraffin *s.* pétrole *m.*; ♤ paraffine = **paraffin wax;** (*med.*) **liquid ~,** (huile de) paraffine *f.*
paragon *s.* modèle *m.*
paragraph *s.* paragraphe *m.*, alinéa *m.*; **new ~,** à la ligne.
Paraguay *s.* (*geog.*) Paraguay *m.*; **~an** *adj.* & *s.m.f.* paraguayen (ne).
parakeet, paroquet *s.* perruche *f.*
parallax *s.* parallaxe *f.*
parallel *s.* (*line of latitude, comparison*) parallèle *m.*; (*math.*) parallèle *f.*; *adj.* parallèle; (*similar*) analogue (à); *v.t.* mettre en parallèle; (*compare*) comparer (à); (*correspond to*) égaler, être comparable à; **~ogram** *s.* parallélogramme *m.*
paraly/se *v.t.* (*lit.* & *fig.*) paralyser; **~sis** *s.* paralysie *f.*; **~tic** *adj.* & *s.m.f.* paralytique.
paramount *adj.* (*lord, chief*) souverain; (*importance, etc.*) suprême.
paramour *s.* amant *m.*, maîtresse *f.*
paranoi/a *s.* paranoïa *f.*; **~ac** *adj.* & *s.m.f.* paranoïque; **~d** *adj.* paranoïde.
parapet *s.* parapet *m.*
paraphernalia *s.* attirail *m.*
paraphrase *s.* paraphrase *f.*; *v.t.* paraphraser.
parapleg/ia *s.* paraplégie *f.*; **~ic** *adj.* & *s.m.f.* paraplégique.
parasit/e *s.* (*animal, plant, inseet, person*) parasite *m.*; **~ic** *adj.* parasite.
parasol *s.* ombrelle *f.*
paratroop/s *s.pl.* parachutistes *m.pl.*; (*abbrev.*) paras *m.pl.*; **~er** *s.* parachutiste *m.*; para *m.*
paravane *s.* paravane *m.*
parboil *v.t.* (*boil partially*) faire cuire à demi; (*overheat*) surchauffer.
parcel *s.* paquet *m.*, colis *m.*; (*of land*) parcelle *f.* (♤ *this meaning only*); (*heap, pile*) tas *m.*; **to be**

part and ~ of, faire partie intégrante de; **~ post,** service des colis postaux *m.*; *v.t.* (*make into ~*) emballer; (*divide*) morceler.
parch *v.t.* & *i.* (se) dessécher; **~ing** *adj.* brûlant.
parchment *s.* parchemin *m.*
pard *s.* (*archaic*) léopard *m.*
pardon *s.* (*eccles.* & *forgiveness*) pardon *m.*; (*remission of punishment*) grâce *f.*; (*forbearance*) indulgence *f.*; **I beg your ~,** je vous demande pardon; *v.t.* (*forgive*) pardonner (qch. à qn.); (*excuse*) excuser; **~able** *adj.* pardonnable; **~ably** *adv.* d'une manière pardonnable.
par/e *v.t.* (*fruit*) peler; (*nails*) rogner; **~ings** *s.* épluchures *f.pl.*
parent *s.* père *m.*, mère *f.*; parents *m.pl.*; ⚠ un parent = **a relative; ~age** *s.* naissance *f.*; **~al** *adj.* paternel, maternel, des parents.
parenthe/sis *s.* parenthèse *f.*; **~tic** *adj.* intercalé; **~tically** *adv.* entre parenthèses.
pariah *s.* paria *m.*
Paris *s.* (*geog.*) Paris *m.*; **~ian** *adj.* & *s.m.f.* parisien(ne).
parish *s.* (*eccles.*) paroisse *f.*; (*local govt.*) commune *f.*; *adj.* communal; **~ council,** conseil municipal *m.*; **~ioner** *s.* paroissien(ne) *m.f.*
parisyllabic *adj.* parisyllabique.
parity *s.* (*equality, being at par*) parité *f.*; (*equivalence*) égalité *f.*
park *s.* (*grounds*) parc *m.*; (*for cars*) parc de stationnement *m.*; **game ~,** parc national *m.*; **~land,** parc *m.*; *v.t.* (*car*) garer; *v.i.* stationner; **~ing** *s.* stationnement *m.*; **no ~ing!,** stationnement interdit!; **~ing-meter** *s.* parcomètre *m.*
parlance *s.* parler *m.*
parley *s.* pourparlers *m.pl.*; *v.i.* parlementer (avec).
parliament *s.* parlement *m.*; **~arian** *s.* parlementaire *m.*; **~ary** *adj.* parlementaire.
parlour *s.* petit salon *m.*; ⚠ parloir *only in institutions, e.g. prison.*
parlous *adj.* périlleux, alarmant.
Parmesan (*cheese*), parmesan *m.*
Parnass/us *s.* Parnasse *m.*; **~ian** *adj.* & *s.* parnassien.
parochial *adj.* (*eccles.*) paroissial; (*admin.*) communal; (*fig. very local*) de clocher; **~ism** *s.* esprit de clocher *m.*
parody *s.* parodie *f.*; *v.t.* parodier.
parole *s.* parole (d'honneur) *f.*; **on ~,** sur parole.
paroxysm *s.* paroxysme *m.*
parquet *s.* parquet *m.*; **~ry** *s.* parquetage *m.*
parricide *s.* parricide *m.*
parrot *s.* (*bird, person*) perroquet *m.*; *v.t.* répéter comme un perroquet.
parry *s.* (*fencing*) parade *f.*; *v.t.* (*blow*) parer; (*difficulty*) tourner.
pars/e *v.t.* faire l'analyse grammaticale de; **~ing** *s.* analyse grammaticale *f.*
parsec *s.* (*astron.*) parsec *m.*
Parsee *s.m.f.* parsi(e); (*lang.*) parsi *m.*
parsimon/ious *adj.* parcimonieux; **~iously** *adv.**; **~y** *s.* parcimonie *f.*
parsley *s.* persil *m.*
parsnip *s.* panais *m.*
parson *s.* (*R.C.*) curé *m.*; (*protestant*) pasteur *m.*; **~age** *s.* presbytère *m.*
part *s.* (*some but not all*) partie *f.*; (*share, portion*) part *f.*; (*rôle*) rôle *m.*; (*mus.*) partie *f.*; (*region*) région *f.*; (*side in dispute*) parti *m.*; (*mech.*) pièce *f.*, **spare ~,** pièce de rechange *f.*; **~s** *s.pl.* (*ability*) talent *m.*, (*place*) **in these ~s,** dans ces parages; **~ and** PARCEL; **in ~,** en partie; **for the most ~,** pour la plupart; **for my ~,** pour ma part; **on my ~,** de ma part; **on the ~ of,** de la part de; **to play a ~,** jouer un rôle; **to take ~ in,** prendre part à; **to take s.o.'s ~,** prendre parti pour qn.; **to take sth. in good ~,** ne pas s'offenser de qch.; *adv.* en partie; **~ly** *adv.* partiellement; **~-exchange** *s.* reprise *f.*; **~-owner** *s.* co-propriétaire *m.*; **~-payment** *s.* acompte *m.*; **~-song** *s.* chant à plusieurs voix *m.*; **~ time** *s.* emploi à mi-temps *m.*; **~-time** *adj.* à mi-temps; *v.t.* & *i.* (*divide*) (se) diviser; (*separate*) (se) séparer; *v.t.* (*share out*) partager; (*hair*) faire une raie (dans les cheveux); *v.i.* (*quit one another's company*) se quitter; **~** COMPANY **with s.o.; ~ from,** quitter, se séparer de; **~ with sth.,** se défaire de qch.
partake *v.t.* (*take share in*) participer à; **~ of,** manger, boire.
parterre *s.* (*hort., theat.*) parterre *m.*
partial *adj.* **1.** (*biased*) partial (*to*—envers); **2.** (*incomplete*) partiel; **to be ~ to,** avoir un faible pour; **~ity** *s.* (1) partialité *f.*, prédilection *f.* (pour); **~ly** *adv.* (1)*; (2)*.
particip/ant *s.* participant(e) *m.f.*; **~ate** *v.i.* participer (*in*—à); **~ation** *s.* participation *f.*; **workers' ~ation,** auto-gestion *f.*; **~ator** *s.* participant(e) *m.f.*
participle *s.* participe *m.*
particle *s.* (*minute portion of matter*) molécule *f.*; (*smallest possible amount*) parcelle *f.*; (*fig.*) brin *m.*; (*part of speech, prefix, suffix*) particule *f.*
particoloured *adj.* bigarré.
particular *s.* détail *m.*; **~s** détails *m.pl.*; **in ~,** en particulier; *adj.* **1.** (*relating to one only, special*) particulier; **2.** (*meticulous*) méticuleux; **3.** (*fastidious*) difficile; **~ity** *s.* (1) particularité *f.*; (2) méticulosité *f.*; (3) difficulté *f.*; **~ize** *v.t.* (1) particulariser; (2) détailler; **~ization** *s.* (1) particularisation *f.*; **~ly** *adv.* (*very*) extrêmement; (*specially*) particulièrement, exceptionnellement; (*in detail*) en détail.
parting *s.* (*departure*) départ *m.*; (*leave-taking*) séparation *f.*; (*in hair*) raie *f.*; *adj.* de départ, d'adieu.
partisan *s.* partisan *m.*; **~ship** *s.* esprit de parti *m.*
partition *s.* **1.** (*division into parts*) division *f.*, partage *m.*; (*of country*) démembrement *m.*; **2.** (*constr.*) cloison *f.*; **3.** (*compartment*) compartiment *m.*; *v.t.* (1) diviser, partager, démembrer; (2) cloisonner.
partitive *adj.* & *s.m.* partitif.
partner *s.* partenaire *m.*; (*comm.*) associé *m.*; **senior ~,** associé principal *m.*; **sleeping ~,** commanditaire *m.*; (*dancing*) cavalier *m.*, danseuse *f.*; *v.t.* être le partenaire de; **~ship** *s.* association *f.*
partridge *s.* perdrix *f.*; (*young, usu. cook.*) perdreau *m.*
parturition *s.* parturition *f.*
party *s.* (*body of people travelling, working, etc. together*) groupe *m.*; (*polit.*) parti *m.*; (*reception*) réunion *f.*, réception *f.*; (*law*) partie *f.*; THIRD **~; to be a ~ to sth.,** y être pour quelque chose; **~ line** *s.* (*telephone*) ligne de postes groupés *f.*, (*polit.*) directives du parti *f.pl.*; **~ politics** *s.* politique de parti *f.*; **~-wall** *s.* mur mitoyen *m.*
paschal *adj.* pascal.
pasha *s.* pacha *m.*
pass[1] *s.* (*in exam.*) moyenne *f.*, mention passable *f.*; (*critical state*) situation *f.*; (*written permission*) laissez-passer *m.*, FREE **~**; (*football*) passe *f.*; (*in mountains, etc.*) col *m.*, défilé *m.*; **to bring to ~,** occasionner; **to come to ~,** arriver; **to make a ~ at s.o.,** faire des avances à qn.; **to be in a pretty ~,** être dans de beaux draps; **~book** *s.* carnet de banque *m.*, (*South Africa*) carnet d'identité *m.*; **~key** *s.* passe-partout *m.*; **~word** *s.* mot de passe *m.*
pass[2] *v.t.* (*cause to go, hand round, spend*) passer; (*exam.*) être reçu à, ⚠ passer un examen = **to sit an exam.;** (*surpass*) dépasser; (*approve*) approuver; (*utter*) émettre; (*auto.*) doubler; (*judgement*) prononcer; (*law*) voter; *v.i.* (*die,*

proceed, change, go by, come to an end, be adequate) passer; (*be sanctioned*) avoir cours; (*happen*) se passer; ~ **along** *v.t.* longer, *v.i.* circuler; ~ **away** *v.i.* mourir, disparaître; ~ **by** *v.t.* & *i.* passer à côté (de); ~ **for,** passer pour; ~ **off** *v.i.* se passer, *v.t.* faire passer; ~ **off for** *v.t.* faire passer pour; ~ **on** *v.i.* mourir, *v.t.* transmettre; ~ **out** *v.i.* s'évanouir; ~ **over** *v.i.* s'éloigner, *v.t.* passer, faire passer, passer sous silence; ~ **through** *v.t.* passer par; ~ **up** *v.t.* (*fam.*) manquer; ~**able** *adj.* passable, (*road*) praticable; ~**ably** *adv.* passablement; ~**er-by** *s.* passant *m.*

passage *s.* (*passing*) passage *m.*; (*crossing*) traversée *f.*; (*fare*) voyage *m.*; (*corridor*) couloir *m.*; (*of book*) passage *m.*; **bird of** ~, oiseau de passage *m.*

passenger *s.* passager *m.*; (*fig. ineffective person*) parasite *m.*

passing *s.* passage *m.*; *adj.* (*transient*) passager; (*fortuitous*) fortuit; ~**-bell** *s.* glas *m.*; *adv.* extrêmement.

passion *s.* (*eccles., strong emotion, sexual love*) passion *f.*; (*anger*) courroux *m.*; **to have a ~ for sth.,** avoir la passion de qch.; ~**-flower** *s.* passiflore *f.*; ~**-fruit** *s.* grenadille *f.*; ~**-play** *s.* mystère *m.*; ~**ate** *adj.* passionné; ~**ately** *adv,**; ~**ateness** *s.* caractère passionné *m.*; ~**less(ly)** *adj. adv.* sans passion.

passiv/e *s.* (*ling.*) passif *m.*; *adj.* (≠ *active*) passif; (*inert*) inactif; (*submissive*) soumis; ~**e resistance,** résistance passive *f.*; ~**ely** *adv.**;*; avec soumission; ~**eness** *s.* & ~**ity** *s.* passivité *f.*; inertie *f.*

Passover *s.* Pâque *f.*; ⚠ Pâques = **Easter.**

passport *s.* passeport *m.*

past *s.* passé *m.*; *adj.* passé; (*just over*) dernier (*after noun*); ~ MASTER; *prep.* (*beyond, after*) au delà de, plus loin que; (*more than*) plus de; **half ~ seven, etc.,** sept heures et demie; **quarter ~ seven, etc.,** sept heures et quart; ~ **belief,** incroyable; ~ **endurance,** insupportable; ~ **it** (*pop.*) sénile; **I would not put it ~ him to,** je le croirais tout à fait capable de; *adv.* **to go** ~, passer; **to run, etc.** ~, passer en courant, etc.

pasta *s.* (*cook.*) pâtes *f.pl.*

paste *s.* (*cook.*) pâte *f.*; (*fish, etc.*) beurre *m.* (d'anchois, etc.); (*glue*) colle de pâte *f.*; (*jewellery*) strass *m.*; **tooth~**, pâte dentifrice *f.*; ~**board** *s.* carton-pâte *m.*; *v.t.* (*stick*) coller; (*pop.* = *thrash*) rosser.

pastel *s.* pastel *m.*; *adj.* ~ **colours,** tons pastels *m.pl.*

pasteuriz/e *v.t.* pasteuriser; ~**ation** *s.* pasteurisation *f.*

pastille *s.* pastille *f.*

pastime *s.* passe-temps *m.*

pastor *s.* pasteur *m.*; ~**ate** *s.* pastorat *m.*

pastoral *adj.* & *s.f.* pastoral(e).

pastry *s.* (*dough*) pâte *f.*; (*cakes*) pâtisserie *f.*; ~**-cook** *s.* pâtissier *m.*

pastur/e *s.* pâture *f.*; *v.t.* & *i.* (faire) paître; ~**age** *s.* pâturage *m.*

pasty *s.* pâté *m.*; *adj.* pâteux.

pat *s.* (*touch or sound*) tape *f.*; (*of butter*) coquille *f.*; **to give s.o. a ~ on the back,** passer la main dans le dos à qn.; *v.t.* taper; (*dog, etc.*) caresser; *adv.* **off** ~, à propos.

Patagonia *s.* (*geog.*) Patagonie *f.*

patch *s.* (*repair*) pièce *f.*; (*over wound*) tampon *m.*; (*over eye*) bandeau *m.*; (*spot*) tache *f.*; (*of ground*) parcelle *f.*; **not to be a ~ on,** ne pas venir à la cheville de; ~**work** *s.* rapiéçage *m.*; ~**y** *adj.* fait de pièces et de morceaux, (*fig.*) inégal; *v.t.* (*mend*) rapiécer; ~ **up** *v.t.* (*fig.*) arranger.

pate *s.* (*fam.*) ciboulot *m.*; **bald** ~ (*fam.*) caillou *m.*

paten *s.* (*eccles.*) patène *f.*

patent *s.* brevet d'invention *m.*; ⚠ patente = **trading licence; letters** ~, lettres patentes *f.pl.*; *adj.* **1.** (*obvious*) patent; **2.** (~*ed*) breveté; ~ LEATHER; ~ **medicine** *s.* spécialité pharmaceutique *f.*; ~**ly** *adv.* (1) manifestement; *v.t.* (2) faire breveter; ~**ee** *s.* détenteur d'un brevet *m.*

patern/al *adj.* paternel; ~**ally** *adv.**; ~**alism** *s.* paternalisme *m.*; ~**ity** *s.* paternité *f.*

paternoster *s.* pater *m.*

path *s.* sentier *m.*; (*in garden*) allée *f.*; (*track* & *fig.*) chemin *m.*; **to lead s.o. up the** GARDEN ~; ~**finder** *s.* pionnier *m.*; ~**way** *s.* sentier *m.*, chemin *m.*, (*in street*) trottoir *m.*

path/etic *adj.* pathétique; ~**etically** *adv.**; ~**os** *s.* pathétique *m.*; ⚠ pathos = **sentimental rhetorical bombast.**

patholog/y *s.* pathologie *f.*; ~**ical** *adj.* pathologique; ~**ist** *s.* pathologiste *m.f.*

patience *s.* patience *f.*; **to lose ~ with s.o.,** être à bout de patience avec qn.; **to have no ~ with,** ne pas pouvoir supporter.

patient *s.* malade *m.f.*; **in-~** *s.* hospitalisé(e) *m.f.*; **out-~** *s.* malade externe *m.f.*; *adj.* patient; ~**ly** *adv.* patiemment; **to wait ~ly,** patienter.

patina *s.* patine *f.*

patio *s.* patio *m.*

patriarch *s.* patriarche *m.*; ~**al** *adj.* patriarcal.

patrician *adj.* & *s.m.f.* patricien(ne).

patrimon/y *s.* patrimoine *m.*; ~**ial** *adj.* patrimonial.

patriot *s.* patriote *m.f.*; ~**ic** *adj.* patriotique; ~**ically** *adv.**; ~**ism** *s.* patriotisme *m.*

patrol *s.* patrouille *f.*; ~ **car** (*police*) voiture de police *f.*; *v.t.* surveiller par des patrouilles; *v.i.* patrouiller.

patron *s.* **1.** (*supporter*) protecteur *m.*; ~**ess** *s.* protectrice *f.*; **2.** (*customer*) client *m.*; (*of restaurant, cinema, etc.*) habitué *m.*; ~ **saint,** patron(ne) *m.f.* ⚠ *otherwise* patron = **master, chief, boss;** ~**age** *s.* (1) patronage *m.*; (2) clientèle *f.*; **3.** (*right to appoint*) droit de disposer *m.* (d'un bénéfice); **under the ~age of,** sous les auspices de; ~**al** *adj.* patronal; ~**ize** *v.t.* (1) protéger, (*support*) appuyer, patronner; (2) donner sa clientèle à; **4.** (*treat condescendingly*) traiter avec condescendance; ~**izing** *adj.* (1) protecteur; (4) hautain.

patronymic *s.* patronyme *m.*; *adj.* patronymique.

patten *s.* socque *m.*

patter *s.* (*chat*) bavardage *m.*; (*sound*) bruit *m.* (de pas, de pluie); *v.i.* (*rain*) fouetter; (*run quickly*) trottiner.

pattern *s.* (*example*) exemple *m.*; (*model*) modèle *m.*; (*dressm.*) patron *m.*; (*sample*) échantillon *m.*; (*design*) motif *m.*; *v.t.* prendre pour modèle; ~ **oneself on,** se modeler sur.

paucity *s.* (*small no. or infrequent occurrence*) rareté *f.*; (*shortage*) pénurie *f.*; (*lack*) manque *m.*

paunch *s.* bedaine *f.*; *v.t.* (*disembowel an animal*) étriper.

pauper *s.* indigent *m.*; **~'s grave,** fosse commune *f.*; ~**ism** *s.* paupérisme *m.*; ~**ize** *v.t.* réduire à l'indigence.

pause *s.* pause *f.*; *v.i.* faire une pause.

pav/e *v.t.* paver; ~**e the way for** (*fig.*) préparer le chemin pour; ~**ement** *s.* trottoir *m.*; ~**ing-stone,** pavé *m.*

pavilion *s.* pavillon *m.*

paw *s.* patte *f.*; *v.t.* donner un coup de patte à; (*fam.*) tripoter; ~ **the ground,** piaffer.

pawn *s.* **1.** (*chess* & *fig.*) pion *m.*; **2.** (*thing ~ed*) gage *m.*; **in** ~, en gage, (*fam.*) chez ma tante; ~**broker** *s.* prêteur sur gages *m.*; ~**shop** *s.* mont-de-piété *m.*, crédit municipal *m.*; ~**-ticket** *s.* reconnaissance *f.*; *v.t.* (2) mettre en gage.

pay *s.* (*gen.*) salaire *m.*; (*monthly or annually*)

appointements *m.pl.*; (*of civil servants, etc.*) traitement *m.*; (*mil., of workmen*) paye *f.*; **in the ~ of,** à la solde de; **~-day** *s.* jour de paye *m.*; **~load** *s.* (*aviat.*) charge utile *f.*; **~master** *s.* (*naut.*) commissaire *m.*, (*mil.*) trésorier *m.*; **~-roll** *s.* livre de paie *m.*; *v.t.* payer; (*attention, visit*) faire; (*homage*) rendre; (*bill*) régler; ROB **Peter to ~ Paul;** *v.i.* (*bear cost, suffer penalty*) payer; (*comm. yield adequate return*) rapporter; **you will ~ through the nose,** cela vous coûtera les yeux de la tête; **~ back** *v.t.* (*money*) rendre, (*person*) rembourser, (*be revenged on s.o.*) se venger de qn.; **~ for sth.** *v.t.* payer qch. (*with*—de); **~ in** *v.t.* verser (à); **~ off** *v.t.* rembourser (qn.), (*debt*) acquitter, (*sack*) licencier; **~ off** *v.i.* (*fam.*) avoir du succès; **~-off** *s.* rentabilité *f.*; **~ out** *v.t.* payer, (*rope*) laisser filer; **~ up** *v.t.* régler; *see* PAID; **~-as-you-earn,** *see* P.A.Y.E.; **~able** *adj.* payable (à); **~able at sight,** payable à vue; **~able to bearer,** payable au porteur; **~ee** *s.* bénéficiaire *m.*; **~er** *s.* payeu/r, -se *m.f.*; **~ing guest** *s.* pensionnaire *m.f.*; **~ment** *s.* paiement *m.*, (*fig.*) récompense *f.*

P.A.Y.E. (*Pay-as-you-earn*) s. mensualisation de l'impôt *f.*

pea *s.* pois *m.*; **green ~s,** petits pois *m.pl.*; **sweet ~,** pois de senteur *m.*; **to be as like as two ~s,** se ressembler comme deux gouttes d'eau; **~nut** *s.* cacahouette, cacahuète *f.*, (*agric.*) arachide *f.*; **~pod, ~shell** *s.* cosse *f.*; **~-shooter** *s.* sarbacane *f.*

peace *s.* paix *f.*; **~ of mind,** tranquillité d'âme *f.*; BREACH **of the ~; to hold one's ~,** se taire; **to make ~ with,** se réconcilier avec; **~maker** *s.* pacificateur *m.*; **~-offering,** offrande propitiatoire *f.*; **~-time,** temps de paix *m.*; **~able** *adj.* pacifique; **~ably** *adv.**; **~ful** *adj.* paisible; **~fully** *adv.**; **~fulness** *s.* tranquillité *f.*

peach[1] *s.* pêche *f.*; (*tree*) pêcher *m.*; **clingstone ~,** alberge *f.*

peach[2] *v.i.* (*pop.*) moucharder.

pea/cock *s.* paon *m.*; **~hen** *s.* paonne *f.*; **~-chick** *s.* paonneau *m.*; **~cock blue,** bleu paon *invar.*

pea-jacket *s.* vareuse *f.*

peak[1] *s.* (*of mountain*) cime *f.*; (*of curve*) pointe *f.*; (*of cap*) visière *f.*; (*fig.*) maximum *m.*, comble *m.*; **~ hours,** heures de pointe *f.pl.*; **~-load** *s.* maximum de charge *m.*; OFF-**~.**

peak[2] *v.i.* dépérir; **~ed** *adj.* (*of features*) tiré; **~y** *adj.* pâlot.

peal *s.* (*ringing*) sonnerie *f.*; (*bells*) carillon *m.*; (*outburst of sound*) éclat *m.*; *v.t.* faire retentir; *v.i.* retentir, carillonner, éclater.

pear *s.* poire *f.*; (*tree*) poirier *m.*; AVOCADO **~;** PRICKLY **~; ~-shaped,** en forme de poire.

pearl *s.* (*lit.* & *fig.*) perle *f.*; MOTHER-**of-~; to cast ~s before swine,** jeter des perles aux pourceaux; **~** BARLEY; **~ grey,** gris perle *invar.*; *v.i.* (*fish for ~s*) pêcher des perles; (*form ~s*) perler; **~y** *adj.* nacré.

peasant *s.* paysan(ne) *m.f.*; **~ry** *s.* paysannat *m.*, classe paysanne *f.*

peat *s.* tourbe *f.*; **~bog** *s.* tourbière *f.*

pebble *s.* (*stone* & *lens*) caillou *m.*; (*on beach*) galet *m.*

peccadillo *s.* peccadille *f.*

peck *s.* **1.** (*measure*) picotin *m.*; (*fam., fig.* **~** *of troubles*) tas *m.*; **2.** (*with beak*) coup de bec *m.*; **3.** (*fam. kiss*) bécot *m.*; *v.t.* (2) becqueter; (3) bécoter; **4.** (*dab at, nibble food*) picoter; **~er** (*fam.*) **to keep one's ~er up,** tenir bon; **~ish** *adj.* (*fam.*) affamé.

pectin *s.* pectine *f.*

pectoral *adj.* & *s.m.* pectoral.

peculat/e *v.t.* détourner (des fonds); **~ion** *s.* détournement (de fonds) *m.*; **~or** *s.* concussionnaire *m.*

peculiar *adj.* **1.** (*individual, exclusive* (*to*)) particulier (à); **2.** (*special*) spécial; **3.** (*odd*) bizarre; **~ity** *s.* (1) particularité *f.*, singularité *f.*; (2) trait distinctif *m.*; (3) bizarrerie *f.*; (*habit*) manie *f.*; **~ly** *adv.* (1)*, (2)*, (3)*.

pecuniar/y *adj.* pécuniaire; **~ily** *adv.**.

pedagog/ue *s.* pédagogue *m.*; **~ic** *adj.* pédagogique; **~y** *s.* pédagogie *f.*

pedal *s.* pédale *f.*; ACCELERATOR **~;** SOFT **~;** *v.t.* & *i.* pédaler.

pedant *s.* pédant(e) *m.f.*; **~ic** *adj.* pédant; **~ically** *adv.* en pédant; **~ry** *s.* pédantisme *m.*, pédanterie *f.*

peddle *v.t.* colporter.

pedestal *s.* (*lit.* & *fig.*) piédestal *m.*; (*block*) socle *m.*

pedestrian *s.* piéton *m.*; *adj.* pédestre; (*fig., dull*) prosaïque; **~ crossing** *s.* passage clouté *m.*; **~ precinct** *s.* voie piétonne *f.*

pediatric *see* PAEDIATRIC.

pedicure *s.* (*person*) pédicure *m.f.*; (*care*) soins de pédicure *m.pl.*

pedigree *s.* généalogie *f.*; (*ancestral line*) arbre généalogique *m.*; (*of animal only*) pedigree *m.*; *adj.* de race.

pediment *s.* fronton *m.*

pedlar *s.* colporteur *m.*

pee *s.* (*fam.*) pipi *m.*; *v.i.* (*fam.*) faire pipi.

peel *s.* pelure *f.*; (*outer skin of orange, lemon*) écorce *f.*; **candied ~,** zeste confit *m.*; *v.t.* peler; (*potato*) éplucher; *v.i.* (*shed bark, skin, etc.*) s'écailler; **~ing** *s.* épluchure *f.*

peep[1] *s.* **1.** (*glance*) regard furtif *m.*; **2.** (*first light*) point du jour *m.*; **~-hole** *s.* judas *m.*; **~-show** *s.* stéréoscope *m.*; *v.i.* (1) regarder furtivement (*also* **~** *at*); (2) poindre.

peep[2] *s.* (*cheep*) pépiement *m.*, (*squeak*) petit cri aigu *m.*; *v.i.* pépier, pousser de petits cris aigus.

peer[1] *s.* (*equal*) pair *m.*, égal *m.*; (*noble*) pair *m.*; **~ess** *s.* pairesse *f.*; **~age** *s.* pairie *f.*; **~less** *adj.* sans pareil; **~lessly** *adv.* incomparablement.

peer[2] *v.i.* (*look narrowly* (*at*)) regarder de près; **~ at s.o.,** dévisager qn.; (*peep out*) poindre.

peev/e *v.t.* irriter; **~ed** *adj.* agacé; **~ish** *adj.* hargneux, maussade; **~ishly** *adv.* avec humeur; **~ishness** *s.* mauvaise humeur *f.*

peewit *s.* vanneau *m.*

peg *s.* (*wood or metal pin*) cheville *f.*; (*for clipping together*) pince *f.*; (*to hang hats, etc.*) patère *f.*; (*for cask*) fausset *m.*; (*drink*) doigt *m.*; (*marker*) fiche *f.*; **clothes-~,** pince (à linge) *f.*; **tent-~,** piquet *m.*; **off the ~,** prêt à porter; **to be a square ~ in a round hole,** ne pas être taillé pour cela; **to take s.o. down a ~,** rabattre le caquet de qn.; *v.t.* (*fix*) cheviller; (*hang out clothes*) étendre; (*comm. prices, etc.*) stabiliser; **~ away** *v.i.* persévérer; **~ out** *v.i.* (*pop.*) claquer.

pejorative *adj.* péjoratif.

Pekin(g) *s.* (*geog.*) Pékin *m.*; **~ese** *adj.* & *s.m.f.* pékinois(e); **~ese** (*dog*) pékinois *m.*

pelargonium *s.* pélargonium *m.*

pelf *s.* (*pop.*) pèze *m.*

pelican *s.* pélican *m.*

pellet *s.* (*small ball of paper, etc.*) boulette *f.*; (*pill*) pilule *f.*; (*small shot*) petit plomb *m.*

pell-mell *adv.* pêle-mêle.

pellucid *adj.* transparent; (*fig.*) lucide; **~ity** *s.* transparence *f.*; (*fig.*) lucidité *f.*

pelmet *s.* lambrequin *m.*

pelt[1] *s.* (*undressed skin*) peau *f.*

pelt[2] *s.* **at full ~,** à toute vitesse; *v.t.* (*with missiles*) lancer une grêle (de pierres, etc.) à; (*with abuse*) cribler (*with*—de); *v.i.* (*rain*) tomber à verse; (*run fast*) courir à toute vitesse; **~ing** *adj.* (*rain*) (pluie) battante.

pelv/is *s.* bassin *m.*; **~ic** *adj.* pelvien.

pemmican *s.* pemmican *m.*

pen *s.* **1.** (*for writing*) plume *f.*, stylo *m.*; BALL-**-point** ~; **felt-tipped** ~, stylo-feutre *m.*; FOUNTAIN-~; **2.** (*enclosure*) parc *m.*; **3.** (*female swan*) cygne femelle *f.*; **~-friend** *s.* correspondant(e) *m.f.*; **~holder** *s.* porte-plume *m.*; **~knife** *s.* canif *m.*; **~manship** *s.* écriture *f.*: **~-name** *s.* pseudonyme *m.*; **~-nib** *s.* plume *f.*; **~wiper** *s.* essuie-plume *m.*; *v.t.* (1) écrire; (2) parquer.

pen/al *adj.* (*law, code, clause*) pénal; (*colony, system, régime*) pénitentiaire; (*punishable*) passible d'une peine; **~al servitude** *s.* travaux forcés *m.pl.*; **~alize** *v.t.* (*sport*) pénaliser; (*law*) infliger une pénalité à; **~alty** *s.* (*fine, punishment, disadvantage*) pénalité *f.*; (*football*) pénalisation *f.*; **~alty kick,** coup de pied de pénalité *m.*; **~ology** *s.* criminologie *f.*

penance *s.* pénitence *f.*; **to do ~ for,** faire pénitence de.

pence *see* PENNY.

pencil *s.* (*for writing*) crayon *m.*; (*set of lines*) faisceau *m.*; **in ~,** au crayon; **~-box** *s.* plumier *m.*; **~-case** *s.* trousse *f.*; **~-sharpener** *s.* taille-crayon *m.*; *v.t.* crayonner; (*art*) dessiner au crayon.

pend/ant, (**ent**) *s.* (*ornament*): (*on chandelier*) pendeloque *f.*, (*of necklace*) pendentif *m.*; (*complement*) complément *m.*; *adj.* suspendu.

pending *adj.* en suspens; *prep.* (*during*) pendant; (*until*) en attendant.

pendul/um *s.* balancier *m.*; **~ous** *adj.* suspendu; (*lip*) pendant.

penetr/ate *v.t.* pénétrer (*into*—dans; *with*—de); (*fig. find out*) découvrir; **~able** *adj.* (*lit.* & *fig.*) pénétrable; **~ability** *s.* pénétrabilité *f.*; **~ation** *s.* pénétration *f.*; **~ating** *adj.* & **~ative** *adj.* (*discerning*) pénétrant, (*piercing*) perçant.

penguin *s.* (*arctic*) pingouin *m.*; (*antarctic*) manchot *m.*

penicillin *s.* pénicilline *f.*

peninsula *s.* péninsule *f.*; (*small*) presqu'île *f.*; **~r** *adj.* péninsulaire.

penis *s.* pénis *m.*

peniten/ce *s.* pénitence *f.*; **~t** *adj.* & *s.m.f.* pénitent(e); **~tly** *adv.* d'un air contrit; **~tial** *adj.* de pénitence; **~tiary** *s.* pénitencier *m.*, *adj.* pénitenciaire.

pennant *s.* flamme *f.*, fanion *m.*

pennon *s.* pennon *m.*

Pennsylvania *s.* Pennsylvanie *f.*

penny *s.* penny *m.* (*pl.* pence *or* pennies *m.pl.*); **like a bad ~,** toujours importun; **the ~ drops** (*fam.*) tu (*or person addressed or intended*) commences à piger; **a pretty ~,** (*cost*) une jolie somme *f.*, (*profit*) de jolis bénéfices *m.pl.*; **~farthing** *s.* vélocipède *m.*; **~-in-the-slot-machine** *s.* distributeur automatique *m.*; **to be ~ wise and pound foolish,** faire des économies de bouts de chandelle; **~worth** *s.* **to buy a ~worth,** en acheter pour deux sous;

penniless *adj.* sans le sou.

pension *s.* pension *f.*; **to take one's ~,** prendre sa retraite; *v.t.* pensionner; **~ off** *v.t.* mettre à la retraite; **~able** *adj.* (*post*) donnant droit à une retraite, (*person*) ayant droit à une retraite; **~er** *s.* retraité *m.*

pensive *adj.* pensif; (*melancholy*) mélancolique; **~ly** *adv.* d'un air pensif; **~ness** *s.* rêverie *f.*

pentagon *s.* pentagone *m.*

pentameter *s.* pentamètre *m.*

Pentateuch *s.* pentateuque *m.*

pentathlon *s.* pentathlon *m.*

Pentecost *s.* Pentecôte *f.*

penthouse *s.* (*shed*) appentis *m.*; (*roof flat*) appartement sur toit *m.*

penultimate *adj.* & *s.f.* pénultième.

penumbra *s.* pénombre *f.*

penur/y *s.* (*shortage*) pénurie *f.*; (*poverty*) misère *f.*; **~ious** *adj.* (*mean*) mesquin; (*poor*) pauvre; **~iously** *adv.* de façon mesquine, pauvrement.

peony, paeony *s.* pivoine *f.*

people *s.* (*race, nation*) peuple *m.*; (*subjects*) sujets *m.pl.*; (*relatives*) parents *m.pl.*; (*persons in general*) (*when counted*) personnes *f.pl.*, **four ~,** quatre personnes, **how many ~?,** combien de personnes?; (*without a numeral*) gens ⚠ *adj. placed before s. is fem.*, **old ~ are brave,** les vieilles gens sont courageux; **there were a lot of ~,** il y avait beaucoup de monde; **~ say,** on dit; *v.t.* (*populate*) peupler; (*inhabit*) habiter.

pep *s.* (*fam.*) allant *m.*; **~ pill** *s.* excitant *m.*; **~ talk** *s.* mot d'encouragement *m.*; *v.t.* animer, ragaillardir.

pepper *s.* (*condiment*) poivre *m.*; (*plant*) poivron *m.*, piment *m.*; **~corn** *s.* grain de poivre *m.*; **~corn rent** *s.* loyer nominal *m.*; **~mint** *s.* menthe poivrée *f.*; **~-pot** *s.* poivrière *f.*; **~y** *adj.* poivré, (*fig.*) irascible; *v.t.* poivrer, pimenter; (*fig.*) cribler (*with*—de).

per *prep.* (*by means of*; *for each*) par; **~ annum,** par an; **~ capita,** par tête; **~ cent,** pour cent; **as ~ instructions,** selon les directives.

peradventure *adv.* par hasard.

perambulat/e *v.t.* parcourir; **~ion** *s.* parcours *m.*; **~or** *s.* voiture d'enfant *f.*

perceiv/e *v.t.* (*become aware of*) s'apercevoir de, que; (*apprehend*) apercevoir; (*understand*) comprendre; **~able** *adj.* perceptible; **~ably** *adv.* d'une manière perceptible.

percentage *s.* pourcentage *m.*

percep/tion *s.* perception *f.*; (*awareness*) sensibilité *f.*; **~tible** *adj.* perceptible; **~tibly** *adv.* d'une manière perceptible; **~tive** *adj.* perceptif, sensible; **~tivity** *s.* faculté de percevoir *f.*

perch *s.* **1.** (*of bird*; *fam. elevated position*) perchoir *m.*; **2.** (*measure*) perche *f.*; **3.** (*fish*) perche *f.*; *v.i.* (1) (se) percher.

perchance *adv.* peut-être.

percheron *s.* percheron(ne) *m.f.*

percipient *adj.* percepteur.

percolat/e *v.t.* & *i.* filtrer; **~ion** *s.* filtrage *m.*; **~or** *s.* percolateur *m.*

percuss/ion *s.* (*act*; *mus.*) percussion *f.*; (*sound*) choc *m.*; **~ion cap** *s.* capsule de fulminate *f.*; **~ive** *adj.* percutant..

perdition *s.* perdition *f.*

peregrinat/e *v.i.* voyager; **~ion** *s.* pérégrination *f.*

peremptor/y *adj.* (*imperious*) péremptoire; (*urgent*) pressant; **~ily** *adv.**; de manière pressante.

perennial *s.* (*hort.*) plante vivace *f.*; *adj.* perpétuel; **~ly** *adv.**.

perfect *s.* (*ling.*) parfait *m.*; *adj.* **1.** (*faultless*) parfait; **2.** (*complete*) complet; **3.** (*skilled*) achevé; **4.** (*exact, precise*) exact, précis; **5.** (*unqualified*) absolu; **~ly** *adv.* (1)*; (2)*; (4)*; (5)*; *v.t.* (1) rendre parfait; (2) achever; (3) & (4) perfectionner; **~ible** *adj.* perfectible; **~ibility** *s.* perfectibilité *f.*; **~ion** *s.* perfection *f.*, **to ~ion,** à souhait; **~ionist** *s.* perfectionniste *m.f.*

perfid/ious *adj.* perfide; **~iously** *adv.**; **~y** *s.* perfidie *f.*

perforat/e *v.t.* perforer; **~ion** *s.* perforation *f.*

perforce *adv.* forcément.

perform *v.t.* **1.** (*carry into effect*) mettre à exécution; **2.** (*accomplish* (*task*)) accomplir; **3.** (*execute* (*duty*)) s'acquitter de; **4.** (*mus.*) exécuter; **5.** (*theat.*) représenter; *v.i.* jouer; **~ance** *s.* (1) exécution *f.*; (2) accomplissement *m.*; (3), (4) exécution *f.*; (5) (*theat.*) représentation *f.*, (*cinema*) séance *f.*; COMMAND **~ance**; **6.** (*techn.*) fonctionnement *m.*; **7.** (*sport*) performance *f.* ⚠ *this meaning only*; **~er** *s.* (*stage*) artiste *m.f.*,

acteur *m.*, actrice *f.*, (*mus.*) exécutant *m.*; **~ing dog** *s.* chien savant *m.*
perfume *s.* parfum *m.*; *v.t.* parfumer; **~ry** *s.* parfumerie *f.*
perfunctor/y *adj.* négligent; **~ily** *adv.* négligemment, pour la forme.
pergola *s.* pergola *f.*
perhaps *adv.* peut-être.
peril *s.* péril *m.*; **at one's ~**, à ses risques et périls; **~ous** *adj.* périlleux; **~ously** *adv.**.
perimeter *s.* périmètre *m.*
period *s.* (*time*; *complete sentence*) période *f.*; (*era*) époque *f.*; (*full stop*) point *m.*; (*med.*) règles *f.pl.*; BRIGHT ~; *adj.* (*of furniture, etc.*) d'époque; **~ic** *adj.* périodique; **~ical** *adj.* & *s.m.* périodique; **~ically** *adv.**; **~icity** *s.* périodicité *f.*
peripatetic *adj.* ambulant.
peripher/y *s.* périphérie *f.*; **~al** *adj.* périphérique.
periphras/is *s.* périphase *f.*; **~tic** *adj.* périphrastique.
periscope *s.* périscope *m.*
perish *v.i.* (*lose life*) périr; (*lose natural qualities*) se détériorer; **be ~ed with cold,** *etc.* mourir de froid, etc.; **~able** *adj.* périssable; **~ables** *s.pl.* (*goods*) denrées périssables *f.pl.*; **~er** *s.* (*pop.*) type *m.*
peristyle *s.* péristyle *m.*
peritonitis *s.* péritonite *f.*
periwig *s.* perruque *f.*
periwinkle *s.* (*flower*) pervenche *f.*; (*shellfish*) bigorneau *m.*
perjur/e (*oneself*) *v.refl.* se parjurer; **~ed** *adj.* parjure; **~er** *s.* parjure *m.f.*; **~y** *s.* parjure *m.*; (*law*) **to commit ~y,** faire un faux serment.
perk[1] *s.* (*pop.*) à-côté *m.*
perk[2] *v.i.* se ranimer; **~ up** *v.i.* (*fam.*) se requinquer; **~y** *adj.* éveillé, effronté.
permafrost *s.* pergélisol *m.*
permanen/ce *s.* permanence *f.*; **~cy** *s.* (*thing*) chose fixe *f.*, (*post*) emploi permanent *m.*; **~t** *adj.* permanent; **~t wave** *s.* permanente *f.*; **~t way** *s.* (*rail.*) voie ferrée *f.*; **~tly** *adv.* de façon permanente.
permanganate *s.* (*chem.*) permanganate *m.*; **potassium ~** *s.* permanganate de potassium *m.*
permea/te *v.t.* pénétrer; (*fig.*) imprégner; *v.i.* (*filter through*) filtrer à travers; **~bility** *s.* perméabilité *f.*; **~ble** *adj.* perméable; **~tion** *s.* pénétration *f.*
permiss/ible *adj.* permis; **~ion** *s.* permission *f.*; **~ive** *adj.* qui permet, tolérant.
permit *s.* permis *m.*; (*comm. law*) passavant *m.*; *v.t.* permettre (à qn. de faire qch.); **~ of,** admettre.
permut/e *v.t.* permuter; **~ation** *s.* permutation *f.*
pernicious *adj.* pernicieux; **~ly** *adv.**.
pernickety *adj.* pointilleux, difficile.
perorat/e *v.i.* pérorer; **~ion** *s.* péroraison *f.*
peroxide *s.* peroxyde *m.*; *v.t.* (*hair*) oxygéner.
perpendicular *s.* (*line*) perpendiculaire *f.*; (*arch.*) style perpendiculaire *m.*; *adj.* perpendiculaire; **~ly** *adv.**.
perpetrat/e *v.t.* (*be guilty of*) perpétrer; (*commit* (*offence*)) commettre; **~ion** *s.* perpétration *f.*; **~or** *s.* auteur *m.*
perpetu/al *adj.* perpétuel; **~ally** *adv.**; **~ate** *v.t.* perpétuer; **~ation** *s.* perpétuation *f.*; **~ity** *s.* perpétuité *f.*; **in ~ity,** à perpétuité.
perplex *v.t.* (*bewilder*) rendre perplexe, embarrasser; (*complicate*) embrouiller; **~ity** *s.* perplexité *f.*
perquisites *s.pl.* petits profits *m.pl.*
perry *s.* poiré *m.*
persecut/e *v.t.* persécuter; **~ion** *s.* persécution *f.*; **~or** *s.* persécut/eur, -rice *m.f.*
persever/e *v.i.* persévérer (*in or at sth.*—dans qch.; *in doing sth.*—à faire qch.); **~ance** *s.* persévérance *f.*; **~ing** *adj.* persévérant; **~ingly** *adv.* avec persévérance.
Persia *s.* (*geog.*) Perse *f.*; **~n** *adj.* & *s.m.f.* (*hist.*) perse, (*mod.*) persan(e); *s.m.* (*lang.*) persan; **~n carpet,** tapis persan *m.*; **~n cat,** chat persan *m.*
persiflage *s.* persiflage *m.*
persist *v.i.* persister (*in sth.*—dans qch.; *in doing sth.*—à faire qch.); **~ence** *s.* persistance *f.*; **~ent** *adj.* persistant.
person *s.* (*individual, bodily presence*; *ling.*) personne *f.*; (*character in book*) personnage *m.*; **~a (non) grata,** persona (non) grata; **~able** *adj.* beau; **~age** *s.* personnage *m.*; **~ate** *v.t.* se faire passer pour; (*theat.*) jouer le rôle de; **~ify** *v.t.* personnifier; **~ification** *s.* personnification *f.*
personal *adj.* personnel; (*law*) **~ property,** biens meubles *m.pl.*; **~ity** *s.* (*identity, prominent person*) personnalité *f.*; (*character*) caractère propre *m.*; **~ize** *v.t.* personnaliser; **~ly** *adv.* (*in ~*) en personne; (*for one's own part*) personnellement, pour ma, sa (etc.) part.
personnel *s.* personnel *m.*
perspective *s.* perspective *f.*; **in ~**, en perspective; *adj.* perspectif.
Perspex *s.* plexiglas *m.*
perspicac/ious *adj.* perspicace; **~ity** *s.* perspicacité *f.*
perspir/e *v.i.* transpirer; **~ation** *s.* transpiration *f.*; **to be bathed in ~ation,** être en nage; ⚠ perspiration *is a med. term.*
persua/de *v.t.* **1.** (*convince*) convaincre (*of*—de); **2.** (*impel by argument*) persuader (*s.o. of sth.*—qn. de qch.; *s.o. to sth.*—qn. de faire qch.; *s.o. that*—qn. que); **I am ~ded that,** je suis convaincu que; **~sion** *s.* (1) conviction *f.*; (2) persuasion *f.*; **3.** (*relig. belief*) croyance *f.*, (*sect*) secte *f.*; **~sive** *adj.* persuasif; **~sively** *adv.* d'une manière persuasive.
pert *adj.* impertinent; **~ly** *adv.* avec impertinence.
pertain *v.i.* (*to*) (*be part of*) appartenir (à); (*relate*) avoir rapport (à).
pertinac/ious *adj.* opiniâtre; **~iously** *adv.**; **~ity** *s.* opiniâtreté *f.*
pertinen/t *adj.* **1.** (*to the point*) pertinent; **2.** (*relevant*) à propos; approprié (à); **~ce** *s.* (1) justesse *f.*; (2) à-propos *m.*; **~tly** *adv.* (1) pertinemment; (2) avec à-propos.
perturb *v.t.* **1.** (*disquiet*) troubler; **2.** (*agitate*) agiter; **3.** (*disrupt*) perturber; **~ation** *s.* (1) trouble *m.*; (2) agitation *f.*; (3) perturbation *f.*
Peru *s.* (*geog.*) le Pérou *m.*; **~vian** *adj.* & *s.m.f.* péruvien(ne).
peruke *s.* perruque *f.*
perus/e *v.t.* lire attentivement; **~al** *s.* lecture *f.*
perva/de *v.t.* pénétrer, imprégner; (*fig.*) s'emparer de; **~sive** *adj.* pénétrant.
pervers/e *adj.* **1.** (*contrary*) obstiné; **2.** (*wayward*) entêté; **3.** (*peevish*) revêche; **4.** (*wicked*) pervers; **~ely** *adv.* (1)*; (2) avec entêtement; (3) d'un air revêche; (4) avec perversité; **~ion** *s.* perversion *f.*; **~ity** *s.* (1) obstination *f.*; (2) entêtement *m.*; (3) caractère revêche *m.*; (4) perversité *f.*
pervert *s.* perverti(e) *m.f.*; (*eccles.*) apostat *m.*; *v.t.* pervertir; (*misinterpret*) dénaturer.
peseta *s.* peseta *f.*
peso *s.* peso *m.*
pessim/ism *s.* pessimisme *m.*; **~ist** *s.* pessimiste *m.f.*; **~istic** *adj.* pessimiste.
pest *s.* (*disease*) peste *f.*; (*insect, fungus*) insecte nuisible *m.*, parasite *m.*; (*anything destructive, person*) fléau *m.*; **~icide** *s.* pesticide *m.*
pester *v.t.* importuner.

pestiferous *adj.* nuisible; (*fam.*) assommant.
pestilen/ce *s.* peste *f.*; **~t** *adj.* pernicieux; (*fam.*) assommant; **~tial** *adj.* pestilentiel; (*fam.*) assommant.
pestle *s.* pilon *m.*
pet[1] *s.* (*child*) enfant gâté *m.*; (*animal*) animal favori *m.*; (*favourite*) favori(te) *m.f.*; *adj.* familier, favori; **~** AVERSION; *v.t.* gâter, choyer; *v.i.* (*fam.*) peloter.
pet[2] *s.* (*ill-humour*) mauvaise humeur *f.*
petal *s.* pétale *m.*
petard *s.* pétard *m.*; **to be** HOIST **with one's own ~.**
Peter *s.* (*name*) Pierre; **Blue ~,** (*naut.*) pavillon de partance *m.*; **to** ROB **~ to pay Paul.**
peter, out *v.i.* s'épuiser, se tarir.
petersham *s.* gros-grain *m.*
petition *s.* pétition *f.*, requête *f.*, demande *f.*; *v.t.* adresser une pétition à; **~er** *s.* solliciteu/r, -se *m.f.*
petrel *s.* (*stormy*) pétrel *m.*
petrif/y *v.t.* (*lit.* & *fig.*) pétrifier (*with*—de); **~action** *s.* pétrification *f.*
petro- (*in combination*) **~chemical** *adj.* pétrochimique *or* pétrolochimique; **~chemistry** *s.* pétrochimie *f.* *or* pétrolochimie *f.*; **~dollar** *s.* pétrodollar *m.*
petrol *s.* essence *f.*; ⚠ pétrole = **oil**; **~-pump** *s.* pompe à essence *f.*; **~ station** *s.* station-service *f.*; **~ tank** *s.* réservoir d'essence *m.*
petroleum *s.* pétrole *m.*
petticoat *s.* jupon *m.*
pettifogg/er *s.* chicaneur *m.*; **~ing** *adj.* chicanier.
pettish *adj.* maussade.
pett/y *adj.* (*trivial*) petit; (*small-minded*) mesquin; (*minor*) insignifiant; **~y cash,** petite monnaie *f.*; **~y officer** *s.* maître *m.*; **~ily** *adv.* petitement; **~iness** *s.* petitesse *f.*, mesquinerie *f.*
petulan/ce *s.* irritabilité *f.*; ⚠ pétulance = **exuberance**; **~t** *adj.* irritable; ⚠ pétulant = **exuberant**; **~tly** *adv.* de façon irritable.
petunia *s.* pétunia *m.*
pew *s.* banc *m.* (d'église).
pewter *s.* étain *m.*
phaeton *s.* phaéton *m.*
phalanx *s.* phalange *f.*
phall/us *s.* phallus *m.*; **~ic** *adj.* phallique.
phant/asm & **phantom** *s.* fantôme *m.*; **~asmagoria** *s.* fantasmagorie *f.*
Pharaoh *s.* Pharaon *m.*
Pharis/ee *s.* pharisien(ne) *m.f.*; (*hypocrite*) hypocrite *m.f.*; **~aic** *adj.* pharisaïque.
pharmac/y *s.* pharmacie *f.*; **~eutical** *adj.* pharmaceutique; **~eutics** *s.* pharmaceutique *f.* ⚠ *sing. in French*; **~ist** *s.* pharmacien *m.*; **~ology** *s.* pharmacologie *f.*; **~opoeia** *s.* pharmacopée *f.*
phase *s.* phase *f.*; *v.t.* (*electr.*) mettre en phase; **~ in** *v.t.* introduire par étapes; **~ out** *v.t.* supprimer par étapes.
Ph.D. *s.* doctorat *m.* (ès lettres, ès sciences, en droit, en médecine); (*person*) docteur *m.*
pheasant *s.* faisan *m.*; faisane *f.*; (*young*) faisandeau *m.*
phenacetin *s.* phénacétine *f.*
phenobarbitone *s.* phénobarbiturique *m.*
phenomen/al *adj.* phénoménal; **~ally** *adv.**; **~on** *s.* phénomène *m.*
phial *s.* flacon *m.*
philander *v.i.* faire la cour (*with*—à); **~er** *s.* coureur *m.*
philanthrop/y *s.* philanthropie *f.*; **~ic** *adj.* philanthropique; **~ist** *s.* philanthrope *m.f.*
philatel/y *s.* philatélie *f.*; **~ic** *adj.* philatélique; **~ist** *s.* philatéliste *m.f.*
Philippin/es *s.* (*geog.*) Philippines *f.pl.*; **~o** *adj.* & *s.m.f.* philippin(e).
Philistine *adj.* & *s.m.f.* philistin(e).
philolog/y *s.* philologie *f.*; **~ist** *s.* philologue *m.f.*
philosoph/y *s.* philosophie *f.*; **~er** *s.* philosophe *m.f.*; **~ical** *adj.* philosophique; (*resigned*) philosophe; **~ically** *adv.* philosophiquement; **~ize** *v.i.* philosopher.
philtre *s.* philtre *m.*
phlebitis *s.* (*med.*) phlébite *f.*
phlegm *s.* (*lit.* & *fig.*) flegme *m.*; **~atic** *adj.* flegmatique.
phlox *s.* phlox *m.*
phobia *s.* phobie *f.*
phoenix *s.* phénix *m.*
phone *s.* (*fam.*) téléphone *m.*; *v.t.* & *i.* téléphoner.
phone/tic *adj.* phonétique; **~tics** *s.* phonétique *f.* ⚠ *sing. in French*; **~me** *s.* phonème *m.*
phon(e)y *s.* charlatan *m.*; *adj.* (*pop.*) (*person*) à la gomme; (*thing*) drôle de, **~ war,** drôle de guerre; (*person* & *thing, shady*) louche.
phono- (*in combination*) **~gram** *s.* sténogramme *m.*; **~graph** *s.* phonographe *m.*; **~logy** *s.* phonologie *f.*
phosphate *s.* phosphate *m.*
phosphoresen/ce *s.* phosphorescence *f.*; **~t** *adj.* phosphorescent.
phosphor/us *s.* phosphore *m.*; **~ic** *adj.* phosphorique.
photo- (*in combination*) **~chemical** *adj.* photochimique; **~copy** *s.* photocopie *f.*; **~electric** *adj.* photo-électrique; **~ finish** *s.* photo-finish *m.*; **~genic** *adj.* photogénique; **~meter** *s.* photomètre *m.*; **~phobia** *s.* photophobie *f.*; **~stat** *s.* photostat *m.*; **~synthesis** *s.* photosynthèse *f.*; **~therapy** *s.* photothérapie *f.*
photograph *s.* photographie *f.*; *v.t.* photographier; **~er** *s.* photographe *m.f.*; **~ic** *adj.* photographique; **~y** *s.* photographie *f.*
phrase *s.* (*group of words*) locution *f.*; (*expression*) expression *f.*; ⚠ phrase = **sentence,** *exc.* (*mus.*) phrase *f.*; **~-book** *s.* manuel de conversation *m.*; *v.t.* exprimer; **~ology** *s.* phraséologie *f.*
phrenolog/y *s.* phrénologie *f.*; **~ist** *s.* phrénologiste *m.f.*
phthis/is *s.* phtisie *f.*; **~ical** *adj.* phtisique.
phylloxera *s.* phylloxéra *m.*
physic *s.* (*science*) médecine *f.*; (*fam. drug*) médicament *m.*; *v.t.* droguer; **~s** *s.* physique *f.* ⚠ *sing. in French*; **~al** *adj.* physique; **~ally** *adv.**; **~ian** *s.* médecin *m.*; **~ist** *s.* physicien *m.*
physiognomy *s.* physionomie *f.*
physiolog/y *s.* physiologie *f.*; **~ical** *adj.* physiologique; **~ist** *s.* physiologiste *m.f.*
physiotherap/y *s.* physiothérapie *f.*; **~ist** *s.* physiothérapiste *m.f.*
physique *s.* physique *m.*
piano (**forte**) *s.* piano *m.*; **grand ~,** piano à queue *m.*; *adj. adv.* piano; **pianist** *s.* pianiste *m.f.*
pica *s.* (*type*) cicéro *m.*
picador *s.* picador *m.*
picaresque *adj.* picaresque.
piccolo *s.* piccolo *m.*
pick *s.* **1.** (*tool*) pic *m.*, pioche *f.*; **tooth~,** cure-dent *m.*; **2.** (*selection*) choix *m.*; *v.t.* (1) piocher; (*bone*) ronger; (*lock*) crocheter; (*teeth*) (se) curer (les dents); (2) choisir; **3.** (*gather*) cueillir; **4.** (*tear*) déchirer; **have a** BONE **to ~ with s.o.**; **~ s.o.'s brains,** exploiter l'intelligence de qn.; **~ a** QUARREL; **~ off** *v.t.* enlever, cueillir; **~ on** (*s.o., sth.*) prendre (qn. qch.) pour cible; **~ out** *v.t.* choisir; **~ over** *v.t.* trier; **~ up** *v.t.* ramasser, prendre; **~ up** *v.i.* reprendre ses forces; **~-up** *s.* (*act*) ramassage *m.*, (*recovery*) reprise *f.*, (*radio*) pick-up *m.*; **~-a-back** *adv.* sur le dos; **~axe** *s.* pioche *f.*; **~pocket** *s.* voleur à la tire *m.*; **~ings** *s.pl.* restes *m.pl.*
picket *s.* **1.** (*stake*) pieu *m.*; **2.** (*police, mil., striker*) piquet *m.*; *v.t.* (1) (*an animal*) mettre au piquet; (2) (*a place*) entourer de piquets.

pickle *s.* **1.** (*brine*) saumure *f.*; **2.** (*fam.*) pétrin *m.*; **~s** *s.pl.* conserves de légumes au vinaigre *f.pl.*; *v.t.* (1) mariner, saler, conserver dans le vinaigre.
picnic *s.* pique-nique *m.*; *v.i.* faire un pique-nique; **~ker** *s.* pique-niqueu/r, -se *m.f.*
pictorial *s.* illustré *m.*; *adj.* (*illustrated*) illustré; (*picturesque*) pittoresque.
picture *s.* (*work of art, beautiful object, scene*) tableau *m.*; (*portrait*) portrait *m.*; (*mental image*) image *f.*; **to put s.o. in the ~,** mettre qn. au courant; (*film*) film *m.*; **~s** *pl.* (= *cinema*) cinéma *m.*; **~-gallery** *s.* musée de peinture *m.*; **~ postcard** *s.* carte postale illustrée *f.*; *v.t.* (*represent*) dépeindre; (*describe*) décrire; (*imagine*) s'imaginer; **~sque** *adj.* pittoresque; **~squely** *adv.**; **~squeness** *s.* pittoresque *m.*
pidgin (**English**) *s.* petit nègre *m.*
pie *s.* (*meat*) pâté *m.*; (*fruit*) tarte *f.*; HUMBLE **~**; MINCE **~**; **to have a** FINGER **in the ~**; **~dish** *s.* (*meat*) terrine *f.*, (*fruit*) tourtière *f.*
piebald *adj.* pie.
piece *s.* (*part*) partie *f.*; (*fragment*) morceau *m.*; (*specimen*) échantillon *m.*; (*theat.*) pièce de théâtre *f.*; (*chess, coin*) pièce *f.*; **~ of** FURNITURE; **~ of** NEWS; **~ of** WORK; **to give s.o. a ~ of one's mind,** faire savoir à qn. de quel bois on se chauffe; **in ~s,** en morceaux; **to go to ~s,** s'effondrer; **to take to ~s,** défaire, démonter; **~-goods** *s.* tissus à la pièce *m.pl.*; **~meal** *adv.* pièce à pièce; **~-work** *s.* travail à la pièce *m.*; *v.t.* (*make of ~s*) assembler; (*mend*) rapiécer; (*decipher*) déchiffrer; **~ together** *v.t.* (*bits*) rassembler, (*facts*) coordonner.
pied *adj.* bigarré.
pier *s.* (*of bridge*) pile *f.*; (*pillar*) pied-droit *m.*; (*at sea*) jetée *f.*; (*for pleasure*) promenade *f.*; **~-glass** *s.* trumeau *m.*
pierc/e *v.t.* percer; **~ing** *adj.* perçant.
piet/y *s.* piété *f.*; **~ism** *s.* piétisme *m.*; **~ist** *s.* piétiste *m.f.*
piffl/e *s.* (*pop.*) balivernes *f.pl.*; **~ing** *adj.* futile, insignifiant.
pig *s.* (*animal & person*) cochon *m.*; GUINEA-**~**; **sucking ~,** cochon de lait *m.*; **to buy a ~ in a poke,** acheter chat en poche; **~headed** *adj.* entêté; **~-iron** *s.* gueuse *f.*, saumon *m.* (de fonte); **~skin** *s.* peau de porc *f.*; **~sticking** *s.* chasse au sanglier *f.*; **~sty** *s.* porcherie *f.*, (*fam.*) bouge *f.*; **~tail** *s.* natte *f.*; **~wash** *s.* (*fam.*) lavasse *f.*; **~gery** *s.* porcherie *f.*; **~let** *s.* porcelet *m.*; *v.i.* (*litter*) mettre bas; **~ it** *v.i.* vivre comme des cochons.
pigeon *s.* pigeon(ne) *m.f.*; **carrier ~,** pigeon voyageur *m.*; **clay ~,** pigeon artificiel *m.*; ROCK **~**; STOOL **~**; **wood ~,** ramier *m.*; **young ~,** pigeonneau *m.*; **to put the** CAT **among the ~s**; **~-hole** *s.* case *f.*, (*set of*) casier *m.*, *v.t.* classer; **~-house, ~-loft** *s.* colombier *m.*
pigment *s.* pigment *m.*; *v.t.* pigmenter; **~ation** *s.* pigmentation *f.*
pike *s.* **1.** (*weapon*) pique *f.*; **2.** (*toll-bar*) barrière de péage *f.*; **3.** (*fish*) brochet *m.*; **~staff** *s.* hampe de pique *f.*; **plain as a ~staff,** clair comme le jour.
pilaff, pilau *s.* (*cook.*) pilaf *m.*
pilaster *s.* pilastre *m.*
pilchard *s.* pilchard *m.*, sardine *f.*
pile *s.* **1.** (*heap*) tas *m.*; (*pop.* = *fortune*) **to make a ~,** faire sa pelote; **2.** (*building*) édifice *m.*; **3.** (*stake or post*) pieu *m.*, (*collection of stakes*) pilotis *m.*; **4.** (*of carpet*) poil *m.*; **5.** (*electr.*) pile *f.*; **~s** (*med.*) hémorroïdes *f.pl.*; **~-driver** (3) *s.* mouton *m.*, sonnette *f.*; *v.t.* (1) entasser, empiler; (*wealth*) amasser; **~ up** *v.i.* (*auto.*) se télescoper; **~-up** *s.* télescopage *m.*
pilfer *v.t.* (*fam.*) chaparder; **~er** *s.* chapardeu/r, -se *m.f.*; **~ing** *s.* chapardage *m.*
pilgrim *s.* pèlerin(e) *m.f.*; **~age** *s.* pèlerinage *m.*
pill *s.* pilule *f.*; **the ~** (*oral contraceptive*) la pilule *f.*; **~box** *s.* (*hat*) toque *f.*, (*mil.*) abri en béton *m.*
pillage *s.* pillage *m.*; *v.t.* piller.
pillar *s.* (*lit. & fig.*) pilier *m.*; (*of smoke, fire, water*) colonne *f.*; **~-box** *s.* boîte aux lettres *f.*
pillion *s.* (*saddle*) selle de femme *f.*; (*of motor-cycle*) tan-sad *m.* (*pl.* tan-sads); **to ride ~,** monter en passager.
pillory *s.* (*hist.*) pilori *m.*; *v.t.* mettre au pilori; (*ridicule*) exposer au ridicule.
pillow *s.* oreiller *m.*; **~case, ~slip** *s.* taie d'oreiller *f.*; *v.t.* (*serve as ~*) servir d'oreiller à; (*rest* (*head, etc.*)) reposer (la tête).
pilot *s.* (*naut., aviat.*) pilote *m.*; (*guide*) guide *m.*; **~-boat** *s.* bateau-pilote *m.*; **~-light** *s.* veilleuse *f.*; **~ officer** *s.* sous-lieutenant *m.*; *adj.* (*experimental*) pilote; **~ scheme,** *etc.* projet (etc.)-pilote; **~age** *s.* pilotage *m.*; *v.t.* piloter.
pimento *s.* piment *m.*
pimpernel *s.* mouron *m.*
pimpl/e *s.* bouton *m.*; **~y** *adj.* boutonneux.
pin *s.* **1.** (*for fastening*) épingle *f.*; HAIR**~**; **hat-~,** épingle à chapeau *f.*; **safety-~,** épingle de sûreté *f.*; **2.** (*wood or metal peg*) cheville *f.*; **drawing-~,** punaise *f.*; **rolling-~,** rouleau à pâtisserie *m.*; **3.** (*skittle*) quille *f.*; **to have ~s and needles,** avoir des fourmis (dans les membres); **~cushion** *s.* pelote à épingles *f.*; **~-money** *s.* argent de poche *m.*; **~-point** *v.t.* pointer; **~prick** *s.* piqûre d'épingle *f.*, (*fam.*) coup d'épingle *m.*; **~-stripe** *adj.* fil-à-fil; *v.t.* (1) épingler; (2) cheviller; (*transfix*) clouer; **~ down** *v.t.* (*bind*) lier, (*specify*) repérer; **~-up** *s.* pin-up *f.*
pinafore *s.* tablier *m.*
pincer/s *s.* (*tool*) tenailles *f.pl.*; (*of lobster, etc.*) pinces *f.pl.*; **~ movement,** mouvement convergent *m.*
pinch *s.* **1.** (*nip*) pinçon *m.*; **2.** (*small amount*) (*salt*) pincée *f.*, (*snuff*) prise *f.*; **at a ~,** au besoin; **to feel the ~,** tirer le diable par la queue; **to take sth. with a ~ of** SALT; *v.t.* (1) (& *shrivel*; & *pop.* = *arrest*) pincer; (*injure*) blesser; (*pop.* = *steal*) chiper; *v.i.* lésiner; **where the shoe ~es,** où le bât blesse.
Pindaric *adj.* pindarique.
pine[1] *s.* **1.** (*tree*) pin *m.*; **2.** (= *~apple*) ananas *m.*; **~-**CONE; **~-**NEEDLE.
pine[2] *v.i.* languir; **~ for,** désirer fortement.
ping *s.* sifflement *m.*; *v.i.* siffler; **~-pong** *s.* ping-pong *m.*
pinion *s.* **1.** (*of wing*) aileron *m.*; **2.** (*mech.*) pignon *m.*; *v.t.* (1) (*bird*) couper le bout de l'aile; (*person*) lier.
pink *s.* (*flower*) œillet *m.*; (*colour*) rose *m.*; *adj.* rose; *v.t.* (*stab*) toucher; (*cut with serrated edge*) denteler; *v.i.* (*of engine*) avoir des ratés.
pinnace *s.* grand canot *m.*
pinnacle *s.* (*lit. & fig.*) pinacle *m.*; (*geol.*) cime *f.*
pint *s.* (*measure*) pinte *f.*; (*fam.*) quart *m.*
pioneer *s.* pionnier *m.*; *v.t.* frayer le chemin pour; (*inaugurate*) inaugurer.
pious *adj.* pieux; **~ly** *adv.**.
pip *s.* (*seed*) pépin *m.*; (*on card, etc.*) point *m.*; (*mil. on uniform*) cabochon *m.*, (*mil. fig.*) galon *m.*; (*pop.*) cafard *m.*; (*radio*) top *m.*; *v.t.* (*fam. defeat*) battre; (*fam. fail candidate in exam*) recaler; (*fail exam*) rater.
pipe *s.* (*gas, water; organ*) tuyau *m.*; EXHAUST **~**; (*mus. instrument*) chalumeau *m.*; **~s** (*bag~s*) cornemuse *f.*; (*naut.*) sifflet *m.*; (*of bird*) pépiement *m.*; (*anat.*) tube *f.* (respiratoire, etc.); (*for smoking; cask*) pipe *f.*; **clay ~,** pipe en terre *f.*; **~clay** *s.* terre de pipe *f.*; **~-cleaner** *s.* cure-pipe *m.*; **~-dream** *s.* chimère *f.*; **~line** *s.* pipeline *m.*, **in the ~line** (*fig.*) en cours; **~-rack** *s.* ratelier à pipes *m.*; *v.t.* (*convey*) trans-

porter par tuyau; (*summon*; *utter shrilly*) siffler; (*trim*) garnir; *v.i.* (*mus.*) jouer du chalumeau, de la cornemuse; (*bird*) pépier; ~ **down** (*fam.*) mettre la sourdine (à); **~d music** *s.* musique en conserve *f.*; **~r** *s.* joueur de cornemuse *m.*; **to pay the ~r** (*fig.*) payer les violons; **piping** *s.* (*~s*) tuyauterie *f.*, (*trimming*) passepoil *m.*; **piping hot,** tout chaud.

pipette *s.* pipette *f.*

pippin *s.* reinette *f.*

piquan/cy *s.* goût piquant *m.*; (*fig.*) piquant *m.*; **~t** *adj.* (*lit.* & *fig.*) piquant.

pique *s.* ressentiment *m.*; *v.t.* (*wound pride*) froisser; (*stir curiosity*) exciter.

piquet *s.* piquet *m.*

pira/cy *s.* piraterie *f.*; (*fig.*) plagiat *m.*; **~te** *s.* pirate *m.*; (*fig.*) plagiaire *m.*; *v.t.* (*infringe copyright*) contrefaire, plagier.

Piraeus *s.* (*geog.*) le Pirée *m.*

pirouette *s.* pirouette *f.*; *v.i.* pirouetter.

Pisa *s.* (*geog.*) Pise *f.*

pisciculture *s.* pisciculture *f.*

pistachio *s.* (*nut*) pistache *f.*; (*tree*) pistachier *m.*

pistol *s.* pistolet *m.*

piston *s.* piston *m.*; **~-ring** *s.* segment de piston *m.*; **~-rod** *s.* tige de piston *f.*

pit *s.* (*hole in ground, in garage*) fosse *f.*; (*mine*) mine *f.*; (*trap*) piège *m.*; (*depression, of stomach, etc.*) creux *m.*; (*theat.*) parterre *m.*; (*motor-racing*) stand *m.*; **~fall** *s.* (*lit.* & *fig.*) piège *m.*; **~-head** *s.* carreau de mine *m.*; *v.t.* (*make holes in*) trouer; (*oppose to*) opposer à; ~ **oneself against,** se mesurer contre; **~ted with** *adj.* grêlé de.

pit-a-pat *adv.* **to go ~,** (*feet*) trottiner; (*heart*) palpiter; (*rain*) crépiter.

pitch *s.* **1.** (*substance*) poix *f.*; **2.** (*act*) lancement *m.*; **3.** (*height, degree*) degré *m.*, **highest ~,** comble *m.*; **4.** (*tone*) ton *m.*, **concert ~,** diapason de concert *m.*; **5.** (*in market, etc.*) place *f.*; **6.** (*sport*) terrain *m.*; **to** QUEER **the ~ for s.o.**; **~-black** *adj.* noir d'ébène; **~blende** *s.* pechblende *f.*; **~fork** *s.* fourche *f.*; **~-pine** *s.* pitchpin *m.*; **~-and-toss,** pile ou face; *v.t.* (1) enduire de poix; (2) lancer; (4) donner le ton; **7.** (*tent*) dresser, (*camp*) établir; *v.i.* (*naut.*) tanguer; (*fall*) tomber; **~ed battle,** bataille rangée *f.*; **~ing** *s.* (*naut.*) tangage *m.*

pitcher *s.* cruche *f.*

piteous *adj.* (*deplorable*) piteux; (*strirring pity*) pitoyable; **~ly** *adv.**;*.

pith *s.* **1.** (*of orange, etc.*) moelle *f.*; **2.** (*chief part*) essence *f.*; **3.** (*energy*) vigueur *f.*; ~ **helmet** *s.* casque colonial *m.*; **~y** *adj.* (3) vigoureux; **~ily** *adv.* avec vigueur; **~iness** *s.* vigueur *f.*

pitiable *adj. see* PITY.

pitiful *adj. see* PITY.

pitiless *adj. see* PITY.

piton *s.* piton *m.*

pittance *s.* pitance *f.*

pituitary *adj.* pituitaire.

pit/y *s.* **1.** (*sorrow for another*) pitié *f.*; **to take ~y on,** prendre pitié de; **out of ~y, for ~y's sake,** par pitié; **2.** (*regrettable fact*) dommage *m.*; **what a ~y!,** quel dommage!; *v.t.* (1) avoir pitié de, plaindre; **~iable** *adj.* (*deserving ~*) pitoyable, (*deserving contempt*) piteux; **~iably** *adv.**;*; **~iful** *adj.* (*compassionate*) compatissant, (*stirring ~*) pitoyable, (*contemptible*) piteux; **~ifully** *adv.* avec compassion,*,*; **~ifulness** *s.* état pitoyable *m.*; **~iless** *adj.* impitoyable; **~ilessly** *adv.* sans pitié; **~ying** *adj.* compatissant; **~yingly** *adv.* avec compassion.

Pius *s.* Pie *m.*

pivot *s.* pivot *m.*; *v.t.* & *i.* (faire) pivoter; **~al** *adj.* essentiel.

pixie, pixy *s.* lutin *m.*

placab/le *adj.* doux; **~ility** *s.* douceur *f.*

placard *s.* affiche *f.*; *v.t.* afficher; ⚠ placard = **cupboard.**

placat/e *v.t.* apaiser; **~ory** *adj.* apaisant.

place *s.* (*point in space*) lieu *m.*, endroit *m.*; (*space for s.o. or sth.*) place *f.*; (*city, etc.*) localité *f.*; (*public office, employment*) poste *m.*, emploi *m.*; (*rank*) rang *m.*; (*at table*) couvert *m.*; **watering ~,** ville d'eau *f.*, station balnéaire *f.*; ~ **of residence,** domicile *m.*; ~ **of worship,** édifice religieux *m.*; **in ~,** à sa place; **out of ~,** déplacé, (*fig.*) mal à propos; **in ~ of,** au lieu de; **to give ~ to,** faire place à; **to take ~,** avoir lieu; **to take the ~ of,** remplacer; **to put s.o. in his ~,** remettre qn. à sa place; *v.t.* placer; (*an order*) passer; (*appoint*) nommer; **placing** *s.* (*act*) mise en place *f.*, (*position*) position *f.*

placenta *s.* placenta *m.*

placid *adj.* placide; **~ity** *s.* placidité *f.*; **~ly** *adv.**.

placket *s.* fente *f.*

plagiar/ism *s.* plagiat *m.*; **~ist** *s.* plagiaire *m.*; **~ize** *v.t.* plagier.

plague *s.* peste *f.*; (*fam.*) fléau *m.*; *v.t.* (*fam.*) tourmenter, embêter.

plaice *s.* carrelet *m.*

plaid *s.* plaid *m.*

plain *s.* (*level country*) plaine *f.*; (*stitch in knitting*) maille à l'endroit *f.*; *adj.* **1.** (*clear, evident*) clair, évident; ~ **as a** PIKE**staff**; **2.** (*frank*) franc; **3.** (*ordinary*) ordinaire; **4.** (≠ *fancy*) simple; **5.** (≠ *pretty*) laid; *adv.* & **~ly** *adv.* (1) clairement; (2) franchement; (4)*; **to make oneself ~,** se faire comprendre; ~ CLOTHES; ~ SAIL**ing**; **~song** *s.* plain-chant *m.*; **~-speaking** *s.* franchise *f.*; **~-spoken** *adj.* franc; **~ness** *s.* (1) clarté *f.*; (4) simplicité *f.*; (5) laideur *f.*

plaint *s.* plainte *f.*; **~iff** *s.* demand/eur, -eresse *m.f.*; **~ive** *adj.* plaintif; **~ively** *adv.**.

plait *s.* natte *f.*; *v.t.* tresser.

plan *s.* plan *m.*; (*project*) projet *m.*; **according to ~,** comme prévu; *v.t.* faire le plan de; (*intend*) projeter; **~ner** *s.* planificateur *m.*; **~ning** *s.* planification *f.*, programme *m.*; FAMILY **~ning**; TOWN **~ning.**

plane *s.* **1.** (*tree*) platane *m.*; **2.** (*surface*) plan *m.*; **3.** (*aircraft*) avion *m.*; **4.** (*level*) niveau *m.*; **5.** (*tool*) rabot *m.*; *adj.* plan, plat; *v.t.* (5) raboter; *v.i.* (3) descendre en vol plané.

planet *s.* planète *f.*; **~ary** *adj.* planétaire; **~arium** *s.* planétarium *m.*

plank *s.* planche *f.*; (*fig. polit.*) article *m.*; *v.t.* planchéier; **~ing** *s.* planchéiage *m.*

plankton *s.* plancton *m.*

plant *s.* (*bot.*) plante *f.*; (*techn.*) matériel *m.*, installation *f.*; (*pop.* = *hoax*) coup monté *m.*; *v.t.* (*agric., hort.*) planter; (*establish*) fonder, implanter; (*deliver blow, etc.*) flanquer, (*pop.*) planquer; ~ **out** (*agric.*) repiquer; **~er** *s.* colon *m.*, planteur *m.*

plantain *s.* (*herb*) plantain *m.*; (*banana*) banane *f.*; (*tree*) bananier *m.*

plantation *s.* plantation *f.*

plaque *s.* plaque *f.*

plash *see* SPLASH.

plasm(a) *s.* plasma *m.*

plaster *s.* **1.** (*med.*) (*dressing*) emplâtre *m.*; **sticking-~,** taffetas anglais *m.*, taffetas gommé *m.*; ~ **of Paris,** plâtre *m.*; **2.** (*constr.*) plâtre *m.*; ~ **cast** *s.* plâtre *m.*; *v.t.* (1) & (2) plâtrer; **~er** *s.* (2) plâtrier *m.*; **~ing** *s.* plâtrage *m.*

plastic *adj.* & *s.m.* plastique; *adj.* (*made of ~*) en plastique; (*fig.*) malléable; ~ **surgery** *s.* autoplastie *f.*; **~ine** *s.* pâte à modeler *f.*; **~ity** *s.* plasticité *f.*

plate *s.* **1.** (*flat sheet of metal, glass, etc.*) plaque *f.*; **hot ~** *s.* plaque-chauffante *f.*; NUMBER-**~**; **2.** (*engraved metal; print.; illustration*) planche *f.*; **3.** (*dish*) assiette *f.*, (*collective, table-ware*) argenterie *f.*; CHROMIUM ~; **4.** (*denture*) dentier *m.*; **5.** (*racing*) coupe *f.*; ~ **armour** *s.* blindage *m.*; ~ **glass** *s.* glace de vitrage *f.*; ~**-rack** *s.* égouttoir *m.*; ~**-warmer** *s.* chauffe-plats *m.*; ~**ful** *s.* assiettée *f.*; *v.t.* (1) plaquer, nickeler, argenter; (*armour*) blinder; ~**d** *adj.* plaqué, nickelé, argenté.

plateau *s.* plateau *m.*

platen *s.* (*print.*) platine *f.*; (*typewriter*) rouleau *m.*

platform *s.* (*dais*) estrade *f.*; (*rail.*) quai *m.*; (*polit.*) programme électoral *m.*; ~ **shoes** *s.* chaussures à semelles compensées *f.pl.*; ~ **ticket** *s.* billet de quai *m.*

platinum *s.* platine *f.*

platitude *s.* platitude *f.*

Plato *s.* Platon *m.*; ~**nic** *adj.* platonicien; ~**nic love,** amour platonique.

platoon *s.* peloton *m.*

platter *s.* plat *m.*; (*mil.*) gamelle *f.*

plaudit *s.* (*usu. pl.*) applaudissements *m.pl.*

plausib/le *adj.* (*argument, excuse*) plausible; (*specious*) spécieux; (*person*) enjôleur; ~**ility** *s.* plausibilité *f.*; ~**ly** *adv.**;*.

play[1] *s.* **1.** (*light movement, freedom of movement, operation*) jeu *m.*; **2.** (*recreation*) divertissement *m.*; **3.** (*trifling*) plaisanterie *f.*; **4.** (~*ing of game*) jeu *m.*; **5.** (*theat.*) spectacle *m.*; FAIR ~; FULL ~; CHILD'**s** ~; **to bring into** ~, mettre en jeu; **in** ~, pour rire; **in** ~ (*sport*) en jeu; **out of** ~ (*sport*) hors jeu; ~**-acting** *s.* comédie *f.*; ~**-actor** *s.* acteur *m.*; ~**bill** *s.* affiche *f.* (de théâtre); ~**boy** *s.* viveur *m.*; ~**fellow** *s.*, ~**mate** *s.* camarade *m.* (de jeu); ~**goer** *s.* amateur de théâtre *m.*; ~**ground** *s.* cour de récréation *f.*; ~**house** *s.* théâtre *m.*; ~**-pen** *s.* parc *m.* (pour enfants); ~**room** *s.* salle de récréation *f.*; ~**thing** *s.* jouet *m.*; ~**time** *s.* récréation *f.*; ~**wright** *s.* dramaturge *m.f.*; ~**ful** *adj.* enjoué, badin; ~**fully** *adv.* en jouant; ~**fulness** *s.* enjouement *m.*

play[2] *v.t.* & *i.* (*nos. refer to* PLAY[1]) (1) jouer; (2) s'amuser; (3) folâtrer; (4) (*game*) jouer à, (*instrument*) jouer de, (*card, ball*) jouer, (*have as opponent*) jouer contre; (5) jouer; ~ FAIR; ~ FALSE; ~ **ball** *v.i.* (*fig.*) coopérer; ~ **the game,** jouer le jeu; ~ **at sth.** (*fig.*) faire qch. pour rire; ~ **back** (*taped material*) repasser; ~**-back** *s.* play-back *m.*; ~ **down** *v.t.* minimiser; ~ **s.o. off against s.o.,** opposer qn. à qn.; ~ **over** *v.t.* (*smile, light*) errer sur; ~ **up** *v.t.* (*fam.*) agacer; ~ **up to s.o.,** flatter qn.; ~**er** *s.* jouer *m.*, (*mus.*) exécutant *m.*, (*theat.*) act/eur, -rice *m.f.*; ~**ing-**CARD; ~**ing-field** *s.* terrain *m.* (de sports).

plea *s.* (*request*) demande *f.*; (*excuse*) excuse *f.*; (*law*) défense *f.*; **on the** ~ **of,** sous prétexte de.

plead *v.t.* alléguer; *v.i.* plaider; ~ **guilty, not guilty,** plaider coupable, non coupable; ~ **with s.o.,** intercéder auprès de qn. (*for s.o.*—pour qn.); ~**ing** *s.* plaidoirie *f.*; ~**ing** *adj.* suppliant; ~**ingly** *adv.* d'un ton suppliant.

pleasant *adj.* agréable; ~**ly** *adv.**; ~**ness** *s.* agrément *m.*; ~**ry** *s.* plaisanterie *f.*

pleas/e *interj.* s'il vous plaît, veuillez + *inf.*, **open the door** ~**e,** ouvrez la porte, s'il vous plaît; **will you** ~**e open the door,** veuillez ouvrir la porte; *v.t.* plaire (à qn.), faire plaisir (à qn.), contenter (qn.); (*with 'it' as subject*) plaire à, **it** ~**es him to think that,** il lui plaît de croire cela; **as you** ~**e,** comme vous voudrez; **if you** ~**e,** s'il vous plaît; ~**ed** *adj.* content (*with*—de); **be** ~**ed with,** être content de; **be** ~**ed to,** être heureux de, se plaire à; ~**ing** *adj.* agréable.

pleasure *s.* plaisir *m.*; ~**-boat,** bateau de plaisance *m.*; ~**-garden,** ~**-ground,** jardin d'agrément *m.*; ~**-trip,** voyage d'agrément *m.*; **pleasurable** *adj.* agréable; **pleasurably** *adv.**.

pleat *s.* pli *m.*; **accordion** ~**s,** plissé soleil *m.*; **box-**~, pli creux *m.*; *v.t.* plisser.

plebeian *adj.* & *s.m.f.* plébéien(ne).

plebiscite *s.* plébiscite *m.*

plectrum *s.* plectre *m.*

pledge *s.* **1.** (*security, token*) gage *m.*; **2.** (*promise*) vœu *m.*; **3.** (*toast*) santé *f.*; *v.t.* (1) mettre en gage; (2) (s')engager (à); (3) boire à la santé de.

Pleiad *s.* (*astron., liter.*) Pléiade *f.*

plenary *adj.* plénier.

plenipotentiary *adj.* & *s.* plénipotentiaire.

plenitude *s.* (*completeness*) plénitude *f.*; (*abundance*) abondance *f.*; (*fulness*) ampleur *f.*

plent/y *s.* (*abundance*) abondance *f.*; (*enough*) suffisance *f.*; *adv.* (*fam.*) suffisamment, ~**y large enough,** suffisamment grand; ~**eous** *adj.* & ~**iful** *adj.* abondant; ~**eously** *adv.* & ~**ifully** *adv.* abondamment; ~**eousness** *s.* & ~**ifulness** *s.* abondance *f.*

pleonas/m *s.* pléonasme *m.*; ~**tic** *adj.* pléonastique.

plethora *s.* (*lit.* & *fig.*) pléthore *f.*

pleurisy *s.* pleurésie *f.*

pliab/le *adj.* **1.** (*easily bent, lit.* & *fig.*) flexible; **2.** (*supple, yielding*) souple, malléable; **3.** (*accommodating*) docile; ~**ility** *s.* (1) flexibilité *f.*; (2) souplesse *f.*; (3) docilité *f.*

plian/t *adj.* **pliancy** *s. as* PLIABLE, PLIABILITY.

pliers *s.* pinces *f.pl.*

plight *s.* état *m.*; **in a sorry** ~, dans de beaux draps; *v.t.* (*archaic*) engager.

Plimsoll line *s.* (*naut.*) ligne de flottaison *f.*

plimsolls *s.pl.* espadrilles *f.pl.*

plinth *s.* plinthe *f.*

plod *v.i.* **1.** (*walk heavily*) marcher lourdement; **2.** (*fam. work laboriously*) bûcher; ~**der** *s.* (2) travailleur *m.*, bûcheur *m.*; ~**ding** *s.* (2) travail assidu *m.*; *adj.* (*step*) lourd; (*person*) persévérant.

plot *s.* **1.** (*of land*) parcelle *f.*; **2.** (*of story, etc.*) intrigue *f.*; **3.** (*conspiracy*) complot *m.*; *v.t.* (2) tracer; (3) comploter; *v.i.* (3) comploter; ~**ter** *s.* conspirat/eur, -rice *m.f.*

plough *s.* (*agric.*) charrue *f.*; **snow-**~, chasse-neige *m.*; (*astron. the P*~) la Grande Ourse *f.*; ~**man** *s.* laboureur *m.*; ~**share** *s.* soc de charrue *m.*; *v.t.* & *i.* (*agric.*) labourer; (*pop. fail candidate*) recaler; ~ **back** (*fin.*) réinvestir; ~ **through** *v.t.* fendre, sillonner; ~**ing** *s.* labourage *m.*

plover *s.* pluvier *m.*

ploy *s.* (*fam.*) truc *m.*

pluck *s.* (*fam.*) cran *m.*; *v.t.* (*bird* & *fig.*) plumer; (*gather*) cueillir; (*pull at*) tirer (par); ~ **out** *v.t.* arracher; ~ **up courage,** prendre son courage à deux mains; ~**y** *adj.* courageux; ~**ily** *adv.**.

plug *s.* **1.** (*stopper*) bouchon *m.*; **2.** (*wedge*) cheville *f.*, tampon *m.*; **3.** (*electr.*) prise *f.*, fiche *f.*; **4.** (*of tobacco*) chique *f.*; **5.** (*of W.C.*) chasse d'eau *f.*; **sparking-**~, bougie *f.*; *v.t.* (1) boucher; (2) tamponner; (3) ~ **in,** brancher; **6.** (*pop.* = *advertise*) faire la réclame pour.

plum *s.* prune *f.*; (*tree*) prunier *m.*; (*fig.*) morceau de choix *m.*

plumage *s.* plumage *m.*

plumb *s.* **1.** (*ball of lead*) plomb *m.*; ~**-line** *s.* fil à plomb *m.*; **2.** (*for sounding*) sonde *f.*; **3.** (*perpendicularity*) aplomb *m.*; *adv.* (*vertically*) d'aplomb; (*exactly*) exactement; *v.t.* (1) (re)-mettre d'aplomb; (2) (*lit.* & *fig.*) sonder; **4.** (*work as* ~*er*) effectuer les travaux de plomberie; ~**er** *s.* plombier *m.*; ~**ing** *s.* (*work*) plomberie *f.*, (*pipes*) tuyauterie *f.*

plume *s.* plume *f.*, plumet *m.*; (*of smoke*) panache *m.* (de fumée); *v.t.* orner de plumes; (*fig.*) se piquer (de).

plummet *s.* plomb *m.*, sonde *f.*; ⚠ plumet = **feather**; *v.i.* plonger.

plump *adj.* potelé, bien arrondi; *v.t.* (*pillow*)

secouer; (*fam.*) se remplumer; *v.i.* tomber lourdement; ~ **for** *v.t.* choisir; **~ness** *s.* embonpoint *m.*

plunder *s.* (*act*) pillage *m.*; (*booty*) butin *m.*; *v.t.* piller; **~er** *s.* pillard *m.*

plunge *s.* plongeon *m.*; *v.t.* & *i.* plonger; (*pop. gamble*) risquer le tout pour le tout; **~r** *s.* piston *m.*

pluperfect *s.* plus-que-parfait *m.*

plural *adj.* & *s.m.* pluriel; **in the ~,** au pluriel; **~ity** *s.* pluralité *f.*

plus *s.* (*symbol* +) plus *m.*; (*additional quality*) supplément *m.*, avantage *m.*; *prep.* plus; *adj.* en plus; (*positive*) positif.

plush *s.* peluche *f.*; *adj.* pelucheux; (*pop.* & **~y**) rupin.

plutocra/cy *s.* ploutocratie *f.*; **~t** *s.* ploutocrate *m.f.*; **~tic** *adj.* ploutocratique.

ply[1] *s.* pli *m.*; **~wood** *s.* contre-plaqué *m.*

ply[2] *v.t.* (*wield*) manier; (*a trade*) exercer (un métier); (*with questions*) presser (qn. de questions); (*with drink, etc.*) offrir à boire (etc.) avec insistance; *v.i.* faire le trajet, faire la navette (*between*—entre).

p.m. *s.* (*afternoon*) après-midi *m.*; **6 p.m.,** six heures de l'après-midi.

pneumatic *adj.* pneumatique.

pneumonia *s.* pneumonie *f.*

poach *v.t.* (*cook.*) pocher; (*game*) braconner; *v.i.* **~ on,** empiéter sur; **~ on s.o.'s preserves,** marcher sur les plates-bandes de qn.; **~er** *s.* braconnier *m.*

pocket *s.* (*in garment*; *fig. resources*; *geol.*; *mil.*) poche *f.*; (*in billiard table*) blouse *f.*; **air ~,** trou d'air *m.*; **to be in ~,** être en veine; **to be out of ~,** en être de sa poche; **to put one's pride in one's ~,** mettre son orgueil dans sa poche; **~-book** *s.* porte-feuille *f.*; **~ handkerchief** *s.* mouchoir *m.* (de poche); **~-knife** *s.* canif *m.*; **~-money** *s.* argent de poche *m.*; *v.t.* empocher; (*take dishonestly*) chiper; (*suppress emotion*) avaler.

pock-marked *adj.* grêlé.

pod *s.* cosse *f.*; *v.t.* écosser.

podgy *adj.* potelé.

poe/m *s.* poème *m.*; **~sy** *s.* poésie *f.*

poet *s.* poète *m.*; **~aster** *s.* rimailleur *m.*; **~ess** *s.* femme-poète *f.* ⚠ poétesse *is pej.*; **~ic(al)** *adj.* poétique; **~ically** *adv.**; **~ize** *v.i.* poétiser; **~ry** *s.* poésie *f.*; **to write ~ry,** écrire des vers.

pogrom *s.* pogrom(e) *m.*

poignan/cy *s.* acuité *f.*; **~t** *adj.* (*pungent, penetrating*) piquant; (*moving*) poignant.

point[1] *s.* (*dot*; *place*; *moment*; *score*; *degree*; *detail*) point *m.*; (*salient feature*) trait *m.*; (*tip*) pointe *f.*; (*electr.*) prise *f.*; (*promontory*) promontoire *m.*; (*fig. effectiveness*) poids *m.*; **~s** *pl.* (*rail.*) aiguillage *m.*; COMPASS **~**; DECIMAL **~**; **~ of no** RETURN; VANTAGE **~**; **boiling, flash, freezing, melting- -~,** point d'ébullition, d'ignition, de congélation, de fusion *m.*; **~ of view,** point de vue *m.*; **on the ~ of,** sur le point de; **to** CARRY **a ~**; **to come to the ~,** venir au fait; **to make a ~ of,** se faire un devoir de; **~-blank** *adj.* catégorique, *adv.* de but en blanc; **on ~-duty,** de service; **~less** *adj.* inutile; **~lessly** *adv.**; **~sman** *s.* (*rail.*) aiguilleur *m.*

point[2] *v.t.* (*sharpen to* ~) tailler en pointe, aiguiser; (*constr.*) jointoyer; (*fig. give* ~ *to*) donner du piquant à; (*direct*): (*finger*) tendre, (*gun*) braquer (sur); **~ at** *v.t.* montrer du doigt; **~ out** *v.t.* montrer du doigt, (*fig.*) faire remarquer; **~ to** *v.t.* désigner, indiquer; **~ed** *adj.* pointu, à pointe, (*fig.*) mordant; **~edly** *adv.* d'un ton mordant; **~er** *s.* (*rod*) baguette *f.*, (*dog*) chien d'arrêt *m.*, (*fam. hint*) tuyau *m.*; **~ing** *s.* (*constr.*) jointoiement *m.*

poise *s.* (*equilibrium*) équilibre *m.*; (*way sth. hangs*) port *m.*; (*ease of manner*) assurance *f.*; *v.t.* tenir en équilibre; *v.i.* être en équilibre; (*hover, hang*) se maintenir en l'air, être suspendu; **~d** *adj.* équilibré.

poison *s.* (*lit.* & *fig.*) poison *m.*; ~ GAS; **to take ~,** s'empoisonner; **~ous** *adj.* (*plants*) vénéneux, (*snakes, etc.* & *fig.*) venimeux, (*gas*) asphyxiant; *v.t.* (*lit.* & *fig.*) empoisonner; **~er** *s.* empoisonneur *m.*; **~ing** *s.* empoisonnement *m.*

poke *s.* (*act*) coup *m.*; (*nudge*) bourrade *f.*; **to buy a** PIG **in a ~**; *v.t.* (*push*) pousser; (*thrust into*) enfoncer dans; (*fire*) attiser; *v.i.* tâtonner; **~ fun at s.o.,** se payer la tête de qn.; **~ one's nose into,** fourrer le nez dans; **~r** *s.* (*for fire*) tisonnier *m.*, (*card game*) poker *m.*; **~r-face** *s.* visage impassible *m.*

poky *adj.* étroit, misérable.

Pol/and *s.* (*geog.*) Pologne *f.*; **~e** *s.m.f.* Polonais(e); **~ish** *s.m.* (*lang.*) polonais; *adj.* polonais.

pole *s.* (*rigid post*) poteau *m.*; (*flexible rod, for punt, jump, etc.*) perche *f.*; (*North P~, South P~, of magnet*) pôle *m.*; **to be ~s apart,** être aux antipodes (l'un de l'autre); **~cat** *s.* putois *m.*; **~-star** *s.* étoile polaire *f.*; **~-vault** *s.* saut à la perche *m.*; **polar** *adj.* polaire; **polar bear** *s.* ours blanc *m.*; **polarize** *v.t.* polariser; **polarization** *s.* polarisation.

polemic *adj.* polémique; **~s** *s.* polémique *f.* ⚠ *sing. in French.*

police *s.* police *f.*; (*rural only*) gendarmerie *f.*; **~ court** *s.* tribunal de police *m.*, tribunal correctionnel *m.*; **~ dog** *s.* chien policier *m.*; **~man** *s.* agent *m.*, (*rural only*) gendarme *m.*; **~-officer** *s.* agent *m.*; **~ state** *s.* régime policier *m.*; **~ station** *s.* poste de police *m.*; **~woman** *s.* femme-agent *f.*

policy *s.* politique *f.*; INSURANCE ~.

polio *s.* (*abbrev. fam.*) polio *f.*

poliomyelitis *s.* poliomyélite *f.*

polish *s.* (*shine*) lustre *m.*; (*substance*): (*for shoes*) cirage *m.*, (*for floor*) cire *f.*, (*for furniture*) encaustique *f.*; FRENCH ~; (*fig.*) politesse *f.*; *v.t.* polir; (*shoes, floor, furniture*) cirer; (*leather*) astiquer; (*fig.*) polir, raffiner; **~ off** *v.t.* (*work*) expédier, (= *kill*) régler son compte à qn.; **~ up** *v.t.* astiquer; **~er** *s.* (*techn. machine*) polissoir *m.*, (*floor-*) cireuse *f.* (à parquet).

Polish *adj.* & *s.m.* (*lang.*) *see* POLAND.

polite *adj.* poli; **~ly** *adv.* poliment; **~ness** *s.* politesse *f.*

politic *adj.* (*of action, etc.*) judicieux; (*of person*) prudent; **~s** *s.* politique *f.* ⚠ *sing. in French*; **~al** *adj.* politique; **~ally** *adv.**; **~ian** *s.* politique *m.*, (*pej.*) politicien *m.*

polity *s.* état *m.*

polka *s.* polka *f.*; ~ DOT.

poll *s.* **1.** (*head*) tête *f.*; **2.** (*votes*) vote *m.*, scrutin *m.*; **3.** (*public opinion* ~) sondage *m.*; *v.t.* (1) *crop hair*) couper les cheveux à; (*cut top off tree*) étêter; (2) *v.t.* & *i.* (*vote, receive votes*) voter, recueillir des voix; **~ing booth** *s.* isoloir *m.*

pollard *s.* (*tree*) têtard *m.*; *v.t.* étêter.

poll/en *s.* pollen *m.*; **~en count** *s.* indice de pollen *m.*; **~inate** *v.t.* féconder, polliniser; **~ination** *s.* pollinisation *f.*

pollut/e *v.t.* polluer; (*fig.*) profaner; **~ion** *s.* pollution *f.*; (*fig.*) profanation *f.*

polo *s.* polo *m.*; **~-neck** *s.* polo *m.*; **~-necked** *adj.* à col roulé.

poltergeist *s.* esprit frappeur *m.*

poltroon *s.* poltron *m.*; **~ery** *s.* poltronnerie *f.*

poly- (*in combination*) **~androus** *adj.* polyandre; **~andry** *s.* polyandrie *f.*; **~ester** *s.* polyester *m.*; **~gamist** *s.* polygame *m.*; **~gamous** *adj.* polygame; **~gamy** *s.* polygamie *f.*; **~glot** *adj.* & *s.m.f.* polyglotte; **~gon** *s.* polygone *m.*; **~gonal** *adj.* polygonal; **~styrene** *s.* polystyrène *m.*; **~syllabic** *adj.* polysyllabe, polysyllabique; **~syllable** *s.* polysyllabe *m.*;

~urethane *s.* polyuréthanne *m.*; **~valent** *adj.* polyvalent.
polyanthus *s.* primevère *f.*
Polynesia *s.* (*geog.*) Polynésie *f.*; **~n** *adj.* & *s.m.f.* polynésien(ne).
polyp *s.* polype *m.*
polytechnic *s.* école des arts et métiers *f.*, institut universitaire technique (I.U.T.) *m.*
polythene *s.* polythène *m.*
pomade *s.* pommade *f.*
pomegranate *s.* grenade *f.*; (*tree*) grenadier *m.*
pommel *s.* pommeau *m.*; *v.t.* rosser.
pomp *s.* pompe *f.*; **~osity** *s.* suffisance *f.*; **~ous** *adj.* (*person*) prétentieux, suffisant; (*thing*) fastueux, pompeux; **~ously** *adv.* pompeusement.
Pompeii *s.* Pompéi *f.*
pom-pom *s.* (*tuft*) pompon *m.*; (*gun*) canon--mitrailleuse *m.*
poncho *s.* poncho *m.*
pond *s.* (*natural*) étang *m.*; (*artificial*) bassin *m.*; FISH-~; MILL-~.
ponder *v.t.* (*on, over*) peser; *v.i.* méditer; **~able** *adj.* pondérable; **~ous** *adj.* (*heavy*) lourd; (*unwieldly*) pesant; (*laborious*) laborieux; **~ously** *adv.* pesamment.
pong *s.* (*fam.*) puanteur *f.*; *v.i.* puer.
pontif/f *s.* pontife *m.*; **~ical** *adj.* pontifical; **~icate** *s.* pontificat *m.*; *v.i.* (*fam.*) pontifier.
pontoon *s.* ponton *m.*
pony *s.* poney *m.*; **~-tail** *s.* queue de cheval *f.*; SHANKS' ~.
poodle *s.* caniche *m.*
pooh-pooh *v.t.* faire fi de.
pool *s.* (*water*) mare *f.*; (*swimming*) piscine *f.*; (*at cards, etc.*) cagnotte *f.*; (*comm.*) syndicat *m.*; (*fin.*) consortium *m.*; (*common fund*) pool *m.*, réserve *f.*; **~s** (*football*) *s.* concours de pronostics de football *m.*; *v.t.* mettre en commun; (*merge*) fusionner; (*share*) partager.
poop *s.* poupe *f.*
poor *s.* **the ~**, les pauvres *m.pl.*; *adj.* **1.** (*fin.*; *soil*; *despicable*) pauvre (*in*—en); **2.** (*inadequate*) piètre, médiocre; **3.** (*pitiable*) malheureux; **~-box** *s.* tronc *m.* (pour les pauvres); **~ly** *adj.* (*ill*) souffrant; **~ly** *adv.* pauvrement; **~ness** *s.* (1) pauvreté *f.*, (2) médiocrité *f.*
pop[1] *s.* (*sound*) crac *m.*, bruit sec *m.*; (*fam.* = *father*) papa *m.*; *v.t.* crever; *v.i.* éclater, sauter; **~ in,** entrer en passant; **~ out,** sortir brusquement; **~corn** *s.* grains de maïs grillés *m.pl.*; **~gun** *s.* fusil à air comprimé *m.*
pop[2] *adj.* (*fam.*) populaire.
pop/e *s.* (*R.C.*) pape *m.*; (*Greek orthodox*) pope *m.*; **~ery** *s.* papisme *m.*; **~ish** *adj.* papiste.
popinjay *s.* fat *m.*
poplar *s.* peuplier *m.*
poplin *s.* popeline *f.*
poppy *s.* pavot *m.*; (*wild*) coquelicot *m.*; **~cock** *s.* (*pop.*) balivernes *f.pl.*
populace *s.* populace *f.*
popular *adj.* populaire; **~ity** *s.* popularité *f.*; **~ize** *v.t.* (*make known*) populariser; (*vulgarize*) vulgariser; **~ly** *adv.**.
populat/e *v.t.* peupler; **~ion** *s.* population *f.*
populous *adj.* populeux.
porcelain *s.* porcelaine *f.*; *adj.* fragile comme la porcelaine.
porch *s.* porche *m.*
porcupine *s.* porc-épic *m.*
por/e[1] *s.* pore *m.*; **~osity** *s.* porosité *f.*; **~ous** *adj.* poreux.
pore[2] *v.i.* **~ over,** s'absorber dans.
pork *s.* porc *m.*; **~-butcher** *s.* charcutier *m.*; **~-butcher's shop,** charcuterie *f.*; ~ CHOP.
porno *adj.* (*fam.*) porno.
pornograph/y *s.* pornographie *f.*; **~ic** *adj.* pornographique.
porphyry *s.* porphyre *m.*
porpoise *s.* marsouin *m.*
porridge *s.* bouillie d'avoine *f.*
porringer *s.* écuelle *f.*
port *s.* (*harbour, town*) port *m.*; (*side of ship*) bâbord *m.*; (*wine*) porto *m.*; **~ of call** *s.* port d'escale *m.*; **~ of** REGISTRY; *adj.* portuaire; **~hole** *s.* hublot *m.*
portable *adj.* portatif; *s.* (*radio, TV*) portable *m.*
portage *s.* (*transport*) port *m.*; (*between rivers*) portage *m.*
portal *s.* portail *m.*
portcullis *s.* herse *f.*
porten/d *v.t.* (*foreshadow*) présager; (*be omen of*) augurer; **~t** *s.* (*omen*) présage *m.*; (*prodigy*) prodige *m.*; **~tous** *adj.* (*indicating ill*) de mauvais augure; (*solemn, pompous*) prodigieux, prétentieux.
port/er *s.* (*door-keeper*) portier *m.*; (*rail.*) porteur *m.*; (*beer*) bière brune *f.*; **~ress** *s.* portière *f.*; **~erage** *s.* factage *m.*
portfolio *s.* (*case*) serviette *f.*; (*fin.*; *parl.*) portefeuille *f.*
portico *s.* portique *m.*
portion *s.* portion *f.*; (*destiny*) sort *m.*; MARRIAGE ~; *v.t.* répartir.
portl/y *adj.* corpulent; **~iness** *s.* corpulence *f.*
portmanteau *s.* valise *f.*; ⚠ portemanteau = **coat-hanger.**
portrait *s.* portrait *m.*; **half length ~**, portrait en buste; **full length ~**, portrait en pied; **~-painter** *s.* portraitiste *m.*; **~ure** *s.* portrait *m.*
portray *v.t.* dépeindre; (*describe*) décrire.
Portug/al *s.* (*geog.*) Portugal *m.*; **~uese** *adj.* & *s.m.f.* portugais(e); *s.m.* (*lang.*) portugais.
pose *s.* pose *f.*; *v.t.* (*propound*) poser; (*arrange*) faire prendre une pose à; *v.i.* prendre une pose; **~ as,** se faire passer pour; **~r** *s.* question embarrassante *f.*; (*fam.*) colle *f.*
posh *adj.* (*pop.*) chic, chouette.
position *s.* position *f.*; (*job*) emploi *m.*, poste *f.*; (*rank*) rang *m.*; (*mental attitude*) point de vue *m.*; **in ~**, à sa place; **out of ~**, déplacé; **to be in a ~ to,** être à même de; *v.t.* mettre en position, situer.
positive *s.* positif *m.*; *adj.* (≠ *negative*; *definite*) positif; (*formally ruled*) formel; (*absolute*) absolu; (*confident*) assuré, convaincu, certain; **~ly** *adv.**;*;*;*; **~ness** *s.* certitude *f.*, assurance *f.*
posse *s.* détachement *m.* (de police, etc.).
possess *v.t.* posséder; (*master*) maîtriser; (*seize,* ~ *oneself of*) s'emparer de; **what ~ed you to do that?,** qu'est-ce qui vous a pris de faire cela?; **~ed by,** sous le coup de; **~ed of,** doué de; **~ed with,** obsédé de; **~ion** *s.* (*~ing, being ~ed, thing ~ed*) possession *f.*; (*occupancy*) jouissance *f.*, VACANT **~ion**; **~ions** *s.pl.* biens *m.pl.*; **take ~ion of,** (*become owner of*) acquérir, (*forcibly*) s'emparer de, (*occupy*) entrer en jouissance de; **~ive** *adj.* & *s.m.* possessif; **~iveness** *s.* caractère possessif *m.*; **~or** *s.* possesseur *m.*, détenteur *m.*
possib/le *adj.* possible; **as far as ~le,** dans la mesure du possible; **~ility** *s.* possibilité *f.*, (*event*) éventualité *f.*; **~ly** *adv.* peut-être; **I may ~ly be late,** il est possible, il se peut, que je sois en retard; **it may ~ly rain,** il se peut qu'il pleuve, peut-être qu'il pleuvra.
post[1] (*of wood or metal*) poteau *m.*; DEAF **as a ~**; *v.t.* (~ *up*) afficher.
post[2] *s.* (*mail*) courrier *m.*; (*service*) poste *f.*; **~**CARD; **~-chaise** *s.* chaise de poste *f.*; **~-code** *s.* code postal *m.*; **~-free,** franco; **~-**HASTE; **~man** *s.* facteur *m.*; **~mark** *s.* cachet d'oblitération *m.*; **~master** *s.* receveur *m.*; **P~-master General** *s.* directeur-général des Postes *m.*; **~mistress** *s.* receveuse *f.*; **P~**

Office *s.* Administration des P. et T. (Postes et Télécommunications) *f.*; ~ **office** *s.* bureau de poste *m.*; **~-office box** *s.* boîte postale *f.*; **~-paid,** port payé; **~age** *s.* affranchissement *m.*; **~age stamp** *s.* timbre-poste *m.*; **~al** *adj.* postal; **~al order** *s.* mandat-poste *m.*; *v.t.* (*mail*) mettre à la poste; (*hurry*) expédier; (*enter in ledger*) reporter; **keep s.o. ~ed,** tenir qn. au courant.

post[3] *s.* (*station, place of duty, employment*) poste *m.*; **last** ~ *s.* (*mil.*) sonnerie aux morts *f.*; *v.t.* (*station*) poster; (*appoint*) nommer.

post- (*in combination*) **~-date** *v.t.* postdater; **~-graduate** *s.* licencié *m.*, *adj.* du troisième cycle; **~prandial** *adj.* d'après le repas; **~-war** *s.* (*period*) après-guerre *m.*; *adj.* d'après-guerre.

poster *s.* affiche *f.*; FOUR-~ (*bed*).

posterior *s.* postérieur *m.*; *adj.* postérieur.

posterity *s.* postérité *f.*

postern *s.* poterne *f.*

posthumous *adj.* posthume; **~ly** *adv.* à titre posthume.

postilion, postillion *s.* postillon *m.*

post-mortem *s.* autopsie *f.*

postpone *v.t.* remettre, renvoyer à plus tard; **~ment** *s.* remise *f.* (à plus tard).

postcript *s.* post-scriptum *m.*

postulate *s.* (*basis of argument*) postulat *m.*; (*prerequisite*) condition préalable *f.*; *v.t.* (*take for granted*) considérer comme admis; (*demand as necessary condition*) stipuler.

posture *s.* posture *f.*; *v.i.* prendre une posture.

posy *s.* bouquet *m.* (de fleurs).

pot[1] *s.* (*vessel, contents of*) pot *m.*; (*cooking* ~) marmite *f.*; (*chamber-*~) pot de chambre *m.*; COFFEE-~; CRACK~; MUSTARD-~; PEPPER-~; TEA~; **~-bellied** *adj.* ventru; **~-boiler** *s.* littérature alimentaire *f.*; **~-herbs** *s.pl.* herbes potagères *f.pl.*; POT-HOLE; **~-hook** *s.* crémaillière *f.*; **take ~ luck,** manger à la fortune du pot; **~sherd** *s.* tesson *m.*; **take a ~-shot,** tirer au jugé; *v.t.* (*cook.*) conserver; (*hort.*) mettre en pot; **~ted** *adj.* condensé; **~ter** *s.* potier *m.*; **~tery** *s.* poterie *f.*; **~ting-shed** *s.* serre *f.*

pot[2] *s.* (*pop. marijuana*) hasch *m.*, kif *m.*

potable *adj.* potable.

potash *s.* potasse *f.*

potassium *s.* potassium *m.*

potato *s.* pomme de terre *f.*; **boiled ~es,** pommes de terre à l'anglaise; **baked, jacket ~es,** pommes de terre en robe de chambre; **mashed ~es,** pommes de terre en purée; SEED ~; **sweet ~,** patate *f.*

poten/t *adj.* (*powerful, influential*) puissant; (*cogent*) convaincant; (*strong*) fort; (*effective*) efficace; **~cy** *s.* puissance *f.*, force *f.*; **~tate** *s.* potentat *m.*; **~tial** *adj.* & *s.m.* potentiel; **~tiality** *s.* potentialité *f.*; **~tly** *adv.* puissamment, avec force.

pot-hol/e *s.* marmite *f.*; (*in road*) trou *m.*; **~er** *s.* spéléologue *m.f.*; (*fam.*) spéléo *m.*; **~ing** *s.* spéléologie *f.*

potion *s.* potion *f.*

pottage *s.* potage *m.*

potter[1] *v.i.* lambiner; ~ **about,** bricoler.

potter[2] *s.* & **pottery** *s. see* POT.

pouch *s.* petit sac *m.*; (*tobacco*) blague *f.*; (*under eyes*) poche *f.*; (*of marsupials*) poche ventrale *f.*

poultice *s.* cataplasme *m.*; *v.t.* mettre un cataplasme à.

poult/ry *s.* volaille *f.*; **~erer** *s.* marchand de volaille *m.*; **~ry-yard** *s.* basse-cour *f.*

pounce *s.* serre *f.*; *v.i.* fondre, se jeter (*on*—sur).

pound *s.* (*weight, money*) livre *f.*; (*enclosure for strays*) fourrière *f.*; PENNY **wise and ~ foolish**; **~age** *s.* commission *f.*; **~er, ten-~er,** *etc.*, de dix (etc.) livres; *v.t.* (*crush, bruise*) piler, broyer; (*thump*) bourrer de coups; *v.i.* avancer d'un pas lourd.

pour *v.t.* verser; (*fig.*) épancher; *v.i.* tomber à verse; **it never rains but it ~s,** un malheur ne vient jamais seul; ~ **down** *v.i.* tomber à flots; ~ **out** *v.t.* verser, *v.i.* sortir à flots; **~ing** *adj.* (*rain*) torrentiel.

pout *s.* moue *f.*; *v.i.* faire la moue; (*sulk*) bouder; **~ing** *adj.* boudeur.

poverty *s.* (*want*) misère *f.*; (*deficiency in*) manque *m.* (de); (*inferiority*) pauvreté *f.*; **~-stricken** *adj.* indigent.

P.O.W. *s.* (*prisoner of war*) P.G. *m.* (prisonnier de guerre).

powder *s.* poudre *f.*; ~ COMPACT; **~-magazine** *s.* poudrière *f.*; **~-puff** *s.* houppe *f.*; **~y** *adj.* poudreux, friable; *v.t.* (*reduce to* ~) pulvériser; (*sprinkle with* ~) saupoudrer (de); (*one's face, etc.*) (se) poudrer.

power *s.* (*ability*) pouvoir *m.*; (*vigour*) force *f.*; (*control, influence, person*) autorité *f.*; (*country*) puissance *f.*; (*mech.*) énergie *f.*; (*mental*) faculté *f.*, talent *m.*; ~ CUT; ~ **drive** *s.* transmission *f.*; **~-station** *s.* centrale électrique *f.*; **~ed** *adj.* motorisé, électrique; **high-~ed** *adj.* puissant; **low-~ed** *adj.* faible; **~ful** *adj.* puissant; **~fully** *adv.* puissamment; **~less** *adj.* impuissant; **to be ~less to,** être dans l'impossibilité de; **~lessness** *s.* impuissance *f.*

pox *s.* vérole *f.*

practicab/le *adj.* faisable, réalisable; (*road*) praticable; **~ility** *s.* praticabilité *f.*

practical *adj.* pratique; (*virtual*) quasi; **~ly** *adv.**; pour ainsi dire.

practic/e *s.* **1.** (≠ *theory*) pratique *f.*; **2.** (*habit*) habitude *f.*; **3.** (*custom*) usages *m.pl.*; **4.** (*exercise*) exercice *m.*, entraînement *m.*; **5.** (*law*) étude *f.*; (*med.*) clientèle *f.*; **in ~e** (1) pratiquement; (4) bien entraîné; **out of ~e** (4) rouillé; **~ian** *s.* praticien(ne) *m.f.*

practis/e *v.t.* (*carry out*) pratiquer, mettre en pratique; (*profession*) exercer; (*exercise*) s'entraîner (à qch.); **~ed** *adj.* expérimenté; **~ing** *adj.* (*in religion*) pratiquant.

practitioner *s.* praticien(ne) *m.f.*

pragmat/ic *adj.* **1.** (*meddlesome*) officieux; **2.** (*dictatorial*) dogmatique; **3.** (*giving priority to action*) pragmatique; ⚠ *this meaning only*; **~ically** *adv.* (1) avec suffisance; (2) avec dogmatisme; (3) de façon pragmatique; **~ism** *s.* (2) dogmatisme *m.*; (3) pragmatisme *m.*

prairie *s.* savane *f.*; (*in N. America*) la Prairie; ⚠ *otherwise* prairie = **meadow.**

praise *s.* éloge *m.*, louanges *f.pl.*; **in ~ of,** à la louange de; *v.t.* louer, faire l'éloge de; **~-worthy** *adj.* louable.

pram *s.* voiture d'enfant *f.*

prance *v.i.* piaffer.

prank *s.* (*act*) fredaine *f.*; (*joke*) farce *f.*

prate *v.i.* jacasser.

prattle *s.* **1.** (*of children*) babil *m.*; **2.** (*gossip*) bavardage *m.*; *v.i.* (1) babiller; (2) bavarder; **~r** *s.* (1) babillard *m.*; (2) bavard *m.*

prawn *s.* crevette *f.*

pray *v.t.* & *i.* prier (pour qch., qn. de faire qch.); **~er** *s.* prière *f.*; LORD**'s ~er**; **~er-book** *s.* livre de prières *m.*; **~ing** MANTIS.

pre- (*in combination*) **~-arrange** *v.t.* organiser à l'avance; **~-cast** (*concrete*) *adj.* & *s.m.* précontraint, *v.t.* faire subir une précontrainte à; **~-condition** *s.* condition préalable *f.*; **~-date** *v.t.* antidater; **~-digested** *adj.* prédigéré; **~-ordain** *v.t.* destiner (à); **~-packed** *adj.* prêt à emporter; **~-tax income,** revenu brut *m.*; **~-war** *adj.* d'avant-guerre.

preach *v.t.* & *i.* prêcher; **~er** *s.* prédicateur *m.*; **~ing** *s.* prédication *f.*

preamble *s.* préambule *m.*

prebend *s.* prébende *f.*; **~ary** *s.* prébendier *m.*
precarious *adj.* précaire; (*uncertain*) douteux; **~ly** *adv.**;*; **~ness** *s.* état précaire *m.*
precaution *s.* précaution *f.*; **~ary** *adj.* de précaution.
preced/e *v.t.* précéder; (*in rank*) avoir la préséance sur; **~ence** *s.* priorité *f.*; préséance *f.*; **~ent** *adj.* & *s.m.* précédent; **~ing** *adj.* précédent.
precentor *s.* premier chantre *m.*, maître de chapelle *m.*
precept *s.* précepte *m.*; **~or, ~ress** *s.* (*private tutor* & *fig.*) précept/eur, -rice *m.f.*; (*school teacher*) institut/eur, -rice *m.f.*
precinct *s.* enceinte *f.*; **~s** *pl.* environs *m.pl.*; PEDESTRIAN ~.
precious *adj.* (*lit.* & *fig.*) précieux; **~ly** *adv.**.
precip/ice *s.* précipice *m.*; **~itous** *adj.* escarpé; **~itously** *adv.* à pic.
precipitat/e *adj.* précipité; (*rash*) irréfléchi; **~ely** *adv.* précipitamment; *v.t.* précipiter; (*chem.*) condenser; **~ion** *s.* précipitation *f.*
précis *s.* abrégé *m.*
precis/e *adj.* précis; (*exact*) exact; (*particular*) méticuleux; **~ely** *adv.* avec précision; exactement; précisément; **at 2 o'clock ~ely,** à deux heures précises; **~eness** *s.* & **~ion** *s.* précision *f.*; **~ion tool,** instrument de précision *m.*
preclude *v.t.* (*prevent*) empêcher; (*make impracticable*) exclure.
precocious *adj.* précoce; **~ly** *adv.**; **~ness** *s.* précocité *f.*
preconc/eive *v.t.* préconcevoir; **~eption** *s.* préjugé *m.*
precursor *s.* précurseur *m.*; **~y** *adj.* précurseur.
predator *s.* (*animal*) prédateur *m.*; (*person*) pillard *m.*; **~y** *adj.* (*animal*) de proie; (*insect*) prédateur; (*person*) pillard.
predecease *v.t.* mourir avant (qn.).
predecessor *s.* prédécesseur *m.*
predestin/e *v.t.* prédestiner; **~ate** *v.t.* prédestiner; **~ation** *s.* prédestination *f.*
predetermin/e *v.t.* déterminer à l'avance; (*eccles.*) prédéterminer; **~ation** *s.* détermination antérieure *f.*; (*eccles.*) prédétermination *f.*
predicament *s.* mauvaise passe *f.*
predicat/e *s.* prédicat *m.*; *v.t.* affirmer; **~ion** *s.* affirmation *f.*
predict *v.t.* prédire; **~able** *adj.* à prédire, à prévoir; **~ably** *adv.* comme on aurait pu prédire; **~ion** *s.* prédiction *f.*
predilection *s.* prédilection *f.*
predispos/e *v.t.* prédisposer (à); **~ition** *s.* prédisposition *f.*
predomina/te *v.i.* prédominer; (*prevail*) prévaloir; **~nce** *s.* prédominance *f.*, prépondérance *f.*; **~nt** *adj.* prédominant; **~ntly** *adv.* de manière prédominante; **~ting** *adj.* prédominant.
pre-eminen/ce *s.* prééminence *f.*; **~t** *adj.* prééminent; **~tly** *adv.* de façon prééminente.
pre-empt *v.t.* acheter, acquérir, d'avance; **~ion** *s.* préemption *f.*; **~ive bid** *s.* enchère *f.*
preen *v.t.* (*feathers*) se lisser; (*oneself, lit.*) s'attifer; (*oneself, fig.—on*) se faire un orgueil de.
prefab *s.* maison préfabriquée *f.*; **~ricate** *v.t.* préfabriquer.
prefa/ce *s.* (*to book*) préface *f.*; (*to speech*) exorde *m.*, préambule *m.*; *v.t.* (*book*) préfacer; (*event*) servir de prélude à; (*words*) faire précéder de; **~tory** *adj.* préliminaire.
prefect *s.* préfet *m.*; **~ure** *s.* préfecture *f.*
prefer *v.t.* & *i.* (*like better*) préférer, aimer mieux; (*make claim, etc.*) intenter; (*promote*) élever; **~able** *adj.* préférable; **~ably** *adv.* de préférence; **~ence** *s.* préférence *f.*, (*prior right*) droit de priorité *m.*; **~ential** *adj.* (*claim, debt, dividend*) privilégié, (*tariff*) préférentiel; **~ment** *s.* avancement *m.*
prefix *s.* préfixe *m.*; *v.t.* préfixer, faire précéder de.
pregnan/cy *s.* grossesse *f.*; **~t** *adj.* enceinte; (*fig.*) fertile en, gros de.
prehensile *adj.* préhensile.
prehistor/y *s.* préhistoire *f.*; **~ic** *adj.* préhistorique.
prejudge *v.t.* préjuger (de qch.); **~ment** *s.* jugement prématuré *m.*
prejudic/e *s.* **1.** (*bias*) préjugé *m.*, parti-pris *m.*; **2.** (*detriment*) préjudice *f.*; **without ~e to,** sans préjudice de; *v.t.* (1) prévenir (*against*—contre); (2) porter préjudice à; **~ial** *adj.* préjudiciable.
prelate *s.* prélat *m.*
preliminar/y *adj.* préliminaire, préalable; **~ies** *s.pl.* préliminaires *m.pl.*
prelude *s.* prélude *m.*; *v.t.* préluder (à).
premature *adj.* prématuré; **~ly** *adv.**.
premeditat/e *v.t.* préméditer; **~ion** *s.* préméditation *f.*
premier *s.* premier ministre *m.*, président du conseil *m.*; *adj.* premier.
première *s.* première *f.*
premises *s.pl.* lieux *m.pl.*, immeubles *m.pl.*
premisses *s.pl.* prémisses *f.pl.*
premium *s.* prime *f.*; **to be at a ~,** faire prime; **to put a ~ on,** offrir une prime pour.
premonit/ion *s.* prémonition *f.*; (*presentiment*) pressentiment *m.*; **~ory** *adj.* prémonitoire.
preoccup/y *v.t.* préoccuper; **~ation** *s.* préoccupation *f.*
prepar/e *v.t.* & *i.* préparer; **~e for sth.,** préparer qch.; **to be ~ed to,** être prêt à; **~ation** *s.* (*act*) préparation *f.*, (*school*) devoir *m.*, (*substance*) produit *m.*; **~ations** *s.pl.* préparatifs *m.pl.*; **~atory** *adj.* préparatoire; (*introductory*) préalable.
prepay *v.t.* payer d'avance; (*post*) affranchir; **prepaid** (*post*) port payé; **~ment** *s.* paiement d'avance *m.*; (*post*) affranchissement *m.*
prepondera/nce *s.* prépondérance *f.*; **~nt** *adj.* prépondérant; **~te** *v.i.* être prépondérant.
preposition *s.* préposition *f.*; **~al** *adj.* prépositif.
prepossess *v.t.* (*imbue with*) imprégner de; (*take possession of*) posséder, obséder; (*prejudice* (*usu.*) *favourably*) prévenir (en faveur de); **~ing** *adj.* aimable, engageant; **~ion** *s.* prévention *f.*
preposterous *adj.* (*absurd*) absurde; (*perverse*) extravagant; (*unreasonable*) déraisonnable; **~ly** *adv.* absurdement; **~ness** *s.* absurdité *f.*
prerequisite *s.* condition préalable *f.*; *adj.* préalablement nécessaire.
prerogative *s.* prérogative *f.*
presage *s.* présage *m.*; *v.t.* présager.
Presbyterian *adj.* & *s.m.f.* Presbytérien(ne).
presbytery *s.* presbytère *m.*
prescien/ce *s.* prescience *f.*; **~t** *adj.* prescient.
prescri/be *v.t.* prescrire; *v.i.* **~be for** (*med.*) faire une ordonnance pour; **~ption** *s.* (*act*) prescription *f.*; (*med.*) ordonnance *f.*; **~ptive** *adj.* de prescription.
presence *s.* présence *f.*; **in ~ of,** en présence de; **~ of mind,** présence d'esprit *f.*;
present[1] *s.* (*gift*) cadeau *m.*, don *m.*; **make ~ a of,** faire cadeau de.
present[2] *s.* (*time*) présent *m.*; **at ~,** à présent; **for the ~,** pour le moment; *adj.* (≠ *absent*) présent; (*ready*) prêt; (*attentive*) attentif; (≠ *past or future*) actuel; **~ly** *adv.* (*at ~*) actuellement, (*before long*) tout à l'heure.
present[3] *v.t.* (*introduce, exhibit, offer to public*) présenter; (*offer as gift*) offrir (qch. à qn.), faire cadeau de (qch. à qn.); **~ s.o. with sth.,** faire cadeau de qch. à qn.; **~ arms!,** présentez armes!; **~able** *adj.* présentable, sortable; **~ation** *s.* présentation *f.*, (*gift*) souvenir *m.*
presentiment *s.* pressentiment *m.*
preserv/e *s.* (*cook.*) conserve *f.*; (*game*) chasse

gardée *f.*; to POACH **on s.o.'s ~es;** *v.t.* (*keep safe, alive*) préserver; (*maintain*) maintenir; (*keep from decay*) conserver; (*game*) garder; **~ation** *s.* (*act*) préservation *f.*, (*state*) conservation *f.*; **~ative** *s.* agent *m. or* moyen *m.*, de conservation; *adj.* qui conserve, antiseptique; **~ing-pan** *s.* bassine à confitures *f.*

preside *v.i.* présider; **~ over** *v.t.* présider.

presiden/cy *s.* présidence *f.*; **~t** *s.* président *m.*; (*comm.*) président-directeur-général *m.*; **~tial** *adj.* présidentiel.

presidium *s.* præsidium *m.*

press *s.* (*crowd*; *affairs*; *mech.*; *newspapers*) presse *f.*; (*for wine, etc.*) pressoir *m.*; (*cupboard*) armoire *f.*; **~-box** *s.*, **~-gallery** *s.* tribune de la presse *f.*; **~ cutting** *s.* coupure de presse *f.*; **~-gang** *s.* presse *f.*; **~man** *s.* journaliste *m.*; **~ release** *s.* communiqué *m.*; **~-stud** *s.* bouton-pression *m.*; *v.t.* (*crowd*; *shape*; *influence*) presser; (*squeeze*) serrer; (*grapes*) pressurer; (*clothes*) repasser; (*on button, etc.*) appuyer sur; (*mil., naut., hist.*) enrôler de force; (*force sth. on s.o.*) imposer qch. à qn.; *v.i.* presser; (*hurry*) se presser; **~ on,** presser le pas; **~ on** REGARD**less; be ~ed for,** être à court de; **~-up** *s.* (*exercise*) traction *f.*; **~ing** *s.* pression *f.*, *adj.* urgent.

pressure *s.* (*force*; *meteor.*) pression *f.*; (*urgency*) presse *f.*; (*of tyre*) gonflage *m.*; (*electr., med.*) tension *f.*, **blood ~,** tension artérielle *f.*; **bring ~ to bear on s.o.,** faire pression sur qn.; **~-cooker** *s.* marmite autoclave *f.*; **~ group** *s.* groupe de pression *m.*; **~ lubrication** *etc.*, graissage (etc.) sous pression *m.*; **pressurize** *v.t.* pressuriser; **pressurized** *adj.* (*aviat.*) pressurisé.

prestig/e *s.* prestige *m.*; **~ious** *adj.* prestigieux.

presum/e *v.t.* présumer; *v.i.* être présomptueux; (*take liberties with*) abuser de; **~e to do sth.,** se permettre de faire qch.; **~able** *adj.* probable; **~ably** *adv.* vraisemblablement; **~ing** *adj.* présomptueux; **~ption** *s.* présomption *f.*; **~ptive** *adj.* présumé; **heir ~ptive,** héritier présomptif; **~ptuous** *adj.* présomptueux; **~ptuously** *adv.**; **~ptuousness** *s.* présomption *f.*

presuppose *v.t.* présupposer; (*involve, imply*) entraîner .

pretence *s.* **1.** (*make-believe*) simulation *f.*; **2.** (*ostentation*) affectation *f.*; **3.** (*pretext*) prétexte *m.*; **4.** (*claim*) prétention *f.*; FALSE **~s.**

preten/d *v.t.* (*nos. refer to* PRETENCE) (1) simuler; (3) feindre; (4) prétendre (*to*—à); *v.i.* (1) faire semblant (de), se faire passer pour; **~der** *s.* (4) prétendant(e) *m.f.*; **~sion** *s.* prétention *f.*; **~tious** *adj.* prétentieux.

pretext *s.* prétexte *m.*; *v.t.* prétexter.

prett/y *adj.* joli; (*fine, good*) fameux; **a ~y** PENNY; **to be sitting ~y,** avoir trouvé un bon filon; *adv.* assez; **~ily** *adv.**; **~iness** *s.* gentillesse *f.*

prevail *v.i.* (*be victorious*) l'emporter (*against, over*—sur); (*attain one's object*) prévaloir (contre, sur); (*predominate*) prédominer; (*be usual*) régner; **~ on s.o. to do sth.,** décider qn. à faire qch.; **~ing** *adj.* prédominant, régnant.

prevalen/ce *s.* prédominance *f.*, généralité *f.*; **~t** *adj.* répandu.

prevaricat/e *v.i.* tergiverser; **~ion** *s.* tergiversation *f.*, faux-fuyants *m.pl.*; ⚠ prévarication = **embezzlement.**

prevent *v.t.* empêcher (qn. de faire qch.); (*avert*) prévenir; **~ion** *s.* prévention *f.*; **~ive** & **~ative** *adj.* préventif.

preview *s.* avant-première *f.*

previous *adj.* (*before in time or order*) antérieur (à); (*prior to*) précédent; **~ly** *adv.* antérieurement; auparavant.

prevision *s.* prévision *f.*

prey *s.* proie *f.*; **bird, beast of ~,** oiseau rapace *m.*, prédateur *m.*; **to be a ~ to,** être en proie à; *v.t.* **~ upon,** faire sa proie de; (*fig.*) miner, obséder.

price *s.* (*lit.* & *fig.*) prix *m.*; (*fin.*) cours *m.*; **cost ~,** prix coûtant, de revient *m.*; **half-~,** (à) moitié prix; **retail ~,** prix de détail *m.*; **wholesale ~,** prix de gros *m.*; **at a ~,** à prix d'or; **at any ~,** à aucun prix; **what ~?,** eh bien?, que dites-vous de?; *v.t.* (*fix ~ of*) établir le prix de; (*ask ~ of*) demander le prix de; (*estimate*) évaluer; **~less** *adj.* inestimable; (*pop.*) impayable.

prick *s.* piqûre *f.*; *v.t.* (*pierce*) percer; (*sting*) piquer; (*spur*) éperonner; (*burst*) crever; **~ out,** (*hort.*) repiquer; **~ up,** (*ears*) dresser; *v.i.* piquer; **~ing** *s.* picotement, *m.*, fourmillement *m.*; **~le** *s.* épine *f.*, piquant *m.*; **~le** *v.i.* fourmiller; **~ly** *adj.* (*lit.* & *fig.*) épineux; **~ly heat** *s.* lichen vésiculaire *m.*; **~ly pear,** oponce *m.*

pride *s.* (*arrogance*) orgueil *m.*; (*elation, pleasure*) fierté *f.*; **to take ~ in,** être fier de; (*of lions*) troupe *f.*; (*fig.*) sommet *m.*; *v.refl.* **~ oneself on,** se vanter de.

priest *s.* prêtre *m.*; **~ess** *s.* prêtresse *f.*; **~hood** *s.* prêtrise *f.*; **~ly** *adj.* de prêtre.

prig *s.* petit saint *m.*; **~gish** *adj.* suffisant.

prim *adj.* **1.** (*formal*) méticuleux; **2.** (*prudish*) guindé; **~ness** *s.* (1) ordre méticuleux *m.*; (2) allure compassée *f.*

primac/y *s.* (*office*) primatie *f.*; (*preeminence*) primauté *f.*; **~te** *s.* (*eccles.*) primat *m.*; (*mammal*) primate *m.*

primar/y *adj.* **1.** (*original*) primitif; **2.** (*first in time, rank*) principal; **3.** (*colour, education, school*) primaire; **~ily** *adv.* (1) primitivement; (2)*.

prime *s.* (*eccles.*) prime *f.*; (*best part*) le meilleur *m.*; (*perfect state*) fine fleur *f.*; (*of life*) fleur de l'âge *f.*; *adj.* (*primary*) primitif; (*chief*) principal; (*of highest quality*) de première qualité; **~ minister** *s.* premier ministre *m.*; **~ number** *s.* nombre premier *m.*; *v.t.* (*gun, pump*) amorcer; (*wood, etc.*) apprêter; (*fig. inform person*) mettre au courant; **~r** *s.* premier livre *m.*, (*manual*) manuel *m.*, (*for wood, etc.*) couche d'apprêt *f.*

primeval *adj.* primitif; **~ forest,** forêt vierge.

primitive *adj.* primitif; **~ly** *adv.**; **~ness** *s.* nature primitive *f.*

primogeniture *s.* primogéniture *f.*

primordial *adj.* primordial.

primrose *s.* primevère *f.*

primus *s.* (*stove*) réchaud à pétrole *m.*

prince *s.* prince *m.*; **~ss** *s.* princesse *f.*; **~ly** *adj.* princier.

principal *s.* (*of institution*) direct/eur, -rice *m.f*; (*actor*) premier rôle *m.*; (*fin.*) principal *m.*; (*of agent*) commettant *m.*; *adj.* principal; **~ly** *adv.**; **~ity** *s.* principauté *f.*

principle *s.* principe *m.*; **in ~,** en principe; **on ~,** par principe.

print *s.* **1.** (*mark*) empreinte *f.*; **2.** (*on paper*) impression *f.*; SMALL **~;** **3.** (*~ed matter*) imprimé *m.*; **4.** (*photo.*) épreuve *f.*; **5.** (*text.*) (tissu) imprimé *m.*; **out of ~,** épuisé; *v.t.* (1) faire une empreinte sur; (2), (3) imprimer; (4) tirer; **6.** (*write like ~ing*) écrire en caractères d'imprimerie; **~er** *s.* imprimeur *m.*; **~ing** *s.* impression *f.*; **~ing-press** *s.* presse *f.*

prior[1] *s.* (*eccles.*) prieur *m.*; **~ess** *s.* prieure *f.*; **~y** *s.* prieuré *m.*

prior[2] *adj.* (*earlier*) antérieur (à); (*antecedent*) précédent; **~ to** *adv.* avant (de), préalablement à; **~ity** *s.* (*in time*) antériorité *f.*, (*in order*) priorité *f.*, (*thing claiming early attention*) devoir *m.*, question *f.*, prioritaire.

prism *s.* prisme *m.*; **~atic** *adj.* prismatique.

prison *s.* prison *f.*; **~ camp,** camp de prisonniers *m.*; **~er** *s.* prisonnier *m.*; (*law*) accusé *m.*; **to take ~er,** faire prisonnier.

pristine *adj.* primitif.

privacy *s.* retraite *f.*, isolement *m.*; (*of ceremony*) intimité *f.*
private *s.* (*mil.*) simple soldat *m.*; *adj.* (≠ *public*) privé; (≠ *official*) particulier; (*place*) isolé, retiré; (*personal*) personnel; (*secret*) secret, confidentiel; ~ VIEW; **in** ~, dans l'intimité; **~ly** *adv.* en particulier, personnellement.
privateer *s.* corsaire *m.*
privation *s.* privation *f.* (*often pl.*).
privet *s.* troène *m.*
privilege *s.* privilège *m.*; (*monopoly*) monopole *m.*; **~d** *adj.* privilégié.
privy *s.* (*archaic, W.C.*) cabinets *m.pl.*; *adj.* privé, secret; **to be ~ to,** être au courant de; **P~ Council,** conseil privé *m.*; **~ purse** *s.* cassette royale *f.*; **~ seal** *s.* petit sceau *m.*; **privily** *adv.* secrètement.
prize *s.* prix *m.*; (*in lottery, etc.*) lot *m.*; (*naut.*) prise *f.*; *adj.* (*animal, book, etc.*) primé; **~-fighter** *s.* boxeur *m.*; **~-money** *s.* prix *m.*; **~winner** *s.* lauréat(e) *m.f.*, (*in lottery, etc.*) gagnant *m.*; *v.t.* (*value*) estimer; (*force open*) ouvrir au levier.
pro[1] *s.* (*fam.* = *professional*) professionnel *m.*
pro[2] *s.* **~s and cons,** les pour et les contre *m.pl.*
P.R.O. (*abbrev. public relations officer*) responsable des relations publiques *m.*
probab/le *adj.* & *s.m.* probable; **~ility** *s.* probabilité *f.*; (*~le event*) éventualité *f.*; **in all ~ility,** selon toute probabilité; **~ly** *adv.**.
probate *s.* homologation *f.*
probation *s.* **1.** (*trial period*) stage *m.*; **2.** (*eccles.*) probation *f.*; **3.** (*law*) liberté surveillée *f.*; **on ~** (1) stagiaire; (3) en liberté surveillée, sous contrôle judiciaire; **~ officer** *s.* délégué à la liberté surveillée *m.*; **~er** *s.* (1) stagiaire *m.f.*; (*novice*) novice *m.f.*; (3) délinquant en liberté surveillée *m.*; **~al, ~ary** *adj.* de stage, de probation.
probe *s.* sonde *f.*; *v.t.* sonder; (*fig.*) scruter.
probity *s.* probité *f.*
problem *s.* problème *m.*; **~ child,** enfant difficile; **~atic(al)** *adj.* problématique.
proboscis *s.* trompe *f.*
procedure *s.* procédé *m.*
proceed *v.i.* (*go on*) poursuivre, continuer (*on one's way*—son chemin); (*make one's way to*) se rendre à; (*act*) agir; (*continue*) se poursuivre, avoir lieu; (*resume*) reprendre; (*issue from*) provenir de; (*originate from*) dériver de; **~ to do sth.,** se mettre à faire qch.; **~ to sth. else,** passer à autre chose; **~ with,** continuer; **~ing** *s.* procédé *m.*; **~ings** *s.pl.* débats *m.pl.*, (*publication*) compte-rendu *m.*; **to take ~ings against,** poursuivre en justice; **~s** *s.pl.* produit *m.sing.*
process *s.* **1.** (*progress*) développement *m.*; **2.** (*comm.*) procédé *m.*, (*operation*) transformation *f.*; **3.** (*law*) procès *m.*, (*writ*) mandat *m.*; **in ~,** en cours; **in the ~ of,** au cours de; *v.t.* (2) traiter, transformer; **~ed** *adj.* traité; **~ing** *s.* traitement *m.*, transformation *f.*
process/ion *s.* cortège *m.*, défilé *m.*; (*eccles.*) procession *f.*; **~ional** *adj.* processionnel; **~** *v.i.* (*fam. go in ~ion*) aller en procession, en cortège.
procla/im *v.t.* proclamer; (*banns*) publier; (*war*) déclarer; **~mation** *s.* proclamation *f.*
proclivity *s.* penchant *m.* (à).
proconsul *s.* proconsul *m.*; **~ar,** *adj.* proconsulaire.
procrastinat/e *v.i.* temporiser; **~ion** *s.* temporisation *f.*
procreat/e *v.t.* procréer; **~ion** *s.* procréation *f.*
proctor *s.* (*acad.*) censeur *m.*; (*law*) avoué *m.*
procur/e *v.t.* (*obtain*) (se) procurer (qch. à qn.); (*cause*) procurer; **~able** *adj.* trouvable; **~ation** *s.* acquisition *f.*; (*law*) procuration *f.*; **~ator** *s.* (*law*) procureur *m.*
prod *s.* (*touch*) coup *m.*; (*instrument*) aiguillon *m.*; *v.t.* pousser; (*fig.*) aiguillonner.
prodigal *adj.* & *s.m.* prodigue (de); **~ity** *s.* prodigalité *f.*; **~ly** *adv.* prodigalement.
prodig/ious *adj.* prodigieux; (*fam.*) formidable; **~iously** *adv.**;*; **~y** *s.* prodige *m.*
produce *s.* (*yield*) produit *m.*; (*agric.*) denrées *f.pl.*; *v.t.* produire; (*theat.*) mettre en scène; (*cause*) provoquer; (*manufacture*) fabriquer; **~r** *s.* producteur *m.*; (*theat.*) metteur en scène *m.*
product *s.* produit *m.*; **~ion** *s.* (*act*) production *f.*, rendement *m.*; (*thing produced*) produit *m.*; (*liter., art*) production *f.*; (*theat.*) mise en scène *f.*; **~ive** *adj.* productif; (*agric.*) fertile; (*fig.*) fécond; **~iveness** *s.* **~ivity** *s.* productivité *f.*
profan/e *adj.* **1.** (*secular*) profane; **2.** (*heathen*) impie; **3.** (*irreverent*) sacrilège; **~ity** *s.* (*blasphemy*) blasphème *m.*, (*oath*) juron *m.*, (3) (*irreverent speech*) sacrilège *m.*; **~ely** *adv.* (1) de façon profane; (2) avec impiété; (3) grossièrement; **~eness** *s.* (1) caractère profane *m.*; (2) impiété *f.*; *v.t.* (*pollute*) polluer; (*violate*) violer; (*treat irreverently*) profaner; **~ation** *s.* profanation *f.*
profess *v.t.* (*pretend to feel*) professer; (*pretend to be or do*) (se) déclarer; (*follow trade*) exercer; *v.i.* professer; **~ed** *adj.* (*avowed*) avéré; (*alleged*) soi-disant; (*eccles.*) profès; **~edly** *adv.* ouvertement, de son propre aveu; soi-disant.
profession *s.* profession *f.*; **~al** *s.* professionnel *m.*; **~al** *adj.* professionnel; de profession, de métier; **~ally** *adv.* par profession, dans l'exercice de sa profession.
professor *s.* professeur *m.f.* (d'université); **~ial** *adj.* professoral; **~ship** *s.* professorat *m.*, chaire *f.*
proffer *v.t.* offrir.
proficien/cy *s.* compétence *f.*; **~t** *adj.* expert (*in, at*—en).
profile *s.* (*of face*) profil *m.*; silhouette *f.*; (*biographical sketch*) portrait *m.*; *v.t.* (se) profiler.
profit *s.* (*advantage*) avantage *m.*; (*benefit*) profit *m.*; (*pecuniary gain*) bénéfice *m.*; **at a ~,** à profit; **~-sharing** *s.* participation (des employés) aux bénéfices *f.*; **~less** *adj.* inutile, sans profit; *v.t.* profiter à; *v.i.* **~ by, from,** profiter de; **~able** *adj.* (*useful*) profitable, (*gainful*) rentable; **~ability** *s.* rentabilité *f.*; **~ably** *adv.* avantageusement; **~eer** *s.* affairiste *m.*, (*pej.*) profiteur *m.*; **~eer** *v.i.* agir en affairiste.
profliga/cy *s.* débauche *f.*; (*lavishness*) prodigalité *f.*; **~te** *adj.* débauché.
profound *adj.* profond; (*intense, detailed*) approfondi; **~ly** *adv.* profondément; **~ness** *s.* & **profundity** *s.* profondeur *f.*
profus/e *adj.* **1.** (*person*) prodigue (*in or of*—de); **2.** (*thing*) abondant (*in*—en); **~ely** *adv.* (1) à profusion; (2) abondamment; **~ion** *s.* profusion *f.*
progenitor *s.* (*human*) aïeul *m.* (*pl.*—aïeux); (*gen. fig.*) ancêtre *m.*
progeny *s.* progéniture *f.*
prognos/is *s.* & **~tic** *s.* pronostic *m.*; **~ticate** *v.t.* pronostiquer.
programme *s.* programme *m.*; *v.t.* programmer; **~r** *s.* programmeu/r, -se *m.f.*
progress *s.* **1.** (*forward movement*) marche en avant *m.*; **2.** (*improvement*) progrès *m.*; (*development*) développement *m.*; **in ~,** en cours; *v.i.* (1) s'avancer; (2) faire des progrès; **~ion** *s.* progression *f.*; **~ive** *s.* progressiste *m.f.*; **~ive** *adj.* progressif; (*reforming*) progressiste; **~ively** *adv.* progressivement.
prohibit *v.t.* (*forbid*) interdire, défendre (à qn. de faire qch.); (*prevent*) empêcher (qn. de faire qch.); **~ion** *s.* interdiction *f.*; (*hist. USA*) prohibition *f.*; **~ive** *adj.* prohibitif.
project *s.* projet *m.*; *v.t.* (*plan*) projeter; (*throw*) lancer; (*draw*) faire la projection de; *v.i.* saillir; **~ile** *s.* projectile *m.*; **~ing** *adj.* en saillie; **~ion**

s. projection *f.*, (~*ing part*) saillie *f.*; **~or** *s.* projecteur *m.*
prolapse *s.* prolapsus *m.*; *v.i.* tomber.
prole *s.* (*pop. abbrev. for proletarian*) prolo *m.*
proletari/an *adj.* & *s.m.f.* prolétaire; **~at** *s.* prolétariat *m.*
proliferat/e *v.i.* proliférer; **~ion** *s.* prolifération *f.*
prolific *adj.* prolifique.
prolix *adj.* prolixe; **~ity** *s.* prolixité *f.*
prologue *s.* prologue *m.*; *v.t.* faire un prologue à.
prolong *v.t.* prolonger; **~ation** *s.* (*time*) prolongation *f.*; (*space*) prolongement *m.*
promenade *s.* promenade *f.*; *v.i.* se promener; *v.t.* faire étalage de.
prominen/ce *s.* proéminence *f.*; (*fig.*) importance *f.*; **~t** *adj.* (*projecting*) proéminent; (*conspicuous*) éminent; (*distinguished*) distingué; **~tly** *adv.* éminemment.
promiscu/ous *adj.* fait au hasard; (*Eng. fam.*) très libre; **~ity** *s.* promiscuité *f.*; **~ously** *adv.* au hasard.
promis/e *s.* promesse *f.*; (*favourable indication*) espérance *f.*; **to show ~e,** donner des espérances; **a** LICK **and a ~e;** *v.t.* promettre (qch. à qn.); **~e to do sth.,** promettre de faire qch.; *v.i.* se révéler très prometteur; **~ing** *adj.* prometteur; **~sory** *adj.* qui promet; **~sory note,** billet à ordre *m.*
promontory *s.* promontoire *m.*
promot/e *v.t.* **1.** (*advance*) promouvoir (⚠ *inf.* & *p.p.* (promu) *only*), avancer, nommer; **2.** (*help*) encourager; **3.** (*comm.*) faire la réclame pour; **~er** *s.* (*esp. fin.*) fondateur *m.*; **~ion** *s.* (1) promotion *f.*; (2) encouragement *m.*; (3) réclame *f.*, promotion des ventes *f.*; (*fin.*) fondation *f.*
prompt *s.* (*theat.*) réplique soufflée *f.*; *adj.* prompt (à); *v.t.* (*theat.*) souffler; (*incite*) inciter, pousser (à); **~er** *s.* (*theat.*) souffleur *m.*; **~itude** *s.* promptitude *f.*; **~ly** *adv.**.
promulgat/e *v.t.* (*laws, etc.*) promulguer; (*news*) répandre; **~ion** *s.* promulgation *f.*
prone *adj.* **1.** (*lying face down*) couché sur le ventre; **2.** (*inclined to*) enclin à; **~ness** *s.* (2) inclination *f.*
prong *s.* fourchon *m.*, dent *f.*; **two-, three-~ed** *adj.* à deux, trois dents; *v.t.* enfoncer la fourche dans.
pron/oun *s.* pronom *m.*; **~ominal** *adj.* pronominal.
pronounce *v.t.* (*articulate; pass judgement*) prononcer; (*state*) déclarer; *v.i.* (*give as opinion*) se prononcer sur; **~able** *adj.* prononçable; **~d** *adj.* marqué; **~ment** *s.* déclaration *f.*
pronunciation *s.* prononciation *f.*
proof *s.* (*evidence*) preuve *f.*; (*of alcohol*) preuve *f.*; **~ spirit,** alcool à preuve *m.*; **over, under, ~,** au dessus de, au dessous de, preuve; (*test; print.*) épreuve *f.*; **~-reader** *s.* correct/eur, -rice *m.f.* (d'épreuves); *adj.* résistant (*against*—à); (*fig.*) à l'abri de; *v.t.* rendre résistant; (*against water*) imperméabiliser; **~ing** *s.* imperméabilisation *f.*
prop *s.* **1.** (*support*) appui *m.*; **2.** (*arch.*) étai *m.*; **3.** (*hort.*) tuteur *m.*; **4.** (*supporter*) soutien *m.*; **5.** (*theat.*) accessoire *m.*; **~ forward** (*rugby*) *s.* pilier *m.*; *v.t.* (1), (4) (*~ up*) soutenir; (2) étayer; (3) tuteurer.
propagand/a *s.* propagande *f.*; (*eccles.*) propagation *f.*; **~ist** *s.* propagandiste *m.f.*
propagat/e *v.t.* & *i.* (se) propager; **~ion** *s.* propagation *f.*; **~or** *s.* (*person*) propagat/eur, -rice *m.f.*; (*hort.*) germoir *m.*
propane *s.* propane *m.*
propel *v.t.* propulser; (*fam.*) pousser; **~lant** *s.* propulseur *m.*; **~lent** *adj.* propulseur; **~ler** *s.* hélice *f.*
propensity *s.* propension *f.* (à).
proper *adj.* **1.** (*suitable*) propre (à); **2.** (*right*) juste, exact; **3.** (*decent*) convenable; **4.** (*fam.* = *thorough*) parfait; **to think ~ to,** juger bon de; **~ly** *adv.* (1)*; (2) bien; (3)*; (4)*; **~ly so-called,** proprement dit.
propert/y *s.* (*owning, possession*) propriété *f.*; biens *m.pl.*; (*quality*) propriété *f.*; **~ies** *s.* (*theat.*) accessoires *m.pl.*
prophecy *s.* prophétie *f.*
prophesy *v.t.* & *i.* prophétiser.
prophet *s.* prophète *m.*; **~ess** *s.* prophétesse *f.*; **~ic** *adj.* prophétique; **~ically** *adv.**.
prophyla/ctic *adj.* & *s.m.* prophylactique; **~xis** *s.* prophylaxie *f.*
propinquity *s.* (*place*) proximité *f.*; (*kinship*) parenté *f.*
propitiat/e *v.t.* rendre propice; (*appease*) apaiser; **~ion** *s.* (*eccles.*) propitiation *f.*; apaisement *m.*; **~ory** *adj.* propiatoire.
propitious *adj.* propice (à); **~ly** *adv.* favorablement.
proponent *s.* auteur *m.* (d'une proposition, etc.).
proportion *s.* proportion *f.*; **in ~ to,** par rapport à; **in ~ as,** à mesure que; **out of ~,** disproportionné; *v.t.* proportionner (à); **~al** *adj.* en proportion (de); proportionnel; **~ally** *adv.* proportionnellement (à); **~ate** *adj.* proportionné à; **~ately** *adv.* en proportion de.
propos/e *v.t.* proposer; *v.i.* (*intend*) se proposer de; (*marriage*) faire une demande en mariage; **~al** *s.* proposition *f.*, (*scheme*) projet *m.*, (*of marriage*) demande en mariage *f.*; **~al form** (*insurance*) demande d'assurance *f.*; **~ition** *s.* proposition *f.*, (*pop. problem*) affaire *f.*; *v.t.* (*fam.*) faire une proposition douteuse à qn.
propound *v.t.* proposer; **~er** *s.* auteur *m.* (d'une proposition).
propriet/or *s.* & **~ress** *s.* propriétaire *m.f.*; **~ary** *adj.* de propriété; (*person*) possédant; **~ary brand,** marque déposée *f.*; **~orial** *adj.* de propriétaire.
propriet/y *s.* propriété *f.*; (*correct behaviour*) convenance *f.*; **~ies** *s.pl.* convenances *f.pl.*
propuls/ion *s.* propulsion *f.*; **~ive** *adj.* propulsif.
pro rata *adv.* au prorata de, proportionnellement à.
prorog/ue *v.t.* (*parl.*) proroger; **~ation** *s.* prorogation *f.*
proscenium *s.* avant-scène *f.*
proscri/be *v.t.* proscrire; **~ption** *s.* proscription *f.*; **~ptive** *adj.* de proscription.
pros/e *s.* prose *f.*; **~aic** *adj.* prosaïque; **~y** *adj.* ennuyeux.
prosecut/e *v.t.* (*carry on, pursue*) poursuivre; (*law*) poursuivre en justice; TRESPASSERS **will be ~ed; ~ion** *s.* (*of studies*) poursuite *f.*, (*of duty, profession*) exercice *m.*, (*legal proceedings*) poursuites *f.pl.*, (*law*) accusation *f.*; **~or** *s.* plaignant(e) *m.f.*, (*official*) procureur *m.*, **public ~or** *s.* procureur de la République *m.*, (*of a kingdom*) procureur du Roi, de la Reine.
proselyt/e *s.* prosélyte *m.f.*; **~ize** *v.t.* faire du prosélytisme.
prosody *s.* prosodie *f.*
prospect *s.* perspective *f.*; (*fam. comm.*) client éventuel *m.*; *v.t.* & *i.* prospecter; **~ive** *adj.* futur, en perspective, éventuel; **~ively** *adv.* en perspective; **~or** *s.* prospecteur *m.*; **~us** *s.* prospectus *m.*
prosper *v.i.* prospérer; **~ity** *s.* prospérité *f.*; **~ous** *adj.* prospère; (*wind*) favorable; **~ously** *adv.* avec prospérité.
prostate *s.* prostate *f.*
prostitut/e *s.* prostituée *f.*; *v.t.* (se) prostituer; **~ion** *s.* prostitution *f.*
prostrat/e *adj.* **1.** (*lying face down*) prosterné; **2.** (*overthrown*) effondré; **3.** (*exhausted*) prostré;

v.t. (1) (se) prosterner; (2) abattre; (3) accabler, épuiser; **~ion** *s.* (1) prosternation *f.*; (2) accablement *m.*; (3) prostration *f.*
protagonist *s.* protagoniste *m.f.*
protect *v.t.* (*defend, shield*) protéger (*from*—de, contre); (*keep safe, guard against*) sauvegarder; **~ion** *s.* protection *f.*, (*comm.*) provision *f.*; **~ionist** *s.* protectionniste *m.f.*; **~ive** *adj.* protecteur; **~or** *s.* protect/eur, -rice *m.f.*; **~orate** *s.* protectorat *m.*
protégé *s.* protégé(e) *m.f.*
protein *s.* protéine *f.*
pro tem *adv.* par intérim.
protest *s.* protestation *f.*; (*comm. law*) protêt *m.*; **under ~**, à son corps défendant; (*law*) sous réserve; *v.t.* & *i.* protester (*against*—contre); **~ one's innocence** *etc.*, protester de son innocence, etc.; **~ation** *s.* protestation *f.*, contestation *f.*
Protestant *adj.* & *s.m.f.* protestant(e); **~ism** *s.* protestantisme *m.*
protocol *s.* protocole *m.*
proton *s.* proton *m.*
protoplasm *s.* protoplasme *m.*
prototype *s.* prototype *m.*
protract *v.t.* **1.** (*prolong*) prolonger; **2.** (*math.*) établir un plan (de qch.) à l'échelle; **~ion** *s.* (1) prolongation *f.*; **~or** *s.* (2) rapporteur *m.*
protru/de *v.t.* pousser en avant; *v.i.* déborder, faire saillie; **~sion** *s.* saillie *f.*; **~sive** *adj.* saillant.
protuberan/ce *s.* protubérance *f.*; **~t** *adj.* protubérant.
proud *adj.* **1.** (*arrogant*) orgueilleux, hautain; **2.** (*feeling proper pride, honoured*) fier; **3.** (*imposing*) imposant; **~ly** *adv.* (1) orgueilleusement; (2) fièrement; **to do s.o. ~**, faire beaucoup d'honneur à qn.
prov/e *v.t.* (*give proof of*) prouver; (*demonstrate*) démontrer; (*test*) éprouver; (*will*) homologuer; *v.i.* (*person*) se montrer; (*thing*) se révéler; **~able** *adj.* prouvable; **~en** *adj.* prouvé.
provenance *s.* provenance *f.*
provender *s.* (*agric.*) fourrage *m.*; (*food*) vivres *m.pl.*
proverb *s.* proverbe *m.*; **~ial** *adj.* proverbial; **~ially** *adv.**.
provid/e *v.t.* (*equip*) pourvoir (*with*—de); (*supply*) fournir (*with*—de); (*stipulate*) stipuler; *v.i.* (*take precautions against*) prendre des précautions contre, se prémunir contre; (*make preparations for*) assurer, prévoir; **~ed, ~ing, that** *conj.* pourvu que, à condition que; **~er** *s.* pourvoyeur *m.*
providen/ce *s.* **1.** (*of God*) Providence *f.*; **2.** (*foresight*) prévoyance *f.*; **3.** (*thrift*) économie *f.*; **~t** *adj.* (2) (*person*) prévoyant; (*society, etc.*) de prévoyance; (3) économe; **~tial** *adj.* providentiel; **~tially** *adv.**.
provinc/e *s.* (*admin. division*) province *f.*; (*sphere of action*) domaine *m.*; **in my ~e,** de mon ressort; **~es** *pl.* (≠ *capital*) province *f.sing.*; **~ial** *adj.* & *s.m.* provincial.
provision *s.* provision *f.*; (*stipulation*) clause *f.*, disposition *f.*; **~s** *s.pl.* provisions *f.pl.*; **~ dealer** *s.* épicier *m.*; *v.t.* approvisionner; **~al** *adj.* provisoire; **~ally** *adv.**.
proviso *s.* condition *f.*; clause restrictive *f.*; **~ry** *adj.* conditionnel.
provo/ke *v.t.* (*incite*) inciter, pousser (à); (*irritate*) agacer; (*call forth*) provoquer; **~cation** *s.* provocation *f.*; **~cative** *adj.* provocateur, provocant; **~catively** *adv.* de façon provocante; **~king** *adj.* (*annoying*) agaçant.
provost *s.* (*Scotland*) maire *m.*; (*mil. police*) prévôt *m.*
prow *s.* proue *f.*
prowess *s.* prouesse *f.*
prowl *v.i.* rôder; (*hunt*) chasser; **~er** *s.* rôdeur *m.*
proxim/ate *adj.* proche, immédiat; **~ity** *s.* proximité *f.*
proxy *s.* (*agency*) procuration *f.*; (*authorized agent*) fondé de pouvoir *m.*; (*vote*) vote émis par mandataire *m.*; **by ~**, par procuration.
prud/e *s.* prude *f.*; **~ery** *s.* pruderie *f.*; **~ish** *adj.* prude.
pruden/ce *s.* prudence *f.*; **~t** *adj.* prudent; **~tly** *adv.* prudemment; **~tial** *adj.* de prudence.
prune[1] *s.* pruneau *m.* ⚠ prune = **plum.**
prun/e[2] *v.t.* (*hort.*) élaguer; (*fig.*) couper, faire des coupures dans; **~ing** *s.* taille *f.*; **~ing-knife** *s.* serpette *f.*
prurien/ce *s.* luxure *f.*; **~t** *adj.* lascif.
Prussia *s.* (*geog.*) Prusse *f.*; **~n** *adj.* & *s.m.f.* prussien(ne); **~n blue,** bleu de Prusse.
prussic *adj.* prussique.
pry[1] *v.i.* fureter; **~ into,** fourrer le nez dans; **~ing** *adj.* indiscret.
pry[2] *v.t.* **~ open,** soulever au levier.
P.S. (*postscript*) P.S. (post scriptum) *m.*
psalm *s.* psaume *m.*; **~ist** *s.* psalmiste *m.*; **~ody** *s.* psalmodie *f.*
psalter *s.* psautier *m.*
pseudo- (*in combination*) pseudo-.
pseudonym *s.* pseudonyme *m.*
pshaw! *interj.* (*contempt*) peuh!; (*impatience*) bah!
psittacosis *s.* psittacose *f.*
psych/e *s.* psyché *f.*; **~edelic** *adj.* psychédélique; **~iatry** *s.* psychiatrie *f.*; **~iatric** *adj.* psychiatrique; **~iatrist** *s.* psychiatre *m.f.*; **~ic** *adj.* psychique; *s.* médium *m.*
psycho- (*in combination*) **~-analysis** *s.* psychanalyse *f.*; **~-analyse** *v.t.* psychanalyser; **~-analyst** *s.* psychanalyste *m.f.*; **~path** *s.* psychopathe *m.f.*; **~pathic** *adj.* mentalement malade; **~somatic** *adj.* psychosomatique; **~therapy** *s.* psychothérapie *f.*
psycholog/y *s.* psychologie *f.*; **~ical** *adj.* psychologique; **~ist** *s.* psychologue *m.f.*
psycho/sis *s.* psychose *f.*; **~tic** *adj.* & *s.m.f.* psychotique.
P.T.O. (*abbrev., please turn over*) T.S.V.P. (tournez s'il vous plaît).
ptomaine *s.* ptomaine *f.*
pub *s.* (*fam.*) bistro *m.*
puberty *s.* puberté *f.*
public *s.* public *m.*; **in ~**, en public; *adj.* public (publique); **~-address system,** système de diffusion publique *m.*; **~ house,** café *m.*; **~ relations officer,** responsable des relations publiques *m.*; **~ school,** collège d'enseignement libre *m.*; **~-spirited** *adj.* qui fait preuve d'esprit social; **~ utilities,** commodités *f.pl.*; **~an** *s.* cabaretier *m.*; **~ation** *s.* publication *f.*; **~ist** *s.* publiciste *m.*; **~ity** *s.* publicité *f.*, *adj.* publicitaire; **~ize** *v.t.* faire connaître (du public); **~ly** *adv.* publiquement.
publish *v.t.* publier; **~ abroad,** crier sur les toits; **~er** *s.* éditeur *m.*
puce *s.* puce *m.*
pucker *s.* fronce *f.*, ride *f.*; *v.t.* & *i.* froncer.
pudding *s.* pudding *m.*
puddle *s.* flaque *f.*
pudgy *adj.* (*fam.*) rondouillard.
pueril/e *adj.* puéril; **~ity** *s.* puérilité *f.*
puff *s.* (*breath*) souffle *m.*; (*of smoke*) bouffée *f.*; (*of steam*) jet *m.*; POWDER-~; **~-adder** *s.* vipère clotho *f.*; **~-ball** *s.* vesse de loup *f.*; **~ pastry,** pâte feuilletée *f.*; *v.t.* (*pipe*) tirer sur; (*advertise*) faire du battage pour; (*inflate*) gonfler; *v.i.* émettre des bouffées de; (*pant*) souffler; **~ out** *v.t.* & *i.* (faire) bouffer; **~ up** *v.t.* gonfler; **~ed up** (*fig.*) bouffi (*with*—de); **~iness** *s.* bouffissure *f.*; **~y** *adj.* (*swollen*) enflé, bouffi, (*out of breath*) essoufflé (*also* **~ed**).
puffin *s.* macareux *m.*

pug *s.* (*~-dog*) carlin *m.*; **~ marks,** (*of wild animal*) piste *f.*, traces *f.pl.*
pugil/ism *s.* boxe *f.*; **~ist** *s.* pugiliste *m.*
pugnaci/ous *adj.* combatif; **~ty** *s.* pugnacité *f.*
puke *v.t.* & *i.* (*fam.*) dégobiller.
pukka *adj.* vrai, véritable.
pule *v.i.* (*whine*) piauler; (*complain*) rouspéter.
pull *s.* (*tug*) traction *f.*; (*fig. influence*) piston *m.*; **to have the ~ over s.o.,** avoir barre sur qn.; (*rough proof*) épreuve *f.*; (*drink*) lampée *f.*; (*handle*) poignée *f.*; *v.t.* & *i.* tirer, traîner; (*pluck*) arracher; (*on oar*) manier; **~ a face,** faire une grimace; **~ a** FAST **one; ~ s.o.'s** LEG; **~ one's** PUNCHES; **~** STRINGS; **~ one's** WEIGHT; **~** WOOL **over s.o.'s eyes; ~ about** *v.t.* tirailler; **~ away** *v.t.* entraîner (qn.), arracher (qch. à qn.); **~ back** *v.t.* & *i.* retirer; **~ down** *v.t.* démolir, (*fig.*) abattre; **~ in** *v.t.* rentrer, (*horse*) retenir, (*fam.*) arrêter; *v.i.* (*train*) entrer en gare, (*vehicle*) se ranger; **~-in** *s.* auberge de routiers *f.*; **~ off** *v.t.* ôter, (*prize*) remporter; **~ it off,** l'emporter; **~ on** *v.t.* enfiler; **~-on** *adj.* (*garment*) facile à enfiler; **~ out** *v.t.* (*teeth, plants*) arracher; *v.i.* (*train*) sortir (de gare), (*withdraw*) se retirer; (*auto. move out of lane*) déboîter; **~-out** *s.* supplément détachable *m.*; **~ over** *v.t.* renverser; **~over** *s.* pull(over) *m.*; **~ round** *v.t.* & *i.* (se) ranimer; **~ through** *v.t.* tirer (qn.) d'affaire, mener (qch.) à terme; *v.i.* s'en tirer; **~ together,** coopérer; **~ oneself together,** se reprendre; **~ up** *v.t.* hisser; **~ one's** SOCKS **up; ~ up** *v.t.* (*agric.*) arracher, (*reprimand*) réprimander; *v.i.* s'arrêter net; **~-up** *s.* arrêt *m.*, (*café*) auberge de routiers *f.*
pullet *s.* poularde *f.*
pulley *s.* poulie *f.*
pullover *see* PULL.
pullulate *v.i.* pulluler.
pulmonary *adj.* pulmonaire.
pulp *s.* (*of fruit*) pulpe *f.*; (*for paper*) pâte *f.*; (*fig.*) marmelade *f.*; *v.t.* réduire en pâte; **~y** *adj.* pulpeux.
pulpit *s.* chaire *f.*
puls/e *s.* (*of arteries*) pouls *m.sing.*; (*beat*) pulsation *f.*; (*edible*) légumineuses *f.pl.*; **to feel s.o.'s ~e,** tâter le pouls à qn.; **~ate** *v.i.* battre; **~ation** *s.* pulsation *f.*
pulveriz/e *v.t.* pulvériser; **~ation** *s.* pulvérisation *f.*
puma *s.* puma *m.*
pumice (*~-stone*) *s.* pierre ponce *f.*
pummel *v.t.* bourrer de coups.
pump *s.* **1.** (*mech.*) pompe *f.*; **2.** (*shoe*) escarpin *m.*; *v.t.* (1) pomper; (*fig. fam.*) tirer les vers du nez à qn.; **~ up** *v.t.* gonfler.
pumpkin *s.* potiron *m.*
pun *s.* jeu de mots *m.*; *v.i.* faire des jeux de mots.
punch *s.* **1.** (*blow*) coup de poing *m.*; **to pull one's ~es** (*fig.*) y aller doucement; **2.** (*tool*) poinçon *m.*, (*mech.*) poinçonneuse *f.*; **3.** (*drink*) punch *m.*; **4.** (*buffoon*) polichinelle *f.*; **P~ and Judy show** *s.* guignol *m.*; **~-bowl** *s.* bol à punch *m.*, (*geol.*) cuvette *f.*; **~** CARD; *v.t.* (1) donner des coups de poing à; (2) poinçonner, (*automatic*) composter; **~-up** *s.* rixe *f.*
puncheon *s.* gros tonneau *m.*
punctilious *adj.* pointilleux; **~ly** *adv.* d'une manière pointilleuse.
punctual *adj.* ponctuel; **~ity** *s.* ponctualité *f.*; **~ly** *adv.**.
punctuat/e *v.t.* ponctuer; **~ion** *s.* ponctuation *f.*
puncture *s.* **1.** (*pricking*) perforation *f.*; **2.** (*med.*) ponction *f.*; **3.** (*of tyre*) crevaison *f.*, pneu crevé *m.*; *v.t.* (1) perforer; (2) ponctionner; (3) *v.t.* & *i.* crever.
pundit *s.* (*title*) pandit *m.*; (*fam.*) ponte *m.*
pungen/cy *s.* **1.** (*taste, smell*) âcreté *f.*; **2.** (*sting*) acuité *f.*; **3.** (*causticity*) causticité *f.*; **~t** *adj.* (1) âcre; (2) piquant; (3) mordant, caustique.
punish *v.t.* punir; (*boxing*) malmener; **~able** *adj.* punissable; (*law*) **~able by,** passible de; **~ing** *adj.* épuisant; **~ment** *s.* punition *f.*; **corporal ~ment,** châtiment corporel *m.*
punitive *adj.* punitif; *rare except in* **~ expedition,** expédition punitive *f.*
Punjab *s.* (*geog.*) Pendjab *m.*; **~i** *adj.* du Pendjab; *s.m.f.* habitant du Pendjab; *s.m.* (*lang.*) Pendjabi.
punt *s.* bachot *m.*; *v.i.* conduire à la perche.
puny *adj.* chétif.
pup(**py**) *s.* petit chien *m.*, chiot *m.*; *v.i.* mettre bas.
pupil *s.* (*learner*) élève *m.f.*; (*in guardianship*) pupille *m.f.*; (*of eye*) pupille *f.*
puppet *s.* marionette *f.*; (*toy*) pantin *m.*; (*fig.*) fantoche *m.*; **~ state,** gouvernement fantoche *m.*
purblind *adj.* (*short-sighted*) myope; (*fig.*) aveugle.
purchas/e *s.* achat *m.*; (*leverage*) point d'appui *m.*; (*grip*) prise *f.*; *v.t.* acheter; **~able** *adj.* achetable; **~er** *s.* acheteu/r, -se *m.f.*
purdah *s.* moucharabieh *m.*; (*curtain*) jalousie *f.*
pur/e *adj.* pur; **~ify** *v.t.* purifier, (*techn.*) rectifier; **~ification** *s.* purification *f.*; **~ist** *s.* puriste *m.*; **~ely** *adv.**; **~ity** *s.* & **~eness** *s.* pureté *f.*
purée *s.* purée *f.*
purgatory *s.* purgatoire *m.*
purg/e *s.* purge *f.*; (*polit.*) épuration *f.*; (*med.*) purgatif *m.*; *v.t.* (*lit.* & *fig.*) purger; (*polit.*) épurer; (*clear of charge*) disculper de; **~ative** *adj.* & *s.m.* purgatif.
purify *see* PURE.
puritan *adj.* & *s.m.f.* puritain(e); **~ical** *adj.* puritain; **~ism** *s.* puritanisme *m.*
purity *see* PURE.
purl *s.* (*knitting*) maille à l'envers *f.*; *v.t.* faire une maille à l'envers; *v.i.* (*stream*) gazouiller.
purlieu *s.* (*usu. pl.*) environs *m.pl.*
purloin *v.t.* soustraire.
purpl/e *s.* pourpre *f.*, violet *m.*; *adj.* pourpre, violet; **~ish** *adj.* violacé.
purport *s.* sens *m.*; *v.i.* laisser entendre; **~ to be,** se présenter comme.
purpose *s.* (*object*) but *m.*; (*firmness*) résolution *f.*; **for the ~ of,** dans le but de; **for this ~,** dans ce but; **to the ~,** à propos; **to what ~?;** à quoi bon?; **on ~,** exprès; **to serve the ~,** faire l'affaire; **to serve no ~,** être inutile; **at** CROSS **~s; to all** INTENTS **and ~s; ~-built, ~-made,** construit, fait, dans un but précis; **~ful** *adj.* réfléchi, résolu; **~fully** *adv.* résolument; **~ly** *adv.* exprès; *v.i.* avoir l'intention de.
purr *s.* **1.** (*of cat*) ronron *m.*; **2.** (*of engine*) ronflement *m.*; *v.i.* (1) ronronner; (2) ronfler.
purse *s.* (*container*) porte-monnaie *m.*; (*funds, prize*) bourse *f.*; PRIVY **~; ~-strings,** cordons de la bourse *m.pl.*; **~r** *s.* (*naut.*) commissaire *m.* (de bord); *v.t.* (*lips*) pincer.
pursuan/ce, in ~ce of, conformément à; **~t to,** par suite de.
pursu/e *v.t.* poursuivre; (*proceed along*) suivre; (*follow profession*) exercer; *v.i.* continuer; **~er** *s.* poursuivant *m.*
pursuit *s.* poursuite *f.*; (*fig.*) recherche *f.*; (*profession*) profession *f.*; (*recreation*) occupation *f.*
purvey *v.t.* fournir; **~or** *s.* fournisseur *m.*
purview *s.* limites *f.pl.*
pus *s.* pus *m.*
push *s.* (*act*) poussée *f.*; (*shove*) coup *m.*; (*effort*) effort *m.*; (*enterprise*) initiative *f.*, dynamisme *m.*; **at a ~,** au moment critique; **~-bike** *s.* vélo *m.*; **~-cart** *s.*, **~-chair** *s.* poussette *f.*; *v.t.* & *i.* (se) pousser; (*impel, urge*) presser, encourager; **~ away, ~ back** *v.t.* repousser; **~-**

-button *adj.* actionné par un bouton; ~ **forward** *v.t.* & *i.* (faire) avancer; ~ **in** *v.t.* enfoncer; ~ **off** *v.t.* & *i.* (*naut.*) pousser au large, (*fam.*) filer; ~ **on** *v.t.* pousser à, *v.i.* avancer; pousser jusqu'à; ~ **out** *v.t.* pousser (dehors); ~ **over** *v.t.* faire tomber; ~**-over** *s.* (*fam.*) jeu d'enfant *m.*; ~**-pull** *adj.* actionné par un levier; ~ **through** *v.t.* & *i.* (faire) traverser, (*fig.*) amener à bonne fin; ~ **up** *v.t.* relever, (*fig.*) pistonner; ~ **up the** DAISIES; ~**ed for,** à court de; ~**ing** *adj.* arriviste.

pusillanim/ous *adj.* pusillanime; ~**ity** *s.* pusillanimité *f.*

puss(**y**) *s.* minet(te) *m.f.*; **to** ~**foot** *v.i.* répondre en normand.

pustule *s.* pustule *f.*

put *v.t.* (*set in place*) mettre; (~ *in order, to flight, etc.*) mettre (en ordre, en fuite, etc.); (*express*) exprimer; (*question*) poser; (*proposal*) soumettre; (*estimate*) estimer; (*hurl*) lancer; (*translate*) traduire; **I** ~ **it to you,** je vous le demande; **let's** ~ **it that,** mettons que; ~ **an** END **to;** ~ **a good** FACE **on;** ~ **to** FLIGHT; ~ **in** MIND **of;** ~ **nose out of** JOINT; ~ SHOULDER **to wheel;** ~ SPOKE **in wheel;** ~ **about** *v.t.* (*circulate*) faire courir; (*inconvenience*) déranger; (*worry*) inquiéter; (*naut.*) *v.i.* faire virer de bord; ~ **it across s.o.,** (*fam.*) faire avaler qch. à qn.; ~ **aside** *v.t.* mettre de côté; (*fig.*) renoncer à; ~ **away** *v.t.* ranger; mettre de côté; (*fam.*) coffrer; ~ **back** *v.t.* remettre (en place); (*clock*) retarder; ~ **by** *v.t.* mettre de côté; ~ **down** *v.t.* déposer; (*suppress*) supprimer; (*repress*) réprimer; (*ascribe to*) attribuer à; (*write down*) inscrire; ~ **forth** *v.t.* émettre; (*bot.*) pousser; (*show*) déployer; ~ **forward** *v.t.* avancer; (*fig.*) pousser; ~ **one's best** FOOT **forward;** ~ **in** *v.t.* (*write down*) inscrire; (*introduce*) introduire; (*instal*) installer; (*agric.*) planter; ~ **off** *v.t.* (*remove*) enlever; (*disconcert*) dérouter; (*disgust*) dégoûter; (*divert*) détourner; (*postpone*) remettre, différer; (*naut.*) pousser au large; ~ **on** *v.t.* (*clothes*) mettre; (*electr.*) allumer; (*brakes*) serrer; (*clock*) avancer; (*pretend*) simuler; (*theat.*) monter; (*speed, weight*) prendre; (*record, tape*) passer; ~ **s.o. on to** (*telephone*) mettre en communication avec; ~ **out** *v.t.* mettre dehors; (*extend*) tendre; (*boat*) mettre à l'eau; (*publish*) publier; (*bone*) démettre; (*annoy*) déranger, contrarier; (*fire, light*) éteindre; ~ **through** *v.t.* (*telephone*) mettre en communication avec; (*cause to undergo*) faire subir (qch. à qn.); (*fig.*) mener à bonne fin; **be hard** ~ **to it to,** trouver difficile de; ~ **together** *v.t.* assembler; (*mech.*) monter; ~ **up** *v.t.* mettre, poser; (*lodge*) loger; (*notice*) afficher; (*parcel*) emballer; (*money*) avancer; (*price*) augmenter, majorer; (*umbrella*) ouvrir; (*prayer*) faire; (*building*) construire; ~**-up job** *s.* (*fam.*) coup monté *m.*; ~ **up to** (*fig.*) inciter à; ~ **up with** *v.t.* supporter; ~ **upon** *v.t.* imposer à, abuser de; **stay** ~, rester en place.

putative *adj.* putatif.

putr/efaction *s.* putréfaction *f.*; ~**efy** *v.t.* & *i.* (se) putréfier; ~**escence** *s.* putrescence *f.*; ~**escent** *adj.* putrescent; ~**id** *adj.* putride.

puttee *s.* bande molletière *f.*

putty *s.* mastic *m.*; *v.t.* mastiquer.

puzzle *s.* (*toy*) puzzle *m.*; (*problem*) problème *m.*; (*enigma*) énigme *f.*; MONKEY-~ **tree;** *v.t.* embarasser; ~ **out** *v.t.* déchiffrer, résoudre.

PVC *s.* (*abbrev. polyvinyl chloride*) chlorure de polyvinyle *f.*; *adj.* polyvinylique.

pygmy, pigmy *s.* (*tribe*) pygmée *m.*; (*dwarf, person or thing*) nain *m.*; *adj.* nain.

pyjamas *s.* pyjama *m.* ⚠ *sing.*

pylon *s.* pylône *m.*

pyramid *s.* pyramide *f.*; ~**al** *adj.* pyramidal.

pyre *s.* bûcher *m.*

Pyrene/es *s.* (*geog.*) Pyrénées *f.pl.*; ~**an** *adj.* & *s.m.f.* pyrénéen(ne).

pyrethrum *s.* pyrèthre *m.*

pyrites *s.* pyrite *f.*

pyro- (*in combination*) ~**mania** *s.* pyromanie *f.*; ~**meter** *s.* pyromètre *m.*; ~**technic** *adj.* pyrotechnique; ~**technics** *s.* (*science*) pyrotechnique *f.* ⚠ *sing. in French*; (*display*) feu d'artifice *m.*

Pyrrhic *adj.* pyrrhique; ~ **victory,** victoire à la Pyrrhus.

python *s.* python *m.*; ~**ess** *s.* pythonisse *f.*

pyx *s.* (*eccles.*) ciboire *m.*

Q

Q.E.D. (*quod erat demonstrandum*) C.Q.F.D. (ce qu'il fallait démontrer).

qua *conj.* en tant que.

quack *s.* **1.** (*of duck*) coin-coin *m.invar.*; **2.** (*charlatan, esp. med.*) charlatan *m.*; *v.i.* (1) faire coin-coin; (*fig.*) jacasser.

quadragenarian *adj.* & *s.m.f.* quadragénaire.

Quadragesima *s.* quadragésime *f.*

quadrang/le *s.* (*figure*) quadrilatère *m.*; (*court*) cour *f.*; ~**ular** *adj.* quadrangulaire.

quadrant *s.* ($\frac{1}{4}$ *circle*) quadrant *m.*, quart de cercle *m.*; (*instrument*) octant *m.*

quadratic *adj.* quadratique.

quadrilateral *adj.* & *s.m.* quadrilatère.

quadrille *s.* (*mus.*) quadrille *m.*; (*card game*) hombre *m.*

quadruped *adj.* & *s.m.* quadrupède.

quadrupl/e *adj.* & *s.m.* quadruple; *v.t.* & *i.* quadrupler; ~**et** *s.* quadruplé(e) *m.f.*; ~**icate** *v.t.* quadrupler; **in** ~**icate,** en quatre exemplaires.

quaff *v.t.* & *i.* lamper.

quagmire *s.* marécage *m.*; (*in road*) fondrière *f.*

quail^1 *s.* caille *f.*

quail^2 *v.i.* trembler, reculer (devant).

quaint *adj.* (*odd*) bizarre, original; (*old-fashioned*) vieillot; ~**ly** *adv.* bizarrement; ~**ness** *s.* bizarrerie *f.*, originalité *f.*

quake *s.* (*fam.*) tremblement de terre *m.*; *v.i.* trembler (*with*—de).

Quaker *s.* quaker *m.*; ~**ess** *s.* quakeresse *f.*

qualif/y *v.t.* **1.** (*describe as*) qualifier de; **2.** (*make fit*) rendre apte (*for sth.*—à qch., *to do sth.*—à faire qch.); **3.** (*modify*) modifier; **4.** (*moderate*) atténuer; *v.i.* **5.** (*fulfil conditions*) être éligible (*for*—à), (*pass test*) être reçu; ~**y as a doctor etc.,** être reçu médecin, etc.; ~**ication** *s.* (1) qualification *f.*; (2) aptitude *f.*, compétence *f.*; (3) modification *f.*, réserve *f.*, restriction *f.*; (5) diplôme *m.*; ~**ied** *adj.* (2) apte (à), compétent (pour); (3) modifié, restreint, sous condition; (5) diplômé.

qualit/y *s.* qualité *f.*; *adj.* de premier choix; ~**ative** *adj.* qualitatif.

qualm *s.* (*misgiving*) appréhension *f.*; (*scruple*) scrupule *m.*; (*sickly feeling*) nausée *f.*

quandary *s.* embarras *m.*, dilemme *m.*

quantify *v.t.* quantifier.

quantit/y *s.* quantité *f.*; **unknown ~y** (*lit.* & *fig.*) inconnue *f.*; **~y surveyor** *s.* métreur (vérificateur) *m.*; **~ative** *adj.* quantitatif.
quantum *s.* quantum *m.* (*pl.* quanta).
quarantine *s.* quarantaine *f.*; *v.t.* mettre en quarantaine.
quarrel *s.* **1.** (*complaint*) sujet de plainte *m.*; **2.** (*contention*) querelle *f.*; **3.** (*rupture*) différend *m.*, (*fam.*) brouille *f.*; **I have no ~ with him,** je n'ai rien à lui reprocher; **to pick a ~ with s.o.,** chercher querelle à qn.; *v.i.* (1) se plaindre (*with*—de); (2) se quereller; (3) se brouiller; **~ with** (1) trouver à redire à qch., faire des reproches à qn.; **~some** *adj.* querelleur, irascible; **~someness** *s.* caractère querelleur *m.*, caractère irascible *m.*
quarry *s.* **1.** (*object of pursuit*) proie *f.*; **2.** (*excavation*) carrière *f.*; *v.t.* (2) extraire (d'une carrière); **~man** *s.* carrier *m.*
quart *s.* (*approx.*) litre *m.*
quarter *s.* (*fourth part*; *measure*; *point of compass*; *time*) quart *m.*; (*of moon*; *mercy*; *district*) quartier *m.*; (*period of year*) trimestre *m.*; (*direction*) direction *f.*; (*locality*) milieu *m.*; (*source of supply, help*) côté *m.*; **~s** *s.pl.* domicile *m.*, (*mil.*) quartiers *m.pl.*; **at close ~s,** corps à corps; **~-day** *s.* terme *m.*; **~deck** *s.* gaillard d'arrière *m.*; **~master** *s.* (*naut.*) second maître *m.*, (*mil.*) intendant *m.*, quartier-maître *m.*; **C.Q.M.S.** sergent-fourrier *m.*; **~ly** *s.* revue trimestrielle *f.*, *adj.* trimestriel; *v.t.* diviser en quatre; (*lodge*) installer; (*mil.*) cantonner; **~ing** *s.* (*herald.*) écartelure *f.*
quartet(**te**) *s.* quatuor *m.*
quarto *s.* in-quarto *m.*
quartz *s.* quartz *m.*
quasar *s.* quasar *m.*
quash *v.t.* (*annul*) annuler; (*reject*) rejeter; (*suppress*) étouffer.
quasi- (*in combination*) quasi-.
quatercentenary *s.* quatrième centenaire *m.*
quatrain *s.* quatrain *m.*
quaver *s.* (*trill*) *m.*; (*in speech*) trémolo *m.*; (*mus.*) croche *f.*; *v.i.* (*vibrate*) vibrer; (*tremble*) trembler, chevroter; **~ing,** *adj.* chevrotant.
quay *s.* quai *m.*
queas/y *adj.* **1.** (*liable to nausea*) nauséeux; **2.** (*liable to qualms*) scrupuleux; **~iness** *s.* (1) nausée *f.*; (2) scrupules *m.pl.*
Quebec *s.* (*geog.*) Québec *f.*; (*inhabitant*) **of ~** *adj.* & *s.m.f.* québecois(e).
queen *s.* (*king's wife, sovereign*; *bee*; *chess*; *fig.*) reine *f.*; (*cards, draughts*) dame *f.*; ⚠ **Q~ Elizabeth,** la reine Elisabeth; **~ mother** *s.* reine-mère *f.*; **~like** *adj.*, **~ly** *adj.* de reine; *v.t.* (*draughts*) damer; **~ it,** prendre des airs de reine.
queer *s.* (*pop.*) tante *f.*; *adj.* (*quaint*) bizarre; (*suspicious*) suspect; (*mad*) excentrique; (*ill*) souffrant; **in Q~ Street** (*pop.*) dans le pétrin; **~ly** *adv.* étrangement; **~ness** *s.* bizarrerie *f.*; *v.t.* (*pop.*) gâcher; **~ the pitch for s.o.,** mettre des bâtons dans les roues à qn.
quell *v.t.* réprimer.
quench *v.t.* (*thirst*) étancher; (*fire*) éteindre; (*fig.*) étouffer; **~less** *adj.* inextinguible.
querulous *adj.* grognon; **~ly** *adv.* en ronchonnant; **~ness** *s.* mauvaise humeur *f.*
query *s.* question *f.*; *v.t.* questionner (qn.); mettre en doute (qch.); *v.i.* chercher à savoir (si).
quest *s.* enquête *f.*; **in ~ of,** en quête de.
question *s.* question *f.*; (*doubt*) doute *m.*; **in ~,** en question; **out of the ~,** hors de doute, **it is out of the ~ to,** il n'est pas question de; **to call in ~,** mettre en doute; **~ mark** *s.* point d'interrogation *m.*; **~ time** *s.* (*parl.*) séance réservée aux interpellations *f.*; *v.t.* interroger; (*throw doubt upon*) mettre en doute; **~able** *adj.* discutable, (*dishonest*) suspect.
questionnaire *s.* questionnaire *m.*
queue *s.* queue *f.*; *v.i.* faire la queue; **to** JUMP **the ~.**
quibble *s.* (*play on words*) calembour *m.*; (*equivocation*) faux-fuyant *m.*; *v.i.* user de faux--fuyants, ergoter.
quick *s.* vif *m.*; **to the ~,** au vif; **to bite one's nails to the ~,** se ronger les ongles jusqu'au sang; **the ~** *s.pl.* les vivants *m.pl.*; *adj.* **1.** (*living*) vivant, vif; **2.** (*prompt*) prompt (à); **3.** (*intelligent*) vif; **4.** (*rapid*) rapide; **~ on the draw** (*fig.*) impulsif; **~lime** *s.* chaux vive *f.*; **~sands** *s.* sables mouvants *m.pl.*; **~set hedge** *s.* haie vive *f.*; **~silver** *s.* vif-argent *m.*; **~step** *s.* pas accéléré *m.*; **~-tempered** *adj.* emporté; **~--witted** *adj.* à l'esprit vif; **~en** *v.t.* (*give life to*) animer, (*inspire*) stimuler, (*accelerate*) accélérer; **~en** *v.i.* se ranimer; **~ie** *s.* (*fam.*) question éclair *f.*; **~ly** *adv.* vite, rapidement; ⚠ vite *is not an adj.*; **~ness** *s.* (2) promptitude *f.*; (3) vivacité *f.*; (4) vitesse *f.*, rapidité *f.*
quid *s.* (*pound*) livre sterling *f.*; (*of tobacco*) chique *f.*
quiddity *s.* qualité essentielle *f.*
quidnunc *s.* (*hist.*) nouvelliste *m.*
quid pro quo *s.* équivalent *m.*, compensation *f.*; ⚠ quiproquo = **misunderstanding.**
quiescen/ce *s.* tranquillité *f.*; **~t** *adj.* (*inert*) inactif; (*dormant*) en repos; (*silent*) silencieux.
quiet *s.* **1.** (*silence*) silence *m.*; **2.** (*calmness*) calme *m.*; **3.** (*peacefulness*) tranquillité *f.*; *adj.* (1) silencieux; **to be ~, to keep ~,** se taire; (2) (*gentle*) doux; (3) tranquille; **4.** (*unobtrusive*) sobre; **~ism** *s.* quiétisme *m.*; **~ist** *s.* quiétiste *m.f.*; **~ly** *adv.* (1) silencieusement; (2)*; (3)*; (4)*; **~ness** *s.* tranquillité *f.*; **~ude** *s.* quiétude *f.*; *v.t.* & *i.* & **~en** (se) calmer, (s')apaiser.
quietus *s.* coup de grâce *m.*
quiff *s.* (*of hair*) mèche *f.*
quill *s.* (*feather*; *pen*) plume *f.*; (*wing or tail feather*) penne *f.*; (*for fishing*) flotteur *m.*; (*of hedgehog*) piquant *m.*
quilt *s.* édredon *m.*, courtepointe *f.*; *v.t.* piquer; (*pad*) ouater; **~ing** *s.* (*text.*) piqué *m.*; (*padding*) ouatage *m.*
quince *s.* coing *m.*; **~ tree** *s.* cognassier *m.*
quincentenary *s.* cinquième centenaire *m.*
quincunx *s.* quinconce *f.*
quinine *s.* quinine *m.*
quinquagenarian *adj.* & *s.m.f.* quinquagénaire.
Quinquagesima *s.* quinquagésime *f.*
quinquennial *adj.* quinquennal.
quinsy *s.* amygdalite *f.*
quintessence *s.* quintessence *f.*
quintet *s.* quintette *m.*
quintupl/e *adj.* & *s.m.* quintuple; *v.t.* quintupler; **~et** *s.* quintuplé(e) *m.f.*; **in ~icate,** en cinq exemplaires.
quip *s.* quolibet *m.*; *v.i.* railler.
quire *s.* (*of paper*) main *f.*; *see* CHOIR.
quirk *s.* caprice *m.*
quisling *s.* collaborateur *m.*
quit *adj.* quitte (de); *v.t.* (*give up*) abandonner; (*leave*) quitter; *v.i.* partir.
quite *adv.* (*completely*) tout à fait; (*rather*) plutôt, assez; **~ so,** parfaitement.
quits, quitte; DOUBLE **or ~.**
quittance *s.* (*fin., comm.*) quittance *f.*; (*fig.*) rétribution *f.*
quiver *s.* carquois *m.*; **~full of children,** ribambelle *f.*, d'enfants; *v.i.* trembler; (*eyelids*) battre; (*wings*) palpiter; **~ing** *s.* tremblement *m.*
Quixot/e *s.* Don Quichotte *m.*; **q~ic** *adj.* de don Quichotte; **q~ically** *adv.* à la don Quichotte; **q~ism** *s.* don-quichottisme *m.*

quiz *s.* série de questions *f.*; (*radio, TV*) jeu radiophonique, jeu télévisé *m.*; *v.t.* (*fam. question*) poser des colles à qn.; (*look at*) lorgner; **~zical** *adj.* railleur.
quoin *s.* pierre d'angle *f.*
quoit *s.* palet *m.*; **~s** (*game*) marelle *f.*
quondam *adj.* d'autrefois.
quorum *s.* quorum *m.*
quota *s.* (*fin., fig.*) quote-part *f.*; (*comm., admin.*) quota *m.*
quot/e *v.t.* (*cite*) citer; (*repeat*) répéter; (*state price*) coter; **~es** *pl.* (*fam.*) guillemets *m.pl.*; **~able** *adj.* citable; **~ation** *s.* citation *f.*; (*price*) cote *f.*; **~ation-marks,** guillemets *m.pl.*
quoth *v.t.* (*archaic. third person*) dit-il.
quotient *s.* quotient *m.*

R

rabbet *s.* rainure *f.*; *v.t.* rainurer.
rabbi *s.* rabbin *m.*; **~nate** *s.* rabbinat *m.*; **~nical** *adj.* rabbinique.
rabbit *s.* lapin(e) *m.f.*; **to be a ~ at** (*tennis, etc.*), jouer comme un sabot; **~-hutch** *s.* clapier *m.*; **~ punch** *s.* coup sur la nuque *m.*; **~-warren** *s.* garenne *f.*, (*fig.*) dédale *m.*; WELSH ~; *v.i.* chasser le lapin.
rabble *s.* (*mob*) cohue *f.*; (*inferior people*) peuple *m.*; (*lowest classes*) canaille *f.*; **~-rouser** *s.* agitateur *m.*; **~-rousing** *s.* incitation à la révolte *f.*
rabid *adj.* (*vet.*) enragé; (*unreasoning*) effréné; **~ity** *s.* (*lit.* & *fig.*) violence *f.*
rabies *s.* rage *f.*
rac(c)oon *s.* raton laveur *m.*
race[1] *s.* **1.** (*contest*) course *f.*; **2.** (*sea current*) raz *m.*; **3.** (*channel*) cours *m.*; MILL-~; **4.** (*mech.*) voie *f.* (de roulement); **~course** *s.* champ de courses *m.*; **~horse** *s.* cheval de course *m.*; **~-meeting** *s.* réunion de courses *f.*; *v.t.* (1) (*compete with*) lutter de vitesse avec; (*cause to go fast*) faire marcher à toute allure; (*horse*) faire courir; *v.i.* marcher à toute allure; (*engine*) s'emballer.
rac/e[2] *s.* (*group, posterity, division of living things, ethnic stock*) race *f.*; (*descent*) lignée *f.*; **~e-riot,** bagarre entre Noirs et Blancs *f.*; **~ial** *adj.* racial; **~ism, ~ialism** *s.* racisme *m.*; **~ist, ~ialist** *s.* raciste *m.f.*; **~y** *adj.* vif, piquant.
raceme *s.* racème *m.*
rachitic *adj.* rachitique.
rack[1] *s.* **1.** (*framework*) étagère *f.*; (*agric.*) râtelier *m.*; **bomb-~**, lance-bombes *m.*; (*auto.*) **roof-~**, galerie *f.*; LUGGAGE-~; PIPE-~; PLATE-~; **2.** (*mech.*) crémaillère *f.*; **3.** (*instrument of torture*) chevalet *m.*; **to be on the ~** (*fig.*) être à la torture, (*fam.*) être sur le gril; *v.t.* (*brains*) se creuser la cervelle; **~ed by,** travaillé par; **~ing** *adj.* fou.
rack[2] *s.* (*driving clouds*) moutons *m.pl.*; (*destruction*) destruction *f.*; **to go to ~ and ruin,** tomber en ruines, (*fig.*) s'en aller à vau l'eau.
racket[1] *s.* (*tennis, etc.*) raquette *f.*; **~s** *s.* (*game*) rackets *m.*
racket[2] *s.* **1.** (*uproar*) (*fam.*) chahut *m.*; **2.** (*business*) affaire *f.*, combine *f.*; **3.** (*dubious dealings*) racket *m.*; *v.i.* (1) faire du boucan; (*live gay life*) faire la noce; (3) faire du chantage; **~eer** *s.* racketteur *m.*; **~y** *adj.* bruyant, tapageur.
radar *s.* radar *m.*; **~-operator** *s.* radariste *m.f.*
radial *adj.* radial; **~(-ply) tyre** *s.* pneu à structure radiale *m.*
radian/ce *s.* éclat *m.*; **~t** *s.* radiant *m.*; **~t** *adj.* rayonnant; (*dazzling*) éclatant; (*with joy, etc.*) rayonnant de (joie, etc.); **to be ~t with,** rayonner de; (*heat, etc.*) radiant; **~tly** *adv.* avec éclat, d'un air radieux.
radiat/e *v.t.* & *i.* (*from centre*) rayonner; (*emit rays*) dégager; (*wireless*) transmettre, diffuser; **~ion** *s.* (*light*) rayonnement *m.*; (*heat*) irradiation *f.*; (*radium*) radiation *f.*; **~ion sickness** troubles dûs aux radiations *m.pl.*; **~or** *s.* radiateur *m.*
radical *s.* radical *m.*; *adj.* radical; **~ism** *s.* radicalisme *m.*; **~ly** *adv.**.
radicle *s.* radicule *f. or* radicelle *f.*
radio *s.* radio *f.*; (*set*) poste de radio *m.*; *adj.* radio-; *v.t.* transmettre par radio.
radio- (*in combination*) **~active** *adj.* radioactif; **~activity** *s.* radioactivité *f.*; **~-astronomy** *s.* radioastronomie *f.*; **~-carbon** *s.* radiocarbone *m.*; **~-element** *s.* radioélément *m.*; **~gram** *s.* (*message*) radiogramme *m.*; **~graph** *v.t.* radiographier; **~graphy** *s.* radiographie *f.*; **~grapher** *s.* radiologue *m.f.*; **~graphic** *adj.* radiographique; **~isotope** *s.* radio-isotope *m.*; **~logist** *s.* radiologue *m.f.*; **~logy** *s.* radiologie *f.*; **~phonic** *adj.* radiophonique; **~scopy** *s.* radioscopie *f.*; **~-telegraphy** *s.* radiotélégraphie *f.*; **~-telescope** *s.* radiotélescope *m.*; **~-therapy** *s.* radiothérapie *f.*
radish *s.* radis *m.*
radium *s.* radium *m.*
radius *s.* (*geom.*) rayon *m.*; (*bone*) radius *m.*
radix *s.* base *f.*
R.A.F. *s.* Armée de l'air britannique *f.*; (*fam.*) Raf *f.*
raffia *s.* raphia *m.*
raffish *adj.* débauché.
raffle *s.* tombola *f.*; *v.t.* mettre en tombola.
raft *s.* radeau *m.*; (*for logging*) train de bois *m.*; **~sman** *s.* flotteur *m.*
rafter *s.* chevron *m.*
rag[1] *s.* (*of material*) chiffon *m.*, lambeau *m.*; RED **~ to a bull;** (*pej. newspaper*) feuille de chou *f.*; **~s** *s.pl.* haillons *m.pl.*; **in ~s,** en haillons; **in one's glad ~s,** sur son trente-et-un; **~-and--bone man** *s.* chiffonnier *m.*; **-amuffin** *s.* garnement *m.*; **~tag (and bobtail)** *s.* racaille *f.*; **~time** *s.* (*mus.*) air syncopé *m.*; **~ trade** *s.* (*pop.*) chiffons *m.pl.*; **~ged** *adj.* (*person*) déguenillé, (*thing*) déchiré, (*fig.*) inégal; **~gedly** *adv.* en haillons, (*fig.*) inégalement; **~ged robin** *s.* (*bot.*) œillet des prés *m.*
rag[2] *s.* (*pop.*) (*spree*) farce *f.*; (*practical joke*) canular *m.*; (*students'*) monôme *m.*; *v.t.* (*tease*) taquiner; (*play jokes on*) brimer.
rag/e *s.* **1.** (*anger*) fureur *f.*; **2.** (*fashion*) vogue *f.*; **to be all the ~e,** faire fureur; *v.i.* (1) être furieux, tempêter (*against*—contre); (*war, epidemic*) sévir; (*wind, storm*) faire rage; **~ing** *adj.* furieux.
raglan *adj.* & *s.m.* raglan.
ragout *s.* (*cook.*) ragoût *m.*
raid *s.* **1.** (*mil., air*) raid *m.*; **2.** (*bandits*) incursion *f.*; **3.** (*police*) rafle *f.*, descente (de police) *f.*; *v.t.* (1) faire une incursion dans; (*air*) bombarder; (2) piller; (3) faire une rafle, une descente, dans; **~er** *s.* (1) commando *m.*; avion ennemi *m.*; (2) pillard *m.*
rail[1] *s.* (*bird*) râle *m.*

rail[2] *s.* **1.** (*bar on gate, window, etc.*) barreau *m.*, (*on bridge*) garde-fou *m.*; (*on stairs*) rampe *f.*, (*hand*~) barre *f.*, TOWEL-~; **2.** (*rail. track*) rail *m.*, (*rail. transport*) chemin de fer *m.*; **by ~,** par chemin de fer; **to go off the ~s** (*lit.* & *fig.*) dérailler; **~ head** *s.* tête de ligne *f.*; **~road, ~way** *s.* chemin de fer *m.*; **~way** *adj.* ferroviaire; **~way** CARRIAGE; **~way** STATION; **~wayman** *s.* cheminot *m.*; *v.t.* (2) envoyer par chemin de fer; **~ in,** fermer avec une grille.

rail[3] *v.t.* invectiver (*at*—contre); ⚠ railler = **to mock.**

raiment *s.* vêtements *m.pl.*

rain *s.* (*lit.* & *fig.*) pluie *f.*; **in the ~,** sous la pluie; (*season*) **the ~s,** saison des pluies *f.*; **as right as ~,** en parfait état; **~bow** *s.* arc-en-ciel *m.*; **~ coat** *s.* imperméable *m.*; **~drop** *s.* goutte de pluie *f.*; **~fall** *s.* chute de pluie *f.*, (*meteor.*) régime des pluies *m.*; **~ forest** *s.* forêt vierge *f.*; **~-gauge** *s.* pluviomètre *m.*; **~-proof** *adj.* imperméable; **~-water** *s.* eau de pluie *f.*; **~-water pipe** *s.* tuyau de descente pluviale *m.*; **~y** *adj.* pluvieux; **to save up for a ~y day** (*fig.*) garder une poire pour la soif; *v.impers.* pleuvoir; **it is ~ing,** il pleut; **it looks like ~,** on dirait qu'il va pleuvoir; **it never ~s but it** POURS; *v.t.* (*send down like* ~) verser; *v.i.* (*fall like* ~) tomber.

raise *s.* (*increase in salary*) augmentation *f.*; *v.t.* **1.** (*lift up from lower position; hand, eyes, head, etc.*) lever; **2.** (*anchor, troops, taxes, siege*) lever; **3.** (*set upright; move up blind, window, etc.*) relever; **4.** (*lift* (*weight*) *from below; cause dust to rise; incite crowd; bring up question*) soulever; **5.** (*erect;* ~ *higher* (*lit.* & *fig.*); *protest, temperature*) élever; **6.** (*breed, rear, bring up* (*children, cattle*) élever; **7.** (*produce crops*) cultiver; **8.** (*increase prices, etc.*) augmenter; **9.** (*extract from ground*) extraire; **10.** (*obtain funds, etc.*) se procurer; **~ money on sth.,** emprunter sur qch.; **11.** (*utter*) pousser; **12.** (*ghosts, etc.*) évoquer; **13.** (*from dead*) ressusciter; **~ Cain, ~ hell,** (*trouble*) causer du grabuge, (*noise*) faire un boucan de tous les diables; **~ the wind** (*fig.*) trouver l'argent; **raising** *s.* (1) & (3) relèvement *m.*; (2) levée *f.*; (5) élévation *f.*; (6) élevage *m.*; (7) culture *f.*; (8) augmentation *f.*; (9) extraction *f.*; (13) résurrection *f.*

raisin *s.* raisin sec *m.*

raj *s.* souveraineté *f.* (britannique, aux Indes); **~ah** *s.* rajah *m.*

rake *s.* **1.** (*implement*) râteau *m.*, râtissoire *f.*; **2.** (*person*) débauché *m.*; **3.** (*of ship*) quête *f.*; *v.t.* (1) (*make smooth*) râtisser, (*pick up*) râteler; (*ransack, search*) fouiller; (*sweep with eyes, fire, etc.*) balayer; *v.i.* (3) être incliné; **~-off** *s.* ristourne *f.*; **to take a ~-off** (*pop.*) faire de la gratte; **~ over** *or* **up** *v.t.* attiser, (*fig.*) réveiller; **raking** *adj.* (*mil. fire*) d'enfilade; **rakish** *adj.* (*naut.*) élancé, (*person*) débauché, (*air*) cavalier.

rally *s.* **1.** (*act*) ralliement *m.*; **2.** (*recovery, comm.*) reprise *f.*; **3.** (*meeting*) réunion *f.*; **4.** (*tennis*) passe de jeu *f.*; **5.** (*auto*) rallye *m.*; *v.t.* & *i.* (1) (se) réunir, rassembler; (2) (se) ranimer; reprendre courage; **6.** (*chaff*) railler.

ram *s.* (*animal; astron.; mil.*) bélier *m.*; (*mech.*) piston *m.*; *v.t.* (*beat firm*) battre; (*force home*) enfoncer; (*pack closely*) fourrer; (*butt*) cogner; (*crash into*) heurter; (*fig. impress*) pousser à fond; **~rod** *s.* (*of rifle*) baguette *f.*, (*of artillery*) écouvillon *m.*; **straight as a ~rod** (*fig.*) droit comme un i.

Ramadan *s.* ramadan *m.*

rambl/e *s.* (petite) promenade *f.*; *v.i.* (*walk*) se promener, vagabonder; (*talk*) divaguer; **~er (rose)** *s.* rosier grimpant *m.*; **~ing** *adj.* (*speech*) décousu; (*arch.*) bâti sans plan.

ramekin *s.* ramequin *m.*

ramif/y *v.i.* se ramifier; **~ication** *s.* ramification *f.*

ramp *s.* (*slope*) pente *f.*; (*sloping floor*) plan incliné *m.*; (*aviat.*) passerelle *f.*; (*pop. swindle*) escroquerie *f.*; *v.i.* (*be ~ant*) sévir; (*be furious*) tempêter; **~ant** *adj.* (*herald.*) rampant; (*unrestrained*) déchaîné.

rampage *s.* rage *f.*; **on the ~,** dans une colère bleue; *v.i.* tempêter, se démener comme un fou.

rampart *s.* rempart *m.*

ramshackle *adj.* délabré.

ran *see* RUN.

ranch *s.* ranch *m.* (*pl.* ranchs *or* ranches); *v.i.* diriger un ranch.

rancid *adj.* rance; **to go ~,** rancir.

ranco/ur *s.* (*hate*) rancune *f.*; (*bitterness*) ressentiment *m.*; **~rous** *adj.* rancunier.

rand *s.* (*geog.*) le Rand *m.*; (*money*) rand *m.*

random *s.* **at ~,** au hasard, à l'aveuglette; *adj.* fait au hasard, fortuit; **~ check,** contrôle par sondage *m.*; **~ shot,** balle perdue *f.*

range *s.* **1.** (*row, series*): (*of buildings*) rangée *f.*, (*of mountains*) chaîne *f.*; **2.** (*freedom*) champ libre *m.*; **3.** (*for shooting*) champ de tir *m.*; **4.** (*sphere, scope*) étendue *f.*, domaine *m.*; **5.** (*compass*) portée *f.*, (*of choice*) fourchette *f.*, (*of gun*) portée *f.*, (*of colours*) gamme *f.*; **to give free ~ to,** donner libre essor à; **within ~,** à (la) portée (de), **out of ~,** hors de portée (de); **6.** (*cooking*) fourneau *m.*; **~-finder** *s.* télémètre *m.*; *v.t.* (1) ranger, aligner; **7.** (*wander over*) parcourir; *v.i.* (4), (5) s'étendre, varier (*from . . . to*—de . . . à); **~r** *s.* garde forestier *m.*

rank[1] *s.* (*row, queue, social class, station; mil.*) rang *m.*; (*officer*) grade *m.*; (*taxis*) station *f.*; **~s** *pl.* rangs *m.pl.*; **~ and** FILE; **to reduce to the ~s** casser; *v.t.* (*arrange in ~s*) ranger; (*assign to* ~) classer; *v.i.* se ranger; se classer; **~ above, below s.o.,** être supérieur, inférieur à qn.

rank[2] *adj.* **1.** (*over-luxuriant*) luxuriant; **2.** (*coarse, gross*) grossier; **3.** (*offensive*) immonde, puant, rance; **4.** (*flagrant*) flagrant; **~ness** *s.* (1) luxuriance *f.*; (2) grossièreté *f.*; (3) odeur fétide *f.*, ranci *m.*

rankle *v.i.* s'enflammer; (*fig.*) s'envenimer; **it ~d with him,** cela l'a ulcéré.

ransack *v.t.* (*search*) fouiller; (*pillage*) piller.

ransom *s.* rançon *f.*; **to hold to ~,** rançonner; *v.t.* (*pay ~ for*) racheter, payer rançon pour; (*set free for payment*) rançonner.

rant *v.i.* (*talk aimlessly*) divaguer; (*be angry*) tempêter; (*talk exaggeratedly*) déclamer avec extravagance; **~ing** *adj.* extravagant.

ranunculus *s.* renoncule *f.*

rap *s.* (*blow*) tape *f.*; (*sound*) coup sec *m.*; **to take the ~** (*pop.*) payer les pots cassés; **not to care a ~,** s'en moquer comme de l'an quarante; *v.t.* frapper.

rapac/ious *adj.* rapace; **~ity** *s.* rapacité *f.*; **~iously** *adv.* avec rapacité.

rape[1] *s.* **1.** (*forcible removal*) rapt *m.*; **2.** (*violation*) viol *m.*; *v.t.* (1) enlever; (2) violer.

rape[2] *s.* (*agric.*) colza *m.*

rapid *s.* rapide *m.*; *adj.* rapide; **~ity** *s.* rapidité *f.*; **~ly** *adv.**.

rapier *s.* rapière *f.*

rapine *s.* rapine *f.*

rapport *s.* rapport *m.*

rapt *adj.* (*attention*) profond; (*look*) ravi; (*in thought, etc.*) absorbé.

raptur/e *s.* transport *m.*, extase *f.*; **to go into ~es over sth.,** s'extasier sur qch.; **~ous** *adj.* (*person*) transporté; (*applause, etc.*) frénétique.

rar/e *adj.* (≠ *dense*; ≠ *common*) rare; (*excellent*) fameux; (*of meat*) saignant; **~efy** *v.t.* (se) raréfier; **~efaction** *s.* raréfaction *f.*; **~ity** *s.* objet rare *m.*; **~ely** *adv.* rarement; **~eness** *s.* rareté *f.*

rascal *s.* coquin *m.*; **~ly** *adj.* de coquin.
rash[1] *s.* (*on skin*) éruption *f.*; (*fig.*) épidémie *f.*
rash[2] *adj.* (*action*) inconsidéré, irréfléchi; (*person*) impétueux, téméraire; **~ly** *adv.* sans réflexion, à la légère, imprudemment; **~ness** *s.* précipitation *f.*, impétuosité *f.*, imprudence *f.*, témérité *f.*
rasher *s.* tranche de lard *f.*
rasp *s.* **1.** (*file*) râpe *f.*; **2.** (*sound*) grincement *m.*; *v.t.* (1) râper; (2) grincer; (*fig.*) irriter.
raspberry *s.* framboise *f.*; **~-cane** *s.* framboisier *m.*; **to give s.o. a ~** (*pop.*) envoyer péter qn.
rat *s.* (*animal*) rat *m.*; (*person*) rénégat *m.*; **to smell a ~** (*fig.*) soupçonner quelque anguille sous roche; **~ race** (*fig.*) concurrence acharnée *f.*; **~-trap** *s.* ratière *f.*; **~ty** *adj.* (*full of ~s*) infesté de rats, (*pop. angry*) de mauvaise humeur; *v.i.* attraper des rats; (*desert*) abandonner le navire, tourner casaque.
ratafia *s.* ratafia *m.*
ratchet *s.* cliquet *m.*
rate *s.* **1.** (*proportion, standard*) taux *m.*; (*percentage*) pourcentage *m.*; (*of exchange*) cours *m.* (de change); BIRTH **~**; **2.** (*value*) classe *f.*; (*tariff*) taux *m.*; (*speed*) allure *f.*; **3.** (*local tax*) taxes municipales *f.pl.*; **at any ~**, en tout cas, de toute façon; **at the ~ of,** à raison de; **first-~, second-~,** de premier, de second, ordre; **~payer** *s.* contribuable *m.f.*; *v.t.* (2) (*estimate*) estimer; (*consider as*) considérer comme; (*deserve*) mériter; (3) (*tax*) taxer; **4.** (*scold*) passer un savon à (qn.); *v.i.* (2) (*be ~ed as*) être classé comme; **~able** *adj.* (3) imposable; **~able value** *s.* loyer imposable *m.*; **rating** *s.* (2) estimation *f.*; (*school, auto., naut.*) classement *m.*, classe *f.*; (*sailor*) matelot *m.*
rather *adv.* (*more*) plutôt; (*somewhat*) un peu, assez; (*for choice*) de préférence; **I would ~ do sth.,** je préférerais *or* j'aimerais mieux faire qch.; **~ than,** plutôt que; **you should work ~ than be idle,** vous devriez travailler plutôt que de rester à ne rien faire; *interj.* (*fam.*) plutôt.
ratif/y *v.t.* ratifier; **~ication** *s.* ratification *f.*
rating *s. see* RATE.
ratio *s.* proportion *f.*
ration *s.* ration *f.*; **~** CARD; *v.t.* rationner.
rational *adj.* (*sane, sensible, moderate*) raisonnable; (*based on reasoning*) raisonné, rationnel; **~ism** *s.* rationalisme *m.*; **~ist** *s.* rationaliste *m.f.*; **~ity** *s.* rationalité *f.*; **~ize** *v.t.* rationaliser; **~ly** *adv.* raisonnablement.
ratline(s) *s.* (*naut.*) enfléchure(s) *f.*(*pl.*).
rattle *s.* **1.** (*instrument*) crécelle *f.*; **2.** (*toy*) hochet *m.*; **3.** (*of rattlesnake*) sonnette *f.*; **4.** (*sound*) bruit *m.*, cliquetis *m.*; **5.** (*med.*) râle *m.*; **~snake** *s.* serpent à sonnettes *m.*; *v.t.* & *i.* (1) & (2) (faire) résonner, agiter, trembler; (4) cliqueter, crépiter; **6.** (*pop.* = *fluster*) ébranler; **~ off** *v.t.* débiter à toute vitesse; **~ on** *v.i.* jacasser; **rattling** *s. as* (4); **rattling** *adj.* (*pop.* = *good*) épatant; SABRE **rattling.**
raucous *adj.* rauque.
ravage *s.* (*usu. pl.*) ravage *m.*; *v.t.* ravager.
rav/e *v.i.* **1.** (*talk wildly*) divaguer; **2.** (*howl, roar*) être déchaîné; **3. ~e about,** s'extasier sur; **~e at,** fulminer contre; **~ing** *s.* (1) divagation *f.*, délire *m.*; (2) (*of wind*) fureur *f.*; (3) (*fam. enthusiasm*) extase *m.*; **~ing** *adj.* **~ing mad,** fou à lier.
ravel *v.t.* embrouiller.
raven[1] *s.* (*bird*) corbeau *m.*; *adj.* noir comme un corbeau.
raven[2] *v.i.* vivre de rapine; **~ous** *adj.* (*appetite*) vorace; (*person*) affamé; **~ously** *adv.**; **to be ~ously hungry,** avoir une faim de loup.
ravine *s.* ravin *m.*, ravine *f.*
ravioli *s.* ravioli *m.*
ravish *v.t.* **1.** (*abduct, rape*) enlever, violer; **2.** (*delight*) ravir, transporter; **~ing** *adj.* (2) ravissant; **~ingly** *adv.* de façon ravissante.
raw *adj.* **1.** (*uncooked*) cru; **2.** (*in natural state*) (*spirit*) pur, (*metal*) brut; **3.** (*crude, inexperienced*) (*mil.*) non aguerri, (*fig.*) novice, inexpérimenté; **4.** (*sore*) à vif; **5.** (*weather*) froid et humide; **in the ~,** cru, crûment; **to touch s.o. on the ~,** toucher qn. au vif; **~** DEAL; **~hide** *adj.* de cuir vert; **~** MATERIALS; **~** RECRUIT; **~ness** *s.* (1) crudité *f.*; (3) inexpérience *f.*; (5) froid humide *m.*
ray *s.* (*of light* & *fig.*) rayon *m.*; **X-~,** rayon X *m.*; (*fish*) raie *f.*
rayon *s.* (*text.*) rayonne *f.*
raze, rase *v.t.* (*demolish*) démolir; (*efface*) effacer.
razor *s.* rasoir *m.*; SAFETY **~**; **~-back** *s.* (*ridge*) colline en dos d'âne *f.*, (*whale*) rorqual *m.* (*pl.*—als); **~-bill** *s.* manchot *m.*; **~-blade** *s.* lame de rasoir *f.*; **~-edge** *adj.* en lame de couteau; **to be on a ~-edge** (*fig.*) être sur la corde raide.
R.C. (*abbrev. Roman Catholic*) catholique romain *m.f.*
R.C. (*abbrev. Red Cross*) Croix-Rouge *f.*
re, ray *s.* (*mus.*) ré *m.*
re *prep.* au sujet de, concernant.
re- *prefix* re (retourner); ré (réexporter); r' (rengager); *see under relevant entries.* ⚠ *in some cases it is necessary to use* de nouveau *with a verb.*
reach *s.* (*act*) atteinte *f.*; (*range, scope*) portée *f.*; (*extent*) étendue *f.*; (*naut.*) bordée *f.*; **out of ~,** hors de portée; **within ~,** à portée (de main); *v.t.* & *i.* (*extend*) (s')étendre; (*put out, hand, etc.*) tendre, avancer; (*pass*) passer; (*get as far as*) atteindre, arriver à; (*amount to*) aboutir à; (*naut.*) courir une bordée; **~ down,** descendre; **~ for,** chercher à prendre.
react *v.i.* réagir (*to*—à, *against*—contre); **~ on,** agir sur; **~ion** *s.* réaction *f.*; **~ionary** *adj.* & *s.m.f.* réactionnaire; **~or** *s.* réacteur *m.*; ⚠ **re-act** = rejouer.
read *v.t.* (*with eyes*) lire; (*study*) étudier; (*record, indicate*) marquer, indiquer; (*proofs*) corriger; (*foretell*) lire dans; (*interpret*) interpréter; (*understand*) comprendre; (*mus.*) déchiffrer; *v.i.* lire, se lire; **~ for,** préparer; **~ off, ~ out,** lire à haute voix; **~ over,** relire; **~ over and over again,** lire et relire; **~ to s.o.,** faire la lecture à qn.; **~ up,** étudier, se documenter sur; **to be ~,** se lire; **well-~,** instruit; **~able** *adj.* (*legible*) lisible, (*pleasant to ~*) agréable à lire; **~er** *s.* lect/eur, -rice *m.f.*, (*one who ~s a lot*) liseur *m.*, (*acad.*) maître de conférences *m.*, (*book*) recueil *m.*, PROOF-**~er**; **~ing** *s.* lecture *f.*, (*scholarship*) culture *f.*, (*rendering*) interprétation *f.*, (*on instrument*) cote *f.*, (*parl.*) discussion *f.*; **~ing age** *s.* degré d'instruction *m.*; **~ing-desk** *s.* pupitre *m.*; **~ing-lamp** *s.* lampe *f.* (de bureau); **~ing matter** *s.* lecture *f.*; **~ing-room** *s.* salle de lecture *f.*
readjust *v.t.* rajuster.
ready *adj.* **1.** (*prepared, fit for use*) prêt (à); **2.** (*willing*) disposé (à), (*inclined to*) porté à; **3.** (*quick*) prompt (à), facile; **4.** (*within reach*) à portée, sous la main; ROUGH **and ~**; **~ money** *s.* argent comptant *m.*; **~ reckoner** *s.* barème *m.*; **to get ~,** (se) préparer; **to come to the ~** (*mil.*) apprêter l'arme; **~, steady, go!,** à vos marques! prêts? partez!; **readily** *adv.* (2) volontiers; (3) facilement; **readiness** *s.* (1) fait d'être prêt *m.*; (2) bonne volonté *f.*, disposition *f.*; (3) promptitude *f.*; *adv.* tout; **~-made** *adj.* tout fait, (*clothes*) prêt à porter; *v.t.* préparer.
reagent *s.* réactif *m.*
real[1] *s.* (*coin*) réal *m.*
real[2] *adj.* (*existing*) réel, vrai; (*objective*) matériel; (*genuine*) véritable, authentique; **~ estate** *s.*

biens immobiliers *m.pl.*; **for ~** (*pop.*) pour de vrai; **~ism** *s.* réalisme *m.*; **~ist** *s.* réaliste *m.f.*; **~istic** *adj.* réaliste; **~ity** *s.* réalité *f.*; **in ~ity,** en réalité; **~ly** *adv.* vraiment, véritablement.

realiz/e *v.t.* **1.** (*convert into fact, into money*) réaliser; **2.** (*understand*) comprendre, se rendre compte de; ⚠ réaliser *in sense* (2) *is an anglicism*; **~able** *adj.* (1) réalisable; (2) perceptible; **~ation** *s.* (1) réalisation *f.*; (2) perception *f.*

realm *s.* royaume *m.*; (*fig.*) domaine *m.*

ream *s.* rame *f.*; *v.t.* (*techn.*) aléser.

reanimate *v.t.* ranimer.

reap *v.t.* (*agric.*) moissonner; (*fig.*) récolter; **~er** *s.* (*person*) moissonneur *m.*; (*machine*) moissonneuse *f.*

reappear *v.i.* reparaître; **~ance** *s.* réapparition *f.*

rear[1] *s.* arrière *f.*; **to bring up the ~,** fermer la marche; *adj.* de derrière, d'arrière; **~-admiral,** contre-amiral *m.*; **~guard** *s.* arrière-garde *f.*; **~guard action,** combat d'arrière-garde *m.*; **~-lamp, ~-light,** feu arrière *m.*; **~-view mirror** *s.* rétroviseur *m.*

rear[2] *v.t.* (*raise*) relever; (*build, bring up*) élever; *v.i.* (*horse*) se cabrer.

rearm *v.t.* réarmer; **~ament** *s.* réarmement *m.*

rearrange *v.t.* réarranger, remettre en ordre; **~ment** *s.* réarrangement *m.*

reason *s.* raison *f.*; **by ~ of,** en raison de; **the ~ why,** la raison pour laquelle; **it stands to ~,** cela va de soi; **with ~,** avec raison; **without** RHYME **or ~**; **~able** *adj.* raisonnable, modéré; **~ableness** *s.* modération *f.*; **~ably** *adv.**; *v.t.* & *i.* raisonner; **~ with s.o.,** discuter avec qn., raisonner qn.; **~ing** *s.* raisonnement *m.*

reassemble *v.t.* rassembler; (*techn.*) remonter; *v.i.* (se) rassembler.

reassume *v.t.* reprendre.

reassur/e *v.t.* rassurer; **~ing** *adj.* rassurant; ⚠ réassurer = **to re-insure.**

rebarbative *adj.* rébarbatif.

rebate *s.* rabais *m.*, escompte *m.*; *v.t.* rabattre.

rebec(k) *s.* rebec *m.*

rebel *adj.* & *s.m.f.* rebelle, insurgé(e); *v.i.* se rebeller, s'insurger (*against*—contre); **~lion** *s.* rébellion *f.*; **~lious** *adj.* rebelle; **~liously** *adv.* en rebelle.

rebid *s.* (*at cards*) nouvelle annonce *f.*; *v.t.* & *i.* annoncer de nouveau.

rebirth *s.* renaissance *f.*

rebore *v.t.* (*auto.*) réaléser.

rebound *s.* rebond *m.*; (*fig.*) rebondissement *m.*; **on the ~,** (*fig.*) faute de mieux; *v.i.* rebondir.

rebuff *s.* rebuffade *f.*; *v.t.* repousser.

rebuild *v.t.* reconstruire; **~ing** *s.* reconstruction *f.*

rebuke *s.* reproche *m.*; *v.t.* reprocher (qch. à qn.).

rebut *v.t.* repousser; (*disprove*) réfuter; **~tal** *s.* réfutation *f.*; ⚠ rebuter = **to repel.**

recalcitrant *adj.* & *s.m.f.* récalcitrant(e).

recall *s.* rappel *m.*; *v.t.* (*call back*) rappeler; (*remember*) se rappeler; (*revive*) ranimer; (*annul*) révoquer.

recant *v.t.* & *i.* (se) rétracter; **~ation** *s.* rétractation *f.*

recap *v.t.* (*fam.*) récapituler.

recapitulat/e *v.t.* récapituler; **~ion** *s.* récapitulation *f.*

recapture *s.* reprise *f.*; *v.t.* reprendre.

recast *s.* refonte *f.*; *v.t.* (*lit.* & *fig.*) refondre; (*theat.*) redistribuer.

reced/e *v.i.* (*shrink back*) reculer, s'éloigner; (*slope back*) fuir; (*retreat*) se retirer; (*decline in value*) baisser; **~ing** *adj.* (*tide*) descendant; (*forehead, chin, etc.*) fuyant; (*hair*) clairsemé.

receipt *s.* (*act of receiving*) réception *f.*; (*document*) quittance *f.*; **to** ACKNOWLEDGE **~ of**; **~s** *s.pl.* recettes *f.pl.*; *v.t.* quittancer.

receiv/e *v.t.* recevoir; (*stolen goods*) receler; (*money, salary*) toucher; (*refusal, etc.*) essuyer; (*radio*) capter; (*accept as true*) accepter pour vrai; **~er** *s.* (*law*) liquidateur *m.*, (*of stolen goods*) receleur *m.*, (*radio*) poste récepteur *m.*, (*telephone*) récepteur *m.*, **to lift the ~er,** décrocher; **to replace the ~er,** raccrocher, (*of letter*) destinataire *m.*, (*of goods*) consignataire *m.*; **~ing-station** *s.* poste de réception *m.*

recent *adj.* récent; (*modern*) nouveau; **~ly** *adv.* récemment.

receptacle *s.* réceptacle *m.*

recept/ion *s.* (*receiving, being received*; *ceremony*; *radio*) réception *f.*; (*welcome*) accueil *m.*; **~ionist** *s.* employé à la réception *m.*; **~ive** *adj.* réceptif; **~ivity** *s.* réceptivité *f.*

recess *s.* (*break*) ajournement *m.*; (*parl.*) vacances *f.pl.*; (*niche, alcove*) niche *f.*, alcôve *f.*; (*secret place*) recoin *m.*; *v.t.* mettre en retrait; *v.i.* être ajourné; **~ion** *s.* (*withdrawal*) recul *m.*; (*decline*) récession *f.*

recharge *v.t.* recharger.

recidiv/ism *s.* récidive *f.*; **~ist** *s.* récidiviste *m.f.*

recipe *s.* (*cook.* & *fig.*) recette *f.*

recipient *s.* (*receptacle*) récipient *m.*; (*of letter*) destinataire *m.f.*; (*of cheque*) bénéficiaire *m.f.*; (*of honour*) récipiendaire *m.f.*; *adj.* récepteur, réceptif.

reciproc/al *adj.* réciproque; **~ally** *adv.**; **~ate** *v.t.* & *i.* (*exchange*) échanger; (*requite*) donner en retour; **~ity** *s.* réciprocité *f.*

recit/e *v.t.* & *i.* réciter; **~al** *s.* (*narrative*) récit *m.*; (*mus.*) récital *m.*; **~ation** *s.* récitation *f.*; **~ative** *s.* récitatif *m.*

reckless *adj.* (*person*) insouciant, imprudent; (*act*) inconsidéré; **~ly** *adv.* avec insouciance, imprudemment; **~ness** *s.* insouciance *f.*, imprudence *f.*

reckon *v.t.* & *i.* (*calculate*) calculer; (*count*) compter; (*think*) croire; **~ on,** compter sur; **~ to,** compter + *inf.*; **~ with,** tenir compte de; **to be ~ed with,** non-négligeable, significatif; READY **~er**; **~ing** *s.* compte *m.*; (*judgement*) estimation *f.*; (*bill*) note *f.*, addition *f.*

reclaim *v.t.* (*reform*) réformer; (*civilize*) régénérer; (*land*) amender; **~able** *adj.* amendable.

reclamation *s.* réclamation *f.*; (*agric., fig.*) amendement *m.*

reclin/e *v.t.* & *i.* (se) reposer, (s')appuyer; **~ing** *adj.* couché.

recluse *s.* reclus *m.*

recognition *s.* reconnaissance *f.*

recogniz/e *v.t.* reconnaître (*by*—à; *as*—pour); (*identify*) identifier (par); (*realize*) se rendre compte de/que; **~able** *adj.* reconnaissable; **~ançe** *s.* (*law*) caution *f.*

recoil *s.* recul *m.*; *v.i.* reculer (devant).

recollect *v.t.* (*recall*) se rappeler; **~ion** *s.* souvenir *m.*; **to the best of my ~ion,** autant que je m'en souvienne; ⚠ récollection = **meditation.**

re-collect *v.t.* rassembler.

recommence *v.t.* recommencer.

recommend *v.t.* recommander; **~ s.o. to do sth.,** recommander à qn. de faire qch.; **~ation** *s.* recommandation *f.*

recompense *s.* **1.** (*reward*) récompense *f.*; **2.** (*requital*) châtiment *m.*; **3.** (*compensation*) compensation *f.*; *v.t.* (1) récompenser; (2) châtier; (3) compenser, dédommager.

reconcil/e *v.t.* & *i.* (*make or become friendly or resigned*) (se) réconcilier (*with, to*—à); (*harmonize*) accorder (*with*—à); (*make compatible*) concilier (*with*—avec); **~e oneself to sth.,** se résigner à qch.; **~able** *adj.* (*person*) réconciliable, (*thing*) conciliable (*with*—avec); **~iation** *s.* réconciliation *f.*, conciliation *f.*

recondite *adj.* abstrus.
recondition *v.t.* remettre à neuf, rénover.
reconnaissance *s.* reconnaissance *f.*; *adj.* de reconnaissance.
reconnoitre *v.t.* reconnaître, faire une reconnaissance.
reconsider *v.t.* examiner de nouveau; (*decision*) revenir sur; **~ation** *s.* nouvel examen *m.*; révision *f.*
reconstitut/e *v.t.* reconstituer; (*cook.*) réhydrater; **~ion** *s.* reconstitution *f.*
reconstruct *v.t.* reconstruire; (*crime*) reconstituer; **~ion** *s.* reconstruction *f.*; (*crime, historical*) reconstitution *f.*
record *s.* (*document, report*) document *m.*, rapport *m.*, mention *f.*; (*disc, tape*) disque *m.*, bande *f.*; (*of s.o.'s past*) dossier *m.*; (*best performance*) record *m.*; **~s** *s.pl.* (*public*) archives *f.pl.*; **on ~,** enregistré; **off the ~,** à titre officieux; **~-breaking** *adj.* record; **~-player** *s.* tourne-disque *m.*; *adj.* record; *v.t.* enregistrer; **~er** *s.* (*official*) juge *m.*, greffier *m.*, (*mus.*) flûte à bec *f.*, (*recording apparatus*) magnétophone *m.*; **crash-~er, flight-~er,** enregistreur d'accident, de vol *m.*; **~ing** *s.* enregistrement *m.*
recount *v.t.* raconter.
re-count *s.* compte de vérification *m.*; (*at election*) second dépouillement de contrôle *m.*; *v.t.* recompter.
recoup *v.t.* (*losses*) récupérer (ses pertes); **~ oneself** *v.refl.* se dédommager (de).
recourse *s.* recours *m.*; **have ~ to,** avoir recours à.
recover *v.t.* **1.** (*regain possession of*) regagner; (*lost time*) rattraper; (*appetite*) retrouver; (*money*) récupérer; (*breath, consciousness*) reprendre; **2.** (*reclaim*) reprendre; **3.** (*bring back to life, etc.*) faire revenir; **4.** (*law, fin.*) recouvrer; *v.i.* (3) (*return to health*) se remettre, revenir à soi; (*fig.*) se ressaisir (*from*—de); **~able** *adj.* récupérable; **~y** *s.* (1) récupération *f.*; (2) (& *of business*) reprise *f.*; (3) rétablissement *m.*; réanimation *f.*; (4) recouvrement *m.*
re-cover *v.t.* recouvrir.
recreant *adj.* & *s.m.* traître.
recreat/e *v.t.* amuser, divertir; **~ion** *s.* récréation *f.*, divertissement *m.*; **~ive** *adj.* récréatif.
re-create *v.t.* recréer.
recriminat/e *v.t.* récriminer; **~ion** *s.* récrimination *f.*
recrudesc/e *v.i.* subir une recrudescence; **~ence** *s.* recrudescence *f.*; **~ent** *adj.* recrudescent.
recruit *s.* (*mil.* & *gen.*) recrue *f.*; **raw ~** (*fam.*) bleu *m.*; *v.t.* & *i.* recruter; (*fig.*) se réapprovisionner en; (*med.*) se remettre; **~ing** *s.* & **~ment** *s.* recrutement *m.*; **~ing-officer** *s.* sergent-recruteur *m.*
rectang/le *s.* rectangle *m.*; **~ular** *adj.* rectangulaire.
rectif/y *v.t.* (*amend* & *chem.*) rectifier; (*electr.*) redresser; **~iable** *adj.* rectifiable; **~ication** *s.* rectification *f.*
rectilineal, rectilinear *adj.* rectiligne.
rectitude *s.* rectitude *f.*
recto *s.* recto *m.*
rector *s.* (*parson*) curé *m.*; (*head of institution*) directeur *m.*; **~y** *s.* presbytère *m.*
rectum *s.* rectum *m.*
recumbent *adj.* couché.
recuperat/e *v.t.* recouvrer; *v.i.* se rétablir; **~ion** *s.* rétablissement *m.*; ⚠ récupérer = **to recover.**
recur *v.i.* (*return to mind*) revenir (à); (*occur again*) se reproduire; **~rence** *s.* retour *m.*, réapparition *f.*; **~rent** *adj.* qui revient.
recycl/e *v.t.* recycler; **~ing** *s.* recyclage *m.*
red *s.* (*colour, polit.*) rouge *m.*; (*debit account*) déficit *m.*; **in the ~,** en déficit; *adj.* rouge; (*hair*) roux; **to see ~,** voir rouge; **to go or turn ~,** rougir; **~breast** *s.* rouge-gorge *m.*; **~cap** *s.* police militaire *f.*; **put out the ~ carpet** (*fig.*) mettre les petits plats dans les grands; **R~ Crescent,** le croissant rouge *m.*; **R~ Cross,** la Croix-Rouge *f.*; ~ CURRANT; ~ DEER; **~-handed,** sur le fait; **~ herring** (*fig.*) prétexte à digression *m.*; **~-hot** *adj.* chauffé au rouge; **R~ Indian** *s.*, **~skin** *s.* peau-rouge *m.*; **~ lead** *s.* minium *m.*; **~-letter day** *s.* jour mémorable *m.*; **see the ~ light** (*fig.*) voir venir le danger; **be like a ~ rag to a bull,** avoir l'effet du rouge sur un taureau; **~start** *s.* rouge-queue *m.*; **~ tape** (*fig.*) formalités *f.pl.*; **~den** *v.t.* & *i.* rougir; **~dish** *adj.* rougeâtre; **~ness** *s.* rougeur *f.*; (*hair*) rousseur *f.*
redeem *v.t.* (*buy back* & *eccles.*) racheter; (*from pawn*) dégager; (*mortgage*) purger; (*promise*) tenir; (*rescue*) sauver; (*make amends for*) compenser; (*lost time*) rattraper; **~able** *adj.* rachetable, (*debt*) amortissable; **~er** *s.* racheteur *m.*, (*eccles.*) Rédempteur *m.*
redempt/ion *s.* (*redeeming*) rachat *m.*; (*of mortgage*) purge *f.*; (*from pawn*) dégagement *m.*; (*of debt*) amortissement *m.*; (*eccles.*) rédemption *f.*; **beyond ~ion,** (*act*) irréparable, (*person*) incorrigible; **~ive** *adj.* rédempt/eur, -rice.
redirect *v.t.* (*letter*) faire suivre.
redistribute *v.t.* répartir de nouveau.
redolent (*of*) parfumé (de), qui sent . . .; (*fig.*) évocateur (de).
redouble *v.t.* (*intensify*) redoubler de; (*double again*) redoubler; (*bridge*) surcontrer.
redoubt *s.* redoute *f.*
redoubtable *adj.* redoutable.
redound *to v.i.* contribuer à, rejaillir sur.
redress *s.* redressement *m.*; (*compensation*) réparation *f.*; *v.t.* redresser; (*remedy*) réparer.
reduc/e *v.t.* (*lower, diminish, subdue, convert to another form*) réduire (en); (*weaken*) affaiblir; (*impoverish*) appauvrir; *v.i.* (*slim*) maigrir; **~e speed,** ralentir; **~e to** RANKS; **~ible** *adj.* réductible; **~tion** *s.* réduction *f.*; (*comm.*) remise *f.* (sur); (*of speed*) ralentissement *m.*
redundan/ce (cy) *s.* surplus *m.*, excédent *m.*; (*style*) verbiage *m.*; **~t** *adj.* superflu, en surnombre; (*style*) verbeux; **~tly** *adv.* en surnombre.
reduplicat/e *v.t.* redoubler; **~ion** *s.* redoublement *m.*
re-echo *v.t.* renvoyer; *v.i.* retentir.
reed *s.* (*plant*) roseau *m.*; (*mus. instrument*) chalumeau *m.*; (*of wind instrument*) anche *f.*; BROKEN **~**; **~y** *adj.* couvert de roseaux; (*sound*) nasillard.
reef *s.* **1.** (*naut. in sail*) ris *m.*; **2.** (*of rocks*) récif *m.*; *v.t.* (1) prendre un ris dans (une voile); **~-knot** *s.* nœud plat *m.*; **~er** *s.* (*jacket*) caban *m.*, (*pop.*) cigarette (à la marijuana) *f.*
reek *s.* odeur *f.*; (*of smoke*) fumée *f.*; *v.i.* puer; fumer; **~ of,** sentir.
reel *s.* **1.** (*winding apparatus*) dévidoir *m.*; **2.** (*of cotton, tape, ribbon, etc.*) bobine *f.*; **3.** (*of film*) bande *f.*, rouleau *m.*; **4.** (*motion*) vacillement *m.*; **5.** (*mus.*) branle *m.*; *v.t.* (1) (*~ off*) dévider; *v.i.* (4) (*be dizzy*) avoir le vertige; (*stagger*) tituber.
re-embark *v.t.* & *i.* rembarquer; **~ation** *s.* rembarquement *m.*
re-engage *v.t.* rengager; **~ment** *s.* rengagement *m.*
re-ent/er *v.t.* & *i.* rentrer; **~rant** *adj.* & *s.m.* rentrant; **~ry** *s.* rentrée *f.*; (*at bridge*) carte maîtresse *f.*
re-examin/e *v.t.* réexaminer; **~ation** *s.* nouvel examen *m.*
ref *s.* (*fam.* = *referee*) arbitre *m.*
refectory *s.* réfectoire *m.*

refer *v.t.* & *i.* **1.** (*trace, assign, to*) attribuer à; **2.** (*consult*) se référer à, consulter; **3.** (*direct to another person*) renvoyer à; **4.** (*relate to*) se rapporter à; **5.** (*allude to*) faire allusion à; **6.** (*apply to*) s'adresser à; **7.** (*hand over to*) soumettre à; **~ence** *s.* (1) (*~ring back to*) renvoi *m.*; (4) rapport *m.*; (5) allusion *f.*; **8.** (*scope*) compétence *f.*; **9.** (*person*) référence *f.*, (*documents*) références *f.pl.*; TERMS **of ~ence**; **~ence book** *s.* ouvrage à consulter *m.*, manuel *m.*; **to have ~ence to,** se rapporter à; **with ~ence to,** (*letter*) comme suite à, (*subject*) à propos de.

referee *s.* **1.** (*sport*) arbitre *m.*; **2.** (*person giving reference*) répondant *m.*; *v.t.* (1) arbitrer.

referendum *s.* référendum *m.*

refill *s.* objet de rechange *m.*, *e.g.* **cartridge (for pen), lead, film, battery,** cartouche, mine, pellicule, pile, de rechange; *v.t.* remplir de nouveau.

refine *v.t.* **1.** (*metal*) affiner; **2.** (*liquid*) épurer; **3.** (*sugar*) raffiner; **4.** (*fig.*) raffiner; **~d** *adj.* raffiné; **~ment** *s.* (1) affinage *m.*; (2) épuration *f.*; (3) raffinage *m.*; (4) raffinement *m.*; (*of person*) distinction *f.*; **~r** *s.* raffineur *m.*; **~ry** *s.* (1) affinerie *f.*; (3) raffinerie *f.*

refit *s.* **1.** (*naut.*) radoub *m.*; **2.** (*techn.*) remontage *m.*, rajustement *m.*; *v.t.* & *i.* (1) (se) radouber; (2) remonter, rajuster.

reflat/e *v.t.* (*econ.*) relancer; **~ion** *s.* relance *f.*

reflect *v.t.* **1.** (*light*) réfléchir; **2.** (*heat, sound*) renvoyer; **3.** (*image* & *fig.*) refléter; **4.** (*bring discredit on*) blâmer, critiquer; **5.** (*bring credit on*) honorer; **6.** *v.i.* (*meditate*) réfléchir; **~ion** *s.* (1) réflexion *f.*; (2) reflet *m.*; (3) image *f.*; (4) critique *f.*; (5) louange *f.*; (6) réflexion *f.*; **~ive** *adj.* réfléchi; **~or** *s.* réflecteur *m.*, (*auto.*) rétroviseur *m.*

reflex *s.* (*light, image*) reflet *m.*; (*action*) réflexe *m.*

reflexive *adj.* réfléchi.

refloat *v.t.* (*naut.*) renflouer; (*comm.* & *fig.*) remettre à flot.

refluent *s.* reflux *m.*; *adj.* qui reflue.

reflux *s.* reflux *m.*

reform *s.* réforme *f.*; *v.t.* & *i.* (se) réformer; **~able** *adj.* réformable; **~ation** *s.* réforme *f.*; (*eccles.*) la Réforme *f.*; ⚠ réformation = **amendment; ~atory** *s.* maison de correction *f.*; *adj.* réformateur; **~er** *s.* réformat/eur, -rice *m.f.*; (*polit.*) réformiste *m.f.*

re-form *v.t.* & *i.* (se) reformer.

refract *v.t.* réfracter; **~ion** *s.* réfraction *f.*

refractory *adj.* (*resistant to heat; unmanageable*) réfractaire; (*rebellious*) rebelle.

refrain[1] *s.* refrain *m.*

refrain[2] *v.i.* se retenir (*from*—de).

refresh *v.t.* & *i.* (se) rafraîchir; **~er** *s.* (*law*) honoraires d'encouragement *m.pl.*; **~er course** *s.* cours de perfectionnement *m.*; **~ing** *adj.* rafraîchissant; **~ment** *s.* rafraîchissement *m.*; **~ments** *s.pl.* rafraîchissements *m.pl.*; **~ment room,** buffet *m.*, buvette *f.*

refrigerat/e *v.t.* réfrigérer; (*meat*) frigorifier; **~ion** *s.* réfrigération *f.*; frigorification *f.*; **~or** *s.* réfrigérateur *m.*, (*fam.*) frigidaire *m.*

refuel *v.t.* & *i.* (se) ravitailler en carburant.

refuge *s.* refuge *m.*; **to take ~,** se réfugier (dans); **~e** *s.* réfugié(e) *m.f.*

refulgen/ce *s.* éclat *m.*; **~t** *adj.* éclatant.

refund *s.* remboursement *m.*; *v.t.* rembourser.

refurnish *v.t.* remeubler; (*with supplies*) refournir (en).

refus/e[1] *v.t.* & *i.* refuser; **~al** *s.* refus *m.*; **first ~al,** première offre *f.*

refuse[2] *s.* ordures *f.pl.*, déchets *m.pl.*

refut/e *v.t.* réfuter; **~able** *adj.* réfutable; **~ation** *s.* réfutation *f.*

regain *v.t.* regagner; (*get back*) recouvrer; (*consciousness*) reprendre.

regal *adj.* royal; **~ly** *adv.**.

regale *v.t.* & *v.refl.* (se) régaler.

regalia *s.pl.* insignes *m.pl.* (de la royauté).

regard *s.* **1.** (*look*) regard *m.*; **2.** (*attention, care*) attention *f.*; égard *m.*; **3.** (*esteem*) estime *f.*; **4.** (*subject*) sujet *m.*; **~s** *s.pl.* amitiés *f.pl.*, compliments *m.pl.*; **with ~ to,** à l'égard de, quant à; **having ~ to,** eu égard à; *v.t.* (1) regarder; (2) faire attention à; (3) respecter; (4) concerner; **5.** (*consider as*) considérer comme; **~ful of,** attentif à, soigneux de; **~ing,** quant à, touchant; **~less,** (*of*) inattentif (à), insouciant (de); *adv.* sans se soucier de; **to press on ~less,** y aller tête baissée.

regatta *s.* régates *f.pl.*

regen/cy *s.* régence *f.*; **~t** *s.* régent *m.*

regenerat/e *v.t.* régénérer; *adj.* régénéré; **~ion** *s.* régénération *f.*

regicide *s.* régicide *m.*

regime *s.* régime *m.*

regiment *s.* régiment *m.*; *v.t.* enrégimenter; **~al** *adj.* régimentaire; **~als** *s.* uniforme *m.*

region *s.* région *f.*; **to cost in the ~ of £200,** coûter dans les deux cents livres; **~al** *adj.* régional.

regist/er *s.* **1.** (*book, record, list*) registre *m.*; **2.** (*of voice or instrument*) registre *m.*; **3.** (*indicator*) compteur *m.*, enregistreur *m.*; **4.** (*draught regulator*) bouche de chaleur *f.*; *v.t.* (1) enregistrer; (*note*) prendre note de; *v.refl.* se faire inscrire; (*car, etc.*) immatriculer; (*birth, etc.*) déclarer; (3) marquer; **5.** *v.i.* (*make an impression*) faire une impression; **6.** *v.t.* (*show emotion, etc.*) exprimer; **7.** (*post*) recommander; **~rar** *s.* (*acad.*) directeur du secrétariat *m.*, (*court*) greffier *m.*, (*law*) officier de l'état civil *m.*; **~ration** *s.*; (1) enregistrement *m.*, inscription *f.*, (7) (*post*) recommandation *f.*; **~ration book** (*vehicle*) carte grise *f.*; **~ry** *s.* (*act*) enregistrement *m.*; **~ry office** *s.* bureau de l'état civil *m.*; **port of ~ry** *s.* (*naut.*) port d'attache *m.*

regnant *adj.* régnant.

regress *v.i.* régresser; **~ion** *s.* régression *f.*

regret *s.* regret *m.*; *v.t.* regretter; **~able** *adj.* regrettable; **~fully** *adv.* avec regret.

regular *s.* (*mil., eccles.*) régulier *m.*; (*fam. customer, visitor*) habitué *m.*; *adj.* (*consistent,* ≠ *casual,* ≠ *amateur*) régulier; (*in due form*) en règle; (*systematic*) régulier; (*person*) réglé, ponctuel; (*habitual*) habituel; (*fam.*) vrai, véritable; **~ as** CLOCK**work**; **~ity** *s.* régularité *f.*; **~ize** *v.t.* régulariser; **~ization** *s.* régularisation *f.*; **~ly** *adv.* régulièrement.

regulat/e *v.t.* régler; **~ing** *s.* réglage *m.*; **~ion** *s.* (*act*) réglementation *f.*; (*rule*) règlement *m.*; *adj.* habituel; **~or** *s.* régulateur *m.*

regurgitate *v.t.* régurgiter.

rehabilitat/e *v.t.* réhabiliter; **~ion** *s.* réhabilitation *f.*

rehash *s.* rabâchage *m.*; *v.t.* rabâcher.

rehears/e *v.t.* **1.** (*recite*) raconter; **2.** (*give list of*) énumérer; **3.** (*practise*) répéter; **~al** *s.* (1) relation *f.*, récit *m.*; (2) énumération *f.*; (3) répétition *f.*; DRESS **~al.**

rehous/e *v.t.* reloger; **~ing** *s.* relogement *m.*

reign *s.* règne *m.*; **in the ~ of,** sous le règne de; *v.t.* régner (sur); **~ing** *adj.* régnant.

reimburse *v.t.* rembourser; **~ment** *s.* remboursement *m.*

rein *s.* rêne *f.*, bride *f.*; ⚠ rein = **kidney; to give (free) ~ to** (*lit.* & *fig.*) lâcher la bride à, (*fig.*) donner libre cours à; *v.t.* retenir.

reincarnation *s.* réincarnation *f.*

reindeer *s.* renne *m.*

reinforce *v.t.* renforcer; **~d concrete,** béton armé; **~ment** *s.* (*act*) renforcement *m.*; (*material*) renfort *m.*

reinstate *v.t.* rétablir (dans); **~ment** *s.* rétablissement *m.*
reinsur/e *v.t.* réassurer; **~ance** *s.* réassurance *f.*
reinvest *v.t.* replacer; **~ment** *s.* replacement *m.*
reissue *s.* nouvelle édition *f.*; *v.t.* rééditer.
reiterat/e *v.t.* réitérer; **~ion** *s.* réitération *f.*
reject *s.* (*person*) inadapté *m.*, (*thing*) article de rebut *m.*; **export ~**, article impropre à l'exportation *m.*; *v.t.* rejeter; (*candidate*) refuser; **~ion** *s.* refus *m.*, (*of bill, etc.*) rejet *m.*
rejoic/e *v.t.* & *i.* (*cause, feel, joy*) (se) réjouir (de); (*make merry*) fêter; **~ing(s)** *s.* réjouissance(s) *f.*
rejoin[1] *v.t.* (*reply*) répondre; (*retort*) répliquer; **~der** *s.* riposte *f.*
rejoin[2] *v.t.* rejoindre.
rejuvenat/e *v.t.* rajeunir; **~ion** *s.* rajeunissement *m.*
rekindle *v.t.* rallumer.
relapse *s.* rechute *f.*; **to have a ~**, faire une rechute; *v.i.* rechuter; **~ into,** retomber dans.
relat/e *v.t.* (*narrate*) raconter; (*bring into relation*) établir un rapport (*with*—entre); *v.i.* (*have reference to*) se rapporter à; **be ~ed to,** être apparenté à; **~ing to,** relatif à.
relation *s.* **1.** (*narration*) récit *m.*; **2.** (*family connection*) parent(e) *m.f.*; **3.** (*connection*) rapport *m.*; **~s** *s.pl.* (2) parents *m.pl.*; (3) rapports *m.pl.*; **~ship** *s.* (2) parenté *f.*; (3) rapport *m.*
relativ/e *s.* (*person*) parent(e) *m.f.*; (*ling.*) relatif *m.*; *adj.* (*in connection with*) relatif à; (*compared with*) par rapport à; **~ely** *adv.* relativement; **~ity** *s.* relativité *f.*
relax *v.t.* & *i.* (se) relâcher; (*fig.*) se détendre; (*med.*) relaxer; ⚠ *otherwise* relaxer = **to free a prisoner**; ⚠ se relaxer *is an anglicism*; **~ation** *s.* (*of pressure*) relâchement *m.*; (*recreation*) récréation *f.*, détente *f.*; (*of penalty*) mitigation *f.*; **~ing** *adj.* (*of climate*) débilitant.
relay *s.* **1.** (*horses*) relais *m.*; **2.** (*gang of men*) relève *f.*; **3.** (*electr.*) relais *m.*; **4.** (*radio*) émission relayée *f.*; **~ race,** course de relais *f.*; *v.t.* (1) relayer; (3) munir de relais; (4) relayer; *v.i.* (2) se relayer.
release *s.* **1.** (*liberation*) libération *f.*; **2.** (*written discharge*) dispense *f.*, décharge *f.*; **3.** (*first production of film, book*) mise en vente, en circulation *f.*; **4.** (*techn.*) déclenchement *m.*, déclic *m.*; **press ~**, communiqué de presse *m.*; *v.t.* (1) libérer; (*prisoner*) relâcher; (*unfasten*) dégager; (2) dispenser (de), décharger (de); (3) mettre en vente, faire sortir; (4) déclencher; (*bombs*) lâcher.
relegat/e *v.t.* reléguer; (*sport*) déclasser; **~ion** *s.* relégation *f.*; (*sport*) renvoi à la division inférieure *m.*
relent *v.i.* se laisser attendrir; **~less** *adj.* impitoyable; **~lessly** *adv.**.
relevan/t *adj.* pertinent; approprié; **~ce** *s.* pertinence *f.*
reliab/le *adj.* (*person*) digne de confiance; (*things*) bon, sûr; **~ility** *s.* sûreté *f.*
relian/ce *s.* confiance *f.* (*on, in*—en); **have, feel, place, ~ce in,** faire confiance à; **~t** *adj.* confiant (en), (*dependent*) dépendant (de).
relic *s.* (*eccles.*) relique *f.*; (*what survives*) restes *m.pl.*; **~s** *s.pl.* (*dead body*) dépouille *f.*
relict *s.* veuve *f.*
relief *s.* (*from pain, etc.*) soulagement *m.*; (*aid*) secours *m.*; (*of siege*) délivrance *f.*; (*person taking over*) relève *f.*; (*distinctness of outline*; *art*) relief *m.*; *adj.* supplémentaire; **~ road** *s.* voie de dégagement *f.*
relieve *v.t.* (*from pain, etc.*) soulager; (*help*) secourir; (*siege*) délivrer; (*sentry, etc.*) relever; (*cause to stand out*) mettre en relief; (*enliven*) égayer; **~ s.o. of sth.** (*fam.*) soutirer qch. à qn.
religi/on *s.* religion *f.*; **~ous** *adj.* religieux, de religion; *s.* religieux *m.*; **~ously** *adv.**; **~ousness** *s.* piété *f.*
relinquish *v.t.* abandonner; (*rights, claim*) renoncer à.
reliquary *s.* reliquaire *m.*
relish *s.* (*flavour or taste*) saveur *f.*; (*enjoyment*) goût *m.*; (*zest*) esprit *m.*; (*sauce*) assaisonnement *m.*; *v.t.* goûter; *v.i.* avoir un goût de.
relive *v.t.* revivre.
reload *v.t.* recharger.
reluctan/ce *s.* répugnance *f.* (à); **with ~ce**, à contre-cœur; **~t** *adj.* (*person*) peu disposé à; (*act*) fait à contre-cœur; **to be ~t to do sth.,** répugner à faire qch., *or impers.* **he was ~t to beg,** il lui répugnait de mendier; **~tly** *adv.* à contre-cœur.
rely *v.t.* (*on*) compter sur, se fier à.
remain *v.i.* rester; **~der** *s.* reste *m.*; (*people*) autres *m.pl.*; **~s** *s.pl.* restes *m.pl.*; (*body*) dépouille mortelle *f.*
remake *v.t.* refaire.
remand *s.* renvoi *m.*; **on ~**, en prévention; *v.t.* renvoyer (à une audience ultérieure).
remark *s.* remarque *f.*; *v.t.* (*notice*) remarquer; (*observe*) observer; (*comment*) faire remarquer; **~able** *adj.* remarquable; **~ably** *adv.**.
remarry *v.i.* se remarier.
remed/y *s.* (*med.* & *fig.*) remède *m.*; (*law*) recours *m.*; *v.t.* remédier à; **~iable** *adj.* remédiable; **~ial** *adj.* (*med.*) curatif; réparateur.
rememb/er *v.t.* se rappeler, se souvenir de; **~er me to your parents,** rappelez-moi au bon souvenir de vos parents; **~rance** *s.* souvenir *m.*, mémoire *f.*
remind *v.t.* rappeler (qch. à qn.); (*put in mind of*) faire penser à; **~er** *s.* mémorandum *m.*
reminisce *v.i.* raconter des souvenirs; **~nce** *s.* réminiscence *f.*; **~nt of** *adj.* qui fait penser à.
remiss *adj.* négligent.
remission *s.* (*of sins, etc.*) rémission *f.*; (*of debt, etc.*) remise *f.*; (*diminution of force, etc.*) diminution *f.*
remit *v.t.* (*pardon sins*; *transmit money*; *send back*) remettre; (*refrain from punishment*) renvoyer; *v.t.* & *i.* (*abate*) (se) relâcher; **~tance** *s.* (*money*) versement *m.*; **~ter** *s.* remettant *m.*; **~tent** *adj.* (*med.*) rémittent.
remnant *s.* reste *m.*, bout *m.*; (*of cloth*) coupon *m.*
remodel *v.t.* (*techn.*) remodeler; (*fig.*) remanier.
remonstra/nce *s.* remontrance *f.*; **~te with** *v.t.* faire des remontrances à.
remorse *s.* remords *m.*; **~ful** *adj.* plein de remords; **~less** *adj.* sans remords; **~lessly** *adv.* sans remords.
remote *adj.* (*in place, time*) reculé, éloigné, lointain; (*not closely related*) distant; (*secluded*) retiré; (*vague, slight*) vague, faible; **the ~st idea,** la moindre idée; **~ control** *s.* télécommande *f.*; **~-controlled** *adj.* télécommandé; **~ly** *adv.* au loin; vaguement; **~ness** *s.* éloignement *m.*
remould *s.* (*tyre*) pneu rechapé *m.*
remount *s.* cheval de rechange *m.*; *v.t.* remonter sur; *v.i.* remonter à cheval.
remov/e *s.* (*stage, degree*) degré *m.*; *v.t.* **1.** (*take away*) enlever, (*obstacle*) éloigner, écarter, (*difficulty*) supprimer; **2.** (*to another place*) transporter, (*house*) déménager; **3.** (*dismiss*) renvoyer, déplacer; **4.** (*med.*) opérer l'ablation de; *v.i.* (2) déménager; **~e oneself,** s'en aller; **~able** *adj.* (2) transportable, (*part*) détachable, (*official*) amovible; **~al** *s.* (1) enlèvement *m.*, suppression *f.*; (2) déménagement *m.*; (3) déplacement *m.*; (4) ablation *f.*
remunerat/e *v.t.* rémunérer; **~ion** *s.* rémunération *f.*; **~ive** *adj.* rémunérateur.
Renaissance *s.* Renaissance *f.*
renal *adj.* rénal.

renascent *adj.* renaissant.
rend *v.t.* déchirer; ~ **asunder,** déchirer en deux; HEART-~**ing.**
render *v.t.* rendre; (*fat*) faire fondre; (*constr.*) plâtrer; ~**ing** *s.* interprétation *f.*, traduction *f.*
rendezvous *s.* rendez-vous *m.*
rendition *s.* (*mil.*) reddition *f.*; (*mus. etc.*) interprétation *f.*; (*translation*) traduction *f.*
renegade *s.* rénégat *m.*
renege, renegue *v.i.* renoncer.
renew *v.t.* renouveler; (*subscription*) se réabonner; ~**al** *s.* & ~**ing** *s.* renouvellement *m.*; (*of activity, etc.*) reprise *f.*; (*of subscription*) réabonnement *m.*
rennet *s.* présure *f.*; (*apple*) reinette *f.*
renounce *v.t.* (*abandon formally*) renoncer à; (*give up*) abandonner; (*repudiate*) répudier; (*withdraw from, treaty*) dénoncer.
renovat/e *v.t.* rénover; ~**ion** *s.* rénovation *f.*
renown *s.* renommée *f.*; ~**ed** *adj.* renommé.
rent[1] *s.* (*tear*) déchirure *f.*; (*gap*) fissure *f.*
rent[2] *s.* (*payment*) loyer *m.*, terme *m.*; GROUND-~; ~**-collector** *s.* receveur *m.* (de loyers); *v.t.* & *i.* (se) louer; ~**able** *adj.* qu'on peut louer; ⚠ rentable = **viable;** ~**al** *s.* loyer *m.*
renunciation *s.* renonciation *f.*
reopen *v.t.* rouvrir; ~**ing,** *s.* réouverture *f.*
rep(p) *s.* (*text.*) reps *m.*
repair[1] *s.* (*restoring*) réparation *f.*, raccommodage *m.*; (*condition*) état *m.*; **out of** ~, en mauvais état; *v.t.* réparer, raccommoder; ~**-shop** *s.* atelier de réparations *m.*
repair[2] *v.i.* (*go to*) se rendre à.
repar/able *adj.* réparable; ~**ation** *s.* réparation *f.*
repartee *s.* repartie *f.*
repast *s.* repas *m.*
repatriat/e *v.t.* rapatrier; ~**ion** *s.* rapatriement *m.*
repay *v.t.* **1.** (*pay back*) rembourser; **2.** (*return blow, etc.*) rendre; **3.** (*requite*) récompenser; *v.i.* faire un remboursement; ~**able** *adj.* remboursable; ~**ment** *s.* (1) remboursement *m.*; (3) récompense *f.*
repeal *s.* abrogation *f.*; *v.t.* abroger.
repeat *s.* répétition *f.*; (*mus.*) reprise *f.*; *v.t.* répéter; (*reproduce*) reproduire; (*divulge*) redire; ~**edly** *adv.* à plusieurs reprises; ~**er** *s.* montre *f.*, fusil *m.*, à répétition.
repel *v.t.* repousser; ~**lent** *adj.* répulsif, (*fig.*) repoussant; ~**lent** *s.* produit antimite, antimoustique, etc. *m.*
repent *v.t.* & *i.* se repentir (*of*—de); ~**ance** *s.* repentir *m.*; ~**ant** *adj.* repentant.
repeople *v.t.* repeupler.
repercussion *s.* (*lit.* & *fig.*) répercussion *f.*
repertory, repertoire *s.* répertoire *m.*; ~ **company** *s.* (*theat.*) troupe à demeure *f.*
repetit/ion *s.* répétition *f.*; (*by heart*) récitation *f.*; ~**ious** *adj.* & ~**ive** *adj.* plein de répétitions.
repine *v.i.* se plaindre (*at, against*—de).
replace *v.t.* **1.** (*put back*) remettre en place; **2.** (*put in place of*) remplacer (*by*—par), substituer à; **3.** (*take place of*) remplacer; ~**ment** *s.* (1) remise en place *f.*; (2) remplacement *m.*; (*techn.*) pièce de rechange *f.*; (3) remplaçant *m.*
replay *s.* match rejoué *m.*; *v.t.* rejouer.
replenish *v.t.* (*refill*) remplir (de); (*restock*) (se) réapprovisionner (en); ~**ment** *s.* remplissage *m.*; réapprovisionnement *m.*
replet/e *adj.* rempli (*with*—de); ~**ion,** *s.* satiété *f.*; ⚠ replet = **plump.**
replica *s.* double *m.*; (*copy*) copie *f.*; (*of painting*) réplique *f.*
reply *s.* réponse *f.*; *v.t.* & *i.* répondre.
report *s.* **1.** (*rumour*) bruit *m.*; **2.** (*repute*) renom *m.*; **3.** (*formal account*) rapport *m.*, compte-rendu *m.*; **4.** (*school*) bulletin *m.*; **5.** (*newspaper*) reportage *m.*; **6.** (*explosion*) détonation *f.*; *v.t.* (1) raconter; (3) faire un rapport sur; (5) faire un reportage sur; **7.** (*inform against*) dénoncer; ~**er** *s.* journaliste *m.f.*; ⚠ report = **postponement** & (*fin.*) **amount carried forward;** reporter = **to postpone.**
repose *s.* (*rest, sleep*) repos *m.*; (*calm*) calme *m.*; *v.t.* reposer; (*place trust, etc. in*) placer; *v.i.* se reposer; (*be lying*) reposer; (*be supported on*) reposer sur; ~**ful** *adj.* reposant.
repository *s.* (*receptacle*) dépôt *m.*; (*store*) magasin *m.*; (*of secrets, etc.*) dépositaire *m.*
repossess (*oneself of*) *v.t.* reprendre possession de.
reprehen/d *v.t.* réprimander; ~**sible** *adj.* répréhensible; ~**sibly** *adv.* de façon répréhensible; ~**sion** *s.* réprimande *f.*
represent *v.t.* représenter; (*act part*) jouer; ~**ation** *s.* représentation *f.*; **to make** ~**ations to,** faire des démarches auprès de; ~**ative** *s.* (*sample*) modèle *m.*, (*type*) type *m.*, (*agent*) représentant *m.*; *adj.* représentatif.
re-present *v.t.* représenter.
repress *v.t.* réprimer; (*med.*) refouler; ~**ion** *s.* répression *f.*; (*med.*) refoulement *m.*; ~**ive** *adj.* répressif.
reprieve *s.* (*law*) sursis *m.*; (*of condemned man*) commutation de peine *f.*; (*fig.*) répit *m.*; *v.t.* accorder un sursis à; (*condemned man*) grâcier.
reprimand *s.* réprimande *f.*; *v.t.* réprimander.
reprint *s.* (*of book*) réimpression *f.*; (*art*) reproduction *f.*; *v.t.* réimprimer.
reprisal *s.* (*usu. pl.*) représailles *f.pl.* **to take** ~**s,** user de représailles.
reproach *s.* (*censure*) reproche *m.*; (*thing bringing discredit*) honte *f.*; *v.t.* faire des reproches à qn. (au sujet de qch.); ~ **s.o. with sth.** reprocher qch. à qn., reprocher à qn. d'avoir fait qch.; ~**ful** *adj.* réprobat/eur, -rice; ~**fully** *adv.* d'un air de reproche.
reprobate *s.* **1.** (*eccles.*) réprouvé *m.*; **2.** (*fam.*) vaurien *m.*; *adj.* (1) réprouvé; (2) dépravé.
reproduc/e *v.t.* & *i.* (se) reproduire; ~**tion** *s.* reproduction *f.*; ~**tive** *adj.* reproduct/eur, -rice.
reproof *s.* réprimande *f.*
reproof *v.t.* réimperméabiliser.
reprov/e *v.t.* réprimander; ~**ingly** *adv.* d'un ton réprobateur.
reptil/e *s.* reptile *m.*; ~**ian** *adj.* reptilien.
republic *s.* république *f.*; ~**an** *s.* & *adj.* républicain; ~**anism** *s.* républicanisme *m.*
republish *v.t.* rééditer.
repudiat/e *v.t.* **1.** (*disown*) désavouer; **2.** (*deny*) renier; **3.** (*wife*) répudier; **4.** (*order*) rejeter; **5.** (*debt, etc.*) refuser d'honorer; **6.** (*offer*) repousser; ~**ion** *s.* (1), (2), (4), (5), (6) rejet *m.*; (3) répudiation *f.*
repugnan/ce *s.* **1.** (*aversion*) répugnance *f.* (*to*—pour); **2.** (*incompatibility*) incompatibilité *f.*; ~**t** *adj.* (1) répugnant; (2) incompatible; **to be** ~**t,** répugner à.
repuls/e *s.* (*mil.*) échec *m.*; (*fig.*) rebuffade *f.*; *v.t.* repousser; ~**ion** *s.* répulsion *f.*; ~**ive** *adj.* repoussant, dégoûtant.
reput/e *s.* (*general opinion*) réputation *f.*; (*fame*) renommée *f.*; *v.t.* réputer; **to be** ~**ed for,** être réputé pour; **to be** ~**ed to be,** passer pour être; ~**ed** *adj.* supposé; ~**edly** *adv.* soi-disant; ~**able** *adj.* honorable, estimable; ~**ation** *s.* réputation *f.*; **to have the** ~**ation of,** avoir la réputation de.
request *s.* requête *f.*; **at the** ~ **of,** à la demande de; **to be in** ~, être très recherché; ~ **stop,** arrêt facultatif *m.*; *v.t.* demander (qch. à qn., à qn. de faire qch.); prier (qn. de faire qch.).
requiem *s.* requiem *m.*
require *v.t.* **1.** (*demand*) demander, réclamer; **2.** (*as condition*) exiger; **3.** (*need*) avoir besoin de; ~**ment** *s.* (1) demande *f.*; (2) exigence *f.*; (3) besoin *m.*

requisite *s.* article nécessaire *m.*; *adj.* nécessaire.
requisition *s.* réquisition *f.*; *v.t.* réquisitionner.
requit/e *v.t.* **1.** (*reward*) récompenser; **2.** (*repay*) payer de retour; **3.** (*avenge*) venger; **~al** *s.* (1) récompense *f.*; (3) vengeance *f.*
reread *v.t.* relire.
reredos *s.* retable *m.*
re-route *v.t.* envoyer par un autre itinéraire.
resale *s.* revente *f.*
rescind *v.t.* (*an act*) révoquer; (*a decision*) annuler.
rescue *s.* **1.** (*setting free*) délivrance *f.*; **2.** (*help*) secours *m.*; **3.** (*saving*) sauvetage *m.*; *adj.* de sauvetage; *v.t.* (1) délivrer (de); (2) secourir; (3) sauver; **~r** *s.* (1) libérat/eur, -rice *m.f.*; (3) sauveteur *m.*
research *s.* recherche *f.*; *v.i.* faire des recherches; **~er** *s.* & **~-worker** *s.* chercheur *m.*
reseda *s.* réséda *m.*
resell *v.t.* revendre.
resembl/e *v.t.* ressembler à; **~ance** *s.* ressemblance *f.* (avec).
resent *v.t.* (*show or feel indignation*) s'offenser de; (*feel injured by*) être blessé de; **~ful** *adj.* rancunier; **~ment** *s.* ressentiment *m.*
reserv/e *s.* réserve *f.*; (*sport*) joueur de réserve *m.*; **~es** *pl.* (*mil.*) réserves *f.pl.*; *adj.* de réserve; *v.t.* réserver; **~ation** *s.* (*limitation*) réserve *f.*; (*land*) réserve *f.*, terrain réservé *m.*; (*booking*) location *f.*; (*seat*) place retenue *f.*; **central ~ation** (*on motorway*) terre-plein central *m.*; **~ed** *adj.* réservé; **~edly** *adv.* avec réserve; **~ist** *s.* (*mil.*) réserviste *m.*
reservoir *s.* (*tank*) réservoir *m.*; (*landscaped*) lac artificiel *m.*
reshuffle *s.* (*polit.*) remaniement *m.* (ministériel); *v.t.* remanier.
resid/e *v.i.* résider (dans); **~ence** *s.* résidence *f.*; PLACE **of ~ence; ~ent** *s.* habitant *m.*; (*official*) résident *m.*; *adj.* résident, à demeure; **~ential** *adj.* résidentiel.
residu/e *s.* reste *m.*; (*chem.*) résidu *m.*; (*law, fin.*) reliquat *m.*; **~al** *adj.* restant; (*chem.*) résiduel.
resign *v.t.* **1.** (*surrender*) abandonner; **2.** (*give up office*) résigner, se démettre de; *v.i.* donner sa démission, démissionner; **3. ~ oneself to sth.,** se résigner à qch.; **~ation** *s.* (1) abandon *m.*; (2) démission *f.*; (3) résignation *f.*; **~ed** *adj.* résigné; **~edly** *adv.* avec résignation.
resilien/ce *s.* élasticité *f.*; (*fig.*) ressort *m.*; **~t** *adj.* élastique; énergique.
resin *s.* résine *f.*; **~ous** *adj.* résineux.
resist *v.t.* & *i.* (*withstand*) résister (à); (*oppose*) s'opposer (à); **~ance** *s.* résistance *f.*; **~ant** *adj.* résistant; **~ible** *adj.* à qui on peut résister; **~less** *adj.* irrésistible, sans résistance; **~lessly** *adv.**, sans résistance.
resit *s.* examen de repêchage *m.*; *v.i.* se représenter (à).
resolut/e *adj.* résolu; **~ely** *adv.**; **~ion** *s.* résolution *f.*; (*solving*) solution *f.*
resolve *s.* résolution *f.*; *v.t.* & *i.* (*disintegrate*) (se) résoudre (en); (*analyse, solve*) résoudre; (*decide upon*) (se) résoudre à.
resonan/ce *s.* résonance *f.*; **~t** *adj.* résonnant.
resonat/e *v.i.* résonner; **~or** *s.* résonateur *m.*
resort *s.* **1.** (*recourse*) recours *m.* (à); **2.** (*frequenting*) fréquentation *f.*; **3.** (*haunt*) rendez-vous *m.*; **4.** (*seaside, mountain, health, holiday*) station *f.* balnéaire, de sports d'hiver, climatique, estivale; *v.i.* **~ to** (1) avoir recours à; (2) fréquenter.
resound *v.t.* & *i.* (faire) résonner, (faire) retentir; **~ing** *adj.* retentissant.
resource *s.* (*~fulness; expedient, device*) ressource *f.*; (*pastime*) distraction *f.*; **~s** *s.pl.* réserve *f.*; (*fin.*) ressources *f.pl.*; **~ful** *adj.* plein de ressources; (*fam.*) débrouillard; **~fulness** *s.* ressource *f.*

respect *s.* **1.** (*esteem*) respect *m.*; **2.** (*heed to*) considération *f.* (pour); **3.** (*reference to*) rapport *m.* (à); **in ~ of,** en ce qui concerne; **with ~ to,** quant à; **4.** (*aspect*) rapport *m.*, égard *m.*; **in this ~,** sous ce rapport; **in every ~,** à tous égards; **~s** *s.pl.* respects *m.pl.*, hommages *m.pl.*; **~able** *adj.* (*deserving ~*) estimable, (*reasonably large, good, etc.*) passable, (*presentable*) convenable, (*decent*) honnête, brave (*before noun*); **~ably** *adv.* honorablement, passablement, convenablement, comme il faut; **~ability** *s.*, respectabilité *f.*, convenance *f.*; **~ful** *adj.* respectueux (à l'égard de); **~fully** *adv.**; **~fulness** *s.* caractère respectueux *m.*; *v.t.* (1) respecter; (2) avoir égard à; (3) concerner, avoir rapport à; **~ing** *prep.* quant à.
respective *adj.* respectif; **~ly** *adv.**.
respir/e *v.t.* & *i.* respirer; **~ation** *s.* respiration *f.*; **~ator** *s.* respirateur *m.* (*gas mask*) masque à gaz *m.*; **~atory** *adj.* respiratoire.
respite *s.* (*permitted delay*) répit *m.*; (*interval*) délai *m.*
resplenden/ce *s.* éclat *m.*; **~t** *adj.* resplendissant; **~tly** *adv.* avec éclat.
respond *v.i.* (*answer*) répondre (à); (*react*) réagir (à); **~ent** (*law*) défend/eur, -eresse *m.f.*
response *s.* (*answer*) réponse *f.*; (*reaction*) réaction *f.*; (*liturgy*) répons *m.*
responsib/le *adj.* (*accountable*) responsable (*for*—de, *to*—envers); (*trustworthy*) digne de confiance; (*involving ~ility*) comportant des responsabilités; **~ility** *s.* responsabilité *f.*
responsive *adj.* sensible (à).
rest *s.* **1.** (*repose, sleep*) repos *m.*, sommeil *m.*, (*break*) pause *f.*; **2.** (*prop, support*) appui *m.*; **3.** (*mus.*) pause *f.*; **4.** (*~-home*) asile *m.*; **5.** (*what remains*) reste *m.*, restant *m.*; **the ~,** les autres *m.pl.*; **for the ~,** pour le reste; **at ~,** au repos; **to set at ~,** tranquilliser; **to come to ~,** s'immobiliser; **to lay to ~,** enterrer; **~-cure** *s.* cure de repos *f.*; **~-room** *s.* foyer *m.*; **~ful** *adj.* reposant; **~less** *adj.* inquiet, agité, (*child*) remuant, (*sea*) agité, (*night*) nuit blanche; **~lessly** *adv.* sans repos, fébrilement; **~lessness** *s.* agitation *f.*, (*child*) turbulence *f.*, (*sleeplessness*) insomnie *f.*; *v.t.* (1) reposer, tranquilliser; (2) appuyer, fonder (sur); *v.i.* (1) se reposer, (*sleep, die*) reposer; (2) s'appuyer, (*be based on*) être fondé sur; (5) rester, demeurer; **it ~s with you to,** c'est à vous de; **~ing-place** *s.* tombe *f.*
restaur/ant *s.* restaurant *m.*; **~ateur** *s.* restaurateur *m.*
restitution *s.* restitution *f.*; **to make ~ of,** restituer.
restive *adj.* (*horse, child*) rétif; (*uneasy*) nerveux.
restor/e *v.t.* **1.** (*give or put back*) rendre, remettre (à sa place); **2.** (*repair*) remettre en état, restaurer; **3.** (*to health, etc.*) rétablir; **~ation** *s.* (1) restitution *f.*, remise en place *f.*; (2) restauration *f.*; (3) rétablissement *m.*; **the R~ation,** la Restauration *f.*; **~ative** *adj.* & *s.m.* (3) fortifiant; **~er** *s.* restaurat/eur, -rice *m.f.*
restrain *v.t.* (*prevent*) empêcher (*from*—de); (*emotions*) contenir; (*suppress*) réprimer; *v.refl.* se contenir, se retenir (de); **~t** *s.* contrainte *f.*; (*self-control*) retenue *f.*; (*reserve*) réserve *f.*
restrict *v.t.* restreindre; **~ed area** (*auto.*) zone à vitesse limitée *f.*; **~ion** *s.* restriction *f.*; **~ive** *adj.* restrictif; **~ive practices,** pratiques restrictives de la production *or* de la concurrence *f.pl.*
result *s.* résultat *m.*; **as a ~ of,** par suite de; *v.i.* résulter (*from*—de); **~ in,** avoir pour résultat, aboutir à; **~ant** *adj.* résultant.
resum/e *v.t.* & *i.* (*take back*) reprendre; (*begin again*) recommencer; (*make résumé of*) résumer ⚠ *this meaning only*; **to ~e one's seat,** se rasseoir; **~ption** *s.* reprise *f.*

resurgen/t *adj.* renaissant; **~ce** *s.* résurrection *f.*
resurrect *v.t.* (*bring back to life*) ressusciter; (*fam. revive memory of*) déterrer; **~ion** *s.* résurrection *f.*
resuscitat/e *v.t.* ressusciter; **~ion** *s.* résurrection *f.*
retail *s.* détail *m.*; **~ trade,** commerce au détail *m.*; ~ PRICE; *v.t.* & *i.* (*sell*) détailler, vendre au détail; (*be sold*) se détailler, se vendre au détail; (*fam. recount*) colporter; **~er** *s.* détaillant(e) *m.f.*
retain *v.t.* retenir; (*keep in mind*) garder en mémoire; **~er** *s.* (*law*) provisions *f.pl.*, (*hist.*) suivant *m.*, **~ers** *s.pl.* suite *f.*; **~ing wall,** mur de soutènement *m.*
retaliat/e *v.t.* payer de retour; *v.i.* user de représailles; **~ion** *s.* revanche *f.*, représailles *f.pl.*
retard *v.t.* retarder; **~ed** *adj.* (*med.*) arriéré.
retch *v.i.* avoir des haut-le-cœur.
retent/ion *s.* (*med.*) rétention *f.*; conservation *f.*, maintien *m.*; **~ive** *adj.* fidèle; **~iveness** *s.* fidélité *f.*
reticen/ce *s.* réticence *f.*; **~t** *adj.* réticent.
reticul/ate *adj.* réticulé; *v.t.* & *i.* diviser en réseau; **~ar** *adj.* réticulaire.
reticule *s.* réticule *m.*
retina *s.* rétine *f.*
retinue *s.* suite *f.*
retir/e *v.i.* **1.** (*withdraw, recede*) se retirer; **2.** (*from job*) prendre sa retraite; **3.** (*retreat*) se replier; **4.** (*go to bed*) aller se coucher; *v.t.* (2) mettre à la retraite; **~ed** *adj.* (1) retiré; (2) en retraite, à la retraite; **~ing** *adj.* (1) (*shy*) réservé; (2) en retraite, (*pension*) de retraite, (*person leaving office*) sortant; **~ement** *s.* retraite *f.*
retort *s.* **1.** (*vessel*) cornue *f.*; **2.** (*reply*) riposte *f.*; *v.i.* (2) riposter; (*retaliate*) payer de retour.
retouch *v.t.* (*photo.*) retoucher.
retrace *v.t.* remonter à la source de; **~ one's steps,** revenir sur ses pas.
retract *v.t.* **1.** (*withdraw, pull back*) rentrer; **2.** (*recant*) rétracter, revenir sur; **~ion** *s.* (1) rétraction *f.*; (2) rétractation *f.*; **~ile** *adj.* rétractile.
retread *s.* (*tyre*) pneu rechapé *m.*; *v.t.* rechaper.
retreat *s.* (*mil.*; *secluded place*; *eccles.*) retraite *f.*; (*withdrawal*) recul *m.*; *v.i.* (*mil.*) battre en retraite; (*retire*) se retirer; (*recede*) reculer.
retrench *v.t.* **1.** (*mil.*) retrancher; **2.** (*expenses*) réduire; *v.i.* (2) faire des économies; **~ment** *s.* (1) retranchement *m.*; (2) économies *f.pl.*
retribution *s.* (*reward*) récompense *f.*; (*punishment*) châtiment *m.*
retriev/e *v.t.* **1.** (*regain possession of*) récupérer; **2.** (*restore*) recouvrer; **3.** (*repair, fig.*) réparer; **4.** (*game*) rapporter; **~able** *adj.* (1) récupérable; (2) recouvrable; (3) réparable; **~er** *s.* (*dog*) chien d'arrêt *m.*
retro- (*in combination*) **~active** *adj.* rétroactif; **~cession** *s.* (*law*; *med.*) rétrocession *f.*; **~-rocket** *s.* rétrofusée *f.*; **~verted** *adj.* (*med.*) rétroversé.
retrograde *adj.* rétrograde; *v.i.* rétrograder.
retrogress *v.i.* rétrograder; **~ion** *s.* mouvement rétrograde *m.*; **~ive** *adj.* rétrograde.
retrospect *s.* examen rétrospectif *m.*, étude rétrospective *f.*; **in ~,** en rétrospective; **~ion** *s.* examen rétrospectif *m.*; **~ive** *adj.* rétrospectif; **~ively** *adv.**.
return *s.* **1.** (*coming or going back*) rentrée *f.*, retour *m.*; **2.** (*sending back*) renvoi *m.*; **3.** (*giving back*) restitution *f.*, (*money*) remboursement *m.*; **4.** (*putting back*) remise en place *f.*; **5.** (*reward*) récompense *f.*; **6.** (*ticket*) (billet) aller et retour *m.*; **7.** (*parl.*) élection *f.*; **8.** (*statistics*) statistique *f.*; **9.** (*income tax*) déclaration *f.*; **~s** *s.pl.* (*comm.*) bénéfices *m.pl.*, rapport *m.*; **many happy ~s (of the day),** heureux anniversaire *m.*; **in ~ for,** en échange de; **~ match,** match retour *m.*; **to reach the point of no ~,** brûler ses vaisseaux; *v.t.* & *i.* (1) revenir, rentrer, retourner; (*revert to*) revenir à; (2) renvoyer, (*sport*) renvoyer (la balle); (3) rendre, rembourser; (4) remettre (en place); (7) élire; (*reply*) répondre; **~able** *adj.* restituable.
reunion *s.* réunion *f.*
reunite *v.t.* réunir; *v.i.* être réunis; ⚠ se réunir = **to assemble.**
rev *s.* (*fam. auto*) tour *m.*; *v.t.* & *i.* **~ up,** (*fam.*) s'emballer.
revalue *v.t.* réévaluer.
revamp *v.t.* rénover.
reveal *v.t.* révéler.
reveille *s.* réveil *m.*
revel *s.* fête *f.*; (*pej.*) orgie *f.*; *v.i.* s'ébattre; (*fam.*) faire bombance; **~ in,** se délecter à, faire ses délices de; **~ler** *s.* noceur *m.*; **~ry** *s.* réjouissances *f.pl.*
revelation *s.* révélation *f.*; **the R~(s),** (*New Testament*) l'Apocalypse *f.*
revenge *s.* vengeance *f.*; **to take ~ for sth. on s.o.** se venger de qch. sur qn.; ⚠ revanche = **retaliation;** *v.t.* venger; se venger de qch. sur qn.; **~ful** *adj.* vindicatif; (*avenging*) veng/eur, -eresse; **~fully** *adv.* par vengeance.
revenue *s.* revenu *m.*; (*of State*) fisc *m.*, trésor public *m.*; INLAND ~; **~ officer** *s.* agent des douanes *m.*
reverberat/e *v.t.* & *i.* **1.** (*light, heat*) (se) réverbérer; **2.** (*sound*) (se) répercuter; **~ion** *s.* (1) réverbération *f.*; (2) répercussion *f.*; **~ory** *adj.* à réverbère.
rever/e *v.t.* révérer; **~ence** *s.* respect *m.*, vénération *f.*; (*title*) révérence *f.*; **~end** *adj.* révérend; **the R~end J. Smith** (*C. of E.*) le révérend J. Smith, (*R.C.*) M. l'abbé Smith; **most ~end,** révérendissime; **~ent** *adj.* respectueux, (*pious*) pieux; **~ently** *adv.**,*.
reverie *s.* rêverie *f.*
revers *s.* revers *m.*
revers/e *s.* (*contrary*) contraire *m.*; (*of coin*) revers *m.*; (*of page*) verso *m.*; (*misfortune*) revers *m.*; (*motion*) marche arrière *f.*; **in ~e,** en marche arrière; *adj.* contraire, inverse; **~ely** *adv.* inversement; *v.t.* renverser; (*transpose*) intervertir; (*revoke*) annuler; **~e the charges** (*telephone*) P.C.V. (prise en charge volontaire); *v.i.* faire marche arrière; **~al** *s.* renversement *m.*, revirement *m.*, (*law*) annulation *f.*; **~ible** *adj.* réversible, (*text.*) à double face, (*law*) révocable; **~ing light** (*auto.*) feu de marche arrière *m.*
rever/t *v.i.* revenir à; **~sion** *s.* retour *m.*; (*law*; *biol.*) réversion *f.*
review *s.* **1.** (*revision*) révision *f.*; **2.** (*survey, inspection*) examen *m.*; revue *f.*; **3.** (*of book, etc.*) critique *f.*, compte-rendu *m.*; **4.** (*periodical*) revue *f.*; *v.t.* (1) revoir; (2) examiner; passer en revue; (3) faire la critique de; **~er** *s.* critique *m.f.*
revile *v.t.* injurier.
revis/e *v.t.* (*go over again, learn*) revoir; (*go over again, amend*) réviser; **~al** *s.* & **~ion** *s.* révision *f.*
reviv/e *v.t.* **1.** (*med.*; *feelings, conversation*) ranimer; **2.** (*fashion, custom*) remettre en vogue; **3.** (*memories, etc.*) faire revivre, réveiller; **4.** (*theat.*) reprendre; **5.** (*law*) remettre en vigueur; *v.i.* (1) se ranimer, reprendre vie; (*trade*) reprendre; (*hopes*) renaître; **~al** *s.* (1) retour à la vie *m.*; (2) remise en vogue *f.*; (3) réveil *m.*; (4) reprise *f.*; (5) remise en vigueur *f.*; (*trade*) reprise *f.*; (*arts*) renaissance *f.*; (*eccles.*) retour à la foi *m.*
revoca/ble *adj.* révocable; **~tion** *s.* (*of edict*) révocation *f.*; (*of law*) abrogation *f.*; (*of licence*) retrait *m.*
revoke *v.t.* (*law*) abroger; (*edict*) révoquer;

(*order*) annuler; (*licence*) retirer; *v.i.* (*cards*) renoncer.

revolt *s.* **1.** (*rebellion*) révolte *f.*; **2.** (*sense of loathing*) dégoût *m.*; *v.t.* (2) révolter; *v.i.* (1) se révolter, se soulever (contre); (2) se révolter; **~ing** *adj.* révoltant.

revolution *s.* (*complete orbit*) tour *m.*; (*polit.*; *astron.*) révolution *f.*; **~ary** *s.m.f.* & *adj.* révolutionnaire; **~ize** *v.t.* révolutionner.

revolv/e *v.t.* & *i.* (faire) tourner; (*fig. in mind*) ruminer; **~er** *s.* revolver *m.*; **~ing** *adj.* (*door, light*) tournant; (*techn.*) rotatif, pivotant.

revue *s.* (*theat.*) revue *f.*

revulsion *s.* (*med.*) révulsion *f.*; (*fig.*) dégoût *m.*

reward *s.* récompense *f.*; *v.t.* récompenser; **~ing** *adj.* rémunérat/eur, -rice.

rewrite *v.t.* récrire; *s.* adaptation *f.*

rexine *s.* cuir artificiel *m.*

rhapsod/y *s.* rhapsodie, rapsodie *f.*; **~ical** *adj.* rhapsodique; **~ize** *v.t.* s'extasier sur.

Rhenish *adj.* rhénan, du Rhin.

rheostat *s.* rhéostat *m.*

rhesus *s.* rhésus *m.*; **R~ factor,** facteur rhésus *m.*

rhetoric *s.* rhétorique *f.*; **~al** *adj.* de rhétorique; (*question*) de pure forme.

rheum *s.* (*in eyes*) chassie *f.*; (*in nose*) mucosité *f.*

rheumat/ism *s.* rhumatisme *m.*; **~ic** *adj.* (*disease*) rhumatismal; (*person*) rhumatisant; **~oid** *adj.* rhumatoïde.

Rhine *s.* (*geog.*) Rhin *m.*; *adj.* du Rhin; **~land** *s.* Rhénanie *f.*

rhinitis *s.* rhinite *f.*

rhinoceros *s.* rhinocéros *m.*

rhizome *s.* rhizome *m.*

Rhodesia *s.* (*geog.*) Rhodésie *f.*; **~n** *adj.* & *s.m.f.* Rhodésien(ne).

rhododendron *s.* rhododendron *m.*

rhomb(us) *s.* rhombe *m.*; **~ic** *adj.* rhombique; **~oid** *adj.* & *s.m.* rhomboïde.

Rhone *s.* (*geog.*) Rhône *m.*; *adj.* rhodanien.

rhubarb *s.* rhubarbe *f.*

rhyme *s.* rime *f.*; **~s** *s.pl.* vers *m.pl.*; **without ~ or reason,** sans rime ni raison; NURSERY **~**; *v.t.* & *i.* (faire) rimer (avec); **~r** *s.* rimeur *m.*; **~ster** *s.* rimailleur *m.*

rhythm *s.* rythme *m.*; **~ic(al)** *adj.* rythmique, cadencé; **~ically** *adv.* en cadence.

rib *s.* **1.** (*anat.*) côte *f.*; **2.** (*ridge, support*) nervure *f.*; (*arch.*) ogive *f.*; (*naut.*) membrure *f.*; **3.** (*of umbrella*) baleine *f.*; **4.** (*knitting*) côte *f.*; *v.t.* (2) garnir de nervures, de membrures; (4) tricoter à côtes; (*fam. = tease*) taquiner; **~bed** *adj.* côtelé.

ribald *adj.* grivois; **~ry** *s.* grivoiserie *f.*

ribbon *s.* (*text.*; *decoration*; *fig.*) ruban *m.*; (*tatter*) lambeau *m.*; **in ~s,** en lambeaux; **~ development,** extension urbaine (*f.*) en bordure de route.

rice *s.* riz *m.*; **ground ~,** farine de riz, *f.*; **~-field** *s.* rizière *f.*; **~-paper** *s.* papier de riz *m.*

rich *adj.* riche (en); (*valuable*) luxueux; **to grow ~,** s'enrichir; **~ly** *adv.* richement, abondamment; **~ness** *s.* richesse *f.*, abondance *f.*; **~es** *s.pl.* richesses *f.pl.*

rick[1] *s.* meule *f.*

rick[2]**, wrick** *s.* (*sprain*): (*of neck*) torticolis *m.*, (*of limb*) foulure *f.*; *v.t.* se tordre (le cou, le pied, etc.); se fouler (la jambe, etc.).

ricket/s *s.* (*med.*) rachitisme *m.*; **~y** *adj.* (*med.*) rachitique; (*shaky*) branlant, boiteux; (*weak*) chancelant.

rickshaw *s.* pousse-pousse *m.*

ricochet *s.* ricochet *m.*; *v.i.* ricocher.

rictus *s.* rictus *m.*

rid *v.t.* débarrasser (de); **get ~ of,** se débarrasser de; **~dance** *s.* débarras *m.*; **good ~dance,** bon débarras!

riddle *s.* **1.** (*puzzle*) énigme *f.*; **2.** (*sieve*) crible *m.*; *v.t.* (2) cribler, passer au crible; (*with holes, as of gunshot*) cribler (de); *v.i.* (1) parler par énigmes.

rid/e *s.* (*journey by horse, bicycle, car, etc.*) promenade *f.* (à cheval, à bicyclette, en auto, etc.); (*path in wood*) allée cavalière *f.*; **to take s.o. for a ~e** (*fam. fig.*) faire marcher qn.; *v.t.* (*horse, etc.*) monter; *v.i.* faire du cheval; monter (à cheval, etc.); (*naut.*) être mouillé (à l'ancre); **~e across, over** *v.t.* traverser (à cheval, etc.); **~e up** *v.i.* (*collar, etc.*) remonter; **~e roughshod over** (*fig.*) piétiner toute opposition; **~e to death** (*fig.*) ressasser; **~e for a fall** (*fig.*) courir à l'échec; **let sth. ~e,** laisser aller qch.; **-~den** *adj.* (*by fear, etc.*) hanté, (*by prejudice*) dominé (par les préjugés); **~er** *s.* cavali/er, -ère *m.f.*, (moto)cycliste *m.f.*, (*bus*) voyageur *m.*; **~erless** *adj.* (*intentionally*) haut-le-pied, (*by accident*) non-monté.

ridge *s.* **1.** (*hill-top*) crête *f.*, arête *f.*; **2.** (*of roof*) faîte *m.*; **3.** (*agric.*) billon *m.*; **4.** (*of sand*) ride *f.*; **5.** (*elevation*) arête *f.*; **~ of high pressure** (*meteor.*) crête barométrique *f.*; **~-pole** *s.* faîtage *m.*; *v.t.* (2) enfaîter; (3) sillonner; *v.i.* (4) se rider.

ridicul/e *s.* dérision *f.*; *v.t.* tourner en ridicule; **~ous** *adj.* ridicule; **~ously** *adv.**; **~ousness,** ridicule *m.*

riding *s.* (*track*) allée *f.*; (*in Yorkshire*) division administrative *f.*; (*sport*) équitation *f.*; **~-boots,** bottes de cheval *f.pl.*; **~-habit** *s.* amazone *f.*; **little red ~** HOOD; **~-light** *s.* (*naut.*) feu de position *m.*; **~ school** *s.* manège *m.*; **~-whip** *s.* cravache *f.*

rife, to be ~ *v.i.* sévir.

riff-raff *s.* canaille *f.*

rifle[1] *s.* fusil *m.*; **~man** *s.* fusilier *m.*; **~-range** *s.* champ de tir *m.*; **~-shot** *s.* coup de fusil *m.*

rifle[2] *v.t.* (*drawer, etc.*) vider; (*person*) dévaliser.

rift *s.* fente *f.*; (*geol.*) faille *f.*; (*in clouds*) éclaircie *f.*; (*fig.*) malentendu *m.*; **~-valley** *s.* fossé d'effondrement *m.*

rig *s.* **1.** (*naut.*) gréement *m.*; **2.** (*oil ~*) tour de forage *f.*; **3.** (*fam.*) accoutrement *m.*; *v.t.* (1) gréer; **4.** (*manipulate*) truquer; **~ out** *v.t.* équiper; **~-out** *s.* toilette *f.*; **~ up** *v.t.* monter; **~ging** *s.* (*naut.*) gréement *m.*

right[1] *s.* (≠ *wrong*) bien *m.*; (≠ *left*) droite *f.*; (*polit.*) droite *f.*; (*justification, claim, privilege, entitlement*) droit *m.*; **~s** *s.pl.* droits *m.pl.*; **to set to ~s,** remettre en ordre, en bon état; **by ~s,** de droit; **to the ~,** à droite; **keep to the ~!,** gardez votre droite!; **to be in the ~,** avoir raison; **~ of way** *s.* (*traffic*) priorité *f.*, (*law*) droit de passage *m.*; **~ful** *adj.* légitime; **~fully** *adv.**, à bon droit.

right[2] *adj.* (*morally good*) bon; (*proper, correct*) juste, exact; (≠ *left*) droit; (*in good condition*) en ordre, en bon état; ALL **~**; (≠ *wrong*) juste; **the ~ man for the job,** l'homme qu'il faut; **is this the ~ train for Rouen?,** est-ce bien le train pour Rouen?; **the ~ thing,** ce qu'il faut (fallait); **the ~ road,** le bon chemin; **to be ~,** avoir raison; **~ angle** *s.* angle droit *m.*; **~ bank** *s.* rive droite *f.*; **~-handed** *adj.* droitier; **to be in one's ~ mind,** être sain d'esprit; **~ side** (*of material*) endroit *m.*; **~ wing** *s.* aile droite *f.*, (*football*) ailier droit *m.*; **~ about turn,** demi-tour à droite; **~ly** *adv.* (*well*) bien; (*correctly*) justement, exactement; **~ness** *s.* justesse *f.*, rectitude *f.*

right[3] *adv.* (*straight*) droit; (*all the way to*) jusqu'à; (*completely*) tout à fait; (*justly*) avec justice; (*properly*) bien, convenablement; (≠ *left*) à droite; **it serves you ~,** c'est bien fait pour vous; **~ away,** tout de suite; **~ here,** ici même; ~ **at the back,** tout au fond; ~ **in the middle,** en plein milieu.

right[4] *v.t.* (*restore to proper position*) redresser; (*a wrong*) réparer; (*vindicate*) faire justice à (qn.); (*correct*) corriger.

righteous *adj.* juste, vertueux; (*anger, etc.*) justifié; ~**ly** *adv.**,*, avec justice; ~**ness** *s.* vertu *f.*, droiture *f.*

rigid *adj.* (*lit.* & *fig.*) rigide; ~**ity** *s.* rigidité *f.*; ~**ly** *adv.**.

rigmarole *s.* galimatias *m.*

rigor *s.* (*med.*) frissons *m.pl.*; ~ **mortis** *s.* rigidité cadavérique *f.*

rigo/ur *s.* rigueur *f.*; ~**rous** *adj.* rigoureux; ~**rously** *adv.**.

rile *v.t.* (*fam.*) agacer.

rill *s.* ruisseau *m.*

rim *s.* (*of wheel*) jante *f.*; (*of spectacles*) monture *f.*; (*edge, border*) bord *m.*, rebord *m.*; ~**less** *adj.* sans bords; (*spectacles*) sans monture.

rime *s.* **1.** *see* RHYME; **2.** (*hoar frost*) givre *m.*

rind *s.* (*bark*) écorce *f.*; (*peel*) pelure *f.*; (*bacon*) couenne *f.*; (*cheese*) croûte *f.*

ring[1] *s.* (*circular metal band, gen.*) anneau *m.*; (*for finger*) bague *f.*; (*wedding-~*) alliance *f.*; SIGNET--~; (*circular object*; *serviette-~*) rond *m.*; (*under eyes*) cerne *m.*; (*left by stain-remover*) auréole *f.*; (*for riding*) piste *f.*; (*for boxing*) ring *m.*; (*of people, etc.*) cercle *m.*; (*comm.*) cartel *m.*; PISTON--~; **to run ~s round s.o.,** courir deux fois plus vite que qn.; ~**-dove** *s.* ramier *m.*; ~--FINGER; ~**leader** *s.* meneur *m.*; ~**-master** *s.* Monsieur Loyal *m.*; ~ **road** *s.* boulevard périphérique *m.*; **to have a ~side seat,** être au premier rang; ~**worm** *s.* teigne *f.*; *v.t* encercler; entourer (*with*—de); (*bird, tree*) baguer; ~**let** *s.* bouclette *f.*

ring[2] *s.* (*sound*) son *m.*, coup de sonnette *m.*; (*act*) sonnerie *f.*; (*telephone call*) coup de téléphone *m.*; *v.t.* & *i.* (faire) sonner; (*resound*) résonner; téléphoner; ~ **false,** ~ **true,** sonner faux, sonner juste; ~ **the changes** (*lit.*) carillonner, (*fig.*) ressasser; **that ~s a bell,** cela évoque quelque chose; ~ **back,** rappeler; ~ **for** *v.t.* appeler; ~ **off** *v.i.* raccrocher; ~ **up** *v.t.* & *i.* donner un coup de téléphone (à); ~**er** *s.* sonneur *m.*; ~**ing** *s.* sonnerie *f.*, (*in ears*) bourdonnement *m.*

rink *s.* patinoire *f.*, skating *m.*

rinse *s.* **1.** (*rinsing*) rinçage *m.*; **2.** (*hair*) teinture *f.*; *v.t.* (1) rincer; (2) teindre.

riot *s.* (*disorder*) émeute *f.*; (*over-indulgence*) débauche *f.*; (*fam.*) **he (or it) is a ~,** il est (c'est) marrant; **to run ~,** être déchaîné, (*of weeds*) pousser follement; **to read the R~ Act,** faire les trois sommations légales, (*fig. fam.*) passer un savon (à qn.); ~ **squad** *s.* (*for minor troubles*) police-secours *f.*, (*for major ~s*) les C.R.S. *m.pl.*; *v.i.* s'ameuter; (*be noisy*) faire du tapage; ~**er** *s.* émeutier *m.*; ~**ous** *adj.* séditieux, turbulent, tapageur; ~**ously** *adv.**, tumultueusement, bruyamment.

rip *s.* déchirure *f.*; *v.t.* & *i.* (se) déchirer; **let ~,** (*in anger*) exploser, (*not check*) laisser courir; ~ **away,** ~ **off,** arracher; ~ **up,** déchirer; ~**-cord** *s.* cordelette de déclenchement *f.*; ~**-tide** *s.* retour de marée *m.*; ~**per** *s.* (*techn.*) défonçeuse *f.*, (*pop.*) type formidable *m.*; ~**ping** *adj.* (*pop.*) épatant.

riparian *adj.* riverain.

ripe *adj.* (*fruit*; *fig.*) mûr; (*cheese*) fait; ~**n** *v.t.* & *i.* mûrir; ~**ness** *s.* maturité *f.*; ~**ning** *s.* maturation *f.*

riposte *s.* riposte *f.*

ripple *s.* **1.** (*on water*) ride *f.*; **2.** (*of stream*) gazouillement *m.*; **3.** (*of hair*) ondulation *f.*; **4.** (*of conversation*) murmure *m.*; **5.** (*of laughter*) cascade (de rires) *f.*; *v.t.* & *i.* (1) (se) rider; (2) gazouiller; (3) onduler; (4) murmurer.

rise *s.* (*upward slope*) montée *f.*; (*advancement*) avancement *m.*, promotion *f.*; (*increase*) hausse *f.*, augmentation *f.*; (*in bank rate*) relèvement *m.*; (*origin*) source *f.*; (*of water*) crue *f.*; **to give ~ to,** donner lieu à, susciter; **to take a ~ out of s.o.** (*fam.*) se payer la tête de qn.; *v.i.* (*get up, out of bed*) se lever; (*parl.*) lever (la séance); (*revolt*) se soulever; (*ascend*) monter; (*project upwards*) s'élever; (*come to surface*) monter; (*have origin in*) avoir sa source dans; (*river*) prendre sa source dans; (*increase*) augmenter; (*fish*) mordre; (*dough*) lever; (*emotions*) croître; ~ **again,** se relever, ressusciter; ~ **up,** se lever; s'élever; (*revolt*) se soulever; ~**r** *s.* (*of staircase*) contre--marche *f.*; **to be an early ~r,** être matinal.

risib/le *adj.* risible; ~**ility** *s.* risibilité *f.*

rising *s.* (*revolt*) révolte *f.*; (*of sun, etc.*) lever *m.*; (*of session*) clôture *f.*; (~ *again*) résurrection *f.*; *adj.* (*road*) qui monte; (*wind*) qui se lève; (*anger, etc.*) croissant; (*generation*) nouveau.

risk *s.* risque *m.*; **at your own ~,** à vos risques et périls; **to run the ~ of,** courir le risque de; *v.t.* risquer; ~ **it,** tenter le coup; ~**y** *adj.* risqué, hasardeux.

rissole *s.* rissole *f.*

rit/e *s.* rite *m.*; ~**ual** *s.* rituel *m.*; *adj.* rituel; ~**ualism** *s.* ritualisme *m.*

rival *adj.* & *s.m.f.* rival(e); *v.t.* rivaliser avec; ~**ry** *s.* rivalité *f.*; (*competition*) concurrence *f.*

riven *adj.* fendu.

river *s.* (*flowing into sea* & *fig.*) fleuve *m.*; (*flowing into another ~*) rivière *f.*; *adj.* (*riparian*) riverain; (*fish*) d'eau douce; (*port, etc.*) fluvial; ~**ine** *adj.* riverain, fluvial.

rivet *s.* rivet *m.*; *v.t.* (*nail*) river; (*rivet*) riveter; (*concentrate*) river; (*engross attention*) retenir; ~**er** *s.* (*person*) riveur *m.*; (*machine*) riveteuse *f.*

rivulet *s.* ruisselet *m.*

R.N.L.I. (*Royal National Lifeboat Institution*) S.N.S.M. *f.* (Société nationale de Sauvetage sur Mer).

roach *s.* (*fish*) gardon *m.*

road *s.* route *f.*; (*in town*) rue *f.*; (*fig.*) voie *f.*, chemin *m.*; (*route*) route *f.*; ~**s** *s.pl.* (*naut.*) rade *f.sing.*; ~ **up,** ~**-works** (*sign*) travaux!; ~ **clear** (*sign*) fin de chantier!; ~-HOG; ~**-house** *s.* relais routier *m.*; ~**man** *s.* cantonnier *m.*; ~**-map** *s.* carte routière *f.*; ~**side** *s.* bord de la route *m.*, *adj.* (situé) au bord de la route; ~**stead** *s.* (*naut.*) rade *f.*; ~**way** *s.* chaussée *f.*; ~**worthy** *adj.* en état de marche, (*official*) conforme aux normes de la sécurité routière.

roam *v.t.* parcourir; *v.i.* errer; ~**er** *s.* vagabond *m.*

roan[1] *adj.* (*horse*) rouan.

roan[2] *s.* (*leather*) basane *f.*

roar *s.* **1.** (*of voices*) hurlement *m.*; **2.** (*of laughter*) éclat *m.*; **3.** (*of bull, sea, wind*) mugissement *m.*; **4.** (*of lion*) rugissement *m.*; **5.** (*of guns, thunder*) grondement *m.*; **6.** (*of fire*) ronflement *m.*; *v.i.* (1) hurler; (2) éclater (*with laughter*—de rire); (3) mugir; (4) rugir; (5) gronder; (6) ronfler; ~**ing** *adj.* (*fire*) ronflant; **to do a ~ing trade** (*fam.*) faire des affaires du tonnerre.

roast *s.* rôti *m.*; *v.t.* & *i.* rôtir; (*fam. fig.*) griller; ~ **beef,** (*joint*) rôti de bœuf *m.*; (*meat*) rosbif *m.*

rob *v.t.* voler (qch. à qn.); ~ **Peter to pay Paul,** faire un trou pour en boucher un autre; ~**ber** *s.* voleur *m.*; **to play** COPS **and ~bers;** ~**bery** *s.* vol *m.*

robe *s.* (*dressing gown, wrap*) robe (de chambre) *f.*; (*of office*) robe *f.*; *v.t.* revêtir d'une robe; *v.i.* se vêtir d'une robe.

robin *s.* rouge-gorge *m.*

robot *s.* robot *m.*; (*traffic lights*) signaux automatiques *m.pl.*

robust *adj.* robuste, vigoureux; **~ly** *adv.**,*; **~ness** *s.* robustesse *f.*, vigueur *f.*

rock[1] *s.* (*mass*) roc *m.*; (*geol.*) roche *f.*, rocher *m.*; **on the ~s** (*fam.*) à la côte, (*pop, drink*) avec des glaçons; **~-bottom** *s.* (*fam.*) fin fond *m.*, adj. le plus bas; **~ climbing** *s.* alpinisme *m.*; **~--garden** *s.* jardin alpestre *m.*; **~-pigeon** *s.* biset *m.*; **~-rose** *s.* hélianthème *m.*; **~-salt** *s.* sel gemme *m.*; **~ery** *s.* jardin alpestre *m.*; **~y** *adj.* rocheux.

rock[2] *v.t.* & *i.* (se) balancer; (*shake*) (s')ébranler; (*techn.*) basculer; *v.i.* osciller, trembler; **~ing** *s.* balancement *m.*, tremblement *m.*, basculage *m.*; **~ing-chair** *s.* chaise à bascule *f.*; **~ing-horse** *s.* cheval à bascule *m.*; **~ and roll** *s.* rock'n roll *m.*

rocket *s.* fusée *f.*; (*pop.*) **to give s.o. a ~,** passer un savon à qn.; *v.i.* s'élancer comme un éclair; (*prices*) monter en flèche.

rococo *s. adj.* & *s.m.* rococo.

rod *s.* (*wood or metal bar*) baguette *f.*; (*symbol of office*) verge *f.*; (*cane*) verges *f.pl.*; (*fishing*) canne (à pêche) *f.*; (*measure*) perche *f.*; (*curtain, etc.*) tringle *f.*; PISTON-~; **to rule with a ~ of** IRON.

rodent *adj.* & *s.m.* rongeur.

rodeo *s.* rodéo *m.*

roe *s.* (*of fish*) (*hard*) œufs *m.pl.*, (*soft*) laitance *f.*; **~-deer,** chevreuil *m.*

Rogation days (*eccles.*) les Rogations *f.pl.*

roger *interj.* (= *message received*) entendu, compris; **the Jolly R~,** le pavillon noir.

rogu/e *s.* **1.** (*rascal*) coquin *m.*; **2.** (*swindler*) bandit *m.*; **3.** (*elephant, etc.*) solitaire *m.*; **~ery** *s.* & **~ishness** *s.* (1) coquinerie *f.*, espièglerie *f.*; (2) malhonnêteté *f.*; **~ish** *adj.* (1) coquin; (2) malhonnête; **~ishly** *adv.* (1) malicieusement; (2) malhonnêtement.

roister *v.i.* faire du tapage; **~er** *s.* tapageur *m.*

rôle *s.* rôle *m.*

roll *s.* (*cylinder of paper, cloth, etc.*) rouleau *m.*; (*register, list*) tableau *m.*, liste *f.*; (*of bread*) petit pain *m.*; (*gait*) balancement *m.*; (*of thunder, drums*) roulement *m.*; (*naut.*) roulis *m.*; **to call the ~,** faire l'appel; **~-call** *s.* appel *m.*; *v.t.* (*cause to ~*) rouler; (*make into ~*) enrouler; (*flatten with ~er*) étendre au rouleau, (*lawn*) passer (la pelouse) au rouleau; *v.i.* rouler, se balancer; (*sound*) gronder; **~ down** *v.i.* (*tears, etc.*) couler; **~-on** *s.* gaine *f.*; **~ over** *v.t.* & *i.* (se) retourner; **~ up** *v.t.* enrouler, (*sleeves*) retrousser; **~ up** *v.i.* (*fam.*) s'amener; **~ed gold,** or laminé; **~er** *s.* (*mech.*) rouleau *m.*, (*wave*) lame de houle *f.*, (*techn.*) laminoir *m.*; **~er-skates,** patins à roulettes *m.pl.*; **~er towel** *s.* essuie-mains à rouleau *m.invar.*; **~ing** *adj.* roulant, (*country*) ondulé; **to be ~ing in money,** rouler sur l'or; **to keep the** BALL **~ing**; **~ing-mill** *s.* laminerie *f.*, (*machine*) laminoir *m.*; **~ing-**PIN; **~ing-stock** *s.* (*rail.*) matériel roulant *m.*; **a ~ing stone gathers no moss,** pierre qui roule n'amasse pas mousse.

rollicking *adj.* exubérant.

roman/ce *s.* (*medieval tale*) roman de chevalerie *m.*; (*fiction*) histoire romanesque *f.*; (*love affair*) idylle *f.*; (*falsehood*) conte *m.*; (*mus.*) romance *f.* ⚠ *this sense only*; *adj.* (*ling.*) roman; *v.i.* exagérer; **~cer** *s.* blagueur *m.*; **~tic** *adj.* romanesque; (*arts*) romantique; **~ticism** *s.* romantisme *m.*; **~ticist** *s.* romantique *m.*

Romania *s.* (*geog.*) Roumanie *f.*; **~n** *adj.* & *s.m.f.* roumain(e); *s.m.* (*lang.*) roumain.

Romany *s.* tsigane *m.f.*; (*pej.*) romanichel *m.*; (*lang.*) langue tsigane *f.*

Rom/e *s.* Rome *f.*; **~an** *adj.* & *s.m.f.* romain(e); **~an nose,** nez aquilin *m.*; **~anesque** *adj.* (*arch.*) roman; ⚠ romanesque = **romantic.**

romp *s.* jeu bruyant *m.*; *v.i.* s'ébattre; **~ home** (*fig.*) gagner dans un fauteuil; **~er(s),** barboteuse *f.*

rondavel *s.* hutte circulaire *f.*

roneo *s.* ronéo *f.*; *v.t.* ronéotyper.

Röntgen *adj.* & *s.m.* röntgen.

rood *s.* (*eccles.*) croix *f.*; **~-screen** *s.* jubé *m.*

roof *s.* (*of building, vehicle*) toit *m.*; (*of mouth*) palais *m.*; (*fig. upper limit*) plafond *m.*; **~-**RACK; **~less** *adj.* sans abri; *v.t.* couvrir; **~ing** *s.* toiture *f.*

rook *s.* (*chess*) tour *f.*; (*bird*) freux *m.*; *v.t.* escroquer; **~ery** *s.* colonie de freux *f.*

room *s.* (*space, spaciousness*) place *f.*; (*opportunity*) lieu *m.*, occasion *f.*; (*in house*) pièce *f.*, (*reception ~*) salle *f.*, (*bed~*) chambre *f.*; **~s** *s.pl.* appartement *m.*; ELBOW-~; REFRESHMENT ~; *v.i.* **~ with,** partager une chambre avec; **~y** *adj.* spacieux.

roost *s.* perchoir *m.*; **to rule the ~** (*fig.*) faire la loi, faire la pluie et le beau temps; *v.i.* se jucher; **~er** *s.* coq *m.*

root *s.* (*bot.*; *anat.*; *math.*; *ling.*) racine *f.*; (*source, basis*) origine *f.*, base *f.*; **~s** *s.pl.* (*vegetables*) racines comestibles *f.pl.*; GRASS **~s**; TAP-~; *v.t.* enraciner; *v.i.* s'enraciner, prendre racine; **~ for** (*fam.*) appuyer; **~ out, ~ up,** déraciner; **~ed** *adj.* enraciné; **~edly** *adv.* profondément.

rope *s.* corde *f.*; (*of bell*) cordon *m.*; (*naut.*) cordage *m.*; (*of pearls*) collier *m.*; TOW-~; **to know the ~s** (*fig.*) connaître les ficelles; *v.t.* corder, encorder, attacher avec une corde; **~ in** *v.t.* (*pop.*) enrôler; **ropy** *adj.* (*pop.*) de camelote.

rosary *s.* (*rose garden*) roseraie *f.*; (*prayer beads*) chapelet *m.*

ros/e *s.* (*flower*) rose *f.*; ROCK-**~e**; (*bush*) rosier *m.*; (*shape*) rosace *f.*; (*nozzle*) pomme *f.*; (*colour*) rose *m.*; **under the ~e** (*fig.*) sous le manteau; **the Wars of the R~es,** la Guerre des deux Roses; **~e-window** *s.* rosace *f.*; **~ewood** *s.* palissandre *m.*; *adj.* rosé, couleur de rose; **~aceous** *adj.* rosacé; **~eate** *adj.* rosé; **~y** *adj.* de rose, rosé, (*cheeks*) vermeil, (*fig.*) riant.

rosemary *s.* romarin *m.*

rosette *s.* rosette *f.*

rosin *s.* colophane *f.*; *v.t.* colophaner.

roster *s.* tableau de service *m.*

rostrum *s.* tribune *f.*

rot *s.* (*decay*) pourriture *f.*; DRY ~; (*med.*) carie *f.*; (*pop.* = *nonsense*) blague *f.*; **what ~!,** quelle blague !; (*failure*) échec *m.*; (*fig.*) démoralisation *f.*; *v.t.* & *i.* (se) carier, pourrir; **~ten** *adj.* pourri, gâté, carié; (*corrupt*) corrompu; (*pop.* = *beastly*) horrible; **~ten to the** CORE; **~tenness** *s.* pourriture *f.*, carie *f.*; **~ter** *s.* (*pop.*) salaud *m.*

rota *s.* liste *f.*; (*eccles.*) rote *f.*

rotary *adj.* rotatif.

rotat/e *v.i.* pivoter; *v.t.* tourner; (*agric.*) alterner; **~ion** *s.* rotation *f.*; (*agric.*) assolement *m.*; **in ~ion,** à tour de rôle; **~ory** *adj.* rotatoire.

rote *s.* routine *f.*; **by ~,** machinalement; (*by heart*) par cœur.

rotor *s.* rotor *m.*

rotten *adj. see* ROT.

rotter *s. see* ROT.

rotund *adj.* **1.** (*figure*) arrondi; **2.** (*person*) rondelet; **3.** (*style*) ronflant; **~ity** *s.* (1) rotundité *f.*; (2) embonpoint *m.*; (3) redondance *f.*

rotunda *s.* rotonde *f.*

rouble *s.* rouble *m.*

rouge *s.* rouge *m.*; *v.t.* mettre du rouge à.

rough *s.* (*golf, etc.*) terrain accidenté *m.*; (*hardship*) malheur *m.*; (*hooligan*) voyou *m.*; *adj.* **1.** (*uneven surface*) accidenté; **2.** (≠ *smooth*) inégal, rude; **3.** (*shaggy*) à poil dur; **4.** (*coarse*) grossier; **5.** (*violent, riotous*) violent, brutal; **6.** (*unfinished*) rude, brut; **7.** (*approximate*) sommaire, approximatif; **8.** (*to taste*) âpre; **9.** (*sea*) gros; **10.** (*weather*) mauvais; **~cast** *s.* crépi *m.*, *v.t.* crépir; **~ copy, ~ draft** *s.* brouillon *m.*; **~-and--ready** *adj.* (*thing*) fait à la hâte, (*person*) sans façons; **~shod** *adj.* ferré à glace; **to** RIDE **~shod over s.o.**; **~ sketch** *s.* ébauche *f.*; **~en** *v.t.* & *i.* rendre, devenir, rude; **~ly** *adv.* (2) rudement; (4)*; (5) violemment; (7) approximativement; **to handle ~ly,** malmener; **~ness** *s.* (1), (2) inégalité *f.*, rudesse *f.*; (4) grossièreté *f.*; (5) violence *f.*; (8) âpreté *f.*; (9) agitation *f.*; *v.t.* (*make* ~) ébourriffer; **~ it** (*fig. fam.*) manger de la vache enragée; **~ out** *v.t.* ébaucher; **~age** *s.* aliment non-assimilable *m.*

roulette *s.* roulette *f.*

round *s.* (*object*) rond *m.*; (*of bread*) tranche *f.*; (*circuit, turn in competition*) tour *m.*; (*cycle*) cycle *m.*; (*series*) série *f.*; (*of drinks, of golf, of inspection*) tournée *f.*; (*mil.*) ronde *f.*; (*mus.*) canon perpétuel *m.*; (*boxing*) round *m.*; (*shot*) cartouche *f.*, coup *m.*; **daily ~,** routine *f.*, train-train *m.*; **in the ~** (*fig.*) dans l'ensemble; *adj.* (*spherical*) rond; (*circular*) circulaire; (*~ed*) arrondi; (*tone*) sonore; (*complete, frank*) rond; **square** PEG **in a ~ hole; ~ish** *adj.* rondelet; **~ly** *adv.* rondement; **~ness** *s.* rondeur *f.*; **R~head** *s.* Tête-ronde *f.*; **~sman** *s.* livreur *m.*; *v.t.* (*make* ~) arrondir; (*naut.*) doubler; **~ off** *v.t.* (*make* ~) arrondir, (*complete*) achever; **~ on** *v.t.* s'en prendre à qn.; **~ up** *v.t.* rassembler, (*police*) rafler; **~-up** *s.* rassemblement *m.*, (*police*) rafle *f.*; *prep.* autour de; *adv.* (*in a circle*) en rond, à la ronde; **~ and ~,** en rond; (*by circuitous way*) en faisant un détour; *see also* GO, PASS, SHOW, TAKE, TURN, *etc.*; **to get ~ to doing sth.,** arriver à faire qch.; **~about** *s.* (*at fair*) manège *m.*, (*traffic*) rond-point *m.*; **~about** *adj.* indirect, détourné.

rous/e *v.t.* (*from sleep*) réveiller; (*provoke to anger, etc.*) provoquer; (*indignation*) soulever; (*evoke feelings*) susciter; (*from indifference*) secouer; **~ing** *adj.* (*appeal*) émouvant, (*applause*) chaleureux, (*cheers*) frénétique, (*speech*) vibrant.

rout *s.* **1.** (*defeat*) déroute *f.*; **2.** (*party*) bande *f.*; *v.t.* (1) mettre en déroute; **~ out** *v.t.* déterrer.

route *s.* route *f.*, itinéraire *m.*; (*of bus, etc.*) direction *f.*, parcours *m.*; **~ march** *s.* marche d'entraînement *f.*; *v.t.* router, acheminer, diriger (par).

routine *s.* routine *f.*; *adj.* routinier, normal, courant.

rov/e *v.t.* parcourir; *v.i.* errer; **~er** *s.* vagabond *m.*; **~ing** *adj.* vagabond, errant.

row¹ *s.* (*line*) rang *m.*; (*of seats, etc.*) rangée *f.*; **in a ~,** (*in succession*) de suite.

row² *s.* (*in boat*) promenade en canot *f.*; *v.t.* (*boat*) faire aller à la rame; (*person*) faire passer en canot; *v.i.* ramer; (*race*) faire une course d'aviron; **~er** *s.* rameur *m.*; **~ing-boat** *s.* bateau à rames *m.*; **~lock** *s.* tolet *m.*

row³ *s.* (*fam.*) (*noise*) vacarme *m.*; (*fight*) querelle *f.*; **to kick up a ~,** faire du vacarme; **to have a ~ with,** se disputer avec; *v.t.* (*fam. = reprimand*) sonner les cloches à qn.; *v.i.* se disputer.

rowan *s.* sorbier *m.*

rowd/y *adj.* & *s.m.* tapageur; **~iness** *s.* tapage *m.*, turbulence *f.*

royal *adj.* royal; **~ sail,** catacatois *m.*; **~ist** *s.* royaliste *m.*; **~ly** *adv.**; **~ty** *s.* royauté *f.*; (*author's*) droits d'auteur *m.pl.*; (*comm.*) redevance *f.*

R.S.M. (*abbrev. Regimental Sergeant-Major*) adjutant-chef *m.*

R.S.P.C.A. (*abbrev. Royal Society for the Prevention of Cruelty to Animals*) S.P.A. *f.* (Société protectrice des Animaux).

R.S.V.P. (*please answer*) R.S.V.P. (répondez s'il vous plaît).

rub *s.* frottement *m.*; (*with duster*) coup de torchon *m.*; (*snag*) hic *m.*; *v.t.* & *i.* frotter; (*med.*) frictionner; **~ along** *v.i.* vivoter; **~ down** *v.t.* (*horse*) bouchonner; **~ out, off,** effacer; **~ up** *v.t.* astiquer; (*fig.*) rafraîchir; **~ s.o. up the wrong way,** prendre qn. à rebrousse-poil; **~bing** *s.* frottement *m.*; (*brass*) calque *m.*

rubber *s.* (*substance*) caoutchouc *m.*; (*india~*) gomme *f.*; (*person*) frotteur *m.*; (*machine*) frottoir *m.*; (*at cards*) robre *m.*; *adj.* en caoutchouc; **~ band** *s.* élastique *m.*; **~ stamp** *s.* tampon *m.*, (*fig.*) coup de tampon *m.*; **~-stamp** *v.t.* (*fig.*) donner un coup de tampon à; **~ize** *v.t.* caoutchouter.

rubbish *s.* déchets *m.pl.*; (*of building*) décombres *m.pl.*; (*trashy goods*) camelote *f.*; (*fam.*) sottises *f.pl.*; **~ bin** *s.* poubelle *f.*; **~ dump** *s.* décharge *f.*; **~y** *adj.* sans valeur.

rubble *s.* blocage *m.*

Rubicon *s.* Rubicon *m.*; **to cross the ~,** franchir le Rubicon.

rubicund *adj.* rubicond.

rubric *s.* rubrique *f.*

ruby *s.* (*stone*) rubis *m.*; (*colour*) couleur de rubis *f.*; (*type*) corps $5\frac{1}{2}$ *m.*; *adj.* couleur de rubis, vermeil.

ruche *s.* ruche *f.*

ruck *s.* **1.** (*fam. crowd*) le vulgum pecus; **2.** (*crease*) pli *m.*; **3.** (*rugby*) mêlée ouverte *f.*; *v.t.* & *i.* (2) plisser, (se) froisser.

rucksack *s.* sac à dos *m.*, sac tyrolien *m.*

ructions *s.* (*pop.*) grabuge *m.*

rudder *s.* (*naut., aviat.*) gouvernail *m.*

ruddy *adj.* **1.** (*healthily red*) rougeâtre, au teint vermeil; **2.** (*pop. = bloody*) sacré (*before noun*); *adv.* (2) rudement.

rude *adj.* **1.** (*primitive*) primitif; **2.** (*in natural state*) rude; **3.** (*uncivilized*) mal élevé; **4.** (*roughly made*) rude; **5.** (*coarse*) grossier; **6.** (*vigorous*) vigoureux; **7.** (*insolent*) impoli; **8.** (*abrupt*) brusque; **9.** (*violent*) violent; **~ly** *adv.* (1)*; (2)*; (3) de façon mal élevée; (4)*; (5)*; (6)*; (7)*; (8)*; (9) violemment; **~ness** *s.* (1) caractère primitif *m.*; (2), (3), (4) rudesse *f.*; (5) grossièreté *f.*; (7) impolitesse *f.*, insolence *f.*; (9) violence *f.*

rudiment/s *s.pl.* (*first principles*) rudiments *m.pl.*; (*germ of sth.*) rudiment *m.*; **~ary** *adj.* rudimentaire.

rue¹ *s.* (*shrub*) rue *f.*

rue² *v.t.* se repentir de, regretter; **~ful** *adj.* triste; **~fully** *adv.**.

ruff *s.* **1.** (*frill*) fraise *f.*, (*on bird or animal*) collier *m.*; **2.** (*bird*) pigeon capucin *m.*; **3.** (*at cards*) coupe *f.*; *v.t.* & *i.* (3) couper.

ruffian *s.* bandit *m.*; **~ly** *adj.* de bandit.

ruffle *s.* (*frill*) ruche *f.*; (*ripple*) rides *m.pl.*; *v.t.* & *i.* (*hair, feathers*) ébouriffer; (*water*) rider; (*clothes*) (se) chiffonner; (*fig.*) froisser (qn.).

rug *s.* (*on floor*) tapis *m.*; (*cover, wrap*) couverture *f.*; **bedside ~,** descente de lit *f.*

Rugby (*football*) & (*fam.*) **rugger** *s.* rugby *m.*

rugged *adj.* **1.** (*uneven*): (*bark*) rugueux, (*road*) raboteux; **2.** (*austere*) austère; **~ness** *s.* (1) aspérité *f.*; (2) rudesse *f.*

rugosity *s.* rugosité *f.*

ruin *s.* ruine *f.*; RACK **and ~;** *v.t.* ruiner; (*cause to fall*) causer la perte de; (*damage*) abîmer; (*fig.*) gâcher; **~ation** *s.* ruine *f.*; **~ous** *adj.* (*in ~s*) ruiné, (*causing ~*) ruineux; **~ously** *adv.**.

rul/e *s.* **1.** (*principle; standard; normal state*) règle *f.*; **2.** (*government*) autorité *f.*; **3.** (*for measuring*) mètre *m.*, règle graduée *f.*; **4.** (*regulation*) règlement *m.*; **as a ~e,** généralement; **by ~e of** THUMB; **to work to ~e,** faire la grève du zèle; *v.t.* (2) gouverner, diriger; (3) régler; *v.i.*; **5.** (*give decision*) décider; **6.** (*be current*) régner; **~e**

out *v.t.* exclure; **~e over,** régner sur; **~e the** ROOST; **be ~ed by,** être dominé par; **~er** *s.* (2) (*king*) souverain *m.*, (*leader*) chef *m.*, **~s** *s.pl.* dirigeants *m.pl.*; **~er** (3) règle *f.*; **~ing** *s.* (5) décision *f.*; **~ing** *adj.* dirigeant, dominant, (*comm.*) (6) actuel.
rum[1] *s.* rhum *m.*
rum[2] *adj.* & **~my** *adj.* (*pop.*) rigolo, bizarre.
Rumania *see* ROMANIA.
rumba *s.* rumba *f.*
rumbl/e *s.* & **~ing** *s.* (*of traffic*) roulement *m.*; (*of thunder, etc.*) grondement *m.*; *v.i.* rouler, gronder; (*pop.* = *to see through*) voir venir (qn.), subodorer (qch.).
rumina/te *v.i.* (*lit.* & *fig.*) ruminer; **~nt** *adj.* & *s.m.* ruminant; **~tion** *s.* rumination *f.*
rummage *s.* fouille *f.*; *v.t.* & *i.* fouiller.
rumour *s.* rumeur *f.*; *v.t.* répandre le bruit que; **~ has it that,** on dit que; **it is ~ed that,** le bruit court que.
rump *s.* (*of bird*) croupion *m.*; (*of animal*) croupe *f.*; (*cook.*) culotte *f.*; **~ steak,** romsteck *m.*
rumple *v.t.* (*hair*) ébouriffer; (*clothes*) chiffonner; (*fig.*) contrarier.
rumpus *s.* (*pop.*) chahut *m.*
run[1] *s.* **1.** (*act*) course *f.*; **at a ~,** au pas de course; **2.** (*direction*) direction *f.*; **3.** (*mus., speech*) cadence *f.*; **4.** (*stretch*) durée *f.*; **5.** (*journey*) voyage *m.*, (*distance, auto., naut.*) trajet *m.*, (*distance, mil., aviat.*) parcours *m.*, (*short trip*) promenade *f.*; **6.** (*series*) série *f.*, suite *f.*; **7.** (*general type*) généralité *f.*, commun *m.*, **~ of the mill** *adj.* ordinaire, habituel; **8.** (*for chickens*) poulailler *m.*; **9.** (*licence to use*) libre accès *m.* (à), disposition *f.* (de) **10.** (*in stocking*) maille filée *f.*; **11.** (*ski*) piste *f.*; **12.** (*on bank*) descente *f.*; **13.** (*theat.*) **to have a long ~,** rester à l'affiche; **in the long ~,** à la longue; **on the ~,** (*escaping*) en fuite, (*busy*) affairé; **to be on the ~,** être recherché par la police; **to have a ~ for one's** MONEY.
run[2] *v.i.* **1.** (*move fast*) courir, (*rush*) se précipiter, (*slide*) glisser; **2.** (*flee*) fuir; **~ for it,** se sauver; **3.** (*flow*) couler, (*stream*) ruisseler, (*colour*) déteindre, (*stocking*) se démailler; **4.** (*spread, extend*) s'étendre, se répandre; **5.** (*suppurate*) suppurer, (*eyes*) pleurer; **6.** (*be worded*) être conçu, être rédigé; **7.** (*auto.*) rouler, (*bus, etc.*) faire le service; **8.** (*theat.*) se jouer, rester à l'affiche; **9.** (*mech.*) marcher, fonctionner; **10.** (*be valid*) être en vigueur, courir; **11.** (*agric.*) grimper, ramper, **~ to seed,** monter en graine, (*fig.*) s'avachir; **~ dry,** s'épuiser, se tarir; **~ short,** s'épuiser; **~ short of,** être à court de; **~ round in** CIRCLES; HIT **and ~ driver**; *v.t.* **1.** (*distance*) couvrir; **2.** (*a risk, a race, etc.*) courir; **3.** (*train, bus, ship*) mettre en service; **4.** (*blockade*) forcer; **5.** (*horse*) faire courir; **6.** (*temperature*) avoir; **7.** (*direct*): (*business*) gérer, diriger, (*mine, etc.*) exploiter, (*hotel*) tenir, (*newspaper*) éditer; **8.** (*mech.*) faire marcher, faire fonctionner; **9.** (*fam.* ~ *a car*) posséder (une auto); **10.** (*smuggle*) faire la contrebande de; **~ aground,** s'échouer, faire échouer; **~ to earth,** (*game*) forcer, (*s.o.*) déterrer (qn.); **~ about,** courir çà et là; **~-about** *s.* (*auto.*) voiturette *f.*; **~ across** *v.t.* traverser en courant, (*meet*) rencontrer par hasard; **~ after,** courir après; **~ against,** se heurter contre; **~ along** *v.t.* longer; *v.i.* (*fam.*) filer; **~ away** (*horse*) s'emballer, (*person*) se sauver, s'enfuir; **~away** *s.* fugitif *m.*, (*mil.*) fuyard *m.*; **~away** *adj.* fugitif, (*horse*) emballé, (*car*) parti à la dérive, (*marriage*) clandestin, (*victory*) facile; **~ away with,** enlever, (*prize, etc.*) emporter; **~ down** *v.i.* descendre en courant, couler, (*watch, etc.*) s'arrêter, (*person*) s'épuiser; **~ down** *v.t.* (*with car*) écraser, renverser, (*disparage*) dénigrer, (*discover*) découvrir la retraite de qn.; (*reduce nos.*) réduire (le personnel); **~-down** *s.* (*analysis*) analyse *f.*, (*reduction*) réduction *f.*; **~-down** *adj.* délabré, (*person*) épuisé; **~ high** (*passion*) être déchaîné, (*temper*) être échauffé; **~ in** *v.t.* (*auto.*) roder, (*fam. arrest*) fourrer au bloc; **~ning-in,** en rodage; **~ into** (*danger, etc.*) s'exposer à, (*collide with*) entrer en collision avec; (*debt*) s'endetter; **~ off** *v.i.* (*flee*) se sauver, (*liquid*) s'écouler, *v.t.* (*liquid*) faire écouler, (*write*) rédiger en vitesse; **~ on** (*print.*) faire suivre, *v.i.* continuer, (*time*) passer, (*verse*) enjamber; **~ out** *v.t.* (*line*) laisser filer, *v.i.* sortir en courant (*leak*) couler, fuir, (*come to an end*) s'épuiser, tirer à sa fin; **~ out of,** épuiser sa provision de; **~ over** *v.i.* déborder, *v.t.* (*scan*) parcourir des yeux, (*touch*) promener les doigts sur, (*with vehicle*) écraser; **~ through** *v.i.* (*one's head*) trotter (dans la tête), *v.t.* (*rehearse*) faire répéter, (*with sword, etc.*) transpercer, (*cross out*) biffer; **~ to,** monter à, (*fam. afford*) se payer; **~ up** *v.t.* (*flag*) hisser, (*debts*) laisser accumuler, (*house, etc.*) construire; **~ up against,** rencontrer; **~-up** *s.* (*sport*) pas d'approche *m.pl.*; (*fig.*) travaux d'approche *m.pl.*, période préparatoire *f.*
rune *s.* rune *f.*
rung *s.* (*of ladder*) échelon *m.*; (*of chair*) barreau *m.*
runner *s.* (*racer*) coureur *m.*; (*messenger*) courrier *m.*; (*of plant*) coulant *m.*; (*ring on rod*) anneau *m.*; (*on sledge*) patin *m.*; (*of skate*) lame *f.*; (*groove or rod*) coulisseau *m.*; (*strip of carpet*) tapis de couloir *m.*; **~-up** *s.* second *m.*; **~ bean** *s.* haricot grimpant *m.*
running *s.* (*movement*) course *f.*; (*management*) direction *f.*; (*med.*) suppuration *f.*; (*techn.*) marche *f.*, fonctionnement *m.*; **to make the ~,** mener le jeu; **to be in the ~,** avoir des chances d'arriver; **to be out of the ~,** ne plus compter; *adj.* (*successive*) de suite; (*flowing*) coulant, vif; **~-board** *s.* (*auto.*) marche-pied *m.*; **~ commentary** *s.* reportage en direct *m.*; **~ fight** *s.* bataille en retraite *f.*; **~ fire** *s.* feu coulant *m.*; **~ jump** *s.* saut avec élan *m.*; **~ title** *s.* titre courant *m.*
runny *adj.* liquide; (*nose*) qui coule.
runt *s.* (*horse*) rosse *f.*; (*person*) nabot *m.*
runway *s.* piste *f.*
rupee *s.* roupie *f.*
rupture *s.* rupture *f.*; (*hernia*) hernie *f.*; *v.t.* & *i.* (se) rompre; se donner une hernie.
rural *adj.* rural.
ruse *s.* ruse *f.*
rush[1] *s.* (*bot.*) ajonc *m.*; (*for chairs, etc.*) paille *f.*
rush[2] *s.* (*act*) ruée *f.*; (*sudden movement*) course précipitée *f.*; (*onslaught*) assaut *m.*; (*of blood, etc.*) afflux *m.*; (*cinema*) projection d'essai *f.*; **~es** *s.pl.* (*cinema*) épreuves de tournage *f.pl.*; *v.t.* (*impel*) pousser vivement; (*take by storm*) prendre d'assaut; (*to hospital, etc.*) transporter d'urgence; (*work*) exécuter d'urgence; *v.i.* se précipiter, se ruer; (*blood, etc.*) affluer; *adj.* (*fam.*) (*order*) urgent; (*moment*) de presse; **~ hour,** heure de pointe *f.*; **~ing** *s.* précipitation *f.*, *adj.* jaillissant; (*fig.*) impétueux.
rusk *s.* biscotte *f.*
russet *adj.* roussâtre.
Russia *s.* (*geog.*) Russie *f.*; **~ leather,** cuir de Russie *m.*; **~n** *adj.* & *s.m.f.* russe; *s.m.* (*lang.*) russe.
rust *s.* rouille *f.*; *v.t.* & *i.* (se) rouiller; **~less** *adj.* inoxydable; **~y** *adj.* (*lit.* & *fig.*) rouillé; **~iness** *s.* rouille *f.*
rustic *s.* paysan *m.*, campagnard *m.*; *adj.* rural; (*uncouth*) rustre; (*untrimmed, timber*) rustique.
rusticat/e *v.t.* renvoyer temporairement; *v.i.*

se retirer à la campagne; ~ion s. renvoi temporaire m., retraite f.
rustle s. (*also* ~*ing*) (*of dress*) frou-frou m.; (*of leaves*) bruissement m.; (*of paper*) froissement m.; v.i. frou-frouter, bruire; v.t. (*steal cattle*) voler (le bétail).

rut s. (*track, groove*) ornière f.; (*of animal*) rut m.; **to be in a ~**, (*fig.*) s'encroûter.
ruthless adj. impitoyable; **~ly** adv.*.
rye s. (*cereal*) seigle m.; (*whisky*) whisky m.; **~-bread** s. pain de seigle m.; **~-grass** s. ray-grass m.

S

sabbat/h s. (*Jewish*) sabbat m.; (*Christian*) dimanche m.; **Witches' ~h,** sabbat m.; **S~arian** adj. & s. (celui, celle) qui observe la loi du repos dominical; **~ical** adj. sabbatique; **~ical year,** année de congé sabbatique f.
sable s. (*animal & fur*) zibeline f.; (*herald.*) sable m.; adj. (*black*) noir; (*gloomy*) lugubre; (*herald.*) de sable.
sabot s. sabot m.
sabot/age s. sabotage m.; v.t. saboter; **~eur** s. saboteur m.
sabre s. sabre m.; **~-rattling** s. (*fig.*) bruit de sabre m.; **~-rattling people,** traîneurs de sabre m.pl.
saccharin s. saccharine f.; **~e** adj. sacchariné.
sacerdotal adj. sacerdotal.
sachet s. sachet m.
sack s. **1.** (*bag*) sac m.; **2.** (*fam. dismissal*) congé m.; **to get the ~,** se faire congédier; **to give s.o. the ~,** congédier qn.; **3.** (*wine*) vin de Xérès m.; **4.** (*plunder*) sac m., pillage m.; **~cloth** s. toile à sac f., (*fig.*) bure f.; **~ful** s. un plein sac m.; **~-race** s. course en sac f.; v.t. (1) mettre en sac; (2) congédier; (4) mettre à sac; **~ing** s. (1) toile à sac f.; (4) pillage m.
sacrament s. sacrement m.; **~al** adj. sacramentel.
sacred adj. (*consecrated, dedicated, to*) consacré à; (*holy, hallowed*) saint; (*inviolable*) sacré (*after the noun*) exc. **S~ College,** le sacré collège, **S~ Heart,** le Sacré Cœur; **~ cow** (*fig.*) vache sacrée f.; (*mus. etc.*) religieux.
sacrific/e s. (*act*) sacrifice m.; (*victim, gift*) victime f., offrande f.; **~ial** adj. sacrificiel, (*comm.*) à perte; v.t. sacrifier; (*comm.*) vendre à perte.
sacrileg/e s. sacrilège m.; **~ious** adj. sacrilège.
sacrist(an) s. sacristain m.; **~y** s. sacristie f.
sacrosanct adj. sacro-saint; (*lit. before noun; pej. after noun*)
sacrum s. sacrum m.
sad adj. **1.** (*feeling, causing, sorrow*) triste; (*loss*) cruel; (*news, event*) déplorable, fâcheux, désolant; **2.** (*cook. = heavy*) mal levé; **~den** v.t. attrister; **~ly** adv. (1) tristement; cruellement, pitoyablement; (*fam.*) sérieusement, bigrement, étrangement; **~ness** s. tristesse f.
saddle s. (*of horse, bicycle, etc.; cook.*) selle f.; (*ridge*) col m.; **in the ~,** en selle; **to be in the ~** (*fig.*) être bien en selle; **~back** s. dos d'âne m., colline en dos d'âne f.; **~-bag** s. sacoche de selle f.; **~-cloth** s. housse f.; v.t. seller; (*burden with*) charger de; **~r** s. sellier m.
sadis/m s. sadisme m.; **~t** s. sadique m.f.; **~tic** adj. sadique.
s.a.e. (*abbrev. stamped addressed envelope*) enveloppe timbrée pour la réponse f.
safari s. safari m.
safe s. (*for food*) garde-manger m.; (*for valuables*) coffre-fort m.; adj. **1.** (*unharmed*), **~ and sound,** sain et sauf; **2.** (*out of danger*) en sûreté, à l'abri; **3.** (*secure*) sûr; **4.** (*reliable*) sûr, certain; **~ conduct** s. sauf-conduit m.; **~ deposit** s. cave des coffres f.; **~guard** s. sauvegarde f., v.t. sauvegarder; **in ~ keeping,** en sécurité; FAIL **~**; **~ly** adv. (1) sain et sauf, sans mal; (2), (3) en sûreté, sans danger; (4) sans hésitation.
safety s. sûreté f.; **to play for ~,** agir avec prudence; **~-**BELT; **~-catch** s. cran de sûreté m.; **~ curtain** s. rideau de fer m.; **~ lamp** s. lampe de sûreté f.; **~ match** s. allumette suédoise f.; **~-**PIN; **~ razor** s. rasoir de sûreté m., rasoir mécanique m.; **~-valve** s. soupape de sûreté f.
saffron s. safran m.; **~-coloured,** safrané.
sag s. affaissement m.; v.i. (*sink*) s'affaisser, fléchir; (*bulge*) bomber.
saga s. (*Scandinavian epic*) saga f.; (*series of books*) roman-fleuve m.
sagac/ious adj. sagace; **~ity** s. sagacité f.
sage[1] s. (*herb*) sauge f.
sage[2] s. (*wise man*) sage m.; adj. sage, prudent.
Sagittarius s. (*astron.*) Sagittaire m.
sago s. sagou m.; **~-palm,** sagoutier m.
said adj. dit, susdit.
sail s. (*piece of canvas*) voile f.; ROYAL **~**; (*collective*) voilure f.; (*ships*) navires m.pl.; (*of windmill*) aile f.; (*trip*) promenade à voile f.; **to set ~,** mettre à la voile; **in full ~,** toutes voiles dehors; **to take the wind out of s.o.'s ~s** (*fig.*) rabattre le caquet à qn,; **~cloth** s. toile à voile f.; **~maker** s. voilier m.; v.i. naviguer; (*start voyage*) partir; (*move easily*) glisser; **~ close to the** WIND; v.t. (*control ship*) commander; (*travel over*) naviguer sur; **~ing** s. navigation f., (*departure*) départ m.; **to be plain ~ing,** ne pas faire un pli; **~or** s. matelot m., marin m.; **to be a good ~or,** avoir le pied marin; **to be a bad ~or,** être sujet au mal de mer.
sainfoin s. sainfoin m.
saint s. saint(e) m.f.; PATRON **~**; **~ed** adj. (*person*) pieux; (*place*) sacré (*after the noun*); **~ly** adj. (*person*) saint; (*thing*) de saint.
sake s. **for the ~ of,** (*out of consideration for*) par égard pour; (*in the interest of*) pour l'amour de; (*in order to get, etc.*) dans le but de; **for God's ~,** pour l'amour de Dieu.
salaam(s) s. salamalec(s) m.pl.; v.i. faire des salamalecs.
salaci/ous adj. lubrique; **~ty** s. lubricité f.
salad s. salade f.; **~ bowl,** saladier m.; **~ days,** vertes années f.pl.; **~-dressing,** vinaigrette f.
salamander s. salamandre f.
salar/y s. appointements m.pl.; ⚠ salaire = **wages** (*for manual workers*); **~ied** adj. rétribué; **~ied class,** les employés m.pl.
sale s. vente f.; (*auction ~*) vente aux enchères f.; (*bargain ~*) solde f.; **on ~,** en vente; **for ~,** à vendre; **in the ~,** en solde; **~able** adj. vendable; **~sman,** (*shop*) vendeur m.; **~swoman,** vendeuse f.; (*dealer*) marchand m.; (*traveller*) voyageur de commerce m.; **~smanship** s. art de vendre m.
Salic adj. salique.
salient adj. & s.m. saillant.
salin/e adj. salin; **~ity** s. salinité f.

saliva *s.* salive *f.*; **~ry** *adj.* salivaire; **~te,** *v.i.* saliver; **~tion** *s.* salivation *f.*
sallow[1] *s.* saule *m.*
sallow[2] *adj.* blafard; **~ness** *s.* teint blafard *m.*
sally *s.* **1.** (*mil.*) sortie *f.*; **2.** (*banter*) saillie *f.*; *v.i.* (1) faire une sortie; **~ forth,** se mettre en route.
salmi *s.* (*cook.*) salmis *m.*
salmon *s.* saumon *m.*; **~-pink,** saumon (*invar.*) **~ trout** *s.* truite saumonée *f.*
salon *s.* salon *m.*
saloon *s.* salon *m.*; **~ bar,** bar *m.*; **~ car,** conduite intérieure *f.*
salsify *s.* salsifis *m.*
salt *s.* (*lit.* & *fig.*) sel *m.*; **cooking ~,** gros sel *m.*; **table ~,** sel fin *m.*; **bath ~s,** sels pour bains *m.pl.*; ROCK-~; SMELL**ing-~s; he's not worth his ~,** il ne vaut pas le pain qu'il mange; **to take sth. with a grain or pinch of ~,** en prendre et en laisser; **old ~,** (*sailor*) vieux loup de mer *m.*; **~-cellar** *s.* salière *f.*; ~-MARSH; ~-SPOON; *adj.* salé; **~ meadow** *s.* pré salé *m.*; **~ water** *s.* eau salée *f.*; **~-water** *adj.* d'eau salée; *v.t.* saler; (*mining*) forcer; **~ away,** mettre de côté; **~ down,** conserver dans le sel; **~er** *s.* (*of fish*) saleur *m.*, (*merchant*) saunier *m.*; **~ing** *s.* salaison *f.*; **~ings** *s.pl.* marais salants *m.pl.*; **~ness** *s.* salure *f.*, (*of sea*) salinité *f.*; **~y** *adj.* salé.
saltpetre *s.* salpêtre *m.*
salubri/ous *adj.* salubre; **~ty** *s.* salubrité *f.*
salutary *adj.* salutaire.
salutation *s.* salutation *f.*
salute *s.* (*greeting*) salut *m.*; (*mil.*) salut militaire *m.*; (*of guns*) salve *f.*; **to take the ~,** passer (les troupes, etc.) en revue; *v.t.* & *i.* saluer.
salvage *s.* **1.** (*rescue*) sauvetage *m.*; **2.** (*of waste material*) récupération *f.*; **3.** (*property ~d*) biens sauvés *m.pl.*; *v.t.* (1) sauver; (2) récupérer.
salvation *s.* (*eccles.* & *fig.*) salut *m.*; (*preservation*) préservation *f.*; **S~ Army,** Armée du Salut *f.*; **~ist** *s.* salutiste *m.f.*
salve *s.* **1.** (*ointment*) onguent *m.*; **2.** (*fig.*) baume *m.*; *v.t.* (1) appliquer un onguent sur; (2) panser; **3.** (*salvage*) sauver.
salver *s.* plateau *m.*
salvo *s.* salve *f.*
sal volatile *s.* sel volatil *m.*, sels anglais *m.pl.*
S.A.M. (*surface-to-air missile*) engin sol-air (Sam) *m.*
Samaritan *s.* samaritain *m.*; **the good ~,** le bon samaritain; **the ~s,** (*equivalent*) S.O.S. Amitié.
same *s.* la même chose; *pron.* le, la, les, même(s); **just, all, the ~,** quand même; **I would have done the ~,** j'aurais fait de même; **it's all the ~ to me,** ça m'est égal; *adj.* même; (*aforesaid*) ledit; **at the ~ time,** en même temps, (*simultaneously*) à la fois; **in the ~ way,** de même; **~ness** *s.* monotonie *f.*
Samoa *s.* (*geog.*) (*W. Samoa*) l'état des Samoa occidentales *m.*; (*E. Samoa*) les Samoa orientales *or* américaines *f.pl.*; **~n** *adj.* & *s.m.f.* (habitant) des Samoa.
samovar *s.* samovar *m.*
sampan *s.* sampan *m.*
sample *s.* échantillon *m.*; (*specimen*) spécimen *m.*; *v.t.* échantillonner; (*food, drink*) goûter; **~r** *s.* broderie de jeune fille *f.*
samurai *s.* samouraï *m.*
sanatorium *s.* sanatorium *m.*; (*pl.* —s).
sancti/fy *v.t.* sanctifier; **~fication** *s.* sanctification *f.*; **~ty** *s.* (*saintliness*) sainteté *f.*; (*sacredness*) caractère sacré *m.*
sanctimonious *adj.* bigot; **~ly,** *adv.* d'une manière bigote; **~ness** *s.* bigoterie *f.*
sanction *s.* sanction *f.*; *v.t.* sanctionner.
sanctity *see* SANCTIFY.
sanctuary *s.* (*inviolable place*) asile *m.*; (*in church*; *private retreat*) sanctuaire *m.*; (*bird, etc.*) refuge *m.*; **to take, to give ~,** chercher, offrir un asile.
sanctum *s.* sanctuaire *m.*
sanctus *s.* sanctus *m.*
sand *s.* sable *m.*; (*fine*) sablon *m.*; **~s** (*beach*) plage *f.*; QUICK**~s; to bury one's head in the ~,** pratiquer la politique de l'autruche; **~bag** *s.* sac de sable *m.*; **~bag** *v.t.* garnir de sacs de sable; **~bank** *s.* banc de sable *m.*; **~-glass** *s.* sablier *m.*; **~-hill, ~-dune** *s.* dune *f.*; **~man** *s.* (*fam.*) marchand de sable *m.*; **~paper** *s.* papier de verre *m.*; **~paper** *v.t.* passer au papier de verre; **~piper** *s.* chevalier *m.*; **~shoes** *s.pl.* espadrilles *f.pl.*; **~stone** *s.* grès *m.*; **~storm** *s.* tempête de sable *f.*; **~y** *adj.* sablonneux, de sable; (*hair*) blond roux; *v.t.* sabler.
sandal *s.* sandale *f.*
sandalwood *s.* bois de santal *m.*
sandwich *s.* sandwich *m.*; **~-board** *s.* panneau d'homme sandwich *m.*; **~ course** *s.* enseignement en alternance *m.*; **~-man** *s.* homme sandwich *m.*; *v.t.* mettre en sandwich; **to be ~ed between,** être pris en sandwich entre.
sane *adj.* sain d'esprit; (*reasonable*) raisonnable.
sanguinary *adj.* (*involving bloodshed*) sanglant; (*bloodthirsty*) sanguinaire.
sanguine *adj.* (*hopeful*) sanguin; (*optimistic*) confiant, optimiste; (*florid*) rubicond; **~ly** *adv.* avec confiance; **~ness** *s.* confiance *f.*, optimisme *m.*
sanita/ry *adj.* sanitaire; **~ry towel** *s.* serviette hygiénique *f.*; **~tion** *s.* hygiène *f.*; (*drainage, sewage, etc.*) aménagements sanitaires *m.pl.*
sanity *s.* (*med.*) santé mentale *f.*; (*reasonableness*) jugement sain *m.*, modération *f.*
Sanskrit *adj.* & *s.m.* sanscrit, sanskrit.
Santa Claus *s.* le père Noël *m.*
sap[1] *s.* (*lit.* & *fig.*) sève *f.*; **~wood** *s.* aubier *m.*; **~less** *adj.* sans sève, desséché; **~ling** *s.* jeune arbre *m.*; **~piness** *s.* richesse en sève *f.*; **~py** *adj.* plein de sève; *v.t.* tirer la sève de; (*fig.*) épuiser.
sap[2] *v.t.* (*undermine, destroy*) saper; **~per** *s.* sapeur *m.*; **~pers** *pl.* (*mil.*) génie *m.*
sapien/ce *s.* sagesse *f.*; **~t** *adj.* (*pej.*) pédant.
saponaceous *adj.* saponacé.
sapphire *s.* saphir *m.*; *adj.* bleu saphir (*invar.*)
saraband *s.* sarabande *f.*
Saracen *adj.* & *s.m.f.* Sarrazin(e).
sarcas/m *s.* sarcasme *m.*; **~tic** *adj.* sarcastique; **~tically** *adv.**.
sarcophagus *s.* sarcophage *m.*
sardine *s.* sardine *f.*; **packed like ~s,** serrés comme des harengs en caque.
Sardinia *s.* (*geog.*) Sardaigne *f.*; **~n** *adj.* & *s.m.f.* sarde.
sardonic *adj.* sardonique; **~ally** *adv.**.
sargasso *s.* sargasse *f.*
sari, saree *s.* sari *m.*
sarong *s.* sarong *m.*
sarsenet *s.* (*text.*) taffetas léger *m.*
sartorial *adj.* de tailleur; (*elegance*) vestimentaire.
sash *s.* **1.** (*uniform*) écharpe *f.*; (*dress*) ceinture *f.*; **2.** (*window*) châssis *m.*; **~-window,** fenêtre à guillotine *f.*
Satan *s.* Satan *m.*; **s~ic** *adj.* satanique.
satchel *s.* cartable *m.*
sat/e *v.t.* (*satisfy*) assouvir; (*surfeit*) rassasier (qn.); **~iate** *v.t.* rassasier; **~iety** *s.* satiété *f.*
sateen *s.* (*text.*) satinette *f.*
satellite *s.* satellite *m.*; (*polit.*) pays satellite *m.*; **~ town,** ville satellite *f.*
satin *s.* satin *m.*; **~wood** *s.* bois de citronnier *m.*
satir/e *s.* satire *f.*; **~ic(al)** *adj.* satirique; **~ist** *s.* auteur satirique *m.*; **~ize** *v.t.* faire la satire de.
satisfact/ion *s.* (*state*) satisfaction *f.*; (*thing which satisfies*) plaisir *m.*; (*payment of debt*)

règlement *m.*; (*amends*) réparation *f.*, dédommagement *m.*; **to give ~ion to,** contenter; **~ory** *adj.* satisfaisant; **~orily** *adv.* de manière satisfaisante.

satisfy *v.t.* (*meet expectations, be adequate*) satisfaire, répondre à; (*be enough*) suffire; (*content*) contenter; (*convince*) convaincre; (*pay creditor*) satisfaire; (*fulfil*): (*condition*) remplir, (*obligation*) s'acquitter de; **to be satisfied with,** se contenter de; **~ing** *adj.* satisfaisant.

satrap *s.* satrape *m.*

saturat/e *v.t.* (*lit.* & *fig.*) saturer; (*with bombs*) écraser (sous les bombes); **~ion** *s.* saturation *f.*

Saturday *s.* samedi *m.*

Saturn *s.* saturne *m.*; **s~alia** *s.* saturnales *f.pl.*

saturnine *adj.* sombre; ⚠ saturnin = **of lead.**

satyr *s.* satyre *m.*

sauc/e *s.* **1.** (*cook.*) sauce *f.*; **2.** (*fam.* = *cheek*) culot *m.*; **to have the ~e to,** avoir le culot de; **~e-boat** *s.* saucière *f.*; **~epan** *s.* casserole *f.*; **~ily** *adv.* insolemment; **~iness** *s.* impertinence *f.*; **~y** *adj.* impertinent; *v.t.* (1) assaisonner; (2) être insolent avec.

saucer *s.* soucoupe *f.*; **eyes like ~s** (*fig. fam.*) des yeux en boules de loto.

Saudi Arabia *s.* (*geog.*) Arabie Saoudite *f.*; **Saudi** *adj.* & *s.m.f.* saoudi(te).

sauerkraut *s.* choucroute *f.*

sauna *s.* sauna *m. or f.*

saunter *s.* petite promenade *f.*; *v.i.* flâner.

saurian *adj.* & *s.m.* saurien.

sausage *s.* (*to be cooked*) saucisse *f.*; (*to be eaten uncooked*) saucisson *m.*; **~-meat,** chair à saucisse *f.*

savage *s.* sauvage *m.*; *adj.* (*uncivilized*) sauvage; (*cruel*) cruel, féroce; (*pop.* = *angry*) furieux; **~ly** *adv.**;*,*;*; **~ness** *s.*, **~ry** *s.* sauvagerie *f.*; *v.t.* attaquer (férocement); (*bite*) mordre.

savanna(h) *s.* savane *f.*

save[1] *s.* (*at football*) arrêt *m.* (du ballon); *v.t.* **1.** (*rescue, protect*) sauver (*from*—de); **~ one's** BACON; **2.** (*eccles.*) sauver; **God ~ the Queen!,** vive la Reine!; **3.** (*keep for future use*) garder; **4.** (*use sparingly*) *v.t.* & *i.* économiser; *v.t.* ménager; **5.** (*relieve of need of expending money, trouble, etc.*) épargner, (*time*) gagner; **6.** (*at football*) arrêter; **~ up,** faire des économies; **~ up for a** RAINY **day**; **~r** *s.* (4) personne qui économise; **saving** *s.* (1) sauvetage *m.*; (2) salut *m.*; (4) économie *f.*; (5) épargne *f.*; **savings** *s.pl.* économies *f.pl.*; **savings bank,** caisse d'épargne *f.*; **savings book,** livret de caisse d'épargne *m.*; **saving** *adj.* (*person*) économe, (*thing*) économique.

save[2] *prep.* (& **saving**) sauf, excepté, à l'exception de.

saveloy *s.* cervelas *m.*

saviour *s.* sauveur *m.*

savory *s.* sarriette *f.*

savour *s.* (*taste, flavour*) saveur *f.*, goût *m.*; (*hint of*) soupçon *m.*, arrière-goût *m.*, pointe *f.* (de); *v.t.* savourer; *v.i.* avoir un goût de, sentir; **~y** *s.* canapé *m.*; *adj.* savoureux.

Savoy *s.* (*geog.*) Savoie *f.*; **s~** (*cabbage*) chou frisé *m.*

saw *s.* **1.** (*maxim*) dicton *m.*; **2.** (*tool*) scie *f.*; FRET-~; HACK-~, **~dust** *s.* sciure *f.*; **~-horse** *s.* chevalet *m.*; **~mill** *s.* scierie *f.*; *v.t.* & *i.* (2) scier; **~bones** *s.* (*pop.*) charcutier *m.*; **~n-off shot-gun,** fusil à canon tronqué *m.*; **~yer** *s.* scieur *m.*

saxifrage *s.* saxifrage *f.*

Saxon *adj.* & *s.m.f.* saxon(ne); (*arch.*) teutonique roman.

Saxony *s.* (*geog.*) Saxe *f.*

saxophone *s.* saxophone *m.*

say *s.* (*chance to speak*) mot *m.*; (*share in decision*) voix *f.*; **to have a ~ in sth.** avoir son mot à dire (sur qch.); *v.t.* (*utter*) dire; (*state*) affirmer; (*tell*) raconter; (*express*) exprimer; (*repeat*) réciter, répéter; **let's ~,** disons, mettons; **that is to ~,** c'est à dire; **I ~!,** dites-donc!; **what do you ~ to that?** qu'en dites-vous?; **it is said,** on dit; **~ing** *s.* proverbe *m.*, maxime *f.*

scab *s.* **1.** (*med.*) croûte *f.*; **2.** (*agric.*) gale *f.*; **3.** (*blackleg*) jaune *m.*; **~by** *adj.* (1) croûteux; (2) galeux.

scabbard *s.* fourreau *m.*

scabies *s.* gale *f.*

scabious *s.* scabieuse *f.*

scaffold *s.* (*for execution*) échafaud *m.*; (*constr.*) *also* **~ing** *s.* échafaudage *m.*

scald *s.* brûlure *f.*; *v.t.* (*injure with hot liquid*) échauder; (*clean with boiling water*) ébouillanter; (*milk*) faire chauffer presqu'à ébullition.

scal/e[1] *s.* **1.** (*of fish, etc.*) écaille *f.*; **2.** (*thin plate or film*) écaille *f.*; **3.** (*scab*) croûte *f.*; **4.** (*deposit of lime, etc.*) dépôt calcaire *m.*; **5.** (*on teeth*) tartre *m.*; *v.t.* & *i.* (1) (s')écailler; (4), (5) détartrer; **~y** *adj.* écailleux.

scale[2] *s.* (*balance pan*) plateau *m.*; **~s** *s.pl.* balance *f.sing.*; *v.t.* peser.

scale[3] *s.* (*graduated series*) échelle *f.*, série *f.*; **sliding ~,** échelle mobile *f.*; (*mus.*) gamme *f.*; (*of map*) échelle *f.*; (*instrument*) cadran gradué *m.*; (*scope, range*) étendue *f.*; **on a large, a small, ~,** à grande, à petite échelle; **on a national ~,** à l'échelon national; **full-~,** de grande envergure; *v.t.* (*climb up*) faire l'ascension de; (*climb over*) escalader; (*represent to ~*) tracer à l'échelle; **~ down,** réduire l'échelle de.

scallop *s.* **1.** (*fish*) coquille *f.*; **2.** (*dressm.*) feston *m.*; *v.t.* (1) faire gratiner en coquilles; (2) festonner.

scallywag *s.* (*pop.*) garnement *m.*

scalp *s.* **1.** (*anat.*) cuir chevelu *m.*; **2.** (*trophy, lit.* & *fig.*) scalp *m.*; *v.t.* (2) scalper.

scalpel *s.* scalpel *m.*

scamp *s.* garnement *m.*; (*child*) polisson *m.*; *v.t.* (*fig. fam.*) bâcler.

scamper *v.i.* courir au galop; **~ away,** détaler.

scampi *s.pl.* langoustines *f.pl.*

scan *v.t.* & *i.* **1.** (*vers.*) (se) scander; *v.t.* **2.** (*examine*) scruter, (*horizon*) sonder; **3.** (*TV, radar*) balayer; **~sion** *s.* (1) scansion *f.*; **~ner** *s.* (*radar*) antenne *f.*, (*med.*) tomographe *m.*; **~ning** *s.* (3) balayage *m.*

scandal *s.* scandale *m.*; (*gossip*) médisance *f.*, cancans *m.pl.*; **to talk ~,** cancaner; **~ize** *v.t.* scandaliser; **~ous** *adj.* scandaleux; **~ously** *adv.**; **~monger** *s.* médisant *m.*; *adj.* cancanier.

Scandinavia *s.* (*geog.*) Scandinavie *f.*; **~n** *adj.* & *s.m.f.* scandinave.

scant *adj.* (*clothing*) sommaire; (*success, etc.*) maigre; (*vegetation*) pauvre; **~y** *adj.* (*meal*) maigre; (*vegetation*) rare; **~ily** *adv.* sommairement; maigrement; **~iness** *s.* insuffisance *f.*; exiguïté *f.*; pauvreté *f.*

scapegoat *s.* bouc émissaire *m.*

scapegrace *s.* garnement *m.*

scapular *s.* scapulaire *m.*

scar *s.* (*lit.* & *fig.*) cicatrice *f.*; (*on face*) balafre *f.*; (*geol.*) rocher escarpé *m.*; *v.t.* laisser une cicatrice; balafrer; *v.i.* se cicatriser.

scarab *s.* scarabée *m.*

scarc/e *adj.* (*food, money*) peu abondant; (*rare*) rare; **to make oneself ~,** s'esquiver; **~ely** *adv.* à peine; ne . . . guère; **~ity** *s.* manque *m.*; (*of food*) disette *f.*

scare *s.* panique *f.*; **to give s.o. a ~,** faire une peur terrible à qn.; *v.t.* & *i.* (s')effrayer; **~crow** *s.* épouvantail *m.*; **~monger** *s.* alarmiste *m.f.*, semeur de panique *m.*

scarf *s.* (*techn.*) enture *f.*; (*dress*) (*official*) écharpe *f.*, (*gen.*) cravate *f.*, foulard *m.*

scarify *v.t.* (*surg.*) scarifier; (*agric.*) écroûter; (*fig. fam.*) éreinter.
scarlatina *s.* scarlatine *f.*
scarlet *adj.* & *s.f.* écarlate; ~ **fever,** scarlatine *f.*
scarp *s.* escarpement *m.*; (*mil.*) escarpe *f.*
scathing *adj.* cinglant, mordant.
scatter *v.t.* (*place at intervals*) éparpiller; (*sprinkle*) parsemer (*with*—de); *v.t.* & *i.* (*disperse*): (*people*) (se) disperser, (*clouds*) (se) dissiper; ~**ed** *adj.* dispersé, (*sporadic*) sporadique; ~**-brain** *s.* étourdi *m.*; ~**-brained** *adj.* étourdi.
scavenge *v.t.* balayer (les rues); vider (les poubelles); ~**r** *s.* (*rubbish collector*) éboueur *m.*; (*animal*) *adj.* nécrophage.
scen/e *s.* (*place of action*) lieu *m.*, cadre *m.*; (*mil.*) théâtre *m.*; (*theat.*; *sight*; *fit of anger*) scène *f.*; **behind the ~es,** dans les coulisses; ~**e-shifter** *s.* machiniste *m.*; ~**ario** *s.* scénario *m.*; ~**ery** *s.* (*theat.*) décor *m.*, (*natural*) paysage *m.*; ~**ic** *adj.* scénique.
scent *s.* **1.** (*characteristic odour*) parfum *m.*, odeur *f.*; **2.** (*fragrance*) senteur *f.*; **3.** (*trail*) piste *f.*; **4.** (*liquid perfume*) parfum *m.*; **5.** (*sense of smell*) odorat *m.*, (*of dogs*) flair *m.*; **to throw off the ~** *v.t.* dépister, (*police*) dérouter; *v.t.* (3) flairer; (2), (4) parfumer; (**sweet**)**-~ed** *adj.* parfumé, odorant, odoriférant; ~**less** *adj.* inodore.
sceptic *s.m.f.* sceptique; ~**al** *adj.* sceptique; ~**ally** *adv.* avec scepticisme; ~**ism** *s.* scepticisme *m.*
sceptre *s.* sceptre *m.*
schedule *s.* **1.** (*list*) liste *f.*, inventaire *m.*, (*of prices*) barème *m.*, (*of taxes*) cédule *f.*; **2.** (*timetable*) horaire *m.*; **on ~,** selon l'horaire, selon les prévisions; *v.t.* (1) classer; (2) (*organize in advance*) prévoir; ~**ed flight** (*aviat.*) service régulier *m.*
schema *s.* schéma *m.*; ~**tic** *adj.* schématique; ~**tize** *v.t.* schématiser.
schem/e *s.* **1.** (*outline*) exposé *m.*; **2.** (*plan*) plan *m.*, projet *m.*; **3.** (*plot*) intrigue *f.*, combine *f.*; ⚠ schème = **form**; *v.t.* & *i.* (2) projeter, former des projets; (3) intriguer, combiner, comploter; ~**er** *s.* (3) intrigant *m.*; ~**ing** *adj.* (3) intrigant.
schism *s.* schisme *m.*; ~**atic** *adj.* schismatique.
schist *s.* schiste *m.*
schizo *adj.* & *s.m.f.* (*fam.*) schizoïde.
schizo/id *adj.* schizoïde; ~**phrenia** *s.* schizophrénie *f.*; ~**phrenic** *adj.* schizophrène.
schnorkel *s.* schnorchel, schnorkel *m.*
scholar *s.* **1.** (*obs. pupil*) écoli/er, -ère *m.f.*; **2.** (*learned person*) savant *m.*; **3.** (*holder of ~ship*) boursier *m.*; ~**ly** *adj.* (2) (*person*) érudit, (*work*) savant; ~**ship** *s.* (2) érudition *f.*; (3) bourse *f.*
scholastic *adj.* (*of schools*) scolaire; (*pedantic*) pédant.
school[1] *s.* (*of whales, etc.*) banc *m.*, bande *f.*
school[2] *s.* (*acad.* & *fig.*) école *f.*; (*of university*) faculté *f.*; DRIVING-~; **grammar ~,** lycée *m.*; PUBLIC ~; SUNDAY ~; TECHNICAL ~; *adj.* scolaire; ~ **age** *s.* âge scolaire *m.*; ~**-book** *s.* livre de classe *m.*; ~**boy** *s.* écolier *m.*; ~ **bus** *s.* autobus scolaire *m.*; ~**girl** *s.* écolière *f.*; ~**fellow** *s.* condisciple *m.*; ~**-leaver** *s.* élève qui a terminé sa scolarité *m.*; ~ **report** *s.* carnet scolaire *m.*; ~**-room** *s.* salle de classe *f.*; ~**teacher** (~**master,** ~**mistress**) (*primary*) institut/eur, -rice *m.f.*; (*secondary*) professeur *m.f.*; *v.t.* (*discipline*) discipliner; (*train*) former, entraîner (qn. à faire qch.); (*accustom to*) (s')habituer à; ~**ing** *s.* enseignement *m.*, études *f.pl.*, scolarité *f.*
schooner *s.* (*naut.*) goélette *f.*; (*glass*) chopine *f.*
sciatica *s.* sciatique *f.*
scien/ce *s.* science *f.*; (*skill*) savoir *m.*; ~**ce fiction** *s.* science-fiction *f.*; ~**tific** *adj.* scientifique; ~**tifically** *adv.**; ~**tist** *s.* savant *m.*, homme de science *m.*
Scill/y islands *s.* (*geog.*) îles Scilly *or* Sorlingues *f.pl.*; ~**onian** *adj.* des îles Scilly; *s.m.f.* habitant des îles Scilly.
scimitar *s.* cimeterre *m.*
scintillat/e *v.i.* scintiller; (*fig.*) pétiller; ~**ion** *s.* scintillation *f.*, (*fig.*) pétillement *m.*
scion *s.* (*hort.*) scion *m.*; (*of family*) rejeton *m.*
scission *s.* division *f.*; (*fig.*) scission *f.*
scissors *s.* ciseaux *m.pl.*; NAIL-~; **scissor** *v.t.* couper.
sclero/sis *s.* sclérose *f.*; ~**tic** *adj.* sclérotique.
scoff *v.i.* **1.** (*mock*) se moquer (de); **2.** (*pop. eat greedily*) bouffer; ~**er** *s.* (1) railleur *m.*; ~**ing** *adj.* (1) moqueur, railleur.
scold *s.* mégère *f.*; *v.t.* gronder; ~**ing** *s.* gronderie *f.*
sconce *s.* bougeoir *m.*
scone *s.* galette (au lait) *f.*
scoop *s.* **1.** (*for flour, etc.*) pelle à main *f.*; (*ladle*) louche *f.*; **2.** (*fam. news*) reportage exclusif *m.*, exclusivité *f.*; *v.t.* ~ **out,** évider; ~ **up,** ramasser à la pelle.
scooter *s.* (*toy*) trottinette *f.*; (*motor ~*) scooter *m.*
scope *s.* (*outlook*) perspective *f.*; (*reach, range*) portée *f.*, envergure *f.*; (*outlet*) carrière *f.*
scorch *v.t.* & *i.* (*burn, become burnt*) (se) brûler; (*clothes*) roussir; (*be very hot*) se griller; (*pop. go very fast*) aller à pleins gaz; ~**ed earth,** terre brûlée *f.*; ~**er** *s.* journée torride *f.*; (*auto.*) chauffard *m.*; ~**ing** *adj.* torride; (*fig.*) mordant.
score *s.* **1.** (*notch*) entaille *f.*; (*techn.*) rayure *f.*; **2.** (*reckoning*) compte *m.*; **3.** (*in game*) total *m.* (des points); ~**-board** *s.* tableau *m.*; **4.** (*mus.*) partition *f.*; **5.** (*twenty*) vingt, vingtaine *f.*; **6.** (*category*) question *f.*; **on that ~,** à cet égard; **on the ~ of,** à cause de; **to pay off old ~s,** régler de vieux comptes; *v.t.* (1) entailler; (*techn.*) gratteler; (2) enregistrer; (3) gagner (des points), (*a goal*) marquer (un but), (*a try*) faire (un essai); (4) orchestrer; ~ **off s.o.** (*pop.*) faire marcher qn.; ~ **out** *v.t.* rayer; ~ **over s.o.,** l'emporter sur qn.; ~**r** *s.* marqueur *m.*
scoria *s.* scorie *f.*
scorn *s.* mépris *m.*; *v.t.* mépriser; *v.i.* (~ *to do sth.*) trouver indigne de soi de faire qch.; ~**ful** *adj.* méprisant; ~**fully** *adv.* avec mépris.
Scorpio *s.* (*astron.*) scorpion *m.*
scorpion *s.* scorpion *m.*
scot-free *adv.* sain et sauf.
Scot *s.* écossais(e) *m.f.*
Scotch[1] *s.* (*whisky*) scotch *m.*; (*lang.*) écossais *m.*; *adj.* écossais; ~**man,** ~**woman** *s.* écossais(e) *m.f.*; ~ **tape** *s.* ruban adhésif *m.*; ~ **terrier** *s.* scottish terrier *m.*
scotch[2] *v.t.* annuler; (*crush*) supprimer.
Scotland *s.* (*geog.*) Écosse *f.*; **S~ Yard** (*equivalent*) la Sûreté *f.*
Scots *adj.* & *s.m.* (*lang.*) écossais.
Scottish *adj. see* SCOTCH.
scoundrel *s.* malfaiteur *m.*; ~**ly** *adj.* scélérat.
scour *v.t.* (*clean*) nettoyer; (*pan*) récurer; (*remove grease*) dégraisser; (*country*) parcourir.
scourge *s.* fouet *m.*; (*fig.*) fléau *m.*; *v.t.* fouetter, flageller.
scout *s.* (*mil.*) éclaireur *m.*; (*boy*) scout *m.*; ~ **car** *s.* engin de reconnaissance *m.*; *v.i.* aller en reconnaissance; *v.t.* repousser avec dédain; ~ **about** *or* **around for,** chercher.
scowl *s.* mine renfrognée *f.*, air maussade *m.*; *v.i.* se renfrogner.
scrabble *v.i.* gratter çà et là; ~ **for,** chercher à quatre pattes.
scragg/y *adj.* décharné; ~**iness** *s.* maigreur *f.*
scram *v.i.* (*pop.*) décamper; ~**!** (*command, pop.*) fiche(z) le camp!
scramble *s.* **1.** (*rough walk*) escalade *f.*; **2.** (*auto.*) moto-cross *m.*; **3.** (*competition*) bousculade *f.*; *v.t.* & *i.* (1) escalader, ramper; (3) se battre

(pour); **4.** (*cook.*) brouiller; **~d** EGGS; **5.** (*telephone*) brouiller.

scrap *s.* **1.** (*small piece*) morceau *m.*; **2.** (*waste material*) bout *m.*; **~s** *pl.* restes *m.pl.*, bouts *m.pl.*; **3.** (*press cutting*) coupure *f.*; **4.** (*pop.* = *fight*) *bagarre f.*; **to sell for ~,** vendre à la casse; **~-book** *s.* album *m.*; **~-heap** *s.* tas de ferraille *m.*; **~-merchant** *s.* ferrailleur *m.*; **~-metal** *s.* ferraille *f.*; **~py** *adj.* fragmenté, plein de lacunes, (*style*) décousu; *v.t.* (2) mettre au rebut, mettre au rancart; *v.i.* (4) se bagarrer.

scrape *s.* (*act*) grattage *m.*; (*sound*) grincement *m.*; (*awkward situation*) mauvais pas *m.*; *v.i.* (*sound*) grincer; **bow and ~,** faire des courbettes; *v.t.* (*clean*) gratter, racler; (*pass closely*) frôler; *v.i.* (*economize*) vivoter; **~ off** *or* **out,** racler; **~ through** *v.i.* réussir de justesse; **~ together,** amasser sou à sou; **~r** *s.* racloir *m.*, (*for shoes*) décrottoir *m.*

scratch *s.* **1.** (*wound*) égratignure *f.*, (*of nail*) coup d'ongle *m.*, (*of claw*) coup de griffe *m.*; **2.** (*sound*) grincement *m.*; **3.** (*sport*) scratch *m.*; **to come up to ~,** s'exécuter; **to start from ~,** partir de rien; **from ~,** à partir de zéro; *adj.* (*team*) de fortune, (*improvised*) improvisé, sommaire; *v.t.* (1) égratigner, griffer, (*rub*) gratter; (3) scratcher; *v.i.* (1) griffer, se gratter; (3) renoncer (à concourir); **~ out** *v.t.* rayer.

scrawl *s.* griffonnage *m.*; *v.t.* griffonner.

scrawny *adj.* décharné.

scream *s.* **1.** (*cry*) cri *m.*; (*of pain*) hurlement *m.*; **2.** (*pop. sth. comic*) truc tordant *m.*; **it's a ~,** c'est marrant; *v.t.* & *i.* (1) crier; hurler; (*with laughter*) rire aux larmes; **~ing** *s.* cris *m.pl.*; hurlements *m.pl.*; **~ing** *adj.* (*sound*) perçant; (*colours*) voyant.

scree *s.* éboulis *m.*

screech *s.* cri perçant *m.*; *v.i.* pousser des cris perçants; ~-OWL.

screed *s.* tirade *f.*; (*fam.*) tartine *f.*

screen *s.* **1.** (*partition*) paroi *m.*, clôture *f.*; ROOD-~; **2.** (*shield*) écran *m.*, (*mil.*, *naut.*) rideau *m.*; **smoke-~,** rideau de fumée *m.*; WIND~; **3.** (*movable piece of furniture*) paravent *m.*; **4.** (*cinema*, *TV*, *for display*, *etc.*) écran *m.*; **5.** (*sieve*) claie *f.*; **6.** (*grid or mesh*) treillage *m.*; **~-play** *s.* (*cinema*) texte *m.*; *v.t.* (1), (2), (3) (*shelter*) abriter, (*hide*) cacher, (*protect*) protéger (par un écran), (*fig. from blame*) soustraire à; **~ off,** abriter derrière un paravent; (4) projeter, (*a novel*, *etc.*) porter à l'écran; (5) cribler, (*fig. persons*) trier; **~ing** *s.* (*med.*) dépistage *m.*

screw *s.* **1.** (*for wood etc.*) vis *f.*; **2.** (*naut.*, *aviat.*) hélice *f.*; **3.** (*miser*) grippe-sou *m.*; **4.** (*of paper*, *etc.*) cornet *m.*; **5.** (*pop. salary*) salaire *m.*; **6.** (*poor horse*) rosse *f.*; **he has a ~ loose,** il lui manque une case; **~driver** *s.* tournevis *m.*; *v.t.* & *i.* (1) (se) visser; **~ down** *or* **in,** visser; **~ sth. out of s.o.,** extorquer qch. à qn.; **~ up** *v.t.* (*face*) contracter, (*courage*) rassembler, (*paper*, *etc.*) froisser.

scribble *s.* griffonnage *m.*; *v.t.* griffonner; **~r** *s.* écrivailleur *m.*

scribe *s.* scribe *m.*

scrimmage *s.* mêlée *f.*; *v.i.* se bousculer.

scrimpy *adj.* chiche.

scrip *s.* (*obs. wallet*) besace *f.*; (*fin.*) certificat provisoire *m.* (d'actions).

script *s.* (*handwriting*, ≠ *print*) écriture *f.*; (*exam paper*) copie *f.*; (*manuscript*) manuscrit *m.*; (*of play*) texte *m.*; (*of film*) scénario *m.*

scriptur/e *s.* écriture sainte *f.*; **~al** *adj.* biblique; ⚠ scriptural *is gen. a financial term.*

scrivener *s.* (*hist.*) écrivain public *m.*, notaire *m.*, changeur *m.*

scroful/a *s.* scrofule *f.*; **~ous** *adj.* scrofuleux.

scroll *s.* rouleau *m.*; (*arch.*) volute *f.*

scroop *s.* grincement *m.*; *v.i.* grincer.

scrotum *s.* scrotum *m.*

scrounge *v.t.* & *i.* (*pop.*) (*steal*) chiper; (*sth. out of s.o.*) écornifler qch. à qn.

scrub[1] *s.* broussailles *f.pl.*; **~by** *adj.* (*land*) broussailleux; (*animal*) rabougri.

scrub[2] *v.t.* frotter, nettoyer à la brosse; (*pop.* = *cancel*) annuler; **~bing-brush,** brosse de chiendent *f.*

scruff *s.* nuque *f.*; **by the ~ of the neck,** (*person*) au collet; (*animal*) par la peau du cou; **~y** *adj.* (*pop.*) miteux.

scrum *s.* (*rugby*; *pop. crowd*) mêlée *f.*; ~-HALF.

scrummage *s.* mêlée *f.*; *v.i.* se mettre en mêlée.

scrumptious *adj.* (*pop.*) épatant.

scrup/le *s.* (*weight*; *doubt*) scrupule *m.*; (*minute quantity*) grain *m.*; *v.i.* se faire scrupule de; **~ulous** *adj.* scrupuleux; **~ulously** *adv.**; **~ulousness** *s.* esprit scrupuleux *m.*

scrutin/ize *v.t.* scruter; **~eer** *s.* scrutat/eur, -rice *m.f.*; **~izing** *adj.* scrutateur; **~y** *s.* examen rigoureux *m.*; ⚠ scrutin = **vote.**

scud *s.* rafale *f.*; *v.i.* galoper, fuir; (*naut.*) avoir vent arrière.

scuff *v.t.* érafler; *v.i.* traîner les pieds.

scuffle *s.* bagarre *f.*; *v.i.* se bagarrer.

scull *s.* **1.** (*light oar*) aviron *m.*; **2.** (*stern oar*) godille *f.*; *v.i.* (1) ramer; (2) avancer à la godille; **~er** *s.* rameur *m.*

scullery *s.* arrière-cuisine *f.*

scullion *s.* marmiton *m.*

sculpt/ure *s.* sculpture *f.*; *v.t.* sculpter; **~or** *s.* sculpteur *m.*; **~ress** *s.* femme sculpteur *f.*; **~ural** *adj.* sculptural.

scum *s.* (*lit.* & *fig.*) écume *f.*; *v.t.* écumer.

scupper *s.* dalot *m.*; *v.t.* (*sink ship*) saborder; (*pop. do for*) massacrer; (*fig.*) saboter.

scurf *s.* pellicules *f.pl.*

scurril/ity *s.* **1.** (*of action*) grossièreté *f.*; **2.** (*of person*) bassesse *f.*; **~ous** *adj.* (1) grossier; (2) ignoble.

scurry *s.* **1.** (*rush*) débandade *f.*; **2.** (*of snow*, *etc.*) tourbillon *m.*; *v.i.* (1) courir à la hâte; (*fam.*) se cavaler.

scurv/y *s.* scorbut *m.*; *adj.* bas, vil; **~ily** *adv.* bassement.

scut *s.* couette *f.*

scuttle *s.* **1.** (*for coal*) seau à charbon *m.*; **2.** (*auto.*) tablier *m.*; **3.** (*naut.*) hublot *m.*; **4.** (*flight*) galopade *f.*; *v.t.* (*naut.*) saborder; *v.i.* (4) courir; **~ away, off,** détaler.

scythe *s.* faux *f.*; *v.t.* faucher.

sea *s.* (*lit.* & *fig.*) mer *f.*; OPEN ~; (*large no.*) multitude *f.*; **to be (all) at ~,** (*lit.*) être en mer (*fig.*) avoir perdu le nord; **to put to ~,** prendre le large; **between the** DEVIL **and the deep blue ~;** *adj.* (*battle*) naval; (*transport*) maritime; (*air*, *life*, *etc.*) marin; **~ anchor** *s.* ancre flottante *f.*; **~ anemone** *s.* actinie *f.*; **~board** *s.* littoral *m.*; **~-chest** *s.* coffre de bord *m.*; **~ coal** *s.* houille *f.*; **~-dog** *s.* (*person*) loup de mer *m.*; **~farer** *s.* marin *m.*; **~faring** *adj.* marin; **~food** *s.* fruits de mer *m.pl.*; **~ front** *s.* esplanade *f.*; **~going** *adj.* (*person*) marin, (*ship*) de long cours, (*trade*) maritime; **~-green,** vert de mer; **~-gull** *s.* mouette *f.*; **~-kale** *s.* chou marin *m.*; **~-legs** *s.* pied marin *m.*; **~-level** *s.* niveau de la mer *m.*; **~-lion** *s.* otarie *f.*; **~man** *s.* marin *m.*; **~manship** *s.* matelotage *m.*; **~plane** *s.* hydravion *m.*; **~port** *s.* port *m.* (de mer); **~scape** *s.* marine *f.*; **~ shell** *s.* coquillage *m.*; **~-shore** *s.* plage *f.*; **to be ~sick,** avoir le mal de mer; **~sickness** *s.* mal de mer *m.*; **~side** *s.* bord de la mer *m.*; **~side** RESORT; **~ trout** *s.* truite saumonée *f.*; **~-urchin** *s.* oursin *m.*; **~-wall** *s.* digue *f.*; **~ward** *adj.* du large, *adv.* vers le large; **~weed** *s.* algue *f.*; **~worthy** *adj.* en état de naviguer; **~worthiness** *s.* navigabilité *f.*

seal[1] *s.* **1.** (*wax impression; metal stamp; of office*) sceau *m.*; (*private*) cachet *m.*; **2.** (*to close aperture*) plomb *m.*; (*techn.*) joint étanche *m.*; PRIVY ~; *v.t.* (1) sceller, cacheter; (2) sceller, boucher; **3.** (*ratify*) confirmer; **~ing-wax** *s.* cire à cacheter *f.*

seal[2] *s.* (*animal*) phoque *m.*; **~skin** *s.* peau de phoque *f.*, phoque *m.*

seam *s.* **1.** (*sewing, naut.*) couture *f.*; **2.** (*joint*) joint *m.*; **3.** (*geol.*) couche *f.*, gisement *m.*; **~less** *adj.* sans couture; **~stress** *s.* couturière *f.*; **~y side** *s.* (*fig.*) le revers de la médaille *m.*; *v.t.* (1) faire une couture à.

seance *s.* séance *f.*

sear *v.t.* (*med.*) cautériser; (*agric.*) dessécher.

search *s.* **1.** (*quest*) recherche *f.*; **in ~ of,** à la recherche de; **2.** (*customs*) visite *f.*; **3.** (*law*) perquisition *f.*; **4.** (*of prisoner*) fouille *f.*; **~light** *s.* projecteur *m.*; **~-party** *s.* expédition de secours *f.*; **~-warrant** *s.* mandat de perquisition *m.*; *v.t.* (1) chercher; (2) visiter; (4) fouiller; (*fig. memory etc.*) scruter; *v.i.* fouiller, faire des recherches; **~ for,** chercher; **~er** *s.* chercheur *m.*; **~ing** *adj.* (*look*) pénétrant, (*study*) approfondi, (*inspection*) rigoureux; **~ingly** *adv.* de façon approfondie, rigoureusement.

season *s.* saison *f.*; (*period of time*) période *f.*, temps *m.*; **in ~** (*agric.*) de saison, (*fig.*) opportun; **~-ticket** *s.* carte d'abonnement *f.*; *v.t.* (*troops*) aguerrir; conditionner; (*wood*) dessécher; (*cook.*) assaisonner, épicer; (*fig.*) tempérer; **~able** *adj.* de saison, opportun; **~ably** *adv.* à propos; **~al** *adj.* des saisons, (*greetings, etc.*) de la saison; **~ing** *s.* assaisonnement *m.*

seat *s.* (*for sitting on*) siège *m.*; (*theat.*) place *f.*; (*auto., rail*) banquette *f.*; (*on council, in parl.*) siège *m.*; (*rump*) derrière *m.*; (*of garment*) siège *m.*; (*site*) siège *m.*; (*of war*) théâtre *m.*; (*country house*) maison de campagne *f.*; (*riding*) assiette *f.*; WINDOW-~; **to take a ~,** s'asseoir; **take your ~s,** en voiture!; ~-BELT; *v.t.* asseoir; (*provide with ~s*) fournir de chaises; *v.i.* (*action*) s'asseoir; **be ~ed,** être assis; **two,** *etc.* **-~er,** (auto, avion, etc.) à deux (etc.) places; **~ing** *s.* (*of guests*) disposition *f.*, (*capacity*) nombre de places assises *m.*

S.E.A.T.O. (*South-East Asia Treaty Organization*) OTASE *f.* (Organisation du Traité de l'Asie du Sud-Est).

secateurs *s.pl.* sécateur *m.sing.*

secede *v.i.* faire sécession.

secession *s.* sécession *f.*

seclude *v.t.* tenir éloigné (du monde); *v.refl.* se tenir éloigné, se tenir à l'écart; **~d** *adj.* retiré.

seclusion *s.* retraite *f.*

second[1] *s.* (*supporter*) (*in duel*) témoin *m.*, (*at boxing*) second *m.*; (*unit of time, measurement; class, gear, etc.; mus.*) seconde *f.*; **~s** *s.pl.* (*goods*) marchandises de deuxième qualité *f.pl.*; *adj.* (*after first*) second, deuxième; ⚠ (*with dates, kings, chapters*) deux; (*additional*) autre, nouveau; (*of lesser importance*) secondaire; (*inferior*) inférieur; **~-best** *adj.* numéro deux, *s.* pis-aller *m.*; **~-class** *adj.* de deuxième qualité, de seconde classe; **~ cousin** *s.* cousin issu de germain *m.*; ~ FIDDLE; **~-hand** *adj.* d'occasion; ~ OFFENCE; **~-rate** *adj.* de second ordre; **~ sight** *s.* seconde vue *f.*; **on ~** THOUGHTS; **~ly** *adv.* deuxièmement.

second[2] *v.t.* **1.** (*support*) appuyer; **2.** (*remove to other post*) détacher; (*mil.*) mettre en disponibilité; **~er** *s.* (1) celui qui appuie; **~ment** *s.* (2) détachement *m.*

secondary *adj.* (*of minor importance; not original*) secondaire; (*subordinate*) subordonné; **~ education** *s.* le secondaire *m.*; **~ school** *s.* établissement d'éducation secondaire *m.*

secrecy *s.* secret *m.*, discrétion *f.*

secret *s.* secret *m.*; **in ~,** en secret; *adj.* secret; (*place*) retiré; **~ive** *adj.* cachottier; **~ly** *adv.**

secretar/y *s.* secrétaire *m.f.*; (*minister*) & **S~y of State,** ministre *m.*; **~y-bird** *s.* serpentaire *m.*; **~ial** *adj.* de secrétaire; **~iat** *s.* secrétariat *m.*

secret/e *v.t.* **1.** (*conceal*) cacher; **2.** (*produce by ~ion*) sécréter; **~ion** *s.* (1) recel *m.*; (2) sécrétion *f.*

sect *s.* secte *m.*; **~arian** *adj.* sectaire.

section *s.* section *f.*; **~al** *adj.* de section.

sector *s.* secteur *m.*

secular *adj.* **1.** (≠ *eccles.*) séculier, laïque; **2.** (≠ *sacred*) temporel; **3.** (*lasting for centuries*) séculaire; **~ize** *v.t.* (1) séculariser, laïciser; **~ization** *f.* (1) sécularisation *f.*, laïcisation *f.*

secure *adj.* **1.** (*free from fear or danger*) en sûreté, à l'abri (*from*—de); **2.** (*impregnable*) ferme, solide; **3.** (*safe, reliable, firm*) sûr, assuré, ferme; **~ly** *adv.* (1) sûrement, sans danger, en sûreté; (2) fermement; (3) avec confiance; **~ness** *s.* sécurité *f.*; *v.t.* (*fortify*) fortifier; (*make safe*) mettre en sûreté; (*fasten firmly*) bien fermer, attacher solidement; (*obtain*) s'emparer de, se procurer; (*guarantee*) garantir.

security *s.* (*state*) sûreté *f.*; (*feeling*) sécurité *f.*; (*guarantee*) garantie *f.*; (*guarantor*) garant *m.*, caution *f.*; (*surety*) cautionnement *m.*; (*stock certificate*) valeurs *f.pl.*; **S~ Council,** Conseil de Sécurité *m.*; **~ risk** *s.* homme peu sûr *m.*

sedan *s.* (*chair*) chaise à porteurs *f.*; (*auto.*) conduite intérieure *f.*

sedat/e *adj.* (*composed*) rassis; (≠ *lively*) calme, posé; **~ely** *adv.* calmement; **~eness** *s.* calme *m.*; *v.t.* tranquilliser; **~ion** *s.* sédation *f.*; **~ive** *adj.* & *s.m.* sédatif.

sedentary *adj.* sédentaire.

sedge *s.* laîche *f.*

sediment *s.* (*dregs*) lie *f.*, dépôt *m.*; (*geol.*) sédiment *m.*; **~ary** *adj.* sédimentaire; **~ation** *s.* sédimentation *f.*

sediti/on *s.* sédition *f.*; **~ous** *adj.* séditieux; **~ously** *adv.**.

seduc/e *v.t.* **1.** (*corrupt*) corrompre; **2.** (*woman* & *fig.*) séduire; **~er** *s.* séduct/eur, -rice *m.f.*; **~tion** *s.* (1) corruption *f.*; (2) séduction *f.*; **~tive** *adj.* séduisant.

sedul/ous *adj.* assidu; **~ity** *s.* assiduité *f.*; **~ously** *adv.* assidûment.

see[1] *s.* (*eccles.*) évêché *m.*; **the Holy S~,** le Saint-Siège *m.*

see[2] *v.t.* & *i.* voir; (*look at*) regarder; (*understand*) comprendre; (*give audience to*) recevoir; (*escort*) accompagner, raccompagner; **~ double,** voir double; **~ which way the** WIND **blows; let us ~!,** voyons!; **~ about,** s'occuper de; **~ s.o. home,** reconduire qn.; **~ s.o. off,** venir dire au revoir à qn.; **~ out,** reconduire; **~ over,** visiter; **~ through,** (*plan, disguise*) pénétrer, (*accomplish*) mener (qch.) à bonne fin; **~ to,** s'occuper de; **~ to it that,** veiller à ce que; **~ that,** s'assurer que; **~ing that,** vu que.

seed *s.* (*for sowing*) semence *f.*; (*of plant; ~like thing*) graine *f.*; (*pip*) pépin *m.*; (*fig.*) germe *m.*; (*tennis*) tête de série *f.*, **no. 2 etc. ~,** tête de série numéro deux, etc.; **to go** *or* **run to ~** (*lit.* & *fig.*) monter en graine; *adj.* de semence; **~-bed** *s.* (*lit.* & *fig.*) pépinière *f.*; **~-corn** *s.* blé de semence *m.*; **~-pearl** *s.* petite perle *f.*; **~-potato** *s.* pomme de terre de semence *f.*; **~sman** *s.* grainetier *m.*; **~-time** *s.* semailles *f.pl.*; **~ling** *s.* semis *m.*; **~y** *adj.* plein de graines, (*clothes*) râpé, (*person*) miteux, (*ill*) souffrant; *v.i.* monter en graine; *v.t.* (*sow*) semer; (*remove ~s from*) épépiner; (*sport*) trier.

seek *v.t.* & *i.* (*look for*) chercher; (*request*) demander; HIDE **and ~**; **~ for,** rechercher; **~ out,** chercher; **~ to do,** s'efforcer de, chercher

à, faire; **sought after** *adj.* recherché; **~er** *s.* chercheur *m.*
seem *v.i.* (*have appearance of*) sembler, avoir l'air; **he ~s honest,** il semble être honnête; **he ~s tired,** il a l'air fatigué; (*appear to be*) paraître; **that ~s fair to me,** cela me paraît juste; (*have a feeling of*) avoir l'impression de/que; **I ~ to know him,** j'ai l'impression que je le connais; **or so it ~s,** du moins à ce qu'il me semble; **~ing** *adj.* apparent; **~ingly** *adv.* en apparence.
seeml/y *adj.* bienséant; **~iness** *s.* bienséance *f.*
seep *v.i.* suinter; **~age** *s.* suintement *m.*
seer *s.* prophète *m.f.*
seersucker *s.* (*text.*) cloqué *m.*
see-saw *s.* bascule *f.*; *adj.* en bascule; *v.i.* jouer à la bascule; (*fig.*) balancer.
seethe *v.i.* bouillonner.
segment *s.* (*math.*, *arch.*) segment *m.*; (*of orange, etc.*) tranche *f.*; **~ary** *adj.* segmentaire.
segregat/e *v.t.* séparer; **~ion** *s.* ségrégation *f.*
seine *s.* (*fishing net*) seine *f.*
seism/ic *adj.* sismique; **~ograph** *s.* sismographe *m.*; **~ology** *s.* sismologie *f.*; **~ologist** *s.* sismologue *m.f.*
seiz/e *v.t.* (*lit.* & *fig.*; *law*) saisir; *v.i.* (*mech.*) (se) gripper; **~e up,** caler; **~ure** *s.* (*capture*) prise *f.*; (*med.*) attaque *f.*
seldom *adv.* rarement.
select *adj.* (*choice*) choisi, de choix; (*exclusive*) d'élite; *v.t.* choisir, sélectionner; **~ion** *s.* choix *m.*, sélection *f.*; **~ive** *adj.* sélectif.
self *s.* individualité *f.*, le moi *m.*; *adj.* (*colour*) uniforme, de même; *pron. see* HER~, HIM~, **etc.**
self- *prefix* **~-abasement** *s.* humiliation *f.*; **~-adjusting** *adj.* à réglage automatique; **~-assertion** *s.* arrogance *f.*; **~-assertive** *adj.* arrogant; **~-assurance** *s.* assurance *f.*; **~-centred** *adj.* egocentrique; **~-closing** *adj.* à fermeture automatique; **~-coloured** *adj.* de couleur naturelle; **~-command** *s.* maîtrise de soi *f.*; **~-conceit** *s.* suffisance *f.*; **~-confidence** *s.* confiance en soi *f.*; **~confident** *adj.* sûr de soi, de lui etc.; **~-conscious** *adj.* gêné; **~-consciousness** *s.* gêne *f.*; **~-contained** *adj.* (*person*) peu communicatif, (*flat*) avec entrée particulière; **~-control** *s.* maîtrise de soi *f.*; **~-defence** *s.* défense légitime *f.* **~-denial** *s.* abnégation *f.*; **~-determination** *s.* libre disposition *f.*; **~-effacing** *adj.* discret; **~-effacement** *s.* discrétion *f.*; **~-employed** *adj.* qui travaille à son propre compte; **~-esteem** *s.* amour-propre *m.*; **~-evident** *adj.* évident; **~-explanatory** *adj.* qui s'explique de soi-même; **~-expression** *s.* expression spontanée *f.*; **~-government** *s.* autonomie *f.*; **~-governing** *adj.* autonome; **~-help** *s.* effort personnel *m.*; **~-important** *adj.* suffisant; **~-imposed** *adj.* volontaire; **~-indulgent** *adj.* qui ne se refuse rien; **~-interest** *s.* égoïsme *m.*; **~-made** *adj.* parti de rien; **~-opinionated** *adj.* entêté; **to indulge in ~-pity,** s'apitoyer sur son propre compte; **~-portrait** *s.* auto-portrait *m.*; **~-possessed** *adj.* calme; **~-possession** *s.* sang-froid *m.*; **~-preservation** *s.* instinct de conservation *m.*; **~-propelling** *adj.* autopropulsé; **~-raising flour,** farine avec levure incorporée *f.*; **~-regulating** *adj.* à autoréglage; **~-reliant** *adj.* indépendant; **~-respect** *s.* dignité *f.*; **~-sacrifice** *s.* sacrifice de soi *m.*; **~-satisfied** *adj.* suffisant; **~-seeking** *adj.* égoïste; **~-service,** libre service; **~-starter** *s.* démarreur automatique *m.*; **~-styled** *adj* soi-disant; **~-sufficiency** *s.* suffisance *f.*; **~-sufficient** *adj.* indépendant; **~-taught** *adj.* autodidacte; **~-will** *s.* obstination *f.*; **~-willed** *adj.* entêté; **~-winding** (*watch*) à remontage automatique.
self/ish *adj.* égoïste; **~ishly** *adv.* par égoïsme; **~ishness** *s.* égoïsme *m.*; **~less** *adj.* altruiste; **~lessly** *adv.* de façon altruiste; **~lessness** *s.* altruisme *m.*
selfsame *adj.* identique.
sell *s.* (*fam. hoax*) blague *f.*; (*disappointment*) déception *f.*; *v.t.* & *i.* (se) vendre; **~ like hot** CAKES; (*advertise*) faire de la réclame pour; **~ at/for,** (se) vendre à/pour; **~ off** *v.t.* liquider; **~ out** *v.t.* (*exhaust stock*) épuiser, (*fin.*) réaliser; **~ up** (*law*) faire saisir; **~able** *adj.* vendable; **~er** *s.* vend/eur, -euse *m.f.*; **best ~er** *s.* succès de librairie *m.*; **~ing price** *s.* prix de vente *m.*
sellotape *s.* ruban adhésif *m.*
selvage, selvedge *s.* lisière *f.*
semantic *adj.* sémantique; **~s** *s.* sémantique *f.* ⚠ *sing. in French.*
semaphore *s.* sémaphore *m.*; *v.t.* & *i.* transmettre par sémaphore.
semblance *s.* apparence *f.*
sem/en *s.* sperme *m.*; **~inal** *adj.* séminal.
semi- *prefix* (*half*) demi-, semi-; (*barely*) à peine; **~breve** *s.* ronde *f.*; **~circle** *s.* demi-cercle *m.*; **~circular** *adj.* semi-circulaire; **~-civilized** *adj.* à peine civilisé; **~colon** *s.* point-virgule *m.*; **~-conscious** *adj.* à demi conscient; **~-detached** *adj.* jumelé; **~final** *s.* demi-finale *f.*; **~quaver** *s.* double-croche *f.*; **~-skilled workman,** ouvrier spécialisé *m.*; **~tone** *s.* demi-ton *m.*
seminar *s.* colloque *m.*, séminaire *m.*
seminar/y *s.* séminaire *m.*; **~ist** *s.* séminariste *m.*
Semit/e *s.* sémite *m.f.*; **~ic** *adj.* sémitique.
semolina *s.* semoule *f.*
sempiternal *adj.* sempiternel.
senat/e *s.* sénat *m.*; **~or** *s.* sénateur *m.*; **~orial** *adj.* sénatorial.
send *v.t.* (*sth.*) expédier; (*s.o.*) envoyer; (*drive* (*mad, etc.*)) rendre (fou, etc.); **~ word of sth. to s.o.,** faire savoir qch. à qn.; **~ away** *v.t.* renvoyer, chasser; **~ back** *v.t.* renvoyer; **~ down** (*from Univ.*) exclure; **~ for** *v.t.* envoyer chercher, faire venir; **~ forth** *v.t.* émettre; **~ off** *v.t.* expédier; **~-off** *s.* départ *m.*; **~ on** *v.t.* (*letters, etc.*) faire suivre; **~ out** *v.t.* répandre; **~-up** *s.* (*fam.*) démystification *f.*; **~er** *s.* expéditeur *m.*; **~ing** *s.* envoi *m.*, expédition *f.*
Senegal *s.* (*geog.*) Sénégal *m.*; **~ese** *adj.* & *s.m.f.* sénégalais(e).
senescen/t *adj.* sénescent; **~ce** *s.* sénescence *f.*
seneschal *s.* sénéchal *m.*
senil/e *adj.* sénile; **~ity** *s.* sénilité *f.*
senior *s.* (*in age*) aîné *m.*; (*in rank*) supérieur *m.*; *adj.* (*in age*) aîné; (*in rank*) supérieur; (*clerk, etc.*) premier; (*partner, etc.*) principal; **~ citizen** *s.* personne du troisième âge; **~ity** *s.* ancienneté *f.*, (*right*) droit d'ancienneté *m.*
senna *s.* séné *m.*
sensation *s.* sensation *f.*; **~al** *adj.* sensationnel.
sense *s.* **1.** (*faculty*); **2.** (*perception*); **3.** (*meaning*) sens *m.*; **~ of** HEAR**ing; ~ of** HUMOUR; **~ of** SMELL; **~ of** TASTE; **4.** (*practical wisdom*) jugement *m.*; COMMON **~**; **5.** (*feeling*) sentiment *m.*; **6.** (*prevailing view*) opinion *f.*; **~s** *s.pl.* (*sanity*) équilibre mental *m.*, (*med.*) connaissance *f.*; **~less** *adj.* insensé, (*med.*) sans connaissance; **~lessly** *adv.* de façon insensée; **~lessness** *s.* absurdité *f.*; *v.t.* (1) percevoir; (5) pressentir.
sensib/le *adj.* **1.** (*having good sense*): (*person*) sensé, (*thing*) judicieux; **2.** (*not unaware of*) conscient (de); **3.** (*perceptible by senses*) sensible; **~ly** *adv.* (1) raisonnablement; (3) sensiblement; **~ility** *s.* (3) sensibilité *f.*
sensit/ive *adj.* (*affected*) sensible (*to*—à); (*touchy*) ombrageux; **~iveness** *s.*, **~ivity** *s.* sensibilité *f.*; **~ize** *v.t.* sensibiliser.
sensor *s.* détecteur *m.*

sensory *adj.* sensoriel.
sensual *adj.* sensuel; **~ity** *s.* sensualité *f.*; **~ly** *adv.* de manière sensuelle.
sensuous *adj.* voluptueux.
sentence *s.* **1.** (*ling.*) phrase *f.*; **2.** (*law*) jugement *m.*; *v.t.* (2) condamner; ⚠ sentence = **verdict.**
sententious *adj.* sentencieux; **~ly** *adv.**.
sentien/t *adj.* sensible; **~ce** *s.* **~cy** *s.* sensibilité *f.*
sentiment *s.* (*mental attitude, feeling*) sentiment *m.*; (*tendency to be emotional*) sensiblerie *f.*; **~al** *adj.* sentimental; **~alist** *s.* personne sentimentale *f.*; **~ally** *adv.* d'une manière sentimentale; **~ality** *s.* sentimentalité *f.*
sentinel, sentry *s.* sentinelle *f.*; **sentry-box** *s.* guérite *f.*; **to be on sentry-go,** être de faction.
sepal *s.* sépale *m.*
separ/ate *adj.* séparé, à part; (*independent*) particulier, indépendant; **~ately** *adv.* séparément; **~ateness** *s.* séparation *f.*; **~atism** *s.* séparatisme *m.*; **~atist** *s.* séparatiste *m.f.*; **~ates** *s.pl.* (*dress*) coordonnés *m.pl.*; *v.t.* & *i.* (se) séparer; (*part from*) (se) détacher (de); (*cream*) écrémer; **~able** *adj.* séparable; **~ation** *s.* séparation *f.*; **~ator** *s.* (*mech.*) séparateur *m.*
sepia *s.* sépia *f.*
sepoy *s.* cipaye *m.*
sepsis *s.* septicémie *f.*
September *s.* septembre *m.*
septen/ary *adj.* septénaire; **~nial** *adj.* septennal.
septet *s.* (*mus.*) septuor *m.*
septic *adj.* septique; **~ tank** *s.* fosse septique *f.*; **~æmia** *s.* septicémie *f.*
septuagenarian *adj.* & *s.m.f.* septuagénaire.
Septuagesima *s.* septuagésime *f.*
septuple *adj.* & *s.m.* septuple; *v.t.* septupler; **~t** *s.m.f.* septuplé(e).
sepulchr/e *s.* sépulcre *m.*; **~al** *adj.* sépulcral, caverneux.
sepulture *s.* sépulture *f.*
sequel *s.* (*of story, etc.*) suite *f.*; (*result*) conséquence *f.*
sequence *s.* (*succession, series*) suite *f.*; (*set*) série *f.*; (*cinema*; *cards*) séquence *f.*
sequest/er *v.t.* **1.** (*isolate*) isoler; **2.** (*confiscate*) séquestrer; **~ered** *adj.* (1) écarté; (2) séquestré; **~rate** *v.t.* (*law*) mettre sous séquestre; **~ration** *s.* (1) retraite *f.*; (2) (*of person*) séquestration *f.*; (*of property*) séquestre *m.*
sequin *s.* sequin *m.*
seraglio *s.* sérail *m.*
seraph *s.* séraphin *m.*; **~ic** *adj.* séraphique.
Serb/ia *s.* (*geog.*) Serbie *f.*; **~(ian)** *adj.* & *s.m.f.* serbe; *s.m.* (*lang.*) serbe; **~o-Croat,** serbo-croate *m.*
sere *adj.* desséché.
serenade *s.* sérénade *f.*; *v.t.* donner une sérénade à.
seren/e *adj.* serein; (*title*) sérénissime; **~ity** *s.* sérénité *f.*; **~ly** *adv.* avec sérénité.
serf *s.* serf *m.*, serve *f.*; **~dom** *s.* servage *m.*
serge *s.* serge *f.*
sergeant *s.* (*cavalry, artillery*) maréchal des logis *m.*; (*infantry, aviat.*) sergent *m.*; (*police*) brigadier *m.*; **~-major,** adjudant *m.*; ⚠ sergent-major = **N.C.O. in charge of accounts.**
serial *s.* feuilleton *m.*; *adj.* en série; **~ize** *v.t.* faire paraître en feuilleton.
seriatim *adv.* successivement.
series *s.* série *f.*; (*of books*) collection *f.*; **in ~,** en série.
serif *s.* (*print.*) empattement *m.*
serious *adj.* sérieux; (*important*) important; (*error*) gros; (*illness*) grave; **~ly** *adv.* sérieusement, (*ill*) gravement; **to take sth. ~ly,** prendre qch. au sérieux; **~ness** *s.* sérieux *m.*
sermon *s.* sermon *m.*; (*Protestant*) prêche *m.*; **~ize** *v.t.* sermonner.
serpent *s.* serpent *m.*; **young ~,** serpenteau *m.*; **~ine** *s.* serpentine *f.*, *adj.* de serpent, (*fig.*) sinueux.
serrated *adj.* dentelé; (*roof*; *geol.*) en dents de scie.
serried *adj.* serré.
serum *s.* sérum *m.*
servant *s.* serviteur *m.*, servante *f.*; (*domestic*) domestique *m.f.*; (*of company*) employé *m.*; CIVIL ~.
serve *v.t.* & *i.* (*be servant to*) être au service de; (*be useful to*) rendre service à; (*in forces*; *food*; *in shop*; *tennis*) servir; (*be suitable to*) répondre à; (*be sufficient*) faire l'affaire; (*meet needs of, bus, train*; *priest, doctor, etc.*) desservir; (*writ*) notifier (*on*—à); (*sentence*) purger (sa peine); (*treat*) traiter; **~ as/for,** servir de; **a sofa ~s him as/for a bed,** un divan lui sert de lit; **~ to do,** servir à faire; **it ~s to show the futility of the process,** cela sert à montrer la futilité du procédé; **~ out** *v.t.* distribuer; **~ up** *v.t.* servir; **it ~s you** RIGHT; **~r** *s.* celui (celle) qui sert; *s.* (*tennis*) servant(e) *m.f.*
service *s.* (*being servant*; *benefit to s.o.*; *bus, train*; *tableware*; *tennis*) service *m.*; (*public ~*) administration *f.*, fonction publique *f.*; (*church ~*) office *m.*; (*assistance*) assistance *f.*; (*maintenance, auto, etc.*) entretien *m.*; (*tennis*) service *m.*; **~s** *s.pl.* forces armées *f.pl.*, armée *f.*; **senior ~,** marine *f.*; (*supply of water, gas, etc.*) commodités *f.pl.*; SELF-~; *v.t.* (*for machine*) entretenir; **~able** *adj.* (*person*) serviable, (*thing*) utile, (*lasting*) durable; **servicing** *s.* (*auto.*) service après-vente *m.*, entretien courant *m.*
serviette *s.* serviette (de table) *f.*
servil/e *adj.* servile; (*slavish*) asservi; **~ity** *s.* servilité *f.*; **~ely** *adv.* avec servilité.
servitor *s.* serviteur *m.*
servitude *s.* servitude *f.*; PENAL ~.
sesame *s.* sésame *m.*
session *s.* séance *f.*
set[1] *s.* **1.** (*of sun*) coucher *m.*; **2.** (*of wind*) direction *f.*; **3.** (*configuration*) configuration *f.*; **4.** (*fit*) disposition *f.*; **5.** (*of hair*) mise en plis *f.*; **6.** (*hort.*) plant *m.*; **7.** (*theat., cinema*) décor *m.*; **8.** (*paving block*) pavé *m.*; **9.** (*of badger*) terrier *m.*; **10.** (*of teeth*) dentition *f.*, (*of false teeth*) dentier *m.*; **11.** (*of people*) groupe *m.*, (*pej.*) bande *f.*; **12.** (*of things*) (*dishes*) service *m.*, (*jewels*) parure *f.*, (*tools*) trousse *f.*; **13.** (*series, collection*) série *f.*, assortiment *m.*, collection *f.*; **14.** (*tennis*) set *m.*; **15.** (*radio, TV*) poste *m.*; **16.** (*clothes*) ensemble *m.*, TWIN ~.
set[2] *v.t.* **1.** (*put, lay*) mettre; **2.** (*cause to stand*) placer, mettre debout; **3.** (*place ready*) disposer; **4.** (*cause to work*) mettre en marche; **5.** (*propose for solution*) proposer; **6.** (*give edge to, saw, etc.*) affiler; **7.** (*bones*) remettre; **8.** (*hort.*) planter; **9.** (*type*) composer; **10.** (*scene*) disposer, dresser; **11.** (*to music*) mettre en musique; **12.** (*gems*) monter; **13.** (*hair*) faire une mise en plis; **14.** (*clock*) régler; **15,** (*trap*) tendre; **16.** (*seal, hand, to sth.*) apposer (à); **17.** (*example*) donner; **18.** (*fashion*) lancer; *v.i.*; **19.** (*solidify*) se figer, (*cook.*) prendre; **20.** (*take shape, fruit, etc.*) se nouer; **21.** (*develop*) développer; **22.** (*sun*) se coucher; **~ one's** CAP **at; ~ on** FIRE, **~** FIRE **to; ~ on** FOOT; **~ to** RIGHTS; **~** SAIL; **~ one's** TEETH; **~ about sth.,** se mettre à qch.; **~ about s.o.,** attaquer qn,; **~ against,** opposer à; **~ oneself, one's face, against,** s'opposer à; **~ apart, ~ aside, ~ by,** mettre de côté; **~ back,** retarder, empêcher; **~-back** *s.* déception *f.*, revers *m.*; **~ down,** déposer; **~ forth** *v.t.* exposer, *v.i.* se mettre en route; **~ off** *v.t.* mettre en valeur, (*cause to explode*) faire exploser, *v.i.* se mettre en route; **~-off** *s.* compensation *f.*; **~ on** *v.t.* pousser à; **~ out** *v.t.* disposer, étaler,

v.i. se mettre en route; **~-out** *s.* étalage *m.*; **~ to,** se mettre à; **~-to** *s.* bagarre *f.*; **~ up** *v.t.* fonder, établir, dresser, *v.i.* s'établir; **~-up** *s.* organisation *f.*; **~ up for, ~ up as,** se donner pour; *adj.* (*prescribed*) prescrit; (*deliberate*) délibéré; (*formal*) formel; (*rigid*) fixe, immobile, (*fig.*) figé; (*ready*) prêt; (*mature*) mûr; (*fruit*) formé, **~ books,** livres *or* auteurs au programme; **~ fair** (*of weather*) beau fixe; **~ square** *s.* équerre *f.*

settee *s.* canapé *m.*

setter *s.* (dog) setter *m.*; (*mech.*) poseur *m.*; (*type-~*) compositeur *m.*

setting *s.* (*mus.*) mise en musique *f.*; (*of gem*) monture *f.*; (*environment*) cadre *m.*, milieu *m.*; (*theat.*) mise en scène *f.*; (*of limb*) remboîtement *m.*; (*at table*) couvert *m.*; *adj.* (*sun*) couchant.

settle[1] *s.* banc à haut dossier *m.*

settle[2] *v.t.* (*establish*) établir; (*agree on*) décider; (*colonize*) coloniser; (*deal with*) arranger; (*pay bill*) régler, payer; (*calm*) calmer, apaiser; (*fix*) fixer; (*date*) arrêter; (*solve*) résoudre; *v.i.* (*become established*) s'établir; (*cease wandering*) s'installer; (*sink, subside*) (*arch.*) se tasser, (*fig.*) s'apaiser; (*weather*) se mettre au beau; (*bird*) se poser; **~ down** *v.i.* s'établir; **~ in** *v.t.* & *i.* (s')installer; **~ (money) on,** assigner à; **~ up,** régler le compte; **~ with s.o.,** régler son compte à qn,; **~d** *adj.* arrangé; **~r** *s.* colon *m.*

settlement *s.* (*marriage*) contrat de mariage *m.*; (*group*) colonie *f.*; (*payment*) règlement *m.*; (*arrangement*) arrangement *m.*; (*arch.*) tassement *m.*

seven *s.* sept *m.*; **at** SIXES **and ~s; ~fold,** sept fois; **~th** *adj.* septième; **~teen,** dix-sept; **~teenth** *adj.* dix-septième; **~ty,** soixante-dix; **~tieth,** soixante-dixième.

sever *v.t.* & *i.* (se) séparer, (se) détacher; (*break, fig.*) rompre; **~ance** *s.* séparation *f.*; rupture *f.*; **~ance pay** *s.* indemnité de licenciement *f.*

several *adj.* (*a moderate number*) plusieurs; (*separate*) différent; *pron.* plusieurs; **~ly** *adv.* séparément.

sever/e *adj.* **1.** (*strict*) sévère; **2.** (*vehement*) violent; **3.** (*hard, weather, winter*) rigoureux; **4.** (*unadorned*) austère; **5.** (*med.*) (*illness*) grave, (*pain*) aigu; **~ity** *s.* (1) sévérité *f.*; (2) rudesse *f.*; (3) rigueur *f.*; (4) sobriété *f.*; (5) gravité *f.*, acuité *f.*; **~ely** *adv.* (1)*; (2) violemment; (3)*; (4)*; (5) (*ill*) gravement, (*wounded*) grièvement.

sew *v.t.* & *i.* coudre; **~ on,** coudre; **~ up** (*pop.*) agencer; **~er** *s.* couseu/r, -se, *m.f.*; **~ing** *s.* couture *f.*; **~ing-**MACHINE.

sew/age *s.* eaux d'égouts *f.pl.*; **~age-**FARM; **~er** *s.* égout *m.*; **~erage** *s.* système d'égouts *m.*

sex *s.* sexe *m.*; (*desire*) désir *m.*; (*copulation*) rapport sexuel *m.*; **~ appeal** *s.* sex-appeal *m.*; **~ual** *adj.* sexuel; **~ually** *adv.**; **~uality** *s.* sexualité *f.*; **~y** *adj.* (*pop.*) capiteux; *v.t.* déterminer le sexe de.

sexagenarian *adj.* & *s.m.f.* sexagénaire.

Sexagesima *s.* sexagésime *f.*

sextant *s.* sextant *m.*

sextet *s.* (*mus.*) sextuor *m.*

sexton *s.* sacristain *m.*

sextuple *adj.* & *s.m.* sextuple; *v.t.* sextupler; **~t** *s.* sextuplé(e) *m.f.*

sexual *see* SEX.

sexy *see* SEX.

shabb/y *adj.* **1.** (*worn, faded*) usé; **2.** (*badly dressed*) pauvrement vêtu, misérable; **3.** (*fig.*) vilain, mesquin; **~ily** *adv.*; (2) pauvrement, misérablement; (3) vilainement; **~iness** *s.* (1) état râpé *m.*; (2) pauvreté *f.*; (3) mesquinerie *f.*

shack *s.* cabane *f.*; *v.i.* (*pop.*) **~ up with,** cohabiter avcc.

shackle *s.* **1.** (*metal loop, staple*) maillon *m.*, anse *f.*; **2. ~s** *s.pl.* fers *m.pl.*, (*fig.*) entraves *f.pl.*; *v.t.* (1) mailler; (2) entraver.

shad/e *s.* **1.** (*darkness*) ombre *f.*; **2.** (*cool retreat*) ombrage *m.*; **3.** (*of colour*) nuance *f.*; **4.** (*small amount*) trace *f.*, soupçon *m.*; **5.** (*ghost*) ombre *f.*; **6.** (*screen*) écran *m.*, (*for lamp*) abat-jour *m.*; **7.** (*glass cover*) globe de verre *m.*; *v.t.* (1), (2) ombrager, (*art*) ombrer; (3) nuancer; (6) voiler, protéger; *v.i.* (3) se fondre (*into*—en); **~ed** *adj.* ombragé, (*art*) ombré, (*map*) hachuré; **~ing** *s.* ombres *f.pl.*; **~y** *adj.* ombragé, (*pop.* = *dishonest*) véreux.

shadow *s.* ombre *f.*; (*obscurity*) obscurité *f.*; (*shelter*) abri *m.*; **S~** CABINET; **~y** *adj.* ombragé, sombre, (*fig.*) chimérique, vague; *v.t.* obscurcir; (*follow*) filer.

shaft *s.* (*of spear, etc.*) hampe *f.*; (*mech.*) arbre *m.*; (*stem, stalk*) tige *f.*; (*arch.*) fût *m.*; (*arrow*) trait *m.*; (*of light, etc.*) trait *m.*; (*of harness*) brancart *m.*; (*of mine*) puits *m.*; (*of lift, etc.*) cage *f.*

shaggy *adj.* poilu; (*eyebrows*) en broussailles; (*hair*) ébouriffé; **~-dog story,** histoire de fous *f.*

shagreen *s.* peau de chagrin *f.*

shah *s.* schah *m.*

shak/e 1. *s.* (*jolt, jerk, shock*) secousse *f.*; (*mus.*) trille *f.*; (*of hand*) poignée (de main) *f.*; (*of head*) hochement *m.*; **~y** *adj.* branlant, tremblant, (*voice*) tremblotant, (*health*) détraqué, (*fig.*) mal assuré; **~ily** *adv.* en tremblant, d'une main tremblante, à pas chancelants.

shake[2] *v.t.* (*move violently, jolt, jar*) secouer; (*hands*) serrer (la main à qn.); (*cause to rock*) ébranler; (*brandish*) brandir; (*weaken*) ébranler; (*disturb*) bouleverser; **that shook him** (*fig.*) cela l'a fait tiquer; *v.i.* trembler (violemment), chanceler; (*voice*) trembloter; **~ down** *v.t.* faire tomber, *v.i.* (*fam.*) s'étendre; **~-down** *s.* (*pop.*) plumard de fortune *m.*; **~ off** *v.t.* (*get rid of*) se débarasser de, (*recover from*) se remettre de; **~ out** *v.t.* secouer; **~ up** (*lit.* & *fig.*) secouer; **~-up** *s.* (*fam.*) grand remaniement *m.*; **~r** *s.* (*cocktail*) shaker *m.*

shako *s.* shako *m.*

shale *s.* schiste *m.*

shall (*past. should*) *v. aux.* **1.** (*1st. person, future or conditional*) *use future or conditional tense*; **I ~ go, we ~ go,** j'irai, nous irons; **I should go,** j'irais; **2.** (*command, 2nd. or 3rd. person*) *use future or conditional tense*; **he ~ go,** il ira; **he should go,** il irait; **3.** (*obligation, any person*) devoir + *inf.*; **he ~ pay,** il doit payer; **we should go,** nous devrions aller; **you should have gone,** vous auriez dû aller; **4.** (*intention*) vouloir *or* aller + *inf.*; **I ~ go,** je veux (je vais) aller; **5.** (*in polite formulae*) **~ I go with you?,** voulez-vous que je vous accompagne?; **~ we dance?,** si nous dansions?

shallot *s.* échalote *f.*

shallow *s.* bas-fond *m.*; *adj.* peu profond; (*fig.*) superficiel, sans profondeur; **~ness** *s.* manque de profondeur *m.*; (*fig.*) caractère superficiel *m.*

sham *s.* **1.** (*pretence*) feinte *f.*, imposture *f.*; **2.** (*person*) imposteur *m.*; **3.** (*counterfeit thing*) faux *m.*, camelote *f.*; *adj.* (1) feint; (3) faux, de camelote, en toc; *v.t.* & *i.* simuler, faire semblant de.

shambl/e *v.i.* marcher en traînant les pieds; **~ing** *adj.* traînant.

shambles *s.* (*slaughter-house*) abattoir *m.*; (*scene of carnage*) scène de carnage *f.*; (*fam. confusion*) pagaille *f.*; **in a ~,** sens dessus-dessous.

shame *s.* honte *f.*; **for ~! what a ~!** (*how disgraceful*) quelle honte!; **what a ~!** (*how unlucky*) quel dommage!; **to put to ~,** faire honte à; **~faced** *adj.* timide; **~facedness** *s.* timidité *f.*; **~ful** *adj.* honteux; **~fully** *adv.**; **~less**

adj. éhonté, effronté; **~lessly** *adv.* effrontément; **~lessness** *s.* effronterie *f.*; *v.t.* faire honte à.
shampoo *s.* (*act* & *product*) shampooing *m.*; *v.t.* faire un shampooing à.
shamrock *s.* trèfle *m.*
shandy *s.* bière panachée *f.*, panaché *m.*
shank *s.* (*leg*) jambe *f.*; (*of horse*) canon *m.*; (*of key, etc.*) tige *f.*; **to go on S~'s pony,** prendre le train onze.
shantung *s.* shant(o)ung *m.*
shanty *s.* (*hut*) baraque *f.*; (*sea-song*) chanson (de bord) *m.*; **~ town** *s.* bidonville *f.*
shape *s.* (*form*) forme *f.*; **in the ~ of,** en forme de, sous la forme de; (*orderly arrangement*) bon état *m.*; (*pattern, mould*) moule *m.*; **to take ~,** prendre forme; **~less** *adj.* sans forme; **~ly** *adj.* bien tourné; **~liness** *s.* beauté de forme *f.*; *v.t.* former, façonner; (*plan*) esquisser; *v.i.* (*develop into*) se développer; **~ well,** promettre.
SHAPE (*abbrev. Supreme Headquarters Allied Powers in Europe*) Shape *m.*
shard *s.* tesson *m.*
share[1] *s.* (*plough*) soc *m.*
share[2] *s.* (*portion, contribution*) part *f.*; FAIR ~; **to have a ~ in,** contribuer à; **to go ~s in,** partager avec; (*fin.*) action *f.*; **~holder** *s.* actionnaire *m.f.*; *v.t.* & *i.* partager; **~ out** *v.t* répartir; **~-out** *s.* répartition *f.*
shark *s.* (*zool.* & *fig.*) requin *m.*; **~-skin** *s.* peau de requin *f.*
sharp *s.* (*mus.*) dièse *m.*; *adj.* **1.** (*≠ blunt*) tranchant; **2.** (*pointed*) aigu, pointu; **3.** (*steep*) raide; **4.** (*taste, smell*) âcre; **5.** (*voice, sound*) perçant, aigre; **6.** (*harsh*) (*wind*) pénétrant, piquant, (*words*) acerbe, sévère, (*criticism*) cinglant; **7.** (*pain*) violent; **8.** (*senses*) fin, perçant, pénétrant, vif; **9.** (*alert*) éveillé, malin, vigilant; **~shooter** *s.* tireur d'élite *m.*; **10.** (*unscrupulous*) (*person*) rusé, (*practice*) malhonnête; **11.** (*speedy*) rapide; **12.** (*mus.*) dièse; **13.** (*well-defined*) net; **14.** (*sudden*) brusque; **~ly** *adv.* (2) en pointe; (3) à pic; (5) d'un ton perçant; (6) d'un ton acerbe, sévèrement; (7) violemment; (8) vivement; (11)*; (13)*; (14)*; **~ness** *s.* (1), (2) acuité *f.*; (3) raideur *f.*; (4) âcreté *f.*, acidité *f.*; (5) âpreté *f.*, aigreur *f.*; (6) rigueur *f.*, acerbité *f.*, sévérité *f.*; (7) violence *f.*; (8) vivacité *f.*, finesse *f.*; (9) vivacité *f.*; (11) rapidité *f.*; (13) netteté *f.*; (14) brusquerie *f.*; *adv.* (*abruptly*) net, brusquement; **to pull up ~,** s'arrêter net; (*punctually*) exactement; **at 10 o'clock ~,** à dix heures précises; **~en** *v.t.* (*blade, appetite*) aiguiser, (*pencil*) tailler; **~er** *s.* escroc *m.*; CARD-**~er.**
shatter *v.t.* & *i.* (se) fracasser; (*fig.*) déranger; (*health*) détraquer; (*hopes*) anéantir.
shav/e *s.* **1.** (*act*) action de raser *f.*; **to have a ~e,** se raser; **2.** (*near miss*) effleurement *m.*; **to have a close ~e** (*fig.*) échapper de justesse; **3.** (*tool*) plane *f.*; *v.t.* & *i.* (1) (se) raser; (2) effleurer; (3) planer; **~eling** *s.* tonsuré *m.*; **~er** *s.* (*mech.*) rasoir électrique *m.*, (*pop.*) gosse *m.*; **~ing** *s.* (*of wood*) copeau *m.*; **~ing-brush** *s.* blaireau *m.*; LATHER **~ing-cream; ~ing-soap** *s.* savon à barbe *m.*
shawl *s.* châle *m.*
she *s.* femelle *f.*; *pron.* elle; **~ who,** celle qui; *adj.* **~-bear, etc.** *see* BEAR *etc.*
sheaf *s.* (*of corn, etc.*) gerbe *f.*; (*of arrows*) faisceau *m.*; (*of papers, etc.*) liasse *f.*
shear *v.t.* tondre; **~er** *s.* tondeur *m.*; **~ing** *s.* tonte *f.*; **~ing time** *s.* tondaison *f.*; *v.i.* se briser.
shears *s.* cisailles *f.pl.*
sheath *s.* (*sword, umbrella*) fourreau *m.*; (*scissors, etc.*) étui *m.*; **~e** *v.t.* (*sword*) rengainer; (*wrap*) envelopper.
sheave *v.t.* mettre en gerbes.
shed[1] *s.* hangar *m.*; (*lean-to*) appentis *m.*; (*store*) remise *f.*
shed[2] *v.t.* (*leaves*) perdre; (*shell, skin*) laisser tomber; (*tears, blood*) verser; (*light*) répandre.
sheen *s.* éclat *m.*
sheep *s.* mouton *m.*; (*eccles. pl.*) ouailles *f.pl.*; **black ~,** brebis galeuse *f.*; **~-dog** *s.* chien de berger *m.*; **~-fold** *s.* bergerie *f.*; **~-shearing** *s.* tonte *f.*; **~skin** *s.* mouton *m.*; **~ish** *adj.* penaud; **~ishly** *adv.* d'un air penaud.
sheer *adj.* **1.** (*absolute*) pur; **2.** (*diaphanous*) diaphane; **3.** (*steep*) à pic; *adv.* (1) complètement; (3) à pic; (*directly*) tout à fait; *v.i.* (*naut.*) faire des embardées; **~ off,** prendre le large.
sheet *s.* (*for bed*) drap *m.*; **white as a ~,** pâle comme un linge; (*of glass, paper, etc.*) feuille *f.*; (*of water, flame*) nappe *f.*; (*sail, rope*) écoute *f.*; GROUND~; **~-anchor** *s.* (*lit.*) ancre de veille *m.*, (*fig.*) ancre de salut *m.*; ~ LIGHTNING; **~ music** *s.* partition *f.*; **~ing** *s.* toile *f.*
sheik(h) *s.* cheik *m.*; **~dom** *s.* principauté *f.*
shekel *s.* sicle *m.*
shelf *s.* (*furniture*) rayon *m.*; (*on cliff*) rebord *m.*; (*reef*) récif *m.*, (*bank*) banc *m.*; **to be on the ~** (*fig.*) avoir coiffé Sainte Catherine.
shell *s.* **1.** (*of egg, nut*) coque *f.*; **in a** NUT~; (*of peas*) cosse *f.*; (*of lobster*) carapace *f.*; (*of crustaceans*) coquille *f.*; (*of tortoise*) écaille *f.*; (*sea ~*) coquillage *m.*; **to come out of one's ~** (*fig.*) sortir de sa coquille; **2.** (*of building*) carcasse *f.*; **3.** (*artillery*) obus *m.*; **~fish** *s.* crustacé *m.*, fruits de mer *m.pl.*; **~-proof** *adj.* (3) blindé; *v.t.* (1) (*nuts*) écaler, (*peas*) écosser; (3) bombarder; **~ out** (*pop.*) casquer.
shellac *s.* laque *f.*
shelter *s.* (*shield or barrier*) abri *m.*; (*screen*) écran *m.*; (*cabin*) asile *m.*; (*safe place*) lieu de refuge *m.*; (*home*) asile *m.*; **to take ~,** s'abriter; **to give ~,** abriter, donner asile à; *v.t.* & *i.* (s')abriter (*from*—de); **~ed** *adj.* à l'abri, à couvert; **~less** *adj.* sans abri.
shelve *v.t.* (*put on shelf*) mettre sur un rayon; (*fit with ~s*) garnir de rayons; (*fig. defer*) remettre; *v.i.* aller en pente.
shepherd *s.* berger *m.*; (*eccles.*) pasteur *m.*; **~ess** *s.* bergère *f.*; *v.t.* (*sheep*) garder; (*people*) guider.
sherbet *s.* sorbet *m.*
sheriff *s.* shérif *m.*
sherry *s.* xérès *m.*
Shetland Isles *s.* (*geog.*) archipel des Shetland *m.*
shibboleth *s.* schibboleth *m.*
shield *s.* (*armour*) bouclier *m.*; (*mech.*) écran *m.*; (*fig.*) bouclier *m.*; (*herald.*) écusson *m.*; (*sports trophy*) trophée *m.*; *v.t.* protéger (*from*—de); (*techn.*) masquer; (*fig.*) couvrir (qn.).
shift *s.* **1.** (*change*) (*of place*) changement *m.*, (*of character*) modification *f.*; **2.** (*expedient, trick*) moyen *m.*, expédient *m.*; **to make ~ to do sth.,** trouver le moyen de faire qch., s'arranger pour faire qch.; **3.** (*obs. dress*) chemise *f.*; **4.** (*gang of workmen*) équipe *f.*, (*period of work*) période de relève *f.*; **~ work** *s.* travail par roulement *m.*; **5.** (*typewriter*) touche *f.*; **~less** *adj.* peu débrouillard; **~y** *adj.* rusé; *v.t.* (1) déplacer; *v.i.* (1) changer de place, se déplacer; **~ for oneself** (2) se débrouiller.
shilling *s.* shilling *m.*
shilly-shally *v.i.* tourner autour du pot.
shimmer *s.* lueur *f.*; *v.i.* luire.
shin *s.* tibia *m.*; *v.i.* **~ up,** grimper.
shindy *s.* (*noise*) boucan *m.*; (*quarrel*) bagarre *f.*
shin/e *s.* (*brightness*) éclat *m.*; (*sheen*) brillant *m.*; (*pop.*) **to take a ~e to s.o.** s'enticher de qn,; *v.t.* faire reluire; *v.i.* luire; (*be bright, lit.* & *fig.*) briller; **to make** HAY **while the sun ~es; the sun is ~ing,** il fait du soleil; **~ing, ~y** *adj.* brillant.

shingle *s.* **1.** (*roof-tile*) bardeau *m.*; **2.** (*hair*) coupe à la garçon *f.*; **3.** (*pebbles*) galets *m.pl.*; **~s** *s.* (*med.*) zona *m.*; *v.t.* (1) couvrir de bardeaux; (2) couper les cheveux à la garçon.

ship *s.* (*naut.*) navire *m.*, vaisseau *m.*; (*aviat.*) appareil *m.*; (*space*) vaisseau spatial *m.*; **~-builder, ~wright** *s.* constructeur de navires *m.*; **~load** *s.* cargaison *f.*; **~owner** *s.* armateur *m.*; **~shape** *adj.* en bon ordre; **~wreck** *s.* naufrage *m.*, *v.t.* faire naufrager, *v.i.* faire naufrage; **~yard** *s.* chantier *m.*; **~ment** *s.* (*act*) expédition *f.*, (*cargo*) chargement *m.*; **~per** *s.* expéditeur *m.*; *v.t.* (*put on* ~) embarquer; (*send by* ~) expédier; (*fix mast, etc.*) monter; (*oars*) armer; (*water*) embarquer; *v.i.* s'embarquer; **~ping** *s.* (*act*) embarquement *m.*, (*of cargo*) mise à bord *f.*, (= ~*s*) navires *m.pl.*; (*profession*) marine marchande *f.*; **~ping** *adj.* (*routes*) de navigation, (*affairs*) maritime; **~ing-agent** *s.* agent maritime *m.*; **~ing-company** *s.* compagnie de navigation *f.*

shire *s.* comté *m.*; **~-horse** *s.* cheval de gros trait *m.*

shirk *v.t.* se dérober à, esquiver; **~er** *s.* (*pop.*) tire-au-flanc *m.*

shirt *s.* (*man's*) chemise *f.*; (*woman's*) chemisier *m.*; STUFF**ed ~**; SWEAT-**~**; **~waister** *s.* robe chemisier *f.*; **to be in one's ~-sleeves,** être en bras de chemise.

shiver *s.* **1.** (*trembling*) frisson *m.*; **2.** (*broken piece*) éclat *m.*; *v.i.* (1) frissonner, grelotter (*with*—de); (2) voler en éclats; *v.t.* (2) fracasser; **~ing** *s.* (1) tremblement *m.*; **~y** *adj.* (1) frissonnant.

shoal *s.* (*of fish*) banc *m.*; (*sandbank*) haut-fond *m.*; (*fig.*) piège *m.*

shock *s.* **1.** (*of corn*) meulon *m.*; **2.** (*of hair*) tignasse *f.*; **3.** (*impact*) choc *m.*, heurt *m.*; **4.** (*sudden mental or physical impression*) choc *m.*, coup *m.*; **5.** (*electric*) choc *m.*; **6.** (*med.*) traumatisme *m.*; **~** ABSORB**er; ~-troops,** troupes de choc *f.pl.*; *v.t.* (4) choquer, scandaliser; (5), (6) choquer; **~er** *s.* (*fam.*) horreur *f.*; **~ing** *adj.* choquant, (*frightening*) affreux, (*bad*) abominable; **~ingly** *adv.* affreusement, horriblement.

shoddy *adj.* de camelote.

shoe *s.* soulier *m.*, chaussure *f.*; (*for horse*) fer *m.*; (*brake-*~) sabot *m.*; (*mech.*) patin *m.*; SNOW-**~**; **where the ~** PINCH**es; ~horn** *s.* chausse-pied *m.*; **~-lace** *s.* lacet *m.*; **~maker** *s.* cordonnier *m.*; **to run on a ~-string** (*fig.*) marcher avec de minces capitaux; **~-tree** *s.* forme *f.*; *v.t.* chausser; (*horse*) ferrer; ROUGH**shod;** SLIP**shod.**

shoo *interj.* eh!, filez!; *v.t.* chasser.

shoot *s.* (*hort.*) rejeton *m.*; (*sport*) partie de chasse *f.*; *v.t.* & *i.* (*with gun*) tirer, **~ at,** tirer sur, **~ straight,** tirer juste; (*football*) marquer un but; *v.t.* (*wound*) blesser, atteindre; (*kill*) tuer; (*rapids*) franchir; (*a bolt*) pousser à fond; (*film*) tourner; (*hunt*) chasser; **~ a** LINE; *v.i.* (*move swiftly*) s'élancer; (*bot.*) pousser; (*show buds*) bourgeonner; (*pain*) élancer; **~ down** *v.t.* abattre, descendre; **~ up** *v.i.* jaillir; **~ing** *s.* (*with gun*) tir *m.*, (*sport*) chasse *f.*; **~ing-box** *s.* pavillon de chasse *m.*; **~ing star** *s.* étoile filante *f.*; **~ing-stick** *s.* canne-siège *f.*; **~ing** *adj.* (*pain*) lancinant.

shop *s.* (*small*) boutique *f.*; (*large*) magasin *m.*; **travelling ~,** camion-magasin *m.*; (*work*~) atelier *m.*; CLOSED **~**; **all over the ~** (*pop.*) (*in disorder*) en désordre, (*everywhere*) partout; **to talk ~,** parler affaires; **~ assistant** *s.* employé *m.*, commis *m.*, vendeur *m.*, vendeuse *f.*; **~-lifter** *s.* voleur à l'étalage *m.*; **~-lifting** *s.* vol à l'étalage *m.*; **~keeper** *s.* marchand *m.*, commerçant *m.*; **~-soiled** *adj.* défraîchi; **~-steward** *s.* délégué syndical *m.*; **~-window** *s.* vitrine *f.*; *v.i.* faire des achats; *v.t.* (*pop. inform against*) faire coffrer; **~ around** *v.i.* prospecter; **~ping** *s.* achats *m.pl.*; **to go ~ping,** faire ses courses, aller au marché; **~ping centre** *s.* (*street*) galerie marchande *f.*, (*building*) centre commercial *m.*; WINDOW-**~ping.**

shore[1] *s.* (*by water*) rivage *m.*, bord *m.*; **in ~** *adj.* côtier.

shore[2] (*prop.*) étai *m.*; *v.t.* **~ up,** étayer.

short *s.* (*electr. fam.*) court-circuit *m.*; (*film*) court métrage *m.*; **~s** *s.* short *m.*, (*underwear*) slip *m.*; **in ~,** bref; *adj.* **1.** (≠ *long, space or time*) court; **2.** (≠ *tall*) petit; **3.** (*soon over*) bref; **4.** (*insufficient*) insuffisant; **5.** (*concise*) bref; **6.** (*curt*) brusque, sec; **7.** (*cook. pastry*) brisé; **to be ~ of,** manquer de; **~bread** *s.* biscuit sablé *m.*; **~** CIRCUIT; **~** CUT; **~coming** *s.* défaut *m.*, faiblesse *f.*; **~fall** *s.* déficit *m.*; **~hand** *s.* sténographie *f.*; **~hand typist** *s.* sténodactylographe *m.f.*; **~-handed** *adj.* à court de personnel; **~ list** *s.* liste étroite *f.*; **~-lived** *adj.* éphémère; **~ sight** *s.* myopie *f.*; **~-sighted** *adj.* myope; **~ story** *s.* nouvelle *f.*; **~-tempered** *adj.* emporté; **~-term** *adj.* à courte échéance; **~age** *s.* manque *m.*, déficit *m.*, (*famine*) disette *f.*; **~en** *v.t.* & *i.* (se) raccourcir, abréger; **~ly** *adv.* brièvement, (*soon*) sous peu; **~ness** *s.* (1), (3), (5) brièveté *f.*; (2) petitesse *f.*; (4) insuffisance *f.*, manque *m.*; (6) brusquerie *f.*; *adv. see under verbs* FALL, RUN, STOP, *etc.*; *v.t.* (*electr. fam.*) court-circuiter.

shot *s.* (*attempt to hit*) coup *m.*; (*attempt to solve*) tentative *f.*; (*person*) tireur *m.*; (*missile*) trait *m.*, balle *f.*; (*pellets*) plombs *m.pl.*; (*of drug*) piqûre *f.*; (*scene*) plan *m.*; (*range*) portée *f.*; **like a ~,** comme une flèche; **to have a ~ at sth.** (*fig.*) essayer (qch., de faire qch.); **big ~** (*fam.*) gros bonnet *m.*; **a long ~,** une chance sur mille; **a** POT **~**; **~-gun** *s.* fusil de chasse *m.*; *adj.* (*silk*) changeant.

should *v. aux. see* SHALL.

shoulder *s.* (*anat., cook.*) épaule *f.*; (*projection*) contrefort *m.*; (*of road, hard* ~) accotement *m.*, (*on motorway*) bande d'arrêt d'urgence *f.*; COLD **~**; **to put one's ~ to the wheel,** pousser à la roue; **to have a** CHIP **on one's ~**; **~ to ~,** coude à coude; **~-strap** *s.* (*of bag*) bandoulière *f.*, (*of garment*) bretelle *f.*, (*of uniform*) patte d'épaule *f.*; *v.t.* (*push*) pousser de l'épaule; (*hoist*) charger sur les épaules; (*fig.*) endosser, se charger de; **~ arms!,** portez armes!

shout *s.* cri *m.*; (*of applause*) acclamations *f.pl.*; *v.t.* & *i.* crier; **~ing** *s.* clameur *f.*

shove *s.* poussée *f.*; *v.t.* & *i.* pousser, bousculer; (*fam. push sth. into drawer, etc.*) fourrer.

shovel *s.* pelle *f.*; **~ful** *s.* pelletée *f.*; *v.t.* pelleter.

show *s.* (*showing*) apparence *f.*; (*outward appearance*) semblant *m.*; (*ostentation*) parade *f.*; (*spectacle*) spectacle *m.*; (*theat., cinema*) pièce *f.*, film *m.*; (*fam.* = *business*) affaire *f.*; (*display*): (*trade*) étalage *m.*, (*dog, flower*) exposition *f.*, (*horse*) concours *m.* (hippique), (*agric.*) comice agricole *m.*, (*auto.*) salon de l'auto *m.*; FLOOR **~**; **side-~,** attraction secondaire *f.*, (*at fair*) spectacle forain *m.*; **by ~ of hands,** à main levée; **good ~!,** bravo!; **bad ~!,** dommage!; **~ business** *s.* le monde du spectacle *m.*; **~-case** *s.* étalage *m.*, vitrine *f.*; **~-down** *s.* moment décisif *m.*; **~-jumping** *s.* concours de sauts d'obstacles *m.*; **~man** *s.* organisateur de spectacles *m.*; **~manship** *s.* abattage *m.*; **~-piece** *s.* modèle *m.*; **~-room** *s.* salon d'exposition *m.*; **~y** *adj.* voyant, fastueux; **~ily** *adv.* d'une manière voyante, avec ostentation; **~iness** *s.* caractère voyant *m.*, prétention *f.*; *v.t.* (*cause to be seen*) montrer; (*disclose*) manifester, révéler; (*exhibit*) exposer, étaler; (*demonstrate to s.o.*) montrer à qn., expliquer à qn,; (*hands on dial*) marquer; (*theat., cinema*) présenter, projeter; (*gratitude, etc.*) témoigner de; (*courage, etc.*) faire preuve de; (*prove, math.*) démontrer;

v.i. se montrer, (*slip*) dépasser; ~ **forth** *v.t.* exposer; ~ **in** *v.t.* faire entrer; ~ **off** *v.t.* étaler, faire parade de; *v.i.* faire le malin; ~ **out** *v.t.* reconduire; ~ **up** *v.t.* (*expose*) faire monter (qn.), (*make visible*) mettre en relief, (*uncover*) démasquer; *v.i.* (*become visible*) se dessiner.

shower *s.* **1.** (*of rain, etc.*) averse *f.*; APRIL ~; **2.** (*of missiles, gifts, etc.*) avalanche *f.*, (*of blows*) grêle *f.*; **3.** (~*-bath*) douche *f.*; **~-proof** *adj.* imperméable; *v.t.* (2) combler (*with*—de); *v.i.* (3) prendre une douche; **~y** *adj.* pluvieux.

shrapnel *s.* shrapnel *m.*

shred *s.* lambeau *m.*; (*fig.*) parcelle *f.*; **to tear to ~s,** déchiqueter; (*fig.*) démolir complètement; *v.t.* déchiqueter; (*paper, rags*) effilocher.

shrew *s.* (*zool.*) musaraigne *f.*; (*woman*) mégère *f.*; **~ish** *adj.* acariâtre.

shrewd *adj.* (*person*) sagace; (*argument, etc.*) judicieux, subtil; **~ly** *adv.* avec perspicacité; **~ness** *s.* sagacité *f.*

shriek *s.* cri perçant *m.*; *v.i.* pousser un cri perçant; ~ **with laughter,** rire aux éclats.

shrift *s.* **to make short ~ of,** expédier.

shrill *adj.* (*cry*) aigu; (*sound*) aigre; (*voice*) perçant; **~y** *adv.* sur un ton aigu; d'une voix perçante.

shrimp *s.* crevette *f.*

shrine *s.* (*casket*) châsse *f.*; (*place*) lieu saint *m.*; (*tomb*) tombeau *m.*; (*fig.*) sanctuaire *m.*

shrink *v.t.* & *i.* **1.** (*make or become smaller*) (se) contracter; (*contract when wet*) (se) rétrécir; (*fig.*) diminuer; **2.** (*recoil from*) reculer devant; **~-proof, ~-resistant** *adj.* irrétrécissable; **~age** *s.* (1) rétrécissement *m.*; **~ing** *adj.* (2) timide.

shrive *v.t.* absoudre.

shrivel *v.t.* & *i.* (se) dessécher; **~led** *adj.* desséché.

shroud *s.* linceul *m.*; **~s** *s.pl.* (*naut.*) haubans *m.pl.*; *v.t.* envelopper (d'un linceul); (*fig.*) voiler.

Shrove Tuesday *s.* mardi gras *m.*

shrub *s.* arbrisseau *m.*, arbuste *m.*; **~bery** *s.* bosquet *m.*

shrug *s.* haussement d'épaules *m.*; *v.t.* hausser (les épaules); ~ **sth. off,** se débarasser de qch.

shudder *s.* **1.** (*with cold*) frisson *m.*; **2.** (*with fear, horror*) frémissement *m.*; *v.i.* (1) frissonner; (2) frémir.

shuffle *s.* **1.** (*gait*) pas traînant *m.*; **2.** (*change of position*) déplacement *m.*; *v.t.* (1) traîner (les pieds); (2) déplacer, (*cabinet*) remanier, (*cards*) battre; *v.i.* (1) marcher d'un pas traînant.

shun *v.t.* éviter.

shunt *v.t.* faire manœuvrer; **~ing** *s.* manœuvre *m.*

shush *interj.* chut!; *v.t.* faire taire.

shut *v.t.* & *i.* (se) fermer; OPEN **and** ~; ~ **down,** fermer; ~ **in,** enfermer; ~ **off,** (*water, current, etc.*) couper; ~ **out,** exclure, fermer la porte à, (*obscure*) empêcher de voir; ~ **up** *v.t.* enfermer, (*fam. v.t.* & *i.*) faire taire, se taire; ~ **up like a** CLAM; ***p.p.*** *adj.* fermé.

shutter *s.* (*window*) volet *m.*; (*camera*) obturateur *m.*

shuttle *s.* navette *f.*; ~ **service** *s.* navette *f.*; **~cock** *s.* volant *m.*

shy[1] *adj.* timide; (*wary*) craintif; **once** BITTEN **twice ~; to** FIGHT ~ **of; ~ly** *adv.**; *; **~ness** *s.* timidité *f.*; *v.i.* (*horse*) faire un écart; (*fig.*) avoir peur (*at*—de).

shy[2] *v.t.* (*throw*) lancer.

Siam *s.* (*geog.*) Siam *m.*; **~ese** *adj.* & *s.m.f.* siamois(e); *s.m.* (*lang.*) siamois; **~ese** TWINS.

Siberia *s.* (*geog.*) Sibérie *f.*; **~n** *adj.* & *s.m.f.* sibérien(ne).

sibilant *adj.* sifflant; *s.* (*ling.*) sifflante *f.*

sibyl *s.* sibylle *f.*

Sicil/y *s.* (*geog.*) Sicile *f.*; **~ian** *adj.* & *s.m.f.* sicilien(ne).

sick *adj.* (*vomiting*) nauséeux; (*ill*) malade; (*disordered*) détraqué; (*disgusted*) dégoûté; **to be** *or* **feel ~,** avoir mal au cœur; **to fall ~,** tomber malade; **to be ~ of sth.,** en avoir assez de qch.; **~-bay** *s.* infirmerie *f.*; **~-leave** *s.* congé de maladie *m.*; **~-list** *s.* liste des malades *f.*; **~en** *v.t.* rendre malade, (*fig.*) écœurer; *v.i.* tomber malade; **~ening** *adj.* écœurant; **~ly** *adj.* (*person*) maladif, (*climate, etc.*) malsain; **~ness** *s.* nausées *f.pl.*, maladie *f.*, mal *m.* (de mer, de l'air, etc.).

sickle *s.* faucille *f.*; HAMMER **and ~.**

side *s.* (*of object*) côté *m.*; (*edge*) bord *m.*; RIGHT ~; WRONG ~; (*of hill*) versant *m.*; (*of bacon*) flèche *f.*; ~ **by ~,** côte à côte; **by the ~ of,** à côté de; **to split one's ~s laughing,** se tenir les côtes de rire; **a thorn in one's ~,** une épine au pied; **on the ~** (*fam.*) par dessus le marché; **to put on one ~,** mettre de côté; **on the short, long, etc. ~,** plutôt court, long, etc.; (*set of people*) parti *m.*; **to take the ~ of,** prendre le parti de; (*team*) équipe *f.*; (*pop. swagger*) suffisance *f.*; **to put on ~** (*fam.*) faire des manières; *adj.* de côté; (*indirect*) latéral; (*subordinate*) secondaire; **~-arms** *s.* baïonnette *f.*; **~board** *s.* buffet *m.*; **~burns** *s.pl.* favoris *m.pl.*; **~-car** *s.* side-car *m.*; **~-effect** *s.* effet secondaire *m.*; ~ **face** *adj.* de profil; **~lights** *s.* (*auto.*) feux de position *m.pl.*; **~long** *adj.* oblique; **~-saddle** *s.* selle de femme *f.*; **to ride ~-saddle** *v.i.* monter en amazone; ~-SHOW; **~sman** *s.* quêteur *m.*; **~-step** *s.* écart *m.*, *v.t.* éviter; **~-street** *s.* petite rue *f.*; **~-table** *s.* desserte *f.*; **~ways** *adv.* de côté, latéralement; **~-track** *v.t.* détourner; **~-whiskers** *s.pl.* favoris *m.pl.*; **~d** *adj.* à (deux, trois, etc.) côtés; **siding** *s.* (*rail.*) voie de garage *f.*; *v.i.* ~ **with,** se ranger du côté de.

sidle (*up to*) *v.i.* avancer de biais (vers).

siege *s.* siège *m.*; **to lay ~ to,** assiéger.

Sienna *s.* (*geog.*) Sienne *f.*; (*s~*) terre de Sienne *f.*

sierra *s.* sierra *f.*

Sierra Leone *s.* (*geog.*) Sierra Leone *f.*

siesta *s.* sieste *f.*

sieve *s.* (*coarse*) crible *m.*; (*fine*) tamis *m.*; *v.t.* passer au crible; tamiser.

sift *v.t.* passer au crible, tamiser; (*sprinkle with sugar, etc.*) saupoudrer (de); (*fig.*) trier; **~er** *s.* tamis *m.*

sigh *s.* soupir *m.*; *v.i.* soupirer (*for*—après).

sight *s.* (*faculty, view, vision*) vue *f.*; **second ~,** seconde vue *f.*; LONG ~; SHORT ~; **on ~, at ~,** à vue; **by ~,** de vue; **within ~,** en vue; **out of ~,** hors de vue; **in s.o.'s ~,** aux yeux de qn.; **to catch ~ of,** apercevoir; **to keep in ~,** garder à vue; **love at first ~,** coup de foudre *m.*; (*scene*) spectacle *m.*; (*of gun*) mire *f.*; **~s** *s.pl.* curiosités *f.pl.*; **~seeing** *s.* tourisme *m.*; **~seer** *s.* touriste *m.f.*, curieux *m.*; **long-~ed** *adj.* presbyte; **short-~ed** *adj.* myope, (*fig.*) peu prévoyant; **~ing** *s.* (*rifle*) visée *f.*, (*artillery*) pointage *m.*; **~less** *adj.* aveugle; **~ly** *adj.* charmant; *v.t.* apercevoir; (*rifle*) pointer.

sign *s.* signe *m.*; (*omen*) présage *m.*; (*of shop*) enseigne *f.*; **~board** *s.* enseigne *f.*, panneau *m.*; **~post** *s.* poteau indicateur *m.*; *v.t.* & *i.* signer; (*make ~s*) faire signe, indiquer par signes; ~ **on** *v.t.* embaucher, *v.i.* s'engager; ~ **off** (*radio*) terminer la transmission; **~ing** *s.* signature *f.*

signal *s.* signal *m.*, avertisseur *m.*; (*message*) transmission *f.*; (*corps of*) **~s,** les transmissions *f.pl.*; **~-box** *s.* poste à signaux *m.*; **~man** *s.* (*mil.*) signaleur *m.*, (*rail.*) aiguilleur *m.*; *v.t.* signaler, faire signe à; *adj.* remarquable; **~ize** *v.t.* signaler, marquer.

signatory *s.* signataire *m.f.*

signature *s.* signature *f.*; KEY ~; ~ **tune** *s.* indicatif musical *m.*
signet *s.* cachet *m.*; **~-ring** *s.* chevalière *f.*
signif/y *v.t.* **1.** (*be sign of*) signifier; *v.i.* **2.** (*be of importance*) importer; **it doesn't ~y,** peu importe; **~icance** *s.* (1) signification *f.*; (2) importance *f.*; **~icant** *adj.* (1) significatif; (2) important; **~ication** *s.* (1) signification *f.*
Sikh *s.* & *adj. invar.* Sikh.
silage *s.* ensilage *m.*
silen/ce *s.* silence *m.*; *v.t.* faire taire; (*suppress*) étouffer; **~cer** *s.* silencieux *m.*; **~t** *adj.* silencieux; (*ling., cinema*) muet; **to keep ~t,** se taire; **~ly** *adv.**.
silex *s.* silex *m.*
silhouette *s.* silhouette *f.*; *v.t.* silhouetter.
silic/a *s.* silice *f.*; **~(e)ous** *adj.* siliceux; **~osis** *s.* silicose *f.*
silicon *s.* silicium *m.*; **~e** *s.* silicone *f.*
silk *s.* (*text.*) soie *f.*; (*Q.C.*) avocat *m.*; **to take ~,** s'inscrire au barreau; **~worm** *s.* ver à soie *m.*; *adj.* de soie, en soie; **~en** *adj.* de soie, en soie; **~y** *adj.* soyeux.
sill *s.* (*of door*) seuil *m.*; (*of window*) rebord *m.*
sillabub, syllabub *s.* sorbet *m.*
sill/y *adj.* (*foolish*) sot, bête; (*feeble-minded*) idiot; **~iness** *s.* sottise *f.*, bêtise *f.*
silo *s.* silo *m.*
silt *s.* vase *f.*; ⚠ vase *m.* = **vase**; *v.t.* & *i.* **~ up,** (s')envaser.
silver *s.* (*metal*) argent *m.*; (*vessels, etc.*) argenterie *f.*; (*coins*) monnaie *f.*; QUICK~; *adj.* en argent; (*colour*) argenté; (*sound*) argentin; **~ gilt** *s.* vermeil *m.*; **~ lining** (*fig.*) rayon d'espoir *m.*; **every cloud has a ~ lining,** après la pluie le beau temps; **~ paper** *s.* feuille d'argent *f.*; **~ plate** *s.* argenterie *f.*; **~-plated** *adj.* plaqué argent; **~smith** *s.* orfèvre *m.*; **to be born with a ~ spoon in one's mouth,** être né coiffé; **~y** *adj.* argenté, argentin; *v.t.* argenter.
simian *s.* simien *m.*; *adj.* (*zool.*) simien; (*fig.*) simiesque.
similar *adj.* similaire; **~ to,** semblable à; **~ity** *s.* similitude *f.*, ressemblance *f.*; **~ly** *adv.* semblablement, de même.
simile *s.* comparaison *f.*
similitude *s.* similitude *f.*
simmer *v.t.* & *i.* (*cook.*) (faire) mijoter; (*fig. with anger, etc.*) frémir (de); **~ down** *v.i.* se calmer.
simoon, simoom *s.* simoun *m.*
simper *s.* sourire affecté *m.*; *v.i.* minauder.
simpl/e *adj.* **1.** (≠ *compound*; ≠ *complicated*; ≠ *elaborate*) simple; **2.** (*unsophisticated*) naïf; **3.** (*half-witted*) simple d'esprit; **4.** (*easily done*) facile (à faire); **~eness** *s.* **~icity** *s.* (1) simplicité *f.*; (2) naïveté *f.*; (4) facilité *f.*; **~ify** *v.t.* simplifier; **~ification** *s.* simplification *f.*; **~y** *adv.* (1)*; (2)*; (4)*; **~eton** *s.* niais *m.*
simulacrum *s.* simulacre *m.*
simulat/e *v.t.* simuler; **~ion** *s.* simulation *f.*; **~or** *s.* (*flight, etc.*) simulateur *m.* (de vol, etc.).
simultaneous *adj.* simultané; **~ly** *adv.**.
sin *s.* péché *m.*; **to live in ~,** vivre ensemble; **~ful** *adj.* coupable; **~ful person** *s.* pécheur *m.*, pécheresse *f.*; **~fulness** *s.* culpabilité *f.*; **~fully** *adv.**; **~less** *adj.* sans péché, innocent; **~ner** *s.* péch/eur, -eresse *m.f.*; *v.i.* pécher.
since *adv.* depuis; (*later*) plus tard; **long ~,** depuis longtemps; **ever ~,** depuis lors; *prep.* depuis; *conj.* (*time*) depuis que; **nothing has happened ~ I spoke to you,** rien n'est arrivé depuis que je vous ai parlé; (*reason*) puisque; **nothing has happened ~ I forbade them to act,** rien n'est arrivé puisque je leur ai défendu d'agir; **it is a long time ~ I saw you,** il y a longtemps que je ne vous ai vu.
sincer/e *adj.* sincère; **~ely** *adv.**; **yours ~ely,** cordialement votre; **~ity** *s.* sincérité *f.*
sine *s.* (*math.*) sinus *m.*
sinecure *s.* sinécure *f.*
sine die *adv.* sine die.
sine qua non *s.* condition sine qua non *f.*
sinew *s.* (*animal tissue*) nerf *m.*; (*anat.*) tendon *m.*; **~s** *s.pl.* (*fig.*) nerf *m.sing.*; **~y** *adj.* (*meat*) tendineux.
sing *v.t.* & *i.* chanter; (*ears*) bourdonner; **~ out,** crier; **~ in/out of** TUNE; **~ another** TUNE; **~er** *s.* chanteur *m.*; cantatrice *f.*; **~ing** *s.* chant *m.*; (*in ears*) bourdonnement *m.*; **~song** *s.* chant *or* ton monotone *m.*; *adj.* monotone.
Singapore *s.* (*geog.*) Singapour *m.*
singe *v.t.* & *i.* (se) roussir.
Sin(g)halese *adj.* & *s.m.f.* cingalais(e).
single *s.* (*ticket, game*) simple *m.*; *adj.* (*one only*) seul, unique; (*individual*) particulier; (≠ *double*) simple; (*solitary*) seul; (*unmarried*) célibataire; (*sport, ticket*) simple; (*combat*) singulier; **~ bed** *s.* lit pour une personne *m.*; **~-breasted** *adj.* droit; **in ~ file,** à la file (indienne); **~-handed** *adj.* tout seul; **~ness** *s.* (*of purpose*) sincérité *f.*; **singly** *adv.* un à un; *v.t.* **~ out,** choisir, distinguer.
singlet *s.* maillot *m.*
singleton *s.* (*cards*) singleton *m.*
singular *s.* (*ling.*) singulier *m.*; **in the ~,** au singulier; *adj.* (*extraordinary*) remarquable; (*strange*; *ling.*) singulier; **~ity** *s.* singularité *f.*; **~ize** *v.t.* singulariser; **~ly** *adv.**;*.
sinister *adj.* sinistre; (*herald.*) sénestre.
sink[1] *s.* évier *m.*; (*fig.*) cloaque *m.*; **~-unit** *s.* bloc-évier *m.*
sink[2] *v.t.* (*cause to penetrate*) enfoncer; (*cause to fall*) faire tomber; (*ship*) couler; (*mine*) foncer; (*well*) creuser; (*fin.*) placer à fonds perdus; (*fig. fam. ruin*) couler; *v.i.* (*penetrate*) s'enfoncer (dans); (*disappear*) disparaître; (*under water*) sombrer, couler; (*level of water, prices*) baisser; (*collapse*) s'affaisser; (*grow less*) diminuer; (*person*) (*to knees, etc.*) tomber (à genoux, etc.), (*into a chair, etc.*) se laisser tomber; (*sun, moon*) baisser; (*med.*) s'affaiblir, se mourir; (*succumb*) succomber; (*fig. spirits*) s'abattre; (*heart*) se serrer; **~ in,** pénétrer; **~er** *s.* (*fishing*) plomb *m.*; **~ing** *s.* (*penetration*) enfoncement *m.*; (*lowering*) abaissement *m.*; (*fin.*) placement (à fonds perdus) *m.*
sinner *see* SIN.
sinolog/y *s.* sinologie *f.*; **~ist** *s.* sinologue *m.f.*
sinu/ous *adj.* sinueux; **~osity** *s.* sinuosité *f.*
sinus *s.* sinus *m.invar.*; **~itis** *s.* sinusite *f.*
sip *s.* goutte *f.*; *v.t.* siroter.
siphon *s.* siphon *m.*; *v.t.* siphonner; *v.i.* se transvaser.
sippet *s.* (*cook.*) croûton *m.*
sir *s.* (*title*) sir *m.*; (*form of address*) monsieur *m.*; (*to king*) sire *m.*
sire *s.* (*king*) sire *m.*; (*male ancestor*; *stallion*) père *m.*; *v.t.* engendrer.
siren *s.* sirène *f.*
sirloin *s.* (*cook.*) aloyau *m.*
sirocco *s.* sirocco *m.*
sisal *s.* sisal *m.*
sister *s.* (*family*) sœur *f.*; (*fellow member*) consœur *f.*; (*eccles.*) sœur *f.*; religieuse *f.*; (*nursing*) infirmière (en chef) *f.*; **~-in-**LAW; **~hood** *s.* communauté *f.*; **~ly** *adj.* de sœur.
sit *v.t.* (*exam*) passer; (*horse*) monter; *v.i.* (*take position*) s'asseoir; (*be in position*) être assis; (*judge*) siéger; (*pose*) poser; (*parl.*) être en séance; (*on eggs*) couver; **~ down** *v.i.* s'asseoir; **~-down strike** *s.* grève sur le tas *f.*; **~ down under sth.,** encaisser qch.; **~ for,** se présenter à; **~ in** *v.i.* occuper les lieux; **~-in** *s.* occupation *f.*; **~ in on,** assister à; **~ (up)on,** (*committee, etc.*) faire partie de, *v.t.* (*suppress*) étouffer; **~ on**

the FENCE; ~ **sth. out,** rester jusqu'à la fin de qch.; ~ **up,** se dresser, (*stay up late*) veiller; ~ **tight,** ne pas céder; **~ter** *s.* (*art*) modèle *m.f.*, (*hen*) poule couveuse *f.*; BABY-**~ter**; **~ting** *s.* (*of assembly*) séance *f.*, (*of court*) audience *f.*, (*art*) pose *f.*, (*eggs*) couvée *f.*; (*in canteen, etc.*) service *m.*; **~ting-room** *s.* salle de séjour *f.*; **~ting** *adj.* (*fig. target*) cible facile *f.*, (*M.P., etc.*) en exercice, (*tenant*) en place.

site *s.* emplacement *m.*; (*for building*) terrain *m.*; (*of works*) chantier *m.*; *v.t.* situer.

situat/e *v.t.* situer; **~ed** *adj.* situé; **~ion** *s.* situation *f.*; (*job*) place *f.*, emploi *m.*

six *s.* six *m.*; **at ~es and sevens,** sens dessus dessous; **~th** *s.* & *adj.* sixième; **~thly** *adv.**; **~teen** *s.* seize *m.*; **~teenth** *adj.* & *s.* seizième; **~ty** *s.* soixante *m.*; **~tieth** *adj.* soixantième.

size *s.* **1.** (*dimensions*) grandeur *f.*, (*of person*) taille *f.*; **2.** (*class*) numéro *m.*, taille *f.*, (*of gloves, shoes*) pointure *f.*; **3.** (*substance*) colle *f.*; **~able** *adj.* (*fig.*) assez important; *v.t.* (2) trouver la dimension voulue; (3) coller; ~ **up** *v.t.* estimer la taille de, (*fig.*) juger.

sizzle *v.i.* grésiller.

skate[1] *s.* (*fish*) raie *f.*

skate[2] *s.* (*for skating*) patin *m.*; ROLLER-**~s**; **~board** *s.* planche à roulettes *f.*; *v.i.* patiner; ~ **over** (*fig.*) glisser, passer sur; **~r** *s.* patin/eur, -euse *m.f.*; **skating** *s.* patinage *m.*; **skating-rink** *s.* patinoire *f.*; ⚠ skating = **roller skating** *or* **roller skating rink.**

skein *s.* (*of yarn*) écheveau *m.*; (*of geese*) vol *m.*

skeleton *s.* squelette *m.*; (*outline*) plan *m.*; (*of building*) carcasse *f.*; ~ **in the cupboard** (*fig.*) secret de famille *m.*; ~ **key** *s.* crochet *m.*, (*burglar's*) rossignol *m.*; ~ **staff,** personnel réduit *m.*; **skeletal** *adj.* squelettique.

skep, skip *s.* panier d'osier *m.*; (*of bees*) ruche *f.*

sketch *s.* (*rough drawing*) croquis *m.*; (*rough draft*) esquisse *f.*; (*short play*) sketch *m.*; **~-book** *s.* album *m.*; *v.t.* esquisser; **~y** *adj.* sommaire, imprécis, vague.

skew *adj.* biais; **~bald** *adj.* pie.

skewer *s.* brochette *f.*; *v.t.* embrocher.

ski *s.* ski *m.*; *v.i.* aller à/en skis; **to go ~ing,** faire du ski; **~er** *s.* skieu/r, -se *m.f.*; **~-lift** *s.* remonte-pente *m. invar.*; **water-~ing** *s.* ski nautique *m.*

skid *s.* (*act*) dérapage *m.*; (*on wheel*) sabot (de roue) *m.*; (*aviat.*) patin *m.*; **~-pan** *s.* piste d'essai sur verglas *f.*; *v.i.* déraper.

skiff *s.* skif(f) m.

skil/l *s.* (*ability*) habileté *f.*, adresse *f.*; (*techn.*) compétence *f.*; (*craft*) métier *m.*; **~led** *adj.* habile, expérimenté; **~led** LABOUR; **~ful** *adj.* habile, adroit; **~fully** *adv.**,*; **~fulness** *s.* habileté *f.*, adresse *f.*

skim *v.t.* (*milk*) écrémer; (*other liquids*) écumer; (*read quickly*) parcourir; (*pass over*) effleurer; ~ **milk,** lait écrémé *m.*; **~mer** *s.* écumoire *f.*

skimp *v.t.* (*supply meagrely*) lésiner sur; (*be parsimonious with*) être chiche de; (*work badly*) bâcler; *v.i.* faire des économies; **~y** *adj.* maigre.

skin *s.* (*anat., complexion, of animal*) peau *f.*; (*thin film*) peau *f.*, pellicule *f.*; (*peel or rind*) pelure *f.*; (*naut.*) carène *f.*; (*aviat.*) revêtement *m.*; THICK ~; THIN ~; **wet to the ~,** trempé jusqu'aux os; **by the ~ of one's teeth,** de justesse; **to get sth.** *or* **s.o. under one's ~,** avoir qch. *or* qn. dans la peau; **to get under s.o.'s ~,** agacer qn.; **nothing but ~ and** BONES; **~-deep** *adj.* superficiel; **~flint** *s.* grippe-sou *m.*; **~-graft** *s.* greffe *f.*; **~-tight** *adj.* collant; **~ny** *adj.* (*lean*) décharné, (*mean*) grippe-sou; *v.t.* (*strip bare*) écorcher; (*fruit*) peler; (*cook.*) éplucher; **~ner** *s.* peaussier *m.*

skip *s.* saut *m.*; *v.t.* (*in reading*) sauter; (*fam. omit*) omettre; *v.i.* sauter; (*with rope*) sauter à la corde; (*pop. decamp*) décamper; **~ping-rope** *s.* corde à sauter *f.*

skipper *s.* patron *m.*

skirmish *s.* escarmouche *f.*; *v.i.* se livrer à des escarmouches.

skirt *s.* **1.** (*dress*) jupe *f.*; **2.** (*border*) abords *m.pl.*; (*of wood*) lisière *f.*; **3.** (*pop.*) poupée *f.*; **4.** (*of meat*) fressure *f.*; *v.t.* (2) contourner; **~ing-board** *s.* plinthe *f.*

skit *s.* satire *f.*, pastiche *m.*; **~tish** *adj.* (*horse*) ombrageux; (*person*) volage.

skittle *s.* quille *f.*; **~s** (*game*) jeu de quilles *m.*

skivvy *s.* (*fam.*) bonne à tout faire *f.*

skulk *v.i.* (*hide*) se cacher; (*move stealthily*) rôder.

skull *s.* crâne *m.*; **~-cap** *s.* calotte *f.*; ~ **and cross-bones,** tête de mort *f.*

skunk *s.* mouffette *f.*; (*fur*) sconse *m.*; (*fam.*) salaud *m.*

sky *s.* (*heaven*) ciel *m.* (*pl.* cieux); (*climate*) ciel *m.* (*pl.* ciels); **to praise to the skies,** porter aux nues; **~-blue** *s.* bleu-ciel *m.*; **~-high** *adv.* jusqu'aux nues; **~lark** *s.* alouette *f.*; **~lark** *v.i.* (*fam.*) faire le fou; **~light** *s.* lucarne *f.*; **~line** *s.* horizon *m.*; **~-rocket** *v.i.* monter en flèche; **~scraper** *s.* gratte-ciel *m.*

slab *s.* (*stone*) dalle *f.*; (*of cake, etc.*) grosse tranche *f.*; (*of chocolate*) tablette *f.*

slack *s.* (*of rope*) battant *m.*; **~s** *s.pl.* pantalon *m.sing.*; *adj.* **1.** (*sluggish*) mou; **2.** (*comm.*) dans le marasme; **3.** (*remiss*) négligent; **4.** (*loose*) lâche, desserré; **5. to be ~** (*techn.*) avoir du jeu; **~en** *v.t.* & *i.* (*loosen*) (se) relacher, (se) desserrer; (*slow*) ralentir; (*grow less*) diminuer; **~ly** *adv.* (1) mollement; (3) négligemment; (4) lâchement; **~ness** *s.* (1) mollesse *f.*, désœuvrement *m.*; (2) stagnation *f.*; (3) négligence *f.*; (4) détente *f.*; (5) jeu *m.*; *v.i.* flemmarder; **~er** *s.* flemmard *m.*

slag *s.* scories *f.pl.*; **~-heap,** *s.* crassier *m.*

slake *v.t.* (*thirst*) étancher.

slalom *s.* (descente en) slalom *m.*

slam *s.* **1.** (*sound*) claquement *m.*; **2.** (*cards*) chelem *m.*; *v.t.* (1) (faire) claquer; (*put down violently*) flanquer par terre.

slander *s.* médisance *f.*; (*law*) diffamation *f.*; *v.t.* calomnier; diffamer; **~ous** *adj.* calomnieux; **~ously** *adv.**.

slang *s.* argot *m.*; *adj.* argotique; *v.t.* (*pop.*) engueuler; **to have a ~ing-match with s.o.,** (*fam.*) s'enguirlander.

slant *s.* **1.** (*slope*) pente *f.*, (*bias*) biais *m.*; **2.** (*point of view*) point de vue *m.*; *v.t.* & *i.* (1) (s')incliner, être en pente; (2) présenter qch. sous un certain jour; **~ing** *adj.* en pente, oblique.

slap *s.* claque *f.*; (*in face*) gifle *f.*; *v.t.* donner une claque à, gifler; **~dash** *adj.* (*person*) impétueux, (*work*) bâclé, *adv.* sans soin, à la six-quatre-deux; **~stick** *adj.* d'arlequinade; **~-up** *adj.* (*pop.*) chic.

slash *s.* entaille *f.*; (*hist. dress*) crevé *m.*; *v.t.* taillader; (*whip*) faire claquer; (*prices*) sacrifier.

slat *s.* lame *f.*

slate *s.* ardoise *f.*; **a** CLEAN ~; **~-coloured** *adj.* ardoisé; *v.t.* couvrir d'ardoises; (*criticise*) critiquer; (*scold*) éreinter.

slattern *s.* souillon *f.*; **~ly** *adj.* malpropre.

slaughter *s.* **1.** (*of animals*) abattage *m.*; **2.** (*of people*) massacre *m.*; **~house** *s.* abattoir *m.*; *v.t.* (1) abattre; (2) massacrer.

Slav *adj.* & *s.m.f.* slave; **~onic** *adj.* slave.

slav/e *s.* (*lit.* & *fig.*) esclave *m.f.*; **~e-driver** *s.* (*fig.*) négrier *m.*; **~e-trade** *s.* traite *f.* (des noirs); **~er** *s.* (*ship* & *person*) négrier *m.*; **~ery** *s.* esclavage *m.*, (*fig.*) asservissement *m.*, (*drudgery*) besogne *f.*; **~ish** *adj.* d'esclave, (*fig.*) servile; **~ishly** *adv.* en esclave, servilement; *v.i.* bûcher, besogner.

slaver *v.i.* baver.

slay *v.t.* tuer; **~er** *s.* tueur *m.*
sleazy *adj.* (*fam.*) de camelote.
sledge, sled, sleigh *s.* traîneau *m.*; *v.i.* aller en traîneau.
sledge-hammer *s.* marteau de forgeron *m.*; masse *f.*
sleek *adj.* (*soft, smooth, glossy*) lisse, poli, luisant; (*well-fed*) dodu; (*plausible*) onctueux; *v.t.* lisser, polir.
sleep *s.* sommeil *m.*; (*short*) somme *m.*; **to go to ~,** s'endormir; **to put to ~,** endormir; **~-walker** *s.* somnambule *m.f.*; **~less** *adj.* sans sommeil, (*night*) blanche; **~y** *adj.* somnolent; **to be ~y,** avoir sommeil; **~ily** *adv.* d'un air endormi; *v.t.* & *i.* dormir; **~ like a** LOG; **~ like a** TOP; (*stay overnight*) coucher; (*provide beds for*) loger; **~ around** (*fam.*) découcher; **~ in** (*at one's work*) coucher à son lieu de travail, (**~** *late*) faire la grasse matinée; **~er** *s.* dormeur *m.*, (*rail.*) traverse *f.*, (*berth*) couchette *f.*; **~ing-bag** *s.* sac de couchage *m.*; **~ing-**CAR; **~ing** DOGS; **~ing** PARTNER; **~ing-pill** *s.* somnifère *m.*; **~ing sickness** *s.* maladie du sommeil *f.*, encéphalite *f.*
sleet *s.* grésil *m.*; **it is (was) ~ing,** il y a (avait) du grésil.
sleeve *s.* (*dress.*) manche *f.*; (*mech.*) manchon *m.*; (*gram. record*) pochette *f.*; **to have sth. up one's ~,** avoir un atout en réserve; **~less** *adj.* sans manches.
sleigh *see* SLEDGE.
sleight *s.* **~-of-hand,** prestidigitation *f.*
slender *adj.* **1.** (*slim*) svelte; **2.** (*scanty*): (*hope*) faible, (*resources*) modeste; **~ness** *s.* (1) sveltesse *f.*; (2) faiblesse *f.*, modicité *f.*
sleuth *s.* limier *m.*; *v.t.* & *i.* filer.
slew *v.t.* & *i.* (faire) pivoter.
slice *s.* **1.** (*of bread, meat, etc.*) tranche *f.*; **2.** (*share*) part *f.*; **3.** (*stroke*) coup qui fait dévier *m.*; **4.** (*implement*) truelle *f.*; *v.t.* (1) découper en tranches; (3) faire dévier (la balle); **~ off** *v.t.* découper; **~r** *s.* machine à découper *f.*
slick *s.* (*oil*) marée noire *f.*; *adj.* (*quick, cunning*) habile, adroit; (*plausible*) fin; *v.t.* lisser.
slide *s.* (*act*) glissade *f.*, glissement *m.*; (*track*) toboggan *m.*; (*mech.*) coulisse *f.*; (*photo.*) diapositive *f.*; (*hair*) barrette *f.* (à cheveux); **~-rule** *s.* règle à calcul *f.*; *v.t.* & *i.* (se) glisser; **sliding door** *s.* porte à coulisse *f.*; **sliding** SCALE.
slight *s.* affront *m.*; *v.t.* manquer d'égards envers qn.; (*disdain*) dédaigner; *adj.* (*slender*) mince; (*flimsy, weak*) léger, faible; (*small in amount*) menu; (*unimportant*) insignifiant; **the ~est,** le (la) moindre; **~ly** *adv.* légèrement.
slim *adj.* svelte; (*fig.*) léger; *v.t.* & *i.* (faire) maigrir; **~ming** *s.* régime (pour maigrir) *m.*; **~ness** *s.* sveltesse, *f.*; (*fig.*) faiblesse *f.*
slim/e *s.* vase *f.*; (*of snail*) bave *f.*; **~iness** *s.* nature vaseuse *f.*, viscosité *f.*; **~y** *adj.* vaseux, visqueux; (*fig.*) mielleux.
sling *s.* (*weapon*) fronde *f.*; (*rope for hoisting*) élingue *f.*; (*bandage*) écharpe *f.*; *v.t.* (*throw*) lancer; (*suspend*) suspendre; (*hammock*) accrocher.
slink *v.i.* aller furtivement; **~ away, s'en aller** furtivement.
slip *s.* (*hort.*) bouture *f.*; (*of paper, etc.*) bout *m.*, fiche *f.*; (*act*) glissade *f.*; (*error*) faux pas *m.*; (*petticoat*) combinaison *f.*; PILLOW**~**; **many a ~ twixt** CUP **and lip; to give s.o. the ~,** dérouter qn.; *v.t.* (*let go*) lâcher; (*escape from*) se dégager de; **~ on,** enfiler; **~ off,** ôter; **~ into,** passer; *v.i.* glisser; (*make mistake*) faire une erreur; (*move quietly*) se glisser, se faufiler; **~ up** (*fig. fam.*) faire une erreur; **~-up** *s.* contretemps *m.*, (*fam.*) gaffe *f.*; **let ~,** laisser échapper; **~ped** DISC; **~-coach** *s.* (*rail.*) wagon détaché *m.*; **~-knot** *s.* nœud coulant *m.*; **~-road** *s.* (*motorway*) bretelle d'accès *f.*; **~shod** *adj.* négligé; **~-stream** *s.* sillage *m.*; **~way** *s.* cale *f.*
slipper *s.* pantoufle *m.*
slipper/y *adj.* **1.** (*insecure*) glissant, incertain; **2.** (*fig.*) rusé; **~iness** *s.* (1) nature glissante *f.*; (2) ruse *f.*
slit *s.* fente *f.*; *v.t.* & *i.* (se) fendre.
slither *v.i.* glisser.
sliver *s.* éclat *m.*
slobber *s.* bave *f.*; (*fig.*) sentimentalisme fade *m.*; *v.i.* baver; (*fig.*) larmoyer.
sloe *s.* prunelle *f.*
slog *s.* (*fam.*) corvée *f.*; *v.t.* & *i.* (*hit*) frapper dur; (*work*) bûcher.
slogan *s.* slogan *m.*
sloop *s.* sloop *m.*
slop *s.* fange *f.*; **~s** *s.pl.* (*water*) eaux de vaisselle *f.pl.*; (*pop. food*) eau de vaisselle *f.*; **~-basin** *s.* vide-tasses *m.*; **~-pail** *s.* seau de toilette *m.*; **~py** *adj.* (*muddy*) boueux, (*work*) bâclé, négligé, (*fam.*) larmoyant; *v.t.* & *i.* (se) répandre; (*spill*) renverser; **~ over** *v.i.* déborder.
slop/e *s.* pente *f.*, biais *m.*; *v.t.* pencher; *v.i.* être en pente; **~e arms!,** armes sur l'épaule!; **~ing** *adj.* en pente.
slosh *s. see* SLUSH; *v.t.* & *i.* (*splash about*) patauger; *v.t.* (*pop.*) (*pour clumsily*) verser maladroitement; (*hit*) flanquer un coup à.
slot *s.* fente *f.*; (*TV, place in programme*) rubrique *f.*; **~-machine** *s.* distributeur automatique *m.*
sloth *s.* (*animal*) ai *m.*, (*fam.*) paresseux *m.*; (*laziness*) paresse *f.*; **~ful** *adj.* paresseux; **~fulness** *s.* paresse *f.*
slouch *s.* démarche lourde *f.*; *v.i.* marcher d'un pas traînant.
slough *s.* **1.** (*swamp*) bourbier *m.*; (*fig.*) abîme *m.*; **2.** (*cast skin*) dépouille *f.*; *v.t.* (2) se dépouiller de; *v.i.* muer.
Slov/ak *adj.* & *s.m.f.* slovaque; **~ene** *adj.* & *s.m.f.* slovène.
sloven *s.* souillon *f.*; **~ly** *adj.* malpropre, mal tenu; **~liness** *s.* négligence *f.*
slow *adj.* **1.** (≠ *quick*) lent; **2.** (*dull-witted*) peu intelligent; **3.** (*tedious*) ennuyeux; **4.** (*time*) en retard; **to be ~ to do sth.,** être long à faire qch.; (*of clock or watch*) **to be 5 minutes ~,** retarder de cinq minutes; **~coach** *s.* lambin *m.*; **~ motion** *s.* ralenti *m.*; **~ train** *s.* train omnibus *m.*; **~ness** *s.* (1) lenteur *f.*; (2) intelligence lente *f.*; (3) lourdeur *f.*, manque d'entrain *m.*; (4) retard *m.*; *adv.* & **~ly** *adv.* lentement; **go-~** *s.* (*strike*) grève perlée *f.*; *v.t.* & *i.* **~ down** *or* **up,** ralentir.
sludge *s.* vase *f.*
slug *s.* (*zool.*) limace *f.*; (*pop. bullet*) pruneau *m.*; **~gard** *s.* paresseu/x, -se *m.f.*; **~gish** *adj.* paresseux, lent; **~gishly** *adv.**,*; **~gishness** *s.* paresse *f.*, lenteur *f.*
sluice *s.* écluse *f.*; **~-gate** *s.* vanne *f.*; *v.t.* rincer.
slum *s.* (*dwelling*) taudis *m.*; **~s** *s.pl.* bas quartiers *m.pl.*; **~ clearance** *s.* démolition des îlots insalubres *f.*; *v.i.* visiter les pauvres.
slumber *s.* sommeil *m.*; *v.i.* sommeiller.
slump *s.* (*comm.*) dépression *f.*, crise *f.*; *v.i.* (*price*) s'effondrer; (*sit down heavily*) tomber lourdement, s'écrouler.
slur *s.* (*discredit*) tache *f.*; (*sound*) bredouillement *m.*; (*mus.*) liaison *f.*; *v.t.* (*smudge*) maculer; (*pronounce indistinctly*) mal articuler.
slurry *s.* (*cement*) coulis de ciment *m.*; (*mud*) boue *f.*
slush *s.* neige fondue *f.*; (*fig.*) sentimentalité larmoyante *f.*
slut *s.* souillon *f.*; **~tish** *adj.* malpropre.
sly *adj.* **1.** (*cunning*) rusé; **2.** (*secret*) sournois; **on the ~,** en tapinois; **~ly** *adv.* (1) adroitement; (2)*; **~ness** *s.* (1) ruse *f.*; (2) sournoiserie *f.*

smack *s.* **1.** (*sound*) claquement *m.*; **2.** (*blow*) claque *f.*, gifle *f.*; **3.** (*taste*) arrière-goût *m.*, (*fig.*) soupçon *m.*; **4.** (*boat*) bateau de pêche *m.*; **5.** (*fam.*) **to have a ~ at sth.,** tenter le coup; *v.t.* (1), (2) (faire) claquer, gifler; **~ of** (3) avoir un arrière-goût de.

small *s.* (*of the back*) chute des reins *f.*; *adj.* **1.** (≠ *large*) petit; **2.** (*space*) exigu; **3.** (*income*) modique; **4.** (≠ *important*) peu important; **5.** (*petty, mean*) mesquin; **6.** (*humble*) humble; **to feel ~** (*fig.*) ne pas être fier; **to look ~** (*fig.*) avoir l'air penaud; **~ ads** *s.pl.* petites annonces *f.pl.*; **~** CHANGE; **~ fry** *s.* menu fretin *m.*; **~**HOLD**ing**; **~ hours,** petit matin *m.*; **~pox** *s.* petite vérole *f.*; **~ print** *s.* paragraphes en petits caractères *m.pl.*; **~-scale,** de portée limitée; **~ talk** *s.* papotage *m.*; **~ish** *adj.* plutôt petit; **~ness** *s.* (1) petitesse *f.*; (2) exiguïté *f.*; (3) modicité *f.*; (4) insignifiance *f.*; (5) mesquinerie *f.*; *adv.* (*into ~ pieces*) menu.

smarm *v.t.* (*fam.*) **~ down,** aplatir; (*flatter s.o.*) être aux petits soins pour qn.; **~y** *adj.* doucereux.

smart *adj.* **1.** (*severe, sharp*) cinglant, (*pain*) cuisant; **2.** (*brisk*) vif, vigoureux; **look ~!** (*pop.*) grouillez-vous!; **3.** (*clever*) alerte, habile, (*witty*) spirituel, (*resourceful*) débrouillard; **4.** (*well--dressed*) élégant, chic; **~en** (*up*) *v.t.* (4) embellir, se faire beau; **~ly** *adv.* (2) vivement; (3) habilement, spirituellement; (4) élégamment; **~ness** *s.* (1) violence *f.*; (2) vivacité *f.*; (3) habileté *f.*, finesse *f.*; (4) élégance *f.*, chic *m.*; *v.i.* (1) éprouver une douleur cuisante, (*wound, etc.*) cuire; **~ under** (*fig.*) souffrir de.

smash *s.* **1.** (*breaking*) fracas *m.*; **2.** (*collision*) collision *f.*; **3.** (*disaster*) débâcle *f.*, (*bankruptcy*) faillite *f.*; **4.** (*tennis*) smash *m.*; **~-and-grab** *s.* vol avec effraction *m.*; **~ hit** *s.* (*pop.*) succès à tout casser *m.*; *v.t.* & *i.* (1) (se) briser, (se) fracasser; (*record*) pulvériser; (2) entrer en collision avec; (3) ruiner, (*fig.*) écraser; *v.i.* faire faillite; (4) smasher; **~ing** *adj.* (*pop.*) formidable.

smattering *s.* connaissance superficielle *f.*; **to have a ~ of,** avoir des notions de.

smear *s.* tache *f.*; (*med. on slide*) échantillon sur lamelle *m.*; (*fig.*) diffamation *f.*; **~ campaign** *s.* campagne de diffamation *f.*; *v.t.* tacher; (*daub*) enduire (*with*—de); (*fig.*) diffamer.

smell *s.* (*sense*) odorat *m.*; (*scent*) odeur *f.*; (*bad ~*) mauvaise odeur *f.*; **~y** *adj.* malodorant; *v.t.* sentir; (*of animals*) flairer; *v.i.* (*have sense of*) avoir bon odorat; (*emit ~*) sentir; (*stink*) sentir mauvais; **~ of,** sentir; **~ a** RAT; **~ing** *adj* odorant; **~ing-salts** *s.pl.* sels (volatils) *m.pl.*

smelt[1] *s.* (*fish*) éperlan *m.*

smelt[2] *v.t.* fondre; **~ing** *s.* fonte *f.*

smile *s.* sourire *m.*; **with a ~,** en souriant; *v.i.* sourire; (*be propitious*) être favorable; **~ at,** sourire de; **~ on,** sourire à; **smiling** *adj.* souriant.

smirch *v.t.* (*lit.* & *fig.*) tacher, noircir.

smirk *s.* sourire affecté *m.*; *v.i.* sourire d'un air affecté.

smit/e *v.t.* (*hit*) frapper; (*defeat*) vaincre; **to be ~ten with,** (*desire*) être pris de; (*remorse*) être affligé de; (*s.o.*) être épris de qn.

smith *s.* forgeron *m.*; (*for horses*) maréchal ferrant *m.*; GOLD~; **tin~,** ferblantier *m.*; **~y** *s.* forge *f.*

smithereens, to smash to ~, briser en mille morceaux.

smock *s.* (*artist's*) sarrau *m.*; (*peasant's*) blouse *f.*; **~ing** *s.* fronces brodées *f.pl.*; *v.t.* broder des fronces.

smog *s.* brouillard fumeux *m.*

smok/e *s.* fumée *f.*; (*cigar*(*ette*)) cigare *f.*, cigarette *f.*; **to have a ~e,** fumer; **to go up in ~e** (*fig.*) n'aboutir à rien; **~e-**SCREEN; **~eless** *adj.* sans fumée; **~y** *adj.* qui fume, enfumé; *v.t.* & *i.* fumer; (*spoil with ~e, ~e out*) enfumer; CHAIN-**~e**; **~er** *s.* fumeur *m.*, (*rail.*) compartiment pour fumeurs *m.*; **~ing** *adj.* fumant; **no ~ing!,** défense de fumer!

smooth *adj.* **1.** (*even*) uni, (*sea*) calme; **2.** (≠ *rough to touch*) lisse, poli; **3.** (≠ *harsh to taste, sound, etc.*) doux; **4.** (*without obstacles*) sans heurts; **5.** (≠ *hairy*) imberbe; **6.** (*plausible*) doucereux; **7.** (*style*) coulant, facile; **~-tongued** *adj.* enjôleur; **~ly** *adv.* (2), (3) doucement; (4) sans secousses; (6) d'une manière doucereuse; (7) facilement; **~-ness** *s.* (1) égalité *f.*; (2), (3) douceur *f.*; (4) égalité *f.*; (6) ton doucereux *m.*; (7) facilité *f.*; *v.t.* & *i.* (1) (s')aplanir; (2) lisser, (*brow*) dérider; (3) adoucir; (4) enlever les obstacles de; **~ away,** aplanir; **~ down** (*fig.*) apaiser.

smother *v.t.* (*suffocate, suppress, cover up*) étouffer; (*cover with*) couvrir de; (*fig.*) accabler de.

smoulder *v.i.* (*lit.* & *fig.*) couver.

smudge *s.* tache *f.*; *v.t.* tacher, brouiller.

smug *adj.* suffisant; **~ly** *adv.* d'un air suffisant; **~ness** *s.* suffisance *f.*

smuggl/e *v.t.* faire passer (qch.) en contrebande *or* faire la contrebande de (qch.); *v.i.* faire de la contrebande; **~er** *s.* contrebandier *m.*; **~ing** *s.* contrebande *f.*

smut *s.* **1.** (*of soot*) flocon de suie *m.*; **2.** (*obscene lang.*) grivoiseries *f.pl.*; **~ty** *adj.* (1) noirci; (2) grossier.

snack *s.* casse-croûte *f.*; **to have a ~,** (*pop.*) manger un morceau sur le pouce; **~-bar** *s.* snack-bar *m.*

snaffle *s.* filet *m.*; *v.t.* (*pop.*) chiper, s'annexer.

snag *s.* (*projection*) chicot *m.*; (*obstacle*) écueil *m.*, anicroche *f.*; (*in stocking*) accroc *m.*; *v.t.* heurter (un obstacle); faire un accroc.

snail *s.* escargot *m.*; **to go at a ~'s pace,** aller comme un escargot.

snake *s.* serpent *m.*; (*common, grass*) couleuvre *m.*; **~ in the grass,** serpent caché sous les fleurs; **~s and ladders,** jeu de l'oie *m.*; **~--charmer** *s.* charmeur de serpent *m.*; *v.t.* & *i.* serpenter.

snap *s.* (*sound*) bruit sec *m.*; (*catch*) agrafe *f.*, bouton-pression *m.*; (*of bag, etc.*) fermoir *m.*; (*spell of cold, etc.*) courte période *f.* (de froid, etc.); (*photo.*) (cliché) instantané *m.*; (*card game*) jeu de cartes enfantin *m.*; (*fig.*) vivacité *f.*, brio *m.*; *adj.* (*of decision, etc.*) pris sans réflexion; **~-dragon** *s.* gueule de loup *f.*; **~-fastener** *s.* bouton-pression *m.*; **~shot** *s.* instantané *m.*; **~pish** *adj.* hargneux; **~py** *adj.* vif; *v.t.* (*bite*) happer; (*break*) casser net; (*close*) fermer brusquement; (*photo.*) prendre un instantané de; *v.i.* (*sound*) claquer; (*break*) se briser; (*speak harshly*) parler avec aigreur; **~ at,** happer, (*fig.*) parler d'un ton hargneux à qn.; **~ off** *v.t.* & *i.* (s')enlever, (se) briser; **~ up** *v.t.* enlever; **~ one's fingers,** faire claquer les doigts; **~ one's fingers at,** se moquer de.

snare *s.* (*lit.* & *fig.*) piège *m.*; *v.t.* prendre au piège.

snarl *s.* **1.** (*act or sound*) grognement *m.*; **2.** (*tangle*) enchevêtrement *m.*, (*traffic*) embouteillage *m.*; *v.i.* (1) grogner; *v.t.* & *i.* (2) **~ up,** (s')embrouiller, embouteiller; **~ing** *adj.* hargneux.

snatch *s.* (*catch*) geste pour saisir *m.*; (*short spell*) courte période *f.*; (*brief view*) coup d'œil *m.*; (*small amount*) bribe *f.*; *v.t.* saisir, s'emparer de; **~ at,** saisir; **~ away (from)** arracher (à); **~ up,** ramasser.

sneak *s.* mouchard *m.*; *v.i.* (*tell tales*) moucharder; (*slink*) se glisser furtivement; **~ away/off,** s'esquiver; **~ in** (*to*), se faufiler dans; **~-thief** *s.* chapardeur *m.*; **~ing** *adj.* furtif; secret, caché.

sneer *s.* ricanement *m.*; (*disdainful*) sourire

méprisant *m.*; *v.i.* ricaner; ~ **at,** se moquer de; ~**ing** *adj.* ricaneur.
sneeze *s.* éternuement *m.*; *v.i.* éternuer; **it's not to be ~d at** (*fig.*) ce n'est pas à dédaigner.
snick *s.* petite entaille *f.*; *v.t.* faire une entaille dans.
snide *adj.* (*pop.*) narquois.
sniff *s.* **1.** (*act, sound*) reniflement *m.*; **2.** (*amount ~ed up*) bouffée *f.*; *v.t.* & *i.* (1) renifler; (2) aspirer.
sniffle *s.* enchifrènement *m.*; *v.i.* être enchifrené.
snigger *s.* rire narquois *m.*; *v.i.* ricaner.
snip *s.* (*act*) coup de ciseaux *m.*; (*small piece*) petit bout *m.*; (*pop. certainty*) affaire avantageuse *f.*; (*pop. bargain*) occasion *f.*; *v.t.* couper.
snipe *s.* bécassine *f.*; *v.i.* chasser la bécassine; ~ **at** *v.t.* canarder; ~**r** *s.* tireur embusqué *m.*
snippet *s.* petit morceau *m.*; (*fig.*) bribe *f.*
snivel *v.i.* être morveux; (*complain*) pleurnicher.
snob *s.* snob *m.*, poseur *m.*; ~**bery** *s.* snobisme *m.*, affectation *f.*; ~**bish** *adj.* poseur, prétentieux.
snood *s.* résille *f.*
snook *s.* **to cock a ~ at s.o.,** faire un pied de nez à qn.
snooker *s.* billard russe *m.*
snoop *v.i.* (*fam.*) fouiner; ~**er** *s.* fouineur *m.*
snoot/y *adj.* arrogant; ~**ily** *adv.* avec arrogance; ~**iness** *s.* arrogance *f.*
snooze *s.* petit somme *m.*; *v.i.* sommeiller.
snore *s.* ronflement *m.*; *v.i.* ronfler.
snorkel *see* SCHNORKEL.
snort *s.* **1.** (*horse*) ébrouement *m.*; **2.** grognement *m.*; *v.i.* (1) s'ébrouer; (2) renifler.
snout *s.* museau *m.*; (*pig's*) groin *m.*
snow *s.* neige *f.*; (*pop. cocaine*) neige *f.*; ~**ball** *s.* boule de neige *f.*; ~**ball** *v.i.* (*fig.*) faire boule de neige; ~**-blindness** *s.* cécité des neiges *f.*; ~**-drift** *s.* congère *f.*; ~**drop** *s.* perce-neige *f.*; ~**flake** *s.* flocon de neige *m.*; ~**-line** *s.* limite des neiges perpétuelles *f.*; ~**man** *s.* bonhomme de neige *m.*; ~-PLOUGH; ~**-shoe** *s.* raquette *f.*; **S~-White,** Blanche-Neige *f.*; ~**y** *adj.* de neige, (*weather*) neigeux; *v.i.* neiger; ~**ed up,** bloqué par la neige; ~**ed under with** (*fig.*) accablé de.
snub *s.* rebuffade *f.*; *v.t.* rabrouer; ~**-nosed** *adj.* camus.
snuff *s.* tabac à priser *m.*; **to take ~,** priser; ~**box** *s.* tabatière *f.*; *v.t.* éteindre, moucher; ~**ers** *s.* mouchettes *f.pl.*
snug *adj.* (*house, position*) confortable; (*bed*) douillet; (*person*) bien au chaud; (*site*) bien abrité; ~**gery** *s.* sanctuaire *m.*; ~**gle** *v.t.* dorloter, *v.i.* se pelotonner (dans, contre); ~**ly** *adv.* confortablement, chaudement.
so *adv.* (*in this or that manner*) ainsi; **why do you speak ~?,** pourquoi parlez-vous ainsi?; **it is better ~,** il vaut mieux ainsi; (*to this or that extent*) si, tellement; ~ **bad,** si mauvais; ~ **beautiful a thing,** une si belle chose; (*likewise*) de même; ~ **be it,** ainsi soit-il; **and ~ forth, and ~ on,** et ainsi de suite; ~ **long!** (*fam.*) à bientôt!; ~ **long as,** pourvu que; ~ **many, ~ much,** tant de; ~ **that** *conj.* afin de (+ *inf.*), afin que, de sorte que (+ *subj.*) **I came early ~ that I could see you,** je suis venu de bonne heure, afin de vous voir; **I came early ~ that you could go,** je suis venu de bonne heure afin que (de sorte que) vous puissiez partir; *adv.* & *conj.* (*therefore*) donc; **he says he is ill, ~ he cannot come,** il dit qu'il est malade, donc il ne peut pas venir; *adv.* (*also, as well*) aussi; **and ~ did I,** et moi aussi; *adv.* & *pron.* (*obj. of verbs of saying, thinking, etc.*) le, **I think ~,** je le pense; **we hope ~,** nous l'espérons; **I told you ~,** je vous l'ai dit; ~**-called** *adj.* prétendu; ~ **to speak,** pour ainsi dire; ~**-and-~,** un tel; ~-~ *adj. adv.* comme ci, comme ça; **or ~,** environ, à peu près; **six or ~,** environ six; **an hour or ~,** à peu près une heure.
soak *v.t.* & *i.* tremper; ~ **in,** ~ **up,** absorber; ~**ed to the skin,** trempé jusqu'aux os; ~**-away** *s.* puisard *n.*; ~**ing** *s.* trempe *f.*; **to get a ~ing,** se faire tremper.
soap *s.* savon *m.*; ~**-box orator** *s.* orateur de carrefour *m.*; ~**-dish** *s.* porte-savon *m.*; ~ **manufacturer** *s.* savonnier *m.*; ~**stone** *s.* stéatite *f.*; ~ **suds** *s.* eau de savon *f.*; ~**-works** *s.* savonnerie *f.*; ~**y** *adj.* savonneux, (*fig.*) onctueux; *v.t.* savonner; **soft ~** (*fam. fig.*) passer de la pommade à qn.
soar *v.i.* (*rise, lit.* & *fig.*) monter, s'élever; (*hover*) planer.
sob *s.* sanglot *m.*; *v.i.* sangloter; ~**-stuff** *s.* littérature larmoyante *f.*
sober *adj.* (≠ *drunk*) pas ivre; (*moderate*) modéré; (*quiet, of colour*) sobre; (*simple*) simple; ⚠ sobre = **frugal;** ~**ly** *adv.* sobrement, modérément, discrètement; *v.t.* & *i.* (*up or down*) (se) dégriser, (se) calmer.
sobriety *s.* modération *f.*, sobriété *f.*
soccer *s.* football *m.*
sociab/le *adj.* sociable; ~**ility** *s.* sociabilité *f.*; ~**ly** *adv.* amicalement.
social *s.* réunion *f.*; *adj.* social; ~ **security,** sécurité sociale *f.*; ~ **worker,** assistante sociale *f.*; ~**ly** *adv**; ~**ism** *s.* socialisme *m.*; ~**ist** *s.* socialiste *m.f.*; ~**ite** *s.* mondain(e) *m.f.*; ~**ize** *v.t.* socialiser.
society *s.* société *f.*; (*companionship*) compagnie *f.*; (*upper class*) beau monde *m.* (*fam.*) gratin *m.*
sociolog/y *s.* sociologie *f.*; ~**ical** *adj.* sociologique; ~**ist** *s.* sociologue *m.f.*
sock[1] *s.* chaussette *f.*; (*for shoe*) semelle *f.*; **to pull one's ~s up,** se dégourdir, se remuer.
sock[2] *s.* (*pop. blow*) coup *m.*; *v.t.* flanquer un coup à qn.
socket *s.* (*mech., electr.*) douille *f.*; (*tooth*) alvéole *m.*; (*eye*) orbite *f.*
Socrat/es *s.* Socrate *m.*; ~**ic** *adj.* socratique.
sod *s.* motte *f.* (de gazon).
soda *s.* soude *f.*; ~**-water** *s.* soda *m.*
sodden *adj.* détrempé.
sodium *s.* sodium *m.*; ~ **carbonate** *s.* carbonate de sodium *m.*; ~ **chloride** *s.* chlorure de sodium *f.*
sodomy *s.* sodomie *f.*
sofa *s.* divan *m.*, canapé *m.*
soft *adj.* (≠ *hard, malleable, feeble*) mou (molle); (≠ *loud, mild, gentle, luxurious, water*) doux; (*smooth*) lisse; (*easily moved*) tendre, compatissant; (*silly*) niais, faible; (*pop.* = *easy*) facile; (*drinks*) sucré; ~ COLLAR; ~ **goods,** tissus *m.pl.*; ~ JOB; ~**pedal** *v.t.* atténuer; ~ SOAP; ~ SPOT; ~ **sugar,** sucre en poudre *m.*; ~**wood,** bois blanc *m.*; ~**en** *v.t.* & *i.* (*make or become less hard*) (s')amollir, (*fig.*) (s')adoucir; (*relieve*) atténuer; ~**ly** *adv.* doucement; ~**ness** *s.* mollesse *f.*, douceur *f.*
soggy *adj.* détrempé; (*cook.*) pâteux.
soh *s.* (*mus.*) sol *m.*
soil *s.* **1.** (*ground*) sol *m.*; (*fig.*) pays *m.*; **2.** (*dirty mark*) saleté *f.*; (2) *v.t.* souiller; *v.i.* se salir.
sojourn *s.* séjour *m.*; *v.i.* séjourner.
solace *s.* consolation *f.*; *v.t.* consoler.
solar *adj.* solaire; ~**ium** *s.* solarium *m.*
solder(ing) *s.* soudure *f.*; *v.t.* souder; ~**ing-iron** *s.* fer à souder *m.*
soldier *s.* soldat *m.*, militaire *m.*; ~**ly** *adj. adv.* de soldat; ~**y** *s.* (*pej.*) soldatesque *f.*; *v.i.* ~ **on** (*fam.*) persévérer.
sole[1] *s.* (*of foot*) plante *f.*; (*of shoe*) semelle *f.*; (*of plough*) cep *m.*; ~**d** *adj.* à semelles; *v.t.* ressemeler.
sole[2] *s.* (*fish*) sole *f.*; **lemon ~,** limande *f.*

sole[3] *adj.* (*one and only*) seul, unique; (*exclusive*) exclusif; **~ly** *adv* uniquement.
solecism *s.* solécisme *m.*
solemn *adj.* solennel; (*grave*) sérieux, grave; **~ly** *adv.**;*,*; **~ity** *s.* solennité *f.*; gravité *f.*, sérieux *m.*; (*occasion*) fête solennelle *f.*; **~ize** *v.t.* solenniser; (*marriage*) célébrer; **~ization** *s.* célébration *f.*
solenoid *s.* (*electr.*) solénoïde *m.*
sol-fa *s.* (*mus.*) solfège *m.*
solicit *v.t.* **1.** (*ask urgently*) solliciter (qch. à qn.); **2.** (*importune*) importuner; **3.** (*request, invite*) demander, inviter; **4.** (*accost immorally*) racoler; **~ation** *s.* (1) sollicitation *f.*; (4) racolage *m.*; **~or** *s.* (*law*) avoué *m.*; **~ous** *adj.* (*concerned*) inquiet (*about*—de), (*anxious*) soucieux (*to*—de); **~ude** *s.* sollicitude *f.*, souci *m.*
solid *s.* solide *m.*; *adj.* (≠ *liquid*) solide; (*hard*) massif; (≠ *hollow*) plein; (*unalloyed, silver, etc.*) pur; (*substantial*) effectif; (*person*) posé; (*unanimous*) unanime, solidaire; **~arity** *s.* solidarité *f.*; **~ify** *v.t.* & *i.* (se) solidifier; **~ification** *s.* solidification *f.*; **~ity** *s.* solidité *f.*; **~ly** *adv.* solidement.
soliloqu/y *s.* monologue *m.*; **~ize** *v.i.* monologuer.
solitaire *s.* (*diamond*) solitaire *m.*; (*card game*) jeu de patience *m.*
solitar/y *s.* solitaire *m.*; *adj.* **1.** (*alone*) solitaire; **2.** (*single*) unique; **3.** (*secluded*) retiré; **4.** (*lonely*) isolé; **~iness** *s.* (1) solitude *f.*; (4) isolement *m.*
solitude *s.* solitude *f.*
solo *s.* (*mus., dance*) solo *m.*; (*cards*) whist *m.*; *adj. adv.* seul, en solo; **~ist** *s.* soliste *m.f.*
solstice *s.* solstice *m.*
solub/le *adj.* soluble; **~ility** *s.* solubilité *f.*
solution *s.* solution *f.*
solv/e *v.t.* résoudre; **~ent** *s.* dissolvant *m.*; **~ent** *adj.* **1.** (*fin.*) solvable; **2.** (*that dissolves*) dissolvant; **~ency** *s.* (1) solvabilité *f.*
Somali/a *s.* (*geog.*) Somalie *f.*; **~** *adj.* & *s.m.f.* somali(e).
sombre *adj.* sombre.
sombrero *s.* sombrero *m.*
some *adj.* (*particular but unspecified*) quelque(s); (*quantity*) du, de, la, des; **~ milk,** du lait; **~ good milk,** du bon lait; **~ meat,** de la viande; **~ bad meat,** de la mauvaise viande; **~ boys,** des garçons; **~ naughty boys,** de mauvais garçons; *indef. pron.* en, un peu de, quelques-un(e)s; **give me ~,** donne-m'en; **do you want ~?,** en voulez-vous?; **~ of the time,** une partie du temps; **~ of my friends,** quelques-uns de mes amis; **~ left, ~ stayed,** les uns sont partis, les autres sont restés; (*approximation*) **~ 5000 people,** quelque cinq mille personnes; **~ 20, 30, etc.,** une vingtaine, une trentaine, etc. (de); (*expressing admiration*) **~ meal!,** quel repas!; **~body** *pron.* quelqu'un, on; **~body** *s.* (*fam.*) personnage *m.*, quelqu'un *m.*; **~how** *adv.* (*indifferently*) tant bien que mal, (*in a way*) dans un certain sens; **~how or other,** d'une manière ou d'une autre; **~one,** quelqu'un; **~thing,** quelque chose; ⚠ + *adj. m.* **~thing good,** quelque chose de bon; **~thing or other,** je ne sais quoi; **~time** (*formerly*) autrefois; (*future*) un de ces jours; **~times,** quelquefois, parfois; **~times . . . ~times,** tantôt . . . tantôt; **~what,** quelque peu, un peu; **~where,** quelque part.
somersault *s.* culbute *f.*; **to turn a ~,** faire la culbute; *v.i.* culbuter.
somnambul/ism *s.* somnambulisme *m.*; **~ist** *s.* somnambuliste *m.f.*
somnolen/ce *s.* somnolence *f.*; **~t** *adj.* somnolent.
son *s.* fils *m.*; **~-in-law,** gendre *m.*; **~ny** (*fam.*) mon garçon.
sonar *s.* (*naut.*) sonar *m.*
sonat/a *s.* sonate *f.*; **~ina** *s.* sonatine *f.*
song *s.* (*singing*) chant *m.*; (*piece of music*) chanson *f.*; (*eccles.*) cantique *f.*; **for a ~** (*fig.*) pour une bouchée de pain; **~-bird,** oiseau chanteur *m.*; **~ster, ~stress** chanteur *m.*, chanteuse *f.*
sonic *adj.* sonique; **~ boom** *s.* bang (supersonique) *m.*
sonnet *s.* sonnet *m.*
sonor/ous *adj.* sonore; **~ity** *s.*, **~ousness** *s.* sonorité *f.*
soon *adv.* bientôt; **so ~,** si tôt; **too ~,** trop tôt; **as ~ as,** aussitôt que; **~er** *adv.* (*time*) plus tôt, (*rather*) plutôt; **he would ~er walk home than stay here,** il aimerait mieux rentrer à pied que de rester ici; **~er or** LATER; **no ~er . . . than,** à peine . . . que; **no ~er said than done,** aussitôt dit, aussitôt fait.
soot *s.* suie *f.*; *v.t.* & *i.* **~ up** (s')encrasser de suie; **~y** *adj.* couvert de suie.
sooth *s.* **in ~,** en vérité; **~sayer** *s.* devin *m.*, devineresse *f.*
soothe *v.t.* calmer.
sop *s.* pain trempé *m.*; (*fig.*) offrande propitiatoire *f.*; *v.t.* & *i.* (*soak*) (faire) tremper; (*absorb*) absorber; **~ping wet** *adj.* trempé; **~py** *adj.* (*fam.*) fadasse.
soph/ism *s.* sophisme *m.*; **~ist** *s.* sophiste *m.f.*; **~istical** *adj.* sophistique; **~istry** *s.* sophisme *m.*
sophisticat/e, *v.t.* altérer, dénaturer; **~ed** *adj.* sophistiqué, (*fig.*) raffiné; **~ion** *s.* sophistication *f.*, (*fig.*) raffinement *m.*
soporific *adj.* & *s.m.* soporifique.
soprano *s.* soprano *m.*
sorbet *s.* sorbet *m.*
sorcer/er *s.* sorcier *m.*; **~ess** *s.* sorcière *f.*; **~y** *s.* sorcellerie *f.*
sordid *adj.* **1.** (*squalid, mean*) sordide; **2.** (*ignoble*) bas, vil; **3.** (*avaricious*) mesquin; **~ly** *adv.* (1)*; (2)*; (3)*; **~ness** *s.* (1) saleté *f.*; (2) bassesse *f.*; (3) mesquinerie *f.*
sore *s.* plaie *f.*; (*ulcer*) ulcère *m.*; *adj.* (*painful*) douloureux; (*sensitive*) sensible; (*irritated*) enflammé; (*fig.*) cruel, urgent; (*fam. fig. angry*) fâché; **to have a ~ throat, etc.,** avoir mal à la gorge, etc.; **a ~ point** (*fig.*) point sensible *m.*; **a** BEAR **with a ~ head; ~ly** *adv.* (*fig.*) cruellement; **~ness** *s.* sensibilité *f.*; (*fig.*) peine *f.*
sorrel *s.* (*herb*) oseille *f.*; *adj.* & *s.m.* (*horse*) alezan.
sorrow *s.* chagrin *m.*, peine *f.*; *v.i.* avoir du chagrin, s'affliger (de); (*mourn for*) regretter; **~ful** *adj.* (*look, person*) triste, (*news*) pénible; **~fully** *adv.* tristement.
sorr/y *adj.* (*pained at*) peiné; (*regretful, pitying*) désolé (*about*—de); (*wretched, mean*) pauvre, misérable; **to be ~y about,** regretter (qch.); **to be ~y for,** plaindre (qn.); (*I'm*) **~y!,** pardon!; **a ~y** PLIGHT; **~ily** *adv.* tristement, pauvrement.
sort *s.* sorte *f.*, genre *m.*; **after a ~,** en quelque sorte; **an artist** (*etc.*) **of a ~,** une espèce d'artiste (etc.); **a good ~,** un brave type *m.*; **to be out of ~s,** être mal en train; *v.t.* classer; (*mail*) trier; **~er** *s.* trieur *m.*; (*machine*) trieuse *f.*; **~ing** *s.* tri *m.*; **~ing office** *s.* centre de tri *m.*
SOS *s.* S.O.S. *m.*
sot *s.* ivrogne *m.*; **~tish** *adj.* abruti (par l'alcool).
sotto voce *adv.* en sourdine.
S(o)udan *s.* (*geog.*) Soudan *m.*; **~ese** *adj.* & *s.m.f.* soudanais(e); (*hist.*) *until 1956* = Soudan anglo-égyptien *m.*; ⚠ Soudan français = Mali *since 1960.*
soufflé *s.* (*cook.*) soufflé *m.*
sough *v.i.* soupirer.
soul *s.* âme *f.*; **I don't see a (living) ~,** je ne vois pas âme qui vive; **the life and ~ of the**

party, le boute-en-train (de la fête); **to be the ~ of discretion, etc.,** être la discrétion (etc.) même; **~-destroying** *adj.* abrutissant; **~-searching** *s.* examen de conscience *m.*; **~-stirring** *adj.* émouvant; **~ful** *adj.* expressif, sentimental; **~less** *adj.* bas.

sound[1] *s.* (*vibrations*) son *m.*, bruit *m.*; (*fig.*) impression *f.*; **not to like the ~ of sth.,** avoir une mauvaise impression de qch.; **~ barrier** *s.* mur du son *m.*; **~-proof** *adj.* insonorisé; **~-proof** *v.t.* insonoriser; **~-track** *s.* bande sonore *f.*; **~-wave** *s.* onde acoustique *f.*; **~less** *adj.* silencieux; *v.t.* & *i.* sonner; (*praises*) chanter; **~ing** *adj.* sonore, sonnant, (*fig.*) imposant; **~ing-board** *s.* abat-voix *m.*

sound[2] *adj.* **1.** (*healthy*) sain; **2.** (*fin. safe*) solide, solvable; **3.** (*correct, valid*) valable, juste, droit; **4.** (*thorough*) vigoureux; **5.** (*sleep*) profond; **6.** (*naut.*) solide, en bon état; **~ly** *adv.* (1)*; (2)*; (3), (4) bien; (5) profondément; **~ness** *s.* (1) bonne santé *f.*; (2) solidité *f.*; solvabilité *f.*; (3) justesse *f.*; (5) profondeur *f.*; (6) bon état *m.*

sound[3] *s.* (*strait*) détroit *m.*

sound[4] *s.* (*probe*) sonde *f.*; *v.t.* sonder; (*med.*) ausculter; **~ing** *s.* sondage *m.*; **~less** *adj.* insondable.

soup *s.* soupe *f.*, potage *m.*, consommé *m.*; **to be in the ~** (*fig.*) être dans le pétrin; **~-spoon** *s.* cuiller à soupe *f.*; **~-tureen** *s.* soupière *f.*

sour *adj.* (*taste*) aigre; (*milk*) tourné; (*smell*) acide; (*fig.*) acariâtre; **to turn ~** *v.i.* (*milk*) tourner; *v.t.* & *i.* (s')aigrir; **~ly** *adv.* aigrement; **~ness** *s.* aigreur *f.*

source *s.* source *f.*; (*of infection, revolt, etc.*) foyer *m.*

souse *v.t.* faire mariner.

south *s.* sud *m.*; (*part of country*) midi *m.*; *adj.* sud (*invar.*), du sud, méridional; *adv.* vers le sud; **~-east,** sud-est; **~-west,** sud-ouest; **~-eastern** *adj.* du sud-est; **~-western** *adj.* du sud-ouest; **S~ Africa, S~ America,** Afrique, Amérique, du sud; **S~ Pole** *s.* pôle sud *m.*; **~erly** *adj.* du sud; **~ern** *adj.* du sud, méridional; **~erner** *s.* méridional *m.*; **~ward** *adv.* vers le sud.

souvenir *s.* souvenir *m.*

sou'wester *s.* (*wind* & *hat*) suroît *m.*

sovereign *s.* souverain *m.*; *adj.* souverain; (*very good*) suprême; **~ty** *s.* souveraineté *f.*

soviet *s.* soviet *m.*; **S~ Union** *s.* Union Soviétique *f.* ; **~ize** *v.t.* soviétiser.

sow[1] *s.* (*pig*) truie *f.*

sow[2] *v.t.* (*seed* & *fig.*) semer; (*a field*) ensemencer; **~ wild** OATS; **~er** *s.* semeur *m.*; **~ing** *s.* semailles *f.pl.*

soya *s.* (*bean*) soja, soya *m.*

spa *s.* station thermale *f.*

space *s.* espace *m.*; (*continuous expanse*) étendue *f.*; *adj.* spatial; **~-bar** *s.* (*typewriter*) barre d'espacement *m.*; **~man** *s.* astronaute *m.*; **~ship** *s.*, **~craft** *s.* astronef *m.*; **~suit** *s.* scaphandre *m.*; **spacious** *adj.* spacieux; **spaciously** *adv.**; **spaciousness** *s.* étendue *f.*, vastes dimensions *f.pl.* *v.t.* espacer; **spacing** *s.* espacement *m.*

spade *s.* (*tool*) bêche *f.*; (*child's*) pelle *f.*; (*cards*) pique *m.*; (*pop. coloured person*) bougnoule *m.f.*; **to** CALL **a ~ a ~**; **~ful** *s.* pelletée *f.*

spaghetti *s.* spaghetti *m.pl.*; ~ JUNCTION.

spahi *s.* spahi *m.*

Spa/in *s.* (*geog.*) Espagne *f.*; CASTLES **in ~in**; **~niard** *s.m.f.* Espagnol(e); **~nish** *adj.* espagnol; *s.m.* (*lang.*) espagnol; **~nish fly** *s.* cantharide *f.* **~nish Main** *s.* mer des Antilles *f.*

span *s.* **1.** (*space*) empan *m.*; **2.** (*time*) espace de temps *m.*, séjour *m.*, durée *f.*; **3.** (*of bridge*) travée *f.*, (*of wings*) envergure *f.*; **4.** (*of horses, oxen*) paire *f.*; *v.t.* (1) mesurer à l'empan, (*extend*) étendre; (2) (*cover period*) comprendre; (3) traverser; (4) accoupler; SPICK **and ~.**

spandrel *s.* (*arch.*) tympan *m.*

spangle *s.* paillette *f.*; *v.t.* pailleter; STAR-**~d banner.**

Spaniard *see* SPAIN.

spaniel *s.* épagneul *m.*

Spanish *see* SPAIN.

spank *v.t.* **1.** (*slap*) fesser, donner une fessée à; **2.** *v.i.* (*horse*) galoper; **~er** *s.* (2) cheval rapide *m.*; (*sail*) brigantine *f.*; **~ing** *s.* (1) fessée *f.*; **~ing** *adj.* (*pop.*) (*very large*) fameux, (*dashing*) épatant.

spanner *s.* clef *f.*; **to throw a ~ in the works** (*fig.*) mettre des bâtons dans les roues.

spar[1] *s.* (*naut.*) espart *m.*

spar[2] *v.i.* se battre, s'entraîner (à la boxe); (*dispute*) se disputer; **~ring partner** *s.* entraîneur *m.* (à la boxe), (*fig.*) antagoniste *m.*

spare *adj.* (*scanty, frugal*) maigre, frugal; (*lean*) maigre; (*not required*) disponible; (*emergency*) de réserve, de rechange; **~ part** *s.* pièce de rechange *f.*; **~-rib** *s.* (*meat*) côte découverte *f.*; **~ room** *s.* chambre d'amis *f.*; **~ time** *s.* moments perdus *m.pl.*, loisir *m.*; **~ wheel** *s.* roue de secours *f.*; **~ly** *adv.* maigrement, frugalement; **~ness** *s.* maigreur *f.*; *v.t.* (*refrain from punishing, etc.*) épargner; (*dispense with*) se passer de; (*be frugal with*) économiser, ménager; (*part with*) se priver de; (*avoid*) éviter; **~ no expense,** ne pas regarder à la dépense; **~ no effort** *or* **trouble,** ne pas marchander sa peine; **have to ~,** avoir à revendre; **sparing** *adj.* frugal, économe, (*fig.*) avare (*with*—de); **sparingly** *adv.* frugalement.

spark *s.* (*fiery particle; electr.; auto.*) étincelle *f.*; (*fig.*) lueur *f.*, souffle *m.*; (*person*) **gay ~,** joyeux drille *m.*; *v.t.* & *i.* jeter des étincelles; **~ off** *v.t.* déclencher; **~ing**-PLUG.

sparkl/e *s.* étincelle *f.*; (*of eyes*) pétillement *m.*; *v.i.* (*lit.* & *fig.*) étinceler; pétiller; **~ing** *adj.* étincelant; (*wines*) mousseux.

sparrow *s.* moineau *m.*; **~-hawk** *s.* épervier *m.*; **~**-OWL.

sparse *adj.* épars; **~ly** *adv.* peu, **~ly populated,** qui a une population clairsemée.

Sparta *s.* (*geog.*) Sparte *f.*; **~n** *adj.* & *s.m.f.* spartiate.

spasm *s.* (*muscular*) spasme *m.*; (*fig.*) accès *m.*; **~odic** *adj.* (*sudden, violent*) spasmodique, convulsif; (*intermittent*) fait par à-coups; **~odically** *adv.* d'une façon spasmodique, irrégulièrement.

spastic *adj.* & *s.m.f.* paraplégique.

spat *s.* demi-guêtre *f.*

spate *s.* (*of river*) crue *f.*; (*rush, outpouring*) flot *m.*, marée *f.*

spatial *adj.* spatial.

spatter *v.t.* éclabousser (*with*—de).

spatula *s.* spatule *f.*; **~te** *adj.* spatulé.

spawn *s.* **1.** (*of fish*) frai *m.*; **2.** (*of mushrooms*) blanc *m.*; **3.** (*brood*) progéniture *f.*; *v.t.* & *i.* (1) frayer; (*fig.*) (se) multiplier.

spay *v.t.* châtrer.

speak *v.t.* (*words*) prononcer; (*say*) dire; (*reveal*) révéler; (*lang.*) parler; ⚠ parler *is v.t. only with lang.*; **to ~ French,** parler français; **to ~ the truth,** *etc.*, dire la vérité, *etc.*; *v.i.* parler; **so to ~,** pour ainsi dire; **~ for,** plaider en faveur de qn.; **~ of,** parler de; **~ out,** parler net; **~ up,** parler fort; **~er** *s.* (*orator*) orateur *m.*; (*parl.*) président *m.*; (*loud~er*) haut-parleur *m.*; **~ing** *s.* art oratoire *m.*; *adj.* parlant; (*telephone*) **John ~ing,** Jean à l'appareil; **not on ~ing terms,** brouillé; **~ing-trumpet** *s.* porte-voix *m.*; **~ing-tube** *s.* tuyau acoustique *m.*

spear *s.* (*weapon*) lance *f.*; (*fishing*) harpon *m.*; (*of grass*) brin *m.*; (*of plant*) tige *f.*; **~head** *s.* fer-de-lance *m.*; **~head** *v.t.* être le fer-de-lance

de; **~mint** *s.* menthe verte *f.*; *v.t.* percer d'une lance.
special *adj.* (*restricted*) spécial; (≠ *general*) particulier; (*exceptional*) exceptionnel; **S~ Branch,** Renseignements généraux *m.pl.*; ~ CONSTABLE; ~ **licence** *s.* dispense spéciale *f.*; **~ist** *s.* spécialiste *m.f.*; **~ity** *s.* spécialité *f.*, (*feature*) particularité *f.*; **~ize** *v.i.* se spécialiser (dans); **~ly** *adv.* spécialement, particulièrement, (*on purpose*) dans un but particulier.
specie *s.* espèces *f.pl.*
species *s.* espèce *f.*
specif/ic *s.* spécifique *m.*; *adj.* spécifique; (*definite*) explicite, précis; **~ically** *adv.**;*,*; **~ication** *s.* devis descriptif *m.*; (*of product*) spécification *f.*; (*of work to be done*) prescriptions *f.pl.*; **~y** *v.t.* spécifier; (*set down as necessary*) préciser.
specimen *s.* spécimen *m.*; (*sample*) échantillon *m.*; (*copy*) exemplaire *m.*
specious *adj.* spécieux; (*plausible*) captieux; **~ly** *adv.**;*; **~ness** *s.* nature spécieuse *f.*
speck *s.* (*of dust*) grain *m.*; (*of colour, mud, etc.*). tache *f.*; **~less** *adj.* sans tache; **~le** *s.* tache *f.*; *v.t.* tacheter.
spectac/le *s.* spectacle *m.*; (*pair of*) **~les** *s.pl.* lunettes *f.pl.*; **~ular** *adj.* spectaculaire, impressionnant.
spectator *s.* spectat/eur, -rice *m.f.*; (*witness*) témoin *m.*; **~s** *s.pl.* assistance *f.*, public *m.*
spectr/e *s.* spectre *m.*; **~al** *adj.* spectral.
spectr/um *s.* spectre *m.*; **~oscope** *s.* spectroscope *m.*; **~oscopic** *adj.* spectroscopique.
speculat/e *v.i.* (*meditate*; *fin.*) spéculer (*on, about, in*—sur); **~ion** *s.* spéculation *f.*; **~ive** *adj.* spéculatif; **~or** *s.* (*fin.*) spéculat/eur, -rice *m.f.*, (*theorist*) penseur *m.*
speculum *s.* spéculum *m.*
speech *s.* (*act or faculty of speaking*) parole *f.*; (*manner of speaking*) élocution *f.*; (*dialect*) langue *f.*, langage *m.*; (*things said*) discours *m.*, paroles *f.pl.*; (*address*) discours *m.*, conférence *f.*, allocution *f.*; **~-day** *s.* distribution des prix *f.*; ~ **defect** *s.* défaut d'élocution *m.*; ~ **therapy** *s.* orthophonie *f.*; **~ify** *v.i.* pérorer; **~less** *adj.* muet (*with*—de).
speed *s.* vitesse *f.*; **at full or top ~,** à toute vitesse; **engine-~** *s.* régime *m.*; **more** HASTE **less ~**; **~boat** *s.* hors-bord *m.*; ~ **limit** *s.* vitesse maximum *f.*; **~-**MERCHANT; **~way** *s.* piste *f.*; **~well** *s.* véronique *f.*; **~ometer** *s.* indicateur de vitesse *m.*; **~y** *adj.* rapide, prompt; **~ily** *adv.**,*; *v.i.* se presser; (*drive too fast*) faire de la vitesse; *v.t.* (*bid farewell to*) souhaiter bon voyage à; (*help*) aider; ~ **up** *v.t.* & *i.* accélérer.
speleolog/y *s.* spéléologie *f.*; **~ist** *s.* spéléologue *m.f.*
spell[1] *s.* **1.** (*charm*) incantation *f.*, charme *m.*; **2.** (*fascination*) charme *m.*; **3.** (*turn of work*) tour *m.*; **4.** (*short period*) intervalle *m.*, BRIGHT ~; **~bound** *adj.* (1) ensorcelé; (2) sous le charme de; *v.t.* (3) relever, relayer.
spell[2] *v.t.* & *i.* (*form words*) épeler; (*in writing*) orthographier; (*mean*) signifier; ~ **out,** expliquer en détail; **~ing** *s.* orthographe *f.*
spend *v.t.* (*money*) dépenser; (*time*) passer; (*waste*) dissiper, gaspiller; (*exhaust*) épuiser; **~thrift** *adj.* prodigue.
spent *adj.* épuisé; (*bullet*) (balle) morte.
sperm *s.* sperme *m.*; ~ **whale** *s.* cachalot *m.*
spermatozoon *s.* spermatozoïde *m.*
spew *v.t.* & *i.* vomir.
sphagnum *s.* sphaigne *f.*
spher/e *s.* sphère *f.*; (*fig.*) domaine *m.*, compétence *f.*; **~ical** *adj.* sphérique; **~oid** *adj.* & *s.m.* sphéroïde.
sphincter *s.* sphincter *m.*
sphinx *s.* sphinx *m.*
spic/e *s.* (*herb*) épice *f.*; (*fig.*) grain *m.*, pointe *f.*; *v.t.* épicer; (*fig.*) pimenter; **~y** *adj.* épicé, relevé; (*fig.*) salé, pimenté.
spick (and span) *adj.* (*room, etc.*) bien astiqué; (*person*) tiré à quatre épingles.
spider *s.* araignée *f.*; **~'s web** *s.* toile d'araignée *f.*; **~y** *adj.* qui ressemble à une araignée; **~y writing,** écriture en pattes de mouches *f.*
spigot *s.* fausset *m.*
spike *s.* pointe *f.*; (*large nail*) clou *m.* (à large tête); (*of flower*) épi *m.*; *v.t.* clouer; ~ **s.o.'s guns,** damer le pion à qn.
spikenard *s.* nard *m.*
spill *s.* **1.** (*fall*) chute *f.*; **2.** (*strip of wood or paper*) allumette *f.* (de copeau, de papier); *v.t.* & *i.* (1) (se) renverser; (*shed blood, etc.*) (se) répandre; (*from horse*) désarçonner; ~ **the beans,** vendre la mèche; **it's no use crying over spilt milk,** ce qui est fait est fait.
spin *s.* (*motion*) tournoiement *m.*; (*aviat.*) vrille *f.*; (*short trip*) promenade *f.*; **to be in a flat ~** (*fig.*) avoir la tête qui tourne; *v.t.* & *i.* (*like a top*) (faire) tourner, pivoter; (*yarn, web*) filer; ~ **a yarn,** raconter une histoire; **~-off** *s.* (*comm.*) à-côté *m.*; ~ **out** *v.t.* faire traîner en longueur; **~-**DRIER; **~ner** *s.* fileu/r, -se *m.f.*; **~ning** *s.* (*by hand*) filage *m.*, (*by machine*) filature *f.*; **~ning-wheel** *s.* rouet *m.*
spina bifida *s.* spina-bifida *m.*
spinach *s.* épinards *m.pl.*; ~ **beet** *s.* épinard *m.*
spinal *adj.* *see* SPINE.
spindl/e *s.* (*in spinning*) fuseau *m.*; (*axis*) axe *m.*, pivot *m.*; **~y** *adj.* long et maigre.
spindrift *s.* embrun *m.*
spin/e *s.* (*backbone*) épine dorsale *f.*; (*thorn*) épine *f.*; (*zool.*) piquant *m.*; (*ridge*) arête *f.*; (*of book*) dos *m.*; **~al** *adj.* (*nerve, muscle*) spinal; **~al column** *s.* colonne vertébrale *f.*; **~al cord** *s.* moelle épinière *f.*; **~eless** *adj.* (*fig.*) mou; **~y** *adj.* (*lit.* & *fig.*) épineux.
spinet *s.* épinette *f.*
spinnaker *s.* spinnaker *m.*
spinney *s.* boqueteau *m.*
spinster *s.* vieille fille *f.*; (*law*) célibataire *f.*; **~hood** *s.* célibat *m.*
spiræa *s.* spirée *f.*
spiral *s.* spirale *f.*; *adj.* en spirale; (*staircase*) en colimaçon; *v.i.* tourner en spirale; (*prices*) monter en flèche.
spire *s.* flèche *f.*; ⇧ spire = **whorl.**
spirit *s.* (*vital principle*; *tone, mood*) esprit *m.*; **Holy S~,** saint Esprit *m.*; (≠ *flesh*) âme *f.*; (*person*) âme *f.*; (*ghost*) spectre *m.*; (*fairy*) fée *f.*, lutin *m.*; (*courage*) cœur *m.*, ardeur *f.*, courage *m.*; **~s** *s.pl.* alcool *m.*, spiritueux *m.pl.*; METHYLATED **~s; high ~s,** entrain *m.*; **low ~s,** abattement *m.*; **~-lamp** *s.* lampe à alcool *f.*; **~-**LEVEL; **~ed** *adj.* animé, (*horse*) fougueux, (*brave*) courageux; **~less** *adj.* sans courage, sans caractère, sans vigueur, sans entrain, abattu; **~uous** *adj.* spiritueux; *v.t.* ~ **away** *v.t.* faire disparaître.
spiritual *s.* chant religieux des Noirs *m.*; *adj.* spirituel, de l'esprit; (≠ *temporal*) spirituel; (*law*) ecclésiastique; **~ly** *adv.**; **~ism** *s.* spiritualisme *m.*, spiritisme *m.*; **~ist** *s.* (*philos.*) spiritualiste *m.f.*; spirite *m.*; **~ity** *s.* spiritualité *f.*; **~ize** *v.t.* spiritualiser.
spit *s.* **1.** (*for roasting*) broche *f.*; **2.** (*of land*) pointe de terre *f.*; **3.** (*spittle*) crachat *m.*; **4. he is the (dead) ~ and image (***or* **the ~ting image) of his father,** c'est son père tout craché; *v.t.* & *i.* (1) embrocher; (3) cracher, (*with rain*) crachiner; **~fire** *s.* rageu/r, -se *m.f.*; **~ting** *s.* crachement *m.*; **~tle** *s.* crachat *m.*; **~toon** *s.* crachoir *m.*
spite *s.* rancune *f.*; (*bitterness*) dépit *m.*; **in ~ of,** malgré; **~ful** *adj.* rancunier; **~fully** *adv.* par

rancune; **~fulness** *s.* rancune *f.*; *v.t.* contrarier; **cut off one's** NOSE **to ~ one's face.**

spiv *s.* (*pop.*) chevalier d'industrie *m.*, escroc *m.*

splash *s.* (*sound*) éclaboussement *m.*; (*mark*) éclaboussure *f.*; (*water*) tache *f.*; (*fam.*) **to make a ~,** faire sensation; *v.t.* éclabousser (*with*—de); (*fam.*) mettre en manchette; *v.i.* barboter; **~-down** *s.* (*space*) amérissage *m.*

splay *v.t.* & *i.* (s')évaser.

spleen *s.* (*anat.*) rate *f.*; (*moroseness*) humeur noire *f.*

splend/id *adj.* splendide; (*fam.*) épatant; **~idly** *adv.**, d'une façon épatante; **~our,** *s.* splendeur *f.*

splice *s.* épissure *f.*; *v.t.* épisser.

splint *s.* éclisse *f.*; *v.t.* éclisser.

splinter *s.* éclat *m.*; (*of bone*) esquille *f.*; *v.t.* & *i.* (faire) voler en éclats; **~ group,** groupe dissident *m.*

split *s.* (*fissure*) fente *f.*; (*schism*) rupture *f.*; (*bun*) petit pain *m.*; **~s** *s.pl.* grand écart *m.*; **to do the ~s,** faire le grand écart; *v.t.* & *i.* (se) fendre, (se) diviser; (*share out*) partager; (*pop.*) cafarder; **~ asunder** *v.t.* & *i.* (se) fendre en deux; **~ up** *v.t.* partager, *v.i.* se séparer; se fractionner; **~ the difference,** couper la poire en deux; ~ HAIRS; **~ one's** SIDES; **~-level** *adj.* sur deux niveaux; **~ pin** *s.* goupille *f.*; **~ second** *adj.* ultra-rapide; **~ting** *adj.* (*headache*) atroce.

splotch *s.* tache *f.*

splutter *v.i.* (*talk indistinctly*) bredouiller; (*fly into pieces*) pétiller; (*sound*) crachoter.

spoil *s.* (*usu. pl.*) butin *m.*; *v.t.* (*plunder*) piller; (*destroy*) abîmer; (*impair*) avarier; (*over-indulge*) gâter; *v.i.* se gâter, s'abîmer; **~er** *s.* spoliat/eur, -rice *m.f.*; **~-sport** *s.* rabat-joie *m.*; **to be ~ing for,** brûler de désir de (se battre, etc.).

spoke *s.* (*of wheel*) rayon *m.*; (*rung of ladder*) échelon *m.*; **~shave** *s.* racloir *m.*; **to put a ~ in s.o.'s wheel,** mettre des bâtons dans les roues à qn.

spokes/man *s.* porte-parole *m.* (*also ~woman*).

spoliation *s.* spoliation *f.*

spondee *s.* spondée *m.*

sponge *s.* éponge *f.*; (*cake*) pâte molle *f.*; **to throw up the ~,** abandonner la partie; **~-bag** *s.* nécessaire de toilette *m.*; **~-cake** *s.* gâteau de Savoie *m.*; **spongy** *adj.* spongieux; *v.t.* éponger; **~ on s.o.** vivre aux crochets de qn.; **~r** *s.* (*fig.*) parasite *m.*; **sponging** *s.* nettoyage à l'éponge *m.*, (*fig.*) parasitisme *m.*

sponsor *s.* **1.** (*godfather, mother*) parrain *m.*, marraine *f.*; **2.** (*guarantor*) garant *m.*; **3.** (*of entertainment, etc.*) commanditaire *m.*; *v.t.* (1) parrainer; (2) être le garant de; (3) subventionner; **~ship** *s.* (1) parrainage *m.*; (2), (3) patronage *m.*

spontane/ous *adj.* spontané; **~ously** *adv.**; **~ity** *s.* & **~ousness** *s.* spontanéité *f.*

spook *s.* fantôme *m.*

spool *s.* (*reel, film, etc.*) bobine *f.*; (*sewing machine*) canette *f.*

spoon *s.* cuiller *f.*; **coffee~, dessert-~, soup--~, tea~,** *etc.*, cuiller à café, *etc.*; **to be born with a** SILVER **~ in one's mouth; ~ful** *s.* cuillerée *f.*; **~-feed** *v.t.* (*fig.*) mâcher la besogne pour qn.; *v.t.* prendre avec une cuiller; *v.i.* (*fam.*) se faire des mamours.

spoor *s.* trace *f.*

sporadic *adj.* sporadique; **~ally** *adv.**.

spore *s.* spore *f.*

sport *s.* (*amusement*) divertissement *m.*; (*games*) sport *m.*; (*pop. person*) chic type *m.*; (*laughing stock*) jouet *m.*; **~s** *s.pl.* concours athlétiques *m.pl.*; **~s car** *s.* voiture sport *f.*; **~s coat** *s.* veston sport *m.*; **~sman, ~swoman** *s.* sport/if, -ive *m.f.*; **~smanlike** *adj.* sportif; **~ing** *adj.* de sport, (*person*) sportif; **~ive** *adj.* gai; *v.t.* (*wear*) arborer; *v.i.* jouer, badiner, se divertir; **~ with,** se moquer de, badiner avec.

spot *s.* (*stain, lit.* & *fig.*) tache *f.*; (*pimple*) bouton *m.*; (*place*) endroit *m.*; (*fam. small amount*) goutte *f.*, brin *m.*; **soft ~,** (*fig.*) faible *m.*; **on the ~** (*time*) sur-le-champ, (*place*) sur les lieux, sur place; **in a ~** (*fam. fig.*) dans le pétrin; **~-on** (*fam.*) exactement; **~ cash** *s.* argent comptant *m.*; **~ check** *s.* contrôle-surprise *m.*; **~light** *s.* projecteur *m.*; **~light** *v.t.* (*fig.*) monter en épingle; **~less** *adj.* immaculé; **~-lessness** *s.* propreté *f.*; **~ted** *adj.* taché; **~ty** *adj.* tacheté; *v.t.* & *i.* (*mark*) (se) tacher, tacheter; (*fam. pick out*) repérer.

spouse *s.* épou/x, -se *m.f.*

spout *s.* (*of roof*) gouttière *f.*; (*of vessel*) bec *m.*; (*of liquid*) jet *m.*; **up the ~** (*fig. fam.*) chez ma tante; *v.t.* & *i.* (faire) jaillir; (*declaim*) déclamer.

sprain *s.* entorse *f.*; *v.t.* fouler.

sprat *s.* sprat *m.*

sprawl *s.* attitude affalée *f.*; *v.i.* s'étaler.

spray[1] *s.* (*mist*) écume *f.*; (*instrument*) vaporisateur *m.*; (*preparation for ~ing*) produit pour atomiseur *m.*; *v.t.* vaporiser; (*with water*) arroser; **~-gun** *s.* pistolet pulvérisateur *m.*

spray[2] *s.* (*bot.*) branche *f.*, brindille *f.*; (*jewel*) barrette *f.*

spread *s.* (*expanse*) étendue *f.*; (*fam. feast*) festin *m.*; (*paste, etc.*) pâté *m.*; (*bedcover*) couverture *f.*; (*expansion*) propagation *f.*, diffusion *f.*, développement *m.*; (*of wings, etc.*) envergure *f.*; **middle-age(d) ~,** embonpoint de la cinquantaine *m.*; *v.t.* & *i.* (*extend*) (s')étendre; (*cover*) couvrir (*with*—de); (*flag, wings, sails*) (se) déployer; (*net*) tendre; (*diffuse*) répandre; (*for show*) étaler; (*disease*) propager; (*news*) (faire) circuler; (*panic, etc.*) semer; **~ out** *v.t.* & *i.* (s')étendre, (se) déployer, (se) répandre, (se) développer; **~er** *s.* (*mech.*) épandeuse *f.*; **~ing** *s.* propagation *f.*, diffusion *f.*; **~ing** *adj.* qui s'étend.

spree *s.* (*fam.*) bamboche *f.*; **to go on the ~,** faire la noce.

sprig *s.* (*nail*) petit clou *m.*; (*branch*) brin *m.*, brindille *f.*; (*fam. pej.*) rejeton *m.*

sprightl/y *adj.* enjoué, vif; **~iness** *s.* enjouement *m.*, vivacité *f.*

spring *s.* **1.** (*leap*) bond *m.*, saut *m.*; **2.** (*elasticity*) élasticité *f.*; **3.** (*mech.*) ressort *m.*; **4.** (*moving agency*) mobile *m.*; **5.** (*source, origin*) source *f.*; **6.** (*of water, etc.*) source *f.*; **7.** (*season*) printemps *m.*; HAIR~; *adj.* (3) à ressort; (6) de source; (7) du printemps, printanier; **~board** *s.* tremplin *m.*; **~-cleaning** *s.* grand nettoyage du printemps *m.*; ~ MATTRESS; **~ tide** *s.* grande marée *f.*; **~time** *s.* printemps *m.*; **~y** *adj.* élastique; *v.i.* (1) bondir, sauter; (5) naître, provenir (*from*—de), (*family*) descendre (de); *v.t.* (*produce unexpectedly*) proposer, présenter, à l'improviste; (*mine*) faire sauter; (*leak*) contracter; **~ a** LEAK; **~ forth** *v.i.* jaillir, pousser; **~ up** *v.i.* se lever vivement, (*storm, wind*) s'élever.

sprinkl/e *v.t.* répandre; (*with liquid*) asperger (de); (*with sugar etc.*) saupoudrer (de); (*fig.*) parsemer (de); **~er** *s.* (*agric., hort.*) appareil d'arrosage *m.*, (*eccles.*) goupillon *m.*; **~ing** *s.* petit nombre *m.*, bribes *f.pl.*, (*with water*) arrosage *m.*, aspersion *f.*

sprint *s.* sprint *m.*; *v.i.* courir à toute vitesse; (*sport*) sprinter; **~er** *s.* sprinter *m.*

sprite *s.* lutin *m.*

sprocket *s.* dent *f.*; **~-wheel** *s.* pignon (*m.*) de chaîne.

sprout *s.* pousse *f.*; **Brussels ~s,** choux de Bruxelles *m.pl.*; *v.t.* & *i.* (*seed*) germer; (*begin* *to grow*) pousser; (*produce new growth*) bourgeonner.

spruce *s.* (*tree*) sapin *m.*; *adj.* pimpant; *v.t.* ~ **oneself up,** se faire beau (belle).

spry *adj.* alerte.

spud *s.* (*fam. cook.*) patate *f.*

spume *s.* écume *f.*

spur *s.* (*for horse, on flower; ridge; branch*) éperon *m.*; (*of cock*) ergot *m.*; (*incentive*) aiguillon *m.*; **on the ~ of the moment,** sous l'inspiration du moment; *v.t.* éperonner; (*fig.*) pousser, inciter (à).

spurious *adj.* (≠ *genuine*) faux; (*simulated*) feint, simulé; (*ms.*) apocryphe; **~ly** *adv.* faussement; **~ness** *s.* fausseté *f.*

spurn *v.t.* (*with foot*) repousser du pied; (*reject*) dédaigner.

spurt *s.* **1.** (*sudden effort*) effort soudain *m.*, coup de collier *m.*; **2.** (*jet*) jet *m.*; *v.t.* & *i.* (1) faire un effort, donner un coup de collier; (2) (faire) jaillir.

sputnik *s.* spoutnik *m.*

sputter(ing) *s.* **1.** (*stammer*) bredouillement *m.*; **2.** (*fire, etc.*) pétillement *m.*; *v.i.* (1) bredouiller; (2) pétiller.

sputum *s.* crachat *m.*

spy *s.* espion(ne) *m.f.*; *v.t.* & *i.* espionner; (*perceive*) apercevoir; ~ **on** *v.t.* épier; ~ **out** *v.t.* explorer; **~glass** *s.* longue-vue *f.*; **~hole** *s.* judas *m.*

squab *s.* (*pigeon*) pigeonneau *m.*; (*cushion*) coussin *m.*; *adj.* trapu.

squabble *s.* chamaillerie *f.*, prise de bec *f.*; *v.i.* se chamailler.

squad *s.* escouade *f.*, peloton *m.*; (*sports*) équipe *f.*; **~ron** *s.* escadron *m.*; (*naut.*) escadre *f.*; (*aviat.*) escadrille *f.*; **~ron leader** *s.* commandant *m.*

squal/id *adj.* sale, misérable; **~idness** *s.* **~or** *s.* saleté *f.*, misère *f.*

squall *s.* **1.** (*storm*) rafale *f.*; **2.** (*scream*) braillement *m.*; *v.i.* (2) brailler; **~y** *adj.* à rafales.

squander *v.t.* gaspiller.

square *s.* (*shape, math.*) carré *m.*; (*open space*) (*in city*) place *f.*, (*with garden*) square *m.*; (*instrument*) équerre *f.*; (*on chess-board, etc.*) case *f.*; (*pop. person*) formaliste *m.f.*; *adj.* (*shape, solid*) carré; (*fair, honest*) honnête, franc; (*fig.*) catégorique; (*pop.*) arriéré; (*even, equal, level*) en bon ordre, en règle; (*meal*) solide; **to get ~ with s.o.,** régler ses comptes avec qn.; ~ **deal** *s.* affaire honnête *f.*; ~ PEG **in round hole; ~ly** *adv.* (*shape*) en carré; (*honestly*) honnêtement; (*fig.*) catégoriquement; **~ness** *s.* forme carrée *f.*; (*honesty*) franchise *f.*; *v.t.* (*shape, math.*) carrer; (*reconcile*) ajuster, accommoder, cadrer (avec); (*settle account*) régler; (*score*) rendre égal; (*bribe*) acheter; (*techn.*) équarrir.

squash *s.* **1.** (*state*) écrasement *m.*; (*crowd*) presse *f.*; **2.** (*sport*) squash *m.*; **3.** (*drink*) citron etc. pressé *m.*; **4.** (*plant*) courge *f.*; *v.t.* (1) écraser; (*snub*) réduire au silence.

squat *v.i.* (*sit on heels*) s'accroupir; (*crouch*) être accroupi; (*animal*) se tapir; (*fam.*) occuper une propriété sans titre légal; *adj.* trapu; **~ter** *s.* squatter *m.*

squaw *s.* femme peau-rouge *f.*

squawk *v.i.* pousser un cri rauque.

squeak *s.* petit cri aigu *m.*; **to have a narrow ~** (*fig.*) échapper de justesse; *v.i.* pousser un cri aigu; (*door, etc.*) grincer.

squeal *s.* cri perçant *m.*; *v.i.* pousser un cri perçant, piailler.

squeamish *adj.* délicat, difficile; **~ness** *s.* délicatesse *f.*

squeeze *s.* (*pressure*) compression *f.*; (*crowd*) presse *f.*; (*econ.*) récession *f.*; (*embrace*) étreinte *f.*; (*of hands*) serrement *m.*; *v.t.* comprimer, serrer; (*fruit*) presser; (*extort*) extorquer (à); (*bring pressure on*) exercer une pression sur; ~ **into** *v.t.* & *i.* (s')introduire de force dans; ~ **out** *v.t.* faire sortir, soutirer (qch.) à (qn.); **~r** *s.* (*fruit*) presse-agrumes *f.*

squelch *s.* (*of mud*) giclement *m.*; (*sound*) flic-flac *m.*; *v.i.* gicler, patauger; faire flic-flac.

squib *s.* pétard *m.*; (*lampoon*) brocard *m.*

squid *s.* calmar *m.*

squiggle *s.* tortillement *m.*; (*signature*) parafe *m.*; *v.i.* se tortiller.

squint *s.* **1.** (*set of eyes*) strabisme *m.*; **2.** (*fam. glance*) coup d'œil *m.*; **to have a ~ at,** jeter un coup d'œil sur; *v.i.* (1) loucher; **~-eyed** *adj.* louche.

squire *s.* (*hist.*) écuyer *m.*; (*country gentleman*) propriétaire terrien *m.*; (*attending lady*) cavalier *m.*; **~archy** *s.* les hobereaux *m.pl.*

squirm *v.i.* se tordre; (*fam.*) se crisper.

squirrel *s.* écureuil *m.*

squirt *s.* **1.** (*syringe*) seringue *f.*; **2.** (*jet*) jet *m.*; **3.** (*pop. person*) freluquet *m.*; *v.t.* (1) seringuer; (2) *v.t.* & *i.* (faire) gicler.

S.R.N. (*abbrev. State Registered Nurse*) infirmière diplômée *f.*

stab *s.* (*wound*) coup de couteau *m.*; (*pain*) douleur lancinante *f.*; (*fam. try*) coup d'essai *m.*; **to have a ~ at sth.,** s'essayer à qch.; *v.t.* poignarder, percer.

stab/le[1] *adj.* stable; **~ility** *s.* stabilité *f.*; **~ilize** *v.t.* stabiliser; **~ilization** *s.* stabilisation *f.*; **~ilizer** *s.* (*naut., aviat.*) stabilisateur *m.*

stabl/e[2] *s.* (*for horses*) écurie *f.*; **~e-boy** *s.* garçon d'écurie *m.*; **~ing** *s.* écuries *f.pl.*; *v.t.* mettre à l'écurie.

staccato *adj.* & *adv.* (*mus.*) staccato; (*fig.*) saccadé.

stack *s.* **1.** (*of hay*) meule *f.*; **2.** (*chimney-*) cheminée *f.*; **3.** (*for books*) bibliothèque *f.*; **4.** (*heap*) tas *m.*; **5.** (*aviat.*) file d'attente *f.*; *v.t.* (1) mettre en meule; (4) entasser; (5) (s')échelonner.

stadium *s.* stade *m.*

staff *s.* (*stick*) bâton *m.*; (*pilgrim's*) bourdon *m.*; (*bishop's*) crosse *f.*; FLAG~; (*mus.*) portée *f.*; (*mil.*) état-major *m.*; (*comm.*) personnel *m.*; ~ **meeting** *s.* (*acad.*) réunion de professeurs *f.*, (*gen.*) réunion de service *f.*; ~ **officer** *s.* officier d'état-major *m.*; *v.t.* pourvoir de personnel.

stag *s.* cerf *m.*; **~-beetle** *s.* cerf-volant *m.*; **~-party** *s.* réunion d'hommes *f.*

stage *s.* (*platform*) estrade *f.*, échafaudage *m.*; (*in theatre*) scène *f.*; (*the theatre*) théâtre *m.*; (*scene of action*) champ *m.*; (*division of journey*) étape *f.*, (*bus*) section *f.*, (*stopping place*) relais *m.*; (*point reached*) degré *m.*, période *f.*; ⚠ stage = **period of training**; **~-coach** *s.* diligence *f.*; ~ **door** entrée des artistes *f.*; ~ **fright** *s.* trac *m.*; **~-manager** *s.* régisseur *m.*; **old ~r** *s.* vieux routier *m.*; **staging** *s.* échafaudage *m.*, (*in greenhouse*) rayonnage à claire-voie *m.*; *v.t.* (*theat.*) mettre en scène; (*organize*) monter.

stagger *v.t.* (*arrange in overlaps*) disposer en quinconces; (*hours of work, etc.*) échelonner; (*fam.*) bouleverser; *v.i.* chanceler; (*be unsettled*) vaciller.

stagn/ant *adj.* stagnant; **~ate** *v.i.* stagner; **~ation** *s.* stagnation *f.*

staid *adj.* sérieux, posé; **~ly** *adv.**,*.

stain *s.* **1.** (*mark*) tache *f.*; **2.** (*dye*) couleur *f.*; **3.** (*fig. blot*) tache *f.*; *v.t.* (1) tacher; (2) colorer; (3) souiller; **~ed glass window,** vitrail (vitraux) *m.* (*pl.*); **~less** *adj.* sans tache; (*steel*) inoxydable.

stair *s.* marche *f.*; **~s** *s.pl.* escalier *m.*; **~case** *s.* escalier *m.*; **down~s** *adv.* en bas; **up~s** *adv.* en haut.

stake *s.* **1.** (*post*) pieu *m.*, poteau *m.*; **2.** (*for* *burning alive*) bûcher *m.*; **3.** (*wager*) enjeu *m.*; **~s** *s.pl.* (*race*) prix *m.*; **at ~,** en jeu; **I have a ~ in this,** cela me concerne; **~-boat** *s.* bateau--balise *m.*; *v.t.* (1) garnir, étayer, de pieux; (3) hasarder; (*supply with money*) subventionner; **~ out,** jalonner; **~ a claim to,** réclamer.

stalactite *s.* stalactite *f.*

stalagmite *s.* stalagmite *f.*

stale *adj.* (*bread*) rassis; (*beer, wine*) éventé; (*goods*) défraîchi; (*fig. subject*) rebattu; (*sport*) surentraîné; **~mate,** *s.* pat *m.*; (*fig.*) impasse *f.*; **~ness,** *s.* (*fig.*) banalité *f.*

stalk[1] *s.* (*of flower*) tige *f.*; (*of cabbage, etc.*) trognon *m.*

stalk[2] *v.t.* (*game*) traquer; (*person*) filer; *v.i.* marcher dignement.

stall *s.* (*for animal*; *in church*) stalle *f.*; (*theat.*) fauteuil *m.*; (*in market*) étal *m.*, éventaire *m.*; (*auto.*) arrêt subit, *m.*; *v.i.* (*auto.*) caler; (*aviat.*) se mettre en perte de vitesse; (*pop.*) différer, temporiser.

stallion *s.* étalon *m.*

stalwart *s.* costaud *m.*; (*fig. esp. polit.*) partisan *m.*; *adj.* vigoureux; (*fig.*) résolu.

stamen *s.* étamine *f.*

stamina *s.* force *f.* (de résistance).

stammer *s.* bégayement *m.*; *v.i.* bégayer.

stamp *s.* **1.** (*with foot*) coup de pied *m.*; **2.** (*impression*) empreinte *f.*; **3.** (*instrument*) estampe *f.*; **4.** (*postage*) timbre (-poste) *m.*; **5.** (*mark, label*) estampille *f.*; **6.** (*characteristic mark*) empreinte *f.*; **7.** (*character, kind*) catégorie *f.*, nature *f.*; TRADING **~**; **~-duty** *s.* droit de timbre *m.*; *v.t.* (1) **~ on,** frapper du pied; (2), (3) (*metal, paper, leather*) estamper; (4) timbrer; (5) estampiller; (6) signaler, marquer; (*on memory*) graver; *v.i.* (1) trépigner; **~ out** *v.t.* écraser, supprimer; **~ing-ground** *s.* (*fig.*) terrain favori *m.*

stampede *s.* **1.** (*flight*) sauve-qui-peut *m.*; **2.** (*attack*) charge *f.*; *v.t.* & *i.* (1) (faire) fuir à la débandade; (2) charger.

stance *s.* position *f.*

stanch, staunch *v.t.* étancher.

stanchion *s.* étançon *m.*; (*naut.*) épontille *f.*

stand[1] *s.* (*position*) position *f.*; (*resistance*) résistance *f.*; (*for taxis*) station *f.*; (*market stall*) étalage *m.*; (*at exhibition*) stand *m.*; (*platform*) estrade *f.*; (*for spectators*) tribune *f.*; (*support*) pied *m.*, socle *m.*; (*small table*) guéridon *m.*; (*for clothes, umbrellas, etc.*) portemanteau *m.*, porte--parapluies *m., etc.*

stand[2] *v.t.* (*place upright*) mettre debout; (*endure*) supporter; (*bear*) soutenir; (*undergo*) subir; (*pay for*) payer; **~ a chance of,** avoir des chances de; **I can't ~ him,** je ne peux pas le voir; **I can't ~ it any longer,** j'en ai assez; *v.i.* (*be upright*) se tenir (debout); (*remain, stop*) rester, arrêter; (*rise*) se lever; (*be placed*) se trouver, être; (*remain firm*) tenir bon; (*remain valid*) tenir, rester valable; (*present firm front*) (se) maintenir; (*for election*) se présenter comme candidat; **it ~s to reason that,** il va sans dire que; **~ to gain,** avoir des chances de gagner; **~ to lose,** risquer de perdre; **it ~s out a mile,** cela crève les yeux; **~ on one's own feet,** voler de ses propres ailes; **~ still** *v.i.* rester immobile; **~still** *s.* arrêt complet *m.*; **~ aloof, away, off** *v.i.* s'écarter (*from*—de); **~ alone** *v.i.* être unique; **~ back** *v.i.* se tenir en retrait; **~ by** *v.i.* se tenir prêt; **~-by** *s.* réserve *f.*; **~ by** *v.t.* (*promise*) rester fidèle à, (*s.o.*) prendre le parti de qn.; **~ down** *v.i.* se retirer, (*as candidate*) se désister; **~ for** *v.t.* signifier (qch.), représenter (qn.); (*tolerate*) supporter; **~ in for,** remplacer; **~-in** *s.* remplaçant *m.*; **~-off half** *s.* (*rugby*) demi d'ouverture *m.*; **~-offish** *adj.* distant; **~ out** *v.i.* se détacher, faire saillie; **~ up** *v.i.* se lever; **~ s.o. up** (*pop.*) poser un lapin à qn.; **~ up for s.o.,** prendre le parti de qn.; **~ up to,** faire face à.

standard *s.* (*flag*) étendard *m.*; (*measure*) taux *m.*, (*money*) étalon *m.*; (*quality*) type *m.*, norme *f.*; (*degree*) degré *m.*, niveau *m.*; **~ of living** *s.* niveau de vie *m.*; (*in school*) classe *f.*; (*support*) pied *m.*; (*tree*) arbre de plein vent *m.*; **~-bearer** *s.* porte-étendard *m.*; **~ lamp** *s.* lampadaire *m.*; *adj.* standard (*invar.*); (*normal*) courant; (*average*) moyen, ordinaire; **~ize** *v.t.* standardiser.

standing *s.* (*reputation, position*) rang *m.*, position *f.*; standing *m.* (*anglicism*); **a friend of long ~,** un ami de longue date; *adj.* (*permanent*) permanent; (*ready*) prêt; (*position*) debout; (*water*) stagnant; (*corn, etc.*) sur pied; (*joke*) classique; **~ orders,** règlements *m.pl.*; **~ room,** places debout *f.pl.*

stand-pipe *s.* tuyau *m.* (vertical).

standpoint *s.* point de vue *m.*

stanza *s.* strophe *f.*

staple[1] *s.* (*wire or metal*) crampon *m.*; (*paper fastener*) agrafe *f.*; *v.t.* cramponner, fixer avec une agrafe; **~r** *s.* agrafeuse *f.*

staple[2] *s.* (*comm. principal product*) denrée principale *f.*; (*text.*) fibre *f.*; *adj.* (*standard*) régulier, normal; (*principal*) principal.

star *s.* **1.** (*astron.*) étoile *f.*, astre *m.*; **2.** (*shape*) étoile *f.*; **3.** (*asterisk*) astérisque *m.*; **4.** (*person*) vedette *f.*, étoile *f.*; **to see ~s,** voire trente-six chandelles; **S~s and Stripes,** drapeau américain *m.*; **~-spangled banner** *s.* drapeau étoilé *m.*; **~board** *s.* tribord *m.*; **~fish** *s.* étoile de mer *f.*; **~-gazer** *s.* (*fam.*) rêvasseur *m.*; **~shell** *s.* fusée éclairante *f.*; **~dom** *s.* succès *m.*; **~let** *s.* starlette *f.*; **~ry** *adj.* étoilé; **~ry--eyed** *adj.* peu pratique; *v.t.* & *i.* (2) étoiler; (3) marquer d'un astérisque; (4) mettre/être en vedette.

starch *s.* **1.** (*in food*) fécule *f.*; **2.** (*for linen*) amidon *m.*; **3.** (*fig.*) raideur *f.*; **~-reduced** *adj.* à féculence réduite; **~y** *adj.* (1) féculent; (3) raide; *v.t.* (2) amidonner; **~ed** *adj.* amidonné.

star/e *s.* regard fixe *m.*; *v.i.* ouvrir de grands yeux; **~e at** *v.t.* regarder fixement; **it's ~ing you in the face,** cela vous crève les yeux; **~ing** *adj.* (*eyes*) grand ouvert; (*colour*) voyant; **stark ~ing mad,** fou à lier.

stark *adj.* (*rigid*) rigide; (*downright*) résolu; (*fam.*) absolu; *adv.* tout à fait; **~ naked** *adj.* tout nu; **~** STARING **mad.**

starling *s.* étourneau *m.*

start *s.* **1.** (*sudden movement*) sursaut *m.*; **2.** (*beginning*) commencement *m.*, début *m.*, (*of journey*) départ *m.*; **3.** (*place*) point de départ *m.*; **4.** (*opportunity*) départ *m.*; **5.** (*advantage*) avance *f.*; **to make a ~,** commencer; **for a ~** (*fam.*) pour commencer; **by** FITS **and ~s**; FLY**ing ~**; *v.t.* (1) lever, lancer; (2) commencer, se mettre à, (*comm.*) lancer, (*fig.*) faire naître, (*mech. auto.*) mettre en marche, (*signal*) donner le signal du départ; *v.i.* (1) sursauter; (2) commencer, partir, (*auto.*) démarrer; **~ back** *v.i.* faire un bond en arrière; **~ out** *v.i.* se mettre en route; **~ up** *v.i.* (*techn.*) démarrer; **~er** *s.* (*person who ~s*) starter *m.*, (*beginner*) débutant *m.*, (*originator* auteur *m.*, (*apparatus*) démarreur *m.*; **~ing** *s.* départ *m.*; **~ing-point** *s.* point de départ *m.*

startl/e *v.t.* surprendre; **~ing** *adj.* saisissant.

starv/e *v.t.* faire mourir de faim; (*deprive of*) priver de; *v.i.* mourir de faim; (*fam.*) être affamé; **be ~ed of,** (*fig.*) manquer de; **~ation** *s.* (*med.*) inanition *f.*; famine *f.*; *adj.* de famine; **~eling** *adj.* & *s.m.f.* affamé(e).

state[1] *s.* **1.** (*condition*) état *m.*; **2.** (*stage*) degré *m.*; **3.** (*rank*) rang *m.*; **4.** (*pomp*) pompe *f.*; **5.** (*community*) état *m.*; **the S~s,** les Etats-Unis *m.pl.*; **to get into a ~,** se mettre dans tous ses états; **to** LIE **in ~**; **in ~,** en grande pompe;

adj. (4) de parade, de cérémonie; (5) d'état; **~craft** *s.* politique *f.*; **~room** *s.* (*apartment*) suite royale *f.*, (*on ship*) cabine de luxe *f.*; **~sman** *s.* homme d'état *m.*; **~smanlike** *adj.* d'homme d'état; **~smanship** *s.* habileté politique *f.*; **~less** *adj.* sans nationalité; **~ly** *adj.* majestueux; **~liness** *s.* majesté *f.*

state[2] *v.t.* affirmer, déclarer, spécifier; (*math.*) poser; **~ment** *s.* (*speech*) déclaration *f.*; (*written*) rapport *m.*; (*of account*) relevé *m.*

static *s.* (*radio*) parasites *m.pl.*; *adj.* statique; **~s** *s.pl.* statique *f.sing.*

station *s.* (*post*) poste *m.*; (*rank*) rang *m.*; (*rail.*) gare *f.*; (*radio*) émetteur *m.*; (*meteor.*) station *f.*; FILLing ~; FIRE ~; PETROL ~; POLICE ~; POWER-~; **~-master** *s.* chef de gare *m.*; **~-wagon** *s.* (*auto.*) commerciale *f.*; *v.t.* poster; ⚠ stationner = **to park**; **~ary** *adj.* stationnaire, fixe, (*auto.*) en stationnement.

stationer *s.* papetier *m.*; **~'s shop,** papeterie *f.*; **~y** *s.* papeterie *f.*

statistic *s.* statistique *f.*; **~s** *s.pl.* (*science*) statistique *f.sing.*; *adj.* & **~al** *adj.* statistique; **~ian** *s.* statisticien(ne) *m.f.*

statu/e *s.* statue *f.*; **~ary** *s.* (*statues*) statuaire *f.*; (*artist*) statuaire *m.*; **~ette** *s.* statuette *f.*; **~esque** *adj.* sculptural.

stature *s.* (*lit.* & *fig.*) stature *f.*

status *s.* position *f.*, rang *m.*; (*law*) statut *m.*; **~ symbol** *s.* marque de standing *m.*

status quo *s.* statu quo *m.*

statut/e *s.* ordonnance *f.*, décret *m.*; ⚠ statut = **status**; **~ory** *adj.* réglementaire.

staunch[1] *adj.* ferme; (*person*) loyal.

staunch[2] *v.t. see* STANCH.

stave *s.* (*stick*) bâton *m.*; (*side of cask*) douve *f.*; (*mus.*) portée *f.*; *v.t.* **~ in,** défoncer, crever; **~ off,** détourner.

stay *s.* **1.** (*naut.*; *cross-piece*) étai *m.*; **2.** (*prop, support*) soutien *m.*; **3.** (*time spent*) séjour *m.*; **~s** *s.pl.* corset *m.sing.*; *v.t.* (2) étayer; **4.** (*check, stop*) différer, arrêter; *v.i.* (*remain*) rester; (*pause*) attendre; (*endure*) tenir le coup; (*in hotel*) descendre à; (*in place*) séjourner; **~-at--home** *adj.* casanier; **~ away** *v.i.* s'absenter; **~ behind** *v.i.* rester en arrière; **~ in** *v.i.* rester chez soi; **~ put** *v.i.* rester en place; **~ up** (*late*) veiller; **~ing-power** *s.* persistance *f.*

S.T.D. (*abbrev. Subscriber Trunk Dialling*) automatique *m.*

stead *s.* place *f.*; **in my/his ~**, à ma/sa place; **to stand s.o. in good ~**, être utile à qn.; **~fast** *adj.* ferme, constant; **~fastly** *adv.**. constamment; **~fastness** *s.* fermeté *f.*, constance *f.*

stead/y *adj.* **1.** (*firm*) ferme; **2.** (*hand*) sûr; **3.** (*comm.*) stable; **4.** (*resolute*) sérieux; **5.** (*regular*) régulier, (*work, etc.*) soutenu, (*person*) persévérant; **6.** (*mil. fire*) nourri; (*command*) **~y!,** attention!; **~ily** *adv.* (1)*; (2)*; (3)*; (4)*; (5)*; de façon soutenue, avec persévérance; **~iness** *s.* (1) fermeté *f.*; (3) stabilité *f.*; (4) sérieux *m.*; (5) régularité *f.*, persévérance *f.*; *v.t.* (1) affermir; (*calm*) calmer.

steak *s.* (*of meat or fish*) tranche *f.*; (*beef*) bifteck *m.*

steal *s.* vol *m.*; (*bargain*) occasion *f.*; *v.t.* & *i.* voler; *v.i.* (*move silently*) se glisser; **~ away/off** s'esquiver; **~ in/out,** entrer/sortir, furtivement; **~ a glance at,** jeter un coup d'œil sur; **~ a march on s.o.,** gagner de vitesse sur qn.

stealth *s.* **by ~** & **~ily** *adv.* à la dérobée; **~y** *adj.* furtif.

steam *s.* vapeur *f.*; **to get up ~**, chauffer, (*fig.*) rassembler ses forces; **to let off ~**, ouvrir les soupapes, (*fig.*) se détendre; **to run out of ~** (*fig.*) s'épuiser; **under one's own ~**, par ses propres moyens; *adj.* à vapeur; **~boat** *s.* bateau à vapeur *m.*; **~-engine** *s.* machine à vapeur *f.*; **~-hammer** *s.* marteau-pilon *m.*; **~-roller** *s.* rouleau compresseur *m.*; **~er** *s.*, **~ship** *s.* paquebot *m.*; *v.t.* (*cook.*) cuire à l'étuvée *or* à l'étouffée; *v.i.* marcher à la vapeur; (*emit ~*) fumer; (*become covered with ~, ~ up*) s'embuer.

steed *s.* coursier *m.*

steel *s.* (*metal*) acier *m.*; (*weapon, tool*) fer *m.*; (*for knives*) fusil *m.*; *adj.* d'acier; **~ wool** *s.* paille de fer *f.*; **~works** *s.* aciérie *f.*; **~yard** *s.* (*balance*) romaine *f.*; **~y** *adj.* d'acier; *v.t.* aciérer; (*fig.*) endurcir.

steep[1] *adj.* **1.** (*sloping sharply*) raide, à pic; **2.** (*fam. price*) exorbitant; **3.** (*fam. incredible*) invraisemblable; **~ly** *adv.* (1) en pente, à pic; **~ness** *s.* (1) raideur *f.*

steep[2] *v.t.* & *i.* tremper; (*fig.*) plonger dans; **~ed in** *adj.* (*fig.*) imprégné de.

steeple *s.* clocher *m.*; **~chase** *s.* steeple(-chase) *m.*

steer[1] *s.* jeune bœuf *m.*

steer[2] *v.t.* & *i.* (*vessel*) gouverner; (*auto.*) conduire; (*steps*) diriger; **~ clear of** *v.t.* éviter; **~ for,** faire route sur; **~age** *s.* troisième classe *f.*; **~ing** *s.* (*naut.*) manœuvre de la barre *f.*, (*auto.*) conduite *f.*; **~ing-gear** *s.* timonerie *f.*; **~ing--wheel** *s.* (*naut.*) roue du gouvernail *f.*, (*auto.*) volant *m.*; **~sman** *s.* homme de barre *m.*

stellar *adj.* stellaire.

stem[1] *s.* (*of flower, etc.*) tige *f.*; (*of fruit*) queue *f.*; (*of glass, of letter*) pied *m.*; (*of pipe*) tuyau *m.*; (*ling.*) radical *m.*; (*of ship*) proue *f.*; **from ~ to stern,** de bout en bout; *v.t.* équeuter; *v.i.* **~ from,** naître de, dériver de.

stem[2] *v.t.* (*check flow*) refouler.

stench *s.* puanteur *f.*

stencil *s.* **1.** (*plate*) pochoir *m.*; **2.** (*paper*) stencil *m.*; *v.t.* (1) peindre au pochoir; (2) tirer au stencil.

stenograph/er *s.* sténographe *m.f.*, (*fam.*) sténo *m.f.*; **~y** *s.* sténographie *f.*

stentorian *adj.* de stentor.

step[1] *s.* (*movement, distance, sound*) pas *m.*; (*on ladder*) échelon *m.*; (*degree in scale*) grade *m.*; (*of stairs*) marche *f.*; (*measure to be taken*) démarche *f.*; **take ~s to,** faire des démarches pour; **~ by ~**, pas à pas; **in ~ with,** au pas avec; **to be out of ~**, ne pas être au pas, (*fig.*) être déphasé; **~-ladder** *s.* escabeau *m.*; *v.i.* marcher, faire un pas; **~ aside** *v.i.* s'écarter; **~ back** *v.i.* reculer; **~ down** *v.i.* descendre; **~ forward** *v.i.* s'avancer; **~ in** *v.i.* entrer, (*fig.*) intervenir; **~ on it** (*fig. fam.*) se grouiller; **~ on the** GAS; **~ out** *v.i.* sortir, (*fam.*) allonger le pas; **~ up** *v.i.* monter, *v.t.* intensifier; **~ping-stone** *s.* marchepied *m.*; *v.t.* (*erect mast*) arborer.

step-[2] *prefix* **~father,** beau-père *m.*; **~mother,** belle-mère *f.*; **~brother,** demi-frère *m.*; **~-sister,** demi-sœur *f.*

steppe *s.* steppe *m.*

stereo *s.* (*radio*) stéréo *f.*; (*in combination*) **~phonic** *adj.* stéréophonique; **~scope** *s.* stéréoscope *m.*; **~scopic** *adj.* stéréoscopique; **~type** *s.* stéréotype *m.*; *v.t.* stéréotyper.

steril/e *adj.* stérile; **~ity** *s.* stérilité *f.*; **~ize** *v.t.* stériliser; **~ization** *s.* stérilisation *f.*

sterling *adj.* & *s.m.* sterling; (*genuine, excellent*) de bon aloi.

stern[1] *s.* (*naut.*) arrière *m.*; (*rump*) derrière *m.*

stern[2] *adj.* (*severe, strict*) sévère, austère; (*hard, grim*) rigoureux, triste; **~ly** *adv.**,*;*,*; **~ness** *s.* sévérité *f.*, austérité *f.*; rigueur *f.*

sternum *s.* sternum *m.*

stertorous *adj.* stertoreux.

stet *v.i.* à maintenir.

stethoscope *s.* stéthoscope *m.*

stevedore *s.* arrimeur *m.*, entrepreneur de manutention *m.*

stew *s.* (*cook.*) ragoût *m.*; (*fam.*) **to be in a ~,** être dans tous ses états; *v.t.* (*cook.*) (*fruit*) faire une compote de; (*meat*) faire un ragoût de; *v.i.* étouffer.

steward *s.* (*agent, manager*) régisseur *m.*; (*waiter*) steward *m.*; SHOP-~; **~ess** *s.* (*naut.*) femme de chambre *f.*; (*aviat.*) hôtesse de l'air *f.*; **~ship** *s.* intendance *f.*; (*fig.*) charge *f.*

stick[1] *s.* (*piece of wood*) bâton *m.*; (*walking-~ etc.*) canne *f.*; BROOM~; FIDDLE~S; SHOOTing-~; (*twig*) brindille *f.*; (*of celery*) branche *f.*; (*of rhubarb*) tige *f.*; (*of bombs*) chapelet *m.*; **~s** (*firewood*) bois sec *m.*; **in the ~s,** dans le bled; **in a** CLEFT **~; to get the wrong end of the ~,** mal comprendre.

stick[2] *v.t.* (*thrust into*) enfoncer, piquer; (*fix with glue, etc.*) coller; (*pop. endure*) souffrir; (*fam. put into*) fourrer (dans); *v.i.* (*adhere*) se coller; (*techn.*) se coincer; (*in mud*) s'embourber; ~-in-the-MUD; (*stay*) rester; (*cook.*) attacher; (*persevere*) persévérer; **~ at sth.,** s'acharner sur qch.; **~ at nothing,** être capable de tout; **~ by s.o.,** rester fidèle à qn.; **~ on** *v.t.* coller, attacher; **~ out** *v.t.* (*head*) passer, (*tongue*) tirer, *v.i.* faire saillie, bomber; (*fam.*) s'obstiner; **~ out for,** insister sur; **~ up** *v.t.* (*poster*) afficher, (*ears*) dresser; *v.i.* se dresser; **~ up for,** prendre le parti de; **~er** *s.* étiquette *f.*; **~ing**-PLASTER; **~iness** *s.* viscosité *f.*; **~y** *adj.* gluant, adhésif, (*fam.*) épineux; **come to a ~y end,** finir mal; **stuck-up** *adj.* prétentieux; **stuck on** (*pop.*) entiché de; **be stuck with sth.,** rester avec qch. sur les bras; **stuck for,** à court de.

stickleback *s.* épinoche *f.*

stickler *s.* **to be a ~ for,** être à cheval sur.

stiff *s.* (*pop. corpse*) macchabée *m.*; *adj.* (≠ *flexible*) raide; (≠ *supple*) rigide; (≠ *fluid*) dur; (*difficult*) dur, difficile; (*ungraceful, haughty*) raide; **to bore s.o. ~,** ennuyer qn. mortellement; **to scare ~,** faire une peur bleue à; **~ upper** LIP; **~ neck** *s.* torticolis *m.*; **~-necked** *adj.* hautain; **~en** *v.t.* & *i.* (se) raidir, (se) durcir; **~ly** *adv.* avec raideur; **~ness** *s.* (*lit.* & *fig.*) raideur *f.*

stifl/e *v.t.* & *i.* (*lit.* & *fig.*) étouffer; **~ing** *adj.* étouffant.

stigma *s.* stigmate *m.*; (*eccles. pl.*) stigmates *m.pl.*; **~tize** *v.t.* stigmatiser.

stile *s.* échalier *m.*

stiletto *s.* stylet *m.*; **~ heel** *s.* talon-aiguille *m.*

still *s.* (*apparatus*) alambic *m.*; (*silence*) calme *m.*, silence *m.*; (*photo.*) photographie *f.*; *adj.* (*silent*) silencieux; (*motionless*) immobile; (*peaceful*) calme, tranquille; (*wine*) non-champagnisé; **~born** *adj.* mort-né; **~** LIFE; **~ waters run deep,** il n'est pire eau que l'eau qui dort; *adv.* (*silently*) sans bruit; (*motionlessly*) sans bouger; (*always*) toujours; (*as before*) encore; (*yet, even + comparative*) encore, **~ greater,** encore plus grand; (*nevertheless*) cependant; **~ness** *s.* silence *m.*; *v.t.* calmer, apaiser.

stilt *s.* échasse *f.*; **~ed** *adj.* guindé.

stimul/ant *s.* stimulant *m.*; **~ate** *v.t.* stimuler; **~ation** *s.* stimulation *f.*; **~ative** *adj.* stimulateur; **~us** *s.* stimulant *m.*

sting *s.* (*of insect*) aiguillon *m.*, dard *m.*; (*of plant*) poil urticant *m.*; (*wound*) piqûre *f.*, douleur cuisante *f.*; (*fig.*) mordant *m.*; *v.t.* & *i.* piquer; (*feel pain*) cuire; (*pop.*) voler; **~-ray** *s.* vive *f.*; **~ing-nettle** *s.* ortie *f.*

sting/y *adj.* avare; **~ily** *adv.* chichement; **~iness** *s.* avarice *f.*

stink *s.* puanteur *f.*; *v.i.* puer; **~er** *s.* (*fam. person*) sale type *m.*; (*fam. problem*) casse-tête *m.*; **~ing** *adj.* puant.

stint *s.* **1.** (*limitation*) restriction *f.*; **2.** (*amount of work, etc.*) besogne *f.*; *v.i.* (1) lésiner sur, mesurer qch. à qn.

stipend *s.* traitement *m.*; **~iary** *s.* salarié *m.*; *adj.* appointé.

stipple *v.t.* pointiller.

stipulat/e *v.t.* stipuler; **~ion** *s.* stipulation *f.*

stir *s.* (*sound*) mouvement *m.*; (*bustle*) agitation *f.*; (*fig.*) sensation *f.*; (*pop. prison*) violon *m.*; *v.t.* (*set in motion*) remuer; (*agitate*) agiter; (*excite, animate*) exciter, émouvoir; *v.i.* bouger; **~ up** *v.t.* agiter; (*trouble, etc.*) susciter; (*excite*) exciter; **~ring** *adj.* émouvant.

stirrup *s.* étrier *m.*; **~-cup** *s.* coup de l'étrier *m.*

stitch *s.* **1.** (*sewing*) point *m.*; (*knitting*) maille *f.*; **2.** (*pain*) point au côté *m.*; **3.** (*of clothing*) vêtement *m.*; *v.t.* & *i.* (1) coudre.

stoat *s.* hermine *f.*

stock *s.* (*hort.*) souche *f.*; (*mech. base, handle*) base *f.*, manche *m.*; (*animals, live~*) bétail *m.*; (*family*) famille *f.*; (*cook.*) bouillon *m.*; (*fund, store*) réserve *f.*, (*fig.*) fonds *m.*; (*fin.*) actions *f.pl.*; (*comm.*) stock *m.*; **~-in-trade** *s.* stock en magasin *m.*; (*neckband*) col *m.*; (*flower*) giroflée *f.*; **rolling-~** (*rail.*) matériel (ferroviaire) *m.*; **~s** *s.pl.* (*hist.*) pilori *m.*, (*naut.*) chantier *m.*; **in ~,** en magasin; **to take ~ of,** faire l'inventaire de, (*fig.*) toiser; **~broker** *s.* agent de change *m.*; **S~ Exchange** *s.* bourse *f.*; **~holder** *s.* actionnaire *m.f.*; **~-market** *s.* bourse *f.*, marché *m.*; **~pile** *s.* stockage *m.*, *v.t.* stocker; **~-pot** *s.* pot-au-feu *m.*; **~-still** *adj.* immobile comme une borne; **~-taking** *s.* inventaire *m.*; **~y** *adj.* trapu; **~** *adj.* (*size, etc.*) courant, (*fig.*) classique, banal; *v.t.* (*equip*) approvisionner (*with*—en); (*keep in ~*) stocker; **~ist** *s.* stockiste *m.*

stockade *s.* palissade *f.*

stocking *s.* (*women's*) bas *m.*; (*boy's*) chaussette *f.*

stodgy *adj.* (*food*) lourd; (*fig.*) indigeste.

stoic *s.* (*hist.*) stoïcien *m.*; (*fig.*) stoïque *m.*; **~al** *adj.* stoïque; **~ally** *adv.**; **~ism** *s.* stoïcisme *m.*

stoke *v.t.* (*up*) (*boiler*) chauffer; (*fire*) entretenir; **~r** *s.* chauffeur *m.*

S.T.O.L. (*abbrev. short take-off and landing (aircraft)*) ADAC *m.* (avion à décollage et à atterrissage courts).

stole *s.* étole *f.*

stolid *adj.* flegmatique; (*not easily moved*) impassible; (*dull*) lourd; **~ity** *s.* flegme *m.*; **~ly** *adv.**;*;*.

stomach *s.* estomac *m.*; (*appetite*) appétit *m.*, (*fig.*) goût *m.*; (*courage*) cran *m.*; BUTTERFLIES **in one's ~; ~-ache** *s.* mal d'estomac *m.*; **~-pump** *s.* pompe stomacale *f.*; **~ upset** *s.* colique *f.*; **~ic** *adj.* stomachique; *v.t.* supporter; (*fam.*) digérer.

stone *s.* pierre *f.*; (*in fruit*) noyau *m.*; (*weight*) stone *m.*; FLAG~; FOUNDATION ~; GALL~; GRAVE~; MILE~; MILL~; SOAP~; TOMB~; STEPPING-~; WHET~; **kill two** BIRDS **with one ~; a** ROLLing **~ gathers no moss; leave no ~ unturned,** remuer ciel et terre; **a ~'s throw,** quelques pas; **S~ Age** *s.* âge de la pierre *m.*; **~-cold** *adj.* complètement froid; **~-dead** *adj.* raide mort; **~-deaf** *adj.* sourd comme un pot; **~wall** *v.i.* faire de l'obstruction; **stony** *adj.* de pierre, pierreux, (*fig.*) dur; **stony-**BROKE; *v.t.* (*pelt with ~s*) lapider; (*remove ~ from fruit*) dénoyauter.

stooge *s.* fantoche *m.*; *v.i.* être le fantoche de qn.

stook *s.* moyette *f.*; *v.t.* mettre en moyettes.

stool *s.* tabouret *m.*; (*fæces*) selles *f.pl.*; **to fall between two ~s,** s'asseoir entre deux chaises; **~-pigeon** *s.* (*sport*) appeau *m.*; (*fam.*) mouchard *m.*

stoop *s.* dos voûté *m.*; *v.i.* se baisser, avoir le dos rond; (*condescend*) daigner; **~ to,** descendre à.

stop *s.* (*halt*) arrêt *m.*; REQUEST ~; (*pause*) halte *f.*; (*punctuation*) point *m.*; (*peg or block*) arrêt *m.*; (*organ*) jeu *m.*; **come to a ~,** s'arrêter; **put a ~**

to, mettre fin à; *v.t.* (*close*) boucher; (*teeth*) plomber; (*block, road, etc.*) barrer; (*bring to a halt*) arrêter; (*hinder, prevent*) empêcher (qn. de faire qch.); (*payment*) suspendre; (*wages*) retenir; (*cheque*) faire opposition à; (*breath, electr., gas, etc.*) couper; (*ling.*) ponctuer; (*cease*) cesser; *v.i.* (*cease from*) cesser de; (*halt*) s'arrêter; ~ DEAD; (*remain, stay*) rester, passer du temps à; ~ **thief!,** au voleur!; ~ **it!,** assez!; ~ **at** (*boat, train*) desservir; ~ **off,** ~ **over,** descendre (à); **~cock** *s.* robinet d'arrêt *m.*; **~gap** *s.* bouche-trou *m.*; **~-go** *s.* intermittence *f.*; **~--press,** dernière heure; **~-watch** *s.* chronomètre *m.*; **~page** *s.* (*of work. etc.*) arrêt *m.*, (*blockage*) obstruction *f.*, (*fin.*) suspension *f.*; **~per** *s.* bouchon *m.*; **~ping** *s.* arrêt *m.*; **~ping** *s.* (*tooth*) plombage *m.*; **~ing train** *s.* train omnibus *m.*

store *s.* (*abundance*) abondance *f.*; (*stock*) provision *f.*, fonds *m.*; (*large shop*) grand magasin *m.*; **~s** *s.pl.* provisions *f.pl.*, vivres *m.pl.*; **in** ~, en réserve; **to set great ~ by,** faire grand cas de; **to set no ~ by,** faire peu de cas de; *adj.* **~ cattle,** bétail à l'engrais *m.*; ⚠ store = **blind; ~house** *s.* magasin *m.*; **~keeper** *s.* magasinier *m.*; **~-room** *s.* dépôt *m.*; *v.t.* (*equip with*) approvisionner (de); (*lay up for future*) mettre en réserve; (*deposit*) emmagasiner; (*fig.*) meubler (de); **storage** *s.* emmagasinage *m.*; COLD **storage; storage heater** *s.* radiateur à accumulation *m.*

storey *s.* étage *m.*; **two, three** (*etc.*) **storied,** à deux, à trois (etc.) étages.

stork *s.* cigogne *f.*

storm *s.* (*weather*) orage *m.*; (*shower*) (*of blows*) pluie *f.*, (*of abuse*) torrent *m.*; (*tumult*) tempête *f.*; (*dispute*) troubles *m.pl.*; (*mil.*) assaut *m.*; **take by** ~, prendre d'assaut; **~-cloud** *s.* nuage orageux *m.*; **~-troops** *s.* troupes de choc *f.pl.*; **~y** *adj.* (*lit. & fig.*) orageux; **to be ~y,** être à l'orage; **~ily** *adv.**; **~iness** *s.* caractère orageux *m.*; *v.t.* (*mil.*) prendre d'assaut; *v.i.* (*rush*) se précipiter; (*rage*) tempêter (contre); **~ing** *s.* assaut *m.*

story *s.* histoire *f.*; (*narrative*) récit *m.*, conte *m.*; (*legend*) légende *f.*; (*plot of play, etc.*) intrigue *f.*; (*newspaper*) article *m.*; (*fam. lie*) histoire *f.*; **~-teller** *s.* conteur *m.*; (*fam. liar*) menteur *m.*

stoup *s.* bénitier *m.*

stout *s.* stout *m.*; *adj.* **1.** (*resolute*) résolu, ferme; **2.** (*thick, strong*) solide, fort; **3.** (*corpulent*) gros, corpulent; **4.** (*brave*) intrépide; **~ly** *adv.* (1) fermement; (2)*,*; **~ness** *s.* (1) vigueur *f.*; (3) corpulence *f.*

stove *s.* (*cooking*) fourneau *m.*; (*heating*) poêle *m.*

stow *v.t.* fourrer; (*naut.*) arrimer; **~age** *s.*, **~ing** *s.* arrimage *m.*; **~away** *s.* passager clandestin *m.*

straddle *v.t. & i.* (*spread legs*) écarter les jambes; (*stand across sth.*) enjamber; (*with bombs*) encadrer.

straf/e *v.t.* (*with guns, bombs*) pilonner; (*with light weapons*) mitrailler; **~ing** *s.* pilonnage *m.*, mitraillage *m.*

straggl/e *v.i.* (*stray*) s'écarter; (*be scattered*) s'éparpiller; (*grow wildly*) pousser en branches gourmandes; **~er** *s.* traînard *m.*; **~ing** *adj.* éparpillé; **~y** *adj.* épars.

straight *adj.* (≠ *curved or crooked, direct*) droit; (*parallel or perpendicular to*) d'aplomb; (*in order*) en ordre; (*undiluted, neat*) sec; (*upright, honest*) franc, honnête; **to put** ~, arranger; **to set** ~, rectifier; **to keep a ~ face,** rester impassible; **~ fight,** campagne à deux candidats *f.*; **~-forward** *adj.* droit, franc; **~forwardly** *adv.* sans détours; **~forwardness** *s.* droiture *f.*, franchise *f.*; *adv.* (*in ~ line*) droit; (*shoot*) juste; **to go ~** (*fig.*) vivre honnêtement; **~away** *adv.* tout de suite; **~ off** *adv.* (*immediately*) immédiatement, (*without hesitation*) tout-de-go; **~ on,** tout droit; **~ out** *adv.* (*frankly*) carrément; **~en** *v.t.* rectifier, arranger; **~ness** *s.* rectitude *f.*, (*fig.*) droiture *f.*

strain *s.* **1.** (*breed, stock*) race *f.*, lignée *f.*; **2.** (*inherited quality*) tendance inhérente *f.*; **3.** (*injury*) foulure *f.*; **4.** (*tension*) tension *f.*, (*mental*) surmenage *m.*; **5.** (*air*) mélodie *f.*; **6.** (*tone, style*) ton *m.*, style *m.*; **~s** *pl.* (*mus.*) accords *m.pl.*; (*poetry*) accents *m.pl.*; *v.t.* (3) (*limb*) se fouler, (*eyes*) s'abîmer; (4) tendre, (*mental*) se surmener; **7.** (*liquid*) passer, filtrer, (*veg.*) faire égoutter; **8.** (*clasp*) serrer; **9.** (*fig. exaggerate*) forcer; *v.i.* s'efforcer, tirer (sur); **~ed** *adj.* contraint, forcé; (*tense*) tendu; **~er** *s.* passoire *f.*

strait *s.* étroit *m.*; **~s** *pl.* gêne *f.*; *adj.* prude; **~-laced** *adj.* collet monté; ~-JACKET; **~ened circumstances,** besoin *m.*

strand *s.* (*shore*) grève *f.*; (*of wire or rope*) toron *m.*; (*of beads* fil *m.*; (*of hair*) tresse *f.*; *v.t.* (*run aground*) échouer; **~ed** *adj.* abandonné.

strange *adj.* (*foreign, alien*) étranger; (*unfamiliar*) inconnu; (*unexpected*) étrange, singulier; (*fresh*) étranger, nouveau; **~ly** *adv.* étrangement; **~ness** *s.* singularité *f.*, nouveauté *f.*; **~r** *s.* étrang/er, -ère *m.f.*, inconnu(e) *m.f.*

strang/le *v.t.* étrangler; (*hinder growth, suppress*) étouffer; **~lehold** *s.* (*fig.*) étau *m.*; **~ulate** *v.t.* étrangler; **~ulation** *s.* strangulation *f.*; (*med.*) étranglement *m.*

strap *s.* courroie *f.*; (*of watch*) bracelet *m.*; SHOULDER-~; **~hanger** *s.* voyageur debout *m.*; *v.t.* (*fasten*) lier avec une courroie; (*thrash*) fouetter avec une courroie; **~ping** *s.* (*plaster*) sparadrap *m.*; (*beating*) fouettée *f.*; *adj.* bien découplé.

strat/agem *s.* stratagème *m.*; **~egic** *adj.* stratégique; **~egist** *s.* stratège *m.*; **~egy** *s.* stratégie *f.*

stratify *see* STRATUM.

stratosphere *s.* stratosphère *f.*

strat/um *s.* (*lit. & fig.*) couche *f.*; **~ify** *v.t. & i.* stratifier; **~ification** *s.* stratification *f.*

straw *s.* paille *f.*; (*for drinking*) chalumeau *m.*; **man of ~,** fantoche *m.*; **the last ~ (that breaks the camel's back)**, la goutte d'eau qui fait déborder le vase; **you can't make** BRICKS **without ~;** *adj.* en paille, de paille; **~-bottomed** *adj.* paillé; **~-coloured** *adj.* paille (invar.); **~ poll, ~ vote** *s.* vote d'essai *m.*

strawberry *s.* fraise *f.*; (*wild*) fraise des bois *f.*; (*plant*) fraisier *m.*; **~-tree** *s.* arbousier *m.*

stray *s.* animal errant *m.*; enfant abandonné *m.*; *adj.* errant, perdu; (*sporadic*) isolé; (*occasional*) fortuit; *v.i.* errer; (*get lost*) s'égarer, s'éloigner.

streak *s.* (*thin line*) raie *f.*; (*flash*) éclair *m.*; (*strain, element*) trace *f.*, trait *m.*; **~y** *adj.* rayé, (*bacon*) entrelardé; *v.t.* rayer (*with*—de); *v.i.* s'élancer.

stream *s.* ruisseau *m.*; (*current*) courant *m.*; (*fig.*) torrent *m.*; (*of light*) flot *m.*; (*acad.*) groupe de niveau *m.*; **up~**, en amont; **down~**, en aval; **~let** *s.* filet d'eau *m.*; **~line** *s.* profil aérodynamique *m.*; **~line** *v.t.* (*auto.*) profiler, caréner, (*fig.*) rationaliser; **~lined** *adj.* (*auto.*) aérodynamique; *v.i.* couler; (*run with liquid*) ruisseler; (*float in wind, etc.*) flotter; *v.t.* (*acad.*) répartir en groupes de niveau; **~er** *s.* banderole *f.*

street *s.* rue *f.*; **man in the ~,** homme de la rue *m.*; **it's right up my ~,** c'est tout à fait de mon rayon; **to be ~s ahead of,** dépasser de beaucoup; **to be in** QUEER **~.**

strength *s.* force *f.*; TOWER **of ~;** (*personnel*) effectifs *m.pl.*; **to be on the ~,** être sur les contrôles; **on the ~ of,** sur la foi de; **~en** *v.t.* fortifier, renforcer.

strenuous *adj.* (*person*) énergique; (*effort, life*) intense; (*work*) ardu; **~ly** *adv.* énergiquement; **~ness** *s.* énergie *f.*

streptococcus *s.* streptocoque *m.*

streptomycin *s.* streptomycine *f.*

stress *s.* **1.** (*pressure*) pression *f.*; (*tension*) tension *f.*; (*strain*) contrainte *f.*; **2.** (*force*) force *f.*, charge *f.*; **3.** (*emphasis*) accent *m.*; **4.** (*mental*) commotion *f.*; **to lay ~ on** (3) insister sur, mettre l'accent sur; *v.t.* (2) (*mech.*) fatiguer; (3) insister sur.

stretch *s.* (*~ing*) allongement *m.*, effort *m.*; (*space*) étendue *f.*; (*time*) période *f.*; (*pop. to do a a ~*) faire de la taule; **at a ~,** tout d'une traite; *v.t.* & *i.* (*make larger*) (s')élargir; (*extend*) (s')étendre; (*legs*) allonger; (*arms*) étendre; (*wings*) déployer; (*tauten, strain*) tendre; (*exaggerate*) forcer; **~ out** *v.t.* allonger, (*hand*) tendre; **~ one's legs,** se dégourdir les jambes; **~er** *s.* (*brick*) panneau *m.*, (*chair rod*) bâton *m.*, (*rowing*) marchepied *m.*, (*med.*) brancard *m.*, (*for canvas*) châssis *m.*; **~er-bearer** *s.* brancardier *m.*

strew *v.t.* semer, joncher (*with*—de).

striated *adj.* strié.

stricken *adj.* (*disease*) atteint (de); (*grief, etc.*) affligé (de); (*wounded*) blessé.

strict *adj.* **1.** (*exact, precise*) exact, précis; **2.** (*rigorous*) strict, rigoureux; **3.** (*severe*) sévère; **~ly** *adv.* (1)*,*; (2)*,*; (3)*; **~ness** *s.* (1) précision *f.*; (2) rigueur *f.*; (3) sévérité *f.*

stricture *s.* (*usu. pl.*) critiques *f.pl.*

stride *s.* enjambée *f.*; **to take sth. in one's ~,** faire qch. sans effort; *v.i.* marcher à grands pas; *v.t.* **~ over,** enjamber.

strident *adj.* strident; **~ly** *adv.* avec un bruit strident.

strife *s.* lutte *f.*, conflit *m.*

strike *s.* **1.** (*refusal to work*) grève *f.*; **on ~,** en grève; **~bound** *adj.* fermé pour cause de grève; **~-breaker** *s.* jaune *m.*; **~ pay** *s.* allocation aux grévistes *f.*; **2.** (*discovery of oil, etc.*) découverte *f.*; **3.** (*sudden success*) coup de veine *m.*; **4.** (*attack, raid*) coup *m.*, assaut *m.*, descente *f.*; *v.i.* (1) se mettre en grève; *v.t.* (2) rencontrer, découvrir; (3) **~ lucky,** avoir de la veine; **~ oil** (*fig.*) trouver le filon; (4) *v.t.* & *i.* (*hit, deliver blow*) frapper, porter un coup à; (*lightning*) frapper, foudroyer; (*bottom*) toucher; **~ while the iron is** HOT; **~ home,** frapper juste; **~ at,** porter un coup à; **~ against,** heurter; **~ back,** rendre le coup; **5.** *v.t.* & *i.* (*produce or record by striking*) (*clock*) sonner; (*mus. instrument*) toucher; **~ a** CHORD; (*money*) frapper; (*bargain*) conclure; (*match*) frotter, allumer, *v.i.* prendre; (*make blind, dumb*) frapper de cécité, de mutisme; **~ down,** abattre; **~ off,** rayer; **struck off,** rayé des cadres; **~ out** *v.t.* rayer, biffer; **~ up** (*mus.*) *v.i.* préluder, *v.t.* entonner, (*conversation*) entamer, (*acquaintance*) lier; **6.** (*produce impression on*) frapper; **7.** (*lower flag*) amener, (*tents*) plier; **8.** (*pierce, stab*) percer, (*stick into*) enfoncer, (*penetrate*) pénétrer, (*with terror, etc.*) frapper de, (*hort.*) *v.t.* & *i.* (faire) prendre; **9.** (*turn in new direction*) se diriger; **10.** (*balance*) établir; **11.** (*attitude*) prendre; **~r** *s.* gréviste *m.f.*; **striking** *adj.* frappant, remarquable.

string *s.* (*twine, cord*) ficelle *f.*; (*mus.*) corde *f.*; (*fibre*) fil *m.*; (*of beads*) collier *m.*; (*eccles.*; *onions, etc.*) chapelet *m.*; (*of horses*) écurie *f.*; (*series*) file *f.*; **~s** *s.pl.* (*mus.*) cordes *f.pl.*; **first/second ~,** (*sport*) meilleur/second, athlète *m.*; **with (no) ~s attached,** à (sans) conditions; **to pull ~s** (*fig.*) tirer les ficelles, (*fam.*) pistonner; APRON-**~s; to have two ~s to one's bow,** avoir deux cordes à son arc; **~ed** *adj.* (*mus.*) à cordes; **~y** *adj.* filandreux; *v.t.* (*tie*) ficeler; (*thread*) enfiler; (*connect*) faire la liaison; (*remove ~s from*) enlever les fils de; **~ along** *v.t.* faire marcher, *v.i.* **~ along with,** suivre; **~ out** *v.t.* & *i.* (s')espacer; **~ up** *v.t.* pendre haut et court; **strung up, highly-strung** *adj.* nerveux.

stringen/t *adj.* rigoureux; **~cy** *s.* rigueur *f*; **~tly** *adv**.

strip *s.* bande *f.*; (*cartoon*) bande dessinée *f.*; TEAR **s.o. off a ~; ~ lighting** *s.* éclairage par tubes *m.*; **~ling** *s.* adolescent *m.*; *v.t.* & *i.* (*denude*) dénuder; (*deprive of*) dépouiller de; (*undress*) (se) déshabiller; **~ off** *v.t.* arracher; **~-tease** *s.* strip-tease *m.*; **~per** *s.* strip-teaseuse *f.*

stripe *s.* raie *f.* PIN **~**; (*mil.*) galon *m.*; *v.t.* rayer; **~ed** *adj.* rayé.

strive *v.i.* s'efforcer (de); **~ against,** lutter contre; **~ for,** disputer qch. à qn.; **~ with,** rivaliser avec.

stroke *s.* (*blow*; **~** *of luck*; *sound of clock*; *sport*) coup *m.*; (*seizure*) attaque *f.*, infarctus *m.*; (*of pen, etc.*; *fig.*) trait *m.*; (*swimming*) brasse *f.*; (*rowing*) chef de nage *m.*; **at a ~,** d'un coup; *v.t.* (*with hand*) caresser; (*rowing*) être chef de nage de; **~ s.o. up the wrong way,** prendre qn. à rebrousse-poil.

stroll *s.* tour *m.*; **to take a ~,** faire un tour; *v.i.* flâner; **~ing** *adj.* ambulant.

strong *adj.* (*powerful, physically, morally, mentally*; *taste, smell, etc.*; *drink*) fort; (*energetic*) vigoureux, énergique; **~ arm,** force armée *f.*; **~-box,** coffre-fort *m.*; **~ drink,** boisson alcoolisée *f.*; **~hold** *s.* forteresse *f.* **~ly** *adv.* fortement.

strontium *s.* strontium *m.*

strop *s.* cuir à rasoir *m.*; *v.t.* affiler sur le cuir.

strophe *s.* strophe *f.*

structur/e *s.* structure *f.*; (*building*) édifice *m.*; **~al** *adj.* structural; *v.t.* construire, organiser.

struggl/e *s.* lutte *f.*; (*brawl*) mêlée *f.*; *v.i.* lutter, combattre, (contre); (*physically*) se débattre; (*fig.*) s'efforcer; **~e along** *v.i.* avancer péniblement; **~e in,** se frayer un passage; **~e up,** grimper péniblement; **~ing** *adj.* qui vit péniblement.

strum *v.t.* (*on*) tapoter.

strut *s.* **1.** (*constr.*) entretoise *f.*; **2.** (*gait*) démarche orgueilleuse *f.*; *v.i.* (2) se pavaner; *v.t.* (1) entretoiser.

strychnine *s.* strychnine *f.*

stub *s.* (*of tree*) souche *f.*; (*of tooth*) chicot *m.*; (*of cigar, etc.*) mégot *m.*; (*of pencil*) bout *m.*; (*of cheque, etc.*) talon *m.*; *v.t.* (*bump against*) buter contre; **~ out** (*cigar, etc.*) écraser.

stubbl/e *s.* (*agric.*) chaume *m.*; (*beard*) barbe de plusieurs jours *f.*; **~y** *adj.* couvert de chaume.

stubborn *adj.* (*person*) têtu; (*effort, etc.*) tenace; **~ly** *adv.* obstinément; **~ness** *s.* entêtement *m.*, obstination *f.*

stucco *s.* stuc *m.*

stuck *see* STICK.

stud 1. (*nail-head*) clou *m.*; (*on boots*) crampon *m.*; **2.** (*for shirt*) bouton *m.*; **3.** (*of horses*) écurie *f.*; **~-farm** *s.* haras *m.*; *v.t.* (1) clouter; **~ded with,** parsemé de.

student *s.* étudiant(e) *m.f.*; *adj.* d'étudiant, pour étudiant, estudiantin; **~ship** *s.* bourse d'études *f.*

studio *s.* (*artist's*) atelier *m.*; (*radio, etc.*) studio *m.*

stud/y *s.* étude *f.*; (*room*) bureau *m.*, cabinet de travail *m.*; BROWN **~y**; *v.t.* étudier; *v.i.* faire des études; **~y for an exam,** préparer un examen; **~y under s.o.,** être l'élève de qn,; **~ied** *adj.* étudié, (*deliberate*) voulu; **~ious** *adj.* studieux, appliqué, (*anxious to*) empressé de; **~iously** *adv.* studieusement.

stuff *s.* (*material*) étoffe *f.*; (*fabric*) tissu *m.*; (*inferior goods*) fatras *m.*; (*nonsense*) balivernes *f.pl.*; **to do one's ~**, se montrer à la hauteur de sa tâche; *v.t.* (*pack, cram*) remplir, bourrer (*with*—de); (*cram into*) fourrer dans; (*bird*) empailler; (*cook.*) farcir; (*block up*) boucher; (*furniture*) rembourrer; *v.i.* se gaver; **~ed shirt** *s.* (*fam.*) poseur *m.*; **~ing** *s.* (*cook.*) farce *f.*; (*furniture*) rembourrage *m.*, bourre *f.*; **~y** *adj.* mal ventilé; (*fig.*) lourd; (*prudish*) collet monté; **~iness** *s.* manque d'air *m.*

stultify *v.t.* (*make worthless*) réduire à néant; (*make ridiculous*) rendre ridicule.

stumbl/e *s.* faux pas *m.*; *v.i.* trébucher, buter (contre); **~e upon** tomber sur; **~ing-block** *s.* pierre d'achoppement *f.*

stump *s.* (*of tree*) souche *f.*; (*of tooth*) chicot *m.*; (*of limb*) moignon *m.*; (*art*) estompe *f.*; *v.t.* & *i.* (*walk clumsily*) clopiner; (*nonplus*) coller; (*parl.*) faire une tournée électorale; **~ up** (*fam.*) casquer; **to be ~ed,** sécher; **~y** *adj.* trapu.

stun *v.t.* étourdir; (*fig.*) abasourdir; **~ning** *adj.* (*pop.*) épatant.

stunt[1] *s.* tour de force *m.*; (*publicity device*) montage publicitaire *m.*; (*aviat.*) acrobatie *f.*; **~ man** *s.* (*cinema*) cascad/eur, -euse *m.f.*

stunt[2] *v.t.* arrêter; **~ed** *adj.* rabougri.

stupef/y *v.t.* stupéfier; **~action** *s.* stupéfaction *f.*

stupendous *adj.* prodigieux; (*fam.*) formidable; **~ly** *adv.**;*.

stupid *adj.* stupide; **~ly** *adv.**; **~ity** *s.* stupidité *f.*

stupor *s.* stupeur *f.*

sturd/y *adj.* vigoureux, robuste; **~ily** *adv.**,*; **~iness** *s.* vigueur *f.*

sturgeon *s.* esturgeon *m.*

stutter *s.* bégaiement *m.*; *v.i.* bégayer.

sty *s.* (*for pigs*) porcherie *f.*; (*fig.*) taudis *m.*

sty(e) *s.* (*on eye*) orgelet *m.*

Stygian *adj.* ténébreux.

styl/e *s.* (*hist. writing tool*; *bot.*; *manner*) style *m.*; (*title*) titre *m.*; (*kind, type*) genre *m.*, manière *f.*; (*fashion*) mode *f.*; (*distinction*) distinction *f.*, cachet *m.*; **to** CRAMP **s.o.'s ~e; to do sth. in ~e,** faire qch. vraiment bien; *v.t.* (*name*) qualifier; (*make in certain ~e*) façonner qch. à la façon de; **~ish** *adj.* élégant; **~ishly** *adv.* élégamment; **~ist** *s.* styliste *m.f.*; **~istic** *adj.* stylistique; **~istics** *s.* stylistique *f. sing.*; **~ize** *v.t.* styliser.

stylus *s.* (*hist.*) style *m.*; (*for gramophone*) aiguille *f.*

stymied *adj.* **to be ~** (*fig.*) rester le bec dans l'eau.

styptic *adj.* & *s.m.* styptique.

Styx *s.* Styx *m.*

suav/e *adj.* **1.** (*perfume*) suave; **2.** (*manner*) aimable; **~ely** *adv.* d'une manière aimable; **~ity** *s.* (1) suavité *f.*; (2) amabilité *f.*

sub *s.* (*fam.*) (*subaltern*) (sous-) lieutenant *m.*; (*submarine*) sousmarin *m.*; (*subscription*) abonnement *m.*; (*substitute*) remplaçant *m.*; (*advance of money*) contribution *f.*; *v.i.* (*money*) verser une contribution; (*act as substitute*) agir comme substitut de.

sub- *prefix* (*usu.*) sous-, (*sometimes*) sub-; **~agency** *s.* succursale *f.*; **~agent** *s.* sous-agent *m.*; **~aqueous** *adj.* sous l'eau; **~arctic** *adj.* boréal; **~committee** *s.* sous-comité *m.*; **~conscious** *adj.* & *s.m.* subconscient; **~consciousness** *s.* subconscience *f.*; **~consciously** *adv.* de façon subconsciente; **~continent** *s.* péninsule *f.*, **the Indian ~continent,** la péninsule des Indes; **~contract** *s.* sous-traité *m.*, *v.t.* & *i.* sous-traiter; **~contractor** *s.* sous-entrepreneur *m.*; **~cutaneous** *adj.* sous-cutané; **~divide** *v.t.* subdiviser; **~division** *s.* subdivision *f.*; **~-edit** *v.t.* mettre au point; **~fusc** *adj.* sombre; **~human** *s.* sous-homme *m.*; **~join** *v.t.* adjoindre; **~let, ~lease** *v.t.* sous-louer; *s.* sous-location *f.*; **~-lieutenant** *s.* sous-lieutenant *m.*; **~liminal** *adj.* subconscient; **~lunary** *adj.* sublunaire; **~-machine-gun** *s.* mitraillette *f.*; **~normal** *adj.* au-dessous de la normale; **~-plot** *s.* intrigue secondaire *m.*; **~section** *s.* subdivision *f.*; **~soil** *s.* sous-sol *m.*; **~sonic** *adj.* sous-sonique; **~standard** *adj.* inférieur; **~-station** *s.* gare *f.*, poste *m.*, station *f.*, secondaire; **~stratum** *s.* substrat *m.*; **~structure** *s.* infrastructure *f.*; **~tenant** *s.* sous-locataire *m.*; **~title** *s.* sous-titre *m.*; **~tropical** *adj.* subtropical; **~way** *s.* souterrain *m.*; **~zero** *adj.* au-dessous de zéro.

subaltern *s.* (*mil.*) sous-lieutenant *m.*, lieutenant *m.*

subdue *v.t.* subjuguer; (*colour*) atténuer; (*voice*) baisser.

subject *s.* (*person*; *theme*; *ling.*) sujet *m.*; (*citizen*) citoyen *m.*; (*mus.*) motif *m.*; **~-matter** *s.* thème *m.*; *adj.* (*dependent*) assujetti (à); (*owing obedience to*) soumis à; (*liable to*) porté à; (*conditional on*) sous réserve de; **~ive** *adj.* subjectif; **~ively** *adv.**; *v.t.* assujettir (à); (*cause to suffer*) exposer à; **~ion** *s.* subjugation *f.*

sub judice *adv.* en cours d'instruction.

subjugat/e *v.t.* subjuguer; **~ion** *s.* (*act*) subjugation *f.*; (*state*) assujettissement *m.*

subjunctive *adj.* & *s.m.* subjonctif.

sublim/e *adj.* sublime; (*awe-inspiring*) majestueux; (*extreme*) sans pareil; **~ate** *v.t.* sublimer; **~ation** *s.* sublimation *f.*; **~ity** *s.* sublimité *f.*; **~ely** *adv.**;*.

submarine *adj.* & *s.m.* sous-marin.

submerge *v.t.* submerger; *v.i.* plonger.

submersion *s.* submersion *f.*

submiss/ion *s.* soumission *f.*; **~ive** *adj.* soumis, docile; **~ively** *adv.* avec soumission.

submit *v.t.* soumettre; (*point out*) faire remarquer; *v.i.* se soumettre (à).

subordinat/e *s.* subordonné(e) *m.f.*; *adj.* subordonné; *v.t.* subordonner (à); **~ion** *s.* subordination *f.*

suborn *v.t.* suborner.

subpœna *s.* citation *f.*; *v.t.* citer.

sub rosa *adv.* sous le manteau, en cachette.

subscrib/e *v.t.* souscrire (à); (*sign name*) apposer; *v.i.* (*to society, etc.*) verser une cotisation à; (*to periodical*) s'abonner à; **~er** *s.* souscripteur *m.*; abonné *m.*

subscription *s.* (*contribution*) souscription *f.*; (*to society, etc.*) cotisation *f.*; (*to periodical, etc.*) abonnement *m.*

subsequent *adj.* (*law*) subséquent; suivant, postérieur; **~ly** *adv.* par la suite.

subservien/t *adj.* **1.** (*serving as means to end*) utile (à); **2.** (*subordinate*) soumis (à); **3.** (*obsequious*) obséquieux; **~ce** *s.* (1) utilité *f.*; (2) asservissement *m.*; (3) servilité *f.*

subsid/e *v.i.* **1.** (*sink*) s'affaisser, s'écrouler; **2.** (*go down*) baisser; **3.** (*into chair, etc.*) se laisser tomber; **4.** (*abate*) s'apaiser, tomber, se calmer; **~ence** *s.* (1) affaissement *m.*; (2) baisse *f.*; (4) apaisement *m.*

subsidiary *s.* (*comm.*) filiale *f.*; *adj.* subsidiaire.

subsid/ize *v.t.* subventionner; **~y** *s.* subvention *f.*

subsist *v.i.* subsister; **~ence** *s.* subsistance *f.*

substan/ce *s.* (*main part of sth.*) substance *f.*; (*purport*) fond *m.*; (*theme*) matière *f.*; (*reality*) réalité *f.*; **~tial** (≠ *illusory*) substantiel; (≠ *inconsiderable*) considérable; (*solid*) solide; (*well-to-do*) cossu; **~tially** *adv.**;*;*; **~tiate** *v.t.* (*give form to*) établir; (*justify*) justifier.

substantive *s.* substantif *m.*; *adj.* (*independent*) autonome; (*not subsidiary*) propre.

substitut/e *s.* (*person*) remplaçant *m.*, suppléant *m.*; (*product*) succédané *m.*, produit de remplacement *m.*; (*imitation*) contrefaçon *f.*; *v.t.* substituer (*for*—à); *v.i.* suppléer; **~ion** *s.* substitution *f.*

subterfuge *s.* subterfuge *m.*
subterranean *adj.* souterrain.
subt/le *adj.* **1.** (*pervasive, fine, delicate*) subtil; **2.** (*ingenious*) ingénieux; **3.** (*crafty, cunning*) rusé, habile; **~ilize** *v.t.* & *i.* subtiliser; **~ly** *adv.* subtilement; **~lety** *s.* (1) subtilité *f.*; (2), (3) finesse *f.*
subtract *v.t.* soustraire (à); **~ion** *s.* soustraction *f.*
suburb *s.* faubourg *m.*; DORMITORY **~**; **~s** *pl.* banlieue *f.*; **~ia** *s.* (*London*) les faubourgs de Londres; **~an** *adj.* suburbain, de banlieue.
subvention *s.* subvention *f.*
subver/t *v.t.* renverser; **~sion** *s.* subversion *f.*; **~sive** *adj.* subversif.
succeed *v.t.* (*come after, inherit from*) succéder à; (*follow*) suivre; (*take place of*) remplacer; *v.i.* (*have success*) réussir (*in sth.*—réussir qch.; *in doing sth.*, à faire qch.).
success *s.* (*favourable result*) succès *m.*; (*attainment of object*) réussite *f.*; **to be a ~**, avoir du succès, réussir; **~ful** *adj.* (*person*) heureux; (*thing*) réussi, couronné de succès; **~fully** *adv.* avec succès.
success/ion *s.* succession *f.*; (*series*) série *f.*; **in ~ion,** de suite; **~ive** *adj.* successif; **~ively** *adv.**; **~or** *s.* successeur *m.*
succinct *adj.* succinct; **~ly** *adv.**; **~ness** *s.* concision *f.*
succour *s.* secours *m.*; *v.t.* secourir.
succulen/t *s.* plante grasse *f.*; *adj.* succulent; (*fruit*) juteux; **~ce** *s.* succulence *f.*
succumb *v.i.* succomber (à); (*die*) mourir.
such *adj.* (*of kind, degree, extent, described*) tel; **~ a man,** un tel homme; **~ a thing,** une telle chose; **~ kindness,** une telle bonté; (*previously described*) pareil, semblable; **there has never been ~ a party,** il n'y a jamais eu de fête pareille; (**~** *a* + *adj.* + *s.*) aussi, si; **~ a beautiful child,** un si bel enfant; **~ a stupid affair,** une affaire aussi stupide; (*with following effect*) **there was ~ a noise that I was deafened,** il y avait un tel bruit que j'en fus étourdi; **they are ~ rich people that everybody envies them,** ce sont des gens si riches que tout le monde les envie; **~ knowledge as he has,** les connaissances qu'il a; **~ money as I have,** l'argent que j'ai; **~-and-~**, un(e) certain(e); **~ as to,** suffisant pour; *pron.* ceux, celles; **~ as wish, may remain,** ceux (celles) qui le désirent, peuvent rester; **as ~**, comme tel; **~like,** de cette sorte, de ce genre; (*fam.*) **and ~like,** et autres choses du même genre.
suck *s.* (*action*) suction *f.*; (*result*) sucée *f.*; **to give ~**, allaiter; *v.t.* & *i.* sucer; (*baby*) téter; **~ at,** tirer sur; **~ down** *v.t.* engloutir; **~ in** *v.t.* aspirer, absorber; **~ up,** absorber; **~ up to s.o.** (*pop.*) lécher les bottes de qn.; **teach grandmother to ~** EGGS; **~er** *s.* (*hort.*) surgeon *m.*, (*pop.*) poire *f.*; **~ing**-PIG.
suckl/e *v.t.* allaiter; **~ing** *s.* nourrisson *m.*
sucrose *s.* saccharose *m.*
suction *s.* aspiration *f.*
Sudan *see* SOUDAN.
sudden *adj.* soudain; **all of a ~**, tout à coup; **~ly** *adv.* soudain; **~ness** *s.* soudaineté *f.*
suds *s.* mousse de savon *f.*
sue *v.t.* poursuivre (qn.) en justice; *v.i.* intenter un procès (à qn.); **~ for,** demander (qch. à qn.); solliciter (qch. de qn.).
suede *s.* (*gloves*) suède *m.*; (*shoes, etc.*) daim *m.*
suet *s.* graisse de rognon *f.*
suffer *v.t.* & *i.* (*experience*) souffrir; (*pain*) ressentir; (*loss*) subir; (*tolerate*) supporter; (*permit*) permettre (à qn. de faire qch.); **~ance** *s.* tolérance *f.*; **on ~ance,** par tolérance; **~er** *s.* victime *f.*, (*sick person*) malade *m.f.*; **~ing** *s.* souffrance *f.*; **~ing** *adj.* souffrant.
suffice *v.i.* suffire (à).
sufficien/t *adj.* suffisant; **to be ~t,** suffire; **to have ~**, en avoir assez; **~cy** *s.* suffisance *f.*; **~tly** *adv.* suffisamment.
suffix *s.* suffixe *m.*
suffocat/e *v.t.* & *i.* suffoquer, étouffer; **~ion** *s.* suffocation *f.*; **~ing** *adj.* suffocant, étouffant.
suffragan *adj.* & *s.m.* suffragant.
suffrage *s.* suffrage *m.*; **~tte** *s.* suffragette *f.*
suffuse *v.t.* se répandre sur.
sugar *s.* sucre *m.*; **granulated ~**, sucre semoule; **icing ~**, sucre glace; **lump ~**, sucre en morceaux; **~-beet** *s.* betterave sucrière *f.*; **~-bowl** *s.* sucrier *m.*; **~-candy** *s.* sucre-candi *m.*; **~**-CANE; **~-loaf** *r.* pain de sucre *m.*; **~-tongs** *s.* pince à sucre *f.*; *adj.* sucrier; **~y** *adj.* sucré; *v.t.* sucrer; (*fig.*) dorer.
suggest *v.t.* suggérer; (*give hint of*) évoquer; **~ible** *adj.* suggestible; **~ion** *s.* suggestion *f.*; (*hint*) nuance *f.*; **~ive,** *adj.* suggestif; **~ive of** faisant penser à.
suicid/e *s.* suicide *m.*; (*person*) suicidé(e) *m.f.*; **to commit ~e,** se suicider; **~al** *adj.* suicidaire.
suit *s.* (*petition*) requête *f.*; (*for marriage*) cour *f.*, demande en mariage *f.*; (*law*) procès *m.*; (*cards*) couleur *f.*; (*clothes*) complet *m.*, costume *m.*, (*woman's*) tailleur *m.*; SWIM-**~**; **to** FOLLOW **~**; **~**CASE; *v.t.* (*adapt to*) adapter à; (*agree with, meet requirements*) convenir à; *v.i.* (*be agreeable*) convenir; (*be convenient*) faire l'affaire; (*be becoming*) aller (à); **~able** *adj.* convenable, adapté à; **~ability** *s.* convenance *f.*; **~ably** *adv.**; **~ing** *s.* tissu *m.*; **~or** *s.* prétendant *m.*
suite *s.* (*retinue*; *mus.*) suite *f.*; (*of rooms*) appartement *m.*; (*of furniture*) mobilier *m.*
sulk *v.i.* bouder; **~s** *s.pl.* bouderie *f.*; **~y** *adj.* boudeur; **~ily** *adv.* en boudant; **~iness** *s.* bouderie *f.*
sullen *adj.* maussade, morose; (*sky*) menaçant; **~ly** *adv.* maussadement; **~ness** *s.* humeur sombre *f.*; taciturnité *f.*
sully *v.t.* souiller.
sulphanilamide *s.* sulfamide *m.*
sulph/ate *s.* sulfate *m.*; **~ide** *s.* sulfure *m.*; **~ite** *s.* sulfite *m.*
sulphur *s.* souffre *m.*; **~ic** *adj.* sulfurique.
sultan *s.* sultan *m.*; **~a** *s.* (*~'s wife*) sultane *f.*; (*dried fruit*) raisin de Smyrne *m.*; **~ate** *s.* sultanat *m.*
sultr/y *adj.* (*weather*) lourd, étouffant; (*fig.*) chaud; (*lurid*) voyant; **it is ~y,** il fait lourd; **~iness** *s.* chaleur étouffante *f.*
sum *s.* (*total*; *amount of money*) somme *f.*; (*summary*) fond *m.*; (*math.*) problème *m.*; **~ total** *s.* somme totale *f.*, montant *m.*; *v.t.* **~ up,** résumer.
summar/y *s.* résumé *m.*; *adj.* sommaire; **~ily** *adv.**; **~ize** *v.t.* résumer.
summer *s.* été *m.*; (*fig. year of age*) printemps *m.*; *adj.* d'été, estival; **~-house** *s.* pavillon *m.*; **~-time** *s.* heure d'été *f.*
summit *s.* (*lit.* & *fig.*) sommet *m.*
summon *v.t.* (*call together*) convoquer; (*call upon to*) sommer (de); (*law*) citer; (*call to appear*) appeler; (*doctor, etc.*) faire venir; **~ up** *v.t.* rassembler; **~s** *s.* appel *m.*; (*law*) citation *f.*; *v.t.* citer.
sump *s.* (*auto.*) carter *m.*; (*techn.*) puisard *m.*
sumptu/ary *adj.* somptuaire; **~ous** *adj.* somptueux; **~ously** *adv.**; **~ousness** *s.* somptuosité *f.*
sun *s.* soleil *m.*; **~bathe** *v.i.* prendre un bain de soleil; **~-beam** *s.* rayon de soleil *m.*; **~-blind** *s.* store *m.*; **~burn** *s.* hâle *m.*; **~burnt, ~-tanned** *adj.* hâlé; **~dial** *s.* cadran solaire *m.*; **~down** *s.* coucher du soleil *m.*; **~flower** *s.* tournesol *m.*; **~-glasses** *s.* lunettes de soleil *f.pl.*; **~-helmet** *s.* casque colonial *m.*; **~light** *s.* lumière du soleil *f.*; **~lit** *adj.* ensoleillé;

~-proof *adj.* à l'épreuve du soleil; **~rise** *s.* lever du soleil *m.*; **~set** *s.* coucher du soleil *m.*; **~shade** *s.* ombrelle *f.*, parasol *m.*; **~shine** *s.* soleil *m.*; **~spot** *s.* tache solaire *f.*; **~stroke** *s.* insolation *f.*; **~-tan** *s.* hâle *m.*; **~ny** *adj.* (*day, place*) ensoleillé, exposé au soleil, (*fig.*) rayonnant; **it is ~ny, the ~ is shining,** il fait (du) soleil; *v.t.* **~ oneself,** se chauffer au soleil.
sundae *s.* glace (aux fruits) *f.*
Sunday *s.* dimanche *m.*; *adj.* dominical; **a month of ~s,** une éternité; **in one's ~ best,** endimanché; **~ school** *s.* catéchisme *m.*
sunder *v.t.* séparer.
sundr/y *adj.* divers; **all and ~y,** tout un chacun; **~ies** *s.pl.* articles divers *m.pl.*; (*fin.*) frais divers *m.pl.*
sunken *adj.* (*road, eyes*) creux; (*naut.*) submergé.
sup *v.t.* & *i.* (*drink*) siroter; *v.i.* (*eat supper*) souper.
super *s.* (*fam.*) (*actor*) figurant *m.*; (*superintendent*) surveillant *m.*; *adj.* (*pop.*) formidable.
super- (*in combination*) **~abundant** *adj.* surabondant; **~abundance** *s.* surabondance *f.*; **~-add** *v.t.* surajouter; **~cargo** *s.* subrécargue *m.*; **~charger** *s.* surcompresseur *n.*; **~eminent** *adj.* prééminent; **~fine** *adj.* surfin; **~human** *adj.* surhumain; **~impose** *v.t.* superposer; **~incumbent** *adj.* superposé; **~man** *s.* surhomme *m.*; **~market** *s.* supermarché *m.*; **~natural** *adj.* surnaturel; **~numerary** *adj.* surnuméraire; **~phosphate** *s.* superphosphate *m.*; **~pose** *v.t.* superposer; **~power** *s.* supergrand *m.*; **~scription** *s.* inscription *f.*, en-tête *f.*; **~structure** *s.* superstructure *f.*; **~sonic** *adj.* supersonique; **~tax** *s.* surtaxe (progressive) *f.*
superannuat/e *v.t.* mettre à la retraite; (*fam.*) mettre au rancart; **~ion** *s.* mise à la retraite *f.*
superb *adj.* superbe; **~ly** *adv.**.
supercilious *adj.* hautain; **~ly** *adv.* avec hauteur; **~ness** *s.* hauteur *f.*, arrogance *f.*
supererogation *s.* surérogation *f.*
superficial *adj.* superficiel; **~ly** *adv.**.
superflu/ous *adj.* superflu; **~ity** *s.* superfluité *f.*; (*quantity*) superflu *m.*
superintend *v.t.* surveiller; **~ence** *s.* surveillance *f.*; **~ent** *s.* surveillant *m.*; **police ~ent** *s.* commissaire divisionnaire *m.*
superior *s.* supérieur *m.*; *adj.* supérieur; (*supercilious*) condescendant; **~ to,** insensible à; **~ity** *s.* supériorité *f.*
superlative *s.* superlatif *m.*; *adj.* suprême; **~ly** *adv.* au suprême degré.
supernal *adj.* céleste.
supersede *v.t.* (*replace by*) remplacer (par); (*take place of*) supplanter.
superstit/ion *s.* superstition *f.*; **~ious** *adj.* superstitieux.
supervene *v.i.* survenir.
supervis/e *v.t.* surveiller; **~ion** *s.* surveillance *f.*; **~or** *s.* surveillant *m.*; **~ory** *adj.* de surveillance.
supine *s.* (*ling.*) supin *m.*; *adj.* (*lying face upwards*) couché sur le dos; (*lazy*) indolent.
supper *s.* souper *m.*; **the Last S~,** la Cène *f.*
supplant *v.t.* supplanter.
supple *adj.* souple; (*servile*) servile; **~ness** *s.* souplesse *f.*
supplement *s.* supplément *m.*; *v.t.* compléter; **~ary** *adj.* supplémentaire.
suppliant *adj.* & *s.m.* suppliant.
supplicat/e *v.t.* supplier; **~ion** *s.* supplication *f.*
suppl/y *s.* **1.** (*provision, stock*) provision *f.*; **2.** (*substitute*) suppléant *m.*; **3.** (*~ying*) approvisionnement *m.*; **~y and demand** (*comm.*) l'offre et la demande; **~ies** *s.pl.* (*mil.*) fournitures *f.pl.*, (*fin.*) crédits *m.pl.*, (*fam.*) vivres *m.pl.*; *v.t.* (1), (3) fournir (de), approvisionner (*with*—en); (2) suppléer (à); (*a need*) répondre à (un besoin); **~ier** *s.* fournisseur *m.*
support *s.* support *m.*, appui *m.*; (*fig.*) soutien *m.*; **in ~ of,** en faveur de; *v.t.* (*bear weight; tolerate*) supporter; (*prop up; encourage*) soutenir; (*supply*) subvenir aux besoins de; (*second*) appuyer; (*corroborate*) corroborer; **~able** *adj.* (*theory*) soutenable; (*bearable*) supportable **~er** *s.* partisan *m.*, (*sport*) supporter *m.*
suppos/e *v.t.* (*as hypothesis*) supposer; (*assume*) imaginer, présumer; (*involve*) présupposer; **~ed** *adj.* présumé; **to be ~ed to do sth.,** être censé faire qch.; **~ing** *conj.* en supposant que; **~ition** *s.* supposition *f.*; **~itious** *adj.* supposé.
suppository *s.* suppositoire *m.*
suppress *v.t.* **1.** (*put down*) supprimer; **2.** (*prevent publication*) interdire; **3.** (*keep secret*) dissimuler, taire; **4.** (*laugh, revolt*) réprimer; **5.** (*yawn, cough, sob, news*) étouffer; **6.** (*emotions*) dominer; **~ion** *s.* (1) suppression *f.*; (3) dissimulation *f.*; (4) répression *f.*; (6) domination *f.* **~or** *s.* (*electr.*) silencieux *m.*, (*radio*) antiparasite *m.*
suppurat/e *v.i.* suppurer; **~ion** *s.* suppuration *f.*
suprem/e *adj.* suprême; **~acy** *s.* suprématie *f.*; **~ely** *adv.**.
surcharge *s.* surcharge *f.*; (*on letter*) surtaxe *f.*; *v.t.* (*overload*) surcharger; (*charge extra*) taxer; (*on stamp*) surcharger.
sure *adj.* (*certain, reliable, faithful*) sûr; (*convinced*) convaincu; **to be ~ to do sth.,** ne pas manquer de faire qch., **to be ~ not to do sth.,** se garder de faire qch.; **to make ~ of/that,** s'assurer de/que; **~ly** *adv.* sûrement; **~ty** (*security*) caution *f.*, (*guarantor*) garant *m.*
surf *s.* ressac *m.*; **~-board** *s.* planche *f.* (de surf); **~ing** *s.*, **~-riding** *s.* surf *m.*; *v.i.* surfer.
surface *s.* surface *f.*; *adj.* de surface, superficiel; (*mail*) par terre, par voie maritime; *v.t.* revêtir (*with*—de); *v.i.* faire surface.
surfeit *s.* satiété *f.*; **to have a ~ of,** être rassasié de; *v.t.* rassasier de.
surge *s.* (*waves*) houle *f.*, (*motion*) bouillonnement *m.*; *v.i.* (*sea*) être houleux; (*techn.*) galoper; (*fig.*) bouillonner.
surg/eon *s.* chirurgien *m.*; ⚠ surgeon = (*hort.*) **sucker**; VETERINARY **~eon; ~ery** *s.* chirurgie *f.*; (*room*) cabinet *m.*; **~ical** *adj.* chirurgical; (*appliance*) orthopédique.
surl/y *adj.* hargneux; **~iness** *s.* caractère hargneux *m.*
surmise *s.* conjecture *f.*; *v.t.* & *i.* conjecturer.
surmount *v.t.* surmonter; **~able** *adj.* surmontable.
surname *s.* nom de famille *m.*; ⚠ surnom = **nickname.**
surpass *v.t.* surpasser (en); (*s.o.*) l'emporter sur qn.; (*exceed hopes, etc.*) dépasser; **~ing** *adj.* incomparable; **~ingly** *adv.* extrêmement.
surplice *s.* surplis *m.*
surplus *s.* surplus *m.*, excédent *m.*; *adj.* en surplus.
surpris/e *s.* surprise *f.*; *v.t.* surprendre; *adj.* inattendu; **~ing** *adj.* surprenant, étonnant; **~ingly** *adv.* étonnamment.
surreal/ism *s.* surréalisme *m.*; **~ist** *s.* surréaliste *m.f.*; **~istic** *adj.* surréaliste.
surrender *s.* **1.** (*giving up*) abandon *m.*, cession *f.* (de); **2.** (*mil.*) reddition *f.*; **3.** (*insurance*) rachat *m.*; *v.t.* (1) abandonner, renoncer à; (2) rendre; (3) racheter; *v.i.* (2) se rendre; (*submit*) se soumettre à.
surreptitious *adj.* subreptice; **~ly** *adv.**.
surround *s.* bordure *f.*; *v.t.* entourer (*with*—de); (*mil.*) cerner; **~ing** *adj.* environnant; **~ings** *s.pl.* (*of place*) environs *m.pl.*; (*of person*) entourage *m.*, milieu *m.*
surtax *s.* surtaxe *f.*

surveillance *s.* surveillance *f.*
survey *s.* **1.** (*general view*) vue *f.*; **2.** (*detailed inspection*) examen *m.*, étude *f.*; **3.** (*of land*) arpentage *m.*; **4.** (*dept.*) service topographique *m.*; ORDNANCE ~; *v.t.* (1) contempler; (2) surveiller, inspecter; (3) arpenter, cadastrer; **~ing** *s.* arpentage *m.*; **~or** *s.* arpenteur *m.*, ingénieur topographe *m.*; QUANTITY **~or.**
surviv/e *v.t.* & *i.* survivre (à), subsister; **~al** *s.* survie *f.*; **~or** *s.* survivant(e) *m.f.*
susceptib/le *adj.* **1.** (*admitting of*) susceptible de; **2.** (*sensitive to*) sensible à; **3.** (*impressionable*) facilement froissé; **4.** (*med.*) prédisposé à; **~ility** *s.* (1) susceptibilité *f.*; (2) sensibilité *f.*; (4) prédisposition *f.*
suspect *adj.* & *s.m.f.* suspect(e); *v.t.* & *i.* (*have suspicions about, think guilty of*) soupçonner; (*mistrust*) se méfier de; (*imagine*) se douter.
suspend *v.t.* suspendre; **~ers** *s.pl.* jarretelles *f.pl.*; **~er belt** *s.* porte-jarretelles *m.*
suspense *s.* (*canon law*) suspense *f.*; (*uncertainty*) incertitude *f.*; (*emotion*) attente angoissée *f.*, tension *f.*, suspense *m.* (*anglicism*); **in ~**, en suspens.
suspension *s.* suspension *f.*; **~ bridge** *s.* pont suspendu *m.*
suspic/ion *s.* soupçon *m.*; **~ious** *adj.* **1.** (*having ~s*) soupçonneux, méfiant; (2) (*seeming ~ious*) suspect; **~iously** *adv.* (1) avec méfiance; (2) de façon suspecte.
sustain *v.t.* (*hold up, support*) soutenir; (*keep in being*) entretenir; (*undergo*) subir, éprouver.
sustenance *s.* subsistance *f.*; (*food*) nourriture *f.*
sutler *s.* cantinier *m.*, vivandière *f.*
suture *s.* suture *f.*; *v.t.* suturer.
suzerain *s.* suzerain *m.*; **~ty** *s.* suzeraineté *f.*
swab *s.* **1.** (*naut.*) faubert *m.*; **2.** (*mil., med.*) écouvillon *m.*; *v.t.* (1) fauberter; (2) écouvillonner.
swaddl/e *v.t.* emmailloter; **~ing-clothes** *s.* langes *f.pl.*
swagger *s.* (*gait*) allure cavalière *f.*; (*appearance*) air fanfaron *m.*; *v.i.* se pavaner; (*fam.*) crâner; **~er** *s.* fanfaron *m.*
Swahili *adj.* & *s.m.* souahili, souahéli.
swain *s.* berger *m.*; (*fam.*) soupirant *m.*
swallow[1] *s.* (*bird*) hirondelle *f.*; **~-dive** *s.* saut de l'ange *m.*
swallow[2] *s.* gorgée *f.*, bouchée *f.*; *v.t.* avaler; (*engulf, ~ up*) engloutir; (*pop. believe*) avaler, gober; (*repress*) réprimer.
swamp *s.* marécage *m.*, marais *m.*; *v.t.* (*inundate*) inonder; (*sink*) submerger; (*fig.*) noyer; **~y** *adj.* marécageux.
swan *s.* cygne *m.*; **~'sdown** *s.* cygne *m.*; **~-neck** *s.* (*techn.*) col de cygne *m.*; **~-song** *s.* chant du cygne *m.*; *v.i.* **~ around** (*pop.*) voyager aux frais de la princesse.
swank *s.* (*fam.*) esbroufe *f.*; (*person*) poseur *m.*; *v.i.* faire de l'esbroufe.
swap *see* SWOP.
swarm *s.* **1.** (*of bees*) essaim *m.*; **2.** (*fig.*) foule *f.*; *v.i.* (1) essaimer; (2) s'attrouper; **~ with,** fourmiller de.
swarthy *adj.* bistré.
swashbuckler *s.* matamore *m.*
swastika *s.* svastika *m.*, croix gammée *f.*
swat *v.t.* écraser.
swath *s.* andain *m.*
swathe *v.t.* emmailloter.
sway *s.* **1.** (*motion*) oscillation *f.*; **2.** (*rule*) domination *f.*, empire *n.*; *v.t.* (1) faire osciller; (2) gouverner; (*influence*) influencer; *v.i.* (1) osciller, se balancer; (*waver*) hésiter.
swear *v.t.* & *i.* **1.** (*take oath*) (faire) prêter serment; **2.** (*state on oath*) jurer; **3.** (*use profane language*) jurer; **~ at** *v.t.* injurier; **~ by,** jurer par; **~ in,** assermenter; **~ to** *v.t.* déclarer sous serment; **~ like a** TROOPER; **~ing** *s.* (1), (2) serment *m.*; (3) jurons *m.pl.*; **~-word** *s.* juron *m.*
sweat *s.* sueur *f.*; (*fam.* = *chore*) corvée *f.*; **~-band** *s.* serre-tête *m.*; **~-shirt** *s.* tricot *m.*; **~-shop** *s.* atelier où les ouvriers sont exploités *m.*; *v.t.* exploiter; *v.i.* suer; (*work hard*) suer sang et eau; **~er** *s.* chandail *m.*; **~ing** *s.* transpiration *f.*
swede *s.* (*veg.*) rutabaga *m.*
Swed/en *s.* (*geog.*) Suède *f.*; **~e** *s.m.f.* suédois(e); **~ish** *s.* (*lang.*) suédois *m.*; *adj.* suédois.
sweep *s.* (*brushing*) coup de balai; (*movement*) grand geste *m.*; (*aviat.*) randonnée *f.*; (*curve in road*) courbe *f.*; (*oar*) aviron de queue *m.*; (*chimney-~*) ramoneur *m.*; (*range*) portée *f.*; (*~stake*) loterie *f.*; **to make a clean ~ of,** faire place nette de; *v.t.* & *i.* (*glide*) aller majestueusement; (*extend*) s'étendre; (*carry along*) emporter; (*pass over*) effleurer; (*clean with brush*) balayer; (*chimney*) ramoner; (*mines*) draguer; **~ away, ~ out, ~ up,** balayer, abolir; **~ down on,** fondre sur; **~ past,** passer vite; **~ under the** CARPET; **be swept off one's** FEET; **~er** *s.* balayeur *m.*, (*mech.*) balai mécanique *m.*; MINE **~er;** **~ing** *adj.* (*statement*) catégorique; **~ings** *s.pl.* balayures *f.pl.*, (*fig.*) rebut *m.*; **~stake** *s.* sweepstake *m.*
sweet *s.* bonbon *m.*; (*pudding*) dessert *m.*; (*term of affection*) chéri(e) *m.f.*; **~s** *s.pl.* délices *f.pl.*; *adj.* doux; (*sugary*) sucré; (*pleasant*) agréable; (*dear*) chéri; (*kind*) aimable, gentil; **to have a ~ tooth,** aimer les friandises; **~bread** *s.* ris de veau *m.*; **~ chestnut** *s.* marron *m.*; **~ corn** *s.* maïs doux *m.*; **~heart** *s.* bon(ne) ami(e) *m.f.*; **~** PEA; **~** POTATO; **~-william** *s.* œillet de poète *m.*; **~en** *v.t.* sucrer, (*fig.*) adoucir; **~ly** *adv.* doucement; **~ness** *s.* douceur *f.*
swell *s.* (*~ing*) gonflement *m.*; (*sea*) houle *f.*; (*mus.*) crescendo *m.*; (*organ*) accent majestueux *m.*; (*ground*) ondulation *f.*; (*fam. person*) rupin *m.*; *adj.* (*fam.*) chic; *v.t.* & *i.* (*dilate, expand*) (se) gonfler, (s')enfler; (*raise up*) élever; (*rise up*) se soulever; (*increase in volume*) grossir; **~ing** *s.* gonflement *m.*, (*med.*) enflure *f.*, (*of river*) crue *f.*
swelter *v.t.* étouffer; *v.i.* être étouffant; **~ing** *adj.* étouffant.
swerve *s.* écart *m.*, déviation *f.*; *v.i.* (*horse*) faire un écart; (*auto.*) faire une embardée; (*person*) dévier (de).
swift[1] *s.* (*bird*) martinet *m.*
swift[2] *adj.* rapide, prompt; **~ly** *adv.**,*; **~ness** *s.* rapidité *f.*, promptitude *f.*
swig *s.* (*fam.*) lampée *f.*; *v.t.* (*fam.*) lamper.
swill *s.* eaux grasses *f.pl.*; *v.t.* laver à grande eau; (*fam.*) lamper.
swim *s.* bain de mer *m.*; **to have a ~,** (aller) nager; **to be in the ~** (*fig.*) être à la page; **~-suit** *s.* maillot *m.*; *v.t.* & *i.* (faire) nager; traverser à la nage; (*float*) flotter; (*of head*) tourner; **~mer** *s.* nageu/r, -se *m.f.*; **~ming** *s.* natation *f.*; **to go ~mingly** (*fig.*) aller comme sur des roulettes; **~ming-bath, ~ming-pool** *s.* piscine *f.*
swindl/e *s.* escroquerie *f.*; *v.t.* escroquer; **~er** *s.* escroc *m.*
swin/e *s.* (*lit.* & *fig.*) cochon *m.*; **cast** PEARLS **before ~e;** **~e-herd** *s.* porcher *m.*; **~ish** *adj.* de pourceau, (*fig.*) immonde.
swing *s.* (*act*) balancement *m.*; (*oscillation*) oscillation *f.*; (*rhythm*) rythme *m.*; (*seat*) balançoire *f.*; (*fig.*) libre carrière *f.*; **to be in full ~,** battre son plein; **to go with a ~** (*pop.*) chauffer; **~ bridge** *s.* pont tournant *m.*; **~-door** *s.* porte va-et-vient *f.*; **~ music** *s.* swing *m.*; **~-wing** (*aircraft*) (avion) à géométrie *or* à flèche, variable; *v.t.* & *i.* (se) balancer, osciller; (*mus. pop.*) swinguer; **~ the** LEAD; **room**

to ~ a CAT; **~ing** *s.* balancement *m.*; **~ing** *adj.* rythmé, oscillant, (*pop.*) swing.
swingeing *adj.* cinglant; (*fam.*) énorme.
swipe *s.* coup *m.*; **to take a ~ at,** frapper à toute volée; *v.t.* frapper; (*pop.*) chiper.
swirl *s.* tourbillonnement *m.*; (*of dust, etc.*) tourbillon *m.*; (*of water*) remous *m.*; *v.i.* tourbillonner.
swish *s.* **1.** (*of whip*) sifflement *m.*; **2.** (*of silk, etc.*) frou-frou *m.*; **3.** (*of water*) bruissement *m.*; *v.i.* (1) siffler; (2) froufrouter; (3) bruire.
Swiss *adj.* suisse; *s.m.f.* Suisse(sse).
switch *s.* **1.** (*whip*) badine *f.*; **2.** (*branch*) canne *f.*; **3.** (*electr.*) commutateur *m.*, interrupteur *m.*; TIME-~; **4.** (*rail.*) aiguille *f.*; **5.** (*false hair*) postiche *m.*; **6.** (*change*) changement *m.* (de position, de direction, etc.); **~back** *s.* montagnes russes *f.pl.*; **~board** *s.* standard *m.*; **~board operator** *s.* standardiste *m.f.*; *v.t.* (1) cingler; (2) brandir; (3) **~ on** (*light*) allumer, (*radio*) mettre, (*auto.*) mettre le contact; (4) aiguiller; (6) changer (de); **~ off,** éteindre, couper.
Switzerland *s.* (*geog.*) Suisse *f.*
swivel *s.* pivot *m.*; *v.t.* & *i.* (faire) pivoter; **~ chair** *s.* fauteuil-pivotant *m.*
swoon *s.* évanouissement *m.*; *v.i.* s'évanouir.
swoop *s.* attaque *f.*; **at one (fell) ~,** d'un seul coup (fatal); *v.i.* fondre (sur).
swop, swap *s.* troc *m.*; *v.t.* troquer.
sword *s.* épée *f.*; (*cavalry*) sabre *m.*; (*fig.*) glaive *m.*; **to cross ~s with s.o.** se mesurer contre qn.; **~-belt** *s.* ceinturon *m.*; **~fish** *s.* espadon *m.*; **~-stick** *s.* canne-épée *f.*
swot *s.* (*pop. hard work*) boulot *m*; (*person*) bûcheur *m.*; *v.i.* bûcher.
sybarit/e *s.* sybarite *m.*; **~ic** *adj.* sybarite.
sycamore *s.* sycamore *m.*
sycophan/t *s.* flagorneur *m.*; **~cy** *s.* flagornerie *f.*; **~tic** *adj.* flagorneur.
syllab/le *s.* syllabe *f.*; **~ic** *adj.* syllabique.
syllabus *s.* programme *m.*
syllogism *s.* syllogisme *m.*
sylph *s.* sylphe *m.*, sylphide *f.*
sylvan *adj.* sylvestre.
symbio/sis *s.* symbiose *f.*; **~tic** *adj.* symbiotique.
symbol *s.* symbole *m.*; **~ic** *adj.* symbolique; **~ically** *adv.**; **~ism** *s.* symbolisme *m.*; **~ize** *v.t.* symboliser.
symmetr/y *s.* symétrie *f.*; **~ic(al)** *adj.* symétrique; **~ically** *adv.**.
sympath/y *s.* (*sharing emotion of s.o.*) sympathie *f.*; (*compassion*) compassion *f.*; **~etic** *adj.* (*feeling ~y*) compatissant; (*congenial*) sympathique, ⚠ *this meaning only*; (*approving of*) bien disposé à; **~etically** *adv.* avec compassion; **~ize** *v.i.* **~ize with,** (*feel or express ~y*) compatir à; **~ize with s.o.,** partager la douleur de qn.; (*share ideas*) comprendre, s'associer à; **~izer** *s.* partisan *m.*
symphon/y *s.* symphonie *f.*; *adj.* **~y concert,** concert symphonique; **~ic** *adj.* symphonique.
symposium *s.* conférence *f.*
symptom *s.* (*med.*) symptôme *m.*; (*fig.*) signe *m.*; **~atic** *adj.* symptomatique.
synagogue *s.* synagogue *f.*
synchromesh *adj.* & *s.f.* (à) vitesse synchronisée.
synchron/ous *adj.* synchrone; **~ize** *v.t.* synchroniser; *v.i.* être synchronisé.
syncopat/e *v.t.* syncoper; **~ion** *s.* syncope *f.*
syncope *s.* syncope *f.*
syndic *s.* syndic *m.*
syndicalism *s.* syndicalisme *m.*
syndicate *s.* syndicat *m.*; *v.t.* (se) syndiquer.
syndrome *s.* syndrome *m.*
synod *s.* synode *m.*
synonym *s.* synonyme *m.*; **~ous** *adj.* synonyme (de).
synop/sis *s.* précis *m.*; (*cinema*) synopsis *f.*; **~tic** *adj.* synoptique.
synt/ax *s.* syntaxe *f.*; **~actic** *adj.* syntaxique.
synthesis *s.* synthèse *f.*
synthetic *adj.* synthétique.
syphili/s *s.* syphilis *f.*; **~tic** *adj.* syphilitique.
Syria *s.* Syrie *f.*; **~n** *adj.* & *s.m.f.* syrien(ne).
syringa *s.* seringa *m.*
syringe *s.* seringue *f.*; *v.t.* seringuer.
syrup *s.* sirop *m.*; GOLD**en ~**; **~y** *adj.* sirupeux.
system *s.* système *m.*; (*method*) méthode *f.*; (*rail. techn.*) réseau *m.*; **~atic** *adj.* systématique; **~atically** *adv.**; **~atize** *v.t.* systématiser.

T

T, to a T, exactement, absolument; **to cross one's t's,** barrer ses t; **T-shirt** *s.* tee-shirt *m.*; **T-square** *s.* equerre en T *f.*
ta *interj.* (*fam.*) merci!
tab *s.* (*strap, loop*) attache *f.*; (*label*) étiquette *f.*; (*on packet*) languette *f.*; **to keep ~s on s.o.,** ne pas perdre qn. de vue.
tabard *s.* tabard *m.*
tabby *adj.* moucheté; *s.* (*cat*) chat tigré *m.*; (*gossip*) vieille chipie *f.*
tabernacle *s.* (*Jewish; arch.*) tabernacle *m.*; (*non-conformist chapel*) temple *m.*
table *s.* (*furniture; food; flat surface; tabulated list*) table *f.*; (*geol.*) plateau *m.*; TIME~; NEST **of ~s**; **to lay the ~,** mettre le couvert; **to clear the ~,** desservir; **to turn the ~s on s.o.,** renverser la situation; *adj.* de table; **~-cloth** *s.* nappe *f.*; **~land** *s.* plateau *m.*; **~-mat** *s.* dessous de plat *m.*; **~ salt** *s.* sel fin *m.*; **~spoon** *s.* cuiller à soupe *f.*; **~ tennis** *s.* ping-pong *m.*; *v.t.* (*lay on ~*) déposer; (*propose*) proposer; (*tabulate*) classer.
tableau *s.* tableau *m.*; (*group of people*) tableau vivant *m.*
tablet *s.* (*of ivory or wood, for writing*) tablette *f.*; (*pad of paper*) bloc-notes *m.*; (*for inscription*) plaque *f.*; (*sweet*) tablette *f.*; (*med.*) comprimé *m.*; (*of soap*) pain *m.*
tabloid *s.* (*med.*) comprimé *m.*; (*newspaper*) journal de petit format *m.*; *adj.* en comprimé.
taboo, tabu *adj.* & *s.m.* tabou; *v.t.* déclarer qch. tabou.
tabor *s.* tambourin *m.*
tabul/ar *adj.* tabulaire; **~ate** *v.t.* disposer en tables, en tableaux; **~ator** *s.* (*typewriter*) tabulateur *m.*
tacit *adj.* tacite; **~ly** *adv.**.
taciturn *adj.* taciturne; **~ity** *s.* taciturnité *f.*
tack *s.* **1.** (*small nail*) semence *f.*; **to get down to brass ~s,** (*fig.*) en venir au fait; **2.** (*stitch*) point de bâti *m.*; **3.** (*rope for sail*) amure *f.*; **4.** (*naut. course*) bordée *f.*; **5.** (*fig.*) voie *f.*; *v.t.* & *i.* (1) clouer; (2) bâtir; (4) virer de bord, louvoyer; (5) (*fam.*) changer ses batteries; **~ on to,** annexer à.
tackle *s.* (*fishing, etc.*) attirail *m.*; (*naut.*) palan *m.*; (*football*) plaquage *m.*; *v.t.* (*lay hold of*) saisir; (*grapple with*) être aux prises avec; (*begin to deal with*) s'attaquer à; (*football*) plaquer.

tacky *adj.* gluant.
tact *s.* tact *m.*; **~ful** *adj.* délicat, plein de tact; **to be ~ful,** avoir du tact; **~fully** *adv.* délicatement, avec tact; **~less** *adj.*, **~lessly** *adv.* sans tact; **to be ~less,** manquer de tact; **~lessness** *s.* manque de tact *m.*
tactic/s *s.* tactique *f.sing.*; **~al** *adj.* tactique, stratégique; **~ian** *s.* tacticien *m.*
tactile *adj.* tactile.
tadpole *s.* têtard *m.*
taffeta *s.* taffetas *m.*
taffrail *s.* lisse *f.*
tag *s.* (*of shoelace, etc.*) ferret *m.*; (*small part, loose end*) bout *m.*; (*label*) étiquette *f.*; (*trite quotation*) cliché *m.*; *v.t.* ~ **on(to)**, attacher (à); ~ **together,** lier (ensemble); *v.t.* & *i.* (*fam. follow*) filer; ~ **along,** suivre.
Tahiti *s.* (*geog.*) Tahiti *f.*; **~an** *adj.* & *s.m.f.* tahitien(ne).
tail *s.* queue *f.*; (*of shirt*) pan *m.*; (*of coin, usu. pl.*) pile *f.*; **~s** (*fam. evening dress*) jaquette *f.*; **to turn ~**, tourner les talons; **with ~ between legs,** l'oreille basse; **make neither** HEAD **nor ~ of sth.**; **~-board** *s.* hayon *m.*; **~coat** *s.* jaquette *f.*; **~-end** *s.* bout *m.*; **~-gate** *s.* hayon *m.*; **~-light** *s.* feu arrière *m.*; **~piece** *s.* (*arts*) cul-de-lampe *m.*, (*of violin*) cordier *m.*; **~plane** *s.* plan fixe *m.*; **~-skid** *s.* béquille *f.*; **~-spin** *s.* vrille *f.*; ~ **wind** *s.* vent arrière *m.*; *v.t.* (*add ~ to sth.*) mettre une queue à; (*follow*) filer; (*remove ~ from fruit, etc.*) équeuter; ~ **away** *v.i.* s'égrener.
tailor *s.* tailleur *m.*; **~ess** *s.* couturière *f.*; **~-made** *adj.* fait sur mesure; *v.t.* & *i.* être tailleur; (*furnish with clothes*) habiller (qn.).
taint *s.* (*lit.* & *fig.*) tache *f.*; (*of infection, etc.*) trace *f.*; *v.t.* & *i.* infecter; (*food*) (se) gâter.
take *s.* (*amount of fish, etc. caught*) prise *f.*; (*takings*) recette *f.*; (*cinema*) prise de vue(s) *f.*; GIVE **and ~**; *v.t.* (*seize, grasp*) saisir, prendre; (*capture, catch*) prendre, capturer; (*remove*) enlever, emporter; (*steal*) prendre, enlever; (*receive*) prendre, recevoir; (*accept*) prendre, accepter; (*obtain, get*) obtenir, se procurer; (*hold*) contenir; (*bear*) supporter; (*consume, eat*) prendre; (*convey sth.*) porter, emporter, apporter; (*conduct s.o.*) emmener, conduire; (*captivate*) captiver; **to be taken with,** être épris de; (*need certain size*) porter, (*of shoes*) chausser; (*win*) gagner, (*a prize*) remporter; (*photo.*) faire; (*study subject*) étudier; (*necessitate*) exiger, demander, mettre; (*consider*) considérer; *v.i.* (*be successful*) prendre, réussir; ~ **into** ACCOUNT; ~ AIM; ~ CHARGE; ~ CARE; ~ COVER; ~ **it** EASY; ~ HOLD; ~ PLACE; ~ POSSESSION; **~-home pay** *s.* salaire net *m.*; ~ **after,** ressembler à; ~ **against,** avoir de l'aversion pour ou contre qn.; ~ **away,** enlever, emporter (qch.), emmener (qn.), retirer (qch. à qn.); ~ **back,** reprendre; ~ **down** (*make note of*) noter, (*demolish*) démolir, (*remove from higher place*) descendre, (*mech.*) démonter; ~ **s.o. down a** PEG; ~ **from,** prendre à; **you can ~ it from me,** vous pouvez m'en croire; ~ **in** (*reduce in size*) rétrécir, (*bring in*) rentrer, (*understand; include*) comprendre, (*deceive*) tromper, (*shelter*) loger; **~-in** *s.* attrape-nigaud *m.*; ~ **off** (*remove*) ôter, enlever, (*mimic*) imiter, (*fin.*) rabattre, *v.i* (*jump*) prendre son élan, (*aviat.*) décoller; **~-off** *s.* (*mimicry*) caricature *f.*, (*sport*) élan *m.*, (*aviat.*) décollage *m.*; ~ **on** (*undertake*) entreprendre, se charger de, (*acquire*) prendre, (*engage*) embaucher, (*sport*) se mesurer contre, *v.i.* (*fam.*) se mettre dans tous ses états; ~ **out,** sortir, (*insurance*) contracter, (*teeth*) arracher; ~ **sth. out of a drawer, etc.,** prendre qch. dans un tiroir, etc.; ~ **it out of** (*exhaust*) éreinter; ~ **it out on,** s'en prendre à; ~ **over** (*comm.*) absorber; **~-over** *s.* absorption *f.*; **~-over bid** *s.* offre d'absorption *m.*; ~ **to** (*begin to*) se mettre à, se livrer à; ~ **a liking to sth.,** prendre goût à qch.; ~ **a liking to s.o.,** se prendre de sympathie pour qn.; ~ **up** (*pick up*) ramasser, (*occupy space or time*) occuper, (*begin to do*) se livrer à; ~ **up with,** se lier avec; **~r** *s.* preneur *m.*; **taking** *adj.* séduisant; **takings** *s.* recette *f.*
talc *s.* & **talcum** (*powder*) *s.* talc *m.*
tale *s.* conte *m.*, histoire *f.*; (*gossip*) ragot *m.*; **to tell ~s,** rapporter; (*fam.*) cafarder; **~-bearer** *s.* rapporteur *m.*, (*fam.*) cafard *m.*; **~teller** *s.* conteur *m.*; (*fam.*) cafard *m.*
talent *s.* talent *m.*; (*gift*) don *m.*; **~ed** *adj.* doué.
talisman *s.* talisman *m.*
talk *s.* (*conversation*) conversation *f.*; (*lecture*) causerie *f.*; (*rumour, gossip*) bruit *m.*, racontar *m.*; SMALL **~**; *v.t.* dire; (*a language*) parler; *v.i.* parler; (*gossip*) bavarder; ~ **of the** DEVIL; ~ **hind leg off a** DONKEY; ~ **about,** parler de; ~ **down,** (*silence*) faire taire, (*aviat.*) donner des instructions d'atterrissage à; ~ **down to,** se mettre à la portée de; ~ **into,** persuader; ~ **out of,** dissuader; ~ **over** (*discuss*) discuter, (*persuade*) persuader; ~ **round,** convaincre; ~ **to** (*fam.*) passer un savon à; **~ing-to** *s.* savon *m.*; **~ative** *adj.* bavard; **~ativeness** *s.* loquacité *f.*; **~er** *s.* causeur *m.*, (*pej.*) bavard *m.*; **~ie** *s.* cinéma parlant *m.*; **~ing** *s.* paroles *f.pl.*, bavardage *m.*; **~ing of** *prep.* à propos de.
tall *adj.* (*above average height*) grand; (*high*) haut, élevé; **how ~ are you?,** quelle est votre taille?; **he is six feet ~,** il mesure six pieds; (*fig. pop.*) outré, exagéré; **it's a ~ order,** ce n'est pas une petite affaire; **~boy** *s.* commode *f.*; **~ness** *s.* (*person*) taille élevée *f.*; (*thing*) hauteur *f.*
tallow *s.* suif *m.*
tally *s.* (*account, score*) taille *f.*; (*ticket, label*) étiquette *f.*; *v.i.* concorder (avec), correspondre (à).
tally-ho! *interj.* taïaut!
Talmud *s.* talmud *m.*
talon *s.* serre *f.*; ⚠ talon = **heel.**
tamarind *s.* tamarin *m.*; (*tree*) tamarinier *m.*
tamarisk *s.* tamaris *m.*
tambour *s.* tambour *m.*
tambourine *s.* tambourin *m.*
tame *v.t.* **1.** (*animal*) apprivoiser; **2.** (*subdue*) dompter; **~r** *s.* dompteur *m.*; *adj.* (1) apprivoisé; (2) soumis, dompté; **3.** (*uninteresting*) plat, insipide; **~able** *adj.* domptable; **~ly** *adv.* (2) servilement; (3) platement; **~ness** *s.* (2) docilité *f.*; (3) banalité *f.*
Tamil *adj.* & *s.m.* tamoul *or* tamil.
tamp *v.t.* (*plug*) bourrer; (*block up*) boucher; (*ram down*) damer.
tamper with *v.i.* **1.** (*corrupt*) tenter de corrompre (qn.); **2.** (*sth.*) tripoter qch.; **3.** (*document*) altérer; **~ing** *s.* (1) subornation *f.*; (3) altération *f.*
tampon *s.* tampon *m.*; *v.t.* tamponner.
tan *s.* **1.** (*crushed bark*) tan *m.*; **2.** (*colour of leather*) couleur havane *f.*; **3.** (*of skin*) bronzage *m.*; *adj.* (2) jaune havane; *v.t.* (1) tanner; (3) bronzer; **~ner** *s.* (1) tanneur *m.*; **~nery** *s.* tannerie *f.*
tandem *s.* tandem *m.*
tang *s.* (*part of tool*) queue *f.*; (*smell, taste; characteristic*) saveur *f.*; (*trace of*) arrière-goût *m.*
tangent *s.* tangente *f.*; *adj.* tangent, tangentiel; **to go off at a ~,** prendre la tangente.
tangerine *s.* (*orange*) mandarine *f.*
tangib/le *adj.* tangible; **~le asset** (*comm.*) actif corporel *m.*; **~le cost** *s.* (*comm.*) investissement récupérable *m.*; **~ility** *s.* tangibilité *f.*
Tangier *s.* (*geog.*) Tanger *f.*
tangle *s.* enchevêtrement *m.*; *v.t.* & *i.* (s')enchevêtrer.
tango *s.* tango *m.*

tank *s.* (*container*) réservoir *m.*, citerne *f.*; (*auto.*) réservoir *m.*; SEPTIC ~; (*part of locomotive*) locomotive-tender *f.*; (*mil.*) char (d'assaut) *m.*; **~er** *s.* (*auto.*) camion-citerne *m.*, (*naut.*) bateau-citerne *m.*, pétrolier *m.*
tankard *s.* chope *f.*
tann/in *s.* tanin *m.*; **~ic** *adj.* tannique.
tansy *s.* tanaisie *f.*
tantaliz/e *v.t.* tourmenter; **~ing** *adj.* tentant, provocant.
tantalus *s.* coffret à liqueurs *m.*
tantamount, to be ~ to, équivaloir à.
tantrum *s.* accès de colère *m.*
Tanzania *s.* (*geog.*) Tanzanie *f.*; **~n** *adj.* & *s.m.f.* tanzanien(ne).
tap[1] *s.* (*for liquid*) robinet *m.*; **on ~,** (*lit.*) en perce, (*fig.*) disponible; **~-root** *s.* pivot *m.*; *v.t.* (*liquid*) tirer; (*cask*) mettre en perce; (*pop. for information*) pomper; (*electr.*) brancher (sur).
tap[2] *s.* (*light blow*) tape *f.*; (*sound*) petit coup *m.*; **~s** *pl.* (*mil.*) extinction des feux *f.*; *v.t.* & *i.* taper, frapper légèrement; **~-dance** *s.* danse à claquettes *f.*
tape *s.* **1.** (*narrow strip*) ruban *m.*; **2.** (*measure*) mètre (à ruban) *m.*; **3.** (*recording*) bande *f.*; **red ~,** bureaucratie *f.*; SCOTCH ~; **~-machine** *s.* téléscripteur *m.*; **~-measure** *s.* mètre (à ruban) *m.*; **~-recorder** *s.* magnétophone *m.*; **~worm** *s.* ver solitaire *m.*; *v.t.* (1) (*fasten*) ficeler; (2) mesurer; (3) enregistrer; **have sth. ~d,** avoir la situation bien en main; **have s.o. ~d,** bien connaître qn.
taper *s.* (*for lighting*) bougie *f.*; (*in church*) cierge *f.*; (*thin candle*) longue chandelle *f.*; (*shape*) fuseau *m.*; *v.t.* & *i.* (s')effiler; **~ing** *adj.* effilé.
tapestry *s.* tapisserie *f.*
tapioca *s.* tapioca *m.*
tappet *s.* (*techn.*) taquet *m.*; (*auto.*) culbuteur *m.*
tar *s.* goudron *m.*; (*fam. sailor*) loup de mer *m.*; **~ry** *adj.* goudronneux; **to have a touch of the ~-brush,** avoir un peu de sang nègre; **~mac** (~ *macadam*) *s.* macadam *m.*, (*aviat.*) piste d'envol *f.*, *v.t.* macadamiser; *v.t.* goudronner; **~ and feather s.o.,** emplumer qn.; **to be ~red with the same brush,** être du même acabit; **~ring** *s.* (*roadmaking*) macadamisage *m.*
taradiddle *s.* (*fam.*) blague *f.*
tarantella *s.* tarantelle *f.*
tarantula *s.* tarentule *f.*
tarboosh *s.* tarbouch *m.*
tard/y *adj.* **1.** (*slow*) lent, peu empressé; **2.** (*belated*) tardif; **~ily** *adv.* (1)*; (2)*; **~iness** *s.* (1) lenteur *f.*, manque d'empressement *m.*; (2) retard *m.*
tare *s.* (*bot.*) ivraie *f.*; (*weight*) tare *f.*
target *s.* (*lit.* & *fig.*) cible *f.*; (*aim*) but *m.*
tariff *s.* tarif *m.*
tarlatan *s.* tarlatane *f.*
tarmac *see* TAR.
tarn *s.* petit lac (de montagne) *m.*
tarnish *s.* ternissure *f.*; *v.t.* & *i.* (se) ternir.
taro *s.* taro *m.*
tarot cards *s.* tarots *m.pl.*
tarpaulin *s.* bâche *f.*
tarragon *s.* estragon *m.*
tarry *v.i.* (*stay*) demeurer; (*delay*) s'attarder; (*be late*) tarder.
tarsus *s.* tarse *m.*
tart[1] (*cook.*) (*fruit, etc. without crust*) tarte *f.*, (*meat, etc. with crust*) tourte *f.*; (*pop. prostitute*) poule *f.*; **~let** *s.* tartelette *f.*; *v.t.* & *i.* **~ up** (*fam.*) enjoliver, s'attifer.
tart[2] *adj.* aigre, acide; (*fig.*) mordant; (*character*) aigre; **~ly** *adv.* avec aigreur; **~ness** *s.* (*lit.* & *fig.*) aigreur *f.*
tartan *s.* tartan *m.*
Tartar[1] *s.* (*native of T~y*) Tartare *m.*; (*violent person*) dur de dur *m.*, virago *f.*; **~ sauce,** tartare *m.*
tartar[2] *s.* (*on teeth, etc.*) tartre *m.*; **cream of ~,** tartrate *m.*; **~ic** *adj.* tartrique.
task *s.* tâche *f.*; (*school*) devoir *m.*; **to take to ~,** réprimander; **~ force** *s.* détachement spécial *m.*; **~master** *s.* tyran *m.*; *v.t.* mettre à l'épreuve.
Tasmania *s.* (*geog.*) Tasmanie *f.*; **~n** *adj.* & *s.m.f.* tasmanien(ne).
tassel *s.* (*on curtain, etc.*) gland *m.*; (*on cap*) pompon *m.*; (*on maize*) aigrette *f.*
taste *s.* **1.** (*flavour*) saveur *f.*, goût *m.*; **2.** (*sense of*) goût *m.*; **3.** (*sample of food*) bouchée *f.*; **4.** (*liking for*) penchant *m.* (pour); **5.** (*sense of fitness*) goût *m.*; **6.** (*act of ~ing*) dégustation *f.*; **~-buds** *s.* papilles gustatives *f.pl.*; **~ful** *adj.* de bon goût; **~fully** *adv.* avec goût; **~less** *adj.* (1) sans saveur, (5) de mauvais goût; **~lessly** *adv.* sans goût; **~lessness** *s.* manque de goût *m.*; **tasty** *adj.* savoureux; *v.t.* (2), (3) & *fig.* goûter; (*sample*) goûter à; (*try, experience*) goûter de; (4) apprécier; *v.i.* (1) avoir un goût (aigre, etc.); **~ good,** avoir bon goût; **~ of,** avoir un goût de; **~r** *s.* dégustateur *m.*
tat *see* TIT.
ta-ta *interj.* (*fam.*) à bientôt.
tatter *s.* lambeau *m.*; **~s** *s.pl.* haillons *m.pl.*; **~ed** *adj.* en lambeaux; **~demalion** *s.* loqueteux *m.*
tattle *s.* commérage *m.*; *v.i.* bavarder; **~r** *s.* bavard *m.*
tattoo *s.* **1.** (*mil.*) carrousel *m.*; **2.** (*drumming*) tambourinage *m.*; **3.** (*on skin*) tatouage *m.*; *v.t.* (2) tambouriner; (3) tatouer.
tatty *adj.* (*ragged*) en lambeaux; (*shabby*) râpé.
taunt *s.* sarcasme *m.*; *v.t.* railler.
Taurus *s.* (*astron.*) le Taureau *m.*
taut *adj.* (*drawn tight*) raide; (*stiff, tense*) tendu; **~en** *v.t.* raidir.
tautolog/y *s.* tautologie *f.*; **~ical** *adj.* tautologique.
tavern *s.* taverne *f.*
tawdr/y *adj.* clinquant; **~ily** *adv.* d'un faux éclat; **~iness** *s.* clinquant *m.*
tawny *adj.* fauve; ~ OWL.
tax *s.* **1.** (*levied by State*) impôt *m.*; **2.** (*burden*) charge *f.*; **3.** (*strain*) épreuve *f.*; **~-collector** *s.* percepteur *m.*; **~-**FREE; **~payer** *s.* contribuable *m.f.*; ~ RETURN; *v.t.* (1) imposer; (2) charger; (3) mettre à l'épreuve; **4.** (*accuse of*) taxer (*with*—de); **~able** *adj.* imposable; **~able horsepower** *s.* puissance fiscale *f.*; **~ation** *s.* taxation *f.*
taxi *s.* taxi *m.*; *v.i.* aller en taxi; (*aviat.*) rouler au sol; **~meter** *s.* taximètre *m.*
taxiderm/ist *s.* empailleur *m.*; **~y** *s.* taxidermie *f.*
T.B. *s.* (*fam.* = *tuberculosis*) tuberculose *f.*
te, ti *s.* (*mus.*) la (note) sensible *f.*
tea *s.* (*leaves, drink*) thé *m.*; (*plant*) théier *m.*; (*meal*) goûter *m.*; (*infusion*) infusion *f.*; **beef ~,** consommé *m.*; **another cup of ~** (*fig.*) une autre paire de manches; **it's (not) my** (*etc.*) **cup of ~,** c'est (ce n'est pas) mon (etc.) rayon; **~-bag** *s.* sachet (de thé) *m.*; **~-break** *s.* pause-café *f.*; **~-chest** *s.* coffret à thé *m.*; **~-cloth** *s.*, **~-towel** *s.* torchon *m.*; ~CUP; **~-leaf** *s.* feuille de thé *f.*; **~-party** *s.* thé *m.*; **~pot** *s.* théière *f.*; ~SPOON.
teach *v.t.* enseigner (qch.); instruire (qn.); apprendre (qch. à qn.); *v.i.* enseigner; **~ one's grandmother to suck** EGGS; **~ s.o. a** LESSON; **~able** *adj.* apte à apprendre; **~er** *s.* enseignant(e) *m.f.*, (*primary*) institut/eur, -rice *m.f.*, (*secondary*) professeur *m.*; **~ing** *s.* enseignement *m.*; **~-in** *s.* carrefour *m.*
teak *s.* teck *m.*
teal *s.* sarcelle *f.*

team *s.* (*of horses*) attelage *m.*; (*sport, workers, etc.*) équipe *f.*; **~-mate** *s.* co-équipier *m.*; **~ spirit** *s.* esprit de corps *m.*; **~-work** *s.* travail en équipe *m.*; *v.t.* & *i.* **~ up** (*with*) (se) lier (à).
tear[1] *s.* (*in eye*) larme *f.*; **to burst into ~s,** fondre en larmes; **~-drop** *s.* larme *f.*; **~-duct** *s.* glande lacrymale *f.*; **~-**GAS; **~-stained** *adj.* éploré; **~ful** *adj.* en larmes, (*pej.*) larmoyant; **~fully** *adv.* en pleurant.
tear[2] *s.* (*rent*) déchirure *f.*; **wear and ~,** usure *f.*; *v.t.* déchirer; **~ away, ~ out, ~ off,** arracher; **~ up,** déchirer; *v.i.* se déchirer; (*move quickly*) se précipiter; **~ one's** HAIR; **~ a strip off s.o.** (*pop.*) passer un savon à qn.; **~ing** *adj.* violent, furieux.
tease *s.* taquin(e) *m.f.*; *v.t.* taquiner; (*wool*) carder; **~r** *s.* (*fam.*) casse-tête *m.*
teasel, teazle *s.* cardère *f.*
teat *s.* (*human*) mamelon *m.*; (*animal; on bottle*) tétine *f.*; (*techn.*) téton *m.*
techn/ics *s.* technique *f.sing.*; **~ical** *adj.* technique; **~ical school,** lycée/collège d'enseignement technique *m.*; **~ical college,** institut universitaire de technologie *m.*; **~icality** *s.* technicité *f.*; **~ically** *adv.**; **~ician** *s.* technicien(ne) *m.f.*; **~icolour** *s.* technicolor *m.*; **~ocracy** *s.* technocratie *f.*; **~ology** *s.* technologie *f.*; **~ologist** *s.* technologue *m.f.*; **~ological** *adj.* technologique.
technique *s.* technique *f.*
Teddy *s.* (*bear*) ours en peluche *m.*; (*in childish talk*) nounours *m.*; **~ boy** *s.* zazou *m.*
tedi/ous *adj.* ennuyeux; **~ously** *adv.* de façon ennuyeuse; **~ousness** *s.* & **~um** *s.* ennui *m.*
tee *s.* **1.** (*t-shaped thing*) té *m.*; **2.** (*golf*) tee *m.*; *v.t.* (2) **~ off** commencer à jouer.
teem *v.i.* fourmiller (*with*—de); (*rain*) faire une pluie torrentielle.
teen/s *s.pl.* années d'adolescence *f.pl.*; **~ager** *s.* adolescent(e) *m.f.*; **~-age boy, girl,** adolescent(e) *m.f.*; **~-age** *adj.* pour adolescents.
teeter *v.i.* chanceler.
teeth/e *v.i.* faire ses dents; **~ing** *s.* dentition *f.*; **~ing troubles** *s.* (*fig.*) inconvénients de rodage *m.pl.*
teetotal *adj.* anti-alcoolique; **~ler** *s.* personne qui ne boit pas d'alcool *f.*
teg *s.* (agneau) antenais *m.*
tegument *s.* tégument *m.*
tele-, *in combination*; **~camera** *s.* appareil de téléphotographie *m.*; **~cast** *s.* émisssion de télévision *f.*; **~communications,** télécommunications *f.pl.*; **~control,** téléguidage *m.*; **~printer** *s.* téléscripteur *m.*
telegram *s.* télégramme *m.*, dépêche *f.*
telegraph *s.* télégraphe *m.*; *v.t.* télégraphier; **~-pole/-wire,** poteau (*m.*), fil (*m.*) télégraphique; **~ic** *adj.* télégraphique; **~er, ~ist** *s.* télégraphiste *m.f.*; **~y** *s.* télégraphie *f.*; **wireless ~y** *s.* télégraphie sans fil *f.*
telepath/y *s.* télépathie *f.*; **~ic** *adj.* télépathique.
telephon/e *s.* téléphone *m.*; **to be on the ~e,** être abonné au téléphone; **~e booth, ~e-box, ~e kiosk** *s.* cabine téléphonique *f.*; **~e call** *s.* appel téléphonique *m.*, (*fam.*) coup de téléphone *m.*; **~e directory** *s.* annuaire *m.*; **~e exchange** *s.* central téléphonique *m.*; **~e operator** *s.* standardiste *m.f.*; *v.t.* & *i.* téléphoner; **~ic** *adj.* téléphonique; **~ist** *s.* standardiste *m.f.*
telephoto *adj.* téléphotographique.
telescop/e *s.* télescope *m.*; *v.t.* & *i.* (se) télescoper; **~ic** *adj.* télescopique.
televis/ion *s.* télévision *f.*; (*set*) appareil *m.* *or* poste *m.* de télévision, téléviseur *m.*; **~ion-viewer** *s.* téléspectateur *m.*; **~e** *v.t.* téléviser.
telex *s.* télex *m.*
tell *v.t.* (*say; betray secret; order; ~ beads; ~ fortunes*) dire; (*relate*) raconter; (*inform*) faire savoir; (*reveal*) révéler; (*distinguish*) distinguer; (*show*) indiquer; (*count*) compter; *v.i.* (*be important*) importer; (*affect*) avoir un effet; **~ off** *v.t.* (*select*) désigner, (*rebuke*) rabrouer; **~ on** *v.t.* affecter, (*fam.*) dénoncer; **you're ~ing me!,** à qui le dites-vous!; **all told,** tout compris; **~er** *s.* (*vote-counter*) scrutateur *m.*, (*bank-clerk*) caissier *m.*; **~ing** *adj.* efficace; **~-tale** *s.* rapporteur *m.*, *adj.* révélateur.
Telstar *s.* telstar *m.*
temerity *s.* témérité *f.*
temper *s.* (*of metal, etc.*) trempe *f.*; (*disposition*) tempérament *m.*; (*anger*) colère *f.*; (*mood*) humeur *f.*; **to lose one's ~,** se mettre en colère; **to be out of ~,** être de mauvaise humeur; *v.t.* (*metal, glass*) tremper; (*modify*) tempérer, adoucir.
tempera *s.* détrempe *f.*
temperament *s.* tempérament *m.*; **~al** *adj.* d'humeur instable.
temperance *s.* modération *f.*; (*of food* & *drink*) tempérance *f.*; *adj.* de tempérance.
temperate *adj.* sobre, modéré; (*climate*) tempéré; **~ly** *adv.* sobrement; **~ness** *s.* modération *f.*, tempérance *f.*
temperature *s.* température *f.*; (*fever*) fièvre *f.*; **to have a ~,** avoir de la fièvre; **to have a ~ of . . . degrees,** avoir . . . degrés de fièvre.
tempest *s.* tempête *f.*; **~uous** *adj.* tempétueux; **~uously** *adv.* orageusement.
Templar *s.* templier *m.*
template *s.* patron *m.*
temple *s.* (*building*) temple *m.*; (*of head*) tempe *f.*
tempo *s.* tempo *m.*
temporal *adj.* (*of time, secular*) temporel; (*of the temples*) temporal.
temporar/y *adj.* temporaire, provisoire; **~ily** *adv.**,*.
temporize *v.i.* temporiser.
tempt *v.t.* (*entice*) tenter; (*allure*) séduire; **~ation** *s.* tentation *f.*; **~er** *s.* tentateur *m.*; **~ress** *s.* tentatrice; **~ing** *adj.* séduisant; (*food*) appétissant.
ten *adj.* & *s.m.* dix; **~fold,** dix fois; **~th** *adj.* & *s.* dixième; **~thly** *adv.**.
tenable *adj.* (*mil.*) tenable; (*that can be maintained*) soutenable; (*to be held for a period*) pour une durée de.
tenaci/ous *adj.* tenace; (*adhesive*) attaché (à); **~ously** *adv.* avec ténacité; **~ity** *s.* ténacité *f.*
tenan/t *s.* locataire *m.f.*; (*farmer*) tenancier *m.*; ⚠ tenant = **defender, holder**; **~cy** *s.* (*period*) durée de location *f.*; (*property*) location *f.*; **~try** *s.* locataires *m.pl.*
tench *s.* tanche *f.*
tend[1] *v.t.* (*care for*) soigner; (*cattle*) garder.
tend[2] *v.i.* (*move towards*) se diriger vers; (*be inclined to*) incliner, tendre, à; **~ency** *s.* tendance *f.*; **~entious** *adj.* tendancieux.
tender[1] *s.* (*naut.*) allège *f.*; (*rail.*) tender *m.*
tender[2] *s.* (*offer for work*) soumission *f.*, offre d'achat publique *m.*; LEGAL **~**; *v.t.* & *i.* soumissionner; **~ for sth.,** soumissionner qch. auprès de qn.; (*offer services, etc.; as payment*) offrir.
tender[3] *adj.* **1.** (≠ *hard,* ≠ *tough*) tendre; **2.** (*easily touched*) sensible; **3.** (*delicate*) délicat; **4.** (*considerate*) soucieux; **5.** (*loving*) affectueux; **~foot** *s.* novice *m.*; **~-hearted** *adj.* compatissant; **~loin** *s.* filet *m.*; **~ly** *adv.* (1)*; (2)*; (3)*; (4)*; (5)*; **~ness** *s.* (1) tendresse *f.*; (2) sensibilité *f.*; (3) délicatesse *f.*; (4) souci *m.*; (5) affection *f.*; **~ize** *v.t.* (*meat*) attendrir.
tendon *s.* tendon *m.*
tendril *s.* vrille *f.*
tenement *s.* H.L.M. *m.* (habitation à loyer modéré).
tenet *s.* principe *m.*

tennis *s.* tennis *m.*; TABLE ~; ~-BALL; **~-court** *s.* court *m.*; ~ **player** *s.* tennisman *m.*; ~-RACKET.
tenon *s.* tenon *m.*; *v.t.* assembler à tenons.
tenor *s.* (*prevailing course*) direction *f.*, cours *m.*; (*purport*) sens *m.*; (*mus.*) ténor *m.*; ⚠ teneur = (*law*) **exact wording**; ~ OBOE.
tense[1] *s.* (*ling.*) temps *m.*
tens/e[2] *adj.* tendu; **~ile** *adj.* extensible; **~ion** *s.* tension *f.*; **~ely** *adv.* de façon tendue; **~eness** *s.* tension *f.*; *v.t.* & *i.* (se) raidir.
tent *s.* tente *f.*; ~-PEG; **~-pole,** mât *m.*
tentacle *s.* tentacule *m.*
tentative *s.* tentative *f.*; *adj.* à titre d'essai, provisoire; **~ly** *adv.* à titre d'essai.
tenterhooks, to be on ~, être sur des charbons ardents.
tenuous *adj.* (*slender*) ténu; (*subtle*) subtil; **~ly** *adv.* subtilement; **~ness** *s.* & **tenuity** *s.* ténuité *f.*; (*of air*) raréfaction *f.*; (*of style*) faiblesse *f.*
tenure *s.* (*possession*) jouissance *f.*; (*of post*) titularisation *f.*
tepid *adj.* tiède; **~ly** *adv.**; **~ity** *s.* & **~ness** *s.* tiédeur *f.*
tercentenary *adj.* & *s.m.* tricentaire.
tergiversat/e *v.i.* tergiverser; **~ion** *s.* tergiversation *f.*
term *s.* (*symbol*; *period*) terme *m.*; (*courts*) session *f.*; (*school*) trimestre *m.*; **~s** *s.pl.* (*conditions*) conditions *f.pl.*, (*relations*) rapports *m.pl.*, (*language*) paroles *f.pl.*; **~s of reference** *s.pl.* attributions *f.pl.*; **to come to ~s with,** composer avec; **to be on speaking ~s with,** être en relations avec; **to be on** BAD **~s with**; *v.t.* appeler.
termagant *s.* harpie *f.*
termin/al *s.* bout *m.*; (*electr.*) borne *f.*; (*terminus*) terminus *m.*; *adj.* (*at end*) terminal; (*occurring each term*) trimestriel; **~able** *adj.* (*law*) résiliable; **~ate** *v.t.* & *i.* (se) terminer; **~ation** *s.* fin *f.*
terminology *s.* terminologie *f.*
terminus *s.* terminus *m.*
termite *s.* termite *m.*
tern *s.* hirondelle de mer *f.*
ternary *adj.* ternaire.
terrace *s.* terrasse *f.*; (*of houses*) rangée de maisons *f.*; *v.t.* terrasser.
terracotta *s.* terre cuite *f.*
terra firma *s.* terre ferme *f.*
terrain *s.* terrain *m.*
terrestrial *adj.* terrestre.
terribl/e *adj.* terrible; **~y** *adv.**.
terrier *s.* terrier *m.*
terrif/y *v.t.* terrifier; **~ic** *adj.* terrifiant; (*fam.*) époustouflant.
terrine *s.* terrine *f.*
territor/y *s.* territoire *m.*; (*fig. sphere, province*) domaine *m.*; **~ial** *adj.* & *s.m.* territorial; **~ial waters,** eaux territoriales *f.pl.*
terror *s.* terreur *f.*; (*child*) enfant terrible *m.*; **~ism** *s.* terrorisme *m.*; **~ist** *s.* terroriste *m.f.*; **~ize** *v.t.* terroriser.
terse *adj.* concis; **~ly** *adv.* avec concision.
tertiary *adj.* tertiaire.
terylene *s.* (*text.*) térylène *m.* **[P.]**
tesselated *adj.* en mosaïque.
test *s.* **1.** (*trial*) épreuve *f.*; ACID ~; **to put to the ~,** mettre à l'épreuve; **2.** (*acad., med.*) test *m.*, examen *m.*; **driving ~,** examen du permis de conduire *m.*; **3.** (*fig.*) pierre de touche *f.*; **4.** (*chem.*) (*reagent*) réactif *m.*, (*trial*) analyse (chimique) *f.*; ~ **case** *s.* précédent *m.*; ~ **flight** *s.* vol d'essai *m.*; ~ **match** *s.* championnat international de cricket *m.*; ~ **pilot** *s.* pilote d'essai *m.*; **~-tube** *s.* éprouvette *f.*; *v.t.* (1) éprouver; (2) examiner; (4) traiter au réactif, analyser; **~ing** *s.* essai *m.*, *adj.* éprouvant.
testament *s.* testament *m.*; (*Bible*) **Old/New T~,** Ancien/Nouveau Testament *m.*; **New T~,** Evangiles *m.pl.*; **~ary** *adj.* testamentaire.
testat/or, -rix *s.* testat/eur, -rice *m.f.*
tester *s.* ciel de lit *m.* (*pl.* ciels de lit).
testicle *s.* testicule *m.*
testify *v.t.* (*bear witness*) déclarer; (*give evidence*) témoigner de; (*affirm*) affirmer; *v.i.* (*law*) déposer; (*be evidence of*) témoigner.
testimon/ial *s.* (*reference*) certificat *m.*; (*gift*) cadeau en témoignage d'estime *m.*; **~y** *s.* témoignage *m.*, déposition *f.*
test/y *adj.* irritable; **~ily** *adv.**.
tetanus *s.* tétanos *m.*
tether *s.* longe *f.*; **to be at the end of one's ~,** être au bout de son rouleau; *v.t.* attacher (à la longe).
tetra- (*in combination*), **~chord** *s.* tétracorde *m.*; **~gon** *s.* quadrilatère *m.*; **~hedron** *s.* tétraèdre *m.*; **~meter** *s.* tétramètre *m.*
tetrarch *s.* tétrarque *m.*
Teutonic *adj.* teutonique.
text *s.* texte *m.*; **~book** *s.* manuel *m.*; **~ual** *adj.* (*error*) de texte, (*quotation*) textuel.
textile *adj.* & *s.m.* textile.
texture *s.* texture *f.*; (*of fabric*) tissu *m.*; *v.t.* tisser.
Thai/land *s.* (*geog.*) Thaïlande *f.*; ~ *adj.* & *s.m.f.* thaïlandais(e); *s.m.* (*lang.*) thaï.
thalidomide *s.* thalidomide *f.*; ~ **child,** enfant victime de la thalidomide.
Thames *s.* (*geog.*) Tamise *f.*
than *conj.* que; (*with nos.*) de.
thank *v.t.* remercier (qn. de qch.); être obligé (à qn. de qch.); ~ **you!,** merci!; **~s** *s.pl.* remerciements *m.pl.*; **~s to** *prep.* grâce à; **~ful** *adj.* reconnaissant; **~fully** *adv.* avec reconnaissance; **~fulness** *s.* reconnaissance *f.*; **~less** *adj.* ingrat; **~lessly** *adv.* avec ingratitude; **~lessness** *s.* ingratitude *f.*; **~sgiving** *s.* action de grâces *f.*
that (*pl.* **those**) *dem. adj.* ce (cet), cette, ces; ce (etc.) . . . là; *dem. pron.* (*referring to s. already mentioned*) celui, celle, ceux, celles; celui (etc.) . . . là; (*referring to unnamed person or thing*) ce, cela, ça; **like ~,** comme cela; **~'s it, ~'s right,** c'est cela; **and all ~,** et le reste; **at ~, besides ~,** par dessus le marché; **~'s all, ~'s ~,** et voilà; *rel. pron.* qui, que; lequel, laquelle, lesquels, lesquelles; où, **the day ~ he came,** le jour où il est venu; *conj.* que; **I think** (~) **you are right,** je crois que vous avez raison; (= *in order ~, so ~*) afin que, pour que; **I am writing ~ you may know,** j'écris pour que vous sachiez.
thatch *s.* chaume *m.*; *v.t.* couvrir de chaume; **~ed cottage** *s.* chaumière *f.*
thaw *s.* (*lit.* & *fig.*) dégel *m.*; (*of snow*) fonte *f.*; *v.t.* & *i.* dégeler.
the *def. art.* le, la, l', les; **to/at ~,** au, à la, à l', aux; **of ~,** du, de la, de l', des; (*emphatic = this*) ce, cet, cette, ces; **it is ~ place,** c'est le lieu par excellence; **this is ~ book,** c'est le livre qui s'impose; *adv.* ~ **more he gets,** ~ **more he wants,** plus il en a, plus il en veut; **so much ~ worse** (**for him,** *etc.*), tant pis (pour lui, etc.).
theatr/e *s.* (*building*; *art*; *field of operations*) théâtre *m.*; **lecture ~e,** amphithéâtre *m.*; **operating-~e,** salle d'opération *f.*; **~ical** *adj.* théâtral; **~icals** *s.* spectacle *m.*
thee *pron.* te, toi.
theft *s.* vol *m.*
their *adj.* leur(s) ⚠ *no feminine*; **~s** *pron.* le leur, la leur, les leurs; **it is ~s,** c'est à eux, à elles.
the/ism *s.* théisme *m.*; **~ist** *s.* théiste *m.f.*
them *pron.* les; **to ~,** leur; (*after prep.*; *after c'est*; *after comparative*; *alone*) eux, elles; **I work for ~,** je travaille pour eux; **it was ~ I saw,** c'est eux que j'ai vus; **I love you more than ~,** je vous

aime plus qu'eux; **I saw ~ at the station,** je les ai vus, eux, à la gare; **one of ~,** un d'entre eux; **~selves** (*refl.*) se; eux- (elles-) mêmes.

them/e *s.* (*subject*) sujet *m.*; (*acad. exercise*; *mus.*) thème *m.*; **~e song** *s.* leitmotiv *m.*; **~atic** *adj.* thématique.

then *adv.* (*at that time*) alors; NOW **and ~**; **~ and there,** séance tenante; (*next*) puis, ensuite; *conj.* (*in that case*) donc, alors; *adj.* d'alors.

thence *adv.* (*place*) de là; (*reason*) par conséquent; **~forth, ~forward,** désormais.

theo- (*in combination*) **~cracy** *s.* théocratie *f.*; **~cratic** *adj.* théocratique; **~logian** *s.* théologien *m.*; **~logical** *adj.* théologique; **~logy** *s.* théologie *f.*; **~sophist** *s.* théosophe *m.*; **~sophy** *s.* théosophie *f.*

theodolite *s.* théodolite *m.*

theorem *s.* théorème *m.*

theor/y *s.* théorie *f.*; **~etical** *adj.* théorique; **~etically** *adv.**; **~ist** *s.* théoricien *m.*; **~ize** *v.i.* faire des théories.

therap/y *s.* thérapie *f.*; SPEECH **~y**; **~eutic(al)** *adj.* thérapeutique; **~eutics** *s.* thérapeutique *f. sing.*

there *adv.* là; (*with a verb*) y; **do you want to go ~?,** voulez-vous y aller?; **I found it ~,** je l'y ai trouvé; **~ is, ~ are,** il y a; **~ he** (*etc.*) **is,** le (etc.) voilà; **down ~,** là-bas; **over ~,** là-bas; **under ~,** là-dessous; **up ~,** là-dessus, là-haut; **~at,** là-dessus; **~about,** à peu près; **~abouts,** aux environs; **~after,** par la suite; **~by,** par là, par ce moyen; **~fore,** donc; **~in,** là-dedans; **~of,** de cela; (*with a verb*) en; **~upon,** là--dessus; **~with,** en outre.

therm *s.* thermie *f.*, unité de chaleur *f.*; **~al** *s.* thermique *m.*, *adj.* (*heat*) thermique, (*spring*) thermal.

thermo- (*in combination*) **~chemistry** *s.* thermochimie *f.*; **~chemical** *adj.* thermochimique; **~dynamics** *s.* thermodynamique *f.sing.*; **~electricity** *s.* thermoélectricité *f.*; **~nuclear** *adj.* thermonucléaire.

thermometer *s.* thermomètre *m.*

thermos *s.* thermos *m.* **[P.]**

thermostat *s.* thermostat *m.*; **~ic** *adj.* à thermostat.

thesaurus *s.* recueil *m.*

these *see* THIS.

thesis *s.* thèse *f.*

thews *s.pl.* nerfs *m.pl.*

they *pron.* ils, elles; (*after c'est*; *after comparative*; *alone*) eux, elles; **it is ~ who want it,** ce sont eux qui le veulent; **he is older than ~,** il est plus vieux qu'eux; **~ want to go, we want to stay,** eux, ils veulent partir, nous, nous voulons rester; **~ say,** on dit.

thick *s.* **in the ~ of it,** au fort de, au cœur de; **through ~ and thin,** contre vents et marées; *adj.* **1.** (≠ *fine*, ≠ *thin*, ≠ *clear*) épais; **2.** (*closely set*) dru, touffu; **3.** (*numerous*, *dense*) dense; **4.** (*packed with*) rempli de; **5.** (*stupid*) bête; **6.** (*voice*) pâteux; **7.** (*fam. intimate with*) très lié avec; **8.** (*pop. intolerable*) fort; **it's a bit ~,** c'est un peu fort; **~set** *adj.* trapu; **~-skinned** *adj.* (*lit.*) à la peau dure, (*fig.*) peu sensible; *adv.* (2) dru; **~en** *v.t.* & *i.* (s')épaissir; **~ly** *adv.* (1) épais; (2) dru; **~ness** *s.* (1) épaisseur *f.*, (*of liquid*) consistance *f.*; (3) densité *f.*; (6) empâtement *m.*

thicket *s.* fourré *m.*

thief *s.* voleur *m.*; SNEAK **~**; **set a ~ to catch a ~,** à trompeur, trompeur et demi.

thiev/e *v.t.* & *i.* voler; **~ish, ~ing** *adj.* voleur; **~ery** *s.* penchant au vol *m.*

thigh *s.* cuisse *f.*; **~-bone** *s.* fémur *m.*

thimble *s.* dé *m.*; **~ful** *s.* doigt *m.*

thin *adj.* **1.** (≠ *thick*; *narrow*; *slender*) mince; **2.** (≠ *plump*) maigre; **3.** (*lacking volume*) léger; **4.** (*weak*, *tea*, *etc.*); (*flimsy*, *excuse*, *etc.*) faible; **5.** (≠ *numerous*) clairsemé, peu nombreux; **through** THICK **and ~**; **to have a ~ time,** en voir de grises; **to vanish into ~ air,** disparaître; **~ end of** WEDGE; **~-skinned** *adj.* (*lit.*) à la peau mince, (*fig.*) susceptible; **~ly** *adv.* (1), (2) maigrement; (5) peu; **~ness** *s.* (1) minceur *f.*; (2) maigreur *f.*; (3) légèreté *f.*, (*of liquid*) fluidité *f.*; (4) faiblesse *f.*; (5) rareté *f.*; *v.t.* & *i.* (s')éclaircir; **~ out** (*hort.*) repiquer.

thine *pron.* le tien, la tienne, les tiens, les tiennes.

thing *s.* chose *f.*; (*object*) objet *m.*; **a** NEAR **~**; (*pej. person*) créature *f.*; OLD **~**; **~s** *pl.* (*clothes*) affaires *f.pl.*; (*utensils*) ustensiles *f.pl.*; (*affairs*) biens *m.pl.*; **the ~ is to,** ce qu'il faut, c'est; **it's not the ~,** cela ne se fait pas; **to do one's own ~,** vivre à sa guise; **to have a ~ about sth.,** tenir à qch.; **to make a ~ of,** insister sur; **~amy, ~umajig, ~ummy** *s.* truc *m.*, machin *m.*

think *v.t.* & *i.* penser; (*consider*) estimer; (*conceive*) concevoir; (*contemplate*) penser à; (*believe*) croire; **~ about,** penser à; **~ again, ~ better of,** se raviser; **~ little of,** faire peu de cas de; **~ much of,** avoir bonne opinion de; **~ of,** penser (à qn.), penser (à faire qch.), envisager; **~ out,** (*plan*) élaborer, (*question*) considérer; **~ over,** peser, réfléchir à; **~ up** (*fam.*) inventer; **~able** *adj.* concevable; **~er** *s.* penseur *m.*; **~ing** *s.* fait de penser *m.*, (*opinion*) avis *m.*, *adj.* qui pense.

third *s.* tiers *m.*; (*mus.*) tierce *f.*; *adj.* troisième; **~ degree** *s.* interrogatoire en règle *m.*; **~ party** *s.* tiers *m.*; **~-party insurance,** assurance au tiers *f.*; **T~ World** *s.* Tiers Monde *m.*; **~ly** *adv.**.

thirst *s.* (*lit.* & *fig.*) soif *f.*; *v.i.* avoir soif (*for*—de); **~y** *adj.* altéré, (*fig.*) avide (*for*—de), (*land*) sec; **to be ~y,** avoir soif; **~ily** *adv.* avidement.

thirteen *s.* & *adj.* treize; **~th** *adj.* treizième.

thirt/y *s.* & *adj.* trente; **~ieth,** trentième.

this (*pl.* **these**) *dem. adj.* ce, cet, cette, ces; ce ... ci, etc.; *dem. pron.* (*referring to s. already mentioned*) celui, celle, ceux, celles; (*referring to unnamed s.*) ceci; **~ is what you must do,** voici ce qu'il faut faire; *adv.* (*fam.* = *so*) si.

thistle *s.* chardon *m.*; **~down** *s.* duvet de chardon *m.*

thither *adv.* là; HITHER **and ~**.

thole *s.* (*naut.*) tolet *m.*

thong *s.* lanière *f.*

thora/x *s.* thorax *m.*; **~cic** *adj.* thoracique.

thorn *s.* épine *f.*; (*-tree*) buisson d'épines *m.*; **to be a ~ in the flesh of s.o.,** agacer qn.; **~y** *adj.* épineux.

thorough *adj.* **1.** (*complete*) complet; **2.** (*entire*) absolu, entier; **3.** (*scrupulous*) minutieux, approfondi; **~bred** *adj.* (*person*) racé, (*dog*, *cat*) de race pure, (*horse*) *adj.* & *s.m.* pur sang; **~fare** *s.* grande rue *f.*, artère *f.*; **no ~fare,** rue sans issue; **~going** *adj.* parfait; **~ly** *adv.* (1)*; (2)*,*; (3) à fond; **~ness** *s.* (1), (2) perfection *f.*; (3) minutie *f.*, méticulosité *f.*

those *see* THAT.

thou *pron.* tu, toi.

though *conj.* quoique, bien que (+ *subjunctive*); *adv.* tout de même; **as ~,** comme si; **what ~,** qu'importe que.

thought *s.* pensée *f.*; (*idea*) idée *f.*; (*consideration*) réflexion *f.*; (*intention*) dessein *m.*; (*opinion*) avis *m.*; (*care*) souci *m.*; **on second ~s,** réflexion faite; **~ful** *adj.* pensif, attentif, soucieux; **~fully** *adv.* pensivement; avec prévenance; **~fulness** *s.* rêverie *f.*; réflexion *f.*; prévenance *f.*; **~less** *adj.* irréfléchi, insouciant, étourdi; **~lessly** *adv.* étourdiment, avec insouciance; **~lessness** *s.* étourderie *f.*; insouciance *f.*

thousand *adj.* & *s.m. invar.* mille; **~s,** des milliers de; **~th,** millième.
thral/l *s.* & **~dom** *s.* esclavage *m.*
thrash *v.t.* (*beat*) rosser; (*conquer*) battre; **~ out** discuter à fond; **~ing** *s.* rossée *f.*
thread *s.* (*lit.* & *fig.*) fil *m.*; (*of screw*) filet *m.*; **~bare** *adj.* râpé, (*fig.*) rebattu; *v.t.* enfiler; (*pick way through*) se faufiler à travers.
threat *s.* menace *f.*; **~en** *v.t.* & *i.* menacer; (*with*—de; *to*—de + *inf.*); **~ening** *adj.* menaçant; **~eningly** *adv.* avec menaces.
three *s.* & *adj.* trois; **~-CORNERed; ~-dimensional** *adj.* à trois dimensions; **~fold,** triple; **~-legged** *adj.* à trois pieds; **~-point turn** *s.* demi-tour *m.*; **~-quarter(s)** *s.* trois-quarts *m.*, (*rugby*) trois-quarts *m.*; **~score,** soixante.
threnody *s.* thrène *m.*
thresh *v.t.* battre; **~er** *s.* (*person*) batteur *m.*; (*machine*) batteuse *f.*
threshold *s.* (*lit.* & *fig.*) seuil *m.*
thrice *adv.* trois fois.
thrift *s.* (*bot.*) statice *m.*; (*economy*) économie *f.*; **~y** *adj.* économe; **~ily** *adv.* économiquement; **~iness** *s.* économie *f.*; **~less** *adj.* prodigue; **~lessness** *s.* prodigalité *f.*
thrill *s.* frisson *m.*; *v.t.* & *i.* (faire) frémir; émouvoir; **~ing** *adj.* saisissant, bouleversant; **~er** *s.* roman policier *m.*
thriv/e *v.i.* (*lit.*) grandir; (*fig.*) prospérer; **~ing** *adj.* vigoureux; prospère.
throat *s.* gorge *f.*; **to have a FROG in one's ~.**
throb *s.* **1.** palpitation *f.*; **2.** (*techn.*) vrombissement *m.*; *v.i.* (1) battre, palpiter; (2) vrombir; **~bing** *s. as* ~ (1), (2).
throes *s.pl.* (*anguish*) douleurs *f.pl.*; (*violent struggle*) tourments *m.pl.*; (*of death*) affres *m.pl.* (de la mort); **to be in the ~ of,** être en train de faire qch., être au beau milieu de qch., être aux prises avec qch.
thrombosis *s.* thrombose *f.*
throne *s.* trône *m.*
throng *s.* foule *f.*; *v.t.* encombrer; *v.i.* affluer; se presser (autour de).
throstle *s.* grive *f.*
throttle *s.* **1.** (*throat*) gosier *m.*; **2.** (*mech.*) régulateur *m.*; **at full ~,** à pleins gaz; *v.t.* (1), (2) étrangler; **~ down,** mettre au ralenti.
through *adj.* (*train, etc.*) direct; (*traffic*) en transit; *adv.* **~ and ~,** d'un bout à l'autre; **to go ~,** traverser; **to walk, run,** *etc.* **~,** traverser à pied, en courant, etc.; **to be ~ with,** en avoir fini avec; **wet ~,** trempé jusqu'aux os; *prep.* à travers; (*by means of*) par; (*by reason of*) grâce à, à cause de; **~out,** d'un bout à l'autre, partout.
throw *s.* (*~ing*) jet *m.*; (*of dice*) coup *m.*; (*in wrestling*) mise à terre *f.*; *v.t.* (*propel, cast dice*) jeter; (*as missile*) lancer, projeter; (*bring to ground*) renverser; (*horseman*) désarçonner; (*shadow*) projeter; (*blame, etc.*) rejeter; (*pop.* = *give*) donner, offrir; **~ oneself at s.o.,** se jeter à la tête de qn.; **~ about, ~ around,** jeter çà et là, éparpiller, (*money*) gaspiller; **~ one's WEIGHT about; ~ away,** (*discard*) jeter, (*time, life*) perdre, (*money*) gaspiller; **~ back,** rejeter, (*ball*) renvoyer, (*image*) réfléchir; **~-back** *s.* recul *m.*, régression *f.*; **~ down,** abattre, renverser; **~ in,** introduire, (*comm.*) ajouter par-dessus le marché; **~ oneself into,** se jeter dans; **~ off,** se débarrasser de, (*clothes*) ôter; **~ out** (*heat, etc.*) répandre, (*reject*) rejeter, (*person*) chasser; **~ over,** abandonner; **~ up** jeter en l'air, (*accentuate*) faire ressortir, (*vomit*) vomir, (*fig.*) renoncer à, (*job*) démissionner.
thrush *s.* (*bird*) grive *f.*; (*med.*) muguet *m.*
thrust *s.* poussée *f.*; (*stab, lunge*) coup de pointe *m.*; *v.t.* & *i.* pousser; (*with weapon*) porter une botte à qn.; **~ in,** fourrer, enfoncer, plonger; **~ sth. on s.o.,** obliger qn. à accepter qch.; **~ oneself on to s.o.,** imposer sa présence à qn.; **~ out** (*hand*) allonger, (*person*) chasser.
thud *s.* bruit sourd *m.*; *v.i.* tomber avec un bruit sourd.
thug *s.* bandit *m.*
thumb *s.* pouce *m.*; TOM **T~; to twiddle one's ~s,** se tourner les pouces; **by rule of ~,** approximativement; **to be under s.o.'s ~,** être sous la coupe de qn.; **~-nail sketch** *s.* croquis *m.*; **~screw** *s.* poucettes *f.pl.*; *v.t.* manier; **~ through,** feuilleter; **~ a lift,** faire de l'auto-stop.
thump *s.* coup violent *m.*; *v.t.* cogner; **~ing** *adj.* (*fam.*) énorme.
thunder *s.* tonnerre *m.*; (*fig.*) foudre *f.*; **to steal s.o.'s ~,** couper l'herbe sous les pieds de qn.; **~bolt** *s.* (*lit.* & *fig.*) coup de foudre *m.*; **~ clap** *s.* coup de tonnerre *m.*; **~storm** *s.* orage *m.*; **~struck** *adj.* foudroyé; **~ous** *adj.* (*weather*) orageux, (*noise*) tonnant; **~y** *adj.* orageux; *v.t.* & *i.* fulminer, tonner; **~ing** *adj.* de tonnerre, (*fam.*) *adj.* formidable, *adv.**.
thurible *s.* encensoir *m.*
Thursday *s.* jeudi *m.*
thus *adv.* ainsi.
thwart *s.* (*in boat*) banc *m.*; *v.t.* contrecarrer.
thy *adj.* ton, ta, tes; **~self,** toi-même.
thyme *s.* thym *m.*
thyroid *adj.* & *s.f.* thyroïde.
tiara *s.* diadème *m.*; (*papal*) tiare *f.*
Tibet *s.* (*geog.*) Tibet *m.*; **~an** *adj.* & *s.m.f.* tibétain(e); *s.m.* (*lang.*) tibétain.
tibia *s.* tibia *m.*
tic *s.* tic *m.*
tick *s.* **1.** (*sound*) tic-tac *m.*; **2.** (*fam.*) instant *m.*; **3.** (*mark*) coche *f.*; **4.** (*insect*) tique *f.*; **5.** (*mattress-case*) toile à matelas *f.*; **6.** (*fam. on* ~) à crédit; *v.t.* (3) cocher; *v.i.* (1) faire tic-tac; **~ off** (3) pointer, (*pop. reprimand*) rabrouer; **~ over** *v.i.* (*auto.*) tourner au ralenti, (*fig.*) marcher au ralenti; **~er** *s.* (*fam. watch*) tocante *f.*, (*heart*) cœur *m.*, (*tape-machine*) transmetteur (télégraphique) *m.*; **~ing** *s.* (5) toile à matelas *f.*
ticket *s.* **1.** (*for admission, train, ship, etc.*) billet *m.*, (*bus, metro*) ticket *m.*; **2.** (*label*) étiquette *f.*; **3.** (*naut. aviat. pilot's certificate*) brevet *m.*; PAWN **~; that's the ~** (*pop.*) c'est ça; **~-collector** *s.* contrôleur *m.*; **~-office** *s.* guichet *m.*; *v.t.* (2) étiqueter.
tickl/e *s.* chatouillement *m.*; *v.t.* & *i.* chatouiller; (*amuse*) donner envie de rire à; **~ish** *adj.* chatouilleux; (*fig.*) épineux.
tide *s.* (*of sea*) marée *f.*; FLOOD-**~**; NEAP-**~**; (*fig. of opinion*) courant *m.*; (*of events*) cours *m.*; (*season*) saison *f.*; **~-mark** *s.* ligne des hautes eaux *f.*; **~way** *s.* lit de marée *m.*; **tidal** *adj.* de marée; **tidal wave** *s.* raz de marée *m.*; *v.t.* (*fig.*) **~ over,** remettre à flot.
tidings *s.pl.* nouvelles *f.pl.*
tid/y *adj.* (*person*) ordonné, soigneux; (*place, thing*) net, propre, bien tenu, rangé; (*fam.*) fameux; (*sum*) important; **~ily** *adv.* proprement; **~iness** *s.* ordre *m.*, propreté *f.*; *v.t.* mettre en ordre.
tie[1] *s.* (*for fastening*) corde *f.*, chaîne *f.*; (*neck~*) cravate *f.*; (*connection*) lien *m.*; (*mus.*) liaison *f.*; (*hindrance*) entrave *f.*; (*sport, draw*) partie égale *f.*; **cup-~,** match de championnat *m.*; **~-beam** *s.* entrait *m.*; **~-clip** *s.* fixe-cravate *m.*; **~-pin** *s.* épingle de cravate *f.*
tie[2] *v.t.* (*fasten*) attacher, lier; (*knot*) nouer; (*arch.*) relier; (*mus.*) lier; (*restrict*) enchaîner; *v.i.* (*sport*) être à égalité; **~ down,** lier (à); **~ up** (*dog, etc.*) attacher, (*parcel*) emballer, (*person*) ligoter, (*dress wound*) bander, (*fin.*) bloquer, (*fig.*) entraver; **to be tied,** être empêché, être

retenu; **to be tied to s.o.'s** APRON**strings; to be tongue-tied,** avoir la langue liée.
tier *s.* gradin *m.*, rangée *f.*; **two-~ed** *adj.* à deux niveaux.
tierce *s.* tierce *f.*
tiff *s.* pique *f.*
tig/er *s.* tigre *m.*; **~ress** *s.* tigresse *f.*; **~er-cat** *s.* chat-tigre *m.*; **~er-lily** *s.* lis-tigré *m.*; **~rish** *adj.* de tigre.
tight *adj.* **1.** (*close-textured*) serré; **2.** (*close-fitting*) collant; **3.** (*tense, taut*) tendu; **4.** (*fam. miserly*) mesquin; **5.** (*difficult to obtain*) rare, (*difficult to deal with*) délicat; **6.** (*pop. drunk*) saoûl; **7.** (*water-~*) étanche; **8.** (*air~*) hermétique; **to be in a ~ corner** (*fig.*) se trouver dans une mauvaise passe; **~-fisted** *adj.* serré; **~rope** *s.* corde raide *f.*; **~en** *v.t.* & *i.* (se) serrer, (se) tendre; **~en one's** BELT; **~ly** *adv.* étroitement; **~ness** *s.* (1), (2) étroitesse *f.*; (3) raideur *f.*, tension *f.*; (5) rareté *f.*; (7) imperméabilité *f.*, étanchéité *f.*; (8) herméticité *f.*; *adv.* bien, fort; *s.pl.* collant(s) *m.* (*pl.*).
tilde *s.* tilde *m.*
tile *s.* **1.** (*roof*) tuile *f.*; **2.** (*floor*) carreau *m.*; *v.t.* (1) couvrir de tuiles; (2) carreler; **~r** *s.* (1) couvreur *m.*; (2) carreleur *m.*
till[1] *s.* (*cashbox*) caisse *f.*
till[2] *v.t.* cultiver; **~age** *s.*, **tilth** *s.* culture *f.*; couche arable *f.*; **~er** *s.* cultivateur *m.*
till[3] *prep.* jusqu'à; *conj.* (*time*) jusqu'à ce que; (*degree*) jusqu'au point où.
tiller *s.* (*naut.*) barre *f.*
tilt *s.* **1.** (*hist. combat*) joute *f.*; **2.** (*slope*) inclinaison *f.*; **at full ~,** à fond de train; *v.i.* (1) jouter; *v.t.* & *i.* (2) (se) pencher, (s')incliner; (*heel over*) (se) renverser; basculer; **~ up,** redresser.
timber *s.* (*for building*) bois de construction *m.*; (*piece of wood*) poutre *f.*; (*standing trees*) arbres (de haute futaie) *m.pl.*; **~ merchant** *s.* marchand de bois *m.*; **~-yard** *s.* chantier de bois *m.*; *v.t.* boiser.
timbre *s.* timbre *m.*
timbrel *s.* tambourin *m.*
Timbuctoo *s.* (*geog.*) Tombouctou *m.*
time *s.* (*duration, season, ~ available*) temps *m.*; (*moment*) moment *m.*; (*period*) époque *f.*; (*allotted portion of ~*) délai *m.*, (bout de) temps *m.*; (*occasion*) fois *f.*; (*o'clock; ~ worked*) heure *f.*; (*rhythm*) mesure *f.*; **~s** *pl.* temps *m.pl.*; **another ~,** une autre fois; **every ~,** chaque fois (que); **at all ~s,** à tout moment; **all the ~,** tout le temps; **at no ~,** jamais; **in no ~,** en moins de rien; **at the present ~,** à l'heure actuelle; **at the same ~,** en même temps; **against ~,** contre la montre; **ahead of ~,** prématuré; **at ~s, from ~ to ~,** de temps en temps; **by the ~ that,** avant que; **for the ~ being,** provisoirement; **in ~ for,** à temps pour, assez tôt pour; **on ~,** à l'heure; **what ~ is it?,** quelle heure est-il?; **to have a good ~,** s'amuser (bien); **to keep good ~,** marcher bien; **to have a** THIN **~; to mark ~,** marquer le pas; **to do ~,** (*pop.*) être sous les verrous; **in the** NICK **of ~; to play for ~,** temporiser; **to take one's ~,** prendre son temps; **behind the ~s,** arriéré; **~ bomb** *s.* bombe à retardement *f.*; **~-consuming** *adj.* interminable; **~-honoured** *adj.* consacré par l'usage; **~keeper** *s.* pointeur *m.*; **~-lag** *s.* retard *m.*; **~-limit** *s.* délai *m.*; **~-piece** *s.* pendule *f.*, montre *f.*; **~-server** *s.* routinier *m.*; **~-sheet** *s.* feuille de présence *f.*; **~-switch** *s.* minuterie *f.*; **~table** *s.* horaire *m.*, emploi du temps *m.*, (*rail.*) indicateur *m.*; **~less** *adj.* éternel; **~ly** *adj.* opportun; **~liness** *s.* opportunité *f.*; *v.t.* faire à propos; (*record*) chronométrer; (*regulate*) régler; **timing** *s.* (*recording*) chronométrage *m.*, (*regulating*) réglage *m.*
timid *adj.* timide; **~ly** *adv.**; **~ity** *s.* timidité *f.*
timorous *adj.* craintif; **~ly** *adv.**.
tin *s.* (*metal*) étain *m.*; (*can*) boîte (en fer blanc) *f.*; (*cake, etc.*) moule *f.*; MESS **~**; *adj.* d'étain, en étain; (*soldier*) de plomb; **~** FOIL; **that puts the ~ hat on it,** il ne manquait plus que ça; **~-opener** *s.* ouvre-boîte *m.*; **~pot** *adj.* (*fig.*) misérable; **~smith** *s.* ferblantier *m.*; **~-tack** *s.* semence *f.*; **~ny** *adj.* (*sound*) grêle, (*taste*) d'étain; *v.t.* (*coat with ~*) étamer; (*preserve*) conserver; **~ned** *adj.* de conserve.
tincture *s.* (*med.*) teinture *f.*; (*tinge*) teinte *f.*; *v.t.* donner une teinture (de . . . à); (*colour*) teinter.
tinder *s.* amadou *m.*
tine *s.* (*of fork*) dent *f.*; (*of antler*) andouiller *m.*
tinge *s.* teinte *f.*; *v.t.* teinter.
tingl/e *v.i.* **1.** (*ears*) tinter; **2.** (*skin*) fourmiller; **~ing** *s.* (1) tintement *m.*; (2) fourmillement *m.*
tinker *s.* rétameur *m.*; *v.i.* **~ with,** bricoler.
tinkl/e *v.t.* & *i.* (faire) tinter; **~ing** *s.* teintement *m.*
tinsel *s.* (*lit.* & *fig.*) clinquant *m.*; *adj.* clinquant, voyant.
tint *s.* teinte *f.*; *v.t.* teinter.
tiny *adj.* tout(e) petit(e), minuscule.
tip *s.* **1.** (*end*) bout *m.*, (*tapered*) pointe *f.*; **2.** (*mouthpiece, of cigarette, etc.*) bout *m.*; **on the ~ of one's tongue,** sur le bout de la langue; **3.** (*money*) pourboire *m.*; **4.** (*information*) tuyau *m.*; **5.** (*dodge*) truc *m.*; **6.** (*for refuse*) décharge publique *f.*; **on ~toe,** sur la pointe des pieds; **~top** *adj.* parfait; *v.t.* & *i.* (1) mettre un bout à; (3) donner un pourboire à; (4) tuyauter; **7.** ((*cause to*) *overturn*) renverser; (*discharge*) verser; **8.** (*touch lightly*) effleurer; **~ off** *v.t.* (*fam.*) tuyauter; **~-off** *s.* tuyau *m.*; **~ up** *v.t.* & *i.* (faire) basculer); **~-up** *adj.* à bascule; **~ster** *s.* tuyauteur *m.*
tippet *s.* collet *m.*
tipple *s.* boisson alcoolique *f.*; *v.i.* (*pop.*) picoler.
tipsy *adj.* ivre.
tirade *s.* tirade *f.*
tire[1] *s. see* TYRE.
tire[2] *v.t.* & *i.* (se) fatiguer; **~d** *adj.* fatigué; **to be ~d of sth.,** être las de qch.; **to be ~d out,** être épuisé; **~dness** *s.* fatigue *f.*; **~less** *adj.* infatigable; **~lessly** *adv.**; **~some** *adj.* agaçant, assommant; **~someness** *s.* caractère assommant *m.*
tiro, tyro *s.* novice *m.*
tissue *s.* tissu *m.*; (*paper handkerchief*) mouchoir de papier *m.*; **~-paper** *s.* papier de soie *m.*
tit *s.* (*bird*) mésange *f.*; **~ for tat,** à bon chat bon rat.
titanic *adj.* titanesque.
titbit *s.* friandise *f.*
tithe *s.* dixième *m.*; (*eccles.*) dîme *f.*
Titian *s.* le Titien.
titillate *v.t.* chatouiller.
titivate *v.t.* & *i.* (*fam.*) (se) pomponner.
title *s.* titre *m.*; (*cinema, credit ~s*) générique *f.*; **~d** *adj.* titré; **~-deed** *s.* titre de propriété *m.*; **~-page** *s.* page de titre *f.*
titmouse *s.* mésange *f.*
titter *v.i.* ricaner.
tittle *s.* (*obs.*) iota *m.*
tittle-tattle *s.* cancans *m.pl.*; *v.i.* faire des cancans.
titular *adj.* titulaire.
tizzy *s.* (*pop.*) **to be in a ~,** être dans tous ses états.
T.N.T. *s.* T.N.T. *m.*
to *prep.* **1.** (*with pron. as ind. obj. of verb*) me, te, se, lui, nous, vous, leur; **2.** (*gen. in direction of, as far as*) (jusqu')à; **3.** (*gen. purpose, in order ~*) pour; **4.** *some examples with other prepositions, but see under relevant adj., verb, etc.*: à: (*towns*) à Paris, à Londres; (*m.sing. countries*) au Portugal, au Canada; (*m.* & *f.pl. countries*) aux Etats-Unis,

aux Indes; *see also* en (*below*); (*after some adjs.*) **useful to know, right to say, ready to wear,** utile à savoir, propre à dire, prêt-à-porter; (*sth. to do, etc.*) qch. à faire, etc.; **a man to know,** un homme à connaître; avec: **a resemblance to,** une ressemblance avec; **to be nice to s.o.,** être aimable avec qn.; contre: (*proportion*) **ten to one,** dix contre un; de: (*after some adjs.*) **happy to, pleased to,** heureux de, content de; **in proportion to,** en proportion de; **the road to Paris,** la route de Paris; en: (*f.sing. countries*) en France, en Angleterre; envers, à l'égard de: (*fig. towards*) **he was very attentive to her, to his mother,** il s'est montré plein d'attentions envers elle, à l'égard de sa mère; pour (*after some adjs.*) **good to,** bon pour, **a friend to,** un ami pour; (*before inf.*) (**in order**) **to see her,** pour la voir; selon: (*according to*) **to all appearances,** selon toute apparence; sur: (*on to*) **to leap to one's feet,** se dresser sur ses jambes; ⚠ **to** *as part of the Eng. inf. is not translated in French*; **to be** = être, **to have** = avoir, *etc.*

toad *s.* crapaud *m.*; **~flax** *s.* monnaie du pape *f.*; **~stool** *s.* champignon vénéneux *m.*; **~y** *s.* flagorneur *m.*, *v.i.* flagorner.

toast *s.* **1.** (*bread*) pain grillé *m.*, toast *m.*; **2.** (*drink*) toast *m.*; **~-master** *s.* annonceur des toasts *m.*; *v.t.* & *i.* (1) griller; (2) porter un toast à; **~er** *s.* grille-pain (électrique) *m.invar.*

tobacco *s.* tabac *m.*; **~nist** *s.* marchand de tabac *m.*; **~-pouch** *s.* blague *f.* (à tabac).

toboggan *s.* toboggan *m.*; *v.i.* faire du toboggan.

toccata *s.* toccata *f.*

tocsin *s.* tocsin *m.*

today *s. adv.* aujourd'hui.

toddle *v.i.* avancer à pas chancelants; **~r** *s.* (tout petit) enfant *m.*

toddy *s.* grog *m.*

to-do *s.* (*bustle*) remue-ménage *m.*; (*fuss*) cérémonies *f.pl.*

toe *s.* orteil *m.*, doigt de pied *m.*; (*of shoe, etc.*) bout *m.*; **from top to ~,** de pied en cap; **to tread on s.o.'s ~s,** marcher sur les plates-bandes de qn.; **~-cap** *s.* bout de chaussure *m.*; *v.t.* botter; **~ the** LINE.

toff *s.* (*pop.*) gommeux *m.*

toffee *s.* caramel *m.*

toga *s.* toge *f.*

together *adv.* (*in company*) ensemble; (*simultaneously*) en même temps; **~ness** *s.* caractère collectif *m.*, (*friendliness*) camaraderie *f.*

toggle *s.* cabillot *m.*

Togo *s.* (*geog.*) Togo *m.*; **~lese** *adj.* & *s.m.f.* togolais(e).

toil *s.* **1.** (*labour*) travail *m.*; **2.** (*drudgery*) peine *f.*; *v.i.* (1) travailler (dur); (2) peiner; **~ along, up,** avancer, monter, péniblement; **~er** *s.* travailleur *m.*; **~some** *adj.* pénible.

toilet *s.* toilette *f.*; (*lavatory*) toilettes *f.pl.*; **~-paper** *s.* papier hygiénique *m.*; **~ powder** *s.* poudre *m.*; **~-roll** *s.* rouleau de papier hygiénique *m.*; **~-ries** *s.pl.* (*comm.*) produits de beauté *m.pl.*

toils *s.pl.* (*net, snare*) rets *m.pl.*

token *s.* (*symbol*) signe *m.*, marque *f.*; (*evidence*) témoignage *m.*; (*keepsake*) souvenir *m.*; (*coin*) jeton *m.*; (*voucher*) bon *m.*; **book, gift, record, ~,** bon pour livre, pour cadeau, pour disque; **~ payment** *s.* somme symbolique *f.*; **~ strike** *s.* grève d'avertissement *f.*

toler/ate *v.t.* supporter; (*med.*) tolérer; **~able** *adj.* supportable; (*fairly good*) passable; **~ably** *adv.**; *; **~ant** *adj.* tolérant; résistant; **~ance** *s.*, **~ation** *s.* tolérance *f.*

toll[1] *s.* **1.** (*charge*) péage *m.*; **2.** (*fig. cost*) prix *m.*; **take ~ of** (2) infliger de grosses pertes à; **~-bar, ~-gate** *s.* barrière à péage *f.*; **~-bridge** *s.* pont à péage *m.*; **~-road** *s.* route à péage *f.*

toll[2] *s.* (*sound, also* **~ing**) tintement *m.*; *v.t.* & *i.* tinter.

Tom *s.* **~, Dick and Harry,** Pierre ou Paul; (**t~**, *male animal*) mâle *m.*; **t~boy** *s.* garçon manqué *m.*; **t~fool** *s.* nigaud *m.*; **t~foolery** *s.* sottises *f.pl.*; **~ Thumb,** le petit Poucet; **t~tit** *s.* mésange *m.*

tomahawk *s.* tomahawk *m.*

tomato *s.* tomate *f.*

tomb *s.* tombeau *m.*; **~stone** *s.* pierre tombale *f.*

tombola *s.* tombola *f.*

tome *s.* tome *m.*

tommy *s.* soldat anglais *m.*; **~-gun** *s.* mitraillette *f.*; **~ rot** *s.* (*pop.*) balivernes *f.pl.*

tomorrow *s.* lendemain *m.*; *adv.* demain.

tom-tom *s.* tam-tam *m.*

ton *s.* (*weight*) tonne *f.*; (*naut.*) tonneau *m.*; **~s of** (*fig.*) des milliers de, des . . . à la pelle; **~nage** *s.* tonnage *m.*

tone *s.* ton *m.*; **~-deaf** *adj.* qui n'a pas d'oreille; **~-poem** *s.* poème symphonique *m.*; **tonal** *adj.* tonal; **tonality** *s.* tonalité *f.*; *v.t.* & *i.* (*mus.*) accorder; (*photo.*) virer; (*art*) adoucir; **~ down** *v.t.* & *i.* (s')adoucir; **~ with,** s'harmoniser avec.

tongs *s.pl.* (*for fire*) pincettes *f.pl.*; (*cook.*) pince *f.*; (*techn.*) tenailles *f.pl.*; SUGAR **~**; HAMMER **and ~s.**

tongue *s.* (*lit.* & *fig.*) langue *f.*; **~**-TIED; **~-twister** *s.* acrobatie verbale *f.*; **with ~ in cheek,** en pince-sans-rire.

tonic *s.* (*med.*) tonique *m.*; (*mus.*) tonique *f.*; *adj.* tonique.

tonight *adv.* ce soir, cette nuit.

tonsil *s.* amygdale *f.*; **~lectomy** *s.* amygdalectomie *f.*; **~litis** *s.* amygdalite *f.*

tonsure *s.* tonsure *f.*; *v.t.* tonsurer.

tontine *s.* tontine *f.*

too *adv.* (*also, as well*) aussi, également; (*in excess*) trop; (*fam. extremely*) très; ⚠ **~ much** = trop.

tool *s.* outil *m.*; (*fig.*) instrument *m.*; MACHINE **~**; **~-chest** *s.* coffre à outils *m.*; **~-kit** *s.* jeu d'outils *m.*, trousse à outils *f.*

toot *v.i.* klaxonner, corner.

tooth *s.* dent *f.*; **to be long in the ~,** prendre de la bouteille; **to escape by the** SKIN **of one's teeth; to take the** BIT **between one's teeth; to gnash one's teeth,** grincer des dents; **to set one's teeth,** serrer les dents; **to set s.o.'s teeth on edge,** faire grincer les dents à qn.; **in the teeth of,** malgré; **~ and nail,** avec acharnement; SWEET **~**; **~ache** *s.* mal de dents *m.*; **~-brush** *s.* brosse à dents *f.*; **~**PASTE; **~**PICK; **~-powder** *s.* poudre dentifrice *m.*; **~ed** *adj.* denté; **~less** *adj.* édenté; **~some** *adj.* savoureux; **~y** *adj.* bien pourvu de fortes dents.

top *s.* (*summit*) sommet *m.*, faîte *f.*; (*upper part*) haut *m.*, dessus *m.*; (*highest place*) cime *f.*; (*cover*) couvercle *m.*; (*of bottle*) bouchon *m.*; (*toy*) toupie *f.*; (*of bus*) impériale *f.*; (*of carrots, etc.*) fanes *f.pl.*; (*naut.*) hune *f.*; (*of class*) premier *m.*, première *f.*; **at the ~ of one's voice,** à tue-tête; **to sleep like a ~,** dormir comme un loir; **from ~ to** BOTTOM; **big ~** *s.* chapiteau de cirque *m.*; *adj.* (*highest*) le plus haut; (*on ~*) d'en haut; **~coat** *s.* pardessus *m.*; **~-dressing** *s.* revêtement *m.*; **~ hat** *s.* haut-de-forme *m.*; **~-heavy** *adj.* trop lourd en haut; **~mast** *s.* mât de hune *m.*; **~sail** *s.* hunier *m.*; **~ secret** *adj.* secret; **~soil** *s.* couche arable *f.*; **~less** (*dress*) à grand décolleté; **~less bathing costume,** monokini *m.*; **~most** *adj.* le plus haut; *v.t.* couronner de; (*remove ~ of*) étêter; (*be at ~ of*) dépasser; **~ up,** remplir; **~ping** *adj.* (*fam.*) formidable.

topaz *s.* topaz *f.*

toper *s.* (*fam.*) soiffard *m.*

topi, topee *s.* casque colonial *m.*

topiary *s.* taille ornamentale (des arbres) *f.*
topic *s.* sujet *m.*, thème *m.*; ⚠ topique *is a philos. term*; **~al** *adj.* d'actualité; ⚠ topique = (*med.*) **topical; ~ality** *s.* actualité *f.*
topograph/y *s.* topographie *f.*; **~ic(al)** *adj.* topographique.
topple *v.t.* & *i.* (faire) tomber; **~ over** *v.i.* dégringoler.
topsy-turvy *adv.* sens dessus dessous.
tor *s.* pic rocheux *m.*
torch *s.* (*piece of wood, etc.*) torche *f.*; (*electr.*) lampe de poche *f.*; **~-bearer** *s.* porte-flambeau *m.*
toreador *s.* toréador *m.*
torment *s.* supplice *m.*; ⚠ tourment *is obs. in this sense*; *v.t.* tourmenter; **~or** *s.* bourreau *m.*
tornado *s.* tornade *f.*
torpedo *s.* **1.** (*missile*) torpille *f.*; **2.** (*fish*) poisson torpille *m.*; ⚠ torpédo = (*obs.*) **fast racing car; ~-boat** *s.* torpilleur *m.*; **~-tube** *s.* (tube) lance-torpilles *m.*; *v.t.* (1) (*lit.* & *fig.*) torpiller.
torp/id *adj.* engourdi; **~or** *s.* **~idity** *s.* torpeur *f.*
torque *s.* (*hist.*) torque *f.*; (*mech.*) couple *m.*
torrent *s.* torrent *m.*; **~ial** *adj.* (*rain*) torrentiel; (*fig.*) torrentueux.
torrid *adj.* torride.
torsion *s.* torsion *f.*; **~al** *adj.* de torsion.
torso *s.* torse *m.*
tort *s.* (*law*) acte dommageable *m.*
tortoise *s.* tortue *f.*; **~-shell** *s.* écaille *f.*; *adj.* en écaille.
tortuous *adj.* (*lit.* & *fig.*) tortueux; **~ly** *adv.**; **~ness** *s.* caractère tortueux *m.*
torture *s.* torture *f.*, supplice *m.*; *v.t.* torturer, mettre au supplice; **~r** *s.* bourreau *m.*
Tory *adj.* & *s.m.* Tory.
toss *s.* (*~ing*) lancement *m.*; (*of head*) mouvement dédaigneux *m.*; (*fall from horse*) chute *f.*; **to win the ~,** gagner à pile ou face; **to argue the ~,** ergoter; PITCH **and ~**; *v.t.* lancer; (*head*) relever dédaigneusement; (*coin*) jouer à pile ou face; (*sea, etc.*) ballotter; *v.i.* s'agiter; **~ off,** expédier; **~ up** *v.t.* lancer en l'air; **~-up** *s.* (coup de) pile ou face *m.*
tot *s.* (*child*) gamin(e) *m.f.*; (*drink*) goutte *f.*; *v.t.* **~ up,** additionner.
total *adj.* & *s.m.* total; **~ly** *adv.**; *v.t.* (*add up*) totaliser; *v.i.* (*add up to*) se monter à; **~itarian** *adj.* totalitaire; **~itarianism** *s.* totalitarisme *m.*; **~ity** *s.* totalité *f.*; **~ize** *v.t.* totaliser; **~izator** *s.* pari-mutuel *m.*
tote *s.* (*abbrev. for totalizator*) pari-mutuel *m.*; *v.t.* (*fam.*) porter.
totem *s.* totem *m.*
totter *v.i.* chanceler; **~ing** *adj.* chancelant.
touch *s.* (*act of ~ing*) attouchement *m.*; (*contact*) contact *m.*; (*sense*) toucher *m.*; (*sensation*) sensation *f.*; (*with pencil, brush, etc.*) touche *f.*; (*mus.*) toucher *m.*; (*football*) touche *f.*; **~-line** *s.* ligne de touche *f.*; (*tinge*) trait *m.*, soupçon *m.*; FINISH**ing ~; personal ~,** note personnelle *f.*; **~-and-go** *adj.* hasardeux; **it was ~-and-go for him,** c'était moins cinq pour lui; **to get in ~ with,** prendre contact avec; **to** KEEP **in ~ with; to put in ~ with,** mettre en contact avec; **~stone** *s.* (*lit.* & *fig.*) pierre de touche *f.*; *v.t.* & *i.* (*come into, be, in contact with*) (se) toucher; (*stroke*) toucher à, effleurer; (*tint with*) teinter de; (*concern*) se rapporter à; (*affect*) toucher; (*reach, approach*) atteindre; **~ wood,** toucher du bois; **~ down** *v.i.* (*aviat.*) se poser; **~down** *s.* (*rugby*) but *m.*; **~ s.o. for** (*pop.*) faire casquer qn.; **~ on,** toucher à; **~ up** *v.t.* retoucher; **~ed** *adj.* (*fam.*) timbré; **~ing** *adj.* touchant; **~y** *adj.* susceptible; **~iness** *s.* susceptibilité *f.*
tough *s.* voyou *m.*; *adj.* **1.** (*resistant*) solide, résistant; **2.** (*hard to chew*) coriace; **3.** (*not easily broken*) dur; **4.** (*hard to overcome*) rude; **5.** (*hardy*) robuste, costaud; **6.** (*pop. ruffianly*) voyou; **~ guy** *s.* dur *m.*; **~ luck** (*fam.*) déveine *f.*; **~en** *v.t.* & *i.* (se) durcir; (*fig.*) (s')endurcir; **~ly** *adv.* (1) solidement; (3)*; (4)*; **~ness** *s.* (1) solidité *f.*; (2), (3) dureté *f.*; (4) rudesse *f.*, difficulté *f.*; (5) robustesse *f.*
toupee *s.* postiche *m.*
tour *s.* (*journey*) voyage *m.*; (*guided*) voyage organisé *m.*; (*visit*) excursion *f.*; (*spell of duty*) tournée *f.*; **on ~,** en voyage, (*theat.*) en tournée; *v.t.* visiter; *v.i.* voyager; **~ing** *s.*, **~ism** *s.* tourisme *m.*; **~ist** *s.* touriste *m.f.*, *adj.* touristique.
tournament *s.* tournoi *m.*; (*sport*) championnat *m.*
tourniquet *s.* garrot *m.*
tousled *adj.* ébouriffé.
tout *s.* racoleur *m.*; *v.t.* & *i.* racoler.
tow[1] *s.* (*flax*) étoupe *f.*; **~-coloured** *adj.* comme de l'étoupe.
tow[2] *s.* (*being ~ed*) remorque *f.*; **on/in ~,** à la remorque; *v.t.* remorquer; **~-path** *s.* chemin de halage *m.*; **~-rope** *s.* remorque *f.*
toward(s) *prep.* (*in direction of, near*) vers; (*fig.*) envers; (*as regards*) en vue de.
towel *s.* serviette *f.*; **hand ~,** essuie-mains *m.*; ROLLER **~; ~-horse** *s.*, **~-rail** *s.* porte-serviettes *m.*; *v.t.* essuyer; **~ling** *s.* tissu-éponge *m.*
tower *s.* tour *f.*; CONTROL **~; watch-~,** tour de guet *f.*; **~ of strength,** puissant soutien *m.*; ⚠ tour de force = **exploit;** *v.i.* s'élever; **~ above/over** *v.t.* dominer; **~ing** *adj.* élevé, (*violent*) violent.
town *s.* ville *f.*; **to go to ~** (*fig.*) mettre les petits plats dans les grands; **~ clerk** *s.* secrétaire de mairie *m.*; **~ council** *s.* conseil municipal *m.*; **~ crier** *s.* tambour de ville *m.*; **~ hall** *s.* hôtel de ville *m.*; **~ planner** *s.* urbaniste *m.f.*; **~ planning** *s.* urbanisme *m.*; **~sman, ~swoman** *s.* citadin(e) *m.f.*; **~ee** *s.* (*pej.*) bourgeois *m.*; **~ship** *s.* commune *f.*
toxæmia *s.* toxémie *f.*
tox/in *s.* toxine *f.*; **~ic** *adj.* toxique; **~icity** *s.* toxicité *f.*; **~icology** *s.* toxicologie *f.*; **~icological** *adj.* toxicologique; **~icologist** *s.* toxicologue *m.f.*; **~icomania** *s.* toxicomanie *f.*
toy *s.* jouet *m.*; *adj.* d'enfant; petit, minuscule, miniature; *v.i.* **~ with,** jouer avec, badiner avec.
trac/e *s.* (*mark left behind*) trace *f.*; (*indication*) marque *f.*; (*small amount*) brin *m.*; (*part of harness*) trait *m.*; **to kick over the ~es,** ruer dans les brancards; *v.t.* (*mark out*) tracer; (*copy*) calquer; (*follow track*) suivre la piste de; (*find*) retrouver; **~eable** *adj.* retraçable; **~e element** *s.* élément décelable *m.*; **~er bullet** *s.* balle traçante *f.*; **~ery** *s.* réseau *m.*; **~ing** *s.* tracé *m.*; **~ing-paper** *s.* papier-calque *m.*
trache/a *s.* trachée *f.*; **~otomy** *s.* trachéotomie *f.*
trachoma *s.* trachome *m.*
track *s.* **1.** (*marks left*) traces *f.pl.*, piste *f.*, empreintes *f.pl.*; **on the ~s of,** sur la piste de; **keep ~ of,** suivre; **stop in one's ~s,** s'arrêter net; **2.** (*path, rough road*) chemin (de terre) *m.*; **3.** (*line of travel*) cours *m.*; **4.** (*racing*) piste *f.*; **5.** (*rail.*) voie *f.*; **6.** (*mech.*) chenille *f.*; **7.** (*naut.*) sillage *m.*; **8.** (*on disc or tape*) piste *f.*; **sound-~,** bande sonore *f.*; **~ suit** *s.* survêtement *m.*; **~less** *adj.* sans chemin; *v.t.* (1) (*follow*) suivre à la piste, poursuivre; (6) munir de chenilles; **~ down** *v.t.* dépister; **~er dog** *s.* chien policier *m.*; **~ing** *s.* poursuite *f.*, dépistage *m.*
tract *s.* (*extent*) étendue *f.*; (*anat.*) voies *f.pl.*; (*pamphlet*) tract *m.*
tractable *adj.* traitable.
traction *s.* traction *f.*; **~-engine** *s.* tracteur *m.*

tractor *s.* tracteur *m.*; CATERPILLAR ~.
trade *s.* (*buying & selling*) commerce *m.*; (*business, craft*) métier *m.*; **~ mark** *s.* marque de fabrique *f.*; **~sman** *s.* commerçant *m.*; **~(s) union** *s.* syndicat *m.*; **~-unionism** *s.* syndicalisme *m.*; **~-unionist** *s.* syndicaliste *m.f.*; **~ winds** *s.* alizés *m.pl.*; *v.i.* (*engage in* ~) faire du commerce; **~ in sth.,** faire le commerce de qch.; **~ sth. in,** donner qch. en reprise; **~ on s.o.,** exploiter qn.; **~r** *s.* commerçant *m.*; **trading** *s.* commerce *m.*; **trading stamp** *s.* bon-prime *m.*
tradition *s.* tradition *f.*; **~al** *adj.* traditionnel; **~ally** *adv.**.
traduce *v.t.* calomnier; **~r** *s.* calomniateur *m.*
traffic *s.* **1.** (*illicit trade*) trafic *m.*; **2.** (*movement of vehicles*) circulation *f.*; (*of trains only*) trafic *m.* (ferroviaire); **3.** (*amount of persons or goods conveyed, use of service*) circulation *f.*; **~ jam** *s.* (2) embouteillage *m.*; **~ island** *s.* refuge *m.*; ~-LIGHTS; **~ policeman** *s.* agent chargé de la circulation *m.*; **~ sign** *s.* signalisation (routière) *f.*; **~ warden** *s.* contractuel(le) *m.f.*; **~ator** *s.* clignotant *m.*; *v.i.* (1) trafiquer (*in*—de).
traged/y *s.* tragédie *f.*; **~ian** *s.* tragédien(ne) *m.f.*
tragic *adj.* tragique; **~ally** *adv.**.
trail *s.* (*~ing growth, etc.*) traînée *f.*; (*track, scent, path*) trace *f.*, piste *f.*; *v.t.* & *i.* (*draw, be drawn, behind*) traîner; (*walk wearily*) se traîner; (*hang loosely*) pendre; (*track*) filer; **~er** *s.* (*plant*) plante grimpante *f.*, (*vehicle*) remorque *f.*, roulotte *f.*, (*cinema*) film-annonce *m.*
train[1] *s.* (*of dress*) traîne *f.*; (*string of people, etc.*) file *f.*; (*retinue*) suite *f.*; (*of events*) suite *f.*, série *f.*; (*rail.*) train *m.*; SLOW ~; **in ~,** en train; **in the ~ of,** à la suite de; **~-bearer** *s.* porte--queue *m.*; **~-ferry** *s.* train-ferry *m.*
train[2] *v.t.* **1.** (*instruct*) former; **2.** (*animal*) dresser; **3.** (*child*) élever; **4.** *v.t.* & *i.* (*physically*) (s') entraîner; **5.** (*plant*) faire grimper; **6.** (*aim*) pointer; **~ee** *s.* (1) stagiaire *m.f.*; (4) poulain *m.*; **~er** *s.* (2) dresseur *m.*; (4) entraîneur *m.*; **~ing** *s.* (1) formation *f.*; (2) dressage *m.*; (4) entraînement *m.*; **~ing-college** *s.* école normale *f.*; **in ~ing,** en pleine forme; **out of ~ing,** rouillé.
trait *s.* trait *m.*
trait/or *s.* traître *m.*; **~ress** *s.* traîtresse *f.*; ⚠ traiteur = **caterer; ~orous** *adj.* traître; **~orously** *adv.* traîtreusement.
trajectory *s.* trajectoire *f.*
tram *s.* tram *m.*; **~-line** *s.* ligne de tramway *f.*; **~-lines** *s.pl.* (*tennis*) ligne de côté (simple/double) *f.*
trammel *s.* **1.** (*fishing-net*) trémail *m.*; **2.** (*shackle*) entrave *f.*; *v.i.* (2) entraver.
tramp *s.* (*sound*) bruit de pas lourds *m.*; (*long walk*) marche à pied *f.*; (*person*) chemineau *m*,; (*ship*) cargo *m.*; *v.t.* & *i.* marcher lourdement.
trample *v.t.* (*lit.* & *fig.*) fouler aux pieds, écraser.
trampoline *s.* trampolino *m.*
trance *s.* (*spiritualism*) trance *f.*; (*fig., eccles.*) extase *f.*
tranquil *adj.* tranquille; **~ly** *adv.**; **~lity** *s.* tranquillité *f.*; **~lize** *v.t.* tranquilliser; **~lizer** *s.* tranquillisant *m.*
trans- (*in combination*) **~alpine** *adj.* transalpin; **~atlantic** *adj.* transatlantique; **~continental** *adj.* transcontinental; **~pacific** *adj.* transpacifique; **~-ship** *v.t.* transborder; **~-shipment** *s.* transbordement *m.*; **~vestism** *s.* travestisme *m.*
transact *v.t.* traiter; **~ion** *s.* transaction *f.*; **~ions** *s.pl.* (*proceedings*) affaires *f.pl.*; (*records of learned soc.*) actes *m.pl.*; **~or** *s.* négociateur *m.*
transcend *v.t.* dépasser; **~ence** *s.*, **~ency** *s.* transcendance *f.*; **~ent** *adj.* transcendant; **~ental** *adj.* transcendantal.
transcri/be *v.t.* transcrire; **~ption** *s.*, **~pt** *s.* transcription *f.*
transept *s.* transept *m.*
transfer *s.* **1.** (*act*) transfert *m.*; (*ticket*) titre *m.* (de propriété); (*thing ~red*) objet du transfert *m.*; **2.** (*design*) report *m.*; **3.** (*of official*) déplacement *m.*; **4.** (*of funds*) virement *m.*; **5.** (*of player*) mutation *f.*; *v.t.* (1) transférer; (2) reporter; (3) déplacer; (4) virer; (5) muter; **6.** (*change, train, etc.*) changer de; **~able** *adj.* (*law*) cessible, (*fin.*) négociable; **~ence** *s.* transfèrement *m.*
transfigur/e *v.t.* transfigurer; **~ation** *s.* transfiguration *f.*
transfix *v.t.* transpercer; (*fig.*) pétrifier.
transform *v.t.* & *i.* (se) transformer (*into*—en); **~ation** *s.* transformation *f.*; **~er** *s.* (*electr.*) transformateur *m.*
transfus/e *v.t.* transfuser; **~ion** *s.* transfusion *f.*
transgress *v.t.* transgresser; *v.i.* pécher; **~ion** *s.* transgression *f.*; **~or** *s.* transgresseur *m.*, pécheur *m.*
transien/t *adj.* passager, transitoire; **~tly** *adv.**,*; **~ce** *s.* nature éphémère *f.*
transistor *s.* transistor *m.*; *adj.* à transistors; **~ize** *v.t.* munir de transistors.
transit *s.* passage *m.*; **in ~,** en transit; *v.t.* & *i.* transiter; **~ion** *s.* transition *f.*; **~ional** *adj.* de transition; **~ive** *adj.* transitif; **~ively** *adv.**; **~ory** *adj.* transitoire; **~orily** *adv.**.
translat/e *v.t.* **1.** (*convey*) transporter; **2.** (*eccles.*) transférer; **3.** (*into another language*) traduire (en); **~able** *adj.* (3) traduisible; **~ion** *s.* (1) transport *m.*; (2) translation *f.*; (3) traduction *f.*; **~or** *s.* traduct/-eur, -rice *m.f.*
transliterat/e *v.t.* transcrire; **~ion** *s.* transcription *f.*
translucen/t *adj.* translucide; **~ce** *s.* translucidité *f.*
transmigration *s.* transmigration *f.*
transmiss/ion *s.* transmission *f.*; **~ible** *adj.* transmissible; **~ibility** *s.* transmissibilité *f.*
transmit *v.t.* (*send*) transmettre; (*electr., radio*) émettre; **~ter** *s.* (*radio*) émetteur *m.*, (*telegr.*) manipulateur *m.*, (*telephone*) microphone *m.*
transmut/e *v.t.* transmuer; **~able** *adj.* transmuable; **~ation** *s.* transmutation *f.*
transom *s.* linteau *m.*
transparen/t *adj.* transparent; **~ce** *s.* transparence *f.*; **~cy** *s.* (*photo.*) diapositive *f.*; (*abbrev.*) diapo *f.*; **~tly** *adv.* de façon transparente.
transpire *v.i.* transpirer; (*happen*) arriver.
transplant *s.* greffe *f.*; *v.t.* (*hort.*) transplanter; (*med.*) greffer; **~ation** *s.* transplantation *f.*
transport *s.* (*lit.* & *fig.*) transport *m.*; *v.t.* transporter; **~ation** *s.* deportation *f.*; **~ing** *adj.* ravissant; **~er** *s.* transporteur *m.*
transpos/e *v.t.* transposer; **~al** *s.* **~ition** *s.* transposition *f.*
transsubstantiation *s.* transsubstantiation *f.*
transverse *adj.* transversal; (*anat.*) transverse; **~ly** *adv.* transversalement.
trap *s.* (*device, plan*) piège *m.*; MOUSE ~; (*racing*) box de départ *m.*; (*carriage*) cabriolet *m.*; (*U pipe*) siphon *m.*; **~door** *s.* trappe *f.*; *v.t.* prendre au piège; **~per** *s.* trappeur *m.*; **~pings** *s.* atours *m.pl.*, (*of horse*) harnachement *m.*
trapeze *s.* trapèze *m.*
Trappist *s.* Trappiste *m.*
trash *s.* (*waste*) rebut *m.*; (*nonsense*) niaiseries *f.pl.*; (*people*) racaille *f.*; (*goods*) camelote *f.*; **~y** *adj.* de camelote.
trauma *s.* (*wound*) trauma *m.*; (*condition*) traumatisme *m.*; **~tic** *adj.* traumatique.
travail *s.* travail *m.*; *v.i.* être en travail.
travel *s.* voyages *m.pl.*; *v.t.* & *i.* voyager (en);

(*journey through*) parcourir; (*eyes*) se promener; (*news*) circuler; **~led** *adj.* qui a beaucoup voyagé; **~ler** *s.* voyageur *m.*; COMMERCIAL **~ler**; **~ler's cheque** *s.* chèque de voyage *m.*; **~ler's joy** *s.* (*bot.*) clématite *f.*; **~ling** *s.* voyage *m.*; **~ling** *adj.* (*library, etc.*) mobile, (*accessory*) de voyage, (*techn.*) roulant; **~ogue** *s.* documentaire sur un voyage *m.*

traverse *s.* (*constr.*) traverse *f.*; (*climbing*) traversée *f.*; *v.t.* traverser.

travesty *s.* travestissement *m.*; *v.t.* travestir.

trawl *s.* chalut *m.*; *v.i.* pêcher au chalut; **~er** *s.* chalutier *m.*

tray *s.* plateau *m.*; (*in cabinet, trunk, etc.*) casier *m.*

treacher/y *s.* trahison *f.*; **~ous** *adj.* traître; (*blow*) déloyal; (*memory*) infidèle; (*unreliable*) trompeur; (*dangerous*) dangereux; **~ously** *adv.* traîtreusement.

treacle *s.* mélasse *f.*

tread *s.* (*walk*) pas *m.*; (*of tyre*) chape *f.*; (*of stair*) giron *m.*; **~mill** *s.* moulin de discipline *m.*; *v.i.* marcher; *v.t.* marcher sur, piétiner; (*grapes*) fouler; **~ on, ~ down,** fouler aux pieds; **~ out,** étouffer; **~ water,** nager debout; **~ on s.o.'s** CORNS, TOES.

treadle *s.* pédale *f.*; *adj.* à pédale; *v.i.* pédaler.

treason *s.* trahison *f.*; **high ~,** (*against sovereign*) lèse-majesté *m.*, (*against state*) haute trahison *f.*; **~able** *adj.* de trahison; **~ous** *adj.* de traître.

treasur/e *s.* trésor *m.*; *v.t.* priser; **~e up,** thésauriser; **~er** *s.* trésorier *m.*; **~y** *s.* (*place, funds*) trésor *m.*; (*dept.*) trésorerie *f.*; (*ministry*) ministère des finances *m.*

treat *s.* fête *f.*, régal *m.*; **to give s.o. a ~,** offrir un bon dîner (etc.) à qn.; *v.t.* traiter; *v.i.* traiter (de, avec); **~ like** DIRT; **~ise** *s.* traité *m.*; **~ment** *s.* traitement *m.*; **~y** *s.* traité *m.*

treble[1] *s.* soprano *m.*; *adj.* de soprano.

trebl/e[2] *adj.* & *s.m.* triple; **~ly** *adv.**; *v.t.* tripler.

tree *s.* arbre *m.*; *adj.* arborescent; **~-fern,** fougère arborescente *f.*; SHOE **~.**

trefoil *s.* trèfle *m.*

trek *s.* voyage *m.* (en char à bœufs); *v.i.* voyager, émigrer; (*fam.*) faire route.

trellis *s.* treillis *m.*

trembl/e *v.i.* trembler; **~ing** *s.* tremblement *m.*; *adj.* tremblant.

tremendous *adj.* effrayant; (*fam.*) (*v. large*) énorme, (*excellent*) sensationnel; **~ly** *adv.* terriblement.

tremolo *adj.* & *s.m.* (*mus.*) trémolo.

tremor *s.* tremblement *m.*; (*thrill*) frisson *m.*

tremulous *adj.* tremblant; (*excitement*) fébrile; (*voice*) tremblotant; **~ly** *adv.* en tremblant; **~ness** *s.* tremblement *m.*

trench *s.* (*mil.*) tranchée *f.*; (*agric.*) fossé *m.*; *v.t.* creuser un fossé; **~ant** *adj.* tranchant; **~er** *s.* tranchoir *m.*

trend *s.* tendance *f.*; *v.i.* avoir tendance (à); **~y** *adj.* dernier cri.

trepan *s.* trépan *m.*; *v.t.* trépaner.

trepidation *s.* trépidation *f.*

trespass *s.* **1.** violation de propriété *f.*; **2.** (*obs. eccles.*) offense *f.*; *v.i.* (1) entrer sans permission; (2) pécher; **~ against** (*law*) enfreindre; **~ on** (*rights*) empiéter sur; (*time, etc.*) abuser de; **~er** *s.* (1) intrus(e) *m.f.*; (2) pécheur *m.*; **~ers will be prosecuted,** défense d'entrer sous peine d'amende.

tress *s.* tresse *f.*

trestle *s.* tréteau *m.*

tri- (*in combination*) **~centenary** *s.* tricentenaire *m.*; **~ennial** *adj.* triennal; **~lateral** *adj.* trilatéral; **~lingual** *adj.* trilingue; **~-partite** *adj.* tripartite; **~reme** *s.* trirème *f.*; **~sect** *v.t.* diviser en trois parties.

triad *s.* triade *f.*

trial *s.* (*test*) essai *m.*; (*law*) procès *m.*; (*fig.*) épreuve *f.*; **on ~,** à l'essai; *adj.* d'essai; **~ balance** *s.* balance de vérification *f.*

triang/le *s.* triangle *m.*; **~ular** *adj.* triangulaire; **~ulate** *v.t.* trianguler.

trib/e *s.* tribu *f.*; (*pej.*) gent *f.*; **~al** *adj.* de la tribu; **~alism** *s.* tribalisme *m.*

tribulation *s.* tribulation *f.*

tribunal *s.* tribunal *m.*

tribune *s.* (*hist.*) tribun *m.*; (*platform*) tribune *f.*

tributary *s.* affluent *m.*; *adj.* tributaire.

tribute *s.* tribut *m.*; **to pay ~ to,** rendre hommage à.

trice, in a ~, en un clin d'œil.

trick *s.* (*crafty device*) ruse *f.*; (*hoax*) tour *m.*; **to play a ~ on s.o.,** jouer un tour à qn.; CONFIDENCE **~**; CONJUR**ing** **~**; DIRTY **~**; MONKEY **~s**; (*clever device*) truc *m.*; (*knack*) chic *m.*, astuce *m.*; (*mannerism*) tic *m.*, manie *f.*; (*cards*) levée *f.*; (*naut.*) tour *m.*; *v.t.* tromper, duper; **~ out/up** (*fam.*) (s')attifer; **~ery** *s.* tromperie *f.*, supercherie *f.*; **~ster** *s.* escroc *m.*; **~y** *adj.* rusé, malin, (*fam.*) délicat, compliqué.

trickle *s.* filet *m.*; *v.i.* dégoutter.

tricolour *s.* (drapeau) tricolore *m.*; *adj.* tricolore.

tricycle *s.* tricycle *m.*

trident *s.* trident *m.*

trier *see* TRY.

trifl/e *s.* (*sth. of slight value or importance*) bagatelle *f.*; (*small amount*) petite somme *f.*, rien *m.*; (*cook.*) charlotte (à la crème fouettée) *f.*; **a ~e** + *adj.* tant soit peu + *adj.*; *v.i.* badiner, jouer (avec); agir légèrement; **~er** *s.* farceur *m.*; **~ing** *s.* légèreté *f.*, *adj.* frivole, insignifiant.

trigger *s.* gâchette *f.*; **~-happy** *adj.* à la gâchette facile; *v.t.* & *i.* **~ off,** provoquer.

trigonometr/y *s.* trigonométrie *f.*; **~ic(al)** *adj.* trigonométrique.

trilby *s.* chapeau mou *m.*

trill *s.* trille *m.*; *v.i.* faire des trilles.

trillion *s.* trillion *m.*

trilogy *s.* trilogie *f.*

trim *s.* **1.** (*readiness*) état *m.*; **2.** (*naut.*) arrimage *m.*; (*aviat.*) équilibrage *m.*; **3.** (*good order*) ordre *m.*, tenue *f.*; **4.** (= **~ming**) garniture *f.*; **5.** (*haircut*) coupe *f.*; *adj.* (3) bien tenu; (≠ *loose*) net; **~ly** *adv.* nettement; **~ness** *s.* netteté *f.*; *v.t.* (1), (3) mettre en ordre, arranger; (2) (*sail*) orienter, (*ship, plane*) équilibrer; (4) garnir; (5) couper, tailler; **~ming** *s.* garniture *f.*; (*of hedges, etc.*) taille *f.*

trimaran *s.* trimaran *m.*

Trinidad *s.* (*geogr.*) Ile de la Trinité *f.*

trinity *s.* trinité *f.*; **T~ Sunday,** la Trinité.

trinket *s.* breloque *f.*

trio *s.* (*mus.*) trio *m.*

trip *s.* **1.** (*excursion*) excursion *f.*; **2.** (*short journey*) trajet *m.*; (*naut.*) voyage *m.*; **3.** (*stumble*) faux pas *m.*; **4.** (*mech.*) déclic *m.*; **5.** (*light step*) pas léger *m.*; *v.t.* & *i.* (3) *also* **~ up,** (faire) tomber, (faire) trébucher; (*fig.*) *v.t.* prendre en faute, *v.i.* faire un faux pas; (4) *v.t.* déclencher; (5) *v.i.* aller d'un pas léger; **~per** *s.* excursionniste *m.f.*; **~ping** *adj.* léger.

tripe *s.* (*cook.*) tripes *f.pl.*; (*pop.*) foutaise *f.*

triple *adj.* & *s.m.* triple; *v.t.* tripler; **~t** *s.* trio *m.*, (*mus.*) triolet *m.*, (*children*) triplé(e)s *m.f.*

triplex *s.* triplex *m.*

triplicate *adj.* & *s.m.* triple; **in ~,** en trois exemplaires.

tripod *s.* trépied *m.*

triptych *s.* triptyque *m.*

trite *adj.* rebattu, banal; **~ly** *adv.* d'une manière banale.

Triton *s.* triton *m.*

triumph *s.* **1.** (*victory*) triomphe *m.*; **2.** (*rejoicing*) jubilation *f.*; *v.i.* (1) triompher (*over*—de); (2) jubiler; **~al** *adj.* (*arch.*) de triomphe, (*march,*

etc.) triomphal; **~ant** *adj.* triomphant; **~antly** *adv.* triomphalement.
trivet *s.* trépied *m.*
trivial *adj.* banal, insignifiant; ⚠ trivial = **unseemly, vulgar**; **~ity** *s*, banalité *f.*, insignifiance *f.*; **~ly** *adv.* d'une manière banale.
trochee *s.* trochée *m.*
troglodyte *s.* troglodyte *m.*
troika *s.* troïka *m.*
Trojan *adj.* & *s.m.f.* troyen(ne); (*horse*) de Troie.
troll *v.i.* (*sing.*) chantonner; (*fish*) pêcher à la cuiller.
trolley *s.* (*truck*) chariot *n.*; (*table*) table roulante *f.*; **~bus** *s.* trolleybus *m.*
trombon/e *s.* trombone *m.*; **~ist** *s.* tromboniste *m.*
troop *s.* bande *f.*; (*mil.*) troupe *f.*; **~s** *s.pl.* troupes *f.pl.*; *v.i.* s'attrouper; **~er** *s.* cavalier *m.*; **to swear like a ~er,** jurer comme un charretier; **~-ship** *s.* transport *m.*
trophy *s.* (*lit.* & *fig.*) trophée *m.*; (*sport*) coupe *f.*
tropic(s) *s.* (*pl.*) tropique(s) *m.* (*pl.*); **~al** *adj.* tropical.
trot *s.* trot *m.*; *v.t.* & *i.* (faire) trotter; **~ out,** faire parade de.
troth *s.* foi *f.*; **to plight one's ~,** engager sa foi.
trouble *s.* **1.** (*cause of affliction*) malheur *m.*, peine *f.*; **2.** (*discontent*) ennui *m.*; **3.** (*pains, effort*) peine *f.*, souci *m.*; **4.** (*inconvenience*) dérangement *m.*; **5.** (*med.*) troubles *m.pl.*; TEETHING **~s**; ⚠ trouble = **disorder**; troubles = **uprising, disturbance**; **to be in ~,** être dans le pétrin; **it's no ~,** il n'y a pas de quoi; **to go to** *or* **take the ~ to** *or* **of,** se donner la peine de; **what's your ~?,** qu'avez-vous?, quel est votre problème?; **~-maker** *s.* trublion *m.*; **~-shooter** *s.* dépanneur *m.*; **~-spot** *s.* point névralgique *m.*; *v.t.* & *i.* (1) (s')affliger; (2) ennuyer; (3) se déranger, se donner de la peine; (4) déranger; ⚠ troubler = **to disturb, to perplex**; **~ s.o. for sth.,** demander qch. à qn.; **~ to do sth.,** se donner la peine de faire qch.; **be troubled with,** souffrir de; **~some** *adj.* (*person*) importun, (*thing*) ennuyeux; **troublous** *adj.* troublé.
trough *s.* (*drinking*) abreuvoir *m.*; (*feeding*) auge *f.*; (*meteor.*) zone de dépression *f.*; (*of wave*) creux *m.*
trounce *v.t.* rosser.
trousers *s.pl.* pantalon *m.sing.*; **to wear the ~,** (*of a woman*) porter la culotte.
trousseau *s.* trousseau *m.*
trout *s.* truite *f.*; SALMON **~.**
trowel *s.* (*for mortar*) truelle *f.*; (*hort.*) déplantoir *m.*
Troy *s.* (*geog.*) Troie *f.*; (*t~ weight*) poids du système troy *m.*
truan/t *s.* absentéiste *m.f.*; **to play ~t,** faire l'école buissonnière; **~cy** *s.* absentéisme *m.*
truce *s.* trêve *f.*
truck[1] *s.* camion *m.*; (*rail.*) wagon *m.*; CATTLE **~.**
truck[2] *v.t.* & *i.* marchander, échanger; **to have no ~ with,** n'avoir rien à faire avec.
truckle *v.i.* ramper (devant qn./qch.); **~-bed** *s.* lit à roulettes *m.*
truculen/t *adj.* violent, brutal; ⚠ truculent = **highly-coloured**; **~ce** *s.* violence *f.*, brutalité *f.*
trudge *s.* marche pénible *f.*; *v.t.* & *i.* parcourir, marcher, péniblement.
tru/e *adj.* (*in accordance with fact*) vrai, exact; (*genuine, real*) véritable; (*loyal*) sincère, fidèle (à); (*well-placed or fitted*) d'aplomb, droit; **to come ~e,** se réaliser; *adv.* juste; **~ly** *adv.* vraiment, en vérité; (*properly, faithfully*) bien, fidèlement; **yours ~ly** (*ending of letter*) veuillez agréer, Monsieur/Madame, l'expression de mes sentiments distingués; **~eness** *s.* vérité *f.*, fidélité *f.*; **~ism** *s.* truisme *m.*
truffle *s.* truffe *f.*
trug *s.* corbeille *f.* (en bois éclaté).
trump *s.* (*card* & *fig.*) atout *m.*; **no ~s,** sans atout; (*fam.*) chic type *m.*; **to turn up ~s** (*fam.*) réussir; *v.t.* (*cards*) couper; **~ up** (*fam.*) inventer.
trumpery *adj.* & *s.m.* (de) clinquant.
trumpet *s.* trompette *f.*; (*sound of elephant*) barrissement *m.*; **ear-~** *s.* cornet acoustique *m.*; SPEAK**ing-~**; **to** BLOW **one's ~**; *v.t.* proclamer; *v.i.* (*elephant*) barrir; **~er** *s.* trompette *m.*
truncat/e *v.t.* tronquer; **~ion** *s.* mutilation *f.*
truncheon *s.* bâton *m.*
trundle *v.t.* pousser.
trunk *s.* (*of tree, of body*) tronc *m.*; (*of elephant*) trompe *f.*; (*luggage*) malle *f.*; **~s** *pl.* slip *m.sing.*; **~-call** *s.* appel interurbain *m.*; **~-road** *s.* grand-route *f.*
truss *s.* **1.** (*of hay*) botte *f.*; **2.** (*arch.*) cintre *m.*; **3.** (*surg.*) bandage herniaire *m.*; **4.** (*of fruit, etc.*) touffe *f.*; *v.t.* (1) botteler; (2) renforcer; **5.** (*tie up*) lier, ligoter; (*fowl*) trousser.
trust *s.* **1.** (*confidence, reliance*) confiance *f.*, espoir *m.*; **2.** (*credit*) crédit *m.*; **3.** (*obligation, charge*) charge *f.*; **4.** (*person, property*) dépôt *m.*; **5.** (*comm.*) trust *m.*; **in ~,** en dépôt; **to take sth. on ~,** prendre qch. de confiance, *or,* à crédit; *v.t.* (1) se fier à; (2) faire crédit à; (3) confier à; **6.** (*hope*) espérer; **~ in,** compter sur; **~ to,** se fier à; **~ee** *s.* dépositaire *m.*, (*of fund*) administrateur *m.*, (*law*) curat/eur, -rice *m.f.*; **~ful** *adj.*, **~ing** *adj.* confiant; **~fully** *adv.* avec confiance; **~worthy** *adj.* digne de confiance; **~y** *adj.* sûr, loyal.
truth *s.* (*what is true, reality*) vérité *f.*; (*loyalty*) sincérité *f.*; (*accuracy*) exactitude *f.*; (*techn.*) aplomb *m.*; **in ~,** en vérité; **to tell the ~,** à vrai dire; **to tell s.o. a few home ~s,** dire ses quatre vérités à qn.; GOSPEL **~**; **~ful** *adj.* sincère, vrai, fidèle; **~fully** *adv.**,*,*; **~fulness** *s.* (*of person*) sincérité *f.*, (*of statement*) véracité *f.*
try *s.* essai *m.*, tentative *f.*; (*rugby*) essai *m.*; *v.t.* & *i.* essayer, tenter (de); (*law*) juger; (*make demands on*) éprouver; **~ for,** essayer d'obtenir; **~ on,** essayer; **~-on** *s.* ballon d'essai *m.*; **~ it on with s.o.,** bluffer; **it's no use ~ing it on with me,** ça ne prend pas avec moi; **~ out,** essayer; **~-out** *s.* essai à fond *m.*; **~ing** *adj.* (*exhausting*) fatigant, (*annoying*): (*person*) agaçant, (*thing*) ennuyeux; **trier** *s.* personne qui tente l'expérience.
tryst *s.* rendez-vous *m.*
tsar, czar *s.* tsar *m.*
tsetse (**fly**) *s.* mouche tsé-tsé *f.*
T-shirt, T-square *see* T.
tub *s.* (*vessel*) baquet *m.*; (*mining*) berline *f.*; (*boat*) canot lourd *m.*; **~-thumper** *s.* orateur de carrefour *m.*; **~by** *adj.* rondelet.
tuba *s.* tuba *m.*
tub/e *s.* tube *m.*; (*of tyre*) chambre *f.* (à air); (*underground rail.*) métro *m.*; TEST-**~e**; **~ular** *adj.* tubulaire.
tuber *s.* tubercule *m.*; **~ous** *adj.* tubéreux.
tuber/cle *s.* tubercule *m.*; **~cular** *adj.*, **~culous** *adj.* tuberculeux; **~culin** *s.* tuberculine *f.*; **~culin test** *s.* tuberculination *f.* *or* tuberculinisation *f.*, *v.t.* tuberculiner *or* tuberculiniser; **~culin-tested** *adj.* tuberculinisé; **~culosis** *s.* tuberculose *f.*
tuberose *s.* tubéreuse *f.*
T.U.C. (*Trades Union Congress*) C.G.T. (Confédération générale du Travail) *f.* (*approx. equivalent*).
tuck *s.* **1.** (*in garment*) pli *m.*; **2.** (*pop. food*) mangeaille *f.*; *v.t.* (1) plisser; **~ in** *v.t.* fourrer, *v.i.* (2) bouffer; **~ up,** replier, retrousser; **~ up in bed,** border (qn., un lit); **~er** *s.* **best** BIB **and ~er.**

Tuesday *s.* mardi *m.*; SHROVE ~.
tuft *s.* touffe *f.*; (*of bird*) huppe *f.*; (*of hair*) toupet *m.*; **~ed** *adj.* (*birds*) huppé.
tug *s.* **1.** (*pull*) saccade *f.*; **2.** (*boat*) remorqueur *m.*; *v.t.* (1) tirer (fort); (2) remorquer; *v.i.* tirer sur; ~ **of war** *s.* lutte à la corde (de traction) *f.*
tuition *s.* enseignement *m.*
tulip *s.* tulipe *f.*; **~-tree** *s.* tulipier *m.*; **~-wood** *s.* bois de rose *m.*
tulle *s.* tulle *m.*
tumble *s.* (*fall*) chute *f.*; (*heap*) amas *m.*; *v.t.* & *i.* ((*cause to*) *fall*) (faire) tomber; (*roll, toss*) (s')agiter; (*overthrow*) renverser; (*disorder*) bouleverser; (*stumble*) trébucher; (*acrobat*) faire des culbutes; ~ **to** (*fig. pop.*) piger; **~down** *adj.* délabré; **~r** *s.* (*acrobat*) acrobate *m.*, (*glass*) verre *m.*, (*mech.*) culbuteur *m.*, (*pigeon*) pigeon culbutant *m.*; **~(r)-drier** *s.* essoreuse *f.*
tumbrel, -il *s.* tombereau *m.*
tumef/y *v.t.* & *i.* tuméfier; **~action** *s.* tuméfaction *f.*
tumid *adj.* (*med.*) enflé; (*fig.*) ampoulé.
tummy *s.* ventre *m.*
tumour *s.* tumeur *f.*
tumult *s.* tumulte *m.*; **~uous** *adj.* tumultueux; **~uously** *adv.**.
tumulus *s.* tumulus *m.*
tun *s.* tonne *f.*
tuna *s.* thon *m.*
tundra *s.* toundra *f.*
tune *s.* (*melody*) air *m.*; (*pitch*) accord *m.*; (*temper*) humeur *f.*; **in** ~, juste; **out of** ~, faux; **in** ~ **with** (*fig.*) en harmonie avec; **to call the** ~, mener la danse; **to change one's** ~ (*fig.*) changer de ton; **to** DANCE **to s.o.'s** ~; **to the** ~ **of,** pour la somme de; **~ful** *adj.* harmonieux; *v.t.* (*mus.*) accorder; (*mech., radio*) régler; ~ **in,** accorder sur; ~ **up,** s'accorder; **tuning-fork** *s.* accordoir *m.*, diapason *m.*; **~r** *s.* accordeur *m.*
tungsten *s.* tungstène *m.*
tunic *s.* tunique *f.*
Tunis *s.* (*geog.*) Tunis *f.*; **~ia** *s.* Tunisie *f.*; **~ian** *adj.* & *s.m.f.* tunisien(ne).
tunnel *s.* tunnel *m.*; *v.t.* & *i.* percer un tunnel (dans/sous).
tunny *s.* thon *m.*
turban *s.* turban *m.*
turbid *adj.* trouble.
turbine *s.* turbine *f.*
turbo- (*in combination*) **~-jet,** turboréacteur *m*; **~-prop(eller)** turbopropulseur *m.*
turbot *s.* turbot *m.*
turbulen/t *adj.* **1.** (*unruly*) turbulent; **2.** (*sea, etc.*) agité; **3.** (*disorderly*) indiscipliné; **~ce** *s.* (1) trouble *m.*; (2) agitation *f.*; (3) indiscipline *f.*
tureen *s.* soupière *f.*
turf *s.* gazon *m.*; (*one piece*) motte de gazon *f.*; (*peat*) tourbe *f.*; (*sport*) turf *m.*; *v.t.* gazonner.
turg/id *adj.* boursouflé; **~escence** *s.* (*med.*) turgescence *f.*; (*fig.*) boursouflure *f.*
Turk/ey *s.* (*geog.*) Turquie *f.*; ~ *s.m.f.* Turc, Turque; **~ish** *adj.* turc; *s.m.* (*lang.*) turc; **~ish bath** *s.* bain turc *m.*; **~ish delight** *s.* (rahat) loukoum *m.*
turkey *s.* dindon *m.*; dinde *f.*
turmoil *s.* agitation *f.*, trouble *m.*
turn[1] *s.* (*one rotation; coil; service; short walk; opportunity*) tour *m.*; (*change of direction*) détour *m.*; (*angle, bend*) tournant *m.*, virage *m.*; (*character, tendency*) penchant *m.*, disposition *f.*; (*of mind, of events*) tournure *f.*; (*fam. shock*) coup *m.*; (*theat.*) numéro *m.*; (*of tide*) changement *m.*; **in** ~, **by ~s,** à tour de rôle; **to take ~s at sth.,** faire qch. à tour de rôle; **to do a good** ~ **to s.o.,** rendre service à qn.
turn[2] *v.t.* & *i.* (*rotate; mech.*) tourner; (*give, take, new direction*) détourner, se tourner vers; (*change sides*) tourner casaque; (*change form, etc.*) (se) changer (*into*—en); (*become*) devenir; ~ RED, *etc.*; (*nauseate stomach*) (se) soulever; (*translate*) traduire (en); (*garment, ground*) retourner; ~ **the** TABLES **on**; ~ TURTLE; ~ **a** DEAF **ear to**; ~ **about** *v.t.* tourner (dans le sens opposé), *v.i.* se tourner, faire demi-tour; **~-about** *s.* (*fig.*) volte-face *f.*; ~ **aside** *v.t.* & *i.* (se) détourner (*from*—de); ~ **away** *v.t.* congédier, renvoyer; ~ **back** *v.t.* retourner, *v.i.* se retourner, rebrousser chemin; ~ **down** *v.t.* (*fold down*) rabattre, (*light, etc.*) baisser, (*reject*) repousser; ~ **in** *v.t.* replier, *v.i.* (*fam.*) se coucher; ~ **into** *v.t.* & *i.* (se) changer en; ~ **off** *v.t.* (*gas, tap, radio*) fermer, (*water*) couper, (*light*) éteindre, *v.i.* se détourner, (*road*) bifurquer; ~ **on** *v.i.* dépendre de; ~ **on** *v.t.* attaquer (qn.), se retourner contre, (*tap*) ouvrir, (*light*) allumer; ~ **out** *v.t.* expulser, (*produce*) fabriquer, (*empty*) vider, *v.i.* devenir, se révéler, tourner; **~-out** *s.* foule *f.*; ~ **over** *v.t.* & *i.* (se) retourner, (*page*) tourner, (*auto.*) capoter, ~ **over a new** LEAF; **~over** *s.* (*cook.*) chausson *m.*, (*comm.*) chiffre d'affaires *m.*; ~ **round** *v.t.* & *i.* (se) retourner; ~ **to,** se tourner vers, s'adresser à (qn.), avoir recours à (qch.); ~ **up** *v.t.* retourner, relever, (*sleeves*) retrousser, *v.i.* se retrousser, (*fam.*) arriver, se présenter; ~ **up** TRUMPS; **~-up** *s.* revers *m.*; ~ **upside down,** renverser, mettre sens dessus dessous; **~coat** *s.* renégat *m.*; **~key** *s.* porte-clefs *m.invar.*; **~pike** *s.* barrière à péage *f.*; **~stile** *s.* tourniquet *m.*; **~table** *s.* (*rail.*) plaque tournante *f.*, (*record player*) tourne-disques *m.invar.*; **~er** *s.* tourneur *m.*; **~ing** *s.* tournant *m.*, virage *m.*; **~ing-point** *s.* (*fig.*) moment décisif *m.*
turnip *s.* navet *m.*
turpentine *s.* térébenthine *f.*; **~-tree** *s.* térébinthe *m.*
turpitude *s.* turpitude *f.*
turquoise *s.* turquoise *f.*; ~ **blue,** bleu turquoise *invar.*
turret *s.* tourelle *f.*
turtle *s.* (*bird*) tourterelle *f.*; (*tortoise*) tortue de mer *f.*; MOCK ~; **to turn** ~, chavirer; **~-necked sweater,** pull ras-de-cou, (=*polo-necked*) à col roulé.
Tuscan/y *s.* (*geog.*) Toscane *f.*; ~ *adj.* & *s.m.f.* toscan(e).
tush *interj.* peuh!
tusk *s.* défense *f.*
tussle *s.* bagarre *f.*; *v.i.* se bagarrer.
tussock *s.* touffe *f.*
tussore *s.* tussor *m.*
tut *interj.* ta, ta, ta!
tutel/age *s.* tutelle *f.*; **~ary** *adj.* tutélaire.
tutor *s.* (*private*) précepteur *m.*; ⚠ tuteur = **legal guardian**; *v.t.* instruire; **~ial** *s.* groupe d'études *m.*, *adj.* de précepteur.
T.V. (*abbrev. television*) télé *f.*
twaddle *s.* fariboles *f.pl.*
twain *s.* les deux *m.pl.*
twang *s.* son vibrant *m.*; **to speak with a** ~, nasiller; *v.t.* & *i.* (faire) résonner; (*pej.*) gratter de.
tweak *v.t.* pincer.
tweed *s.* tweed *m.*
tweezers *s.* pince *f.sing.*
twelfth *adj.* & *s.* douzième; **T~-night,** fête des Rois *f.*
twelve *adj.* & *s.* douze; **~month** *s.* une année *f.*, *adj.* d'une année.
twent/y *adj.* & *s.m.* vingt; **~ieth,** vingtième.
twerp *s.* (*pop.*) idiot *m.*
twice *adv.* deux fois.
twiddle *v.t.* tortiller, jouer avec; ~ **one's** THUMBS.
twig *s.* brindille *f.*; *v.t.* & *i.* (*pop.*) piger.
twilight *s.* crépuscule *m.*; *adj.* crépusculaire.

twill *s.* croisé *m.*
twin *s.* jumeau *m.*, jumelle *f.*; **Siamese ~s,** frères *or* sœurs siamois(es) *m.f.pl.*; (*astron.*) les Gémeaux *m.pl.*; *adj.* jumelé; *v.t.* jumeler; **~ set** *s.* twin-set *m.*; **~ning** *s.* jumelage *m.*
twine *s.* ficelle *f.*; *v.t.* & *i.* (s')entrelacer, (s') enrouler.
twinge *s.* (*med.*) élancement *m.*; (*fig.*) brûlure *f.*
twinkl/e *s.* & **~ing** *s.* scintillement *m.*, pétillement *m.*; **with a ~e in his eye,** les yeux brillants de malice; *v.i.* scintiller; (*fig.*) pétiller.
twirl *s.* tournoiement *m.*; (*of smoke, etc.*) volute *f.*; (*dance*) pirouette *f.*; *v.t.* faire tournoyer, tortiller; *v.i.* pirouetter.
twist *s.* (*being ~ed*) torsion *f.*; (*tendency*) tournure *f.*, tendance *f.*; (*strain*) foulure *f.*; (*thread*) cordonnet *m.*; (*of tobacco*) carotte *f.*; (*of paper, etc.*) cornet *m.*; *v.t.* tordre (en spirale); (*wrench*) déformer; (*ankle, etc.*) se fouler (la cheville, etc.); *v.i.* s'enrouler, s'entortiller, se tordre; (*road, river*) serpenter; TONGUE-**~er.**
twit *s.* (*pop.*) imbécile *m.*; *v.t.* reprocher (*s.o. with sth.*—qch. à qn.).
twitch *s.* (*of hands*) crispation *f.*; (*of face*) tic *m.*; *v.t.* tirer; *v.i.* se crisper.
twitter *s.* gazouillement *m.*; *v.i.* gazouiller.
two *adj.* & *s.m.* deux; **~fold** *adj.* double, *adv.* doublement; **~-edged** *adj.* à deux tranchants; **~-faced** *adj.* à double face; **~-handed** *adj.* à deux mains; **~-piece** *s.* deux-pièces *m.*; **~-ply** *adj.* double; **~-seater** *s.* voiture à deux places *f.*; **~-stroke engine** *s.* moteur à deux temps *m.*; **~-time** *v.t.* (*pop.*) duper; **~-way** *adj.* à deux sens; **~-wheeler** *s.* deux-roues *m.sing.*
tycoon *s.* magnat *m.*
tympanum *s.* tympan *m.*
typ/e *s.* (*specimen, class, model*) type *m.*; (*print.*) caractères d'imprimerie *n.pl.*; **~escript** *s.* texte dactylographié *m.*; **~e-setter** *s.* compositeur *m.*; **~ewriter** *s.* machine à écrire *f.*; **~e-written** *adj.* dactylographié; **~ical** *adj.* typique; **~ify** *v.t.* symboliser, être le type de; **~ist** *s.* dactylo (graphe) *m.f.*; **~ographer** *s.* typographe *m.f.*; **~ography** *s.* typographie *f.*; **~ographical** *adj.* typographique; *v.t.* & *i.* (*typify*) représenter; (*classify*) classer; (*write*) taper à la machine.
typhoid *s.* typhoïde *f.*
typhoon *s.* typhon *m.*
typhus *s.* typhus *m.*
tyran/t *s.* tyran *m.*; **~nical** *adj.* tyrannique; **~ically** *adv.**; **~nize** *v.t.* tyranniser; *v.i.* agir en tyran; **~nous** *adj.* tyrannique; **~ny** *s.* tyrannie *f.*
tyre *s.* pneu *m.*
tyro *s. see* TIRO.
Tyrol *s.* (*geog.*) Tyrol *m.*; **~ean** *adj.* & *s.m.f.* tyrolien(ne).
tzar *s. see* TSAR.

U

U *adj.* (*fam. upper class*) sélect, distingué; **that's non-U,** cela n'est pas sélect, cela manque de distinction.
ubiquit/ous *adj.* omniprésent; **~y** *s.* ubiquité *f.*
U-boat *s.* sous-marin (allemand) *m.*
udder *s.* mamelle *f.*
U.D.I. (*abbrev. unilateral declaration of independence*) proclamation unilatérale d'indépendance *f.*
U.F.O. (*abbrev. unidentified flying object*) O.V.N.I. (objet volant non identifié) *m.*
Uganda *s.* (*geog.*) Ouganda *f.*; **~n** *adj.* & *s.m.f.* ougandais(e).
ugl/y *adj.* laid; (*fig.*) dangereux; (*abusive*) vilain; **~y** DUCKLING; **~iness** *s.* laideur *f.*
U.H.F. (*abbrev. ultra-high frequency*) à très haute fréquence.
U.K. (*abbrev. United Kingdom*) R.U. (Royaume-Uni) *m.*
ukase *s.* ukase *m.*
Ukrain/e *s.* (*geog.*) Ukraine *f.*; **~ian** *adj.* & *s.m.f.* ukrainien(ne).
ukulele *s.* ukulélé *m.*
ulcer *s.* (*lit.* & *fig.*) ulcère *m.*; **~ate** *v.t.* & *i.* (s')ulcérer; **~ation** *s.* ulcération *f.*; **~ed** *adj.* ulcéré; **~ous** *adj.* ulcéreux.
ullage *s.* vidange *f.*; (*customs*) manquant *m.*
Ulster *s.* (*geog.*) Ulster *m.*; (*obs. overcoat u~*) ulster *m.*
ulterior *adj.* ultérieur; (*motive*) inavoué.
ultimate *adj.* dernier, ultime; (*fundamental*) fondamental; **~ly** *adv.* finalement.
ultimatum *s.* ultimatum *m.*
ultra- (*in combination*) **~marine,** outremer; **~-modern** *adj.* ultramoderne; **~montane** *adj.* ultramontain; **~sonic** *adj.* ultrasonique; **~-violet** *adj.* ultraviolet.
ululat/e *v.i.* ululer; **~ion** *s.* ululement *m.*
umbel *s.* ombelle *f.*; **~late** *adj.* ombellé; **~liferous** *adj.* ombellifère.
umber *s.* terre d'ombre *f.*; *adj.* couleur d'ombre.
umbilical *adj.* ombilical; **~ cord** *s.* cordon ombilical *m.*
umbra *s.* (*astron.*) ombre *f.*
umbrage *s.* (*poet.* = *shade*; *mod.* = *offence*) ombrage *m.*; **to give, to take ~,** porter, prendre, ombrage; **~ous** *adj.* ombragé.
umbrella *s.* parapluie *m.*; (*fig.*) protection *f.*; (*aviat.*) écran de protection *m.*; ⚠ ombrelle = **sunshade.**
umpire *s.* arbitre *m.*; *v.t.* & *i.* arbitrer.
umpteen *adj.* je ne sais combien (de).

---

un- *prefix. In view of the almost unlimited possibility, in English, of composing words with the prefix un-, only some of the more common compounds can be given here. It should be noted that the same possibility does not exist in French. The following indications may be helpful:—* **1.** *adj.* il- (illimité); in- (inattendu); im- (impitoyable); ir- (irréprochable). *But it is important to remember that these prefixes cannot be used at will to form words, as with un- in English. It is advisable to cross-check any such word, which does not appear below, in the French–English dictionary. Also* non + *adj.* (*usu. part.*) non préparé (**unprepared**); sans + *inf.* sans broncher (**unflinching**); *or use the relevant positive adj.* pur (**unblemished**); *or* peu + *adj.* peu intéressant (**uninteresting**); *or* mal + *adj.* malpropre (**unclean**); **2.** *adv. as for adj.*; **3.** *verb. the most common negative prefix is* dé-, défaire (**undo**); **4.** *s. sometimes the same prefix as adj.* irréalité (**unreality**), *or use* manque de + *s.*

U.N. (*abbrev. United Nations*) O.N.U. (Organisation Nations Unies) *f.*
unabashed *adj.* impassible; *adv.* sans se déconcerter.
unabated *adj.* (*undiminished*) non diminué; (*unweakened*) non affaibli; *adv.* sans répit.
unable *adj.* incapable; **to be ~ to do sth.** (*inability*) ne pas pouvoir faire qch.; (*impossibility*) être dans l'impossibilité de faire qch.; (*inadequacy*) ne pas être en mesure de faire qch.

unabridged *adj.* non abrégé, intégral.
unaccented *adj.* non accentué.
unacceptable *adj.* inacceptable, inadmissible.
unaccompanied *adj.* non accompagné, seul.
unaccountabl/e *adj.* **1.** (*person not accountable*) qui ne doit de comptes à personne; **2.** (*strange*) inexplicable; **~y** *adv.* (2)*.
unaccustomed *adj.* inaccoutumé, peu habituel; **~ to,** peu habitué à.
unacknowledged *adj.* non reconnu; (*letter*) resté sans réponse.
unacquainted *adj.* ignorant (*with*—de); qui n'est pas au courant (de); **to be ~ with,** ignorer (qch.); ne pas connaître (qn.).
unadorned *adj.* sans ornements, naturel; (*fig.*) sans fard.
unadulterated *adj.* non frelaté, pur.
unadvisable *adj.* imprudent, à déconseiller.
unadvisedly *adv.* imprudemment.
unaffected *adj.* (*resistant to*) qui résiste à; (*untouched*) insensible (*by*—à); (*plain, sincere*) naturel, sincère; *adv.* sans affectation.
unaided *adj.* & *adv.* sans aide, seul.
unalarmed *adj.* sans inquiétude, calme.
unalienable *adj.* (*law*) inaliénable.
unalloyed *adj.* sans mélange, pur.
unalterable *adj.* immuable.
unaltered *adj.* inchangé.
unambitious *adj.* peu ambitieux.
unamiable *adj.* peu aimable; **~ness** *s.* manque d'amabilité *m.*
unanim/ity *s.* unanimité *f.*; **~ous** *adj.* unanime; **~ously** *adv.* à l'unanimité.
unanswer/able *adj.* irréfutable; **~ed** *adj.* sans réponse.
unapparent *adj.* peu évident.
unappealing *adj.* déplaisant.
unappeased *adj.* inapaisé.
unappetizing *adj.* peu appétissant.
unappreciat/ed *adj.* méconnu; **~ive** *adj.* insensible (*of*—à).
unapproachable *adj.* inaccessible; (*person*) inabordable.
unappropriated *adj.* disponible, sans destination précise.
unarmed *adj.* sans armes.
unashamed *adj.* sans honte; **~ly** *adv.* sans rougir.
unasked *adj.* non demandé, non invité, sans être invité.
unassailable *adj.* inattaquable.
unassisted *adj.* & *adv.* sans aide.
unassuming *adj.* sans prétentions.
unattached *adj.* non attaché; (*mil.*) disponible; (*disengaged*) libre; (*not married*) seul.
unattainable *adj.* inaccessible (*by*—à).
unattended *adj.* seul, sans escorte, sans suite; (*neglected*) négligé.
unattractive *adj.* peu attirant.
unauthorized *adj.* non autorisé, sans autorisation.
unavailable *adj.* non disponible.
unavailing *adj.* inutile, infructueux.
unavoidabl/e *adj.* inévitable; **~y** *adv.**.
unaware *adj.* ignorant (de); **to be ~ of,** ignorer; **~s** *adv.* (*unexpectedly*) à l'improviste; (*by surprise*) au dépourvu.
unbalanced *adj.* déséquilibré.
unbearabl/e *adj.* insupportable; **~y** *adv.**.
unbeat/en *adj.* non battu; **~able** *adj.* invincible.
unbecoming *adj.* malséant, inconvenant; (*clothes*) peu seyant.
unbeknown *adj.* inconnu (*to*—de); *adv.* **~ to,** à l'insu de.
unbelief *s.* manque de foi *m.*; (*incredulity*) incrédulité *f.*
unbelievabl/e *adj.* incroyable; **~y** *adv.**.
unbeliever *s.* incroyant *m.*, incrédule *m.f.*
unbend *v.t.* & *i.* (*lit.* & *fig.*) (se) détendre; (*fig. fam.*) se dégeler; **~ing** *adj.* inflexible.
unbiased *adj.* impartial.
unbidden *adj.* non invité; (*spontaneous*) spontané; *adv.* spontanément.
unbind *v.t.* délier.
unbleached *adj.* écru.
unblemished *adj.* sans tache, pur.
unblushing *adj.* éhonté; **~ly** *adv.* sans rougir.
unbolt *v.t.* déverrouiller.
unborn *adj.* à naître, futur.
unbosom oneself *v.refl.* ouvrir son cœur.
unbound *adj.* délié; (*book*) broché; **~ed** *adj.* démesuré, sans bornes.
unbreakable *adj.* incassable.
unbridled *adj.* débridé.
unbroken *adj.* (*whole*) intact; (*unsurpassed*) non battu; (*uninterrupted*) ininterrompu; (*horse*) non dressé.
unbrotherly *adj.* peu fraternel.
unbuckle *v.t.* déboucler.
unburden *v.t.* décharger; **~ oneself,** se confier (à).
unbusinesslike *adj.* dépourvu de sens commercial; (*untidy*) qui manque de méthode.
unbutton *v.t.* déboutonner.
uncalled-for *adj.* déplacé; injustifié.
uncann/y *adj.* surnaturel, mystérieux; **~ily** *adv.**,*.
uncared-for *adj.* négligé.
unceasing *adj.* incessant; **~ly** *adv.* sans cesse.
unceremonious *adj.* **1.** (*informal*) peu cérémonieux; **2.** (*off-hand*) sans façons; **~ly** *adv.* (1) sans cérémonie; (2) sans gêne.
uncertain *adj.* (≠ *certain*) incertain, douteux; (*unreliable*) peu sûr; (*changeable*) variable, hésitant; **~ly** *adv.* d'une façon incertaine; **~ty** *s.* incertitude *f.*
unchangeabl/e *adj.* immuable; **~y** *adv.**.
unchang/ing *adj.* invariable; **~ed** *adj.* inchangé.
uncharitabl/e *adj.* peu charitable; **~y** *adv.**.
unchecked *adj.* (*unhindered*) non réprimé; (*unverified*) non vérifié.
uncircumcised *adj.* incirconcis.
uncivil *adj.* impoli.
uncivilised *adj.* non-civilisé.
unclaimed *adj.* non réclamé; (*goods*) laissé pour compte.
unclasp *v.t.* (*hook*) dégrafer; (*release*) déserrer.
unclassified *adj.* non classé.
uncle *s.* oncle *m.*; GREAT **~**; **at ~'s** (*pop.*) chez ma tante.
unclean *adj.* malpropre; **~ness** *s.* malpropreté *f.*
unclothe *v.t.* déshabiller.
uncoil *v.t.* & *i.* (se) dérouler.
uncoloured *adj.* incolore.
uncomfortabl/e *adj.* (*person*) mal à l'aise; (*chair, etc.*) peu confortable; **~y** *adv.* peu confortablement; (*fig.*) fâcheusement, désagréablement.
uncommon *adj.* peu commun, rare; **~ly** *adv.* remarquablement.
uncommunicative *adj.* peu communicatif.
uncomplaining *adj.* qui ne se plaint pas, résigné; **~ly** *adv.* sans se plaindre.
uncomplimentary *adj.* peu flatteur.
uncompromising *adj.* intransigeant.
unconcern *s.* insouciance *f.*; (*indifference*) indifférence *f.*; **~ed** *adj.* sans inquiétude; indifférent; **~edly** *adv.* avec insouciance; avec indifférence.
unconditional *adj.* inconditionnel; **~ly** *adv.**.
unconfined *adj.* illimité.
unconfirmed *adj.* non confirmé.
uncongenial *adj.* (*person*) peu sympathique; (*work, etc.*) désagréable.
unconnected *adj.* sans rapport (avec), décousu.
unconquerable *adj.* invincible.

unconscionable *adj.* (*unscrupulous*) peu scrupuleux; (*unreasonable*) déraisonnable; (*inordinate*) exorbitant.
unconscious *s.* inconscient *m.*; *adj.* (*unaware of*) sans conscience de; (*not conscious*) sans connaissance; (*done* **~***ly*) inconscient; **~ly** *adv.* inconsciemment, sans se rendre compte; **~ness** *s.* inconscience *f.*; évanouissement *m.*
unconsidered *adj.* (*rash*) irréfléchi; (*unimportant*) insignifiant.
unconstitutional *adj.* inconstitutionnel; **~ly** *adv.**.
uncontested *adj.* incontesté.
uncontrollabl/e *adj.* irrésistible; indomptable; (*child*) indiscipliné; **~y** *adv.**;*, de façon indisciplinée.
unconventional *adj.* peu conventionnel.
unconvert/ed *adj.* non converti; **~ible** *adj.* inconvertible.
unconvinc/ed *adj.* non convaincu; **~ing** *adj.* peu convaincant.
uncooked *adj.* non cuit, cru.
unco-operative *adj.* individualiste, peu prêt à contribuer à l'effort commun.
uncork *v.t.* déboucher.
uncorrected *adj.* non corrigé.
uncouple *v.t.* découpler.
uncouth *adj.* **1.** (*ill-mannered*) gauche; **2.** (*vulgar*) grossier; **~ness** *s.* (1) gaucherie *f.*; (2) grossièreté *f.*
uncover *v.t.* & *i.* (se) découvrir; (*fig.*) dévoiler.
uncritical *adj.* peu critique.
uncrossed *adj.* (*cheque*) non barré.
UNCTAD (*abbrev. United Nations Conference on Trade & Development*) C.N.U.C.E.D. (Conférence des Nations Unies pour le Commerce et le Développement) *f.*
unct/ion *s.* (*lit.* & *fig.*) onction *f.*; **~uous** *adj.* onctueux; **~uousness** *s.* onctuosité *f.*
uncultivated *adj.* (*land*) inculte; (*person*) sans culture.
uncurtailed *adj.* non abrégé.
uncut *adj.* (*book*) non rogné.
undamaged *adj.* indemne, en bon état.
undated *adj.* sans date.
undaunted *adj.* intrépide; *adv.**.
undeceive *v.t.* détromper, désabuser.
undecided *adj.* indécis.
undecipherable *adj.* indéchiffrable.
undefended *adj.* sans défense; (*law*) non défendu.
undefiled *adj.* sans tache.
undefin/ed *adj.* indéterminé; **~able** *adj.* indéfinissable.
undemanding *adj.* peu exigeant.
undemonstrative *adj.* peu expansif, réservé.
undeniabl/e *adj.* incontestable; **~y** *adv.**.
under *adj.* de dessous, inférieur; (*dose*) insuffisant; *adv.* au-dessous, en-dessous; *see* GO **~**; KEEP **~**, *etc.*; *prep.* (*below*) sous, au-dessous de; (*in accordance with*; *in the time of*) sous; (*inferior to, subject to, bound by*) sous, subordonné à; **~ age** *adj.* mineur; **~ the circumstances,** dans les circonstances; **~ examination,** à l'examen; **~ repair,** en réparation; **~most** *adj.* le plus en-dessous; *prefix* (*in combination*) sous- (*see below*).
underarm *adv.* par en-dessous.
underbid *v.i.* faire une offre inférieure (à celle de qn.).
undercarriage *s.* (*aviat.*) train d'atterrissage *m.*
underclothes *s.pl.* & **~clothing** *s.* sous--vêtements *m.pl.*
undercoat *s.* (*paint*) première couche *f.*
undercover *adj.* clandestin.
undercurrent *s.* courant sous-marin *m.*; (*fig.*) courant *m.*
undercut *s.* (*cook.*) filet *m.*; *v.t.* prendre/vendre moins cher (que qn.).
underdeveloped *adj.* sous-développé; (*countries*) en voie de développement.
underdog *s.* le plus faible *m.*
underdone *adj.* pas assez cuit; (*meat*) saignant.
underestimate *s.* sous-estimation *f.*; *v.t.* sous--estimer.
underexpose *v.t.* (*photo.*) sous-exposer.
underfed *adj.* sous-alimenté.
underfoot *adv.* sous les pieds.
undergarment *s.* sous-vêtement *m.*
undergo *v.t.* subir.
undergraduate *s.* étudiant(e) *m.f.*; *adj.* estudiantin, étudiant.
underground *s.* (*rail.*) métro *m.*; (*polit.*) résistance *f.*; *adj.* souterrain; (*secret*) clandestin; *adv.* sous terre.
undergrowth *s.* sous-bois *m.*
underhand *adj.* clandestin; (*person*) sournois; *adv.* en sous-main; sournoisement.
underline *v.t.* souligner.
underling *s.* subalterne *m.*
underlying *adj.* sous-jacent; (*fig.*) latent, caché.
undermine *v.t.* (*lit.* & *fig.*) miner.
underneath *adv.* en-dessous; *prep.* sous.
underpants *s.* caleçon *m.sing.*, slip *m.sing.*
under-part *s.* dessous *m.*
underpass *s.* passage souterrain *m.*
underpay *v.t.* mal rétribuer.
underpin, ~prop *v.t.* étayer.
underprivileged *adj.* défavorisé.
underproduction *s.* sous-production *f.*
underrate *v.t.* sous-estimer.
undersell *v.t.* vendre moins cher (que qn).
undersigned *adj.* soussigné.
undersized *adj.* rabougri.
understand *v.t.* & *i.* (*comprehend*) comprendre; (*know how to deal with*) s'entendre à; (*infer*) sous-entendre; (*take for granted*) convenir; **~able** *adj.* compréhensible; **~ing** *s.* compréhension *f.*, (*intelligence*) intelligence *f.*, (*agreement*) entente *f.*, accord *m.*, (*sympathy*) compréhension *f.*; **~ing** *adj.* compréhensif, intelligent.
understate *v.t.* atténuer en exposant; **~ment** *s.* atténuation des faits *f.*; euphémisme *m.*
understudy *s.* doublure *f.*; *v.t.* doubler.
undertak/e *v.t.* (*bind oneself to*) s'engager à; (*engage in*) entreprendre; (*promise*) promettre; (*guarantee*) garantir; **~er** *s.* entrepreneur de pompes funèbres *m.*; **~ing** *s.* entreprise *f.*, engagement *m.*
undertone *s.* ton atténué *m.*; (*fig.*) courant *m.*
undertow *s.* ressac *m.*
undervalue *v.t.* sous-évaluer; déprécier (qn.)
underwater *adj.* sous-marin.
underwear *s.* sous-vêtements *m.pl.*
underworld *s.* (*myth.*) les enfers *m.pl.*; (*of society*) bas-fonds *m.pl.*, le milieu *m.*
underwrit/e *v.t.* souscrire; **~er** *s.* assureur *m.*; **~ing** *s.* assurance *f.*
undeserv/ed *adj.* immérité; **~edly** *adv.* injustement; **~ing** *adj.* (*person*) peu méritant; (*thing*) peu méritoire.
undesigned *adj.* involontaire; **~ly** *adv.**.
undesirable *adj.* (*person*) indésirable; (*thing*) peu souhaitable.
undeterred *adj.* non ébranlé; *adv.* sans broncher.
undeveloped *adj.* non-développé, sous-développé.
undeviating *adj.* direct, constant.
undigested *adj.* non digéré, mal digéré.
undignified *adj.* peu digne, sans dignité.
undiluted *adj.* non dilué.
undiplomatic *adj.* peu diplomatique.
undischarged *adj.* non libéré; (*bankrupt*) non réhabilité; (*debt*) non acquitté.
undisciplined *adj.* indiscipliné.
undiscriminating *adj.* peu judicieux.
undisguised *adj.* non déguisé, franc, ouvert.

undismayed *adj.* & *adv.* sans peur.
undisputed *adj.* incontesté.
undistinguished *adj.* indiscernable (de); (*mediocre*) médiocre, sans distinction.
undisturbed *adj.* paisible, tranquille; *adv.**,*.
undivided *adj.* non divisé, entier, complet; (*law*) indivis.
undo *v.t.* défaire; (*annul*) annuler; (*unfasten*) dénouer; (*open*) ouvrir.
undone *adj.* (*unfinished*) inachevé; (*untied, opened*) défait, déficelé, ouvert; (*fig.*) perdu.
undoubted *adj.* indubitable, certain; **~ly** *adv.**,*.
undreamed of *adj.* inimaginé, qui dépasse l'imagination.
undress *s.* déshabillé *m.*; *v.t.* & *i.* (se) déshabiller.
undrinkable *adj.* imbuvable.
undu/e *adj.* (*attention*) excessif; (*demand*) injuste; (*reward*) immérité; **~ly** *adv.* excessivement.
undulat/e *v.i.* onduler; **~ing** *adj.* ondulé; (*country*) accidenté; **~ion** *s.* ondulation *f.*
undutiful *adj.* irrespectueux.
undying *adj.* immortel.
unearned *adj.* immérité; **~ income,** revenus d'un capital investi *m.pl.*
unearth *v.t.* déterrer; **~ly** *adj.* surnaturel; (*fam.*) infernal.
uneas/e *s.* **1.** (*discomfort*) malaise *f.*, gêne *f.*; **2.** (*anxiety*) inquiétude *f.*; **~ily** *adv.* (1) difficilement; (2) avec inquiétude; **~iness** *s. as* **~e** (1), (2); **~y** *adj.* (1) mal à l'aise, gêné; (2) inquiet; (*situation*) difficile, gênant.
uneatable *adj.* immangeable.
uneconomic(al) *adj.* peu économique, non rémunérateur.
unedifying *adj.* peu édifiant.
uneducated *adj.* illettré, sans instruction.
unemploy/ed *adj.* (*thing*) inemployé; (*person*) sans travail; **~ed person** *s.* chômeur *m.*; **the ~ed** *s.pl.* les chômeurs *m.pl.*; **~able** *adj.* (*thing*) inutilisable; (*person*) inapte; **~ment** *s.* chômage *m.*
unending *adj.* interminable; **~ly** *adv.**.
unendurable *adj.* intolérable.
unengaged *adj.* libre.
un-English *adj.* peu anglais.
unenjoyable *adj.* désagréable.
unenterprising *adj.* peu entreprenant.
unenviable *adj.* peu enviable.
unequal *adj.* inégal; **to be ~ to** (*fig.*) ne pas être à la hauteur de; **~led** *adj.* inégalé; **~ly** *adv.**.
unequivocal *adj.* sans équivoque; **~ly** *adv.* carrément.
unerring *adj.* infaillible.
UNESCO (**Unesco**) (*abbrev. United Nations Educational, Scientific and Cultural Organization*) Unesco *m.*
unethical *adj.* immoral; **~ly** *adv.**.
uneven *adj.* inégal, irrégulier; (*ground*) accidenté; (*no.*) impair; **~ly** *adv.**,*; **~ness** *s.* inégalité *f.*
uneventful *adj.* tranquille, sans incidents.
unexceptionable *adj.* irréprochable.
unexpected *adj.* inattendu; **~ly** *adv.* à l'improviste.
unexplored *adj.* inexploré.
unexpressed *adj.* inexprimé.
unfading *adj.* impérissable.
unfailing *adj.* inépuisable; (*fig.*) infaillible.
unfair *adj.* injuste; (*competition, etc.*) déloyal; (*wages*) inéquitable; **~ly** *adv.**;*;*; **~ness** *s.* injustice *f.*; déloyauté *f.*
unfaithful *adj.* infidèle; **~ly** *adv.**; **~ness** *s.* infidélité *f.*
unfamiliar *adj.* peu familier, étranger, inaccoutumé; **~ity** *s.* étrangeté *f.*
unfashionable *adj.* démodé.
unfasten *v.t.* détacher, ouvrir.
unfathomable *adj.* insondable.
unfavourabl/e *adj.* défavorable; **~y** *adv.**.
unfeeling *adj.* insensible.
unfeigned *adj.* sincère; **~ly** *adv.**.
unfilial *adj.* peu digne d'un fils.
unfinished *adj.* inachevé.
unfit *adj.* **1.** (*unsuitable*) peu propre (*for*—à), incapable (*to*—de); **2.** (*sick*) souffrant; **to be ~,** être souffrant; **~ness** *s.* (1) incapacité *f.*; (2) faiblesse *f.*; **~ting** *adj.* peu convenable.
unflagging *adj.* infatigable.
unflattering *adj.* peu flatteur.
unflinching *adj.* impassible; *adv.* sans broncher.
unfold *v.t.* & *i.* (*open out*) déplier (se) dérouler; (*reveal*) (se) révéler; (*develop*) (se) développer.
unforced *adj.* libre, spontané.
unforesee/n *adj.* imprévu; **~able** *adj.* imprévisible.
unforgettable *adj.* inoubliable.
unforgivable *adj.* impardonnable.
unfortified *adj.* (*town*) ouvert.
unfortunate *adj.* malheureux; (*event*) fâcheux; **~ly** *adv.**.
unfounded *adj.* sans fondement.
unfreeze *v.t.* & *i.* (faire) fondre, dégeler.
unfrequented *adj.* peu fréquenté.
unfriendl/y *adj.* inamical; **~iness** *s.* inimitié *f.*
unfrock *v.t.* défroquer.
unfruitful *adj.* stérile; (*fig.*) infructueux; **~ness** *s.* stérilité *f.*
unfulfilled *adj.* (*desire, etc.*) inassouvi; (*condition*) non rempli.
unfurl *v.t.* déployer.
unfurnished *adj.* non meublé.
ungainl/y *adj.* gauche; **~iness** *s.* gaucherie *f.*
ungentlemanly *adj.* mal élevé.
unget-at-able *adj.* inaccessible.
ungodly *adj.* & *s.m.f.* impie.
ungovernable *adj.* (*country, etc.*) ingouvernable; (*fig.*) irrépressible.
ungraceful *adj.* disgracieux; **~ly** *adv.**.
ungracious *adj.* peu aimable; **~ly** *adv.* sans amabilité; **~ness** *s.* manque d'amabilité *m.*
ungrateful *adj.* ingrat; **~ly** *adv.* avec ingratitude; **~ness** *s.* ingratitude *f.*
ungrounded *adj.* sans fondement.
ungrudgingly *adv.* de bon cœur.
unguarded *adj.* non gardé; (*moment*) d'inadvertance; (*fig.*) impudent.
unguent *s.* onguent *m.*
unguided *adj.* sans guide, tout seul.
ungulate *adj.* & *s.m.* ongulé.
unhallowed *adj.* profane.
unhand *v.t.* lâcher.
unhapp/y *adj.* malheureux; **~ily** *adv.**; **~iness** *s.* malheur *m.*
unharmed *adj.* indemne, sain et sauf.
unhealth/y *adj.* **1.** (*diseased*) maladif; **2.** (*harmful to health*) insalubre; **3.** (*unwholesome*) malsain; **~ily** *adv.* (1)*; (3) de façon malsaine; **~iness** *s.* (1) mauvaise santé *f.*; (2) insalubrité *f.*
unheard-of *adj.* inouï.
unheeded *adj.* (*not noticed*) inaperçu; (*not attended to*) négligé.
unhelpful *adj.* peu secourable.
unhesitatingly *adv.* sans hésitation.
unhinge *v.t.* démonter; (*fig. fam.*) déséquilibrer.
unholy *adj.* (*profane*) profane; (*person*) impie; (*fam.*) infernal.
unhook *v.t.* (*unfasten*) dégrafer; (*remove from hook*) décrocher.
unhoped-for *adj.* inespéré.
unhurt *adj.* indemne, sain et sauf.
uni- (*in combination*) **~cameral** *adj.* n'ayant qu'une seule chambre (législative); **~cellular** *adj.* unicellulaire; **~lateral** *adj.* unilatéral.

UNICEF (*abbrev. United Nations Children's Emergency Fund*) Unicef *m.*
unicorn *s.* licorne *f.*
UNIDO (*abbrev. United Nations Industrial Development Organization*) ONUDI *f.* (Organisation des Nations Unies pour le Développement Industriel).
uniform *adj.* & *s.m.* uniforme; **~ity** *s.* uniformité *f.*; **~ly** *adv.* uniformément.
unif/y *v.t.* unifier; **~ication** *s.* unification *f.*
unimagin/able *adj.* inimaginable; **~ative** *adj.* peu imaginatif.
unimpaired *adj.* intact.
unimpeded *adj.* & *adv.* sans obstacle.
unimportant *adj.* peu important, sans importance.
unimpressive *adj.* peu impressionnant.
uninformed *adj.* (*not aware of sth.*) ignorant (de); (*uneducated*) sans instruction.
uninhabit/able *adj.* inhabitable; ⚠ *Eng. inhabitable* = habitable; **~ed** *adj.* inhabité.
uninhibited *adj.* sans inhibitions.
uninitiated *adj.* non initié.
uninjured *adj.* indemne.
uninspir/ed *adj.* sans inspiration; **~ing** *adj.* plat.
unintellig/ent *adj.* inintelligent; **~ible** *adj.* inintelligible.
unintentional *adj.* involontaire; **~ly** *adv.**.
uninterest/ing *adj.* peu intéressant, sans intérêt; **~ed** *adj.* désintéressé.
uninterrupted *adj.* ininterrompu; **~ly** *adv.* sans interruption.
uninvit/ed *adj.* non invité; **~ing** *adj.* peu attirant.
union *s.* union *f.*; TRADE ~; **U~ Jack** *s.* pavillon britannique *m.*; **~ist** *s.* unioniste *m.f.*, TRADE-**~ist.**
unique *adj.* unique; **~ly** *adv.**.
unison *s.* unisson *m.*; **in ~,** à l'unisson.
unit *s.* unité *f.*; SINK ~; **~arian** *s.* Unitarien *m.*
unit/e *v.t.* & *i.* (s')unir; **~ed** *adj.* uni; **~edly** *adv.* ensemble; **~y** *s.* unité *f.*, (*harmony*) union *f.*
universal *adj.* universel; **~ity** *s.* universalité *f.*; **~ly** *adv.**.
universe *s.* univers *m.*
university *s.* université *f.*; *adj.* universitaire.
unjust *adj.* injuste; **~ly** *adv.**; **~ifiable** *adj.* injustifiable; **~ifiability** *adv.**.
unkempt *adj.* dépeigné, hirsute.
unkind *adj.* peu aimable; **~ly** *adv.* sans amabilité; **~liness** *s.* & **~ness** *s.* manque d'amabilité *m.*
unknow/n *s.* & *adj.* inconnu(e) *m.f.*; **~ingly** *adv.* sans le savoir.
unlace *v.t.* délacer.
unladen *adj.* non chargé.
unladylike *adj.* indigne d'une dame.
unlatch *v.t.* lever le loquet de.
unlawful *adj.* **1.** (*law*) illégal; **2.** (*gen.*) illicite; **~ly** *adv.* (1)*; (2)*; **~ness** *s.* illégalité *f.*
unleash *v.t.* lâcher.
unleavened *adj.* (*bread*) azyme.
unless *conj.* à moins que (+ *subjunctive*); à moins de (+ *inf.*).
unlicensed *adj.* sans autorisation, sans permis.
unlike *adj.* peu ressemblant, différent; **~ly** *adj.* improbable; **~lihood** *s.* improbabilité *f.*
unlimited *adj.* illimité.
unlisted *adj.* (*fin.*) non inscrit; (*telephone no.*) qui ne se trouve pas dans l'annuaire.
unload *v.t.* décharger; (*get rid of*) se décharger de.
unlock *v.t.* ouvrir.
unlooked-for *adj.* imprévu, inattendu.
unlov/ely *adj.* & **~able** *adj.* peu aimable.
unluck/y *adj.* malchanceux, malheureux; (*omen*) funeste; **~ily** *adv.**,*.
unman *v.t.* affaiblir; (*fig.*) décourager; **~ly** *adj.* peu viril; **~ned** *adj.* (*space capsule*) robot.
unmanageable *adj.* (*child*) indocile; (*person*) intraitable; (*thing*) peu maniable.
unmannerly *adj.* mal élevé.
unmarried *adj.* célibataire; ~ **mother,** mère célibataire *f.*
unmask *v.t.* démasquer.
unmentionable *adj.* innommable.
unmerciful *adj.* impitoyable; **~ly** *adv.**.
unmerited *adj.* immérité.
unmindful *adj.* insouciant (de).
unmistakabl/e *adj.* qui ne laisse aucun doute, qui ne prête à aucune erreur; **~y** *adv.* incontestablement.
unmitigated *adj.* (*fam.*) parfait.
unmixed *adj.* sans mélange, pur.
unmoved *adj.* impassible, insensible (*by*—à).
unnatural *adj.* peu naturel, dénaturé, anormal.
unnecessar/y *adj.* peu nécessaire, superflu; **~ily** *adv.* sans nécessité, inutilement.
unneighbourly *adj.* & *adv.* de mauvais voisinage.
unnerve *v.t.* décourager.
unnoticed *adj.* inaperçu.
unnumbered *adj.* innombrable.
U.N.O. (*abbrev. United Nations Organization*) O.N.U. *f.* (Organisation des Nations Unies).
unobjectionable *adj.* irréprochable.
unobserv/ed *adj.* inaperçu; **~ant** *adj.* peu attentif.
unobtainable *adj.* impossible à obtenir.
unobtrusive *adj.* discret; **~ly** *adv.**.
unoccupied *adj.* inoccupé, libre.
unoffending *adj.* innocent, inoffensif.
unofficial *adj.* officieux; **~ly** *adv.**.
unopposed *adj.* sans opposition.
unorthodox *adj.* peu orthodoxe.
unostentatious *adj.* sans ostentation; **~ly** *adv.* sans ostentation.
unpack *v.t.* défaire; *v.i.* défaire ses malles.
unpaid *adj.* (*bill*) impayé; (*work*) bénévole.
unpalatable *adj.* peu agréable au goût.
unparalleled *adj.* incomparable.
unpardonabl/e *adj.* impardonnable; **~y** *adv.* de façon impardonnable.
unpatriotic *adj.* (*person*) peu patriote; (*action*) peu patriotique.
unpick *v.t.* défaire.
unpitying *adj.* impitoyable.
unplanned *adj.* spontané.
unpleasant *adj.* désagréable; **~ly** *adv.**; **~ness** *s.* caractère désagréable *m.*; (*incident*) mésentente *f.*
unpolished *adj.* non poli; (*fig.*) grossier.
unpopular *adj.* impopulaire; **~ity** *s.* impopularité *f.*
unpractical *adj.* peu pratique.
unprecedented *adj.* sans précédent.
unpredictable *adj.* imprévisible.
unprejudiced *adj.* sans préjugés, impartial.
unpremeditated *adj.* non prémédité; impromptu.
unprepared *adj.* non préparé, improvisé.
unprepossessing *adj.* peu attirant.
unpresentable *adj.* peu présentable.
unpretentious *adj.* sans prétention(s).
unprincipled *adj.* sans principes.
unproductive *adj.* improductif.
unprofessional *adj.* contraire aux usages de la profession.
unprofitabl/e *adj.* peu profitable; **~y** *adv.* sans profit.
unpromising *adj.* peu prometteur.
unpronounceable *adj.* imprononçable.
unpropitious *adj.* peu propice.
unprovoked *adj.* sans provocation.
unpublished *adj.* inédit.
unpunctual *adj.* inexact.
unpunished *adj.* impuni.
unqualified *adj.* (*person*) incompétent (à), non

qualifié, non diplômé; (*approval etc.*) sans réserve.
unquenchable *adj.* inextinguible.
unquestion/able *adj.* indiscutable, incontestable; **~ably** *adv.**,*; **~ed** *adj.* incontesté.
unquiet *adj.* agité, inquiet.
unravel *v.t.* démêler.
unreadable *adj.* illisible.
unread/y *adj.* pas prêt; (*unwilling*) peu disposé (à); **~ily** *adv.* à contre-cœur.
unreal *adj.* irréel; **~istic** *adj.* peu réaliste; **~ity** *s.* irréalité *f.*; **~izable** *adj.* irréalisable.
unreasonabl/e *adj.* déraisonnable; **~y** *adv.**.
unrecognizable *adj.* méconnaissable.
unrecorded *adj.* non enregistré.
unregistered *adj.* non enregistré.
unrehearsed *adj.* non préparé, impromptu.
unrelated *adj.* (*kinship*) non apparenté; (*without relevance*) sans rapport (à).
unrelenting *adj.* impitoyable.
unreliab/le *adj.* instable, douteux; **~ility** *s.* instabilité *f.*
unrelieved *adj.* monotone, plat.
unremitting *adj.* (*endless*) incessant; (*untiring*) infatigable.
unremunerative *adj.* non rentable.
unrepeatable *adj.* qu'on ne peut répéter.
unrepentant *adj.* impénitent.
unrepresentative *adj.* peu typique.
unrequited *adj.* non récompensé; (*love*) non partagé.
unreserved *adj.* (*seat*) non retenu; (*person*) expansif; (*without reservations*) sans réserve; **~ly** *adv.* sans réserve.
unrest *s.* agitation *f.*, troubles *m.pl.*
unrestrained *adj.* sans contrainte, libre.
unrestricted *adj.* sans restriction.
unreward/ed *adj.* non récompensé; **~ing** *adj.* non rentable.
unrighteous *adj.* injuste.
unripe *adj.* pas mûr, vert.
unrivalled *adj.* sans rival, sans égal.
unroll *v.t.* & *i.* (se) dérouler.
unruly *adj.* (*child*) indiscipliné; déchaîné.
unsafe *adj.* dangereux.
unsaleable *adj.* invendable.
unsatisfactor/y *adj.* peu satisfaisant, insuffisant; **~ily** *adv.* de façon peu satisfaisante.
unsatisfied *adj.* peu satisfait, mécontent (de); (*appetite*) inassouvi.
unsavoury *adj.* désagréable; (*fig.*) déplaisant.
unsay *v.t.* se dédire de.
unscathed *adj.* indemne.
unscientific *adj.* peu scientifique.
unscrew *v.t.* dévisser.
unscrupulous *adj.* sans scrupule(s); **~ly** *adv.* sans scrupule(s).
unseal *v.t.* décacheter.
unseasonabl/e *adj.* hors de saison; (*fig.*) inopportun; **~y** *adv.* hors de saison.
unseaworthy *adj.* pas en état de prendre la mer.
unsecured *adj.* (*fin.*) non garanti.
unseeded *adj.* (*tennis, etc.*) non classé.
unseeing *adj.* aveugle.
unseemly *adj.* malséant.
unseen *s.* (*other world*) au-delà *m.*; (*translation*) version *f.*; *adj.* inaperçu.
unselfish *adj.* désintéressé; **~ly** *adv.* sans égoïsme **~ness** *s.* désintéressement *m.*
unserviceable *adj.* inutilisable.
unsettl/e *v.t.* déranger; **~ed** *adj.* (*restless*) agité; (*disturbed*) troublé; (*changeable*) variable, indécis; (*unpaid*) non payé; **~ing** *adj.* troublant.
unshakeable *adj.* inébranlable.
unshapely *adj.* difforme.
unsheathe *v.t.* dégaîner.
unshod *adj.* nu-pieds.
unshrinkable *adj.* irrétrécissable.
unsightly *adj.* laid.
unskilled *adj.* inexpert (dans); non-spécialisé, non-qualifié.
unsociable *adj.* insociable, farouche.
unsold *adj.* invendu.
unsolicited *adj.* non sollicité, spontané.
unsolved *adj.* non résolu.
unsophisticated *adj.* ingénu, simple.
unsound *adj.* (*diseased*) malade; (*mentally*) dérangé; (*rotten*) gâté, avarié; (*erroneous*) erroné; (*unreliable*) peu sûr, défectueux.
unsparing *adj.* prodigue (de); **~ly** *adv.* avec prodigalité.
unspeakabl/e *adj.* inexprimable; **~y** *adv.* indiciblement.
unspecified *adj.* non spécifié.
unspoken *adj.* non prononcé, sous-entendu, tacite.
unsporting *adj.* peu sportif.
unstable *adj.* instable.
unstead/y *adj.* **1.** (*hand, light, etc.*) tremblant; **2.** (*wind*) changeant; **3.** (*thing*) chancelant; **4.** (*fig.*) inconstant; **~ily,** *adv.* (1) en tremblant; (2) en changeant; (3) en chancelant; (4) inconstamment; **~iness** *s.* instabilité *f.*, variabilité *f.*
unstinted *adj.* sans bornes.
unstuck *adj.* **to come ~** (*fam.*) n'aboutir à rien, échouer.
unstressed *adj.* sans accent.
unstudied *adj.* naturel.
unsubstantial *adj.* immatériel, peu solide.
unsuccessful *adj.* (*person*) malheureux; (*attempt, etc.*) infructueux; **to be ~**, échouer, ne pas avoir de succès; **~ly** *adv.* sans succès.
unsuitabl/e *adj.* inopportun; (*person*) inapte; peu propre à; **~y** *adv.* de façon inconvenante.
unsupported *adj.* sans support; (*fig.*) non appuyé.
unsure *adj.* peu certain, douteux.
unsurpassed *adj.* sans pareil.
unsuspecting *adj.* sans méfiance.
unswerving *adj.* constant.
unsympathetic *adj.* peu compatissant.
untangle *v.t.* démêler.
untenable *adj.* (*position*) intenable; (*theory, etc.*) insoutenable.
unthankful *adj.* ingrat.
unthink/able *adj.* inconcevable; **~ing** *adj.* irréfléchi.
untid/y *adj.* en désordre; (*person*) négligé; **~ily** *adv.* en désordre, sans soin; **~iness** *s.* désordre *m.*
untie *v.t.* (*knot*) dénouer; (*parcel, etc.*) déficeler.
until *prep.* jusqu'à; *conj.* jusqu'à ce que (+ *subjunctive*).
untimely *adj.* inopportun, prématuré.
untiring *adj.* infatigable.
unto *prep.* jusqu'à.
untold *adj.* incalculable.
untouchable *s.* paria *m.*
untoward *adj.* malencontreux, fâcheux.
untrained *adj.* (*without training or qualifications*) sans formation, non qualifié; (*undisciplined*) indiscipliné.
untransferable *adj.* (*law*) inaliénable.
untranslatable *adj.* intraduisible.
untried *adj.* (*thing*) non essayé; (*person*) non éprouvé.
untroubled *adj.* calme, tranquille.
untru/e *adj.* faux, inexact; (*unfaithful*) infidèle; **~th** *s.* mensonge *m.*; **~thful** *adj.* faux, inexact.
untrustworth/y *adj.* indigne de confiance; **~iness** *s.* caractère douteux *m.*
unturned *adj.* **to leave no** STONE **~**.
unusual *adj.* peu commun, rare; **~ly** *adv.* (*not often*) rarement; (+ *adj.*) extraordinairement.
unused *adj.* inutilisé, neuf; (*unaccustomed to*) inaccoutumé à.

unutterable *adj.* inexprimable.

unvarnished *adj.* non verni; (*fig.*) sans fard.

unvarying *adj.* invariable.

unveil (*lit.* & *fig.*) *v.t.* dévoiler; (*statue, etc.*) inaugurer.

unversed *adj.* peu versé (dans).

unviab/le *adj.* peu rentable; **~ility** *s.* manque de rentabilité *m.*

unvoiced *adj.* pas prononcé.

unwanted *adj.* pas voulu, importun.

unwarrant/ed *adj.* injustifié; **~able** *adj.* injustifiable.

unwar/y *adj.* imprudent; **~ily** *adv.* imprudemment.

unwelcome *adj.* (*guest*) mal venu; (*news, etc.*) fâcheux.

unwell *adj.* souffrant.

unwholesome *adj.* malsain.

unwieldy *adj.* pesant, peu maniable.

unwilling *adj.* peu disposé (à); **~ly** *adv.* à contre-cœur.

unwind *v.t.* & *i.* (se) dérouler.

unwise *adj.* imprudent; **~ly** *adv.* imprudemment.

unwitting *adj.* inconscient; **~ly** *adv.* inconsciemment, sans le savoir.

unwomanly *adj.* peu féminin.

unwonted *adj.* inhabituel.

unworkable *adj.* peu pratique.

unworth/y *adj.* indigne; **~ily** *adv.**; **~iness** *s.* indignité *f.*

unwrap *v.t.* déballer.

unwritten *adj.* non écrit, oral; (*law*) coutumier.

unyielding *adj.* inflexible.

unzip *v.t.* & *i.* (s')ouvrir.

up *adv.* (*to or in higher place*) en haut; **further ~,** plus haut; **~ there,** là-haut; ⚠ **go, come, mount ~** = monter; **prices are ~,** les prix ont monté; ⚠ *with verbs often* re-, **lift ~,** relever, **roll, ~,** retrousser; **the curtain is ~,** le rideau est levé; **the game is ~,** tout est perdu; **time is ~,** c'est le moment de finir; **the river is ~,** la rivière est haute; **road ~!,** travaux!; **~ to,** jusqu'à, **~ to the door,** jusqu'à la porte; ⚠ **come** *or* **go ~ to,** s'approcher de; (*in erect position*) debout; (*out of bed*) levé; **get ~, stand ~,** se lever; *see* PUMP, PUT, SCREW, STIR, TURN, WIND, *etc.*; **to be well ~ in,** être calé dans; **what's ~?,** (*fam.*) qu'est-ce qu'il y a?; (*expressing completion*) *see* DIG, SAVE, TEAR, USE, WASH, *etc.*; **it's all ~ with him,** c'en est fait de lui; *see* BRING, GIVE, MAKE, *etc.*; **~ against,** contre; **to be ~ against** (*fig.*) avoir affaire à, être aux prises avec; **~ and down,** de long en large; **~ to the present,** jusqu'à présent; **it's ~ to you, us,** *etc.* **to,** c'est à vous, nous, etc. de; **to be ~ to sth.,** avoir qch. en tête; **to be ~ to doing sth.,** être en mesure, être capable, de faire qch.; **~ to date** *adj.* moderne, (*fam.*) à la page; *prep.* **go ~ the hill, a ladder, the street,** *etc.* monter (la colline, une échelle, la rue, etc.); *adj.* (*train, etc.*) montant; **~-and--coming** *adj.* progressif, (*successful*) en voie d'arriver; **on the ~-and-~** (*fam.*) (*improving*) en voie d'amélioration, (*honestly*) à dire vrai; **~s and downs,** les hauts et les bas *m.pl.*

upbraid *v.t.* réprimander.

upbringing *s.* éducation *f.*

update *v.t.* moderniser; mettre à jour.

upgrade *s.* pente montante *f.*; **to be on the ~,** remonter, se relever; *v.t.* avancer en rang.

upheaval *s.* soulèvement *m.*

uphill *adj.* montant; (*fig.*) pénible; *adv.* en montant.

uphold *v.t.* soutenir.

upholster/y *s.* capitonnage *m.*, tapisserie *f.*; **~er** *s.* tapissier *m.*

upkeep *s.* entretien *m.*

uplands *s.pl.* hautes terres *f.pl.*

uplift *v.t.* soulever; *s.* (*fam.*) inspiration *f.*

upon *prep.* sur; **to take it ~ oneself to** (*undertake*) se charger de; (*presume*) se permettre de.

upper *s.* (*of shoe*) empeigne *f.*; *adj.* supérieur, haut; **~-cut** *s.* uppercut *m.*; **~** CASE; **~** HAND; **keep a stiff ~** LIP; **~most** *adj.* le plus haut.

upright *s.* montant *m.*; *adj.* **1.** (*erect*) debout, droit; **2.** (*honest*) droit, honnête; **~ly** *adv.* (1) droit; (2) honnêtement; **~ness** *s.* (1) droiture *f.*; (2) rectitude *f.*

uprising *s.* rébellion *f.*

uproar *s.* vacarme *m.*; **~ious** *adj.* tumultueux.

uproot *v.t.* déraciner.

upset *s.* (*being overturned*) renversement *m.*; **2.** (*fig.*) bouleversement *m.*; **3.** (*disorder*) branle--bas *m.*; **4.** (*med.*) indisposition *f.*; *v.t.* & *i.* (1) (se) renverser, (*auto.*) (faire) verser, (*boat*) (faire) chavirer; (2) bouleverser; (3) déranger; (4) rendre malade.

upshot *s.* résultat *m.*

upside-down *adv.* sens dessus dessous.

upstage *adv.* (*theat.*) au second plan; *adj.* (*pop.*) hautain.

upstairs *adv.* en haut; *adj.* d'en haut.

upstart *s.* parvenu(e) *m.f.*

upstream see STREAM.

uptake *s.* **to be slow in the ~,** avoir la comprenette un peu dure; **to be quick in the ~,** comprendre à demi-mot.

uptight *adj.* (*fam.*) énervé; **to get ~,** s'énerver.

upward *adj.* montant, ascensionnel; *adv.* vers le haut; **~ of,** plus de, au dessus-de.

uræmia *s.* urémie *f.*; **~ic** *adj.* urémique.

uranium *s.* uranium *m.*

urban *adj.* urbain; **~ize** *v.t.* urbaniser.

urban/e *adj.* courtois; **~ity** *s.* urbanité *f.*

urchin *s.* gamin *m.*; SEA-~.

Urdu *adj.* (*no f.*) & *s.m.* ourdou.

urge *s.* poussée *f.*; **to feel the ~ to do sth.,** se sentir poussé à faire qch.; *v.t.* (*impel*) pousser, inciter (à); (*entreat*) prier vivement (de); (*advocate*) soutenir avec vigueur, recommander instamment.

urgen/t *adj.* urgent, pressant; **~cy** *s.* urgence *f.*; **~tly** *adv.* d'urgence.

urin/e *s.* urine *f.*; **~al** *s.* urinoir *m.*; **~ate** *v.i.* uriner.

urn *s.* urne *f.*

urticaria *s.* urticaire *f.*

us *pron.* nous.

U.S.A. (*abbrev. United States of America*) États-Unis (d'Amérique) *m.pl.*; (*fam.*) U.S.A. *m.pl.*

usage *s.* (*treatment*) traitement *m.*; (*custom*) usage *m.*

use[1] *s.* (*employment*) emploi *m.*; (*right or power of using, availability*) usage *m.*; (*custom*) habitude *f.*; (*utility*) utilité *f.*; (*enjoyment*) jouissance *f.*; **out of ~,** inusité; **to be of ~ to,** rendre service à; **to make ~ of,** se servir de; **to have no ~ for s.o.** *or* **sth.,** n'avoir que faire de qn. *or* qch., ne pas pouvoir souffrir qn. *or* qch.; **what's the ~?,** à quoi bon?

use[2] *v.t.* (*employ*) se servir de; (*avail oneself of*) utiliser, profiter de; (*treat*) traiter; *v.i.* (*be accustomed to, usu. in past tense*) avoir l'habitude de, *or, use the imperfect alone*; **I used to go to Church every Sunday,** j'allais à l'église tous les dimanches; **~d to** *adj.* habitué à; **to be used for,** servir à; **~ up,** consommer; **usable** *adj.* utilisable; **~r** *s.* usager *m.*; **~ful** *adj.* utile; **~fully** *adv.**; **~fulness** *s.* utilité *f.*; **~less** *adj.* inutile; **~lessly** *adv.**; **~lessness** *s.* inutilité *f.*

usher *s.* huissier *m.*; *v.t.* **~ in,** introduire; **~ette** *s.* ouvreuse *f.*

U.S.S.R. (*abbrev. Union of Soviet Socialist Republics*) U.R.S.S. *f.* (Union des Républiques socialistes soviétiques).

usual *adj.* habituel; **~ly** *adv.* d'habitude.
usufruct *s.* usufruit *m.*
usurp *v.t.* usurper; **~ation** *s.* usurpation *f.*; **~er** *s.* usurpat/eur, -rice *m.f.*
usur/y *s.* usure *f.*; **~er** *s.* usurier *m.*; **~ious** *adj.* usuraire.
utensil *s.* ustensile *f.*
uterus *s.* utérus *m.*
utilitarian *adj.* utilitaire.
utility *s.* utilité *f.*; PUBLIC **utilities**; *adj.* (*clothes, etc.*) utilitaire, d'usage courant.
utiliz/e *v.t.* utiliser; **~ation** *s.* utilisation *f.*
utmost *s.* maximum *m.*; *adj.* (*biggest*) le plus grand; (*furthest*) le plus éloigné.
Utopia *s.* utopie *f.*; **~n** *adj.* utopique.
utter[1] *adj.* complet, total; **~ly** *adv.**,*; **~most** *see* UTMOST.
utter[2] *v.t.* (*cry, sigh*) pousser; (*word*) prononcer; (*money, etc.*) émettre; **~ance** *s.* expression *f.*, articulation *f.*
uvula *s.* luette *f.*
uxorious *adj.* très attaché à sa femme.

V

vac/ancy *s.* **1.** (*being ~ant*) vacuité *f.*; **2.** (*empty space, place, job*) vide *m.*, vacance *f.*, place disponible *f.*; **3.** (*emptiness of mind*) vide mental *m.*, manque d'idées *m.*; **~ant** *adj.* (1) vide; (2) (*seat*) libre, disponible, (*job*) vacant, (*time*) de loisir; (3) (*mind*) vide, (*face*) sans expression; **with ~ant possession,** avec jouissance immédiate; **~antly** *adv.* (3) d'un air vague.
vacat/e *v.t.* (*leave empty*) laisser libre; (*give up*) quitter; (*annul*) annuler; **~ion** *s*, vacances *f.pl.*
vaccinat/e *v.t.* vacciner; **~ion** *s.* vaccination *f.*
vaccine *s.* vaccin *m.*
vacillat/e *v.i.* (*lit.* & *fig.*) vaciller; **~ing** *adj.* vacillant; **~ion** *s.* vacillation *f.*
vacu/ity *s.* vide *m.*, vacuité *f.*; **~ous** *adj.* vide, vague.
vacuum *s.* (*empty space*) vide *m.*; (*empty of air*) vacuum *m.*; **~ brakes** *s.* freins à vide *m.pl.*; ~ CLEANer; ~ FLASK; **~-packed** *adj.* fermé sous vide; *v.t.* (*fam.*) passer l'aspirateur sur.
vagabond *adj.* & *s.m.f.* vagabond(e).
vagary *s.* caprice *m.*
vagina *s.* vagin *m.*; **~l** *adj.* vaginal.
vagran/t *adj.* & *s.m.f.* vagabond(e); **~cy** *s.* vagabondage *m.*
vague *adj.* (*not clearly expressed or identified*) vague; (*ill-defined*) imprécis; (*inexact*) inexact; (*indefinite*) indéterminé; **~ly** *adv.**; de façon imprécise;*; de façon indéterminée; **~ness** *s.* vague *m.*, imprécision *f.*
vain *adj.* **1.** (*unavailing*) vain, inutile; **2.** (*empty, trivial*) frivole, futile; **3.** (*conceited*) vaniteux; **in ~,** en vain; **~ly** *adv.* (1) en vain, inutilement; (2)*,*; (3)*; **~ness** *s.* (1) inutilité *f.*; (2) & (3) vanité *f.*; **~glory** *s.* vanité *f.*; **~glorious** *adj.* vaniteux; **~gloriously** *adv.**.
valance, valence *s.* cantonnière *f.*
vale *s.* vallée *f.*
valedict/ory *s.* discours d'adieu *m.*; *adj.* d'adieu; **~ion** *s.* adieu *m.*
valent/ine *s.* carte pour la Saint-Valentin *f.*; **St. V~'s day,** la Saint-Valentin.
valerian *s.* valériane *f.*
valet *s.* valet de chambre *m.*; *v.t.* servir qn. comme valet de chambre.
valetudinarian *adj.* & *s.m.f.* valétudinaire.
valian/t *adj.* vaillant; **~cy** *s.* vaillance *f.*; **~tly** *adv.* vaillamment.
valid *adj.* **1.** (*sound*) solide, irréfutable; **2.** (*having legal force*) valide; **~ate** *v.t.* (2) valider; **~ity** *s.* (1) valeur *f.*, force *f.*; (2) validité *f.*; **~ly** *adv.* (1) solidement; (2) validement.
valise *s.* valise *f.*
valley *s.* vallée *f.*; LILY **of the ~**; RIFT-**~**.
val/our *s.* vaillance *f.*; **~orous** *adj.* valeureux; **~orously** *adv.**.
valu/e *s.* valeur *f.*; (*price*) prix *m.*; FACE **~e; good ~e** *adj.* avantageux; **~e-added tax** *s.* taxe sur la valeur ajoutée *f.*; **~able** *adj.* de valeur, précieux; **~ables** *s.pl.* objets de valeur *m.pl.*; **~eless** *adj.* sans valeur; *v.t.* (*evaluate*) évaluer; (*esteem*) estimer, priser, faire cas de; **~ation** *s.* évaluation *f.*; **~ed** *adj.* estimé; **~er** *s.* appréciateur *m.*, (*official*) commissaire-priseur *m.*
valv/e *s.* (*techn.*) soupape *f.*; (*of tyre*) valve *f.*; (*anat.*) valvule *f.*; (*organ*) soupape *f.*; (*other instruments*) clé *f.*; (*radio*) lampe *f.*; **~ular** *adj.* valvulaire.
vamp *s.* **1.** (*of shoe*) empeigne *f.*; **2.** (*mus.*) accompagnement improvisé *m.*; *v.t.* & *i.* (1) (*repair, patch*) rafistoler; (2) improviser un accompagnement.
vampire *s.* vampire *m.*
van *s.* (= *~guard*) avant-garde *f.*; (*auto.*) fourgonnette *f.*; (*rail.*) fourgon *m.*; GUARD**'s ~**; LUGGAGE **~**.
vandal *s.* vandale *m.f.*, casseur *m.*; **~ism** *s.* vandalisme *m.*; **~ize** *v.t.* détruire, saccager.
vane *s.* (*weathercock*) girouette *f.*; (*blade of propeller*) pale *f.*
vanguard *s.* avant-garde *f.*
vanilla *s.* vanille *f.*; *adj.* à la vanille, vanillé.
vanish *v.i.* disparaître; (*fig.*) s'évanouir; **~ing** *s.* disparition *f.*; **~ing-point** *s.* point de fuite *m.*
vanity *s.* (*vain or worthless thing*) vanité *f.*; (*futility*) futilité *f.*; (*pride*) prétention *f.*; **~ bag, ~ case** *s.* réticule *m.*
vanquish *v.t.* vaincre; **~er** *s.* vainqueur *m.*
vantage *s.* (*tennis*) avantage *m.*; **~-point** *s.* position avantageuse *f.*
vapid *adj.* fade; **~ity** *s.* fadeur *f.*
vaporiz/e *v.t.* & *i.* (se) vaporiser; **~er** *s.* vaporisateur *m.*
vapour *s.* vapeur *f.*; **~ous** *adj.* vaporeux.
variable *see* VARY.
variance *see* VARY.
variant *see* VARY.
variation *see* VARY.
varicose *adj.* variqueux; **~ vein** *s.* varice *f.*
varied *see* VARY.
variety *see* VARY.
various *see* VARY.
varnish *s.* (*lit.* & *fig.*) vernis *m.*; NAIL **~**; *v.t.* vernir; (*fig.*) enjoliver; **~er** *s.* vernisseur *m.*; **~ing** *s.* (*act*) vernissage *m.*, (*result*) vernis *m.*; **~ing-day** *s.* (*private view*) vernissage *m.*
var/y *v.t.* & *i.* varier, (se) modifier; **~iable** *s.* variable *f.*, *adj.* variable, changeant; **~iability** variabilité *f.*; **~iably** *adv.* variablement; **~iance** *s.* désaccord; **at ~iance,** en désaccord; **~iant** *s.* variante *f.*, *adj.* différent; **~iation** *s.* variation *f.*; **~ied** *adj.* varié; **~iegate** *v.t.* diversifier, bigarrer; **~iegated** *adj.* divers; bigarré, diapré; **~iety** *s.* variété *f.*, (*theat.*) music-hall *m.*; **~ious** *adj.* divers, différent; **~iously** *adv.* diversement.

vascular *adj.* vasculaire.
vase *s.* vase *m.*; ⚠ vase *s.f.* = **mud.**
vaseline *s.* vaseline *f.*
vaso- (*in combination*) **~-constrictive** *adj.* vaso-constricteur *m.*; **~-dilating** *adj.* vaso-dilatateur *m.*; **~-motor** *adj.* vaso-mot/eur, -rice.
vassal *s.* vassal *m.*; **~age** *s.* vassalité *f.*
vast *adj.* vaste, énorme; **~ly** *adv.**,*; (*fam.*) infiniment, énormément; **~ness** *s.* immensité *f.*
vat *s.* cuve *f.*
V.A.T. *s.* (*abbrev. value-added tax*) T.V.A. *f.* (taxe sur la valeur ajoutée).
Vatican *s.* Vatican *m.*
vaticinat/e *v.i.* vaticiner; **~ion** *s.* vaticination *f.*
vault[1] *s.* (*arch.* & *fig.*) voûte *f.*; (*cellar*) cave *f.*; (*tomb*) caveau *m.*; (*of bank*) chambre forte *f.*; **~ed** *adj.* voûté; **~ing** *s.* voûtes *f.pl.*
vault[2] *s.* (*leap*) saut *m.*; *v.t.* & *i.* sauter; **~ing** *s.* exercice du saut *m.*
vaunt *v.t.* & *i.* se vanter (de).
veal *s.* veau *m.*
vector *s.* (*math.*, *aviat.*) vecteur *m.*; (*med.*) porteur *m.*
veer *v.i.* (*naut.*) virer; (*wind*) tourner.
veget/able *s.* (*edible*) légume *m.*; (≠ *animal*) végétal *m.*; (*person*) personne réduite à une vie végétative *f.*; ⚠ une grosse légume (*pop.*) = **a big noise**; *adj.* végétal, **~able** GARDEN; **~able** MARROW; **~arian** *adj.* & *s.m.f.* végétarien(ne); **~ate** *v.i.* végéter; **~ation** *s.* végétation *f.*
vehemen/t *adj.* véhément; **~ce** *s.* véhémence *f.*; **~tly** *adv.* avec véhémence.
vehic/le *s.* véhicule *m.*; (*mil.*) engin *m.*; **~ular** *adj.* véhiculaire.
veil *s.* (*of nun*; *disguise*) voile *m.*; (*dress*) voilette *f.*; **to take the ~,** prendre le voile; **to draw a ~ over** (*fig.*) jeter un voile sur; *v.t.* voiler.
vein *s.* (*lit.* & *fig.*) veine *f.*; VARICOSE **~**; **~ed** *adj.* veiné.
veld(t) *s.* veld(t) *m.*
vellum *s.* vélin *m.*
veloci/ty *s.* vélocité *f.*; **~pede** *s.* vélocipède *m.*
velour(s) *s.* (*text.*) velours de laine *m.*
velvet *s.* velours *m.*; *adj.* de velours; **~een** *s.* velvet *m.*; **~y** *adj.* velouté.
venal *adj.* vénal; **~ity** *s.* vénalité *f.*
vend *v.t.* vendre; **~ible** *adj.* vendable; **~or** *s.* vendeur *m.*; **~ing-machine** *s.* distributeur automatique *m.*
vendetta *s.* vendetta *f.*
veneer *s.* (*on furniture*) placage *m.*; (*wood*) bois de placage *m.*; (*fig.*) vernis *m*,; *v.t.* plaquer; **~ing** *s.* placage *m.*
vener/able *adj.* vénérable; **~ate** *v.t.* vénérer; **~ation** *s.* vénération *f.*
venere/al *adj.* vénérien; **~ology** *s.* vénér(é)-ologie *f.*; **~ologist** *s.* spécialiste des maladies vénériennes *m.f.*
Venetian *adj.* & *s.m.f.* vénitien(ne); **~** BLIND.
Venezuela *s.* (*geog.*) Venezuela *m.*; **~n** *adj.* & *s.m.f.* vénézuélien(ne).
venge/ance *s.* vengeance *f.*; **with a ~ance,** furieusement; **~ful** *adj.* vindicatif.
venial *adj.* véniel.
Venice *s.* Venise *f.*
venison *s.* venaison *f.*
venom *s.* (*lit.* & *fig.*) venin *m.*; **~ous** *adj.* (*zool.* & *fig.*) venimeux, (*bot.*) vénéneux.
vent *s.* (*slit*) fente *f.*; (*air outlet*) ouverture *f.*, trou *m.*; (*fig.*) libre cours *m.*; **to give ~ to** (*fig.*) donner libre cours à; *v.t.* décharger.
ventilat/e *v.t.* ventiler; (*fig.*) faire connaître; **~ion** *s.* ventilation *f.*; **~or** *s.* ventilateur *m.*
ventricle *s.* ventricule *m.*
ventriloqu/ism *s.* ventriloquie *f.*; **~ist** *s.* ventriloque *m.f.*
venture *s.* aventure *f.*; (*comm.*) spéculation *f.*; **at a ~,** au hasard; *v.t.* risquer, hasarder; *v.i.* **~ to,** oser; **~ on,** se risquer à; **venturous** *adj.* & **~some** *adj.* (*person*) aventureux; (*thing*) hasardeux.
venue *s.* rendez-vous *m.*
Venus *s.* Vénus *f.*
verac/ious *adj.* véridique; **~ity** *s.* véracité *f.*
veranda(h) *s.* véranda *f.*
verb *s.* verbe *m.*; **~al** *adj.* verbal, (*translation*) littéral; **~ally** *adv.**,*, mot à mot; **~atim** *adv.* mot pour mot; **~iage** *s.* verbiage *m.*; **~ose** *adj.* verbeux; **~osity** *s.* verbosité *f.*
verbena *s.* verveine *f.*
verd/ant *adj.* verdoyant; **~ure** *s.* verdure *f.*
verdict *s.* verdict *m.*
verdigris *s.* vert-de-gris *m.*
verge *s.* (*brink*, *border*) bord *m.*; (*grass edge*) bordure *f.*; (*limits*) confins *m.pl.*; **on the ~ of,** sur le point de (faire qch.), à deux doigts (de qch.); ⚠ verge = **staff**; *v.i.* tendre (vers); **~ on,** approcher de, tirer sur.
verger *s.* suisse *m.*; ⚠ verger = **orchard.**
verif/y *v.t.* (*check*) vérifier; (*confirm*) confirmer; **~ication** *s.* vérification *f.*
verily *adv.* en vérité.
verisimilitude *s.* vraisemblance *f.*
veritabl/e *adj.* véritable; **~y** *adv.**.
verity *s.* vérité *f.*
vermicelli *s.* vermicelle *m.*
vermi/cide *s.* vermicide *m.*; **~cular** *adj.* vermiculaire; **~culated** *adj.* vermiculé, (*worm-eaten*) vermoulu; **~culite** *s.* vermiculite *f.*; **~form** *adj.* vermiculaire; **~fuge** *adj.* & *s.m.* vermifuge.
vermilion *s.* vermillon *m.*; *adj.* vermeil.
vermin *s.* vermine *f.*; **~ous** *adj.* plein de vermine.
vermouth *s.* vermouth *m.*
vernacular *s.* dialecte *m.*; *adj.* indigène.
vernal *adj.* printanier.
veronica *s.* véronique *f.*
versatil/e *adj.* aux talents variés, souple; ⚠ versatile = **fickle**; **~ity** *s.* souplesse d'esprit *f.*
vers/e *s.* (*poetry*) vers *m.pl.*; ⚠ un vers = **a line of poetry**; (*stanza*) strophe *f.*; (*of Bible*) verset *m.*; CHAPTER **and ~e**; **~ify** *v.t.* & *i.* versifier; **~ification** *s.* versification *f.*; **~ifier** *s.* versificat/eur, -rice *m.f.*
versed *adj.* **~ in,** versé dans.
version *s.* version *f.*
verso *s.* verso *m.*
versus *prep.* contre.
vertebr/a *a.* vertèbre *f.*; **~al** *adj.* vertébral; **~ate** *adj.* & *s.m.* vertébré.
vertex *s.* sommet *m.*; (*astron.*) zénith *m.*
vertical *adj.* vertical; **~ly** *adv.**.
vertig/o *s.* vertige *m.*; **~inous** *adj.* vertigineux.
vervain *s.* verveine *f.*
verve *s.* verve *f.*
very *adj.* vrai; **the ~ man,** l'homme qu'il nous fait; **in the ~ middle,** au beau milieu; **at the ~ moment,** au moment même; *adv.* très; (*extremely*) extrêmement; (*precisely*) précisément; **the ~ last,** le tout dernier; **the ~ best,** tout ce qu'il y a de mieux; **~ much,** beaucoup; **~ well!,** bien!
vesicle *s.* vésicule *f.*
vesper *s.* soir *m.*; **~s** *s.pl.* vêpres *f.pl.*
vessel *s.* (*naut.*; *anat.*) vaisseau *m.*; (*receptacle*) récipient *m.*
vest *s.* maillot de corps *m.*, tricot de corps *m.*; ⚠ veste = **jacket**; *v.t.* **~ in** *or* **with,** attribuer à, investir de; **~ed** *adj.* dévolu; **~ed interests,** droits acquis *m.pl.*, intérêts *m.pl.*; **~ment** *s.* vêtement (sacerdotal) *m.*
vestal *adj.* vestal; **~ virgin** *s.* vestale *f.*
vestibule *s.* vestibule *m.*
vestig/e *s.* vestige *m.*, trace *f.*; **~ial** *adj.* (*biol.*) rudimentaire; (*gen.*) résiduel.

vestry *s.* (*room*) sacristie *f.*; (*assembly*) conseil de fabrique *m.*
Vesuvius *s.* Vésuve *m.*
vet *s.* (*fam.*) vétérinaire *m.*; *v.t.* (*treat*) traiter; (*examine*) examiner, scruter.
vetch *s.* vesce *f.*
veteran *s.* vétéran *m.*; *adj.* (*of long service*) aguerri; (*experienced*) expérimenté; ~ **car,** véhicule ancien *m.*
veterinar/y *adj.* vétérinaire; **~y surgeon** & **~ian** *s.* vétérinaire *m.f.*
veto *s.* veto *m.*; *v.t.* opposer son veto à.
vex *v.t.* vexer, fâcher; **~ed question,** question épineuse; **~ation** *s.* ennui *m.*, contrariété *f.*; **~atious** *adj.* contrariant.
V.H.F. (*abbrev. very high frequency*) très haute fréquence *f.*
via *prep.* via.
viab/le *adj.* rentable; **~ility** *s.* rentabilité *f.*
viaduct *s.* viaduc *m.*
vial *s.* fiole *f.*
viands *s.pl.* aliments *m.pl.*
viaticum *s.* viatique *m.*
vibran/t *adj.* vibrant; **~cy** *s.* résonance *f.*
vibrat/e *v.i.* (*quiver*) osciller; (*sound*) retentir; (*thrill*) frémir (de); **~ion** *s.* vibration *f.*; **~ory** *adj.* vibratoire.
viburnum *s.* viorne *f.*
vicar *s.* (*R.C.*) curé *m.*; (*protestant*) pasteur *m.*; ⚠ vicaire = **curate**; **~age** *s.* presbytère *m.*; **~ious** *adj.* délégué; **~iously** *adv.* par procuration.
vice[1] *s.* (*evil*) vice *m.*; (*fault*) défaut *m.*
vice[2] *s.* (*tool*) étau *m.*
vice- *prefix.* vice-; **~-president,** *etc.* vice-président; **~roy** *s.* vice-roi *m.*; **~regal** *adj.* de vice-roi.
vice versa *adv.* vice versa.
vicinity *s.* voisinage *m.*
vicious *adj.* **1.** (*evil*) vicieux; **2.** (*depraved*) dépravé; **3.** (*spiteful*) méchant; **4.** (*horse*) rétif; **5.** (*thing*) dépravant; ~ **circle,** cercle vicieux *m.*; **~ly** *adv.* (1)*; (3) méchamment; **~ness** *s.* (1) nature vicieuse, *f.*; (3) méchanceté *f.*
vicissitude *s.* vicissitude *f.*
victim *s.* victime *f.*; **~ize** *v.t.* prendre pour victime.
victor *s.* vainqueur *m.*; **~ious** *adj.* victorieux; **~iously** *adv.**; **~y** *s.* victoire *f.*
victual(s) *s.pl.* victuailles *f.pl.*; *v.t.* ravitailler; **~ler** *s.* fournisseur *m.*; **licensed ~ler** *s.* débitant de boissons *m.*
vicuna *s.* vigogne *f.*
video *adj.* ~ **tape,** magnétoscope *m.*
vie *v.t.* ~ **with s.o. in sth.,** rivaliser de qch. avec qn.
Vienn/a *s.* Vienne *f.*; **~ese** *adj.* & *s.m.f.* viennois(e).
Vietnam *s.* (*geog.*) Vietnam *m.*; **~ese** *adj.* & *s.m.f.* vietnamien(ne).
view *s.* **1.** (*range of vision*) vue *f.*; **2.** (*inspection*) vue *f.*, inspection *f.*; **3.** (*scene*) perspective *f.*; **4.** (*mental attitude*) avis *m.*; **with a ~ to,** en vue de; **to have in ~,** avoir en vue, envisager; **in ~ of,** vu; **take a** DIM **~ of**; **on ~,** exposé; **point of ~, ~point** *s.* point de vue *m.*; **private ~** *s.* vernissage *m.*; **~finder** *s.* viseur *m.*; *v.t.* (1) regarder; (2) examiner; (4) envisager; **~er** *s.* (*TV*) téléspectat/eur, -rice *m.f.*; (*device for ~ing transparencies*) visionneuse *f.*
vigil *s.* veille *f.*; **to keep ~,** veiller; **~ance** *s.* vigilance *f.*; **~ant** *adj.* vigilant; **~antly** *adv.* avec vigilance; **~ante** *s.* membre d'un comité de vigilance *m.*
vigorous *adj.* vigoureux; **~ly** *adv.**; **~ness** *s.* vigueur *f.*
vigour *s.* vigueur *f.*
Viking *s.* viking *m.*
vile *adj.* (*despicable, worthless*) vil; (*depraved*) ignoble; (*disgusting*) abominable, infect; (*shameful*) infâme; **~ly** *adv.**;*; abominablement; de façon infâme; **~ness** *s.* bassesse *f.*
vilif/y *v.t.* diffamer; **~ication** *s.* diffamation *f.*
villa *s.* villa *f.*
village *s.* village *m.*; *adj.* du village, campagnard; **~r** *s.* villageois(e) *m.f.*
villain *s.* (*hist.*) vilain *m.*; (*guilty person*) scélérat *m.*; ⚠ vilain (*adj.*) = **ugly**; **~ous** *adj.* (*act*) de scélérat; (*person*) ignoble; (*fam.*) abominable; **~y** *s.* (*action*) vilenie *f.*; infamie *f.*
vim *s.* (*fam.*) vigueur *f.*
vinaigrette *s.* flacon de sels *m.*; (*sauce*) vinaigrette *f.*
vindicat/e *v.t.* justifier; **~ion** *s.* justification *f.*
vindictive *adj.* vindicatif; **~ly** *adv.* d'une manière vindicative; **~ness** *s.* caractère vindicatif *m.*
vine *s.* vigne *f.*; ~ **branch** *s.* sarment *m.*; **~-grower** *s.* vigneron *m.*; **~yard** *s.* vignoble *m.*; **~ry** *s.* serre à vigne *f.*
vinegar *s.* vinaigre *m.*; **~y** *adj.* de vinaigre; (*fig.*) aigre.
vintage *s.* (*crop*) vendange *f.*; (*season*) vendanges *f.pl.*; (*year*) cru *m.*; ~ **car** *s.* voiture de la belle époque *f.*
vintner *s.* négociant en vins *m.*
vinyl *s.* vinyle *m.*
viol *s.* viole *f.*
viola *s.* **1.** (*mus.*) viole *f.*; ~ **da gamba,** viole de gambe *f.*; **2.** (*bot.*) pensée *f.*
violat/e *v.t.* **1.** (*transgress*) violer; **2.** (*infringe*) enfreindre; **3.** (*rape*) violer; **4.** (*break into*) (*sanctuary*) profaner, (*peace*) troubler; **~ion** *s.* (1) violation *f.*; (2) infraction *f.*; (3) viol *m.*; (4) profanation *f.*, intrusion *f.*; **~or** *s.* violat/eur, -rice *m.f.*
violen/ce *s.* violence *f.*; **~t** *adj.* violent; **~tly** *adv.* violemment.
violet *s.* violette *f.*; *adj.* violet.
violin *s.* violon *m.*; **~ist** *s.* violoniste *m.f.*
violoncell/o *s.* violoncelle *m.*; **~ist** *s.* violoncelliste *m.f.*
V.I.P. *s.* notabilité *f.*; (*pop.*) grosse légume *f.*
viper *s.* (*lit.* & *fig.*) vipère *f.*; **~ish** *adj.* de vipère.
virago *s.* virago *f.*
virgin *s.* vierge *f.*; *adj.* vierge; **~al** *s.* (*mus.*) virginal *f.*; **~al** *adj.* de vierge, virginal; **~ity** *s.* virginité *f.*
Virginia *s.* Virginie *f.*; ~ **creeper** *s.* vigne vierge *f.*
Virgo *s.* Vierge *f.*
viril/e *adj.* viril; **~ity** *s.* virilité *f.*
virolog/y *s.* science des virus *f.*; **~ist** *s.* spécialiste des virus *m.f.*
virtual *adj.* **1.** (*in effect*) vrai, de fait; **2.** (*potential*) virtuel; **~ly** *adv.* (1) en fait, effectivement; (2) virtuellement.
virtu/e *s.* (*moral goodness*) vertu *f.*; (*good point*) qualité *f.*, avantage *m.*; (*chastity*) honnêteté *f.*; **by ~e of,** en vertu de; **~oso** *s.* virtuose *m.f.*; **~osity** *s.* virtuosité *f.*; **~ous** *adj.* vertueux; **~ously** *adv.**; **~ousness** *s.* vertu *f.*
virulen/ce *s.* virulence *f.*; **~t** *adj.* virulent; (*poisonous*) venimeux.
virus *s.* virus *m.*
visa *s.* visa *m.*
visage *s.* visage *m.*
viscera *s.pl.* viscères *m.pl.*; **~l** *adj.* viscéral.
viscose *s.* viscose *f.*
viscosity *see* VISCOUS.
viscount *s.* vicomte m.; **~ess** *s.* vicomtesse *f.*
visc/ous *adj.* visqueux; **~osity** *s.* viscosité *f.*
visib/le *adj.* visible; **~ility** *s.* visibilité *f.*; **~ly** *adv.**.
vision *s.* (*faculty*; *dream*) vision *f.*; (*foresight*)

prévoyance *f.*; (*apparition*) apparition *f.*; **~ary** *s.* visionnaire *m.f.*; *adj.* imaginaire.
visit *s.* **1.** (*call*) visite *f.*; **2.** (*temporary stay*) séjour *m.*; FLYing **~**; *v.t.* (1) visiter; (2) faire un séjour chez; **3.** (*attack*) atteindre; **4.** (*punish*) punir; *v.i.* (1) faire des visites; (2) être en visite; **~ation** *s.* visite *f.*, (*apparition*) apparition *f.*, (*test*) épreuve *f.*; **~ing** *s.* visites *f.pl.*; **~ing-**CARD; **~or** *s.* visiteur *m.*, (*in hotel*) voyageur *m.*
visor, vizor *s.* visière *f.*; (*auto.*) pare-soleil *m.*
vista *s.* perspective *f.*
visual *adj.* visuel; **~ize** *v.t.* rendre visible; (*imagine*) se représenter.
vital *adj.* vital; **~ statistics** *s.pl.* (*particulars*) état-civil *m.*, (*fam.* = *measurements*) mesures *f.pl.*; **~s** *s.pl.* organes vitaux *m.pl.*; **~ity** *s.* vitalité *f.*; **~ly** *adv.* de façon vitale; **~ize** *v.t.* donner de la vie à.
vitamin *s.* vitamine *f.*; **~ized** *adj.* vitaminé.
vitiate *v.t.* vicier.
viticulture *s.* viticulture *f.*
vitr/eous *adj.* vitreux; **~ify** *v.t.* & *i.* (se) vitrifier.
vitriol *s.* (*lit.* & *fig.*) vitriol *m.*; **~ic** *adj.* vitriolique.
vituperat/e *v.t.* injurier; **~ion** *s.* injures *f.pl.*; **~ive** *adj.* injurieux.
viva *s.* (*fam.*) oral *m.*; **~ voce** *s.* examen oral *m.*, soutenance de thèse *f.*; *adj.* oral; *adv.* de vive voix.
vivaci/ous *adj.* vif, animé; ⚠ vivace = (*bot.*) **long-lived**; **~ty** *s.* vivacité *f.*
vivid *adj.* (*bright, intense, lively*) vif; (*dazzling*) éclatant; (*graphic*) vivant; **~ly** *adv.* vivement; **~ness** *s.* vivacité *f.*, éclat *m.*
viviparous *adj.* vivipare.
vivisection *s.* vivisection *f.*; **~ist** *s.* personne qui pratique la vivisection *f.*
vixen *s.* renarde *f.*; (*fig.*) mégère *f.*
viz à savoir.
vizier *s.* vizir *m.*
vocabulary *s.* vocabulaire *m.*
vocal *adj.* vocal; (*eloquent*) éloquent; (*fam.*) braillard; **~ist** *s.* chanteu/r, -se *m.f.*; **~ize** *v.t.* vocaliser; **~ly** *adv.* vocalement.
vocation *s.* vocation *f.*; **~al** *adj.* professionel.
vocative *s.* vocatif *m.*
vocifer/ate *v.i.* vociférer; **~ation** *s.* vocifération *f.*; **~ous** *adj.* criard.
vodka *s.* vodka *f.*
vogue *s.* vogue *f.*; **in ~**, en vogue.
voice *s.* voix *f.*; **in a loud ~**, à haute voix; **in a low ~**, à voix basse; **with one ~**, à l'unanimité; **~less** *adj.* muet; *v.t.* exprimer; (*ling.*) sonoriser.
void *s.* vide *m.*; *adj.* (*empty*) vide; (*vacant*) vacant; (*invalid*) nul; *v.t.* (*invalidate*) annuler; (*discharge*) évacuer.
voile *s.* (*text.*) voile *m.*
volatil/e *adj.* **1.** (*readily evaporating*) volatil; **2.** (*changeable, lively*) volage, vif, inconstant; **3.** (*transient*) transitoire; **~ity** *s.* (1) volatilité *f.*; (2) inconstance *f.*; **~ize** *v.t.* & *i.* (se) volatiliser.
volcan/o *s.* volcan *m.*; **~ic** *adj.* volcanique.
vole *s.* campagnol *m.*
volition *s.* volition *f.*; **of one's own ~**, de son propre gré.
volley *s.* (*of missiles*) volée *f.*, rafale *f.*; (*tennis*) volée *f.*; **half-~**, demi-volée *f.*; *v.t.* (*project*) lancer une volée de; (*return shot*) reprendre à la volée.
volt *s.* volt *m.*; **~age** *s.* voltage *m.*; **~meter** *s.* voltmètre *m.*
volub/le *adj.* (*person*) volubile; (*speech*) facile; **~ility** *s.* volubilité *f.*; **~ly** *adv.* avec volubilité.
volum/e *s.* (*book; space; size; sound*) volume *m.*; (*of water*) flots *m.pl.*; (*of smoke*) nuage *m.*; (*quality of sound*) ampleur *f.*; **~etric** *adj.* volumétrique; **~inous** *adj.* volumineux.
voluntar/y *s.* (*organ*) morceau d'orgue *m.*; *adj.* volontaire; **~ily** *adv.**.
volunteer *s.* volontaire *m.*; *adj.* volontaire; (*army*) de volontaires; *v.t.* & *i.* (*offer to do sth.*) s'offrir à faire qch.; (*give*) donner volontairement; (*mil.*) s'engager volontairement.
voluptu/ary *s.* épicurien(ne) *m.f.*; **~ous** *adj.* voluptueux; **~ously** *adv.**; **~ousness** *s.* sensualité *f.*
vomit *s.* (*act*) vomissement *m.*; (*matter*) vomissure *f.*; *v.t.* & *i.* vomir.
voodoo *s.* vaudou *m.*; *v.t.* envoûter; **~ism** *s.* vaudou *m.*
voraci/ous *adj.* vorace; **~ously** *adv.**; **~ty** *s.* voracité *f.*
vortex *s.* (*lit.* & *fig.*) tourbillon *m.*
votar/y *s.* partisan *m.*, amateur *m.*; **~ess** *s.* partisane *f.*, dame amateur *f.*
vot/e *s.* (*right to ~*) suffrage *m.*; (*number of ~es*) vote *m.*; (*expression of choice*) voix *f.*; (*opinion, decision*) motion *f.*; (*by ballot*) scrutin *m.*; *v.t.* & *i.* voter; (*fam.*) déclarer; (*suggest*) proposer; **~er** *s.* votant *m.*, élect/eur, -rice *m.f.*; **~ing** *s.* vote *m.*
votive *adj.* votif.
vouch *v.t.* confirmer; *v.i.* **~ for,** (*s.o.*) répondre de qn.; (*sth.*) garantir qch.; **~safe** *v.t.* & *i.* condescendre à, daigner; **~er** *s.* (*token*) bon *m.* (pour); (*receipt*) quittance *f.*
vow *s.* vœu *m.*; *v.t.* & *i.* vouer, jurer.
vowel *s.* voyelle *f.*
voyage *s.* voyage *m.*; *v.i.* voyager (par mer); **~r** *s.* voyageur *m.*
V.S.O. (*abbrev. Voluntary Service Overseas*) service de coopération *m.* (*approx. equivalent*).
V.T.O.(L.) (*abbrev. vertical take-off* (& *landing*)) ADAV *m.* (avion à décollage et atterrissage vertical).
vulcan/ite *s.* vulcanite *f.*; **~ize** *v.t.* vulcaniser.
vulcanology *s.* volcanologie *f.*
vulgar *adj.* **1.** (*plebeian, low*) vulgaire, bas; **2.** (*in common use*) commun; **3.** (*in bad taste*) de mauvais goût; **~ism** *s.* expression vulgaire *f.*; **~ity** *s.* vulgarité *f.*; **~ize** *v.t.* vulgariser; **~ly** *adv.* (1)*,*; (2) communément; (3) grossièrement.
Vulgate *s.* vulgate *f.*
vulnerab/le *adj.* vulnérable; **~ility** *s.* vulnérabilité *f.*
vulpine *adj.* (*of fox*) de renard; (*crafty*) rusé.
vulture *s.* (*lit.* & *fig.*) vautour *m.*
vulva *s.* vulve *f.*

W

W.A.C. (*abbrev. Women's Army Corps*) AFAT *f.pl.* (Auxiliaires Féminines de l'Armée de terre).
wad *s.* tampon *m.*, bouchon *m.*; (*mil.*) bourre *f.*; (*of bank notes*) liasse *f.*; *v.t.* presser, faire une boulette de; (*plug*) bourrer; **~ding** *s.* ouate *f.*
waddle *s.* dandinement *m.*; *v.i.* se dandiner.
wade *v.i.* (*in water, etc.*) patauger; **~ into** (*fam.*) s'attaquer à; **~ through** (*fig.*) avancer péniblement dans; **~r** *s.* (*bird*) échassier *m.*; **~rs** *s.pl.* bottes de pêche *f.pl.*
wadi *s.* oued *m.*
wafer *s.* (*biscuit*) gaufrette *f.*; (*for Eucharist*) hostie *f.*; (*seal*) cachet de papier *m.*, pain à cacheter *m.*; **~-thin** *adj.* mince comme du papier à cigarettes.
waffle *s.* (*cook.*) gaufre *f.*; *v.i.* (*fam.*) divaguer.
waft *s.* bouffée *f.*; *v.t.* porter; *v.i.* souffler.
wag *s.* **1.** (*motion*): (*of head*) hochement *m.*, (*of tail*) frétillement *m.*; **2.** (*joker*) farceur *m.*; *v.t.* & *i.* (1) hocher, remuer, (s')agiter; **~tail** *s.* bergeronnette *f.*; **~gish** *adj.* (2) farceur, badin.
wage(s)[1] *s.* salaire *m.*; (*of servants*) gages *m.pl.*; (*fig.*) salaire *m.*; LIVING ~; MINIMUM ~; **~-earner** *s.* salarié *m.*
wage[2] *v.t.* (*war, etc.*) faire.
wager *s.* pari *m.*; *v.t.* parier.
waggle *v.t.* agiter.
wag(g)on *s.* chariot *m.*; (*mil.*) fourgon *m.*; (*rail.*) wagon *m.*; (*auto.*) camion *m.*; **to be on the ~** (*pop.*) boire de l'eau; **~er** *s.* roulier *m.*; **~ette** *s.* break *m.*
waif *s.* épave *f.*, enfant abandonné *m.*
wail *s.* (& **~ing**) **1.** (*cry of pain; wind*) gémissement *m.*; **2.** (*of grief*) plainte *f.*; **3.** (*of child*) vagissement *m.*; *v.i.* (1) gémir; (2) se plaindre; (3) vagir.
wainscot *s.* lambris *m.*; *v.t.* lambrisser; **~ing** *s.* lambris *m.*; (*act*) lambrissage *m.*
waist *s.* taille *f.*; (*techn.*) étranglement *m.*; **~band** *s.* ceinture *f.*; **~coat** *s.* gilet *m.*; **~line** *s.* (tour de) taille *f.*; **~ed** *adj.* à taille pincée.
wait *s.* (*period of time*) attente *f.*; (*carol singer*) chanteur de noëls *m.*; **to lie in ~ for,** guetter; *v.t.* attendre; *v.i.* attendre (*till*—que); (*pause*) faire une pause; (*be on watch*) être aux aguets; (*act as ~er*) servir; **~ for** *v.t.* attendre; **~ (up)-on,** servir, accompagner; **~ and see,** être dans l'expectative; **~ and see!,** attendez (la suite)!; **~er** *s.* garçon *m.*, WINE **~er**; **~ress** *s.* serveuse *f.*; **~ing** *s.* attente *f.*; **~ing-room** *s.* salle d'attente *f.*
waive *v.t.* renoncer à, ne pas insister sur; **~r** *s.* (*law*) renonciation *f.*; (*fin.*) dispense *f.*
wake *s.* (*of ship*) sillage *m.*; **in the ~ of,** dans le sillage de, (*fig.*) par suite de; (*funeral*) veillée mortuaire *f.*; (*annual holiday, usu. pl.*) fêtes *f.pl.*; *v.t.* & *i.* & **~ up,** (se) réveiller; (*excite*) (se) ranimer; **~n** *v.t.* & *i.* (se) réveiller; **~ful** *adj.* (*person*) éveillé, (*night*) blanc, (*alert*) vigilant; **~fulness** *s.* insomnie *f.*, vigilance *f.*
Wales *s.* (*geog.*) Pays de Galles *m.*
walk *s.* (*pace*) pas *m.*; (*gait*) démarche *f.*; (*journey*) promenade *f.*; **it is ten minutes ~ from here,** c'est à dix minutes à pied; (*path*) avenue *f.*, allée *f.*; **~ of life** *s.* carrière *f.*; **to go for a ~,** (aller) faire une promenade; *v.t.* (*cover distance on foot*) faire à pied; (*cause to ~*) faire marcher, promener; *v.i.* (*gen.*) marcher; (≠ *drive, ride, etc.*) aller à pied; (*for pleasure*) se promener; (*horse*) marcher au pas; **~ away with** (*fig. win easily*) arriver dans un fauteuil; **~ down,** descendre, **~ in(to),** entrer (dans); **~ into (a trap)** tomber dans; **~ off** (*fam.*) filer; **~ off with** (*fam.*) chiper; **~ on** (*theat.*) faire de la figuration; **~ out,** sortir, (*fam. strike*) se mettre en grève; **~-out** *s.* débrayage *m.*; **~ out on,** abandonner; **~ over,** gagner d'office; **~-over** *s.* (*racing*) walk-over *m.*; **~ up,** monter (à pied); **~ing** *s.* marche *f.*; **~ing** *adj.* ambulant; **~-ing-stick** *s.* canne *f.*
walkie-talkie *s.* radio portative *f.*
wall *s.* (*of building*) mur *m.*; **with one's** BACK **to the ~**; (*rampart, mountain*) muraille *f.*; (*med.*) paroi *m.*; *adj.* mural; **~flower** *s.* giroflée *f.*; **be a ~flower** (*fig.*) faire tapisserie; **~paper** *s.* papier peint *m.*; **~ unit** *s.* éléments muraux *m.pl.*; *v.t.* (*town*) fortifier; **~ in,** entourer de murs; **~ off,** cloisonner; **~ up,** murer.
wallaby *s.* petit kangourou *m.*
wallet *s.* (*pouch*) besace *f.*; (*notecase*) portefeuille *f.*
Walloon *adj.* & *s.m.f.* wallon(ne).
wallop *v.t.* (*pop.*) rosser.
wallow *v.i.* se vautrer; (*fig.*) nager (dans).
walnut *s.* (*tree, wood*) noyer *m.*; (*fruit*) noix *f.*
walrus *s.* morse *m.*; **~ moustache,** moustache à la gauloise *f.*
waltz *s.* valse *f.*; *v.i.* valser.
wan *adj.* (*complexion*) blême; (*light*) blafard; (*smile*) pâle.
wand *s.* (*of office*) verge *f.*; (*fairy's*) baguette *f.*
wander *v.i.* (*move idly*) flâner; (*go from place to place*) errer; (*go astray*) s'égarer; (*wind, meander*) serpenter; (*mentally*) divaguer; **~er** *s.* voyageur sans but *m.*, (*pej.*) vagabond *m.*; **~ing** *s.* voyage à l'aventure *m.*, (*pej.*) vagabondage *m.*, (*med.*) délire *m.*, (*straying*) déviation *f.* (de), (*dreaming*) rêverie *f.*; **~ing** *adj.* errant, (*tribe*) nomade, (*med.*) délirant, (*speech*) incohérent, (*attention*) distrait.
wane *s.* (*astron.*) décours *m.*; (*fig.*) déclin *m.*; **to be on the ~,** être sur son déclin; *v.i.* (*decrease in brilliance, size, etc.*) décroître; (*lose power, etc.*) diminuer.
wangle *s.* (*pop.*) *m.*, resquille *f.*; *v.t.* resquiller.
want *s.* **1.** (*lack of*) manque (de) *m.*; **2.** (*need of, thing needed*) besoin *m.*; **3.** (*penury*) misère *f.*; **4.** (*desire*) désir *m.*; **for ~ of,** faute de; *v.t.* (1) manquer de; (2) avoir besoin de; (4) vouloir, désirer; (*ask for*) demander; (*look for*) rechercher; *v.i.* (3) être dans la gêne; **~ for,** manquer de; **~ed** *adj.* recherché (par la police); **~ing** *adj.* dépourvu (de), déficient; **to be ~ing,** manquer, faire défaut.
wanton *s.* femme légère *f.*; *adj.* **1.** (*capricious*) capricieux; **2.** (*wild*) déréglé, (*of growth*) luxuriant; **3.** (*licentious*) licencieux; **4.** (*reckless*) imprudent, étourdi; **5.** (*motiveless*) gratuit; **~ly** *adv.* (1) de gaité de cœur; (2) avec surabondance; (3) de façon licencieuse; (4) imprudemment; (5)*; **~ness** *s.* (1) gaité de cœur *f.*; (2) exubérance *f.*; (3) licence *f.*; (4) étourderie *f.*
war *s.* guerre *f.*; **~ of attrition,** guerre d'usure *f.*; CIVIL **~**; **cold ~,** guerre froide *f.*; **W~s of the** ROSES; TUG **of ~**; **to make ~ on,** faire la guerre contre; **to have been in the ~s** (*fam.*) être endommagé; **~-cry** *s.* cri de guerre *m.*; **~fare** *s.* guerre *f.*; **~head** *s* (cône de) charge

m.; ~**-horse** *s.* cheval de bataille *m.*; ~**monger** *s.* agitateur *m.*, belliciste *m.*; **W~ Office** *s.* ministère de la guerre *m.*; ~**-paint** *s.* peinture de guerre *f.*; ~**-path** *s.* sentier de la guerre *m.*; **to be on the ~-path** (*fig.*) se faire agressif; ~**ship** *s.* navire de guerre *m.*; ~**like** *adj.* (*act*) guerrier, martial, (*mood*) belliqueux; ~**ring** *adj.* combattant; *v.i.* faire la guerre.

warbl/e *v.i.* gazouiller; ~**er** *s.* fauvette *f.*; ~**ing** *s.* gazouillement *m.*

ward *s.* (*guardianship*) tutelle *f.*; (*minor*) pupille *m.f.*; (*in hospital*) salle *f.*, service *m.*; (*admin. division*) circonscription *f.*; (*of key*) garde *f.*; ~**room** *s.* (*naut.*) carré des officiers *m.*; *v.t.* ~ **off,** parer; (*fig.*) détourner.

warden *s.* gouverneur *m.*, directeur *m.*; CHURCH-~; GAME-~; TRAFFIC ~.

ward/er *s.* gardien *m.*; ~**ress** *s.* gardienne *f.*

wardrobe *s.* (*cupboard, clothes*) garde-robe *f.*; (*theat.*) costumes *m.pl.*; ~ **mistress** *s.* habilleuse *f.*

ware *s.* (*merchandise, usu. pl.*) marchandises *f.pl.*; (*pottery*) faïence *f.*; ~**house** *s.* entrepôt *m.*; ~**housing** *s.* entreposage *m.*

warm *s.* chaud *m.*, chaleur *f.*; *adj.* **1.** (*fairly hot*) chaud; **2.** (*with exercise*) échauffé; **3.** (*clothes*) chaud; **4.** (*feelings*) ardent, cordial, chaleureux; **5.** (*dangerous*) dangereux; **to be ~** (*person*) avoir chaud, (*weather*) faire chaud; ~**-hearted** *adj.* généreux; ~**ly** *adv.* (1), (3) *; (4) cordialement, chaleureusement; ~**th** *s.* chaleur *f.*; *v.t.* & *i.* (se) chauffer; (*cook.*) faire chauffer; (*fig.*) échauffer; ~ **up,** réchauffer, (*cook.*) faire réchauffer; (*sport*) se mettre en train; PLATE-~**er;** ~**ing-pan** *s.* bassinoire *f.*

warn *v.t.* prévenir (*against*—contre), avertir (*of*—de); ~ **against,** mettre en garde contre; ~ **off,** détourner; ~**ing** *s.* avertissement *m.*, préavis *m.*; **without ~ing,** sans prévenir.

warp *s.* **1.** (*in loom*) chaîne *f.*; **2.** (*tow-rope*) (h)aussière *f.*; **3.** (*distortion*) (*techn.*) gauchissement *m.*, (*fig.*) distortion *f.*; *v.t.* (2) haler; (3) gauchir, déformer.

warrant *s.* (*authority*) autorisation *f.*; (*document*) mandat *m.*; (*mil.*) brevet *m.*; ~**-officer** *s.* sous-officier breveté *m.*; ~**y** *s.* garantie *f.*; *v.t.* garantir, justifier; ~**able** *adj.* soutenable, légitime.

warren *s.* garenne *f.*

warrior *adj.* & *s.m.* guerrier.

Warsaw *s.* (*geog.*) Varsovie *f.*

wart *s.* verrue *f.*; ~**-hog** *s.* phacochère *m.*

war/y *adj.* prudent; ~**ily** *adv.* prudemment; ~**iness** *s.* prudence *f.*

wash *s.* (*act*) toilette *f.*, ablutions *f.pl.*, lavage *m.*; (*laundry*) lessive *f.*, blanchissage *m.*; (*paint*) couche *f.*; (*waves*) remous *m.*; (*of ship*) sillage *m.*; (*pig-food*) eaux-grasses *f.pl.*; *v.t.* & *i.* (*with liquid; of material, bear ~ing*) (se) laver; (*laundry*) faire la lessive; (*purify*) purifier; (*beat against*) baigner, arroser; **that won't ~** (*fam.*) ça ne marche pas; ~ **away,** enlever, emporter; ~ **down** (*meal*) arroser; ~ **off,** enlever; ~ **out,** laver; ~ **over,** baigner, balayer; ~ **up,** faire la vaisselle; ~ **one's hands of sth.,** se laver les mains de qch.; BRAIN~; ~**-basin** *s.* cuvette *f.*; ~**-day** *s.* jour de lessive *m.*; ~-LEATHER; ~**-out** *s.* (*pop.*) fiasco *m.*; ~**-stand** *s.* lavabo *m.*; ~**eteria** *s.* laverie automatique *f.*; ~**able** *adj.* lavable; ~**er** *s.* lav/eur, -euse *m.f.*, (*machine*) lessiveuse *f.*; DISH~**er;** ~**erwoman** *s.* blanchisseuse *f.*; ~**ed out** *adj.* (*fam.*) éreinté; ~**ing** *s.* lessive *f.*; ~**ing-machine** *s.* machine à laver *f.*; ~**ing-up** *s.* vaisselle *f.*; ~**ing-up machine** *s.* machine à laver la vaisselle *f.*

washer *s. see* WASH; (*mech.*) rondelle *f.*; (*plumbing*) joint *m.*

wasp *s.* guêpe *f.*; ~**'s nest** *s.* guêpier *m.*; ~**-waisted** *adj.* à taille de guêpe; ~**ish** *adj.* (*fig.*) irascible.

wastage *s.* gaspillage *m.*

waste[1] *s.* (*region*) désert *m.*; (*loss from wear & tear*) perte *f.*, déperdition *f.*; (*extravagance*) gaspillage *m.*; (~ *matter*) ordures *f.pl.*; (*industrial* ~) déchets *m.pl.*; ~**ful** *adj.* (*person*) gaspilleur, (*cost*) ruineux; ~**fully** *adv.* en gaspillant; ~**fulness** *s.* gaspillage *m.*, prodigalité *f.*

waste[2] *adj.* (*desert*) désert; ~ **land** *s.* terrain vague *m.*; (*left over*) de rebut, de déchet; (*superfluous*) inutile; **to lay ~,** ravager; ~ **paper** *s.* papier de rebut *m.*; ~**-paper basket** *s.* corbeille (à papier) *f.*; ~**-pipe** *s.* trop-plein *m.*

waste[3] *v.t.* (*lay* ~) ravager; (*squander*) gaspiller; (*time*) perdre; *v.i.* s'épuiser; ~ **away,** dépérir; ~ **not, want not,** qui épargne gagne; ~**r** *s.* gaspilleur *m.*; **wasting** *adj.* (*med.*) de langueur.

watch *s.* **1.** (*staying awake*) veille *f.*; **2.** (*naut.*) quart *m.*, (*crew*) bordée *f.*; **3.** (*look-out*) guet *m.*; **4.** (*timepiece*) montre *f.*; STOP-~; WRIST-~; ~**-dog** *s.* chien de garde *m.*; ~**maker** *s.* horloger *m.*; ~**man** *s.* gardien *m.*; ~**-strap** *s.* bracelet *m.*; ~-TOWER; ~**word** *s.* mot de passe *m.*, mot d'ordre *m.*, slogan *m.*; ~**ful** *adj.* vigilant; ~**fully** *adv.* avec vigilance; *v.t.* (1) veiller; (3) guetter; (*observe*) observer; ~ **over** surveiller, garder.

water *s.* eau *f.*; (*tide*) marée *f.*; **drinking ~,** eau potable *f.*; STILL ~**s run deep;** TREAD ~; **to hold ~** (*fig.*) tenir debout; *adj.* d'eau, aquatique; **hot**~-BOTTLE, ~**-butt** *s.* citerne *f.*; ~**-cannon** *s.* lance à eau *f.*; ~**-closet** *s.* cabinets *m.pl.*; ~**-colour** *s.* aquarelle *f.*; ~**course** *s.* cours d'eau *m.*; ~**cress** *s.* cresson *m.*; ~**-diviner** *s.* sourcier *m.*; ~**fall** *s.* chute d'eau *f.*; ~**fowl** *s.* gibier d'eau *m.*; ~**front** *s.* quai *m.*; ~**-glass** *s.* silicate de potasse *m.*; ~**-heater** *s.* chauffe-eau *m.*; ~**-jump** *s.* rivière *f.*; ~**-lily** *s.* nénuphar *m.*; ~**-line** *s.* (*naut.*) ligne de flottaison *f.*; ~**logged** *adj.* rempli d'eau, (*wood, land*) détrempé d'eau; ~**man** *s.* batelier *m.*; ~**mark** *s.* (*in paper*) filigrane *m.*, (*naut.*) laisse *f.*; ~**-melon** *s.* pastèque *f.*; ~**-mill** *s.* moulin à eau *m.*; ~ **polo** *s.* water-polo *m.*; ~**proof** *adj.* & *s.m.* imperméable; ~**proof** *v.t.* imperméabiliser; ~**-ram** *s.* bélier hydraulique *m.*; ~**shed** *s.* ligne de partage des eaux *f.*, (*fig,*) moment décisif *m.*; ~**-ski** *v.i.* faire du ski nautique; ~**spout** *s.* trombe *f.*; ~**-table** *s.* niveau hydrostatique *m.*; ~**tight** *adj.* étanche; ~**-way** *s.* voie navigable *f.*; ~**-weed** *s.* plante aquatique *f.*; ~**works** *s.* service des eaux *m.*; ~**less** *adj.* désert; ~**y** *adj.* aqueux, (*eyes*) humide; *v.t.* (*sprinkle with* ~) arroser; (*animals*) faire boire; (*dilute*) couper d'eau; *v.i.* (*eyes*) se mouiller; **make one's** MOUTH ~; ~**ing** *s.* arrosage *m.*; ~**ing-can** *s.* arrosoir *m.*; ~**ing**-PLACE.

watt *s.* (*electr.*) watt *m.*

wattle *s.* clayonnage *m.*

wave *s.* (*on water*) vague *f.*, flot *m.*; (*line*) ondulation *f.*; (*fig.*) vague *f.*, flot *m.*; (*gesture*) geste *m.*; (*radio*) onde *f.*; **heat ~** *s.* vague de chaleur *f.*; PERMANENT ~; **shock ~,** onde de choc *f.*; **sound ~,** onde acoustique *f.*; TIDAL ~; ~**-length** *s.* longueur d'onde *f.*; *v.t.* agiter; (*hand*) faire signe de la main; (*make wavy*) onduler; *v.i.* onduler; (*flag*) flotter; ~ **down** *v.t.* arrêter d'un signe de la main; ~ **goodbye,** faire un signe d'adieu; **wavy** *adj.* (*hair*) ondulé, (*corn*) ondulant, (*surface*) onduleux.

waver *v.i.* **1.** (*flicker*) vaciller; **2.** (*be irresolute*) défaillir; **3.** (*falter*) hésiter, balancer; ~**ing** *adj.* (1) vacillant; (2) défaillant; (3) hésitant.

wax[1] cire *f.*; ~ **candle** *s.* bougie *f.*; ~**work** *s.* figure de cire *f.*; ~**works** *s.* musée de figures de cire *m.*; ~**en** *adj.* de cire, en cire, (*complexion*) cireux; ~**y** *adj.* cireux, malléable; *v.t.* cirer.

wax² *v.i.* (*moon*) croître.
way *s.* (*road, path; distance*) chemin *m.*; DUAL **carriage**~; PERMANENT ~; (*route*) route *f.*; (*passage*) passage *m.*; (*direction*) côté *m.*; **two-**~ *adj.* bilatéral, (*traffic*) à double sens; ~ **in** *s.* entrée *f.*; ~ **out** *s.* sortie *f.*; **by** ~ **of,** en passant par; (*fig.*) en guise de; **by the** ~, en passant, à propos; **on the** ~, en route; **out of the** ~, (*secluded*) retiré, (*unusual*) extraordinaire; **under** ~, en route, (*naut.*) appareillé; **to be in the** ~, encombrer, être de trop; **to have one's own** ~, faire à sa guise; **to give** ~, céder (*to*—à), (*collapse*) s'effondrer; **to make** ~ **for,** livrer passage à; **to make one's** ~, faire son chemin; **make one's** ~ **to,** prendre la direction de; **to lead the** ~, montrer le chemin; **to lose one's** ~, s'égarer; STROKE **up the wrong** ~; **where there's a will, there's a** ~, vouloir, c'est pouvoir; **see which** ~ **the** WIND **blows;** (*manner*) manière *f.*; (*means*) moyen *m.*; ~**s and means,** moyens *m.pl.*, **in a** ~, dans une certaine mesure; **in some** ~**s,** à certains égards; **to pay one's** ~, se suffire; **to see one's** ~ **to,** trouver le moyen de; (*condition*) état *m.*; **in a** BAD ~; ~**-bill** *s.* feuille de route *f.*; ~**farer** *s.* voyageur *m.*; ~**lay** *v.t.* guetter, (*fam.*) accrocher au passage; ~**side** *s.* bord de la route *m.*, *adj.* du bord de la route; ~**ward** *adj.* capricieux, entêté; ~**wardly** *adv.**; ~**wardness** *s.* caprice *f.*, entêtement *m.*; *adv.* ~ **back,** il y a longtemps; ~**-out** *adj.* avant-garde.
W.C. *s.* W.C. *m.*
we *pron.* nous; (*emphat.*) nous autres.
weak *adj.* faible; (*fragile*) fragile; ~**-kneed** *adj.* (*fig.*) pusillanime; ~**en** *v.t.* & *i.* (s')affaiblir; ~**ening** *s.* affaiblissement *m.*; ~**ling** *s.* personne chétive *f.*; ~**ly** *adj.* chétif, débile; ~**ly** *adv.* faiblement; ~**ness** *s.* faiblesse *f.*, point faible *m.*; (*liking*) faible *m.*
weal *s.* (*mark*) zébrure *f.*; (*obs. welfare*) bien-être *m.*
wealth *s.* richesse *f.*, fortune *f.*; (*abundance*) abondance *f.*; **national** ~, patrimoine national *m.*; ~ **tax** *s.* impôt sur le capital *m.*; ~**y** *adj.* riche.
wean *v.t.* sevrer; (*fig.*) détacher (de).
weapon *s.* arme *f.*
wear *s.* (*clothes*) vêtements *m.pl.*; (*resistance*) usage *m.*; (*damage*) usure *f.*; ~ **and** TEAR; *v.t.* (*clothes*) porter; (*damage*) user; ~ **a hole in,** faire un trou à; **if the cap** FITS ~ **it;** *v.i.* (*endure*) faire de l'usage, se conserver; (~ *out*) s'user; ~ **away** *v.t.* & *i.* (s')effacer; ~ **down** *v.t.* user; ~ **off** *v.i.* s'effacer; ~ **out** *v.t.* & *i.* (s')user, (s')épuiser; ~ **well,** faire de l'usage; ~**able** *adj.* mettable; ~**er** *s.* personne qui porte *f.*; *see* WORN.
wear/y *adj.* (*tired*) las, fatigué; (*tiring*) fatigant; **to grow** ~**y of,** se lasser de; *v.t.* & *i.* (se) lasser, (se) fatiguer; ~**ily** *adv.* d'un air las, péniblement; ~**iness** *s.* lassitude *f.*, fatigue *f.*; ~**isome** *adj.* fatigant, (*fig.*) ennuyeux.
weasel *s.* belette *f.*
weather *s.* temps *m.*; **to make heavy** ~ **of sth.,** avoir beaucoup de peine à faire qch.; **under the** ~ (*fam.*) patraque; ~ **permitting,** si le temps le permet; ~**-beaten** *adj.* hâlé; ~**-board** *s.* jet *m.*; ~**cock** *s.* girouette *f.*; ~ **forecast** *s.* bulletin météorologique *m.*; ~**-glass** *s.* baromètre *m.*; *v.t.* user par les intempéries; (*wear away*) user; (*come safely through*) doubler (le cap); ~**ed** *adj.* décoloré par les intempéries.
weave *v.t.* (*fabric*) tisser; (*baskets, flowers*) tresser; *v.i.* tituber; ~ **one's way,** se frayer un chemin; ~**r** *s.* tisserand *m.*
web *s.* (*fabric* & *fig.*) tissu *m.*; (*spider's*) toile (d'araignée), *f.*; (*of bird*) palme *f.*; ~**bed** *adj.* palmé; ~**bing** *s.* toile de sangle *f.*
wed *v.t.* (*marry*) épouser; (*unite in marriage*) marier; *v.i.* se marier; **newly-**~**s** *s.pl.* nouveaux mariés *m.pl.*; ~**ded to** (*fig.*) attaché à; ~**ding** *s.* (*eccles.*) mariage *m.*, (*function*) noces *f.pl.*; ~**ding** *adj.* de mariage, nuptial; ~**ding ring** *s.* alliance *f.*; ~**lock** *s.* mariage *m.*
wedge *s.* (*for wood*) coin *m.*; (*for casks*) cale *f.*; **it's the thin end of the** ~, c'est un pied de pris; ~**-heeled** *adj.* à semelles compensées; *v.t.* (*force open*) fendre au coin; (*pack together*) coincer.
Wednesday *s.* mercredi *m.*; ASH ~.
wee *adj.* minuscule.
weed *s.* mauvaise herbe *f.*; SEA~; ~**-killer** *s.* herbicide *m.*; ~**y** *adj.* plein de mauvaises herbes; *v.t.* (*garden*) sarcler, (*pull out* ~*s*) arracher; ~ **out,** éliminer; ~**ing** *s.* sarclage *m.*
week *s.* semaine *f.*; (*period*) huit jours *m.pl.*; **today** ~, aujourd'hui en huit; ~**day** *s.* jour de semaine *m.*; ~**-end** *s.* week-end *m.*; ~**ly** *adj.* & *s.m.* hebdomadaire; ~**ly** *adv.* toutes les semaines.
weep *v.t.* (*s.o.*) pleurer sur qn.; (*tears*) verser; *v.i.* pleurer, couler; (*drip*) suinter; ~**ing** *adj.* en pleurs; ~**ing willow** *s.* saule pleureur *m.*
weevil *s.* charançon *m.*
w.e.f. (*abbrev. with effect from*) à partir de.
weft *s.* trame *f.*
weigh *v.t.* & *i.* (*lit.* & *fig.*) peser; (*anchor*) lever; (*have influence*) avoir du poids; (*in hand*) soupeser; ~ **down,** surcharger, (*fig.*) accabler; ~ **in** (*boxing*) se faire peser; ~ **(up)on,** peser sur; ~ **up,** peser; ~**bridge** *s.* pont-bascule *m.*; ~**ing-machine** *s.* bascule *f.*
weight *s.* (*lit.* & *fig.*) poids *m.*; (*phys.*) pesanteur *f.*; **to** CARRY ~; **to pull one's** ~, y mettre du sien, tenir son rôle; **to put on** ~, prendre du poids; **to throw one's** ~ **about** (*fig. fam.*) faire du volume; ~**-lifter** *s.* haltérophile *m.*; ~**-lifting** *s.* haltérophilie *f.*; ~**y** *adj.* pesant, important, de poids; *v.t.* (*attach* ~ *to*) plomber; (*burden*) charger; (*fig.*) accabler; (*adjust figures*) ajouter un coefficient à, pondérer.
weir *s.* barrage *m.*
weird *adj.* étrange, surnaturel.
welcome *s.* accueil *m.*, réception *f.*; *adj.* (*person*) bienvenu; (*news, etc.*) agréable; **to be** ~ **to do sth.,** être libre de faire qch.; **you are** ~ **to use my car,** ma voiture est à votre disposition; **you're** ~, (*response to thanks*) je vous en prie; *v.t.* souhaiter la bienvenue à qn.; accueillir (avec joie); *interj.* soyez le (la, les) bienvenu(e)s) !
weld *s.* soudure *f.*; *v.t.* souder; ~**er** *s.* soudeur *m.*
welfare *s.* bien-être *m.*; ~ **officer** *s.* assistant(e) social(e) *m.f.*; **child** ~ **officer** *s.* magistrat délégué à la protection de l'enfance *m.*; **W**~ **State** *s.* état providence *m.*; ~ **work** *s.* assistance sociale *f.*
well¹ *s.* puits *m.*; (*of stairs, lift*) cage *f.*; (*ink-*~) encrier *m.*; (*fig.*) source *f.*; *v.i.* ~ **up,** jaillir.
well² *adj.* (*in health*) en bonne santé; (*satisfactory*) bon, opportun; *adv.* (*rightly, carefully, probably*) bien; (*properly*) comme il faut; (*kindly*) aimablement; **as** ~, aussi; **you might as** ~ **go,** autant vaudrait partir; **as** ~ **as,** aussi bien que; **to do** ~, prospérer; **you did** ~ **to,** vous avez bien fait de; **to** MEAN ~; **to let** ~ ALONE; ALL**'s** ~ **that ends** ~; **hail-**FELLOW**-**~**-met;** ~ **off,** ~**-to-do,** cossu, aisé; *interj.* **very** ~**!,** eh bien; (*resignation*) soit!
well- (*in combination*) ~**-advised** *adj.* judicieux; ~**-balanced** *adj.* bien équilibré ; ~**-behaved** *adj.* bien élevé; ~**-being** *s.* bien-être *m.*; ~**-bred** *adj.* (*person*) bien élevé, (*animal*) racé; ~**-groomed** *adj.* soigné; ~**-heeled** *adj.* (*fam.*) riche; ~**-informed** *adj.* bien documenté; ~**-meaning** *adj.* bien intentionné; ~ **timed** *adj.*

opportun; **~-wisher** *s.* partisan *m.*; **~-worn** *adj.* usé, (*fig.*) rebattu.
wellingtons *s.pl.* bottes (en caoutchouc) *f.pl.*
Welsh *adj.* gallois; **~man, ~woman** *s.* Gallois(e) *m.f.*; *s.m.* (*lang.*) gallois; **~ rabbit** *s.* (*cook.*) croque-monsieur *m.*
welt *s.* (*of shoe*) trépointe *f.*; (*of garment*) bordure *f.*; (*mark of blow*) zébrure *f.*
welter *v.i.* se vautrer; **~-weight** *s.* poids mi- -moyen *m.*
wench *s.* fille *f.*
werewolf *s.* loup-garou *m.*
west *s.* (*compass point*) ouest *m.*: (*region*) occident *m.*; **to go ~** (*fam. of people*) passer l'arme à gauche; *adj.* (*wind*) d'ouest; (*geog.*) occidental; *adv.* à l'ouest; **W~ Indies** *s.* (*geog.*) Antilles *f.pl.*; **W~ Indian** *adj.* & *s.m.f.* antillais(e); **~erly** *adj.* d'ouest; **~erlies** *s.* (*meteor.*) zone des vents d'ouest *f.*; **~ern** *adj.* d'ouest, occidental; **~ern** *s.* western *m.*, film de cowboys *m.*; **~erner** *s.* occidental *m.*; **~ernize** *v.t.* occidentaliser; **~ward** *adv.* vers l'ouest.
wet *s.* **1.** (*liquid*) humidité *f.*; **2.** (*weather*) temps pluvieux *m.*; **3.** (*pop. person*) chiffe *f.*; *adj.* (1) humide (*soaked*) mouillé; (2) pluvieux; (3) mou; **~ through,** mouillé jusqu'aux os; **~** BLANKET; **~ suit** *s.* combinaison de plongée *f.*; **~ness** *s.* humidité *f.*; *v.t.* mouiller.
wether *s.* bélier châtré *m.*
whack *s.* (*fam. blow*) coup *m.*; (*pop. share*) part *f.*; *v.t.* (*fam.*) cogner; **~ed** *adj.* (*pop.*) épuisé; **~ing** *adj.* (*pop.*) formidable.
whale *s.* baleine *f.*; SPERM **~**; **we had a ~ of a time** (*fam.*) on s'est follement amusé; **~bone** *s.* baleine *f.*; **~r** *s.* baleinier *m.*; **whaling** *s.* pêche à la baleine *f.*; *adj.* baleinier.
wharf *s.* quai *m.*, appontement *m.*
what *rel. pron.* ce qui, ce que, ce dont, ce à quoi; **tell me ~ is happening,** dites-moi ce qui se passe; **tell me ~ you want,** dites-moi ce que vous voulez; **tell me ~ you need,** dites-moi ce dont vous avez besoin; **tell me ~ you're thinking about,** dites-moi ce à quoi vous pensez; *interrog. adj.* quel, quelle, quels, quelles; *exclam. adj.* **~ luck!,** quelle chance!; **~ a fool you are!,** que vous êtes bête!; *interrog. pron.* qu'est-ce qui, qu'est ce que, de quoi, que; **~ is happening?,** qu'est-ce qui se passe?; **~ do you want?,** qu'est-ce que vous voulez?; **~ do you need?,** de quoi avez-vous besoin?; **~ am I to do?,** que faire?; (*as interj.*) (*fam.*) quoi?, comment?; **~ use is it?,** à quoi ça sert?; **to know ~'s ~,** savoir ce dont il s'agit; **and ~ not,** et que sais-je?; **~ about?,** que pensez-vous de?, que diriez-vous de?; **~ for?,** pourquoi donc?; **~ if,** et si?; **~ then, so ~?,** et après?; **~ though,** même si; **~ with,** étant donné (que); **~ is more,** qui plus est; **~ever** *pron.* & *adj.* **do ~ever you like,** faites tout ce qui vous plaira; **~ever you do,** quoi que vous fassiez; **~ever ideas you may have,** quelques idées que vous ayez; **~ever may be his terms,** quelles que soient ses conditions; **~soever** *pron.* & *adj.* **he has no ability ~soever,** il n'a pas le moindre talent; **it will be no trouble ~soever,** cela ne nous dérangera en aucune façon.
wheat *s.* (*gen.*) blé *m.*; (*agric.*) froment *m.*; **~en** *adj.* de blé, de froment; **~-meal** *s.* farine de froment *f.*
wheedl/e *v.t.* & *i.* cajoler; **~e sth. out of s.o.,** soutirer qch. à qn. par des cajoleries; **~er** *s.* cajoleur *m.*; **~ing** *s.* cajolerie *f.*
wheel *s.* roue *f.*; (*auto. steering-~*) volant *m.*; (*naut.*) barre *f.*; (*spinning-~*) rouet *m.*; (*potter's*) tour *m.*; (*mil.*) conversion *f.*; **~s** (*fig.*) rouages *m.pl.*; **~s within ~s,** rouages *m.pl.*; **cart-~** (*sport*) roue *f.*, *v.i.* faire la roue; **free-~** *v.i.* marcher en roue libre; **spare ~,** roue de rechange *f.*; **to set ~s in motion** (*fig.*) faire le nécessaire pour; **to put one's** SHOULDER **to the ~**; **to put a** SPOKE **in s.o.'s ~**; **~barrow** *s.* brouette *f.*; **~base** *s.* (*auto.*) empattement *m.*; **~chair** *s.* fauteuil roulant *m.*; **~wright** *s.* charron *m.*; *v.t.* (*barrow, chair*) rouler; (*bicycle*) pousser; *v.i.* tourner en rond, (*mil.*) faire une conversion.
wheez/e *s.* (*med.*) respiration sifflante *f.*; (*fam.*) idée *f.*; *v.i.* siffler; **~y** *adj.* asthmatique.
whelk *s.* buccin *m.*
whelp *s.* chiot *m.*; (*of lion*) lionceau *m.*; (*of wolf*) louveteau *m.*
when *adv.* & *conj.* quand; ⚠ *followed by future if v. in main clause is future*) **~ he arrives, he will tell us,** quand il arrivera, il nous dira; **~ever** *adv.* & *conj.* à n'importe quel moment, toutes les fois que.
whence *conj.* d'où.
where *adv.* & *conj.* où; **~abouts** *s.* endroit où se trouve (qch. *or* qn.) *m.*; **~as** *conj.* tandis que, vu que; **~at,** sur quoi; **~by,** par quoi; **~ever, ~soever,** partout où; **~ever he may be,** où qu'il soit; **~fore,** pourquoi; **~in,** en quoi; **~of,** de quoi, dont; **~upon,** sur quoi; **~withal** *s.* moyens *m.pl.*; **to have the ~withal to do sth.,** avoir de quoi faire qch.
wherry *s.* bachot *m.*
whet *v.t.* (*lit.* & *fig.*) aiguiser; **~stone** *s.* pierre à aiguiser *f.*
whether *conj.* si; **he asked ~ it was true,** il demanda si c'était vrai; **~ he takes the train, or the bus,** (soit) qu'il prenne le train, ou l'autobus; **~ . . .** OR.
whew! *interj.* oh là, là!
whey *s.* petit-lait *m.*
which *rel. pron.* qui, que, dont; **the book ~ is on the table,** le livre qui est sur la table; **the book ~ you want,** le livre que vous cherchez; **the book of ~ I told you,** le livre dont je vous ai parlé; (*with prep.*) lequel, *etc.*; **in ~,** où; **from ~,** d'où; **the book in ~ I read that,** le livre dans lequel (*or* où) j'ai lu cela; **the work to ~ I have devoted all my time,** le travail auquel j'ai consacré tout mon temps; (*referring to complete clauses*) ce qui, ce que, ce dont, ce à quoi; **he refused, ~ didn't surprise me,** il refusa, ce qui ne m'étonna pas; **he refused, ~ I couldn't believe,** il refusa, ce que je ne croyais pas possible; **he gave me some apples, ~ I didn't need,** il me donna des pommes, ce dont je n'avais pas besoin; **he refused, ~ I didn't expect,** il refusa, ce à quoi je ne m'attendais pas; *interrog. pron.* lequel, laquelle, lesquels, lesquelles; *interrog. adj.* quel(le)s); **~ever, ~soever** *adj.* & *pron.* n'importe (le)-quel.
whiff *s.* (*puff of air, smoke, etc.*) bouffée *f.*; (*boat*) skiff *m.*; (*small cigar*) cigarillo *m.*
while *s.* temps *m.*; **all the ~,** tout le temps; **once in a ~,** de temps en temps; **to be worth ~,** en valoir la peine; *adv.* & *conj.* (*also whilst*) (*during time that*) pendant que; (*for as long as*) tant que; (*although*) tandis que; (*and at the same time*) alors que; *v.t.* **~ away,** passer; (*time*) tuer.
whim *s.* caprice *m.*; **~sical** *adj.* (*person*) capricieux; (*thing*) fantasque.
whimper *s.* pleurnichement *m.*; *v.i.* pleurnicher; **~ing** *s.* pleurnichement *m.*
whine *s.* **1.** (*cry*) gémissement *m.*; **2.** (*querulous tone*) pleurnichement *m.*; **3.** (*complaint*) geignement *m.*; *v.i.* (1) gémir; (2) pleurnicher; (3) geindre.
whip *s.* (*instrument*) fouet *m.*; (*motion, fig.*) fouettement *m.*; (*hunt official*) piqueur *m.*; (*parl.*) chef de file *m.*; **~cord** *s.* whipcord *m.*;

~**-saw** *s.* scie à chantourner *f.*; *v.t.* **1.** fouetter, (*urge on*) pousser du fouet; **2.** (*beat*) (*eggs*) battre, (cream) fouetter; **3.** (*bind with twine*) surlier; **4.** (*snatch*) saisir; **5.** (*bind seam*) surjeter; ~ **out of** *v.t.* & *i.* sortir brusquement; ~ **up** *v.t.* fouetter, (*fig.*) exciter; ~**-round** *s.* collecte *f.*; ~**per--snapper** *s.* freluquet *m.*; ~**ping** *s.* (1) fouet *m.*, (*fig.*) fouettement *m.*; fouettée *f.*; (3) surliure *f.*; (5) surjet *m.*

whippet *s.* lévrier de course *m.*

whirl *s.* (*violent movement*) tourbillonnement *m.*; (*rush*) tourbillon *m.*; **to be in a** ~, avoir la tête qui tourne; *v.t.* & *i.* (*swing round*) (faire) tournoyer; (*send fast*) entraîner à toute vitesse; (*go fast*) filer; (*head*) tourner; ~**igig** *s.* (*toy*) tourniquet *m.*, (*at fair*) manège *m.*; ~ **pool** *s.*, ~**wind** *s.* tourbillon *m.*

whir(r) *s.* ronflement *m.*; *v.i.* ronfler.

whisk *s.* **1.** (*brush*) époussette *f.*; **2.** (*for eggs, etc.*) fouet *m.*; **3.** (*movement*) effleurement rapide *m.*; *v.t.* & *i.* (1) chasser; (2) battre, fouetter; (3) (3) passer/envoyer à toute vitesse.

whisker *s.* (*human*) favori *m.*; (*of cat, etc.*) moustache *f.*

whisky *s.* whisky *m.*

whisper *s.* **1.** (*vocal sound*) chuchotement *m.*; **2.** (*murmur*) murmure *m.*; **3.** (*rumour*) bruit *m.*; *v.t.* & *i.* (1) chuchoter; (2) murmurer; (3) faire courir (un bruit); ~**ing** *s.* chuchotement *m.*

whist *s.* whist *m.*

whistle *s.* (*sound*) sifflement *m.*; (*instrument*) sifflet *m.*; *v.t.* & *i.* siffler.

whit *s.* brin *m.*

white *s.* (*colour, of egg, of eye. etc.*; *person*) blanc *m.*; *adj.* blanc; (*pale*) pâle; (*unstained*) pur; ~ **ant** *s.* termite *f.*; ~**bait** *s.* blanchaille *f.*; ~**-collar work(er)** *s.* travail (employé) de bureau *m.*; ~ CURRANT; ~ ELEPHANT; ~ FEATHER; ~ **flag** *s.* drapeau parlementaire *m.*; ~**-haired** *adj.* à cheveux blancs; ~**-hot** *adj.* chauffé à blanc; ~ HORSE; ~ LEAD; ~ **lie** *s.* pieux mensonge *m.*; ~ **sauce,** béchamel *f.*; ~**thorn** *s.* aubépine *f.*; ~**wash** *s.* badigeon *m.*, *v.t.* badigeonner, (*fig.*) blanchir; ~**n** *v.t.* blanchir; **whitish** *adj.* blanchâtre; ~**ness** *s.* blancheur *f.*

whither *adv.* où

whiting *s.* merlan *m.*

whitlow *s.* panaris *m.*

Whitsun/tide *s.* Pentecôte *f.*; ~**day** *s.* dimanche de la Pentecôte *m.*

whittle *v.t.* tailler (au couteau); ~ **away,** ~ **down,** rogner.

whiz(z) *s.* sifflement *m.*; *v.t.* & *i.* siffler.

who *rel.* & *interrog. pron.* qui, qui est-ce qui; ~**ever,** ~**soever,** quiconque, qui que ce soit; ~**ever you are,** qui que vous soyez; **W~'s W~** *s.* bottin mondain *m.*

W.H.O. (*World Health Organization*) O.M.S. *f.* (Organisation Mondiale de la Santé).

whoa *interj.* ho!

whodun(n)it *s.* (*fam.*) roman/film policier *m.*

whole *s.* (*full amount*) totalité *f.*; (*complete thing*) tout *m.*; **on the** ~, à tout prendre; **as a** ~, dans l'ensemble; *adj.* (*intact, complete*) entier, intact; (*all* (*of*)) tout(e) le (la); (*uninjured*) sain et sauf; ~**-hearted** *adj.* sincère; **go the** ~ HOG; ~**meal** *s.* pain complet *m.*; ~**sale** *s.* gros *m.*, *adj.* en gros; ~**sale** PRICE; ~**some** *adj.* sain, (*climate*) salubre; ~**someness** *s.* caractère sain *m.*, salubrité *f.*; ~**-time** *adj.* à temps complet; **wholly** *adv.* entièrement.

whom *rel. pron.* que; (*after prep.*) qui; *interrog. pron.* qui, qui est-ce que; **the man ~ you see,** l'homme que vous voyez; **the man to ~ you are speaking,** l'homme à qui vous parlez; **the man for ~ I work,** l'homme pour qui je travaille; ~ **did you see?,** qui avez-vous vu?

whoop *s.* hourra *m.*; *v.i.* crier hourra; ~**ee!** *interj.* hourra!; ~**ing cough** *s.* coqueluche *f.*

whopp/er *s.* (*pop.*) monstre *m.*; (*lie*) énormité *f.*; ~**ing** *adj.* (*pop.*) énorme.

whore *s.* putain *f.*

whorl *s.* spirale *f.*

whose *rel. pron.* dont, de qui, duquel, etc.; *interrog. pron.* de qui?, à qui?

why *adv.* & *s.m.* pourquoi; *interj.* tiens!, tenez!

wick *s.* mèche *f.*

wicked *adj.* méchant; (*painful*) mauvais; (*mischievous*) malicieux; ~**ly** *adv.* méchamment; ~**ness** *s.* méchanceté *f.*

wicker *s.* osier *m.*; *adj.* d'osier, en osier; ~**work** *s.* vannerie *f.*

wicket *s.* guichet *m.*

wide *adj.* (≠ *narrow*) large; (*of great extent*) étendu; (≠ *tight*) ample; (*fig.*) vaste, large; **to be two feet** ~, être large de deux pieds, avoir deux pieds de large; FAR **and** ~; ~ **apart,** très espacé, (*legs*) écarté; ~ **awake** *adj.* éveillé; ~ OPEN; ~**spread** *adj.* répandu; ~**ly** *adv.* largement; ~**n** *v.t.* & *i.* (s')élargir.

widow *s.* veuve *f.*; ~**er** *s.* veuf *m.*; ~**ed** *adj.* veu/f, -ve; ~**hood** *s.* veuvage *m.*

width *s.* largeur *f.*; (*of cloth*) lé *m.*

wield *v.t.* (*tool*) manier; (*weapon*) brandir; (*fig. influence, etc.*) exercer.

wife *s.* femme *f.*, épouse *f.*; ~**ly** *adj.* d'épouse.

wig *s.* perruque *f.*

wigging *s.* semonce *f.*; **to give s.o. a** ~, passer un savon à qn.

wiggle *s.* secousse *f.*; *v.t.* agiter.

Wight *see* ISLE **of** ~.

wigwam *s.* wigwam *m.*

wild *s.* désert *m.*; *adj.* **1.** (*in natural state,* ≠ *tame*) sauvage; **2.** (≠ *cultivated*) inculte; **3.** (*uncivilized*) farouche; **4.** (*tempestuous*) furieux; **5.** (*uncontrolled*) déréglé, indiscipliné, (*look*) égaré; **6.** (*excited*) fou (*with*—de); **7.** (*enthusiastic*) enthousiaste, frénétique; **8.** (*rash*) imprudent, extravagant; ~**cat** *adj.* risqué, (*strike*) non--officielle; ~**fire** *s.* feu grégeois *m.*; **like ~fire,** comme une traînée de poudre; ~-GOOSE **chase;** ~ OATS; **to run** ~, se dévergonder, (*plant*) pousser à la diable; ~**ly** *adv.* (3)*; (4)*; (5) de façon déréglée; (6) follement; (7) avec enthousiasme, *; (8) imprudemment; ~**ness** *s.* (1), (2), (3) nature sauvage *f.*, état sauvage *m.*; (4) fureur *f.*; (5) indiscipline *f.*; (6) folie *f.*; (7) frénésie *f.*; (8) imprudence *f.*, extravagance *f.*

wilderness *s.* désert *m.*

wil/e *s.* ruse *f.*; ~**y** *adj.* rusé; ~**iness** *s.* astuce *f.*

wilful *adj.* **1.** (*intentional*) voulu, délibéré; **2.** (*self-willed*) entêté; **3.** (*wayward*) déréglé; ~**ly** *adv.* (1) délibérément; (2) avec entêtement; ~**ness** *s.* (1) préméditation *f.*; (2) entêtement *m.*

will[1] *s.* **1.** (*faculty, action*) volonté *f.*; **2.** (*intention*) intention *f.*; **3.** (*desire*) gré *m.*, désir *m.*; **4.** (*testament*) testament *m.*; **at** ~, à volonté; **of one's own free** ~, de son plein gré; **against one's** ~, contre son gré; **to bear s.o. ill** ~, en vouloir à qn.; **where there's a ~ there's a** WAY; ~**-power** *s.* volonté *f.*; *v.t.* (1) vouloir; (2) avoir l'intention de; (3) désirer, vouloir; (4) léguer; *v.i.* vouloir; (*consent, wish*) vouloir (*fut.* & *cond.*) **I hope he ~ come,** j'espère qu'il voudra bien venir; (*be accustomed to*) avoir l'habitude de, *or, use imperfect tense*; **they would go to the beach every day,** ils allaient à la plage tous les jours.

will[2] *v.aux.* (*fut.* & *cond.*) *use fut. or cond. of verb or* aller + *inf.*; **I ~ explain,** je vous expliquerai, *or*, je vais vous expliquer.

William *s.* Guillaume *m.*

willing *adj.* (*ready to help*) disposé à, prêt à; (*done*

~*ly*) spontané, fait de bon cœur; (*full of goodwill*) courageux, obligeant; **~ly** *adv.* de plein gré, spontanément, volontiers, avec plaisir; **~ness** *s.* bonne volonté *f.*, empressement *m.*
will-o'-the-wisp *s.* feu follet *m.*
willow *s.* saule *m.*; WEEP**ing ~**; **~-herb** *s.* épilobe *m.*; **~-warbler** *s.* pouillot *m.*
willy-nilly *adv.* bon gré mal gré.
wilt *v.t.* & *i.* (se) flétrir.
wimple *s.* guimpe *f.*
win *s.* victoire *f.*; *v.t.* (*money, prize, race*) gagner; (*victory*) remporter; (*reputation*) se faire; *v.i.* gagner; **~** HANDS **down; ~ back** *v.t.* regagner; **~ over** *v.t.* gagner, rallier; **~ through** *v.i.* arriver au but; **~ner** *s.* gagnant *m.*; **~nings** *s.pl.* gains *m.pl.*; **~ning** *adj.* gagnant, (*attractive*) séduisant; **~ning-post** *s.* poteau d'arrivée *m.*
wince *v.i.* broncher.
winceyette *s.* tiretaine *f.*
winch *s.* manivelle *f.*; treuil *m.*; *v.t.* hisser au treuil.
wind[1] *s.* (*current of air; med.*) vent *m.*; TRADE **~**; (*breath*) souffle *m.*; (*mus.*) instruments à vent *m.pl.*; **to get ~ of sth.,** avoir vent de qch.; **to get the ~ up** (*pop.*) avoir la frousse; **to** RAISE **the ~; close to the ~,** (*naut.*) au plus près du vent; **to sail close to the ~,** friser l'illégalité; **to take the ~ out of s.o.'s** SAILS**; to see which way the ~ blows,** voir d'où vient le vent; GONE **with the ~; ~bag** *s.* (*pop.*) phraseur *m.*; **~-break** *s.* abat-vent *m.*; **~-cheater** *s.* blouson *m.*; **~-**DEFLECT**or; ~fall** *s.* fruit tombé *m.*, (*fig.*) aubaine *f.*; **~ instrument** *s.* instrument à vent *m.*; **~mill** *s.* moulin (à vent) *m.*; **~pipe** *s.* trachée-artère *f.*; **~screen** *s.* pare-brise *m.*; **~screen** WIPE**r; ~-sock** *s.* manche à air *f.*; **~ward** *s.* côté du vent *m.*, *adj.* exposé au vent; **~y** *adj.* (*place, weather*) venteux, (*fam.* = *long-~ed*) verbeux (*pop.*) froussard; *v.t.* (*detect by scent*) avoir vent de; (*deprive of breath*) essouffler; **~ed** *adj.* essoufflé; LONG-**~ed.**
wind[2] (*move sinuously*) *v.t.* faire tourner, *v.i.* serpenter; (*coil round*) *v.t.* & *i.* (s')enrouler, dévider; (*haul, hoist*) *v.t.* hisser (au treuil); **~ up** (*clock*) remonter, (*debate*) *v.t.* clore, *v.i.* se terminer, (*comm.*) *v.t.* & *i.* (se) liquider; **~er** *s.* dévidoir *m.*, remontoir *m.*; **~ing** *s.* (*of river, road*) détour *m.*, méandre *m.*; **~ing** *adj.* (*river, road*) sinueux, (*staircase*) tournant; **~ing-up** *s.* (*comm.*) liquidation *f.*
windlass *s.* treuil *m.*
window *s.* (*house*) fenêtre *f.*; (*shop*) devanture *f.*, vitrine *f.*; (*rail., auto.*) glace *f.*; BAY **~**; FRENCH **~**; ROSE-**~**; SASH-**~**; STAINED GLASS **~**; **~-box** *s.* caisse à fleurs *f.*; **~-dressing** *s.* (*fig.*) trompe l'œil *m.*; **~-frame** *s.* châssis *m.*; **~-pane** *s.* vitre *f.*, carreau *m.*; **~-sill** *s.* rebord (de fenêtre) *m.*; **to go ~-shopping,** faire du lèche-vitrine.
wine *s.* vin *m.*; **good ~ needs no bush,** à bon vin point d'enseigne; **~-cellar** *s.* cave (à vin) *f.*; **~-glass** *s.* verre à vin *m.*; **~-grower** *s.* viticulteur *m.*; **~-merchant** *s.* négociant en vins *m.*; **~press** *s.* pressoir *m.*; **~-waiter** *s.* sommelier *m.*
wing *s.* (*anat., aviat., auto., mil., sport, polit., constr.*) aile *f.*; (*flight*) vol *m.*; **~s** *s.pl.* (*theat.*) coulisses *f.pl.*; **on the ~,** en vol; **to take ~,** prendre son essor; **to take s.o. under one's ~,** prendre qn. sous son aile; **to** CLIP **s.o.'s ~s; ~ commander,** lieutenant-colonel (de l'armée de l'air) *m.*; **~-span** *s.* envergure *f.*; **~ed** *adj.* ailé; **~er** *s.* (*sport*) ailier *m.*; *v.t.* & *i.* voler; (*arrow*) décocher; (*wound in ~*) blesser à l'aile.
wink *s.* clin d'œil *m.*; **not to sleep a ~,** ne pas fermer les yeux de la nuit; **to tip s.o. the ~,** cligner de l'œil à qn,; FORTY **~s;** *v.i.* clignoter; **~ at** (*fig.*) fermer les yeux sur.
winkle *s.* bigorneau *m.*; *v.t.* **~ out** dénicher.
winnow *v.t.* vanner; (*fig.*) trier; **~er** *s.* (*person*) vanneur *m.*; (*techn.*) van *m.*; **~ing** *s.* vannage *m.*; (*fig.*) tri *m.*
winsome *adj.* séduisant.
winter *s.* hiver *m.*; *adj.* & **wintry** *adj.* d'hiver, hivernal; **~-green** *s.* gaulthérie *f.*, (essence de) wintergreen *m.*; **~ sports** *s.pl.* sports d'hiver *m.pl.*; *v.i.* hiverner; *v.t.* faire passer l'hiver à.
wipe *s.* coup de torchon, de mouchoir, *etc. m.*; *v.t.* essuyer; **~ away** *v.t.* essuyer; **~ out** *v.t.* effacer, (*destroy*) anéantir; **~ up** *v.t.* nettoyer; **~r** *s.* (*auto.*) essuie-glace *m.invar.*
wire *s.* fil (métallique) *m.*, fil de fer *m.*; BARBED **~**; (*fam.* = *telegram*) dépêche *f.*; **live ~** (*fig. person*) personne dynamique *f.*; **to pull the ~s** (*fig.*) tirer les ficelles; *adj.* de fil, en fil; **~-haired** *adj.* (*dog*) à poil dur; **~less** *s.* T.S.F. *f.*, radio *f.*, *adj.* radiophonique; **~less set** *s.* poste de radio *m.*; **~ netting** *s.* treillis métallique *m.*; **~ wool** *s.* paille de fer *f.*; **~-worm** *s.* larve d'élatère *m.*; **wiry** *adj.* (*fig.*) nerveux; *v.t.* & *i.* (*support, secure, with ~s*) monter sur fil, grillager; (*electr.*) équiper (un bâtiment); (*fam.*) télégraphier.
wisdom *s.* sagesse *f.*; (*learning*) connaissances *f.pl.*; **~ tooth** *s.* dent de sagesse *f.*
wise[1] *adj.* (*archaic*) sage; (*prudent, sensible*) prudent, judicieux; (*having knowledge*) savant; PENNY **~**; **~crack** *s.* (*fam.*) bon mot *m.*; **~ man** *s.* sage *m.*; **be/put ~ to,** être/mettre, au courant de; **~ly** *adv.* sagement, prudemment.
wise[2] *s.* (*manner*) guise *f.*, façon *f.*
wish *s.* désir *m.*; **good, best ~es,** vœux *m.pl.*; **~bone** *s.* fourchette *f.*; **~ful** *adj.* désireux (de), (*look*) d'envie; **that's ~ful thinking,** c'est prendre ses désirs pour des réalités; *v.t.* (*want*) désirer, souhaiter (qch. à qn.); vouloir (*often in cond.*); **~ for,** souhaiter.
wishy-washy *adj.* fade.
wisp *s.* (*of straw*) bouchon *m.*; (*of smoke*) ruban *m.*; **~y** *adj.* petit.
wistaria *s.* glycine *f.*
wistful *adj.* **1.** (*dreamy*) rêveur, pensif; **2.** (*covetous look, etc.*) d'envie; **~ly** *adv.* (1) pensivement; (2) avec envie.
wit *s.* esprit *m.*; (*person*) homme d'esprit *m.*; **to be at one's ~s'** END**; to keep one's ~s about one,** ne pas perdre la tête; **~less** *adj.* (*person*) inintelligent; (*action*) stupide; **to ~,** à savoir.
witch *s.* sorcière *f.*; **~craft** *s.* sorcellerie *f.*; **~-doctor** *s.* sorcier-guérisseur *m.*; **~-hunt** *s.* (*fig.*) chasse aux sorcières *f.*
with *prep.* **1.** (*in company of, against*) avec; **come ~ me,** venez avec moi; **to discuss ~ s.o., to fight ~ s.o.,** discuter avec qn., se battre avec qn.; **2.** (*having, carrying*) à; **the man ~ the red beard, ~ the bowler hat,** l'homme à la barbe rousse, au chapeau melon; *also after some verbs e.g.* parler à qn.; **3.** (*near, in the presence of*) auprès; **to find peace ~ s.o.,** trouver la paix auprès de qn.; **4.** (*against*) contre; **to be furious ~ s.o.,** être furieux contre qn.; **5.** (*at the house of, in the case of*) chez; **he lives ~ us,** il habite chez nous; **it's normal ~ him,** c'est normal chez lui; **6.** (*by means of*) de; **he followed her ~ his eyes,** il la suivit des yeux; **I did it ~ all my might,** je l'ai fait de toutes mes forces; *also after some adjs. e.g.* content de, malade de; **7.** (*despite*) malgré; **~ all his learning, he is humble,** malgré toutes ses connaissances, il est humble; **8. to begin, to end ~,** commencer, finir, par; **9.** (*not expressed in French*) **~ his hat on his head,** le chapeau sur la tête; **~ tears in her eyes,** les larmes aux yeux; **~ one's mouth open,** la bouche ouverte; **to be ~ it,** (*fam. fig.*) être dans le vent; **~al,** de plus.

withdraw *v.t.* & *i.* (se) retirer; **~al** *s.* (*of person*) retraite *f.*, (*of sth.*) retrait *m.*
wither *v.t.* & *i.* (se) faner; **~ing** *adj.* (*fig.*) foudroyant.
withers *s.pl.* garrot *m.*
withhold *v.t.* retenir.
within *adv.* à l'intérieur, à la maison; *prep.* à l'intérieur de, dans; (*time*) en (l'espace de) un an, trois mois, *etc.*; (*distance*) à trois milles; (*approximately*) à vingt francs près, à deux mètres près.
without *adv.* à l'extérieur, dehors; *prep.* (≠ *with*) sans; (≠ *within*) en dehors de; **to do/go ~**, se passer de.
withstand *v.t.* résister à.
witness *s.* **1.** (*testimony*) témoignage *m.*; **2.** (*person giving ~*) témoin *m.*; **3.** (*person ~ing signature*) témoin *m.*; **4.** (*spectator*) témoin *m.*; **to bear ~ to, to call to ~**, témoigner de; **~-box** *s.* banc des témoins *m.*; *v.t.* (2) témoigner; (3) signer; (4) assister à; *v.i.* témoigner.
witt/y *adj.* spirituel; **~icism** *s.* bon mot *m.*; **~ily** *adv.* avec esprit; **~ingly** *adv.* sciemment.
wizard *s.* sorcier *m.*; *adj.* (*fam.*) épatant.
wizened *adj.* desséché.
W.M.O. (*World Meteorological Organization*) OMM *f.* (Organisation Météorologique mondiale).
woad *s.* guède *f.*
wobbl/e *v.i.* **1.** (*person*) chanceler; **2.** (*car*) zigzaguer; **3.** (*table*) branler; **4.** (*fig.*) hésiter; **~y** *adj.* (1) chancelant; (2) zigzaguant; (3) bancal; (4) hésitant.
woe *s.* chagrin *m.*; **~s** *s.pl.* malheurs *m.pl.*; **~ to, ~ betide,** malheur à; **~begone** *adj.* désolé; **~ful** *adj.* (*person*) désolé; (*thing*) déplorable; **~fully** *adv.* tristement, lamentablement.
wold *s.* lande vallonnée *f.*
wolf *s.* loup *m.*, louve *f.*; **to keep the ~ from the door** (*fig.*) (se) mettre à l'abri du besoin; **to cry ~**, crier au loup; **~-cub** *s.* louveteau *m.*; **~hound** *s.* chien-loup *m.*; **~ish** *adj.* de loup; *v.t.* dévorer.
woman *s.* femme *f.*; **~-hater** *s.* misogyne *m.*; **~hood** *s.* état de femme *m.*; **~kind** *s.* femmes *f.pl.*; **~ish** *adj.* efféminé; **~ly** *adj.* de femme.
womb *s.* matrice *f.*; (*fig.*) sein *m.*
wond/er *s.* (*marvel, strange thing*) merveille *f.*, prodige *m.*; (*emotion*) étonnement *m.*, surprise *f.*, admiration *f.*; **to promise ~ers,** promettre monts et merveilles; **~erful** *adj.* étonnant, merveilleux; **~erfully** *adv.* étonnamment, *; **~rous** *adj.* & **~rously** *adv. as* **~erful(ly)**; *v.i.* (*admire*) s émerveiller (*at*—à); (*be surprised*) s'étonner (*at*—de, *that*—que); (*want to know*) se demander.
wonky *adj.* (*pop.*) (*person*) patraque; (*chair, etc.*) bancal.
wont *s.* (*obs.*) habitude *f.*; **to be ~ to,** avoir l'habitude de; **~ed** *adj.* habituel.
woo *v.t.* faire la cour à; (*fig.*) solliciter; **~er** *s.* soupirant *m.*; **~ing** *s.* cour *f.*
wood *s.* (*trees, substance*) bois *m.*; PLY~; (*wine cask*) fût *m.*; **he can't see the ~ for the trees,** les arbres lui cachent la forêt; **to be out of the ~**, (*fig.*) arriver au bout du tunnel; *adj.* en bois, de bois, (*birds, flowers*) des bois; **~bine** *s.* chèvrefeuille *m.*; **~cock** *s.* bécasse *f.*; **~cut** *s.* gravure sur bois *f.*; **~cutter** *s.* bûcheron *m.*; **~land** *s.* terrain boisé *m.*; **~-louse** *s.* cloporte *m.*; **~pecker** *s.* pivert *m.*; ~-PIGEON; **~-pulp** *s.* pâte de bois *f.*; **~-wind** *s.* (*mus.*) bois *m.*; **~work** *s.* boiserie *f.*; **~worm** *s.* ver *m.*; **~ed** *adj.* boisé; **~en** *adj.* de bois, en bois, (*fig.*) de bois; **~y** *adj.* boisé.
woof *s.* (*obs.*) trame *f.*
wool *s.* laine *f.*; COTTON **~**; STEEL **~**; **to pull the ~ over s.o.'s eyes,** endormir la vigilance de qn.; **dyed in the ~** *adj.* (*fig.*) pur sang, convaincu; **~-gathering** *s.* distraction *f.*, *adj.* distrait; **~** *adj.* lainier; **~len** *adj.* de laine; **~ly** *s.* pull-over *m.*, *adj.* laineux, (*fig.*) confus, vague.
word *s.* (*symbol*) mot *m.*; (*spoken; promise*) parole *f.*; (*pass~*) mot d'ordre *m.*; (*news*) nouvelle *f.*; (*order*) ordre *m.*; **my ~!**, ma parole!; **~s** *s.pl.* (*speech*) paroles *f.pl.*; (*text of song, play*) texte *m.*; (*fam. = quarrel*) mots *m.pl.*; **~ for ~**, mot à mot; **in other ~s,** autrement dit; **to break one's ~**, manquer à sa parole; **to** KEEP **one's ~**; **to get a ~ in,** glisser un mot; **not to breathe a ~,** ne pas souffler mot; **to have a ~ with,** dire un mot (de qch. à qn.); **to eat one's ~s,** revenir sur ce qu'on a dit; **to send ~**, faire savoir; **you can take my ~ for it,** vous pouvez m'en croire; **~-blindness** *s.* cécité verbale *f.*; *v.t.* rédiger, exprimer; **~ing** *s.* expression *f.*, (*text of document, etc.*) libellé *m.*; **~y** *adj.* verbeux.
work[1] *s.* (*activity*) travail *m.*; (*job*) tâche *f.*, besogne *f.*; (*employment*) emploi *m.*; (*product*) ouvrage *m.*; (*book, etc.*) œuvre *f.*; FRET~; **~s** *s.pl.* (*liter.*) œuvres *f.pl.*, (*operations*) travaux *m.pl.*, (*mech.*) mécanisme *m.*, (*factory*) usine *f.*; **to be out of ~**, chômer; **to set to ~** *v.t.* & *i.* (se) mettre au travail; **to put a** SPANNER **in the ~s**; **~aday** *adj.* de tous les jours; **~-basket** *s.* corbeille à ouvrage *f.*; **~-bench** *s.* établi *m.*; **~-force** *s.* main d'œuvre *f.*; **~house** *s.* asile *m.*; **~man** *s.* ouvrier *m.*; **~manship** *s.* travail *m.*, habileté *f.*; **~shop** *s.* atelier *m.*; **~-table** *s.* table à ouvrage *f.*
work[2] *v.t.* (*person*) faire travailler; (*mech.*) faire fonctionner; (*mine*) exploiter; (*effect*) produire, causer; (*cook. knead*) travailler; (*agric. land*) cultiver; (*clay*) pétrir; (*iron*) forger; (*wood*) ouvrager; (*embroider*) broder; *v.i.* travailler; (*operate*) fonctionner, agir; (*be in motion*) marcher; (*ferment*) fermenter; (*become loose*) se desserrer; **~ to** RULE; **~ oneself into a rage,** se mettre en fureur; **~ on** *v.t.* agir sur; **~ out** *v.t.* (*plan*) développer, (*problem*) résoudre, (*project*) étudier; *v.i.* aboutir; **~ out at** *v.i.* se monter à; **~ up** *v.t.* préparer, élaborer; monter la tête à qn.; (*trouble*) fomenter; **~able** *adj.* practicable; **~er** *s.* travailleur *m.*, (= *~man*) ouvrier *m.*, (*bee*) abeille ouvrière *f.*; MANUAL **~er.**
working *s.* (*method*) fonctionnement *m.*; (*action*) travail *m.*, effet *m.*; (*of mine*) exploitation *f.*; **~s** *s.pl.* (*mine*) chantier *m.*; *adj.* (*that works*) en marche; (*at work*) laborieux, ouvrier; **~ class** *s.* classe ouvrière *f.*; **~ day** *s.* jour ouvrable *m.*; **~ man** *s.* travailleur *m.*; **~ model** *s.* modèle de travail *m.*; **~ majority** *s.* majorité suffisante *f.*; **in ~ order,** en état de marche; **~ party** *s.* commission *f.*
world *s.* (*this life*) monde *m.*; (*secular ≠ eccles.*) siècle *m.*; (*earth*) terre *f.*; (*universe*) univers *m.*; (*sphere of interest*) milieu *m.*; **for all the ~**, pour rien au monde; **out of this ~**, inouï; **~ without end,** dans les siècles des siècles; **man of the ~**, homme qui connaît la vie *m.*; **it will do you a ~ of good,** cela vous fera un bien énorme; *adj.* mondial; **W~ Bank,** banque mondiale *f.*; **~-famous** *adj.* connu partout dans le monde; **~ war** *s.* guerre mondiale *f.*; **~-wide** *adj.* mondial; **~ly** *adj.* (*temporal, earthly*) matériel; mondain, attaché aux biens terrestres; **~liness** *s.* mondanité *f.*
worm *s.* ver *m.*; (*of screw*) filet *m.*; **the** EARLY **bird catches the ~**; **~eaten** *adj.* vermoulu; **~-hole** *s.* trou de ver *m.*; **~wood** *s.* absinthe *f.*, (*fig.*) fiel *m.*; *v.t.* enlever les vers de; *v.refl.* **~ onself into,** s'insinuer dans; **~ sth. out of s.o.,** tirer les vers du nez à qn.
worn *adj.* usé; **~ out** *adj.* épuisé.
worry *s.* (*trouble*) inquiétude *f.*, tracas *m.*; (*cause of ~*) souci *m.*; *v.t.* (*with teeth*) mordiller; (*harass,*

pester) agacer, importuner; (*trouble*) tracasser, inquiéter; *v.i.* se tracasser, s'inquiéter; **don't ~!,** ne vous en faites pas!
worse *s.* pire *m.*; **from bad to ~,** de mal en pire; *adj.* pire; (*med.*) plus malade; *adv.* plus mal; **to get ~,** empirer; **to get ~ and ~,** aller de mal en pis; **for** BETTER **or for ~; to be none the ~ for sth.,** ne pas s'en trouver plus mal; **~n** *v.t.* rendre pire; *v.t.* empirer.
worship *s.* (*homage*) adoration *f.*; (*rites*) culte *m.*; PLACE **of ~; Your W~,** votre Honneur; **~ful** *adj.* honorable; *v.t.* adorer; **~per** *s.* adorat/eur, -rice *m.f.*; **~ping** *s.* adoration *f.*
worst *s.* le plus mauvais *m.*; *adj.* le (la) pire; le (la) plus malade; *adv.* le plus mal; **at the ~,** en mettant les choses au pire; **to get the ~ of sth.,** avoir le dessous; *v.t.* battre.
worsted *s.* (*text.*) peigné *m.*
worth *s.* (*value*) valeur *f.*; (*equivalent of*) prix *m.*; **to get one's money's ~,** en avoir pour son argent; *adj.* (*worthy*) méritant; (*possessed of*) riche de; **to be ~,** valoir; **this is ~ ten francs,** cela vaut dix francs; **~less** *adj.* sans valeur; (*person*) indigne; **~lessness** *s.* inutilité *f.*, (*person*) bassesse *f.*; **~while** *adj.* qui en vaut la peine; **~y** *s.* notable *m.*, *adj.* digne (de); **~ily** *adv.* dignement; **~iness** *s.* mérite *m.*
would *v.aux. see* WILL; **~-be** *adj.* soi-disant, prétendu (*before the noun*).
wound *s.* (*lit.* & *fig.*) blessure *f.*; *v.t.* blesser.
W.R.A.C. (*abbrev. Women's Royal Army Corps*) AFAT *f.pl.* (Auxiliaires féminines de l'Armée de terre).
W.R.A.F. (*abbrev. Women's Royal Air Force*) (*approx.*) Auxiliaires féminines de l'Armée de l'air *f.pl.*
wraith *s.* fantôme *m.*, spectre *m.*
wrangle *s.* dispute *f.*; *v.i.* se disputer.
wrap *s.* (*blanket*) couverture *f.*; (*shawl*) fichu *m.*, châle *m.*; *v.t.* & *i.* **~ up** (s')envelopper; **~ up** (*fig.*) conclure; **to be ~ped up in** (*fig.*) être absorbé par; **~per** *s.* (*paper*) bande *f.*, (*person*) emballeur *m.*, (*material*) toile d'emballage *f.*, (*dress*) peignoir *m.*
wrath *s.* courroux *m.*; **~ful** *adj.* courroucé; **~fully** *adv.* avec courroux.
wreak *v.t.* **~ vengeance,** se venger (de).
wreath *s.* (*of flowers*) guirlande *f.*; (*for funeral*) couronne *f.*; (*of smoke, etc.*) volute *f.*
wreathe *v.t.* & *i.* (s')entrelacer; (*garland*) orner de guirlandes.
wreck *s.* (*ship~*) naufrage *m.*; (*remains*) épave *f.*; (*arch.*) débris *m.pl.*; (*person* & *fig.*) ruine *f.*; *v.t.* faire naufrager; causer la perte de; (*fig.*) ruiner, faire échouer; **to be** (*ship*)**~ed,** faire naufrage; **~age** *s.* épaves *f.pl.*; **~er** *s.* naufrageur *m.*
wren *s.* roitelet *m.*
Wren *s.* personnel auxiliaire féminin de l'Armée de mer *m.* (*fam.*) marinette *f.*
wrench *s.* **1.** (*violent twist*) torsion *f.*; **2.** (*med.*) foulure *f.*; **3.** (*tool*) clef *f.*; **4.** (*fig.*) arrachement *m.*; *v.t.* (1) tordre; (2) fouler; **~ off,** arracher brutalement.
wrest *v.t.* (*twist, pervert*) dénaturer, fausser; (*remove by force*) arracher violemment (à).
wrestl/e *v.i.* (*lit.* & *fig.*) lutter; **~er** *s.* lutteur *m.*; **~ing** *s.* lutte *f.*
wretch *s.* **1.** (*unhappy person*) malheureux *m.*; **2.** (*shameless person*) misérable *m.*; **~ed** *adj.* (1) malheureux; (2) méchant; **3.** (*of poor quality*) mauvais; **4.** (*pitiful*) pitoyable, misérable; **5.** (*fam. before noun*) sacré; **~edly** *adv.* misérablement; **~edness** *s.* (1) malheur *m.*; (3) médiocrité *f.*; (4) tristesse *f.*
wriggle *v.i.* se tortiller; **~ out of sth.,** se retirer de qch.
wring *v.t.* (*squeeze*) tordre; (*distress*) serrer; (*extort*) extorquer (à); (*s.o.'s hand*) serrer fortement (la main à qn.); (*one's hands*) se tordre (les mains); **~ out,** faire sortir l'eau en tordant; **~er** *s.* essoreuse *f.*; **~ing wet** *adj.* trempé.
wrinkle *s.* (*in skin*) ride *f.*; (*in cloth*) faux pli *m.*; (*hint*) truc *m.*, (*fam.*) tuyau *m.*; *v.t.* & *i.* rider; (*clothes*) (se) froisser; (*eyebrows*) froncer (les sourcils); **~d** *adj.* ridé.
wrist *s.* poignet *m.*; **~band** *s.* manchette *f.*; **~-watch** *s.* montre-bracelet *f.*
writ *s.* (*law*) exploit (d'huissier) *m.*
write *v.t.* & *i.* écrire; (*record*) inscrire; (*as profession*) être écrivain; **~ back,** répondre (à une lettre); **~ down,** noter; **~ off** *v.t.* (*fin.*) amortir, déduire; (*cancel*) rayer; (*destroy*) détruire; **~-off** *s.* annulation *f.*; perte totale *f.*; **~ out** *v.t.* transcrire, rédiger; **~ up** *v.t.* rédiger, (*fam.*) prôner; **~-up** *s.* reportage *m.*; **~r** *s.* celui (celle) qui écrit, (*professional*) écrivain *m.*; **writing** *s.* écriture *f.*, (*document*) écrit *m.*, (*profession*) métier d'écrivain *m.*; **in writing,** par écrit; **writing-paper** *s.* papier à lettres *m.*; **writing-table** *s.* bureau *m.*; **written** *adj.* écrit.
writhe *v.i.* se tordre.
W.R.N.S. (*abbrev. Women's Royal Naval Service*) personnel auxiliaire féminin de l'armée de mer *m.*
wrong *s.* (*morally ~*) mal *m.*; (*action*) tort *m.*; (*injustice*) injustice *f.*; **in the ~,** dans son tort; *adj.* (≠ *right, morally*) méchant; (≠ *correct*) erroné; (≠ *true*) faux; (*not in good order*) dérangé détraqué; (*not what is required*) mauvais; **to take the ~ road, train, etc.,** se tromper de route, de train, etc.; **it's the ~ book,** ce n'est pas le livre qu'il faut; **to sing a ~ note,** chanter une fausse note; **there's sth. ~ with him,** il y a qch. qui ne va pas chez lui; **to** RUB/STROKE **up the ~ way; to be ~,** avoir tort, (*mistaken*) se tromper; **~doer** *s.* méchant *m.*, (*law*) délinquant *m.*; **~doing** *s.* méfaits *m.pl.*; **~ful** *adj.* injuste; **~ side** *s.* envers *m.*; **get out of** BED **on the ~ side;** *adv.* & **~ly** *adv.* mal, à tort; **to go ~,** se détraquer, mal marcher; *v.t.* faire tort à; (*dishonour*) nuire à.
wrought *adj.* (*iron*) (fer) forgé.
wry *adj.* tordu; (*smile*) forcé.

X

xenophob/ia *s.* xénophobie *f.*; **~e** *s.* xénophobe *m.f.*
Xmas *s.* (*abbrev.*) Noël *m.*
X-ray *s.* (*photograph*) radiographie *f.*; (*pl.* **~s**) rayons X *m.pl.*; *v.t.* (*photograph*) radiographier; (*examine*) faire une radioscopie; (*treat*) traiter par radiothérapie.
xylophone *s.* xylophone *m.*

Y

yacht *s.* yacht *m.*; *v.i.* faire du yachting; **~ing** *s.* yachting *m.*; **~sman** *s.* yachtman *m.*
yahoo *s.* (*pop.*) brute *f.*
yak *s.* ya(c)k *m.*
yam *s.* igname *f.*
yank *s.* coup brusque *m.*; *v.t.* tirer brusquement.
Yank(ee) *adj.* & *s.m.* yankee.
yap *s.* **1.** (*barking*) jappement *m.*; **2.** (*talk*) jacassement *m.*; *v.t.* (1) japper; (2) jacasser.
yard[1] *s.* (*measure*) yard *m.*; (*naut.*) vergue *f.*; **~-arm** *s.* bout de vergue *m.*; **~stick** *s.* critère *m.*
yard[2] *s.* (*enclosure*) cour *f.*; CHURCH-~; COURT-~; DOCK-~; **farm-~**, basse-cour *f.*; GRAVE-~; VINE~; (*rail.*) dépôt *m.*; **Scotland Y~** (*approx.*) la Sûreté *f.*
yarn *s.* **1.** (*fibre*) fil *m.*; **2.** (*fam. tale*) histoire à dormir debout *f.*; *v.i.* (2) raconter des histoires.
yarrow *s.* mille-feuille *f.*
yashmak *s.* litham *m.*
yaw *v.i.* (*naut.*) faire une embardée.
yawl *s.* (*naut.*) yole *f.*
yawn *s.* bâillement *m.*; *v.i.* bâiller; (*gape*) béer; **~ing** *adj.* béant.
year *s.* an *m.*, (*whole period*) année *f.*; (*fin.*) exercice *m.*; **~s** *s.pl.* ans *m.pl.*, âge *m.*; LEAP ~; **~ in ~ out,** bon an mal an; **~-book** *s.* annuaire *m.*; **~ling** *s.* animal d'un an *m.*; **~ly** *adj.* annuel, *adv.**.
yearn *v.i.* **~ for,** aspirer à, soupirer après; **~ to,** brûler de, avoir envie de; **~ing** *s.* aspiration *f.*, envie *f.*
yeast *s.* levure *f.*
yell *s.* hurlement *m.*; *v.t.* & *i.* hurler.
yellow *s.* jaune *m.*; *adj.* jaune; (*cowardly*) froussard; **~ fever** *s.* fièvre jaune *f.*; **~hammer** *s.* bruant jaune *m.*; **~ press** *s.* presse à sensation *f.*; **~ish** *adj.* jaunâtre; **~ness** *s.* couleur jaune *f.*, teint jaune *m.*; *v.t.* & *i.* jaunir.
yelp *s.* **1.** (*of dog*) jappement *m.*; **2.** (*of other animals, of person*) glapissement *m.*; *v.i.* (1) japper; (2) glapir.
yen *s.* (*pop.*) désir *m.*, envie *f.*
yeoman *s.* (*farmer*) franc tenancier *m.*; (*mil.*) yeoman *m.* (*pl.* yeomen); **to do ~ service** (*fig.*) rendre des services inestimables; **~ry** *s.* troupes territoriales *f.pl.*
yes *s.* oui *m.*; (*in answer to negative question*) si; **you didn't see him, did you? ~ I did,** vous ne l'avez pas vu, n'est-ce pas; Mais si, je l'ai vu; **~-man** *s.* (*fam.*) béni-oui-oui *m.*
yesterday *s.* & *adv.* hier; **day before ~**, avant-hier; **~'s** *adj.* d'hier, d'autrefois.
yet *adv.* encore; *conj.* néanmoins; **as ~**, jusqu'ici; **not ~**, pas encore.
yeti *s.* yeti *m.*
yew *s.* if *m.*
Y.H.A. (*abbrev. Youth Hostels Association*) A.J. *f.pl.* (Auberges de la Jeunesse).
Yiddish *adj.* & *s.m.* yiddish, yddisch.
yield *s.* rendement *m.*; *v.t.* (*produce*) produire; (*concede*) céder; *v.i.* céder; **~ing** *adj.* accommodant.
yob *s.* (*pop.*) voyou *m.*
yodel *s.* tyrolienne *f.*; *v.t.* & *i.* jodler, iodler.
yog/a *s.* yoga *m.*; **~i** *s.* yogi *m.*
yog(h)urt, yaourt *s.* yog(h)ourt, yaourt *m.*
yoke *s.* (*for oxen; tie*) joug *m.*; (*pair of oxen*) paire *f.*; (*servitude*) servitude *f.*; (*dressm.*) empiècement *m.*; *v.t.* mettre au joug; (*fig.*) unir.
yokel *s.* (*pej.*) péquenot *m.*, péquenaud(e) *m.f.*
yolk *s.* jaune *m.*
yonder *adj.* de là-bas; *adv.* là-bas.
yore *adv.* **of ~**, jadis.
you *pron.* (*sing.* & *pl. subj.* & *obj.*) vous; (*sing. fam. subj.*) tu; (*sing. fam. obj.*) te; (*sing. fam. emphatic*) toi; (*impers. subj. only*) on.
young *s.* (*collective*) les jeunes *m.pl.*, la jeunesse *f.*; **with ~** *adj.* enceinte, grosse; *adj.* (≠ *old*) jeune; (*newly formed*) jeune, nouveau; (*youthful*) de jeunesse; **~er** *adj.* & *s.m.f.* cadet(te); **~ish** *adj.* assez jeune; **~ster** *s.* adolescent *m.*
your *adj.* ton, ta, tes; votre, vos; **~s** *pron.* à toi; à vous; le (la) tien(ne), les tien(ne)s; le, la (les) vôtre(s); **~s** TRULY *etc.*; **~self** *pron.* vous-même, toi-même; *refl. pron.* te, vous; **~selves**, vous-mêmes.
youth *s.* jeunesse *f.*; (*young man*) jeune homme *m.*; **~ hostel** *s.* auberge de la jeunesse *f.*; **~ful** *adj.* jeune, de jeunesse; **~fully** *adv.* comme un jeune; **~fulness** *s.* jeunesse *f.*
yucca *s.* yucca *m.*
Yugoslav/ia, Jugoslavia *s.* (*geog.*) Yougoslavie *f.*; **~** *adj.* & *s.m.f.* yougoslave.
yule *s.* Noël *m.*; **~-log** *s.* bûche de Noël *f.*

Z

zabaglione *s.* (*cook.*) sabayon *m.*
Zaire *s.* (*geog.*) Zaïre *f.*; **~ian** *adj.* & *s.m.f.* zaïrois(e).
Zambesi *s.* (*geog.*) Zambèze *m.*
Zambia *s.* (*geog.*) Zambie *f.*; **~n** *adj.* & *s.m.f.* zambien(ne).
zany *adj.* & *s.m.f.* (*of person*) bêta(sse); (*idea, etc.*) farfelu.
Zanzibar *s.* (*geog.*) Zanzibar *m.*; **~i** *adj.* de Zanzibar; *s.m.f.* habitant de Zanzibar.
zeal *s.* zèle *m.*; **~ot** *s.* (*hist. eccles.*) zélote *m.*; (*fig.*) fanatique *m.*; **~ous** *adj.* zélé; **~ously** *adv.* avec zèle.
zebra *s.* zèbre *m.*; **~ crossing** *s.* passage clouté *m.*
zebu *s.* zébu *m.*
zenith *s.* (*lit.* & *fig.*) zénith *m.*
zephyr *s.* zéphyr *m.*
zero *s.* zéro *m.*; **~ hour,** heure H *f.*
zest *s.* (*piquancy*) piquant *m.*; (*gusto*) allant *m.*; (*piece of orange or lemon peel*) zeste *m.*
zigzag *s.* zigzag *m.*; *adj.* & *adv.* en zigzag; *v.i.* zigzager.
zinc *s.* zinc *m.*
zinnia *s.* zinnia *m.*
Zion *s.* Sion *f.*; **~ism** *s.* sionisme *m.*; **~ist** *s.* sioniste *m.f.*

zip *s.* (*sound*) crissement *m.*; (*of bullet*) sifflement *m.*; (*energy*) allant *m.*; (*-fastener*) fermeture éclair *f.*; *v.t.* & *i.* fermer avec une fermeture éclair; ~ **past,** passer comme un éclair.
zither *s.* cithare *f.*
zodiac *s.* zodiaque *m.*
zombie *s.* (*voodoo*) zombi *m.*; (*fam.*) crétin *m.*
zon/e *s.* zone *f.*; (*belt*) ceinture *f.*; *v.t.* répartir en zones; ~**ing** *s.* zonage *m.*
zoo *s.* zoo *m.*; ~**logical** *adj.* zoologique; ~**logist** *s.* zoologiste *m.f.*; ~**logy** *s.* zoologie *f.*; ~**-morphic** *adj.* zoomorphique; ~**phyte** *s.* zoophyte *m.*
zoom *v.t.* & *i.* (*sound*) vrombir; (*aviat.*) monter en flèche; (*TV, cinema*) faire un gros-plan; ~ **lens** *s.* objectif à focale variable *m.*
Zulu *adj.* & *s.* zoulou (*usu. invar.*); *s.m.* (*lang.*) zoulou.

NOTES

NOTES